Britannica CONCISE ENCYCLOPEDIA

Britannica CONCISE ENCYCLOPEDIA

ENCYCLOPÆDIA
Britannica

ENCYCLOPÆDIA BRITANNICA, INC.

Chicago • London • New Delhi • Paris • Seoul • Sydney • Taipei • Tokyo

Britannica CONCISE ENCYCLOPEDIA

Encyclopædia Britannica

First published in 1768, the *Encyclopædia Britannica* has long been the standard by which all other reference works are judged. It represents a tradition of excellence that was built, over the centuries, on meticulous scholarship and unmatched attention to detail. Today, Encyclopædia Britannica, Inc., produces a range of fine products for reference, education, and learning in different media and in many different languages. Wherever you see the Britannica name—in print, on the Internet, CD-ROM, or DVD—it is your guarantee of quality, accuracy, and authority.

Library of Congress Control Number: 2002100913
International Standard Book Number: 0-85229-964-8

The original edition of this book, created in conjunction with Merriam-Webster, Incorporated, was published in 2000 as Merriam-Webster's Collegiate Encyclopedia.

Encyclopædia Britannica and other fine products are available on the Internet at http://www.britannica.com.

(Trademark Reg. U.S. Pat. Off.) Printed in U.S.A.

Contents

ENCYCLOPÆDIA Britannica

Foreword

It is hard to think of a more cherished source of history and general information than the encyclopedia. For more than 2,000 years, in virtually every land, in countless languages and various forms—from ancient papyrus rolls and codices of folded parchment to multivolume print sets, laser-burned discs, and Internet-accessible online databases—encyclopedias have been a common point of departure for readers the world over wanting a comprehensive look at life and its many wonders, past and present.

Since the publication of its first edition in 1768, Encyclopædia Britannica has been a leader in this field of publishing. Its 44-million word encyclopedia is often cited as the most authoritative reference work in the world, and its 32-volume print set—the equivalent of a library of several hundred books—is the oldest continuously published and revised work in the English language.

And so it is with great pleasure that we offer today yet another way to access Britannica's wealth of information. *Britannica Concise Encyclopedia* is the only single-volume, general desk reference work published exclusively by Encyclopædia Britannica. Portable and designed for quick reference and based on *Merriam-Webster's Collegiate Encyclopedia*, published in conjunction with Encyclopædia Britannica in 2000, this updated and enhanced edition covers in abridged form in a new, color format the chief subjects of academic study and topics of popular interest, from sports to world history, from film to the hard sciences. Like Britannica's core encyclopedia, the scope of *Britannica Concise* is global and far-reaching, reflecting both the shrinking world we live in and the quickly expanding base of knowledge we desire as a result. Whether the user is a young reader wanting to know about J.K. Rowling, a college student needing a list of the rulers of the Russian Empire, or simply a family at the dinner table wanting to quell debate over the height of Mt. Everest, the origins of the Taliban, or the method of calculating the wind chill temperature, *Britannica Concise* should serve as a convenient and reliable place to turn for cogent answers and general information.

Because the entries derive largely from their longer counterparts in *Encyclopædia Britannica*, they reflect the same standards of quality for which Britannica is famous. Ideally, *Britannica Concise* will meet the readers' needs of the moment while whetting their appetite for the extended treatment of people, places, and ideas found in Britannica's many other products.

The over 28,000 entries in *Britannica Concise* vary in length from about 50 to 1,000 words, with the shortest entries being helpful cross-references. There are more than 2.6 million words of text, 1,800 photographs, 190 maps, 150 line drawings, and 30 tables. The new 16-page section of color plates presents useful information on the world, from maps on countries and population density to maps on world religions and the international time zones; there are even plates with a sampling of official World Heritage sites.

A wealth of information is also found in the many tables throughout *Britannica Concise*, from descriptions of the geologic time periods or months in the Muslim calendar to the various measurements in the International System of Units; there is a table listing every winner of a Nobel Prize as well as tables delineating the gods and goddesses of Greek and Roman mythology. Whatever the subject or issue at hand, *Britannica Concise*, we trust, will enrich the reader's understanding of the matter while serving as a quick and authoritative guide to the many other manifestations of life and human endeavor.

So, on behalf of Encyclopædia Britannica's editorial staff, whose hard work and devotion make Britannica products possible, we welcome you to the latest addition to the Britannica family of reference works.

Theodore Pappas
Editor

Explanatory Notes

Alphabetization. The articles are alphabetized word by word, with further alphabetizing letter by letter within a word. A "word" is here defined as a unit of one or more characters set off from other words by spaces, dashes, hyphens, or other symbols. Entry titles consisting of more than one word are arranged in alphabetical order of the succeeding words. Titles with identical spellings are arranged in the order (1) persons, (2) places, and (3) things. The following list illustrates the word-by-word principle:

horn
Horn, Cape
Horn of Africa
hornbill
Horne, Lena
horned toad
Hornsby, Rogers

Further alphabetization rules include the following: (1) Diacritics, apostrophes, hyphens, dashes, periods, and ampersands are ignored in alphabetization. (2) Names of monarchs and popes that are identical except for the Roman numeral following the name are ordered numerically. (3) Names beginning with *Mac-* and *Mc-* are ordered literally, all names beginning with *Mac-* preceding (by a number of pages) all names beginning with *Mc-*.

Entry headword style. Variant spellings or versions of the encyclopedia's entry headwords are printed in boldface type when they are in common use; more obscure variants are printed in ordinary roman type and are not provided with pronunciations. No effort has been made to be exhaustive in listing variants, and rare variants have been ignored.

Several italicized terms are used to discriminate among the variants. The label *or* simply indicates a common alternative name or spelling. The label *orig.* precedes the birth name of a person who is entered under a name that was adopted or acquired subsequently. When a person's original surname is different from the name in the principal headword, the entire birth name is given, not enclosed in parentheses. The label *known as* precedes a common way of referring to a person that may never have had formal status. The label *later* generally precedes a title bestowed on a person in the course of his or her lifetime. The label *formerly* indicates an older and generally discarded name for an entity, usually a geographical locale. The label *officially* indicates a formal or legal version of a name. The label *in full* precedes a fully spelled-out version of a name that is usually encountered in its shorter form. A label consisting of a language name precedes a native version or spelling of a name or term.

Biographical entry headwords in particular may employ parentheses in several ways. Parentheses may enclose portions of a person's name that are rarely used, a person's original given name or names, a later addition such as a title, or translations of titles or epithets.

drum *or* **croaker**
Odin *or* **Wotan**
Bacall, Lauren *orig.* **Betty Joan Perske**
O'Donnell, Daniel *known as* **the Liberator**
Heath, Edward (Richard George) *later* **Sir Edward**
Iqaluit *formerly* **Frobisher Bay**
Latvia *officially* **Republic of Latvia**
OCR *in full* **optical character recognition**
fax *in full* **facsimile**
Magellan, Strait of *Spanish* **Estrecho de Magellanes**
Odysseus *Roman* **Ulysses**
Connelly, Marc(us Cook)
Doctorow, E(dgar) L(aurence)
Hughes, (James Mercer) Langston
Basil II *known as* **Basil Bulgaroctonus ("Slayer of the Bulgars")**

Pronunciations. Entries for terms and names whose pronunciation the encyclopedia's likely users might hesitate over are supplied with pronunciations. Foreign names or terms that are pronounced in a markedly different way by native speakers and English-speakers are frequently provided with two pronunciations, one of them preceded by a language label (e.g., *English, French, Spanish*). Thus, for Hassan II we provide the pronunciations \ˈhá-sán, *English* ha-ˈsän\. The symbols employed and the sounds they represent are listed on page x.

Romanization of foreign languages. Words from languages that do not use the Western (Roman) alphabet generally reflect the spellings most commonly seen in English-language contexts.

Chinese names are almost always transcribed according to the Pinyin system. Where a Chinese name or term appears as a headword, the older Wade-Giles spelling is given as an *or* variant. Taiwanese place-names and biographical names, however, are generally listed in their Wade-Giles spelling, with the Pinyin spelling as a variant. A few Chinese words widely used in English (e.g., *Taoism*) retain their traditional English spelling.

Japanese names and terms are generally transcribed according to the Hepburn system but without macrons to indicate vowel length.

Russian names and terms generally observe traditional Western spellings and follow the diacritic-free system employed by the U.S. Board on Geographic Names.

Arabic names and terms generally follow the best-established Western usage. Ayns and hamzas have generally been omitted. Except in a few well-established Western transliterations, the *l* in the article *al-* or *el-* ("the") is not assimilated to a following consonant (thus, we employ the spelling *Harun al-Rashid,* not *Harun ar-Rashid*), even though such assimilation reflects Arabic pronunciation and is sometimes encountered in English sources.

Cross-references. Cross-references to other articles are indicated by small capitals for the alphabetized element of the term or name. Thus, "J. VON NEUMANN"; sends the reader to the V's, "J. W. von GOETHE" to the G's; CAPE BRETON ISLAND"sends the reader to the C's, "Cape of GOOD HOPE" to the G's; and so on. In the case of personal names in which there is no ambiguity as to alphabetical placement, the entire name appears in small capitals.

A term is cross-referenced only when it is likely that the reader of the article within which the cross-reference appears would want to be notified about the additional article. Hence many terms for which there are corresponding entries are not highlighted as references. For instance, in the article on Tim Berners-Lee, we have cross-referenced "World Wide Web" (whose invention was his principal achievement) but not "Internet," which is naturally cross-referenced within the "World Wide Web" article. Because cross-referencing of this kind is discretionary, readers should not assume that a noun lacks its own entry simply because it is not referenced within the article being read.

For the sake of saving space, many people who receive their own entries have their given names abbreviated and their surnames in small capitals when they are mentioned in an article, regardless of how likely the reader of the article is to want to be alerted to the biographical entry. The names of countries, U.S. states, and Canadian provinces, by contrast, are virtually never referenced, regardless of their centrality to a given article, on the presumption that readers will correctly assume that the encyclopedia contains articles on all such entities.

Some 3,000 cross-references are provided at their own alphabetical place, to direct the reader who has looked up a variant version of the name or has expected an entry to be alphabetized according to an element other than the one actually used.

Abbreviations

AD	anno Domini
Adm.	Admiral
Ala.	Alabama
Amer.	American
Ariz.	Arizona
Ark.	Arkansas
BC	before Christ
C	Celsius
c.	circa
Cal.	California
Capt.	captain
cc	cubic centimeter(s)
cent.	century, centuries
cm	centimeter(s)
Co.	Company, County
Col.	Colorado, Colonel
Conn.	Connecticut
Corp.	Corporation
cu	cubic
D.C.	District of Columbia
Del.	Delaware
Dr.	Doctor
E	East
e.g.	exempli gratia (for example)
est.	estimate, estimated
F	Fahrenheit
fl.	flourished
Fla.	Florida
ft	foot, feet
g	gram(s)
Ga.	Georgia
Gen.	General
Gov.	Governor
i.e.	id est (that is)
Ill.	Illinois
in.	inch(es)
Ind.	Indiana
Jr.	Junior
K	Kelvin
Kan.	Kansas
kg	kilogram(s)
km	kilometer(s)
kph	kilometers per hour
Ky.	Kentucky
La.	Louisiana
lb, lbs	pound, pounds
m	meter(s)
MA	Master of Arts
Maj.	Major
Mass.	Massachusetts
Md.	Maryland
Me.	Maine
mi	mile(s)
Mich.	Michigan
Minn.	Minnesota
Miss.	Mississippi
ml	milliliter(s)
mm	millimeter(s)
Mo.	Missouri
Mont.	Montana
mph	miles per hour
N	North
N.C.	North Carolina
N.D.	North Dakota
NE	northeastern
Neb.	Nebraska
Nev.	Nevada
N.H.	New Hampshire
N.J.	New Jersey
N.M.	New Mexico
NW	northwestern
N.Y.	New York
Okla.	Oklahoma
Ore.	Oregon
oz	ounce(s)
Pa.	Pennsylvania
PhD	Doctor of Philosophy
Pres.	President
r.	reigned, ruled
Rev.	Reverend
R.I.	Rhode Island
S	South
S.C.	South Carolina
S.D.	South Dakota
SE	southeastern
Sen.	Senator
sq	square
St.	Saint
SW	southwestern
Tenn.	Tennessee
U.N.	United Nations
U.S.	United States
Va.	Virginia
vs.	versus
Vt.	Vermont
W	West
W.V.	West Virginia
Wash.	Washington
Wisc.	Wisconsin
Wy.	Wyoming

Pronunciation Symbols

ə	banana, collide, abut, humdrum
ᵊ	preceding \l\, \n\, \m\, \ŋ\, as in battle, mitten, eaten, lock and key \-ᵊŋ-\; following \l\, \m\, \r\, as in French table, prisme, titre
ər	further, merger, bird
a	mat, gag
ā	day, fade, aorta
ä	bother, cot, father, cart
ȧ	father as pronounced by speakers who do not rhyme it with *bother*; French patte
au̇	now, loud, out
b	baby, rib
ch	chin, nature \ˈnā-chər\
d	did, adder
e	bet, bed, peck
ē	beat, easy
f	fifty, cuff
g	go, big
h	hat, ahead
i	tip, banish
ī	site, buy
j	gem, judge
k	kin, cook, ache
k̲	German ich, Buch
l	lily, pool
m	murmur, dim
n	no, own
ⁿ	indicates that a preceding vowel or diphthong is pronounced with the nasal passages open, as in French *un bon vin blanc* \œⁿ-bōⁿ-vaⁿ-bläⁿ\
ŋ	sing\ˈsiŋ\, singer\ˈsiŋ-ər\, finger\ˈfiŋ-gər\, ink\ˈiŋk\
ō	bone, know, beau
ȯ	saw, all, caught
œ	French boeuf, German Hölle
œ̄	French feu, German Höhle
ȯi	coin, destroy
p	pepper, lip
r	red, car, rarity
s	source, less
sh	shy, mission, machine, special
t	tie, attack, late, latter
th	thin, ether
t̲h̲	then, either, this
ü	rule, youth, union \ˈyün-yən\, few \ˈfyü\
u̇	pull, wood, book
ue	German füllen, hübsch
ue̅	French rue, German fühlen
v	vivid, give
w	we, away
y	yard, cue \ˈkyü\, union \ˈyün-yən\
ʸ	indicates that during the articulation of the sound represented by the preceding character the front of the tongue has substantially the position it has when pronouncing *y*, as in French *digne* \dēnʸ\
z	zone, raise
zh	vision, azure \ˈa-zhər\
ˈ	precedes a syllable with primary (strongest) stress: \ˈpen-mən-ˌship\
ˌ	precedes a syllable with secondary (medium) stress: \ˈpen-mən-ˌship\
-	marks syllable division
( )	indicate that what is enclosed is pronounced by some but not by others: *factory* \ˈfak-t(ə-)rē\

Guide to Plates

Map Legend

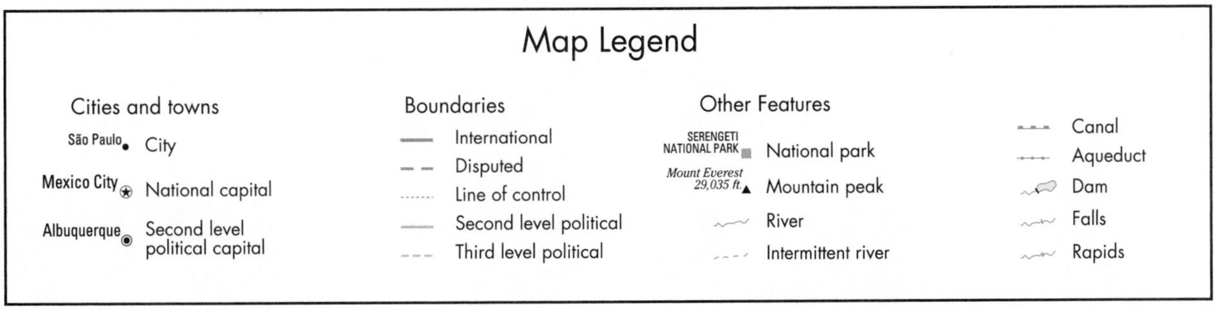

A&P See GREAT ATLANTIC & PACIFIC TEA CO.

a posteriori See A PRIORI

a priori \ˌä-prē-ˈōr-ē, ˌā-prī-ˈōr-ī\ In EPISTEMOLOGY, knowledge that is independent of all particular experiences, as opposed to a posteriori (or empirical) knowledge, which derives from experience. The terms have their origins in the medieval Scholastic debate over Aristotelian concepts (see SCHOLASTICISM). IMMANUEL KANT initiated their current usage, pairing the ANALYTIC–SYNTHETIC DISTINCTION with the a priori–a posteriori distinction to define his theory of knowledge.

Aachen \ˈä-k̲ən\ *French* **Aix-la-Chapelle** \ˌeks-lȧ-shȧ-ˈpel\ City (pop., 1995 est.: 247,000), western Germany, southwest of Cologne. It was inhabited by Romans in the 1st century AD. A center of Carolingian culture, and the second city of CHARLEMAGNE's empire, it was the site of his great palace. The cathedral built by Charlemagne c. 800 saw the coronation of most German kings of the 10th–16th century; his chapel, with his tomb, remains as part of the larger Gothic cathedral today. Aachen was part of France 1801–15. It is famous for its many spas.

Aaiun, El See EL AAIUN

Aalto \ˈäl-tȯ\, **(Hugo) Alvar (Henrik)** (1898–1976) Finnish architect and designer. He graduated from the Technical Institute of Helsinki, and in 1925 married Aino Marsio (died 1949), who served as his collaborator. His reputation rests on a distinctive style that blends classic modernism, indigenous materials (especially timber), and personal expression. His unique blending of modernism and informal regional character was perhaps best expressed in his civic center at Säynätsalo (1950–52), with its simple forms in red brick, wood, and copper. He remains one of the Modern movement's most popular architects; reproductions of his bent laminated wood furniture appear in households worldwide.

aardvark *or* **African ant bear** Heavily built mammal *(Orycteropus afer)* of sub-Saharan forests and plains. Its stout, piglike body ("aardvark" is Afrikaans for "earth pig") may be as long as 6 ft (1.8 m), including a 2-ft (60-cm) tail. It has a long snout, rabbitlike ears, short legs, and long toes with large, flattened claws. It feeds at night by ripping open ant and termite nests and lapping up the insects with a long (1-ft, or 30-cm), sticky tongue. Though not aggressive, it uses claws to fight off attackers. Its classification with regard to other mammals is uncertain.

Aare River \ˈär-ə\ *or* **Aar River** River, central and northern Switzerland. The longest river entirely within Switzerland, it flows northwest from the BERNESE ALPS and passes through the Gorge of the Aare and by the city of BERN before flowing northeast to enter the RHINE at Koblenz, after a course of 183 mi (294 km).

Aarhus See ARHUS

Aaron (fl. c. 13th century BC) Brother of MOSES and first high priest of ancient Israel. Acting as a spokesman for Moses, he played a central role in forcing the pharaoh to allow the Israelites to leave Egypt. God charged Aaron and Moses with commemorating the event at Passover, and Aaron and his sons were given priestly authority by Moses. Though Aaron is a pivotal figure in EXODUS, he nearly fades from view thereafter. He is mentioned as the one responsible for the Israelites' idolatrous worship of the golden calf while Moses was on Mount Sinai receiving the Law from God. His death at 123 is noted in Numbers.

Hank Aaron.
PICTORIAL PARADE

Aaron, Hank *orig.* **Henry Louis** (born 1934) U.S. baseball player. Born in Mobile, Ala., he played briefly in the Negro and minor leagues before joining the Milwaukee Braves in 1954. He would play outfield most of his career. By the time the Braves moved to Atlanta in 1965, he had hit 398 home runs; in 1974 he hit his 715th, breaking BABE RUTH's record. He played his final two seasons (1975–76) with the Milwaukee Brewers. His records for career home runs (755), extra-base hits (1,477), and runs batted in (2,297) remain unbroken, and only TY COBB and PETE ROSE exceeded him in career hits (3,771). He is renowned as one of the greatest hitters of all time.

AARP *formerly* **American Association of Retired Persons** Nonprofit, nonpartisan organization that addresses the needs and interests of Americans aged 50 and older. It was founded in 1958 by a retired teacher, Ethel Andrus, and merged in 1982 with the National Retired Teachers Assn., also founded by Andrus (1947). Its bimonthly magazine, *Modern Maturity,* has the largest circulation of any U.S. periodical. Its membership of more than 30 million and its members' reliably high voting turnout have made it one of the most powerful lobbying groups in the U.S.

abacus Calculating instrument that uses beads that slide along a series of wires or rods set in a frame to represent the decimal places. Probably of Babylonian origin, it is the ancestor of the modern digital calculator. Used by merchants in the Middle Ages throughout Europe and the Arabic world, it was gradually replaced by arithmetic based on HINDU-ARABIC NUMERALS. Though rarely used in Europe past the 18th century, it is still used in the Middle East, China, and Japan.

Abahai See HONGTAIJI

Abakanowicz \ˌä-bä-ˈkän-ō-ˌwits\, **Magdalena** (born 1930) Polish sculptor. A descendant of nobility, she graduated from Warsaw's Academy of Fine Arts in 1955. She became the pioneer and leading exponent of sculpture made of woven fabrics, calling her three-dimensional weavings "Abakans" (from her surname). She produced series of fabric forms called *Heads* (1975), *Backs* (1976–80), *Embryology* (1980), and *Catharsis* (1986). She has also exhibited paintings, drawings, and sculptures in other media internationally, and has been widely imitated in Europe and the U.S. She has taught in Poznan since 1965.

abalone \ˌa-bə-ˈlō-nē\ Any of several marine SNAIL species (genus *Haliotis,* family Haliotidae), found in warm seas worldwide. The outer surface of the single shell has a row of small holes, most of which fill in as the animal grows; some remain open as outlets for waste products. Abalones range from 4 to 10 in. (10–25 cm) across and up to 3 in. (8 cm) deep. The largest is the 12 in. (30 cm) abalone *(H. rufescens).* The shell's lustrous, iridescent interior is used in ornaments, and the large muscular foot is eaten as a delicacy. Commercial abalone fisheries exist in California, Mexico, Japan, and South Africa.

Abbado \ä-ˈbä-dō\, **Claudio** (born 1933) Italian conductor. Born in Milan, he studied piano at its conservatory before beginning to conduct in Vienna. He was long associated with LA SCALA (1968–86), as principal conductor and ultimately as artistic director, as well as with the Vienna Philharmonic. In 1989 he succeeded H. VON KARAJAN as permanent conductor and artistic director of the Berlin Philharmonic. He is known for his commitment to adventurous programming, including much modern music.

Abbas, Ferhat (1899–1985) Algerian political leader who served as first president of the provisional government of the Algerian Republic (1958). Originally a Francophile, he became disillusioned with France and during World War II issued a condemnation of French rule, demanding a constitution that would grant equality to all Algerians. He joined the NATIONAL LIBERATION FRONT (FLN), which helped achieve independence from France 1958–62. He was elected president of the Algerian Constituent Assembly in 1962, but resigned in 1963 following a dispute within the FLN. See also YOUNG ALGERIANS.

Abbas I *known as* **Abbas the Great** (1571–1629) Shah of Persia 1587–1629. Succeeding his father, Sultan Muhammad Shah, he strengthened the SAFAVID DYNASTY by expelling Ottoman and Uzbek troops and creating a standing army. He made ESFAHAN Persia's capital, and under Abbas it became one of the world's most beautiful cities. Persian artistic achievement reached a high point during his reign, when illuminated manuscripts, ceramics, and painting all flourished, and the

Portuguese, Dutch, and English competed for trade relations with Persia. Tolerant in public life (he granted privileges to Christian groups) and concerned for his people's welfare, his fear for his personal security and ruthlessness led him to blind or execute many of his immediate family.

Abbas I, detail of a painting by the Mughal school of Jahangir, c. 1620; in the Freer Gallery of Art, Washington, D.C.

BY COURTESY OF THE SMITHSONIAN INSTITUTION, FREER GALLERY OF ART, WASHINGTON, D.C.

Abbas Hilmy I \âb-'bas-'hil-mē\ (1813–1854) Viceroy of Egypt (1848–54) under the OTTOMAN EMPIRE. He succeeded his uncle, Ibrahim, and worked to undo the Westernizing reforms begun by his grandfather, MUHAMMAD ALI. He distrusted the French, who had worked closely with his grandfather. Though he opposed Ottoman-imposed reforms, he sent troops to help the Ottomans in the Crimean War (1853) and in 1851 granted the British the right to construct a railroad between Alexandria and Cairo, thus countering the French-inspired Suez Canal project. He died when strangled by two servants at his palace in Banha.

Abbasid dynasty \ə-'ba-səd\ (750–1258) Second dynasty of the Muslim Empire of the Caliphate, succeeding the UMAYYAD DYNASTY. It was named after al-Abbas (566–c. 633), uncle of MUHAMMAD, from whom all its CALIPHS were descended. The Abbasids refocused their attention to the east of Arabia, moving the capital city to BAGHDAD and taking over much of the Persian tradition of government. Under their rule, Arab culture and empire reached new heights and Islam gained non-Arab converts. The greatest Muslim contributions to science and philosophy were made during this period, sometimes regarded as the golden age of Islam. The Abbasids' hold on power began to weaken when non-Muslim mercenaries were recruited into the army and invaders from the east demanded civil autonomy for areas they controlled. Gradually the caliphate's power became largely spiritual. The dynasty fell to the MONGOLS after a siege of Baghdad.

Abbate \äb-'bä-tā\, **Niccolo dell'** *or* **Niccolo dell'Abate** (1509/12–1571) Italian painter. He was trained in Modena and developed his mature style under the influence of his contemporaries CORREGGIO and PARMIGIANINO in Bologna (1544–52). There he painted portraits and decorated palaces with frescoes of landscapes and figure compositions in the Mannerist style. In 1552 he was invited by Henry II of France to work under PRIMATICCIO at the Palace of FONTAINEBLEAU, where he executed immense murals (most now lost). He remained in France the rest of his life. His mythological landscapes were a principal source of the French classical landscape tradition, and he was a precursor of CLAUDE LORRAIN and NICOLAS POUSSIN.

Abbe \'ab-ē\, **Cleveland** (1838–1916) U.S. meteorologist. Born in New York City, he was trained as an astronomer and appointed director of the Cincinnati Observatory in 1868. His interest turned to meteorology, and he inaugurated a public weather service that served as a model for the national weather service, which was organized shortly thereafter as a branch of the (U.S. Army) Signal Service. In 1871 he was appointed chief meteorologist of the branch, which in 1891 was reorganized under civilian control as the U.S. Weather Bureau (later the National Weather Service), and he served in that capacity more than 45 years.

abbey Complex of buildings housing a MONASTERY or convent under the direction of an abbot or abbess, serving the needs of a self-contained religious community. The first abbey was MONTE CASSINO in Italy, founded in 529 by St. BENEDICT OF NURSIA. The CLOISTER linked the most important elements of an abbey together. The dormitory was often built over the dining hall on the eastern side of the cloister and linked to the central church. The western side of the cloister provided for public dealings, with the gatehouse controlling the only opening to the outer, public courtyard. On the southern side of the cloister were a central kitchen, brewery, and workshops. The novitiate and infirmary were housed in a building with its own chapel, bathhouse, dining hall, kitchen, and garden. In the 12th–13th century, many abbeys were built throughout Europe, especially in France.

The ruins of Fountains Abbey, a Cistercian monastery founded in the 12th century, near Ripon, North Yorkshire, England.

ANDY WILLIAMS

Abbey, Edward (1927–1989) U.S. writer and environmentalist. Born in Home, Pa., he earned degrees from the University of New Mexico, then worked as a park ranger and fire lookout for the National Park Service. He wrote on consumer culture's encroachment on the wilderness of southeastern Utah in *Desert Solitaire* (1968). His 1975 novel *The Monkey Wrench Gang*, describing the exploits of a band of guerrilla environmentalists, inspired numerous real-life activists. His many other works include its posthumously published sequel, *Hayduke Lives!* (1990).

Abbey Theatre Dublin theater. It developed from the Irish Literary Theatre, founded in 1899 by WILLIAM BUTLER YEATS and Lady AUGUSTA GREGORY to foster Irish drama. After moving the troupe to a renovated theater on Abbey Street in 1904, they codirected its productions with JOHN MILLINGTON SYNGE, staged their own plays, and commissioned works by SEAN O'CASEY and others. Important premieres included Synge's *The Playboy of the Western World* (1907) and O'Casey's *The Plough and the Stars* (1926). The Abbey became the first state-subsidized theater in the English-speaking world in 1924. A fire destroyed the original playhouse in 1951, and a new theater was built in 1966.

Abbott, Berenice (1898–1991) U.S. photographer. Born in Springfield, Ohio, she left in 1918 to study in New York, Paris, and Berlin. In Paris she became an assistant to MAN RAY and EUGENE ATGET. In 1925 she set up her own studio and made portraits of Parisian expatriates, artists, writers, and collectors. She retrieved and catalogued Atget's prints and negatives after his death. In the 1930s, she photographed New York's neighborhoods for the WPA FEDERAL ART PROJECT, documenting its changing architecture; many of the photographs were published in *Changing New York* (1939).

Abbott, George (Francis) (1887–1995) U.S. theater director, producer, and playwright. Born in Forestville, N.Y., he began his career in 1913 as an actor in Broadway plays. He began writing and directing plays, achieving the first of many hits with *The Fall Guy* (1925). He also wrote, directed, or produced the popular musicals *The Boys from Syracuse* (1938), *Pal Joey* (1940), *Where's Charley* (1948), *Wonderful Town* (1953), and *Damn Yankees* (1955). He was active in the theater into the 1980s, directing a revival of *On Your Toes* at age 95.

Abbott, Grace (1878–1939) U.S. social worker, public administrator, educator, and reformer. Born in Grand Island, Neb., she did graduate work at the University of Chicago and began working at JANE ADDAMS Hull House in 1908. That same year she cofounded the Immigrants' Protective League in Chicago. As director of the U.S. Children's Bureau 1921–34, she fought to end child labor through legislation and federal contract policies, and proposed a constitutional amendment prohibiting child labor. Her best-known book is *The Child and the State* (2 vols., 1938).

Abbott, John (Joseph Caldwell) *later* **Sir John** (1821–1893) Canadian prime minister (1891–92). Born in St. Andrews, Lower Canada (now St.-André-Est, Quebec), he practiced law from 1847 and became dean of McGill University law school (1855–80). He was elected to the legislative assembly (1857–74, 1880–87). In 1887 he was appointed to the Senate and became government leader. After JOHN MACDONALD's death, Abbott became the compromise choice for prime minister. Ill health forced his resignation in 1892.

Abbott, Lyman (1835–1922) U.S. minister. Son of the writer Jacob Abbott (1803–1879), in 1881 he became editor in chief of HENRY WARD BEECHER's weekly *Christian Union.* In 1888 he succeeded to Beecher's pulpit in Brooklyn. A leading exponent of the SOCIAL GOSPEL movement, he worked to apply Christianity to social and industrial problems, rejected both socialism and laissez-faire economics, and sought to interpret rather than condemn the effect of the theory of evolution on religion, in such books as *Christianity and Social Problems* (1897).

Lyman Abbott, 1901.
BY COURTESY OF THE LIBRARY OF CONGRESS, WASHINGTON, D.C.

Abbott and Costello U.S. comedy team, prominent in VAUDEVILLE from 1931 and on radio from 1938. Bud (originally William Alexander) Abbott (1895–1974) was born in Asbury Park, N.J.; Lou (originally Louis Francis) Costello (1906–1959) was born in Woodland Hills, Cal. Their first successful film, *Buck Privates* (1941), was followed by over 30 other SLAPSTICK comedies, with tall, thin Abbott playing straight man to short, plump Costello, the buffoon. Their famous routine "Who's on First?" was first performed in the film *The Naughty Nineties* (1945).

abbreviation Shortened form of a written word or phrase used in place of the whole. Abbreviations have proliferated in the 19th and 20th century; they are employed to reduce the time required for writing or speaking, especially when referring to new organizations, bureaucratic entities, and technological products. An abbreviation can easily become a word, either an initialism in which the letter names are pronounced individually (e.g., TV or FBI) or an acronym in which the letters are combined into syllables (e.g., scuba, laser, or NAFTA).

ABC *in full* **American Broadcasting Co.** Major U.S. television network. It began when the expanding national radio network NBC split into the separate Red and Blue networks in 1928. To avoid a communications monopoly, NBC was forced to sell the Blue network in 1941. Its buyer, Edward J. Noble, maker of Life-Savers candies, gave the company its present name. After merging with United Paramount Theaters in 1953, ABC expanded into the emerging television industry and soon became one of the three top networks. It was bought by Capital Cities Communications in 1985 and by the Walt Disney Co. in 1995.

Abd al-Krim \ˌab-dəl-ˈkrēm\ *in full* **Muhammad ibn Abd al-Karim al Khattabi** (1882–1963) BERBER resistance leader against Spanish and French rule in northern Morocco. As chief Muslim judge for Morocco's Melilla district, he became disillusioned with Spanish policies and eventually led a resistance movement with his brother. He set up the Republic of the RIF in 1921 and became its president. In 1926 France and Spain amassed 250,000 men to force his surrender. Exiled to Réunion, in 1947 he received permission to live in France, but took asylum in Egypt while en route to France. When Morocco became independent (1956), MUHAMMAD V invited him to return, but he refused because of the continued presence of French troops in North Africa.

Abd al-Malik ibn Marwan \ˌab-dəl-ˈmal-ik-ˌib-ən-mär-ˈwan\ (646/67–705) Fifth caliph (685–705) of the UMAYYAD DYNASTY. Raised in Medina, he was forced out with his father in 683 by rebels against Damascus-based Umayyad rule. Two years later he succeeded to the caliphate and began a seven-year campaign to defeat all rebellions against the Umayyads and reunify the Muslim world. He resumed the conquest of North Africa, winning the Berbers to his side and capturing Carthage (697). His good relations with the Medina clergy led many to abandon their opposition to the Umayyads. He made Arabic the language of government throughout his domains, struck new, Islamic gold coins to replace Byzantine ones, and built the DOME OF THE ROCK in Jerusalem.

Abd al-Mumin ibn Ali \ˌab-dəl-ˈmu̇-min-ˌib-ən-ȧ-ˈlē\ (died 1163) BERBER caliph (1130–63) of the ALMOHAD DYNASTY. Around 1117 he fell under the sway of Ibn Tumart, founder of the Almohad religious movement, and joined him in opposing the ruling ALMORAVID DYNASTY. He succeeded Ibn Tumart on the latter's death in 1130 and for the next 17 years carried on the struggle against the Almoravids. After defeating them at Marrakech in 1147, he massacred the city's inhabitants, then made Marrakech his home and conquered all of North Africa west of Egypt.

Abd al-Rahman III \ˌab-dəl-räk-ˈmän\ (891–961) First CALIPH and greatest ruler of the Umayyad Arab Muslim dynasty of Spain. He succeeded his grandfather Abdullah as emir of CÓRDOBA in 912. He set out to subdue Muslim rebels in their mountain fortresses, which became an annual task until the fall of Toledo in 933. Addressing the Christian threat to the north, he led the campaigns of Muez (920) and Navarre (924). In 928 he declared himself caliph. By 958 he had Christian kings paying him homage. During his rule, Córdoba was exemplary for its social, political, and cultural development; Christian and Jewish communities flourished, and the city's fame rivaled that of Constantinople.

Abd al-Samad (fl. 16th century) Persian miniature painter. Born in Iran, he traveled to India and became one of the first members of the imperial atelier there. Through their teachings in India, he and fellow countryman MIR SAYYID ALI played a strong role in the foundation of the school of MUGHAL PAINTING. Abd al-Samad supervised the majority of illustrations in the Mughal manuscript *Dastan-e Amir Hamzeh* ("Stories of Amir Hamzeh"), which included about 1,400 paintings. Favored at court, in 1576 he was appointed master of the mint, and in 1584 he was made *dewan* (revenue commissioner) of Multan.

Abd Allah (ibn Muhammad al-Taiishi) \ˌäb-du̇l-ˈlä\ *or* **Abdullahi** \əb-ˌdu̇l-ä-ˈhē\ (1846–1899) Political and religious leader who succeeded Muhammad Ahmad (al-Mahdi) as head of the MAHDIST MOVEMENT in Sudan in 1885. He launched attacks against the Ethiopians and invaded Egypt, securing his position by 1891. In 1896 Anglo-Egyptian forces began to reconquer the Sudan. Abd Allah resisted until 1898, when he was forced to flee OMDURMAN. He died in battle one year later.

Abdelqadir al-Jazairi \ˌab-dəl-ˈkäd-ər-al-jaz-ˈa-i-rē\ (1808–1883) Founder of Algeria and leader of its struggle against the French. His father, Mahieddin, had led a harassment campaign against the French, who invaded Algeria in 1830. Abdelqadir succeeded his father as emir in 1832; by 1837, through battles and treaties, he had established his rule over most of Algeria's interior. He organized a true state, imposing equal taxes and suppressing the privileges of the warlike tribes. He fortified the interior towns, opened arsenals and workshops, and expanded education. The French overpowered him by 1846. Revered for his exemplary life and ideals, he died respected by both French and Algerians, and he remains the Algerian national hero.

Abdera \ab-ˈdir-ə\ City of ancient THRACE on the Aegean Sea nearly opposite THASOS. First settled in the 7th century BC, it was colonized a second time c. 540 BC. A prosperous member of the DELIAN LEAGUE, it was crippled in the 4th century BC by Thracian invasions.

abdominal cavity Largest hollow space of the body, between the DIAPHRAGM and the top of the pelvic cavity and surrounded by the spine and the ABDOMINAL MUSCLES and others. It contains most of the ALIMENTARY CANAL, the LIVER and PANCREAS, the SPLEEN, the KIDNEYS, and the ADRENAL GLANDS. It is lined by the peritoneum, a membrane covering the cavity's inside wall (parietal peritoneum) and each organ or structure in it (visceral peritoneum). Disorders include ascites (fluid in the peritoneal cavity) and PERITONITIS.

abdominal muscle Any of the muscles of the front and side walls of the ABDOMINAL CAVITY. Three flat layers—the external oblique, internal oblique, and transverse abdominis muscles—extend from each side of the spine between the lower ribs and the hipbone. The abdominal muscles attach to aponeuroses, connective tissue sheaths that merge toward the midline, sheathing the rectus abdominis muscle on each side of the midline. The abdominal muscles support and protect the internal organs, and take part in exhaling, coughing, urinating, defecating, childbirth, and motion of the trunk, groin, and lower limbs.

Abduh \ˈab-dü\, **Muhammad** (1849–1905) Egyptian religious scholar, jurist, and liberal reformer. As a student in Cairo he came under the influence of JAMAL AL-DIN AL-AFGHANI. He was exiled for political radicalism 1882–88; he began his judicial career when he returned to Egypt. He rose from judge to mufti (legal counselor) in 1899. In his *Treatise on the Oneness of God,* he argued that Islam was superior to Christianity because it was more receptive to science and civilization. He liberalized Islamic law and administration, promoting considerations of equity, welfare, and common sense, even when this meant disregarding the literal texts of the Quran.

Abdul-Jabbar \ˌab-dəl-jə-ˈbär\, **Kareem** *orig.* **(Ferdinand) Lew(is) Alcindor** (born 1947) U.S. basketball player. Born in New York City, he reached a height of 7 ft 1⅜ in. (2 m 17 cm). During his college career at UCLA, the team lost only two games, and he led it to three national championships (1966–68). He then joined the Milwaukee Bucks; in 1975 he was traded to the Los Angeles Lakers. The dominant center of his time, in 1984 he surpassed WILT CHAMBERLAIN's career scoring total of 31,419 points, and by the time he retired in 1989 he had scored a record 38,387 points. He also holds the record for most field goals (15,837), ranks second for most blocked shots (3,189) and games played (1,560), and ranks third for rebounds (17,440). He was voted Most Valuable Player a record six times.

Abdul Rahman Putra Alhaj \ˈab-dül-rä-ˈmän-ˈpu̇t-rə-al-ˈhaj\, **Tunku (Prince)** (1903–1990) First prime minister of independent Malaya (1957–63) and then of Malaysia (1963–70). He was educated in England and served in the Malayan Federal Legal Department (1949–51) before pursuing a career in politics. As president of the United Malays National Organization, Abdul Rahman brought Chinese and Indian political groups into the Alliance Party, which won an overwhelming majority in the 1955 election. He negotiated for Malayan independence from Britain (achieved in 1957); the federation of Malaysia was formed in 1963.

Abdülhamid II \ˌab-dəl-ha-ˈmēd\ (1842–1918) Ottoman sultan (1876–1909) under whose rule the TANZIMAT reform movement reached its climax. After initially promoting the first Ottoman constitution (primarily to ward off foreign intervention), he suspended it 14 months later and ruled thereafter as a despot. He used Pan-Islamism to rally Muslim opinion outside his empire; the Hejaz Railway was built with foreign contributions. Discontent with his absolutist rule and resentment over European intervention in the Balkans resulted in his overthrow by the YOUNG TURKS in 1908. See also MUSTAFA KEMAL ATATURK, ENVER PASA, MIDHAT PASA.

Abdullahi See ABD ALLAH

Abel See CAIN AND ABEL

Abelard, Peter (1079–1142) French theologian and philosopher. The son of a knight, he abandoned his inheritance to study philosophy. He became private tutor to Héloïse, niece of a canon in Paris, c. 1114. They fell in love and married secretly. Her wrathful uncle had Abelard castrated, after which he became a monk and Héloïse became a nun. Abelard's *Theologia* was condemned as heretical in 1121. He accepted election as abbot of a monastery in Brittany in 1125, but his relations with the community deteriorated and he had to flee for his life. From c. 1135 Abelard taught and wrote at Mont-Sainte-Geneviève, where he wrote *Ethica,* in which he analyzed the notion of sin. In 1140 he was again condemned for heresy, and he withdrew to the monastery at CLUNY. His other works include *Sic et non,* a collection of contradictory writings by church fathers.

Abenaki \ˌa-bə-ˈnä-kē\ *or* **Abnaki** Confederacy of ALGONQUIAN-speaking Indian peoples in northeastern North America organized to resist the IROQUOIS CONFEDERACY, especially the MOHAWK. It consisted principally of the Malecite, Passamaquoddy, and Penobscot peoples. In the 17th century the Abenaki sided with the French against the English, but after severe defeats they withdrew to Canada, eventually settling at Saint-François-du-Lac in Quebec. Their current population is about 1,000.

Abeokuta \ä-ˈbā-ō-ˌkü-tä\ City (pop., 1996 est.: 424,000), southwestern Nigeria. Located about 60 mi (96 km) north of LAGOS, Abeokuta was established c. 1830 as a refuge from slave hunters. It was the chief town of the Egbas, who long maintained a working relationship with the British; not until 1914 was it incorporated into British Nigeria. The modern town is an agricultural and exporting center.

Aberdeen City (pop., 1995 est.: 219,000) and commercial port on the North Sea, eastern Scotland. Situated at the mouths of the Dee and Don rivers, it is the chief port of northern Scotland. It was a royal burgh from the 12th century and a Scottish royal residence in the 12th–14th century. It supported ROBERT THE BRUCE in wars for Scottish independence, and for a time was the headquarters of EDWARD I. From the 1970s Aberdeen developed rapidly as the principal British center of the North Sea oil industry and its associated service and supply industries. It is the headquarters for the administrative region of GRAMPIAN.

Aberdeen, Earl of *orig.* **George Gordon** *or* **George Hamilton-Gordon** (1784–1860) British foreign secretary and prime minister (1852–55). As special ambassador to Austria in 1813, he helped form the coalition that defeated NAPOLEON. As foreign secretary (1828–30, 1841–46), he settled boundary disputes between Canada and the U.S. with the WEBSTER-ASHBURTON TREATY and the Oregon Treaty (see OREGON QUESTION). As prime minister, he formed a coalition government, but his indecision hampered peacekeeping efforts, and led to Britain's involvement in the CRIMEAN WAR. Constitutionally responsible for the mistakes of British generals in the war, he resigned in 1855.

Aberhart \ˈā-bər-ˌhärt\, **William** (1878–1943) Canadian politician, first SOCIAL CREDIT PARTY premier (Alberta, 1935–43). Born in Kippen, Ontario, he was a high-school principal in Calgary (1915–35). An active lay preacher, he founded the Calgary Prophetic Bible Institute (1918). In 1932 he used his evangelical rhetoric to promote monetary-reform theories to solve Alberta's economic problems of the Great Depression, proposing to issue dividends (social credit) to each person, based on the real wealth of the province. When his party won a majority in the 1935 provincial election, he became premier and minister of education, but his social-credit proposals were disallowed by the federal government.

Abernathy \ˈab-ər-ˌnath-ē\, **Ralph David** (1926–1990) U.S. pastor and civil-rights leader. Born in Linden, Ala., he was ordained a Baptist minister in 1948 and led a church in Montgomery, Ala., where he met MARTIN LUTHER KING. In 1955–56 the two men organized a nonviolent boycott of the city bus system, which marked the beginning of the civil-rights movement. In 1957 they founded the SOUTHERN CHRISTIAN LEADERSHIP CONFERENCE. Abernathy became its president on King's assassination in 1968; in 1977 he resigned to resume work as a pastor in Atlanta.

aberration Deviation of light rays by LENSES or mirrors which causes the images to be blurred. Spherical aberration occurs because curvature in a lens or mirror causes rays falling on the outer edges to be brought to a focus at a different point from those from the middle. This makes the images formed appear blurred. Chromatic aberration, which occurs in lenses but not mirrors, is the failure of a lens to focus all colors (WAVELENGTHS) of light in the same plane; the image appears blurred and shows rainbow-colored fringes around the edges. See also ASTIGMATISM.

aberration of starlight Apparent displacement of a star or other celestial body resulting from earth's orbital motion around the sun. The maximum displacement is about 20.49 seconds of arc. It depends on the ratio of earth's orbital speed to the speed of light and the earth's direction of motion, and thus provides confirmation that the earth orbits the sun rather than the reverse.

Aberystwyth \ˌa-bə-ˈris-ˌtwith\ Municipal borough (pop., 1985 est.: 12,600), western Wales, on CARDIGAN BAY. The medieval walled town was built around a 13th-century fortress. It later became the exporter for the once-flourishing local lead mines. A principal stronghold of Welsh culture, in recent years it has grown as a seaside resort.

Abhayagiri \äb-ˈyä-gə-rē\ THERAVADA Buddhist monastic center built at Anuradhapura, then capital of Ceylon, by King Vattagamani Abhaya (r.29–17 BC). Originally associated with the nearby Mahavihara ("Great Monastery"), it soon seceded in a dispute over the relations between monks and the lay community and the use of Sanskrit works to augment Pali texts as scripture. It gained wealth and power under the patronage of Gajabahu I (AD 113–35) and flourished until Anuradhapura was abandoned in the 13th century. Two of its main colleges operated into the 16th century.

Abhidhamma Pitaka \ˌä-bi-ˈdä-mə-ˈpē-tə-kə\ Third and latest collection of texts comprising the Pali canon (see TRIPITAKA) of THERAVADA Buddhism. The first two collections, SUTTA PITAKA and VINAYA PITAKA, are attributed to the BUDDHA. Abhidhamma Pitaka texts are ascribed to later disciples and scholars; they deal with ethics, psychology, and epistemology.

Abhidharmakosa \ˌä-bi-ˌdär-mə-ˈkō-sə\ Buddhist scholarly work that provides an introduction to the seven Abhidharma treatises in the SARVASTIVADA canon and a digest of their contents. It was composed by the Buddhist monk Vasubandhu (fl. 4th or 5th century), who lived in northwestern India. It systematizes Sarvastivada doctrine and shows the influence of MAHAYANA, to which Vasubandhu later converted. It provides much information on doctrinal differences among the ancient Buddhist schools.

abhijna \ə-ˈbij-nə\ In Buddhist philosophy, the miraculous powers obtained through meditation and wisdom. They include the ability to travel any distance or take any form at will, to see everything, to hear everything, to read minds, and to recall former existences. A sixth miraculous power, available only to BUDDHAS and ARHATS (saints), is freedom by undefiled wisdom (Enlightenment). The powers are signs of spiritual progress but their indulgence is a distraction from the path toward Enlightenment.

Abidjan \ˌä-bē-ˈjän\ Largest city (pop., 1996 est.: 2,500,000) and chief port of Ivory Coast. Abidjan was a rail terminus from 1904; after its lagoon was opened to the sea to create a port (1950), the city became the financial center of FRENCH WEST AFRICA. Though it was once the country's capital and remains its seat of government, the official capital was moved to YAMOUSSOUKRO in 1983. Abidjan has a museum of traditional Ivorian art, a national library, and several research institutes.

Abilene Town (pop., 1996 est.: 6,500), Kansas. It lies on the Smoky Hill River east of Salina. Settled in 1858, it gained importance when it became the railway terminus for Texas cattle drives, and acquired a reputation for lawlessness; Wild Bill HICKOK was its marshal in 1871. Pres. DWIGHT D. EISENHOWER spent his boyhood there and is buried at the Eisenhower Center, which includes his family home and library.

Abilene City (pop., 1994 est.: 110,000), northwestern Texas. Founded in 1881 as the new railhead for the overland Texas cattle drives, it took the business of the previous railhead, Abilene, Kan. It is the site of several educational institutions, the West Texas Fair, and the reconstructed Old Abilene Town.

Abnaki See ABENAKI

abnormal psychology *or* **psychopathology** Branch of psychology concerned with mental and emotional disorders (e.g., NEUROSIS, PSYCHOSIS, mental deficiency) and with certain incompletely understood normal phenomena (such as DREAMS and HYPNOSIS). The chief tool used in classifying psychological disorders is the American Psychiatric Assn.'s *Diagnostic and Statistical Manual of Mental Disorders,* 4th edition *(DSM-IV).*

ABO blood-group system Classification of human BLOOD according to whether red blood cells (ERYTHROCYTES) have or lack the inherited ANTIGENS called A (including A1 and A2) and B on their surface. Blood can be type O (lacking both), type A (having only A), type B (having only B), or type AB (having both). The ABO antigens make certain blood types incompatible for transfusion. They are developed well before birth and remain through life. The frequencies of blood groups vary among different racial groups and in different geographic areas. Certain diseases are rarer in persons with particular blood groups.

abolitionism (c. 1783–1888) Movement to end the SLAVE TRADE and emancipate slaves in western Europe and the Americas. Antislavery sentiment gradually gained support in England in the 18th century, but initially had little impact on the centers of slavery—the West Indies, South America, and the southern U.S. In 1807 British and U.S. abolitionists successfully banned the importation of African slaves, and turned their attention to winning the emancipation of slaves already in captivity. The 11 Southern states of the U.S., however, clung to slavery as a social and economic institution. The AMERICAN ANTI-SLAVERY SOCIETY fueled the abolitionist movement in the North. Major American abolitionist figures included WILLIAM LLOYD GARRISON, FREDERICK DOUGLASS, and HARRIET BEECHER STOWE. The election of ABRAHAM LINCOLN, who opposed the spread of slavery into the West, marked the issue's turning point; the resulting SECESSION of the Southern states led to the AMERICAN CIVIL WAR, which in turn led to the EMANCIPATION PROCLAMATION (1863) and the 13th Amendment to the U.S. Constitution (1865), freeing all slaves in the nation. Slavery was finally abolished in Latin America by 1888.

Abominable Snowman *Tibetan* **Yeti** Mythical monster believed to inhabit the HIMALAYAS near the snow line. The Yeti is thought to resemble an oversized man covered with shaggy fur. Reported sightings are rare; evidence of its existence consists largely of unusual footprints left in the snow, probably the tracks of bears. At certain gaits, bears place the hindfoot partly over the imprint of the forefoot, thus creating tracks that resemble the footprints of a very large primate heading in the opposite direction.

Aborigine See AUSTRALIAN ABORIGINE

abortion Expulsion of a fetus from the uterus before it can survive on its own. Spontaneous abortions are called MISCARRIAGES. Induced abortions occur today through intentional medical intervention and are performed to preserve the mother's life or health, to prevent the completion of a pregnancy resulting from rape or incest, to prevent the birth of a child with serious medical problems, or because the mother does not believe she is in a position to rear a child properly. The drug RU 486, if taken within a few weeks of conception, will trigger a miscarriage. Up to about 19 weeks of pregnancy, injections of saline solutions or hormones may be used to stimulate uterine contractions that will expel the fetus. Hysterotomy, the surgical removal of the contents of the uterus, may be used in the second trimester or later. Dilation and extraction procedures, known as partial-birth abortions, have been very controversial and may occur in the third trimester. The social acceptability of abortion as a means of population control has varied from time to time and place to place throughout history. It was apparently a common method of family limitation in the Greco-Roman world, but Christian theologians early and vehemently condemned it. It became widely accepted in Europe in the Middle Ages. Severe criminal sanctions to deter abortion became common in the 19th century, but in the 20th century those sanctions were gradually modified in many countries. In the U.S., the 1973 *ROE V. WADE* decision had the effect of legalizing abortion on demand through the first three months of pregnancy; the decades since have seen fierce debate between supporters and opponents of a liberalized abortion policy. In 1995 Norma McCorvey, the "Jane Roe" of that case, reversed her position by saying she no longer supported the right to abortion.

Abraham (fl. early 2nd millennium BC) First of the Hebrew PATRIARCHS, revered by JUDAISM, CHRISTIANITY, and ISLAM. GENESIS tells how Abraham, at 75, left UR with his barren wife Sarai (later SARAH) and others to found a new nation in CANAAN. There God made a COVENANT with him, promising that his descendants would inherit the land and become a great nation. Abraham fathered Ishmael by Sarah's maidservant Hagar; Sarah herself bore Isaac, who inherited the covenant. Abraham's faith was tested when God ordered him to sacrifice Isaac; he was prepared to obey but God relented. In Judaism he is a model of virtue, in Christianity he is the father of all believers, and in Islam he is an ancestor of MUHAMMAD and a model (in SUFISM) of generosity.

Abraham, Karl (1877–1925) German psychoanalyst. He helped establish the first branch of the International Psychoanalytic Institute in 1910, and pioneered the psychoanalytic treatment of manic-depressive psychosis. He suggested that the sexual drive develops in six stages and that if development is arrested at any of the earlier stages, mental disorders will likely result from fixation at that level. His most important work was *A Short Study of the Development of the Libido* (1924).

Abraham, Plains of Plateau located southwest of the old walled city of QUEBEC, Canada. On September 13, 1759, it was the scene of the decisive battle of the FRENCH AND INDIAN WAR, in which the British under JAMES WOLFE defeated the French under the Marquis de MONTCALM. U.S. forces held the plateau (1775–76) in their siege of Quebec during the AMERICAN REVOLUTION. It is now a park within Quebec city limits.

abrasion platform See WAVE-CUT PLATFORM

abrasives Sharp, hard materials used to wear away the surface of softer, less resistant materials. Abrasives are indispensable to the manufacture of the highly precise components and ultrasmooth surfaces required in the manufacture of automobiles, airplanes and space vehicles, mechanical and electrical appliances, and machine tools. Abrasives may be natural (e.g., DIAMOND, CORUNDUM, EMERY) or synthetic (e.g., silicon CARBIDE or CARBORUNDUM, synthetic diamond, alumina—a synthetic form of corundum). They range from the relatively soft particles used in household cleansers and jeweler's polish to diamonds.

Abruzzi \ä-ˈbrüt-sē\ Autonomous region (pop., 1996 est.: 1,271,000), central Italy. Its capital is L'Aquila. Most of the region is mountainous or hilly and includes the Apennines. The ancient Italic tribes of the region long resisted conquest by the Romans. The Normans established themselves in the 12th century, and the region later sided with the Hohenstaufens against the papacy. As Abruzzi e Molise, the area became part of the Kingdom of Italy in 1861; in 1965 it was divided into the separate regions of Abruzzi and Molise. The economy is primarily agricultural.

Absalom (fl. c. 1020 BC) In ancient Israel, the third and most beloved son of David. His story is told in II Samuel 13–19. An attractive but lawless man, he killed his half-brother Amnon as revenge for the latter's rape of Tamar, Absalom's sister, and was banished from the kingdom for a time. He later raised a rebellion against his father, capturing Jerusalem but meeting defeat in the forest of Ephraim, where he was killed by his cousin Joab, who found him caught by the hair in an oak tree. Despite Absalom's treachery, David greatly lamented his death.

Absaroka Range \ab-ˈsär-ə-kə\ Range of the Rocky Mtns. It extends from southern Montana across Yellowstone National Park into northwestern Wyoming, crossing portions of Gallatin, Shoshone, and Custer national forests. It is about 175 mi (280 km) long; its highest point is Franks Peak, at 13,140 ft (4,005 m).

abscess \ˈab-ˌses\ Localized collection of pus in a cavity on the skin surface or within the body, formed from tissues broken down by white blood cells (leukocytes) in response to inflammation caused by bacteria. A wall develops, separating the thick yellowish pus (formed from broken-down tissues, dead bacteria, and leukocytes) from the extracellular fluid of nearby healthy tissues. Rupture of the abscess allows the pus to escape and relieves swelling and pain. Treatment consists of cutting into the wall to drain the pus and giving antibiotics and perhaps antihistamines. If infective contents enter the bloodstream, they may be carried to surrounding tissues, seeding new abscesses.

absentee ownership Ownership of land by those who do not live on it but who enjoy income from it. Criticized for centuries as an economic injustice, absentee ownership was a feature of pre-Revolutionary France and English rule of Ireland. Ending the practice continues to be a goal of land-reform programs in many developing countries.

absolute value Measure of the magnitude of a real number, complex number, or vector. Geometrically, the absolute value of any real number is its distance from zero. Thus if the number a is positive or zero, its absolute value is itself; if a is negative, its absolute value is $-a$. The absolute value of the complex number $a + bi$ (also called the *modulus*) is the real number $\sqrt{a^2 + b^2}$. This is also a distance from the origin when the complex number is represented by the ordered pair (a,b). The absolute value of a vector is its length, which in Euclidean space is the square root of the sum of the squares of its components. In all three cases, absolute value is symbolized by vertical bars, as in $|x|$, $|z|$, or $|\mathbf{v}|$. Such expressions are always nonnegative and obey the properties $|a \cdot b| = |a| \cdot |b|$ and $|a + b| \leq |a| + |b|$.

absolute zero Temperature at which a thermodynamic system (see thermodynamics) has the lowest energy, 0 kelvin (K). It corresponds to −459.67°F (−273.15°C) and is the lowest possible temperature theoretically achievable by a system. A gas at constant pressure contracts as the temperature is decreased. A perfect gas would reach zero volume at absolute zero. However, a real gas condenses to a liquid or a solid at a temperature higher than absolute zero. At absolute zero, the system's molecular energy is minimal and none is available for transfer to other systems. The Kelvin temperature scale has absolute zero as its zero point, and its fundamental unit is the kelvin.

absolution In Christianity, a pronouncement of forgiveness of sins made to a person who has repented. This rite is based on the forgiveness that Jesus extended to sinners during his ministry. In the early church, the priest absolved repentant sinners after they had confessed and performed their penance in public. During the Middle Ages, it became the custom for priests to hear confession and grant absolution privately. In Roman Catholicism penance is a sacrament, and the priest has the power to absolve a contrite sinner who promises to make satisfaction to God. In Protestant churches, the confession of sin is usually made in a formal prayer by the whole congregation, after which the minister announces their absolution.

absolutism Political doctrine and practice of unlimited, centralized authority and absolute sovereignty, especially as vested in a monarch. Its essence is that the ruling power is not subject to regular challenge or check by any judicial, legislative, religious, economic, or electoral agency. Though it has been used throughout history, the form that developed in early modern Europe (16th–18th century) became the prototype; Louis XIV is seen as the epitome of European absolutism. Religious authority was assumed by the monarch, who became the head of the church as well as the state, on the basis that the right to rule came from God (see divine kingship). See also authoritarianism, dictatorship, totalitarianism.

absorption Transfer of energy from a wave to the medium through which it passes. The energy of the wave can be reflected, transmitted, or absorbed. If the medium absorbs only a fraction of the energy, it is said to be transparent to that energy. When all energy is absorbed, the medium is opaque. All substances absorb energy to some extent. For instance, the ocean appears transparent to sunlight near the surface, but becomes opaque with depth. Substances absorb specific types of radiation. Rubber is transparent to infrared radiation and X rays, but opaque to visible light. Green glass is transparent to green light but absorbs red and blue light. Absorption of sound is fundamental to acoustics; a soft material absorbs sound energy as the waves strike it.

abstract art *or* **nonobjective art** *or* **nonrepresentational art** Art, including painting, sculpture, and graphic art, that does not represent recognizable objects. In the late 19th century, the traditional European conception of art as the imitation of nature was abandoned in favor of the imagination and the unconscious. Abstraction developed in the early 20th century with such movements as Fauvism, Expressionism, Cubism, and Futurism. Vassily Kandinsky is credited as the first modern artist to paint purely abstract pictures, c. 1910. The Dada group in Zurich and Piet Mondrian and the Netherlands' De Stijl group widened the spectrum c. 1915–20. Abstraction continued to flourish between the two world wars, and after the 1930s it was the most characteristic feature of 20th-century art. After World War II, Abstract Expressionism emerged in the U.S. and had a great influence on European and American painting and sculpture.

Abstract Expressionism Movement in U.S. painting that began in the late 1940s. It had two notable forerunners, Arshile Gorky and Hans Hofmann. The arrival in the late 1930s and early 1940s of many European avant-garde artists greatly influenced the New York painters, most prominent among them Jackson Pollock, Willem de Kooning, Franz Kline, and Mark Rothko. The movement comprised many styles but shared several characteristics. The works were usually abstract (i.e., they depicted forms not found in the natural world); they emphasized freedom of emotional expression, technique, and execution; they displayed a single unified, undifferentiated field, network, or other image in unstructured space; and the canvases were large, to enhance the visual effect and project monumentality and power. The movement had a great impact on U.S. and European art in the 1950s; it marked the shift of the creative center of modern painting from Paris to New York. See also abstract art, action painting.

absurd, theater of the Body of dramatic works of the 1950s and '60s that expressed the existentialist philosophy of meaninglessness and the absurdity of life. Such playwrights as Arthur Adamov, Edward Albee, Samuel Beckett, Jean Genet, Eugene Ionesco, and Harold Pinter created absurdist plays without traditional plots and with characters who engaged in circular, purposeless conversations. Beckett's *Waiting for Godot* (1953), in which two tramps wait for a mysterious man who never arrives, is a classic of the genre.

Abu al-Hasan al-Ashari See Abu al-Hasan al-Ashari

Abu Bakr \ə-ˌbü-ˈbä-kər\ (573?–634) Muhammad's father-in-law, adviser, and close companion. Some Muslim traditions say he was the first male convert to Islam after Muhammad. He became the first caliph after Muhammad's death in 632, and during his two years as caliph he consolidated central Arabia under Muslim control, ending the resistance to Muslim hegemony that ensued. He also realized the urgency of rapidly expanding the regions under Muslim control if peace was to be maintained among Arab tribes.

Abu Dhabi Largest constituent emirate (pop., 1995 est.: 928,000) of the UNITED ARAB EMIRATES. Its rich oil fields make it, after DUBAYY, the federation's most prosperous emirate. It fronts the PERSIAN GULF for about 280 mi (450 km) and borders Qatar, Saudi Arabia, and Oman. Since the 18th century the Al bu Falah clan of the Bani Yas has held power. In 1761 they found wells of potable water at the site of ABU DHABI city, and they made their headquarters there from 1795. In the 19th century territorial conflicts between Abu Dhabi, MASQAT and Oman, and the ancestors of the present ruling class of Saudi Arabia led to border disputes, most still unsettled. Abu Dhabi signed an agreement with Great Britain in 1892 placing foreign affairs under British control. When Britain withdrew from the Persian Gulf in 1968, Abu Dhabi and the other Trucial States formed the United Arab Emirates.

Abu Dhabi City (pop., 1989 est.: 363,000), capital of ABU DHABI emirate and national capital of the United Arab Emirates. It occupies most of the small island of Abu Dhabi, which is connected to the mainland by bridge. Settled in 1761, it was of little importance until the discovery in 1958 of the emirate's rich oil fields. Oil royalties revolutionized its political and economic position, and it has ambitiously modernized.

Abu Hanifah (al-Numan ibn Thabit) \ə-ˌbü-hä-'nē-fə\ (699–767) Muslim jurist and theologian. The son of a merchant in Kufah, Iraq, he gained wealth in the silk trade and studied law under the noted jurist Hammad. After Hammad's death (738), Abu Hanifah became his successor. He was the first to develop systematic legal doctrines from the accumulated Islamic legal tradition. Primarily a scholar, he neither accepted a judgeship nor took direct part in court politics; he supported the successors of ALI over the ruling UMAYYAD and ABBASID dynasties. His doctrinal system became one of four canonical schools of Islamic law (SHARIA) and is still widely followed in India, Pakistan, Turkey, Central Asia, and Arab countries.

Abu Muslim \ə-ˌbü-'mu̇s-lim\ (died 755) Leader of a revolutionary movement in KHORASAN who brought down the UMAYYAD DYNASTY. Born a *mawali* (non-Arab Muslim) of humble origins, he met an Abbasid agent while in prison (741). After his arranged release he was sent to Khorasan (745–46) to instigate a revolt. Recruiting from various discontented groups, he succeeded in overthrowing the last Umayyad caliph, Marwan II, killed in battle in 750. He was rewarded with the governorship of Khorasan. His popularity led the second Abbasid caliph, Abu al-Mansur, to view him as a threat and have him put to death. See also ABBASID DYNASTY.

Abu Qir Bay \ˌä-bü-'kēr\ Inlet of the Mediterranean Sea, lying near the Rosetta mouth of the NILE in Lower Egypt. It was the scene of the Battle of the NILE (1798), in which an English fleet under HORATIO NELSON defeated the Napoleonic fleet.

Abu Simbel Site of two temples built by RAMSES II in the 13th century BC. The area, anciently at the southern frontier of pharaonic Egypt, lies near the modern Sudanese frontier. The temples were unknown to the outside world until their rediscovery in 1813. The larger temple displays four 67-ft (20-m) seated figures of Ramses; the smaller was dedicated to Queen Nefertari. When the reservoir created by the building of ASWAN HIGH DAM threatened to submerge the site in the early 1960s, an international team disassembled both temples and reconstructed them 200 ft (60 m) above the riverbed.

Sandstone figures of Ramses II in front of the main temple at Abu Simbel near Aswan, Egypt.

BY COURTESY OF AIR FRANCE

Abuja \ä-'bü-jä\ City (pop., 1995 est.: 423,000), federal capital of Nigeria. Construction of the city, at a site chosen for its central location and healthful climate about 300 mi (480 km) northwest of LAGOS, began in 1976 under the architect KENZO TANGE. It officially replaced Lagos as capital in 1991.

Abydos \ə-'bī-dəs\ Sacred city, one of the most important archaeological sites of ancient Egypt. It was a royal necropolis of the first two dynasties, and later a pilgrimage center for the worship of OSIRIS. The pharaohs, including THUTMOSE III and RAMSES III, embellished the temple to Osiris, and some pharaohs had CENOTAPHS at Abydos. The temple of Seti I, one of the most beautiful, has helped decode Egyptian history: in a long gallery is a relief, the so-called Abydos list of kings, showing Seti and his son Ramses making offerings to the cartouches of 76 dead predecessors.

Abydos Ancient Anatolian town northeast of modern Canakkale, Turkey, on the eastern side of the DARDANELLES. It was colonized c. 670 BC by the Milesians (see MILETUS). XERXES crossed the strait on a bridge of boats to invade Greece in 480 BC. Abydos is celebrated for its resistance to PHILIP V of Macedon in 200 BC and for the legend of HERO AND LEANDER.

abyssal plain \ə-'bis-əl\ Flat seafloor area at a depth of 10,000–20,000 ft (3,000–6,000 m), generally adjacent to a continent. The larger plains are hundreds of miles wide and thousands of miles long. The plains are largest and most common in the Atlantic Ocean, less common in the Indian Ocean, and even rarer in the Pacific Ocean, where they occur mainly as small, flat floors of marginal seas or as long, narrow bottoms of trenches. They are thought to be the upper surfaces of land-derived sediment that accumulates in abyssal depressions.

Abyssinia See ETHIOPIA

Abyssinian cat \ˌab-ə-'si-nē-ən\ Breed of DOMESTIC CAT, considered more similar to the sacred cat of ancient Egypt than any other living cat. It is lithe and has slender legs and a long, tapering tail. Its short, finely textured coat is ruddy reddish brown, with individual hairs distinctively ticked, or tipped, with bands of black or brown. The nose is red, and the tail tip and backs of the hindlegs are black. The Abyssinian is affectionate and quiet, though generally shy with strangers.

Abzug \'ab-zəg\, **Bella** *orig.* **Bella Savitzky** (1920–1998) U.S. lawyer and politician. Born in New York City, she studied law at Columbia University and subsequently took on numerous union, civil-liberties, and civil-rights cases, representing several people charged by Sen. JOSEPH MCCARTHY. She founded and chaired (1961–70) the antiwar Women Strike for Peace and later the National Women's Political Caucus. In the House of Representatives (1971–77), she was known for her flamboyant style and outspoken support for the Equal Rights Amendment, abortion rights, and child-care legislation and opposition to the Vietnam War.

AC See ALTERNATING CURRENT

acacia \ə-'kā-shə\ Any of the approximately 800 species of trees and shrubs that make up the genus *Acacia,* of the MIMOSA family, native to tropical and subtropical regions of the world, particularly Australia and Africa. Sweet acacia *(A. farnesiana)* is native to the southwestern U.S. Acacias have distinctive, finely divided leaflets, and their leafstalks may bear thorns or sharp spines at their base. Their small, often fragrant, yellow or white flowers have many stamens apiece, giving each a fuzzy appearance. On the plains of southern and eastern Africa, acacias are well-known landmarks. Several species are important economically, yielding substances such as gum arabic and tannin, as well as valuable timber.

Spreading wattle (*Acacia genistifolia*), an Australian acacia in which the leafstalks are flattened and function as leaves.

© RALPH AND DAPHNE KELLER/AUSTRALASIAN NATURE TRANSPARENCIES

academic degree See academic DEGREE

Académie Française \à-kà-dā-'mē-frä^n-'sez\ French literary academy established by Cardinal de RICHELIEU in 1634 to maintain standards of literary taste and to establish the literary language. In modern times it has endeavored (somewhat absurdly) to purify French of foreign loanwords. Its membership is limited to 40. Despite its conservatism, most of France's great writers, including

Pierre Corneille, Jean Racine, Voltaire, and Victor Hugo, have been members.

academy Society of learned individuals organized to advance art, science, literature, music, or some other cultural or intellectual area of endeavor. The word comes from the name of an olive grove outside ancient Athens, the site of Plato's famous school of philosophy in the 4th century BC. Academies appeared in Italy in the 15th century and reached their greatest influence in the 17th–18th century. Most European countries now have at least one academy sponsored by or otherwise connected with the state. See also Académie Française.

Academy Awards Annual awards of merit presented by the Academy of Motion Picture Arts and Sciences. The Academy was formed in 1927 by Louis B. Mayer and others to raise the standards of film production, and its first awards were presented in 1929. The awards (nicknamed Oscars when, supposedly, an Academy librarian joked that the gold-plated statuette looked like her Uncle Oscar) recognize excellence in acting, directing, screenwriting, and other activities related to film production.

Acadia North American possession of France in the 17th–18th century, centered in what is now Nova Scotia. Acadia was probably intended to include the other present Maritime Provinces as well as parts of Maine and Quebec. The first European settlement was made by the French colonizer Sieur de Monts in 1604. The area at times was also claimed by the British and was contested often in the 18th-century colonial wars; in 1713 Nova Scotia came under British rule. In 1755 many French-speaking Acadians were deported by the British because of imminent war with France; several thousand settled in French-ruled Louisiana, where their descendants were known as Cajuns. The event was the theme for Henry W. Longfellow's *Evangeline*.

Acadia National Park Preserve on the coast of Maine. It has an area of 65 sq mi (168 sq km). Originally established as Sieur de Monts National Monument (1916), it became the first national park in the eastern U.S. as Lafayette National Park (1919) and was renamed Acadia in 1929. It consists mainly of a forested area on Mount Desert Island, dominated by Cadillac Mtn.

Acadia University Privately endowed university in Wolfville, Nova Scotia. Founded in 1838, it took its current name and status in 1891. It has faculties of arts, professional studies, science, theology, education, and graduate studies. Enrollment is about 3,400.

Acadian orogeny \ə-ˈkā-dē-ən-ȯ-ˈrä-jə-nē\ Mountain-building event that affected the northern portion of the Appalachian Geosyncline from present-day New York to Newfoundland during the Devonian period. The orogeny was most intense in northern New England. Its origin has been ascribed to the collision of the northeastern portion of the North American Plate with western Europe. Evidence for the orogeny includes deformation of pre-Devonian and Devonian rocks.

acanthus \ə-ˈkan-thəs\ Any of the plants that make up the family Acanthaceae, of the figwort order, found mostly in tropical and subtropical regions. Most are herbaceous plants or shrubs; some are climbers (vines) or trees. Most grow in damp tropical forests. Acanthus have simple leaves arranged in opposite pairs on the twigs, enlarged cells called cystoliths in streaks or protuberances in the vegetative parts, and bilaterally symmetrical, bisexual flowers usually crowded together in clusters and individually enclosed by leaflike bracts, often colored and large. They are mainly of horticultural interest and include some ornamentals.

Acapulco (de Juárez) Seaport (pop., 1990: 592,000), southwestern Mexico. Situated on a deep semicircular bay, it has the best harbor on Mexico's Pacific coast. It was discovered by Hernan Cortes in 1531, and a settlement was founded in 1550. Until 1815 it was a main depot for Spanish colonial fleets going to East Asia, and especially to Manila. It has become a major international resort for tourists attracted by its scenic beauty, climate, and excellent beaches.

Acarnania \ˌa-kər-ˈnā-nē-ə\ District, ancient Greece bounded by the Ionian Sea, the Ambracian Gulf, and the Achelous River. First settled in the 7th–6th century BC, it developed into a federal state by the late 5th century; its capital was Stratus. It later came under Athenian, Theban, and Macedonian rule. Part of Acarnania recovered its independence in 231 BC and began an alliance with Philip V of Macedon. Rome overthrew the Macedonian dynasty in 167 BC, and Acarnania survived until Augustus incorporated many Acarnanians into his new city Nicopolis Actia.

acceleration Rate of change of velocity. Acceleration, like velocity, is a vector quantity: it has both magnitude and direction. The velocity of an object moving on a straight path can change in magnitude only, so its acceleration is the rate of change of its speed. On a curved path, the velocity may or may not change in magnitude, but it will always change in direction, which means that the acceleration of an object moving on a curved path can never be zero. If velocity is stated in meters per second (m/s) and the time interval in seconds (s), then the units of acceleration are meters per second per second (m/s/s, or m/s^2). See also centripetal acceleration.

accelerator, particle See particle accelerator

accelerometer \ik-ˌse-lə-ˈrä-mə-tər\ Instrument that measures acceleration. Because it is difficult to measure acceleration directly, the device measures the force exerted by restraints placed on a reference mass to hold its position fixed in an accelerating body. The output is usually either a varying electrical voltage or displacement of a moving pointer over a fixed scale. Specially designed accelerometers are used in varied applications: control of industrial vibration test equipment, detection of earthquakes (seismographs), and input to navigational and inertial guidance systems.

accent In prosody, rhythmically significant stress on the syllables of a verse, usually at regular intervals. Though the term is often used interchangeably with "stress," some prosodists use accent to mean the emphasis determined by normal language usage and stress to mean emphasis determined by metrical pattern.

acceptance Short-term credit instrument consisting of a written order that requires a buyer to pay a specified sum to the seller at a given date, signed by the buyer as a promise to honor the obligation. Acceptances are often used in export/import transactions: an exporter may require a buyer to sign and return an acceptance, which the exporter can then sell to the bank at a discount, thereby obtaining payment promptly. The buyer then has until the bill's maturity date to dispose of the goods and pay the promised sum (now owed to the bank). See also bill of exchange, promissory note.

acclimatization Any of numerous gradual, long-term responses of an individual organism to changes in its environment. The responses are more or less habitual and reversible should conditions revert to an earlier state. These criteria differentiate acclimatization from homeostasis; from growth and development (which cannot be reversed); and from evolutionary adaptation (which occurs in a population over generations). Acclimatization can occur in anticipation of a change and enable organisms to survive conditions beyond their natural experience. Examples include adaptations to seasonal changes and adjustments to changes in altitude.

accordion Portable musical instrument that uses a hand-pumped bellows and two keyboards to sound free reeds, small metal tongues that vibrate when air flows past them. The keyboards on either side of the bellows effectively resemble individual reed organs. The right-hand keyboard plays the treble line or lines. Most of the keys on the left-hand (bass) keyboard sound three-note chords; "free-bass" accordions permit the playing of single-note lines. A prototype accordion, using buttons rather than keys, was patented in 1822 by Friedrich Buschmann in Berlin (also inventor of the harmonica). The instrument gained wide popularity in dance bands and as a folk instrument. See also concertina.

Italian accordion, 19th century.
RICHARD SAUNDERS–SCOPE ASSOCIATES, INC.

account payable Any amount owed as the result of a purchase of goods or services on a credit basis. Though the purchaser issues no written promise of payment, it enters the amount owed as a current liability in its accounts. Companies often incur this type of short-term debt in order to finance their inventories, especially in industries where inventory turnover is rapid. See also account receivable.

account receivable Any amount owed as the result of a purchase of goods or services from it on a credit basis. Though the seller receives no written promise of payment, it enters the amount due as a current asset in its books. Accounts receivable constitute a major portion of the assets of many companies, and they may even be sold or pledged as collateral to obtain loans. See also ACCOUNT PAYABLE, FACTORING.

accounting Systematic development and analysis of information about the economic affairs of an organization. The actual recording and summarizing of financial transactions is known as BOOKKEEPING. When the data thus produced are abstracted in reports (usually quarterly or annual) for the use of persons outside the organization, the process is called financial accounting. Three reports are typically generated in financial accounting: the BALANCE SHEET, which summarizes the firm's assets and liabilities; the income statement, which reports the firm's gross proceeds, expenses, and profit or loss; and the statement of CASH FLOW, which analyzes the flow of cash into and out of the firm. The creation of reports (usually monthly) for internal managerial use is called managerial accounting. Its aim is to provide managers with reliable information on the costs of operations and on standards with which those costs can be compared, to assist them in budgeting.

Accra \'ä-krə, ə-'krä\ Capital and largest city (pop., 1988 est.: 949,000) of Ghana, on the Gulf of GUINEA. When the Portuguese first settled on the coast in 1482, the site was occupied by villages of the Ga tribe. In 1650–80 the Europeans built three fortified trading posts, sponsored by the English, the Danes, and the Dutch. The Danes and Dutch left the region in 1850 and 1872, respectively, and in 1877 Accra became the capital of the British GOLD COAST colony. In the later 20th century it became Ghana's administrative, economic, and educational center. Tema, 17 mi (27 km) east, has taken over Accra's former port functions.

acculturation See CULTURE CONTACT

accused, rights of the In law, the rights and privileges of a person accused of a crime. In most modern legal systems these include the presumption of innocence until proved guilty, trial by JURY, representation by counsel, the right to present witnesses and evidence to establish one's innocence, and the right to cross-examine one's accusers. Also important are prohibitions against unreasonable SEARCHES AND SEIZURES, the right to a speedy trial, and guarantees of freedom from DOUBLE JEOPARDY and of the right to APPEAL. In the U.S. a person accused of a crime must be notified immediately of the right to secure counsel and the right to refuse to answer questions if answering might be incriminating (*MIRANDA VS. ARIZONA*).

acetaminophen \ə-ˌsē-tə-'min-ə-fən\ Organic compound, a drug used to relieve mild headache or muscle and joint pain and to reduce fever. It relieves pain by raising the body's pain threshold and reduces fever by acting on the temperature-regulating center of the brain, though details of its modes of action remain unclear. Unlike ASPIRIN, it has no anti-inflammatory effect. It is also much less likely to irritate the stomach and cause ULCERS, is not linked with REYE'S SYNDROME, and can be taken by persons using ANTICOAGULANTS or allergic to aspirin. Overdosages can cause fatal liver damage. The most familiar brand name in the U.S. is Tylenol. See also IBUPROFEN.

acetate $C_2H_3O_2^-$ ion, a SALT, ESTER, or acylal derived from ACETIC ACID. Acetates are important in the biochemical synthesis of fats from carbohydrates in plants and animals. Industrially, metal acetates are used in printing, vinyl acetate in plastic production, cellulose acetate in photographic films and TEXTILES (one of the first synthetic fibers, often called simply acetate), and volatile organic esters as solvents.

acetic acid \ə-'sē-tik\ Most important CARBOXYLIC ACID (CH_3COOH). Pure ("glacial") acetic acid is a clear, syrupy, corrosive liquid that mixes readily with water. VINEGAR is its dilute solution, from FERMENTATION and oxidation (see OXIDATION-REDUCTION) of natural products. Its SALTS and ESTERS are ACETATES. It occurs naturally as a metabolic intermediate in body fluids and plant juices. Industrial production is either synthetic, from ACETYLENE, or biological, from ETHANOL. Industrial chemicals made from it are used in printing and as plastics, photographic films, textiles, and solvents.

acetone \'a-sə-ˌtōn\ *or* **dimethyl ketone** \dī-'me-thəl-'kē-ˌtōn\ Simplest and most important KETONE (CH_3COCH_3). It is a colorless, flammable liquid, boiling at 133°F (56.2°C). Many fats, RESINS, and organic materials dissolve easily in it, so it is used to make artificial fibers, explosives, resins, paints, inks, cosmetics (including nail-polish remover), coatings, and adhesives. Acetone is used as a chemical intermediate in pharmaceuticals and many other compounds.

acetylcholine \ə-ˌsē-tᵊl-'kō-lēn\ Ester of CHOLINE and ACETIC ACID, a NEUROTRANSMITTER active at many nerve SYNAPSES and at the motor end plate of vertebrate voluntary MUSCLES (where its activity is blocked in MYASTHENIA GRAVIS). It affects several of the body's systems, including the CARDIOVASCULAR (decreases heart rate and contraction strength, dilates blood vessels), gastrointestinal (increases PERISTALSIS in the stomach and amplitude of digestive contractions), and URINARY (decreases bladder capacity, increases voluntary voiding pressure) systems. It also affects the RESPIRATORY SYSTEM and stimulates secretion by all GLANDS that receive parasympathetic nerve impulses (see AUTONOMIC NERVOUS SYSTEM). It is important in memory and learning and is deficient in the brains of those with ALZHEIMER'S DISEASE.

acetylene *or* **ethyne** \'e-ˌthīn\ Simplest alkyne, C_2H_2. A colorless, flammable, explosive gas, it is used as a fuel in welding and cutting metals and as a raw material for many organic compounds and plastics. It is produced by reaction of water with calcium carbide, passage of a hydrocarbon through an electric arc, or partial combustion of methane. Decomposing it liberates heat; depending on degree of purity, it is also an explosive. An acetylene torch reaches about 6,000°F (3,300°C), hotter than combustion of any other known gas mixture. See also HYDROCARBON.

Achaean League \ə-'kē-ən\ 3rd-century-BC confederation of towns of Achaea, an area in the northern Peloponnese of ancient Greece. Twelve cities had joined together by the 4th century BC to combat piracy, but they disbanded after the death of ALEXANDER THE GREAT. Ten cities renewed the league in 280 BC, later admitting non-Achaean cities to defend themselves against Macedonia, then Sparta, and finally Rome. Rome dissolved the league after defeating it in 146 BC. Later a smaller league was formed that existed into the Roman imperial age.

Achaeans Ancient Greek people identified in HOMER as those who, with the Danaoi and the Argeioi, attacked Troy. Some identify them with the MYCENAEANS of the 14th–13th century BC; others say that they arrived in the 12th-century DORIAN invasions. They may have held power only a few generations before being replaced by the Dorians. HERODOTUS claims the later Achaeans of the northern Peloponnese (see ACHAEAN LEAGUE) were descended from these earlier Achaeans.

Achaemenian dynasty \ˌa-kə-'mē-nē-ən\ (7th century BC–330 BC) Persian dynasty. Achaemenes, its founder, is thought to have lived in the early 7th century BC. From his son Teispes were descended two lines of kings. The older line included Cyrus I, Cambyses I, CYRUS II (the Great), and Cambyses II; the junior line began with DARIUS I and ended with the death of Darius III after his defeat by ALEXANDER THE GREAT (330 BC). Its greatest rulers were Cyrus II (r.559–529? BC), who actually established the Persian empire and from whose reign it is dated; Darius I, who secured the borders from external threats; and XERXES I, who completed many of Darius's public works. At its height, the Achaemenian empire reached from Macedonia to northern India and from the Caucasus Mountains to the Persian Gulf. The ruins of PERSEPOLIS survive from its golden age.

Achebe \ä-'chā-bā\, **(Albert) Chinua(iumogu)** (born 1930) Nigerian Igbo novelist. Concerned with emergent Africa at its moments of crisis, he is acclaimed for depictions of the disorientation accompanying the imposition of Western customs and values on traditional African society. *Things Fall Apart* (1958) and *Arrow of God* (1964) portray traditional Igbo life as it clashes with colonialism. *No Longer at Ease* (1960), *A Man of the People* (1966), and *Anthills of the Savannah* (1988) deal with corruption and other aspects of postcolonial African life.

Achelous River \ˌa-kə-'lō-əs\ Longest river in Greece. It rises in the Pindus Mountains and flows south 140 mi (220 km) to the Ionian Sea. Hydroelectric dams harness its waters at Kastraki and Kremasta. In ancient mythology, Achelous was a protean river god, who was vanquished by Hercules.

Acheson \'a-chə-sən\, **Dean (Gooderham)** (1893–1971) U.S. secretary of state (1949–53). Born in Middletown, Conn., he practiced law in Washington, D.C., before joining the State Department (1941), where he later served as undersecretary (1945–47). In 1947 he helped design the TRUMAN DOCTRINE and the MARSHALL PLAN. As secretary of state under HARRY TRUMAN, he promoted the formation of NATO and was a principal creator of U.S. foreign policy in the Cold War. During the hearings held by Sen. JOSEPH MCCARTHY, he refused to fire any State Department subordinates, including ALGER HISS. He established the policies of nonrecognition of Red China and aid to the regime of CHIANG KAI-SHEK in Taiwan, and he supported U.S. aid to the French colonial regime in Indochina. After leaving office, he continued to advise successive presidents. His memoir *Present at the Creation* won a 1970 Pulitzer Prize.

Acheson, Edward Goodrich (1856–1931) U.S. inventor. He was born in Washington, Pa. He helped develop the INCANDESCENT LAMP, and in 1881 installed the first electric lights for THOMAS ALVA EDISON in Italy, Belgium, and France. Attempting to produce artificial diamonds, he created instead the highly effective ABRASIVE material CARBORUNDUM. He later found that the silicon vaporizes from Carborundum at 7500°F (4150°C), leaving graphitic carbon, and patented his GRAPHITE-making process in 1896.

Acheulian industry \ə-'shü-lē-ən\ STONE-TOOL INDUSTRY of the Lower PALEOLITHIC PERIOD characterized by bifacial stone tools with round cutting edges, and typified especially by an almond-shaped (amygdaloid) flint hand ax measuring 8–10 in. (20–25 cm) in length and flaked over its entire surface. Other implements include cleavers, borers, knives, and choppers. The name derives from the site near St. Acheul in northern France where such tools were first discovered. Acheulian industry was extremely long-lived (1.5 million–110,000 years ago) and is associated with both *HOMO ERECTUS* and archaic *HOMO SAPIENS*.

Achilles \ə-'ki-lēz\ In GREEK MYTHOLOGY, the bravest and strongest of the Greek warriors in the TROJAN WAR. Because his mother dipped him into the River STYX, he was invulnerable except at the heel by which she held him. During the war against Troy Achilles took 12 nearby cities, but after a quarrel with AGAMEMNON he refused further service. He allowed his beloved cousin Patroclus to fight in his armor, and when HECTOR slew Patroclus, Achilles returned to battle, killed Hector, and dragged his body around the walls of Troy. HOMER mentions Achilles' funeral but not the circumstances of his death; the later poet Arctinus relates that PARIS killed Achilles with an arrow guided by APOLLO.

Achilles Painter (fl. 5th century BC) Greek vase painter, named for an amphora decorated with a painting of Achilles and Briseis attributed to him. He was active in Athens in the time of PERICLES, and was a contemporary of PHIDIAS. His Achilles vase (c. 450 BC) is among the finest surviving examples of RED-FIGURE POTTERY from the Classical period. He is also known for his *lekythoi* (funerary vases with colored figures on a white background), regarded as the most reliable documentation of monumental Greek paintings. Some 300 extant vase paintings are attributed him.

Achinese \ˌa-chə-'nēz\ One of the main ethnic groups on the island of Sumatra, Indonesia. In the 13th century the Achinese became the first people in the archipelago to adopt Islam. After expelling the Portuguese in the 17th century, the sultanate of Acheh was dominant in northern Sumatra until it was conquered by the Dutch in 1904 (see ACHINESE WAR). Now part of the Indonesian republic, they are restive and are administered within a special district. They trace their descent through both maternal and paternal lines, and the position of women is high. They number roughly 2.1 million.

Achinese War (1873–1904) Armed conflict between the Netherlands and the Muslim sultanate of Acheh in northern Sumatra. Considering the sultanate of Acheh to be within their northern Sumatran sphere of influence, the Dutch invaded, but despite the capitulation of the Achinese sultan, the people engaged the Dutch in a prolonged and costly guerrilla war, which the Dutch were only able to win by researching the area and devising a new "castle strategy" that relied on fortified bases.

acid Any substance that in water solution tastes sour, changes the color of acid-base indicators (e.g., LITMUS), reacts with some METALS (e.g., iron) to yield HYDROGEN gas, reacts with BASES to form SALTS, and promotes certain CHEMICAL REACTIONS (e.g., acid CATALYSIS). Acids contain one or more hydrogen atoms that, in solution, dissociate as positively charged hydrogen IONS. Inorganic, or mineral, acids include SULFURIC ACID, NITRIC ACID, HYDROCHLORIC ACID, and phosphoric acid. Organic acids include CARBOXYLIC ACIDS, PHENOLS, and sulfonic acids. Broader definitions of acids cover situations in which water is not present. See also ACID-BASE THEORY.

acid and basic rocks Division of IGNEOUS ROCKS on the basis of their SILICATE MINERAL content, these minerals usually being the most abundant in such rocks. Rocks are described as acid, intermediate, basic, and ultrabasic, in order of decreasing silica content, because it was earlier thought that silica is present in rock MAGMAS in the form of silicic acid. In modern usage the terms do not refer to acidity in the chemical sense. In general, the gradation from acid to basic corresponds to an increase in color (i.e., light to dark).

acid-base theory Any of several theories that give rise to alternative definitions of ACIDS and BASES. The original theory was based on SVANTE ARRHENIUS's electrolytic theory of solutions and involved the DISSOCIATION water into hydrogen and hydroxide IONS. To explain the behavior of a chemical, particularly if water is not present, two other theories were developed. The most widely accepted and useful is the Brønsted-Lowry definition (1923): An acid is a chemical that tends to lose a PROTON (H^+), and a base is a chemical that tends to gain a proton. Another is the Lewis definition (also 1923): An acid (see ELECTROPHILE) is a chemical that can accept an ELECTRON pair from a base (see NUCLEOPHILE), which they share to form a COVALENT BOND. The three theories have superficial similarities but subtle and important differences for certain applications.

acid rain Any precipitation, including snow, that contains a heavy concentration of SULFURIC and NITRIC acids. This form of pollution is a serious environmental problem in many areas of North America and Europe. Automobiles, certain industrial operations, and electric power plants that burn FOSSIL FUELS emit the gases sulfur dioxide and nitrogen oxides into the atmosphere, where they combine with water vapor in clouds to form sulfuric and nitric acids. The highly acidic precipitation from these clouds may contaminate lakes and streams, damaging fish and other aquatic species; damage vegetation, including agricultural crops and trees; and corrode the outsides of buildings and other structures. Though usually most severe around large urban and industrial areas, acid precipitation may also occur at great distances from the source of the pollutants.

Ackermann, Konrad Ernst (c. 1710–1771) German actor-manager. He joined a theater company in 1740 and acted in German adaptations of French plays. In the 1750s he led a troupe on tour throughout Europe. He developed German domestic drama and a technique for combining the comic and the sentimental. In 1765 he opened a theater in Hamburg, considered the first German national theater. He later turned its management over to his stepson, Friedrich L. Schröder (1744–1816), who brought Shakespeare to the German stage. See also ACTOR-MANAGER SYSTEM.

ACLU See AMERICAN CIVIL LIBERTIES UNION

acne \'ak-nē\ Any of some 50 inflammatory diseases of the oil glands of the skin. Acne vulgaris, probably the most frequent chronic skin disorder, results from an interplay of hereditary factors, hormones, and bacteria, beginning in the teen years when overactive SEBACEOUS GLANDS are stimulated by high levels of ANDROGENS. Its primary lesion, the blackhead, may be open or closed; it consists of a plug of skin oil (sebum), cell debris, and microorganisms in a hair follicle. Acne has four grades of severity, with increasing degrees of spread, inflammation, pustule formation, and scarring. Lower grades generally respond to treatment, which may include skin medication, sunlight, antibiotics, and hormones; many cases eventually resolve spontaneously.

Acoma \'ä-kō-mə\ Indian pueblo, western central New Mexico. It is located on a reservation west of ALBUQUERQUE and is known as the "Sky City." Its people live in terraced dwellings made of stone and adobe atop a sandstone butte 357 ft (109 m) high. Settled in the 10th century, it is believed to be the oldest continuously inhabited place in the U.S. In 1540 Spanish explorer FRANCISCO VAZQUEZ DE CORONADO described it as the strongest defensive position in the world.

Aconcagua \ˌä-kōn-'kä-gwä\, **Mount** Mountain, western Argentina, on the Chilean border. At 22,834 ft (6,960 m) high, it is the highest peak of the ANDES and of the Western Hemisphere. It is of volcanic origin but is not itself a volcano. The summit was first reached in 1897.

aconite \'a-kə-ˌnīt\ Any member of two genera of perennial herbaceous plants of the BUTTERCUP family: *Aconitum* (monkshood or wolfsbane), consisting of summer-flowering poisonous plants, and *Eranthis* (winter aconite), consisting of spring-flowering ornamentals. The dried tuberous root of *A. napellus* was formerly used as a sedative and a painkiller.

acorn Nut of the oak. Acorns are usually seated in or surrounded by a woody cupule. They mature within one to two seasons, and their appearance varies depending on the species of oak. Acorns provide food for small game animals and are used to fatten swine and poultry.

Acosta \ä-'kō-stä\, **Uriel** *orig.* **Gabriel da Costa** (c. 1585–1640) Portuguese Jewish freethinker. Born into a Marrano family, he came to feel that there was no salvation through the Roman Catholic church, and converted to Judaism. His mother and brother also converted, and he and his family fled to Amsterdam. In 1616 he attacked rabbinic Judaism as nonbiblical and was excommunicated. When he enlarged on his criticisms in 1623–24, denying the immortality of the soul, he was arrested and fined. He recanted, but was later excommunicated again. He recanted publicly in 1640, after which he wrote a short autobiography, *Example of a Human Life,* and shot himself.

acoustics \ə-'kü-stiks\ Science of production, control, transmission, reception, and effects of sound. Its principal branches are architectural, environmental, musical, and engineering acoustics, and ultrasonics. Environmental acoustics focuses on controlling noise produced by aircraft engines, factories, construction machinery, and general traffic. Musical acoustics deals with the design and use of musical instruments and how musical sounds affect listeners. Engineering acoustics concerns sound recording and reproduction systems. Ultrasonics deals with ultrasonic waves, which have frequencies above the audible range, and their applications in industry and medicine.

acoustics, architectural Relationship between sound produced in a space and its listeners, of particular concern in the design of concert halls and auditoriums. Good acoustic design takes into account such issues as reverberation time; sound absorption of the finish materials; echoes; acoustic shadows; sound intimacy, texture, and blend; and external noise. Architectural modifications (e.g., orchestral shells, canopies, and undulating or angled ceilings and walls) may act as focusing elements to improve sound quality.

acquired immunodeficiency syndrome See AIDS

Acre \'ä-krə, 'ä-kər\ *or* **Akko** \'ä-kō\ Seaport city (pop., 1993 est.: 44,000), northwestern Israel on the Mediterranean coast. First mentioned in an Egyptian text from the 19th century BC, it was ruled by Egyptians, Romans, Persians, and Arabs; under Phoenician rule it was called Ptolemais. It was a Syrian town under the Seljuq Turks when the crusaders captured it in 1104; the Crusaders renamed the city St. Jean d'Acre and made it their last capital (see Crusades). Except for brief intervals, it was under the rule of Ottoman Turks from 1516 until British forces took it in 1918. It was part of Palestine under the British mandate and became part of Israel in 1948. Notable structures include the Great Mosque and the Crypt of St. John.

acrobatics Art of jumping, tumbling, and balancing. The art is of ancient origin; acrobats performed leaps, somersaults, and vaults at Egyptian and Greek events. Acrobatic feats were featured in the commedia dell'arte theater and in the Peking Opera. The later use of such apparatuses as poles, tightropes, and flying trapezes made acrobatics a major attraction in circus performances. Its popularity increased in the 20th century with such performers as the Flying Wallendas (see Karl Wallenda).

acromegaly \ˌa-krō-'me-gə-lē\ Growth and metabolic disorder in which the skeletal extremities enlarge when a pituitary gland tumor causes overproduction of growth hormone after maturity. It is often associated with pituitary gigantism. Acromegaly is characterized by gradual enlargement of hands and feet, exaggeration of facial features, skin thickening, and enlargement of most internal organs, along with headaches, excessive sweating, and high blood pressure. Acromegalic individuals are likely to develop congestive heart failure, muscle weakness, joint pain, osteoporosis, and often diabetes mellitus and visual problems, including blindness. If treatment with surgery and/or radiation fails, then hormone therapy is used. Treatment can cause hormone deficiency, necessitating hormone replacement therapy; spontaneous events may also cause hormone deficiency.

acropolis (Greek: "city at the top") Central, defensively oriented district in ancient Greek cities, located on the highest ground and containing the chief municipal and religious buildings. The renowned Athens Acropolis (5th century BC), atop a craggy walled hill, is home to four main edifices—the Propylaea (see propylaeum), Parthenon, Erechtheum (Ionic temple noted for its caryatid porch), and Temple of Athena Nike—all built from white marble plentiful in the region.

The Acropolis, Athens, second half of the 5th century BC, with the Parthenon at centre and the Erechtheum at left.
TONI SCHNEIDERS

acrostic Originally, a short verse composition, constructed so that one or more sets of letters (such as the initial, middle, or final letters of the lines), taken consecutively, form words. An acrostic in which the initial letters form the alphabet is called an abecedarius. Ancient Greek and Latin writers, medieval monks, and Renaissance poets are among those who devised acrostics. Today the term is used for a type of word puzzle utilizing the acrostic principle. A popular form is double acrostics, puzzles constructed so that the middle or last, as well as initial, letters of lines may form words.

acrylic compound Any of a class of synthetic plastics, resins, and oils used to manufacture many products. By varying the starting reagents (such as acrylic acid, $C_3H_4O_2$, or acrylonitrile, C_3H_3N) and the process of forming, a material may be produced that is hard and transparent, soft and resilient, or a viscous liquid. Acrylic compounds are used to make molded structural and optical parts, jewelry, adhesives, coating compounds, and textile fibers. Lucite and Plexiglas are trademarks used for glasslike acrylic materials.

acrylic painting \ə-'kri-lik\ Painting executed in the medium of acrylic resins, synthetic resins that dry rapidly, are water-soluble, and serve as a vehicle for any pigment. Its effects may range from the transparent brilliance of watercolor to the density of oil paint. Acrylics are less affected by heat and deterioration than oils. They were first used by artists in the 1940s, but became popular with such artists as David Hockney when they were produced commercially in the 1960s.

Act of Union See Act of Union (1707), Act of Union (1800)

Acta (Latin: "Acts") In ancient Rome, the daily minutes of public business and a record of political and social events. Julius Caesar in 59 BC ordered that the Senate's daily doings *(acta diurna, commentaria Senatus)* be made public; Augustus later prohibited publication, though the Senate's acts continued to be recorded and could be read with special permission. There were also public registers (*acta diurna urbis,* "daily minutes of the city") of the acts of the popular assemblies and the courts as well as births, deaths, marriages, and divorces. These constituted a daily gazette, a prototype of the modern newspaper.

ACTH *in full* **adrenocorticotropic hormone** \ə-'drē-nō-ˌkȯr-ti-kō-'trō-pik\ Polypeptide hormone made in the pituitary gland. It regulates the activity of part of the cortex of the adrenal glands, the production site of important steroid hormones that affect electrolyte and water balance and the metabolism of fats, carbohydrates, and proteins. ACTH is found in vertebrates (except jawless fishes); in mammals it contains 39 amino acids. Overproduction of ACTH is one cause of Cushing's syndrome.

actin One of two PROTEINS responsible for contraction of MUSCLE cells and the motility of other cells. It occurs as a MONOMER, G-actin, a globular protein, and in living cells as a POLYMER, F-actin, which resembles two strings of beads twisted around each other into thin filaments. The filaments occur in regular structures, alternated and interwoven with thick filaments that contain myosin, the other major muscle protein. The thick and thin filaments slide past each other, under the control of CALCIUM ions, resulting in contraction (shortening) and relaxation (lengthening) of the muscle cells.

acting Art of representing a character on a stage or before a camera by means of movement, gesture, and intonation. Acting in the Western tradition originated in Greece in the 6th century BC; the tragedian THESPIS is traditionally regarded as founder of the profession. ARISTOTLE defined acting as "the right management of the voice to express various emotions" and declared it a natural gift that he doubted could be taught. Acting declined as an art in the Middle Ages, when Christian LITURGICAL DRAMA was performed by craft guilds and amateurs. Modern professional acting emerged in the 16th century with Italy's COMMEDIA DELL'ARTE troupes. It flourished during the era of WILLIAM SHAKESPEARE. Not until the 18th century, however, was acting considered a profession to be taken seriously, through the efforts in England of the actor-manager DAVID GARRICK and the talents of such actors as SARAH SIDDONS, EDMUND KEAN, and HENRY IRVING. Modern acting styles have been influenced by KONSTANTIN STANISLAVSKY's emphasis on the actor's identification with his role and by BERTOLT BRECHT's insistence on the objectivity and discipline of the actor. The STANISLAVSKY METHOD was adapted in the U.S. by LEE STRASBERG and Stella Adler (1901–1992) and is the basis of most contemporary training, which features the cultivation of emotional and sense memory, physical and vocal training, and improvisation.

actinide \'ak-tə-ˌnīd\ Any of the series of 15 consecutive chemical ELEMENTS in the PERIODIC TABLE from actinium to lawrencium (ATOMIC NUMBERS 89–103). All are radioactive heavy METALS; and only the first four (actinium, thorium, protactinium, and URANIUM) occur in nature in appreciable quantities. The other 11 (the TRANSURANIUM ELEMENTS) are unstable and are produced only artificially. Actinides are TRANSITION ELEMENTS, so their ATOMS have similar configurations and similar physical and chemical behavior; the most usual VALENCES are 3 and 4.

actinolite \ak-'ti-nᵊl-ˌīt\ Colorless to green AMPHIBOLE mineral, darkening with increased iron content from green to black. It has a prismatic and splintery texture and is abundant in regionally metamorphosed (see METAMORPHISM) rocks such as SCHISTS. Actinolite has a monoclinic crystal structure, and it may alter to chlorite. See also ASBESTOS.

actinomycete \ˌak-ti-nō-'mī-sēt\ Any of a group of generally low-oxygen-utilizing BACTERIA identified by a branching growth pattern that results in large threadlike structures. The filaments may break apart to form rods or spheroidal shapes. Some actinomycetes can form spores. Many species occur in soil and are harmless to animals and higher plants; others are important disease-causing agents. For diagnostic purposes in human infections, the presence of sulfur granules is used.

Action Française \àk-sē-'ōⁿ-fräⁿ-'sez\ ("French Action") Influential right-wing antirepublican group in early-20th-century France, whose views were promoted in a newspaper of the same name. The Action Française movement, led by CHARLES MAURRAS, espoused the antiparliamentarian, anti-Semitic, and strongly nationalist views inspired by the ALFRED DREYFUS Affair. The movement peaked after World War I, when nationalist feeling was strong. It was denounced by the papacy in 1926, and ceased to exist after World War II because of its association with the collaborationist Vichy government (see VICHY FRANCE).

action painting Direct, instinctual, dynamic style of painting that involves the spontaneous application of vigorous, sweeping brush strokes and the chance effects of dripping and spilling paint onto the canvas. The term characterizes the work of JACKSON POLLOCK, WILLEM DE KOONING, and FRANZ KLINE. The "automatic" techniques developed in Europe by the Surrealists in the 1920s and '30s had great influence on U.S. artists, who regarded a picture not merely as a finished product but as a record of the process of its creation. It was a major force in ABSTRACT EXPRESSIONISM in the 1950s. See also AUTOMATISM, TACHISM.

action potential Brief (about one-thousandth of a second) reversal of electric polarization of the membrane of a nerve or muscle cell. Stimulation of the cell by certain chemicals or by sensory receptor cells causes depolarization of the membrane, permitting an impulse to move along the nerve fiber (in nerve cells) or causing the cell to contract (in muscle cells).

action theory Subfield of philosophy of MIND that is specially important for ETHICS; it concerns the distinction between things that happen to a person and things one does or makes happen. Action theorists consider issues such as motive, desire, purpose, deliberation, decision, INTENTION, trying, and free will (see FREE WILL PROBLEM). A central problem is the question of volition, or what connects intention with bodily movement; in LUDWIG WITTGENSTEIN's formulation, "What is left over if I subtract the fact that my arm goes up from the fact that I raise my arm?"

Actium \'ak-shē-əm\, **Battle of** (31 BC) Naval battle off ACARNANIA, Greece, between Octavian (later AUGUSTUS) and Mark ANTONY. With 500 ships and 70,000 infantry, Antony camped at Actium, between the Ionian Sea and the Ambracian Gulf. Octavian, with 400 ships and 80,000 infantry, cut Antony's line of communication from the north. Desertion by allies and a lack of supplies forced Antony to act. Outmaneuvered on land, he followed CLEOPATRA's advice to attack Octavian at sea. Antony's larger fleet included his own and Cleopatra's ships. In the heat of battle Cleopatra fled with her galleys, and Antony followed with a few ships. His fleet surrendered immediately, his army a week later. Octavian's victory left him undisputed ruler of the Roman world.

activation energy Minimum amount of ENERGY (HEAT, ELECTROMAGNETIC RADIATION, or electrical energy) required to activate ATOMS or MOLECULES to a condition in which it is equally likely that they will undergo chemical reaction or transport as it is that they will return to their original state. Chemists posit a transition state between the initial conditions and the product conditions and theorize that the activation energy is the amount of energy required to boost the initial materials "uphill" to the transition state; the reaction then proceeds "downhill" to form the product materials. CATALYSTS (including ENZYMES) lower the activation energy by altering the transition state. Activation energies are determined by experiments that measure them as the constant of proportionality in the equation describing the dependence of REACTION RATE on temperature, proposed by SVANTE ARRHENIUS. See also ENTROPY, heat of REACTION.

active galactic nucleus Small region at the center of a GALAXY that emits a prodigious amount of energy in the form of radio, optical, X-ray, or gamma radiation or high-speed particle jets. Many classes of "active galaxies" have been identified; they appear similar in many respects to QUASARS. Astronomers suspect that the observed energy is generated as matter accretes onto a supermassive BLACK HOLE with a mass millions or even billions of times that of the sun. The accreting matter can outshine the rest of the galaxy as it is heated in very high-speed collisions outside the black hole's EVENT HORIZON. It is believed that many galaxies harbor these central black holes, and that they might have been quasars in their early history, but now appear to be dormant unless orbiting matter is accreting onto the black hole.

activity coefficient Number expressing the ratio of a substance's chemical activity to its molar concentration (see MOLE). The measured concentration of a substance may not be an accurate indicator of its chemical effectiveness as represented by the equation for a particular reaction; in such cases, the activity is calculated by multiplying the concentration by the activity coefficient. In SOLUTIONS, the activity coefficient is a measure of how much the solution differs from an ideal solution.

Acton (of Aldenham), Baron *orig.* **John Emerich Edward Dalberg Acton** (1834–1902) English historian. He served in the House of Commons 1859–65. Editor of the Roman Catholic monthly *The Rambler* (1859–64), he resigned because of papal criticism of his scientific approach to history. An adviser to WILLIAM E. GLADSTONE from 1865, he was raised to the peerage in 1869. In 1895 he was appointed Regius professor of modern history at Cambridge University. He later coordinated the massive publication project of *The Cambridge Modern History*. A critic of nationalism, he coined the familiar aphorism "Power tends to corrupt, and absolute power corrupts absolutely."

actor-manager system Method of theatrical production prevalent in 19th-century England and the U.S. An actor formed a theater company, chose the plays he wanted to produce, played the leading roles in them, and managed the company's business arrangements. The first actor-managers emerged in the 17th century, and in the 18th century actor-managers such as COLLEY CIBBER and DAVID GARRICK gained prominence. The system produced high performance standards, typified by such 19th-century figures as WILLIAM MACREADY, HENRY IRVING, and HERBERT TREE. It waned as actor-managers were replaced first by stage managers and later by directors.

Actors Studio Professional actors' workshop based in New York. Founded in 1947 by the directors CHERYL CRAWFORD, ELIA KAZAN, and Robert Lewis as a leading center of the STANISLAVSKY METHOD, it was directed by LEE STRASBERG from 1948 to 1982. In 1962 it launched a company, and a workshop was established in Los Angeles in 1966. Actors work together without the pressures of commercial production. Membership is by invitation; six or seven new members are chosen yearly from 1,000 auditions. Members have included MARLON BRANDO, MARILYN MONROE, PAUL NEWMAN, and ROBERT DE NIRO.

actuary One who calculates insurance risks and premiums. Actuaries compute the probability of the occurrence of such events as birth, marriage, illness, accidents, and death. They also evaluate the hazards of property damage or loss and the legal liability for the safety and well-being of others. Usually employed by insurance companies, actuaries set premium rates based on statistical studies, establish underwriting procedures, and determine the amounts of money required to assure the payment of benefits.

Acuff \'ā-kəf\, **Roy (Claxton)** (1903–1992) U.S. singer, songwriter, and fiddler. Born in Maynardsville, Tenn., he turned to music after an aborted baseball career and gained immediate popularity with "The Great Speckled Bird" and "The Wabash Cannonball." Reasserting the mournful musical traditions of Southeastern rural whites, he became a national radio star on the GRAND OLE OPRY. In 1942 he and FRED ROSE founded Acuff-Rose Publishing, the first publishing house exclusively for country music. In 1962 Acuff was elected the first living member of the Country Music Hall of Fame.

acupressure *or* **shiatsu** \shē-'ät-sü\ ALTERNATIVE-MEDICINE practice in which pressure is applied to points on the body aligned along 12 main meridians (pathways), usually for a short time, to improve the flow of vital force (QI). Though often referred to by its Japanese name, shiatsu, it originated in China thousands of years ago. A single point may be pressed to relieve a specific symptom or condition, or a series of points can be worked on to promote overall well-being. Some studies suggest that acupressure can be effective for certain health problems, including nausea, pain, and stroke-related weakness. Risks are minimal with cautious use. See also ACUPUNCTURE.

acupuncture Medical technique in which needles are inserted into the skin and underlying tissues, devised in China before 2500 BC. One or more small metal needles are inserted at precise points along 12 meridians (pathways) in the body, through which the vital life force (QI) is believed to flow, in order to restore YIN-YANG balance and treat disease caused by yin-yang imbalance. Acupuncture appears to relieve pain and is used as an ANESTHETIC for surgery. Theories to explain its effects include stimulation of release of natural opiates, blockage of pain-signal transmission, and a placebo effect. See also ACUPRESSURE.

Ada \'ā-də\ High-level computer PROGRAMMING LANGUAGE whose development was initiated in 1975 by the U.S. Dept. of Defense and standardized in 1983. Ada (named for the countess of LOVELACE) was intended to be a common language for use on the department's computers, which were produced by many different manufacturers. It is similar to PASCAL but contains many additional features convenient for the development of large-scale, multiplatform programs. The 1995 revision, called Ada 95, supports object-oriented design methodology (see OBJECT-ORIENTED PROGRAMMING).

Adad \ä-'däd\ Babylonian and Assyrian god of weather, the son of ANU (sometimes called the son of BEL). He was known as the Lord of Abundance for rains that made the land bloom, but he sent death-dealing storms to his enemies. He was also the god of oracles and divination. Though widely worshiped, he was a minor god and appears to have had no cult center of his own.

Adal \'ä-dəl\ Historic Islamic state, eastern Africa, southwest of the Gulf of ADEN, with its capital at Harer (now in Ethiopia). Its rivalry with Christian Ethiopia began in the 14th century. In the 16th century Adal launched a series of attacks, led by Ahmed Gran, who succeeded by 1533 in gaining control of most of central Ethiopia. Gran was killed in battle in 1543, and the OROMO invasions of the later 16th century ended Adal's power.

Adalbert \'ad-ᵊl-ˌbərt\, **St.** *orig.* **Vojtech** (956–997) Czech prelate. Descended from the princes of Bohemia, he was trained in theology at Magdeburg (Germany). Elected the first native bishop of Prague in 982, he promoted the political aims of the Bohemian prince by extending the influence of the church beyond the Czech kingdom. Failing to convert his people, he retired in 988 to a monastery near Rome. On papal orders he returned in 992 to find little change. Disillusioned, he left Bohemia in 994 to become a missionary along the Baltic coast, where he was martyred in 997. An account of his life was written by his friend and disciple St. BRUNO.

Adam, Robert (1728–1792) Scottish architect and designer. Son of the architect William Adam, he apprenticed in his father's offices. He traveled in Europe 1754–58, studying architectural theory and Roman ruins. On his return to London, he and his brother James (1732–1794) developed an essentially decorative style that synthesized elements from various sources and employed classical forms with a new lightness and freedom. Their style is most remembered for its interiors, with their contrasting room shapes and delicate classical ornaments. Adam's executed works consisted mainly of the remodeling of houses, including Osterley Park (1761–80) in Middlesex and Kedleston Hall (c. 1765–70) in Derbyshire. Other works included the Adelphi development in London (1768–72) and the University of Edinburgh (1789). He was also a leading furniture designer; his style, popularized by GEORGE HEPPLEWHITE, was meant to harmonize with his interior architecture down to the last detail.

Adam and Eve In the Judeo-Christian and Islamic traditions, the parents of the human race. GENESIS gives two versions of their creation. In the first, God creates "male and female in his own image" on the sixth day. In the second, Adam is placed in the Garden of Eden, and Eve is later created from his rib to ease his loneliness. For succumbing to temptation and eating the fruit of the forbidden tree of knowledge of good and evil, God banished them from Eden, and they and their descendants were forced to live lives of hardship. CAIN AND ABEL were their children. Christian theologians developed the doctrine of ORIGINAL SIN based on the story of their transgression; in contrast, the QURAN teaches that Adam's sin was his alone and did not make all people sinners.

Adamawa \ˌä-dä-'mä-wä\ Traditional emirate centered in what is now Adamawa state, eastern Nigeria. It was founded by Modibbo Adama in the early 19th century. He moved the capital several times before finally settling it in 1841 in Yola. The colonialist British established trading posts there; when the emir tried to force them out in 1901, they captured the town. Adamawa was partitioned in 1901 between British Northern Nigeria and German Kamerun (Cameroon). In 1919 the Cameroon portion was divided between the French and the British. The emirate's territories eventually came to form almost all of northern Cameroon and part of eastern Nigeria.

Adamawa-Ubangi languages \ˌad-ə-'mä-wə-ü-'baŋ-gē\ *formerly* **Adamawa-Eastern languages** Branch of the huge NIGER-CONGO family of African languages. Adamawa-Ubangi has two divisions, Adamawa in the west and Ubangi in the east. Adamawa may comprise more than 70 languages, most poorly known and nearly all with fewer than 100,000 speakers, in eastern Nigeria, northern Cameroon, southwestern Chad, and western Central African Republic. Ubangi includes about the same number of languages as Adamawa and extends across a much broader region, from northern Cameroon across the Central Africa Republic to adjacent parts of southern Sudan and northern Congo (former Zaire). Ubangi languages with over half a million speakers include Banda, Gbaya, Ngbaka, and Zande (see AZANDE). Sango, a restructured form of one or more languages of the Ngbandi group of Ubangi, has become a lingua franca of the Central African Republic.

Adamov \ə-'dä-məv\, **Arthur** (1908–1970) Russian-French playwright. He settled in Paris in 1924, and his first major work, written after suffering a nervous breakdown, was his autobiography, *The Confession* (1938–43). Influenced by AUGUST STRINDBERG and FRANZ KAFKA, he began writing plays in 1947. *Le professeur Taranne* (1953) and *Le ping-pong* (1955) expressed the view of life's meaninglessness characteristic of the theater of the ABSURD. In *Paolo Paoli* (1957) and later plays, he abandoned absurdism for radical political theater influenced by BERTOLT BRECHT. He died from a drug overdose, an apparent suicide.

Adams, Abigail *orig.* **Abigail Smith** (1744–1818) U.S. first lady. Born in Weymouth, Mass., she received a meager education but became an avid reader of history. She married John Adams in 1764 and raised four children, including John Quincy Adams, in Quincy, Mass. In 1774 she began a prolific correspondence with her husband when he was at the Continental Congress in Philadelphia, describing daily life and discussing public affairs during the American Revolution with wit and political acuity. She continued her letters to family and friends while in Europe (1784–88) and Washington, D.C. (1789–1801), during her husband's diplomatic and presidential careers.

Adams, Ansel (1902–1984) U.S. photographer. Born in San Francisco, in 1927 he published *Parmelian Prints of the High Sierras*, photographs that imitated Impressionist painting by suppressing detail in favor of soft, misty effects achieved in the darkroom. Adams was known for his dramatic images of mountain landscapes. He became one of the outstanding technicians in the history of photography; *Making a Photograph* (1935) was the first of his many books on photographic technique. He worked consistently to foster public awareness of photography as a fine art. In 1940 he helped organize the first public collection of photographs, at the Museum of Modern Art, and in 1946 he established, at the California School of Fine Arts, the first academic photography department.

Adams, Charles Francis (1807–1886) U.S. diplomat. Born in Boston, the son of John Quincy Adams and grandson of John Adams, he served in the Massachusetts legislature and edited a Whig journal. He helped form the antislavery Free Soil Party and in 1848 was chosen its candidate for U.S. vice president. As ambassador to Britain (1861–68) he was instrumental in securing Britain's neutrality during the Civil War, and in promoting the arbitration of the *Alabama* claims.

Charles Francis Adams.

BY COURTESY OF THE LIBRARY OF CONGRESS, WASHINGTON, D.C.

Adams, Gerry *orig.* **Gerard** (born 1948) Irish nationalist and leader of Sinn Féin. Allegedly a member of the Irish Republican Army (IRA) and its commander in Belfast, he was interned without trial as a suspected terrorist in 1972 and 1973–77. He became vice president of Sinn Féin in 1978 and persuaded the group to enter candidates in the 1981 elections. Elected to the British Parliament in 1983, he refused to take the oath of allegiance and never took his seat. As Sinn Féin's president (from 1983), in 1991 he began to shift its strategy toward negotiation; his efforts led to indirect talks with the British government and a 1993 agreement (the Downing Street Declaration) by the British and Irish prime ministers to consider Northern Ireland's future. He was credited with the IRA's 1994 announcement of its first cease-fire.

Adams, Henry (Brooks) (1838–1918) U.S. historian and man of letters. A product of Boston's elite Brahmin class and a descendant of two presidents, he was infused with disgust for American politics of his own time. As a young newspaper correspondent and editor, he called for social and political reforms, but he later became disillusioned with a world he characterized as devoid of principle. That loss of faith was reflected in his novel *Democracy* (1880). His study of U.S. democracy culminated in his nine-volume *History of the United States of America* (1889–91), which received immediate acclaim. In *Mont-Saint-Michel and Chartres* (1913) he described the medieval worldview as reflected in its architecture. *The Education of Henry Adams* (1918), his best-known work and one of the outstanding autobiographies of Western literature, traces his confrontations with the uncertainties of the 20th century.

Adams, John (1735–1826) U.S. politician, first vice president (1789–97) and second president (1797–1801) of the U.S. Born in Braintree, Mass., he practiced law in Boston. In 1764 he married Abigail Smith (A. Adams). Active in the American independence movement, he was elected to the Massachusetts legislature and served as a delegate to the Continental Congress (1774–78), where he was appointed to a committee with Thomas Jefferson and others to draft the Declaration of Independence. In 1776–78 he was appointed to many congressional committees, including one to create a navy and another to review foreign affairs. He served as a diplomat in France, the Netherlands, and England (1778–88). In the first U.S. presidential election, he received the second-largest number of votes and became vice president under George Washington. Adams's term as president was marked by controversy over his signing the Alien and Sedition Acts in 1798 and by his alliance with the conservative Federalist Party. In 1800 he was defeated for reelection by Jefferson and retired to live a secluded life in Massachusetts. In 1812 he was reconciled with Jefferson, with whom he began an illuminating correspondence. Both men died on July 4, 1826, the Declaration's 50th anniversary. John Quincy Adams was his son.

John Adams, oil painting by Gilbert Stuart, 1826; in the National Collection of Fine Arts, Washington, D.C.

BY COURTESY OF THE NATIONAL COLLECTION OF FINE ARTS, SMITHSONIAN INSTITUTION, WASHINGTON, D.C.

Adams, John (Coolidge) (born 1947) U.S. composer. He studied at Harvard Univ., and has since worked as a professional clarinetist, taught at the San Francisco Conservatory, and conducted widely. His style, though strongly influenced by minimalism, has become richer with time. His *Nixon in China* (1987) and *The Death of Klinghoffer* (1991) are two of the best-known operas of recent decades. Other celebrated works include *Harmonium* (1980), *Grand Pianola Music* (1982), and *Harmonielehre* (1985).

Adams, John Quincy (1767–1848) Sixth president of the U.S. (1825–29). Born in Braintree, Mass., he was the eldest son of John Adams and Abigail Adams. He accompanied his father to Europe on diplomatic missions (1778–80). He was appointed U.S. minister to the Netherlands (1794) and to Prussia (1797). In 1801 he returned to Massachusetts and served in the U.S. Senate (1803–8). Resuming his diplomatic service, he became U.S. minister to Russia (1809–11) and Britain (1815–17). Appointed secretary of state (1817–24), he was instrumental in acquiring Florida from Spain and in drafting the Monroe Doctrine. In the 1824 presidential election, he was one of three candidates; none received a majority of the electoral votes, though Andrew Jackson received a plurality. The decision went to the House of Representatives, where Adams received crucial support from Henry Clay and the electoral votes necessary to elect him president. He appointed Clay secretary of state, which further angered Jackson. Adams's presidency was unsuccessful; when he ran for reelection, Jackson defeated him. In 1830 he was elected to the House, where he served until his death. He was outspoken in his opposition to slavery and in 1839 proposed a constitutional amendment forbidding slavery in any new state admitted to the Union. Southern congressmen prevented discussion of antislavery petitions by passing gag rules (repealed in 1844 as a result of Adams's persistence). In 1841 he successfully defended the slaves in the Amistad Mutiny case.

Adams, Samuel (1722–1803) American Revolutionary leader. Born in Boston, he was a cousin of John Adams. He became a strong opponent of British taxation measures and organized resistance to the Stamp Act. He was a member of the state legislature (1765–74), and in 1772 he helped found the Committees of Correspondence. He influenced reaction to the Tea Act of 1773, organized the Boston Tea Party, and led opposition to the Intolerable Acts. A delegate to the Continental Congress (1774–81), he continued to call for separation from Britain and signed the Declaration of Independence. He helped draft the Massachusetts constitution in 1780 and served as the state's governor (1794–97).

Adams, Walter S(ydney) (1876–1956) U.S. (Syrian-born) astronomer. He returned to the U.S. with his missionary parents when he was 8 and studied at Dartmouth College, the University of Chicago, and the University of Munich. Using the spectroscope, he investigated sunspots and the rotation of the sun, the velocities and distances of thousands of stars, and planetary atmospheres. In 1904 he joined the original staff of Mount Wilson Observatory, where he served as director 1923–46. He took an important part in planning the 200-in. (5-m) telescope for the Palomar Observatory.

Adam's Peak Mountain, southern central Sri Lanka. Standing 7,360 ft (2,243 m) high, it is sacred and a place of pilgrimage to Buddhists, Muslims, and Hindus. On its summit, it has a large hollow, 5 ft (1.5 m) long, that is venerated as the footprint of Buddha, Adam, and Shiva, respectively. Many pilgrims of all faiths visit the peak every year.

Adamson, Joy *orig.* **Joy-Friederike Victoria Gessner** (1910–1980) Czech-British naturalist. Educated in Vienna, she moved to Kenya in 1939. She became known worldwide for books describing how she and her husband raised a lion cub, Elsa, and returned it to its natural habitat: *Born Free* (1960), *Living Free* (1961), and *Forever Free* (1962). She later repeated her rehabilitation success with cheetah and leopard cubs. She founded the Elsa Wild Animal Appeal (1961), an international conservation fund. She was killed by a disgruntled employee.

Adamson, Robert See Hill, David Octavius, and Robert Adamson

Adana \ˌä-dä-ˈnä\ City (pop., 1995: 1,066,000), southern central Turkey, on the Seyhan River. An agricultural and industrial center and one of Turkey's largest cities, it probably overlies a Hittite settlement that dates from c. 1400 BC. Conquered by Alexander the Great in 335–334 BC, it was later a Roman military station. It came under the rule of the Abbasid Arabs at the end of the 7th century AD and changed hands intermittently until the establishment of the Turkmen dynasty in 1378. Adana's prosperity has long derived from the fertile valleys behind it and its position as a bridgehead on the Anatolian-Arabian trade routes.

Adanson \á-däⁿ-sōⁿ\, **Michel** (1727–1806) French botanist. He studied theology, classics, and philosophy in Paris before traveling to Senegal, where he lived several years. He returned with a large collection of plant specimens, now in the National Museum of Natural History. In *Familles des plantes* (1763; "Families of Plants"), he described his classification system; it was opposed by Carolus Linnaeus, whose system eventually prevailed. He was the first to classify mollusks. He also studied electricity in torpedo fish and the effects of electrical current on regenerating frog legs and heads. He is now known mainly for introducing the use of statistical methods in botanical studies.

Adapa \ə-ˈdä-pə\ Legendary sage of the Sumerian city of Eridu. Endowed with great intelligence by Ea but still mortal, he was the hero of the Sumerian myth of the Fall of Man. Adapa was fishing when he was blown into the sea by the southern wind, whose wings he broke in rage. The heavenly doorkeepers Tammuz and Ningishzida interceded for him when he was summoned before Anu for punishment, but when Anu offered him the bread and water of eternal life, he refused, and humankind thus became mortal.

adaptation In biology, the process by which an animal or plant becomes fitted to its environment. It is the result of natural selection acting on inherited variation. Even simple organisms must be adapted in many ways, including structure, physiology, and genetics; movement or dispersal; means of defense and attack; and reproduction and development. To be useful, adaptations must often occur simultaneously in different parts of the body.

ADD See attention deficit disorder

Adda River \ˈäd-dä\ River, Lombardy region, Italy. It flows southward 194 mi (313 km) through Lake Como and across the Lombardy Plain before joining the Po River above Cremona. It is used extensively for hydroelectric power in its upper course and for irrigation on the plain. Historically, it has served as a strategic defense line in wars dating back to the Roman period.

Addams, Charles (Samuel) (1912–1988) U.S. cartoonist. Born in Westfield, N.J., he worked briefly as a commercial artist before selling his first cartoon to *The New Yorker* in 1933. He became famous for cartoons depicting morbid behavior by sinister-looking characters, especially a family of ghouls whose activities travestied those of a conventional family; in one popular image, they prepare to pour boiling oil on a group of Christmas carolers. These evolved into *The Addams Family,* a 1960s television series that generated two Hollywood films.

Addams, Jane (1860–1935) U.S. social reformer. Born in Cedarville, Ill., she became interested in social reform and she traveled in Europe and visited the Toynbee Hall settlement house in London. In 1889 she cofounded Hull House in Chicago, one of the first settlement houses in North America to provide practical services and educational opportunities for the poor. She championed such social reforms as juvenile-court law, justice for immigrants and blacks, worker's rights and compensation, and the women's suffrage movement. In 1910 she became the first female president of the National Conference of Social Work. An ardent pacifist, she served in 1915 as chair of the International Congress of Women and helped form the Women's International League for Peace and Freedom and the American Civil Liberties Union. In 1931 she shared the Nobel Peace Prize with Nicholas M. Butler.

adder Any of several venomous snakes of the viper family (Viperidae) and the death adder, a viperlike elapid. Vipers include the common adder, puff adders, and night adders. Adders occur in Europe, Asia, Africa, and Australia. They range in length from 18 in. to 5 ft (45 cm–1.5 m). The puff adder of Africa and the death adder of Australia and the nearby islands are particularly venomous, with a bite often lethal to humans. The name is also used for other snakes (e.g., the hognose snake).

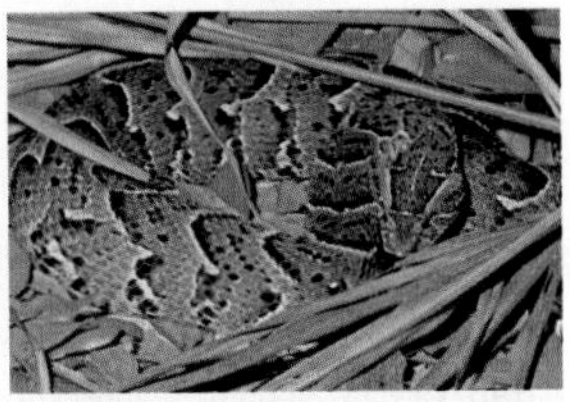

Puff adder (*Bitis arietans*).

Adderley, Cannonball *orig.* **Julian Edwin** (1928–1975) U.S. saxophonist, one of the most popular jazz musicians of the 1950s and '60s. Adderley was born in Tampa, Fla., and worked as a music teacher before moving to New York in 1955. Arriving shortly after the death of Charlie Parker, he was hailed as Parker's stylistic successor. He performed with Miles Davis 1957–59, then led an ensemble with his brother, cornetist Nat Adderley (1931–2000). Also influenced by Benny Carter, Adderley's playing showed a strong blues inspiration, and his music in the 1960s reflected the introduction of gospel-music harmonies. He died following a stroke at age 46.

Addis Ababa \ˈäd-dis-ˈä-bä-ˌbä, ˈa-dəs-ˈa-bə-bə\ Capital and largest city (pop., 1994: 2,113,000), Ethiopia. It lies on a plateau in the country's geographic center at an altitude of about 8,000 ft (2,450 m). The capital was moved there in 1896 because of the unsatisfactory location of its predecessor, Entoto. It was the capital of Italian East Africa 1935–41. It has become the national center for higher education, banking and insurance, and trade. Several international organizations have their headquarters there, including the Organization of African Unity. In recent decades it has suffered unrest and extensive damage as a result of the country's political instability.

Addison, Joseph (1672–1719) English essayist, poet, and dramatist. His poem on the Battle of Blenheim, *The Campaign* (1705), brought him to the attention of leading Whigs and paved the way to important government posts (including secretary of state) and literary fame. With Richard Steele, he was a leading contributor to and guiding spirit of the periodicals *The Tatler* (1709–11) and *The Spectator* (1711–12, 1714). One of the most admired masters of English prose, he brought to perfection the periodical essay. His *Cato* (1713), a highly successful play with political overtones, is one of the important tragedies of the 18th century.

Joseph Addison, oil painting by M. Dahl, 1719; in the National Portrait Gallery, London.

Addison's disease Disease in which gradual atrophy of the cortex of the adrenal glands causes them to produce insufficient quantities of the steroid hydrocortisone while causing the pituitary gland to produce excess quantities of pituitary hormones. Most of the cortex tissue is destroyed by the time symptoms (including weakness, abnormal coloration, weight loss, and hypotension) appear. Hydrocortisone replacement therapy is often successful, usually with hormones to stabilize sodium levels. More than half of cases are believed to be due to an autoimmune reaction (see AUTOIMMUNE DISEASE); the remainder are caused by destruction of the adrenal gland by granuloma (e.g., TUBERCULOSIS).

additive In foods, any of various chemical substances added to produce desirable effects. Additives include such substances as artificial or natural colorings and flavorings; stabilizers, emulsifiers, and thickeners; preservatives and humectants (moisture-retainers); and supplementary nutrients. Though many additives are harmless or even beneficial, others reduce nutritional value or conceal inferior raw materials or processing.

Adelaide City (pop., 1995: 1,081,000) and capital, S. AUSTRALIA. The city lies at the base of the Mount Lofty Ranges on the Torrens River, near its harbor facilities at Port Adelaide. Founded in 1837, it was incorporated in 1840 as Australia's first municipal government. Its rise as an agricultural marketing center and the proximity of natural mineral deposits contributed to its economic growth. It is an industrial center and has petroleum refineries as well as connections by pipeline to natural-gas fields. Landmarks include the University of Adelaide, parliament and government houses, and two cathedrals.

Aden \'ä-dən, 'ā-dən\ Seaport city (pop., 1995: 562,000), southern Yemen, on the Gulf of ADEN. It was a principal terminus of the spice road of western Arabia for about 1,000 years before the 3rd century AD. It then became a trading center under Yemeni, Ethiopian, and Arab control. The Turks captured the city in 1538, and the British governed it as part of India 1839–1937. It grew in importance as a coaling station and transshipment point after the opening of the SUEZ CANAL. It was separated from India and made a crown colony in 1937, incorporated in the Federation of South Arabia (1963–67), and served as the capital of South Yemen until that republic's merger with North Yemen in 1990.

Aden, Gulf of Arm of the Indian Ocean between the ARABIAN PENINSULA and Somalia. To the west, it narrows into the Gulf of Tadjoura; its eastern limit is the meridian of Cape Guardafui. In these terms it is about 550 mi (885 km) long; geologically, it extends a total of 920 mi (1,480 km), to the eastern limits of the continental shelf beyond the Kuria Muria islands and the island of SOCOTRA. Its marine life is rich in quantity and variety. Its coastline lacks large-scale fishing facilities but supports many fishing towns, as well as the major ports ADEN and DJIBOUTI.

Adena culture \ə-'dē-nə\ Culture of various communities of ancient North American Indians, c. 500 BC–AD 100, occupying the middle Ohio River Valley. The Adena usually lived in villages containing circular houses constructed of poles and bark. They subsisted by hunting, fishing, and gathering wild plant foods and used a variety of stone tools and simple pottery. Adena ornaments of copper, mica, and seashells indicate trade with faraway peoples. See also WOODLAND CULTURES.

Adenauer \'a-dᵊn-au̇r\, **Konrad** (1876–1967) German statesman, first chancellor of the Federal Republic of Germany (West Germany). Elected to the Cologne city council (1906), he served as the city's lord mayor 1917–33. He was elected to the Prussian Staatsrat (state council) in 1920 and served as its speaker 1928–33. He lost his posts when the Nazis came to power, and in 1944 he was sent to a concentration camp. As World War II drew to a close, he played an important role in the formation of the CHRISTIAN DEMOCRATIC UNION. As chancellor from 1949, Adenauer stressed individualism under the rule of law. His fear of Soviet expansion made him a strong supporter of NATO. He worked hard to reconcile Germany with its former enemies, especially France and Russia. He retired in 1963.

Adenauer.

adenine \'a-dᵊn-ˌēn\ Organic compound of the PURINE family, often called a base, consisting of two rings, each containing both nitrogen and carbon atoms, and an amino group. It occurs free in tea and in combined form in NUCLEIC ACIDS, ATP, VITAMIN B_{12}, and several COENZYMES. In DNA its complementary base is THYMINE. It or its corresponding NUCLEOSIDE or NUCLEOTIDE may be prepared from nucleic acids by selective techniques of HYDROLYSIS.

adenoids \'a-dᵊn-ˌȯidz\ *or* **pharyngeal tonsils** \ˌfar-ən-'jē-əl, fə-'rin-jē-əl\ Mass of LYMPHOID TISSUE, similar to the (palatine) TONSILS, on the back wall of the nasal PHARYNX. If the adenoids become infected in childhood, their inflammation can obstruct nasal breathing and SINUS drainage (promoting SINUSITIS) and block the eustachian tubes that connect to the middle ear (setting the stage for OTITIS). Surgical removal of enlarged or infected adenoids is frequently recommended.

adenosine triphosphate See ATP

adenovirus \ˌa-dᵊn-ō-'vī-rəs\ Any of a group of spheroidal VIRUSES, made up of DNA wrapped in a protein coat, that cause sore throat and fever in humans, HEPATITIS in dogs, and several diseases in fowl, mice, cattle, pigs, and monkeys. An adenovirus develops within the nucleus of an infected cell. In humans, adenoviruses, like cold viruses, may cause infections of the upper respiratory tract, the eyes, and frequently the lymph nodes. Like cold viruses, adenoviruses are often found in inactive infections in clinically healthy persons. Because only a few adenoviruses commonly cause illness in humans, vaccines against them are possible.

Adès \'ad-əs\, **Thomas** (born 1971) British composer. Trained as a pianist at the Guildhall School, he later attended King's College, Cambridge. Initial recognition came for his virtuoso piano playing, but he started to write music in 1990 (*Five Eliot Landscapes*) and was instantly acclaimed a major composer for his inventiveness and remarkably secure technique. His controversial opera *Powder Her Face* (1995), about a 20th-century divorce scandal, attracted international attention, as did his large symphonic work *Asyla* (1997).

ADHD See ATTENTION DEFICIT DISORDER

Adi Granth \ˌä-dē-'grănth\ (Punjabi: "First Book") Sacred scripture of SIKHISM. Composed of nearly 6,000 hymns of the Sikh GURUS and Hindu and Islamic saints, it is the central object of worship in all GURDWARAS (temples). It is ritually opened and closed daily and is read continuously on special occasions. First compiled in 1604 by ARJAN, it included his own hymns and those of his predecessors and the devotional songs of saints. In 1704 the last Guru, GOBIND SINGH, added more hymns and decreed that after his death the Granth would take the place of the Guru. Written mostly in Punjabi or Hindi, it contains the *Mul Mantra* (basic prayer), *Japji* (the most important scripture, written by NANAK), and hymns arranged according to the RAGAS in which they are to be sung.

Adige River \'ä-dē-ˌjā\ River, 255 mi (410 km) long, the longest in Italy after the PO. It rises below the Resia Pass and flows southeast through the Venosta Valley. After receiving the Isarco River at Bolzano, it turns south across the Po lowlands to enter the ADRIATIC SEA south of Chioggia. It supplies hydroelectric power in its upper alpine section and irrigation for the VENETO. Its floods, including those of 1951 and 1966, do great damage and require constant control of the riverbank. The Adige has been the scene of many battles, notably in the Austrian-Italian campaign of 1916.

adipose tissue *or* **fatty tissue** CONNECTIVE TISSUE consisting mainly of fat cells, specialized to synthesize and contain large globules of FAT, with a structural network of fibers. It is found mainly under the skin but also in deposits between the muscles, among the intestines and in their membrane folds, around the heart, and elsewhere. The fat stored in this tissue comes from dietary fats or is produced in the body. It acts as a fuel reserve for times of starvation or great exertion, helps conserve body heat, and forms pads between organs.

Adirondack Mountains \ˌa-də-'rän-ˌdak\ Mountains in northeastern New York state. They extend south from the ST. LAWRENCE RIVER valley and Lake CHAMPLAIN to the MOHAWK RIVER valley. The Adirondack region covers more than 6 million acres (2.4 million hectares). It has more than 40 summits higher than 4,000 ft (1,219 m); the tallest, Mount Marcy (5,344 ft, or 629 m), is the state's highest. SAMUEL DE CHAMPLAIN became the first European to sight the Adirondacks in 1609. The area was sparsely settled when in 1892 the state legislature created Adirondack Park, which has grown over the years to become, at over 5 million acres

(2 million hectares), the largest U.S. state or national park outside of Alaska.

Adler, Alfred (1870–1937) Austrian psychiatrist. He earned his medical degree in Vienna, and from his earliest years as a physician he stressed consideration of the individual in relation to his or her total environment. A student and associate of SIGMUND FREUD (1902–11), he eventually broke with Freud over the importance of early-childhood sexual conflicts in the development of psychopathology. With his followers he developed the school of individual psychology, the humanistic study of drives, feelings, emotions, and memory in the context of the individual's overall life plan. Adler advanced the theory of the INFERIORITY COMPLEX to explain cases of psychopathology; Adlerian psychotherapy sought to direct patients emotionally disabled by inferiority feelings toward maturity, common sense, and social usefulness. He established the first child-guidance clinic in 1921 in Vienna. He taught in the U.S. (at Columbia University and the Long Island College of Medicine) from 1927 until his death. His works include *Understanding Human Nature* (1927) and *What Life Should Mean to You* (1931).

Adler, Guido (1855–1941) Austrian musicologist. After studies at the Vienna Conservatory, he studied music history at the University of Vienna under Eduard Hanslick (1825–1904), whom he succeeded as professor. He worked with Philipp Spitta (1841–1894) and FRIEDRICH CHRYSANDER in founding MUSICOLOGY as an academic discipline. He wrote an early survey of methods of musical scholarship (1919). Among his distinguished students were Karl Geiringer (1899–1989), Knud Jeppesen (1892–1974), ANTON WEBERN, and Egon Wellesz (1885–1974).

Adler, Larry *orig.* **Lawrence Cecil** (1914–2001) U.S. harmonica player. Born in Baltimore, Adler became the first person to perform concert music on the harmonica (though he had only learned to read music in his mid-twenties). His musicality attracted many composers to write especially for him, including DARIUS MILHAUD and RALPH VAUGHAN WILLIAMS. His political activities caused him to be blacklisted in the early 1950s, and he lived in England for a number of years.

Adler, Mortimer J(erome) (1902–2001) U.S. philosopher, educator, and editor. Born in New York City, he earned a doctorate from Columbia University and taught philosophy of law at the University of Chicago from 1930, where he joined with ROBERT M. HUTCHINS to promote the idea of liberal education based on great books. Together they edited the 54-volume *Great Books of the Western World* (1952), and Adler later edited other series. In 1969 he became director of planning for *ENCYCLOPÆDIA BRITANNICA*, and he served as chairman of its board of editors 1974–95. His many books include *How to Read a Book* (1940) and *The Paideia Proposal* (1982).

administrative law Law regulating the powers, procedures, and acts of public administration. It applies to all public officials and public agencies. As distinguished from legislative and judicial authority, administrative authority entails the power to issue rules and regulations based on statutes, grant licenses and permits to facilitate the conduct of government business, initiate investigations of and provide remedies for complaints or problems, and issue orders directing parties to conform to governing statutes or rules. An administrative-law judge is a government official with quasi-judicial powers, including the authority to conduct hearings, make findings of fact, and recommend resolution of disputes concerning the agency's actions.

admiral butterfly Any of several species of BUTTERFLIES (family Nymphalidae) that are colorful, fast-flying, and much prized by collectors. The migratory red admiral *(Vanessa atalanta),* widespread in Europe, Scandinavia, North America, and North Africa, feeds on stinging nettles. The Indian red admiral *(V. indica)* is found in the Canary Islands and India. The white admiral *(Limenitis camilla,* or *Basilarchia arthemis),* a Eurasian and North American species, feeds on honeysuckle.

Admiralty, High Court of See HIGH COURT OF ADMIRALTY

Admiralty Islands Extension of the BISMARCK ARCHIPELAGO. The group lies about 190 mi (300 km) north of Papua New Guinea in the South Pacific Ocean and comprises about 40 islands. Manus Island contains most of its land area and is the site of Lorengau, the islands' principal settlement. First sighted by the Dutch explorer Willem Schouten in 1616, it was named by the British captain Philip Carteret in 1767. Subsequently ruled by the Germans, Australians, and Japanese, the islands were made part of the U.N. Trust Territory of New Guinea in 1946. When Papua New Guinea attained independence in 1975, the islands became part of that country.

admiralty law See MARITIME LAW

adobe \ə-ˈdō-bē\ Handmade sun-dried bricks formed from a mixture of heavy clay and straw found in arid regions. As a building material, adobe dates back thousands of years and is found in many parts of the world. Molds for shaping the bricks were brought to the New World by the Spanish. Excellent insulating properties make adobe an ideal material for both dwellings and ovens; home interiors retain heat in winter and stay cool in summer. The adobe buildings at Taos, N.M., are typical of Native American PUEBLO dwellings.

adolescence Period of life from PUBERTY to ADULTHOOD (roughly ages 12–20) characterized by marked physiological changes, development of sexual feelings, efforts toward the construction of identity, and a progression from concrete to abstract thought. Adolescence is sometimes viewed as a transitional state, during which youths begin to separate themselves from their parents but still lack a clearly defined role in society. It is generally regarded as an emotionally intense and often stressful period.

Adonis \ə-ˈdä-nəs\ In GREEK MYTHOLOGY, a youth of remarkable beauty, the favorite of APHRODITE. As a child he was put in the care of PERSEPHONE, who refused to allow him to return from the underworld. ZEUS ruled that he should spend a third of the year with Persephone, a third with Aphrodite, and a third on his own. He became a hunter and was killed by a boar. In answer to Aphrodite's pleas, Zeus allowed him to spend half the year with her and half in the underworld. Mythically, Adonis represents the cycle of death and resurrection in winter and spring. He is identified with the Babylonian god TAMMUZ.

adoption Act of transferring parental rights and duties to someone other than a minor's biological parents. The practice is ancient and occurs in all cultures. Traditionally, its goal was to continue the male line for the purposes of inheritance and succession; most adoptees were male (and sometimes adult). Contemporary laws and practices aim to promote child welfare and the development of families. A decline in the number of children available for legal adoption in the late 20th century loosened traditional restrictions on adult-child age differential, level of income, mother's employment outside the home, and placement across religious and ethnic lines. Single-parent adoptions and adoptions by same-sex couples also became more acceptable.

Adorno \ä-ˈdȯr-nō\, **Theodor (Wiesengrund)** (1903–1969) German philosopher. He was educated at Johann Wolfgang Goethe University and taught briefly at the University of Frankfurt before emigrating to England in 1934 to escape Nazism. He lived 10 years in the U.S. (1938–48) before returning to Frankfurt, where he taught and headed the Frankfurt Institute for Social Research (see FRANKFURT SCHOOL). He is notable for his books and essays on philosophy, literature, psychology, sociology, and music (which he studied with ALBAN BERG). For Adorno, the great task of modernist music, literature, and art was to keep alive the possible social alternatives to capitalism, which philosophy and political theory could no longer imagine. His works include *Dialectic of Enlightenment* (1947; with MAX HORKHEIMER), *Minima Moralia* (1951), and *Notes to Literature* (4 vols., 1958–74).

Adour River \ə-ˈdür\ River, southwestern France. Flowing northwest from the PYRENEES, it traverses the scenic Campan Valley; beyond Tarbes it feeds irrigation canals, most importantly the Canal d'Alaric. After a course of 208 mi (335 km), it empties into the Bay of BISCAY below Bayonne.

Adowa \ˈäd-ə-wə\, **Battle of** *or* **Battle of Adwa** Military clash (March 1, 1896) at Adowa, in northern central Ethiopia, between the Ethiopian army of King MENILEK II and Italian forces. The decisive Ethiopian victory produced independence for Ethiopia and checked Italy's attempt to build an empire in Africa comparable to that of the French or British. The colony of ERITREA was carved out in the ensuing peace negotiations.

adrenal gland \ə-ˈdrē-nᵊl\ *or* **suprarenal gland** \ˌsü-prə-ˈrē-nᵊl\ Either of two small, triangular endocrine GLANDS over the kidneys. In humans, each gland weighs about 0.15 oz (4.5 g) and consists of an inner medulla, which produces the catecholamine hormones EPINEPHRINE and norepinephrine, and an outer cortex (about 90% of the gland), which secretes the STEROID hormones aldosterone, cortisol, and ANDROGENS (the last two in response to ACTH from the PITUITARY GLAND). Diseases of the adrenal glands include pheochromocytoma (a tumor of the medulla), and the cortical disorders ADDISON'S DISEASE, adrenal hypertrophy, CUSHING'S SYNDROME, ADRENOGENITAL SYNDROME, and primary aldosteronism.

adrenaline See EPINEPHRINE

adrenogenital syndrome \ə-ˌdrē-nō-ˈje-nit-əl\ Complex of symptoms resulting from excessive secretion of androgenic 17-ketosteroid hormones by the adrenal cortex. In infants and children, the cause is genetic: the ADRENAL GLANDS produce too little cortisol and too much ANDROGEN. Results are masculine secondary sexual characteristics, possibly with malelike genital changes (pseudohermaphroditism) in females, or early development of secondary sexual characteristics and excessive penile development with small testes in males; dark skin; and disorders of metabolism, homeostasis, and hormonal status. Adult females exhibit male physical characteristics and lack of menstruation and ovulation.

Adrian, Edgar Douglas *later* **Baron Adrian of Cambridge** (1889–1977) British electrophysiologist. He amplified electrical potential variations in nerve impulses from sense organs to record ever smaller changes, eventually recording impulses from single sensory endings and motor nerve fibers. His work clarified the physical basis of sensation and the mechanism of muscular control. Adrian's later studies of brain electrical activity included investigations into epilepsy and the location of cerebral lesions. He shared a 1932 Nobel Prize with CHARLES SHERRINGTON.

Adrian IV \ˈā-drē-ən\ *orig.* **Nicholas Breakspear** (1100?–1159) Pope (1154–59), the only Englishman ever to hold the office. He served in France and Italy before a successful mission to Scandinavia led to his election as pope. Adrian crowned FREDERICK I BARBAROSSA emperor in 1155, but his policy toward the Normans of southern Italy soon aroused the emperor's anger. His controversial bull *Laudabiliter* supposedly gave Ireland to HENRY II of England, a claim that was later refuted. Adrian's refusal to recognize the king of Sicily, William I, stirred revolt in the Campania.

Adrianople, Battle of *or* **Battle of Hadrianopolis** (AD 378) Battle fought in present-day Edirne, Turkey, that marked the beginning of serious Germanic incursions into Roman territory. It pitted the Roman army under the emperor VALENS against the horsemen of the VISIGOTHS, OSTROGOTHS, and other Germanic tribes. The Roman army was annihilated and Valens died on the battlefield. His successor, THEODOSIUS I, and the GOTHS agreed in 382 that the Goths would help with imperial defenses in exchange for food subsidies. The treaty set the pattern for later barbarian intrusions.

Adrianople, Treaty of See Treaty of EDIRNE

Adriatic Sea Arm of the MEDITERRANEAN SEA, lying between Italy and the Balkan Peninsula. It is about 500 mi (800 km) long, with an average width of 110 mi (175 km), a maximum depth of 4,035 ft (1,324 m), and an area of 50,590 sq mi (131,050 sq km). The Italian coast is relatively straight and continuous, having no islands, but the Balkan coast is full of large and small islands, generally running parallel to the shore. The Strait of Otranto at its southeasterly limit links it with the Ionian Sea.

adsorption Capability of a SOLID substance (adsorbent) to attract to its surface MOLECULES of a GAS or SOLUTION (adsorbate) with which it is in contact. Physical adsorption depends on VAN DER WAALS FORCES of attraction between molecules and resembles condensation of liquids. In chemical adsorption (often called chemisorption; see CATALYSIS), the gas is held to the surface by chemical forces specific to the chemicals involved, and formation of the bond may require an ACTIVATION ENERGY.

Adullam \ə-ˈdəl-əm\ Ancient village, Israel, 15 mi (24 km) southwest of Jerusalem. A cave in its vicinity was from early times a place of refuge; it is mentioned several times in the Bible, including as the place where David hid from Saul. In modern Israel the name Adullam is given to a development center west of Jerusalem.

adult education See CONTINUING EDUCATION

adultery Sexual relations between a married person and someone other than the spouse. Prohibitions against adultery are found in virtually every society; Jewish, Islamic, and Christian traditions all condemn it. Attitudes toward adultery in different cultures have varied widely. In ancient Rome, for example, an offending female could be killed, but men were not severely punished. In Western Europe and North America, adultery by either spouse is a ground for divorce. The spread of Western ideas of equality in marriage has resulted in pressure for equal marital rights for women in traditional African and Southeast Asian societies.

adulthood Period in the human life span in which full physical and intellectual maturity have been attained. Adulthood is commonly thought of as beginning at age 20 or 21. It includes middle age (commencing around age 40) and old age (from about age 60). Physically, it is characterized by the peaking (around age 30) and gradual decline of bodily functioning; the post-peak phase includes diminished acuity of the senses, reduction in muscular and skeletal mass, buildup of cholesterol in the arteries, weakening of the heart muscle, and diminished production of hormones. Some slowing in the rate of central-nervous-system processing also begins with middle age, but is generally compensated for by an increased capacity to retain practical information and apply accumulated cultural knowledge. In old age, most individuals experience a significant decline in physical capacity, and many eventually also suffer impaired mental function.

Advaita \əd-ˈvī-tə\ (Sanskrit: "Nondualism") Most influential school of VEDANTA. It originated with Gaudapada's 7th-century commentary on the Mandukya UPANISHAD. Gaudapada builds on the MAHAYANA Buddhist philosophy of emptiness, asserting that there is no duality; the mind, awake or dreaming, moves through MAYA (illusion). The mind's ignorance conceals the truth that there is no becoming and no individual soul or self (JIVA), only a temporary delineation from the ATMAN (all-soul). In the 8th century SANKARA developed Advaita further, arguing that the world is unreal and that the Upanishads teach the nature of BRAHMAN, the only reality. The extensive Advaita literature influences modern Hindu thought.

Advent In the Christian calendar, the first season of the church year, a period of preparation for the birth of JESUS. Advent begins on the Sunday nearest to November 30 and continues until CHRISTMAS. Viewed as a penitential season, it is also considered a time of preparation for the Second Coming of Christ. The origin of Advent is unknown, but it was observed as early as the 6th century. In many countries it is celebrated with popular customs such as the lighting of Advent candles.

Adventist Member of any of a group of Protestant churches that arose in the U.S. in the 19th century and assert that the Second Coming of Christ is close at hand. Adventism was founded during a period marked by MILLENNIALISM by William Miller (1782–1849), a former U.S. army officer, who asserted that Christ would return to separate saints from sinners and inaugurate his 1,000-year kingdom on earth sometime in the year before March 21, 1844. After that date passed, Miller and his followers set a new date, October 22, 1884. The "Great Disappointment" was followed by a Mutual Conference of Adventists in 1845. Those who persisted concluded that Miller had misinterpreted the signs and that, though Christ had begun the "cleansing of the heavenly sanctuary," he would not appear until he had completed that task. These Millerites founded the Seventh-Day Adventists in 1863; other Adventist groups include the Evangelical Adventists and the Advent Christian Church. Seventh-Day Adventists observe Saturday as the SABBATH and avoid eating meat and using narcotics and other stimulants.

adversary procedure In Anglo-American law, the principal method of offering evidence in court. It requires the opposing sides to present pertinent information and to introduce and cross-examine witnesses before a jury and/or a judge. Each side must conduct its own investigation. In criminal proceedings, the prosecution represents the government and has at its disposal the police department with its investigators and laboratories; the defense must arrange and pay for its own investigation. (Legal aid is available for the poor.) In civil (noncriminal) proceedings the adversary system works similarly, except that both sides engage private attorneys to prepare their cases. Skillful questioning often produces testimony that can be interpreted in various ways; in cross-examination, lawyers seek to alter the jury's initial perception of the testimony.

adverse possession In Anglo-American property law, holding of real property (see REAL AND PERSONAL PROPERTY) with the knowledge and against the will of one who has a superior ownership interest in it. Statutes of limitation in most U.S. states allow an adverse possessor to acquire legal title if the owner does not seek timely possession.

advertising Techniques and practices used to bring products, services, opinions, or causes to public notice for the purpose of persuading the public to respond in a certain way. Weekly newspapers in London first carried advertisements in the 17th century; by the 18th century such advertising was flourishing. The first advertising agencies were established in the 19th century to broker for space in newspapers, and by the early 20th century agencies were producing the advertising message itself, including copy and artwork. Most advertising promotes goods for sale, but similar methods are used in public-service messages, to promote causes, charities, or political candidates. In many countries, advertising is the most important source of income for the media through which it is conducted. In addition to newspapers, magazines, and broadcast media, advertising media include direct mail (see DIRECT-MAIL MARKETING), billboards and posters, transit advertising, the Internet, and promotional items such as matchbooks or calendars. Advertisers attempt to choose media that are favored by the advertisers' target audience. See also MARKETING, MERCHANDISING.

adze *or* **adz** Hand tool for shaping wood. A handheld stone chipped to form a blade, it is one of the earliest tools, and was used widely in the PALEOLITHIC and NEOLITHIC periods. By Egyptian times, it had acquired a wooden haft (handle) with a copper or BRONZE blade set flat at the top of the haft to form a T. In this form but with a steel blade, it continued to be the prime hand tool for shaping and trimming wood; the carpenter stands on or astride a log or other piece of timber, swinging the adze like a pick, down and between the legs.

Æ \'ā-'ē\ *orig.* **George William Russell** (1876–1935) Irish poet and mystic. A leading figure in the IRISH LITERARY RENAISSANCE, he published many books of verse, including *Homeward* (1894). Though initially considered by many to be the equal of WILLIAM BUTLER YEATS, he did not develop as a poet, and many critics found him facile, vague, and monotonous. His pseudonym arose from a proofreader's query about an earlier pseudonym, Æon.

Aegean civilizations \ē-'jē-ən\ BRONZE AGE civilizations c. 3000–1000 BC in the area of the Aegean Sea. They included CRETE, the CYCLADES, the Greek mainland south from Thessaly, including the Peloponnese, and MACEDONIA, THRACE, and western Anatolia. The most significant were the MINOAN and MYCENAEAN civilizations. The term also sometimes refers to NEOLITHIC civilizations in the same region c. 7000–3000 BC.

Aegean Islands \ē-'jē-ən\ Greek islands, AEGEAN SEA, particularly the CYCLADES, Sporades, and Dodecanese groups. The Cyclades consist of about 220 islands. The Dodecanese, or Southern Sporades, include Kalymnos, Karpathos, Kos, Leros, Patmos, RHODES, and Simi; some geographers also include SAMOS, Ikaria, CHIOS, and LESBOS. The Sporades, or Northern Sporades, include Skyros, Skopelos, and Skiathos. All the islands have to some extent shared Greece's history through the centuries.

Aegean Sea Arm of the MEDITERRANEAN SEA, lying between Greece and Turkey. About 380 mi (610 km) long and 186 mi (300 km) wide, it has a total area of some 83,000 sq mi (214,000 sq km) and a maximum depth of 11,627 ft (3,543 m). The straits of the DARDANELLES, the Sea of MARMARA, and the BOSPORUS connect it with the BLACK SEA. The Aegean was the cradle of the great early civilizations of Crete and Greece. THÍRA, one of its numerous islands, has been linked with the legend of ATLANTIS.

Aegina \ē-'jī-nə\ Island in the Saronic group of Greece. Located 16 mi (26 km) southwest of Piraeus, it has an area of 32 sq mi (83 sq km). Its chief town and port, Aegina, lies over the ancient town of the same name. Inhabited since c. 3000 BC, it became a maritime power after the 7th century BC; its period of glory, reflected in PINDAR's poetry, was in the 5th century BC. Its economic rivalry with Athens led to frequent warfare, and in 431 BC the Athenians deported all its population. It came under Roman rule in 133 BC. It was briefly the capital of independent Greece (1826–28). See photograph opposite.

aegirine \'ā-gə-ˌrēn\ PYROXENE mineral, sodium and iron silicate ($NaFe^{+3}Si_2O_6$), commonly found in alkaline igneous rocks, particularly in syenites (composed of an alkali feldspar and a ferromagnesian mineral) and syenite PEGMATITES. It also occurs in SCHISTS. Aegirine is generally dark green to greenish black.

aegis \'ē-jəs\ In ancient Greece, the leather cloak or breastplate associated with ZEUS. It was worn most prominently by Zeus's daughter ATHENA (whose aegis bore the head of MEDUSA) but occasionally also by other gods (e.g., APOLLO in the *Iliad*).

Aegospotami \ˌē-gə-'spä-tə-ˌmī\, **Battle of** (405 BC) Naval victory of Sparta over Athens in the final battle of the PELOPONNESIAN WAR. The Spartans under LYSANDER surprised the Athenians at anchor off Aegospotami, in Thrace, and defeated them decisively. The Athenians escaped with only 20 of 180 ships, and the Spartans put almost 4,000 captured Athenians to death. The victory led to the Spartan march on Athens and the Athenian surrender in 404.

Aehrenthal \'e-rən-ˌtäl\, **Aloys, Graf (Count) Lexa von** (1854–1912) Austro-Hungarian diplomat. As foreign minister of Austria-Hungary (1906–12), he aggressively revived the empire's dormant foreign policy. His proclamation of the annexation of Bosnia and Herzegovina in 1908 provoked fears of war with Russia, inflamed Serbia's Austrophobe passions, and drew international censure, leading to the BOSNIAN CRISIS.

Aeneas \i-'nē-əs\ Mythical hero of Troy and Rome. He was the son of APHRODITE and Anchises, a member of Trojan royal family. According to HOMER, he was second only to his cousin HECTOR in defending Troy during the TROJAN WAR. VIRGIL's *Aeneid* tells of Aeneas's escape after Troy's fall, carrying his elderly father on his back, and of his journey to Italy, where his descendants became the rulers of Rome. See also DIDO.

Aeolian harp \ē-'ō-lē-ən\ Stringed instrument played by the wind (named for the wind god AEOLUS). It is usually a long, narrow, shallow box with soundholes and 10 or 12 strings strung lengthwise between two bridges. The strings are of the same length but different thicknesses and are all tuned to the same pitch; the wind makes them vibrate in successively higher HARMONICS. The harp may be hung, or set horizontally under a window sash. The first known Aeolian harp was constructed c. 1650 by Athanasius Kircher (1601–1680).

Aeolus \'ē-ə-ləs\ Greek god of the winds. In the *Odyssey*, HOMER represents Aeolus as the mortal ruler of the floating island of Aeolia. He gives ODYSSEUS a favorable wind for his voyage and a bag in which the unfavorable winds are confined, but Odysseus' careless companions open the bag, releasing the winds and driving their ship back to shore. Later writers depicted Aeolus as a minor god rather than a human being. The AEOLIAN HARP is named for him.

aeon *or* **eon** \'ē-ˌän\ In GNOSTICISM or MANICHAEISM, one of the orders of spirits, or spheres of being, emanating from the godhead. The first aeon emanated directly from unmanifested divinity and was charged with divine force. Aeons increased in number and decreased in divine energy with increased remoteness from the divinity. At sufficient remoteness, error became possible and was the source of the material universe. Aeons may be viewed positively, as embodiments of the divine, or nega-

The temple of Aphaea, Aegina, Greece.
SUSAN MCCARTNEY—PHOTO RESEARCHERS

A–B

tively, as media through which the soul must pass to reach its divine origin.

aepyornis \ˌē-pē-ˈȯr-nəs\ *or* **elephant bird** Any of a group of giant flightless birds in the extinct genus *Aepyornis,* found as fossils in Pleistocene and post-Pleistocene deposits on Madagascar. Most were massively constructed (some stood more than 10 ft, or 3 m, high) and had a small skull and a long slim neck. Remains of aepyornis and its eggs (as large as 3 ft, or 1 m, in circumference) are common. Its ancestry is uncertain.

aerarium (Saturni) Central treasury of ancient Rome, housed in the Temple of Saturn. During the republic (509–27 BC), two QUAESTORS managed the treasury and the Senate controlled it. All revenues were paid into the aerarium, and approved payments were made from it. Under the principate (27 BC–AD 305) the aerarium lost funds and importance, as emperors and magistrates bypassed Senate control and drew directly from the *fisci* (provincial treasuries). From AD 6 AUGUSTUS used taxes to fund the *aerarium militare,* a public treasury, to reward veterans, and the aerarium Saturni became the treasury of the city of Rome.

aerial See ANTENNA

aerial perspective Method of producing a sense of depth in a painting by imitating the effect of atmosphere that makes objects look paler, bluer, and hazier or less distinct in the middle and far distance. The term was coined by LEONARDO DA VINCI, but the technique can be seen in ancient Greco-Roman wall paintings (e.g., at POMPEII). It was discovered that dust and moisture in the atmosphere caused the scattering of light passing through it; short-wavelength light (blue) is scattered most and long-wavelength light (red) least. Italian painters in Leonardo's time used the device; it was exploited by 15th-century northern European artists and later by J.M.W. TURNER.

aerobatics Sport of performing spectacular flying feats and maneuvers, such as rolls, loops, stalls, spins, and dives. As an organized sport, rather than as an air-show attraction ("stunt flying"), aerobatics began international competition in 1964. The annual contest of the Experimental Aircraft Assoc. (U.S.) is one of the largest.

aerobics System of physical conditioning for increasing the efficiency of the body's intake of oxygen. Aerobic exercises (e.g., running, jogging, swimming, dancing) stimulate heart and lung activity. To produce a benefit, aerobic training must raise the heart rate (pulse) to the exerciser's training level for at least 20 minutes and include at least three sessions a week. The concept of aerobics was pioneered by Kenneth H. Cooper and popularized in his books *Aerobics* (1968) and *The Aerobics Way* (1977).

aerodynamics Branch of physics concerned with the forces acting on bodies passing through air and other gaseous fluids. It explains the principles of flight of aircraft, rockets, and missiles. It is also involved in the design of automobiles, trains, and ships, and even stationary structures such as bridges and tall buildings, which must withstand high winds. Aerodynamics emerged as a discipline around the time of WILBUR AND ORVILLE WRIGHT's first powered flight in 1903. Developments in the field have led to major advances in turbulence theory and supersonic flight.

Aeroflot \ˌar-ə-ˈflȯt\ State airline of the former Soviet Union. Founded in 1928 as Dobroflot, it was reorganized as Aeroflot in 1932. During the Soviet era Aeroflot was the world's largest airline, with about 15% of all civil air traffic. After the 1991 breakup of the Soviet Union, Aeroflot surrendered its monopoly over commercial air travel in the former Soviet states while remaining Russia's national airline.

aerosol System of tiny liquid or solid particles evenly distributed in a finely divided state through a gas, usually air. Aerosol particles participate in chemical processes and influence the electrical properties of the atmosphere. Though true aerosol particles range in diameter from a few millimicrometers to about 1 micrometer, the term is commonly used to refer to fog or cloud droplets and dust particles, which can have diameters of more than 100 micrometers. See also COLLOID, EMULSION.

aerospace engineering Field concerned with the development, design, construction, testing, and operation of AIRPLANES and SPACECRAFT. The field has its roots in BALLOON flight, GLIDERS, and AIRSHIPS, and in the 1960s was broadened to include space vehicles. Principal technologies are those of AERODYNAMICS, propulsion, structure and stability, and control. Aerospace engineers in academic, industrial, and government research centers cooperate in designing new products. Flight testing of prototypes follows, and finally quantity production and operation. Important developments in aerospace engineering include the metal monocoque fuselage, the cantilevered monoplane wing, the JET ENGINE, supersonic flight, and space flight.

aerospace medicine Branch of medicine, pioneered by PAUL BERT, dealing with atmospheric flight (aviation medicine) and space flight (space medicine). Intensive preflight simulator training and attention to design of equipment and spacecraft promote the safety and effectiveness of humans exposed to the stresses of flight and can prevent some problems. The world's first unit for space research was established in the U.S. in 1948. Physicians trained in aerospace medicine are known as flight surgeons.

Aeschines \ˈes-kə-ˌnēz\ (390–314? BC) Athenian orator and advocate of PHILIP II of Macedonia's expansion into Greece. He and DEMOSTHENES, who later became his bitter opponent, participated in 346 BC in forging a peace between Athens and Macedonia. Demosthenes later accused Aeschines of treason because he had promoted the Macedonian cause during the negotiations. At a trial (343) Aeschines was acquitted by a narrow majority. In 339 he helped incite the war that led to the Battle of CHAERONEA and to Macedonian control of central Greece. In 336 he opposed as illegal a motion to honor Demosthenes; the matter came to trial in 330, and Aeschines suffered an overwhelming defeat.

Aeschylus \ˈes-kə-ˌləs\ (525–456 BC) Greek tragic dramatist. He fought with the Athenian army at Marathon (490 BC) and won the first of several major dramatic competitions in Athens in 484 BC. He wrote over 80 plays, but only seven are extant; the earliest of these, the *Persians,* was performed in 472 BC. Other plays that survive are the *Oresteia* trilogy *(Agamemnon, The Libation Bearers,* and *The Eumenides), Seven Against Thebes, The Suppliants,* and *Prometheus Bound.* Considered the father of Greek tragic drama, he added a second actor to the performance, an innovation that enabled the later development of dialogue and created true dramatic action. He was the first of the three great Greek tragedians, preceding SOPHOCLES and EURIPIDES.

Aesculapius See ASCLEPIUS

Aesir \ˈā-zir\ In GERMANIC RELIGION, one of the two main groups of deities, the other being the VANIR. ODIN, his wife FRIGG, Tyr (the god of war), and THOR were the four Aesir common to the Germanic nations. BALDER and LOKI were considered Aesir by other peoples. The Aesir were a warlike race and were originally dominant over the Vanir, but after numerous defeats in battle they were forced to grant the Vanir equal status. The poet-god KVASIR was born out of the peace ritual in which the two races mingled their saliva in the same vessel.

Aesop \ˈē-ˌsäp\ Supposed author of a collection of Greek FABLES, almost certainly a legendary figure. Though HERODOTUS, in the 5th century BC, said that he was an actual personage, "Aesop" was probably no more than a name invented to provide an author for fables centering on beasts. Aesopian fables emphasize the social interactions of human beings, and the morals they draw tend to embody advice on how to deal with the competitive realities of life. The Western fable tradition effectively begins with these tales. Modern editions list some 200 Aesopian fables.

Aesop, with a fox, from the central medallion of a kylix, c. 470 BC; in the Gregorian Etruscan Museum, the Vatican.

ALINARI—ART RESOURCE/EB INC.

Aestheticism \es-ˈthet-ə-ˌsiz-əm\ Late-19th-century European arts movement that centered on the doctrine that art exists for the sake of its beauty alone. It began in reaction to prevailing utilitarian social philosophies and to the perceived ugliness and philistinism of the industrial age. Its philosophical foundations were laid by IMMANUEL KANT, who proposed that aesthetic standards could be separated from morality, utility, or pleasure. JAMES M. WHISTLER, OSCAR WILDE, and STEPHANE MALLARME raised the movement's ideal of the cultivation of refined sensibility to perhaps its highest point. Aestheticism had affinities with French Symbolism and was a precursor of Art Nouveau.

aesthetics \es-'thet-iks\ Philosophical study of the nature and evaluation of art, also concerned with beauty and taste. Defining what counts as an aesthetic object or experience is a central project of aesthetics. Though aesthetics is broader in scope than the philosophy of art, art is often taken as the prime example of the nature and importance of aesthetic interest. G. W. F. Hegel considered the study of the various forms of art and of the spiritual content peculiar to each to be the main task of aesthetics. Seminal works include Edmund Burke's *On the Sublime and Beautiful* (1757), Immanuel Kant's *Critique of Judgment* (1790), and Ludwig Wittgenstein's *Philosophical Investigations* (1953).

Aethelberht I See Ethelbert I

Aethelred Unraed See Ethelred II

Aetolia \ē-'tō-lē-ə\ District north of the Gulf of Corinth, ancient Greece. Aetolia figures prominently in early legend. By 367 BC it had been organized by various tribes into a federal state comprising the Aetolian League. Coming under Roman rule, it was incorporated into the province of Achaea (see Achaean League) in 27 BC by Augustus. Governed later by Albania and Venice, it came under Turkish rule in AD 1450. It was the scene of fierce fighting in the War of Greek Independence (1821–29). Modern Aetolia is linked with Acarnania as a department of Greece.

Aetolian League \ē-'tō-lē-ən\ Federal state of Aetolia in central ancient Greece, probably based on a looser tribal community. A leading power by c. 340 BC, it resisted invasions by Macedonia in 322 and 314–311, expanded into Delphi, and allied with Boeotia c. 300. It fended off the Gauls in 279 and formed and alliance with Macedonia (c. 270–240). The league's power in central Greece was confirmed with the defeat of the Boeotians (245). From the late 3rd century Aetolia began to lose power and territory to Macedonia, culminating in the sacking of the league's federal capital, Thermum, by Philip V in 220. The league then allied with Rome against Macedonia, resulting in the defeat of Philip at Cynoscephalae (197). Rome later forced it into a permanent alliance (189) that cost it territory, power, and independence.

Afars and Issas, French Territory of the See Djibouti

affections, doctrine of the *German* **Affektenlehre.** Aesthetic theory of music in the Baroque period. Under the influence of classical rhetoric, it was held that the primary aim of music was to move the emotions. By the end of the 17th century, individual movements were customarily organized around a single emotion ("unity of affection"), resulting in the lack of strong contrasts and the repetitive rhythms characteristic of Baroque music. Several attempts at systematic lists of the emotional effects of different scales and figures were made, but to no general agreement.

affective disorder Mental disorder characterized by dramatic changes or extremes of mood. Affective disorders may include manic or depressive episodes less severe than those of bipolar disorder. Symptoms include elevated, expansive, or irritable mood, with hyperactivity, pressured speech, and inflated self-esteem; and/or dejected mood, with lack of interest in life, sleep disturbances, agitation, and feelings of worthlessness or guilt.

affenpinscher \'a-fən-ˌpin-chər\ Sturdy breed of toy dog, known since the 17th century. Standing 10 in. (26 cm) high or less and weighing 7–8 lbs (3–3.5 kg), it is a terrier-like dog with small, erect ears, round black eyes, and a short, docked tail. Its wiry, preferably black coat is short on parts of the body but longer on the legs and face, where it produces the monkeylike expression for which the breed is named (from German *Affe*, "ape").

affidavit \ˌa-fə-'dā-vət\ Written statement made voluntarily, confirmed by the oath or affirmation of the party making it, and signed before an officer empowered to administer such oaths. It usually names the place of execution and certifies that the person making it states certain facts and appeared before the officer on a certain date and "subscribed and swore" to the statement.

affirmative action In the U.S., an active effort to improve employment or educational opportunities for women and members of minority groups. It was undertaken at the federal level following passage of the landmark Civil Rights Act of 1964. Designed to counteract the effects of past discrimination, it consists of policies and programs that give preferences to minorities and women in job hiring, college admissions, government contract awards, and the allocations of other social benefits. The main criteria are race, sex, ethnic origin, religion, disability, and age. The most important challenge to the program came in the U.S. Supreme Court's 1978 ruling in *Regents of the University of California vs. Bakke*. Several recent Supreme Court decisions placed further restrictions on these programs, as in *Adarand Constructors vs. Pena* (1995) and *Texas vs. Hopwood* (1996).

Affleck, Thomas (1740–1795) U.S. (Scottish-born) cabinetmaker. Trained in England, he moved to Philadelphia, where he produced outstanding furniture in the Chippendale style for Gov. John Penn and other leading citizens. The Marlborough-style leg (straight, grooved, with a block foot) and elaborate carving characterize his work.

afforestation See deforestation

Afghan hound Breed of dog developed as a hunter in the hill country of Afghanistan. It was brought to Europe in the late 19th century by British soldiers returning from the Indian-Afghan border wars. It hunts by sight; in Afghanistan it has been used to pursue leopard and gazelle. Its high, wide hipbones are well adapted to rough country. It stands 24–28 in. (61–71 cm) high and weighs 50–60 lbs (23–27 kg). It has floppy ears, a long topknot, and a long silky coat of various colors.

Afghan hound.
SALLY ANNE THOMPSON

Afghan wars Series of wars in Afghanistan during the 19th, 20th, and early 21st centuries. In the 19th century Britain twice invaded Afghanistan (the first and second Anglo-Afghan Wars; 1839–40 and 1878–80). The British were unable fully to subdue the country, and the third Anglo-Afghan War (1919) led to its full independence. The outbreak of civil war in 1978 led to an invasion by the Soviet Union the following year (the Afghan War). For the next 10 years the Soviets supported the communist government against a coalition of Islamic insurgents, the Mujahidin, who toppled the regime in 1992. A group of disaffected fighters known as the Taliban had taken control of most of the country by 1996. The ensuing stalemate was broken in 2001 when the U.S. overthrew the Taliban because of its support for international terrorism.

Afghani, Jamal al-Din al- See Jamal al-Din al-Afghani

Afghanistan Country, southern central Asia. Area: 251,825 sq mi (652,225 sq km). Population (2001 est.: 26,813,000). Capital: Kabul. About two-fifths of the people belong to the Pashtun ethnic group; other ethnic groups include Tajiks, Uzbeks, and Hazaras. Languages: Pashto, Persian (Dari) (official). Religion: Islam (official). Currency: Afghani. Afghanistan has three distinctive regions: the northern plains are the major agricultural area; the southwestern plateau consists primarily of desert and semiarid landscape; the central highlands, including the Hindu Kush, separates these regions. Afghanistan has a developing economy based largely on agriculture; its significant mineral resources remain largely untapped because of the Afghan War of the 1980s and subsequent fighting. Traditional handicrafts remain important; woolen carpets are a major export. The area was part of the Persian empire in the 6th century BC and was conquered by Alexander the Great in the 4th century BC. Hindu influence entered with the Hephthalites and Sasanians; Islam became entrenched during the rule of the Saffarids, c. AD 870. Afghanistan was divided between the Mughal empire of India and the Safavid empire of Persia until the 18th century, when other Persians under Nadir Shah took control. Britain fought several wars in the area in the 19th century. From the 1930s the country had a stable monarchy; it was overthrown in the 1970s. Marxist reforms sparked rebellion, and Soviet troops invaded. Afghan guerrillas prevailed, and the Soviets withdrew in 1989. In 1992 rebel factions overthrew the government and established an Islamic republic. In 1996 the Taliban militia took power and enforced a harsh Islamic order. The militia's unwillingness to extradite extremist leader Osama bin Laden and members of his al-Qaeda organization fol-

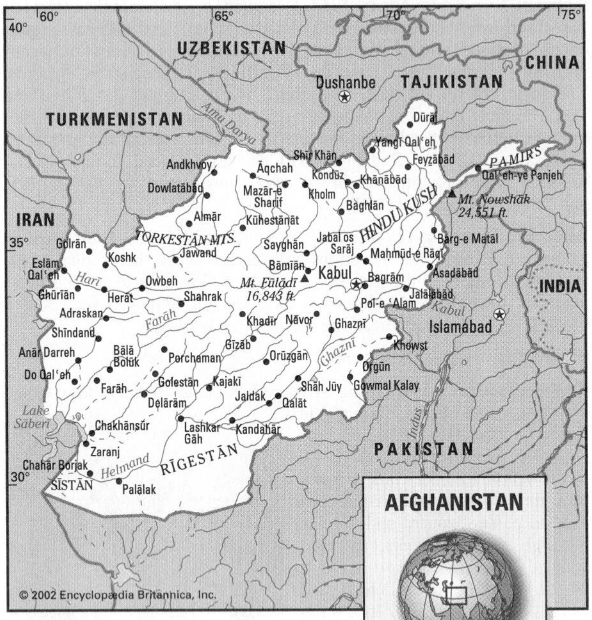

lowing the SEPTEMBER 11 ATTACKS in 2001 led to military conflict with the U.S. and allied nations, the overthrow of the Taliban, and the establishment of an interim government.

AFL-CIO *in full* **American Federation of Labor–Congress of Industrial Organizations** U.S. federation of labor unions formed in 1955 by the merger of the AFL and the CIO. The AFL was founded in 1886 as a loose federation of craft unions under the leadership of SAMUEL GOMPERS. Member unions retained autonomy and received protection of their workers and jurisdiction over a certain industrial territory. The CIO was founded in 1935 as the Committee for Industrial Organization by a splinter group of AFL unions whose leaders believed in organizing skilled and unskilled workers across entire industries; at its first convention in 1938, it adopted its current name and elected JOHN L. LEWIS president. For two decades the AFL and CIO were bitter rivals for the leadership of the U.S. labor movement, but they formed an alliance in the increasingly conservative, antilabor climate of the postwar era, and in 1955 they merged under the leadership of GEORGE MEANY. AFL-CIO membership reached 17 million in the late 1970s but declined from the 1980s as the U.S. manufacturing sector shrank. AFL-CIO activities include recruiting and organizing members, conducting educational campaigns, and supporting political candidates and legislation deemed beneficial to labor. See also LANE KIRKLAND, KNIGHTS OF LABOR, WALTER REUTHER.

Aflaq \'äf-läk\, **Michel** (1910–1989) Syrian social and political leader. While studying at the University of Paris (1929–34) he came to believe that the Arab nationalist struggle had to oppose both the native elite and foreign rulers. Hoping to unite all the Arab states into a single socialist nation through nonviolence, he established the BAATH PARTY in 1946 and served as its teacher, theorist, and organizer. He persuaded the Syrian government to form the United Arab Republic with Egypt in 1958, from which Syria withdrew in 1961. His career in Syrian politics ended in 1966 when he moved to Lebanon. See also PAN-ARABISM.

aflatoxin \,a-flə-'täk-sən\ Complex of toxins formed by MOLDS of the genus *Aspergillus,* which frequently contaminate improperly stored nuts (especially peanuts), grains, meals, and certain other foods. Discovered after an outbreak of "turkey X disease" in England in 1960, aflatoxins may cause liver disease and cancer and may trigger REYE'S SYNDROME.

Afonso I *known as* **Afonso the Conqueror** (c. 1110–1185) First king of Portugal (1139–85). He defeated his mother to take the throne (1128), ruling first as a vassal of his cousin Alfonso VII of León but later securing Portuguese independence and gaining the title of king (1139). He defeated nearby Muslims and imposed tribute on them, then took Lisbon (1147) with the help of crusaders. Afonso eventually extended Portugal beyond the TAGUS RIVER. He shared power with his son SANCHO I and left him a stable, independent monarchy.

Afonso III (1210–1279) King of Portugal (1248–79). He emigrated to France and became, by marriage, count of Boulogne. He gained the Portuguese crown when his older brother SANCHO II was deposed by order of the pope. As king, Afonso regained control of the district of Faro (1249) and completed the reconquest of Algarve from the Muslims. His reign saw the first admission of commoners to the Portuguese Cortes (parliament). Afonso's assertion of the royal right to repossess church lands led to his excommunication by the pope.

Afonso the Great See Afonso de ALBUQUERQUE

Africa Second-largest continent on earth. It is bounded by the Mediterranean Sea, the Atlantic Ocean, the Red Sea, and the Indian Ocean; it is divided almost equally by the equator. Area: 11,724,300 sq mi (30,365,700 sq km). Population (2001 est.): 816,524,000. Africa is composed largely of a rigid platform of ancient rocks that underlies vast plateau regions in the interior. Its average elevation is about 2,200 ft (670 m), but elevations range from 19,340 ft (5,895 m) at Mount KILIMANJARO to 515 ft (157 m) below sea level at Lake ASSAL. The SAHARA, the world's largest contiguous desert, occupies more than one-fourth of the total land area. The continent's hydrology is dominated by the NILE RIVER in the north and the CONGO in central Africa. Only about 6% of the continent is arable, while nearly one-fourth is forested or wooded. The peoples of Africa probably speak more languages than those of any other continent. Arabic is predominant from Egypt to Mauritania and in the Sudan. The sub-Sahara is inhabited by peoples speaking a number of languages known collectively as BANTU, while a smaller number use languages from the KHOISAN LANGUAGE family of Southwest Africa. Peoples of European descent are found in the south; Dutch (Boer) migrations began in the 17th century, and the English first settled in what is now Zambia and Zimbabwe in the 19th century. Africa as a whole is a developing region. Agriculture is the most important sector of the economy in most countries. Diamond and gold mining are especially important in the south, while other areas produce petroleum and natural gas. Most African governments are controlled by a single clique. Many legal systems are based on laws introduced by European powers during the colonial era, though North African countries derive many laws from Islam. African leaders have sought to develop a pan-African approach to the continent's political and military affairs through the ORGANIZATION OF AFRICAN UNITY. Human beings are widely thought to have originated in Africa. The oldest known hominid remains are thought to date to about 6 million years ago. *HOMO HABILIS* and *HOMO ERECTUS* inhabited Africa before and during the Pleistocene epoch (1.6 million–10,000 years ago), and forms of *HOMO SAPIENS* began appearing 500,000–300,000 years ago. By the end of the Pleistocene, distinct African races of modern humans had emerged. Africa's first great historical kingdom, Egypt, arose along the Nile c. 3000 BC and flourished for nearly 3,000 years. The PHOENICIANS established a colony at CARTHAGE and controlled the western Mediterranean for nearly 600 years. While northern Africa was dominated by the Romans for several centuries, the first known empire in western Africa was GHANA (5th–11th century AD). Muslim empires included those of MALI (c. 1250–1400) and the SONGHAI of Gao (c. 1400–1591). In eastern and central Africa the emphasis was on trade with Arabia, and several powerful city-states, including MOGADISHU and MOMBASA, were established. The Portuguese explored the coast in the 15th century. Before the late 19th century, Europe showed little interest in colonizing Africa, but by 1884 European countries had begun a scramble to partition the continent, and by 1920 much of it was under colonial rule. Anticolonial sentiment developed gradually, becoming widespread after 1950, and one by one the colonies became independent. See map on following page.

Africa, Horn of See HORN OF AFRICA

Africa, Roman Proconsular Roman province. It was founded after the Roman defeat of CARTHAGE in 146 BC. It was subsequently extended to include NUMIDIA and the northern part of modern Libya. Between 30 BC and AD 180, other parts of northern Africa, including CYRENAICA, Marmarica, and Mauretania, became part of the Roman empire. In the 5th century the region was taken by the VANDALS; the Muslims conquered the area in 641.

African ant bear See AARDVARK

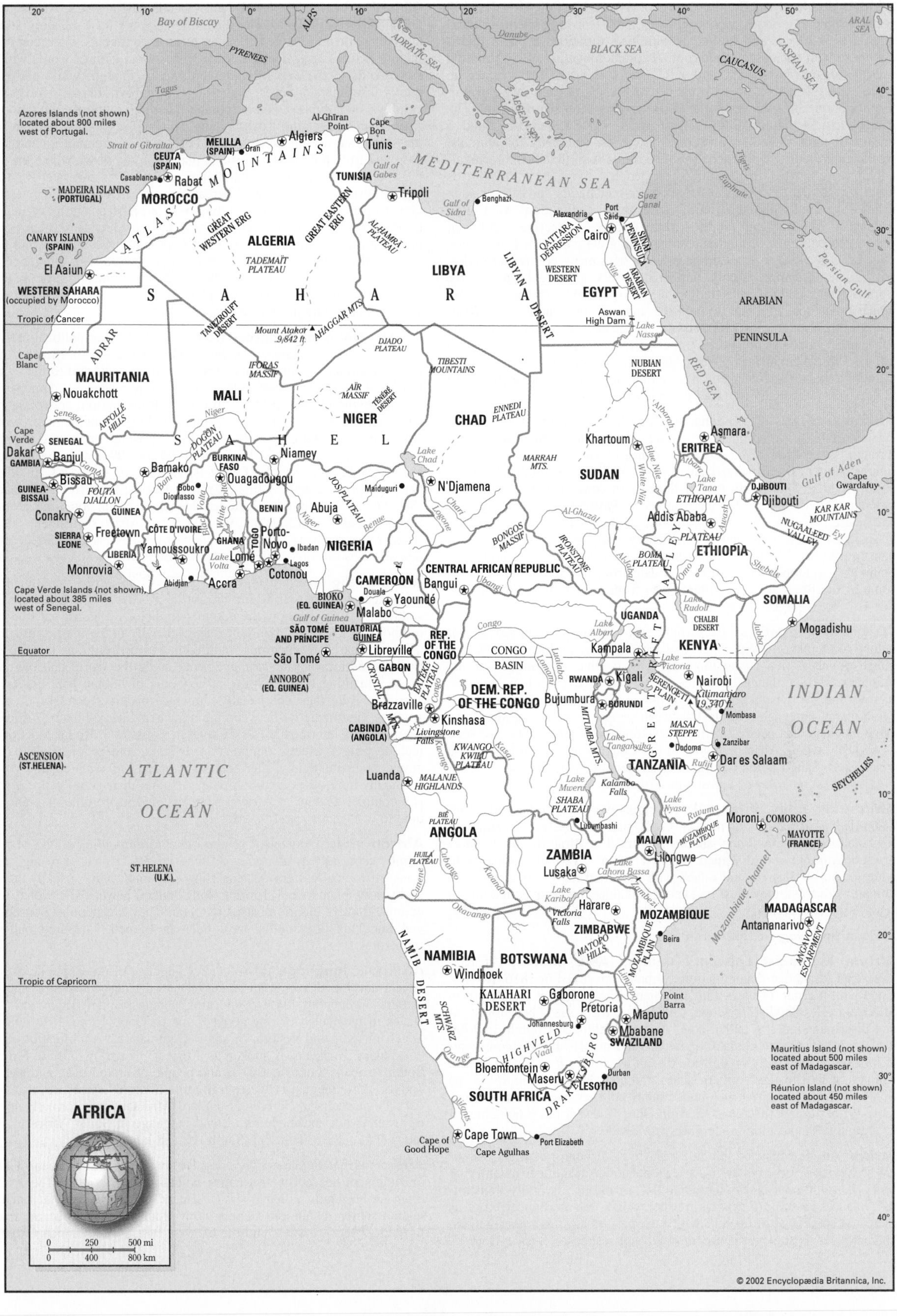
AFRICA
Bay of Biscay
PYRENEES
Tagus
ALPS
ADRIATIC SEA
Danube
BLACK SEA
CAUCASUS
CASPIAN SEA
ARAL SEA
AEGEAN SEA
MEDITERRANEAN SEA
Tigris
Euphrates
Persian Gulf
Azores Islands (not shown) located about 800 miles west of Portugal.
Strait of Gibraltar
MELILLA (SPAIN)
Oran
Algiers
Al-Ghīran Point
Cape Bon
Tunis
CEUTA (SPAIN)
Casablanca
Rabat
ATLAS MOUNTAINS
Gulf of Gabes
TUNISIA
MADEIRA ISLANDS (PORTUGAL)
MOROCCO
Tripoli
Gulf of Sidra
Benghazi
Alexandria
Port Said
Suez Canal
CANARY ISLANDS (SPAIN)
GREAT WESTERN ERG
GREAT EASTERN ERG
ALGERIA
AL-HAMRĀ' PLATEAU
QATTARA DEPRESSION
Cairo
SINAI PENINSULA
TADEMAÏT PLATEAU
LIBYA
LIBYAN DESERT
WESTERN DESERT
Nile
ARABIAN DESERT
El Aaiun
WESTERN SAHARA (occupied by Morocco)
SAHARA
EGYPT
ARABIAN
Tropic of Cancer
TANEZROUFT DESERT
Mount Atakor 9,842 ft.
AHAGGAR MTS.
Aswan High Dam
Lake Nasser
PENINSULA
ADRAR
DJADO PLATEAU
Cape Blanc
IFORAS MASSIF
TIBESTI MOUNTAINS
NUBIAN DESERT
RED SEA
MAURITANIA
Nouakchott
MALI
AÏR MASSIF
TÉNÉRÉ DESERT
Niger
NIGER
ENNEDI PLATEAU
CHAD
'Atbarah
Senegal
AFFOLLÉ HILLS
DOGON PLATEAU
Asmara
Cape Verde
SENEGAL
SAHEL
Khartoum
ERITREA
Dakar
GAMBIA
Banjul
Gambia
Niamey
Lake Chad
MARRAH MTS.
Blue Nile
White Nile
SUDAN
Albara
Gulf of Aden
BURKINA FASO
Bamako
Bani
Ouagadougou
Lake Tana
DJIBOUTI
Cape Gwardafuy
GUINEA-BISSAU
Bissau
Bobo Dioulasso
JOS PLATEAU
Maiduguri
N'Djamena
ETHIOPIAN
Djibouti
FOUTA DJALLON
GUINEA
Black Volta
White Volta
BENIN
Chari
Al-Ghazāl
Addis Ababa
Awash
KAR KAR MOUNTAINS
NUGAALEED VALLEY
Conakry
Abuja
Logone
Benue
BONGOS MASSIF
SIERRA LEONE
Freetown
CÔTE D'IVOIRE
GHANA
TOGO
Porto-Novo
Ibadan
NIGERIA
IRONSTONE PLATEAU
PLATEAU
ETHIOPIA
LIBERIA
Yamoussoukro
Lake Volta
Lomé
Lagos
BOMA PLATEAU
Omo
Shebele
Eyl
Monrovia
Abidjan
Accra
Cotonou
CAMEROON
CENTRAL AFRICAN REPUBLIC
Bangui
Ubangi
Cape Verde Islands (not shown) located about 385 miles west of Senegal.
BIOKO (EQ. GUINEA)
Douala
Yaoundé
Malabo
Lake Rudolf
SOMALIA
Gulf of Guinea
UGANDA
CHALBI DESERT
Jubba
SÃO TOMÉ AND PRÍNCIPE
EQUATORIAL GUINEA
REP. OF THE CONGO
Congo
Lake Albert
GREAT RIFT VALLEY
KENYA
Mogadishu
Equator
São Tomé
Libreville
CONGO BASIN
Kampala
Lake Victoria
ANNOBÓN (EQ. GUINEA)
GABON
BATÉKÉ PLATEAU
CRYSTAL MTS.
Lualaba
Lomami
RWANDA
Kigali
SERENGETI PLAIN
Nairobi
DEM. REP. OF THE CONGO
Kilimanjaro 19,340 ft.
INDIAN OCEAN
Brazzaville
Bujumbura
BURUNDI
MITUMBA MTS.
Mombasa
CABINDA (ANGOLA)
Kinshasa
Livingstone Falls
MASAI STEPPE
Dodoma
Zanzibar
ASCENSION (ST.HELENA)
KWANGO-KWILU PLATEAU
Kwango
Kasai
Lake Tanganyika
Dar es Salaam
ATLANTIC OCEAN
TANZANIA
Rufiji
SEYCHELLES
Luanda
MALANJE HIGHLANDS
Lake Mweru
Kalambo Falls
SHABA PLATEAU
Lake Nyasa
Ruvuma
Moroni
COMOROS
BIÉ PLATEAU
ANGOLA
Lubumbashi
MALAWI
MOZAMBIQUE PLATEAU
MAYOTTE (FRANCE)
ZAMBIA
Lilongwe
HUILA PLATEAU
ST.HELENA (U.K.)
Cubango
Kwando
Lusaka
Lake Cahora Bassa
Mozambique Channel
Cunene
Lake Kariba
Zambezi
Harare
Okavango
Victoria Falls
MOZAMBIQUE
MADAGASCAR
ZIMBABWE
Antananarivo
Beira
NAMIB DESERT
NAMIBIA
BOTSWANA
MATOPO HILLS
MOZAMBIQUE PLAIN
ANGAVO ESCARPMENT
Windhoek
Limpopo
Tropic of Capricorn
KALAHARI DESERT
Gaborone
Point Barra
Pretoria
Maputo
SCHWARZ MTS.
Johannesburg
Mbabane
SWAZILAND
HIGHVELD
Vaal
Orange
Mauritius Island (not shown) located about 500 miles east of Madagascar.
Bloemfontein
Durban
Maseru
DRAKENSBERG
LESOTHO
Réunion Island (not shown) located about 450 miles east of Madagascar.
SOUTH AFRICA
Olifants
Cape of Good Hope
Cape Town
Port Elizabeth
Cape Agulhas
0 250 500 mi
0 400 800 km
20° 10° 0° 10° 20° 30° 40° 50°
40° 30° 20° 10° 0° 10° 20° 30° 40°

African architecture Building styles of Africa. Most of Africa's 5,000 peoples build in grasses, wood, and clay. A prevalent form in southern Africa, West Africa, and the Sudan, with local variations, is the cylindrical house with conical thatched roof. A common method of construction uses a ring of posts with mud infill (see POLE CONSTRUCTION). Where wood is less available, houses may be constructed of mud in a coil pottery technique. In some areas the KRAAL serves a defensive function. The characteristic settlement form in West Africa is the walled compound, a cluster of units including dwellings, granaries, and pens for animals. Rectangular houses with pitched roofs covered with thatch (or corrugated iron) are used by many rain-forest peoples. Many pastoral nomads build TENT STRUCTURES. The MASAI construct rectangular huts using stick frames plastered with cattle dung. Earlier urban civilizations were often influenced by Arab and North African traditions, erecting rectilinear, flat-roofed buildings of mud and stone. The great palace of Benin City, Nigeria, was as large as a European town, with many courts and galleried buildings, shingled roofs, and high towers sporting bronze birds. Yoruba towns maintain the traditional *afin* (palace) at the center, from which broad roads radiate; though the architecture is now often Westernized, traditional courtyards and high surrounding walls persist; the substantial palace buildings had open verandas supported by caryatid pillars. Prominent in many West African towns are the mosques, bristling with wood reinforcement. Though monumental temple architecture is rare, spiritual symbolism may pervade dwellings.

African arts Arts of sub-Saharan Africa. Sub-Saharan Africa has diverse cultures, but all their arts have adapted to outside influences through the centuries. The earliest evidence of visual art is provided by figures scratched and painted on rocks c. 3000 BC. Architecture dominates the arts of the north and of the eastern coast, where Islamic and Oriental Christianity exerted their influence. Pastoral cultures in the east emphasize personal adornment; sculpture predominates in the agricultural societies in the west and south. Pottery sculptures found in Nigeria date to 500 BC. Metalworking was practiced from the 9th century AD. Sculptures in stone, ivory, and wood date from the 16th–17th century; some of the finest wood sculptures date from as recently as the 1920s. See also BULI STYLE, DÉBLÉ, SEGONI-KUN.

African languages Languages indigenous to sub-Saharan Africa that belong to the NIGER-CONGO, NILO-SAHARAN, KHOISAN, and AFROASIATIC language phyla. Africa is the most polyglot continent; estimates of the number of African languages range from 1,000 to 1,200. Many have numerous dialects. Distinctions in TONE play a significant role in nearly all sub-Saharan languages. Contact between people who do not speak the same language has necessitated the development of LINGUA FRANCAS such as SWAHILI in East Africa, Lingala in the Congo River basin (see BANTU LANGUAGES), Sango in the Central African Republic (see ADAMAWA-UBANGI LANGUAGES), and ARABIC across much of the SAHEL.

African lily *or* **lily of the Nile** Perennial evergreen herbaceous plant *(Agapanthus africanus)* of the LILY FAMILY, native to Africa. In summer, long stalks bear many funnel-shaped flowers. The attractive, thick, dark-green leaves are sword-shaped. There are many varieties, some with white or purple flowers and others with patterned leaves. If grown in a climate with frost, they must be kept in containers and moved indoors to survive the cold weather.

African lion dog See RHODESIAN RIDGEBACK

African Methodist Episcopal Church (AME Church) African-American Methodist denomination, formally organized in 1816. It originated with a group of black Philadelphians who withdrew in 1787 from St. George's Methodist Episcopal Church (see METHODISM) because of racial discrimination and built Bethel African Methodist Church. In 1799 RICHARD ALLEN became minister of Bethel, and in 1816 he was consecrated bishop of the newly organized African Methodist Episcopal Church. Limited at first to the Northern states, the church spread rapidly in the South after the Civil War. It founded many colleges and seminaries, notably Wilberforce University (1856) in Ohio. Today it has 3,600 churches and more than a million members worldwide.

African music Music of sub-Saharan Africa. Though a vast geographical area with diverse cultures, Africa's music has a number of unifying traits. Its traditional music, including its "art music," is orally transmitted; thus, pieces do not exist as finished works, but are conceived of as recreated somewhat differently with each performance. Another general characteristic is the prevalence of "call and response." Aside from its spiritual and celebratory and dance-accompanying roles, African music has a distinctly political role; the GRIOT sings the tribe's history and creates songs of praise for the leader, or mocking songs when community feeling is running against the leader. The association of words with music extends to the existence of words to be thought while performing purely instrumental pieces. Being largely improvisational, African music employs only limited counterpoint (including roundlike imitation that may be an outgrowth of overlapping calls and responses), though melodies are often accompanied in parallel intervals, creating a chordal texture, and truly polyphonic music is played on the MBIRA, where the melodies performed by the two hands are conceived as separate. Rhythm is highly developed in Africa. Whereas Westerners tend to perceive simultaneous patterns as sharing a common meter, Africans think of such patterns as cycles with different starting points. Outside influences have played a role in African music, most importantly Islam. In recent times, compatible elements of Western music have mixed with indigenous elements, though in popular music these Western influences more likely arrived via Arabic and Indian examples. The music of North Africa represents a separate tradition (see MIDDLE EASTERN MUSIC).

African National Congress (ANC) South African political party and black nationalist organization. Founded in 1912 (as the South African Native National Congress), the ANC was long dedicated to the elimination of APARTHEID. In response to government massacres of demonstrators at Sharpeville (1960) and Soweto (1976), it carried out acts of sabotage and guerrilla warfare. The campaign was largely ineffective, owing to stringent South African internal-security measures, including an official ban on the ANC between 1960 and 1990. In 1991, with the ban lifted, NELSON MANDELA succeeded OLIVER TAMBO as ANC president. In 1994 the party swept the country's first all-race elections; the ANC led a coalition government that initially included members of its longtime rival, the NATIONAL PARTY, and Mandela became South Africa's president. In 1999 THABO MBEKI replaced him as president of the ANC and of South Africa. See also INKATHA FREEDOM PARTY, ALBERT LUTULI, PAN-AFRICAN MOVEMENT.

African religions Indigenous religions of the African continent. The introduced religions of Islam (in northern Africa) and Christianity (in southern Africa) are now the continent's major religions, but traditional religions still play an important role, especially in the interior of sub-Saharan Africa. The numerous traditional African religions have in common the notion of a creator god, who made the world and then withdrew, remaining remote from the concerns of human life. Prayers and sacrificial offerings are usually directed toward secondary divinities, who are intermediaries between the human and sacred realms. Ancestors also serve as intermediaries (see ANCESTOR WORSHIP). Ritual functionaries include priests, elders, rainmakers, diviners, and prophets. Rituals are aimed at maintaining a harmonious relationship with cosmic powers, and many have associated myths that explain their significance. ANIMISM is a common feature of African religions, and misfortune is often attributed to WITCHCRAFT AND SORCERY.

African violet Any plant of the genus *Saintpaulia,* of the GESNERIAD family, especially *S. ionantha.* African violets are native to high elevations in tropical eastern Africa. They are small, hairy, usually stemless herbaceous plants with crowded, long-stalked leaves. The violet, white, or pink flowers bloom most of the year. They are popular houseplants, and hundreds of varieties have been developed, including half-sized miniatures.

Afrikaans language \ˌaf-ri-ˈkänz\ Language of the Republic of South Africa developed from 17th-century Dutch by descendants of European settlers, indigenous KHOISAN-speaking peoples, and African and Asian slaves in the Dutch colony at the Cape of Good Hope. It differs from Dutch in its sound system, in some grammatical simplification, and in vocabulary. Afrikaans is spoken as a first language by close to 6 million South Africans, both AFRIKANERS and people of mixed race, and as a second or third language by several million more; there are also about 150,000 speakers in Namibia. Standard Afrikaans was formally separated from Dutch and made an official language in South Africa in 1925; today it is one of 11 official South African languages.

Afrikaner \ˌaf-ri-ˈkän-ər\ *formerly* **Boer** Any South African of Dutch or Huguenot descent whose native language is AFRIKAANS. The Afrikaners were originally called Boers ("farmers"), since many Dutch and Huguenot settlers of the old Cape Colony (founded 1652) became frontier farmers in the TRANSVAAL and the ORANGE FREE STATE. Staunch Calvinists, they saw themselves as children of God in a pagan wilderness. They established self-sufficient patriarchal communities, developed their own language and subculture, and were committed to a policy of APARTHEID. They fought a bitter war with the British (the SOUTH AFRICAN WAR, 1899–1902) over the right to govern the frontier territories. Though defeated, they retained their old language and culture and eventually attained politically the power they had failed to win militarily. Having dominated South African politics for most of the century, they were obliged to give up national power after the first all-race elections in 1994. Much of the country's economic wealth remains in Afrikaner hands. Today they number about 6.4 million. See also CAPE TOWN, GREAT TREK, NATIONAL PARTY OF SOUTH AFRICA.

Afro-Caribbean, Afro-Brazilian, and Afro-American religions Religions among persons of African ancestry in the Caribbean, Brazil, and U.S. These include Haitian VODUN, the Jamaican RASTAFARIAN movement, SANTERÍA, and CANDOMBLÉ and other MACUMBA sects in Brazil. Similarly syncretistic religions appeared in the U.S. during the era of slavery. The Nation of ISLAM combines black nationalism with an unorthodox version of ISLAM. Black Protestant churches (especially Baptist and Pentecostal) have imported some forms of lively worship from Africa.

Afroasiatic languages *formerly* **Hamito-Semitic languages** Superfamily of about 250 languages presently spoken by an estimated 250–300 million ethnically and physically diverse people in North Africa and parts of sub-Saharan African and in South Asia. The major branches of Afroasiatic are SEMITIC, Berber, EGYPTIAN, Cushitic, Omotic, and Chadic. Berber is a group of closely related languages spoken by perhaps 15 million people in enclaves scattered across North Africa from Morocco to northwestern Egypt and in parts of the western Sahara. Cushitic is a family of about 30 languages spoken by more than 30 million people in northeastern Sudan, Eritrea, Ethiopia, Somalia, Djibouti, Kenya, and a few areas of northeastern Tanzania. Omotic, formerly classified as part of Cushitic, is a cluster of perhaps more than 30 languages spoken by 2–3 million people, most of whom live near the Omo River in southwestern Ethiopia. Chadic comprises about 140 languages, most poorly known to linguists, spoken in northern Nigeria, southern Niger, southern Chad, and northern Cameroon; except for HAUSA, probably no individual Chadic language has more than half a million speakers.

Afrocentrism Cultural, political, and ideological movement, predominantly comprised of African Americans, which regards all blacks as syncretic Africans and which believes that their worldview should positively reflect traditional African values. Afrocentrism argues that for centuries blacks and other nonwhites have been dominated, through slavery and colonization by Europeans, and that European culture ignores or devalues efforts by non-Europeans to achieve self-determination. Rooted in historical black nationalist movements such as ETHIOPIANISM, PAN-AFRICANISM, and NEGRITUDE, Afrocentrism asserts the cultural primacy of ancient Egypt and is seen as a spur to political activism. In addition to emphasizing cooperation and spirituality, it champions contemporary African-American expressive culture (language, cuisine, music, dance, and clothing). Coined by Molefi Asante in the 1980s, the term "Afrocentrism" was popularized by such books as *Black Athena: The Afroasiatic Roots of Classical Civilization*, 2 vol. (1987–91), by Martin Bernal. However, it has encountered opposition from mainstream scholars who charge it with historical innacuracy, scholarly ineptitude, and racism—prompting countercharges of racism from some of its defenders.

afterburner Second combustion chamber in a TURBOJET or turbofan engine, immediately in front of the engine's exhaust nozzle. The injection and combustion of extra fuel in this chamber provide additional thrust for takeoff or supersonic flight; in most cases, the afterburner can nearly double the thrust of a turbojet engine. The jet nozzle must be larger when using the afterburner, so an automatic, adjustable nozzle is an essential component of the afterburner system. Because the afterburner sharply increases fuel consumption and is generally less effective at subsonic speeds, its use is usually restricted to supersonic military aircraft.

afterpiece Supplementary entertainment offered after a full-length play in 18th-century England. A short comedy, farce, or pantomime was presented to lighten the five-act neoclassical tragedy that was commonly performed. A reduced admission price for latecomers, usually after the third act, enabled less sophisticated playgoers and working people to see the end of the drama and the one-act afterpiece.

aftosa See FOOT-AND-MOUTH DISEASE

Aga Khan \ˌä-gə-ˈkän\ Title of the IMAMS of the Nizari ISMAILI sect of SHIITE Islam. It was first granted in 1818 to Hasan Ali Shah (1800–1881) by the shah of Iran. Aga Khan I later revolted against Iran (1838) and, defeated, fled to India. His eldest son, Ali Shah (died 1885), was briefly Aga Khan II; Ali Shah's son Sultan Sir Mohammed Shah (1877–1957) became Aga Khan III. He acquired a leading position among India's Muslims, served as president of the All-India Muslim League, and played an important part in the Round Table conferences on Indian constitutional reform (1930–32); in 1937 he was appointed president of the LEAGUE OF NATIONS. He chose as his successor his grandson Karim al-Hussain Shah (born 1937), who, as Aga Khan IV, became a strong leader; he founded the Aga Khan Foundation and other agencies offering educational and other services in South Asia and East Africa.

Agadir \ˌä-gä-ˈdir\ Seaport (pop., 1994 est.: 155,000), southwestern Morocco. It was occupied in the 16th century by the Portuguese, but later became an independent Moroccan port. After the 1911 MOROCCAN CRISIS when a German gunboat appeared offshore to protect perceived German interests, it was occupied by French troops in 1913. Modern growth began with the port's construction in 1914, and the development of the fishing industry. Destroyed in 1960 by earthquakes, tidal wave, and fire, it was rebuilt south of its original location. In addition to its port functions, it is a market place for the surrounding agricultural area.

Agamemnon \ˌa-gə-ˈmem-ˌnän\ In Greek legend, the son of ATREUS, brother of MENELAUS, and king of MYCENAE and commander of the Greek forces that attacked Troy. By his wife, Clytemnestra, Agamemnon had a son, ORESTES, and three daughters. When PARIS carried off Menelaus's wife, HELEN, Agamemnon called on the Greeks to unite in a war of revenge against the Trojans. ARTEMIS sent a calm or contrary winds to prevent the Greek fleet from sailing, and Agamemnon sacrificed his daughter IPHIGENEIA to appease the goddess. After the TROJAN WAR he returned home, where he was killed by his wife and her lover, Aegisthus. His murder was avenged by Orestes. These events formed the basis of AESCHYLUS' great dramatic trilogy the *Oresteia.*

Agana \ä-ˈgän-yä\ Town (pop., 1990: 1,100), capital of GUAM. It lies on Guam's western coast on Agana Bay. A town of 10,000 in 1940, it was completely destroyed in World War II and has come back slowly. Nearby Latte Stone Park features pillars (latte stones) that supported houses of the prehistoric Latte culture.

agape \ä-ˈgä-pā\ In the New Testament, the fatherly love of God for humans and their reciprocal love for God. The term extends to the love of one's fellow humans. The Church Fathers used the Greek term to designate both a rite using bread and wine and a meal of fellowship that included the poor. The historical relationship between this meal, the Lord's Supper, and the EUCHARIST, the meal of fellowship and the sacrament, is uncertain.

agaric \ˈa-gər-ik\ Any FUNGUS of the family Agaricaceae, including the familiar commercially grown MUSHROOM. Agarics have SPORE-bearing cells (basidia) located on thin sheets called gills. Best known of the agarics is the genus *Agaricus (Psalliota),* which includes some 60 species, the most prominent being the edible meadow or field mushroom, *A. campestris,* and the common cultivated mushroom, *A. bisporus.*

Agartala \ə-ˈgər-tə-lə\ City (pop., 1991: 158,000), capital of TRIPURA state, India. It lies near the Bangladesh border on the Haroa River in an intensively cultivated plain. The commercial center of the area, it also contains a maharaja's palace, a temple, and four colleges affiliated with the University of Calcutta.

Agassi \ˈa-gə-sē\, **Andre (Kirk)** (born 1970) U.S. tennis player. Born in Las Vegas, he won the Wimbledon men's singles in 1992, the U.S. Open in 1994, and the Australian Open in 1995. By 1997 he had dropped to 122 in the international rankings, but he recovered to become the world's top-ranked player by 2000. He is known for his aggressive style and demeanor on and off the court.

Agassiz \ˈa-gə-sē\, **Alexander (Emmanuel Rodolphe)** (1835–1910) Swiss-U.S. marine zoologist, oceanographer, and mining engineer. The son of LOUIS AGASSIZ, he emigrated in 1849 to the U.S., where he conducted significant systematic zoology work on ECHINODERMS (e.g., STARFISH). He developed and supervised what became the world's foremost copper mine (Calumet, Mich.). He also pursued marine and CORAL-REEF studies. He challenged CHARLES DARWIN's theory of coral-reef formation based on observations made on an 1875 trip to the western coast of South America.

Agassiz, Elizabeth Cabot *orig.* **Elizabeth Cabot Cary** (1822–1907) U.S. naturalist and educator. Born in Boston, she was educated at home. In 1850 she married LOUIS AGASSIZ. She helped organize and manage several of his field expeditions, and together they founded a marine laboratory in Buzzards Bay, Mass. After his death she pursued her idea of a college for women to be taught by the HARVARD UNIVERSITY faculty. She was instrumental in launching the Society for the Collegiate Instruction of Women (1882); she served as its president until 1894, when it was renamed Radcliffe College, and she continued as president until 1899.

Agassiz \'a-gə-sē\, **(Jean) Louis (Rodolphe)** (1807–1873) Swiss-U.S. naturalist, geologist, and teacher. After studies in Switzerland and Germany, he moved to the U.S. in 1848. He did landmark work on glacier activity and extinct fishes. He became famous for his innovative teaching methods, which encouraged learning through direct observation of nature, and his term as a zoology professor at Harvard University revolutionized the study of natural history in the U.S.; every notable American teacher of natural history in the late 19th century was a pupil either of Agassiz or of one of his students. In addition, he was an outstanding science administrator, promoter, and fund-raiser. He was a lifelong opponent of CHARLES DARWIN's theory of evolution. His second wife, ELIZABETH AGASSIZ (1822–1907), cofounder and first president of Radcliffe College, and his son, ALEXANDER AGASSIZ (1835–1910), were also noted naturalists.

agate \'a-gət\ Common semiprecious silica mineral, a variety of CHALCEDONY that occurs in bands of varying color and transparency. Varieties are characterized by peculiarities in the shape and color of the bands, which are seen in sections cut at right angles to the layers. Agate is found throughout the world, commonly in cavities in eruptive rocks and in GEODES. Brazil and Uruguay are major producers of agates; they are also found in Oregon, Washington, Idaho, Montana, and other western U.S. states. Agate is essentially QUARTZ. Much commercial agate is artificially dyed to make the naturally dull-gray stones more colorful.

Banded agate.
B.M. SHAUB

Agate Fossil Beds National Monument Natural "depository" of an extinct animal community on the Niobrara River, northwestern Nebraska. The beds, laid down as sedimentary deposits 20 million years ago, bear the remains of prehistoric mammals. Discovered c. 1878, the site was named for its proximity to rock formations containing agates. A national monument since 1965, it covers 2,269 acres (918 hectares).

Agatha, St. (fl. 3rd century AD) Legendary Christian martyr. Born in Palermo or Catania, she resisted the advances of a Roman prefect sent to govern Sicily. After brutal torture she was sent to the stake, but as the fire was lighted a great earthquake occurred, and the crowd demanded her release. She was led away to prison, where she died. Though she appears in lists of martyrs as early as the 6th century, the legend may be unfounded.

Agathocles \ə-'ga-thə-klēz\ (361–289 BC) Tyrant of SYRACUSE (317–304?) and self-styled king of Sicily (304?–289). Born at Thermae in Sicily, he moved to Syracuse as a youth and served in its army. After two failed attempts, he overthrew the Syracusan oligarchy (317) and took power. He waged wars with other Sicilian Greek cities (316–313?) and with Carthage (311), almost capturing Carthage itself before he was defeated (307). He concluded a favorable treaty (306) that curtailed Carthaginian expansion in Sicily. Harsh domestic measures kept him in power, and he declared himself king of Sicily; his reign was peaceful thereafter. He restored Syracusan liberty in his will, but his death was followed by a renewal of Carthaginian power in Sicily.

agave family \ə-'gä-vē\ Family Agavaceae of the order Liliales, composed of short-stemmed, often woody plants found in tropical, subtropical, and temperate areas. They have narrow, lance-shaped, sometimes fleshy or toothed leaves clustered at the base of the plant. Most species have large flower clusters. The fruit is a CAPSULE or BERRY. Plants of the genus *Agave* are important primarily for the fibers obtained from their leaves. Sisal HEMP, from *A. sisalana,* is the most valuable hard fiber. Some species of *Agave* contain a sap that is fermented to produce the intoxicating drinks known as pulque and mescal. Many species of YUCCA are popular as ornamentals; other ornamentals in the agave family include plants of the genera *Dasylirion, Nolina, Cordyline, Dracaena,* and *Sansevieria.*

age set Formally organized social group consisting of every male (or female) of comparable age. In societies where the practice traditionally occurs (e.g., the NUER of the southern Sudan or the Nandi of Kenya), a person belongs, either from birth or from a determined age, to a named age set that passes through a series of life stages, or age grades, each of which has a distinctive status or social and political role. See also rite of PASSAGE, SOCIAL STATUS.

Agee \'ā-jē\, **James** (1909–1955) U.S. poet and novelist. Born in Knoxville, Tenn., he attended Harvard University. In the 1930s and '40s, his film reviews in *Time* and the *Nation* made him a pioneer in serious film criticism. His lyrical *Let Us Now Praise Famous Men* (1941), with photographs by WALKER EVANS, documents the daily lives of poverty-stricken Alabama sharecroppers. After 1948 Agee worked mainly as a screenwriter, notably on *The African Queen* (1951) and *The Night of the Hunter* (1955). He is best known for his autobiographical novel *A Death in the Family* (1957, Pulitzer Prize).

Agenais \àzh-'ne, à-zhə-'nā\ *or* **Agenois** \à-zhe-'nwä\ Historical region, southwestern France. In ancient GAUL, Agenais was the country of the Nitrobriges, then a Gallo-Roman *civitas,* whose limits became those of the diocese of Agen. It was acquired by the dukes of AQUITAINE in 1036. When ELEANOR OF AQUITAINE married the future HENRY II of England in 1152, Agenais became the possession of the English kings. It alternated between French and British rule until it was reunited to the French crown in 1615.

Agence France-Presse \à-zhä^{n}s-frä^{n}s-'pres\ **(AFP)** French cooperative NEWS AGENCY. Based in Paris, it has roots in the Bureau Havas, created in 1832, which in 1835 became the Agence Havas, the world's first true news agency. The Agence Havas was active until the German occupation of France in 1940, when many of its personnel went underground. After the liberation of Paris in 1944, underground journalists emerged to form AFP. The French government assigned the assets of Agence Havas to AFP, which quickly became one of the world's great wire news services.

agency In law, a relationship in which one party (the agent) acts on behalf of and under the control of another (the principal) in dealing with third parties. It has its roots in ancient servant-master relations. Agency becomes a legal issue when the agent injures or wrongs a third party. In Anglo-American law, principals are bound by and liable for the acts of such agents as stockbrokers, business agents, contractors, real-estate agents, lawyers, union representatives, managing partners, and private detectives. See also REGULATORY AGENCY.

agenesis \ā-'je-nə-səs\ Failure of all or part of an organ to develop during embryonic growth. Many forms of agenesis are lethal, such as absence of the entire brain (anencephaly), but agenesis of one of a paired organ may cause little problem. Agenesis of a kidney, bladder, testicle, ovary, thyroid, and lung are known. Agenesis of the arms or legs is called meromelia (absence of one or both hands or feet), phocomelia (normal hands and feet but no arms or legs), and amelia (complete absence of a limb or limbs). Agenesis may be caused by absence of embryonic tissue or by chemical exposure in the uterus, and is often associated with other congenital disorders.

Agent Orange Mixture of HERBICIDES. It contains approximately equal amounts of ESTERS of 2,4-D (2,4-dichlorophenoxyacetic acid) and 2,4,5-T (2,4,5-trichlorophenoxyacetic acid) and trace amounts of DIOXIN. About 13 million gallons were sprayed by U.S. military forces onto Vietnam's forests and crops during the Vietnam War, with the dual purpose of destroying cover for enemy movements and destroying food sources. Exposure to Agent Orange has been blamed for an abnormally high incidence of miscarriages, skin diseases, cancers, birth defects, and malformations among Vietnamese and of cancers and other disorders in U.S., Australian, and New Zealand servicemen and their families.

ageratum \ˌa-jə-'rā-təm\ Any plant of the genus *Ageratum,* of the COMPOSITE FAMILY, native to tropical South America. Ageratums have toothed, oval leaves that are opposite each other on the stem; compact clusters of blue, pink, lilac, or white flowers; and small, dry fruits. Dwarf varieties are used as edging plants. Some ageratums are variously known as floss-flower and pussy-foot.

Agesilaus II \ə-ˌje-sə-ˈlā-əs\ (444?–360 BC) King of SPARTA (399–360) and commander of its army during most of the era of Spartan supremacy (404–371). A member of the Eurypontid family, he took the throne with LYSANDER's help while Sparta was fighting Persia. He defeated the allied Thebes, Athens, Argos, and Corinth in the Corinthian War (395–387), despite losing some ground in central Greece and a battle with the Persian fleet in 394. He dissolved the Boeotian League, but battles against the Boeotian Confederacy (371) and Thebes (370, 361) ended Sparta's ascendancy. He died returning from a mercenary engagement in Egypt.

agglomerate \ə-ˈglä-mə-rət\ Large, coarse, angular rock fragments associated with lava flow that are ejected during explosive volcanic eruptions. Although they may appear to resemble sedimentary CONGLOMERATES, agglomerates are IGNEOUS ROCKS that consist almost wholly of angular or rounded lava fragments of varying size and shape. Some geologists sort agglomerates into BOMBS, blocks, and BRECCIA. Bombs are ejected in a molten state, becoming rounded upon solidification, and blocks are erupted as solid fragments. Upon accumulation and solidification of the angular fragments (also known as pyroclastics), they form agglomerates.

aggressive behavior Any action of an animal intended to injure an opponent or prey animal or to cause an opponent to retreat. Aggression may be caused by various stimuli. Within its own group, an animal must display aggressive postures to maintain its position within the hierarchy (e.g., the PECKING ORDER of chickens). A threat by itself, as in ruffled feathers or teeth revealed in a snarl, is usually sufficient to maintain an already established social order. Aggression often occurs just before mating season, when males win their choice of females and territories.

Aghlabid dynasty \ˈäg-lə-bid\ (800–909) Arab Muslim dynasty that ruled Ifriqiyah (Tunisia and eastern Algeria) through a succession of 11 emirs. Nominally subject to the ABBASID DYNASTY, they in fact were independent. High points of Aghlabid rule included the conquest of Sicily (827–29), the flowering of their capital city, KAIROUAN (9th century), and naval control of the central Mediterranean. Public works included a system for conserving and distributing water.

Agiads \ˈā-jē-ədz\ Line of Spartan kings named after Agis I (11th century BC?). Agis was traditionally held to be the son of one of the legendary twins who founded SPARTA. Agis II (died 400/398 BC) commanded the Spartan army during most of the PELOPONNESIAN WAR (431–404) against Athens. Agis III (died 331 BC) led the Greek cities in an unsuccessful revolt against ALEXANDER THE GREAT. Agis IV (died 241 BC) failed in his attempt to reform the unequal distribution of land and wealth in Sparta, losing his crown and his life to Leonidas II.

Agincourt \ˈa-jin-kōrt**, Battle of** (October 25, 1415) Battle resulting in the decisive victory of the English over the French in the HUNDRED YEARS' WAR. In pursuit of his claim to the French throne, HENRY V invaded Normandy with an army of 11,000 men in August 1415. The English took Harfleur in September, but with their forces cut in half by battle and disease, they resolved to return to England. At Agincourt they were cornered by a French army of 20,000–30,000 men, including many mounted knights in heavy armor. On a cramped battlefield where the superior French numbers offered little advantage, Henry made skillful use of his lightly equipped, mobile archers. The French were disastrously defeated, losing over 6,000 men, while the English lost fewer than 450.

aging Gradual change in an organism that leads to increased risk of weakness, disease, and death. It takes place in a cell, an organ, or the total organism over the entire adult life span of any living thing. There is a decline in biological functions and in ability to adapt to metabolic stress. Changes in organs include the replacement of functional cardiovascular cells with fibrous tissue. Overall effects of aging include reduced IMMUNITY, loss of muscle strength, decline in memory and other aspects of cognition, and loss of color in the hair and elasticity in the skin. In women, the process accelerates after MENOPAUSE. See also GERONTOLOGY AND GERIATRICS, OLD AGE.

agitprop \ˈa-jət-ˌpräp\ Political strategy in which techniques of agitation and propaganda are used to influence public opinion. Originally described by the Marxist theorist GEORGY PLEKHANOV and then by VLADIMIR ILICH LENIN, it called for both emotional and reasoned arguments. The term, a shortened form for the Agitation and Propaganda Section of the COMMUNIST PARTY in the former Soviet Union, has been used in English, typically with a negative connotation, to describe any work—especially in drama and other art forms—that aims to indoctrinate the public and achieve political goals.

Agnes, St. (fl. early 4th century) Legendary Christian martyr, the patron saint of girls. According to tradition, she was a beautiful virgin in Rome who turned away all suitors, declaring that she could have no spouse but Jesus. The rejected suitors informed Roman officials that she was a Christian, and she was punished by being exposed in a brothel. There she was left miraculously unharmed; the only man who attempted to violate her was struck blind, and she healed him with prayer. She was later murdered during the persecutions ordered by DIOCLETIAN.

Agnew, Spiro T(heodore) (1918–1996) U.S. politician, the only vice president forced to resign. Born in Baltimore, he earned a law degree and served as Baltimore Co. executive (from 1962). He was elected governor of Maryland in 1967. In 1968 and 1972 he was elected vice president on the Republican ticket headed by RICHARD NIXON. His speeches denouncing Vietnam War protesters and television news coverage brought him much attention. Investigated for extortion, bribery, and income-tax violations during his governorship, he resigned in 1973 and pleaded no contest to a single income-tax charge. He was fined $10,000 and sentenced to three years of unsupervised probation. Disbarred in 1974, he became a consultant to foreign businesses.

Agni Hindu god of fire, second only to INDRA in Vedic mythology. He is the fire of the sun, of lightning, and of the hearth of worship, and is the divine personification of the fire of sacrifice. He is thus the messenger between human and divine orders. Agni is described as ruddy-hued and with two faces, one beneficent and one malignant. In the RIG VEDA he is sometimes identified with Rudra, the forerunner of SHIVA.

Agnon \äg-ˈnōn**, S. Y.** *orig.* **Shmuel Yosef Halevi Czaczkes** (1888–1970) Ukrainian-Israeli writer. Born into a Polish Galician family, he moved to Palestine in 1907 and chose Hebrew as his literary language. *The Day Before Yesterday* (1945), perhaps his greatest novel, examines the problem facing the westernized Jew who immigrates to Israel. Other works include the novels *The Bridal Canopy* (1919) and *A Guest for the Night* (1938). He is regarded as one of the greatest modern Hebrew novelists and short-story writers. In 1966 he and NELLY SACHS shared the Nobel Prize.

agnosticism \ag-ˈnäs-tə-ˌsiz-əm\ Doctrine that one cannot know the existence of anything beyond the phenomena of experience. It is popularly equated with religious skepticism, and especially with the rejection of traditional Christian beliefs under the impact of modern scientific thought. T.H. HUXLEY popularized philosophical agnosticism after coining the term agnostic (as opposed to gnostic) in 1869, to designate one who repudiated traditional Judeo-Christian THEISM but was not a doctrinaire atheist (see ATHEISM). Agnosticism may mean no more than the suspension of judgment on ultimate questions because of insufficient evidence, or it may constitute a rejection of traditional Christian tenets.

agora \ˈa-gə-rə\ In ancient Greek cities, an open space serving as an assembly area and backdrop for commercial, civic, social, and religious activities. Use of the agora varied in different periods. Located in the

Plaster model of the Agora, Athens, as it might have appeared in the 2nd century AD.

AMERICAN SCHOOL OF CLASSICAL STUDIES AT ATHENS

middle of the city or near the harbor, it was often enclosed by public buildings, COLONNADES containing shops, and STOAS for protection from sun and bad weather. The highest honor for a citizen was to be granted a tomb in the agora.

Agoracritus *or* **Agorakritos** \ˌa-gə-ˈrak-rə-təs\ (fl. 5th century BC) Greek sculptor. A student of PHIDIAS, his most notable work was the colossal marble statue of Nemesis at Rhamnus. A fragment of the head is in the British Museum, and fragments of the pedestal reliefs are in Athens.

agouti \ə-ˈgü-tē\ Any of about half a dozen species of rabbit-sized rodents (genus *Dasyprocta*) that occur in the American tropics (S Mexico to northern South America). Agoutis are 16–24 in. (40–60 cm) long and have a long body, small ears, vestigial tail or none at all, and slender feet with long, hooflike claws. Their wiry fur is reddish brown to blackish, with individual hairs banded in what is called the agouti pattern. Agoutis generally live in forests and eat roots, leaves, and fruit.

Agouti (*Dasyprocta*).
WARREN GARST—TOM STACK & ASSOCIATES

Agra \ˈä-grə\ City (pop., 1991: 892,000), western central UTTAR PRADESH, India. It was founded by Sikander Lodi in the early 18th century on the Yumana River southeast of New Delhi, and was intermittently the MUGHAL capital. The city fell successively to the Jats and the MARATHAS in the late 18th century, and finally to the British in 1803. It is the site of the TAJ MAHAL and the imperial palace of AKBAR.

Agramonte (y Simoni) \ä-grä-ˈmōn-tā\, **Aristides** (1868–1931) U.S. (Cuban-born) physician, pathologist, and bacteriologist. Reared in New York City, he received his MD from Columbia University. He was a member of the U.S. Army's Reed Yellow Fever Board, which discovered in 1901 the role of mosquitoes in transmitting YELLOW FEVER. As a professor at the University of Havana (1900–30), he became an influential leader of scientific medicine in Cuba.

agribusiness Agriculture operated by business; specifically, that part of a modern national economy devoted to the production, processing, and distribution of food and fiber products and by-products. Commercial farming has largely supplanted the family farm in production of cash crops. Some food-processing firms that operate farms have begun to market fresh produce under their brand names. In recent years, conglomerates involved in nonagricultural businesses have entered agribusiness by buying and operating large farms.

Agricola \ə-ˈgri-kə-lə\, **Georgius** *orig.* **Georg Bauer** (1494–1555) German scholar and scientist known as the father of mineralogy. A town physician in Saxony (1527–33), he was among the first to found a natural science upon observation as opposed to speculation. His *De re metallica* (1556) dealt chiefly with mining and smelting; his *De natura fossilium* (1546), considered the first mineralogy textbook, presented the first scientific classification of minerals (based on their physical properties) and described many new minerals, their occurrence, and mutual relationships.

Agricola \ə-ˈgrik-ə-lə\, **Gnaeus Julius** (AD 40–93) Roman general. After serving as TRIBUNE and QUAESTOR in Britain and Asia, he was appointed by VESPASIAN governor of Britain (77/78–84). He conquered parts of Wales and northern England, then advanced into Scotland and set a frontier between the Clyde and Forth rivers. In 83 he crossed the Forth and defeated the Caledonians at Mons Graupius; he then occupied Scotland to the fringe of the highlands, with forts at the main passes and a fortress at Inchtuthil. Recalled to Rome, Agricola was offered the proconsulship of Asia, but chose retirement. His life is known through the writings of his son-in-law TACITUS.

Agricultural Adjustment Administration (AAA) NEW DEAL program to restore U.S. agricultural prosperity during the GREAT DEPRESSION. Established by an act of Congress in 1933, the AAA sought to curtail farm production of certain staples, in order to raise prices. It also established the Commodity Credit Corp., to make loans to farmers and to purchase and store crops in order to maintain farm prices. The program had limited success before it was declared unconstitutional in 1936.

Agricultural Revolution Gradual transformation of the traditional agricultural system that began in Britain in the 18th century. Aspects of this complex transformation, which was not completed until the 19th century, included the reallocation of land ownership to make farms more compact and an increased investment in technical improvements, such as new machinery, better drainage, scientific methods of breeding, and experimentation with new crops and systems of crop rotation. The agricultural revolution was an essential prelude to the INDUSTRIAL REVOLUTION.

agriculture Science or art of cultivating the SOIL, growing and harvesting CROPS, and raising LIVESTOCK. Agriculture probably first developed in South Asia and Egypt, then spread to Europe, Africa, the rest of Asia, the islands of the central and South Pacific, and finally to North and South America. Agriculture in the Middle East is believed to date from 9000–7000 BC. Early cultivated crops include wild barley (Middle East), domesticated beans and water chestnuts (Thailand), and pumpkins (the Americas). Domestication of animals occurred during roughly the same period. Slash-and-burn land-clearing methods and CROP ROTATION were early agricultural techniques. Steady improvements in tools and methods over the centuries increased agricultural output, as did mechanization, selective breeding and hybridization, and, in the 20th century, the use of HERBICIDES and INSECTICIDES. More of the world's aggregate manpower is devoted to agriculture than to all other occupations combined.

Agriculture, U.S. Department of (USDA) Federal executive division in charge of programs and policies relating to the farming industry and the use of NATIONAL FORESTS and grasslands. Formed in 1862, the USDA works to stabilize or improve domestic farm income, develop foreign markets, curb poverty and hunger, protect soil and water resources, make credit available for rural development, and ensure the quality of food supplies.

agrimony \ˈa-grə-ˌmō-nē\ Any plant of the genus *Agrimonia,* of the ROSE family, especially *A. eupatoria,* an herbaceous, hardy perennial native to Europe but widespread in other northern temperate regions, where it grows in hedge banks and the borders of fields. Its leaves yield a yellow dye. The leaflets are oval with toothed margins; the small, stalkless yellow flowers are borne in a long terminal spike. The fruit is a tiny bur. *A. gryposepala,* a similar species, is widespread in the U.S.

Agrippa \ə-ˈgrip-ə\, **Marcus Vipsanius** (63?–12 BC) Powerful deputy of AUGUSTUS. He helped Octavian (later Augustus) take power after Julius CAESAR'S MURDER (44), defeating Sextus POMPEIUS in 36 and Mark ANTONY at the Battle of ACTIUM in 31. He went on to quell rebellions, found colonies, administer parts of the empire, and give funds for public works and buildings to Rome. In 23 Augustus seemed to make him heir, and Agrippa married Augustus' daughter JULIA. His administrative and military skills were particularly directed to the eastern empire, where in 15 BC he met with and made an ally of HEROD of Judaea. Agrippa's writings (now lost) influenced STRABO and PLINY THE ELDER. His daughter Agrippina the Elder (14? BC–AD 33) was the wife of GERMANICUS CAESAR, mother of CALIGULA and AGRIPPINA THE YOUNGER, and grandmother of NERO.

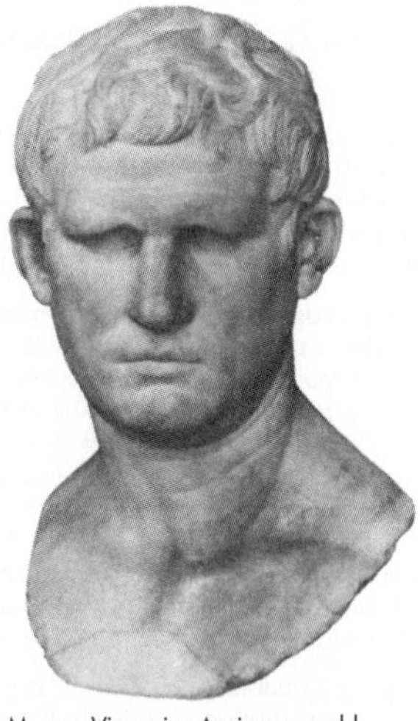
Marcus Vipsanius Agrippa, marble portrait bust, early 1st century BC; in the Louvre, Paris.
CLICHE MUSEES NATIONAUX, PARIS

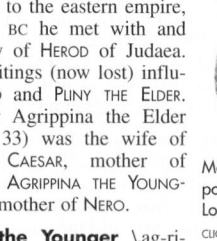

Agrippina the Younger \ˌag-ri-ˈpī-nə\ (AD 15–59) Mother of NERO and a major influence in the early years of his reign. She was the daughter of Agrippina the Elder (c. 14 BC–AD 33) and the sister of CALIGULA. She was exiled (39–41) for conspiring against Caligula. Her first husband, Gnaeus Domitius Ahenobarbus, was Nero's father. Accused of poisoning her second husband (49), she married CLAUDIUS, her uncle, and had him adopt Nero as his heir instead of his own son. She poisoned her son's rivals, and when Claudius died in 54 she was suspected of having poisoned him. She became regent when Nero took the throne at 16, but gradually lost power; he tried to murder her when she opposed one of his affairs, and finally had her put to death at her country house.

agrochemical Any chemical used in AGRICULTURE, including chemical FERTILIZERS, HERBICIDES, and INSECTICIDES. Most are mixtures of two or more chemicals; active ingredients provide the desired effects, and inert ingredients stabilize or preserve the active ingredients or aid in application. Together with other technological advances, including tractors, mechanical harvesters, and irrigation pumps, agrochemicals have increased the per-acre productivity of regions such as the Great Plains by 200–300% since the 1930s. Their long-term effects on the environment and the stability of agricultural systems that use them are hotly debated.

agronomy Branch of AGRICULTURE that deals with field CROP production and soil management. Agronomists generally work with crops that are grown on a large scale (e.g., small grains) and that require relatively little management. Agronomic experiments focus on a variety of factors relating to crop plants, including yield, diseases, cultivation, and sensitivity to factors such as climate and soil.

Aguán River \ä-'gwän\ River, northern Honduras. It rises in the central highlands west of Yoro, descends northeast to the coastal lowlands, and empties into the Caribbean Sea near Santa Rosa de Aguán, for a total course of 150 mi (240 km). The lands along the river are used primarily for agriculture but are susceptible to floods and hurricanes.

Aguascalientes \ˌä-gwäs-käl-'yen-tās\ State (pop., 2000: 943,506), central Mexico. One of the country's smallest states (2,112 sq mi, or 5,471 sq km), it occupies part of the central plateau. Explored by Spaniards in the 16th century, it was a coal mining center. During the revolution of 1919–20 it was the scene of bitter fighting. It is a fertile agricultural area, and is noted for its mineral production. Its capital is AGUASCALIENTES.

Aguascalientes City (pop., 2000: 594,056), capital of AGUASCALIENTES state, Mexico. Located on the Aguascalientes River, it was founded as a mining settlement in 1575, and became the state capital in the 1850s. It is sometimes called La Ciudad Perforada ("The Perforated City") because of an underground labyrinth of tunnels built by an unknown pre-Columbian people. It is an agricultural center, with several industries. Several churches possess outstanding examples of colonial religious art.

Aguinaldo \ˌä-gē-'näl-dō\, **Emilio** (1869–1964) Philippine independence leader. Of Chinese and Tagalog parentage, he was educated at the University of Santo Tomás, Manila, and became a leader of the Katipunan, a revolutionary society that fought the Spanish. Philippine independence was declared in 1898 and Aguinaldo became president, but within months Spain signed a treaty ceding the islands to the U.S. Aguinaldo fought U.S. forces until he was captured in 1901. After taking an oath of allegiance to the U.S., he was induced to retire from public life. He collaborated with the Japanese during World War II; after the war he was briefly imprisoned; released by presidential amnesty, he was vindicated by his appointment to the Council of State in 1950. In his later years he promoted nationalism, democracy, and improvement of relations with the U.S.

Aguinaldo.
BROWN BROTHERS

Agulhas \ə-'gəl-əs\, **Cape** Cape, southernmost point of the African continent. Its name, Portuguese for "needles," refers to the rocks and reefs that have wrecked many ships. The cape's meridian of 20°E is the official boundary between the Indian and Atlantic oceans.

Agusan River \ə-'gü-ˌsän\ River, MINDANAO, Philippines. Rising in the southeast and flowing north 240 mi (390 km) to enter Butuan Bay of the Bohol Sea, it forms a fertile valley 40–50 mi (65–80 km) wide between the Central Mindanao Highlands and the Pacific Cordillera. It is navigable for 160 mi (260 km). Despite early Spanish contacts in the 17th century, most of the valley has remained sparsely settled by native peoples.

Ahab \'ā-ˌhab\ (fl. 9th century BC) Seventh king of the northern kingdom of Israel (r.c. 874–853 BC). He inherited a realm that included territory east of the Jordan River, in GILEAD and probably BASHAN, and also the tributary kingdom of MOAB. His marriage to JEZEBEL revived an alliance with the PHOENICIANS, but her efforts to establish BAAL worship provoked bitter opposition from ELIJAH. Ahab's reign was dominated by a fierce border war with Syria; he died in an attempt to recover Ramoth-Gilead from the Syrians.

Ahaggar Mountains \ə-'hä-gər, ˌä-hə-'gär\ *or* **Hoggar Mountains** \'häg-ər, ō-'gär\ High plateau region, southern Algeria. Located in the central SAHARA, it extends about 970 mi (1,550 km) north–south and 1,300 mi (2,100 km) east–west. Its elevation is higher than 3,000 ft (900 m); its highest peak is Mount Tahat (9,573 ft, or 2,918 m). The main caravan route to KANO (Nigeria) passes along its western margin.

Ahidjo \ä-'hi-jō\, **Ahmadou** (1924–1989) First president of Cameroon, 1960–82. He presided over one of the few successful attempts at African unity: the joining of the southern half of the former British Cameroons with the larger French-speaking Cameroun. In 1982, after managing to build up a stable, relatively prosperous nation (through single-party rule), he went into exile after being implicated in a plot against his successor, Paul Biya.

ahimsa \ə-'him-sä\ (Sanskrit: "noninjury") Fundamental ethical virtue of JAINISM, also respected in BUDDHISM and HINDUISM. In Jainism ahimsa is the standard by which all actions are judged. It requires a householder observing the small vows *(anuvrata)* to refrain from killing any animal life. An ascetic observing the great vows *(mahavrata)* is expected to take the greatest care not to injure any living substance, even unknowingly. To do so interrupts that being's spiritual progress and increases one's own KARMA, delaying liberation from the cycle of rebirth. In the 20th century MOHANDAS K. GANDHI extended ahimsa into the political sphere as SATYAGRAHA.

Ahmad, Mirza Ghulam See Mirza GHULAM AHMAD

Ahmad ibn Hanbal \'äḵ-məd-ˌib-ən-'ḵan-bəl\ (780–855) Muslim theologian and jurist. Born in Baghdad, he began to study the HADITH at 15. He traveled widely to study with the great masters, and made five pilgrimages to Mecca. In 833–35 he bravely endured floggings and imprisonment rather than subscribe to the MUTAZILA doctrine of a created (rather than eternal) Quran, and he is remembered as a staunch upholder of Muslim traditionalism. He compiled the Traditions of Muhammad and is the eponym of the Hanbali school, the most traditional of the four orthodox Islamic schools of law. Opposing codification of the law, he believed jurists needed the freedom to derive legal solutions from the Quran and the SUNNA. He is revered as one of the fathers of Islam.

Ahmad Khan \'am-ad-'ḵän\, **Sayyid** *later* **Sir Sayyid** (1817–1898) Indian educator and jurist. Born into a family of officials in the Mughal dynasty, he worked for the British East India Co. and held various judicial posts. He supported the British in the 1857 Indian Mutiny but criticized their errors in his influential pamphlet "Causes of the Indian Revolt." His other works include *Essays on the Life of Mohammed* (1870) and commentaries on the Bible and Quran. He founded schools at Muradabad and Ghazipur, established the Scientific Society, sought to strengthen the Muslim community through the reform journal *Tahdhib al-Akhlaq,* and was active in founding a Muslim college, the Anglo-Mohammedan Oriental College, in 1877 at Aligarh.

Ahmad Shah Durrani \'äḵ-məd-'shä-dür-'ä-nē\ (1722?–1772) Founder of Afghanistan. The son of an Afghan chief, he became shah in 1747 on the death of NADIR SHAH. He proceeded to invade India nine times over the next 22 years in an attempt to control the trade routes between northern India and central and western Asia, and became ruler of an empire that extended from the AMU DARYA to the Indian Ocean and from Khorasan to present-day northern India. His hold on the Punjab, governed by his son Timur Shah, was weakened by his distractions in the west, and he ultimately lost control of it to the Sikhs. Much of his empire disintegrated after his death.

Ahmadabad \'ä-mə-də-ˌbäd\ *also* **Ahmedabad** City (metro. area pop., 2001 prelim.: 4,519,278), GUJARAT state, western central India. It is located on the Sabarmati River 290 miles (467 km) north of Mumbai

(Bombay). Founded in 1411 by Sultan Ahmad Shah, Ahmadabad reached its height later that century but subsequently declined. It was revived under MUGHAL emperors in the 17th century and came under British rule in 1818. With the opening of cotton mills in 1859, it became India's largest inland industrial center. The city is associated with Indian nationalism; MOHANDAS K. GANDHI's political agitation began there in 1930. The city was struck by a violent earthquake in 2001 that took many lives.

Ahmadiya \ˌäh-mə-ˈdē-ə\ Modern Islamic sect, founded in India in 1889 by MIRZA GHULAM AHMAD. It holds that Jesus feigned death and resurrection and escaped to India, and that JIHAD is a peaceful battle against nonbelievers. Following the death of Ghulam Ahmad's successor (1914), the Ahmadiya split. The Qadianis, based in Rabwah, Pakistan, recognize Ghulam Ahmad as a prophet; they are zealous missionaries, preaching Ahmadi beliefs as the one true ISLAM. A Lahore-based sect regards Ghulam Ahmad merely as a reformer and seeks to make converts to Islam generally. The term Ahmadiya is also used to describe various Sufi orders (see SUFISM), particularly that founded by Ahmad al-Badawi (died 1276). One of the most popular orders in Egypt, it has branches throughout the Islamic world.

Ahmadu Seku \a-ˈmad-ü-ˈsā-kü\ (died 1898) Second and last ruler of the TUKULOR empire in West Africa, celebrated for his resistance to French occupation. Succeeding his father, al-Hajj Umar, in 1864, Ahmadu ruled over a great empire centered on the ancient BAMBARA kingdom of Segu, in present Mali. In 1887 he was forced to abandon Segu and accept French protectorate status. By 1891 most of his strongholds had been seized.

Ahmed Yesevi \äk̲-ˈmet-ˌye-se-ˈvē\ *or* **Ahmad Yasawi** \äk̲-ˈmed-ˌyä-sä-ˈvē\ (died 1166) Turkish poet and Sufi mystic. He was born in Sayram (now in Kazakhstan) and his family moved to Yasi, where he began his teaching. The *Book of Wisdom*, a collection of mystical poetry, is traditionally attributed to him. He established a mystical order whose rituals preserved Islamic and ancient Turco-Mongol customs, and promoted the spread of mysticism throughout the Turkish-speaking world. His poetry influenced Turkish literature and led to the development of mystical folk literature. He was revered as a saint, and TIMUR erected a magnificent mausoleum over his grave in 1397/98.

Ahsai \äk̲-ˈsä-ē\, **Ahmad al-** *in full* **Shaykh Ahmad ibn Zayn al-Din Ibrahim al-Ahsai** (1753–1826) Founder of the heterodox Shiite Muslim Shaykhi sect of Iran. Born in Arabia, he traveled widely in Persia and the Middle East. In 1808 he settled in Yazd, Persia, where he attracted followers with his interpretation of Shiism. He claimed knowledge from visions of MUHAMMAD and the IMAMS, and contended that the imams were originally beings of divine light who participated in the creation of the world. Orthodox Shiite theologians declared him an apostate in 1824; he died two years later on pilgrimage to Mecca, but the Shaykhi sect survived him.

Ahura Mazda \ˈä-hu̇r-ə-ˈmäz-də\ Supreme god of ancient Iranian religion, especially ZOROASTRIANISM. Ahura Mazda was worshiped by DARIUS I and his successors as the greatest god and the protector of the just king. ZOROASTER taught that Ahura Mazda created the universe and maintains the cosmic order, and that the history of the world consists of the battle between two spirits he created—the beneficent Spenta Mainyu and the destructive Angra Mainyu. The AVESTA identifies Ahura Mazda himself with the beneficent spirit and represents him as bountiful, all-knowing, and the creator of everything good. In late sources (from the 3rd century), Zurvan ("Time") is the father of the twins Ormazd (Ahura Mazda) and Ahriman (Angra Mainyu), who in orthodox Mazdaism (Zoroastrianism and Parsiism) reign alternately over the world until Ormazd's ultimate victory.

Ai \ˈā-ˌī\ Town, eastern CANAAN, ancient PALESTINE. In the Bible (Joshua 7–8), it was destroyed by the Israelites under JOSHUA. Biblical references agree in locating Ai just east of BETHEL (modern Baytin), at the Early Bronze Age site now called At-Tall. Excavations at Ai in 1933–35 uncovered a temple of the 3rd millennium BC. The biblical events at Ai are assigned to the period c. 1400–1200 BC, when evidence indicates it was not in fact occupied; early tradition may have identified the Canaanite town under Bethel with the nearby ruins of At-Tall.

Aidan \ˈād-ᵊn\, **St.** (died 651) Apostle of Northumbria and founder of LINDISFARNE. He was a monk at Iona in Scotland when King Oswald of Northumbria requested that he be made bishop of the newly converted Northumbrians. He established his church, see, and monastery on the island of Lindisfarne. From there he evangelized northern England, founding churches, monasteries, and a school. BEDE praised him for his learning, charity, and simplicity of life.

aide-de-camp \ˌād-di-ˈkamp\ Officer on the personal staff of a general, admiral, or other high-ranking commander who acts as a confidential secretary. Today they are usually of junior rank, and their duties are largely social. The term also denotes a high-ranking military officer who acts as an aide to a chief of state.

AIDS *in full* **acquired immunodeficiency syndrome** Fatal transmissible disorder caused by HIV. AIDS, the last stage of HIV infection, is defined by the appearance of potentially lethal opportunistic infections. The first AIDS cases were identified in 1981, HIV was isolated in 1983, and blood tests were developed by 1985. In 2002 approximately 40 million people worldwide were living with HIV, and over 25 million had died of AIDS. In the U.S., some 2 million people had been infected with HIV, 800,000 had been diagnosed with AIDS, and 450,000 had died. Sub-Saharan Africa remains the focus of infection, but the number of cases in South and Southeast Asia and elsewhere continues to mount at an alarming rate as well. An initial acute illness usually resolves within weeks. Infected persons then generally have few or no symptoms for about 10 years. As the IMMUNE SYSTEM deteriorates, they develop diseases such as *Pneumocystis carinii* PNEUMONIA, CYTOMEGALOVIRUS, LYMPHOMA, or KAPOSI'S SARCOMA.

Aiken \ˈā-kən\, **Conrad (Potter)** (1889–1973) U.S. writer. Born in Savannah, Ga., he was traumatized as a child when his father killed his mother and then himself. Educated at Harvard University he wrote most of his fiction in the 1920s and '30s. His works are influenced by early psychoanalytic theory. Generally more successful than his novels were his short stories, notably "Strange Moonlight" from *Bring! Bring!* (1925) and "Silent Snow, Secret Snow" and "Mr. Arcularis" from *Among the Lost People* (1934). His best poetry, including "Preludes to Definition," is in his *Collected Poems* (1953).

Aiken, Howard H(athaway) (1900–1973) U.S. mathematician and inventor. Born in Hoboken, N.J., he received his PhD from Harvard University. With three other engineers, he began work in 1939 on an automatic calculating machine that could perform any selected sequence of five arithmetical operations (addition, subtraction, multiplication, division, and reference to previous results) without human intervention. The first such machine, the Harvard Mark I (1944), was 51 ft (15 m) long and 8 ft (2.4 m) high, and weighed 35 tons (31,500 kg).

aikido \ˌī-ki-ˈdō, ī-ˈkē-dō\ Japanese art of self-defense employing locks and holds and utilizing the principle of nonresistance to cause an opponent's own momentum to work against him. Aikido was developed to subdue rather than (as in JUJITSU and KARATE) to maim or kill. It especially emphasizes the importance of achieving complete mental calm and control of one's own body to master an opponent's attack. There are no offensive moves. It traces its origins to Japanese martial (samurai) traditions dating to the 14th century, and it was developed as a modern form in the early 20th century by Ueshiba Morihei. See MARTIAL ART.

ailanthus \ā-ˈlan-thəs\ Any of the flowering plants that make up the genus *Ailanthus*, in the quassia family (Simaroubaceae), native to eastern and southern Asia and northern Australia, and naturalized in subtropical and temperate regions elsewhere. Ailanthus leaves alternate along the stem and are composed of multiple leaflets arranged along an axis. The most familiar species is the TREE OF HEAVEN.

Ailey \ˈā-lē\, **Alvin, Jr.** (1931–1989) U.S. dancer and choreographer. Born in Rogers, Texas, he moved to Los Angeles in 1942, where he studied dance and choreography (1949–54). He then moved to New York, where he performed in various theatrical productions. In 1958 he founded the Alvin Ailey American Dance Theater, composed

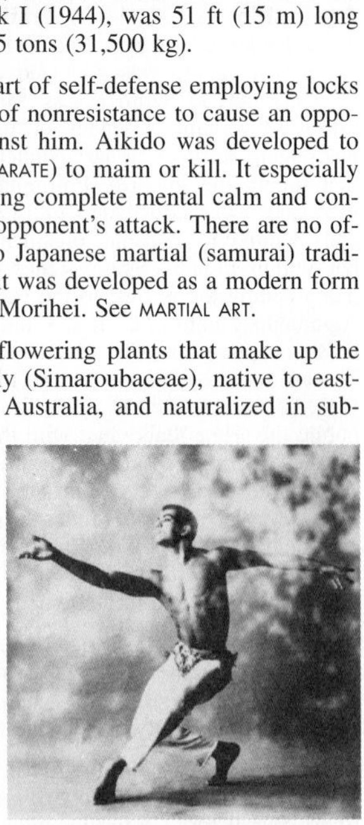
Ailey, 1960.
BY COURTESY OF ZACHARY FREYMAN

primarily of blacks. The numerous works he choreographed for the company included its signature *Revelations* (1960), set to black spirituals. From the 1960s to the 1980s the company toured worldwide, making Ailey one of the best-known U.S. choreographers. After his death from AIDS, JUDITH JAMISON assumed the title of artistic director of the company.

Ailly \ȧ-'yē\, **Pierre d'** (1350–1420) French theologian and cardinal. D'Ailly worked to end the Western SCHISM. He advocated the doctrine of conciliarism (see CONCILIAR MOVEMENT). He was active at the Council of Pisa (1409), which deposed both pope and ANTIPOPE in favor of the new conciliar pope, Alexander V, and at the Council of Constance (1414–18), which called for the abdication of the antipope John XXIII (r.1410–15) and the election of yet another pope (MARTIN V). His writings included a geographical treatise, *Image of the World*, used by CHRISTOPHER COLUMBUS.

Aintab See GAZIANTEP

Ainu \'ī-nü\ People of Japan, originally residing throughout its four major islands. Pushed north by the Japanese people over the last 2,000 years, the few remaining pure Ainu today live principally in northern Hokkaido, Sakhalin, and the Aleutians. Originally physically and culturally distinct from the Japanese, their language and origins and their role in Japanese history and prehistory have been the subject of scholarly debate. The Ainu were traditionally hunters, fishermen, and trappers; their religion centered on spirits believed to be present in animals and the natural world.

Ainu couple in ceremonial dress, Hokkaido Island, Japan.
COURTESY OF THE CONSULATE GENERAL OF JAPAN, NEW YORK CITY

air Mixture of gases constituting the earth's atmosphere. Some gases occur in steady concentrations. The most important are molecular nitrogen (N_2), 78% by volume, and molecular oxygen (O_2), 21%. Small amounts of argon (Ar; 1.9%), neon (Ne), helium (He), methane (CH_4), krypton (Kr), hydrogen (H_2), nitrous oxide (N_2O), and xenon (Xe) are also present in almost constant proportions. Other gases occur in variable concentrations: water vapor (H_2O), ozone (O_3), carbon dioxide (CO_2), sulfur dioxide (SO_2), and nitrogen dioxide (NO_2). Air also contains trace amounts of ammonia and hydrogen sulfide. The variable constituents are important for maintaining life. Water vapor is the source for all forms of precipitation and is an important absorber and emitter of infrared radiation. Carbon dioxide is necessary for photosynthesis and is also an important absorber and emitter of infrared radiation. Ozone in the STRATOSPHERE (see OZONE LAYER) is an effective absorber of ultraviolet radiation from the sun, but at ground-level is a corrosive pollutant and a major constituent of smog.

air brake Either of two kinds of braking systems. The first, used by trains, trucks, and buses, operates by a piston driven by compressed air from reservoirs connected to BRAKE cylinders (see PISTON AND CYLINDER). When air pressure in the brake pipe is reduced, air is automatically admitted into the brake cylinder. The first practical air brake for railroads was invented in the 1860s by GEORGE WESTINGHOUSE. The second type, used by aircraft and race cars, consists of a flap or surface that can be mechanically projected into the airstream to increase the resistance of the vehicle to air and lower its speed.

air-conditioning Control of temperature, humidity, purity, and motion of air in an enclosed space, independent of outside conditions. In a self-contained air-conditioning unit, air is heated in a boiler unit or cooled by being blown across a refrigerant-filled coil and then distributed to a controlled indoor environment. Central air-conditioning in a large building generally consists of a main plant located on the roof or mechanical floor and intermittently spaced air-handling units, or fans that deliver air through ducts to zones within the building. The air then returns to the central air-conditioning machinery through spaces called plenums to be recooled (or reheated) and recirculated. Alternate systems of cooling use chilled water, with water cooled by a refrigerant at a central location and circulated by pumps to units with fans that circulate air locally.

air-cushion vehicle *or* **hovercraft** Vehicle supported above the surface of land or water by an air cushion, produced by downwardly directed fans, enclosed within a flexible skirt beneath the hull. The concept was first proposed by John Thornycroft in the 1870s, but a working model was not produced until 1955, when Christopher Cockerell solved the problem of keeping the air cushion from escaping from under the vehicle, and formed Hovercraft Ltd. to manufacture prototypes. Problems with skirt design and engine maintenance have restricted the vehicle's commercial application; today hovercraft are used mainly as ferries.

air force Military organization of a nation that has the primary responsibility for conducting AIR WARFARE. The air force must gain control of the air, support ground forces (e.g., by bombing enemy ground forces), and accomplish strategic-bombing objectives. Its basic weapons are FIGHTER AIRCRAFT, BOMBERS, attack aircraft (which operate at lower altitudes than bombers), and reconnaissance craft. The army and naval branches of a nation's armed forces may also operate aircraft.

Air France *in full* **Compagnie Internationale Air France** French passenger and cargo airline with more than 200 destinations in 90 countries. It introduced supersonic CONCORDE service in 1976. As of 2002 the French government planned to privatize the company.

air mass In meteorology, a large body of air having nearly uniform conditions of temperature and humidity at any given altitude. Such a mass has distinct boundaries and may extend hundreds or thousands of miles horizontally and sometimes as high as the top of the TROPOSPHERE. An air mass forms whenever the atmosphere remains in contact with a large, relatively uniform land or sea surface long enough to acquire its temperature and moisture properties. The earth's major air masses all originate in polar or subtropical latitudes. The middle latitudes constitute essentially a zone of modification, interaction, and mixing of the polar and tropical air masses.

air pollution Release into the atmosphere of gases, finely divided solids, or finely dispersed liquid aerosols at rates that exceed the capacity of the atmosphere to dissipate them or to dispose of them through incorporation into the BIOSPHERE. Dust storms in desert areas and smoke from forest and grass fires contribute to particulate and chemical air pollution. Volcanic activity is the major natural source of air pollution, pouring huge amounts of ash and toxic fumes into the atmosphere. Air pollution may affect humans directly, causing irritation of the eyes or coughing. More indirectly, its effects can be measured far from the source, as, for example, the fallout of tetraethyl lead from automobile exhausts, which has been observed in the oceans and on the Greenland ice sheet. Still less direct are possible effects on global climates. See also SMOG.

air warfare Military operations conducted by airplanes, helicopters, or other aircraft against aircraft or targets on the ground and in the water. Hot-air balloons were used in the 19th century to observe enemy troop movements, but air warfare did not become important until the 20th century. By World War I, the British, French, German, Russian, and Italian armed forces had flying units, including biplanes made of wood and fabric and armed with machine guns for "dogfights" with enemy FIGHTER AIRCRAFT. ZEPPELINS and Allied airplanes also carried out bombing raids. The 1920s and '30s saw important advances, including development of the monoplane, the all-metal fuselage, and the AIRCRAFT CARRIER.

airbrush PNEUMATIC DEVICE for developing a fine, small-diameter spray of paint, protective coating, or liquid color (see AEROSOL). The airbrush can be a pencil-shaped atomizer used for various highly detailed activities such as shading drawings and retouching photographs; in contrast, a spray gun is usually used for covering large surfaces with paint.

Airbus Industrie European aircraft-making consortium that is the world's second largest maker of commercial aircraft (after BOEING CO.). Full members include the German-French-Spanish-owned EUROPEAN AERONAUTIC DEFENCE AND SPACE COMPANY (EADS), with an 80-percent interest, and Britain's BAE SYSTEMS, with 20 percent. Belgium's Belairbus and Italy's Alenia are risk-sharing associate members in selected programs. Airbus was formed in 1970 by French and German aerospace firms (later joined by Spanish and British companies) to fill a market niche for short- to medium-range, high-capacity jetliners and compete with long-established American manufacturers. Its first product, the A300, entered service in 1974. It was the first wide-body jetliner equipped with only two engines for more economical operation. The twin-engine A320 (entered service 1988) incorporated numerous technical innovations, notably fly-by-wire (electric rather than mechanically linked), computer-based flight controls. The four-engine A340 (1993) and smaller, twin-engine A330 (1994) were long-range airliners. In 2000 Airbus launched development of the A380, intended to be the world's largest airliner with a typical seating of 555 passengers.

aircraft carrier Naval vessel equipped with a platform that allows airplanes to take off and land. Takeoffs are facilitated by turning the ship into the wind and through the use of catapults in the flight deck. For landing, aircraft are fitted with retractable hooks that engage transverse wires on the deck, braking them to a quick stop. The British navy developed the first true aircraft carrier near the end of World War I, and carriers first saw in combat in World War II. The Japanese attack on Pearl Harbor was conducted by carrier-based planes, and the carrier played leading roles in such Pacific naval engagements as the Battles of MIDWAY and the Coral Sea.

Airedale terrier Dog breed that is the largest of the TERRIERS, probably descended from the otterhound and the extinct Old English terrier. It stands about 23 in. (58 cm) high, weighs 40–50 lbs (18–23 kg), and has a boxy appearance, with a long, squared muzzle. Its coat is dense and wiry, with a black saddle and tan legs, muzzle, and underparts. Intelligent and courageous, powerful and affectionate (though reserved with strangers), the Airedale has been used as a wartime dispatch carrier, police dog, guard, and big-game hunter.

Airedale terrier.
WALTER CHANDOHA

airfoil Shaped surface, such as an AIRPLANE wing, tail, or PROPELLER blade, that produces LIFT and DRAG when moved through the air. An airfoil produces a lifting FORCE that acts at right angles to the airstream and a dragging force that acts in the same direction as the airstream. High-speed aircraft usually employ thin, low-drag, low-lift airfoils; slow aircraft that carry heavy loads use thicker airfoils with high drag and high lift.

airline, national Air transportation services owned and operated by national governments. All U.S. airlines are privately owned, but many other countries have government-owned airlines. Often national airlines were founded as private services and later purchased by the government. The oldest airline in the English-speaking world, Qantas Airways, was founded privately in Australia in 1920 to provide taxi services and joy flights; it was purchased by the Australian government in 1947. Air France was formed in 1933 by the merger of four private airlines. British Airways was formed in 1974 through the merger of Britain's European and overseas airlines, both already government-owned, in 1987 the British government sold it off through a huge stock offering. Other national airlines include Ireland's Aer Lingus and Russia's AEROFLOT.

airplane Fixed-wing aircraft that is heavier than air, propelled by a screw PROPELLER or a high-velocity jet, and supported by the dynamic reaction of the air against its wings. An airplane's essential components are the body or fuselage, a flight-sustaining wing system, stabilizing tail surfaces, altitude-control devices such as rudders, a thrust-providing power source, and a landing support system. Beginning in the 1840s, several British and French inventors produced designs for engine-powered aircraft, but the first powered, sustained, and controlled flight was only achieved by WILBUR AND ORVILLE WRIGHT in 1903. Later airplane design was affected by the development of the JET ENGINE; most airplanes today have a long nose section, swept-back wings with jet engines placed behind the plane's midsection, and a tail stabilizing section. Most airplanes are designed to operate from land; SEAPLANES are adapted to touch down on water, and carrier-based planes are modified for high-speed short takeoff and landing. See also air foil, AVIATION, GLIDER, HELICOPTER. See illustration opposite.

airport Site and installations for the takeoff and landing of aircraft. Early airports were open, grass-covered fields, called landing fields, that allowed a pilot to head directly into the wind to aid a plane's lift on takeoff and to decrease its speed on landing. In the 1930s heavier airplanes required paved runway surfaces. Larger planes needed longer runways, which today can reach 15,000 ft (4,500 m) to accommodate the largest jet aircraft. Air traffic is regulated from control towers and regional centers. Passenger and cargo terminals include baggage-movement and passenger-transit operations.

airship *or* **dirigible** Lighter-than-air aircraft with steering and propulsion systems. Airships could be nonrigid (blimps), semirigid, or rigid. They all included a large cigar-shaped bag or balloon filled with a gas such as HYDROGEN or HELIUM, a car or gondola suspended below the balloon that held the crew and passengers, engines to drive the propellers, and rudders for steering. Attempts to control the flight of balloons began soon after their invention in the 1780s. The first propeller-driven airship, built by Henri Giffard, flew in 1852 in France; design improvements led to construction of the rigid ZEPPELIN (1900). The nonrigid helium-filled blimp was principally developed by Alberto Santos-Dumont (1873–1932). In 1928 Germany began regular transatlantic airship passenger service. Several explosions, particularly the 1937 *HINDENBURG* DISASTER,

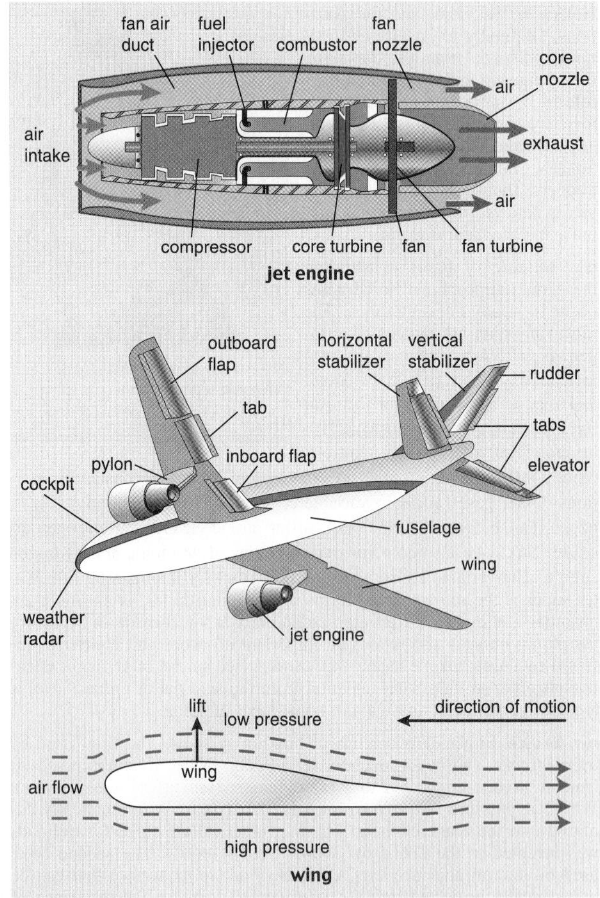

Four physical forces act on an airplane in flight: gravity (weight), thrust, lift, and drag. Jet engines, such as the turbofan shown, provide thrust by the rearward discharge of a jet of air. Air is taken into the front of the engine, compressed, and used to burn fuel in the combustor. Hot exhaust gases and air are expelled in a high-speed jet from the rear, providing forward thrust. Lift is generated by the shape of the wings and their angle of attack to the oncoming air. Because of its shape, air flowing over the top of a wing moves faster than that flowing beneath it; as a result, the air above exerts a lower pressure on the wing than that below, producing an upward force on the wing.

and AIRPLANE developments made the airship commercially obsolete. See also BALLOON.

Aisha (bint Abi Bakr) \'ä-ē-shə\ (614–678) Third wife of MUHAMMAD. The daughter of his supporter ABU BAKR, she became Muhammad's favorite wife. Left a childless widow at 18, she became politically active during the reign of the third caliph, UTHMAN IBN AFFAN, leading the opposition that resulted in his murder in 656. She led an army against his successor, ALI, who defeated her. She was allowed to live her remaining years quietly in Medina and is credited with transmitting more than a thousand HADITH.

Aitken, William Maxwell See Baron BEAVERBROOK

Aix-en-Provence \ˌeks-äⁿ-prō-'väⁿs\ City (pop., 1990: 127,000), southeastern France. Founded as a military colony by the Romans c. 123 BC, it was the scene of the defeat of the Teutons by MARIUS in 102 BC. Visigoths, Franks, Lombards, and finally Muslim invaders from Spain successively plundered the town. As the capital of PROVENCE, it was a center of culture during the Middle Ages; it became part of France in 1486. It is now a residential suburb of MARSEILLE; its industries include tourism, food processing, and the manufacturing of electrical machinery.

Aix-la-Chapelle See AACHEN

Aix-la-Chapelle \ˌeks-lȧ-shȧ-'pel\, **Congress of** (1818) First of four congresses held by Britain, Austria, Prussia, Russia, and France to address European problems following the NAPOLEONIC WARS. At Aix-la-Chapelle (now Aachen, Germany), the participants accepted an offer by France to pay most of the war indemnity owed to the allies in exchange for the withdrawal of their armies of occupation. France was also admitted to the new Quintuple Alliance.

Aix-la-Chapelle, Treaty of (1748) Treaty that ended the War of the AUSTRIAN SUCCESSION. The treaty, negotiated largely by Britain and France, was marked by the mutual restitution of conquests, including the fortress of Louisbourg (in Nova Scotia) to France and Madras (now Chennai; in India) to England. It preserved MARIA THERESA's right to the Austrian lands, but the Habsburgs were weakened by Prussia's retention of SILESIA. The treaty did not resolve any issues in the commercial struggle between England and France and thus did not lead to a lasting peace.

Aizawl \ī-'zau̇l\ City (pop., 1991: 154,000), capital of MIZORAM state, India. The surrounding region is part of the Assam-Myanmar geologic province, with steeply inclined hill ranges. Many in the population are from Myanmar. In the 1970s Aizawl was the scene of an armed attack on the government treasury by members of the Mizo National Front. Poultry raising supplements an agricultural economy.

Ajax Greek hero of the TROJAN WAR. In the *Iliad* HOMER described him as of great stature and second only to ACHILLES in strength and bravery. He fought HECTOR in single combat and rescued the body of Achilles from the hands of the Trojans. When Achilles' armor was awarded to ODYSSEUS, he was so enraged that he went mad. According to several Greek and Roman poets, Ajax slaughtered a flock of sheep he mistook for his enemies, then returned to his senses and killed himself out of shame.

Ajodhya \ə-'jōd-yə\ *or* **Ayodhya** \ə-'yōd-yə\ Former city, northern India. Lying on the banks of the GHAGHARA RIVER just east of Faizabad, of which it is now a part, Ajodhya in ancient times was one of India's greatest cities, and it is one of the seven holy cities of HINDUISM. It was the capital of KOSALA, as described in the *RAMAYANA*. It became an important Buddhist center in BUDDHISM's early years (6th–4th century BC); the BUDDHA is said to have lived there. It is also sacred to followers of JAINISM. In the 16th century the Mughal emperor BABUR built a mosque on a site traditionally associated with an ancient Hindu temple marking the birthplace of the god RAMA. The storming of the mosque by Hindus in 1990, amid religious tensions, was followed by riots, and the ensuing crisis brought down the government. In 1992 the mosque was demolished by Hindu fundamentalists; more than 1,000 people may have died in the rioting that subsequently swept through India.

AK-47 \'ā-'kā\ Soviet ASSAULT RIFLE. Designed by Mikhail T. Kalashnikov (its name stands for "automatic Kalashnikov 1947"), it had both semiautomatic and automatic capabilities and fired intermediate-power 7.62-mm ammunition. It was manufactured in the former Soviet Union and Soviet-bloc countries as well as in China and North Korea. In the 1980s it was replaced by the AKM, a modernized version with better sights. Both versions were the basic shoulder weapon for virtually all communist armies as well as for many guerrilla and nationalist movements. See also M16 RIFLE.

Akal Takht \ə-'käl-'tək-tə\ Chief center of religious authority for Indian Sikhs, located in Amritsar opposite the GOLDEN TEMPLE. It also serves as the headquarters of the AKALI PARTY. Since the line of GURUS came to an end in 1708, the Sikh community has settled religious and political disputes at meetings in front of the Akal Takht. In the 20th century local congregations began to pass resolutions on matters of Sikh doctrine and rules of conduct; disputed resolutions may be appealed to the Akal Takht. It was badly damaged during the assault on the Golden Temple by the Indian army in 1984 and had to be rebuilt. See also SIKHISM.

Akali Party \ə-'kä-lē\ Sikh political party in India. The term Akali was first applied to suicide squads that appeared in the Sikh armies c. 1690 in response to Mughal persecution. The Akali name was revived in the 1920s during the GURDWARA reform movement to refer to a semimilitary corps of volunteers opposed to British rule. Akalis took the lead in agitation for a Punjabi-speaking Sikh-majority state, a goal achieved in 1966 with the establishment of the Indian state of PUNJAB. The modern Akali Party participates in national elections but is mainly concerned with the status of the Sikhs in Punjab.

Akan \'ä-ˌkän\ Cluster of peoples inhabiting southern Ghana, eastern Ivory Coast, and parts of Togo. Their languages are of the KWA branch of the NIGER-CONGO family. In the 14th–18th century several Akan states, notably the FANTE confederacy and the ASHANTI empire, formed in regions where gold was produced and traded. Today many of the Akan, who number about 5 million, work in urban districts.

Akbar *in full* **Abu-ul-Fath Jalal-ud-Din Muhammad Akbar** (1542–1605) Greatest of the Mughal emperors (see MUGHAL DYNASTY) of India (r.1556–1605). Akbar, whose ancestors included TIMUR and GENGHIS KHAN, ascended the throne as a youth. Initially his rule extended only over the Punjab and the area around Delhi. The Rajput raja of Amber (Jaipur) acknowledged his suzerainty in 1562, and other Rajput rajas followed suit. Akbar included Rajput princes and other Hindus in the highest ranks of his government and reduced discrimination against non-Muslims. He continued his conquests, taking Gujarat in the west (1573) and Bengal in the east (annexed in 1576). Toward the end of his reign he conquered Kashmir (1586) and moved south into the Deccan. Administratively, he strengthened central power, establishing that all military officers and civil administrators were to be appointed by the emperor. He encouraged scholars, poets, painters, and musicians, making his court a center of culture. He had Sanskrit classics translated into Persian and was enthusiastic about the European paintings presented to him by Jesuit missionaries. His reign was often portrayed as a model by later governments—strong, benevolent, tolerant, and enlightened. See also BABUR.

Ake \'ä-kē\, **Claude** (1939–1996) Nigerian political scientist and activist. He received his PhD from Columbia University in 1966. He founded the Center for Advanced Social Science in Port Harcourt, Nigeria, and was active in efforts to uncover environmental and human-rights abuses by the Nigerian government. His books on African development and politics made him one of Africa's leading political scientists. He served as a consultant to ROYAL DUTCH/SHELL GROUP, but angrily resigned in 1995 to protest the execution of the activist KEN SARO-WIWA. He died the next year in a plane crash, whose cause has been disputed.

Akhenaton *or* **Akhnaton** \äk-'nä-tᵊn\ *orig.* **Amenhotep IV** \'ä-mən-'hō-ˌtep\ (r.1353–36 BC) Egyptian pharaoh of the 18th dynasty (1539–1292 BC). He came to power during a period of Egyptian preeminence, with Egypt controlling Palestine, Phoenicia, and Nubia. Shortly after his reign began, he began to encourage

Akhenaton, detail of the sandstone pillar statue from the Aton temple at Karnak, c. 1370 BC; in the Egyptian Museum, Cairo.
HIRMER FOTOARCHIV, MUNCHEN

the exclusive worship of the little-known deity ATON. Assuming the name Akhenaton ("One Useful to Aton"), he moved his capital from Thebes to present-day Tell el-Amarna to escape established religious powers. A new art style that focused on the details of actual life rather than on timeless conditions became popular. In government, Akhenaton tried to recapture the old authority of the ruler, which had been largely diverted to bureaucrats and officials, but his focus on his new religion to the exclusion of affairs of state resulted in the disintegration of Egypt's Asian empire. He was succeeded by two of his sons-in-law, Smenkhkare and TUTANKHAMEN, but on Tutankhamen's early demise the army took over the throne and Akhenaton's new religion was abandoned.

Akhmatova \ək-'mä-tə-və\, **Anna** *orig.* **Anna Andreyevna Gorenko** (1889–1966) Russian poet. She won fame with her first poetry collections (1912, 1914). Soon after the Revolution of 1917, Soviet authorities condemned her work for what they perceived as its narrow preoccupation with love and God, and in 1923, after the execution of her former husband on conspiracy charges, she entered a long period of literary silence. After World War II she was again denounced and expelled from the Writers Union. After JOSEPH STALIN's death in 1953, she was slowly rehabilitated. In her later years she became the influential center of a circle of younger Russian poets. Her longest work, *Poem Without a Hero*, is considered one of the great poems of the 20th century. Regarded today as one of the greatest of all Russian poets, she is also admired for her translations of other poets' works and for her memoirs.

Anna Akhmatova.
NOVOSTI PRESS AGENCY

Akiba ben Joseph \ä-'kē-vä-ben-'jō-zəf\ (c. AD 40–c. 135) Jewish sage, one of the founders of RABBINIC JUDAISM. Born in Caesarea, Palestine, he is said to have been an illiterate shepherd who began to study after age 40. He believed that Scripture contained many implied meanings in addition to its overt meaning, and he regarded written law (Torah) and oral law (Halakah) as ultimately one. He collected and systematized the oral traditions concerning the conduct of Jewish social and religious life, thus laying the foundation of the MISHNA. He may have been involved in BAR KOKHBA's rebellion against Rome. He was imprisoned by the Romans and martyred for his public teaching. See also ISHMAEL BEN ELISHA.

Akihito \ä-'kē-hē-ˌtō\ *or* **Heisei emperor** \'hā-'sā\ (born 1933) Emperor of Japan from 1989. Because his father, HIROHITO, renounced the quasi-divine status previously enjoyed by Japan's emperors, Akihito's role has been largely ceremonial. He is the first Japanese emperor to have married a commoner, and his marriage was hailed at the time for being a love match rather than an arranged marriage.

Akita \ə-'kē-tə\ Breed of working dog that originated in the mountains of northern Japan. In 1931 the Japanese government designated the breed as a national treasure. It is a powerful, muscular dog with a broad head, erect pointed ears, and a large curved tail carried over the back or curled against the flank. Colors and markings vary, including all-white, brindle, and pinto. All but the white akitas bear a distinct mask (dark area around the muzzle). Males stand 26–28 in. (66–71 cm) high, females 24–26 in. (60–66 cm).

Akkad \'a-kad\ Ancient region, central Iraq. Akkad was the northern division of ancient BABYLONIA (SUMER was the southern division). Its name was taken from the city of Agade, founded by the conqueror SARGON c. 2300 BC. Sargon and Naram-Sin united the city-states in the region and extended the empire to much of MESOPOTAMIA, including Sumer, ELAM, and the upper TIGRIS. The empire waned in the 22nd century BC. Under the kings of Akkad, their Semitic language, AKKADIAN, became a literary language, and great art was fostered.

Akkadian language \ə-'kā-dē-ən\ *or* **Assyro-Babylonian language** SEMITIC LANGUAGE spoken in Mesopotamia in the 3rd–1st millennium BC and known from a great many inscriptions, seals, and clay tablets in CUNEIFORM WRITING. It supplanted Sumerian as the major spoken language of southern Mesopotamia by 2000 BC and from this time split into an Assyrian dialect spoken in the northeast and a Babylonian dialect spoken in the south. Akkadian died out as a vernacular in the first half of the 1st millennium BC, being effectively replaced by ARAMAIC in Mesopotamia, though it was written until about the 1st century AD.

Akko See ACRE

Akmola See ASTANA

Akron City (pop., 2000: 217,074), northeastern Ohio, on the CUYAHOGA RIVER. At 1,200 ft (370 m) above sea level, Akron was named for its "high place" (Greek: *acros*) on the watershed between the MISSISSIPPI RIVER and the GREAT LAKES. Laid out in 1825, the town was assured substantial growth by the completion of two canals (1827, 1840). The abundant water supply and the arrival of the railroads prompted B. F. Goodrich to move a rubber factory there in 1871. Akron became known as "rubber capital of the world," although by the 21st century much production had moved from the area.

Aksum *or* **Axum** \'äk-ˌsüm\ Ancient kingdom, northern Ethiopia. At its apogee (3rd–6th century AD), Aksum merchants traded as far as ALEXANDRIA and beyond the NILE RIVER. The modern town of Aksum (population 1994: 27,148), once the kingdom's capital, is a religious center best known for its antiquities. It has long been regarded as a holy city for the ETHIOPIAN ORTHODOX CHURCH; according to tradition, King Menilek I, son of SOLOMON and the Queen of SHEBA, brought the ARK OF THE COVENANT there from Jerusalem. Aksum is a tourist center.

Akwamu \'äk-wä-mü\ State of western Africa's GOLD COAST. Founded by an AKAN people c. 1600, it grew rich on the sale of gold. At its height in the early 18th century, Akwamu stretched more than 250 mi (400 km) along the coast, from Whydah (now Ouidah, Benin) in the east to beyond Winneba (now in Ghana) in the west. By 1710 the state was being pressured by other groups (including the ASHANTI) that had grown powerful in the area, and by 1731 it had ceased to exist.

al-Azhar University See AZHAR UNIVERSITY, al-

Al-Hanafi \al-'han-ə-fē\, **Alam al-Din** (1178?–1251) Egyptian mathematician, astronomer, and engineer. He wrote a treatise on EUCLID's postulates, built water mills and fortifications on the ORONTES RIVER, and constructed the second-oldest existing Arabic celestial globe.

Al-Jazeera *also* **al-Jazirah** Arabic-language cable news network founded in QATAR in 1996. It was established by the emir of Qatar and was transmitted from its capital, Doha, and from bureaus around the world. It began continuous programming in 1999. The editorial freedom exercised by its staff was unique in the Middle East, and its broadcasts were occasionally blocked by Arab states. It was the only network to broadcast from Kabul during the 2001 U.S.-led campaign in AFGHANISTAN.

Al-Jazirah See GEZIRA

Al Kharj \ˌäl-'kärj\ Oasis, eastern central Saudi Arabia. It lies southeast of RIYADH and is administered with that city. Situated around a series of deepwater pools, it was chosen as the site of a government experimental farm in 1938. Its traditional dairy industry was greatly expanded in 1981 with inauguration of a meat and dairy combine.

al-Khwarizmi \al-'kwär-iz-mē\ *Arabic* **Muhammad Ibn Musa al-Khwarizmi** (c. 780–c. 850) Muslim mathematician and astronomer. He lived in Baghdad during the first golden age of Islamic science and, like EUCLID, wrote mathematical books that collected and arranged the discoveries of earlier mathematicians. His *Kitab al-jabr wa al-muqabalah* ("The Book of Integration and Equation") is a compilation of rules for solving linear and QUADRATIC EQUATIONS, as well as problems of geometry and PROPORTION. Its translation into Latin in the 12th century provided the link between the great Hindu and Arab mathematicians and European scholars. A corruption of the book's title resulted in the word *algebra;* a corruption of the author's own name resulted in the term *algorithm.*

Al-Manamah See MANAMA

Al-Qaeda *also* **al-Qa'idah** (Arabic: "the Base") Broad-based Islamic militant organization founded in Afghanistan by OSAMA BIN LADEN. Its members supported Muslim fighters during the AFGHAN WAR; afterward, the organization dispersed but continued to oppose secularized Muslim regimes and foreign (namely U.S.) presence in Islamic lands. It staged numerous terrorist attacks, including the bombing of the WORLD TRADE CENTER in 1993, the destruction of two U.S. embassies in Africa in 1998, and a suicide bomb attack against the U.S. warship *Cole* in 2000. During that time it merged with other Islamic extremist organizations and eventually reestablished its headquarters in TALIBAN-controlled Afghanistan, where it trained thousands of Muslim militants. In 2001, 19 such militants staged the SEPTEMBER 11 ATTACKS. The U.S. and allied forces responded by attacking Taliban and Al-Qaeda forces in Afghanistan, killing and capturing thousands and driving the remainder into hiding.

Al-Uqab, Battle of See Battle of LAS NAVAS DE TOLOSA

Alabama State (pop., 2000: 4,447,000), southern central U.S. Covering 51,718 sq mi (133,950 sq km), its capital is MONTGOMERY. Its original inhabitants included CHEROKEE, CHICKASAW, CHOCTAW, and CREEK Indians; evidence of their activity can be found near Tuscaloosa. HERNANDO DE SOTO traveled here, and the French founded a settlement at Fort Louis in 1702. The Alabama Territory was created in 1817, and statehood was granted in 1819. Alabama seceded from the Union in 1861, becoming part of the Confederacy; it was readmitted in 1868. Efforts during RECONSTRUCTION to include blacks in government failed, and Alabama remained segregationist until the 1960s. Dependent on cotton until the early 20th century, the state has since diversified its agricultural production and developed industrially, especially at BIRMINGHAM; MOBILE has become a major ocean terminal.

Alabama claims U.S. maritime grievances against Britain in the AMERICAN CIVIL WAR. Though Britain had declared official neutrality in the war, it allowed the Confederate cruiser *Alabama*, which later destroyed 68 Union ships, to be constructed in England. U.S. ambassador CHARLES FRANCIS ADAMS demanded that the British take responsibility for these damages, and advocated arbitration to settle the matter. In May 1871 the parties signed the Treaty of Washington, which established certain wartime obligations of neutrals. The tribunal also held Britain liable for losses and awarded the U.S. damages of $15.5 million.

Alabama River River, southern Alabama. Formed by the COOSA and TALLAPOOSA rivers northeast of MONTGOMERY, it winds westward to Selma and then flows south, for a length of 318 mi (512 km). It is joined above MOBILE by the TOMBIGBEE to form the Mobile and Tensaw rivers, which flow into the Gulf of MEXICO. Mobile and Montgomery became major cities largely because they were on this important artery.

alabaster Fine-grained GYPSUM that has been used for centuries for statuary, carvings, and other ornaments. It normally is snow-white and translucent but can be artificially dyed; it may be made opaque and similar in appearance to marble by heat treatment. Florence, Livorno, Milan, and Berlin are important centers of the alabaster trade. The alabaster of the ancients was a brown or yellow onyx marble.

Alacahöyük \ˌä-lä-ˈjä-hœ-ˌyᵫk\ Ancient Anatolian site, northern central Turkey. It lies northeast of the old HITTITE capital of Bogazköy. Traces of a Hittite building were found in the early 20th century, and below them a royal necropolis of tombs dating from c. 2500 BC. There is evidence of the advanced accomplishments of Copper Age metallurgy in the form of jewelry, bowls, and jugs. Though the ethnic identity of the preliterate inhabitants is uncertain, they probably belonged to the non-Indo-European population that preceded the Hittites.

Aladdin Hero of a well-known story in *The THOUSAND AND ONE NIGHTS*. The son of a poor widow, Aladdin is a lazy, careless boy who meets an African magician claiming to be his uncle. He sends Aladdin into a cave to find a magic lamp, but Aladdin refuses to hand over the lamp until he is safely out of the cave. The angry magician shuts the boy in the cave and departs, but Aladdin discovers that he can summon powerful genies (jinn) by rubbing the lamp. The genies grant his every wish, and Aladdin becomes rich, marries the sultan's beautiful daughter, and reigns for many years.

Alamein, Battles of El See Battles of EL ALAMEIN

Alamgir II \ˈäl-əm-ˌgēr\ *in full* **Aziz-ud-Din Alamgir II** (1699–1759) Mughal emperor of India (1754–59). He was placed on the throne by the imperial vizier Imad ul-Mulk Ghazi-ud-Din and was always the puppet of more powerful men, including the Afghan ruler AHMAD SHAH DURRANI, whose agents occupied Delhi in 1757 and made Alamgir the nominal emperor of Hindustan. He was murdered by Ghazi-ud-Din, who feared Alamgir might be captured and used against him in another Afghan invasion.

Alamo 18th-century mission in San Antonio, Texas, site of a historic resistance in 1836 by a small group of Texans besieged by a Mexican army during the MEXICAN WAR. The abandoned mission was occupied occasionally by Spanish troops, who named it the Alamo ("cottonwood") after the surrounding trees. At the start of the Texas war for independence in December 1835, volunteers occupied the Alamo and vowed to fight to the death any attempt to recapture it. In February 1836 a Mexican army of several thousand began a siege that lasted 13 days. The Texas force of about 180, led by JIM BOWIE and including DAVY CROCKETT, was overrun; all were killed. "Remember the Alamo!" became a rallying cry in Texas's fight for independence.

Alanbrooke, Viscount See Alan F. BROOKE

Åland Islands \ˈō-ˌlän\ Archipelago, southwestern Finland, constituting Ahvenanmaan autonomous *kunta* (commune). It consists of about 35 inhabited islands (pop., 2002 est.: 26,008), and over 6,000 uninhabited ones, with a total land area of 599 sq mi (1,552 sq km). Åland, the largest island, is the location of Mariehamn, the administrative capital and chief seaport. The islands were Christianized by 12th-century Swedish missionaries. When Finland declared its independence in 1917, the Ålanders sought to become part of Sweden. Though the archipelago remains with Finland, it has been given unique autonomy.

alanine \ˈa-lə-nēn\ Either of two organic compounds. Alpha-alanine is one of the nonessential AMINO ACIDS, found in most PROTEINS and particularly abundant in fibroin, the protein in SILK. It is used in research and as a dietary supplement. Beta-alanine is a naturally occurring amino acid not found in proteins. It is an important constituent of the vitamin PANTOTHENIC ACID and is used in its synthesis, as well as in biochemical research, electroplating, and organic synthesis.

Alaric I \ˈa-lə-rik\ (c. 370–410) Chief of the VISIGOTHS (395–410). He commanded Gothic troops in the Roman army before leaving to become chief of the Visigoths. He led his tribe into Greece, sacking cities until placated by the Eastern emperor (397). He twice led invasions of Italy, the second time extorting a large payment from the Roman Senate. Alaric's forces grew after the Romans massacred the wives and children of Visigoths serving in the Roman army. He besieged Rome (408, 409), proclaiming Priscus Attalus as Western emperor. In 410 Alaric occupied and plundered Rome, the first time the city had been captured by a foreign enemy in 800 years. See also GOTHS.

Alaska State (pop., 2000: 626,932) of the U.S., lying at the extreme northwest of North America. It is the largest in area of the U.S. states and covers 587,875 sq mi (1,522,595 sq km), most of it in land. Facing SIBERIA across the Bering Strait and Sea to the west, it has the highest point on the continent, Mount MCKINLEY. Its capital is JUNEAU. The original inhabitants, Indians and Eskimos, are thought to have migrated over the Bering Land Bridge. The first European settlement was established in the late 18th century by Russian fur traders on KODIAK ISLAND. HUDSON'S BAY CO. traders were also interested in the same area, and Russian-Canadian trade rivalry lasted well into the 19th century. In 1867 WILLIAM SEWARD negotiated Alaska's sale from the Russians to the U.S., and the subsequent discovery of gold stimulated American settlement. Alaska was a U.S. Territory from 1912 until it was admitted as the 49th state in 1959. Its economy has become increasingly centered on oil and natural gas: since the opening of the TRANS-ALASKA PIPELINE in 1977, Alaska has become second only to Texas in the U.S. production of crude oil.

Alaska, Gulf of Gulf, southern Alaska. Situated between the ALASKA PENINSULA and the ALEXANDER ARCHIPELAGO, it receives the Susitna and Copper rivers. Ports on the gulf include ANCHORAGE, Seward, and Valdez; the last is North America's northernmost ice-free harbor and the TRANS-ALASKA PIPELINE's terminal. Capt. JAMES COOK, its European discoverer, entered the gulf in 1778 and proceeded as far north as Prince William Sound.

Alaska, University of State university system with campuses in Fairbanks, Anchorage, and Juneau (University of Alaska S.E.). It was founded in Fairbanks in 1917; instruction began in 1922. All three campuses offer master's degree programs in business and education; Fairbanks and Anchorage also have schools of engineering and arts and sciences. Fairbanks offers doctorates in the natural sciences. Research groups include the Geophysical Institute and the Institute of Marine Science. Total enrollment is about 25,000.

Alaska Highway *formerly* **Alcan Highway** Road through the Yukon, connecting Dawson Creek, British Columbia, with Fairbanks, Alaska, a distance of 1,523 mi (2,451 km). It was constructed by U.S. Army engineers in 1942 as an emergency war measure to provide an overland military supply route to Alaska. It is a scenic route now open year-round.

Alaska Peninsula Peninsula, southwestern Alaska. It stretches about 500 mi (800 km) between the Pacific Ocean and Bristol Bay. The volcanic Aleutian Range runs along its entire length. It is the site of KATMAI NATIONAL PARK AND PRESERVE, ANIAKCHAK NATIONAL MONUMENT, and Becherof, Alaska Peninsula, and Izembek national wildlife refuges.

Alaska Pipeline See TRANS-ALASKA PIPELINE

Alaska Purchase Acquisition in 1867 by the U.S. from Russia of 586,412 sq mi (1.5 million sq km) at the northwestern tip of North America, comprising the current state of Alaska. The territory, held by Russia since 1741, had become an economic liability, and in 1866 it was offered for sale. Pres. ANDREW JOHNSON's secretary of state, WILLIAM SEWARD, negotiated its purchase for $7.2 million, or about two cents an acre. Critics labeled the purchase "Seward's Folly." Congressional opposition delayed the appropriation until 1868, when extensive lobbying and bribes by the Russians secured the required votes.

Alaska Range Mountain range, southern Alaska. An extension of the Coast Mountains, it extends in a semicircle from the ALASKA PENINSULA to the YUKON boundary. Mount MCKINLEY, in DENALI NATIONAL PARK, is the highest point in North America. Many nearby peaks exceed 13,000 ft (3,960 m), including Mounts Silverthrone, Hunter, Hayes, and Foraker. The range is crossed at Isabel Pass by the TRANS-ALASKA PIPELINE.

Alaskan king crab See KING CRAB

Alaskan malamute Sled dog developed by the Malemiut, an Eskimo group. It is a strongly built dog with a broad head, erect ears, and a plumelike tail carried over its back. Its thick coat is usually gray and white or black and white, the colors frequently forming a caplike or masklike marking on the head. It stands 23–25 in. (58–64 cm) high and weighs 75–85 lbs (34–39 kg). Characteristically loyal and friendly, it has served on expeditions to the Antarctic.

Alaungpaya dynasty \ä-ˌlä-ůŋ-ˈpī-ə\ *or* **Konbaung dynasty** \ˌkȯn-bȧ-ˈůŋ\ (1752–1885) Last ruling dynasty of Myanmar. In the face of the fragmentation of the TOUNGOO DYNASTY, Alaungpaya (1714–1760), headman in a village near Mandalay, raised an army and subdued the separatist MON people in southern Myanmar and then conquered the northeastern Shan states. He attacked the Siamese kingdom of AYUTTHAYA (now in Thailand), but was forced to retreat. His son Hsinbyushin, the third king of the dynasty (r.1763–76), sent armies into neighboring kingdoms and successfully rebuffed four retaliatory Chinese invasions. The sixth king, BODAWPAYA (r.1782–1819), mounted a number of unsuccessful campaigns against the Siamese and moved the capital to Amarapura. He also conquered the kingdom of Arakan. His incursions in Assam aroused the ire of the British, and under BAGYIDAW (r.1819–37), Myanmar was defeated in the first ANGLO-BURMESE WAR. From then on the dynasty's hold on Myanmar gradually declined, ending in total annexation by the British in 1885.

Alawi \ˈä-lȧ-wē\ *or* **Alawite** \a-lə-ˈwēt\ *or* **Nusayri** \nü-sī-rē\ Member of a minority sect of SHIITE Islam. The sect, which exists mainly in Syria, traces its roots to the teachings of Muhammad ibn Nusayr al-Namiri (fl. 850) and was chiefly established by Husayn ibn Hamdan al-Khasibi (died 957/958). Its basic doctrine includes a deification of ALI and an interpretation of the five Pillars of Islam as symbolic. Some of its religious practices are secret; it celebrates some Islamic and some Christian holidays.

Alba, Fernando Álvarez de Toledo (y Pimentel), duque (Duke) de (1507–1582) Spanish soldier. He commanded CHARLES V's imperial armies to defeat the SCHMALKALDIC LEAGUE in 1547, and served as viceroy of Naples 1556–59. As a chief minister to PHILIP II, Alba became notorious for his tyranny as governor-general of the Netherlands (1567–73), where he instituted the Council of Troubles. That court set aside local laws and condemned some 12,000 people for rebellion. Recalled to Spain in 1573, Alba later conducted a brilliant campaign against Portugal (1580) but never regained Philip's favor.

Alba, oil painting by Sir Antony More, 1549; in the Musées Royaux des Beaux-Arts, Brussels.

BY COURTESY OF THE MUSEES ROYAUX DES BEAUX-ARTS, BRUSSELS

albacore Large oceanic TUNA *(Thunnus alalunga)* that is noted for its fine flesh. The streamlined bodies of these voracious predators are adapted to fast and continuous swimming. They occur in both the Atlantic and Pacific oceans and migrate long distances. The bluefin tuna is also sometimes called albacore.

Albani, Francesco *or* **Francesco Albano** (1578–1660) Italian painter. He trained with CARRACCI FAMILY in Bologna, then moved to Rome in 1601 and collaborated with Annibale CARRACCI and DOMENICHINO on the decoration of the Farnese Palace. While in Rome he established his own studio and painted frescoes in various churches and palaces. In 1617 he returned to Bologna and produced altarpieces, allegorical paintings, and idyllic landscapes. His best-known paintings are of mythological and poetic subjects.

Albania *officially* **Republic of Albania** Nation, western Adriatic coast of the BALKAN PENINSULA. Area: 11,000 sq mi (28,700 sq km). Population (1992 est.): 3,400,000. Capital: TIRANË. Ethnic Albanians are the Ghegs and the Tosks. Language: Albanian (official). Religions: Islam; minority, Christianity (Greek Orthodoxy, Roman Catholicism). Currency: lek. Albania may be divided into two major regions, a mountainous highland region and a western coastal lowland region that contains the country's agricultural lands and most of its population. It has a developing economy that until 1991 was shaped by a socialist system of state

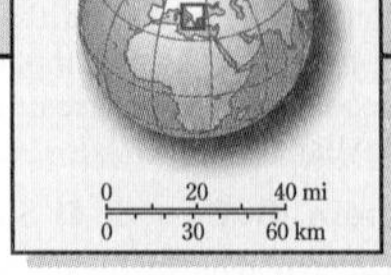

ownership. In 1992 the government introduced economic reforms encouraging a free-market economy. The Albanians are descended from the Illyrians, an ancient Indo-European people who lived in central Europe and migrated south by the beginning of the Iron Age (see ILLYRIA). Of the two major Illyrian migrating groups, the Ghegs settled in the north and the Tosks in the south, along with Greek colonizers. The area was under Roman rule by the 1st century BC; after AD 395 it was connected administratively to Constantinople. Turkish invasion began in the 14th century and continued into the 15th century; though the national hero, Skanderbeg, was able to resist them for a time, after his death (1468) the Turks consolidated their rule. The country achieved independence in 1912 and was admitted into the League of Nations in 1920. It was briefly a republic (1925–28), then became a monarchy under Zog I, whose initial alliance with Benito Mussolini led to Italy's invasion of Albania in 1939. After the war a socialist government under Enver Hoxha was installed, and gradually Albania cut itself off from the nonsocialist international community, and eventually from all nations, including China, its last political ally. By 1990 economic hardship had produced antigovernment demonstrations, and in 1992 a non-Communist government was elected and Albania's international isolation ended. In 1997 it plunged into chaos, brought on with the collapse of pyramid investment schemes. In 1999 it was overwhelmed by ethnic Albanians seeking refuge from Yugoslavia (see Kosovo conflict).

Albanian language Indo-European language spoken by 5–6 million people in Albania, Kosovo in Yugoslavia, western Macedonia, and enclaves elsewhere, including southern Italy and southern Greece. There are two main dialect groups, Gheg (Geg) in the north, including Kosovo and Macedonia, and Tosk in the south. Albanian is the only extant representative of a distinct branch of Indo-European, whose pre-Roman Balkan ancestry is uncertain. The earliest written attestation is from the 15th century, though a standard orthography using the Latin alphabet was not adopted until 1909. The core vocabulary of Albanian is native, though in the course of its history it has absorbed many loanwords from Greek, Latin, Balkan Romance (see Romanian), Slavic languages, and Turkish.

Albany \'ȯl-bə-nē\ City (pop., 1996 est.: 103,000), capital of New York state. It lies along the Hudson River 145 mi (230 km) north of New York City. The first permanent settlement, named Beverwyck, was built in 1624 by the Dutch. When the British took the area in 1664, the village was renamed to honor the Duke of York and Albany. In 1754 the Albany Congress adopted Benjamin Franklin's "Plan of Union." In the 19th century Albany became a major transportation center. Its focal point today is Empire State Plaza, a governmental, cultural, and convention complex.

Albany Congress Conference in 1754 at Albany, N.Y., that advocated a union of the British colonies in North America. It was convened by the British colonial government in part to secure a defensive union against the French before the outbreak of the French and Indian War. Colonial delegates such as Benjamin Franklin supported a plan to unify the seven colonies, but it was never adopted. The plan became a model for later proposals made during the American Revolution.

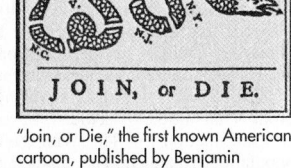

"Join, or Die," the first known American cartoon, published by Benjamin Franklin in his *Pennsylvania Gazette*, 1754, to support his plan for colonial union presented at the Albany Congress.
THE GRANGER COLLECTION

albatross Any of more than a dozen species of large seabirds (family Diomedeidae). Albatrosses are among the most spectacular gliders of all birds; in windy weather they can stay aloft for hours without flapping their wings. They drink seawater and usually eat squid. Albatrosses come ashore only to breed, in colonies typically established on remote oceanic islands. Adults of common species attain wingspans of 7–11 ft (200–350 cm). Albatrosses live long and may be among the few birds to die of old age. They were once held in awe by seamen, who held that killing one would bring bad luck.

albedo \al-'bē-dō\ Fraction of light reflected by a body or surface, commonly used in astronomy to describe the reflective properties of planets, natural satellites, and asteroids. "Normal" albedo (the relative brightness of a surface when illuminated and observed from directly above) is often used to determine the surface compositions of satellites and asteroids. The albedo, diameter, and distance of such objects together determine their brightness.

Albee \'ȯl-bē\, **Edward (Franklin)** (born 1928) U.S. playwright. Born in Virginia, he was the adopted grandson and namesake of a well-known vaudeville theater manager. His first one-act play, *The Zoo Story* (1959), and other early plays, including *The Sandbox* (1960) and *The American Dream* (1961), were characteristic of the theater of the absurd. His *Who's Afraid of Virginia Woolf* (1962; film, 1966) was widely acclaimed. He won Pulitzer Prizes for *A Delicate Balance* (1966), *Seascape* (1975), and *Three Tall Women* (1991). He has also adapted other writers' works for the stage, including Vladimir Nabokov's *Lolita* (1981).

Albemarle Sound \'al-bə-ˌmärl\ Coastal inlet, northeastern North Carolina. Protected from the Atlantic Ocean by the Outer Banks, it is about 50 mi (80 km) long and 5–14 mi (8–23 km) wide. It is connected with Chesapeake Bay by the Dismal Swamp and the Albemarle and Chesapeake Canal. Elizabeth City is its chief port. Explored by Ralph Lane in 1585, it was later named for George Monck, Duke of Albemarle.

Albéniz \äl-'bā-nēs\, **Isaac (Manuel Francisco)** (1860–1909) Spanish composer. A piano prodigy by age 4, he later studied in Leipzig and Brussels, returned to Spain to teach in Barcelona and Madrid, then moved to France in 1893. His fame rests on his piano pieces, which, under the influence of Felipe Pedrell, utilize the melodic styles, rhythms, and harmonies of Spanish folk music. *Iberia* (1905–9) is a set of 12 virtuoso piano pieces; other piano works include the *Suite española*, *Cantos de España*, and five sonatas. He also wrote several operas.

Albers, Josef (1888–1976) German-U.S. painter, poet, teacher, and theoretician. He studied and taught at the Bauhaus, and in 1933 became one of the first Bauhaus teachers to emigrate to the United States, where he taught at Black Mountain College and later at Yale. He developed a painting style characterized by abstract rectilinear patterns and primary colors as well as black and white. He is known for his series of paintings titled *Homage to the Square*, begun in 1950. His research into color theory was published in the influential *Interaction of Color* (1963).

Josef Albers, photograph by Arnold Newman, 1948.
© ARNOLD NEWMAN

Albert *orig.* **Franz Albrecht August Karl Emanuel, Prinz (Prince) von Sachsen-Coburg-Gotha** *known as* **Prince Albert** (1819–1861) Prince consort of Queen Victoria of Britain and father of Edward VII. Albert married Victoria, his first cousin, in 1840 and became in effect her private secretary and chief confidential adviser. Their domestic happiness helped assure the continuation of the monarchy, which had been somewhat uncertain. Though the German-born Albert was undeservedly unpopular, the British public belatedly recognized his worth after his death at 42 from typhoid fever. In the ensuing years, the grief-stricken queen made policy decisions based on what she thought Albert would have done.

Albert, Lake Lake, eastern central Africa. Lying at an altitude of 2,021 ft (616 m), it is 100 mi (160 km) long and has an average width of about 20 mi (32 km). In the southwest, the Semliki River brings into the lake the waters of Lake Edward; at its northeastern corner, just below Murchison Falls, it receives the Victoria Nile from Lake Victoria. In 1864 the lake's first European visitor, Samuel Baker, named it after Queen Victoria's consort. Initially part of Uganda, it now forms part of the Uganda-Congo border.

Albert I (1875–1934) King of the Belgians (1909–34). He succeeded his uncle, King Leopold II, in 1909. He strengthened the army and reaffirmed Belgian neutrality in 1914, rejecting William II's demand (August 2, 1914) for free passage of German troops across Belgium. Following the German invasion on August 5, Albert assumed leadership of the Belgian army and remained with his troops throughout World War I. He later spent 15 years guiding the country's postwar rebuilding effort.

Albert National Park See Virunga National Park

Alberta Province (pop., 1996: 2,847,000), Canada, westernmost of three Prairie Provinces. Alberta is bounded by Saskatchewan, British Columbia, the Northwest Territories, and the U.S. Its capital is Edmonton. Long inhabited by various Indian peoples, the area was explored by Europeans in the 1750s. It eventually came under the rule of the Hud-

SON'S BAY CO., which transferred it to the Dominion of Canada in 1870. It was made part of the Northwest Territories in 1882. Its population grew with the coming of the railroads, and the expansion of wheat farming. Alberta was made a province in 1905. Once dependent on agriculture, it underwent economic growth with the discovery of oil in 1947, and the ensuing discovery of other major oil and gas deposits.

Alberta, University of Public university in Edmonton, Alberta. Opened in 1908, it is one of Canada's five largest research universities. It offers undergraduate and graduate programs in liberal arts, agriculture and forestry, science and engineering, business, law, education, and the health professions. Special programs include French-language teaching and a School of Native Studies. Total enrollment is about 30,000.

Alberti, Leon Battista (1404–1472) Italian architect, art theorist, and humanist. After pursuing a literary career as papal secretary, Alberti was encouraged (1438) to direct his talents toward the field of architecture. The Palazzo Rucellai (c. 1445–51) and the facade of Santa Maria Novella (1456–70), both in Florence, are noted for their harmonic proportions. His central-plan church of Sant'Andrea, Mantua (begun 1472), with its triumphal-arch motif, is an early Renaissance masterpiece. Unconcerned with the practical aspects of building, Alberti was one of the foremost theorists on Renaissance architecture and art, known for codifying the principles of linear perspective (in *On Painting,* 1436). A prototype of the Renaissance man, he also made contributions to moral philosophy, cartography, and cryptography.

Albertus Magnus, St. (c. 1200–1280) German cleric and philosopher. Son of a wealthy German lord, he studied at Padua, where he joined the Dominican order (1223). At the University of Paris he was introduced to the works of ARISTOTLE and to AVERROËS' commentaries. For 20 years he worked on his *Physica,* which encompassed natural science, logic, rhetoric, mathematics, astronomy, ethics, economics, politics, and metaphysics. He believed that many points of Christian doctrine were recognizable both by faith and by reason. In 1248 he organized the first Dominican seminary in Germany at Cologne, where THOMAS AQUINAS was his chief disciple. His works represented the entire body of European knowledge of his time, and he contributed greatly to the development of natural science.

Albertus Magnus, detail of a fresco by Tommaso da Modena, c. 1352; in the Church of San Nicolo, Treviso.
ALINARI—ART RESOURCE/EB INC.

Albigensian Crusade \ˌal-bə-ˈjen-shən\ (1209–29) Crusade called by Pope INNOCENT III against the heretical CATHARI of southern France. The war pitted the nobility of northern France against that of southern France, and it led to the extirpation of the Albigensian heresy (named for its center in the town of Albi, France) but at the price of much devastation and injustice, which Innocent came to regret. The crusade ended with the Treaty of PARIS (1229), which took away the independence of the southern princes and largely destroyed the culture of PROVENCE. The heresy lingered on into the 13th–14th century and became the object of the INQUISITION.

Albigensians See CATHARI

albinism \ˈal-bə-ˌni-zəm, al-ˈbī-ˌni-zəm\ Absence of the pigment melanin in the eyes, skin, hair, scales, or feathers. It arises from a genetic defect and occurs in humans and other vertebrates. Because they lack the pigments that normally provide protective coloration and screen against the sun's ultraviolet rays, albino animals rarely survive in the wild. Humans have long intentionally bred certain albino animals (e.g., rabbits) for their appearance. In humans with generalized, or total, albinism, the affected person has milk-white skin and hair; the iris of the eye appears pink, the pupil red. Vision abnormalities such as astigmatism, nystagmus (rapid involuntary oscillation of the eye), and photophobia (extreme sensitivity to light) are common. Generalized albinism occurs in all races in about one in 20,000 persons.

Albinoni \ˌal-bə-ˈnō-nē\, **Tomaso (Giovanni)** (1671–1751) Italian composer. Born to a wealthy Venetian family, he was not obliged to work for a living, and he became a highly prolific composer. He had more than 50 operas successfully produced between 1694 and 1741, though few survive. His approximately 60 concertos became popular; he also wrote more than 80 sonatas for various instrumental combinations and over 40 solo cantatas. The famous Adagio in G minor was actually written by Remo Giazotto.

Albinus \äl-ˈbē-nəs\, **Bernard Siegfried** (1697–1770) German-Dutch anatomist. A professor at the University of Leiden, he is best known for the excellent drawings in his *Tables of the Skeleton and Muscles of the Human Body* (1747). He was the first to show the connection of the vascular systems of mother and fetus. With HERMANN BOERHAAVE, he edited the works of ANDREAS VESALIUS and WILLIAM HARVEY.

albite Common FELDSPAR mineral, a sodium aluminosilicate ($NaAlSi_3O_8$) that occurs most widely in PEGMATITES and acid igneous rocks such as granites. It may also be found in low-grade metamorphic rocks (those formed under relatively low temperature and pressure conditions) and in certain sedimentary rocks. Albite usually forms brittle, glassy crystals that may be colorless, white, yellow, pink, green, or black. It is used in the manufacture of glass and ceramics, but its primary geologic importance is as a rock-forming mineral.

Albright, Ivan (Le Lorraine) (1897–1983) U.S. painter. He was born in North Harvey, Ill., the son of a painter. Independently wealthy, he studied at various institutions, developing a meticulously detailed style and often spending several years of painstaking work on a single painting. With pinpoint exactness and hallucinatory hyperclarity, he repeatedly depicted decay, corruption, and the wreckage of age, often with great emotional intensity. His important works include *That Which I Should Have Done I Did Not Do* (1931–41) and *The Picture of Dorian Gray* (1943), painted for a film of OSCAR WILDE's story, which brought him fame.

albumin \al-ˈbyü-mən\ Any of a diverse class of PROTEINS historically defined by their ability to dissolve in water and in a half-saturated (see SATURATION) solution of ammonium sulfate. They are readily coagulated by heating. Examples include serum albumin, a major component of PLASMA; α-lactalbumin, found in milk; ovalbumin, which makes up about half the proteins of egg white; and conalbumin, another egg-white protein. Ovalbumin is used commercially in the food, wine, adhesives, paper coatings, pharmaceutical, and other industries and in research.

Albuquerque \ˈal-bə-ˌkər-kē\ City (pop., 1996 est.: 419,000), New Mexico. The state's largest city, it lies on the RIO GRANDE southwest of Santa Fe. Founded by the governor of New Mexico, it was named for the Duque de Alburquerque (the first *r* was later dropped), the viceroy of NEW SPAIN. After 1800 growing commerce on the SANTA FE TRAIL brought an influx of settlers; an army post was established following U.S. occupation in 1846. With the coming of the railroad in 1880, the population expanded. The characteristically Spanish "old town" and its mission church (1706) have survived. Since the 1930s many defense-related federal agencies have been established there.

Albuquerque \ˌäl-bü-ˈkər-kə\, **Afonso de** *or* **Afonso the Great** (1453–1515) Portuguese soldier, conqueror of Goa (1510) and of Melaka (1511). He gained early military experience during 10 years of service in North Africa, but his reputation came from his service in South and Southeast Asia. His efforts to gain control of all the main maritime trade routes of the East and to build permanent fortresses with settled populations paved the way for Portuguese domination in S.East Asia. He was inspired by the crusading spirit of King John II and others, and considerations of mercantile gain did not divert him from his schemes.

Alcaeus \al-ˈsē-əs\ *or* **Alkaios** \al-ˈkā-əs\ (c. 620–c. 580 BC) Greek lyric poet. Only fragments and quotations survive from his work, consisting of hymns in honor of gods and heroes, love poetry, drinking songs, and political poems. Many reflect Alcaeus' vigorous involvement in the life of his native Mytilene, particularly its political life. His poetry was a favorite model for HORACE, who adapted from him his own alcaic stanza.

Alcalá Zamora, Niceto (1877–1949) Spanish politician. After serving as minister of works (1917) and minister of war (1922), he opposed the dictatorship of MIGUEL PRIMO DE RIVERA and joined the republican movement. As leader of the revolutionary committee that successfully demanded the abdication of ALFONSO XIII, he became head of the government in 1931 and was elected president of Spain's Second Republic that same year. He tried to moderate the policies of the extremist factions, but he was deposed in 1936 after the election of the Popular Front and went into exile to France and then to Argentina.

Alcamenes *or* **Alkamenes** \al-'kam-ə-,nēz\ (fl. late 5th century BC) Greek sculptor. Probably the leading sculptor in Athens after the death of PHIDIAS, he is noted for the delicacy and finish of his works. Several are known from copies; a mutilated marble statue of *Procne with Itys* in the Acropolis Museum is considered an original.

Alcan Highway See ALASKA HIGHWAY

Alcatraz Island Rocky island in SAN FRANCISCO BAY, California. It has an area of 22 acres (9 hectares) and is located 1.5 mi (2 km) offshore from the city of SAN FRANCISCO. The site of the first lighthouse (1854) on the California coast, it became an army garrison (1859) and a military prison (1868). From 1934 to 1963 it served as a federal prison for dangerous civilian prisoners. Its famous inmates included AL CAPONE, George "Machine Gun" Kelly, and Robert Stroud, the "Birdman of Alcatraz." It is now open to the public.

alcázar \al-'kä-zər\ Form of military architecture of medieval Spain, generally rectangular with defensible walls and massive corner towers. Inside was an open space (patio) surrounded by chapels, salons, hospitals, and sometimes gardens. The finest surviving example from the Moorish period is Seville's Alcázar Palace; begun in 1181 under the ALMOHADS and continued by the Christians, it exhibits both Moorish and Gothic features, including a decagonal brick tower, the Torre del Oro.

Toledo *alcázar,* 14th century, renovated 16th century, severely damaged during the Spanish Civil War and later restored.
ALFONSO GUTIERREZ—ESCERA

Alcestis \al-'ses-təs\ In Greek legend, the beautiful daughter of Pelias, king of Iolcos. Admetus, son of the king of Pherae, sought her hand. To win her he was required to harness a lion and a boar to a chariot, and he succeeded with the aid of APOLLO. When Apollo learned that Admetus had not long to live, he persuaded the FATES to prolong his life, on condition someone else die in his stead. As a loyal wife Alcestis consented to do so, but was rescued by HERACLES, who wrestled with Death at her grave. Her story is told in EURIPIDES' *Alcestis*.

alchemy Pseudoscience focused on the attempt to change base metals into gold. Ancient alchemists believed that, under the correct astrological conditions, lead could be "perfected" into gold. They tried to hasten this transformation by heating and refining the metal in a variety of chemical processes, most of which were kept secret. Alchemy was practiced in much of the ancient world, from China and India to Greece. It migrated to Egypt during the Hellenistic period and was later revived in 12th-century Europe through translations of Arabic texts into Latin. Medieval European alchemists made some useful discoveries, including mineral acids and alcohol. The revival led to the development of PHARMACOLOGY under the influence of PARACELSUS and to the rise of modern CHEMISTRY. Not until the 19th century were the gold-making processes of alchemists finally discredited.

Alcibiades \,al-sə-'bī-ə-,dēz\ (c. 450–404 BC) Brilliant but unscrupulous Athenian politician and commander. PERICLES was his guardian, his father having died in battle. Lacking personal attention in his upbringing, he became associated with SOCRATES, who was attracted to the youth's physical beauty and intellectual promise. They served together in the PELOPONNESIAN WAR, saving each other's lives in battle, yet Alcibiades failed to acquire Socrates' personal integrity. By 420 he was a general. Recalled from a Sicilian expedition in 415 on charges of sacrilege for mutilating statues of Hermes, he fled to Sparta. Though he aided the Spartan cause against Athens, he was eventually rejected and sought haven with the Persian king. The Athenian fleet eventually recalled him, and he directed Athenian victories 411–408. Though he achieved hero status, his enemies again forced him to leave. From Thrace he warned Athens presciently of danger at the Battle of AEGOSPOTAMI. He fled from Thrace to Phrygia, where the Spartans conspired to have him murdered. His political agitation was a decisive factor in Athens's defeat in the Peloponnesian War. His notorious behavior helped strengthen the charges brought against Socrates in 399.

Alcmaeon *or* **Alcmeon** \alk-'mē-ən\ In GREEK MYTHOLOGY, the son of the seer Amphiaraus. The seer had been persuaded by his wife to join the expedition of the Seven Against THEBES. On realizing that he would die, he charged Alcmaeon and his other sons with avenging his death. Alcmaeon led the sons of the seven in the destruction of Thebes and then obeyed his father's injunction to kill his mother, a crime for which the FURIES drove him mad. He was purified by King Phegeus of Psophis, whose daughter he married but subsequently killed. Following the advice of an oracle, he settled on an island at the mouth of the Achelous River, where he married again, but was killed by Phegeus and his sons.

Alcmaeonid family \alk-'mē-ən-id\ Athenian family important in the 6th–5th century BC. During the archonship (magistracy) of the Alcmaeonid Megacles (632? BC), the family was banished for murder; it returned twice to oust the tyrant PEISISTRATUS before again being exiled. Megacles' son CLEISTHENES became archon in 525/524, but in 514 Peisistratus' son Hippias again exiled the family for murdering his brother. The family reestablished itself after the Spartans drove out the Peisistratids in 510. The next generation may have aided the Persians at the Battle of MARATHON (490). ALCIBIADES and PERICLES were both Alcmaeonids.

Alcoa U.S. company, the world's largest producer of aluminum. Established in Pittsburgh in 1888, it adopted the name Aluminum Co. of America in 1907. Alcoa introduced aluminum foil in 1910 and found uses for aluminum in the emerging aviation and automobile industries. In 1913 it established the town of Alcoa in eastern Tennessee as a planned industrial community. A 1945 federal antitrust ruling obliged it to sell its Canadian subsidiary (now Alcan Aluminum Ltd., its strongest competitor). In 1998 Alcoa acquired Alumax Inc.; the combined companies have 100,000 employees and an annual output of nearly 4 million tons of aluminum.

alcohol Any of a class of common organic compounds that contain one or more hydroxyl groups (—OH) attached to one or more of the carbon atoms in a HYDROCARBON chain. The number of other substituent groups (R) on that carbon atom make the alcohol a primary (RCH_2OH), secondary (R_2CHOH), or tertiary (R_3COH) alcohol. Many alcohols occur naturally and are valuable intermediates in the synthesis of other compounds because of the characteristic CHEMICAL REACTIONS of the hydroxyl group. Oxidation (see OXIDATION-REDUCTION) of primary alcohols yields ALDEHYDES and (if taken further) CARBOXYLIC ACIDS; oxidation of secondary alcohols, KETONES. Tertiary alcohols break down on oxidation. Alcohols generally react with carboxylic acids to produce ESTERS. They may also be converted to ETHERS and OLEFINS. Products of these numerous reactions include fats and waxes, detergents, plasticizers, emulsifiers, lubricants, emollients, and foaming agents. ETHANOL (grain alcohol) and METHANOL (wood alcohol) are the best-known alcohols with one hydroxyl group. GLYCOLS (e.g., ethylene glycol, or antifreeze) contain two hydroxyl groups, GLYCEROL three, and polyols three or more. See also ALCOHOLIC BEVERAGE, ALCOHOLISM.

Alcohol, Tobacco and Firearms, Bureau of (ATF) Agency of the U.S. Department of the Treasury. Established in 1972, it enforces and administers laws covering the production, taxation, and distribution of alcohol and tobacco products, as well as laws relating to the use of firearms and explosives. It inspects plants, issues licenses, oversees tax collection on alcohol and tobacco, monitors advertising and labeling practices, and investigates violations. It also investigates the illegal use of firearms and explosives, as well as illicit trafficking in firearms, distilled spirits, and contraband cigarettes.

alcoholic beverage Any fermented liquor, such as wine, beer, or distilled liquor, that contains ethyl alcohol, or ethanol, as an intoxicating agent. When an alcoholic beverage is ingested, the alcohol is rapidly absorbed in the stomach and intestines because it does not undergo any digestive processes. It is distributed to the rest of the body through the blood, and has a pronounced depressant action on the brain. Under the influence of alcohol, the drinker is less alert, less able to discern objects in the environment, slower in reacting to stimuli, and generally prone to sleep.

Alcoholics Anonymous (AA) Voluntary fellowship of people suffering from alcoholism who seek to become and stay sober through mutual self-help by meeting in local, independent groups to share their common experience. Anonymity, confidentiality, and understanding of alcoholism as a disease free members to speak frankly. Many consider AA to be the most successful method of coping with alcoholism; participation raises the chances of success of other treatments. Its 12 steps to recovery include acknowledgment of the problem, faith in a "higher power" as understood by each individual, self-examination, and a desire to change for the better and to help others recover. Begun in 1935 by two alcoholics, AA has grown to some 2 million members worldwide. Similar organizations for abusers of other substances and for habitual gamblers and debtors are based on its principles.

alcoholism Excessive habitual consumption of alcoholic beverages despite physical, mental, social, or economic harm (e.g., cirrhosis, drunk driving and accidents, family strife, frequently missing work). Persons who drink large amounts of alcohol over time become tolerant to its effects. Alcoholism is usually considered an addiction and a disease. The causes are unclear, but there may be a genetic predisposition. It is more common in men, but women are more likely to hide it. Treatment may be physiological (with drugs that cause vomiting and a feeling of panic when alcohol is consumed; not an effective long-term treatment), psychological (with therapy and rehabilitation), and/or social (with group therapies). Group therapies such as Alcoholics Anonymous are the most effective treatments. Suddenly stopping heavy drinking can lead to withdrawal symptoms, including delirium tremens.

Alcott, (Amos) Bronson (1799–1888) U.S. teacher and philosopher. Born in Wolcott, Conn., the self-educated son of a poor farmer, he worked as a peddler before establishing a series of innovative but ultimately unsuccessful schools for children. He traveled to Britain with money borrowed from Ralph Waldo Emerson and returned with the mystic Charles Lane, with whom he founded the short-lived utopian community Fruitlands outside Boston. Returning to Concord, Mass., he is credited with establishing the first parent-teacher association while superintendent of schools. A prominent member of the Transcendentalists, he wrote a number of books, but did not become financially secure until his daughter Louisa May Alcott achieved success.

Louisa May Alcott, portrait by George Healy; in the Louisa May Alcott Memorial Association collection, Concord, Massachusetts.

BY COURTESY OF LOUISA MAY ALCOTT MEMORIAL ASSOCIATION

Alcott, Louisa May (1832–1888) U.S. author. Born in Germantown, Pa., the daughter of Bronson Alcott, she grew up in Transcendentalist circles in Boston and Concord, Mass. She began writing to help support her mother and sisters. An ardent abolitionist, she volunteered as a nurse during the American Civil War, where she contracted the typhoid that damaged her health the rest of her life; her letters, published as *Hospital Sketches* (1863), first brought her fame. With the huge success of the autobiographical *Little Women* (1868–69), she finally escaped debt. *An Old-Fashioned Girl* (1870), *Little Men* (1871), and *Jo's Boys* (1886) also drew on her experiences as an educator.

Alcuin \'al-ˌkwēn\ (732?–804) Anglo-Latin poet, educator, and cleric. As head of the Palatine school established by Charlemagne at Aachen, he introduced the traditions of Anglo-Saxon humanism into western Europe and was the foremost scholar of the revival of learning known as the Carolingian Renaissance. He also made important reforms in the Roman Catholic liturgy and left more than 300 Latin letters, a valuable source for the history of his time.

Alda \'ȯl-də\, **Alan** *orig.* **Alphonso Joseph d'Abruzzo** (born 1936) U.S. actor, director, and screenwriter. Born in New York City, the son of actor Robert Alda (1914–1986), he acted in such Broadway plays as *The Apple Tree* and *The Owl and the Pussycat* and starred in the long-running television series *M*A*S*H* (1972–83), cowriting and directing many episodes and winning numerous Emmy awards. He has appeared in such films as *Same Time, Next Year* (1978) and *Flirting with Disaster* (1996); films he has directed include *Sweet Liberty* (1986) and *Betsy's Wedding* (1990).

aldehyde Any of a class of organic compounds that contain a carbonyl group (—C=O; see functional group) in which the carbon atom is bonded to at least one hydrogen atom. Many have characteristic odors. Oxidation (see oxidation-reduction) of aldehydes yields acids; reduction produces alcohols. They participate in many chemical reactions and readily undergo polymerization into chains containing tens of thousands of the monomer molecule. The combination of aldehydes (e.g., formaldehyde) with other molecules results in several familiar plastics. Many aldehydes are large-scale industrial materials, useful as solvents, monomers, perfume ingredients, and intermediates. Many sugars are aldehydes, as are several natural and synthetic hormones and compounds such as retinal (a derivative of vitamin A, important in vision) and pyridoxal phosphate (a form of vitamin B_6).

Alden, John (1599?–1687) American (British-born) pilgrim. He was hired as a cooper by the London merchants who funded the *Mayflower*'s expedition to the New World in 1620. Alden signed the Mayflower Compact and held various civic positions in the colony, including assistant to the governor (1623–41, 1650–86). He was mythologized as the first Pilgrim to set foot on Plymouth Rock and in Henry W. Longfellow's poem as the stand-in for Myles Standish in his suit for Priscilla Mullens's hand in marriage. Alden in fact married Mullens in 1623.

alder Any of about 30 species of ornamental shrubs and trees in the genus *Alnus,* of the birch family, found throughout the Northern Hemisphere and western South America on cool, wet sites. Alders are distinguished from birches by their usually stalked winter buds and by cones that remain on the branches after the small, winged nutlets are released. Alders have scaly bark, oval leaves that fall without changing color, and separate male and female flowers (catkins) borne on the same tree. Some familiar North American alders are the red alder *(A. rubra* or *A. oregona);* the white, or Sierra, alder *(A. rhombifolia);* and the speckled alder *(A. rugosa).* Alder wood is fine-textured and durable, even under water; it is useful for furniture, cabinetry, lathe work, and in charcoal manufacture and millwork. Alders' spreading root systems and tolerance of moist soils lend them to planting on stream banks for flood and erosion control.

Alder (*Alnus glutinosa*).

EARL L. KUBIS—ROOT RESOURCES

Aldrich, Nelson W(ilmarth) (1841–1915) U.S. senator and financier. Born in Foster, R.I., he served in the U.S. House of Representatives (1879–81) and Senate (1881–1911). His work as chair of the National Monetary Commission (1908–12) helped prepare the way for the Federal

RESERVE SYSTEM (1913). Along the way he invested profitably in banking, electricity, gas, rubber, and sugar.

Aldrich \'ȯl-drich\, **Robert** (1918–1983) U.S. film director and producer. Born in Cranston, R.I., he held various jobs at RKO from 1941, working under such directors as JEAN RENOIR and CHARLIE CHAPLIN. After directing his first feature film, *The Big Leaguer* (1953), he formed his own production company and earned a reputation for tough, often violent films, including *Apache* (1954), *The Big Knife* (1955), *What Ever Happened to Baby Jane?* (1962), *Hush . . . Hush, Sweet Charlotte* (1964), and *The Dirty Dozen* (1967).

Aldrich \'ȯl-drich\, **Thomas Bailey** (1836–1907) U.S. poet, short-story writer, and editor. Born in Portsmouth, N.H., he left school at 13 and soon began to contribute to newspapers and magazines. He was editor of *The* ATLANTIC MONTHLY 1881–90. He drew on his childhood for his classic children's novel *The Story of a Bad Boy* (1870). His use of the surprise ending influenced the development of the short story in the U.S. His poems reflect New England culture and his experiences visiting Europe.

Aldrin \'ȯl-drən\, **Edwin Eugene, Jr.** *known as* **Buzz Aldrin** (born 1930) U.S. astronaut. Born in Montclair, N.J., he graduated from West Point and flew 66 combat missions in the Korean War. In 1963 he received a PhD from MIT and was chosen as an astronaut. In 1966 he joined James A. Lovell, Jr. (born 1928), on the four-day GEMINI 12 flight. Aldrin's 5½-hour walk in space proved that humans can function effectively in the vacuum of space. In July 1969, on the APOLLO 11 mission, he became the second human on the moon.

ale Fermented MALT beverage, full-bodied and somewhat bitter, with strong flavor of HOPS. Until the 17th century it was an unhopped brew of YEAST, water, and malt, BEER being the same brew with hops added. Modern ale (now largely synonymous with beer) is made with top-fermenting yeast and processed at higher temperatures than lager beer. Pale ale has up to 5% alcohol content; the darker strong ale contains up to 6.5%.

Alea \ä-'lā-ə\, **Tomás Gutiérrez** (1928–1996) Cuban film director. After earning a law degree in Cuba, he studied filmmaking in Rome (1951–53). A supporter of FIDEL CASTRO, he helped develop Cuba's film industry after 1959 and made the Communist regime's first official feature film, *Stories of the Revolution* (1960). Later he worked within the restrictions of the regime to satirize and explore various aspects of life in postrevolutionary Cuba in such internationally acclaimed films as *Death of a Bureaucrat* (1966), *Memories of Underdevelopment* (1968), *The Survivors* (1978), and *Strawberry and Chocolate* (1993). He is regarded as the finest director Cuba has produced.

aleatory music \'ā-lē-ə-ˌtōr-ē\ (from Latin, *alea:* "dice game") Any music, particularly that of the 1950s and '60s, whose composition or performance incorporates elements of chance. Such aspects as the ordering of a piece's sections, its rhythms, and even its pitches are decided at the moment of performance. When not purely improvising, players follow lists of arbitrary rules or interpreted "graphic" notation that merely suggest the sounds. C. IVES and H. COWELL had used such techniques, but J. CAGE became the principal figure in aleatory; other aleatory composers included Earle Brown (born 1926), Morton Feldman (1926–1987), and P. BOULEZ.

Aleichem, Sholem See SHOLEM ALEICHEM

Aleixandre \ˌä-lā-'sän-drā\, **Vicente** (1898–1984) Spanish poet. A member of the group of Spanish writers known as the Generation of 1927, he was strongly influenced by Surrealism. His first major book, *Destruction or Love* (1935), won the National Prize for Literature. Other works include *Historia del corazón* (1954; "History of the Heart"), *En un vasto dominio* (1962; "In a Vast Domain"), and *Diálogos del conocimiento* (1974; "Dialogues of Insight"). He received the Nobel Prize in 1977.

Aleksandrovsk See ZAPORIZHZHYA

Alemán \ˌä-lā-'män\, **Mateo** (1547–1614?) Spanish novelist. Descended from Jews who had been forcibly converted to Roman Catholicism, he expressed many aspects of the experiences and feelings of the New Christians in 16th-century Spain. His most important literary work is *Guzmán de Alfarache* (1599, 1604), one of the earliest PICARESQUE NOVELS, which brought him fame throughout Europe but little profit.

Alembert \à-läⁿ-'ber\, **Jean Le Rond d'** (1717–1783) French mathematician, scientist, philosopher, and writer. In 1743 he published a treatise on DYNAMICS containing "d'Alembert's principle," relating to ISAAC NEWTON's laws of motion. He developed PARTIAL DIFFERENTIAL EQUATIONS and published findings of his research on INTEGRAL CALCULUS. He was associated with the *ENCYCLOPÉDIE* of DENIS DIDEROT from c. 1746 as editor of its mathematical and scientific articles; he contributed articles on music as well, and he also published treatises on acoustics. He was elected to the French Academy in 1754.

Alentejo \à-lāⁿn-'tā-zhü\ *formerly* **Alemtejo** Historical province, Portugal. Lying southeast of the TAGUS RIVER, it borders Spain and the Atlantic Ocean. The region produces two-thirds of the world's cork. Until the Portuguese revolution of 1974, Alentejo contained vast estates, mostly owned by absentee landlords; many have since been divided among the Alentejanos.

alenu \à-'lā-nü\ (Hebrew: "it is our duty") Opening words of a Jewish prayer recited at the end of the three periods of daily prayer since the Middle Ages. The first section is a prayer of thanks for Israel's being chosen for God's service; the second expresses hope for the coming messianic age. Though traditionally ascribed to JOSHUA, it is often credited to Abba Arika, a Jewish scholar in Babylonia in the 3rd century AD.

Aleppo \ə-'le-pō\ *Arabic* **Halab** \'ḥà-làb\ City (pop., 1994 est.: 1,591,000), northwestern Syria. Syria's second-largest city, it is about 30 mi (48 km) from the Turkish border. Lying at the crossroads of great commercial routes, it has long been inhabited, and is first mentioned at the end of the 3rd millennium BC. It subsequently came under the control of many kingdoms, including the HITTITES (17th–14th century BC). Controlled by the Persians in the 6th–4th century BC, it later fell to the SELEUCIDS, who renamed it Beroea. Absorbed into the Roman empire in the 1st century BC, it prospered for several centuries. In AD 637 it was conquered by the Arabs, under whom it reverted to its old name, Halab. The city successfully defended itself from the Crusaders (1124), fell to the MONGOLS (1260), and finally was incorporated into the OTTOMAN empire (1516). Modern Aleppo is an industrial and intellectual center rivaling DAMASCUS.

Alessandri Palma \ä-lā-'sän-drē-'päl-mä\, **Arturo** (1868–1950) President of Chile (1920–25, 1932–38). Son of an Italian immigrant, his election in 1920 represented the urban classes' first successful challenge to Chile's oligarchy. When he defended workers' groups and attempted liberal reforms, he encountered stiff opposition in Congress. A coup led by CARLOS IBANEZ forced him into exile, but he was soon recalled and drafted a new constitution that increased the president's power. He became president again in 1932 during the Great Depression, dependent for support on the political right. His declaration of a state of siege in response to widespread strikes cost him his labor and middle-class support.

Aleut \ˌa-lē-'üt\ Native of the Aleutian Islands and western portion of the Alaska Peninsula. Aleuts speak two main dialects and are physically and culturally closely related to the ESKIMO. Traditional Aleut villages were located on the seashore near fresh water, where the people hunted marine mammals, fish, birds, caribou, and bear. Aleut women wove fine grass basketry; stone, bone, and ivory were also worked. After the arrival of the Russians in the 18th century, their population declined drastically, and today the Aleut number only about 3,500.

Aleutian Islands \ə-'lü-shən\ Chain of small islands (pop., 1990: 12,000), Alaska. They form a border of the BERING SEA, extending in an arc about 1,100 mi (1,800 km) west from the tip of the ALASKA PENINSULA to Attu Island. The major island groups, from east to west, are the Fox Islands (including Unimak and Unalaska), Islands of the Four Mountains, Andreanof Islands (including Adak), and Near Islands (including Attu). The main settlements are on Unalaska and Adak. Originally inhabited by ALEUTS, the islands were explored by Russian-sponsored ships in 1741. As Siberian fur hunters moved eastward through the islands, the Russians gained a foothold in North America but nearly caused the extinction of the Aleuts. Russia sold the islands, with the rest of Alaska, to the U.S. in 1867.

alewife Important North American food fish *(Pomolobus,* or *Alosa, pseudoharengus)* of the HERRING family. The alewife grows to about 1 ft (30 cm). Most populations spend several years along North America's Atlantic coast before ascending freshwater streams to spawn each spring in ponds or sluggish rivers.

Alexander, Harold (Rupert Leofric George) *later* **Earl Alexander (of Tunis)** (1891–1969) British field marshal in World War II.

In 1940 he helped direct the Dunkirk Evacuation and was the last man to leave the beaches. Appointed British commander in chief in the Mediterranean theater in 1942, he helped lead the North Africa Campaign against the Germans. He directed the invasions of Sicily and Italy, then became commander in chief of Allied forces in Italy. After the war, he served as governor-general of Canada (1946–52) and as Britain's minister of defense (1952–54).

Alexander, Severus See Severus Alexander

Alexander, William *later* **Earl of Stirling, Viscount of Canada** (1576?–1640) Scottish poet and colonizer of Canada. He was a member of the court of James I, where he wrote his sonnet sequence *Aurora* (1604). In 1621 he obtained a grant for territory in North America that he named New Scotland (Nova Scotia), despite French claims to part of the land. He offered baronetcies to Scotsmen who would sponsor settlers, but the region was not colonized until his son established a settlement at Port Royal (Annapolis Royal). Alexander was compelled to surrender the territory under the Treaty of Susa (1629), which ended an Anglo-French conflict. Scottish settlers were ordered to withdraw by 1631.

Alexander I *Russian* **Aleksandr Pavlovich** (1777–1825) Czar of Russia (1801–25). He became czar in 1801 after the assassination of his father, Paul I. He and his advisers corrected many of the injustices of the preceding reign, but failed to carry out the abolition of serfdom. During the Napoleonic Wars he alternately fought and befriended Napoleon and helped form the coalition that finally defeated him. He also participated in the Congress of Vienna (1814–15) and formed the Holy Alliance (1815). After his sudden death in 1825, a legend sprang up that he had simply "departed" to a Siberian retreat.

Alexander I (1888–1934) King of Yugoslavia (1921–34). After commanding Serbian forces in World War I, Alexander succeeded his father, Peter I, as king of the Kingdom of Serbs, Croats, and Slovenes in 1921. In 1929 he abolished the constitution and established a royal dictatorship. As part of his efforts to unify his subjects, he changed the name of the country to Yugoslavia; outlawed political parties based on ethnic, religious, or regional distinctions; reorganized the state; and standardized legal systems, school curricula, and national holidays. In 1934 he was assassinated by an agent of Croatian separatists.

Alexander II *Russian* **Aleksandr Nikolayevich** (1818–1881) Czar of Russia (1855–81). Succeeding to the throne at the height of the Crimean War, which was demonstrating Russia's backwardness, he responded to a general desire for drastic change with various reforms, most importantly the emancipation of the serfs (1861). He also improved communications and administrative institutions. His reforms reduced class privilege and fostered humanitarian progress and economic development. Though sometimes described as a liberal, Alexander was in reality a firm upholder of autocratic principles, and an assassination attempt in 1866 strengthened his commitment to conservatism. A period of repression after 1866 led to a resurgence of revolutionary terrorism, and in 1881 he was killed in a plot sponsored by the terrorist organization People's Will.

Alexander II (1198–1249) King of Scotland (1214–49). He came to the throne on the death of his father, William I the Lion. In 1215 he supported the rebellious English barons against King John, hoping to regain land in northern England. After the rebellion collapsed (1217), he did homage to Henry III and in 1221 married Henry's sister, Joan. He consolidated royal authority in Scotland and subdued Argyll in 1222. In 1237 he concluded the Peace of York with Henry by which he abandoned his claim to land in England and received in exchange several English estates.

Alexander III *orig.* **Rolando Bandinelli** (c. 1105–1181) Pope (1159–81). A member of the group of cardinals who feared the growing strength of the Holy Roman Empire, he helped draw up an alliance with the Normans (1156). He angered Frederick I Barbarossa by referring to the Empire as a "benefice," implying that it was a gift of the pope. On Alexander's election as pope in 1159, a minority of cardinals supported by Frederick elected the first of several antipopes, and imperial opposition obliged Alexander to flee to France (1162). A vigorous defender of papal authority, he supported St. Thomas Becket against Henry II of England. He returned to Rome in 1165 but was exiled again the following year. He gained support with the formation of the Lombard League, which defeated Frederick at Legnano in 1176, paving the way for the Peace of Venice. Alexander stood in the reform tradition and presided at the third Lateran Council (1179).

Alexander III *Russian* **Aleksandr Aleksandrovich** (1845–1894) Czar of Russia (1881–94). He assumed the throne after the assassination of his father, Alexander II. The internal reforms he instituted were designed to correct what he saw as the too-liberal tendencies of his father's reign. He thus opposed representative government and ardently supported Russian nationalism. His political ideal was a nation containing a single nationality, language, religion, and form of administration, and accordingly he instituted programs such as the Russification of national minorities in the Russian empire and the persecution of non-Orthodox religious groups.

Alexander III (1241–1286) King of Scotland (1249–86). Son of Alexander II, he came to the throne at age 7. In 1251 he was married to Margaret, daughter of England's King Henry III, who sought to gain control over Scotland. In 1255 Alexander was seized by a pro-English party in Scotland; in 1257 the anti-English party gained control of the government until he came of age (1262). In 1263 he repulsed a Norwegian invasion, and in 1266 he acquired the Hebrides and the Isle of Man from Norway. His reign was later viewed as a golden age by Scots caught up in the long conflict with England.

Alexander VI *orig.* **Rodrigo de Borja y Doms** (1431–1503) Pope (1492–1503). Born into the Spanish branch of the Borgia family, he amassed great wealth and lived scandalously, fathering four illegitimate children prior to his election as pope, which resulted chiefly from Spanish influence. He warred against the Ottoman Turks and forced the French to abandon their effort to seize Naples. The murder of his son Juan (1497) prompted Alexander's short-lived attempt to restrain the corruption of the papal court. He concluded an alliance with Spain and negotiated the Treaty of Tordesillas (1494). A patron of the arts, he embellished the Vatican palaces and commissioned Michelangelo to draw up plans for the rebuilding of St. Peter's Basilica.

Alexander VI, detail of a fresco by Pinturicchio, 1492–94; in the Vatican.
ALINARI—ART RESOURCE/EB INC.

Alexander Archipelago Group of about 1,100 islands (pop., 1991 est.: 39,000), southeastern Alaska. Extending southward from Glacier Bay, the chief islands are Chichagof, Admiralty, Baranof, Kupreanof, Prince of Wales, and Revillagigedo. The chief towns are Sitka (on Baranof) and Ketchikan (on Revillagigedo). The islands are separated from the mainland by deep, narrow channels that form part of the Inside Passage. The archipelago's name, given in 1867, honors Czar Alexander II.

Alexander Island Island in Bellingshausen Sea, separated from the Antarctica mainland by George VI Sound. An extremely rugged region with peaks as high as 9,800 ft (3,000 m), it is 270 mi (435 km) long and up to 125 mi (200 km) wide, with an area of 16,700 sq mi (43,250 sq km). The Russian F. G. von Bellingshausen discovered the land in 1821 and named it after Czar Alexander. It was believed part of the mainland until 1940, when a U.S. expedition proved it to be an island, connected to the continent by a huge floating ice shelf. It has been claimed by Britain (since 1908), Chile (1940), and Argentina (1942).

Alexander Nevsky \'nev-skē\, **St.** (c. 1220–1263) Prince of Novgorod (1236–52) and Kiev (1246–52) and grand prince of Vladimir (1252–63). He fought off invading Swedes in 1240 at the Neva River (resulting in the epithet Nevsky). He was called back to service to defeat the Teutonic Knights in 1242, and also won victories over the Lithuanians and Finns. He collaborated with the Golden Horde in imposing Mongol rule on Russia, and the Great Khan made him grand prince of Vladimir. Alexander continued to rule Novgorod through his son. He helped the Mongols impose taxes, interceding with the Khan to prevent reprisals when rebellions broke out. A national hero, he was canonized by the Russian Orthodox Church.

Alexander the Great *or* **Alexander III** (356–323 BC) Greatest military leader of antiquity. The son of Philip II of Macedonia, he was taught by Aristotle. He soon showed military brilliance, helping win the Battle of Chaeronea at 18. He succeeded his assassinated father in 336 and promptly took Thessaly and Thrace; he brutally razed Thebes except for its temples and the house of Pindar. Such destruction was to be his standard method, and other Greek states submitted meekly. In 334 he crossed to Persia and defeated a Persian army at the Granicus River. He is said to have cut the Gordian knot in Phrygia (333), by which act, according to legend, he was destined to rule all Asia. At the Battle of Issus in 333, he defeated another army, this one led by the Persian king Darius III, who managed to escape. He then took Syria and Phoenicia, cutting off the Persian fleet from its ports. In 332 he completed a seven-month siege of Tyre, considered his greatest military achievement, and reached and took Egypt. There he received the pharaohs' double crown, founded Alexandria, and visited the oracle of the god Amon, the basis of his claim to divinity. In control of the eastern Mediterranean coast, in 331 he defeated Darius in a decisive battle at Gaugamela, though Darius again escaped. He next took the province of Babylon. In Persia he burnt Xerxes' palace at Persepolis in 330, and he envisioned an empire ruled jointly by Macedonians and Persians. He continued eastward, quashing real or imagined conspiracies among his men and taking control to the Oxus and Jaxartes rivers, founding cities (most named Alexandria) to hold the territory. Taking present-day Tajikistan, he married the princess Roxana and embraced Persian absolutism, adopting Persian dress and enforcing Persian court customs. By 326 he reached the Hyphasis in India, where his weary men mutinied; he turned back, marching and pillaging down the Indus, and reached Susa with much loss of life. He continued to promote his unpopular policy of racial fusion, a seeming attempt to form a Persian-Macedonian master race. On the death of his favorite, Hephaestion (324), he gave him a hero's funeral and demanded that divine honors be given at his own funeral. He fell ill at Babylon after long feasting and drinking and died at 33. He was buried in Alexandria, Egypt. His empire, the greatest that had existed to that time, extended from Thrace to Egypt and from Greece to the Indus Valley.

Alexanderson, Ernst F(rederik) W(erner) (1878–1975) Swedish-U.S. electrical engineer and television pioneer. He emigrated to the U.S. in 1901 and spent most of the next five decades at General Electric; from 1952 he worked for RCA. He developed a high-frequency alternator that was capable of producing continuous radio waves, revolutionizing radio communication. His completed alternator (1906) greatly improved transoceanic communication and firmly established the use of wireless devices in shipping and warfare. He also developed a sophisticated control system (1916) used to automate intricate manufacturing processes and operate antiaircraft guns. He was awarded his 321st patent in 1955 for the color TV receiver he developed for RCA.

Alexandra *Russian* **Aleksandra Fyodorovna** *orig.* **Alix, Prinzessin (Princess) von Hesse-Darmstadt** (1872–1918) Consort of Russia's Czar Nicholas II. A granddaughter of Queen Victoria, she married Nicholas in 1894 and sought to restore absolute power in the monarchy. Desperate for help for her hemophiliac son, Alexis, she turned to the hypnotic powers of Grigory Rasputin, who became her spiritual adviser. In 1915 Nicholas left Moscow to command Russian forces in World War I, and Alexandra dismissed capable ministers and replaced them with nonentities favored by Rasputin. Her misrule contributed to the collapse of the imperial government. After the Bolshevik takeover in the Russian Revolution of 1917, the royal family was imprisoned and later executed.

Alexandria City (metro. area pop., 1996 est.: 3,700,000) and chief seaport, northern Egypt. It lies on a strip of land between the Mediterranean Sea and Lake Mareotis. The ancient island of Pharos, whose lighthouse was one of the Seven Wonders of the World, is now a peninsula connected to the mainland. Alexandria's modern harbor is west of the peninsula. The city was founded in 332 BC by Alexander the Great, and was noted as a center of Hellenistic culture; its library was the greatest in ancient times. The city was captured by the Arabs in AD 640 and by the Turks in 1517. After a long period of decline, caused by the rise of Cairo, Alexandria was revived commercially when Muhammad Ali joined it by a canal to the Nile in the early 19th century. Modern Alexandria is a thriving commercial community; cotton is its chief export and important oil fields lie nearby. See also Museum of Alexandria.

Alexandria City (pop., 1992 est.: 115,000), northern Virginia, on the Potomac River. The site was settled in 1695, and in 1749 it was named for John Alexander, the land's original grantee. It was part of Washington, D.C., 1791–1847, after which it was ceded back to Virginia. Many colonial buildings survive in "Old Alexandria"; George Washington's estate, Mount Vernon, is nearby.

Alexandria, Library of Most famous library of classical antiquity. It was part of the Alexandrian Museum, a research institute at Alexandria, Egypt. The museum and library were founded and maintained by a succession of Ptolemies from the early 3rd century BC. It aspired to the ideal of an international library—incorporating all Greek literature and also translations into Greek—but it is uncertain how close this ideal came to being realized. A bibliography of the library compiled by Callimachus, lost in the Byzantine period, was long a standard reference work. The museum and library were destroyed in the late 3rd century AD; a subsidiary library was destroyed in AD 391.

Alexandrina \\,a-lig-,zan-'drē-nə\\, **Lake** Lagoon, southeastern South Australia. It covers 220 sq mi (570 sq km) and is about 23 mi (37 km) long and 13 mi (21 km) wide. With Lake Albert and the Coorong lagoon, it forms the mouth of the Murray River. In 1830 the explorer Charles Sturt named it after Princess Alexandrina (later Queen Victoria). Five barrages across the lake's exits prevent the intrusion of seawater upstream; irrigated agriculture has developed in the upstream area.

alexandrine \\,al-ek-'zan-drən\\ Verse form that is the most popular measure in French poetry. It consists of a line of 12 syllables with a pause after the sixth syllable, major stresses on the sixth and the last syllable, and one secondary accent in each half line. It is a flexible form, adaptable to a wide range of subjects. It became the preeminent French verse form for dramatic and narrative poetry in the 17th century and reached its highest development in the tragedies of Pierre Corneille and Jean Racine.

Alexandrists Italian Renaissance philosophers, led by Pietro Pomponazzi (1462–1525), who followed the explanation of Aristotle's *De Anima* given by Alexander of Aphrodisias (2nd–3rd century AD). Alexander held that *De Anima* denied individual immortality, considering the soul a material and therefore a mortal entity, organically connected with the body. The Alexandrists disagreed with Thomas Aquinas and his followers, who interpreted Aristotle as saying that the individual soul is immortal, and with the Latin Averroists (see Averroës), who held that the individual intellect is reabsorbed after death into the eternal intellect.

Alexeyev \\ə-lyi-'ksyā-yif\\, **Vasiliy** (born 1942) Soviet weight lifter. A superheavyweight, he broke 80 world records between 1970 and 1977 and won Olympic gold medals in 1972 and 1976. He was the first man ever to lift more than 500 lbs (227 kg) in the clean and jerk. He retired after failing to win a third gold medal in 1980.

Alexis *Russian* **Aleksey Mikhaylovich** (1629–1676) Czar of Russia (1645–76). Son of Michael, the first Romanov monarch of Russia, Alexis acceded to the throne at 16. He encouraged trade with the West, which brought an upsurge in foreign influences. During his reign the peasants were finally enserfed, the land assemblies fell into gradual disuse, the professional bureaucracy and regular army grew in importance, and Nikon's reforms of the Russian Orthodox church were adopted. Though reportedly warm-hearted and popular, Alexis was a weak ruler who entrusted matters of state to sometimes incompetent favorites.

Alexius I Comnenus \\käm-'nē-nəs\\ (1048–1118) Byzantine emperor (1081–1118). An experienced military leader, he seized the Byzantine throne in 1081, driving back the invading Normans and Turks and founding the Comnenian dynasty. Alexius increased Byzantine strength in Anatolia and in the eastern Mediterranean but failed to curb the power of the landed

Alexius I Comnenus, detail of an illumination from a Greek manuscript; in the Vatican Library (Cod. Vat. Gr. 666).
BIBLIOTECA APOSTOLICA VATICANA

magnates who had divided the empire in the past. He protected the Eastern Orthodox church but did not hesitate to seize its assets when in financial need. His appeal for Western support in 1095 was a factor in Pope URBAN II's call for the First CRUSADE. Alexius's relations with the crusaders were difficult and, from 1097 onward, the Crusades frustrated his foreign policy.

Alexius V Ducas Murtzuphlus \thü-käs-'mu̇rt-su̇-flȯs\ (died 1204) Byzantine emperor. In 1204 he led a Greek revolt against his co-emperors ISAAC II and Alexius IV, who had been reinstated by Latin crusaders, and he became the last Greek emperor of united Byzantium before its overthrow and partition by the crusaders. He imprisoned Alexius IV and demanded the crusaders leave Constantinople, but they instead besieged the city. He fled to join the fugitive Alexius III (his father-in-law), who, instead of allying with him, had him blinded. Captured by the crusaders, he was thrown from the top of a column to his death.

alfalfa Perennial, CLOVER-like LEGUME *(Medicago sativa),* widely grown primarily for HAY, pasturage, and SILAGE. It is known for its tolerance of drought, heat, and cold, and for its value in soil improvement. The plant, which grows 1–3 ft (30–90 cm) tall, develops numerous stems that arise from a much-branched crown at soil level, each bearing many three-leaved leaflets. Its long primary root—as long as 50 ft (15 m) in some plants—accounts for its unusual ability to tolerate drought. Its remarkable capacity for regeneration of dense growths of new stems and leaves following cutting makes possible as many as 13 crops of hay in one growing season. Alfalfa hay is very nutritious and palatable, high in protein, minerals, and vitamins.

Alfasi \äl-'fä-sē\, **Isaac ben Jacob** (1013–1103) Moroccan Jewish scholar. He spent most of his life in Fez, but in 1088 he was denounced to the government and was obliged to flee to Spain. He became head of the Jewish community in Lucena and established a noted Talmudic academy, provoking a rebirth of Talmudic study in Spain. His codification of the Talmud, *Sefer ha-Halakhot* ("Book of Laws"), deals with Hebrew Law and ranks with the works of MAIMONIDES and KARO. It was crucial in establishing the primacy of the Babylonian Talmud over the Palestinian Talmud.

Alferov, Zhores (Ivanovich) (b. 1930) Soviet physicist. Born in Vitebsk, Belorussia, he received a Ph.D. (1970) from the A.F. Ioffe Physico-Technical Institute; he became director of the institute in 1987. With a research team, he developed the first practical heterostructure electronic device in 1966 and went on to pioneer electronic components made from heterostructures, including the first heterostructure laser. His work led to great advances in communications technology. In 2000 he shared the Nobel Prize for Physics with HERBERT KROEMER and JACK S. KILBY.

Alfieri \äl-'fyā-rē\, **Vittorio, conte (Count)** (1749–1803) Italian tragic poet and playwright. Through his lyrics and dramas he helped revive the national spirit of Italy. After a period of travel in which he experienced English political liberty and read the works of MONTESQUIEU and other French writers, he left the military and began writing. His tragedies almost always present the struggle between a champion of liberty and a tyrant. Of the 19 tragedies that he approved for publication in an edition of 1787–89, the best are *Filippo*, *Antigone*, *Oreste*, *Mirra*, and his masterpiece, *Saul,* often considered the most powerful drama in the Italian theater. His autobiography (1804) is his chief prose work.

Alfonsín (Foulkes) \äl-fȯn-'sēn\, **Raúl (Ricardo)** (born 1926/27) Civilian president of Argentina (1983–1989). He took a degree in law and founded a newspaper before entering politics in 1953. After Argentina lost the FALKLAND ISLANDS WAR, the discredited military permitted free elections, and Alfonsín defeated the PERONIST candidate. He prosecuted members of the armed forces for human-rights violations, but military pressure (including several armed revolts) led him to pardon most convicted officers. His presidency was plagued by high inflation, a huge national debt, labor disputes, and a discontented military. Constitutionally barred from a second term, he was succeeded by CARLOS MENEM.

Alfonso I (Portugal) See AFONSO I

Alfonso III (Portugal) See AFONSO III

Alfonso V *known as* **Alfonso the Magnanimous** (1396–1458) King of ARAGON (1416–58) and of NAPLES (as Alfonso I, 1442–58). He followed a policy of Mediterranean expansion, pacifying Sardinia and Sicily and attacking Corsica (1420). Taken prisoner by the Genoese (1435) while preparing to attack Naples, he persuaded his captors into an alliance and conquered Naples (1442), to which he transferred his court. He engaged in much diplomatic and military activity in Africa, the Balkans, and the eastern Mediterranean in order to protect his commerce with the East and defend Christendom against the Turks. He died during an assault on Genoa.

Alfonso VI *known as* **Alfonso the Brave** (1040–1109) King of LEÓN (1065–70) and of CASTILLA Y LEÓN (1072–1109). He inherited Leon from his father, Ferdinand I, and warred with his envious brother SANCHO II. On Sancho's death he inherited Castile (1072); he also occupied Galicia and imprisoned his brother García, its rightful ruler. In 1077 Alfonso proclaimed himself emperor of all Spain. He took Toledo from the Muslims, but his demands for tribute led to the invasion of Spain by the North African ALMORAVIDS, and he was defeated at Zallaqah (1086). El CID became an ally and defended eastern Spain, but Alfonso continued to lose ground against the Berber armies.

Alfonso X *known as* **Alfonso the Wise** (1221–1284) King of Castilla y León (1252–84). He crushed revolts by Muslims (1252) and nobles (1254), and he annexed Murcia after repelling an invasion by Morocco, Granada, and Murcia (1264). He claimed the title of Holy Roman Emperor (1256), but GREGORY X persuaded him to renounce the claim. His second son became his successor as SANCHO IV. Alfonso's court was a center of culture, producing an influential law code, the *Siete partidas,* and establishing the form of modern Castilian Spanish.

Alfonso XII (1857–1885) Spanish king whose reign (1874–85) inspired hopes for a constitutional monarchy in Spain. Alfonso followed his mother, ISABELLA II, into exile following her deposition by the revolution of 1868. He was proclaimed king in 1874 and returned to Spain the next year. His reign was marked by unaccustomed tranquillity. The most urgent problems—ending the civil war with the Carlists (see CARLISM) and drafting a constitution—were settled in 1876. Alfonso was popular, and his early death from tuberculosis disappointed those who desired a constitutional monarchy.

Alfonso XIII (1886–1941) Spanish king (1886–1931). The posthumous son of ALFONSO XII, he was immediately proclaimed king under his mother's regency and assumed full authority at 16. He relished power, and after World War I he moved toward a system of more personal rule, even seeking to rid himself of Parliament. He associated himself with the dictatorship of MIGUEL PRIMO DE RIVERA (1923–30), but after the latter's fall the freely elected Republicans demanded Alfonso's abdication, and he was forced to leave Spain in 1931.

Alfred *known as* **Alfred the Great** (849–899) King of Wessex (871–99) in southwestern England. He joined his brother Ethelred I in confronting a Danish army in Mercia (868). Succeeding his brother as king, Alfred fought the Danes in Wessex in 871 and again in 878, when he was the only West Saxon leader to refuse to submit to their authority. He defeated the Danes at the Battle of Edington (878) and saved Kent from another Danish invasion in 885. The next year he took the offensive and captured London, a success that brought all the English not under Danish rule to accept him as king. The conquest of the DANELAW by his successors was enabled by his strategy. Alfred drew up an important code of laws (see ANGLO-SAXON LAW) and promoted literacy and learning, personally translating Latin books into Anglo-Saxon. The compilation of the Anglo-Saxon Chronicle was begun under his reign.

algae \'al-jē\ Any of a group of mostly aquatic, photosynthetic organisms (see PHOTOSYNTHESIS) that defy precise definition. They range in size from the microscopic flagellate *Micromonas* to giant KELP that reach 200 ft (60 m) in length. Algae provide much of the earth's oxygen, serve as the food base for almost all aquatic life, and provide foods and industrial products, including petroleum products. Their photosynthetic pigments are more varied than those of plants, and their cells have features not found among plants and animals. The classification of algae is changing rapidly as new taxonomical information is discovered. Algae were formerly classified into three major groups—the red, brown, and green seaweeds—based on the pigment molecules in their CHLOROPLASTS. Many more than three groups are now recognized, each sharing a common set of pigment types. Algae are not closely related to each other in an evolutionary sense. Specific groups can be distinguished from PROTOZOANS and fungi (see FUNGUS) only by the presence of chloroplasts and their ability to carry out photosynthesis, and thus have a closer evolutionary relationship with the protozoa or fungi than with other algae. Use of algae is perhaps as old as mankind; seaweeds are eaten by coastal societies, and algae are served in many restaurants. They are common on "slimy" rocks in streams (see DIATOMS) and as green sheens on pools and ponds.

Algardi, Alessandro (1598–1654) Italian sculptor. He trained in Bologna under CARRACCI FAMILY and in 1625 moved to Rome, where he designed the stucco decorations in San Silvestro al Quirinale. He later became the most outstanding sculptor in Rome after GIAN LORENZO BERNINI. He was a prolific sculptor of portrait busts in the baroque style and his colossal marble relief of the *Meeting of Attila and Pope Leo* (1646–53) in St. Peter's Basilica influenced the development and popularity of illusionistic reliefs. His work as a restorer of antique statuary brought him some notoriety.

"Meeting of Attila and Pope Leo," colossal marble relief by Alessandro Algardi, 1646–53; in St. Peter's, Rome.

ALINARI—ANDERSON FROM ART RESOURCE/EB INC.

algebra, fundamental theorem of Theorem of equations proved by CARL FRIEDRICH GAUSS in 1800. It states that every POLYNOMIAL equation has at least one solution, which may be a REAL NUMBER or an IMAGINARY NUMBER.

algebra, linear See LINEAR ALGEBRA

algebra and algebraic structures Generalized version of arithmetic that uses VARIABLES to stand for unspecified numbers. Its purpose is to solve ALGEBRAIC EQUATIONS or SYSTEMS OF EQUATIONS. Examples of such solutions are the quadratic formula (for solving a QUADRATIC EQUATION) and Gauss-Jordan elimination (for solving a SYSTEM OF EQUATIONS in MATRIX form). In higher mathematics, an "algebra" is a structure consisting of a class of objects and a set of rules (analogous to addition and multiplication) for combining them. Basic and higher algebraic structures share two essential characteristics: (1) calculations involve a finite number of steps and (2) calculations involve abstract symbols (usually letters) representing more general objects (usually numbers). Higher algebra (also known as modern or abstract algebra) includes all of elementary algebra, as well as GROUP THEORY, theory of RINGS, FIELD THEORY, MANIFOLDS, and VECTOR SPACES.

algebraic equation Mathematical statement of equality between algebraic expressions. An expression is algebraic if it involves a finite combination of numbers and VARIABLES and algebraic operations (addition, subtraction, multiplication, division, raising to a power, and extracting a root). Two important types of such equations are linear equations, in the form $y = ax + b$, and QUADRATIC EQUATIONS, in the form $y = ax^2 + bx + c$. A solution is a numerical value that makes the equation a true statement when substituted for a variable. In some cases it may be found using a formula; in others the equation may be rewritten in simpler form. Algebraic equations are particularly useful for modeling real-life phenomena.

algebraic geometry Study of geometric objects expressed as equations and represented by graphs in a given COORDINATE SYSTEM. In contrast to EUCLIDEAN GEOMETRY, algebraic geometry represents geometric objects using ALGEBRAIC EQUATIONS (e.g., a circle of radius r is defined by $x^2 + y^2 = r^2$). Objects so defined can then be analyzed for symmetries, intercepts, and other properties without having to refer to a graph.

algebraic topology Field of mathematics that uses algebraic structures to study transformations of geometric objects. It uses FUNCTIONS (often called maps in this context) to represent continuous transformations (see TOPOLOGY). Taken together, a set of maps and objects may form an algebraic group, which can be analyzed by GROUP-THEORY methods. A well-known topic in algebraic topology is the FOUR-COLOR MAP PROBLEM.

Algeciras Conference \ˌal-jə-ˈsir-əs\ (1906) Conference held at Algeciras, Spain, that resolved the first of the MOROCCAN CRISES. In 1905 WILLIAM II objected to France's efforts to exert influence in Morocco, prompting a conference of the European powers and the U.S. Superficially, the Act of Algeciras (1906) seemed to limit French penetration, but the conference's real significance was the diplomatic support that Britain and the U.S. gave France, foreshadowing their roles in World War I.

Alger \ˈal-jər\, **Horatio, Jr.** (1832–1899) U.S. writer. Born in Chelsea, Mass., the son of a Unitarian minister, he graduated from Harvard with honors, then earned a degree from its divinity school. Forced to leave his pulpit after two years because of allegations of improper activities with youths, he took up writing. Beginning with *Ragged Dick* (1868), he wrote over 100 books that were almost alike in preaching that through honesty, cheerful perseverance, and hard work, a poor but virtuous lad would have his just reward (though it was almost always precipitated by good luck). His books sold more than 20 million copies, despite consistently weak plots and dialogue, and Alger was one of the most popular and socially influential writers of the late 19th century.

Algeria *officially* **Democratic and Popular Republic of Algeria** Nation, northern Africa. Area: 918,497 sq mi (2,378,907 sq km). Population (1997 est.): 29,476,000. Capital: ALGIERS. Most of the population is Arabic; Berbers are the main minority group. Languages: Arabic (official), French, Berber. Religion: Islam (official). Currency: Algerian dinar. Algeria has the second-largest land area (after Sudan) on the continent. The coastline has few inlets and the rivers are small. It is traversed in the north by the ATLAS and Saharan Atlas Mtns.; its highest peak is Djebel Chélia, at 7,648 ft (2,331 m). Central and southern Algeria occupy much of the northern SAHARA DESERT. Algeria has a centrally planned developing economy based primarily on the production and export of oil and natural gas. Since achieving independence, the country has nationalized much of its economy. It is a republic with two legislative bodies; its chief of state is the president, and its head of government is the prime minister. Phoenician traders settled there early in the 1st millennium BC; several centuries later the Romans invaded, and by AD 40 they had control of the Mediterranean coast. The fall of Rome in the 5th century led to invasion by the VANDALS, and later by Byzantium. The Islamic invasion began in the 7th century; by 711 all of northern Africa was under the control of the UMAYYAD caliphate. Several Islamic Berber empires followed, most prominently the ALMORAVID (c. 1054–1130), which extended its domain to Spain, and the ALMOHAD (c. 1130–1269). The BARBARY COAST pirates, operating in the area, had menaced Mediterranean trade for centuries, and France seized this pretext to enter Alge-

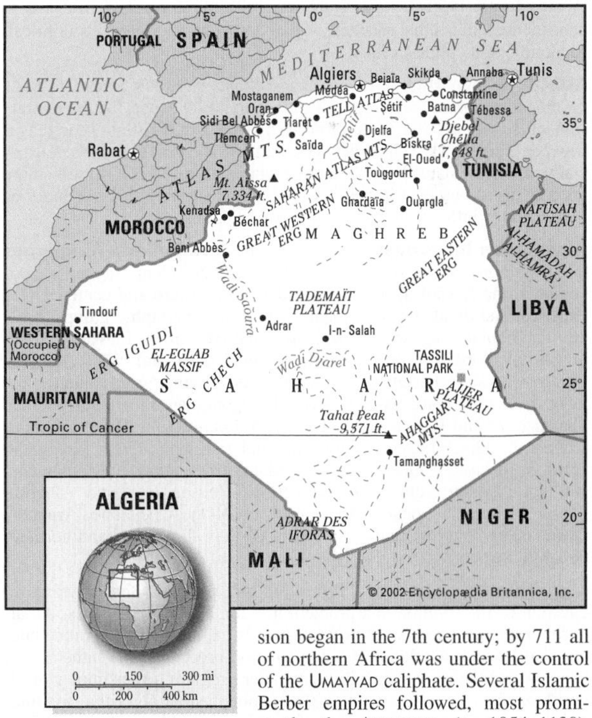

ria in 1830. By 1847 France had established control in the region, and by the late 19th century had instituted civil rule. Popular movements resulted in the bloody ALGERIAN WAR (1954–61); independence was achieved following a referendum in 1962. In the 1990s Islamic fundamentalists opposing the military brought Algeria to a state of virtual civil war.

Algerian Reformist Ulama \u̇-lä-'mä\, **Association of** Group of Muslim religious scholars founded in 1931 that worked to create an Algerian Muslim identity. The Ulama opened schools and promoted the teaching of Arabic. It was opposed by the French-educated elite and the traditional Muslim establishment, which felt threatened by its purist tendencies. It joined the NATIONAL LIBERATION FRONT during the war of independence (1954–62) and later had a seat in Algeria's provisional government. See also YOUNG ALGERIANS.

Algerian War (1954–1962) War for Algerian independence from France. The movement for independence began in World War I and gained momentum after promises of greater self-rule went unfulfilled after World War II. In 1954 the National Liberation Front (FLN) began a guerrilla war against France and sought diplomatic recognition at the U.N. to restore a sovereign Algerian state. In 1959 CHARLES DE GAULLE declared that the Algerians had the right to determine their own future. Despite terrorist acts by European Algerians opposed to independence, a truce was signed in 1962 and Algeria became independent.

Algiers *French* **Alger** \al-'zhā\ City (pop., 1995 est.: 2,168,000), chief seaport, and capital of Algeria. Located along the Bay of Algiers, and first settled by Phoenicians, it was later ruled by the Romans. It was destroyed by the VANDALS in the 5th century AD but revived under a Berber dynasty in the 10th century. When the Spanish threatened it in the early 16th century, the emir appealed to BARBAROSSA, who expelled the Spanish and placed Algiers under the OTTOMAN sultanate. Algiers became the major base for the BARBARY COAST pirates for 300 years; their activities were finally curtailed in 1818 by an American force led by STEPHEN DECATUR. The French took the city in 1830 and made it headquarters for their African colonial empire. In World War II, it became the Allied headquarters in northern Africa and for a time the provisional capital of France. In the 1950s it was the focal point in the drive for Algeria's independence; after independence, Algiers grew as the country's political, economic, and cultural center.

ALGOL \'al-ˌgȯl\ High-level algebraic computer PROGRAMMING LANGUAGE developed in the late 1950s as an international language for the expression of ALGORITHMS (its name is derived from ALGOrithmic Language) between humans as well as between humans and machines. Used especially in mathematical and scientific applications, ALGOL was more popular in Europe than in the U.S., but it was an important precursor of PASCAL and it influenced the development of C language.

Algonquian languages \al-'gän-kwē-ən\ *or* **Algonkian languages** \al-'gäŋ-kē-ən\ Family of 25–30 North American Indian languages, spoken or formerly spoken across a broad area of eastern and central North America, and divided conventionally into three geographic groups. Eastern Algonquian languages, spoken from the Gulf of St. Lawrence south to coastal North Carolina, include Micmac, East and West Abenaki, Delaware, Massachusett, and Powhatan (or Virginia Algonquian)—the latter two now long extinct. Central Algonquian languages include Shawnee, Miami-Illinois, Sauk, Kickapoo, Potawatomi, Menominee (all around the Great Lakes), Ojibwa (around the upper Great Lakes and north from eastern Quebec through Manitoba), and Cree-Montagnais-Naskapi (spoken from Labrador west to Hudson Bay and Alberta). Plains Algonquian includes the languages of the Cheyenne, Arapaho, Atsina (Gros Ventres), and Blackfeet (spoken in the central and northern Great Plains).

algorithm \'al-gə-ˌri-t͟həm\ Procedure that produces the answer to a question or the solution to a problem in a finite number of steps. An algorithm that produces a yes or no answer is called a decision procedure; one that leads to a solution is a computation procedure. A mathematical formula and the instructions in a computer program are examples of algorithms. EUCLID's *Elements* (c. 300 BC) contained an algorithm for finding the greatest common divisor of two integers. Manipulation of lists (searching for, inserting, and removing items) can be done efficiently by using algorithms.

algorithms, analysis of Basic computer-science discipline that aids in the development of effective programs. Analysis of ALGORITHMS provides proof of the correctness of algorithms, allows for the accurate prediction of program performance, and can be used as a measure of COMPUTATIONAL COMPLEXITY. See also DONALD KNUTH.

Algren \'ȯl-grən\, **Nelson** *orig.* **Nelson Ahlgren Abraham** (1909–1981) U.S. writer. Born in Detroit, the son of a machinist, he grew up in Chicago and worked his way through the University of Illinois during the Depression. His novels of the poor skillfully capture the mood of the city's underside and are lifted from routine naturalism by his vision of his characters' pride, humor, and unquenchable yearnings. Among his popular successes were *The Man with the Golden Arm* (1949; film, 1956) and *A Walk on the Wild Side* (1956; film, 1962). He also published an admired short-story collection, *The Neon Wilderness* (1947).

Alhambra \al-'am-brə\ Palace of the Moorish monarchs of Granada, Spain, built 1238–1358 on a plateau above the city. Its name (Arabic: "the red") may refer to the color of the sun-dried bricks used in its outer walls. The Alhambra, only three parts of which remain intact, is made up of a series of rooms and gardens clustered around three principal courts, with extensive use of fountains and water basins. Its surfaces are astoundingly ornate and varied, with outstanding examples of stalactite work.

Ali (ibn Abi Talib) (c. 600–661) Son-in-law of the prophet MUHAMMAD and fourth CALIPH. Ali had been a ward of Muhammad, just as Muhammad had been a ward of Ali's father. An early convert to Islam, he helped Muhammad foil an assassination plot and fought beside him against his enemies. Since some claimed Muhammad did not name any successor and others claimed he named Ali, the controversy over Ali's claim to the caliphate resulted in the first FITNAH (656–61). His brief reign as caliph (656–61) was spent fighting corruption and the rebellions that stemmed from his reforms. See also HUSAYN IBN ALI, Battle of KARBALA, al-MUAWIYAH I.

Ali, Muhammad *orig.* **Cassius (Marcellus) Clay** (born 1942) U.S. boxer. Born in Louisville, Ky., he rose through the amateur ranks to win the Olympic light heavyweight crown in 1960. His first professional heavyweight title win was against Sonny Liston in 1964. After defending the title nine times between 1965 and 1967, he was stripped of it for refusing induction into the armed forces following his conversion to Islam. He regained it in 1974 after defeating the former champion Joe Frazier and the then-current champion GEORGE FOREMAN. He lost to Leon Spinks in 1978 but later that year regained the title a third time, becoming the first heavyweight champion ever to do so. He retired in 1979, having lost only three of 59 fights. Attempted comebacks in 1980 and 1981 failed. Throughout his career Ali was known for his aggressive charm, invincible attitude, and colorful boasts, often expressed in doggerel verse. "I am the greatest" was his personal credo. He was diagnosed in 1984 with Parkinson's disease, but has remained a beloved public figure.

Muhammad Ali (right) fighting Ernie Terrell, 1967.
UPI COMPIX

Aliákmon River \äl-'yäk-mȯn\ River, northern Greece. Rising in the Grammos Mountains and flowing southeast and northeast for 185 mi (297 km) into the upper Gulf of Salonika, it is the longest river in Greek Macedonia. Throughout history it has served as a natural line of defense against invaders from the north.

Alicante \ˌä-lē-'kän-tā\ City (pop., 1995 est.: 276,000), southeastern Spain, located on Alicante Bay of the Mediterranean Sea. Founded as a Greek colony in 325 BC, it was captured in 201 BC by the Romans, who called it Lucentum. It was ruled by the Moors 718–1249 and was incorporated into the kingdom of ARAGON in 1265. The city was besieged by the French in 1709 and by the Federalists of CARTAGENA in 1873. Its economy is based on tourism and the export of wine and produce.

Alice Springs Town (pop., 2001 prelim.: 26,990), Northern Territory, Australia. It lies between DARWIN and ADELAIDE, virtually in the center of the continent. It originated in the 1870s as a station on the Overland Telegraph Line. Because of its location, it has become a major shipping point. Its mild winter climate makes it a popular tourist destination.

alien In law, one who resides in a country without becoming naturalized, retaining instead the citizenship of another country. The laws of most nations have long afforded aliens certain minimum standards of civilized treatment but have also restricted their employment and ownership of property. Under U.S. law, all aliens have had to register since 1940. Registration cards ("green cards") entitle them to obtain employment. Like citizens, aliens are protected by the U.S. Constitution, including the Bill of Rights and the due-process clause of the 14th Amendment. They remain subject to limitations under local laws, and residence in the U.S. is not a right but a privilege granted by Congress.

Alien and Sedition Acts Four laws passed by the U.S. Congress in 1798, in anticipation of war with France after the XYZ AFFAIR, which restricted aliens and curtailed press criticism of the government. The laws, aimed at French and Irish immigrants (who were mostly pro-France), increased the waiting period for naturalization and authorized expulsion of aliens considered dangerous. The laws, which led to the first STATES' RIGHTS movement, were opposed by THOMAS JEFFERSON and others and helped propel Jefferson to the presidency. They were repealed or had expired by 1802.

alienation In the social sciences, the state of feeling estranged from one's milieu, work, or self. The concept appears implicitly or explicitly in the works of ÉMILE DURKHEIM, FERDINAND TÖNNIES, MAX WEBER, and GEORG SIMMEL, but is most famously associated with KARL MARX, who spoke of workers being alienated from their work under CAPITALISM. In other contexts the term alienation, like ANOMIE, can suggest a sense of powerlessness, meaninglessness, normlessness, or social isolation brought on by the lack of fit between individual expectations and the social order.

alimentary canal *or* **digestive tract** Pathway along which food travels when it is eaten and from which solid wastes are expelled. It includes the MOUTH, PHARYNX, ESOPHAGUS, STOMACH, SMALL and LARGE intestines, and ANAL CANAL. See also DIGESTION.

alimony See MARRIAGE LAW

Alitalia Italian international airline with headquarters in Rome. Although the airline no longer commands monopoly status, as of 2002 the Italian government still owned a majority share of the company.

aliyah \ä-'lē-yä\ (Hebrew: "ascending") Jewish immigration to Israel. The first two waves occurred in 1882–1914, the next three in 1919–39. The sixth aliyah (1945–48) brought many HOLOCAUST survivors. Waves of immigration continue to this day (e.g., Ethiopian FALASHAS, émigrés from the former Soviet Union). In a religious sense, aliyah is the honor of being called to read a passage from the Torah at sabbath-morning services. See also ZIONISM.

Alkaios See ALCAEUS

Alkalai \ˌal-kə-'lī\, **Judah ben Solomon Hai** (1798–1878) Bosnian-born Sephardic rabbi. Raised in Jerusalem, he became rabbi at Semlin, Croatia. He argued that a physical return to Israel, rather than a symbolic return through repentance and practice, was necessary for the salvation of the Jewish people, a view that put him at odds with Jewish orthodoxy. He saw the anti-Semitic Damascus Affair of 1840 as part of a divine plan to reawaken Jews to the reality of their condition in exile. Unsuccessful in gaining support for emigration, he himself settled in Palestine in 1871. His writings helped pave the way for ZIONISM.

alkali \'al-kə-ˌlī\ Inorganic compound, any soluble HYDROXIDE (—OH) of the ALKALI METALS: LITHIUM, SODIUM, POTASSIUM, rubidium, and CESIUM. More broadly, ammonium hydroxide (see AMMONIA) and soluble hydroxides of the ALKALINE EARTH METALS are also called alkalies. Strong BASES that turn LITMUS paper blue, they react with ACIDS to yield SALTS, are caustic, and in concentrated form corrode tissues. Sodium hydroxide (CAUSTIC SODA) and potassium hydroxide (caustic potash) are very important industrial chemicals, used in the manufacture of soaps, glass, and many other products.

alkali feldspar Any of several common SILICATE MINERALS that often occur as whitish to variously colored, glassy crystals. The alkali FELDSPARS may be regarded as mixtures of sodium aluminosilicate ($NaAlSi_3O_8$) and potassium aluminosilicate ($KAlSi_3O_8$). Both the sodium and potassium aluminosilicates have several distinct forms, each with a different structure. Alkali feldspars are used in the manufacture of glass and ceramics; transparent, highly colored, or iridescent varieties are sometimes used as gemstones. They are primarily important, however, as constituents of rocks (see PLAGIOCLASE).

alkali metal Any of the six chemical ELEMENTS in the leftmost group of the PERIODIC TABLE (LITHIUM, SODIUM, POTASSIUM, rubidium, CESIUM, and francium). They form ALKALIES when they combine with other elements. Because their ATOMS have only one ELECTRON in the outermost shell, they are very reactive chemically (they react rapidly, even violently, with water), form numerous compounds, and are never found free in nature.

alkaline earth metal Any of the six chemical ELEMENTS in the second leftmost group of the PERIODIC TABLE (BERYLLIUM, MAGNESIUM, CALCIUM, STRONTIUM, BARIUM, and RADIUM). Their name harks back to medieval ALCHEMY. Their ATOMS have two ELECTRONS in the outermost shell, so they react readily, form numerous compounds, and are never found free in nature.

alkaloid Basic (see BASE) organic compounds of plant origin, containing combined NITROGEN. Alkaloids are AMINES, so their names usually end in "ine" (e.g., CAFFEINE, NICOTINE, MORPHINE, QUININE). Most have complex chemical structures of multiple ring systems. They have diverse, important physiological effects on humans and other animals, but their functions in the plants that produce them are poorly understood. Some plants (e.g., OPIUM POPPY, ERGOT fungus) produce many different alkaloids, but most produce only one or a few. Certain plant families, including the POPPY FAMILY (Papaveraceae) and the NIGHTSHADE FAMILY (Solanaceae), are particularly rich in them. Alkaloids are extracted by dissolving the plant in dilute ACID.

Alkamenes See ALCAMENES

alkane *or* **paraffin** Any of a class of HYDROCARBONS whose MOLECULES consist only of carbon and hydrogen atoms joined by single COVALENT BONDS (general formula $C_nH_{(2n+2)}$). The simplest is METHANE (CH_4). Alkanes with more than three carbon atoms may have straight and branched ISOMERS. Cycloalkanes have ring structures (but are not AROMATIC COMPOUNDS) with two fewer hydrogen atoms per molecule than the corresponding alkane; many have more than one ring. Commercial sources include PETROLEUM and NATURAL GAS. Uses, often as mixtures, include as fuels, SOLVENTS, and raw materials. See also PARAFFIN.

alkene See OLEFIN

All Saints' Day In Christianity, a day commemorating all the saints of the church, known and unknown. It is celebrated on November 1 in the Western churches and on the first Sunday after PENTECOST in the Eastern churches. The first general observance of All Saints' Day was ordered by Pope Gregory IV in 837. In medieval England the festival was called All Hallows, and its eve is still known as HALLOWEEN.

All Souls' Day In the Roman Catholic church, a day commemorating all the Christians believed to be in PURGATORY. Celebrated on November 2, it was first established by Odilo (died 1048), abbot of Cluny, in the 11th century, and it was widely celebrated by the 13th century. The date follows ALL SAINTS' DAY, with the idea that remembering the saints in heaven should be followed by remembering the souls awaiting release from purgatory. Roman Catholic doctrine holds that the prayers of the faithful on earth will help cleanse these souls in order to prepare them for heaven.

Allah (Arabic: "God") Standard Arabic word for God, used by Arab Christians as well as by Muslims. According to the QURAN, Allah is the creator and judge of mankind, omnipotent, compassionate, and merciful. The Muslim profession of faith affirms that there is no god but Allah and emphasizes that he is inherently one: "nothing is like unto him." Everything that happens occurs by his commandment; submission to God is the basis of ISLAM. The Quran and the HADITH contain the 99 "most beautiful names" of God, including the One and Only, the Living One, the Real Truth, the Hearer, the Seer, the Benefactor, and the Constant Forgiver.

Allahabad See PRAYGRAJ

Allbutt, Thomas Clifford *later* **Sir Thomas** (1836–1925) English physician. He introduced the modern clinical thermometer (the thermometer had previously been a foot-long instrument that required 20 minutes to register temperature) and outlined the use of the ophthalmoscope to inspect the interior of the eye. He demonstrated the aortic origin of angina pectoris. His investigations improved treatment of arterial diseases and resulted in, among other works, *Diseases of the Arteries* (1915). His chief publication was *Systems of Medicine* (8 vols., 1896–99).

Alleghenian orogeny \ˌal-ə-ˈgā-nē-ən-ȯ-ˈrä-jə-nē\ *formerly* **Appalachian Revolution** Mountain-building event that affected the APPALACHIAN GEOSYNCLINE in the late PERMIAN PERIOD (c. 290–248 million years ago). The Alleghenian orogeny is most pronounced in the central and southern Appalachian Mountains and produced the different effects in various subregions: compressional folding and faulting of the Valley and Ridge Province, westward thrusting of the Blue Ridge, and folding and minor metamorphism and igneous intrusion in the Piedmont Province. It may have resulted from the collision (see PLATE TECTONICS) of the central and southern Appalachian continental margin with that of North Africa in the Permian period.

Allegheny Mountains \ˌal-ə-ˈgā-nē\ Ranges of the APPALACHIAN system in Pennsylvania, Maryland, Virginia, and West Virginia, west of and generally parallel with the BLUE RIDGE MTNS. They extend some 500 mi (800 km) south-southwestward, with heights of over 4,800 ft (1,460 m). The eastern slope is sometimes called the Allegheny Front, while the Allegheny Plateau spans the entire upland area from the CUMBERLAND PLATEAU to the Mohawk Valley in New York.

Allegheny River River in Pennsylvania and New York. It rises in Potter Co., Pa., loops northwest into New York, turns back into Pennsylvania, and unites with the MONONGAHELA to form the OHIO RIVER at PITTSBURGH. It is 325 mi (523 km) long; its chief tributaries are the Clarion, the Kiskiminetas, and French Creek. Several dams make the river navigable from Pittsburgh to East Brady.

allegory Work of written, oral, or visual expression that uses symbolic figures, objects, and actions to convey truths or generalizations about human conduct or experience. It encompasses such forms as the FABLE and parable. Characters often personify abstract concepts or types, and the action of the narrative usually stands for something not explicitly stated. Symbolic allegories, in which characters may also have an identity apart from the message they convey, have frequently been used to represent political and historical situations and have long been popular as vehicles for SATIRE. EDMUND SPENSER's long allegorical poem *The Faerie Queen* is a famous example.

allele \ə-ˈlēl\ Any one of two or more alternative forms of a GENE that may occur alternatively at a given site on a CHROMOSOME. Alleles may occur in pairs, or there may be multiple alleles affecting the expression of a particular trait. If paired alleles are the same, the organism is said to be homozygous for that trait; if they are different, the organism is heterozygous. A dominant allele will override the traits of a recessive allele in a heterozygous pairing (see DOMINANCE and RECESSIVENESS). In some traits, alleles may be codominant (i.e., neither acts as dominant or recessive). An individual cannot possess more than two alleles for a given trait. All genetic traits are the result of the interactions of alleles.

allemande \ˈal-ə-ˌmand\ Processional couple dance with stately flowing steps, fashionable in the 16th century, especially in France. A line of couples extended their paired hands forward and paraded back and forth the length of the ballroom. It was revived in the 18th century as a figure dance for four couples, in which each pair performed intricate turns under each other's arms, a figure that partly survives in the "allemand" of the U.S. SQUARE DANCE. In the late 17th century a stylized version of the dance in 4/4 time began to be used by composers as the first movement of the SUITE.

Allen, Ethan (1738–1789) American soldier and frontiersman. Born in Litchfield, Conn., he fought in the FRENCH AND INDIAN WAR (1754–63), then settled in what is now Vermont. In 1770 he organized a force he called the Green Mountain Boys, which in the AMERICAN REVOLUTION helped win the Battle of TICONDEROGA (1775). As a volunteer with Gen. PHILIP SCHUYLER's troops, he attempted to take Montreal but was captured by the British and held prisoner until 1778. He returned to Vermont, where he worked for statehood.

Allen, Fred *orig.* **John Florence Sullivan** (1894–1956) U.S. comedian. Born in Cambridge, Mass., he began his career in VAUDEVILLE as a juggler and ventriloquist, then turned to comedy and appeared in revues in the 1920s. He entered radio in 1932 and was featured on *Town Hall Tonight* (1934–39), which became the popular *Fred Allen Show* (1939–49). He and his wife, Portland Hoffa (1906–1990), played the principal roles along with other characters of "Allen's Alley." He wrote nearly all the 273 episodes, which displayed his laconic style, dry wit, and flawless timing.

Allen, Mel *orig.* **Melvin Allen Israel** (1913–1996) U.S. sports broadcaster. He was born in Birmingham, Ala. As head announcer for the New York Yankees baseball team (1940–64), he was known for his congeniality and his catchphrase "How about that!" He hosted the television program *This Week in Baseball* (1977–95). He was elected to the Baseball Hall of Fame in 1978.

Allen, Richard (1760–1831) U.S. religious leader. He was born to slave parents in Philadelphia, and his family was sold to a Delaware farmer. A Methodist convert at 17, he was licensed to preach five years later. By 1786 he had purchased his freedom and settled in Philadelphia, where he joined St. George's Methodist Episcopal Church. Racial discrimination prompted him to withdraw in 1787, and he turned an old blacksmith shop into the first black church in the U.S. Allen and his followers built the Bethel African Methodist Church, and in 1799 he was ordained as its minister. In 1816 he organized a conference of black leaders to form the AFRICAN METHODIST EPISCOPAL CHURCH, of which he was named the first bishop.

Allen, Steve *orig.* **Stephen Valentine Patrick William** (1921–2000) U.S. entertainer and songwriter. Born in New York City, the son of vaudevillians, he appeared as a comedian on radio in the 1940s before moving to late-night television, where he created and hosted *The Tonight Show* (1953–57) and *The Steve Allen Show* (1957–60). He hosted several other television shows, including *Meeting of Minds* (1977–81). He composed over 3,000 songs, including "Picnic," "This Could Be the Start of Something Big," and "Impossible," and appeared in films such as *The Benny Goodman Story* (1956) and *The Sunshine Boys* (1975).

Allen, Woody *orig.* **Allen Stewart Konigsberg** (born 1935) U.S. film director, screenwriter, and actor. His middle-class Jewish family in Brooklyn and his chronic neuroticism became the source of much of his comic material. After writing routines for comedians and performing as a nightclub comic, he wrote the Broadway play *Don't Drink the Water* (1966). His first film, *What's New, Pussycat?* (1965), was followed by *Take the Money and Run* (1969), *Bananas* (1971), and *Sleeper* (1973), combining highbrow comedy and slapstick in a style influenced by the MARX BROTHERS. Later romantic comedies such as *Annie Hall* (1977), which won him three Academy Awards, and *Manhattan* (1979) offered a bittersweet view of New York life. His other films include *Zelig* (1983), *Hannah and Her Sisters* (1986, Academy Award), *Crimes and Misdemeanors* (1989), *Bullets over Broadway* (1994), and *Sweet and Lowdown* (1999).

Allenby, Edmund Henry Hynman *later* **Viscount Allenby (of Megiddo and of Felixstowe)** (1861–1936) British field marshal. He fought in the SOUTH AFRICAN WAR and served as inspector general of cavalry 1910–14. In World War I, he commanded with distinction in the Middle East. His victory over the Turks at Gaza (1917) led to the capture of Jerusalem, and his victory at Megiddo, along with his capture of Damascus and Aleppo, ended Ottoman power in Syria. His success was partly due to his innovative use of cavalry and other mobile forces, and he is remembered as the last great British leader of mounted cavalry. As high commissioner for Egypt (1919–25), he steered that country to recognition as a sovereign state (1922).

Allende (Gossens) \ä-ˈyen-dā\, **Salvador** (1908–1973) Socialist president of Chile (1970–73). Of upper-middle-class background, Allende took a degree in medicine and in 1933 helped found Chile's Socialist Party. He ran for president unsuccessfully three times before winning narrowly in 1970. He attempted to restructure Chilean society along socialist lines while retaining democracy, civil liberties, and due process of law, but his efforts to redistribute wealth resulted in stagnant production, food shortages, rising inflation, and widespread strikes. His inability to control his radical supporters further alienated the middle class. His policies dried up foreign credit and led to a covert campaign by the U.S. CENTRAL INTELLIGENCE AGENCY to destabilize the government. He was overthrown in a violent military coup, during which he died by gunshot, reportedly self-inflicted. He was replaced by Gen. AUGUSTO PINOCHET. See also EDUARDO FREI.

Allentown City (pop., 1996 est.: 102,000), eastern Pennsylvania. It was laid out along the Lehigh River in 1762 and named Northampton by William Allen, later the state's chief justice; its name was changed in 1838 to honor Allen. During the AMERICAN REVOLUTION, the Liberty Bell was removed there for safekeeping. It is a major iron and mining center.

allergy Hypersensitive reaction by the body to foreign substances (allergens or ANTIGENS), such as POLLENS, DRUGS, dusts, and foods, that are harmless to most people. Immediate allergic reactions result from genetic predisposition or sensitization by previous exposure; blood vessels dilate and bronchial air passages constrict. A severe reaction (ANAPHYLAXIS) can obstruct breathing and may be fatal. Delayed allergic responses (e.g., contact DERMATITIS) appear 12 hours or more after exposure. Avoiding allergens and taking ANTIHISTAMINES can prevent or treat allergies. When avoidance is not feasible and antihistamines do not relieve symptoms, DESENSITIZATION can be attempted.

alliance In international politics, a union for joint action of various powers or states, such as the alliance of the European powers and the U.S. against Germany and its allies during World War II, or of the NATO states against the Soviet Union and its allies. Many alliances rest on the principle of collective security, through which an attack on one member is considered an attack on all members. Major 20th-century alliances have included the ANZUS PACT, ARAB LEAGUE, ASSOCIATION OF S.EAST ASIAN NATIONS, ORGANIZATION OF AMERICAN STATES, S.EAST ASIA TREATY ORGANIZATION, and WARSAW PACT.

Alliance for Progress International development program initiated by the U.S. and joined by 22 Latin American countries in 1961 to strengthen democratic government and promote social and economic reforms in Latin America. The program, which provided loans and aid from the U.S. and the international financial community, built some schools and hospitals but was widely viewed as a failure. Significant LAND REFORM was not achieved, population growth outstripped gains in health and welfare, and the U.S. willingness to support military dictators to prevent communism from gaining a foothold sowed distrust and undermined the reforms the Alliance was intended to promote.

Alliance Israélite Universelle \äl-'yäⁿs-is-rä-el-'ēt-ᵫ-nē-ver-'sel\ Political organization founded in France in 1860 for the purpose of providing assistance to Jews. Its founders were a group of French Jews who had the resources to help those who were poor, offering political support, helping individuals emigrate, and eventually setting up Jewish education programs in eastern Europe, the Middle East, and North Africa. In 1945 it expressed support for political ZIONISM, and in 1946 its diplomatic activities were taken over by the Consultative Council of Jewish Organizations in New York City.

Allied Powers *or* **Allies** Nations allied in opposition to the CENTRAL POWERS in WORLD WAR I or to the AXIS POWERS in WORLD WAR II. The original Allies in World War I—the British empire, France, and the Russian empire—were later joined by many other countries, including Portugal, Japan, and Italy. Nations joining the Allies after 1917, including the U.S., were called Associated Powers, a term emphasized by Pres. WOODROW WILSON to preserve the U.S.'s free hand in the war. In World War II, the major Allied Powers were Britain, France, the Soviet Union, the U.S., and China. More generally, the Allies included all the wartime members of the UNITED NATIONS, the 1942 signatories to the Declaration of the U.N.

alligator Either of two species of long-snouted reptiles constituting the genus *Alligator* (family Alligatoridae, order Crocodilia). Alligators differ from CROCODILES in snout shape and tooth placement. Living in large bodies of water such as lakes, swamps, and rivers, these lizardlike carnivores use their powerful tail for defense and swimming. The eyes, ears, and nostrils, located on top of the long head, project above the water's surface. Alligators dig burrows in which they shelter from danger and hibernate in cold weather. The once-endangered American alligator of the southeastern U.S. may grow to 19 ft (5.7 m) long but usually ranges from 6 to 12 ft (2–3.5 m). The Chinese alligator of the Chang (Yangtze) River region, which grows to 5 ft (1.5 m), is considered endangered or extinct. See photograph opposite.

Allingham \'al-iŋ-əm\, **Margery (Louise)** (1904–1966) British detective-story writer. She published her first story at 8, her first novel at 19, and her first detective story in her early 20s. Her stories about the fictional detective Albert Campion became very popular, and such novels as *Tiger in the Smoke* (1952) and *The China Governess* (1962), with their intellectual style and psychological insight, helped win detective fiction consideration as a serious literary genre.

alliteration *or* **head rhyme** Repetition of consonant sounds in two or more neighboring words or syllables. A frequently used poetic device, it is often discussed with assonance (the repetition of stressed vowel sounds within words with different end consonants) and consonance (the repetition of end or medial consonants).

allium Any plant of a large genus *(Allium)* of bulbous, onion- or garlic-scented herbs of the LILY FAMILY, including the ONION, GARLIC, CHIVE, LEEK, and SHALLOT. *Allium* species are found in most regions of the world except the tropics and New Zealand and Australia. Some are cultivated as ornamental border plants.

allocation of resources Apportionment of productive assets among different uses. The issue of resource allocation arises as societies seek to balance limited resources (CAPITAL, LABOR, LAND) against the various and often unlimited wants of their members. Mechanisms of resource allocation include the price system in free-market economies and government planning in state-run economies or in the public sectors of mixed economies. The aim is always to allocate resources in such as way as to obtain the maximum possible output from a given combination of resources.

Allosaurus \,al-ə-'sȯr-əs\ Large carnivorous dinosaur of a group similar to the TYRANNOSAURS, found as fossils primarily in Late Jurassic rocks of North America. It weighed 2 tons (1,800 kg) and grew to 35 ft (10.5 m) long. Its well-developed tail, half of its total body length, probably functioned as a counterbalance for the body. *Allosaurus* walked on its two hind limbs and probably used the much smaller forelimbs for grasping. Equipped with powerful, flexible jaws, allosaurs likely preyed on medium-sized dinosaurs; they were possibly scavengers that hunted in groups. Some related allosaurs (*Giganotosaurus, Carcharodonotosaurus*) may have been larger than *Tyrannosaurus rex.*

allosteric control \,a-lō-'ster-ik\ Inhibition or activation of an ENZYME by a small regulatory molecule that interacts with the enzyme at a site (allosteric site) other than the active site (at which catalytic activity occurs). The interaction changes the shape of the enzyme, thus affecting the active site of the usual complex between the enzyme and its substrate (the substance on which the enzyme acts). As a result, the enzyme's ability to catalyze a reaction (see CATALYSIS) is either inhibited or enhanced. If the regulatory molecule inhibits an enzyme in the pathway of its own synthesis, the control is said to be FEEDBACK INHIBITION. Allosteric control enables the cell to regulate needed substances rapidly.

allotrope \'a-lə-,trōp\ Any of two or more forms of the same chemical ELEMENT. They may have different arrangements of ATOMS in CRYSTALS of the solid—for example, GRAPHITE and DIAMOND for CARBON—or different numbers of atoms in their MOLECULES—for example, ordinary OXYGEN (O_2) and OZONE (O_3). Other elements that have allotropes include TIN, SULFUR, ANTIMONY, ARSENIC, SELENIUM, and PHOSPHORUS.

Alligator (*Alligator mississippiensis*).
P. MORRIS—WOODFIN CAMP AND ASSOCIATES

alloy Metallic substance composed of two or more elements, as either a mixture, compound, or solid solution. The components of alloys are ordinarily themselves METALS, though CARBON is an essential nonmetal component of STEEL. Alloys are usually produced by melting the mixture of ingredients. The value of alloys was discovered in very ancient times; BRASS (copper and zinc) and BRONZE (copper and tin) were especially important. Today the most important are the alloy steels, which have a wide range of special properties, including hardness, toughness, corrosion resistance, magnetizability, and workability.

Allport, Gordon W(illard) (1897–1967) U.S. psychologist. Born in Montezuma, Ind., he taught at Harvard University 1930–67, becoming noted for his theory of personality, which focused on the adult self rather than on childhood or infantile emotions and experiences, set forth in such books as *Personality* (1937). In *The Nature of Prejudice* (1954) he made important contributions to the analysis of prejudice.

allspice Tropical EVERGREEN tree *(Pimenta diocia)* of the MYRTLE family, native to the West Indies and Central America and valued for its berries, the source of a highly aromatic spice. Allspice was so named because the flavor of the dried berry resembles a combination of cloves, cinnamon, and nutmeg. It is widely used in baking. The name is applied to several other aromatic shrubs as well, including Carolina allspice *(Calycanthus floridus)*, Japanese allspice *(Chimonanthus praecox)*, and wild allspice, or SPICEBUSH.

Allspice (*Pimenta diocia*).
J.E. CRUISE

Allston, Washington (1779–1843) U.S. painter and writer. Born on his family's plantation in South Carolina, he studied at Harvard University and at London's Royal Academy with BENJAMIN WEST. He settled in Massachusetts in 1830 and became the most important first-generation U.S. Romantic painter. His large landscapes depicted the mysterious and dramatic aspects of nature. He later relied on mood and reverie in smaller, more dreamlike images. His writings include poetry, a novel, and art theory, published posthumously in *Lectures on Art* (1850).

alluvial deposit Material deposited by rivers. It consists of SILT, SAND, CLAY, and GRAVEL, as well as much organic matter. Alluvial deposits are usually most extensive in the lower part of a river's course, forming floodplains and DELTAS, but they may form at any point where the river overflows its banks or where the flow of a river is checked. They yield very fertile soils, such as those of the deltas of the Mississippi, Nile, Ganges and Brahmaputra, and Huang (Yellow) rivers. They contain most of the world's supply of tin ore, as well as, in some regions, gold, platinum, and gemstones.

Alma-Tadema \'al-mə-'ta-də-mə\, **Lawrence** *later* **Sir Lawrence** (1836–1912) Dutch-British painter. After studies at the Antwerp Academy, he visited Italy (1863) and became enamored of Greco-Roman antiquity and Egyptian archaeology; the ancient world was to provide his primary themes. He settled in London in 1870. He excelled at the accurate re-creation of ancient scenes, exotic costumes, and the sensuous depiction of beautiful women against backgrounds of marble, bronze, and silk. His figurative images combined sentimentality and anecdote. He enjoyed immense popularity and flaunted a sumptuous personal style. He was elected to the Royal Academy in 1879 and knighted in 1899. His success encouraged several imitators, but his work went out of favor after his death, only to be revived in the late 20th century.

Almagest \'al-mə-ˌjest\ Astronomical and mathematical encyclopedia compiled c. AD 140 by PTOLEMY. It served as the basic guide for Arab and European astronomers until the 17th century. The name derives from the Arabic for "the greatest." Its 13 books cover such topics as the geocentric (earth-centered), or Ptolemaic, plan of the solar system; eclipses; the coordinates and sizes of certain fixed stars; and the distances to the sun and the moon.

Almagro \äl-'mä-grō\, **Diego de** (1475–1538) Spanish soldier who played a leading role in the Spanish conquest of Peru. Following service in the Spanish navy, he arrived in South America in 1524 and, with FRANCISCO PIZARRO, led the expedition that conquered the INCA empire in what is now Peru. Bitter enmity arose between the two men, and Almagro imprisoned Pizarro's two brothers for insubordination during an Indian rebellion. Pizarro then defeated Almagro's army and had his former friend put to death.

almanac Book or table containing a calendar of a given year, with a record of various astronomical phenomena, often with weather prognostications, seasonal suggestions for farmers, and other information. The first printed almanac appeared in the mid-15th century. BENJAMIN FRANKLIN began his famous *Poor Richard's* almanacs in 1732. A form of folk literature, 18th-century almanacs furnished useful and entertaining information where reading matter was scarce; a surviving example is the *Old Farmer's Almanac*. Modern almanacs are often annual publications containing statistical, tabular, and general information.

Almaty \əl-'mä-tē\ *or* **Alma-Ata** \əl-'mä-ə-'tä\ City (pop., 1995 est.: 1,150,000), southeastern Kazakhstan. Formerly the capital of Kazakhstan, it lost its capital status in 1995 to Aqmola (now ASTANA). The modern city was founded in 1854 when the Russians established a military fortification on the site of the ancient city of Almaty, destroyed by the MONGOLS in the 13th century. With the coming of the railroad in 1930, its population grew rapidly. In World War II, heavy industry expanded widely as factories were evacuated to the site from Russian Europe. The city remains a major industrial center.

Almendros \äl-'men-drōs\, **Nestor** (1930–1992) Spanish cinematographer. In 1948 he emigrated from Spain to Cuba, where he worked with documentary filmmakers. After moving to France in 1961, he collaborated with ERIC ROHMER on *My Night at Maud's* (1969) and *Claire's Knee* (1970) and with FRANCOIS TRUFFAUT on *The Wild Child* (1970). His many films in the U.S. include *Days of Heaven* (1978, Academy Award), *The Last Metro* (1980), *Sophie's Choice* (1982), and *Billy Bathgate* (1991).

Almohad dynasty \'al-mō-ˌhad\ (1130–1269) Dynasty created by a BERBER confederation born out of religious opposition to the Islam of the ALMORAVIDS. The Almohad leader, Ibn Tumart, began his rebellion in the 1120s. Marrakech was captured in 1147 under the leadership of his successor ABD AL-MUMIN. By the 1170s all of the MAGHREB was under unified control for the only time in its history, and the Almohads also controlled Muslim Spain. Their rule was marked by, on the one hand, the cultivation of science and philosophy, and, on the other, efforts at religious unification by compelling Jews and Christians to convert or leave. They lost control of Spain to the Christians in 1212, and their North African provinces to the Hafsid dynasty in Tunis (1236) and the MARINIDS in Marrakech (1269).

almond Tree *(Prunus dulcis)* in the ROSE family, native to South Asia; also its edible seed, or NUT. The tree, growing somewhat larger and living longer than the PEACH, is strikingly beautiful when in flower. The nuts are either sweet or bitter. Sweet almonds are the edible type consumed as nuts and used in cooking. The extracted oil of bitter almonds is used to make flavoring extracts for foods and liqueurs. Almonds provide small amounts of protein, iron, calcium, phosphorus, and B vitamins and are high in fat. They are commonly used in confectionery baking and in marzipan, a traditional European candy.

Almoravid dynasty \ˌal-mə-'rä-vəd\ BERBER dynasty that succeeded the FATIMID DYNASTY in the MAGHREB. It flourished in the 11th and early 12th century. Its founder, Abdallah ibn Yasin, was a religious scholar who used religious reform as his means to gain followers in the mid-11th century. As the Fatimids lost political control in the aftermath of the Arab invasion, the Almoravids took over Morocco, the rest of the Maghrib, and eventually Muslim Spain. By 1082 their rule reached ALGIERS. By 1110 they also controlled Muslim Spain, but the Christians began to win back territory in 1118. In the 1120s the ALMOHADS began their rebellion, eventually displacing the Almoravids.

aloe Any shrubby SUCCULENT plant of the genus *Aloe* in the LILY FAMILY, containing about 200 species native to Africa. Most aloes have a rosette of leaves at the base but no stem. Several species are cultivated as ornamentals. The juice of some species, especially the popular pot plant known as true aloe *(Aloe vera)*, is used as an ingredient in cosmetics, as a purgative, and as a treatment for burns.

aloe, American See CENTURY PLANT

Alonso, Alicia *orig.* **Alicia Martínez Hoyo** (born 1921) Cuban ballerina, choreographer, and director. She studied in Havana and New York, where she danced with the Ballet (later AMERICAN BALLET) THEATRE

(1940–41, 1943–48, 1950–55, 1958–59). In 1948 she formed her own company, Ballet Alicia Alonso (renamed Ballet Nacional de Cuba in 1959), with which she performed frequently on tour in Latin America. Despite failing eyesight, she continued for many years to dance leading roles as a guest artist with the American Ballet Theatre and other companies.

Alp-Arslan \'älp-är-'slän\ (c. 1030–1072/73) Second sultan of the SELJUQ DYNASTY who added Georgia, Armenia, and much of Asia Minor to his domains of KHORASAN and western Iran. He preferred conquest to governing, and left the administration of his empire to his vizier, NIZAM AL-MULK. In 1071 his victory over the Byzantines resulted for the first time in a Byzantine emperor being held captive by the Muslims. Alp-Arslan's Byzantine expeditions paved the way for the Turkish conquest of Asia Minor. He died a year later when mortally wounded by a prisoner during a quarrel.

alpaca \al-'pa-kə\ South American species *(Lama pacos)* in the CAMEL family (Camelidae); closely related to the GUANACO, LLAMA, and VICUÑA, known collectively as lamoids. Domesticated several thousand years ago by Indians of the Andes Mtns., the alpaca has a slender body, a long neck and legs, a small head, a short tail, and large, pointed ears. Alpacas stand about 35 in. (90 cm) at the shoulder and weigh 120–145 lbs (54–65 kg). They are found in central and southern Peru and western Bolivia, on marshy ground at high altitudes. They are the most important of the lamoids for wool production.

Alpha Centauri Triple star in the constellation Centaurus, the faintest component of which, Proxima Centauri, is currently the closest star to the sun (about 4.3 light-years away). The two brighter components are about 0.1 light-year farther from the sun. As seen from earth, the system is the third brightest star (after SIRIUS and Canopus); Proxima is indistinguishable as a separate star to the unaided eye. Alpha Centauri can be seen from the earth's surface only from points south of about 40° northern latitude.

alpha decay Type of radioactive disintegration (see RADIOACTIVITY) in which some unstable atomic nuclei dissipate excess energy by spontaneously ejecting an alpha particle. Alpha particles have two positive charges and a MASS of four atomic mass units; they are identical to helium nuclei. Though they are emitted at speeds about one-tenth that of light, they are not very penetrating and have ranges in air of about 1–4 in. (2.5–10 cm). Alpha decay commonly occurs in elements with ATOMIC NUMBERS greater than 83 (bismuth), but can occur in some rare-earth elements in the atomic-number range of 60 (neodymium) to 71 (lutetium). Alpha decay HALF-LIVES range from about a microsecond (10^{-6} second) to billions of years (10^{17} seconds).

alphabet Set of symbols or characters that represent language's sounds in WRITING. Each character usually represents a simple VOWEL, a diphthong (two vowels), or one or two CONSONANTS. A writing system in which one character represents a whole syllable is called a syllabary. The first alphabet is believed to have been the North Semitic, which originated in the eastern Mediterranean region between 1700 and 1500 BC. Alphabets that arose in the next 500 years included the Canaanite and Aramaic, from which the modern Hebrew and Arabic alphabets descended, and the Greek (ancestor of the LATIN ALPHABET), considered the first true alphabet because it includes both CONSONANTS and VOWELS. Scholars have attempted to establish an exact correspondence between each sound and its symbol in new alphabets such as the INTERNATIONAL PHONETIC ALPHABET.

Alpheus River \al-'fē-əs\ River, southern Greece. About 75 mi (120 km) long, it is the longest river in the PELOPONNESE. It rises in Arcadia and flows northwest through southern Elias into the Ionian Sea. OLYMPIA is on its northern bank. It shares its name with the ancient river god, and it figures in Greek legend, including Hercules' cleaning of the Augean stables, and in SAMUEL TAYLOR COLERIDGE's poem "Kubla Khan."

Alpine orogeny \ō-'rä-jə-nē\ Mountain-building event that affected a broad segment of southern Europe and the Mediterranean region during the middle TERTIARY PERIOD. It produced intense METAMORPHISM, crumpling of rock strata, and uplift accompanied by faulting. It was responsible for the elevation of the present Alps, from which the name derives, the uplifting of plateaus in the Balkan Peninsula and in Corsica and Sardinia, and volcanic activity in England, France, Iceland, and parts of Italy.

Alpine skiing Class of competitive ski events consisting of SLALOM and downhill racing. The latter includes speed events contested in single runs down longer, steeper, faster courses, with fewer turns, than those featured in the technical, or slalom, events. Alpine events were first included in the Olympic Games in 1936. See also CROSS-COUNTRY SKIING, NORDIC SKIING.

Alps Mountain system, southern central Europe. The Alps extend in a crescent about 750 mi (1,200 km) from the Mediterranean coast between France and Italy to Vienna, and cover more than 80,000 sq mi (207,000 sq km). Several peaks rise above 10,000 ft (3,000 m); the highest is Mont BLANC. The Alps form a divide between the Atlantic, the Mediterranean, and the Black Sea, and give rise to several major European rivers, including the RHÔNE, DANUBE, and PO. Glaciers cover about 1,500 sq mi (3,900 sq km), mostly at elevations above 10,000 ft (3,000 m). The ST. GOTTHARD PASS is one of the Alps' notable tunnels. GRENOBLE, INNSBRUCK, and Bolzano are major alpine cities.

Alsace-Lorraine \al-'sas-lō-'rān\ Area, eastern France. It is now usually considered to include the present-day French departments of Haut-Rhin, Bas-Rhin, and Moselle. The area was ceded by France to Germany in 1871 after the FRANCO-PRUSSIAN WAR. It was returned to France after World War I, occupied by the Germans in World War II, then again restored to France. French prewar governmental policies that had clashed with the region's particularism have since been modified. The German dialect known as Alsatian remains the lingua franca, and both French and German are taught in the schools.

Alsatian See GERMAN SHEPHERD

Altai Mountains *Russian* **Altay** \al-'tī\ *Chinese* **Altay Shan** \al-'tī-'shän\ *Mongol* **Altayn Nuruu** Mountain system, central Asia. The mountains extend about 1,200 mi (2,000 km) southeast-northwest from the GOBI DESERT to the western Siberian plain, through Chinese, Mongolian, Russian, and Kazakh territory. The highest point is the Russian peak Belukha, at approx. 15,000 ft (4,600 m). The mountains are the source of the IRTYSH and OB rivers, and are notable for their mining and hydroelectrical potential.

Altaic languages \al-'tā-ik\ Group of about 40 languages, comprising the TURKIC, MONGOLIAN, and MANCHU-TUNGUS families, spoken across Eurasia by more than 140 million people (the overwhelming majority of whom speak Turkic languages). Most scholars consider Altaic itself to be a family, of proven genetic relationship, though a minority attribute similarities in the languages to borrowings and areal convergence. A still remoter relationship with KOREAN and JAPANESE is regarded by some as probable though not yet demonstrated, while some see Altaic as a component of the huge NOSTRATIC phylum.

Altamira \,al-tə-'mir-ə\ Cave near SANTANDER, northern Spain, famous for its magnificent prehistoric paintings and engravings dating to 14,000–12,000 BC, first described in 1880. The cave is 890 ft (270 m) long. The roof of the main chamber is covered with paintings, chiefly of bison, in vivid red, black, and violet. There are also wild boars, horses, a hind, and other figures in a simpler style, as well as eight engraved anthropomorphic figures and various handprints and hand outlines. Engraved artifacts and other material remains suggest that the site may have been a center for seasonal gatherings. See also MAGDALENIAN CULTURE, ROCK ART.

Altan \'äl-tän\ *or* **Anda** \'än-dä\ (died 1583) Mongol KHAN who terrorized China in the 16th century. He established a Chinese-style government in his homeland and concluded a peace treaty with MING-DYNASTY China in 1571. He converted the MONGOLS to the reformed, or DGE-LUGS-PA, sect of Tibetan Buddhism. In 1578 Altan granted the head of the sect the title of DALAI LAMA. With Mongol military aid, later Dalai Lamas crushed the more established Karma-pa (Red or Black Hat) sect in Tibet to become Tibet's spiritual and temporal rulers. See also GTSANG DYNASTY.

altar Raised structure or place used for sacrifice, worship, or prayer. Altars probably originated with the belief that objects or places (e.g., a tree or spring) were inhabited by spirits or deities worthy of prayers or gifts. SACRIFICE to deities required a structure on which the victim could be killed and blood channeled off or flesh burned. In ancient Israel, the altar was a rectangular stone with a hollowed-out basin on top. The ancient Greeks placed altars (see BAETYLUS) in homes, marketplaces, public buildings, and sacred groves. Roman altars were similarly ubiquitous and were often decorated with relief sculptures. Christians at first did not use altars, but by the 3rd century the table on which the EUCHARIST was celebrated was regarded as an altar. It became the focus of the MASS in Christian churches and in Western churches was often adorned by a BALDACHIN and an ALTARPIECE.

altarpiece Painting, relief, sculpture, screen, or decorated wall standing on or behind an altar in a Christian church. The images depict holy personages, saints, and biblical subjects. There are two types of altarpieces: the reredos, which rises from the floor behind the altar, and the retable, which stands on the altar itself or on a pedestal behind it. The diptych is an altarpiece consisting of two panels; a triptych, three panels; and a polyptych, four or more panels. Altarpieces vary in size; some are small and portable, some are huge and stationary, and some have movable wings that can be opened and closed. The practice of erecting sculptural altarpieces dates from the 11th century; altar paintings became common in the 14th century.

Altdorfer \'ält-ˌdȯr-fər\, **Albrecht** (c. 1480–1538) German painter and printmaker. He was the leading artist of the DANUBE SCHOOL. Most of his works depict religious subjects, but he was one of the first artists to develop landscape painting as an independent genre, specializing in sunset lighting and ruins in twilight. His drawings demonstrate these skills in black with white highlights on dark paper. The influence of ALBRECHT DURER is evident in his miniature engravings and woodcuts. From 1526 until his death he was town architect of Regensburg; no architectural work of his is known to have survived.

Alte Pinakothek \'äl-tə-ˌpē-nä-kō-'tek\ (German: "Old Museum of Painting") Art museum, one of several collections within the Bavarian State Picture Galleries in Munich and one of the great museums of the world. It specializes in European painting from the Middle Ages through the late 18th century; its core collections once belonged to several early Bavarian electors palatine. The building is a 1957 reconstruction of the original 19th-century gallery, destroyed in World War II. Other state museums include the Neue ("New") Pinakothek, based on the private collections of Bavarian kings of 18th–20th-century European paintings and sculpture; the Schack Gallery collection of late-Romantic German painting; and the State Gallery of Modern Art.

alternating current (AC) Flow of ELECTRIC CHARGE that reverses periodically, unlike DIRECT CURRENT. It starts from zero, grows to a maximum, decreases to zero, reverses, reaches a maximum in the opposite direction, returns again to zero, and repeats the cycle indefinitely. The time taken to complete one cycle is called the period (see PERIODIC MOTION), and the number of cycles per second is the FREQUENCY; the maximum value in either direction is the current's amplitude. Low frequencies (50–60 cycles per second) are used for domestic and commercial power, but frequencies of around 100 million cycles per second (100 megahertz) are used in television and of several thousand megahertz in RADAR and MICROWAVE communication. A major advantage of alternating current is that the voltage can be increased and decreased by a transformer for more efficient transmission over long distances. Direct current cannot use transformers to change voltage. See also ELECTRIC CURRENT.

alternation of generations In biology, alternation of a sexual phase (GAMETOPHYTE) and a nonsexual phase (SPOROPHYTE) in the life cycle of an organism. The two phases, or generations, are often distinct in structure, and sometimes in CHROMOSOME makeup. Alternation of generations is common in ALGAE, fungi (see FUNGUS), MOSSES, FERNS, and SEED PLANTS. The character and extent of the two phases vary greatly among different groups of plants and algae. During the course of evolution, the gametophyte stage has been progressively reduced. Thus in higher (VASCULAR) plants, the sporophyte is the dominant phase; in more primitive, nonvascular plants the gametophyte is dominant. Among animals, many invertebrates (e.g., PROTOZOANS, jellyfish, flatworms) have an alternation of sexual and asexual generations.

alternative education Education that diverges in some way from that offered by conventional schools. Publicly funded schools, private schools, and homeschooling curricula may all be alternative. The focus may be on alternative structures (e.g., open classrooms), alternative subject matter (e.g., religious instruction), or alternative relationships (e.g., more informal relations between students and teachers or between students of different ages). Alternative education aims to supply what is seen to be lacking in conventional education, whether moral or ethical principles or recognition of children's individual learning styles and innate creativity.

alternative energy Any of various renewable POWER sources to use in place of FOSSIL FUELS and URANIUM. Fusion devices (see NUCLEAR FUSION) are believed by some to be the best long-term option, because their primary energy source would be DEUTERIUM, abundant in ordinary water. Other technologies include SOLAR ENERGY, WIND POWER, tidal power, wave power, HYDROELECTRIC POWER, and GEOTHERMAL ENERGY. The amount of energy in such renewable and virtually pollution-free sources is large in relation to world energy needs, yet at present only a small portion of it can be converted to electric power at reasonable cost.

alternative medicine *or* **complementary medicine** Any of a broad range of healing approaches not used in conventional Western medicine. Many are holistic (see HOLISTIC MEDICINE); many also emphasize prevention and education. Alternative therapies include ACUPUNCTURE, AROMATHERAPY, AYURVEDA medicine, CHINESE MEDICINE, CHIROPRACTIC, herbal medicine, HOMEOPATHY, MASSAGE, MEDITATION, naturopathy, therapeutic touch, and YOGA. Though considered alternative in the West, such medicine is the main source of health care for up to 80% of people in less-developed countries. Some alternative-medicine practices are useless or harmful; others are effective and may offer treatments in areas where conventional approaches have not succeeded (e.g., chronic disorders).

alternator Source of direct ELECTRIC CURRENT in modern vehicles for ignition, lights, fans, and other uses. The electric power is generated by an alternator mechanically coupled to the engine, with a rotor field coil supplied with current through slip rings, and a stator with a three-phase winding. A rectifier converts the power from alternating to direct form. A regulator ensures that the output voltage is properly matched to the battery voltage as engine speed varies. An inductor alternator is a special kind of synchronous generator in which both the field and the output winding are on the stator.

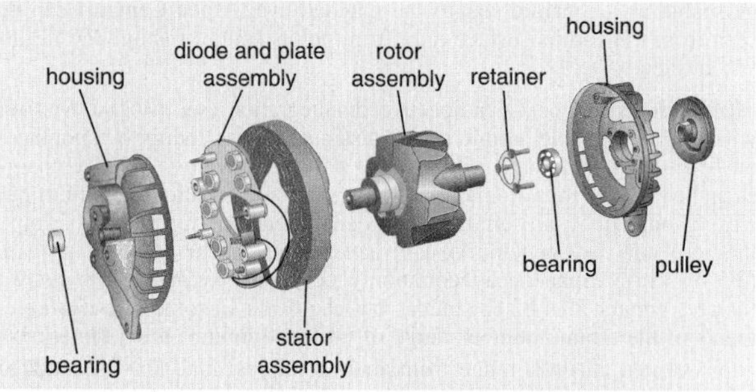

Exploded view of an automotive alternator. The engine's turning crankshaft, connected to the alternator's pulley by a belt, turns the magnetic rotor inside the stationary stator assembly, generating an alternating current. The diode assembly rectifies the alternating current, producing direct current, which is used to meet the demands of the vehicle's electrical system, including recharging the battery.

Altgeld, John Peter (1847–1902) U.S. (German-born) politician, governor of Illinois (1893–97). He emigrated from Germany as a child and in the 1870s moved to Chicago, where he became wealthy in real estate and active in Democratic Party politics. In 1892 he won the governorship as a reformist candidate. In 1893, at the insistence of CLARENCE DARROW and labor leaders, he pardoned participants in the HAYMARKET RIOT. The controversial pardon provoked an outcry from conservatives and contributed to his defeat for reelection in 1896, though Altgeld's decision later gained wide approval in judicial circles.

altimeter \al-'tim-ət-ər\ Instrument that measures the altitude of the land surface or of any object, such as an airplane. The mechanical pressure altimeter measures atmospheric pressure relative to sea level through a series of bellows, gears, and springs, which move pointers on a dial. Radio altimeters measure the distance of an aircraft above the ground rather than above sea level by indicating the time a pulse of RADIO energy takes to travel from the aircraft to the ground and back; they are used in automatic navigation and blind-landing systems.

Altiplano \ˌal-ti-'plä-nō\ Region, southeastern Peru and western Bolivia. Comprising a series of high plains, it originates northwest of Lake TITICACA in southern Peru and extends southeast to southwestern Bolivia.

The region's wildlife originally included the alpaca and the llama, both now bred for wool. The cities of Puno and Julaca (Peru) and LA PAZ (Bolivia) lie along the shores of Lake Titicaca. The area has been populated since ancient times.

altitude and azimuth \'az-məth\ Two coordinates describing the position of an object above earth in a COORDINATE SYSTEM called the altazimuth, or horizon, system, and used in astronomy, gunnery, navigation, surveying, and other fields. Altitude in this sense is expressed as angle of elevation (up to 90°) above the horizon. Azimuth, in astronomical measurement, is the number of degrees clockwise from due north to the point on the horizon most directly below the object.

altitude sickness *or* **mountain sickness** Acute reaction to a change from low altitudes to altitudes above 8,000 ft (2,400 m). Most people gradually adapt, but some have a severe reaction that can be fatal unless they return to low altitude. Normal adaptations to the reduced oxygen at high altitude (e.g., breathlessness, racing heartbeat) are exaggerated; other manifestations include headache, gastrointestinal upsets, and weakness. Pulmonary EDEMA is quickly reversed with oxygen and evacuation to a lower area.

Altman \'ȯlt-mən\, **Robert (B.)** (born 1925) U.S. film director. Born in Kansas City, he learned filmmaking by directing industrial films, then directed several television series before making his first feature film, *Countdown* (1967). The successful antiwar comedy *M*A*S*H* (1970) established his reputation as an independent director whose work emphasizes character and atmosphere over plot. His other films include *Brewster McCloud* (1970), *McCabe and Mrs. Miller* (1971), *Nashville* (1976), *Popeye* (1980), the critically acclaimed *The Player* (1992), *Short Cuts* (1993), *The Gingerbread Man* (1998), and *Cookie's Fortune* (1999).

Altman, Sidney (born 1939) Canadian-U.S. molecular biologist. Born in Montreal, he studied at MIT and the University of Colorado and has taught at Yale University since 1971. Working independently, Altman and THOMAS CECH discovered that RNA, previously believed to be simply a passive carrier of genetic codes between different parts of the living cell, could also initiate and carry out (i.e., catalyze) some reactions, opening up new fields of research and biotechnology. The two shared the 1989 Nobel Prize for Chemistry.

alto *or* **contralto** Voice or register that extends approximately from the F below middle C to the second D above. The second-highest part in four-part music, it is normally sung by women. The name derives from *contratenor altus,* the part above the tenor part. It is used for some instruments that play principally in the alto range (alto saxophone, alto flute, etc.).

Altona Former city, Germany. It was a fishing village when it passed to Denmark in 1640. It grew into a city, and was granted customs privileges with the intention of making it a rival to HAMBURG. Despite the NAPOLEONIC WARS, it prospered until 1853, when it lost its privileges. Altona was occupied in 1864 and became Prussian in 1866; in 1937 it was incorporated into Hamburg.

altruism Ethical theory that regards the good of others as the end of moral action; by extension, the disposition to take the good of others as an end in itself. The term (French, *altruisme,* derived from Latin *alter:* "other") was coined in the 19th century by AUGUSTE COMTE and adopted generally as a convenient antithesis to EGOISM. Most altruists have held that each person has an obligation to further the pleasures and alleviate the pains of other people. The same argument holds if happiness, rather than pleasure, is taken as the end of life.

alum \'a-ləm\ Inorganic compound, any of a class of hydrated double SALTS, usually consisting of ALUMINUM sulfate, water of hydration (an essential part of the CRYSTAL makeup), and the SULFATE of another element. The most important alums are those of potassium sulfate (potassium alum, or potash alum, $K_2SO_4 \cdot Al_2(SO_4)_3 \cdot 24H_2O$), ammonium sulfate, and sodium sulfate. Alums occur naturally in various minerals and can be prepared and purified by crystallization from their solutions. Most are white crystals with an astringent, acid taste. They are used as paper-sizing agents, flocculating agents in water treatment, mordants in dyeing, and in pickles, baking powder, fire extinguishers, and medicines.

aluminum Metallic chemical ELEMENT, chemical symbol Al, atomic number 13. A lightweight, silvery-white METAL, it is so reactive chemically that it always occurs in compounds. It is the most abundant metallic element in the earth's crust, chiefly in BAUXITE (its principal ORE), FELDSPARS, MICAS, CLAY MINERALS, and LATERITE. It also occurs in gemstones, such as TOPAZ, GARNET, and chrysoberyl; EMERY, CORUNDUM, RUBY, and SAPPHIRE are crystalline aluminum OXIDE. Aluminum was first isolated in 1825, became commercially available in the late 19th century, and is now the most widely used metal after IRON. Its surface oxidizes at once to a hard, tough film, deterring further corrosion. Uses include building and construction, corrosion-resistant chemical equipment, auto parts, power transmission lines, photoengraving plates, magnets, and tubes for ointments and pastes. Important compounds include ALUMS; alumina (aluminum oxide), useful as corundum and as a carrier for many catalysts; aluminum chloride, a widely used catalyst for organic syntheses; and aluminum hydroxide, used to waterproof fabrics.

Alvarado \ˌäl-vä-'rä-t͟hō\, **Pedro de** (1485?–1541) Spanish soldier and colonial administrator. In 1519 he accompanied the army led by HERNAN CORTES that conquered Mexico. In 1522 he became the first mayor of Tenochtitlán (Mexico City). In 1523 he conquered the native peoples of Guatemala and founded the city (modern Antigua) that became the first capital of the Guatemala region, which later included much of Central America. He was governor of Guatemala 1527–31. In 1539 he began an exploration of central Mexico, but died while quelling an Indian uprising.

Alvarez \'al-və-ˌrez\, **Luis W(alter)** (1911–1988) U.S. experimental physicist. Born in San Francisco, he joined the faculty of UC-Berkeley in 1936, where he would remain until 1978. In 1938 he discovered that some radioactive elements decay when an orbital electron merges with the atom's nucleus, producing an element with an atomic number smaller by 1, a form of beta decay. In 1939 he and Felix Bloch (1905–1983) made the first measurement of the magnetic moment of the neutron. During World War II he developed a radar guidance system for landing aircraft and participated in the Manhattan Project to develop the atomic bomb. He later helped construct the first proton linear accelerator and constructed the liquid hydrogen bubble chamber. With his son, the geologist Walter Alvarez (born 1940), he helped develop the theory that links the dinosaurs' extinction with a giant asteroid or comet impact. For work that included the discovery of many subatomic particles, he received a Nobel Prize in 1968.

Luis Alvarez.

BY COURTESY OF THE LAWRENCE RADIATION LABORATORY, THE UNIVERSITY OF CALIFORNIA, BERKELEY

alveolus See PULMONARY ALVEOLUS

Alzheimer's disease \'älts-ˌhī-mərz\ Degenerative brain disorder of middle to late adult life that destroys neurons and connections in the CEREBRAL CORTEX, resulting in significant loss of brain mass. The most common form of DEMENTIA, Alzheimer's disease progresses from short-term memory impairment to further memory loss; deterioration of language, perceptual, and motor skills; mood instability; and, in advanced stages, unresponsiveness, with loss of mobility and control of body functions; death typically ensues in 5–10 years. Originally described in 1906 by the German neuropathologist Alois Alzheimer (1864–1915) in a 55-year-old and regarded as a presenile dementia, Alzheimer's disease is now recognized as accounting for much of the SENILE DEMENTIA once thought normal with aging. The 10% of cases that begin before age 60 result from an inherited mutation. Neuritic plaques and neurofibrillary tangles in the brain on autopsy are the primary features used for diagnosis. No cure has been found. Most treatment targets the depression, behavioral problems, and sleeplessness that often accompany the disease.

AM *in full* **amplitude modulation** Variation of the amplitude of a carrier wave (commonly a RADIO WAVE) in correspondence to fluctuations in the audio or video signal being transmitted. AM is the oldest method of broadcasting radio programs. Commercial AM stations operate in the frequency range of 535 kilohertz (kHz) to 1605 kHz. Because radio waves of these frequencies are reflected back to the earth's surface by the ionosphere, they can be detected by receivers hundreds of miles away. In addition to commercial radio broadcasting, AM is also employed in short-wave radio broadcasts, and in transmitting the video portion of television programs. See also FM.

AMA See AMERICAN MEDICAL ASSN.

Amadeus VI \ˌam-ə-ˈdā-əs\ *known as* **Amadeus the Green Count** (1334–1383) Count of SAVOY (1343–83). Ruler of Savoy from age 9, he significantly extended his kingdom's territory and power. By the 1350s, after adding lands on the Italian side, he held nearly the entire western Alps. He joined a crusade against the Turks (1366) and restored JOHN V PALAEOLOGUS to the Byzantine throne. A mediator of quarrels among Italian powers, he set out to rescue Queen JOAN I of Naples from her enemies (1382) but died of plague during the expedition.

Amado \ä-ˈmä-dü\, **Jorge** (1912–2001) Brazilian novelist. Born and reared on a cacao plantation, he published his first novel at 20. His early works, including *The Violent Land* (1942), explore the exploitation and suffering of plantation workers. Despite imprisonment and exile for leftist activities, he continued to produce novels, many of which have been banned in Brazil and Portugal. Later works such as *Gabriela, Clove and Cinnamon* (1958), *Dona Flor and Her Two Husbands* (1966), and *The War of the Saints* (1993) preserve Amado's political attitude in their more subtle satire.

Amalfi \ä-ˈmäl-fē\ Town (pop., 1993 est.: 5,600), southern Italy, on the Gulf of Salerno. It was of little importance until the mid-6th century, when it fell under Byzantine control. It grew into one of the first Italian maritime republics in the 9th century, becoming a rival of VENICE and GENOA. Annexed by ROGER II of Sicily in 1131, it was sacked by PISA in 1135 and 1137 and rapidly declined in importance, though its maritime code, the Tavola Amalfitano, was recognized in the Mediterranean until 1570. Amalfi is now a notable tourist resort.

amalgam \ə-ˈmal-gəm\ ALLOY of MERCURY and one or more other METALS. Those of silver, gold, and palladium occur naturally. Those with a very high mercury content are liquid; others are crystalline. Amalgams of silver and tin, with minor amounts of copper and zinc, are used in dentistry to fill teeth. Sodium amalgam is used in manufacturing chlorine and sodium hydroxide by electrolysis of brine. Amalgams are used to recover silver and gold from their ores: The ore is shaken with mercury, the amalgam is separated and heated until the mercury distills off (see DISTILLATION), and the precious metal is the residue. Amalgams are also used to silver mirrors and apply other metal coatings.

Amalric I \ə-ˈmal-rik, ˈam-əl-rik\ (died 1174) King of Jerusalem (1163–74). Amalric was a strong ruler who helped break the unity of Muslims surrounding the Holy Land. He passed a law giving vassals the right to appeal to the High Court against unjust treatment by their lords. His invasion of Egypt (1163) led to a war with Nureddin of Syria, which Amalric lost despite help from MANUEL I COMNENUS. Though the effort to conquer Egypt failed, the Palestinian-Byzantine alliance continued.

Amalric II (c. 1155–1205) King of Cyprus (1194–1205) and of Jerusalem (1198–1205). Amalric inherited the kingdom of Cyprus on the death of his brother, Guy of Lusignan, and formed a close alliance with the ruler of Palestine. He also became the vassal of Holy Roman Emperor HENRY VI. When the ruler of Palestine died, Amalric married his widow and became king of Jerusalem. He administered Jerusalem separately from his other lands and made peace with his Muslim neighbors after SALADIN's death (1193).

Fly agaric (*Amanita muscaria*).
LARRY C. MOON—TOM STACK & ASSOCIATES

amanita \ˌam-ə-ˈnē-tə\ Any MUSHROOM of the genus *Amanita,* containing about 100 species, some of which are poisonous to humans. Among the deadliest of all mushrooms are the large white destroying angels *(A. bispongera, A. ocreata, A. verna,* and *A. virosa),* which are found in forests during wet periods in summer and autumn. The green or brown death cap *(A. phalloides),* also deadly, is found in woods in summer or early autumn. The poisonous fly agaric *(A. muscaria),* found in pastures and fields in summer, was once used as a fly poison. Common edible species include *A. caesarea, A. rubescens,* and *A. vaginata.*

Amar Das \ˈəm-är-ˈdäs\ (1479–1574) Third Sikh GURU. Much revered for his wisdom and piety, he became Guru at age 73. He was noted for his missionary efforts to spread SIKHISM and for the division of the PUNJAB into 22 dioceses. To strengthen the faith, he ordered three great Sikh festivals each year, and he made the city of Goindwal a center of Sikh learning. He extended the casteless *langar* ("community kitchen") and required that anyone wanting to see him must first eat there. Advocating a middle way between the extremes of asceticism and sensuous pleasure, he purified Sikhism of Hindu practices, encouraged intercaste marriages, allowed widows to remarry, and prohibited suttee.

amaranth family \ˈa-mə-ˌranth\ Family Amaranthaceae, which contains about 60 genera and more than 800 species of herbaceous plants and a few shrubs, trees, and vines, native to tropical America and Africa. Globe amaranth *(Gomphrena)* and cockscomb *(Celosia)* are cultivated as ornamentals. The large genus *Amaranthus* contains the ornamentals love-lies-bleeding *(A. caudatus)* and Joseph's-coat *(A. tricolor),* as well as many weedy plants known as pigweed, especially *A. retroflexus.* Some *Amaranthus* species are TUMBLEWEEDS, and some are potential high-protein grain crops.

Amaravati sculpture \ˌä-mə-ˈrä-və-tē\ (fl. c. 2nd century BC–3rd century AD) Style of sculpture found in the Andhra region of southeastern India. Carved in relief on greenish-white limestone, these sculptures depict events in the life of BUDDHA. The compositions are dynamic, sensuous, and dramatic, with overlapping figures and diagonals suggesting depth. The style spread from the Amaravati ruins west to Maharashtra Pradesh, to Sri Lanka (Ceylon), and to much of South Asia. The Amaravati stupa was one of the largest in Buddhist India; it was largely destroyed in the 19th century by building contractors to make lime mortar.

Amarillo City (pop., 1996 est.: 169,000), northern Texas. The chief city of the Texas Panhandle, it originated in 1887 with the coming of the railroad, and grew after 1900 as agriculture became important in the region. The discovery of petroleum and natural gas in the 1920s further promoted its development.

Amarna, Tell el- See TELL EL-AMARNA

amaryllis family \ˌam-ə-ˈril-əs\ Family Amaryllidaceae of the order Liliales, containing about 65 genera and at least 835 species of perennial herbaceous plants, found mostly in tropical and subtropical regions and prized for their showy flowers, which are borne on smooth, hollow stalks with few or no leaves. Many species are cultivated as garden ornamentals. Many tropical lilylike plants also belong to the family, including the genera *Haemanthus* (Cape tulip, or blood lily), *Alstroemeria* (Peruvian lily), and *Hippeastrum.* Some are grown as houseplants.

Amaterasu (Omikami) \ˌam-ə-ˈter-ə-sü\ In SHINTO, the sun goddess from whom the Japanese royal family traditionally claims descent. She was given domain over heaven while her brother, the storm god Susanoo, was set to rule over the sea. The two produced children together, but Susanoo began to behave rudely and destructively, and Amaterasu withdrew in protest into a cave, plunging the world into darkness. She was lured out by the other gods and goddesses and a rope was placed over its entrance to prevent her return. Her chief place of worship is the Grand Shrine of ISE, Shinto's most important shrine.

Amati, Nicola (1596–1684) Italian violin maker. His grandfather, Andrea (before 1511–before 1580), set the form of the modern violin, and his father, Girolamo (1561–1630), gained an international reputation for his instruments. Nicola, who like his forebears worked in Cremona, is regarded as the family's finest craftsman. Among his famous pupils were ANDREA GUARNERI, A. STRADIVARI, and his son Girolamo (1649–1740).

Amazon In GREEK MYTHOLOGY, a member of a race of women warriors. One of the labors of HERACLES was to obtain the girdle of the Amazon queen Hippolyte. In another tale, THESEUS attacked the Amazons, and they responded by invading Attica, where they were defeated; Theseus married the Amazon Antiope. In ancient Greek art, Amazons resembled

Athena (with weapons and helmet) and later Artemis (in a thin dress girded high for speed).

Amazon River *Portuguese* **Rio Amazonas** River, northern South America. It is the largest river in the world in volume and area of drainage basin, and second only to the Nile in length. It originates within 100 mi (160 km) of the Pacific Ocean in the Peruvian Andes and flows almost 4,000 mi (6,400 km) across northern Brazil into the Atlantic Ocean. Its Peruvian length is often called the Marañón; the Brazilian portion to the mouth of the Negro is often called the Solimões. Its more than 1,000 known tributaries rise in the Guiana Highlands, the Brazilian Highlands, and (principally) the Andes; seven are longer than 1,000 mi (1,600 km), and the Madeira is longer than 2,000 mi (3,200 km). The Amazon can accommodate large freighters as far as Manaus, 1,000 mi (1,600 km) upriver. The first European descent was made by Francisco de Orellana in 1541; he is said to have given the river its name after reporting battles with tribes of women, whom he likened to the Amazons. Pedro Teixeira achieved the first ascent in 1637–39, but the river remained little explored until the mid-19th century. Many indigenous peoples originally lived along the river, but they moved inland as exploring parties sought to enslave them. The river was opened to world shipping in the 1860s; traffic increased exponentially with the coming of the rubber trade, which reached its height c. 1910 but soon declined. It is the site of the world's greatest rain forest and hosts an extraordinary diversity of birds and wildlife. Since the 1960s, the effects of economic exploitation on the region's ecology have generated worldwide concern.

Amazonia National Park Park, northern central Brazil, about halfway between Manaus and Belém, along the Tapajós River. Established in 1974, it has gradually expanded to cover about 2.5 million acres (1 million hectares) and contains an immense diversity of flora and fauna.

amban (Manchu: "minister") Representative of China's Qing emperor who lived in the territory of a tributary state or dependency. In 1793 the Qing emperor Qianlong changed the procedure for selecting the Dalai Lama, and the Tibetans had to persuade the amban that they had complied. In 1904, when the British were trying to force Tibet to sign a trade treaty, the amban said he was powerless to negotiate for the Tibetans, an admission that called into question the degree of control China exercised over Tibet. The ambans' role and authority continues to be debated by the Chinese government and advocates of Tibetan independence in the attempt to support their conflicting claims for Tibet's status.

ambassador Highest-ranking diplomatic representative of one government to another or to an international organization. As formally defined and recognized at the Congress of Vienna (1815), ambassadors were originally regarded as personal representatives of their country's chief executive rather than of the whole country, and their rank entitled them to meet personally with the head of state of the host country. Originally, only the principal monarchies exchanged ambassadors; the U.S. did not appoint ambassadors until 1893. Since 1945 all nations have been recognized as equals, and ambassadors or their equivalents are sent to all countries with which diplomatic relations are maintained. Before the development of modern communications, ambassadors were entrusted with extensive powers; they have since been reduced to spokespeople for their foreign offices.

amber Fossil tree resin that occurs as irregular nodules, rods, or droplike shapes in all shades of yellow with nuances of orange, brown, and, rarely, red. Milky-white opaque varieties are called bone amber. Hundreds of species of insects and plants are found as fossils in amber. Deeply colored translucent to transparent amber is prized as gem material, and numerous ornamental carved objects and beads are made from amber. Amber has been found throughout the world, but the largest deposits occur along the shores of the Baltic Sea.

ambergris \'am-bər-ˌgris, 'am-bər-ˌgrē\ Waxy substance (about 80% cholesterol) formed in the intestine of sperm whales, used chiefly as a spice in the East and for fixing the scent of fine perfumes in the West. It is thought to form as a collection of feces around indigestible parts of squid and other prey of the whale. Fresh ambergris is soft, black, and smelly; exposed to sun, air, and seawater, it hardens, fades, and develops a pleasant scent. It may wash ashore or be found floating or in the bodies of slaughtered whales. Pieces are usually small, but the largest have weighed almost 1,000 lbs (450 kg).

amberjack Any of various popular marine game fishes (genus *Seriola*), members of the jack family (Carangidae). Amberjacks are found worldwide. The greater amberjack of the tropical Atlantic is one of the largest jack species, often attaining a length of 6 ft (1.8 m).

Ambler, Eric (1909–1998) British author of espionage and crime novels. Among his early works are *The Dark Frontier* (1936), *Epitaph for a Spy* (1938), *A Coffin for Dimitrios* (1939), and *Journey into Fear* (1940; film, 1942). Following wartime service as a film director for the British Army, he wrote screenplays and such novels as *Judgment on Deltchev* (1951), *The Light of Day* (1962), and *Dirty Story* (1967).

Ambon \äm-'bȯn\ Island of the Moluccas, Indonesia. Located in the Malay Archipelago, it is 31 mi (50 km) long and 10 mi (16 km) wide, with an area of 294 sq mi (761 sq km). Its chief port is also called Ambon (pop., 1990: 277,000). The island is subject to earthquakes and volcanic activity; Mount Salhatu (3,405 ft, or 1,038 m) is its highest point. The clove trade first attracted the Portuguese, who founded a settlement in 1521. The Dutch ousted the Portuguese in 1605, took over the spice trade, and in 1623 killed English settlers in the Amboina Massacre. The British captured Ambon in 1796 and 1810, but it was restored to the Dutch in 1814. It was a separate residency until it was united with Ternate to form the Government of the Moluccas (1927). The Japanese occupied it during World War II. A short-lived independence movement in 1950 was soon suppressed.

Ambrose, St. (339?–397) Bishop of Milan. Born in Gaul, he was raised in Rome and became a Roman provincial governor. As a compromise candidate he was unexpectedly elevated from unbaptized layman to bishop of Milan in 374. He established the medieval concept of the Christian emperor as subject to episcopal advice and censure, and he opposed tolerance for adherents of Arianism. He wrote theological treatises influenced by Greek philosophy, including *On the Holy Spirit* and *On the Duties of Ministers,* as well as a series of hymns. His sermons converted St. Augustine.

St. Ambrose, detail of a fresco by Pinturicchio, 1480s; in Sta. Maria del Popolo, Rome.

Alinari–Art Resource/EB Inc.

AMC See American Motors Corp.

AME Church See African Methodist Episcopal Church

Amelung glass \'am-ə-ləŋ\ U.S. glass produced between 1784 and c. 1795 by John Frederick Amelung. Born in Bremen, Germany, he founded the New Bremen Glassmanufactory in Frederick, Md., with financial support from German and U.S. promoters. He attempted to set up a crafts community, importing glassworkers and other craftsmen from Germany, but the industry failed when Congress defeated Amelung's petition for a loan in 1790. Few authentic pieces of Amelung glass survive, most of them presentation pieces decorated with restrained engraving.

amen Expression of agreement or confirmation used in worship by Jews, Christians, and Muslims. The word derives from a Semitic root meaning "fixed" or "sure." The Greek Old Testament usually translates it as "so be it"; in the English Bible it is often translated as "verily" or "truly." By the 4th century BC, it was a common response to a doxology or other prayer in the Jewish temple liturgy. By the 2nd century AD, Christians had adopted it in the liturgy of the Eucharist, and in Christian worship a final amen now often sums up and confirms a prayer or hymn. Though less common in Islam, it is used after reading of the first sura.

Amen See Amon

Amenemhet I \'ä-mə-nəm-'het\ Egyptian pharaoh (r.1938–1908 BC) who founded the 12th dynasty and, with provincial governors, restored unity to Egypt after the civil war that followed the death of his predecessor, Montuhotep IV. He moved the capital from Thebes to near modern-day al-Lisht, south of Memphis. He extended Egyptian control up the Nile and fortified the delta. Reaffirming the Egyptian monarchy's claim to divinity, he also enlarged the Temple of AMON at Thebes. In 1918 BC he made his son, Sesostris I, his coruler. He was assassinated 10 years later.

Amenhotep II \'ä-mən-'hō-ˌtep\ Egyptian pharaoh (r.1514–1493 BC), son and successor of Ahmose I. Amenhotep extended Egyptian rule southward to the Third Cataract of the Nile while also maintaining rule in the northeast. He pioneered the transition away from pyramidal tombs to rock-cut tombs in the Valley of the Kings in western Thebes. The royal mortuary temples were erected at the edge of the desert during his reign, though the location of his own tomb is unknown.

Amenhotep II offering sacrifices, statue, 15th century BC; in the Egyptian Museum, Cairo.

BY COURTESY OF THE EGYPTIAN MUSEUM; PHOTOGRAPH, HIRMER FOTOARCHIV, MUNCHEN

Amenhotep III Egyptian pharaoh (r.1390–1353 BC) during a time of prosperity. Early in his reign he led a military campaign south of Egypt, but otherwise his rule was peaceful. His reign is noted for the expansion of diplomacy with Syria, Cyprus, Babylon, and Assyria, and the construction of public buildings in Memphis, Thebes, and Nubia, including portions of the temples at Luxor and Karnak. He broke with tradition by marrying Tiy, a commoner, with whom he shared his rule. He was succeeded by his son AKHENATON.

Amenhotep III, head of a statue from western Thebes, c. 1390 BC.

REPRODUCED BY COURTESY OF THE TRUSTEES OF THE BRITISH MUSEUM

Amenhotep IV See AKHENATON

amenorrhea \ˌā-ˌmen-ə-'rē-ə\ Lack of MENSTRUATION. Signs of primary amenorrhea (failure to start menstruating by age 16) include infantile reproductive organs, lack of breasts and pubic hair, dwarfism, and deficient muscle development. In secondary amenorrhea (abnormal cessation of cycles once started), the genitals atrophy and pubic hair diminishes. Not itself a disease, amenorrhea reflects a failure in the balance among the hypothalamus, pituitary gland, ovaries, and uterus; tumors, injuries, or diseases of these can lead to amenorrhea. Other causes include systemic diseases, emotional shock, stress, hormone over- or underproduction, anorexia, absence of ovaries or uterus, pregnancy, lactation, and menopause. Infrequent menstruation or amenorrhea not resulting from organic disease is not harmful.

America See CENTRAL AMERICA, NORTH AMERICA, SOUTH AMERICA

America Online, Inc. (AOL) Company that provides on-line services and Internet access. Founded in 1985 as Quantum Computer Services, it offered E-mail, electronic bulletin boards, and news and information services. It changed its name to America Online in 1991, when it first offered its services to Macintosh and Apple computer users. By the mid 1990s it was the world's largest on-line service, having surpassed rivals CompuServe and Prodigy. In 2000 it had over 20 million members. It went on to acquire CompuServe (1997), Netscape Communications Corp. (1998), Mirabilis (makers of ICQ, 1998), MovieFone, Inc. (1999), and Digital Marketing Services, Inc. (1999). In 2001 AOL merged with Time Warner Inc. to create a fully integrated media and communications company, AOL Time Warner, with combined revenues of over $30 billion.

American Airlines Major U.S. airline. American was created through a merger of several smaller U.S. airlines and incorporated in 1934. It continued to buy the routes of other airlines, becoming an international carrier in the 1970s; its routes today include South America, the Caribbean, Europe, and the western Pacific. Its parent company, AMR Corp., also has holdings in food services, hotels, and airport ground services. The company acquired bankrupt TRANS WORLD AIRLINES in 2001.

American aloe See CENTURY PLANT

American Anti-Slavery Society Activist arm of the abolition movement that sought an immediate end to slavery in the U.S. Cofounded in 1833 by WILLIAM LLOYD GARRISON and ARTHUR TAPPAN, it promoted the formation of state and local auxiliaries to agitate for abolition. Despite violent opposition, by 1840 the group had 2,000 auxiliaries and over 150,000 members, including THEODORE WELD and WENDELL PHILLIPS. Its most effective public meetings featured testimony of former slaves, including FREDERICK DOUGLASS and WILLIAM WELLS BROWN. In 1839 it split into two factions: a radical group led by Garrison that denounced the Constitution as supportive of slavery, and a moderate faction led by Tappan that led to the birth of the LIBERTY PARTY.

American Association of Retired Persons See AARP

American Ballet Theatre Prominent ballet company based in New York. It was founded in 1939 as the Ballet Theatre (the name was changed in 1958) by Lucia Chase and Richard Pleasant to promote works "American in character." Oliver Smith replaced Pleasant as codirector in 1945; MIKHAIL BARYSHNIKOV served as artistic director from 1980 to 1989 after dancing with the company in the 1970s. New ballets were created for the company by AGNES DE MILLE, JEROME ROBBINS, TWYLA THARP, and ANTONY TUDOR; MICHEL FOKINE revived many of his earlier works for them as well. Principal dancers have included ALICIA ALONSO, ERIK BRUHN, ANTON DOLIN, and NATALIA MAKAROVA.

American Bar Association (ABA) Voluntary association (founded 1878) of U.S. lawyers, judges, and other legal professionals. The largest bar association in the U.S., it seeks to improve the legal profession, ensure the availability of legal services to all citizens, and improve the administration of justice. It conducts educational and research projects, sponsors professional meetings, and publishes a monthly journal. At the turn of the 21st century it had about 375,000 members.

American Broadcasting Co. See ABC

American Civil Liberties Union (ACLU) Organization founded by ROGER BALDWIN and others in New York City in 1920 to champion constitutional liberties in the U.S. It works for three basic concepts: freedom of expression, conscience, and association; DUE PROCESS of law; and EQUAL PROTECTION under the law. From its founding it has initiated test cases and intervened in cases already in the courts. It may provide legal counsel, or it may file an AMICUS CURIAE brief. The SCOPES TRIAL was one of its test cases; it provided counsel for the SACCO-VANZETTI CASE. In the 1950s and '60s it opposed the blacklisting of supposed left-wing subversives and worked to guarantee freedom of worship and the rights of the ACCUSED. Its work is performed by volunteers and full-time staff, including lawyers who provide free legal counsel. See also CIVIL LIBERTY.

American Civil War *or* **Civil War** *or* **War Between the States** (1861–65) Conflict between the U.S. federal government and 11 Southern states that fought to secede from the Union. It arose out of disputes over the issues of slavery, trade and tariffs, and the doctrine of states' rights. In the 1840s and '50s, Northern opposition to slavery in the western territories caused the Southern states to fear a threat to their slaveholdings, which formed the economic base of their large cotton plantations. By the 1850s ABOLITIONISM was growing in the North, and when the antislavery Republican candidate ABRAHAM LINCOLN was elected president in 1860, the Southern states seceded to protect their right to keep slaves. They were organized as the CONFEDERATE STATES OF AMERICA under JEFFERSON DAVIS, while the Northern states were led by Lincoln. The war began in Charleston, S.C., when Confederate artillery fired on FORT SUMTER on April 12, 1861. Both sides quickly raised armies. In July 1861, 30,000 Union troops marched toward the Confederate capital at Richmond, Va., but were stopped by Confederate forces in the Battle of BULL RUN and forced to retreat to Washington, D.C. The defeat shocked the Union, which called for 500,000 more recruits. The war's first major campaign began in February 1862, when Union troops under ULYSSES S. GRANT captured Confederate forts in western Tennessee. Union victories at the Battles of SHILOH and NEW ORLEANS followed. In the East, ROBERT E. LEE won several Confederate victories in the SEVEN DAYS' BATTLES and, after defeat at the Battle of ANTIETAM, in the Battle of FREDERICKSBURG (December 1862). After the Confederate victory at the Battle of CHANCELLORSVILLE, Lee invaded the North and engaged Union forces under GEORGE MEADE at the momentous Battle of GETTYSBURG. The war's turning point in the West occurred in July 1863 with Grant's success in the VICKSBURG CAMPAIGN, which brought the entire Mississippi River under Union control. Grant's command was expanded after the Union defeat at the Battle of CHICKAMAUGA, and in March 1864 Lincoln gave him supreme command of the Union armies. He began a strategy of attrition and, despite heavy Union casualties at the Battles of the WILDERNESS and Spotsylvania, began to surround Lee's troops in Petersburg, Va. (see PETERSBURG CAMPAIGN). Meanwhile WILLIAM T. SHERMAN captured Atlanta in September (see ATLANTA CAMPAIGN), set out on a destructive march through Georgia, and soon captured Savannah. Grant captured Richmond on April 3, 1865, and accepted Lee's surrender on April 9 at APPOMATTOX COURT HOUSE. On April 26 Sherman received the surrender of JOSEPH JOHNSTON, thereby ending the war. The mortality numbers were staggering—about 620,000 deaths out of a total of 2.4 million soldiers. The South was devastated. But the Union was preserved, and slavery was abolished.

American Express Co. U.S. financial-services company. Founded in 1850 as an express-transportation company, American Express originally provided rapid transport of goods across New York and the Midwest. The company introduced traveler's checks in 1891 and opened its first European office in Paris in 1895. Today it offers credit cards, provides services for travelers (including tour packages and car-rental reservations), and owns banking and investment-services firms.

American Federation of Labor–Congress of Industrial Organizations See AFL-CIO

American Federation of Teachers (AFT) Trade union for classroom educators in the U.S. It was formed in 1916 as an affiliate of the American Federation of Labor (see AFL-CIO). Through COLLECTIVE BARGAINING and teachers' strikes, it has obtained for teachers better wages, pensions, sick leaves, academic freedom, and other benefits. Under the leadership of Albert Shanker (1928–97; pres. 1974–97), it instituted national certification tests and other reforms. Membership is about 940,000. See also NATIONAL EDUCATION ASSN.

American Fur Co. Enterprise formed by JOHN J. ASTOR in 1808 that dominated the U.S. fur trade early in the 19th century. The company, considered the first U.S. business monopoly, absorbed or drove out rivals throughout the central and western U.S. Exploration by its trappers and traders helped open the frontier to settlement. By 1834, when Astor sold his company, it had become the largest commercial organization in the U.S.

American Indian *or* **Native American** *or* **Amerindian** Member of any of the aboriginal peoples of the Western Hemisphere, with the exception of the ESKIMOS and ALEUTS. Though the term Native American is today often preferred over American Indian, particularly in North America, many Native American peoples continue to prefer American Indian (or Indian). The ancestors of the American Indians were nomadic hunters of northeastern Asia who migrated over the Bering Strait land bridge into North America probably during the last glacial period (20,000–30,000 years ago). By c. 10,000 BC they had occupied much of N., Middle, and South America. See also ANASAZI CULTURE, ANDEAN CIVILIZATION, CLOVIS COMPLEX, EASTERN WOODLANDS INDIANS, FOLSOM COMPLEX, HOHOKAM CULTURE, HOPEWELL CULTURE, MESOAMERICAN CIVILIZATION, MISSISSIPPIAN CULTURE, MOGOLLON and Mimbres, NORTHWEST COAST INDIANS, PLAINS INDIANS, PUEBLO INDIANS, SOUTHEASTERN INDIANS, SOUTHWEST INDIANS, WOODLAND CULTURES.

American Indian languages Languages spoken by the original inhabitants of the Americas and the West Indies and by their modern descendants. They display an extraordinary structural range, and no attempt to unite them into a small number of genetic groupings has won general acceptance. Before Columbus, more than 300 distinct languages were spoken in North America north of Mexico by an estimated population of 2–7 million. Today there are fewer than 170 languages, of which the great majority are spoken fluently only by older adults. A few widespread language families (ALGONQUIAN, IROQUOIAN, SIOUAN, MUSKOGEAN, ATHABASKAN, UTO-AZTECAN, SALISHAN) account for many of the languages of eastern and interior North America, though the far west was an area of extreme diversity (see HOKAN, PENUTIAN). In Mexico and northern Central America (Mesoamerica), an estimated 15–20 million people spoke more than 300 languages before Columbus. The large OTO-MANGUEAN and MAYAN families and a single language, NAHUATL, shared Mesoamerica with many smaller families and language isolates. More than 10 of these languages and language complexes still have over 100,000 speakers. South America and the West Indies had an estimated pre-Columbian population of 10–20 million, speaking more than 500 languages. Important language families include Chibchan in Colombia and southern Central America, QUECHUAN and Aymaran in the Andean region, and ARAWAKAN, CARIBAN, and TUPIAN in northern and central lowland South America. Aside from Quechuan and Aymaran, with about 10 million speakers, and the TUPIAN language Guaraní, most remaining South American Indian languages have very few speakers, and some face extinction before linguists can adequately record them.

American Indian Movement (AIM) Civil-rights organization founded in 1968, originally to help urban American Indians displaced by government programs. It later broadened its efforts to include demands for economic independence, autonomy over tribal areas, restoration of illegally seized lands, and protection of Indian legal rights and traditional culture. Some of its protest activities were highly publicized (see WOUNDED KNEE). Internal strife and the imprisonment of some leaders led to the disbanding of its national leadership in 1978, though local groups have continued to function.

American Indian religions, North Religious beliefs and practices of the indigenous peoples of North America. They are characterized by a conviction that spirit moves through all things, animate and inanimate, and that the living are intimately connected with the souls of the dead. They discover recognizable beings in the natural world of animals, plants, and trees, as well as in natural features such as mountains, lakes, and clouds. Because North American religions were so highly localized, it is impossible to determine how many have existed, and their beliefs have varied widely. Whereas IROQUOIS elders speak of a perfectly wise and good Creator who planned the universe, the Koyukon envision the creator as Raven, a trickster god who is only one of many powerful spirits. Whereas nearly all NAVAJO ceremonies are performed on behalf of individuals in response to specific needs, most PUEBLO ceremonies are performed communally and scheduled according to the cycles of nature. However, all native North American religions share certain features: ancestral lands and locally sacred spots are important; access to some knowledge is restricted, and initiation is required to acquire it; kinship obligations are central; the oral tradition includes narratives that record human interaction with nonhuman powers; and generosity is a religious act. Contact with Europeans led to development of new religious movements, including the GHOST DANCE tradition and the NATIVE AMERICAN CHURCH. See also MESOAMERICAN RELIGIONS.

American Indian religions, South Religious beliefs and practices of the indigenous peoples of South America. The ancient ANDEAN CIVILIZATIONS of the CHIMU and the INCA had highly developed religions. The Inca religion combined complex ceremonies, animistic beliefs, belief in objects having magical powers, nature worship, and sun worship. The Incas built monumental temples, occupied by priests and Chosen Women. Priests conducted divination, and sacrifices were offered on every important occasion. Human sacrifice was offered when the need was extreme. In present-day South America, as many as 1,500 distinct native cultures have been described, and religious beliefs vary greatly. Creation mythologies are of major importance, often describing the origin of the first world and its fate as well as the creation and destruction of subsequent worlds. Ceremonial initiation into adulthood is widely practiced, both for males and females, with the initiation ceremony often acting out events from the dawn of creation. Initiations are also used to mark the ascent of individuals into positions of religious authority, with priests, diviners, and spirit mediums playing special roles. The SHAMAN specializes in inducing states of ecstasy, controlling the passage of the soul out of and back into the body. Ritual fires, musical instruments (especially the rattle), esoteric languages, and sacred songs may be used in a theatrical performance designed to demonstrate the shaman's command of invisible powers. Christianity has come to be a strong component of folk belief among many native peoples, but it continues to be interpreted in the light of local tradition, and elements of traditional religion continue to survive. See also MESOAMERICAN RELIGIONS.

American Labor Party Minor political party organized in New York in 1936 by the labor leaders SIDNEY HILLMAN and DAVID DUBINSKY and by liberal Democrats. The party supported FRANKLIN ROOSEVELT's NEW DEAL programs and backed candidates who endorsed liberal social legislation. The party was influential in New York City elections, though after 1940 it was often divided by pro- and anti-Communist issues. It was dissolved in 1956.

American League With the NATIONAL LEAGUE, one of two associations in the U.S. and Canada of professional, major-league BASEBALL teams. The league was founded in 1900. There are now three divisions: Eastern (comprising the Baltimore Orioles, Boston Red Sox, New York Yankees, Tampa Bay Devil Rays, and Toronto Blue Jays), Central (Chicago White Sox, Cleveland Indians, Detroit Tigers, Kansas City Royals, and Minnesota Twins), and Western (Anaheim Angels, Oakland Athletics, Seattle Mariners, and Texas Rangers).

American Legion Organization of U.S. war veterans. Founded in 1919, it focuses on the care of disabled and sick veterans, and advocates for compensation and pensions for the disabled, widows, and orphans. Nonpolitical and nonsectarian, its membership requirement is honorable service and an honorable discharge. It was instrumental in establishing veteran hospitals, and sponsored the creation of the U.S. Veterans Administration in 1930 (see U.S. Department of VETERANS AFFAIRS). In 1944 it played an important role in the passage of the GI BILL. At its height the Legion had about 3 million members in 16,000 local posts, or groups.

American Medical Association (AMA) Organization of U.S. physicians founded in 1847 "to promote the science and art of medicine and the betterment of public health." It has about 250,000 members, about half of all practicing U.S. physicians. It disseminates information to its members and the public, operates as a lobbying group, and helps set medical education standards. Its publications include *Journal of the American Medical Association, American Medical News,* and journals on medical specialties.

American Motors Corp. (AMC) U.S. automobile manufacturer. AMC was formed in 1954 from the merger of two pioneering auto manufacturers, Nash-Kelvinator Corp. (successor to Nash Motor Co., founded 1916) and Hudson Motor Car Co. (founded 1909). AMC produced AMC compact cars, AM General trucks and buses, and, until 1968, Kelvinator appliances. Jeeps joined the product line after AMC purchased the Kaiser-Jeep Corp. (dating to 1903) in 1970. AMC became a subsidiary of CHRYSLER CORP. in 1987, which in turn merged with DAIMLER-BENZ in 1998.

American Museum of Natural History Major center of research and education on the natural sciences, established in New York City in 1869. It pioneered in staging field expeditions and in creating dioramas and other lifelike exhibits showing natural habitats and their plant and animal life. Its research collections contain tens of millions of specimens, and its fossil and insect collections are among the largest in the world. It conducts research in anthropology, astronomy, entomology, herpetology, ichthyology, invertebrate biology, mammalogy, mineralogy, ornithology, and vertebrate paleontology, and maintains permanent research stations in the Bahamas, New York, Florida, and Arizona. It also contains one of the world's largest planetariums.

American Party See KNOW-NOTHING PARTY

American Protective Association Secret anti-Catholic, anti-immigrant society formed in Iowa in 1887. Its membership rose to over 2 million in the 1890s, consisting mainly of farmers who feared the growth and political power of immigrant-populated cities. Membership dwindled after the election of 1896 and the return of agricultural prosperity in the Midwest. By 1911 the society had disappeared.

American Renaissance *or* **New England Renaissance** Period from the 1830s roughly until the end of the American Civil War in which U.S. literature came of age as an expression of a national spirit. The literary scene was dominated by New England Brahmin writers, notably HENRY W. LONGFELLOW, OLIVER WENDELL HOLMES, and JAMES RUSSELL LOWELL. Also influential were the Transcendentalists (see TRANSCENDENTALISM), including RALPH WALDO EMERSON and HENRY DAVID THOREAU, as well as the great imaginative writers NATHANIEL HAWTHORNE, HERMAN MELVILLE, WALT WHITMAN, and EDGAR ALLAN POE.

American Revolution *or* **United States War of Independence** (1775–83) War that won political independence for 13 of Britain's North American colonies, forming the United States of America. After the end of the costly FRENCH AND INDIAN WAR (1763), Britain imposed new taxes on the colonies (see STAMP ACT, SUGAR ACT) and trade restrictions, which fueled growing resentment and added to the colonists' objection to their lack of representation in the British Parliament. Determined to achieve independence, the colonies formed the Continental Army, composed chiefly of MINUTEMEN, to challenge Britain's large, organized militia. The war began when Britain sent a force to destroy rebel military stores at Concord, Mass. After fighting broke out on April 19, 1775 (see Battles of LEXINGTON AND CONCORD), rebel forces began a siege of Boston that ended when American forces under HENRY KNOX forced out the British troops under WILLIAM HOWE on March 17, 1776 (see Battle of BUNKER HILL). Britain's offer of pardon in exchange for surrender was refused by the Americans, who declared themselves independent on July 4, 1776. British forces retaliated by driving the army of GEORGE WASHINGTON from New York to New Jersey. On Christmas night, Washington crossed the Delaware River and won the Battles of TRENTON AND PRINCETON. The British army split to cover more territory, a fatal error. In engaging the Americans in Pennsylvania, notably in the Battle of the BRANDYWINE, they left the troops in the north vulnerable. Despite a victory in the Battle of TICONDEROGA, British troops under JOHN BURGOYNE were defeated by HORATIO GATES and BENEDICT ARNOLD in the Battle of SARATOGA (October 17, 1777). Washington quartered his 11,000 troops through a bleak winter at VALLEY FORGE, where they received training from FREDERICK STEUBEN that gave them victory in Monmouth, N.J., on June 28, 1778. British forces in the north thenceforth chiefly concentrated near New York. France, which had been secretly furnishing aid to the Americans since 1776, finally declared war on Britain in June 1778. French troops assisted American troops in the south, culminating in the successful Siege of YORKTOWN, where CHARLES CORNWALLIS's forces surrendered on October 19, 1781, bringing an end to the war on land. War continued at sea, fought chiefly between Britain and the U.S.'s European allies. The navies of Spain and the Netherlands contained most of Britain's navy near Europe and away from the fighting in America. The last battle of the war was won by the American navy under JOHN BARRY in March 1783 in the Straits of Florida. With the Treaty of Paris (September 3, 1783), Britain recognized the independence of the U.S. east of the Mississippi River and ceded Florida to Spain.

American saddlebred *or* **American saddle horse** Breed of light HORSE that originated in the U.S., formed by crossing THOROUGHBREDS, MORGANS, and STANDARDBREDS on native mares having an easy gait. It stands 15–16 hands (5–5.3 ft, or 1.5–1.6 m) high, and its colors are bay, brown, black, gray, and chestnut. There are two distinct types, three-gaited and five-gaited. The three natural gaits are walk, trot, and canter; the five-gaited horse also has two trained gaits, the rack and the slow gait, or running walk. Three-gaited saddle horses often have slightly less style and finish than the five-gaited horse. The American saddlebred is also used as a fine harness horse mainly for show.

American Samoa *officially* **Territory of American Samoa** Unincorporated U.S. territory (pop., 1995 est.: 57,000), southwestern central Pacific Ocean, including the islands of Tutuila (the largest, with over two-thirds of the territory's land area and 95% of the population), Aunuu, Rose, Swains, and the Manua group. Area: 77 sq mi (199 sq km). Capital: PAGO PAGO (on Tutuila). Languages: Samoan, English (both official). Currency: U.S. dollar. Most of the islands are rocky, were formed from extinct volcanoes, and are surrounded by coral reefs. Tutuila and the islands of Manua are dominated by central mountain ranges. Fishing and tourism are major industries, but the U.S. administration is the main employer. The majority of the population is of Samoan ancestry. The islands were probably inhabited by Polynesians 2,500 years ago. Dutch explorers became the first Europeans to visit the islands in 1722. A haven for runaway sailors and escaped convicts, the islands were ruled by native chiefs until c. 1860. The U.S. gained the right to establish a naval station at PAGO PAGO in 1872, and the U.S., Britain, and Germany administered a tripartite protectorate in 1889–99. The high chiefs ceded the eastern islands to the U.S. in 1904 (Britain ceded Swains in 1925). American Samoa was administered by the U.S. Department of the Navy until 1951 and afterwards by the Department of the Interior. Its first constitution was approved in 1960, and in 1978 the territory's first elected governor took office.

American Stock Exchange (AMEX) Second-largest stock exchange in the U.S. Originally known as "the Curb," it began as an outdoor marketplace in New York City c. 1850. It moved indoors to its present location in the Wall Street area in 1921. Once a marketplace for SECURITIES not reputable enough for the NEW YORK STOCK EXCHANGE, it became equally respectable, with its own listing admissions requirements. In 1999 it merged with NASDAQ to form the Nasdaq-Amex Market Group.

American System of manufacture Production of many identical parts and their assembly into finished products. Though ELI WHITNEY has been credited with this development, the ideas had appeared earlier in Europe and were being practiced in arms factories in the U.S. (see ARMORY PRACTICE). MARC BRUNEL, while working for the British Admiralty (1802–8), devised a process for producing wooden pulley blocks by sequential machine operations, whereby 10 men (rather than the 110 needed previously) could make 160,000 pulley blocks per year. Not until London's CRYSTAL PALACE exhibition (1851) did British engineers, viewing exhibits of machines used in the U.S. to produce INTERCHANGEABLE PARTS, begin to apply the system. Within 25 years, the American System was being widely used in making a host of industrial products. See also ASSEMBLY LINE, FACTORY.

American Telephone and Telegraph Co. See AT&T

American University Private university in Washington, D.C. It was incorporated by act of Congress in 1891 as a graduate school and research center, but courses did not begin until 1914. An undergraduate division was founded in 1925. It includes a law school and a business school as well as schools of international service and public affairs. It has a strong government and public-services orientation. Total enrollment is about 11,000.

America's Cup Most prestigious trophy in international yachting competition. First offered under another name in Britain in 1851, the cup was won easily by the *America* from New York and subsequently became known as the America's Cup. The America's Cup race, held about every four years, is between one defending vessel and one challenging vessel; each must be designed and built in the country it represents. The 22.6-mi (36.4-km) racecourse is divided into eight legs. The U.S. completely dominated the competition until recently, when it has been defeated by Australia (1983) and New Zealand (1995). From 1936 until the 1983 loss, the race was held off Newport, R.I.; the more recent U.S. site has been San Diego.

americium \ˌam-ə-ˈri-shē-əm\ Synthetic radioactive chemical ELEMENT, chemical symbol Am, atomic number 95. The fourth TRANSURANIUM element discovered, it was first produced in 1944 from PLUTONIUM-239 in a nuclear reactor. The ISOTOPE americium-241 has been prepared in kilogram quantities and is used in a variety of measuring applications that utilize its gamma radiation. Its most familiar use is in household smoke detectors.

Amerindian See AMERICAN INDIAN

Ames, Fisher (1758–1808) U.S. essayist and politician. Born in Dedham, Mass., he initially worked as a teacher and lawyer. Supporting a strong central government and arguing for property rights and protection of commercial interests, he defeated SAMUEL ADAMS for a seat in the first session of the U.S. House of Representatives (1789–97), where he was active as a Federalist who opposed Jeffersonian democracy. His eloquent support of the treaty negotiated by JOHN JAY to preserve peace with England (1794) convinced the House to pass an enabling appropriation.

Ames, Winthrop (1870–1937) U.S. theatrical producer and manager. Born in North Easton, Mass., into a wealthy New England family, he traveled to Europe in 1904 to study the management of 60 opera and theater companies. After comanaging a Boston theater, he became managing director of New York's New Theatre (1908–11). He founded the Little Theatre and the Booth Theatre, where he produced and directed such successful plays as *The Philanderer* (1913), *Beggar on Horseback* (1924), and a series of Gilbert and Sullivan revivals (1926–29). His *Snow White* (1913) was the first play produced in the U.S. especially for children.

amesha spenta \ä-ˈmesh-ə-ˈspen-tə\ In ZOROASTRIANISM, any of the six divine beings (three male, three female) created by AHURA MAZDA to help govern creation. They are worshiped separately, and each has a special month, festival, and flower. The most important are Asha Vahishta ("Truth"), who presides over the sacred fire and holds out the path of justice and spiritual knowledge, and Vohu Manah ("Good Mind"), who welcomes the blessed into paradise. Khshathra Vairya ("Desirable Dominion") presides over metal, Spenta Armaiti ("Beneficent Devotion") over earth, and Haurvatat ("Wholeness") and Ameretat ("Immortality") over water and plants. In later Zoroastrianism, each is opposed by a specific archfiend.

amethyst Transparent, coarse-grained variety of QUARTZ that is valued as a semiprecious gem for its violet color. It contains a little more iron oxide (Fe_2O_3) than any other variety of quartz, and its color probably arises from this iron content. Heating removes the color or changes it to the yellow of CITRINE; most commercial citrine is made in this manner. Notable deposits are found in Brazil, Uruguay, Ontario, and North Carolina. The birthstone for February, amethyst is usually faceted with step cuts or emerald cuts but also has been used since ancient times for carved intaglios.

White-tipped amethyst from Guerrero, Mexico.

LEE BOLTIN

AMEX See AMERICAN STOCK EXCHANGE

Amhara \am-ˈhä-rə\ People of the Ethiopian central highlands who, numbering about 17 million, compose close to one-third of Ethiopia's population. Their language is AMHARIC, their religion ETHIOPIAN ORTHODOX. The Amhara, who have dominated the history of their country, descend from ancient Semitic conquerors who mingled with indigenous Cushitic peoples. They are agriculturalists and place great value on land ownership.

Amharic language \am-ˈhä-rik\ SEMITIC LANGUAGE of Ethiopia, spoken by over 17 million people as a first language, and used as a LINGUA FRANCA throughout much of central highland Ethiopia. Its status as a de facto national language is largely due to the long dominance of the Ethiopian monarchy by AMHARA sovereigns. Amharic is written in a modified form of the partly syllabic, partly alphabetic script used to write Ge'ez, the classical language of Christian Ethiopian civilization (see ETHIOPIC LANGUAGES). Though manuscripts in Amharic are known from the 14th century, the language has only recently been used as a general medium for literature, journalism, and education.

Amherst, Jeffery *later* **Baron Amherst** (1717–1797) British army commander. In the FRENCH AND INDIAN WAR, he took the French fort at Louisbourg, Cape Breton Island, in 1758, and was promoted to chief of command in America. In 1760 he directed the campaign that captured Quebec and Montreal, and in 1761 he quelled the Indian uprising under Pontiac. Having secured Canada for Britain, he remained there as governor-general until 1763. Returning to England, he served as commander in chief of the British army (1772–95), but his tenure was marred by failure in the war with the American colonies and by serious abuses in the army. He was created a baron in 1776 and a field marshal in 1796. Several U.S. towns and AMHERST COLLEGE are named for him.

Amherst College \ˈam-ərst\ Private liberal-arts college in Amherst, Mass., chartered in 1825. NOAH WEBSTER was one of its founders. Consistently ranked as one of the finest colleges in the U.S., it offers a wide range of courses in the humanities, social sciences, and natural sciences. Originally a men's college, it became coeducational in 1975. It participates in an exchange program with nearby Hampshire, MOUNT HOLYOKE, and SMITH colleges and the University of MASSACHUSETTS. Enrollment is about 1,600.

amicus curiae \ə-ˈmē-kəs-ˈkyu̇r-ē-ī, ə-ˈmī-kəs-ˈkyu̇r-ē-ē\ (Latin: "friend of the court") One who assists a court by furnishing information or advice regarding questions of law or fact. A person (or other entity, such as a state government) who is not a party to a particular lawsuit but nevertheless has a strong interest in it may be allowed, by leave of the court, to file an amicus curiae brief, a statement of particular views on the subject matter of the lawsuit. Such briefs are often filed in cases involving public-interest matters (e.g., entitlement programs, consumer protection, civil rights).

Amida See AMITABHA

amide \ˈa-ˌmīd\ Any member of either of two classes of NITROGEN-containing organic compounds related to AMMONIA and AMINES and containing a carbonyl group (—C=O; see FUNCTIONAL GROUP). The first class, covalent amides are formed by replacing the hydroxyl group (—OH) of an ACID with an amino group (—NR$_2$, in which R may represent a HYDROGEN atom or an organic combining group, such as methyl). Amides formed from CARBOXYLIC ACIDS, called carboxamides, are solids except for the simplest, formamide, a liquid. They do not conduct electricity, have high boiling points, and (when liquid) are good SOLVENTS. There are no practical natural sources of simple covalent amides, but the PEPTIDES and PROTEINS in living systems are long chains (POLYMERS) with peptide bonds (see COVALENT BOND), which are amide linkages. UREA is an amide with two amino groups. Commercially important covalent amides include several used as solvents; others are the SULFA DRUGS and NYLON. The second class, ionic (salt-like) amides (see IONIC BOND), are made by treating a covalent amide, an amine, or ammonia with a reactive metal (e.g., sodium) and are strongly alkaline.

Amiens \äm-ˈye^{n}\ *ancient* **Samarobriva** *later* **Ambianum.** City (pop., 1990: 136,000), northern France. Located on the SOMME RIVER, it became a Roman stronghold. The chief city of a medieval county, it passed to BURGUNDY in 1435 and was captured by the Spanish in 1597. Recovered by HENRY IV, it served as the capital of PICARDY until 1790. The Prussians captured the city in 1870, and the Germans held it briefly in 1914; it gave its name to a successful Allied counteroffensive against Germany in 1918. The Germans occupied it during World War II. It has been a major center of the French textile industry since the 16th century and is the site of the Gothic cathedral of Notre Dame, the largest church in France.

Amiens \äm-ˈya^{n}\, **Treaty of** (1802) Agreement signed at Amiens, France, by Britain, France, Spain, and the Batavian Republic (the Netherlands). By the treaty France and its allies recovered most of their colonies, despite their military reverses overseas. The treaty ignored continuing trade differences between Britain and France, but it achieved a peace in Europe for 14 months during the NAPOLEONIC WARS.

Amin (Dada Oumee) \ä-ˈmēn\, **Idi** (born 1924/25) Military officer and president (1971–79) of Uganda. A member of the small Kakwa ethnic group and a Muslim, he was closely associated during his military career with MILTON OBOTE, Uganda's first prime minister and president. In 1971 he staged a coup against Obote. In 1972 he expelled all Asians from Uganda, reversed Uganda's amicable relations with Israel, was personally involved in the Palestinian hijacking of a French airliner to Entebbe (see ENTEBBE INCIDENT), and ordered the torture and murder of 100,000–300,000 Ugandans. When Ugandan nationalist and Tanzanian troops invaded in 1979, Amin fled to Libya and eventually settled in Saudi Arabia.

Amin.

JANET GRIFFITH/BLACK STAR

amine \ə-ˈmēn\ Any of a class of NITROGEN-containing organic compounds derived, either in principle or in practice, from AMMONIA (NH_3). Almost all their chemical names end in "ine." Replacement of one, two, or all three of the HYDROGEN atoms in ammonia with organic groups yields primary, secondary, or tertiary amines, respectively. Addition of a fourth hydrogen with an accompanying positive charge on the nitrogen atom results in a quatenary amine. Naturally occurring amines include ALKALOIDS, present in certain plants; some NEUROTRANSMITTERS, including DOPAMINE and EPINEPHRINE; and HISTAMINE. Industrially important amines include ANILINE, ethanolamine, and others, used in making rubber, dyes, pharmaceuticals, synthetic resins and fibers, and in a host of other applications. A nitrogen atom with one or two hydrogens is often referred to as an amino group.

amino acid \ə-ˈmē-nō\ Any of a class of organic compounds in which a CARBON atom has bonds to an amino group (—NH$_2$), a carboxyl group (—COOH), a hydrogen atom (—H), and an organic side group (called —R). They are therefore both CARBOXYLIC ACIDS and AMINES. The physical and chemical properties unique to each result from the properties of the R group, particularly its tendency to interact with water and its charge (if any). Amino acids joined linearly by peptide bonds (see COVALENT BOND) in a particular order make up PEPTIDES and PROTEINS. Of over 100 natural amino acids, each with a different R group, only 20 make up the PROTEINS of all living organisms. Humans can synthesize 10 of them (by interconversions) from each other or from other molecules of intermediary METABOLISM, but the other 10 (essential amino acids: ARGININE, HISTIDINE, ISOLEUCINE, LEUCINE, LYSINE, METHIONINE, PHENYLALANINE, THREONINE, TRYPTOPHAN, and VALINE) must be consumed in the diet.

Amis, Kingsley (William) *later* **Sir Kingsley** (1922–1995) British novelist, poet, critic, and teacher. His first novel, *Lucky Jim* (1954; film, 1957), was a hugely successful comic masterpiece. He was often characterized as an ANGRY YOUNG MAN, a label he rejected. Notable among his more than 40 books (including four volumes of poetry) are the mordantly humorous novels *That Uncertain Feeling* (1955; film, *Only Two Can Play*, 1962), *The Green Man* (1959; film, 1957), *Jake's Thing* (1978), and *The Old Devils* (1986, Booker Prize). He was the father of MARTIN AMIS.

Amis \ˈā-mis\, **Martin** (born 1949) British writer and critic. The son of KINGSLEY AMIS, he graduated from Oxford University in 1971. He worked for the *Times Literary Supplement* and the *New Statesman* before becoming a full-time writer. His works—including the novels *The Rachel Papers* (1973), *Money* (1984), *London Fields* (1989), *Time's Arrow* (1991), *The Information* (1995), and *Night Train* (1998), and the short-story collection *Heavy Water* (1999)—feature inventive word play and often scabrous humor as they satirize the horrors of modern urban life.

Amish \ˈä-mish\ Member of a conservative Christian group in North America known as the Old Order Amish Mennonite Church. The Amish originated in 1693–97 as followers of the MENNONITE elder Jakob Ammann (1644?–c. 1730) in Switzerland, Alsace, and Germany. He taught that lying was grounds for excommunication (which meant being shunned by all other Mennonites), that clothing should be uniform and beards untrimmed, and that the state church should be avoided. Migration to North America and assimilation eliminated the Amish in Europe. They settled in Pennsylvania in the 18th century. After 1850 they split into "Old Order" (traditional) and "New Order" (now the Mennonite churches). Old Order Amish now live in Pennsylvania, Ohio, Indiana, Iowa, Illinois, and Kansas. Adults are baptized and admitted to formal church membership at age 17 to 20. Services are in Pennsylvania Dutch (a German dialect) and some English. Though similar in theology to Mennonites, Amish wear modest, old-fashioned clothing and reject modern technology, including automobiles and telephones.

Amistad Mutiny Revolt by 53 African slaves aboard the schooner *Amistad* near Cuba in 1839. The slaves, abducted from Africa, seized control of the ship, killed the captain and cook, and ordered the navigator to sail for Africa. Pretending to do so, he sailed northward instead, and the ship was intercepted off New York. Despite attempts by Pres. MARTIN VAN BUREN to send the Africans to Cuba, abolitionists demanded a trial, contending the men were free under international law. A federal judge agreed, and the government appealed to the U.S. Supreme Court, where in 1841 defending counsel JOHN QUINCY ADAMS successfully argued that the men should be freed. The 35 survivors arrived in Sierra Leone in 1842.

Amitabha \ˌam-i-ˈtä-bə\ *Japanese* **Amida** Savior deity worshiped by followers of PURE LAND BUDDHISM in Japan. According to the Sukhavati-vyuha-sutra (Pure Land SUTRA), the monk Dharmakara vowed many ages ago that once he attained buddhahood, all who believed in him and called upon his name would be

Great bronze Amida (Daibutsu) at Kamakura, Japan, 1252.

ASUKA-EN

born into his paradise (the Pure Land) and reside there until achieving NIRVANA. The cult of Amitabha came to the forefront in China c. 650 and then spread to Japan, where it led to the formation of the Pure Land and True Pure Land sects. In Tibet and Nepal, Amitabha is regarded as one of the five eternal buddhas (rather than as a savior), who manifested himself as the earthly BUDDHA Gautama and as the BODHISATTVA AVALOKITESVARA.

Amman \ä-ˈman\ City (pop., 1994 est.: 963,000), capital of Jordan. It lies 25 mi (40 km) northeast of the DEAD SEA. Amman is by far the largest city of Jordan. Fortified settlements have existed in the area from remote antiquity; the earliest date from the Chalcolithic period (c. 4000–3000 BC). As Rabbah, it became the capital of the Ammonites. It was conquered by Egypt's PTOLEMY II PHILADELPHUS, who renamed it Philadelphia, a name retained through Roman times. Taken by the Arabs in AD 635, it later went into decline and subsequently disappeared. In 1878 the Ottoman Turks resettled it. When the British set up Transjordan in 1921, Amman became its capital. Its modern development was furthered by Jordanian independence in 1946. Amman has since often had to deal with refugee problems exacerbated by the continuing unrest between Israelis and Palestinians.

Ammannati \ˌäm-än-ˈnä-tē\, **Bartolommeo** *or* **Bartolommeo Ammanati** (1511–1592) Italian sculptor and architect active chiefly in Florence. He trained under BACCIO BANDINELLI in Florence and JACOPO SANSOVINO in Venice. In 1550 he went to Rome, where he collaborated with GIORGIO VASARI and Giacomo da Vignola on the Villa Giulia. In 1555 he returned to Florence, where he spent the rest of his career working for the MEDICIS. He finished the Laurentian Library, begun by MICHELANGELO, but is best known for the Bridge of Santa Trinità and his additions to FILIPPO BRUNELLESCHI's Pitti Palace, including the courtyard. His Fountain of Neptune in the Piazza della Signoria features a colossal marble statue surrounded by bronze deities, nymphs, and satyrs.

ammonia \ə-ˈmō-nyə\ Colorless, pungent gas composed of NITROGEN and HYDROGEN, chemical formula NH_3. Easily liquefied by compression or cooling for use in refrigerating and air-conditioning equipment, it is manufactured in huge quantities. Ammonia is made by the HABER-BOSCH PROCESS (see FRITZ HABER). Its major use is as a FERTILIZER, applied directly to soil from tanks of the liquefied gas. SALTS of ammonia, including ammonium phosphate and ammonium nitrate (also a high explosive), are used as fertilizers too. Ammonia has many other industrial uses as a raw material, CATALYST, and ALKALI. It dissolves readily in water to form ammonium hydroxide, an alkaline solution (see BASE) familiar as a household cleaner.

ammonia-soda process See SOLVAY PROCESS

ammonite \ˈa-mə-ˌnīt\ Extinct shelled CEPHALOPOD whose FOSSILS are often used to correlate rocks, especially of the CRETACEOUS PERIOD (144–65 million years ago). Most shells were coiled, but some were straight. Unusual ammonites called heteromorphs were shaped like fat corkscrews and fat hairpins and probably had difficulty moving about. Ammonites preyed on other aquatic invertebrates and were themselves prey to many larger animals, including marine reptiles. See also AMMONOID.

ammonoid \ˈam-ə-ˌnȯid\ Any of a group of extinct shelled CEPHALOPODS, related to the modern pearly nautilus, that are commonly found as fossils in marine rocks of the DEVONIAN through CRETACEOUS periods (417–65 million years ago). Most ammonoids were predators. The shells, either straight or coiled, served as protective and supportive structures and enabled the animals to compensate for varying water depths. Ammonoids are important index FOSSILS because of their wide geographic distribution in shallow marine waters, rapid evolution, and easily recognizable features. See also BELEMNOID.

amnesia \am-ˈnē-zhə\ Loss of MEMORY as a result of brain injury or deterioration, shock, fatigue, senility, drug use, alcoholism, anesthesia, illness, or neurotic reaction. Amnesia may be anterograde (in which events following the causative trauma or disease are forgotten) or retrograde (in which events preceding the trauma or disease are forgotten). It can often be traced to a severe emotional shock, in which case personal memories (e.g., identity) rather than less-personal material (e.g., language skills) are affected. Such amnesia seems to represent an escape from disturbing memories, and is thus an example of REPRESSION; these memories can generally be recovered through PSYCHOTHERAPY or after the amnesiac state has ended. Amnesia may occasionally last for weeks, months, or even years, a condition known as fugue. See also HYPNOSIS.

amnesty In criminal law, a sovereign act of oblivion or forgetfulness (from Greek *amnestia*, "forgetfulness") granted by a government, especially to a group of persons who are guilty of (usually political) crimes in the past. It is often conditional upon the group's return to obedience and duty within a prescribed period. See also PARDON.

Amnesty International (AI) International HUMAN-RIGHTS organization. It was founded in 1961 by Peter Benenson, a London lawyer who organized a letter-writing campaign calling for amnesty for "prisoners of conscience." AI seeks to inform the public about violations of human rights, especially abridgments of freedom of speech and religion and the imprisonment and torture of political dissidents. It actively seeks the release of political prisoners, and support of their families when necessary. Its members and supporters are said to number 1 million in 162 countries. Its first director, SEAN MACBRIDE, won the 1974 Nobel Peace Prize; AI itself won the award in 1977.

amniocentesis \ˌam-nē-ō-sen-ˈtē-səs\ Surgical insertion of a hollow needle through the abdominal wall into the UTERUS of a pregnant female to extract fluid from the amniotic sac for analysis of fluid and fetal cells. This can reveal the fetus's sex (important when sex-linked genetic disease is possible), chromosomal disorders, and other problems. First performed in the 1930s, amniocentesis is generally done under local anesthesia in the 15th–17th week of gestation.

amoeba \ə-ˈmē-bə\ One-celled PROTOZOAN that can form temporary extensions of CYTOPLASM (pseudopodia) in order to move about. Some amoebas are found on the bottom of freshwater streams and ponds. Others live in the human digestive system; one type causes amebic DYSENTERY in humans. Each amoeba contains a small mass of jellylike cytoplasm with VACUOLES and a NUCLEUS. Food is taken in and material is excreted at any point on the cell surface. Amoebas are used extensively in cell research for determining the relative functions and interactions of the nucleus and the cytoplasm.

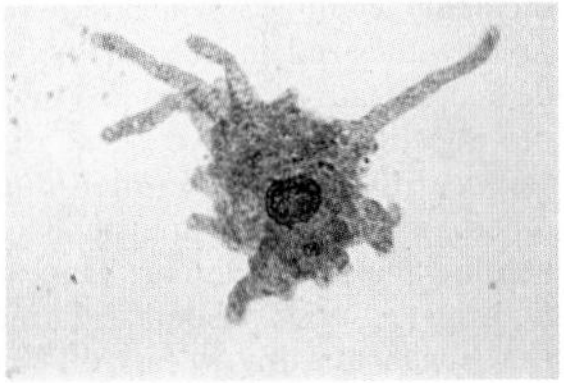

Amoeba (magnified).
RUSS KINNE—PHOTO RESEARCHERS

Amon \ˈä-ˌmän\ *or* **Amen** Egyptian deity revered as king of the gods. Amon may have originated as a local deity at Khmun in Middle Egypt. His cult spread to Thebes, where he became patron of the pharaohs by Mentuhotep I's reign (2008–1957 BC) and was identified with the sun god RE. Represented as a human, a ram, or both, Amon-Re was worshiped with the goddess MUT and the youthful god KHONS. AKHENATON directed his reforms against the cult of Amon, but with little success, and Amon's status was restored in the 14th–13th century BC. In the New Kingdom, Amon came to be seen as one of a triad with PTAH and Re, and in the 11th–10th century BC as a universal god who intervened in affairs of state by speaking through oracles.

amortization \ˌam-ər-ti-ˈzā-shən\ In finance, the systematic repayment of a DEBT; in accounting, the systematic writing off of some account over a period of years. An example of the first meaning is a home mortgage, which may be repaid in monthly installments that include interest and a gradual reduction of the principal. Such systematic reduction is safer for the lender, since it is easier for the borrower to repay a series of small amounts than a single lump sum. In the second sense, a firm may gradually reduce the balance-sheet valuation of a depreciable asset such as a building, machine, or mine. The U.S. government has sometimes permitted accelerated amortization of assets, which encourages industrial development by decreasing a company's tax burden in the years immediately after a purchase.

Amos (fl. 8th century BC) Earliest Hebrew PROPHET (one of the 12 Minor Prophets) to have a biblical book named for him. Born in Tekoa in Judah, he was a shepherd. According to the Book of Amos, he traveled to the richer and more powerful kingdom of Israel to preach his visions of divine destruction and the message that God's absolute sovereignty required justice for rich and poor alike and that God's chosen people were not exempt from the moral order. He foretold the destruction of the northern kingdom of Israel and anticipated the predictions of doom by later Old Testament prophets.

Amos 'n' Andy See Freeman and Charles Correll GOSDEN

amosite \'a-mə-ˌsīt\ Variety of the silicate mineral cummingtonite, which is a source of asbestos. Cummingtonite is an AMPHIBOLE mineral, an iron and magnesium silicate that occurs in metamorphic rocks in the form of long needlelike, fibrous crystals.

Ampère \äⁿ-'per\, **André-Marie** (1775–1836) French physicist, founder of the science of electromagnetism. A prodigy who mastered the entire known field of mathematics by age 12, he became a professor of physics, chemistry, and mathematics. He formulated a law of electromagnetism, called AMPÈRE'S LAW, that describes the magnetic force between two electric currents. An instrument he devised to measure the flow of electricity was later refined as the GALVANOMETER. His chief published work was *Memoir on the Mathematical Theory of Electrodynamic Phenomena* (1827). The ampere (A) unit of electric current was named for him.

Ampère's law Law of ELECTROMAGNETISM that describes mathematically the MAGNETIC FORCE between two ELECTRIC CURRENTS. It was named after A.-M. AMPÈRE, who discovered that such forces exist. If two currents flow in the same direction, the force between the two wires is attractive; if they flow in opposite directions, the force is repulsive. In each case, the force is directly proportional to the currents.

amphetamine \am-'fe-tə-ˌmēn\ Organic compound, prototype of a class of synthetic amphetamine drugs (e.g., Benzedrine, Dexedrine, methamphetamine), which stimulate the central NERVOUS SYSTEM. It was first synthesized in 1887. Amphetamines cause wakefulness, euphoria, decreased fatigue, and increased ability to concentrate. Since they dull the appetite, they have been used for weight reduction. Often called "speed," they are used (often illicitly) by pilots, truckers, soldiers, and others to stay awake. In hyperactive children, they have a calming effect, helping them concentrate. Undesirable effects include overstimulation, with restlessness, insomnia, tremor, and irritability, and a deep DEPRESSION when the drug wears off. This, along with rapid development of tolerance requiring increased doses, can lead to DRUG ADDICTION. Large doses can bring on a psychosis resembling paranoid SCHIZOPHRENIA.

amphibian Any member of a class (Amphibia) of cold-blooded VERTEBRATE animals that includes more than 4,400 species in three groups: FROGS and TOADS (order Anura), SALAMANDERS (order Caudata), and CAECILIANS (order Apoda). Probably evolved from certain fish species of the Early DEVONIAN PERIOD (417–391 million years ago), amphibians were the first vertebrates to move from an aquatic environment to land. Most species have an aquatic larval, or TADPOLE, stage that metamorphoses into a terrestrial adult, but a few species spend their entire life in water. Amphibians are found worldwide, the majority in the tropics.

amphibious warfare Military operations directed against hostile shores and characterized by attacks launched from the sea by naval and landing forces. It may be used to seize a strategic site from the enemy or as a prelude to further combat operations ashore. It has been conducted since ancient times. The Greeks attacking Troy (1200 BC) had to make a shore landing, as did the Persian invaders of Greece prior to the Battle of MARATHON (490 BC). The British-led landings at GALLIPOLI (1915) were the main amphibious assault in World War I. The Allies of World War II found amphibious tactics essential in the Pacific campaign against numerous Japanese-held islands. The NORMANDY CAMPAIGN (1944) ranks as the greatest amphibious assault in history. Amphibious warfare's greatest advantage is its mobility and flexibility; its greatest limitation is that the attacker must start from nothing to build up strength ashore.

amphibole \'am-fə-ˌbōl\ Any of a group of common rock-forming hydrous SILICATE MINERALS. Amphiboles occur in many igneous rocks as minor and major constituents and form the major component in many GNEISSES and SCHISTS. Some highly fibrous forms are collectively called ASBESTOS.

amphibole asbestos Collective term for three highly fibrous (asbestiform) varieties of amphibole: CROCIDOLITE, AMOSITE, and ACTINOLITE. All have long, silky to splintery fibers with appreciable tensile strength and are of economic importance as ASBESTOS.

amphibolite \am-'fi-bə-ˌlīt\ Igneous or metamorphic rock composed largely or dominantly of AMPHIBOLE minerals. For igneous rocks, the term hornblendite is usually used and is more restrictive; HORNBLENDE is the most common amphibole. Metamorphic amphibolites are more widespread and variable than igneous ones. Typically, they are medium- to coarse-grained and are composed of hornblende and PLAGIOCLASE. Basic igneous rocks such as basalts and gabbros (see ACID AND BASIC ROCKS) can be the parent rocks of amphibolite.

amphibolite facies \'fā-shēz\ One of the major divisions of the mineral facies classification of METAMORPHIC ROCKS, encompassing rocks that formed under conditions of moderate to high temperatures (950°F, or 500°C, maximum) and pressures. Less-intense temperatures and pressures form rocks of the EPIDOTE-AMPHIBOLITE FACIES, and more-intense temperatures and pressures form rocks of the GRANULITE FACIES. Amphibole, diopside, epidote, plagioclase, certain types of garnet, and wollastonite are minerals typically found in amphibolite facies rocks. They are widely distributed in Precambrian gneisses and probably formed in the deeper parts of folded mountain belts.

Amphion and Zethus \'am-fē-ən...'zē-thəs\ In GREEK MYTHOLOGY, twin sons of ZEUS by the mortal Antiope. As infants the two were left to die on Mount Cithaeron, but were found and raised by a shepherd. Amphion grew up to become a great musician and singer, while Zethus became a hunter and herdsman. According to legend, they built the city of THEBES after the stone blocks arranged themselves into walls at the sound of Amphion's lyre. Amphion became king of Thebes, and he married NIOBE, with whom he had six sons and six daughters. When their children were killed by the gods, he committed suicide.

amphioxus \ˌam-fē-'äk-səs\ *or* **lancelet** \'lan-slət\ Any of certain small marine CHORDATES (invertebrate subphylum Cephalochordata) found widely on tropical and subtropical coasts and less commonly in temperate waters. Seldom more than 3 in. (8 cm) long, they resemble small, slender fishes without eyes or a definite head. They are grouped in several species in two genera *(Branchiostoma* or *Amphioxus,* and *Epigonichthyes* or *Asymmetron).* They spend much of their time buried in gravel or mud on the ocean bottom, though they are able to swim, and feed by filtering food particles from water passing through their gill slits. They have no brain or distinct heart.

Amphipolis \am-'fi-pə-ləs\ Ancient city, eastern Macedonia, near the mouth of the STRUMA RIVER. Amphipolis was a strategic transportation center, controlling the bridge over the river and the route from northern Greece to the Dardanelles. Colonized by ATHENS in 437 BC, it was taken by SPARTA in 424 BC. It soon received its independence, only to be taken by PHILIP II of Macedon in 358 BC. Later, under Roman rule, it was the headquarters of the Roman governor of Macedonia.

amphitheater Freestanding, open-air round or oval structure with a central arena and tiers of concentric seats. The amphitheater originated in ancient Italy (Etruria and Campania) and reflects the entertainment forms popular there, including gladiatorial games and contests of animals with one another or of men with animals. The earliest extant amphitheater is one built at POMPEII (c. 80 BC). Examples survive throughout the former provinces of the Roman empire, the most famous being Rome's COLOSSEUM.

amplifier Device that responds to a small input signal (voltage, current, or power) and delivers a larger output signal with the same waveform features. Amplifiers are used in radio and television receivers, high-fidelity audio equipment, and computers. Amplification can be provided by electromechanical devices (e.g., TRANSFORMERS and GENERATORS) and VACUUM TUBES, but most electronic systems now employ solid-state microcircuits. One amplifier is usually insufficient, so its output is fed into a second, whose output is fed to a third, and so on, until the output level is satisfactory.

amplitude modulation See AM

amputation Removal of any part of the body, usually surgical removal of part or all of a limb. Congenital amputation means lack of a limb at birth (see AGENESIS). Surgical amputation may be a lifesaving measure to prevent excessive blood loss from injury or to check the spread of infection, gangrene, or malignant soft-tissue or bone tumors. Reconstructive surgery and rehabilitation, and prompt treatment with blood and plasma, have made amputation rarer than in the past. Prostheses reduce handicaps for amputees, whose surgery may have been designed with the PROSTHESIS in mind.

Amr ibn al-As \'äm-ər-,ib-ən-əl-'äs\ (died 663) Arab conqueror of Egypt. After accepting Islam (c. 630) his first proselytizing mission was in Oman, where he converted its rulers. He also gained southwestern Palestine in the 630s before deciding on his own initiative to conquer Egypt, succeeding (642) after a two-year campaign. A good administrator and politician, late in his career he aided the governor of Syria, al-MUAWIYAH I, against ALI, Islam's fourth caliph. He was rewarded with the governorship of Egypt at the beginning of the UMAYYAD DYNASTY (661).

Amritsar \,əm-'rit-sər\, **Massacre of** (1919) Incident in which British troops fired on a crowd of Indian protesters. In 1919 the British government of India enacted the Rowlatt Acts, extending its World War I emergency powers to combat subversive activities. On April 13th a large crowd gathered to protest the measures and troops opened fire, killing about 379 and wounding about 1,200. The massacre was the prelude to MOHANDAS K. GANDHI's noncooperation movement of 1920–22.

Amsterdam City (pop., 2000 est.: 731,288), western Netherlands. It lies at the head of the IJSSELMEER. It is the nominal capital of the Netherlands, whose seat of government is at THE HAGUE. Originally a fishing village, it received its charter as a town in 1300. It joined the HANSEATIC LEAGUE in 1369 and grew steadily in the 14th and 15th centuries. After the decline of ANTWERP at the end of the 16th century, Amsterdam became the source of growing Dutch commercial and naval power. It was the center for the DUTCH EAST INDIA and West India companies, and became the leading trade metropolis of Europe. It became part of the Kingdom of Holland, which entered the Kingdom of the Netherlands in 1815. It suffered a partial decline in the 18th century, but its prosperity increased when it was connected by canal to the North Sea in 1875. It was occupied by Germany in World War II. After the war Amsterdam became known as a place of tolerance and liberalism. The city is now a major European port and a hub for international finance and trade.

Amtrak *formally* **National Railroad Passenger Corp.** Federally supported corporation that operates nearly all intercity passenger trains in the U.S. It was established by Congress in 1970 in the face of private railroads' heavy financial losses. Routes were cut back severely, and service is now maintained only in highly populated areas and between the largest cities. Amtrak pays the railroads to run passenger trains and compensates them for the use of tracks and terminals. Amtrak bears all administrative costs and manages scheduling, route planning, and ticket sales. Despite income from tickets and mail-carrying services, Amtrak has required large federal subsidies to cover its operating losses, though in recent years its revenues have covered an increasing percentage of its costs. See also CONRAIL, RAILWAY EXPRESS AGENCY, national RAILWAYS.

Amu Darya \'ä-mü-'där-yə\ *ancient* **Oxus** River, central Asia. It is one of the longest rivers in central Asia, at 1,578 mi (2,540 km), measured from the remotest sources of the Panj River; its other headstream is the Vakhsh. It flows west-northwest to its mouth on the ARAL SEA. It forms part of Afghanistan's border with Tajikistan, Uzbekistan, and Turkmenistan, and of Uzbekistan's border with Turkmenistan.

Roald Amundsen, 1923.
UPI/BETTMANN

Amundsen \'ä-mün-sən\, **Roald (Engelbregt Gravning)** (1872–1928?) Norwegian explorer, leader of the first group to reach the South Pole. In 1897 he took part in a Belgian expedition that was the first to winter in the Antarctic. In 1903–5 he was the first to navigate the Northwest Passage. He planned an expedition to the North Pole, but after learning that ROBERT E. PEARY had reached that goal, he set off for the South Pole in 1910. He prepared his trip carefully and in October 1911 set out with four men, 52 dogs, and four sledges. He reached the South Pole in December 1911, one month before ROBERT FALCON SCOTT's ill-fated attempt. He returned to Norway and established a successful shipping business. In 1926 he and Umberto Nobile (1885–1978) passed over the North Pole in a dirigible. Amundsen disappeared in 1928 while flying to rescue Nobile from a dirigible crash.

Amundsen Gulf \'ä-mən-sən\ SE extension of the BEAUFORT SEA. Extending about 250 mi (400 km), the gulf is bordered by VICTORIA ISLAND on the east, and separates BANKS ISLAND from the Canadian mainland. In 1850 the gulf was entered from the west by the British explorer Robert McClure. It is named for ROALD AMUNDSEN.

Amur River \ä-'mür\ *Chinese* **Heilong** *or* **Hei-lung** \'hā-'lùng\ River, northeastern Asia. The Amur proper begins at the confluence of the Shilka and ARGUN rivers and is 1,755 mi (2,824 km) long. It flows east-southeast along the Russian-Chinese border to Khabarovsk, Siberia, then northeast across Russian territory to empty into the TATAR STRAIT. Among its tributaries are the Zeya, Bureya, and USSURI rivers. From the 18th century, Russians have settled to the north of the river and Chinese to the south, a situation which at times has provoked border clashes.

amygdule \ə-'mig-,dyül\ Secondary deposit of minerals found in a rounded, elongated, or almond-shaped cavity in volcanic rock. The cavities (vesicles) were created by the expansion of gas bubbles or steam within lava. Because gas bubbles tend to rise through the lava, amygdules are most common near the tops of flows. Many minerals have been found as amygdules, including some spectacular museum specimens of ZEOLITES.

amyotrophic lateral sclerosis (ALS) \,ā-,mī-ə-'trō-fik...sklə-'rō-səs\ *or* **Lou Gehrig's disease** Degenerative NERVOUS-SYSTEM disorder causing muscle wasting and paralysis. The disease usually occurs after age 40, more often in men. Most victims die within two to five years from respiratory muscle ATROPHY. ALS affects motor NEURONS; the muscles they control become weak and atrophied, with debility usually beginning in the hands and creeping slowly up to the shoulders. The lower limbs become weak and spastic. Variants include progressive muscular atrophy and progressive bulbar palsy. In 1993 the defective gene that accounts for 5–10% of cases was discovered; it produces an ineffective version of an enzyme that neutralizes free radicals, which destroy motor neurons.

An Lushan Rebellion \'än-'lü-'shän\ Rebellion in 755 in China led by An Lushan (703–757), a general of non-Chinese origin. An Lushan rose through the ranks of the TANG-DYNASTY army in the 740s, becoming a military governor and a favorite of the emperor, XUANZONG. In 755 he turned his troops on the eastern capital city, Luoyang, and after taking it he proclaimed himself emperor. Six months later his forces took CHANG-AN, the western capital. He was murdered in 757, and the rebellion was put down in 763. The Tang government was much weakened, however, and the second half of the Tang dynasty and the subsequent FIVE DYNASTIES period were troubled by chronic warlordism.

An Yu \'än-'yü\ *or* **An Hyang** \'än-'hyäŋ\ (1243–1306) Korean Neo-Confucian scholar and educator. In 1287 he accompanied King Chungnyol to the Mongol court in Peking, where he encountered the texts of ZHU XI. Returning to Korea, An Yu used Neo-Confucian thought as the basis for promoting education. He helped reconstitute the National Academy and established a state treasury for national education. Eventually he became director of the Munmyo, the Korean national shrine to culture. Known as an opponent of Zen Buddhism in Korea, he was the most famous Confucian scholar of his era. See also NEO-CONFUCIANISM.

Anabaena \,an-ə-'bē-nə\ Genus of blue-green algae (CYANOBACTERIA) that are capable of NITROGEN FIXATION. Found as PLANKTON in shallow water and on moist soil, they occur in both solitary and colonial forms. In northern latitudes in summer, extensive growth of *Anabaena* may form water blooms that remain suspended instead of forming a surface scum. A toxic substance produced is fatal to cattle and other animals if present in drinking water in sufficient concentration.

Anabaptist Member of a radical movement of the 16th-century Protestant REFORMATION characterized by adult BAPTISM. Following HULDRYCH ZWINGLI, Anabaptists held that infants were not punishable for SIN since they had no awareness of good and evil and thus could not yet exercise free will, repent, and accept baptism. Confident of living at the end of time, early Anabaptists sought to restore the institutions and spirit of the primitive church. The first adult baptisms took place outside Zurich in early 1525. Most Anabaptists were pacifists and refused to swear civil oaths. They were expelled from one city after another, and many were martyred. Thomas Muntzer emphasized the end-time and was executed after leading the Thuringian peasant revolt (1525). Many Anabaptists settled in Moravia, where they stressed the community of goods modeled on the primitive church at Jerusalem. This branch continues as the Hutterite movement, primarily in the western U.S. and Canada. Increasingly persecuted throughout Europe, Anabaptists in the Netherlands and northern Germany rallied under the leadership of Menno Simonsz and survive as the Mennonites.

anabolic steroids \ˌa-nə-ˈbä-lik\ Steroid hormones that increase tissue growth. They are given to elderly or postoperative patients to promote muscle growth and tissue regeneration. Unsupervised use by athletes to build muscle and improve strength can have serious harmful effects, including coronary heart disease, sexual and reproductive disorders, immunodeficiencies, liver damage, stunted growth, aggressive behavior, susceptibility to connective-tissue injury, and (in girls) irreversible masculinization.

Anacletus II \ˌan-ə-ˈklēt-əs\ *orig.* **Pietro Pierleoni** (died 1138) Antipope (1130–38). Named a cardinal at Rome in 1116, he was elected pope by a majority of cardinals in 1130, while a minority created a schism by choosing Innocent II. Anacletus forced the rival pope to flee to France, where Innocent was declared legitimate by the Council of Étampes (1130). Innocent's supporters, including the Holy Roman and Byzantine emperors, invaded Italy in an unsuccessful effort to restore him. A second expedition in 1136 eroded support for Anacletus, who died before the issue was resolved.

anaconda Either of two South American snake species in the genus *Eunectes* (family Boidae) that constrict their prey. The heavily built giant anaconda, or great water boa, is usually not more than 16 ft (5 m) long but can be longer than 24 ft (7.5 m), rivaling the largest pythons in length. The yellow anaconda is much smaller. Typically dark green with alternating oval black spots, the giant anaconda lives along tropical rivers east of the Andes and in Trinidad. It kills at night by lying in wait in water; it constricts prey as large as young pigs or caimans and occasionally forages in trees for birds. It may bear 75 live young at a time.

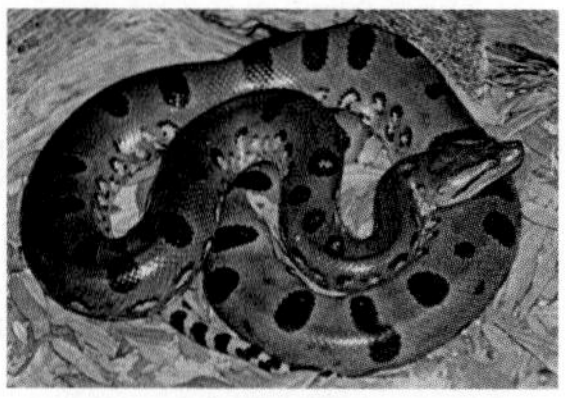

Giant anaconda (*Eunectes murinus*).

Anacreon *or* **Anakreon** \ə-ˈnak-rē-ən\ (582?–485? BC) Last great lyric poet of Asian Greece. Only fragments of his poetry have survived. Though he may have written serious poems, the poems quoted by later writers are chiefly in praise of love and wine. His sentiments and style were widely imitated, and the anacreontic meter in poetry was named for him.

Anaheim City (pop., 1992 est.: 276,000), southwestern California. Lying on the plain of the Santa Ana River 25 mi (40 km) southeast of Los Angeles, it was founded by German immigrants in 1857 as a cooperative agricultural community. After 1950 its citrus groves and vineyards had all but disappeared in the Los Angeles-Orange Co. urban-industrial expansion. Walt Disney's first amusement park, Disneyland, opened there in 1955. Today it is a prominent convention site.

anal canal End portion of the alimentary canal, distinguished from the rectum by the transition from an internal mucous membrane layer to one of skinlike tissue and by its narrower diameter. Waste products move from the rectum to the anal canal. The human anal canal is 1–1.5 in. (2.5–4 cm) long and has three parts: upper, with longitudinal folds (rectal columns); lower, with involuntary and voluntary constrictive muscles (sphincters) to control discharge of feces; and the anal opening itself. Enlargements of the ends of rectal and anal veins are called hemorrhoids.

Analects See Lunyu

analgesic \ˌan-əl-ˈjē-zik\ Drug that relieves pain without blocking nerve impulse conduction or markedly altering sensory function (see nervous system). Two classes are defined by the type of pain-relieving action. Opioids (opiates and synthetic narcotics; see opium) act on brain receptors to inhibit pain impulses. They may be used for short- or long-term pain relief, usually by prescription, but carry a risk of drug addiction. Nonopioids, used mostly for short-term relief, are available without prescription. They include NSAIDs (including aspirin and ibuprofen), acetaminophen, and phenacetin; all act by inhibiting synthesis of prostaglandins, molecules involved in the peripheral perception of pain.

analog computer Computer in which continuously variable physical quantities such as electrical potential, fluid pressure, or mechanical motion are represented in a way analogous to the corresponding quantities in the problem to be solved. The analog system is set up according to initial conditions and then allowed to change freely. Answers to the problem are obtained by measuring the variables in the analog model. Analog computers are especially well suited to simulating dynamic systems; such simulations may be conducted in real time or at greatly accelerated rates, allowing experimentation by performing many runs with different variables. They have been widely used in simulating the operation of aircraft, nuclear power plants, and industrial chemical processes. See also digital computer.

analysis In chemistry, the determination of the properties and composition of samples of materials; qualitative analysis establishes what is there, and quantitative analysis measures how much. A large body of systematic procedures (analytical chemistry) has evolved in close association with other branches of the physical sciences since their beginnings. A sample of a single compound may be analyzed to establish its elemental composition (see element, molecular weight) or molecular structure; many measurements use spectroscopy and spectrophotometry. A mixed sample is usually analyzed by separating, detecting, and identifying its components by methods that depend on differences in their properties (e.g., volatility, mobility in an electric or gravitational field, distribution between liquids that do not mix). The many types of chromatography are increasingly useful, particularly with biological and biochemical samples.

analysis Field of mathematics that incorporates the methods of algebra and calculus—specifically of limits, continuity, and infinite series—to analyze classes of functions and equations having general properties (e.g., differentiability). Analysis builds on the work of G. W. Leibniz and Isaac Newton by exploring the applications of the derivative and the integral. Several distinct but related subfields have developed, including the calculus of variations, differential equations, Fourier analysis (see Fourier transform), complex analysis, vector and tensor analysis, real analysis, and functional analysis. See also numerical analysis.

analytic geometry Investigation of geometric objects using coordinate systems. Because Rene Descartes was the first to apply algebra to geometry, it is also known as Cartesian geometry. It springs from the idea that any point in two-dimensional space can be represented by two numbers and any point in three-dimensional space by three. Because objects like lines, circles, ellipses, and spheres can be thought of as collections of points in space that satisfy certain equations, they can be explored via equations and formulas rather than graphs. Most of analytic geometry deals with the conic sections. Because these are defined using the notion of fixed distance, each section can be represented by a general equation derived from the distance formula.

analytic philosophy Philosophical tradition that defines the primary goal of philosophy to be analysis of concepts and of the language in which thoughts are expressed. A predominantly Anglo-American tradition, analytic philosophy is commonly opposed to Continental philosophy, but the significance of the opposition is open to serious doubt. Analytic philosophers primarily pursue issues in logic, language, epistemology, and the philosophy of mind, but apply their ideas to other topics, such as metaethics (see ethics), metaphysics, and the philosophy of religion. The tradition, which has its roots in British empiricism, began in the early 20th century, with work by G. E. Moore, Alfred North Whitehead, and Bertrand Russell. It also has strong connections to the Vienna Circle, logical positivism, Gottlob Frege, and the early work of Ludwig Wittgenstein. Later major contributions include those of A. J. Ayer, Gilbert Ryle, W. V. O. Quine, and J. L. Austin.

analytic psychology Psychoanalytic method of Carl Gustav Jung as he distinguished it from that of Sigmund Freud. Jung attached less importance than did Freud to the role of childhood sexual conflicts in the development of neurosis. He defined the unconscious to include both the individual's own unconscious and that inherited, partly in the form of archetypes, from his or her ancestors (the "collective unconscious"). He classified people into introvert and extrovert types, and further distinguished them according to four primary functions of the mind—thinking, feeling, sensation, and intuition—one or more of which predominated in any given person.

analytic–synthetic distinction In both LOGIC and EPISTEMOLOGY, the distinction (derived from KANT) between statements whose predicate is included in the subject (analytic statements) and statements whose predicate is not included in the subject (synthetic statements). Some philosophers prefer to define as analytic all statements whose denial would be self-contradictory, and to define the term synthetic as meaning "not analytic." The distinction aroused extensive debate in the mid-20th century, particularly in view of objections raised by W.V.O. QUINE.

anamorphosis \ˌan-ə-ˈmȯr-ˈfō-sis\ Drawing or painting technique that gives a distorted image of the subject when seen from the usual viewpoint, but when viewed from a particular angle or reflected in a curved mirror shows it in true proportion. Its purpose is to amuse or mystify. It was a curious by-product of the discovery of PERSPECTIVE in the 14th–15th century and was regarded as a display of technical virtuosity. The first examples appear in LEONARDO DA VINCI's notebooks.

Ananda \ˈä-nən-də\ (fl. 6th century BC) First cousin and disciple of the BUDDHA. A monk who served as the Buddha's personal attendant, he became known as the "beloved disciple." By tradition, he was the only intimate disciple of the Buddha who had not attained enlightenment before his master's death; he attained that state just before the first Buddhist Council (c. 544 or 480 BC), when he recited from memory the SUTTA PITAKA. He is represented as the author of several Buddhist discourses.

anaphylaxis \ˌan-ə-fī-ˈlak-sis\ Severe, immediate, potentially fatal bodily reaction to contact with a substance (ANTIGEN) to which the individual has become sensitized by a prior exposure that provoked no reaction. Often triggered by antiserum, antibiotics, or insect stings, symptoms include skin flushing, bronchial swelling (with difficulty breathing), and loss of consciousness. SHOCK may follow. Milder cases may involve HIVES and severe headache. Treatment, consisting of injection of EPINEPHRINE, followed by ANTIHISTAMINES, CORTISONE, or similar drugs, must begin within minutes. Anaphylaxis may be caused by extremely small amounts of antigen.

anarchism \ˈan-ər-ˌkiz-əm\ Political theory holding all forms of governmental authority to be unnecessary and undesirable and advocating a society based on voluntary cooperation and free association of individuals and groups. The word was used only pejoratively until P.-J. PROUDHON, now regarded as the founder of anarchism, adopted it in *What is Property?* (1840). The anarchist MIKHAIL BAKUNIN clashed with KARL MARX at the FIRST INTERNATIONAL; when it was dissolved in 1872, Bakunin's followers retained control of workers' organizations in Latin countries such as Spain and Italy. Even anarchists who believed that the transition to a government-free society required violent revolution disagreed on the nature of the transition. Anarcho-SYNDICALISM, which grew up in the late 1880s, based its ideology on labor unions *(syndicats)* rather than the individual, calling for general strikes to paralyze the state. In the 19th and 20th century, anarchism also inspired experimental communities, including New Lanark in Britain and BROOK FARM in the U.S. During the early months of the SPANISH CIVIL WAR, anarchist militias were in virtual control of much of eastern Spain, where they established hundreds of anarchist collectives. Suppressed as an organized movement by fascism in the 1930s, anarchism reemerged in the 1950s and '60s through its influence on the CIVIL RIGHTS MOVEMENT and the student movements in the U.S. and Europe. The radical ECOLOGY movement in the 1970s also was inspired by anarchist ideas. Beginning in 1999, anarchist-led street demonstrations against the policies of the WORLD BANK and INTERNATIONAL MONETARY FUND received unprecedented publicity and inspired a proliferation of new anarchist groups, periodicals, and Internet sites. Anarchist themes are reflected in the work of many 20th century artists, writers, and musicians, including PABLO PICASSO, the poets of the American BEAT MOVEMENT, the Spanish surrealist filmmaker LUIS BUÑUEL, and the American composer JOHN CAGE.

Anasazi culture \ˌä-nə-ˈsä-zē\ North American civilization that developed from c. AD 100 to historic times, centering on the area where the boundaries of Arizona, New Mexico, Colorado, and Utah intersect. *Anasazi* (Navajo for "Ancient Ones") is used to refer to the ancestors of contemporary PUEBLO INDIAN peoples. Anasazi civilization is customarily divided into five periods: Basketmaker (AD 100–500), Modified Basketmaker (500–700), Developmental Pueblo (700–1050), Classic Pueblo (1050–1300), and Regressive Pueblo (1300–1550). As among present-day Pueblo peoples, religion was highly developed and centered on rites partly conducted in underground circular chambers called KIVAS. The best-known Anasazi ruins are the great cliff dwellings at MESA VERDE (Col.) and Chaco Canyon (N.M.).

Anastasia *Russian* **Anastasiya Nikolayevna** (1901–1918) Grand duchess of Russia and youngest daughter of Czar NICHOLAS II. She was executed at age 17 with the other members of her immediate family by the Bolsheviks in the RUSSIAN REVOLUTION OF 1917. After the executions several women outside Russia claimed her identity, making her the subject of periodic popular conjecture and publicity. Some also claimed to be heir to the Romanov fortune held in Swiss banks. The most famous was Anna Anderson (died 1984), a Pole married to a U.S. history professor; her claim was finally rejected in 1970, and later genetic tests proved there was no connection between Anderson and the Romanovs.

Anastasius I \ˌan-ə-ˈstā-zhəs\ (430?–518) Byzantine emperor (491–518). Originally a bodyguard to ZENO, he succeeded Zeno as emperor and married his widow. Anastasius reformed the monetary and taxation systems and expelled rebel tribes from Constantinople, building a wall to protect the capital against raiders. He recognized THEODORIC's rule in Italy (497) but later sent a fleet to ravage the Italian coast. War with Persia (502–5) ended when he agreed to pay tribute to the Persian king. Anastasius accepted the MONOPHYSITE doctrine, a stand that caused unrest in Byzantium but fostered peace with Egypt and Syria.

Anatolia See ASIA MINOR

Anatolian languages Branch of the INDO-EUROPEAN LANGUAGE family spoken in Anatolia in the 2nd–1st millennium BC. The attested Anatolian languages are Hittite, Palaic, Luwian (Luvian), Hieroglyphic Luwian, Lycian, and Lydian. Hittite, by far the most copiously attested of the group, is known chiefly from a vast archive of CUNEIFORM tablets found in 1905 at Hattuša (now Boğazköy, in northern central Turkey), the capital of the HITTITE Empire; Hittite texts date from the 16th–13th century BC. By the late Roman or early Byzantine period at the latest, Anatolian languages had all become extinct. Several non-Indo-European languages of ancient Anatolia, all known from cuneiform texts, are also sometimes considered Anatolian languages: Hattic, spoken in central Anatolia before the coming of the Hittites and known solely from words and texts preserved by Hittite scribes; Hurrian, spoken in the 2nd millennium BC in northern Mesopotamia and southeastern Anatolia; and Urartian (Urartean), known from northwestern Anatolian texts of the 9th–7th century BC.

anatomy Biological field that deals with body structures as revealed by dissection. HEROPHILUS first laid the factual groundwork for gross anatomy, the study of structures large enough to see without a microscope. GALEN's ideas were the authority for anatomy in Europe until ANDREAS VESALIUS methods placed it on a firm foundation of observed fact. The microscope permitted the discovery of tiny structures (e.g., capillaries and cells), the subject of microscopic anatomy. Crucial advances in this area, including the microtome, which slices specimens into extremely thin sections, and staining (e.g., GRAM STAIN), led to the new fields of CYTOLOGY and HISTOLOGY. ELECTRON MICROSCOPY opened up the study of subcellular structures, and X-RAY DIFFRACTION gave rise to the new subspecialty of molecular anatomy. Comparative anatomy compares structures in different animals to see how they have changed with EVOLUTION.

Anaxagoras \ˌan-ak-ˈsag-ə-rəs\ (c. 500–428? BC) Greek philosopher. Though only a few fragments of his writings have been preserved, he is remembered for his cosmology and for his discovery of the true cause of eclipses. His cosmology grew out of the efforts of earlier PRE-SOCRATICS to explain the physical universe in terms of a single element. The most original aspect of his system was his doctrine of *nous* ("mind"), according to which the growth of living things depends on the power of *nous* that enables them to extract nourishment from surrounding substances.

Anaximander \ə-ˈnak-sə-ˌman-dər\ (610–546/545 BC) Greek philosopher, often called the founder of astronomy. He apparently wrote treatises on geography, astronomy, and cosmology that survived for several centuries and made a map of the known world. He was the first thinker to develop a COSMOLOGY. A rationalist, he prized symmetry and used geometry and mathematical proportions to help map the heavens; his theories thus departed from earlier, more mystical conceptions and foreshadowed the achievements of later astronomers. Whereas earlier theories had suggested earth was suspended or supported from elsewhere in the heavens, Anaximander asserted that earth remained unsupported at the center of the universe because it had no reason to move in any direction.

Anaximander, represented with a sundial, mosaic, 3rd century AD; in the Rhineland Museum, Trier, Ger.

BY COURTESY OF THE LANDESMUSEUM, TRIER, GER

Anaximenes \ˌan-ak-ˈsim-ə-ˌnēz\ (fl. c. 545 BC) Greek philosopher of nature. With Thales and Anaximander, he is one of three Milesian thinkers (see Miletus) traditionally considered the first philosophers in the Western world. He defined the essence of matter as *aer* ("air") and explained the densities of various types of matter in terms of varying degrees of condensation of moisture. His writings no longer exist except as quoted by later authors.

ANC See African National Congress

ancestor worship Religious beliefs or practices that involve addressing prayers or offerings to the spirits of dead relatives. It existed among the ancient Greeks, other Mediterranean peoples, and the ancient Europeans; it also plays a major role in traditional African religions. The dead are related to the family, clan, tribe, or village; mythical ancestors may be included. They may be friendly, or they may be displeased and require propitiation. Commemorative ceremonies are sometimes held at graves or monuments and may include prayers, offerings, sacrifices, and festivals of honor. Worship of individual ancestors is common; it may be combined with communal forms of worship, as in the case of the Roman emperor cult. An ancestor whose deeds are heroic may attain the status of a god. In China and Japan, ancestor worship (more accurately, ancestor reverence) has declined with the decline in the size and importance of kinship groups.

Anchorage Seaport, largest city (pop., 1996 est.: 250,000), and chief commercial center of Alaska. It lies at the head of Cook Inlet near the base of the Kenai Peninsula. It was founded in 1914 as a construction camp for the building of a railroad to Fairbanks. It became a key aviation and defense center in World War II and is now a regular stop on air routes from the U.S. to East Asia. Anchorage experienced rapid population growth in the late 20th century. In 1964 a severe earthquake caused a number of deaths and extensive property damage.

anchovy Any of more than 100 species of schooling saltwater fishes (family Engraulidae) related to the herring. Anchovies are distinguished by a large mouth, almost always extending behind the eye, and by a pointed snout. Most species live in shallow tropical or warm temperate seas, where they often enter brackish water around river mouths. Adults are 4–10 in. (10–25 cm) long. Temperate-water species such as the northern and European anchovies are important food fishes; tropical species such as the tropical anchovy, or anchoveta, are important bait fishes. See also schooling behavior.

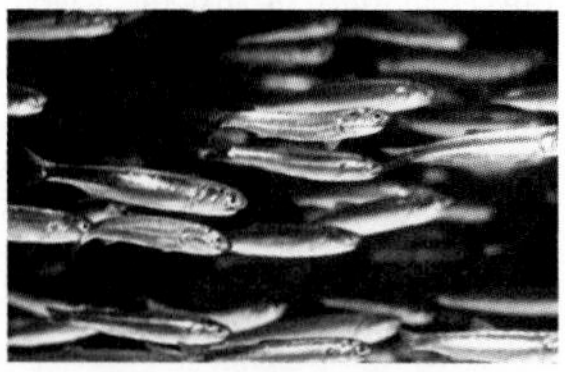

Anchovies (*Engraulis mordax*).

TOM MCHUGH—PHOTO RESEARCHERS

ancien régime \ä^{n}s-ya^{n}-rā-ˈzhēm\ (French: "old order") Political and social system of France before the French Revolution. Under the regime, everyone was a subject of the king of France as well as a member of an estate and province. All rights and status flowed from the social institutions, divided into three orders: clergy, nobility, and others (the Third Estate). France was not truly a unit of government and there was no national citizenship.

Ancona Seaport (pop., 1991: 101,000), central Italy, and capital of the Marche region. Founded by colonists from Syracuse c. 390 BC, it was taken by Rome in the 2nd century BC. It became a flourishing port particularly favored by Trajan, who enlarged the harbor. It was attached to the Holy Roman Empire in the 12th century; in the 16th century it came under papal protection, which was largely maintained until Ancona became part of Italy in 1861. It underwent severe bombing in World War II, but many notable Roman and medieval landmarks survive.

Anda See Altan

Andalusia \ˌan-də-lü-ˈsē-ə\ Autonomous community (pop., 1996 est.: 7,235,000) and historic region, southern Spain. It occupies an area of 33,694 sq mi (87,267 sq km); the capital is Seville. It is traversed by mountain ranges, including the Sierra Morena and Sierra Nevada; its main river is the Guadalquivir. It has a long history of inhabitation: by the Phoenicians (at what is now Cádiz, c. 1100 BC), the Carthaginians (480 BC), and the Romans. The Arabic name Al-Andalus was originally applied by the Moors to the whole Iberian Peninsula. When the Umayyad dynasty established its court at Córdoba, this area became the peninsula's intellectual and political center. It returned to Spanish rule in 1492, and remained a province until divided in 1833 into the eight modern provinces. A mining and agricultural region, its beaches along the Costa del Sol attract a growing tourist trade.

Andaman and Nicobar Islands \ˈan-də-mən...ˈnik-ō-ˌbär\ Union territory (pop., 1994 est.: 322,000), India. It consists of two groups of islands in the Bay of Bengal about 400 mi (650 km) west of Myanmar. The chief islands are North Andaman, Middle Andaman, and South Andaman (known collectively as Great Andaman), and Little Andaman. The Nicobar group includes Car Nicobar, Camorta (Kamorta) and Nancowry, and Great Nicobar. Most of the population lives in the Andaman group. The first European settlement was at Port Blair, South Andaman, now the union territory capital. In the Nicobar group there are remnants of inhabitation dating to AD 1050.

Andaman Sea Sea, part of the Bay of Bengal. Bounded by the Andaman and Nicobar Islands, Myanmar, the Malay Peninsula, and the Strait of Malacca and Sumatra, it covers some 218,000 sq mi (565,000 sq km). Trading vessels have plied the sea since ancient times. Part of the early coastal trade route between India and China, from the 8th century it formed a route between India (and Sri Lanka) and Myanmar. Its largest modern ports are Pinang (Malaysia) and Yangon (Myanmar).

Andania mysteries Ancient Greek mystery cult, held in honor of the goddess Demeter and her daughter Kore (Persephone) at Andania in Messenia. It was performed by "holy ones" of both sexes from various tribes. Initiation was open to all. Costumes were plain and inexpensive, except for those costumed as deities. There was a procession, and a pageant or drama may have been performed; sacrifices were made to several deities before the main ceremony.

Andean bear See spectacled bear

Andean civilization Complex of aboriginal cultures that evolved in the Andean region (see Andes Mtns.) of western South America before the arrival of the Spanish conquistadores in the 16th century. Unlike the peoples of the Mesoamerican civilization to the north, none of the aboriginal Andean peoples developed a system of writing, though the Incas devised a sophisticated system of recording numbers. In its level of cultural development and technical expertise in the arts and crafts, however, this civilization constitutes a New World counterpart to those of ancient Egypt, China, and Mesopotamia. See also Chibcha, Chimu, Moche, Tiahuanaco.

Andean Geosyncline Linear trough in the earth's crust in which rocks were deposited in South America in the Mesozoic era (248–65 million years ago) and Cenozoic era (65 million years ago to the present). A complex history of volcanism, uplift, block faulting, and erosion led eventually to the present configuration of the Andes Mountains.

Hans Christian Andersen.

THE BETTMANN ARCHIVE

Andersen, Hans Christian (1805–1875) Danish writer of fairy tales. Though reared in poverty, he received a university education. In his many collections of tales, published 1835–72, he broke with literary tradition and employed the idioms and constructions of spoken language. His stories are imaginative combinations of universal elements from folk legend and include such favorites as "The Ugly Duckling" and "The Emperor's New Clothes." While some reveal an optimistic belief in the ultimate triumph of goodness and beauty (e.g., "The Snow Queen"), others are deeply pessimistic. Part of what makes his tales compelling is the way they identify with the unfortunate and outcast. He also wrote plays, novels, poems, travel books, and several autobiographies.

Anderson, Elizabeth Garrett (1836–1917) British physician. Refused admission to medical schools, she studied privately with physicians and in London hospitals and was licensed to practice in 1865. Appointed general medical attendant to St. Mary's Dispensary (1866), later the New Hospital for Women, she worked to create a medical school for women. In 1918 the hospital was named for her.

Anderson, Judith *orig.* **Frances Margaret** *later* **Dame Judith** (1898–1992) Australian-U.S. actress. She made her stage debut in Sydney in 1915 and first appeared in New York in 1918. She was noted for such roles as Lavinia in *Mourning Becomes Electra* (1932), Gertrude in *Hamlet* (1936), and Lady Macbeth in *Macbeth* (1937, 1941), and for the title role in *Medea* (1947). She appeared in over 25 films, usually playing an evil or sinister figure, including Mrs. Danvers in *Rebecca* (1940) and Ann Treadwell in *Laura* (1944).

Anderson, Laurie (born 1947) U.S. performance artist. Born in Chicago, she studied at Columbia University and began giving New York performances in 1973 while teaching art history. Combining elements of music, theater (dance, mime), film, technology, and speech, she has satirized media and mass culture, using the tools they themselves provide. The pop-music success of her "O Superman" (1980) led to her recording two albums, *Big Science* (1982) and *Mister Heartbreak* (1984). Her major 1980s piece was *United States*. Other works include *Stories from the Nerve Bible* (1993) and a multimedia work based on *Moby-Dick* (1999).

Anderson, Leroy (1908–1975) U.S. composer of light orchestral music. Born in Cambridge, Mass., he studied at Harvard; fluent in nine languages, he was an army interpreter in two wars. In 1936 he began a long association with A. FIEDLER and the Boston Pops Orchestra, and such pieces as "Syncopated Clock," "Sleigh Ride," "Bugler's Holiday," and the *Irish Suite* became standards. A 1953 survey determined that Anderson was the most frequently performed American composer.

Anderson, Lindsay (1923–1994) English critic and director. He was a founding editor of the film magazine *Sequence*, and from 1948 he directed a series of documentaries, including *Thursday's Children* (1955, Academy Award). He coined the term "Free Cinema" for the British cinematic movement inspired by JOHN OSBORNE's play *Look Back in Anger*. His first feature film, *This Sporting Life* (1963), is a classic of the British social-realist cinema. He directed several theatrical productions before making his next film, *If . . .* (1968). After directing the premieres of David Storey's plays, he went on to make such films as *O Lucky Man!* (1973) and *The Whales of August* (1987).

Anderson, Marian (1897–1993) U.S. singer. Born in Philadelphia, she was immediately recognized for the beauty of her voice and her artistry at her New York debut in 1924, but the fact that she was black made a concert or opera career in the U.S. impossible. Her London debut in 1930 and tours of Scandinavia established her in Europe, where she worked exclusively until 1935. S. HUROK convinced her to again try to make a career in her native land. When she was denied use of Constitution Hall in Washington, D.C., by the Daughters of the American Revolution in 1939, ELEANOR ROOSEVELT arranged for her to sing at the Lincoln Memorial, and the concert was broadcast to great acclaim. Her debut at the Metropolitan Opera, the first performance there by a black singer, took place in 1955, when she was in her late fifties.

Marian Anderson.
BY COURTESY OF RCA RECORDS

Anderson, (James) Maxwell (1888–1959) U.S. playwright. Born in Atlantic, Pa., he worked as a journalist before cowriting his first successful play, *What Price Glory?* (1924), which was followed by *Saturday's Children* (1927). His verse dramas *Elizabeth the Queen* (1930) and *Mary of Scotland* (1933) were later adapted for film. He returned to prose for *Both Your Houses* (1933, Pulitzer Prize) and *Winterset* (1935), then turned to verse again for *High Tor* (1936). He collaborated with K. WEILL on the musicals *Knickerbocker Holiday* (1938) and *Lost in the Stars* (1949). His last play, *The Bad Seed* (1954), became a successful film.

Anderson, Sherwood (1876–1941) U.S. author. Born in Camden, Ohio, he was irregularly schooled. Having married, he abruptly left his family and business career to become a writer in Chicago. *Winesburg, Ohio* (1919), a collection of interrelated sketches and tales about the obscure lives of the citizens of a small town, was his first mature book and made his reputation. His short stories were collected in *The Triumph of the Egg* (1921), *Horses and Men* (1923), and *Death in the Woods* (1933). His prose style, based on everyday speech and influenced by the experimental writing of GERTRUDE STEIN, in turn influenced such writers as ERNEST HEMINGWAY and WILLIAM FAULKNER.

Andersonville Village, southwestern central Georgia. It was the site of a Confederate military prison in 1864–65 during the AMERICAN CIVIL WAR. Notorious for its dreadful conditions, it provided only makeshift shelter for the Union prisoners, more than a quarter of whom died. The Andersonville National Cemetery, which includes the prison site, contains the graves of 12,912 Union prisoners who perished there. In 1865 Capt. Henry Wirz, commander of the prison, was tried by a military commission and hanged.

Andes Mountain system, western South America. One of the great natural features of the globe, the Andes extend north-south about 5,500 mi (8,850 km). They run parallel to the Caribbean coast in Venezuela before turning southwest and entering Colombia. There they form three distinct massifs: the Cordilleras Oriental, Central, and Occidental. In Ecuador they form two parallel cordilleras, one facing the Pacific and the other descending toward the Amazon basin. These ranges continue southward into Peru; the highest Peruvian peak is Mount Huascarán, at 22,205 ft (6,768 m), in the Cordillera Blanca. In Bolivia, the Andes again form two distinct regions; between them lies the ALTIPLANO. Along the Chile-Argentina border, they form a complex chain that includes their highest peak, Mount ACONCAGUA. In southern Chile part of the cordillera descends beneath the sea, forming innumerable islands. The Andes are studded with numerous volcanoes that form part of the RING OF FIRE. They also are the source of many rivers, including the ORINOCO, AMAZON, and PILCOMAYO.

andesite \'an-də-ˌzīt\ Any member of a large family of rocks that occur in most of the world's volcanic areas, mainly as surface deposits and to a lesser extent as dikes and small plugs. The Andes, where the name was first applied, and most of the cordillera (parallel mountain chains) of Central and North America consist largely of andesites. They also occur in abundance in volcanoes along practically the entire margin of the Pacific basin. Andesites are most often porphyritic (having distinct crystals in a fine-grained base) rocks.

Andhra Pradesh \ˌän-drə-prə-'desh\ State (pop., 1994 est.: 71,800,000), southeastern India. Located on the Bay of BENGAL, and covering 106,272 sq mi (275,244 sq km), it was formed in 1953 from part of MADRAS state; its capital is HYDERABAD. Its name derives from the Telugu-speaking Andhra people, who have long inhabited the area. Many dynasties have flourished here, dating back to the 3rd century BC. The area came under British influence in the 17th century; in the 19th century the Andhras played a decisive role in the rise of Indian nationalism. The state's economy is primarily agricultural.

Andizhan \ˌan-di-'zhan\ *or* **Andijon** \ˌan-di-'jän\ City (pop., 1993 est.: 313,000), eastern Uzbekistan. Dating back to at least the 9th century AD, it was an important trading center in the 15th century because of its location on the SILK ROAD. Part of the khanate of Kokand (see QUQON) in the 18th century, it was captured by the Russians in 1876. The surrounding area is the most densely populated part of Uzbekistan and the country's main petroleum-producing region.

Andocides \an-'dä-si-,dēz\ (c. 440–after 391 BC) Athenian orator and politician. He went into exile (415–403) after being implicated in and having informed on those responsible for the mutilation of the sacred busts of Hermes just before Athens's expedition to Sicily, returning after the restoration of democracy. He helped arrange a treaty with Sparta in the Corinthian War (392), but Athens rejected it and exiled him and the other ambassadors.

Andorra *officially* **Principality of Andorra** Independent coprincipality, southeastern Europe. Lying on the southern slopes of the Pyrenees Mtns., it consists of a cluster of mountain valleys whose streams form the Valira River; it is bounded by Spain and France. Area: 180 sq mi (480 sq km). Population (1997 est.): 65,000. Capital: Andorra la Vella. Much of the population is Spanish; a minority is Andorran. Language: Catalan (official). Religion: Roman Catholicism. Currency: Spanish peseta, French franc. Andorra's independence is traditionally ascribed to Charlemagne, who recovered the region from the Muslims in 803. It was placed under the joint suzerainty of the French counts of Foix and the Spanish bishops of the See of Urgell in 1278, and it was subsequently governed jointly by the Spanish bishop of Urgell and the French head of state. This feudal system of government, the last in Europe, lasted until 1993, when a constitution was adopted that transferred most of the coprinces' powers to the Andorran General Council, a council elected by universal suffrage. Andorra has long had a strong affinity with Catalonia; its institutions are based in Catalonian law and it is part of the diocese of the See of Urgell (Spain). The traditional economy was based on sheepraising, but from the 1950s tourism has become very important.

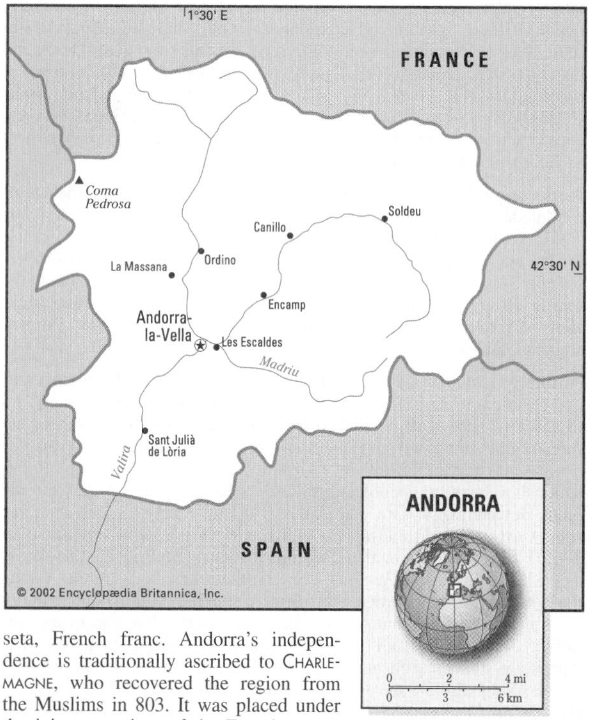

Andorra la Vella \an-'dȯr-ə-lä-'vel-yä\ Town (pop., 1995: 22,000), capital of Andorra. It lies near the confluence of the Valira and Valira del Norte rivers. The town long remained relatively isolated from the outside world, but its population began to grow after World War II as tourists began arriving at the nearby sports areas. Because of its country's duty-free status, the town has become a retail shopping center for other Europeans.

Andrada e Silva \a^{n}-'drá-thá-ē-'sil-vá\, **José Bonifácio de** *known as* **José Bonifácio** \zhü-'ze-,bō-ni-'fä-sē-ō\ (1763?–1838) Chief architect of Brazil's independence from Portugal. Andrada was born in Brazil but educated in Portugal, where he became a distinguished scholar. On returning to Brazil in 1819, he became chief minister of the Portuguese prince regent (later the emperor Pedro I), who had fled Portugal with the rest of the royal family to escape Napoleon. He became the leading intellectual advocate of independence. After Pedro I declared Brazil independent in 1822, Andrada served as prime minister and as tutor to the child emperor Pedro II, who became an effective and enlightened monarch.

Andrássy \'än-,drá-sē\, **Gyula, Gróf (Count)** (1823–1890) Hungarian politician. A follower of Lajos Kossuth, Andrássy helped lead the unsuccessful revolt of 1848–49, then fled into exile until 1857. He supported the creation of an Austro-Hungarian dual monarchy and played a major role in negotiating the Compromise of 1867. He served as Hungary's first prime minister (1867–71), and later as foreign minister (1871–79), in which roles he helped strengthen Austria-Hungary's international position. Just before resigning, he signed the fateful Austro-German alliance that linked those two powers until the end of World War I.

Andre, Carl (born 1935) U.S. sculptor. He grew up in Quincy, Mass., the son of a draftsman for a shipbuilding firm, and attended Phillips Andover Academy and Northeastern University. He moved to New York in 1957 and soon was producing large-scale horizontal configurations out of steel plates, slabs of granite, styrofoam planks, bricks, and cement blocks, using a grid system based on simple mathematical principles. In the late 1960s he was among the pioneers of Minimalism. In 1988 he was tried for murder after his wife, the sculptor Ana Mendiata, fell to her death from their apartment window, but was acquitted.

André \'an-drē\, **John** (1750–1780) British army officer and spy. From 1774 he was chief intelligence officer to the British commander Henry Clinton at New York. In 1779 André began corresponding with Gen. Benedict Arnold, who had become disillusioned with the American cause. In 1780 he obtained Arnold's agreement to surrender the West Point fort. André was captured while returning to New York, and incriminating papers were found in his boot; he was found guilty of espionage and hanged.

André, Maurice (born 1933) French trumpeter. He worked, like his father, in a mine for four years before going to the Paris Conservatory in 1951. Too poor to pay the tuition, he became eligible for a scholarship by first joining a military band. He has specialized impressively in the Baroque repertoire, playing a specially made trumpet (with four valves) for high-lying parts. He has released more than 300 recordings, more than any other classical trumpeter.

Andrea del Sarto \än-'drā-ə-del-'sär-tō\ *orig.* **Andrea d'Agnolo** (1486–1530) Italian painter active in Florence. His name derives from his father's profession (*del sarto,* "of the tailor"). After an apprenticeship with Piero di Cosimo, he became established as one of the outstanding painters of the city, most notably as a fresco decorator and painter of altarpieces. His feeling for color and atmosphere was unrivaled among Florentine painters. One of his most striking achievements was the series of grisaille frescoes on the life of St. John the Baptist (1511–26) in the Chiostro dello Scalzo. Among his students and followers were Jacopo da Pontormo and Giorgio Vasari.

"Marriage of St. Catherine," oil on panel by Andrea del Sarto, 1512–13; in the Gemäldegalerie Alte Meister, Dresden, Ger.

SACHSISCHE LANDESBIBLIOTHEK/ABTEILUNG DEUTSCHE FOTOTHEK/A. ROUS

Andreanof Islands \,an-drē-'a-nȯf\ Group of the Aleutian Islands, southwestern Alaska. Lying between the Pacific Ocean and the Bering Sea, the islands extend east to west about 270 mi (430 km) between the Fox and Rat island groups. They were strategically important in World War II, when U.S. military bases were developed, especially on Adak Island. Other islands in the group include Atka, Tanaga, and Kanaga.

Andreini family \,än-drā-'ē-nē\ Italian actors. After their marriage, Francesco Andreini (1548–1624) and Isabella Canali Andreini (1562–1604) founded the Compagnia dei Gelosi, one of the earliest and most famous of the commedia dell'arte troupes. Their son Giovambattista Andreini (1579?–1654) acted in his parents' company until c. 1601, when he formed his own troupe, the Compagnia dei Fedeli. The troupe was invited to the French court in Paris, where Andreini wrote the play *Adamo* (1613), supposedly the inspiration for JOHN MILTON's *Paradise Lost.*

Andretti, Mario (Gabriel) (born 1940) Italian-U.S. automobile racing driver. He was born in Montona, Italy, where he became interested in racing before coming to the U.S. in 1955. His notable wins include the USAC championship-car race (1965–66, 1969), the Daytona Beach stock-car race (1967), the Sebring Grand Prix sports-car race (1967, 1970), the INDIANAPOLIS 500 race (1969), and the Formula I world driving championship (1978). He retired from competition in 1994.

Andrew, St. (died AD 60/70) One of the 12 APOSTLES, brother of St. PETER, and patron saint of Scotland and Russia. According to the Gospels, he was a fisherman and a disciple of JOHN THE BAPTIST. Early Byzantine tradition calls Andrew *protokletos,* "first called." He and Peter were called from their fishing by JESUS, who promised to make them fishers of men. Early church legends tell of Andrew's missionary work around the Black Sea. A 4th-century tradition says he was crucified; 13th-century tradition states that the cross was X-shaped. His relics were moved several times after his death; his head was kept in St. Peter's in Rome from the 15th century until 1964, when the pope returned it to Greece as a gesture of goodwill.

Andrew II *Hungarian* **Endre** (1175–1235) King of Hungary (1205–35). His reign was marked by controversy with the landed nobility, who drained royal funds and reduced Hungary to a state of near anarchy. Rebellious nobles murdered his first wife, Gertrude of Meran, in 1213. Andrew led a CRUSADE to the Holy Land in 1217. On his return he agreed to the Golden Bull of 1222, limiting royal rights, guaranteeing justice, promising improved coinage, and giving nobles the right to resist royal decrees. His daughter was St. ELIZABETH OF HUNGARY.

Andrews, Julie *later* **Dame Julie** *orig.* **Julia Elizabeth Wells** (born 1935) British-U.S. actress and singer. She made her London debut at 12 in a revue, and her New York stage debut in *The Boy Friend* (1954). A major star of the Broadway musical, she originated the roles of Eliza Doolittle in *My Fair Lady* (1956) and Guinevere in *Camelot* (1960). She also starred in such films as *Mary Poppins* (1964, Academy Award), *The Sound of Music* (1965), *Star!* (1968), and *Victor/Victoria* (1982), and returned to the stage in 1995 in an adaptation of *Victor/Victoria* directed by her husband, BLAKE EDWARDS.

Andrews, Roy Chapman (1884–1960) Naturalist, explorer, and author. Born in Beloit, Wis., in 1906 he joined the staff of the American Museum of Natural History, where he would spend much of his working life. There he assembled one of the best collections of cetaceans in the world before turning his attention to Asiatic exploration. He led expeditions to Tibet, southwestern China, and Burma (1916–17); northern China and Outer Mongolia (1919); and central Asia. Important discoveries included the first known dinosaur eggs, skeleton parts of *Baluchitherium* (the largest known land mammal), and evidence of prehistoric human life. His many books for the general public include *Across Mongolian Plains* (1921) and *This Amazing Planet* (1940).

Andrić \'än-drich\, **Ivo** (1892–1975) Bosnian writer. He established his reputation with *Ex Ponto* (1918), which he wrote while interned for nationalist political activities in World War I. He later served as a Yugoslavian diplomat. Collections of his short stories were published from 1920 onward. Of his three novels, written during World War II, two—*The Bridge on the Drina* (1945) and *Bosnian Story* (1945)—are about the history of Bosnia. He was awarded the Nobel Prize in 1961.

androgen \'an-drə-jən\ Any of a group of HORMONES that mainly influence the development of the male REPRODUCTIVE SYSTEM. The main and most active androgen is TESTOSTERONE, produced by cells in the TESTES. Androgens produced in smaller quantities, mainly by the ADRENAL GLAND but also by the testes, support the functions of testosterone. Androgens cause the normal changes of PUBERTY in boys' bodies and then influence sperm-cell formation, sexual interest and behavior, and male pattern baldness. Females produce trace quantities of androgens, mostly in the adrenal glands, as well as in the ovaries.

Andromeda \an-'drä-mə-də\ In GREEK MYTHOLOGY, the wife of PERSEUS. She was the daughter of King Cepheus and Queen Cassiope of Joppa in Palestine (called Ethiopia). Her mother boasted that Andromeda was more beautiful than the NEREIDS, and POSEIDON punished her by sending a sea monster to devastate Joppa. To appease the gods, Andromeda was chained to a rock and left to be devoured by the monster. Perseus flew by on PEGASUS, fell in love with Andromeda, and slew the monster. She married him and bore him six sons and a daughter. After her death she became a constellation.

Andromeda galaxy \an-'drò-mə-də\ *or* **M31** Great spiral galaxy in the constellation Andromeda. It is the nearest spiral galaxy outside the MILKY WAY and one of the few visible to the unaided eye, appearing as a milky blur. About 2 million light-years from earth, it has a diameter of about 200,000 light-years, which makes it the largest galaxy in the LOCAL GROUP. For centuries astronomers considered it part of the Milky Way; only in the 1920s did EDWIN HUBBLE determine conclusively that it was a separate galaxy.

Andronicus I Comnenus \ˌan-drə-'nī-kəs...käm-'nē-nəs\ (1118–1185) Byzantine emperor (1183–85), the last of the Comnenus dynasty. A cousin of MANUEL I COMNENUS, he raised an army and seized power in 1182, causing a massacre of Westerners in Constantinople. He was crowned co-emperor with Alexius II in 1183; two months later he had Alexius strangled and married his 13-year-old widow. Andronicus reformed the Byzantine government and asserted the independence of the Eastern Church, provoking a Sicilian Norman invasion. News of the Normans' approach led to a revolt, in which Andronicus was killed by a mob and ISAAC II ANGELUS was declared emperor.

Andronicus II Palaeologus \ˌpā-lē-'äl-ə-gəs\ (1260–1332) Byzantine emperor (1282–1328). The son of MICHAEL VIII PALAEOLOGUS, he was an intellectual and theologian rather than a soldier and statesman, and during his reign the BYZANTINE EMPIRE declined to the status of a minor state. Ottoman Turks controlled Anatolia by 1300, and Serbs dominated the Balkans. By siding with Genoa in the war between Genoa and Venice, Andronicus provoked an attack by the Venetian navy. Despite the rising political disorder, he promoted Byzantine art and the independence of the Eastern Orthodox Church. Deposed by his grandson ANDRONICUS III PALAEOLOGUS, he entered a monastery.

Andronicus III Palaeologus (1296–1341) Byzantine emperor (1328–41). He forced his grandfather ANDRONICUS II PALAEOLOGUS to make him co-emperor (1325) and then to abdicate (1328). He relied on JOHN VI CANTACUZENUS to reform the courts and rebuild the imperial navy. He ceded control of Macedonia to Serbia (1334) and lost land to the Ottoman Turks in Anatolia, but he regained some Aegean islands from the Genoese and reasserted control of Epirus and Thessaly.

Andropov \än-'drō-ˌpòf\, **Yury (Vladimirovich)** (1914–1984) Soviet leader. He joined the Communist Party in 1939 and rose rapidly in the party hierarchy. His tenure as head of the KGB (1967–82) was noted for its suppression of political dissidents. In 1982 he succeeded LEONID BREZHNEV as general secretary of the party's Central Committee, but ill health quickly overtook him, and he accomplished little before his death 15 months later.

Andros \ˌan-drəs\ Island (pop., 1995 est.: 9,000), Bahamas. The Bahamas' largest island, it extends about 100 mi (160 km) north to south and about 45 mi (72 km) east to west; its area is 2,300 sq mi (6,000 sq km). Just off its eastern coast is the third-largest barrier reef in the world.

Andros \'an-drəs\, **Edmund** *later* **Sir Edmund** (1637–1714) English governor of the Dominion of New England. Appointed governor of New York and New Jersey in 1674, he was recalled in 1681 following complaints from colonists. He returned in 1686 as governor of the Dominion, a kind of supercolony imposed by Britain. He again attempted to stem growing colonial independence and his interference in local government again antagonized the colonists. In 1688 they revolted and imprisoned him. He was recalled to England but returned as governor of Virginia (1692) and Maryland (1693–94).

anemia Condition in which ERYTHROCYTES are reduced in number or volume or are deficient in HEMOGLOBIN. The patient is usually noticeably pale. Close to 100 varieties exist (including APLASTIC ANEMIA, PERNICIOUS ANEMIA, and SICKLE-CELL ANEMIA), distinguished by cause; erythrocyte size, shape, and hemoglobin content; and symptoms. Anemia may result from blood loss; increased destruction, reduced production, or inhibited formation of red cells; or hormone deficiency. Treatment may involve nutrition, toxin removal, drugs, surgery, or transfusion. See also FOLIC-ACID-DEFICIENCY ANEMIA, IRON-DEFICIENCY ANEMIA.

anemia of bone-marrow failure See APLASTIC ANEMIA

anemometer \ˌan-ə-ˈmä-mə-tər\ Instrument for measuring the speed of airflow. The most familiar instruments for measuring wind speeds are the revolving cups that drive an electric generator (useful range approximately 5–100 knots). For very low airspeeds, a unit in which revolving vanes operate a counter measures the airspeed. For strong, steady wind speeds (in wind tunnels and aboard aircraft in flight), a PITOT-TUBE anemometer is often used; the pressure difference between the interior of the tube and the surrounding air can be measured and converted to airspeed.

anemone \ə-ˈne-mə-nē\ Any of about 120 species of perennial plants that make up the genus *Anemone,* in the BUTTERCUP family, many of which are cultivated for their colorful flowers. Though found throughout the world, anemones occur most commonly in woodlands and meadows of the northern temperate zone. Many colorful varieties of the tuberous poppylike anemone *A. coronaria* are grown for the garden and florist trade. Popular spring-flowering species include *A. apennina, A. blanda,* and *A. pavonina.* Other species, such as the Japanese anemone *(A. hupehensis),* are favorite border plants for autumn flowering. The European wood anemone, *A. nemorosa,* causes blistering of the skin and was once used as an ingredient in medicines. Anemones are also known colloquially as pasqueflowers or windflowers.

anesthesiology \ˌa-nəs-ˌthē-zē-ˈäl-ə-jē\ Medical specialty dealing with anesthesia and related matters, including resuscitation and pain. Originally concerned only with general anesthesia in the operating room, anesthesiology now includes epidural anesthesia (injection of local ANESTHETICS into the spinal fluid, cutting off feeling below the point of injection); artificial respiratory support during operations requiring paralyzing drugs that render patients unable to breathe; clinical management of all unconscious patients; management of pain relief, and cardiac and respiratory resuscitation problems; respiratory therapy; and treatment of fluid, electrolyte, and metabolic disturbances. Progress in anesthesiology has made possible more complex operations and surgery for more critically ill patients. The anesthesiologist's role has become increasingly important and complex.

anesthetic \ˌan-es-ˈthet-ik\ Agent that produces a local or general loss of sensation, including pain, and therefore is useful in SURGERY and DENTISTRY. General anesthesia induces loss of consciousness, most often using HYDROCARBONS (e.g., cyclopropane, ethylene); halogenated (see HALOGEN) hydrocarbons (e.g., CHLOROFORM, ethyl chloride, trichloroethylene); ETHERS (e.g., ethyl ether or vinyl ether); or other compounds, such as tribromoethanol, NITROUS OXIDE, or BARBITURATES. Local anesthesia induces loss of sensation in one area of the body by blocking nerve conduction (see NERVOUS SYSTEM, NEURON), usually with ALKALOIDS such as COCAINE or synthetic substitutes (e.g., lidocaine). See also ANESTHESIOLOGY.

aneuploidy See PLOIDY

aneurysm \ˈan-yə-ˌriz-əm\ Blood-filled protrusion in the wall of a blood vessel (usually an ARTERY, and particularly the AORTA). Disease or injury weakens the wall so that normal BLOOD PRESSURE makes it balloon out. Typically, the two inner layers rupture and the outer layer bulges. In a false aneurysm, all three layers rupture and surrounding tissues hold the blood in place. Symptoms vary with size and location. Aneurysms tend to enlarge over time, and blood-vessel walls weaken with age. Many aneurysms eventually burst, causing serious, even massive, internal bleeding; aortic aneurysm rupture causes severe pain and immediate collapse. Rupture of an aneurysm in the brain is a major cause of STROKES. Treatment can consist of simply tying off a small vessel; more serious aneurysms require surgery to replace the diseased section of artery with a plastic graft.

Angara River \ən-ˌgə-ˈrä\ River, southeastern central Russia. The outlet for Lake Baikal, it is a major tributary of the Yenisey River, which it joins near Yeniseysk. It is about 1,150 mi (1,850 km) long, and with its many rapids, it provides great potential for hydroelectric power. Some existing dams and power stations provide power in the Irkutsk industrial area.

angel Primarily in Western religions, any of numerous benevolent spiritual beings who mediate between heaven and earth. They often serve as messengers or servants of God or as guardians of an individual or nation. In Zoroastrianism, the AMESHA SPENTA are arranged in a hierarchy of seven. Judaism and Christianity base their notion of angels on Old Testament references to divine servants and to the heavenly hosts. Two archangels (Michael and Gabriel) are mentioned in the Old Testament and two others (Raphael and Uriel) in the Apocrypha. Islam's hierarchy of angels descends from the four throne bearers of Allah to the cherubim who praise Allah, the four archangels, and lesser angels such as the *hafazeh* (guardian angels). See also CHERUB, SERAPH.

Angel Falls (Salto Ángel), La Gran Sabana region of Bolívar state, Venezuela.

G. DE STEINHEIL—SHOSTAL ASSOC./EB INC.

Angel Falls Waterfall, southeastern Venezuela. It lies on the Churún River, a tributary of the Caroní, southeast of Ciudad Bolívar. The highest waterfall in the world, it drops 3,212 ft (979 m) and is 500 ft (150 m) wide at its base. It was named for James Angel, an American who crash-landed his plane nearby in 1937.

An aquarium angelfish (*Pterophyllum*).

JANE BURTON—BRUCE COLEMAN LTD.

angelfish Any of various unrelated fishes of the order Perciformes. The best-known angelfishes are freshwater CICHLIDS popular in home aquariums (genus *Pterophyllum*): thin and deep-bodied fishes that are usually silver with vertical dark markings but may be solid or partially black. These species may grow to 6 in. (15 cm) long. Brightly colored marine angelfishes are in the family Pomacanthidae. They are found among tropical reefs in the Atlantic and the Indo-Pacific, where they eat algae and marine invertebrates and reach a maximum length of 18 in. (46 cm).

Angelico \an-ˈjel-i-kō\, **Fra** *orig.* **Guido di Piero** (c. 1395–1455) Italian painter and Dominican friar active in Florence. He entered the convent of San Domenico at Fiesole sometime between 1417 and 1425 and began his artistic career by painting illuminated manuscripts and altarpieces. He was influenced by Masaccio's use of architectural perspective. Among his earliest masterpieces is a large triptych, the Linaiuoli Altarpiece (1433–36), executed for the linen merchants' guild; it is enclosed in a marble shrine designed by Lorenzo Ghiberti. His most notable works are frescoes at the convent of San Marco, Florence (c. 1440–45), and in the chapel of Pope Nicholas V in the Vatican (c. 1448–49). One of the outstanding fresco painters of the 15th century, he influenced such masters as Fra Filippo Lippi; Benozzo Gozzoli was among his students.

Angelou \ˈan-jə-ˌlō\, **Maya** *orig.* **Marguerite Johnson** (born 1928) U.S. poet. Born in St. Louis, she was raped at age 8 and went through a period of muteness. Her varied jobs before she became a writer included waitress, prostitute, cook, dancer, and actress. Her autobiographical works, which explore themes of economic, racial, and sexual oppression, include *I Know Why the Caged Bird Sings* (1970), *The Heart of a Woman* (1981), and *All God's Children Need Traveling Shoes* (1986). Her poetry collections include *Just Give Me a Cool Drink of Water 'fore I Diiie* (1971), *And Still I Rise* (1978), and *I Shall Not Be Moved* (1990). Her recitation of a poem she wrote for William Jefferson Clinton's first inauguration (1993) brought her widespread fame.

Ångermanland \ˈȯŋ-ər-mən-ˌland\ Region, eastern Sweden, on the Gulf of Bothnia. A former province of Sweden, it is approximately coextensive with the modern provinces of Västernorrland and Västerbotten. Consisting of vast forests with large rivers, including the Fax and Ångerman rivers, the region was inhabited as early as the Stone Age.

Angevin dynasty \ˈan-jə-vən\ Descendants of a 10th-century count of Anjou (the source of the adjective Angevin). The Angevin dynasty overlaps with the House of Plantagenet, but is usually said to consist of only the English kings HENRY II, RICHARD I, and JOHN. Henry established the Angevin empire when he took control of Normandy, Anjou, Maine, and Aquitaine, thus extending the Angevin holdings in the late 12th century from Scotland to the Pyrenees. English claims to French territory led to the HUNDRED YEARS' WAR; by 1558 the English had lost all their former French lands.

Angilbert \'aŋ-gəl-ˌbərt\, **St.** (c. 740–814) Frankish poet and prelate at the court of CHARLEMAGNE. Of a noble family, he was educated at the palace school at Aachen and was a student of ALCUIN. In 800 he accompanied Charlemagne to Rome. He was made lay abbot of Centula (St.-Riquier), Picardy, in 794. His graceful and sophisticated Latin poems offer a picture of life in the imperial circle.

angina pectoris \an-'jī-nə-'pek-tə-rəs\ Spasm of chest pain, caused when the heart's oxygen demand temporarily outpaces its blood supply, usually because of CORONARY HEART DISEASE. A deep, viselike pain in the heart and stomach area commonly spreads to the left arm. Exertion or emotional stress can bring on angina, obliging the victim to rest until the pain subsides. If rest does not help, drugs can dilate the blood vessels. As heart disease worsens, angina recurs with less exertion.

angiocardiography \ˌan-jē-ō-ˌkär-dē-'äg-rə-fē\ Method of DIAGNOSTIC IMAGING that shows the flow of blood through the HEART and great vessels to evaluate patients for surgery on the cardiovascular system. A CONTRAST MEDIUM is introduced through a catheter into a heart chamber. A series of X-ray images shows where the flow narrows, signaling blockage of a blood vessel by ARTERIOSCLEROSIS.

angiography \ˌan-jē-'äg-rə-fē\ *or* **arteriography** \är-ˌtir-ē-'äg-rə-fē\ X-RAY examination of arteries and veins with a CONTRAST MEDIUM to differentiate them from surrounding organs. The contrast medium is introduced through a catheter to show the blood vessels and the structures they supply, including organs. Angiography of diseased leg, brain, or heart arteries is necessary before corrective surgery. See also ANGIOCARDIOGRAPHY.

Angiolini \ˌan-jə-'lē-nē\, **Gasparo** *or* **Angelo Gasparini** (1731–1803) Italian choreographer, among the first to integrate dance, music, and plot in dramatic ballets. In 1757 he became ballet master of the Vienna court opera house; in 1761 he collaborated with C.W. GLUCK to produce *Don Juan* and later choreographed other ballets to Gluck's music. In 1765 Angiolini became ballet master of the Imperial Theatre in St. Petersburg. He maintained a rivalry with J.-G. NOVERRE and disagreed with his interpretation of the innovative *ballet d'action.*

angioplasty \'an-jē-ə-ˌplas-tē\ Opening of a blocked blood vessel, often by flattening plaques (see ARTERIOSCLEROSIS) against an artery's wall by inflation of a balloon near the end of a catheter (see CATHETERIZATION). Performed on a coronary artery, angioplasty is a less invasive alternative to CORONARY BYPASS surgery in the treatment of CORONARY HEART DISEASE. Complications, including EMBOLISMS and tearing, are rare, and results are excellent, but plaques tend to build up again after the procedure. Angioplasty is also used to expand a severely obstructed heart valve.

angiosperm See FLOWERING PLANT

Angkor Archaeological site, northwestern Cambodia. Located 4 mi (6 km) north of the modern town of Siem Reap, it was the capital of the KHMER (Cambodian) empire in the 9th–15th century. Its most imposing monuments are ANGKOR WAT, a temple complex built in the 12th century by King SURYAVARMAN II, and Angkor Thom, a temple complex built c. 1200 by King JAYAVARMAN VII. During the period of great construction that lasted more than 300 years, there were many changes in architecture as the religious focus changed from Hindu to Buddhist cults. After the Siamese conquest of the Khmers in the 15th century, the ruined city and its temples were buried in the jungle. When the French colonial regime was established in 1863, the entire site became the focus of scholarly interest. During Cambodia's political upheavals of the late 20th century there was some war damage, but the major problem was one of neglect.

Angkor Wat \'aŋ-kȯr-'wät\ Temple complex in Angkor (now in northwestern Cambodia), the crowning work of Khmer architecture. About 1,700 yards (1,550 m) long by 1,500 yards (1,400 m) wide, it is the world's largest religious structure. Dedicated to VISHNU, it was built in the 12th century by SURYAVARMAN II. The Wat, an artificial mountain originally surrounded by a vast external wall and moat, rises in three enclosures toward a flat summit. The five remaining towers (shrines) at the summit are composed of the repetitive diminishing tiers typical of Asian architecture.

angle In geometry, a pair of rays (see LINE) sharing a common endpoint (the vertex). An angle may be thought of as the rotation of a single ray from an initial to a terminal position. Clockwise rotation is considered negative and counterclockwise rotation positive. Either may be measured in degrees (one full rotation = 360°) or radians (one full rotation 2π rad). A 90° angle is called a right angle. Any angle less than 90° is an acute angle; any angle more than 90° but less than 180° is an obtuse angle.

anglerfish Any of about 210 species of marine fishes (order Lophiiformes) named for their method of "fishing" for prey. The foremost spine of the dorsal fin is located on the head and is modified into a "fishing rod" tipped with a fleshy "bait." Prey fishes attracted to this lure stray close enough for the anglerfish to swallow them. Often bizarre in form, anglerfishes are also characterized by small gill openings and by limblike pectoral and (in some species) pelvic fins. Most species inhabit the sea bottom. In some species the small male bites into the larger female's body, his mouth fuses with the skin, and the bloodstreams of the two become permanently connected.

Angles Germanic people who, with the Jutes and SAXONS, invaded England in the 5th century AD. According to BEDE, their homeland was Angulus, traditionally identified as the Angeln district in Schleswig. They abandoned this area when they invaded Britain, where they settled in the kingdoms of Mercia, Northumbria, and East and Middle Anglia. Their language is known as Englisc, and they gave their name to England.

Anglesey \'aŋ-gəl-sē\ *ancient* **Mona** Island (pop., 1995 est.: 67,000), Wales. The largest island in England or Wales, at 276 sq mi (715 sq km), Anglesey is known for its ancient history and its prehistoric and Celtic remains. By 100 BC the Celts had colonized the island, which became a famous DRUID center and later a stronghold of resistance to the Romans. It finally fell to AGRICOLA in AD 78. It was ruled by the princes of Wales in the 7th–13th century, when it was taken by EDWARD I. Tourism is now an important part of the economy.

Anglia See ENGLAND

Anglican Communion See Church of ENGLAND

Anglo-Afghan Wars See AFGHAN WARS

Anglo-Burmese Wars (1824–26, 1852, 1885) Conflicts between the British and the Burmese in present-day Myanmar. The Burmese king BODAWPAYA's conquest of the kingdom of Arakan, which bordered on British-controlled territory in India, led to border conflicts between Arakan freedom fighters and the Burmese. When the Burmese crossed the border into Bengal, the British responded in force, taking Rangoon. The resulting two-year conflict ended with a treaty that gave Britain Arakan and Assam and required the Burmese to pay an indemnity. Another war erupted 25 years later when a British naval officer seized a ship that belonged to the Burmese king; this war resulted in the British occupation of Lower Burma. The third war was sparked by threats to the British teak monopolies in Lower Burma and Burmese overtures to the French; it resulted in the British annexation of Upper Burma (formalized in 1886), thus ending Burmese independence.

Anglo-Dutch Wars *or* **Dutch Wars** Four naval conflicts between England and the Dutch Republic in the 17th–18th century. The First (1652–54), Second (1665–67), and Third (1672–74) Anglo-Dutch Wars all arose from commercial rivalry between the two nations, and victories by England established its naval might. The two countries had been allied for a century when the Fourth Anglo-Dutch War (1780–84) broke out over Dutch interference in the AMERICAN REVOLUTION. By 1784 the Dutch Republic had declined dramatically in power and prestige.

Anglo-French Entente See ENTENTE CORDIALE

Anglo-French War See OPIUM WARS

Anglo-German Naval Agreement (1935) Bilateral concord between Britain and Germany countenancing a German navy but limiting it to 35% of the size of the British navy. Part of the process of APPEASEMENT before World War II, the agreement allowed Germany to violate restrictions imposed by the Treaty of VERSAILLES, prompting international criticism and driving a wedge between the French and the British.

Anglo-Japanese Alliance (1902–23) Alliance between Britain and Japan to protect their respective interests in China and Korea. Directed against Russian expansionism, the alliance helped Japan in the RUSSO-JAPANESE WAR by discouraging France from entering the war on the Russian side. The alliance later prompted Japan to enter World War I on the side of the Allies. Britain allowed the alliance to lapse after the war, when it no longer feared Russian encroachment in China.

Anglo-Russian Entente \än-'tänt\ (1907) Pact in which Britain and Russia settled their colonial disputes in Persia, Afghanistan, and Tibet. It delineated spheres of influence in Persia, stipulated that neither country would interfere in Tibet's internal affairs, and recognized Britain's influence over Afghanistan. The agreement led to the formation of the TRIPLE ENTENTE.

Anglo-Saxon See OLD ENGLISH

Anglo-Saxon art Painting, sculpture, and architecture produced in Britain from the late 5th century to the NORMAN CONQUEST. Before the 9th century, manuscript illumination was the predominant art form, with two schools: Canterbury produced works in the classical tradition brought by Roman missionaries; a more influential school in Northumbria produced works inspired by the revival of learning encouraged by Irish missionaries. The curvilinear forms, spirals, and interlaced patterns of the Celtic tradition brought by Irish monks were integrated with the abstract ornamentation and bright colors of the Anglo-Saxon metalwork tradition. After the destructive effects of the 9th-century Danish invasions, the monasteries were revived and interest in architecture developed. Building activity consisted of small churches influenced by continental types, notably from Norman France (e.g., the original WESTMINSTER ABBEY, c. 1045–50, rebuilt 1245). The monastic revival resulted in the production of many books and the formation of the Winchester school of illumination (late 10th century). See also HIBERNO-SAXON art.

Anglo-Saxon law Body of legal principles that prevailed in England from the 6th century until the NORMAN CONQUEST (1066). It was directly influenced by early Scandinavian law as a result of the Viking invasions of the 8th and 9th century and indirectly influenced (primarily through the church) by ROMAN LAW. Anglo-Saxon law had three components: laws promulgated by the king, customary practices such as those regulating kinship relations, and private compilations. The primary emphasis was on criminal law, though certain material dealt with problems of public administration, public order, and ecclesiastical matters.

Anglo-Saxon literature Literature written in OLD ENGLISH c. 650–c. 1100. Anglo-Saxon poetry survives almost entirely in four manuscripts. BEOWULF is the oldest surviving Germanic epic and the longest Old English poem; other great works include *The Wanderer, The Seafarer, The Battle of Maldon,* and the *Dream of the Rood.* The poetry is alliterative; one of its features is the kenning, a metaphorical phrase used in place of a common noun (e.g., "swan road" for "sea"). Notable prose includes the *Anglo-Saxon Chronicle,* a historical record, begun about the time of King ALFRED's reign (871–899) and continuing for more than three centuries. See also CAEDMON, CYNEWULF.

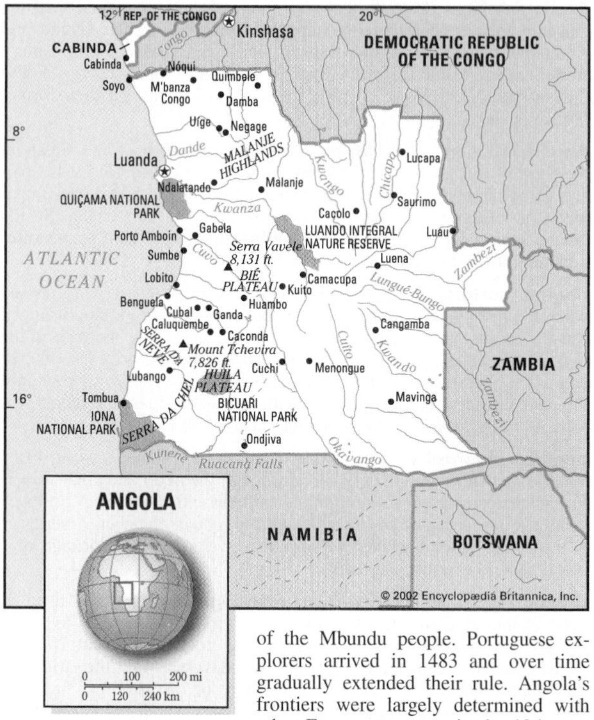

Angola *officially* **Republic of Angola** *formerly* **Portuguese West Africa** Nation, South Africa. Its northernmost section of coastland, the Cabinda exclave, is separated from Angola proper by a narrow corridor of Congo territory. Area: 481,354 sq mi (1,246,700 sq km). Population (2002 est.) 10,593,000. Capital: LUANDA. The population is made up of mostly BANTU-speaking peoples; the main ethnic groups are the OVIMBUNDU and the MBUNDU, while the Khoisan-speaking SAN (Bushmen) inhabit southeastern Angola. Languages: Portuguese (official), indigenous languages. Religions: Christianity (Roman Catholicism, Protestantism), traditional beliefs. Currency: kwanza. The country contains several plateau regions, which separate it into three distinct drainage systems. One in the northeast drains into the CONGO RIVER basin; another in the southeastern sector drains into the ZAMBEZI system; the remaining drainage, westward into the Atlantic, provides most of Angola's hydroelectric power. About 40% of the land area is forest; less than 10% is arable. Despite substantial petroleum reserves, Angola's economy has been unable to take advantage of its resources because of the devastation caused by its protracted civil war. It is nominally a republic with one legislative house; its head of state and government is the president. An influx of Bantu-speaking peoples in the 1st millennium AD led to their dominance in the area by c. 1500. The most important Bantu kingdom was the KONGO; south of the Kongo was the Ndongo kingdom of the Mbundu people. Portuguese explorers arrived in 1483 and over time gradually extended their rule. Angola's frontiers were largely determined with other European powers in the 19th century, but not without severe resistance by the indigenous peoples. Its status as a Portuguese colony was changed to that of an overseas province in 1951. Resistance to colonial rule led to the outbreak of fighting in 1961, which led ultimately to independence in 1975. Rival factions continued fighting after independence. Although a peace accord was reached in 1994, forces led by JONAS M. SAVIMBI continued to resist government control until his death in 2002, after which a peace accord was signed.

Angora See ANKARA

Angora cat See TURKISH ANGORA CAT

Angora goat Breed of domestic GOAT that originated in the district of Angora in Asia Minor. Its silky coat yields commercial mohair. Angora goats are generally smaller than other domestic goats and have long, drooping ears. Both sexes are horned. The Western mohair industry developed after the animal was established in South Africa in the mid-19th century. Importation to the U.S. followed shortly; breeding has centered in the Southwest. The coat, with its strong elastic fibers, differs from WOOL primarily in its smoothness and luster.

Angora goat.
GRANT HEILMAN PHOTOGRAPHY, INC.

Angoulême \ˌäⁿ-gü-'lām\ City (pop., 1999: 43,171), southwestern France, on the CHARENTE RIVER. CLOVIS captured the town from the VISIGOTHS in 507, and from the 9th century it was the center of a countship. Fought over by the French and English in the HUNDRED YEARS' WAR, it was ceded to England in 1360 but restored to France in 1378. It passed to the house of Orleans in 1394. The city is noted for papermaking and is the site of the 12th-century cathedral of St. Pierre.

angry young men Group of mid-20th-century young British writers whose works express the bitterness of the lower classes toward the established sociopolitical system and the mediocrity and hypocrisy of the middle and upper classes. The label came from a press agent's description of JOHN OSBORNE, whose play *Look Back in Anger* (1956) is the movement's representative work. The group was said to include John Wain (1925–1994), KINGSLEY AMIS, ALAN SILLITOE, and Bernard Kops (born 1926). A dominant literary force in the 1950s, the movement had faded by the early 1960s.

Ångström \'äŋ-strœm\, **Anders Jonas** (1814–1874) Swedish physicist. From 1839 he taught at the University of Uppsala. He devised a method of measuring thermal conductivity, showing it to be proportional to electrical conductivity, and deduced that an incandescent gas emits rays of the same refrangibility as those it can absorb. A founder of SPECTROSCOPY, he discovered that hydrogen is present in the sun's atmosphere, published a map of the normal solar spectrum, and was the first to examine the spectrum of the aurora borealis and to detect and measure the characteristic bright line in its yellow-green region. The angstrom (10^{-10} m), a unit of length, was named in his honor.

Anguilla \aŋ-'gwi-lə\ Island (pop., 1995 est.: 7,000), LEEWARD ISLANDS, West Indies. A dependent territory of the United Kingdom, it is the most northerly of the Leeward Islands, and covers about 35 sq mi (90 sq km). Its territory includes nearby Scrub, Seal, Dog, and Sombrero islands and Prickly Pear Cays. Most of its people are descendants of African slaves. The official language is English, and most of the population is Protestant. First colonized in 1650 by settlers from ST. KITTS, it was administered by the British. From 1825 it was closely associated with St. Kitts, a situation Anguilla protested. It was united with St. Kitts and Nevis in 1882. When a nation consisting of the three was formed in 1967, Anguilla proclaimed its independence. The British intervened, and Anguilla was separated in 1980; while retaining some autonomy, it consented to remain under British rule.

angular momentum Property that describes the rotary INERTIA of a system in motion about an axis. It is a VECTOR quantity, having both magnitude and direction. The magnitude of the angular momentum of an object is the product of its linear MOMENTUM (mass m × velocity v) and the perpendicular distance r from the center of rotation, or mvr. The direction is that of the axis of rotation. The angular momentum of an isolated system is constant. This means that a rigid spinning object continues to spin at a constant rate unless acted upon by an external TORQUE. This means that a spinning GYROSCOPE in an airplane remains fixed in its orientation, independent of the airplane's motion, because of the conservation of direction as well as magnitude.

Angus Breed of black, hornless beef cattle. Formerly known as Aberdeen Angus, it originated in northeastern Scotland, but its ancestry is obscure. Angus have a compact and low-set body. The fine quality of the flesh and the high dressing percentage make it a beef breed of the highest rank. Introduced into the U.S. in 1873, its influence there and in other countries spread widely thereafter.

Anhalt \'än-,hält\ Former German state in what is now central Germany. The area around the upper ELBE RIVER from which Anhalt was constituted was in the 11th century still part of the duchy of SAXONY. It achieved separate territorial status in 1212. Subdivided and reunited frequently, it was finally reconstituted as the duchy of Anhalt by Leopold IV in 1863. It became part of the German empire in 1871. Reconstituted after World War II as Saxony-Anhalt, it subsequently became part of East Germany, and, in 1990, part of reunified Germany.

Anheuser-Busch Co., Inc. \'än-hòi-zər\ Largest producer of BEER and second-largest beverage producer in the world. Headquartered in St. Louis, Mo., its origins can be traced to a small brewery founded in 1852 and bought in 1860 by the soap manufacturer Eberhard Anheuser. In 1861 his daughter married Adolphus Busch, a brewery supplier. Busch pioneered the use of refrigerated railcars and of PASTEURIZATION in the brewing industry. In 1876 the company introduced a light-colored beer called Budweiser; under August Anheuser Busch, Jr. (president 1946–75), and A. A. Busch III (president from 1975), it became the best-selling U.S. beer brand. The company also produces the Michelob brand. Among its other holdings are beverage-container manufacturing and recycling plants, media and advertising groups, and amusement parks, including the Sea World theme parks and Busch Gardens (Tampa, Fla.).

anhinga *or* **snakebird** Any fish-eating bird of the family Anhingidae (order Pelecaniformes), sometimes considered a single species *(Anhinga anhinga)* with geographical variants. Anhingas are about 35 in. (90 cm) long, slender, and long-necked. They are mostly black, with silvery wing markings. Males, glossed with green, develop pale head plumes and a dark "mane" in breeding season. Anhingas live in small colonies along lakes and rivers in tropical to warm temperate regions except in Europe. They swim nearly submerged; the head and neck show above water, darting snakelike from side to side.

Anhui *or* **Anhwei** \'än-'hwā\ Province (pop., 1996 est.: 60,130,000), eastern central China. It is one of China's smallest provinces; its capital is HEFEI. Anhui was the first part of southern China to be settled by the HAN, in the later part of the 1st millennium BC. Well-watered by the Huai and CHANG (Yangtze) rivers, it was the empire's major agricultural area for several centuries. Anhui was ruled by the MING DYNASTY in the 14th–17th century. It was occupied by the Japanese in World War II; after the war, the Nationalists held it briefly before the Communists took over. It is a notable agricultural producer.

anhydride \,an-'hī-,drīd\ Any chemical COMPOUND obtained, either in practice or in principle, by eliminating WATER (H_2O) from another compound. Examples of inorganic anhydrides are sulfur trioxide, SO_3, which is derived from sulfuric acid, H_2SO_4, and calcium oxide, CaO, which is derived from calcium hydroxide $Ca(OH)_2$. The most important organic anhydride is acetic anhydride, $(CH_3CO)_2O$, an important raw material for cellulose acetate (the base of magnetic tapes), textile fibers, and ASPIRIN. It can be thought of as ACETIC ACID minus water. Organic anhydrides are very important starting materials for organic synthesis, as they can give rise to CARBOXYLIC ACIDS, ESTERS, or AMIDES under the proper conditions.

anhydrite Rock-forming mineral, anhydrous calcium sulfate ($CaSO_4$), which differs chemically from gypsum (to which it changes in humid conditions) by having no water of crystallization. Anhydrite occurs most often with salt deposits in association with gypsum, as in the cap rock of the Texas-Louisiana salt domes. Anhydrite is one of the major minerals in EVAPORITE deposits; it is also present in dolomites and limestones, and in ore veins. It is used in plasters and cement as a drying agent.

Aniakchak National Monument \,an-ē-'ak-chak\ Park, southern shore of the ALASKA PENINSULA. Situated in the volcanically active Aleutian Range, it consists primarily of a great dry caldera, which last erupted in 1931. The crater has an average diameter of 6 mi (10 km). Declared a national monument in 1978, it covers 942 sq mi (2,440 sq km).

Aniene River \än-'yā-nā\ River, central Italy. It rises in the Simbruini Mountains southeast of Rome and meanders 67 mi (108 km) to join the TIBER RIVER north of Rome. NERO created a group of artificial lakes in its upper course and built a villa there, the remains of which survive.

aniline \'a-nə-,līn\ One of the most important organic BASES, parent substance for many dyes and drugs. Pure aniline is a highly poisonous, oily, colorless liquid with a distinctive odor. First obtained (1826) from INDIGO, it is now prepared synthetically. It is a weakly basic primary aromatic AMINE and participates in many reactions with other compounds. It is used to make chemicals used in producing rubber, dyes and intermediates, photographic chemicals, urethane foams, pharmaceuticals, explosives, herbicides, and fungicides as well as to make chemicals used in petroleum refining.

animal Any member of the kingdom Animalia (see TAXONOMY), a group of many-celled organisms that differ from members of the two other many-celled kingdoms, the PLANTS and the fungi (see FUNGUS), in several ways. Animals have developed muscles, making them capable of spontaneous movement (see LOCOMOTION), more elaborate sensory and nervous systems, and greater levels of general complexity. Unlike plants, animals cannot manufacture their own food, and thus are adapted for securing and digesting food. In animals, the cell wall is either absent or composed of material different from that of the plant cell wall. Animals account for about three-quarters of living species. Some one-celled organisms display both plant and animal characteristics. See also ALGAE, ARTHROPOD, BACTERIA, CHORDATE, INVERTEBRATE, PROTIST, PROTOZOAN, VERTEBRATE.

animal communication Transmission of information from one animal to another by means of sound, visible sign or behavior, taste or odor, electrical impulse, touch, or a combination of these. Most animal communication uses sound (e.g., birds calling, crickets chirping). Visual communication usually indicates an animal's identity (species, sex, age, etc.) or other information through specific characteristics (e.g., horns, patches of color) or behavior (e.g., the bee's "dance" describing a source of food). Chemical communication involves pheromones (chemical signals) produced by the animal's endocrine system. EELS and some other fishes use electrical impulses to communicate.

animal husbandry Controlled cultivation, management, and production of domestic animals, including improvement of the qualities considered desirable by humans by means of BREEDING. Animals are bred and raised for utility (e.g., food, fur), sport, pleasure, and research. See also BEEKEEPING, DAIRY FARMING.

animal rights rights, primarily against being killed and being treated cruelly, that are thought to be possessed by higher nonhuman animals (e.g., chimpanzees) and many lower ones by virtue of their sentience. Respect for the welfare of animals is a precept of some ancient Eastern religions, including JAINISM, which enjoins *ahimsa* ("noninjury") toward all living things, and BUDDHISM, which forbids the needless killing of animals, especially (in India) of cows. In the West, traditional JUDAISM and CHRISTIANITY taught that animals were created by God for human use, including as food, and many Christian thinkers argued that humans had no moral duties of any kind to animals, even the duty not to treat them cruelly, because they lacked rationality or because they were not, like Man, made in the image of God. This view prevailed until the late 18th century, when ethical philosophers such as JEREMY BENTHAM applied the principles of UTILITARIANISM to infer a moral duty not to inflict needless suffering on animals. In the latter half of the 20th century, the ethical philosopher Peter Singer and others attempted to show that a duty not to harm animals follows straightforwardly from simple and widely accepted moral principles, such as "It is wrong to cause unnecessary suffering." They also argued that there is no "morally relevant difference" between humans and animals that would justify raising animals, but not humans, for food on "FACTORY FARMS" or using them in scientific experiments or for product testing (e.g., of cosmetics). An opposing view held that humans have no moral duties to animals because animals are incapable of entering into a hypothetical "moral contract" to respect the interests of other rational beings. The modern animal-rights movement was inspired in part by Singer's work. At the end of the 20th century, it had spawned a large number of groups dedicated to a variety of related causes, including protecting endangered species, protesting against painful or brutal methods of trapping and killing animals (e.g., for furs), preventing the use of animals in laboratory research, and promoting what adherents considered the health benefits and moral virtues of VEGETARIANISM.

animal-rights movement Organized social effort promoting the fair and humane treatment of animals (see cruelty to ANIMALS). The movement is rooted in the ancient teachings of PYTHAGORAS. Perhaps the world's first anticruelty law, addressing treatment of domesticated animals, was included in the legal code of the Massachusetts Bay Colony (1641); similar legislation was passed in Britain in 1822. Many specialized animal advocacy groups appeared in the late 20th century, including groups dedicated to protecting ENDANGERED SPECIES and others that protest against painful or brutal methods of trapping and killing animals and the use of animals in medical and scientific research and in product testing (e.g., of cosmetics).

animals, cruelty to Willful or wanton infliction of pain, suffering, or death upon an animal or the intentional or malicious neglect of an animal. Perhaps the world's first anticruelty law, which addressed the treatment of domesticated animals, was included in the legal code of the Massachusetts Bay Colony (1641); similar legislation was passed in Britain in 1822. The world's first animal welfare society, the Society for the Protection of Animals, was established in England in 1824; the American Society for the Prevention of Cruelty to Animals was chartered in 1866. In varying degrees, cruelty to animals is illegal in most countries, and interest in ENDANGERED SPECIES gave further impetus to the anticruelty movement in the late 20th century. Reflecting such interest, many laws have been passed, though they are seldom enforced unless public pressure is brought to bear. Acts targeted by the movement have ranged from the mistreatment of domesticated animals to BULLFIGHTING and VIVISECTION. FACTORY FARMING, which involves various evidently cruel practices, has remained largely exempt from legal scrutiny. See also ANIMAL RIGHTS.

animals, master of the Supernatural figure regarded as the protector of game animals in the traditions of hunting peoples. In some traditions he is the ruler of the forest and guardian of all species; in others, he is the guardian of a single species—usually a large and valuable animal—and may have both human and animal characteristics. He requires that hunters treat slain animals with respect; if they fail to do so, he may withhold game until he is placated through a ceremony or by a SHAMAN.

animation Process of giving the illusion of movement to drawings, models, or inanimate objects. From the mid-1850s, such optical devices as the zoetrope produced the illusion of animation. Stop-action photography enabled the production of cartoon films. The innovative design and assembly techniques of WALT DISNEY soon moved him to the forefront of the animation industry, and he produced a series of classic animated films, beginning with *Snow White and the Seven Dwarfs* (1937). In reaction against the naturalistic style of Disney's cartoons, a group of artists formed United Productions of America (UPA) and created such characters as Mr. Magoo and Howdy Doody. Computer animation, as seen in the first fully computer-generated animated feature, *Toy Story* (1995), moved the art to a new level.

animé Style of animation popular in Japanese films. Animé films are meant primarily for the Japanese market and, as such, employ many cultural references unique to Japan. For example, the large eyes of animé characters are commonly perceived in Japan as multifaceted "windows to the soul." Much of the genre is aimed at the children's market, but animé films are sometimes marked by adult themes and subject matter. Modern animé began in 1956 and found lasting success in 1961 with the establishment of Mushi Productions by Osamu Tezuka, a leading figure in modern "manga" (Japanese comics). Such animé as *Akira* (1988), *Mononoke Hime* (1997; *Princess Mononoke*), and the *Pokémon* series of films have attained international popularity.

animism Belief in the existence of spirits separable from bodies. Such beliefs are traditionally identified with small-scale ("primitive") societies, though they also occur in major world religions. They were first competently surveyed by EDWARD BURNETT TYLOR in *Primitive Culture* (1871). Classic animism, according to Tylor, consists of attributing conscious life to natural objects or phenomena, a practice that eventually gave rise to the notion of a SOUL. See also SHAMAN.

anion \'a-ˌnī-ən\ Atom or group of atoms carrying a negative ELECTRIC CHARGE, indicated by a superscript minus sign after the chemical symbol. Anions in a liquid subjected to an electric field migrate toward the positive electrode (ANODE). Examples include hydroxyl ($—OH^-$; see HYDROXIDE), CARBONATE ($—CO_3^{2-}$), and PHOSPHATE ($—PO_4^{3-}$). See also ION.

anise Annual herb (*Pimpinella anisum*) of the PARSLEY family, cultivated chiefly for its fruit, called aniseed, which tastes like LICORICE. Native to Egypt and the eastern Mediterranean region, anise is cultivated throughout the world. Aniseed is used as a flavoring and as a soothing herbal tea. Star anise is the dried fruit of the EVERGREEN tree *Illicium verum* (MAGNOLIA family), native to southeastern China and Vietnam. Its flavor and uses are similar to those of anise.

Anjou \'an-jü\ Historical region, lower LOIRE valley, northwestern France. Organized in the Gallo-Roman period as the Civitas Andegavensis, it later became the countship, and from 1360 the duchy, of Anjou. Its capital was Angers. Under the CAROLINGIAN DYNASTY, it was nominally administered by a count representing the French king. The area came under the English king HENRY II when he married ELEANOR OF AQUITAINE in 1152, thus founding the Anglo-Angevin empire of the PLANTAGENET dynasty. The French recovered Anjou in 1259, and it was united with France in 1487. It ceased to exist as a department in 1790.

Anjou, House of See House of PLANTAGENET

Ankara \'äŋ-kə-rə\ *formerly* **Angora** City (pop., 1995: 2,838,000), capital of Turkey. Located about 220 mi (355 km) southeast of ISTANBUL on the Ankara River, it has been inhabited at least since the Stone Age. Conquered by ALEXANDER THE GREAT in 334 BC, it was incorporated into the Roman empire by AUGUSTUS. As a city of the Byzantine empire, Ankara fell to the Turks in

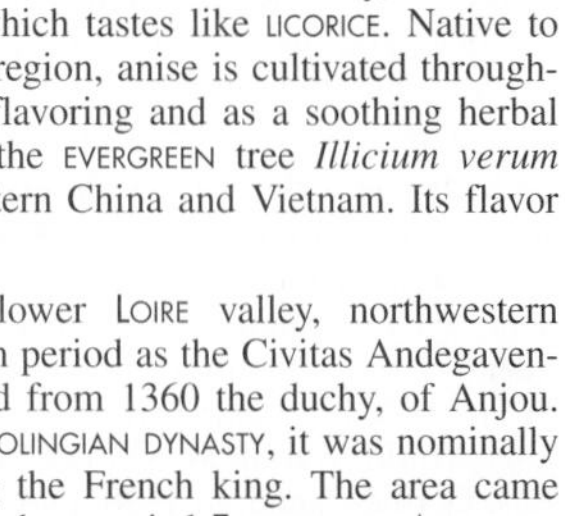

The Atatürk Mausoleum, Ankara, Turkey.

ROBERT HARDING PICTURE LIBRARY, LONDON

1073, but the crusader RAYMOND IV of Toulouse drove them out in 1101. In 1403 it came under Ottoman rule. After World War I, MUSTAFA KEMAL ATATURK made Ankara the center of resistance to both the Ottomans and the invading Greeks, and it became the capital of Turkey in 1923. The city today is Turkey's chief industrial center after Istanbul. Its history is displayed in its Roman, Byzantine, and Ottoman architecture and ruins and in its important historical museums.

ankh \'äŋk\ Ancient Egyptian HIEROGLYPH signifying life, consisting of a cross surmounted by a loop. In tomb inscriptions, gods and pharaohs are often pictured holding the ankh, which forms part of the hieroglyph for concepts such as health and happiness. It is used as a cross in the COPTIC ORTHODOX CHURCH.

Ankobra River River, southern Ghana. It rises northeast of Wiawso and flows about 130 mi (209 km) south to the Gulf of GUINEA, just west of Axim. Its chief tributaries are the Mansi and Bonsa rivers; much of its basin is shared with the Tano River to the west.

Ann, Cape Cape northeast of Boston, Mass. Sheltering Ipswich Bay, it includes Annisquam Harbor on the north and Gloucester Harbor on the south. The rocky, picturesque promontory, named for Queen Anne (wife of JAMES I), is noted for its old fishing villages and artists' colonies. Gloucester and Rockport are its main towns.

Ann Arbor City (pop., 1996 est.: 109,000), southeastern Michigan. Founded in 1824, it became an agricultural center with the coming of the railroad in 1839. The University of MICHIGAN, which moved there from DETROIT in 1837, has played a major role in Ann Arbor's growth. Private industrial research and the university's institutes of science and technology make the city a major Midwest center for space and nuclear research.

Anna *in full* **Anna Ivanovna** (1693–1740) Empress of Russia (1730–40). After the death of PETER II, the Supreme Privy Council, Russia's actual ruling body, offered Anna the throne (as the daughter of IVAN V) if she agreed to conditions placing the real power in the council's hands. She initially agreed but later tore up the conditions, abolished the council, and reestablished the autocracy, countenancing a severely repressive regime. She occupied herself primarily with extravagant amusements and relied on her lover, Ernst Johann Biron (1690–1772), and a group of German advisers to manage the state. Shortly before her death, Anna named as her successor her grand-nephew Ivan (later IVAN VI).

Anna Comnena \käm-'nē-nə\ (1083–1148?) Byzantine historian. Daughter of the emperor ALEXIUS I COMNENUS, she conspired with her mother against her brother JOHN II COMNENUS; when the plot was discovered, she was forced to enter a convent. There she wrote the *Alexiad*, a biography of her father and a pro-Byzantine account of the early CRUSADES.

Annaba \à-'nä-bə\ *formerly* **Bône** \'bōn\ Seaport (pop., 1987: 223,000), northeastern Algeria. Identified with the port of ancient Hippo (or Hippo Regius) to the south, it was a rich city of Roman Africa until c. AD 300. It was home to St. AUGUSTINE 396–430. Severely damaged by the VANDALS in 431, it was rebuilt by the Arabs in the 7th century and named Bona. It was occupied by the French in 1832 when they took over the area. Modern Annaba is Algeria's chief exporter of minerals; it also serves as a trading port and port of call.

Annales school \ä-'näl\ School of history established by Lucien Febvre (1878–1956) and FERNAND BRAUDEL. Its roots were in the journal *Annales: économies, sociétés, civilisations,* Febvre's reconstituted version of a journal he had earlier formed with MARC BLOCH. Under Braudel's direction the Annales school promoted a new form of history, replacing the study of leaders with the lives of ordinary people and replacing examination of politics, diplomacy, and wars with inquiries into climate, demography, agriculture, commerce, technology, transportation, and communication, as well as social groups and mentalities. While aiming at a "total history," it also yielded dazzling microstudies of villages and regions. Its international influence on historiography has been enormous.

Annam \a-'nam\ Historic kingdom, eastern Vietnam. The area was conquered c. 200 BC by the Chinese, who gave it its name (which has never been used by the indigenous inhabitants). It became independent in the 15th century AD, opening the way for steady Vietnamese movement toward the MEKONG RIVER delta. When Vietnam was united in 1802, the city of HUE became the capital, and the area was ruled by the emperor of Annam. Central Vietnam gradually came under French control in the 19th century; it became a protectorate in 1883–85, leaving the court at Hue with only nominal power. The area was partitioned between North and South Vietnam in 1954, and Annam's last emperor was deposed in 1955.

Annan \ä-'nan\, **Kofi (Atta)** (born 1938) Seventh secretary-general of the UNITED NATIONS (from 1997) who shared, with the U.N., the 2001 Nobel Prize for Peace. He was born in Ghana, the son of a provincial governor and hereditary paramount chief of the Fante people. He did graduate work at Geneva's Institute for Advanced International Studies and at MIT. He has spent almost his entire career within the U.N., beginning at the WORLD HEALTH ORGANIZATION (1962). As undersecretary-general for peacekeeping (from 1993), he transferred peacekeeping operations in Bosnia from the U.N. to NATO. Elected in December 1996, he became the first U.N. secretary-general from sub-Saharan Africa, with a mandate to reform the U.N. bureaucracy. He has criticized the U.N.'s failure to prevent or minimize genocide in Rwanda (1994) and unsettled many by declaring that the U.N. should address human-rights violations perpetrated by governments on their own people. His priorities have included a comprehensive program of reform, efforts to restore public confidence in the organization, and work to strengthen the U.N.'s activities for peace and development. Annan was appointed to a second term in 2001.

Annapolis \ə-'na-pə-ləs\ City (pop., 1994 est.: 35,000), capital of Maryland. It lies along the Severn River on CHESAPEAKE BAY. Settled in 1649 as Providence by Virginia Puritans, it was later known as Ann Arundel Town. It became the state capital in 1694, and was later renamed to honor Princess (later Queen) ANNE. Its economy is tied to government services, and it is home to the U.S. NAVAL ACADEMY.

Annapolis Convention Meeting in Annapolis, Md., in 1786 that led to the convening of the CONSTITUTIONAL CONVENTION. Delegates from five states gathered to discuss problems in maritime commerce but found they could not solve them without changes in the ARTICLES OF CONFEDERATION. They issued a call to all states to meet in Philadelphia in 1787 to resolve the difficulties.

Annapurna Mountain range, Nepal. It forms a ridge 30 mi (48 km) long and contains four main summits. Annapurna I (26,545 ft, or 8,091 m) was first scaled in 1950 by a French expedition; it was the first peak of more than 26,000 ft (8,000 m) to be ascended to the summit. In 1970 an all-woman Japanese team climbed Annapurna III (24,786 ft, or 7,555 m).

Anne (1665–1714) Queen of Great Britain (1702–14) and the last STUART monarch. Second daughter of JAMES II, who was overthrown by WILLIAM III in 1688, Anne became queen on William's death (1702). Though she wished to rule independently, her intellectual limitations and poor health led her to rely on advisers, including the duke of MARLBOROUGH. Her reign was marked by the Act of UNION with Scotland (1707) and by bitter rivalries between Whigs and Tories.

Anne of Austria (1601–1666) Queen consort (1615–43) of LOUIS XIII of France and regent (1643–51) for her son LOUIS XIV. Daughter of PHILIP III of Spain and MARGARET OF AUSTRIA, Anne married the 14-year-old Louis XIII in 1615. He treated her coolly, and the powerful Cardinal de RICHELIEU attempted to limit her influence over her husband. After Louis XIII died and she was declared sole regent, she strove to ensure that her son would succeed to the absolute power Richelieu had won for Louis XIII. Together with her first minister, Cardinal MAZARIN, she faced the series of revolts known as the FRONDE. Her regency ended in 1651, when Louis XIV was proclaimed of age to rule.

Anne of Austria, detail of a portrait by Peter Paul Rubens, in the Rijksmuseum, Amsterdam.

BY COURTESY OF THE RIJKSMUSEUM, AMSTERDAM

Anne of Brittany (1477–1514) Duchess of Brittany and twice queen consort of France. After succeeding to her father's duchy in 1488, Anne allied herself with MAXIMILIAN I of Austria. She was then forced to break with him and in 1491 marry CHARLES VIII of France, thus beginning the process of the union of Brittany with the French crown. After Charles's death (1498), she married his successor, LOUIS XII. Throughout her life Anne devoted herself to safeguarding Brittany's autonomy within the kingdom.

Anne of Cleves (1515–1557) Fourth wife of HENRY VIII of England. Henry married Anne, whom he found homely, to form an alliance with her brother William, duke of Cleves, a leader of the Protestants of western Germany. The alliance, arranged by THOMAS CROMWELL, seemed necessary because it appeared that the major Roman Catholic powers, France and the Holy Roman Empire, intended to attack Protestant England. When that threat dissipated, the marriage became a political embarrassment and was annulled by an Anglican convocation in 1540.

annealing Treatment of a METAL, ALLOY, or other material by heating to a predetermined temperature, holding for a certain time, and then cooling to room temperature, done to improve DUCTILITY and reduce brittleness. Process annealing is carried out intermittently during the working of a piece of metal to restore ductility lost through repeated hammering or other working, if several cold-forming operations are required but the metal is so hardened after the first operation that further cold working would cause cracking (see HARDENING). Full annealing is done to give workability to such parts as forged blanks destined for use in the machine-tool industry. Annealing is also done for relief of internal stresses in metal and glass. Annealing temperatures and times differ for different materials and with properties desired; steel is usually held for several hours at about 1,260°F (680°C) and then cooled for several hours. See also HEAT TREATING, SOLID SOLUTION.

annelid \'a-nə-ˌlid\ Any member of a phylum (Annelida) of INVERTEBRATE animals that possess a body cavity (coelom), movable bristles (setae), and a body divided into segments by crosswise rings. Known as segmented WORMS, annelids are divided into three classes: marine worms (Polychaeta; see POLYCHAETE), EARTHWORMS (Oligochaeta), and LEECHES (Hirudinea). See illustration opposite.

Anne's War, Queen See QUEEN ANNE'S WAR

annihilation In physics, a reaction in which a particle and its antiparticle (see ANTIMATTER) collide and disappear. The annihilation releases energy equal to the original mass m multiplied by the square of the speed of light c, or $E = mc^2$, in accordance with ALBERT EINSTEIN's special theory of RELATIVITY. The energy can appear directly as GAMMA RAYS or can convert back to particles and antiparticles (see PAIR PRODUCTION).

annual Any plant that completes its life cycle in a single GROWING SEASON. The dormant SEED is the only part of an annual that survives from one growing season to the next. Annuals include many WEEDS, WILDFLOWERS, garden flowers, and VEGETABLES. See also BIENNIAL, PERENNIAL.

annual ring See GROWTH RING

annuity Payment made at a fixed interval. A common example is the payment received by retirees from their PENSION plan. There are two main classes of annuities: annuities certain and contingent annuities. Under an annuity certain, a specified number of payments are made, after which the annuity stops. With a contingent annuity, each payment depends on the continuance of a given status; for example, a life annuity continues only as long as the recipient survives. Contingent annuities such as pension plans or LIFE INSURANCE depend on shared risk. Everyone pays in a fixed amount until the annuity begins; some will not live long enough to receive back all the money they have paid, while others will live long enough to collect more than they have paid.

annulment Legal invalidation of a MARRIAGE. It announces the invalidity of a marriage that was void from its inception. It is to be distinguished from dissolution or DIVORCE. To justify annulment, the marriage contract must have a defect (e.g., incompetence of one party because of age, insanity, or a preexisting marriage). Continued absence of one party may also justify annulment. Generally, annulment is easier if the marriage is unconsummated. Both secular law and Christian CANON LAW have annulment procedures.

anode Terminal or ELECTRODE from which ELECTRONS leave a system. In a BATTERY or other source of DIRECT CURRENT, the anode is the negative terminal. In a passive load it is the positive terminal. In an electron tube, electrons from the CATHODE travel across the tube toward the anode; in an electroplating cell, negative ions are deposited at the anode.

anodizing Method of coating metal for corrosion resistance, electrical insulation, thermal control, abrasion resistance, sealing, improving paint adhesion, and decorative finishing. Anodizing consists of electrically depositing an OXIDE film from aqueous solution onto the surface of a metal, often ALUMINUM, which serves as the ANODE in an electrolytic cell. In the most common type of anodizing, which uses a 15% sulfuric-acid bath, dyes can be introduced into the oxidation process to achieve a colored surface. Aluminum thus anodized and colored is used widely in giftware, home appliances, and architectural decoration.

anomie \'a-nə-mē\ In the social sciences, a condition of social instability or personal unrest resulting from a breakdown of standards and values or from a lack of purpose or ideals. The term was introduced in 1897 by É. DURKHEIM, who believed that one type of SUICIDE (anomic) resulted from the breakdown of social standards that people need and use to regulate their behavior. ROBERT K. MERTON studied the causes of anomie in the U.S., finding it severest in persons who lack acceptable means of achieving their cultural goals. Delinquency, crime, and suicide are often reactions to anomie. See also ALIENATION.

anorexia nervosa \ˌa-nə-'rek-sē-ə-nər-'vō-sə\ Failure to maintain one's body weight at the normal level, resulting from an intense desire to be thin, a fear of gaining weight, or a disturbance in body image. Anorexia nervosa usually starts in late adolescence and occurs mostly in young women. One will go to great lengths to resist eating and to lose weight, including BULIMIA and vigorous exercise. A usual symptom is

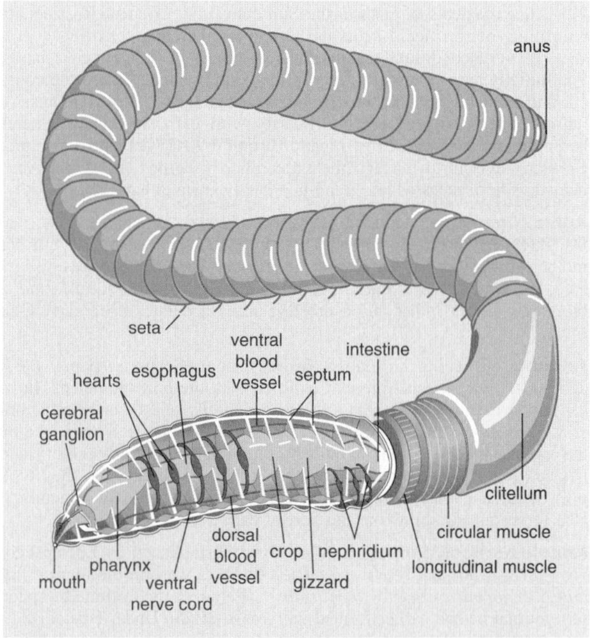

Body plan of an earthworm. Partitions (septa) divide the body cavity (coelom) into more than 100 segments. The circular and longitudinal muscles work with the setae to move the worm forward. Soil is pulled into the mouth by the sucking action of the pharynx; the crop releases food slowly into the gizzard, where the soil is ground to release and break up any organic matter. The cerebral ganglion, or "brain," controls all body functions and movement via a ventral nerve cord. Contraction of the hearts (aortic arches) and ventral blood vessel forces blood through the body, after which it returns via the dorsal blood vessel. Nitrogenous waste is eliminated through the tubules of the nephridia. The clitellum secretes mucus for mating and a cocoon in which eggs are deposited.

AMENORRHEA. Medical complications can be life-threatening. Treatment includes psychological and social therapy.

anorthite FELDSPAR mineral, calcium aluminosilicate ($CaAl_2Si_2O_8$), that occurs as white or grayish, brittle, glassy crystals. Primarily a rock-forming mineral, it is used in the manufacture of glass and ceramics. Anorthite occurs in basic igneous rocks (see ACID AND BASIC ROCKS).

anorthosite Type of IGNEOUS ROCK composed predominantly of calcium-rich FELDSPAR. It is considerably less abundant than either basalt or granite, but the complexes in which it occurs are often immense. All anorthosites found on the earth consist of coarse crystals, but some from the moon are finely crystalline.

Anouilh \á-'nüy\, **Jean (-Marie-Lucien-Pierre)** (1910–1987) French playwright. After studying law, he wrote his first play, *The Ermine* (1932), followed by the successful *Traveler Without Luggage* (1937). He is best remembered for *Antigone* (1944), *The Lark* (1953), and *Becket* (1959), in which he used such techniques as the play within the play, flashbacks and flash-forwards, and the exchange of roles. A skillful exponent of the WELL-MADE PLAY, he rejected naturalism and realism in favor of a return to THEATRICALISM.

Ansar (Arabic: "Helper") Term originally applied to some of the COMPANIONS OF THE PROPHET. When MUHAMMAD left Mecca for MEDINA, the Ansar were the Medinese who aided him and who became his devoted followers. The term was revived in the 19th century to refer to the followers of al-MAHDI, al-Mahdi's successor, or his descendants.

Anschluss \'än-ˌshlu̇s\ (German: "union") Political union of Austria with Germany, which occurred when ADOLF HITLER annexed Austria. In 1938 the Austrian chancellor KURT VON SCHUSCHNIGG was bullied into canceling a plebiscite on union with Germany, which he expected Austrians to oppose. He resigned his office and ordered the Austrian army not to resist the Germans. The Germans invaded on March 12, and the enthusiasm shown by Austrians persuaded Hitler to annex Austria outright the next day. Though France and Britain protested Hitler's methods, they and other countries accepted the fait accompli.

Anselm of Canterbury, St. (1033–1109) Founder of SCHOLASTICISM. Born in Lombardy, Anselm entered the Benedictine monastery at Bec (in Normandy) in 1057 and became abbot in 1078. In 1077 he wrote the *Monologium* to demonstrate God's existence and attributes by reason alone. He then wrote *Proslogium,* which established the ONTOLOGICAL ARGUMENT for the existence of God. In 1093, he became archbishop of Canterbury. In the INVESTITURE CONTROVERSY, he asserted that only an ecclesiastical authority—not a secular one—could invest him with the symbols of office. In 1099 he completed *Cur Deus homo?* ("Why Did God Become Man?"), on Jesus' redemption of humankind. Anselm was declared a Doctor of the Church in 1720.

Ansgar \'ans-ˌgär\, **St.** (801?–865) Missionary, first archbishop of Hamburg, and patron saint of Scandinavia. He was sent by LOUIS I the Pious to help King Harald Christianize Denmark and King Bjorn Christianize Sweden. He initiated a mission to all Scandinavians and Slavs and was appointed archbishop of Hamburg (832). But Sweden and Denmark returned to paganism by 845 and Ansgar had to repeat all his work. He thwarted another pagan rebellion and was canonized soon after his death.

Anshan \'an-ˌshan\ City and territory of ancient ELAM, north of modern SHIRAZ, Iran. Anshan came to prominence c. 2350 BC, but its greatest period was in the 13th–12th century BC, when, as kings of Anshan and Susa, Elamite rulers periodically raided the cities of BABYLONIA. The area apparently came under the control of Persia c. 675 BC. Its ruins have yielded major finds, including examples of early Elamite writing.

Anshan *or* **An-shan** \'än-'shän\ City (pop., 1990 est.: 1,285,849), LIAONING province, northeastern China. Established as a post station in 1387, it was fortified in 1587 as part of the defenses set up by the MING DYNASTY against the rising power of the MANCHUS. It was destroyed by fire during the BOXER REBELLION and badly damaged during the RUSSO-JAPANESE WAR (1904–5). In the 1930s the Japanese occupied Anshan and made it a steelmaking center. The city was bombed by U.S. aircraft in 1944 and looted by the Soviets following World War II. The Chinese later redeveloped it into an industrial center that produces steel, cement, and chemicals.

ant Any member of approximately 8,000 species of the social insect family Formicidae. Ants are found worldwide but are especially common in hot climates. They range from 0.1 to 1 in. (2–25 mm) long and are usually yellow, brown, red, or black. Ants eat both plant and animal substances; some even "farm" fungi for food, cultivating them in their nests, or "milk" APHIDS. Ant colonies consist of three castes (queens, males, and workers, including soldiers) interacting in a highly complex society paralleling that of the HONEYBEES. Well-known ant species are the carpenter ants of North America, the voracious army ants of tropical America, and the stinging FIRE ANT.

Carpenter ant (*Camponotus*).
GRACE THOMPSON FROM THE NATIONAL AUDUBON SOCIETY COLLECTION–PHOTO RESEARCHERS

antacid Any substance, such as sodium bicarbonate, magnesium hydroxide, or aluminum hydroxide, used to relieve the discomfort caused by indigestion, gastritis, and several forms of ulcers. Antacids counteract or neutralize gastric acidity for up to three hours after a single dose. Antacids should be taken when gastric acidity is most likely to be increasing, namely, between one and three hours after each meal and at bedtime.

Antakya See ANTIOCH

Antarctic Circle Parallel of latitude approximately 66.5° south of the equator that circumscribes the southern frigid zone. It marks the northern limit of the area within which, for one day or more each year, the sun does not set or rise. The length of continuous day or night increases southward from the Antarctic Circle, mounting to six months at the SOUTH POLE.

Antarctic Regions ANTARCTICA and the southern waters of the Pacific, Atlantic, and Indian oceans (the term *Antarctic Ocean* is sometimes used, inappropriately). Much of the area is characterized by subpolar conditions; ice shelves and sea ice extend well beyond the borders of the continent. The greatest recorded depth is 21,043 ft (6,414 m). Water cooled by the coastal ice masses of the Antarctic continent sinks and flows northward along the ocean bottom and is replaced at the surface by warmer water flowing south from the Indian, Pacific, and Atlantic oceans. The meeting point of these currents is the Antarctic Convergence, an area rich in phytoplankton and krill, which are important to various species of fish as well as penguins and other seabirds.

Antarctica Fifth-largest continent on earth. Antarctica lies concentrically about the SOUTH POLE, its landmass almost wholly covered by a vast ice sheet averaging 6,500 ft (2,000 m) thick. It is divided into two subcontinents: East Antarctica, consisting mainly of a high, ice-covered plateau, and West Antarctica, consisting largely of an archipelago of mountainous islands covered with ice. Its land area is about 5.5 million sq mi (14.2 million sq km). The southern portions of the Atlantic, Pacific, and Indian oceans form the surrounding Antarctic Ocean (see ANTARCTIC REGIONS). Antarctica would be circular except for the outflaring Antarctic Peninsula and two principal bays, the Ross Sea and the Weddell Sea. East and West Antarctica are separated by the long chain (1,900 mi, or 3,000 km) of the Transantarctic Mountains. The ice sheet overlaying the continent represents about 90% of the world's glacial ice. By far the coldest continent, it has the world's lowest recorded temperature, −128.6°F (−89.2°C), measured in 1983. The climate supports only a small community of land plants, but the rich offshore food supply promotes immense seabird rookeries. The Russian F. G. von Bellingshausen (1778–1852), the Englishman Edward Bransfield (1795?–1852), and the American Nathaniel Palmer (1799–1877) all claimed first sightings of the continent in 1820. The period to c. 1900 was dominated by the exploration of Antarctic and sub-Antarctic seas. The early 20th century, the "heroic era" of Antarctic exploration, produced expeditions deep into the interior by ROBERT FALCON SCOTT and later ERNEST SHACKLETON. The South Pole was reached by ROALD AMUNDSEN in December 1911, and by Scott in January 1912. The first half of the 20th century was also Antarctica's colonial period. Seven nations claimed sectors of the continent, while many other nations carried out explorations. In the International Geophysical Year of 1957–58, 12 nations established over 50 stations on the continent for cooperative study. In 1961 the Antarctic Treaty, reserving Antarctica for free and nonpolitical scientific study, en-

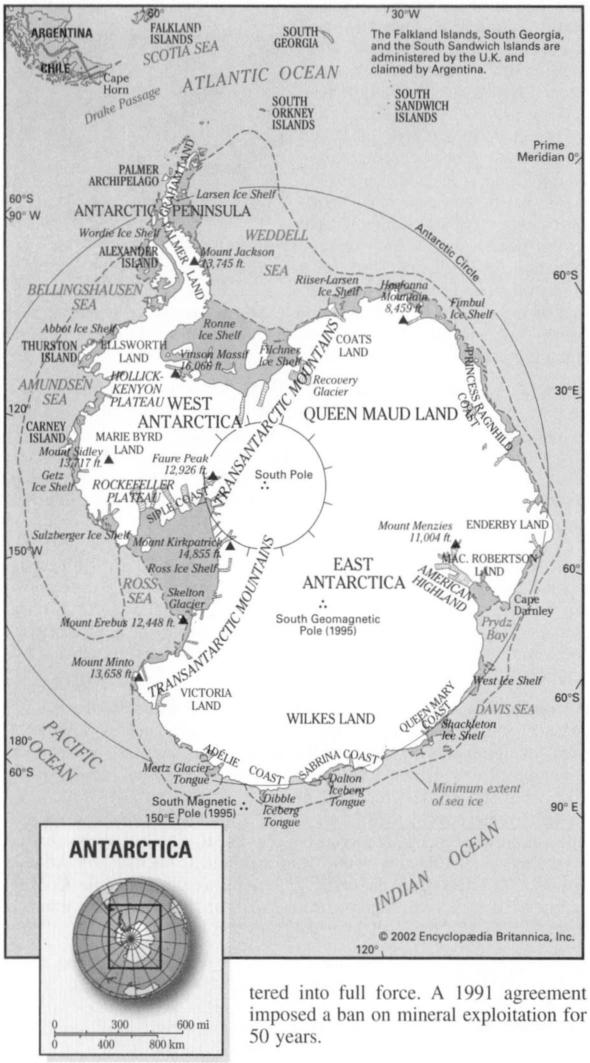

tered into full force. A 1991 agreement imposed a ban on mineral exploitation for 50 years.

anteater Any of four species of toothless, insect-eating placental mammals. Found in tropical savannas and forests from Mexico to northern Argentina and Uruguay, anteaters have a long tail, dense fur, a long skull, and a tubular muzzle. Their mouth opening is small, and the tongue is long and wormlike. They live alone or in pairs and feed mainly on ants and termites, which they obtain by inserting their sticky tongue into a nest torn open by the long, sharp, curved claws of their forefeet. The species range in length from 15 in. (37 cm) to 6 ft (1.8 m). Once grouped together, anteaters are now considered as separate from ECHIDNAS and PANGOLINS.

Antelami \ˌän-te-ˈlä-mē\, **Benedetto** (fl. 1178–c. 1230) Italian sculptor and architect. He probably belonged to the Magistri Antelami, a civic builders' guild in the Lake Como region. An early signed marble relief, *The Descent from the Cross* (1178), is in Parma Cathedral; his extensive cycle of sculpture on the Baptistery at Parma was begun in 1196. He is credited with the sculptural decorations of Fidenza Cathedral, the church of Sant'Andrea at Vercelli, and Ferrara Cathedral.

antelope Any of numerous species of Old World grazing or browsing BOVIDS that typically are swift, slender, and graceful plains dwellers. The North American PRONGHORN is also sometimes referred to as an antelope. Most antelope are African; the others, except for the pronghorn, are Eurasian. They range in shoulder height from 10 to 70 in. (25–175 cm). The male, and sometimes the female, bears distinctive, backwardly curved horns. See also BONGO, DIK-DIK, DUIKER, ELAND, GAZELLE, GNU, HARTEBEEST, IMPALA, KUDU, NYALA, ORYX, SPRINGBOK, WATERBUCK.

antenna *or* **aerial** Component of RADIO, TELEVISION, and RADAR systems that directs incoming and outgoing radio waves. Usually of metal, antennas range in shape and size from the mastlike devices used for radio and television broadcasting to the large parabolic reflectors used to focus satellite signals and the radio waves generated by distant astronomical objects and reflect them toward the centrally located receiver. Antennas were invented in the 1880s by HEINRICH HERTZ; GUGLIELMO MARCONI made many improvements.

antenna In zoology, one of a pair of slender, segmented sensory organs on the head of INSECTS, myriapods (e.g, CENTIPEDES, MILLIPEDES), and CRUSTACEANS. Antennae of insects, which are movable, are believed to serve as both tactual and smell receptors; in some species, the development of elaborate antennal plumes and brushlike terminations has led to the suggestion that they also serve for hearing. Evidence supports this idea only for the MOSQUITO, whose antennae are attached to specialized structures stimulated by vibrations of the antennal shaft. In social insects (e.g., ANTS), antennae movements may serve as communication.

Antenor \an-ˈtē-ˌnȯr\ (fl. c. 530–510 BC) Greek sculptor active in Athens. In antiquity he was famous for his bronze group of the *Tyrannicides* (c. 510 BC) made for the Athenian AGORA; no copies exist. A large marble KORE (c. 520 BC) from the Acropolis, found in 1886, is also attributed to him.

anthem Choral composition with English words used in church services. It developed in the mid-16th century as the Anglican version of the Catholic Latin MOTET. The full anthem is for unaccompanied chorus throughout; the verse anthem employs one or more soloists, and generally instrumental accompaniment. Both often employ antiphonal singing, the alternation of two half-choirs ("anthem" derives from "antiphon"). W. BYRD, T. TALLIS, H. PURCELL, and G.F. HANDEL wrote well-known anthems. A national anthem is the national patriotic song of a country, ideally sung chorally by its citizens.

Anthesteria \ˌan-thə-ˈstir-ē-ə\ Athenian festival in honor of DIONYSUS, held during the month of Anthesterion (Feb.-Mar.) to celebrate the beginning of spring and the maturing of the wine stored at the previous vintage. It lasted three days and included libations to the god from newly opened casks, popular merrymaking, a secret ceremony of marriage between Dionysus and the wife of the king, and underworld rites.

Anthony, Susan B(rownell) (1820–1906) U.S. pioneer in the WOMEN'S SUFFRAGE MOVEMENT. Born in Adams, Mass., she was sent to boarding school and then taught at a female academy in upstate New York (1846–49). Discouraged by the limited role for women in social movements, from 1852 she joined ELIZABETH CADY STANTON and AMELIA BLOOMER in campaigning for women's rights, helping found the Woman's State Temperance Society of New York and the New York Working Women's Association. In 1872, demanding equal voting rights, she twice led a group of women to the polls, and was subsequently arrested and fined for violating voting laws. She served as president of the National American Woman Suffrage Association, 1892–1900, and lectured throughout the country for a federal women's-suffrage amendment.

Susan B. Anthony.
BY COURTESY OF THE LIBRARY OF CONGRESS, WASHINGTON, D.C.

Anthony of Egypt, St. (251?–356) Egyptian hermit, considered the founder of organized Christian MONASTICISM. He began his practice of asceticism at age 20 and lived in solitude on Mount Pispir from 286 to 305. He emerged from his retreat to organize the monastic life of the hermits who had settled nearby. When the Edict of Milan (313) ended the persecution of Christians, Anthony moved to the desert between the Nile and the Red Sea. His monastic rule was compiled from writings and discourses attributed to him in Athanasius' *Life of St. Anthony* and the *Apophthegmata patrum* and was still observed in the 20th century by Coptic and Armenian monks. The hellish temptations he endured as a hermit became a popular subject for artists.

Anthony of Padua, St. (1195–1231) Franciscan friar, Doctor of the Church, and patron saint of Portugal. Born in Lisbon, he joined the Augustinian order in 1210 and was probably ordained a priest. He joined the Franciscans in 1220 with the goal of seeking martyrdom among the Saracens but instead became a teacher of theology at Bologna and in southern France. The most beloved of the followers of St. FRANCIS, he was known as a great preacher and miracle worker. He was buried in Padua, Italy, and he is the patron of that city. He is also invoked for the return of lost property.

anthophyllite \ˌan-thə-ˈfi-ˌlīt\ AMPHIBOLE mineral, a magnesium and iron silicate that occurs in altered rocks, such as the crystalline schists of Kongsberg, Norway; southern Greenland; and Pennsylvania. Anthophyllite is commonly produced by regional METAMORPHISM of ultrabasic rocks (see ACID AND BASIC ROCKS).

anthracite *or* **hard coal** Coal containing more fixed carbon than any other form of coal and the lowest amount of volatile (quickly evaporating) material, giving it the greatest heat value. The most valuable of the coals, it is also the least plentiful, making up less than 2% of all coal reserves in the U.S., with most of the known deposits occurring in the East. Anthracites are black and have a brilliant, almost metallic luster. Hard and brittle, they can be polished and used for decorative purposes. They are difficult to ignite but burn with a pale-blue flame and require little attention to sustain combustion. They are sometimes mixed with BITUMINOUS COAL to heat commercial buildings but are seldom used alone for heating because of their high cost.

anthracnose \an-ˈthrak-ˌnōs\ Plant disease of warm humid areas, caused by a FUNGUS (usually *Colletotrichum* or *Gloeosporium*), that infects various plants from trees to grasses. Symptoms include sunken spots of various colors in leaves, stems, fruits, or flowers, often leading to wilting and dying of tissues. Dogwood anthracnose, caused by the fungus *Discula destructiva,* thrives in cool climates; in the U.S. it has caused severe losses to natural stands of DOGWOODS in mountainous regions. It is controlled by destroying diseased tree tissue, using disease-free seed and disease-resistant varieties, applying FUNGICIDES, and controlling insects and mites that spread anthracnose fungi from plant to plant.

anthrax \ˈan-ˌthraks\ Infectious disease of warm-blooded animals, caused by *Bacillus anthracis*, a bacterium that, in spore form, can retain its virulence in contaminated soil or other material for many years. A disease chiefly of herbivores, the infection may be acquired by persons handling the wool, hair, hides, bones, or carcasses of affected animals. Infection may lead to death from respiratory or cardiac complications (within 1–2 days if acute), or the animal may recover. In humans, anthrax occurs as a cutaneous, pulmonary, or intestinal infection. The most common type, which occurs as an infection of the skin, may lead to fatal septicemia (blood poisoning). The pulmonary form of the disease is usually fatal. Sanitary working environments for susceptible workers are critical to preventing anthrax; early diagnosis and treatment are also of great importance. In recent decades, various countries have attempted to develop anthrax as a weapon of BIOLOGICAL WARFARE; many factors, including its extreme potency (vastly greater than any chemical-warfare agent), make it the preferred biological-warfare agent. Concerns about anthrax mounted in 2001 after it was found in letters mailed to members of the U.S. government and news agencies.

anthropology Study of human beings, particularly their evolutionary history, biological variation, social relationships, and cultural history. Established as an academic discipline near the beginning of the 20th century, anthropology as practiced in the U.S. consists of four major disciplines: PHYSICAL ANTHROPOLOGY, ARCHAEOLOGY, CULTURAL ANTHROPOLOGY, and anthropological LINGUISTICS. In Europe the arrangement of the disciplines differs somewhat. Some specialists use the term *ethnology* to refer to comparative and historical anthropology.

anthroposophy \ˌan-thrə-ˈpä-sə-fə\ Philosophy based on the view that the human intellect has the ability to contact spiritual worlds. It was formulated in the early 20th century by RUDOLF STEINER and was influenced by THEOSOPHY. Steiner wanted to develop a faculty for spiritual perception independent of the senses, which he believed was latent in all human beings, and to this end he founded the Anthroposophical Society in 1912. Now based in Dornach, Switzerland, the society has branches worldwide.

anthurium \an-ˈthu̇r-ē-əm\ Any plant of the genus *Anthurium*, containing about 600 tropical herbaceous species, in the ARUM FAMILY, many of which are popular foliage plants. A few species are widely grown for the florist trade for their showy, long-lasting blossoms; these include the flamingo lily *(A. andraeanum),* which boasts a salmon-red flower, and the flamingo flower, or pigtail plant *(A. scherzeranum),* which has a scarlet flower.

Anti-Comintern Pact Agreement concluded first between Germany and Japan (1936) and later between Italy, Germany, and Japan (1937). The pact, sought by ADOLF HITLER, was ostensibly directed against the COMINTERN but was specifically directed against the Soviet Union. It was one of a series of agreements leading to the formation of the AXIS POWERS. Japan renounced the pact in 1939 but later acceded to the Tripartite Pact of 1940, which pledged Germany, Japan, and Italy to mutual assistance.

Anti-Corn Law League British organization founded in 1839, devoted to fighting England's CORN LAWS, regulations governing the import and export of grain. It was led by RICHARD COBDEN, who saw the laws as both morally wrong and economically damaging. The league mobilized the industrial middle classes against the landlords, and Cobden won over the prime minister, SIR ROBERT PEEL. The Corn Laws were repealed in 1846.

Anti-Federalists U.S. leaders who opposed the strong central government envisioned in the U.S. CONSTITUTION of 1787 and whose agitation led to the addition of a BILL OF RIGHTS. While admitting the need for changes in the ARTICLES OF CONFEDERATION, they feared that a strong federal government would infringe on states' rights. The group's adherents, including GEORGE MASON, PATRICK HENRY, THOMAS PAINE, SAMUEL ADAMS, and GEORGE CLINTON, were as numerous as the FEDERALISTS, but their influence was weak in urban areas, and only Rhode Island and North Carolina voted against ratification. Anti-Federalists were later powerful during THOMAS JEFFERSON's presidency and formed the nucleus of what later became the DEMOCRATIC PARTY.

Anti-Lebanon Mountains Mountain range along the Syria-Lebanon border. Running parallel to the LEBANON MTNS., the range averages 6,500 ft (2,000 m) above sea level. Because of poor soil and steep slopes, it is sparsely populated.

Anti-Masonic Movement Popular movement in the U.S. in the 1830s opposed to FREEMASONRY. The disappearance and presumed murder, in New York in 1826, of a former Mason who had supposedly revealed the order's secrets ignited reaction against the Masons in the northeastern U.S. In 1831 the Anti-Masonic Party became the first U.S. third party and the first party to hold a national convention. It condemned Freemasonry for its secrecy and undemocratic character. Its candidate won Vermont in the 1832 election. By the late 1830s it had been absorbed into the WHIG PARTY.

anti-Semitism Hostility toward or discrimination against Jews as a religious or racial group. Although the term *anti-Semitism* has wide currency, it is a misnomer, implying discrimination against all Semites. Arabs and other peoples are also Semites yet not the targets of anti-Semitism as it is usually understood. Nazi anti-Semitism, which culminated in the HOLOCAUST, had a racist dimension, targeting Jews because of their supposed biological characteristics. This variety of anti-Jewish racism dates from the so-called "scientific racism" in the 19th century and is different in nature from earlier anti-Jewish prejudices. By the 4th century, Christians tended to see Jews as an alien people whose repudiation of Christ had condemned them to perpetual migration. Jews were denied citizenship and its rights in much of Europe in the Middle Ages (though some societies were more tolerant), and there were forced expulsions of Jews from several regions in that period. The Enlightenment and the French Revolution brought a new religious freedom to Europe in the 18th century, but in the 19th century violent discrimination intensified (see POGROM), and race rather than religion became the primary basis for anti-Semitism. In the 20th century, the economic and political dislocations caused by World War I intensified anti-Semitism. Under the Nazis during World War II, an estimated six million Jews were exterminated.

A
B

Anti-Slavery Society, American See AMERICAN ANTI-SLAVERY SOCIETY

antiaircraft gun ARTILLERY piece fired from the ground or shipboard in defense against aerial attack. They were first used in combat in World War I, when field artillery were converted to antiaircraft use by mountings that enabled them to fire nearly vertically. RANGE FINDERS and searchlights, developed in the 1920s and '30s, increased their effectiveness. Advances in World War II included rapid-firing and automatic weapons, RADAR for target tracking, and radio-operated fuses. British and U.S. forces used a 40-mm gun that fired ammunition to a height of 2 mi (3.2 km). Heavier GUNS, up to 120 mm, were used against high-flying bombers. For most of the war, the most effective was the German 88-mm *Fliegerabwehrkanone*; its abbreviated name, flak, became a universal term for antiaircraft fire. With the introduction of GUIDED MISSILES in the 1950s and '60s, heavy antiaircraft guns were phased out, though lighter radar-guided automatic guns remained effective against low-flying aircraft and helicopters.

antiballistic missile (ABM) Weapon designed to intercept and destroy ballistic MISSILES. Ballistic missiles are guided in the ascent phase of a high-arch trajectory but freely falling in the descent. In the late 1960s both the U.S. and the Soviet Union developed two-part, nuclear-armed ABM systems that combined a high-altitude interceptor missile (the U.S. Spartan and Soviet Galosh) with a terminal-phase interceptor (the U.S. Sprint and Soviet Gazelle). Such systems were subsequently limited by the 1972 Treaty on Antiballistic Missile Systems, under which each side was allowed one ABM location with 100 interceptor missiles. In 2002 the U.S. formally withdrew from the treaty in order to develop a missile defense program (see STRATEGIC DEFENSE INITIATIVE).

Antibes \ä^{n}-'tēb\ *ancient* **Antipolis** Seaport (pop., 1999: 72,412), southeastern France. Located on the Mediterranean coast southwest of NICE, it was a Greek trading post established by Phocaeans c. 340 BC. It became a Roman town and eventually a fief of the Grimaldi family (see MONACO) from 1384 to 1608. It is noted as a winter resort and for its Roman ruins.

antibiotic Chemical substance that in dilute solutions can inhibit the growth of microorganisms or destroy them with little or no harm to the infected host. Early antibiotics were natural microbial products, but chemists have modified the structures of many to produce semisynthetic and even wholly synthetic ones. Since the discovery of PENICILLIN (1928), antibiotics have revolutionized the treatment of BACTERIAL, FUNGAL, and some other diseases. They are produced by many ACTINOMYCETES (e.g., STREPTOMYCIN, TETRACYCLINE) and other BACTERIA (e.g., polypeptides such as bacitracin) and by fungi (e.g., PENICILLIN). Antibiotics may be broad-spectrum (active against a wide range of pathogens) or specific (active against one, or one class). Drawbacks include activity against beneficial microorganisms, often causing DIARRHEA; ALLERGIES; and development of drug-resistant strains of the targeted microorganisms.

antibody Protective molecule in the IMMUNE SYSTEM that circulates in blood and LYMPH in response to invasion by an ANTIGEN. Antibodies are GLOBULINS formed in LYMPHOID TISSUES by B CELLS, whose receptors are specialized to bind to a specific antigen. These receptors are copied as antibodies that attack the target antigens by binding to them, either neutralizing them or triggering a COMPLEMENT reaction. Antibodies have widely varying binding sites, providing protection from a wide range of infectious agents and toxic substances. Antibodies derived from the blood serum of infected people or animals are often given in an antiserum for quick immunization against fast-acting toxins or microbes. In 1975 CESAR MILSTEIN and colleagues developed a process for producing specific antibodies in virtually limitless amounts; these monoclonal antibodies can deliver radiation or drugs directly to specific antigens. See also ANTITOXIN, RETICULOENDOTHELIAL SYSTEM.

Antichrist Chief enemy of Christ who would reign at the end of time, first mentioned in the epistles of St. JOHN. The idea of a mighty ruler who will appear at the end of time to fight against the forces of good was adapted from Judaism; the Jewish concept in turn had been influenced by Iranian and Babylonian myths of the battle of God and the DEVIL at the end of time. In the Book of DANIEL the evil one is a military leader modeled on ANTIOCHUS IV EPIPHANES, who persecuted the Jews. In several books of the New Testament, the Antichrist is a tempter who works by signs and wonders and seeks divine honors. It was a potent concept in medieval Christianity that received the attention of many commentators including Adso of Montier-en-Der, whose work became the basic medieval treatise on the Antichrist. During the Middle Ages, popes and emperors struggling for power often denounced each other as the Antichrist, and during the Reformation, MARTIN LUTHER and other Protestant leaders identified the papacy itself as the Antichrist.

anticoagulant Substance that prevents blood from clotting by suppressing the synthesis or function of various clotting factors (see COAGULATION). Anticoagulants are given to prevent THROMBOSIS and used in drawing and storing blood. There are two main types of anticoagulants: HEPARIN and vitamin K antagonists (e.g., WARFARIN). The latter have longer-lasting effects, interfering in the liver's metabolism of VITAMIN K to cause production of defective clotting factors. Anticoagulant therapy carries a high risk of uncontrollable HEMORRHAGE.

Anticosti Island Island, Gulf of ST. LAWRENCE. Lying at the mouth of the ST. LAWRENCE RIVER in southeastern Quebec, it is 140 mi (225 km) long; its greatest width is 35 mi (56 km). Visited by JACQUES CARTIER in 1534, it became part of Quebec province in 1774. Port-Menier is its present-day settlement. It is now primarily a recreation area. Port-Menier is the island's only settlement.

antidepressant Any drug used to treat DEPRESSION. The three main types inhibit the metabolism of SEROTONIN and NOREPINEPHRINE in the brain. The aim is to keep these monoamine NEUROTRANSMITTERS from dropping to levels associated with depression. The drugs may take a few weeks to show any effect. Tricyclic antidepressants, which inhibit inactivation of norepinephrine and serotonin, help more than 70% of patients. Monoamine oxidase (MAO) inhibitors apparently block the action of MAO, an enzyme that helps break down norepinephrine, serotonin, and DOPAMINE in neurons. They have unpredictable side effects and are usually given only when tricyclic drugs do not help. Selective serotonin reuptake inhibitors (SSRIs) apparently block reabsorption only of serotonin, allowing its levels to build up in the brain. One of the best-known antidepressants, fluoxetine (trade name Prozac), often helps with depression unrelieved by tricyclics or MAO inhibitors and has milder side effects.

antidote Remedy to counteract the effects of a POISON or TOXIN. Administered by mouth, intravenously, or sometimes on the skin, it may work by directly neutralizing the poison; causing an opposite effect in the body; binding to the poison to prevent its absorption, inactivate it, or keep it from fitting a receptor at its site of action; or binding to a receptor to prevent the poison's binding there, blocking its action. Some poisons are not active until converted to a different form in the body; their antidotes interrupt that conversion.

Antietam \an-'tē-təm\, **Battle of** (September 17, 1862) Decisive and bloody battle of the AMERICAN CIVIL WAR that halted the Confederate advance on Maryland to gain military supplies. Following victory at the Second Battle of BULL RUN, Gen. ROBERT E. LEE moved his troops into Maryland with an eye to capturing Washington, D.C. They were stopped by Union troops under GEORGE B. MCCLELLAN at Antietam Creek, Md. Confederate casualties numbered some 13,700, and Union losses were about 12,400. McClellan was criticized for allowing Lee's forces to retreat to Virginia, but the victory encouraged Pres. ABRAHAM LINCOLN to issue a preliminary EMANCIPATION PROCLAMATION.

antifreeze Any substance that lowers the FREEZING POINT of WATER, protecting a system from the ill effects of freezing. In automobile cooling systems, mixing water with ETHYLENE GLYCOL or propylene glycol can lower its freezing point to 0°F (−17.8°C) and does not damage radiators. Additives to prevent freezing of water in gasoline (e.g., Drygas) usually contain METHANOL or isopropanol. Organisms that must survive freezing temperatures use various chemicals: GLYCEROL or DIMETHYL SULFOXIDE in insects, glycerol or trehalose in other invertebrates (NEMATODES, ROTIFERS), and PROTEINS in antarctic fishes.

antigen \'an-ti-jən\ Foreign substance in the body that induces an immune response by stimulating LYMPHOCYTES to produce ANTIBODIES or to attack the antigen directly (see IMMUNITY). Virtually any large foreign molecule can act as an antigen, including those of bacteria, viruses, parasites, foods, venoms, blood components, and cells and tissues of various species, including humans. Sites on the antigens' surface fit and bind to receptor molecules on the lymphocytes' surface, stimulating the latter to multiply and initiate an immune response that neutralizes or destroys the antigens.

Antigone \an-'ti-gə-nē\ In Greek legend, the daughter born of the incestuous relationship between OEDIPUS and his mother, Jocasta. After Oedipus had blinded himself in self-punishment, Antigone and her sister Ismene served as his guides, following him into exile. When he died, Antigone returned to THEBES, where her brothers Eteocles and Polyneices were at war. Both were killed, and Creon, the new king, declared that because Polyneices was a traitor, his corpse should remain unburied. Unwilling to let the body be defiled, Antigone buried him; when Creon condemned her to death, she hanged herself. Her story was dramatized by SOPHOCLES and EURIPIDES (in Euripides' version she escapes and joins her beloved, Haemon).

Antigonid dynasty Ruling house of ancient Macedonia (300–168 BC). ANTIGONUS I was proclaimed king in 306 BC after his son Demetrius conquered Cyprus, thus giving his father control of the Aegean, the eastern Mediterranean, and most of the Middle East. Under Demetrius II (r.239–229 BC), Macedonia was weakened by war with the Greek ACHAEAN and AETOLIAN leagues. Antigonus III (died 221) reestablished the Hellenic Alliance, restoring Macedonia to a strong position in Greece. Under PHILIP V, Macedonia first clashed with Rome in 215. Philip's defeat upset the old balance of power, and Rome became the decisive force in the eastern Mediterranean. The defeat of his successor, PERSEUS, at Pydna in 168 BC marked the end of the dynasty.

Antigonus I Monophthalmus ("One-Eyed") \an-'tig-ə-nəs...-,män-əf-'thal-məs\ *or* **Antigonus I Cyclops** (382–301 BC) Founder of the Macedonian dynasty of the ANTIGONIDS. He served as a general under ALEXANDER THE GREAT. From the plots, alliances, and wars among Alexander's successors, he emerged in control of Asia Minor and Syria, though he soon relinquished the lands east of the Euphrates to SELEUCUS I NICATOR. In 307 his son DEMETRIUS I ousted the governor of Athens and conquered Cyprus, giving Antigonus control of the eastern Mediterranean, the Aegean, and Asia Minor. In 306 he was proclaimed king of the empire by the assembled army. In 302 he and his son renewed the Panhellenic League (consisting of all the Hellenic states except Sparta, Messenia, and Thessaly), in order to ensure peace in Hellas and protect Antigonus. His dreams of taking Macedonia itself and Alexander's entire former empire died with him at the Battle of IPSUS (301), the only battle he ever lost.

Antigonus II Gonatas \'gän-ət-əs\ (319?–239 BC) King of Macedonia (276–239 BC). The son of DEMETRIUS I POLIORCETES, he defeated the Gauls in Greece (279) and in Asia Minor (277), occupied key cities, and made alliances. He defeated PYRRHUS of Epirus in Greece (272) to solidify his control in Macedonia. In the Chremonidean War (267–261), he achieved lasting victory over Egypt, Sparta, and Athens. He allied with the AETOLIAN LEAGUE and local tyrants to stave off incursions of the ACHAEAN LEAGUE. His defeat of the Egyptian fleet at Andros (244?) assured Macedonian hegemony in the Aegean.

Antigua and Barbuda \an-'tə-gə...bär-'byü-də\ Island nation, Lesser ANTILLES. It consists of three islands, Antigua, Barbuda, and Redonda. Area: 171 sq mi (443 sq km). Population (1997 est.): 65,000. Capital: ST. JOHN'S (on Antigua). The majority of the population are descendants of African slaves brought in during colonial times. Language: English (official). Religion: Christianity. Currency: Eastern Caribbean dollar. The largest of the islands is Antigua (108 sq mi, or 280 sq km). It lacks forests, mountains, and rivers, and is subject to droughts. The main anchorage is the deepwater harbor of St. John's. Barbuda, 25 mi (40 km) north of Antigua, is a 62-sq-mi (161-sq-km) game reserve inhabited by a variety of wildlife, including wild deer; its only settlement is Codrington, on its western coast. Redonda, an uninhabited rock (0.5 sq mi, or 1.3 sq km), lies southwest of Antigua. Tourism is the mainstay of the country's economy; offshore banking is growing. CHRISTOPHER COLUMBUS visited Antigua in 1493 and named it after a church in SEVILLE, Spain. It was colonized by English settlers in 1632, who imported African slaves to grow tobacco and sugarcane. Barbuda was colonized by the English in 1678. In 1834 its slaves were emancipated. Antigua (with Barbuda) was part of the British colony of the Leeward Islands from 1871 until that colony was defederated in 1956. The islands achieved full independence in 1981. See map opposite.

antihistamine \,an-ti-'his-tə-,mēn, ,an-ti-'his-tə-mən\ Synthetic drug that counteracts the effects of released HISTAMINE in the body. Antihistamines compete with histamine at one of the two types of histamine receptors, preventing allergic attacks (see ALLERGY) or INFLAMMATION. Some of the more than 100 antihistamines available also prevent MOTION SICKNESS and VERTIGO. Drowsiness is a frequent side effect. H_2 antihistamines, which bind to the second receptor type, are used to control gastric-acid secretion (see STOMACH) and treat PEPTIC ULCERS.

Antilles \an-'til-ēz\, **Greater and Lesser** Two groups of islands in the WEST INDIES, bounding the Caribbean Sea on the north and east, respectively. The Greater Antilles include the largest islands (Cuba, Jamaica, Hispaniola, and Puerto Rico), the Lesser Antilles all being much smaller. The name Antilia originally referred to semimythical lands located somewhere west of Europe across the Atlantic. After CHRISTOPHER COLUMBUS's discoveries, the Spanish name Antillas was commonly assigned to the new lands; "Sea of the Antilles" in various European languages is used as an alternative name for the Caribbean Sea.

antimatter Substance composed of elementary particles having the MASS and ELECTRIC CHARGE of ordinary matter (such as ELECTRONS and PROTONS), but for which the charge and related magnetic properties are opposite in sign. The existence of antimatter was a consequence of the electron theory of P. A. M. DIRAC. In 1932 the POSITRON (antielectron) was detected in COSMIC RAYS, followed by the antiproton and the antineutron using PARTICLE ACCELERATORS. Positrons, antiprotons, and antineutrons, collectively called antiparticles, are the antiparticles of electrons, protons, and neutrons, respectively. When matter and antimatter are in close proximity, ANNIHILATION occurs within a fraction of a second, releasing large amounts of ENERGY.

antimetabolite \,an-ti-mə-'ta-bə-,līt\ Substance that competes with, replaces, or inhibits a specific compound within a CELL, whose functioning is thereby disrupted. Because its structure resembles the compound's, it is taken up by the cell, but it does not react in the same way with the ENZYME that acts on the usual compound. It may inhibit the enzyme or be converted into an aberrant chemical. Many antimetabolites are useful in treating disease, including SULFA DRUGS, which disrupt bacterial but not human METABOLISM for bacterial diseases, and others (e.g., methotrexate, 5-fluorouracil) for various cancers.

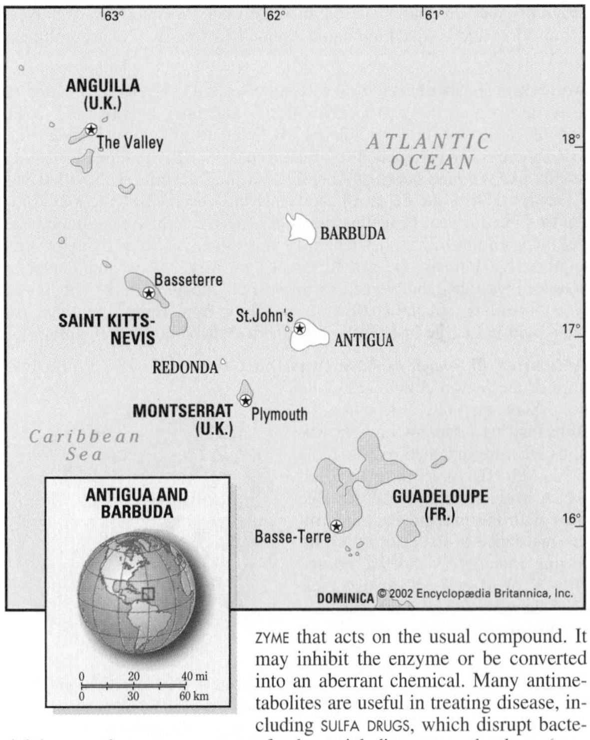

antimony \'an-tə-,mō-nē\ Semimetallic to metallic chemical ELEMENT (see METAL), chemical symbol Sb, atomic number 51. Of its various ALLOTROPES, the most common is a lustrous, bluish, brittle, flaky solid. In nature antimony occurs chiefly as the gray SULFIDE MINERAL STIBNITE, Sb_2S_3. Pure antimony metal has no important uses, but its ALLOYS and COMPOUNDS are extremely useful. Some antimony alloys have the rare quality of expanding on solidifying; these are used for castings and for type metal. Alloys with lead are used in car BATTERIES, bullets, and cable sheaths. Antifriction alloys with tin and lead (babbitt metals) are used as components of machine bearings. Antimony COMPOUNDS (VALENCES 3, 4, and 5) are widely used as flame retardants in paints, plastics, rubber, and textiles; others are used as paint pigments.

antinovel Type of avant-garde novel that departs from traditional novelistic conventions by ignoring such elements as plot, dialogue, and human interest. Seeking to overcome reader's habits and challenge their expectations, antinovelists deliberately avoid any intrusion of authorial personality, preferences, or values. Though the term was coined by J.-P. SARTRE in 1948, the approach is at least as old as the works of the 18th-century writer LAURENCE STERNE. Writers of such works include NATHALIE SARRAUTE, CLAUDE SIMON, ALAIN ROBBE-GRILLET, Uwe Johnson, and Rayner Heppenstall.

Antioch \'an-tē-ˌäk\ *Turkish* **Antakya** \ˌän-tä-'kyä\ City (pop., 1994 est.: 137,000), southern Turkey. Founded in 300 BC by Greeks, Antioch was the center of the SELEUCID kingdom until 64 BC, when the Romans made it the capital of their province of Syria. An early center of Christianity, the city was the headquarters of St. PAUL c. AD 47–55. It came under Persian domination in the 6th century and Arab domination in the 7th century, and was captured by the Crusaders in 1098. It finally fell to the Ottoman Turks in 1517 and remained in their control until World War I.

Antioch University Private university founded in 1852 as Antioch College in Yellow Springs, Ohio. Horace MANN was its first president (1852–59). From its founding it was coeducational, nonsectarian, and open to black students. It is noted for its experimental curricula. Students alternate between academic work and full-time jobs, to give them experience of "actual living." In 1978 Antioch consolidated its various programs and campuses (in Ohio, California, Washington, and New Hampshire) and adopted the name Antioch University. Total enrollment is about 3,200.

Antiochus I Soter \an-'tī-ə-kəs...'sō-ter\ (324–262/261 BC) King of SELEUCID Syria in the east (292?–281 BC) and later overall (281–261). Son of SELEUCUS I, he consolidated the Seleucid kingdom, founded numerous cities, and expanded its trade routes. In 281 he contended with revolts in Syria and northern Anatolia and fought a war with ANTIGONUS II GONATAS. With the defeat of the Gauls in Greece (279), he and Antigonus signed a pact of nonintervention. The Gauls in Asia Minor were not defeated until 275, after which he was hailed as Soter ("Savior") by appreciative Ionians. He settled Greeks in Asia Minor and Persia to counter invasions, and worked to revive Babylonian culture. Though he won Phoenicia and the coast of Asia Minor from Egypt, he soon lost them, and in 261 he lost much of northern Asia Minor to Pergamum.

Antiochus III *known as* **Antiochus the Great** (242–187 BC) SELEUCID king of the Syrian empire (223–187 BC). After quelling a rebellion by Achaeus, his governor in Asia Minor (213), he marched east to India (212–205). He forged a peaceful alliance with Armenia, and forcible ones with Parthia and Bactria, stilling resistance to his campaign. Following Ptolemy IV's death, he and PHILIP V of Macedonia divided most of Ptolemy's empire, Antiochus taking the southern and eastern lands, including Palestine (c. 202). He then marched against Egypt, concluding a peace in 195, through which he acquired southern Syria and Ptolemy's territories in Asia Minor. Rome grew angry with him after he admitted HANNIBAL of Carthage to his court; when he took a force to defend the Aetolians against Rome, Rome struck against him, eventually defeating him at Magnesia (189). He gave up lands in Europe and western Asia Minor but kept Syria, Mesopotamia, and western Iran. He was murdered while exacting much-needed tribute near Susa.

Antiochus III, coin, late 3rd–early 2nd century BC; in the British Museum.

BY COURTESY OF THE TRUSTEES OF THE BRITISH MUSEUM; PHOTOGRAPH, J.R. FREEMAN & CO. LTD.

Antiochus IV Epiphanes \i-'pif-ə-ˌnēz\ **("God Manifest")** (c. 215–164 BC) SELEUCID king of the Hellenistic Syrian kingdom (175–164 BC). Son of ANTIOCHUS III, he was taken hostage in Rome (189–175), where he learned about Roman institutions. On his release, he ousted a usurper to take over Syria. He conquered Egypt except Alexandria (169) and ruled Egypt as regent for his nephew Ptolemy VI. The Roman defeat of his Macedonian allies neutralized his victories in Cyprus and Egypt (168), and he was forced to leave both, though he kept southern Syria. He took Jerusalem (167) and enforced its Hellenization; Jewish rites were forbidden on pain of death. In 164 JUDAS MACCABAEUS and the anti-Greek Jews conquered Judaea except for the Acra in Jerusalem (164), tore down the altar of Zeus, and reconsecrated the Temple. Antiochus then turned to defending his empire against the Parthians in the east, regained Armenia, and went on to the Arabian coast before dying in Persis.

antioxidant Any of various COMPOUNDS added to certain foods, natural and synthetic rubbers, gasolines, and other products to retard autoxidation (combination with OXYGEN in the air at room temperature) and its effects. AROMATIC COMPOUNDS such as aromatic AMINES, PHENOLS, and aminophenols delay loss of elasticity in rubber and gummy deposits in gasoline. Preservatives such as tocopherol (VITAMIN E), propyl gallate, butylated hydroxytoluene (BHT), and butylated hydroxyanisole (BHA) prevent rancidity in FATS, OILS, and fatty foods. In the body, antioxidants such as VITAMINS C and E and SELENIUM may reduce oxidation caused by FREE RADICALS.

Antipater \an-'tip-ə-tər\ (died 43 BC) Founder of the Herodian dynasty in Palestine. Born in Idumaea, a region of southern JUDAEA, he gained power by helping the Romans, and in return, Julius CAESAR appointed him procurator of Judaea in 47 BC. He was assassinated by a rival four years later, but his son, HEROD THE GREAT, was made king of Judaea.

Antiphon \'an-ti-ˌfän\ (c. 480–411 BC) Orator and statesman. The first Athenian known to practice rhetoric professionally, he wrote speeches for others to give in court but was reluctant to appear in public debate. He may have instigated the revolution of the oligarchic Council of the FOUR HUNDRED, an attempt to seize the Athenian government in the midst of war. When the oligarchy fell, he defended his role in the overthrow in a speech called by THUCYDIDES the greatest defense ever made, but he was nonetheless executed for treason.

antipope In ROMAN CATHOLICISM, a person who tries to take the place of the legitimately elected pope. Some antipopes were elected by factions in doctrinal disagreements, and others were chosen in double elections arbitrated by secular authorities or picked as third candidates in an effort to resolve such disputes. The principal age of the antipope came after the papal court was moved from Rome to Avignon in the 14th century (see AVIGNON PAPACY), an event that led to the Western SCHISM of 1378–1417. During this era, the popes now considered canonical were elected in Rome, and the antipopes were elected in Avignon.

Antirent War Civil protest from leaseholding farmers in upper New York state in the 1840s. The farmers resented outdated laws based on semifeudal leaseholding practices of the early Dutch estate owners. In 1839, when they revolted against attempts to collect back rent in Albany Co., the governor called out the militia to quell the violence. Sporadic acts of resistance against rent and tax collection spread across the state, and in 1845 the governor was forced to declare martial law. In 1846 a new state constitution abolished the leasehold system.

antiseptic Agents applied to living tissue to destroy or inhibit growth of infectious microorganisms. Disinfectants are used to destroy microorganisms on surfaces; ANTIBIOTICS and other antimicrobial agents are given in shots or orally for infections but may also be applied locally for superficial infections. An antiseptic's efficiency depends on concentration, time, and temperature. Many antiseptics destroy specific types or forms of microorganisms (e.g., BACTERIA but not SPORES). Among the major families of antiseptics are ALCOHOLS, PHENOLS, CHLORINE and IODINE compounds, MERCURY-based tinctures, certain acridine DYES, and some ESSENTIAL OILS.

antitank weapon Any of several GUNS, MISSILES, and mines intended for use against TANKS. LAND MINES, ordinary ARTILLERY, and other projectiles were used to destroy tanks in World War I. By World War II antitank guns had been developed; they frequently fired special ammunition such as the hollow charge shell, which exploded on impact with great penetrating force. Various antitank missiles and launching devices, including the BAZOOKA, were also used in the war.

antitoxin ANTIBODY formed in the body in reaction to a bacterial TOXIN, which it can neutralize. People who have recovered from bacterial diseases often develop specific antitoxins that give them IMMUNITY against recurrence. Injecting an animal (usually a horse) with increasing doses of toxin produces a high concentration of antitoxin in the blood. The resulting highly concentrated preparation of antitoxins is called an antiserum. The first antitoxin developed (1890) was specific to DIPHTHERIA; today, antitoxins are also used to treat BOTULISM, DYSENTERY, gas GANGRENE, and TETANUS.

antitrust law Any law restricting business practices considered unfair or monopolistic. Among U.S. laws, the best known is the SHERMAN ANTITRUST ACT of 1890, which declared illegal "every contract, combination . . . or conspiracy in restraint of trade or commerce." The Clayton Antitrust Act of 1914, as amended in 1936 by the Robinson-Patman Act, prohibits discrimination among customers through prices or other means; it also prohibits mergers or acquisitions whenever the effect may be "to substantially lessen competition." Labor unions are also subject to antitrust laws.

antlion Insect (family Myrmeleontidae) known in its larval stage for its aggressive capture of prey. The antlion LARVA digs a funnel-shaped sandy pit by using its oval, bristled abdomen, then buries itself in the pit with only its powerful jaws uncovered. Any small insect that ventures over the pit's edge slips to the bottom and is seized by the antlion, which sucks the contents of its victim and throws out the empty skin. The adult antlion does not feed. The best known of the 65 described species occurs in North America and Europe.

Antlion.

WILLIAM E. FERGUSON

Antofagasta \ˌän-tō-fä-ˈgäs-tä\ Seaport (pop., 1995: est.: 219,000), capital of Antofagasta region, northern Chile. Located on Moreno Bay, it was a Bolivian city until it was ceded to Chile in 1879. Its early growth resulted from the nitrate boom that began in 1866 and from the Caracoles silver discovery in 1870. The largest city of northern Chile, it remains a supply source for the mines and is a communications center on the PAN-AMERICAN HIGHWAY.

Antonello da Messina \ˌan-tō-ˈnel-ō-dä-mā-ˈsē-nə\ (c. 1430–1479) Italian painter. Born in Messina, Sicily, and trained in Naples, then a cosmopolitan art center, he studied the Flemish artists, notably JAN VAN EYCK. He introduced oil painting into Venetian art. His major works were altarpieces and portraits. In Venice he executed the San Cassiano altarpiece, of which three fragments remain. His portrait busts in three-quarter view, combining Flemish detail with Italian grandeur, became fashionable. See also VENETIAN SCHOOL.

"Portrait of a Man," panel painting by Antonello da Messina, c. 1472; in the National Gallery, London.

BY COURTESY OF THE TRUSTEES OF THE NATIONAL GALLERY, LONDON

Antonescu \ˌan-tə-ˈnes-kü\, **Ion** (1882–1946) Romanian general. He rose in the Romanian army to the rank of general and chief of staff (1934) and later became minister of defense (1937–38). Appointed prime minister in 1940, he established a fascist dictatorship and openly supported the Axis Powers. Initially he won broad support for his domestic reforms and declaration of war against the Soviet Union (1941), but that support eroded. His regime was overthrown in 1944, and he was later executed as a war criminal.

Antonine Wall Roman frontier barrier in Britain. It ran 37 mi (59 km) across Scotland between the Clyde River and the Firth of Forth. Ordered by ANTONINUS PIUS and built in AD 142 by the governor of Britain, it was about 15 ft (5 m) wide and 10 ft (3 m) high; a ditch 40 ft (12 m) wide and 12 ft (4 m) deep ran in front of it and a road behind. It was controlled by 19 forts spaced at 2-mi (3-km) intervals. Its construction moved the northern boundary of Roman Britain into Scotland, providing defense against the northern tribes beyond HADRIAN'S WALL, which lay to the south. The wall was abandoned by 196, but traces remain.

Antoninus Pius \ˌan-tə-ˈnī-nəs-ˈpī-əs\ *in full* **Caesar Titus Aelius Hadrianus Antoninus Augustus Pius** (AD 86–161) Roman emperor (AD 138–61). Of Gallic origins, he served as consul (120) before being assigned judicial administrative duties in Italy. He later governed the province of Asia (c. 134). He became an adviser to HADRIAN, and in 138 was made Hadrian's heir. On accession, he had the deceased emperor declared a god; for such dutiful acts he was named Pius ("pious"). He quelled rebellions in Britain and in other provinces and built the ANTONINE WALL.

Antoninus Pius, marble bust; in the British Museum.

REPRODUCED BY COURTESY OF THE TRUSTEES OF THE BRITISH MUSEUM

Antonioni \ˌan-ˌtō-nē-ˈō-nē\, **Michelangelo** (born 1912) Italian film director and producer. He wrote film reviews and studied filmmaking before directing his short film *The People of the Po Valley* (1947). His first major film, *The Girl Friends* (1955), was followed by the international successes *L'avventura* (1960), *Eclipse* (1962), and *Blow-up* (1966). His other films include *The Red Desert* (1964), *Zabriskie Point* (1970), and *The Passenger* (1974). In Antonioni's films, plot and dialogue are subordinated to the visual image, which becomes a metaphor of human existence rather than a record of it.

Antony, Mark *Latin* **Marcus Antonius** (82/81–30 BC) Roman general. After military service (57–54), he joined the staff of his relative Julius CAESAR. He helped Caesar drive POMPEY from Italy in 49, and in 44 was made co-consul. After Caesar's assassination, Octavian (later AUGUSTUS) initially opposed Antony, but later formed the Second TRIUMVIRATE with Antony and Lepidus. Antony helped defeat republican forces at PHILIPPI and took control of Rome's eastern provinces. On a mission to Egypt to question CLEOPATRA about her loyalty, he became her lover (41–40). He returned to Italy in 40 to settle differences with Octavian, whereupon he received command of the eastern provinces. To strengthen his position, he agreed to marry Octavian's sister Octavia. When relations with Octavian again collapsed, he headed for Syria and sent for Cleopatra for aid. Octavian sent Octavia to him, and when Antony ordered her back to Rome a fatal breach opened. The triumvirate ended in 32, leaving Antony little support in Rome. He divorced Octavia, and Octavian declared war on Cleopatra. Antony lost the Battle of ACTIUM, and he and Cleopatra fled to Egypt pursued by Octavian. When resistance became futile, they committed suicide.

Mark Antony, detail of a marble bust; in the Vatican Museum.

ALINARI—ART RESOURCE/EB INC.

Antrim Town (pop., 1981: 22,000) and district (pop., 1995 est.: 49,000), Northern Ireland. The town borders Lough NEAGH. In 1798 it was the scene of a battle in which several thousand nationalist insurgents led by Henry J. McCracken were defeated by the British. A busy market center, Antrim town was formerly an important locale for the linen industry. Also the name of a former Northern Ireland county, the area it covered has evidence of human inhabitation dating to c. 6000 BC. Anglo-Norman adventurers arrived in the 12th century AD, and the area became part of the earldom of Ulster. The invasion by Edward Bruce from Scotland in 1315 caused the decline of British power. In Northern

Ireland's 1973 administrative reorganization, the county was divided into several districts.

Antwerp *French* **Anvers** \äⁿ-'ver\ *Flemish* **Antwerpen** \'änt-ˌver-pən\ City (pop., 1995 est.: 456,000), capital of Antwerp province, Belgium. One of the world's major seaports, it is located 55 mi (88 km) southeast of the North Sea. Because it lies in the Flemish-speaking part of Belgium, it plays the role of unofficial capital of FLANDERS. It received municipal rights in 1291 and became a member of the HANSEATIC LEAGUE by 1315. As a distribution center for Spanish and Portuguese trade, it became the commercial and financial capital of Europe in the 16th century. Following destructive invasions it went into decline, but began to revive after NAPOLEON's improvement of the harbor c. 1803. It was part of the Kingdom of the Netherlands (1815–30), then was ceded to Belgian nationalists. Its current economic life centers around shipping, port-related activities, and major manufacturing.

antyesti \ant-'yes-tē\ Hindu funeral rites. They generally involve cremation followed by disposal of the ashes in a sacred river. As soon as possible after death, the body is removed to the cremation grounds, usually on the riverbank. The eldest son of the deceased and a priest perform the final rites. For 10 days, the mourners are considered impure as they perform rites intended to provide the soul of the deceased with a new spiritual body for the next life. At a prescribed date, the bones are collected and buried or immersed in a river.

Anu \'ä-ˌnü\ Mesopotamian sky god. He belonged to a triad that included BEL and EA. Though he was the highest god, his role in mythology, hymns, and cult was small. The father of all gods, evil spirits, and demons, and the god of kings and the calendar, he was depicted with headdress and horns signifying strength. His Sumerian counterpart, An, was originally envisaged as a great bull; he probably began as a god of herders.

Anu \'ä-ˌnü\, **Chao** (1767–1835) Ruler of the central Lao kingdom of Vientiane (r.1804–29). In his youth Anu fought with the Siamese against the Burmese and won Siamese respect for his military prowess. Chosen by them to be king of Vientiane, he undertook major public works and cultivated good relations with Vietnam. He had the Siamese appoint his son ruler of the southern Lao principality of Champassak and began to plot a rebellion for Lao independence. His armies nearly reached Bangkok, but the revolt was quelled and Vientiane was sacked and later razed. Anu fled to the forests but was captured, punished, and killed.

Anubis \ə-'nü-bəs\ Ancient Egyptian god of the dead, represented as a jackal or as a man with the head of a jackal. In the Early Dynastic period and the Old Kingdom he was preeminent as lord of the dead, but he was later overshadowed by OSIRIS. Anubis was associated with the care of the dead and was credited with the invention of embalming, an art he first practiced on the corpse of Osiris. Later assigned the role of conducting souls into the underworld, he was sometimes identified in the Greco-Roman world with HERMES.

Anuradhapura \ə-'nu̇r-ə-də-ˌpu̇r-ə\ Sinhalese kingdom centered at Anuradhapura in Sri Lanka (Ceylon) c. 3rd century BC–AD 10th century. Though plagued by invasions from southern India (which took actual control of the kingdom several times) and internal strife among warring clans, the kingdom of Anuradhapura developed a high degree of culture. Its complex irrigation system is often considered its major achievement. The city of Anuradhapura contains vast Buddhist ruins and a bo tree grown from a slip of the tree under which the historical BUDDHA obtained enlightenment.

anvil Iron block on which metal is placed for shaping, originally by hand with a hammer. The blacksmith's anvil is usually of wrought iron (sometimes of cast iron), with a smooth working surface of hardened steel. A projecting conical beak, or horn, at one end is used for hammering curved pieces of metal. When power hammers are used, the anvil is supported on a heavy block, which in turn rests on a strong foundation of timber and masonry or concrete. See also SMITHING.

anxiety In psychology, a feeling of dread, fear, or apprehension, often with no clear justification. Anxiety differs from true fear in that it is typically the product of subjective, internal emotional states rather than a response to a clear and actual danger. It is marked by physiological signs such as sweating, tension, and increased pulse, by doubt concerning the reality and nature of the perceived threat, and by self-doubt about one's capacity to cope with it. Some anxiety inevitably arises in the course of daily life and is normal; but persistent, intense, chronic, or recurring anxiety not justified by real-life stresses is usually regarded as a sign of an emotional disorder. See also STRESS.

Anzio \'änt-sē-ˌō\ Seaport and resort town (pop., 1991: 32,000) southeast of Rome, Italy. It was founded, according to legend, by Anteias, son of ODYSSEUS and CIRCE. It was a stronghold of the VOLSCI in the 5th century BC. Conquered by Rome in 338 BC, Antium (as it was then known) became a resort for wealthy Romans. NERO and CALIGULA were born there. Destroyed by the SARACENS in the 9th–10th century, it remained virtually deserted until 1698, when Pope Innocent XII built a new port nearby. In 1944 it was the scene of a bloody but successful amphibious landing by Allied forces.

ANZUS Pact *officially* **Pacific Security Treaty** Security pact for the South Pacific, signed in 1951 by Australia, New Zealand, and the U.S. (hence its acronym). The U.S. first suggested a pact to Australia in the wake of the U.S.-Japan Security Treaty and fears of Japanese rearmament. The signatories agreed to maintain a consultative relationship for their collective security. In the 1980s New Zealand refused to let ships carrying nuclear weapons dock at its ports; the U.S., refusing to identify its nuclear-armed ships, suspended its treaty obligations to New Zealand in 1986, and the treaty has since been nonoperative with reference to New Zealand.

AOL See AMERICA ONLINE

aorta ARTERY that carries blood from the heart to all the organs and structures of the body. Where the left ventricle opens into the aorta, a valve prevents backflow of blood into the heart. The aorta ascends from the heart, arches over it to the left, then descends into the trunk. Arteries branch off along its length until it divides at hip level into arteries that go to the legs.

aorta, coarctation of the Congenital disorder involving narrowing of a short section of the aorta's arch over the heart. It causes a characteristic murmur, abnormally high blood pressure in the arms, and reduced blood flow to the abdomen, pelvis, and legs. It increases the workload of the left ventricle, which usually becomes enlarged. Surgical reconstruction or replacement (depending on the person's age) of the narrowed area is most effective in the young.

aortic arch syndrome Group of disorders in which the vessels that branch off from the aortic arch are blocked. It is most common in middle-aged or elderly persons with atherosclerosis (see ARTERIOSCLEROSIS). It impairs circulation to the brain, which can lead to blindness and paralysis. Congenital aortic-arch defects include patent DUCTUS ARTERIOSUS and coarctation of the AORTA. Treatment is surgical.

aortic stenosis \stə-'nō-səs\ Narrowing of the passage from the left ventricle of the heart to the AORTA, in or near the aortic valve. It may be a congenital disorder or may result from rheumatic heart disease or valve degeneration. It is detected by characteristic heart sounds. Exertion may cause fainting or ANGINA PECTORIS. Stenosis may lead to CONGESTIVE HEART FAILURE and makes patients susceptible to ENDOCARDITIS. Medical treatment focuses on these complications. Surgical treatment repairs the valve or replaces it with a synthetic or transplanted valve.

Aosta \ä-'ȯs-tä\ City (pop., 1989: 36,000), capital of VALLE D'AOSTA region, northwestern Italy. Located at the juncture of the Great and Little St. Bernard Pass roads through the ALPS, it was a stronghold of the Salassi, a Celtic tribe subdued by the Romans in 25 BC. A Roman town was founded there by AUGUSTUS in 24 BC, and many Roman structures survive, including the walls, two gates, and a triumphal arch in honor of Augustus. Aosta was the birthplace of St. ANSELM. See photograph opposite on following page.

AP See ASSOCIATED PRESS

Apache American Indians of the southwestern U.S. Culturally, the Apache are divided into Eastern Apache, which include the Mescalero, Jicarilla, Chiricahua, and Lipan, and Western Apache, which include the Cibecue. The Eastern Apaches were predominantly HUNTING AND GATHERING SOCIETIES, while their Western counterparts relied more on farming. Their ancestors had come down from the north to settle the Plains, but with the introduction of the horse they were pressed south and west by the COMANCHE and UTE. They attempted to be friends of the Spanish, the Mexicans, and later the Americans. In 1861, however, there began a quarter-century confrontation between U.S. military forces and the

Apache and NAVAJO. The Apache wars were among the fiercest fought on the frontier. The last ended in 1886 with the surrender of GERONIMO. The Chiricahua Apache were evacuated from the West and held successively in Florida, Alabama, and Oklahoma. The Apache today total about 11,000 and live largely on or near reservations in Arizona and New Mexico. See also COCHISE.

Apamea Cibotus \ˌa-pə-ˈmē-ə-si-ˈbō-təs\ Ancient city, southern PHRYGIA. The city was built by ANTIOCHUS I SOTER in the 3rd century BC on the Maeander (MENDERES) River. Superseding Celaenae, it was placed in a commanding position on the great east-west trade route of the Seleucid kingdom. In the 2nd century BC, Apamea passed to Roman rule and became an important center for Italian and Jewish traders. Declining after the 3rd century AD, it was captured by the Turks in 1070 and finally destroyed by an earthquake. The remains are partly covered by the modern city of Dinar, Turkey.

apartheid \ə-ˈpär-ˌtāt\ (Afrikaans: "apartness" or "separateness") Policy of SEGREGATION and political and economic discrimination against non-European groups in South Africa. The term was first used as the name of the official policy of the NATIONAL PARTY in 1948, though racial segregation, sanctioned by law, was already widely practiced. The Group Areas Act of 1950 established residential and business sections in urban areas for each race and strengthened the existing "pass" laws, which required nonwhites to carry identification papers. Other laws forbade most social contacts between the races, authorized segregated public facilities, established separate educational standards, restricted each race to certain types of jobs, curtailed nonwhite labor unions, denied nonwhite participation in the national government, and established various black African "homelands," partly self-governing units that were nevertheless politically and economically dependent on South Africa. Apartheid was always subject to internal criticism, and led to many violent protests, strikes, and acts of sabotage; it also received international censure. In 1990–91 most apartheid legislation was repealed, though segregation remains deeply entrenched in South African society. See also AFRICAN NATIONAL CONGRESS, RACISM.

apatite A member of the PHOSPHATE group of minerals, the world's major source of phosphorus, found as variously colored, glassy crystals, masses, or nodules. Much of it has a chemical composition approximating $Ca_5(PO_4)_3(F,Cl,OH)$. If not for its softness, apatite would be a popular gemstone; some of the material found is clear, but it is fragile and difficult to cut and polish.

Apatosaurus \ə-ˌpa-tə-ˈsȯr-əs\ Genus of giant herbivorous dinosaur, one of the largest land animals of all time. *Apatosaurus* lived between 147 million and 137 million years ago during the Late Jurassic and Early Cretaceous Periods in North America and Europe. It weighed as much as 30 tons and was as long as 70 ft (21 m), including the very long neck and tail. Formerly known as *Brontosaurus* because of incomplete fossil evidence, its head was depicted until 1978 as massive and snub-nosed, with spoonlike teeth; scientists now know the animal had a slender, elongated skull and long, peglike teeth. Skeletal evidence indicates that, despite their great bulk, apatosaurs were primarily land animals.

Ruins of Roman theatre, Aosta, Italy.
MARZARI—SCALA FROM ART RESOURCE

ape Any of the tailless, anthropoid PRIMATES of two families: Hylobatidae (the lesser apes: GIBBONS and siamangs) and Pongidae (the great apes: CHIMPANZEES, BONOBOS, ORANGUTANS, and GORILLAS). Apes are found in the tropical forests of western and central Africa and South Asia. They are distinguished from monkeys by having no tail, having an appendix, and having a more complex brain. Apes typically move about by swinging, and they tend to stand erect, occasionally walking on two feet. Highly intelligent animals, apes are more closely related to humans than are any other living primates. As a result of habitat destruction and hunting, all the apes are now regarded as endangered.

APEC *in full* **Asia-Pacific Economic Cooperation** Trade group established in 1989 to promote the economic development of its members. The original members were Australia, Brunei, Canada, China, Indonesia, Japan, Malaysia, New Zealand, the Philippines, Singapore, South Korea, Thailand, and the U.S., as well as Taiwan and Hong Kong (since membership was based on "economies" rather than nations). The original 15 represented nearly 2 billion people and the world's leading exporters. APEC's first summit was held in Seattle in 1993. Mexico, Chile, and Papua New Guinea joined APEC in 1994. The APEC group now represents about 40% of the world's population, 40% of global trade, and 50% of the world's gross national product. See also NORTH AMERICAN FREE TRADE AGREEMENT, TRADE AGREEMENT, WORLD TRADE ORGANIZATION.

apella \ə-ˈpe-lə\ Ancient Spartan assembly, similar to the ECCLESIA of other Greek states. The apella, whose monthly meetings were open to citizens over 30, did not initiate proposals, and could only consider matters submitted by the EPHORS or the GEROUSIA; voting was by shouts. Its business included treaties, wars, and succession; it named commanders, elected elders and ephors, and voted on changes in the laws.

Apelles \ə-ˈpe-ˌlēz\ (fl. late 4th century–early 3rd century BC) Greek painter. He studied under Pamphilus and was court painter to PHILIP II of Macedonia and his son, ALEXANDER THE GREAT. Notable works included a portrait of Alexander, an allegorical picture of Calumny, and a painting of Aphrodite rising from the sea. A master of composition and chiaroscuro, he was noted for his technical improvements; he used a dark glaze to preserve his paintings and soften their color. Though no copies of his works survive, he was considered in antiquity the greatest of Greek painters.

Apennines \ˈa-pə-ˌnīnz\ Mountain range, central Italy. It stretches some 840 mi (1,350 km) from near Savona in the northwest to REGGIO DI CALABRIA in the south, its width varying from 25 to 80 mi (40–130 km). Monte Corno is its highest peak, at 9,560 ft (2,915 m). The range is the source of most of Italy's rivers, including the ARNO, TIBER, Volturno, and Garigliano. It is famous for its hill towns, including FLORENCE, Arezzo, L'AQUILA, and Benevento.

Apgar Score System Rating procedure to identify newborns needing life-sustaining medical assistance. It was developed in 1952 by Virginia Apgar (1909–1974). Five signs, keyed to Apgar's name—Appearance (color), Pulse, Grimace (reflex irritability), Activity (muscle tone), and Respiration—measure adaptation to leaving the uterus. The maximum score is 10. If the total score at one and then five minutes after birth is less than 7, the infant is reevaluated every five minutes for 20 minutes or until two consecutive scores of 7 or more are obtained.

aphasia \ə-ˈfā-zhə\ *or* **dysphasia** \dis-ˈfā-zhə\ Brain-generated defect in saying words, unrelated to physical ability to produce sounds. Symptoms vary with the brain area involved: the ability to say words in a specific category or to put words in a meaningful order may be lost. The term also covers related disturbances, including agraphia (inability to write) and agnosias (perceptual aphasias, inability to recognize what is perceived through one of the senses; e.g., DYSLEXIA). Aphasias show that the apparent unity of "the mind" rests on the interaction of independent parts of the brain.

aphid \'ā-fəd', a-fəd\ Any of several species of sapsucking, soft-bodied INSECTS (order Homoptera) that are about the size of a pinhead, with tubelike projections on the abdomen. Serious plant pests, they stunt plant growth, produce plant GALLS, transmit plant viral diseases, and deform leaves, buds, and flowers. ANTS may take care of aphids, protecting them from weather and natural enemies and transferring them from wilted to healthy plants. The ants in turn obtain honeydew, a sweet product excreted by aphids, which the ants retrieve by "milking" the aphids (stroking their abdomens).

aphorism Terse formulation of any generally accepted truth or sentiment conveyed in a pithy, memorable statement. The term was first used in the *Aphorisms* of HIPPOCRATES, a long series of propositions concerning disease and the art of healing. Aphorisms were used especially in dealing with subjects for which principles and methodology developed relatively late, including art, agriculture, medicine, jurisprudence, and politics, but in the modern era they have usually been vehicles of wit and pithy wisdom. Celebrated modern aphorists include FRIEDRICH NIETZSCHE and OSCAR WILDE.

aphrodisiac \ˌa-frə-'dē-zē-ˌak\ Any of various forms of stimulation thought to arouse sexual excitement. They may be psychophysiological (arousing the senses of sight, touch, smell, or hearing) or internal (e.g., foods, alcoholic drinks, drugs, love potions, medicinal preparations). Most foods traditionally believed to be aphrodisiacs have no chemical components that would have such an effect. In some cases, their reputation may be based on a supposed resemblance to genitalia (e.g., ginseng root, rhinoceros horn). Drugs such as alcohol or marijuana may lead to sexual excitation by lessening the user's inhibitions. Few medical studies have been conducted; the only substances medically recognized as aphrodisiacs are extremely hazardous to the health.

Aphrodite \ˌa-frə-'dī-tē\ Greek goddess of sexual love and beauty. She is also associated with the sea and, according to legend, was born of sea foam arising from the genitals of URANUS. Sparta, Thebes, and Cyprus honored her as a goddess of war. Many scholars believe that her cult is Semitic rather than Greek in origin. According to Homer, she was the daughter of ZEUS and his consort Dione, and she married HEPHAESTUS, but betrayed him with ARES. She had many mortal lovers. Her main centers of worship were on the islands of Cyprus and Cythera and at Corinth. As a fertility goddess, she is associated with EROS, the GRACES, and the Horae (seasons). VENUS is her Roman counterpart.

Apia \ä-'pē-ä\ Seaport town (pop., 1995 est.: 33,000) and capital, Samoa. It lies on the northern coast of Upolu Island. Its economy centers on the export of goods to AMERICAN SAMOA. ROBERT LOUIS STEVENSON is buried at nearby Mount Vaea; Vailima, his former home, is now the residence of the head of state.

apiculture See BEEKEEPING

Apis \'ā-pəs\ In ancient Egyptian religion, a sacred bull deity worshiped at Memphis. The cult originated at least as early as the 1st dynasty (c. 2925–c. 2775 BC). Apis was probably at first a fertility god but became associated with PTAH and also with OSIRIS and Sokaris, gods of the dead. When an Apis bull died, it was buried with great pomp, and the calf that was to be its successor was installed at Memphis. Apis's priests drew omens from the bull's behavior, and his ORACLE had a wide reputation. The worship of Serapis (a combination of Osiris and Apis) probably arose at Memphis in the 3rd century BC and became one of the most widespread oriental cults in the Roman empire.

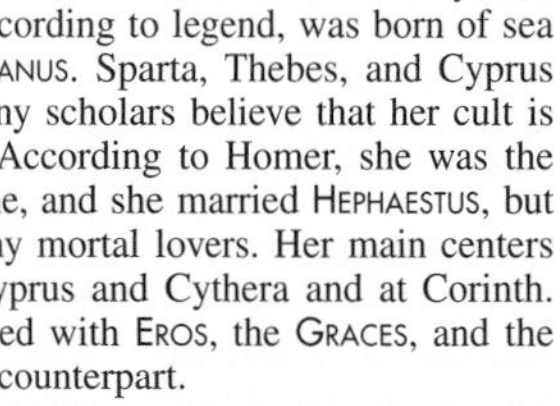

Apis, bull deity, painted on the bottom of a wooden coffin, c. 700 BC; in the Roemer und Pelizaeus Museum, Hildesheim, Ger.
BAVARIA VERLAG

APL Computer PROGRAMMING LANGUAGE based on (and named with the initials of) the book *A Programming Language,* by Kenneth E. Iverson of IBM (1962). It has been adapted for use in many different computers and fields because of its concise syntax. Statements are expressed with simple notations that have powerful built-in operational functions such as looping, sorting, and selection. Once a popular language, it is not used often today for new programs.

aplastic anemia \ā-'plas-tik\ *or* **anemia of bone-marrow failure** Inadequate BLOOD-CELL FORMATION by BONE MARROW. Pancytopenia is lack of all cell types (ERYTHROCYTES, LEUKOCYTES, and PLATELETS), but any combination may be missing. Drug, chemical, or radiation exposure most often causes the disease, but about half of cases have no known cause. It may occur at any age. Acute disease may be quickly severe, even fatal; chronic disease has symptoms including weakness, shortness of breath, headache, fever, and pounding heart. There is usually a waxy pallor. Hemorrhages occur in mucous membranes, skin, and other organs. Lack of white blood cells lowers resistance to infection and becomes the major cause of death. Very low platelet count may lead to severe bleeding. The treatment of choice is bone-marrow transplantation. Otherwise, treatment involves avoiding any known toxic agent, and giving fluids, glucose, and proteins (often intravenously) as well as blood components and antibiotics.

aplite *or* **haplite** Any IGNEOUS ROCK of simple composition, such as granite composed only of alkali feldspar, muscovite mica, and quartz; in a more restricted sense, uniformly fine-grained (less than 0.08 in., or 2 mm), light-colored igneous rocks that have a characteristic granular texture. Unlike PEGMATITE, which is similar but much coarser-grained, aplite occurs in small bodies that rarely contain zones of different minerals. The two rocks may occur together and are assumed to have formed at the same time from similar MAGMAS.

Apo \'ä-pō\, **Mount** Active volcano, MINDANAO, Philippines. Located west of Davao City, it is the highest point in the Philippines, at 9,690 ft (2,954 m). In 1939 its slopes and immediate vicinity were incorporated into Mount Apo National Park, which includes numerous peaks and valleys as well as Malasita Falls and Sibulao Lake.

apocalypse \ə-'pä-kə-ˌlips\ In many Western religious traditions, the period of catastrophic upheaval expected to occur just before the end of the world, when God will come to sit in judgment on mankind. The belief that the world will come to a violent and cataclysmic end exists in Judaism and Christianity as well as in Zoroastrianism. Several of the prophetic works of the Old Testament, notably the Book of DANIEL, include visions of the apocalypse. The Book of REVELATION (or Apocalypse) gives a dark and dramatic picture of the end of time, when the wicked will be punished and the good will triumph through God's intervention. The approach of the Last Days is expected to be marked by famines, wars, earthquakes, plagues, and other natural disasters, along with signs in the heavens. Today apocalyptic themes are emphasized by various religious groups (e.g., fundamentalist Christians) and have also been taken up by science-fiction writers. See also ESCHATOLOGY, MILLENNIALISM.

Apocrypha \ə-'pä-krə-fə\ In biblical literature, works outside an accepted canon of SCRIPTURE. In modern usage the Apocrypha refers to ancient Jewish books that are not part of the Hebrew BIBLE but are considered canonical in ROMAN CATHOLICISM and EASTERN ORTHODOXY. Among the various books included are Tobit, Judith, Baruch, and the Maccabees as well as Ecclesiasticus and the Wisdom of Solomon. Protestant churches follow Jewish tradition in judging these works apocryphal or noncanonical. The term deuterocanonical is used to refer to works accepted in one canon but not all. Pseudepigrapha are spurious works for which biblical authorship is claimed.

Apollinaire, drawing by Pablo Picasso from the frontispiece to *Calligrammes,* 1918.
H. ROGER-VIOLLET

Apollinaire \á-pò-lē-'ner\, **Guillaume** *orig.* **Guillelmus (or Wilhelm) Apollinaris de Kostrowitzky** (1880–1918) Italian?-French poet. He arrived in Paris at 20, but always kept his early life obscure. In his short life he took part in all the avant-garde movements that flourished at the beginning of the 20th century. His poetry was characterized by daring, even outrageous, technical experiments. Because of his efforts to create an effect of surprise by means of unusual verbal associations and word patterns, he is often considered the herald of Surrealism. His poetic masterpiece was *Alcools* (1913). His death resulted from a head wound received in World War I.

Apollo Most widely revered of the Greek gods. He communicated the will of his father Zeus, made humans aware of their guilt and purified them of it, presided over religious and civil law, and foretold the future. His bow symbolized distance, death, terror, and awe; his lyre symbolized music, poetry, and dance. As a patron of the arts, he was often associated with the Muses. He was also a god of crops and herds. He became associated with the sun, and was even identified with Helios, the sun god. Also associated with healing, he was the father of Asclepius. By tradition, Apollo and his twin, Artemis, were born at Delos to Leto. Apollo's oracle was established at Delphi; the Pythian Games commemorated his killing (while still an infant) of the serpent Python to take the shrine. His many lovers fared poorly: the fleeing Daphne became a laurel tree; the unfaithful Coronis was shot by Artemis, and Cassandra, who rejected him, was doomed to utter true prophecies no one would believe.

Apollo Belvedere, restored Roman copy of the Greek original attributed to Leochares, 4th century BC; in the Vatican Museum, Rome.
ALINARI—ART RESOURCE/EB INC.

Apollo NASA moon-landing project of the 1960s and '70s. The Apollo spacecraft, supplied with their own low-powered rockets, could brake on approach to the Moon and go into lunar orbit. They also could release part of the spacecraft, the lunar module, with its own rocket power, to land Astronauts on the moon and bring them back to the lunar orbiter. In July 1969 Apollo 11 made the first lunar landing (see Edwin Aldrin, Neil Armstrong). In 1970 Apollo 13 was damaged by an explosion in an oxygen tank but returned safely to earth. Later Apollo missions explored the lunar surface extensively, collecting samples of moon rocks and installing instruments for research. Apollo 17, the program's final flight, took place in 1972.

Apollo asteroid See Earth-crossing asteroid

Apollo Theatre Center of African-American popular culture on 125th Street in New York's Harlem district. Built in 1914, it hosted musical performers such as Bill Robinson, Billie Holiday, Bessie Smith, Ethel Waters, Duke Ellington, and others in the 1930s and '40s; such stars as Ella Fitzgerald, Sarah Vaughan, and James Brown were discovered on Wednesday amateur nights. In the 1960s the Apollo featured soul artists such as the Supremes, S. Wonder, and Marvin Gaye. Converted into a movie theater in 1975, it was reopened as a performance venue in 1983.

Apollonius Dyscolos \ˌap-ə-ˈlō-nē-əs-ˈdis-kə-ləs\ (fl. 2nd century AD) Greek grammarian considered the founder of the systematic study of Grammar. Priscian based his work on the writings of Apollonius. Four of Apollonius' works survive: *On Syntax* and the shorter treatises *On Pronouns, On Conjunctions*, and *On Adverbs.*

Apollonius of Perga (c. 240–c. 190 BC) Anatolian mathematician known as "The Great Geometer." His *Conics,* one of the greatest scientific treatises of the ancient world, built on the work of Euclid. In it he introduced the terms parabola, ellipse, and hyperbola. He also improved on Archimedes' approximation of π. Much of his work is lost, known only through references in works of his followers.

Apollonius of Rhodes (born c. 295 BC) Greek poet and grammarian. He served as librarian of the famous Library of Alexandria. His *Argonautica*, a romantic epic in four books about the Argonauts, is derived from Homer and is noted for its fresh handling of old episodes, suggestive similes, and vivid descriptions of nature.

apologetics Branch of Christian Theology devoted to the intellectual defense of faith. In Protestantism, apologetics is distinguished from polemics, the defense of a particular sect. In Roman Catholicism, apologetics refers to the defense of the whole of Catholic teaching. Apologetics has traditionally argued positively to quell believers' doubts and negatively against opposing beliefs to remove obstacles to conversion. It attempts to take objections to Christianity seriously without giving ground to skepticism. Biblical apologetics defended Christianity as the culmination of Judaism, with Jesus as the Messiah. John Calvin's "natural theology" attempted to establish religious truths by rational argument. The late-18th-century argument that a universe exhibiting design must have a designer continues to be used to the present; apologists have also dealt with the challenges of Darwinism, Marxism, and psychoanalysis. See also Apologist.

Apologist Any of the Christian writers, primarily in the 2nd century, who attempted to provide a defense of Christianity against Greco-Roman culture. Many of their writings were addressed to Roman emperors and were submitted to government secretaries in order to defend Christian beliefs and practices. The Apologists tried to prove the antiquity of Christianity as the fulfillment of Old Testament prophecy, and they argued that the worshipers of the mythological gods were truly godless. They also insisted on the philosophical nature of their faith and its high ethical standards. Greek Apologists include Justin Martyr and Clement of Alexandria. Latin Apologists of the 2nd century include Tertullian. See also apologetics.

apology In literature, an autobiographical form in which a defense is the framework for the author's discussion of his or her personal beliefs. Examples include Plato's *Apology* (4th century BC), in which Socrates answers his accusers by giving a history of his life and moral commitment, and John Henry Newman's *Apologia pro Vita Sua* (1864), an examination of the principles that inspired his conversion to Catholicism.

apomixis \ˌa-pə-ˈmik-səs\ Reproduction by special tissues without fertilization. Examples include parthenogenesis in animals (in which a new individual develops from an unfertilized egg) and apogamy in plants (in which the generating tissue may be either the gametophyte or the sporophyte). Apomixis provides for the preservation of traits favorable to individual survival, but it eliminates the longer-term evolutionary advantage of genetic contribution from two parents.

apoptosis \ˌa-pəp-ˈtō-səs\ *or* **programmed cell death** Mechanism that allows cells to self-destruct when stimulated by the appropriate trigger. It may be initiated when a cell is no longer needed, when a cell becomes a threat to the organism's health, or for other reasons. The aberrant inhibition or initiation of apoptosis contributes to many disease processes, including cancer. Though embryologists had long been familiar with the process of programmed cell death, not until 1972 was the mechanism's broader significance recognized. Apoptosis is distinguished from necrosis, a form of cell death that results from injury.

Apostle Any of the 12 disciples chosen by Jesus. They were Peter, James and John (sons of Zebedee), Andrew, Philip, Bartholomew, Matthew, Thomas, James (son of Alphaeus), Thaddaeus or Judas (son of James), Simon the Cananaean or Zealot, and Judas Iscariot. The 12 were privileged to attend Jesus continually and receive his teaching. Peter, James, and John formed an inner circle and were allowed to witness such events as the Transfiguration and the agony of Jesus at Gethsemane. After the defection and death of Judas Iscariot, Matthias was elected an Apostle. Paul also claimed the title on the ground that he had seen the Lord and been commissioned by him.

Apostolic succession \ˌa-pə-ˈstä-lik\ In Christianity, the doctrine that bishops represent an uninterrupted line of descent from the Apostles of Jesus. This succession gives bishops special powers, including the right to confirm church members, ordain priests, consecrate bishops, and rule over the clergy and church members of a diocese. Clement, bishop of Rome, stated the doctrine as early as AD 95, and it is accepted by Roman Catholic, Eastern Orthodox, Old Catholic, and several other churches. Some Protestant churches maintain that succession is spiritual and doctrinal rather than ritual and historical.

apotheosis \ə-ˌpä-thē-ˈō-səs\ Elevation to the status of a god. The term recognizes that some individuals cross the dividing line between human and divine. Ancient Greek religion was disposed to belief in heroes and demigods, and historical figures were sometimes worshiped as gods.

Until the end of the republic the Romans accepted only one apotheosis, identifying the god QUIRINUS with ROMULUS. The emperor AUGUSTUS ordered Julius CAESAR recognized as a god and thus began a tradition of deifying emperors.

apotropaic eye \ˌa-pə-trō-ˈpā-ik\ Painting of a large eye or eyes used to ward off evil. The symbol appears most commonly on Greek drinking vessels from the 6th century BC and was perhaps thought to keep dangerous spirits from entering the mouth with the wine. It is also used in Turkish and Egyptian art.

Appalachian Geosyncline Great downbuckle in the earth's crust in the region of the present APPALACHIAN MTNS. It was in the Appalachians that JAMES HALL first worked out the geosynclinal theory of mountain building (see GEOSYNCLINE).

Appalachian Mountains Mountain system, eastern North America. The Appalachians, among the oldest mountains on earth, extend almost 2,000 mi (3,200 km) from Newfoundland, Quebec, and New Brunswick southwest to Alabama, and include the WHITE MTNS. in New Hampshire, the GREEN MTNS. in Vermont, the CATSKILL MTNS. in New York, the ALLEGHENY MTNS. in Pennsylvania, the BLUE RIDGE MTNS. in Virginia and North Carolina, the GREAT SMOKY MTNS. in North Carolina and Tennessee, and the CUMBERLAND PLATEAU in Tennessee. Their highest peak is Mount MITCHELL. See also APPALACHIAN GEOSYNCLINE, APPALACHIAN NATIONAL SCENIC TRAIL.

Appalachian National Scenic Trail Footpath, APPALACHIAN MTNS. Extending over 2,000 mi (3,200 km) from Mount Katahdin, Me., to Springer Mtn., Ga., along the crest of the mountains, the trail passes through 14 states, eight national forests, and two national parks. Hikers and volunteers maintain the shelters and campsites. The trail's highest point is Clingmans Dome (6,643 ft, or 2,025 m) in the GREAT SMOKY MTNS. Originally established by hikers in the 1930s, it became part of the National Trail System established by the U.S. Congress in 1968.

Appalachian orogenic belt \ˌȯr-ə-ˈje-nik\ Mountain range that extends more than 1,860 mi (3,000 km) along the eastern margin of North America, from Alabama to Newfoundland. It was formed by the progressive eastward addition of material to the continental margin of North America. The earliest Appalachian sediments were deposited near the start of the Cambrian period.

Appalachian Revolution See ALLEGHENIAN OROGENY

Appaloosa Color breed of horse popular in the U.S., said to have descended in the Nez Percé Indian territory of North America from wild mustangs, which in turn descended from the horses of Spanish explorers. The Appaloosa has several distinctive color patterns and all the regular coat colors of horses. They stand 14–16 hands (about 57–64 in., or 144–163 cm) tall and weigh 1,000–1,100 lbs (450–500 kg). Though light, they are also sturdy.

Appaloosa.
SALLY ANNE THOMPSON

appanage \ˈa-pə-nij\ In France, primarily from the 13th to the 16th century, the giving of lands or pensions to children of the royal family. Established to provide for the younger brothers and sisters of the king, appanages also helped develop royal administration within the lands concerned. The Ordinance of Moulins (1566) made royal lands inalienable, so all appanages would eventually revert to the crown. They were abolished during the French Revolution but were briefly reestablished between 1810 and 1832.

appeal Resort to a higher court to review the decision of a lower court, or to any court to review the order of an administrative agency. Its scope is usually limited. In the U.S., the higher court will review only matters in the record of the original trial; no new evidence can be presented. The U.S. Supreme Court hears some appellate cases, but unless cases have an important effect on the public interest, appeal stops with the U.S. COURTS OF APPEALS. See also CERTIORARI.

appeasement Foreign policy of pacifying an aggrieved nation through negotiation in order to prevent war. The prime example is Britain's policy toward Fascist Italy and Nazi Germany in the 1930s. NEVILLE CHAMBERLAIN sought to accommodate Italy's invasion of Ethiopia in 1935 and took no action when Germany absorbed Austria in 1938. When ADOLF HITLER prepared to annex ethnically German portions of Czechoslovakia, Chamberlain negotiated the notorious MUNICH AGREEMENT.

Appel \ˈä-pel\, **Karel** (born 1921) Dutch painter, sculptor, and graphic artist. He attended Amsterdam's Royal Academy of Fine Arts (1940–43) and was cofounder of the COBRA group of northern European Expressionists. In 1950 he moved to Paris; by the 1960s he had settled in New York. An exponent of expressive abstraction, he developed a painting style characterized by thick layering of pigment, violent color and brushwork, and crude, reductive figures. His figurative sculptures are executed in metal and wood. He painted portraits of jazz musicians and a number of public works, including a mural in the Paris UNESCO building.

appendix *in full* **vermiform appendix** Vestigial hollow tube attached to the cecum of the LARGE INTESTINE. The human appendix, usually 3–4 in. (8–10 cm) long and less than 0.5 in. (1.3 cm) wide, has no digestive function. Its muscular walls expel their own mucous secretions or any intestinal contents that enter it. Blockage of the opening may prevent expulsion and cause appendicitis: fluids collect, bacteria propagate, and the appendix becomes distended and inflamed; tissue in the appendix begins to die, and the organ may burst, causing PERITONITIS. Its symptoms may begin with moderate pain in the upper abdomen, about the navel, or all over the abdomen. Nausea and vomiting may then develop. The pain may shift to the right lower abdomen, where the appendix is (unless it is in an abnormal location). Fever is usually present but is seldom high in the early phases. The LEUKOCYTE count is high (12,000–20,000). Differentiating acute appendicitis from other causes of abdominal pain requires careful examination. Treatment is removal of the appendix (appendectomy).

Appian Way \ˈa-pē-ən\ *Latin* **Via Appia.** First and most famous of the ancient Roman roads, running from Rome to Campania and southern Italy. Begun in 312 BC by the censor Appius Claudius Caecus, the road originally ran 132 mi (212 km) to ancient Capua; by 244 BC it extended 230 mi (370 km) to the port of Brundisium (Brindisi) in Italy's heel. Built of smoothly fitted blocks of lava on a heavy stone foundation, the road provided a long-lasting surface for transporting merchandise to these seaports (and thence by ship to Greece and the eastern Mediterranean). Remains can be seen today outside Rome.

apple Fruit of the genus *Malus,* in the ROSE family, the most widely cultivated tree fruit. *Malus* species are native to the temperate zones of both hemispheres. They require a considerable period of dormancy, well-drained soil, careful pruning in early years of growth, and a rigorous pest-management program for mature trees. The apple is one of the pome (fleshy) fruits. Apples at harvest vary widely in size, shape, color, and acidity, but most are roundish and some shade of red or yellow. The thousands of varieties fall into three broad classes: cider, cooking, and dessert varieties. Varieties that ripen in late summer generally do not store well, but those that ripen in late autumn may be stored for as long as a year. The largest producers of apples are the U.S., China, France, Italy, and Turkey. Eaten fresh or cooked in various ways, apples provide vitamins A and C, carbohydrates, and fiber.

Apple Computer Inc. Microcomputer design and manufacturing company, the first successful PERSONAL-COMPUTER company. It was founded in 1976 by STEVEN JOBS and STEPHEN WOZNIAK, whose first computer was manufactured in the Jobs's family garage. The Apple II (1977), with its plastic case and color graphics, launched the company to success, earning Apple over $100 million by 1980, the year the company first offered stock to the public. The 1981 introduction of IBM's PC, running a MICROSOFT CORP. operating system, marked the beginning of long-term competition for Apple in the personal-computer market. The Macintosh, introduced in 1984, was the first personal computer to use a GRAPHICAL USER INTERFACE and a MOUSE. The "Mac" initially sold poorly, and Jobs left the company in 1985, but eventually it found its niche in the desktop publishing market. Stiff competition from Microsoft's WINDOWS interface/operating system led to a steadily declining market share for Apple. After being led by a series of ineffective managers, Apple recalled Jobs in 1997. He formed an alliance with Microsoft, streamlined the product lines, and in 1998 helped introduce the iMac, which quickly became the best selling of all the Macs.

apple scab Disease of APPLE trees caused by the FUNGUS *Venturia inaequalis,* producing dark blotches or lesions on the leaves, fruit, and sometimes young twigs. Affected plants may drop their fruit prematurely, resulting in potentially high crop losses. Apple scab is found wherever apples are grown but is most severe where spring and summer are cool and moist. All species in the genus *Malus* are affected. Regular spraying with FUNGICIDES is the most effective method of controlling the disease.

Appleseed, Johnny *orig.* **John Chapman** (1774–1845) U.S. pioneer and folk hero. Born in Leominster, Mass., he was trained as a nurseryman and began c. 1800 collecting apple seeds from cider presses in Pennsylvania, then traveled west to the Ohio River valley, planting apple seeds along the way. He tended 1,200 acres of his own orchards and was responsible for hundreds of square miles of others, having sold or given away thousands of apple seedlings to pioneers. His kind and generous nature, devout spirituality, affinity for the Indians and the wilderness, and eccentric appearance (including bare feet, a coffee-sack shirt, and a mush pan for a hat) helped make Johnny Appleseed a legendary hero.

applied psychology Branch of psychology concerned with solving practical problems of human behavior by using the findings and methods of psychological science. Intelligence testing, legal problems, industrial efficiency, motivation, and delinquency were among the first areas of application in the early 20th century. World Wars I and II fostered work on vocational testing, teaching methods, evaluation of attitudes and morale, performance under stress, propaganda and psychological warfare, and rehabilitation. The aviation and aerospace industries were important for the development of engineering psychology, the study of human-machine relationships. Other areas include CONSUMER PSYCHOLOGY, SCHOOL PSYCHOLOGY, and community psychology. See also INDUSTRIAL PSYCHOLOGY, PSYCHOMETRICS.

appliqué See QUILTING

Appomattox Court House \ˌa-pə-ˈma-təks\ Former town, southern central Virginia, site of the surrender of ROBERT E. LEE to ULYSSES S. GRANT on April 9, 1865, effectively ending the AMERICAN CIVIL WAR. It was virtually deserted after the removal of the county seat to the new town of Appomattox in 1892. It became a national historical monument in 1940 and a national historical park in 1954.

apprenticeship Training in an art, trade, or craft under a legal agreement defining the relationship between master and learner and the duration and conditions of their relationship. Known from antiquity, apprenticeship became prominent in medieval Europe with the emergence of the craft GUILDS. The standard apprenticeship lasted seven years. During the Industrial Revolution a new kind of apprenticeship developed in which the employer was the factory owner and the apprentice, after a period of training, became a factory worker. The increasing need for semiskilled workers led to the development of vocational and technical schools in Europe and the U.S., especially after World War II. Today in the U.S. some industries, such as the building industry, continue to employ apprenticeship schemes, the trainee advancing by passing qualifying exams and receiving 60–90% of regular pay.

approximation, linear See LINEAR APPROXIMATION

APRA \ˈä-prä\ *in full* **Alianza Popular Revolucionaria Americana (Spanish: "American Popular Revolutionary Alliance")** Party founded by VICTOR RAUL HAYA DE LA TORRE (1924), which dominated Peruvian politics for decades. Largely synonymous with the so-called Aprista movement, it was dedicated to Latin American unity, the nationalization of foreign-owned enterprises, and an end to the exploitation of Indians. Supported by workers and middle-class liberals, the party wielded significant power, but conservative forces took extraordinary measures to prevent Haya de la Torre from ever gaining the presidency. An APRA candidate, Alan García, finally became president in 1985. See also INDIGENISMO.

apraxia \ā-ˈprak-sē-ə\ Disturbance in carrying out skilled acts, caused by a lesion in the CEREBRAL CORTEX; motor power and mental capacity remain intact. Motor apraxia is the inability to perform fine motor acts. Ideational apraxia is loss of the ability to plan even a simple action. In ideokinetic apraxia, there is no coordination between formation of ideas and motor activity; affected persons can do certain things automatically but not deliberately. Constructional apraxia is the inability to put together elements to form a meaningful whole.

apricot Fruit of the tree *Prunus armeniaca,* in the ROSE family, cultivated generally throughout the temperate regions of the world and used fresh, cooked in pastries, or preserved by canning or drying. Apricot trees are large and spreading, with heart-shaped, dark green leaves. Flowers are white. The fruit is nearly smooth and generally similar to the PEACH in shape, but with little to no hairiness when ripe. Apricots are a good source of vitamin A and are high in natural sugars. Dried apricots are an excellent source of iron.

April Fools' Day *or* **All Fools' Day** First day of April, named for the custom of playing practical jokes on that date. Though it has been observed for centuries in several countries, including France and Britain, its origin is unknown. It resembles the Hilaria festival of ancient Rome (March 25) and the HOLI festival of India (ending March 31). The custom of playing April Fools' jokes was brought to America by the British.

April Theses Program developed by VLADIMIR ILICH LENIN during the RUSSIAN REVOLUTION OF 1917, calling for Soviet control of state power. In the theses, published in April 1917, Lenin advocated seizing power from the Provisional Government, withdrawing from World War I, and distributing land among the peasantry. The theses contributed to the JULY DAYS uprising and the Bolshevik coup d'état in October.

apse Semicircular or polygonal termination to the choir, chancel (see CATHEDRAL), or aisle of a public building, first used in pre-Christian Roman architecture. Originally a large niche to hold the statue of a deity in a temple, the apse also appeared in ancient baths and BASILICAS. The domed apse became a standard part of the Christian church plan.

Apse, basilica of S. Vitale, Ravenna, 526–547.

ALINARI—ART RESOURCE

Apuleius \ˌa-pə-ˈlā-əs\, **Lucius** (AD 124?–after 170?) Roman Platonic philosopher, rhetorician, and author. His *The Golden Ass,* a prose narrative of the ribald adventures of a young man who is changed into an ass, was long influential. This novel, considered a revelation of ancient manners, is valuable for its description of the ancient religious mysteries. Apuleius' philosophical treatises include three books on PLATO, two of which survive.

Apulia See PUGLIA

Apure River \ä-ˈpü-rā\ River, western Venezuela. The major navigable tributary of the ORINOCO RIVER, the Apure rises in the Cordillera de Mérida and flows about 510 mi (820 km) northeast and east through the heart of Venezuela's Llanos (plains), its principal cattle-raising area.

Apurímac River \ˌä-pür-ˈē-ˌmäk\ River, southern Peru. Arising in the Peruvian ANDES, it flows northwest to join the URUBAMBA and form the UCAYALI RIVER. For most of its 430-mi (700-km) length it flows through narrow canyons and its course is interrupted by falls and rapids. Short stretches of its lower course are called the Perené and the Tambo.

Aqaba \ˈä-kə-bə\, **Gulf of** NE arm of the RED SEA penetrating between Saudi Arabia and the SINAI Peninsula. It is 100 mi (160 km) long and varies in width from 12 to 17 mi (19–27 km). Its head touches Egypt, Israel, Jordan, and Saudi Arabia. Its only sheltered harbor is Dhahab (Dahab), Egypt; Jordan and Israel created the ports of Aqaba and Elat, respectively, as outlets to the Red Sea and the INDIAN OCEAN.

Aqhat Epic \ˈä-kät\ Ancient West Semitic legend explaining the earth's barrenness during the dry summer months, known only in fragmentary form from three tablets excavated in northern Syria and dating to about the 14th century BC. It records the birth of a prince, Aqhat, in response to prayers. As a youth, Aqhat comes into possession of a bow intended for the goddess ANATH and is killed by her when he refuses to part with it. His death brings famine, and his father and sister set out to avenge him, but there the text ends.

Aqmola See ASTANA

aquaculture *or* **fish farming** *or* **mariculture** \'mar-ə-ˌkəl-chər\ Rearing of fish, shellfish, and some aquatic plants to supplement the natural supply. Fish are reared in controlled conditions worldwide. Though most aquaculture supplies the commercial food market, many governmental agencies engage in it to stock lakes and rivers for sport fishing. It also supplies goldfish and other decorative fish for home aquariums and bait fish for sport and commercial fishing. CARP, TROUT, CATFISH, TILAPIA, SCALLOPS, MUSSELS, LOBSTERS, and OYSTERS are well-known species raised through aquaculture.

aquamarine Pale greenish blue or bluish green variety of BERYL that is valued as a gemstone. The most common variety of gem beryl, it occurs in PEGMATITES, in which it forms much larger and clearer crystals than EMERALD, the dark green variety of beryl. Aquamarine occurs in Brazil, which is the chief source, and in such other sites as the Ural Mtns., Madagascar, Sri Lanka, India, and Maine, New Hampshire, Connecticut, North Carolina, and Colorado in the U.S. Heat treatment is commonly used to improve the color of gem beryls.

aquarium Receptacle for maintaining aquatic organisms, either freshwater or marine, or a facility in which a collection of aquatic organisms is displayed or studied. The first display aquarium opened in Regent's Park, England, in 1853. Many of the world's principal cities now have public aquariums as well as commercial ones; other aquarium facilities serve chiefly as research institutions. Regardless of size—whether a small one-gallon jar or a huge million-gallon tank—aquariums must be constructed with care; many substances, especially plastics and adhesives, that are nontoxic to humans are toxic to water-breathing animals. The primary requirement for maintaining aquatic organisms is water quality.

Aquarius (Latin: "Water carrier") In astronomy, the constellation lying between Capricorn and Pisces; in ASTROLOGY, the 11th sign of the ZODIAC, governing approximately the period January 20–February 18. It is usually represented as a man pouring a stream of water out of a jug, probably because in ancient times the rising of Aquarius coincided in the Middle East with the annual arrival of floods or rainfall. In the astrological concept called the Great Year—the 25,000-year period it takes the earth to pass through the influence of the entire zodiac—the early 19th century was the beginning of the Age of Aquarius.

aquatint Method of ETCHING that produces finely granulated tonal areas rather than lines, so that finished prints often resemble WATERCOLOR or wash drawings. A copper plate is exposed to acid through a layer of granulated resin or sugar, which yields a finely speckled gray tone when the plate is inked and printed. The texture and depth of tone are controlled by the strength of the acid baths and the length of time the plate is exposed to them. Aquatint became the most popular method of producing toned prints in the late 18th century; its most notable practitioner was FRANCISCO GOYA. In the 19th century, EDGAR DEGAS and CAMILLE PISSARRO experimented with it, and in the 20th century the sugar aquatint was employed by PABLO PICASSO, GEORGES ROUAULT, and ANDRE MASSON.

aquavit \'ä-kwə-ˌvēt\ (from Latin, *aqua vitae:* "water of life") Clear Scandinavian DISTILLED LIQUOR flavored with caraway seeds. Distilled from a fermented potato or grain mash, filtered with charcoal, and usually bottled without aging, aquavit has an alcohol content of 42–45% by volume. Most aquavits are sweet and spicy. It is usually served chilled and unmixed, in small glasses.

aqueduct Conduit built to carry water from its source to a main distribution point. Ancient Rome's aqueduct system, an extraordinary feat of engineering, brought water to the city from as far as 57 mi (92 km) away. Only a portion of the Roman aqueducts utilized the familiar stone arch; most were underground conduits made of stone or terra-cotta pipe. Modern aqueduct systems employ cast iron or steel. See also WATER-SUPPLY SYSTEM.

aquifer \'ä-kwə-fər\ In hydrology, a rock layer or sequence that contains water and releases it in appreciable amounts. The rocks contain water-filled pores that, when connected, allow water to flow through their matrix. A confined aquifer is overlain by a rock layer that does not transmit water in any appreciable amount or that is impermeable. There probably are few truly confined aquifers. In an unconfined aquifer the upper surface (water table) is open to the atmosphere through permeable overlying material. An aquifer also may be called a water-bearing stratum, lens, or zone.

Aquinas, St. Thomas See St. THOMAS AQUINAS

Aquitaine Historical region, southwestern France. It was roughly equivalent to Aquitania, the Roman division of southwestern Gaul, which consisted of the area between the PYRENEES Mountains and the GARONNE RIVER. Conquered by CLOVIS in AD 507, it was later made a subkingdom by CHARLEMAGNE in the 8th century. After the Carolingian decline, it became a powerful feudal duchy, which by the 10th century controlled much of France south of the LOIRE. It passed to the Capetian line when ELEANOR OF AQUITAINE married LOUIS VII (1137); on her second marriage, to HENRY II of England (1152), it passed to the English Plantagenets. The name GUIENNE, a corruption of Aquitaine, came into use in the 10th century, and the subsequent history of Aquitaine is merged with that of GASCONY and Guienne.

AR-15 See M16 RIFLE

Ara Pacis (Augustae) \'ä-rä-'pä-sis\ ("Augustan Altar of Peace") State monument built by Caesar AUGUSTUS in Rome's Campus Martius (13–9 BC) to commemorate his victorious return from Spain and Gaul. It consists of an altar on a podium enclosed by walls. Its lavish sculptural decoration is among the finest examples of Roman art; reliefs representing the ceremonial procession at the altar's dedication are the first in Western art that can strictly be called documentary, showing identifiable individuals in a contemporary event.

Arab Any member of the ARABIC-speaking peoples of the Middle East and North Africa. Before the spread of Islam in the 630s, the term referred to the largely nomadic Semitic peoples of the ARABIAN PENINSULA; it came to apply to Arabic-speaking peoples from Africa's Mauritanian and Moroccan coasts east to Iraq and the Arabian Peninsula and south to northern Sudan after their acceptance and promotion of Islam. Traditionally, some Arabs are desert-dwelling pastoral nomads (see BEDOUIN), whereas others live by oases and in small, isolated farming villages. While most Arabs are Muslims, some are Christian. The term may also be used in an ethnic ("the Arab nation") or sociolinguistic sense.

Arab-Israeli Wars Series of wars fought between various Arab countries and Israel 1948–49, 1956, 1967, 1969–70, 1973, and 1982. The first war (1948–49) began when Israel declared itself an independent state following the United Nations' partition of PALESTINE. Protesting this move, five Arab countries—Egypt, Iraq, Jordan, Lebanon, and Syria—attacked Israel. The conflict ended with Israel gaining considerable territory. The 1956 SUEZ CRISIS began after Egypt nationalized the SUEZ CANAL. A French, British, and Israeli coalition attacked Egypt and occupied the canal zone but soon withdrew under international pressure. In the SIX-DAY WAR of 1967, Israel attacked Egypt, Jordan, and Syria. The war ended with the Israel occupying substantial amounts of Arab territory. An undeclared war of attrition (1969–70) was fought between Egypt and Israel along the Suez Canal and ended with the help of international diplomacy. Egypt and Syria attacked Israel in 1973 (the Yom Kippur War), but, despite early Arab success, the conflict ended inconclusively. In 1979 Egypt made peace with Israel. In 1982 Israel invaded Lebanon in order to expel Palestinian guerrillas based there. Israel withdrew from most of Lebanon by 1985 but maintained a narrow buffer zone inside that country until 2000. See also YASIR ARAFAT, HAFIZ AL-ASSAD, MENACHEM BEGIN, DAVID BEN-GURION, CAMP DAVID ACCORDS, MOSHE DAYAN, HIZBULLAH, GAMAL ABDEL NASSER, YITZHAK RABIN, SABRA AND SHATILA MASSACRES, ANWAR AL-SADAT.

Arab League *or* **League of Arab States** Regional organization formed in 1945 and based in Cairo. It initially comprised Egypt, Syria, Lebanon, Iraq, Transjordan (now Jordan), Saudi Arabia, and Yemen; today Libya, Sudan, Tunisia, Morocco, Kuwait, Algeria, Bahrain, Oman, Qatar, the United Arab Emirates, Mauritania, Somalia, the PALESTINE LIBERATION ORGANIZATION, and Djibouti are also members. The league's original aims were to strengthen and coordinate political, cultural, economic, and social programs and to mediate disputes, to which it later added military defense coordination. Members have often split on political issues; Egypt was suspended for ten years (1979–89) following its peace with Israel, and the PERSIAN GULF WAR also caused deep rifts. See also PAN-ARABISM.

arabesque Style of decoration characterized by interlacing plant forms and abstract curvilinear motifs. It is typical of Islamic ornamentation from c. 1000. The word was first used in the 15th or 16th century when Europeans became interested in the Islamic arts, but the motif itself was derived from Hellenistic craftsmen in Asia Minor. Arabesques were also applied to the decoration of illuminated manuscripts, walls, furniture, metalwork, pottery, stonework, majolica, and tapestry from the Renaissance to the 19th century.

Arabesque decoration on the dome of the Madar-i-Shah *madrasah* ("school") built by Husayn I, early 18th century, at Esfahan, Iran.

RAY MANLEY—SHOSTAL ASSOC./EB INC.

Arabian Desert Desert region, Arabian Peninsula. It covers about 900,000 sq mi (2,330,000 sq km), occupying nearly the entire peninsula. It lies largely within Saudi Arabia but extends into Jordan, Iraq, Kuwait, Qatar, the United Arab Emirates, Oman, and Yemen. While sand covers at least one-third of the desert, two water systems, the Tigris-Euphrates in the northeast and the Wadi Hajr in Yemen, flow perennially. Humans have inhabited the area since Pleistocene times.

Arabian horse Earliest improved breed of horse, valued for its speed, stamina, beauty, intelligence, and gentleness. Its long history has been obscured by legend, but it was developed in Arabia by the 7th century AD. It has contributed its qualities to most modern breeds of light horses. It is compact and relatively small, with a small head, protruding eyes, wide nostrils, marked withers, and a short back. Its average height is about 15 hands (60 in., or 152 cm), its average weight 800–1,000 lbs (360–450 kg). Though many colors are possible, gray is most common.

Arabian Nights' Entertainment See The Thousand and One Nights

Arabian Peninsula *or* **Arabia** Peninsular region, South Asia. With its offshore islands, it covers about 1 million sq mi (2.6 million sq km). It is divided among Bahrain, Kuwait, Oman, Qatar, United Arab Emirates, Yemen, and principally Saudi Arabia. Its population (1990) is about 32,138,000. The modern economy is dominated by oil production. In ancient geography the peninsula was divided into Arabia Petraea ("Stony") in the northwest, Arabia Deserta ("Deserted") in the north and center, and Arabia Felix ("Flourishing") in the south and southwest. Its political consolidation was begun by Muhammad and extended after his death. It was the center of the orthodox caliphate until 661, when the Umayyad caliphate, ruling from Damascus, took over. After 1517 much of the region was dominated by the Ottoman Turks, though revolts occurred repeatedly into the 20th century. See also Arabian Desert.

Arabian religions, ancient Polytheistic religions of Arabia prior to the rise of Islam. Most of the deities of the Arab tribes were sky gods, associated with heavenly bodies such as the sun and moon, and they had the power to ensure fecundity, protection, or revenge. At the head of the southern Arabian pantheon was Athtar, a god of thunderstorms and rain. Each kingdom also had a national deity, of whom the nation called itself the progeny. Sanctuaries were carved in rock on high places and held a baetyl ("raised stone") or statue of the god in an open-air enclosure, accessible only to ritually clean persons. In northern Arabia they included a walled enclosure with a covered or enclosed altar, similar to the Muslim Kaaba. Libations, animal sacrifices, and other offerings were made to the gods, and priests interpreted oracles and performed divination. Worshipers made yearly pilgrimages to important shrines, participating in rites that included purification, the wearing of ritual clothing, sexual abstinence, abstention from shedding blood, and circuits performed around the sacred object.

Arabian Sea NW part of the Indian Ocean, lying between India and the Arabian Peninsula. It has an area of about 1,491,000 square miles (3,862,000 square km) and an average depth of 8,970 feet (2,734 meters). The Gulf of Oman connects it with the Persian Gulf via the Strait of Hormuz, while the Gulf of Aden connects it with the Red Sea via the Strait of Bab el-Mandeb. The Indus is the principal river draining into the Arabian Sea. Socotra, Lakshadweep, and other islands lie within it. Chief ports are Mumbai (Bombay), Karachi, and Aden. The sea was part of the principal trade route between Europe and India for centuries.

Arabic alphabet Script used to write Arabic and a number of other languages whose speakers have adopted Islam. The 28-character Arabic alphabet developed from a script used to write Nabataean Aramaic. Because Arabic had more consonants than Aramaic, diacritical dots came to be used to eliminate ambiguous readings of some letters, and these remain a feature of the script. Arabic is written from right to left. The letters denote only consonants, though the symbols for *w, y,* and (historically) the glottal stop do double duty as vowel letters for long *u, i,* and *a*. Additional diacritics, representing short vowels and geminate consonants, are normally employed only for the text of the Quran. Because Arabic script is fundamentally cursive, most letters have slightly different forms depending on whether they occur in the beginning, middle, or end of a word. Non-Semitic languages for which the Arabic alphabet has been or is used include Persian, Kurdish, Pushto, Urdu, Turkic languages, Malay, Swahili, and Hausa.

Arabic language Semitic language spoken across a broad region of South Asia and in North Africa from Egypt and the Sudan west to Morocco and Mauritania. Though Arabic words and proper names are found in Aramaic inscriptions from ancient Palmyra and the Nabataean kingdom centered around Petra, abundant documentation of the language only begins with the rise of Islam. Grammarians from the 8th century on codified it into the form known as Classical Arabic. In the 19th–20th century, expansion of Classical Arabic's stylistic range and vocabulary led to the creation of Modern Standard Arabic, which serves as a lingua franca among contemporary Arabs. Spoken Arabic has long diverged from the classical language, and the more than 200 million speakers of today use an enormous range of dialects, which at their furthest extremes are mutually unintelligible. See also Arabic alphabet.

Arabic literary renaissance 19th-century movement to develop a modern Arabic literature, inspired by contacts with the West and a renewed interest in classical Arabic literature. It began in Egypt with Syrian and Lebanese writers who sought the freer environment there. It spread to other Arab countries as a result of the dismemberment of the Ottoman Empire after World War I and the coming of independence after World War II. Its success in altering the direction of Arabic literature is related to the spread and modernization of education and the emergence of an Arabic press.

Arabic philosophy *or* **Islamic philosophy** Doctrines of the Arabic philosophers of the 9th–12th century who influenced medieval Scholasticism in Europe. The Arabic tradition combines Aristotelianism and Neoplatonism with other ideas introduced through Islam. Influential thinkers include the Persians al-Kindi, al-Farabi, and Avicenna, as well as the Spaniard Averroës, whose interpretations of Aristotle were taken up by both Jewish and Christian thinkers. Muslims, Christians, and Jews participated in the Arabic tradition and separated themselves according to philosophic rather than religious doctrines. When the Arabs dominated Spain, the Arabic philosophic literature was translated into Hebrew and Latin; this contributed to the development of modern European philosophy. In Egypt around the same time, the Arabic tradition was developed by Moses Maimonides and Ibn Khaldun.

Arachne \ə-ˈrak-nē\ In Greek mythology, the daughter of the dyer Idmon of Colophon. She was a weaver who acquired such skill that she ventured to challenge Athena to a contest. Athena wove a tapestry showing the gods in majesty, while Arachne depicted them in their amorous adventures. Enraged at the perfection of her rival's work, Athena tore it to shreds, whereupon Arachne hanged herself. Out of pity Athena loosened the rope, which became a cobweb, and Arachne was changed into a spider.

arachnid \ə-ˈrak-nid\ Any member of the class Arachnida, primarily carnivorous arthropods having a well-developed head, hard external skeleton, and four pairs of walking legs. Most species have a segmented body (but see daddy longlegs); they range in size from the mite (0.003 in., or 0.08 mm, long) to the 8-in. (21-cm) black scorpion of Africa. As arachnids grow, they molt several times (see molting). Most are unable to digest food internally, instead injecting their prey with digestive fluids then sucking the liquefied remains. Arachnids are found worldwide in nearly every habitat. Most groups are free-living, but some mites and ticks are parasitic; these can carry serious animal and human diseases.

Venomous SPIDERS and scorpions also may pose a danger to humans, but most arachnids are harmless and prey on insect PESTS.

Arachosia \ˌar-ə-ˈkō-zhə\ Ancient province, eastern Persian empire, occupying the southern part of modern Afghanistan. It came under ALEXANDER THE GREAT's Macedonian rule c. 330 BC, after the death of the Persian ruler Darius III.

Arafat \ˌar-ə-ˈfat\, **Yasir** *orig.* **Muhammad Abd al-Rauf al-Qudwah al-Husayni** (born 1929) Palestinian leader. Born in Jerusalem, he graduated from the University of Cairo as a civil engineer and served in the Egyptian army during the 1956 war with Israel. That year, working as an engineer in Kuwait, he cofounded the guerrilla organization FATAH, which became the leading military component of the PALESTINE LIBERATION ORGANIZATION (PLO), which he led from 1969. In 1974 the PLO was formally recognized by the U.N., and Arafat became the first leader of a nongovernmental organization to address the U.N. In 1988 he acknowledged Israel's right to exist, and in 1993 he formally recognized Israel during direct talks regarding land controlled by Israel since the SIX-DAY WAR. In 1994 he shared the Nobel Peace Prize with YITZHAK RABIN and SHIMON PERES. In 1996 he became president of the new Palestinian Authority.

Aragon \ˈar-ə-ˌgän\ Autonomous community (pop., 1996 est.: 1,188,000), northeastern Spain. It occupies an area of 18,398 sq mi (47,651 sq km); its capital is at the city of SARAGOSSA. It is roughly coextensive with the historical kingdom of Aragon. Mountains, including the PYRENEES, dominate the relief north and south of the EBRO RIVER, which bisects Aragon. Established in 1035 by Ramiro I, the historical kingdom grew as land was retaken from the Moors: Saragossa, the capital of the ALMORAVID kingdom, fell to Alfonso I of Aragon in 1118, and the reconquest of present-day Aragon was completed by the late 12th century. In the 13th–14th century, it came to rule Sicily, Sardinia, Naples, and Navarre. In the 15th century FERDINAND married ISABELLA of Castile, uniting the kingdoms of Aragon and Castile and forming the nucleus of modern Spain. The old kingdom of Aragon survived as an administrative unit until 1833, when it was divided into provinces. Agriculture, mining, and industry, the latter concentrated at Saragossa, are economically important.

Aragon \á-rá-ˈgōⁿ\, **Louis** *orig.* **Louis Andrieux** (1897–1982) French poet, novelist, and essayist. He was introduced by ANDRE BRETON into avant-garde circles, and the two cofounded the Surrealist review *Littérature* in 1919. From 1927 he was increasingly a political activist and spokesman for communism, which resulted in a break with the Surrealists. Among his works are the novel tetralogy *Le monde réel* (4 vols., 1933–44), describing the class struggle of the proletariat; the huge novel *Les communistes* (6 vols., 1949–51); novels of veiled autobiography; and volumes of poems expressing patriotism and love for his wife. He was editor of the communist weekly of arts and literature *Les lettres françaises* 1953–72.

aragonite \ə-ˈrag-ə-ˌnīt\ A CARBONATE MINERAL, the stable form of calcium carbonate ($CaCO_3$) at high pressures. It is somewhat harder and has a slightly higher specific gravity than CALCITE. Aragonite is found in recent deposits formed at low temperatures near the surface of the earth, as in caves as stalactites, with ore minerals, in serpentine and other basic (see ACID AND BASIC ROCKS) rocks, and in sediments. Aragonite is the mineral normally found in pearls, and it occurs in some animal shells. It is polymorphous (same chemical formula but different crystal structure) with calcite and vaterite, and, with geologic time, changes to calcite even under normal conditions.

Araguaia River \ˌar-ə-ˈgwī-ə\ River, central Brazil. Rising in the Brazilian highlands, it flows north some 1,600 mi (2,620 km) to join the TOCANTINS RIVER at São João do Araguaia. In midcourse it divides into channels on either side of Bananal Island, which is about 200 mi (320 km) long and the site of the National Park of Araguaia. Though the river drains a vast area of interior Brazil, it offers poor transportation because of its many falls.

arahant See ARHAT

Arai Hakuseki \á-rī-há-kü-ˈsä-kē\ (1657–1725) Japanese scholar of CONFUCIANISM and government official of the mid-EDO PERIOD. Arai was tutor and later adviser to Tokugawa Ienobu, the sixth Tokugawa SHOGUN. He wrote on such subjects as Japanese geography, philosophy, and legal institutions and is considered one of Japan's greatest historians. Among his best-known works are *Tokushi yoron* ("Lessons from History") and *Koshi tsu* ("The Understanding of Ancient History"). See also GENROKU PERIOD, TOKUGAWA SHOGUNATE.

Arakcheyev \á-rək-ˈchā-yif\, **Aleksey (Andreyevich), Count** (1769–1834) Russian soldier and statesman. Appointed inspector general of artillery in 1803, he reorganized that branch of the army, then served as minister of war 1808–10. In the Russo-Swedish War of 1808–9, he personally compelled the reluctant Russian forces to cross the frozen Gulf of Finland to attack the Åland Islands, which ultimately resulted in Sweden's cession of Finland to Russia. He was ALEXANDER I's chief military adviser in the NAPOLEONIC WARS. After the wars, he supervised the management of Russia's domestic matters with brutal and ruthless efficiency, which caused the period 1815–25 to be known as *Arakcheyevshchina*, but also took part in the emancipation of serfs in the Baltic provinces and created a system of military-agricultural colonies.

Araks River \ä-ˈräks\ *or* **Aras River** \ä-ˈräs\ River in Turkey, Armenia, and Azerbaijan. It rises in the mountains of Turkish Armenia south of Erzurum and flows east to join the KURA RIVER about 60 mi (95 km) from its mouth. Since a flood in 1897, a separate distributary of the Araks has also emptied into the Caspian Sea. About 570 mi (915 km) long, it forms the boundary between Armenia and Azerbaijan (north) and Turkey and Iran (south). Located on its banks from 180 BC to AD 50 was Armenia's capital, Artaxata.

Aral Sea Large saltwater lake between KAZAKHSTAN and UZBEKISTAN. It once covered 25,659 sq mi (66,457 sq km) and was the fourth largest inland body of water in the world, but diversion of the waters of the SYR DARYA and AMU DARYA rivers for irrigation has shrunk its surface area by half since 1960. Its volume has been reduced by 75%; it has a salinity of 10.7%. Except for the southern shores, it is uninhabited.

Aram \ˈar-əm\ Ancient country, South Asia. It extended from the Lebanon Mountains to beyond the EUPHRATES RIVER. It was named after the ARAMAEANS, who emerged from the Syrian desert to invade Syria and Upper MESOPOTAMIA (c. 14th century BC) and who built numerous city-kingdoms, including DAMASCUS. It lends its name to the ARAMAIC LANGUAGE.

Aramaeans \ˌar-ə-ˈmē-ən\ People belonging to a confederacy of tribes that migrated from the Arabian Peninsula to the FERTILE CRESCENT c. 1500–1200 BC. Among them were the biblical matriarchs Leah and RACHEL, wives of Jacob. The ARAMAIC LANGUAGE and culture spread through international trade. They reached a cultural peak during the 9th–8th century BC. By 500 BC, Aramaic had become the universal language of commerce, culture, and government throughout the Fertile Crescent and remained so through the time of JESUS and into the 7th century in some areas.

Aramaic language \ˌar-ə-ˈmā-ik\ NW SEMITIC LANGUAGE, originally spoken by the ancient ARAMAEANS. The earliest Aramaic texts are inscriptions in an alphabet of Phoenician origin found in the northern Levant dating from c. 850–600 BC. The period 600–200 BC saw a dramatic expansion of Aramaic, leading to the development of a standard form known as Imperial Aramaic. In later centuries, as "Standard Literary Aramaic," it became a linguistic model. Late (or Classical) Aramaic (c. AD 200–1200) has an abundant literature, both in Syriac and in Mandaic (see MANDAEANISM). With the rise of Islam, Arabic rapidly supplanted Aramaic as a vernacular in South Asia. Modern Aramaic (Neo-Aramaic) comprises West Neo-Aramaic, spoken in three villages northeast of Damascus, and East Neo-Aramaic, a group of languages spoken in scattered settlements of Jews and Christians in southeastern Turkey, northern Iraq and northwestern Iran, and by modern Mandaeans in the SHATT AL ARAB. Since c. 1900 persecution has forced most contemporary East Neo-Aramaic speakers, who number several hundred thousand, into diaspora communities dispersed around the world.

Aramco \ə-ˈram-kō\ *in full* **Arabian American Oil Co.** Oil company founded by the Standard Oil Co. of California (Chevron) in 1933, when the Saudi Arabian government granted it a concession. Other U.S. companies joined after oil was found near Dhahran in 1938. In 1950 Aramco opened a pipeline from Saudi Arabia to the Mediterranean port of Sidon, Lebanon. It was closed in 1983 except to supply a refinery in Jordan. A more successful pipeline, with a destination on the Persian Gulf, was finished in 1981. In 1951 Aramco found the first offshore oil field in the Middle East. In the 1970s and 1980s, control gradually passed to the Saudi Arabian government, which eventually took Aramco over and renamed it Saudi Aramco.

Aran Islands \'ar-ən\ Islands (pop., 1991: 600), Galway Bay, western Ireland. The group of small islands, totaling about 18 sq mi (47 sq km), includes Inishmore (or Aranmore), Inishmaan, and Inisheer. Their main town is Kiloran on Inishmore. The islands contain impressive prehistoric and early Christian forts. LIAM O'FLAHERTY was born on Inishmore.

Arany \'ȯr-'ȯnʸ\, **János** (1817–1882) Hungarian epic poet. His main work is the trilogy of *Toldi* (1847), *Toldi szerelme* (1848–79; "Toldi's Love"), and *Toldi estéje* (1854; "Toldi's Evening"). Recounting the adventures of a 14th-century youth of great physical strength, it was received with enthusiasm by a public craving a national literature of quality in a language all could grasp. Other notable works include a fragment of an epic poem, *Bolond Istók* (1850; "Stephen the Fool"), and *The Death of King Buda* (1864), the first part of a projected Hun trilogy. The *Oszikék*, written just before his death, poignantly reflects his sense of unfulfillment and isolation. He is considered Hungary's greatest epic poet.

arap Moi, Daniel See Daniel arap MOI

Arapaho \ə-'ra-pə-,hō\ PLAINS INDIAN people of ALGONQUIAN LANGUAGE stock who lived along the Platte and Arkansas rivers in the 19th century. Like other Plains groups, the Arapaho were nomadic, living in TEPEES and depending on the buffalo for subsistence. They were highly religious and practiced the SUN DANCE. Their social organization included age-graded military societies as well as men's shamanistic societies. They traded with the MANDAN and Arikara and were often at war with the SHOSHONE, UTE, and PAWNEE. A southern branch was long allied with the CHEYENNE and fought with them against Col. GEORGE CUSTER at LITTLE BIGHORN in 1876. Today about 2,000 Arapaho live in Wyoming and another 3,000 Arapaho-Cheyenne in Oklahoma.

Ararat \'ar-ə-,rat\, **Mount** Mountain, eastern Turkey. Located in Agri province, near the Iranian border, Ararat has two peaks, Great Ararat, at almost 17,000 ft (5,300 m) the highest in Turkey, and Little Ararat, almost 13,000 ft (4,000 m). Ararat is traditionally associated with the mountain where Noah's ark came to rest at the end of the biblical flood. A village on its slopes at the site where Noah is said to have built an altar was destroyed in an earthquake in 1840.

Aras River See ARAKS RIVER

Aratus of Sicyon \ə-'rā-təs...'sis-ē-,än\ (271–213 BC) Hellenistic Greek statesman, diplomat, and soldier. He democratized SICYON (251), and, as leader of the ACHAEAN LEAGUE (in alternate years from 245), set up democracies in league cities and helped free Athens from Macedonia (229). Under him, the league opposed Sparta; with Macedonian help, it defeated Aetolia (217). Aratus nevertheless defied the anti-Roman policy of PHILIP V of Macedonia; his death, popularly linked to Philip, was more likely caused by tuberculosis.

Araucanians \ə-,rau̇-'kä-nē-ənz\ South American Indians who are now concentrated in the valleys and basins between the Bío-Bío and Toltén rivers in southern central Chile. When the Spanish CONQUISTADORES arrived in Chile, they encountered three Araucanian populations: the Picunche, who were accustomed to INCA control; the Huilliche, who were too few and scattered to resist the conquistadores; and the MAPUCHE, successful farmers and artisans. The first two were soon assimilated, but the Mapuche managed to resist Spanish and Chilean control for 350 years. Finally subdued in the late 19th century, they were settled on reservations, but now live independently.

araucaria \,ar-ȯ-'kar-ē-ə\ Any pinelike coniferous plant (see CONIFER) of the genus *Araucaria* (family Araucariaceae), found in South America, the Phoenix Islands, and Australia. The trees are magnificent EVERGREENS, with whorled branches and stiff, flattened, pointed leaves. Common araucaria species are the MONKEY PUZZLE TREE and the NORFOLK ISLAND PINE, often grown as a houseplant. Several species are cultivated on the Pacific coast of the U.S. and in southern Florida. See also PINE.

Arawak \'ar-ə-,wäk\ American Indians of the Greater Antilles and South America who spoke languages of the Arawakan linguistic group. The TAINO were one Arawak group. The Arawak were apparently the people who CHRISTOPHER COLUMBUS first encountered in 1492. The South American Arawak inhabited northern and western areas of the Amazon basin, where they farmed, hunted, and fished. Their society was relatively nonhierarchical. The Campa Arawak lived in the foothills of the Andes but remained isolated from influences of the ANDEAN CIVILIZATIONS.

Arawakan languages \,ar-ə-'wä-kən\ *or* **Maipuran languages** \mī-'pü-rən\ Largest family of American Indian languages, comprising an estimated 65 known languages, of which at least 30 are now extinct. They stretch from the Caribbean coast of Central America to the GRAN CHACO and southern Brazil, and from western Peru to the Guianas and central Brazil. Taino, a now extinct Arawakan language of the Antilles, was the first American Indian language encountered by Europeans. Arawakan languages that are still viable include Guajiro in Columbia and Venezuela; Amuesha, Machiguenga, and the Campa languages in Peru; and Terena in Brazil.

Arbenz (Guzmán) \'är-bāns\, **Jacobo** (1913–1971) Soldier and president of Guatemala (1951–54). The son of a Swiss emigré, Arbenz joined the leftist army officers who overthrew the dictator Jorge Ubico (1878–1946) in 1944. Elected president in 1951, he made LAND REFORM his central project. His efforts to expropriate idle land owned by the UNITED FRUIT CO. and his alleged Communist links led to an invasion sponsored by the U.S. CENTRAL INTELLIGENCE AGENCY. When the army refused to defend Arbenz against what appeared to be a superior force, he resigned and went into exile, and the CIA installed the leader of the proxy army, Col. Carlos Castillo Armas (1914–1957), as president.

Arber, Werner (born 1929) Swiss microbiologist. He has taught chiefly at the University of Basel. He shared a 1978 Nobel Prize with DANIEL NATHANS and HAMILTON O. SMITH for the discovery and use of restriction enzymes that break the giant molecules of DNA into pieces small enough to be separated for individual study but large enough to retain meaningful amounts of the genetic information of the original substance. He also observed that bacteriophages cause mutation in their bacterial hosts and undergo hereditary mutations themselves.

Arbiter, Gaius Petronius See Gaius PETRONIUS ARBITER

arbitrage \'är-bə-,träzh\ Business operation involving the purchase of foreign CURRENCY, gold, financial SECURITIES, or commodities in one market and their almost simultaneous sale in another market, in order to profit from price differentials existing between the markets. In the 1980s a form of speculation called risk arbitrage arose, in which speculators tried to identify companies targeted for takeover and buy blocks of their STOCK, to be resold at a profit when the takeover was announced and the company's stock rose in value. See also INSIDER TRADING.

arbitration Process of resolving a dispute or a grievance outside the court system by presenting it to an impartial third party or panel for a decision. Both sides usually must agree in advance as to the choice of arbitrator and must certify that they will abide by the arbitrator's decision. In medieval Europe it was used to settle disputes between merchants; today it is commonly used in commercial, labor-management, and international disputes. The procedures differ from those used in the courts, especially regarding burden of proof and presentation of evidence. Arbitration avoids costly litigation and offers a relatively speedy resolution as well as privacy for the disputants. The disadvantage is that setting guidelines is difficult; therefore the outcome is often less predictable than a court decision. See also MEDIATION.

arbor Garden shelter providing privacy and partial protection from the weather, most commonly a lightweight, latticed framework (trellis) of wood or metal with interlaced branches of vines or climbing shrubs trained over it. If there is a distinction between an arbor and a bower, it is that the bower is an entirely natural recess whereas an arbor is only partially natural.

arboretum \,är-bə-'rē-təm\ Place where trees, shrubs, and sometimes herbaceous plants are cultivated for scientific and educational purposes. An arboretum may be a collection in its own right or a part of a BOTANICAL GARDEN. Important U.S. arboretums include the Arnold Arboretum of Harvard University (Jamaica Plain, Mass.) and the U.S. National Arboretum in Washington, D.C.

arboriculture \'är-bər-ə-,kəl-chər\ Cultivation of trees, shrubs, and woody plants for shading and decorating. Arboriculture includes all aspects of growing, maintaining, and identifying plants, arranging plantings for their ornamental values, and removing trees. The well-being of individual plants is the major concern of arboriculture, in contrast to such related fields as FORESTRY and AGRICULTURE, in which the major concern is the welfare of a large group of plants as a whole.

arborvitae \ˌär-bər-ˈvī-tē\ (Latin: "tree of life") Any of six species (genus *Thuja*) of resinous, EVERGREEN ornamental and timber CONIFERS of the CYPRESS family, native to North America and eastern Asia. Arborvitae trees or shrubs have thin, scaling outer bark and fibrous inner bark; horizontal or ascending branches; and flattened, spraylike branchlets with scalelike leaves. The oriental, or Chinese, arborvitae *(T. orientalis),* a popular ornamental native to Asia, is a gracefully symmetrical shrub. Arborvitae wood is soft and lightweight but very durable, fragrant, and easily worked. The giant arborvitae *(T. plicata)* is the most important timber-producing species, but the wood of the American arborvitae *(T. occidentalis)* is also frequently used. False arborvitae *(Thujopsis dolabrata)* is closely related.

arbovirus \ˌär-bə-ˈvī-rəs\ Any of a large group of viruses that develop in arthropods (chiefly mosquitoes and ticks), in which they cause no apparent harm. (The name derives from "*ar*thropod-*bo*rne *virus*.") The spheroidal virus particle is encased in a fatty membrane and contains RNA. Arboviruses are transmitted by bites to vertebrate hosts, in which they establish infections and complete their growth cycle; they include the agents responsible for YELLOW FEVER and equine ENCEPHALITIS. See also TOGAVIRUS.

Arbus, Diane *orig.* **Diane Nemerov** (1923–1971) U.S. photographer. Born in New York City, the sister of HOWARD NEMEROV, she worked with her husband, Allan Arbus, as a fashion photographer in the 1950s, and published her first photo essay, for *Esquire*, in 1960. She is best known for photographs of the unusual and the extraordinary, including nudists, sideshow freaks, inmates of mental hospitals, and transvestites, in which she employed the square format and flash lighting to achieve theatrical effects. Her suicide followed years of increasing depression.

Arbuthnot \är-ˈbəth-nət\, **John** (1667–1735) Scottish mathematician, physician, and satirist. His satirical writings include a political allegory, *The History of John Bull* (1712), that established John Bull as a personification of England. He was a founding member of the famous Scriblerus Club, which aimed to ridicule bad literature and false learning. He was also chief contributor to and guiding spirit of the *Memoirs of Martinus Scriblerus* (written 1713–14), a mocking exposure of pedantry written by club members.

Arbuthnot, detail of an oil painting by W. Robinson; in the Scottish National Portrait Gallery, Edinburgh.

BY COURTESY OF THE SCOTTISH NATIONAL PORTRAIT GALLERY, EDINBURGH

arbutus \är-ˈbyü-təs\ Any of about 14 species (genus *Arbutus*) of broad-leaved EVERGREEN shrubs or trees, in the HEATH FAMILY. Native to southern Europe and western North America, they are characterized by loosely clustered white or pink flowers and red or orange berries. *A. menziesii* (variously known as the madrona, Pacific madrona, laurelwood, and Oregon laurel) and *A. unedo* (the strawberry tree) are cultivated as ornamentals. The TRAILING ARBUTUS belongs to the genus *Epigaea*.

Arc de Triomphe \ˈärk-də-trī-ˈō^{n}f\ Largest TRIUMPHAL ARCH in the world. A masterpiece of Romantic classicism, it is one of the best-known monuments of Paris. It stands at the center of the Place Charles de Gaulle, at the western terminus of the CHAMPS-ÉLYSÉES. Initiated by NAPOLEON, designed by JEAN-FRANCOIS CHALGRIN, and constructed 1806–36, this monument to Napoleon's military victories is 164 ft (50 m) high and 148 ft (45 m) wide. Decorative relief sculptures cover its surfaces.

arc furnace Type of ELECTRIC FURNACE in which heat is generated by an arc between carbon ELECTRODES above the surface of the material (commonly a metal) being heated. WILLIAM SIEMENS first demonstrated the arc furnace in 1879 at the Paris Exposition by melting iron in crucibles; horizontally placed carbon electrodes produced an electric arc above the container of metal. The first commercial arc furnace in the U.S. (1906) had a capacity of four tons (3.6 metric tons) and was equipped with two electrodes. Modern furnaces range in heat size from a few tons up to 400 tons (360 metric tons), and the arcs strike directly into the metal bath from vertically positioned, graphite electrodes to remelt scrap steel or refine briquettes of direct-reduced iron ore.

arcade Series of arches, supported by columns or piers, joined together end to end in a row. When supporting a roof, an arcade may function as a passageway adjacent to a solid wall, a covered walkway that provides access to adjacent shops, or a transitional element surrounding an open internal court. See also COLONNADE.

Arcadia Ancient country, central PELOPONNESE, Greece. Mountainous and landlocked, it was not overrun by the DORIANS during their occupation of Greece (1100–1000 BC). Its isolation and its pastoral character partly explain why it was represented as a paradise in Greek and Roman bucolic poetry. It was the scene of conflict during the War of GREEK INDEPENDENCE (1821–29). The modern Greek department of Arkadhía is nearly coextensive with the ancient country.

Arcadian League Confederation of ancient Greek city-states of Arcadia. Arcadian towns had been forced to ally with SPARTA by 550 BC, and most Arcadians remained faithful to Sparta during the PELOPONNESIAN WAR (431–404 BC). In an effort to contain Sparta, EPAMINONDAS of Thebes founded the city-state of MEGALOPOLIS in 371–368 BC as the seat of the Arcadian League. The League united the Arcadians for a few decades until internal discord crippled their confederation.

Arcand \är-ˈkä^n\, **Denys** (born 1941) Canadian film director. Born in Deschambault, Quebec, he joined the NATIONAL FILM BOARD OF CANADA in 1963 and directed several short films. His first full-length documentary, *On est au coton* (1970, released 1976), was a controversial exposé of the textile industry. He moved on to feature films with his witty *Decline of the American Empire* (1986) and his burlesque of modern life *Jesus of Montreal* (1989). Later films include *Love and Human Remains* (1993) and *Poverty and Other Delights* (1996).

Arcaro, Eddie *orig.* **George Edward** (1916–1997) U.S. jockey. Born in Cincinnati, he became the first jockey to ride five KENTUCKY DERBY winners (1938, 1941, 1945, 1948, 1952) and the first to ride two TRIPLE CROWN champions (Whirlaway, 1941; CITATION, 1948). In 31 years of riding Thoroughbreds (1931–61), he won 549 stakes events, a total of 4,779 races, and more than $30 million in purses.

arch Curved structure that spans the opening between two piers or columns and supports loads from above. The masonry arch provides the stepping stone from the POST-AND-BEAM SYSTEM to the evolution of the VAULT, and was first widely used by the Romans. Its construction depends on a series of wedge-shaped blocks (voussoirs) set side by side in a semicircular curve or along two intersecting arcs (as in a pointed arch). The central voussoir is called the keystone, and the two points where the arch rests on its supports are known as the spring points. An arch can carry a much greater load than a horizontal beam of the same size and material, because downward pressure forces the voussoirs together instead of apart. The resulting outward thrust must be resisted by the arch's supports. Present-day lightweight monolithic (one-piece) arches of steel, concrete, or laminated wood are highly rigid, and thereby minimize horizontal thrust. See illustration on following page.

archaebacteria \ˌar-kē-ˌbak-ˈtir-ē-ə\ Group of BACTERIA whose members differ from the EUBACTERIA in certain physical, physiological, and genetic features (e.g., cell-wall components). Archaebacteria are aquatic or terrestrial microorganisms that exhibit a diversity of shapes, including spherical, rod-shaped, and spiral forms. They survive in various extreme environments, including very hot or salty ones. Some require oxygen; some do not. Some produce methane as an end product; others depend on sulfur for their metabolism.

archaeology Scientific study of material remains (including fossil relics, artifacts, and monuments) of past human life and activities. Archaeological investigations are a principal source of our knowledge of prehistoric, ancient, and extinct cultures. The field emerged as an academic discipline in the late 19th century, following centuries of haphazard antiquarian collecting. Among the archaeologist's principal activities are the locating, surveying, and mapping of sites and the EXCAVATION, classification, DATING, and interpretation of materials to place them in historical context. Major subfields include classical archaeology, the study of ancient Mediterranean and Middle Eastern civilizations; prehistoric archaeology, or general archaeology; and historical archaeology,

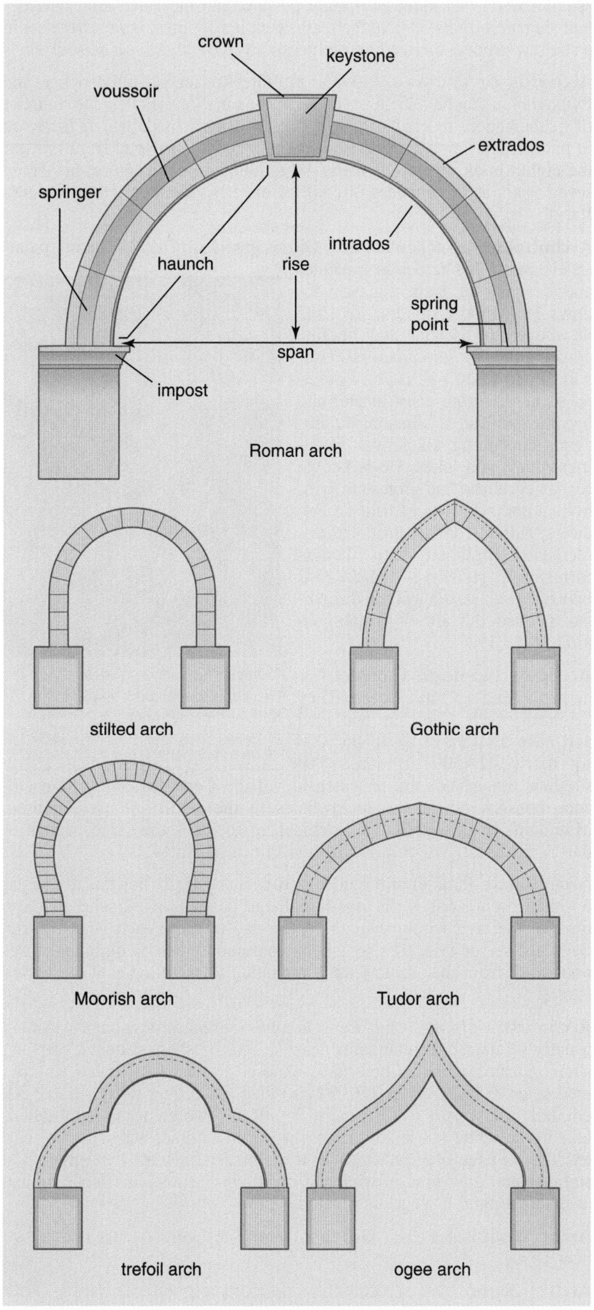

The arch supports a vertical load primarily by axial compression of its wedge-shaped voussoirs. As shown on the Roman arch, the first voussoir, or springer, rests on the impost, at the top of the abutment or pier. The haunch, rising from the impost to the crown (highest point), is defined by the inner curve, or intrados, and outer curve, or extrados. The Roman arch, with its semicircular intrados, has a rise exactly half the width of the span. Below it are shown examples of the curved arch (left) and the pointed arch (right). The stilted arch has vertical sides. A Moorish arch widens above the spring points. The trefoil arch's intrados has three indentations, or foils. A Gothic arch is a pointed arch usually having two haunches of equal radii of curvature. A Tudor arch has greater curvature near the springers than near the point. Each haunch of the ogee arch consists of a double curve.

the study of historic-period remains to augment the written record. See also ANTHROPOLOGY, NUMISMATICS, STONE-TOOL INDUSTRY.

archaeopteryx \ar-kē-'äp-tə-riks\ Oldest known fossil animal that is generally accepted as a bird (classified as genus *Archaeopteryx*). It flourished during the Late JURASSIC PERIOD (159–144 million years ago). Fossil specimens indicate that archaeopteryx ranged in size from as small as a blue jay to as large as a chicken. Archaeopteryx shared anatomical characteristics with both birds (well-developed wings and bird-like skull) and THEROPOD dinosaurs (well-developed teeth and a long tail).

Archangel See ARKHANGELSK

archbishop In Christianity, a BISHOP who has jurisdiction, but not superiority, over the other bishops in a province as well as episcopal authority in his own diocese. Introduced as an honorary title in the Eastern churches in the 4th century, the office did not become common in Western churches until the 9th century. It is now most widely used in the Roman Catholic and Eastern Orthodox churches. It is more rarely used in Protestant denominations, though the Church of England has archbishops of Canterbury and York, and the Lutheran churches of both Sweden and Finland have an archbishop.

Archean eon *or* **Archaean eon** \är-'kē-ən\ *or* **Archeozoic eon** Older of the two divisions of PRECAMBRIAN TIME. The Archean begins with the formation of the earth's CRUST c. 4 billion years ago and extends to c. 2.5 billion years ago, up to the start of the Proterozoic eon, the second division of the Precambrian period. The earliest and most primitive forms of life (BACTERIA and CYANOBACTERIA) originated c. 3.5 billion years ago in the middle of the Archean eon (the Archean's alternative name, Archeozoic, means "ancient life").

archer fish Any of five species (family Toxotidae) of Indo-Pacific fishes noted for their ability to knock their insect prey off overhanging vegetation by shooting it with drops of water expelled from their mouth. Archer fishes are elongated and have a relatively deep body that is almost flat from the dorsal fin forward. The head is pointed, the mouth is large, and the dorsal and anal fins are placed toward the back of the body. Different species are spotted or vertically banded with black. Archer fishes live in both fresh and salt water, usually remaining near the surface. One well-known species *(Toxotes jaculator,* or *jaculatrix)* grows to about 7 in. (18 cm) long.

archery Sport of shooting with BOW AND ARROW. As the bow began to be replaced by the gun as the principal weapon of warfare and the hunt beginning in the 16th century, it increasingly became a sporting device. By the mid-19th century, many archery clubs had sprung up in England and the U.S. Competitions including target-shooting were held at the Olympic Games in the early 20th century, but were then suspended until 1972. Other varieties of archery include field archery, or roving (a simulation of hunting), and flight shooting (a distance event).

Arches National Park Preserve, eastern Utah. Located on the COLORADO RIVER north of Moab, the preserve was established as a national monument in 1929 and as a national park in 1971. Its area is 115 sq mi (298 sq km). Its red limestone has been eroded into unusual shapes, including Courthouse Towers, Fiery Furnace, and Devils Garden, the site of Landscape Arch, at 291 ft (89 m) the longest natural rock bridge in the world.

archetype \'är-ki-ˌtīp\ Primordial image, character, or pattern of circumstances that recurs throughout literature and thought consistently enough to be considered universal. Literary critics adopted the term from CARL GUSTAV JUNG's theory of the collective UNCONSCIOUS. Because archetypes originate in pre-logical thought, they are held to evoke startlingly similar feelings in reader and author. Examples of archetypal symbols include the snake, whale, eagle, and vulture. An archetypal theme is the passage from innocence to experience; archetypal characters include the blood brother, rebel, wise grandparent, and prostitute with a heart of gold.

Archimedean screw \ˌär-kə-'mēd-ē-ən\ *or* **Archimedes' screw** Machine for raising water, said to have been invented by ARCHIMEDES for removing water from the hold of a large ship. One form consists of a circular pipe enclosing a helix and inclined at an angle of about 45°, with its lower end dipped in the water; rotation of the device lifts the water in the pipe. Other forms consist of a helix revolving in a fixed cylinder or a helical tube wound around a shaft.

Archimedes \ˌär-kə-ˈmē-ˌdēz\ (c. 290–212 BC) Legendary Greek inventor and mathematician. His principal discoveries were the Archimedes screw, an ingenious device for raising water, and the hydrostatic principle, or ARCHIMEDES' PRINCIPLE. His main interests were optics, mechanics, pure mathematics, and astronomy. Archimedes' mathematical proofs show both boldly original thought and a rigor meeting the highest standards of contemporary geometry. His approximation of π was not improved on until after the Middle Ages, and translations of his works were important influences on 9th-century Arab and 16th- and 17th-century European mathematicians. In his native city, Syracuse, he was known as a genius at devising siege and countersiege weapons. He was killed by a Roman soldier during the storming of the city.

Archimedes' principle Law of buoyancy, discovered by ARCHIMEDES, which states that any object that is completely or partially submerged in a fluid at rest is acted on by an upward, or buoyant, force. The magnitude of this force is equal to the weight of the fluid displaced by the object. The volume of fluid displaced is equal to the volume of the portion of the object submerged.

Archipenko \ˌär-kə-ˈpeŋ-kō\, **Alexander** (1887–1964) Ukrainian-U.S. sculptor and painter. In 1908 he moved to Paris to study at the École des Beaux-Arts, and he soon became active in the Cubist movement. His abstract sculptures reduced the human figure to geometrical forms with holes and concavities, producing contrasting solids and voids, which revolutionized modern sculpture. In 1923 he moved to New York City, where he worked and taught for most of his life.

architecture Art and technique of designing and building, as distinguished from the skills associated with construction. The practice of architecture emphasizes spatial relationships, ORIENTATION, the support of activities to be carried out within a designed environment, and the arrangement and visual rhythm of structural elements, as opposed to the design of structural systems themselves (see CIVIL ENGINEERING). Appropriateness, uniqueness, a sensitive and innovative response to functional requirements, and a sense of place within its surrounding physical and social context distinguish a built environment as representative of a culture's architecture. See also BUILDING CONSTRUCTION.

archives Repository for an organized body of records produced or received by a public, semipublic, institutional, or business entity in the transaction of its affairs and preserved by it or its successors. The modern institution of archives and archival administration dates from the late 18th century, when national and departmental archives were established in France. In the U.S. the National Archives was established in 1934 to house the retired records of the national government; the Federal Records Act of 1950 authorized regional records repositories. Each state has its own archival agency. Archivists in the 20th century increasingly handled records involving new technologies, such as computer-kept records, and records of businesses, institutions, and individuals.

archon In ancient Greece, the chief magistrate or magistrates in a city-state, from the Archaic period onward. In ATHENS, nine archons divided state duties: the *archon eponymous* headed the BOULE and ECCLESIA, the *polemarch* commanded troops and presided over legal cases involving foreigners, the *archon basileus* headed state religion and the AREOPAGUS, and the six others handled various judicial matters. At first only elected aristocrats could serve, and their term was for life; later, terms were limited to a year. Archons were chosen by a combination of election and lot. In the 5th century BC, the archons' authority declined as elected generals took most of their powers.

Archon \ˈär-ˌkän\ In GNOSTICISM, any of various world-governing powers created with the material world by the DEMIURGE. Because the Gnostics regarded the material world as evil or as the product of error, Archons were considered forces of evil. Seven or 12 in number, they were identified with the seven planets of antiquity or the 12 signs of the ZODIAC. They were thought to have imprisoned the divine spark of human souls in material creation. The gnosis sent from the realms of divine light through Jesus enabled Gnostic initiates to pass through the spheres of the Archons into the realms of light.

archosaur \ˈär-kə-ˌsȯr\ Any of the various advanced REPTILES in the subclass Archosauria ("ruling reptiles"), including all thecodonts, PTEROSAURS, DINOSAURS, bird ancestors, and crocodilians, the only living order. Early archosaurs appeared just before the beginning of the TRIASSIC PERIOD (248–206 million years ago). All early archosaurs possessed an ankle specialization that aided in upright posture, and most had long hindlegs and short forelimbs. Unlike the teeth of earlier reptiles, which were set in a shallow groove, the teeth of archosaurs were (and are) set in sockets.

Archytas \är-ˈkī-təs\ (c. 430–350 BC) Greek scientist, philosopher, and Pythagorean mathematician. Archytas is sometimes called the founder of mathematical mechanics. PLATO, a close friend, made use of his work in mathematics, and there is evidence that EUCLID borrowed from him for the eighth book of his *Elements*. An influential public figure, he served seven years as commander in chief of his city, Tarentum (now Taranto, Italy).

Arcimboldo \ˌär-chēm-ˈbōl-dō\, **Giuseppe** (1527?–1593) Italian painter. He began his career as a painter and designer of stained-glass windows for Milan Cathedral. In 1562 he moved to Prague and became court painter to the emperors Ferdinand I and Rudolf II. He also painted scenery for the court theater and became skillful at illusionistic imagery containing allegorical meanings, puns, and jokes. He is known for his eccentric and grotesque symbolical compositions of fruits, vegetables, animals, landscapes, and implements arranged into human forms. The style was regarded as being in poor taste until the Surrealists revived the art of visual punning in the 1920s.

"Summer," painting on canvas by Giuseppe Arcimboldo, 1563; in the Kunsthistorisches Museum, Vienna.

BY COURTESY OF THE KUNSTHISTORISCHES MUSEUM, VIENNA; PHOTOGRAPH, ERWIN MEYER

Arctic Archipelago Group of Canadian islands, Arctic Ocean. They lie north of the Canadian mainland and have an area of about 550,000 sq mi (1,424,500 sq km). The southeastern islands are an extension of the Canadian Shield; the balance consists of the Arctic lowlands to the south and the Innuitian Mountains to the north. The archipelago includes the large islands of BAFFIN, ELLESMERE, VICTORIA, BANKS, and Prince of Wales.

Arctic Circle Parallel of latitude approximately 66.5° north of the equator that circumscribes the northern frigid zone. It marks the southern limit of the area within which, for one day or more each year, the sun does not set or rise. The length of continuous day or night increases northward from the Arctic Circle, mounting to six months at the NORTH POLE.

Arctic fox Northern FOX *(Alopex lagopus)* found throughout the Arctic, usually on tundra or mountains near the sea. Its short, rounded ears and short muzzle reduce its body area exposed to heat loss; it has fur-covered soles. It is 20–24 in. (50–60 cm) long (excluding the 12-in., or 30-cm, tail) and weighs 7–17 lbs (3–8 kg). It has two color phases. Individuals in the white phase are grayish brown in summer and white in winter; those in the blue phase (blue foxes of the fur trade) are grayish in summer and gray-blue in winter. It dwells in burrows and feeds on any available animal or vegetable material.

Arctic National Park, Gates of the See GATES OF THE ARCTIC NATIONAL PARK

Arctic Ocean Ocean centering approximately on the NORTH POLE. Smallest of the world's oceans, it is almost completely surrounded by the landmasses of Eurasia and North America, and is distinguished by a cover of ice. Lands in it and adjacent to it include Pt. Barrow in Alaska, the ARCTIC ARCHIPELAGO, two-thirds of GREENLAND, SVALBARD, FRANZ JOSEF LAND, and northern SIBERIA. The ocean covers about 5,427,000 sq mi (14,056,000 sq km) and reaches a maximum depth of about 18,000 ft (5,500 m). Various sections are known by specific names, including the BARENTS, BEAUFORT, Chukchi, Greenland, and Kara seas. Areas within the ARCTIC CIRCLE were first explored in the 9th–12th century by the Norse. In the 16th–17th century explorers searching for the NORTHWEST PASSAGE reached the area; MARTIN FROBISHER discovered the southern part of BAFFIN ISLAND (1576–78), and HENRY HUDSON navigated the eastern coast of HUDSON BAY (1610–11). Later explorers included ROALD AMUNDSEN, FRIDTJOF NANSEN, ROBERT E. PEARY, and RICHARD E. BYRD. Development of the area's

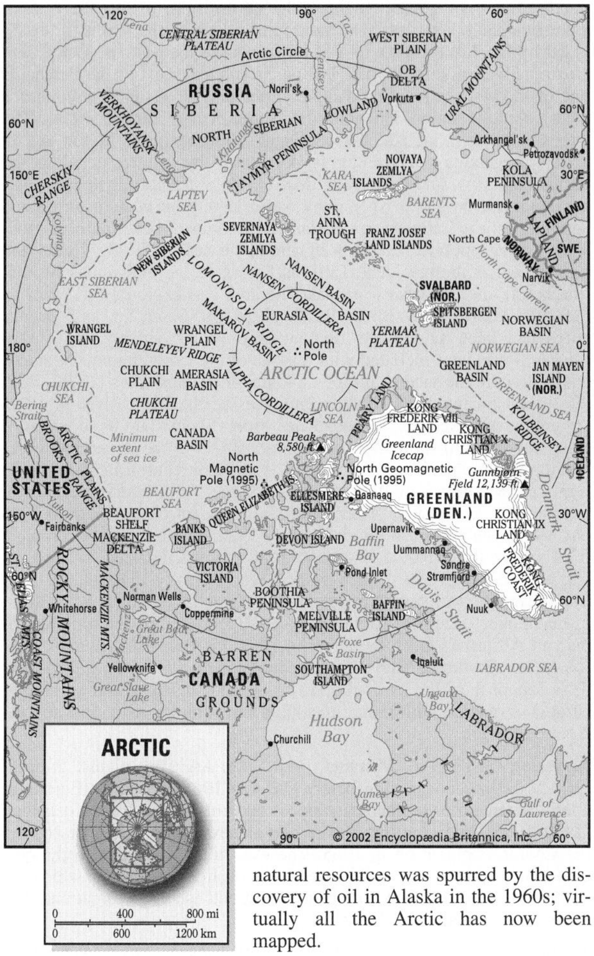

natural resources was spurred by the discovery of oil in Alaska in the 1960s; virtually all the Arctic has now been mapped.

Arctic tern TERN species *(Sterna paradisaea)* that makes the longest annual migration of any bird. It breeds in the southerly reaches of the Arctic and winters in the Antarctic, making its migration a round-trip of nearly 22,000 mi (over 35,000 km). Its appearance—white with a black cap and grayish wings—is similar to that of the common tern *(S. hirundo),* its frequent companion.

Ardea \'är-dē-ə\ Ancient town, Italy. Located south of Rome, Ardea was ruled by the Rutuli people and was an important center for the cult of JUNO. In 444 BC the town signed a treaty with the Romans, who colonized it as a barrier against the VOLSCI. It declined in the Roman civil wars of the 1st century BC.

Arden, Elizabeth *orig.* **Florence Nightingale Graham** (1878–1966) Canadian-U.S. businesswoman. Born in Ontario, she moved to New York c. 1908, where she opened a beauty salon under the name Elizabeth Arden. She was instrumental in making cosmetics acceptable for respectable women. In 1915 she began to market her cosmetics products internationally. At her death there were over 100 Elizabeth Arden salons throughout the world.

Arden, John (born 1930) British playwright. He studied architecture at Cambridge and the Edinburgh College of Art. His plays mix poetry and songs with colloquial speech in a boldly theatrical manner and involve strong conflicts purposely left unresolved. His works include *All Fall Down* (1955), *Serjeant Musgrave's Dance* (1959), *The Workhouse Donkey* (1963), *Vandaleur's Folly* (1978), and the radio series *Whose Is the Kingdom?* (1988).

Ardennes \är-'den\ *or* **Forest of Ardennes** Wooded plateau region, northwestern Europe. It covers over 3,860 sq mi (10,000 sq km) and includes parts of Belgium, Luxembourg, and the MEUSE RIVER valley of France; its average height is about 1,600 ft (488 m). Though half of it is covered with forests, the soil is generally unfertile and supports only heath. It is located in the middle of the heavily populated triangle of PARIS, BRUSSELS, and COLOGNE. During World Wars I and II, the area was the scene of severe fighting in 1914, 1918, and 1944 (see Battle of the BULGE).

Ardhanarisvara \ˌär-də-nä-'rēsh-və-rə\ Composite male-female figure of the Hindu god SHIVA and his consort PARVATI. In many Indian and S.East Asian sculptures, the right half is male and the left female. The figure symbolizes the inseparability of male and female principles.

Ards District (pop., 1995 est.: 67,000), Northern Ireland. Formerly part of Co. Downs, Ards was established as a district in 1973. Much of its land is devoted to crops and pasture. NEWTOWNARDS, settled c. 1608 by Scots, is its administrative seat and manufacturing center. Donaghadee is a popular resort town.

area See LENGTH, AREA, AND VOLUME

Arecibo Observatory \ˌar-ə-'sē-bō\ Astronomical OBSERVATORY near Arecibo, Puerto Rico, site of the world's largest single-unit RADIO TELESCOPE (as opposed to multiple telescope interferometers such as the VERY LARGE ARRAY). The telescope dish, 1,000 ft (300 m) across, is built into a valley; celestial sources are tracked across the sky by moving secondary structures suspended about 500 ft (150 m) above the dish. The observatory has produced detailed radar maps of the surface of Venus and near-earth asteroids, made detailed studies of the earth's ionosphere, and made major contributions to studies of pulsars and hydrogen gas in galaxies.

arena stage See THEATER-IN-THE-ROUND

Arendt \ä-'rent\, **Hannah** (1906–1975) German-U.S. political theorist. She obtained her doctorate from the University of Heidelberg. Forced to flee the Nazis in 1933, she became a social worker in Paris, then fled again, to New York, in 1941. After several jobs related to Jewish culture, she wrote her major work, *Origins of Totalitarianism* (1951), which related totalitarianism to 19th-century anti-Semitism, imperialism, and the disintegration of the traditional nation-state. She taught at the University of Chicago (1963–67) and thereafter at the New School for Social Research. Her controversial *Eichmann in Jerusalem* (1963) suggested that ADOLF EICHMANN's role in the extermination of the Jews epitomized the "banality of evil."

areopagus \ˌar-ē-'ä-pə-gəs\ Supreme tribunal of ancient ATHENS. It was named for the Areopagus ("Ares' Hill"), where it met. It began as the king's council; by DRACO's code of law (c. 621 BC) it consisted of former ARCHONS, but SOLON (594) opened candidacy to any citizen. It had broad judicial powers. Its prestige fluctuated from the mid-6th to the mid-4th century BC, after which its power revived and continued under Roman domination, when it reacquired extensive administrative duties.

Arequipa \ˌä-rā-'kē-pä\ City (pop., 1998 est.: 710,103), southern Peru. Located at an altitude of 7,557 ft (2,303 m) at the foot of Misti Volcano (19,031 ft, or 5,801 m), it has been subject to earthquakes, usually associated with volcanic activity, and was largely destroyed by an earthquake in 1868. In the INCA empire, Arequipa was an important point on the route from CUZCO to the seacoast. Modern Arequipa is the commercial center of southern Peru.

Ares, classical sculpture; in the National Roman Museum, Rome.
ANDERSON–ALINARI FROM ART RESOURCE

Ares \'ar-ēz\ Greek god of war. Unlike his Roman counterpart, MARS, his worship was not extensive. From the time of HOMER, he was one of the Olympian deities, the son of Zeus and Hera, but disliked by the other gods. His worship occurred largely in northern Greece. He was associated from early times with Aphrodite, occasionally portrayed as his legitimate wife and at other times his lover. He was accompanied in battle by his sister Eris (strife) and by two of his children by Aphrodite, Phobos and Deimos (Panic and Rout).

Aretino \ˌä-rā-ˈtē-nō\, **Pietro** (1492–1556) Italian poet, prose writer, and dramatist. He was celebrated throughout Europe in his time for his bold and insolent literary attacks on the powerful. His fiery letters and dialogues are of great biographical and topical interest. His dramas, which are relatively free of venomous assaults, include five comedies and a tragedy, *Orazia* (1546; "The Horatii"), perhaps the best Italian tragedy of the 16th century.

Arévalo (Bermejo) \ˌä-rā-ˈbä-lō\, **Juan José** (1904–1990) President of Guatemala (1945–51). Soon after earning his doctorate, he went to Argentina, where he held various academic positions. After the overthrow of the Guatemalan dictator Jorge Ubico (1878–1946), he was elected president, receiving 85% of the vote. He established freedom of speech and of the press, and his administration inaugurated a social-security system, a labor code, and important education and health programs. His policies favored urban and agricultural workers and the indigenous population. He stepped down voluntarily at the end of his term. A military coup prevented him from running again in 1963.

Argentina *officially* **Argentine Republic** Federal republic, South America. Area: 1,072,156 sq mi (2,776,884 sq km). Population (1997 est.): 35,409,000. Capital: Buenos Aires. The population is largely ethnically Spanish, with other European influences. Language: Spanish (official). Religion: Roman Catholicism (official). Currency: Argentine peso. Argentina can be divided into four general regions: the northeastern plains, the Pampas, Patagonia, and the Andes. The subtropical plains in the northeast are divided by the Paraná River into Mesopotamia to the east and Gran Chaco to the west and north. The Pampas, south and west of the Paraná, is one of the world's most productive agricultural areas and the country's most populous region. Patagonia lies south of the Colorado River. The Argentine Andes include the continent's highest peak, Mount Aconcagua. Argentina's hydrology is dominated by rivers, including the Paraná, Uruguay, and Pilcomayo, that drain into the Río de la Plata. Argentina has a developing economy based largely on manufacturing and agriculture; it is Latin America's largest exporter of beef and beef products. It is a republic with two legislative houses; its head of state and government is the president. Little is known of the indigenous population before the Europeans' arrival. The area was explored for Spain by Sebastian Cabot 1526–30; by 1580, Asunción, Santa Fe, and Buenos Aires had been settled. At first attached to the viceroyalty of Peru (1620), it was later included with regions of modern Uruguay, Paraguay, and Bolivia in the viceroyalty of La Plata, or Buenos Aires (1776). With the establishment of the United Provinces of the Plate River in 1816, Argentina achieved its independence from Spain, but its boundaries were not set until the early 20th century. In 1943 the government was overthrown by the military; Col. Juan Peron took control in 1946. He in turn was overthrown in 1955. He returned in 1973 after two decades of turmoil. His second wife, Isabel, became president on his death in 1974 but lost power after a military coup in 1976. The military government tried to take the Falkland Islands in 1982 but was defeated by the British, with the result that the government returned to civilian rule in 1983. The government of Raul Alfonsin worked to end the human-rights abuses that characterized the former regimes. Hyperinflation led to public riots and Alfonsín's electoral defeat in 1989; his Peronist successor, Carlos Menem, instituted laissez-faire economic policies. In 1999 Fernando de la Rúa of the Alliance coalition was elected president, and his administration struggled with rising unemployment, foreign debt, and government corruption.

Argerich \ˈär-ger-ich\, **Martha** (born 1941) Argentine pianist. A prodigy, she began concertizing before she was 10. She went to Europe in 1955, where her teachers included Arturo Benedetti Michelangeli (1920–1995). She won the Busoni and Geneva competitions at 16, and the Chopin competition in 1965. The exceptionally brilliant technique, emotional depth, and élan displayed in the Romantic works in which she specializes have won her perhaps the most enthusiastic international following of any pianist in the world.

arginine \ˈär-jə-ˌnēn\ One of the essential amino acids, particularly abundant in histones and other proteins associated with nucleic acids. It plays an important metabolic role in the synthesis of urea, the principal form in which mammals excrete nitrogen compounds. Arginine is used in medicine and biochemical research, in pharmaceuticals, and as a dietary supplement.

argon Chemical element, chemical symbol Ar, atomic number 18. Colorless, odorless, and tasteless, it is the most abundant of the noble gases on earth, and the one most used in industry. It constitutes about 1% of air and is obtained by distillation of liquid air. Argon provides an inert gas shield in welding and brazing, in special lightbulbs and lasers, in Geiger counters, and in the production and fabrication of certain metals. Because it is formed by decay of a naturally occurring radioactive potassium isotope, it can be used to date rocks and samples over 100,000 years old.

argon-argon dating See potassium-argon dating

Argonauts In Greek legend, a band of 50 heroes who went with Jason in the ship *Argo* to retrieve the Golden Fleece from the grove of Ares at Colchis. They included such figures as Heracles, Orpheus,

The Argonauts, detail of a painting by Lorenzo Costa in the Civic Museum, Padua, Italy.
SCALA—ART RESOURCE

and THESEUS. They had many adventures before arriving at Colchis, from which they were eventually forced to flee, pursued by MEDEA's father, Aeëtes. The *Argo* eventually returned to Jason's home kingdom (Iolcus), and was placed in a grove sacred to POSEIDON; Jason died when its prow toppled as he was resting in its shadow.

Árgos Ancient city-state, northeastern PELOPONNESE, Greece. Under the Argive king Pheidon, it was the dominant city-state in the PELOPONNESE in the 7th century BC until the rise of SPARTA. After suffering incursions from MACEDONIA, Árgos joined the ACHAEAN LEAGUE in 229 BC. Later it came under Roman rule. The city flourished in Byzantine times, but ultimately fell to the OTTOMAN EMPIRE in the 16th century. During the War of GREEK INDEPENDENCE (1821–29), the first free Greek Parliament was convened at Árgos. The modern town (pop., 1991 est.: 22,300) is an agricultural center.

argument from design *or* **teleological argument** Argument for the existence of God. From the premises that anything complex (appearing designed) must have a creator and that the universe is very intricate, the argument concludes that God exists. Its history traces from ARISTOTLE, who defined God as the unmoved (or prime) mover. THOMAS AQUINAS used the argument in his *Ways*. DAVID HUME discussed it critically at length. Some thinkers, including IMMANUEL KANT, suggest that the reasoning is fallacious because it presupposes its own conclusion.

Argun River *Chinese* **Ergun** \'är-'gün\ *or* **O-erh-ku-na** \'ō-'är-'gü-'nä\ River, northeastern Asia. Rising in the Great Khinggan Mtns., it runs about 450 mi (724 km), forming part of the boundary between northeastern China and Russia, uniting with the Shilka River to form the AMUR RIVER. In its upper course it is called the Hailar.

arhat \'är-hət\ *or* **arahant** \'a-rə-hant\ In BUDDHISM, one who has gained insight into the true nature of existence, has achieved NIRVANA, and will not be reborn again. THERAVADA Buddhism regards becoming an arhat as the goal of spiritual progress. It holds that a seeker must pass through three earlier stages before being reborn in a heaven as an arhat. MAHAYANA Buddhism criticizes the goal of becoming an arhat and considers the BODHISATTVA to be a higher goal. This divergence of opinion is one of the fundamental differences between Theravada and Mahayana Buddhism.

Århus *or* **Aarhus** \'ȯr-,hüs\ Seaport (pop., 1994: 209,000), eastern Jutland, Denmark. It lies along Århus Bay and has an extensive harbor. Its origins are unknown, but it became a bishopric in AD 948 and, with its many religious institutions, prospered during the Middle Ages. In modern times, industrialization and harbor expansion have made it Denmark's second-largest city.

aria Solo song with instrumental accompaniment in OPERA, CANTATA, or ORATORIO. The strophic or stanzaic aria, in which each new stanza might represent a melodic variation on the first, appeared in opera in CLAUDIO MONTEVERDI's *Orfeo* (1607) and was widely used for decades. The standard aria form c. 1650–1775 was the da capo aria, in which the opening melody and text are repeated after an intervening melody-text section (often in a different key, tempo, and meter); the return of the first section was often virtuosically embellished by the singer. Comic operas never limited themselves to da capo form. Even in serious opera, from c. 1750 a variety of forms were used; GIAOCHINO ROSSINI and others often expanded the aria into a complete musical scene in which two or more conflicting emotions were expressed. RICHARD WAGNER's operas largely abandoned the aria in favor of a continuous musical texture, but arias have never ceased to be written.

Ariadne \,ar-ē-'ad-nē\ In GREEK MYTHOLOGY, the daughter of Pasiphaë and King MINOS of Crete. She fell in love with THESEUS, who had promised to slay the MINOTAUR confined in Minos's Labyrinth. She gave Theseus a ball of thread or glittering jewels that enabled him to mark his path and thus to escape the Labyrinth after killing the monster. Endings to the legend vary. In one, Theseus abandons Ariadne and she hangs herself; in others, he carries her to Naxos, where she either dies or marries the god DIONYSUS. See also PHAEDRA.

Arianism Christian HERESY that declared JESUS to be not truly divine but a created being. According to the Alexandrian presbyter ARIUS (4th century), God alone is immutable and self-existent, and the Son is not God, but a creature with a beginning. The Council of NICAEA (AD 325) condemned Arius and declared the Son to be "of one substance with the father." Arianism had numerous defenders for the next 50 years, but eventually collapsed. The Council of CONSTANTINOPLE (381) approved the NICENE CREED and proscribed Arianism. The heresy continued among the Germanic tribes through the 7th century, and similar beliefs are held in the present day by the JEHOVAH'S WITNESSES and by some adherents of UNITARIANISM.

Arias Sánchez \'är-ē-äs-'sän-chās\, **Oscar** (born 1941) President of Costa Rica (1986–90). A moderate socialist born to wealth, Arias worked for the moderate socialist National Liberation Party from the 1960s. He became president at a time when much of Central America was torn by civil war. His 1987 Central American peace plan, signed by the leaders of El Salvador, Guatemala, Honduras, and Nicaragua, included provisions for cease-fires, free elections, and amnesty for political prisoners. He was awarded the 1987 Nobel Peace Prize.

Aries (Latin: "Ram") In astronomy, the constellation lying between Pisces and Taurus; in ASTROLOGY, the first sign of the ZODIAC, governing approximately the period March 21–April 19. It is represented by a ram, which is sometimes identified with the Egyptian god AMON. In Greek mythology Aries was identified with the ram that carried the prince Phrixus out of Thessaly to Colchis. Phrixus sacrificed the ram to Zeus, who placed it in the heavens as a constellation. Its golden fleece was later recovered by JASON.

aril \'ar-il\ Special covering of certain seeds that commonly develops from the seed stalk. It is often a bright-colored fleshy envelope, as in such woody plants as the YEWS and NUTMEG and in members of the ARROWROOT family, OXALIS, and the CASTOR-OIL PLANT. Animals are attracted to arils and eat the seeds, dispersing them in their wastes. The aril of nutmeg is the source of the spice known as mace.

Arion \ə-'rī-ən\ Semilegendary Greek poet and musician. He lived at Methymna on the island of LESBOS and is identified as the inventor of the DITHYRAMB. He was sailing homeward after a performing tour when the sailors decided to kill him and steal his wealth. After singing a dirge for himself, he jumped overboard, but a dolphin charmed by his music carried him to shore. He reached CORINTH before the ship; when the sailors arrived, the ruler Periander forced them to confess and punished them. Arion's lyre and the dolphin were placed in the heavens as the constellations Lyra and Delphinus.

Ariosto \,är-ē-'ó-stō\, **Ludovico** (1474–1533) Italian poet. His epic poem *Orlando Furioso* (1516; "Roland Mad") is regarded as the finest literary expression of the Italian Renaissance. It enjoyed immediate popularity throughout Europe and was highly influential. He also wrote five comedies based on Latin classics but inspired by contemporary life; though minor in themselves, they are among the first of the imitations of Latin comedy in the vernacular that would long characterize European comedy. He also composed seven satires modeled after those of HORACE (1517–25).

Ariosto, woodcut after a drawing by Titian from the third edition of *Orlando furioso*, 1532.

BY COURTESY OF THE TRUSTEES OF THE BRITISH MUSEUM; PHOTOGRAPH, J.R. FREEMAN & CO. LTD.

Aristagoras \,ar-ə-'stag-ə-rəs\ (died 497 BC) Tyrant of MILETUS. He assumed his regency from his father-in-law, Histiaeus (died 494 BC), who had lost the trust of the Persian emperor, DARIUS I. Possibly incited by Histiaeus, and with support from Athens and Eretria, Aristagoras raised the IONIAN REVOLT against Persia. Defeated, he left Miletus to found a colony in Thrace, where he died in battle.

Aristarchus of Samos \,ar-ə-'stär-kəs\ (c. 310–230 BC) Greek astronomer. His advanced ideas on the movement of the earth (which he asserted revolved around the sun) are known from ARCHIMEDES and PLUTARCH. His only surviving work is the short treatise "On the Sizes and Distances of the Sun and Moon"; though the values he obtained are inaccurate, he showed that the sun and stars are at immense distances. A peak in the center of a lunar crater named for him is the brightest formation on the moon.

Aristide \ˌar-i-ˈstēd\, **Jean-Bertrand** (born 1953) First president of Haiti (1991, 1994–96, 2001–) to be elected in free democratic elections. A priest in the Roman Catholic Salesian order, he aligned himself with the poor and opposed the harsh regime of Jean-Claude Duvalier, son of FRANÇOIS DUVALIER, often putting himself at odds with the church hierarchy and the military; expelled by the Salesians in 1988, he formally requested that he be relieved of his priestly duties in 1994. In 1990 progressive-center forces united behind Aristide and swept him into power. He initiated dramatic reforms but was ousted in a military coup after only seven months in office. Though restored to office in 1994 with the help of U.S. occupying troops, he received little aid with which to address his country's endemic ills. Constitutionally prohibited from seeking a consecutive term, he stepped down in 1996 but remained Haiti's most potent political figure. In 2000 he was reelected president amid charges of electoral fraud.

Aristides \ˌar-ə-ˈstī-dēz\ (2nd century AD) Athenian philosopher, one of the earliest Christian APOLOGISTS. His *Apology for the Christian Faith* discussed the harmony in creation and the nature of the divine being and stated that barbarians, Greeks, and Jews were all inadequate in their conception of the deity and their religious practices. Long considered lost, the *Apology* was reconstructed in the late 19th century.

Aristides the Just (5th century BC) Athenian statesman and general. He was ostracized in 482 BC, probably for opposing THEMISTOCLES, but was recalled in 480 and helped defeat the Persians at the battles of SALAMIS and PLATAEA. In 478 he helped Sparta's eastern allies form the DELIAN LEAGUE; allied with Athens and based on Athenian naval power and the trust Aristides inspired, the league effectively became the Athenian empire.

aristocracy \ˌar-ə-ˈstä-krə-sē\ Originally, leadership by a small privileged class or a minority thought to be best qualified to lead. PLATO and ARISTOTLE considered aristocrats to be those who are morally and intellectually superior, and therefore fit to govern in the interests of the people. The term has come to mean the upper layer of a stratified group. Most aristocracies have been hereditary, and many European societies stratified their aristocratic classes by formally titling their members, thereby making the term roughly synonymous with nobility. See also OLIGARCHY.

Aristophanes \ˌar-ə-ˈstä-fə-ˌnēz\ (c. 450–388? BC) Greek playwright. An Athenian, he began his career as a comic dramatist in 427 BC. He wrote about 40 plays, of which 11 survive, including *The Clouds* (423 BC), *The Wasps* (422), *The Birds* (414), *Lysistrata* (411), and *The Frogs* (405). Most of the plays typify the Old Comedy (of which they are the only extant representatives), in which mime, chorus, and burlesque were important features. His satire, wit, and merciless topical commentary made him the greatest comic dramatist of ancient Greece.

Aristotle (384–322 BC) Greek philosopher and scientist. Son of the court physician to ALEXANDER THE GREAT's grandfather, he became a student of PLATO in Athens and taught at Plato's Academy for 20 years. He went back to Macedonia c. 342 to tutor the young Alexander, then returned to Athens in 335 to found his own school, the Lyceum. Aristotle distinguished his philosophy from Plato's by declaring that the assumption of the existence of a separate realm of transcendent Ideas (see FORM) is unnecessary and that the world of perceived things is the real world. He wrote prolifically; his major surviving works include the *Organon, De Anima, Physics, Metaphysics, Nicomachean Ethics, Eudemian Ethics, Magna Moralia, Politics, Rhetoric,* and *Poetics,* as well as other works on natural history and science (most were first edited and published in the 1st century BC). Aristotle divides philosophical topics into ETHICS, PHYSICS, and LOGIC. To him, logic was required for the study of every other topic. He distinguished four kinds of cause—material, formal, efficient, and final—and postulated an unmoved mover (God) as a necessary element of physics. In ethics, he argued that "good" for human beings (or anything else) lies in fulfilling their purpose or function, a view that came to be known as TELEOLOGY. With Plato, Aristotle is considered a founder of Western philosophy, and his influence on later Western science and philosophy has been vast.

arithmetic Branch of mathematics that deals with the properties of NUMBERS and ways of combining them through addition, subtraction, multiplication, and division. Initially, it dealt only with the counting numbers, but its definition has broadened to include not only RATIONAL NUMBERS but IRRATIONAL and COMPLEX numbers. Its divisibility and PRIME NUMBER theorems overlap parts of NUMBER THEORY. Of primary importance in arithmetic is the establishment of the order of operations—multiplication and division before addition and subtraction—and the properties of the operations. In multiplication and addition, for example, order does not matter: $a + b = b + a$ and $ab = ba$ (the COMMUTATIVE LAW), and grouping is arbitrary: $a + (b + c) = (a + b) + c$ and $a(bc) = (ab)c$ (the ASSOCIATIVE LAW). Subtraction and division do not share these properties.

arithmetic, fundamental theorem of Fundamental principle of NUMBER THEORY proved by CARL FRIEDRICH GAUSS in 1801. It states that any integer greater than 1 can be expressed as the product of PRIME NUMBERS in only one way.

Arius \ˈar-ē-əs\ (c. 250–336) Christian priest and heretic, whose teachings gave rise to the doctrine of ARIANISM. He was leader of a Christian community near Alexandria, where he preached doctrines that combined NEOPLATONISM with a literal, rationalist interpretation of biblical texts. By asserting the absolute oneness and immutability of God, he called into question the divinity of Christ. His views were publicized through his major work, *Thalia* (c. 323). In 325 the Council of Nicaea declared him a heretic. He was striving to compromise his views and win readmission to the church when he died suddenly in Constantinople. The Arian HERESY posed a threat to Christian orthodoxy for several centuries.

Arizona State (pop., 1997 est.: 4,555,000), southwestern U.S. It covers 114,000 sq mi (295,260 sq km); its capital is PHOENIX. Its highest point is Humphrey's Peak, at 12,633 ft (3,850 m). The site of GRAND CANYON and PETRIFIED FOREST national parks, Arizona also has almost 40% of U.S. Indian tribal lands. Humans settled the area more than 25,000 years ago. Nomadic APACHE and NAVAJO Indians arrived after the collapse of the ANASAZI and HOHOKAM civilizations. They were followed in the 16th century by Spanish treasure seekers from Mexico, including FRANCISCO VAZQUEZ DE CORONADO, establishing Mexico's claim to the area. In 1776 the Mexican army built the first presidio at TUCSON. After the MEXICAN WAR, Arizona was ceded to the U.S. as part of New Mexico in 1848; the GADSDEN PURCHASE was added in 1853. Organized as a territory in 1863, Arizona became the 48th state in 1912. Though still lightly populated, it has grown rapidly in population in recent decades, largely because of its climate. About one-sixth of the population is Spanish-speaking; another 5% is Indian, including Navajo, HOPI, Apache, PAPAGO, and PIMA. Its diverse economy includes agriculture, mining, aerospace, electronics, and tourism.

Arizona, University of Public university in Tucson. Created in 1885 as a land-grant institution, it later added schools of education and law (1920s), business and public administration (1934), pharmacy (1949), medicine (1961), and nursing (1964). Today it grants bachelor's, master's, and doctoral degrees in most areas of study, and is noted for its programs in astronomy and Southwest archaeology. Total enrollment is about 35,000.

Arjan \ˈər-jən\ (1563–1606) Fifth GURU of the Sikhs (1581–1606) and its first martyr. He compiled the volume of Sikh scripture on which the ADI GRANTH is based, and he completed the GOLDEN TEMPLE at Amritsar. The first Guru to serve as both temporal and spiritual head of SIKHISM, he built up Amritsar as a commercial center and enlarged missionary efforts. He was also a prolific poet and writer of hymns. He prospered under the tolerant Mughal emperor AKBAR, but was tortured to death by Akbar's successor for not altering the Adi Granth to remove passages that gave offense to Hinduism or Islam.

Arjuna \ˈər-jü-nə\ One of the five brothers who are the heroes of the *MAHABHARATA*. His reluctance to go into battle prompts KRISHNA, manifested as his friend and charioteer, to deliver the discourse on duty that constitutes the BHAGAVADGITA. An exemplar of skill, duty, and compassion as well as a seeker of true knowledge, Arjuna is a central figure in Hindu myth and theology.

Ark of the Covenant In Judaism and Christianity, the ornate, gold-plated wooden chest that in biblical times housed the two tablets of the Law given to MOSES by God. The Levites carried the Ark during the Hebrews' wandering in the wilderness. Following the conquest of CANAAN, it was kept at Shiloh, but was sometimes carried into battle by the Israelites. DAVID took it to Jerusalem, and SOLOMON placed it in the Temple of JERUSALEM, where it rested in the HOLY OF HOLIES and was seen only by the high priest on YOM KIPPUR. Its final fate is unknown.

Arkansas State (pop., 1997: 2,523,000), southern central U.S. It covers 53,187 sq mi (137,754 sq km). Its capital is LITTLE ROCK, while its highest point is Magazine Mtn., at 2,753 ft (839 m). The earliest inhabitants were Indian bluff dwellers along the Mississippi River c. AD 500. Mound-building cultures later left sepulchral mounds along the river. Spanish and French explorers traversed the region in the 16th–17th century; the first permanent European settlement was founded at Arkansas Post in 1686. Acquired by the U.S. as part of the LOUISIANA PURCHASE, Arkansas Territory was formed in 1819; the state's current boundaries were fixed in 1828. Arkansas became the 25th state in 1836. It seceded in 1861 to join the Confederacy in the AMERICAN CIVIL WAR; it was readmitted to the Union in 1868. Following RECONSTRUCTION, a rigid policy of segregation lasted until 1957, when court-ordered desegregation of the schools was implemented. Once dominated by agriculture, the state's economy now also includes mining and manufacturing. Tourism is promoted especially by the mineral springs at HOT SPRINGS NATIONAL PARK and resorts in the OZARK MTNS.

Arkansas, University of State university with campuses in Fayetteville (main campus), Little Rock, Pine Bluff, and Monticello. Little Rock is also home to the University of Arkansas for Medical Sciences. The Fayetteville campus was established in 1871 as a land-grant college; the largest of the universities, its enrollment exceeds 14,000, and it is the state's only doctoral degree-granting institution.

Arkansas River River, rising in central Colorado. At 1,450 mi (2,333 km) long, it flows east through southern Kansas and southeast across northeastern Oklahoma and bisects Arkansas, where it empties into the MISSISSIPPI RIVER. Navigable for 650 mi (1,046 km), its largest tributaries are the CANADIAN and CIMARRON rivers. It is believed to have been crossed by FRANCISCO VAZQUEZ DE CORONADO in 1541 near the site of Dodge City, Kan., and by ZEBULON PIKE in 1806.

Arkhangelsk \ˌər-ˈkän-gilsk\ *English* **Archangel** City (pop, 1994 est.: 374,000), northwestern Russia. Located at the head of the Dvina Gulf, it has a large harbor kept open in winter by icebreakers. The area was settled by Norsemen in the 10th century AD. In 1553 it was visited by the English who were looking for the NORTHEAST PASSAGE. Founded in 1584 as a monastery of MICHAEL the archangel, it became a trading station of the Muscovy Co. Opened to European trade by the czar BORIS GODUNOV, it flourished as the sole Russian seaport until ST. PETERSBURG was built in 1703. It was the scene of British, French, and U.S. support of the northern Russian government against the BOLSHEVIKS, 1918–19. In World War II, it received convoys of LEND-LEASE goods from England and the U.S. (1941–45). Now Russia's major timber exporting port, it also has extensive shipbuilding facilities.

Arkona W. Slavic citadel-temple of the war-god Svantovit, built in the 9th–10th century AD and destroyed in 1168/69 by Christian Danes when they stormed the island of Rügen in the southwestern Baltic. According to SAXO GRAMMATICUS, it was a log structure with red roof, surrounded by a yard and fence, carved and painted with symbols. The inner sanctum contained a statue of Svantovit with four heads and throats facing in opposite directions. Excavations in 1921 proved the temple's actual existence.

arkose \ˈär-ˌkōs, ˈär-ˌkōz\ Coarse SANDSTONE that has formed by the disintegration of granite without appreciable decomposition. It thus consists primarily of quartz and feldspar grains. In the absence of stratification, arkose may bear superficial resemblance to granite, and it sometimes has been described as reconstituted granite, or granite wash. Like the granite from which it was formed, arkose is pink or gray.

Arkwright, Richard *later* **Sir Richard** (1732–1792) British TEXTILE industrialist and inventor. His first spinning machine was patented in 1769 (see LEWIS PAUL). His WATER FRAME (so-called because it operated by waterpower) produced a cotton YARN suitable for warp (see WEAVING), stronger than thread made on the SPINNING JENNY, which proved suitable only for weft. He introduced all-cotton calico in 1773. He opened several factories equipped with machinery for carrying out the phases of textile manufacturing from CARDING through spinning (see DRAWING).

Arledge, Roone (born 1931) U.S. television executive. Born in Forest Hills, N.Y., he began work at ABC-TV in 1960 as a sports producer. He later became president of ABC Sports and Monday Night Football (1965–85) and group president of ABC News and Sports (1985–90). He created such programs as *Wide World of Sports, Nightline, 20/20,* and *PrimeTime Live,* produced television coverage of 10 Olympic games, and made many technical and editorial innovations in sports coverage.

Arlen, Harold *orig.* **Hyman Arluck** (1905–1986) U.S. songwriter. Born in Buffalo, N.Y., to a Jewish cantor and a pianist, Arlen left school to form a band, and he made a living until he was 24 chiefly as a performer and arranger. In 1929 he began a successful collaboration with lyricist Ted Koehler (1894–1973) with "Get Happy"; their later songs, including "I've Got the World on a String," were featured in shows at Harlem's COTTON CLUB. Arlen's Broadway musicals included *You Said It* (1931); *Life Begins at 8:40* (1934); *Hooray for What?* (1937); *Bloomer Girl* (1944); *St. Louis Woman* (1946) and *Saratoga* (1959), both with J. MERCER; and *House of Flowers* (1954), with TRUMAN CAPOTE. For Hollywood, Arlen wrote "It's Only a Paper Moon," "Let's Fall in Love," and "That Old Black Magic." His most famous song is perhaps "Over the Rainbow" (lyrics by E.Y. HARBURG) from *The Wizard of Oz* (1939).

Arles \ˈärl, ˈärlz\ City (pop., 1991: 53,000), southeastern France. Occupied and built up by the Romans in the 1st century BC, Arles became, through commerce, a leading city of the ROMAN EMPIRE. In the 10th century AD it became the capital of BURGUNDY, known also as the Kingdom of Arles. Portions of the Roman wall around the old town remain, and a Roman arena of the 1st century BC is still used for bullfights and plays. The city was home to VINCENT VAN GOGH during one of his most productive periods. Arles is still a river port, but its economy is based largely on tourism and agriculture.

Arlington Unincorporated settlement (pop., 1994: 175,000), northern Virginia. Lying across the POTOMAC RIVER from Washington, D.C., the city is the capital of Arlington Co., which was part of Washington, D.C., from 1789 to 1846, when it was returned to Virginia. It is the site of Arlington National Cemetery (located on the former estate of ROBERT E. LEE), Ronald Reagan National Airport, and numerous federal buildings, including the PENTAGON.

arm Upper limb of a biped, particularly a primate. Primate arms have one long bone, the humerus, in the upper arm above the elbow, and two thinner bones, the radius and ulna, in the forearm. The triceps muscle straightens the forearm at the elbow joint; the brachialis and biceps muscles bend it. Forearm and small muscles in the hand move the hand and fingers. The term may also denote the limb or the locomotive or prehensile organ of an invertebrate (e.g., the ray of a starfish or the tentacle of an octopus).

Armada, Spanish Great fleet sent by PHILIP II of Spain in 1588 to invade England in conjunction with a Spanish army from Flanders. Philip was motivated by a desire to restore the Roman Catholic faith in England and by English piracies against Spanish trade and possessions. The Armada, commanded by the duke of Medina-Sidonia, consisted of about 130 ships. In the weeklong battle, the Spanish suffered defeat after the English launched fire ships into the Spanish fleet, breaking the ships' formation and making them susceptible to the English ships' heavy guns. Many Spanish ships were also lost during the long voyage home, and a total of perhaps 15,000 Spaniards died. The defeat of the Armada, in which FRANCIS DRAKE played a principal role, saved England and the Netherlands from possible absorption into the Spanish empire.

armadillo Any of 20 species of armored mammals (family Dasypodidae) related to SLOTHS and ANTEATERS. Armadillos are stout and short-legged, with strong, curved claws and a protective covering of pinkish to brown armor composed of solid plates separated by movable bands. They occur in tropical and subtropical regions, primarily in South America. Most species inhabit open areas, but some live in forests. The species range in size from about 6 in. (16 cm) to 5 ft (1.5 m) long. They live alone, in pairs, or in small groups and feed on termites or other insects, vegetation, small animals, and carrion.

Nine-banded armadillo (*Dasypus novemcinctus*).

APPEL COLOR PHOTOGRAPHY

Armageddon \ˌär-mə-ˈged-ən\ In the NEW TESTAMENT, the place where the kings of the earth under demonic leadership will wage war on the forces of God at the end of history. Armageddon is mentioned only in the Revelation to JOHN. The name may mean "Mountain of Megiddo," a reference to the city of MEGIDDO, which held strategic importance in Palestine. Other biblical references suggest JERUSALEM as the battle site.

Armagh \ˈär-ˌmä\ District (pop., 1999 est.: 54,000), Northern Ireland. Formerly part of Co. Armagh, the district was established in 1973. It lies south of Lough NEAGH. The northern part of the district is the island's main fruit-growing region; the southern part, along the Irish Republic's border, was a hotbed of sectarian violence through the late 20th century. The district seat is Armagh town (pop., 1991: 14,000). According to tradition, St. PATRICK established his principal Irish church here in the 5th century AD. The area was the leading intellectual center of the Western world in the 5th–9th century. Taken by English Protestant forces in the 16th century, Armagh became a prosperous center for Protestant clergy and gentry, a circumstance reflected in its many Georgian monuments and buildings.

Armagnac \ˌär-mä-ˈnyäk\ Small territory in historical GASCONY, southwestern France. A portion was part of the Roman province of Aquitania (see AQUITAINE). From c. 960 it was the separate countship of Armagnac, and grew to occupy a buffer zone between lands controlled by the French kings (Toulouse) and those controlled by the English (GUIENNE). It led the resistance to the English king HENRY V's invasion of France, but suffered a setback at the Battle of AGINCOURT. First annexed to France in 1497, it returned finally by descent through the Navarre family in 1607. Again a countship from 1645, it was dissolved in 1789. It produces the famous Armagnac brandy.

Armani \är-ˈmä-nē\, **Giorgio** (born 1934) Italian fashion designer. He abandoned medical school and worked as a buyer for a department store (1957–64) before training as a fashion designer. In 1974–75 he introduced his own label of ready-to-wear for men and women. In 1980–81 he founded Giorgio Armani USA, Emporio Armani, and Armani Jeans, and in 1989 he opened shops in London. He was a leader in the pared-down, unstructured silhouette in menswear and was responsible for the wide-shouldered look for executive women. His designs are often characterized by understated glamour and luxurious fabrics suitable for urban life.

Armenia *officially* **Republic of Armenia** Nation, South Asia. Area: 11,484 sq mi (29,743 sq km). Population (2001 est.): 3,807,000. Capital: YEREVAN. Armenians constitute nine-tenths of its population; there are also small numbers of Azerbaijanis, Kurds, Russians, and Ukrainians. Languages: Armenian (official), Russian. Religion: Christianity (Armenian Apostolic, Armenian Catholic). Currency: dram. Armenia is a mountainous country with an average elevation of 5,900 ft (1,800 m). The Lesser CAUCASUS ranges lie across its northern portion, and Lake SEVAN lies in the eastern central part. Armenia has a dry and continental climate that changes dramatically with elevation. Though it has become highly industrialized (as a result of the development of hydroelectric power during Soviet rule) and increasingly urbanized, agriculture is still important. Armenia is a successor state to a historical region in CAUCASIA. Historical Armenia's boundaries have varied considerably, but old Armenia extended over what is now northeastern Turkey and the Republic of Armenia. The area was equivalent to the ancient kingdom of VAN, which ruled c. 1270–850 BC. It was later conquered by the Medes (see MEDIA) and MACEDONIA, and still later allied with the Roman empire. Armenia adopted Christianity as its national religion in AD 303. For centuries the scene of strife among Arabs, Seljuqs, Byzantines, and Mongols, it came under the rule of the Ottoman Turks in 1514. Over the next centuries, as parts were ceded to other rulers, nationalism arose among the scattered Armenians; by the late 19th century it was causing widespread disruption. Fighting between Ottomans and Russians escalated when part of Armenia was ceded to Russia in 1878, and it continued through World War I, leading to widespread Armenian deaths (see ARMENIAN MASSACRES). With the Turkish defeat, the Russian part was set up as a Soviet republic in 1921. Armenia became a constituent republic of the U.S.S.R. in 1936. With the latter's dissolution in the late 1980s, Armenia declared its independence in 1990. In the years that followed, it fought Azerbaijan for control over NAGORNO-KARABAKH until a cease-fire in 1994. About one-fifth of the population has left the country since 1993 because of an energy crisis. Political tension escalated, and in 1999 armed dissidents killed the prime minister and several legislators.

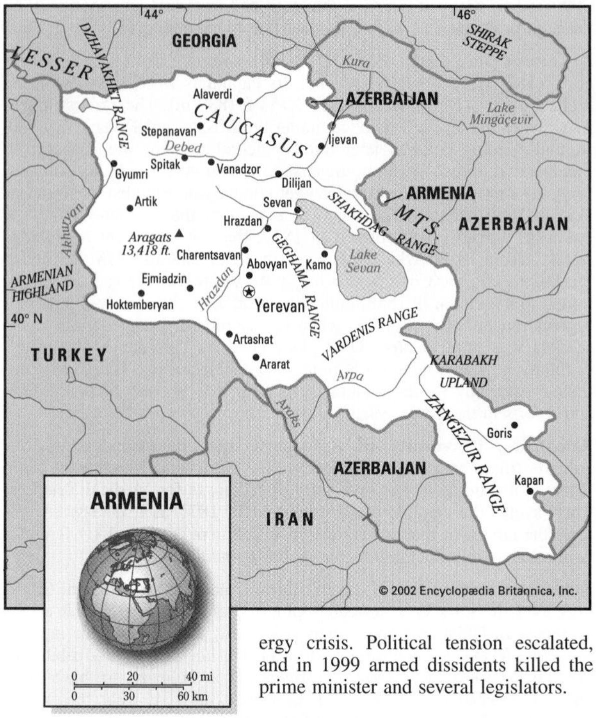

Armenia, Little See LITTLE ARMENIA

Armenian language INDO-EUROPEAN LANGUAGE of the ARMENIANS, spoken by perhaps 5–6 million people worldwide. Armenian has undergone phonetic and grammatical changes that make it completely distinct from other branches of Indo-European; its closest affinity may be with Greek, though this hypothesis has been vigorously disputed. Its long history of contact with IRANIAN LANGUAGES has resulted in the adoption of many PERSIAN loanwords. According to tradition, the unique Armenian alphabet was created by the cleric Mesrop Mashtots in AD 406 or 407. Armenian of the 5th–9th century (Grabar, or Classical Armenian) was employed as the literary language into modern times. A 19th-century cultural revival led to the formation of two new literary languages: West Armenian, based on the speech of Istanbul Armenians, and East Armenian, based on the speech of Transcaucasian Armenians. Because of a long tradition of emigration and the massacres and expulsions during the last decades of Ottoman rule, most speakers of West Armenian live outside Anatolia. East Armenian is the language of the present-day Republic of Armenia.

Armenian massacres Murder and expulsion of Turkish Armenians by the OTTOMAN EMPIRE under ABDÜLHAMID II in 1894–96 and by the YOUNG TURK government in 1915–16. In 1894, when the Armenians began agitating for territorial autonomy and protesting against high taxes, Ottoman troops and Kurdish tribesmen killed thousands. In 1896, hoping to call attention to their plight, Armenian revolutionaries seized the Ottoman Bank in Istanbul. Mobs of Muslim Turks, abetted by elements of the government, killed more than 50,000 Armenians in response. Sporadic killings occurred over the next two decades. In response to Russia's use of Armenian troops against the Ottomans in World War I (1914–18), the government deported 1.75 million Armenians south to Syria and Mesopotamia, in the course of which 600,000 Armenians were killed or died of starvation.

Armenians Indo-European people first recognized in the early 7th century BC when they moved into an area conquered by BABYLONIA and MEDIA that was subsequently conquered by ALEXANDER THE GREAT in 331 BC. Armenian culture reached a high point in the 14th century, producing highly regarded sculpture, architecture, and fine art. Armenian history has been one of off-and-on struggles for independence from foreign domination, first by the BYZANTINE EMPIRE, then by the SELJUQ DYNASTY, the OTTOMAN EMPIRE, Persia, and Russia. The most recent period of foreign domination (1922–90) ended with the collapse of the Soviet Union. Until the 20th century, Armenians were primarily agricultural; now they are highly urbanized. Traditionally they are either Orthodox or Catholic Christians; Armenia was considered the first Christian state. Over 3.5 million live in the Republic of Armenia, and there is an appreciable diaspora in the West. See also ARMENIAN MASSACRES.

Armistice (1918) Agreement between Germany and the Allies ending WORLD WAR I. Allied representatives met with a German delegation in a railway carriage at Rethondes, France, to discuss terms. The agreement was signed on November 11, and the war ended at 11 a.m. that day ("the 11th hour of the 11th day of the 11th month"). The principal term was that Germany would evacuate Belgium, France, and Alsace-Lorraine. Negotiations formalizing the armistice were conducted at the PARIS PEACE CONFERENCE. Later, a "stab in the back" legend developed in Germany asserting that the German military situation had not been hopeless and that traitorous politicians had done the Allies' bidding by signing the Armistice.

armor *or* **body armor** Protective clothing that can shield the wearer from weapons and projectiles. By extension, armor is also protective covering for animals, vehicles, and so on. Prehistoric warriors used leather hides and helmets. Chinese warriors used rhinoceros skin in the 11th century BC, and Greek infantry wore thick, multilayered metal-and-linen cuirasses (armor covering the body from neck to waist) in the 5th century BC. Shirts of CHAIN MAIL were worn throughout the Roman Empire, and mail was the chief armor of Western Europe until the 14th century. Ancient Greeks and Romans used armor made of rigid metal plates, which reappeared in Europe around the 13th century. Plate armor dominated European design until the 17th century, when firearms began to make it obsolete. It began to disappear in the 18th century, but the helmet reappeared in World War I and became standard equipment. Modern body armor (the bulletproof vest) covers the chest and sometimes the groin; it is a flexible garment reinforced with steel plates, fiberglass, boron carbide, or multiple layers of nylon fabric. The synthetic KEVLAR is now widely used for such armor.

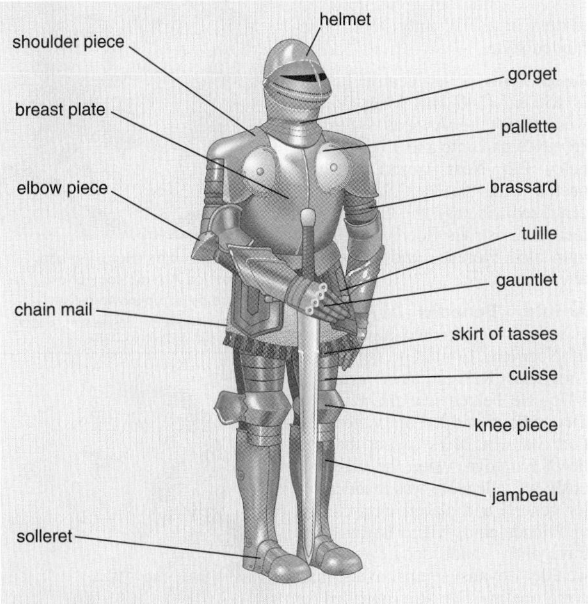

Suit of 15th-century European plate armor.

armored vehicle Motor vehicle with plating for protection against bullets, shells, or other projectiles that moves either on wheels or on two rolling metal belts called tracks. The TANK is the chief armored vehicle for military use. Other military types include armored personnel carriers, armored cars, and mobile weaponry platforms such as tank destroyers and ANTIAIRCRAFT GUNS. First widely used in World War II, personnel carriers are armored tracked vehicles that transport infantry into battle or serve as combat platforms from which soldiers can fight without dismounting. Armored cars are wheeled vehicles generally equipped with machine guns; they move quickly over smooth terrain and are often used for reconnaissance.

armory practice Production system for the assembly of finished products, in this case arms. With the adoption of the Model 1842 musket, the U.S. military achieved the large-scale assembly of weapons from uniform, INTERCHANGEABLE PARTS. By the mid-1850s arms makers around the world were beginning to copy this AMERICAN SYSTEM OF MANUFACTURE, which contributed to the creation of the modern military small arm, especially after the introduction of percussion ignition and rifled barrels.

Armory Show *formally* **International Exhibition of Modern Art** Exhibition of painting and sculpture held in 1913 at the 69th Regiment Armory in New York City. Conceived by its organizers, the Association of American Painters and Sculptors, as a selection of works exclusively by U.S. artists, it evolved into a comprehensive look at current European art movements. Of the 1,300 works assembled, one-third were European, tracing the evolution of modern art from FRANCISCO GOYA to MARCEL DUCHAMP and VASSILY KANDINSKY, with works representative of IMPRESSIONISM, SYMBOLISM, POSTIMPRESSIONISM, FAUVISM, and CUBISM. The U.S. works featured the younger, more radical artists of the ASH CAN SCHOOL and THE EIGHT. The show traveled to Chicago and Boston, introducing the public to advanced European art and establishing itself as a decisive event in the development of U.S. art and art collecting.

Armour, Philip Danforth (1832–1901) U.S. entrepreneur and innovator. Born in Stockbridge, N.Y., he earned his first capital in California mining endeavors. He vastly expanded his family's midwestern grain-dealing and meatpacking business in 1875, originating the use of by-products and the sale of canned meat. When rail-car refrigeration was introduced in the 1880s (see GUSTAVUS FRANKLIN SWIFT), he established distributing plants in eastern states and began exporting Armour meat products to Europe. His Armour & Co. enterprises helped make Chicago the meatpacking capital of the world.

arms, coat of *or* **shield of arms** Heraldic device dating to the 12th century in Europe. It was originally a cloth tunic worn over or in place of armor to establish identity in battle. In the full armorial achievement the distinctively patterned shield is ornamented with a crest, helmet, mantling, motto, crown, wreath, and supporters and rests upon a compartment. Arms were later adopted as emblems for schools, churches, guilds, and corporations to reflect their origins or histories. See also HERALDRY.

arms control Concept of limiting the development, testing, production, deployment, proliferation, or use of weapons through international agreements. Arms control did not arise in international diplomacy until the first HAGUE CONVENTION (1899). The WASHINGTON CONFERENCE (1921–22) and the KELLOGG-BRIAND PACT (1928) were broken without much fear of sanction. U.S.-Soviet treaties to control nuclear weapons were taken more seriously. See also NUCLEAR TEST-BAN TREATY, SALT, START.

Armstrong, Edwin H(oward) (1890–1954) U.S. inventor. Born in New York City, he studied at Columbia Univ., where he devised a feedback circuit that brought in signals with a thousandfold amplification (1912). At its highest amplification, the circuit shifted from being a receiver to being a primary generator of radio waves, and as such it is at the heart of all radio and television broadcasting. It earned him the Franklin Medal, the highest U.S. scientific honor. His 1933 invention of circuits that produced the carrier waves for frequency modulation (FM) made possible the first high-fidelity broadcasting.

Armstrong, Gillian (born 1950) Australian film director. She won an award at the Sydney Film Festival for a short film in 1976, and received international acclaim and numerous awards as the director of *My Brilliant Career* (1979). Her subsequent works include Australian films such as *The Last Days of Chez Nous* (1993) and *Oscar and Lucinda* (1997) as well as U.S. films such as *Mrs. Soffel* (1984), *Little Women* (1994), and *Charlotte Gray* (2001).

Armstrong, Lance (born 1971) American cyclist and four-time winner of the TOUR DE FRANCE (1999–2002). Armstrong began his professional CYCLING career in 1992 when he joined the Motorola team. He won stages of the Tour de France in 1993 and 1995 but withdrew from three of four Tours he attempted from 1993 to 1996. After the 1996 Tour Armstrong fell ill, suffering from testicular cancer that had by that time also spread to his lungs and brain. Months of treatments followed before he could attempt his comeback. In 1998 Armstrong won the Tour of Luxembourg, his first important race since his illness, and on July 25, 1999, Armstrong became the second American ever to win the Tour de France and the first to win it for an American team (three-time winner Greg LeMond had raced with European teams). Armstrong felt his July 23, 2000, win of the Tour to be a vindication of his 1999 victory and an answer to critics who had suspected his use of performance-enhancing substances. Armstrong excelled in the mountain stages in his 2001 and 2002 Tour victories.

Armstrong, Louis (1901–1971) U.S. trumpeter and singer, the first great soloist in jazz and its most popular public figure. Armstrong was born in New Orleans, where he participated in marching, riverboat, and cabaret bands. (A childhood nickname, Satchelmouth, was shortened to Satchmo and used throughout his life.) In 1922 he moved to Chicago to join KING OLIVER's Creole Jazz Band (see DIXIELAND); he made his first records the following year. In 1924 he joined the FLETCHER HENDERSON Orchestra in New York and recorded with BESSIE SMITH and MA RAINEY. In 1925 he switched from cornet to trumpet and began recording under his own name with his Hot Five and Hot Seven ensembles, groups resembling the New Orleans bands of Oliver and Kid Ory. In these recordings the prevailing emphasis on collective improvisation gives way to his developing strength as soloist and vocalist. By the time of his 1928 "West End Blues," Armstrong had established the preeminence of the virtuoso soloist in jazz. His vibrant melodic phrasing, inventive harmonic improvisation, and swinging rhythmic conception established the vernacular of jazz music. His powerful tone, great range, and dazzling velocity set a new technical standard. He also was the first scat singer, improvising nonsense syllables in the manner of a horn. He became something more than a jazz musician: solo attraction, bandleader, film actor, and international star. His later recordings and his role as musical ambassador to the world maintained his celebrity until the end of his life.

Louis Armstrong.

AP/WIDE WORLD PHOTOS

Armstrong, Neil (Alden) (born 1930) U.S. astronaut. Born in Wapakoneta, Ohio, he became a pilot at 16, studied aeronautical engineering, and won three Air Medals in the Korean War. In 1955 he became a civilian research pilot for the forerunner of NASA. He joined the space program in 1962 with the second group of astronauts. In 1966, as command pilot of GEMINI 8, he and David Scott completed the first manual space docking maneuver, with an unmanned Agena rocket. On July 20, 1969, as part of the APOLLO 11 mission, he became the first person to step onto the moon, announcing "That's one small step for a man, one giant leap for mankind."

Neil Armstrong, 1969.

AP/WIDE WORLD

army Large, organized force armed and trained for war, especially on land. The term may be applied to a large unit organized for independent action or to a nation's or ruler's overall military organization for land warfare. The character and organization of armies have varied through history. At various times armies have been built around INFANTRY soldiers or mounted warriors (e.g., CAVALRY) or men in machines, and have been made up of professionals or amateurs, of MERCENARIES fighting for pay or for plunder, or of patriots fighting for a cause. See also AIR FORCE, CONSCRIPTION, GUERRILLA, MILITARY UNIT, MILITIA, U.S. ARMY.

Arndt, Ernst Moritz (1769–1860) German (Swedish-born) prose writer, poet, and patriot. He rejected the Lutheran ministry at 28 and eventually became a professor of history at Greifswald and Bonn. Among his important works is the huge *Geist der Zeit (Spirit of the Times),* a bold call for political reforms which expressed German national awakening during the Napoleonic era (4 vols., 1806–18). Not all his poems were inspired by political ideas; *Gedichte* (1804–18; "Poems") contains many religious poems of great beauty.

Arne, Thomas Augustine (1710–1778) British composer. Son of a London upholsterer, he secretly taught himself instrumental skills and composition with the help of an opera musician. Smitten by the opera, he had an early success with his own first opera, *Rosamond* (1733), and thereafter concentrated almost exclusively on the theater. As composer to Drury Lane Theatre and London's great pleasure gardens, he became Britain's leading theatrical composer and, after G.F. HANDEL, possibly the finest British composer of the century. Of his approximately 90 theatrical works, the best known are *Comus* (1738), *The Judgment of Paris* (1740), and *Artaxerxes* (1762). His song "Rule, Britannia" became an unofficial national anthem. His sister Susannah (1714–1766) was the famous singer and actress known as Mrs. Cibber.

Arnhem Land \'är-nəm\ Region, northeastern NORTHERN TERRITORY, Australia. It extends south from Van Diemen Gulf to the Gulf of CARPENTARIA and Groote Eylandt. Never fully explored, it has a total area of about 37,000 sq mi (96,000 sq km) and contains important bauxite and uranium mines. Occupied by AUSTRALIAN ABORIGINES since the late PLEISTOCENE, it was visited in 1623 by the Dutch explorer Jan Carstensz, who named it for his ship. The name now primarily refers to its large Aboriginal reserves.

Arnim, Bettina von *orig.* **Elisabeth Katharina Ludovica Magdalena Brentano** (1785–1859) German writer. Her best-known works are reworked records of her correspondence with JOHANN W. VON GOETHE, Karoline von Günderode, and her brother CLEMENS BRENTANO, much of it fictitious, but written in a brilliantly vivid, uninhibited style.

Bettina von Arnim, engraving after Armgass von Arnim's copy of a miniature by an unknown artist.

BY COURTESY OF THE TRUSTEES OF THE BRITISH MUSEUM; PHOTOGRAPH, J.R. FREEMAN & CO. LTD.

Arno River River, central Italy. It is 150 mi (240 km) long, flowing west from the APENNINES through FLORENCE and into the Ligurian Sea below PISA. Near Arezzo it is connected with the TIBER RIVER by its canalized tributary, the Chiani. Subject to disastrous floods, in 1966 it inundated Florence and caused extensive damage.

Arnold, Benedict (1741–1801) U.S. army officer and traitor. Born in Norwich, Conn., he joined the American Revolutionary army in 1775. He helped win the Battle of Ticonderoga and led the victories at Fort Stanwix, N.Y., and at the Battle of Saratoga, where he was seriously wounded. He was made a major general and placed in command of Philadelphia, where he lived extravagantly and socialized with wealthy Loyalist sympathizers, marrying one in 1779. Reprimanded for fiscal irregularities in his command, he began secret overtures to the British. After receiving command of the fort at West Point, N.Y. (1780), he offered to surrender it to the British for £20,000. The plot was uncovered after his British contact, JOHN ANDRE, was captured. Arnold escaped on a British ship to England, where he died penniless.

Benedict Arnold, engraving by H.B. Hall, 1865.

BY COURTESY OF THE LIBRARY OF CONGRESS, WASHINGTON, D.C.

Arnold, Eddy *orig.* **Richard Edward** (born 1918) U.S. COUNTRY-MUSIC singer. Born in Henderson, Tenn., Arnold grew up on a farm, made his radio debut in 1936, and in 1940 began appearing on the GRAND OLE OPRY with Pee Wee King's Golden West Cowboys. His smooth crooning gave him vast appeal, and in 1948 he had his first crossover hit with "Bouquet of Roses." Many hits followed over the next 10 years, as well as a TV series, and in the 1960s he recorded such hits as "What's He Doing in My World" and "Make the World Go Away" with lush orchestral backgrounds.

Arnold, Hap *orig.* **Henry Harley** (1886–1950) U.S. air force officer. Born in Gladwyne, Pa., he attended West Point and initially served in the infantry. Volunteering as a flyer, he received instruction from ORVILLE WRIGHT. After World War I, with BILLY MITCHELL he became an eloquent advocate of an expanded air force. He rose through the ranks of the U.S. Army Air Corps to become its commander in 1938, and he commanded the Army Air Forces worldwide during World War II, overseeing a massive buildup and greatly influencing air bombardment strategy. He was named general of the army in 1944 and, after the National Defense Act of 1947 created an independent Air Force, general of the Air Force.

Arnold, Matthew (1822–1888) English poet and literary and social critic. Son of the educator THOMAS ARNOLD, he attended Oxford and then worked as an inspector of schools for the rest of his life. His verse includes "Dover Beach," his most celebrated work; "Sohrab and Rustum," a romantic epic; and "The Scholar Gipsy" and "Thyrsis." *Culture and Anarchy* (1869), his central work of criticism, is a masterpiece of ridicule as well as a searching analysis of Victorian society. In a later essay, "The Study of Poetry," he argued that in an age of crumbling creeds, poetry would replace religion, and therefore readers would have to understand how to distinguish the best poetry from the inferior.

Arnold, Thomas *known as* **Dr. Arnold** (1795–1842) British educator. A classical scholar, he became headmaster in 1828 of Rugby School, which was in a state of decline. He revived Rugby by reforming its curriculum, athletics program, and social structure (in the prefect system he introduced, older boys served as house monitors to keep discipline among younger boys), becoming in the process the preeminent figure in British education. In 1841 he was named Regius Professor of Modern History at Oxford. In addition to several volumes of sermons, he wrote a three-volume *History of Rome* (1838–43). He was the father of MATTHEW ARNOLD and grandfather of the novelist Mrs. Humphry Ward (1851–1920).

Thomas Arnold, detail of an engraving by H. Cousins, 1840, after an oil painting by Thomas Philips.

BY COURTESY OF THE TRUSTEES OF THE BRITISH MUSEUM; PHOTOGRAPH, J.R. FREEMAN & CO. LTD.

Arnolfo di Cambio (c. 1245–1302?) Italian sculptor and architect active in Florence. He studied under NICOLA PISANO and assisted him on the pulpit for Siena Cathedral (1265–68). In 1277 he went to Rome, where he worked for Charles of Anjou. His portrait statue of Charles is one of the earliest since ancient times. He also designed and constructed monuments, including the tomb of Cardinal de Braye (died 1282) in San Domenico, Orvieto. A document from 1300 praises Arnolfo as designer of Florence's Duomo (1296) and sculptor of the statues for its facade (now in the cathedral's museum). Other buildings in Florence attributed to him include the Palazzo Vecchio and the church of Santa Croce.

Arnulf (died 899) King of Germany. Originally duke of Carinthia, he was elected king of the East Franks in 887, deposing his uncle, CHARLES THE FAT. The West Franks, Burgundy, and Italy refused to recognize Arnulf, thus dividing the Carolingian empire. He defeated the Vikings (891), ending their raids up the Rhine River, and maintained control of Lotharingia (now LORRAINE). He invaded Italy at the urging of Pope Formosus, captured Rome (895), and was crowned Holy Roman Emperor in 896. Illness forced him to return to Germany, however, and the previous emperor continued to rule. Arnulf's last years saw invasions by Moravia and Hungary and the collapse of his power.

aromatherapy Therapy using essential oils and water-based COLLOIDS extracted from plant materials to promote physical, emotional, and spiritual health and balance. Single or combined extracts may be diffused into inhaled air, used in massage oil, or added to bathwater. Inhaled molecules of these extracts stimulate the olfactory nerve, sending messages to the brain's limbic system (the seat of memory, learning, and emotion) that are said to trigger physiological responses (e.g., eucalyptus relieves congestion, lavender promotes relaxation). Mainstream medical practitioners question the claim of independent physiological effects; they consider many of the benefits more likely due to the conditioned responses that odors can reinforce or help create. The oils and solutions used have been shown to have certain effects but are not standardized. The few risks involved include allergic reactions.

aromatic compound Any of a large class of organic compounds whose molecular structure includes one or more planar rings of atoms, usually but not always six CARBON atoms. The ring's carbon-carbon bonds (see BONDING) are neither single nor double but a type characteristic of these compounds, in which electrons are shared equally with all the atoms around the ring in an electron cloud. The term was first applied c. 1860 to a class of HYDROCARBONS isolated from coal tar and distinguished by odors much stronger than those of other classes of hydrocarbons. In modern chemistry, aromaticity denotes the chemical behavior, especially low reactivity, of this class of molecules related to their bonding. The parent compound of this class is BENZENE (C_6H_6). See also HYDROGENATION.

Aron \är-'ō^{n}\, **Raymond (-Claude-Ferdinand)** (1905–1983) French sociologist and historian. After receiving his doctorate from the École Normale Supérieure (1930), he taught at the University of Toulouse until 1939. During World War II he joined the FREE FRENCH and edited their newspaper (1940–44). He later taught at the École Nationale d'Administration, the Sorbonne, and the Collège de France. He was also a columnist for *Le Figaro* (1947–77) and *L'Express* (1977–83). His opposition to Marxism put him at odds with France's left-wing intellectuals, including his former classmate J.-P. SARTRE. His books often discuss violence and war, from a rationalist humanist point of view.

Aroostook War \ə-'rü-stu̇k\ (1838–39) Bloodless conflict over the disputed boundary between the U.S. state of Maine and the British Canadian province of New Brunswick. As settlers from both countries moved into the disputed Aroostook area, officials and bands of men from both sides made arrests and took prisoners of "trespassers." In 1839 U.S. and Canadian troops were ordered to the area. A truce allowed joint occupancy of the territory until a treaty settlement in 1842 fixed the boundaries.

Arp, Jean *known as* **Hans Arp** (1886–1966) French painter, sculptor, and poet. After studying in Weimar, Germany, and at the Académie Julian in Paris, he became involved in the most important movements of early 20th-century art: Der Blaue Reiter in Munich (1912), Cubism in Paris (1914), Dada in Zurich during World War I, Surrealism (1925), and Abstraction-Creation (1931). He produced polychrome relief carvings in wood, cut-paper compositions, and, in the 1930s, his most distinctive works in sculpture: abstract forms that suggest animals and plants.

Arrabal \,är-rä-'bäl\, **Fernando** (born 1932) Spanish-French absurdist playwright, novelist, and filmmaker. He turned to writing in the 1950s, and in 1955 he began studying drama in Paris, where he remained. His early plays, in particular *Picnic on the Battlefield*, brought him to the attention of the French avant-garde. After the mid-1960s his plays evolved into what he termed Théâtre Panique ("Panic Theater"); typical of this period is *And They Put Handcuffs on the Flowers*. His dramatic and fictional world is often violent, cruel, and pornographic.

arrastra \ə-'ras-trə\ Drag-stone mill for pulverizing ORES to isolate SILVER by the PATIO PROCESS, apparently used in pre-Columbian America. The silver ore was crushed and ground by mule power in the arrastras (shallow circular pits paved with stone). Large blocks of stone attached by beams to a central rotating post were dragged around the arrastra, reducing the ore to a fine mud. Further steps resulted in the isolating of the silver.

arrest Restraint and seizure of a person by someone (e.g., a police officer) acting under legal authority. An officer may arrest a person who is committing or attempting to commit a crime in the officer's presence.

Arrest is also permitted if the officer reasonably believes that a crime has been committed and that the person arrested is the guilty party. A court or judicial officer may issue an arrest warrant on a showing of probable cause. Most states restrict or prohibit arrest in civil (noncriminal) cases; an example of occasionally permitted civil arrest is the taking into custody of a debtor who might otherwise abscond. In the U.S., suspects must be warned of their rights when they are arrested (see *MIRANDA VS. ARIZONA*). An unlawful arrest is regarded as false imprisonment and usually invalidates any evidence collected in connection with the arrest. See also rights of the ACCUSED, GRAND JURY, INDICTMENT.

Arrhenius \är-ˈā-nē-əs\, **Svante (August)** (1859–1927) Swedish physical chemist. His theories on DISSOCIATION of substances in solution into ELECTROLYTES or IONS, first published in 1884 as his PhD thesis, were initially met with skepticism, but increasing recognition abroad gradually won over the opposition in Sweden. He also did important work on REACTION RATES; the equation describing the dependence of reaction rates on temperature is often called the Arrhenius law, and he was the first to recognize the GREENHOUSE EFFECT. After receiving the Royal Society of London's Davy Medal (1902), he became in 1903 the third recipient of the Nobel Prize for Chemistry. He is regarded as one of the founders of the field of physical chemistry.

Svante Arrhenius, 1918.

BY COURTESY OF THE KUNGLIGA BIBLIOTEKET, STOCKHOLM

arrhythmia See CARDIAC ARRHYTHMIA

arrow See BOW AND ARROW

Arrow, Kenneth J(oseph) (born 1921) U.S. economist. Born in New York City, he received his PhD from Columbia University and taught principally at Stanford and Harvard. His books include *Social Choices and Individual Values* (1951). His most striking claim was that, under certain conditions of rationality and equality, a ranking of societal preferences will not necessarily correspond to the rankings of individual preferences, given more than two individuals and alternative choices. In 1972 he shared the Nobel Prize with JOHN R. HICKS.

Arrow War See OPIUM WARS

arrowroot Any of several plant species of the genus *Maranta* (family Marantaceae), whose RHIZOMES yield an edible starch. Chief among these is the herbaceous perennial *M. arundinacea,* the source of genuine, or West Indies, arrowroot. The powder obtained from the harvested roots is almost pure starch; it is used in cookery as a thickener. Arrowroot is easily digested and is used in diets requiring bland, low-salt, and low-protein foods. Its name is sometimes applied to starches obtained from other plants and used as substitutes for true arrowroot. Brazilian arrowroot, from the CASSAVA plant, is the source of tapioca.

Ars Antiqua \ˈärs-an-ˈtē-kwə\ (Latin: "the Old Art") Musical style of the 13th century, as retrospectively distinguished from that of the 14th cent (ARS NOVA), beginning with the NOTRE-DAME SCHOOL. It is partly characterized by use of the six rhythmic modes, each being a rhythmic pattern that would recur throughout a piece, such as long-short (first mode) or short-long (second). Akin to the "feet" of poetry (see PROSODY), the relative lengths of long and short depended on the mode. The system broke down as composers began to use subdivisions of the short note. The musical genres of the Ars Antiqua included ORGANUM and the early MOTET.

Ars Nova \ˈärs-ˈnō-və\ (Latin: "the New Art") Musical style of the 14th century. As composers began to use ever shorter notes in their music, the old system of rhythmic modes (see ARS ANTIQUA) ceased to be adequate to describe it. In 1323, in his treatise *Ars nova*, Philippe de Vitry (1291–1361) proposed a way of relating longer and shorter notes by a metrical scheme, the ancestor of time signatures, whereby each note value could be subdivided into either two or three of the next-shorter note. Though seemingly abstract, this innovation had a marked effect on the sound of music because composers were better able to control the relative motion of several voices, and 14th-century music consequently sounds much less "medieval" to modern ears. G. DE MACHAUT and F. LANDINI are the principal composers of the Ars Nova. See also FORMES FIXES.

Arsacid dynasty \är-ˈsas-id\ (247 BC–AD 224) Persian dynasty founded by Arsaces (r.c. 250–211? BC) of the Parni tribe, which lived east of the Caspian Sea and entered PARTHIA after the death of ALEXANDER THE GREAT (323 BC), gradually extending control southward. Arsacid power reached its peak under Mithradates I (r.171–138 BC). The government was influenced by that of the SELEUCID DYNASTY and tolerated the formation of vassal kingdoms. The dynasty legitimized its rule over former ACHAEMENIAN territories by claiming descent from the Achaemenian king Artaxerxes II. It controlled trade routes between Asia and the Greco-Roman world and used its resultant wealth to erect many buildings. The dynasty was overthrown in 224 by the SASANIAN DYNASTY.

arsenic Nonmetallic to semimetallic chemical ELEMENT, chemical symbol As, atomic number 33. It exists uncombined in two stable (and several unstable) ALLOTROPES, one gray and one yellow, but is more usually found in nature as the sulfide or OXIDE. The elemental form is used to form ALLOYS of METALS (especially lead), and SEMICONDUCTORS are made from crystals of gallium arsenide (GaAs). Arsenious oxide (arsenic trioxide or white arsenic, As_2O_3), is used in pesticides, as a pigment, and as a preservative of hides and wood; this is the poisonous "arsenic" (see ARSENIC POISONING) in detective stories. Arsenic pentoxide (As_2O_5) is also used in insecticides, herbicides, metal adhesives, and pigments.

Arsenic (gray) with realgar (red) and orpiment (yellow).

BY COURTESY OF THE JOSEPH AND HELEN GUETTERMAN COLLECTION; PHOTOGRAPH, JOHN H. GERARD

arsenic poisoning Harmful effects of ARSENIC compounds (in pesticides, chemotherapy drugs, paints, etc.), most often from INSECTICIDE exposure. Susceptibility varies. Arsenic is believed to combine with certain enzymes, interfering with cellular metabolism. Symptoms of acute arsenic poisoning include nausea and abdominal pain followed by circulatory collapse. Acute exposure to the gas arsine causes destruction of red blood cells and kidney damage; chronic exposure causes weakness, skin disorders, anemia, and nervous-system disorders. Arsenic in urine and hair or nails is the key to diagnosis. Treatment involves washing out the stomach and promptly administering the antidote dimercaprol.

Arsinoe II \är-ˈsin-ō-ē\ (316?–270 BC) Daughter of PTOLEMY I SOTER and queen of THRACE (300–281) and of Egypt (277–270). She married the king of Thrace (300) and tried to have her son made heir instead of Agathocles, the king's son by an earlier marriage. Agathocles sought help from SELEUCIDS, causing a war in which Arsinoe's husband was killed in battle. Her half brother, who took power in Thrace and Macedonia, cajoled her into marrying him and then promptly killed her two younger sons. She fled to Alexandria, ousted the wife of her brother PTOLEMY II, and married him (c. 277); like the pharaohs, the two were called "Philadelphoi" ("Sibling-loving"). She wielded great power and shared many honors with Ptolemy, including deification while alive.

Arsinoe II, coin, 270–250 BC; in the British Museum.

BY COURTESY OF THE TRUSTEES OF THE BRITISH MUSEUM

arson Crime of willfully, wrongfully, and unjustifiably setting property on fire, often for the purpose of committing fraud (e.g., on an insurance company). In nearly all countries but Britain, the arsonist may be charged with murder if arson causes death. Germany and some U.S. states also impose serious penalties for arson if committed to conceal or destroy evidence of another crime. A fire caused by accident or ordinary carelessness is not arson, but people who act in reckless disregard of the consequences of their actions may be guilty of arson.

art Combination of skill and imagination in the creation of objects, environments, or experiences. The term also designates modes of expression such as painting, drawing, sculpture, filmmaking, music, dance, poetry, theater, architecture, ceramics, and decorative arts, collectively known as the arts.

art, academy of Professional institution established by artists and scholars for the instruction and exhibition of its members' works. The first true art academy was the Accademia del Disegno (1563), founded by Cosimo I de' Medici in Florence, with Michelangelo and Cosimo at its head. After the Italian Renaissance, the decline of the church and the aristocracy as patrons gave rise to state-supported academies that came to control public taste and the economic fortunes of artists throughout Europe. 19th-century artists, including eventually the Impressionists, succeeded in winning critical acclaim outside the official institutions. The academy as a place of instruction became synonymous with the modern art school.

art brut \ˌärt-ˈbrüt, ȧr-ˈbrᵫt\ (French: "raw art") Art produced by people outside the established art world, particularly crude, inexperienced, or obscene works created by the psychotic or untrained. The term was coined by Jean Dubuffet, who regarded such works as the purest form of expression. See also naive art.

art collection Works of art accumulated by an individual or institution. Such collections were made in the earliest civilizations; precious objects were stored in temples, tombs, sanctuaries, and palaces. A taste for collecting developed in Greece (4th–1st century BC). The great art collections of the world grew out of private collections formed by royalty, aristocracy, and the wealthy. By the 18th century, collectors were donating their holdings to the public and constructing buildings to house them (e.g., the Louvre Museum, Uffizi Gallery). Wealthy industrialists in the U.S. played a prominent role in the 19th–20th century, and an unprecedented flow of masterpieces from Europe soon filled U.S. museums.

art conservation and restoration Maintenance and preservation of works of art, their protection from future damage, deterioration, or neglect, and the repair or renovation of works that have deteriorated or been damaged. Research in art history has relied heavily on 20th-century technical and scientific advances in art restoration.

art criticism Description, interpretation, and evaluation of works of art, manifested in journal reviews, books, the patronage of artists, and the public and private collection of their works. Art criticism encompasses a wide variety of approaches, from critical commentary to more subjective emotional reactions inspired by viewing works of art. The establishment of commercial art galleries in the 19th century and of newspapers with wide circulations allowed art critics to function as tastemakers for the art-buying middle class. In the 20th century, perceptive critics became champions of new artistic movements.

Art Deco \ˌärt-ˈde-kō, ˌär-dā-ˈkō\ *or* **Style Moderne** \ˈstēl-mȯ-ˈdern\ Movement in design, interior decoration, and architecture in the 1920s and '30s in Europe and the U.S. The name derives from the Exposition Internationale des Arts Décoratifs et Industriels Modernes in Paris in 1925. Influenced by Art Nouveau, Bauhaus, Cubist, Native American, and Egyptian sources, it was initially a luxury style featuring simple geometric shapes and expensive materials (including jade, silver, ivory, lacquer, and chrome) that expressed wealth and sophistication. During the Great Depression, emphasis was also given to materials that could be economically mass-produced, such as Bakelite. Typical motifs included stylized animals, foliage, nude female figures, and sun rays.

Art Ensemble of Chicago U.S. jazz ensemble, innovators in free jazz. The group evolved from the Association for the Advancement of Creative Musicians (AACM), an experimental collective. Saxophonists Roscoe Mitchell and Joseph Jarman, trumpeter Lester Bowie, bassist Malachi Favors, and drummer Don Moye formed the group in 1969, combining freely changing tempos, dynamics, and textures with an often comic theatricality of presentation. Their diversity of inspiration is expressed by their motto, "Great Black Music—Ancient to Modern."

art history Historical study of the visual arts for the purpose of identifying, describing, evaluating, interpreting, and understanding art objects and artistic traditions. Art-historical research involves discovering and collecting biographical data on artists to establish attribution; determining at what stage in a culture's or artist's development an object was made; weighing the influence the object or artist had on the historical past; and documenting an object's previous whereabouts or ownership (provenance). The analysis of symbols, themes, and subject matter is of primary concern.

Art Institute of Chicago Museum in Chicago that houses European, American, Asian, African, and pre-Columbian art. It was established in 1866 as the Chicago Academy of Design and took its current name in 1882. In 1893 it moved to its present building, designed by the architectural firm of Shepley, Rutan, and Coolidge for the World's Columbian Exposition, on Michigan Avenue. The Art Institute, which comprises both a museum and a school, is noted for its extensive collections of 19th-century French painting (Impressionist works and the work of Claude Monet in particular) and 20th-century European and American painting. Among its best-known works are Georges Seurat's *A Sunday Afternoon on La Grand Jatte—1884* (1884–86), Grant Wood's *American Gothic* (1930), and Edward Hopper's *Nighthawks* (1942).

Art Nouveau \ˌärt-nü-ˈvō, ˌär-nü-ˈvō\ ("New Art") Decorative style that flourished in Western Europe and the U.S. c. 1890–1910. The term was derived in 1895 from a gallery in Paris called L'Art Nouveau. Characterized by sinuous, asymmetrical lines based on plant forms, the style was used in architecture, interior design, graphic art and design, jewelry, and glass. It was international in scope, with celebrated exponents in England (A. Beardsley), Paris (A. Mucha), the U.S. (Louis Comfort Tiffany), Scotland (Charles Rennie Mackintosh), Spain (A. Gaudí), and Belgium (V. Horta). The style did not significantly survive the outbreak of World War I. See also Arts and Crafts Movement, Jugendstil.

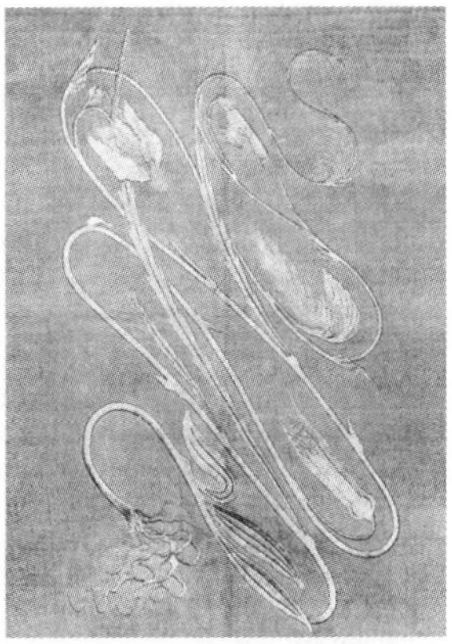
"The Whiplash," Art Nouveau tapestry by Hermann Obrist, silk embroidered on wool, 1895; in the Münchner Stadtmuseum, Munich.
BY COURTESY OF THE MUNCHNER STADTMUSEUM, MUNICH

Arta, Gulf of Inlet of the Ionian Sea, western Greece. It is 25 mi (40 km) long and 4–10 mi (6–16 km) wide. On its shores are the ruins of several cities important in ancient Greece. The seaport of Preveza, founded 290 BC, is to the north; the Battle of Actium took place near the gulf's entrance.

Artaud \ȧr-ˈtō\, **Antonin** (1896–1948) French poet, actor, and drama theorist. He wrote surrealist poetry from 1925 and made his acting debut in surrealist productions in Paris. He described his theory of drama in the *Manifesto of the Theatre of Cruelty* (1932) (see theater of cruelty) and *The Theatre and Its Double* (1938). His own plays (including *Les Cenci*, 1935) were failures, but his theories exerted great influence on playwrights of the theater of the absurd. Lifelong mental illness confined him periodically to asylums from 1936.

Artaud, 1948.
DENISE COLOMB–J.P. ZIOLO

Artemis \ˈär-tə-məs\ In Greek religion, the goddess of wild animals, the hunt, vegetation, chastity, and childbirth. Artemis was the daughter of Zeus and Leto and the twin sister of Apollo. Accompanied by nymphs, she danced in mountains and forests. She both killed game and, as Mistress of Animals (see Master of the Animals), protected it. Stories of her nymphs' love affairs may originally have been told of the goddess herself, but poets after Homer stressed her chastity. She was known for her unpitying wrath when offended. Artemis may have developed out of ISHTAR in the East. Her Roman counterpart was DIANA.

Artemis as a huntress, classical sculpture; in the Louvre.
ALINARI—ART RESOURCE/EB INC.

artemisia \ˌär-tə-ˈmi-zhə\ Any of a genus *(Artemisia)* of aromatic herbs and shrubs in the COMPOSITE FAMILY. Examples include wormwood, SAGEBRUSH, and TARRAGON. Many *Artemisia* species are valued as ornamentals for their attractive silvery-gray foliage, which is frequently used in horticultural plantings to create contrast or smooth the transition between intense colors. The leaves of common wormwood *(A. absinthium)* have been used in medicines and beverages such as absinthe and vermouth. An extract from the Eurasian *A. annua* is used to treat quinine-resistant malaria.

Artemisia I \ˌärt-ə-ˈmiz-ē-ə\ (died c. 450 BC) Queen of HALICARNASSUS and of the island of Cos c. 480 BC. She ruled under the Persian king XERXES, and helped him invade Greece (480–479). She commanded five ships in the Battle of SALAMIS; according to HERODOTUS, she advised Xerxes to retreat from Greece rather than risk another engagement.

Artemisia II (died c. 350 BC) Sister and wife of King MAUSOLUS (r.377?–353? BC) of Caria, southwestern Anatolia, and sole ruler for about three years after his death. She built his tomb, the Mausoleum, considered one of the SEVEN WONDERS OF THE WORLD. She was also known as a botanist and medical researcher; the plant genus *Artemisia* is named for her.

Artemisia II, statue by an unknown artist; in the National Archeological Museum, Naples.
ANDERSON—ALINARI FROM ART RESOURCE

arteriography See ANGIOGRAPHY

arteriosclerosis \är-ˌtir-ē-ō-sklə-ˈrō-səs\ *or* **hardening of the arteries** Chronic disease characterized by abnormal thickening of the walls of the ARTERIES. In atherosclerosis, its major form, fatty deposits (called atheromas) of CHOLESTEROL form on arterial inner walls. These thicken, forming plaques that narrow the vessel channel (lumen) and impede blood flow. Scarring and calcification make the walls less elastic, raising blood pressure. Eventually, plaques may completely block a lumen, or a blood clot (thrombus) may obstruct a narrowed channel. Atherosclerosis of one or more coronary arteries can decrease the heart muscle's blood supply, causing ANGINA PECTORIS. Complete blockage causes MYOCARDIAL INFARCTION. Treatments include CORONARY BYPASS and balloon ANGIOPLASTY. In the brain, arteriosclerosis may result in STROKE. In leg arteries, it may cause intermittent lameness, pain, and ulceration, with increased risk of infection.

arteritis \ˌär-tə-ˈrī-təs\ INFLAMMATION of the ARTERIES. It occurs in diseases including SYPHILIS, TUBERCULOSIS, and LUPUS ERYTHEMATOSUS. Varieties not closely associated with systemic disease or disease of an organ outside the cardiovascular system have been described: thromboangiitis obliterans; temporal arteritis; polymyalgia rheumatica; aortic arch arteritis; and polyarteritis nodosa.

artery Vessel that carries blood from the heart to other parts of the body (see CARDIOVASCULAR SYSTEM). Arterial blood carries oxygen and nourishment to tissues; the one exception is the pulmonary artery, which conveys oxygen-depleted blood from the heart to the lungs for oxygenation and removal of excess carbon dioxide. Arteries are muscular, elastic tubes that transport blood under the pressure of the heart's pumping action, which can be felt as the PULSE. Large arteries branch off from the AORTA and give rise to smaller arteries, down to the threadlike arterioles, which branch into CAPILLARIES. An artery wall's inner layer (tunica intima) consists of an endothelial (cellular) lining, a fine connective tissue network, and a layer of elastic fibers. The middle layer (tunica media) is mostly smooth muscle cells. The outer layer (tunica externa) contains supportive collagen fibers. See also VEIN.

arthritis \är-ˈthrī-təs\ INFLAMMATION of the JOINTS and its effects. Acute arthritis is marked by pain, redness, and swelling. The principal forms are OSTEOARTHRITIS, RHEUMATOID ARTHRITIS, and SEPTIC ARTHRITIS. Several forms of arthritis are part of the symptom complexes of AUTOIMMUNE DISEASES.

arthropod Any member of the largest phylum (Arthropoda) in the ANIMAL kingdom, consisting of more than a million known INVERTEBRATE species in four subphyla: Uniramia (five classes, including INSECTS), Chelicerata (three classes, including ARACHNIDS and HORSESHOE CRABS), Crustacea (CRUSTACEANS), and Trilobita (TRILOBITES). All arthropods are bilaterally symmetrical and possess a segmented body covered by an exoskeleton containing CHITIN, which serves as both armor and a surface for muscle attachment; each body segment may bear a pair of jointed appendages. The phylum includes CARNIVORES, HERBIVORES, OMNIVORES, detritus feeders, filter feeders, and parasites (see PARASITISM) in nearly all environments, both aquatic and terrestrial. See illustration on following page.

Arthur, Chester A(lan) (1829–1886) 21st president of the U.S. (1881–85). Born in North Fairfield, Vt., he practiced law in New York City from 1854. He became active in local Republican politics and a close associate of ROSCOE CONKLING, and was appointed customs collector for the port of New York (1871–78), an office long known for its employment of the spoils system. He conducted the business of the office with integrity but continued to pad its payroll with Conkling loyalists. At the Republican national convention in 1880, Arthur became the compromise choice for vice president on the ticket with JAMES GARFIELD, and became president on Garfield's assassination. As president, Arthur displayed unexpected independence by vetoing measures that rewarded political patronage. He also signed the PENDLETON ACT, which created a civil-service system based on merit. He and his navy secretary recommended the appropriations that initiated the rebuilding of the U.S. Navy toward the strength it achieved in the SPANISH-AMERICAN WAR. He failed to win his party's nomination for a second term.

Arthurian legend Body of stories and medieval romances centering on the legendary English king Arthur. The stories chronicle Arthur's life, the adventures of his knights, and the adulterous love between his knight Sir LANCELOT and his queen, Guinevere. The legend was popular in Wales before the 11th century, was brought into literature by GEOFFREY OF MONMOUTH, and was adapted by other medieval writers, including CHRÉTIEN DE TROYES, WACE, LAYAMON, and SIR THOMAS MALORY, becoming entwined with legends of the GRAIL. From Victorian times, when interest in the legend revived, it has figured in major works by ALFRED TENNYSON *(Idylls of the King)* and T.H. WHITE *(The Once and Future King)*. It is uncertain whether Arthur was a historical figure. Medieval sources say he was a 6th-century warrior and champion of Christianity, who united the British tribes against the Saxon invaders, died in battle at Camlann c. 539, and was buried at Glastonbury. See also GALAHAD, MERLIN, TRISTAN AND ISOLDE.

Arthur's Pass Mountain pass, SOUTHERN ALPS, New Zealand. It lies at the Alps' northern end, at an altitude of 3,031 ft (924 m) and provides the only railway and highway passage, with the rail line passing through the Otira Tunnel (5.3 mi, or 8.6 km). It now forms part of a national park.

Artibonite River \ˌär-tē-bȯ-ˈnēt\ River, Hispaniola Island. Rising in the Cordillera Central of the Dominican Republic, it flows along the Haitian border and then west and northwest into and through Haiti's Artibonite Plain to enter the Gulf of Gonaïves after a course of some 150 mi (240 km). It is the island's longest river.

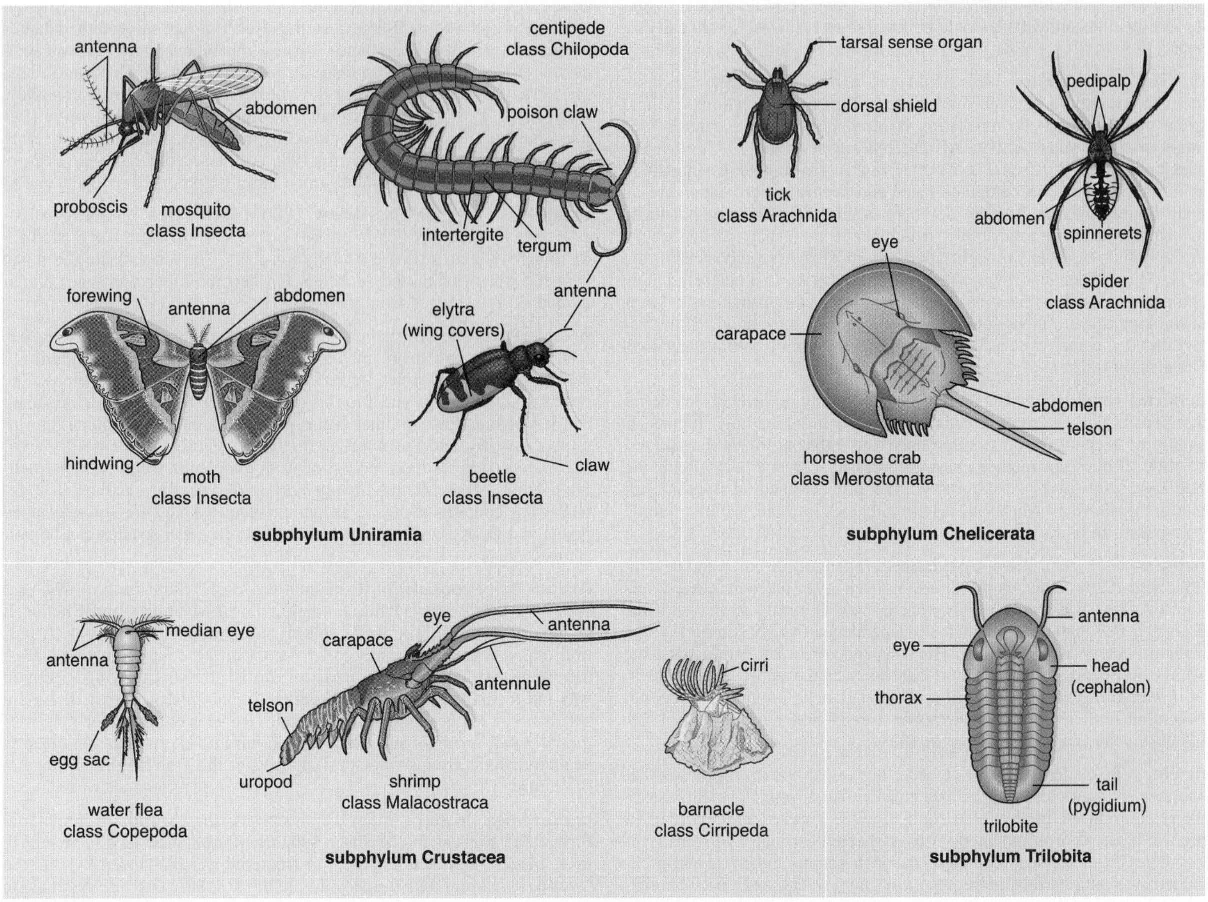

Representative arthropods. Uniramia, the largest of the arthropod subphyla, contains mostly terrestrial insects and myriapods (incl. centipedes and millipedes). The insects, the largest arthropod class, differ from other arthropods in that they are usually winged and have only three pairs of legs. Members of the Crustacea subphylum are mostly marine-dwelling and include the shrimp, lobsters, crabs, and barnacles. The microscopic water fleas are chiefly found in freshwater, and along with other minute members of this subphylum are part of the zooplankton. Most members of the Chelicerata subphylum are arachnids (class Arachnida), incl. the spiders, scorpions, ticks, and mites. The trilobites are extinct marine arthropods that flourished during the Cambrian period. Fossilized remains show a body having three longitudinal lobes divided into three regions consisting of a head, thorax, and tail region.

artichoke Large, coarse, herbaceous, thistlelike perennial plant *(Cynara scolymus)* of the COMPOSITE FAMILY. The thick edible scales and bottom part (heart) of the immature flower heads are a culinary delicacy. The artichoke is native to the Mediterranean and is cultivated extensively in other regions with rich soil and a mild, humid climate. The JERUSALEM ARTICHOKE is a TUBER and does not resemble the artichoke.

Articles of Confederation Early U.S. constitution (1781–89) that bridged the initial government by the First CONTINENTAL CONGRESS and the federal government provided under the U.S. CONSTITUTION of 1787. It provided for a confederation of sovereign states and gave the Congress power to regulate foreign affairs, war, and the postal service, to control Indian affairs, and to borrow money. Under the Articles, Congress settled state claims to western lands and established the NORTHWEST ORDINANCE. But Congress had no power to enforce its requests to the states for money or troops, and governmental effectiveness broke down by late 1786. Delegates to the ANNAPOLIS CONVENTION called a meeting of all the states to amend the Articles.

articulation In PHONETICS, the shaping of the vocal tract (LARYNX, PHARYNX, and oral and nasal cavities) by positioning mobile organs such as the tongue relative to other parts that may be rigid, such as the hard palate, and hence modifying the airstream to produce SPEECH sounds. Articulators include the tongue, lips, teeth and upper gum ridge, hard and soft palate, uvula, pharyngeal wall, and glottis. Primary articulation refers either to where or how the vocal tract is narrowed or blocked to produce a CONSONANT, or to the tongue contour, lip shape, and larynx height that determine the sound of a vowel. Other articulators may be used to produce a secondary articulation such as palatalization (the front of the tongue approaching the hard palate), glottalization (complete or partial closure of the vocal cords), or nasalization (simultaneous passage of air through the nasal and oral tracts).

artificial heart Machine or mechanical pump that maintains blood circulation in the human body. The heart-lung machine, a mechanical pump, can maintain circulation for a few hours while the heart is stopped for surgery. It shunts blood away from the heart, oxygenates it, and returns it to the body. No device has yet been developed for total, long-term replacement of the heart; existing artificial hearts reduce the heart's workload by pumping between beats or acting as an auxiliary ventricle and are suitable only as temporary replacements in patients awaiting transplant. See also PACEMAKER.

artificial insemination Introduction of semen into a female's vagina or cervix by means other than sexual intercourse. First developed for animal breeding in the early 20th century in Russia, it is now also used to induce pregnancy in women whose partners cannot impregnate them. The partner's (or other donor's) semen is inserted with a syringe. Though reasonably successful, artificial insemination in humans raises moral issues that are not yet fully resolved. In livestock, deep-frozen semen from a male animal can be stored for long periods without losing its fertility, thus allowing a single bull to sire as many as 10,000 calves a year.

artificial intelligence (AI) Ability of a machine to perform tasks thought to require human intelligence. Typical applications include game playing, language translation by computers, fault diagnosis (see EXPERT SYSTEMS), and ROBOTICS. AI research began in the 1940s with the development of the DIGITAL COMPUTER. It has grown and developed at about the same rate as computer speed and sophistication, which are its main limiting factors. The development of computer memories containing circuits that are comparable in number to the synaptic connections in the human brain has brought about the most striking advances in the field. The challenge driving AI research today is to understand how computer capabilities must be organized in order to reproduce the kinds of thinking that are thought to be uniquely human, such as visual PATTERN RECOGNITION, complex decision making, and the use of natural language. See also TURING TEST.

artificial respiration Breathing induced by any of several techniques in a person who has stopped or is having difficulty breathing. It consists chiefly of keeping the air passage open and inducing inhalation and exhalation. It does not include chest compressions to maintain circulation (see CARDIOPULMONARY RESUSCITATION). The primary method is mouth-to-mouth breathing, in which the rescuer breathes into the victim's mouth, with pauses to allow exhalation.

Artigas \är-ˈtē-gäs\, **José Gervasio** (1764–1850) Soldier and revolutionary leader regarded as the father of Uruguayan independence. In his youth Artigas was a GAUCHO in what is now Uruguay. Allied with the Buenos Aires junta, he fought for independence from Spain and won a brilliant victory at Las Piedras. His insistence on federalism against the efforts of Buenos Aires to assert control over the entire region led to civil war. He ruled over a portion of what is now Uruguay and central Argentina until a Portuguese invasion forced him into exile in 1820. Uruguay achieved independence in 1828.

artillery In modern military science, big GUNS, howitzers, or MORTARS operated by crews and of a caliber greater than 15 mm. The earliest artillery, introduced in the 14th century, were CANNON and mortars of bronze, brass, or iron mounted on two-wheeled carriages. Modern artillery dates from the second half of the 19th century, when advances included steel gun barrels, more powerful gunpowders, and piston mountings that held artillery carriages steady during recoil. Both powder and projectile were encased in a SHELL, which allowed for faster loading. Since World War II, artillery has been ranked as light (up to 105 mm, for support of ground troops), medium (106–155 mm, for bombardment), and heavy (over 155 mm, for attacking rear installations). See also ANTIAIRCRAFT GUNS.

Arts and Crafts Movement English social and aesthetic movement of the second half of the 19th century, dedicated to reestablishing the importance of craftsmanship in an era of mechanization and mass production. The name derives from the Arts and Crafts Exhibition Society (1888). Inspired by JOHN RUSKIN and other writers who deplored the effects of industrialization, WILLIAM MORRIS founded a firm of interior designers and manufacturers to produce handcrafted textiles, printed books, WALLPAPER, furniture, jewelry, and metalwork. The movement was criticized as elitist and impractical in an industrial society, but in the 1890s its appeal widened and spread to other countries, including the U.S. See also ART NOUVEAU.

Aru Islands \ˈä-ˌrü\ Island group, eastern Indonesia. The easternmost island group of the MOLUCCAS, located off southwestern NEW GUINEA, the Arus consist of one large island and about 90 small ones. The main island, Tanabesan, is about 120 mi (195 km) long and is divided into six sections by narrow channels. Dobo, on Wamar Island, is the principal harbor. The islands became part of Indonesia in 1949.

Aruba Island (pop., 1994: 72,000), Lesser ANTILLES, off northwestern Venezuela. Aruba is an internally self-governing part of the Netherlands. It has an area of 70 sq mi (180 sq km). Its capital is ORANJESTAD. Most of the present-day population is a combination of Amerindian, Spanish, and Dutch, with traces of African stocks. Dutch is its official language; Papiamento, a creole language, is used for daily affairs. The principal religion is Roman Catholicism. Its currency is the Aruban florin. Aruba's lack of water severely limits agriculture. Its petroleum-refining complex, among the world's largest, was the main source of employment until it closed in 1985. Since then, tourism has become the island's economic mainstay. The island's earliest inhabitants were ARAWAK Indians, whose cave drawings can still be seen. Though the Dutch took possession of Aruba in 1636, they did not begin to develop it aggressively until 1816. The Netherlands controls Aruba's defense and foreign affairs, but internal affairs are handled by an island government directing its own judiciary and currency. In 1986 Aruba seceded from the Federation of the NETHERLANDS ANTILLES, in an initial step toward independence.

arugula \ə-ˈrü-gə-lə\ *or* **rocket** Yellowish-flowered European herbaceous plant *(Eruca vesicaria sativa)* of the MUSTARD FAMILY cultivated for its foliage, which is used especially in salads. The leaves taste sharp and peppery when young and succulent but become bitter with age. A medicinal oil is extracted from the seeds.

arum family \ˈar-əm\ Family Araceae, containing about 2,000 species, that is rich in popular ornamentals and foliage plants native primarily to the tropics and subtropics. A few species grow in temperate zones. The genera *Philodendron* and *Monstera* are grown for their vinelike habit and large green leaves. Other arums grown ornamentally include the florist's CALLA lily and the water arum *(Calla palustris)*. JACK-IN-THE-PULPIT *(Arisaema triphyllum)* is well known in woodlands, and the foul-smelling eastern SKUNK CABBAGE *(Symplocarpus foetidus)* in marshes. The genus *Arum* contains about 15 perennial species noted for funnel-shaped bracts and glossy, arrow-shaped leaves. Sap in *Arum* species can be poisonous.

Arunachal Pradesh \ˈär-ü-ˌnä-chəl-prə-ˈdesh\ State (pop., 1994 est.: 965,000), northeastern India, bordering Tibet, Myanmar, and Bhutan. It occupies 32,269 sq mi (83,577 sq km) and its capital is ITANAGAR. A portion of the region was annexed by ASSAM in the 16th century. By 1826 the British had made Assam part of British India. In 1954 the region was known as the North East Frontier Agency and was part of Assam state; in 1987 it became a separate state. It incorporates major ranges of the HIMALAYA foothills and has a rugged terrain. The population consists of many ethnic groups who speak dialects of the Tibeto-Burman linguistic family.

arupa-loka \ä-ˌrü-pə-ˈlō-kə\ In BUDDHISM, the "world of immaterial form," the highest of the three spheres of existence in which rebirth takes place. The others are the "fine-material world" (RUPA-LOKA) and the "world of feeling" *(kama-loka)*. In the arupa-loka, existence depends on the stage of concentration attained in the previous life, of which there are four levels: the infinity of space, the infinity of thought, the infinity of nonbeing, and the infinity of neither consciousness nor nonconsciousness. Beings in the arupa-loka do not have a material body.

Arusha National Park Preserve, northern Tanzania. Established in 1960, the park contains a rich variety of flora and fauna. It is the site of Mount Meru (14,954 ft, or 4,558 m) and Ngurdoto Crater, an extinct volcano. Nearby are Mount KILIMANJARO, OLDUVAI GORGE, and Ngorongoro Crater, whose surrounding area teems with wildlife.

Aryan \ˈar-ē-ən\ Prehistoric people that settled in Iran and northern India. In the 19th century there arose a notion, propagated by the Comte de GOBINEAU and later by his disciple HOUSTON STEWART CHAMBERLAIN, of an "Aryan race": people who spoke INDO-EUROPEAN, especially GERMANIC, languages and lived in northern Europe. These Aryans were considered to be superior to all other races. Though repudiated by numerous scholars, including FRANZ BOAS, the notion was seized on by ADOLF HITLER and made the basis of the Nazi policy of exterminating Jews, Gypsies, and other "non-Aryans." See also RACISM.

Arya Samaj \ˈär-yə-sä-ˈmäj\ Reform sect of HINDUISM, founded in 1875 by DAYANANDA SARASVATI, in order to reestablish the VEDAS as revealed and infallible truth. The Arya Samaj opposes idolatry, ANCESTOR WORSHIP, animal SACRIFICE, a CASTE system based on birth rather than merit, untouchability (see UNTOUCHABLE), child marriage, PILGRIMAGES, and temple offerings. It upholds the sanctity of the cow, SAMSKARAS, oblations to fire, and social reform, including the education of women. Strongest in western and northern India, it is governed by representatives elected to *samajas* ("societies") at the local, provincial, and national levels, and it played an important role in the growth of Indian nationalism.

Asad, Hafiz al- See Hafiz al-ASSAD

ASALA *in full* **Armenian Secret Army to Liberate Armenia** Marxist-Leninist terrorist group formed in 1975 to force the Turkish government to acknowledge the ARMENIAN MASSACRES of 1915 and pay reparations. Its activities have been directed against Turkish government officials and institutions. Its founder, Hagop Hagopian, was killed in 1988. It has been relatively inactive in recent years.

Asam \'äz-äm\, **Cosmas Damian and Egid Quirin** (1686–1739, 1692–1750) Bavarian architects, decorators, and brothers. After studying in Rome (1711–13), Cosmas Damian became a prolific fresco painter and Egid Quirin a sculptor and stuccoist. They developed the effects of dramatic lighting and illusionism originated by GIAN LORENZO BERNINI and Andrea Pozzo. Working as a team, they produced magnificent illusionistic decoration, combining dramatic lighting and color, in ecclesiastical buildings. Their most notable collaboration, the church of St. John Nepomuk in Munich (1729–46)—known as the Asamkirche, as it was owned by them and attached to Egid Quirin's house—is a masterpiece of Bavarian Rococo style.

asbestos Any of several minerals that separate readily into long, flexible fibers. CHRYSOTILE accounts for about 95% of all asbestos still in commercial use. The other types all belong to the AMPHIBOLE group and include the highly fibrous forms of ANTHOPHYLLITE, AMOSITE, CROCIDOLITE, tremolite, and ACTINOLITE. Asbestos fiber was used in brake linings, insulation, roofing shingles, floor and ceiling tiles, cement pipes, and other building materials. Asbestos fabrics were used for safety apparel and theater curtains. In the 1970s, it was found that prolonged inhalation of the tiny asbestos fibers can cause ASBESTOSIS, lung cancer, and/or mesothelioma, all serious lung diseases. The incidence of mesothelioma is most commonly associated with extensive inhalation of AMPHIBOLE ASBESTOS. In 1989 the U.S. government instituted a gradual ban on the manufacture, use, and export of most products made with asbestos.

asbestos, amphibole See AMPHIBOLE ASBESTOS

asbestosis \ˌas-ˌbes-'tō-səs\ Lung disease caused by long-term inhalation of ASBESTOS fibers. A PNEUMOCONIOSIS found primarily in asbestos workers, asbestosis is also seen in people living near asbestos industries. Fibers remain in the lungs and many years later cause extensive scarring and fibrosis. Shortness of breath and inadequate oxygenation result; advanced cases include a dry cough. There is no effective treatment. The associated increased cardiac effort may induce heart disease. Cigarette smoking greatly exacerbates its symptoms. LUNG CANCER and malignant mesothelioma are more common with asbestos inhalation and asbestosis.

Ascanius \as-'kā-nē-əs\ In Roman legend, the son of AENEAS and founder of Alba Longa (probably the site of modern Castel Gandolfo) near Rome. In LIVY's account, his mother was Lavinia, and he was born after Aeneas founded Lavinium. Ascanius was also called Iulus, and he was considered the founder of the line that included Julius CAESAR.

Ascension In Christian belief, the ascent of JESUS into heaven 40 days after the Resurrection. The Book of Acts relates that, after several appearances to the APOSTLES over a period of 40 days, Jesus was taken up in their presence and hidden behind a cloud, a symbol of God's presence. The event is thought to indicate a new relationship between Jesus and God and between Jesus and his followers. The feast of the Ascension is universally observed by Christians, and its celebration emphasizes the kingship of Christ. Since the 4th century, it has been celebrated 40 days after EASTER and 10 days before PENTECOST.

asceticism \ə-'set-ə-ˌsiz-əm\ Practice of the denial of physical or psychological desires in order to attain a spiritual ideal or goal. Most religions have some features of asceticism. The desire for ritual purity in order to come in contact with the divine, the need for atonement, and the wish to earn merit or gain access to supernatural powers all are reasons for ascetic practice. Christian monastic orders, wandering Hindu ascetics, and Buddhist monks all reject worldly goods and practice various forms of self-denial, including celibacy, abstinence, and fasting. Though MONASTICISM is rejected in the Quran, ascetic movements such as ZUHD have arisen in Islam. ZOROASTRIANISM forbids fasting and mortification.

Asch \'äsh\, **Sholem** (1880–1957) Polish-U.S. novelist and playwright. Much of his writing concerns the experience of Jews in Eastern European villages or as immigrants in the U.S. (to which he himself emigrated in 1914). It includes the play *The God of Vengeance* (1907) and the novels *Mottke the Thief* (1916), *Uncle Moses* (1918), *Judge Not* (1926), and *Chaim Lederer's Return* (1927). In later, more controversial works, he explored the common heritage of Judaism and Christianity. His career was outstanding both for output and impact, and he is one of the best-known writers in modern Yiddish literature.

Ascham \'as-kəm\, **Roger** (1515–1568) English humanist, scholar, and writer. He entered Cambridge University at 14 and studied Greek. He became the future Queen ELIZABETH I's tutor in Greek and Latin (1548–50) and continued to serve her after she took the throne. His best-known book is the posthumous *The Scholemaster* (1570), which deals with the psychology of learning, the education of the whole person, and the ideal moral and intellectual personality that education should mold. He is notable also for his lucid prose style and his promotion of the vernacular.

ASCII \'as-ˌkē\ *in full* **American Standard Code for Information Interchange** Standard DATA-TRANSMISSION code used to represent both text (letters, numbers, punctuation marks) and noninput device commands (control characters). It converts information into standardized digital formats that allow computers to communicate with each other and to process and store data efficiently. Standard ASCII uses groups of seven-digit BITS, and can represent 128 characters. Extended ASCII, which uses an 8-bit encoding system, can represent 256 characters, including many useful characters not available in standard ASCII, such as letters with accents. Extended ASCII is the industrywide standard for encoding text on personal computers. See also EBCDIC, UNICODE.

Asclepius \as-'klē-pē-əs\ *Latin* **Aesculapius** \ˌes-kyə-'lā-pē-əs\ Greco-Roman god of medicine. He was the son of APOLLO and the nymph Coronis. He learned the art of healing from the Centaur CHIRON. Fearful that Asclepius would make humans immortal, ZEUS slew him with a thunderbolt. His cult originated in Thessaly and spread throughout Greece. Because he was said to cure the sick in dreams, the practice of sleeping in his temples became common. Asclepius was often represented holding a staff with a serpent coiled around it.

Asclepius, from an ivory diptych, 5th century AD; in the Liverpool City Museum, England.

THE BRIDGEMAN ART LIBRARY/ART RESOURCE, NY

ascorbic acid See VITAMIN C

ASEAN See ASSOCIATION OF SOUTHEAST ASIAN NATIONS

Asgard \'as-ˌgärd\ In Norse mythology, the dwelling place of the gods. It consisted of 12 or more realms, including VALHALLA, home of ODIN; Thrudheim, home of THOR; and Breidablick, home of BALDER. Each Norse god had his own palace in Asgard. This heavenly region could only be reached from earth via the rainbow bridge called Bifrost.

ash Any tree of the genus *Fraxinus,* in the OLIVE family. The genus includes about 70 species of trees and shrubs found mostly in the Northern Hemisphere. The U.S. boasts 18 species of ash, five of which furnish most of the ash cut as lumber. Most important are the white ash *(F. americana)* and the green ash *(F. pennsylvanica),* which yield wood that is stiff, strong, and resilient, yet lightweight. This "white ash" is used for baseball bats, hockey sticks, paddles and oars, tennis and other racket frames, and the handles of agricultural tools. Black ash *(F. nigra),* blue ash *(F. quadrangulata),* and Oregon ash *(F. latifolia)* produce wood of comparable quality that is used for many more purposes, including furniture, interior paneling, and barrels.

Ash Can school Group of U.S. realist painters active in New York City c. 1908–18, who specialized in scenes of everyday urban life. Inspired by ROBERT HENRI, the core group included WILLIAM GLACKENS,

George Luks (1867–1933), Everett Shinn (1876–1953), and JOHN SLOAN. As artist-reporters on the *Philadelphia Press* before moving to New York, they had developed a quick eye and a memory for detail. Though they often depicted slums and outcasts of the city, they were more interested in the picturesque aspects of these subjects than in the social issues they raised. GEORGE WESLEY BELLOWS and EDWARD HOPPER were also associated with the group. See also The EIGHT.

ash cone See CINDER CONE

Ash Wednesday See LENT

Ashanti People of southern Ghana and adjacent areas of Togo and the Ivory Coast. A section of the AKAN peoples, they speak Twi, a language of the KWA group; they number about 5 million. Though some Ashanti now live and work in urban centers, they remain primarily a village people engaged in agriculture. The symbol of Ashanti unity is the Golden Stool, formerly used as a throne by the paramount chief. The Ashanti supplied slaves to British and Dutch traders in exchange for firearms, which they used to build up a large empire in the 18th–19th century. They fought several wars against the British (1824, 1863, 1869, 1874), finally losing their capital, KUMASI, in 1896. Thereafter what remained of the empire went into decline. Ashanti gold work and kente cloth remain prominent items of trade. See also FANTE.

Ashari \'ä-shȧ-rē\, **Abu al-Hasan al-** (873/874–935/936) Muslim Arab theologian. Born at Basra, Iraq, he probably belonged to the family of Abu Musa al-Ashari, one of the COMPANIONS OF THE PROPHET. He joined the MUTAZILA school and compiled scholarly opinions in his *Maqalat al-Islamiyin* ("Theological Opinions of the Muslims"). At about age 40 he concluded that his method had led to sterile concepts of God and humanity, and turned to more orthodox theology. He expanded his *Maqalat* and authored *Kitab al-Luma* ("The Luminous Book"). Reflecting on the ideas of al-MUHASIBI and others, he created his own school, which became known as the Khorasan or Asharite school. See also ASHARIYA.

Ashariya School of Muslim theology founded by Abu al-Hasan al-ASHARI in the 10th century. It supported the use of reason and speculative theology (KALAM) to defend the faith, but was not as extreme in its rationalism as the MUTAZILA school. Followers attempted to demonstrate the existence and nature of God through rational argument, while affirming the eternal, uncreated nature of the QURAN. They were accused by the Mutazila of believing in predestination because they claimed the human capacity for action was only acquired at the very moment of action.

Ashbery, John (Lawrence) (born 1927) U.S. poet. Born in Rochester, N.Y., he earned degrees from Harvard and Columbia and subsequently became well known as an art critic. His poems, noted for their elegance, originality, and obscurity, are characterized by arresting images, exquisite rhythms, intricate form, and sudden shifts in tone and subject. His collection includes *Turandot and Other Poems* (1953), *Some Trees* (1956), *Rivers and Mountains* (1966), *The Double Dream of Spring* (1970), *Self-Portrait in a Convex Mirror* (1975, Pulitzer Prize, National Book Award), *Houseboat Days* (1977), *A Wave* (1984), *April Galleons* (1987), *Flow Chart* (1991), and *Wakefulness* (1998).

Ashcroft, Peggy *orig.* **Edith Margaret Emily** *later* **Dame Peggy** (1907–1991) British actress. She made her debut in 1927 and appeared from 1932 with the OLD VIC company, winning acclaim in *Romeo and Juliet* (1935). She starred in more than 100 stage productions, playing comedy and tragedy with equal success. One of the great actresses of the British stage, she was a founding member of the ROYAL SHAKESPEARE CO. (1961) and later a director. She acted in such films as *The Thirty-nine Steps* (1935) and *A Passage to India* (1984, Academy Award) and in the television series *The Jewel in the Crown* (1984).

Ashe, Arthur (Robert), Jr. (1943–1993) U.S. tennis player. Born in Richmond, Va., he was recognized early as a tennis prodigy despite being restricted by segregation. After a stellar career at UCLA and important amateur victories, including the U.S. Open (1968), he turned professional. The first black member of the U.S. DAVIS CUP team, he helped win five championships (1963, 1968, 1969, 1970, 1978). In 1975 he won the WIMBLEDON and World Championship Tennis singles events and received top world ranking. He retired in 1980 and became captain of the U.S. Davis Cup team (to 1985). In 1985 he became the first black male inducted into the International Tennis Hall of Fame. Off the court he was a critic of racial injustice, including South Africa's apartheid policy. In 1992 he revealed that he had been infected with the AIDS virus by a transfusion following surgery, and he thereafter devoted time to increasing public awareness of the disease. The U.S. Open is now played at Arthur Ashe Stadium, which opened at the National Tennis Center in Flushing, N.Y., in 1997.

Ashford, Evelyn (born 1957) U.S. sprinter. Born in Shreveport, La., she attended UCLA, where she won four national collegiate championships and competed in the 1976 Olympics in Montreal. She went on to win world championship matches (100- and 200-m sprints) in 1979 and 1981, and was named Woman Athlete of the Year both years. She won two gold medals in the 1984 Olympics (100-m dash, 4 × 100-m relay), and a silver and a gold medal in the 1988 Olympics (in the same events). At the 1992 games, her fifth Olympics, she became the oldest woman (at 35) to win a gold medal in track and field (4 × 100-m relay).

Ashgabat \'äsh-gä-ˌbät\ *or* **Ashkhabad** \'ash-kə-ˌbad\ City (pop., 1995 est.: 536,000), capital of Turkmenistan. It lies in an oasis at the northern foot of the Kopet-Dag Range near the Iranian border. Founded in 1881 as a Russian military fort, it was the capital of Turkmenistan S.S.R. 1924–90. A violent earthquake destroyed the city in 1948; it was rebuilt on the same plan. It is now an industrial, transportation, and cultural center.

Ashikaga family \ˌä-shē-'kä-gä\ Japanese warrior family that established the ASHIKAGA SHOGUNATE in 1338. The founder, Ashikaga Takauji (1305–1358), supported the emperor GO-DAIGO's attempt to wrest control of the country from the HOJO FAMILY, but then turned on him and set up an emperor from another branch of the imperial family, who granted Takauji the title of SHOGUN. Takauji's grandson Yoshimitsu (1358–1408), the third Ashikaga shogun, ended the dual imperial courts that had resulted from his grandfather's actions, took an active role in the court bureaucracy, and reorganized civil government. Yoshimitsu reopened formal trade with China and is remembered as a sponsor of the arts; he commissioned the famous Golden Pavilion (Kinkaku-ji) in Kyoto. Ashikaga Yoshimasa (1436–1490), the eighth Ashikaga shogun, was also a great patron of the arts and a devotee of the TEA CEREMONY. He commissioned the Silver Pavilion (Ginkaku-ji), whose understated elegance contrasts with the opulence of the Golden Pavilion. Politically, Yoshimasa's tenure as shogun coincided with increasing loss of control over the countryside as Japan headed toward a century of civil war. See also DAIMYO, ONIN WAR, SAMURAI.

Ashikaga shogunate Military government of Japan established in 1338 by the warrior Ashikaga Takauji that lasted in name until 1573, when the last of the Ashikaga SHOGUNS was deposed, but in fact lost control of Japan during the ONIN WAR (1467–77). Also known as the Muromachi period, the era of Ashikaga rule was, in spite of its turbulence, a time of great cultural growth. It saw the flourishing of ZEN Buddhism, NO DRAMA and other literary forms, and Chinese-style ink painting. See also ASHIKAGA FAMILY, DAIMYO, KANO SCHOOL, SAMURAI.

Ashkenazi \ˌäsh-kə-'nä-zē\ Any of the historically Yiddish-speaking European Jews who settled in central and northern Europe, or their descendants. They lived originally in the Rhineland valley, and their name is derived from the Hebrew word *Ashkenaz* ("Germany"). After the start of the Crusades in the late 11th century, many migrated east to Poland, Lithuania, and Russia to escape persecution. In later centuries Jews who adopted the German-rite synagogue ritual were called Ashkenazim to differentiate them from the Sephardic, or Spanish-rite, Jews (see SEPHARDI), from whom they differ in cultural traditions, pronunciation of Hebrew, and synagogue chanting as well as in the use of the YIDDISH LANGUAGE (until the 20th century). Today they constitute more than 80% of the world's Jews.

Ashley, William Henry (1778?–1838) U.S. fur trader. Born in Powhatan, Va., he arrived in Missouri about 1802 and prospered in mining and land speculation. In 1820 he became the state's first lieutenant governor. With Andrew Henry (1771–1833), he organized the Rocky Mountain Fur Co. in 1822 and established a trading post at the mouth of the Yellowstone River. Forced to abandon the post by Indians, in 1825 he instituted the annual rendezvous, where trappers would trade their furs to him for supplies for the next year. By 1827 he had made a fortune and retired. Elected to the U.S. House of Representatives (1831–37), he championed Western interests.

Ashoka \ə-'shō-kə\ *or* **Asoka** \ə-'sō-kə\ (died 238? BC) Last major emperor (c. 265–238 BC) of the MAURYAN EMPIRE in India and a patron of BUDDHISM. After his bloody conquest of Kalinga in the eighth year of his reign, Ashoka renounced military aggression and resolved to live according to the DHARMA. He spoke of Buddhism only to fellow Buddhists and adopted a policy of toleration for other religions. He spread Buddhist teachings through inscriptions known as the Rock Edicts and Pillar Edicts. He enjoined officials to be aware of the needs of common people and to dispense justice impartially; dharma ministers were appointed to relieve suffering and look to the special needs of other religions, women, outlying regions, and neighboring peoples. He erected stupas and monasteries, developed a course of study for adherents, and sent missionaries to Ceylon. He is remembered as the ideal Buddhist ruler.

Ashqelon \'ash-kə-ˌlän\ *formerly* **Ascalon** Archaeological site, Israel. The historic coastal city-state of Ascalon was traditionally the key to the conquest of southwestern PALESTINE. Its name appears in Egyptian texts c. 1800 BC. It was conquered by several ancient empires, including that of ALEXANDER THE GREAT in 332 BC. Conquered by the Arabs in AD 636, it was taken by Crusaders in 1153 and became one of their principal ports. It was retaken by SALADIN in 1187 and destroyed by BAYBARS I in 1270. Modern Ashqelon (pop., 1990 est.: 56,800), originally an Arab settlement, was resettled by Israelis after 1949 and is now a resort and industrial center.

ashram \'äsh-rəm, 'ash-ˌram\ *or* **ashrama** \'äsh-rə-mə\ In HINDUISM, any of the four stages of life through which a "twice-born" (see UPANAYANA) Hindu ideally will pass. These stages are: the student, who is devoted and obedient to his teacher; the householder, who supports his family and the priests and fulfills duties to the gods and ancestors; the hermit, who withdraws from society to pursue ascetic and yogic practices; and the homeless mendicant, who renounces all possessions and wanders from place to place begging for food. In English the word has come to mean a place for the pursuit of spiritual or religious disciplines, often under a GURU.

Ashtart See ASTARTE

Ashton, Frederick (William Mallandaine) *later* **Sir Frederick** (1904–1988) Principal choreographer and director of England's ROYAL BALLET. After creating ballets from 1925 for the Ballet Club (later Ballet Rambert), he joined the Vic-Wells (later Royal) Ballet in 1933, becoming principal choreographer, assistant director (1953–63), and director (1963–70). At least 30 of his works remain in its repertoire, including *Façade* (1931), *Symphonic Variations* (1946), and *Birthday Offering* (1956). He also choreographed for such companies as the Royal Danish Ballet (*Romeo and Juliet,* 1955) and the NEW YORK CITY BALLET (*Illuminations,* 1950).

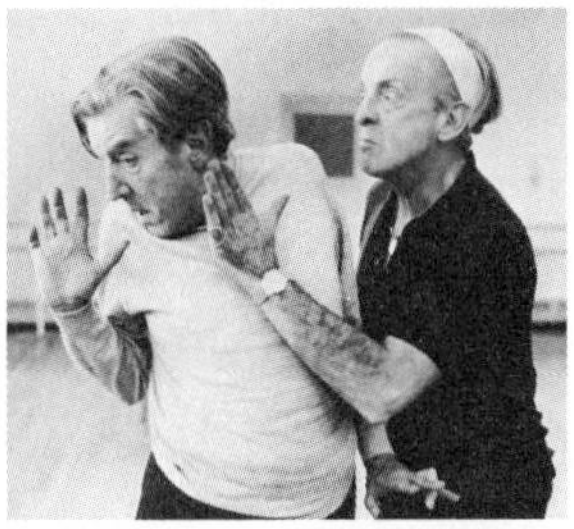

Ashton (left) and Robert Helpmann rehearsing their roles as the Ugly Sisters in *Cinderella,* 1965.

Ashur Ancient religious capital of ASSYRIA, on the TIGRIS RIVER, 60 mi (97 km) south of Mosul, northern Iraq. The name Ashur was applied to the city, to Assyria itself, and to Assyria's principal god. The capital's site was originally occupied c. 2500 BC, and later became part of AKKAD. By the late 12th century BC it was under Assyrian control. Its religious sanctity ensured its continuous upkeep until 614 BC, when it was destroyed by BABYLONIA. The archaeological site has yielded fortifications, temples, and palaces.

Ashurbanipal \ˌä-sər-'bä-ni-ˌpäl\ (r.668–627 BC) Last great Assyrian king. He was appointed crown prince of Assyria in 672 BC; his half-brother was appointed crown prince of Babylonia. On his father's death, Ashurbanipal assumed full power without incident. He quelled a rebellion in Egypt and successfully besieged Tyre. His half-brother, who served him in Babylonia peacefully for 16 years, joined a coalition of peoples from outlying areas of the Assyrian empire and plotted rebellion, but Ashurbanipal discovered the plots and, after a three-year siege, took Babylon. By 639 BC he had the whole known world under his control. A religious zealot, he rebuilt or adorned most of the major shrines of Assyria and Babylonia. His principal intellectual accomplishment was the creation in Nineveh of the first systematically organized library in the Middle East; the clay tablets collected there preserved omen texts, Mesopotamian epics, prayers and incantations, scientific texts, lexicographical texts, and folktales.

Ashurbanipal carrying a basket in the rebuilding of the temple, stone bas-relief from the Esagila, Babylon, 650 BC; in the British Museum.

Asia Largest continent on earth. It is bounded by the Arctic Ocean, the Pacific Ocean, and the Indian Ocean; the western boundary, with Europe, runs roughly north-south along the eastern Ural Mtns.; the Caspian, Black, Aegean, and Mediterranean seas; the Suez Canal; and the Red Sea. The islands of Sri Lanka and Taiwan and the archipelagoes of Indonesia, the Philippines, and Japan also form part of Asia. Area: 17,139,445 sq mi (44,391,162 sq km). Population, excluding Asian Russia and the countries of former Soviet Central Asia (1996 est.): 3,499,626,000. Mountains and plateaus predominate on the continent, with the highest mountains located in Central Asia. Asia's elevations include the earth's highest (Mount EVEREST) and the lowest (the DEAD SEA). The largest of its many desert regions are the THAR and GOBI deserts. Its hydrology is dominated by some of the longest rivers in the world, including the EUPHRATES, TIGRIS, INDUS, GANGES, CHANG (Yangtze), HUANG (Yellow), OB, YENISEY, and LENA. The CASPIAN, ARAL, and Dead seas are major saltwater lakes. More than 15% of Asia's landmass is arable. Asia's principal language groups and languages include SINO-TIBETAN, INDO-ARYAN, JAPANESE, AUSTRONESIAN, AUSTROASIATIC, SEMITIC, and KOREAN. East Asia contains three main ethnic groups: Chinese, Japanese, and Korean. The Indian subcontinent contains a vast diversity of peoples, most of whom speak languages from the Indo-Aryan subgroup of the INDO-EUROPEAN family. Because of the influence of China and the former Soviet Union, Mandarin and Russian are widespread. Asia is the birthplace of all the world's major religions and hundreds of minor ones. HINDUISM is the oldest religion to have originated in southern Asia; JAINISM and BUDDHISM emerged in the 6th and 5th century BC, respectively. South Asia was the cradle of JUDAISM and its offshoots, CHRISTIANITY and ISLAM. TAOISM and CONFUCIANISM, both of which originated in the 6th or 5th century BC, have profoundly influenced Chinese and Chinese-driven culture. Asia is marked by great disparities in wealth, both between and within its countries. A few countries, notably Japan, Singapore, and the oil-rich nations of Arabia, have achieved high standards of living; others, such as Bangladesh and Myanmar, are very poor. Between these two extremes lie Russia, China, and India. Asia's culture is the result of the interaction of five main influences: Chinese, Indian, Islamic, European (including Russia), and Central Asian. China has had great influence in East Asia as the source of Confucianism, a style of art, and the Chinese script. Indian influence has been expressed through Hinduism and Buddhism, affecting Tibet, Indonesia, Cambodia, and Central Asia. Islam spread from its original Arabian home to become important in the Middle East, South Asia, and elsewhere, accompanied by the use of the Arabic alphabet. *Homo erectus* hominids migrated from Africa to East Asia at least 1 million years ago. One of the earliest civilizations to use writing developed in the Tigris and Euphrates river valleys c. 3500–3000 BC (see MESOPOTAMIA). Civilization in the Indus valley and in northern Syria followed c. 2500 BC. Chinese urban civilization began with the SHANG DYNASTY (traditionally, 1766–1122 BC) and continued under the ZHOU (1122–221 BC). Indo-European-speaking peoples (ARYANS) began to invade India from the west c. 1700 BC and developed the VEDIC culture. A succession of empires and charismatic rulers, including ALEXANDER THE GREAT, spread their political mantles as far as military power could carry them. In the 13th century AD, GENGHIS KHAN and his MONGOL successors united much of Asia under their rule. In the 14th century

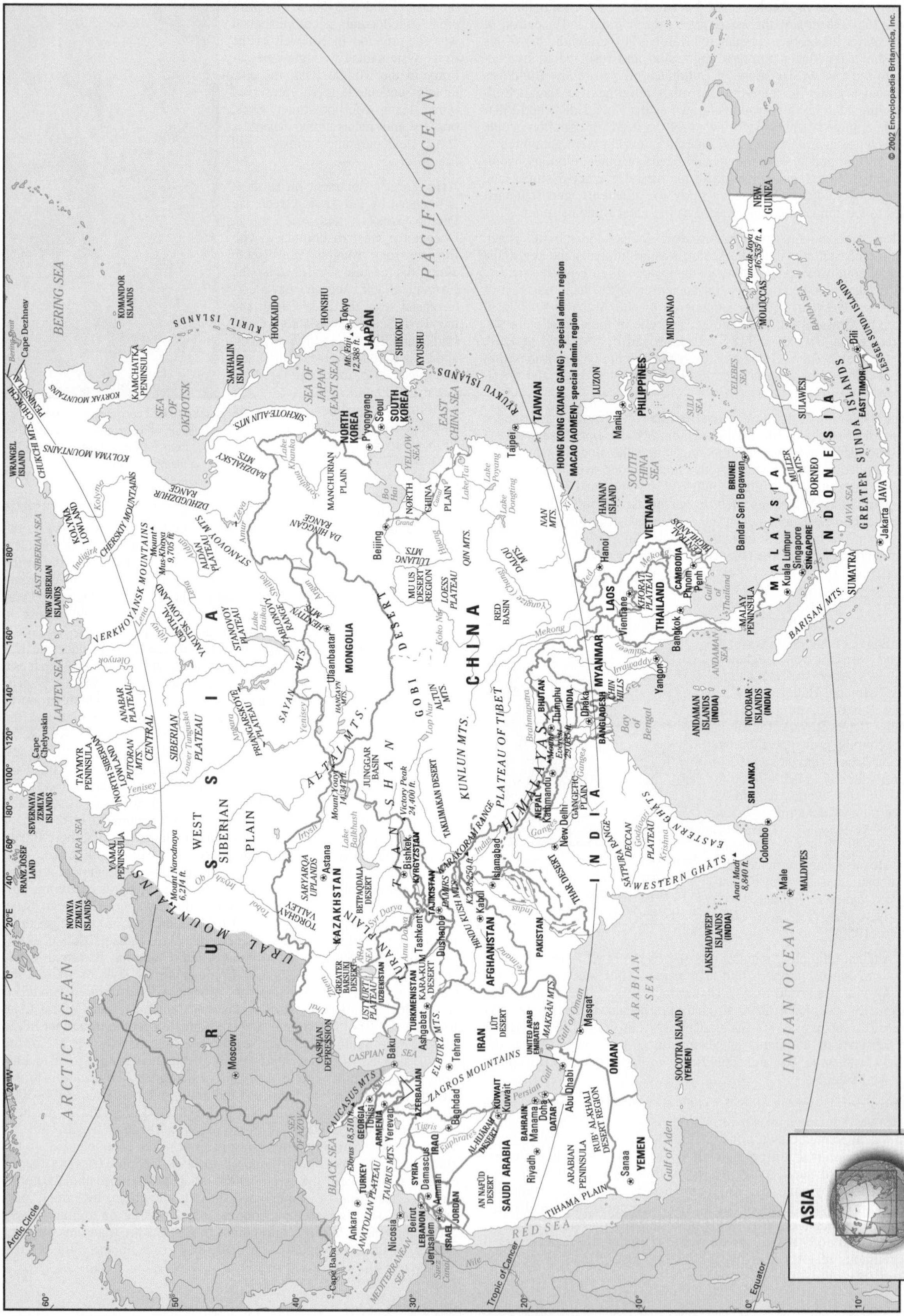
ASIA
ARCTIC OCEAN
PACIFIC OCEAN
INDIAN OCEAN
RUSSIA
URAL MOUNTAINS
WEST SIBERIAN PLAIN
CENTRAL SIBERIAN PLATEAU
KAZAKHSTAN
MONGOLIA
CHINA
GOBI DESERT
PLATEAU OF TIBET
HIMALAYAS
INDIA
PAKISTAN
AFGHANISTAN
IRAN
IRAQ
SAUDI ARABIA
TURKEY
SYRIA
JORDAN
ISRAEL
LEBANON
YEMEN
OMAN
UNITED ARAB EMIRATES
QATAR
BAHRAIN
KUWAIT
TURKMENISTAN
UZBEKISTAN
TAJIKISTAN
KYRGYZSTAN
GEORGIA
ARMENIA
AZERBAIJAN
NEPAL
BHUTAN
BANGLADESH
MYANMAR
THAILAND
LAOS
VIETNAM
CAMBODIA
MALAYSIA
SINGAPORE
INDONESIA
PHILIPPINES
BRUNEI
EAST TIMOR
TAIWAN
JAPAN
NORTH KOREA
SOUTH KOREA
SRI LANKA
MALDIVES
NEW GUINEA
HONG KONG (XIANG GANG) - special admin. region
MACAO (AOMEN)- special admin. region
Moscow
Ankara
Nicosia
Beirut
Jerusalem
Amman
Damascus
Baghdad
Kuwait
Riyadh
Manama
Doha
Abu Dhabi
Masqat
Sanaa
Tehran
Baku
Tbilisi
Yerevan
Ashgabat
Tashkent
Dushanbe
Bishkek
Astana
Kabul
Islamabad
New Delhi
Kathmandu
Thimphu
Dhaka
Colombo
Male
Yangon
Bangkok
Vientiane
Hanoi
Phnom Penh
Kuala Lumpur
Singapore
Jakarta
Bandar Seri Begawan
Manila
Taipei
Beijing
Ulaanbaatar
P'yongyang
Seoul
Tokyo
Dili
ARABIAN SEA
Bay of Bengal
SOUTH CHINA SEA
EAST CHINA SEA
SEA OF JAPAN (EAST SEA)
SEA OF OKHOTSK
BERING SEA
CASPIAN SEA
BLACK SEA
RED SEA
MEDITERRANEAN SEA
Persian Gulf
Gulf of Oman
Gulf of Aden
KARA SEA
LAPTEV SEA
EAST SIBERIAN SEA
Arctic Circle
Tropic of Cancer
Equator
Mount Everest 29,035 ft.
Mt. Fuji 12,388 ft.
Puncak Jaya 16,535 ft.
© 2002 Encyclopædia Britannica, Inc.

TIMUR conquered much of Central Asia. Muslim Turks destroyed the remnants of the Byzantine empire in the 15th century. In the 19th century, European imperialism began to replace Asian imperialism. Czarist Russia pushed to the Pacific Ocean, the British gained control of India, the French moved into Indochina, the Dutch occupied the East Indies, and the Spanish and later the U.S. ruled the Philippines. After World War II, European imperialism largely vanished as former colonies gained independence. Asia has subsequently divided into pro-Western, communist, and nonaligned groups.

Asia Minor *or* **Anatolia** *Turkish* **Anadolu** \ˌä-nä-ˈdō-lü\ The part of Turkey in Asia. The peninsula forms the western extremity of Asia, between the Black Sea and the Mediterranean Sea; it also borders on the Aegean Sea. Because of its location at the point where Asia and Europe meet, it has long been the scene of numerous migrations and conquests. It was the original location of the Kingdom of HITTITES (c. 1950–1200 BC). Later, Indo-European races, possibly Greeks, established the PHRYGIAN kingdom. In the 6th century BC, CYRUS THE GREAT ruled the area; it was invaded by ALEXANDER THE GREAT in 334 BC. In the 1st century BC, the Romans began expanding there, and when the Roman empire was split in AD 395 it fell to the Byzantine empire. The area endured invasions by Arabs, Turks, Mongols, and the Turkic army of TIMUR before Ottoman power was established in the 15th century; its later history to 1920 is that of the OTTOMAN EMPIRE.

Asimov \ˈa-zi-ˌmȯf\, **Isaac** (1920–1992) U.S. (Russian-born) author and biochemist. He arrived in the U.S. at age 3, earned a doctorate from Columbia Univ., and subsequently taught for many years at Boston University. Before embarking on graduate study he had begun publishing his stories. "Nightfall" (1941) is often called the finest science-fiction short story ever written. His *I, Robot* (1950) greatly influenced how later writers treated intelligent machines. A trilogy of novels, *Foundation*, *Foundation and Empire*, and *Second Foundation* (1951–53), has achieved classic status. Asimov's nonfiction science books for lay readers are noted for their lucidity and humor. Immensely prolific, he published over 300 volumes in all.

Askja \ˈäs-kyä\ Caldera, Iceland. The largest crater in the Dyngjufjöl volcanic massif, Askja lies 20 mi (32 km) north of Vatnajökull, Iceland's largest ice field. Its rugged peaks, up to 4,954 ft (1,510 m), encircle a lake of 4.25 sq mi (11 sq km) that occupies the caldera. The volcano erupted in 1875 and again in 1961.

Asmara \ˈäs-mä-rä\ City (pop., 1992: 400,000), capital of Eritrea. It lies on the northern tip of the Ethiopian Plateau at an elevation of 7,765 ft (2,367 m). Its Red Sea port, Mitsiwa, is 40 mi (65 km) northeast. Formerly a hamlet of the TIGRAY people, Asmara became the capital of the Italian colony of Eritrea in 1900. It was under British control from 1941 until Eritrea's federation with Ethiopia in 1952. It became the capital of independent Eritrea in 1993. It is an agricultural marketplace.

Aso \ˈä-sō\ *or* **Asosan** Volcanic mountain, central KYUSHU island, Japan. The highest of its five peaks is about 5,223 ft (1,592 m) tall. It has one of the largest active craters in the world, measuring 71 mi (114 km) in circumference; its caldera marks the original crater and contains an active volcano and hot springs. The crater is inhabited; its pastures are used for cattle raising and dairy farming.

Asoka See ASHOKA

asp Anglicized form of *aspis,* the name used in classical antiquity for a venomous snake, probably the Egyptian COBRA *(Naja haje)*. The asp was the symbol of royalty in Egypt, and its bite was used for the execution of criminals in Greco-Roman times. CLEOPATRA is said to have killed herself with an asp.

asparagine \ə-ˈspar-ə-ˌjēn\ One of the nonessential AMINO ACIDS, widely distributed in plant PROTEINS and closely related to ASPARTIC ACID. First isolated in 1806 from asparagus, it is used in medicine and biochemical research.

asparagus Any plant of the genus *Asparagus* (LILY FAMILY), which contains about 300 species native from Siberia to southern Africa. The best-known and economically most important species is the garden asparagus, *A. officinalis,* cultivated as a green VEGETABLE for its succulent spring stalks. Several African species are grown as ornamental plants. The poisonous species prized for their delicate and graceful foliage are *A. plumosus* (the feathery asparagus fern, or florists' fern—not a true FERN), *A. sprengeri,* and *A. asparagoides.*

aspartame \ˈas-pər-ˌtām\ Synthetic organic compound (a dipeptide) of PHENYLALANINE and ASPARTIC ACID. It is 150–200 times as sweet as cane SUGAR and is used as a nonnutritive tabletop sweetener and in low-calorie prepared foods (brand names NutraSweet, Equal) but is not suitable for baking. Because of its phenylalanine content, persons with PHENYLKETONURIA must avoid it. Though it is approved by the FDA, safety concerns remain even for those without the disease. See also SACCHARIN.

aspartic acid One of the nonessential AMINO ACIDS, found in many PROTEINS and closely related to ASPARAGINE. It is used in medical and biochemical research, as an organic intermediate, and in various industrial applications. It is one of the two components of ASPARTAME.

Aspasia \as-ˈpā-shə\ (5th century BC) Mistress of PERICLES and a vivid figure in Athenian society. Originally from Miletus, she lived with Pericles from c. 445 BC until his death in 429. Because she was not a citizen, their son was initially denied civic rights. Though an intellectual admired by SOCRATES, she endured public attacks, especially in comic theater, for her private life and her supposed influence on Pericles' foreign policy.

Aspen City (pop., 1990: 5,000), western central Colorado. It is located on the Roaring Fork River at the edge of the White River National Forest, at an altitude of 7,907 ft (2,410 m). Founded by prospectors c. 1878, it was a booming silver-mining town by 1887 but declined rapidly after silver prices collapsed in the early 1890s. Its revival as a ski resort began in the late 1930s and it is now a popular tourist town; it is also known for its cultural festivals, notably the Aspen Music Festival.

aspen Any of three trees of the genus *Populus,* of the WILLOW family: *P. tremula* (the common European aspen), *P. tremuloides* (the American quaking, or trembling, aspen), and *P. grandidentata* (the American big-tooth aspen). Native to the Northern Hemisphere, aspens are known for the fluttering of their leaves in the slightest breeze. Aspens grow farther north and higher up the mountains than other *Populus* species. All aspens have a smooth, gray-green bark, random branching, rich green leaves that turn brilliant yellow in fall, and CATKINS that appear before the leaves in spring.

Aspendus \as-ˈpen-dəs\ Ancient city, Pamphylia (now southwestern Turkey). It was a wealthy city by the 5th century BC. Occupied by ALEXANDER THE GREAT in 333 BC, it was taken by the Romans in 133 BC. It is noted for its Roman ruins, including a huge theater designed by the architect Zeno in honor of MARCUS AURELIUS.

aspergillus \ˌas-pər-ˈjil-əs\ Any FUNGUS of the genus *Aspergillus* of the Fungi Imperfecti (form-class Deuteromycetes). Species for which the sexual phase is known are placed in the order Eurotiales. *A. niger* causes black mold of foodstuffs; *A. niger, A. flavus,* and *A. fumigatus* cause aspergillosis in humans. *A. oryzae* is used to ferment SAKE, and *A. wentii* to process SOYBEANS.

asphalt Black or brown petroleum-like material that has a consistency varying from viscous liquid to glassy solid. It is obtained either as a residue from the distillation of petroleum or from natural deposits. Asphalt consists of compounds of hydrogen and carbon with minor proportions of nitrogen, sulfur, and oxygen. It softens when heated and is elastic under certain conditions. Used principally in road surfacing, asphalt is also used for roofs, coatings, floor tilings, and waterproofing, and in industrial products.

asphodel \ˈas-fə-ˌdel\ Any of several flowering plants belonging to the LILY FAMILY. This common name is variously applied and thus much misunderstood. The asphodel of the poets is often a NARCISSUS; that of the ancients is either of two genera, *Asphodeline* or *Asphodelus.* Asphodels are hardy herbaceous perennials with narrow leaves and an elongated stem bearing a handsome spike of white, pink, or yellow flowers. Bog asphodel *(Narthecium ossifragum)* is a small herbaceous plant growing in boggy places in Britain.

asphyxia \as-ˈfik-sē-ə\ Lack of exchange of oxygen and carbon dioxide due to respiratory failure or disturbance, resulting in insufficient brain oxygen, which leads to unconsciousness or death. Causes include strangulation, drowning, and carbon monoxide poisoning. Breathing in food or fluid can cause obstruction of the airway and pulmonary collapse. Emergency resuscitation usually includes CARDIOPULMONARY RESUSCITATION.

aspidistra \ˌas-pə-ˈdis-trə\ Any plant of the genus *Aspidistra* (LILY FAMILY), native to eastern Asia and known for ornamental foliage. The only cultivated species is a HOUSEPLANT commonly known as cast-iron plant *(A. elatior,* or *A. lurida),* which has long, stiff, pointed EVERGREEN leaves that are capable of withstanding temperature extremes, dust, smoke, and other harsh conditions. The solitary, bell-shaped flowers, which are usually lilac in color but sometimes brown or green, are borne at the base of the plant. The fruits are small berries.

aspirin Common name of acetylsalicylic acid, an organic compound introduced in 1899. The ESTER of SALICYLIC ACID and ACETIC ACID, it inhibits production of PROSTAGLANDINS in the body. Its ANALGESIC, fever-reducing, and anti-inflammatory effects make it useful in treating headaches, muscle and joint aches, ARTHRITIS pain, and the symptoms of mild fevers and infections. It also has ANTICOAGULANT activity and is taken in low doses by CORONARY HEART DISEASE patients to prevent MYOCARDIAL INFARCTION. Prolonged use may cause stomach bleeding and PEPTIC ULCER, and its use in children with fever has been linked to REYE'S SYNDROME. See also ACETAMINOPHEN, IBUPROFEN, NSAIDS.

Aspiring, Mount See MOUNT ASPIRING NATIONAL PARK

Asplund, (Erik) Gunnar (1885–1940) Swedish architect. His work shows the historically important transition from neoclassical architecture to modernism. By 1928, influenced by LE CORBUSIER, he had turned from a reminiscent style to the new architecture. He planned the Stockholm Exposition of 1930, a place of futuristic, glassy pavilions that had a significant influence on exhibition architecture to follow. His Woodland Crematorium, Stockholm (1935–40), with its spare Neoclassical colonnade surrounded by meadows, is admired by classicists and modernists alike.

Asquith, H(erbert) H(enry) *later* **Earl of Oxford and Asquith** (1852–1928) British politician and prime minister (1908–16). Elected to the House of Commons in 1886, he served as home secretary 1892–95. A leader of the Liberal Party, he became prime minister in 1908. His plan to limit the powers of the House of Lords was enacted by the PARLIAMENT ACT OF 1911. He led Britain in the early years of World War I, but domestic crises combined with British losses in the war led to widespread dissatisfaction. He resigned in 1916, but remained leader of his party until 1926.

ass *or* **wild ass** Either of two species of small, sturdy EQUINES. Asses are 3–5 ft (90–150 cm) high at the shoulder. The African wild ass, or true ass *(Equus asinus)* is bluish gray to fawn; the Asiatic wild ass, or half-ass *(E. hemionus)* is reddish to yellow-gray. The half-ass differs from the true ass in that it has extremely long, slender legs, shorter ears, and larger hooves. The true ass has the alternating "hee-haw" bray. Desert dwellers, wild asses often inhabit regions that cannot support other large mammals. They are very swift runners. See also DONKEY.

Assad \ˈä-ˌsȧd\, **Hafiz al-** (1930–2000) President of SYRIA (1971–2000). He joined the BAATH PARTY in 1946 and in 1955 became an air-force pilot. He became air-force commander (1963) after helping the Baathists gain power. After participating in a military coup in 1966, he became minister of defense. He led a coup in 1970 to replace his political mentor, Salah al-Jadid, as Syria's leader. He joined Egypt in a surprise attack on Israel (1973), but nearly 20 years later (1991) joined peace negotiations with Israel in an effort to regain the Golan Heights, taken by Israel in the SIX-DAY WAR of 1967. A longtime foe of Saddam HUSSEIN, he supported the Western Alliance against Iraq in the PERSIAN GULF WAR. He was succeeded by his son Bashar.

Assal \ä-ˈsäl\, **Lake** Saline lake, central Djibouti. Situated at 515 ft (157 m) below sea level, it is the lowest point in Africa. It has been used for quarrying salt.

Assam \a-ˈsam\ State (pop., 1994 est.: 24,200,000), northeastern India. With an area of 30,318 sq mi (78,524 sq km), Assam borders Bhutan and Bangladesh; its capital is DISPUR. A strong independent kingdom was founded there in the 13th century by invaders from Myanmar (Burma) and China; it reached its zenith in the early 18th century. The British took control in the early 19th century. In the division of India (1947), Assam lost some territory to Pakistan. Beginning in the 1960s, four new states—NAGALAND, MEGHALAYA, MIZORAM, and ARUNACHAL PRADESH—were created from land within Assam. The BRAHMAPUTRA River valley is its dominant physical feature. The population consists of Indo-Iranian and Asian peoples; the most widely spoken language is Assamese.

Assassin Islamic sect of the 11th–13th century that regarded killing its enemies as a religious duty. From Alamut, his fortress in Iran, the sect's leader, Hasan-e Sabbah (died 1124), commanded a network of strongholds and a corps of terrorists who murdered generals and statesmen of the ABBASID DYNASTY. The MONGOLS finally ended Assassin power when they captured Alamut in 1256. Present-day ISMAILIS are descended from the Assassins.

assassin bug Any of about 4,000 insect species (family Reduviidae) characterized by a thin, necklike structure connecting the narrow head to the body. Many species are common to North and South America. Ranging in size from 0.5 to 1 in. (13–25 mm), assassin bugs use their short, three-segmented beak to suck body fluids from their victims. Most assassin bugs prey on other insects; some, however, suck blood from vertebrates, including humans, and transmit diseases. One species, the large assassin bug, defends itself by accurately "spitting" saliva toxic enough to blind a human.

assassin fly See ROBBER FLY

assault and battery Related but distinct crimes. Battery is the unlawful application of physical force to another; assault is an attempt to commit battery or an act that may reasonably cause fear of imminent battery. With manslaughter and murder (see HOMICIDE), these concepts are articulated to protect against rude and undesired physical contact or the threat of it. Battery requires no minimum degree of force, nor does it need to be applied directly; administering poison and transmitting a disease may both be battery. Accidents and ordinary NEGLIGENCE are not, nor is reasonable force used in the performance of duty (e.g., by a police officer). See also RAPE.

assault rifle Military firearm that is chambered for ammunition of reduced size or propellant charge and has the capacity to switch between semiautomatic and fully automatic fire. Light and portable, yet able to deliver a high volume of fire with reasonable accuracy at modern combat ranges of 1,000–1,600 ft (300–500 m), assault rifles have become the standard infantry weapon of modern armies. Their ease of handling makes them ideal for mobile assault troops crowded into personnel carriers or helicopters, as well as for guerrilla fighters engaged in jungle or urban warfare. Widely used assault rifles are the U.S. M16, the Soviet Kalashnikov (the AK-47 and modernized versions), the Belgian FAL and FNC, and the German G3.

assaying \ˈa-sā-iŋ\ In chemical ANALYSIS, the process of determining proportions of metal, particularly precious metal, in ORES and metallurgical products. The most important assaying technique grew largely out of the experiments of the ancient alchemists and goldsmiths. Precious metals tend to occur as scattered particles randomly distributed, so a large sample of ore is required. Such large samples (typically containing gold, silver, and lead) are still most economically assayed by this ancient method, which involves several steps of heating and cooling. More sophisticated recent methods, such as SPECTROCHEMICAL ANALYSIS, are not suited to assaying precious metal ores because the samples of the inhomogeneous ore that must be used are larger than the instruments can handle. See also PARTING.

assemblage \ˌa-säm-ˈbläzh\ Three-dimensional construction made from household materials such as rope and newspapers or from any found materials. The term, coined by JEAN DUBUFFET in the 1950s, has been applied to COLLAGE, photomontage, and sculptural assemblage. The Dadaists and Surrealists produced READY-MADE assemblages and elevated them to art by simply exhibiting them. Later artists who have worked with the technique include LOUISE NEVELSON and ROBERT RAUSCHENBERG.

Assemblies of God Largest Pentecostal denomination in the U.S. It was formed in 1914 in Hot Springs, Ark., by the union of several small Pentecostal groups. The Assemblies of God emphasize the centrality of the Bible in Christian faith and worship. Instead of SACRAMENTS, the Assemblies have two ordinances, BAPTISM by total immersion and the Lord's Supper. Personal sanctification is believed to happen gradually rather than instantaneously, and millennial doctrines dealing with Christ's Second Coming and the establishment of the Kingdom of God are of great importance. The Assemblies of God have been very active in mission work in the U.S. and overseas. See also MILLENNIALISM, PENTECOSTALISM.

assembly language Type of low-level computer PROGRAMMING LANGUAGE consisting mostly of symbolic equivalents of a particular computer's MACHINE LANGUAGE. Computers produced by different manufacturers have different machine languages and require different assemblers and assembly languages. Some assembly languages can be used to convert the code that programmers write (source code) into machine language (readable by the computer), and have functions to facilitate programming (e.g., by combining a sequence of several instructions into one entity). Programming in assembly languages requires extensive knowledge of COMPUTER ARCHITECTURE.

assembly line Industrial arrangement of machines, equipment, and workers for continuous flow of workpieces in MASS-PRODUCTION operations. An assembly line is designed by determining the sequences of operations for manufacture of each component as well as the final product. Each movement of material is made as simple and short as possible, with no cross flow or backtracking. Work assignments, numbers of machines, and production rates are programmed so that all operations performed along the line are compatible. Automated assembly lines (see AUTOMATION) consist entirely of machines run by other machines and are used in such continuous-process industries as petroleum refining and chemical manufacture and in many modern automobile-engine plants. See also HENRY FORD, INTERCHANGEABLE PARTS, TAYLORISM.

assessment Process of setting a value on real or personal property, usually for the purpose of taxation. It is carried out either by central government agencies or by local officials. Property may be assessed on the basis of its annual rental value, as in Britain, or its capital value, as in the U.S. Various methods are used to determine capital value, including analysis of market data to estimate the property's current market price, estimation of the cost of reproducing the property minus accrued DEPRECIATION, and capitalization of the property's earnings.

assessor One with special knowledge of a subject who is appointed or elected to assist a judge or magistrate in deciding a legal matter. In the U.S. the term also designates an official who evaluates property for the purposes of taxation. Assessors were appointed in the late 19th century throughout Europe to try to limit the influence of the JURY system, which had been introduced in the wake of the French Revolution. Assessors thus represented a return to the CIVIL-LAW traditions of Europe. In England and the U.S., assessors came to be used in labor and maritime courts as well as in some other civil jurisdictions.

assimilation See CULTURE CONTACT

Assiniboia \ə-ˌsin-ə-ˈbȯi-ə\ Early region, western Canada. Named for the ASSINIBOIN Indians, it was an area with indefinite boundaries, controlled by the HUDSON'S BAY CO. c. 1811–70. It included present-day southern Manitoba and until 1818, present-day North Dakota and Minnesota. It was incorporated into Manitoba in 1870. In 1882 the Canadian government created another district of Assininboia as part of the old Northwest Territories. In 1905 this district was divided between Alberta and Saskatchewan.

Assiniboin \ə-ˌsin-ə-ˈbȯi-ən\ PLAINS INDIAN people of SIOUAN LANGUAGE stock who inhabited an area between the upper Missouri and middle Saskatchewan rivers. They were divided into BANDS, each with its own chief and council, and were generally friendly with whites. The bands moved their camps frequently in pursuit of migrating buffalo. Prowess in war consisted of taking scalps and horses and of touching the enemy ("counting coups") during battle. Their numbers were severely reduced by smallpox in the 1820s and '30s, after which most were placed on reservations. Today they number about 1,000 in Canada and about 4,000 in the U.S.

Assiniboin, placating the spirit of a slain eagle, photograph by Edward S. Curtis, 1908; from *The North American Indian.*

BY COURTESY OF THE NEWBERRY LIBRARY, CHICAGO, AYER COLLECTION

Assiniboine River \ə-ˈsin-ə-ˌbȯin\ River, southern Canada. Rising in Saskatchewan, it flows southeast across Manitoba into the RED RIVER OF THE NORTH at WINNIPEG. It is about 590 mi (950 km) long and has two tributaries, the QU'APPELLE and the SOURIS. Explored by PIERRE LA VERENDRYE in 1736, it later served as a route to the plains by colonists from Red River Settlement.

Assis, Joaquim Maria Machado de See Joaquim M. MACHADO DE ASSIS

Assistance, Writs of General search warrants used in the American colonies by the British. The warrants authorized customhouse officers, with the assistance of a sheriff, to search any house or ship for smuggled goods, without specifying the place or the goods. Their legality was challenged by the colonists in the 1760s, and the writs became a major grievance in the years leading up to the AMERICAN REVOLUTION. See also JAMES OTIS.

assize \ə-ˈsīz\ In law, a session, or sitting, of a court. It originally referred to a judicial inquest in which a panel of men conducted an investigation. It was later applied to special sessions of high courts in England and France. Assize courts were abolished in most countries in the 20th century, but in France they are still the courts of first instance in the handling of serious crimes.

Associated Press (AP) Cooperative NEWS AGENCY, the oldest and largest in the U.S. and long the largest in the world. Its beginnings trace to 1848, when six New York City newspapers pooled their efforts to finance a telegraphic relay of foreign news brought by ships to Boston. In 1892 the modern AP was set up under the laws of Illinois; several years later it moved to New York. Its restrictive controls on new memberships were ended with federal antitrust prosecution in the 1940s. The AP today serves more than 15,000 news organizations worldwide.

association In psychology, the process of forming mental connections or bonds between sensations, ideas, or memories. Though discussed by the ancient Greeks (in terms of similarities, contrasts, and contiguities), the "association of ideas" was first proposed by JOHN LOCKE and subsequently examined by DAVID HUME, JOHN STUART MILL, HERBERT SPENCER, and WILLIAM JAMES. IVAN PAVLOV used objective methods to study the phenomenon, resulting in his identification of the conditioned reflex (see CONDITIONING). Within PSYCHOANALYSIS, the therapist encourages "free association" in order to help identify latent CONFLICTS. Practitioners of GESTALT PSYCHOLOGY and others have criticized associationist theories as too all-embracing, while some theorists of COGNITIVE PSYCHOLOGY have made it central to their theory of MEMORY.

association football See FOOTBALL

Association of Caribbean States (ACS) Trading bloc composed of 25 nations of the Caribbean basin. Responding to a proposal by Pres. WILLIAM JEFFERSON CLINTON for a Free Trade Area of the Americas (FTAA), existing Caribbean-area trading blocs joined forces in 1995 to strengthen their economic position and ease future integration into the FTAA. Prominent in the ACS are the Caricom nations (13 English-speaking countries and Suriname), which have been struggling toward a single market and economy along the lines of the European Union. The ACS has addressed such issues as unifying responses to natural disasters, ending the U.S. embargo of Cuba, and ending shipments of nuclear materials through the Panama Canal.

Association of Southeast Asian Nations (ASEAN) International organization established by the governments of Indonesia, Malaysia, the Philippines, Singapore, and Thailand in 1967 to accelerate economic growth, social progress, and cultural development and to promote peace and security in the region. Brunei became a member in 1984, Vietnam in 1995, Laos and Myanmar in 1997, and Cambodia in 1999. ASEAN became a leading voice on regional trade and security issues in the 1990s; in 1992 member nations created the ASEAN Free Trade Area.

associative law Two closely related laws of number operations. In symbols, they are stated: $a + (b + c) = (a + b) + c$, and $a(bc) = (ab)c$. Stated in words: The terms or factors may be associated in any way desired and the result will be the same. This holds for the numbers generally encountered: positive and negative, integral and fractional, rational and irrational, real and imaginary. Exceptions occur (e.g., in nonassociative algebras and divergent INFINITE SERIES). See also COMMUTATIVE LAW, DISTRIBUTIVE LAW.

A
B

Assos *ancient* **Assus** Ancient city, southern TROAS (now northwestern Turkey). It was founded c. 900 BC on the Gulf of Adramyttium (now Edremit), opposite LESBOS. It was long an important city and port. ARISTOTLE taught there 348–45 BC, and it was the birthplace of the philosopher Cleanthes (331?–232? BC). Its ruins now lie in the village of Behramköy.

assumpsit \ə-'səmp-sit\ (Latin: "he has undertaken") In COMMON LAW, an action to recover damages for breach of contract, especially an implied or quasi contract. It developed in early English law as a form of recovery for the negligent performance of an undertaking (e.g., failing to protect from damage another's goods in one's care). Eventually, it came to cover broader claims regarding failure to keep a promise. It remains available as a contractual remedy in some U.S. jurisdictions.

Assyria Ancient empire, western Asia. It grew from a small region around ASHUR (N Iraq) to encompass an area stretching from Palestine to Turkey. Assyria may have originated in the 3rd millennium BC, but it came to power gradually. Its greatest period began in the 9th century BC, when its conquests reached the Mediterranean under Ashurnasipal II, and c. 745–626 BC, when it conquered Israel, Damascus, Babylon, and Samaria. Its greatest rulers during the latter period were TIGLATH-PILESER III, SARGON II, SENNACHERIB, and ASHURBANIPAL. Famous for their cruelty and fighting prowess, the Assyrians were also monumental builders, as shown by archaeological finds at NINEVEH, ASHUR, and CALAH. The opulence of Ashurbanipal's court at Nineveh became legendary. Artistically, the Assyrians were particularly noted for their stone bas-reliefs. It was vanquished between 626 and 612 BC, when Nineveh was destroyed by the kings of MEDIA and BABYLONIA (Chaldea).

Assyro-Babylonian language See AKKADIAN LANGUAGE

Astaire, Fred *orig.* **Frederick Austerlitz** (1899–1987) U.S. dancer and singer of stage and movies. He was born in Omaha. At age 7 he and his sister Adele began their popular vaudeville dance act, making their Broadway debut in 1917; they continued dancing in stage hits until Adele retired in 1932. Astaire's successful film appearances with Ginger Rogers (1911–1995) began with *Flying Down to Rio* (1933) and continued until 1939. In the 1940s and 1950s he danced onscreen with E. Powell, Cyd Charisse, and JUDY GARLAND. His singing, though untrained, was admired by the finest songwriters of his time. He retired in 1971 but occasionally appeared in films and on television. His sophisticated, effortless grace combined with technical virtuosity revolutionized popular-dance performance.

Astaire in *Top Hat*, 1935.
CORBIS-BETTMANN

Astana *formerly (1992–99)* **Aqmola** *or* **Akmola** \äk-'mō-lə\, *(1961–92)* **Tselinograd** \'tsi-'lē-nə-ˌgrät\ City (pop., 1993 est.: 287,000) and capital of Kazakhstan. Lying on the banks of the ISHIM RIVER in northern central Kazakhstan, it was founded in 1824 as a Russian military outpost. The city's importance was enhanced by its location at the junction of the Trans-Kazakhstan and South Siberian railways. It is in the center of a mineral-rich steppe region. In 1994 the Kazakh government began to transfer the national capital from ALMATY to Astana, changing the city's name in 1999.

Astarte \a-'stär-tē\ *or* **Ashtart** \'ash-ˌtärt\ Goddess of the ancient Near East and chief deity of the Mediterranean seaports of Tyre, Sidon, and Elath. Astarte shared many qualities, and perhaps a common origin, with her sister ANATH. The goddess of love and war, she was worshiped in Egypt and among the Hittites as well as in Canaan. Her Akkadian counterpart was ISHTAR. She is often mentioned in the Bible under the name Ashtoreth, and JOSIAH destroyed the shrines dedicated to her. In Egypt she was assimilated with ISIS and HATHOR; in the Greco-Roman world she was assimilated with APHRODITE, ARTEMIS, and JUNO.

aster Any of various chiefly fall-blooming, leafy-stemmed herbaceous plants (*Aster* and closely related genera) in the COMPOSITE FAMILY, often with showy flowers. Included among the asters are many perennial WILDFLOWERS and hundreds of garden varieties.

asteroid Any of the many small rocky astronomical objects found mainly in a "belt" between the orbits of Mars and Jupiter. Also called minor planets, they are thought to have been kept from aggregating into a single planet while the SOLAR SYSTEM was forming by the gravitational influence of what became Jupiter. Smaller than any of the nine major planets, only about 30 are more than 125 mi (200 km) across. CERES is the largest known asteroid. Millions of boulder-sized asteroids are thought to exist in the solar system. A few asteroids or their fragments strike the earth, plunging through the atmosphere as METEORS to reach its surface (see METEORITE). Asteroids appear to be composed of carbonaceous, stony, and metallic (mainly iron) materials. See also EARTH-CROSSING ASTEROID, TROJAN ASTEROIDS.

asthenosphere \as-'the-nə-ˌsfir\ Zone of the earth's MANTLE lying beneath the LITHOSPHERE, believed to be much hotter and more fluid than the lithosphere. The asthenosphere is thought to extend from about 60 mi (100 km) to about 450 mi (700 km) below the earth's surface.

asthma \'az-mə\ Chronic disease with attacks of shortness of breath, wheezing, and coughing from constriction and mucous-membrane swelling in the bronchi (air passageways in the lungs). It is caused primarily by ALLERGY or respiratory infection. Secondhand smoke can cause asthma in children. Asthma is common, runs in families, and affects all races; predisposition may be hereditary. In established asthmatics, exercise, stress, and sudden changes in temperature or humidity can bring on attacks. Attacks usually last from a half hour to several hours; severe attacks can be fatal. Corticosteroids can control asthma; injections of EPINEPHRINE can relieve acute attacks. Prevention involves avoiding exposure to allergens.

astigmatism \ə-'stig-mə-ˌti-zəm\ Lack of symmetry in the curvature of the cornea or, rarely, the lens of the EYE. The unequal curvatures spread light rays, preventing them from being sharply focused at a point on the RETINA, causing blurring of part of the image. The effect of astigmatism can also be produced by misalignment of the lens. Astigmatic vision is corrected by means of lenses (see CONTACT LENS, EYEGLASSES) that refract the light rays to the proper degree in the opposite direction of that produced by the defects in curvature.

Astor, John Jacob (1763–1848) German-U.S. fur magnate and financier. After emigrating from Germany at 17, he opened a fur-goods shop in New York c. 1786. By 1800 he was a leader in the fur trade, and he established the AMERICAN FUR CO. He controlled the fur trade with China (1800–17) and in the Mississippi and Missouri valleys (in the 1820s) before selling his interests in 1834. He invested in New York City real estate that became the foundation of the family fortune. At his death, Astor was the wealthiest person in the U.S.; he willed $400,000 to found what became the NEW YORK PUBLIC LIBRARY. His son, William B. Astor (1792–1875), greatly expanded the family real-estate holdings, building over 700 stores and dwellings in the city.

John Jacob Astor, detail of an oil painting by Gilbert Stuart, 1794; in the Brook Club, New York.
BY COURTESY OF THE FRICK ART REFERENCE LIBRARY

Astrakhan \'as-trə-ˌkan\ City (pop., 1992 est.: 512,000), southwestern Russia. It is situated on several islands in the delta of the VOLGA RIVER. It was the capital of a TATAR khanate that became independent of the GOLDEN HORDE in the 13th century, and its location on caravan and water routes made it a trading center. IVAN THE TERRIBLE conquered Astrakhan in 1556, giving Russia control of the Volga. The Turks burned the city in 1569. It served as the base for PETER THE GREAT's campaign against Persia and was given special trade privileges by CATHERINE II. Sites of interest include a fortress and a cathedral.

astrolabe Type of early scientific instrument used for reckoning time and for observational purposes. They can be traced to the 6th century

AD, came into wide use in Europe and the Islamic world in the early Middle Ages, and were adopted by mariners by the mid-15th century. One widely used variety, the planespheric astrolabe, can be regarded as a kind of basic analog computer. It enabled astronomers to calculate the positions of the sun and other major nearby stars with respect to both the horizon and the meridian.

Rete side of an iron astrolabe made after 1582.

BY COURTESY OF THE PEABODY MUSEUM OF SALEM; PHOTOGRAPH, M.W. SEXTON

astrology DIVINATION that consists of interpreting the influence of stars and planets on earthly affairs and human destinies. In ancient times it was inseparable from ASTRONOMY. It originated in Mesopotamia (c. 3rd millennium BC) and spread to India, but it developed its Western form in Greek civilization during the Hellenistic period. Astrology entered Islamic culture as part of the Greek tradition and was returned to European culture through Arabic learning during the Middle Ages. According to the Greek tradition, the heavens are divided according to the 12 constellations of the ZODIAC, and the bright stars that rise at intervals cast a spiritual influence over human affairs. Astrology was also important in ancient China, and in imperial times it became standard practice to have a HOROSCOPE cast for each newborn child and at all decisive junctures of life. Though the COPERNICAN SYSTEM shattered the geocentric worldview that astrology requires, interest in astrology has continued into modern times and astrological signs are still widely believed to influence personality.

astronaut Person trained to pilot a SPACECRAFT, operate any of its systems, or conduct research aboard it during spaceflights. The term commonly refers to those participating in U.S. space missions; cosmonaut is the Russian equivalent. Extensive training, including classroom study of technical subjects as well as practice in computer-controlled simulators and full-sized mock-ups of spacecraft to experience FREE FALL, prepares astronauts physically and psychologically for space missions. Astronauts also learn to use the control, communication, and life-support systems of any given spacecraft and conduct difficult flight operations. See also EDWIN ALDRIN, NEIL ARMSTRONG, GUION S., JR. BLUFORD, YURY A. GAGARIN, JOHN H., JR. GLENN, MAE JEMISON, SALLY RIDE, ALAN B. SHEPARD, VALENTINA TERESHKOVA.

astronomical unit (AU) Length of the semimajor axis of earth's orbit around the sun: 92,955,808 mi (149,597,870 km), often defined simply as the average distance from earth to the sun. Direct measurement through the PARALLAX method cannot be used for accurate determinations, because the sun drowns out the light of the background stars necessary to make the measurement. The most precise values have been obtained since 1958 by timing radar reflections from Venus. This indirect method is based on Kepler's law relating the relative size of the planets' orbits; thus, if the distance to one planet can be determined, then the distance to the sun can be calculated.

astronomy Science dealing with the origin, evolution, composition, distance, and motion of all bodies and scattered matter in the UNIVERSE. The most ancient of the sciences, it has existed since the dawn of recorded civilization. Much of the earliest knowledge of celestial bodies is often credited to the Babylonians. The ancient Greeks introduced influential cosmological ideas, including theories about the earth in relation to the rest of the universe. PTOLEMY's model of an earth-centered universe (2nd century AD) influenced astronomical thought for over 1,300 years. In the 16th century, NICOLAUS COPERNICUS assigned the central position to the sun (see COPERNICAN SYSTEM), ushering in the age of modern astronomy. The 17th century saw several momentous developments: JOHANNES KEPLER's discovery of the principles of planetary motion, GALILEO's application of the TELESCOPE to astronomical observation, and ISAAC NEWTON's formulation of the laws of motion and gravitation. In the 19th century, SPECTROSCOPY and photography made it possible to study the physical properties of planets, stars, and nebulae, leading to the development of ASTROPHYSICS. In 1927 EDWIN HUBBLE discovered that the universe, hitherto thought static, was expanding. In 1937 the first RADIO TELESCOPE was built. The first man-made satellite, SPUTNIK, was launched in 1957, and the first deep-space probes (see PIONEER) were launched in the 1960s. See also BIG BANG, COSMOLOGY, GAMMA-RAY ASTRONOMY, INFRARED ASTRONOMY, RADIO AND RADAR ASTRONOMY, ULTRAVIOLET ASTRONOMY, X-RAY ASTRONOMY.

astrophysics Branch of ASTRONOMY concerned mainly with the properties and structures of cosmic objects, including the universe as a whole. Starting in the 19th century, SPECTROSCOPY and photography were applied to astronomical research, making it possible to study the brightness, temperature, and chemical composition of cosmic objects. It was soon realized that these bodies' properties could be understood only in terms of the physics of their atmospheres and interiors. X-RAY ASTRONOMY, GAMMA-RAY ASTRONOMY, INFRARED ASTRONOMY, ULTRAVIOLET ASTRONOMY, and RADIO AND RADAR ASTRONOMY are all basically concerned with extending electromagnetic coverage to constrain the physical characteristics of astronomical objects.

Astruc of Lunel \as-trūēk\ *orig.* **Abba Mari ben Moses ben Joseph** (1250?–after 1306) French Jewish scholar. He revered MAIMONIDES but argued that Maimonides' followers undermined faith by reading the Bible allegorically. Through letters he persuaded the powerful Rabbi Solomon ben Abraham Adret (1235–1310) of Barcelona to forbid the study or teaching of science and philosophy by those under 25 (1305). The resulting controversy almost split the Jewish communities of France and Spain. A schism was prevented when Philip IV of France expelled the Jews from France in 1306, and Astruc settled in Majorca.

Asturias \äs-'tu̇r-ē-əs\ Autonomous community (pop., 1996: 1,088,000) and province, on the Bay of BISCAY, northwestern Spain. It occupies an area of 4,079 sq mi (10,565 sq km); its capital is OVIEDO. Coextensive with the historical Principality of Asturias, it is largely covered by mountains that isolate it from other Spanish provinces. Its population and industries are concentrated in the Nalón River valley, whose extensive coalfields make the province Spain's mining center. Conquered by the Romans under AUGUSTUS in 25 BC, it was later ruled by the VISIGOTHS. It became part of the Kingdom of LÉON on the accession of Alfonso III in 866. It was made a principality in 1388, a province in 1838, and an autonomous community in 1981.

Asturias \äs-'tu̇r-ē-əs\, **Miguel Ángel** (1899–1974) Guatemalan poet, novelist, and diplomat. He moved to Paris in 1923 and became a Surrealist under the influence of ANDRÉ BRETON. His first major works appeared in the 1930s. He began his diplomatic career in 1946, which culminated in his serving as ambassador to France 1966–70. His writings combine a Mayan mysticism with an epic impulse toward social protest, especially against U.S. and oligarchic power. In *Men of Maize* (1949), often considered his masterpiece, he depicts the seemingly irreversible wretchedness of the Indian peasant. Other major novels, some of which employ the style of magic realism, are *El Señor Presidente* (1946), a fictional denunciation of Guatemala's dictator; *The Cyclone* (1950); *The Green Pope* (1954); and *The Eyes of the Interred* (1960). He won the Nobel Prize in 1967.

Miguel Ángel Asturias.

CAMERA PRESS

Asunción \ä-ˌsün-'syōn\ *in full* **Nuestra Señora de la Asunción** Capital city (pop., 1992: 502,000) of Paraguay. It lies on the PARAGUAY RIVER near its confluence with the PILCOMAYO RIVER. Founded in 1537 by Spanish conquistadores, it replaced BUENOS AIRES as the headquarters of Spanish colonial activities in eastern South America during the period of the latter's depopulation (1541–80). In 1731 Asunción was the site of one of the first major rebellions against Spanish rule. The city declared independence from both Spain and Argentina in 1811. Today it dominates social, cultural, and economic trends in Paraguay.

Asvaghosa \ˌäsh-və'-gō-shə\ (AD 80?–150?) Indian philosopher and poet, considered the father of Sanskrit drama. Born a Brahman, he opposed Buddhism until a debate with a Buddhist scholar led to his conversion. Asvaghosa became known as a brilliant orator, and he spoke on Mahayana at the fourth Buddhist council. He is considered India's greatest poet before Kalidasa. Works attributed to him include the *Buddhacarita* ("Life of the Buddha") and the *Mahalankara* ("Book of Glory").

asvamedha \ˌäsh-və-ˈmā-də\ Rite of the Vedic religion in ancient India, performed by a king to celebrate his supremacy. A stallion was selected and allowed to roam freely for a year under the protection of a royal guard. It was said to symbolize the progress of the sun and the power of the king. If it was not captured during the year, it was brought back to the capital along with the rulers of lands it had entered. It was then sacrificed at a public ceremony, and the king assumed the title of universal monarch. The Buddha condemned the practice, but it was revived in the 2nd century BC and may have continued as late as the 11th century AD.

Aswan City (pop., 1996 est.: 219,017), southeastern Egypt. It lies on the Nile River just north of Lake Nasser. In ancient times it was the southern frontier of pharaonic Egypt. Later known as Syene, it served as a frontier garrison post for the Romans, Turks, and British. Modern Aswan is located near the old Aswan Dam (completed 1902) and the Aswan High Dam.

Aswan High Dam Dam across the Nile River, north of Aswan, Egypt. Built 4 mi (6 km) upstream from the earlier Aswan Dam (1902), it is 364 ft (111 m) high and 12,562 ft (3,830 m) long. Differences with Gamal Abdel Nasser led the U.S. and Britain to withdraw financial support of the project in 1956, whereupon Nasser turned to the Soviet Union. The dam, completed in 1970, impounds the reservoir Lake Nasser and controls the annual Nile flood, releasing floodwaters for irrigation; it also enables the production of great amounts of electric power. Its construction necessitated the relocation of the ancient Abu Simbel ruins.

asylum Protection from arrest and extradition given to political refugees by a nation or by an embassy that has diplomatic immunity. No one has a legal right to asylum, and the sheltering state, which has the legal right to grant asylum, is under no obligation to give it. It is thus a right of the state, not the individual. Its traditional use has been to protect those accused of such political offenses as treason, desertion, sedition, and espionage. Beginning in the late 20th century it also has been granted to those who can demonstrate a reasonable fear of politically motivated persecution in their home country.

asymmetric synthesis Chemical reaction by which unequal amounts of two product isomers are formed. It is normally not possible to synthesize from materials that do not have optical activity (i.e., are not chiral) one stereoisomer of a chiral compound without the other, but use of a chiral auxiliary, such as an enzyme or other catalyst, a solvent, or an intermediate, can force the reaction to produce predominantly or only one isomer. Asymmetric syntheses are often called stereoselective; if one product forms exclusively, it is stereospecific.

asymptote \ˈa-səm-ˌtōt\ In mathematics, a line or curve that acts as the limit of another line or curve. For example, a descending curve that approaches but does not reach the horizontal axis is said to be asymptotic to that axis, which is the asymptote of the curve.

AT&T Corp. *formerly* **American Telephone and Telegraph Co.** U.S. telecommunications corporation. It was established as a subsidiary of Bell Telephone Co. (founded by Alexander Graham Bell in 1877) to build long-distance telephone lines and later became the parent company of the Bell system. In the early 20th century it gained a virtual monopoly over the U.S. telecommunications industry, and by 1970 it was the world's largest corporation. It developed transoceanic radiotelephone links and telephone cable systems and created the Telstar satellite communications system. Years of federal antitrust litigation resulted in AT&T's 1984 divestment of its 22 regional telephone companies, which were combined to form seven "Baby Bells": Nynex, Bell Atlantic, Ameritech (or American Information Technologies, Inc.), BellSouth, Southwestern Bell Corp., US West, and Pacific Telesis Group. In 1996 AT&T divided its operations into three separate companies: AT&T Corp., Lucent Technologies Inc. (composed of the former operations of Western Electric and Bell Laboratories), and the NCR Corp. AT&T was divided into four units in 2000.

Atacama Desert \ˌä-tä-ˈkä-mä\ Arid area, northern central Chile. Extending north from the city of Copiapó, the area covers most of the Antofagasta region and the northern part of the Atacama region. For much of the 19th century, the desert was the object of conflicts among Chile, Bolivia, and Peru; after the War of the Pacific (1883), Chile emerged with permanent ownership of sectors previously controlled by Peru and Bolivia. For years before the development of synthetic methods of fixing nitrogen, the desert was a chief source of the world's nitrates. It is one of the driest regions in the world.

Atahuallpa \ˌä-tä-ˈwäl-pä\ (1502?–1533) Last free-reigning emperor of the Incas. He became ruler after defeating his half brother in what may have been the greatest military engagement in Inca history. The conquistador Francisco Pizarro met Atahuallpa just before the emperor's triumphal entry into Cuzco and invited him to a feast in his honor. When Atahuallpa and his unarmed retainers arrived, Pizarro ambushed them on horseback with cannons and guns, slaughtered thousands, and took Atahuallpa prisoner. Pizarro accepted Atahuallpa's offer of a ransom of a roomful of gold, then, having received 24 tons of gold and silver, ordered Atahuallpa burned at the stake. The sentence was changed to death by garrote when Atahuallpa agreed to convert to Christianity.

Atalanta \ˌa-tᵊl-ˈan-tə\ In Greek mythology, a swift-footed huntress. Born in Boeotia or Arcadia, she was left to die at birth but was suckled by a bear. As an adult she took part in the famous Calydonian boar hunt and drew first blood. She offered to marry any man who could outrun her in a race, but the losers were required to pay with their lives. One contestant, Hippomenes (or Milanion), obtained three golden apples from Aphrodite to carry in the race. As he dropped them, Atalanta stooped to pick them up, and thus lost the race. The two were later turned into lions after they desecrated a shrine to Cybele or Zeus.

Atalanta, Greek marble statue; in the Louvre.
GIRAUDON—ART RESOURCE

Atanasoff \ə-ˈtan-ə-ˌsȯf\, **John V(incent)** (1903–1995) U.S. physicist. Born in Hamilton, N.Y., he received a PhD from the University of Wisconsin. With Clifford Berry, he developed the Atanasoff-Berry Computer (1937–42), a machine capable of solving differential equations using binary arithmetic; its design components became the basic architecture of computers. In 1941 he joined the Naval Ordnance Laboratory; he participated in the atomic-bomb tests at Bikini Atoll (1946). In 1952 he established the Ordnance Engineering Co., which he later sold to Aerojet Engineering Corp. In 1973, after a judge voided a patent owned by Sperry Rand Corp. on ENIAC, the Atanasoff-Berry Computer was credited as the first electronic digital computer.

Atargatis \ə-ˈtär-gə-tis\ Goddess of northern Syria who was worshiped at Hierapolis, northeast of Aleppo, along with her consort, Hadad. Primarily a goddess of fertility, she was also mistress of the city and its people. She was often depicted wearing a crown and carrying a sheaf of grain, and her throne was supported by lions, suggesting her power over nature. Considered a combination of Anath and Astarte, she also showed kinship with the Anatolian Cybele (Great Mother of the Gods). Merchants and mercenaries carried her cult throughout the Greek world, where she was considered a form of Aphrodite.

Atatürk \ˈat-ə-ˌtərk\, **Mustafa Kemal** (1881–1938) Founder of modern Turkey. Born in Ottoman-controlled Greece and dedicated by his father to military service, he graduated near the top of his class in military school. As a young officer, he was critical of the government and became involved with the Turkish nationalist Committee of Union and Progress. He nevertheless fought for the government during World War I, defeating the Allies at Gallipoli. The eventual Allied victory brought British, French, and Italian troops to Anatolia; appointed to restore order there, he used the opportunity to incite the people against the Allied invaders. Greece and Armenia, territorial beneficiaries of the Ottoman empire's defeat, opposed the Turkish nationalists, but he overcame all opposition, and the Turkish republic was established in 1923. Mustafa Kemal was given the name Atatürk ("father of the Turks") in 1934. He pursued a policy of Westernization, deemphasizing religion, mandating Western fashions, emancipating women, imposing surnames, overhauling the legal system, and replacing the Arabic alphabet with the Roman. See also ENVER PASA, YOUNG TURKS.

ataxia \ā-'tak-sē-ə\ Inability to coordinate voluntary muscular movements; in common usage, unsteady gait. Hereditary ataxias are usually caused by degeneration of the SPINAL CORD, CEREBELLUM, or other parts of the NERVOUS SYSTEM. The most common is Friedreich's ataxia, which begins at ages 3–5, progressing slowly to almost complete incapacity by age 20. There is no specific therapy. Metabolic disorders, brain injuries, and toxins can cause ataxia.

Atbara River \'at-bə-rə\ River, North Africa. Rising in the Ethiopian highlands, it flows about 500 mi (800 km) northwest through eastern Sudan to join the NILE RIVER at Atbara (pop., 1983: 73,000) in Sudan. It is the Nile's northernmost tributary.

Atchafalaya Bay \ə-,cha-fə-'lī-ə\ Inlet of the Gulf of Mexico on the Louisiana coast. With the Four League Bay, it extends about 21 mi (34 km). The ATCHAFALAYA RIVER links the bay with Morgan City on the GULF INTRACOASTAL WATERWAY. The area includes many natural gas and oil fields.

Atchafalaya River River, southern Louisiana. Rising in central Louisiana, it flows south 225 mi (362 km) into ATCHAFALAYA BAY. It is an additional outlet for the RED and MISSISSIPPI rivers during periods of high water. Its name is Choctaw for "long river."

Atchison, Topeka and Santa Fe Railroad Co. Former railway. Chartered in Kansas in 1860 by Cyrus K. Holliday, the founder of Topeka, as the Atchison and Topeka Railroad Co., it was built along the SANTA FE TRAIL and became known as the Santa Fe Railway. Its main line, completed in 1872, extended to the Colorado state border. Further expansion west in the 1880s and early 1890s reached about 9,000 mi (14,500 km) of track. It reached its greatest extent in 1941, with more than 13,000 mi (21,000 km) of track, but gradually shrank thereafter. In 1971 its famously luxurious passenger service was sold to AMTRAK. In the 1990s it merged with Burlington Northern to become Burlington Northern Santa Fe Railway.

atelectasis \,at-ᵊl-'ek-tə-səs\ *or* **lung collapse** Lack of expansion of pulmonary alveoli (see PULMONARY ALVEOLUS). With a large-enough collapsed area, the victim stops breathing. In congenital atelectasis, obstruction or lack of surface tension keeps a newborn's alveoli from expanding. Compression atelectasis is caused by external pressure. Obstructive atelectasis may be caused by blockage of a major airway or when pain from abdominal surgery keeps breathing too shallow to clear bronchial secretions; treatment involves removal of obstruction or fluids, control of infection, and lung reinflation.

Aten See ATON

Atget \àt-'zhe\, **(Jean-) Eugène (-Auguste)** (1857–1927) French photographer. He began his adult life as an itinerant actor. Around age 30 he settled in Paris and became a photographer. With an eye for strange and unsettling images, he recorded shop fronts, statues, trees, fountains, buildings, monuments, and poor tradespeople. After World War I he received a commission to document the brothels of Paris. MAN RAY published four of Atget's photographs in *La révolution surréaliste* (1926), the only recognition he received in his lifetime. After his death, Ray, BERENICE ABBOTT, and the art dealer Julien Lévy bought his remaining collection, which is now in the Museum of Modern Art.

Athabasca, Lake Lake, western central Canada. It extends 208 mi (335 km), crossing the Alberta-Saskatchewan boundary. On the southwest it receives the ATHABASCA RIVER, and on the northwest it discharges into the SLAVE RIVER. It is important for its commercial fishing.

Athabasca River River, western central Canada. A tributary of the MACKENZIE RIVER in Alberta, it rises in the Rocky Mountains in JASPER NATIONAL PARK, and flows northeast and north 765 mi (1,231 km) into Lake ATHABASCA. Its chief tributaries are the Pembina, Lesser Slave, and La Biche rivers. Extensive petroleum deposits lie in oil-impregnated sands (Athabasca Tar Sands) along a 70-mi (113-km) stretch of the river.

Athabaskan languages *or* **Athapaskan languages** Family of North American Indian languages, with perhaps 200,000 speakers today. Northern Athabaskan includes more than 20 languages scattered across an immense region of subarctic North America from western Alaska to Hudson Bay and south to southern Alberta and British Columbia. Pacific Coast Athabaskan consisted of four to eight languages, all now extinct or nearing extinction. Apachean consists of eight closely related languages spoken in the southwestern U.S. and northern Mexico, including Navajo and the various subdivisions of Apache. In 1990 Navajo had close to 150,000 speakers, far more than any other indigenous language of the U.S. or Canada. In 1915 EDWARD SAPIR placed the Athabaskan family together with Tlingit and Haida (languages of Alaska and British Columbia, respectively) in a larger grouping called Na-Dene; this hypothetical relationship continues to be controversial.

Athanasius \,a-thə-'nā-zhəs\, **St.** (293?–373) Early Christian theologian and defender of Christian orthodoxy against ARIANISM. He studied philosophy and theology at Alexandria, Egypt, and in 325 he attended the Council of NICAEA, which condemned the Arian heresy. In 328 he was appointed patriarch of Alexandria, but theological disputes led to the first of several banishments in 336. He returned from exile repeatedly and resumed his office, but Arian opposition continued. After being banished by Constantius II in 356, he lived in a remote desert in Upper Egypt and wrote theological treatises, including his *Four Orations Against the Arians*. The emperor's death in 361 gave him a brief respite under the toleration proclaimed by JULIAN, but a controversy with Julian's heathen subjects forced him to flee into the Theban desert. At the time of his death he again possessed the see at Alexandria.

atheism \'ā-thē-,iz-əm\ Critique and denial of metaphysical beliefs in God or divine beings. Unlike AGNOSTICISM, which leaves open the question of whether there is a God, atheism is a positive denial. It is rooted in an array of philosophical systems. Ancient Greek philosophers such as DEMOCRITUS and EPICURUS argued for it in the context of MATERIALISM. In the 18th century DAVID HUME and IMMANUEL KANT, though not atheists, argued against traditional proofs for God's existence, making belief a matter of faith alone. Atheists such as LUDWIG FEUERBACH held that God was a projection of human ideals and that recognizing this fiction made self-realization possible. MARXISM exemplified modern MATERIALISM. Beginning with FRIEDRICH NIETZSCHE, existentialist atheism proclaimed the death of God and the human freedom to determine value and meaning. Logical POSITIVISM holds that propositions concerning the existence or nonexistence of God are nonsensical or meaningless.

Athena \ə-'thē-nə\ *or* **Athene** \ə-'thē-nē\ In ancient GREEK RELIGION, the goddess of war, handicraft, and wisdom, and patroness of Athens. Her Roman counterpart was MINERVA. HESIOD told how Athena sprang in full armor from ZEUS's forehead. In the *Iliad*, she fought alongside the Greek heroes, and she represented the virtues of justice and skill in warfare as opposed to the blood-lust of ARES. She was associated with birds, especially the owl and the snake, and she was usually represented as a virgin goddess. Her birth and contest with POSEIDON for suzerainty of Athens were depicted on the PARTHENON. Her birthday festival was the PANATHENAEA.

The Varakion, a Roman marble copy (c. AD 130) of the colossal gold and ivory statue of the Athena Parthenos by Phidias (438 BC); in the National Archaeological Museum, Athens.
ALINARI—ART RESOURCE/EB INC.

Athens *Greek* **Athínai** \ä-'thē-ne\ City (pop., 1991: 772,000), capital of Greece. It is located inland near its port, PIRAEUS, on the SARONIC GULF in eastern Greece. The source of many of the West's intellectual and artistic conceptions, including that of democracy, Athens is generally considered the birthplace of Western civilization. An ancient city-state, it had by the 6th century BC begun to assert its influence. It was destroyed by XERXES in 480 BC, but rebuilding began immediately. By 450 BC, led by PERICLES, it was at the height of its commercial prosperity and cultural and political dominance, and over the next 40 years many major building projects, including the Acropolis and PARTHENON, were completed. Athens' "Golden Age" saw the works of the philosophers SOCRATES, PLATO, and ARISTOTLE; the dramatists SOPHOCLES, ARISTOPHANES, and EURIPIDES; the historians HERODOTUS, THUCYDIDES, and XENOPHON; and the sculptors PRAXITELES and PHIDIAS. The PELOPONNESIAN WARS with SPARTA ended in Athens' defeat in 404, but it quickly recovered its independence and prosperity. After 338 BC Athens came under MACEDONIA's hegemony, which was lifted with the aid of Rome in 197 BC in a battle at Cynoscephalae. It became subject to Rome in 146 BC. In the 13th century Athens was taken by the Crusaders. It was conquered in 1456 by the Ottoman Turks, who held it until 1833, when it was declared the capital of independent Greece. Athens is Greece's principal center for business and foreign trade. The city's ruins and many museums make it a major tourist destination. It was selected to host the 2004 Summer Olympic Games.

athlete's foot Form of RINGWORM that affects the feet. In the inflammatory type, the infection may lie inactive much of the time, with occasional acute episodes in which blisters develop, mostly between the toes. The dry type is a chronic condition marked by slight redness of the skin and dry scaling that may involve the sole and sides of the foot and the toenails, which become thick and brittle.

athletics See TRACK AND FIELD

Athos \'ä-ˌthȯs\, **Mount** Mountain, northern Greece. Reaching a height of 6,670 ft (2,033 m), it occupies Aktí, a promontory of the Chalcidice Peninsula. It is the site of a semiautonomous republic of 20 monasteries and dependencies (skítes). Organized monastic life began there in 963, when St. ATHANASIUS the Athonite founded the first monastery. By 1400 there were 40 monasteries. Long regarded as the holy mountain of the GREEK ORTHODOX CHURCH, it was declared a theocratic republic in 1927. Its churches and libraries house a rich collection of Byzantine art and ancient and medieval manuscripts.

Athyr See HATHOR

Atitlán \ˌä-tē-'tlän\, **Lake** Lake, southwestern Guatemala. It lies at an altitude of about 4,700 ft (1,430 m) in the central highlands. Occupying a crater some 1,000 ft (300 m) deep, the lake is 12 mi (19 km) long and 6 mi (10 km) wide. On its borders are three volcanoes: Atitlán, Tolimán, and San Pedro. Main towns along the lake, including Atitlán and San Lucas, cater to the tourist trade.

Atkins, Chet *orig.* **Chester Burton** (1924–2001) U.S. guitarist and recording executive. Born in Luttrell, Tenn., Atkins began his musical career as a fiddler in the early 1940s, but it was his signature style of playing guitar (bass rhythm played with thumb, melody picked with three fingers) that brought him worldwide acclaim. In the early 1950s he began playing electric guitar, pioneering its use in country music. He recorded more than 100 albums for RCA. As an RCA executive, he produced hit recordings for ELVIS PRESLEY, Jim Reeves, and Waylon Jennings.

Atlanta City (pop., 2000: 416,474; metro area pop.: 4,112,198), capital of Georgia. Lying in the foothills of the BLUE RIDGE MTNS., Atlanta is Georgia's largest city. In 1837 a spot was selected here for a railroad terminus that would serve the southeastern U.S. First named Terminus and later Marthasville, it was given the name Atlanta in 1845. An important supply depot during the AMERICAN CIVIL WAR, it was burned by Union forces under WILLIAM T. SHERMAN. Atlanta became the state capital in 1868. As it recovered from the war's destruction, it began to epitomize the spirit of the "New South" in seeking reconciliation with the North. It was the home of MARTIN LUTHER KING, and was the first major Southern city to elect a black mayor (1970). It is the principal trade and transportation center of the southeastern U.S.

Atlanta Campaign Important series of AMERICAN CIVIL WAR battles in Georgia (May–September 1864). Though most of the battles ended in draws, they eventually cut off the main Confederate supply center, Atlanta. Union troops under WILLIAM T. SHERMAN forced the evacuation of the city (August 31–September 1) and then burned it. His victory assured the reelection of Pres. ABRAHAM LINCOLN later that year.

Atlanta Compromise Classic statement on race relations by BOOKER T. WASHINGTON in a speech at the Atlanta Exposition (1895). He asserted that vocational education, which gave blacks a chance for economic security, was more valuable than social equality or political office. Many blacks feared that such a limited goal would keep blacks in subservience to whites; that fear led to the founding of the NAACP.

Atlanta Constitution Daily morning newspaper published in Atlanta. Generally regarded as the "voice of the New South," it is usually counted among the great newspapers of the U.S. It became a leader among Southern papers soon after its founding in 1868, and a succession of outstanding editors contributed to its distinction: Henry W. Grady (1850–1889), in the late 1870s and 1880s; Clark Howell, 1897–1938; and Ralph McGill, editor 1942–60 and publisher 1960–69. In 1950 it was bought by James M. Cox, who already owned the evening *Atlanta Journal* (founded 1883); a merged paper, the *Atlanta Journal-Constitution*, is published on weekends.

Atlantic, Battle of the Contest in WORLD WAR II between Britain (and later the U.S.) and Germany for the control of Atlantic sea routes. Initially the Anglo-French coalition drove German merchant shipping from the Atlantic, but with the fall of France in 1940, Britain was deprived of French naval support. The U.S. then assisted Britain with the LEND-LEASE program. Early in 1942, the Axis began a large-scale submarine offensive against coastal shipping in U.S. waters, and German U-BOATS also operated in force along the South Atlantic ship lanes to India and the Middle East. Allied shipping losses were severe, but the Allies succeeded in tightening their blockade of Axis Europe and combating the Axis war on shipping. By mid-1943 the Allies had recovered control of the sea routes.

Atlantic Charter Joint declaration issued on August 14, 1941, during WORLD WAR II, by WINSTON CHURCHILL and FRANKLIN ROOSEVELT. Among the statements made in this propaganda manifesto, signed when the U.S. had not yet entered the war, were that neither the U.S. nor Britain sought aggrandizement and that both advocated the restoration of self-government to peoples forcibly deprived of it. The charter was incorporated by reference in the Declaration of the U.N. (1942).

Atlantic City City (pop., 2000: 40,517) and resort, southeastern New Jersey. Lying on narrow Absecon Island, the resort began to be developed in the mid-19th century. Amusement piers were constructed, and the first beachfront boardwalk was built there in 1870. The Miss America Pageant was established in Atlantic City in 1921. After World War II the city began to decline. In 1978 the state approved legalized gambling, and extensive development in Atlantic City provided a huge influx of money to the resort, but much of the surrounding area remained impoverished.

Atlantic Intracoastal Waterway Navigable route, coastal eastern U.S. Authorized by Congress in 1919 to provide sheltered passage for both commercial shipping and pleasure craft, and constructed by the Army Corps of Engineers, it was originally planned to form a continuous channel from New York City to Brownsville, Texas. Because the link through Florida was never completed, it remains in two separate sections (see GULF INTRACOASTAL WATERWAY). The Atlantic portion consists of rivers, bays, and canals from CAPE COD to Florida Bay, including the Cape Cod Canal and the Chesapeake and Delaware Canal.

Atlantic languages *formerly* **West Atlantic languages** Branch of the NIGER-CONGO family of African languages. Atlantic comprises more than 40 languages spoken mainly in extreme western West Africa. The most widespread Atlantic language is Fula (see FULANI), with an estimated 18 million speakers spread across West Africa.

Atlantic Monthly, The Monthly journal of literature and opinion, one of the oldest and most respected of U.S. reviews. Published in Boston, it was founded in 1857 by Moses Dresser Phillips. It soon became noted for the quality of its fiction and general articles, contributed by such distinguished editors and authors as JAMES RUSSELL LOWELL, RALPH WALDO EMERSON, HENRY W. LONGFELLOW, and OLIVER WENDELL HOLMES. In the early 1920s it expanded its scope to political affairs, featuring articles by such figures as THEODORE ROOSEVELT, WOODROW WILSON, and BOOKER T. WASHINGTON. In the 1970s, increasing costs nearly shut the magazine down; it was purchased in 1980 by Mortimer B. Zuckerman.

Atlantic Ocean Ocean separating North and South America from Europe and Africa. The second-largest of the world's oceans, the Atlantic has an area of 31,830,000 sq mi (82,440,000 sq km). With its marginal seas, including the BALTIC, NORTH, BLACK, and MEDITERRANEAN to the east, and BAFFIN BAY, HUDSON BAY, the Gulf of ST. LAWRENCE, Gulf of MEXICO, and CARIBBEAN SEA to the west, it covers 41,000,000 sq mi (105,000,000 sq km); including these latter bodies of water, its average depth is 10,925 ft (3,330 m). Its most powerful current is the GULF STREAM.

Atlantic salmon Oceanic TROUT species *(Salmo salar)*, a highly prized game fish. It averages about 12 lbs (5.5 kg) and is marked with round or cross-shaped spots. Found on both sides of the Atlantic Ocean, it enters streams in the fall to spawn. The young enter the sea in about two years and mature in about four. Adults may return to the sea and, after a year or two, spawn again. The ouananiche of rivers and the sebago, or lake, salmon are landlocked subspecies that are also prized for sport. The Atlantic salmon has been successfully introduced into the U.S. Great Lakes.

Atlantis Legendary sunken island in the Atlantic Ocean west of Gibraltar. The main sources for the legend are two of PLATO's dialogues, *Timaeus* and *Critias*. According to Plato, Atlantis had a rich civilization, and its princes made many conquests in the Mediterranean before earthquakes destroyed the island and it was swallowed up by the sea. Plato also supplied a history of its ideal commonwealth, and Atlantis is sometimes imagined as a utopia. The legend may have originated with the eruption c. 1500 BC of a volcano on THÍRA, which was so powerful that it gave rise to earthquakes and tidal waves.

Atlas In GREEK MYTHOLOGY, the strong man who supported the weight of the heavens on his shoulders. He was the son of the TITAN Iapetus and the nymph Clymene (or Asia) and the brother of PROMETHEUS. According to HESIOD, Atlas was one of the Titans who waged war against Zeus, and as punishment he was condemned to hold aloft the heavens.

atlas Collection of maps or charts, usually bound together. The name derives from a custom—initiated by GERARDUS MERCATOR in the 16th century—of using the figure of the Titan ATLAS, holding the globe on his shoulders, as a frontispiece for books of maps. Abraham Ortelius's *Epitome of the Theater of the World* (1570) is generally thought to be the first modern atlas. Atlases often contain pictures, tabular data, facts about areas, and indexes of place-names keyed to coordinates of latitude and longitude or to a locational grid with numbers and letters along the sides of maps.

atlas Male figure used as a column to support an ENTABLATURE, balcony, or other projection, originating in Classical architecture. Such figures are posed as if supporting great weights, like ATLAS bearing the world. The related telamon of Roman architecture, the male counterpart of the CARYATID, is also a weight-bearing figure but does not usually appear in an atlas pose.

Atlas, Charles *orig.* **Angelo Siciliano** (1893–1972) U.S. bodybuilder. Born in Acri, Italy, Atlas emigrated to the U.S. at the age of 10. In 1929 he and the advertiser Charles P. Roman launched a course involving isotonic exercises and nutritional maintenance. Their mail-order bodybuilding course became legendary through advertisements in three generations of pulp comic books, the standard ad depicting scenes in which a skinny boy loses his girlfriend to a well-built lifeguard who kicks sand in his face, and regains her after taking the Atlas course.

Atlas Mountains Mountain system, northwestern and northern Africa. It extends some 1,200 mi (2,000 km) from Cape Dra, Morocco, to Cape BON, Tunisia. It comprises several ranges, including the High Atlas in Morocco, the Maritime or Tell Atlas from Morocco to Tunisia, and the Saharan Atlas in Algeria. Its highest peak is Morocco's Mount Toubkal, at 13,665 ft (4,165 m).

Atlas rocket Booster for space vehicles, particularly the U.S. MERCURY spacecraft series, originally designed as an intercontinental ballistic missile (ICBM). Two of its engines are boosters, jettisoned after about 2½ minutes of operation; the third, a sustainer, operates until orbital speed is attained. Coupled with Agena, an upper-stage rocket, Atlas is used for launching lunar and planetary probes and earth-orbiting satellites.

atman \'ät-mən\ (Sanskrit: "breath" or "self") Basic concept in Hindu philosophy, describing that eternal core of the personality that survives death and transmigrates to a new life or is released from the bonds of existence. Atman became a central philosophical concept in the UPANISHADS. It underlies all aspects of personality, as BRAHMAN underlies the working of the universe. The schools of SAMKHYA, YOGA, and VEDANTA are particularly concerned with atman. See also SOUL.

atmosphere Gaseous envelope that surrounds the earth. Near the surface it has a well-defined chemical composition (see AIR). In addition to gases, the atmosphere contains solid and liquid particles in suspension. Scientists divide the atmosphere into five main layers: in ascending order, the TROPOSPHERE (surface to 6–8 mi, or 10–13 km); the STRATOSPHERE (4–11 mi, or 6–17 km, to about 30 mi, or 50 km); the mesosphere (31–50 mi, or 50–80 km); the thermosphere (50–300 mi, or 80–480 km); and the exosphere (from 300 mi and gradually dissipating). Most of the atmosphere consists of neutral atoms and molecules, but in the IONOSPHERE a significant fraction is electrically charged. The ionosphere begins near the top of the stratosphere but is most distinct in the thermosphere. See also OZONE LAYER.

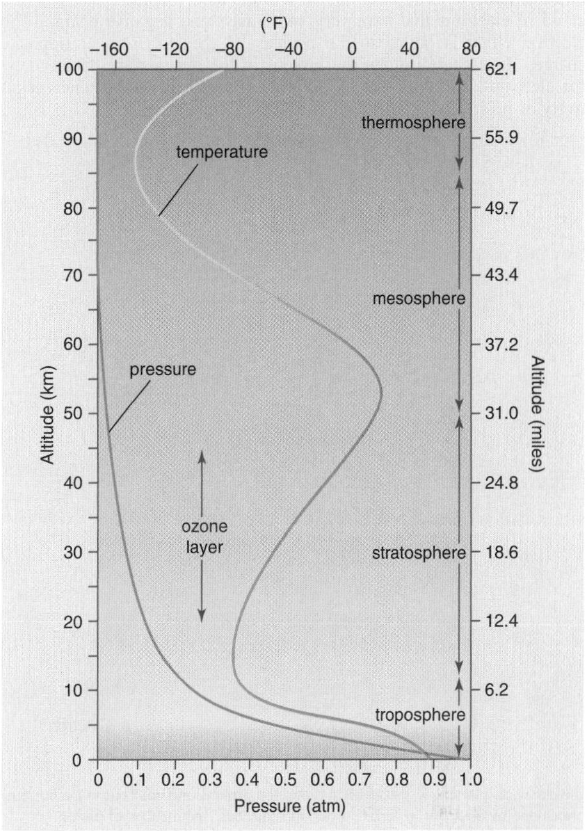

In earth's atmosphere, the limits of the atmospheric layers are approximate and variable, especially with latitude. Most weather occurs within the troposphere. The ozone layer, which absorbs most incoming ultraviolet radiation, forms part of the stratosphere. The thermosphere extends hundreds of miles above earth's surface and is bounded by outer space. Atmospheric pressure drops off steadily with altitude, but temperature rises and falls through successive layers in a more complex manner.

atmospheric pressure *or* **barometric pressure** Force per unit area exerted by the air above the surface of the earth. Standard sea-level pressure, by definition, equals 1 atmosphere (atm), or 29.92 in. (760 mm) of mercury, 14.70 lbs per square in., or 101.35 kilopascals, but pressure varies with elevation and temperature. It is usually measured with a mercury barometer (hence the term barometric pressure), which indicates the height of a column of mercury that exactly balances the weight of the column of atmosphere above it. It may also be measured using an aneroid barometer, in which the action of atmospheric pressure in bending a metallic surface is made to move a pointer.

atoll \'a-ˌtȯl\ Coral reef enclosing a LAGOON. Atolls consist of ribbons of reef that may not be circular but that are closed shapes, sometimes miles across, around a lagoon that may be 160 ft (50 m) deep or more. Most of the reef itself is usually below the water surface; around the rim along the top are usually low, flat islands or more continuous strips of low, flat land.

atom Smallest unit into which matter can be divided and still retain the characteristic properties of an element. The word derives from the Greek *atomos* ("indivisible"), and the atom was believed to be indivisible until the early 20th century, when ELECTRONS and the NUCLEUS were discovered. It is now known that an atom has a positively charged nucleus that makes up more than 99.9% of the atom's MASS but only about 10^{-14} (less than a trillionth) of its volume. The nucleus is composed of positively charged PROTONS and electrically neutral NEUTRONS, each about 2,000 times as massive as an electron. Most of the atom's volume consists of a cloud of electrons that have very small mass and negative charge. The electron cloud is bound to the nucleus by the attraction of opposite charges. In a neutral atom, the protons in the nucleus are balanced by the electrons. An atom that has gained or lost electrons becomes negatively or positively charged and is called an ION.

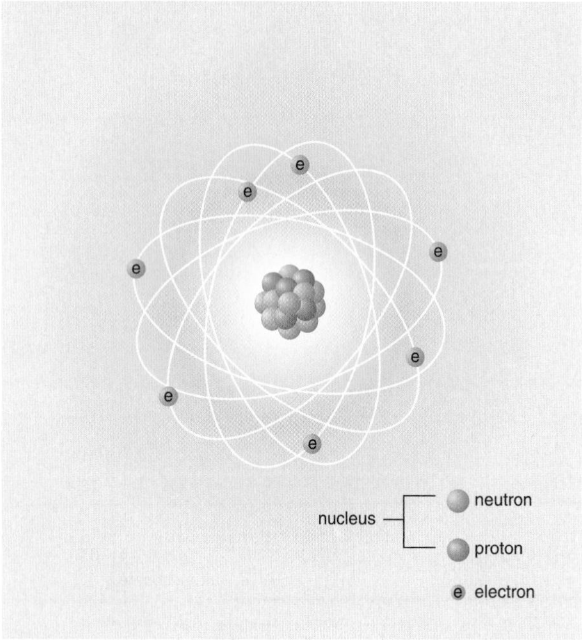

The classical "planetary" model of an atom. The protons and neutrons in the nucleus are circled by electrons in "orbit" around the nucleus. The number of protons determines which element is represented, the number of electrons determines its charge, and the number of neutrons determines which isotope of the element is represented.

atomic bomb Weapon whose great explosive power results from the sudden release of energy upon the splitting, or fission, of the nuclei of such heavy elements as plutonium or uranium (see NUCLEAR FISSION). An atomic bomb containing 2 lbs (1 kg) of uranium-235 will generate a 17-kiloton explosion that creates a huge fireball, a large shock wave, and lethal radioactive FALLOUT. The first atomic bomb, developed by the MANHATTAN PROJECT during World War II, was set off on July 16, 1945, in the New Mexico desert. The first bomb used in warfare was dropped by the U.S. on HIROSHIMA on August 6, 1945; a second bomb was dropped on NAGASAKI three days later. After the war, the U.S. conducted dozens of atomic tests in the Pacific and in Nevada. In 1949 the Soviet Union tested its first atomic bomb, followed by Britain (1952), France (1960), and China (1964), and subsequently India (1974) and Pakistan (1998). Israel and South Africa are also suspected of having tested atomic weapons. See also HYDROGEN BOMB, NON-PROLIFERATION TREATY.

atomic number Number of a chemical ELEMENT in the systematic, ordered sequence shown in the PERIODIC TABLE. The elements are arranged in order of increasing number of PROTONS in the NUCLEUS of the ATOM (the same as the number of ELECTRONS in the neutral atom), and that number for each element is its atomic number.

atomic physics Scientific study of the structure of the ATOM, its energy states, and its interaction with other particles and fields. The modern understanding of the atom is that it consists of a heavy NUCLEUS of positive charge surrounded by a cloud of light, negatively charged ELECTRONS. The physical properties of atoms are largely determined by the laws of QUANTUM MECHANICS and QUANTUM ELECTRODYNAMICS. The primary tools for the study of these properties are SPECTROSCOPY, particle collisions (see PARTICLE ACCELERATOR), and statistical models that simulate complex, many-body interactions (such as gas dynamics). A broad field, atomic physics has applications in the study of condensed matter, gases, chemical-reaction mechanisms, atmospheric science, lasers, NUCLEAR PHYSICS, and the arrangement of elements in the periodic table.

atomic weapon See NUCLEAR WEAPON

atomic weight Ratio of the average MASS of a chemical ELEMENT's atoms to 1⁄12 the mass of an atom of the carbon-12 ISOTOPE. The original standard of atomic weight, established in the 19th century, was hydrogen, with a value of 1. From c. 1900 until 1961, the reference standard was oxygen, with a value of 16, and the unit of atomic mass was defined as 1⁄16 the mass of an oxygen atom. Oxygen, however, contains small amounts of two isotopes that are heavier than the most abundant one, and 16 is actually a weighted average of the masses of the three isotopes of oxygen. Therefore, the standard was changed to one based on carbon-12. The new scale required only minimal changes to the values that had been used for chemical atomic weights.

atomism Philosophical doctrine that material objects are aggregates of simpler parts known as atoms. Atomism in the strict sense is characterized by three points: the atoms are absolutely indivisible, qualitatively identical apart from shape, size, and motion, and combinable with each other only by juxtaposition. Atomism is usually associated with REALISM and MECHANISM; it is mechanistic because it maintains that all observable changes can be reduced to changes in the configuration of the atoms that constitute matter. It is opposed to HOLISM because it holds that the properties of any whole can be explained in terms of those of its parts.

Aton *or* **Aten** \'ä-tən, 'a-tən\ In ancient Egyptian religion, a sun god, depicted as the solar disk emitting rays terminating in human hands. The pharaoh AKHENATON (r.1353–36 BC) declared Aton to be the only god, and in opposition to the Amon-Re priesthood of Thebes, built the city of Akhetaton as the center for Aton's worship, but Aton's religion is poorly understood. After Akhenaton's death, the old religion was restored.

King Akhenaton (left) with his wife, Queen Nefertiti, and three of their daughters under the rays of the sun god Aton, altar relief, mid-14th century BC; in the State Museums at Berlin.

atonality \ˌā-tō-'na-lə-tē\ Literally, the absence of TONALITY. Probably originally a pejorative term applied to music of extreme CHROMATICISM, it has become the most widely used descriptive term for 20th-century music whose connection with tonality is difficult to hear. ARNOLD SCHOENBERG and his students ALBAN BERG and ANTON WEBERN are regarded as the seminal atonal composers; the SERIALISM of their later work is often distinguished from their earlier "free atonality."

atonement Religious concept in which obstacles to reconciliation with God are removed, usually through sacrifice. Most religions have rituals of purification and expiation by which the relation of the individual to the divine is strengthened. In Christianity, atonement is achieved through the death and resurrection of JESUS. In Roman Catholicism, Eastern Orthodoxy, and some Protestant churches, penance is a sacrament that allows for personal atonement (see CONFESSION). In Judaism the annual Day of Atonement, YOM KIPPUR, is the culmination of 10 days centered on repentance.

Atonement, Day of See YOM KIPPUR

ATP *in full* **adenosine triphosphate** \ə-ˈde-nə-ˌsēn-trī-ˈfäs-ˌfāt\ Organic compound, substrate in many enzyme-catalyzed reactions (see CATALYSIS) in the CELLS of animals, plants, and microorganisms. ATP's chemical bonds (see BONDING) store a large amount of chemical energy. ATP therefore functions as the carrier of chemical energy from energy-yielding oxidation (see OXIDATION-REDUCTION) of food to energy-demanding cellular processes. Three such processes of METABOLISM are sources of ATP and stored energy: FERMENTATION, the TRICARBOXYLIC ACID CYCLE, and cellular respiration (also called oxidative phosphorylation). All form ATP from adenosine monophosphate (AMP) or adenosine diphosphate (ADP) and inorganic PHOSPHATE. When the reaction goes in the other direction, ATP is broken down to ADP or AMP and phosphate and the energy is used to perform chemical, electrical, or osmotic work for the cell.

atresia and stenosis \ə-ˈtrē-zhə...ste-ˈnō-səs\ Absence (atresia), usually congenital, or narrowing (stenosis) of almost any normal body cavity or passage. The more important include atresia of the anus, esophagus, aortic arch, heart valves, and urinary passages; and stenosis of the intestine, urinary passages, pyloric valve (stomach outlet), and heart valves. Most must be surgically corrected soon after birth. See also AORTIC STENOSIS, MITRAL STENOSIS.

Atreus \ˈā-trē-əs\ In Greek legend, the son of PELOPS. Atreus became king of Mycenae and drove out his brother Thyestes. Plagued by a curse on the house of Pelops, Atreus murdered his own son Pleisthenes and was eventually killed by the nephew he had raised as a son. Two more sons, AGAMEMNON and MENELAUS, fought in the Trojan War.

atrial fibrillation \ˈā-trē-əl\ Irregular rhythm (arrhythmia) of contraction of the atria (upper heart chambers). The most common major CARDIAC ARRHYTHMIA, it may be caused by chest surgery, pulmonary EMBOLISM, severe infection or fever, or heart malformation or disease. If it continues, it can permit formation of blood clots, which can block blood flow to essential organs. Emergency treatment consists of electric shocks (defibrillation). Atrial fibrillation with ventricular paroxysmal TACHYCARDIA is treated with DIGITALIS. See also VENTRICULAR FIBRILLATION.

atrium \ˈā-trē-əm\ In an ancient Roman house, an open central court that contained the impluvium, a basin where rainwater collected. It originally contained the hearth and functioned as the center of family life. The term later came to be used for the open front courtyard of a Christian BASILICA, where congregants collected before services. The atrium was revived in the 20th century in the form of glass-covered, greenery-filled multistory spaces sometimes found in shopping centers, office buildings, and large hotels.

Atrium of the basilica of S. Ambrogio, Milan, 1088–1128.
ALINARI—ART RESOURCE

atrophy \ˈa-trə-fē\ Decrease from previous normal size of the body or a part, cell, organ, or tissue. An organ or body part's cells may be reduced in number, size or both. Atrophy of some cells and organs is normal at certain points in the life cycle. Other causes include malnutrition, disease, disuse, injury, and hormone over- or underproduction.

atropine \ˈa-trə-ˌpēn\ Anticholinergic drug, a poisonous, crystalline alkaloid from certain nightshade plants, especially Egyptian henbane, used chiefly in ophthalmology to dilate the pupil of the eye or to break up adhesions between the lens and iris. It also dries and relieves hay fever and cold symptoms; relaxes intestinal spasms; is used in treating ENURESIS; inhibits the vagus nerve; and affects the central nervous system. Synthetic substitutes with more specific effects (e.g., dilation of the pupil or antispasmodic action) have been developed.

Atsumi, Kiyoshi (1928–1996) Japanese comic actor. Atsumi grew up in an impoverished section of Tokyo and took odd jobs in the theatre before first portraying the role of Tora-san for a television film in 1968. He went on to play the character until 1996 in the 48-film series *Otoko wa tsurai yo* ("It's Tough Being a Man"), the longest-running series in which the same actor portrayed the central character. Tora-san, a middle-aged peddler, is a charmingly irresponsible rogue who sells trinkets to passersby and unsuccessfully courts pretty women. Atsumi infused the role with witty wordplay and a folksy sincerity.

attainder In English law, the extinction of civil and political rights after a sentence of death or outlawry, usually after a conviction of TREASON. A legislative act attainting a person without trial was known as a bill of attainder. The most important consequences of attainder were forfeiture of property and "corruption of blood," meaning that the attainted person was disqualified from inheriting or transmitting property, thus disinheriting his descendants. All forms of attainder except forfeiture following indictment for treason were abolished in the 19th century. As a result of the English experience, the U.S. Constitution provided that "no Attainder of Treason shall work Corruption of Blood, or Forfeiture except during the Life of the Person attainted." The U.S. Supreme Court has also struck down as bills of attainder such things as the test oaths passed after the Civil War to disqualify Confederate sympathizers from certain professions.

Attalus I Soter ("Savior") \ˈat-ə-ləs...ˈsōt-ər\ (269–197 BC) Ruler of PERGAMUM (241–197). He crushed an attack by the Galatians (c. 230) and won most of Anatolia (228) through victory over the SELEUCID king, though by 222 the Seleucids had won most of it back. With Rome he fought the First and Second MACEDONIAN WARS, but he died shortly before PHILIP V's defeat. He was celebrated as a patron of the arts.

Attenborough, David (Frederick) *later* **Sir David** (born 1926) British television writer. For the BBC, which he joined in 1952, he originated the series *Zoo Quest* (1954–64). As controller of BBC-2 (1965–68) and director of programs (1968–72), he helped produce *The Forsyte Saga*, *The Ascent of Man*, and *Civilisation*. As an independent producer, he made innovative educational programs such as *Life on Earth* (1979) and *The Living Planet* (1984). His brother is RICHARD ATTENBOROUGH.

Attenborough, Richard (Samuel) *later* **Baron Attenborough** (born 1923) The brother of DAVID ATTENBOROUGH, he was a screen actor from 1942, appearing in such films as *Stairway to Heaven* (1946), *I'm All Right, Jack* (1959), *The Great Escape* (1963), and *Elizabeth* (1998). He won acclaim for directing *Oh, What a Lovely War!* (1969), *A Bridge Too Far* (1977), *Gandhi* (1982, Academy Award), *Chaplin* (1992), and *Shadowlands* (1993).

attention In psychology, the act or state of applying the mind to an object of sense or thought. WILHELM WUNDT was perhaps the first psychologist to study attention, distinguishing between broad and restricted fields of awareness. He was followed by WILLIAM JAMES, who emphasized active selection of stimuli, and IVAN PAVLOV, who noted the role attention plays in activating conditioned reflexes. JOHN B. WATSON sought to define attention not as an "inner" process but rather as a behavioral response to specific stimuli. Psychologists today consider attention against a background of "orienting reflexes" or "preattentive processes," whose physical correlates include changes in the voltage potential of the cerebral cortex and in the electrical activity of the skin, increased cerebral blood flow, pupil dilation, and muscular tightening. See also ATTENTION DEFICIT DISORDER.

attention deficit (hyperactivity) disorder (ADD *or* ADHD) *formerly* **hyperactivity** Behavioral syndrome in children, whose major symptoms are inattention and distractibility, restlessness, inability to sit still, and difficulty concentrating on one thing for any period of time. It occurs in about 5% of all schoolchildren, and is three times more common in boys than in girls. It can adversely affect learning, though many

A
B

children with ADD can learn to control their behavior sufficiently to perform satisfactorily in school. It appears to be caused by a combination of genetic and environmental factors. Certain aspects of the syndrome may persist into adulthood. Treatment usually entails counseling and close parental supervision, and may also include medication.

atthakatha \ˌä-tə-ˈkä-tə\ Commentaries on the Pali Buddhist canon from ancient India and Ceylon. Pali commentaries had reached Ceylon by the 3rd century BC and been translated into Sinhalese by the 1st century AD. The scholar Buddhaghosa (5th century) reworked in Pali much of the early material plus Dravidian commentaries and Sinhalese traditions. The earlier atthakatha have disappeared, but the works of Buddhaghosa and his successors provide information on the development of life and thought in the THERAVADA Buddhist community and contain much secular and legendary material as well.

attic Floor of a dwelling contained within the eaves of the roof structure. The word originally denoted any portion of a wall above the main cornice (see ENTABLATURE). Used by the ancient Romans principally for decorative purposes and inscriptions, as in TRIUMPHAL ARCHES, it became an important part of the Renaissance facade, often enclosing an additional story.

Inscribed attic surmounting the main cornice of the Arch of Titus, Rome, AD 81.

A.F. KERSTING

Attica *Greek* **Attiki** \ˌä-tē-ˈkē\ Ancient district, eastern central Greece. It was bordered by the AEGEAN SEA on the south and east and included the island of Salamis; its chief cities were ATHENS, PIRAEUS, and ELEUSIS. Its coastal settlements were enriched by maritime trade. Originally inhabited by Pelasgians, it was a center of MYCENAEAN culture in the 2nd millennium BC; the IONIAN Greeks invaded it c. 1300 BC. The territory was unified under Athens by 700 BC, traditionally through the efforts of King THESEUS.

Attila \ˈa-tᵊl-ə, ə-ˈti-lə\ (died 453) King of the HUNS (434–53, ruling jointly with his elder brother until c. 445). He was one of the greatest of the barbarian rulers who assailed the ROMAN EMPIRE. He and his brother Bleda inherited an empire that stretched from the Alps and the Baltic nearly to the Caspian Sea. The failure of the Romans to pay promised tributes prompted Attila to launch assaults along the Danube in 441 and 443. He murdered his brother in 445 and two years later invaded the Balkan provinces and Greece, a campaign later ended by another peace treaty that exacted heavy damages from the Eastern Romans. He invaded Gaul (451) but was defeated by an alliance of the Roman general Aetius and the Visigoths. His invasion of Italy (452) was ended by famine and plague. His depredations, which seemed to some like divine punishment, earned him the epithet Flagellum Dei ("Scourge of God"). Attila died on his wedding night, possibly murdered by his bride, and was succeeded by his sons, who divided his empire among them.

Attis Mythical consort of the GREAT MOTHER OF THE GODS and vegetation god worshiped in Phrygia and Asia Minor. His worship later spread to the Roman empire, where he became a solar deity in the 2nd century AD. The worship of Attis and the Great Mother included the celebration of mysteries at the beginning of spring.

attitude In psychology, a mental position with regard to a fact or state. Attitudes reflect a tendency to classify objects and events and to react to them with some consistency. Attitudes are not directly observable but rather are inferred from the objective, evaluative responses a person makes. Thus, investigators depend heavily on behavioral indicators of attitudes—what people say, how they respond to questionnaires, or such physiological signs as changes in heart rate. Attitude research is employed by social psychologists, advertising professionals, and political scientists, among others.

Attlee, Clement (Richard) *later* **Earl Attlee (of Walthamstow)** (1883–1967) British Labour Party leader (1935–55) and prime minister (1945–51). Committed to social reform, he lived for much of the years 1907–22 in a settlement house in London's poor district. Elected to Parliament in 1922, he served in several Labour governments and in the wartime coalition government of WINSTON CHURCHILL, whom he succeeded as prime minister in 1945. Attlee presided over the establishment of the WELFARE STATE in Britain, the nationalization of major British industries, and the granting of independence to India, an important step in the conversion of the BRITISH EMPIRE into the COMMONWEALTH OF NATIONS. He resigned when the Conservatives narrowly won the election in 1951.

Attlee, photograph by Yousuf Karsh.

©KARSH FROM RAPHO/PHOTO RESEARCHERS

attorney See LAWYER

attorney, power of Authorization to act as agent or attorney for another. Many of the general powers of attorney important in civil-law countries come under the powers of TRUST in common-law countries (see CIVIL LAW, COMMON LAW). Durable power of attorney becomes effective when the principal becomes unable to manage his or her affairs; general power of attorney authorizes the agent to carry on business for the principal; special power of attorney authorizes the agent to carry out a particular business transaction.

attorney general Chief law-enforcement officer of a state and legal adviser to the chief executive. The office dates to the Middle Ages but did not assume its modern form until the 16th century. In the U.S., the position dates to the Judiciary Act of 1789. Head of the Department of Justice and a member of the CABINET, the attorney general oversees all the government's law business and acts as the president's legal adviser. Every U.S. state also has an attorney general.

Attucks \ˈat-əks\, **Crispus** (1723?–1770) American patriot and martyr of the BOSTON MASSACRE. His early life is unclear, but he was probably a runaway slave of African and Natick Indian ancestry, and may have served on whaling ships. He is the only one of the Massacre's five victims widely remembered.

Atwood, Margaret (Eleanor) (born 1939) Canadian poet, novelist, and critic. Born in Ottawa, she attended the University of Toronto and Harvard University. In the poetry collection *The Circle Game* (1964; Governor General's Award), she celebrates the natural world and condemns materialism. Her novels, several of which have become best-sellers, include *Surfacing* (1972), *Lady Oracle* (1976), *Life Before Man* (1979), *Bodily Harm* (1981), *The Handmaid's Tale* (1985; Governor General's Award), *Cat's Eye* (1988), *The Robber Bride* (1993), and *Alias Grace* (1996). She is noted for her Canadian nationalism and her feminism.

Auburn University Public university founded in 1856 in Auburn, Ala. It offers undergraduate and graduate degree programs in business, education, engineering, agriculture, forestry, architecture, and arts and sciences, as well as degrees in nursing, pharmacy, and veterinary medicine. Auburn is home to the Space Power Institute, a space-technology research and development center. A second campus is in Montgomery. Total enrollment is about 22,000.

Aubusson carpet \ˌō-bə-ˈsōⁿ\ Floor covering produced at the village of Aubusson in central France. A center for the production of tapestries and furniture coverings since the 16th century, Aubusson was granted the title of Royal Manufactory in 1665. In 1743 workshops were established to manufacture pile carpets for the nobility, and soon thereafter carpets were being produced in the flat-woven tapestry technique in floral and chinoiserie patterns. In the 19th–20th century the name Aubusson became synonymous with a flat-woven French carpet.

Auckland City (pop., 2001: 377,382; metro. area pop.: 1,158,891), North Island, New Zealand. Located on WAITEMATA and Manukau harbors, it is the country's principal port and largest city. Founded in 1840 as New Zealand's capital and named for George Eden, Earl of Auckland, it remained the capital until superseded by WELLINGTON in 1865. It is a major manufacturing and shipping center. A bridge links it with the growing northern shore suburbs and with Devonport, New Zealand's chief naval base.

auction Buying and selling of property through open public bidding. Typically, potential purchasers make a succession of increasing bids or offers until the highest (and final) bid is accepted by the auctioneer. At a so-called Dutch auction, by contrast, the seller offers property at successively lower prices until one of his offers is accepted or until the price drops so low as to force the withdrawal of the offered property. Prospective buyers are usually allowed to examine auction items beforehand, and sellers may set a minimum price below which the property will not be sold. Auctions are important in the agricultural markets of many countries, permitting the rapid sale of perishable goods. Other items often sold at auction include artwork and antiques, secondhand goods, and farms and buildings repossessed by banks or the government. Auction selling is also employed on stock and commodity exchanges.

Auden, W(ystan) H(ugh) (1907–1973) British-U.S. poet and man of letters. He attended Oxford University, where he exerted a strong influence on C. DAY-LEWIS, LOUIS MACNEICE, and STEPHEN SPENDER. Throughout his life his varied works would deal with intellectual and moral issues of public concern as well as the inner world of fantasy and dream. In the 1930s he became a hero of the left, pointing up the evils of capitalism while also warning against those of totalitarianism. He collaborated with CHRISTOPHER ISHERWOOD on three verse dramas. Later writing reflects changes in his life (he became a U.S. citizen) and in his religious and intellectual perspective (he embraced Christianity and became disillusioned with the left), and occasionally his homosexuality. His poetic works include the long poem *The Age of Anxiety* (1947, Pulitzer Prize) and the collections *Another Time* (1940) and *Homage to Clio* (1960). With his longtime companion Chester Kallman, he wrote opera librettos, notably *The Rake's Progress* (1951) for IGOR STRAVINSKY. His other writings include commentaries for documentary films, essays, and reviews. After the death of T. S. ELIOT, he was widely considered the foremost poet writing in English.

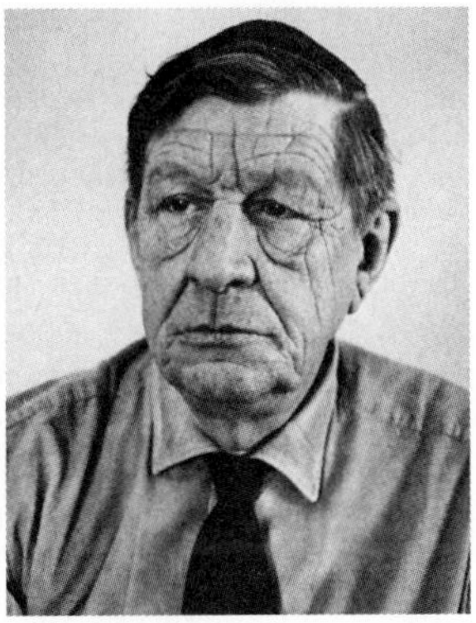

Auden, 1965.
HORST TAPPE

audio card See SOUND CARD

Audion Elementary radio tube developed by LEE DE FOREST (patented 1907). It was the first triode VACUUM TUBE, incorporating a control grid as well as a cathode and an anode. It was capable of more sensitive reception of wireless signals than were the electrolytic and Carborundum detectors then in use. The Audion made possible live radio broadcasting and became the key component of all radio, telephone, radar, television, and computer systems before the invention of the TRANSISTOR.

audit Examination of the records and reports of an enterprise by accounting specialists other than those responsible for their preparation. Public auditing by independent accountants is common in large firms. The auditor performs tests to determine whether the firm's statements were prepared in accordance with acceptable accounting principles and fairly present its financial position and operating results. Personal tax audits are carried out to determine whether people have accurately reported their financial circumstances when filing their taxes. Failing such an audit may result in a fine, or, in cases of extensive and deliberate deception, criminal prosecution. See also INTERNAL REVENUE SERVICE.

auditorium Portion of a theater or hall where an audience sits, as distinct from the stage. The auditorium originated in the theaters of ancient Greece, as a semicircular seating area cut into a hillside. Floor levels in a large auditorium may include stalls, private boxes, dress circle, balcony or upper circle, and GALLERY. A sloping floor and converging walls allow for a clear view of the stage and improve acoustics. The walls and ceilings of contemporary auditoriums usually conceal light, sound, and air-conditioning equipment.

Audubon, John James *orig.* **Fougère Rabin** *or* **Jean Rabin** *later* **Jean-Jacques Fougère Audubon** (1785–1851) French-U.S. ornithologist, artist, and naturalist known for his drawings and paintings of North American birds. Born illegitimately to a French merchant in Haiti, he returned with his father to France, where he studied painting briefly with J.-L. DAVID before moving to the U.S. at 18. From his father's Pennsylvania estate he made the first American bird-banding experiments. After failing in business ventures, he concentrated on drawing and studying birds, which took him from Florida to Labrador. His extraordinary four-volume *Birds of America* was published in London in 1827–38. He simultaneously published the extensive accompanying text *Ornithological Biography* (5 vols., 1831–39). His multivolume *Viviparous Quadrupeds of North America* (1842–54) was completed by his sons. Though his bird poses are sometimes unrealistic (the result of painting dead birds wired into position) and some details are inaccurate, few argue with the excellence of his illustrations as art, and his studies were fundamental to New World ornithology.

Audubon Society, National Organization dedicated to conserving and restoring natural ecosystems; named for JOHN JAMES AUDUBON. Founded in 1905, the society has 550,000 members and maintains 100 wildlife sanctuaries and nature centers throughout the U.S. Its high-priority campaigns include preserving wetlands and endangered forests, protecting corridors for migratory birds, and conserving marine wildlife. Its 300-member staff includes scientists, educators, sanctuary managers, and government-affairs specialists.

Auerstedt, Battle of See Battles of JENA AND AUERSTEDT

auger Tool (or bit) used with a carpenter's brace for drilling holes, usually in wood. It looks like a corkscrew and produces extremely clean holes, almost regardless of how large the bit is. Expansive auger bits have adjustable blades with cutting edges and spurs that can be extended radially to cut large holes. Large augers are used to bore holes in soil for fence posts and telephone poles, or in ice for ice fishing. Horizontal augers as much as 8 ft (2.5 m) in diameter are used in coal mining.

augite \'ȯ-jīt\ Most common PYROXENE mineral, occurring chiefly as blocky crystals in basalts, gabbros, andesites, and various other dark igneous rocks. It also is a common constituent of lunar basalts and meteorites and may be found in certain metamorphic rocks, such as pyroxenites. Because the diopside-hedenbergite series and augite are nearly indistinguishable, the term augite is sometimes used to designate any dark green to black pyroxene with monoclinic symmetry (three unequal crystallographic axes with one oblique intersection).

Augsburg \'au̇ks-ˌbu̇rk\ City (pop., 1996 est.: 260,000), BAVARIA, southern Germany. Founded as a Roman colony by AUGUSTUS c. 14 BC, it was the seat of a bishopric by AD 739. It became an imperial free city in 1276, and joined the Swabian League in 1331. The FUGGER and Welser families made the city a major banking and commercial center in the 15th–16th century. The AUGSBURG CONFESSION was read at the Diet of 1530; the Peace of AUGSBURG was concluded in 1555; and the League of AUGSBURG was formed in 1686. The city became part of Bavaria in 1806. It was heavily bombed during World War II. Sites of interest include the Fuggerei (1519), the world's oldest housing settlement for the poor.

Augsburg \'ȯgz-bərg\, **League of** Coalition formed in 1686 by Emperor LEOPOLD I, the kings of Sweden and Spain, and the electors of Bavaria, Saxony, and the Palatinate. The league was formed to oppose the expansionist plans of LOUIS XIV of France prior to the War of the GRAND ALLIANCE. It proved ineffective because of the reluctance of some princes to oppose France and the absence of provisions for combined military action.

Augsburg, Peace of Convention promulgated in 1555 by the Diet of the Holy Roman Empire, which provided the first permanent legal basis for the existence of LUTHERANISM in addition to Catholicism in Germany. The Diet determined that no member of the empire would make war against another on religious grounds. It recognized just two denominations, the Roman Catholics and the Lutherans, and it stipulated that in each territory of the empire, only one denomination was allowed. However, people were allowed to move to states where their faith was adopted. Despite numerous shortcomings, the accord saved the empire from serious internal conflicts for over 50 years. See also REFORMATION.

Augsburg Confession \'au̇ks-ˌbu̇rk\ Basic doctrinal statement of LUTHERANISM. Its principal author was PHILIPP MELANCHTHON, and it was presented to Emperor CHARLES V at the Diet of Augsburg on June 25, 1530. Its purpose was to defend the Lutherans against misrepresentations of their teachings and to provide a statement of theology that Roman Catholics might accept. It consisted of 28 articles that outlined Lutheran doctrine and listed abuses that had crept into Western Christendom over the centuries. The unaltered document has remained authoritative for Lutherans. Translated into English in 1536, it had a major influence on the Anglican Church's Thirty-nine Articles and the Methodists' Twenty-five Articles of Religion.

Augusta City (pop., 1996 est.: 21,000), capital of Maine. It was established in 1628 by traders from PLYMOUTH COLONY as a post at the head of navigation on the KENNEBEC RIVER. Fort Western was built there in 1754 (restored 1919), attracting settlers. Incorporated in 1797, the town was renamed the next year for the daughter of an American Revolutionary general. It became the state capital in 1832. It is one of Maine's leading vacation centers.

Augustan Age Illustrious period in Latin literary history, c. 43 BC–AD 18. With the preceding period dominated by CICERO, it forms the Golden Age of Latin literature. Marked by civil peace and prosperity, the age reached its highest expression in poetry, with polished, sophisticated verse on themes of patriotism, love, and nature, generally addressed to a patron or to the emperor AUGUSTUS. Writers active in the period include VIRGIL, HORACE, LIVY, and OVID. The term is also applied to "classical" periods in the literature of other nations, especially to late-17th- and 18th-century England.

Augustine (of Hippo), St. (354–430) Roman Catholic theologian. Born in Roman North Africa, he adopted MANICHAEISM, taught rhetoric in Carthage, and fathered a son. After moving to Milan he was converted to Christianity under the influence of St. AMBROSE, who baptized him in 387. He returned to Africa to pursue a contemplative life, and in 396 he became bishop of Hippo (now Annaba, Algeria), a post he held until his death in 430, while the city was under siege by a Vandal army. His best-known works include the *Confessions*, an autobiographical meditation on God's grace, and *The City of God*, on the place of Christianity in history. His theological works *On Christian Doctrine* and *On the Trinity* are also widely read. His sermons and letters show the influence of Neoplatonism and carry on debates with the proponents of Manichaeism, Donatism, and Pelagianism. His views on predestination influenced later theologians, notably JOHN CALVIN. He was declared a Doctor of the Church in the early Middle Ages.

Augustine of Canterbury \'ò-gəs-ˌtēn, ò-'gəs-tən\, **St.** (died 604?) First archbishop of Canterbury. A Benedictine prior in Rome, he was chosen by Pope GREGORY I to lead 40 monks as missionaries to England. They arrived in 597 and were welcomed by King ETHELBERT of Kent, at the behest of his queen, and he gave them a church in Canterbury. Augustine converted the king and thousands of his subjects and was made bishop of the English. On the pope's instructions he purified pagan temples and consecrated 12 other bishops. He founded Christ Church, Canterbury, as his cathedral and made Canterbury the primary see in England. He tried unsuccessfully to unify his churches with the Celtic churches of northern Wales.

Augustinian In the Roman Catholic church, a member of any of the religious orders and congregations whose constitutions are based on the Rule of St. AUGUSTINE. The two main branches of the Augustinians are the Augustinian Hermits and the Augustinian Canons. The former was one of the four great mendicant orders of the Middle Ages, and its members (including MARTIN LUTHER) were active in European university life and ecclesiastical affairs. The latter became in the 11th century the first Roman Catholic order to combine clerical status with full common life. The order declined after the Reformation, but it continues mission, educational, and hospital work. Other notable orders are the Augustinian Recollects (founded in the 16th century) and the Second Order of St. Augustine (1264) for nuns, both still active today.

Augustus, Caesar *or* **Octavian** *orig.* **Gaius Octavius** *later* **Gaius Julius Caesar Octavianus** (63 BC–AD 14) First Roman emperor. Born to a wealthy family, he was named adoptive son and heir of his great-uncle Julius CAESAR at 18. After Caesar's assassination (44 BC) a power struggle ensued, and after several battles he formed the Second TRIUMVIRATE with his chief rivals, LEPIDUS and Mark ANTONY. Continuing battles between the triumvirs ended with his disposing of Lepidus in 32 and Antony (now allied with CLEOPATRA) at the Battle of ACTIUM in 31 to become sole ruler. He was anointed PRINCEPS; the Roman empire is said to begin with his accession. At first he ruled as CONSUL, maintaining republican administration, but in 27 he accepted the title Augustus and in 23 he received imperial power. His rule (31 BC–AD 14) brought changes to every aspect of Roman life and lasting peace and prosperity to the Greco-Roman world. He secured outlying imperial provinces, built roads and public works, established the PAX ROMANA, and fostered the arts. He took steps to rectify Roman morality, even exiling his daughter JULIA for adultery. When he died, the empire stretched from Iberia to Cappadocia and from Gaul to Egypt. He was deified after his death.

Augustus II *Polish* **August Fryderyk** (1670–1733) King of Poland and elector of Saxony (as Frederick Augustus I). He ascended to the Polish throne in 1697, having converted to Catholicism to better his chances. Also called Augustus the Strong, he invaded Livonia in 1700, beginning the Second NORTHERN WAR. Charles XII of Sweden defeated Augustus's army and forced him to abdicate in 1706, but he was restored as king in 1710. Poland declined during Augustus's reign from a major European power to a protectorate of Russia.

Augustus III *Polish* **August Fryderyk** (1696–1763) King of Poland and elector of Saxony (as Frederick Augustus II), whose reign (1733–63) marked a great period of disorder within Poland. He cared more for pleasure than affairs of state and left the administration of Saxony and Poland to his chief adviser, Heinrich von Brühl (1700–1763), and the powerful CZARTORYSKI FAMILY. He gave Saxon support to Austria in the War of the AUSTRIAN SUCCESSION and the SEVEN YEARS' WAR.

auk In general, any of 22 species of diving birds (family Alcidae), especially the little auk and the razorbill, or razor-billed auk. Auks are 6–16 in. (15–40 cm) long, with short wings and legs and webbed feet. They occur only in Arctic, subarctic, and temperate regions (with a few species south to Baja California). Auks nest colonially on cliff ledges or in rock crevices or burrows near the sea; many spend the winter far from land. They feed on fish, crustaceans, mollusks, and plankton. True auks are black and white and stand erect on land. See also GREAT AUK.

aulos \'ò-lōs\ Single- or double-reed pipe usually played in pairs, particularly in ancient Greece. The classical pipes were of equal length, each with three or four fingerholes. The principal wind instrument of most ancient Middle Eastern peoples, it existed in Europe up to the early Middle Ages, often as a single pipe with more fingerholes. Its quavering sound, described by PLATO, was classically associated with the rites of DIONYSUS.

Auloi player with phorbeia, and dancer with krotala, detail from a kylix signed by Epictetus, found at Vulci, Italy, c. 520–510 BC; in the British Museum, London.

BY COURTESY OF THE TRUSTEES OF THE BRITISH MUSEUM, LONDON

Aum Shinrikyo \'aùm-shin-'rik-yō\ Japanese new religious movement founded by Shoko Asahara (born 1955 as Chizuo Matsumoto) in 1987. It contained elements of Hinduism and Buddhism and was founded on the millenarian expectation of a series of disasters that would bring an end to this world and inaugurate a new cosmic cycle. In 1995 its members released nerve gas into the Tokyo subway system, killing 12 and injuring 5,000. The group has been linked with other nerve-gas incidents and violent crimes. It claimed some 50,000 members, mostly in Russia, at the time of the bombing. Membership collapsed in the wake of the bombing, but had grown to some 2,000 members by the early 21st century. The group changed its name to Aleph in 2000.

Aung San \'òŋ-'san\ (1914?–1947) Burmese nationalist leader. He led a student strike in 1936 and became secretary-general of a nationalist group in 1939. He accepted Japanese aid in raising a Burmese military force, which helped the Japanese in their 1942 invasion, but, doubting that the Japanese would truly deliver Burmese independence and displeased with their treatment of Burmese forces, he switched in 1945 to the Allied cause. After the war, he effectively became prime minister, and he negotiated Burmese independence, which was agreed upon in 1947 and achieved in 1948. He was assassinated in 1947.

Aung San Suu Kyi \'òŋ-'san-'sü-'chē\ (born 1945) Opposition leader in Myanmar. Daughter of AUNG SAN, she studied in Burma and India and at Oxford University. She lived a quiet life until, returning to Myanmar in 1988, she was moved by the brutality of U NE WIN's military regime to began a nonviolent struggle for democracy and human rights. The 1990 electoral victory of her National League for Democracy was ignored by Ne Win's government, and she was held under house arrest from 1989 to 1995. She was awarded the Nobel Peace Prize in 1991.

Aurangzeb \ˌau̇-rəŋ-'zeb\ *orig.* **Muhi-ud-Din Muhammad** (1618–1707) Last of the great Mughal emperors of India (r.1658–1707). He was the third son of the emperor SHAH JAHAN and Mumtaz Mahal, for whom the TAJ MAHAL was built. After distinguishing himself early in life with his military and administrative ability, he fought his eldest brother for the right of succession and had several other rival relatives (including a son) executed. During the first half of his reign he proved a capable Muslim monarch of a mixed Hindu-Muslim empire, disliked for his ruthlessness but respected. From c. 1680 his devout religious side came to dominate; he excluded Hindus from public office and destroyed their temples and schools, became embroiled in fruitless warfare with the Marathas in South India, and executed the Sikh guru Tegh Bahadur (1664–1675), starting a Sikh-Muslim feud that continues to the present.

Aurangzeb, Mughal miniature, 17th century; in the Metropolitan Museum of Art, New York City.

BY COURTESY OF THE METROPOLITAN MUSEUM OF ART, NEW YORK, BEQUEST OF GEORGE D. PRATT, 1945

Aurelian \ò-'rā-lē-ən\ *Latin* **Lucius Domitius Aurelianus** (AD c. 215–275) Roman emperor AD 270–75. Probably from the Balkans, he became emperor after Claudius II's death and the brief reign of Claudius' brother. He reunited the empire and restored Roman power in Europe, turning back invaders and quelling revolts, securing provinces in the east and defeating the Germans to the north, for which he took the title *restitutor orbis* ("restorer of the world"). He built a new wall around Rome and increased food distribution to the poor, but his monetary and religious reforms failed. While marching to Persia he was slain by a group of officers who mistakenly believed they had been marked for execution.

Aurelius, Marcus See MARCUS AURELIUS

Aurgelmir \'au̇r-gəl-ˌmir\ *or* **Ymir** \'i-mir\ In Norse mythology, the first being, a giant created from the drops of water that formed when the ice of Niflheim met the heat of Muspelheim. He was the father of all giants; a male and female grew under his arm and his legs produced a six-headed son, whom the cow Audumla nursed. Audumla licked salty frost from stones, which she shaped into the man Buri, grandfather of ODIN and his brothers. The gods killed Aurgelmir and put his body into the void, where his flesh became the earth, his blood the seas, his bones mountains, his teeth stones, his skull the sky, and his brains the clouds. His eyelashes (or eyebrows) became the fence around MIDGARD, home of mankind.

Aurignacian culture \ˌòr-ēn-'yā-shən\ STONE-TOOL INDUSTRY and artistic tradition of Upper PALEOLITHIC Europe, named after the village of Aurignac in southern France where the tradition was first identified. The Aurignacian period dates to 35,000–15,000 BC. Its tools included scrapers, burins (which made the engraving possible), and blades. Points and awls were fashioned from bones and antlers. Aurignacian art represents the first complete artistic tradition, moving from simple engravings of animal forms on small rocks to finer pieces of carved bone and ivory to highly stylized clay figurines of pregnant women (the so-called "Venus figures," presumably fertility figures). By the end of the Aurignacian, hundreds of engravings, reliefs, and paintings had been executed on the walls and ceilings of limestone caves in western Europe, most famously LASCAUX GROTTO.

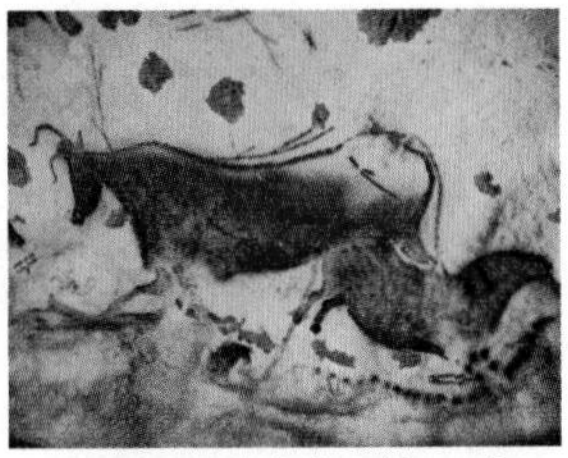

Cave painting of a bull and horse from the late Aurignacian period, in Lascaux Grotto, near Montignac, France.

HANS HINZ, BASEL

aurochs \'au̇r-ˌäks\ *or* **auroch** Extinct wild OX *(Bos primigenius)* of Europe, the species from which CATTLE are probably descended. The aurochs survived in central Poland until 1627. It was black, stood 6 ft (1.8 m) high at the shoulder, and had spreading, forward-curving horns. Some German breeders claim to have re-created this race since 1945, but their animals are smaller and probably lack the aurochs's genetic constitution. The name has sometimes been wrongly applied to the European BISON.

Aurora Roman goddess of dawn. Her Greek counterpart was Eos. HESIOD described her as the daughter of the TITANS Hyperion and Theia. She was the sister of HELIOS, the sun, and SELENE, the moon. By the Titan Astraeus, she became the mother of the winds and of the evening star. In Greek mythology she was also represented as the lover of the hunters Cephalus and ORION.

Aurora City (pop., 1996 est.: 252,000), northern central Colorado. It was founded near DENVER during the silver boom of 1891 and named Fletcher; it was incorporated and renamed in 1907. Though mainly residential, it is also the site of Buckley Air National Guard Base.

aurora Luminous phenomenon of the upper atmosphere that occurs primarily at high latitudes. Auroras in the Northern Hemisphere are called aurora borealis, or northern lights; in the Southern Hemisphere they are called aurora australis, or southern lights. Auroras are caused by the interaction of energetic particles (electrons and protons) from outside the atmosphere with atoms of the upper atmosphere. Such interaction occurs in zones surrounding the earth's magnetic poles. During periods of intense solar activity, auroras occasionally extend to the middle latitudes.

Auschwitz \'au̇sh-ˌvits\ *or* **Auschwitz-Birkenau** Nazi Germany's largest CONCENTRATION CAMP and extermination camp, located in Poland (modern Oswiecim). It consisted of three camps, established in 1940, 1941 (Birkenau), and 1942. Able-bodied Jewish prisoners were sent to a forced-labor camp, while the aged, the weak, and children and their mothers were killed. Some prisoners were also subjected to medical experiments, conducted by JOSEF MENGELE. The total number who died at Auschwitz is estimated at between 1 million and 2.5 million. See also HOLOCAUST.

auscultation \ˌò-skəl-'tā-shən\ Procedure for detecting certain defects or conditions by listening for normal and abnormal heart, breath, bowel, fetal, and other sounds in the body. The invention of the stethoscope in 1819 improved and expanded this practice, still very useful despite the great technological advances in other means of diagnosis.

Ausgleich See COMPROMISE OF 1867

Jane Austen, pencil and watercolor portrait by C. Austen, c. 1810; in the National Portrait Gallery, London.

BY COURTESY OF THE NATIONAL PORTRAIT GALLERY, LONDON

Austen, Jane (1775–1817) English novelist. The daughter of a rector, she lived in the circumscribed world of minor landed gentry and country clergy that she was to use in her writing; her closest companion was her sister, Cassandra. Her earliest known writings are mainly parodies, notably of sentimental fiction. In her six full-length novels—*Sense and Sensibility* (1811), *Pride and Prejudice* (1813), *Mansfield Park* (1814), *Emma*

(1815), *Persuasion* (1817), and *Northanger Abbey* (published 1817, but written before the others)—she created the COMEDY OF MANNERS of middle-class English life in her time. Her writing is noted for its wit, realism, shrewd sympathy, and brilliant prose style. Through her treatment of ordinary people in everyday life, she was the first to give the novel its distinctly modern character. She published her novels anonymously; two only appeared after her death at 41.

Austerlitz, Battle of (December 2, 1805) First engagement of the War of the Third Coalition and one of NAPOLEON's greatest victories. In the battle, fought near Austerlitz in Moravia (now Slavkov u Brna, Czech Republic), Napoleon's 68,000 troops defeated almost 90,000 Russians and Austrians under Russia's ALEXANDER I and MIKHAIL KUTUZOV. Napoleon's resounding victory forced Austria's FRANCIS I to conclude the Treaty of Pressburg, ceding Venetia to the French kingdom in Italy and temporarily ending the anti-French alliance. See also NAPOLEONIC WARS.

Austin City (pop., 2000: 656,600), capital of Texas. It was founded in 1835 as the village of Waterloo on the COLORADO RIVER in southern central Texas. In 1839 it was made capital of the Republic of Texas and renamed to honor STEPHEN AUSTIN; when Texas became a state in 1845, Austin remained its capital. It is the home of the University of TEXAS.

Austin, J(ohn) L(angshaw) (1911–1960) British philosopher. He taught at Oxford from 1945 throughout his professional career. He is best known for his emphasis on the importance of ordinary language in philosophy, particularly as a source of conceptual distinctions. He believed that linguistic analysis could provide solutions to philosophical riddles, but he disapproved of the language of formal logic, believing it contrived and often less complex and subtle than ordinary language. His theoretical essays and lectures were published posthumously in *Philosophical Papers* (1961), *Sense and Sensibilia* (1962), and *How to Do Things with Words* (1962). See also ANALYTIC PHILOSOPHY.

Austin, John (1790–1859) British jurist. Though initially unsuccessful in his law practice (1818–25), his analytical mind and intellectual honesty impressed colleagues, and he was named the first professor of JURISPRUDENCE at University College, London (1826). His writings, especially *The Province of Jurisprudence Determined* (1832), sought to distinguish law from morality. He also helped define jurisprudence as the analysis of fundamental legal concepts, as distinct from the criticism of legal institutions, which he called the "science of legislation." His work, largely unrecognized in his own time, influenced later jurists, including OLIVER WENDELL HOLMES, JR.

Austin, Stephen (Fuller) (1793–1836) U.S. founder of the first legal colony of English-speaking people in Texas when it was still part of Mexico. Born in Austinville, Va., he was raised in Missouri Territory and served in its legislature (1814–19). The economic panic in 1819 led his father to conceive a plan to colonize Texas on land obtained from the Mexican government. Austin continued the project after his father died (1821) and founded a colony of several hundred families on the Brazos River in 1822. He maintained good relations with the Mexican government. He later worked to secure independence for Texas, participating in the Texas Revolution, and is considered one of the state's founders. The city of Austin is named for him.

Austral Islands Group of islands (pop., 1996: 6,563), southern FRENCH POLYNESIA. The southernmost part of French Polynesia (Austral is Latin for "south"), the islands form a chain about 850 mi (1,370 km) long. They were sighted by Capt. JAMES COOK in 1769 and 1777. They were taken over by the French in the late 19th century. The inhabited islands are Rimatara, Rurutu, Tubuai, Raevavae, and Rapa.

Australia *officially* **Commonwealth of Australia** Smallest continent and sixth-largest country (in area) on earth, lying between the Pacific and Indian oceans. Area: 2,967,909 sq mi (7,686,884 sq km). Population (2002 est.): 19,702,000. Capital: CANBERRA. Most Australians are descendants of Europeans; the largest nonwhite minority is the AUSTRALIAN ABORIGINES. The Asian part of the population has grown as a result of relaxed immigration policy. Language: English (official). Religions: Roman Catholicism, Anglicanism. Currency: Australian dollar. Australia has four major physiographic regions. More than half its land area is the Western Australian Shield, which includes the outcrops of Arnhem Land and the Kimberleys in the northwest and the MACDONNELL RANGES in the east. A second region, the Great Artesian Basin, lies east of the shield region. The Eastern Uplands, which includes the GREAT DIVIDING RANGE, is a series of high ridges, plateaus, and basins. The fourth region is the Flinders-Mount Lofty ranges. The country's highest point is Mount KOSCIUSKO in the AUSTRALIAN ALPS; the lowest, Lake EYRE. Major rivers include the MURRAY-DARLING system, the FLINDERS and SWAN rivers, and COOPER CREEK. There are many islands and reefs along the country's coast, including the GREAT BARRIER REEF, MELVILLE ISLAND, KANGAROO ISLAND, and TASMANIA. Australia is rich in mineral resources, including coal, petroleum, and uranium. A vast diamond deposit was found in WESTERN AUSTRALIA in 1979. The country's economy is basically free-enterprise; its largest components include finance, manufacturing, and trade. Formally a constitutional monarchy, its chief of state is the British monarch, represented by the Governor-General. In reality it is a parliamentary state with two legislative houses; its head of government is the prime minister. Australia has long been inhabited by Aborigines, who arrived 40,000–60,000 years ago. Estimates of the population at the time of European settlement in 1788 range from 300,000 to more than 1 million. Widespread European knowledge of Australia began with 17th-century explorations. The Dutch landed in 1616 and the British in 1688, but the first large-scale expedition was that of JAMES COOK in 1770, which established Britain's claim to Australia. The first English settlement, at Port Jackson (1788), consisted mainly of convicts and seamen; convicts were to make up a large proportion of the incoming settlers. By 1859 the colonial nuclei of all Australia's states had been formed, but with devastating effects on the Aborigines, whose population declined sharply with the introduction of European diseases and weaponry. Britain granted its colonies limited self-government in the mid-19th century, and an act federating the colonies into a commonwealth was passed in 1900. Australia fought alongside the British in World War I, notably at GALLIPOLI, and again in World War II, preventing its occupation by the Japanese. It joined the U.S. in the KOREAN and VIETNAM wars. Since the 1960s the government has sought to deal more fairly with the Aborigines, and a loosening of immigration restrictions has led to a more heterogeneous population. Constitutional links allowing British interference in government were formally abolished in 1968, and Australia has assumed a leading role in Asian and Pacific affairs. During the 1990s, it experienced several debates about giving up its British ties and becoming a republic. See map on following page.

Australian Aboriginal languages Group of perhaps 250 languages spoken by the 1–2 million native inhabitants of Australia before the beginning of European conquest in 1788. More than half are now extinct; of the remainder, only about 20, mostly in the North Territory and northern Western Australia, remain in active use by both adults and children. Most Australian languages belong to a single superfamily, Pama-Nyungan, and the remainder, a very diverse group of languages spoken in the Kimberley region of Western Australia and parts of the North Territory, may be remotely akin to Pama-Nyungan.

Australian Aborigine \a-bə-'ri-jə-ˌnē\ Any of the indigenous peoples of Australia and Tasmania that arrived 40,000–60,000 years ago. At one time there were as many as 500 language-named, territorially anchored groups (tribes) of Aborigines. They were hunters and gatherers, limited by distance from fresh water. Groups formed along the male line and centered around a watering place settled by its ancestors. The men were divided into lodges, custodians of the mythology evoked in the DREAMING ritual. The estimated Aboriginal population of 300,000–1,000,000 when European colonization began in the late 18th century was devastated by disease and by the bloody 19th-century "pacification by force." The government established reserves in the 1920s and '30s; however, Aborigines today number fewer than 260,000. Most aspects of their traditional culture have been severely modified; no Aborigines exist who have not had some contact with modern Australian society, and all are now Australian citizens.

Australian Alps Mountain range, southeastern Australia. It forms the southern end of the GREAT DIVIDING RANGE and the watershed between the headstreams of the MURRUMBIDGEE RIVER and the rivers flowing south to the Pacific Ocean. Its highest peak is Mount KOSCIUSKO. Its valleys have been used for grazing, while its highlands have been mined.

Australian Ballet Leading ballet company of Australia. It was sponsored in 1962 by art patrons interested in promoting a national ballet. Peggy van Praagh was the first artistic director (1962-74). Since 1965 the company has made tours of Europe and North America.

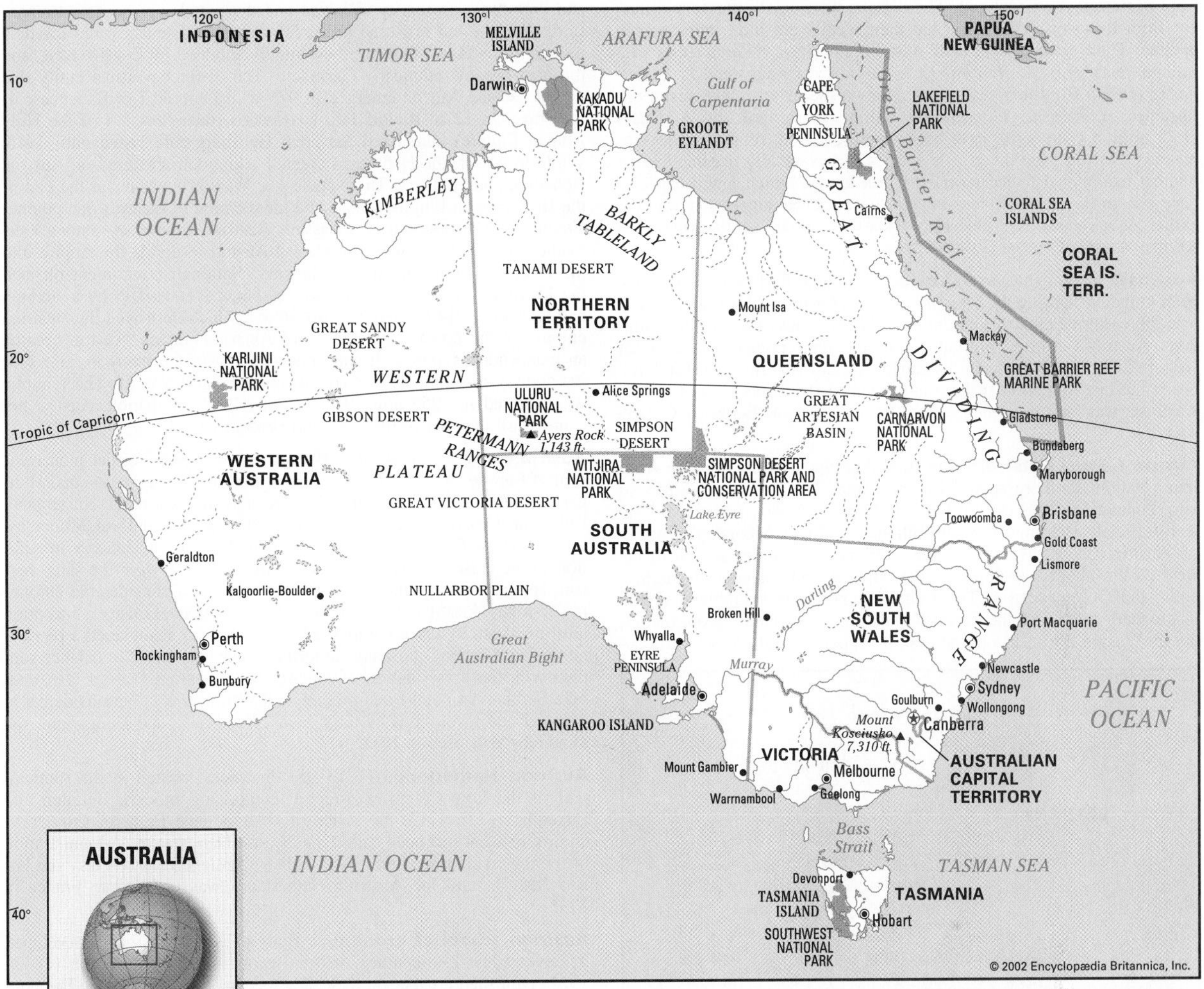

Australian Capital Territory Political entity (pop., 1999 est.: 310,170), southeastern Australia. An area dictated by the 1901 Australian constitution, the site was chosen among competitors, including SYDNEY and MELBOURNE, in 1908. It lies within NEW SOUTH WALES and consists of CANBERRA and the area around JERVIS BAY. Parliament moved there from Melbourne in 1927. In 1989 the Territory received responsibility for self-government.

Australian National University Public university in Canberra, Australia. Founded in 1946, it originally offered only graduate programs. Undergraduates were first admitted in 1960, and today the university offers a wide range of graduate and undergraduate programs. Affiliated with the university are research schools of medicine, physical and biological sciences, social sciences, and Pacific studies. Total enrollment is about 10,000.

Australian religion Religion of Australia's Aborigines, based in the DREAMING. Religion involved living in agreement with the way of life ordained in the Dreaming, through the performance of rituals and obedience to the law. Through dreams and other states of altered consciousness, the living could come into contact with the spiritual realm and gain strength from it; myths, dances, and other rituals bound the human, spiritual, and physical worlds together in a single cosmic order. A child's spirit was held to come from the Dreaming to animate a fetus, and a person's spiritual heritage was more important than the bond between a physical parent and child. Sacred art included TJURUNGA, sand and cave paintings, and paintings on bark.

Australian Rules football Variety of football that is played between two teams of 18 players on an oval field 148–202 yards (135–165 m) long with four posts at each end. A six-point goal is scored when the oval ball is kicked through the two central goalposts. A one-point "behind" is scored when the ball is kicked over the behind line extending between the central and outer goalposts. The game's finest spectacle is the "mark" in which competing players leap, sometimes riding on the back of an opponent, in order to catch the ball directly from the kick of another player. The player making such a catch is awarded a mark, an unhindered kick from behind the spot of the catch. The sport was developed in Melbourne. Victoria Football League, the first professional league, was established in 1897 and was renamed the Australian Football League in 1990, to reflect the addition of franchises outside of that state. It is Australia's foremost sport.

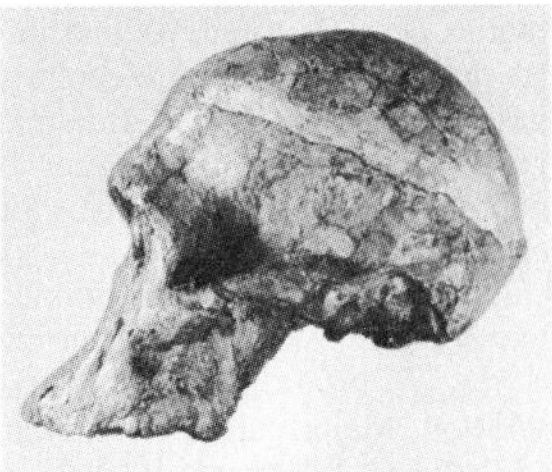
Lateral view of skull of *Australopithecus africanus* found at Sterkfontein, S.Af.

BY COURTESY OF THE TRANSVAAL MUSEUM, PRETORIA, S.AF.

Australopithecus \ȯ-ˌstrā-lō-ˈpi-thə-kəs\ ("southern ape") Genus of extinct HOMINIDS that lived in southern and eastern Africa from the early Pliocene Epoch (beginning c. 5.3 million years ago) to the beginning of the Pleistocene (c. 1.8 million years ago). It is believed to be ancestral to modern human beings. The australopithecines were distinguished from the APES by their upright posture and bipedal gait. Their brains were small, not very different from those of living apes, but their teeth were more human than apelike. Three species of gracile australopithecines, *A. anamensis* (4.2 million years ago), *A. afarensis* (3.75 million years ago) and *A. africanus* (3 million–2 million years ago), and two species of robust australopithecines, *A. robustus* (2 million–1 million years ago) and *A. boisei* (1.75 million years ago), have been identified. Both robust species apparently evolved from the gracile species and eventually became extinct without evolutionary successors. It is not known which gracile species gave rise to the genus *Homo,* though the evidence suggests it was the earlier *A. afarensis.* See also HADAR REMAINS, HUMAN EVOLUTION, LAETOLI FOOTPRINTS, LUCY, OLDUVAI GORGE, STERKFONTEIN.

Austrasia \ȯ-ˈstrā-zhə\ *or* **Ostrasia** \ä-ˈstrā-zhə\ Early medieval European kingdom. During the MEROVINGIAN DYNASTY (6th–8th century AD), it was the eastern Frankish kingdom and NEUSTRIA was the western kingdom. Austrasia covered present-day northeastern France and areas of western and central Germany; its capital was at METZ. In 751 PEPIN III deposed the last Merovingian king and founded the CAROLINGIAN DYNASTY. Austrasia was later consolidated into the HOLY ROMAN EMPIRE by CHARLEMAGNE.

Austria *German* **Österreich** \ˈœ-stər-ˌrīk\ *officially* **Republic of Austria** Nation, southern central Europe. Area: 32,375 sq mi (83,851 sq km). Population (2001 est.): 8,117,770. Capital: VIENNA. Language: German (official). Religion: Roman Catholicism (75%). Monetary unit: euro. Austria can be divided into three regions. The alpine region in the west covers about two-thirds of the country, and includes its highest point, the GROSSGLOCKNER. The Bohemian Forest is a highland region that extends north into the Czech Republic. The lowland region, including the Vienna Basin, lies in the east; it supports mainly agricultural activities. The DANUBE RIVER and its tributaries drain nearly the entire country. Austria has a developed mixed free-market and government-operated economy based on manufacture and commerce; tourism is also important. It is a republic with two legislative houses. Austria's chief of state is the president and its head of government is the chancellor. Its greatest cultural contribution has been in music (see JOSEPH HAYDN, WOLFGANG AMADEUS MOZART, FRANZ SCHUBERT, ALBAN BERG, ANTON WEBERN). Major cultural figures in other fields include OSKAR KOKOSCHKA, SIGMUND FREUD, and LUDWIG WITTGENSTEIN. Settlement in Austria goes back some 3,000 years, when Illyrians were probably the main inhabitants. The CELTS invaded c. 400 BC and established NORICUM. The Romans arrived after 200 BC and established the provinces of RAETIA, Noricum, and PANNONIA; prosperity followed and the population became Romanized. With the fall of Rome in the 5th century AD, many tribes invaded, including the SLAVS; they were eventually subdued by CHARLEMAGNE, and the area became ethnically Germanic. The distinct political entity that would become Austria emerged in 976 with Leopold I of Babenberg as margrave. In 1278, Rudolf IV of HABSBURG (later RUDOLF I of the Holy Roman Empire) conquered the area; Habsburg rule lasted until 1918. While in power, the Habsburgs created a kingdom centered on Austria, Bohemia, and Hungary. The Napoleonic Wars brought about the end of the Holy Roman Empire (1806) and the creation of the Austrian empire. Count von METTERNICH tried to assure Austrian supremacy among Germanic states, but war with Prussia led Austria to divide the empire into the Dual Monarchy of Austria-Hungary. Nationalist sentiment plagued the kingdom, and the assassination of FRANCIS FERDINAND by a Serbian nationalist in 1914 triggered WORLD WAR I, which destroyed the Austrian empire. In the postwar carving up of Austria-Hungary, Austria became an independent republic. It was annexed by Nazi Germany in 1938 (see ANSCHLUSS) and joined the Axis powers in World War II. The republic was restored in 1955 after 10 years of Allied occupation. Austria became a full member of the EUROPEAN UNION in 1995.

Austria-Hungary *or* **Austro-Hungarian Empire** Former monarchy, central Europe. Austria-Hungary at one time included Austria and Hungary, Bohemia, Moravia, Bukovina, Transylvania, Carniola, Küstenland, Dalmatia, Croatia, Fiume, and Galicia. The so-called Dual Monarchy, formed by the COMPROMISE OF 1867, created a king of Hungary in addition to the existing Austrian emperor; though these were the same person, Hungary was granted its own parliament and considerable autonomy. FRANCIS JOSEPH held both titles from Austria-Hungary's inception until his death in 1916. Up to 1914, the monarchy maintained a precarious balance among its many minorities; that year saw the balance toppled with the assassination of the Austro-Hungarian FRANCIS FERDINAND by a Serbian nationalist that precipitated WORLD WAR I. With its defeat in that war and revolutions by the Czechs, Yugoslavs, and Hungarians, the monarchy collapsed in 1918.

Austrian Netherlands (1713–95) Provinces located in the southern part of the Low Countries, roughly comprising modern Belgium and Luxembourg. In 1713, the Peace of UTRECHT gave Emperor CHARLES VI control of what had been called the SPANISH NETHERLANDS. Administration of the region continued under the Habsburg rulers MARIA THERESA and later JOSEPH II, until the Austrian Netherlands was annexed to France in 1795.

Austrian school of economics Body of economic theory developed by several late-19th-century Austrian economists. Carl Menger (1840–1921) published a paper on their new theory of value in 1871. The concept of value was subjective, the source of a product's value being its ability to satisfy human wants. The actual value depended on the utility derived by the consumer from the product in its least important use (MARGINAL UTILITY). The theory was also applied to production and pricing. Other founders of the school included Friedrich von Wieser (1851–1926) and Eugen von Böhm-Bawerk (1851–1914). See also OPPORTUNITY COST, PRODUCTIVITY.

Austrian Succession, War of the (1740–48) Group of related wars that took place after the death (1740) of Emperor CHARLES VI. At issue was the right of Charles's daughter MARIA THERESA to inherit the Habsburg lands. The war began when FREDERICK II of Prussia invaded SILESIA in 1740. His victory suggested that the Habsburg dominions were incapable of defending themselves, prompting other countries to enter the fray. The conflict was ended by the Treaty of AIX-LA-CHAPELLE.

Austro-German Alliance *or* **Dual Alliance** (1879) Pact between Austria-Hungary and the German Reich in which the two powers promised each other support in case of attack by Russia, and neutrality in case of aggression by any other power. Germany's OTTO VON BISMARCK saw the alliance as a way to prevent the isolation of Germany and to preserve peace, as Russia would not wage war against both empires. The addition of Italy in 1882 made it the TRIPLE ALLIANCE. The agreement remained an important element of both German and Austro-Hungarian foreign policy until 1918.

Austro-Prussian War See SEVEN WEEKS' WAR

Austroasiatic languages Superfamily of about 150 languages spoken by close to 90 million physically and culturally very diverse people in South and Southeast Asia. Today most scholars believe that it is subdivided into two families, MUNDA and MON-KHMER. The present fragmented distribution of Austroasiatic languages is most likely the result of relatively recent incursions by INDO-ARYAN, SINO-TIBETAN, TAI, and AUSTRONESIAN-speaking peoples. In prehistoric times Austroasiatic languages most likely extended over a much broader and more continuous area, including much of what is now southeastern China. Other than VIETNAMESE and KHMER, no Austroasiatic language is an official national language.

Austronesian languages *formerly* **Malayo-Polynesian languages** Family of about 1,200 languages spoken by more than 200 million people in Indonesia, the Philippines, Madagascar, the central and southern Pacific island groups (except most of New Guinea; see PAPUAN LANGUAGES), and parts of mainland S.East Asia and Taiwan. Before European colonial expansion, it had the widest territorial extent of any language family. A primary genetic division in the family separates the Austronesian languages of Taiwan from the remaining languages, which are divided into Western and Central-Eastern Malayo-Polynesian. Western Malayo-Polynesian includes Javanese, which is spoken by about 76 million people—more than a third of all Austronesian-speakers. Eastern Malayo-Polynesian includes Oceanic, the best-defined subgroup of Austronesian, comprising nearly all the languages of POLYNESIA, MICRONESIA, and MELANESIA. Typological generalizations about Austronesian languages are difficult because of their enormous number and diversity, though content words tend to be disyllabic, and vowel and consonant inventories tend to be limited, especially in Polynesian. Written records in scripts of S.East Asian provenance (see INDIC WRITING SYSTEM) survive for several languages, including Old Javanese and Cham, the language of the kingdom of CHAMPA.

auteur theory \ō-ˈtœr\ Theory that holds that a film's director is its "author" (French, *auteur*). It originated in France in the 1950s and was promoted by FRANCOIS TRUFFAUT and J.-L. GODARD and the journal *Cahiers du Cinéma*. The director oversees and "writes" the film's audio and visual scenario and therefore is considered more responsible for its content than the screenwriter. Supporters maintain that all the most successful films bear the distinctive imprint of their director.

authoritarianism Principle of unqualified submission to authority, as opposed to individual freedom of thought and action. As a political system, authoritarianism is antidemocratic in that political power is concentrated in a leader or small elite not constitutionally responsible to those governed. It differs from TOTALITARIANISM in that authoritarian governments usually lack a guiding ideology, tolerate some pluralism in social organization, lack the power to mobilize the whole population in pursuit of national goals, and exercise their power within relatively predictable limits. See also ABSOLUTISM, DICTATORSHIP.

autism Neurobiological disorder that affects physical, social, and language skills. First described by Leo Kanner and Hans Asperger in the 1940s, the syndrome usually appears before 2½ years of age. Autistic infants appear indifferent or averse to affection and physical contact. They may be slow in learning to speak and suffer episodes of rage or panic; they may also appear deaf and display an almost hypnotized fascination with certain objects. Autism is often characterized by rhythmic body movements such as rocking or hand-clapping and by an obsessive desire to prevent change in daily routines. Autistic individuals may be hypersensitive to some stimuli (e.g., high-pitched sounds) and abnormally slow to react to others (e.g., physical pain). The disorder is three to four times more common in males. Though postnatal factors such as lack of parental attention were once blamed, it is now known that autism is the result of abnormalities in the brain structure. About 15–20% of autistic adults live and work independently; "high-functioning" autistic people may have special gifts based on their unusual ability for visual thinking. See also IDIOT SAVANT.

auto sacramental \ˈau̇-tō-ˌsä-krä-men-ˈtäl\ Spanish dramatic genre of short plays on sacred or biblical subjects, similar to MIRACLE or MORALITY plays. Performed outdoors as part of Corpus Christi feast-day celebrations, they were verse allegories dealing with some aspect of the mystery of the Holy Eucharist. The form first appeared in the 16th century and reached its height in plays by PEDRO CALDERON DE LA BARCA, who covered a wide range of nonsacramental subjects. Their performance was prohibited by royal decree in 1765 on the ground of irreverence.

autobiography Biography of oneself narrated by oneself. Little autobiographical literature exists from antiquity and the Middle Ages; with a handful of exceptions, the form begins to appear only in the 15th century. Autobiographical works take many forms, from intimate writings made during life that are not necessarily intended for publication (including letters, diaries, journals, memoirs, and reminiscences) to the formal autobiography. Outstanding examples of the genre extend from St. AUGUSTINE'S *Confessions* (c. AD 400) to VLADIMIR NABOKOV'S *Speak, Memory* (1951).

autoclave Vessel, usually of steel, able to withstand high temperatures and pressures. The chemical industry uses various types of autoclaves in manufacturing dyes and in other chemical reactions requiring high pressures. In bacteriology and medicine, instruments, equipment, supplies, and culture media are sterilized by superheated steam in an autoclave. In 1679 Denis Papin (1647–c. 1712) invented a prototype known as a steam digester; still used in cooking, it is now called a pressure cooker.

autograph Any manuscript handwritten by its author; in common usage, a handwritten signature. Aside from its value as a collector's item, an early or corrected draft of a work may show its stages of composition or "correct" final version. The earliest autograph signature of a famous person is probably the CID'S, dated 1096. There exist autographs of most of the great Renaissance figures, including LEONARDO DA VINCI, MICHELANGELO, and LUDOVICO ARIOSTO. From the 18th century, autograph material of notable people in the arts, sciences, or public life becomes more abundant.

autoimmune disease Any disease caused by an immune response (see IMMUNITY) against ANTIGENS in the tissues of one's own body. The IMMUNE SYSTEM has two known ways to prevent such a response: destruction of LYMPHOCYTES in the THYMUS before they leave to attack one's own tissues, and loss of ability to react to their target antigens by any such cells that do leave the thymus. Autoimmune diseases arise when these mechanisms fail and lymphocytes destroy host tissues; examples include insulin-dependent DIABETES MELLITUS, systemic LUPUS ERYTHEMATOSUS, PERNICIOUS ANEMIA, and RHEUMATOID ARTHRITIS. Treatment may replace the function of the affected tissue (e.g., insulin therapy for diabetes) or suppress the immune system (see IMMUNOSUPPRESSION). ALLERGIES are another type of autoimmune reaction.

automata theory \ō-ˈtä-mə-tə\ Body of physical and logical principles underlying the operation of any electromechanical device (an automaton) that converts information input in one form into another, or into some action, according to an ALGORITHM. NORBERT WIENER and ALAN M. TURING are regarded as pioneers in the field. In computer science, automata theory is concerned with the construction of robots (see ROBOTICS) from basic building blocks of automatons. The best example of a general automaton is an electronic DIGITAL COMPUTER with large but fixed memory storage capacity. Networks of automata may be designed to mimic human behavior. See also ARTIFICIAL INTELLIGENCE, TURING MACHINE.

automation Term coined about 1946 by a Ford Motor Co. engineer, used to describe a wide variety of systems in which there is a significant substitution of mechanical, electrical, or computerized action for human effort and intelligence. In general usage, automation can be defined as a technology concerned with performing a process by means of programmed commands combined with automatic feedback control (see CONTROL SYSTEM) to ensure proper execution of the instructions. The resulting system is capable of operating without human intervention.

automatism \ō-ˈtä-mə-ˌtiz-əm\ Method of painting or drawing in which conscious control over the movement of the hand is suppressed so that the subconscious mind may take over. For some Abstract Expressionists, such as JACKSON POLLOCK, the automatic process encompassed the entire process of composition. The Surrealists, having once achieved an interesting image or form by automatic or chance means, exploited the technique with fully conscious purpose. See also ABSTRACT EXPRESSIONISM, ACTION PAINTING, SURREALISM.

automaton \ō-ˈtä-mə-tən\ Mechanical object, either functional (such as a clock) or decorative (such as a miniature singing bird), that is self-operating. Devices set in motion by water, falling weights, and steam were in use in the 1st century. Decorative mechanical objects were made for ecclesiastical use and table ornaments in the Middle Ages and Renaissance. Spectacular fountains and waterworks can be seen in 16th-century Italian gardens; elaborate mechanical devices (pictures, snuffboxes) were popular in the 18th–19th century. Except for some works by CARL

FABERGE, the production of expensive automatons virtually ceased by the 20th century.

automobile Four-wheeled automotive vehicle designed for passenger transportation, commonly propelled by an INTERNAL COMBUSTION ENGINE using a volatile fuel. The modern automobile consists of about 14,000 parts, divided into several structural and mechanical systems. These include the steel body, containing the passenger and storage space, which sits on the chassis or steel frame; the internal combustion gasoline engine, which powers the car by means of a TRANSMISSION; the steering and braking systems, which control the car's motion; and the electrical system, which includes a battery, alternator, and other devices. Subsystems involve fuel, exhaust, lubrication, cooling, suspension, and tires. Though experimental vehicles were built in the 18th and mid-19th century, not until the 1880s did GOTTLIEB DAIMLER and KARL BENZ in Germany begin separately to manufacture cars commercially. In the U.S., James and William Packard (1863–1928, 1861–1923) and Ransom Olds (1864–1950) were among the first auto manufacturers, and by 1898 there were 50 U.S. manufacturers. Some early cars operated by steam engine, such as those made from c. 1902 by FRANCIS E. AND FREELAN O. STANLEY. The internal combustion engine was used by HENRY FORD when he introduced the MODEL T in 1908; Ford would soon revolutionize the industry with his use of the ASSEMBLY LINE. In the 1930s European manufacturers began to make small, affordable cars such as the Volkswagen. In the 1950s and '60s, U.S. automakers produced larger, more luxurious cars with more automatic features. In the 1970s and '80s Japanese manufacturers exported their small, reliable, fuel-efficient cars worldwide, and their increasing popularity spurred U.S. automakers to produce similar models. See also AXLE, BRAKE, BUS, CARBURETOR, ELECTRIC AUTOMOBILE, FUEL INJECTION, MOTORCYCLE, TRUCK.

automobile racing Automobile sport practiced in a variety of forms on roads, tracks, or closed circuits. It includes GRAND PRIX RACING, speedway racing (including the INDIANAPOLIS 500 race), STOCK-CAR RACING, SPORTS-CAR RACING, DRAG RACING, midget-car racing, and KARTING, as well as hill climbs and RALLY DRIVING. A Motor Sports Hall of Fame is located in Talladega, Ala. There is no central governing body for automobile racing in the U.S. as there is in most other countries.

autonomic nervous system \ˌȯt-ə-ˈnäm-ik\ Part of the NERVOUS SYSTEM that is not under conscious control and that regulates the internal organs. It includes the sympathetic and parasympathetic nervous systems. The first, which connects the internal organs to the brain via spinal nerves, responds to stress by increasing heart rate and blood flow to the muscles and decreasing blood flow to the skin. The second comprises the cranial nerves and the lower spinal nerves, which increase digestive secretions and slow the heartbeat. Both have sensory fibers that send feedback on the condition of internal organs to the central nervous system, information that helps maintain HOMEOSTASIS. A third division, the enteric nervous system, embedded in the walls of the stomach and intestines, controls digestive movement and secretions. See illustration opposite.

autopsy \ˈȯ-ˌtäp-sē\ *or* **necropsy** *or* **postmortem** Dissection and examination of a dead body to determine cause of death and learn about disease processes in ways that are not possible with the living. Autopsies have contributed to the development of medicine since at least the Middle Ages. Beyond revealing causes of individual deaths, autopsy is crucial to the accuracy of disease and death statistics, the education of medical students, the understanding of new and changing diseases, and the advancement of medical science.

Autry, (Orvon) Gene (1907–1998) U.S. actor and singer. Born on a ranch in Tioga, Texas, he worked as a radio telegrapher in Oklahoma and made his debut on a local radio show in 1928, hosting his own radio program from 1931. His first film, *In Old Santa Fe* (1934), launched his career as a cowboy actor. Known as "the Singing Cowboy," he starred in 18 movies, ending with *Alias Jesse James* (1959). His recordings, including "Rudolph the Red-Nosed Reindeer" (1949), sold millions of copies. The televised *Gene Autry Show* ran from 1950 to 1954.

autumn crocus Any plant of the genus *Colchicum* (LILY FAMILY), sometimes called meadow saffron, consisting of about 30 species of herbaceous plants native to Eurasia. The stemless, crocuslike flowers bloom in autumn. Several species are cultivated as ornamentals for their pink, white, or bluish-purple tubelike flowers, especially *C. autumnale, C. bornmuelleri,* and *C. speciosum.* The swollen underground stem of *C. autumnale* contains colchicine, a substance used to relieve the pain of GOUT.

Auvergne \ō-ˈvernʸ\ Region (pop., 1990: 1,321,000), southern central France. It was once inhabited by the Arverni, a Gallic people led by VERCINGETORIX and defeated by Julius CAESAR. It was yielded to the VISIGOTHS in AD 475 and conquered by the FRANKS under CLOVIS I in 507. It became part of AQUITAINE, and in the 8th century was made a countship. It passed to the BOURBONS in 1416 and to France c. 1530.

auxiliary In GRAMMAR, a verb that is subordinate to the main lexical verb in a clause. Auxiliaries can convey distinctions of TENSE, aspect, MOOD, person, and number. In GERMANIC LANGUAGES such as English and ROMANCE LANGUAGES such as French, an auxiliary verb occurs with the main verb in the form of an infinitive or participle.

auxin Any of a group of HORMONES that regulate plant growth, particularly by stimulating cell elongation in STEMS and inhibiting it in ROOTS. Auxins influence the growth of stems toward light (phototropism) and against the force of gravity (geotropism). Auxins also play a role in cell division and differentiation, fruit development, the formation of roots from CUTTINGS, the inhibition of lateral branching, and leaf fall. The most important naturally occurring auxin is beta-indolylacetic acid.

Ava \ˈä-vä\ Ruined city, Myanmar. The city, located on the IRRAWADDY RIVER southwest of MANDALAY, was founded in the 14th century by the SHANS, who made it their capital. It was destroyed in 1527, but again became the capital in 1634 under the Toungoo dynasty. When Alaungpaya founded the Konbaung dynasty in the 18th century, Ava served as its

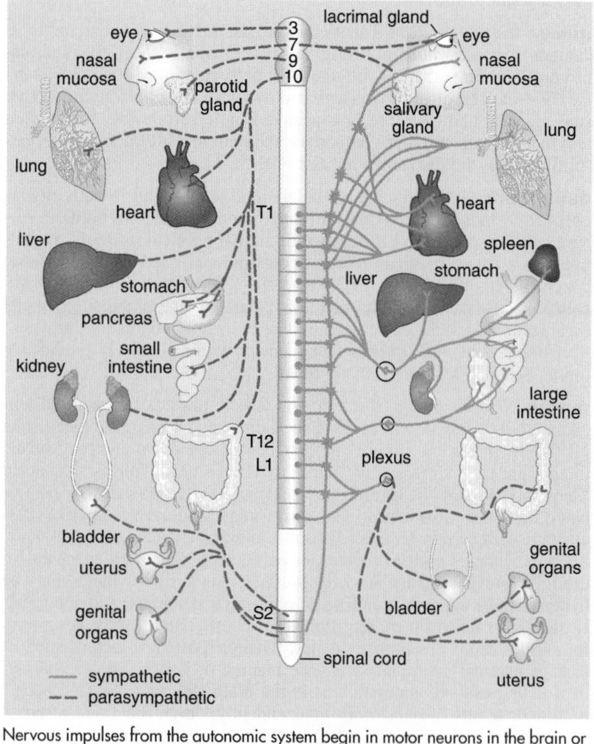

Nervous impulses from the autonomic system begin in motor neurons in the brain or spinal cord. Each motor neuron connects with a second motor neuron outside the central nervous system to carry the impulse to the glands and smooth muscles. These second motor neurons are found in ganglia (masses of neurons), which are interconnected with nerves to form two chains along either side of the spinal cord. Other ganglia form large clusters (plexuses) elsewhere in the body. Preganglionic fibers of the sympathetic division emerge along the thoracic (T) and first three lumbar (L) segments of the spinal cord. Fibers of parasympathetic neurons originating in the brain stem arise from the third, seventh, ninth, and tenth cranial nerves. Other parasympathetic fibers emerge from the second, third, and fourth sacral (S) segments of the spinal cord.

capital for a time, and even after the dynasty built Amarapura and Mandalay, its seat was often referred to as the "Court of Ava."

avalanche Large mass of rock debris or snow that moves rapidly down a mountain slope, sweeping and grinding everything in its path. Avalanches begin when a mass of material overcomes the frictional resistance of the sloping surface, often after its foundation is loosened by spring rains or is partially melted by a warm, dry wind. Vibrations caused by loud noises, such as gunfire or thunder, can start the mass moving. Some avalanches develop during heavy snowstorms and slide while the snow is still falling, but more often they occur after snow has accumulated at a given site. Avalanche control consists largely of detonating explosives in the upper reaches of avalanche zones, intentionally causing the snow to slide before accumulations become very great.

Avalokitesvara \ˌə-və-ˌlō-ki-ˈtāsh-və-rə\ *Chinese* **Guanyin** \ˈgwän-ˈyin\ *Japanese* **Kannon** \ˈkän-ˈnȯn\ BODHISATTVA of infinite compassion and mercy, the most popular of MAHAYANA Buddhist deities. He is the earthly manifestation of AMITABHA, guarding the world between the departure of the historical BUDDHA, Gautama, and the appearance of the future Buddha, MAITREYA. He is the creator of the fourth world, the actual living universe. In China and Japan his gender became ambiguous; he is sometimes called a goddess. For PURE LAND BUDDHISTS, he forms a ruling triad with Amitabha and the bodhisattva Mahasthamaprapta. The most popular deity in Tibet, he is thought to be reincarnated in each DALAI LAMA.

Avalokitesvara, bronze figure from Kurkihar, Bihar, 9th century; in Patna Museum, Patna, Bihar.

BY COURTESY OF PATNA MUSEUM, PATNA (BIHAR); PHOTOGRAPH, ROYAL ACADEMY OF ARTS, LONDON

Avalon Island to which Britain's legendary King ARTHUR was taken after he was mortally wounded in his last battle. First described by GEOFFREY OF MONMOUTH, it was said to be ruled by MORGAN LE FAY and her eight sisters, all of whom were skilled in the healing arts. Legend held that when Arthur was healed he would return to rule Britain. The tale may have originated in Celtic myths of an elysium for fallen heros. Avalon has sometimes been identified with Glastonbury in Somerset.

Avanti Historic kingdom, northern India. Located on the overland trade routes between northern and southern India, it lay within present-day MADHYA PRADESH. Its capital was at Ujjain. It flourished in the 6th–4th century BC as one of the great powers of northern India. In the 4th century BC it was conquered and annexed by Candra Gupta Maurya of Magadha. Ujjain, one of the seven holy cities of HINDUISM, was renowned for its beauty and wealth; it also became a center of early BUDDHISM and JAINISM.

Avars \ˈä-värz\ People of undetermined origin who built an empire in eastern Europe between the Adriatic and Baltic seas and the Elbe and Dnieper rivers in the 6th–9th century. Mounted nomads, possibly from Central Asia, they made the Hungarian plain the center of their empire, from which they intervened in Germanic tribal wars, helped the Lombards overthrow allies of Byzantium, and nearly succeeded in occupying Constantinople in 626. They also fought the MEROVINGIANS and helped push the Serbs and Croats southward. Weakened by revolts and internal dissent, they submitted to CHARLEMAGNE in 805.

Avatamsaka-sutra \ˌə-və-ˈtəm-sə-kə-ˈsü-trə\ *or* **Garland Sutra** MAHAYANA Buddhist SUTRA that explores the teachings of the BUDDHA Gautama. It speaks of the deeds of the Buddha and the resulting merits that blossom like a garland of flowers. It begins with the Buddha's Enlightenment attended by a chorus of BODHISATTVAS and divine beings. It describes an assembly in the palace of INDRA, where the Buddha teaches that all beings have the Buddha nature. Around AD 400 a Chinese translation appeared, *Huayan jing,* which gave rise in the 6th century to the Huayan sect, which became in Japan the KEGON school. See also VAIROCANA.

avatar \ˈa-və-ˌtär\ In HINDUISM, the incarnation of a deity in human or animal form to counteract an evil in the world. It usually refers to 10 appearances of VISHNU, including an incarnation as the BUDDHA Gautama. The doctrine appears in the BHAGAVADGITA in the words of Lord Krishna to ARJUNA: "Whenever there is a decline of righteousness and rise of unrighteousness then I send forth Myself."

Avebury \ˈāv-bə-rē\ Village, WILTSHIRE, England, lying partly within one of the largest prehistoric sites in Europe. The site occupies 28.5 acres (11.5 hectares) and contains vast megalithic remains, including chalk blocks and sandstone pillars placed in circles. Its date and origin are uncertain. Kennet Avenue, a route into the interior of the great circle, linked Avebury with a temple 1 mi (1.6 km) away.

Avedon \ˈa-və-ˌdän\, **Richard** (born 1923) U.S. photographer. Born in New York City, he began studying photography in the U.S. Merchant Marine. In 1945 he became a regular contributor to *Harper's Bazaar*; he later was closely associated with *Vogue*. He is noted for his celebrity portraits and fashion photographs, which are characterized by strong black-and-white contrast and confrontational poses. His many books include *Observations* (1959; text by TRUMAN CAPOTE), *Nothing Personal* (1964; text by JAMES BALDWIN), *Portraits* (1976), *Evidence* (1994), and *The Sixties* (1999).

avens \ˈa-venz\ Any of the low-growing, perennial flowering plants (approximately 50 species) of the genus *Geum,* in the ROSE family. Most occur in the northern or southern temperate zones or in the Arctic. Several species are cultivated for their solitary or clustered white, red, orange, or yellow flowers. The plants grow no more than 2 ft (60 cm) tall. Most of the compound, deeply lobed or cut leaves arise from the base of the stem.

average See MEAN, MEDIAN, AND MODE

Avernus \ə-ˈvər-nəs\, **Lake** *ancient* **Lacus Avernus** Lake, southern Italy. It lies west of Naples in the crater of an extinct volcano. Because of its sulfurous vapors, it was considered an entrance to the underworld by the ancient Romans, including VIRGIL. According to legend, the grove of HECATE and the grotto of the Cumaean SIBYL lay nearby. In the 1st century BC it was transformed into a naval base, Portus Iulius, by AGRIPPA and linked to the sea. Its impressive Roman ruins include baths, temples, and villas.

Averroës \ə-ˈver-ə-ˌwēz\ *Arabic* **Ibn Rushd** \ˌib-ən-ˈrüsht\ *in full* **Abu al-Walid Muhammad ibn Ahmad ibn Muhammad ibn Rushd** (1126–1198) Spanish Arabic philosopher. He worked as a judge and physician in Córdoba, Seville, and Morocco. His interpretations of ARISTOTLE (often in reaction against AVICENNA) consisted of three series of commentaries: (1) the "little commentaries," short epitomes providing a brief analysis of the treatises, (2) the "middle commentaries," explaining the texts literally, and (3) the "great commentaries," a more advanced and profound exegesis. While mostly faithful to Aristotle's thought, he endowed the Aristotelian "prime mover" with the characteristics of the Plotinian (see PLOTINUS) and Islamic transcendent God, the universal First Cause, and partially synthesized Greek and Arabic philosophical thought. See also ARABIC PHILOSOPHY.

Avery, Oswald (Theodore) (1877–1955) Canadian-U.S. bacteriologist. Born in Halifax, Nova Scotia, he studied at Colgate University before taking a post at New York's Rockefeller Institute Hospital. There he discovered transformation, a process by which a change could be introduced into bacteria and passed on to later generations of transformed cells. He and his coworkers reported in 1944 that the substance that caused the transformation was DNA, the cell's genetic material. The discovery thus opened the door to deciphering the GENETIC CODE.

Avesta \ə-ˈves-tə\ *or* **Zend-Avesta** Sacred book of ZOROASTRIANISM. It contains hymns, prayers, and appeals to righteousness ascribed to ZOROASTER. The present text was assembled in the 3rd–7th century AD from the remains of a larger body of scripture that was destroyed when ALEXANDER THE GREAT conquered Persia. It has five parts: the *Gatha*s, hymns in what are thought to be Zoroaster's own words; *Visp-rat,* containing homages to spiritual leaders; *Vendidad,* the main source for Zoroastrian law; the *Yashts*, 21 hymns to angels and ancient heroes; and the *Khurda avesta,* composed of minor texts.

Avestan language \ə-'ves-tən\ Old IRANIAN LANGUAGE of the AVESTA. The oldest portion of the Avesta, the Gathas, are now commonly thought to data from around the end of the 2nd millennium BC, and are thus contemporary with Vedic SANSKRIT. Not until the mid-SASANIAN period (5th–6th century AD) was the Avesta committed to writing, in an alphabetic script invented for the purpose on the basis of existing Middle Persian scripts. The oldest manuscripts date only from the 13th century.

aviary Structure for keeping captive birds, usually spacious enough for the aviculturist to enter. Aviaries range from small enclosures to large flight cages 100 ft (30 m) or more long and up to 50 ft (15 m) high. Enclosures for birds that fly only little or weakly (e.g., RAILS, PHEASANTS) may be only about 3 ft (1 m) high. In cold climates the aviary is usually enclosed and heated. Most aviculturists prefer to place birds in natural, planted surroundings. Many aviaries are maintained for pleasure by private aviculturists; others, especially large ones, are found in ZOOS or research institutions.

aviation Development and operation of heavier-than-air aircraft. In 1783 the BALLOON became the first aircraft to carry humans. Production of a successful GLIDER in 1891 and refinement of the INTERNAL COMBUSTION ENGINE led to the first successful engine-powered AIRPLANE flight by WILBUR AND ORVILLE WRIGHT in 1903. World War I accelerated the expansion of aviation, and in the 1920s the first small airlines began carrying mail and passengers. World War II was another period of innovation in aircraft size, speed, and range. In the late 1940s the JET ENGINE made possible the subsequent development of commercial airlines throughout the world. See also AIRSHIP, HELICOPTER, SEAPLANE.

Avicenna \ˌa-və-'se-nə\ *Arabic* **Ibn Sina** \'ib-ən-'sē-nä\ *in full* **Abu Ali al-Husayn ibn Abd Allah ibn Sina** (980–1037) Islamic philosopher and scientist. Born in Bukhara (now in Uzbekistan), he became physician to several sultans and also twice served as vizier. His *Canon of Medicine* was long a standard work in the field. He is also known for his great encyclopedia of philosophy, *The Book of Healing (Kitab al-shifa).* His other writings include *The Book of Salvation* and *The Book of Directives* and *Remarks.* His ideas, especially his interpretations of ARISTOTLE, influenced the medieval European Scholastics. His system rests on a conception of God as the necessary existent: only in God do essence (*what* he is) and existence (*that* he is) coincide.

Avignon \ˌà-vē-'nyō^n\ *ancient* **Avennio** City (pop., 1990: 89,000), southeastern France. Founded as a Phocaean colony, it was conquered by the Romans, Goths, Burgundians, Ostrogoths, and finally the Franks. It was part of the kingdom of ARLES and briefly became a republic (1135–46). It belonged to Venaissin before being sold by JOAN I of Naples to Pope CLEMENT VI in 1348, and it was the capital of the papacy (1309–77) and seat of the Avignonese popes during the Western SCHISM. France annexed the city in 1791. Landmarks include a Romanesque cathedral, the papal palace, and Saint-Bénézet bridge, made famous by the song "Sur le pont d'Avignon."

Avignon papacy Roman Catholic papacy during the period 1309–77, when the popes resided at AVIGNON, France. Elected pope through the machinations of Philip IV of France, CLEMENT V moved the papal capital to Avignon four years later primarily for political reasons. All seven popes of this period were French, as were most of the cardinals, which aroused English and German animosity. During the Avignon papacy the cardinals began to play a stronger role in church government, church and clergy were reformed, missionary efforts were expanded, and popes tried to settle royal rivalries and establish peace. The heavy French influence damaged the prestige of the papacy, however, and in 1377 Gregory XI returned to Rome. The cardinals elected a new pope who took the Avignon seat, becoming the first of a line of ANTIPOPES and beginning the Western SCHISM.

Avignon school School of late Gothic painting associated with the city of Avignon, France, during the AVIGNON PAPACY, when many Italian artists worked there. Under the direction of SIMONE MARTINI, the papal palace and secular buildings in nearby towns were decorated with frescoes. The city was one of the channels by which Italian 14th-century art reached France. By the early 15th century, Flemish influences had reached the city, consolidating the Italian and northern styles. The Avignon Pietà (c. 1460), attributed to Enguerrand Charonton, is the masterpiece of the school. The artistic activity at Avignon greatly influenced French painting in the late 15th and 16th century. See also GOTHIC ART.

Avilés, Pedro Menéndez de See Pedro MENENDEZ DE AVILES

Avocado (*Persea americana*).
S.A. SCIBOR—SHOSTAL

avocado Fruit of *Persea americana,* of the LAUREL FAMILY, a tree native to the Western Hemisphere from Mexico south to the Andean regions. Avocados are extremely variable in shape, size, and color (green to dark purple). The outer skin may be thin, or coarse and woody. The greenish or yellowish flesh has a buttery consistency and a rich, nutty flavor. In some varieties the flesh contains as much as 25% unsaturated oil. Avocados are the principal ingredient of the Mexican sauce guacamole. They provide thiamine, riboflavin, and vitamin A.

American avocet (*Recurvirostra americana*).
MILDRED GLUECK FROM ROOT RESOURCES—EB INC.

avocet \'a-və-ˌset\ Any of several large shorebirds (genus *Recurvirostra*) with boldly contrasting plumage, long bluish legs, and a long black bill upturned at the tip. Avocets inhabit fresh and salt marshes that have areas of open shallow water and mudflats, and feed by sweeping the partly open bill in the shallows. They often wade together to corral minnows and crustaceans. Four avocet species are found in temperate and tropical regions worldwide. The American avocet is about 18 in. (45 cm) long, including the bill.

Avogadro's law \ˌä-və-'gä-drōz\ Statement that under the same conditions of TEMPERATURE and PRESSURE, equal volumes of different GASES contain an equal number of molecules (see AVOGADRO'S NUMBER). First proposed by the Italian scientist Amedeo Avogadro (1776–1856) in 1811, it became accepted c. 1860. From the law, it follows that the volume occupied by one MOLE of gas (at standard conditions of 32°F, or 0°C, and 1 atmosphere of pressure) is the same for all gases (22.4 liters).

Avogadro's number Number of units in one MOLE of any substance (defined as its MOLECULAR WEIGHT in grams), equal to 6.0221367×10^{23}. The units may be ELECTRONS, ATOMS, IONS, or MOLECULES, depending on the nature of the substance and the character of the reaction (if any). See also AVOGADRO'S LAW, law of MASS ACTION, STOICHIOMETRY.

avoidance, zone of Region of apparent absence of GALAXIES near the plane of the MILKY WAY GALAXY. Millions of external galaxies are in this region of the sky but are obscured by interstellar dust within the Milky Way. The zone's obscuration can be penetrated at the infrared portion of the ELECTROMAGNETIC SPECTRUM.

avoidance behavior Type of activity exhibited by animals exposed to adverse stimuli in which the tendency to flee or to act defensively is stronger than the tendency to attack. Vision is the sense that most often produces avoidance behavior (e.g., small birds react to the sight of an owl), but sound (e.g., a warning cry) may do so as well.

Avon Former county, southwestern England. Bordering the SEVERN Estuary and the BRISTOL CHANNEL, it was created in the 1974 government reorganization; its capital was BRISTOL. During the Roman era, major roads were built and BATH became known for its medicinal waters. From the 7th century, Avon was incorporated into the Kingdom of WESSEX. In the 18th century Bristol was an important seaport and Bath again became fashionable. The region has a diversified economy, including agriculture and manufacturing; tourism is also important.

Avon River, Lower River, southwestern England. Rising in GLOUCESTERSHIRE, it flows 75 mi (121 km) southwest through BRISTOL and into the BRISTOL CHANNEL at Avonmouth, Bristol's port. Below Bristol it has cut through a limestone ridge to form Clifton Gorge, noted for its suspension bridge.

Avon River, Upper River, central England. Rising in NORTHAMPTONSHIRE, it flows 96 mi (154 km) southwest into the SEVERN RIVER at Tewkesbury. It is known for its scenic beauty, notably in the Vale of Evesham. Important towns along it include STRATFORD, where WILLIAM SHAKESPEARE was born.

AWACS (Airborne Warning and Control System) \'ā-waks\ Mobile, long-range RADAR surveillance-and-control center for air defense. Used by the U.S. Air Force since 1977, AWACS is mounted in a specially modified Boeing 707 aircraft, with its main radar antenna affixed to a rotating dome. It can detect, track, and identify low-flying aircraft at a distance of 200 nautical mi (370 km) and high-level targets at much greater distances. It can also track maritime traffic and operate in any weather. The computer system can assess enemy action and track the location and availability of any aircraft within range. Operators of its secure communications system can guide friendly aircraft against enemy planes.

Awakening, Great See GREAT AWAKENING

Awolowo \ä-'wü-lō-ˌwō\, **Obafemi** (1909–1987) Nigerian nationalist politician and leader of the YORUBA ethnic group. While studying law in London he wrote the influential *Path to Nigerian Freedom* (1947) and laid the basis for the first Yoruba political party, the Action Group. As premier of Nigeria's Western Region (1954–59) he worked to improve education, social services, and agriculture. He remained a major figure in national politics but never won high elective office.

ax Hand tool used for chopping, splitting, chipping, and piercing. Stone Age hand axes originated in simple stone implements that acquired wooden hafts, or handles, about 30,000 BC. Copper-bladed axes appeared in Egypt about 4000 BC and were followed by axes with blades of BRONZE and eventually iron. The development of the iron-bladed felling ax in the Middle Ages made possible the vast forest clearances of Europe, North and South America, and elsewhere. Though the ax has lost much of its historic role to powered saws and other machinery, it remains a widely used tool with many uses.

axiology Philosophical theory of value. Axiology is the study of goodness, or value, in their widest senses. JOHN DEWEY distinguished between instrumental and intrinsic value—between what is good as a means and what is good as an end—in *Human Nature and Conduct* (1922) and *Theory of Valuation* (1939). In normative ETHICS, particularly CONSEQUENTIALISM, the distinction between intrinsic and extrinsic value is central. Something has intrinsic value if it is valuable in its own right (e.g., pleasure for a hedonist); something has extrinsic value if it is valuable only as a means to something else that has intrinsic value (e.g., paper money). See also EUDAEMONISM, FACT-VALUE DISTINCTION.

axiom In mathematics or logic, an unprovable rule or first principle accepted as true because it is self-evident or particularly useful (e.g., "Nothing can both be and not be at the same time and in the same respect"). The term is often used interchangeably with *postulate,* though the latter term is sometimes reserved for mathematical applications (such as the postulates of EUCLIDEAN GEOMETRY). It should be contrasted with a THEOREM, which requires a rigorous proof.

axiomatic method In LOGIC, the procedure by which an entire science or system of theorems is deduced in accordance with specified rules by logical deduction from certain basic propositions (AXIOMS), which in turn are constructed from a few terms taken as primitive. These terms may be either arbitrarily defined or conceived according to a model in which some intuitive warrant for their truth is felt to exist. The oldest examples of axiomatized systems are Aristotle's SYLLOGISTIC and EUCLIDEAN GEOMETRY. Early in the 20th century, BERTRAND RUSSELL and ALFRED NORTH WHITEHEAD attempted to formalize all of mathematics in an axiomatic manner. Scholars have even subjected the empirical sciences to this method, as in J. H. Woodger's *The Axiomatic Method in Biology* (1937) and Clark Hull's *Principles of Behavior* (1943).

Axis Powers Coalition headed by Germany, Italy, and Japan that opposed the ALLIED POWERS in World War II. The alliance originated in a series of agreements between Germany and Italy, followed in 1936 by the ROME–BERLIN AXIS declaration and the German–Japanese ANTI-COMINTERN PACT. The connection was strengthened by the formal PACT OF STEEL (1939) between Germany and Italy and by the Tripartite Pact signed by all three powers in 1940. Several other countries, including Hungary, Romania, Bulgaria, Croatia, and Slovakia, later allied themselves with the original Axis Powers.

axle Pin or shaft on or with which wheels revolve; with fixed wheels, one of the basic simple MACHINES for amplifying FORCE. Combined with the WHEEL, in its earliest form it was probably used for raising weights or water buckets from wells. Its principle of operation can be illustrated in the attachment of large and small GEARS to the same shaft; the tendency of a force applied at the radius on the large gear to turn the shaft is sufficient to overcome a larger force at the radius on the small gear. The MECHANICAL ADVANTAGE is equal to the ratio of the two forces and also equal to the ratio of the radii of the two gears.

Axminster carpet Floor covering produced in a factory founded at Axminster, England, in 1755 by the cloth weaver Thomas Whitty. The carpets were knotted in wool on woolen warps, with wefts of flax or hemp, and featured Renaissance architectural or floral patterns. The factory closed in 1835 with the advent of industrial weaving machines. The name survives as a generic term for all machine-made carpets with pile similar to velvet or chenille.

Axum See AKSUM

ayatollah \ˌī-ə-'tō-lə\ In the SHIITE branch of Islam, a high-ranking religious authority regarded by his followers as the most learned person of his age. The ayatollah's authority rests on the infallible IMAM. His legal decisions are accepted as binding by his personal followers and (in the present day) by the wider community.

Ayckbourn \'āk-ˌbȯrn\, **Alan** *later* **Sir Alan** (born 1939) British playwright. He began acting with the Stephen Joseph Co. in Scarborough, Yorkshire, where he also wrote his earliest plays under the pseudonym Roland Allen (1959–61). Most of his plays premiered at its theater, where he was artistic director from 1970, before winning acclaim in London and New York. He has written over 50 plays, mostly farces and comedies that deal with marital and class conflicts, including *Relatively Speaking* (1967), *Absurd Person Singular* (1972), the trilogy *The Norman Conquests* (1973), *Intimate Exchanges* (1982), and *Communicating Doors* (1995).

Aydid \ī-'dēd\, **Muhammad Farah** (c. 1930–1996) Somali faction leader, the dominant clan leader at the center of the Somalian civil war (1991–95). He received military training in Italy and the U.S.S.R., and served in posts under MOHAMED SIAD BARRE (1978–89) before overthrowing him in 1991. Losing the interim presidency to another factional leader, Aydid continued warring on rival clans. When U.N. and U.S. troops arrived in Somalia (1992), Aydid ambushed a U.N. contingent and was declared an outlaw. The attempt to capture him led to many deaths, and the foreign troops were withdrawn. He then intensified his campaign against his rivals, but reportedly died of a heart attack after being wounded in battle.

Ayer \'a(ə)r, 'e(ə)r\, **A(lfred) J(ules)** *later* **Sir Alfred** (1910–1989) British philosopher. He taught at University College London (1946–59) and later at Oxford (1959–78). A proponent of LOGICAL POSITIVISM, he gained international notice in 1936 with his first book, *Language, Truth and Logic,* which drew on the ideas of the VIENNA CIRCLE and EMPIRICISM. His interests are reflected in the titles of his later works: *The Foundations of Empirical Knowledge* (1940), *The Problem of Knowledge* (1956), *The Origins of Pragmatism* (1968), *Russell and Moore* (1971), *The Central Questions of Philosophy* (1973), and *Wittgenstein* (1985).

Ayers Rock \'arz\ Rock outcrop, southwestern Northern Territory, Australia. Called Uluru by the AUSTRALIAN ABORIGINES and located in Uluru National Park, it is 1,100 ft (335 m) high and may be the world's largest monolith. Its arkosic sandstone changes color according to the height of the sun. Shallow caves at the base of the rock are sacred to several Aboriginal tribes and contain carvings and paintings. In 1985, ownership of Ayers Rock was officially returned to the Aborigines.

Aying *or* **A-ying** \'ä-'yiŋ\ *orig.* **Qian Xingcun** (1900–1977) Chinese critic and historian of modern Chinese literature. A member of the Communist Party and of the standing committee of the League of Left-Wing Writers, he began c. 1930 to gather and study materials on the literature of modern times and of the Ming and Qing dynasties. His published works, including *Women Writers in Modern China* (1933) and *Two Talks* *on the Novel* (1958), contributed greatly to the record of modern culture in China.

Aylesbury \'ālz-bə-rē\ Town (pop., 1995 est.: 61,000), southeastern central England. The county seat of BUCKINGHAMSHIRE, it lies northwest of London in the THAMES valley known as the Vale of Aylesbury, noted for its rich clay. Once an important market town, it is now an industrial center. Its historic buildings include an 18th-century county hall and a 15th-century inn.

Aymara \ˌī-mə-'rä\ Large South American Indian group living on the Titicaca plateau of the central Andes in present-day Peru and Bolivia. The Aymara were conquered by the INCAS and the Spanish, though they rebelled against both. Traditional Aymara now live in an area of poor soil and harsh climate, where they herd llamas and alpacas, grow crops, and fish using giant-reed boats. Numbering 1.5–2 million, they are among the poorest people in the hemisphere.

Aymé \e-'mā\, **Marcel** (1902–1967) French novelist, essayist, and playwright. His novels include *The Hollow Field* (1929), *The Fable and the Flesh* (1943), and *The Transient Hour* (1946). He delighted a vast public with witty tales of talking farm animals (reflecting his own farm upbringing), some of which were published in English as *The Wonderful Farm* (1951). Though his extravagant creations mingling fantasy and reality were long dismissed as minor, he was belatedly recognized as a master of light irony and storytelling.

Ayodhya See AJODHYA

Ayrshire \'er-ˌshir\ Breed of hardy dairy CATTLE (see DAIRY FARMING) that originated in the county of Ayr, Scotland, in the late 18th century. It is considered the only special dairy breed to have originated in the British Isles. Its body color varies from almost pure white to nearly all cherry red or brown. Exported widely to other countries, it is especially common in Britain, the U.S., and Canada.

Ayub Khan \ä-'üb-'kän\, **Mohammad** (1907–1974) President of Pakistan (1958–69). After studies at Aligarh Muslim University and at the British Royal Military College, he became an officer in the Indian army (1928). He fought in Burma (present-day Myanmar) in World War II, and afterward rose through the ranks in the military in newly independent Pakistan. In 1958 Pakistan's Pres. Iskander Mirza abrogated the nation's constitution, and Ayub became chief martial-law administrator. He declared himself president the same year, exiling Mirza. He established close ties to China and in 1965 went to war with India over control of Jammu and Kashmir. The failure to take Kashmir combined with unrest over suffrage restrictions led to riots, and Ayub resigned in 1969.

Ayurveda \'ä-yər-ˌvā-də\ *or* **Ayurvedic medicine** Traditional system of Indian medicine. It is attributed to Dhanvantari, the physician to the gods in Hindu mythology, who received it from BRAHMA. Its earliest concepts were set out in the portion of the VEDAS known as the Atharvaveda (c. 2nd millennium BC). The most important Ayurvedic texts are the *Caraka samhita* and *Susruta samhita* (1st–4th century AD). These texts analyze the human body in terms of earth, water, fire, air, and ether as well as the three bodily humors (wind, bile, and phlegm). To prevent illness, Ayurvedic medicine emphasizes hygiene, exercise, herbal preparations, and yoga. To cure ailments, it relies on herbal medicines, physiotherapy, and diet. Ayurvedic medicine is still a popular form of health care in India, where it is taught in roughly 100 colleges, and it has gained currency in the West as a form of alternative medicine.

Ayutthaya \ˌä-yü-'tī-ə\ *in full* **Phra Nakhon Si Ayutthaya** Former Thai capital located northeast of Bangkok. Political Thailand (formerly Siam) is said to date from its founding (between 1347 and 1351). The kingdom of Ayutthaya was once one of the most powerful in S.East Asia, and the city flourished for more than 400 years. Much of its architecture, art, and literature was destroyed in the 1767 sack of the city by Hsinbyushin of the ALAUNGPAYA DYNASTY. Modern Ayutthaya is set among the ruins of the ancient city.

Ayyubid dynasty \ä-'yü-bid\ (1173–1250) Kurdish dynasty founded by SALADIN that ruled over Egypt, most of Syria, upper Iraq, and Yemen. After overthrowing the FATIMID DYNASTY, Saladin united the Muslims to defend Palestine against the CRUSADES and made Egypt the most powerful Muslim state in the world. After Saladin's death the Ayyubid regime became decentralized. The Ayyubids introduced the madrasah, an academy of religious sciences. In 1250 the MAMLUK REGIME exploited a palace feud to take over the empire.

azalea Any plant of certain species of the genus *Rhododendron* (HEATH FAMILY), formerly given the generic name *Azalea.* Though some gardeners consider azaleas distinct from RHODODENDRONS, distinguishing characteristics of the two groups are not consistent enough to separate them into two genera. Azaleas typically are deciduous (see DECIDUOUS TREE), with flowers that are funnel-shaped, somewhat two-lipped, and often fragrant. Cultivated varieties have been bred from species native to the hilly regions of Asia and North America. Well-known North American kinds include the smooth, or sweet, azalea *(R. arborescens);* the flame azalea *(R. calendulaceum);* and the pinxter flower *(R. periclymenoides).*

Azali \á-zá-'lē\ Any member of the Babi movement who remained faithful to the teachings of the BAB and his chosen successor, Mirza Yahya, known as Sobh-e Azal, after the movement split in 1863. For 13 years after the Bab's execution, followers recognized Sobh-e Azal as their leader. Then Sobh-e Azal's half-brother, BAHA ULLAH, privately declared himself to be the prophet whose coming the Bab had foretold. The Azalis rejected him, but most Babis followed him, establishing the BAHA'I faith in 1867. Now located almost exclusively in Iran, the Azalis probably number no more than a few thousand.

Azaña (y Díaz) \ə-'thän-yə\, **Manuel** (1880–1940) Spanish prime minister and president. As prime minister from 1931 to 1933, he attempted to fashion a moderately liberal government. Elected president in May 1936, he was able to accomplish little before the SPANISH CIVIL WAR broke out in July. He lost control of policy and remained in office as only a figurehead until 1939, when the Nationalist forces won and he went into exile.

Azaña y Díaz, detail of an oil painting by J.M. López Mezquita, 1937; in the Hispanic Society of America collection.

BY COURTESY OF THE HISPANIC SOCIETY OF AMERICA, NEW YORK

Azande \ə-'zan-dē\ *or* **Zande** \'zan-dē\ People of central Africa who speak an ADAMAWA-UBANGI LANGUAGE of the NIGER-CONGO family. They live partly in Sudan, partly in Congo (Zaire), and partly in the Central African Republic. They occupy widely scattered family homesteads, subsisting through agriculture and hunting. Patrilineal CLANS are numerous. Witchcraft, magic, and divination are major features of social life. The Azande number about 3.7 million.

Azerbaijan \ˌa-zər-bī-'jän\ *officially* **Republic of Azerbaijan** Nation, South Asia. Area: 33,400 sq mi (86,600 sq km). Population (1997 est.): 7,617,000. Capital: BAKU. The Azerbaijanis have a Turkic strain dating from the 11th century AD, while SELJUQ migrations brought further mixtures, including Iranian; Russians are a minority. Languages: Azerbaijani (official), Russian. Religions: Islam, minority Orthodox Christianity. Currency: manat. Azerbaijan is characterized by a variety of landscapes. More than 40% of its territory is lowlands, while areas above 5,000 ft (1,500 m) occupy some 10% of the total area. The central part of the country is a plain through which flow the KURA RIVER and its tributaries, including the Araks, whose upper course forms part of the boundary with Iran. The CASPIAN SEA serves Baku as a trade outlet. Agriculture, petroleum refining, and light manufacturing are economically important. It is a republic with one legislative body; its head of state and government is the president assisted by the prime minister. Azerbaijan adjoins the Iranian region of the same name, and the origin of their respective inhabitants is the same. By the 9th century AD it had come under Turkish influence, and in ensuing centuries it was fought over by Arabs, Mongols, Turks, and Iranians. Russia acquired what is now independent Azerbaijan in the early 19th century. After the RUSSIAN REVOLUTION OF 1917, Azerbaijan declared its independence; it was subdued by the Red Army in 1920 and became a Soviet Socialist Republic. It declared independence from the collapsing Soviet Union in 1991. Azerbaijan has two geographic peculiarities. The exclave Naxçivan (Nakhichevan) is separated from the rest of Azerbaijan by Armenian

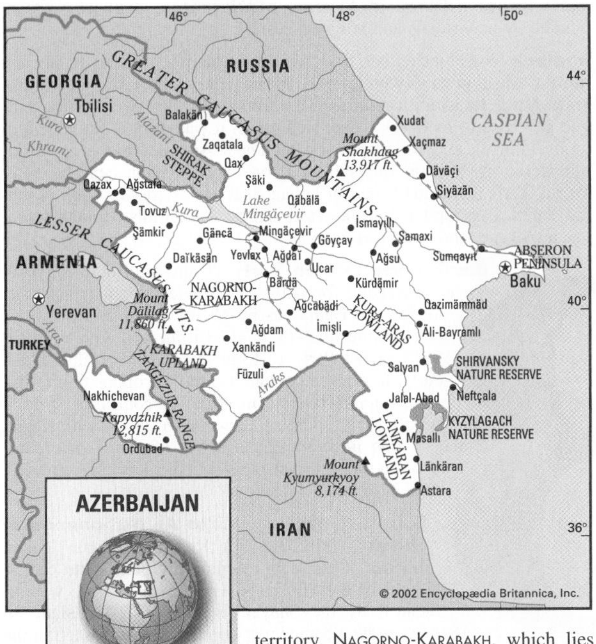

territory. NAGORNO-KARABAKH, which lies within Azerbaijan and is administered by it, has a Christian Armenian majority. Azerbaijan and Armenia went to war over both territories in the 1990s, causing great economic disruption. Though a cease-fire was declared in 1994, the political situation remained unresolved.

Azhar University \'äz-,hàr\, **al-** Chief center of Islamic and Arabic learning in the world, centered on the al-Azhar Mosque in the medieval quarter of Cairo. It was founded by the Fatimids in 970. The basic program has always focused on Islamic law, theology, and Arabic. Philosophy and medical studies were added during the Middle Ages but were eventually withdrawn as being too conducive to independent thinking. Philosophy was restored at the end of the 19th century, and social sciences were added at a branch campus in the 20th century. Women were first admitted in 1962. Total enrollment is about 90,000.

Azikiwe \ə-'zik-wā\, **Nnamdi** (1904–1996) President of Nigeria (1963–66) and leader of southern Nigerian (especially IGBO) nationalism. Azikiwe's National Council party won the important 1959 federal elections and helped stimulate Nigerian independence. In the Biafran Civil War (1967–70) Azikiwe first backed his fellow Ibo but then threw his support to the federal government. Thereafter he was a leading opponent of the ruling party.

azimuth See ALTITUDE AND AZIMUTH

azo dye \'ā-zō\ Any of a large class of synthetic organic compounds, DYES containing two nitrogen atoms joined by a double bond (see BONDING, COVALENT BOND) in the form —N═N— as part of their molecular structure. More than half the dyes in commercial use are azo dyes. They are usually classed according to the fibers for which they are useful or the methods by which they are applied; direct dyes are absorbed from solution by the fibers, but others require a second solution (a mordant) or a second step before the color is fast.

Azores \ə-'zōrz\ *Portuguese* **Açores** \ə-'sō-rish\ Archipelago (pop., 1992 est.: 237,000), northern Atlantic Ocean, constituting an autonomous region of Portugal. Its islands are Flores, Corvo, Terceira, São Jorge, Pico, Faial, Graciosa, São Miguel, and Santa Maria; the capital is Ponta Delgada (on São Miguel). It covers an area of 868 sq mi (2,247 sq km). Subject to earthquakes and volcanic eruptions, the islands lie some 1,000 mi (1,600 km) west of mainland Europe. The uninhabited Azores were reputedly discovered c. 1427 by Portuguese pilot Diogo de Sevilha. Settlement began c. 1432; by the end of the 15th century, all the islands were inhabited and trade with Portugal was well established. They were subject to Spain in 1580–1640, and a famous sea battle between the British and Spanish occurred off Flores in 1591. The Portuguese installed a governor and captain general for the whole group in 1766; the islands were given limited autonomy in 1895. Important air and naval bases were set up there during World War II; in 1951 the U.S. established a NATO base on Lajes.

Azov \ə-'zòf, 'ā-,zòf\, **Sea of** Inland sea in Europe between Ukraine and Russia. It is connected to the BLACK SEA by Kerch Strait. About 210 mi (340 km) long and 85 mi (135 km) wide, it occupies an area of 14,500 sq mi (37,600 sq km). With a maximum depth of only about 46 ft (14 m), it is the world's shallowest sea. It is fed by the DON and KUBAN rivers, and at their entrance in the Taganrog Gulf, its depth is 3 ft (1 m) or less. In the west lies the Arabat Spit, a 70-mi- (113-km-) long sandbar that separates the Sea of Azov from the Syvash, a system of marshy inlets dividing the CRIMEAN Peninsula from the Ukrainian mainland.

AZT *in full* **azidothymidine** Drug that has had success in delaying the development of AIDS in patients with HIV. Since its introduction in the mid-1980s, it has prolonged the lives of millions of patients. It is particularly effective in preventing transmission of HIV from infected pregnant women to their fetuses. Since it has a greater effect on the replication of VIRUSES than of body cells, it has fewer side effects than most other AIDS drugs, though many patients nevertheless cannot tolerate it. Its beneficial effects tend to decrease as treatment progresses, so it is now usually given with other drugs.

Aztec Ruins National Monument Archaeological site, northwestern New Mexico. Located on the Animas River just north of the town of Aztec, it was established in 1923, and has an area of 0.5 sq mi (1.3 sq km). Mistakenly called Aztec by early settlers, the site actually contains the excavated ruins of a 12th-century PUEBLO town. It was designated a WORLD HERITAGE SITE in 1987.

Aztecs NAHUATL-speaking people who in the 15th and early 16th century ruled a large empire in what is now central and southern Mexico. They may have originated on the northern Mexican plateau before migrating to their later location. Their migration may have been linked to the collapse of the TOLTEC civilization. Their empire, which at its height comprised 5–6 million people spread over 80,000 sq mi (200,000 sq km), was made possible by their successful agricultural methods, including intensive cultivation, irrigation, and reclamation of wetlands. The Aztec state was despotic, militaristic, and sharply stratified according to class and caste. Aztec religion was syncretic, drawing especially on the beliefs of the MAYA. The Aztecs practiced HUMAN SACRIFICE; in a particularly gruesome episode, 20,000–80,000 prisoners were said to have been killed in four days. The empire came to an end when HERNAN CORTES took the emperor MONTEZUMA II prisoner and conquered the great city TENOCHTITLÁN (present-day Mexico City). See also NAHUA.

azulejo \,ä-zü-'lā-hō\ Spanish and Portuguese glazed, polychromed tile produced from the 14th century. Introduced into Spain by the Arabs during the Moorish occupation, azulejos were used in Islamic architecture for facing walls and paving floors. Early designs were geometrical and 5–6 in. (13–15 cm) square. In the 15th–16th century, Portugal imported the tiles from Spain for use in religious and private buildings. The Portuguese exported them in the 17th century to the Azores, Madeira, and Brazil, and the Spaniards introduced them to their American colonies. In the 18th century, interiors and exteriors in Puebla, Mexico, were covered with azulejos in brilliant colors on a scale unequaled elsewhere.

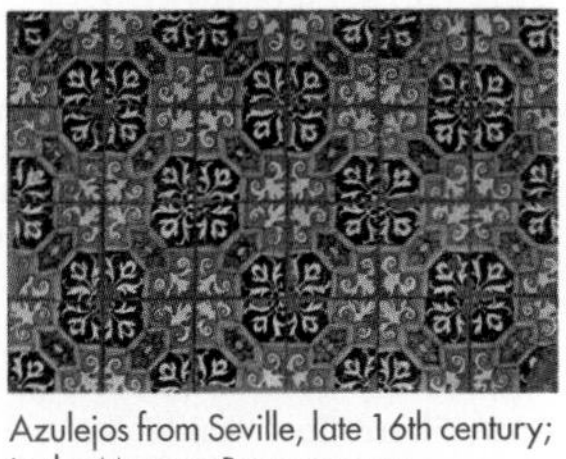
Azulejos from Seville, late 16th century; in the Museum Boymans-van Beuningen, Rotterdam.
BY COURTESY OF MUSEUM BOYMANS-VAN BEUNINGEN, ROTTERDAM

B-17 *or* **Flying Fortress** U.S. heavy bomber used in World War II. Designed by the Boeing Aircraft Co. in 1934, it cruised at 35,000 ft (10,700 m) at a maximum speed of 287 mph (462 kph). It was called the Flying Fortress because of the .50-caliber machine guns, 13 in all, at every corner. It could carry 3 tons (2.7 metric tons) of bombs in its bays and more on racks under its wings. More than 12,000 B-17s were produced during World War II, and most were used for high-level bombing over Europe.

B-52 *or* **Stratofortress** U.S. long-range heavy bomber, designed in 1948 and first flown in 1952. Originally intended as an atomic-bomb carrier capable of reaching the Soviet Union, it proved highly adaptable and remained in service at the end of the 20th century. It has a wingspan of 185 ft (56 m) and a length of more than 160 ft (49 m). Powered by eight jet engines, its maximum speed at 55,000 ft (17,000 m) is 595 mph (960 kph). It carries a crew of six, and its sole defensive armament is a gun turret in the tail.

B cell One of the two types of lymphocytes (the others being T cells). All lymphocytes begin their development in the bone marrow. B cells are involved in so-called humoral immunity; on encountering a foreign substance (antigen), the B lymphocyte differentiates into a plasma cell, which secretes immunoglobulin (see antibody).

Baader-Meinhof Gang \'bä-dər-'mīn-ˌhōf\ *or* **Red Army Faction** West German leftist terrorist group formed in 1968 and popularly named after two of its early leaders, Andreas Baader (1943–1977) and Ulrike Meinhof (1934–1976). The members initially supported themselves by bank robberies and engaged in terrorist bombings and arson, especially of West German and U.S. targets in West Germany. Baader, Meinhof, and 18 others were arrested in 1972; Meinhof eventually hanged herself, and Baader apparently also died a suicide. By the mid-1970s the group had turned to international terrorism; two members took part in the 1976 Palestinian airplane hijacking in the Entebbe incident. After the collapse of communism in East Germany (1989–90), it was discovered that East Germany's secret police had provided training and supplies to the gang. The group announced an end to its terrorist campaign in 1992.

Baal \'bāl\ God worshiped in many ancient Middle Eastern communities, especially among Canaanites, for whom he was a fertility deity. In the mythology of Canaan, he was locked in combat with Mot, the god of death and sterility; depending on the outcome of their struggles, seven-year cycles of fertility or famine would ensue. Baal was also king of gods, having seized the kingship from the sea god, Yamm. Baal worship was popular in Egypt from the later New Kingdom to its end (1400–1075 BC). The Aramaeans used the Babylonian pronunciation Bel; Bel became the Greek Belos, identified with Zeus. The Old Testament often refers to a specific local Baal or multiple Baalim.

baal shem \bäl-'shām\ In Judaism, a title bestowed on men who worked wonders and cures through secret knowledge of the names of God. The practice dates to the 11th century AD, long before the term was applied to certain rabbis and Kabbalists. They were numerous in 17th- and 18th-century eastern Europe, where they exorcised demons, inscribed amulets, and performed cures using herbs, folk remedies, and the Tetragrammaton. Because they combined faith healing with use of the Kabbala, they clashed with physicians, rabbis, and followers of the Haskala. See also Baal Shem Tov.

Baal Shem Tov \'bāl-'shem-'tȯv\ *orig.* **Israel ben Eliezer** (c. 1700–1760) Polish founder of Hasidism (c. 1750). An orphan, he worked in synagogues and yeshivas, and when he retired to the Carpathian Mountains to engage in mystical speculation he gained a reputation as a baal shem. From c. 1736 he lived in the village of Medzhibozh and devoted himself to spiritual pursuits. He was widely known as the Besht, an acronym of Baal Shem Tov. He rejected the asceticism of older rabbis and focused on communion with God, service of God in everyday tasks, and rescue of the sparks of divinity that, according to the Kabbala, are trapped in the material world. His discourses during Sabbath meals have been preserved; he left no writings of his own. He made a point of conversing with simple working people. Hasidism brought about a social and religious upheaval in Judaism, establishing a mode of worship marked by new rituals and religious ecstasy.

Baalbek \'bā-əl-ˌbek, 'bäl-ˌbek\ Village, eastern Lebanon. In ancient times it was a great city built on the lower western slope of the Anti-Lebanon Mtns. Its identification with the worship of Baal as a Semitic sun-god gave rise to its Greek name, Heliopolis. It was made a Roman colony by Julius Caesar. In AD 637 it came under Arab control, and was administered by Muslim rulers from Syria until the 20th century. After World War I it was made part of Lebanon. It has extensive ruins, including temples of Jupiter, Bacchus, and Venus, town walls, Roman mosaics, a mosque, and Arab fortifications.

Baath Party *or* **Bath Party** \'bäth\ Arab political party that advocates formation of a single Arab socialist state. Founded in Damascus by Michel Aflaq and Salah al-Din al-Bitar in 1943, in 1953 it merged with the Syrian Socialist Party to form the Arab Socialist Baath Party. It espoused nonalignment and opposition to imperialism and colonialism. It gained control of Syria in 1963 after the failure of a short-lived union with Egypt, and of Iraq in 1968 after a series of coups. The party also has branches in other Middle Eastern countries. See also Pan-Arabism.

Bab \'bȧb\, **the** *orig.* **Mirza Ali Muhammad of Shiraz** (1819/20–1850) Iranian religious leader, founder of the Babi religion and one of the central figures of Baha'i. The son of a merchant, he was influenced by the Shaykhi school of Shiite Islam. In 1844 he wrote a commentary on the sura of Joseph in the Quran and declared himself the Bab (Arabic: "gateway") to the hidden imam. Later he would claim to be the imam himself, and finally a divine manifestation. The same year he assembled 18 disciples, who spread the new faith in the various Persian provinces. He had popular support but was opposed by members of the religious class, and he was arrested near Tehran in 1847 and imprisoned. Meeting at Badasht in 1848, his followers, the Azali, formally broke with Islam. Mirza was executed by a firing squad at Tabriz in 1850.

Bab el-Mandeb \'bȧb-ȧl-'mȧn-deb\ *or* **Strait of Mandeb** Strait between the southwestern Arabian Peninsula and the Africa coast. It connects the Red Sea with the Gulf of Aden and the Indian Ocean. It is 20 mi (32 km) wide and is divided into two channels by Perim Island. Its name means "the gate of tears," referring to the dangers that formerly attended its navigation.

Babashoff, Shirley (born 1957) U.S. swimmer. Born in Whittier, Cal., she won two silver medals (100- and 200-m freestyle) and a team gold medal (400-m freestyle relay) in the 1972 Olympics. At the 1976 Olympics she again won a team gold medal and added silver medals in one medley and three freestyle events. Overall she set six world records.

Babbage \'bab-ij\, **Charles** (1791–1871) British mathematician and inventor. Educated at Cambridge Univ., he devoted himself from c. 1812 to devising machines capable of calculating mathematical tables. His first small calculator could perform certain computations to eight decimals. In 1823 he obtained government support for the design of a projected machine with a 20-decimal capacity. In the 1830s he developed plans for the so-called analytical engine, capable of performing any arithmetical operation on the basis of instructions from punched cards, a memory unit in which to store numbers, sequential control, and most of the other basic elements of the present-day computer. The forerunner of the modern digital computer, the analytical engine was never completed. In 1991 British scientists built Difference En-

Babbage, detail of an oil painting by Samuel Lawrence, 1845; in the National Portrait Gallery, London.

BY COURTESY OF THE NATIONAL PORTRAIT GALLERY, LONDON

gine No. 2 (accurate to 31 digits) to Babbage's specifications. His other contributions included establishing the modern postal system in England, compiling the first reliable actuarial tables, and inventing the locomotive cowcatcher.

Babbitt, Milton (Byron) (born 1916) U.S. composer. Born in Philadelphia but raised in Mississippi, he studied mathematics and music. At Princeton University he studied with R. SESSIONS and later joined the faculty, where he remained throughout his career. He became one of the first U.S. twelve-tone composers, and by 1947 he became (in his *Three Compositions for Piano*) perhaps the first composer to write totally serialized music based on ordered structures not only of pitch but of elements such as rhythm and dynamics. The first composer to work with RCA's Mark II synthesizer, he became one of the first Americans to write electronically synthesized music. He wrote various works combining live performers and tape; his best-known works include *Composition for Synthesizer* (1961) and *Philomel* (1964). He also composed popular songs, film music, and a musical.

Babel \'bá-bʸil\, **Isaak (Emmanuilovich)** (1894–1941) Russian short-story writer. Born Jewish in Ukraine, Babel grew up in an atmosphere of persecution that is reflected in his stories. MAXIM GORKY encouraged him to travel abroad to expand his horizons. Out of his experience as a soldier in the war with Poland came the stories in *Red Cavalry* (1926). His *Odessa Tales* (1931) include realistic and humorous sketches of the Jewish ghetto outside Odessa. Initially well regarded in the Soviet Union, in the late 1930s Babel's writing was found incompatible with official literary doctrine. He was arrested in 1939 and died in a Siberian prison camp. He is often thought of as Russia's greatest writer of short stories after ANTON CHEKHOV.

Babel \'bā-bəl, 'ba-bəl\, **Tower of** In the Old Testament, a high tower built in Shinar (BABYLONIA). According to GENESIS 11:1–9, the Babylonians wanted to build a tower "with its top in the heavens." Angry at their presumption, God disrupted the enterprise by confusing the languages of the workers so that they could no longer understand each other. The tower was left unfinished and the people dispersed over the face of the earth. The myth may have been inspired by a tower temple located north of the MARDUK temple and known as Bab-ilu ("Gate of God").

"The Tower of Babel," oil painting by Pieter Bruegel the Elder, 1563; in the Kunsthistorisches Museum, Vienna.

BY COURTESY OF THE KUNSTHISTORISCHES MUSEUM, VIENNA

Babenberg \'bä-bən-ˌberk\, **House of** Austrian ruling house in the 10th–13th century. Leopold I of Babenberg became margrave of Austria in 976. The Babenbergs' power was modest until the 12th century, when they came to dominate the Austrian nobility. With the death of Duke Frederick II in 1246, the male line ended, and the family's power declined rapidly.

Babeuf \ba-'bəf\, **François-Noël** (1760–1797) French political journalist and agitator. During the era of the French Revolution he advocated an equal distribution of land and income. For his part in a conspiracy to overthrow the DIRECTORY and institute a return to the Constitution of 1793, he was guillotined. His tactical strategies provided a model for left-wing movements of the 19th century.

Babeuf, engraving by an unknown artist, 18th century.

BY COURTESY OF THE BIBLIOTHEQUE NATIONALE, PARIS

Babington, Anthony (1561–1586) English conspirator. Raised secretly as a Catholic, Babington was joined by the priest John Ballard in the unsuccessful "Babington Plot" to assassinate Queen ELIZABETH I and install her prisoner, MARY, QUEEN OF SCOTS, on the English throne. The conspiracy included many Roman Catholics, and PHILIP II of Spain promised to provide immediate assistance after the assassination. After letters to Mary explaining his plans were intercepted, Babington was imprisoned and executed. The letters were also used as evidence against Mary at her trial.

Babism \'bab-ˌiz-əm\ Religion that developed in Iran around Mirza Ali Muhammad's claim (1844) to be the BAB. Its beliefs are set forth in the *Bayan*, a holy book written by the Bab, which proclaims a universal law in place of all existing religious legal codes. Babism originated as a messianic movement in SHIITE Islam. In 1867 the movement split, with the AZALIS remaining faithful to the original teachings of the Bab and those of his successor Sobh-e Azal. Most Babis accepted the leadership of Sobh-e Azal's half-brother BAHA ULLAH, and under him the BAHA'I faith was developed.

baboon Any of five species of robust MONKEYS (genus *Papio*) of Arabia and sub-Saharan Africa. Baboons have a large head, cheek pouches, and a long, doglike muzzle. They walk on all fours, carrying the tail in a characteristic arch. They weigh 30–90 lbs (14–40 kg) and are about 20–45 in. (50–115 cm) long, excluding the tail (18–28 in., or 45–70 cm, long). Found mainly in drier savanna and rocky areas, they feed on a variety of plants and animals. Highly social and intelligent, they travel in large noisy troops, communicating by calls. They may destroy crops, and their enormous canine teeth and powerful limbs make them dangerous opponents.

Anubis, or olive, baboon (*Papio anubis*).

NORMAN MYERS—PHOTO RESEARCHERS

Babur \'bä-bər\ *orig.* **Zahir-ud-Din Muhammad** (1483–1530) Emperor (1526–30) and founder of the MUGHAL DYNASTY of India. A descendant of GENGHIS KHAN and TIMUR, he came from a tribe of Mongol origin but was Turkish in language and upbringing. In his youth he tried for 10 years (1494–1504) to gain control of Samarkand, Timur's old capital. Those efforts ended in his losing his own principality in Fergana, but he consoled himself by seizing and holding Kabul (1504). After four failed attempts, he successfully occupied Delhi (1525). Surrounded by enemy states, Babur (the name is Arabic for "Tiger") persuaded his homesick troops to stand their ground, and over the next four years he defeated his foes. His grandson AKBAR consolidated the new empire. Babur was also a gifted poet and a lover of nature who constructed gardens wherever he went. His prose memoirs, the *Babur-nameh,* have become a world classic of autobiography.

Babuyan Islands \ˌbä-bü-'yän\ Island group (pop., 1980: 9,000), northern Philippine Islands. Lying north of LUZON, the Babuyans consist of about 24 islands with a total area of 225 sq mi (583 sq km). The chief islands are Babuyan, Camiguin, Calayan, Fuga, and Dalupiri. Calayan is the largest town and only port.

baby boom Generation born in the U.S. between 1946 and 1964. The hardships and uncertainties of the GREAT DEPRESSION and WORLD WAR II led many unmarried couples to delay marriage and many married couples to delay having children. The war's end, followed by a sustained period of economic prosperity (the 1950s and early 1960s), led to a surge in population. The sheer size of the baby-boom generation (76 million) has magnified its impact on society: when "boomers" were young, the youth culture they defined took center stage; as they age, their consumer patterns dominate the market; and as they begin to retire, their needs are expected to strain public resources.

Baby Yar \ˌbä-bē-ˈyär\ Large ravine near Kiev in Ukraine, the site of a mass grave of more than 100,000 people killed by German Nazi SS squads between 1941 and 1943. Most of the victims were Jews, but some were communist officials and Russian prisoners of war. A symbol of Jewish suffering in the HOLOCAUST, the site came to world attention after the 1961 publication of YEVGENY YEVTUSHENKO's poem *Baby Yar.*

Babylon Ancient ruined city on the EUPHRATES RIVER, Iraq. It lay about 55 mi (89 km) south of Baghdad, near the modern city of Al Hillah. Babylon was one of the most famous cities in antiquity. Probably settled in the 3rd millennium BC, it came under the Amoritic kings around 2000 BC. It became the capital of BABYLONIA and was the chief commercial city of the TIGRIS-Euphrates valley. Destroyed by SENNACHERIB in 689 BC, it was later rebuilt. It attained its greatest glory as capital of the Neo-Babylonian empire under NEBUCHADNEZZAR II (r.605–c. 561 BC). Taken by ALEXANDER THE GREAT in 331 BC, it was where he died. Evidence of its topography comes from excavations, CUNEIFORM texts, and descriptions by HERODOTUS. Most of the ruins are from the city built by Nebuchadnezzar. The largest city in the world at the time, it contained many temples, including the great temple of MARDUK with its associated ZIGGURAT, apparently the basis for the story of the Tower of BABEL. The Hanging Gardens, a simulated hill of vegetation-clad terracing, was one of the SEVEN WONDERS OF THE WORLD.

Babylonia Ancient country, EUPHRATES RIVER valley, South Asia. The area was divided into SUMER (in the southeast) and AKKAD (northwest) when the first Babylonian line of Amorites took power after 2000 BC, largely because of HAMMURABI (c. 1790–1750). The empire declined after his death; the Kassites from the east eventually assumed power (c. 1595) and established a dynasty that lasted 400 years. After ELAM conquered Babylonia (c. 1157 BC), a series of wars established a new Babylonian dynasty whose outstanding member was Nebuchadnezzar I (r.1124?–1103 BC). Following his rule, a three-way struggle developed among ASSYRIA, Aram (see ARAMAEANS), and CHALDEA. The Assyrians ruled the area most frequently in the 9th–7th century BC. In the 7th–6th century BC the Chaldean NEBUCHADNEZZAR II instituted the last and greatest period of Babylonian supremacy, conquering SYRIA and PALESTINE and rebuilding BABYLON, the capital city. Conquered in 539 BC by the Persian CYRUS THE GREAT, and in 331 BC by ALEXANDER THE GREAT, the area was later gradually abandoned.

Babylonian Exile *or* **Babylonian Captivity** Forced detention of Jews in Babylonia following its conquest of Judah in 598/7 and 587/6 BC. The first deportation may have occurred after King Jehoiachin was deposed in 597 BC or after NEBUCHADNEZZAR destroyed JERUSALEM in 586. In 538 BC, the Persian CYRUS THE GREAT conquered Babylonia and allowed the Jews to return to Palestine. Some Jews chose to remain in Babylonia, initiating the Jewish DIASPORA. During the Captivity the Jews maintained their national spirit and religious identity, with EZEKIEL and other prophets keeping hope alive, despite cultural pressures in a foreign land.

baby's breath Either of two species of herbaceous plants of the genus *Gypsophila* (PINK FAMILY), having profuse small blossoms. Both *G. elegans,* an annual, and *G. paniculata,* a perennial, are cultivated for their fine misty effect in rock gardens and flower borders and in floral arrangements. They are native to Eurasia.

Bacall, Lauren *orig.* **Betty Joan Perske** (born 1924) U.S. actress. Born in New York City, she worked as a model while seeking Broadway roles; her photo on a magazine cover led to her casting in the film *To Have and Have Not* (1944) with HUMPHREY BOGART, whom she soon married. An instant success, she made three more films with Bogart: *The Big Sleep* (1946), *Dark Passage* (1947), and *Key Largo* (1948). After his death she appeared in such films as *Harper* (1966), *Murder on the Orient Express* (1974), and *Misery* (1990), and starred on Broadway in *Goodbye Charlie* (1959), *Cactus Flower* (1965), *Applause* (1970, Tony award), and *Woman of the Year* (1981, Tony award).

baccarat Card game resembling CHEMIN DE FER in which three hands of two or three cards each are dealt and players may bet either or both hands against the dealer's. In a two-handed version, players may bet on or against the dealer. Baccarat's popularity in France and England, and eventually in other countries, dates from the 19th century. Players aim for a count of 9. Face (court) cards and 10s are counted as 0. The cards in each hand are added to obtain the value, but only the last digit is significant. Thus, in a hand of 6 and 7, the sum is 13, but only the 3 of that number counts. Though a glamorous game that attracts high rollers, baccarat is mostly a game of luck.

Baccarat glass Glassware manufactured since 1765 in Baccarat, France. The firm originally produced soda glass for windows and industrial use. In 1816 it was acquired by a Belgian manufacturer of lead crystal; since then it has specialized in this type of glass, especially paperweights. Baccarat exhibited works in the important 1925 Exposition des Arts Décoratifs et Industriels Modernes in Paris. Today the company produces tableware in both historical and modern designs.

Bacchanalia \ˌba-kə-ˈnāl-yə\ *or* **Dionysia** In Greco-Roman religion, any of the festivals of the wine god Bacchus (DIONYSUS), which probably originated as fertility rites. The most famous Greek festivals included the Greater Dionysia, with its dramatic performances; the ANTHESTERIA; and the Lesser Dionysia, characterized by simple rites. Bacchanalia were introduced from lower Italy into Rome, where they were at first secret, open only to women, and held three times a year. They later admitted men and became as frequent as five times a month. In 186 BC their reputation as orgies led the Senate to prohibit them throughout Italy, except in special cases.

bacchantes See MAENADS AND BACCHANTES

Bacchus See DIONYSUS

Bach, Alexander, Freiherr (Baron) von (1813–1893) Austrian politician noted for instituting a system of centralized control. He served as minister of the interior (1849–59); after the death of FELIX, FURST ZU SCHWARZENBERG in 1852, he largely dictated policy in the regime. Bach centralized administrative authority for the Austrian empire, but he also endorsed reactionary policies that reduced freedom of the press and abandoned public trials.

Bach, Carl Philipp Emanuel (1714–1788) German composer. Second son of J.S. BACH, he received a superb musical education from his father. In 1740 he became harpsichordist at the court of FREDERICK II the Great, where he remained for 28 years, after which he moved to Hamburg to take the city's leading musical position. He was the preeminent exponent of the *empfindsamer Stil* ("expressive style"), which emphasized rhapsodic freedom and sentiment. A founder of the Classic style, he is one of the first composers in whose works sonata form becomes clearly evident. He wrote some 200 works for harpsichord, clavichord, and piano (including dozens of sonatas), some 50 keyboard concertos, some 20 symphonies, and several oratorios and Passions. His *Essay on the True Manner of Playing Keyboard Instruments* (1753) was a highly important practical music treatise.

C.P.E. Bach, engraving by A. Stöttrup.

BY COURTESY OF HAAGS GEMENTEMUSEUM, THE HAGUE

Bach, Johann Christian (1735–1782) German-British composer. Youngest son of J.S. BACH, he studied with his brother C.P.E. BACH in Berlin before moving to Italy. In 1762 he became composer to the King's Theatre in London, where he would remain the rest of his life, becoming music teacher to the queen, and later the impresario (with C. F. Abel) of an important series of concerts (1765–81). He wrote some 50 symphonies, some 35 keyboard concertos, and much chamber music. His music, melodious and well formed but far from profound and with no trace of his father's influence, became an important prototype of the Classic style and influenced W.A. MOZART.

Bach, Johann Sebastian (1685–1750) German composer. Born in the village of Eisenach to a musical family, he became a superbly well-rounded musician; from 1700 he held positions as singer, violinist, and organist. His first major appointment, in 1708, was as organist at the ducal court at Weimar. This was followed by a six-year stay (1717–23) as kapellmeister at the princely court of Cöthen, which was in turn followed by his appointment as cantor at the great church of St. Thomas in Leipzig, where he would remain the rest of his life. Imbued with the northern German contrapuntal style from early childhood, he encountered the lively Italian style, especially in the works of A. VIVALDI, around 1710, and much of his music embodies an immensely convincing melding of the two styles. At St. Thomas he wrote over 200 church cantatas. His orchestral works include the six Brandenburg Concertos, the four orchestral suites, and many harpsichord concertos, a genre he invented. His solo keyboard works include the great didactic set *The Well-Tempered Clavier,* the huge but unfinished *Art of the Fugue,* the superb *Goldberg Variations,* numerous suites, and many organ preludes and fugues. His surviving choral works include (in addition to the sacred cantatas) over 30 secular cantatas, two monumental Passions, and the Mass in B Minor. His works, never widely known in his lifetime, went into near-total eclipse after his death, and only in the early 19th century were they revived, to enormous acclaim. He was perhaps the greatest organist and harpsichordist of his time. Today Bach is regarded as the greatest composer of the baroque era, and, by many, as the greatest composer of all time.

Bach, Wilhelm Friedemann (1710–1784) German composer and organist. Eldest son of J.S. BACH, he was trained by his father. One of the finest organists of his time, he held important organist posts in Dresden (1723–46) and Halle (1746–64), but thereafter lived an unsettled life and drifted into drinking and poverty. Though a highly gifted composer, his compositions veered confusingly between the old contrapuntal style and the new pre-Classic styles. He wrote over 30 church cantatas, several keyboard concertos, and many solo keyboard works.

Bacharach \'bak-ə-,rak\, **Burt** (born 1929) U.S. songwriter and pianist. He was born in Kansas City, the son of a syndicated fashion columnist. He studied under D. MILHAUD, B. MARTINU, and H. COWELL. In the 1950s he wrote arrangements for Steve Lawrence and Vic Damone, and later toured with MARLENE DIETRICH. In the late 1950s he began his long association with lyricist Hal David (born 1921), which would produce many hits especially for Dionne Warwick (born 1940), including "Walk On By," "I Say a Little Prayer," and "Do You Know the Way to San Jose?" He and David collaborated on the successful musical *Promises, Promises* (1968).

Bachchan, Amitabh (born 1942) Indian film actor. Bachchan's first film success was *Zanjeer* (1973); by the end of the 1970s he was something of a cultural phenonemon in India and was regarded as the most popular star in the history of Indian films. He is often compared to such American action stars as CLINT EASTWOOD, although his talents also extend to singing, dancing, and comedy. After a brief stint in politics in the mid-1980s, Bachchan gained a new generation of fans in the next decade as host of the television game show *Kaun banega crorepati*, the Indian version of the U.S. and U.K. hit *Who Wants to Be a Millionaire?*

bachelor's button *or* **cornflower** Herbaceous, hardy annual plant *(Centaurea cyanus)* of the COMPOSITE FAMILY, having flower heads with blue, pink, or white rays. It is native to the Mediterranean region and widely cultivated in North America. A common garden plant, it often also appears as a weed.

Bacillariophyta See DIATOM

bacillus \bə-'si-ləs\ Any of the rod-shaped, gram-positive bacteria (see GRAM STAIN) that make up the genus *Bacillus,* widely found in soil and water. The term is sometimes applied to all rodlike bacteria. Bacilli frequently occur in chains and can form SPORES under unfavorable environmental conditions. Resistant to heat, chemicals, and sunlight, these spores may remain capable of growing and developing for long periods of time. One type sometimes causes spoilage in canned foods. Another, widespread bacillus contaminates laboratory cultures and is often found on human skin. Most strains do not cause disease in humans, infecting them only incidentally in their role as soil organisms; a notable exception is *B. anthracis,* which causes ANTHRAX. Some bacilli produce medically useful ANTIBIOTICS.

backbone See VERTEBRAL COLUMN

backgammon Board game played with two dice and counter-pieces (called stones) in which the two players try to be the first to gather their pieces into one corner (home) and then systematically remove them from the board. The board has four sections (called tables), each marked with six narrow wedges (points) in two alternating colors. Fifteen white and fifteen black stones represent the two opposing sides. Stones are moved from point to point in opposite directions according to the number of points shown on the dice. Most commonly played in the eastern Mediterranean, it is one of the most ancient games, dating from 3000 BC.

backpacking Sport of HIKING while carrying clothing, food, and CAMPING equipment in a pack on the back. As practiced in the earlier 20th century, backpacking was primarily a means of getting to wilderness areas inaccessible by car or by day hike. It subsequently became associated with general touring by foot in urban as well as wilderness settings. Types of packs range from the frameless rucksack to the contour frame pack, with a frame of aluminum tubing and often a waistband that transfers most of the pack's weight to the hips.

Backus, John W(arner) (born 1924) U.S. mathematician. Born in Philadelphia, he received his bachelor's and master's degrees from Columbia University. He was head of a small group that in 1957 developed the computer language FORTRAN for numerical analysis. He contributed to the development of ALGOL and developed a notation known as the Backus Normal (or -Naur) Form for defining the syntax of a programmable language (1959). He received the Turing Award in 1977.

Bacolod \bə-'kō-,lōd\ City (pop., 2000: 429,076), Philippine Islands. It lies on the Guimaras Strait in the north of the island of Negros, opposite Guimaras Island. It is regarded as the Philippine sugar capital. Its port, to the south, is important for fishing.

Bacon, Francis *later* **Viscount St. Albans** (1561–1626) British statesman and philosopher, father of modern SCIENTIFIC METHOD. Nephew of WILLIAM CECIL, he studied at Cambridge and Gray's Inn. A supporter of the Earl of ESSEX, he turned against him when Essex was tried for treason. Under JAMES I he rose steadily, becoming successively solicitor general (1607), attorney general (1613), and lord chancellor (1618). Convicted of accepting bribes from those being tried in his court, he was briefly imprisoned and permanently lost his public offices; he died deep in debt. As a scientist, he attempted to put natural science on a firm empirical foundation rather than allow it to rest on citations of ancient authorities. His method was set forth in *Novum Organum* (1620). Philosophically, he was an early empiricist (see EMPIRICISM), considering experience the only source of knowledge. His elaborate classification of the sciences inspired the 18th-century French Encyclopedists, and his empiricism inspired 19th-century British philosophers of science. Other works include *The Advancement of Learning* (1605), a *History of Henry VII* (1622), and several important legal and constitutional works.

Bacon, Francis (1909–1992) Irish-British painter. Born in Dublin, he lived in Berlin and Paris before settling in London (1929) to begin a career as an interior decorator. With no formal art training, he started painting, drawing, and participating in gallery exhibitions, with little success. In 1944 he achieved instant notoriety with a series of controversial paintings, *Three Studies for Figures at the Base of a Crucifixion.* His images depict distorted figures in isolation and despair with nightmarish horror, and his skill in handling paint, smeared with violent color, won the admiration of critics and peers. He destroyed many of his early works, but some can be found in U.S. and European museums.

Bacon, Nathaniel (1647–1676) British-American colonial planter, leader of Bacon's Rebellion. He emigrated from England in 1673 and acquired land in Virginia, where he was appointed to the council of WILLIAM BERKELEY, the British governor. After a dispute over Indian policy, he defied Berkeley's orders and organized an expedition against the Indians in 1676. He then turned his forces against Berkeley,

Nathaniel Bacon, detail of an engraving.
BY COURTESY OF THE LIBRARY OF CONGRESS, WASHINGTON, D.C.

captured Jamestown, and briefly controlled most of Virginia. His death at 29 of influenza, at the height of his power, ended the rebellion.

Bacon, Roger (c. 1220–1292) English scientist and philosopher. Educated at Oxford and the University of Paris, he joined the Franciscan order in 1247. He speculated about lighter-than-air flying machines, land and sea transportation, and microscopes and telescopes; the term "experimental science" was popularized through his writings. His philosophical thought is essentially Aristotelian; he was critical of the methods of theologians such as ALBERTUS MAGNUS and THOMAS AQUINAS, arguing that a more accurate experimental knowledge of nature would be of great value in confirming the Christian faith. He also wrote on mathematics and logic. He was condemned to prison c. 1277 by his fellow Franciscans because of "suspected novelties" in his teaching.

bacteremia \\,bak-te-'rē-mē-ə\\ Presence of bacteria in the blood. Short-term bacteremia follows dental or surgical procedures, especially if local infection or very high-risk surgery releases bacteria from isolated sites. In some cases, prior antibiotic therapy can prevent this. It causes little problem to a healthy immune system but can be serious for those with prostheses (where infection can center) or high susceptibility to bacterial invasion. Extensive bacteremia can release toxins into the blood (SEPTICEMIA), leading to shock and vascular collapse. Antibiotic-resistant bacteria have increased the rate of severe bacteremia.

bacteria Group of microscopic, single-celled organisms that are PROKARYOTES. They may have spherical, rodlike, or spiral shapes. They inhabit virtually all environments, including soil, water, organic matter, and the bodies of multicellular animals. Different types are distinguished in part by the structure of their cell walls, which is determined by GRAM STAIN. Many bacteria swim by means of flagella (see FLAGELLUM). The DNA of most bacteria is found in a single circular CHROMOSOME and is distributed throughout the CYTOPLASM rather than contained within a membrane-enclosed nucleus. Though some bacteria can cause food poisoning and infectious diseases in humans, most are harmless and many are beneficial. They are used in various industrial processes, especially in the food industry (e.g., the production of yogurt, cheeses, and pickles). Bacteria are divided into EUBACTERIA and ARCHAEBACTERIA. See also BUDDING BACTERIA, COLIFORM BACTERIA, CYANOBACTERIA, DENITRIFYING BACTERIA, NITRIFYING BACTERIA, SHEATHED BACTERIA, SULFUR BACTERIA.

bacterial diseases Diseases caused by BACTERIA. The most common infectious diseases, they range from minor skin infections to bubonic PLAGUE and TUBERCULOSIS. Until the mid-20th century, bacterial PNEUMONIA was probably the leading cause of death among the elderly. Improved sanitation, VACCINES, and ANTIBIOTICS have all decreased the mortality rates from bacterial infections, though antibiotic-resistant strains have caused a resurgence in some illnesses. Bacteria cause disease by secreting or excreting TOXINS (as in BOTULISM), by producing toxins internally, which are released when the bacteria disintegrate (as in TYPHOID), or by inducing sensitivity to their antigenic properties (as in tuberculosis). Other serious bacterial diseases include CHOLERA, DIPHTHERIA, bacterial MENINGITIS, and SYPHILIS.

bacteriology Study of bacteria. Modern understanding of bacterial forms dates from FERDINAND COHN's classifications. Other researchers, such as LOUIS PASTEUR, established the connection between bacteria and fermentation and disease. The modern methods of bacteriological technique began in the late 19th century with the use of stains and the development of methods of cultivating organisms on plates of nutrients. Important discoveries came when Pasteur succeeded in immunizing animals against two bacterial diseases, which led to the development of IMMUNOLOGY. See also MICROBIOLOGY.

bacteriophage \\bak-'tir-ē-ə-,fāj\\ *or* **phage** Any of a group of usually complex VIRUSES that infect bacteria. Discovered in the early 20th century, bacteriophages were used to treat human bacterial diseases such as bubonic plague and cholera, but were not successful; they were abandoned with the advent of ANTIBIOTICS in the 1940s. The rise of drug-resistant bacteria in the 1990s focused renewed attention on the therapeutic potential of bacteriophages. Thousands of varieties exist, each of which may infect only one or a few types of bacteria. The core of a bacteriophage's genetic material may be either DNA or RNA. On infecting a host cell, bacteriophages known as lytic or virulent phages release replicated viral particles by lysing (bursting) the host cell. Other types, known as lysogenic or temperate, integrate their nucleic acid into the host's chromosome to be replicated during cell division. During this time they are not virulent. The viral genome may later become active, initiating production of viral particles and destruction of the host cell. A. D. HERSHEY and Martha Chase used a bacteriophage in a famous 1952 experiment that supported the theory that DNA is the genetic material. Because bacteriophage genomes are small and because large quantities can be prepared in the laboratory, they are a favorite research tool of molecular biologists. Studies of phages have helped illuminate genetic RECOMBINATION, nucleic-acid replication, and protein synthesis.

Bactria Ancient country, South Asia. It was between the HINDU KUSH and the AMU DARYA in present-day Afghanistan, Uzbekistan, and Tajikistan. Its capital was the city of Bactra. From the 6th century BC it was controlled by the ACHAEMENIAN DYNASTY; conquered by ALEXANDER THE GREAT, the area was ruled after his death (323 BC) by the SELEUCID DYNASTY. It formed an independent kingdom c. 250 BC. It was long important as a crossroads for East-West overland trade as well as for religion and art. The area ultimately came under Muslim control in the 7th century AD.

Baden \\'bäd-ᵊn\\ Former German state, southern Germany. The name (meaning "baths") refers to the warm mineral springs, particularly in the town of Baden-Baden (pop., 1989: 51,000), valued since Roman times. Baden first became a political unit when Frederick, son of the margrave of Verona, took the title of Margrave of Baden in 1112. Subsequently split up many times, the territory was finally reunited under Margrave Charles Frederick in 1771. A center of 19th-century liberalism, it was active in the revolutions of 1848–50. It joined the German empire in 1871, and it became part of the Weimar Republic in 1919. The southern part became a state of West Germany in 1949, while the northern part was incorporated into the West German state of Württemberg-Baden. Following a referendum, the two states merged to form Baden-Württemberg in 1952.

Baden and Rastatt, Treaties of See Treaties of RASTATT AND BADEN

Baden-Powell \\'bā-dᵊn-'pō-əl\\, **Robert (Stephenson Smyth)** *later* **Baron Baden-Powell (of Gilwell)** (1857–1941) British army officer and founder of the Boy Scouts and Girl Guides (see SCOUTING). He was noted for his use of observation balloons in warfare in Africa (1884–85). In the SOUTH AFRICAN WAR, he became a national hero in the siege of MAFIKENG. Having learned that his military textbook *Aids to Scouting* (1899) was being used to train boys in woodcraft, he wrote *Scouting for Boys* (1908) and that same year established the Boy Scout movement. In 1910, with his sister Agnes and his wife, Olave, he founded the Girl Guides.

badger Any of eight species of stout-bodied carnivores (family Mustelidae) that possess an anal scent gland, powerful jaws, and large, heavy claws on their forefeet. Most species are brown, black, or gray, with markings on the face or body, and are found in South Asia. Badgers dig to find food and to construct burrows and escape routes. The American badger *(Taxidea taxus),* the only New World species, lives in the open, dry country of western North America. Badgers feed mostly on small animals, especially rodents. Species may be 9–12 in. (23–30 cm) high and 13–32 in. (33–81 cm) long, excluding the 2- to 10-in. (5- to 23-cm) tail, and may weigh 2–48 lbs (1–22 kg). Badgers can be savage fighters.

Badlands Barren region covering some 2,000 sq mi (5,200 sq km) of southwestern South Dakota. It has an extremely rugged landscape almost devoid of vegetation. It was created by cloudbursts that have cut deep gullies in poorly cemented bedrock; its extensive fossil deposits have yielded the remains of such animals as the three-toed horse, camel, saber-toothed tiger, and rhinoceros. Badlands National Park (379 sq mi, or 982 sq km), lying mostly between the CHEYENNE and White rivers, was established as a national monument in 1939 and a national park in 1978.

badminton Court or lawn game played with light long-handed rackets and a shuttlecock volleyed over a net. The game is named after the residence of Britain's duke of Beaufort, where it supposedly originated c. 1873. Officially sanctioned badminton matches are played indoors to protect the shuttlecock from winds. Play consists entirely of hitting the shuttlecock back and forth without letting it touch the floor or ground. The best-known match is the All-England Championships. It became a full-medal sport at the 1992 Olympics. The world governing body is the International Federation of Badminton, in Cheltenham, Gloucestershire.

Badoglio \bə-'dōl-yō\, **Pietro** (1871–1956) Italian general and politician. An army officer, he served as chief of the general staff 1919–21 and 1925–28, and was made a field marshal in 1926. He governed Libya 1928–34, and commanded the Italian forces in Ethiopia 1935–36. In 1940 he resigned as chief of staff in disagreement with BENITO MUSSOLINI, and in 1943 he helped organize Mussolini's downfall. As prime minister (1943–44), Badoglio extricated Italy from World War II by arranging for an armistice with the Allies.

BAE Systems British manufacturer of aircraft, missiles, avionics, naval vessels, and other aerospace and defense products. BAE Systems was formed (1999) from the merger of British Aerospace (BAe) with Marconi Electronic Systems. BAe, in turn, dates to the merger (1977, with two other firms) of British Aircraft Corporation (BAC) and Hawker Siddeley Aviation, both having been nationalized a year earlier owing to unprofitable financial situations. Through its BAe antecedents, BAE Systems carries the legacy of some 20 British aircraft firms (e.g., Bristol, Avro, Gloster, De Havilland, Supermarine), several dating to the first decades of flight. In the 1960s and early '70s, BAC and Hawker Siddeley each produced significant aircraft. BAC built the Vickers-Armstrongs VC10 and BAC One-Eleven jetliners and, in partnership with Aerospatiale of France, the Concorde supersonic transport. Hawker Siddeley developed the HS 121 Trident jetliner, Vulcan bomber, and Harrier vertical/short-takeoff-and-landing (V/STOL) fighter. In 1979 British Aerospace joined the AIRBUS INDUSTRIE jetliner-manufacturing consortium, and during the early 1980s it became privatized. In the 1990s it became a partner with firms in Germany, Italy, and Spain in the Eurofighter Typhoon program. It also joined a venture led by LOCKHEED MARTIN to develop the Joint Strike Fighter.

Baeck \'bek\, **Leo** (1873–1956) Prussian-Polish rabbi, spiritual leader of German Jewry during the Nazi period. After earning his PhD in philosophy at the University of Berlin, he served as a rabbi in Silesia, Düsseldorf, and Berlin, becoming the leading liberal Jewish religious thinker of his time. He synthesized Neo-Kantianism and rabbinic ethics in *The Essence of Judaism* (1905) and considered the Christian gospels as rabbinic literature in *The Gospel as a Document of Jewish Religious History* (1938). He negotiated with the Nazis to buy time for the German Jews; finally arrested, he was sent to the Theresienstadt concentration camp, where he wrote and lectured on Plato and Kant. Liberated in 1945, the day before he was to be executed, he settled in England.

Baedeker \'bed-ə-kər\, **Karl** (1801–1859) German publisher. The son of a printer and bookseller, Baedeker started a firm at Koblenz in 1827 that became known for its guidebooks. His aim was to give travelers the practical information necessary to enable them to dispense with paid guides. A notable feature of the books was the use of "stars" to indicate objects and views of special interest and to designate reliable hotels. By the time of his death much of Europe had been covered by his guidebooks. Under the ownership of his sons the firm expanded to include French and English editions.

Karl Baedeker, oil painting by an unknown artist.
POPPERFOTO

Baekeland \'ba-kə-,länt, *Engl* 'bāk-lənd\, **Leo (Hendrik)** (1863–1944) Belgian-U.S. industrial chemist. A teacher of chemistry in Belgium, he emigrated to the U.S. in 1889. He invented Velox, the first commercially successful photographic paper, which could be developed under artificial light, and sold the rights to GEORGE EASTMAN for $1 million in 1899. His search for a substitute for shellac led to the discovery in 1909 of a method of forming a hard thermosetting plastic, which he named Bakelite, produced from formaldehyde and phenol. His discovery helped found the modern plastics industry.

Baer \'ber\, **Karl Ernst, Ritter (Knight) von** (1792–1876) Prussian-Estonian embryologist. Studying chick development with his friend Christian Pander (1794–1865), Baer expanded Pander's concept of germ-layer formation to all vertebrates, thereby laying the foundation for comparative embryology. He emphasized that embryos of one species could resemble embryos (but not adults) of another, and that the younger the embryo the greater the resemblance, a concept in line with his belief that development proceeds from simple to complex, from like to different. He also discovered the mammalian ovum. His *On the Development of Animals* (2 vols., 1828–37) surveyed all existing knowledge on vertebrate development and established embryology as a distinct subject of research.

baetylus *or* **baetulus** \'bē-tə-ləs, 'bē-tyə-ləs\ In GREEK RELIGION, a sacred stone or pillar. In antiquity there were numerous holy stones, most associated with a deity. The most famous example is the holy stone known as the Omphalos in the temple of Apollo at DELPHI. Sometimes the stones were formed into pillars or into groups of three pillars.

Baeyer \'bā-ər\, **(Johann Friedrich Wilhelm) Adolf von** (1835–1917) German research chemist. He synthesized INDIGO and formulated its structure, discovered the phthalein DYES, and investigated such chemical families as the polyacetylenes, oxonium salts, and uric-acid derivatives (discovering barbituric acid, parent compound of the BARBITURATES). He also made contributions to theoretical chemistry. He received the Nobel Prize in 1905.

Baeyer, 1905.
HISTORIA-PHOTO

Baez \'bī-ez\, **Joan (Chandos)** (born 1941) U.S. folksinger and activist. Born on Staten Island, N.Y., she moved often as a child, receiving little musical training. While still in her teens, her luminous soprano voice brought her to the forefront of the 1960s folk-song revival. An active participant in the protest movements of the 1960s and '70s, Baez made free concert appearances at civil-rights and anti-Vietnam War rallies. In 1964 she refused to pay federal taxes that went toward war expenses, and she was jailed twice in 1967. She published two books of memoirs.

Baffin Bay Large inlet, Atlantic Ocean, between western GREENLAND and eastern BAFFIN ISLAND. With an area of 266,000 sq mi (689,000 sq km), it extends 900 mi (1,450 km) southward from the Arctic, and is connected to the Atlantic by DAVIS STRAIT. It was visited by the English captain Robert Bylot in 1615 and named for his lieutenant, William Baffin. Its climate is severe, and icebergs are dense even in August.

Baffin Island Largest island in Canada and fifth-largest island in the world (183,810 sq mi, or 476,068 sq km), lying between Greenland and the Canadian mainland. Located west of BAFFIN BAY and DAVIS STRAIT, it is part of NUNAVUT. It was probably visited by Norse explorers in the 11th century. It was sighted by MARTIN FROBISHER during his search for a NORTHWEST PASSAGE (1576–78). It is uninhabited except for a few coastal settlements. The world's northernmost mines are at Nanisvik. In 1972 Auyuittuq National Park was created on the eastern coast.

Baganda See GANDA

bagasse \bə-'gas\ Fiber remaining after the extraction of the sugar-bearing juice from SUGARCANE. The term was once applied more generally to various waste residues from processing plant materials. Bagasse may be used as fuel in the sugarcane mill or as a source of CELLULOSE for manufacturing animal FEEDS. Paper is produced from bagasse in several Latin-American countries, in the Middle East, and in all sugar-producing countries that are deficient in forest resources. It is the essential ingredient for the production of pressed building board, acoustical tile, and other construction materials.

Bagehot \'baj-ət\, **Walter** (1826–1877) English economist, political analyst, and journalist. While working in his uncle's bank, Bagehot wrote literary essays and economic articles that led to his involvement with *The* ECONOMIST. As its editor from 1860, he helped make it one of the leading business and political journals in the world. His classic *The English Constitution* (1867) describes how the British system of government really operates behind its facade. His other works include *Physics* *and Politics* (1872), one of the earliest attempts to apply the concept of evolution to societies, and *Lombard Street* (1873), a study of banking methods. His literary essays have been continually republished.

Walter Bagehot, mezzotint by Norman Hirst, after a photograph.
BY COURTESY OF THE TRUSTEES OF THE BRITISH MUSEUM; PHOTOGRAPH, J.R. FREEMAN & CO. LTD.

Baggara \bä-'gär-ə\ *or* **Baqqarah** \bä-'kär-ə\ Nomadic Arab people, numbering about 600,000, probably descended from the Arabs who migrated west out of Egypt in the Middle Ages. Today they live in a region of Sudan extending from Lake Chad east to the Nile, migrating with their cattle herds south to the river lands in the dry season and north to the grasslands during the rains. They also raise sorghum and millet. Association with the FULANI and others have given them a distinct dialect of Arabic.

Baghdad *or* **Bagdad** City (metro. area pop., 1999 est.: 4,689,000), capital of Iraq. Located on the TIGRIS RIVER, the site has been settled from ancient times. It rose to importance after being chosen in AD 762 by Caliph al-Mansur (r.754–775) as the capital of the ABBASID DYNASTY. Under HARUN AL-RASHID it achieved its greatest glory, reflected in the *THOUSAND AND ONE NIGHTS*, as one of the world's largest and richest cities. A center of Islam, it was second only to CONSTANTINOPLE in trade and culture. It began to decline when the capital was moved to Samarra in 809. It was sacked by the Mongols under Hülegü in 1258, taken by TIMUR in 1401, and captured by the Persian SULEYMAN I in 1524. It was a shadow of its former self in 1638, when it was absorbed by the Ottoman empire. In 1921 it became capital of the kingdom of Iraq. In 1958 a coup d'état in Baghdad ended the monarchy. Severely damaged by bombing in the PERSIAN GULF WAR, it has since suffered under international trade sanctions.

bagpipes Wind instrument consisting of two or more single- or double-reed pipes, the reeds being vibrated by wind fed by arm pressure on a skin or cloth bag. The pipes are held in wooden sockets tied into the bag, which is inflated either by the mouth or by bellows strapped to the body. Melodies are played on the fingerholes of the melody pipe, or chanter, while the remaining pipes, or drones, sound single notes. Bagpipes existed by c. AD 100. The early bag was an animal bladder or a nearly whole sheepskin or goatskin. Bagpipes have always been folk instruments. An important related instrument is the Irish union (or uilleann) pipes.

Baguirmi *or* **Bagirmi** \bȧ-gēr-'mē\ Former sultanate, now part of southwestern Chad. Located southeast of Lake CHAD, it was probably established in the 16th century. The king ruled from the capital city of Massenya. Though the 17th century brought prosperity as a result of the slave trade, Baguirmi became a pawn in conflicts between rival empires to the east and west. It was repeatedly sacked in the 19th century, and ultimately came under French control in the late 19th century.

bagworm moth Any insect of the MOTH family Psychidae, found worldwide, named for the baglike cases the larvae (see LARVA) carry with them. The bag, which ranges in size from 0.25 to 6 in. (6–150 mm), is constructed from silk and bits of leaves, twigs, and other debris. The strong-bodied male has broad, fringed wings with a wingspread averaging 1 in. (25 mm). The wormlike female lacks wings. Bagworm larvae often damage trees, especially evergreens.

Bagyidaw \'bäg-yi-ˌdau̇\ (died 1846) Seventh monarch of the ALAUNGPAYA DYNASTY (r.1819–37) of Myanmar. Bagyidaw was an ineffectual king, but his general, Maha Bandula, convinced him to pursue a policy of expansion in northeastern India. His conquest of Assam and Manipur angered the British, who launched the first of the ANGLO–BURMESE WARS. Bagyidaw spent the rest of his reign trying to mitigate the harsh terms of the Treaty of Yandabo (1826), which concluded that conflict.

Baha Ullah \bä-'hä-u̇l-'lä\ *orig.* **Mirza Hoseyn Ali Nuri** (1817–1892) Iranian religious leader, founder of the BAHA'I faith. A Shiite Muslim who allied himself with the BAB, he joined his half-brother Mirza Yahya (known as Sobh-e Azal) in leading the Babi movement after the Bab's execution. Sunni Muslims exiled him to Baghdad, Kurdistan, and finally Constantinople, where in 1867 he declared himself the imam-mahdi foretold by the Bab and sent by God. This pronouncement split BABISM into two factions, with a small group (the AZALI) adhering to its original beliefs and a larger group following him into what became the Baha'i faith. The Ottoman government banished him to Acre where, as Baha Ullah, he developed Baha'i into a teaching that advocated the unity of all religions and universal human brotherhood.

Baha'i \bä-'hä-ē\ Religion founded in Iran in the mid-19th century by BAHA ULLAH. It emerged from BABISM when in 1863 Baha Ullah asserted that he was the messenger of God predicted by the Bab. Before his death in 1892, he appointed his son Abd ol-Baha to lead the community. The writings of the Bab, Baha Ullah, and Abd ol-Baha form the sacred literature. Worship consists of readings from scriptures of all religions. Baha'i faith proclaims the essential unity of all religions and the unity of humanity. It is concerned with social ethics and has no priesthood or sacraments. Because of its 19 initial disciples, it considers the number 19 sacred, and the calendar consists of 19 months of 19 days (with four additional days). Adherents are expected to pray daily, fast 19 days a year, and keep to a strict ethical code. Baha'i has experienced major growth since the 1960s but has been persecuted in Iran since the fundamentalist revolution of 1979.

Bahamas *officially* **Commonwealth of the Bahamas** Archipelago and nation consisting of about 700 islands and numerous cays, northwestern edge of the WEST INDIES, lying southeast of Florida and north of Cuba. Area: 5,386 sq mi (13,950 sq km). Population (1997 est.): 287,000. Capital: NASSAU (on New Providence Island). The people are a blend of African and European ancestry, the former a legacy of the slave trade. Language: English (official). Religion: Christianity. Currency: Bahamian dollar. Chief among the islands, from north to south, are Grand Bahama, Abaco, Eleuthera, New Providence, Andros, Cat, and Inagua;

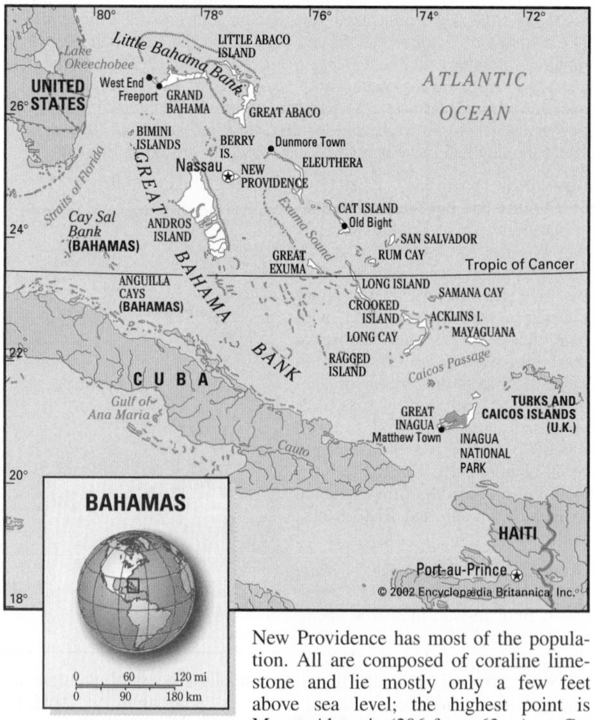

New Providence has most of the population. All are composed of coraline limestone and lie mostly only a few feet above sea level; the highest point is Mount Alvernia (206 ft, or 63 m) on Cat Island. There are no rivers. Its market economy is heavily dependent on tourism, for which gambling is a particular attraction, and on international financial services. Most foodstuffs are imported from the U.S.; fish and rum are significant exports. It is a constitutional monarchy with two legislative houses; its chief of state is the British monarch, represented by a governor-general, and the head of government is the prime minister. The islands were inhabited by Lucayan Indians when CHRISTOpher Columbus sighted them on October 12, 1492. He is thought to have landed on San Salvador (Watling) Island. The Spaniards made no attempt to settle, but carried out slave raids that depopulated the islands; when English settlers arrived in 1648 from Bermuda, the islands were uninhabited. They became a haunt of pirates and buccaneers, and few of the ensuing settlements prospered. The islands enjoyed some prosperity following the American Revolution, when Loyalists fled the U.S. and established cotton plantations there. They were a center for blockade runners during the American Civil War. Not until the development of tourism after World War II did permanent economic prosperity arrive. The Bahamas was granted internal self-government in 1964, and became independent in 1973.

Bahia \bä-'ē-ä\ State (pop., 2000 prelim.: 13,066,764), eastern Brazil. Its capital is Salvador. The major river is the São Francisco. The Portuguese first entered the region in 1501 through the bay where Salvador is now located. Colonization began in the coastal region; the discovery of gold and gems in the Diamantina Upland attracted more settlers in the 18th century. A state since 1889, Bahia is rich in mineral resources, including petroleum, natural gas, lead, copper, chrome, and tin. Its heavy industries include petroleum refining and ironworks. It is also an important agricultural producer.

Bahia See Salvador

Bahr al-Ghazal \ˌbär-äl-gȧ-'zäl\ River, southwestern Sudan. Formed by the confluence of the Bahr el Arab and Jur rivers in a swampy area of southern Sudan, it is 445 mi (716 km) long. It flows east to unite at Lake No with the Bahr el Jebel and form the White Nile River. It was mapped in 1772 by the French geographer J.-B. Bourguignon d'Anville.

Bahr el Jebel \ˌbär-el-'je-bel\ River, southern central Sudan. The river flows northward 594 mi (956 km) over the Fula Rapids, past Juba (the head of navigation), and through a vast swampy region. It receives the Bahr al-Ghazal at Lake No and then turns east to join the Sobat River of western Ethiopia, thereafter forming the White Nile River.

Bahrain \bä-'rān\ *officially* **Kingdom of Bahrain** Country, constitutional monarchy, occupying an archipelago consisting of Bahrain Island and about 30 smaller islands, lying along the Arabian Peninsula in the Persian Gulf. Area: 268 sq mi (694 sq km). Population (2001 est.): 701,000. Capital: Manama. Most of the population is Arab. Language: Arabic (official). Religion: Islam (official), divided between Sunnite and Shiite. Currency: Bahraini dinar. Bahrain Island accounts for seven-eighths of the country's total area and, with the islands of Al-Muharraq and Sitrah off its northeastern coast, constitutes the population and economic center of the country. Bahrain Island is 27 mi (43 km) long and 10 mi (16 km) wide, and is connected to Saudi Arabia by a 15-mi (25-km) causeway completed in 1986. The highest elevation is Ad-Dukhan Hill at 440 ft (132 m). The country has a developing mixed state and private-enterprise economy based largely on natural gas and petroleum refining. The chief of state is the king and head of government is the prime minister. The area has long been an important trading center and is mentioned in Persian, Greek, and Roman references. It was ruled by Arabs from the 7th century AD, but then occupied by the Portuguese 1521–1602. Since 1783 it has been ruled by the Khalifah family, though through a series of treaties its defense remained a British responsibility 1820–1971. After Britain withdrew its forces from the Persian Gulf (1968), Bahrain declared its independence in 1971. It served as a center for the allies in the Persian Gulf War. Since 1994 it has experienced bouts of political unrest mainly by Shiites. A constitution ratified in 2002 declared Bahrain a constitutional monarchy, enfranchised women, and set a date for the election of a new parliament (the first since 1975) later that year.

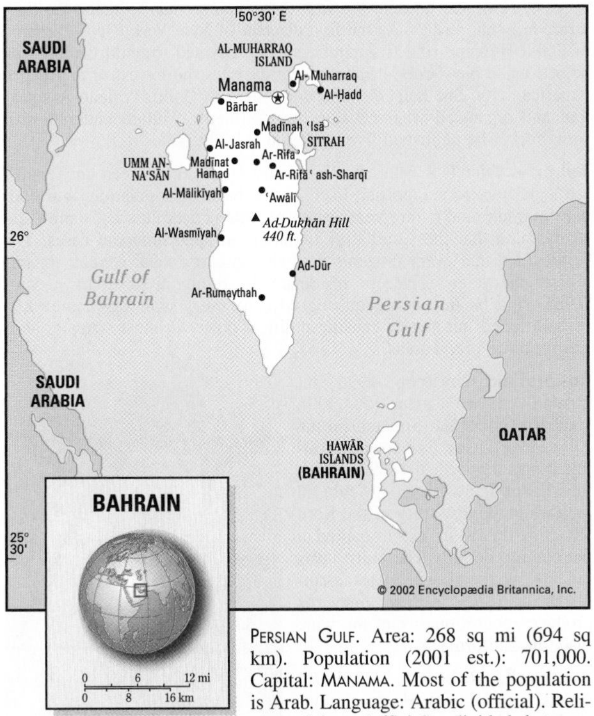

Bai Juyi See Bo Juyi

Bai River *or* **Pai River** \'bī\ River, northeastern China. It rises beyond the Great Wall in Hebei province and flows southeastern through Beijing municipality. It continues through Tianjin municipality where it becomes known as the Hai River from its junction with the Grand Canal to its mouth at Bo Hai. About 300 mi (483 km) long, it is navigable for some 100 mi (160 km).

Baibars I See Baybars I

Baikal, Lake *or* **Lake Baykal** \bī-'käl\ Lake, southern Siberia, Russia in Asia. At 395 mi (636 km) long, with an area of some 12,200 sq mi (31,500 sq km), it is the largest freshwater basin in Eurasia. The deepest continental body of water on earth (5,315 ft, or 1,620 m), it contains one-fifth of the fresh water on the earth's surface. Over 330 rivers flow into it; on its east it receives the Barguzin and Selenga rivers, and most of its outflow is through the Angara at the northern end. The island of Olkhon is in its center. Plant and animal life are rich and various; more than 1,200 species are unique to the lake. Growing industrialization along its shores has produced threatening pollution.

bail Temporary release of a prisoner in exchange for security given to guarantee the prisoner's appearance at a later hearing. It also refers to the actual security given (e.g., cash). Its main use today is to secure the freedom, pending trial, of someone arrested and charged with a criminal offense. Its use in civil (noncriminal) cases is far less common, as most do not involve imprisonment. The amount of bail is generally set in relation to the gravity of the offense, though other factors, such as the strength of the evidence, the character of the accused, and the accused's ability to secure bail may also be considered. See also bond, recognizance.

Bailey, Pearl (Mae) (1918–1990) U.S. singer and entertainer. Born in Newport News, Va., she began her career at 15, appearing in nightclubs and theaters and with jazz bands, including the Count Basie band. Her first Broadway musical was *St. Louis Woman* in 1946; her first film was *Variety Girl* in 1947. She became known for her lively and earthy style. In 1952 she married the drummer and bandleader Louis Bellson, with whom she later often appeared. The most memorable of her Broadway roles, which included Carmen Jones (1954), was as Dolly Levi in an all-black production of *Hello, Dolly!* (1967–69).

bailiff Officer of some U.S. courts whose duties include keeping order in the courtroom and guarding prisoners or jurors in deliberation. In medieval Europe, it was a title of some dignity and power, denoting a manorial superintendent or royal agent who collected fines and rent, served writs, assembled juries, made arrests, and executed the monarch's orders. The bailiff's authority was gradually eroded by the increasing need to use administrators with legal or other specialized training.

Bailly \bȧ-'yē\, **Jean-Sylvain** (1736–1793) French astronomer and politician. Noted for his computation of an orbit for Halley's Comet (1759), he turned to politics with the outbreak of the French Revolution. He was chosen president of the Third Estate in May 1789 and was proclaimed the first mayor of Paris in July. He later lost popularity, particularly after his order to disperse a riotous crowd led to the massacre of the Champ de Mars (1791). He retired but was subsequently arrested, taken before the revolutionary tribunal, and guillotined.

Baily's beads Arc of bright spots seen during a total ECLIPSE of the sun, named for Francis Baily (1774–1844), the English astronomer who first called attention to them. Just before the moon's disk completely covers the sun, the narrow crescent of sunlight may be broken in several places by mountains and valleys on the edge of the moon's disk; the resulting spots resemble a string of beads. The "diamond-ring effect" occurs when the very last rays of the sun to be obscured look like a bright diamond on the solar CORONA.

Baird, Bil and Cora (1904–1987, 1912–1967) U.S. puppeteers. Born in Grand Island, Neb., Bil (originally William Britton) Baird worked under the puppeteer Tony Sarg for five years, then produced his own puppet shows from the mid-1930s. He and Cora Eisenberg (born in New York City) married in 1937 and began to create original puppets, scenery, and music for their shows. They produced a series of television shows in the 1950s and opened their own MARIONETTE theater in New York in 1966. Bil wrote *The Art of the Puppet* (1965) and trained such puppeteers as JIM HENSON.

Baird, John L(ogie) (1888–1946) Scottish engineer. Plagued by ill health, he gave up his job as an electric-power engineer in 1922 and devoted himself to television research. He produced televised objects in outline in 1924 and recognizable human faces in 1925, and in 1926 became the first person to televise pictures of objects in motion. He demonstrated color television in 1928. The German post office gave him facilities to develop a television service in 1929. When the BBC television service began (1936), his system competed with that of Marconi Electric and Musical Industries; the BBC adopted the latter exclusively in 1937. Baird was reported to have completed research on stereoscopic television at the time of his death.

Bairiki \'bī-ˌrē-kē\ Islet (pop., 1990: 2,000) and administrative center, Kiribati. It is located on TARAWA atoll, northern GILBERT ISLANDS. It has port facilities as well as an extension center of the University of the South Pacific.

Baja California \'bä-ˌhä\ *or* **Lower California** Peninsula, northwestern Mexico. Bounded by the U.S., the Pacific Ocean, and the Gulf of California, it is about 760 mi (1,220 km) long, and has an area of 55,366 sq mi (143,396 sq km). Politically it is divided into the states of BAJA CALIFORNIA and BAJA CALIFORNIA SUR. It has over 2,000 mi (3,200 km) of coastline, with sheltered harbors on both the western coast and the Gulf. The area had been inhabited for 9,000 years when the Spanish arrived in 1533. Jesuit missionaries established permanent settlements in the late 17th century, but the native Indians were practically exterminated in epidemics unwittingly introduced by the Spanish. The area was separated from what is now the U.S. state of California by treaty in 1848 following the MEXICAN WAR.

Baja California State (pop., 1995 est.: 2,112,000), northern BAJA CALIFORNIA peninsula, northern Mexico. Formerly called Baja California Norte, it covers an area of 27,071 sq mi (70,114 sq km). Although long inhabited, it remained sparsely populated until the 1950s, when it experienced phenomenal growth. This was partly due to its proximity to the U.S. border where several foreign companies established factories in the region. Its capital is Mexicali.

Baja California Sur State (pop., 1995 est.: 375,000), southern BAJA CALIFORNIA peninsula, northern Mexico. Occupying an area of 28,447 sq mi (73,678 sq km), it became a state in 1974. It is sparsely populated and remains relatively neglected. Much new acreage of cotton has been planted near LA PAZ, the capital, but subsistence agriculture is the norm. Tourism and improved communications are alleviating the state's isolation.

Baker, Chet *orig.* **Chesney** (1929–1988) U.S. trumpeter and singer, whose delicate tone and gentle phrasing made him the epitome of the cool jazz (see BEBOP) of the 1950s. Born in Oklahoma, his early musical experience was in army bands, after which engagements with CHARLIE PARKER and GERRY MULLIGAN in 1952 and 1953 assured his reputation. His recording of "My Funny Valentine" established his detached, reserved approach as a vocalist, which mirrored his trumpet style. Much of his later career, interrupted several times by legal problems stemming from drug addiction, was spent in Europe.

Baker, Josephine *orig.* **Freda Josephine McDonald** (1906–1975) U.S.-French entertainer. Born in St. Louis, Mo., she joined a dance troupe at 16 and soon moved to New York, where she performed in Harlem nightclubs and on Broadway in *Chocolate Dandies* (1924). She went to Paris in 1925 to dance in *La revue nègre.* To French audiences she personified the exoticism and vitality of African-American culture, and she became Paris's most popular MUSIC-HALL entertainer, receiving star billing at the FOLIES BERGÈRE. In World War II she worked with the Red Cross and entertained FREE FRENCH troops. From 1950 she adopted numerous orphans of all nationalities as "an experiment in brotherhood," returning periodically to the U.S. to advance the cause of civil rights.

Josephine Baker.
H. ROGER-VIOLLET

Baker, Newton D(iehl) (1871–1937) U.S. secretary of war. Born in Martinsburg, Va., he practiced law from 1897. After moving to Cleveland, he was elected mayor (1912–16) and helped obtain the 1912 presidential nomination for WOODROW WILSON, who appointed him secretary of war (1916–21). Though a pacifist, Baker developed a plan for the military draft and oversaw the mobilization of over 4 million men during the war. In 1928 he was appointed to the International Court of Arbitration at The Hague.

Baker, Philip John Noel- See Philip NOEL-BAKER

Baker, Russell (Wayne) (born 1925) U.S. newspaper columnist. A native of Virginia, Baker joined the *Baltimore Sun* in 1947. In 1954 he moved to the Washington bureau of the *New York Times*, and in the early 1960s he began his syndicated "Observer" column. Initially concentrating on political satire, he later found other subjects to skewer as well. In 1979 he won the Pulitzer Prize for commentary. His books include the autobiographies *Growing Up* (1982, Pulitzer Prize) and *The Good Times* (1989). In 1993 he became host of the television program *Masterpiece Theatre*.

Baker, Sara Josephine (1873–1945) U.S. physician. Born in Poughkeepsie, N.Y., she became the first American woman to receive a doctorate in public health. As the first director of New York City's Division of Child Hygiene (the first public agency devoted to child health), she helped make New York's infant-mortality rates the lowest of any major American city. She helped found the American Child Hygiene Association and organized what became the Children's Welfare Federation of New York. She published five books on child hygiene.

Baker v. Carr U.S. Supreme Court case (1962) that forced the Tennessee legislature to reapportion itself on the basis of population, thus ending the traditional overrepresentation of rural areas in the legislature and establishing that the Court may intervene in apportionment cases. The Court ruled that every citizen's vote should carry equal weight, regardless of the voter's place of residence. Its ruling in *Reynolds* v. *Sims* (1964) built on *Baker* by requiring virtually every state legislature to be reapportioned, ultimately causing political power in most states to shift from rural to urban areas.

Bakersfield City (pop., 1996 est.: 205,000; metro. area: 564,000), southern California. Situated on the Kern River in the San Joaquin Valley, it was founded in 1869 by Thomas Baker. It was in an agricultural area when the discovery of the Kern River oil fields in 1899 sparked a petroleum boom. The city was quickly rebuilt after a major earthquake in 1952. Nearby vineyards produce about a quarter of the wine made in California.

Bakewell, Robert (1725–1795) English agriculturist. He revolutionized English sheep and cattle breeding by methodical selection, inbreeding, and culling. He was one

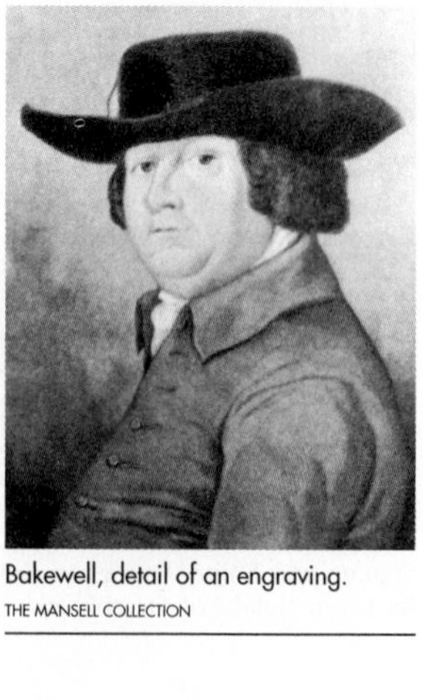

Bakewell, detail of an engraving.
THE MANSELL COLLECTION

of the first to breed sheep and cattle for meat, and the first to establish on a large scale the practice of letting animals for stud. His farm became famous as a model of scientific management.

Bakhtin \bək-'tēn\, **Mikhail (Mikhailovich)** (1895–1975) Russian literary theorist and philosopher of language. His works frequently offended the Soviet authorities, and in 1929 he was exiled from Vitsyebsk to Kazakhstan. He is especially known for *Problems of Dostoevsky's Poetics* (1929), which advanced theories that he further developed in *The Dialogic Imagination* (1975). His wide-ranging ideas significantly influenced Western thinking in cultural history, linguistics, literary theory, and aesthetics.

Bakhtiyari *or* **Bakhtyari** \bäk-'tē-ə-rē\ Nomadic pastoral tent dwellers of western Iran. They number about 880,000. They speak the Luri dialect of Persian and are Shiite Muslims. Their two tribal groups are the Chahar Lang and Haft Lang; the position of leader of all the Bakhtiyari alternates every two years between the chiefs of the two tribal groups. Many chiefs have been influential in national public affairs and have held office. Bakhtiyari women are normally better-educated and freer than other Muslim women in Iran.

baking Process of cooking by dry heat, especially in an oven. Baked products include BREAD, cookies, pies, and pastries. Ingredients used in baking include FLOUR, water, leavening agents (baker's yeast, baking soda, baking powder), shortening (fats, butter, oils), eggs, milk, and sugars. These are mixed together to create dough or batter, which is then transferred to a metal pan or sheet and heated. Leavening agents produce gas that becomes trapped in the dough, causing it to rise. Shortening makes doughs more easily workable and the final product tenderer. Egg whites are used to produce a light, airy texture, and yolks contribute color, flavor, and texture. Milk is used for flavoring, and sugars to sweeten and to aid FERMENTATION.

baking soda See BICARBONATE OF SODA

Bakke case See *REGENTS OF THE UNIVERSITY OF CALIFORNIA VS. BAKKE*

Bakongo See KONGO

Bakst \'bȧkst\, **Leon** *orig.* **Lev Samuilovich Rosenberg** (1866–1924) Russian painter and stage designer. He attended the Imperial Academy of Arts at St. Petersburg and studied in Paris. In 1898 he cofounded the journal *Mir Iskusstva* ("World of Art") with SERGEY DIAGHILEV. He began designing scenery for the imperial theaters in 1900. In Paris he designed sets and costumes for Diaghilev's new BALLETS RUSSES. His bold designs and sumptuous colors, conveying an exotic orientalism, won him international fame. His work played a major role in the impact of the Ballet Russes, revolutionized European stage design, and strongly influenced European high fashion.

Baku \bä-'kü\ City (pop., 1995 est.: 1,740,000), capital of Azerbaijan. Located on the western shore of the CASPIAN SEA at the sea's best harbor, Baku has long been inhabited. By the 11th century AD, it was in the possession of the Shirvan shahs, who made it their capital in the 12th century. In 1723 PETER THE GREAT took Baku, but returned it to Persia in 1735; Russia captured the town finally in 1806. It was the capital of the BOLSHEVIK government in 1917, and became the capital of the new Soviet republic of Azerbaijan in 1920. The basis of Baku's economy is petroleum.

Baku rug *or* **Chilia rug** \'kēl-yə\ Handwoven floor covering made near BAKU, Azerbaijan. It is a pile rug with warps of wool and wefts of cotton, of modified Persian design. The ground pattern displays rows of geometric pear or leaf forms; the border is of narrow diagonal stripes. The colors are muted. Also ascribed to Baku are finely woven prayer rugs, the warp and weft a combination of cotton and silk or cotton and wool.

bakufu \bä-'kü-fü\ (Japanese: "tent government") Military rule of the country by a hereditary SHOGUN, as opposed to rule by the imperial court and the emperor. Japanese history has seen three periods of bakufu government: MINAMOTO YORITOMO established the Kamakura bakufu (KAMAKURA SHOGUNATE) at the end of the 12th century, Ashikaga Takauji established the Muromachi bakufu (ASHIKAGA SHOGUNATE) in the early 14th century, and TOKUGAWA IEYASU established the Edo bakufu (TOKUGAWA SHOGUNATE) at the beginning of the 17th century. The Edo bakufu was the most successful, a time of peace and prosperity that lasted over 250 years. See also DAIMYO, HOJO FAMILY, JITO.

Bakunin \bə-'kün-yən\, **Mikhail (Aleksandrovich)** (1814–1876) Russian anarchist and political writer. He traveled in Western Europe and was active in the REVOLUTIONS OF 1848. After attending the Slav congress in Prague, he wrote the manifesto *An Appeal to Slavs* (1848). Arrested for revolutionary intrigues in Germany (1849), he was sent to Russia and exiled to Siberia. He escaped in 1861 and returned to Western Europe, where he continued his militant anarchist teachings. At the FIRST INTERNATIONAL (1872) he engaged in a famous quarrel with KARL MARX, which split the European revolutionary movement.

Balaguer (y Ricardo) \ˌbä-lä-'ger\, **Joaquín (Vidella)** (born 1907) President of the Dominican Republic (1960–62, 1966–78, 1986–96). He held numerous government posts during Gen. RAFAEL TRUJILLO's 30-year dictatorship. He was vice president under Trujillo's brother Hector and became president when Hector resigned, but Gen. Trujillo continued to wield actual power until his assassination in 1961. Balaguer's subsequent attempts at liberalization caused his overthrow by the military. Elected president in 1966 after the U.S. military intervention in 1965, he achieved steady economic growth and modest social reforms. He was reelected repeatedly, but his last term was shortened by two years amid political violence and charges of electoral fraud and corruption.

Balakirev \bə-'lá-kyi-ryif\, **Mily (Alekseyevich)** (1837–1910) Russian composer. Taken in hand early by M. GLINKA, he himself later became the mentor of César Cui (1835–1918) and M. MUSSORGSKY. In 1861–62 their group expanded to become the MIGHTY FIVE. In 1862 he cofounded the Free School of Music. After a nervous breakdown in 1871, he adopted a fervent and bigoted form of Orthodoxy, and was thereafter involved in musical life only sporadically. His works include two symphonies, the piano fantasy *Islamey* (1869), music for *King Lear* (1861, 1905), and a piano concerto. With his brilliant color and use of folk themes, he was perhaps the most influential proponent of Russian nationalism.

Balaklava \bə-lə-'klä-və\, **Battle of** (October 1854) Indecisive military engagement of the CRIMEAN WAR. The Russians sought to capture the Black Sea supply port of Balaklava, which was controlled by the British, French, and Turks. They occupied positions on the heights above a nearby valley. To disrupt the Russian troop movements, BARON RAGLAN gave an ambiguous order for Lord CARDIGAN's Light Brigade to attack. Instead of leading his cavalry against the Russian guns on the heights, Cardigan swept down the valley after the retreating Russian cavalry. The battle ended with the loss of 40% of the Light Brigade.

balalaika \ˌba-lə-'lī-kə\ Russian stringed instrument with a triangular body, three strings, and movable frets on its fingerboard. It comes in six sizes, from piccolo to double bass. It developed in the 18th century from the dombra. It has been primarily a solo folk instrument for accompanying song and dance, but is also played in large balalaika orchestras.

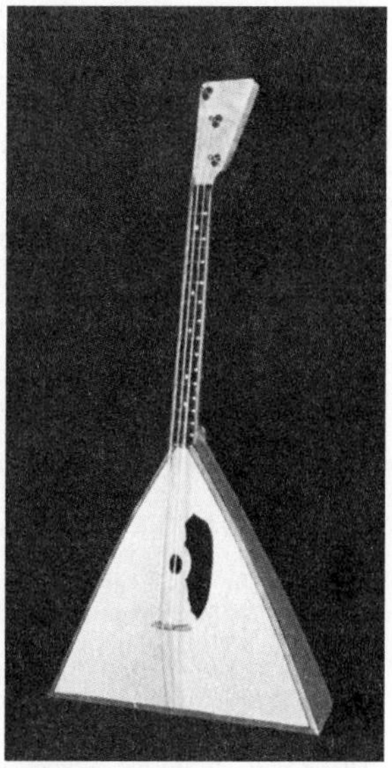

Russian tenor balalaika, 20th century; in the Metropolitan Museum of Art, New York City.

BY COURTESY OF THE METROPOLITAN MUSEUM OF ART, NEW YORK CITY, THE CROSBY BROWN COLLECTION OF MUSICAL INSTRUMENTS, 1889

balance Instrument for comparing the weights of two bodies, usually for scientific purposes, to determine the difference in MASS. The equal-arm balance dates back to the ancient Egyptians, possibly as early as 5000 BC. By the early 20th century, it had been developed into an exquisitely precise measuring device. Electronic balances today depend on electrical compensation rather than mechanical deflection. The ultramicrobalance is any weighing device that serves to determine the weight of even smaller samples than can be weighed with the microbalance (which can weigh samples as small as a few milligrams), that is, total amounts as small as a few micrograms.

A
B

balance of payments Systematic record of all economic transactions during a given period between residents (including the government) of one country and residents (including the governments) of other countries. The transactions are presented in the form of double-entry bookkeeping. The U.S. balance of payments, for example, records the various ways in which dollars are made available to foreigners through U.S. imports, U.S. tourist spending abroad, foreign lending, and so on. These expenditures are shown on the debit side of the balance. The credit side shows the various uses to which foreigners put their dollars, including paying for U.S. exports, servicing debts to the U.S., and the like. Foreign countries may acquire more dollars than they need to spend on U.S. goods and services and may hold the surplus or purchase gold or securities; or they may have fewer dollars than they need to purchase U.S. goods and services, and may acquire additional dollars by transferring gold, selling holdings in the U.S., and so on. Certain forms of transferring funds (e.g., large outflows of gold) are less desirable as a way of settling foreign debts than others (e.g., transfers of currency acquired through international trade). The INTERNATIONAL MONETARY FUND helps address problems relating to balance of payments. See also BALANCE OF TRADE.

balance of power In international relations, an equilibrium of power sufficient to discourage or prevent one nation or party from imposing its will on or interfering with the interests of another. The term came into use at the end of the Napoleonic Wars to denote the power relationships in the European state system. Until World War I, Britain played the role of balancer in a number of shifting alliances. After World War II, a Northern Hemisphere balance of power pitted the U.S. and its allies (see NATO) against the Soviet Union and its satellites (see WARSAW PACT) in a bipolar balance of power backed by the threat of nuclear war. China's defection from the Soviet camp to a nonaligned but covertly anti-Soviet stance produced a third node of power. With the Soviet Union's collapse (1991), the U.S. and its NATO allies were recognized universally as the world's paramount military power.

balance of trade Difference in value over a period of time between a nation's imports and exports of goods and services. The balance of trade is part of a larger economic unit, the BALANCE OF PAYMENTS, which includes all economic transactions between residents of one country and those of other countries. If a nation's exports exceed its imports, the nation has a favorable balance of trade, or a trade surplus. If imports exceed exports, an unfavorable balance of trade, or a trade deficit, exists. Under MERCANTILISM a favorable balance of trade was an absolute necessity, but in CLASSICAL ECONOMICS it was more important for a nation to utilize its economic resources fully than to build a trade surplus. The idea of the undesirability of trade deficits persisted into the 20th century, however, and is often advanced by advocates of PROTECTIONISM.

balance sheet Financial statement that describes the resources under a company's control on a specified date and indicates where they have come from. It consists of three major sections: assets (valuable rights owned by the company), liabilities (funds provided by outside lenders and other creditors), and the owners' EQUITY. On the balance sheet, total assets must always equal total liabilities plus total owners' equity.

Balanchine \bá-läⁿ-'shēn\, **George** *orig.* **Georgy (Melitonovich) Balanchivadze** (1904–1983) Russian-U.S. choreographer, and co-founder and artistic director of the NEW YORK CITY BALLET (1948–82). After studying at the Imperial Ballet school, he left the Soviet Union in 1925 to join the BALLETS RUSSES, where his choreography of *Apollo* (1928) exemplified the spare neoclassical style that became his trademark. His work impressed LINCOLN KIRSTEIN, who in 1933 invited "Mr. B." to form the School of American Ballet and its performing group, the American Ballet. The group became the Metropolitan Opera's resident company (1935–38) but disbanded in 1941. In 1946 Kirstein and Balanchine founded the Ballet Society, from which emerged the New York City Ballet in 1948. Balanchine created over 150 works for the company, including *The Nutcracker* (1954), *Don Quixote* (1965), and *Jewels* (1967), and also choreographed musicals and operas. He collaborated closely with I. STRAVINSKY, setting over 30 works to the latter's music. Balanchine's work remains in the repertoires of many companies worldwide, and he is widely considered the greatest choreographer of the 20th century.

Balanchine.
©1983 MARTHA SWOPE

Balaton \'bȯ-lȯ-ˌtōn\, **Lake** Lake, Hungary. Southwest of Budapest, and the largest lake in central Europe, it covers 232 sq mi (601 sq km), with a maximum depth of about 35 ft (11 m). It contains two wildlife reserves. While agriculture remains important in the area, the tourist industry has become significant, and resorts, including Siófok and Balatonfüred, have been developed.

Balbo, Italo (1896–1940) Italian aviator and politician. He led the Fascist BLACKSHIRTS in the March on ROME (1922) and served under BENITO MUSSOLINI as general of militia (1923) and air minister (1929–33). Balbo developed Italian military and commercial aviation, and became famous for promoting mass international flights to demonstrate Italy's air power. He was appointed governor of Libya in 1933 and died when his plane was accidentally shot down by Italian guns over Tobruk.

Balboa, Vasco Núñez de (1475–1519) Spanish conquistador and explorer. In 1500 he explored the coast of modern Colombia, then settled in Hispaniola. Forced to flee creditors, he joined an expedition to assist a colony in Colombia. He persuaded the settlers to move across the Gulf of Urabá to Darién, where in 1511 they founded the first stable settlement on the South American continent. In 1513 he became the first European to see the Pacific Ocean and took possession of the Mar del Sur (South Sea) and adjacent lands for Spain. He became governor of the Mar del Sur and of the provinces of Panamá and Coiba but remained subject to a rival, Pedro Arias Dávila, or Pedrarias (1440?–1531). Fearing Balboa's influence, Pedrarias had him seized and charged with rebellion, treason, and other misdeeds. After a farcical trial, Balboa was beheaded.

Balch \'bȯlch\, **Emily Greene** (1867–1961) U.S. sociologist and peace activist. Born in Jamaica Plain, Mass., she studied at Bryn Mawr College and taught at Wellesley College from 1896. She founded a settlement house in Boston and served on state commissions on industrial relations (1908–9) and immigration (1913–14). She lost her professorship in 1918 because of her opposition to U.S. entry into World War I. In 1919, with JANE ADDAMS, she helped found the Women's International League for Peace and Freedom. In 1946 she shared the Nobel Peace Prize with John R. Mott (1865–1955).

bald cypress Either of two large SWAMP trees (*Taxodium distichum* and *T. ascendens;* family Taxodiaceae) of the southern U.S. that are related to the sequoias. The hard red wood of cypress is often used for roofing shingles. The so-called deciduous cypress family (see DECIDUOUS TREE) consists of 10 genera with 15 species of ornamental and timber EVERGREEN trees, native to eastern Asia, Tasmania, and North America. The leaves on a single tree may be scalelike, needlelike, or a mixture of both. Both male and female CONES are borne on the same tree. The Tasmanian cedar *(Athrotaxis),* Japanese cedar *(Cryptomeria japonica),* China fir *(Cunninghamia lanceolata),* umbrella pine *(Sciadopitys verticillata),* BIG TREE, REDWOOD, DAWN REDWOOD, and bald cypress are economically important timber trees in this family.

bald eagle Species of SEA EAGLE *(Haliaeetus leucocephalus)* that occurs inland, along rivers and large lakes. Strikingly handsome, it is the only EAGLE solely native to North America and has been the U.S. national bird since 1782. The adult, about 40 in. (1 m) long, is dark brown with white head and tail, a wingspan of 6.5 ft (2 m), and yellow beak, eyes, and feet. Bald eagles snatch fish from the water surface, rob OSPREY of fish, and eat carrion. They nest in lone trees, often on river islands. Though protected in the U.S. since 1940, the eagle population has been depleted by river pollution, pesticides, and loss of nesting sites.

Bald eagle (*Haliaeetus leucocephalus*).
ALEXANDER SPRUNT, IV

baldachin \'bȯl-də-kən\ Freestanding canopy of stone, wood, or metal over an altar or tomb. The Italian term *baldacchino* originally referred to brocaded material from Baghdad hung as a canopy over an altar or throne. The characteristic architectural form consists of four columns supporting ENTABLATURES, which carry miniature COLONNADES topped by a pyramidal or gabled roof. GIAN LORENZO BERNINI's famous bronze baldachin (1624–33) stands at ST. PETER'S BASILICA in Rome.

Baldachin, St. Peter's, Vatican City, by Gian Lorenzo Bernini, 1624–33.
SCALA—ART RESOURCE/EB INC.

Balder \'bȯl-dər, 'bäl-dər\ In Norse mythology, the just and beautiful son of ODIN and FRIGG. He could be harmed by nothing except mistletoe. Knowing he was invulnerable, the gods amused themselves by throwing things at him. Deceived by LOKI, the blind god Höd hurled mistletoe at Balder and killed him. The giantess Thökk, probably Loki in disguise, refused to weep the tears that would have released Balder from the underworld.

baldness *or* **alopecia** \ˌal-ə-'pē-shə\ Lack or loss of HAIR, either permanent (from destruction of hair follicles) or temporary (from short-term follicle damage). Male pattern baldness is inherited and affects up to 40% of men; treatments are transplanting of follicles from areas where hair still grows and application of drugs (e.g., minoxidil) to the scalp. Other causes of permanent baldness are skin diseases and injuries, inborn lack of hair development, and severe follicle injury. Temporary hair loss may follow high fever or come from X rays, drugs, malnutrition, or endocrine disorders. Alopecia areata, with sharply outlined patches of sudden complete baldness, is also usually temporary.

Baldovinetti \ˌbäl-dō-vē-'nāt-tē\, **Alesso** (c. 1425–1499) Italian artist active in Florence. Little is known of his early training, but his style shows the influence of Fra ANGELICO and DOMENICO VENEZIANO. His masterpiece, *The Nativity* (1460–62), a fresco in the church of the Santissima Annunziata, Florence, and a *Madonna and Child* (1460s) in the Louvre both depict views of the Arno River valley in the background; they are among the earliest European paintings of landscapes. He designed the mosaic decoration over LORENZO GHIBERTI's doors on the Baptistery in Florence (1453–55) and also produced designs for stained glass and intarsia.

"Madonna and Child," oil on canvas by Alesso Baldovinetti, c. 1465; in the Louvre, Paris.
GIRAUDON—ART RESOURCE/EB INC.

Baldung \'bäl-du̇ŋ\, **Hans** *or* **Hans Baldung Grien** \'grēn\ (1484–1545) German painter and graphic artist. He was assistant to ALBRECHT DURER in Nuremberg and was active in Strasbourg as official painter to the episcopate. He is best known for the high altar of the cathedral at Freiburg, where he lived 1512–17. His output was varied and extensive: religious paintings, allegories, mythologies, portraits, designs for stained glass, tapestry, and book illustration. His paintings are equaled in importance by his drawings, engravings, and woodcuts, frequently depicting the themes of the Dance of Death and Death and the Maiden. In his taste for the gruesome, Baldung is close in style and spirit to MATTHIAS GRUNEWALD.

Baldwin I (1172–1205) First Latin emperor of Constantinople (1204–5). Count of Flanders and Hainaut, he was a leader of the Fourth CRUSADE against the Byzantine Christians. He helped capture Constantinople and install a pro-Latin emperor (1203). When crusaders and their Venetian allies seized power, he was made emperor (1204) and recognized by the pope. He created a feudal government on the Western European model, granting Greek lands to his knights, but was defeated and executed by invading Bulgars.

Baldwin I *known as* **Baldwin of Boulogne** \bü-'lȯn-yə\ (1058?–1118) King of Jerusalem (1100–18). The son of a French count, he joined the First CRUSADE and gained control of EDESSA (now in Turkey) in 1098. In 1100 his brother Godfrey died in Jerusalem, and Baldwin was summoned by nobles to succeed him as king of the crusader state and defender of the Holy Sepulchre. He expanded the kingdom by conquering coastal cities such as Arsuf and Caesarea and built an administration that served for 200 years as the basis for Frankish rule in Syria and Palestine.

Baldwin II *known as* **Baldwin of Bourg** \'bürk\ (died 1131) King of Jerusalem (1118–31). A French nobleman, he joined the First CRUSADE and was made count of EDESSA (now in Turkey) by his cousin BALDWIN I in 1100. Captured by Seljuq Turks in 1104, he was ransomed four years later and reclaimed Edessa from the regent by force. He became king of Jerusalem in 1118 on the death of Baldwin I. He was held hostage by the Turks 1123–24. He later expanded his kingdom and attacked Damascus with the aid of the KNIGHTS OF MALTA and TEMPLARS. He arranged the marriage of his daughter Melisend to Fulk V of Anjou and made them his successors.

Baldwin II Porphyrogenitus \ˌpōr-fə-rō-'jen-ət-əs\ (1217–1273) Fifth and last Latin emperor of Constantinople (1228–61). The son of the third Latin emperor (Porphyrogenitus means "born to the purple," thus "of royal birth"), Baldwin inherited the throne on the death of his brother. Invasions by Greeks and Bulgars reduced the empire to the area around Constantinople, and Baldwin's empty treasury obliged him to travel twice to Western Europe to ask for aid. He sold sacred relics to LOUIS IX of France and broke up parts of the imperial palace for firewood. He lost the throne in 1261 when MICHAEL VIII PALAEOLOGUS captured Constantinople and restored Greek rule. Baldwin fled to Europe and later died in Sicily.

Baldwin IV *known as* **Baldwin the Leper** (1161–1185) King of Jerusalem (1174–85). He was crowned at age 13 on the death of his father, but the kingdom was ruled by a series of regents. Baldwin was afflicted with leprosy throughout his short life, which contributed to power struggles among the nobility. His defeat of SALADIN in 1177 led to a two-year truce, but in 1183 Saladin captured Aleppo and completed the encirclement of Jerusalem. Baldwin crowned his nephew king in 1183.

Baldwin, James (Arthur) (1924–1987) U.S. essayist, novelist, and playwright. He grew up in poverty in Harlem, New York City, and became a preacher while in his teens. After 1948 he lived alternately in France and the U.S. His semiautobiographical first novel, *Go Tell It on the Mountain* (1953), regarded as his finest, was followed by the essay collections *Notes of a Native Son* (1955) and *Nobody Knows My Name* (1961); the novels *Giovanni's Room* (1956), a story of homosexual life, and *Another Country* (1962); the long polemical essay *The Fire Next Time* (1963), prophesying widespread racial violence; and the play *Blues for Mister Charlie* (produced 1964). His eloquence and passion on the subject of race made him for years perhaps the country's most prominent black writer.

James Baldwin.
UPI

Baldwin, Robert (1804–1858) Canadian politician. Born in York (Toronto), he became a lawyer and held provincial political positions. In 1842–43 he and LOUIS HIPPOLYTE LAFONTAINE formed the first Liberal Party administration; when the Liberals returned to power in 1848, they were able to establish responsible, or cabinet, government. He resigned in 1851.

Baldwin, Roger (Nash) (1884–1981) U.S. civil-rights leader. Born in Wellesley, Mass., he taught sociology at Washington University (1906–9) in St. Louis, where he also was chief probation officer of the city's juvenile court and secretary of its Civic League. When the U.S. entered World War I, he directed the pacifist American Union Against Militarism, the predecessor of the American Civil Liberties Union (ACLU). As the ACLU's director (1920–50) and national chairman (1950–55), he made civil rights, once a leftist cause, a universal one.

Baldwin, Stanley *later* **Earl Baldwin (of Bewdley)** (1867–1947) British politician. After managing his family's diversified heavy industries, he became a Conservative Party member of the House of Commons (1908–37). He served as financial secretary of the treasury (1917–21) and president of the Board of Trade (1921–22), then was appointed prime minister (1923–24, 1924–1929, 1935–37). He proclaimed a state of emergency in the general strike of 1926 and later secured passage of the antiunion Trade Disputes Act. As prime minister after 1935, he began to strengthen the British military while showing little public concern about the aggressive policies of Germany and Italy. He was criticized for not protesting the Italian conquest of Ethiopia. In 1936 he procured the abdication of Edward VIII, whose desire to marry Wallis Simpson Baldwin felt threatened the prestige of the monarchy.

Stanley Baldwin, 1932.
BASSANO AND VANDYK

Balearic Islands \'ba-lē-'ar-ik\ *Spanish* **Islas Baleares** Archipelago, (pop., 1996 est.: 760,000), western Mediterranean Sea, constituting an autonomous community and province, Spain. It occupies an area of 1,936 sq mi (5,014 sq km); its capital is Palma. The most important islands are Majorca, Minorca, Ibiza, Formentera, and Cabrera. Long inhabited, the islands were ruled by Carthage in the 5th century BC, by Rome from c. 120 BC, and by the Byzantine empire from AD 534. Raided by the Arabs, the area was finally conquered in the 10th century by the Umayyad dynasty at Córdoba. It was reconquered by the Spanish and united with the kingdom of Aragon in 1344. Fought over in the 18th century by the Spanish, British, and French, the islands came under Spain in 1802. Their modern economy is fueled by tourism.

baleen whale \bə-'lēn, 'ba-ˌlēn\ Any of about 13 species of cetaceans in the suborder Mysticeti. They are distinguished by a specialized feeding structure, the baleen, which strains plankton and small crustaceans from the water. It consists of two horny plates attached to the roof of the mouth. Each plate (as long as 12 ft, or 3.6 m, in the right whale) is composed of parallel slats with fringes that mat together to form a sieve. Other baleen whales are the blue, fin, gray, humpback, and sei whales and the rorqual. Baleen was once used for corset stays and is still used in some industrial brushes.

Balenciaga \bäl-en-'thyäg-ə\, **Cristóbal** (1895–1972) Spanish-French fashion designer. He studied dressmaking as a child and was inspired to become a couturier by a visit to Paris. By age 20 he had his own firm in San Sebastián. In 1937 the Spanish Civil War drove him back to Paris, where his business flourished for the next 30 years. His fashion line featured sumptuous dresses and suits; in the 1950s he popularized the cape and flowing clothes without waistlines, and, in the 1960s, plastic rainwear.

Balfour, Arthur James *later* **Earl Balfour (of Whittingehame)** (1848–1930) British statesman. The nephew of Marquess of Salisbury, Balfour served in Parliament 1874–1911, and in his uncle's government as secretary for Ireland 1887–91. From 1891 he was the Conservative Party's leader in Parliament and succeeded his uncle as prime minister (1902–5). He helped form the Entente Cordiale (1904). His most famous action came in 1917 when, as foreign secretary (1916–19), he wrote the so-called Balfour Declaration, which expressed official British approval of Zionism. He served as lord president of the council (1919–22, 1925–29) and drafted the Balfour Report (1926), which defined relations between Britain and the dominions expressed in the Statute of Westminster.

Arthur James Balfour, c. 1900.
BASSANO AND VANDYK

Balfour Declaration (November 2, 1917) Statement issued by the British foreign secretary, Arthur James Balfour, in a letter to Lionel Walter Rothschild (1868–1937), a leader of British Jewry, as urged by the Russian Jewish Zionist leaders Chaim Weizmann and Nahum Sokolow (1861–1936). The Declaration promised the establishment of a homeland for the Jewish people in Palestine that would not disturb the non-Jewish groups already residing there. The British anticipated gaining a mandate over Palestine after World War I and hoped to win over Jewish public opinion to the side of the Allies. They also hoped that pro-British settlers would help protect the approaches to the Suez Canal.

Bali \'bä-lē, 'ba-lē\ Island (pop., 1995 est.: 2,900,000), Indonesia. Located in the Lesser Sunda Islands, off the eastern coast of Java, it constitutes, with minor adjacent islands, a province of Indonesia. The main towns are Singaraja, and Denpasar, the provincial capital. The island is mountainous; its highest peak is Mount Agung (10,308 ft, or 3,142 m). Colonized by India in early times and supplemented by emigrés from Java in the 16th century, Bali is the remaining stronghold of Hinduism in the Indonesian archipelago. Visited by the Dutch in the late 16th century, it only came under Dutch rule in the late 19th century. It was occupied by the Japanese in World War II. It became part of Indonesia in 1950. Tourism is increasingly important to its modern economy.

Balinese People of the island of Bali, Indonesia. They differ from other Indonesians in adhering to the Hindu religion, though their culture has been heavily influenced by the Javanese. In Balinese villages each family lives in its own compound, surrounded by earthen or stone walls; all villages have temples and an assembly hall. Balinese religion fuses Hindu Saivism with Buddhism, ancestor cults, and belief in spirits and magic. Marriage is often limited to members of the same kinship organization, and family relationships are reckoned through the male line.

Balkan League \'bȯl-kən\ (1912–13) Alliance of Bulgaria, Serbia, Greece, and Montenegro, which fought the first Balkan War against the Ottoman empire. Ostensibly created to limit Austrian power in the Balkans, the league was actually formed at the instigation of Russia to expel the Turks from the Balkans. The league disintegrated when its members quarreled over the division of territorial spoils after their victory in the first Balkan War.

Balkan Mountains *Bulgarian* **Stara Planina** \'stä-rä-ˌplä-nē-'nä\ Mountain range, eastern Europe. It extends east to west across central Bulgaria from the Yugoslav border to the Black Sea; the highest point is Botev Peak, at 7,793 ft (2,375 m). The range forms the major divide between the Danube River in the north and the Maritsa River in the south. It is crossed by about 20 passes (notably Shipka Pass), several railway lines, and the Iskur River.

Balkan Peninsula Peninsula, southeastern Europe. Located between the Adriatic Sea, the Mediterranean Sea, and the Aegean and Black seas, it contains many countries, including Slovenia, Croatia, Bosnia and Herzegovina, Macedonia, Yugoslavia, Romania, Bulgaria, Albania, Greece, and Turkey in Europe. From 168 BC to AD 107, part of the area was incorporated into Roman provinces, including Epirus, Moesia, Pannonia, Thrace, and Dacia. It was subsequently settled by Slavic invaders, Serbs, Croats, Slovenes, and Slavonized Bulgars, the last of whom were pushed into the Balkan region in the 6th century. It was gradually organized into kingdoms, many of which were overrun by the Ottoman Turks in the 14th–15th century. The factional strife that occurred there from the early 20th century, provoking the continual breakups and regroupings of different states, introduced the word *balkanize* into English.

Balkan Wars (1912–13) Two military conflicts that deprived the Ottoman empire of almost all its remaining territory in Europe. In the First Balkan War, the BALKAN LEAGUE defeated the OTTOMAN empire, which, under the terms of the peace treaty (1913), lost Macedonia and Albania. The Second Balkan War broke out after Serbia, Greece, and Romania quarreled with Bulgaria over the division of their joint conquests in Macedonia. Bulgaria was defeated, and Greece and Serbia divided up most of Macedonia between themselves. The wars heightened tensions in the Balkans and helped spark World War I.

Balkhash, Lake *or* **Lake Balqash** \'bäl-'käsh\ Lake, eastern Kazakhstan. It is about 375 mi (600 km) long, with a maximum depth of 85 ft (26 m). Its chief feeder is the Ili River, which enters at the southeast in a wide delta. Harsh climate affects its size greatly; its area has varied from about 6,000 sq mi (15,500 sq km) to 7,300 sq mi (19,000 sq km) depending on rainfall. It is frozen from November to March. In recent decades, damming and industrial pollution have caused severe ecological damage.

Ball, Lucille (Désirée) (1911–1989) U.S. actress and television comedy star. Born in Jamestown, N.Y., she studied drama and worked as a model, playing minor roles in films from 1933. She starred in a comedy radio series from 1947. With her bandleader husband, Desi Arnaz (1917–1986), she created the very successful television comedy series *I Love Lucy* (1951–57), and later the *Lucy-Desi Comedy Hour* (1957–60). After their divorce in 1960, Ball appeared in *The Lucy Show* (1962–68) and *Here's Lucy* (1968–74). With her red hair and rasping voice and a comic persona alternately brassy and feminine, she was the preeminent female star of the early decades of television.

Lucille Ball and Desi Arnaz.
PHOTOFEST

ball bearing One of the two types of rolling, or antifriction, BEARINGS (the other is the ROLLER BEARING). Its function is to connect two machine members that move relative to one another so that the frictional resistance to motion is minimal. In many applications, one of the members is a rotating shaft and the other a fixed housing. Each ball bearing has three main parts: two grooved, ringlike races and a number of balls. The balls fill the space between the two races and roll with negligible FRICTION in the grooves. The balls may be loosely restrained and separated by means of a retainer or cage.

ballad Form of short narrative folk song. Its distinctive style crystallized in Europe in the late Middle Ages as part of the oral tradition and has been preserved as a musical and literary form. The oral form has persisted as the folk ballad, and the written, literary ballad evolved from the oral tradition. The folk ballad typically tells a compact tale with deliberate starkness, using devices such as repetition to heighten effects. The modern literary ballad (e.g., those by W. H. AUDEN, BERTOLT BRECHT, and ELIZABETH BISHOP) recalls in its rhythmic and narrative elements the traditions of folk balladry.

ballad opera English 18th-century comic opera in which songs and musical interludes, usually consisting of existing popular tunes or opera melodies with new words, are interspersed with spoken dialogue. The first ballad opera, *The Beggar's Opera* (1728), by JOHN GAY and J. C. Pepusch (1667–1752), was a sharply satirical work that became wildly popular and led to numerous similar works. Ballad opera led directly to the German SINGSPIEL and can be seen as the source of the modern MUSICAL.

ballade \bä-'läd\ One of several FORMES FIXES in French lyric poetry and song, cultivated particularly in the 14th–15th centuries. It consists of three stanzas, all having the same rhyme scheme and identical final refrain lines, and a shortened final dedicatory stanza. The texts were often solemn and formal, containing elaborate symbolism and classical references. Though present in the poetry of many ages and regions, the ballade in its purest form was found only in France and England. Its precursors can be found in the songs of the TROUBADOURS and TROUVÈRES.

Ballard \'bal-ərd\, **J(ames) G(raham)** (born 1930) British (Chinese-born) writer. Ballard spent four years of his childhood in a Japanese prison camp, an experience described in *Empire of the Sun* (1984; film, 1987). His science fiction is often set in ecologically unbalanced landscapes caused by decadent technological excess. His apocalyptic novels, often shockingly violent, include *Crash* (1973; film, 1996), *Concrete Island* (1974), and *High Rise* (1975). His later works include the short-story collection *War Fever* (1990) and the novels *The Kindness of Women* (1991) and *Cocaine Nights* (1998).

Ballard \'ba-lərd\, **Robert D(uane)** (born 1942) U.S. oceanographer and marine geologist. Born in Wichita, Kan., he grew up near San Diego, Cal. As a marine scientist at the Woods Hole (Mass.) Oceanographic Research Institution, he pioneered the use of deep-diving submersibles, participated in the first manned exploration of the MID-ATLANTIC RIDGE, and discovered warm water springs and their unusual animal communities in the Galápagos Rift. He is best known for his dramatic discovery of the wreck of the *TITANIC* in 1985. Since then he has gone on to discover ships lost in battle during World War II.

Ballesteros \,bal-əs-'ter-ōs\, **Seve(riano)** (born 1957) Spanish golfer. One of four professional golfing brothers, he repeatedly won the British Open (1979, 1984, 1988) and the Masters (1980, 1983), and captained the 1997 European Ryder Cup team to victory. Known for his flamboyant and imaginative style of play, by the late 1990s he had accumulated more than 70 wins in international tournaments.

ballet Theatrical dance in which a formal academic technique (the *danse d'école*) is combined with music, costume, and stage scenery. Developed from court productions of the Renaissance, ballet was renewed under Louis XIV, who established France's Académie Royale de Danse in 1661, where Pierre Beauchamp developed the five BALLET POSITIONS. Early ballets were often accompanied by singing and were often incorporated into opera-ballets by such composers as J.-B. LULLY. In the 18th century J.-G. NOVERRE and GASPARO ANGIOLINI separately developed the dramatic ballet *(ballet d'action)* to tell a story through dance steps and mime, a reform echoed in C.W. GLUCK's music. Significant developments in the early 19th century included pointe work (balance on the extreme tip of the toe) and the emergence of the prima ballerina, exemplified by MARIE TAGLIONI and FANNY ELSSLER. In the late 19th and early 20th century Russia became the center of ballet production and performance, through such innovators as SERGEY DIAGHILEV, ANNA PAVLOVA, VASLAV NIJINSKY, MARIUS PETIPA, and MICHEL FOKINE; great ballets were composed by P. TCHAIKOVSKY and I. STRAVINSKY. Since then, ballet schools

Arabesque executed by Natalya Bessmertnova, with Nikolay Fadeychev, of the Bolshoi Ballet; *Swan Lake.*
NOVOSTI–SOVFOTO

in Great Britain and the U.S. have elevated ballet in those countries to Russia's level and greatly increased its audience. See also AMERICAN BALLET THEATRE, BALLET RUSSE DE MONTE CARLO, BALLETS RUSSES, BOLSHOI BALLET, NEW YORK CITY BALLET, ROYAL BALLET.

ballet position Any of the five positions of the feet fundamental to all classical BALLET. First codified by Pierre Beauchamp (1636–1705) in 1680, the positions form the base from which a dancer achieves stability or aplomb, the basic law of ballet. Fundamental to all the positions is the turnout, or rotation of the dancer's legs out from the hips, which creates a firm basis for movement in any direction. Various positions of the arms and hands *(port de bras)* complete the figures.

Ballet Russe de Monte Carlo \bá-lā-'rūes-də-mōⁿ-tā-'kär-lō\ Ballet company formed in Monte Carlo in 1932. The name derived from SERGEY DIAGHILEV'S BALLETS RUSSES, which dissolved after his death in 1929. Under René Blum and Col. Wassili de Basil, the company presented works by LEONID MASSINE and GEORGE BALANCHINE and featured ALEXANDRA DANILOVA, ANDRE EGLEVSKY, and David Lichine. In 1938 clashes split the company into two groups: the Original Ballet Russe, led by de Basil, which toured internationally before dissolving in 1947; and the Ballet Russe de Monte Carlo, led by Massine, which toured mainly in the U.S. with Danilova, ALICIA MARKOVA, and MARIA TALLCHIEF until 1963.

Ballets Russes \bá-lā-'rūes\ Ballet company founded in Paris in 1909 by SERGEY DIAGHILEV. Considered the source of modern ballet, the company employed the most outstanding creative talent of the period. Its choreographers included MICHEL FOKINE, LEONID MASSINE, BRONISLAVA NIJINSKA, and GEORGE BALANCHINE, and among its dancers were YEKATERINA GELTZER, TAMARA KARSAVINA, and VASLAV NIJINSKY. Music was commissioned from such composers as I. STRAVINSKY, M. RAVEL, D. MILHAUD, S. PROKOFIEV, and C. DEBUSSY, and ballets featured stage designs by ALEXANDRE BENOIS, PABLO PICASSO, GEORGES ROUAULT, HENRI MATISSE, and ANDRE DERAIN. Among its many influential productions were *Les sylphides* (1909), *The Firebird* (1910), *The Rite of Spring* (1913), *Parade* (1917), *Les noces* (1923), and *The Prodigal Son* (1929). The avant-garde company revolutionized 20th-century ballet, and its influence lasted well beyond its cessation after Diaghilev's death in 1929.

Ballinger \'bal-in-jər\, **Richard A(chilles)** (1858–1922) U.S. secretary of the interior (1909–11). Born in Boonesboro, Iowa, he moved to Washington and served as the reform mayor of Seattle (1904–6) before being appointed federal commissioner of the land office. As secretary of the interior, he sought to make public resources more available for private exploitation. Implicated in a fraudulent Alaskan land-claims scheme, he was cleared after a congressional investigation but resigned in 1911. The episode split the Republicans between conservatives led by Pres. WILLIAM H. TAFT and progressives loyal to THEODORE ROOSEVELT.

Balliol, John de See JOHN (SCOTLAND)

ballista \bə-'lis-tə\ Ancient missile launcher designed to hurl long arrows or heavy balls. The Greek version was basically a huge CROSSBOW fastened to a mount. The Roman ballista was powered by torsion derived from two thick skeins of twisted cords through which were thrust two separate arms joined at their ends by the cord that propelled the missile. The largest could accurately hurl 60-lb (27-kg) weights up to about 500 yards (450 m).

ballistics Science of propulsion, flight, and impact of projectiles. Internal ballistics deals with propulsion of projectiles, such as within the barrel of a gun or at a rocket launch. Guns and rocket engines convert CHEMICAL ENERGY of propellants into KINETIC ENERGY of projectiles. External ballistics deals with projectile flight. The trajectory, or path, of a projectile is subject to the forces of gravity (see GRAVITATION), DRAG, and LIFT. Terminal ballistics deals with the impact of projectiles on a target. Wound ballistics deals with the mechanisms and medical implications of trauma caused by bullets and explosively driven fragments, such as shrapnel.

balloon Large airtight bag filled with hot air or a lighter-than-air gas such as HELIUM or HYDROGEN that can rise and float in the atmosphere. Experimental attempts may have begun by 1709, but not until 1783 did J.-M. and J.-É. MONTGOLFIER develop a fabric-bag balloon that would rise when filled with hot air. Balloons provided military aerial observation sites in the 19th century and were used in the 20th century by scientists such as AUGUSTE PICCARD to gather high-altitude data. The first round-the-world balloon flight was achieved in 1999 by Bertrand Piccard and Brian Jones. See also AIRSHIP.

ballooning Riding of a BALLOON in competition or for recreation. Sport ballooning began in the early 20th century and became popular in the 1960s. The balloons used are of lightweight synthetic materials (e.g., polyester coated in aluminized mylar) and are filled with hot air or lighter-than-air gas. Balloon races often involve tasks such as changing elevations or landing on or near a target. Competitions are regulated by the International Aeronautical Federation. The first transatlantic, transcontinental, and transpacific balloon flights were achieved in 1978, 1980, and 1981, respectively. In 1997–98 international teams began competing to become the first to balloon around the world, a feat finally accomplished in 1999 by the Swiss psychiatrist Bertrand Piccard and his British copilot Brian Jones, who spent 19 days in the air.

Ballot Act (1872) British law that introduced the secret ballot for all parliamentary and municipal elections. The secret ballot was also called the Australian ballot, because it was first used in Australian elections (1856). The British law, which was designed to protect voters from bribery and coercion, was one of the important achievements of WILLIAM E. GLADSTONE's first administration.

ballot initiative See REFERENDUM AND INITIATIVE

ballroom dance European and American social dancing performed by couples. It includes standard dances such as the fox-trot, WALTZ, POLKA, TANGO, rumba, CHARLESTON, JITTERBUG, and MERENGUE. Ballroom dance became popularized by VERNON AND IRENE CASTLE, FRED ASTAIRE, and later by Arthur Murray (1895–1991), who established ballroom dance studios throughout the U.S. Ballroom dance contests, especially popular in Europe, feature both amateur and professional dancers.

Ballycastle Town (pop., 1981: 3,000), district seat of MOYLE, Northern Ireland. It is situated along Ballycastle Bay, opposite an island where Scotland's king ROBERT I is said to have hidden from enemies in a cave. It is a market center, fishing harbor, and resort.

Ballymena \,ba-lē-'mē-nə\ District (pop., 1995 est.: 58,000), Northern Ireland. Established in 1973, it is an agricultural and farming area. The Antrim Mountains, which reach a height of 1,430 ft (435 m), traverse the eastern part of the district, sloping toward the River MAIN valley. Ballymena town (pop., 1985 est.: 25,000), the district seat, is a marketing center for the surrounding area; it has long been known for its linen and woolen production.

Ballymoney \,ba-lē-'mə-nē\ District (pop., 1995 est.: 25,000), Northern Ireland. Established in 1973, it is an agricultural area. The town of Ballymoney (pop., 1981: 6,000), the district seat, was the birthplace of James McKinley, the father of U.S. president WILLIAM MCKINLEY.

balm Any of several fragrant herbs of the MINT family, particularly *Melissa officinalis* (balm gentle, or lemon balm), cultivated in temperate climates for its fragrant leaves, which are used as a scent in perfumes and as a flavoring. The name is also applied to *Melittis melissophyllum* (bastard balm), *Monarda didyma* (BERGAMOT, or BEE BALM), *Collinsonia canadensis* (horse balm), *Glecoma hederacea* and *Satureja (Calamintha) nepeta* (field balm), and *Molucella laevis* (Molucca balm, or bells of Ireland), as well as to aromatic substances from species of *Commiphora* (trees and shrubs of the incense-tree family).

Balmain \bál-'maⁿ\, **Pierre (-Alexandre-Claudius)** (1914–1982) French fashion designer. He gave up architectural studies to become a designer in 1934. He worked briefly with CHRISTIAN DIOR, who became his rival after World War II. The House of Balmain produced elegant evening wear for clients who included film stars and royalty. He later opened branches in New York and Caracas and expanded into perfume and accessories.

Balochis See BALUCHIS

Balochistan See BALUCHISTAN

Balqash, Lake See Lake BALKHASH

balsa Tree *(Ochroma pyramidale,* or *O. lagopus)* of the bombax family (Bombacaceae), native to tropical South America and noted for its extremely light wood, which resembles clear white pine or BASSWOOD. Because of its buoyancy (about twice that of cork), balsa is well adapted for making floats for lifelines and life preservers. Its resiliency makes it an excellent shock-absorbing packing material. Its insulating properties make it a good lining material for incubators, refrigerators, and cold-storage rooms. Because it combines lightness and high insulating power, it is a valuable construction material for transportation containers for solidified carbon dioxide. It is also used in the construction of airplane passenger compartments and in model airplanes and boats.

balsam Aromatic resinous substance that flows from a plant, either spontaneously or from an incision, and is used chiefly in medicinal preparations. Some of the more aromatic varieties are used in incense. Balsam of Peru, a fragrant, thick, deep brown or black fluid used in perfumes, is a true balsam, from a lofty leguminous tree, *Myroxylon pereirae,* native to and introduced into Sri Lanka. Balsam of Tolu (Colombia) is used in perfumes and in cough syrups and lozenges; it hardens with age. Canada balsam and Mecca balsam are not true balsams.

balsam poplar North American POPLAR *(Populus balsamifera),* native from Labrador to Alaska and across the extreme northern U.S. Often cultivated as a shade tree, it has buds thickly coated with an aromatic resin that is used to make cough syrups. It grows best in northwestern Canada.

Balthus \bäl-'tēs\ *orig.* **Balthazar Klossowski** (1908–2001) French painter. Born in Paris to Polish parents, he was considered a child prodigy and was encouraged by family friends PIERRE BONNARD and ANDRÉ DERAIN. Without formal training, he supported himself through commissions for stage sets and portraits. He had his first one-man show in 1934. His paintings are characterized by large, mysterious interiors and austere, muted landscapes peopled with isolated, pensive adolescent girls. From 1961 to 1977 he served as director of the French Academy in Rome. His disturbing and erotic images, including the scandalous *The Guitar Lesson,* and his carefully cultivated persona made him an international cult figure.

Baltic languages Branch of the INDO-EUROPEAN LANGUAGE family whose three attested languages, LITHUANIAN, LATVIAN, and Old Prussian, were or are spoken along the eastern and southeastern shore and hinterlands of the Baltic Sea. Medieval chronicles report four other Baltic-speaking peoples in the region, though by the 16th century these peoples had been completely assimilated. Baltic has certain striking features in common with SLAVIC LANGUAGES, including the development of the syllabic sonorants, similarities in the accentuation system for nouns, the rise of the category of definiteness in adjectives, and some common vocabulary, though the deep divisions within Baltic itself, among other factors, make the hypothesis of a common Balto-Slavic protolanguage difficult to defend.

Baltic religion Ancient beliefs and practices of the Balts of Eastern Europe. They are believed to give evidence of a common source with VEDIC and IRANIAN RELIGION. The most important Baltic divinities were sky gods: DIEVS (the sky), Perkons (the thunderer), SAULE (sun goddess), and Meness (moon god). A forest divinity, the Mother of the Forest, was common to all Baltic peoples and was differentiated into goddesses that personified various aspects of nature. Destiny or luck was personified as the goddess Laima, who determined a person's fate at the moment of birth. The dead were thought to revisit the world as good or evil spirits; evil was also done by the devil, Velns, and by a werewolf-like creature known as Vilkacis or Vilkatas. The structure of the world, with the WORLD TREE at its center, and the enmity between Saule and Meness are important themes. Festivals marked the summer solstice, the harvest, marriages, and funerals. Worship was conducted at holy groves and small hills; excavations have also revealed circular wooden temples.

Baltic Sea Sea, northern Europe. An arm of the Atlantic Ocean, connecting with the North Sea, it is 1,056 mi (1,699 km) long, covers an area of 163,050 sq mi (422,300 sq km), and has a maximum depth of 1,539 ft (469 m). It receives the VISTULA and ODER rivers and many other rivers. It is enclosed by Denmark, Sweden, Finland, Estonia, Latvia, Lithuania, Poland, and Germany. It has two large arms, the Gulf of BOTHNIA and the Gulf of FINLAND. The modifying effect of the North Atlantic Current is scarcely felt; its waters contain only about one-fourth as much salt as the oceans, and it freezes readily.

Baltic States Republics of Lithuania, Latvia, and Estonia, situated on the eastern shore of the BALTIC SEA. The name has sometimes been used to include Finland and Poland. They were created as independent states in 1917 from the Baltic provinces of Russia, the city of Kovno, and part of the Polish department of Wilno (later Lithuania). With the aid of German and Allied forces, the Baltic states repelled a BOLSHEVIK invasion in 1919. In 1940 they were forcibly occupied by the Soviet Union and incorporated as constituent republics. In 1944 Soviet troops recovered the territory overrun by German forces in 1941. The Baltic states gained independence on the breakup of the Soviet Union in 1991.

Baltimore City (pop., 1996 est.: 675,000), northern central Maryland. Located at the head of the Patapsco River estuary, 15 mi (24 km) above CHESAPEAKE BAY, it is Maryland's largest city and economic hub. Established in 1729, it was named after the Irish barony of Baltimore (seat of the Calvert family, proprietors of the colony of Maryland). It became the first U.S. Roman Catholic diocese in 1789. In 1827 the nation's first railroad began operations here. In World War I, Baltimore began to develop industrially, and it has since become a major seaport.

Baltimore, David (born 1938) U.S. virologist. Born in New York City, he received his doctorate from the Rockefeller Institute. He and Howard Temin (1934–1994), working independently, discovered an enzyme that synthesizes DNA from RNA, the reverse of the usual process. This enzyme, reverse transcriptase, has become an invaluable tool in recombinant-DNA technology. The research of Baltimore, Temin, and RENATO DULBECCO helped illuminate the role of viruses in cancer; the three men shared a Nobel Prize in 1975. In 1990 Baltimore became president of Rockefeller University; in 1997 he became president of the California Institute of Technology.

Baltimore and Ohio Railroad (B&O) First steam-operated railway in the U.S. to be chartered as a common carrier of freight and passengers (1827). The B&O was established by Baltimore merchants to foster trade with the West. By 1852 the railroad extended to Wheeling, Va. (now W.V.), and in the next two decades it reached Chicago and St. Louis. The B&O's long-distance passenger trains were discontinued in 1971 after AMTRAK was established, but the company (now part of CSX Corp.) still runs limited commuter service and hauls freight.

Baltimore Sun Daily newspaper published in Baltimore. It was begun as a four-page penny tabloid in 1837 by Arunah Shepherdson Abell, a journeyman printer from Rhode Island. Known through much of its history for its coverage of national and international news, the paper was run by Abell's family until 1910, when control passed to a group of Baltimore businessmen, including H. Crawford Black. Members of Black's family were chairmen of the board until 1984. In 1986 the *Sun* was acquired by the Times Mirror Company. H.L. MENCKEN was for years prominently associated with the paper.

Baluba See LUBA

Baluchis \bə-'lü-chēz\ *or* **Balochis** \bə-'lō-chēz\ Group of tribes speaking the Baluchi language and inhabiting the province of BALUCHISTAN in Pakistan and neighboring areas of Iran, Afghanistan, Bahrain, and the Punjab (India). Some 70% of the total Baluchi population live in Pakistan, where they are divided into two groups, the Sulaimani and the Makrani. They probably came originally from the Iranian plateau, and are mentioned in 10th-century Arabic chronicles. Traditional Baluchis are nomads, but settled agricultural existence is becoming more common. They raise camels and other livestock and engage in carpet making and embroidery.

Baluchistan \bə-ˌlü-chi-'stän\ *or* **Balochistan** \bə-ˌlō-chi-'stän\ Province (pop., 1983 est.: 4,611,000), southwestern Pakistan. Its capital is Quetta (pop., 1981: 286,000). Its landscape includes mountains, notably the SULAIMAN and Kithar ranges; barren, flat plains; arid desert; and marshy swamps. In ancient times, it was part of GEDROSIA. ALEXANDER THE GREAT traversed it in 325 BC. It was included in the Bactrian kingdom, then was ruled by Arabs in the 7th–10th century AD. It was ruled by Persia for centuries, with the exception of a period when it belonged to the Mughal empire (1594–1638). It became a British dependency in 1876 and a British province of India in 1887. It was made part of Pakistan in 1947–48 and was designated a separate province in 1970. Wheat, sorghum, and rice are staple crops; industries include cotton and woolen manufacturing.

Balzac \bäl-'zak\, **Honoré de** *orig.* **Honoré Balssa** (1799–1850) French writer. Born in Tours, he began working as a clerk in Paris around age 16. An early attempt at a business career left him with huge debts, and for decades he toiled incessantly to improve his worsening financial condition. In 1829 his novels and stories began to achieve some success, and his early masterpieces soon followed. In a vast series he collectively called *The Human Comedy*, eventually numbering some 90 novels and novellas, he sought to produce a comprehensive picture of contemporary society by presenting all the varieties of human nature. Among his masterpieces are *Eugénie Grandet* (1833), *Père Goriot* (1835), *Lost Illusions* (1837–43), *A Harlot High and Low* (1843–47), and *Cousin Bette* (1846). His novels are notable for their great narrative drive, their large casts of vital and diverse characters, and their obsessive interest in and examination of virtually all spheres of life. His best-known story collection is his *Droll Stories* (3 vols., 1832–37). His tumultuous life was one of mounting debts and almost incessant toil, with frequent bouts of writing feverishly for 15 hours at a stretch (his death has been attributed to overwork and excessive coffee consumption). He is generally considered the major early influence on REALISM, or NATURALISM, in the novel and one of the greatest fiction writers of all time.

Honoré de Balzac, daguerreotype, 1848.

J.E. BULLOZ

Bamako \'bä-mä-ˌkō\ City (metro. area pop., 1995 est.: 800,000), capital of Mali. Located in southwestern Mali on the NIGER RIVER, it was a settlement of a few hundred inhabitants when it was occupied for the French in 1880. It became the capital of the former colony of French Sudan in 1908. Now spanning both sides of the river, it has several colleges and most of Mali's industrial enterprises. The city more than tripled in size in the 1960s, largely because of rural migration from drought-stricken areas of the countryside.

Bambara \bam-'bär-ə\ People of the upper Niger region of Mali who speak a MANDE LANGUAGE of the NIGER-CONGO family. Numbering 3.1 million, the Bambara have their own writing system and are noted for their sculpture in wood and metal. In the 17th–18th century the Bambara developed two separate empires, one based in Ségou (and including TIMBUKTU) and the other in Kaarta.

bambocciati \ˌbȧm-bō-'chät-ē\ (Italian: "childishnesses") Small, anecdotal paintings of everyday life made in Rome in the mid-17th century. The genre's originator and most noteworthy exponent was the Dutch painter Pieter van Laer (1599–1642); the word derives from his nickname, Il Bamboccio ("Little Clumsy One," reflecting his physical deformity). Van Laer arrived in Rome from Haarlem c. 1625 and influenced various other northern European painters active in Rome. Their images depicting the lower classes in humorous or grotesque ways were condemned by the leading critics and painters. The *bamboccianti* (painters of *bambocciati*) influenced the Dutch genre painters ADRIAEN BROUWER and ADRIAEN VAN OSTADE.

bamboo Any of the tall, treelike GRASSES found in tropical and subtropical to mild temperate regions that make up the subfamily Bambusoideae, family Poaceae (or Gramineae). Bamboos are giant, fast-growing grasses with woody stems. A few species of the genus *Arundinaria* are native to the southern U.S., where they form dense canebrakes along riverbanks and in marshy areas. The woody, hollow aerial stems grow in branching clusters from a thick RHIZOME, often forming a dense undergrowth that excludes other plants. All parts of the bamboo are used, for purposes including food, livestock fodder, fine-quality paper, construction materials, and medicines, and as ornamentals in landscape gardens.

banana Fruit of the genus *Musa* (family Musaceae), a gigantic herbaceous plant spread by RHIZOMES, and one of the most important food crops of the world. The banana is consumed extensively throughout the tropics, where it is grown, and is valued in the temperate zone for its flavor, nutritional value, and constant availability. Hundreds of varieties are cultivated. Perhaps the most important species is the common banana, *M. sapientum*. The ripe fruit is high in carbohydrates (mainly sugar), potassium, and vitamins C and A, and low in protein and fat. Though usually eaten fresh, bananas may also be cooked. The U.S. imports more bananas than does any other country. See also PLANTAIN.

Banbridge District (pop., 1995 est.: 37,000), Northern Ireland, established in 1973. The area includes the Legananny Hills, which reach an altitude of 1,745 ft (532 m) in eastern Banbridge district, and slope southwestward to lowlands that are bisected by the River BANN. Located on the Bann, Banbridge town (pop., 1981: 10,000), the district seat, was established in 1712. It is the main agricultural and population center of the region.

Banco, Nanni di See NANNI DI BANCO

Bancroft, George (1800–1891) U.S. historian. Born in Worcester, Mass., he was educated at Harvard and several German universities and held such political posts as minister to England (1846–49), Prussia (1867–71), and the German empire (1871–74). He was the first scholar to plan a comprehensive study of the U.S. from the colonial days through the end of the Revolutionary War. His 10-volume *History of the United States* (1834–40, 1852–74) reflected his belief that the U.S. represented humanity's closest approximation yet to the perfect state and earned him his reputation as the "father of U.S. history."

George Bancroft, photograph by Mathew Brady.

BY COURTESY OF THE LIBRARY OF CONGRESS, WASHINGTON, D.C.

band Type of human social organization consisting of a small number of nuclear families (see FAMILY) or related subgroups who are loosely organized for purposes of subsistence or security. Bands may be integrated into a larger community or TRIBE. They generally exist in sparsely populated areas and possess relatively simple technologies; their habitats range from the desert (AUSTRALIAN ABORIGINES) to the African rain forest (MBUTI, Aka) to the northern tundra (Kaska Indians). Bands may occasionally coalesce for broader community ceremonies, hunting, or warfare. See also HUNTING AND GATHERING SOCIETIES, SOCIOCULTURAL EVOLUTION.

band Musical ensemble that generally excludes STRINGED INSTRUMENTS. Ensembles of WOODWIND, BRASS, and PERCUSSION instruments originated in 15th-century Germany, taking on particularly a military role; these spread to France, Britain, and eventually the New World. In the 15th–18th century, many European towns had town musicians, or waits, who performed especially for ceremonial occasions in wind bands often consisting primarily of SHAWMS and sackbuts (trombones). In the 18th–19th century, the English amateur brass band, largely consisting of the many newly developed brass instruments, took on the important nonmilitary function of representing organizations of all kinds. In America, P. GILMORE's virtuoso band became famous in the mid-19th century; his greatest successor, J.P. SOUSA, bequeathed a repertory of marches that has remained very popular. The "big band," under such leaders as DUKE ELLINGTON and COUNT BASIE, was central to American popular music in the 1930s and '40s. In the rock band, unlike most other bands, stringed instruments (electric guitars and electric bass) are paramount.

band theory In chemistry and physics, a theoretical model describing the states of ELECTRONS in solid materials, which can have energy values only within certain specific ranges, called bands. Ranges of energy between two allowed bands are called forbidden bands. As electrons in an atom move from one energy level to another, so can electrons in a solid move from an energy level in one band to another in the same band or in another band. The band theory accounts for many of the electrical and thermal properties of solids and forms the basis of the technology of devices such as SEMICONDUCTORS, heating elements, and capacitors (see CAPACITANCE).

Banda, Hastings (Kamuzu) (1902?–1997) First president of Malawi (1963–94). Banda became involved in politics when white settlers demanded the federation of Nyasaland (later Malawi) and the Rhodesias in 1949. In the 1950s he toured the country making anti-federation speeches, for which he was imprisoned by British colonial officials. In 1963, when the federation was dissolved, he became prime minister. He concentrated on building his country's infrastructure and increasing agricultural productivity. Declared president for life in 1971, his rule became increasingly autocratic and austere. He was voted out of office in 1994.

Bandama River \bän-'dä-mä\ River, central Ivory Coast. The longest and commercially most important river in the Ivory Coast, it and its tributaries drain half the country's surface area. It rises in the highlands and flows southward 497 mi (800 km) to enter the Gulf of GUINEA and the Taga Lagoon. A major hydroelectric plant is sited at Kossou.

Bandar Seri Begawan \'bän-där-'ser-ē-be-'gä-wän\ *formerly* **Brunei** Town (pop., 1991: 22,000; metro area population 1999 est.: 85,000), capital of Brunei. Lying along the Brunei River near its mouth on Brunei Bay, it is a trade center and river port. Heavily damaged during World War II, it was largely rebuilt; newer buildings include the largest mosque in East Asia.

Bandaranaike \,bən-də-rə-'nī-kə\, **S(olomon) W(est) R(idgeway) D(ias)** (1899–1959) Statesman and prime minister of Ceylon (present-day Sri Lanka) 1956–59. Educated at Oxford University, he became a prominent member of Ceylon's Western-oriented United National Party. In 1952 he founded the nationalist Sri Lanka Freedom Party, becoming the leader of the opposition in the legislature. He later formed an alliance of four nationalist-socialist parties that swept elections in 1956 and made him prime minister. Under Bandaranaike, Sinhalese replaced English as the country's official language, Buddhism (the majority religion) was given a prominent place in the affairs of state, and Ceylon established diplomatic relations with communist states. He was assassinated in 1959. His widow, Sirimavo Ratwatte Dias Bandaranaike (1916–2000), became the world's first woman prime minister in 1960, serving until 1965, and twice more served as prime minister (1970–77 and 1994–2000). Her terms saw adoption of a new constitution proclaiming a republic (1972) and the change of the country's name to Sri Lanka. She was appointed to a third term as prime minister when her daughter, Chandrika Bandaranaike Kumaratunga (born 1945), became president in 1994.

S.W.R.D. Bandaranaike.
CAMERA PRESS

bandeira \bän-'der-ə\ Any of several 17th-century Brazilian expeditions into the interior in search of precious metals and Indians to enslave. Bandeiras consisted of 50 to several thousand men *(bandeirantes)*, usually from São Paulo, organized and controlled by wealthy entrepreneurs. The *bandeirantes* explored unmapped regions, built roads, established settlements, laid the basis for ranching and agriculture in the interior, and helped Brazil define and extend its boundaries. The bandeiras netted large profits and inflicted untold injury on the Indian tribes. See also PAULISTA.

Bandelier National Monument \,ban-də-'lir\ Archaeological area, northern central New Mexico. Lying along the RIO GRANDE 20 mi (32 km) northwest of SANTA FE, it was established in 1916. It occupies an area of 51 sq mi (132 sq km) and was named for Adolph Bandelier, a Swiss-American archaeologist. The monument contains many cliff and open-pueblo ruins of pre-Columbian Indians (mostly 13th-century) in Frijoles Canyon. Stone sculptures and man-made caves have also been unearthed.

bandicoot Any of about 22 species of MARSUPIALS (family Peramelidae) found in Australia, Tasmania, New Guinea, and nearby islands. Bandicoots are 12–30 in. (30–80 cm) long, including the 4- to 12-in. (10- to 30-cm) sparsely haired tail. They have a stout, coarse-haired body, a tapered muzzle, and hindlimbs longer than their forelimbs. Unlike other marsupials, bandicoots have a placenta. They are terrestrial, solitary animals that dig pits to search for insect and plant food. Farmers consider them pests. All species have declined, and some are now endangered.

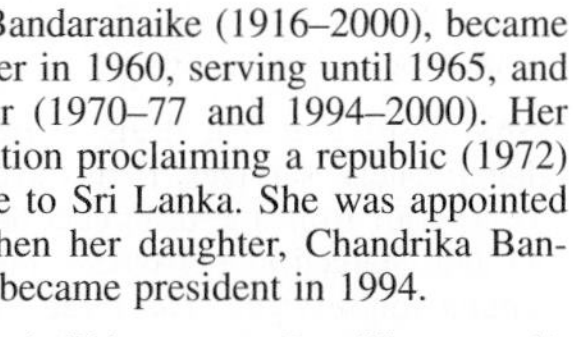
Bandicoot (*Perameles nasuta*).
WARREN GARST—TOM STACK AND ASSOCIATES

Bandinelli, Baccio (1488–1560) Italian sculptor and painter active in Florence. Though trained as a goldsmith by his father, he soon became one of the principal sculptors at the Medici court. He often failed to complete his commissions, and was accused of jealousy and incompetence by BENVENUTO CELLINI and GIORGIO VASARI. He is remembered more for his unattractive character than for the quality of his work. His most famous sculpture is *Hercules and Cacus* (1534), in the Piazza della Signoria.

Bandung \'bän-du̇ŋ\ City (pop., 1996 est.: 2,429,000), Indonesia. The capital of West Java province, it was founded by the Dutch in 1810 in the interior of JAVA on a 2,400-ft (730-km) plateau. It is surrounded by beautiful scenery. It is the center of cultural life for the Sundanese, who compose most of West Java's population and differ in customs and language from their Javanese neighbors. It is a center for the study and preservation of Sundanese culture and an educational center.

bandwidth Measurement of the capacity of a communications signal. For digital signals, the bandwidth is the data speed or rate, measured in bits per second (bps). For analog signals, it is the difference between the highest and lowest frequency components, measured in hertz (cycles per second). For example, a MODEM with a bandwidth of 56 kilobits per second (Kbps) can transmit a maximum of about 56,000 bits of digital data in one second. The human voice, which produces analog sound waves, has a typical bandwidth of three kilohertz between the highest and lowest frequency sounds it can generate.

Banerjea \'bä-nər-jē\, **Surendranath** *later* **Sir Surendranath** (1848–1925) Indian statesman, one of the founders of modern India. As a young man, he attempted unsuccessfully to serve in the Indian Civil Service, at the time virtually closed to ethnic Indians. He then became a teacher and founded a college in Calcutta (now Kolkata), which was later named after him. Banerjea attempted to bring Hindus and Muslims together for political action, and for 40 years he put forward a nationalist viewpoint in his newspaper, *The Bengalee*. Twice elected president of the Indian National Congress, he advocated for an Indian constitution on the Canadian model. He was elected in 1913 to two legislative councils and later knighted (1921); in 1924 he was defeated by an independence candidate, whereupon he retired to write his autobiography, *A Nation in the Making* (1925).

Banff National Park Park, southwestern Alberta. Established in 1885 as Canada's first national park, it lies on the eastern slopes of the ROCKY MOUNTAINS and includes mineral springs, ice fields, and glacial lakes, including Lake Louise. It has been greatly expanded to its present area of 2,564 sq mi (6,641 sq km). Banff is famed for its spectacular beauty, and visitors are so numerous that it is now more a recreation than a conservation area.

Bangalore \'baŋ-gə-,lōr\ City (metro. area pop., 2001 prelim.: 5,686,844), capital of KARNATAKA state, southern India. It is a cultural meeting place for Kannada-, Telugu-, and Tamil-speaking peoples. Founded in the 17th century, it was later a possession of the MARATHAS. It became a fief of the Indian ruler HYDER ALI in 1758, but was taken by the British in 1791. It was the headquarters of the British administration 1831–81, when it was restored to the raja of MYSORE (now Karnataka). Today, it is one of India's largest cities and an industrial and educational center.

Banghazi See BENGHAZI

Bangka *or* **Banka** Island, Indonesia. Located off the eastern coast of SUMATRA across the Bangka Strait, it is separated from BELITUNG island by Gaspar Strait. Its area is 4,609 sq mi (11,937 sq km); the chief town is Pangkalpinang. The sultan of PALEMBANG ceded Bangka to the British in 1812; they in turn exchanged it with the Dutch in 1814 for property in India. Occupied by Japan during World War II, it became part of Indonesia in 1949. Bangka is one of the world's chief tin-producing centers.

Bangkok *Thai* **Krung Thep** \'kru̇ŋ-'tep\ City (pop., 2000: 6,320,174), capital of Thailand. Lying 25 mi (40 km) above the mouth of the CHAO PHRAYA, it is the country's major port and also its cultural, financial, and educational center. Established as a fort before 1767 as a stronghold against the Burmese, it became the capital in 1782. Seized by the Japanese in World War II, it subsequently suffered heavy Allied bombing. In 1971–72 it incorporated several outlying districts to form a single city-province, and has since experienced phenomenal growth. Throughout the city, walled Buddhist temples and monasteries serve as focal points for its religious life.

Bangladesh *officially* **People's Republic of Bangladesh** Country, southern central Asia. Area: 55,126 sq mi (142,776 sq km). Population (1997 est.): 125,340,000. Capital: DHAKA. The vast majority of the population are Bengalis. Language: Bengali (official). Religions: Islam (official; mainly Sunni), Hinduism (over 10%). Currency: taka. Bangladesh is generally flat, its highest point being only 660 ft (200 m). It is characterized by alluvial plains dissected by numerous connecting rivers. The southern part consists of the eastern sector of the Ganges-Brahmaputra Delta. The chief rivers are the GANGES and the BRAHMAPUTRA (here known as the Jamuna), which unite to form the Padma. Though primarily agricultural, the country has been unable to feed itself. The monsoons that occur from May to October produce extreme flooding over much of Bangladesh, often causing severe crop damage and great loss of life; a cyclone in 1991 left 130,000 Bengalis dead, and several in 1997 were

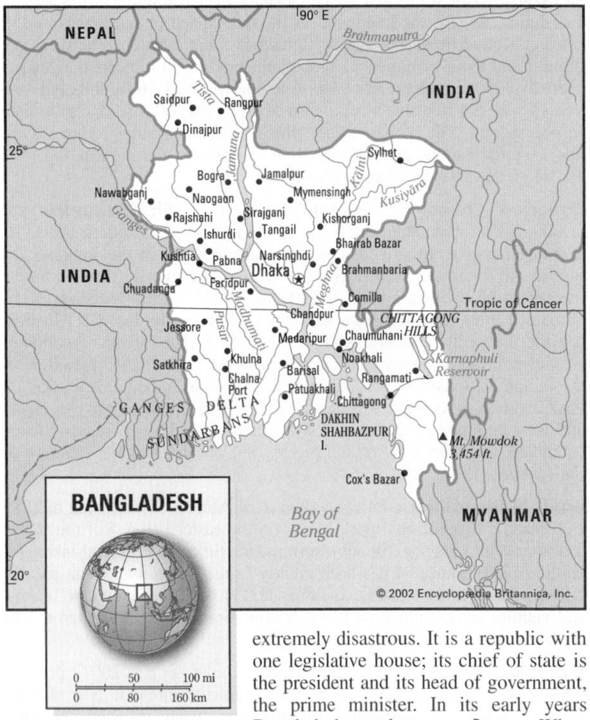

extremely disastrous. It is a republic with one legislative house; its chief of state is the president and its head of government, the prime minister. In its early years Bangladesh was known as BENGAL. When the British left the subcontinent in 1947, the area that was East Bengal became the part of Pakistan called East Pakistan. Bengali nationalist sentiment increased after the creation of an independent Pakistan. In 1971 violence erupted; some 1 million Bengalis were killed, and millions more fled to India, which finally entered the war on the side of the Bengalis, ensuring West Pakistan's defeat. East Pakistan became the independent nation of Bangladesh. Little of the devastation caused by the war has been repaired, and political instability, including the assassination of two presidents, has continued.

Bangor Town (pop., 1981: 47,000), seat of NORTH DOWN district, Northern Ireland. It lies on the southern shore of Belfast Lough, 12 mi (19 km) northeast of BELFAST. St. Comgall founded a monastery at Bangor c. 555, which became a celebrated seat of learning. The town was sacked by the Danes in the 9th century; it was partially rebuilt by St. Malachy in the 12th century. It is now a seaside resort.

Bangui \'bäŋ-gē\ City (pop., 1994: 524,000), capital of the Central African Republic. A major port on the UBANGI RIVER, it is connected by an extended 1,100-mi (1,800-km) river and rail transport system with the Congolese cities of POINTE-NOIRE and BRAZZAVILLE. Chiefly a commercial and administrative center, Bangui is also the site of a university and research institutes.

Bangweulu \ˌbäŋ-gwā-'ü-lü\, **Lake** Lake, northern Zambia. Located southeast of Lake MWERU and southwest of Lake TANGANYIKA at an elevation of 3,740 ft (1,140 m), it is about 45 mi (72 km) long and, with its adjacent swamps, covers an area of 3,800 sq mi (9,840 sq km). Its outlet is the Luapul, a headstream of the CONGO. It has three inhabited islands. DAVID LIVINGSTONE, the first European to visit the lake, died there in 1873.

Banja Luka \'bän-yä-'lü-kä\ City (pop., 1991: 195,000), northeastern Bosnia and Herzegovina. It was an important military center under the Turks and the seat (1583–1639) of the Bosnian territory governed by a pasha. A battlefield between the Austrians and Turks in the 16th–18th century, it played an important part in the 19th-century Bosnian uprisings against Turkey as well as in the revolts of the Serbs. It was a center of resistance in the Axis-dominated country of CROATIA during World War II. In 1992 it became the capital of the autonomous Serbian Republic of Bosnia and Herzegovina. It was a center of fighting during the BOSNIAN CONFLICT.

banjo Plucked stringed musical instrument of African origin. It has a tambourine-like body, four or five strings, and a long fretted neck. The fifth string (if present) is pegged at the fifth fret and acts primarily as a drone plucked by the thumb. In its original form, the banjo had only four strings and lacked frets. It was brought by slaves to the U.S., where it was popularized in 19th-century MINSTREL SHOWS, and thence exported to Europe. It has been an important American folk instrument, especially in BLUEGRASS, and was used in early jazz.

Banjul \'bän-ˌjül\ *formerly (1816–1973)* **Bathurst** Seaport (metro. area pop., 1993: 270,500), capital of Gambia. Located on the Island of St. Mary in the GAMBIA RIVER, it is the country's largest city. Founded by the British in 1816 to suppress the slave trade, it subsequently became the capital of the British colony of Gambia. With Gambia's independence in 1965, it became the national capital. Tourism is of increasing importance, while Banjul serves as a transportation center with connections to the interior and to Senegal.

bank Institution that deals in MONEY and its substitutes and provides other financial services. Banks accept deposits and make loans and derive a PROFIT from the difference in the interest paid to lenders (depositor) and charged to borrowers, respectively. They also profit from fees charged for services. The three major classes of banks are COMMERCIAL BANKS, INVESTMENT BANKS, and CENTRAL BANKS. Banking depends entirely on public confidence in the system's soundness; no bank could pay all its depositors should they simultaneously demand cash, as may happen in a PANIC. See also CREDIT UNION, FEDERAL RESERVE SYSTEM, SAVINGS AND LOAN ASSOCIATION, SAVINGS BANK.

Bank of the United States Bank chartered in 1791 by the U.S. Congress. It was conceived by ALEXANDER HAMILTON to pay off debts from the AMERICAN REVOLUTION and provide a stable currency. Its establishment, opposed by THOMAS JEFFERSON, led to the first U.S. political parties, the FEDERALISTS and the Democratic-Republicans. The national bank restrained private state banks from overexpansion, a restriction opposed by states'-rights advocates, and came to represent privilege and wealth against agrarian populism. Criticism reached its height in Pres. ANDREW JACKSON's administration and led to the BANK WAR. The bank's charter expired in 1836. Its reorganization as the Bank of the U.S. of Pennsylvania ended its regulation of private banks.

bank rate See DISCOUNT RATE

Bank War Controversy in the 1830s over the existence of the BANK OF THE U.S., at that time the only national banking institution. Pres. ANDREW JACKSON objected to the concentration of economic power in the bank's small group of financiers. Its president, NICHOLAS BIDDLE, obtained the support of HENRY CLAY and DANIEL WEBSTER in an effort to renew the bank's charter, and the issue became central to the 1832 presidential election. After his reelection Jackson forbade the deposit of government funds in the bank. Biddle retaliated by calling in loans, which precipitated a credit crisis. Denied renewal of its federal charter, the bank secured a Pennsylvania charter in 1836. Faulty investment decisions forced it to close in 1841.

Bankhead, Tallulah (Brockman) (1902–1968) U.S. film and stage actress. Born in Huntsville, Ala., to a socially prominent family (her father became a prominent Congressman), she made her Broadway debut in 1918 and achieved fame on the London stage in *The Dancer* (1923). Her vivid presence and throaty voice contributed to her singular performances in the hit plays *The Little Foxes* (1939), *The Skin of Our Teeth* (1942), and *Private Lives* (1946). She made such films as *A Woman's Law* (1928) and ALFRED HITCHCOCK's *Lifeboat* (1944), but remained primarily a stage performer. Her final appearance was in *The Milk Train Doesn't Stop Here Anymore* (1964).

bankruptcy Status of a DEBTOR who has been declared by judicial process to be unable to pay his or her debts. It also refers to the legal process involved: the administration of an insolvent debtor's property by the court for the benefit of the debtor's creditors. Filing by a debtor is called voluntary bankruptcy; involuntary bankruptcy is declared by the court upon petition by a creditor. The U.S. Bankruptcy Code makes four types of relief available to bankrupt individuals or corporations: liquidation (under Chapter 7), reorganization (Chapter 11), debt adjustment for a family farmer (Chapter 12), and debt adjustment for an individual with a regular income (Chapter 13). Municipalities may file under Chapter 9. Generally, not all debts are paid in a bankruptcy. The court determines which debts are to be repaid, and the debtor is typically granted a discharge of the rest. See also INSOLVENCY.

Banks, Ernie *orig.* **Ernest** (born 1931) U.S. baseball player. Born in Dallas, he played shortstop and later first base for the Chicago Cubs from 1953 to 1971. Batting right-handed, he became known as one of the finest power hitters in history, earning career batting totals of 512 home runs and 1,636 runs batted in, and hitting more than 40 home runs in each of five seasons. He was elected to the Baseball Hall of Fame in his first year of eligibility.

Banks, Joseph *later* **Sir Joseph** (1743–1820) British explorer and naturalist. After studying at Oxford, Banks inherited a fortune that allowed him to travel extensively, collecting plant and natural-history specimens. He outfitted and accompanied JAMES COOK's voyage around the world (1768–71). Particularly interested in economic plants and their introduction from one country to another, he was the first to suggest the identity of the wheat rust and barberry fungus (1805); he was also the first to show that marsupial mammals are more primitive than placental mammals. He served as president of the Royal Society from 1778 to 1820, and as unofficial director of KEW GARDENS transformed it into a major botanical institution. His HERBARIUM, one of the most important in existence, and his library, a major collection of works on natural history, are now at the British Museum.

Banks, Russell (born 1940) U.S. novelist. Born in Newton, Mass., he was associated in the 1960s with Lillabulero Press and has taught at various colleges and universities. He attracted wide attention with *Continental Drift* (1985), inspired by a stint in Jamaica; his later novels, which, like his earlier works, often portray characters trapped by economic and social forces they do not understand, include *Affliction* (1989; film, 1998), *The Sweet Hereafter* (1991; film, 1997), and *Cloudsplitter* (1998), a historical novel about the abolitionist JOHN BROWN.

Banks Island Island, Northwest Territories, Canada. The westernmost island in the Canadian ARCTIC ARCHIPELAGO, it lies northwest of VICTORIA ISLAND and is separated from the mainland by AMUNDSEN GULF. About 250 mi (400 km) long, it has an area of 27,038 sq mi (70,028 sq km). First sighted by Sir William Parry's expedition in 1820, it was named for the naturalist JOSEPH BANKS.

Banks Peninsula Peninsula, South Island, New Zealand, extending about 35 mi (55 km) into the Pacific. Originally an island formed by two contiguous volcanic cones, it was visited in 1770 by Capt. JAMES COOK, who named it for JOSEPH BANKS. CHRISTCHURCH is situated at its base.

Bann River River, Northern Ireland. The Upper Bann flows northwest 25 mi (40 km) into Lough NEAGH, while the Lower Bann flows north out of the lake 33 mi (53 km) into the Atlantic Ocean.

Banna \ban-'na\, **Hasan al-** (1906–1949) Egyptian political and religious leader. He began teaching Arabic at a primary school in Ismailia in 1927. In 1928 he established the MUSLIM BROTHERHOOD, which aimed at rejuvenating Islam and Egyptian society and expelling the British from Egypt. By 1940 it was attracting students, civil servants, and urban laborers to its ranks. He tried to maintain an alliance with the Egyptian government, but many members saw the government as betraying Egyptian nationalism, and after the war, members were implicated in several political assassinations, including that of Prime Minister al-Nuqrashi in 1948. Hasan al-Banna was assassinated with government involvement the next year.

Banneker, Benjamin (1731–1806) American astronomer, compiler of almanacs, and inventor. He was born a free black in Ellicott's Mills, Md., and owned a farm near Baltimore. He taught himself astronomy and mathematics and began astronomical calculations in 1773. He accurately predicted a solar eclipse in 1789. In 1790 he was appointed to the commission that surveyed the site for Washington, D.C. From 1791 to 1802 he published annual almanacs; he sent an early copy to THOMAS JEFFERSON to counter a contention that blacks were intellectually inferior. He also wrote essays denouncing slavery and war.

Banner System Military organization used by the MANCHU tribes of Manchuria (now northeastern China) to conquer and control China in the 17th century. The system was developed by the Manchu leader NURHACHI, who in 1601 organized his warriors into four companies, each known for its banner of a distinguishing color. More Banners (as the companies were known) were soon established, and as the Manchus began to conquer their Chinese and MONGOL neighbors they organized their captives into similar companies. With these troops the Manchus conquered China and established the QING DYNASTY in 1644. Over time, the Banners' fighting qualities deteriorated, until by the end of the 19th century the System had become largely ineffective.

Bannister, Roger (Gilbert) *later* **Sir Roger** (born 1929) British runner. He attended Oxford University before earning a medical degree. In 1954 he became the first person to complete a mile in less than four minutes (3 minutes 59.4 seconds). Many authorities had previously regarded the four-minute mile "barrier" as unbreakable. A neurologist, he wrote papers on the physiology of exercise, and he is said to have achieved his speed through scientific training methods.

Bannockburn, Battle of (June 23–24, 1314) Decisive battle in Scottish history, at which the Scots under Robert the Bruce (later ROBERT I) defeated the English under EDWARD II. The Scots were outnumbered three to one by the English soldiers, but they triumphed through masterly use of terrain, forcing the English onto a cramped, marshy battlefield with little room to maneuver. The English forces were put to flight, and many were slaughtered by the pursuing Scots. The victory cleared the last English troops from Scotland and secured Scottish independence, establishing Bruce on the throne as Robert I.

Banpo *or* **Pan-p'o** \'bän-'pō\ Site of a Neolithic village located on the Wei River in China, dating to the earlier part of the YANGSHAO CULTURE, 5000–4000 BC. A huge number of artifacts have been uncovered, including 8,000 stone and bone tools, pottery fragments, and clay figurines. The main cultivated crop was foxtail millet; the diet was supplemented through hunting and gathering. Pigs and dogs were domesticated, and evidence of hemp and silkworm cultivation point to textile manufacture. 250 graves have been excavated. See also NEOLITHIC PERIOD.

Bantam Former city and sultanate, JAVA. It was located at the western end of Java between the Java Sea and the Indian Ocean. In the early 16th century it became a powerful Muslim sultanate, which extended its control over parts of SUMATRA and BORNEO. Invaded by the Dutch, Portuguese, and British, it ultimately recognized Dutch sovereignty in 1684. The city was Java's most important port for the European spice trade until its harbor silted up in the late 18th century. It suffered severely from the eruption of KRAKATAU in 1883.

Banting, Frederick Grant *later* **Sir Frederick** (1891–1941) Canadian physician. Born in Alliston, Ontario, he taught at the University of Toronto from 1923. With CHARLES BEST, he was first to obtain a pancreatic extract of insulin (1921), which they isolated in the laboratory of J. J. R. MACLEOD in a form effective against diabetes. Banting and Macleod received a 1923 Nobel Prize for the discovery of insulin; Banting voluntarily shared his portion of the prize with Best.

Bantu languages Family of perhaps close to 500 languages spoken by more than 200 million people in Africa, from roughly below the continent's westward bulge to its southern tip. About 35 Bantu languages, including Kongo (Kikongo), Rundi (Kirundi), Rwanda (Kinyarwanda), Gikuyu (Kikuyu), Chewa (Chichewa), North and South Sotho, Zulu, and Xhosa, have a million or more speakers. The Bantu family belongs to the BENUE-CONGO branch of the huge NIGER-CONGO LANGUAGE family.

The best-known grammatical feature of Bantu languages is their division of nouns into classes (see GENDER)—in part on semantic grounds, in part arbitrarily—which are marked by prefixes on nouns and which require agreeing prefixes on parts of speech such as adjectives and verbs that are governed by nouns.

Bantu peoples Speakers of some 500 distinct BANTU LANGUAGES, numbering more than 200 million, occupying almost the entire southern projection of Africa. The classification is primarily linguistic, for the cultural patterns of Bantu-speakers are extremely diverse. Included in the group are the Bemba, Bena, Chaga, Chewa, Embu, FANG, GANDA, Gusii, Hehe, HERERO, HUTU, Kagwe, KIKUYU, Luba, LUHYA, Lunda, Makonde, Meru, Nayamwezi, NDEBELE, Nkole, NYAKYUSA, NYORO, Pedi, SHONA, SOTHO, SWAZI, Tsonga, TSWANA, TUTSI, Venda, XHOSA, YAO, Zaramo, and ZULU.

banyan Unusually shaped tree *(Ficus benghalensis,* or *F. indica)* of the FIG genus in the MULBERRY FAMILY, native to tropical Asia. Aerial ROOTS that develop from its branches descend and take root in the soil to become new trunks. The banyan reaches a height of up to 100 ft (30 m) and spreads laterally indefinitely. One tree may in time assume the appearance of a very dense thicket as a result of the tangle of roots and trunks.

Bánzer Suárez \'bän-ser-'swä-res\, **Hugo** (1926–2002) Soldier and president of Bolivia (1971–78, from 1997). After an education in Bolivian and U.S. Army training schools, Bánzer served in various government posts. He became president after participating in the overthrow of two Bolivian governments in 1970 and 1971. A conservative, he encouraged foreign investment and severely repressed all opposition. His restrictions of union activities and constitutional liberties led to opposition by labor, the clergy, peasants, and students. A 1978 coup d'état overthrew him, but he was democratically elected in 1997. He resigned in 2001.

Bao Dai \'bau̇-'dī\ *orig.* **Nguyen Vinh Thuy** (1913–1997) Last reigning emperor of Vietnam (r. 1926–45, 1949–55). He was educated in France and in 1926 succeeded to a throne that was dominated by the French. Retained as a powerless ruler under the Japanese during World War II, he fled the country after the VIET MINH drove the Japanese out. In 1949 the French, having agreed to the principle of an independent Vietnam, invited him to return as sovereign. He did, but he accomplished little and retired to France in 1955 when a national referendum called for the country to become a republic.

baobab \'bau̇-ˌbab\ Tree *(Adansonia digitata)* of the bombax family (Bombacaceae), native to Africa. The barrel-like trunk may reach a diameter of 30 ft (9 m) and a height of 60 ft (18 m). The large, gourdlike, woody fruit contains a tasty pulp. A strong fiber from the bark is used locally for rope and cloth. The trunks are often excavated to serve as water reserves or temporary shelters. For its extraordinary shape the baobab is grown as a curiosity in areas of warm climate, such as Florida. A related species, *A. gregorii,* occurs in Australia, where it is called baobab or bottle tree.

baojia *or* **pao-chia** \'bau̇-'jē-ə\ Chinese village militia system created by WANG ANSHI as part of his reforms of 1069–76. Units of 10 families were regularly trained and supplied with arms, thereby reducing the government's dependence on mercenaries. Members were mutually responsible for each other. The system was resurrected in the 19th century to help put down the TAIPING REBELLION and was imitated by both the GUOMINDANG and the CHINESE COMMUNIST PARTY in the 20th century.

baptism In Christianity, the SACRAMENT of admission to the church, symbolized by the pouring or sprinkling of water on the head or by immersion in water. The ceremony is usually accompanied by the words "I baptize you in the name of the Father, and of the Son, and of the Holy Spirit." In the doctrine originated by St. PAUL, it signifies the wiping away of past SINS and the rebirth of the individual into a new life. Judaism practiced ritual purification by immersion, and the Gospels report that JOHN THE BAPTIST baptized JESUS. Baptism was an important ritual in the early church by the 1st century, and infant baptism appeared by the 3rd century. Roman Catholic, Orthodox, and most Protestant churches practice infant baptism. The ANABAPTIST reformers insisted on adult baptism after a confession of faith; modern BAPTISTS and the DISCIPLES OF CHRIST also practice adult baptism.

Baptist Member of a group of Protestant Christians who hold that only adult believers should be baptized and that it must be done by immersion. During the 17th century two groups of Baptists emerged in England: General Baptists, who held that Christ's atonement applied to all persons, and Particular Baptists, who believed it was only for the elect. Baptist origins in the American colonies can be traced to ROGER WILLIAMS, who established a Baptist church in Providence, R.I., in 1639. Baptist growth in the U.S. was spurred by the GREAT AWAKENING in the mid-18th century. The 1814 General Convention showed divisions among U.S. Baptists over slavery; a formal split occurred when the Southern Baptist Convention was organized in 1845 and was confirmed when the Northern (American) Baptist Convention was organized in 1907. African-American Baptist churches provided leadership in the 1960s CIVIL RIGHTS MOVEMENT, notably through the work of MARTIN LUTHER KING. Baptist belief emphasizes the authority of local congregations in matters of faith and practice; worship is characterized by extemporaneous prayer and hymn-singing as well as by the exposition of scripture in sermons.

baptistery *or* **baptistry** Domed hall or chapel, adjacent to or part of a church, for the administration of BAPTISM. By the 4th century, the baptistery had assumed an eight-sided shape (eight in Christian numerology being the symbol for a new life), as had the baptismal font within. The font itself was set beneath a dome-shaped BALDACHIN and encircled by columns and an ambulatory (aisle), features first used by the Byzantines.

Battistero (baptistery) San Giovanni, Florence, begun 7th century.
ALINARI—ART RESOURCE

Baqqarah See BAGGARA

bar association Group of lawyers organized primarily to deal with issues affecting the legal profession. In general, they are concerned with furthering the interests of lawyers through advocating reforms in the legal system, sponsoring research projects, and regulating professional standards. Bar associations sometimes administer the examinations required for admission to practice law. The largest U.S. bar association is the AMERICAN BAR ASSOCIATION.

bar code Printed series of parallel bars of varying width used for entering data into a computer system, typically for identifying the object on which the code appears. The width and spacing of the bars represent binary information that can be read by an optical (laser) SCANNER that is part of a computer system. The coding is used in many different areas of manufacturing and marketing, including inventory control and tracking systems. The bar codes printed on supermarket and other retail merchandise are those of the UNIVERSAL PRODUCT CODE (UPC).

bar graph See HISTOGRAM

Bar Kokhba \ˌbär-'kȯk̲-bä\ *orig.* **Simeon bar Kosba** (died AD 135) Leader of an unsuccessful Jewish revolt against Roman rule in Palestine. In 131 HADRIAN forbade circumcision and built a temple to Jupiter on the ruins of the Temple of JERUSALEM. The Jews rebelled in 132, led by Simeon bar Kosba, who, according to one story, was hailed as a messiah by AKIBA BEN JOSEPH. He was called Bar Kokhba ("Son of the Star"), a messianic allusion. His army captured Aelia and inflicted heavy casualties, but Hadrian visited the battlefield and summoned reinforcements, and the Romans retook Jerusalem. Bar Kokhba was killed at Betar in 135, and the remnant of the Jewish army was soon crushed, with total Jewish losses numbering 580,000. Surviving Jews were exiled and barred from Jerusalem.

Bar Mitzvah \ˌbär-'mits-və\ Jewish ritual celebrating a boy's 13th birthday and his entry into the community of JUDAISM. It usually takes place during a Sabbath service, when the boy reads from the TORAH and may give a discourse on the text. The service is often followed by a festive KIDDUSH and a family dinner on the same day or next day. REFORM JUDAISM substituted confirmation of boys and girls for the Bar Mitzvah celebration after 1810, but many congregations restored the Bar Mitzvah in the 20th century. A separate ceremony for girls, Bat Mitzvah, has been instituted in Reform and CONSERVATIVE JUDAISM.

Bara \'bar-ə\, **Theda** *orig.* **Theodosia Goodman** (1885–1955) U.S. film actress. Born in Cincinnati, Ohio, she had a brief stage career before going to Hollywood. Her first major picture, *A Fool There Was* (1915), was accompanied by a publicity campaign, billing her as the daughter of an Eastern potentate, that made her an instant success. Establishing a sultry, exotic persona, she became the prototype of the screen "vamp." She made more than 40 films within a few years, but her popularity soon declined, and she retired in the 1920s.

Barabbas \bə-ˈra-bəs\ In the New Testament, a prisoner or criminal freed to please the mob before the crucifixion of Jesus. Described as a thief or an insurrectionist, Barabbas is mentioned in all four Gospels. Following the custom of setting free one prisoner chosen by popular demand before Passover, Pontius Pilate suggested pardoning Jesus, but the crowd protested and demanded the release of Barabbas. Pilate gave in and sent Jesus to his death.

Barada River \ˈbär-ə-də\ *ancient* **Chrysorrhoas.** River, western Syria. It flows about 45 mi (72 km) from the Anti-Lebanon Mountains past Damascus. Throughout history, channels have been cut at different levels parallel to the main branch of the river to divert its flow. The channels (of Nabataean, Aramaean, and especially Roman origin) fan out as they reach Damascus, irrigating a large area. This system created the site of Damascus, an artificial oasis of extreme fertility.

Barak River See Surma River

Baraka \bä-ˈrä-kə\, **(Imamu) Amiri** *orig.* **(Everett) LeRoi Jones** (born 1934) U.S. playwright and black nationalist. He was born in Newark, N.J., and educated at Howard University. His first play, *Dutchman* (1964), produced off-Broadway, explored the suppressed hostility of U.S. blacks toward the dominant white culture. *The Slave* and *The Toilet,* also produced in 1964, aroused controversy. He founded the Black Arts Repertory Theater in Harlem and in 1968 founded the Black Community Development and Defense Organization, a Black Muslim group, to affirm black culture and promote black political power. He has also written volumes of poetry and essays.

barangay \ˌbar-ən-ˈgī\ Type of early Filipino settlement. Sailboats called *balangay* brought Malay settlers to the Philippines from Borneo. Each boat carried a family group that established a village. These villages, which sometimes grew to include 30–100 families, remained isolated from one another; the fact that no larger political grouping emerged (except on Mindanao) facilitated the 16th-century Spanish conquest. The Spanish retained the barangay as a unit of local administration.

Barataria Bay \ˌbar-ə-ˈtar-ē-ə\ Inlet of the Gulf of Mexico, southeastern Louisiana. About 15 mi (24 km) long and 12 mi (19 km) wide, its entrance is a narrow channel, navigable through connecting waterways into the Gulf Intracoastal Waterway system. The area is noted for its shrimp industry and natural-gas and oil wells. Jean Laffite and his brother organized a colony of pirates around its coast in 1810–14, and it is sometimes called Laffite Country.

Barbados \bar-ˈbā-dəs\ Island nation, West Indies. The most easterly of the Caribbean islands, it lies about 270 mi (430 km) northeast of Venezuela. Area: 166 sq mi (430 sq km). Population (1997 est.): 265,000. Capital: Bridgetown. More than 90% of the population is black. Language: English (official). Religion: Christianity. Currency: Barbados dollar. Composed of coral accumulation, Barbados is low and flat except in its northern central part; its highest point is Mount Hillaby, at 1,104 ft (336 m). There is little surface water. It is almost encircled by coral reefs and lacks good natural harbors. The economy is based on tourism and sugar, while the offshore financial sector is growing. It is a constitutional monarchy with two legislative houses; its chief of state is the British monarch, represented by a governor-general, and the head of government is the prime minister. The island was probably inhabited by Arawaks who originally came from South America. Spaniards may have landed by 1518, and by 1536 they had apparently wiped out the Indian population. Barbados was settled by the English in the 1620s. Slaves were brought in to work the sugar plantations, which were especially prosperous in the 17th–18th century. The British empire abolished slavery in 1834, and all the Barbados slaves were freed by 1838. In 1958 Barbados joined the West Indies Federation. When the latter dissolved in 1962, Barbados sought independence from Britain; it achieved Commonwealth status in 1966. See map opposite.

Barbara, St. (died c. AD 200) Early Christian martyr and patroness of artillerymen. She was the daughter of a pagan, Dioscorus, who kept her guarded to protect her beauty and virginity. When she converted to Christianity he became enraged and took her to the Roman prefect, who ordered her to be tortured and beheaded. Her father performed the execution himself, and on the way home he was struck by lightning and reduced to ashes. Barbara was a popular saint during the Middle Ages and was invoked for aid in thunderstorms. She was dropped from the church calendar in 1969.

Barbarossa \ˌbär-bə-ˈrä-sə\ *orig.* **Khidr** *later* **Khayr al-Din** (died 1546) Greek-Ottoman pirate and admiral. He and his brother Aruj (or Horuk), sons of a Turk from Lesbos, hated the Spanish and Portuguese for their attacks on North Africa and took up piracy on the Barbary Coast in hopes of seizing an African domain for themselves. When Aruj was killed in 1518, Khidr took the title Khayr al-Din. He offered homage to the Ottoman sultan and in return received military aid that enabled him to capture Algiers in 1529. Appointed admiral in chief of the Ottoman Empire (1533), he conquered all of Tunisia. Charles V captured Tunis in 1535, but Khayr al-Din defeated his fleet at the Battle of Preveza (1538), securing the eastern Mediterranean for the Turks for 33 years. His red beard was the source of the epithet Barbarossa, used by Europeans.

Barbary ape Tailless, terrestrial macaque *(Macaca sylvana)* found in bands in Algeria and Morocco and on the Rock of Gibraltar. It is about 24 in. (60 cm) long and has yellowish brown fur and a naked, pale-pink face. It is the only wild monkey in Europe and may have been taken westward during the medieval Muslim Arab territorial expansion. According to legend, British dominion over Gibraltar will end when the Barbary ape departs.

Barbary macaque (*Macaca sylvana*).
TOM MCHUGH—PHOTO RESEARCHERS

Barbary Coast Mediterranean coastal region, North Africa. It extends from Egypt to the Atlantic Ocean. The region was overrun by Vandals in the 5th century AD. Conquered by the Byzantines c. AD 533, it was overcome by Arabs during the 7th century and was eventually broken up into the independent Muslim states known as the Barbary States (Morocco, Algeria, Tunisia, and Libya). For centuries the coast was notorious for the pirates who ravaged shipping and collected tribute from leading European states. After the U.S. war with Tripoli (see Tripolitan War), the U.S. expedition to Algiers (1815), and the bombardment of Algiers by the British (1816), the pirates abandoned the exaction of tribute.

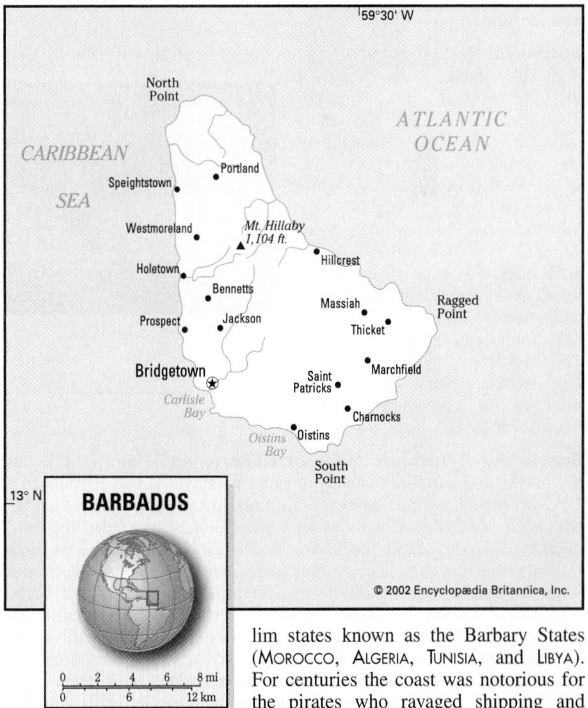

Barber, Red *orig.* **Walter Lanier** (1908–1992) U.S. sports broadcaster. Born in Columbus, Miss., he became the radio and television announcer for the baseball games of the Cincinnati Reds (1934–39), Brooklyn Dodgers (1939–53), and New York Yankees (1954–66). He combined technical expertise with homespun comments; his signature exclamation was "Oh-ho, Doctor!" He provided weekly commentary on National Public Radio from 1981.

Barber, Samuel (1910–1981) U.S. composer. Born in West Chester, Pa., he studied piano, voice, conducting, and composition at the Curtis Institute, where he began a close lifelong association with G.C. MENOTTI. His style, frequently lyrical and neo-Romantic, proved highly attractive to the public. His works include *Dover Beach* (1931), the *Adagio for Strings* (1936), two orchestral *Essays* (1937, 1942), *Knoxville: Summer of 1915* (1947), a piano sonata (1949), the *Hermit Songs* (1953), a piano concerto (1962, Pulitzer Prize), and the operas *Vanessa* (1957, Pulitzer Prize), *A Hand of Bridge* (1958), and *Antony and Cleopatra* (1966).

barberry Any of the almost 500 species of thorny evergreen or deciduous shrubs constituting the genus *Berberis*, the largest and most important genus of the family Berberidaceae, in the buttercup order. Most are native to the northern temperate zone, particularly Asia. *Berberis* species have yellow wood and yellow flowers. The fruit of several species is made into jellies.

American barberry (*Berberis canadensis*).

WALTER CHANDOHA

barbershop quartet Popular vocal ensemble consisting of four unaccompanied male voices. The voice parts are tenor, lead, baritone, and bass, with the lead normally singing the melody and the tenor harmonizing above. Barbershop apparently originated in the U.S. in the late 19th century, when American barbershops formed social and musical centers for neighborhood males, though the term may derive from "barber's music," the British term for an extemporized performance by patrons waiting to be shaved and referring to a barber's traditional role as a musician.

barbet \'bär-bət\ Any of about 75 species of tropical birds (family Capitonidae) named for the bristles at the base of their stout, sharp bill. They are big-headed and short-tailed, 3.5–12 in. (9–30 cm) long, and greenish or brownish, with splashes of bright colors or white. Barbets are found throughout Central America to northern South America, in sub-Saharan Africa, and in South Asia. They all fly weakly, and they sit in treetops when not feeding on insects, lizards, birds' eggs, fruit, and berries. They call loudly, jerking the head or tail. Maddeningly vocal or repetitious species are sometimes called brain-fever birds.

Crimson-headed barbet (*Capito bourcieri*).

C. LAUBSCHER—BRUCE COLEMAN INC.

Barbie *in full* **Barbara Millicent Roberts** An 11½-inch- (29-cm-) tall plastic doll with the figure of an adult woman that was introduced in 1959 by Mattel, Inc., a southern California toy company. Ruth Handler, who cofounded Mattel with her husband, Elliot, spearheaded the introduction of the doll. Since the 1970s, Barbie has been criticized for materialism (amassing cars, houses, and clothes) and unrealistic body proportions. In fact, in 1994 researchers in Finland announced that if Barbie were a real woman she would not have enough body fat to menstruate. Yet many women who had played with the doll as girls credit Barbie with providing an alternative to restrictive 1950s gender roles. Today the doll has come to symbolize consumer capitalism and is as much a global brand as Coca-Cola, with key markets in Europe, Latin America, and Japan. Barbie never caught on in the Muslim world, however. In 1995 the Kingdom of Saudi Arabia stopped its sale because it violated the Islamic dress code. Similar dolls, complete with *hijabs* (head coverings), were eventually marketed to Muslim girls.

Barbie, Klaus (1913–1991) Nazi leader. As head of the Gestapo in Lyon, France (1942–44), he pursued members of the French RESISTANCE and promoted the torture and execution of thousands of prisoners. After World War II he was seized by U.S. authorities in Germany, who recruited him for counterintelligence work (1947–51) and then moved him and his family to Bolivia. He lived there as a businessman from 1951 until he was extradited to France in 1983 to stand trial. Throughout his trial "the Butcher of Lyon" remained unrepentant and proud of his service to the Nazis. Held responsible for the death of some 4,000 persons and the deportation of some 7,500 others, he was sentenced to life imprisonment.

barbiturate \bär-'bi-chə-rət\ Any of a class of HETEROCYCLIC COMPOUNDS based on the parent structure, uric acid, and used in medicine. They depress the central NERVOUS SYSTEM, acting particularly on certain parts of the BRAIN, though they tend to depress the functioning of all the body's tissues. Long-acting barbiturates (e.g., barbital and phenobarbital) are used to treat EPILEPSY. Intermediate ones (e.g., amobarbital) are used to treat INSOMNIA, short-acting ones (e.g., pentobarbital) to overcome difficulty in falling asleep (one aspect of insomnia), and ultrashort-acting ones (e.g., thiopental sodium) to induce unconsciousness in surgical patients before administration of other ANESTHETICS. Prolonged use of barbiturates may lead to addiction. Sudden withdrawal can be fatal; addicts must be weaned from the drug under medical supervision. Overdoses can result in coma and even death; barbiturates are particularly dangerous, even at normal doses, when combined with alcoholic beverages.

Barbizon school \,bär-bə-'zōn\ Group of 19th-century French landscape painters. They were part of a larger European movement toward NATURALISM that made a significant contribution to REALISM in French landscape painting. Led by THEODORE ROUSSEAU and J.-F. MILLET, they attracted a large following of painters who came to live at Barbizon, a village near Paris: C.-F. DAUBIGNY, Narcisse-Virgile Díaz de la Peña (1806–1876), Jules Dupré (1811–1889), Charles-Émile Jacque (1813–1894), and Constant Troyon (1810–1865). Each had his own style, but all emphasized painting out-of-doors directly from nature, using a limited palette, and creating atmosphere or mood in their landscapes.

Barbuda See ANTIGUA AND BARBUDA

Barca, Pedro Calderón de la See Pedro CALDERON DE LA BARCA

Barcelona \bär-sə-'lō-nə\ Seaport city (metro. area pop., 2000 est.: 1,496,266), capital of CATALONIA autonomous region, northeastern Spain. Spain's largest port and second-largest city, it is the country's principal industrial and commercial center. Traditionally said to have been founded in the 3rd century BC by the Carthaginian Hamilcar Barca (270?–229/28), for whom it may have been named, it was later ruled by the Romans and Visigoths. It was taken by the Moors c. AD 715, but retaken by the Franks under CHARLEMAGNE in 801 and made capital of the Spanish March (Catalonia). After Catalonia united with ARAGON in 1137, Barcelona became a flourishing commercial center and the rival of Italian ports. In the 19th century it was a center for radical social movements and Catalonian separatism. It was the Loyalist capital in 1937–39 (see SPANISH CIVIL WAR); its capture by FRANCISCO FRANCO brought the collapse of Catalonian resistance and Catalonia's reintegration into Spain. Modern Barcelona is known for its handsome architecture, including buildings by ANTONI GAUDI, and is an educational and cultural center for the CATALAN LANGUAGE.

Barclay de Tolly \bär-'klī-də-'tò-lē\, **Mikhail (Bogdanovich)** *later* **Prince Barclay de Tolly** (1761–1818) Russian field marshal prominent in the NAPOLEONIC WARS. A member of a Scottish family that had settled in Livonia, Barclay entered the Russian army in 1786. In 1812 he took command of one of two Russian armies operating against NAPOLEON. His strategy of avoiding decisive action and retreating into Russia proved unpopular and he was forced to resign his command. He took part in the invasion of France in 1814, and in 1815 he was commander in chief of the Russian army that invaded France after Napoleon's return from Elba.

Barcoo River See COOPER CREEK

bard Celtic tribal poet-singers gifted in composing and reciting verses of eulogy and satire or of heroes and their deeds. The institution died out in Gaul but survived in Ireland, where bards have preserved a tradition of chanting poetic eulogy, and in Wales, where the bardic order was codified into distinct grades in the 10th century. Despite a decline in the late Middle Ages, the Welsh tradition is celebrated in the annual National Eisteddfod.

Bard College Private liberal-arts college founded in 1860 in Annandale-on-Hudson, N.Y. It was founded as an Episcopal college for men by a family of teachers named Bard. Between 1928 and 1944 it served as Columbia University's undergraduate school. It became coeducational in 1944. Its undergraduate curriculum includes courses in the social sciences, languages and literature, arts, and natural sciences and mathematics. Enrollment is about 1,200.

Bardeen, John (1908–1991) U.S. physicist. Born in Madison, Wis., he earned a PhD in mathematical physics from Princeton University. He worked for the U.S. Naval Ordnance Laboratory during World War II, after which he worked for Bell Telephone Laboratories. His work there led to his sharing a 1956 Nobel Prize with William B. Shockley and Walter H. Brattain for the invention of the transistor. In 1972 he again shared a Nobel Prize, this time with Leon Cooper and J. Robert Schrieffer (born 1931) for developing the theory of superconductivity (1957); this theory (called the BCS theory, for Bardeen-Cooper-Schrieffer) is the basis for all later theoretical work in superconductivity. Bardeen was also the author of a theory explaining certain properties of semiconductors.

Bardeen.
BY COURTESY OF UNIVERSITY OF ILLINOIS AT URBANA-CHAMPAIGN

Bardesanes \ˌbär-də-ˈsā-nēz\ *or* **Bardaisan** \ˌbär-dī-ˈsän\ (AD 154–c. 222) Syrian Christian missionary. Born in Edessa, Syria (now in Turkey), he converted to Christianity in 179 and became a missionary. He attacked the fatalism of the Greek philosophers and, showing the influence of Gnosticism, ascribed the creation of the world, the devil, and evil to a hierarchy of gods rather than to the supreme God. His chief written work, *The Dialogue of Destiny,* is the oldest known example of Syriac literature. He is also remembered for his Syriac hymns.

Bardot \bär-ˈdō\, **Brigitte** (born 1934) French film actress. She was discovered by Roger Vadim when she appeared on a magazine cover at 15, and made her film debut in 1952. Vadim crafted her "sex kitten" image for his films *And God Created Woman* (1956) and *The Night Heaven Fell* (1958), which set box-office records and made her an international star. She displayed her acting ability in *The Truth* (1960), *Contempt* (1963), and *Viva Maria!* (1965). An animal-rights activist, she established an animal-welfare organization in 1987.

Barenboim \ˈbar-ən-ˌbȯim\, **Daniel** (born 1942) Israeli (Argentinian-born) pianist and conductor. A prodigy, he made his debut at 8. His family moved to Israel in 1952, and he first performed in the U.S. with L. Stokowski in 1957. As conductor, he led the English Chamber Orchestra (1964–75) and the Orchestre de Paris (1975–89), while pursuing brilliant careers as piano soloist and chamber musician. In 1967 he married the cellist Jacqueline Du Pré (1945–1987). In 1991 he became principal conductor of the Chicago Symphony Orchestra. He has been a prominent advocate for peace in the Middle East.

Barents Sea Outlying portion of the Arctic Ocean. Bounded by the Norwegian and northwestern Russian mainland and the Greenland Sea, it is 800 mi (1,300 km) long and 650 mi (1,050 km) wide, and covers 542,000 sq mi (1,405,000 sq km). Its average depth is 750 ft (229 m), with a maximum depth of 2,000 ft (600 m) in the major Bear Island Trench.

bargello \bär-ˈje-lō\ *or* **Florentine canvas work** Type of 17th-century embroidery, named for the upholstery of a set of Italian chairs at Florence's Bargello Museum. It consists of a wavy, zigzag pattern of flat vertical stitches laid parallel with the canvas weave, rather than crossing the intersections diagonally as in most canvas stitches, in gradating tones of the same color or in contrasting colors. The characteristic stitch is called Florentine, cushion, Hungarian, or flame stitch (an allusion to the flamelike gradation of color).

Bari \ˈbä-rē\ *ancient* **Barium.** Seaport city (pop., 1996: 337,000), and capital of Puglia region, southeastern Italy. Evidence shows that the site may have been inhabited since 1500 BC. Under the Romans it became an important port. In the 9th century AD it was a Moorish stronghold, but it was taken by the Byzantines in 885. Peter the Hermit preached the First Crusade there in 1096. Razed by the Sicilians in 1156, it acquired new greatness in the 13th century under Frederick II. It became an independent duchy in the 14th century, passed to the Kingdom of Naples in 1558, and became part of the Italian kingdom in 1861.

barite \ˈbar-ˌīt\ *or* **barytes** \bə-ˈrī-tēz\ *or* **heavy spar** Most common barium mineral, barium sulfate ($BaSO_4$). It commonly forms as platy crystals (known as crested barite). Barite is abundant in parts of Spain, Germany, and the U.S. Commercially, ground barite is used in oil well and gas well drilling muds; in the preparation of barium compounds; as a filler for paper, cloth, and phonograph records; as a white pigment; and as an inert material in colored paints.

Sample of crested barite from Missouri.
JOSEPH AND HELEN GUETTERMAN COLLECTION; PHOTOGRAPH, JOHN H. GERARD

baritone In vocal music, the voice or register between bass and tenor, the most common category of male voice. Its range is approximately from the A a 10th below middle C to the F above middle C. The term *baritonus* was first employed in 15th-century five- and six-voice part music; when four-part settings became standard, the baritone part was dropped, and natural baritones were forced to develop either their bass or tenor register. Instruments that play principally in the baritone register include the baritone saxophone and the baritone horn.

barium \ˈbar-ē-əm\ Chemical element, one of the alkaline earth metals, chemical symbol Ba, atomic number 56. It is very reactive and in compounds always has valence 2. In nature it is found chiefly as the minerals barite (barium sulfate) and witherite (barium carbonate). The element is used in metallurgy, and its compounds are used in fireworks, petroleum mining, and radiology and as pigments and reagents. All soluble barium compounds are toxic. Barium sulfate, one of the most insoluble salts known, is given in a "barium meal" as a contrast medium for X-ray examination of the gastrointestinal tract.

bark In woody plants, tissues outside of the vascular cambium. The term is also used more popularly to refer to all tissues outside the wood. The inner soft bark is produced by the vascular cambium; it consists of secondary phloem (food-conducting) tissue whose innermost layer transports food from the leaves to the rest of the plant. The layered outer bark contains cork and old, dead phloem. The bark is usually thinner than the woody part of the stem or root.

bark beetle Any member of the beetle family Scolytidae, many of which severely damage trees. Bark beetles are cylindrical, brown or black, and usually less than 0.25 in. (6 mm) long. A male and females (as many as 60 females with each male) bore into a tree and form a chamber where each female deposits her eggs. The emerging larvae bore away from the chamber, forming a characteristic series of tunnels. Different species attack particular trees, damaging roots, stems, seeds, or fruits. Some species transmit disease (e.g., elm bark beetles carry spores of the fungal Dutch elm disease).

Bark beetle (*Dendroctonus valens*).
WILLIAM E. FERGUSON

bark painting Abstract and figurative designs applied to nonwoven fabric made from bark, also called *tapa*, by scratching or painting. The most popular material is the inner bark of the paper mulberry tree. The bark is stripped off, soaked, and beaten until it is thin. Today hand-painted bark cloth is made in northern Australia, New Guinea, and parts of Melanesia. Styles and imagery vary by location, from naturalistic and stylized representations of human and animal forms to mythical beings, spirals, circles, and abstract motifs.

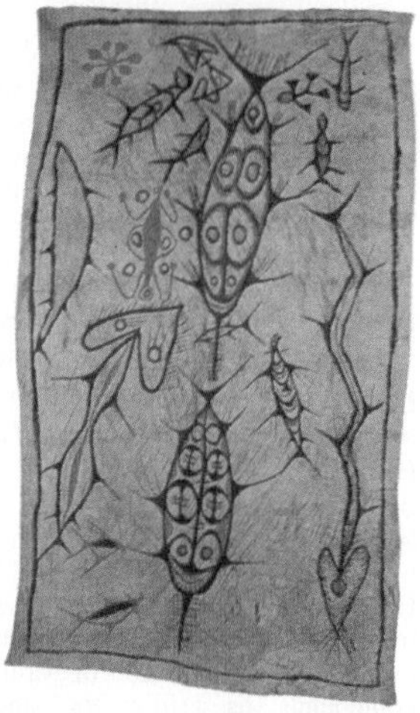
Tapa wall drapery painted with animal clan emblems, from the Teluk Jos Sudarso (Humboldt Bay) area, Irian Jaya (West New Guinea), Indonesia, in the Rijksmuseum voor Volkenkunde Justinus van Nassau, Breda, Neth.
HOLLE BILDARCHIV, BADEN-BADEN, GER

Barker, Harley Granville- See Harley GRANVILLE-BARKER

barking deer See MUNTJAC

Barkley, Alben W(illiam) (1877–1956) U.S. politician. Born in Graves Co., Ky., he practiced law from 1898. A Democrat, he was elected to the U.S. House of Representatives (1913–27) and the Senate (1927–49), where he served as majority leader 1937–47 and was a leading spokesman for the domestic and international policies of Pres. FRANKLIN ROOSEVELT. He served as vice president under Pres. HARRY TRUMAN (1949–53). He later returned to the Senate (1954–56).

Barkley, Charles (Wade) (born 1963) U.S. basketball player. Born in Leeds, Ala., he spent his collegiate career as a forward at Auburn University. He played for the Philadelphia 76ers (1984–91), the Phoenix Suns (1992–95), and the Houston Rockets (from 1996). He is known for his all-around abilities on the court and for his unapologetic outspokenness.

Barlach \'bär-läk\, **Ernst** (1870–1938) German sculptor, graphic artist, and writer. He studied in Hamburg, Dresden, and Paris. He achieved fame in the 1920s and '30s with the execution of several war memorials for the Weimar Republic. He became an outstanding exponent of German Expressionism, though his prints and sculpture were also strongly influenced by medieval German wood carving. He also wrote Expressionist plays, which he illustrated with woodcuts and lithographs. His studio at Güstrow was opened posthumously as a museum.

barley CEREAL plant of the genus *Hordeum,* in the family Poaceae (or Gramineae), and its edible grain. The three cultivated species are *Hordeum vulgare, H. distichum,* and *H. irregulare*. Barley is adaptable to a greater range of climate than any other cereal. About half of the world's crop is used as livestock feed, the rest for human food and for malting. Most BEER is made from malted barley, which is also used in distilled beverages (see MALT). Barley has a nutlike flavor and is high in carbohydrates, with moderate quantities of protein, calcium, and phosphorus. Barley flour is used to make unleavened bread and porridge. Pearl barley, the most popular form in many parts of the world, is often added to soups.

Barlow, Joel (1754–1812) U.S. writer and poet. He was a member of the group of young writers known as the Hartford (or Connecticut) Wits, whose patriotism led them to attempt to create a national literature. He became famous for his *Vision of Columbus* (1787), a poetic paean to America, but is remembered primarily for *The Hasty Pudding* (1796), a mock-heroic epic poem inspired by homesickness for New England.

Barmakids \'bär-mə-ˌkidz\ *or* **Barmecides** \'bär-mə-ˌsīdz\ Priestly family of Persian origin that achieved prominence in the 8th century as scribes and VIZIERS to the Abbasid caliphs (see ABBASID DYNASTY). They supported the arts and sciences, tolerated explorations of religion and philosophy, and promoted public works. The first notable Barmakid, Khalid ibn Barmak (died 781/82), helped establish the Abbasid caliphate; he became governor of Tabaristan and later Fars. His son Yahya (died 805) and grandsons Al-Fadl (died 808) and Jafar (died 803) held power as viziers but died in prison or were executed in a reversal of fortune, largely because their excessive power, wealth, and liberalism made them a threat to the caliph.

Barmen, Synod of Meeting of German Protestant leaders at Barmen in May 1934 to organize Protestant resistance to Nazism. Representatives came from Lutheran, Reformed, and United churches. Some church leaders had already chosen to limit their efforts to passive resistance, and others had been co-opted by the Nazi regime. The Pastors' Emergency League, headed by MARTIN NIEMOLLER, was the backbone of active resistance. The Synod was of major importance in the founding of the CONFESSING CHURCH by KARL BARTH and others.

barn Farm building used for sheltering animals, their feed and other supplies, farm machinery, and farm products. Barns are named according to their purpose (e.g., hog barns, dairy barns, tobacco barns, and tractor barns). The principal type in the U.S. is the general-purpose barn, used for housing LIVESTOCK and for storing HAY and grain. Most North American and European farms have one or more barns. They usually consist of two stories, though one-story barns gained in popularity in the late 20th century.

barn owl Any of several species of nocturnal BIRDS OF PREY (genus *Tyto*), sometimes called monkey-faced owls because of their heart-shaped facial disk and absence of ear tufts. Barn owls are about 12–16 in. (30–40 cm) long, white to gray or yellowish to brownish orange. Their dark eyes are smaller than those of other OWLS. They hunt mainly small rodents, often on cultivated land, and nest in hollow trees, buildings, towers, and old hawk nests. The common barn owl is found worldwide except in Antarctica and Micronesia. Other species occur only in the Old World.

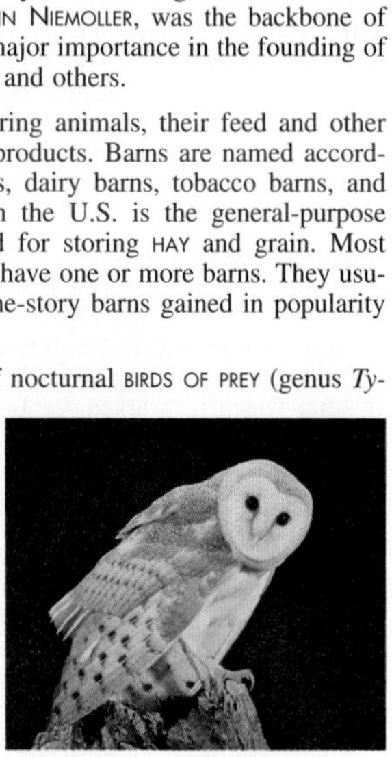
Common barn owl (*Tyto alba*).
KARL MASLOWSKI—PHOTO RESEARCHERS

Barnabas \'bär-nə-bəs\, **St.** *orig.* **Joseph the Levite** (fl. 1st century AD) Apostolic Father and early Christian missionary. Born in Cyprus, he was a hellenized Jew who joined the church in Jerusalem shortly after its founding. According to the Acts of the Apostles, he helped found the church in Antioch, calling on St. PAUL to assist him. A conflict eventually separated them, and Barnabas returned to the island of his birth. One legend holds that he was martyred in Cyprus. His reputed tomb is near the Monastery of St. Barnabas at Salamis, whose Christian community Paul and Barnabas founded.

barnacle Any of a majority of the 1,000 species of the subclass Cirripedia of marine CRUSTACEANS that, as adults, are covered with a shell made of hard calcium-containing plates and are permanently cemented, head down, to rocks, pilings, ships' hulls, driftwood, or seaweed or to the bodies of larger sea creatures, from clams to whales. Barnacles trap tiny particles of food with their cirri, feathery retractable organs that emerge from openings between the shell plates. Adult barnacles commonly are hermaphrodites.

Barnacle.
ANTHONY MERCIECA, FROM ROOT RESOURCES—EB INC.

barnacle goose Species *(Branta leucopsis)* of waterbird that resembles a small CANADA GOOSE, with dark back, white face, and black neck and bib. It winters in the northern British Isles and on the coasts of Denmark, Germany, and the Netherlands. In the Middle Ages, it was thought to hatch from BARNACLES, and thus was considered "fish" and could be eaten on Fridays.

Barnard \'bär-nərd\, **Christiaan (Neethling)** (born 1922) South African surgeon. He showed that intestinal atresia is caused by deficient fetal blood supply, which led to development of a surgical procedure to correct the formerly fatal defect. He introduced open-heart surgery to South Africa, designed a new artificial heart valve, and did animal heart transplant experiments. In 1967 Barnard's team performed the first human heart transplant, replacing the heart of Louis Washkansky with one from an accident victim. The transplant was successful, but Washkansky, given immunity-suppressing drugs to prevent rejection of the heart, died 18 days later from pneumonia.

Barnard, Henry (1811–1900) U.S. educator. Born in Hartford, Conn., he studied law and entered the state legislature, where he helped create a state board of education and the first teachers' institute (1839). With HORACE MANN, he undertook to reform the country's common schools; he was an innovator in instituting school inspections, textbook reviews, and parent-teacher organizations. As Rhode Island's first commissioner of education (from 1845) he worked to raise teachers' wages, repair buildings, and obtain higher-education appropriations. In 1855 he helped found the *American Journal of Education*. He was chancellor of the University of Wisconsin 1858–61. In 1867 he became the first U.S. commissioner of education, in which post he established a federal agency to collect national educational data.

Henry Barnard, detail of a portrait by an unknown artist; in the University of Wisconsin collection, Madison.

BY COURTESY OF THE UNIVERSITY OF WISCONSIN, MADISON

Barnard's star \'bär-nərdz\ Star about six light-years away from the sun, next nearest the sun after the ALPHA CENTAURI system, in the constellation Ophiuchus. Named for Edward Emerson Barnard (1857–1923), who discovered it in 1916, it has the largest PROPER MOTION of any known star. It is gradually nearing the solar system. The star is of special interest to astronomers because its proper motion was claimed to show periodic deviations attributed to the gravitational pull of two planets.

Barnburners See HUNKERS AND BARNBURNERS

Barnes, Albert C(oombs) (1872–1951) Pharmaceutical manufacturer and art collector. Born in Philadelphia, he obtained a medical degree and later studied in Germany. In 1902 he made a fortune with his invention of the antiseptic Argyrol. In 1905 he built a mansion in Merion, Pa., and began collecting seriously, amassing some 180 paintings by AUGUSTE RENOIR, 66 by PAUL CEZANNE, and 35 by PABLO PICASSO, and an extraordinary collection of 65 works by HENRI MATISSE. In 1922 he established the Barnes Foundation in a building next to his mansion. He himself wrote and lectured on art. In 1961, after extensive litigation, his galleries were opened to the public. An even more controversial ruling in 1991 overturned stipulations in his will, resulting in a worldwide traveling exhibition of paintings from the foundation and the first publication of color reproductions of them.

Barnes, Djuna (1892–1982) U.S. writer. Born in Cornwall-on-Hudson, N.Y., she worked as an artist and journalist in her youth. She went to Paris in 1920, where she became a well-known figure in the literary scene. She wrote plays, short stories, and poems; her masterpiece, the novel *Nightwood* (1936), tells of the homosexual and heterosexual loves of five extraordinary people. After returning to New York in 1940, she wrote little and lived reclusively.

Barnet \bär-'net\, **Charles (Daly)** (1913–1991) U.S. saxophonist and leader of one of the most popular big bands of the SWING era. Born to a wealthy New York family, Barnet took up the saxophone as a child and eventually performed on tenor, alto, and soprano. His was among the first racially integrated big bands, and his unabashed admiration for DUKE ELLINGTON and COUNT BASIE resulted in an effective synthesis of their styles. His best-known recording was "Cherokee."

Barnett, Ida B. Wells- See Ida B. WELLS

Barnsley Town (pop., 1991: 217,000), northern England. Located on the Dearne River northeast of Manchester, it is the administrative seat of SOUTH YORKSHIRE. Its major growth came in the 19th century as a coal-mining town in the heart of the Yorkshire coalfield. Local coal production has declined since the early 20th century, and light industries have been promoted.

Barnum, P(hineas) T(aylor) (1810–1891) U.S. showman. Born in Bethel, Conn., in 1841 he bought the American Museum, a collection of conventional exhibits in New York City, and transformed it into a carnival of live freaks and dramatic curiosities, which he promoted with sensational publicity. He exhibited the midget Tom Thumb with great international success, and brought JENNY LIND (billed as the "Swedish Nightingale") to the U.S. for a profitable concert tour in 1850. By the time his museum closed in 1868 after several fires, he had enticed 82 million visitors there. In 1871 he started a circus and in 1881 joined a rival, James A. Bailey (1847–1906), to form the three-ring Barnum and Bailey's Circus, which featured the elephant Jumbo as part of the "Greatest Show on Earth."

Barocci \bä-'rȯt-chē\, **Federico** (c. 1535–1612) Italian painter. Except for two visits to Rome (mid-1550s, 1560–63), where he painted frescoes for Pope Pius IV's casino in the Vatican Gardens, he seems to have spent his whole life in and near Urbino. He executed altarpieces and devotional paintings in a style characterized by subtle color harmonies and warmth of feeling. His patrons included the duke of Urbino and Emperor Rudolf II (1552–1612), and he received commissions from the cathedrals of Genoa and Perugia. His famous works include the *Deposition* (1567–69) and the *Madonna del Popolo* (1579). A prolific draftsman, he was one of the first artists to use colored chalks. He enjoyed a long and productive career, becoming one of the leading painters in central Italy.

Baroda See VADODARA

Baroja (y Nessi) \bȧ-'rō-hä\, **Pío** (1872–1956) Basque writer. He wrote 11 trilogies dealing with contemporary social problems, the best known of which is *The Struggle for Life* (1904). His most ambitious project was a long cycle of works about a 19th-century insurgent and his era. He wrote almost 100 novels, including *Zalacaín el aventurero* (1909). Because of his anti-Christian views, stubborn insistence on nonconformity, and somewhat pessimistic tone, he never achieved great popularity. He is considered the foremost Spanish novelist of his time.

barometer Device used to measure ATMOSPHERIC PRESSURE. Because atmospheric pressure changes with distance above or below sea level, a barometer can also be used to measure altitude. In the mercury barometer, atmospheric pressure balances a column of MERCURY, the height of which can be precisely measured. Normal atmospheric pressure is about 14.7 lb per square inch, equivalent to 30 in. (760 mm) of mercury. Other liquids can be used in barometers, but mercury is the most common because of its great density. An aneroid barometer indicates pressure on a dial using a needle that is mechanically linked to a partially evacuated chamber, which responds to pressure changes.

barometric pressure See ATMOSPHERIC PRESSURE

baron Title of nobility, ranking in modern times immediately below a VISCOUNT or a COUNT (in countries without viscounts). The wife of a baron is a baroness. Originally, in the early Middle Ages, the term designated a tenant of whatever rank who held a tenure of barony direct from the king. Gradually, it came to mean a powerful personage, and therefore a magnate. The rights and title may be conferred for military or other honorable service.

baronet British hereditary rank of honor, first created by JAMES I in 1611 to raise money, ostensibly for support of troops in Ulster. The baronetage is not part of the peerage, nor is it an order of knighthood. A baronet ranks below a BARON but above all KNIGHTS except a Knight of the Garter (see Order of the GARTER). The baronetcy is inherited by the male heirs of a baronet.

Baroque, Late See ROCOCO STYLE

baroque architecture \bə-'rōk\ Architectural style originating in late-16th-century Italy and lasting in some regions, notably Germany and colonial South America, until the 18th century. It had its origins in the COUNTER-REFORMATION, when the Catholic Church launched an overtly emotional and sensory appeal to the faithful. Complex plan shapes, often based on the oval, and the dynamic opposition and interpenetration of spaces were favored to heighten the feeling of motion and sensuality. Other characteristic qualities are grandeur, drama and contrast (especially in lighting), curvaceousness, and an often dizzying array of rich surface treatments, twisting elements, and gilded statuary. Architects unabashedly applied bright colors and illusory, vividly painted ceilings. Outstanding practitioners in Italy include Gian Lorenzo Bernini, Carlo Maderno (1556–1629), Francesco Borromini, and Guarino Guarini (1624–1683). Classical elements subdued baroque architecture in France. In Central Europe, the baroque arrived late but flourished in the works of such architects as the Austrian J. B. Fischer von Erlach (1656–1723). Its impact in Britain can be seen in the works of Christopher Wren. The Late Baroque style is often referred to as Rococo or, in Spain and Spanish America, as Churrigueresque.

baroque period Era in the arts that originated in Italy in the 17th century and flourished elsewhere well into the 18th century. It embraced painting, sculpture, architecture, the applied arts, and music. The word, derived from a Portuguese term for an irregularly shaped pearl, and originally used derogatorily, has long been employed to describe a variety of characteristics, from dramatic and bizarre to overdecorated. The style was embraced by countries absorbed in the Counter-Reformation; artworks commissioned by the Roman Catholic Church were overtly emotional and sensory. The period's most notable practitioners were the Carracci family, Caravaggio, and Gian Lorenzo Bernini. A spectacular example of the baroque arts is the Palace of Versailles. In music, the baroque era is usually considered to extend from c. 1600 to c. 1750, when such significant new vocal and instrumental genres as opera, oratorio, cantata, sonata, and concerto were introduced, and such towering composers as C. Monteverdi, J.S. Bach, and G.F. Handel flourished.

Barotse See Lozi

Barquisimeto \ˌbär-kē-sē-ˈmā-tō\ City (pop., 1992: 693,000), northwestern Venezuela. The capital of Lara state, it is located at the northern end of the Cordillera Mérida, at an altitude of 1,856 ft (566 m). Founded in 1552 as Nueva Segovia, it is one of the country's oldest cities. It was almost destroyed by an earthquake in 1812, and was further damaged in 19th-century civil wars. It is a hub of transport and commerce, and the center of an agricultural region.

Barr, Roseanne *later* **Roseanne Arnold** (born 1952) U.S. comedian. Born in Salt Lake City, she performed in comedy clubs in Denver and Los Angeles from 1981. Known for her salty, working-class persona, she starred in the hugely successful comedy series *Roseanne* (1988–97).

barracuda Any of about 20 species of predaceous marine fishes (family Sphyraenidae) found in all warm and tropical regions and in some more temperate areas. Swift and powerful, barracudas are slender and have small scales, a jutting lower jaw, and a large mouth with many large, sharp teeth. They vary in size from relatively small to 4–6 ft (1.2–1.8 m) long. They are primarily fish eaters. They are popular sport fishes and are caught for food, though in certain seas they may become contaminated with a toxic substance. Bold and inquisitive, they are potentially dangerous to humans when large.

Barracuda (*Sphyraena*).
C. LEROY FRENCH—TOM STACK & ASSOCIATES

Barranquilla \ˌbä-rän-ˈkē-yä\ City (pop., 1993: 1,091,000), northern Colombia. Founded in 1629, 10 mi (16 km) from the mouth of the Magdalena River, it remained unimportant until the 1930s, when the clearing of sandbars enabled it to thrive as a Caribbean seaport. It has since been rivaled by the Pacific port of Buenaventura, but it still handles goods from the interior and is the terminus of natural-gas pipelines from northern Colombia.

Barraqué \bà-rà-ˈkā\, **Jean** (1928–1973) French composer. A student of Jean Langlais (1907–1991) and O. Messiaen, his major work (employing a radically nonrepetitive style) was a planned five-part reflection on Hermann Broch's *Death of Virgil*, of which he completed three parts— *. . . au-delà du hasard* (1959), *Chant après chant* (1966), and *Le temps restitué* (1968)—before his early death. He also composed a huge piano sonata (1952) and a clarinet concerto (1968).

Barras \bà-ˈràs\, **Paul-François-Jean-Nicolas, vicomte (Viscount) de** (1755–1829) French revolutionary. A Provençal nobleman, Barras became disenchanted with the royal regime and welcomed the French Revolution. Elected to the National Convention (1792), he played a key role in the overthrow of Maximilien Robespierre and emerged as the commander of the army of the interior and the police. In 1795 he and Napoleon defended the regime against a royalist insurrection and established the Directory, with Barras as chief among the five directors. The Coup of 18 Fructidor brought him greater power, but he was overthrown in 1799 and exiled from Paris on suspicion of conspiracy to restore the monarchy.

Barrault \bà-ˈrō\, **Jean-Louis** (1910–1994) French actor and director. He made his acting debut in Paris (1931) and joined the Comédie-Française (1940–46) as an actor and director. He and his wife, Madeleine Renaud, formed their own company (1946–58) at the Théâtre Marigny. There they performed a mixture of French and foreign classics and modern plays that helped revive French theater after World War II. He was appointed director of the Théâtre de France (1959–68) and later directed at several other Paris theaters (1972–81). He appeared in over 20 films and was best known for his role in *The Children of Paradise* (1945).

Barre, Mohamed Siad See Mohamed Siad Barre

Barrès \bà-ˈres\, **(Auguste-) Maurice** (1862–1923) French writer and politician. He served in the Chamber of Deputies 1889–93 and became a strong nationalist. With Charles Maurras, he expounded the doctrines of the French Nationalist Party in two newspapers, and in his novels he expressed an individualism that included a deep-rooted attachment to his native region and a fervent nationalism. His series of novels titled "Les Bastions de l'Est" earned success as French propaganda during World War I.

Barrès, 1906.
H. ROGER-VIOLLET

Barrie, James (Matthew) *later* **Sir James** (1860–1937) British playwright and novelist. After moving to London, he wrote *Auld Licht Idylls* (1888) about his native Scotland. His best-selling novel *The Little Minister* (1891) was made into a play in 1897. *Quality Street* (1901) and *The Admirable Crichton* (1902) ran successfully in London. After creating the stories of Peter Pan for a friend's sons, he won great success with his classic children's play *Peter Pan, the Boy Who Wouldn't Grow Up* (1904). His other plays include *What Every Woman Knows* (1908), *The Twelve-Pound Look* (1910), and *Dear Brutus* (1917).

barrier penetration See tunneling

barrister \ˈbar-ə-stər\ One of two types of practicing lawyers in Britain (the other is the solicitor). Barristers engage in advocacy (trial work), and only they may argue cases before a high court. A barrister must be a member of one of the four Inns of Court. In Canada, all lawyers are both barristers and solicitors, though individual lawyers may describe themselves as one or the other. In Scotland trial lawyers are called advocates.

Barrow, Clyde and Bonnie Parker *known as* **Bonnie and Clyde** (1909–1934, 1911–1934) U.S. robbers. Clyde, born in Telico, Texas, had been a robber long before meeting Bonnie (born in Rowena, Texas) in 1930. After Clyde spent time in prison (1930–32), he and Bonnie began their 21-month criminal spree, robbing gas stations, restaurants, and small-town banks in Texas, Oklahoma, New Mexico, and Missouri and killing a number of people. Their exploits received wide coverage by newspapers. In 1934 they were betrayed by a friend and shot by police in a roadblock ambush.

Barry, comtesse du See comtesse DU BARRY

Barry, John (1745–1803) U.S. (Irish-born) naval officer. He emigrated to America in 1760 and was a merchant shipmaster out of Philadelphia at age 21. He outfitted the first American fleet in 1776 and as captain of a frigate captured several British ships. He fought the last battle of the Revolution in March 1783 in the Straits of Florida, where he defeated three British ships. After the war he was recalled to active service as senior captain of the new U.S. Navy. He was often called the "Father of the Navy" because he trained many future naval officers.

Barrymore family U.S. theatrical family. Maurice Barrymore (born Herbert Blythe) (1847–1905) made his stage debut in London before moving to New York (1875), where he adopted Barrymore as his stage name. He joined Augustin Daly's company and in 1876 married Georgiana Drew, of the theatrical DREW FAMILY. Their eldest child, Lionel (1878–1954), became a leading Broadway actor in such plays as *Peter Ibbetson* (1917) and *The Copperhead* (1918), then moved to Hollywood in 1926, where he appeared in such films as *A Free Soul* (1931, Academy Award) and *Grand Hotel* (1932). Famous as a character actor, he made some 200 films, including 15 "Dr. Kildare" pictures. His sister Ethel (1879–1959) appeared in London in *The Bells* and *Peter the Great* (1898) and on Broadway in *Captain Jinks of the Horse Marines* (1901). She opened the New York theater named for her in 1928 in *The Kingdom of God* and later starred in *The Corn Is Green* (1940). She appeared in over 30 films, including *None but the Lonely Heart* (1944, Academy Award) and *The Spiral Staircase* (1946). Their brother John (1882–1942) was acclaimed in such plays as *Justice* (1916), *Richard III* (1920), and especially *Hamlet* (1922). His films include *Dr. Jekyll and Mr. Hyde* (1920) and *Dinner at Eight* (1933). An alcoholic, he was known for his flamboyant behavior. John's granddaughter Drew Barrymore (born 1975) first won notice at age 7 in *E.T.* (1982).

barter Direct exchange of goods or services without the use of money or any other intervening medium of exchange. Barter is conducted either according to established rates of exchange or by bargaining. It is common in nonliterate societies. See also CURRENCY, GIFT EXCHANGE.

Barth, John *orig.* **John Simmons Barth, Jr.** (born 1930) U.S. writer. Born in Cambridge, Md., he grew up on Maryland's eastern shore, the locale of much of his writing, and from 1953 he taught principally at Johns Hopkins University. Apart from the experimental pieces in *Lost in the Funhouse* (1968), his best-known works are the novels *The Floating Opera* (1956), *The End of the Road* (1958), *The Sot-Weed Factor* (1960), *Giles Goat-Boy* (1966), and *The Tidewater Tales* (1987), most of which play with and parody traditional narrative forms, combining philosophical depth with biting satire and boisterous, often bawdy humor.

Barth \'bärt\, **Karl** (1886–1968) Swiss theologian. Born in Basel, he studied at the Universities of Berlin, Tübingen, and Marburg. In 1911–21 he was a pastor at Safenwil, Switzerland. The tragedy of World War I made him question the liberal theology of his teachers, rooted in post-Enlightenment ideas. With *The Epistle to the Romans* (1919) he inaugurated a radical turnaround in Protestant thought, initiating a trend toward neoorthodoxy. The work led to his appointment as professor at Göttingen (1921), Münster (1925), and Bonn (1930). He was a founder of the CONFESSING CHURCH, which opposed the Nazi regime; when his refusal to take the oath of allegiance to Hitler cost him his chair at Bonn, he returned to Basel. He spoke at the opening of the World Council of Churches in 1948 and visited Rome following the Second Vatican Council.

Barthelme \'bärt-əl-mē\, **Donald** (1931–1989) U.S. writer. Born in Philadelphia, he worked as a journalist, journal editor, and museum director before his fiction began to be published. He is known for modernist "collages" marked by technical experimentation and melancholy gaiety. His story collections include *Come Back, Dr. Caligari* (1964), *City Life* (1970), *Sadness* (1972), *Sixty Stories* (1981), and *Overnight to Many Distant Cities* (1983); his novels include *Snow White* (1967), *The Dead Father* (1975), *Paradise* (1986), and *The King* (1990). His brother Frederick (born 1943) is also a novelist (*Second Marriage*, 1984) and short-story writer (*Moon Deluxe*, 1983).

Barthes \'bärt\, **Roland (Gérard)** (1915–1980) French social and literary critic. His early books examined the arbitrariness of the constructs of language and applied similar analyses to popular-culture phenomena. He analyzed mass culture in *Mythologies* (1957). *On Racine* (1963) set off a literary furor, pitting him against more traditional French literary scholars. His later contributions to SEMIOTICS included the even more radical *S/Z* (1970); *The Empire of Signs* (1970), his study of Japan; and other significant works that brought his theories wide (if belated) attention in the 1970s and helped establish STRUCTURALISM as one of the leading intellectual movements of the 20th century. In 1976 he became the first person to hold the chair of literary semiology at the Collège de France.

Bartholdi \bär-'tòl-dē\, **Frédéric-Auguste** (1834–1904) French sculptor. He studied sculpture and painting in Paris. In 1865 he and several others conceived the idea for a monument to the Franco-American alliance of 1778, which resulted in his design and execution of the STATUE OF LIBERTY (1875–86). His masterpiece is the *Lion of Belfort* (1871–80), carved out of the red sandstone of a hill overlooking Belfort in eastern France.

Bartholomaeus (Anglicus) \bär-ˌtòl-ə-'mā-əs\ *or* **Bartholomew the Englishman** (fl. c. 1220–1240) Franciscan encyclopedist. Though primarily interested in scripture and theology, in his 19-volume encyclopedia *On the Properties of Things* he covered all customary knowledge of his time and was the first to make readily available the views of Greek, Jewish, and Arabic scholars on medical and scientific subjects. The encyclopedia was printed in English translation c. 1495.

Bartholomew, St. (fl. 1st century AD) One of the 12 APOSTLES of JESUS. He is mentioned only briefly in the New Testament, and his Hebrew name may have been Nathanael bar Tolmai. By tradition he was a missionary to Ethiopia, Mesopotamia, Parthia (in modern Iran), Lycaonia (in modern Turkey), and Armenia. He was supposedly martyred at the command of the Armenian king Astyages, who had him flayed and beheaded.

Barthou \bär-'tü\, **(Jean-) Louis** (1862–1934) French politician. Elected to the Chamber of Deputies in 1889, he served in various conservative governments. He was appointed premier (1913) and secured the passage of a bill requiring three years' compulsive military service. He represented France at the Conference of GENOA, entered the Senate, and became chairman of the reparations commission. Named foreign minister in 1934, he was assassinated with King ALEXANDER of Yugoslavia during the latter's visit to France.

Bartlett, Frederic C(harles) *later* **Sir Frederic** (1886–1969) British psychologist best known for his studies of memory. The first professor of experimental psychology at Cambridge University (1931–52), he also directed the university's psychological laboratory. His major work, *Remembering* (1932), described memories not as direct recollections but rather as mental reconstructions colored by cultural attitudes and personal habits.

Bartlett, John (1820–1905) U.S. bookseller and editor. Born in Plymouth, Mass., Bartlett was an employee and then owner of the Harvard University Bookstore. In 1855 he published the work for which he is best known, *Familiar Quotations* (1855), based largely on a notebook he kept for his customers. It was greatly expanded in later editions; the 16th edition appeared in 1992. He also wrote a *Complete Concordance to Shakespeare's Dramatic Works and Poems* (1894), outstanding for the number and fullness of its citations.

John Bartlett.
BY COURTESY OF LITTLE, BROWN AND CO.

Bartók \'bär-tōk\, **Béla** (1881–1945) Hungarian composer and ethnomusicologist. He developed a superb piano technique at an early age. In 1904 he set about researching Hungarian folk music, having discovered that the folk-music repertory generally accepted as Hungarian was in fact largely urban Gypsy music. His fieldwork with Z. KODALY formed the basis for all later research in the field, and he published major studies of Hungarian, Romanian, and Slovakian folk music. He worked folk themes and rhythms insistently into his own music, giving it its most characteristic aspect. He also toured widely as a virtuoso pianist. He emigrated to the U.S. in 1940, where he was inadequately recognized. His works include the opera *Bluebeard's Castle* (1911), the ballet *The Miraculous Mandarin* (1923), six celebrated string quartets (1908–39), the didactic piano set *Mikrokosmos* (1926–39), *Music for Strings, Percussion and Celesta* (1936), *Concerto for Orchestra* (1943), *Sonata for Two Pianos and Percussion* (1937), two violin concertos (1908, 1938), three piano concertos (1926, 1931, 1945), and a viola concerto (1945). The greatest composer Hungary ever produced, Bartók was one of the giants of 20th-century music.

Bartolomé de Cárdenas See Bartolome BERMEJO

Bartolomeo \ˌbär-tō-lō-ˈmā-ō\, **Fra** *orig.* **Baccio della Porta** (1472–1517) Italian painter active in Florence. His early works, such as the *Annunciation* (1497) in Volterra Cathedral, were influenced by PERUGINO and LEONARDO DA VINCI. In 1500 he joined the Dominican order. He visited Venice in 1508 and Rome in 1513. He painted religious subjects, primarily the Madonna and Child in various settings, with monumental figures grouped in balanced compositions, and became the leading painter in Florence, rivaled only by ANDREA DEL SARTO. He was a brilliant draftsman; his drawings include figure studies and landscape and nature studies.

Barton, Clara *orig.* **Clarissa Harlowe** (1821–1912) U.S. nurse, founder of the American RED CROSS. Born in Oxford, Miss., she initially worked as a schoolteacher. During the Civil War she organized the distribution of supplies for wounded soldiers and set up a bureau of records to help search for missing men, becoming known as the "angel of the battlefield." She later helped with relief work for victims of the Franco–Prussian War and became associated with the International Red Cross. In 1881 she founded the American Red Cross. She lobbied Congress to sign the GENEVA CONVENTION, and wrote the U.S. amendment to the constitution of the Red Cross, which provides for relief not only in war but also in natural disasters. She served as president of the American Red Cross until 1904.

Barton, Derek H(arold) R(ichard) *later* **Sir Derek** (1918–1998) British chemist. Unsatisfied in his father's carpentry business, he entered London's Imperial College and received his doctorate in 1942. His studies revealed that organic molecules have a preferred three-dimensional form from which their chemical properties can be inferred. This research earned him the 1969 Nobel Prize for Chemistry, shared with Odd Hassel of Norway.

Bartram \ˈbär-trəm\, **John** (1699–1777) U.S. naturalist and explorer, considered the "father of American botany." Largely self-educated, he was a friend of BENJAMIN FRANKLIN and the botanist for the American colonies to GEORGE III. He was the first North American experimenter to hybridize flowering plants, and he established near Philadelphia a botanical garden that became internationally famous. He explored the Alleghenies and the Carolinas and in 1743 was commissioned by the British crown to explore the wilderness north to Lake Ontario in Canada. In 1765–66 he explored extensively in Florida with his son WILLIAM BARTRAM.

Bartram, William (1739–1823) U.S. naturalist and botanist. Born in Kingsessing, Pa., the son of JOHN BARTRAM, he described the abundant river swamps of the southeastern U.S. in their primeval condition in his *Travels through North and South Carolina, Georgia, East and West Florida* (1791). He was a major precursor of J.J. AUDUBON, and his book was influential among the English and French Romantics.

Baruch \bə-ˈrük\, **Bernard (Mannes)** (1870–1965) U.S. financier and adviser to presidents. Born in Camden, S.C., he went to work in Wall Street brokerage houses, where he amassed a fortune as a speculator. During World War I he was appointed chairman of the War Industries Board by Pres. WOODROW WILSON. In 1919 he was a member of the economic council at the Versailles peace conference and one of Wilson's advisers on the treaty. In World War II he was an unofficial adviser on economic mobilization to Pres. FRANKLIN ROOSEVELT. Later he was instrumental in setting U.N. policy on the international control of atomic energy.

Barye \bȧ-ˈrē\, **Antoine-Louis** (1796–1875) French sculptor. The son of a goldsmith, he was apprenticed at 13 to an engraver. He studied at the École des Beaux-Arts (1818–23), and began to sculpt animal forms c. 1819. Influenced by THEODORE GERICAULT, he had a unique talent for rendering dynamic tension and exact anatomical detail. His most famous works depict wild animals devouring their prey; he also executed groups of domestic animals. His notable bronzes include *Lion Devouring a Gavial Crocodile* (1831) and an equestrian statue of Napoleon at Ajaccio, Corsica (1860–65).

baryon \ˈbar-ē-ˌän\ Any member of one of two classes of HADRONS. Baryons are heavy SUBATOMIC PARTICLES made up of three QUARKS. They are characterized by a baryon number, *B*, of 1, and have half-integer spin values. Their antiparticles (see ANTIMATTER), called antibaryons, have a baryon number of −1. Both PROTONS and NEUTRONS are baryons.

Baryshnikov \bə-ˈrish-nə-ˌkȯf\, **Mikhail (Nikolayevich)** (born 1948) Russian-U.S. dancer preeminent in the 1970s and 1980s. After entering the Kirov Ballet's training school in St. Petersburg in 1963, he joined the company as a soloist in 1966. There he quickly became popular with Soviet audiences, dancing leading roles created for him in such ballets as *Gorianka* (1968) and *Vestris* (1969). He defected while on tour in Canada in 1974. He danced with the AMERICAN BALLET THEATRE until 1978, winning enormous acclaim, and served as its artistic director from 1980 to 1989. He has danced and acted in several movies and on television. In 1990 he cofounded the White Oak Dance Project.

barytes See BARITE

Barzakh \ˈbär-ˌzäk\, **al-** In Islam, the period between the burial of the dead and the final judgment. According to the 14th-century *Book of the Soul,* the Angel of Death appears when a person dies and instructs the soul to depart either to "the wrath of God" or to his mercy. After this accounting the soul is returned to the body in the grave, and the deceased is questioned about Islamic doctrine. At the final judgment, all are resurrected and endowed with physical bodies to suffer or enjoy whatever lies in store for them.

bas-relief \ˌbä-ri-ˈlēf\ *or* **low relief** Sculptural form in which figures are carved in a flat surface and project only slightly from the background rather than standing freely. Depending on the degree of projection, reliefs may also be classified as high or medium relief.

basalt \bə-ˈsȯlt\ Dark IGNEOUS ROCK that is low in silica content and comparatively rich in iron and magnesium. Some basalts are glassy (have no visible crystals), and many are very fine-grained and compact. Basaltic lavas may be spongy or pumice-like. Olivine and augite are the most common minerals in basalts; PLAGIOCLASE is also present. Basalts may be broadly classified into two main groups. Calc-alkali basalts predominate among the lavas of mountain belts; the active volcanoes of Mauna Loa and Kilauea in Hawaii erupt calc-alkali lavas. Alkali basalts predominate among the lavas of the ocean basins and are also common in mountain belts.

base In chemistry, any substance that in water solution is slippery to the touch, tastes bitter, changes the color of acid-base indicators (e.g., LITMUS paper), reacts with ACIDS to form SALTS, and promotes certain chemical reactions (e.g., base CATALYSIS). Examples of bases are the HYDROXIDES of the ALKALI METALS and alkaline earth metals (SODIUM, CALCIUM, etc.) and the water solutions of AMMONIA or its derivatives (AMINES). Such substances produce hydroxide IONS (OH^-) in water solutions. Broader definitions of bases cover situations in which water is not present. See also ACID-BASE THEORY, ALKALI, NUCLEOPHILE.

baseball Game played with a bat and fist-sized ball between two teams of nine or ten (if a designated hitter is used) players each on a large field having four bases laid out in a square, or diamond, whose outlines mark the course a runner must take to score. Teams alternate positions as batters and fielders, exchanging places when three members of the batting team are put out. Batters try to hit a pitched ball out of reach of the fielding team and run a complete circuit around the bases for a run (1 point). The team that scores the most runs in nine innings (times at bat) wins the game. If the game is tied, extra innings are played until the tie is broken. Baseball is traditionally considered the national pastime of the U.S. It was once thought to have been invented in

1839 by ABNER DOUBLEDAY in Cooperstown, N.Y., but it is more likely that baseball developed from an 18th-century English game called rounders, as modified by ALEXANDER CARTWRIGHT. The first professional association, comprising teams from eight cities, was formed in 1871; in 1876 it became the NATIONAL LEAGUE. A rival AMERICAN LEAGUE was founded in 1900, and since 1903 the winning teams of each league have played a postseason championship known as the WORLD SERIES. Canadian teams were admitted to the major leagues in 1968 and 1976. In the early 20th century there were separate NEGRO LEAGUES, but they began to disband in the 1940s as black players became integrated into the majors (see JACKIE ROBINSON). The regular baseball season extends from early April to early October, followed by division playoffs and the World Series. A Baseball Hall of Fame is located in Cooperstown.

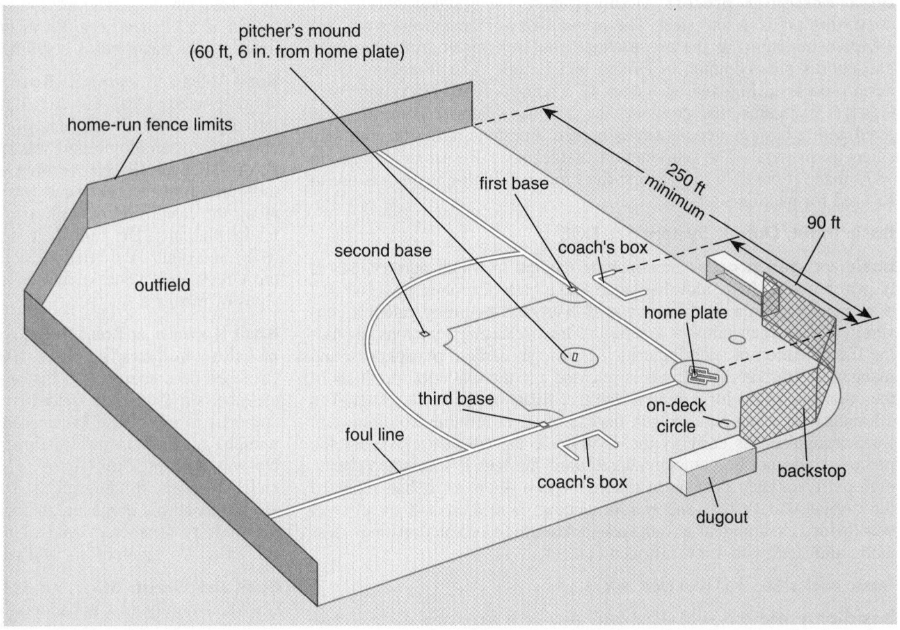

A typical college or professional baseball field. The batter stands at home plate, the pitcher at the pitcher's mound. When a hit falls outside the foul lines, the batter may not run. Any ball over the fence represents a home run for the batter. Coaches at first and third base tell runners when to run. Players wait to bat in their team's dugout. Home-run fence distances and configurations vary from field to field. Softball is played on a similar field, but with bases closer together (typically 60 ft apart) and the pitcher's mound closer to the plate (40 ft for women, 46 ft for men), and the home-run fence may be as close as 200 ft.

© 2002 MERRIAM-WEBSTER INC.

Basel \'bä-zəl\ *or* **Basle** \'bäl\ *French* **Bâle** \'bål\ City (pop., 1996: 174,000; metro. area pop.: 404,000), northwestern Switzerland. It straddles the RHINE at the point where France, Germany, and Switzerland meet. It was originally a settlement of the Celtic Rauraci tribe. Its university, the first in Switzerland, was founded by Pope Pius II while attending the Council of BASEL (1431–49). In 1501 Basel was admitted into the Swiss Confederation. When DESIDERIUS ERASMUS taught at the university 1521–29, the city became a center of humanism and of the REFORMATION. Primarily German-speaking and Protestant, it is an important trading and industrial city and river port.

Basel, Council of (1431–49) Council of the Roman Catholic Church held in Basel, Switzerland. Called during the Western SCHISM, it addressed the question of papal supremacy and the problem of the HUSSITE heresy. Its members renewed the decree *Sacrosancta* (issued by the Council of CONSTANCE), which declared the council's authority greater than the pope's, and voted to receive most Hussites back into the church. In 1437 Pope Eugenius IV transferred the council to Ferrara, but several members remained in Basel as a rump council. They were later excommunicated by Eugenius, and they responded by electing a new pope, Felix V. On the death of Eugenius, his successor, NICHOLAS V, obliged Felix to abdicate and ended the rump council.

basenji \bə-'sen-jē\ Ancient breed of HOUND native to central Africa, where it is used to point and retrieve and to drive quarry into a net. Known as the barkless dog, it produces a variety of sounds other than barks. Its finely wrinkled forehead, erect ears, and tightly curled tail give it a characteristic alert expression. It has a short, silky reddish brown, black, or black-and-tan coat and white feet, chest, and tail tip. It stands 16–17 in. (41–43 cm) high and weighs 22–24 lbs (10–11 kg). It is clean and gentle.

Basenji.

SALLY ANNE THOMPSON—EB INC.

BASF AG German chemical and plastics manufacturing company. Founded in 1865, BASF (the full German name means "Baden Aniline and Soda Factory") was part of the chemical cartel IG FARBEN from 1925 until 1945, when the latter was dissolved by the Allies. Refounded in 1952, BASF today operates in some 30 countries. Its products include oil and natural gas, fertilizers, synthetic fibers, dyes and pigments, inks and printing accessories, electronics, and pharmaceuticals. Its headquarters are in Ludwigshafen am Rhein.

Bashan \'bā-shən\ Ancient country, eastern PALESTINE. Frequently cited in the Old Testament and later important in the Roman empire, it was located in what is now Syria. In New Testament times, Bashan ranked as one of the great granaries of the Roman empire. One of its towns, Bozrah (Roman Bostra), was important to both Nabataea and Rome. AUGUSTUS made HEROD THE GREAT ruler of Bashan, and in AD 106 TRAJAN brought the whole Nabataean kingdom under the empire in creating the province of Arabia, with Bostra (see BUSRA) as its capital. The country went into decline in the 7th century.

Basho \ˌbäsh-'ō\ *or* **Matsuo Basho** \mä-'tsü-ō\ *orig.* **Matsuo Munefusa** (1644–1694) Japanese HAIKU poet, the greatest practitioner of the form. Following the Zen philosophy he studied, he attempted to compress the meaning of the world into the simple pattern of his poetry, disclosing hidden hopes in small things and showing the interdependence of all objects. His *The Narrow Road to the Deep North* (1694), a poetic prose travelogue, is one of the loveliest works of Japanese literature.

BASIC *in full* **Beginner's All-purpose Symbolic Instruction Code** Computer PROGRAMMING LANGUAGE developed by JOHN G. KEMENY and Thomas E. Kurtz (born 1928) at Dartmouth College in the mid-1960s. One of the simplest high-level languages, with commands similar to English, it can be learned with relative ease even by schoolchildren and novice programmers. Since c. 1980, BASIC has been popular for use on PERSONAL COMPUTERS.

basic action In ACTION THEORY, an action that is not performed by performing any other action. If someone turns on the light by flipping the switch, flipping the switch is more basic than turning on the light (because one cannot flip the switch by turning on the light), but moving one's finger is unqualifiedly basic, since one does not do it by doing anything else. Contemporary philosophers have debated how to individuate acts—whether flipping the switch and turning on the light represent one act or two closely related acts (see INDIVIDUATION).

basic Bessemer process Modification of the BESSEMER PROCESS for converting pig iron into steel. The original Bessemer converter was not effective in removing the PHOSPHORUS from iron made from the high-phosphorus ores common in Britain and Europe. The invention of the basic process in England by Sidney G. Thomas (1850–1885) and PERCY GILCHRIST overcame this problem; the Thomas-Gilchrist converter was lined with a basic material such as burned limestone rather than an acid siliceous material. The introduction of the basic Bessemer process in 1879 made it possible for the first time for such high-phosphorus ore to be used for making STEEL.

Basic Input/Output System See BIOS

basic oxygen process Steelmaking method in which pure OXYGEN is blown through a long, movable lance into a bath of molten BLAST-FURNACE IRON and scrap, in a steel furnace with a REFRACTORY lining called a converter. The oxygen initiates a series of heat-releasing reactions, including the oxidation of such impurities as silicon, carbon, phosphorus, and manganese; carbon-dioxide gas is released and the oxidation products of the other impurities form molten slag that floats on the molten STEEL. The advantages of using pure oxygen instead of air in refining iron into steel were recognized as early as the 1850s (see BESSEMER PROCESS), but the process could not be commercialized until the late 1940s, when cheap, high-purity oxygen became available. Within 40 years it had replaced the OPEN-HEARTH PROCESS and was producing more than half of all steel worldwide. Commercial advantages include high production rates, less labor, and steel with a low nitrogen content.

basic rocks See ACID AND BASIC ROCKS

basidiomycete \bə-ˌsi-dē-ō-ˈmī-ˌsēt\ Any of a large and diverse class of fungi (division Mycota), including jelly and shelf, or bracket, fungi; MUSHROOMS, PUFFBALLS, and stinkhorns; and the rusts and SMUTS. The club-shaped, SPORE-bearing organ (basidium) is borne on a usually large and conspicuous fruiting body. Basidiomycetes include bird's-nest fungi, whose hollow fruiting bodies resemble nests containing eggs; the 15 species of the order Exobasidiales, which are parasitic on higher plants, particularly AZALEAS and RHODODENDRONS; and jelly fungi, so called because they have jellylike, often colorful fruiting bodies. See also FUNGUS.

Basie \ˈbā-sē\, **Count** *orig.* **William Allen** (1904–1984) U.S. jazz pianist and bandleader, whose band became the most refined exponent of SWING. Born in Red Bank, N.J., Basie was influenced by the Harlem pianists JAMES P. JOHNSON and FATS WALLER, receiving informal tutelage on the organ from the latter. He formed his band in Kansas City in 1936. Its rhythm section, including guitarist Freddie Green, bassist Walter Page, and drummer Jo Jones, quickly became noted for its lightness, precision, and relaxation; on this foundation, the brass and reed sections developed a vocabulary of riffs and motifs on such recordings as "One O'Clock Jump" and "Jumpin' at the Woodside." Basie's piano style became increasingly spare, a distillation of the stride tradition and a model of economy. His soloists included singer JIMMY RUSHING, trumpeters Buck Clayton and Harry "Sweets" Edison, and saxophonist LESTER YOUNG. Basie's reorganized band of the 1950s placed greater emphasis on ensemble work, as arrangers such as Neal Hefti and Ernie Wilkins codified a more powerful style built from the riffs and buoyant rhythm of the earlier group. The band achieved renewed popularity for recordings featuring vocalist JOE WILLIAMS and became recognized as a jazz institution.

Count Basie, 1969.
RON JOY—GLOBE PHOTOS

basil Herb consisting of the dried leaves of *Ocimum basilicum,* an annual herb of the MINT family, native to India and Iran. The dried large-leaf varieties have a fragrant aroma faintly reminiscent of ANISE, and a warm, sweet, aromatic, mildly pungent flavor. The dried leaves of common basil are less fragrant and more pungent in flavor. Basil is widely grown as a kitchen herb. TEA made from basil leaves is a stimulant. The heart-shaped basil leaf is a symbol of love in Italy.

Basil I \ˈba-zəl\ *known as* **Basil the Macedonian** (c. 830–886) Byzantine emperor (867–86) and founder of the Macedonian dynasty. Born into a peasant family in Macedonia, he won employment in official circles in Constantinople and was made chamberlain by the reigning emperor, Michael III. He became co-emperor with Michael in 866 and murdered him the next year. Basil won victories against Muslim forces along the eastern borders of Asia Minor and asserted control over Slavs in the Balkans. He gained ground in southern Italy but lost Syracuse (878) and other key cities in Sicily to the Muslims. He also formulated the Greek legal code known as the Basilica. In later life Basil showed signs of madness.

Basil II *known as* **Basil Bulgaroctonus** \ˌbu̇l-gə-ˈräk-tə-nəs\ **("Slayer of the Bulgars")** (957?–1025) Byzantine emperor (976–1025). Crowned co-emperor with his brother in 960, he had to exile the grand chamberlain (985) and defeat rival generals (989) in order to gain the authority to rule. Basil became one of the strongest Byzantine emperors, winning territory in the Balkans, Mesopotamia, Armenia, and Georgia. He was noted for his victory (1014) in the war with Bulgaria, which ended with his blinding all the soldiers in the defeated Bulgarian army. He increased his domestic authority by attacking the landed interests of the military aristocracy and of the church. Because Basil left no able successor, the gains of his rule were soon undone.

Basil the Great, St. (c. AD 329–379) Early church father. Born into a Christian family in Cappadocia, he studied at Caesarea, Constantinople, and Athens and later established a monastic settlement on the family estate at Annesi. He opposed Arianism, which was supported by the emperor VALENS and his own bishop Dianius, and organized resistance to it after 365. He succeeded EUSEBIUS as bishop of Caesarea in 370. He died shortly after Valens, whose death in battle opened the way for the victory of Basil's cause. More than 300 of his letters survive; several of his Canonical Epistles have become part of canon law in EASTERN ORTHODOXY.

Saint Basil, detail of a mosaic, 12th century; in the Palatine Chapel, Palermo.
ALINARI—ART RESOURCE

basilica Originally a secular public building in ancient Rome, typically a large rectangular structure with an open hall and a raised platform at one or both ends. In one type, the central hall was flanked by side aisles set off by COLONNADES, and the raised platform was enclosed by an APSE. The early Christians adopted this type for their churches. In the typical early Christian basilica, the columns separating the NAVE from the lower side aisles carried either arches or ENTABLATURES, above which rose CLERESTORY walls that supported the roof. The long nave came to be crossed just before the apse by a shorter TRANSEPT, creating the cross-shaped plan that remains a standard church form to the present. "Basilica" is also a title of honor given to a Roman Catholic or Greek Orthodox church distinguished by its antiquity or its role as an international center of worship. See also CATHEDRAL.

Basilicata \bä-ˌzē-lē-ˈkä-tä\ Autonomous region (pop., 1996 est.: 609,000), southern Italy. Roughly divided into a western mountainous region and an eastern section of low hills and wide valleys, its capital is POTENZA. Known in ancient times as Lucania, the area was under LOMBARD LEAGUE rule in the early Middle Ages. Until the fall of the Swabian HOHENSTAUFENS (1254), it played a significant part in the affairs of southern Italy; later it followed the variable fortunes of the Kingdom of NAPLES until united with Italy in 1861. The region suffered severe damage in a disastrous earthquake in 1980. Agriculture is an economical mainstay.

Basilides \ˌba-sə-ˈlī-dēz\ (fl. 2nd century AD) Founder of the Basilidian school of GNOSTICISM. According to CLEMENT OF ALEXANDRIA, Basilides claimed to base his teaching on a secret tradition of PETER THE APOSTLE. He wrote psalms, odes, commentaries on the Gospels, and his own gospel. Fragments of these writings and varying accounts by Clement, St. IRENAEUS, and others suggest that his system of belief included elements from Neoplatonism as well as the New Testament. The school survived in Egypt until the 4th century.

Baskerville, John (1706–1775) British typographer. In 1757 he set up a printing house and published his first work, an edition of VIRGIL. His editions of the Latin classics, JOHN MILTON's poems (1758), and a folio Bible (1763) are characterized by clear and careful presswork rather than ornament. He served as printer to Cambridge University 1758–68, and he created the widely used Baskerville typeface.

Baskerville, detail of a portrait after James Millar, 1774; in the National Portrait Gallery, London.

BY COURTESY OF THE NATIONAL PORTRAIT GALLERY, LONDON

basketball Court game between two teams of five players each who score by tossing, or shooting, an inflated ball through a raised hoop, or basket, located in their opponent's end of the court. A goal is worth two points, three if shot from outside a specified limit. A free throw worth one point is awarded to any player fouled (through unwarranted physical contact) by another, two free throws if the foul occurs during the act of shooting. Professional games are divided into 12-minute quarters, collegiate games into 20-minute halves. Introduced in 1891 by JAMES A. NAISMITH in Springfield, Mass., basketball quickly became a popular collegiate sport. The NATIONAL COLLEGIATE ATHLETIC ASSOCIATION (NCAA) tournament following the regular college season pits 64 select teams in a series of elimination rounds to determine a national champion; so frenzied and unpredictable is the play that the tournament has earned the nickname "March Madness." Women's collegiate play is similarly organized. A men's professional league was organized in 1898 but did not gain much of a following until 1949, when it was reconstituted as the NATIONAL BASKETBALL ASSOCIATION (NBA). An American Basketball Association (ABA) was set up in 1967, but was merged with the NBA in 1976. The Women's Basketball Association (WNBA) was organized in 1997. The professional basketball season runs from October to April, with play-offs and championship matches extending into June. A Basketball Hall of Fame is located in Springfield.

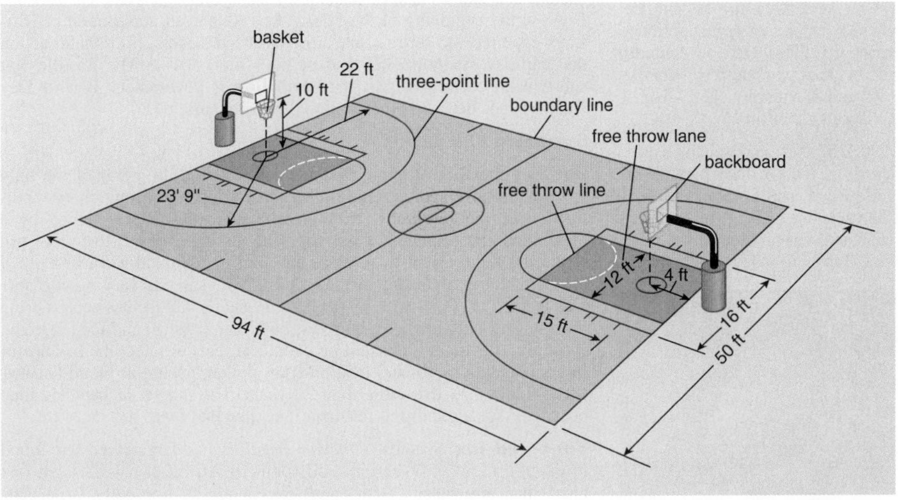

The U.S. professional court is shown. The U.S. college court has similar dimensions, but has shallower (19-ft 9-in) three-point line. International courts are slightly smaller and have 20-ft 6-in three-point lines and trapezoidal free-throw lanes that are wider at the boundary line than at the free-throw line. The basket height is 10 ft on all courts.

basketry Art and craft of making containers and other objects from interwoven flexible fibers such as grasses, twigs, bamboo, and rushes. It is primarily a functional rather than a decorative art. The type of basketry in a given geographic region is determined by the type of vegetation available there. Numerous Asian, African, Oceanic, and Native American cultures have excelled in basketry.

Baskin, Leonard (1922–2000) U.S. sculptor and graphic artist. Born in New Brunswick, N.J., he studied in Europe and the U.S. In 1939 he had his first one-man exhibition in New York City, and he later taught for many years at Smith College. He is known for his bleak portrayals of the human figure. His sculptures in bronze, limestone, and wood are dominated by themes of death, vulnerability, and spiritual decay. In his woodcuts he developed a distinctive linear style, depicting figures resembling those in anatomical charts.

basking shark Huge, sluggish SHARK (family Cetorhinidae) named for its habit of floating or slowly swimming at the surface. Possibly comprising more than one distinct species, it inhabits northern and temperate regions of the Atlantic, Pacific, and Indian oceans. It may grow as large as 46 ft (14 m); among fishes, only the WHALE SHARK grows larger. Despite its size, the basking shark feeds on plankton. It is gray-brown or blackish, with tiny teeth and very long gill slits. It is generally harmless and is hunted sporadically for fish meal and liver oil.

Basle See BASEL

Basque \'bask\ *Spanish* **Vasco** Member of a people of unknown origin living in Spain and France along the Bay of Biscay and in the western Pyrenees mountains in the region of the BASQUE COUNTRY. About 850,000 true Basques live in Spain and another 130,000 in France. Physically the Basques are similar to other Western European peoples; the BASQUE LANGUAGE, however, is not Indo-European. The Basques have sought autonomy from Spain since the 19th century. A national government was proclaimed in the SPANISH CIVIL WAR, which saw the brutal bombing of Guernica (1937). After the war, the government and many Basques went into exile as FRANCISCO FRANCO abolished their special privileges. The Basque separatist movement was rekindled after Franco's death and the establishment of a liberal Spanish monarchy in 1975. Despite the granting of limited autonomy in 1978, the more militant separatists, including the terrorist ETA (Basque Homeland and Liberty), continued a campaign for complete independence.

Basque Country *French* **Pays Basque** \pe-'ē-'bäsk\ Cultural region, extreme southwestern France. It extends from the Anie Peak of the PYRENEES to the coast around BIARRITZ on the Bay of BISCAY. The region has been largely spared the problems associated with Basque separatism in Spain's BASQUE COUNTRY. Fishing and tourism are economic mainstays.

Basque Country *Spanish* **País Vasco** \'pīs-'bäs-kō\ Autonomous community (pop., 1996 est.: 2,098,000) and historical region, northern Spain. Bounded by the Bay of BISCAY, it consists of the modern provinces of Vizcaya, Alava, and Guipúzcoa, and has an area of 2,803 sq mi (7,260 sq km); its capital is VITORIA. Inhabited by BASQUES, the area retained virtual autonomy until the 19th century, when it suffered repression under ALFONSO XII. A separatist movement succeeded in regaining Basque autonomy in 1936 under the short-lived Republican government, but autonomy was withdrawn by FRANCISCO FRANCO in 1939. Though limited autonomy was granted in 1980, a campaign of terrorism against the Spanish government continued. Alava is an agricultural region, while metallurgical industry is concentrated around BILBAO.

Basque language Language spoken by an estimated 660,000 Basque people living in the BASQUE COUNTRY of northern central Spain and southwestern France. The only remnant of the languages spoken in western Europe before incursions by INDO-EUROPEAN-speaking peoples, Basque has no known linguistic relatives. Its grammar is markedly distinct from that of all other western European languages. Typologically, it is ergative in nominal and verbal MORPHOLOGY (see ERGATIVITY). Basque is sparsely attested before the 16th century, when the first book in the language was printed (1545), though it has maintained a continuous literary tradition since then.

Basra City (pop., 1987 est.: 407,000), southeastern Iraq. It lies at the head of the SHATT AL ARAB, about 75 mi (120 km) from the Persian Gulf. Founded in AD 638, it became famous under the ABBASID DYNASTY; in *The THOUSAND AND ONE NIGHTS* it was the city from which Sinbad set out. In the 17th–18th century it became a trading center. Occupied by the British in World War I, the town and port underwent many improvements and grew in importance. After World War II, the growth of Iraq's petroleum industry turned Basra into a major refining center. It suffered heavy damage in the IRAN-IRAQ and PERSIAN GULF WARS.

bass \'bas\ In zoology, any of numerous fish species, many valued for food or sport. Most are placed in three families (all in the order Perciformes): 400 species of SEA BASS and GROUPER; the family Moronidae, which contains about 12 species, including striped and European basses; and SUNFISHES, including the BLACK and largemouth basses, prized by fishermen. Many other species are also known as bass, including the channel bass (a DRUM) and the calico bass (a CRAPPIE).

bass \'bās\ Lowest musical voice or register. In vocal music, its range is approximately from the second E below middle C to middle C itself. A basso profundo emphasizes a lower register, a basso cantante a somewhat higher one. Outside of Russia, the solo bass voice has generally been relegated to certain standard operatic character roles. The lowest-pitched member of most instrumental families is usually called the bass (bass clarinet, DOUBLE BASS, etc.). In Western tonal music, the bass part is usually second in importance only to the melody, being the chief determiner of harmonic movement, a tendency that became particularly notable after the appearance of the basso CONTINUO c. 1600.

Bass Strait \'bas\ Strait separating Australia from TASMANIA. It is 150 mi (240 km) wide at its widest point and 185 mi (298 km) long. It was named in 1798 for the British surgeon-explorer George Bass. Development of its offshore petroleum resources began in the 1960s.

Bassano \bä-'sä-nō\, **Jacopo** *orig.* **Jacopo da Ponte** (c. 1517–1592) Italian painter. He was the most celebrated member of a family of artists from the small town of Bassano, near Venice, where he worked for most of his life. He trained with Bonifacio de' Pitati in Venice and was influenced by other Venetian painters. He became known for his biblical themes, lush landscapes, and rustic scenes. Four painter sons continued the Bassano workshop tradition: Francesco (1549–1592), Leandro (1557–1622) (both of whom worked in the workshop's Venetian branch), Giovanni Battista (1553–1613), and Gerolamo (1566–1621). Many products of the workshop were collaborative efforts.

Basse-Terre \bås-'ter\ Island (pop., 1990: 152,000) and seaport (pop., 1990: 14,000), GUADELOUPE, West Indies. It is the western part of the French department of Guadeloupe (whose eastern part is Grande-Terre). Located north of Dominica, it is about 35 mi (56 km) long. Its extremely rugged terrain culminates in the volcanic summit of Mount Soufrière, at 4,813 ft (1,467 m). The town of Basse-Terre (founded 1643; metro. area pop., 1990: 53,000), on the southwestern coast, is the capital of Guadeloupe.

Basset hound.
SALLY ANNE THOMPSON

basset hound Centuries-old breed of dog developed in France and maintained, chiefly in France and Belgium, as a hunting dog of the aristocracy. Originally used to trail hares, rabbits, and deer, it has also been used for hunting birds, foxes, and other game. It is a slow, deliberate hunter, with a deep voice and a nose exceeded in keenness only by the BLOODHOUND's. Short-legged and heavy-boned, the basset hound has long, dangling ears and a short coat in any combination of black, tan, and white. It stands 12–15 in. (30–38 cm) high and weighs 40–60 lbs (18–27 kg).

Basseterre \bås-'ter\ Seaport (pop., 1994 est.: 13,000), St. Kitts Island. Chief town of St. Kitts and capital of the federated state of St. Kitts and Nevis, it lies on the southwestern coast, west of St. John's, Antigua. Founded in 1627, it serves as a depot distributing merchandise to neighboring islands.

Bassi \'bås-ē\, **Agostino** (1773–1856) Pioneer Italian bacteriologist. Born in Lodi, he attended Pavia University. In 1807 he began an investigation of the silkworm disease muscardine, which was causing serious economic losses in Italy and France. After 25 years of research, he demonstrated that the disease was contagious and was caused by a microscopic parasitic fungus spread among the silkworms by contact and infected food. He announced his discoveries in 1835 and theorized that many plant, animal, and human diseases are caused by animal or vegetable parasites, thus preceding both LOUIS PASTEUR and ROBERT KOCH in formulating a germ theory of disease.

basso continuo See CONTINUO

bassoon Large double-reed WOODWIND INSTRUMENT whose bore doubles back on itself (to keep its length manageable). The principal tenor-bass instrument of the orchestral woodwind family, it developed from the older curtal (or dulzian) in the 17th century. It has a range of 3½ octaves, starting at B-flat two octaves below middle C. It is an agile instrument with a mild tone. The contrabassoon, a large metal instrument whose tubing doubles back four times, has a range an octave lower.

basswood Any of certain species of LINDEN common to North America. The name refers especially to *Tilia americana,* found in a vast area of eastern North America but centered in the Great Lakes region, and to *T. caroliniana* and *T. georgiana,* found in the southeastern U.S.

bast See PHLOEM

Bastet \'bas-ˌtet\ *or* **Bast** *or* **Ubasti** In EGYPTIAN RELIGION, a goddess worshiped first as a lioness and later as a cat. Her nature changed after the domestication of the cat c. 1500 BC. She had cults at Bubastis in the Nile delta and at Memphis. In the Late and Ptolemaic periods, large cemeteries of mummified cats were created at both sites, and thousands of bronze statuettes of the goddess were deposited as votive offerings. Bastet is represented as a lioness or a woman with a cat's head, usually holding a bag, a breastplate, and a sistrum (wire rattle). The Romans carried her cult to Italy.

Bastille \bas-'tēl\ Medieval fortress in Paris that became a symbol of despotism. In the 17th–18th century, the Bastille was used as a French state prison and a place of detention for important persons. On July 14, 1789, at the beginning of the FRENCH REVOLUTION, an armed mob of Parisians captured the fortress and released its prisoners, a dramatic action that came to symbolize the end of the ANCIEN RÉGIME. The Bastille was subsequently demolished by the Revolutionary government. Bastille Day (July 14) has been a French national holiday since 1880.

Basutoland See LESOTHO

bat Any member of about 900 species (order Chiroptera) of the only MAMMALS to have evolved true flight. Their wings are evolutionary modification of the forelimbs, with greatly elongated fingers joined by a membrane that extends down the side of the body. Most bats use ECHOLOCATION to orient themselves and find prey. Found worldwide, they are particularly abundant in the tropics. Wingspreads vary among species from 6 in. (15 cm) to 5 ft (1.5 m). Nearly all species roost during the day (in caves, crevices, burrows, building, or trees) and feed at night. Most are INSECTIVORES, consuming enough insects to affect the balance of insect populations. Others feed on fruit, pollen, nectar, or blood (VAMPIRE BATS). Some may live more than 20 years. The GUANO of bats has long been used for agricultural fertilizer. See also FREE-TAILED BAT, FRUIT BAT.

bat-eared fox Species *(Otocyon megalotis)* of large-eared FOX found in open, arid areas of eastern and southern Africa. It has 48 teeth (six more than any other CANINE) and, except for its unusually large ears, looks like the RED FOX. It grows to a length of about 32 in. (80 cm), including a 12-in. (30-cm) tail, and weighs 7–10 lbs (3–4.5 kg). It lives alone or in small groups and feeds primarily on insects, especially termites. See photograph on following page.

Bat-eared fox (*Otocyon megalotis*).

MARK BOULTON FROM THE NATIONAL AUDUBON SOCIETY COLLECTION/PHOTO RESEARCHERS—EB INC.

BAT Industries PLC British conglomerate formed in 1976 by the merger of Tobacco Securities Trust Co. Ltd. (TST) and British-American Tobacco Co. Ltd. (BAT). It is today the world's largest manufacturer of tobacco products; its other operations include retailing, paper, and financial services. Its international headquarters are in London. Its U.S. subsidiary, BATUS Inc., headquartered in Louisville, Ky., owns Brown & Williamson Tobacco, whose brands include Kool, Raleigh, Pall Mall, and Lucky Strike.

Bat Mitzvah See Bar Mitzvah

Bataan Death March \bə-ˈtan\ (April 1942) Forced march of 70,000 U.S. and Filipino prisoners of war (World War II) captured by the Japanese in the Philippines. From the southern end of the Bataan Peninsula, the starving and ill-treated prisoners were force-marched 63 mi (101 km) to a prison camp. Only 54,000 prisoners lived to reach the camp; up to 10,000 died on the way and others escaped in the jungle. In 1946 the Japanese commander of the march was convicted by a U.S. military commission and executed.

Bataille \bä-ˈtäy\, **Georges** (1897–1962) French librarian and writer. He trained as an archivist and worked at the Bibliothèque Nationale and at the Orléans library. He wrote a number of novels under pseudonyms before publishing *Le Coupable* (1944; "The Guilty One") under his own name. His novels, essays, and poetry show a fascination with eroticism, mysticism, violence, and an ideal of excess and waste. In 1946 he founded the influential literary review *Critique,* which he edited until his death.

Batak \bə-ˈtäk\ Several closely related ethnic groups of central Sumatra, Indonesia. The Batak are descendants of a powerful Proto-Malayan people who until 1825 lived in relative isolation in the highlands surrounding Lake Toba in Sumatra. They have their own written language. In their traditional religion, ancestors, plants, animals, and inanimate objects are considered to possess souls or spirits; today about a third of the 3.1 million Batak adhere to traditional beliefs, while the rest profess Christianity or Islam.

Batavian Republic Republic of the Netherlands after it was conquered by France in 1795. Its government, set up in 1798, was bound to France by alliance. In 1805 Napoleon renamed it the Batavian Commonwealth and placed executive power in the hands of a dictator. In 1806 it was replaced by the Kingdom of Holland under the rule of Louis Bonaparte; it was incorporated into the French empire in 1810.

Bateman, Hester *orig.* **Hester Needham** (1708–1794) British silversmith. In 1760, after the death of her husband, John Bateman, she took over the family business. Assisted by her two sons, she executed designs commissioned by other silversmiths. Her shop later became well known for its tableware, such as spoons, sugar bowls, saltcellars, and teapots. Bateman's designs were restrained and graceful, characterized by beaded edges. In addition to domestic silver, she produced large presentation pieces.

Silver coffee pot by Hester Bateman, 1773–74; in the Victoria and Albert Museum, London.

BY COURTESY OF THE VICTORIA AND ALBERT MUSEUM, LONDON

Bates College Private liberal-arts college in Lewiston, Me. It was founded in 1855 as an independent academy committed to egalitarian education; it was renamed in 1863 after a benefactor, Benjamin E. Bates. Research facilities include the coastal Bates-Morse Mountain Conservation Area. Enrollment is about 1,700.

Bateson, Gregory (1904–1980) British-U.S. anthropologist. Son of William Bateson, he studied anthropology at Cambridge University but soon thereafter moved to the U.S. His first important book, *Naven* (1936), was a groundbreaking study of cultural symbolism and ritual based on fieldwork in New Guinea. From 1936 to 1950 he was married to Margaret Mead, with whom he studied the connection between culture and personality, publishing *Balinese Character* in 1942. His interests broadened to include problems of learning and communication among schizophrenics. His last book, *Mind and Nature* (1978), synthesized many of his ideas.

Bateson, William (1861–1926) British biologist. In 1900, while studying inheritance of traits, he was drawn to the research of Gregor Mendel, which explained perfectly the results of his own plant experiments. He was the first to translate Mendel's major work into English. With Reginald Crundall Punnett, he published the results of a series of breeding experiments that not only extended Mendel's principles to animals but also showed that, contrary to Mendel, certain features were consistently inherited together, a phenomenon that came to be termed linkage (see linkage group). In 1908 he became Britain's first professor of genetics, and in 1909 he introduced the term genetics. He opposed Thomas Hunt Morgan's theory of chromosomes. Gregory Bateson was his son. See also Carl Erich Correns, Hugo de Vries, Erich Tschermak von Seysenegg

William Bateson, drawing by Sir William Rothenstein, 1917; in the National Portrait Gallery, London.

BY COURTESY OF THE NATIONAL PORTRAIT GALLERY, LONDON

Bath City (pop., 1995 est.: 84,000), southwestern England. Situated on the Avon River, it was founded as Aquae Sulis by the Romans, who were attracted to its hot mineral springs. The Anglo-Saxons arrived in the 6th century AD, followed by the Normans c. 1100. In the Middle Ages it was a prosperous center for the cloth trade. When the Roman baths were rediscovered in 1755, Bath had already revived as a spa; its popularity is reflected in the works of Jane Austen, Richard Brinsley Sheridan, and Tobias Smollett. It was rebuilt and extended in the Palladian style during the 18th century. Bath today retains many of its 18th-century structures.

Bath Party See Baath Party

batholith Large body of igneous rock formed beneath the earth's surface by the intrusion and solidification of magma. Batholiths are usually composed of coarse-grained rocks (e.g., granite or quartz diorite) and often have an irregular shape, with side walls that incline steeply. They may have a surface exposure of 40 sq mi (100 sq km) or more and may be 6–9 mi (10–15 km) thick. A well-known batholith is located in the Sierra Nevada range of California.

Báthory, Stephen See Stephen Báthory

Bathurst See Banjul

Bathurst Island Island, Nunavut. Located in the Arctic Ocean between Cornwallis and Melville islands, it is 160 mi (260 km) long and 50–100 mi (80–160 km) wide. The coastline is fringed with inlets, and several islands stretch from its western tip. Discovered in 1819 by Sir William Parry, it was named for the Earl of Bathurst. The northern magnetic pole lies off the island's northern coast.

bathypelagic zone \ˌbath-i-pə-ˈla-jik\ Worldwide zone of deep ocean waters, about 3,000–13,000 ft (1,000–4,000 m) below the surface. It is inhabited by a wide variety of marine forms, including eels, fishes, mollusks, and others.

bathyscaphe \ˈba-thi-ˌskaf\ Navigable diving vessel developed by Auguste Piccard (assisted by his son Jacques), designed to reach great depths in the ocean. The first bathyscaphe, the *FNRS 2,* was built in 1946–48 in Belgium. A later version, the *Trieste,* was acquired by the

U.S. Navy; in 1960 it dived to a record 35,810 ft (10,916 m) in the MARIANA TRENCH. The bathyscaphe consists of two main components: a steel cabin, heavier than water and resistant to sea pressure, to accommodate the observers; and a light container called a float, filled with gasoline, which, being lighter than water, provides the necessary lifting power (replacing cables, which had previously been used to support descending chambers but had proven unreliable at great depths).

batik \bə-ˈtēk\ Method of dyeing textiles, principally cottons, in which patterned areas are covered with wax so that they will not receive color. Multicolored effects are achieved by repeating the dyeing process several times, the initial pattern of wax being boiled off and another design applied before redyeing. Wax was applied with bamboo strips in Indonesia, where the technique originated. A small copper pot with a handle and narrow applicator spout for applying the wax came into use in Java by the mid-18th century; a wood-block wax applicator was developed in the 19th century. Dutch traders imported the cloth and the technique to Europe. Today machines for applying wax in traditional Javanese patterns reproduce the same effects as the hand-dyeing process.

Batiniya \ˌbä-ti-ˈnē-yə\ School of Islamic thought that interpreted religious texts exclusively on the basis of hidden rather than literal meanings. Such interpretation gained currency around the 8th century among esoteric SHIITE sects, especially the schismatic ISMAILIS, who believed that beneath every obvious meaning lay a hidden, true meaning, which the IMAM was empowered to interpret. While influenced by speculative philosophy and theology, the Batiniya remained proponents of esoteric knowledge. Sunni Muslims condemned the Batiniya as enemies of Islam for rejecting literal truth and producing confusion and controversy through their multiple textual readings.

Batista (y Zaldívar) \bá-ˈtēs-tä\, **Fulgencio** (1901–1973) Soldier, president, and dictator who twice ruled Cuba (1933–44, 1952–59). A poor mulatto, Batista worked his way up through the army and came to power as a strongman, ruling first through associates, then as president himself from 1940. During his first term he cultivated the support of the U.S., the army, organized labor, and the civil service, and he achieved gains in the educational system, public works, and the economy as a whole while enriching himself and his associates. He lost the 1944 election but returned by way of an army revolt in 1952. His second rule was a corrupt and brutal dictatorship that set the stage for his overthrow by FIDEL CASTRO on January 1, 1959.

Batlle y Ordóñez \ˈbät-yā-ē-ȯr-ˈth̲ōn-yās\, **José** (1856–1929) President of Uruguay (1903–7, 1911–15). The son of a former president of Uruguay, he was involved in politics from the 1880s. His narrow victory in the 1903 presidential election led to a brief civil war, but when he held new elections in 1905 he won again. He stepped down at the end of his term and was reelected in 1911. He inaugurated labor reforms, limited the profits of foreign-owned businesses, encouraged migration, nationalized and developed public works, ended the death penalty, and protected children born out of wedlock. He is credited with transforming Uruguay into a stable, democratic welfare state.

Baton Rouge \ˈbat-ᵊn-ˈrüzh\ City (pop., 1996 est.: 216,000), capital of Louisiana. Located on the Mississippi River, it is the state's second-largest city. Settled by the French in 1719, it was named for a red cypress pole that marked a boundary between Indian tribes. The area was ceded to Britain in 1763, then taken by the Spanish in the American Revolution. Spain ceded Louisiana to France in 1800, but tried to retain Baton Rouge at the time of the LOUISIANA PURCHASE (1803). In 1810 the city was annexed to the U.S., and it became the state capital in 1849. The capital was transferred to other towns when Baton Rouge was occupied by Federal troops during the AMERICAN CIVIL WAR; in 1882 it regained its capital status. It has deepwater port facilities and is an important petroleum refining center.

battalion Tactical military organization composed of a headquarters and two or more companies, batteries, or similar units and usually commanded by a field-grade officer such as a lieutenant colonel. The term has been used in nearly every Western army for centuries and has had many meanings. In the 16th–17th century, it denoted a unit of infantry used in a line of battle and was loosely applied to any large body of men. During the Napoleonic Wars, battalions were fighting units of the French army under the administrative unit of the REGIMENT. In the armies of the British Commonwealth nations, infantry battalions are tactical units within regiments. The typical U.S. Army battalion is a unit of 800–900 soldiers, divided into a headquarters company and three rifle companies; two to five battalions form the combat elements of a tactical BRIGADE. See also MILITARY UNIT.

Battenberg family *or* **Mountbatten family** Family that rose to international prominence in the 19th–20th century. The first Battenbergs were a family of German counts that died out c. 1314; the title was revived in 1851. In 1917 the family members who lived in England renounced the German title of prince of Battenberg and adopted Mountbatten as a surname ("Mount" being a translation of "Berg"). Prominent members of the family included PHILIP, DUKE OF EDINBURGH, and LOUIS MOUNTBATTEN.

battered woman syndrome Psychological and behavioral pattern displayed by female victims of domestic violence. Explanations have evolved since the late 1970s from LEARNED HELPLESSNESS to a "cycle of violence" theory and then a form of POST-TRAUMATIC STRESS DISORDER. The term is a legal concept rather than a psychiatric diagnosis, and lacks clearly defined criteria. It has been used to support legal arguments of SELF-DEFENSE, DIMINISHED CAPACITY, or INSANITY when a woman is accused of murdering or assaulting her batterer, committing a crime under his coercion, or provoking the behavior the batterer is on trial for. Critics say the term creates a stereotyped image inadequate to describe individual experiences.

battering ram Medieval weapon consisting of a heavy timber with a metal knob or point at the front. Rams were used to beat down the gates or walls of a besieged city or castle. Usually suspended by ropes from the roof of a movable shed, the timber was swung back and forth by its operators so that it banged against the structure under siege. The shed's roof was covered with animal skins to protect the operators inside it from bombardment with stones or fiery materials.

Battersea enamelware Painted enamelware made by Stephen Theodore Janssen at York House in London's Battersea district 1753–56. The ware is composed of soft white enamel over a copper ground. The designs were applied by hand painting or by transfer printing: an impression from an engraved metal plate brushed with enamel colors is made on paper, and the design was then transferred to the object to be decorated. Most of the objects (e.g., snuffboxes, watch cases) were decorated with mottoes, portraits, landscapes, or flowers. The transfer printing technique was first used for large-scale production at Battersea.

battery Any of a class of devices, consisting of a group of electric cells, that convert chemical ENERGY into electrical energy. A wet cell (e.g., a car battery) contains free liquid ELECTROLYTE; in a dry cell (e.g., a flashlight battery), the electrolyte is held in an absorbent material. Chemicals are arranged so that ELECTRONS released from the battery's negative electrode flow (see ELECTRIC CURRENT) through a CIRCUIT outside the battery (in the device powered by it) to the positive electrode. The voltage depends on the chemicals used and the number of cells (in series); the current depends on the resistance in the total circuit (including the battery—and thus on electrode size). Multiple batteries may be connected in series (the positive electrode of one to the negative electrode of the next), increasing total voltage, or in parallel (positive to positive and negative to negative), increasing total current. Standard dry cells used in flashlights and certain wet cells for marine, mine, highway, and military use are not rechargeable; car batteries, many dry cells used in cordless appliances, and batteries for certain military and aerospace uses may be recharged repeatedly. See illustration on following page.

battery See ASSAULT AND BATTERY

battlement Parapet (portion above the roof) of the exterior wall of a fortification, consisting of alternating low portions (crenels) and high portions (merlons). Rooftop defenders would shoot from behind the merlons during times of siege. Medieval battlements were often bracketed out (see CORBEL) to form a machicolation (overhang) with holes in its floor through which objects could be dropped on encroachers below.

battleship Capital ship of the world's navies from c. 1860, when it began to replace the wooden-hulled SHIP OF THE LINE, until World War II, when it was superseded by the AIRCRAFT CARRIER. They combined large size, powerful guns, and heavy armor with fairly high speed and great cruising radius. The most powerful could hit targets at a range of more than 20 mi (30 km) and absorb heavy damage while remaining afloat and continuing to fight. It originated in early IRONCLAD vessels with mixed sail and steam propulsion, such as the French armored frigate

Gloire (1859). In 1906 the HMS DREADNOUGHT revolutionized battleship design by introducing steam-turbine propulsion and an array of ten 12-in. (305-mm) guns. In World War II battleships were used mainly for specialized tasks such as bombarding enemy coastal defenses in AMPHIBIOUS WARFARE. After the Persian Gulf War, the U.S. decommissioned its last two active battleships.

Batu \'bä-tü\ (died 1255?) Grandson of GENGHIS KHAN and founder of the GOLDEN HORDE. In 1235 Batu was elected commander in chief of the western part of the Mongol empire and given responsibility for the invasion of Europe. His troops burned and sacked Kiev in 1240, and by the end of 1241 he had conquered Russia, Poland, Bohemia, Hungary, and the Danube valley. Only the death of ÖGÖDEI prevented him from invading Western Europe. Batu established the state of the Golden Horde in southern Russia, which was ruled by his successors for the next 200 years.

Baudelaire \bōd-'ler\, **Charles (-Pierre)** (1821–1867) French poet. While a law student, he became addicted to opium and hashish and contracted syphilis. His early reckless spending on fine clothes and furnishings would lead to a life dogged by debt. In 1844 he formed an association with a black woman, Jeanne Duval, who would inspire some of his finest poetry. He published a single novel, *La fanfarlo,* in 1847. His discovery of the works of EDGAR ALLAN POE in 1852 led to many years of work on Poe, which produced many masterly translations and critical articles. His reputation rests primarily on the extraordinary poetry collection *Les fleurs du mal* (1857; *The Flowers of Evil*), which dealt with erotic, aesthetic, and social themes in ways that appalled many of his middle-class readers, and he was convicted of obscenity and blasphemy. Though the title became a byword for depravity, the book became perhaps the most influential collection of lyrics published in Europe in the 19th century. His *Petits poèmes en prose* (1868) was an important and innovative experiment in prose poetry. He also wrote provocative essays in art criticism. His later years were darkened by disillusionment, despair, and mounting debt; his death at 46 resulted from syphilis. He is regarded as the earliest and finest poet of modernism in French.

Baudelaire, photograph by Étienne Carjat, 1863.

BY COURTESY OF THE BIBLIOTHEQUE NATIONALE, PARIS

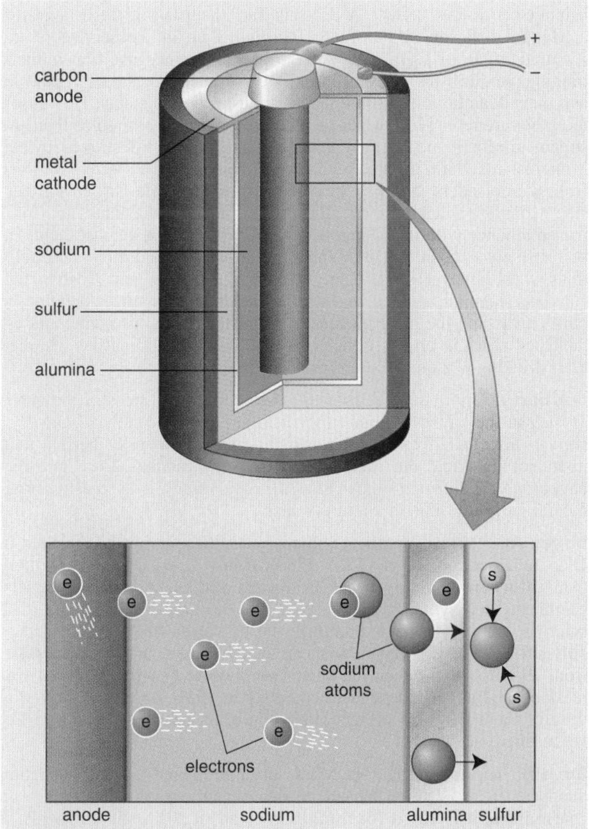

The sodium-sulfur (NaS) battery, still under development, has been used in some electric cars. During discharge, the sodium reacts with the ceramic alumina electrolyte, losing electrons, which travel out the anode to the circuit the battery is powering. The ionic sodium then combines with sulfur, which has acquired electrons from the cathode. The reaction is reversible, so the battery can be recharged. The advantage of this battery over other rechargeables (e.g., lead-acid, nickel-cadmium, or nickel-metal hydride batteries) is that it can provide the same amount of power with a smaller, lighter battery. However, since the chemicals must be heated to a molten state and pure sodium is very reactive, failure of the battery casing or ceramic electrolyte is potentially dangerous.

Baudot \bō-'dō\, **Jean Maurice Émile** (1845–1903) French engineer. In 1874 he patented a telegraph code that by the mid-20th century had supplanted Morse code as the standard telegraphic alphabet. In Baudot's code, each letter is represented by a five-unit combination of current-on or current-off signals of equal duration, providing 32 permutations (sufficient for the Roman alphabet, punctuation, and control of the machine's mechanical functions). Baudot also invented (1894) a distributor system for multiplex (simultaneous) transmission of several messages on the same telegraphic circuit or channel. The baud, a unit of data transmission speed, is named for him.

Baudouin I \bōd-'waü\ (1930–1993) King of the Belgians (1951–93). The son of King LEOPOLD III, Baudouin lived with his family under house arrest in German-occupied Belgium during World War II. After postwar exile in Switzerland, Baudouin became king on his father's abdication (1951). He helped restore confidence in the monarchy after the stormy reign of his father and became a unifying force in a country divided between Flemish- and French-speaking factions. Because Baudouin and his wife, Fabiola, were childless, he was succeeded by his brother, Albert II.

Baudrillard \bō-drē-'yär\, **Jean** (born 1929) French philosopher. A professor of sociology at the University of Paris, he examines in his writings the world and its fixed destiny with irony. In *America* (1986) he praises the U.S. for its transcendent banality; in other works he has argued that electronic media shape reality. He is regarded as a principal exponent of POSTMODERNISM.

Baugh \'bȯ\, **Sammy** *orig.* **Samuel Adrian** (born 1914) First outstanding quarterback of U.S. professional football. Born in Temple, Texas, he led the NFL in forward passing in 6 of 16 seasons (1937–52) with the Washington Redskins. He also excelled as a punter and as a defensive halfback.

Bauhaus \'baů-,haůs\ (German: "House of Building") Influential, forward-looking German school of architecture and applied arts (1919–33) founded by WALTER GROPIUS with the ideal of integrating art, craftsmanship, and technology. Realizing that mass production had to be the precondition of successful design in the machine age, its members rejected the ARTS AND CRAFTS MOVEMENT's emphasis on individually executed luxury objects. The Bauhaus is often associated with a severe but elegant geometric style carried out with great economy of means, though in fact the works produced by its members were richly diverse. Its faculty included JOSEF ALBERS, L. Moholy-Nagy, LYONEL FEININGER, PAUL KLEE, VASSILY KANDINSKY, and MARCEL BREUER. The school was based in Weimar until 1925, Dessau through 1932, and Berlin in its final months, when its last director, LUDWIG MIES VAN DER ROHE, closed the school in anticipation of the Nazis' doing so. See also INTERNATIONAL STYLE.

Baum \'bäm\, **L(yman) Frank** (1856–1919) U.S. writer of children's books. Born in Chittenango, N.Y., he achieved commercial success with his first book, *Father Goose* (1899), and followed it the next year with the even more popular *Wonderful Wizard of Oz*. He wrote 13 more Oz books, which acquired a huge readership. The series was continued by Ruth Plumly Thompson after his death.

bauxite Most important ALUMINUM ore, of varying compositions in which aluminum hydroxide or aluminum oxide predominate (named for Les Baux in southern France, where the ore was identified in 1821). The other constituents are largely iron oxide, silica, and titania. Bauxite has been found in all the continents except Antarctica. Known deposits can supply the world with aluminum for hundreds of years at present production levels.

Bavaria *German* **Bayern** \'bī-ərn\ State (pop., 1996 est.: 11,996,000), southern Germany. Conquered by the Romans in the 1st century BC (see NORICUM and RAETIA), the area was taken by CHARLEMAGNE and incorporated into his empire in 788. It became one of the great duchies of the HOLY ROMAN EMPIRE. Under MAXIMILIAN I, Bavaria led the CATHOLIC LEAGUE in the THIRTY YEARS' WAR. It was overrun repeatedly in the context of larger wars in the 18th century. It joined the German empire in 1871, while remaining a kingdom. The king was overthrown in 1918; after a brief period of instability, Bavaria joined the WEIMAR REPUBLIC in 1919. ADOLF HITLER had his first power base there in the 1920s. It adopted a new constitution in 1946, and became a state of the Federal Republic of Germany in 1949. It has long been Germany's most Roman Catholic area. Its largest cities are MUNICH (its capital), AUGSBURG, and NUREMBERG. Notable regions include the Bavarian ALPS, the BLACK FOREST, and the BOHEMIAN FOREST. Bavaria is famous for the beauty of its rolling landscape and the charm of its villages.

Bavarian Succession, War of the (1778–79) Conflict in which FREDERICK II of Prussia prevented JOSEPH II of Austria from acquiring Bavaria. After the death of the Bavarian elector Maximilian Joseph (1727–1777), his successor, Charles Theodore (1724–1799), ceded Lower Bavaria to Austria. Frederick II responded by declaring war (1778). There was little fighting because each force was concerned with cutting its opponent's communications and denying it supplies; as a result, the conflict was nicknamed the "potato war." In 1779 Austria and Prussia signed a treaty giving Austria a fraction of the territory originally occupied.

Bax, Arnold (Edward Trevor) *later* **Sir Arnold** (1883–1953) British composer. Born into a wealthy family, he was free to compose throughout his life and consequently wrote prolifically. His early works, influenced by the poetry of WILLIAM BUTLER YEATS, frequently evoke Celtic legend. His compositions include seven symphonies, the orchestral works *Spring Fire* (1913), *November Woods* (1917), and *Tintagel* (1919), four piano sonatas, three string quartets, and numerous vocal works.

bay In architecture, any division of a building between vertical lines or planes, especially the entire space included between the centerlines of two adjacent vertical supports. The space between two columns or PILASTERS, or from PIER to pier in a church, including that part of the vaulting (see VAULT) or ceiling between them, is thus called a bay.

bay Any of several small trees with aromatic leaves, especially the sweet bay, or bay laurel *(Laurus nobilis),* source of the bay leaf used in cooking. The California laurel *(Umbellularia californica)* is an ornamental tree also called the bay tree. The bay rum tree, or simply bay *(Pimenta racemosa),* has leaves and twigs that yield, when distilled, oil of bay, which is used in perfumery and in the preparation of bay rum, a fragrant cosmetic and medicinal liquid.

bay Semicircular or nearly circular concavity, similar to a GULF but usually smaller. Bays may range from a few hundred yards to several hundred miles from side to side. They are usually located where easily eroded rocks, such as clays and sandstones, are bounded by harder, more erosion-resistant formations of igneous rocks, such as granite, or hard calcareous rocks, such as massive limestones. Some bays form excellent harbors.

Bay \'bī\, **Laguna de** Lake, central LUZON, Philippine Islands. Located southeast of MANILA, the lake, about 32 mi (52 km) long, is the largest in the Philippines. Its outlet is the Pasig River. It is dotted with islands, the largest being densely settled Talim.

Bay of Pigs invasion (April 17, 1961) Abortive invasion of Cuba directed by the CENTRAL INTELLIGENCE AGENCY and carried out by Cuban exiles. The invasion was intended to spark a rebellion that would topple FIDEL CASTRO, who was considered a threat to U.S. interests in the region. The rebellion never materialized. The invasion began with the bombing of Cuban military bases; two days later a force of about 1,500 landed at several sites along the coast, including the Bay of Pigs. The invasion force was quickly defeated and more than 1,100 men were imprisoned. The result was a huge propaganda victory for Castro and a severe embarrassment for the administration of JOHN F. KENNEDY.

Bayamón \ˌbī-ä-'mōn\ Town (pop., 1995 est.: 231,000), northeastern Puerto Rico, part of the metropolitan area of SAN JUAN. Puerto Rico's first settlement, Caparra, was founded nearby in 1508 by Spanish explorer JUAN PONCE DE LEON. Established as a town in 1772, it is now a manufacturing center for clothing, furniture, automotive parts, and metal products. Educational institutions include Bayamón Central Univ.

Bayard \'bā-ərd\, **Thomas Francis** (1828–1898) U.S. statesman, diplomat, and lawyer. Born in Wilmington, Del., to a family prominent in Delaware politics, he succeeded his father in the U.S. Senate (1869–85). He served as secretary of state 1885–89 and as ambassador to Britain 1893–97, the first to hold that title. A champion of arbitration, he was critical of the aggressive position of Pres. GROVER CLEVELAND in the dispute with Britain over the Venezuelan boundary (1895).

Baybars I *or* **Baibars I** \'bī-bärs\ (1223–1277) Most eminent Mamluk sultan (see MAMLUK REGIME). A Kipchak Turk, he was sold as a slave after a Mongol invasion in the 1240s. He ended up in the service of the Ayyubid sultan of Egypt (see AYYUBID DYNASTY), who gave him military training. In 1250 his army captured the crusader king LOUIS IX, and he and other Mamluk officers murdered the last Ayyubid sultan. He himself took the throne in 1260, when he murdered the third Mamluk sultan. As sultan he rebuilt the Syrian fortresses that had been destroyed by the Mongols and built up the sultanate's armaments. He seized territory from the crusaders that they were never to recover. He harried the Persian Mongols, attacking their allies, the Christian Armenians, and forging an alliance with the Mongols of the GOLDEN HORDE against them. He sent military expeditions into Nubia and Libya. He had diplomatic relations with James I of Aragon, Alfonso X of León and Castile, and Charles of Anjou, as well as with the Byzantine emperor. At home he built canals and the great mosque in Cairo that bears his name, and established efficient postal service between Cairo and Damascus. He died after drinking poison prepared for someone else.

bayberry Any of several aromatic shrubs and small trees of the genus *Myrica* in the bayberry family (Myricaceae), but especially *M. pennsylvanica,* also called candleberry, which has grayish waxy berries that, upon boiling, yield the wax used in bayberry candles. The California bayberry, or California wax myrtle *(M. californica),* is used as an ornamental on sandy soils in warm climates.

Bayer AG German chemical and pharmaceutical company. Founded in 1863 by Friedrich Bayer (1825–1880), it now operates plants in more than 30 countries. Bayer has originated scores of pharmaceuticals, chemicals, and synthetic materials; it was the first developer and marketer of ASPIRIN (1899); of Prontosil, the first SULFA DRUG (1935); and of polyurethane (1937). Bayer was part of the chemical cartel IG FARBEN from 1925 to 1945, when the latter was dissolved by the Allies; it was reestablished as an independent company in 1951. Its most noteworthy drug of the 1990s was the antibiotic Cipro. Its headquarters are in Leverkusen.

Bayeux Tapestry \bá-'yœ\ Medieval embroidered TAPESTRY depicting the NORMAN CONQUEST. Woven in woolen threads of eight colors on coarse linen, it is 224 ft (68.4 m) long by about 20 in. (50 cm) wide. It consists of 79 consecutive scenes, with Latin inscriptions and decorative borders. Stylistically it resembles English illuminated manuscripts. It was probably woven within a few years of 1066 and possibly commissioned by Odo, bishop of Bayeux, brother of WILLIAM I THE CONQUEROR. The most famous of all pieces of needlework, it hung for centuries in the Bayeux Cathedral (Normandy) and now hangs in the tapestry museum there. See photograph opposite on following page.

Bayezid I \bī-ə-'zēd\ (c. 1360–1403?) Sultan of the OTTOMAN EMPIRE (1389–1402). After succeeding his father, Murad II (killed in the Battle of Kosovo, 1389), Bayezid expanded Ottoman control of the shrinking Byzantine empire, dominating vast Balkan territories and securing his rule south of the Danube. From 1391 to 1398 he blockaded Constantinople, and he crushed the Hungarian crusaders at NICOPOLIS in 1396. He then sought to widen Ottoman control over Anatolia. Overwhelmed by TIMUR near Ankara in 1402, Bayezid was defeated and died in captivity. His son, SÜLEYMAN I, succeeded him.

Bayezid II \ˌbī-ə-ˈzēd\ (1448?–1512) Ottoman sultan who consolidated control of the empire begun by his father, MEHMED II. After taking the throne in 1481, he reversed his father's policies of expropriating Muslim religious properties and rejected his pro-European orientation but continued the policy of territorial conquest. Under him, Herzegovina came under Ottoman control, and the Ottoman hold over the Crimea and Anatolia was strengthened. He fought the SAFAVID DYNASTY in the east, the MAMLUK REGIME in the south, and the Venetians in the west. At home he built mosques, colleges, hospitals, and bridges, and supported jurists, scholars, and poets. He abdicated in favor of his son Selim a month before his death.

Baykal, Lake See Lake BAIKAL

Bayle \ˈbel\, **Pierre** (1647–1706) French philosopher. Educated at a Jesuit school, he converted to Catholicism but later reverted to his original Calvinist faith. His religious views led to his losing professorships first at Sedan and later at Rotterdam. He was convinced that philosophical reasoning led to universal SKEPTICISM, but that nature compelled mankind to accept blind faith. The bulk of his *Historical and Critical Dictionary* (1697) consists of quotations, anecdotes, commentaries, and erudite annotations that cleverly undo whatever orthodox Christian beliefs the articles express, and it was condemned by religious authorities. Bayle's oblique method of subversive criticism was later adopted by the contributors to DENIS DIDEROT's *ENCYCLOPÉDIE*.

Baylis, Lilian (Mary) (1874–1937) British theatrical manager and founder of the OLD VIC. She assisted her aunt, Emma Cons, in the operation of the Royal Victoria Hall and Coffee Tavern, and on Cons's death in 1912 she converted the hall into the Old Vic, which became famous for its Shakespearean productions. Between 1914 and 1923 the theater staged all of WILLIAM SHAKESPEARE's plays, a feat no other playhouse had attempted. In 1931 she took over the derelict Sadler's Wells Theatre and made it a center of opera and ballet.

Bayliss, William Maddock *later* **Sir William** (1860–1924) British physiologist. He and ERNEST H. STARLING studied nerve-controlled blood-vessel contraction and dilation and discovered the peristaltic wave. In 1902 they showed that dilute hydrochloric acid mixed with partly digested food activates a chemical in the duodenum that they called secretin, because it stimulates secretion of pancreatic juice. This marked the discovery of hormones, a term the men coined. Bayliss also showed how the enzyme trypsin was formed from inactive trypsinogen and measured precisely the time it took to digest protein. His recommendation of gum-saline injections for wound shock saved many lives in World War I.

English axman in combat with Norman cavalry during the Battle of Hastings, detail from the Bayeux Tapestry; in the Musée de la Tapisserie de la Reine-Mathilde, in the former Bishop's Palace, Bayeux, Fr.

GIRAUDON—ART RESOURCE

Baylor, Elgin (born 1934) U.S. basketball player. Born in Washington, D.C., the 6-ft 5-in (1-m 96-cm) Baylor played for the Minneapolis (later, Los Angeles) Lakers from 1958 to 1971. With a career scoring average (27.4) that ranks him third behind MICHAEL JORDAN and WILT CHAMBERLAIN, he is regarded as one of the game's greatest forwards.

Baylor University Private university in Waco, Texas. It is the world's largest Baptist university and the oldest college (founded 1845) in Texas; it is named for one of its founding missionaries, Judge R. E. B. Baylor. It comprises a college of arts and sciences and schools of business, education, music, medicine, nursing, law, and graduate studies. Total enrollment is about 12,000.

bayonet Short, sharp-edged, sometimes pointed weapon, designed for attachment to the muzzle of a firearm. According to tradition, it was developed in Bayonne, France, early in the 17th century and soon spread throughout Europe. The earliest design, the plug bayonet, was inserted into the muzzle of a musket, thus preventing the musket from being fired until the bayonet was removed. Later designs, including the socket bayonet invented by SEBASTIEN LE PRESTRE DE VAUBAN (1688), slipped it over the muzzle. Repeating firearms greatly reduced its combat value. By World War I it had become an all-purpose knife.

bayou \ˈbī-ü\ Still or slow-moving section of marshy water, usually a creek, secondary watercourse, or minor river that is a tributary of another river or channel. It may occur in the form of an OXBOW LAKE. Bayous are typical of the Louisiana's Mississippi River DELTA.

Bayreuth \bī-ˈrȯit\ City (pop., 1992 est.: 73,000), eastern central Germany. It is situated northeast of NUREMBERG. Founded in 1194 under Bishop Otto II of Bamberg, it came under the burgrave of NUREMBERG in 1248–1398 and the margraves of Brandenburg-Kulmbach in 1603–1769. The margraves patronized the arts and commissioned many baroque buildings that still exist. It was ceded to Prussia in 1791, captured by NAPOLEON in 1806, and passed to BAVARIA in 1810. Composer RICHARD WAGNER settled there in 1872 and designed the Festspielhaus, where Wagner festivals have been held since its opening in 1876. Manufactures include machinery, textiles, chemicals, pianos, porcelain, and glassware.

Bazin \bä-ˈza^{n}\, **Henri-Émile** (1829–1917) French engineer. As an assistant to H.-P.-G. Darcy (1803–1858), he completed his program of tests on resistance to water flow in channels after Darcy's death, producing the classic study of the subject. He later studied the problem of wave propagation (see WAVE) and the contraction of fluid flowing through an orifice. In 1854 he enlarged the Canal de Bourgogne and made it profitable for commercial navigation. In 1867 he suggested the use of pumps for dredging rivers, leading to the construction of the first suction dredgers.

bazooka Shoulder-type rocket launcher adopted by the U.S. Army in World War II. It consisted of a smoothbore steel tube, originally about 5 ft (1.5 m) long, open at both ends and equipped with a hand grip, shoulder rest, trigger mechanism, and sights. Officially named the M9A1 Rocket Launcher, it was called bazooka after the crude horn of that name used by a popular radio comedian. It was developed chiefly for attacking tanks and fortified positions at short range. The U.S. Army abandoned it during the Vietnam War in favor of lighter-weight ANTITANK WEAPONS.

BBC *in full* **British Broadcasting Corp.** Publicly financed broadcasting system in Britain. A private company at its founding in 1922, it was replaced by a public corporation under royal charter in 1927. The BBC World Service began in 1932, and by the 1990s was broadcasting programs in 38 languages to 120 million people worldwide. BBC television service, which kept its monopoly on television service until a commercial channel began broadcasting in 1954, introduced regular color broadcasts in Europe in 1967. The BBC radio monopoly ended in 1972. The BBC today offers five radio networks and two national television channels.

BBS See BULLETIN-BOARD SYSTEM

BCS theory Comprehensive theory that explains the behavior of superconducting materials. It was developed in 1957 by JOHN BARDEEN, LEON COOPER, and J. Robert Schrieffer (born 1931), whose surname initials provide its name. Cooper discovered that ELECTRONS in a superconductor are grouped in pairs (Cooper pairs), and that the motions of all the pairs within a single superconductor constitute a system that functions as a single entity. An electric voltage applied to the superconductor causes all Cooper pairs to move, forming an ELECTRIC CURRENT. When the voltage is removed, the current continues to flow because the pairs encounter no opposition. See also SUPERCONDUCTIVITY.

beach Sediments that accumulate along sea or lake shores. One type of beach occurs as a sediment strip bordering a rocky or cliffy coast. A second type is the outer margin of a marine plain. The third type consists of narrow sediment barriers stretching for dozens or even hundreds of miles parallel to the general direction of the coast. These barriers separate LAGOONS from the open sea and generally are dissected by tidal inlets. Certain sediment forelands, such as spits, points, and tombolos (which connect an island with a mainland), occasionally are called beaches.

Beach, Amy *orig.* **Amy Marcy Cheney** *known as* **Mrs. H. H. A. Beach** (1867–1994) U.S. composer and pianist. Born in Henniker, N.H., to a distinguished family, she was a precociously brilliant and mostly self-taught musician, and she performed as soloist with major orchestras in the U.S. and Europe. As a composer, she was devoted to German Romanticism rather than American themes or sources. Her best-loved works were her songs. Her *Gaelic Symphony* (1894) was the first symphony written by an American woman. Other works include a piano concerto (1899), the choral pieces *The Chambered Nautilus* (1907) and *Canticle of the Sun* (1928), the opera *Cabildo* (1932), and a piano quintet (1907).

Beach Boys U.S. rock group, formed in California in 1961 by brothers Brian Wilson (born 1942) on keyboards and bass, Dennis Wilson (1944–1983) on drums, and Carl Wilson (1946–1998) on guitar; their cousin Mike Love (born 1941) on drums; and Alan Jardine (born 1942) on guitar. Within a year they launched a string of surf-oriented hits marked by close vocal harmony, including "Surfin' Safari" and "California Girls." By 1966 they had released over 10 albums, including *Pet Sounds* (1966), considered their best. After Dennis's death by drowning, they continued touring into the 1990s.

beach flea See SAND FLEA

bead Small round object made of wood, shell, bone, seed, nut, metal, stone, glass, or plastic. It is usually pierced for stringing so that it can be worn for decorative or, in some cultures, magical purposes. The earliest Egyptian beads (from c. 4000 BC) were made of stone, feldspar, lapis lazuli, carnelian, turquoise, hematite, or amethyst and were variously shaped (sphere, cone, shell, animal head). By 3000–2000 BC, gold beads in tubular shapes were in use. From the Middle Ages to the 18th century, trade in beads was enormous. Today the richness of BEADWORK varies with fashion.

Beadle, George Wells (1903–1989) U.S. geneticist. Born in Wahoo, Neb., he earned his PhD from Cornell University. While studying drosophila, he realized that genes must influence heredity chemically, and designed a complex technique to determine the nature of those effects, showing that something as apparently simple as eye color results from a long series of chemical reactions, which are affected by genes. With EDWARD L. TATUM, he found that the total environment of a bread mold could be varied so that researchers could locate and identify mutations relatively easily, concluding that each gene determines the structure of a specific enzyme, which in turn allows a single chemical reaction to proceed. For the "one gene, one enzyme" concept, they shared a 1958 Nobel Prize with JOSHUA LEDERBERG. He later served as president of the University of Chicago (1960–68).

beadwork Ornamental work in beads. In the Middle Ages beads were used to embellish embroidery work. In Renaissance and Elizabethan England, clothing, purses, fancy boxes, and small pictures were adorned with beads. In the 19th–20th century beadwork proliferated in dress decoration. Beads are used as ornamentation on a variety of objects (clothing, masks, weapons, dolls) in many cultures, including the Native American, African, and Oceanic.

beagle Breed of small HOUND, popular as both a pet and a hunter. It looks like a small FOXHOUND, with large brown eyes, hanging ears, and a short coat that is usually a combination of black, tan, and white. Beagles are solidly built and heavy for their height. Two sizes are recognized: those standing less than 13 in. (33 cm) and weighing about 18 lbs (8 kg), and those standing about 15 in. (38 cm) and weighing about 30 lbs (13.5 kg). Beagles generally excel as rabbit hunters and are typically alert and affectionate.

Beagle.
SALLY ANNE THOMPSON—EB INC.

Beagle Channel Channel, southern tip of South America. Separating the TIERRA DEL FUEGO Islands and a group of Chilean islands, it is about 150 mi (240 km) long and 3–8 mi (5–13 km) wide. The eastern portion forms part of the Chile-Argentina border, while the western portion lies entirely within Chile. It was named for the ship in which CHARLES DARWIN explored the area.

beak *or* **bill** Stiff, projecting oral structure of birds and turtles (both of which lack teeth) and certain other animals (e.g., CEPHALOPODS and some insects, fishes, and mammals). The term bill is preferred for the beak of a bird, composed of upper and lower jaws covered by a horny sheath of skin, with the nostrils on top, usually at the base. The shapes and sizes of bills are adapted for obtaining food, preening, building nests, and other functions; they range from the long, slim bill of nectar-sipping hummingbirds to the sturdy, curved, nut-cracking bill of parrots.

Beaker culture Culture of the Late NEOLITHIC and early BRONZE AGE in northern and western Europe, known for its distinctive bell-shaped earthenware beakers decorated with toothed stamps, probably used in rituals of consumption. The people buried their dead in simple graves, but also in megalithic tombs in western Europe. They used the bow and arrow as well as copper daggers and spearheads. As they searched for gold and copper, they spread metallurgy into other parts of Europe. They eventually mixed with the Battle-Ax culture and spread from central Europe to eastern England.

beam In building construction, a horizontal member spanning an opening and carrying a load. The load may be a wall above the opening (see POST-AND-BEAM SYSTEM) or it may be a floor or roof. Beams may be of wood, steel or other metals, reinforced or prestressed concrete, plastic, or even brick with steel reinforcement. For weight reduction, metal beams are I-shaped, having a thin vertical web and thicker horizontal flanges where greater stress occurs. A joist is any of a series of small parallel beams supporting a floor or roof. See also GIRDER, SPANDREL.

bean SEED or pod of certain leguminous plants (see LEGUME). The mature seeds of the principal food beans, except SOYBEANS, are similar in composition, though they differ widely in eating quality. Rich in protein and providing moderate amounts of iron and vitamins B_1 and B_2, fresh or dried beans are used worldwide for cooking. Varieties differ greatly in size, shape, color, and tenderness of the immature pods. The common string, snap, or green bean *(Phaseolus vulgaris)* of Central and South American origin is the dominant edible-podded bean in the U.S., second to the soybean in importance. Third in importance is the broad, or fava, bean *(Vicia faba),* the principal bean of Europe. The lima bean *(P. limensis)*, of Central American origin, is commercially important in few countries outside the Americas. The scarlet runner bean *(P. coccineus)* is native to the New World tropics and is grown in Europe for its attractive flowers and fleshy immature pods. The mung bean, or green gram *(P. aureus),* is native to India and grown extensively in the Orient for food.

Bean, Roy (1825?–1903) U.S. justice of the peace and saloonkeeper. Born in Mason Co., Ky., he left Kentucky in 1847 and moved from town to town, killing at least two men in duels, before settling in Texas. He became prosperous as a blockade runner in the Civil War. In 1882 he moved to a site on the lower Pecos River that he named for LILLIE LANGTRY, opened a saloon, and dispensed hard, commonsensical, and prankish rulings as an unofficial magistrate, styling himself the "law west of the Pecos."

bear Generally massive, short-legged mammal (family Ursidae), the most recently evolved carnivore, found in Europe, Asia, North and South America, and North Africa. Closely related to the dog and the raccoon, most bears climb with ease and are strong swimmers. As a family, they are omnivores, but dietary preferences vary among species (POLAR BEARS feed mainly on seals, the SPECTACLED BEAR on vegetation, etc.). Though they do not truly hibernate, bears often sleep fitfully through much of the winter. They live 15–30 years in the wild, but much longer in captivity. They have been hunted as trophies, for hides, and for food. See also BLACK BEAR, BROWN BEAR, SUN BEAR.

bear cat See lesser PANDA

Bear Flag Revolt Short-lived rebellion in 1846 by American settlers in California against Mexican authorities. In June a small group captured Sonoma, a settlement north of San Francisco, and declared independence, raising a flag that featured a grizzly bear. Capt. JOHN C. FREMONT soon arrived to give his support and was elected to head the "republic." In July U.S. forces occupied San Francisco and Sonoma and claimed California for the U.S. The bear flag later became the state flag.

bear grass Either of two species of North American plants that make up the genus *Xerophyllum,* in the LILY FAMILY. The western species, *X. tenax,* also known as elk grass, squaw grass, and fire lily, is a smooth, light-green mountain perennial with a stout, unbranched stem and grasslike, rough-edged leaves at the bottom. It flowers at five to seven years, bearing a large cluster of small, creamy white flowers at the top of the stem. The turkey beard *(X. asphodeloides)* of southern North America is a similar plant that grows in dry pine barrens. In the southern and southwestern U.S., the name bear grass is given to various kinds of YUCCA and to the camas *(Camassia scilloides)* and the aloelike *Dasylirion texanum.*

bear market In securities and commodities trading, a declining market. A bear is an investor who expects prices to decline and, on this assumption, sells a borrowed SECURITY or commodity in the hope of buying it back later at a lower price, a speculative transaction called selling short. See also BULL MARKET.

bearberry Flowering, prostrate, EVERGREEN shrub *(Arctostaphylos uva-ursi)* of the HEATH FAMILY, occurring widely throughout North America in rocky and sandy woods and open areas. It has woody stems that are often 5–6 ft (1.5–1.8 m) long. Roots develop from stem joints, and the plant spreads, forming a broad, massive ground cover. The foliage turns bronzy in winter. The white, pink, or pink-tipped flowers are shaped like a narrow-mouthed bell. The berries are red.

Beard, Charles A(ustin) (1874–1948) U.S. historian. Born and reared in Indiana, Beard taught at Columbia University (1904–17) and cofounded New York's New School for Social Research (1919). He is best known for iconoclastic studies of the development of U.S. political institutions, emphasizing the dynamics of socioeconomic conflict and change and analyzing motivational factors in the founding of institutions. His works include *An Economic Interpretation of the Constitution of the United States* (1913), claiming that the Constitution was formulated to serve the economic interests of the founders; *The Economic Origins of Jeffersonian Democracy* (1915); and, with his wife, Mary R. Beard (1876–1958), *The Rise of American Civilization* (1927).

Beard, James (1903–1985) U.S. chef and cookbook author. Born in Portland, Ore., he started a catering business when he could not find regular employment as an actor. In 1945 he became the first chef to demonstrate cooking on network television. Through his Greenwich Village cooking school he influenced such future chefs as JULIA CHILD and Craig Claiborne (1920–2000). He championed simple American and English dishes and wrote one of the first serious books on outdoor cooking. His more than 20 cookbooks include *James Beard's American Cookery* (1972) and *Beard on Bread* (1973).

Bearden, Romare (Howard) (1914–1988) U.S. painter. Born in Charlotte, N.C., he studied with GEORGE GROSZ at the Art Students League and Columbia University. After military service in World War II, he attended the Sorbonne and traveled in Europe. During this time he achieved recognition for his complex, semiabstract collages of photographs and painted paper on canvas. The narrative structure of his work was simple; aspects of African-American culture, including ritual, music, and family, were his predominant themes. By the 1960s Bearden was recognized as the preeminent collagist in the U.S. He is regarded as one of the most important African-American artists of the 20th century.

Beardsley, Aubrey (Vincent) (1872–1898) British illustrator. His only formal training was a few months of evening classes at the Westminster School of Art. His style was based on the work of EDWARD BURNE-JONES and Japanese woodcuts, and he quickly became a master of the curvilinear black-and-white ornamental illustration popularized by the ART NOUVEAU movement. In 1893 he illustrated an edition of SIR THOMAS MALORY's *Morte D'Arthur,* and in 1894 achieved notoriety with his erotic illustrations for the English version of OSCAR WILDE's *Salome.* He became art editor and illustrator of the new quarterly *The Yellow Book* that same year. He died at 25 of tuberculosis.

bearing In machine construction, a connector (usually a support) that permits the connected members to rotate or to move in a straight line relative to one another. Often one of the members is fixed, and the bearing acts as a support for the moving member. Most bearings support rotating shafts against either transverse (radial) or thrust (axial) loads. To minimize FRICTION, the contacting surfaces in a bearing may be separated by a film of oil or gas; these are sliding bearings (see OIL SEAL). In BALL BEARINGS and ROLLER BEARINGS, the surfaces are separated by balls or rollers.

bearing wall *or* **load-bearing wall** Wall that carries the load of floors and roof above in addition to its own weight. The traditional masonry bearing wall is thickened in proportion to the forces it has to resist: its own weight, the dead load of floors and roof, the live load of people, as well as the lateral forces of ARCHES, VAULTS, and wind. Such walls may be much thicker toward the base, where maximum loads accumulate. Bearing walls may also be framed and sheathed or constructed of reinforced concrete.

Béarn \bā-'ärn\ Historical region and former province, southwestern France. It was bounded by GASCONY and the PYRENEES; its capital was Pau. It formed part of Aquitania under the Romans; it was later devastated by the VANDALS and VISIGOTHS. Held as the countship of Béarn by the future HENRY IV, it became a holding of the French crown when he became king in 1589. In the 16th century Pau was an important cultural center under the patronage of MARGARET OF ANGOULÊME.

Beas River \'bē-ˌäs\ *ancient* **Hyphasis.** River, northwestern India. One of the "five rivers" that give the PUNJAB its name, it rises in the HIMALAYAS east of Dharmsala in HIMACHAL PRADESH and flows west-southwest 290 mi (467 km) to the SUTLEJ RIVER southwest of Kapurthala. It was the approximate limit of ALEXANDER THE GREAT's invasion of India in 326 BC.

beat In physics, the pulsation resulting from a combination of two waves of slightly different FREQUENCY. Beat frequency is the difference between the frequencies of the combining waves. When the interfering frequencies are in the audible range, the beats are heard as alternating soft and loud pulses. The human ear can detect beats with frequencies up to 10 hertz, or 10 beats per second. Piano tuners listen for beats when comparing the pitch of a tuning fork to that of a vibrating string; when no beats are heard, the fork and string are at the same frequency. Ultrasonic or inaudible frequencies can be superimposed to produce audible beats, allowing the detection of vocal sounds produced by bats or dolphins.

Beat movement American social and literary movement of the 1950s and '60s, associated with bohemian artists' communities in San Francisco, Los Angeles, and New York. Its adherents expressed alienation from conventional society and advocated personal release and illumination through heightened sensory awareness and altered states of consciousness. Beat poets, including LAWRENCE FERLINGHETTI, ALLEN GINSBERG, Gregory Corso (1930–2001), and GARY SNYDER, sought to liberate poetry from academic refinement, creating verse that was frequently chaotic and sprinkled with obscenities but sometimes powerful and moving. JACK KEROUAC and WILLIAM S. BURROUGHS developed an unstructured, spontaneous, sometimes hallucinatory approach to prose writing that was designed to convey the immediacy of experience. Though it faded by c. 1970, the movement paved the way for acceptance of other unorthodox and previously ignored writers.

Beatles British musical group that ushered in the climactic phase of rock music. Its members, all born in Liverpool, were PAUL MCCARTNEY, JOHN LENNON, George Harrison (1943–2001), and Ringo Starr (born 1940). It began in the pairing of McCartney and Lennon in 1956, joined by Harrison in 1957, along with Stu Sutcliffe (1940–1962) and later Pete Best (born 1941). In 1960 they adopted the name The Beatles. In 1962 they signed a recording contract and replaced Best with Starr. The release in 1962–63 of such songs as "Please Please Me" and "I Want to Hold Your Hand" made them England's most popular rock group, and in 1964 "Beatlemania" struck the U.S. Originally inspired by CHUCK BERRY, ELVIS PRESLEY, and BILL HALEY, their direct and energetic songs kept them at the top of popularity charts. Their long hair and tastes in dress proved influential throughout the world, as did their experimentation with hallucinogenic drugs and Indian mysticism. Guaranteed huge sales, they felt free to experiment with a mix ranging from ballads ("Yesterday") to complex rhythm tunes ("Paperback Writer"), from children's songs ("Yellow Submarine") to songs of social comment ("Eleanor Rigby"). Their public performances ended in 1966. Albums such as *Rubber Soul* (1965), *Revolver* (1966) and *The Beatles* ("White Album," 1968) set new trends in rock. In 1967 they produced *Sgt. Pepper's Lonely Hearts Club Band,* an album novel for its conception as a dramatic whole, use of electronic music, and character as a studio work unreproducible on stage. They appeared in the films *A Hard Day's Night* (1964) and *Help!* (1965). The group dissolved in 1971.

Beaton, Cecil (Walter Hardy) *later* **Sir Cecil** (1904–1980) British photographer and designer. When he received his first camera at age 11, he began making portraits of his sisters. In the 1920s he became staff photographer at *Vanity Fair* and *Vogue.* In Beaton's exotic and bizarre portraits, the sitter is only one element of an overall decorative composition dominated by flamboyant backgrounds. His photographs of the siege of Britain were published in *Winged Squadrons* (1942). After the war, he designed costumes and stage sets, including those for the movies *Gigi* (1958) and *My Fair Lady* (1964).

Beatrix (Wilhelmina Armgard) \bā-ȧ-'trēks\ (born 1938) Queen of the Netherlands. Beatrix went into exile with her family when the Germans invaded the Netherlands in World War II, and she spent the war years in Britain and Canada. In 1965 her betrothal to a German diplomat sparked controversy because of his past membership in the Hitler Youth and the German army. They were married in 1966, and the hostility waned with the births of the first male heirs in the House of ORANGE since 1890. Beatrix became queen in 1980 after the abdication of her mother, JULIANA.

Beatrix.

BY COURTESY OF THE ROYAL NETHERLANDS EMBASSY; PHOTOGRAPH, MAX KOOT

Beatty \'bāt-ē\, **(Henry) Warren** *orig.* **Henry Warren Beaty** (born 1937) U.S. film actor, producer, director, and screenwriter. Born in Richmond, Va., he and his sister, SHIRLEY MACLAINE, studied acting with their mother, a drama coach. After appearing on Broadway in WILLIAM INGE's *A Loss of Roses* (1960), he made his film debut in *Splendor in the Grass* (1961) and later starred in and produced the successful *Bonnie and Clyde* (1967) and *Shampoo* (1975). Often cowriting, directing, or producing his own films, he later starred in *Heaven Can Wait* (1978), *Reds* (1981, Academy Award), *Dick Tracy* (1990), *Bugsy* (1991), and *Bulworth* (1998).

Beaubourg Center See POMPIDOU CENTER

Beaufort Sea \'bō-fərt\ Part of the ARCTIC OCEAN northeast of Alaska, northwest of Canada, and west of BANKS ISLAND in the ARCTIC ARCHIPELAGO. Its surface area is about 184,000 sq mi (476,000 sq km), its average depth is 3,239 ft (1,004 m), and its greatest depth is 15,360 ft (4,680 m). It is frozen over almost year-round; only in August and September does the ice break up. The MACKENZIE RIVER flows into the sea; the chief settlement is PRUDHOE BAY, Alaska.

Beauharnais \bō-är-'ne\, **Alexandre, vicomte (Viscount) de** (1760–1794) French politician and general, first husband of JOSÉPHINE. A liberal noble, he became a prominent figure during the FRENCH REVOLUTION. He presided over the Constituent Assembly in 1791, served with gallantry in the army, and was named general in chief of the Army of the Rhine in 1793. He was guillotined during the REIGN OF TERROR, largely because he was a noble. He was the father of E. and H. de Beauharnais (see EUGENE DE BEAUHARNAIS and HORTENSE DE BEAUHARNAIS) and the grandfather of NAPOLEON III.

Beauharnais, Eugène de (1781–1824) French administrator and general. Son of JOSÉPHINE and ALEXANDRE, VICOMTE DE BEAUHARNAIS, he became a useful military aide to his stepfather, NAPOLEON. In 1804 he received the title of prince and was appointed archchancellor of state. He was named Napoleon's viceroy in Italy (1805), where he reorganized public finances, built roads, and introduced the French legal system. As commander of the Italian army, he fought admirably in various conflicts. In 1814 he held out in Italy against the Austrians and the Neapolitans, but was forced to conclude an armistice. He retired to the Bavarian court of his wife's family.

Beauharnais, (Eugénie-) Hortense de (1783–1837) French-born queen of Holland (1806–10). Daughter of JOSÉPHINE and ALEXANDRE, VICOMTE DE BEAUHARNAIS, and stepdaughter of NAPOLEON, Hortense married Napoleon's brother, Louis BONAPARTE. When he became king of Holland, she was named queen. The marriage was unhappy but produced three children, including the future NAPOLEON III. When Napoleon was exiled in 1814, Hortense became the center of Bonapartist intrigue, and her support of Napoleon during his return led to her banishment from France in 1815, after which she settled in Switzerland.

Beaujolais \,bō-zhȯ-'lā\ Region in northern Rhône and northeastern Loire departments, eastern central France. It is located east of the MASSIF CENTRAL and west of the SAÔNE RIVER. The region is wooded and supports a local forestry industry; its highest point is Mount Saint-Rigaud, at 3,310 ft (1,009 m). East of the mountain are the limestone escarpments of the Côte Beaujolaise, which support a world-famous red wine industry.

Beaujoyeulx \bōzh-wȧ-'yœ̄\, **Balthazar de** *orig.* **Baltazarini di Belgioioso** (died 1587) Italian-French composer and choreographer. In 1555 he left Italy for Paris and joined the court of CATHERINE DE MÉDICIS as a violinist. There he organized unofficial court fetes and became valet de chambre to the royal family. In 1581 he staged the lavish *Ballet comique de la reine;* considered the first *ballet de cour,* it was emulated by other European courts and was the precursor of developments in ballet for the next century.

Beaumarchais \,bō-mär-'shā\, **Pierre-Augustin Caron de** (1732–1799) French playwright. Son of a watchmaker, he invented a clockwork mechanism and became embroiled in lawsuits over its patent; a series of witty pamphlets he wrote in his defense established his reputation as a writer. His comedy *The Barber of Seville* (1772) was kept off the stage for three years because it criticized the aristocracy. His *Marriage of Figaro* (1784) similarly criticized the nobility and it too was initially banned. The plays became famous operas by G. ROSSINI and W.A. MOZART, respectively. He founded the Société des Auteurs (1777) to enable playwrights to obtain royalty payments. His wealth led, ironically, to his temporary imprisonment during the French Revolution, an event his plays were sometimes said to have sparked.

Pierre Beaumarchais, oil painting by Jean-Marc Nattier.

GIRAUDON–ART RESOURCE

Beaumont \'bō-,mänt\ City (pop., 1996 est.: 111,000), southeastern Texas. Lying at the head of navigation on the Neches River, it is connected to the Gulf of Mexico by the Sabine-Neches Canal and is a major port of entry. It was founded in 1835. When Spindletop, the first major oil field in Texas, was discovered in 1901, the city grew rapidly. With Port Arthur and Orange, it forms the "Golden Triangle" petrochemical and industrial complex.

Beaumont \'bō-,mänt\, **Francis** (1584?–1616) British playwright. He is known chiefly for the 10 very popular plays on which he collaborated with John Fletcher (1579–1625) c. 1606–13. These included the tragicomedies *The Maides Tragedy, Phylaster,* and *A King and No King.* Forty other plays attributed to them were later found to have been written by others. Their independent work includes Beaumont's poetry and his parody *The Knight of the Burning Pestle* (1607) and Fletcher's pastoral *The Faithful Shepherdess* (1608). After Beaumont retired in 1613, Fletcher collaborated with other playwrights, possibly including WILLIAM

SHAKESPEARE, with whom he may have written *King Henry the Eighth* and *The Two Noble Kinsmen.*

Beaumont, William (1785–1853) U.S. surgeon. Born in Lebanon, Conn., he served many years as an army surgeon. When treating a trapper whose abdomen had been perforated by a shotgun blast, Beaumont collected gastric juice for analysis, and showed that it contained hydrochloric acid, which supported his belief that digestion was a chemical process. He also reported on the effects of different foods on the stomach and established alcohol as a cause of gastritis.

Beauregard \'bō-rə-ˌgärd\, **P(ierre) G(ustave) T(outant)** (1818–1893) U.S. military leader. Born near New Orleans, he graduated from West Point in 1838. He served in the Mexican War. After Louisiana seceded in 1861, he resigned his commission and became a general in the Confederate army. He commanded the forces that bombarded Fort Sumter, S.C., and was in command at the battles of BULL RUN and SHILOH. He conducted the defenses of Charleston, S.C., and Richmond, Va. He was a controversial commander, often questioning orders, and after the war he quarreled with other generals' accounts of his role in the war.

Beauvoir \'bō-ˌvwär\, **Simone (Lucie-Ernestine-Marie-Bertrand) de** (1908–1986) French writer and feminist. As a student at the Sorbonne, she met J.-P. SARTRE, with whom she would form a lifelong intellectual and romantic bond. She is known primarily for her treatise *The Second Sex* (1949), a scholarly and passionate plea for the abolition of what she called the myth of the "eternal feminine" that became a major classic of feminist literature. She also wrote four admired volumes of autobiography (1958–72), philosophical works that explore themes of EXISTENTIALISM, and fiction, notably *The Mandarins* (1954, Prix Goncourt). *The Coming of Age* (1970) is a bitter reflection on society's indifference to the elderly.

Beaux-Arts \bō-'zär\, **École (Nationale Supérieure) des** School of fine arts *(beaux arts)* in Paris. It was founded by the merger in 1793 of the Académie de Peinture et de Sculpture, founded by CHARLES LE BRUN in 1648, and the Académie d'Architecture, founded in 1671 by J.-B. COLBERT. It has traditionally provided instruction in drawing, painting, sculpture, engraving, and (until 1968) architecture. The BEAUX-ARTS STYLE in architecture has been particularly influential.

Beaux-Arts style \bō-'zär\ *or* **Second Empire style** *or* **Second Empire Baroque** Architectural style developed at the École des BEAUX-ARTS in Paris. It enjoyed international dominance in the late 19th century (see SECOND EMPIRE) and rapidly became an official style for many of the new public buildings demanded by expanding cities and their national governments. Buildings are typically massive and have a symmetrical plan with rooms arranged axially, profuse classicist detail, and often pavilions that extend forward at the ends and center. Among the most admired Beaux-Arts structures is the PARIS OPERA.

beaver Either member of the aquatic rodent family Castoridae (genus *Castor*), well known for their dam-building. Beavers are heavyset and have short legs and large, webbed hind feet. They grow as large as 4 ft (1.3 m) long (including the 1-ft, or 30-cm, tail) and as heavy as 66 lbs (30 kg). Beavers build their dams of sticks, stones, and mud in small rivers, streams, and lakes, often producing sizable ponds. With their powerful jaws and large teeth, they can fell medium-sized trees, whose branches they use in their dams and whose tender bark and buds they eat. One or more family groups share a dome-shaped stick-and-mud lodge built in the water, with tunnel entrances below water level. American beavers range from northern Mexico to the Arctic. Their prized pelts stimulated the exploration of western North America, and by 1900 beavers were nearly trapped to extinction. Eurasian beavers are now found only in a few locations, including the Elbe and Rhône drainages of Europe. The mountain beaver of the Pacific Northwest is unrelated.

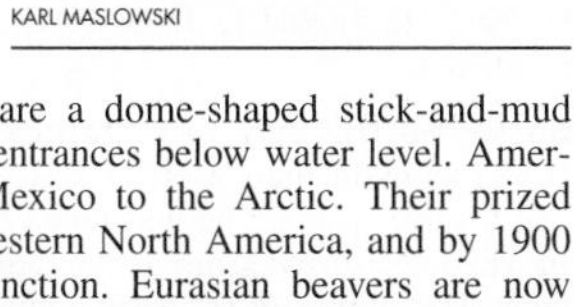

Beaver (*Castor canadensis*).
KARL MASLOWSKI

Beaverbrook (of Beaverbrook and of Cherkley), Baron *orig.* **William Maxwell Aitken** *known as* **Lord Beaverbrook** (1879–1964) Canadian-British politician and newspaper proprietor. After making a fortune in Montreal as a financier, he moved to England and became active in politics as a Conservative. Beginning in 1916, he took over or founded newspapers, including the London *Daily Express, Sunday Express,* and *Evening Standard.* Idiosyncratic and very successful, he became a "press lord" and a champion of individual enterprise and British imperial interests. He held various high government appointments, including positions in the British Cabinet during both World Wars, but never fully achieved the political power he sought.

Bebel \'bā-bəl\, **August** (1840–1913) German socialist and writer. A turner by trade, Bebel joined the Leipzig Workers' Educational Association (1861) and became its chairman (1865). Influenced by the ideas of WILHELM LIEBKNECHT, in 1869 he helped found the Social Democratic Labor Party (later the SOCIAL DEMOCRATIC PARTY) and became its most influential and popular leader for more than 40 years. He served in the Reichstag in 1867, 1871–81, and 1883–1913. He spent a total of nearly five years in prison on such charges as "libel of Bismarck." He wrote a number of works, including *Woman and Socialism* (1883), a powerful piece of Social Democratic propaganda.

Bebey, Francis (1929–2001) Cameroonian-born French writer and singer-songwriter. He went to Paris and New York to study and settled in Paris in 1960. He worked for UNESCO researching and documenting traditional African music meanwhile composing and recording his own highly experimental music that incorporated elements typical of the musics of other cultures. Because of this, he is sometimes considered "The Father of WORLD MUSIC." He also wrote two books about African music and several works of fiction that were translated into English.

bebop *or* **bop** JAZZ characterized by harmonic complexity, convoluted melodic lines, and frequent shifting of rhythmic accent. In the mid-1940s, a group of musicians, including DIZZY GILLESPIE, THELONIOUS MONK, and CHARLIE PARKER, rejected the conventions of SWING to pioneer a self-consciously artistic extension of improvised jazz, which set new technical standards of velocity and harmonic subtlety. Two genres grew out of bebop in the 1950s: the delicate, dry, understated approach that came to be known as cool jazz, and the aggressive, BLUES-tinged earthiness of hard bop.

Beccafumi \ˌbek-ə-'fü-mē\, **Domenico** *orig.* **Domenico di Giacomo di Pace** *known as* **Mecherino** \ˌmāk-kā-'rē-nō\ (1484–1551) Italian painter and sculptor active in Siena. He adopted the name of his patron, Lorenzo Beccafumi. In 1510 he went to Rome to study the work of RAPHAEL and MICHELANGELO. In 1512 he returned to Siena, where most of his best work can be found. He is noted for his sense of fantasy and striking effects of light, as in *The Birth of the Virgin* (c. 1543). He painted decorations for the Siena town hall (1529–35) and executed designs for the marble pavement of Siena Cathedral. He is considered the outstanding Sienese painter of the Mannerist style.

"The Birth of the Virgin," panel painting by Domenico Beccafumi, 1544; in the Pinacoteca Nazionale, Siena, Italy.
SCALA—ART RESOURCE

Beccaria \ˌbäk-kä-'rē-ə\, **Cesare** (1738–1794) Italian criminologist and economist. He became an international celebrity in 1764 with the publication of *Dei delitti e delle pene* ("Crime and Punishment"), the first systematic statement of principles governing criminal punishment, in which he argued that the effectiveness of criminal justice depended more on the certainty of punishment than on its severity. The book greatly influenced criminal-law reform in Western Europe. In later years, Beccaria lectured at Milan's Palatine School and served as a public official, dealing with such issues as monetary reform, labor relations, and public education.

Bechet \bə-'shā\, **Sidney** (1897–1959) U.S. saxophonist, one of the first great soloists in jazz. Born in New Orleans, Bechet took up the clarinet at age 6, later switching to the more powerful soprano saxophone. His emergence as a soloist from the New Orleans tradition of collective improvisation (see DIXIELAND) established his reputation in the mid-1920s, but his lack of exposure with prominent groups caused his influence on others to be indirect, most notably through the playing of JOHNNY HODGES. Bechet moved to France in 1951.

Bechtel \'bek-tᵊl\, **Stephen D(avison)** (1900–1989) U.S. construction engineer and president (1936–60) of W. A. Bechtel Co. and its successor, Bechtel Corp. Born in Aurora, Ind., he became a vice president in the San Francisco-based family firm of W. A. Bechtel Co. in 1925. In 1937 he and John McCone formed Bechtel-McCone Corp., a builder of refineries and chemical plants. The companies built ships and made aircraft parts during World War II. After the war, the newly formed Bechtel Corp. became one of the world's largest construction and engineering firms, building pipelines in Canada, the Middle East, and elsewhere and constructing power plants all over the world. The Bechtel companies helped construct the Hoover Dam, the Alaska oil pipeline, and the city of Al-Jubayl in Saudi Arabia. Bechtel retired as its president in 1960 but remained senior director of what became known as the Bechtel Group.

Bechuanaland See BOTSWANA

Beck, Ludwig (1880–1944) German general. After serving with the army general staff in World War I, he was later chief of the general staff (1935–38). He opposed ADOLF HITLER's occupation of the Rhineland and resigned to protest the decision to conquer Czechoslovakia. He helped plan the unsuccessful JULY PLOT to assassinate Hitler; when it failed, Beck committed suicide.

Beckenbauer, Franz (born 1945) German football (soccer) player. He is credited with inventing the modern attacking sweeper. Nicknamed "Der Kaiser," Beckenbauer is the only man to both captain and manage World Cup-winning teams (1974 and 1990, respectively). He spent most of his career with Bayern Munich (1958–77), leading the team to three European Cup championships (1974–76) and four national titles. He was named European Footballer of the Year in 1972 and 1976. After brief stints in New York and Hamburg, he retired in 1984 and turned to managing.

Becker, Boris (Franz) (born 1967) German tennis player. He left school in the 10th grade to concentrate on tennis. In 1985 he became the youngest winner (at 17) of the WIMBLEDON's men's singles title and the youngest ever to win a men's Grand Slam tournament, as well as the only unseeded player and the first German ever to win the title. He was victorious at Wimbledon again in 1986 and 1989, and also won singles titles in the 1989 U.S. Open and the 1991 and 1996 Australian Open competitions. In 1997 he announced his retirement from Grand Slam play, though he played again at Wimbledon in 1999.

Becker, Gary S(tanley) (born 1930) U.S. economist. Born in Pottsville, Pa., he studied at Princeton University and the University of Chicago. As a professor at Columbia University and the University of Chicago, he applied the methods of economics to aspects of human behavior previously considered the domain of sociology and demography. In *Human Capital* (1964) and *A Treatise on the Family* (1981), he advanced the theory that rational economic choices, based on self-interest, govern most human activities, even apparently noneconomic activities such as the formation of families. He won the Nobel Prize in 1992.

Murder of Thomas Becket, illustration from an English psalter, c. 1200; in the British Library.

BY COURTESY OF THE TRUSTEES OF THE BRITISH LIBRARY

Becket, St. Thomas *or* **Thomas à Becket** (1118?–1170) Archbishop of Canterbury (1162–70). The son of a Norman merchant, he served as chancellor of England (1155–62) under HENRY II, whose entire trust he won. A brilliant administrator, diplomat, and military strategist, he aided the king in increasing the royal power. Resistant to the Gregorian reform movement that asserted the autonomy of the church, Henry hoped to reinforce royal control of the church by appointing Becket archbishop of Canterbury in 1162. Becket, however, embraced his new duties devoutly and opposed royal power in the church, especially proclaiming the right of offending clerics to be tried in ecclesiastical courts. The king issued the Constitutions of CLARENDON (1164) listing royal rights over the church, and he summoned the archbishop to trial. Becket fled to France and remained in exile until 1170, when he returned to Canterbury and was murdered in the cathedral by four of Henry's knights. His tomb became a site of pilgrimage, and he was canonized in 1173.

Beckett, Samuel (Barclay) (1906–1989) Irish playwright. After studying in Ireland and traveling, he settled in Paris in 1937. During World War II he supported himself as a farmworker and joined the underground resistance. In the postwar years he wrote, in French, the narrative trilogy *Molloy* (1951), *Malone Dies* (1951), and *The Unnamable* (1953). His play *Waiting for Godot* (1952) was an immediate success in Paris and gained worldwide acclaim when he translated it into English. Marked by minimal plot and action, it typifies the theater of the ABSURD. His later plays, also abstract works with minimal sets that deal with the mystery and despair of human existence in a comic spirit, include *Endgame* (1957), *Krapp's Last Tape* (1958), and *Happy Days* (1961). In 1969 he was awarded the Nobel Prize.

Samuel Beckett, 1965.

© GISELE FREUND

Beckford, William (1760–1844) English dilettante, novelist, and eccentric. He is remembered for his gothic novel *Vathek* (1786), about an impious voluptuary who builds a tower so high that he challenges Muhammad in heaven and so brings about his fall to the kingdom of the prince of darkness; though unevenly written, the story is full of invention and bizarre detail. Beckford and his family were forced to leave England for 10 years by a scandal involving a youth. On his return he built Fonthill Abbey, the most sensational building of the English GOTHIC REVIVAL, whose own 270-ft (82-m) tower later twice collapsed.

Beckmann \'bek-,män\, **Max** (1884–1950) German Expressionist painter and graphic artist. He was trained at the conservative Weimar Academy. In 1903 he moved to Berlin and joined the Berlin SEZESSION. His experience as a medical orderly in World War I changed his outlook, and his work became full of horrifying imagery, with deliberately repulsive colors and erratic forms. He considered his work to be a combination of brutal realism and social commentary. In 1933 the Nazis declared his art "degenerate" and forced him to resign his professorship at the Frankfurt Städelsches Kunstinstitut. In 1937 he fled to Amsterdam and in 1947 moved to the U.S., where he taught in St. Louis and New York.

Becknell \'bek-nᵊl\, **William** (1796?–1865) U.S. trader. Born in Amherst Co., Va., he settled in Missouri, where he became involved in trade with the Southwest. When the Spanish prohibition on trade with New Mexico was lifted in 1821, he followed the customary route through the Colorado Rocky Mountains south to Santa Fe, where he sold his goods at great profit. The next year he pioneered a new route through the mountains of northeastern New Mexico that became known as the SANTA FE TRAIL. He moved to Texas c. 1834, where he fought for Texas's independence.

Beckwourth, Jim *orig.* **James Pierson Beckwith** (1798–1867?) U.S. mountain man. Born a slave in Virginia, the son of a white man and a slave woman, he was taken by his father to St. Louis and set free. In 1823–24 he was hired by trading expeditions in the Rocky Mountains. He married a series of Indian women and lived among the Crow for about six years. During the California gold rush (1848) he established a route through the Sierra Nevada. In California he met Thomas D. Bonner, who in 1856 published many of Beckwourth's stories and recollections.

Becquerel \be-'krel\, **(Antoine-) Henri** (1852–1908) French physicist. His grandfather, Antoine-César (1788–1878), was one of the founders of the field of electrochemistry, and his father, Alexandre-Edmond (1820–1891), made important studies of light phenomena. Henri likewise studied phosphorescent materials as well as uranium compounds, and employed photography in his experiments. He is remembered for his discovery of RADIOACTIVITY, which occurred when he found that the element uranium (in a sample of pitchblende) emitted invisible rays that could darken a photographic plate. His 1901 report of a burn caused by a sample of MARIE CURIE's radium that he carried in his vest pocket led to investigations by physicians and ultimately the medical use of radioactive substances. In 1903 he shared a Nobel Prize with the Curies. The unit of radioactivity, the becquerel (Bq), is named for him.

bed Piece of furniture on which a person may recline or sleep. Beds of simple construction appear in medieval manuscripts, as well as more decorative beds with carving and inlay, embroidered coverlets, and elaborate hangings. The canopy, or tester, was introduced in the 15th century. In the 1820s, the development of coiled springs fitted into mattresses revolutionized the bed. In the Middle East, beds consisted of rugs piled up on the floor. In China, raised and canopied beds were used 2,000 years ago. The traditional Japanese bed (futon) consist of quilted padding and a coverlet arranged on the floor.

Great Bed of Ware, carved, inlaid, and painted wood, English, late 16th century; in the Victoria and Albert Museum, London.

BY COURTESY OF THE VICTORIA AND ALBERT MUSEUM, LONDON, CROWN COPYRIGHT RESERVED

bedbug Any member of approximately 75 species of nocturnal insects (family Cimicidae) that feed by sucking the blood of humans and other warm-blooded animals. The reddish brown adult is broad and flat and less than 0.2 in. (4–5 mm) long. Among the most cosmopolitan of human parasites, they are found in every kind of dwelling. They digest meals slowly; adults have lived for at least a year without food. Though the bite is irritating, it is not known to transmit diseases to humans.

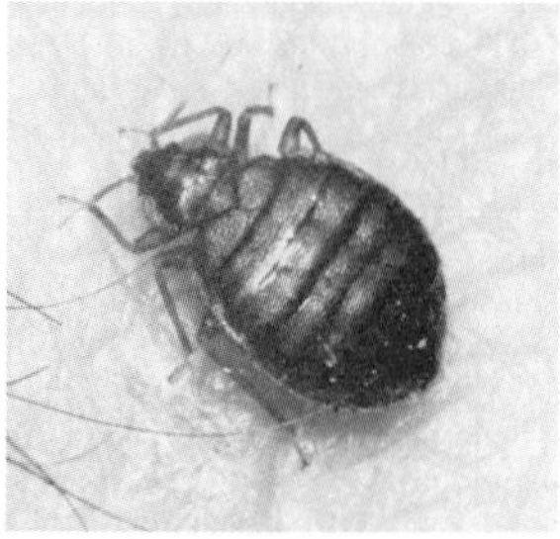

Bedbug (*Cimex lectularius*) magnified 5×.

WILLIAM E. FERGUSON

bedding plant Plant that is grown, usually in quantity, in pots or flats in a GREENHOUSE or similar structure, and that is intended to be transplanted to a flower garden, hanging basket, window box, or other outdoor planter. Most bedding plants are annuals. They are transplanted outdoors after all danger of frost has passed. Some important bedding plants are IMPATIENS, MARIGOLDS, and PETUNIAS.

Bede, St. *known as* **the Venerable Bede** (672/673–735) Anglo-Saxon theologian, historian, and chronologist. Raised in a monastery, he was ordained a priest at 30. He is best known for his *Ecclesiastical History of the English People* (732?), tracing Britain's history from 55 BC to AD 597, a source vital to the history of the conversion to Christianity of the Anglo-Saxon tribes in Britain. His method of dating events from the time of Christ's birth (AD) came into general use through the popularity of the *Historia ecclesiastica* and two works on chronology.

Bedford City (pop., 1995 est.: 81,000), southeastern central England. The administrative seat of BEDFORDSHIRE, it lies on the OUSE RIVER northwest of London. It was a Roman fording station and a Saxon town. It was recaptured by the Anglo-Saxons from the Danes in 914. JOHN BUNYAN is thought to have written *A Pilgrim's Progress* while imprisoned there.

Bedfordshire \'bed-fərd-ˌshir\ County (pop., 1995 est.: 364,000), southeastern central England. Much of the county is occupied by the OUSE RIVER valley; its capital is BEDFORD. Settled c. 1800 BC by the BEAKER CULTURE, the valley was resettled by the Romans in the 1st–5th century AD. First mentioned as a political unit in 1010, the county has survived virtually unchanged within its present boundaries. Its architectural masterpiece is Woburn Abbey, seat of the dukes of Bedford.

Bedlington terrier Breed of dog developed in the 19th century in Northumberland, England, and named for Bedlingtonshire, a mining district in the area. Initially established as a fighting dog and hunter of vermin, the breed later became a popular pet. Lamblike in appearance, it has an arched back, a topknot, and a thick, curly coat that is blue-gray, deep reddish brown, or pale sandy, often with tan markings. The breed stands 15–16 in. (38–40 cm) tall and weighs 22–24 lbs (10–11 kg).

Bedlington terrier.

SALLY ANNE THOMPSON—EB INC.

Bedouin \'bed-win\ Arabic-speaking desert nomads of the Middle East. Ethnically, the Bedouin are identical to other ARABS. Bedouin social rank is determined by the animals they herd: camel nomads are most prestigious, followed by sheep and goat herders and finally cattle nomads. Traditionally, Bedouin migrated into the desert during the rainy season and returned to cultivated areas during the dry season, but since World War II some national governments have nationalized their range lands and conflicts over land use have arisen, and many groups have settled. Most, however, retain pride in the nomadic heritage.

Bedouin with a young goat in central Qatar.

M. ERICSON—OSTMAN AGENCY

bedstraw Any low perennial herbaceous plant of the genus *Galium,* in the MADDER FAMILY, found in damp woods and swamps and along stream banks and shores. Bedstraws bear finely toothed, often needle-shaped leaves in whorls of four to eight; clusters of small green, yellow, or white flowers; and fruit composed of two rounded NUTS joined together. Northern bedstraw *(G. boreale),* marsh bedstraw *(G. palustre),* and goosegrass *(G. aparine)* are common throughout Europe and have become naturalized in parts of North America. Sweet woodruff *(G. odoratum)* smells like freshly mown HAY; its dried shoots are used in perfumes, sachets, and beverages. The roots of several species yield a red dye.

bee Any member of some 20,000 INSECT species (superfamily Apoidea, order Hymenoptera), including the familiar BUMBLEBEE. Adults range in size from about 0.08 to 1.6 in. (2 mm–4 cm). Bees are related to WASPS, but, unlike wasps, which can eat other insects, most bees are entirely dependent on flowers for their food. Male bees are usually short-lived and never collect pollen; female bees make and provision the nest and usually have special anatomical structures for carrying pollen. Most species are solitary. The so-called killer bee, an Africanized subspecies of *Apis mellifera* (see HONEYBEE), reached the U.S. from Mexico c. 1990; killer bees react quickly and attack in number. See also KARL VON FRISCH.

Leaf-cutting bee (*Anthidium*).

M.W.F. TWEEDIE FROM THE NATURAL HISTORY PHOTOGRAPHIC AGENCY—EB INC.

bee balm Any of 12 North American annual or perennial plants in the genus *Monarda,* variously known as BERGAMOT, horsemint, and bee balm, belonging to the MINT family and having showy flowers. Wild bergamot

(*M. fistulosa*) has a minty aroma. The more sharply scented Oswego tea (*M. didyma;* a bergamot variety) is native in eastern North America but is widely cultivated elsewhere.

bee-eater Any of about 25 species of brightly colored birds (family Meropidea) that feed on bees, wasps, and other insects. They are found throughout tropical and subtropical Eurasia, Africa, and Australasia (one species occasionally reaches the British Isles). Bee-eaters range in length from 6 to 14 in. (15–35 cm). Their bill is moderately long, slightly downcurved, and pointed. Their brilliant plumage is usually predominantly green, but many species are partially colored with red, yellow, blue, or purple.

Bee-eater (*Merops apiaster*).
S.C. PORTER–BRUCE COLEMAN LTD.

beech Any of several different types of trees, especially about 10 species of deciduous ornamental and timber trees constituting the genus *Fagus* (family Fagaceae), native to temperate and subtropical regions of the Northern Hemisphere. About 40 species of superficially similar trees, known as false beech (genus *Nothofagus*), are native to cooler regions of the Southern Hemisphere. A beech of the family Fagaceae is tall, round-headed, and wide-spreading, with smooth, steel-gray bark and toothed, shiny green leaves. The American beech *(F. grandifolia),* native to eastern North America, and the European beech *(F. sylvatica),* found throughout England and Eurasia, are the most widely known species. Both are economically important timber trees, often planted as ornamentals. Beech wood is durable under water and is valued for indoor use, tool handles, and shipping containers. The nuts provide forage for game animals, are used in fattening poultry, and yield an edible oil. Beeches are slow-growing but may live to 400 years or more.

Beecham, Thomas *later* **Sir Thomas** (1879–1961) British conductor. Born to an aristocratic family and educated at Oxford, he was self-taught as a conductor. Devoted to broadening British musical tastes, he created the Beecham Symphony Orchestra in 1909, and programmed many British premieres not only of the concert repertoire but of operas as well. In 1932 he founded the London Philharmonic Orchestra, and in 1947 the Royal Philharmonic Orchestra; he also founded opera companies. Though he had significant gaps in his technique, he was an incomparable interpreter of the music he loved, especially W.A. MOZART; of his contemporaries, he particularly championed R. STRAUSS and F. DELIUS.

Beecher, Catharine (Esther) (1800–1878) U.S. educator who popularized and shaped a conservative movement to both elevate and entrench woman's role in the domestic sphere. Daughter of the minister and temperance activist Lyman Beecher and sister of HARRIET BEECHER STOWE and HENRY WARD BEECHER, she helped found the Hartford Female Seminary (1823) and other organizations devoted to women's education. Her *Treatise on Domestic Economy* (1841) went through 15 editions and helped standardize domestic practices and reinforce the belief that a woman's proper place was in the home.

Beecher, Henry Ward (1813–1887) U.S. Congregational clergyman. Born in Litchfield, Conn., the son of a minister, he was the brother of HARRIET BEECHER STOWE and CATHARINE ESTHER BEECHER. After graduating from Amherst College and later studying at Lane Theological Seminary, he served as pastor to congregations in Indiana. In 1847 he was called to Plymouth Church in Brooklyn, N.Y. A famous orator and one of the most influential preachers of his time, he opposed slavery and supported women's suffrage, Darwin's theory of evolution, and scientific biblical criticism. He gained unfavorable publicity in 1874 when he was put on trial for adultery, but he was acquitted and returned to his church.

Henry Beecher, photographed by Napoleon Sarony.
THE GRANGER COLLECTION

beef Flesh of mature CATTLE, as distinguished from VEAL, the flesh of calves. The best beef is obtained from steers (castrated males) and heifers (female COWS that have not calved). Tenderness and flavor are improved by aging; in one common method, the carcass is hung for about two weeks at approx. 36°F (2°C). The world's primary beef producers and consumers are the U.S., the European Union, Brazil, China, Argentina, and Australia. Grading standards are relatively uniform; in the U.S., grades range from prime and choice to utility and canner. Beef provides protein and B vitamins; it also contains saturated fat, an excess of which can contribute to heart disease and other health problems. Beef is not eaten by Hindus because of the sacred status of the cow.

beehive tomb *or* **tholos** \'thō-,läs\ Large, beehive-shaped ceremonial tomb, sometimes built into the side of a hill. The Treasury of Atreus, a surviving tholos (c. 1300–1250 BC) of the Mycenaean civilization, is a pointed dome built up of stepped blocks of conglomerate masonry cut and polished to give the impression of a true VAULT. A small side chamber contained the burials, while the main chamber was probably reserved for ritual use.

beekeeping *or* **apiculture** \'ā-pə-,kəl-chər\ Care and manipulation of HONEYBEES to enable them to produce and store more honey than they need so that the excess can be collected. Beekeeping is one of the oldest forms of animal husbandry. Early efforts at collecting the honey required destroying the hive; modern beekeepers use an extractor that empties the cells of the honeycomb without damaging them. To collect honey, beekeepers need a veiled helmet for protection, a tool for cutting comb, and a smoker for tranquilizing the bees. Maintaining the hive includes protecting the colony against diseases, parasites, and predators.

beer ALCOHOLIC BEVERAGE made usually from malted BARLEY, flavored with HOPS, and brewed by slow FERMENTATION. Known from ancient times, beer was especially common in northern climates not conducive to grape cultivation for WINE. It is produced by employing either a bottom-fermenting YEAST, which falls to the bottom of the container when fermentation is completed, or a top-fermenting yeast, which rises to the surface. Lager beers (from *lagern,* "to store"), of German origin, are bottom-fermented and stored at a low temperature for several months; most are light in color, with high carbonation, medium hop flavor, and alcohol content of 3–5% by volume. Top-fermented beers, popular in Britain and including ALE, stout, and porter, are characterized by a prominent head of released carbon dioxide and a sharper, more strongly hopped flavor than lagers; alcohol content is 4–6.5% by volume. See also MALT.

Beer Hall Putsch *or* **Munich Putsch** \'pu̇ch\ (1923) Unsuccessful attempt by ADOLF HITLER to start an insurrection in Germany against the WEIMAR REPUBLIC. On November 8, Hitler and his men pushed their way into a right-wing political meeting in a Munich beer hall and obtained agreement that the leaders there should join in carrying the "revolution" to Berlin. The next day, some 3,000 Nazis marched toward the Marienplatz, but were met by police gunfire. Hitler was subsequently sentenced to five years in prison for treason; he only served eight months, time he spent writing *Mein Kampf.*

Beerbohm, (Henry) Max(imilian) *later* **Sir Max** (1872–1956) English caricaturist, writer, and dandy. His sophisticated drawings and parodies were unique in capturing, usually without malice, whatever was pretentious, affected, or absurd in his famous and fashionable contemporaries. His first literary collection, *The Works of Max Beerbohm* (1896), and his first book of drawings, *Caricatures of Twenty-five Gentlemen* (1896), were followed by the charming fable *The Happy Hypocrite* (1897) and his only novel, *Zuleika Dobson* (1911), a burlesque of Oxford life. His story collection *Seven Men* (1919) is considered a masterpiece.

Beersheba City (pop., 1992 est.: 128,000), southern Israel. Historically it marked the extreme southern limit of Palestine, hence the biblical phrase "from Dan to Beersheba" (Dan is in far northern Israel). It fell to the Arabs in the 7th century and to the Turks in the 16th century. It was a watering place for the nomadic Bedouin tribes of the NEGEV desert. Held by the British from 1917, it was taken by Israel in 1948. It has since developed as the administrative, cultural, and industrial center of the Negev.

Beery, Wallace (Fitzgerald) (1885–1949) U.S. film and stage actor. Born in Kansas City, he initially worked in the circus and later in the choruses of New York theatrical productions. After playing the lead in *The Yankee Tourist,* he spent several years as a dramatic actor in touring and stock companies. He started his film career in 1913, first as a comedian in MACK SENNETT's Keystone comedies. He is best known for his performances in *The Champ* (1931, Academy Award), *Min and Bill* (1931), and *Tugboat Annie* (1933).

beeswax Commercially useful wax secreted by worker HONEYBEES to make the cell walls of the honeycomb. A bee consumes an estimated 6–10 lbs (3–4.5 kg) of honey for each pound of the wax it secretes in small flakes from glands on the underside of its abdomen. After honey removal, the comb is melted to produce the beeswax, which ranges from yellow to almost black. It is used for candles (often for churches), artificial fruit and flowers, modeling wax, and as an ingredient of furniture and floor waxes, leather dressings, waxed paper, lithographic inks, cosmetics, and ointments.

beet Cultivated form of the plant *Beta vulgaris* of the goosefoot family (Chenopodiaceae), one of the most important VEGETABLES. Four distinct types are cultivated: the garden beet, as a garden vegetable; the SUGAR BEET, a major source of sugar and commercially the most important type; the mangel-wurzel, a succulent feed for livestock; and the leaf beet, or Swiss CHARD, for its edible leaves. Beet greens are a source of riboflavin, iron, and vitamins A and C. Beets are grown most extensively in temperate to cool regions or during the cooler seasons.

Beet (*Beta*).
GRANT HEILMAN

Beethoven \'bā-ˌtō-vən\, **Ludwig van** (1770–1827) German-Austrian composer. Born in Bonn to a musical family, he was a precociously gifted pianist and violist. After nine years as a court musician in Bonn, he moved to Vienna to study with F.J. HAYDN and remained there the rest of his life. He was soon well known as both a virtuoso and a composer, and he became the first important composer to earn a successful living while forsaking employment in the church or court (though three noblemen, recognizing his brilliance, paid him an unconditional annual annuity). He uniquely straddled the Classical and Romantic eras. His astonishing *Eroica Symphony* (1803) was the thunderclap that announced the Romantic century, and it embodies the titanic but rigorously controlled energy that was the hallmark of his style. Physically, he was short and unattractive, and he grew increasingly eccentric with age. His increasing deafness from c. 1795 led to near-suicidal depression; from c. 1819 he was totally deaf. Despite several hopeless loves, he remained single. For his last 15 years he was unrivaled as the world's most famous composer. His works include the celebrated nine symphonies (1800–24); 16 string quartets (1798–1826); 32 piano sonatas (1796–1822); the opera *Fidelio* (1805, rev. 1814); two masses, including the *Missa Solemnis* (1823); five piano concertos; a violin concerto (1806); six piano trios; 10 violin sonatas; five cello sonatas; and several concert overtures.

beetle Any of at least 250,000 species of insects constituting the order Coleoptera (the largest order in the animal kingdom), characterized by special forewings, called elytra, which are modified into hardened covers over a second pair of functional wings. Beetles occur in almost all environments except Antarctica and the peaks of the highest mountains. Temperate zones have fewer beetle species than the tropics but in greater numbers. The smallest species are less than 0.04 in. (1 mm) long; the largest can exceed 8 in. (20 cm). Most beetles eat either other animals or plants; some eat decaying matter. Some species destroy crops, timber, and textiles and spread parasitic worms and diseases. Others are valuable predators of insect pests. Some beetles are known by other common names (e.g., borer, CHAFER, curculio, FIREFLY, WEEVIL). Beetles are preyed on by other insects and by bats, swifts, and frogs.

Begin \be-'gēn\, **Menachem (Wolfovitch)** (1913–1992) Prime minister of Israel 1977–83. Born in Russia, he earned a law degree from the University of Warsaw. During World War II he was captured by the Russians and sent to Siberia in 1940. Released in 1941, he joined the Polish army in exile. He escaped to Palestine, where he became leader of the IRGUN ZVAI LEUMI in 1943. From 1948 to 1977 he led the opposition in the Israeli Knesset, except for three years when he sat in the Government of National Unity (1967–70). As head of the LIKUD coalition, he became prime minister in 1977. He shared the 1978 Nobel Peace Prize with ANWAR AL-SADAT for negotiations that resulted in the 1979 Israel-Egypt peace treaty. His 1982 invasion of Lebanon turned world opinion against Israel, and he resigned in 1983. See also ARAB-ISRAELI WARS, VLADIMIR JABOTINSKY, SABRA AND SHATILA MASSACRES.

Menachem Begin, 1987.
RALPH CRANE/CAMERA PRESS FROM GLOBE PHOTOS

begonia \bi-'gōn-yə\ Any of about 1,000 species (genus *Begonia*) of mostly SUCCULENT, tropical or subtropical plants, many with colorful flowers or leaves and used as pot plants indoors or as garden plants. Begonias come in a bewildering array of cultivated varieties. The wax begonia *(B. semperflorens)* is the most popular for use as a summer BEDDING PLANT; angelwing begonias are characterized by their tall stems; hairy begonias have feltlike leaves. Most begonias are tender and intolerant of dry conditions; they require protection from strong sunlight.

Behan \'bē-ən\, **Brendan (Francis)** (1923–1964) Irish author. An alcoholic from age 8 and an anti-English rebel, he was repeatedly arrested. *Borstal Boy* (1958) is an account of his detention in an English reform school, which combines earthy satire and powerful political commentary. His first play, *The Quare Fellow* (1954), is an explosive statement on capital punishment and prison life. His second, *The Hostage* (produced 1958), is considered his masterwork. He also wrote poetry, short stories, radio scripts, anecdotes, memoirs, and a novel.

behavior genetics Study of the influence of an organism's genetic composition on its behavior and of the interaction of HEREDITY and environment ("nature" and "nurture") in determining behavior. The first scientist to explore the area was FRANCIS GALTON, who sought to show that mental powers run in families. His work was followed by huge numbers of studies seeking to establish a link between IQ and genetics, none of them conclusive. Other human characteristics or behaviors studied for their possible hereditary nature include SCHIZOPHRENIA, ALCOHOLISM, DEPRESSION, INTROVERT AND EXTROVERT behavior, and general activity level (including sleep disorders). Many such studies are based on long-term observation of identical (monozygotic) twins raised in different environments. In animal studies, which examine such topics as LEARNING, sexual activity, and aggressive behavior, selective breeding is used to produce groups of genetically similar individuals that may be compared to other, dissimilar individuals or groups. See also GENETICS, HUMAN NATURE.

behavior therapy *or* **behavior modification** Application of experimentally derived principles of LEARNING to the treatment of psychological disorders and the control of behavior. The concept, which has its roots in the work of EDWARD L. THORNDIKE, was popularized in the U.S. by theorists of BEHAVIORISM, including B. F. SKINNER. Behavior-therapy techniques are based on the principle of operant CONDITIONING, in which desired behaviors are rewarded. There is little or no concern for conscious experience or unconscious processes. Such techniques have been applied with some success to such disturbances as ENURESIS, TICS, PHOBIAS, STUTTERING, OBSESSIVE-COMPULSIVE DISORDER, and various neuroses. Behavior modification more generally refers to the application of reinforcement techniques for shaping individual behavior toward some desired end or for controlling behavior in classrooms or institutional situations. See also PSYCHOTHERAPY.

behaviorism Highly influential academic school of psychology that dominated psychological theory in the U.S. between the two World Wars. Classical behaviorism concerned itself exclusively with the objective evidence of behavior (measured responses to stimuli) and excluded ideas, emotions, and inner mental experience (see CONDITIONING). It emerged in the 1920s from the work of JOHN B. WATSON (who borrowed from IVAN PAVLOV) and was developed in subsequent decades by CLARK L. HULL and B. F. SKINNER. Through the work of EDWARD C. TOLMAN, strict behaviorist doctrines began to be supplemented or replaced by those admitting such variables as reported mental states and differences in PERCEPTION. A natural outgrowth of behaviorist theory was BEHAVIOR THERAPY.

Behn \'bān\, **Aphra** (1640–1689) English dramatist, novelist, and poet, the first Englishwoman known to earn her living by writing. Her early life is obscure (as is her original surname), but she spent most of it in South America. She married an English merchant named Behn in 1658. Her novel *Oroonoko* (1688), the story of an enslaved African prince who Behn knew in South America, influenced the development of the English novel. Her first play, *The Forc'd Marriage*, was produced in 1671; her later witty comedies, such as the two-part *The Rover* (1677, 1681), were highly successful, and toward the end of her life she wrote many popular novels.

Behrens \'bā-rens\, **Peter** (1868–1940) German architect. He became director of Düsseldorf's arts and crafts school in 1903, and in 1907 he was appointed artistic adviser for the large electrical company AEG. His AEG Works turbine factory in Berlin (1909–12), with its sweeping glass CURTAIN WALL, became the most significant building in Germany at that time. He was an influential pioneer of modernism; WALTER GROPIUS, LE CORBUSIER, and LUDWIG MIES VAN DER ROHE all worked in his office.

Behrens, painting by Max Liebermann.
ARCHIV FUR KUNST UND GESCHICHTE, BERLIN

Behrman \'ber-mən\, **S(amuel) N(athaniel)** (1893–1973) U.S. playwright. Born in Worcester, Mass., he contributed to New York newspapers and magazines and studied drama at Harvard University. His successful first play, the light comedy *The Second Man* (1927), was followed by the popular *Meteor* (1929), *Brief Moment* (1931), and *Biography* (1932). His more serious plays include *Rain from Heaven* (1934) and *No Time for Comedy* (1939). Noted for addressing complex social and moral issues, he wrote over 25 comedies in his 40-year career, and nearly every one was a hit.

Beiderbecke \'bī-dər-ˌbek\, **Bix** *orig.* **Leon** (1903–1931) U.S. jazz cornetist and composer, noted for his gentle, clear tone and introspective approach. Born in Davenport, Iowa, Beiderbecke developed a style independent of the influence of LOUIS ARMSTRONG and became the leading player of the Chicago style of jazz in the 1920s. His interest in the harmonies of impressionist composers such as CLAUDE DEBUSSY was reflected in both his playing and his compositions. With saxophonist Frankie Trumbauer, Beiderbecke worked in the bands of Jean Goldkette and PAUL WHITEMAN. His alcoholism and early death contributed to his status as one of the early romantic legends of jazz.

Bix Beiderbecke.
BROWN BROTHERS

Beijing \'bā-'jiŋ\ *or* **Pei-ching** *or* **Peking** \'pē-'kiŋ\ *formerly (1928–49)* **Peiping** \'pā-'piŋ\ City, municipality with provincial status, and capital of China (pop., 1999 est.: city, 6,633,929; municipality, 12,570,000). Lying on a broad plain in northeastern China, the city has been settled since ancient times and has been known by various names, including Khanbalik (or Cambaluc) when it became the royal residence of KUBLAI KHAN in AD 1264, and was visited by MARCO POLO. It was chosen as the capital in 1421, which it remained under the MANCHUS. It suffered heavy damage when it was occupied by European forces in 1860 and 1900 (see BOXER REBELLION). In 1928 the capital was moved to NANJING, and the name Peiping was given the former capital. Nearby, in 1937, the MARCO POLO BRIDGE INCIDENT took place. Beijing's capital status and its former name were restored following the communist victory in 1949. It is China's cultural and educational center. The old FORBIDDEN CITY contains the former imperial palace. Abutting it is TIANANMEN SQUARE, the world's largest public square. Beijing's 15th-century walls were partly demolished in the CULTURAL REVOLUTION. In 2001 the city was selected as the site for the 2006 Summer Olympic Games.

Beijing Opera (Chinese *jingxi*: "opera of the capital") Traditional Chinese theater, originally devised in 1790 as part of the Qianlong Emperor's birthday celebration. Highly formal and symbolic, it combines orchestral music, speech, song, dance, and acrobatics. The performers enact dramas based on historical epics, legend, and myth. The characters' roles and social ranks are conveyed through elaborate costumes and stylized makeup. The Beijing Opera traditionally employed an all-male cast with female impersonators, but has recently expanded its scope to admit female actors. The actor Mei Lanfang brought its influence to the West through his tours of Russia and the U.S. in the 1930s.

Beijing University One of the oldest and most important universities in China. It was founded as Capital College in 1898 and became a university in 1911. By 1920 it had become a center for progressive thought. During the Japanese invasion of China (1937–45) it was temporarily relocated to YUNNAN province. The first disturbances of the CULTURAL REVOLUTION began at Beijing University in 1966; education there ceased between 1966 and 1970. The university has since reasserted its position as China's foremost nontechnical university. It has about 25 academic departments and several research institutes, and has the largest university library in China. Total enrollment is about 13,000.

Beilstein \'bīl-ˌshtīn\, **Friedrich Konrad** (1838–1906) Russian chemist. From 1866 to his retirement he taught at St. Petersburg's Technical Institute. His *Handbuch der organischen Chemie* ("Handbook of Organic Chemistry"; 1st ed., 1880–83) fully described 15,000 organic compounds. The fourth edition (27 vols., 1937) is periodically supplemented, and remains indispensable for workers in organic chemistry.

Beira \'bā-rə\ Coastal city (pop., 1997: 412,588), southeastern Mozambique. Located near the mouth of the ZAMBEZI RIVER, it is the chief port for central Mozambique, Zimbabwe, and Malawi. Founded in 1891 as a trading company's headquarters, it passed to Portuguese administration in 1942 and then to independent Mozambique in 1975. It is the terminus of railways from South Africa, Zimbabwe, Congo, Zambia, and Malawi.

Beirut \bā-'rüt\ City (metro area pop., 1998 est.: 1,500,000), capital of Lebanon. The country's chief port and largest city, it lies at the foot of the Lebanon Mountains. Initially settled by the Phoenicians, it gained prominence under Roman rule in the 1st century BC. It was captured by the Arabs in AD 635. Christian Crusaders held Beirut 1110–1291, after which it was dominated by the Saracens, Druze, and Ottoman Turks. It became the capital of the new state of Lebanon (under French mandate) in 1920, and capital of an independent Lebanon in 1941. It went on to flourish as the chief banking and cultural center of the Middle East. It lost that status after the LEBANESE CIVIL WAR broke out in 1975; it became a main target, and suffered heavy damage over many years. With the cessation of war in 1990, the city slowly began to rebuild.

Béjart \bā-'zhär\, **Maurice** *orig.* **Maurice Jean Berger** (born 1927). French-Belgian dancer, choreographer, and opera director. Born in Marseille, he studied in Paris, then toured with various companies before founding his own, Les Ballets de l'Étoile (later Ballet Théâtre de Maurice Béjart), in Paris in 1954. In 1959 it moved to Brussels; renamed the Ballet of the 20th Century, it became one of the world's foremost troupes. His productions have been noted for reworking tradition in unusual and often controversial ways. Since 1961 he has also worked in opera, staging *Tales of Hoffmann* and Berlioz's *Damnation of Faust,* among other works. In 1987 the company moved to Switzerland and took the new name Béjart Ballet Lausanne.

Béjart family \bā-'zhär\ 17th-century French theatrical family. Joseph (1617?–1659), Louis (1630–1678), and their sisters Madeleine (1618–1672) and Geneviève (1622?–1675) were members of a traveling company directed by Madeleine. They joined MOLIÈRE's first company, the Illustre Théâtre, in 1643 and created many parts in his plays. Madeleine's sister, or possibly daughter, Armande Béjart (1642–1700), joined the company in 1653. She married Molière in 1662 and played most of his heroines. After his death, she led the company until it merged with another troupe to become the COMÉDIE-FRANÇAISE in 1680.

Bekáa Valley \be-'kä\ *or* **Al Biqa** \,äl-be-'kä\ *ancient* **Coele-Syria** Valley, Lebanon. Located between the LEBANON and ANTI-LEBANON mountain ranges, it is about 80 mi (130 km) long and 10 mi (15 km) wide. Traversed by the upper ORONTES and Litani rivers, it is an agricultural area. BAALBEK, in ancient times a city of great size, is located there. In recent decades the valley has been the scene of continued skirmishes between Syrian and Lebanese and Palestine Liberation Organization forces.

Békésy \'bā-,kā-shē\, **Georg von** (1899–1972) Hungarian-U.S. physicist and physiologist. He emigrated to the U.S. in 1947 and taught at Harvard University 1947–66. He discovered that sound vibrations travel along a membrane in the cochlea in waves, peaking at different places, where nerve receptors determine pitch and loudness. His research resulted in greatly expanded understanding of the hearing process, partly through instrumentation Békésy had helped design, and the differentiation of forms of deafness, which permitted the selection of proper treatment. He received a 1961 Nobel Prize.

Bekhterev \'byāk-tir-yif\, **Vladimir (Mikhaylovich)** (1857–1927) Russian neurophysiologist and psychiatrist. A competitor of IVAN PAVLOV, Bekhterev independently developed a theory of conditioned reflexes. His most lasting work was in brain structure research and descriptions of nervous symptoms and illnesses. He discovered the superior vestibular nucleus (Bekhterev nucleus) and other brain formations, and described spinal numbness (spondylitis deformans, or Bekhterev's disease) and other diseases. He founded the first Russian journal on nervous diseases. His approach to the study of behavior influenced the growing movement toward behaviorism in the U.S.

Bel Akkadian god of the atmosphere and member of a triad including ANU (An) and EA (Enki). His Sumerian counterpart was Enlil. His breath brought both severe storms and gentle spring winds. He was the god of agriculture and as such was more important than the high god Anu. As Bel he was known as the god of order and destiny. As Enlil, he was banished to the underworld for raping his consort Ninlil (BELIT), in a myth that explains the cycle of the seasons.

Bel See MARDUK

Belafonte \,bel-ə-'fän-tā\, **Harry** *orig.* **Harold (George) Belafonte, Jr.** (born 1927) U.S. singer, actor and producer. He was born in New York City to immigrants from Martinique and Jamaica, and he lived with his mother in Jamaica 1935–40. In the early 1950s he initiated a fad for CALYPSO music with such songs as "Day-O (Banana Boat Song)" and "Jamaica Farewell." He starred in the films *Carmen Jones* (1954) and *Island in the Sun* (1957), and later became the first black television producer. In the 1960s and '70s he was a prominent civil-rights activist.

Belarus *or* **Byelarus** \,byā-lə-'rüs\ *formerly* **Belorussia** Republic, northern central Europe. Area: 80,154 sq mi (207,599 sq km). Population (1997 est.): 10,360,000. Capital: MINSK. The population is mainly Belarusan, with Russian and Ukrainian minorities. Languages: Belarus, Russian (both official). Religion: predominantly Eastern Orthodoxy. Currency: ruble. The northern part is crossed by the Western DVINA RIVER; the DNIEPER flows through its eastern portion; the south has extensive marshy areas along the PRIPYAT; the upper course of the NEMAN flows in the west; and the BUG forms part of the boundary with Poland in the southwest. The chief settlements, in addition to Minsk, are HOMYEL, MAHILYOW, and VITSYEBSK. The economy is predominantly agricultural. It is a republic with two legislative houses; its head of state and government is the president. While Belarusans share a distinct identity and language, they never previously enjoyed political sovereignty. The territory that is now Belarus underwent partition and changed hands often; as a result its history is entwined with its neighbors'. In medieval times the region was ruled by Lithuanians and Poles. Following the Third Partition of POLAND it was ruled by Russia. After World War I, the western part was assigned to Poland and the eastern part became U.S.S.R. territory. After World War II, the Soviets expanded what had been the Belorussian S.S.R. by annexing more of Poland. Much of the area suffered contamination from the CHERNOBYL ACCIDENT in 1986, forcing many to evacuate. Belarus declared its independence in 1991 and later joined the COMMONWEALTH OF INDEPENDENT STATES. Amid increasing political turmoil in the 1990s, it proposed a union with Russia in 1997, which was still in debate at the start of the 21st century.

Belarusian language \,byā-lə-'rü-se-ən\ *or* **Belarusan language** \,byā-lə-'rüs-ən\ *or* **Byelorussian language** \,byā-lə-'rə-shən\ *or* **Belorussian language** \,be-lə-'rə-shən\ East SLAVIC LANGUAGE of Belarus, spoken by 10.2 million people worldwide. Belarusian features begin to appear in Church Slavic manuscripts from the 14th century (see OLD CHURCH SLAVIC LANGUAGE). The chancery language of the Grand Duchy of Lithuania, used in the 15th–16th century, contains a substantial Belarusian element, mixed with Church Slavic, UKRAINIAN, and POLISH. Belarusian was not fully elaborated as a modern literary language until the early 20th century, when orthographic norms for writing it in CYRILLIC were established. It has long struggled to maintain itself against RUSSIAN, particularly in Belarusian urban centers, where there is a high degree of Russification and Belarusian-Russian bilingualism.

Belasco \bə-'las-kō\, **David** (1853–1931) U.S. theatrical producer and playwright. Born in San Francisco, he acted with traveling companies before becoming a theater manager, first in San Francisco and later in New York (from 1880). An independent producer from 1890, he built his own theater in 1906; there he introduced changes in stage lighting, used realistic scenery, and demanded high production standards. He successfully fought against the monopolistic Theatrical Syndicate. He wrote or collaborated on numerous plays, including *Madame Butterfly* (1900) and *The Girl of the Golden West* (1905), which became operas by G. PUCCINI.

Belau See PALAU

Belém \be-'lem\ City (pop., 1991: 765,000; metro. area pop: 1,574,000), northern Brazil. The capital of Pará state, the port of Belém lies on the PARÁ RIVER in the vast AMAZON RIVER delta 90 mi (145 km) from the Atlantic Ocean. It began in 1616 as a fortified settlement; as it gradually became established, it helped consolidate Portuguese supremacy in northern Brazil. It was made the state capital in 1772. It enjoyed prosperity in the late 19th century as the main exporting center of the

Amazon rubber industry. After the rubber era ended in 1912, it continued to be northern Brazil's commercial center and a main port for Amazon River craft.

belemnoid \'bel-əm-ˌȯid\ *or* **belemnite** Member of an extinct group of CEPHALOPODS, possessing a large internal shell, that first appeared c. 345 million years ago, in the Early Carboniferous period, and became extinct during the Eocene epoch, which ended c. 36.6 million years ago. The internal shell of most species is straight, but that of some species is loosely coiled. The shell served for support and muscle attachment and enabled the animal to compensate for depth and its own body weight. See also AMMONOID.

Reconstruction of squidlike belemnoid cephalopods from the Cretaceous System, southern Tennessee.

BY COURTESY OF THE AMERICAN MUSEUM OF NATURAL HISTORY, NEW YORK

Belfast District, seaport, and capital (pop., 1995 est: 297,000) of Northern Ireland. On the River Lagan, the site was occupied in the Stone and Bronze ages, and the remains of Iron Age forts can still be seen. Belfast's modern history began in the early 17th century when Sir Arthur Chichester developed a plan for colonizing the area with English and Scottish settlers. Having survived the Irish insurrection of 1641, the town grew in economic importance, especially after a large immigration of French HUGUENOTS arrived after the rescinding of the Edict of NANTES (1685) and strengthened the linen trade. It became a center of Irish Protestantism, setting the stage for sectarian conflict in the 19th–20th century. The latest conflicts broke out in the 1960s and continued into the 1990s; a provisional peace agreement was reached in 1998. The city is Northern Ireland's educational and commercial center.

belfry Bell tower, either freestanding or attached to another structure. More particularly it refers to the room, usually at the top of such a tower, where the bells and their supporting timberwork are hung. The belfry is a prominent feature of Belgian Gothic architecture, especially in Flanders. The Halles (Market Hall) and belfry in Brugge (late 13th century) is a typical example. The term derives from the medieval siege tower *(berfrei)*, a tall wooden structure that could be rolled up to a fortification wall so that the warriors hidden inside could storm the battlements.

Belgae \'bel-ˌgī\ Inhabitants of GAUL north of the Sequana (SEINE) and Matrona (MARNE) rivers. The term was apparently first applied by Julius CAESAR, whose Gallic victories (54–51 BC) sent many Belgae into Britain, where they formed kingdoms, the most important of which were at Colchester, St. Albans, and Silchester.

Belgian Congo See Democratic Republic of the CONGO

Belgica \'bel-ji-kə\ Ancient country, northeastern Gallia (GAUL). One of the administrative areas into which AUGUSTUS divided Gaul, it stretched from the SEINE RIVER to the RHINE and included the LOW COUNTRIES. Its capital was Durocortorum Remorum (now REIMS). Part of the area became Germania Inferior and Germania Superior under DOMITIAN, and later, under DIOCLETIAN, the remainder was divided into Belgica Prima and Belgica Secunda. In the 5th century AD, Belgica was absorbed by the FRANKS. See also BELGIUM.

Belgium *French* **Belgique** \bel-'zhēk\ *Flemish* **België** \'bel-k̲ē-ə\ Kingdom, northwestern Europe. Area: 11,787 sq mi (30,528 sq km). Population (2000 est.): 10,249,000. Capital: BRUSSELS. The population consists mostly of Flemings and Walloons. The Flemings, more than half the population, speak Flemish (Dutch) and live in the northern half of the country; the Walloons, about one-third of the population, speak French and inhabit the southern half. Languages: Dutch, French, German (all official). Religions: Roman Catholicism (90%), Islam, Protestantism. Monetary unit: euro. Belgium can be divided into several geographic regions. The southeast consists of the forested ARDENNES highland, which extends south of the MEUSE RIVER valley and includes Belgium's highest point, Mount Botrange (2,277 ft, or 694 m). Middle Belgium is a fertile region crossed by tributaries of the SCHELDE RIVER. Lower Belgium comprises the flat plains of FLANDERS in the northwest with their many canals. Maritime Flanders borders the North Sea and is agriculturally prosperous; the chief North Sea port is Oostende, but

ANTWERP, near the mouth of the Schelde, has much greater trade. Belgium has minimal natural resources, so the manufacture of goods from imported raw materials plays a major role in the economy, and the country is highly industrialized. It is a monarchy with a parliament composed of two legislative houses; the chief of state is the monarch, and the head of government is the prime minister. Inhabited in ancient times by the Belgae, a Celtic people, the area was conquered by CAESAR in 57 BC; under AUGUSTUS it became the Roman province of BELGICA. Conquered by the Franks, it later broke up into semi-independent territories, including BRABANT and LUXEMBOURG. By the late 15th century the territories of the Netherlands, of which the future Belgium was a part, gradually united and passed to the HABSBURGS. In the 16th century it was a center for European commerce. The basis of modern Belgium was laid in the southern Catholic provinces that split from the northern provinces after the Union of Utrecht in 1579 (see NETHERLANDS). Overrun by the French and incorporated into France in 1801, it was reunited to Holland and with it became the independent kingdom of the Netherlands in 1815. After the revolt of its citizens in 1830, it became the independent kingdom of Belgium. Under LEOPOLD II, it acquired vast lands in Africa. Overrun by the Germans in World Wars I and II, it was the scene of the BATTLE OF THE BULGE. Internal discord led to legislation in the 1970s and 1980s that created three nearly autonomous regions in accordance with language distribution: Flemish FLANDERS, French Wallonia, and bilingual Brussels. In 1993 it became a federation comprising the three regions. It is a member of the EUROPEAN UNION.

Belgrade *Serbian* **Beograd** \bā-'ȯ-ˌgräd\ City (pop., 1991: 1,168,000), capital of Yugoslavia. Lying at the juncture of the DANUBE and SAVA rivers, it is one of the Balkans' most important commercial and transportation centers. Inhabited by Celts in the 4th century BC, it was later taken by the Romans and named Singidunum. It was destroyed by the Avars in the 6th century. In the 11th century AD it became a frontier town of Byzantium, and in the 13th century came under the rule of SERBIA. The Ottoman Turks besieged the city in the 15th century, and SULEYMAN's forces finally took it in 1521; it was held almost continuously by the Turks into the 19th century. In 1882 it became the capital of the kingdom of Serbia and, after World War I, of the new Kingdom of Serbs, Croats, and Slovenes (renamed Yugoslavia in 1929). It suffered severely under Nazi occupation 1941–44. It was damaged by NATO bombers in the KOSOVO CONFLICT (1999).

Belgrade, Peace of (1739) Either of two peace settlements that ended the Ottoman empire's four-year war with Russia and its two-year war with Austria. In 1735 Russia had attempted to establish itself on the northern Black Sea. Austria entered the war as Russia's ally in 1737, but military failures prompted it to make a separate peace in September 1739, ceding northern Serbia (including Belgrade) and Little Walachia to the Ottomans. With Austria's defection, the Russians had to make a disappointing peace that same month. Under its terms, Russia could not have warships on the Black Sea and had to depend on Ottoman shipping for its Black Sea commerce.

Belhadj \bel-'häj\, **Ali** (born 1956) Deputy leader of the Islamic Salvation Front (FIS), Algeria's main opposition group. Born in Tunisia to Algerian parents, he became a high-school teacher and imam. He and the more moderate Abassi Mandani registered FIS as a political party in 1989. In 1990 FIS won a majority of votes in local elections; in 1991 the Algerian government announced martial law and imprisoned Belhadj and Mandani. In 1994 Belhadj was transferred to house arrest.

Belidor \bā-lē-'dȯr\, **Bernard Forest de** (1698–1761) French military and civil engineer. After serving in the French army, he worked on measuring an arc of the earth. As professor of artillery at a French military school, he wrote notable books on engineering, artillery, ballistics, and fortifications, but his fame rests primarily on his classic *Architecture hydraulique* (4 vols., 1737–53), covering engineering mechanics, mills and waterwheels, pumps, harbors, and sea works.

Belinsky \byəl-'yēn-skē\, **Vissarion (Grigoryevich)** (1811–1848) Russian literary critic. Expelled from the University of Moscow in 1832, he worked as a journalist, making his reputation with critical articles that expounded nationalist doctrine. His argument that literature should express political and social ideas had a major impact on Soviet literary criticism, and he was often called the father of the Russian radical intelligentsia.

Belisarius (c. 505–565) Byzantine general. While serving in the bodyguard of Emperor Justinian I, he was appointed (c. 525) to command in the eastern armies, and he defeated the Persians in the Battle of Dara (530). He led expeditions to overthrow the Vandals in North Africa (533) and regain Sicily and southern Italy from the Ostrogoths (535–537), defending Rome 537–538. He was offered a kingship by the Goths, which caused Justinian to recall him in disfavor. He was sent again to Rome (544–548) but with inadequate forces, and he was replaced by Narses in 548. Still loyal to Justinian, he was recalled in 559 to repel Hun invaders.

Belit \'bā-lit\ Akkadian goddess of destiny, consort of Bel, and mother of the moon god, Sin. Her Sumerian counterpart was Ninlil. Assyrians sometimes identified her with Ishtar. Ninlil was a grain goddess, and the story of her rape by Enlil, the Lord of the Wind, reflects the seasonal cycle of pollination, ripening, and withering.

Belitung \bā-'lē-ˌtu̇ŋ\ *or* **Billiton** \bē-'lē-ˌtōn\ Island (pop., 1980: 164,000), Indonesia. Lying between the China Sea and Java sea southwest of Borneo, it is 55 mi (88 km) long and 43 mi (69 km) wide, with an area of 1,866 sq mi (4,833 sq km). The main town and port is Tanjungpandan. Belitung was ceded to the British in 1812 by the sultan of Palembang, Sumatra, but Britain recognized the Dutch claim in 1824. The island became part of Indonesia after World War II. It is important for its tin mines, discovered in 1851.

Beliveau \'bel-i-vō\, **Jean (Marc A.)** (born 1931) Canadian ice-hockey center. Born in Trois-Riviéres, Quebec, he played for the Montreal Canadiens from 1953 to 1971. His career record of 79 goals and 176 points made during play-off games, including 17 Stanley Cup championships, stood until 1987.

Belize \bə-'lēz\ *Spanish* **Belice** \bā-'lē-sā\ *formerly (1840–1973)* **British Honduras** Country, Central America. It is bounded by Mexico, the Caribbean Sea, and Guatemala. Area: 8,867 sq mi (22,966 sq km). Population (1997 est.): 228,000. Capital: Belmopan. Much of the population is racially mixed: Creoles of mixed African and European ancestry, Maya Indians, Mayan-European mestizos, and Black Caribs. Languages: English (official), Creole, Spanish. Religions: Roman Catholicism, Methodism, Anglicanism. Currency: Belize dollar. Belize is a land of mountains, swamps, and tropical jungle. The northern half consists of swampy lowlands drained by the Belize and Hondo rivers; the latter forms the boundary with Mexico. The southern half is more mountainous and contains the country's highest peak, Victoria (3,681 ft, or 1,122 m). Off the coast lies the world's second-largest barrier reef. Belize is relatively prosperous and has a developing free-market economy with

some government participation. It is a constitutional monarchy with two legislative houses; its head of state is the British monarch represented by the governor-general, and the head of government is the prime minister. The area was inhabited by the Maya c. 300 BC–AD 900; the ruins of their ceremonial centers, including Caracol and Xunantunich, can still be seen. The Spanish claimed sovereignty from the 16th century but never tried to settle Belize, though they regarded as interlopers the British who did. British logwood cutters arrived in the mid-17th century; Spanish opposition was finally overcome in 1798. When settlers began to penetrate the interior they met with Indian resistance. In 1862 British Honduras became a crown colony, but an unfulfilled provision of a 1859 British-Guatemalan treaty led Guatemala to claim the territory. The situation had not been resolved when Belize was granted its independence in 1981. A British force, stationed there to ensure the new nation's security, was withdrawn after Guatemala officially recognized the territory's independence in 1991.

Belize City City (pop., 1996: 53,000), Belize. The chief seaport and former capital of Belize, it lies at the mouth of the Belize River, which was until the 10th century a heavily populated trade artery of the Maya empire. The British settled the area in the 17th century. The city, built on ground only slightly above sea level, has been ravaged by hurricanes, so the capital was moved to Belmopan in 1970.

bell Hollow vessel, usually of metal, that produces a ringing sound when struck by an interior clapper or a mallet. In the West, open bells have acquired a standard "tulip" shape. Though the vibrational patterns of such open bells are basically nonharmonic, they can be tuned so that the lower overtones produce a recognizable chord. Forged bells have existed for many thousands of years. Bells were first cast, or founded, in the Bronze Age; the Chinese were the first master founders. Bells have carried a wide range of cultural meanings. They are particularly important in religious ritual in East and South Asia. In Christianity, especially Russian Orthodoxy, bells have also been used ritually. They have tolled the hours from monastery and church steeples, originally to govern monastic routine and later also to fill a similar role for the secular world.

Bell, Alexander Graham (1847–1922) Scottish-U.S. audiologist and inventor. Born in Edinburgh, he moved to the U.S. in 1871 to teach the visible-speech system developed by his father, Alexander Melville Bell (1819–1905). He opened his own school in Boston for training teachers of the deaf (1872), and was influential in disseminating these methods. In 1875 he became the first person to transmit intelligible words through electric wire ("Watson, come here, I want you," spoken to his assistant

Thomas Watson). He patented the telephone the next year, and in 1877 he cofounded Bell Telephone Co. With the proceeds from France's Volta Prize, he founded Volta Laboratory in Washington, D.C., in 1880. His experiments there led to the invention of the photophone (which transmitted speech by light rays), the audiometer (which measured acuteness of hearing), the Graphophone (an early practical sound recorder), and working wax recording media, both flat and cylindrical, for the Graphophone. He was chiefly responsible for founding the journal *Science,* founded the American Association to Promote Teaching of Speech to the Deaf (1890), and continued his significant research on deafness throughout his life.

Alexander Graham Bell.
CULVER PICTURES

Bell, (Arthur) Clive (Heward) (1881–1964) British art critic. He studied at Cambridge University and in Paris. In 1907 he married Vanessa Stephen, sister of VIRGINIA WOOLF; with Virginia's husband, Leonard Woolf, and ROGER FRY, they formed the core of the BLOOMSBURY GROUP. Bell's most important aesthetic ideas were published in *Art* (1914) and *Since Cézanne* (1922), in which he promoted his theory of "significant form" (the quality that distinguishes works of art from all other objects). His assertion that art appreciation involves an emotional response to purely formal qualities, independent of subject matter, was influential for several decades.

Bell, Cool Papa *orig.* **James Thomas** (1903–1991) U.S. baseball player. Born in Starkville, Miss., he was a switch-hitting outfielder for most of his career. Playing primarily in the NEGRO LEAGUES, he is said to have stolen 175 bases in a 200-game season, and is reputed to be the fastest base runner of all time. Also a fine hitter, he once batted .391 over a five-year period. He was inducted into the Baseball Hall of Fame in 1972.

Bell, Gertrude (1868–1926) British traveler, writer, and colonial administrator. After graduating from Oxford, she traveled throughout the Middle East. After World War I, she wrote a well-received report on the administration of Mesopotamia between the end of the war and the Iraqi rebellion of 1920 and later helped determine postwar boundaries. In 1921 she helped place a son of the sharif of Mecca, FAISAL I, on the Iraqi throne. In helping create the National Museum of Iraq, she promoted the idea that excavated antiquities should stay in their country of origin.

Bell, John (1797–1869) U.S. politician. Born near Nashville, Tenn., he served in the U.S. House of Representatives (1827–41) and Senate (1847–59). Though a large slaveholder, he opposed efforts to expand slavery to U.S. territories and voted against admitting Kansas as a slave state. His defense of the Union brought him the 1860 nomination for president on the Constitutional Union ticket, but he carried only three states. He later supported the South in the Civil War.

Bell Burnell, (Susan) Jocelyn *orig* **Susan Jocelyn Bell** (born 1943) English astronomer. As a research assistant at Cambridge Univ., she assisted in constructing a large radio telescope and discovered peculiar pulsating radio signals that were dubbed PULSARS. These were subsequently determined to be rapidly spinning NEUTRON STARS, providing the first direct evidence for the existence of the latter. The 1974 Nobel Prize was awarded for the discovery of pulsars to ANTONY HEWISH (her adviser) and MARTIN RYLE, sparking a controversy over the omission of Bell Burnell. She subsequently became a professor at The Open University and vice president of the Royal Astronomical Society.

bell curve See NORMAL DISTRIBUTION

Bell Laboratories U.S. research and development company (founded 1925) that develops telecommunications equipment and carries out defense-related research. Formerly part of AT&T, it now belongs to Lucent Technologies, Inc., which spun off from AT&T in 1996. Bell Labs has produced thousands of inventions, including the first synchronous-sound MOTION-PICTURE system, the electrical-relay DIGITAL COMPUTER, the LASER, the SOLAR CELL, UNIX, and the C and C++ programming languages. Several Bell researchers have won Nobel Prizes: Clinton Davisson, for demonstrating the wave nature of matter; JOHN BARDEEN, WALTER H. BRATTAIN, and WILLIAM B. SHOCKLEY, for inventing the TRANSISTOR; and ARNO PENZIAS and ROBERT W. WILSON, for discovering cosmic microwave background radiation. It operates today in some 20 countries.

bell ringing See CHANGE RINGING

Bella, Ahmed Ben See Ahmed BEN BELLA

belladonna Tall, bushy, herbaceous plant, the deadly nightshade *(Atropa belladonna)* of the NIGHTSHADE FAMILY; also, the crude drug consisting of its dried leaves or roots. The plant is a native of wooded or waste areas in central and southern Eurasia. It has dull green leaves, violet or greenish flowers, shiny black berries about the size of cherries, and a large tapering root. Belladonna is highly poisonous and is cultivated for medicinal substances (ALKALOIDS) that are derived from the crude drug and used in sedatives, stimulants, and antispasmodics. Because of toxicity and undesirable side effects, however, these substances are being replaced by synthetic drugs.

Bellamy \'bel-ə-mē\, **Edward** (1850–1898) U.S. writer. A native of Chicopee Falls, Mass., Bellamy first became aware of the plight of the urban poor at 18 while studying in Germany. He engaged throughout his life in progressive causes and wrote several books reflecting his concerns, but is known chiefly for his utopian novel *Looking Backward* (1888), which describes the U.S. in the year 2000 as an ideal socialist state featuring cooperation, brotherhood, and industry geared to human need. It sold more a million copies; a sequel, *Equality* (1897), was less successful.

Bellamy.
BY COURTESY OF THE LIBRARY OF CONGRESS, WASHINGTON, D.C.

Bellarmine \'bel-,är-mən\, **St. Robert** *Italian* **Roberto Francesco Romolo Bellarmino** (1542–1621) Italian cardinal and theologian. He joined the Jesuits in 1560, and after ordination in the Spanish Netherlands (1570) he began to teach theology. He was made a cardinal in 1599 and an archbishop in 1602. He took a prominent part in the first examination of GALILEO's writings; though somewhat sympathetic to Galileo, he thought it best to have the COPERNICAN SYSTEM declared "false and erroneous," which was done in 1616. He gave impartial attention to Protestant works and was regarded as an enlightened theologian. He died a pauper, having given all his funds to the poor. In 1931 he was named a Doctor of the Church.

Belle Isle, Strait of Channel, eastern Canada. The northern entrance from the Atlantic Ocean to the Gulf of ST. LAWRENCE, it is 90 mi (145 km) long and 10–20 mi (16–32 km) wide. It flows between the northern tip of Newfoundland and southeastern LABRADOR and is the most direct route from the SAINT LAWRENCE SEAWAY and GREAT LAKES ports to Europe. The cold Labrador Current flows through the strait, extending the period of ice cover and limiting shipping to between June and late November.

Bellerophon \bə-'ler-ə-fən\ Legendary Greek hero. The son of GLAUCUS and grandson of SISYPHUS, as a youth in Corinth he tamed and rode the winged horse PEGASUS. The wife of King Proteus of Argos fell in love with him, and when he rejected her, she falsely accused him of attempted rape. Proteus sent him to the king of Lycia with a message asking that he be killed. The king instead ordered him to kill the monster CHIMERA, and with the aid of Pegasus he succeeded. He married the king's daughter but later lost the favor of the gods and became an unhappy wanderer. Another version of the legend holds that he tried to fly up to heaven and was thrown from Pegasus and lamed.

bellflower Any of about 300 annual, perennial, and biennial herbaceous plants of the genus *Campanula* (family Campanulaceae) that bear bell-shaped, usually blue flowers. They are native mainly to northern temperate regions in both hemispheres, Mediterranean areas, and tropical mountains. Distribution and habitat may be quite diverse. Species

Bellflower (*Campanula*).

W.H. HODGE

native to northern Eurasia and eastern North America but also grown in gardens are the bluebell *(C. rotundifolia)* and the tall bellflower *(C. americana)*. The creeping bellflower *(C. rapunculoides)* is a notorious garden weed. Among the few food plants in the bellflower family, which includes a total of 40 genera and 700 species, are the rampion *(C. rapunculus)*, eaten as a vegetable in parts of Europe, and some robust members—especially *Canarina, Clermontia,* and *Centropogon*—that produce edible berries.

Bellini, Vincenzo (1801–1835) Italian composer. Born into a musical family in Sicily, he was educated at the Naples Conservatory. He wrote his first opera at 24, and went on to complete nine more before his death at 33. The most famous are *Il pirata* (1827), *I Capuleti e i Montecchi* (1830), *La sonnambula* (1831), *Norma* (1831), and *I Puritani* (1835). His works, which rely strongly on beautiful vocal melody ("bel canto"), rivaled those of his contemporaries G. ROSSINI and G. DONIZETTI in popularity.

Bellini family \bāl-'lē-nē\ Family of Italian artists. Jacopo Bellini (c. 1400–1470/71) was trained under GENTILE DA FABRIANO, and by c. 1440 he had a thriving studio in Venice. More important than his paintings are his two surviving sketchbooks, which total nearly 300 drawings. He was the father-in-law of ANDREA MANTEGNA. His son Gentile (c. 1429–1507) inherited his father's sketchbooks and took over as head of the studio. His most important extant works are two huge canvases, *Procession of the Relic of the True Cross* (1496) and *Miracle at the Bridge of San Lorenzo* (1500), depicting scenes of contemporary Venetian life. Gentile's brother Giovanni (called Giambellino, c. 1430–1516) was the greatest and most prolific artist of the family. He transformed Venice into a Renaissance center rivaling Florence and Rome. Giovanni was an early master of oil painting. Primarily a religious painter, he also excelled at portraits, of which *Doge Leonardo Loredan* (c. 1501) is his best known. TITIAN and GIORGIONE were probably trained in his workshop. See also VENETIAN SCHOOL.

Belloc \'bel-ˌäk\, **(Joseph-Pierre) Hilaire** (1870–1953) French-British poet, historian, Catholic apologist, and essayist. A highly versatile writer, he is best remembered for his light verse, particularly for children, and for his lucid and graceful essays. His works include *Verses and Sonnets* (1895), *The Bad Child's Book of Beasts* (1896), *The Modern Traveller* (1898), *Mr. Burden* (1904), and *Cautionary Tales* (1907). He also wrote several historical works, including a four-volume *History of England* (1925–31).

Bellotto \bel-'lȯt-tō\, **Bernardo** *known as* **Canaletto** (1721–1780) Italian painter of topographical views, known as *vedute* ("view paintings"). He was the nephew of CANALETTO, with whom he studied and from whom he took the name by which he is sometimes known. In 1747 he left Italy to spend the rest of his life working at various European courts, most notably at Dresden for Frederick Augustus II (1747–66) and at Warsaw for STANISLAW II (1767–80). His detailed views of the Polish capital were used as guides to reconstruct the historic sections of the city after their destruction in World War II. His style is distinguishable from his uncle's by its Dutch characteristics (e.g., cast shadows, massed clouds, somber tone and color).

Bellow, Saul (born 1915) U.S. (Canadian-born) novelist. Born near Montreal to a immigrant Russian-Jewish family, he was fluent in Yiddish from childhood. His family moved to Chicago when he was 9; he grew up and attended college there, and after some years in New York returned to teach in Chicago. His works, which make him representative of the Jewish-American writers whose works became central to American literature after World War II, deal with the modern urban dweller, disaffected by society but not destroyed in spirit; his originality lies partly in his combination of cultural sophistication and street wisdom. His novels include *The Adventures of Augie March* (1953; National Book Award), *Seize the Day* (1956), *Henderson the Rain King* (1959), *Herzog* (1964, National Book Award), *Mr. Sammler's Planet* (1970, National Book Award), *Humboldt's Gift* (1975, Pulitzer Prize), and *The Dean's December* (1982). He won the Nobel Prize in 1976.

bellows Mechanical contrivance for creating a jet of air, consisting usually of a hinged box with flexible sides, which expands to draw in air through an inward opening valve and contracts to expel the air through a nozzle. Invented in medieval Europe, the bellows was commonly used to speed combustion, as in a blacksmith's or ironworker's FORGE, or to operate reed or pipe ORGANS.

Bellows, George Wesley (1882–1925) U.S. painter and lithographer. Born in Columbus, Ohio, he studied with ROBERT HENRI at the New York School of Art and became associated with the artists of the ASH CAN SCHOOL. Best known for his boxing scenes, he achieved notoriety with his painting *Stag at Sharkey's* (1909), depicting an illegal boxing match. He was one of the organizers of the ARMORY SHOW. From 1916 until his death he produced a series of some 200 lithographs, including the well-known *Dempsey and Firpo* (1924).

"Stag at Sharkey's," oil on canvas by George Bellows, 1909; in the Cleveland Museum of Art, Ohio.

BY COURTESY OF THE CLEVELAND MUSEUM OF ART, OHIO, HINMAN B. HURLBUT COLLECTION

Bell's palsy See PARALYSIS

Belmondo \bel-mōⁿ-'dō\, **Jean-Paul** (born 1933) French film actor. After studying in Paris and performing with provincial stage companies, he appeared in minor film roles before achieving international fame in J.-L. GODARD'S *Breathless* (1960). Though not conventionally handsome, he became the leading antihero of NEW WAVE films, acting in 25 films by 1963, then went on to appear in such international films as *The Thief of Paris* (1967), *Borsalino* (1970), *Stavisky* (1974), and *Les misérables* (1995).

Belmont family U.S. family prominent in banking and finance, politics, and patronage of the arts. Its founder in the U.S. was August Belmont (1816–1890), a Prussian-born Jewish banker and diplomat. Belmont entered the ROTHSCHILDS' Frankfurt banking house at age 14. In 1837 he moved to New York, where he acted as the Rothschilds' agent and laid the foundation for his own banking house, which became one of the largest in the country. He took an active interest in politics. Strongly opposed to slavery, he influenced merchants and financiers in England and France in favor of the Union during the Civil War. He introduced Thoroughbred horse racing into the U.S. (see BELMONT STAKES). He married the daughter of Commodore MATTHEW PERRY. His son Perry (1850–1947) became a U.S. Congressman and wrote books on U.S. history and politics. Another son, August Belmont, Jr. (1853–1924), took over the banking house and financed the building of New York's subway, while his wife supported the METROPOLITAN OPERA.

Belmont Stakes Oldest of the three U.S. horse races that constitute the TRIPLE CROWN. The Belmont originated in 1867 and is named after August Belmont (see BELMONT FAMILY). The stakes is held in early June at Belmont Park, near Garden City, Long Island; the course is 1.5 mi (2,400 m).

Belmopan \ˌbel-mō-'pän\ City (pop., 1996: 6,500), capital of Belize. It lies in the Belize River valley, 50 mi (80 km) inland from the former capital, BELIZE CITY. After a hurricane did extensive damage to the low-lying Belize City, the new capital site was chosen far enough inland to avoid flooding. Construction began in 1966, and Belmopan became the capital in 1970.

Belo Horizonte \'bā-lō-rē-'zō^{n}n-tē\ City (pop., 1991, city: 1,530,000; metro. area: 3,899,000), eastern Brazil. Capital of Minas Gerais state, it lies on the western slope of the Serra do Espinhaço, at an elevation of 2,811 ft (857 m). The site was chosen in the late 19th century to accommodate expansions that the former capital could not. Brazil's first planned city, it was laid out on a radiating pattern following the models of WASHINGTON, D.C., and LA PLATA, Argentina. It is the hub of a large agricultural region and the area's commercial and industrial center.

Belorussia See BELARUS

Belorussian language See BELARUSIAN LANGUAGE

Belsen See BERGEN-BELSEN

Belshazzar \bel-'sha-zər\ (died c. 539 BC) Coregent of BABYLON. Though he is referred to in the Book of DANIEL as the son of Nebuchadnezzar, Babylonian inscriptions suggest that he was the eldest son of King Nabonidus. When the king went into exile in 550 BC, the kingdom and most of its army were entrusted to Belshazzar. In the biblical story Belshazzar holds a last great feast at which he sees a hand writing on a wall the words "mene, mene, tekel, upharsin," which Daniel interprets as a judgment from God foretelling the fall of Babylon. Belshazzar died after Babylon fell to the Persians in 539 BC.

belt drive Pair of PULLEYS attached to usually parallel shafts and connected by an encircling flexible belt (band) that can serve to transmit and modify rotary MOTION from one shaft to the other. Most belt drives consist of flat leather, rubber, or fabric belts running on cylindrical pulleys or of belts with a V-shaped cross section running on grooved pulleys. Another type of belt, used on some INTERNAL-COMBUSTION ENGINES for connecting the crankshaft and camshafts, is the toothed (or timing) belt, a flat belt with evenly spaced transverse teeth that fit in matching grooves on the periphery of the pulley.

Beltane \'bel-tān, 'bel-tin\ *or* **Beltine** \'bel-tin\ *or* **Cétsamain** \'ket-ˌsaù-in\ In CELTIC RELIGION, a festival held on the first day of May, celebrating the beginning of summer and open pasturing. Beltane was one of two turning points in the year, the other being November 1 (Samhain), the start of winter. At both, the bounds between the human and supernatural worlds were erased. On May Eve, witches and fairies roamed freely, and measures had to be taken against their enchantments. As late as the 19th century in Ireland, cattle were driven between two bonfires on Beltane as a magical means of protecting them from disease. See also HALLOWEEN.

Belter, John Henry *orig.* **Johann Heinrich** (1804–1863) German-U.S. cabinetmaker and designer. Trained in Germany, he settled in New York in 1833. He opened a fashionable shop specializing in rosewood, walnut, and mahogany furniture. In 1854 he patented his invention of processing rosewood in many layers to achieve thin panels that, once shaped in molds through steam heating, could be finely carved. In 1858 he opened a large factory, but soon competitive French imports and economic troubles associated with the Civil War impaired his business, and the firm closed in 1867.

beluga \bə-'lü-gə\ *or* **hausen** \'haù-z^{ə}n\ Large species of STURGEON *(Huso huso,* or *Acipenser huso)* that inhabits the Caspian and Black seas and the Sea of Azov. It reaches a length of 25 ft (7.5 m) and a weight of 2,900 lbs (1,300 kg), but its flesh and CAVIAR are less valuable than those of smaller species.

beluga *or* **white whale** Species *(Delphinapterus leucas)* of WHALE found in the Arctic Ocean and adjacent seas, in both deep offshore and coastal waters. It may also enter rivers that empty into far northern seas. A TOOTHED WHALE with a rounded forehead and no dorsal fin, the beluga is about 13 ft (4 m) long. Born dark blue-gray or blackish, it fades to white or cream at 4–5 years of age. It feeds on fish, cephalopods, and crustaceans and usually lives in groups of five to 10. It has been hunted commercially for its oil, hide, and flesh, and is used in the Arctic as food for humans and dogs. See photograph opposite.

belvedere Roofed architectural structure, freestanding or attached, and open on one or more sides, built in an elevated position to provide a view and capture daylight and fresh air. Used in Italy since the Renaissance, it often assumes the form of a LOGGIA. The term is often used for a GAZEBO on top of a building, esp. the glazed viewing room of a Victorian dwelling.

Belvedere Torso Hellenistic marble torso of a male figure 5 ft 3 in. (1.6 m) high seated on a rock. It is named after the Belvedere court in Vatican City, where it once stood; it is now in the Vatican Museum. It is signed by the Greek sculptor Apollonius and possibly dates from the 1st century BC. Well known by 1500, it had a profound influence on MICHELANGELO and other Renaissance artists.

bema \'bē-mə\ (Greek: "step") Raised stone platform originally used in Athens as a tribunal where orators addressed the citizens and courts of law. In modern times it is usually a rectangular wooden platform. The bema became a standard fixture in Eastern Orthodox churches, functioning as a stage for the altar and clergy. In synagogues, the bema (or *bimah*) is a raised platform with a reading desk from which the Torah and passages from the Prophets are read.

Bembo \'bem-ˌbō\, **Pietro** (1470–1547) Italian prelate and linguist. Born into an aristocratic family in Venice, he became librarian of St. Mark's Cathedral and was created a cardinal in 1539. After writing lyric poetry in Latin, he turned to the vernacular, producing Italian poems in imitation of PETRARCH and an Italian history of Venice. His *Discussions of the Vernacular Language* (1525) was one of the earliest books to codify Italian spelling and grammar, and it helped establish the Italian literary language. Bembo successfully advocated the adoption of 14th-century Tuscan as a model for literary Italian.

Ben Ali \ben-'ä-lē\, **Zine al-Abidine** (born 1936) President of Tunisia (from 1987). Trained as a soldier, he headed the defense ministry's military intelligence for 10 years (1964–74) before entering the foreign service, serving as ambassador to Poland before returning home to hold several domestic government posts, which culminated in a dual appointment as prime minister and interior minister. In 1987 he replaced Pres. HABIB BOURGUIBA, who had been declared medically unfit. He was elected and reelected in 1989 and 1994.

Ben Bella, Ahmed (born 1916?) First elected president of Algeria. After a French education, he entered the army, and was decorated by the French during World War II. After the war he took up arms to fight French rule. In 1954 he helped found the NATIONAL LIBERATION FRONT (FLN) and became its political leader. He was imprisoned 1956–62 while the FLN fought to expel the French. He took control of the FLN's Bureau Politique after his release, and was elected president in 1963. He was deposed in a coup in 1965 and imprisoned until 1980. He spent ten years in exile, returning to Algeria in 1990. See also MUHAMMAD BOUDIAF, HOUARI BOUMEDIENNE.

Ben-Gurion \ben-'gùr-ē-ən\, **David** *orig.* **David Gruen** (1886–1973) First prime minister of Israel. Born in Poland to a Zionist father, he emigrated to Ottoman-ruled Palestine in 1906, hoping to fulfill the Zionist aspiration of rebuilding the Jewish state. Expelled from the Ottoman empire at the outbreak of World War I, he traveled to New York, where he married. Following the BALFOUR DECLARATION, he joined the British ar-

Beluga, or white whale (*Delphinapterus leucas*).

E.R. DEGGINGER

my's Jewish Legion and returned to the Middle East. In the 1920s and '30s he led several political organizations, including the Jewish Agency, world Zionism's highest directing body. As Britain became more sympathetic to Palestinian Arabs, restricting Jewish immigration to Palestine, he called on the Jewish community to rise against Britain. On the establishment of the state of Israel, he became prime minister and minister of defense. He succeeded in fusing the underground armies that had fought the British into a national army, which he used successfully against Arab attacks. Unpopular with Britain and the U.S., he found an ally in France during the Algerian War and the Suez Crisis. He resigned in 1963. See also Arab–Israeli Wars.

Ben Nevis Highest mountain, British Isles. It is located in the Scottish Highlands; its summit, which reaches 4,406 ft (1,343 m), is a plateau of about 100 acres (40 hectares). Snow lies in some parts all year. It consists of a superstructure of volcanic rocks surmounting the ancient schists of the Highlands.

Benares See Varanasi

Benavente y Martínez \ˌbe-nə-ˈven-tē-ē-mär-ˈtē-nəs\, **Jacinto** (1866–1954) Spanish dramatist. His most celebrated work, *The Bonds of Interest* (1907), was based on the Italian commedia dell'arte; his 1913 tragedy *La malquerida* ("The Passion Flower") was also popular. During the Spanish Civil War he was detained by the authorities for a time, but he reestablished himself in official favor with *Lo increíble* (1941). One of the foremost Spanish dramatists of the 20th century, he continued to write until the end of his life, producing more than 150 plays. He received the Nobel Prize in 1922.

Bench, Johnny (Lee) (born 1947) U.S. baseball player. Born in Oklahoma City, he joined the Cincinnati Reds in 1967. In 17 seasons as catcher with the Reds (1967–83), he helped lead the team (with Pete Rose and Joe Morgan) to four National League pennants (1970, 1972, 1975, 1976) and two World Series victories (1975, 1976). Batting right-handed, he led the National League in runs batted in three times (1970, 1972, 1974) and twice in home runs (1970, 1972). He is regarded as one of the greatest defensive catchers ever to play the game.

Benchley, Robert (Charles) (1889–1945) U.S. drama critic, actor, and humorist. Born in Worcester, Mass., he graduated from Harvard University and joined the staff of *Life* magazine in 1920. A regular member of the Algonquin Round Table, he was drama critic for the *New Yorker* 1929–40, for which he also wrote "The Wayward Press" column under the pseudonym Guy Fawkes. He acted in 46 short films, including *How to Sleep* (1934, Academy Award). His writing was warmly humorous, his satire sharp but not cruel.

bends See decompression sickness

Bene-Israel \ˈben-ē-ˌiz-rā-ˈel\ (Hebrew: "Sons of Israel") one of three groups of Jews in India. The origins of the Bene-Israel are uncertain, but because of their observance of certain traditions and lack of observance of others, they are believed to have escaped persecution in Galilee before the 2nd century BCE and to have shipwrecked on the coast of India. Seven couples are believed to have survived, without the benefit of a material culture. Isolated from other Jews, they largely assimilated into India's caste system, though they practiced Jewish dietary laws, circumcised male children on the eighth day, and did not work on Saturday. Present-day Bene-Israel bear a physical resemblance to the Marathi people and speak Marathi and English. Many have emigrated to Israel.

Benedetto da Maiano \bā-nā-ˈdāt-tō-dä-mä-ˈyä-nō\ (1442–1497) Italian sculptor active in Florence. He was influenced by Bernardo Rossellino, and his marble tomb designs are variants on Rossellino's patterns. His masterpiece is a pulpit in Santa Croce in Florence (completed 1485), consisting of five narrative reliefs. He often worked with his brothers, Giovanni and Giuliano, in the design and execution of such architectural features as pilasters, capitals, friezes, and niches. He was also a master of naturalistic portrait busts.

Benedict, Ruth *orig.* **Ruth Fulton** (1887–1948) U.S. anthropologist. Born in New York City, she received her PhD under Franz Boas at Columbia University in 1923 and taught at Columbia from 1930 until her death. In *Patterns of Culture* (1934), her most famous work, she emphasized how small a part of the range of possible human behavior is elaborated or emphasized in any one society. She described how these forms of behavior are integrated into patterns or configurations, and she supported cultural relativism, or the judging of cultural phenomena in the context of the culture in which they occur. In *The Chrysanthemum and the Sword* (1946), she applied her methods to Japanese culture. Her theories had a profound influence on cultural anthropology.

Ruth Benedict.
BY COURTESY OF COLUMBIA UNIVERSITY, NEW YORK

Benedict XII *orig.* **Jacques Fournier** (died 1342) Pope (1334–42). A French cardinal and theologian, he became the third pontiff to reign at Avignon (see Avignon papacy), succeeding John XXII. Benedict devoted himself to the reform of the church and its religious orders; he also tried unsuccessfully to prevent the outbreak of the conflict between England and France that became the Hundred Years' War. His bull *Benedictus Deus* (1336) set forth the doctrine of the Beatific Vision as a vision of God granted to the souls of the just immediately after death.

Benedict XII, detail from a bust by Paolo da Siena, 1342; in the Grotto of the Vatican, Rome.
ALINARI—ANDERSON/ART RESOURCE

Benedict XIII *orig.* **Pedro de Luna** (1328?–1423) Antipope (1394–1423). A French professor of canon law, he was named a cardinal in 1375, and when the Western Schism began in 1378 he supported the antipope Clement VII. Elected pope at Avignon (see Avignon papacy), he refused French pressure to abdicate and was besieged in the papal palace (1398). Benedict escaped to Provence in 1403 and won back the obedience of France. He refused to yield when deposed by the councils of Pisa (1409) and Constance (1417).

Benedict XIV *orig.* **Prospero Lambertini** (1675–1758) Pope, 1740–58. Nobly born, he received a doctorate in theology and law. Typical of his pontificate were his promotion of scientific learning and his admonition to those drawing up the *Index of Forbidden Books* to act with restraint. In the Papal States he reduced taxation, encouraged agriculture, and supported free trade. He maintained conciliatory relations with neighboring kingdoms. A lifelong active scholar, he founded several learned societies and laid the groundwork for the present Vatican Museum. Bernard Garnier, a French cleric who was counter-antipope (1425–1433) while Martin V was pope and Clement VIII was antipope, was also called Benedict XIV.

Benedict XV *orig.* **Giacomo Della Chiesa** (1854–1922) Pope (1914–22). Ordained a priest in 1878, he entered the papal diplomatic service. He was made archbishop of Bologna in 1907 and cardinal in 1914. Elected pope a month after the outbreak of World War I, he tried to follow a policy of strict neutrality and concentrated the church's efforts on relief. He later made positive efforts toward reestablishing peace, though his principal attempt to mediate (1917) was unsuccessful.

Benedict XV, 1921.
UPI

Benedict of Nursia, St. (c. AD 480–547?) Founder of the BENEDICTINE monastery at MONTE CASSINO, Italy, and father of Western MONASTICISM. Born into a prominent family at Nursia in central Italy, he rejected the immoral and profligate life of the rich and became a hermit outside Rome, where he attracted disciples. At his monastery at Cassino he formulated the Benedictine Rule, which became standard in monasteries throughout Europe. The Rule includes a probationary year prior to the vow of obedience and lifelong residence at the one monastery, a ban on personal property, an abbot elected for life who appoints all other officers, and a precisely ordered day that includes five to six hours of liturgy and prayer, five hours of manual work, and four hours of scriptural and spiritual reading.

Benedictine Member of the Order of St. Benedict, the confederated autonomous congregations of monks and lay brothers who follow the Benedictine Rule, created by St. BENEDICT OF NURSIA in the 6th century. The Rule spread slowly in Italy and Gaul. By the 9th century it was nearly universal in northern and western Europe, where Benedictine monasteries became repositories of learning, literature, and wealth. The order declined during the 12th–15th century, when it was revived with reforms that limited abbots to fixed terms and required monks to make their vows to the congregation rather than a particular house. The REFORMATION virtually eliminated Benedictines from northern Europe, and they declined elsewhere. In the 19th century another revival strengthened the order in Europe, especially in France and Germany, and led to the establishment of new congregations worldwide.

benefice \'be-nə-fəs\ System of land tenure first used by the Franks during the 8th century. A Frankish lord leased an estate to a freeman *in beneficium* (Latin: "for the benefit (of the tenant)"), normally until the death of the lord or tenant, though tenants often succeeded in turning benefices into hereditary holdings. By the 12th century benefice was dying out as a term for land tenure; instead it referred to a church office that carried with it the right of receiving income. A lord or bishop chose a priest, who was granted the benefice in return for the performance of spiritual duties.

beneficiary \ˌbe-nə-'fi-shē-ˌer-ē, ˌbe-nə-'fi-shə-rē\ Person or entity (e.g., a charity or estate) that receives a benefit from something (e.g., a TRUST, life-insurance policy, or CONTRACT). A primary beneficiary receives proceeds from a trust or insurance policy before any other. A contingent beneficiary receives proceeds upon the occurrence of a specified event, such as the death of the primary beneficiary. A direct beneficiary is a third party whom contracting individuals intend to benefit from a contract; an incidental beneficiary benefits without that being the contracting individuals' intention.

beneficiation \ˌbe-nə-ˌfi-shē-'ā-shən\ Treatment of raw material (such as pulverized ORE) to improve physical or chemical properties in preparation for further processing. Beneficiation techniques include washing, sizing of particulates, and concentration (which involves the separation of valuable minerals from the other raw materials received from a grinding mill). In large-scale operations, various distinguishing properties of the minerals to be separated (e.g., magnetism, wettability, density) are exploited to concentrate the desirable components. Beneficiation is also used in the ceramics and clay industries. See also FLOTATION, MINING, ORE DRESSING.

Benelux Economic Union \'be-nə-ˌləks\ Economic union of Belgium, the Netherlands, and Luxembourg. The three countries formed a customs union in 1948, and in 1958 they signed the Treaty of the Benelux Economic Union, which became operative in 1960. Benelux became the first completely free international labor market and contributed to the establishment of the EUROPEAN ECONOMIC COMMUNITY.

Beneš \'be-ˌnesh\, **Edvard** (1884–1948) Czechoslovakian statesman. A disciple of TOMAS MASARYK, Beneš was a founder of modern Czechoslovakia. He served as its first foreign minister (1918–35) and president (1935–38). Forced to capitulate to ADOLF HITLER's demands over the SUDETENLAND, he resigned. He headed the Czech government-in-exile in England (1940–45), then reestablished a government on his native soil in 1945. Recognizing the need to cooperate with the Soviet Union, he nevertheless refused to sign a new communist constitution and resigned in 1948 shortly before his death.

Benét \bə-'nā\, **Stephen Vincent** (1898–1943) U.S. poet, novelist, and short-story writer. Born in Bethlehem, Pa., he is best known for *John Brown's Body* (1928, Pulitzer Prize), a long narrative poem on the Civil War. *A Book of Americans* (1933), poems written with his wife, the former Rosemary Carr, brought many historical characters to life for American schoolchildren. His story "The Devil and Daniel Webster" (1937) was the basis for a play, an opera (by Douglas Moore), and a film.

benevolent despotism See ENLIGHTENED DESPOTISM

Bengal \ben-'gȯl\ Former province, northeastern British India. Generally corresponding to the area inhabited by speakers of the BENGALI LANGUAGE, it is now divided between the Indian state of West Bengal and Bangladesh. Bengal formed part of most of the early empires that controlled northern India. In the 8th–12th century it was under a Buddhist dynasty, and from 1576 it belonged to the Mughal empire. In the 18th century it was dominated by the nawabs of Bengal; they came into conflict with the British, who had established themselves at Calcutta (now KOLKATA) in 1690. By 1764 the British had taken possession, and from then on Bengal was the base for British expansion in India. With the end of British rule in 1947, the area was divided. West Bengal, BIHAR, and ORISSA became part of India. East Bengal went to Pakistan; in 1971 it became Bangladesh.

Bengal, Bay of Part of the INDIAN OCEAN. Occupying about 839,000 sq mi (2,172,000 sq km), it is bordered by Sri Lanka, India, Bangladesh, Myanmar, and the northern MALAY PENINSULA. It is about 1,000 mi (1,600 km) wide, with an average depth of more than 8,500 ft (2,600 m). Many large rivers, including the Godavari, Krishna, Kaveri, Ganges, and Brahmaputra, flow into it. The ANDAMAN AND NICOBAR ISLANDS, the bay's only islands, separate it from the ANDAMAN SEA. It has long been crossed by Indian and Malaysian traders; Chinese maritime trading dates from the 12th century. VASCO DA GAMA led the first European voyage into the bay in 1498.

Bengal, Partition of (1905) Division of Bengal carried out by Lord CURZON, the British viceroy in India. The British province of BENGAL, which also included BIHAR and ORISSA, had by the beginning of the 20th century grown too large to handle under a single administration. Curzon chose to unite eastern Bengal with ASSAM, leaving western Bengal with Bihar and Orissa. The partition went through despite widespread protests, unrest, and boycotts, but in 1911 eastern and western Bengal were reunited. Assam resumed its old status, and Bihar and Orissa were separated to form a new province.

Bengali language \ben-'gä-lē\ INDO-ARYAN LANGUAGE spoken principally in Bangladesh and the Indian state of West Bengal. Bengali has more speakers—close to 190 million—than all but a handful of other languages of the world. Like other Modern Indo-Aryan languages, Bengali has drastically reduced the complex inflectional system of Old Indo-Aryan (see SANSKRIT LANGUAGE). It has virtually dropped grammatical GENDER and fixed stress on the initial syllable of a word or phrase. Bengali was the first of the Indian languages to adopt Western secular literary styles, such as fiction and drama.

Benghazi \ben-'gä-zē\ *or* **Banghazi** \bän-'gä-zē\ Coastal city (metro area, pop., 1995: 804,000), northeastern Libya. Located on the Gulf of SIDRA, it is Libya's second-largest city and was once its capital. Founded by Greeks as Hesperides, it received from PTOLEMY III the additional name Berenice in honor of his wife. After the 3rd century AD it superseded CYRENE and Barce as the chief city of the region. After its importance waned, it remained a small town until it was extensively developed during the Italian occupation of Libya (1912–42). In World War II it suffered considerable damage before being captured by the British in 1942. It is now an administrative and commercial center, and the site of one of the world's largest desalinization plants.

Beni River \'bā-nē\ River, Bolivia. Rising in the eastern cordillera of the ANDES, it flows north and unites with the MAMORÉ to form the MADEIRA RIVER at Villa Bella. Near its mouth it receives the MADRE DE DIOS. It is 994 mi (1599 km) long.

Benigni \bā-'nēn-yē\, **Roberto** (born 1952) Italian film comedian and director. He came to the attention of Italians in TV programs such as *L'altra Domenica,* where his wildly mischievous approach to such sensitive topics as God, politics, and sex earned him a wide audience. He debuted as a film actor in *Berlingeur, Ti voglio bene* (1977) and as director in *Tu mi trubi* (1983). Later films such as *Down by Law* (1986) and *Il mostro* (1994) were popular across Europe and in the U.S. He is best known for his performance in the controversial *Life Is Beautiful* (1998, Academy Award).

Benin \bə-ˈnēn\ *officially* **Republic of Benin** *formerly* **Dahomey** Country, western Africa. Area: 43,483 sq mi (112,621 sq km). Population (1997): 5,902,000. Capital: PORTO-NOVO (official), COTONOU (de facto). The FON people and related groups constitute three-fifths of the population; minorities include the YORUBA, FULANI, and a Voltaic-speaking group. Languages: French (official), Fon. Currency: CFA franc. Religion: traditional religions (two-thirds of the population), Islam and Christianity (one-third). Extending about 420 mi (675 km) inland from the Gulf of GUINEA, the republic consists of a hilly region in the northwest, where the maximum elevation is 2,150 ft (650 km). There are plains in the east and north, and a marshy region in the south, where the coastline extends about 75 mi (120 km). Benin's longest river, the

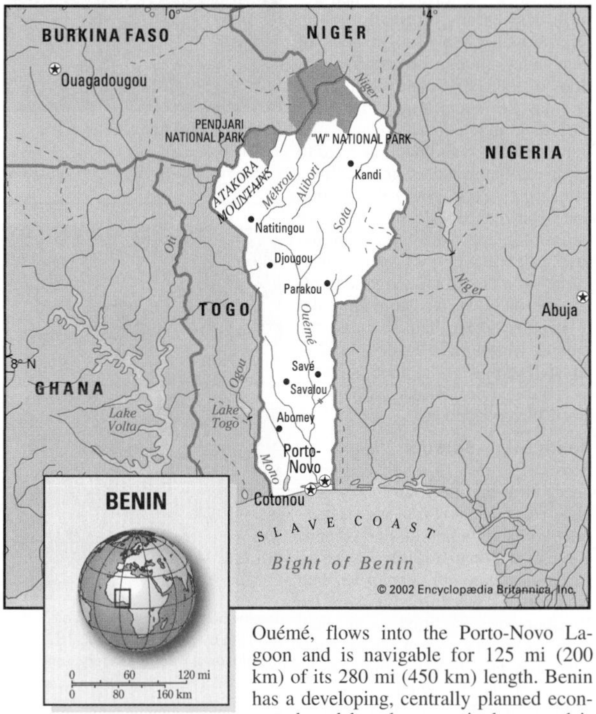

Ouémé, flows into the Porto-Novo Lagoon and is navigable for 125 mi (200 km) of its 280 mi (450 km) length. Benin has a developing, centrally planned economy based largely on agriculture, and is developing its offshore oil field. It is a republic with one legislative house; the head of state and government is the president, assisted by the prime minister. In southern Benin, the Dahomey, or Fon, established the Abomey kingdom in 1625. In the 18th century the kingdom expanded to include Allada and Ouidah, where French forts had been established in the 17th century. In 1857 the French reestablished themselves in the area, and eventually fighting ensued. In 1894 Dahomey became a French protectorate; it was incorporated into the federation of FRENCH WEST AFRICA in 1904. It achieved independence in 1960. Dahomey was renamed Benin in 1975. At the end of the 20th century, its chronically weak economy produced tension between laborers and the government.

Benin, Bight of Bay, northern section of Gulf of GUINEA. It extends along the West African coast about 400 mi (640 km) from Cape St. Paul, Ghana, past Togo and Benin to an outlet of the NIGER RIVER in Nigeria. Major ports include LOMÉ, COTONOU, and LAGOS. It was the scene of extensive slave trading during the 16th–19th century, and the region of coastal lagoons west of the Niger delta became known as the Slave Coast. By the 1830s trade in palm oil had become the major economic activity. Petroleum was discovered in the Niger delta in the 1950s.

Benin, kingdom of One of the principal historic kingdoms (13th–19th century) of the western African forest region, centered on present-day Benin City in southern Nigeria. With the accession of Ewuare the Great in the mid-15th century, the kingdom became highly organized, trading in ivory, palm oil, pepper, and slaves with Portuguese and Dutch traders. In the 18th and early 19th century it was weakened by succession struggles and the end of the slave trade. When the British burned Benin City in 1897, the kingdom was incorporated into British Nigeria.

Benjamin, Judah P(hilip) (1811–1884) British-U.S. lawyer and Confederate cabinet member. Born in St. Croix, he moved with his parents to South Carolina. In 1832 he began to build a successful law practice in New Orleans. He was the first Jew elected to the U.S. Senate (1853–61), and was noted for his proslavery speeches. After the South seceded, JEFFERSON DAVIS appointed him attorney general (1861), secretary of war (1861–62), and secretary of state (1862–65). His unpopular proposal to arm slaves for the Confederate army forced him to flee to England in 1865.

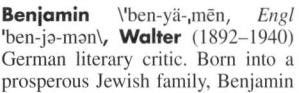

Judah Benjamin.
BY COURTESY OF THE LIBRARY OF CONGRESS, WASHINGTON, D.C.

Benjamin \ˈben-yä-ˌmēn, *Engl* ˈben-jə-mən\, **Walter** (1892–1940) German literary critic. Born into a prosperous Jewish family, Benjamin studied philosophy and worked as a literary critic and translator in Berlin from 1920 until 1933, when he fled to France to avoid persecution. The Nazi takeover of France led him to flee again in 1940; he committed suicide at the Spanish border on hearing that he would be turned over to the Gestapo. Posthumous publication of his essays has won him a reputation as the leading German literary critic of the first half of the 20th century, as well as one of the first serious writers about film and photography. His independence and originality are evident in the essays collected in *Illuminations* (1961) and *Reflections* (1979). His writings on art reflect his reading of KARL MARX and his friendships with BERTOLT BRECHT and THEODOR ADORNO.

Benn, Gottfried (1886–1956) German poet and essayist. He received military medical training and was made medical supervisor of jail inmates and prostitutes in occupied Brussels during World War I. His early poems, including those in *Fleisch* (1917; "Flesh"), contain allusions to degeneracy and medical aspects of decay. Because of his Expressionism and despite his right-wing views, he was penalized during the Nazi era. He regained literary attention with *Statische Gedichte* (1948; "Static Poems") and the reappearance of his old poems. A broad selection of his poetry and prose was published in English as *Primal Vision* (1961).

Bennett, Alan (born 1934) British dramatist, screenwriter, and actor. He first gained success with the brilliant satirical revue *Beyond the Fringe* (1960), which he cowrote and performed with Dudley Moore, Peter Cook, and JONATHAN MILLER. He later wrote works for television, including *An Englishman Abroad* (1982) and *Talking Heads* (1988), marked by his characteristic mixture of wry comedy and sadness. His first stage play, *Forty Years On* (1968), was followed by *Getting On* (1971), *Habeas Corpus* (1973), *The Old Country* (1977), *Enjoy* (1980), and the successful *The Madness of King George* (1991; film, 1994). His screenplays include *Prick Up Your Ears* (1987).

Bennett, (Enoch) Arnold (1867–1931) British novelist, playwright, critic, and essayist. His major works, inspired by GUSTAVE FLAUBERT and HONORE DE BALZAC, form an important link between the English novel and the mainstream of European realism. He is best known for his highly detailed novels of the "Five Towns"—the Potteries in his native Staffordshire—which are the setting of *Anna of the Five Towns* (1902), *The Old Wives' Tale* (1908), and the three novels that make up *The Clayhanger Family* (1925). He was also a well-known critic.

Bennett, James Gordon (1795–1872) Scottish-U.S. editor. He emigrated to the U.S. in 1819 and was employed on various newspapers until 1835, when he started the *New York Herald*. The paper became very successful and introduced many of the methods of modern news reporting. Among other innovations, Bennett published the first Wall Street financial article (1835), established the first correspondents in Europe (1838), maintained a staff of 63 war correspondents during the Civil War, was a leader in using illustrations, introduced a society department, and published the first account in U.S. journalism of a love-nest murder (1836).

Bennett, Michael *orig.* **Michael Bennett Difiglia** (1943–1987) U.S. dancer, choreographer, and stage musical director. Born in Buffalo, N.Y., he began dancing at 3 and left high school to tour in a production of *West Side Story*. His major contribution to dance was as choreographer-director of such Broadway musicals as *Promises, Promises* (1968), *Company* (1970), *Follies* (1971), and *Dreamgirls* (1981). His most remarkable musical was *A Chorus Line* (1975, Pulitzer Prize), which he conceived, directed, and choreographed. Bennett personally received eight Tony awards during his career. His early death resulted from AIDS.

Bennett, Richard B(edford) *later* **Viscount Bennett (of Mickleham and of Calgary and Hopewell)** (1870–1947) Canadian prime minister (1930–35). Born in Hopewell, New Brunswick, he served in the legislatures of the Northwest Territories and Alberta, and in the Canadian House of Commons (1911). He was named director general of national service (1916) and later minister of justice (1921). He became head of the Conservative Party in 1927 and, having promised relief from the Great Depression, prime minister in 1930. He underestimated the severity of the crisis, and his measures were superficial. He was defeated by the Liberals and W.L. MACKENZIE KING. In 1939 he retired to England, where he was made a viscount in 1941.

Bennett, Robert Russell (1894–1981) U.S. composer, conductor, and Broadway orchestrator. Born in Kansas City, he studied music in Berlin, London, and Paris. Beginning in the 1920s, he scored some 300 Broadway musicals over 40 years, including the works of J. KERN, C. PORTER, R. RODGERS, IRVING BERLIN, GEORGE GERSHWIN, and F. LOEWE, and such hit shows as *Show Boat, Anything Goes, Kiss Me Kate, South Pacific, My Fair Lady,* and *The Sound of Music.*

Bennett, Tony *orig.* **Anthony (Dominick) Benedetto** (born 1926) U.S. popular singer. The son of a grocer in Queens, N.Y., his first job was as a singing waiter, and he later sang under the name Joe Bari. In 1949 Pearl Bailey asked him to join her nightclub revue, and in 1950 BOB HOPE suggested his new name. He had many hits in the 1950s, but his signature song became "I Left My Heart in San Francisco" (1962). His style became increasingly jazz-oriented over the years, and in the mid-1990s a special appearance on MTV heralded a comeback.

Bennington College Private liberal-arts college in Bennington, Vt. It was founded in 1932 as a women's college; men were first admitted in the late 1960s. It has divisions of literature and languages, social sciences, visual arts, music, dance, drama, and natural sciences and mathematics. Master's degree programs are offered in the fine arts. Enrollment is about 400.

Benny, Jack *orig.* **Benjamin Kubelsky** (1894–1974) U.S. comedian. Born in Chicago, he took up the violin as a boy, and he played it in vaudeville from 1912. After discovering a talent for comedy while in the navy, he returned to vaudeville as a comedian. He made his film debut in 1927 and appeared in 18 films in the years 1930–45. His weekly *Jack Benny Program* on radio (1932–55) and television (1950–65) won loyal audiences, and he became famous for a unique comic style characterized by subtle verbal inflection, meaningful pauses, seriocomic violin playing, and the stage image of a vain, stingy man.

Benois \'byi-nȯi\, **Alexandre (Nikolayevich)** (1870–1960) Russian theater art director, painter, and influential ballet set designer. With SERGEY DIAGHILEV he cofounded the avant-garde art magazine *Mir Iskusstva* ("World of Art") in 1899. He began his scenic-design career in 1901 and designed many of the innovative BALLETS RUSSES decors from 1909 to 1929. He designed sets for numerous other ballet companies in the 1940s and 1950s.

Bénoué River See BENUE RIVER

bent grass Any of the annual or perennial GRASSES that make up the genus *Agrostis,* in the family Poaceae (or Gramineae), found in temperate and cool regions and at high altitudes in subtropical and tropical areas. At least 40 species are found in the U.S.; some are weeds, others FORAGE and TURF plants. They have slender stems and flat blades. Many spread by creeping STOLONS. Redtop *(A. gigantea)* is a HAY and pasture grass. Creeping bent *(A. stolonifera* variety *palustris)* and colonial bent *(A. tenuis)* are popular lawn grasses; the many strains of both species are planted in golf courses and bowling greens, where they are closely cut to develop a fine, spongy, firm turf.

Creeping bent (*Agrostis stolonifera* variety *palustris*).

R.G. DOORD FROM THE NATURAL HISTORY PHOTOGRAPHIC AGENCY—EB INC.

Bentham \'ben-thəm\, **Jeremy** (1748–1832) British social and political theorist. Precociously brilliant, he graduated from Oxford at 15. He was an atheist and an exponent of the new laissez-faire economics of ADAM SMITH and DAVID RICARDO. The first great exponent of UTILITARIANISM, he wrote that government should promote "the greatest happiness." He inspired much reform legislation, especially prison reform, and was a vocal advocate of democracy, though he attacked notions of the social contract and natural law as superfluous. Believing society could advance by calculation of pleasure and pain, he tried to compare the relative gratifications of health, wealth, power, friendship, and benevolence, as well as those of "irascible appetite" and "antipathy." He thought of punishment purely as a deterrent, and graded offenses solely by the harm they did to happiness. He helped found the radical *Westminster Review* (1823). He willed that his clothed skeleton be exhibited permanently at University College London.

Jeremy Bentham, detail of an oil painting by H.W. Pickersgill, 1829; in the National Portrait Gallery, London.

BY COURTESY OF THE NATIONAL PORTRAIT GALLERY, LONDON

Bentham, Samuel *later* **Sir Samuel** (1757–1831) British engineer, naval architect, and navy official. He was the brother of JEREMY BENTHAM and father of the botanist George Bentham (1800–1884). An early advocate of explosive-shell weapons for warships, Bentham led Russian vessels fitted with shell guns to victory over a larger Turkish force in 1788. In England, he developed the Arrow class of sloops used against France. He served as commissioner of the navy 1807–12.

Bentinck, William (Henry Cavendish), Lord (1774–1839) British colonial administrator. Born to wealth and rank, he was appointed governor of Madras in 1803. Recalled in 1807 after a mutiny of Indian troops at Vellore, he pressed for the next 20 years for a chance to vindicate his name. In 1828 he was named governor-general of Bengal (in effect, of all India), and he served until 1835. He reformed the country's finances, opened up administrative and judicial posts to Indians, suppressed the bands of Thugs, and abolished SUTTEE. His policies helped pave the way to independence more than a century later.

Bentley, Eric (Russell) (born 1916) British-U.S. drama critic and translator. He was a stage director in several European cities (1948–51); in Munich, after working with BERTOLT BRECHT on *Mother Courage,* he translated Brecht's plays into English. His reporting on European theater for several magazines helped introduce many European playwrights to the U.S. He wrote numerous critical works, including *Life of the Drama* (1964), and taught at Columbia University (1953–69) and elsewhere.

Bentley, Richard (1662–1742) British clergyman and classical scholar. He was appointed Boyle lecturer at Oxford in 1692, became keeper of the Royal Library in 1694, and was named master of Trinity College, Cambridge, in 1700. He displayed his skill in textual emendation and his knowledge of ancient meter in *Epistola ad Joannem Millium* (1691). In *Dissertation on the Epistles of Phalaris* (1699), he proved the epistles' spuriousness; his dispute with Charles Boyle over their authenticity was satirized by JONATHAN SWIFT in *The Battle of the Books* (1704). He also published critical texts of classical authors, including HORACE, and made linguistic contributions to the study of ancient Greek.

Benton, Thomas Hart (1782–1858) U.S. politician. Born near Hillsborough, N.C., he moved to St. Louis in 1815 and edited the *St. Louis Enquirer*. Appealing to agrarian and commercial interests, he was elected to the U.S. Senate in 1820. He became a crusader for the distribution of public lands to settlers, and was soon acknowledged as the Democratic Party's chief spokesman in the Senate. His opposition to the extension of slavery into the West cost him his Senate seat in 1851, though he later served in the House of Representatives (1853–55). His grandnephew was the artist THOMAS HART BENTON.

Thomas Hart Benton, c. 1845–50.

BY COURTESY OF THE LIBRARY OF CONGRESS, WASHINGTON, D.C.

Benton, Thomas Hart (1889–1975) U.S. painter and muralist. Born in Neosho, Mo., he studied at the Art Institute of Chicago and at the Académie Julian in Paris, where he came into contact with Synchronism and Cubism. In 1912 he returned to New York, but, failing in his attempts at modernism, he set out to travel through the rural heartland, sketching people and places. In the 1930s he painted several notable murals, including *America Today* (1930–31) at the New School for Social Research. He often transposed biblical and classical stories to rural American settings, as in *Susanna and the Elders* (1938). His style, which quickly became influential, is characterized by undulating forms, cartoonlike figures, and brilliant color. He taught at the Art Students League in New York, where JACKSON POLLOCK was his best-known student.

Benton, William (Burnett) (1900–1973) U.S. publisher, advertising executive, and government official. Born in Minneapolis, a descendant of missionaries and educators, he founded, with CHESTER BOWLES, the successful New York advertising agency of Benton & Bowles. He later became a vice president at the University of Chicago; through his efforts, the university acquired *Encyclopædia Britannica,* which he managed and later purchased. In 1945 he became assistant secretary of state, and he later briefly served in the U.S. Senate (1949–52). Thereafter he devoted sustained attention to the encyclopedia; he died shortly before publication of its 15th edition.

bentwood furniture Type of furniture made of wooden rods bent into shape after being heated with steam. The method was used on the 18th-century Windsor chair, but its principal exponent was MICHAEL THONET, who exploited its possibilities in the 1840s. His bentwood chairs are among the most successful examples of early mass-produced furniture. Bentwood is light, comfortable, and inexpensive, as well as strong and graceful.

Bent beechwood armchair by the Thonet brothers, Austria, c. 1870; in the Museum of Modern Art, New York City.

BY COURTESY OF THE MUSEUM OF MODERN ART, NEW YORK, GIFT OF THONET INDUSTRIES

Benue-Congo languages \'bā-nwā\ Largest branch of the NIGER-CONGO family of languages, both in numbers of languages and speakers. Its major divisions are Defoid, including Yoruba and Itsekiri, with more than 23 million speakers; Edoid, including Edo (see kingdom of BENIN), Etsako, Isoko, and Urhobo; Nupoid, including Nupe, Ebira, and Gbari; Idomoid, including Idoma; Igboid, including the many dialects of the approximately 19 million IGBO people; Kainji and Platoid, a congeries of more than 50 languages; Cross River, a group of more than 55 languages; and Bantoid. Bantoid, the largest branch, includes over 600 languages and is divided into Northern Bantoid and Southern Bantoid. The BANTU LANGUAGES make up the largest subgroup of Southern Bantoid.

Benue River \'bā-nwā\ *or* **Bénoué River** \bā-'nwā\ River, western Africa. Rising in northern Cameroon (as the Bénoué), the river flows west across eastern central Nigeria (as the Benue). About 870 mi (1,400 km) long, it is the chief tributary of the NIGER RIVER and transports a considerable volume of trade.

Benz \'bents\, **Karl (Friedrich)** (1844–1929) German mechanical engineer who designed and built the first practical AUTOMOBILE powered by an INTERNAL COMBUSTION ENGINE. The original car, his three-wheeled *Motorwagen,* first ran in 1885. Benz's company produced its first four-wheeled car in 1893 and the first of its series of racing cars in 1899. Benz left the company in 1906 to form another group with his sons. In 1926 the Benz company merged with the company started by GOTTLIEB DAIMLER.

benzene Simplest aromatic HYDROCARBON (see AROMATIC COMPOUND), parent substance of a large class of chemical compounds. It was discovered in 1825 by MICHAEL FARADAY. The chemical formula is C_6H_6; AUGUST KEKULE VON STRADONITZ in 1865 was the first to propose the correct structure, a six-membered ring of CARBON atoms, each with one HYDROGEN atom bonded to it (see BONDING). Although benzene is often represented with alternating single and double bonds between carbon atoms, the electrons in the bonds are shared or delocalized in such a way as to make all carbon atoms alike. Benzene is a colorless, mobile liquid with a characteristic odor. An excellent solvent, it is also widely used as a starting material for many plastics, dyes, detergents, insecticides, and other industrial chemicals. Benzene is highly toxic, and long exposure may cause LEUKEMIA.

Benzer, Seymour (born 1921) U.S. molecular biologist. Born in New York City, he received his PhD from Purdue University. He developed a method for determining the detailed structure of viral genes and coined the term cistron to denote functional subunits of genes. He did much to explain the nature of genetic oddities, called nonsense mutations, in terms of the nucleotide sequence of DNA, and discovered a reversal, or suppression, of these mutations in certain bacteria.

Beowulf \'bā-ə-,wu̇lf\ Heroic poem considered the highest achievement of Old English literature and the earliest European vernacular EPIC. It deals with events of the early 6th century and was probably composed c. 700–750. It tells the story of the Scandinavian hero Beowulf, who gains fame as a young man by vanquishing the monster Grendel and Grendel's mother; later, as an aging king, he kills a dragon but dies soon after, honored and lamented. *Beowulf* belongs metrically, stylistically, and thematically to the Germanic heroic tradition but shows a distinct Christian influence.

Berain \bā-'ra^{n}\, **Jean, the Elder** (1640–1711) French decorator and designer. Trained under CHARLES LE BRUN, he was appointed chief designer to the court of LOUIS XIV in 1674. He was skilled in designing tapestries, accessories, furniture, costumes, and elaborate stage settings for operas and extravagant theatrical productions, filled with fantastic iconography. He satisfied the king's appetite for splendor and inspired such other cabinetmakers as A.-C. BOULLE.

Berar \bā-'rär\ Historical region, central India. Located north of HYDERABAD, Berar emerged as a distinct political entity after the incursions of Muslim armies in the 13th century AD. It formed part of several Muslim kingdoms until, on the breakup of the Mughal empire, it fell to the ruler of Hyderabad. Coming under British control in 1853, it was subsequently assigned to various provinces; it has been part of MAHARASHTRA state since 1960. The region includes a rich cotton-growing area in the Purna River basin.

Berbers Speakers of the various Berber languages of the MAGHREB, including Tamazight, Tashahit, and Tarifit. Berber-speakers were the original inhabitants of North Africa, though many regions succumbed first to Roman colonization and later to the ARAB conquests beginning in the 7th century AD. Berbers gradually accepted Islam, and many switched to Arabic or became bilingual, though the Berber languages are still spoken in some rural and mountain areas of Morocco and Algeria and by some inhabitants of Tunisia and Libya. Since the 1990s Berber intellectuals have sought to revive interest in the language. The Berber-speaking ALMORAVID and ALMOHAD dynasties built empires in North Africa and Spain in the 11th–13th century. See also ABD AL-KRIM, KABYLE, RIF.

Berbice River \bər-'bēs\ River, eastern Guyana. Rising in Guyana's highlands, it flows northward 370 mi (595 km) through dense forests to the Atlantic Ocean. Its basin is restricted by the proximity of the larger ESSEQUIBO and COURANTYNE rivers. Its name derives from a Dutch colony that became part of British Guiana (now Guyana) in 1831.

Berchtesgaden \'berk-təs-ˌgäd-ᵊn\ Town (pop., 1992 est.: 8,000), southern Germany. Located in the Bavarian Alps south of SALZBURG, it is surrounded on three sides by Austrian territory. Once part of Austria, it passed to BAVARIA in the early 19th century. It was the site of ADOLF HITLER's villa retreat before and during World War II. In 1938 he met there with NEVILLE CHAMBERLAIN. Destroyed by bombing in 1945, the villa was leveled in 1952. Mountain climbing and skiing make the area a popular destination.

Berchtold \'berk-ˌtōlt\, **Leopold, Graf (Count) von** (1863–1942) Austro-Hungarian politician. One of the richest men in Austria-Hungary, he entered the diplomatic service in 1893 and became foreign minister in 1912. After the assassination of Archduke FRANCIS FERDINAND in 1914, Berchtold delivered an ultimatum to Serbia that led to the outbreak of WORLD WAR I. He was forced to resign in 1915.

Berengar of Tours \'ber-ən-ˌgär...'tu̇r\ (999?–1088) French theologian. He became canon of Tours Cathedral and archdeacon of Angers (c. 1040). He rejected the prevailing view of TRANSUBSTANTIATION, espoused by LANFRANC, in favor of transsignification and was excommunicated (1050) by Pope LEO IX. He was condemned by the Council of Vercelli (1050) and the Synod at Paris (1051). After a compromise, he was again condemned in 1076, 1078, 1079, and 1080 and spent the rest of his life in ascetic solitude.

Berenson \'ber-ən-sən\, **Bernard** (1865–1959) U.S. (Lithuanian-born) art historian, critic, and connoisseur. Born in Vilnius, he grew up in Boston and attended Harvard University. He lived in Italy most of his life, where he built a reputation as an authority on Italian Renaissance painting. He was adviser to the art dealer Joseph Duveen (1869–1939) and to Isabella Stewart Gardner (1840–1924), founder of Boston's Gardner Museum. He bequeathed his villa, I Tatti, near Florence, with its art collection and outstanding library, to Harvard to be administered as the Harvard Center for Italian Renaissance Studies. His books include *The Drawings of the Florentine Painters* (1903, 1938, 1961) and *Italian Painters of the Renaissance* (1952).

Beresford \'bērz-fərd\, **Bruce** (born 1940) Australian film director. After studies in Sydney he went to London, where he helped produce documentaries for the British Film Institute (1966–71). Back in Sydney, he directed three films before his widely acclaimed *Breaker Morant* (1980), which helped establish the Australian film industry. He later directed such U.S. films as *Tender Mercies* (1983), *Crimes of the Heart* (1986), *Driving Miss Daisy* (1989), and *Double Jeopardy* (1999).

Berezina River \bə-'rāz-ᵊn-ə\ River, Belarus. It is 365 mi (587 km) long and flows southeast into the DNIEPER RIVER. During NAPOLEON's retreat from Moscow in 1812, a bitter engagement was fought on the Berezina at the crossroads of the river near Baryslaw, and Russian forces inflicted enormous losses on Napoleon's army. In 1941 it was the scene of fierce fighting during the German advance on SMOLENSK.

Berg \'berk\ Former duchy, HOLY ROMAN EMPIRE. Located on the RHINE RIVER, the area now lies in the districts of DÜSSELDORF and COLOGNE, Germany. In the 11th century the counts of Berg acquired Westphalian lands east of Cologne; these were incorporated into a duchy in 1380. Berg became a leading iron and textile manufacturing center in the 17th–18th century. In 1806 NAPOLEON made it a grand duchy in his CONFEDERATION OF THE RHINE. Following the Congress of VIENNA in 1814–15, it became part of PRUSSIA.

Berg \'berk\, **Alban (Maria Johannes)** (1885–1935) Austrian composer. Born in Vienna, he was largely self-taught musically until he met A. SCHOENBERG at 19. This would prove the decisive event in his life, and Schoenberg would remain his teacher for eight years. Under his influence, Berg's early late-Romantic tonal works give way to increasing atonality and finally (1925) to twelve-tone composition. His Expressionist opera *Wozzeck* (1922) would become the most universally acclaimed post-Romantic opera. His second opera, *Lulu*, on which he worked six years, remained unfinished at his death at 50, which resulted from septicemia caused by an abscess. His other works include two string quartets, including the *Lyric Suite* (1926); *Three Pieces for Orchestra* (1915); and a violin concerto (1935).

Berg, Paul (born 1926) U.S. biochemist. Born in New York City, he received his PhD from Western Reserve University. While studying the actions of isolated genes, he devised methods for splitting DNA molecules at selected sites and attaching the resulting segments to the DNA of a virus or plasmid, which could then enter bacterial or animal cells. The foreign DNA was incorporated into the host and caused the synthesis of proteins not ordinarily found there. One of the earliest practical results of this research was the development of a strain of bacteria that contained the gene for producing insulin. In 1980 Berg shared a Nobel Prize with Walter Gilbert (born 1932) and FREDERICK SANGER.

bergamot \'bər-gə-ˌmät\ Any of several North American perennial plants of the MINT family, also known as BEE BALM, fragrant balm, and Indian's plume. The leaves are used as an herb to flavor tea, punches, lemonade, and other cold drinks. *Monarda didyma,* native to the U.S., is made into Oswego tea, a beverage used by the American Indian Oswego tribe and said to be the drink adopted by the 18th-century colonists during their boycott of British tea. The pear-shaped fruit of the bergamot orange *(Citrus bergamia),* found chiefly in Calabria, Italy, is valued by the flavoring and perfume industries for the ESSENTIAL OIL extracted from its peel. The bergamot pear, a popular winter pear cultivated in Britain, is a large, round fruit with yellowish-green skin.

Bergen City (municipality pop., 2000 est.: 229,496), southwestern Norway. It is Norway's second-largest city and most important port. Founded in 1070 by King Olaf III, it was Norway's capital in the 12th–13th century. In the 14th century, German HANSEATIC LEAGUE merchants acquired control over its trade; their influence in a weakened Norway lasted into the 16th century. Repeatedly destroyed by fire (most notably in 1702 and 1916), Bergen has been resurrected each time. Its economy is based largely on fishing and shipbuilding. It was the birthplace of EDVARD GRIEG and the violinist OLE BULL.

Bergen, Edgar *orig.* **Edgar John Bergren** (1903–1978) U.S. comedian and ventriloquist. As a boy in his native Chicago he developed the skill in VENTRILOQUISM that he later used to earn his tuition at Northwestern University. After stints in vaudeville and nightclubs, he took his act to radio, where the *Edgar Bergen-Charlie McCarthy Show* (with his caustic and irrepressible dummy Charlie McCarthy) was one of the most popular programs for 20 years (1937–57). His daughter Candice (born 1946), a successful screen actress, achieved her greatest fame in the television series *Murphy Brown* (1988–98).

Bergen-Belsen *or* **Belsen** Nazi CONCENTRATION CAMP near Bergen and Belsen, villages in what was then Prussian Hanover, Germany. Established in 1943 partly as a prisoner-of-war camp and partly as a Jewish transit camp, it was designed for 10,000 prisoners but eventually held 41,000. It contained no gas chambers, but some 37,000 prisoners died there, including ANNE FRANK. As the first such camp to be liberated by the Western Allies (April 15, 1945), it received instant notoriety.

Berger, Victor (Louis) (1860–1929) German-U.S. cofounder of the U.S. Socialist Party. He emigrated to the U.S. from Austria-Hungary in 1878, founded a German-language newspaper in 1892, and edited the *Social Democratic Herald* (later *Milwaukee Leader*) 1898–1929. With EUGENE V. DEBS he founded the Social Democratic Party, which became the Socialist Party in 1901. He served in the U.S. House of Representatives (1911–13) as the first Socialist ever elected to Congress. Elected again in 1918, he was denied his seat after being convicted under the Espionage Act for opposing U.S. participation in World War I. His conviction was overturned, and he again served in the House (1923–29) and succeeded Debs as Socialist Party chairman (1927–29).

Bergerac, Savinien Cyrano de See Savinien CYRANO DE BERGERAC

Bergey \'bər-gē\, **David Hendricks** (1860–1937) U.S. bacteriologist. Born in Skippack, Pa., he taught school before attending the University of Pennsylvania, where he earned a doctorate in public health. He subsequently became director of biological research for the National Drug Company in Philadelphia. He is best remembered as the primary author of *Bergey's Manual of Determinative Bacteriology,* an invaluable reference for classification, and researched such varied topics as tuberculosis, food preservatives, phagocytosis (engulfment of particles by cells), and allergic reactions.

Bergman, (Ernst) Ingmar (born 1918) Swedish film writer-director. The rebellious son of a Lutheran pastor, he worked in the theater before directing his first film, *Crisis* (1945). He won a reputation as one of the world's great filmmakers with *Smiles of a Summer Night* (1955), *The Seventh Seal* (1956), and *Wild Strawberries* (1957). He assembled a group of actors, including Max von Sydow and Liv Ullmann, and a cinematographer, Sven Nykvist, with whom he made powerful films often marked by bleak depictions of human loneliness, including *Through a Glass Darkly* (1961), *Persona* (1966), *Cries and Whispers* (1972), *Scenes from a Marriage* (1973), *Autumn Sonata* (1978), and *Fanny and Alexander* (1982). He later wrote screenplays for *The Best Intentions* (1992) and *Private Confessions* (1996). Throughout his career Bergman has continued to direct stage productions, usually at Stockholm's Royal Dramatic Theater.

Bergman, Ingrid (1915–1982) Swedish film and stage actress. After appearing in *Intermezzo* in Sweden, she came to the U.S. to act in the English-language version (1939). Her radiance and unaffected charm made her a star in films such as *Casablanca* (1942), *For Whom the Bell Tolls* (1943), *Gaslight* (1944, Academy Award), and Alfred Hitchcock's *Spellbound* (1945) and *Notorious* (1946). The scandal caused by her love affair with Roberto Rossellini (1949) kept her off the U.S. screen for seven years, and she made films in Europe before being welcomed back to Hollywood in *Anastasia* (1956, Academy Award). Her later films include *Indiscreet* (1958), *Cactus Flower* (1969), *Murder on the Orient Express* (1974, Academy Award), and *Autumn Sonata* (1978).

Bergonzi \ber-'gōnt-sē\, **Carlo** (born 1924) Italian singer. Born near Parma, he studied at its conservatory and made his debut as a baritone in 1948. Three years later he made a second debut as a tenor. His La Scala debut followed in 1953, his U.S. debut at the Chicago Lyric Opera in 1955. From 1956 to 1983, his beautiful voice was a fixture in the 19th-century Italian and French repertoire at the Metropolitan Opera. He gave a farewell recital in New York in 1994.

Bergson \berk-'sō^{n}\, **Henri (-Louis)** (1859–1941) French philosopher. His major books include *Time and Free Will* (1889), on the difference between the subjective and objective perception of time; *Matter and Memory* (1896), on the mind-body problem, taking a position opposed to scientific determinism; and *Creative Evolution* (1907), which argued that evolution, which he accepted as scientific fact, is not mechanistic but driven by *élan vital* ("vital impulse"). He was the first to elaborate a process philosophy, rejecting static values and embracing dynamic values such as motion, change, and evolution. His writing style has been widely admired for its grace and lucidity, and he won the Nobel Prize for Literature in 1927. Very popular in his time, he remains influential in France.

Bergson, 1928.
ARCHIV FUR KUNST UND GESCHICHTE, WEST BERLIN

Beria \'ber-ē-ə\, **Lavrenty (Pavlovich)** (1899–1953) Soviet politician and director of the Soviet secret police. He worked in intelligence and counterintelligence activities from 1921. As Communist Party head of the Transcaucasian republics (1932–38), he personally oversaw the political purges initiated by Joseph Stalin (see Purge Trials). He was head of the Soviet secret police 1938–53, and after Stalin's death he became one of four deputy prime ministers and the head of the Ministry of Internal Affairs. After attempting to succeed Stalin as sole dictator, he was arrested and executed.

beriberi \ˌber-ē-'ber-ē\ *or* **vitamin B_1 deficiency** Nutritional disorder (its name is from the Sinhalese for "extreme weakness"), with nerve and heart impairment, caused by thiamine deficiency. Symptoms include fatigue, digestive problems, and limb numbness and weakness. Dry beriberi involves gradual long-nerve degeneration, with muscle atrophy and loss of reflexes. Wet beriberi is more acute, with edema from cardiac failure and poor circulation. Vitamin B_1 occurs widely in food but is lost in processing; a well-balanced diet high in unprocessed foods can prevent beriberi. In Western countries, chronic alcoholism is the most common cause.

Bering, Vitus (Jonassen) (1681–1741) Danish-Russian navigator. He joined the fleet of the Russian czar Peter I and in 1724 was appointed leader of an expedition to determine whether Asia and North America were connected by land. In 1728 he set sail from the Siberian peninsula and passed through what would later be named the Bering Strait. His plan for a second expedition was expanded into Russia's Great Northern Expedition (1733–43), which mapped much of the Arctic coast of Siberia. After exploring the Alaskan coast, he fell ill from scurvy and died after his ship was wrecked. His exploration paved the way for a Russian foothold in North America.

Bering Sea Body of water, northern Pacific Ocean. Enclosed by Alaska, the Aleutian Islands, the Kamchatka Peninsula, and eastern Siberia, it covers 885,000 sq mi (2,292,150 sq km). It has numerous islands, including the Aleutians, Nunivak, St. Lawrence, and the Pribilofs. It is crossed diagonally by the International Date Line. The sea is connected to the Arctic Ocean by the Bering Strait, which separates Asia from North America and is believed to have been a land bridge during the Ice Age that enabled migration from Asia to North America. Vitus Bering's exploration of the sea and strait in 1728 and 1741 formed a basis for Russian claims to Alaska.

Bering Sea Dispute Dispute between the U.S. and Britain (and Canada) over the international status of the Bering Sea. In an attempt to control seal hunting off the Alaskan coast, the U.S. in 1881 claimed authority over the Bering Sea and the right to seize sealing vessels. When several Canadian ships were seized in the late 1880s, Britain protested the U.S. claim. An agreement in 1891 permitted both countries to police the area. In 1893 an international tribunal determined that the area was part of the high seas and that no nation had jurisdiction over it.

Berio, Luciano (born 1925) Italian composer. He has been an important innovator in electronic music, the combining of live and taped music, aleatory music, graphic notation, musical "collage" using borrowed material, and (perhaps most significantly) in musical "performance pieces." His wife, the singer Cathy Berberian (1925–1983), was his principal collaborator. His best-known works include *Omaggio a Joyce* (1958), *Visage* (1961), *Sinfonia* (1968), *Opera* (1970), and his ongoing series of *Sequenze* (1958–).

Berkeley City (pop., 1996 est.: 103,000), western California. Located on San Francisco Bay, the city was founded as Oceanview in 1853 and selected as a campus site by the College (later Univ.) of California. The college, named for the philosopher George Berkeley, opened in 1873. See also University of California.

Berkeley, Busby *orig.* **William Berkeley Enos** (1895–1976) U.S. film director and choreographer. Born in Los Angeles, the son of itinerant actors, he acted and danced in comedies from age 5. After choreographing over 20 Broadway musicals, he was summoned to Hollywood to direct dance numbers for *Whoopee* (1930). His elaborate production numbers, innovative camera techniques, and opulent sets in such films as *Gold Diggers of 1933* and *Footlight Parade* (1933) revolutionized the musical and offered escapist fare for moviegoers during the Great Depression. When rising production costs made such extravaganzas unfeasible, he directed less innovative but still popular films such as *The Gang's All Here* (1943).

Berkeley \'bärk-lē\, **George** *known as* **Bishop Berkeley** (1685–1753) Irish bishop, philosopher, and social activist. He worked principally at Trinity College, Dublin (to 1713), and as bishop of Cloyne (1734–52). He is best known for his contention that, for material objects, to be is to be perceived ("Esse est percipi"). His religious calling may have facilitated his qualifying his position by claiming that, even if no human perceives an object, God does, thereby ensuring the continued existence of the physical world when not perceived by any finite being. With John Locke and David Hume, he was one of the founders of modern empiricism. Unlike Locke, he did not believe that there exists any material substance external to the mind, but rather that objects exist only as collections of sense-data. His works include *An Essay Towards a New Theory of Vision* (1709), *Treatise Concerning the Principles of Human Knowledge* (1710), and *Three Dialogues between Hylas and Philonous* (1713). He spent part of his career in America, where he advocated educating Indians and blacks. Berkeley, Cal., is named for him.

Berkeley, William *later* **Sir William** (1606–1677) British colonial governor of Virginia. Appointed governor in 1641, he introduced successful programs in crop diversification and manufacturing and promoted peace with the Indians. A strong monarchist, he was forced to retire to his Virginia plantation during the Commonwealth period in England (1652–59). He was reappointed in 1660, but was faced with crop failures and Indian attacks on the frontier. In 1676 NATHANIEL BACON mounted an expedition against the Indians in defiance of Berkeley's policy of fostering trade. Berkeley fought Bacon for control of the colony, which he eventually regained.

Berkshire \'bərk-shər\ County (population 1998 est.: 800,200), southern England. Established in 1974, it occupies the valleys of the middle THAMES immediately west of LONDON; its capital is READING. Settlement of the area dates from the Iron Age, and the Belgic site at Silchester later became a Roman route center. With the NORMAN CONQUEST the Thames valley's strategic importance became recognized, and the first WINDSOR CASTLE was built. Windsor and ETON, on Berkshire's eastern boundary, contain the county's most noted structures. In 1998 it ceased to exist as an administrative county.

Berkshire Hills Segment of the APPALACHIAN MTNS., western Massachusetts. Many of its summits exceed 2,000 ft (600 m), including Mount Greylock (3,491 ft, or 1,064 m), the highest point in the state. The wooded hills are a continuation of the GREEN MTNS. of Vermont; they include the Hoosac and TACONIC RANGES. Crossed by the APPALACHIAN NATIONAL SCENIC TRAIL, the Berkshires contain state parks and forests and are the home of the Tanglewood summer music festival (in Lenox).

Berlage \'ber-läk-ə\, **Hendrik Petrus** (1856–1934) Dutch architect. After studies in Zurich, he began his practice in Amsterdam (1889). His best-known work is the Amsterdam Stock Exchange (1897–1903), notable for its forthright use of structural steel and traditional Dutch brickwork. While visiting the U.S. (1911), he was exposed to the work of LOUIS SULLIVAN and FRANK LLOYD WRIGHT and later introduced their methods and ideas to Europe. His work was characterized by the honest use of materials based on their fundamental properties and the avoidance of meaningless ornamentation.

Berle \'bərl\, **Milton** *orig.* **Milton Berlinger** (1908–2002) U.S. comedian. Born in New York City, he appeared in VAUDEVILLE from age 10 and later acted in over 50 silent films. He worked chiefly as a nightclub comedian (1939–49) while vainly seeking a radio audience, but his slapstick routines and facial contortions were more suited to a visual medium, and he appeared in 19 movies (1937–68). His greatest success came with the television variety show *Texaco Star Theater* (1948–54), later called *The Milton Berle Show* (1954–56, 1958–59), a show so popular that many people are said to have bought television sets just to watch "Uncle Miltie."

Berlin City and state (pop., 1999 est.: 3,392,900), capital of reunified Germany. Founded in the early 13th century, it was a member of the HANSEATIC LEAGUE in the 14th century. It became the residence of the HOHENZOLLERNS and the capital of BRANDENBURG. It was successively the capital of PRUSSIA (from 1701), of the German empire (1871–1918), of the WEIMAR REPUBLIC (1919–32), and of the THIRD REICH (1933–45). In World War II much of the city was destroyed by Allied bombing. In 1945 it was divided into four occupation zones: American, British, French, and Soviet. The three Western powers integrated their sectors into one economic entity in 1948; the Soviets responded with the BERLIN BLOCKADE. When independent governments were established in eastern and western Germany in 1949, East Berlin was made the capital of East Germany, and West Berlin, though surrounded by East Germany, became part of West Germany. Continuing immigration from East to West Berlin through the 1950s prompted the 1961 erection of the BERLIN WALL. The area immediately became the most vivid focal point of the COLD WAR. The dramatic dismantling of the wall in 1989 marked the international upheaval that accompanied the end of the Soviet Union. Berlin became reunified as Germany's official capital in 1991; the transfer of government from BONN was completed in 1999. It is the site of the University of BERLIN, Charlottenburg Palace, the BRANDENBURG GATE, and the Berlin Zoo, and is home to the Berlin Opera and the Berlin Philharmonic Orchestra.

Berlin, Congress of (1878) Diplomatic meeting of the major European powers at which the Treaty of Berlin replaced the Treaty of SAN STEFANO. Dominated by OTTO VON BISMARCK, the congress solved an international crisis by revising the peace settlement to satisfy the interests of Britain and Austria-Hungary. By humiliating Russia and failing to adequately acknowledge the aspirations of the Balkan peoples, it laid the foundation for future Balkan crises.

Berlin, Irving *orig.* **Israel Baline** (1888–1989) U.S. songwriter. He was born to the family of a Russian Jewish cantor that emigrated to New York in 1893. With only two years of formal education, he worked as a street singer and singing waiter. His first published song, "Marie from Sunny Italy," appeared in 1907; a printer's error named him Irving Berlin. Unable to read or write music, he learned and played by ear. In 1911 he wrote the great hit of TIN PAN ALLEY's RAGTIME vogue, "Alexander's Ragtime Band." In 1919 he founded the publishing house Irving Berlin Music Corp. He may have written more than 1,500 songs, including "Oh, How I Hate to Get Up in the Morning," "Always," "Cheek to Cheek," "Puttin' on the Ritz," and "God Bless America." His film scores include *Top Hat* (1935), *Easter Parade* (1948), and *White Christmas* (1954); his score for *Holiday Inn* (1942) introduced "White Christmas," one of the best-selling songs of all time. Altogether Berlin wrote the scores for 19 Broadway shows (including *Annie Get Your Gun,* 1946, and *Call Me Madam,* 1950) and 18 films. He died at 101.

Berlin, Isaiah *later* **Sir Isaiah** (1909–1997) British (Latvian-born) historian and writer. His family emigrated to Britain in 1920. Educated at Oxford Univ., Berlin taught there 1950–67, serving as president of Wolfson College 1966–75 and thereafter teaching at All Souls College. He is noted for his writings on political philosophy; his most important works include *Karl Marx* (1939), *The Hedgehog and the Fox* (1953), *Historical Inevitability* (1955), *The Age of Enlightenment* (1956), and *Four Essays on Liberty* (1969).

Berlin, University of *or* **Humboldt University of Berlin** Public university in Berlin, founded (as Friedrich Wilhelm Univ.) in 1809–10 by WILHELM, FREIHERR VON HUMBOLDT. By the mid-1800s it had attained world renown for its modern curriculum and its scientific research institutes. Among its faculty were G. W. F. HEGEL, JOHANN GOTTLIEB FICHTE, ARTHUR SCHOPENHAUER, LEOPOLD RANKE, HERMANN VON HELMHOLTZ, FRIEDRICH SCHLEIERMACHER, and JACOB AND WILHELM GRIMM. In the 1930s it was Nazified and many of its faculty fled abroad. Under the German Democratic Republic after World War II, it was renamed Humboldt-Universität and given a Marxist-Leninist orientation. It was reorganized after reunification in 1990. Total enrollment is about 37,600.

Berlin blockade and airlift (1948–49) International crisis that arose from an attempt by the Soviet Union to force the Allied powers (U.S., Britain, and France) to abandon their postwar jurisdictions in West Berlin. The Soviets, regarding the economic consolidation of the three Allied occupation zones in Germany in 1948 as a threat to the East German economy, blockaded all transportation routes between Berlin and West Germany. The U.S. and Britain responded by supplying the city with food and other supplies by military air transport and airlifting out West Berlin exports. An Allied embargo on exports from the Eastern bloc forced the Soviets to lift the blockade after 11 months.

Berlin Painter (fl. 500–460 BC) Greek vase painter, the outstanding vase painter of the late Archaic period. He is best known as the decorator of an amphora now in Berlin. Whereas it had been customary to frame the groups of figures on each side of the vase with pattern bands, the Berlin Painter eliminated the frame, allowing the figures to dominate and stand out sharply against the black background. Nearly 300 vases are attributed to him.

Berlin Wall Barrier surrounding West Berlin that closed off East Germans' access to West Berlin from 1961 to 1989 and served as a symbol of the COLD WAR's division of East and West Germany. The barrier was built in response to the flight of about 2.5 million East Germans to West Germany in the years 1949–61. First erected on the night of August 12–13, 1961, it developed into a system of concrete walls topped with barbed wire and guarded with watchtowers, gun emplacements, and mines. It was opened in the 1989 democratization that swept through Eastern Europe and has been largely torn down.

Berlin West Africa Conference Series of negotiations (1884–85) at Berlin in which the major European nations met to determine the future of central Africa. The participants declared the region to be neutral, guaranteed freedom of trade and shipping for all colonial powers, forbade slave trading, and recognized Belgium's interests in developing the independent Congo Free State.

Berlinguer \ˌber-lin-ˈgwer\, **Enrico** (1922–1984) Italian politician. Born into a middle-class Sardinian family, he joined the Communist Party in 1943 and held a series of party posts before becoming secretary-general in 1972, a post he would keep until his death. He became a leading advocate of "national communism," seeking independence from Moscow and favoring the adaptation of MARXISM to local requirements. His proposal for a coalition government of Christian Democrats and communists was never realized.

Berlioz \ˈber-lē-ˌōz\, **(Louis-) Hector** (1803–1869) French composer. He studied guitar in his early years, but had to fight to be permitted to study music seriously. His *Symphonie fantastique* (1830), written at 27 in the frenzy of an infatuation, had a stormy premiere and became a landmark of the Romantic era. He became a brilliant conductor, with an unsurpassed knowledge of the orchestra. Impulsive and passionate, he was a contentious critic and gadfly constantly at war with the musical establishment. Though he was the most compelling French musical figure of his time, his idiosyncratic compositional style kept almost all his music out of the repertory until the mid-20th century. His works include the operas *Benvenuto Cellini* (1837), *Les Troyens* (1858), and *Béatrice et Bénédict* (1862); the program symphonies *Harold in Italy* (1834) and *Romeo and Juliet* (1839); and the choral *Requiem* (1837), *La damnation de Faust* (1846), *Te Deum* (1849), and *L'enfance du Christ* (1854). His orchestration treatise (1843) is the most influential such work ever written, and his memoirs (1870) were widely read.

Berlusconi, Silvio (born 1936) Italian media tycoon and prime minister in 1994 and from 2001. After graduating from the University of Milan, he became a real estate developer, amassing a considerable fortune by the 1970s. By the 1990s, he owned more than 150 businesses, including three television networks and Italy's largest publishing house. In 1994, he founded Forza Italia, a conservative political party, and was elected prime minister. Faced with conflict of interest and other charges, he resigned in December 1994. He was later convicted of fraud and corruption, though he was acquitted of tax evasion. Despite the convictions and criticism of his control of much of the Italian media, he remained the leader of Forza Italia and again became prime minister in 2001.

Bermejo \ber-ˈmā-hō\, **Bartolomé** *or* **Bartolomé de Cárdenas** \ˈkär-dā-näs\ (c. 1440–1495) Spanish painter. He was active in Valencia (1468) and Aragon, and in Barcelona from 1486. His earliest masterpiece is the panel painting *Santo Domingo de Silos* (1474). His signed and dated *Pietà* (1490) in Barcelona Cathedral is considered a masterpiece of early Spanish oil painting; the influence of ROGIER VAN DER WEYDEN can be seen in the rich detail and color. Bermejo cultivated the Flemish style and was considered the most outstanding painter in Spain before El GRECO.

Bermejo River \ber-ˈmā-hō\ River, northern Argentina. Rising on the Bolivian frontier, it flows southeast 650 mi (1,045 km) into the PARAGUAY RIVER on the Paraguay–Argentina border. The abundant silt it carries in suspension is the source of its name (meaning "reddish"). It is navigable for small craft along its central course, known as the Teuco.

Bermuda British colony (pop., 1995 est.: 58,000), western Atlantic Ocean. Comprising about 300 islands, of which only some 20 are inhabited, it lies about 640 mi (1,030 km) southeast of Cape HATTERAS, N.C. The archipelago has a total land area of about 20 sq mi (52 sq km). Its capital is HAMILTON, on Bermuda Island. It was named for Juan de Bermúdez, who may have visited the islands in 1503. Colonized by the English in 1612, Bermuda became a crown colony in 1684. Its economy is based on tourism and international finance; its per-capita gross national product is among the world's highest.

Bermuda Triangle Triangular area, Atlantic Ocean, whose apexes are usually said to be BERMUDA, MIAMI, Fla., and SAN JUAN, Puerto Rico. It has been the site of numerous disappearances of planes and ships, and various abandoned ships have been discovered there. Reports of unexplained occurrences in the region date to the mid-19th century. Non-supernatural explanations cite the area's violent freak storms, the local turbulence of the GULF STREAM, and the quickly shifting topology of the area's seabed. It is also one of the rare regions where magnetic north coincides with true north, which could disorient inexperienced pilots.

Bern City (pop., 1996: 127,000; metro area pop.: 320,000), capital of Switzerland. Lying along a loop of the AARE RIVER, it was founded as a military post in 1191 by Berthold V, duke of Zähringen. It became a free imperial city in 1218. Gradually extending its power, it became an independent state, and in 1353 it entered the Swiss Confederation. It was a scene of disputation in 1528 between Roman Catholics and reformers, which led to its subsequent championing of Protestant doctrines. It became a member of the Helvetic Republic, and in 1848 was made the capital of Switzerland. It is headquarters of the international postal, railway, and copyright unions.

Bern Convention *officially* **International Convention for the Protection of Literary and Artistic Works** International agreement adopted in Bern, Switzerland, in 1886 to protect COPYRIGHTS on an international basis. It was modified several times throughout the 20th century. Its signatories constitute the Bern Copyright Union. Each member country grants the authors of other member countries the same rights that its laws grant its own nationals. Protected works include every kind of literary, scientific, and artistic production, regardless of mode of expression, including paintings, sculpture, architectural plans, and musical arrangements. Copyright is now protected for 70 years after the creator's death.

Bernadette of Lourdes, St. *orig.* **Marie-Bernarde Soubirous** (1844–1879) French visionary. The daughter of a miller, she had a poverty-stricken childhood and was often ill. In 1858 she had a series of visions of Mary; she defended their authenticity against the doubts of her parents, the clergy, and civil authorities. She joined the Sisters of Charity at Nevers (1866) and remained in seclusion until her death at 35. The grotto at LOURDES became a pilgrimage site; its waters are reputed to have healing powers. Bernadette was canonized in 1933.

Bernadotte (af Wisborg) \ber-nȧ-ˈdȯt\, **Folke, Greve (Count)** (1895–1948) Swedish soldier, humanitarian, and diplomat. A nephew of King GUSTAV V, Bernadotte headed the Swedish Red Cross in World War II and was credited with saving some 20,000 concentration-camp inmates. In 1948 he was appointed mediator in Palestine by the U.N. Security Council and secured a cease-fire between Israel and the Arab states. He made enemies by proposing that Arab refugees be allowed to return to their homes in what had become Israel, and was assassinated by Jewish extremists.

Bernanos \ber-nȧ-ˈnōs\, **Georges** (1888–1948) French novelist and polemical writer. One of the most original and independent Roman Catholic writers of his time and a man of humor and humanity, he abhorred materialism and compromise with evil. His masterpiece, *The Diary of a Country Priest* (1936), is the story of a young priest's war against sin. *Dialogues of the Carmélites* (1949), a screenplay about 16 nuns martyred during the French Revolution, was the basis for an opera by FRANCIS POULENC (1957).

Bernard \ber-ˈnär\, **Claude** (1813–1878) French physiologist. He taught at several major French institutions, and was named a senator in 1869. He discovered the role of the pancreas in digestion, the glycogenic function of the liver in carbohydrate metabolism, and blood-supply regulation by the vasomotor nerves. He helped establish the principles of experimentation in the life sciences, including the need for a hypothesis to be confirmed or refuted. His concept of the internal environment of the organism led to the present understanding of HOMEOSTASIS. Bernard also studied the effects of such poisons as carbon monoxide and curare. He was awarded the grand prize in physiology three times by the Académie des Sciences.

Bernard de Clairvaux \kler-ˈvō\, **St.** (1090–1153) French CISTERCIAN monk mystic, and Doctor of the Church. Born into an aristocratic family near Dijon, he turned away from a literary education for a life of renunciation, entering an austere religious community at Cîteaux in 1112. He established an abbey at Clairvaux, Champagne, in 1115, and served as its abbot. Between 1130 and 1145 he mediated civil and ecclesiastical councils and theological debates; he was the confidant of five popes and became perhaps the most renowned religious figure in Europe. He opposed the rationalism of PETER ABELARD and defended the cult of the Virgin Mary.

Bernardine See Cistercian

Bernardine of Siena, St. \'bər-nər-dēn\ (1380–1444) Franciscan priest and theologian. Born into a noble family but orphaned early, he entered the Observants (1402), a strict branch of the Franciscan order that he later helped to spread throughout Europe. In 1417 he began preaching tours in Italy, seeking to combat the lawlessness, strife, and immorality resulting from the Western Schism. Through the Council of Florence he worked to unite the Greek and Roman churches. Numerous miracles are said to have occurred at his tomb.

Bernays, Edward L. (1891–1995) U.S. publicist, the "father of public relations." A nephew of Sigmund Freud, he was born in Vienna but brought up in New York. In organizing endorsements for a play on the taboo subject of venereal disease, he found his calling as a publicist. His early clients included the U.S. War Department and the Lithuanian government. He took credit for persuading women to smoke in public, boasted that his books were favored by the Nazi propagandist Joseph Goebbels, and claimed to have convinced the U.S. government to overthrow Guatemala's elected government in 1954. He edited *The Engineering of Consent* (1955), whose title is his often-quoted definition of public relations. He died at the age of 103.

Berners-Lee, Tim (born 1955) British physicist. The son of computer scientists, he graduated from Oxford University and in 1980 accepted a fellowship at CERN in Geneva. In 1989 he suggested a global hypertext project. He and his CERN colleagues created a communications protocol called HyperText Transfer Protocol (HTTP) that standardized communication between computer servers and clients. Their text-based Web browser was released to the public in 1991, marking the beginnings of the World Wide Web and general public use of the Internet. He declined all opportunities to profit from his immensely valuable innovation. In 1994 he joined MIT's Laboratory for Computer Science as director of the World Wide Web Consortium.

Bernese Alps *German* **Berner Oberland** \ˌbər-nər-'ō-bər-ˌlänt\ Segment of the Alps, Switzerland. Lying north of the Rhone River and south of the Brienzersee and Thunersee, the mountains extend east from Martigny-Ville to Grimsel Pass and the valley of the upper Aare River. Many peaks, including the Finsteraarhorn, Jungfrau, and Aletschhorn, rise to more than 12,000 ft (3,660 m). They are crossed by the Lötschen, Gemmi, and Pillon passes and the Lötschberg railway tunnel. Many resorts, including Interlaken, Grindelwald, and Gstaad, dot the area.

Bernese mountain dog Breed of Swiss working dog brought to Switzerland over 2,000 years ago by invading Romans. The hardy breed was widely used to pull carts and to drive cattle to and from their pastures. It has a broad chest, hanging V-shaped ears, and a long, silky, black coat. Markings include brown spots on the chest and forelegs and over the eyes, and sometimes white on the chest, nose, feet, and tail tip. The breed stands 21–28 in. (53–70 cm) high and weighs about 90 lbs (40 kg).

Bernhard \'bern-ˌhärt\ (born 1911) Prince of the Netherlands. Born in Germany, the son of Prince Bernhard Casimir of Lippe-Biesterfeld, in 1937 Bernhard married the Dutch crown princess Juliana and took Dutch citizenship. He opposed Germany's invasion of the Netherlands and took his family to Britain after the Dutch surrender (1940). In World War II he served as the Dutch liaison with the British armed forces, flew with the Royal Air Force (1942–44), and led Dutch troops in the Allied offensive in the Netherlands (1945). After the war and Juliana's accession as queen (1948–80), he became the Netherlands' goodwill ambassador.

Bernhardi \'bern-ˌhär-dē\, **Friedrich von** (1849–1930) German soldier and military writer. He fought in the Franco–Prussian War and became commander of the Seventh Army corps in 1909. In 1911 he published *Germany and the Next War*, arguing that Germany had a right and responsibility to wage war to gain the power it deserved. The Allies later considered his book a contributing cause of World War I, in which Bernhardi served as a corps commander.

Bernhardt \ber-'när, *Engl* 'bərn-ˌhärt\, **Sarah** *orig.* **Henriette-Rosine Bernard** (1844–1923) French actress. The illegitimate child of a courtesan, she was encouraged in a theatrical career by one of her mother's lovers, the duc de Morny. After a brief appearance at the Comédie-Française (1862–63), she joined the Odéon Theatre (1866–72), where she acted in Alexandre Dumas's *Kean* and Victor Hugo's *Ruy Blas*, charming audiences with her "golden voice." Returning to the Comédie-Française (1872–80), she starred in *Phèdre* to great acclaim in Paris and London. She formed her own company in 1880 and toured the world in *La dame aux camélias* by Alexandre Dumas (*fils*), *Adrienne Lecouvreur*, four plays written for her by Victorien Sardou, and Edmond Rostand's *L'aiglon*. After an injury to her leg forced its amputation (1915), she strapped on a wooden leg and chose roles she could play largely seated. One of the best-known figures in the history of the stage, she was made a member of France's Legion of Honor in 1914.

Sarah Bernhardt, photograph by Napoleon Sarony, 1880.

BY COURTESY OF THE LIBRARY OF CONGRESS, WASHINGTON, D.C.

Bernicia \ber-'ni-shə\ Ancient northern Anglo-Saxon kingdom. It stretched northward from perhaps as far south as the River Tees, ultimately reaching the Firth of Forth. By the end of the 7th century AD it had united with its neighbor Deira to form the kingdom of Northumbria. It had a royal residence at coastal Bamburgh. The first recorded king, Ida, was crowned there in 547; his grandson Aethelfrith (r.593–616) united Bernicia and Deira.

Bernini, Gian Lorenzo (1598–1680) Italian architect and artist credited with the invention of baroque sculpture. He began his career working for his father, a sculptor. Among his early sculptures are *Apollo and Daphne* (1622–24) and an active *David* (1623–24). Under the patronage of Urban VIII, the first of eight popes he was to serve, he created the baldachin over the tomb of St. Peter in Rome. He was appointed architect of St. Peter's Basilica and the Palazzo Barberini in 1629. His works often represent a fusion of architecture and sculpture, as in the Cornaro Chapel, in Santa Maria della Vittoria, Rome, with its celebrated theatrical sculpture *The Ecstasy of St. Teresa* (1645–52). His greatest architectural achievement is the colonnade enclosing the piazza before St. Peter's. Among his many other contributions to Rome are his marble fountains, noted for their architectural composition and detail.

"Apollo and Daphne," marble sculpture by Gian Lorenzo Bernini, 1622–24; in the Borghese Gallery, Rome.

SCALA/ART RESOURCE, NEW YORK CITY

Bernoulli family \ber-'nü-lē\ Two generations of distinguished Swiss mathematicians. Jakob (1655–1705) and Johann (1667–1748) were the sons of a pharmacist who wanted one boy to study theology and the other medicine. Over his objections, both pursued careers in mathematics, making important discoveries in calculus, the calculus of variations, and differential equations. They sometimes worked together, but not without friction. Johann's son Daniel (1700–1782) made important contributions to fluid dynamics (see Bernoulli's principle) and probability theory. Widely admired throughout Europe, he also studied and lectured on medicine, physics, astronomy, and botany.

Bernoulli's principle *or* **Bernoulli's theorem** Principle that relates pressure, velocity, and height for a nonviscous fluid with steady flow. A consequence is that, for horizontal flow, as the speed of a fluid increases, the pressure it exerts decreases. Derived by Daniel Bernoulli (see Bernoulli family), the principle explains the lift of an airplane in motion. As the speed of the plane increases, air flows faster over the curved top of the wing than underneath. The upward pressure exerted by the air under the wing is thus greater than the pressure exerted downward above the wing, resulting in a net upward force, or lift. Race cars use the principle to keep their wheels pressed to the ground as they accelerate. A race car's spoiler—shaped like an upside-down wing, with the curved surface at the bottom—produces a net downward force.

Bernstein \'bern-shtīn\, **Eduard** (1850–1932) German politician and writer. He joined the German SOCIAL DEMOCRATIC PARTY in 1872, then spent years in exile as an editor of socialist journals. In London he met FRIEDRICH ENGELS and was influenced by the FABIAN SOCIETY. Returning to Germany in 1901, Bernstein became the political theorist of the revisionists and was one of the first socialists to modify such Marxist tenets as the imminent collapse of capitalism. He envisaged a type of social democracy that combined private initiative with social reform. As a member of the Reichstag (1902–6, 1912–16, 1920–28), he inspired much of the reformist programs of the Social Democrats.

Bernstein \'bərn-stīn\, **Elmer** (born 1922) U.S. composer. Born in New York City and trained at Juilliard, a student of Stefan Wolpe (1902–1972) and R. SESSIONS, he started working in radio after World War II. He is known for his outstanding film music, often employing a jazz idiom. His scores include *The Man with the Golden Arm* (1955), *The Magnificent Seven* (1960), *Walk on the Wild Side* (1962), *Thoroughly Modern Millie* (1967, Academy Award), *True Grit* (1969), *Ghostbusters* (1984), and *The Grifters* (1990).

Bernstein, Leonard (1918–1990) U.S. conductor, composer, and writer. Born in Lawrence, Mass., he resolved on a music career only after graduating from Harvard University. After studying conducting at the Curtis Institute with FRITZ REINER, he became a fixture at Tanglewood (in Lenox, Mass.), where he met A. COPLAND and became S. KOUSSEVITZKY's assistant. Fame came abruptly when he substituted on short notice at a concert broadcast in 1943. In 1944 he triumphed with his music for JEROME ROBBINS's ballet *Fancy Free* and the hit Broadway show *On the Town*. As conductor, his closest associations were with the Israel, New York, and Vienna Philharmonics; he premiered much contemporary music and was instrumental in the G. MAHLER revival. His best-known composition was the hit musical *West Side Story* (1957); other works include the musicals *Wonderful Town* (1952) and *Candide* (1956), three symphonies, the *Chichester Psalms* (1965), and the theatrical *Mass* (1971). Well known as a television lecturer, he was also a prominent political activist.

Leonard Bernstein.
LAUTERWASSER, COURTESY DEUTSCHE GRAMMOPHON

Bernstorff \'bern-shtȯrf\, **Johann-Heinrich, Graf (Count) von** (1862–1939) German diplomat. After entering the diplomatic service (1899), he represented Germany in London and Cairo before serving as ambassador to the U.S. (1908–17). During World War I he worked to facilitate mediation of the conflict by WOODROW WILSON but did not receive the support he expected from authorities in Berlin. He served as chairman of the German League of Nations Union until 1933, when he went into exile in Geneva.

Berra \'ber-ə\, **Yogi** *orig.* **Lawrence Peter** (born 1925) U.S. baseball player, manager, and coach. Born in St. Louis, he joined the New York Yankees in 1946 and served as the team's regular catcher from 1949 until his retirement in 1963. He was named the American League's Most Valuable Player in 1951, 1954, and 1955. He caught in more World Series games (75) than any other catcher, and hit 20 or more home runs a season through 1958. He managed the Yankees in 1964, but was fired and became a coach and manager (1965–75) with the New York Mets. He returned to the Yankees as a coach (1976–82) and later manager (1983–85). He was known for idiosyncratic remarks such as "It ain't over till it's over," and the cartoon character Yogi Bear was named for him.

Berrigan, Daniel (Joseph) and Philip (Francis) (born 1921, 1923) U.S. activist priests. Born in Two Harbors, Minn., the brothers both became Catholic priests (Daniel a Jesuit, Philip a Josephite). They soon became involved in nonviolent activism, carrying out campaigns of civil disobedience to oppose racism, nuclear war, and the Vietnam War. They are best known for their Vietnam-era raid of draft-board files in Catonsville, Md., which they destroyed with chicken blood and napalm. They are also known for the persistence of their activism, which continues to the present, though Philip later left the priesthood. Both have written numerous books on their work and beliefs; Daniel has written poetry and plays as well.

Berruguete \ˌber-ü-'gā-tā\, **Pedro** *or* **Pedro Español** *or* **Pietro Spagnuolo** \ˌspän-yə-'wō-lō\ (c. 1450–c. 1500) Spanish painter. After a sojourn in Italy, he returned to Spain, where he painted numerous altarpieces and also worked as a fresco painter in Toledo Cathedral from 1483. The influence of Flemish and Italian art is evident in his panel paintings, which are characterized by luxurious ornament and gold decoration. He was his country's first great Renaissance painter. His son Alonso (c. 1488–1561), a sculptor and painter, worked in Florence and Rome c. 1508–16. In 1516 he returned to Spain, and in 1518 he became court painter to CHARLES V, but succeeded primarily as a sculptor. His best-known work is a set of wooden reliefs with highly expressive figures for choir stalls in Toledo Cathedral (1539–43). He is considered the greatest Spanish sculptor of the 16th century.

Berry \be-'rē\ Historical region and former province, central France. It was originally inhabited by the Bituriges Cubi, who opposed VERCINGETORIX. Under Roman rule it was part of Aquitania Prima. A countship in the Carolingian period, it fell to the French crown in the 11th century. When AQUITAINE was acquired by HENRY II of England, Berry became a matter of dispute between England and France. As a duchy, at one time it came under Jean de France, duc de Berry, an important patron of the arts. It returned to France in 1601 and remained a province until 1798.

berry Simple, fleshy FRUIT that usually has many seeds (e.g., the BANANA, TOMATO, or CRANBERRY). The middle and inner layers of the fruit wall often are not distinct from each other. Any small, fleshy fruit is popularly called a berry, especially if it is edible. RASPBERRIES, BLACKBERRIES, and STRAWBERRIES are not true berries, but rather aggregate fruits—fruits that consist of multiple smaller fruits. The DATE is a one-seeded berry whose stone is hard nutritive tissue.

Berry, Chuck *orig.* **Charles Edward Anderson** (born 1926) U.S. singer-songwriter, one of the first to shape big-beat BLUES into what came to be called rock and roll (see ROCK MUSIC) and to achieve widespread popularity with white audiences. Though first interested in country music, in the early 1950s Berry led a blues trio that played in black nightclubs around his native St. Louis. In 1955 he traveled to Chicago and made his first hit record, "Maybellene," which was soon followed by "Sweet Little Sixteen," "Johnny B. Goode," "Rock and Roll Music," and "Roll Over, Beethoven." In 1959 he began a five-year prison sentence for immoral behavior, and in 1979 he was convicted of income-tax evasion. He was the subject of the documentary *Hail! Hail! Rock and Roll* (1987). He continued to perform into the 1990s.

Berry \be-'rē\, **duc (Duke) de** *orig.* **Charles-Ferdinand de Bourbon** (1778–1820) French nobleman. Son of the future CHARLES X, he left France at the outbreak of the French Revolution and lived abroad until 1815. His assassination by a Bonapartist fanatic marked a turning point in the BOURBON RESTORATION, hastening the downfall of the moderate Decazes government and the polarization into liberal and royalist groups.

Berry, Jean de France, duc de (1340–1416) French nobleman and patron of the arts. Son of King JOHN II of France, as duke of Berry and Auvergne he controlled at least one-third of France during the middle period of the HUNDRED YEARS' WAR. Berry shared in the administration of France and worked for peace with England and within France, acting as diplomat and mediator. He invested fortunes in the art treasures that became his monument—paintings, tapestries, jewelry, and illuminated manuscripts that included the famous *Très riches heures du duc de Berry*.

John Berryman.
BY COURTESY OF THE UNIVERSITY OF MINNESOTA

Berryman, John (1914–1972) U.S. poet. Born in McAlester, Okla., he attended Columbia and Cambridge Univs. and later taught at various universities. *Homage to Mistress Bradstreet* (1956), one of his first experimental poems, assured his importance. His technical daring was also evident in *77 Dream Songs* (1964, Pulitzer Prize), augmented to form a sequence of 385 "Dream Songs" by *His Toy, His Dream, His Rest* (1968). Later works include the deceptively offhand *Love & Fame* (1970) and *Recovery* (1973), an account of his struggle against alcoholism. He is noted for his confessional poetry laced with humor. Subject to deep depression, he committed suicide by jumping from a bridge.

berserkers *Old Norse* **beserkr** ("bearskin") In premedieval and medieval Norse and Germanic history and folklore, unruly warrior gangs that worshiped ODIN and attached themselves to royal and noble courts as bodyguards and shock troops. They raped and murdered at will in their host communities, and their savagery in battle and animal-skin attire contributed to the development of the WEREWOLF legend in Europe.

Bert \'ber\, **Paul** (1833–1886) French physiologist, founder of modern AEROSPACE MEDICINE. He taught many years at the Sorbonne, and served as a deputy in the government 1872–86. His research on the effects of air pressure on the body helped make possible the exploration of space and the ocean depths. Bert found the main cause of altitude sickness to be low atmospheric oxygen content and showed decompression sickness to be due to nitrogen bubbles formed in the blood during rapid drops in external pressure.

Bertelsmann AG German media company. Beginning as a religious printer and publisher in 1835, the company grew steadily over the next century. Though virtually destroyed by Allied bombing in 1945, it recovered quickly after World War II. By 1998 Bertelsmann AG had grown to include more than 300 media companies, with more than half its employees in countries other than Germany. Its worldwide acquisitions have included the U.S. publishers Bantam Doubleday Dell and RANDOM HOUSE. By 2000 the company claimed to be the world's third-largest media conglomerate.

Berthelot \ber-tə-'lō\, **(Pierre-Eugène-) Marcellin** (1827–1907) French chemist. The first professor of organic chemistry at the Collège de France (from 1865), he later also held high government offices, including that of foreign minister (1895–96). He did research in ALCOHOLS and CARBOXYLIC ACIDS, the synthesis of HYDROCARBONS, and REACTION RATES, studied the mechanism of explosion, discovered many coal-tar derivatives, and wrote on the history of early chemistry. He was a pioneer in the use of chemical analysis as a tool of archaeology. His work helped break down the traditional division between organic and inorganic compounds. He opposed the then-current idea that a "vital force" is responsible for synthesis and was one of the first to prove that all chemical phenomena depend on physical forces that can be measured.

Berthoud \ber-'tü\, **Ferdinand** (1727–1807) Swiss-French clockmaker and writer on timekeeping. Working in Paris from 1748, his inventiveness and many publications soon made him influential. His interest in the problem of determining longitude at sea (see LATITUDE AND LONGITUDE) led to his major achievement, an improved, less expensive marine CHRONOMETER. Berthoud's improvements were retained in modern instruments. See also JOHN HARRISON.

Bertoia \bər-'tȯi-ə\, **Harry** (1915–1978) Italian-U.S. sculptor and designer. He attended the Cranbrook Academy of Art and later taught there (1937–43). He worked in California with CHARLES EAMES before joining Knoll Associates in New York in 1950. He achieved notoriety with the Bertoia chair, made of polished steel wire with elastic Naugahyde upholstery. He also produced "sound sculptures" that were activated by the wind and numerous works for corporations and public spaces.

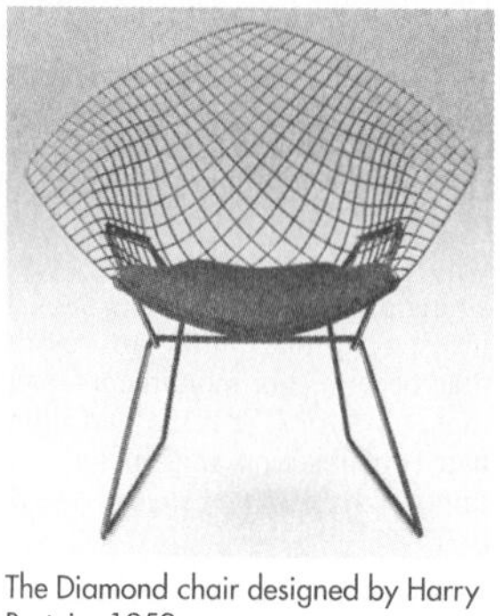

The Diamond chair designed by Harry Bertoia, 1952.

BY COURTESY OF THE KNOLL GROUP

Bertolucci \ˌber-tə-'lü-chē\, **Bernardo** (born 1940) Italian film director. After writing poetry and an award-winning book, he entered filmmaking as an assistant to PIER PAOLO PASOLINI in 1961. His first films as a director, *The Grim Reaper* (1962) and *Before the Revolution* (1964), were followed by the well-received *The Spider's Stratagem* and *The Conformist* (1970). The erotic *Last Tango in Paris* (1972) made him an international and commercial sensation. He later directed such films as *1900* (1976), *The Last Emperor* (1987, Academy Award), *Little Buddha* (1994), *Stealing Beauty* (1996), and *Besieged* (1998).

beryl \'ber-əl\ Mineral composed of beryllium aluminum silicate, $Be_3Al_2(SiO_3)_6$, a commercial source of BERYLLIUM. Several varieties are valued as gemstones: AQUAMARINE (pale blue-green); EMERALD (deep green); heliodor (golden yellow); and morganite (pink). Before 1925 beryl was used only as a gemstone, but since then many important uses have been found for beryllium (e.g., in nuclear reactors, space vehicles, and X-ray tubes). No large deposits have been found, and most production is a by-product of the mining of feldspar and mica. Brazil is a major producer; others include Zimbabwe, South Africa, Namibia, and the U.S.

beryllium \bə-'ril-ē-əm\ Chemical ELEMENT, lightest of the ALKALINE EARTH METALS, chemical symbol Be, atomic number 4. It does not occur uncombined in nature but chiefly as the mineral BERYL (of which emerald and aquamarine are gemstone varieties). Beryllium METAL, particularly in ALLOYS, has many structural and thermal applications; it is used in nuclear reactors. Beryllium has VALENCE 2 in all its compounds, which are generally colorless and taste distinctly sweet. All soluble beryllium compounds are toxic. Beryllium oxide is used in specialized ceramics for nuclear devices, and beryllium chloride is a CATALYST for organic reactions.

Jöns Jacob Berzelius, detail of an oil painting by Olof Johan Södermark, 1843; in the Royal Swedish Academy of Sciences, Stockholm.

BY COURTESY OF SVENSKA PORTRATTARKIVET, STOCKHOLM

Berzelius \ber-'sā-lē-əs\, **Jöns Jacob** *later* **Baron Berzelius** (1779–1848) Swedish chemist. As a professor in Stockholm (1807–32) he achieved an immensely important series of innovations and discoveries. He is especially noted for his intruduction of basic laboratory equipment that remains in use today; his determination of ATOMIC WEIGHTS; his creation of the modern system of CHEMICAL SYMBOLS; his theory of ELECTROCHEMISTRY; his discovery of the elements CERIUM, SELENIUM, and thorium and his isolation of SILICON, ZIRCONIUM, and TITANIUM; his contribution to the classical techniques of ANALYSIS; and his investigations of ISOMERISM and CATALYSIS, both of which he named. He published more than 250 original research papers. He is regarded as one of the founders of modern chemistry.

Bes Minor Egyptian god with a grotesque appearance. His figure was intended to inspire joy or drive away pain and sorrow, and his ugliness was probably thought to frighten off evil spirits. He was associated with music and childbirth. The name Bes is now used to designate a group of deities of similar appearance with various ancient names.

Bes represented as a dwarf, statue; in the Louvre.

GIRAUDON—ART RESOURCE

Besant \'be-sᵊnt\, **Annie** *orig.* **Annie Wood** (1847–1933) British social reformer. She was a prominent Fabian socialist in the 1880s before becoming an adherent of THEOSOPHY in 1889. She served as international president of the Theosophical Society from 1907 until her death, and her writings are still considered some of the best expositions of theosophical belief. After emigrating to India, she became an Indian independence leader and established the Indian Home Rule League in 1916.

Bessarabia \ˌbe-sə-ˈrā-bē-ə\ Region, eastern Europe. It is bounded by the Prut and DNIESTER rivers, the BLACK SEA, and the DANUBE RIVER delta. Greek colonies were founded on its Black Sea coast in the 7th century BC, and it was probably part of DACIA in the 2nd century AD. It became part of MOLDAVIA in the 15th century; the Turks later annexed the southern portion into the Ottoman empire. The remainder fell to them in the 16th century when Moldavia submitted to the Turks; Bessarabia remained under Turkish control until the 19th century. Russia acquired it and half of Moldavia in 1812 and retained control until World War I. A nationalist movement developed, and after the RUSSIAN REVOLUTION IN 1917 Bessarabia declared its independence and voted to unite with Romania. The Soviet Union never recognized Romania's right to the province and in 1940 demanded that it cede Bessarabia; when Romania complied, the U.S.S.R. set up the Moldavian Soviet Socialist Republic (see MOLDOVA), and incorporated the northern region into the Ukrainian S.S.R. Bessarabia remained divided after Ukraine and Moldavia declared independence in 1991.

Bessel \ˈbe-səl\, **Friedrich Wilhelm** (1784–1846) German astronomer. He was the first to measure (by means of parallax) the distance to a star other than the sun. One of his major discoveries was that the bright stars Sirius and Procyon make tiny motions explainable only by the existence of invisible companions disturbing their motions. His observation of tiny irregularities in the orbit of Uranus, which he concluded were caused by an unknown planet beyond, led to the discovery of Neptune. His mathematical functions for studying planetary motions became widely used in solving a wide range of differential equations.

Friedrich Wilhelm Bessel, engraving by E. Mandel after a painting by Franz Wolf.

THE BETTMANN ARCHIVE

Bessemer process Technique for converting pig iron to steel invented by HENRY BESSEMER in England in 1856 and brought by him into commercial production in 1860. Air blown through liquid pig iron in a refractory-lined converter oxidizes the carbon and silicon in the iron. Heat released by the oxidation keeps the metal molten. R.F. MUSHET contributed the technique for deoxidizing the converted metal that made the process a success. WILLIAM KELLY conducted experiments with an air-blown converter between 1856 and 1860 in Kentucky and Pennsylvania, but failed to make steel. ALEXANDER L. HOLLEY built the first successful Bessemer steel plant in the U.S. in 1865. High-volume production of low-cost steel in Britain and the U.S. by the Bessemer process soon revolutionized building construction and provided steel to replace iron in railroad rails and many other uses. The Bessemer process was eventually superseded by the OPEN-HEARTH PROCESS. See also BASIC BESSEMER PROCESS.

Henry Bessemer, detail of an oil painting by Rudolf Lehmann; in the Iron and Steel Institute, London.

BY COURTESY OF THE IRON AND STEEL INSTITUTE, LONDON; PHOTOGRAPH, THE SCIENCE MUSEUM, LONDON

Bessemer, Henry *later* **Sir Henry** (1813–1898) British inventor and engineer. Son of a metallurgist, he set up his own casting business at 17. At that time the only iron-based construction materials were CAST IRON and WROUGHT IRON. So-called steel was made by adding CARBON to pure forms of wrought iron (see WOOTZ); the resulting material was used almost entirely for cutting tools. During the Crimean War Bessemer worked to devise a stronger cast iron for cannon. The result was a process for the inexpensive production of large, slag-free ingots of steel as workable as any wrought iron. He eventually also discovered how to remove excess oxygen from the iron. The BESSEMER PROCESS (1856) led to the development of the Bessemer converter. See also BASIC BESSEMER PROCESS, R.F. MUSHET, PUDDLING PROCESS.

Bessey, Charles E(dwin) (1845–1915) U.S. botanist. Born in Ohio, he taught at Iowa State Agricultural College (1870–84) before joining the faculty of the University of Nebraska. By then he had so developed the experimental study of plant morphology that the recently founded university immediately became one of the nation's outstanding centers for botanical research. He wrote widely popular textbooks that dominated U.S. botanical instruction for more than 50 years.

Charles E. Bessey, c. 1910.

COURTESY OF HUNT INSTITUTE FOR BOTANICAL DOCUMENTATION, CARNEGIE MELLON UNIVERSITY, PITTSBURGH, PA.

Besson \bes-ˈō^{n}\, **Jacques** (1540–1576) French engineer. His improvements in the LATHE were of great importance in the development of the MACHINE-TOOL industry and of scientific instrumentation. His designs, published in 1569, introduced CAMS and templates (patterns used to guide the form of a piece being made) to the screw-cutting lathe, thus increasing the operator's control of tool and workpiece and permitting production of more accurate and intricate work in metal. He also improved the drive and feed mechanism of the ornamental lathe and described a more efficient form of WATERWHEEL, considered a prototype of the water TURBINE.

Best, Charles H(erbert) (1899–1978) U.S.-Canadian physiologist. Born in West Pembroke, Me., he was a professor and administrator at the University of Toronto 1929–67. With FREDERICK BANTING, he was first to obtain a pancreatic extract of INSULIN in a form useful for controlling DIABETES MELLITUS (1921). He did not share Banting's and J. J. R. MACLEOD's 1923 Nobel Prize because he did not yet have his MD degree. Best also discovered the vitamin choline and the enzyme histaminase, and introduced anticoagulants to treat thrombosis.

bestiary Medieval European work in verse or prose, often illustrated, consisting of a collection of stories, each based on a description of certain qualities of the subject, usually an animal or a plant. The stories were allegories, used for moral and religious instruction and admonition. They ultimately were derived from the Greek *Physiologus*, a text compiled by an unknown author before the mid-2nd century AD. Many traditional attributes of real or mythical creatures derive from bestiaries, such as the phoenix's burning itself to be born again and the parental love of the pelican, which, believed to feed its young by gashing its own breast, became a symbol of Christ.

beta-blocker \ˈbā-tə\ *in full* **beta-adrenergic blocking agent** Any of a class of synthetic drugs used to treat a wide range of diseases and conditions of the sympathetic NERVOUS SYSTEM (see AUTONOMIC NERVOUS SYSTEM). They block beta-adrenergic receptors in HEART and other smooth MUSCLE cells, which respond to EPINEPHRINE by causing excitation of the sympathetic nervous system. By preventing that excitation, beta-blockers are useful in controlling ANXIETY, HYPERTENSION, and a variety of heart conditions (see HEART DISEASE). They reduce the risk of a second MYOCARDIAL INFARCTION.

beta decay Any of three processes of radioactive disintegration in which a beta particle is spontaneously emitted by an unstable atomic NUCLEUS in order to dissipate excess energy. Beta particles are either ELECTRONS or POSITRONS. The three beta-decay processes are electron emission, positron emission, and electron capture. The process of beta decay increases or decreases the positive charge of the original nucleus by one unit without changing the mass number. Though beta decay is in general a slower process than GAMMA or ALPHA decay, beta particles can penetrate hundreds of times farther than alpha particles. Beta decay HALF-LIVES are a few milliseconds or more. See also RADIOACTIVITY.

Betancourt \ˌbe-ˌtän-ˈkůr\, **Rómulo** (1908–1981) President of Venezuela (1945–48, 1959–64). As a youth he was active against the dictatorial regime of Juan Vincente Gómez (1857/64–1935). After a brief period in the Communist Party, he turned against it and helped found the left-wing anticommunist party Acción Democrática, which came to power in 1945 after a coup. As provisional president, he pursued a policy of moderate social reform before resigning to permit election of a successor. Elected to a second term in 1959, he steered a middle course between pro-Cuban Communists and frightened conservatives, initiating an ambitious public-works program and fostering industrial development, mostly financed by Venezuela's vast oil exports. He retired in 1964.

betel \ˈbē-tᵊl\ Either of two different plants that are widely used in combination for chewing purposes in southern Asia and the East Indies. The betel nut is the seed of the areca, or betel, PALM *(Areca catechu),* family Palmae; the betel leaf is from the betel pepper, or pan plant *(Piper betle),* family Piperaceae. For chewing, a small piece of the areca palm's fruit is wrapped in a leaf of the betel pepper, along with a pellet of lime to cause salivation and release the stimulating ALKALOIDS. Chewing results in a heavy flow of brick-red saliva, which may temporarily dye the mouth, lips, and gums orange brown. Betel nuts yield an alkaloid that veterinarians use as a worming agent.

The betel nut, seed of the areca palm *(Areca catechu).*

WAYNE LUKAS–GROUP IV—THE NATIONAL AUDUBON SOCIETY COLLECTION/PHOTO RESEARCHERS

Betelgeuse \ˈbē-tᵊl-ˌjüs\ (from Arabic *bat al-dshauza*: "the giant's shoulder") Brightest star in the constellation Orion, marking the hunter's eastern shoulder. About 430 light-years from earth, Betelgeuse is easily identifiable by its brightness, its position in brilliant Orion, and its deep reddish color. It is a red SUPERGIANT STAR, one of the largest known; its diameter varies between about 500 and 800 times that of the sun somewhat irregularly within a period of four to six years.

Bethe \ˈbā-tə\, **Hans (Albrecht)** (born 1906) German-U.S. theoretical physicist. He fled Germany in 1933 and taught at Cornell University 1937–75. He showed how the electric field surrounding an atom in a crystal affects the atom's energy states, work that helped shape quantum mechanics and increased understanding of the forces governing the structures of atomic nuclei. He was the first to propose the carbon cycle as a source of energy production in stars (1939). He headed the theoretical physics division of the MANHATTAN PROJECT, but worked in the postwar era to publicize the threat of nuclear warfare. He was awarded the Max Planck Medal (1955) and the Enrico Fermi Award (1961), and received the 1967 Nobel Prize for Physics.

Bethel Ancient city, PALESTINE. Now an archaeological site and town (Baytin) located in Israeli-occupied territory, it lies about 10 mi (16 km) north of Jerusalem. Important in Old Testament times, it was associated with ABRAHAM and JACOB. After the division of Israel, Bethel was made the chief sanctuary of the northern kingdom (Israel), and was later the center for the prophetic ministry of AMOS.

Bethlehem Town (pop., 1987 est.: 34,000), southwest of JERUSALEM. An ancient town of JUDAEA, it was the early home of King DAVID. A Roman garrison was stationed there during the Second Jewish Revolt (AD 135). Christians regard it as the birthplace of JESUS; the Church of the Nativity, built in the 3rd century over a cave identified as the site of the Nativity is one of the oldest Christian churches extant. Bethlehem was included in the British mandate of Palestine (1923–48); after the ARAB–ISRAELI WAR (1948–49), it was annexed by Jordan in 1950. After the SIX-DAY WAR (1967), it became part of the WEST BANK territory under Israeli administration. It was turned over to Palestine in 1995 under an Israeli–Palestinian self-rule agreement. Long an important pilgrim and tourist center, it is also an agricultural market town closely linked to Jerusalem.

Bethlehem City (pop., 1994 est.: 73,000), eastern Pennsylvania. With ALLENTOWN and Easton it forms an urban industrial complex. Founded in 1741 by MORAVIAN missionaries, it was the site of a hospital for Continental soldiers during the AMERICAN REVOLUTION. Industrialization began with the opening of the Lehigh Canal (1829) and the founding of the forerunner of BETHLEHEM STEEL CORP. (1857); the city became a major steel-producing center. Its economy has since diversified to include textiles, metal products, furniture, and chemicals.

Bethlehem Steel Corp. U.S. corporation created in 1904 to consolidate Bethlehem Steel Co., the Union Iron Works, and a few smaller companies. Its principal founder was CHARLES M. SCHWAB. In its early decades Bethlehem Steel (based in Bethlehem, Pa.) produced primarily coal, iron ore, and steel. In recent decades it has diversified into plastics, chemicals, and nonferrous ores. It is today the second-largest steel producer in the U.S.

Bethmann Hollweg \ˈbāt-ˌmän-ˈhȯl-ˌvek\, **Theobald von** (1856–1921) German politician and chancellor (1909–17). A member of the civil service, he was appointed Prussian minister of the interior in 1905 and became German chancellor in 1909. Before World War I, he allowed the militarist factions to dominate the government; in 1914 he supported a "blank check" to Austria-Hungary for measures against Serbia. In 1916 he tried to secure the mediation of the U.S. to end the war, but he also failed to restrict submarine warfare. In 1917 he angered conservatives by promises of electoral reforms in Prussia and was forced to resign.

Bethmann Hollweg, detail from a portrait by Brant, 1909.

ARCHIV FUR KUNST UND GESCHICHTE, WEST BERLIN

Bethune \be-ˈthün\, **Louise Blanchard** *orig.* **Jennie Louise Blanchard** (1856–1913) First U.S. professional woman architect. Born in Waterloo, N.Y., she opened an independent office in Buffalo in 1881. Her firm designed several hundred buildings throughout New York State, many of them in the Romanesque Revival style popular in the late 19th century. She was the first woman elected to the American Institute of Architects (1888).

Bethune \bā-ˈth(y)ün\, **Mary (Jane) McLeod** *orig.* **Mary Jane McLeod** (1875–1955) U.S. educator. Born to former slaves in Mayesville, S.C., she made her way through college and in 1904 founded a school that later became part of Bethune-Cookman College in Daytona Beach, Fla. She was president of the college 1923–42 and 1946–47, also serving as a special adviser to Pres. FRANKLIN ROOSEVELT. Prominent in African-American organizations, particularly women's groups, she directed the Division of Negro Affairs of the National Youth Administration 1936–44.

Bethune \bə-ˈthün\, **(Henry) Norman** (1890–1939) Canadian surgeon and political activist. Born in Gravenhurst, Ontario, he began his medical career in 1917, serving with Canadian forces in World War I. During the Spanish Civil War he was a surgeon with the loyalist forces, setting up the first mobile blood-transfusion service. A Communist, he left Canada in 1938 to serve as a surgeon with the Chinese army in its war with Japan, organizing field hospitals and setting up medical schools, and became a national hero of China.

Betjeman \ˈbech-ə-mən\, **John** *later* **Sir John** (1906–1984) British poet. His poetry volumes include *Mount Zion* (1933), *High and Low* (1966), and *A Nip in the Air* (1974), and his prose works include guidebooks to English counties and essays on places and buildings. His nostalgia for the near past, his exact sense of place, and his precise rendering of social nuance made him widely read at a time when much of what he wrote about was vanishing. From 1972 until his death he served as poet laureate of England.

Bettelheim \ˈbe-təl-ˌhīm\, **Bruno** (1903–1990) Austrian-U.S. psychologist. Trained in Vienna, he was arrested by the Nazis and interned in concentration camps 1938–39. He emigrated to the U.S., where from 1944 he directed the University of Chicago's Orthogenic School, a laboratory school for disturbed children, and became known especially for his work with autistic children. He applied psychoanalytic principles to social problems, especially in child rearing. His works include an influential paper on adaptation to extreme stress (1943), *Love Is Not Enough* (1950), *The Informed Heart* (1960), *The Empty Fortress* (1967), *Children of the Dream* (1967), and *The Uses of Enchantment* (1976). He died a suicide, depressed after the death of his wife and after suffering a stroke. His reputation was later clouded by revelations that he had invented his academic credentials and had abused and misdiagnosed children at his school.

Better Business Bureau Any of several U.S. and Canadian organizations formed to protect communities from unfair, misleading, or fraudulent advertising and selling practices. Organized at the local level, Better Business Bureaus investigate and set standards for business practices, receive complaints of improper practices, and conduct educational campaigns alerting the public to methods of deceit and fraud in advertising and selling.

Betti \'bāt-tē\, **Ugo** (1892–1952) Italian playwright. He pursued a legal career, serving as a judge and as librarian of the Ministry of Justice in Rome. He wrote three volumes of poetry, three collections of short stories, and 26 plays. His first play, *The Landlady* (1927), drew mixed reviews, but later works were more successful. Several were translated into French and English and performed in Paris, London, and New York, including *Landslide* (1933), *Corruption in the Palace of Justice* (1949), *The Queen and the Rebels* (1951), and *The Fugitive* (1953).

Betwa River \'bā-twä\ River, northern India. Rising in western MADHYA PRADESH, it flows northeast 360 mi (579 km) through UTTAR PRADESH into the YAMUNA RIVER near Hamirpur. Nearly half its course is unnavigable. It feeds a large irrigation area; the Jamni and Dhasan rivers are its main tributaries.

Beust \'bȯist\, **Friedrich Ferdinand, Graf (Count) von** (1809–1886) German statesman. A career diplomat in Saxony from 1830, he served as its foreign minister 1849–53 and its interior minister 1853–66. Often opposed to OTTO VON BISMARCK, Beust was forced to resign in 1866. He was then appointed by Saxony's ally and Habsburg emperor FRANCIS JOSEPH as the Austrian minister for foreign affairs (1866) and imperial chancellor (1867–71). As chancellor Beust negotiated the COMPROMISE OF 1867 and helped restore the Habsburgs' international position. He later served as ambassador to London (1871–78) and Paris (1878–82).

Beuve, Charles-Augustin Sainte- See C.-A. SAINTE-BEUVE

Beuys \'bȯis\, **Joseph** (1921–1986) German avant-garde sculptor and performance artist. He served in the German air force in World War II and later studied art in Düsseldorf (1947–51); in 1961 he was appointed professor of sculpture at its Art Academy. In the 1960s he worked with the international group FLUXUS, whose emphasis was not on what an artist makes but on his personality, actions, and opinions. His most famous and controversial performance was *How to Explain Pictures to a Dead Hare* (1965), in which he walked around an art gallery with his face covered in honey and gold leaf, talking to a dead hare about human and animal consciousness. He succeeded in creating a popular personal mythology and was one of the most influential artists and teachers of the later 20th century.

Bevan \'bev-ən\, **Aneurin** (1897–1960) British politician. As a young man, he entered Labour Party politics and was elected to the House of Commons in 1929. He overcame a speech impediment to become a brilliant orator. As minister of health in CLEMENT R. ATTLEE's government (1945–51), "Nye" Bevan established the NATIONAL HEALTH SERVICE. He was minister of labor (1951) but resigned in protest against rearmament expenditures that reduced spending on social programs. A controversial figure in the Labour Party, he headed its left-wing (Bevanite) group and was the party's leader until 1955.

Beveridge \'bev-ˌrij\, **Albert J(eremiah)** (1862–1927) U.S. senator and historian. Born in Highland Co., Ohio, he became a lawyer in Indianapolis. He served in the U.S. Senate 1900–12, where he supported progressive legislation proposed by Pres. THEODORE ROOSEVELT. He broke with the conservative wing of the Republican Party and served as chairman of the 1912 convention that organized the PROGRESSIVE PARTY and nominated Roosevelt for president. He retired from public life to write several historical works, including the four-volume *Life of John Marshall* (1916–19, Pulitzer Prize).

Beveridge, William Henry *later* **Baron Beveridge (of Tuggal)** (1879–1963) British economist. He took a lifelong interest in the problem of unemployment and served as director of labor exchanges (1909–16). He directed the London School of Economics (1919–37), then became master of University College, Oxford (1937–45). Invited by the government to become the architect of the new British WELFARE STATE, he helped shape Britain's social policies and institutions through the Beveridge Report (1942). His books included *Insurance for All* (1924), *Full Employment in a Free Society* (1944), and *Pillars of Security* (1948).

Beverly Hills City (pop., 1992 est.: 33,000), southwestern California. It is surrounded by the city of LOS ANGELES and adjoining HOLLYWOOD. It was established in 1906 as a residential area called Beverly. The Beverly Hills Hotel was built in 1912. Movie stars MARY PICKFORD and DOUGLAS FAIRBANKS built their estate there in 1919, beginning the fashion among Hollywood celebrities of building lavish homes in Beverly Hills. Occupying an area of 5.7 sq mi (14.8 sq km), the city is crossed by the famous streets of Sunset Boulevard, Santa Monica Boulevard, and Rodeo Drive.

Bevin, Ernest (1881–1951) British labor leader and statesman. Active in labor organizations from 1905, he became head of the Dockers' Union. In 1921 he merged several unions into the Transport and General Workers' Union, which became the world's largest trade union, and served as its general secretary until 1940. He was a forceful minister of labor and national service in WINSTON CHURCHILL's wartime coalition government (1940–45). As foreign secretary in CLEMENT R. ATTLEE's Labour government (1945–51), he negotiated the BRUSSELS TREATY and helped establish NATO.

Bewick, Thomas (1753–1828) British wood engraver. At 14 he was apprenticed to a metal engraver, with whom he later went into partnership in Newcastle, where he remained most of his life. He rediscovered the technique of wood engraving, which had declined into a reproductive technique, and brought to it brilliant innovations, such as the use of parallel lines instead of cross-hatching to achieve a wide range of tones and textures, and developing a method of printing gray backgrounds to heighten the effect of atmosphere and space. Some of his finest works are illustrations for books on natural history. He established a school of engraving in Newcastle.

"The Tawny Owl," wood engraving by Thomas Bewick, from his *History of British Birds,* 1797–1804.

Bezos \'bā-zōs\, **Jeff(rey P.)** (born 1964) U.S. Internet entrepreneur. Born in Albuquerque, N.M., and educated at Princeton Univ., he worked in banking and investment at Bankers Trust and D. E. Shaw & Co. before founding Amazon.com in 1995. The Internet company began as a bookseller and later expanded into recorded music, videos, electronic equipment, tools, and other areas, and also began conducting on-line auctions. It became famous for the extraordinary rise in its stock-market valuation despite its losing significant sums of money every year, reflecting investor confidence in the future of on-line retailing.

Bhadracarya-pranidhana \ˌbäd-rə-chär-'yä-ˌprä-nē-də-'nä\ MAHAYANA Buddhist text that is also important to TIBETAN BUDDHISM. It is related to the AVATAMSAKA-SUTRA and is considered by some to be its final section. It presents ten vows of the bodhisattva Samantabhadra. These became daily lessons in Chinese monasteries. By keeping the vows, including inexhaustible service to all buddhas and the embracing of all universes, the faithful can realize the universe of interdependent phenomena manifested in the BUDDHA and enter into the Pure Land of AMITABHA.

Bhagavadgita \'bä-gə-ˌväd-'gē-tə\ (Sanskrit: "Song of God") One of the greatest of the Hindu scriptures, constituting part of the *MAHABHARATA*. It is written in the form of a dialogue between the warrior Prince ARJUNA and the charioteer KRISHNA, an incarnation of VISHNU. It was proba-

A
B

bly composed in the 1st or 2nd century AD, later than much of the epic. Concerned over the suffering the impending battle will cause, Arjuna hesitates, but Krishna explains that the higher way is the dispassionate discharge of duty without concern for personal triumph. The Bhagavadgita considers the nature of God and ultimate reality and offers three disciplines for transcending the limitations of this world: *jnana* (knowledge or wisdom), KARMA (dispassionate action), and BHAKTI (love of God). It has inspired numerous commentaries over the centuries, including those by RAMANUJA and MOHANDAS K. GANDHI.

Bhagavata \'bä-gə-ˌvə-tə\ Member of the earliest recorded Hindu sect, representing the beginnings of theistic, devotional worship and modern VAISHNAVISM. The Bhagavata sect originated in the Mathura region c. 3rd–2nd century BC and spread through western, northern, and southern India. The faith centers on devotion to a personal god, variously called VISHNU, KRISHNA, Hari, or Narayana. The BHAGAVADGITA (1st–2nd century AD) is the earliest exposition of the Bhagavata system, but its central scripture is the Bhagavata PURANA. The sect was prominent within Vaishnavism until the 11th century, when BHAKTI (devotional worship) was revitalized by RAMANUJA.

bhakti \'bək-tē\ Southern Asian devotional movement, particularly in HINDUISM, emphasizing the love of a devotee for his or her personal god. In contrast to ADVAITA, bhakti assumes a dualistic relationship between devotee and deity. Though VISHNU, SHIVA, and Shakti (see SHAKTI) all have cults, bhakti characteristically developed around Vishnu's incarnations as RAMA and KRISHNA. Practices include reciting the god's name, singing hymns, wearing his emblem, and making pilgrimages. The fervor of South Indian hymnists in the 7th–10th century spread bhakti and inspired much poetry and art. Poets such as MIRABAI conceived of the relationship between the worshiper and the god in familiar human terms (e.g., the lover and beloved), while more abstract poets such as KABIR and NANAK portrayed the divinity as singular and ineffable.

bharata natya \'bä-rə-tə-'nät-yə\ Principal classical dance style of India, indigenous to TAMIL NADU. It expresses Hindu religious themes, and its techniques and terminology are found in the treatise *Natya-shastra,* written by the sage Bharata (3rd century AD). One dancer performs the entire two-hour program, accompanied by drums, drone, and singer. Originally performed only by female temple dancers, the art fell into disrepute as temple dancing became associated with prostitution, but it was revived in its original purity in the late 19th century.

Bharatiya Janata Party (BJP) *English* **Indian People's Party** Pro-Hindu political party of India, formally established in 1980. It achieved its first significant electoral success in 1989, though the destruction of the Babri Masjid mosque in Ajodhya in 1992 caused a backlash against it. In 1996 the BJP formed a short-lived government. Two years later, it and its allies formed a majority government with ATAL BIHARI VAJPAYEE as prime minister. Vajpayee again became prime minister in 1999 as head of a coalition of the BJP and other parties.

Bharatpur \'bə-rət-ˌpu̇r\ *or* **Bhurtpore** \'bərt-ˌpōr\ City (pop., 2001 prelim.: 204,456), RAJASTHAN state, northwestern India. Located west of AGRA, it was founded c. 1733 and was the capital of the princely state of Bharatpur. It was so strongly fortified that the British besieged it unsuccessfully in 1805 and did not take it until 1826. The city is renowned for its superb bird sanctuary.

Bharhut sculpture \'bä-rət\ (mid-2nd century BC) Indian sculpture that decorated the great stupa, or relic mound, of Bharhut, in Madhya Pradesh. It is now mostly destroyed; the railings and gateways that remain are in Kolkata's (Calcutta's) Indian Museum. The ornamental medallions depicting legends of the Buddha's previous births and events in his life are labeled and so are indispensable for an understanding of Buddhist iconography.

Bhartrhari \'bä-trə-rē\ (570?–650) Indian Hindu philosopher, poet, and grammarian. He was of noble birth; according to legend, he made seven attempts to renounce the world for monastic life before eventually becoming a yogi and moving into a cave near Ujjain. His *Vakyapadiya* is his major work on the philosophy of language. Also ascribed to him are three collections of poetry: *Shrngara-shataka* (on love), *Niti-shataka* (on ethics and polity), and *Vairagya-shataka* (on dispassion).

Bhasa \'bä-sə\ (2nd or 3rd century AD) Indian dramatist. The earliest known dramatist in Sanskrit, he was known only by the allusions of other Sanskrit dramatists until the texts of 13 of his dramas were discovered in 1912. Most of his works are adaptations of themes of heroism and romantic love borrowed from the *RAMAYANA* and the *MAHABHARATA*. He diverged from the conventions of the time by portraying battles and killings on the stage. His influence is seen in the works of KALIDASA.

Bhaskara I (fl. c. 629) Indian astronomer and mathematician. His fame rests on three treatises he composed on the works of Aryabhata I (born 476). Two of these, known today as *Mahabhaskariya* ("Great Book of Bhaskara") and *Laghubhaskariya* ("Small Book of Bhaskara"), are astronomical works in verse, while *Aryabhatiyabhashya* (629) is a prose commentary on the *Aryabhatiya* of Aryabhata. Bhaskara stressed the importance of proving mathematical rules rather than just relying on tradition or expediency.

bhiksu \'bik-shü\ *Pali* **bhikku** \'bik-ü\ In BUDDHISM, a member of the SANGHA, the ordained order of men established by the Buddha. (Female orders exist in some Mahayana Buddhist traditions). Originally they were mendicant followers of the Buddha who taught Buddhist ways in return for food. Today children may enter monastic life as novices, but candidates for ordination must be 21 years old. There are some 200 rules; sexual relations, taking of life, stealing, or boasting of spiritual attainment will lead to expulsion. A bhiksu shaves his head and face, owns a few essential items, and begs daily for his food. See also VINAYA PITAKA.

Bhopal Former princely state, central India. It is crossed by the Vindhya Mtns.; the NARMADA RIVER is its southern boundary. It was founded in 1723 by an Afghan chieftain who had served under the Mughal emperor AURANGZEB. In its struggles with the Marathas, Bhopal was itself friendly to the British and concluded a treaty with them in 1817. It was the chief state of the Bhopal Agency and the second-largest Muslim principality of the British empire. At India's independence, Bhopal remained a separate Indian province. When it was incorporated into MADHYA PRADESH in 1956, BHOPAL city became the state's capital.

Bhopal \bō-'päl\ City (pop., 2001 prelim.: 1,433,875), capital of MADHYA PRADESH state, India. Situated north of NAGPUR, it is primarily an industrial city and a major rail junction. It is the site of India's largest mosque and home to several colleges. In 1984 Bhopal became the site of one of the worst industrial accidents in history when tons of toxic gas escaped from a Union Carbide insecticide plant and spread over a densely populated area; the final death toll was estimated at 3,800.

Bhubaneswar \ˌbü-bə-'nesh-wər\ City (pop., 2001 prelim.: 647,302), capital of ORISSA, eastern India. Its history from the 3rd century BC is represented in nearby archaeological remains. In the 5th–10th century AD it was the provincial capital of many Hindu dynasties. Its many temples, displaying every phase of Orissan architecture, were built in the 7th–16th century. It became the state capital in 1948.

Bhumibol Adulyadej *or* **Phumiphon Adunlayadet** \'pü-mē-ˌpȯn-ä-'du̇n-lə-ˌdāt\ *or* **Rama IX** (born 1927) Ninth king of the CHAKRI DYNASTY and Thailand's longest-ruling monarch. Born in the U.S., he took the throne in 1946 after the death of his older brother, King Ananda Mahidol (1925–1946). As head of state his role is largely ceremonial, but he moderates between extreme parties and serves as a focus of national unity.

Bhutan \bü-'tän\ *Bhutanese* **Druk-yul** \'drük-'yül\ Kingdom, HIMALAYA MTNS. Area: 16,000 sq mi (41,500 sq km). Population (2002 est.): 721,000 (not including some 100,000 refugees in Nepal). Capital: THIMPHU. There are three main ethnic groups: the Buddhist Sharchops (Assamese) in the east; the Tibetan Buddhist Bhutia, about three-fifths of the population, in the northern, central, and western areas; and the Hindu Nepalese in the southwest. Languages: Dzongkha (official), Tibetan dialects. Religion: Mahayana Buddhism (official). Currency: ngultrum. Its northern part lies in the Great Himalayas, with peaks surpassing 24,000 ft (7,300 m) and high valleys lying at 12,000–18,000 ft (3,700–5,500 m). Spurs radiate southward, forming the Lesser Himalayan ranges. Several fertile valleys there, at elevations of 5,000–9,000 ft (1,500–2,700 m), are fairly well populated and cultivated. South of these mountains lies the Duars Plain, controlling access to the strategic mountain passes; much of it is hot and steamy and covered with dense forest. The Bhutanese economy is mainly agricultural; nearly all exports go to India. It is a monarchy with one legislative house; its head of state and government is the monarch. Bhutan's mountains and forests long made it inaccessible to the outside world, and its feudal rulers banned foreigners until well into the 20th century. It nevertheless became the object of foreign inva-

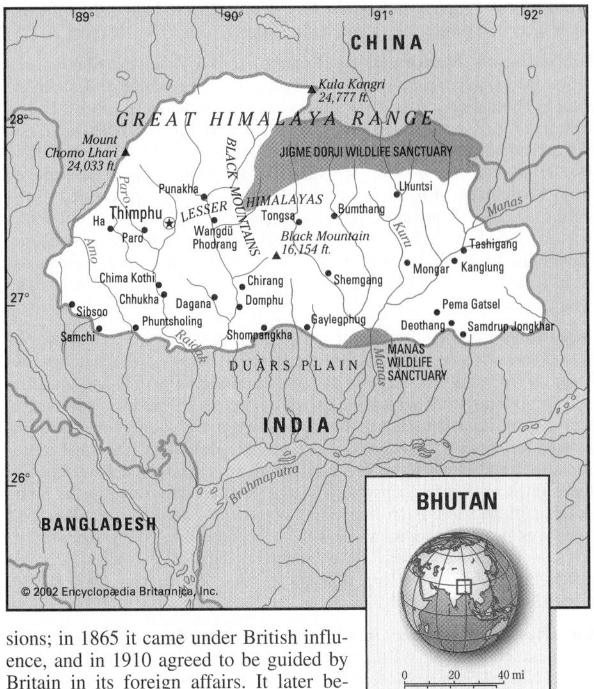

sions; in 1865 it came under British influence, and in 1910 agreed to be guided by Britain in its foreign affairs. It later became oriented toward British-ruled India, though much of its trade continued to be with Tibet. India took over Britain's role in 1949, and Communist China's 1950 occupation of neighboring Tibet further strengthened Bhutan's ties with India. The apparent Chinese threat made its rulers aware of the need to modernize, and it has embarked on a program to build roads and hospitals and to create a system of secular education.

Bhutto \'bü-tō\, **Benazir** (born 1953) Pakistani politician, the first woman leader of a Muslim nation in modern history. After receiving an education at Harvard and Oxford, she led the political opposition to Pres. ZIA-UL-HAQ after the 1979 execution of her father, ZULFIKAR ALI BHUTTO. From 1979 to 1984 she endured frequent house arrest, and she was exiled 1984–86. When Zia died in a plane crash in 1988, she became prime minister of a coalition government. She was unable to do much to combat Pakistan's widespread poverty, governmental corruption, and increasing crime, and her government was dismissed in 1990 on charges of corruption and other malfeasance. A second stint as prime minister (1993–96) ended similarly. In 1999 she was convicted of taking kickbacks from a Swiss company and sentenced in absentia to five years in prison.

Bhutto, Zulfikar Ali (1928–1979) President (1971–73) and prime minister (1973–77) of Pakistan. Son of a prominent politician, he was educated in India, the U.S., and Britain. He served eight years in the government of Mohammad Ayub Khan (1907–1974), then resigned to form the Pakistan People's Party (1967). After the overthrow of the Ayub Khan regime and the Pakistani civil war, Bhutto became president (1971). He nationalized several key industries and taxed landed families. He became prime minister in 1973 and his government, retaining martial law, began a process of Islamization. Bhutto's party won elections in 1977, but the opposition accused him of electoral fraud. Gen. ZIA-UL-HAQ seized power and had Bhutto imprisoned and later executed. BENAZIR BHUTTO is his daughter.

Biafra \bē-'äf-rə\ Former secessionist state, West Africa. It constituted the former Eastern Region of Nigeria, inhabited principally by the IGBO (Ibo). In a period of political and economic instability in the 1960s, the resentment of the HAUSA in the north toward the more prosperous Igbo exploded in fighting and massacres, which led to the secession of the Eastern Region as the state of Biafra in 1967. A costly civil war and the death by starvation of an estimated 1 million civilians ended in Biafra's collapse and reincorporation into Nigeria in 1970.

Biafra, Bight of Inlet of the Atlantic Ocean, West Africa. The innermost bay of the Gulf of GUINEA, it is bounded by Nigeria, Cameroon, Equatorial Guinea, and Gabon, and receives portions of the NIGER and OGOOUÉ rivers. It includes several islands, including BIOKO. Its ports include MALABO, CALABAR, and DOUALA. In the 16th–19th century the bay was the scene of extensive slave dealing. By the 1830s palm-oil trading had surpassed slave trading. Today petroleum is a major economic resource.

Bialystok \byä-'wi-stȯk\ City (pop., 1996 est.; 278,000), northeastern Poland. Founded in the 14th century, it was annexed to Prussia in 1795–1807. It passed to Russia, was captured by Germany in 1915, and was restored to Poland in 1919. During World War II it was overrun by Germans in 1941, then retaken by Soviet troops in 1944. Returned to Poland in 1945, it is now an important rail junction; it has been a major textile producer since 1863.

Biarritz \byä-'rēts\ Town (pop., 1990: 29,000), southwestern France. It lies on the Gulf of Gascogne (Bay of BISCAY) near Bayonne, 11 mi (18 km) from Spain. Once a small fishing village, Biarritz became a fashionable summer resort after 1854 with the visits of NAPOLEON III; visited also by British royalty, it grew additionally as a winter residence. Its mild climate and variety of beaches, and the folklore and traditions of the local BASQUES, continue to draw an international clientele.

biathlon Winter sports event combining CROSS-COUNTRY SKIING with rifle sharpshooting. It originated in Scandinavian hunting. It was first included in the Winter Olympics program in 1960. Competitors cover a 20-km (12.5-mi) course, carrying a single-shot rifle and ammunition and stopping at four points to fire five shots at small targets. Relay and 10-km events were added in 1968 and 1980 respectively.

Bibiena family See GALLI BIBIENA FAMILY

Bible Sacred scriptures of JUDAISM and CHRISTIANITY. The Jewish scriptures consist of the TORAH (or Pentateuch), the Neviim ("Prophets"), and the Ketuvim ("Writings"), which together constitute what Christians call the OLD TESTAMENT. The Pentateuch and Joshua relate how Israel became a nation and came to possess the Promised Land. The Prophets describe the establishment and development of the monarchy and relate the prophets' messages. The Writings include poetry, speculation on good and evil, and history. The Roman Catholic and Eastern Orthodox Bible includes additional Jewish writings called the APOCRYPHA. The NEW TESTAMENT consists of early Christian literature. The GOSPELS tell of the life, person, and teachings of Jesus. The Acts of the Apostles relates the earliest history of Christianity. The Epistles (Letters) are correspondence of early church leaders (chiefly St. PAUL) and address the needs of early congregations. REVELATION is the only canonical representative of a large genre of early Christian apocalyptic literature. See also BIBLICAL SOURCE, BIBLICAL TRANSLATION. See table on following page.

biblical source Any of the original oral or written materials compiled as the BIBLE. While authorship of many biblical books is anonymous or pseudonymous, scholars have used internal evidence and the tools of biblical criticism to identify sources and arrange them in chronological order of composition. There are four sources for the Pentateuch: J (sources in which God is called YHWH, German JHVH), eastern (sources in which God is called Elohim), D (sources in the style of Deuteronomy), and P (for sources with priestly style and content). Parts of lost books have also been identified in the OLD TESTAMENT. NEW TESTAMENT sources include original writings and ORAL TRADITIONS. The first three (synoptic) GOSPELS have a common source, Matthew and Luke being based on Mark and a lost source called Q; John conveys an independent tradition. Biblical sources are studied to uncover the history of the scriptures and to restore texts as closely as possible to their original content. Scholars may also analyze biblical sources in an effort to reconstruct the oral tradition behind them.

biblical translation Art and practice of translating the BIBLE. The OLD TESTAMENT was originally written in Hebrew, with scattered passages of Aramaic. It was first translated in its entirety into Aramaic and then, in the 3rd century AD, into Greek (the SEPTUAGINT). Hebrew scholars created the authoritative Masoretic text (6th–10th century) from Aramaic TARGUMS, the original Hebrew scrolls having been lost. The NEW TESTAMENT was originally in Greek or Aramaic. Christians translated both Testaments into Coptic, Ethiopian, Gothic, and Latin. St. JEROME's Latin Vulgate (405) was the standard Christian translation for 1,000 years. New

Old Testament: Jewish Scripture

Genesis	Isaiah	Nahum	Song of Songs
Exodus	Jeremiah	Habakkuk	Ruth
Leviticus	Ezekiel	Zephaniah	Lamentations
Numbers	Hosea	Haggai	Ecclesiastes
Deuteronomy	Joel	Zechariah	Esther
Joshua	Amos	Malachi	Daniel
Judges	Obadiah	Psalms	Ezra
1 & 2 Samuel	Jonah	Proverbs	Nehemiah
1 & 2 Kings	Micah	Job	1 & 2 Chronicles

Old Testament: Roman Catholic and Protestant Canons

Catholic	Protestant	Catholic	Protestant
Genesis	Genesis	Wisdom	
Exodus	Exodus	Sirach	
Leviticus	Leviticus	Isaiah	Isaiah
Numbers	Numbers	Jeremiah	Jeremiah
Deuteronomy	Deuteronomy	Lamentations	Lamentations
Joshua	Joshua	Baruch	
Judges	Judges	Ezekiel	Ezekiel
Ruth	Ruth	Daniel	Daniel
1 & 2 Samuel	1 & 2 Samuel	Hosea	Hosea
1 & 2 Kings	1 & 2 Kings	Joel	Joel
1 & 2 Chronicles	1 & 2 Chronicles	Amos	Amos
Ezra	Ezra	Obadiah	Obadiah
Nehemiah	Nehemiah	Jonah	Jonah
Tobit		Micah	Micah
Judith		Nahum	Nahum
Esther	Esther	Habakkuk	Habakkuk
Job	Job	Zephaniah	Zephaniah
Psalms	Psalms	Haggai	Haggai
Proverbs	Proverbs	Zechariah	Zechariah
Ecclesiastes	Ecclesiastes	Malachi	Malachi
Song of Songs	Song of Solomon	1 & 2 Maccabees	

Old Testament: Protestant Apocrypha

1 & 2 Esdras	Additions to Esther	Baruch	Bel and the Dragon
Tobit	Wisdom of Solomon	Prayer of Azariah	Prayer of Manasses
Judith	Ecclesiasticus	Susanna	1 & 2 Maccabees

New Testament

Matthew	Romans	Colossians	Hebrews
Mark	1 & 2 Corinthians	1 & 2 Thessalonians	James
Luke	Galatians	1 & 2 Timothy	1 & 2 Peter
John	Ephesians	Titus	1, 2, 3 John
Acts of the Apostles	Philippians	Philemon	Jude
			Revelation

learning in the 15th–16th century generated new translations. Martin Luther translated the entire Bible into German (1522–34). The first complete English translation, credited to John Wycliffe, appeared in 1382, but it was the King James version (1611) that became the standard for more than three centuries. By the late 20th century the entire Bible had been translated into 250 languages and portions of it into more than 1,300.

bibliography Broadly, the systematic study and description of books. The word can refer to the listing of books according to some system (called descriptive, or enumerative, bibliography), to the study of books as tangible objects (called critical, or analytical, bibliography), or to the product of those activities. The purpose of bibliography is to organize information about materials on a given subject so that students of the subject may have access to it. A descriptive bibliography may take the form of information about a particular author's works or about works on a given subject or on a particular nation or period. Critical bibliography, which emerged in the early 20th century, involves meticulous descriptions of the physical features of books, including the paper, binding, printing, typography, and production processes used, to help establish such facts as printing dates and authenticity.

Bibliothèque Nationale de France \‚bib-lē-ō-'tek-‚nȧ-sē-ȯ-'nȧl-də-'frä^{n}s\ Most important library in France and one of the oldest in the world. The nation's first royal library, the Bibliothèque du Roi ("King's Library"), was established under Charles V (r.1364–80) but later dispersed; another was established under Louis XI (r.1461–83). From 1537 the library received a copy of every French publication. It was moved from Fontainebleau to Paris in the late 16th century and opened to the public in 1692. It acquired its current name in 1795, and its collection was expanded through Revolutionary appropriations and Napoleon's acquisitions. In 1995 it moved to a new facility with a controversial design, which now houses all its books (over 12 million), periodicals, and magazines.

bicameral system System of government in which the legislature has two houses. It originated in Britain (see Parliament), where it was devised to represent the interests of both the common people and the elite, and to provide a deliberative legislative process. In the U.S., the bicameral system represents a compromise between the claims for equal representation among the states (in the Senate, each state has equal representation) and equal representation for all its citizens (each member of the House of Representatives is meant to represent roughly the same number of people). Each house has powers not held by the other, and measures need the approval of both to become law. Many federal systems of government today have bicameral legislatures. All U.S. states but Nebraska have bicameral legislatures. See also Canadian Parliament, Congress of the U.S., Diet.

bicarbonate of soda *or* **sodium bicarbonate** *or* **baking soda** Inorganic compound, white, crystalline salt of sodium, chemical formula $NaHCO_3$. It is a weak base and dissociates into water and carbon dioxide gas as it dissolves in the presence of hydrogen ions. In addition to household uses as an antacid, cleaner, and deodorizer, it is used in manufacturing effervescent salts and beverages and baking powder. Industrial uses include production of other sodium salts, treatment of wool and silk, and use in pharmaceuticals, sponge rubber, fire extinguishers, cleaners, lab reagents, mouthwash, and gold and platinum plating.

Bichat \bē-'shȧ\, **(Marie-François-) Xavier** (1771–1802) French anatomist and physiologist. In addition to bedside observations of patients, he conducted autopsies to study the changes disease causes in various organs. With no knowledge of the cell as the functional unit of living things, Bichat was among the first to see the organs of the body as being formed through the specialization of simple, functional units (tissues). Without using a microscope, he distinguished 21 kinds of tissues that, in different combinations, form the organs of the body. His systematic study of human tissues helped create the science of histology.

bichon frise \bē-‚shō^n-frē-'zā\ Breed of small dog noted for its fluffy coat and cheerful disposition. Descended from the water spaniel, it stands about 9–12 in. (23–30.5 cm) tall and has a short, blunt muzzle; silky, drooping ears; a puffy, silky, curled coat; and an undercoat. It is mostly white, but may have shadings of cream, gray, or apricot on the head. It originated in the Mediterranean region.

Bicol Peninsula \'bē-‚kōl\ Peninsula, southeastern Luzon, Philippine Islands. It has a lengthy coastline with large subpeninsulas. Its area is about 4,660 sq mi (12,070 sq km). It includes the Bicol Plain, a large lowland area important in rice production. It is densely populated though largely rural. It is the homeland of the Bicol, the country's fifth-largest ethnolinguistic group, and it has been a stronghold of Philippine communists.

bicycle Lightweight, two-wheeled, steerable machine that is propelled by the rider. The wheels are mounted in a metal frame, and the front wheel is held in a movable fork. The rider sits on a saddle and steers by handlebars attached to the fork, propelling the bicycle by two pedals attached to cranks that turn a driving sprocket. An endless chain transmits power from the driving sprocket to a back-wheel sprocket. A heavy pedalless form built in 1818 was propelled simply by the rider paddling his feet against the ground. In 1839 the Scottish blacksmith Kirkpatrick Macmillan (1813–1878) built a bicycle propelled by pedals, cranks, and drive rods; he is widely credited with inventing the bicycle. Important innovations were introduced by Pierre and Ernest Michaux in France in 1861, and by 1865 their company was manufacturing 400 *vélocipèdes* a

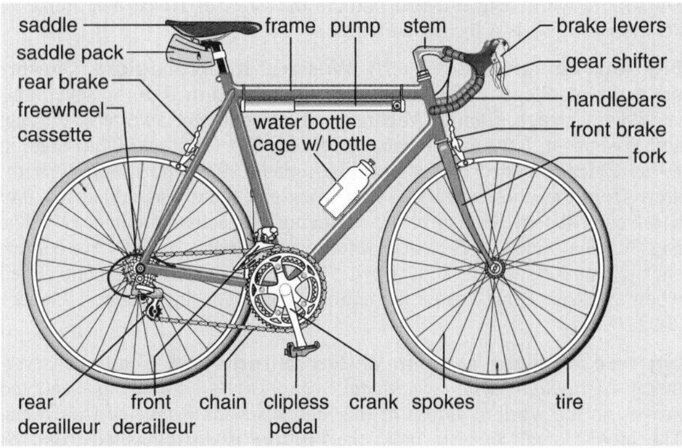

Components of a modern touring bicycle.

year. A lighter version produced in England in 1870 (nicknamed the "penny-farthing") featured a large front wheel and small back wheel. By the 1890s the standard bicycle design was established, and with the smooth ride enabled by the new pneumatic tires its popularity exploded. The so-called mountain bike became the standard design by the early 1990s. The bicycle is used worldwide as a basic means of transportation.

Bidault \bē-'dō\, **Georges (-Augustin)** (1899–1983) French statesman and Resistance leader in World War II. After being imprisoned in Germany (1940), he returned to France (1941) and worked with the National Council of Resistance, which he headed in 1943. He helped found the POPULAR REPUBLICAN MOVEMENT (1944) and supported CHARLES DE GAULLE's wartime government. After the war he briefly served twice as prime minister and three times as minister of foreign affairs. In 1958 he broke with de Gaulle and opposed Algerian independence. He advocated terrorism to prevent independence, went underground, and was forced into exile (1962–68).

Biddle, James (1783–1848) U.S. naval officer. Born in Philadelphia, he entered the navy in 1800. During the War of 1812, he served on the USS *Wasp* when it captured the British ship *Frolic* and commanded the USS *Hornet* in its victory over the *Penguin*. In 1817 his ship entered the Columbia River and claimed the Oregon Territory for the U.S. As commodore of U.S. ships in East Asia, he conducted negotiations with China and in 1846 negotiated the first preliminary trade agreement with China.

Biddle, John (1615–1662) Father of English UNITARIANISM. He studied at Oxford University and became master of a free school in Gloucester. In 1644 he wrote *Twelve Arguments Drawn out of Scripture*, denying the deity of the HOLY SPIRIT. When it reached church authorities, he was arrested and imprisoned for two years. After its publication in 1647 he was again detained and copies of the book were burned. His later writings attacked the doctrine of the Holy TRINITY. Freed from a third imprisonment in 1652, he began to meet for worship with his adherents, who came to be called Unitarians. After he published his *Two-fold Catechism* (1654), OLIVER CROMWELL prevented his execution by exiling him to the Scilly Isles. He returned in 1658; in 1662 he was again put in prison, where he died.

Nicholas Biddle.

Biddle, Nicholas (1786–1844) U.S. financier. Born in Philadelphia, he served as secretary to Pres. JAMES MONROE (1806–7) before being appointed president of the Second Bank of the United States by Monroe (1823). He developed the bank into the first effective U.S. CENTRAL BANK, sponsoring policies that curbed credit, regulated the money supply, and safeguarded government deposits. In 1832 it came under attack from Pres. ANDREW JACKSON, who managed to terminate its national charter in 1836. Biddle later became president of the bank under a Pennsylvania state charter.

Bidwell, John (1819–1900) U.S. political leader. Born in Chautauqua Co., N.Y., he was a member of the first group to travel by wagon train to California from Independence, Mo. In California he supported the BEAR FLAG REVOLT and fought under JOHN C. FREMONT in the Mexican War. He then returned to Sutter's Fort, where he was the first to find gold on the Feather River. Later he bought a large ranch, became a leading agriculturalist, and played a prominent role in state politics. In 1892 he became the PROHIBITION PARTY's presidential candidate.

Biedermeier style \'bē-dər-ˌmī-ər\ Style of German and Austrian art, furniture, and decoration that developed from c. 1815 to 1848. Gottlieb "Papa" Biedermeier was a fictional cartoon character, the comic symbol of middle-class comfort, with an emphasis on family life and the pursuit of hobbies. The subject matter of Biedermeier paintings, which were either genre or historical, was treated sentimentally; Carl Spitzweg (1808–1885) is the best-known of the Biedermeier painters. The simplicity and functionality of Biedermeier furniture were derived from the EMPIRE and DIRECTOIRE styles, but it was characterized by more restrained geometric shapes. The style was revived in the 1960s.

Biel \'bēl\, **Gabriel** (c. 1420–1495) German philosopher, economist, and Scholastic theologian. He became professor at the University of Tübingen (1484). His *Collectorium circa IV libros sententiarum* presented the teachings of William of OCKHAM; the work influenced followers known as Gabrielistae. His economic theories favored fair taxation and price control. See also SCHOLASTICISM.

Bielefeld \'bē-lə-ˌfelt\ City (pop., 1994 est.: 325,000), northwestern Germany. The old town was probably founded and chartered in 1214, and the "new town" arose from a religious settlement around St. Mary's Church in the late 13th century. It joined the HANSEATIC LEAGUE in the 14th century and passed to BRANDENBURG in 1647. The first mechanized textile mills in Germany were established there in 1851. Heavily damaged in World War II, the city has since been rebuilt. It is the center of a linen industry; it also has silk and plush weaving mills.

biennial Any plant that completes its life cycle in two GROWING SEASONS. During the first growing season biennials produce roots, stems, and leaves; during the second they produce flowers, fruits, and seeds, and then die. SUGAR BEETS and CARROTS are examples of biennials. See also ANNUAL, PERENNIAL.

Bienville \byaⁿ-'vēl\, **Jean-Baptiste Le Moyne de** (1680–1767) Canadian-French explorer, founder of New Orleans. Born in Montreal, he served with the French navy in King William's War. He accompanied his brother PIERRE IBERVILLE on expeditions to the mouth of the Mississippi River. They founded a settlement in 1699, and he later commanded the colony of Louisiana (1701–12, 1717–23). He founded New Orleans in 1718 and made it the colony's capital in 1722. Recalled to France in 1723, he returned to serve as governor of Louisiana 1733–43.

Bierce, Ambrose (Gwinnett) (1842–1914?) U.S. newspaperman, satirist, and short-story writer. Born in Meigs Co., Ohio, and reared in Indiana, he became a newspaper columnist and editor in San Francisco, specializing in attacks on frauds of all sorts. Among his books were *Tales of Soldiers and Civilians* (1891; revised as *In the Midst of Life*), which includes "An Occurrence at Owl Creek Bridge"; *Can Such Things Be?* (1893); and *The Devil's Dictionary* (1906), a volume of ironic definitions. Tired of American life, he went to Mexico in 1913, then in the middle of a revolution, and mysteriously disappeared, possibly killed in the 1914 siege of Ojinaga.

Bierstadt \'bēr-ˌshtät\, **Albert** (1830–1902) U.S. (German-born) painter of the HUDSON RIVER SCHOOL. His parents emigrated to the U.S. when Albert was an infant. As a young man he traveled through Europe sketching before returning to the U.S. to join a westward-bound expedition in 1859. Specializing in grandiose pictures of vast mountain scenery, he achieved great popularity in his lifetime with panoramic and often fanciful scenes of the West, including *The Rocky Mountains* (1863) and *Mount Corcoran* (c. 1875–77). His huge paintings were actually executed in his New York studio.

big bang Model of the origin of the UNIVERSE, which holds that it emerged from a state of extremely high temperature and density in an explosive expansion 10–15 billion years ago. Its two basic assumptions—that ALBERT EINSTEIN's general theory of RELATIVITY correctly describes the gravitational interaction of all matter and that an observer's view of the universe does not depend on direction of observation or on location—make it possible to calculate physical conditions in the universe back to a very early time called the Planck time (after MAX PLANCK). According to the model proposed by GEORGE GAMOW in the 1940s, the universe expanded rapidly from a highly compressed early state, with a steady decrease in density and temperature. Within seconds, MATTER predominated over ANTIMATTER and certain nuclei formed. It took another million years before ATOMS could form and RADIATION could travel through space unimpeded. The abundances of hydrogen, helium, and lithium and the discovery of COSMIC BACKGROUND RADIATION support the model, which also explains the RED SHIFTS of galaxies as resulting from the expansion of space.

Big Ben Clock designed by Sir Edmund Beckett (1816–1905), housed in the tower at the eastern end of Britain's Houses of Parliament. Big Ben is famous for its accuracy and its 13-ton bell. The name (for Sir Benjamin Hall, commissioner of works at the time of its installation in 1859) originally applied only to the bell, but eventually came to include the clock itself.

Big Ben, London, designed by Edmund Beckett.
A.F. KERSTING

Big Bend National Park Preserve, southwestern Texas. It lies 250 mi (400 km) southeast of EL PASO, and occupies 1,252 sq mi (3,243 sq km). It was established in 1944 and named for the wide bend in the RIO GRANDE that skirts its southern edge. It has magnificent mountain and desert scenery; it is home to more than 1,000 species of plants, and its wildlife includes coyotes, pumas, and roadrunners.

Big Bertha GUN from either of two different sets of long-range CANNON produced by the Krupp works (see THYSSEN KRUPP STAHL) in Germany during World War I. The first were 420-mm (16.5-in.) howitzers used by German forces advancing through Belgium in 1914. The second were guns specially built to bombard Paris in 1918. About 112 ft (34 m) long, they weighed 200 tons (181 metric tons) and were 210 mm (8 in.) or more in caliber. The Paris guns were moved on railway tracks; they bombarded the city for 140 days. Their unprecedented range of 75 mi (121 km) was achieved by sending the shells on a trajectory 12 mi (19 km) into the stratosphere. They were nicknamed for the Krupp matriarch Bertha von Bohlen.

Big Cypress Swamp Swamp region and national preserve, southern Florida. Covering 2,400 sq mi (6,200 sq km), the region merges into the swampy EVERGLADES on the east. It is dominated by cypress trees, and wildlife is abundant. The SEMINOLE Indians have reservations in the area.

Big Stick Policy Policy named by Pres. THEODORE ROOSEVELT to describe the assertion of U.S. dominance as a moral imperative. It was taken from an African proverb, "Speak softly and carry a big stick; you will go far." Roosevelt first used it when he asked Congress for money to increase U.S. naval preparedness to support his diplomatic objectives. The press used the phrase to describe Roosevelt's Latin America policy and his domestic policy of regulating monopolies.

Big Sur Scenic region along the Pacific coast of western California. It comprises a ruggedly beautiful stretch of seacoast 100 mi (160 km) long. Popular with tourists and naturalists, it extends southward from Carmel to the Hearst Castle at San Simeon. A narrow, mountainous coastal road affords views of the Pacific Ocean and the wilderness areas of the Los Padres National Forest. The Pfeiffer-Big Sur State Park contains the town of Big Sur and borders the Big Sur River. The home of ROBINSON JEFFERS is a local landmark.

Big Ten Conference *formerly* **Western Intercollegiate Conference.** U.S. college football league. It was formed in 1896 by seven universities: Chicago, Illinois, Michigan, Minnesota, Northwestern, Purdue, and Wisconsin. Iowa and Indiana were added in 1899, and Ohio State in 1912. Chicago ended its football program in 1939 and officially withdrew from the conference in 1946. Michigan State was added in 1949 and Pennsylvania State in 1990 (bringing the actual total to 11). The Big Ten had since 1947 sent a representative team, usually its conference champion, to the ROSE BOWL. This exclusive arrangement ended when the Rose Bowl hosted the national championship game in January 2002.

big tree *or* **giant sequoia** *or* **Sierra redwood** Coniferous EVERGREEN (*Sequoiadendron giganteum;* see CONIFER) found in scattered groves on the western slopes of the Sierra Nevada Range of California. The largest of all trees in bulk, the big tree is distinguished from the coastal REDWOOD *(Sequoia)* by having uniformly scalelike, or awl-shaped, leaves that lie close against the branches, scaleless winter buds, and cones requiring two seasons to mature. The pyramidal tree shape, reddish-brown furrowed bark, and drooping branches are common to both genera. The largest specimen (in total bulk) is the General Sherman tree in SEQUOIA NATIONAL PARK—101.5 ft (31 m) in circumference at its base, 272.4 ft (83 m) tall, and weighing an estimated 6,167 tons (5,593 metric tons). Because big-tree lumber is more brittle than redwood lumber and thus less desirable, the big tree has been easier to preserve; though some groves have been cut, most of the 70 remaining groves are now protected by state or national forests or parks.

Bigelow, Erastus Brigham (1814–1879) U.S. industrialist. Born in West Boylston, Mass., he left school at 10. At 23 he invented his first LOOM for LACE manufacture, which he followed with looms for weaving figured fabrics, tapestry carpeting, and ingrain carpeting. In 1843 he and his brother Horatio established a gingham mill, around which grew up the town of Clinton, Mass., and he founded the Bigelow carpet mills there several years later. From 1845 to 1851 he developed his greatest invention, a power loom for the manufacture of Brussels and Wilton carpets. He was a leader of the founding committee of the MASSACHUSETTS INSTITUTE OF TECHNOLOGY (1861).

Bigfoot *or* **Sasquatch** Large, hairy, humanlike creature that reportedly lives in isolated areas of the northwestern U.S. and western Canada. Descriptions of Bigfoot are similar to those of the ABOMINABLE SNOWMAN of the Himalayas. It is said to be a primate 6–15 ft (2–4.5 m) in height, walking upright and either moving silently or emitting a high-pitched cry. Footprints have measured up to 24 in. (60 cm) in length. Despite many reported sightings, there is still no solid evidence that Bigfoot exists.

bighorn *or* **mountain sheep** Stocky, climbing hoofed mammal (*Ovis canadensis*) of western North America. Both sexes have horns that in the male may curve in a spiral more than 39 in. (1 m) long. Their fur is usually brown with a whitish rump patch. The related thinhorn, or Dall's sheep (*O. dalli*), of Alaska and Canada is similar to the bighorn. Both species are about 39 in. (1 m) tall at the shoulder, but the bighorn is heavier, weighing up to 300 pounds (136 kg). They live in small groups among remote crags and cliffs of mountainous areas and feed mainly on grasses. Bighorn rams compete for females by launching themselves at each other from a few yards' distance and clashing horns.

Canadian bighorn sheep (*Ovis canadensis*).
HARRY ENGELS—THE NATIONAL AUDUBON SOCIETY COLLECTION/PHOTO RESEARCHERS

Bighorn Mountains Mountain range, southern Montana and northern Wyoming. A range of the northern ROCKY MTNS. extending 120 mi (193 km), its mountains rise abruptly 4,000–5,000 ft (1,200–1,500 m) above the GREAT PLAINS and Bighorn Basin. The highest summit is Wyoming's Cloud Peak, at 13,165 ft (4,013 m). Bighorn National Forest covers part of the range. On Medicine Mountain is the Medicine Wheel, a prehistoric stone-spoked circle 70 ft (20 m) in diameter.

Bighorn River River, Wyoming and Montana. Formed by the confluence of the Popo Agie and Wind rivers in western central Wyoming, it flows north 336 mi (541 km) into the YELLOWSTONE RIVER in southeastern Montana. The Little Bighorn joins the main stream at Hardin, Mont. The Bighorn Canyon National Recreation Area stretches along the Montana–Wyoming border. See also Battle of the LITTLE BIGHORN.

Bihar \bi-'här\ State (pop., 2001: 82,878,796), northeastern India, on the border with Nepal. It occupies 38,301 sq mi (99,200 sq km) and its capital is PATNA. Its limits are nearly the same as those of the ancient kingdoms of Videha and Magadha, for which records date back to c. 600 BC. In AD 320 the area came under the GUPTA empire, whose capital was at Pataliputra (Patna). Overcome by the Muslims c. 1200, Bihar was annexed to DELHI c. 1497. Taken by the British in 1765, it was made part of BENGAL. The area was the scene of revolts against the British in the mid-19th century and of MOHANDAS K. GANDHI's nonviolent movement in 1917. Bihar was made a province of British India in 1936; it became a state after India's independence in 1947. It is one of India's least urbanized states, and most of its population engages in agriculture. In 2000 the new state of JHARKHAND was created from Bihar's southern provinces.

Bikini Atoll with about 20 islets, MARSHALL ISLANDS, MICRONESIA. It was administered by the U.S. from 1947 as part of the U.S. Trust Territory of the Pacific Islands under a U.N. trusteeship. The U.S. used the atoll for atomic testing 1946–58. The 167 inhabitants were removed before the tests began and returned in 1969, but they were evacuated again in 1978 because of high radiation levels. Cleanup there continued, and in 1997 it was pronounced safe for inhabitation. The atoll became part of the Republic of the Marshall Islands in 1979.

Biko \'bē-kō\, **Stephen** (1946–1977) South African political activist. A former medical student, in 1969 he founded the Black Consciousness Movement, designed to raise black awareness of APARTHEID oppression. He was officially "banned" by the South African government in 1973 and was arrested several times in 1976–77. His death from head injuries suffered in police custody made him an international martyr for South African black nationalism. The initial inquest absolved the police of wrongdoing, but in 1997 five former officers confessed to Biko's murder.

Bilbao \bil-'bä-ˌō, bil-'baủ\ Port city (pop., 1995 est.: 371,000), northern Spain. It is located 7 mi (11 km) inland from the Bay of BISCAY. The largest city in the BASQUE COUNTRY, it originated as a settlement of mariners and ironworkers and was chartered in 1300. In the 18th century it prospered through trade with Spain's New World colonies. The city was sacked by French troops in the PENINSULAR WAR (1808) and besieged during the Carlist Wars (see CARLISM). It is a chief port in Spain and a center of the metallurgical industries and shipbuilding, as well as for banking. Landmarks include the 14th-century Cathedral of Santiago and the Guggenheim Museum Bilbao.

bilberry Low-growing deciduous shrub *(Vaccinium myrtillus)* of the HEATH FAMILY, found in woods and on heaths, chiefly in hilly districts of Britain, northern Europe, and Asia. The stiff stems bear small egg-shaped leaves and small rosy flowers tinged with green. The dark-blue, waxy berries are an important food of the GROUSE and are used for tarts and preserves. They are borne singly, unlike those of the much more productive cultivated BLUEBERRIES of the U.S. *(V. australe),* which are borne in long clusters.

Bilbo, Theodore G(ilmore) (1877–1947) U.S. senator (1935–47). Born near Poplarville, Miss., he was elected to the state senate in 1907, running as an antirailroad populist and supporter of white supremacy. He was later elected lieutenant governor (1911–16) and governor (1916–20). A later term as governor (1928–32) was marked by fiscal irresponsibility and the firing of many state-university faculty members. He is remembered for his racist and demagogic rhetoric, including his advocacy of deportation of blacks to Africa.

bildungsroman \'bil-ˌdủŋz-rō-ˌmän\ (German: "novel of character development") Class of novel in German literature that deals with the formative years of the main character, whose moral and psychological development is depicted. It ends on a positive note, with the hero's foolish mistakes and painful disappointments behind him and a life of usefulness ahead. It grew out of folklore tales in which a dunce goes out into the world seeking adventure. The first novelistic development of the theme, JOHANN W. VON GOETHE's *Wilhelm Meister's Apprenticeship* (1795–96), remains a classic example.

bile *or* **gall** Greenish-yellow liver secretion passed to the GALLBLADDER for concentration, storage, or transport into the duodenum for fat digestion. Bile contains bile acids and salts, cholesterol, and electrolyte chemicals that keep it slightly acidic. In the intestine, products of the acids and salts emulsify fat and reduce its surface tension to prepare it for the action of pancreatic and intestinal fat-splitting enzymes.

bilharziasis See SCHISTOSOMIASIS

bilingualism Ability to speak two languages. It may be acquired early by children in regions where most adults speak two languages (e.g., French and dialectal German in Alsace). Children may also become bilingual by learning languages in two different social settings; for example, British children in British India learned an Indian language from their nurses and family servants. A second language can also be acquired in school. Bilingualism can also refer to the use of two languages in teaching, especially to foster learning in students trying to learn a new language. Advocates of bilingual education argue that it speeds learning in all subjects for children who speak a foreign language at home, and prevents them from being marginalized in English-language schools. Detractors counter that it hinders such children from mastering the language of the larger society and limits their opportunities for employment and higher education.

bill See BEAK

Bill, Max (1908–1994) Swiss painter, sculptor, graphic artist, and industrial designer. He studied architecture, metalwork, stage design, and painting at the Bauhaus. In 1930 he opened his own studio in Zurich, where he spent most of his life, and earned a living designing advertisements. In the 1940s he designed chairs featuring geometric forms. He cofounded and directed the College of Design in Ulm, Germany (1951–55), and also designed its buildings. He is best known for his advertising designs.

bill of exchange Short-term negotiable financial instrument consisting of a written order addressed by the seller of goods to the buyer requiring the latter to pay a certain sum of money on demand or at a future time. Bills of exchange are often used in international transactions, and the holder of such a bill may redeem it in cash immediately by selling it to a bank at a discount. Bills of exchange used in domestic transactions are sometimes called drafts. See also ACCEPTANCE, PROMISSORY NOTE.

Bill of Rights (1689) British law, one of the basic instruments of the British constitution. It incorporated the provisions of the Declaration of Rights, which WILLIAM III and MARY II accepted upon taking the throne. Its main purpose was to declare illegal various practices of JAMES II, such as the royal prerogative of dispensing with the law in certain cases. The result of a long struggle between the STUART kings and the English people and PARLIAMENT, it made the monarchy clearly conditional on the will of Parliament and provided freedom from arbitrary government. It also dealt with the succession to the throne.

Bill of Rights First 10 amendments to the U.S. CONSTITUTION, adopted as a single unit in 1791. They are a collection of guarantees of individual rights and of limitations on federal and state governments, which derived from popular dissatisfaction with the limited guarantees of the Constitution. The first Congress submitted 12 amendments (drafted by JAMES MADISON) to the states, 10 of which were ratified. The 1st Amendment guarantees freedom of religion, speech, and the press, and grants the right to petition for redress and to assemble peaceably. The 2nd Amendment guarantees the right of the people to keep and bear arms. The 3rd prohibits the quartering of soldiers in private dwellings in peacetime. The 4th protects against unreasonable SEARCH AND SEIZURE. The 5th establishes grand-jury indictment for serious offenses, protects against DOUBLE JEOPARDY in criminal cases, and prohibits compelling a person to testify against himself. The 6th establishes the right of the ACCUSED to a speedy trial and an impartial jury, and guarantees the right to legal counsel and to the obtaining of witnesses in his favor. The 7th preserves the right to trial by jury in serious civil suits and prohibits double jeopardy in civil cases. The 8th prohibits excessive bail and cruel and unusual punishment. The 9th states that enumeration of certain rights in the Constitution does not mean the abrogation of rights not mentioned.

The 10th reserves to the states and people any powers not delegated to the national government.

billfish Any of several long-jawed fishes, especially those in the family Istiophoridae, including MARLINS, spearfishes, and SAILFISHES. The name is also applied to the GAR, NEEDLEFISH, and sauries (family Scomberesocidae).

billiards Any of various games played on a cloth-topped, cushion-railed rectangular table by driving small, hard balls against one another or into pockets with a long stick called a cue. Carom, or French billiards, is played with three balls, two white and one red, on a table without pockets. The object is to stroke the white cue ball so that it hits the two object balls in succession, scoring a carom (one point). English billiards is also played with three balls but on a pocketed table; it is scored in various ways. SNOOKER is another popular British billiards game. The principal billiards game in North America is pocket billiards, or POOL. The Billiard Congress of America controls U.S. tournament play, including the U.S. Open Pockets Billiard Championship, regarded as the world championship.

Billings City (pop., 2000: 89,847), southern central Montana. Billings was established on the YELLOWSTONE RIVER in 1882 by the Northern Pacific Railway and named for its president. It is now a trading and shipping point for wool, livestock, and agriculture. Nearby Pictograph Cave State Monument has prehistoric artifacts.

Billings, John Shaw (1838–1913) U.S. surgeon and librarian. Born in Switzerland Co., Ind., Billings worked for the U.S. Army 1861–95. He fostered the growth of the surgeon general's library in Washington, D.C., developing what would become the National Library of Medicine, the world's largest medical reference center. He founded the monthly *Index Medicus* (1879), still one of the primary U.S. medical bibliographies, and published the first *Index Catalogue* (1880–95). He also designed Johns Hopkins Hospital and was its medical adviser, ran national vital statistics programs, led the U.S. effort to end yellow fever, and was the first director of the New York Public Library. His organization of U.S. medical institutions was central to modernization of hospital care and maintenance of public health.

Billings, William (1746–1800) American hymn composer, sometimes called the first American composer. Born in Boston to a poor family, he worked as a tanner and was largely self-taught in music. His robust and primitive style, lacking instrumental parts, has seemed to embody the distinctive virtues of early America. His *New England Psalm-Singer* (1770) was the first published collection of American music; his other works include *The Singing Master's Assistant* (1778) and *The Continental Harmony* (1794).

Billiton See BELITUNG

Billroth \'bil-rōt\, **(Christian Albert) Theodor** (1829–1894) Austrian surgeon. He pioneered the study of bacterial causes of wound fever and adopted early the antiseptic techniques that eradicated the threat of fatal surgical infections. The founder of modern surgery of the abdominal cavity, he altered and removed organs previously considered inaccessible. In 1872 he was the first to remove part of an esophagus, joining the ends together; later he performed the first complete larynx removal. In 1881, when he had made intestinal surgery almost commonplace, he successfully removed a cancerous pylorus (lower end of the stomach).

Billy the Kid *orig.* **William H. Bonney, Jr.** *or* **Henry McCarty** (1859?–1881) U.S. outlaw. Born in New York City, he moved with his family to Kansas, then lived in New Mexico from c. 1868. His career of lawlessness throughout the Southwest began early, and he had allegedly killed 27 men when he was captured in 1880 by Sheriff PAT GARRETT. In New Mexico in 1881 he was convicted and sentenced to hang. He escaped from jail, killing two deputies, and remained at large until Garrett tracked him down and killed him.

Biloxi \bi-'lək-sē, bi-'läk-sē\ Coastal city (pop., 2000: 50,644), southeastern Mississippi. Located east of Gulfport, it grew out of Fort Louis (established 1719); a nearby earlier fort, Fort Maurepashad, was the Mississippi valley's first permanent European settlement (1699). It has been under the flags of France, Spain, Britain, the West Florida Republic, and the Confederacy. By the late 20th century, casino gambling had become its chief industry, augmented by fishing and seafood processing. Beauvoir, JEFFERSON DAVIS's last home, is nearby.

bimetallism Monetary standard or system based on the use of two metals, traditionally gold and silver, rather than one (monometallism). In the 19th century, a bimetallic system defined a nation's monetary unit by law in terms of fixed quantities of gold and silver (thus automatically establishing a rate of exchange between the two metals). The system provided a free and unlimited market for the two metals, imposed no restrictions on the use and coinage of either metal, and made all other MONEY in circulation redeemable in either gold or silver. Because each nation independently set its own rate of exchange between the two metals, the resulting rates of exchange often differed widely from country to country. When the ratio of the official prices proved different from the ratio of prices in the open market, GRESHAM'S LAW operated in such a way that coins of only one metal remained in circulation. A monometallic system using the GOLD STANDARD proved more responsive to changes in supply and demand and was widely adopted after 1867. See also EXCHANGE RATE, SILVER STANDARD.

bin Laden, Osama (born 1957) Leader of a broad-based Islamic extremist movement implicated in numerous acts of TERRORISM against the U.S. and other Western countries. The son of a wealthy Saudi family, he joined the Muslim resistance in Afghanistan after the 1979 Soviet invasion of that country. Following his homecoming, he became enraged at the presence of U.S. troops in Saudi Arabia during the PERSIAN GULF WAR and through a network of like-minded Islamic militants, known as AL-QAEDA, launched a series of terrorist attacks. These acts included the bombings of the WORLD TRADE CENTER in New York City in 1993, the U.S. embassies in Kenya and Tanzania in 1998, and the U.S. warship *Cole* in Aden, Yemen, in 2000. A self-styled Islamic scholar, bin Laden issued several legal opinions calling on Muslims to take up JIHAD against the U.S., and in 2001 a group of militants under his direction launched the SEPTEMBER 11 ATTACKS, which led to the deaths of more than 3,000 people. The U.S. thereafter demanded bin Laden's extradition from Afghanistan, where he was sheltered by that country's TALIBAN militia, and launched attacks on Taliban and Al-Qaeda forces when that ultimatum was not met. With the collapse of the Taliban, bin Laden and his associates went into hiding.

binary code Code used in DIGITAL COMPUTERS, based on a binary number system in which there are only two possible states, off and on, usually symbolized by 0 and 1. Whereas in a decimal system, which employs 10 digits, each digit position represents a power of 10 (100, 1,000, etc.), in a binary system each digit position represents a power of 2 (4, 8, 16, etc.). A binary code signal is a series of electrical pulses that represent numbers, characters, and operations to be performed. A device called a clock sends out regular pulses, and components such as TRANSISTORS switch on (1) or off (0) to pass or block the pulses. In binary code, each decimal number (0–9) is represented by a set of four binary digits, or BITS. The four fundamental arithmetic operations (addition, subtraction, multiplication, and division) can all be reduced to combinations of fundamental Boolean algebraic operations (see BOOLEAN ALGEBRA) on binary numbers.

binary star Pair of stars in orbit around a common center of gravity. Their relative sizes and brightnesses and the distance between them vary widely. Perhaps half of all stars in the Milky Way are binaries or members of more complex multiple systems. Some binaries form a class of VARIABLE STARS (see ECLIPSING VARIABLE STAR), while others are detected only by the motions of a single visible star.

binding energy ENERGY required to separate a particle from a system of particles or to disperse all the particles of a system. Nuclear binding energy is the energy required to separate an atomic NUCLEUS into its constituent PROTONS and NEUTRONS. It is also the energy that would be released by combining individual protons and neutrons into a single nucleus. ELECTRON binding energy, or IONIZATION POTENTIAL, is the energy required to remove an electron from an ATOM, MOLECULE, or ION, and also the energy released when an electron joins an atom, molecule, or ion. The binding energy of a single proton or neutron in a nucleus is about a million times greater than that of a single electron in an atom.

bindweed Any plant of the closely related genera *Convolvulus* and *Calystegia,* mostly twining, often weedy, and producing funnel-shaped flowers. Bellbine, or greater bindweed *(Calystegia sepium),* native in Eurasia and North America, is a twining perennial that grows from creeping, underground stems and is common in hedges and woods and along roadsides. Sea bindweed *(C. soldanella)* creeps along European seaside sand and gravel. Several *Convolvulus* species are widespread or conspicuous. The weedy, perennial field bindweed *(C. arvensis),* European but widely naturalized in North America, twines around CROP plants and along roadsides. Scammony, a purgative, is derived from the RHIZOMES of *C. scammonia,* a trailing perennial native to western Asia. Rosewood oil comes from certain species of *Convolvulus.*

Binet \bi-'nā\, **Alfred** (1857–1911) French psychologist. His interest in J.-M. CHARCOT's work on hypnosis prompted him to abandon a law career and study medicine at the Salpêtrière Hospital in Paris (1878–91). He served as director of a research laboratory at the Sorbonne 1895–1911. A major figure in the development of experimental psychology in France, he founded *L'Année Psychologique*, the first French journal on psychology, in 1895. He developed experimental techniques to measure reasoning ability; between 1905 and 1911 he and Theodore Simon developed influential scales for the measurement of intelligence of children. His works include *Experimental Study of Intelligence* (1903) and *A Method of Measuring the Development of the Intelligence of Young Children* (1915).

Binford, Lewis R(oberts) (born 1930) U.S. archaeologist. Born in Norfolk, Va., he has taught principally at the University of New Mexico. In the mid-1960s he initiated what came to be known as the "New Archaeology," which champions the use of quantitative methods and the practice of archaeology as a rigorous science. He applied the new methodology in an influential study of MOUSTERIAN artifacts, and later extended it to a study of the hunting activities of a living people, the Nunamiut, trying to draw analogies to prehistoric contexts. A chief goal has been to develop a body of "bridging theories" that can help link the archaeological record to understandings about past human activities and the operation of cultural systems.

Bing, Rudolf *later* **Sir Rudolf** (1902–1997) Austrian-British opera impresario. After holding positions in German opera houses, he assumed the position of general manager at the Glyndebourne Opera (1935–49). In 1946 he helped found the Edinburgh Festival. From 1950 until 1972 he served as general manager of the Metropolitan Opera, where, wielding autocratic power, he raised the institution's performance standards, extended its season, encouraged innovations in design and production, ended the exclusion of black singers, and oversaw the company's move to Lincoln Center.

Bingham, George Caleb (1811–1879) U.S. painter and frontier politician. Born in Virginia, he studied briefly at the Pennsylvania Academy of Fine Arts, but was largely self-taught. He entered politics in Missouri and worked as an itinerant portrait painter before turning to the lively routines of frontier life for inspiration. He is known for his incisive characterizations, clear, golden light, and talent for organizing large, dense compositions. His best-known works include *Fur Traders Descending the Missouri* (1845) and *Jolly Flatboatmen* (1846).

bingo Game of chance played with cards having numbered squares corresponding to numbered balls drawn at random and won by covering five such squares in a row (vertically, horizontally, or diagonally). Cards are purchased and proceeds are placed into a common "pot"; winning cards are awarded a portion of the pot. Wildly popular in the mid-1900s, bingo has in recent decades suffered a decline, perhaps due to the increasing popularity of LOTTERY operations and legalized gambling. The earliest name for the game, lotto, was recorded in 1776.

Binh Dinh Vuong See LE LOI

binoculars Optical instrument for providing a magnified view of distant objects, consisting of two similar TELESCOPES, one for each eye, mounted on a single frame. In most binoculars, each telescope has two PRISMS, which reinvert the inverted image provided by the eyepiece of each telescope. Light rays travel along a folded path inside the telescopes, so the instrument has a shorter overall length. The prisms also provide better depth perception at greater distances, by allowing the two objectives (object LENSES) to be set farther apart than the eyepieces. Binocular eyepieces are often fitted to microscopes or other optical instruments.

binomial nomenclature System of naming organisms in which each organism is indicated by two words, the GENUS (capitalized) and SPECIES (lowercase) names, both written in italics. For example, the tea rose is *Rosa odorata;* the common horse is *Equus caballus.* The system was developed by CAROLUS LINNAEUS in the mid-18th century. The number of binomial names proliferated as new species were established and more categories were formed, and by the late 19th century the nomenclature of many groups of organisms was confused. International committees in the fields of zoology, botany, bacteriology, and virology have since established rules to clarify the situation. See also TAXONOMY.

binomial theorem In algebra, a formula for expansion of the binomial $(x + y)$ raised to any positive integer power. A simple case is the expansion of $(x + y)^2$, which is $x^2 + 2xy + y^2$. In general, the expression $(x + y)^n$ expands to the sum of $(n + 1)$terms in which the power of x decreases from n to 0 while the power of y increases from 0 to n in successive terms. The terms can be represented in factorial notation by the expression $[n!/((n - r)!r!)]x^{n-r}y^r$ in which r takes on integer values from 0 to n.

Bío-Bío River \,bē-ō-'bē-ō\ River, southern central Chile. Rising in the ANDES, it flows northwestward 240 mi (380 km) to enter the Pacific Ocean near CONCEPCIÓN. Though one of Chile's longest rivers, it is navigable only by flat-bottomed boats.

biochemistry Field of science concerned with chemical substances and processes that occur in plants, animals, and microorganisms. It involves the quantitative determination and structural ANALYSIS of the organic compounds that make up CELLS (PROTEINS, CARBOHYDRATES, and LIPIDS) and of those that play key roles in CHEMICAL REACTIONS vital to life (e.g., NUCLEIC ACIDS, VITAMINS, and HORMONES). Biochemists study cells' many complex and interrelated chemical changes. Examples include the chemical reactions by which proteins and all their precursors are synthesized, food is converted to ENERGY (see METABOLISM), hereditary characteristics are transmitted (see HEREDITY), energy is stored and released, and all biological chemical reactions are catalyzed (see CATALYSIS, ENZYME). Biochemistry straddles the biological and physical sciences and uses many techniques common in medicine and physiology as well as those of organic, analytical, and PHYSICAL CHEMISTRY.

biochip Small-scale device, analogous to an INTEGRATED CIRCUIT, constructed of or used to analyze organic molecules associated with living organisms. One type of theoretical biochip is a small device constructed of large organic molecules, such as proteins, and capable of performing the functions (data storage, processing) of an electronic computer. The other type of biochip is a small device capable of performing rapid, small-scale biochemical reactions for the purpose of identifying gene sequences, environmental pollutants, airborne toxins, or other biochemical constituents.

biodegradability Capacity of a material to decompose by biological action. The term usually refers to the environmental breakdown of waste by microorganisms. Generally, plant and animal products are biodegradable and mineral substances (e.g., metals, glass, plastics) are not. Local conditions, especially presence or absence of oxygen, affect biodegradability. Disposal of nonbiodegradable waste is a primary source of pollution. Absorbable surgical materials are also called biodegradable.

biodiversity Diversity of plant and animal species in an environment. Sometimes habitat diversity (the variety of places where organisms live) and genetic diversity (diversity of genetic information within a species; that is, the number of distinct populations of a species) are also considered types of biodiversity. The estimated 3–30 million species on earth are divided unequally among the world's habitats, with 50–90% of the world's species diversity occurring in tropical regions. The more diverse a habitat, the better chance it has of surviving a change or threat to it, because it is more likely to be able to make a balancing adjustment. Habitats with little biodiversity (e.g., Arctic tundra) are more vulnerable to change. The 1992 EARTH SUMMIT resulted in a treaty for the preservation of biodiversity.

bioengineering Application of ENGINEERING principles and equipment to BIOLOGY and MEDICINE. It includes the development and fabrication of life-support systems for underwater and SPACE EXPLORATION, devices for medical treatment (see DIALYSIS, PROSTHESIS), and instruments for monitoring biological processes. Development has been particularly rapid in the area of artificial organs, which culminated in the implantation of an ARTIFICIAL HEART into a human being in 1982. Bioengineers also develop equipment that enables humans to maintain body functions in hostile environments, such as the space suits worn by astronauts during extravehicular maneuvers.

biofeedback Information supplied instantaneously about an individual's own physiological processes. Data concerning cardiovascular activity (blood pressure and heart rate), temperature, brain waves, or muscle tension is monitored electronically and returned or "fed back" to the individual through a gauge on a meter, a light, or a sound. The goal is for the patient to use that biological data to learn to voluntarily control the body's reactions to stressful external events. A type of BEHAVIOR THERAPY, biofeedback training is sometimes used in combination with psychotherapy to help patients understand and change their habitual reactions to stress. Complaints treated through biofeedback include migraine headaches, gastrointestinal problems, high blood pressure, and epileptic seizures.

biography Form of nonfictional literature whose subject is the life of an individual. The earliest biographical writings probably were funeral speeches and inscriptions. The origins of modern biography lie with PLUTARCH's moralizing lives of prominent Greeks and Romans and SUETONIUS' gossipy lives of the Caesars. Few biographies of common individuals were written until the 16th century. The major developments of English biography came in the 18th century, with such works as JAMES BOSWELL's *Life of Johnson*. In modern times impatience with Victorian reticence and the development of psychoanalysis have sometimes led to a more penetrating and comprehensive understanding of biographical subjects. See also AUTOBIOGRAPHY.

Bioko \bē-'ō-kō\ *formerly* **Fernando Póo** \fer-'nän-dō-'pō\ Island (pop., 1983: 58,000), Bight of BIAFRA, West Africa. It lies 100 mi (160 km) northwest of continental EQUATORIAL GUINEA, of which it is a part. Bioko became the official name in 1979. Volcanic in origin, with an area of 779 sq mi (2,018 sq km), it rises sharply from the sea; its highest point is Santa Isabel Peak, at 9,869 ft (3,008 m). MALABO, the country's capital, is located on Bioko. The island was visited by the Portuguese explorer Fernão Pó, probably in 1472. Though claimed by Spain after 1778, the first attempt at firm Spanish control came only in 1858. The original inhabitants, the Bubi, are descendants of Bantu-speaking migrants from the mainland. Many FANG have flocked to the island from the continent.

biological psychology Branch of PSYCHOLOGY that deals with the physiological basis of behavior. Traditional areas of study in the field include PERCEPTION, MOTIVATION, EMOTION, LEARNING, MEMORY, COGNITION, and mental disorders. Also considered are other physical factors that affect the nervous system, including heredity, metabolism, hormones, disease, drug ingestion, and diet. An experimental science, biological psychology relies heavily on laboratory research and quantitative data.

biological rhythm Periodic biological fluctuation in an organism corresponding to and in response to periodic environmental change, such as day and night, or high and low tide. The internal mechanism that maintains this rhythm even without the apparent environmental stimulus is a "biological clock." When the rhythm is interrupted, the clock's adjustment is delayed, accounting for such phenomena as JET LAG when traveling across time zones. Rhythms may have 24-hour (CIRCADIAN RHYTHM), monthly, or annual cycles. See also PHOTOPERIODISM.

biological warfare *or* **germ warfare** Military use of disease-producing agents, such as BACTERIA (including those that cause ANTHRAX and BOTULISM) and VIRUSES, and the means for combating such agents. A 1925 Geneva protocol prohibited the use of biological agents in warfare, and in 1972 more than 70 countries signed the Biological and Toxin Weapons Convention, prohibiting the production, stockpiling, or development of biological weapons and requiring the destruction of existing stockpiles. One reason for the ban is to prevent an agent's escaping from control, as is said to have happened at the siege of Caffa in the Crimea in 1347, when the Mongols hurled the bodies of PLAGUE victims over the walls of the Genoese defenders and Genoese ships later carried the bacillus to Europe, causing the BLACK DEATH. The British in the French and Indian War, and U.S. Army units in the 19th century, gave blankets used by SMALLPOX victims to American Indians. In World War I the Germans infected Romanian cavalry horses and U.S. livestock with the bacterial disease glanders. The Japanese used biological agents against China in the 1930s. Despite the international ban, a number of nations, including Iran, Iraq, and Russia and other former Soviet states, are believed to retain stocks of biological-warfare agents.

biology Study of living things and their vital processes. An extremely broad subject, biology is standardly divided into branches. The current approach is based on the levels of biological organization involved (e.g., molecules, cells, individuals, populations) and on the specific topic under investigation (e.g., structure and function, growth and development). According to this scheme, biology's main subdivisions include MORPHOLOGY, PHYSIOLOGY, TAXONOMY, EMBRYOLOGY, GENETICS, and ECOLOGY, each of which can be further subdivided. Alternatively, biology can be subdivided into fields especially concerned with one type of living thing; for example, BOTANY (plants), ZOOLOGY (animals), ORNITHOLOGY (birds), ENTOMOLOGY (insects), MYCOLOGY (fungi), MICROBIOLOGY (microorganisms), and BACTERIOLOGY (bacteria). See also BIOCHEMISTRY, MOLECULAR BIOLOGY.

bioluminescence \ˌbī-ō-ˌlü-mə-'ne-sᵊns\ Emission of light by an organism or biochemical system (e.g., the glow of BACTERIA on decaying meat or fish, the phosphorescence of PROTOZOANS in tropical seas, the flickering signals of fireflies). It occurs in a wide range of protists and animals, including bacteria and fungi, insects, marine invertebrates, and fish. It is not known to exist naturally in true plants or in amphibians, reptiles, birds, or mammals. It results from a chemical reaction that produces radiant energy very efficiently, giving off very little heat. The essential light-emitting components are usually the organic molecule luciferin and the ENZYME luciferase, which are specific for different organisms. In higher organisms, light production is used to frighten predators and to help members of a species recognize each other. Its functional role in lower organisms such as bacteria, dinoflagellates, and fungi is uncertain. Luminous species are widely scattered taxonomically, with no clear-cut pattern, though most are marine.

biomass Weight or total quantity of living organisms of one animal or plant species (species biomass) or of all the species in the community (community biomass), commonly referred to as a unit area or volume of the habitat. The biomass in an area at a given moment is the standing crop.

biome \'bī-ˌōm\ Largest geographic biotic unit, a major community of plants and animals with similar requirements of environmental conditions. It includes various communities and developmental stages of communities and is named for the dominant type of vegetation, such as grassland or coniferous forest. Several similar biomes constitute a biome type; for example, the temperate deciduous forest biome type includes the deciduous forest biomes of Asia, Europe, and North America. The standard European term for biome is "major life zone."

Biondi \bē-'än-dē\, **Matt** (born 1965) U.S. swimmer. Born in Palo Alto, Cal., the 6-ft 7-in. Biondi won 11 medals, including eight gold medals, in three consecutive OLYMPIC GAMES in 1988, 1992, and 1996. His time for the 100-m freestyle in 1988 remains an Olympic record.

biophysics Discipline concerned with applications of the principles and methods of the physical sciences to biological problems. Biophysics deals with biological functions that depend on physical agents such as electricity or mechanical force, with the interaction of living organisms with physical agents such as light, sound, or ionizing radiation, and with interactions between living things and their environment as in locomotion, navigation, and communication. Its subjects include bone, nerve impulses, muscle, and vision as well as organic molecules, using such tools as PAPER CHROMATOGRAPHY and X-ray CRYSTALLOGRAPHY.

biopsy \'bī-ˌäp-sē\ Procedure in which cells or tissues are removed from a patient and examined. The sample may be obtained from any organ, by any of several methods, including suction through a needle, swabbing, scraping, ENDOSCOPY, and cutting out the entire structure (excision) or part of it (incision) to be tested. Biopsy is a standard step in distinguishing malignant from benign tumors and can provide other information for diagnosis, particularly concerning such organs as the liver or pancreas. Slides of the tissue are prepared and examined by microscope.

BIOS \'bī-ˌōs\ *in full* **Basic Input/Output System** Computer PROGRAM that is typically stored in EPROM and used by the CPU to perform start-up procedures when the computer is turned on. Its two major procedures are determining what peripheral devices (keyboard, mouse, disk drives, printers, video cards, etc.) are available and loading the operating system (OS) into main memory. After start-up, the BIOS program manages data flow between the OS and the peripherals, so neither the OS nor the application programs need to know the details of the peripherals (such as hardware addresses).

biosolids Sewage sludge, the residues remaining from the treatment of sewage. For use as a FERTILIZER in agricultural applications, biosolids must first be stabilized through processing, such as digestion or the addition of lime, to reduce concentrations of heavy metals and harmful organisms (certain BACTERIA, VIRUSES, and other pathogens). This processing also reduces the volume of material and stabilizes the organic matter in it, thus reducing the potential for odors. Use of biosolids in agriculture has become controversial, critics claiming that even treated sewage may harbor harmful bacteria, viruses, and heavy metals.

biosphere Relatively thin life-supporting stratum of the earth's surface, extending from a few miles into the atmosphere to the deep-sea vents of the oceans. The biosphere is a global ECOSYSTEM that can be broken down into regional or local ecosystems, or BIOMES. Organisms in the biosphere are classified into trophic levels (see FOOD CHAIN) and communities.

biotechnology Application to industry of advances made in the biological sciences. The growth of the field is linked to the development in the 1970s of GENETIC ENGINEERING and to the 1980 U.S. Supreme Court decision that "a live human-made microorganism is a patentable matter," which resulted in the establishment of numerous commercial biotechnology firms that manufacture genetically engineered substances for a variety of mostly medical, agricultural, and ecological uses.

biotin \'bī-ə-tən\ Organic compound, part of the VITAMIN B COMPLEX, essential for growth and well-being in animals and some microorganisms. A CARBOXYLIC ACID with two rings in its structure, it includes nitrogen and sulfur atoms as well as carbon, hydrogen, and oxygen. Because the bacteria normally present in the LARGE INTESTINE can synthesize biotin, humans do not require it in their diet. A biotin deficiency can be induced by consuming large amounts of raw egg white, which contains a protein (avidin) that combines with biotin and makes it unavailable. Biotin is needed to synthesize FATTY ACIDS and convert AMINO ACIDS to GLUCOSE in the body.

biotite *or* **black mica** SILICATE MINERAL in the common MICA group. It is abundant in metamorphic rocks, in pegmatites, and in granites and other igneous rocks. Biotite is a layer silicate structure in which aluminum and silicon occur in infinitely extending Si-Al-O sheets that alternate with potassium-rich and magnesium- (and iron-) containing sheets.

Biotite mica from the district of Juchitán, Oaxaca, Mex.

BY COURTESY OF THE FIELD MUSEUM OF NATURAL HISTORY, CHICAGO; PHOTOGRAPH, JOHN H. GERARD—EB INC.

Bioy Casares \bē-'ȯi-kä-'sä-rās\, **Adolfo** (1914–1999) Argentine writer and editor. He is known for his use of magic realism both in his own works and in collaborations with JORGE LUIS BORGES. Among his novels are *The Invention of Morel* (1940), *The Dream of Heroes* (1954), and *Diary of the War of the Pig* (1969). In 1990 he received the Cervantes Prize, the highest honor in Hispanic letters.

bipolar disorder *or* **manic-depressive psychosis** Mental illness characterized by the alternation of manic and depressive states. DEPRESSION is the more common symptom, and many patients experience only a brief period of overoptimism and mild euphoria during the manic phase. The condition, which seems to be inheritable, probably arises from malregulation of the amines NOREPINEPHRINE, DOPAMINE, and 5-hydroxytryptamine. It is most commonly treated with LITHIUM carbonate.

birch Any of about 40 species of short-lived ornamental and timber trees and shrubs of the genus *Betula,* the largest genus of the family Betulaceae, which also contains ALDERS, FILBERTS, *Carpinus* (hornbeam), and the genera *Ostrya* and *Ostryopsis.* Birches are found throughout cool regions of the Northern Hemisphere; other members of the family Betulaceae are found in temperate and subarctic areas of the Northern Hemisphere, in tropical mountains, and in South America through the Andes as far south as Argentina. Leaves are simple, serrate, and alternate; male and female flowers (CATKINS) are borne on the same plant. The fruit is a small NUT or short-winged samara (dry, winged fruit). Birches produce economically important timber. Oil obtained from birch twigs smells and tastes like wintergreen and is used in tanning Russian leather (see TANNING).

bird Any member of the warm-blooded VERTEBRATE class Aves, containing about 8,700 living species. A covering of FEATHERS distinguishes birds from all other animals. They have a four-chambered heart (like MAMMALS), forelimbs modified into WINGS, an egg with a calcium-containing shell, and keen vision. Their sense of smell is not highly developed. Birds are found almost worldwide in diverse habitats. Dietary preferences and NEST structure vary widely. Almost all species incubate their eggs. The big flying birds have evolved skeletons in which part of the bone is replaced by air spaces, an adaptation for reducing weight. The crop, an enlarged part of the esophagus used for temporary food storage, enables birds to feed while in flight. Humans use wild and domesticated birds and their eggs for food, hunt wild birds for sport, and use feathers for decoration and insulation. More than 1,000 extinct species of bird have been identified from fossil remains; the earliest known fossil bird is the ARCHAEOPTERYX.

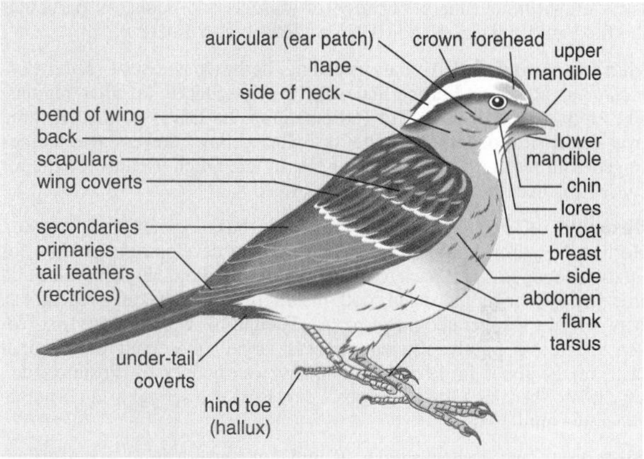

Principal features of a songbird.

Bird, Larry (Joe) (born 1956) U.S. basketball player. Born in Baden, Ind., the 6-ft 9-in. (2-m 6-cm) Bird spent most of his collegiate career at Indiana State University Drafted by the Boston Celtics as a forward, he helped lead that team to NBA championships in 1981, 1984, and 1986 and was named the NBA's most valuable player for three consecutive years (1984–86). He retired in 1992. Named head coach of the Indiana Pacers for the 1997–98 season, he immediately took the team to its best record in franchise history. He is considered one of the best all-around players in basketball history.

bird-of-paradise Any of about 40 species (family Paradisaeidae) of small to medium-sized forest birds that are rivaled by only a few pheasants and hummingbirds in color and in the bizarre shape of the males' plumage. Courting males perform mating rituals for hours on a perch or in a cleared space on the forest floor. Birds-of-paradise are found in the New Guinea highlands and on nearby islands; some species are found also in Australia. Among the most notable species are the plumebirds, 12–18 in. (30–46 cm) long, with central tail feathers elongated as wires or twisted ribbons.

bird-of-paradise *or* **crane flower** Ornamental plant *(Strelitzia reginae)* of the family Strelitziaceae. All five species of the genus *Strelitzia* are native to southern Africa. The large, showy *Strelitzia* flower has two erect, pointed petals and five stamens. One main BRACT, shaped like a boat, is green with red borders. It holds many long-stemmed orange and bright-blue flowers, each resembling the crest and beak of a crane, giving the plant its common name.

bird of prey Any bird that pursues other animals for food. Diurnal birds of prey (order Falconiformes, comprising EAGLES, FALCONS, HAWKS, and VULTURES) are also called RAPTORS. Nocturnal birds of prey (order Strigiformes) are the OWLS. CONDORS and eagles are among the largest and strongest of birds. All birds of prey have a hook-tipped beak and sharp curved claws called talons. (Nonpredatory vultures have atrophied talons.) Despite the similarities between owls and raptors, many authorities believe they are not closely related but developed similar features because of their similar predatory lives.

bird stone Abstract stone carving by the prehistoric cultures of the eastern U.S. and eastern Canada. They resemble birds and are about 6 in. (15 cm) long. Many were carved from black, brown, or dark green slate and polished with sand or other abrasive materials. All feature a pair of conical holes running diagonally through the base. They may have been used as weights or handles on a short rod (known as an *atlatl*) used to hurl spears or arrows.

bird-watching *or* **birding** Observation or identification of wild birds in their natural habitat. Basic equipment includes binoculars, a field guide to aid identification, and a notebook for recording time and place of sightings. The lists of bird observations compiled by members of local bird-watching societies are often useful to scientists in determining dispersal, habitat, and migration patterns of the various species. Bird-watching is primarily a 20th-century phenomenon; before 1900 most students of birds had to shoot them in order to identify them. Its popularity grew through the publication of journals and books, in particular the field guides (beginning in 1934) of ROGER TORY PETERSON.

bird's-foot trefoil Perennial, spreading, herbaceous LEGUME *(Lotus corniculatus)* native to Europe and Asia but introduced to other regions. The stem grows to about 2 ft (60 cm) long. Its leaves consist of three oval leaflets, broadest near the tip. The yellow flowers (sometimes tinged with red) grow in clusters of five to ten. Often used as FORAGE for cattle, it is occasionally a troublesome weed.

Birdseye, Clarence (1886–1956) U.S. businessman and inventor. Born in New York City, he is remembered for developing a process for FREEZING foods in small packages suitable for retailing. He achieved rapid freezing by placing packaged food, including fish, fruits, and vegetables, between two refrigerated metal plates. Though his were not the first frozen foods, his highly efficient process largely preserved the original taste of the food. In 1929 his company was bought by Postum, Inc., which later became GENERAL FOODS CORP. Birdseye served as a corporate executive until 1938.

birdsong Certain vocalizations of birds, characteristic of males during the breeding season, for the attraction of a mate and for territorial defense. Birdsong also reinforces pair bonds, and some species have a flight song. Birdsongs are usually more complex and longer than birdcalls, which are used for communication within a species. Birdsong may be hereditary or learned; a newly hatched male CHAFFINCH, for example, can sing a "subsong" but must learn to sing the true song by listening to and imitating adult males.

birefringence See DOUBLE REFRACTION

Biringuccio \bē-rēŋ-'güt-chō\, **Vannoccio** (1480–1539?) Italian metallurgist and armaments maker. He is chiefly known for the first clear, comprehensive work on METALLURGY, *De la pirotechnia* (published posthumously in 1540). His book, which contrasts strikingly with the obscure alchemical writings of the time, is replete with lavish woodcuts illustrating equipment and processes and includes clear, practical instructions for MINING, SMELTING, and metalworking. It became a standard reference and remains a valuable resource on 15th- and 16th-century technology.

Birkenau See AUSCHWITZ

Birkenhead, Earl of *orig.* **Frederick Edwin Smith** (1872–1930) British politician. Elected to the House of Commons in 1906, he became noted as an orator and soon became a leader of the Conservative Party. As attorney general (1915–18), he successfully prosecuted ROGER CASEMENT. As lord chancellor (1919–22), he secured passage of the Law of Property Act (1922) and subsequent real-property statutes (1925) that replaced a convoluted system of land law. He also helped negotiate the Anglo-Irish treaty of 1921.

Birmingham \'bər-miŋ-əm\ City (pop., 1999: 1,013,200), central England. It lies 100 mi (160 km) northwest of London. Its first charter was granted in 1166. It was a small manufacturing town until the 18th century, when it became a center of the INDUSTRIAL REVOLUTION, counting among its citizens JAMES WATT, JOSEPH PRIESTLEY, and JOHN BASKERVILLE. It suffered heavy bombing during World War II but was subsequently rebuilt. It remains the chief center of Britain's light and medium industry, and is also the cultural center for a wide area. With two universities, it is also the site of a grammar school founded by King Edward VI in 1552.

Birmingham \'bər-miŋ-ˌham\ City (pop., 2000: 249,459), northern central Alabama. It is Alabama's largest city. Founded in 1871 by a land company backed by railroad officials, it was named for the English city. It developed as the South's iron and steel center. From nearby Port Birmingham a barge canal leads south to MOBILE. Birmingham was the scene of civil rights drives by MARTIN LUTHER KING, Jr., in the early 1960s, and in 1963 four black girls were killed in a church bombing; this incident gave major impetus to the CIVIL RIGHTS MOVEMENT.

Birney, (Alfred) Earle (1904–1995) Canadian poet and educator. Born in Calgary, Alberta, he received a PhD from the University of Toronto and brought out his first collection of poetry, *David* (1942, Governor General's Award), during his time there. After serving in World War II, he published *Now Is Time* (1946, Governor General's Award) and other collections and held a number of teaching and editorial positions. His love of language led him to experiment with sound poems and to explore concrete poetry; he also wrote two novels, a drama in verse, and several radio plays.

Birney, James Gillespie (1792–1857) U.S. politician and antislavery leader. Born in Danville, Ky., he practiced law there, then moved to Alabama and was elected to its legislature in 1819. He became active in the anti-slavery societies and in 1837 was elected secretary of the AMERICAN ANTI-SLAVERY SOCIETY. After the group split, he helped lead the faction that became the LIBERTY PARTY, and was its presidential candidate in the 1840 and 1844 elections.

birth See PARTURITION

birth control Voluntary limiting of human reproduction, using such means as CONTRACEPTION, sexual abstinence, surgical STERILIZATION, and induced ABORTION. The term was coined in 1914–15 by MARGARET SANGER. Medically, birth control is often advised when childbirth might endanger the mother's health or substantial risk exists of bearing a severely disabled child. Socially and economically, limitation of reproduction frequently reflects a desire to maintain or improve family living standards. Most religious leaders now generally agree that some form of fertility regulation is desirable, though the means are strongly debated. See also FAMILY PLANNING.

birth defect Genetic or trauma-induced abnormality present at birth. A more restrictive term than CONGENITAL DISORDER, it covers abnormalities that arise during the formation of an EMBRYO's organs and tissues and does not include those caused by diseases (e.g., SYPHILIS) that damage structures after they are formed.

birthmark Unusual mark or blemish on the skin at birth. Most birthmarks are either HEMANGIOMAS or MOLES. They are usually harmless, and many fade in childhood; those that do not can sometimes be removed by laser surgery or abrasion.

birthstone Gemstone associated with the month of one's birth. Wearing one was popularly supposed to bring good luck or health. The ancient belief that supernatural powers could be attributed to gemstones is still held by some people today. The list of genuine stones (e.g., diamond, emerald, sapphire, ruby) was supplemented in the 20th century by a series of synthetic stones for use as less costly substitutes.

Birtwistle, Harrison (Paul) *later* **Sir Harrison** (born 1934) British composer. He began as a clarinetist, only shifting to composition in his twenties. He cofounded the Pierrot Players with P.M. DAVIES (1967), but felt limited by the group's size. He has concentrated on exploring large-scale time structures; his music's form is controlled by complex cyclical principles that he has declined to discuss. His works include the theater pieces *Punch and Judy* (1966–67), *The Mask of Orpheus* (1973–86), and *Gawain* (1991), and the orchestral works *The Triumph of Time* (1972), *Silbury Air* (1977), and *Secret Theater* (1984).

Biruni \bē-'rü-nē\, **al-** (973–1048) Persian scientist and scholar. Some time after 1017, he went to India, of which he wrote an encyclopedic account. Later he settled at Ghazna in Afghanistan, where he was patronized by the GHAZNAVID DYNASTY. Conversant with many languages, he wrote in Arabic, producing works on mathematics, astronomy, astrology, geography, physics, medicine, history, and chronology. His scientific achievements included accurate calculations of latitude and longitude and explanations of natural springs by the laws of hydrostatics. His best-known works are *India* and *Chronology*.

Biscay, Bay of *or* **Gulf of Gascony** *French* **Golfe de Gascogne** \ˌgȯlf-də-gȧ-ˈskȯnʸ\ *Spanish* **Golfo de Vizcaya** \ˈgōl-fō-ˌthā-bēth-ˈkä-yä\ Inlet of the Atlantic Ocean, bounded by southwestern France and northwestern Spain. It has an area of about 86,000 sq mi (223,000 sq km) and a maximum depth of 15,525 ft (4,735 m). It is known for its rough seas. Rivers flowing into the bay include the LOIRE, ADOUR, and GARONNE. Its ports include (in France) Brest, NANTES, and BORDEAUX, and (in Spain) BILBAO, SANTANDER, and Avilés; none can accommodate large vessels. French coastal resorts include La Baule, BIARRITZ, and Saint-Jean-de-Luz.

Biscayne Bay Inlet of the Atlantic Ocean, southeastern U.S. Located along southeastern Florida, it is about 40 mi (64 km) long and 2–10 mi (3–16 km) wide; it forms part of the ATLANTIC INTRACOASTAL WATERWAY. It is bordered by MIAMI on the northwest and the Florida Keys on the east. The bay was named for the early explorer El Biscaino, of Viscaya (Biscaya) province, Spain. See also BISCAYNE NATIONAL PARK.

Biscayne National Park Preserve, southeastern Florida. Located 20 mi (32 km) south of MIAMI, with an area of 172,925 acres (70,035 hectares), it consists mostly of coral reef and water containing some 33 keys that form a north-to-south chain separating BISCAYNE BAY from the Atlantic Ocean. It is noted for a wide variety of sealife. Authorized as Biscayne National Monument in 1968, it became a national park in 1980.

Bischof \ˈbi-shōf\, **Werner** (1916–1954) Swiss photojournalist. He studied at the Zurich Arts and Crafts School 1932–36. In 1942 he began working for the picture magazine *Du*, for which he photographed war-torn France, Germany, and the Netherlands. In 1949 he joined the cooperative photographers' agency Magnum Photos. He died in a car accident while working in Peru. Collections of his photographs were published in *Japan* (1954), *Incas to Indians* (1956), and *The World of Werner Bischof* (1959).

Bishkek \bish-ˈkek\ *or* **Pishpek** \pish-ˈpek\ *formerly (1926–91)* **Frunze** \ˈfrün-zi\ City (pop., 1996 est.: 590,000), capital of Kyrgyzstan. It lies on the Chu River near the Kyrgyz Mountains on the Kazakhstan border. In 1825 the Uzbek khanate of Kokand (see QUQON) established a fortress on the site, which in 1862 was captured by the Russians, who misunderstood it as named Pishpek. When the Kirgiz (Kyrgyz) Autonomous Soviet Socialist Republic was set up in 1926, the city became its capital and was renamed Frunze after a Red Army leader who was born there. It developed as an industrial city, especially in World War II when heavy industries from western Russia were moved there.

bishop In some Christian churches, the chief pastor and overseer of a diocese, an area containing several congregations. From the 4th century AD until the REFORMATION, bishops held broad secular and religious powers, including the settling of disputes, ordination of clergy, and CONFIRMATION of church members. Some Christian churches (notably the Anglican, Roman Catholic, and Eastern Orthodox churches) continue the bishop's office and the doctrine of APOSTOLIC SUCCESSION. Others, including some Lutheran and Methodist churches, retain bishops but not the principle of apostolic succession; still others have abolished the office altogether. POPES, CARDINALS, ARCHBISHOPS, PATRIARCHS, and metropolitans are gradations of bishops. In Roman Catholicism, the pope selects the bishop; in Anglicanism, the dean and chapter of the cathedral of the diocese elect the bishop; in Methodism a synod chooses the bishop. See also EPISCOPACY.

Bishop, Billy *orig.* **William Avery** (1894–1956) Canadian World War I fighter ace. Born in Owen Sound, Ontario, he was educated at the Royal Military College. In 1915 he transferred from the cavalry to the Royal Flying Corps. While serving in France in 1917, he shot down 72 enemy aircraft, including 25 in one 10-day period. He was appointed to the staff of the British Air Ministry and helped form the Royal Canadian Air Force as a separate brigade. After the war he became a businessman and writer.

Bishop, Elizabeth (1911–1979) U.S. poet. Born in Worcester, Mass., she was reared by relatives in Nova Scotia after her father died and her mother was institutionalized. In the 1950s and '60s she lived principally in Brazil with the Brazilian woman she loved. Her first book of poems (1946) contrasts her New England origins and her love of hot climates; reprinted with additions as *North & South: A Cold Spring* (1955), it received the Pulitzer Prize. Her works are celebrated for their formal brilliance and their close observations of everyday reality, and are notable for the admiration they have elicited from other poets. Posthumous publications include *The Collected Prose* (1984) and *One Art* (1994), a much-admired collection of her letters.

Bishop, J(ohn) Michael (born 1936) U.S. virologist. Born in York, Pa., he graduated from Harvard's medical school. In 1970 he and HAROLD VARMUS tested the theory that healthy body cells contain ONCOGENES (cancer-causing genes). Further research showed that such genes can cause cancer even without viral involvement. By 1989, the year Bishop and Varmus shared a Nobel Prize for their research, scientists had identified more than 40 oncogenes in animals.

Bishop's University Privately endowed university in Lennoxville, Quebec, founded in 1843. It offers undergraduate and graduate programs in the humanities, social sciences, natural sciences, business, and education. Total enrollment is about 1,800.

Bisitun \ˌbē-si-ˈtün\ *ancient* **Behestun** Ruined town, western Iran. On a limestone cliff above the present village is a monument of King DARIUS the Great (r.522–486 BC); an inscription in Old Persian, Babylonian, and Elamite records how Darius killed a usurper, defeated the rebels, and assumed the throne. The inscriptions were first copied (1837–47) by Sir Henry Rawlinson (1810–1895), an officer of the EAST INDIA CO. His deciphering of the Old Persian was a major advance in the study of CUNEIFORM WRITING.

bisj pole \ˈbis-ē\ Carved wooden pole used in the religious rites of the South Pacific islands. The poles, 12–26 ft (4–8 m) tall, resemble an upended canoe with an exaggerated prow; they consist of carved figures thought to represent deceased ancestors, placed one atop the other, and terminate in a flat projection of ornate, openwork ornament. They are intended to harbor the souls of the dead, keeping them away from the village, and are also used to transmit magical powers. See also TOTEM POLE.

Bismarck \ˈbiz-ˌmärk\ City (pop., 1994 est.: 53,000), capital of North Dakota. It was settled as a MISSOURI RIVER port in the 1830s. In 1872 a military post was established to protect railway workers, and in 1873 it was named for OTTO VON BISMARCK in the hope of attracting German investment. With the discovery of gold in the nearby BLACK HILLS, it became a prospecting center. In 1883 it was made the capital of Dakota Territory; when the territory was divided into two states in 1889, Bismarck became the capital of the northern state. Today it is the region's business, cultural, and financial center.

Bismarck German BATTLESHIP of World War II. The formidable 52,600-ton (47,700-metric-ton) vessel was launched in 1939. British reconnaissance aircraft sighted it off Bergen, Norway, in May 1941, and almost the entire British home fleet was sent to intercept it. Two cruisers engaged it near Iceland, and the *Bismarck* destroyed the *Hood* before escaping to the open sea. Sighted 30 hours later, it was torpedoed and then bombarded by battleships throughout the night. The *King George V* and the *Rodney* crippled it in an hour-long attack, and it was finally sunk by torpedoes from the cruiser *Dorsetshire*.

Bismarck, Otto (Eduard Leopold) von *later* **Fürst (Prince) von Bismarck** (1815–1898) Prussian statesman who founded the German empire in 1871 and served as its chancellor for 19 years. Born into the Prussian landowning elite, Bismarck studied law and was elected to the Prussian Diet in 1849. In 1851 he was appointed Prussian representative to the federal Diet in Frankfurt. After serving as ambassador to Russia (1859–62) and France (1862), he became prime minister and foreign minister of Prussia (1862–71). When he took office Prussia was widely considered the weakest of the five European powers, but under his leadership Prussia won a war against Denmark in 1864 (see SCHLESWIG-HOLSTEIN QUESTION), the SEVEN WEEKS' WAR (1866), and the FRANCO-PRUSSIAN WAR (1870–71). Through these wars he achieved his goal of political unification of a Prussian-dominated German empire. Once the empire was established, he became its chancellor. The "Iron Chancellor" skillfully preserved the peace in Europe through alliances against France (see THREE EMPERORS' LEAGUE, REINSURANCE TREATY, TRIPLE ALLIANCE). Domestically, he introduced administrative and economic reforms but sought to preserve the status quo, opposing the SOCIAL DEMOCRATIC PARTY and the Catholic church (see KULTURKAMPF). When Bismarck left office in 1890, the map of Europe had been changed immeasurably. However, the German empire, his greatest achievement, survived him by only 20 years because he had failed to create an internally unified people.

Bismarck Archipelago Island group (pop., 1989 est.: 371,000), western Pacific Ocean. Lying northwest of New Guinea, it forms part of Papua New Guinea. It has a total area of 19,173 sq mi (49,658 sq km); its largest components include New Britain, New Ireland, the Admiralty Islands, and New Hanover (Lavongai). Annexed by Germany in 1884, it was named for Otto von Bismarck. Occupied by Australia in 1914, it was made a mandated territory of Australia in 1920. The group became part of the U.N. Trust Territory of New Guinea after World War II, and part of Papua New Guinea when it attained independence in 1975.

bismuth \'biz-məth\ Semimetallic to metallic chemical element, chemical symbol Bi, atomic number 83. Hard, brittle, and lustrous, it has a distinctive gray-white color with a reddish tinge. It is often found free in nature and also occurs in compounds and in mixed ores. Bismuth alloys are used (because of their low melting points) in making metal castings, special solders, automatic sprinkler heads, fuses, and many fire-detection devices. Bismuth phosphomolybdate is a catalyst in the production of acrylonitrile, an important raw material for fibers and plastics. Salts of bismuth are used in making soothing agents for digestive disorders (especially bismuth subsalicylate), in treating skin infections and injuries, and in lipstick, nail polish, and eye shadow, to which they impart a pearlescent quality.

bison \'bī-sᵊn, 'bī-zᵊn\ Species *(Bison bison)* of oxlike bovid that has a convex forehead and a pronounced shoulder hump. Its dark-brown, coarse hair is especially long on the head, which is held low, and on the neck and shoulders. Both sexes bear heavy, curved horns. A mature bull stands about 6.5 ft (2 m) at the shoulder and weighs more than 1,980 lbs (900 kg). Bison live in herds. The American bison, commonly called buffalo, was abundant over most of North America when Europeans arrived. Hunting drove it nearly to extinction by 1900; today managed herds seem to be ensuring its survival. The European bison survives only in a few managed herds.

American bison, or plains buffalo (*Bison bison*).
ALAN G. NELSON—ROOT RESOURCES

Bissau \bis-'aù\ Seaport (pop., 1995: 233,000), capital of Guinea-Bissau. Lying on an estuary of the Gêba River where it flows into the Atlantic Ocean, the port originated in 1687 as a Portuguese fortified post. In 1941 it replaced Bolama as the country's capital, and has since developed as an excellent roadstead for large vessels.

bit *in full* **binary digit** In communication and information theory, a unit of information equivalent to the result of a choice between only two possible alternatives, such as 1 and 0 in the binary code generally used in digital computers. It is also applied to a unit of memory corresponding to the ability to store the result of a choice between two alternatives. A byte consists of a string of eight consecutive bits and makes up the basic information processing unit of a computer. Because a byte includes only an amount of information equivalent to one letter or one symbol (e.g., a comma), the processing and storage capacities of computer hardware are usually given in kilobytes (1,024 bytes), megabytes (1,048,576 bytes), and even gigabytes (about 1 billion bytes) and terabytes (1 trillion bytes).

bit-map Method by which a display space (such as a graphics image file) is defined, including the color of each of its pixels (or bits). In effect, a bit-map is an array of binary data representing the values of pixels in an image or display. A GIF is an example of a graphics image file that has a bit-map. When the GIF is displayed on a computer monitor, the computer reads the bit-map to determine which colors to use to "paint" the screen. In a bit-mapped font, each character is defined as a pattern of dots in a bit-map.

Bithynia \bə-'thin-ē-ə\ Ancient country, northwestern Asia. Bounded by the Sea of Marmara, the Bosporus, and the Black Sea, it was settled by Thracians in the late 2nd millennium BC. They never submitted to Alexander the Great, and by the 3rd century BC a powerful Hellenistic kingship had been established in the area. There followed a century of inept leadership and rapid decline. Bithynia's last king, Nicomedes IV, bequeathed his kingdom to the Romans in 74 BC.

bittern Any of 12 species of solitary marsh birds (family Ardeidae), related to herons but having a shorter neck and a stouter body. Most bitterns bear a camouflage pattern (streaks of variegated brown and buff) that enables them to hide by standing upright with bill pointed upward, imitating the reeds and grasses of their habitat. They feed on fish, frogs, crayfish, and other small swamp and marsh animals, which they spear with their sharp-pointed bills. Bitterns are found almost worldwide. The largest species grow to 30 in. (75 cm), the smallest to about 12–16 in. (30–40 cm).

Bitterroot Range Segment of the northern Rocky Mtns., U.S. Extending north-south 300 mi (480 km) along the Idaho-Montana border, its peaks average about 9,000 ft (2,700 m); Idaho's Scott Peak is the highest, at 11,393 ft (3,473 m). Owing to the mountains' inaccessibility from the east, the Lewis and Clark Expedition (1805) had to travel north more than 100 mi (160 km) to find a route through the range. Bitterroot National Forest extends across the center of the range.

bittersweet Any of several vines with colorful fruit. The genus *Celastrus* (family Celastraceae) includes American bittersweet, or staff vine *(C. scandens),* and Oriental bittersweet *(C. orbiculatus),* woody vines grown as ornamentals. Oriental bittersweet is a more vigorous climber than the American species. Both types climb by twining around supports. Another bittersweet, *Solanum dulcamara*, belongs to the nightshade family.

bitumen \bə-'tyü-mən\ Mixture of tarlike hydrocarbons derived from petroleum. Black or brown, it varies from viscous to solid; the solid form is usually called asphalt. Bitumen occurs in nearly every part of the world and in nearly the whole range of geologic strata. The term may also refer to synthetic hydrocarbon compounds.

bituminous coal \bə-'tyü-mə-nəs\ *or* **soft coal** Most abundant form of coal. It is dark brown to black and has a relatively high heat value. Widely abundant and with the broadest range of commercial uses, it has long been used for steam generation in electric power plants and industrial boiler plants. Certain varieties are also used to make coke, a hard substance of almost pure carbon that is important for smelting iron ore. One major problem is that burning large quantities of bituminous coal that has a medium to high sulfur content contributes to air pollution and produces acid rain. See also anthracite.

bituminous sand See tar sand

bivalve Any member of the mollusk class Bivalvia, or Pelecypoda, characterized by having a two-halved (valved) shell. Clams, cockles, mussels, oysters, scallops, and shipworms are bivalves. Most are completely enclosed by the shell, the two valves of which are joined by an elastic ligament, and by two sheets of tissue called the mantle. Bivalves have no head. They feed on phytoplankton by pumping water across the gills and trapping food particles that are then moved to the mouth. Bivalves are found in most parts of the ocean from the intertidal zone to abyssal depths. See illustration opposite on following page.

Biwa \'bē-wä\, **Lake** Lake, central Honshu, Japan. It is Japan's largest lake, measuring 40 mi (64 km) long and 12 mi (19 km) wide, with an area of 260 sq mi (673 sq km). Its name refers to the musical instrument (see pi-pa) that the lake resembles in shape. Its sole outlet, the Yodo River, flows from its southern tip to Osaka Bay. Lake Biwa is noted for its pearl culture industry. Its great scenic beauty, long a subject of Japanese poetry, makes it one of Japan's major tourist attractions.

Bizet \bē-'zä\, **Georges** *orig.* **Alexandre-César-Léopold** (1838–1875) French composer. Son of a music teacher, he gained admission to the Paris Conservatoire at 9, and at 17 he wrote the precocious Symphony in C major. Intent on success on the operatic stage, he produced *The Pearl Fishers* (1863), *La jolie fille de Perth* (1866), and *Djamileh* (1871). Disgusted with the frivolity of French light opera, he determined to reform the genre of *opéra comique*. In 1875 his masterpiece, *Carmen,* reached the stage. Though its harsh realism repelled many, *Carmen* quickly won international enthusiasm and was recognized as the supreme example of *opéra comique*. Bizet's death at 37, shortly after its premiere, cut short a remarkable career.

Björling \'byœr-liŋ\, **Jussi** *orig.* **Johann Jonaton** (1911–1960) Swedish tenor. He began to sing in public as a child, and toured Europe and the U.S. with his family. Recruited by the Royal Swedish Opera in 1928, he was soon a star performer. He made his Metropolitan Opera debut in 1938 as Rodolfo in *La Bohème*. He remained in Sweden during the war but returned to the Met for several seasons afterward. Though not known as an actor, he became a favorite on stage and in recordings for the sheer beauty and musicality of his singing.

Bjørnson \'byœrn-sȯn\, **Bjørnstjerne (Martinius)** (1832–1910) Norwegian writer, editor, and theater director. He worked to stimulate national pride by linking Norwegian history and legend to modern ideals. Together with HENRIK IBSEN, Alexander Kielland, and JONAS LIE, he is known as one of "the four great ones" of 19th-century Norwegian literature. He won the Nobel Prize in 1903. His poem "Yes, We Love This Land Forever" is the Norwegian national anthem.

Black, Hugo (La Fayette) (1886–1971) U.S. Supreme Court justice (1937–71). Born in Clay Co., Ala., he practiced law in Alabama from 1906. He served in the U.S. Senate 1927–37, where he was a strong supporter of New Deal legislation. Pres. FRANKLIN ROOSEVELT appointed him to the Supreme Court, where he helped reverse earlier court vetoes of New Deal legislation. In the 1960s he was prominent in the liberal majority that struck down mandatory school prayer and guaranteed the availability of legal counsel to suspected criminals. He became best known for his absolutist belief in the Bill of Rights as a guarantee of civil liberties. His last major opinion supported the right of the *New York Times* to publish the PENTAGON PAPERS (1971).

Black, James (Whyte) *later* **Sir James** (born 1924) Scottish pharmacologist. Through studying interactions between receptors on cells and chemicals in the bloodstream that attach to them, Black developed the first of the beta-blocking drugs, to relieve angina pectoris. He used a similar approach to develop drugs for stomach and duodenal ulcers. He shared a 1988 Nobel Prize with GEORGE H. HITCHINGS and GERTRUDE ELION.

black aesthetic movement *or* **black arts movement** Period of artistic and literary development among black Americans in the 1960s and early '70s. Based on the cultural politics of black nationalism, the movement sought to create art forms capable of expressing the varieties of black experience in the U.S. Leading theorists included AMIRI BARAKA, Houston Baker (born 1943), and HENRY LOUIS GATES. Don L. Lee (born 1942), known as Haki R. Madhubuti after 1973, was one of its most popular writers; other notable writers included TONI MORRISON, ALICE WALKER, and Ntozake Shange (born 1948). The movement also produced such autobiographical works as *The Autobiography of Malcolm X* (1965; with ALEX HALEY), Eldridge Cleaver's *Soul On Ice* (1968), and *Angela Davis: An Autobiography* (1974).

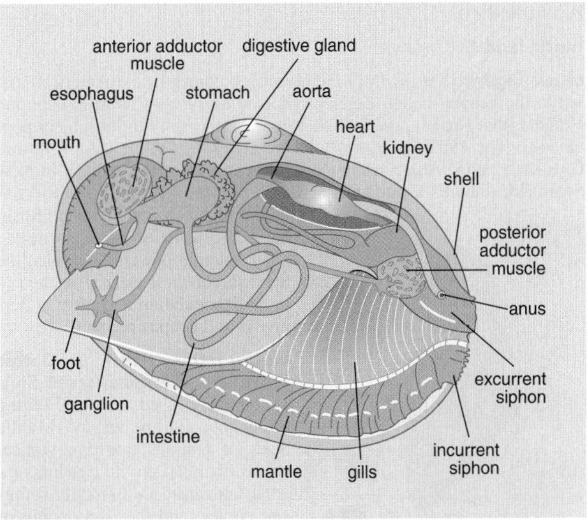

Internal structure of a clam. A ligament hinges the shell's two halves (valves) open, and the beating motion of cilia on the gills causes water to enter through the incurrent siphon. As water moves over the gills, oxygen diffuses into the blood, and food particles become trapped in mucus and are moved to the mouth. A pair of adductor muscles can hold the shell tightly closed. A fold of tissue (mantle) encloses the body's organs and releases the material that forms the shell. A large muscular foot allows the clam to creep and burrow. The circulatory system consists of a heart and blood vessels, and kidneys remove wastes from the blood. Deoxygenated blood and wastes are removed in the water that exits through the excurrent siphon.

Black and Tan Member of a British auxiliary force employed in Ireland against the republicans (1920–21). When Irish nationalist agitation intensified after World War I, many Irish police resigned and were replaced by these temporary English recruits, who dressed in a mixed "black and tan" outfit because of a shortage of uniforms. In their efforts to thwart the terrorism of the IRISH REPUBLICAN ARMY, the Black and Tans themselves engaged in brutal reprisals.

black bass Any of about six species (genus *Micropterus*) of slender freshwater fishes of the SUNFISH family; found in eastern North America. Two, the largemouth and smallmouth black basses, have been introduced into other countries and are prized as hard-fighting game fishes. Black basses are larger and longer-bodied than sunfishes and more predatory. The largemouth bass may grow to 32 in. (80 cm) long and weigh 22 lbs (10 kg); it lives in quiet weedy lakes and streams. The smallmouth bass, which usually grows to 5–6 lbs (2–3 kg), inhabits clear, cool lakes and running streams.

black bear Forest-dwelling BEAR *(Ursus americanus)* that, despite reductions in population and range, is still the most common North American bear. The adult ranges from 5 to 6 ft (150–180 cm) in length and weighs 200–600 lbs (90–270 kg). It has various color phases but always a brown face and usually a white chest mark. It eats animals and vegetation, including pinecones, berries, and roots. It frequently raids campsites and seizes anything edible. Though it may be tamed and taught tricks, it often becomes dangerous when mature.

American black bear (*Ursus americanus*).

LEONARD LEE RUE III

Black Canyon of the Gunnison National Monument Park, western Colorado. Comprising a narrow, deep gorge of the Gunnison River, the preserve, established in 1933, occupies an area of 32 sq mi (83 sq km). The canyon derives its name from its black-stained, lichen-covered walls, which accentuate the gloom of the chasm.

black code Laws enacted in the former Confederate states after the AMERICAN CIVIL WAR that restricted the freedom of former slaves and were designed to assure white supremacy. They originated in the slave codes, which defined slaves as property. In some states these codes included vagrancy laws that targeted unemployed blacks, apprentice laws that made black orphans and dependents available for hire to whites, and commercial laws that excluded blacks from certain trades and businesses and restricted their ownership of property. Northern reaction to the laws helped produce radical RECONSTRUCTION and passage of the 14th and 15th Amendments to the Constitution, as well as creation of the FREEDMEN'S BUREAU. Many provisions of the black codes were reenacted in the JIM CROW LAWS and remained in force until the 1964 CIVIL RIGHTS ACT.

Black Death Fierce and widespread outbreak of PLAGUE that ravaged Europe during the 14th century. The epidemic originated in Asia and was transmitted to Europeans in 1347 when a Turkic army besieging a Genoese trading post in the Crimea catapulted plague-infested corpses into the town. It spread from the Mediterranean ports and ravaged all of Europe between 1347 and 1351. Renewed outbreaks occurred in 1361–63, 1369–71, 1374–75, 1390, and 1400. Towns and cities were more heavily hit than the countryside, and whole communities were sometimes destroyed, and much of Europe's economy was devastated. About one-third of the European population, or a total of 25 million people, died in the Black Death.

black-eyed pea See COWPEA

black-eyed Susan Either of two North American CONEFLOWERS *(Rudbeckia hirta* and *R. serotina)* having flower heads with deep yellow to orange petals and dark conical centers. The stems are rough and hairy;

the leaves are large and ovate at the base of the plant and narrow at the top.

black-figure pottery Type of Greek pottery that originated in Corinth c. 700 BC. The figures were painted in black pigment on the natural red clay ground. Finishing details were then incised into the black pigment, revealing the red ground. The great Attic painters (mid-6th century BC), most notably Exekias, developed narrative scene decoration and perfected the style. It continued to be popular until the advent of red-figure pottery (c. 530 BC).

Dionysus and satyrs, amphora painted in the black-figure style by the Amasis Painter, c. 540 BC; in the Antikenmuseum, Basel, Switz.

BY COURTESY OF THE ANTIKENMUSEUM, BASEL, SWITZ.; PHOTOGRAPH, COLORPHOTO HANS HINZ

Black Forest *German* **Schwarzwald** \'shfärts-,vält\ Mountain region, Baden-Württemberg, southwestern Germany. It extends in a fairly narrow strip about 100 mi (160 km) along the eastern bank of the upper Rhine River, from the Neckar to the Swiss border. Its highest peak is Feldberg, at 4,905 ft (1,495 m). Its name comes from its dark interior, the higher parts being thickly forested with fir and pine. It is the source of the Neckar and Danube rivers. The setting of many of the Grimm brothers' fairy tales, it is famed for the beauty and charm of its villages and rolling hills. Winter sports are prominent in the area, which also has many mineral springs and watering places, including Baden-Baden. The forest has suffered serious damage from acid rain.

Black Friday Day (September 24, 1869) when plunging gold prices precipitated a U.S. stock-market panic. An attempt by Jay Gould and James Fisk to corner the market in gold and drive up its price depended on preventing the sale of government gold, an arrangement assured through the two men's political influence. When Pres. Ulysses S. Grant heard of the scheme, he ordered the government to sell $4 million in gold, which caused the price to drop and produced a panic selling of other stocks.

black gum *or* **sour gum** Most widely distributed tupelo, *Nyssa sylvatica*, also known as black tupelo or pepperidge tree. It is found in moist areas of the eastern U.S. from Maine south to the Gulf Coast and westward to Oklahoma. Its wood is light and soft but tough. The black gum is sometimes grown as an ornamental and is prized for its brilliant scarlet autumnal foliage.

Black Hand Secret Serbian society formed in 1911 primarily by army officers, which used terrorist methods to promote the liberation of Serbs outside Serbia from Habsburg or Ottoman rule. It conducted propaganda campaigns, organized armed bands in Macedonia, and established revolutionary cells throughout Bosnia. Within Serbia it dominated the army and wielded tremendous influence over the government. It gained its greatest notoriety with the assassination of Archduke Francis Ferdinand in 1914. After a trial in 1917, three leaders were executed and more than 200 were imprisoned. The name also referred to several extortion rackets run by immigrant Sicilian and Italian gangsters in the Italian communities of many large U.S. cities c. 1890–1920. Local merchants and wealthy individuals would receive threatening notes printed with black hands, daggers, or other menacing symbols that demanded money on pain of death or destruction of property. It declined with the beginning of Prohibition and large-scale bootlegging.

Black Hawk (1767–1838) Sauk Indian leader of a faction of Sauk and Fox whose defiance of government orders to vacate villages along the Rock River in Illinois resulted in the brief but tragic Black Hawk War of 1832. Long antagonistic to whites, Black Hawk, who had been driven into Iowa from his native Illinois in 1831, led his people back across the Mississippi the following year, only to face military opposition and eventual massacre, though he himself survived. The ruthlessness of the war so affected neighboring Indian groups that by 1837 most had fled to the far West, leaving most of the Northwest Territory to white settlers. See photograph opposite.

Black Hills Group of mountains western South Dakota and northeastern Wyoming. Occupying about 6,000 sq mi (15,540 sq km), they lie between the Cheyenne and Belle Fourche rivers and rise to a maximum elevation of 7,242 ft (2,207 m) at Harney Peak. Their name refers to the dark appearance that their rounded hilltops and well-forested slopes present at a distance. The Sioux Indians were guaranteed treaty rights to the region in 1868; however, the discovery of gold in 1874 led to an influx of white miners and to the Black Hills War (1876), including the Battle of the Little Bighorn. Tourist attractions include the mining town of Deadwood, Mount Rushmore and Jewel Cave national monuments, Wind Cave National Park, and Custer State Park, all in South Dakota, and Devils Tower National Monument in Wyoming.

black hole Cosmic body with gravity (see gravitation) so intense that nothing, not even light, can escape. It is suspected to form in the death and collapse of a star that began with more than 10 times the sun's mass. Stars with less mass evolve into white dwarf stars or neutron stars. Details of a black hole's structure are calculated from Albert Einstein's general theory of relativity: a "singularity" of zero volume and infinite density pulls in all matter and energy that comes within an event horizon, defined by the Schwarzschild radius, around it. Black holes are hard to observe because they are small and emit no light. However, their enormous gravitational fields affect nearby matter, which is drawn in and emits X rays as it collides at high speed outside the event horizon. Some black holes may have nonstellar origins. Astronomers speculate that supermassive black holes at the centers of quasars and many galaxies are the source of energetic activity that is observed. Stephen W. Hawking has theorized the creation of numerous tiny black holes, possibly no more massive than an asteroid, during the big bang. These primordial "mini-black holes" lose mass over time and disappear as a result of Hawking radiation. Technically, black holes are still theoretical, but phenomena have been observed that match their predicted behavior.

black humor Humor marked by the use of morbid, ironic, or grotesquely comic episodes that ridicule human folly. The term came into common use in the 1960s to describe the work of such novelists as Joseph Heller, whose *Catch-22* (1961) is an outstanding example; Kurt Vonnegut, particularly in *Slaughterhouse Five* (1969); and Thomas Pynchon, in *V* (1963) and *Gravity's Rainbow* (1973). A film exemplar is Stanley Kubrick's *Dr. Strangelove* (1963). The term "black comedy" has been applied to some playwrights in the theater of the absurd, especially Eugene Ionesco.

black lead See graphite

black legend Stories from the Spanish colonies in the Americas that led to the general belief, eagerly endorsed by such rivals as Britain and Holland, that Spain exceeded other nations in cruelty to its subject populations. The 16th–17th-century historians Bartolome de Las Casas and Garcilaso de la Vega documented the treatment of the Indians in New Spain (Mexico and Guatemala) and Peru, respectively, and laid the foundation for the legend. Though Spain may not actually have surpassed other colonial powers in cruelty, the Spanish conquest clearly resulted in rapid depopulation and great suffering for indigenous peoples.

Black Hawk, oil painting by George Catlin, 1832; in the National Museum of American Art, Smithsonian Institution, Washington, D.C.

BY COURTESY OF NATIONAL MUSEUM OF AMERICAN ART, SMITHSONIAN INSTITUTION, WASHINGTON, D.C.

black letter script *or* **Gothic script** *or* **Old English script** Style of alphabet used in handwriting throughout Europe in the Middle Ages. It features uniform, vertical strokes that end on the baseline, angular lines instead of smooth curves and circles, and the overlapping of convex forms. Black letter and roman were the dominant letter shapes of medieval typography. The only extant work by Johannes Gutenberg, the 42-line Bible (1450s), was set in black letter type. Roman type largely superseded it in the Renaissance, though it persisted in Germany well into the 20th century. Today black letter is often used for diplomas, Christmas cards, and liturgical writings.

black market Trading in violation of publicly imposed regulations such as rationing laws, laws against the sale of certain goods, and official rates of exchange among currencies. Black-market activity is common in wartime, when scarce goods and services are often strictly rationed (see RATIONING). Black-market foreign-exchange transactions flourish in countries where convertible foreign currency is scarce and foreign exchange is tightly controlled.

Black Muslims See Nation of ISLAM

black nationalism U.S. political and social movement to develop economic power and community and ethnic pride among blacks. It was proclaimed by MARCUS GARVEY in the early 20th century, when many U.S. black nationalists hoped for the eventual creation of a separate black nation in Africa. In the 1960s and '70s, ELIJAH MUHAMMAD and MALCOLM X preached the ideal of black nationalism as an alternative to assimilation to the predominantly white culture of the U.S. In Africa black nationalism developed in the years following World War II, and by the early 1960s most of the European colonies in Africa had achieved independence.

Black Panther Party (for Self-Defense) U.S. black revolutionary party founded in 1966 by HUEY NEWTON and Bobby Seale (born 1936) in Oakland, Cal., to protect black residents from police brutality. It developed into a Marxist revolutionary group that called for the arming of blacks, their exemption from the draft, the release of all black prisoners, and payment of compensation to blacks for centuries of exploitation by white Americans. By the late 1960s it had over 2,000 members, with chapters in several major cities; an early spokesman was Eldridge Cleaver (1935–1998). Conflicts with police in the late 1960s and early 1970s involved shoot-outs in California, New York, and Chicago. Charges of police harassment led to congressional investigations. By the mid-1970s the group had lost support; it turned to providing neighborhood social services, and soon disbanded.

black pepper *or* **pepper** Perennial, woody climbing vine *(Piper nigrum)* of the family Piperaceae, native to India; also, the hotly pungent SPICE made from its berries. One of the earliest spices known, pepper is probably the most widely used spice in the world today. It early became an important article of overland trade between India and Europe. The plant is cultivated throughout Indonesia and has been introduced into tropical areas elsewhere. It has broad, shiny leaves and dense, slender spikes of small flowers. The small berrylike fruits are called peppercorns. See also PEPPER.

black sand Accumulation of fragments of durable, usually dark, heavy minerals (those with a density greater than that of quartz). These accumulations are found in streambeds or on beaches where stream flow and wave energy are sufficient to carry away low-density material but not the heavy minerals. Thus, heavy minerals resistant to weathering and abrasion concentrate in these areas, though they may be only minor constituents of inland rocks. Placer mining of such deposits yields magnetite, cassiterite, and zircon, as well as gold, platinum, and other rare metals.

Black Sea Sea between Europe and Asia. Bordered by Ukraine, Russia, Georgia, Turkey, Bulgaria, and Romania, it occupies an area of about 180,000 sq mi (465,000 sq km) and has a maximum depth of 7,250 ft (2,210 m). It is connected with the AEGEAN SEA through the BOSPORUS, the Sea of MARMARA, and the DARDANELLES, and with the Sea of AZOV by Kerch Strait. It receives many rivers, including the DANUBE, DNIESTER, BUG, DNIEPER, KUBAN, KIZIL IRMAK, and Sakarya. The Crimean Peninsula (see CRIMEA) extends into it from the north. Created when structural upheavals in ASIA MINOR split off the Caspian basin from the Mediterranean Sea, the Black Sea gradually became isolated; salinity is now less than half that of the world's oceans. Though long popular for its resorts, it has suffered severe pollution in recent decades.

black snake Any of several species of all-black or nearly all-black snakes. Australian black snakes are in the ELAPID genus *Pseudeschis*. The black snake of Australian wetlands *(P. porphyriacus)* grows to an average length of 5 ft (1.5 m). If annoyed, it expands its neck, cobra fashion. Its venom is rarely fatal. Other Australian black snakes are the mulga snake *(P. australis)* and the spotted black snake *(P. guttatus)*. North American black snakes include two species in the family Colubridae: the black RACER and the pilot black snake *(Elaphe obsoleta)*.

Black Sox scandal U.S. baseball scandal, centering on the charge that eight members of the Chicago White Sox had been bribed to lose the 1919 World Series to the Cincinnati Reds. Five of those accused admitted to a grand jury that they had thrown the series, but their confessions later disappeared. All eight players were acquitted in 1921, but commissioner KENESAW MOUNTAIN LANDIS banned them from playing for life.

Black Stone of Mecca Muslim object of veneration, built into the eastern wall of the KAABA and probably predating ISLAM. It consists of three large pieces of stone and some fragments, surrounded by a stone ring and held together with a silver band. According to legend, the stone was given to Adam on his fall from paradise and was originally white but has been made black by the sins of the thousands of pilgrims who have touched and kissed it.

black theater In the U.S., a dramatic movement encompassing plays written by, for, and about blacks. The first known play by an American black was James Brown's *King Shotaway* (1823). After the Civil War, blacks began to perform in MINSTREL SHOWS, and musicals written, produced, and acted entirely by blacks appeared by c. 1900. The first real success of a black dramatist was Angelina W. Grimké's *Rachel* (1916). Theater flourished during the HARLEM RENAISSANCE of the 1920s and '30s, and by 1940 the American Negro Theater and the Negro Playwrights' Co. were firmly established. After World War II black theater grew more progressive and militant, seeking to establish its own mythology, abolish racial stereotypes, and integrate black playwrights into the mainstream. Its strongest proponent, AMIRI BARAKA, established the Black Arts Repertory Theatre in 1965. In the 1980s and '90s Charles Fuller and AUGUST WILSON won Pulitzer Prizes.

Black Warrior River Navigable river, western Alabama. Formed by the confluence of the Locust and Mulberry forks in Jefferson county, it flows southwest through coalfields to join the TOMBIGBEE RIVER near Demopolis. The river is 178 mi (286 km) long and furnishes waterpower above Tuscaloosa.

black widow Any member of six known species of SPIDER in the genus *Latrodectus*. They have a venomous bite that is rarely fatal to humans. Black widows occur in North and South America, Africa, South Asia, and southern Europe. Three species are found in the U.S. The female of the most common North American species is shiny black, usually with a reddish hourglass-shaped design on the underside of the spherical abdomen, and with a body about 1 in. (2.5 cm) long. The black widow preys on insects. The male, about one-fourth the female's size, is often killed and eaten by the female after mating (the source of its name).

Blackbeard *orig.* **Edward Teach** (died 1718) English pirate. He was probably a privateer in the West Indies until 1716. With his 40-gun warship, he preyed on shipping off the Virginia and Carolina coasts, sharing his prizes with the governor of the North Carolina colony in return for protection. He was eventually killed by a British naval force, and his head, with its great black beard, was affixed to the end of his bowsprit. According to legend, he left a great buried treasure; it has never been found and probably never existed.

blackberry Usually prickly, fruit-bearing bush of the genus *Rubus*, in the ROSE family, native chiefly to northern temperate regions. The blackberry is abundant in eastern North America and on the Pacific coast; in Europe it is common in thickets and hedges. Its usually BIENNIAL, prickly, erect, semi-erect, or trailing stems bear leaves with usually three or five oval, coarsely toothed, stalked leaflets; white, pink, or red flowers in terminal clusters; and black or red-purple aggregate fruits. The several trailing species are commonly called DEWBERRIES. Blackberries are a fairly good source of iron and vitamin C.

Blackberry (*Rubus*).

DEREK FELL

blackbird In the New World, any of several species of songbirds in the family Icteridae, collectively called icterids; also, an Old World THRUSH

(*Turdus merula,* family Turdidae). The best known icterid is the red-winged blackbird *(Agelaius phoeniceus),* which ranges from Canada to the West Indies and Central America. It is 8 in. (20 cm) long, and the male's black plumage is set off by red shoulder patches. The Old World blackbird, 10 in. (25 cm) long, is common in woods and gardens throughout temperate Eurasia as well as in Australia and New Zealand. See also GRACKLE.

blackbody Theoretical surface that absorbs all radiant energy that falls on it, and radiates electromagnetic energy at all frequencies, from RADIO WAVES to GAMMA RAYS, with an intensity distribution dependent on its temperature. Because all visible light falling on such a surface is absorbed without reflection, the surface will appear black as long as its temperature is such that its emission peak is not in the visible portion of the SPECTRUM. See also ABSORPTION.

blackcap Common WARBLER (*Sylvia atricapilla,* family Sylviidae) from Europe and North Africa to central Asia. It is about 6 in. (14 cm) long and has brownish upper parts, gray underparts and face, and a black (male) or reddish brown (female) crown. Common in woodland borders and rough hedges, it has a rich song.

Male (bottom) and female blackcaps (*Sylvia atricapilla*).
HANS REINHARD—BRUCE COLEMAN LTD.

Blackett \'blak-ət\, **Patrick M(aynard) S(tuart)** *later* **Baron Blackett (of Chelsea)** (1897–1974) British physicist. He graduated from Cambridge University in 1921 and spent 10 years at the Cavendish Laboratory, where he developed the Wilson cloud chamber into an instrument for the study of cosmic radiation. He was awarded a 1948 Nobel Prize for his discoveries, and was made a life peer in 1969.

blackfly Any member of the insect family Simuliidae, comprising 300 species of small, humpbacked DIPTERANS found worldwide. Usually black or dark gray, the blackfly has short mouthparts adapted for sucking blood. The females bite and are sometimes abundant enough to kill chickens and even cattle. Some species carry worms capable of causing human disease, including RIVER BLINDNESS. In subarctic regions blackflies may be so numerous that human habitation is impossible.

Blackfly (Simuliidae).
E.S. ROSS

Blackfoot Group of three ALGONQUIAN-speaking Indian peoples in Alberta and Montana, comprising the Piegan, the Blood, and the Blackfoot proper. They were among the first Algonquians to move westward from timberland to open grassland and, later, among the first to acquire horses and firearms. They were known as the strongest and most aggressive military power on the northwestern plains, and at the height of their power, in the first half of the 19th century, held a vast territory extending from northern Saskatchewan to southwestern Montana. Each group was subdivided into hunting bands led by one or more chiefs. These bands wintered separately but came together in summer to celebrate the SUN DANCE. For three decades beginning in 1806, the Blackfoot prevented white men from settling in their territory. They signed their first treaty with the U.S. in 1855, after which they were forced into farming and cattle-raising. Today about 25,000 Blackfoot live in Montana and Alberta. See photograph opposite.

blackjack *or* **twenty-one** Card game whose object is to be dealt cards having a higher count than those of the dealer, up to but not exceeding 21. The dealer may use a single deck of 52 cards or two or more decks from a holder called a shoe. Aces count as 1 or 11, and face cards as 10. Depending on the rules used, bets may be placed before the deal, after each player has been dealt one card facedown, or after each player has received two cards facedown and the dealer has exposed one of his cards.

blackmail See EXTORTION

Blackmun, Harry (1908–1999) U.S. jurist. Born in Nashville, Ill., he received his law degree from Harvard (1932) and taught law (1935–41) while advancing to general partner in his Minnesota law firm. He served as resident counsel to the Mayo Clinic (1950–59), then was appointed to the Eighth U.S. Circuit Court of Appeals. Pres. R. Nixon named him to the U.S. SUPREME COURT in 1970, where he served until 1994. Perceived as a conservative when he commenced his Supreme Court service, Blackmun became progressively more liberal over the years. He wrote the majority decision in *ROE VS. WADE* (1971).

blackpoll warbler Species *(Dendroica striata)* of WOOD WARBLER. Like all wood warblers, it is a small, active bird that feeds on insects and has a short thin bill. A common species, it is less striking than many other wood warblers, which are known for their brightly colored plumage.

Blackshirts *Italian* **Camicie Nere** Armed squads of Italian Fascists under BENITO MUSSOLINI, who wore black shirts as part of their uniform. The squads, first organized in 1919, targeted socialists, communists, republicans, and others. Hundreds of people were killed as the squads grew in number. In 1922 Blackshirts from all over Italy participated in the March on ROME. In 1923 the private Blackshirts were officially transformed into a national militia. With Mussolini's fall in 1943, the Blackshirts fell into disgrace.

Blackstone, William *later* **Sir William** (1723–1780) British jurist. Orphaned at age 12, he was educated by his surgeon uncle and became a BARRISTER. He served as assessor of the Chancellor's Court, took a doctorate in civil law, and concentrated on teaching law and doing legal work around Oxford. He gave the first university lectures on English COMMON LAW and published a synopsis for students in 1756. He was elected to hold the first chair in common law in 1758. His classic *Commentaries on the Laws of England* (1765–69) is the best known description of the doctrines of English law; it became the basis of university legal education in England and North America. He also served as a member of Parliament (1761–70), as solicitor general to the queen (from 1763), and as judge of the Court of COMMON PLEAS (1770–80).

Blackstone River River, central Massachusetts and Rhode Island. It flows about 40 mi (64 km) past WORCESTER and across northeastern Rhode Island to Pawtucket, where it becomes the Sekonk River. It furnishes power to a highly industrialized area.

Blackwell, Elizabeth (1821–1910) U.S. (British-born) physician. Her family emigrated to the U.S. in 1832, and her father died a few years later. She began her medical education by reading medical books and hiring private instructors. Medical schools rejected her applications until she was accepted at the Geneva Medical (later Hobart) College in 1847.

In a Piegan lodge, photograph by Edward S. Curtis, 1910; from *The North American Indian*.
COURTESY OF THE EDWARD E. AYER COLLECTION, THE NEWBERRY LIBRARY, CHICAGO

Though ostracized, she graduated at the head of her class in 1849, becoming the first woman doctor in modern times and the first to gain her degree from a U.S. medical school. In 1857, despite much opposition, she established the New York Infirmary, staffed entirely by women, and she later added a full course of medical education for women. She was also a founder of the London School of Medicine for Women. Her sister Emily (1826–1910) ran the infirmary for many years and served as dean and professor at the associated medical college.

Blackwell's Island See ROOSEVELT ISLAND

bladder cancer Malignant TUMOR of the bladder. The most significant risk factor associated with bladder cancer is smoking. Exposure to chemicals called arylamines, which are used in the leather, rubber, printing, and textiles industries, is another risk factor. Most bladder cancers are diagnosed after the age of 60; men are affected more than women. Symptoms include blood in the urine, difficulty urinating, excessive urination, or, more rarely, painful urination. Bladder cancer can be treated with surgery, radiation therapy, or chemotherapy.

bladderwort Any of about 120 widespread species of terrestrial and aquatic CARNIVOROUS PLANTS of the genus *Utricularia* (family Lentibulariaceae). They are characterized by small hollow sacs (bladders) that actively capture and digest tiny animals that touch them, including insect larvae, aquatic worms, water fleas, and other small swimmers. Closely related to the bladderworts are the butterworts *(Pinguicula),* 35 species of land plants that capture insects by means of sticky glands on the leaf surfaces.

Blaine, James G(illespie) (1830–1893) U.S. politician and diplomat. Born in West Brownsville, Pa., he moved to Maine in 1854 to become editor of the *Kennebec Journal*, a crusading Republican newspaper. He served in the U.S. House of Representatives 1863–76, becoming speaker in 1868. An advocate for a moderate Republican Party, he opposed the party radicals led by ROSCOE CONKLING. He served in the U.S. Senate 1876–81. As secretary of state in 1881 he took the first steps toward securing U.S. control of the eventual route of the Panama Canal. He was the Republican presidential nominee in 1884 but lost narrowly to GROVER CLEVELAND. He again served as secretary of state (1889–92) and chaired the first Pan-American Conference.

Blair, Henry William (1834–1920) U.S. politician. Born in Campton, N.H., he practiced law from 1859 and served in the state legislature before being elected to the U.S. House of Representatives (1875–79) and Senate (1879–91). In 1876 he proposed to give revenues from the sale of public lands to the nation's schools, and in 1881 he proposed a $120 million grant to the states to "vitalize" their schools; neither effort succeeded. He also advocated women's rights and racial justice.

Blair, Tony *orig.* **Anthony Charles Lynton** (born 1953) British politician who in 1997 became Britain's youngest prime minister since 1812. Born in Edinburgh, Blair was a lawyer before winning election to the House of Commons in 1983. Entering the shadow cabinet of the LABOUR PARTY in 1988 at age 35, Blair urged the party to move to the political center and deemphasize its traditional advocacy of state control and public ownership of certain sectors of the economy. He assumed leadership of his party in 1994 and revamped its platform. He led Labour to landslide victories in the 1997 and 2001 elections.

Blais \'ble\, **Marie-Claire** (born 1939) French-Canadian novelist and poet. She studied at Laval Univ., Quebec. In two early, dreamlike novels, *Mad Shadows* (1959) and *Tête blanche* (1960), she staked out her territory, working-class people doomed to unrelieved sorrow and grinding poverty. *A Season in the Life of Emmanuel* (1965) received the Prix Médicis and was widely translated and discussed. Later works include *The Manuscripts of Pauline Archange* (1968, Governor General's Award) and *Deaf to the City* (1979, Governor General's Award). She has also published poetry collections and several plays.

Blake, Edward (1833–1912) Canadian politician. Born in Adelaide, Ontario, he practiced law from 1856. In 1867 he was elected to the Canadian House of Commons. He served as premier of Ontario (1871–72) and minister of justice (1875–77) in ALEXANDER MACKENZIE's cabinet, where he helped draft the constitution. He was leader of the Liberal Party 1880–87. In 1890 he withdrew from Canadian politics and moved to Ireland, where he served in the British House of Commons 1892–1907.

Blake, Eubie *orig.* **James Hubert** (1883–1983) U.S. songwriter and pianist. Born in Baltimore, Blake played piano in cafés and brothels as a teenager, and in 1899 he composed his first rag, "Sounds of Africa." He and his partner, lyricist and vocalist Noble Sissle (1889–1975), were among the first black performers to appear onstage without minstrel makeup. Their show *Shuffle Along* (1921), which introduced P. ROBESON and JOSEPHINE BAKER, was among the first musicals written, produced, and directed by blacks. In 1925 Blake cowrote the score to *Blackbirds of 1930.* He retired in 1946. He achieved his greatest fame when the musical *Eubie* opened on Broadway (1978). In 1981 he was awarded the Medal of Freedom. He gave his last concert in 1982, and died at the age of 100.

Blake, William (1757–1827) English poet, painter, engraver, and visionary. Though he did not attend school, he was trained as an engraver at the Royal Academy and opened a print shop in London in 1784. He developed an innovative technique for producing colored engravings and began producing his own illustrated books of poetry with his "illuminated printing," including *Songs of Innocence* (1789), *The Marriage of Heaven and Hell* (1793), and *Songs of Experience* (1794). *Jerusalem* (1804–20), his third major epic treating of the fall and redemption of humanity, is his most richly decorated book. His other major works include *The Four Zoas* (1795–1804) and *Milton* (1804–8). A late series of 22 watercolors inspired by the Book of Job includes some of his best-known pictures. He was called mad because he was single-minded and unworldly; he lived on the edge of poverty and died in neglect. His books form one of the most strikingly original and independent bodies of work in the Western cultural tradition. Ignored by the public of his day, he is now regarded as one of the earliest and greatest figures of ROMANTICISM.

William Blake, watercolor portrait by John Linnell; in the National Portrait Gallery, London.

BY COURTESY OF THE NATIONAL PORTRAIT GALLERY, LONDON

Blakelock, Ralph (1847–1919) U.S. painter. Born in New York City, he studied at CCNY but was self-taught as an artist. He developed a highly original and subjective style of landscape painting, characterized by luminous impasto images of moonlit scenes with nocturnal lighting and strangely dappled trees and foliage. Neglected by the public and constantly under the strain of poverty, he suffered a breakdown in 1899, ceased to paint, and spent the rest of his life in an asylum. During his confinement he achieved some fame, and forgeries of his work became common as his popularity continued to rise.

Blakeslee, Albert Francis (1874–1954) U.S. botanist and geneticist. Born in Geneseo, N.Y., he received his PhD from Harvard University. In his dissertation he became the first person to describe sexuality in the lower fungi. His later experimental work focused on higher plants. After a long tenure with the Carnegie Institution's Cold Spring Harbor laboratory (1915–41), he joined the faculty of Smith College, where he published a long series of papers on the genetics and cell biology of jimsonweed. He used the alkaloid colchicine to achieve an increase in the number of chromosomes and thus opened up a new field of artificially produced polyploids.

Blakey, Art *later* **Abdullah Ibn Buhaina** (1919–1990) U.S. jazz drummer. Born in Pittsburgh, Blakey worked with FLETCHER HENDERSON's big band before joining BILLY ECKSTINE's forward-looking ensemble (1944–47). His prodigious technique and thunderous attack assured his role as one of the principal drum stylists in modern jazz. With HORACE SILVER, Blakey formed the Jazz Messengers in 1954, and the group, with its aggressive blues-inflected approach, became the archetypal hard-bop unit (see BEBOP). Many band members became celebrated, and the group became one of the most enduring ensembles in modern jazz.

Blalock \'blā-ˌläk\, **Alfred** (1899–1964) U.S. surgeon. Born in Culloden, Ga., he received an MD from Johns Hopkins University. His research showing that traumatic and hemorrhagic shock resulted from loss of blood volume led to volume-replacement treatment, which saved countless lives during World War II. He is remembered for his development, with HELEN BROOKE TAUSSIG, of a surgical treatment for heart malformations in newborns. In 1944 he performed the first subclavian-pulmonary artery anastomosis operation, which corrected the birth defect.

Blanc \'blän\, **(Jean-Joseph-Charles-) Louis** (1811–1882) French utopian socialist and journalist. In 1839 he founded the socialist newspaper *Revue du progrès* and serially published his *Organisation du travail (The Organization of Labor)*, which described his theory of worker-controlled "social workshops" that would gradually take over production until a socialist society came into being. He was a member of the provisional government of the SECOND REPUBLIC (1848) but was forced to flee to England after workers unsuccessfully revolted. In exile (1848–70), he wrote a history of the French Revolution and other political works.

Louis Blanc.
H. ROGER-VIOLLET

Blanc \'blaŋk\, **Mel(vin Jerome)** (1908–1989) U.S. entertainer. Born in San Francisco, he began his career as a musician on NBC radio, and in 1933 he joined a daily radio program, for which he created several voices to augment the cast. In 1937 he joined the cartoon department of WARNER BROTHERS, and he took part in the development of Looney Tunes and Merrie Melodies, providing the voices of Porky Pig, Daffy Duck, Woody Woodpecker, and Bugs Bunny. In his 50-year career, he supplied the voices for about 3,000 animated cartoons, including 90% of the Warner Brothers cartoons.

Blanc \'blän\, **Mont** *Italian* **Monte Bianco** Mountain massif, Europe. Located in the ALPS on the borders of France, Italy, and Switzerland, it is Europe's highest peak, at 15,771 ft (4,807 m). It was first climbed in 1786 by Michel-Gabriel Paccard and Jacques Balmat. Mont Blanc Tunnel, at 8 mi (13 km), one of the longest vehicular tunnels in the world, connects France with Italy. The region has become a major tourist and winter sports center.

Blanchard \blän-'shȧr\, **Jean-Pierre-François** (1753–1809) French balloonist. In 1785 he made the first aerial crossing of the English Channel, accompanied by John Jeffries, an American doctor. He invented a parachute in 1785. His balloon flights in other European countries and in the U.S. in 1793 spurred an interest in ballooning. He and his wife performed many exhibitions in Europe; they died in separate balloon accidents.

J.-P.-F. Blanchard, engraving by James Newton, 1785, after an oil painting by Richard Livesay.
BY COURTESY OF THE LIBRARY OF CONGRESS, WASHINGTON, D.C.

Blanchard \'blan-chərd\, **Thomas** (1788–1864) U.S. inventor. Born in Sutton, Mass., in 1818 he invented a LATHE capable of turning irregular shapes, such as a gunstock. It duplicated the form of a pattern object by transmitting to the cutting tool the motion of a friction wheel rolling over the pattern. His invention was an essential step in the development of MASS-PRODUCTION techniques. He produced several successful designs of shallow-draft steamboats, and in 1849 invented machinery for bending wood into complex shapes such as plow handles and ship's frames.

Blanda, George (Frederick) (born 1927) U.S. football player. Born in Youngwood, Pa., he played for the University of Kentucky. As a professional quarterback and kicker, he played for the Chicago Bears (1949–58), Houston Oilers (1960–66), and Oakland Raiders (1967–76), setting still-standing records for most seasons played (26), most games played (340), most points scored (2,002), and most points after touchdowns (943). His record for most field goals (335) was broken in 1983, though he still holds the record for most attempts (638).

blank verse Unrhymed verse, specifically unrhymed iambic pentameter, the preeminent dramatic and narrative verse form in English. It is also the standard form for dramatic verse in Italian and German. Adapted from Greek and Latin sources, it was introduced in Italy, then in England, where in the 16th century WILLIAM SHAKESPEARE transformed blank verse into the vehicle for the greatest English dramatic poetry, and its potential for grandeur was confirmed with JOHN MILTON's *Paradise Lost* (1667).

Blanqui \blän-'kē\, **(Louis-) Auguste** (1805–1881) French socialist and revolutionary. A legendary martyr-figure of French radicalism, Blanqui believed that there could be no socialist transformation of society without a temporary dictatorship that would eradicate the old order. His activities, including the formation of various secret societies, caused him to be imprisoned various times for a total of more than 33 years. His disciples, the Blanquists, played an important role in the history of the workers' movement even after his death.

blanquillo See TILEFISH

Blanton, Jimmy *orig.* **James** (1918–1942) U.S. musician whose revolutionary technique changed jazz bass playing and became the major influence on subsequent bassists. Born in Chattanooga, Tenn., Blanton joined DUKE ELLINGTON's orchestra in 1939. His buoyant rhythmic approach and harmonic subtlety provided a supple, relaxed sense of swing for the band. His unprecedented dexterity, tone, and intonation enabled him to execute a melodic conception of the role of the bass in jazz, demonstrated on recordings made with Ellington such as "Jack the Bear" and "Pitter Panther Patter." He died of tuberculosis at age 23.

Blantyre \blan-'tīr\ City (pop., 1998: 502,053), southern Malawi. The largest city in Malawi, it was founded in 1876 as a Church of Scotland mission station and named after DAVID LIVINGSTONE's Scottish birthplace. It became a British consular post in 1883 and attained municipal status in 1895, making it Malawi's oldest municipality. Its colonial trade laid the foundation for its present importance as Malawi's chief commercial center. In 1956 Blantyre was united with nearby Limbe.

Blarney Village (pop., 1995 est.: 3,000), county Cork, Ireland. Situated northwest of CORK, it is famous as the site of Blarney Castle (c. 1446). Below the battlements on the southern castle wall is the Blarney Stone, which is said to make anyone who kisses it proficient in blarney (smooth, flattering talk). This feat can be achieved only by hanging head downward.

Blasco Ibáñez \'bläs-kō-ē-'bän-yāth\, **Vicente** (1867–1928) Spanish writer and politician. An ardent republican, he was elected to the Cortes (parliament) but later settled on the French Riviera because of his opposition to the military dictatorship of MIGUEL PRIMO DE RIVERA. His early novels are primarily intense depictions of life in Valencia. He achieved world renown for his novels dealing with World War I, especially *The Four Horsemen of the Apocalypse* (1916).

Blasis \'blä-sēs\, **Carlo** (1803–1878) Italian ballet teacher and writer on the technique, history, and theory of dance. He danced briefly at the Paris Opéra, before being appointed director of the ballet school at Milan's La Scala in 1837, where he would train many of the most brilliant dancers of the 19th century. Among his many innovations, Blasis discovered the technique of spotting (focusing on one spot and snapping one's head around faster than one's body) to prevent dizziness when turning. Many of his teachings still form the basis of classical ballet.

Blass, Bill *orig.* **William Ralph** (1922–2002) U.S. fashion designer. Born in Fort Wayne, Indiana, Blass left home at age 17 to attend the Parsons School of Design in New York City. After serving in the U.S. Army during World War II, he returned to New York, where in 1959 he became the head designer of Maurice Rentner, Ltd. Building upon the innovations of European designers such as COCO CHANEL, Blass made chic, modern women's clothing designed for ease and comfort. His work became popular among New York high-society women. In 1970 Blass became owner of Rentner, which he renamed after himself. He was a pioneer in employing the business strategy of licensing his designs and name to a huge array of fashion accessories.

blast furnace Vertical shaft furnace that produces liquid METALS by the reaction of air introduced under pressure into the bottom of the furnace with a mixture of metallic ORE, fuel, and FLUX fed into the top. Blast furnaces are used to produce PIG IRON from iron ore for subsequent processing into STEEL; they are also employed in processing lead, copper, and other metals. The current of pressurized air maintains rapid combustion. Blast furnaces were used in China as early as 200 BC, and appeared in Europe in the 13th century, replacing the BLOOMERY PROCESS. Modern blast furnaces are 70–120 ft (20–35 m) high, have 20–45-ft (6–14-m) hearth diameters, use COKE fuel, and can produce 1,000–10,000 tons (900–9,000 metric tons) of pig iron daily. See also METALLURGY, SMELTING.

Blaue Reiter \\ˌblau̇-ə-ˈrī-tər\\, **Der** (German: "The Blue Rider") Organization of Expressionist artists formed in Munich in 1911 by VASSILY KANDINSKY and FRANZ MARC. The name derived from a volume of essays and illustrations they published. Other members included PAUL KLEE and August Macke (1887–1914). Influenced by JUGENDSTIL, CUBISM, and FUTURISM but lacking a specific program or philosophy, they exhibited with an international group, including GEORGES BRAQUE, ANDRE DERAIN, and PABLO PICASSO. The group disintegrated at the outbreak of World War I. See also EXPRESSIONISM.

Blavatsky \\blə-ˈvat-skē\\, **Helena (Petrovna)** *orig.* **Helena Petrovna Hahn** *known as* **Madame Blavatsky** (1831–1891) Russian spiritualist and writer. After a brief marriage, she studied occultism and spiritualism and traveled through Europe, Asia, and the U.S. In 1873 in New York City she became a close companion of Henry Olcott (1832–1907); they and others founded the Theosophical Society (1875; see THEOSOPHY). In 1879 Blavatsky and Olcott went to India and established headquarters at Adyar. The society thrived, and she edited its journal, *The Theosophist.* She claimed psychic powers, but the London Society for Psychical Research in 1885 labeled her a fraud. In poor health, she returned to live in Europe. Her most important work, *The Secret Doctrine* (1888), was an overview of theosophical teachings.

bleach Solid or liquid chemical compound used to whiten or remove the natural color of fibers, yarns, paper, and textile fabrics. Sunlight was the chief bleaching agent up to the discovery of chlorine in 1774 by Karl Wilhelm Scheele (1742–1786) and the demonstration of its bleaching properties in 1785 by Claude-Louis Berthollet (1748–1822). In textile finishing, the bleaching process is used to produce white cloth, to prepare fabrics for other finishes, or to remove discoloration. CHLORINE, sodium hypochlorite, calcium hypochlorite, and hydrogen PEROXIDE are commonly used as bleaches.

bleeding heart Any of several species of *Dicentra,* a genus of herbaceous flowering plants of the fumitory family (Fumariaceae). The old garden favorite is the Japanese *D. spectabilis,* which has small rosy-red and white, heart-shaped flowers dangling from arching stems. The eastern, or wild, bleeding heart *(D. eximia)* produces sprays of small pink flowers from April to September in the Allegheny Mountains region. The Pacific, or western, bleeding heart *(D. formosa),* ranging from California to British Columbia, has several varieties of garden interest.

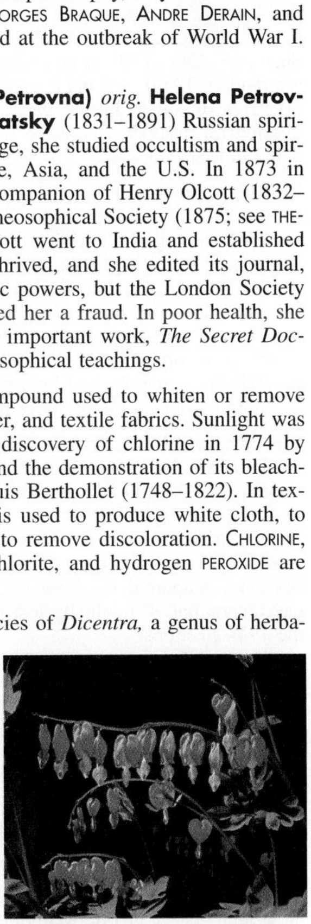

Bleeding heart (*Dicentra spectabilis*).
GRANT HEILMAN

Bleeding Kansas Term applied to a period of civil unrest (1854–59) between proslavery and antislavery advocates for control of the new Kansas Territory. Under the doctrine of POPULAR SOVEREIGNTY, antislavery emigrants from the North clashed with armed proslavery groups from Missouri. In 1856 a proslavery raid and burning of a hotel and newspaper in Lawrence were followed by several murders instigated by antislavery radicals under JOHN BROWN. Sporadic battles continued until Kansas was admitted to the Union as a free state in 1861.

blende See SPHALERITE

Blenheim \\ˈble-nim\\, **Battle of** (1704) Famous victory of the duke of MARLBOROUGH and EUGENE OF SAVOY against the French in the War of the SPANISH SUCCESSION, fought at Blenheim (now Blindheim) on the Danube River in Bavaria. English and Austrian troops led by Marlborough and Eugene surprised the unprepared French and Bavarian forces, broke through their center, and captured 13,000 of their troops; another 18,000 were killed, wounded, or drowned. The French army suffered its first major defeat in over 50 years, and Bavaria was removed from the war.

Blenheim Palace \\ˈble-nim\\ English residence near Woodstock, Oxfordshire, designed by JOHN VANBRUGH and built (1705–24) by the British Parliament as a gift to John Churchill, duke of Marlborough. It is regarded as the finest example of BAROQUE ARCHITECTURE in Britain. In the early 18th century Queen Anne's gardener, Henry Wise, designed its grounds in the formal style of the Palace of VERSAILLES; Capability BROWN later redesigned them in his pastoral style, using natural-looking woods, lawns, and waterways.

blenny Any of numerous and diverse fishes (suborder Blenniodei, order Perciformes) that are mostly small, marine species found from tropical to cold seas. Blennies are slim, ranging from moderately elongated to very long and eel-like. Their habitats range from rocky pools to sandy beaches, reefs, and beds of kelp. Many live in shallow water, but some range to depths of about 1,500 ft (450 m). Some are mainly herbivores; others are partial or complete carnivores. They are generally unobtrusive and of little economic importance.

Shanny (*Blennius pholis*), a common European blenny.
JANE BURTON–BRUCE COLEMAN LTD.

Blessing Way Central ritual in the complex system of ceremonies performed by the NAVAJO to restore equilibrium to the cosmos. Of the major categories of Navajo rituals, the largest group is the Chant Ways, which are concerned with curing. The Chant Ways include a subgroup of chants called the Holy Ways, which are further divided into the Blessing Way and the Wind Ways (used to cure illness). Lasting for two days, the Blessing Way is a simple chant performed for the well-being of the community rather than for a specific curative purpose.

Bleuler \\ˈblȯi-lər\\, **Eugen** (1857–1939) Swiss psychiatrist. He is best known for his studies of schizophrenics and for introducing (1908) the term schizophrenia for the disorder previously called dementia praecox. Bleuler argued (against accepted wisdom) that schizophrenia was more than one disease, was not always incurable, and did not always progress to full dementia. He described the basic symptoms—disordered mental associations and splitting or fragmentation of the personality—but believed that many cases were not apparent. He insisted that psychosis did not need to result from organic brain damage, and could have psychological causes instead. His *Textbook of Psychiatry* (1916) became a standard text.

Bligh, William (1754–1817) English admiral. He went to sea at age 7 and joined the Royal Navy in 1770. He was sailing master on Capt. JAMES COOK's final voyage (1776–80). In 1787 he was named to command HMS *BOUNTY.* While en route from Tahiti to Jamaica, the ship was seized by Fletcher Christian, the master's mate, and Bligh and loyal crew members were set adrift; some two months later, they reached Timor. The mutiny made little difference to Bligh's career, though he had two more encounters with mutineers, including one while he was governor of New South Wales, Australia (1805–8). Described as overbearing, he was unpopular as a commander but was also courageous and a greatly skilled navigator.

blight Any of various plant diseases whose symptoms include sudden and severe yellowing, browning, spotting, withering, or dying of leaves, flowers, fruit, stems, or the entire plant. Usually the shoots and other young, rapidly growing tissues of a plant are attacked. Most blights are caused by BACTERIA or fungi (see FUNGUS); some result from drought. Fungal and bacterial blights are most likely under cool, moist conditions. Most economically important plants are susceptible to one or more blights. Measures taken to fight blight include destroying the infected plant parts; using disease-free seed or stock and resistant varieties; rotating crops (see CROP ROTATION); pruning and spacing plants for better air circulation; controlling pests that carry the fungus from plant to plant;

avoiding overhead watering and working among wet plants; and, where needed, applying FUNGICIDES or ANTIBIOTICS. Maintaining sanitary conditions is the most important measure for stopping the spread of the infestation. See also CHESTNUT BLIGHT.

blind fish Any of various species of sightless fishes, among them several unrelated cave-dwelling species. Blind cave fishes are pale and small, growing to about 4 in. (10 cm) long, and are found in dark limestone caves of the U.S. All have small but nonfunctional eyes and tactile organs that are sensitive to touch, allowing the fish to feel what it cannot see. Other cave-dwelling fishes tending toward blindness are found in Cuba, Mexico's Yucatán, South America, and Africa.

blindness Inability to see with one or both eyes. Transient blindness (blackout) can result from vertical acceleration causing high gravitational forces; glomerulonephritis (a kidney disease); or a clot in a blood vessel of the eye. Continuing blindness may arise from injuries or diseases of the eye (e.g., CATARACT, GLAUCOMA), including the RETINA, the optic nerve, or the brain's visual centers. Many infectious, noninfectious, and parasitic systemic diseases can cause blindness. Sexually transmitted diseases and RUBELLA in pregnant women can cause blindness in their infants. See also MACULAR DEGENERATION, VISUAL-FIELD DEFECT.

Bliss, Arthur (Edward Drummond) *later* **Sir Arthur** (1891–1975) British composer. He studied with R. VAUGHAN WILLIAMS and G. HOLST. Though compositionally adventurous at first, his music turned conservatively Romantic, and he has been seen as the principal successor to E. ELGAR. His works include *A Colour Symphony* (1922), *Pastoral* (1928), the choral symphony *Morning Heroes* (1930), *Music for Strings* (1936), and the ballets *Checkmate* (1937) and *Miracle in the Gorbals* (1944).

Bliss, Tasker (Howard) (1853–1930) U.S. general. Born in Lewisburg, Pa., he attended West Point. After serving in the Spanish-American War, he became the first commandant of the Army War College (1903–5) and later served in the Philippines (1905–9). As army chief of staff in 1917, he upgraded the army to battle-readiness for World War I and resisted attempts to divide the U.S. force among the various Allied commands. He was a delegate to the Paris Peace Conference and an ardent supporter of U.S. participation in the League of Nations.

Bliss, William D(wight) P(orter) (1856–1926) U.S. social reformer. Born in Constantinople to U.S. missionaries, he graduated from Hartford Theological Seminary and held Congregationalist and Episcopalian pastorates. An advocate of CHRISTIAN SOCIALISM, he organized the first such group in the U.S. in 1889. He lectured widely on labor and social reform and compiled many books, including the *Encyclopedia of Social Reform* (1897).

blister Rounded skin elevation in which fluid fills a separation between layers of epidermis or between the epidermis and the dermis. The fluid is usually clear; yellowish fluid contains pus, and red fluid contains blood. Blisters often occur on the palms or soles when pressure and friction cause an upper skin layer to move back and forth over the one under it. A small gap opens between them and becomes filled with fluid. This type generally heals spontaneously, sometimes leaving a thickened callus. Blisters that occur as symptoms of contact DERMATITIS, viral infection, or AUTOIMMUNE DISEASE can appear anywhere on the body and may leave scars.

blister beetle Any of approximately 2,000 species of BEETLES (family Meloidae) that secrete an irritating substance, cantharidin, which is used medically as a topical skin irritant to remove warts. In the past, cantharidin was often used for inducing blisters, a common remedy for many ailments, and the dried remains of Spanish fly *(Lytta vesicatoria)* were a major ingredient in so-called love potions. Adult blister beetles, which are often brightly colored, range between 0.1 and 0.8 in. (3–20 mm) in length. Blister beetles are both helpful and harmful to humans; the larvae eat grasshopper eggs, but the adults destroy crops.

Blister beetle (*Lytta magister*).
PHOTO RESEARCH INTERNATIONAL

blister rust Any of several diseases of PINES, caused by rust fungi (see FUNGUS) of the genus *Cronartium.* Blister rust affects sapwood (see WOOD) and inner bark and produces external blisters from which additional spores of the fungus are released and RESIN oozes, forming characteristic hardened masses on the trunk. It affects pines of all ages and sizes, retarding growth and weakening stems as it spreads along the trunk, sometimes killing the tree; young trees are killed more quickly than older ones. Measures taken to fight blister rust include growing resistant varieties, destroying nearby alternative host plants, observing strict sanitation measures, and spraying with FUNGICIDES.

blitzkrieg \'blits-ˌkrēg\ (German: "lightning war") Military tactic used by Germany in WORLD WAR II, designed to create psychological shock and resultant disorganization in enemy forces through the use of surprise, speed, and superiority in matériel or firepower. The Germans tested the blitzkrieg during the SPANISH CIVIL WAR in 1938 and against Poland in 1939, and used it in the successful invasions of Belgium, the Netherlands, and France in 1940. The German blitzkrieg coordinated land and air attacks—using tanks, dive-bombers, and motorized artillery—to paralyze the enemy principally by disabling its communications and coordination capacities.

Blitzstein \'blit-ˌstīn\, **Marc** (1905–1964) U.S. composer. Born in Philadelphia, he studied at the Curtis Institute, then with N. BOULANGER in Paris and A. SCHOENBERG in Berlin. His best-known works were for the theater: *The Cradle Will Rock* (1937), the circumstances of whose production by ORSON WELLES and JOHN HOUSEMAN became legendary; the opera *Regina* (1949); and his English adaptation of *The Threepenny Opera* (1952), a Broadway hit. He was working on a Metropolitan Opera commission for an opera about the Sacco-Vanzetti case when he was murdered in Martinique.

Blobel, Günter (born 1936) U.S. cellular and molecular biologist. Born in Germany, he earned his MD from Eberhard-Karl University and his PhD from the University of Wisconsin. Working in collaboration with other research groups, Blobel showed that each protein carries a signal sequence that directs it to the proper location inside the cell. He also concluded that proteins enter organelles through a porelike channel that opens in the organelle's outer membrane when the correct protein arrives at the organelle. For his work, Blobel was awarded a Nobel Prize in 1999. His research shed light on such hereditary diseases as CYSTIC FIBROSIS and provided the basis for bioengineered drugs, including INSULIN.

Bloc National \'blȯk-nȧs-yȯ-'nȧl\ Right-wing coalition that controlled the French government from 1919 to 1924. On a wave of nationalist sentiment at the end of World War I, the Bloc gained about 75% of the seats in the French Chamber of Deputies in the 1919 elections. The government tried to ensure French security against Germany through a strict enforcement of the Treaty of VERSAILLES. Its leaders, including RAYMOND POINCARE, supported the RUHR OCCUPATION (1923) to force Germany to pay reparations. It gradually lost public support, and it was defeated in the 1924 elections.

Bloch \'blȯk\, **Ernest** (1880–1959) Swiss-U.S. composer. He conducted and lectured at the Geneva Conservatory before moving in 1916 to the U.S., where he served as director of the San Francisco Conservatory 1925–30 and taught at UC-Berkeley 1942–52. He worked in tonal, atonal, and serialist idioms; his works, many of them Jewish in inspiration, include the opera *Macbeth* (1910), *Schelomo* for cello and orchestra (1916), the huge choral works *America* (1926) and *Avodath hakodesh* (1933), and a violin concerto (1938).

Bloch \'bläk\, **Felix** (1905–1983) Swiss-U.S. physicist. He emigrated to the U.S. in 1933, and taught at Stanford University 1934–71. He worked on atomic energy at Los Alamos and on radar countermeasures at Harvard University during World War II. In 1954 he became the first director general of CERN. For developing the NUCLEAR MAGNETIC RESONANCE method of measuring the magnetic fields of atomic nuclei, he shared with Edward Purcell (1912–1997) a 1952 Nobel Prize.

Bloch \'blȯk\, **Marc (Léopold Benjamin)** (1886–1944) French historian. He served in the French infantry in World War I. From 1919 he taught medieval history at Strasbourg, where he cofounded the important periodical *Annales d'histoire économique et sociale*. He taught economic history at the Sorbonne from 1936. During World War II he joined the French Resistance and was captured and killed by the Germans. Among his major works are *The Royal Touch* (1924), *French Rural History* (1931), and *Feudal Society* (1939). As the founder of the "*Annales* school" of historiography, with its wide-ranging, interdisciplinary approach, Bloch exerted a huge influence on the study of history that is still being felt internationally.

block and tackle Combination of pulleys with a rope or cable, commonly used to augment pulling force. Two or more of the pulleys are attached to a fixed block, and the remaining pulleys are free to move as well as rotate. A block and tackle can be used to lift heavy weights or to exert large forces in any direction. Higher force ratios may be obtained by the use of more pulleys, but this advantage may be offset by increased friction.

Block Island Island, Rhode Island. It lies at the eastern entrance to Long Island Sound, 9 mi (15 km) southwest of Point Judith, R.I. It has an area of about 11 sq mi (29 sq km), and is coextensive with the town of New Shoreham (pop., 1990: 800). Called Manisses by its original Indian inhabitants, Block Island (named for the Dutch explorer Adriaen Block) received its first European settlers in 1661 and was admitted to the colony of Rhode Island in 1664. Once dependent on fishing and farming, it is now primarily a resort.

block mill Earliest mechanized factory for mass production. It was conceived by Samuel Bentham, with machinery designed by Marc Brunel and built by Henry Maudslay, and built at England's Portsmouth naval dockyard. By 1805 it was producing 130,000 pulley blocks per year. It remained in production for over 100 years. See also American System of manufacture.

blockade Act of war whereby one party blocks entry to or departure from an enemy area, often a coast. Blockades are regulated by international law and custom, which require advance warning to neutral states and impartial application. Penalties for breach of blockade are seizure of ship and cargo and their possible condemnation as lawful prizes. Neutral ships may not be destroyed for blockade running.

Bloemfontein \'blüm-ˌfän-ˌtān\ City (pop., 1991: 127,000), Republic of South Africa. It lies on the Modder River in Free State province. Founded in 1846 as a fort, it became the seat of the British-administered Orange River Sovereignty (1848–54), and later that of Orange Free State, an independent Boer republic formed in 1854. The failure of the Bloemfontein Conference (1899) resulted in the outbreak of the South African War. In the 20th century the city became a geographical transportation hub. It is the country's judicial capital. See also Pretoria, Cape Town.

Blok, Aleksandr (Aleksandrovich) (1880–1921) Russian poet and dramatist. He was the principal representative of Russian Symbolism (see Symbolist movement). He later rejected what he termed their sterile bourgeois intellectualism and embraced the Bolshevik movement as essential for the redemption of the Russian people. Influenced by early-19th-century Romantic poetry, he wrote musical verse in which sound was paramount. His preeminent work of impressionistic verse was the enigmatic ballad *The Twelve* (1918), which united the Russian Revolution and Christianity in an apocalyptic vision. In the era of postrevolutionary hardship, he declined into mental and physical illness, possibly brought on by venereal disease, and died at 40.

Blondin \blō^n-'da^n, *Engl* 'blän-dēn\, **Charles** *orig.* **Jean-François Gravelet** (1824–1897) French tightrope walker. After training as an acrobat, he achieved fame, first in 1859, with his many crossings of Niagara Falls on a tightrope 1,100 ft (335 m) long, 160 ft (48 m) above the water. Each time he used a different theatrical variation: blindfolded, in a sack, trundling a wheelbarrow, on stilts, carrying a man on his back, and sitting down midway to cook an omelette. In 1861 he appeared in London at the Crystal Palace, turning somersaults on stilts on a rope stretched across the central transept, 170 ft (52 m) from the ground. He gave his last performance in 1896.

blood Circulatory fluid (see circulation) in multicellular animals. In many species it also carries hormones and disease-fighting substances. Blood picks up oxygen from the lungs and nutrients from the gastrointestinal tract and carries them to cells throughout the body for metabolism. It picks up carbon dioxide and other wastes from those cells and transports them to the lungs and excretory organs. Blood composition varies among species. Mammalian blood consists of plasma, red and white cells (erythrocytes and leukocytes), and platelets (thrombocytes). Blood disorders include polycythemia (abnormal increase in the number of circulating red blood cells), anemia, leukemia, and hemophilia. See also ABO blood-group system, blood analysis, blood bank, blood-cell formation, blood pressure, blood transfusion, blood typing, Rh blood-group system.

blood analysis Laboratory examination of the physical and chemical properties and components of a sample of blood. Analysis includes number of red and white blood cells (erythrocytes and leukocytes); red cell volume, sedimentation (settling) rate, and hemoglobin concentration; blood typing; cell shape and structure; hemoglobin and other protein structure; enzyme activity; and chemistry. Special tests detect substances characteristic of specific infections.

blood bank Organization that collects, stores, processes, and supplies blood. Most blood donations are separated into components, which can be frozen and stored longer than whole blood and used by multiple patients. In hemapheresis, large amounts of one component can be separated from a single donor's blood and the rest returned to the donor. Before World War I, a physician had to find a compatible donor and give an immediate blood transfusion. Safe storage of blood and its components made possible innovations such as heart-lung machines.

blood-cell formation *or* **hematopoiesis** \hi-ˌma-tə-pȯi-'ē-səs\ *or* **hemopoiesis** \ˌhē-mə-pȯi-'ē-səs\ Continuous production of blood cells. Blood cells originate in blood-forming organs, notably bone marrow, which produces all the erythrocytes (red blood cells) and platelets and most of the leukocytes (white blood cells), the rest being produced by the lymphatic and reticuloendothelial systems. Red and white cells develop from undifferentiated stem cells. Platelets are formed from the giant cells of the bone marrow.

blood poisoning See septicemia

blood pressure Force originating when the heart's pumping pushes the blood against the walls of the blood vessels. Their stretching and contraction help maintain blood flow. Usually measured over an arm or leg artery in humans, blood pressure is expressed as two numbers; normal adult blood pressure is about 120/80 mm of mercury. The higher number (systolic) is measured when the heart's ventricles contract and the lower (diastolic) when they relax. See also hypertension, hypotension.

blood transfusion Transfer of blood taken from one person into the circulation of another to restore blood volume, increase hemoglobin levels, or combat shock. Once the blood-group antigens and antibodies (see ABO blood-group system, Rh blood-group system) were discovered, blood typing of donors and recipients rendered transfusion safe. In exchange transfusion, all or most of the blood is removed and replaced with another's blood. Undesirable reactions to transfusion are not uncommon.

blood typing Classification of blood by inherited antigens associated with erythrocytes (red blood cells). The ABO blood-group system and Rh blood-group system are among those most commonly considered. Without identification of these factors, blood transfusion from an incompatible donor may result in destruction of red cells or coagulation. Blood typing also helps identify disorders such as erythroblastosis fetalis.

bloodhound Breed of dog superior to any other in scenting ability, the foundation breed of most scent-hunting hound breeds. They were known, although not in its present form, in the Mediterranean area in pre-Christian times. Calm and affectionate, they are often used to track animals and trail persons. A large, strong dog, the bloodhound stands 23–27 in. (58–69 cm) and weighs 80–110 lbs (35–50 kg). It has short hair and long ears, with loose skin that falls into folds and wrinkles around the head and neck. The coat is black-and-tan, red-brown and tan, or tawny.

Bloodroot (*Sanguinaria canadensis*).
WALTER CHANDOHA

Bloodless Revolution See Glorious Revolution

bloodroot Plant *(Sanguinaria canadensis)* of the poppy family, native throughout eastern and midwestern North America, growing mainly in deciduous woodlands and blooming in early spring. The white, cup-shaped flower with bright yellow stamens in the center is borne on a reddish stalk. Large, veiny, half-opened leaves on red stalks enfold the flower stem and, after the flower has bloomed, open into multilobed, round blue-green leaves. The orange-red sap, once used by American Indians for dye, is found in the RHIZOMES, as is the medical ALKALOID sanguinarine. The species, particularly the variety *S. canadensis* 'Multiplex,' which has showy double flowers, is an interesting plant for the wild garden.

Bloody Sunday (1905) Massacre of peaceful demonstrators in St. Petersburg, marking the beginning of the RUSSIAN REVOLUTION OF 1905. The priest Georgy Gapon (1870–1906), hoping to present workers' request for reforms directly to NICHOLAS II, arranged a peaceful march toward the Winter Palace. Police fired on the demonstrators, killing more than 100 and wounding several hundred more. The massacre was followed by strikes in other cities, peasant uprisings, and mutinies in the armed forces. The term "Bloody Sunday" was also used to describe the murder in Dublin, Ireland (November 21, 1920), of 11 Englishmen suspected of being intelligence agents, by the IRISH REPUBLICAN ARMY; the BLACK AND TANS took revenge and attacked spectators at a soccer match, killing 12 and wounding 60. The term was used again in Derry (January 30, 1972) when 13 participants in a civil rights march were killed by British soldiers, who allegedly had been fired on by the marchers.

Bloom, Harold (born 1930) U.S. literary critic. Born in New York City, he studied at Cornell and Yale and taught at Yale from 1955. In *The Anxiety of Influence* (1973) and *A Map of Misreading* (1975), he suggested that poetry results from poets deliberately misreading the works that both influence and threaten them. In *The Book of J* (1990), he speculated that the earliest known biblical texts were written by a woman with principally literary intentions. His best-selling *The Western Canon* (1994) identifies 26 canonical Western writers and argues against the politicization of literary study.

Bloomer, Amelia *orig.* **Amelia Jenks** (1818–1894) U.S. reformer. Born in Homer, N.Y., she married Dexter Bloomer in 1840. She wrote articles on education, unjust marriage laws, and women's suffrage and published the biweekly *Lily* (1849–54). Among her interests was dress reform, and the full trousers that she wore came to be known as bloomers. This publicity attracted large crowds to her lectures in New York, where she often shared the platform with SUSAN B. ANTHONY and the Rev. Antoinette L. Brown.

bloomery process Process for IRON SMELTING. In ancient times, smelting involved creating a bed of red-hot CHARCOAL in a furnace to which iron ORE mixed with more charcoal was added. The ore was chemically reduced (see OXIDATION-REDUCTION), but, because primitive furnaces could not reach the melting temperature of iron, the product was a spongy mass of pasty globules of metal intermingled with a semiliquid SLAG. This hardly usable product, known as a bloom, may have weighed up to 10 lbs (5 kg). Repeated reheating and hot hammering eliminated much of the slag, creating WROUGHT IRON, a much better product. By the 15th century, many bloomeries used low shaft furnaces with waterpower to drive the bellows, and the bloom, which might weigh over 200 lbs (100 kg), was extracted through the top of the shaft. The final version of this kind of bloomery hearth survived in Spain until the 19th century. Another design, the high bloomery furnace, had a taller shaft and evolved into the Stückofen, which produced blooms so large they had to be removed through a front opening.

Bloomfield, Leonard (1887–1949) U.S. linguist. Born in Chicago, he began his career as a philologist trained in INDO-EUROPEAN, especially GERMANIC LANGUAGES. He taught Germanic philology at the University of Chicago (1927–40) and linguistics at Yale (1940–49). In *Language* (1933), one of the clearest 20th-century presentations of linguistics, he advocated the study of linguistic phenomena in isolation from their nonlinguistic environment and emphasized the need for empirical description. His thinking was influenced by his work on non-Indo-European languages, particularly the ALGONQUIAN family; *The Menomini Language* (1962) is a paragon of linguistic description and American Indian linguistic scholarship.

Bloomsbury group Name given to a coterie of English writers, philosophers, and artists who frequently met to discuss aesthetic and philosophical questions between about 1907 and 1930 at several houses in the Bloomsbury district of London. Among the group were E.M. FORSTER, LYTTON STRACHEY, CLIVE BELL, the painters Vanessa Bell (1879–1961) and Duncan Grant (1885–1978), JOHN MAYNARD KEYNES, the Fabian writer Leonard Woolf (1880–1969), and VIRGINIA WOOLF.

Blount \'blənt\, **William** (1749–1800) U.S. politician. Born in Bertie Co., N.C., he served in the American Revolution before being elected to six terms in the legislature, and was a delegate to the Constitutional Convention. As the first governor of lands ceded to the U.S. by North Carolina, he worked to secure statehood for what would become Tennessee. In 1796 he became one of Tennessee's first two senators, but he was expelled from the Senate in 1797 on charges of plotting to help the British gain control of Spanish Florida and Louisiana.

Blow, John (1649–1708) British composer, organist, and teacher. He was appointed organist at Westminster Abbey in 1668; in 1774 he became master of the children at the Chapel Royal, and he later held various equally prominent posts, in which he influenced many students, including H. PURCELL. Of the abundant music he wrote in his official capacities, about 12 services and over 100 anthems survive. His court masque *Venus and Adonis* (1685) represents a landmark in the development of English opera.

blowfish See PUFFER

blowfly Any member of the DIPTERAN family Calliphoridae, including the SCREWWORM and the bluebottle, greenbottle, and cluster flies. Metallic blue, green, or bronze, and noisy in flight, blowflies resemble the HOUSEFLY in size and habits. The larvae usually feed on decaying flesh and sometimes infest open wounds. They may help prevent infection by cleaning away dead flesh, but may also destroy healthy tissue. Blowflies were once used to treat gangrene and a human bone disease and were used in World War I to clean soldiers' wounds. Some species seriously hurt or kill livestock by massive infestation or by carrying diseases such as ANTHRAX, DYSENTERY, and JAUNDICE.

blowgun Long, narrow pipe through which darts or other projectiles are blown. Primarily a hunting weapon, it is rarely used in warfare. It has been used by aboriginal peoples in Malaysia and elsewhere in South Asia, southern India and Sri Lanka, Madagascar, northwestern South America, and Central America. Blowguns vary in length from 18 in. to more than 23 ft (45 cm to 7 m) and are often made of cane or bamboo. Darts are usually made of palm-leaf midribs or wood or bamboo splinters 1.5–40 in. (4–100 cm). The dart must fit the tube snugly, so that a puff of human breath will cause it to fly from the tube. To be effective against quarry larger than small birds, blowgun darts require poison.

blowing engine Machine for pumping air into a furnace. Bellows driven by a waterwheel were the earliest form of blowing engine, later replaced by reciprocating pumps driven by steam or gas engines and by turbo-blowers. A modern blast furnace requires an enormous blowing engine.

Blücher \'blü-kər\, **Gebhard von** *later* **Fürst (Prince) von Wahlstatt** \'väl-ˌshtät\ (1742–1819) Prussian military leader. He joined the Prussian army in 1760 and commanded troops against the French 1793–94 and in the NAPOLEONIC WARS. In 1813 he came out of retirement to command Prussian troops against the French, defeating them at Wahlstatt and assisting in the allied victory at the Battle of LEIPZIG. In 1815 he again commanded Prussian forces in the Battle of Waterloo, coordinating his army with the allied forces under the duke of WELLINGTON to bring about Napoleon's defeat.

blue (butterfly) Any member of the widely occurring LEPIDOPTERAN family Lycaenidae. Adults, sometimes known as gossamer-winged butterflies, are small and delicate, with a wingspan of 0.75–1.5 in. (18–38 mm). Blues are rapid fliers, and most species have iridescent wings. Larvae are short, broad, and sluglike. Some species secrete honeydew, a sweet by-product of digestion that attracts ants, which stroke the larvae with their legs to stimulate honeydew secretion.

blue asbestos See CROCIDOLITE

blue crab Any member of a genus *(Callinectes)* of DECAPODS, particularly *C. sapidus* and *C. hastatus*, common edible CRABS of the western Atlantic coast prized as delicacies. Their usual habitats are muddy shores, bays, and estuaries. The blue crab shell, greenish on top and dingy white below, is about 3 in. (15–18 cm) long. The legs are bluish. The chelae, or pincers, are large and somewhat unequal in size, and the fifth pair of legs is flattened for swimming. Blue crabs are scavengers. See photograph on following page.

Blue crab (*Callinectes sapidus*).
JOHN H. GERARD FROM THE NATIONAL AUDUBON SOCIETY COLLECTION/PHOTO RESEARCHERS—EB INC.

blue-green algae See CYANOBACTERIA

blue ground See KIMBERLITE

blue law U.S. statute regulating work, commerce, and amusements on Sundays. The name is said to derive from a list of Sabbath regulations published (on blue paper or in blue wrappers) in New Haven, Conn., in 1781. Throughout colonial New England such laws regulated morals and conduct. Most lapsed after the American Revolution, but some, such as prohibitions against the Sunday sale of alcoholic beverages, remain on the books in some areas.

Blue Mountains Part of the GREAT DIVIDING RANGE, Australia. Located in NEW SOUTH WALES, the range rises 2,000–3,000 ft (600–900 m). Once used as a retreat by wealthy SYDNEY residents, it is now accessible by good roads and is a popular tourist area; its growth in population has been dramatic. The city of Blue Mountains (pop., 1991: 69,000) was incorporated in 1947.

Blue Mountains Mountain range, eastern Jamaica. It extends from north of KINGSTON eastward 30 mi (50 km) to the Caribbean Sea. Its highest point is Blue Mountain Peak, at 7,388 ft (2,252 m). It experiences heavy rain and widely divergent temperatures. Blue Mountain coffee is famous for its excellent quality.

Blue Nile See NILE RIVER

Blue Ridge (Mountains) Section of the APPALACHIAN MTNS., eastern U.S. The range extends from near HARPERS FERRY, W.V., southwest across Virginia and North Carolina into Georgia; it is sometimes considered to include a northern extension into Maryland, Pennsylvania, and New York. The highest peaks are in the Black Mountains of North Carolina; the average elevation is 2,000–4,000 ft (600–1,200 m). The scenic Blue Ridge Parkway, established in 1936 and administered by the National Park Service, runs 470 mi (756 km) along the crest.

blue whale Mottled, blue-gray BALEEN WHALE (*Balaenoptera musculus*), also called sulfur-bottom whale because of the yellowish DIATOMS on some individuals. The largest of all animals, the blue whale reaches a maximum length of about 100 ft (30 m) and a maximum weight of 150 tons (136,000 kg). It is found alone or in small groups in all oceans. In summer it feeds on KRILL in polar waters, and in winter it moves toward the equator to breed. It was once the most important of the commercially hunted baleen whales, and its populations were greatly reduced. Listed as an ENDANGERED SPECIES, it is now protected.

Bluebeard *or* **Gilles de Rais** *or* **Gilles de Retz** \zhēl-də-ˈrā\ (1404–1440) Baron and marshal of France renowned for his cruelty. His name was later connected with the story "Bluebeard" by CHARLES PERRAULT. He fought several battles at the side of JOAN OF ARC and was made marshal of France (1429). Back in Brittany he led a dissipated life and eventually turned to alchemy and satanism. Accused of abducting and murdering more than 140 children, he was tried by ecclesiastical and civil courts. Condemned for heresy, he confessed, repented, and died bravely at the gallows; his body was burned. Skeptics have noted irregularities in the trials and the interest of others in his ruin. The fairy-tale Bluebeard takes a wife, who, curious about the one room of the castle to which he denies her the key, discovers there the skeletons of her predecessors.

Bluebeard, illustration by Gustave Doré.
BY COURTESY OF THE TRUSTEES OF THE BRITISH MUSEUM; PHOTOGRAPH, J.R. FREEMAN & CO., LTD.

bluebell Any plant of the genus *Endymion,* in the LILY FAMILY, native to Eurasia. Bluebell, or wild hyacinth *(E. nonscriptus),* and Spanish bluebell *(E. hispanicus),* bearing clusters of bell-shaped blue flowers, are cultivated as garden ornamentals; some authorities place them in the related genus *Scilla* of the same family. Many other plants are commonly known as bluebells, including species of the genera *Campanula, Eustoma, Polemonium,* and *Clematis.* In the U.S. the name bluebell is usually reserved for *Mertensia virginica.*

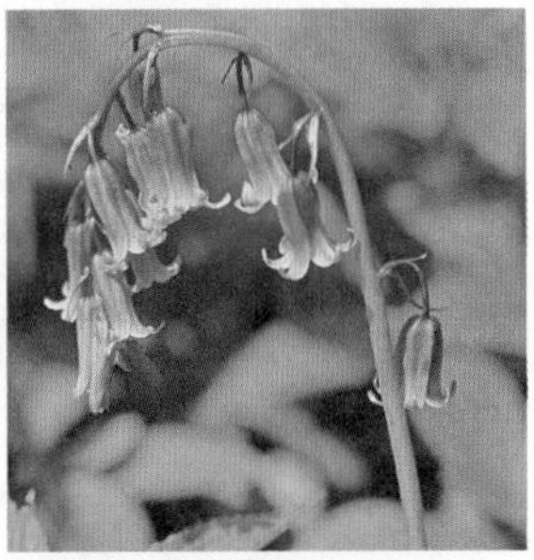
Wild hyacinth (*Endymion nonscriptus*).
M.T. TANTON—THE NATIONAL AUDUBON SOCIETY COLLECTION/PHOTO RESEARCHERS

blueberry Any of several shrubs, native to North America, of the genus *Vaccinium,* in the HEATH FAMILY. They are prized for their sweet edible fruits, a source of vitamin C and iron. Blueberries grow only in highly acidic and well-drained but moist soils. The highbush blueberry *(V. corymbosum),* economically and ornamentally the most important species, is in the U.S. cultivated primarily in Maine, New Jersey, southwestern Michigan, and eastern North Carolina.

Blueberry.
GRANT HEILMAN—EB INC.

bluebird Any of three North American bird species (songbird genus *Sialia*) of the CHAT-THRUSH group. The eastern bluebird *(S. sialis),* which is 5.5 in. (14 cm) long, and the western bluebird *(S. mexicana)* are red-breasted forms found east and west of the Rockies, respectively. The mountain bluebird *(S. currucoides),* also found in the West, is all blue. Bluebirds arrive from the south in earliest spring. They live in open country and woodlands and nest in holes in trees or in fence posts and bird boxes.

Western bluebird (*Sialia mexicana*).
HERBERT CLARKE

bluebonnet Any of several flowering plants, including the Texas bluebonnet *(Lupinus subcarnosus),* a North American annual LEGUME native to the plains of Texas. About 1 ft (0.3 m) tall, it bears silky-haired compound leaves and clusters of purplish-blue flowers marked in the center with white or yellow. In the spring it covers immense areas in southern and western Texas like a blue carpet. It is one of the most popular WILDFLOWERS of Texas. In Scotland the name is given to the bluebottle *(Centaurea cyanus)* and to the blue scabious, or devil's bit *(Succisa pratensis).*

bluefish Swift-moving food and game fish *(Pomatomus saltatrix)* found throughout warm and tropical regions of the Atlantic and Indian oceans. It lives in schools and is a voracious predator of smaller animals, especially other fishes. It is slender and has a forked tail and a large mouth with strong, pointed teeth. It is blue or greenish and grows to a length of about 4 ft (1.2 m) and a weight of 25 lbs (11.5 kg).

bluegill Popular game fish *(Lepomis macrochirus)* and one of the best-known SUNFISHES throughout its original range, the freshwater habitats of the central and southern U.S. It has been introduced throughout the western U.S. and in other parts of the world. Bluegills are usually bluish or greenish and have a characteristic dark flap at the rear of the gill cover. Among the smallest of the food and game fishes, they normally are only 6–9 in. (15–23 cm) long and weigh less than 0.5 lbs (0.25 kg). Bluegills are known as highly spirited fighters on the end of a fishing line.

bluegrass Any of many slender annual and perennial lawn, pasture, and forage GRASSES of the genus *Poa,* in the family Poaceae, or Gramineae. About 250 species are found in temperate and cool climates, more than 50 in the U.S. Most have small spikelets lacking bristles and arranged in open clusters. The narrow leaf blades have boat-shaped tips. Kentucky bluegrass *(P. pratensis),* the best-known U.S. species, is a popular lawn and pasture grass in the northern states with blue-green leaves, common in open areas and along roadsides. Texas bluegrass *(P. arachnifera),* mutton grass *(P. fendleriana),* and plains bluegrass *(P. arida)* are important western forage grasses. Annual bluegrass *(P. annua),* a small, light-green species, is considered a pest in lawns.

bluegrass In music, a country-and-western style that emerged after World War II, a direct descendant of the string-band music played by such groups as the CARTER FAMILY. Bluegrass is distinguished from its predecessors by its more syncopated rhythm, its high-pitched tenor (lead) vocals, its tight harmonies, its driving rhythms, and a strong influence of jazz and blues. A very prominent place is given to the banjo, always played in the unique three-finger style developed by Earl Scruggs (see LESTER FLATT). Mandolin and fiddle are generally featured, and traditional square-dance tunes, religious songs, and ballads furnish much of the repertory. Bluegrass was originated by and got its name from BILL MONROE and his Blue Grass Boys. From the late 1940s on, it continued to grow in popularity; from the 1970s an influx of younger musicians brought some influence from rock music.

Bluegrass region Area of central Kentucky. The region contains Kentucky's best agricultural land, and thus became the first area to be settled. It became known for its abundant BLUEGRASS and famous for breeding fine horses; the calcium-rich soil imparts its minerals to the grass and thence into the horses' bones.

blues Secular musical form incorporating a repeating harmonic structure with melodic emphasis on the flatted or "blue" third and seventh notes of the scale. The specific origins of the blues are not known, but elements of the music of former slaves include the call-and-response pattern and syncopated rhythms of SPIRITUALS and work songs. The codification of the structure of the blues occurred in the early 20th century, most commonly as a 12-bar phrase using the chords of the first, fourth, and fifth degrees of the major scale. Its origins as a primarily vocal form induced instrumental performers to imitate the human voice with "bent" notes. Lyric stanzas are usually in three lines, the words of the second generally repeating those of the first. The elaboration of the rural blues from Texas and the Mississippi delta established both lyric and instrumental traditions, often featuring speech-like inflection and guitar accompaniment. W.C. HANDY's compositions brought blues elements to the popular music of the first decades of the century. The first blues recordings featured singers Ma RAINEY and BESSIE SMITH in the early 1920s using jazz accompanists, performing a style which would become known as classic blues. The highly personal interpretations and improvisation of the blues, combined with elements of its structure and inflection, served as the foundation for JAZZ, RHYTHM AND BLUES, and ROCK MUSIC.

Bluestocking Any of a group of ladies who in mid-18th-century England held "conversations" to which they invited men of letters and members of the aristocracy with literary interests. The term probably originated when Mrs. Elizabeth Vesey invited the learned Benjamin Stillingfleet to one of her parties; he declined, saying he lacked appropriate dress, until she told him to come "in his blue stockings"—the ordinary worsted stockings he was wearing at the time. The word came to be applied derisively to a woman who affects literary or learned interests.

Bluford \'blü-fərd\, **Guion S(tewart), Jr.** (born 1942) U.S. astronaut. Born in Philadelphia, he flew 144 combat missions in the Vietnam War; on his return, he received a PhD in aerospace engineering from the Air Force Institute of Technology. He joined NASA's astronaut program in 1978, and flew on numerous space-shuttle missions, his first being the *Challenger*'s third flight (1983), the first to be launched and land at night. He was the first African-American to fly in space.

Blum \'blüm\, **Léon** (1872–1950) French politician and writer. He made a name as a brilliant literary and drama critic, then entered politics in the FRENCH SOCIALIST PARTY. As a member of the Chamber of Deputies (1919–28, 1929–40), he became a leader of the Socialists from 1921. The chief architect of an electoral alliance of the left, he became the first Socialist (and the first Jewish) premier of France as head of the POPULAR FRONT government (1936–37). He introduced such reforms as the 40-hour workweek and collective bargaining and nationalized the chief war industries and the Bank of France. Arrested by the Vichy government in 1940, he was imprisoned until 1945. In the postwar years he was one of France's leading veteran statesmen.

Blumberg \'bləm-bərg\, **Baruch S(amuel)** (born 1925) U.S. research physician. Born in New York City, he received his MD from Columbia University. His discovery of an ANTIGEN that he later proved to be part of the hepatitis B virus, and which causes the body to produce antibodies to the virus, led to blood-donor screening and a vaccine. He shared a 1976 Nobel Prize with D. CARLETO GAJDUSEK.

Blunt, Anthony (Frederick) (1907–1983) British art historian and spy. He began his espionage for the Soviet Union after meeting GUY BURGESS at Cambridge University in the 1930s. From 1937 Blunt had a brilliant career as an art historian, publishing scores of scholarly works that largely established art history in Britain. In World War II he served in British military intelligence and also gave secret information to the Soviets. In 1945 he was appointed surveyor of the king's (later queen's) pictures, and in 1947 he became director of the prestigious Courtauld Inst. He ceased active intelligence work but in 1951 arranged for the escape of Burgess and Donald Maclean (1913–1983) from Britain. In 1964, after the defection of KIM PHILBY, Blunt was confronted by British authorities and secretly confessed his Soviet connections. When his past as the "fourth man" in the spy ring was made public in 1979, he was stripped of the knighthood awarded him in 1956.

Bly, Nellie *orig.* **Elizabeth Cochrane** (1867–1922) U.S. newspaper writer. Born in Cochrane's Mills, Pa., she started writing for *The Pittsburgh Dispatch* at 18, producing feature articles on such subjects as divorce and slum life. After joining the *New York World,* she feigned insanity to get into an asylum and wrote an exposé that brought about needed reforms. Beginning in 1889, in an attempt to beat the fictional record in JULES VERNE's *Around the World in Eighty Days,* she circled the globe in about 72 days, 6 hours. The much-publicized trip made her byname a celebrated synonym for a female star reporter.

Bly, Robert (Elwood) (born 1926) U.S. poet and translator. Born in Madison, Minn., he attended Harvard University and the University of Iowa. In 1958 he founded *The Fifties* (later *The Sixties*), which published the works of young poets. He helped found American Writers Against the Vietnam War, and he donated his 1968 National Book Award prize money (received for *The Light Around the Body*) to a draft resisters' organization. His best-selling *Iron John* (1990) probed the male psyche, and Bly became the best-known leader of the "men's movement." He is also known for his translations of a wide range of poetry.

Blyton \'blī-tᵊn\, **Enid (Mary)** (1897–1968) English children's writer. Trained as a schoolteacher, she published her first book, *Child Whispers,* in 1922. She went on to produce more than 600 children's books and numerous magazine articles. She is probably best known for several book series, including those featuring Noddy, the Famous Five, and the Secret Seven. Though often criticized for their stereotyped characters, simple writing style, and didactic moralism, her books were widely translated and remained internationally popular long after her death.

BMW *in full* **Bayerische Motoren Werke AG** \'bī-er-ish-ə-mō-'tōr-ən-'ver-kə\ German automaker. Founded in 1929, the company became known for its high-speed motorcycles. During World War II, BMW built the world's first jet airplane engines for the Luftwaffe. It suffered financially in the postwar period but recovered after 1969 with a line of high-priced cars conventional in design but engineered like sports cars.

B'nai B'rith \bə-'nā-'brith\ (Hebrew: "Sons of the Covenant") Oldest and largest Jewish service organization. Founded in New York City in 1843, it now has men's lodges, women's chapters, and youth organizations around the world. Its goals include defending human rights, aiding Jewish college students (mainly through the Hillel Foundation), sponsoring educational programs for adult and youth groups, helping victims of natural disasters, supporting hospitals and philanthropic institutions, and promoting the welfare of Israel. In 1913 it established the Anti-Defamation League to combat ANTI-SEMITISM.

Bo Hai *or* **Po Hai** \'bō-'hī\ *or* **Gulf of Chihli** \'jə-'lē\ Arm of the YELLOW SEA off the northern China coast. With the Gulf of Liaotung (generally considered part of the Bo Hai), the gulf's maximum dimensions are 300 mi (480 km) northeast-southwest and 190 mi (306 km) east-west. The HUANG (YELLOW) RIVER empties into it.

Bo Juyi *or* **Po Chü-i** \'bwȯ-'jᵫ-'ē\ (772–846) Chinese poet of the TANG DYNASTY. He began composing poetry at 5, and at 28 passed the examinations for the Chinese civil service. He rose steadily in official life and became the informal leader of a group of poets who rejected the courtly style of the time, believing that poetry should have a moral and social purpose. His satirical ballads and social-protest poems often took the form of free verse based on old folk ballads. He was revered both in China and in Japan, where his poems, notably the "Song of Everlasting Sorrow," became material for other literary works.

bo tree See BODHI TREE

boa Any of about 60 species of stout-bodied snakes (subfamily Boinae, family Boidae) found in both the Old and New Worlds, mostly in warm regions. Species vary in length from about 8 in. (20 cm) to more than 25 ft (7.5 m). Most are terrestrial or semiaquatic; some live in trees. Most species have blotches and diamonds on their brown, green, or yellowish body. Boas bite their prey, then kill by wrapping their body around the prey and crushing it. Several species have heat-sensitive lip pits for detecting warm-blooded prey, and most bear live young. Contrary to folklore, boas are not dangerous to humans.

Boadicea See BOUDICCA

boar *or* **wild boar** *or* **wild pig** Any wild member of the PIG species *Sus scrofa;* the ancestor of domestic pigs. It is native to forests ranging from western and northern Europe and North Africa to India, the Andaman Islands, and China and has been introduced to New Zealand and the U.S. It has a bristly, blackish or brown coat and stands up to 35 in. (90 cm) tall at the shoulder. Except for old, solitary males, boars live in groups. They are omnivores and are good swimmers. They have sharp tusks and, though normally not aggressive, can be dangerous. Because of its strength, speed, and ferocity, the boar has long been a prized game animal.

Board of Trade See Board of TRADE

Boas \'bō-ˌaz\, **Franz** (1858–1942) German-U.S. anthropologist, largely credited with establishing anthropology as an academic discipline in the U.S. Trained in physics and geography (PhD, 1881), Boas was part of an early scientific expedition to Baffin Island (1883–84), where he turned to studying ESKIMO culture. He later studied native peoples of British Columbia, including the KWAKIUTL. From 1896 to 1905 he directed the Jesup North Pacific Expedition, which investigated the relationships between the aboriginal peoples of Siberia and North America. His achievements in anthropology are virtually unrivaled. Before Boas, most anthropologists adhered to a relatively crude theory of SOCIOCULTURAL EVOLUTION, arguing that some peoples were inherently more civilized or developed than others. Boas argued that such views were ethnocentric, and that all human groups have actually evolved equally but in different ways. It is largely due to Boas that human differences are now attributed by anthropologists to historic "cultural" rather than genetic factors. Teaching at Columbia University from 1896 until his death, he was a leading organizer of the profession in the U.S. and the mentor of RUTH BENEDICT, ALFRED L. KROEBER, MARGARET MEAD, and EDWARD SAPIR. His books include *The Mind of Primitive Man* (1911), *Primitive Art* (1927), and *Race, Language and Culture* (1940).

Boas, 1941.
AP/WIDE WORLD PHOTOS

boat people Refugees fleeing by boat. The term originally referred to the thousands of Vietnamese who fled their country by sea following the collapse of the South Vietnamese government in 1975. Crowded into small vessels, they were prey to pirates, and many suffered dehydration, starvation, and death by drowning. The term was later applied to waves of refugees who attempted to reach the U.S. by boat from Cuba and Haiti.

Bob and Ray U.S. comedian team. Bob (originally Robert Brackett) Elliott (born 1923) was born in Boston, Ray (originally Raymond Walter) Goulding (1922–1990) in Lowell, Mass. They met while working at a Boston radio station and soon established their comedy team in a program of parodies and satire (1946–51). *The Bob and Ray Show* was nationally syndicated (1951–53), and their comedy sketches were popular in the 1950s and '60s on several networks. They also performed in the theater and starred in the Broadway show *The Two and Only* (1970).

bobbin Elongated spool of thread, used in the TEXTILE industry. In modern processes, the spun fibers are wound on bobbins; the weft filling in WEAVING comes off bobbins. Bobbins are essential to the manufacture of bobbin LACE (see LACEMAKING). The first bobbin lace probably originated in Flanders in the early 16th century. Early bobbin lace consisted of rows of deep acute-angled points worked from a narrow band, and the patterns were usually similar to those of the needle laces. It was much used for ruffs and collars in the 16th–17th century. See also TAPESTRY.

bobcat Bobtailed, long-legged North American cat *(Felis rufa)* found in forests and deserts from southern Canada to southern Mexico. It is a close relative of the LYNX and CARACAL. Bobcats have large paws and tufted ears; are 24–40 in. (60–100 cm) long, excluding the 4–8-in. (10–20-cm) tail; stand 20–24 in. (50–60 cm) at the shoulder; and weigh 15–33 lbs (7–15 kg). The fur is pale brown to reddish with black spots. Bobcats are nocturnal and generally solitary. They feed on small mammals and some birds and are important for controlling rodent and rabbit populations. They are sometimes found in suburban areas.

Bobcat (*Felis rufa*).
JOE VAN WORMER—PHOTO RESEARCHERS

bobolink \'bäb-ə-ˌliŋk\ Songbird *(Dolichonyx oryzivorus)* that breeds in northern North America and winters chiefly in central South America. Migrating flocks may raid rice fields, and the fat "ricebirds" were formerly shot as a table delicacy. In the breeding season the 7-in (18-cm) male bobolink (named for his bubbling song) has a black underside, yellow hindneck, white back and rump, and white patches on the wings; in winter he resembles the brown female.

bobsledding Sport of sliding down a winding ice-covered run on a large metal sled (bobsled) equipped with two pairs of runners, a long seat for two or more (usually four) people, a steering wheel, and a hand brake. Bobsledding originated in Switzerland in the 1890s, and was included in the first Olympic Winter Games in 1924. Championship competitions are held each year. The bob run used is usually at least 1,500 m (4,920 ft) long, with 15–20 banked turns. Four-man sleds attain speeds approaching 100 mph (160 kph); two-man sleds are only slightly slower.

bobwhite North American QUAIL species *(Colinus virginianus)* that exists in about 20 subspecies from southern Canada to Guatemala. It is reddish brown and has a gray tail. Its name is suggestive of its two-note call. A popular game bird of the southern and central U.S., it is found in brush, open pinelands, and abandoned fields.

Boccaccio \bōk-'käch-chō\, **Giovanni** (1313–1375) Italian poet and scholar. His life was full of difficulties and occasional bouts of poverty. His early works include *The Love Afflicted* (c. 1336), a prose work in five books, and *The*

Boccaccio, detail of a fresco by Andrea del Castagno; in the Cenacolo di Sant' Apollonia, Florence.
ALINARI—ART RESOURCE

Book of Theseus (c. 1340), an ambitious epic of 12 cantos. He is best known for his *Decameron,* a masterpiece of classical Italian prose that had an enormous influence on literature throughout Europe. A group of 100 earthy tales united by a frame story, it was probably composed 1348–53. After this period, he turned to humanist scholarship in Latin. With PETRARCH, he laid the foundations for Renaissance humanism, and through his writings in Italian he helped raise vernacular literature to the level of the classics of antiquity.

Boccherini \ˌbä-kə-ˈrē-nē\, **Luigi (Rodolfo)** (1743–1805) Italian composer. Son of a musician, he received excellent early training and toured widely in Europe as a cellist. He held positions at the courts of Madrid and Prussia. His huge chamber-music output includes some 125 string quintets (more than any other composer), some 90 string quartets, and some 50 string trios. He also wrote over 25 symphonies and 11 cello concertos. His music's elegance and charm has ensured its continuing popularity.

boccie *or* **bocci** *or* **bocce** \ˈbä-chē\ (from Italian *bocce,* "balls") Game of Italian origin, similar to BOWLS, played on a long, narrow, packed-clay court enclosed with boarded ends and sides. Each player or team in turn rolls four balls (made of wood, metal, or composition material) toward a smaller ball. The object is to bring one's ball nearer the small ball than an opponent's ball; one point is awarded for each such roll. The game usually ends at 12 points.

Boccioni \bōt-ˈchō-nē\, **Umberto** (1882–1916) Italian painter, sculptor, and theorist. He was trained in the studio of Giacomo Balla (1871–1958) in Rome. The most energetic member of the Futurist group (see FUTURISM), Boccioni helped publish *Technical Manifesto of the Futurist Painters* (1910), promoting the representation of modern technology, power, time, motion, and speed. These ideas are best shown in his masterpiece of early modern sculpture, *Unique Forms of Continuity in Space* (1913). His painting *The City Rises* (1910) is a dynamic composition of swirling human figures in a fragmented crowd scene.

Bochco \ˈbäch-kō\, **Steven** (born 1943) U.S. television writer, director, and producer. Born in New York City, he worked as a scriptwriter and producer for Universal Studios (1966–78) and MTM Enterprises (1978–85) before forming his own production company in 1987. He cowrote and produced such successful television dramas as *Hill Street Blues* (1981–86), *L.A. Law* (1986–94), *NYPD Blue* (from 1993), and *Murder One* (1995–97), winning numerous Emmy awards for his scripts.

Bock, Jerry *orig.* **Jerrold Lewis** (born 1928) U.S. composer. Born in New Haven, Conn., he studied at the University of Wisconsin, then collaborated with Larry Holofcener (born 1926) on songs for television's *Your Show of Shows* and the musical *Mr. Wonderful* (1956). With the composer-lyricist Sheldon Harnick (born 1924), he had his greatest successes, *Fiorello!* (1959, Pulitzer Prize) and *Fiddler on the Roof* (1964). Bock and Harnick's other musicals included *The Body Beautiful* (1958), *Tenderloin* (1960), the admired *She Loves Me* (1963), *The Apple Tree* (1966), and *The Rothschilds* (1966).

Böcklin \ˈbœk-lēn\, **Arnold** (1827–1901) Swiss-Italian painter. After studies and work in northern Europe and Paris, he won the patronage of the king of Bavaria with his mural *Pan in the Bulrushes* (1856–58). In 1858–61 he taught at the Weimar Art School and executed mythological frescoes for the Public Art Collection in his native Basel. He settled in Italy, painting nymphs, satyrs, tritons, moody landscapes, and sinister allegories that presaged Symbolism and Surrealism. His later style was somber, mystical, and morbid, as in his five versions of *The Isle of the Dead* (1880–86). Though most of his time was spent in Italy, he was the most influential artist in the German-speaking world in the late 19th century.

"Self-Portrait with Death as a Fiddler," oil on canvas by Arnold Böcklin, 1872; in the Nationalgalerie, Berlin.

BY COURTESY OF THE STAATLICHE MUSEEN PREUSSISCHER KULTURBESITZ, NATIONALGALERIE, BERLIN; PHOTOGRAPH, WALTER STEINKOPF

Bodawpaya \ˌbō-dȯ-ˈpī-ə\ (1740/41–1819) King of Myanmar (r.1782–1819). He was a son of Alaungpaya and the sixth monarch of the ALAUNGPAYA DYNASTY. Bodawpaya deposed his grandnephew to become king. In 1784 he invaded the kingdom of Arakan and deported more than 20,000 of its people as slaves; in 1785 he attempted to conquer Siam. His oppressive rule in Arakan led to rebellion; his pursuit of rebel leaders across the border into British-controlled Bengal nearly resulted in open conflict with the British. His campaigns in Assam heightened tensions. A fervent Buddhist, he proclaimed himself *Arimittya,* the messianic Buddha destined to conquer the world.

Bodensee See Lake CONSTANCE

Bode's law Rule giving the approximate distances of PLANETS from the SUN. First announced in 1766 by the German Johann Daniel Titius (1729–1796), it was popularized, from 1772, by his countryman Johann Elert Bode (1747–1826). It may be given as follows: To each number in the sequence 0, 3, 6, 12, 24, and so on, add 4 and divide the result by 10. The answers closely approximate the distances from the sun, in ASTRONOMICAL UNITS, of the planets (except Neptune) and suggested that a planet should be found between Mars and Jupiter where the asteroid belt was later discovered.

bodhi \ˈbō-dē\ (Sanskrit and Pali: "awakening" or "enlightenment") In BUDDHISM, the final enlightenment that ends the cycle of death and rebirth and leads to NIRVANA. This awakening transformed Siddhartha Gautama into the historical BUDDHA. Bodhi is achieved by ridding oneself of false beliefs and the hindrance of passions through the discipline of the EIGHTFOLD PATH. Though not supported in canonical texts, commentaries give a threefold classification of bodhi: that of a perfectly enlightened one, or a Buddha; that of an independently enlightened one; and that of an ARHAT.

bodhi tree *or* **bo tree** In BUDDHISM, the fig tree under which the BUDDHA sat when he attained enlightenment (BODHI) at Bodh Gaya (near Gaya, India). The tree growing on the site now is believed to be a descendant of the original, planted from a cutting of a tree in Sri Lanka that had been propagated from the original; both trees are sites of pilgrimage for Buddhists. The bo tree or a representation of its leaf has often been used as a symbol of the Buddha.

Bodhidharma \ˌbō-di-ˈdər-mə\ *Chinese* **Damo** *Japanese* **Daruma** (fl. 6th century) Legendary Indian monk credited with the establishment of the Chan or ZEN school of BUDDHISM. Considered the 28th Indian successor in a direct line from the BUDDHA Gautama, he is recognized by the Chinese Chan schools as their first patriarch. Legend states that he traveled from India to Guang (now Guangzhou), China, where he was granted an interview with the emperor Wudi, who was famous for his good works. He told the emperor that meditation, not good deeds, led to enlightenment. He himself was said to have meditated sitting motionless for nine years.

bodhisattva \ˌbō-di-ˈsət-və\ Term for the historical BUDDHA Gautama prior to his enlightenment as well as for other individuals destined to become buddhas. In MAHAYANA Buddhism the bodhisattva postpones attainment of NIRVANA in order to alleviate the suffering of others. The ideal supplanted the THERAVADA Buddhist ideals of the ARHAT and the self-enlightened buddha, which Mahayana deemed selfish. The number of bodhisattvas is theoretically limitless, and the title has been applied to great scholars, teachers, and Buddhist kings. Celestial bodhisattvas (e.g., AVALOKITESVARA) are considered manifestations of the eternal Buddha and serve as savior figures and objects of personal devotion, especially in East Asia.

Bodin \bȯ-ˈdaⁿ\, **Jean** (1530–1596) French political philosopher. He studied and later taught law at the University of Toulouse (1551–61). In 1571 he entered the household of François, duc d'Alençon, the king's brother. He favored negotiation with the Huguenots, with whom the government was engaged in a civil war, and opposed the sale of royal domains. His *Six livres de la république* (*Six Books of the Republic,* 1576) won him immediate fame. In it he suggested that the key to securing order and authority lay in recognition of the state's SOVEREIGNTY, whose validity he did not believe depended on its subjects. He assumed that governments commanded by divine right, and he distinguished three types: monarchy (which he favored), aristocracy, and democracy.

Bodleian Library \bȯd-ˈlē-ən\ Library of the University of Oxford and one of the oldest and most important nonlending reference libraries in Britain. The Bodleian is particularly rich in Oriental manuscripts and collections of English literature, local history, and early printing. Though it was established earlier, it was not secured by the university until 1410. After a period of decline, it was restored by Sir Thomas Bodley (1545–1613), a collector of medieval manuscripts, and reopened in 1602. Under provisions established in 1610 and 1662, it is a legal deposit library entitled to free copies of all books printed in Britain.

Bodmer \'bōd-mər\, **Johann Georg** (1786–1864) Swiss inventor of MACHINE TOOLS and textile-making machinery. In 1824 he established a small factory in England to make textile machinery, and by 1833 he had a shop equipped with his own machine tools. Between 1839 and 1841 he patented more than 40 specialized machine tools that he then set up in an ingenious factory-type arrangement. A gear-making machine that cut teeth of predetermined pitch, form, and depth in a metal blank was especially noteworthy. Bodmer also patented various STEAM-ENGINE devices and is credited with inventing the cylinder with opposed pistons.

Bodoni \bō-'dō-nē\, **Giambattista** (1740–1813) Italian typographer. Son of a printer, he served an apprenticeship at the press of the Roman Catholic Church in Rome. In 1768 he assumed management of the Royal Press of the duke of Parma. By the 1780s he was designing his own typefaces; the Bodoni typeface appeared in 1790, and is still in use today. He became internationally known and collectors sought his books. His many important works include fine editions of HORACE (1791), VIRGIL (1793), and HOMER's *Iliad* (1808).

Bodrum See HALICARNASSUS

body louse See human LOUSE

body modification and mutilation Intentional modification of the human body for religious, aesthetic, or social reasons. It is frequently performed for magical or pseudo-medical purposes, but cosmetic motives are equally common. The variability of the results in different cultures reflects varying ideals of beauty or morality. Modifications include head flattening, insertion of a lip plug, TATTOOS, scarification, and piercing of the ear and other parts of the body. Mutilations include male and female circumcision, foot binding, and amputation.

bodybuilding Developing of the physique through exercise and diet, often for competitive exhibition. Bodybuilding aims at displaying pronounced muscle tone and exaggerated muscle mass and definition for overall aesthetic effect. WEIGHT TRAINING is the principal form of exercise used; high-protein foods and vitamin and mineral supplements contribute to the diet. Bodybuilding competition grew largely out of 19th-century European strongman theatrical and circus acts. The first important international competition was the Mr. Universe contest, founded in 1947. It was followed in 1965 by the even more prestigious Mr. Olympia contest. Competition for women began in the 1970s. In 1998 bodybuilding was granted provisional status by the International Olympic Committee. The use of STEROIDS to enhance performance, though generally forbidden, has long been common among bodybuilders.

Boehm \'bœm\, **Theobald** (1794–1881) German flutist and flute designer. Son of a goldsmith, he was a self-taught virtuoso flutist, who realized that the craft he learned from his father could be put to use to improve the instrument. He created a new kind of key mechanism in 1832. He later studied acoustics, and by 1847 he had completely redesigned the flute, giving it a different internal shape, moving the holes, and extending the use of the keys. His work achieved a stronger and more uniform tone than that of earlier instruments and formed the basis for the modern flute.

Boeing Co. Major U.S. firm that is the world's largest aerospace company and foremost maker of commercial jet transports. It was founded by William E. Boeing (1881–1956) in 1916 (as Aero Products Company). In the late 1920s it became part of United Aircraft and Transport Corp., but it reemerged as an independent entity in 1934 when that company was broken up to comply with antitrust legislation. Boeing pioneered the development of single-wing planes in the 1930s; its B-17 Flying Fortress (first flown 1935) and B-29 Superfortress (1942) played prominent roles in World War II. After the war the company developed the B-52 jet bomber, long a mainstay of U.S. strategic forces. It produced the first U.S. jetliner, the Boeing 707 (in service 1958), and went on to develop a highly successful series of commercial jet transports. By the start of the 21st century these formed seven families—the narrow-body 737 and 757; wide-body 747, 767, and 777; 717 (formerly McDonnell Douglas MD-95); and MD-11. In the 1960s Boeing built the Lunar Orbiters, Lunar Roving Vehicles, and the first stage of the Saturn V rockets (see SATURN) for the U.S. APOLLO program. Beginning in 1993, it served as NASA's prime contractor for the INTERNATIONAL SPACE STATION. In 1996 it purchased the aerospace and defense units of Rockwell International Corp., and a year later it bought MCDONNELL DOUGLAS CORP. It acquired the satellite business of Hughes Electronics in 2000. See also LOCKHEED MARTIN CORP.

Boeotia \bē-'ō-shə\ District and ancient republic, eastern central Greece. Bounded by ATTICA and the Gulf of Corinth, its chief cities were ORCHOMENUS and THEBES. Inhabited by Boeotians, an Aetolian people from Thessaly, it became politically significant after the Boeotian League was formed under Theban leadership c. 600–550 BC. Hostile to ATHENS, the League revolted against it c. 447 BC. In the PELOPONNESIAN WAR, Boeotia defeated Athens at Delium in 424 BC. Led by Thebes, it dominated Greece until Thebes was destroyed by ALEXANDER THE GREAT c. 335 BC.

Boer See AFRIKANER

Boerhaave \'bür-ˌhä-və\, **Hermann** (1668–1738) Dutch physician. As a professor at the University of Leiden, he was renowned as a teacher, and he is often credited with founding the modern system of teaching medical students at the patient's bedside. His reputation as one of the greatest physicians of the 18th century lay partly in his attempts to organize the mass of medical information known at the time, in a series of major texts and encyclopedic works.

Boerhaave, detail of a portrait by Cornelis Troost; in the Rijksmuseum, Amsterdam.

BY COURTESY OF THE RIJKSMUSEUM, AMSTERDAM

Boethius \bō-'ē-thē-əs\ *in full* **Anicius Manlius Severinus Boethius** (c. 480–524) Roman scholar, Christian philosopher, and statesman. Born to a patrician family, he became consul in 510 and subsequently chief minister to the Ostrogothic king THEODORIC. Accused of treason and condemned to death, he wrote his Neoplatonic *The Consolation of Philosophy* while in prison awaiting execution. The book remained extremely popular and influential through the Middle Ages and later. He is also known for his translations of works of Greek logic and mathematics, including Porphyry and ARISTOTLE, and his translations and commentaries became basic texts in medieval SCHOLASTICISM.

bog bodies Informal collection of some 700 variously preserved human remains found over the past 200 years in natural peat bogs, mostly in western Europe. The bodies, including the soft tissues and the stomach contents, remain preserved because of the anaerobic fluid conditions in the bogs. They range chronologically from the early part of the 1st millennium BC to postmedieval times. The condition of some of them (e.g., cut throats, severed limbs, ropes around the neck) suggests the possibility of ritual killings, murders, and ignominious burial (since none received a proper grave).

bog iron ore Iron ore consisting of hydrated iron oxide minerals such as limonite and goethite formed by precipitation of groundwater flowing into wetlands. Bacterial action contributes to formation of the ore. Economically useful deposits can regrow within 20 years after harvesting. Bog iron was widely used as a source of iron in the past.

Bogarde \'bō-ˌgärd\, **Dirk** *orig.* **Derek Niven van den Bogaerde** *later* **Sir Dirk** (1921–1999) British actor. The son of a Dutch-born art critic, he made his stage debut in 1939 and won a film contract from the Rank studios after World War II. After appearing for a decade mainly in light comedies such as *Doctor in the House* (1953), he began demonstrating his acting range in such serious films as *The Doctor's Dilemma* (1958), *Victim* (1961), *The Servant* (1963), *Darling* (1965), *Accident* (1967), *The Damned* (1969), and *Death in Venice* (1971).

Bogart, Humphrey (DeForest) (1899–1957) U.S. actor. Born in New York City, he had minor roles on the stage and in Hollywood before winning success on Broadway as the murderer Duke Mantee in *The Pet-*

rified Forest (1935), a role he reprised in the film version (1936). He appeared in over 25 films, usually as a gangster, before achieving stardom in *High Sierra* (1941). Often playing a sardonic loner who proves capable of love, he appeared in such films as *The Maltese Falcon* (1941), *Casablanca* (1942), *Treasure of the Sierra Madre* (1948), *Key Largo* (1948), *The African Queen* (1951, Academy Award), and *The Caine Mutiny* (1954). He acted in four films with his fourth wife, LAUREN BACALL, beginning with *To Have and Have Not* (1945).

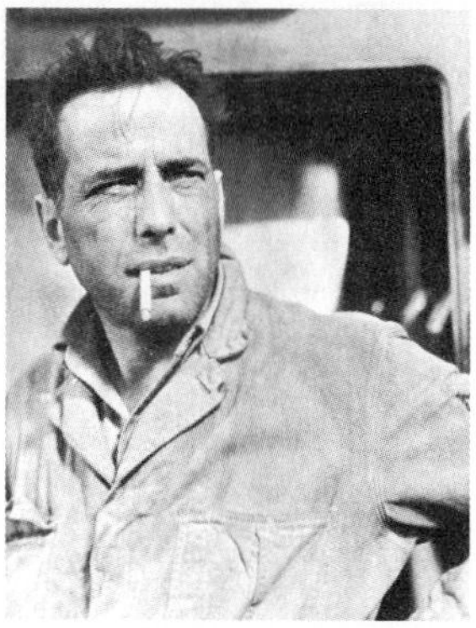

Humphrey Bogart in *Sahara* (1943).
THE BETTMANN ARCHIVE

Bogazköy \bò-'ä-kœi\ *or* **Bogazkale** \bò-'äz-kä-le\ Village, northern central Turkey in Asia. Located about 90 mi (145 km) east of ANKARA, it is on the ruins of the ancient Hittite capital Hattushash. The site contains archaeological remains, including temples, city gates, and walls of a powerful Hattic dynasty which ruled c. 16th–12th century BC, and was later described by HERODOTUS. Excavations conducted throughout the 20th century have uncovered hundreds of CUNEIFORM tablets attesting to the ancient city's importance.

Bogd Gegeen Khan \'bòg-əd-gə-'gen\ (fl. 1911–1924) Urga (now Ulaanbaatar) "Living Buddha" of the Yellow Hat (DGE-LUGS-PA) sect. In 1911 he proclaimed Mongolia independent of China, though true independence was not achieved until 1921. He remained head of state until 1924.

Bogomils \'bä-gə-ˌmilz\ Religious sect that flourished in the Balkans in the 10th–15th century. Founded by the 10th-century Bulgarian priest Bogomil, the sect's beliefs arose from a fusion of dualistic, neo-Manichaean doctrines imported mainly from the Paulicians (a sect of Armenia and Asia Minor) and a local Slavonic movement aimed at reforming the new Bulgarian Orthodox church. Its central teaching was that the visible, material world was created by the devil. The Bogomils denied the doctrine of the incarnation, rejected the Christian conception of matter as a vehicle of grace, and repudiated the whole organization of the Orthodox Church. In the 11th–12th century Bogomilism spread over many European and Asian provinces of the Byzantine empire, and it later spread westward. In Bulgaria it remained a powerful force until the late 14th century. With the Ottoman conquest of southeastern Europe in the 15th century, its influence declined. See also DUALISM.

Bogotá \ˌbō-gō-'tä\ City (pop., 1994 est.: 5,132,000), capital of Colombia. The District Capital area is officially known as Santafé de Bogotá. It lies on a plateau east of the ANDES. European settlement began in 1538 when Spanish conquistadores overran Bacatá, the main seat of the CHIBCHA Indians; the name was soon corrupted to Bogotá. It became the capital of the viceroyalty of NEW GRANADA and a center of Spanish colonial power in South America. It was the scene of revolt against Spanish rule in 1810–11, and SIMON BOLIVAR took the city in 1819. It became the capital of the confederation of GRAN COLOMBIA; when that was dissolved in 1830, it remained the capital of New Granada (later Republic of Colombia). Today Bogotá is an industrial, commercial, educational, and cultural center.

Boguslawski \ˌbò-gü-'slåf-skē\, **Wojciech** (1757–1829) Polish actor, director, and playwright. He joined the Polish National Theater in Warsaw as an actor in 1778 and later became its director (1783–1814). Considered the father of Polish theater, he wrote over 80 plays, including numerous comedies adapted from Western European writers as well as the popular original play *Krakovians and Highlanders* (1794). He helped develop theater companies in Vilna (1785) and L'viv (1794) and toured with the L'viv company in Polish and foreign plays. In 1787 he played Hamlet in his own translation of Shakespeare's play.

Bohai See PARHAE

Bohemia Former kingdom, central Europe. Settled in the 5th century AD by the Czechs, it became tributary to CHARLEMAGNE's empire. It was part of the kingdom of MORAVIA in 870; on the dissolution of Moravia, it became a duchy with an important center at PRAGUE. In the 10th century it expanded to include parts of SILESIA, Slovakia, and KRAKÓW. From the election of FERDINAND I as king in 1526, it remained under HABSBURG rule until 1918. Following World War I, Bohemia declared independence along with Moravia and Slovakia. It was invaded by Germany in 1939 on the pretext that much of the population was German. After World War II it became a province of Czechoslovakia (later the Czech Socialist Republic). On the breakup of the eastern European bloc, it became part of the independent Czech Republic in 1993.

Bohemian Forest *German* **Böhmer Wald** \'bœ̄-mər-ˌvält\ Mountain range, central Europe. It lies along the boundary between BAVARIA (Germany) and BOHEMIA (Czech Republic), extending northwest-southeast from the Ohre River to the DANUBE RIVER valley in Austria. Its highest point, the Arber, rises 4,780 ft (1,457 m). It is the source of the VLTAVA (MOLDAU) RIVER.

Bohemian glass Decorative glass made in Bohemia from the 13th century. In the early 17th century, Caspar Lehmann, gem cutter to Rudolf II in Prague, perfected the technique of gem engraving on glass. By 1700, a heavy, high-luster, richly ornamented potash-lime glass (Bohemian crystal) had become popular. In the late 18th century, black glass with chinoiserie designs was introduced. Ruby glass and an opaque glass with white overlay, both carved and enameled, were introduced in the 19th century.

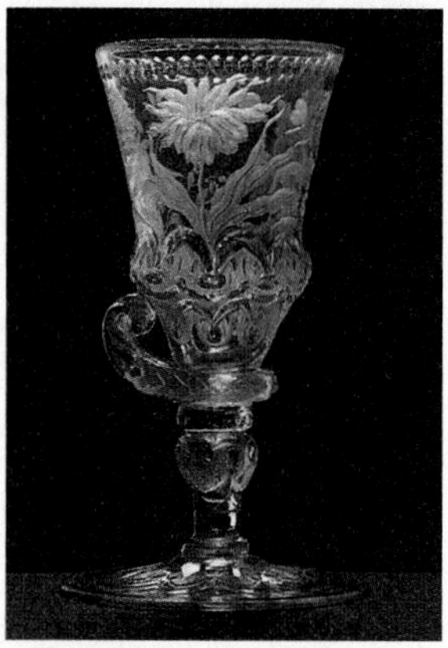

Bohemian glass goblet, relief cut and decorated with intaglio-engraved Baroque flowers, from the workshop of Friedrich Winter in Silesia, about 1710–20; in the Museum of Decorative Arts, Prague.
MUSEUM OF DECORATIVE ARTS, PRAGUE

Bohemian language See CZECH LANGUAGE

Bohemian school School of visual arts that flourished in and around Prague in the later 14th century. CHARLES IV attracted artists and scholars to Prague from all over Europe. French and Italian manuscripts inspired a local school of book illumination. Though most of the painters are anonymous, their achievements in panel painting and fresco had an important influence on German GOTHIC ART. A vital Bohemian tradition in architecture provided the impetus for the great German GOTHIC ARCHITECTURE of the 15th century.

Bohemond I \'bō-ə-mənd\ *orig.* **Marc** (c. 1050–1111) Prince of Otranto (1089–1111) and of Antioch (1098–1101, 1103–4). The son of a duke who held sway in southeastern Italy, he was nicknamed after a legendary giant. He joined his father's army and contested with ALEXIUS I COMNENUS for territory in the Byzantine Empire. In 1095 he joined the First CRUSADE, reconquering Byzantine lands from the Turks and capturing Antioch (1098). Rather than taking part in the battle to gain Jerusalem, Bohemond remained in Antioch, which he ruled as a principality. His efforts to muster French and Italian support against Alexius and the Byzantine Empire were ultimately unsucessful.

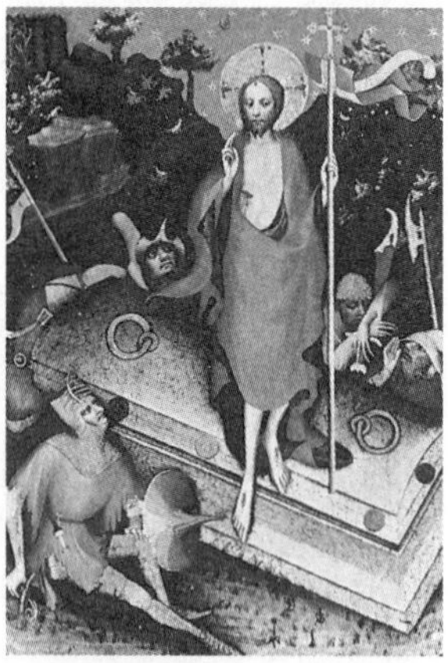

"Resurrection," panel painting by the Master of Wittingau, c. 1380–90; in the Národní Galerie, Prague.
GIRAUDON—ART RESOURCE

Böhm \'bœ̄m\, **Karl** (1894–1981) Austrian conductor. Having risen from rehearsal pianist to chief conductor at Graz, he was invited to conduct at Munich by BRUNO WALTER in 1921. As director of the Dresden

State Opera (1934–42), he conducted numerous premieres, including two by R. Strauss, with whose work he had a strong affinity. He had a long association with the Salzburg Festival (from 1938) and was especially admired for his conducting of W.A. Mozart.

Böhme \'bœ̄-mə\, **Jakob** (1575–1624) German mystic. Originally a cobbler, Böhme had a religious experience in 1600 wherein he gained an insight that he thought would help him resolve the tensions of his age, an insight expounded in *Aurora* (1612). The work of Paracelsus inspired his interest in nature mysticism. In *The Great Mystery* (1623) he explained the Genesis account of creation in terms of Paracelsian principles, and in *On the Election of Grace* he expounded the free will problem, made acute at the time by the spread of Calvinism and its doctrine of predestination. He had a profound influence on such later intellectual movements as idealism and Romanticism, and he is regarded as the father of theosophy.

Bohol \bō-'hȯl\ Island (pop., 1990 est.: 881,000), Philippine Islands. Located in the Visayan group north of Mindanao, it has an area of 1,492 sq mi (3,864 sq km). Visited by the Spanish in 1565, it remained under their rule until the late 19th century. Its character is essentially rural and its economy agricultural. The chief settlements, including Loon and Talibon, are on the coast.

Bohr \'bōr\, **Niels (Henrik David)** (1885–1962) Danish physicist. He studied the structure of the atom with J. J. Thomson and Ernest Rutherford at the Univs. of Cambridge and Manchester. He was among the first to see the importance of an element's atomic number and postulated that any atom could exist only in a discrete set of states characterized by definite values of energy. He became the first to apply the quantum theory to atomic and molecular structure, and his concept of the atomic nucleus was a key step in understanding such processes as nuclear fission. From 1920 to 1962 he directed the newly created Institute for Theoretical Physics in Copenhagen. His work on atomic theory won him a Nobel Prize in 1922. He was president of the Royal Danish Academy from 1939 until his death. Though he contributed to atomic-bomb research in the U.S. during World War II, he later dedicated himself to the cause of arms control. He received the first U.S. Atoms for Peace Award in 1957. Element 107, bohrium, is named in his honor. His son Aage Niels Bohr (born 1922) shared the 1975 Nobel Prize with Ben Mottelson (born 1926) and James Rainwater (1917–1986) for their work on atomic nuclei.

Boieldieu \bȯ-yel-'dyœ̄\, **(François-) Adrien** (1775–1834) French composer. Well known as a concert pianist, he taught piano at the Paris Conservatoire from 1798. His early *opéras comiques* won popularity in Paris, and he wrote several more operas as director of the French Opera in St. Petersburg (1804–10). Of his approximately 40 operas (including many one-act works), the most popular were *Le calife de Bagdad* (1800), *Le petit chaperon rouge* (1818), and *La dame blanche* (1825). He was France's leading opera composer of the early 19th century, but G. Rossini's rise left him increasingly in the shade.

Boigny, Félix Houphouët- See Felix Houphouet-Boigny

boil *or* **furuncle** \'fyu̇r-ˌəŋ-kəl\ *or* **furunculosis** Inflamed pus-filled swelling due to staphylococcus skin infection at a hair follicle. It hurts and feels hard; healing requires discharging the pus. Boils usually occur in hairy areas exposed to friction and maceration. A sty is a boil at the base of an eyelash. A carbuncle occurs when several adjoining boils merge. Boils may arise when scratching an existing skin disorder introduces staphylococci on the skin into hair follicles. Treatment usually involves keeping the area clean and protected from further infection; antibiotics often help severe cases.

Boileau (-Despréaux) \bwȧ-'lō\, **Nicolas** (1636–1711) French poet and literary critic. His *L'art poétique* (1674), a didactic treatise in verse setting out rules of composition of poetry in the classical tradition, provides valuable insight into the literary controversies of the period. He also translated the classical treatise *On the Sublime*, attributed to Longinus, which ironically became a key source of the aesthetics of Romanticism. His works upheld classical standards in both French and English literature.

boiler Apparatus for converting a liquid to vapor. A boiler consists of a furnace in which fuel is burned, surfaces to transmit heat from the combustion products to the water (or other liquid), and a space where steam (or vapor) can form and collect. A conventional boiler burns a fossil fuel or waste fuel; a nuclear reactor may instead supply the heat. There are two types of conventional steam boiler. In a fire-tube boiler, the water surrounds the steel tubes through which hot gases from the furnace flow; easy to install and operate, fire-tube boilers are widely used to heat buildings and to provide power for factory processes, as well as in steam locomotives. In a water-tube boiler, the water is inside tubes, with the hot furnace gases circulating outside the tubes; water-tube boilers, which produce more and hotter steam, are used in ships and factories. The largest are found in the central-station power plants of public utilities; other large units are used in steel mills, paper mills, oil refineries, and chemical plants. See also steam engine.

boiling Cooking of food by immersion in water heated to near its boiling point. Boiling is used primarily to cook meats and vegetables. Scalding, accomplished by heating water to around 185°F (85°C), is commonly used to prepare milk for breads and custards (usually in a double boiler, which suspends a pan containing the food above another containing the water). At just above the scalding temperature, fish and eggs may be poached (also using a type of double boiler). At the simmering point, just below that of boiling, soups, stews, and pot roasts may be prepared. Vegetables are often steamed in a rack placed above boiling water.

boiling point Temperature at which a liquid is converted to vapor when heated. At the boiling point, addition of heat results in the transformation of the liquid into its vapor without an increase in temperature. A liquid's boiling point varies according to the liquid's characteristics and the applied pressure. Water, at standard atmospheric pressure, or sea level, boils at 212°F (100°C), while ethanol boils at about 172°F (78°C). At higher altitudes, boiling points are lower and foods can take longer to cook; pressure cookers can be used to increase the pressure so that the boiling point is raised.

Bois, W. E. B. Du See W. E. B. Du Bois

Bois de Boulogne \ˌbwä-də-bü-'lȯnʸ\ Park, west of Paris, France. In a loop of the Seine River, it was once a forest and a royal hunting preserve. It was acquired by the city of Paris in 1852 and transformed into a recreational area. It occupies 2,155 acres (873 hectares) and contains the famous racetracks of Longchamp and Auteuil.

Boise \'bȯi-zē\ City (pop., 1996 est.: 153,000), capital of Idaho. The largest city in the state, it lies on the Boise River. Following the 1862 gold rush to the river basin, Fort Boise was established in 1863, and a community developed to provide services for the mines. It became the capital of Idaho Territory in 1864, and of the state in 1890. Agricultural expansion and the growth of the lumber industry contributed to its rapid growth. Boise is the headquarters of the Boise National Forest.

Boito \'bȯ-ē-tō\, **Arrigo** *orig.* **Enrico Giuseppe Giovanni** (1842–1918) Italian composer and librettist. As a composer, he is remembered for his opera *Mefistofele* (1868). He wrote the text for G. Verdi's *Inno delle nazioni* (1862) and revised the libretto for his *Simon Boccanegra* (1881), tasks which led to his writing the celebrated texts for Verdi's masterworks *Otello* (1887) and *Falstaff* (1893). He was also the librettist of Amilcare Ponchielli's *La gioconda* (1876). His own opera *Nerone* was left unfinished at his death.

Edward Bok, photograph by Pirie MacDonald, 1909.

BY COURTESY OF THE LIBRARY OF CONGRESS, WASHINGTON, D.C.

Bojador \ˌbȯ-jə-'dȯr\, **Cape** Cape, West Africa. It extends into the Atlantic Ocean off Western Sahara south of the Canary Islands. After 1434 the Portuguese began exploiting the region, particularly for slaves. Later the area was disputed by Spain and Portugal; Spain finally gained control in 1860 and annexed it in 1884. After Spain's withdrawal from Western Sahara in 1976, Morocco claimed the cape, garrisoned troops there, and made the area a province.

Bojangles See Bill Robinson

Bok, Edward (William) (1863–1930) U.S. editor. Raised in a poor Dutch immigrant family in Brooklyn, N.Y., Bok pursued a career in book and magazine publishing. As editor of the *Ladies' Home Journal* (1889–1919), he devised departments to inform women on diverse subjects and led campaigns for public health and beautification. His decision to stop accepting patent-medicine advertising helped lead the way to the Pure Food and Drug Act (1906). He also broke the taboo against the printed mention of venereal disease. His last years were devoted to working for civic improvement and world peace. He wrote a notable autobiography, *The Americanization of Edward Bok* (1920, Pulitzer Prize).

bok choy *or* **Chinese mustard** *Brassica chinensis,* one of two types of Chinese cabbage. It has glossy dark-green leaves and thick, crisp white stalks in a loose head. Its yellow-flowering center is especially prized. See also brassica, mustard.

Bokassa \bō-'kas-ə\, **Eddine Ahmed** *orig.* **Jean-Bédel** (1921–1996) President of the Central African Republic (1966–77) and self-proclaimed emperor of the Central African Empire (1977–79). Son of a village chief, Bokassa joined the French army in 1939, and later received the Croix de Guerre for his service in Indochina. In 1961 he returned to head the army of the newly independent Central African Republic; five years later he overthrew the president, his cousin David Dacko. In 1977 he crowned himself emperor. When he was found to have participated in the massacre of 100 schoolchildren and accused of cannibalism, French paratroops removed him in a coup and reestablished the republic. Bokassa settled in the Ivory Coast. Though sentenced to death in absentia in 1980, he returned in 1986 and was arrested; his death sentence was later commuted, and he was freed in 1993.

Bokhara See Bukhara

Bokn Fjord \'bük-ᵊn-'fyȯrd\ Inlet of the North Sea, Norway. Located north of Stavanger, a commercial center for offshore oil drilling, it is about 35 mi (56 km) long and 10–15 mi (16–24 km) wide. Its branches include other fjords, and it is dotted by many islands and islets.

Boleyn \bu̇-'lin\, **Anne** (1507?–1536) British royal consort. After spending part of her childhood in France, Anne lived at the court of Henry VIII, who soon fell in love with her and began secret proceedings to rid himself of his first wife, Catherine of Aragon. For six years Pope Clement VII refused to grant an annulment. In 1533 Henry and Anne were secretly married, and Henry had the archbishop of Canterbury, Thomas Cranmer, annul his previous marriage. Anne gave birth to the future Elizabeth I, but failed to produce the male heir Henry wanted. He lost interest in her, and in 1536 he had her imprisoned on questionable charges of adultery and incest. She was convicted and beheaded.

Bolingbroke \'bä-liŋ-ˌbrük\, **Viscount** *orig.* **Henry Saint John** (1678–1751) British politician. After entering Parliament in 1701, he became a prominent Tory in the reign of Queen Anne, serving as secretary of war (1704–8) and of state (1710–15). He was dismissed from office by George I and, fearing impeachment because of his intrigues with the Jacobites, he fled to France in 1715. He returned to England in 1725 and became the center of a literary circle that included Jonathan Swift, Alexander Pope, and John Gay. He waged an influential propaganda campaign in opposition to the Whigs and their leader, Robert Walpole, and also wrote several historical and philosophical works, including *The Idea of a Patriot King* (1744, 1749).

Bolívar \bō-'lē-vär\, **Pico** Mountain, Venezuela. Located in Sierra Nevada National Park, it is the highest mountain, at 16,427 ft (5,007 m), in the Cordillera de Mérida (a northeastern spur of the Andes) and in Venezuela.

Bolívar, detail of an engraving by C.G. Childs.

COURTESY OF THE LIBRARY OF CONGRESS, WASHINGTON, D.C.

Bolívar \bō-'lē-vär\, **Simón** *known as* **The Liberator** (1783–1830) South American soldier and statesman who led the revolutions against Spanish rule in New Granada (now Colombia, Venezuela, and Ecuador), Peru, and Upper Peru (now Bolivia). The son of a Venezuelan aristocrat, Bolívar received a European education. Influenced by European rationalism, he joined Venezuela's independence movement and became a prominent political and military leader. The revolutionaries expelled Venezuela's Spanish governor (1810) and declared the nation's independence in 1811. The young republic was defeated by the Spanish in 1814, and Bolívar went into exile. In 1819 he undertook a daring attack on New Granada, leading some 2,500 men over routes considered impassable. Taking the Spanish by surprise, he defeated them quickly. With the help of Antonio Sucre, he secured the independence of Ecuador in 1822. He completed Jose de San Martin's revolutionary work in Peru, freeing that country in 1824. On Bolívar's orders, Sucre liberated Upper Peru (1825). As president of both Colombia (1821–30) and Peru (1823–29), Bolívar oversaw the creation in 1826 of a league of Hispanic-American states, but the new states soon began warring among themselves. Less successful at ruling countries than at liberating them, Bolívar exiled himself and died on his way to Europe.

Bolivia *officially* **Republic of Bolivia** Nation, western South America. Area: 424,162 sq mi (1,098,579 sq km). Population (1997 est.): 7,767,000. Capitals: La Paz (administrative), Sucre (constitutional). The

population consists of three principal groups: Indians, descendants of the Aymara and the Quechua; Indian-Spanish mestizos; and descendants of the Spanish. Languages: Spanish, Aymara, Quechua (all official). Religions: Roman Catholicism (official), vestiges of pre-Columbian religion. Currency: boliviano. Bolivia may be divided into three major regions. The southwestern highlands, or Altiplano, where Lake Titicaca is located, extends through southwestern Bolivia. It is enclosed by the second region, the western and eastern branches of the Andes. Much of the eastern branch is heavily forested terrain, with many deep river valleys; the western branch is a high plateau bordered by volcanoes, including the country's highest peak, Mount Sajama, at 21,463 ft (6,542 m). The third region is a lowland area that comprises the northern and eastern two-thirds of the country; its rivers include the Guaporé, Mamoré, Beni, and upper Pilcomayo. Bolivia has a developing mixed economy based on the production of natural gas and agricultural foodstuffs. A republic with two legislative houses, its head of state and government is the president. The Bolivian highlands were the location of the advanced Tiwanaku culture in the 7th–11th century, and, with its passing, became the home of the Aymara, an Indian group conquered by the Incas in the 15th century. The Incas were overrun by the invading Spanish under Hernando Pizarro in the 1530s. By 1600 Spain had established the cities of Charcas (now Sucre), La Paz, Santa Cruz, and what would become Cochabamba, and had begun to exploit the silver wealth of Potosí. Bolivia flourished in the 17th century, and for a time Potosí was the largest city in the Americas. By the end of the century, the mineral wealth had dried up. Talk of independence began as early as 1809, but not until 1825 were Spanish forces finally defeated. Bolivia shrank in size when it lost Atacama province to Chile in 1884 at the end of the War of the Pacific, and again in 1939 when it lost most of Gran Chaco to Paraguay. One of South America's poorest countries, it was plagued by governmental instability for much of the 20th century. By the 1990s Bolivia had become one of the world's largest producers of coca, from which cocaine is derived. The government subsequently instituted a largely successful program to eradicate the crop, although such efforts were resisted by the many poor farmers who depended on coca.

Böll \'bœl\, **Heinrich (Theodor)** (1917–1985) German writer. As a soldier in World War II, he fought on several fronts, a central experience in the development of his antiwar, nonconformist views. His ironic novels on the travails of German life during and after the war captured the changing psychology of the German nation. He became a leading voice of the German left. Among his works are *Acquainted with the Night* (1953), *Billiards at Half-Past Nine* (1959), *The Clown* (1963), *Group Portrait with Lady* (1971), and *The Lost Honor of Katharina Blum* (1974). He won the Nobel Prize in 1972.

boll weevil \'bōl-'wē-vəl\ Small beetle *(Anthonomus grandis)* found almost everywhere cotton is cultivated. It is the most serious cotton pest in North America. Adults vary in size according to how much food they received as larvae, but they average about 0.25 in. (6 mm), including the long, curved snout. In spring, adults deposit eggs in cotton buds or fruit. After hatching, the larvae live within the cotton boll, destroying the seeds and surrounding fibers. Because the larvae and pupae remain inside the cotton bolls, they cannot be killed with insecticides. The boll weevil destroys an estimated 3–5 million bales of cotton annually.

Boll weevil (*Anthonomus grandis*).
HARRY ROGERS

bollworm \'bōl-ˌwərm\ Any larva of various moth species, including the pink bollworm (family Gelechiidae) and some *Heliothis* species (family Noctuidae; see corn earworm). Bollworms attack corn, tomatoes, cotton, peas, alfalfa, beans, soybeans, flax, peanuts, and other commercial crops. They can be controlled by natural parasites, early crop planting, trap crops, and insecticides.

Bollywood Indian moviemaking industry that began in Bombay (now Mumbai) in the 1930s and developed into an enormous film empire. Bombay Talkies, launched in 1934 by Himansu Rai, spearheaded the growth of Indian cinema. Throughout the years, several classic genres emerged from Bollywood: the historical epic, notably *Mughal-e-azam* (1960); the curry western, such as *Sholay* (1975); the courtesan film, such as *Pakeezah* (1972), which highlights stunning cinematography and sensual dance choreography; and the mythological movie, represented by *Jai Santoshi Maa* (1975). Star actors, rather than the films themselves, have accounted for most box-office success. Standard features of Bollywood films include formulaic story lines, expertly choreographed fight scenes, spectacular song-and-dance routines, emotion-charged melodrama, and larger-than-life heroes. At the beginning of the 21st century, Bollywood produced as many as 1,000 feature films annually, and international audiences began to develop among Asians in the U.K. and the U.S.

Bologna \bō-'lō-nyə\ City (pop., 2000 est.: 381,161), capital of Emilia-Romagna region, northern Italy. Located north of Florence, it lies at the northern foot of the Apennines. Originally the Etruscan town of Felsina, it became a Roman military colony c. 190 BC. It was subject to the Byzantine exarchate of Ravenna from the 6th century AD. It became a free commune in the 12th century. Incorporated into the Papal States in 1506, it was the scene of the crowning of Charles V in 1530. After a brief period of French occupation, it was restored to the Papal States in 1815, and in 1861 was united to the Kingdom of Italy. The University of Bologna is Europe's oldest university. The city is a road and rail center for traffic between northern and southern Italy. It is the site of excellent medieval and Renaissance architecture, and is famous for its cuisine. It has been governed by communists continuously since World War II.

Bologna, Giovanni da See Giambologna

Bologna, University of Oldest university in Europe, founded in Bologna, Italy, in 1088. It became in the 12th–13th century the principal center for studies in civil and canon law, and a model for the organization of universities throughout Europe. Its faculties of medicine and philosophy were formed c. 1200. The faculty of science was developed in the 17th century. In the 18th century women were admitted as students and teachers. Today it includes faculties of law, political science, economics, letters and philosophy, natural sciences, agriculture, medicine, and engineering. Total enrollment is about 64,000.

Bolognese school \ˌbō-lə-'nēz, ˌbō-lə-'nyēz\ Works produced and theories expounded by the Academy of the Progressives, founded in Bologna c. 1582 by Lodovico, Agostino, and Annibale Carracci. In reaction against Mannerism, they advocated drawing directly from life. Among their leading students were Domenichino and Guido Reni. Their clear, simple pictures accorded well with the artistic demands of the Counter-Reformation, which wanted works of art to be immediately comprehensible. What began as a regional movement became one of the most influential forces in 17th-century art.

Bolshevik \'bōl-shə-ˌvik\ (Russian: "member of the majority") Member of the wing of the Russian Social-Democratic Workers' Party led by Vladimir Ilich Lenin that seized control in the Russian Revolution of 1917. The group arose in 1903 when Lenin's followers insisted that party membership be restricted to professional or full-time revolutionaries. Though they joined with their rivals, the Mensheviks ("members of the minority"), in the Russian Revolution of 1905, the two groups later split, and in 1912 Lenin formed his own party. Its appeal grew among urban workers and soldiers during World War I. The Bolshevik consolidation of power after 1917 became one prototype of totalitarianism; the other was fascism of Benito Mussolini and Adolf Hitler. See also Communist Party, Leninism.

Bolshoi Theater complex in Moscow where concerts, opera, ballet, and dramatic works are presented. The institution (whose name means "Large") dates back to 1776, when Catherine II licensed a company to give all theatrical performances in Moscow; its scope soon expanded to include opera and dance as well as drama. The original complex was built in 1825; it was rebuilt after a fire in 1853. The performing companies have changed over time, but the institution and the rebuilt edifice have survived.

Bolshoi Ballet \bȯl-'shȯi\ Leading ballet company of Russia, noted for elaborate productions of 19th-century classical ballets. The company was formed in 1776 and took the name of its home, Moscow's Bolshoi Theater, in 1825. Its influential choreographers included Marius Petipa, Carlo Blasis, Alexander Gorsky, and Rostislav. Zakharov. Yuri Grigorovich was artistic director from 1964 to 1995. Its many successful tours have introduced its outstanding dancers, including Yekaterina Geltzer, Vasily Tikhomirov, Galina Ulanova, and Maya Plisetskaya, to audiences worldwide.

bolt Mechanical fastener, usually used with a nut, for connecting two or more parts. Bolted joints can be readily disassembled and reassembled; hence bolts or screw fasteners are used more than other types of mechanical fastener. A bolt consists of a head and a cylindrical body with screw threads along a portion of its length. Nuts have internal (or female) threads to match those of the bolt. Washers are often used to prevent loosening and crushing.

bolt action Type of breech mechanism that was key to developing an effective repeating rifle. It combines the firing pin, a spring, and an extractor, all housed in or attached to the bolt. A projecting handle with a round knob moves the bolt back and forth. As the bolt is thrust forward, it pushes a cartridge into the chamber and cocks the piece. The trigger releases the spring-driven firing pin inside the bolt. After firing, the extractor on the head of the bolt removes the spent cartridge and ejects it. The bolt then moves a new cartridge from the magazine.

Bolton, Guy (Reginald) (1884–1979) British-U.S. playwright and librettist. Born in England of American parents, Bolton's first play appeared on Broadway in 1911. In collaboration with P.G. Wodehouse and others, he turned out dozens of scripts scored by composers such as J. Kern (*Oh, Boy!* 1917), George Gershwin (*Lady, Be Good!* 1924; *Girl Crazy*, 1930), and C. Porter (*Anything Goes*, 1934).

Boltzmann \'bōlts-ˌmän\, **Ludwig (Eduard)** (1844–1906) Austrian physicist. He obtained his doctorate from the University of Vienna and thereafter taught at several German and Austrian universities. He was one of the first European scientists to recognize the importance of JAMES CLERK MAXWELL's electromagnetic theory. He explained the second law of THERMODYNAMICS by applying the laws of mechanics and the theory of probability to the motions of atoms, and he is remembered as the developer of STATISTICAL MECHANICS. His work was widely attacked and misunderstood; subject to depression after 1900, he eventually committed suicide. Shortly after his death, his conclusions were finally supported by discoveries in atomic physics and by recognition that phenomena such as BROWNIAN MOTION could be explained only by statistical mechanics.

Boltzmann constant Ratio of the universal gas constant (see GAS LAWS) to AVOGADRO'S NUMBER. It has a value of 1.380662×10^{-23} joules per kelvin. Named after LUDWIG BOLTZMANN, it is a fundamental constant of physics, occurring in nearly every statistical formulation of both classical and quantum physics.

bomb In volcanology, any unconsolidated volcanic material that has a diameter greater than 1.25 in. (32 mm). Bombs form from clots of wholly or partly liquid lava ejected during a volcanic explosion; they solidify and become rounded during flight. The final shape is determined by the initial size, viscosity, and flight velocity of the MAGMA.

Bombay See MUMBAI

bomber Military aircraft designed to drop bombs on surface targets. Aerial bombardment can be traced to the Italo-Turkish War (1911), in which an Italian pilot dropped grenades on two Turkish targets. In World War I the Germans used ZEPPELINS as strategic bombers. In the 1930s dive bombers were developed; they caused great destruction in the Spanish Civil War. World War II saw further development of heavy bombers, including the U.S. B-29, which could carry 20,000 lbs (9,000 kg) of bombs. Bombers were a major factor in the Allied victory. After the war, jet-propelled bombers carrying nuclear bombs were important to Cold War strategy, but from the 1960s strategic bombers began to be replaced by nuclear-armed ballistic MISSILES. Late-20th-century efforts to evade increasingly sophisticated radar systems culminated in the development of STEALTH bombers, but their enormous cost (and the end of the Cold War) raised questions about their worth compared to missiles.

Bombon, Lake See Lake TAAL

Bomu River \'bō-mü\ River, central Africa. Flowing west, it forms the boundary between northern Congo and southern Central African Republic (where it is called the Mbomou). It flows in a wide 500-mi (800-km) curve through savannas to join the Uele River and form the UBANGI.

Bon \'bȯn\ Popular annual festival in Japan, usually observed July 13–15, in honor of the spirits of deceased family members and of all the dead. As at the New Year festival, the dead are believed to return to their birthplaces. Memorial stones are cleaned, dances performed, and paper lanterns and fires are lit to welcome the dead and to bid them farewell when their visit ends.

Bon \'pœ̄ⁿ\ Indigenous religion of Tibet. It was originally concerned with magical propitiation of demonic forces, and its practices included blood sacrifices. It later developed a cult of divine kingship (with kings regarded as manifestations of the sky divinity), reformulated in TIBETAN BUDDHISM as the reincarnation of LAMAS. Bon's order of oracular priests had their counterpart in Buddhist soothsayers, and its gods of air, earth, and underworld in the lesser Tibetan Buddhist deities. Though its religious supremacy ended in the 8th century, Bon survives in many aspects of Tibetan Buddhism and as a living religion on Tibet's northern and eastern frontiers.

Bon \'bōⁿ\, **Cape** *Arabic* **Ras at Tib** \ˌrȧs-ȧt-'tēb\ Peninsula, Tunisia. Extending northeast from extreme northeastern Tunisia, it is about 50 mi (80 km) long. During World War II, it was occupied by German troops in retreat from Egypt and Libya (1943); they soon surrendered to the Allies there.

Bon, Gustave Le See Gustave LE BON

Bon Marché \bōⁿ-mȧr-'shā\ (French: "Good Buy") Paris DEPARTMENT STORE. It was founded as a small shop in the early 19th century, and by c. 1865 it had become the world's first true department store. Its 1876 building was designed by Alexandre-Gustave Eiffel (1832–1923). The Bon Marché chain now belongs to Federated Department Stores, Inc.

Bona Dea \ˌbō-nə-'dā-ə\ In ROMAN RELIGION, the deity of fruitfulness, both in the earth and in women. The dedication day of her temple on the Aventine was May 1. Her temple was cared for and attended only by women, though inscriptions show that there was a public side to her worship in which men could participate.

Bonaparte, (Marie-Annonciade-) Caroline (1782–1839) Queen of Naples (1808–15). The youngest sister of NAPOLEON, she married JOACHIM MURAT in 1800. Her ambitious nature was partially responsible for her husband's becoming king of Naples, among other achievements. Her relations with Napoleon became strained as she associated herself with Murat's shifting allegiances in 1814–15, which led to his execution. Caroline then took refuge in Trieste and became comtesse de Lipona.

Bonaparte, Jérôme (1784–1860) French nobleman. He was the youngest brother of NAPOLEON, from whom he became estranged after marrying a U.S. resident (1803) without Napoleon's consent; he later allowed his marriage to be annulled. Napoleon then married Jérôme to Princess Catherine of Württemberg and made him king of Westphalia (1807–13). He served in the Russian campaign of 1812 and at the Battle of WATERLOO. After Napoleon's fall, he lived in Florence; after the rise of his nephew, NAPOLEON III, he returned to France to become a marshal of France and president of the Senate.

Bonaparte, Joseph (1768–1844) French lawyer, diplomat, and soldier. Elder brother of NAPOLEON, he served during Napoleon's reign as king of Naples (1806–8), where he abolished feudalism, reformed the monastic orders, and reorganized the judicial, financial, and educational systems. He was named king of Spain in 1808, but his attempts at reform there were less successful. In 1813 he abdicated and returned to France. After Napoleon's defeat at Waterloo, Joseph lived in the U.S. (1815–32) and later settled in Italy.

Bonaparte, Louis (1778–1846) French nobleman and soldier. A brother of NAPOLEON, he accompanied Napoleon on the Italian campaign of 1796–97 and was his aide-de-camp in Egypt (1798–99). At Napoleon's insistence, he married HORTENSE DE BEAUHARNAIS in 1802, but the union proved unhappy and did not last. Proclaimed king of Holland in 1806, he was criticized by Napoleon for being too easy on his subjects. His unwillingness to join the CONTINENTAL SYSTEM led him into conflict with Napoleon, and in 1810 he fled his kingdom and eventually settled in Italy. NAPOLEON III was his son.

Bonaparte, Lucien (1775–1840) French nobleman and politician. A brother of NAPOLEON, he became president of the Council of Five Hundred and he helped Napoleon seize power in the Coup of 18–19 BRUMAIRE. Lucien's belief that Napoleon's ambition jeopardized the cause of democracy led to strained relations between the brothers. However, he offered Napoleon help during the HUNDRED DAYS and was the last to defend Napoleon's prerogatives at the time of his second abdication, after which he lived in Italy.

Bonaparte, (Marie-) Pauline (1780–1825) French noblewoman. A sister of NAPOLEON, she married one of his staff officers, Gen. C. V. E. Leclerc (1772–1802), in 1797. After Leclerc's death, she married Prince Camillo F. L. Borghese (1803) and went with him to Rome. She soon tired of him and returned to Paris, where her behavior caused some scandal. In 1806 she received the title of duchess of Guastalla. She died of cancer in Florence.

Bonaventure \ˌbä-nə-'ven-chər\, **St.** (1217?–1274) Italian medieval theologian, cardinal, and minister general of the Franciscans. Born in the Papal States, the son of a physician, he recovered from a near-fatal childhood illness through the intercession of St. FRANCIS OF ASSISI. After study at the University of Paris, he entered the Franciscan order in 1244. In 1254 he assumed control of the Franciscan school in Paris. He defended the mendicants against the charge that they defamed the Gospels by begging for alms. Elected Franciscan minister-general in 1257, he healed an incipient rift between those who favored a rigorous approach to poverty and those favoring a looser regimen. Pope Gregory X appointed him cardinal of Albano (Italy) in 1273, and at the Second Council of Lyon he reconciled parish clergy with the mendicant orders.

bond In construction, the systematic arrangement of bricks or other building units (e.g., concrete blocks, glass blocks, or clay tiles) to ensure stability. Units laid with their ends toward the face of a wall are called headers; units with their lengths parallel to the wall are called stretchers. Common types are the English bond (courses of stretchers and headers alternate), the Flemish or Dutch bond (headers and stretchers are laid alternately within each course, each header being centered over the stretcher below it), and the American bond (every fifth or sixth course consists of headers, the rest being stretchers). See also MASONRY.

bond Loan contract issued by local, state, and national governments and by private corporations, specifying an obligation to return borrowed funds. The issuer promises to pay interest on the debt when due (usually semiannually) at a stipulated percentage of the face value and to redeem the face value of the bond at maturity in legal tender. Bonds usually indicate a debt of substantial size and are issued in more formal fashion than PROMISSORY notes, ordinarily under seal. Government bonds may be backed by taxes, or they may be REVENUE BONDS, backed only by revenue from the specific project (toll roads, airports, etc.) to which they are committed. Bonds are rated based on the issuer's creditworthiness. The ratings, assigned by independent rating agencies, generally run from AAA to D; bonds with ratings from AAA to BBB are regarded as suitable for investment. See also JUNK BOND.

bond In law, a formal written agreement by which a person undertakes to perform a certain act (e.g., appearing in court or fulfilling the obligations of a contract); failure to perform obligates the person to pay a sum of money or forfeit money on deposit. It is an incentive to fulfill an obligation; it also provides reassurance that compensation is available if the duty is not fulfilled. A surety usually is involved, and the bond makes the surety responsible for the consequences of the obligated person's behavior. See also BAIL.

Bond, (Horace) Julian (born 1940) U.S. politician and civil-rights leader. Born in Nashville, Tenn., the son of a professor, he attended Morehouse College. In 1960 he helped create the Student Nonviolent Coordinating Committee (SNCC). In 1965 he was elected to the Georgia legislature, but his support of a SNCC statement denouncing U.S. policy in the Vietnam War caused the legislature to deny him his seat. He was twice reelected and refused entry. The U.S. Supreme Court ruled his exclusion unconstitutional in 1967. He later served in the state senate (1975–87). In 1997 he became chairman of the NAACP.

bonding Any of the interactions that account for the association of ATOMS into MOLECULES, IONS, CRYSTALS, METALS, and other stable species. When atoms' nuclei and ELECTRONS interact, they tend to distribute themselves so that the total energy is lowest; if the energy of a group arrangement is lower than the sum of the components' energies, they bond. The physics and mathematics of bonding were developed as part of QUANTUM MECHANICS. The number of bonds an atom can form, its VALENCE, equals the number of electrons it contributes or receives. COVALENT BONDS form molecules: Atoms bond to specific other atoms by sharing an electron pair between them. If the sharing is even, the molecule is not polar; if it is uneven, the molecule is an ELECTRIC DIPOLE. IONIC BONDS are the extreme of uneven sharing: CATIONS give up electrons, ANIONS take them up, and all the ions are held together in a crystal by ELECTROSTATIC FORCES. In crystalline metals, a diffuse electron sharing bonds the atoms (metallic bonding). Other types include HYDROGEN BONDING; bonds in AROMATIC COMPOUNDS; coordinate covalent bonds; multicenter bonds, exemplified by boranes (boron hydrides), in which more than two atoms share electron pairs; and the bonds in coordination complexes (see TRANSITION ELEMENT), still poorly understood. See also VAN DER WAALS FORCES.

Bonds, Barry L(amar) (born 1964) U.S. baseball player. Born in Riverside, California, he was a college All-American at Arizona State University. A left-handed power hitter and a superb base stealer, he played outfield for the Pittsburgh Pirates (1985–92) and the San Francisco Giants (from 1993). He was named Most Valuable Player several times, and by the end of the 1998 season, he had earned eight gold glove awards for fielding. In 2001 he hit 73 home runs, breaking MARK MCGWIRE's single-season record of 70; that year he also had 177 walks to top BABE RUTH's record (170). His father, Bobby Bonds (born 1946), was also an outstanding professional baseball player.

Bône See ANNABA

bone Rigid CONNECTIVE TISSUE of VERTEBRATES consisting of cells embedded in a hard matrix. Bones serve as the body's supporting framework; provide muscle attachment points for movement; protect the internal organs; house the BLOOD-CELL FORMATION system (red BONE MARROW); and hold about 99% of the calcium vital to many body processes. Bone consists of a matrix of calcium, phosphate, and carbonate crystals embedded among COLLAGEN fibers, providing strength and elasticity, and bone cells (less than 5% of its volume). An external layer of compact bone surrounds a central area of spongy bone, except at the marrow cavity. Bone does not grow by cell division; instead, different types of bone cells generate bone matrix, break it down, and maintain it. Bone is remodeled by this process, which strengthens it in areas under greatest stress, permits healing of FRACTURES, and helps regulate calcium levels in body fluid (see CALCIUM DEFICIENCY). The process also causes underutilized bone, as in an immobilized limb, to atrophy. Bone disorders include RHEUMATOID ARTHRITIS, OSTEOARTHRITIS, RICKETS, OSTEOPOROSIS, and TUMORS. Bone can fracture suddenly or over time, as in stress fractures.

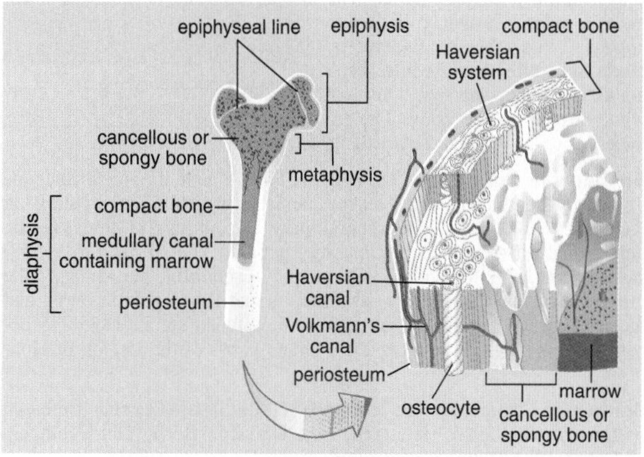

Internal structure of a human long bone, with a magnified cross section of the interior. The periosteum is a connective sheath covering the outer surface of bone. The Haversian system, consisting of inorganic substances arranged in concentric rings around the Haversian canals, provides compact bone with structural support and allows for metabolism of bone cells. Osteocytes (mature bone cells) are found in tiny cavities between the concentric rings. The canals contain capillaries that bring in oxygen and nutrients and remove wastes. Transverse branches are known as Volkmann's canals.

bone china Hard-paste PORCELAIN containing bone ash. It was developed by Josiah Spode (1754–1827) in England c. 1800. The addition of bone ash to china stone and china clay (i.e., hard china) made bone china easier to manufacture; it is stronger, does not chip easily, and has an ivory-white color that lends itself to decoration. Other factories (Minton, Derby, Worcester, WEDGWOOD, Rockingham) adopted the formula in the early 19th century. Bone china remains popular for tableware in Britain and the U.S. See also STONEWARE.

Wedgwood bone china plate, Staffordshire, 1815–20; in the Victoria and Albert Museum, London.

BY COURTESY OF THE VICTORIA AND ALBERT MUSEUM, LONDON; PHOTOGRAPH, EB INC.

bone marrow *or* **myeloid tissue** Soft, gelatinous tissue that fills BONE cavities. Red bone marrow contains stem cells, progenitor cells, percursor cells, and functional blood cells (see RETICULOENDOTHELIAL SYSTEM). LYMPHOCYTES mature in the lymphoid organs (see LYMPHOID TISSUE). All other BLOOD-CELL FORMATION occurs in red marrow, which also takes part in destruction of old ERYTHROCYTES (red blood cells). Yellow bone marrow mainly stores FATS. Because the LEUKOCYTES (white blood cells) produced in bone marrow are involved in immune defenses, marrow transplants can treat some types of IMMUNODEFICIENCY. Radiation and some anticancer drugs can damage marrow and impair IMMUNITY. Bone-marrow examination helps diagnose diseases related to blood and blood-forming organs.

bonefish Marine game fish *(Albula vulpes)* that inhabits coastal and island waters in tropical seas and is admired by anglers for its speed and strength. Its maximum length is about 30 in. (76 cm), and its maximum weight is 14 lbs (6.4 kg). The bonefish has a deeply notched caudal fin (near the tail) and a small mouth beneath a pointed, piglike snout. It grubs on the bottom for worms and other food.

bongo Large, brightly colored ANTELOPE *(Boocercus*, or *Taurotragus, euryceros)* found in dense forests of central Africa. Shy, swift, and elusive, the bongo lives in small groups or in pairs. It stands about 51 in. (1.3 m) at the shoulder and has an erect mane running the length of the back. Both sexes bear heavy, spirally twisted horns. The male is reddish brown to dark mahogany with black underparts, black-and-white legs, white head markings, and narrow, vertical white stripes on the body. The female is similarly marked but usually a brighter reddish brown.

Bongo (*Boocercus euryceros*).
TOM MCHUGH—PHOTO RESEARCHERS

Bonheur \bä-'nər\, **Rosa** (1822–1899) French animal painter. She was trained by her father, an art teacher, and began exhibiting regularly at the Paris Salon in 1841. Her unsentimental paintings of lions, tigers, horses, and other animals became very popular; *The Horse Fair* (1853) gained her an international reputation. A colorful personality, she dressed as a man to study horses at the actual Horse Fair in Paris, and received formal permission from the police to do so. In 1865 she became the first woman to receive the Grand Cross of the Legion of Honor.

Bonhoeffer \'bȯn-ˌhœ-fər\, **Dietrich** (1906–1945) German Lutheran pastor and theologian. He attended the Univs. of Berlin and Tübingen, and from 1931 lectured in theology at the University of Berlin. He became a leading spokesman for the CONFESSING CHURCH and was active in the Resistance movement under the guise of employment in military intelligence. He was arrested and imprisoned in 1943. The discovery of documents connecting him with the 1944 attempt on ADOLF HITLER's life led to his execution a month before the end of World War II. One of the most insightful theologians of the 20th century, he argued for a new vision of Christianity that would abolish the division between the sacred and profane and abandon the traditional privileges of the church in favor of active involvement in the world's problems. His best-known works include *The Cost of Discipleship* (1937), *Ethics* (1949), and *Letters and Papers from Prison* (1951).

Boniface \'bä-nə-fəs\, **St.** (c. 675–754) English missionary and reformer. Born in Wessex, he became a Benedictine monk and then a priest. He made two attempts to convert the Frisian Saxons; in 718 he journeyed to Rome, where Pope Gregory II entrusted him with a mission to the pagans east of the Rhine. In 722 at Hesse he founded the first of many Benedictine monasteries. He was active for 10 years (725–35) in Thuringia. He established four bishoprics in Bavaria, paving the way for its incorporation into the Carolingian Empire. He convened five synods (740–45) to reform the Frankish clergy and Irish missionaries and a council (747) to reform the entire Frankish kingdom. He was killed by a band of Frisians while reading the Bible to recent converts.

Boniface VIII *orig.* **Benedict Caetani** (c. 1235–1303) Pope (1294–1303). Born into an influential Roman family, Caetani studied law in Bologna and rose through the papal government to become cardinal-deacon (1281) and pope. In 1296 his attempt to end hostilities between EDWARD I of England and PHILIP IV of France became embroiled in the issue of taxation of clergy without papal consent. When Boniface issued a bull forbidding such taxation, Philip fought back with economic measures. They clashed again in 1301 over control of the clergy when Philip had a French bishop tried and imprisoned. Eventually, hearing that Boniface planned to excommunicate Philip, Philip's supporters captured the pope; though rescued two days later, he died shortly thereafter.

Boniface of Querfurt, St. See St. BRUNO OF QUERFURT

Bonifácio, José See Jose Bonifacio de ANDRADA E SILVA

Bonin Islands \'bō-nin\ *Japanese* **Ogasawara-gunto** \ō-ˌgä-sä-'wär-ä-'gün-tō\ Island group, western Pacific Ocean. Located about 600 mi (950 km) south of Tokyo and consisting of 27 volcanic islands with a total area of about 40 sq mi (104 sq km), the group includes Chichi-Jima (the largest), Haha-Jima, Muko-Jima, and Yome-Jima. They were colonized in 1830 by a group of Europeans and Hawaiians. The islands were formally annexed by Japan in 1876; they were administered by the U.S. 1945–68.

Bonington \'bä-niŋ-tən\, **Richard Parkes** (1802–1828) British painter active in France. In 1818 he went to Paris to study with A.-J. GROS. His skill in watercolor, a novelty in Paris, attracted many imitators. He exhibited at the famous "English" Salon of 1824 and won a gold medal. With JOHN CONSTABLE and J.M.W. TURNER, he popularized the oil sketch, a rapidly executed record of the transitory effects of nature. He became influential in England and France as a master of the Romantic movement and a technical innovator. His death at 26 cut short a brilliant career.

bonito \bə-'nē-tō\ Swift, predaceous schooling fishes (genus *Sarda*) of the MACKEREL family (Scombridae). Bonitos, found worldwide, have a striped back and silvery belly and grow to about 30 in. (75 cm) long. Like TUNAS, they are streamlined, with a narrow tail base, a forked tail, and a row of small finlets behind the dorsal and anal fins. Bonitos have both commercial and sporting value. The three generally recognized species are found in the Atlantic and Mediterranean, the Indo-Pacific, and the Pacific.

Bonn City (pop., 1996 est.: 291,000), Germany. Located on the RHINE RIVER south of COLOGNE, it was, until 1999, the capital of West Germany. An old settlement that predated the coming of the Romans, its name was continued in Castra Bonnensia, a 1st-century Roman fortress. By the 9th century it had become the Frankish town of Bonnburg. It grew from the 13th century, becoming capital of the Electorate of Cologne. In 1815 Bonn was awarded to PRUSSIA by the Congress of VIENNA, and by the late 19th century it was a fashionable residential town. It was bombed heavily in World War II; its postwar redevelopment was accelerated when in 1949 it was chosen as West Germany's capital. With Germany's reunification in 1990, the national capital was moved to BERLIN. Bonn was the birthplace of LUDWIG VAN BEETHOVEN.

Bonnard \bȯ-'när\, **Pierre** (1867–1947) French painter and printmaker. He studied at the Académie Julian and the École des BEAUX-ARTS (1888–89). In the 1890s he became a leading member of the NABIS group and came under the influence of Art Nouveau and Japanese prints. With his friend EDOUARD VUILLARD, he developed the intimate domestic interior scene, a genre known as Intimist, depicting fashionable Parisian life in the years before World War I. He also produced still lifes, self-portraits, seascapes, and large-scale decorative paintings. In 1910 he discovered the south of France and began a series of luminous landscapes of the Mediterranean region. He was fascinated by perspective, which he employed in such paintings as *The Dining Room* (1913). From the 1920s he specialized in landscapes, interiors, views of gardens, and bathing nudes. He produced illustrations for the celebrated *Revue blanche* and decorative pages for PAUL VERLAINE's *Parallèlement* (1900). He was one of the greatest colorists of modern art.

Bonnefoy, Yves (b. 1923) French poet. A student of mathematics, Bonnefoy moved to Paris and came under the influence of the SURREALISTS. His poetry describes a thought universe brought to life by an intuition of the "real world." Among his poetry collections are *In the Shadow's Light* (1987) and *The Beginning and End of Snow* (1991). Bonnefoy, also a scholar, compiled *Mythologies* (1981), a dictionary of mythologies and religions. He held the chair in comparative poetics at the Collège de France from 1981 to 1994.

Bonnet \bȯ-'nā\, **Georges-Étienne** (1889–1973) French politician. Elected to the Chamber of Deputies (1924–40), he became a leader of the RADICAL-SOCIALIST PARTY. He served as finance minister (1937–38) and foreign minister (1938–39) and was a prominent supporter of appeasement of Nazi Germany. He also supported the Vichy regime. After the liberation, proceedings against him were started but dropped. He was expelled from the Radical Party in 1944, readmitted in 1952, and again expelled in 1955. He later served in the Chamber of Deputies (1956–68).

bonnet monkey Agile Indian MACAQUE *(Macaca radiata)* named for the thatch of long hair forming a cap, or "bonnet," on the crown. It is grayish brown and has a hairless pink face. It is 14–24 in. (35–60 cm) long, excluding its 20–28-in. (50–70-cm) tail, and weighs 7–20 lbs (3–9 kg). It sometimes raids gardens or stores of food.

Bonnet monkey (*Macaca radiata*).
WARREN GARST—TOM STACK & ASSOCIATES

Bonnie and Clyde See BARROW, Clyde, and Bonnie Parker.

Bonnie Prince Charlie See Charles Edward STUART

bonobo \bə-'nō-bō\ Species *(Pan paniscus)* of great APE once considered a subspecies of the CHIMPANZEE, which it closely resembles in size, appearance, and way of life. Its range, the lowland rain forests of central Congo (Zaire), is more restricted than that of the chimpanzee, and it has longer, more slender arms, a more slender body, and a less protruding face. Bonobos eat mainly fruits but also leaves, seeds, grass, and small animals. They form communities of 50–120 individuals. A striking feature of their social lives is that they engage in sexual activity with great frequency, often as a means of settling quarrels, and with little regard for sex or age. Populations are shrinking, largely because of hunting and habitat destruction, and bonobos are listed as vulnerable.

Bononcini \ˌbō-nōn-'chē-nē\, **Giovanni** (1670–1747) Italian composer. His father was Giovanni Maria Bononcini (1642–1678), *maestro di cappella* of Modena Cathedral and the composer of numerous church and chamber sonatas. Giovanni himself served as *maestro di cappella* at San Giovanni in Monte at Modena; he later held desirable positions in various European capitals. In London in the 1720s he had a celebrated operatic rivalry with G.F. HANDEL. He wrote more than 30 operas, some 20 oratorios, and nearly 300 cantatas (most for solo voice and continuo), but they are rarely heard today. His brother Antonio Maria Bononcini (1677–1726) wrote some 20 operas and some 40 cantatas.

bonsai (Japanese: "tray planting") Living dwarf tree or trees; also, the art of training and growing them in containers. Bonsai specimens are ordinary trees and shrubs, not hereditary dwarfs; they are dwarfed by a system of pruning roots and branches and training branches by tying them with wire. The art originated in China but has been pursued and developed primarily by the Japanese. The direct inspiration for bonsai is found in nature, in trees that grow in harsh, rocky places and are dwarfed and gnarled throughout their existence. Prized characteristics are aged-looking trunk and branches and weathered-looking exposed upper roots. Bonsai may live for a century or more and are handed down from one generation to another as valued family possessions. Bonsai pots, usually earthenware and of variable shape, are carefully chosen to harmonize in color and proportion with the tree. A sizable bonsai industry exists as part of the nursery industry in Japan; California is home to a small-scale bonsai industry.

Bonsai pine.
JUDITH GROFFMAN

Bontemps \bän-'täm\, **Arna(ud) (Wendell)** (1902–1973) U.S. writer of the HARLEM RENAISSANCE. Born in Alexandria, La., he moved with his family to California three years later after a racial incident. His poetry began appearing in the black magazines *Crisis* and *Opportunity* in the 1920s. With COUNTEE CULLEN he turned his first novel, *God Sends Sundays* (1931), into the play *St. Louis Woman.* Two later novels dealt with slave revolts. He edited anthologies with LANGSTON HUGHES and wrote prolifically for children, mostly nonfiction works on black Americans and black history. He worked at Fisk University for most of his adult life.

Bonus Army World War I veterans who gathered in Washington, D.C., in summer 1932 to demand payment of their promised bonuses. Over 12,000 veterans and their families camped in tents and shanties near the Capitol, urging support for a bill to force early payment of bonuses already voted by Congress. When the bill was defeated, most of the crowd returned home, but some angry protests caused local authorities to ask Pres. HERBERT HOOVER for federal assistance. Army troops led by Gen. DOUGLAS MACARTHUR drove out the protesters and burned their camps. The resulting public outcry was a factor in Hoover's defeat in the 1932 election. Another group of veterans gathered in 1933, but Congress again rejected bonus legislation. In 1936 Congress finally enacted a bill that paid nearly $2.5 million in veterans' benefits.

bony fish Any member of the VERTEBRATE class Osteichthyes, including the great majority of living FISHES and all the world's sport and commercial fishes. Also called Pisces, the class excludes jawless fishes (HAGFISHES and LAMPREYS) and cartilaginous fishes (SHARKS, SKATES, and RAYS). There are more than 20,000 species worldwide, all with a skeleton at least partly composed of true bone. Other features include, in most species, a swim bladder (an air-filled sac to give buoyancy), gill covers over the gill chamber, bony platelike scales, a skull with sutures, and external fertilization of eggs. Bony fishes occur in all freshwater and ocean environments.

bony pelvis See PELVIC GIRDLE

booby Any of six or seven species of large tropical seabirds (family Sulidae), named for their presumed lack of intelligence. Two common species are wide-ranging in the Atlantic, Pacific, and Indian oceans; another is found in the Pacific from southern California to northern Peru and on the Galápagos Islands. The booby has a long bill, cigar-shaped body, and long, narrow, angular wings. It flies high above the ocean looking for schools of fish and squid, which it snatches in a vertical dive. Boobies vary in length from 25 to 35 in. (65–85 cm). They nest in colonies but are territorial.

book Written (or printed) message of considerable length, meant for circulation and recorded on any of various materials that are durable and light enough to be easily portable. The papyrus roll of ancient Egypt is more nearly the direct ancestor of the modern book than is the clay tablet; examples of both date to c. 3000 BC. Somewhat later, the Chinese independently created an extensive scholarship based on books, many made of wood or bamboo strips bound with cords. Lampblack ink was introduced in China c. AD 400 and printing from wooden blocks in the 6th century. The Greeks adopted the papyrus roll and passed it on to the Romans. The parchment or vellum CODEX superseded the papyrus roll by AD 400. Medieval parchment or vellum leaves were prepared from the skins of animals. By the 15th century, paper manuscripts were common. Printing spread rapidly in the late 15th century. Subsequent technical achievements, such as the development of offset printing, improved many aspects of book culture.

book club Marketing service that chooses suitable books and offers them for sale to subscribers through the mail, often at reduced prices. The first U.S. book club, the Book-of-the-Month Club, was founded in 1926; the rival Literary Guild appeared a year later. By the 1980s nearly 100 book clubs existed in the U.S., most of them specialized (e.g., for religious books, mysteries, etc.). A common incentive for attracting new members is the offer of several free or heavily discounted books; long-standing members often receive bonuses.

Book of Common Prayer See Book of COMMON PRAYER

Book of the Dead Ancient Egyptian collection of mortuary texts made up of spells and charms and placed in tombs to aid the deceased in the next world. It was probably compiled and reedited during the 16th century BC. Later compilations included hymns to RE. Scribes produced and sold copies, often colorfully illustrated, for burial use. Of the many extant copies, none contains all of the approximately 200 known chapters.

bookbinding Joining together of leaves of paper, parchment, or vellum within covers to form a BOOK or CODEX. Bookbinding developed when the codex replaced the roll. Early bindings were often splendidly decorated, but the typical artistic bookbinding is of decorated leather and was first produced in the monasteries of Egypt's Coptic Church. Rare books, historical documents, and manuscripts may be bound by hand. The cover (case) of the typical book is now affixed to the leaves by machine.

bookcase Piece of furniture fitted with shelves, formerly often enclosed by doors. In early times the ambry, or wall cupboard, was used to hold books. Bookcases were included in the medieval fittings of college libraries in Britain. The earliest dated domestic examples were made of oak in 1666 for the diarist SAMUEL PEPYS.

Booker Prize Prestigious British award given annually to a full-length novel. It was established in 1968 by the multinational company Booker McConnell as a counterpart to the French Prix Goncourt. Entries, which are nominated by publishers, must be written by an English-language author from the United Kingdom, the Commonwealth countries, Ireland, or South Africa. Its winners have included KINGSLEY AMIS, A. S. BYATT, RUTH PRAWER JHABVALA, and SALMAN RUSHDIE. In 1992 a Booker Russian Novel Prize was introduced.

bookkeeping Recording of the money values of business transactions. Bookkeeping provides the information from which accounts are prepared but is distinct from ACCOUNTING. Bookkeeping offers information on both the current value, or EQUITY, of an enterprise and on its change in value (due to profit or loss) over a given time period. Managers require such information to examine the results of operations and budget for the future; investors need it to make decisions about buying or selling securities; and credit grantors use it to determine whether to grant a loan. Financial records were kept in Babylon and in ancient Greece and Rome. The double-entry method of bookkeeping began with the development of the Italian commercial republics of the 15th century. The Industrial Revolution stimulated the spread of bookkeeping, and 20th-century taxation and government regulations made it a necessity. Though bookkeeping has become increasingly computerized, two types of records continue to be used in the process—journals and ledgers. The journal contains daily transactions (sales, purchases, etc.); the ledger contains the record of individual accounts. Each month an income statement and a BALANCE SHEET are posted in the ledger.

bookmaking Gambling practice of determining odds and receiving and paying off bets on the outcome of sporting events and other competitions. Horse racing is perhaps most closely associated with bookmaking, but boxing, baseball, football, basketball, and other sports have also long been of interest to bookmakers ("bookies") and gamblers. Morning-line odds, established by legal bookmakers, are printed in the sports sections of newspapers throughout the U.S. Illegal bookmaking operations have often been linked to ORGANIZED CRIME. See also HANDICAP.

bookplate Label with a printed design pasted inside the front cover of a book to identify its owner. It probably originated in Germany in the mid-15th century; the earliest extant dated bookplate (1516) is German. The earliest American example is dated 1749. Bookplate designs include portraits, views of libraries, and landscapes, as well as symbols of the owner's interests or occupation (e.g., military trophies, palettes), and, toward the end of the 19th century, nude figures.

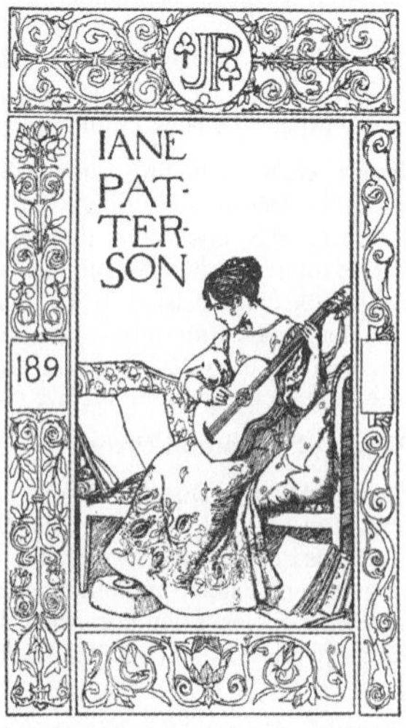

Jane Patterson's bookplate designed by Robert Anning Bell, English, 1890s.

BY COURTESY OF THE VICTORIA AND ALBERT MUSEUM, LONDON

Boole, George (1815–1864) British mathematician. Though basically self-taught and lacking a university degree, in 1849 he was appointed professor of mathematics at Queen's College in Ireland. His original and remarkable general symbolic method of logical inference is fully stated in *Laws of Thought* (1854). Boole argued persuasively that logic should be allied with mathematics rather than with philosophy, and his two-valued algebra of logic, now called BOOLEAN ALGEBRA, is used in telephone switching and by electronic digital computers.

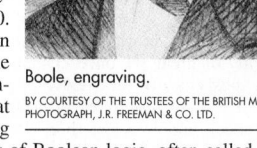

Boole, engraving.

BY COURTESY OF THE TRUSTEES OF THE BRITISH MUSEUM; PHOTOGRAPH, J.R. FREEMAN & CO. LTD.

Boolean algebra Symbolic system used for designing logic circuits and networks for DIGITAL COMPUTERS. Its chief utility is in representing the truth value of statements, rather than the numeric quantities handled by ordinary algebra. It lends itself to use in the binary system employed by digital computers, since the only possible truth values, true and false, can be represented by the binary digits 1 and 0. A circuit in computer memory can be open or closed, depending on the value assigned to it, and it is the integrated work of such circuits that give computers their computing ability. The fundamental operations of Boolean logic, often called Boolean operators, are "and," "or," and "not"; combinations of these make up 13 other Boolean operators.

boomerang Curved throwing stick used chiefly by the aborigines of Australia for hunting and warfare. About 12–30 in. (30–75 cm) in length, the returning boomerang varies in shape from a deep curve to almost straight sides of an angle. The ends are twisted or skewed in opposite directions. It is held at one end, above and behind the thrower's shoulder, and swung forward rapidly. Just before release, the thrower adds spin by flicking the wrist so that the stick will loop around and return to him. Returning boomerangs were used only in eastern and western Australia as playthings, in tournament competition, and by hunters to imitate hawks for driving flocks of game birds into nets. The longer, straighter, and heavier nonreturning boomerang can kill animals and even humans.

boomslang Venomous snake *(Dispholidus typus)* of the savannas of sub-Saharan Africa, the only species of its family that is decidedly dangerous to humans. When hunting, it lies in wait in a bush or tree for chameleons and birds; the forepart of the body often extends motionless into the air. The boomslang's body and eye colors are extremely variable and provide excellent camouflage. In defense it inflates its neck, showing the dark skin between the scales, and then may strike. Its venom causes hemorrhages and is fatal to humans in even minuscule amounts.

Boomslang (*Dispholidus typus*).

DADE THORNTON FROM THE NATIONAL AUDUBON SOCIETY COLLECTION—PHOTO RESEARCHERS/EB INC.

Boone, Daniel (1734?–c. 1820) U.S. frontiersman and legendary hero. Born in Berks Co., Pa., he lived on the North Carolina frontier as a hunter and trapper. He made several trips through the CUMBERLAND GAP into eastern Kentucky (1767, 1769–71) and in 1775 was employed to blaze a permanent trail, called the Wilderness Road. He established the settlements of Boonesboro and Harrodsburg. As a militia captain he defended Boonesboro against Indian attack; he was captured by the Shawnee in 1778 but escaped after five months to warn Boonesboro of an impending attack. After losing his Kentucky land claims in the late 1780s, he moved to Missouri Territory. His exploits were featured in a widely read history of Kentucky and in Lord BYRON's epic poem *Don Juan.*

Boorman, John (born 1933) British film director. He began his television career as a film editor and then became a producer of documentary films. As head of the BBC's documentary film unit in Bristol (1962–64) he produced the acclaimed *Citizen 63* series. After directing his first feature film in 1965, Boorman directed *Point Blank* (1967) and *Hell in the Pacific* (1968) in the U.S. His successful *Deliverance* (1972) was a harrowing tale of endurance and survival. Later films include *Excalibur* (1981), *The Emerald Forest* (1985), and *Hope and Glory* (1987).

Booth, Edwin (Thomas) (1833–1893) U.S. actor. Born near Bel Air, Md., into a noted theatrical family, he played his first starring roles in Boston and New York in 1857. He became famous as Hamlet, appearing in the role for 100 consecutive nights in 1864–65. When his brother JOHN WILKES BOOTH assassinated Pres. ABRAHAM LINCOLN, Edwin withdrew from the stage until 1866. In 1869 he opened his own theater, but mismanagement forced him to sell it in 1873. His interpretations of Hamlet, Iago, and King Lear won great acclaim in England and Germany. He founded the Players' Club in New York in 1888.

Edwin Booth, photograph by Bradley and Rulofson.
BY COURTESY OF THE THEATRE COLLECTION, THE NEW YORK PUBLIC LIBRARY AT LINCOLN CENTER, ASTOR, LENOX AND TILDEN FOUNDATIONS

Booth, John Wilkes (1838–1865) U.S. actor and assassin of Pres. ABRAHAM LINCOLN. Born near Bel Air, Md., into a family of famous actors, he achieved success in Shakespearean roles but resented the greater acclaim for his brother, EDWIN BOOTH. A fanatical believer in slavery and the Southern cause, he made plans with co-conspirators to abduct Lincoln; after several failed attempts, he vowed to destroy the president and his cabinet. On April 14, 1865, he shot Lincoln during a performance at Ford's Theater. He broke his leg jumping from the president's box but escaped on horseback to a Virginia farm. Tracked down, he refused to surrender and was shot, either by a soldier or by himself.

Booth, William (1829–1912) British religious leader, founder and general (1878–1912) of the SALVATION ARMY. At 15 he underwent a religious conversion and became a revivalist preacher. In 1849 he went to London, where he became a regular preacher of the Methodist New Connection (1852–61) and then an independent revivalist. Aided by his wife, Catherine Mumford Booth (1829–1890), a fellow preacher and social worker, he founded the Christian Mission in 1864, which in 1978 became the Salvation Army. He traveled worldwide to lecture and organize branches of the Army. His proposals for remedying social ills received widespread acceptance and the encouragement of EDWARD VII.

Boothia Peninsula Peninsula, Nunavut. Almost an island, it is the northernmost point of the North American mainland, reaching 71°58′N, and was formerly the location of the North Magnetic Pole. With an area of 12,483 sq mi (32,330 sq km), it extends into the ARCTIC OCEAN and is separated from BAFFIN ISLAND by the Gulf of Boothia and from Prince of Wales Island by the Franklin Strait. It was discovered in 1829 by James Clark Ross, who named it Boothia Felix for Sir Felix Booth, the expedition's financier. It is sparsely populated.

bootlegging Illegal traffic in liquor in the U.S. The term was probably first used to describe the practice of concealing flasks of illicit liquor in boot tops when going to trade with Indians. It became widely used in the 1920s when the 18th Amendment to the Constitution and the Volstead Act of 1919 effected the prohibition of liquor manufacturing and sales. Early bootleggers smuggled foreign-made liquor into the U.S. from Canada and Mexico and from ships anchored in international waters. Later sources included medicinal whiskey, denatured alcohol, and the manufacture of corn liquor. Bootlegging led to the rise of ORGANIZED-CRIME syndicates that controlled operations from the manufacture of liquor to its distribution in restaurants and speakeasies. In 1933 PROHIBITION was repealed by the 21st Amendment. Some counties and municipalities continue to ban liquor, and bootlegging is still practiced.

bop See BEBOP

Bophuthatswana \ˌbō-pü-tä-ˈtswä-nä\ Former political entity (pop., 1993 est.: 2,564,000), South Africa. Consisting of a group of noncontiguous black enclaves, it was established by South African authorities as a "homeland" for the TSWANA people and granted its independence in 1977, with its capital at Mmabatho. It was never internationally recognized as independent. Under the 1993 South African constitution, Bophuthatswana was dissolved and the area was reincorporated into South Africa. Its various enclaves became parts of Orange Free State (now Free State) and the newly created North-West and Eastern Transvaal (now Mpumalanga) provinces.

Bopp \ˈbȯp\, **Franz** (1791–1867) German linguist. He published the first lengthy comparative analysis of INDO-EUROPEAN LANGUAGES, his voluminous *Comparative Grammar of Sanskrit, Zend, Latin, Lithuanian, Old Slavic, Gothic, and German* (1833–52). Though the relation of Sanskrit to European languages was known at the time, Bopp was a pioneer in actually isolating common elements in the verbal and nominal MORPHOLOGY of Sanskrit and other older Indo-European languages. Most of his career was spent at the University of Berlin.

borage Large hairy ANNUAL herb *(Borago officinalis)*, an ornamental species with large, rough, oblong leaves and loose, drooping clusters of starlike blue flowers. It is a member of the family Boraginaceae, which contains mostly herbs but also some trees and shrubs, all found in tropical, subtropical, and temperate areas and most concentrated in the Mediterranean region. Several other ornamental species are grown in gardens, including the Virginia bluebell *(Mertensia virginica)*, FORGET-ME-NOTS, HELIOTROPES, and lungworts *(Pulmonaria)*. Borage is also used as an herbal and bee plant and eaten as a vegetable.

Borage (*Borago officinalis*).
A TO Z BOTANICAL COLLECTION

Borah, William E(dgar) (1865–1940) U.S. senator (1907–40). Born in Fairfield, Ill., he practiced law in Boise, Idaho, and in 1892 became the state's Republican Party chairman. In the Senate he was an isolationist in foreign policy; he wielded great power as chairman of the foreign relations committee from 1924, becoming best known for his role in preventing the U.S. from joining the LEAGUE OF NATIONS, and opposed efforts to aid the Allies before the U.S. entered World War II. A maverick Republican, he supported many of the New Deal programs to relieve economic hardship and sponsored bills establishing the Department of Labor as well as the federal Children's Bureau.

borax *or* **tincal** \ˈtiŋ-kəl\ Sodium tetraborate decahydrate ($Na_2B_4O_5(OH)_4{\cdot}H_2O$), a soft, light, colorless crystalline mineral used as a component of glass and pottery glazes in the ceramics industry, as a solvent for metal-oxide slags in metallurgy, as a flux in welding and soldering, and as a fertilizer additive, a soap supplement, a disinfectant, a mouthwash, and a water softener. About 50% of the world's supply comes from southern California deserts, including DEATH VALLEY.

Borch, Gerard ter See Gerard TERBORCH

Bordeaux \bȯr-ˈdō\ City (pop., 1990: 213,000), southwestern France. Lying on the GARONNE RIVER above its junction with the DORDOGNE, Bordeaux has long been noted for its wine production. As Burdigala, it was the chief town of the Bituriges Vivisci, a Celtic people. Under Roman rule it was capital of Aquitania Secunda. As part of the inheritance of ELEANOR OF AQUITAINE, Bordeaux became English in 1154 on her husband's accession to the English throne as HENRY II. It enjoyed great prosperity through a thriving trade with the English until it was united to France on the English defeat in the HUNDRED YEARS' WAR (1453). As a GIRONDIN center, it suffered severely in the FRENCH REVOLUTION. In 1870, during the FRANCO-PRUSSIAN WAR, the French government was transferred to Bordeaux, as it was again in 1914 at the outbreak of World War I. Its university, founded in 1441, educated such figures as MONTESQUIEU.

Borden, Frederick (William) *later* **Sir Frederick** (1847–1917) Canadian politician. Born in Nova Scotia, he returned there to practice medicine after studying at Harvard University. In 1874 he was elected as a Liberal Party member to the House of Commons, where he served almost continuously until 1911. As minister of militia and defense (1896–1911), he improved the training of the armed services and helped create a Canadian navy.

Borden, Lizzie (Andrew) (1860–1927) U.S. murder suspect. Born in Fall River, Mass., she lived there with her wealthy but parsimonious father and stepmother. On August 4, 1892, Mr. Borden and his wife were discovered dead in their home by Lizzie, brutally mutilated with a sharp instrument. Only Lizzie and the maid admitted to being in the house at the time of the murders. Lizzie was arrested and tried for both murders, the maid being suspected as an accomplice. Evidence against Lizzie included her attempt to buy prussic acid the day before the murders. An ax was found in the basement. Acquitted, she remained in Fall River until her death, largely ostracized by the community.

Borden, Robert (Laird) *later* **Sir Robert** (1854–1937) Prime minister of Canada (1911–20). Born in Nova Scotia, he practiced law in Halifax from 1874 and later founded one of the largest law firms in the Maritime Provinces. In 1896 he was elected to the Canadian House of Commons and became leader of the Conservative Party in 1901. As prime minister, he implemented conscription in World War I and represented Canada in Britain's imperial war cabinet. He insisted on separate Canadian membership in the League of Nations, which helped transform Canada from a colony to a nation.

border collie Breed of long-haired SHEEPDOG that has been used along the English–Scottish border for about 300 years. Usually black and white, it stands about 20 in. (50 cm) and weighs 30–50 lbs (14–23 kg). It is the most popular working sheepdog in the British Isles.

Bordet \bȯr-'dā\, **Jules (-Jean-Baptiste-Vincent)** (1870–1961) Belgian bacteriologist and immunologist. In 1895 he found that two blood serum components cause bacteriolysis (bacterial cell-wall rupture), one a heat-stable antibody in animals immune to the bacterium and the other a heat-sensitive complement in all animals. In 1898 he discovered hemolysis (rupture of foreign erythrocytes), a similar process that also requires complement. This research was vital to the foundation of serology, the study of immune reactions in body fluids. His work with Octave Gengou led to serological tests for many diseases, including typhoid, tuberculosis, and syphilis (the Wassermann test). In 1906 they discovered *Bordetella pertussis,* which causes whooping cough. In 1919 Bordet received a Nobel Prize.

Borduas \bȯr-dᵫ̄-'äs\, **Paul-Émile** (1905–1960) Canadian painter. He was trained in Montreal as a church decorator and later studied in Paris. In the early 1940s, influenced by Surrealism, he began to produce "automatic" paintings, and with J.-P. RIOPELLE founded the radical abstract group known as Les Automatistes (c. 1946–51). His later works are reminiscent of those of JACKSON POLLOCK, but the only U.S. influence he acknowledged was that of FRANZ KLINE. See also AUTOMATISM.

boreal forest See TAIGA

Borg, Björn (Rune) (born 1956) Swedish tennis player. He turned professional at age 14. Noted for his powerful serve and two-handed backhand, he became the first man to win the Wimbledon singles championship five successive times (1976–80) since Laurie Doherty (1902–6) and the first to win the French Open four times in a row and six times in all (1974–75, 1978–81). By the time he finally lost at Wimbledon to JOHN MCENROE (1981), he had won a record 41 straight Wimbledon singles matches. He also holds records for consecutive wins in Davis Cup play (33) and at the French Open (28). He won a lifetime total of 11 Grand Slam titles. He retired in 1983.

Borge \'bȯr-gə\, **Victor** *orig.* **Borge Rosenbaum** (1909–2000) Danish-U.S. comedian and pianist. He made his concert stage debut in 1922, first appeared in a musical revue in 1934, then began writing and directing shows, developing a style that combined humor with music. He emigrated to the U.S. in 1940. Though he performed as soloist and guest conductor with many of the world's leading orchestras, his significant pianistic talent was often overshadowed by his highly popular humor.

Borges \'bȯr-hās\, **Jorge Luis** (1899–1986) Argentine poet, essayist, and short-story writer. Educated in Switzerland, he recognized early that he would have a literary career. From the 1920s on he was afflicted by a growing hereditary blindness. In 1938 a severe head wound seemed to free his deepest creative forces. His blindness was total by the mid-1950s and forced him to abandon the writing of long texts and begin dictating his works. From 1955 he held the honorary post of director of Argentina's national library. Much of his work is rich in fantasy and metaphorical allegory, including the story collections *Ficciones* (1944), which won him an international following, and *The Aleph* (1949). *Dreamtigers* (1960) and *The Book of Imaginary Beings* (1967) almost erase the distinctions between prose and poetry. Though he later repudiated it, he is credited with establishing in South America the modernist Ultraist movement, a rebellion against the decadence of the established writers of the Generation of '98.

Jorge Luis Borges.

BY COURTESY OF WELLESLEY COLLEGE, WELLESLEY, MASSACHUSETTS

Borghese family \bōr-'gā-sā\ Noble Italian family, originally from Siena, who first gained fame in the 13th century as magistrates, ambassadors, and other public officials. They moved to Rome in the 16th century and there, after Camillo Borghese was elected (1605) as Pope Paul V, the family rose in wealth and fame. Prominent family members included the adopted Scipione Caffarelli (later Borghese) (1576–1633), a cardinal and patron of the arts, and Camillo F. L. Borghese (1775–1832), who married PAULINE BONAPARTE and played an important role in Franco-Italian relations.

Borgia \'bȯr-jä\, **Cesare** *later* **duc (Duke) de Valentinois** \vå-lä^{n}-tēn-'wä\ (1475?–1507) Italian military leader and illegitimate son of the later Pope Alexander VI and brother of LUCREZIA BORGIA. He was made archbishop of Valencia (1492) and cardinal (1493). After his brother's murder (1497), he took command of the papal armies. In 1498 he resigned his ecclesiastical offices and married the sister of the king of Navarre, a move calculated to win French support for a campaign to regain control of the Papal States. Acting in concert with his father, Cesare won a series of military successes in the Papal States (1499–1503), gaining a reputation for ruthlessness and assassination; his political astuteness led NICCOLO MACHIAVELLI to cite him as an example of the new "Prince." Cesare's gains proved fruitless, however, when his father died (1503) and the new pope, JULIUS II, demanded that he give up his lands. He escaped from prison in Spain and died fighting for Navarre.

Borgia, Lucrezia (1480–1519) Italian noblewoman. The daughter of Pope ALEXANDER VI and sister of CESARE BORGIA, she was probably more an instrument for their ambitious projects than, as has been suggested, an active participant in their many crimes. Her three marriages into prominent families helped augment the political and territorial power of the Borgias. Her child may have been the issue of an incestuous relationship with her father. After her father's death (1503), she ceased to play a political role, and increasingly turned to religion. She died at 39.

Borglum \'bȯr-gləm\, **(John) Gutzon (de la Mothe)** (1867–1941) U.S. sculptor. Born in Bear Lake, Idaho, to Danish immigrant parents, he studied art in Paris. In 1901 he opened a studio in New York. His bronze group *The Mares of Diomedes* was the first U.S. sculpture purchased by the Metropolitan Museum of Art. He carved the head of ABRAHAM LINCOLN in the U.S. Capitol rotunda. In 1916 he was commissioned to sculpt a memorial to the Confederacy on Stone Mtn., Ga., but disputes with his patrons caused him to abandon the project in 1924; it was completed by others. His most notable project was the MOUNT RUSHMORE NATIONAL MEMORIAL.

Borglum.

BY COURTESY OF THE LIBRARY OF CONGRESS, WASHINGTON, D.C.

boring machine MACHINE TOOL for producing smooth and accurate holes in a workpiece by enlarging existing holes with a cutting tool, which may bear a single tip of steel, cemented carbide, or diamond or may be a small grinding wheel. The hole's diameter is controlled by adjusting the boring head. Bored holes are more accurate in roundness, concentricity, and parallelism than drilled holes. Boring machines used in toolmaking shops have a vertical spindle and a work-holding table that moves horizontally in two perpendicular directions so that holes can be accurately spaced. In mass-production plants, boring machines with multiple spindles are common. See also DRILL, DRILL PRESS, LATHE.

Boris I *orig.* **Mikhail** (died 907) Khan of Bulgaria (852–89). He resolved to use Christianity to unite his ethnically divided country, and an unsuccessful war with the Byzantines led to his baptism in the Orthodox faith (864). Boris's attempt to enforce mass baptism set off a pagan rebellion, which he quelled, and he helped establish the Bulgarian church. He sponsored missionaries to foster Slavic learning and the use of the OLD CHURCH SLAVIC LANGUAGE. He abdicated in 889 to become a monk but returned to drive his reactionary son Vladimir from the throne. After installing another son, SIMEON I, as khan, Boris went back to his monastery. He was later made an Orthodox saint.

Boris Godunov See Boris GODUNOV

Borlaug \'bȯr-ˌlȯg\, **Norman (Ernest)** (born 1914) U.S. agricultural scientist and plant pathologist. Born in Cresco, Iowa, he earned his PhD at the University of Minnesota. As a researcher with the Rockefeller Foundation in Mexico (1944–60), he developed strains of grain that tripled Mexican WHEAT production. Later his dwarf wheats raised harvests in Pakistan and India 60%, ending the food shortages that had plagued the subcontinent in the 1960s. For helping lay the groundwork of the GREEN REVOLUTION, he was awarded the Nobel Peace Prize in 1970. He has since worked on improving crop yields in Africa, among many other projects, and since 1984 has taught at Texas A&M Univ.

Bormann \'bȯr-ˌmän\, **Martin** (1900–1945?) German Nazi leader. He joined the Nazi party in 1925 and served as RUDOLF HESS's chief of staff 1933–41. He was appointed head of the party chancellery in 1941 and became one of ADOLF HITLER's closest lieutenants. A shadowy but extremely powerful presence, Bormann controlled all legislation, party promotions and appointments, and the personal access of others to Hitler. He disappeared shortly after Hitler's death. Though some reports allege that he escaped to South America, German authorities have officially declared him dead.

Born, Max (1882–1970) German physicist. He taught theoretical physics at the University of Göttingen from 1921 to 1933, when he fled to Britain where he taught principally at the University of Edinburgh (1936–53). In 1921 he gave a very precise definition of quantity of heat, the most satisfactory mathematical statement of the first law of thermodynamics. In 1926 he collaborated with his student WERNER HEISENBERG to develop the mathematical formulation that would adequately describe Heisenberg's first laws of a new quantum theory. He later showed, in the work for which he is perhaps best known, that the solution of the SCHRÖDINGER EQUATION has a statistical meaning of physical significance. His later work concerned the scattering of atomic particles and calculations dealing with the electronic structures of molecules. In 1954 he shared a Nobel Prize with Walther Bothe (1891–1957).

Max Born.
BY COURTESY OF GODFREY ARGENT; PHOTOGRAPH, WALTER STONEMAN

Borneo Island, MALAY ARCHIPELAGO. Bounded by the CHINA SEA, Sulu, and CELEBES seas, the Makassar Strait, and the Java Sea, it is the third-largest island in the world, measuring 290,320 sq mi (751,929 sq km). The northern part includes the Malaysian states of Sabah and Sarawak and the sultanate of Brunei; the southern section forms part of Indonesia. Borneo is mountainous and largely covered in dense rain forest; its highest point is Mount Kinabalu, at 13,455 ft (4,101 m). Much of it is drained by navigable rivers, including the RAJANG, which are the principal lifelines of trade and commerce. It is mentioned in PTOLEMY's *Guide to Geography* of c. AD 150; Roman trade beads give evidence of an earlier civilization. Brahman and Buddhist images in the Gupta style indicate the influence of Indians who apparently arrived in the 5th century. With the arrival of Islam in the 16th century, various Muslim kingdoms were founded, some of which owed allegiance to JAVA. Around the same time, the Portuguese, followed by the Spanish, set up trading stations. In the early 17th century the Dutch broke the Portuguese-Spanish monopoly, but they in turn had to deal with newly established British interests. After World War II, Sarawak and North Borneo (later Sabah) became British crown colonies. Strong nationalist sentiment in Dutch Borneo resulted in the passing of sovereignty to Indonesia in 1949. The British relinquished Sabah and Sarawak to the Malaysian federation in 1963, while Brunei became independent in 1984.

Bornholm Island (pop., 1993 est.: 45,000), Denmark. Lying in the BALTIC SEA south of Sweden, it has an area of 227 sq mi (588 sq km). Its seat is at Rønne. Once a Viking stronghold, it was seized by the HANSEATIC LEAGUE in 1510. Until 1660 it was held for varying periods by Sweden and Denmark, but it has since been Danish. It is now a popular tourist resort.

bornite Common copper-ore mineral, copper and iron sulfide (Cu_5FeS_4). Typical occurrences are found in Mount Lyell, Tasmania; Chile; Peru; and Butte, Mont. Bornite may form isometric crystals but occurs most commonly as irregular masses. Under appropriate geologic conditions, it alters to chalcocite and other copper minerals.

Bornu Vast plain, northeastern Nigeria. Prominent physical features include the plain, a volcanic plateau, and swamps south of Lake CHAD. Now inhabited chiefly by the Kenuri people, it constituted a Muslim kingdom from about the 11th century. Together with Kanem it later formed an empire (see KANEM-BORNU), which reached the height of its power c. 1570–1600. Visited by Europeans in the 19th century, in 1902 it became part of Nigeria, which was then under British rule. In 1967 it became the state of Borno, Nigeria's largest, and covers 44,942 sq mi (116,400 sq km).

Borobudur \ˌbō-rō-bü-'dür\ Buddhist monument in central Java, built c. 778–850 under the Shailendra dynasty. Constructed with about 2 million cu ft (57,000 cu m) of gray volcanic stone, it resembles a stepped pyramid. Its base and first five terraces are square; the highest three terraces are circular. Reliefs on its terrace walls represent the ascending stages of enlightenment. The simple and spacious upper circular terraces carry 72 bell-shaped STUPAS, each containing a statue of the Buddha.

Borobudur, Java, Indonesia.
ROBERT HARDING PICTURE LIBRARY/PHOTOBANK BKK

Borodin \ˌbȯr-ə-'dēn\, **Aleksandr (Porfiryevich)** (1833–1887) Russian composer. From 1862 he took lessons from M. BALAKIREV; fired by nationalist sentiment, the two men became the core of the MIGHTY FIVE. A professor of chemistry for much of his life, he left a small compositional output, which includes the orchestral suite *In the Steppes of Central Asia* (1880), two string quartets, and three symphonies, the second of which has remained highly popular. The opera *Prince Igor* was left unfinished after 18 years of intermittent work.

Borodin \bə-rə-'dyēn, *Engl* ˌbȯr-ə-'dēn\, **Mikhail (Markovich)** *orig.* **Mikhail Gruzenberg** (1884–1951) Russian diplomat. He joined the BOLSHEVIK faction in 1903, was arrested (1906), and lived in exile in the U.S. He returned to Russia in 1917 and in 1923 was sent to China as an adviser to SUN YAT-SEN. There he built the loosely structured Nationalist Party (GUOMINDANG) into a highly centralized Leninist-style organization and helped the Chinese Nationalists develop their army. After leaving China (1927), he served as deputy director of the Tass news agency and editor of the *Moscow Daily News* (1932–49). He was arrested in a Stalinist purge of Jewish intellectuals and died in a Siberian labor camp.

Borodino, Battle of (1812) Bloody battle of the NAPOLEONIC WARS, fought during NAPOLEON's invasion of Russia, near the town of Borodino, about 70 mi (110 km) west of Moscow. Napoleon's 130,000 troops won a narrow victory over 120,000 Russians under MIKHAIL KUTUZOV. The Russians suffered about 45,000 dead and wounded, while the French lost about 30,000 men. The victory allowed Napoleon to occupy Moscow.

boron Semimetallic chemical ELEMENT, chemical symbol B, atomic number 5. Pure crystalline boron is a black, lustrous, very hard but brittle SEMICONDUCTOR that does not occur naturally. Boron compounds are found widely dispersed as various minerals, including BORAX and the gemstone TOURMALINE. The element is used to harden certain STEELS, among other metallurgical uses, and is also used in semiconductors. Its compounds (borates), in which it has VALENCE 3, are essential to plant growth and have many uses in soaps, mild ANTISEPTICS, and eye ointments. Industrially, they are used as herbicides, fire retardants in fabrics, and CATALYSTS in numerous organic reactions. They are also used in ELECTROPLATING and glass and ceramic formulations. The exceptional hardness and inertness of certain boron compounds, including boron carbide, aluminum boride, and boron nitride (with an electronic structure resembling DIAMOND's), make them useful as abrasives and reinforcing agents, particularly for high-temperature applications.

Borromeo \ˌbōr-rō-ˈmā-ō\, **St. Charles** (1538–1584) Archbishop of Milan and leading figure in the COUNTER-REFORMATION. He earned a doctorate in canon and civil law at the University of Pavia in 1559. His uncle, Pope Pius IV, appointed him cardinal and archbishop of Milan in 1560. He was active in directing the Council of TRENT, and he later helped execute its decrees and draw up the Roman catechism in 1566. He established seminaries and colleges in Milan and nearby cities and gained renown for his heroic behavior during the plague of 1576–78.

Borromini, Francesco *orig.* **Francesco Castelli** (1599–1667) Italian baroque architect. Though he worked with GIAN LORENZO BERNINI on the design of the famous BALDACHIN in ST. PETER'S BASILICA, the two later became bitter rivals. Borromini's first independent commission was the Roman church and monastery of San Carlo alle Quattro Fontane (1638–41), the dome of which appears to float because its spring points (see ARCH) and light sources are concealed below. His works, composed of flowing concave and convex forms, contain spaces that are irregular ovals and polygons, as at Sant'Ivo della Sapienza (1642–60). His fortunes declined in later years, and in 1667 he committed suicide. His influence was felt in northern Italy and central Europe in the next century.

Interior of the dome of the church of S. Ivo della Sapienza, Rome, by Francesco Borromini, 1642–60.
GEKS

Borsippa \bȯr-ˈsi-pə\ Ancient city, BABYLONIA. Located southwest of BABYLON, its proximity to that capital helped it become an important religious center. HAMMURABI built or rebuilt the temple at Borsippa, dedicating it to MARDUK. During NEBUCHADNEZZAR II's reign the city reached its greatest prosperity. Borsippa was destroyed by XERXES I in the early 5th century BC and never fully recovered. The ruins lie south of modern Al Hillah.

borzoi \ˈbȯr-ˌzȯi\ Breed of HOUND developed in Russia. It is descended from the Arabian GREYHOUND and a collielike Russian SHEEPDOG. Formerly known as the Russian wolfhound, it was originally bred to hunt wolves and hares. It is graceful, strong, and swift, attaining a height of about 26–31 in. (66–79 cm) and a weight of 55–105 lbs (25–48 kg). It has a long, narrow head; small ears; a deep but narrow chest; long, muscular hindquarters; and a long, curved tail. Its silky coat is flat or slightly curled and usually is white with darker markings. It is noted for its elegant appearance.

Borzoi.
SALLY ANNE THOMPSON—EB INC.

Bosanquet \ˈbō-zən-ˌket\, **Bernard** (1848–1923) British philosopher. He helped revive in Britain the absolute IDEALISM of G. W. F. HEGEL and sought to apply its principles to social and political problems. His debt to Hegel is most evident in his works on ethics, aesthetics, and metaphysics. His *Some Suggestions in Ethics* (1918) shows a desire to view reality as a synthesis in which are reconciled such traditional oppositions as egoism-altruism. His other works include *Knowledge and Reality* (1885), *Logic* (1888), and *History of Aesthetic* (1892). His idealism was strongly criticized by G. E. MOORE and BERTRAND RUSSELL.

Bosch \ˈbȯsh\, **Hieronymus** *orig.* **Jeroen van Aken** *or* **Jerome van Aken** (c. 1450–1516) Netherlandish painter. He was the son and grandson of accomplished painters; his name comes from his native town of 's Hertogenbosch. He enjoyed a successful career and was widely imitated. Of the numerous works attributed to him, none can be dated precisely. His paintings blend fantasy and reality in apocalyptic scenes of chaos with half-human, half-animal creatures, devils, and demons interacting with human figures in imaginary architecture and landscapes. Among his best-known works is *The Garden of Earthly Delights,* depicting the dreams that afflict people who live in a pleasure-seeking world. One of the most original northern European artists of the late Middle Ages, he was an outstanding draftsman and one of the first to make drawings as independent works. He also produced decorative works, altarpieces, and stained-glass designs.

Bosch (Gaviño) \ˈbȯsh\, **Juan** (1909–2001) Scholar, poet, and president of the Dominican Republic (1963). Born in La Vega, he was raised in a lower-middle-class family. Dismayed by the brutality of the dictator RAFAEL TRUJILLO, he spent 24 years in exile but returned after Trujillo's death to build a leftist anticommunist movement. After winning the first free presidential election in 38 years, he instituted liberal constitutional changes, many of which benefited the country's poor. His reforms, however, alienated landholders and industrialists, and after only seven months in office Bosch was ousted in a military coup. When his supporters revolted against the ruling junta in 1965, U.S. President Lyndon B. Johnson, claiming that Bosch's followers were communists, sent troops to suppress the rebellion. Over the subsequent three decades, Bosch ran repeatedly but unsuccessfully for president.

Bose \ˈbōs\, **Subhas Chandra** (1897–1945) Indian revolutionary. Preparing in Britain for a career in the Indian civil service, he resigned his candidacy on hearing of nationalist turmoil back home. Sent by MOHANDAS K. GANDHI to organize in Bengal, he was deported and imprisoned several times. He favored industrialization, which put him at odds with Gandhi's economic thought, and though elected president of the INDIAN NATIONAL CONGRESS in 1938 and 1939, without Gandhi's support he felt bound to resign. He slipped out of India in 1941 and carried on his struggle against the British from Nazi Germany and later from S.East Asia. In 1944 he invaded India from Myanmar with a small army of Indian nationals and Japanese, but his army was soon forced to retreat. He fled S.East Asia after the Japanese surrender in 1945 and died of burns from a plane crash.

Bose-Einstein statistics One of two possible ways (the other is FERMI-DIRAC STATISTICS) in which a collection of indistinguishable particles may occupy a set of available discrete energy states. The gathering of particles in the same state, which is characteristic of particles that obey Bose-Einstein statistics, accounts for the cohesive streaming of LASER light and the frictionless creeping of superfluid helium (see SUPERFLUIDITY). The theory of this behavior was developed in 1924–25 by Satyendra Nath Bose (1894–1974) and ALBERT EINSTEIN. Bose-Einstein statistics apply only to those particles, called BOSONS, which have integer values of SPIN and so do not obey the PAULI EXCLUSION PRINCIPLE.

Bosna River \ˈbȯs-nä\ River, Bosnia and Herzegovina. Rising at the foot of Mount Igman, it flows northward about 150 mi (241 km) before entering the SAVA RIVER. Major cities along the Bosna include SARAJEVO, Zenica, and Doboj.

Bosnia and Herzegovina \ˈbäz-nē-ə...ˌher-tsə-gō-ˈvē-nə\ *officially* **Republic of Bosnia and Herzegovina** Country, BALKAN PENINSULA, bounded by modern Yugoslavia and Croatia. Area: 19,904 sq mi (51,750 sq km). Population (1997 est.): 3,124,000 (excludes about 1,000,000 refugees in adjacent countries and elsewhere). Capital: SARAJEVO. Major ethnic groups include Bosnian Muslims (about two-fifths of the population), Serbs (about one-third), and Croats (about one-fifth); they are racially indistinguishable. Language: Serbo-Croatian (official). Religions: Islam, Orthodox Christian, Roman Catholic. Currency: dinar. The country's relief is largely mountainous, and elevations of more than 6,000 ft (1,800 m) are common; the land drops abruptly southward toward the

Adriatic Sea; it is drained by the Sava, Drina, and Neretva rivers and their tributaries. Agriculture is a mainstay of the economy; though the area possesses a variety of minerals, it remains one of the poorest regions of the former Yugoslavia. A republic with two legislative houses, its chief of state is the chairman of the tripartite presidency, and the heads of government are the two cochairmen of the Council of Ministers. Habitation long predates the era of Roman rule, when much of the country was included in the province of Dalmatia. Slav settlement began in the 6th century AD. For the next several centuries, parts of the region fell under the rule of Serbs, Croats, Hungarians, Venetians, and Byzantines. The Ottoman Turks invaded Bosnia in the 14th century, and after many battles it became a Turkish province in 1463. Herzegovina, then known as Hum, was taken in 1482. In the 16th–17th century the area was an important Turkish outpost, constantly at war with the Habsburgs and Venice. During this period much of the native population converted to Islam. At the Congress of Berlin after the Russo-Turkish War of 1877–78, Bosnia and Herzegovina was assigned to Austria-Hungary and annexed in 1908. Growing Serb nationalism resulted in the 1914 assassination of the Austrian Archduke Francis Ferdinand at Sarajevo by a Bosnian Serb, an event that precipitated World War I. After the war the area was annexed to Serbia. Following World War II the twin territory became a republic of communist Yugoslavia. With the collapse of communist regimes in eastern Europe, Bosnia and Herzegovina declared its independence in 1992; its Serbian population objected, and conflict ensued among Serbs, Croats, and Muslims (see Bosnian conflict). The 1995 peace accord established a loosely federated government roughly divided between a Muslim Croat federation and a Serb republic. In 1996 a NATO peace-keeping force was installed there.

Bosnian conflict (1992–98) Ethnically rooted war in Bosnia and Herzegovina, a republic of Yugoslavia with a multiethnic population—44% Muslim, 33% Serb, and 17% Croat. Unrest began with Yugoslavia's breakup in 1990; after a 1992 referendum, the European Community recognized Bosnia's independence. Bosnia's Serbs responded violently, seized 70% of Bosnian territory, besieged Sarajevo, and terrorized Muslims and Croats with internment in concentration camps, mass rapes, and summary executions. A 1993 peace plan failed to garner support. After bitter fighting between the Bosnian Croats and the Bosnian government, international pressure forced the two factions to sign a cease-fire and an agreement for a federation. Both then concentrated on their common enemy, the Serbs. After rejected peace plans, attacks and counterattacks, a four-month truce, further multiple offensives, and an intensification of the bombing, the Western nations imposed a final cease-fire negotiated at Dayton, Ohio, in 1995. After 44 months and more than 200,000 deaths, Bosnia-Herzegovina was to become a single state composed of two distinct entities with great autonomy. Sarajevo was assigned to the federation, while other delicate issues were left to international arbitration. Today Bosnia-Herzegovina has three de facto monoethnic entities, three separate armies and police forces, and a very weak national government. Political power is concentrated among hardline nationalists. See also Radovan Karadzic, Franjo Tudjman.

Bosnian crisis (1908) International crisis caused by Austria-Hungary's annexation of the Balkan provinces of Bosnia and Herzegovina. Russia supported Serbia, which protested the annexation and demanded that Austria cede part of the territory to Serbia, but Austria-Hungary, supported by Germany, threatened to invade Serbia if it persisted in its demands. Since Russia could not risk war against both Germany and Austria-Hungary, it was forced to accept the annexation. Though the crisis was resolved without immediate warfare, it contributed to the outbreak of World War I.

boson \'bō-ˌzän\ Subatomic particle with integral spin that is governed by Bose-Einstein statistics. Bosons include mesons, nuclei of even mass number, and the particles required to embody the fields of quantum field theory. Unlike fermions, there is no limit to the number of bosons that can occupy the same quantum state, a behavior that gives rise to the superfluidity of helium-4.

Bosporus \'bäs-pə-rəs\ *Turkish* **Karadeniz Bogazi** \ˌkä-rä-de-'nēz-ˌbō-ä-'zi\ Strait separating Turkey in Europe from Turkey in Asia. Connecting the Sea of Marmara with the Black Sea, it is 19 mi (31 km) long and 2.8 mi (4.4 km) at its widest. Bosporus literally means "ox ford" and is traditionally connected with the legendary figure of Io, who in the form of a heifer crossed the Thracian Bosporus in her wanderings. Because of its strategic importance for the defense of Constantinople, which straddled its southern end, the Byzantine emperors and later the Ottoman sultans constructed fortifications along its shores. With the growing influence of the European powers in the 19th century, rules were codified governing the transit of vessels through the strait. An international commission assumed control of it after World War I; Turkey resumed control in 1936. Two of the world's longest bridges, completed in 1973 and 1988, span the strait.

Bosporus, Cimmerian See Cimmerian Bosporus

Bosra See Busra

Boston Seaport city (pop., 2000: 589,141), capital of Massachusetts. Located on Massachusetts Bay at the mouths of the Charles and Mystic rivers, it is the state's largest city. Settled by Gov. John Winthrop in 1630, it was made the capital of Massachusetts Bay Colony in 1632. As a leader in the opposition to British trade restrictions on its American colonies, Boston was a locus of events leading to the American Revolution: it was the scene of the Boston Massacre (1770) and Boston Tea Party (1773). It was the center for the antislavery movement 1830–65. As the Industrial Revolution took hold in the U.S., Boston grew as an important manufacturing and textile center. Today financial and high-technology industries are basic to its economy. Numerous institutions of higher education are located there, including Boston Univ. See also Cambridge.

Boston College Private institution of higher learning in Chestnut Hill, Mass. Founded in 1863, it is affiliated with the Roman Catholic church. It comprises a college of arts and sciences and schools of education, nursing, management, and law. Total enrollment is about 15,000.

Boston Globe, The Daily newspaper published in Boston, one of the most influential newspapers in the U.S. Founded in 1872, it was purchased in 1877 by Charles H. Taylor. Under his leadership, it began publishing morning and evening editions, increased local and regional coverage, and introduced big headlines, especially on sensational stories. In the 20th century, still headed by the Taylor family, the paper began providing more national and international news while maintaining a generally liberal editorial stance. The New York Times Co. acquired the *Globe* in 1993.

Boston Massacre Skirmish on March 5, 1770, between British troops and a crowd in Boston. After provocation by the colonists, British soldiers fired on the mob and killed five men, including Crispus Attucks. The incident was widely publicized by Samuel Adams, Paul Revere, and others as a battle for American liberty, and it contributed to the unpopularity of the British in the years before the AMERICAN REVOLUTION.

Boston Police Strike Strike in 1919 by most of Boston's police force to protest the police commissioner's decision to deny them the right to unionize. The mayor called in the city militia to restore order and break the strike; Gov. CALVIN COOLIDGE later sent in the state militia, which gave him a reputation as a strong supporter of law and order and led to his nomination as vice president on the 1920 Republican ticket.

Boston Strangler American serial killer who murdered at least 11 and as many as 13 women in the Boston area between 1962 and 1964. His first victim, a 55-year-old woman, was sexually assaulted and strangled in her apartment on June 14, 1962. During the following months, several other elderly women were murdered in similar circumstances, though subsequent victims included young women. In 1965 Albert DeSalvo, an inmate at a state mental hospital, confessed to the murders. Although never charged with the killings because no physical evidence tied him to the murder scenes, he was convicted on separate counts of sexual assault and sentenced to life imprisonment. DeSalvo's guilt remains controversial, in part because his confessions demonstrated ignorance of many aspects of the crimes. In 2001 DNA tests confirmed that it was all but impossible that DeSalvo was guilty of the last of the murders, though it was one of the crimes to which he had confessed.

Boston Tea Party Incident on December 16, 1773, in which 342 chests of tea were thrown from three British ships into Boston Harbor by American patriots disguised as Indians, led by SAMUEL ADAMS. The action was taken to prevent the payment of the British-imposed tax on tea and to protest the British monopoly of the colonial tea trade authorized by the TEA ACT. In retaliation, Parliament passed the INTOLERABLE ACTS, which served to further unite the colonies in their opposition to the British.

Boston terrier Breed of dog developed in the late 19th century in Boston. Bred from the English BULLDOG and a white English TERRIER, the Boston terrier is one of the few breeds to have originated in the U.S. It has a terrier-like build, dark eyes, a short muzzle, and a short, fine coat of black or brindle, with white on the face, chest, neck, and legs. It stands 14–17 in. (36–43 cm) high and ranges in weight from 15 to 25 lbs (7–11 kg). The breed is characteristically gentle and affectionate.

Boston University Private university in Boston. Founded in 1839 (reorganized 1867), it was one of the first American universities to accept black and international students. Today it comprises 15 schools and colleges. Professional degrees are awarded at its schools of law, medicine, dentistry, and management; graduate degrees are awarded in education, engineering, and the arts and sciences. Among its archival collections are the papers of MARTIN LUTHER KING, Jr., THEODORE ROOSEVELT, and ROBERT FROST. Total enrollment is about 30,000.

Boswell, James (1740–1795) Scottish friend and biographer of SAMUEL JOHNSON. Boswell, a lawyer, met Dr. Johnson in 1763 and visited him often in 1772–84, making a superlatively detailed record of Johnson's conversations. His two-volume *Life of Samuel Johnson, LL.D.* (1791), is regarded as the greatest of English biographies. His *Journal of a Tour to the Hebrides* (1785) is mainly an account of Johnson's responses to their 1773 trip to Scotland. The 20th-century publication of Boswell's journals showed him to have been also one of the world's greatest diarists.

Boswell, detail of an oil painting from the studio of Sir Joshua Reynolds, 1786; in the National Portrait Gallery, London.

BY COURTESY OF THE NATIONAL PORTRAIT GALLERY, LONDON

Bosworth Field, Battle of (August 22, 1485) Final battle in the English Wars of the ROSES. It was fought between the forces of King RICHARD III of York and the contender for the crown, Henry Tudor (later HENRY VII) of Lancaster. The battle occurred when Henry returned from exile, landing with an army at Milford Haven and meeting Richard's forces west of Leicester. The king's men were defeated and put to flight, and Richard was unhorsed and killed in a bog (a scene depicted in WILLIAM SHAKESPEARE's *Richard III*). The battle established the TUDOR dynasty on the English throne.

botanical garden *or* **botanic garden** Originally, a collection of living plants designed to illustrate relationships within plant groups. Most modern botanical gardens are concerned primarily with exhibiting ornamental plants in a scheme that emphasizes natural relationships. A display garden of mostly woody plants (shrubs and trees) is often called an ARBORETUM. The botanical garden as an institution can be traced to ancient China and many Mediterranean countries, where such gardens were often centers for raising plants used for food and medicines. Botanical gardens are also reservoirs of valuable heritable characteristics, potentially important in the breeding of new varieties of plants. Still another function is the training of gardeners. The world's most famous botanical garden is KEW GARDENS.

botany Branch of BIOLOGY that deals with plants, including the structure, properties, and biochemical processes of all forms of plant life, as well as plant classification, plant diseases, and the interactions of plants with their physical environment. The science of botany traces back to the ancient Greco-Roman world but received its modern impetus in Europe in the 16th century, mainly through the work of physicians and herbalists, who began to observe plants seriously to identify those useful in medicine. Today the principal branches of botanical study are MORPHOLOGY, PHYSIOLOGY, ECOLOGY, and systematics (the identification and ranking of all plants). Subdisciplines include bryology (the study of MOSSES and LIVERWORTS), pteridology (the study of FERNS and their relatives), paleobotany (the study of FOSSIL plants), and palynology (the study of modern and fossil POLLEN and SPORES). See also FORESTRY, HORTICULTURE.

Botany Bay Inlet of the South Pacific Ocean, southeastern Australia. Lying south of SYDNEY off Port Jackson, it is about 6 mi (10 km) at its widest. It was the scene of the first Australian landing by Capt. JAMES COOK in 1770; he named the bay for its great variety of plants. It was selected in 1787 as the site for a penal settlement, but the settlement was soon transferred inland. Its shores are now ringed by Sydney's suburbs.

Botero, Fernando (born 1932) Colombian painter and sculptor. Born in Medellín, Colombia, Botero began painting as a teenager. By the time he moved to New York in 1960, he had developed his trademark style: the depiction of round, corpulent humans and animals. In these works, his use of flat, bright color and boldly outlined forms reflected the influence of Latin-American folk art, while his strong compositions often emulated the old masters. In 1973 Botero moved to Paris and began creating sculptures that focused on rotund subjects. Exhibitions of his bronze figures were staged around the world at the end of the 20th century.

botfly Any member of several DIPTERAN families with beelike adults and larvae that are parasitic on mammals. Some species are serious pests of horses, cattle, deer, sheep, rabbits, and squirrels, and one species (the human botfly) attacks humans. Adults of several species lay many eggs (nits) on the host's body, and the emerging larvae penetrate its skin. The larvae reemerge through the skin, then mature into egg-laying adults. In the New World tropics, the botfly's infestation of cattle has led to loss of beef and hides. See also WARBLE FLY.

Botha \'bō-tə\, **Louis** (1862–1919) First prime minister (1910–19) of the Union of South Africa. Botha was elected to the South African Republic's parliament in 1897, where he sided with moderates against Pres. PAUL KRUGER's hostile policy toward Uitlanders (non-Boer, mostly English, settlers). In the SOUTH AFRICAN WAR he commanded southern forces besieging Ladysmith and then tried unsuccessfully to defend the TRANSVAAL. As prime minister he sought earnestly to appease the English-speaking population and was bitterly attacked by AFRIKANER nationalists. In World War I he acceded to British requests to conquer German S.West Africa (now Namibia).

Botha, P(ieter) W(illem) (born 1916) Prime minister (1978–84) and first state president (1984–89) of South Africa. Elected to parliament as a NATIONAL PARTY candidate in 1948, Botha served in several posts before replacing JOHN VORSTER as prime minister in 1978. His government faced serious difficulties, including the coming to power of black governments in Mozambique, Angola, and Zimbabwe, an insurgency in S.West Africa (Namibia), and domestic unrest among black students and labor unions. Botha responded by backing antigovernment troops in the bordering states and suppressing rebellion at home. A target of criticism from within and outside his party, he fell ill and resigned in 1989.

Bothnia, Gulf of Northern arm of the BALTIC SEA. Extending between Sweden and Finland, it covers about 45,200 sq mi (117,000 sq km). It is 450 mi (725 km) long and 50–150 mi (80–240 km) wide; its average depth is 965 ft (295 m). Because many rivers drain into it, its salinity is very low; ice cover consequently lasts up to five months of the year.

Botox Trademark for botulinum toxin type A, a drug produced by the bacterium *Clostridium botulinum,* which contains the same toxin that causes severe food poisoning (botulism). When locally injected, Botox blocks the release of the neurotransmitter acetylcholine, interfering with the ability of the muscle to contract. It is used to treat severe muscle spasm or severe, uncontrollable sweating. Botox can also be used for cosmetic purposes to treat facial wrinkles.

Botswana *officially* **Republic of Botswana** *formerly* **Bechuanaland** \ˌbech-ˈwä-nə-ˌland\ Country, southern Africa, bounded by Namibia, Zimbabwe, and South Africa. Area: 219,916 sq mi (569,582 sq km). Population (1997 est.): 1,533,383. Capital: GABORONE. Less than half the population are ethnic TSWANA; other main groups include the Khalagari, Ngwato, Tswapong, Birwa, and Kalanga. Small groups of KHOIKHOI and SAN follow a nomadic way of life and move seasonally across the Namibian border. Languages: English (official), Tswana. Religion: Christian, with a large admixture of traditional African beliefs. Currency: pula. Botswana is essentially a tableland, with a mean elevation of about 3,300 ft (1,000 m). Part of the KALAHARI DESERT is in the southwest and west, while the Okavango Swamp is in the north. The only sources of permanent surface water are the Chobe River, which marks the Namibian boundary; the OKAVANGO RIVER, in the far northwest; and the LIMPOPO RIVER, which marks the South African boundary in the southeast. The economy is traditionally dependent on livestock raising; the development of diamond mining in the 1980s has increased the country's wealth. It is a republic with one legislative body; its head of state and government is the president. The region's earliest inhabitants were the Khoikhoi and San (Bushmen). Sites were settled as early as AD 190 during the southerly migration of Bantu-speaking farmers. Tswana dynasties, which developed in the western TRANSVAAL in the 13th–14th century, moved into Botswana in the 18th century and established several powerful states. European missionaries arrived in the early 19th century, but it was the discovery of gold in 1867 that excited European interest. In 1885 the area became the British Bechuanaland Protectorate. The next year, the region south of the Molopo River became a crown colony, and it was annexed by the Cape Colony 10 years later. Bechuanaland itself continued as a British protectorate until the 1960s. In 1966 the Republic of Bechuanaland (later, Botswana) was proclaimed an independent member of the British COMMONWEALTH. Independent Botswana tried to maintain a delicate balance between its economic dependence on South Africa and its relations with the surrounding black countries; the independence of Namibia in 1990 and South Africa's rejection of apartheid eased tensions.

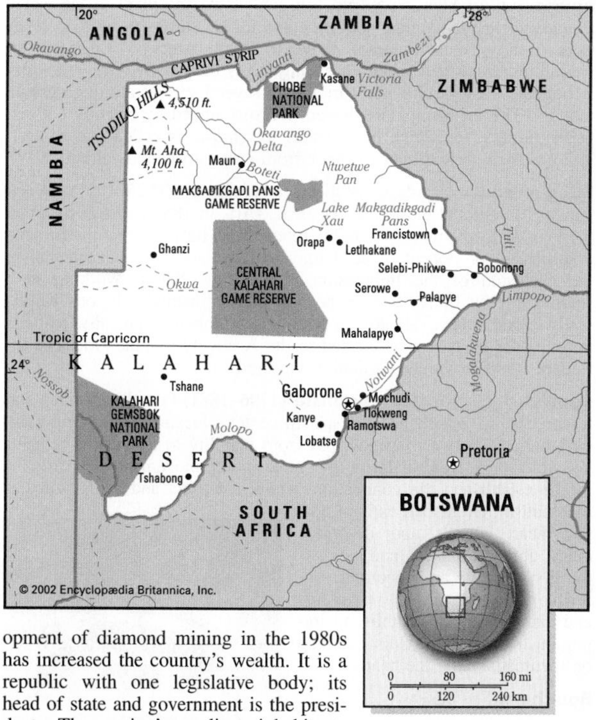

Botticelli \ˌbät-ə-ˈchel-ē\, **Sandro** *orig.* **Alessandro di Mariano Filipepi** (1445–1510) Italian painter active in Florence. As a youth he may have been apprenticed to a goldsmith, and he later trained with FRA FILIPPO LIPPI in Florence. By 1470 he had developed a distinctive style and was established as a master. In 1481 he was among a team of Florentine and Umbrian artists called to Rome to decorate the SISTINE CHAPEL; three of his finest religious frescoes (completed 1482) can be seen there. Though prolific as a painter of religious images, his mythological paintings are his best-known works. His outstanding portraits show the influence of contemporary Flemish art in the placement of the figure in front of a landscape. Among his greatest works are the *Primavera, Pallas and the Centaur, Venus and Mars,* and *The Birth of Venus*, all painted c. 1477–90. About 75 of his paintings survive, many of them in the Uffizi Gallery. Interest in his work revived in the 19th century, and today he is one of the most esteemed painters of the Italian Renaissance.

"The Birth of Venus," oil on canvas by Sandro Botticelli, about 1485; in the Uffizi, Florence.

ANDERSON—ALINARI FROM ART RESOURCE

bottlenose dolphin *or* **bottle-nosed dolphin** Widely recognized species (*Tursiops truncatus,* family Delphinidae) of mammalian DOLPHIN found worldwide in warm and temperate seas. Bottlenose dolphins reach average lengths of 8–10 ft (2.5–3 m) and weights of 300–650 lbs (135–300 kg). Males are generally larger than females. A familiar performer at marine shows, the species is characterized by a "built-in smile" formed by the curvature of its mouth. It has also become the subject of scientific studies because of its intelligence and its ability to communicate with its kind through sounds and ultrasonic pulses.

botulism \ˈbä-chə-ˌli-zəm\ Poisoning by botulinum toxin, one of the most potent TOXINS known, produced by *Clostridium botulinum* bacteria (usually from improperly sterilized canned—mostly home-canned—foods). Heat-resistant spores of these anaerobic bacteria in fresh food may survive canning. The bacteria multiply and secrete toxin, which remains potent if the food is not well heated before it is eaten. Botulism can also result from wound infection. Botulinum toxin blocks nerve-impulse transmission. If botulism is recognized in time, administered ANTITOXINS can neutralize it. The first symptoms of botulism, nausea and vomiting, usually appear six hours or less after the contaminated food is eaten. Fatigue, blurry vision, and general weakness follow. Respiratory paralysis can cause death if not treated with emergency tracheotomy and respiratory aid. Most victims recover completely if they survive paralysis. The bacteria's intense toxicity makes it a potentially deadly biological warfare agent.

Bouaké \bwä-ˈkā\ City (pop., 1995 est.: 330,000), central Ivory Coast. It was established as a French military post in 1899 on the road and railroad line from ABIDJAN to BURKINA FASO (then, Upper Volta). Bouaké is among the nation's largest cities and is the commercial and transportation hub of the interior.

Boucher \bü-ˈshā\, **François** (1703–1770) French painter, engraver, and designer. He was probably trained by his father, a minor painter. In 1723 he won the Prix de Rome, but was unable to travel to Italy until 1728. For his first major commission he produced 125 engravings of drawings by ANTOINE WATTEAU. He executed important decorative commissions for Madame de POMPADOUR at Versailles. His playful style and frivolous subject matter exemplify the Rococo style and embody the elegant superficiality of French court life in the mid-18th century. He became a member of the Royal Academy in 1734, a principal designer for the royal porcelain factories, and director of the Gobelins tapestry factory. In 1765 he became director of the Royal Academy and first painter to LOUIS XV. One of the great painters and draftsmen of the 18th century, he mastered every branch of decorative and illustrative painting.

Boucher \ˈbau̇-chər\, **Jonathan** (1738–1804) English-American clergyman. He went to Virginia in 1759 as a private tutor. As rector of Annapolis, Md., he tutored GEORGE WASHINGTON's stepson and became a family friend. His royalist views cost him his position and he was forced to return to England in 1775. In his retirement he wrote *A View of the Causes and Consequences of the American Revolution* (1779); his glossary of "archaic and provincial words" was later used for NOAH WEBSTER's dictionary.

Boucicault \ˈbü-si-ˌkō\, **Dion** *orig.* **Dionysius Lardner Boursiquot** (1822–1890) Irish-U.S. playwright. He began acting in 1837 and wrote the successful comedy *London Assurance* (1841) and *The Corsican Brothers* (1852). In 1853 he moved to New York, where he was instrumental in obtaining the first copyright law for drama in the U.S. His successful play *The Poor of New York* (1857) was presented elsewhere as, for example, *The Poor of London.* Concerned with social themes, he wrote a veiled attack on slavery in *The Octoroon* (1859). He also wrote a series of popular Irish plays, including *The Colleen Bawn* (1860) and *The Shaughraun* (1874).

Boudiaf \bü-ˈdyáf\, **Muhammad** (1919–1992) Algerian political leader. With AHMED BEN BELLA, he cofounded the Algerian NATIONAL LIBERATION FRONT (FLN), which led the fight for Algerian independence from France (1954–62). He was imprisoned from 1956 until Algerian independence in 1962, whereupon he became deputy premier under Ben Bella. His opposition to Ben Bella's autocratic style led to a 27-year exile. In 1992 he was invited back to head the government and to deal with rising religious influence in political affairs. He was assassinated by a bodyguard shortly thereafter. See also ISLAMIC SALVATION FRONT.

Boudicca \bü-ˈdik-ə\ *or* **Boadicea** \ˌbō-əd-ə-ˈsē-ə\ (died AD 60) Ancient British queen who led a revolt against Roman rule. When her husband, a Roman client king of the Iceni, died in AD 60, he left his estate to his daughters and the emperor NERO, hoping for protection. Instead the Romans annexed his kingdom and mistreated his family and tribesmen. Boudicca raised a rebellion in East Anglia, burning Colchester, St. Albans, and part of London and military posts; according to TACITUS, her forces massacred up to 70,000 Romans and pro-Roman Britons and destroyed the Roman 9th Legion. When the Roman governor rallied his troops and destroyed her huge army, she took poison or died of shock.

Boudin \bü-ˈda^{n}\, **Eugène** (1824–1898) French landscape painter. He was encouraged at an early age by J.-F. MILLET. He became a strong advocate of painting directly from nature. In 1874 he exhibited with the Impressionists, but he was not an innovator, and from 1863 to 1897 he exhibited regularly in the official Salon. His favorite subjects were beach scenes and seascapes, which show remarkable sensitivity to effects of atmosphere; on the backs of his paintings he recorded the weather, light, and time of day. His works link the careful naturalism of the mid-19th century and the brilliant colors and fluid brushwork of Impressionism.

boudinage \ˌbüd-^{ə}n-ˈäzh\ Cylinder-like structures making up a layer of deformed rock. They commonly lie adjacent to each other and are joined by short necks, giving the appearance of a string of sausages (*boudin* is French for "sausage"). The necks may be filled with recrystallized minerals such as quartz, feldspar, or calcite. Boudinage occurs in a variety of rock types and is one of the more common structures found in folded rocks.

Boudinot \ˈbüd-^{ə}n-ō\, **Elias** (1740–1821) American public official. Born in Philadelphia, he became a conservative Whig but supported the Revolution when the war began. He was president of the Continental Congress 1782–83 and later served in the U.S. House of Representatives (1789–95) and as director of the U.S. Mint at Philadelphia (1795–1805).

Bougainville \ˈbü-gən-ˌvil\ Island (pop., 1990 est.: 140,000), Papua New Guinea. The largest of the Solomon Islands, near the northern end of that chain, it has a land area of about 3,880 sq mi (10,050 sq km). The Emperor Range, with its highest peak at Balbi (9,000 ft, or 2,743 m), occupies the northern half of the island, while the Crown Prince Range occupies the southern half. It was visited by L.-A. de BOUGAINVILLE in 1768, and it came under German control in the late 19th century. After World War I it was included in an Australian mandate. Following World War II it was made part of the U.N. Trust Territory of New Guinea, and it passed to Papua New Guinea when that country became independent in 1975. In recent decades there has been an active secessionist group on the island.

Bougainville \bü-ga^{n}-ˈvēl\, **Louis-Antoine de** (1729–1811) French navigator. In 1764 he established a colony for France in the Falkland Islands. Commissioned by the government to circle the earth in a voyage of exploration, he put to sea in 1766; after touching Samoa and the New Hebrides he continued west into waters not previously navigated by any European. He turned north on the fringes of the Great Barrier Reef and did not sight Australia. He stopped in the Moluccas and in Java before returning to Brittany in 1769. His widely read *Voyage Round the World* (1771) helped popularize a belief in the moral worth of man in his natural state. He was secretary to LOUIS XV (1772), led the French fleet in support of the American Revolution, and was named to the Legion of Honor by NAPOLEON. The plant genus *Bougainvillea* is named for him.

bougainvillea \ˌbü-gən-ˈvil-yə, ˌbü-gən-ˈvē-ə\ Any plant of the genus *Bougainvillea,* containing about 14 species of shrubs, vines, or small trees (family Nyctaginaceae) native to South America and hardy in warm climates. Many species are spiny. Only the woody vines are widely popular; showy cultivated varieties of several species are often grown indoors. The inconspicuous flowers are surrounded by brightly colored papery BRACTS, for which one species, *B. glabra,* is called paperflower. The bracts of various species range from purple to lemon yellow.

Bouguereau \bü-gə-ˈrō\, **William (-Adolphe)** (1825–1905) French painter. He entered the École des Beaux-Arts in 1846 and was awarded the Prix de Rome in 1850. On his return from Italy in 1854, he became a successful proponent of academic painting, and was instrumental in the exclusion of the Impressionists from the Salon. Working in a smooth, highly finished style, he painted sentimental religious works, coyly erotic nudes, allegorical scenes, and photographically realistic portraits. In 1876 he was elected to the Academy of Fine Arts. His influence was felt widely, particularly in the U.S.

Bouillaud \bü-ˈyō\, **Jean-Baptiste** (1796–1881) French physician and researcher. He established the speech center's location in the brain and differentiated between speech loss from inability to create and remember word forms from inability to control speech movements. In cardiology, he established the connection between carditis and acute articular rheumatism. He helped explain normal heart sounds and described many abnormal ones, and he was the first to name and accurately describe the endocardial membrane and endocarditis. He published important books on heart diseases and on rheumatism and the heart.

Boukhara See BUKHARA

Boulanger \bü-lä^{n}-ˈzhā\, **Georges (-Ernest-Jean-Marie)** (1837–1891) French general and politician. He entered the army in 1856, helped suppress the PARIS COMMUNE (1871), and rose in rank to brigadier general (1880) and director of infantry (1882). Named minister of war in 1886, he introduced various military reforms and was seen as

Georges Boulanger.
H. ROGER-VIOLLET

the man destined to avenge France's defeat in the Franco–Prussian war. In 1888 he led a short-lived but influential authoritarian movement that threatened to topple the Third Republic. In 1889 the government decided to prosecute him, prompting him to flee Paris. He was convicted in absentia for treason, and in 1891 he committed suicide.

Boulanger \bü-lä^{n}-'zhä\, **Nadia (-Juliette)** (1887–1979) French music teacher and conductor. Having studied composition with Charles-Marie Widor (1844–1937) and G. Fauré, she stopped composing in her twenties and devoted the rest of her life to conducting, playing the organ, and teaching at the École Normale (1920–39), Paris Conservatoire (from 1946), and especially the American Conservatory at Fontainebleau (from 1921). She became the most celebrated composition teacher of the 20th century; her many students included A. Copland, R. Harris, D. Milhaud, V. Thomson, E. Carter, Leonard Bernstein, and P. Glass. Her sister, Lili Boulanger (1893–1918), the first woman composer to win the Prix de Rome (1913), died at 25, having written a remarkable amount of vocal and other music.

Boulder City (pop., 1996 est.: 91,000), northern central Colorado. Located in the Rocky Mtns. northwest of Denver, it was settled by miners in 1858 and grew with the arrival of two railroads in 1873. An extensive government-industrial-educational complex has developed in recent decades. It is the site of the University of Colorado.

Boulder Dam See Hoover Dam

boule \'bü-lē\ Deliberative council in the city-states of ancient Greece. It existed in almost all constitutional city-states, especially from the late 6th century BC. In Athens the boule was created as an aristocratic body by Solon in 594 BC; later, under Cleisthenes, 500 members were elected to represent the 10 tribes (50 each). A certain number, in rough proportion to size, were allotted to each deme. Complementing the work of the ecclesia and Areopagus, the boule controlled finances, managed the fleet and cavalry, evaluated officials, received foreign ambassadors, and advised the strategus. The boule model largely influenced the organization of councils of other cities in the Hellenic period.

boules \'bülz\ French ball game, similar to bowls and boccie. Players take turns throwing or rolling a steel ball as close as possible to a small target ball; an opponent's ball may be knocked away if necessary. The playing field is called a pitch.

boulevard Broad landscaped avenue that typically permits several lanes of vehicular traffic as well as pedestrian walkways. The earliest boulevards originally followed the city walls (the word originally meant "bulwark") and were built in the ancient Middle East, especially at Antioch. In Paris, straight and geometrically precise boulevards were incorporated into design principles taught at the École des Beaux-Arts, and they form a prominent feature of the city. Similar boulevards are found in other cities such as Washington, D.C. Formal curving boulevards are a feature of such cities as Vienna and Prague.

Boulez \bü-'lez\, **Pierre** (born 1925) French composer and conductor. Originally a student of mathematics, he later studied with O. Messiaen at the Paris Conservatoire. He was music director of the Renaud-Barrault theater company 1946–56. Inspired by the works of A. Webern, he began to experiment with total serialism in 1951. He founded the new-music group Domaine Musical in 1954 and directed it until 1967. He was conductor of the New York Philharmonic 1971–78. He conducted Richard Wagner's *Ring* at Bayreuth in 1976 and the premiere of the completed version of A. Berg's *Lulu* in 1979. In 1974 he founded the French national experimental studio IRCAM. His important works include *Le soleil des eaux* (1948), *Structures I* and *II* (1952, 1961), *Le marteau sans maître* (1957), *Pli selon pli* (1962), and three piano sonatas (1946, 1948, 1957). With his greatly varied activities, including his often iconoclastic writings, he was the principal figure of the postwar international musical avant-garde.

Boulle \'bül\, **André-Charles** *or* **André-Charles Boule** (1642–1732) French cabinetmaker. After studying drawing, painting, and sculpture, he achieved fame as the most skillful furniture designer in Paris. In 1672 Louis XIV appointed him royal cabinetmaker at Versailles; his other patrons included Philip V of Spain and the duke of Bourbon. He stretched the technique of marquetry to new heights, and his incorporation of elaborate brasswork and the inlaying of exotic woods (called boulle or buhl work, since his last name sometimes appeared as Buhl) was heavily imitated in the 18th–19th century.

Boullée \bü-'lā\, **Étienne-Louis** (1728–1799) French architect, theorist, and teacher. He studied architecture and opened his own studio by age 19. Through his investigation of the properties of geometric forms, to which he attributed innate symbolic qualities, Boullée achieved a pure, modern classicism. His greatest influence was as a teacher and theorist. In a series of theoretical plans for public monuments, culminating in the design for an immense sphere that would serve as a cenotaph honoring Isaac Newton (1784), he gave imaginary form to his theories.

Boulogne, Jean See Giambologna

Boulsover \'bōl-,zō-vər\, **Thomas** (1706–1788) British inventor of fused plating ("old Sheffield plate"). As a craftsman of the Cutlers Co. in 1743, while repairing a copper-and-silver knife handle, he discovered that the two metals could be fused and that when the fused metals were rolled in a rolling mill they behaved like a single metal. His invention opened the way to economical production of a great variety of plated objects, from buttons and snuffboxes, which he himself made, to hollowware (e.g., tea sets) and utensils, which were soon manufactured in large quantity by other Sheffield workers.

Boulton \'bōlt-^{ə}n\, **Matthew** (1728–1809) British manufacturer and engineer. With James Watt and William Murdock (1754–1839), he established the steam-engine industry by installing pumping engines to drain the Cornish tin mines. Foreseeing great industrial demand for steam power, he urged Watt to make various design improvements. Applying steam power to coining machinery, he made large quantities of coins for the British East India Co. and also supplied machinery to the Royal Mint. By 1800, almost 500 steam engines had been installed in the British Isles and abroad.

Boumédienne \bü-mād-'yen\, **Houari** *orig.* **Muhammad ben Brahim Boukharouba** (1927–1978) Algerian political leader and president (1965–1978). During Algeria's fight for independence, he helped raise an Algerian army in the safety of Morocco and Tunisia. He deposed Pres. Ahmed Ben Bella in 1965. His policies in the 1970s created tensions with Morocco and France, but he also negotiated important industrial contracts with Western nations and cultivated close relations with the Soviet bloc, becoming a leading figure in the nonaligned movement.

boundary layer In fluid mechanics, a thin layer of flowing gas or liquid in contact with a surface (e.g., of an airplane wing or the inside of a pipe). The fluid in the boundary layer is subjected to shear forces. A range of velocities is established across the boundary layer, from zero (provided the fluid is in contact with the surface) to maximum. Flow in boundary layers is more easily described mathematically than is flow in the free stream. Boundary layers are thinner at the leading edge of an aircraft wing and thicker toward the trailing edge; such boundary layers generally have laminar flow in the leading (upstream) portion and turbulent flow in the trailing (downstream) portion. See also drag.

Bounty, HMS British armed transport ship remembered for the mutiny of its crew on April 28, 1789. Commanded by Capt. William Bligh (1754–1817), it had sailed to Tahiti, taken on a cargo of breadfruit trees, and traveled as far as the Friendly Islands (Tonga) on the voyage to Jamaica when it was seized by the master's mate, Fletcher Christian (1764–1790/93?). The causes have been much debated; Bligh's opponents charged him with tyranny, while Bligh argued that the mutineers had become attached to Tahiti and its women. Bligh and 18 loyal crew members were set adrift in a longboat; after a voyage of more than two weeks and some 3,600 mi (5,800 km), they reached Timor. Christian and eight others took the *Bounty* to Pitcairn Island, where the small colony they founded remained undiscovered until 1808 and where their descendants still live. Of the mutineers who later went to Tahiti, three were taken to Britain and hanged.

bourbon See whiskey

Bourbon, Charles-Ferdinand de See duc de Berry

Bourbon \bür-'bō^{n}, *Engl* 'bu̇r-bən\, **House of** One of the most important ruling houses of Europe. Its members were descended from Louis I, duc de Bourbon from 1327 to 1342, grandson of the French king Louis IX. Bourbons subsequently ruled in France (1589–1792, 1814–48); in Spain (1700–1868, 1870–73, 1874–1931, and since 1975); and in Naples and Sicily (1735–1861). Among its prominent members were Henry IV, Louis XIII, Louis XIV, Louis XV, Louis XVI, and Philip V.

Bourbon Restoration (1814–30) In France, the period that began when NAPOLEON abdicated and the BOURBON monarchs were restored to the throne. The First Restoration occurred when Napoleon fell from power and LOUIS XVIII became king. Louis's reign was interrupted by Napoleon's return to France (see HUNDRED DAYS), but Napoleon was forced to abdicate again, leading to the Second Restoration. The period was marked by a constitutional monarchy of moderate rule (1816–20), followed by a return of the ULTRAS during the reign of Louis's brother, CHARLES X (1824–30). Reactionary policies revived the opposition liberals and moderates and led to the JULY REVOLUTION, Charles's abdication, and the end of the Bourbon Restoration.

Bourbonnais \ˌbür-bȯ-ˈne\ Historical region, central France. In Roman times it was part of Celtic GAUL under Julius CAESAR, and later part of Aquitania under AUGUSTUS. It gradually began a separate existence in the 10th century under a lord of Bourbon. It eventually passed to Louis, created duc de Bourbon in 1327, the ancestor of the BOURBON dynasty. Bourbonnais became part of the royal domain in 1527.

Bourdieu \bür-ˈdyœ̄\, **Pierre** (born 1930) French sociologist and anthropologist known for his critical studies on culture and education. Bourdieu introduced the concept of cultural capital, wealth based on SOCIAL STATUS and education, noting that success in school and society depends largely on the individual's ability to absorb the cultural ethos, or *habitus,* of the dominant class. Influenced by STRUCTURALISM, he has suggested that the habitus is similar to yet more fundamental than a language. His works include *Outline of a Theory of Praxis* (1977), *Reproduction in Education, Society and Culture* (1977), and *Distinction* (1984).

Bourgeois \bür-ˈzhwä\, **Léon (-Victor-Auguste)** (1851–1925) French politician. He entered the civil service in 1876 and was elected to the National Assembly in 1888. He served in several ministerial posts and was briefly premier (1895–96). He was a member of the Senate 1905–23, and its president from 1920. An advocate of international cooperation, he was appointed to the INTERNATIONAL COURT OF JUSTICE in 1903. In 1919 he was France's representative to the LEAGUE OF NATIONS, emerging as its champion. In 1920 he was awarded the Nobel Peace Prize.

Bourgeois \bür-ˈzhwä\, **Louise** (born 1911) French-U.S. sculptor. Born in Paris, she studied briefly with FERNAND LEGER and initially worked as a painter and engraver. In the late 1940s, after moving to New York with her American husband, she turned to sculpture. She achieved recognition in the 1950s with wooden constructions painted uniformly black or white. She has also worked in marble, plaster, latex, and glass. Though her works @T:are abstract, they are suggestive of the human figure and express themes of betrayal, anxiety, and loneliness.

bourgeoisie \ˌbu̇rzh-ˌwä-ˈzē\ In socioeconomic theory, the social order dominated by the property-owning class. The term arose in medieval France, referring to craftsmen who occupied the social tier between rural landlords and the peasantry. With the INDUSTRIAL REVOLUTION, economic relationships began to diverge into employer and employee classes, creating a sharp social divide. The class consciousness that arose tended to identify employers (capitalists) as the bourgeoisie and workers as the PROLETARIAT. The term, much employed by 19th-century social reformers, is less commonly used today. See also social CLASS.

Bourges, Pragmatic Sanction of See PRAGMATIC SANCTION OF BOURGES

Bourguiba \bu̇r-ˈgē-bə\, **Habib (ibn Ali)** (1903–2000) President of Tunisia (1957–87). He studied at the Sorbonne, where he met independence-minded Algerians and Moroccans. He founded a nationalist newspaper in 1932. In 1934 he founded the Neo-Destour Party and became central to the Tunisian liberation movement. After imprisoning him three times, the French negotiated independence with him in 1956. The Tunisian monarchy was abolished in 1957, and Bourguiba became president. During his 30 years in office he kept the army small and devoted much of the budget to education and health. Made president for life in 1975, he had to be removed in 1987 because of ill health. See also ZINE AL-ABIDINE BEN ALI.

Bourke-White \ˌbərk-ˈhwīt\, **Margaret** (1904–1971) U.S. photographer. Born in New York City, she began her professional career as an industrial and architectural photographer in 1927. She gained a reputation for originality, and in 1929 was hired by HENRY R. LUCE for his magazine *Fortune*. She covered World War II for *Life* magazine as the first woman photographer to serve with the U.S. armed forces. Several collections of her photographs have been published, including *You Have Seen Their Faces* (1937), about sharecroppers of the American South.

Bournemouth \ˈbōrn-məth\ Seaside resort (pop., 1992 est.: 159,000), DORSET, southern England, located on the ENGLISH CHANNEL. It dates from 1810 but did not grow rapidly until after the coming of the railway in 1870. Predominantly a resort and residential town, it is one of England's main convention centers and is popular with retirees.

Bournonville \ˈbōr-nōn-ˌvē-lə\, **August** (1805–1879) Danish dancer, choreographer, and director of the Royal Danish Ballet for almost 50 years. After studying and performing in Paris and Copenhagen, he became director and choreographer of the Royal Danish Ballet in 1830, where he continued to dance until 1848. He collaborated with Danish composers, and influences absorbed during his European tours blended into his unique style based on bravura dancing and expressive mime. Many of his works, including *La sylphide* (1836), *Napoli* (1842), and *A Folk Tale* (1854), remain in the company's repertoire.

Boutros-Ghali \ˈbü-trōs-ˈgä-lē\, **Boutros** (born 1922) Sixth secretary-general of the UNITED NATIONS (1992–96), the first Arab and first African to hold the office. A descendant of a distinguished Egyptian Coptic family, he was educated at Cairo University and the University of Paris. After teaching at universities around the world, he joined Egypt's foreign ministry in 1977. As foreign minister he accompanied Pres. ANWAR AL-SADAT to Jerusalem. He became Egypt's deputy prime minister in 1991 and was appointed U.N. secretary-general in 1992. During his single term he oversaw peacekeeping operations in Bosnia, Somalia, and Rwanda and led the U.N. in its 50th-anniversary celebration. In 1996 the U.S. blocked his bid for a second term.

Bouts \ˈbau̇ts\, **Dirck** (c. 1415–1475) Netherlandish painter. Born in Haarlem, he was active in Louvain, where he was influenced by ROGIER VAN DER WEYDEN. His best-known works are a triptych altarpiece (1464) for the church of St. Peter in Louvain, its panels representing the Last Supper and four Old Testament scenes, and two huge panels representing a scene of secular justice (1470–75) for the city hall, intended as examples of justice for the Louvain town council. His treatment of his figures ranges from strong emotion expressed through symbolic gesture to great severity and restraint.

Bouvines \bü-ˈvēn\, **Battle of** (July 27, 1214) Decisive victory won by the French king PHILIP II over an international coalition that included Emperor OTTO IV, King JOHN of England, and several powerful French vassals. Fought in the marshy plain between Bouvines and Tournai in Flanders, the battle was furiously contested but ended in a clear French victory. It confirmed Philip's possession of French lands formerly held by the English and added to the power and prestige of the French monarchy. John's defeat increased the opposition of his barons.

bouzouki \bu̇-ˈzü-kē\ Long-necked lute used in Greek popular music. Developed from a Turkish instrument early in the 20th century, it has a pear-shaped body and a fretted fingerboard. The modern instrument usually has four courses of strings, which are plucked with a plectrum, typically in a vigorous and agile style.

Boveri \bō-ˈvā-rē\, **Theodor Heinrich** (1862–1915) German cell biologist. Working with roundworm eggs, Boveri proved that chromosomes are separate units within the nucleus of a cell. With WALTER S. SUTTON, he was the first to propose that genes were located on chromosomes. Boveri proved Edouard von Beneden's theory that the ovum (egg) and sperm cell contribute equal numbers of chromosomes to the new cell created during fertilization. He later introduced the term centrosome and demonstrated that this structure is the division center for a dividing egg cell.

bovid \ˈbō-vid\ Any RUMINANT of the family Bovidae. Bovids have hollow, unbranched, permanently attached horns; they are grazing or browsing animals found in both the Eastern and Western Hemispheres, most often in grasslands, scrublands, or deserts. Most species live in large herds. Species range in shoulder height from a 10-in. (25-cm) ANTELOPE to the 6.5-ft (2-m) BISON. Some of the 138 species (including domestic CATTLE, SHEEP, GOATS) are of economic value to humans. Others (including BIGHORN and some antelope) are hunted for food, sport, horns, or hides. See also BUFFALO, RUMINANT.

Bow \'bō\, **Clara** (1905–1965) U.S. film actress. Born in Brooklyn, N.Y., she escaped poverty at 16 by winning a magazine contest that gave her a bit part in a film. Hired by Paramount Pictures in 1925, she played larger roles in such films as *Mantrap* (1926) and *Kid Boots* (1926). After her starring role as a flapper in the successful silent film *It* (1927), Bow was known as "the It girl," with "It" being understood as the appeal of the liberated young woman. She starred in 20 more films (1927–30), but scandals and nervous breakdowns undermined her career. She retired in 1933 and spent her later years in mental institutions.

Clara Bow.
BROWN BROTHERS

bow and arrow Weapon consisting of a strip of wood or other flexible material, bent and held in tension by a string. The arrow, a long wooden shaft with a pointed tip, is stabilized in flight by a feathered tail. The arrow is fitted to the string by a notch in the end of the shaft and is drawn back to produce tension in the bow, which propels the arrow when the string is released. Bow construction ranges from wood, bone, and metal to plastic and fiberglass; arrowheads have been made from stone, bone, and metal. The origins of the bow and arrow are prehistoric. The bow was a primary military weapon from Egyptian times through the Middle Ages in the Mediterranean world and Europe and even longer in China and Japan. The Huns, Turks, Mongols, and other peoples of the Eurasian steppes excelled in warfare as mounted archers; horse archers were the most deadly weapon system of pre-gunpowder warfare. The CROSSBOW, the compound bow, and the English LONGBOW made the arrow a formidable battlefield missile. The powerful Turkish bow had a great impact on warfare in the late Middle Ages. In many cultures, the bow's importance in warfare has been secondary to its value as a hunting weapon. It is still sometimes used for recreational hunting. See also ARCHERY.

Bow porcelain \'bō\ English soft-paste PORCELAIN made at a factory in Stratford-le-Bow, Essex, c. 1744–76. From 1750 bone ash was used in its production by Thomas Frye, an Irish engraver, who invented the process. Bow varies in appearance and quality, but at its best has a soft, creamy-white tone with a smooth glaze. Bow tablewares were among the first English porcelain to be ornamented with transfer-printed decorations (see BATTERSEA ENAMELWARE). Bow also produced great quantities of figurines (e.g., statesmen, actors, birds, animals) in the ROCOCO STYLE.

Bow River \'bō\ River, Alberta. Rising in BANFF NATIONAL PARK on the eastern slopes of the ROCKY MTNS., it flows 315 mi (507 km) southeast through the park and east past CALGARY to unite with the Oldman River and form the SASKATCHEWAN RIVER. It is important for hydroelectric power and irrigation. Bow Valley Provincial Park is 50 mi (80 km) west of Calgary.

Bowditch \'bau̇d-ich\, **Nathaniel** (1773–1838) U.S. mathematician and astronomer. Born in Salem, Mass., he was largely self-educated. After investigating the accuracy of J. H. Moore's *The Practical Navigator*, he produced a revised edition in 1799. In 1802 he published *The New American Practical Navigator*; adopted by the U.S. Department of the Navy, it was recognized as the best navigation text of its time. He translated and updated four volumes of PIERRE-SIMON LAPLACE's *Celestial Mechanics* (1829–39). He discovered the Bowditch curves (describing the motion of a pendulum), which have important applications in astronomy and physics. He refused professorships at several universities, and instead worked for insurance companies.

Bowdler, Thomas (1754–1825) English physician, philanthropist, and man of letters. He is known for his *Family Shakspeare* (1818), in which, by expurgation and paraphrase, he aimed to provide an edition of the plays suitable for a father to read aloud to his family without fear of offending their susceptibilities or corrupting their minds. The first edition (1807) contained a selection of 20 plays that probably were expurgated by Bowdler's sister, Harriet.

Bowdoin College \'bō-dᵊn\ Private liberal-arts college in Brunswick, Me. Founded in 1794 as a men's college, it was named for James Bowdoin (1726–1790), first president of the American Academy of Arts and Sciences. It became coeducational in 1971. It offers bachelor's degrees in the natural sciences, social sciences, arts, and humanities. Academic facilities include a marine research station and an arctic museum. Its historic buildings include the Walker Art Building, designed by CHARLES F. MCKIM and STANFORD WHITE. Enrollment is about 1,600.

bowel movement See DEFECATION

Bowen \'bō-ən\, **Elizabeth (Dorothea Cole)** (1899–1973) British (Irish-born) novelist and short-story writer. Among her novels are *The House in Paris* (1935), *The Death of the Heart* (1938), and *The Heat of the Day* (1949). Her short-story collections include *The Demon Lover* (1945). Her finely wrought prose style frequently details uneasy and unfulfilling relationships among the upper middle class. Her essays appear in *Collected Impressions* (1950) and *Afterthought* (1962).

Bowen, Norman L(evi) (1887–1956) Canadian geologist. Born in Kingston, Ontario, he worked on and off for more than 35 years for the Geophysical Laboratory in Washington, D.C., where he researched silicate systems. During World War I he made a brief foray into optics, but after the war he returned to his studies of silicate systems. In 1928 he published *The Evolution of the Igneous Rocks,* which had a profound influence on petrologic thought. At the University of Chicago (1937–47) he developed a school of experimental PETROLOGY. His achievements won him honors both in the U.S. and Europe.

bowerbird \'bau̇(-ə)r-ˌbərd\ Any of 17 bird species constituting the PASSERINE family Ptilonorhynchidae, of Australia, New Guinea, and nearby islands. The male builds an elaborate structure (the bower) on the ground, decorates it with bright and shiny objects, and displays and sings loudly above it; females visit him and then lay their eggs in simple nests nearby. The mat, or platform, type of bower is a thick pad of plant material. The maypole type is a hut (sometimes as large as a child's playhouse) of twigs erected around one or more saplings in a cleared court. The avenue type consists of two close-set parallel walls of sticks on a circular mat of twigs. See also CATBIRD.

Bowes, Edward *known as* **Major Bowes** (1874–1946) U.S. radio personality. Born in San Francisco, he became a partner in a real-estate firm that owned theaters in New York and Boston. He promoted attendance at New York's Capitol Theatre by starting a variety show, the *Major Bowes Capitol Family,* which became the radio program *Original Amateur Hour* (1935–46). The show (later revived for television as *The Ted Mack Original Amateur Hour)* gave aspiring singers and comedians, including F. SINATRA and BOB HOPE, a chance to perform before a national radio audience; contestants were sought out by traveling amateur shows.

bowfin \'bō-ˌfin\ Voracious freshwater fish *(Amia calva)* that is the only living representative of the family Amiidae, which dates back to the JURASSIC PERIOD (206–144 million years ago). It is found in sluggish North American waters from the Great Lakes southward to the Gulf of Mexico. Mottled green and brown, it has a long dorsal fin and strong conical teeth. The female, which is larger than the male, reaches a length of 30 in. (75 cm). The bowfin spawns in spring, when the male constructs a crude nest and guards both the fertilized eggs and the newly hatched young. It is sometimes called a dogfish.

Bowie \'bō-ē\, **David** *orig.* **David Robert Jones** (born 1947) British rock singer. In the mid-1960s Bowie sang in a number of bands in his native London. He changed his name in 1966 to avoid confusion with the lead singer of The Monkees. His first hit album, *Space Oddity* (1969), and such later albums as *The Rise and Fall of Ziggy Stardust and the Spiders From Mars* (1972) ushered in the glitter-rock trend, marked by theatricality and androgyny. He collaborated on hit recordings with JOHN LENNON *(Young Americans)* and BING CROSBY *(Peace on Earth),* starred on stage in *The Elephant Man,* and appeared in such films as *The Man Who Fell to Earth* (1976).

Bowie \'bü-ē\, **Jim** *orig.* **James** (1796?–1836) U.S. soldier. Born in Logan Co., Ky., he lived in Louisiana, where he owned a sugar plantation and served in the state legislature. In 1828 he settled in Texas, assumed Mexican citizenship, acquired land grants, and married the vice-governor's daughter. In opposition to Mexican legislation to curb the emigration of white settlers, he joined the Texas revolutionary movement and became a colonel in the Texas army. He is remembered for his death leading the forces at the Alamo. He invented the knife that bears his name and became a legendary hero through Western song and ballad.

Bowles \'bōlz\, **Chester (Bliss)** (1901–1986) U.S. advertising executive and diplomat. Born in Springfield, Mass., he graduated from Yale University. In 1929 he and William Benton established the Benton and Bowles advertising company, which became one of the largest in the world. After selling his interest in 1941, Bowles served as director of the Federal Price Administration 1943–46. Elected governor of Connecticut in 1948, he was defeated in 1950 because of his liberal stand on civil rights. He was ambassador to India 1951–53, served in the U.S. House of Representatives 1953–61, and returned to India as ambassador 1963–69.

Bowles, Paul (Frederick) (1910–1999) U.S.-Moroccan composer, writer, and translator. Born in New York City, he studied composition with A. Copland and wrote music for over 30 plays and films. He moved to Morocco in the 1940s. He set his best-known novel *The Sheltering Sky* (1948; film, 1990) in Tangier; as in that novel, his protagonists are often Westerners maimed by their contact with traditional cultures that bewilder them, and violent events and psychological collapse are recounted in a detached and elegant style. His wife, Jane Bowles (1917–1973), is known for the novel *Two Serious Ladies* (1943) and the play *In the Summer House* (1953).

bowling Game in which a heavy ball is rolled down a long, narrow lane to knock down a group of 10 wooden objects (called pins). Versions of the game have existed since ancient times. Ninepin bowling was brought to the U.S. in the 17th century by Dutch settlers; it became so popular and so associated with gambling that it was outlawed in several states. According to legend, a tenth pin was added in the 18th century to circumvent such laws. The game grew to enormous popularity in the 20th century, both as a recreational activity and (since 1958) as a professional sport. Each game is divided into 10 frames, and each player is allowed to deliver up to two balls per frame. If all the pins are knocked down on the first ball, a strike is recorded (10 points). If pins remain standing, and the second ball knocks them down, the player is awarded a spare (10 points). If a strike is thrown in a frame, the number of pins knocked down by the next two balls bowled count in that frame. After a spare, the score of the next ball counts in the spare's frame. Thus, the maximum point total for a single frame is 30. A perfect score is 300, or 12 strikes in a row. Versions of the game include candlepins, duckpins, and skittles.

bowls *or* **lawn bowls** *or* **lawn bowling** Bowling game similar to the Italian boccie and the French boules played on a green with wooden balls (called bowls) that are rolled at a target ball (the jack). The object is to roll one's bowls so that they come to rest nearer to the jack than those of an opponent, sometimes achieved by knocking aside an opponent's bowl or jack. One point is awarded for each winning bowl. Depending on the game, players use four, three, or two bowls, and games end at 18 or 21 points.

Bowman \'bō-mən\, **William** *later* **Sir William** (1816–1892) English surgeon and histologist. His studies of organ tissues with his teacher Robert Todd led to major papers on the structure and function of voluntary muscle and of the kidneys and on the detailed anatomy of the liver. In the kidneys, he found that the capsule (Bowman's capsule) surrounding each glomerulus (ball of capillaries) in the nephrons is a continuous part of the renal duct. This was of prime importance to his filtration theory of urine formation, key to understanding kidney function. Bowman and Todd published *The Physiological Anatomy and Physiology of Man* (5 vols., 1845–56), a pioneering work in both physiology and histology. Turning to the eye, Bowman became one of the world's foremost ophthalmic research scientists and London's outstanding eye surgeon, and the first to describe several eye structures and their functions.

box In botany, an evergreen shrub or small tree (genus *Buxus*) of the box family (Buxaceae), best known for the ornamental and useful boxwoods. The family comprises seven genera of trees, shrubs, and herbaceous plants, native to North America, Europe, North Africa, and Asia. The plants bear male and female flowers, without petals, on separate plants. The leathery, evergreen leaves are simple and alternate. Fruits are one- or two-seeded capsules or drupes. Three species of the genus *Buxus* provide the widely grown boxwood: the common, or English, box *(B. sempervirens),* used for hedges, borders, and topiary figures; the Japanese box *(B. microphylla);* and the tall boxwood tree *(B. balearica).*

box elder Hardy and fast-growing tree *(Acer negundo),* also called ash-leaved maple, of the maple family, native to the central and eastern U.S. Its compound leaves (rare among maples) consist of three, five, or seven coarsely toothed leaflets. The single seed is borne in a samara (dry, winged fruit). Because of its rapid growth and its drought resistance, it was widely planted for shade by early settlers in the prairie regions of the U.S. Maple syrup and sugar are sometimes obtained from the box elder. Its wood is used for crates, furniture, paper pulp, and charcoal.

box turtle Any of several species of terrestrial turtle (genus *Terrapene*) found in the U.S. and Mexico. Box turtles have a high, rounded upper shell (carapace) that grows to a maximum length of about 7 in. (18 cm). The lower shell (plastron) is hinged across the center and can be drawn very tightly against the carapace to form a protective "box" that completely encloses the turtle's soft parts. They feed on earthworms, insects, mushrooms, and berries. Box turtles are often kept as pets.

Box turtle (*Terrapene carolina*).
JOHN H. GERARD—EB INC.

boxer Smooth-haired breed of working dog named for its manner of "boxing" with its sturdy front paws when beginning to fight. Developed in Germany, it includes strains of bulldog and terrier in its heritage. Because of its reputation for courage, aggressiveness, and intelligence, it has been used in police work; it is also valued as a watchdog and companion. Trim and squarely built, it has a short, square muzzle; a black mask on its face; and a shiny, shorthaired coat of reddish brown or brindle. It stands 21–24 in. (53–61 cm) high and weighs 60–70 lbs (27–32 kg).

Boxer.
SALLY ANNE THOMPSON—EB INC.

Boxer Rebellion Officially supported peasant uprising in 1900 in China that attempted to drive all foreigners from the country. "Boxer" was the English name given to a Chinese secret society that practiced boxing and calisthenic rituals that they believed would make them impervious to bullets. Support for them grew in northern China during the late 19th century, when China's people were suffering from growing economic impoverishment and the nation was forced to grant humiliating concessions to Western powers. In June 1900 an international relief force was dispatched to deal with the growing threat the Boxers posed. The empress dowager, Cixi, ordered imperial forces to block its advance; the conflict escalated and was not resolved until August, when Beijing was captured and sacked. Hostilities were ended with a protocol that required massive reparations to the U.S., Germany, and other foreign powers. See also U.S. Open Door policy.

boxing Sport involving attack and defense with the fists. In the modern sport, boxers wear padded gloves and fight bouts of up to 12 three-minute rounds in a roped-off square known as the ring. In ancient Greece fighters used leather thongs on their hands and forearms, while in Rome gladiators used metal-studded leather hand covering *(cesti)* and usually fought to the death. Not until implementation of the London Prize Ring rules in 1839 were kicking, gouging, butting, biting, and blows below the belt eliminated from the boxer's standard repertoire. In 1867 the Queensberry rules called for the wearing of gloves, though bare-knuckle boxing continued into the late 1880s. The last of the great bare-knuckle fighters was John L. Sullivan. From Sullivan on, the U.S. became the premier boxing venue, partly because immigrants supplied a constantly renewed pool of boxers. Boxing has been included among the Olympic Games since 1904. Today there are 17 primary weight classes in professional boxing: strawweight, to 105 lbs (48 kg); junior flyweight, to 108 lbs (49 kg); flyweight, to 112 lbs (51 kg); junior bantamweight, to 115 lbs (52 kg); bantamweight, to 118 lbs (53.5 kg); junior featherweight, to 122 lbs (55 kg); featherweight, to 126 lbs (57 kg); junior lightweight, to 130 lbs (59 kg); lightweight, to 135 lbs (61 kg); junior welterweight, 140 lbs (63.5 kg); welterweight, to 147 lbs (67 kg); junior middleweight, 154 lbs (70 kg); middleweight, to 160 lbs (72.5 kg); super middleweight, 168 lbs (76 kg); light heavyweight, to 175 lbs (79 kg); cruiserweight, 195 lbs (88 kg); and heavyweight, over 195 lbs. A bout can be won either by knocking out or felling one's opponent for a count of 10 (a KO) or by delivering the most solid blows and thus amassing the most points. The referee can also stop the fight when one boxer is being badly beaten (a technical knockout, or TKO) or he can disqualify a fighter for rules violations and award the fight to his opponent.

Boy Scouts See SCOUTING

boyars \bō-ˈyärz\ Upper class of medieval Russian society and state administration. In KIEVAN RUS (10th–12th century) the boyars belonged to the prince's retinue, holding posts in the army and civil administration and advising the prince in matters of state through a boyar council, or DUMA. In the 13th–14th century, the boyars constituted a privileged class of rich landowners in northeastern Russia. In the 15th–17th century, the boyars of Muscovy ruled the country along with the grand prince (later the CZAR) and legislated through the boyar council. Their importance declined in the 17th century, and the title was abolished by PETER I in the early 18th century.

boycott Collective and organized ostracism applied in labor, economic, political, or social relations to protest and punish practices considered unfair. The tactic was popularized by CHARLES STEWART PARNELL to protest high rents and land evictions in Ireland in 1880 by the estate manager Charles C. Boycott (1832–1897). Boycotts are principally used by labor organizations to win improved wages and working conditions or by consumers to pressure companies to change their hiring, labor, environmental, or investment practices. U.S. law distinguishes between primary boycotts (refusal by employees to purchase the goods or services of their employers) and secondary boycotts (pleas to third parties to also shun the target), the latter being illegal in most states. Boycotts were used as a tactic in the U.S. civil-rights movement of the 1950s and '60s and have also been applied in recent years to influence the conduct of multinational corporation.

Boyden, Seth (1788–1870) U.S. inventor. Born in Foxboro, Mass., he worked in Newark, N.J., inventing processes for making patent leather (1819), malleable cast iron, till then a European trade secret (1825), and sheet iron. He also designed a hat-shaping machine, and he manufactured locomotives and stationary steam engines.

Boyden, Uriah Atherton (1804–1879) U.S. inventor. The brother of SETH BOYDEN, he is known for his improvements to the water TURBINE. To the first successful water turbine (built by BENOIT FOURNEYRON in 1827), Boyden in 1844 added an outlet diffuser to recover part of the kinetic energy exiting the device, greatly improving its efficiency.

Boyer \bwä-ˈyā\, **Charles** (1897–1978) French-U.S. actor. After earning a philosophy degree from the Sorbonne, he made his stage debut in Paris in 1920. He became a popular romantic leading man in French theater and film, and his rich, accented voice and suave manner made him an international star. His first successful U.S. film, *Private Worlds* (1935), was followed by such films as *Algiers* (1938), *Gaslight* (1944), and *Stavisky* (1974). He cofounded Four Star Television in 1951 and starred in many of its productions. His most notable stage appearance was in *Don Juan in Hell*.

Boyle, Kay (1902–1992) U.S. writer. Born in St. Paul, Minn., Boyle married a French student and lived in Europe during the 1920s and '30s. Later she served as a European correspondent for the *New Yorker* (1946–53). Her writing is noted for its elegant style and consistently leftist stance. Her novels, which include *Plagued by the Nightingale* (1931) and *Generation Without Farewell* (1960), are less highly regarded than her short stories, including "The White Horses of Vienna," "Keep Your Pity," and "Defeat."

Boyle, Robert (1627–1691) Irish-English chemist and natural philosopher. The son of Richard Boyle, the "Great Earl of Cork" (1566–1643), he settled in Oxford in 1654 and, with his assistant ROBERT HOOKE, began his pioneering experiments on the properties of GASES, including those expressed in Boyle's law (see GAS LAWS). He demonstrated the physical characteristics of AIR, showing that it is necessary in combustion, respiration, and sound transmission. In *The Sceptical Chymist* (1661) he attacked ARISTOTLE's theory of the four elements (earth, air, fire, and water), espousing a corpuscular view of matter that presaged the modern theory of chemical elements. A founding member of the Royal Society of London, he achieved great renown in his lifetime. His brother Roger Boyle, Earl of Orrery (1621–1679), was a general under OLIVER CROMWELL, but eventually helped secure Ireland for CHARLES II.

Boyne, Battle of the (July 1690) Victory in Ireland for WILLIAM III of England, a Protestant, over the former king JAMES II, a Roman Catholic. James was attempting, with the help of the French and the Irish, to regain his throne. In this battle, fought on the banks of the River Boyne, some 35,000 men under William defeated about 21,000 of James's troops, forcing James to flee the country. The battle is celebrated in Northern Ireland as a victory for the Protestant cause.

boysenberry Very large BRAMBLE fruit, usually considered, along with the LOGANBERRY and the youngberry, a variety of BLACKBERRY *(Rubus ursinus)*. The dark, reddish-black fruit is especially valued for canning and preserving. It is grown chiefly in the southern and southwestern U.S. and on the Pacific Coast from southern California into Oregon. It was developed in the early 1920s by Rudolph Boysen (1895–1950) of Napa, Cal.

BP See BRITISH PETROLEUM CO. PLC

Brabant \ˈbrä-bänt\ Old duchy, northwestern Europe. Located in what is now the southern Netherlands and central and northern Belgium, the region in the 9th century AD was part of the kingdom of Lotharingia. In the late 12th century it became independent; it finally passed to the house of BURGUNDY in 1430. Inherited by the HABSBURGS in 1477, it became a center of culture and commerce (see ANTWERP and BRUSSELS). The northern section of Brabant took part in a revolt from Spain, and in 1609 was awarded to the United Provinces, while the southern section remained part of Spanish (later Austrian) Netherlands. The northern section now forms the Dutch province of North Brabant. The southern section eventually became part of Belgium and is divided between the provinces of Flemish Brabant and Walloon Brabant.

Bracciolini, Gian Francesco Poggio See G. F. POGGIO BRACCIOLINI

bracken *or* **brake** Any FERN of the genus *Pteridium,* represented by a single species *(P. aquilinum)* with 12 varieties found throughout the world in temperate and tropical regions. It has a perennial black rootstock, which creeps extensively underground and at intervals sends up fronds that may reach a height of 15 ft (5 m) or more. Though they die in autumn, the fronds often remain standing throughout winter, in some areas affording cover for game. Humans use the fronds for thatching and as fodder.

bracket fungus *or* **shelf fungus** BASIDIOMYCETE that forms shelflike sporophores (SPORE-producing organs). Bracket fungi are commonly found growing on trees or fallen logs in damp woodlands. They can severely damage cut lumber and stands of timber. Specimens 16 in. (40 cm) or more in diameter are not uncommon.

bract Modified, usually small leaflike structure often positioned beneath a flower or INFLORESCENCE. What are often taken to be the petals of flowers are sometimes bracts—for example, the large, colorful bracts of POINSETTIAS or the showy white or pink bracts of DOGWOOD blossoms.

Bradbury, Ray (Douglas) (born 1920) U.S. author. Born in Waukegan, Ill., he is best known for highly imaginative science-fiction stories and novels that blend social criticism with an awareness of the hazards of runaway technology. *The Martian Chronicles* (1950) is considered a science-fiction classic. His other short-story collections include *The Illustrated Man* (1951; film, 1969), *The October Country* (1955), and *I Sing the Body Electric!* (1969); his novels include *Fahrenheit 451* (1953; film, 1966), *Dandelion Wine* (1957), and *Something Wicked This Way Comes* (1962).

Braddock, Edward (1695–1755) British army commander in the FRENCH AND INDIAN WAR. After service in Europe, he arrived in Virginia in 1755 to command British forces in North America against the French. He undertook an expedition to attack the French-held Fort Duquesne (now Pittsburgh, Pa.); his force, which included British regulars and provincial militiamen such as GEORGE WASHINGTON, cut the first road across the Allegheny Mountains and reached a point on the Monongahela River near the fort. There his army of over 1,400 men was ambushed and defeated by a group of 254 French and 600 Indians, and he was mortally wounded in the ensuing rout.

Bradford City (metro area pop., 1999 est.: 457,344), West Yorkshire, northern England. The manufacture of wool products was important to its economy as early as 1311; the fine worsted trade began in the late 17th century. By 1900 it emerged as the main wool-buying center for Yorkshire. The city remains a center of the textile industry and is the site of the University of Bradford.

Bradford, William (1590–1657) American governor of the Plymouth Colony for 30 years. A member of the Separatist movement within Puritanism, in 1609 he left England and went to Holland seeking religious freedom. Finding a lack of economic opportunity there, in 1620 he helped organize an expedition of about 100 Pilgrims to the New World. He helped draft the Mayflower Compact aboard the group's ship, was unanimously chosen governor, and served as governor of the Plymouth Colony for all but five years from 1621 to 1656. He helped establish and foster the principles of self-government and religious freedom that characterized later American colonial government. His descriptive journal provides a unique source of both the voyage of the *Mayflower* and the challenges faced by the settlers.

Bradlee, Benjamin C(rowninshield) (born 1921) U.S. newspaper editor. Born in Boston, Bradlee was a reporter for the *Washington Post* before joining *Newsweek* in Paris and then in Washington. Returning to the *Post,* he served as its executive editor 1968–91. During his tenure the *Post* published the Pentagon Papers, broke much of the story surrounding the Watergate scandal, and was recognized as one of the most important and influential newspapers in the U.S. His books include *Conversations with Kennedy* (1975) and the memoir *A Good Life* (1995).

Bradley, Bill *in full* **William Warren Bradley** (born 1943) U.S. basketball player and politician. Born in Crystal City, Mo., Bradley attended Princeton University (1961–65), where, as a 6-ft 5-in. (1.96-m) playmaker and high-scoring forward, he was named College Player of the Year in 1964–65. In a semifinal game he scored 58 points, an NCAA play-off record. In 1964 he helped the U.S. team win the Olympic gold medal. He studied at Oxford University as a Rhodes scholar, then returned to play with the New York Knicks until 1977, helping them win two NBA championships (1970, 1973). As a prominent U.S. Senator from New Jersey (1979–97), he sought to raise public awareness of race relations and poverty and was a critic of campaign-financing practices. In 1999–2000 he was an unsuccessful candidate for president.

Bradley, F(rancis) H(erbert) (1846–1924) British idealist philosopher. Influenced by G. W. F. Hegel, he considered mind to be more fundamental than matter. In *Ethical Studies* (1876) he sought to expose the confusions in utilitarianism. In *The Principles of Logic* (1883) he denounced the psychology of the empiricists. His most ambitious work, *Appearance and Reality* (1893), maintained that reality is spiritual, but that that notion cannot be demonstrated because of the fatally abstract nature of human thought. Instead of ideas, he recommended feeling, the immediacy of which could embrace the harmonious nature of reality. He was the first English philosopher awarded the Order of Merit.

Bradley, Omar N(elson) (1893–1981) U.S. Army commander. Born in Clark, Mo., he graduated from West Point. He directed the army's infantry school at the start of World War II. In 1943 he commanded U.S. forces in the North Africa Campaign and contributed directly to the fall of Tunisia to the Allies, then led the successful Sicilian invasion. As commander of the 1st Army, he helped plan the invasion of France and took part in the Normandy Campaign and the liberation of Paris. As commander of the 12th Army, the largest U.S. force ever placed under one general, he oversaw European operations until the German surrender. After the war he was appointed head of veterans' affairs (1945–47) and chief of staff of the army (1948–49). Admired by both officers and men, he was chosen the first chairman of the Joint Chiefs of Staff (1949–53) and promoted to General of the Army (1950).

Bradley, Thomas (1917–1998) Mayor of Los Angeles (1973–93). Born in Calvert, Texas, he was reared in Los Angeles from age 7. In 1940 he began a 22-year tenure with the city's police department, earning a law degree. In 1963 he became the city's first African American council member, and in 1973 he was elected one of the nation's first two African American mayors of a major city (with Coleman Young). During five terms as mayor, he helped transform Los Angeles into a bustling business and trading center, overseeing massive growth and hosting the 1984 Olympic Games. He retired in 1992 after rioting broke out following the acquittal of police officers in the beating of Rodney King.

Bradman, Don (1908–2001) Australian cricketer. One of the greatest run scorers in the history of the game, in Test (international) matches Bradman scored 6,996 runs for Australia and set a record with his average of 99.94 runs per match. In 1948 he was captain of the Australian team that was victorious in England, four matches to none. He retired from first-class cricket in 1949 and was knighted in the same year. Bradman is often judged the greatest cricket player of the 20th century.

Bradstreet, Anne *orig.* **Anne Dudley** (1612?–1672) British-American poet, one of the first poets of the American colonies. At 18 she sailed from England with other Puritans to settle on Massachusetts Bay. She wrote many of her poems while rearing eight children. Without her knowledge, her brother-in-law took her poems to England, where they were published in 1650. She won critical acceptance in the 20th century, particularly for "Contemplations," a sequence of religious poems first published in the mid-19th century.

Brady, Mathew B. (1823–1896) U.S. photographer. Born near Lake George, N.Y., he learned to make daguerreotypes from Samuel F. B. Morse. In 1844 he opened the first of two studios in New York and began photographing famous people (including Daniel Webster, Edgar Allan Poe, and Henry Clay). In 1847 he opened a studio in Washington, D.C., and there created, copied, and collected portraits of U.S. presidents. He achieved international fame with *A Gallery of Illustrious Americans* (1850). In 1861 he set out to make a complete record of the Civil War with a staff of more than 20 photographers, including Timothy H. O'Sullivan and Alexander Gardner. He probably photographed the battles of Bull Run, Antietam, and Gettysburg himself.

Bragg, Braxton (1817–1876) U.S. and Confederate army officer. Born in Warrenton, N.C., he graduated from West Point and served in the Seminole Wars and Mexican War. When North Carolina seceded, he joined the Confederate army in the American Civil War. He was promoted to general in 1862 at the Battle of Shiloh. As commander of the Army of Tennessee, he led his troops to victory at the Battle of Chickamauga. His forces besieged the Union troops at Chattanooga but were eventually routed. He was relieved of his command but appointed military adviser to Jefferson Davis.

Braxton Bragg, engraving by George E. Perine.

BY COURTESY OF THE LIBRARY OF CONGRESS, WASHINGTON, D.C.

Bragg, William (Henry) *later* **Sir William** (1862–1942) Pioneer British scientist in solid-state physics. With his son (William) Lawrence Bragg (1890–1971), he shared a 1915 Nobel Prize for research on the determination of crystal structures and Lawrence's discovery (1912) of the Bragg law of X-ray diffraction. The Bragg ionization spectrometer William designed and built is the prototype of all modern X-ray and neutron diffractometers; the two men used it to make the first exact measurements of X-ray wavelengths and crystal data.

Bragg law Relation between the spacing of atomic planes in crystals and the angles of incidence at which the planes produce the most intense reflections of electromagnetic radiation and particle waves. The law, first formulated by Lawrence Bragg, is useful for measuring wavelengths and for determining the lattice spacings of crystals (see crystal lattice), and is the principal way to make precise energy measurements of X rays and low-energy gamma rays. See also William Bragg.

Brahe \'brä, 'brä-hē\, **Tycho** (1546–1601) Danish astronomer. Kidnapped by his wealthy but childless uncle, he was raised at the latter's castle and educated at the Univs. of Copenhagen and Leipzig. He traveled through Europe 1565–70, acquiring mathematical and astronomical instruments, and on inheriting his father's and uncle's estates he built a small observatory. In 1573 he reported his discovery of a new star, news that shook faith in the immutable heavens. With the aid of Denmark's King Frederick II, he built a new, larger observatory (Uraniborg), which became northern Europe's center of astronomical study and discovery. There he undertook a comprehensive study of the solar system and accurately charted the positions of more than 777 fixed stars. His pupil and assistant Johannes Kepler used the observational data left on Tycho's death to lay the groundwork for Isaac Newton's work.

Tycho Brahe, engraving by H. Goltzius of a drawing by an unknown artist, c. 1586.

BY COURTESY OF DET NATIONALHISTORISKE MUSEUM PAA FREDERIKSBORG, DENMARK

Brahma One of three major gods in late Vedic Hinduism, c. 500 BC–c. AD 500. He was gradually eclipsed by the other two, Vishnu and Shiva. In classical times the doctrine of Trimurti identified the three as aspects of a supreme deity. Brahma was associated with the creator god Prajapati, whose identity he came to assume. All temples of Shiva or Vishnu contain an image of Brahma, but today there is no sect or cult devoted exclusively to him.

brahma-loka \'brä-mə-'lō-kə\ In Hinduism and Buddhism, the realm of pious celestial spirits. In Theravada, it includes the 20 uppermost planes of existence. The lower 16 of these are the *rupa-brahma-loka,* material realms inhabited by progressively radiant gods. The highest four realms, the *arupa-brahma-loka,* are devoid of substance. Rebirth into these realms is the reward for great virtue and meditation; the level attained is determined by faithfulness to the Buddha, the dharma and the sangha. See also arupa-loka, rupa-loka.

Brahmagupta \,brə-mə-'gu̇p-tə\ (598–665) Indian mathematician and astronomer. His principal work, the *Brahma-sphuta-siddhanta* ("The Opening of the Universe"), most of which deals with planetary motion, also contains important proofs of various geometrical theorems on quadratic equations, the geometry of right triangles, and the properties of geometric solids.

Brahman In the Upanishads, the eternal, infinite, and omnipresent spiritual source of the finite and changing universe. The schools of Vedanta differ in interpreting Brahman. The Advaita school defines Brahman as categorically different from any phenomenon, conceiving it as an absolute reality onto which human perceptions of differentiation are projected. The Bhedabheda school maintains that Brahman is not different from the world it produces. The Visistadvaita school holds that phenomenality is a glorious manifestation of Brahman. The Dvaita school maintains that both soul and matter are separate from and dependent on Brahman.

Brahman *or* **Brahmin** Any member of the highest of the four varnas, or social classes, in Hindu India. Their existence as a priestly caste dates to the late Vedic period, and they have long been considered to be of greater ritual purity than members of other castes and alone to be capable of performing certain religious tasks, including preservation of the collections of Vedic hymns. Because of their high prestige and tradition of education, they dominated Indian scholarship for centuries. As the spiritual and intellectual elite, they advised the politically powerful warrior caste, and after Indian independence they supplied many heads of state. They still retain traditional privileges, though these are no longer legally sanctioned. Ritual purity is maintained through taboos, vegetarianism, and abstention from certain occupations.

Brahman \'brā-mən\ *or* **zebu** \'zē-,bü\ Any of several varieties of cattle that originated in India and were crossbred in the U.S. with improved beef breeds, producing the hardy beef animal known as the Santa Gertrudis. Similar blending in Latin America resulted in the breed known as Indo-Brazil. The Brahman is characterized by a pronounced hump over the shoulder and neck, horns that usually curve up and back, and drooping ears. Gray is the prevalent color, with deep shading in the fore and rear quarters of the bull. A red strain has also been developed.

Brahmana \'brä-mə-nə\ Any of a number of discourses on the Vedas that explain their use in ritual sacrifices and the symbolism of the priests' actions. Dating to 900–600 BC, they constitute the oldest historical sources for Indian ritual. The *Aitareya* and *Kausitaki Brahmana,* compiled by followers of the Rig Veda, include discussions of daily sacrifices, the sacrificial fire, new- and full-moon rites, and the rites for installation of kings. The *Pancavimsa, Sadvimsa,* and *Jaiminiya Brahmana* discuss the "going of the cows," soma ceremonies, and atonements for mistakes in ritual. The *Satapatha Brahmana* introduces elements of domestic ritual, and the *Gopatha Brahmana* treats the priests' supervision of sacrifices.

Brahmaputra River \,brä-mə-'pü-trə\ River, central and southern Asia. From its headsprings in Tibet (as the Zangbo River), it flows across southern Tibet to break through the Himalayas in great gorges (where it is known as the Dihang). It flows southwest through the Assam valley and south through Bangladesh (where it is known as the Jamuna). There it merges with the Ganges to form the Ganges-Brahmaputra Delta. About 1,800 mi (2,900 km) long, the river is an important source for irrigation and transportation. Its upper course was long unknown, and its identity with the Zangbo was only established by exploration in 1884–86.

Brahmo Samaj \'brä-mō-sə-'mäj\ Monotheistic movement within Hinduism, founded in Calcutta (now Kolkata) in 1828 by Ram Mohun Roy. It rejected the authority of the Vedas and the doctrine of avatars, did not insist on belief in karma or rebirth, denounced polytheism and the caste system, and adopted some Christian practices. Roy's intention was to reform Hinduism from within, but his successor, Debendranath Tagore, rejected Vedic authority. In 1866 Keshab Chunder Sen organized the more radical Brahmo Samaj of India, which campaigned for the education of women and against child marriages. After Keshab nonetheless arranged a marriage for his underage daughter, a third group, Sadharan Brahmo Samaj, was formed in 1878. It gradually reverted to the teaching of the Upanishads but continued the work of social reform. The movement, always an elite group without significant popular following, lost force in the 20th century.

Brahms, Johannes (1833–1897) German-Austrian composer. Born in Hamburg, son of a musician, he became a piano prodigy. In 1853 he met R. and C. Schumann (see C. Schumann, R. Schumann); Robert immediately proclaimed him a genius, and Clara became the lifelong object of his affections. In 1863 he moved to Vienna, which would remain his principal home until his death. He took several positions as choral and orchestral conductor and performed as a soloist. The success of his *German Requiem* (1868) gave him an international reputation; his first symphony (1876) led to even greater fame, and his violin concerto (1879) and second piano concerto (1882) led many to acclaim him the greatest living composer. His music, grounded in the Classical style, was seen as conservative, especially with respect to that of Richard Wagner and F. Liszt. His orchestral works include four symphonies (1876, 1877, 1883, 1885), two piano concertos (1858, 1881), a violin concerto (1878), and a double concerto (1887), two serenades (1858, 1859), and two overtures (1880). His large chamber-music output included four string quartets, two string sextets, two string quintets, three piano quartets, three piano trios, three violin sonatas, two cello sonatas, and two clarinet sonatas. He also wrote three piano sonatas, choral music, and more than 250 lieder.

Braille \'brāl\ Universal system of writing and printing for the blind. Louis Braille invented the system in 1824. Characters embossed on paper are read by passing the fingers lightly over the manuscript. The system is based on a matrix of six dots arranged in two columns of three. The 63 combinations possible in this framework stand for letters, numbers, punctuation marks, and common words like *and* and *the.* A Braille code for English was not adopted until 1932. Modifications also exist for other languages, for mathematical and technical material, and for musical notation. Braille may be handwritten—from right to left—using a stylus to press dots into a piece of paper between hinged metal plates; when the sheet is turned over, the dots face up and are read from left to right. Braille typewriters and electric embossing machines are also used. See illustration on following page.

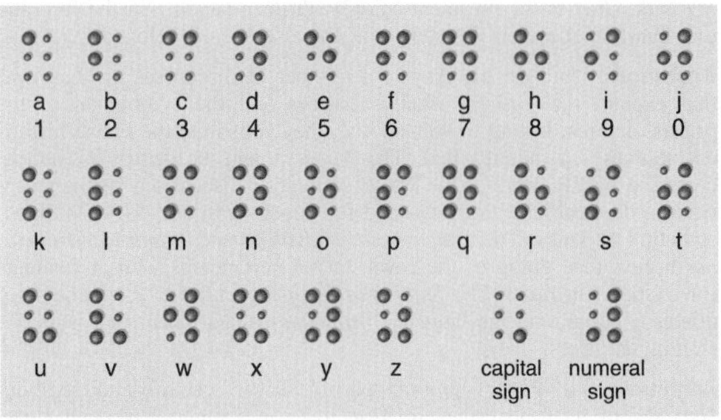

The alphabet and the digits 0–9 in the modern Braille system. Each letter or digit consists of six "cells" that are either embossed or left blank to form a unique pattern. Large dots indicate raised cells; smaller dots indicate cells that are left blank.

Braille \'bräy\, **Louis** (1809–1852) French educator who developed the BRAILLE system of printing and writing for the blind. Himself blinded at the age of 3 in an accident, he went to Paris in 1819 to attend the National Institute for Blind Children, and from 1826 he taught there. Braille adapted a method created by Charles Barbier to develop his own simplified system.

brain Concentration of nerve tissue in the front or upper end of an animal's body that handles sensory information, controls motion, is vital to instinctive acts, and in higher vertebrates is the center of learning. Vertebrate brains consist of the hindbrain (rhombencephalon), midbrain (mesencephalon), and forebrain (prosencephalon). The hindbrain comprises the medulla oblongata and the pons, which connects the SPINAL CORD with higher brain levels and transfers information from the CEREBRAL CORTEX to the CEREBELLUM. The midbrain, a major sensory integration center in other vertebrates, serves primarily to link the hindbrain and forebrain in mammals. Large nerve bundles connect the cerebellum to the medulla, pons, and midbrain. In the forebrain, the two cerebral hemispheres are connected by a thick bundle of nerve fibers (corpus callosum) and are divided by two deep grooves into four lobes (frontal, parietal, temporal, and occipital). The cerebrum, the largest part of the human brain, is involved with its more complex functions. Motor and sensory nerve fibers from each hemisphere cross over in the medulla to control the opposite side of the body.

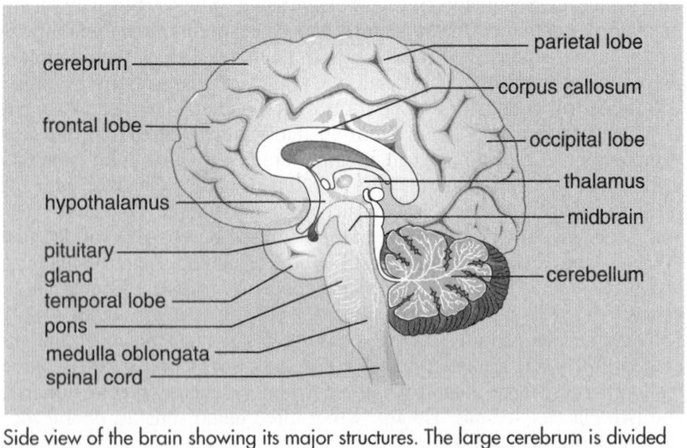

Side view of the brain showing its major structures. The large cerebrum is divided into two halves or hemispheres connected by the corpus callosum, a bundle of nerve fibers. Two grooves divide the hemispheres into four lobes: frontal, temporal, parietal, and occipital. Many nerve cells are found in the convoluted cerebrum's outer surface or cortex, which controls sensory and motor activities. The thalamus relays incoming sensory impulses from the spinal cord to the cortex. The hypothalamus's many functions include control of breathing, blood flow, temperature regulation, and emotions. The pituitary gland is attached to and regulated by the hypothalamus. The midbrain relays signals between the forebrain and hindbrain. The cerebellum, along with the cerebrum, plays a role in voluntary movement as well as balance. The pons serves as a relay point linking the medulla oblongata, midbrain, cerebellum, and cerebrum. The medulla, lying between the pons and the spinal cord and continuous with both, plays a role in essential involuntary regulatory and reflexive responses (incl. breathing, swallowing, and heartbeat) and relays signals between the spinal cord and other brain regions.

brain death State of irreversible destruction of the brain. Before the invention of life-support systems, brain death always led quickly to death of the body. Ethical considerations are crucial to defining criteria for brain death, which in most countries must be met before efforts to extend life may be ended. Such criteria include deep coma with a known cause, absence of any brain-stem functions (e.g., spontaneous respiration, pupil reactions, gag and cough reflexes), and exclusion of hypothermia, drugs, and poison as causes. ELECTROENCEPHALOGRAPHY is useful but not essential in determining brain death. Organ donors must be declared brain-dead before their organs may be removed for transplant. The question of when life support can legally be ended has been the subject of numerous court cases.

brain laterality See LATERALITY

Brain Trust Group of advisers to FRANKLIN ROOSEVELT in his 1932 presidential campaign. Its principal members were the Columbia University professors RAYMOND MOLEY, REXFORD TUGWELL, and Adolf A. Berle, Jr. (1895–1971). They presented Roosevelt with analyses of national social and economic problems and helped him devise public-policy solutions. The group did not meet after Roosevelt became president, but members served in government posts. See also NEW DEAL.

brainwashing Systematic effort to destroy an individual's former loyalties and beliefs and to substitute loyalty to a new ideology or power. It has been used by religious CULTS as well as by radical political groups such as the Chinese Communists in 1949. The techniques of brainwashing usually involve isolation from former associates and sources of information; an exacting regimen calling for absolute obedience and humility; strong social pressures and rewards for cooperation; physical and psychological punishments for noncooperation, including social ostracism and criticism, deprivation of food, sleep, and social contacts, bondage, and torture; and constant reinforcement. Its effects are sometimes reversed through deprogramming, which combines confrontation and intensive psychotherapy.

brake Device for decreasing the speed of a body or stopping its motion. Most brakes act on rotating mechanical elements and absorb KINETIC ENERGY mechanically, hydrodynamically, or electrically. Mechanical

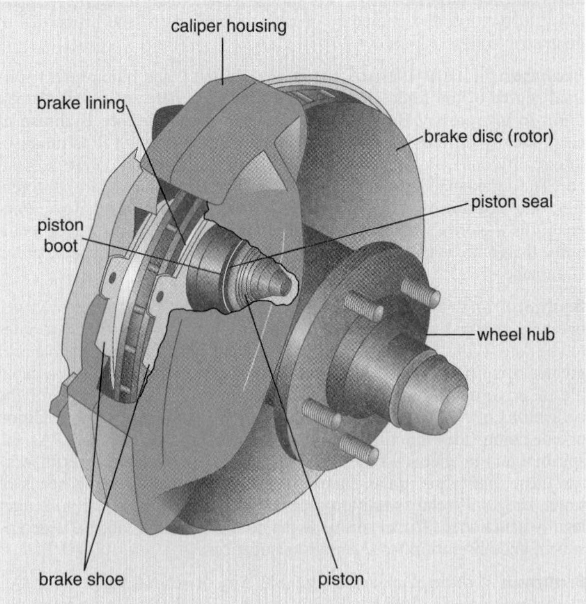

A disk brake assembly. Wheel rotation is slowed by friction when the hydraulic pistons squeeze the caliper, pressing the brake pads against the spinning disk (rotor), which is bolted to the wheel hub.

brakes are the most common; they dissipate the kinetic energy as heat generated by mechanical FRICTION between a rotating drum or disk and a stationary friction element. A hydrodynamic (fluid) brake has a rotor (rotating element) and a stator (stationary element). Resistance to rotation is created by fluid friction and circulation of the liquid (usually water) from a series of pockets in the rotor to a series of complementary pockets in the stator. See also AIR BRAKE.

brake See BRACKEN

Bramah, Joseph (1748–1814) British engineer and inventor. Originally a cabinetmaker, Bramah in 1784 devised a pick-proof lock, which defied all efforts for 67 years. Since the success of his locks depended on their complexity, they could be produced in quantity only after the creation of a set of well-designed and precisely engineered machine tools, for which he hired a brilliant young blacksmith, HENRY MAUDSLAY. Their prototype machines were essential to the founding of the MACHINE-TOOL industry. Bramah's hydraulic press found many industrial uses and led to the development of hydraulic machinery.

Bramante \brä-'män-tā\, **Donato** (1444–1514) Italian architect and perspectivist painter. The son of wealthy peasants, he was working as a painter by 1477. His early architectural works included the church of Santa Maria presso San Satiro (c. 1480), in which the choir is painted in perspective to give an illusion of a much larger space. In 1499 he went to Rome, where he spent the rest of his life. His TEMPIETTO was the first masterpiece of the High Renaissance. Under the patronage of Pope JULIUS II, he drew up plans for the immense Belvedere courtyard in the Vatican (begun c. 1505) and the new ST. PETER'S BASILICA (begun 1506), his greatest work. These ambitious projects were far from complete at the time of his death. Despite the grandiose scale of the St. Peter's undertaking, Bramante continued to work on other projects and played an important role in Julius II's plans for rebuilding Rome.

Tempietto, S. Pietro in Montorio, Rome, designed by Bramante, 1502.
ANDERSON–ALINARI FROM ART RESOURCE

bramble Any plant of the genus *Rubus* (rose family), consisting of usually prickly shrubs, including RASPBERRIES and BLACKBERRIES. Brambles grow wild throughout North America, as well as in Europe and Asia, and are widely cultivated for their fruits.

Brampton City (pop., 1991: 235,000), southeastern Ontario. Located west of TORONTO, it was founded c. 1830. It was incorporated as a town in 1873 and as a city in 1976. Its industries include flower growing, tanning, lumbering, and the manufacture of automobiles, shoes, stationery, furniture, and optical equipment.

Brân \'bran\ In CELTIC RELIGION, a gigantic deity described in the *MABINOGION* as king of Britain. He was so large that he and his court lived in a tent rather than a house. When Brân was mortally wounded, he asked his companions to cut off his head and keep it with them, telling them it would provide entertainment and allow them to forget their sorrows. His companions passed 80 joyous years, eventually following his instructions and burying the head on the White Mount in London, where it protected England from invaders until it was finally unearthed.

bran Edible broken seed coat, or protective outer layer, of WHEAT, RYE, or other CEREAL grain, separated from the kernel. In flour processing, it is normally removed from the ground kernels by sifting them in a rotating, meshed, cylindrical frame; whole-grain flours retain the bran. Wheat bran, the most widely processed, contains 16% protein, 11% natural fiber, and 50% carbohydrate. Most bran is coarsely ground for stock feed. In a more refined form, it is used in breakfast cereal, breads, and muffins for its value to the human digestive system as roughage.

Branagh \'bra-nə\, **Kenneth (Charles)** (born 1960) British actor, director, and writer. After making his London stage debut in 1981, he joined the ROYAL SHAKESPEARE CO. (1984–87), where he won acclaim in *Hamlet* and *Henry V.* He cofounded the Renaissance Theatre Co. (1987), in which he served as actor, director, and writer. He directed and starred in film versions of Shakespeare, including *Henry V* (1989), *Much Ado About Nothing* (1993), and *Hamlet* (1996), as well as *Dead Again* (1991) and *Mary Shelley's Frankenstein* (1994). He was married to EMMA THOMPSON.

Branch Davidians Religious sect that believes in the imminent return of Jesus Christ. It was founded in 1935 near Waco, Texas, by Victor Houteff as a breakaway group from the Seventh-Day Adventists. Under the leadership of Vernon Howell, a charismatic and apocalyptic preacher who would take the name David Koresh (1959–1993), it stockpiled weapons at its compound, where some 130 followers were living by 1993. That year, after a shoot-out in which four federal agents were killed, federal law-enforcement agencies besieged the compound for 51 days. The standoff ended, at the orders of Attorney General Janet Reno, in a conflagration in which some 80 members died, including several children and Koresh himself. Intense controversy about the precise circumstances and the necessity of the final assault led to a Congressional investigation, which in 2000 exonerated federal agents.

Brancusi, Constantin (1876–1957) Romanian-French sculptor. He became adept at carving wooden farm implements as a child and later studied in Bucharest and Munich and at the École des Beaux-Arts in Paris, having walked most of the way from Munich. He first exhibited in Paris in 1906. In 1908 he executed *Sleeping Muse,* influenced by AUGUSTE RODIN, and *The Kiss,* his first truly original work. He developed a style of geometrization that became his hallmark, reducing natural forms to an ultimate abstract simplicity. He exhibited five works, including *Mademoiselle Pogany,* in the 1913 ARMORY SHOW. One of his favorite themes was a bird in flight; his most famous treatment was the celebrated polished-bronze *Bird in Space* (1919). Through numerous exhibitions in the U.S. and Europe, he achieved great fame and success, and he is regarded as a pioneer of modern abstract sculpture.

Brandeis \'bran-ˌdīs\, **Louis (Dembitz)** (1856–1941) U.S. jurist. He was born in Louisville, Ky., the son of Bohemian Jewish immigrants, and attended schools in Kentucky and Germany before obtaining his law degree from Harvard (1877). As a lawyer in Boston (1877–1916), he was known as "the people's attorney" for his defense of the constitutionality of several state hours-and-wages laws, his devising of a savings-bank life-insurance plan for working people, and his efforts to strengthen the government's antitrust power. His work influenced passage in 1914 of the Clayton Anti-Trust Act and the Federal Trade Commission Act. He also developed what came to be called the "Brandeis brief," in which economic and sociological data, historical material, and expert opinion are marshaled to support a legal argument. Appointed to the U.S. Supreme Court (1916), he was noted for his devotion to FREEDOM OF SPEECH. Many of his minority opinions, in which he was often aligned with OLIVER WENDELL HOLMES, Jr., later were accepted by the Court in the New Deal era. His appointment as the first Jewish justice was vigorously opposed by some business interests and anti-Semitic groups. He served until 1939. BRANDEIS UNIV. is named for him.

Brandeis.
BY COURTESY OF THE LIBRARY OF CONGRESS, WASHINGTON, D.C.

Brandeis University \'bran-ˌdīs\ Private university in Waltham, Mass., founded in 1948 as the first Jewish-sponsored nonsectarian university in the U.S. It is named for LOUIS BRANDEIS. Its undergraduate college has programs in the sciences, social sciences, humanities, and creative arts. Its graduate programs include ancient and modern Jewish thought, history, and culture, as well as social policy, international economics, and biomedical research. Total enrollment is about 4,200.

Brandenburg Historical region and province of PRUSSIA. The earliest Germanic inhabitants were replaced by Slavic Wends, who in turn were overcome in the 12th century by Albert the Bear, margrave of Brandenburg. It became one of the seven electorates of the HOLY ROMAN EMPIRE in

1356. Under the Elector Frederick William (1640–88), Brandenburg-Prussia grew to be a leading power. It became a province of Prussia in 1815 and remained such after the unification of Germany (1871) and until the end of World War II. After the war, the eastern portion became part of Poland and the western portion part of East Germany. With Germany's reunification in 1991, the western part became a German state. Brandenburg city, or Brandenburg an der Havel (pop., 1992 est.: 89,000), was formerly the residence of Prussia's reigning family.

Brandenburg Gate Monumental gateway in Berlin, the only remaining town gate, at the western end of the avenue Unter den Linden. Carl G. Langhans (1732–1808), who built the gate (1789–93), modeled it after the Propylaeum of the Athenian Acropolis. On top was the "Quadriga of Victory," a statue of a chariot drawn by four horses. Heavily damaged in World War II, the gate was restored in 1957–58. From 1961 to 1989 the Berlin Wall shut off access to it to both East and West; the gate was reopened in 1989 with the reunification of East and West Berlin.

Brandes \'bran-dəs\, **Georg (Morris Cohen)** (1842–1927) Danish critic and scholar. His published lectures at the University of Copenhagen, *Main Currents in 19th-Century Thought* (6 vols., 1872–90), catalyzed the breakthrough from Romanticism to realism in Danish literature. His calls for writers to work in the service of progressive ideas and the reform of modern society, and his championing of such writers as Henrik Ibsen and August Strindberg, earned strong conservative opposition but exerted enormous influence throughout Scandinavia. His other critical works include *Men of the Modern Breakthrough* (1883) and *Danish Poets* (1877).

Brando (Jr.), Marlon (born 1924) U.S. actor. Born in Omaha, he studied drama and acted in minor roles before winning stardom on Broadway as Stanley Kowalski in *A Streetcar Named Desire* (1947). An early member of the Actors Studio, he brought its Method acting style to his first film, *The Men* (1950). His slurred, mumbling delivery marked his rejection of classical dramatic training, and his true and passionate performances proved him one of the great actors of his generation. After starring in the screen version of *Streetcar* (1951), he appeared in films such as *Viva Zapata!* (1952), *Julius Caesar* (1953), *The Wild One* (1954), *On the Waterfront* (1954, Academy Award), *The Godfather* (1972, Academy Award), *Last Tango in Paris* (1972), *Apocalypse Now* (1979), and *A Dry White Season* (1989).

Brandt, Bill *orig.* **William** (1904–1983) British photographer. In 1929 he worked in the studio of Man Ray in Paris. He returned to England in 1931 and took up photojournalism, documenting English industrial workers in the 1930s and covering the home front during World War II. His work reveals the influence of Eugene Atget, Brassai, and Henri Cartier-Bresson. He is best known for his photographs of British life, and especially for his unconventional nudes photographed in extremely distorted form, which approach abstract designs.

Brandt, Willy *orig.* **Herbert Ernst Karl Frahm** (1913–1992) German statesman. As a young Social Democrat, he fled to Norway to avoid arrest after the rise of the Nazis in the 1930s. There he assumed the name Willy Brandt and worked as a journalist. Returning to Germany after World War II, he was elected to parliament in 1949 and became mayor of West Berlin (1957–66), a post in which he achieved world fame. He led a coalition government as chancellor of the Federal Republic of Germany (1969–74). As chancellor he improved relations with East Germany, other communist nations in Eastern Europe, and the Soviet Union, and helped strengthen the European Economic Community. He remained the leader of the Social Democratic Party until 1987. He received the Nobel Peace Prize in 1971.

Willy Brandt.
AUTHENTICATED NEWS INTERNATIONAL

brandy Alcoholic beverage distilled from wine or a fermented fruit mash. The name comes from the Dutch *brandewijn,* "distilled wine." Most brandies are aged and contain about 50% alcohol by volume. Some are darkened with caramel. They are usually served alone as after-dinner drinks, but are sometimes used in mixed drinks or dessert dishes, or as fuel in flamed dishes such as crêpes suzettes and cherries jubilee. They are also used to produce liqueur. The finest brandy is usually thought to be French cognac.

Brandywine, Battle of the (September 11, 1777) Battle in the American Revolution. The British general William Howe attempted to remove Pennsylvania from the war by engaging George Washington's troops on Brandywine Creek, 25 mi (40 km) from Philadelphia. In the end, the British troops occupied the battlefield but failed to destroy Washington's army or cut it off from the capital at Philadelphia. This failure contributed to the later British defeat at the Battle of Saratoga.

Brant, Henry (Dreyfuss) (born 1913) Canadian-U.S. composer. His eclectic career included work in commercial music and teaching positions at Columbia University and the Juilliard School. Inspired by the music of C. Ives, his compositions employ unusual timbral combinations and frequently require the spatial separation of performing forces, each group generally performing music contrasting sharply with that of the others. His works, numbering over 150, include *Angels and Devils* (1931), *Antiphony I* (1953), and *The Grand Universal Circus* (1956).

Brant, Joseph (1742–1807) Mohawk Indian chief and Christian missionary. Brant was converted to the Anglican Church while attending a school for Indians in Connecticut. He fought for the British in the last French and Indian War (1754–63). He led four of the six Iroquois nations on the British side in the American Revolution, winning several notable battles. After the war Brant was granted land along the Grand River in Ontario, where he ruled peacefully and continued his missionary work.

Joseph Brant, portrait by Charles Willson Peale, 1797; in Independence National Historical Park, Philadelphia.
BY COURTESY OF THE INDEPENDENCE NATIONAL HISTORICAL PARK COLLECTION, PHILADELPHIA

Brant, Sebastian (1458?–1521) German poet. He taught law and later was appointed imperial councillor and court palatine by Maximilian I. His varied writings include works on law, religion, politics, and especially morals. His best-known work is *The Ship of Fools* (1494), an allegory telling of fools on a ship bound for a "fool's paradise." The most famous German literary work of the 15th century, it ridicules the vices of the age and gave rise to a whole school of fool's literature.

Braque \'bräk\, **Georges** (1882–1963) French painter. He studied painting in Le Havre, then in Paris at a private academy and briefly at the École des Beaux-Arts. Though his earliest works were influenced by Impressionism, his first important paintings (1905–7) were in the Fauvist style pioneered by Andre Derain and Henri Matisse; in 1907 he exhibited and sold six of these paintings at the Salon des Indépendants. Abandoning Fauvism in 1907, with Pablo Picasso he invented the revolutionary new style known as Cubism. He painted mostly still lifes featuring geometrical shapes and low-key color harmonies. In 1912 he introduced the collage or *papier collé* (pasted-paper picture) by attaching three pieces of wallpaper to the drawing *Fruit Dish and Glass.* By the 1920s he was a prosperous, well-established modern master. In 1923 and 1925 he designed stage sets for Sergey Diaghilev's Ballets Russes. He enjoyed a long and prestigious career; in his later years he was honored with important exhibitions throughout the world. In 1961 he became the first living artist to have his works exhibited in the Louvre.

Bras d'Or Lake \brä-'dȯr\ Salt lake, Nova Scotia, Canada. Located on Cape Breton Island, it is about 50 mi (80 km) long and has an area of 360 sq mi (932 sq km). Its extension, Little Bras d'Or, connects it to the Atlantic Ocean on the north, while a man-made canal connects it to the Atlantic on the south. The lake is a popular summer resort area.

Brasília City (pop., 1991: 1,493,000; metro area pop.: 1,778,000), capital of Brazil. It lies on the Paraná River. Though the idea of having the country's capital located in the interior was proposed as early as 1789,

Brasília's construction began only in 1956. It was designed by the Brazilian architects Lúcio Costa and Oscar Niemeyer. In 1960 the government began its move from Rio de Janeiro. The city is a governmental rather than an industrial center, while many nationwide companies have headquarters there. Brasília National Park is nearby.

Brasov *or* **Brashov** \brä-'shōv\ *German* **Kronstadt** \'krōn-ˌshtät\ City (pop., 1994 est.: 324,000), Romania. It lies in the foothills of the Transylvanian Alps north of Bucharest. Founded by Teutonic Knights in 1211, it became the center of a Saxon colony trading in cloth and metalwork throughout much of Walachia and Moldavia. The substantial autonomy of its German inhabitants ended in 1876 with the abolition of their separate national status. Brasov is today a center for heavy manufacturing.

brass Alloy of copper and zinc, important for its hardness and workability. Brass was first used c. 1200 BC in the Near East, then extensively in China after 220 BC, and soon thereafter by the Romans. In ancient documents, including the Bible, the term brass is often used to denote bronze (copper/tin alloy). The malleability of brass depends on its zinc content; brasses with more than 45% zinc are not workable. Alpha brasses contain less than 40% zinc; beta brasses (40–45% zinc) are less ductile than alpha brasses but stronger. A third group includes brasses with additional elements. Among these are lead brasses, which are more easily machined; naval and admiralty brasses, in which a small amount of tin improves resistance to corrosion by seawater; and aluminum brasses, which provide strength and corrosion resistance where the naval brasses may fail.

brass instruments Musical wind instruments, usually made of brass or other metal, in which the vibration of the player's lips against a cup- or funnel-shaped mouthpiece causes an air column to vibrate. The trumpet, trombone, French horn, tuba, euphonium, sousaphone, cornet, flugelhorn, and bugle, as well as such historical instruments as the ophicleide, cornett, and serpent, are brass instruments (though the last two were made of wood); the saxophones, though made of brass, are reed instruments classified as woodwind instruments.

Brassai \brà-'sī\ *orig.* **Gyula Halasz** (1899–1984) Hungarian-French photographer, poet, and sculptor. His pseudonym derives from his native city. In 1924 he settled in Paris, where he became acquainted with Pablo Picasso, Joan Miro, and Salvador Dali. He earned his living as a journalist and found it necessary to use a camera for his assignments. In the 1930s he became known for his dramatic photographs of Paris nightlife. Books of his photographs, including *Paris After Dark* (1933) and *Pleasures of Paris* (1935), brought him international fame.

"'Bijoux' in Place Pigalle Bar," by Brassaï, 1932.
BRASSAI—RAPHO/PHOTO RESEARCHERS

brassica Any plant of the large genus *Brassica,* in the mustard family, containing about 40 Old World species and including the cabbages, mustards, and rapes. *B. oleracea* has many edible varieties, such as broccoli, Brussels sprouts, cabbage, cauliflower, kale, and kohlrabi. Also included in this genus are the turnip *(B. rapa),* the rutabaga *(B. napobrassica),* and the Chinese cabbages *(B. pekinensis* and *B. chinensis).*

Bratislava \ˌbrä-ti-'slä-və\ *German* **Pressburg** \'pres-ˌbu̇rk\ *Hungarian* **Pozsony** \'pō-ˌzhōnʸ\ City (pop., 1996: 452,000), capital of Slovakia. Settled first by Celts and Romans, it was ultimately inhabited by Slavs in the 8th century. As Pressburg, it developed as a trade center and became a free royal town in 1291. The first university in what was then Hungary was founded there in 1467. The city served as the Hungarian capital 1541–1784 and was the seat of the Diet until 1848. The Treaty of Pressburg (1805) was signed here by Napoleon and Francis II following the Battle of Austerlitz. After World War I, on the formation of Czechoslovakia, it became capital of the province of Slovakia, and became the national capital on Slovakia's independence in 1992.

Brattain \'bra-tᵊn\, **Walter H(ouser)** (1902–1987) U.S. scientist. Born in China, he was educated in the U.S. and became a researcher at Bell Laboratories in 1929. With John Bardeen and William B. Shockley, he shared the 1956 Nobel Prize for Physics for the development of the transistor and for investigation of the properties of semiconductors. His chief research involved the atomic structure of a material at its surface, which usually differs from the atomic structure of the interior.

Brauchitsch \'brau̇-k̲ich\, **(Heinrich Alfred) Walther von** (1881–1948) German army officer. A member of the general staff in World War I, he rose to become field marshal and army commander in chief (1938). In World War II, he successfully directed Germany's ground war until Adolf Hitler forced his resignation after suffering major losses in Russia in 1941. He survived the war but died shortly before his scheduled trial as a war criminal.

Braudel \brō-'del\, **(Paul Achille) Fernand** (1902–1985) French historian and educator. While a prisoner of the Germans during World War II, Braudel wrote from memory his thesis on the history of the Mediterranean region in the 16th century, later published as *The Mediterranean and the Mediterranean World in the Age of Phillip II* (1949). With Marc Bloch and Lucien Febvre, he became an influential leader of the *Annales* school, which emphasized the effects of factors such as climate, geography, and demographics on history. His second major work was *Civilization and Capitalism, 15th–18th Century* (1967, 1979).

Braun \'brau̇n\, **Eva** (1912–1945) German mistress of Adolf Hitler. A saleswoman in the shop of Hitler's photographer, she became his mistress in the 1930s, living first in a house he provided in Munich, then at his chalet in Berchtesgaden. He never allowed her to be seen in public with him, and she had no influence on his political life. In April 1945 she joined him in Berlin, against his orders. In recognition of her loyalty, he married her in a civil ceremony in the Chancellery bunker on April 29. The next day Eva Hitler ended her life at 33 by taking poison; her husband either poisoned or shot himself at her side. Their bodies were burned.

Eva Braun, 1944.
HEINRICH HOFFMANN, MUNICH

Braun \'brau̇n\, **Wernher von** (1912–1977) German-U.S. rocket engineer. Born into an aristocratic family, he received his doctorate from the University of Berlin. In 1936 he became technical director of the new military development facility at Peenemünde, an essential center for the rearmament of Nazi Germany, forbidden by the Versailles accords. Liquid-fueled rocket aircraft and jet-assisted takeoffs were successfully demonstrated there, and the V-2 long-range ballistic missile and the Wasserfall supersonic antiaircraft missile were developed. By 1944 the sophistication of the rockets and missiles being tested at Peenemünde was many years ahead of that of any other country. After World War II he and his team surrendered to the U.S.; they were immediately set to work on guided missiles by the U.S. Army, and in 1952 he became technical director (later chief) of the Army's ballistic-weapon program. Under his leadership, the Redstone, Jupiter-C, Juno, and Pershing missiles were developed. In 1958 he and his group launched the first U.S. satellite, Explorer 1. After NASA was formed, von Braun led the development of some of the large Saturn space launch vehicles; the engineering success of each of the Saturn class of space boosters remains unmatched in rocket history.

Braunschweig See Brunswick

Brazil *officially* **Federative Republic of Brazil** Nation, central South America. Area: 3,284,426 sq mi (8,506,663 sq km). Population (1997 est.): 159,691,000. Capital: Brasília. Brazil's ethnic groups have intermixed since the earliest days of its colonial history. Unmixed elements are rare, with those Indians untouched by immigration restricted to the most remote parts of the Amazon Basin. Language: Portuguese (official). Religions: Roman Catholicism, traditional Indian and African beliefs. Currency: real. Brazil may be divided into many regions, but the Amazon River Basin and the Brazilian Highlands (or Plateau) dominate the landscape. The Highlands, a plateau with an average elevation of 3,300 ft (1,000 m), lies primarily in the southeast, while the Amazon Basin, which lies at elevations of less than 800 ft (250 m), is in the north. The Amazon Basin, with its more than 1,000 known tributaries, comprises about 45% of the nation's total territory. Brazil's other rivers include the São Francisco, Parnaíba, Paraguay, Alto Paraná, and Uruguay. Except for the islands of Marajó and Caviana at the mouth of the Amazon and Maracá to the north, there are no large islands along the 4,603 mi (7,406 km) of its Atlantic coastline. There are good harbors at Belém, Salvador, Rio de Janeiro, Santos, and Pôrto Alegre. The country's immense forests are a source of many products, while its savannas support cattle raising. Agriculture is important; mineral reserves are large. Brazil has a developing market economy based mainly on manufacturing, financial services, and trade. It is a republic with two legislative houses; its chief of state and government is the president. Little is known about Brazil's early indigenous inhabitants. Though the area was theoretically allotted to Portugal by the 1494 Treaty of Tordesillas, it was not formally claimed by discovery until Pedro Alvares Cabral accidentally touched land in 1500. It was first settled by the Portuguese in the early 1530s on the northeastern coast and at São Vicente (near modern São Paulo); the French and Dutch created small settlements over the next century. A viceroyalty was established in 1640 and Rio de Janeiro became the capital in 1673. In 1808 Brazil became the refuge and seat of the government of John VI of Portugal when Napoleon invaded Portugal; ultimately the Kingdom of Portugal, Brazil, and Algrave was proclaimed, and John ruled from Brazil 1815–21. On John's return to Portugal, Pedro I proclaimed Brazilian independence. In 1889 his successor, Pedro II, was deposed, and a constitution mandating a federal republic was adopted. The 20th century saw increased immigration and growth in manufacturing along with frequent military coups and suspensions of civil liberties. Construction of a new capital at Brasília, intended to spur development of the country's interior, worsened the inflation rate. After 1979 the military government began a gradual return to democratic practices, and in 1989 the first popular presidential election in 29 years was held. The late 1990s brought a severe economic crisis.

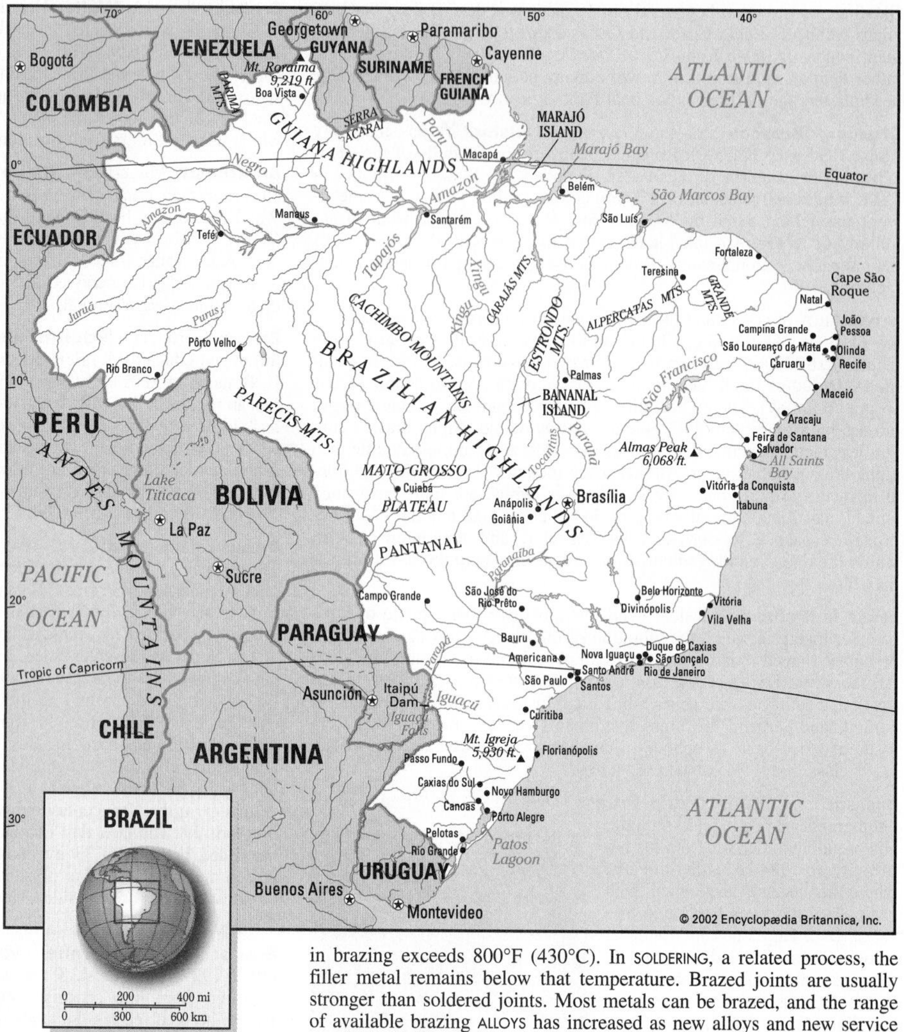

Brazil nut Edible seed of a large South American tree, *Bertholletia excelsa* (family Lecythidaceae), one of the major commercially traded nuts in the world. The hard-walled fruit, resembling a large coconut, contains 8–24 nuts (seeds) arranged in it like sections of an orange. Each nut has a very hard shell and is three-cornered in shape. Brazil nuts are high in fat and protein and taste somewhat like almond or coconut. The tree grows wild in stands in the Amazon River basin, reaching heights of 150 ft (45 m) or more.

brazing Process for joining two pieces of metal by applying heat and adding a filler metal. The filler, which has a lower melting point than the metals to be joined, is either pre-placed or fed into the joint as the parts are heated. In brazing parts with small clearances, the filler is able to flow into the joint by capillarity. The temperature of the molten filler in brazing exceeds 800°F (430°C). In soldering, a related process, the filler metal remains below that temperature. Brazed joints are usually stronger than soldered joints. Most metals can be brazed, and the range of available brazing alloys has increased as new alloys and new service requirements are introduced. Brazed joints are highly reliable and are used extensively on rockets, jet engines, and aircraft parts. See also welding.

Brazos River \'bra-zəs\ River, central Texas. Formed in northern Texas, it flows southeast 840 mi (1,351 km) into the Gulf of Mexico. The city of Waco is one of the largest on the river. Near its mouth it connects with the Gulf Intracoastal Waterway. The river valley was a major site of early Anglo-American settlement in Texas; one of the first English-speaking colonies there was founded by Stephen Austin at San Felipe de Austin in 1822. The river's original name was Brazos de Dios ("Arms of God").

Brazza \brȧ-'zȧ\, **Pierre (-Paul-François-Camille) Savorgnan de** (1852–1905) French explorer and colonial administrator. Born to Italian nobility in Brazil, he joined the French navy. In 1875–78, he explored the Ogooué River (in present-day Gabon). In an attempt to beat Henry Morton Stanley, he was sent up the Congo River; he founded the French (Middle) Congo and explored Gabon, as well as the city of Brazzaville (1883), adding some 200,000 sq mi (500,000 sq km) to the French colonial empire. From 1886 to 1897 he governed a colony there.

Brazzaville \'brä-zə-ˌvil\ River port (pop., 1992 est.: 938,000), capital of Republic of the Congo. Lying on the north bank of the Congo River across from Kinshasa, it was founded in 1883 by Pierre Savorgnan de Brazza. Developed as a European administrative and residential center, it was used as a base for later claims of France to lands to the northeast; it became the capital of French Equatorial Africa. The river port forms the terminus of the Congo-ocean transport system, with steamer service to the Congo's upper reaches and a railroad to Pointe-Noire 245 mi (394 km) west.

bread Baked food product made of flour or meal that is moistened, kneaded into a dough, and often fermented using yeast. A major food since prehistoric times, bread has been made in various forms using a variety of ingredients and methods throughout the world. Flat, unleavened bread, the earliest form, is still eaten in the Middle East, Asia, and Africa. The principal grains used in such breads are corn, barley, millet, buckwheat, wheat, and rye. Raised bread, common in Europe and the U.S., is usually made of wheat or rye. Both contain the elastic protein substance gluten, which traps gas produced during fermentation, helping the bread to rise. Other ingredients include milk or water, shortening (fats, butter, oils), salt, and sugar. Bread is a source of complex carbohydrates and B vitamins (see vitamin B complex); whole-wheat bread contains more protein, vitamins, minerals, and fiber than white-flour bread. See also baking.

breadfruit Fruit of either of two closely related trees belonging to the mulberry family. *Artocarpus communis* (also called *A. incisa* or *A. altilis*) provides a staple food of the South Pacific. Its greenish to brownish-green, roundish ripe fruits have a white fibrous pulp. *Treculia africana,* native to tropical Africa, is less important as a food crop. Cultivated in the Malay Archipelago (where it is thought to be indigenous) since remote antiquity, the breadfruit spread throughout the tropical South Pacific in prehistoric times. It is high in starch and is seldom eaten raw. Unable to tolerate frost, the tree has not been successfully grown in the U.S., even in southernmost Florida. In the South Seas cloth is made from the inner bark, the wood is used for canoes and furniture, and glue and caulking material are obtained from the milky juice.

breakbone fever See dengue fever

bream European food and game fish *(Abramis brama)* of the carp family (Cyprinidae). Found in lakes and slow rivers, the bream lives in schools and eats worms, mollusks, and other small animals. Deep-bodied, with flat sides and a small head, it is silvery with a bluish or brown back. It is usually about 12–20 in. (30–50 cm) long and weighs up to 13 lbs (6 kg). Other species called bream include the silver bream *(Blicca bjoorkna),* the golden shiner, and the sea breams (family Sparidae).

Bream (*Abramis brama*).
W.S. PITT—ERIC HOSKING

breast cancer Tumor in a breast, usually in women after menopause. Risk factors include family history of breast cancer, prolonged menstruation, late first pregnancy (after age 30), obesity, alcohol use, and some benign tumors. Most breast cancers are adenocarcinomas. Any lump in the breast needs investigation because it may be cancer. Treatment may begin with radical or modified mastectomy or lumpectomy (in which only the tumor is removed), followed by radiation therapy, chemotherapy, or removal of the ovaries or adrenal glands.

breathing See respiration

Brébeuf \brā-'bœf\, **St. Jean de** (1593–1649) French Jesuit missionary to New France. Ordained in 1623, he arrived in New France in 1625 to work as a missionary among the Huron. Forced out by the English in 1629, he returned to "Huronia" in 1634 to live and work for 15 years. In 1648 the Iroquois began their war against the Huron, and in 1649 they captured Brébeuf and tortured him to death. He was canonized in 1930. His writings include historical narratives and a Huron grammar. He is regarded as the patron saint of Canada.

breccia \'bre-chə\ Coarse sedimentary rock consisting of angular or nearly angular fragments larger than 0.08 in. (2 mm). Breccia commonly results from processes such as landslides or geologic faulting, in which rocks are fractured. It can also be of igneous explosive origin (e.g., a volcanic breccia).

Brecht \'brekt\, **Bertolt** *orig.* **Eugen Berthold Friedrich** (1898–1956) German playwright and poet. He studied medicine at Munich (1917–21) before writing his first plays, including *Baal* (1922). Other plays followed, including *A Man's a Man* (1926), as well as a considerable body of poetry. With K. Weill he wrote the satirical musicals *The Threepenny Opera* (1928; film, 1931), which gained him a wide audience, and *The Rise and Fall of the City of Mahagonny* (1930), and the dance-drama *The Seven Deadly Sins* (1933). In these years he became a Marxist and developed his theory of epic theater. With the rise of the Nazis he went into exile, first in Scandinavia (1933–41), then in the U.S., where he wrote his major essays and such plays as *Mother Courage and Her Children* (1941), *The Life of Galileo* (1943), *The Good Woman of Sichuan* (1943), and *The Caucasian Chalk Circle* (1948). Harassed for his politics, he returned to East Germany in 1949, where he established the Berliner Ensemble theater troupe and staged his own plays, including *The Resistible Rise of Arturo Ui* (1957). He outlined his theory of drama in *A Little Organum for the Theater* (1949).

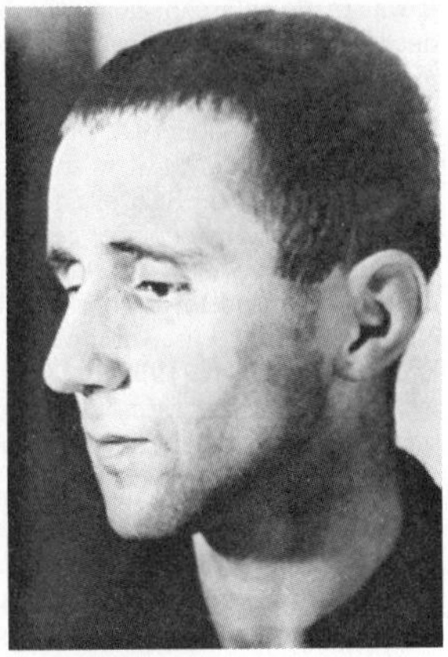

Bertolt Brecht, 1931.
ULLSTEIN BILDERDIENST

Breckinridge, John C(abell) (1821–1875) U.S. politician, vice president (1857–61), and Confederate army officer. Born near Lexington, Ky., he practiced law and later served in the U.S. House of Representatives (1851–55). In 1856 he was elected vice president under James Buchanan. In 1860 the Democratic Party split into factions over the slavery issue, and Breckinridge became the Southern wing's nominee for president. After the election of Abraham Lincoln he worked for compromise; but after the firing on Fort Sumter he urged Kentucky to secede. He became a general in the Confederate army and took part in the Vicksburg, Wilderness, and Shenandoah Valley campaigns. He served as Confederate secretary of war in 1865. After the war he fled to England for three years, then returned to Kentucky to resume his law practice.

Breda \brā-'dä\, **Declaration of** (1660) Document issued by the exiled King Charles II in Breda, the Netherlands, making certain promises in return for his restoration to the English throne. It expressed his desire for a general amnesty, liberty of conscience, an equitable settlement of land disputes, and full payment of arrears to the army. He left the specifics to the Convention Parliament. See also Restoration.

breeding Application of genetic principles in animal husbandry, agriculture, and horticulture to improve desirable qualities. Ancient agriculturists improved many plants through selective cultivation. Modern plant breeding centers on pollination; pollen from the chosen male plant, and no other pollen, must be transferred to the female plant. Animal breeding consists of choosing the ideal trait (e.g., fine wool, high milk production), selecting the breeding stock, and determining the mating system (e.g., whether mating animals are unrelated, mildly related, or highly inbred).

Breisgau \'brīs-ˌgau̇\ Historic region, southwestern Germany. Located between the Rhine River and the Black Forest, it was once part of the Roman empire. From the 3rd century AD it was occupied by the Germanic Alemanni. It became a countship in the early Middle Ages, and in 1120 the town of Freiburg im Breisgau was founded. In the 14th century the Habsburgs incorporated most of it into their domains. Breisgau was subjected to destructive sieges during the Thirty Years' War, and for a time was held by the Swedes. It now forms part of the state of Baden-Württemberg.

Brel, Jacques (1929–1978) Belgian-French singer and songwriter. He first started singing his songs with real-life themes in public in 1953. Frequently sharply satirical and often implicitly religious, they became hugely popular in Europe. He acted in and directed a number of films 1967–73. His U.S. reputation was made by the revue *Jacques Brel Is Alive and Well and Living in Paris* (1968).

Bremen \'brā-mən\ Former duchy, Germany. Lying between the lower Weser and lower Elbe rivers and northwest of the former duchy of Brunswick-Lüneburg, it covered an area of about 2,000 sq mi (5,200 sq km).

It was made an archbishopric in the 13th century, and in 1648 became a duchy under the supremacy of Sweden. In 1715 it became part of the electorate of Hanover.

Bremen City (pop., 1996 est.: 549,000), northwestern Germany. Located on the Weser River, it was established as a diocese in 787 by Charlemagne, and was the seat of an archbishopric from 845. In the 10th century it became an economic center of northern Germany, especially after entering the Hanseatic League in 1358. It joined the German Confederation in 1815 and the reconstituted German empire in 1871. It suffered extensive damage in World War II; after the war Bremen, with nearby Bremerhaven (pop., 1992 est.: 131,000), became a state of West Germany. Today the state forms an integral part of the German economy and serves as headquarters for many industries.

bremsstrahlung \'brem-ˌshträl-əŋ\ (German: "braking radiation") Electromagnetic radiation produced by a sudden slowing down or deflection of charged particles, especially electrons, passing through matter in the vicinity of the strong electric fields of atomic nuclei. It occurs as cosmic rays pass through the earth's atmosphere and accounts for continuous X-ray spectra.

Brendan, St. (c. AD 484–578) Celtic saint and hero of legendary Atlantic voyages. Educated by St. Ita at her school in southwestern Ireland, he became a monk and priest and was put in charge of the abbey at Ardfert. He later founded monasteries in Ireland and Scotland, notably Clonfert (561). A famous traveler, he voyaged to the Hebrides and perhaps to Wales and Brittany. He was immortalized in *Voyage of Brendan*, an Irish epic translated into Latin in the 10th century which told of his journey to a "Promised Land of Saints," and St. Brendan's Island was long sought by explorers.

Brennan, William J(oseph), Jr. (1906–1997) U.S. jurist. Born in Newark, N.J., he studied law under Felix Frankfurter at Harvard and after graduation specialized in labor law. He rose through the ranks of the New Jersey courts, where he was noted for his administrative skill. Though a Democrat, he was named to the U.S. Supreme Court by Pres. Dwight D. Eisenhower in 1956. He came to be regarded as among the most influential jurists in its history. A liberal constructionist and an articulate defender of the Bill of Rights, he is perhaps best remembered for his role in a series of obscenity cases, beginning with *Roth vs. U.S.* (1957), many of which broadened the protection accorded to publishers while seeking to balance individual freedoms with the interests of the community. In *New York Times Co. vs. Sullivan* (1964), he wrote that even false statements about public officials are protected under the 1st and 14th Amendments unless "actual malice" can be demonstrated. He also wrote the majority opinion in *Baker vs. Carr* (1962). He opposed capital punishment and supported abortion rights, affirmative action, and school desegregation. He served until 1990; his decisions numbered more than 1,350.

Brent, Margaret (c. 1600–1671?) British colonial landowner in North America. She arrived in Maryland in 1638 and obtained a patent for 70 acres, becoming the first woman in the colony to hold land in her own right. By 1657 she was among the colony's largest landowners. In a border dispute with Virginia in 1646, she organized a group of armed volunteers to support the Maryland colony's governor, Leonard Calvert. On his death in 1647, she became executor of his estate and settled a dispute over back pay for his soldiers that had nearly led to civil war.

Brentano \bren-'tä-nō\, **Clemens** (1778–1842) German poet, novelist, and dramatist. He was one of the founders of the Heidelberg Romantic school, which emphasized German folklore and history. With his brother-in-law Achim von Arnim (1781–1831) he published *Des Knaben Wunderhorn* (1805–8; *The Youth's Magic Horn*), a collection of German folk lyrics (including successful imitations of folk style) that became an important inspiration to lyric poets and composers such as G. Mahler. Among his most successful works are his fairy tales, particularly *Gockel, Hinkel and Gackeleia* (1838).

Brentano \bren-'tä-nō\, **Franz (Clemens)** (1838–1917) German philosopher. Nephew of Clemens Brentano, he was ordained a priest in 1864 and taught at the University of Würzburg 1866–73. Religious doubts led to his resignation from the priesthood in 1873. To present a systematic psychology that would serve as a science of the soul, he wrote the influential *Psychology from an Empirical Standpoint* (1874). He became the founder of act psychology, or intentionalism, which concerns itself with the mind's "acts" or processes (e.g., perception, judgment, loving, and hating) rather than its contents. He later taught at the University of Vienna (1874–80, 1881–95) and published such works as *Inquiry into Sense Psychology* (1907) and *The Classification of Psychological Phenomena* (1911).

Brescia \'brā-shä, 'bre-shə\ *ancient* **Brixia** City (pop., 1996 est.: 190,000), Lombardy region, northern Italy. Originally a Celtic stronghold, it was occupied by the Romans c. 200 BC and became the seat of a Roman colony in 27 BC. It was devastated by the Goths (AD 412) and plundered by Attila (452). It was a free city in 936–1426. It passed to Venice, France, and Austria before being united with Italy in 1860. Historic structures include Roman ruins and 11th- and 17th-century cathedrals. The art treasures in its numerous churches include works by painters of the 15th- and 16th-century Brescia school.

Breshkovsky, Catherine (1844–1934) Russian revolutionary. After becoming involved with the Narodnik (or Populist) revolutionary group in the 1870s, she was arrested and exiled to Siberia for the years 1874–96. In 1901 she helped organize the Socialist Revolutionary Party, and her involvement again led to her arrest and exile to Siberia (1910–17). Though she became known as the "little grandmother of the Revolution," she opposed the Bolsheviks after their 1917 victory and emigrated to Prague.

Breslau See Wroclaw

Breslin, Jimmy *orig.* **James Earl** (born 1930) U.S. columnist and novelist. During his long newspaper career Breslin became known as a tough-talking voice of his native Queens, a working-class New York borough. Educated at Long Island University he started as a copyboy, then established himself as a sportswriter; later as a syndicated columnist and contributor to numerous publications he wrote with passion and personal involvement on politics and social issues, often focusing on injustice and corruption. He won a 1986 Pulitzer Prize. Among his books are the novel *The Gang That Couldn't Shoot Straight* (1969).

Bresson, Henri Cartier- See Henri Cartier-Bresson

Bresson \brə-'sō^{n}\, **Robert** (1901–1999) French film director. He worked as a painter and photographer before making his first film in 1934. His feature-length *Les anges du péché* (1943) established his austere, intellectual style. Noted for intense psychological probing and the subordination of plot to visual imagery, he also directed *The Diary of a Country Priest* (1950), *A Man Escaped* (1956), *Pickpocket* (1959), *Balthazar* (1966), *Lancelot of the Lake* (1974), and *L'argent* (1983).

Brest-Litovsk \'brest-li-'tȯfsk\, **Treaty of** (March 3, 1918) Peace treaty signed at Brest-Litovsk (now in Belarus) by the Central Powers with Soviet Russia, concluding hostilities between those countries in World War I. Russia lost the Ukraine, its Polish and Baltic territories, and Finland by signing the treaty, which was later annulled by the Armistice.

Brétigny \brā-tēn-'yē\, **Treaty of** (1360) Treaty between England and France that ended the first phase of the Hundred Years' War. Marking a serious setback for the French, the treaty was signed after Edward the Black Prince defeated and captured John II of France at the Battle of Poitiers (1356). The French ceded extensive territories in northwestern France to England and agreed to ransom John at a cost for 3 million gold crowns, while Edward renounced his claim to the French throne. The treaty failed to establish a lasting peace.

Breton \brə-'tōü\, **André** (1896–1966) French writer, critic, and editor. In 1919 he helped found the Dada magazine *Littérature.* Influenced by psychiatry and the Symbolist movement, he wrote poetry using the automatic-writing technique. In 1924 his *Manifeste du surréalisme* provided a definition of Surrealism, of which he was the chief promoter. In the 1930s he joined and then broke with the Communist Party; in 1938 he founded the Fédération de l'Art Revolutionnaire Independant with Leon Trotsky in Mexico. He spent World War II in the U.S. and returned to France in 1946. His *Poèmes* appeared in 1948. He also wrote essays, works of criticism, and novels, including *Nadja* (1928).

Breton language \'bre-t^{ə}n\ Celtic language spoken in Brittany, introduced in the 5th–6th century by immigrants from southern Britain. Breton is attested in glosses in Latin manuscripts of the 8th–10th century, but no continuous text is known before the 15th century. The modern language is divided into four groups of very diverse dialects; this disunity has hindered efforts to form orthographic and literary standards.

Though Breton may have half a million speakers, use of the language is generally thought to be in sharp decline among younger people despite a resurgence of regional particularism in western Europe.

Bretton Woods Conference *officially* **United Nations Monetary and Financial Conference** (July 1–22, 1944) Meeting held at Bretton Woods, N.H., to make financial arrangements for the postwar era after the expected defeat of Germany and Japan. Representatives of 44 countries, including the Soviet Union, agreed to create the INTERNATIONAL BANK FOR RECONSTRUCTION AND DEVELOPMENT (WORLD BANK) and the INTERNATIONAL MONETARY FUND. See also JOHN MAYNARD KEYNES.

bretwalda \bret-'wäl-də\ *or* **brytenwalda** \ˌbri-tən-'wäl-də\ Any of several Anglo-Saxon kings with lordship over kingdoms beyond their own. Used in the Anglo-Saxon Chronicle, the title probably means "ruler of the Britons." It was given to Egbert (died 839) of Wessex and to seven earlier kings: Aelle of Sussex (fl. late 5th century), Ceawlin of Wessex (died 593), Aethelberht of Kent (died 616), Raedwald of East Anglia (died 616/27), Edwin of Northumbria (died 632), Oswald of Northumbria (died 641), and Oswiu of Northumbria (died 670).

Breuer \'brȯi-ər\, **Marcel (Lajos)** (1902–1981) Hungarian-U.S. architect and furniture designer. He studied and then taught at the BAUHAUS (1920–28), where he invented the famous tubular steel chair (1925). He moved to Cambridge, Mass., in 1937 to teach and practice with WALTER GROPIUS. Their synthesis of Bauhaus internationalism with New England regional wood-frame building greatly influenced domestic architecture throughout the U.S. He was one of the most influential exponents of the INTERNATIONAL STYLE. His major commissions include UNESCO's Paris headquarters (1953–58) and the Whitney Museum of American Art (1966).

Brewer, David J(osiah) (1837–1910) U.S. Supreme Court justice (1889–1910). Born to U.S. missionaries in Turkey, he grew up in Connecticut and practiced law in Kansas from 1858. He served in local judgeships (1861–70), on the state supreme court (1870–84), and on the federal circuit court. On the Supreme Court he generally joined conservatives in resisting the trend toward increased federal power and responsibility. In 1895–97 he led the panel that settled the Venezuela–British Guiana boundary dispute.

Brewster, William (1567–1644) British-American Puritan leader of Plymouth Colony in Massachusetts. He studied briefly at Cambridge University and became leader of a small Puritan congregation at Scrooby. Government persecution forced Brewster and his followers to emigrate to Holland in 1608, and he printed religious books in Leiden. In 1620 he joined the first group of Pilgrims aboard the *Mayflower* on the voyage to North America. When the colonists landed at Plymouth, Brewster became the senior elder of the colony, serving as its religious leader and as an adviser to Gov. WILLIAM BRADFORD.

Breyer \'brī-ər\, **Stephen (Gerald)** (born 1938) U.S. jurist. Born in San Francisco, he became a lawyer, clerked for ARTHUR GOLDBERG (1964–65), and taught at Harvard Law School (1967–81). He served as special counsel (1974–75) and chief counsel (1979–81) to the U.S. Senate Judiciary Committee before being appointed to the First U.S. Circuit Court of Appeals (1980); he became chief judge in 1990. He served on the commission that devised guidelines for federal sentencing (1985–89). He was nominated to the U.S. Supreme Court in 1994 by Pres. WILLIAM JEFFERSON CLINTON; as a pragmatic moderate he has usually joined the Court's moderate wing.

Brezhnev \'brezh-ˌnef\, **Leonid (Ilich)** (1906–1982) Soviet leader. He worked as an engineer and director of a technical school in the Ukraine and held local posts in the Communist Party, becoming regional party secretary in 1939. In World War II he was a political commissar in the Red Army and rose to major general (1943). In the 1950s he supported NIKITA KHRUSHCHEV and became a member of the Politburo. After Khrushchev's ouster (1964), Brezhnev emerged as general secretary of the party (1966–82) and the dominant leader in the coalition that ousted Khrushchev. He developed the Brezhnev Doctrine, which asserted the right of Soviet intervention in such WARSAW PACT countries as Czechoslovakia (1968). In the 1970s he attempted to normalize relations with the West and to promote DÉTENTE with the U.S. He was made marshal of the Soviet Union in 1976 and chairman of the Presidium of the Supreme Soviet in 1977, becoming the first to hold the leadership of both the party and the state. He greatly expanded the Soviet Union's military-industrial complex, but in so doing he deprived the rest of the Soviet economy. Despite frail health he retained his hold on power to the end.

Brian Boru \'brēn-bə-'rü\ (941–1014) High king of Ireland (1002–14). He became king of Munster in 976, won control of the southern half of Ireland from the high king Maelsechlainn in 997, and replaced him in 1002. Leinster and the Norsemen of Dublin united against him in 1013 with help from abroad; at the Battle of Clontarf, won by his son Murchad, Brian was killed in his tent by fleeing Norsemen (see VIKINGS). A line of princes, the O'Briens, descended from him.

Briand \brē-'ä^{n}\, **Aristide** (1862–1932) French statesman. He became secretary-general of the FRENCH SOCIALIST PARTY in 1901 and served in the Chamber of Deputies 1902–32. Between 1909 and 1929 he served 11 times as premier of France, and he held 26 ministerial posts between 1906 and 1932. His achievements included the Pact of LOCARNO and the KELLOGG-BRIAND PACT. For his efforts for international cooperation, the LEAGUE OF NATIONS, and world peace, he shared the 1926 Nobel Peace Prize with GUSTAV STRESEMANN.

bribery Crime of giving a benefit (e.g., money) in order to influence the judgment or conduct of a person in a position of trust (e.g., an official or witness). Accepting a bribe also constitutes a crime. Bribery is typically punishable as a FELONY. In any charge of bribery, some element of "corrupt purpose" must be implied or proved. Thus, in the absence of a complete statutory prohibition on the granting of favors to a public official, a gift is not a bribe unless it is given with some intent to influence the recipient's official behavior. See also EXTORTION.

Brice, Fanny *orig.* **Fannie Borach** (1891–1951) U.S. comedian and singer. Born in New York City, she played in vaudeville and burlesque shows, where FLORENZ ZIEGFELD discovered her in 1910. She became a headliner in his *Follies* with her musical numbers and comedy routines, including satiric sketches of ballet dancers and fan dancers as well as affecting torch songs such as "My Man." The character of Baby Snooks, an incorrigible little girl, which she created to amuse her friends, became the basis of a popular radio series (1938–51). The Broadway musical *Funny Girl* (1964; film, 1968) was based on her life.

Fanny Brice as Baby Snooks.
CULVER PICTURES

brick Small building unit in the form of a rectangular block, first produced in a sun-dried form at least 6,000 years ago. Clay, the basic ingredient, is mined from open pits, formed, and then fired in a kiln to produce strength, hardness, and heat resistance. Brick was the chief building material in the ancient Near East. Its versatility was expanded in ancient Rome by improvements in manufacture and by new techniques of bonding. Brick came to be widely used in Western Europe for the protection it offered against fire. See also MASONRY, MORTAR.

Bricker, John W(illiam) (1893–1986) U.S. politician, governor of Ohio (1939–45) and U.S. senator (1947–59). Born in Madison Co., Ohio, he practiced law and served as the state's attorney general 1933–37. Elected governor, he became the first Republican to win three consecutive terms. He was THOMAS DEWEY's running mate in the 1944 presidential race. As a U.S. senator, he led efforts to curb the president's power in foreign affairs. In 1953 he sponsored a constitutional amendment to limit U.S. participation in international treaties; opposed by JOHN FOSTER DULLES, it was narrowly defeated.

bridewealth Payment made by the groom or his kin to the kin of the wife in order to ratify the marriage. The practice is common in most parts of the globe in one form or another, but is perhaps most prevalent in Africa. It is most often a matter of social and symbolic as well as economic reciprocity, being part of a long series of exchanges between the two intermarrying families. It represents a pledge that the wife will be well treated, and serves as compensation for her family's loss. Payment may consist of goods or, less frequently, services, and it may be paid in one sum or regularly over a long period of time. See also DOWRY.

bridge Structure that spans horizontally to allow pedestrians and vehicles to cross a void. Bridge construction has always presented civil engineering with its greatest challenges. The simplest bridge is the beam (or girder) bridge, consisting of straight, rigid beams placed across a span (e.g., a tree trunk laid across a stream). Ancient Roman bridges are famous for their rounded arch form, which permitted spans much longer than those of stone beams and were more durable than wood. A modification of the arch bridge was the drawbridge, developed during medieval times. The lift bridge, another movable type, can change position to allow clearance for ships and boats. Suspension bridges (e.g., BROOKLYN BRIDGE, GOLDEN GATE BRIDGE) are capable of spanning great distances; their main support members are cables composed of thousands of strands of wire supported by two towers and anchored at each end, and the roadway is supported by vertical cables hung from the main cables. Other bridges include the truss bridge, popular (e.g., for railroad bridges) because it uses a relatively small amount of material to carry large loads, and the cantilever bridge, typically made with three spans, with the outer spans anchored down at the shore and the central span resting on the cantilevered arms.

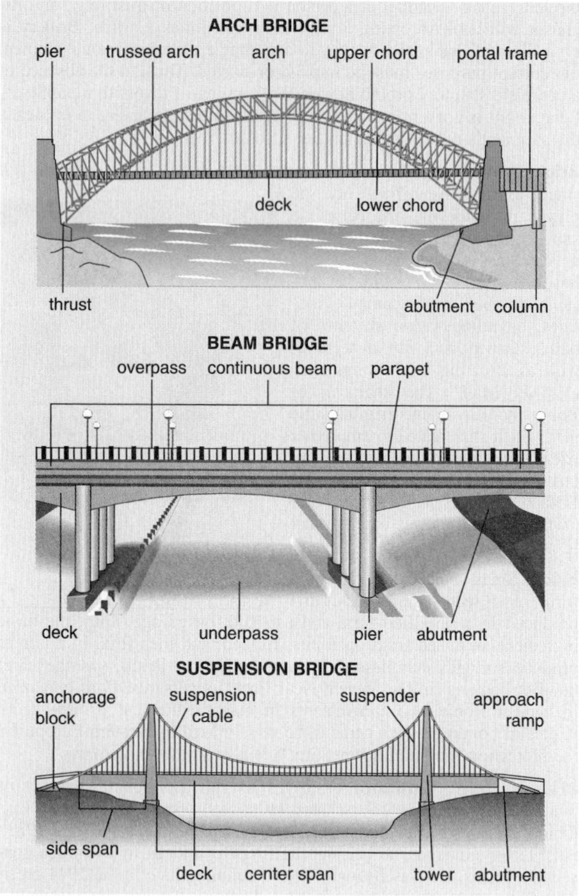

Three common types of bridge design.

bridge Any of various card games similar to WHIST for four players in two partnerships. Bridge is played with a 52-card pack, all of whose cards are dealt face downward one at a time, clockwise. The object is to win tricks, or hands consisting of one card from each player in rotation. The players must, if able, contribute a card of the suit led, and the trick is won by the highest card. Before play begins, a suit may be designated the trump suit, in which case any card in it beats any card of the other suits. The two most popular forms of bridge are contract bridge, in which overtricks (i.e., tricks made in excess of the bid) do not count toward game or slam (single-hand) bonuses, and auction bridge, in which such tricks are scored toward the game. The whist and bridge family of games are of English origin.

Bridgeport City (pop., 2000: 139,529), southwestern Connecticut. Located on LONG ISLAND SOUND at the mouth of the Pequonnock River, it was settled in 1639. Its earlier names included Newfield and Stratford; Bridgeport was chosen in 1800. P. T. BARNUM was once its mayor, and his star attraction "Tom Thumb" was born there. The city evolved into an industrial center following the AMERICAN CIVIL WAR. In the late 20th century, its industrial base eroded, causing financial problems for the city.

Bridger, Jim *orig.* **James** (1804–1881) U.S. frontiersman. Born in Richmond, Va., he grew up in Illinois. From 1822 he led fur-trapping expeditions to Utah and Idaho. He was apparently the first white man to visit the Great Salt Lake (1824) and among the first to explore Wyoming's Yellowstone River region. In 1843 he established Fort Bridger, Wyo., as a fur-trading post on the Oregon Trail. After the 1850s he worked as a government scout. He became legendary for his knowledge of the territory and its Indian inhabitants.

Bridges, Calvin Blackman (1889–1938) U.S. geneticist. Born in Schuyler Falls, N.Y., he entered Columbia University in 1909 and assisted THOMAS HUNT MORGAN in designing experiments using drosophila that showed that variations in the insect could be traced to observable changes in its genes. These experiments led to the construction of gene maps and proved the chromosome theory of heredity. In 1928 Bridges and Morgan moved to Caltech, where Bridges continued gene mapping and later discovered an important class of drosophila mutants caused by gene duplications.

Bridges, Harry *orig.* **Alfred Bryant Renton** (1901–1990) Australian-U.S. labor leader. He arrived in the U.S. as a seaman in 1920, and soon settled in San Francisco and became active in the local branch of the International Longshoremen's Association (ILA). In 1937 he led the Pacific Coast division out of the ILA and reconstituted it as the International Longshoremen's and Warehousemen's Union (ILWU), affiliated with the CIO (see AFL-CIO). His aggressive labor tactics and Communist Party connections led the CIO to expel the ILWU in 1950 during a purge of allegedly communist-dominated unions, and conservatives tried unsuccessfully to have Bridges deported. He retired as president of the ILWU in 1977.

Bridges, Robert (Seymour) (1844–1930) English poet. He published several long poems and poetic dramas, but his reputation rests on the lyrics collected in *Shorter Poems* (1890, 1894), which reveal his mastery of prosody. His 1916 edition of the poetry of his friend GERARD MANLEY HOPKINS rescued it from obscurity. He was poet laureate of England from 1913 until his death.

Robert Bridges, gold-point drawing by W. Strang; in the National Portrait Gallery, London.

Bridget, St. (1303?–1373) Mystic and patron saint of Sweden. She had religious visions from an early age but married and had eight children, including St. Catherine of Sweden. On the death of her husband (1344), she retired to a life of prayer. She lived in Rome after 1350, striving to bring the pope back from Avignon, and died after a visit to the Holy Land. In response to a revelation, she founded a new religious order in 1370.

Bridgetown Capital (pop., 1990: 6,070) of BARBADOS, West Indies. Located on Carlisle Bay at the southwestern end of Barbados, it is the island's only port of entry. Founded in 1628, it was originally called Indian Bridge. The name St. Michael's Town came into favor c. 1660 and remained in use into the 19th century. The town was ravaged repeatedly by fires, and in 1854 a cholera epidemic killed some 20,000 people. Landmarks include St. Michael's Anglican Cathedral, built of coral rock. Economic mainstays include sugar refining, rum distilling, and tourism.

brier HEATH (*Erica arborea*), also called white heath or tree heath, found in southern France and the Mediterranean region. Its roots and knotted stems are used for making briarwood tobacco pipes. Its leaves are needlelike and its flowers almost white. The term brier also applies generally to any plant (as of the genera *Rosa, Rubus,* and *Smilax*) with a woody and thorny or prickly stem.

brig Two-masted sailing ship with square rigging on both masts. Brigs were both naval and mercantile vessels. As merchantmen, they often followed coastal trading routes, but ocean voyages were not uncommon, and some were even used for whaling and sealing. Naval brigs carried 10–20 guns on a single deck. In the 18th–19th century, they served as couriers for battle fleets and as training vessels for cadets. Brigs of the early U.S. Navy won distinction on the Great Lakes in the War of 1812. Because square rigging required a large crew, merchant brigs became uneconomical, and in the 19th century they began to give way to vessels such as the SCHOONER and the bark.

brigade \bri-ˈgād\ MILITARY UNIT commanded by a brigadier general or a colonel and composed of two or more subordinate units, such as REGIMENTS or BATTALIONS. Two or more brigades make up a division.

Brigham Young University \ˌbrig-əm\ Private university in Provo, Utah. Founded in 1875 by the Mormon president BRIGHAM YOUNG, it continues to be supported by the MORMON church. It is composed of nine colleges as well as schools of management and law. Important research facilities include laboratories for nuclear, plasma, and solid-state physics, aquatic ecology, and veterinary pathology and institutes for the study of food and agriculture and of computer-aided manufacturing. Total enrollment is about 31,000.

Bright, John (1811–1889) British reform politician and orator. He entered Parliament in 1843 and served three times as a member of WILLIAM E. GLADSTONE's cabinet. He was active in campaigns for free trade, lower grain prices, and parliamentary reform. His Quaker beliefs shaped his politics, which consisted mainly of demands for an end to inequalities between individuals and between peoples. He denounced the Crimean War, supported the REFORM BILL OF 1867, and was a cofounder (with RICHARD COBDEN) of the ANTI-CORN LAW LEAGUE.

Brighton Town (pop., 1995 est.: 143,000), southern England. Lying on the ENGLISH CHANNEL south of London, it was for several centuries a small fishing village, but gained popularity in the late 18th century when the Prince of Wales (later GEORGE IV) made the first of his many visits. His powerful patronage stamped the town with the distinguished character still seen in its REGENCY STYLE squares. Victorian Brighton grew rapidly with the opening of the railway connecting it to London (1841).

Bright's disease Type of NEPHRITIS without pus formation or EDEMA. It may or may not recur. The acute stage involves severe inflammation and back pain, deficient kidney function, swelling, and HYPERTENSION. In the subacute stage, the kidney enlarges, blood does not reach its surface and red blood cells are damaged (leading to anemia), and its tissue breaks down, releasing excess blood protein into urine. In the chronic stage, a small, shriveled, scarred kidney cannot filter nitrogen compounds from the blood, causing UREMIA. Treatment focuses on symptom relief.

Brigit \ˈbri-jət\ In CELTIC RELIGION, the goddess of poetry, crafts, prophecy, and divination. She was equivalent to the Roman MINERVA and the Greek ATHENA, and substantially the same as the northern British goddess Brigantia. In Ireland she was worshiped by the *filid,* a poetic and priestly class. She was one of three daughters of DAGDA, all named Brigit, the others being associated with healing and the craft of the smith. Some of the lore surrounding Brigit was transferred to the 5th-century Irish abbess St. Brigid. Her feast day, February 1, is the date of the pagan festival Imbolc, when the ewes came into milk. Her great monastery at Kildare was probably founded on a pagan sanctuary, and many holy wells in the British Isles are dedicated to her.

Brillat-Savarin \brē-yá-sá-vá-ˈra^{n}\, **(Jean-) Anthelme** (1755–1826) French lawyer and gastronome. Mayor of the town of Belley, he fled France during the REIGN OF TERROR, but returned to sit on France's highest court, where he remained the rest of his life. His celebrated *Physiologie du goût* ("Physiology of Taste"; translated as *A Handbook of Gastronomy*), published in 1825, is less a treatise on cuisine than a witty compendium of anecdotes and observations intended to enhance the pleasures of the table, with only the occasional recipe included.

brine shrimp Any of several small CRUSTACEANS (genus *Artemia*) inhabiting brine pools and other highly salty inland waters throughout the world. *A. salina,* which occurs in vast numbers in Great Salt Lake, Utah, is commercially important. Young brine shrimp hatched there from dried eggs are used widely as food for fish and other small animals in aquariums. Up to 0.6 in. (15 mm) long, the brine shrimp's body has a distinguishable head and a slender abdomen. It normally swims upside down, and it feeds primarily on green algae, which it filters from the water with its legs.

Brine shrimp (*Artemia salina*).
DOUGLAS P. WILSON

Brinkley, David (McClure) (born 1920) U.S. television news broadcaster. Born in Wilmington, N.C., he joined NBC in 1943 and became Washington correspondent for NBC News (1951–81). With Chet Huntley he coanchored NBC's nightly *Huntley-Brinkley Report* (1956–70). He later hosted a weekly television news and interview program on ABC (1981–97).

Brinkman, Johannes Andreas (1902–1949) Dutch architect. After graduating from the Delft Technical Univ., he helped design the van Nelle tobacco factory (1928–30) in Rotterdam, one of the most architecturally important industrial buildings of the 1920s. An outstanding example of modernist architecture, its unbroken expanses of glass convey a strong feeling of lightness and transparency.

Brisbane \ˈbriz-ˌbān\ City (pop., 1995: 1,489,000), QUEENSLAND, Australia. Lying on the northern bank of the Brisbane River above its mouth at MORETON BAY, the site was first explored by the English in 1823. It was founded as a penal colony in 1824, and declared a town in 1834 when it was named in honor of Sir Thomas Brisbane, former governor of New South Wales. Made the capital of Queensland in 1859, it was joined with South Brisbane in the 1920s to form greater Brisbane. The city, connected by bridges and ferries, is Australia's third-largest; it is the hub of rail lines and highways and a busy port. It is the site of the Queensland Cultural Centre, and a university.

Brisbane, Albert (1809–1890) U.S. social reformer. Born in Batavia, N.Y., to wealthy landowners, he went to Europe in 1828 to study with social reformers, including FRANCOIS GUIZOT, G. W. F. HEGEL, and CHARLES FOURIER. In 1834 he returned to the U.S. and later established a Fourier community in New Jersey. His book *Social Destiny of Man* (1840) attracted widespread attention. In his newspaper column in the *New York Tribune* he explained the Fourier system of self-sustaining communities, which he called Associationism. His son Arthur (1864–1936) was editor of the *New York Evening Journal* (1897–1921) and the *Chicago Herald and Examiner* (from 1918).

brise-soleil \ˌbrēz-sō-ˈlā\ (French: "breaks the sun") Sun baffle of vertical or horizontal louvers outside the windows or extending over the entire surface of a building's facade, especially precast concrete grids of the type developed by LE CORBUSIER. Many traditional methods exist for reducing the effects of the sun's glare, such as the projecting upper-story window of latticework *(mashrabiyah* or *mushrabiyah)* used in Islamic architecture, pierced screens as used at the TAJ MAHAL, or blinds of split bamboo *(sudare)* as used in Japan.

brisling See SPRAT

Brissot (de Warville) \brē-ˈsō\, **Jacques-Pierre** (1754–1793) French revolutionary politician. He founded the popular newspaper *Le Patriote Français* and became a leader of the GIRONDINS (often called Brissotins) in the FRENCH REVOLUTION. Elected to the Legislative Assembly in 1791, he advocated war against Austria, arguing that war would consolidate the Revolution. Along with other Girondins, he was arrested and guillotined during the REIGN OF TERROR.

Bristol City (pop., 1995: 401,000), southwestern England. Lying at the confluence of the AVON and Frome rivers, the city received its first charter in 1155. Long a center of commerce, it was the point of departure in 1497 of JOHN CABOT in his search for a route to Asia. During the 17th–18th century it prospered on the triangular slave trade between West Africa and the West Indian and American plantation colonies. Though Bristol suffered a decline in trade in the early 19th century, it soon rebounded with the coming of the railway. It suffered severe destruction from bombing in World War II, but was rebuilt. Today it is an important shipping center, especially for oil and food products.

Britain Name historically applied to the island of GREAT BRITAIN. Britain is used especially when referring to its pre-Roman and Roman periods and to its early Anglo-Saxon period. It is the Anglicized form of Latin *Britannia.* See also UNITED KINGDOM.

Britain, Battle of (June 1940–April 1941) Series of intense raids directed against Britain by the German air force in WORLD WAR II. The air attacks, intended to prepare the way for a German invasion, were directed against British ports and RAF bases. In September 1940 the attacks turned to London and other cities in a "blitz" of bombings for 57 consecutive nights, which was followed by intermittent raids until April 1941. The RAF was outnumbered but succeeded in blocking the German air force through superior tactics and codebreaking.

British Airways An international passenger airline based in London with destinations in more than 80 countries. Its predecessor companies include the nationalized British Overseas Airways Corporation (BOAC) and British European Airways (BEA). In 1974 BEA and BOAC combined to form British Airways. The airline was privatized in 1987. It merged with British Caledonian later that year.

British Broadcasting Corp. See BBC

British Columbia Province (pop., 1996: 3,933,000), western Canada. It is bounded by Yukon Territory, Northwest Territories, Alberta, the Pacific Ocean, and the U.S. (including Alaska); its capital is VICTORIA. The area was inhabited by indigenous peoples, including Coast Salish, NOOTKA, KWAKIUTL, and HAIDA. It was visited in 1578 by Sir FRANCIS DRAKE and in 1778 by Capt. JAMES COOK, who was searching for the NORTHWEST PASSAGE. Capt. George Vancouver surveyed the coast (1792–94), and overland expeditions were made by several explorers, including ALEXANDER MACKENZIE, MERIWETHER LEWIS and WILLIAM CLARK, and SIMON FRASER. The British and Americans contended over VANCOUVER ISLAND for years, until it was recognized as British and made a crown colony in 1849. The mainland became the Colony of British Columbia in 1858; with the colony of Vancouver, it joined Canada in 1871 as the province of British Columbia. The province has a prosperous economy based on diverse sources, including logging, mining, tourism, agriculture, and shipping.

British Commonwealth See COMMONWEALTH

British East Africa Territory under former British control, Africa. British penetration of the area began in ZANZIBAR in the late 19th century. In 1888 the British East Africa Co. claimed territory in what is now Kenya. British protectorates were established over Zanzibar and the kingdom of Buganda (see UGANDA). In 1919 Britain was awarded the former German territory of Tanganyika as a League of Nations mandate. All these territories achieved political independence in the 1960s.

British empire Worldwide system of dependencies—colonies, protectorates, and other territories—that over a span of three centuries came under the British government. Territorial acquisition began in the early 17th century with a group of settlements in North America and West Indian, East Indian, and African trading posts founded by private individuals and trading companies. In the 18th century the British took GIBRALTAR, established colonies along the Atlantic seacoast, and began to add territory in India. With its victory in the FRENCH AND INDIAN WAR (1763), it secured Canada and the eastern Mississippi Valley and gained supremacy in India. From the late 18th century it began to build power in Malaya and acquired the Cape of Good Hope, Ceylon (see SRI LANKA), and MALTA. The English settled Australia in 1788, and subsequently New Zealand. ADEN was secured in 1839, and HONG KONG in 1842. Britain went on to control the SUEZ CANAL 1875–1956. In the 19th-century European partition of Africa, Britain acquired Nigeria, Egypt, the territories that would become BRITISH EAST AFRICA, and part of what would become the Union (later Republic) of South Africa. After World War I, Britain secured mandates to German East Africa, part of the Cameroons, part of Togo, German South-West Africa, MESOPOTAMIA, PALESTINE, and part of the German Pacific islands. Prior to 1783, Britain claimed full authority over colonial legislatures; after the U.S. gained independence, Britain gradually evolved a system of self-government for some colonies, as set forth in Lord Durham's report of 1839. Dominion status was given to Canada (1867), Australia (1901), New Zealand (1907), the Union of South Africa (1910), and the Irish Free State (1921). Britain declared war on Germany in 1914 on behalf of the entire empire; after World War I the dominions signed the peace treaties themselves and joined the LEAGUE OF NATIONS as independent states. In 1931 the Statute of WESTMINSTER recognized them as independent countries "within the British empire," referring to the "British Commonwealth of Nations." At the time of its founding, the Commonwealth consisted of the United Kingdom, Australia, Canada, the Irish Free State (withdrew in 1949; see IRELAND), NEWFOUNDLAND (became a Canadian province in 1949), New Zealand, and the Union of South Africa (withdrew in 1961). After World War II, with "British" no longer officially used, the Commonwealth was joined by the following countries: India, Pakistan (1947; Pakistan withdrew in 1972, but rejoined in 1989); Ceylon (1948; now Sri Lanka); Ghana (1957); Nigeria (1960); Cypress, Sierra Leone (1961); Jamaica, Trinidad and Tobago, Uganda, Western Samoa (1962); Kenya, Malaysia (1963); Malawi, Malta, Tanzania, Zambia (1964); Gambia, Singapore (1965); Barbados, Botswana, Guyana, Lesotho (1966); Mauritius, Nauru (special status); Swaziland (1968); Tonga (1970); Bangladesh (1972); Bahamas (1973); Grenada (1974); Papua New Guinea (1975); Seychelles (1976); Solomon Islands, Tuvalu (special status), Dominica (1978); St. Lucia, Kiribati, St. Vincent and the Grenadines (1979); Zimbabwe, Vanuatu (1980); Belize, Antigua and Barbuda (1981); Maldives (1982); St. Kitts-Nevis (1983); Brunei (1984); South Africa (rejoined 1994); Cameroon, Mozambique (1995). The last significant British colony, Hong Kong, was returned to Chinese sovereignty in 1997.

British Expeditionary Force (BEF) Home-based regular British army forces sent to northern France at the start of World Wars I and II to support the French armies. Britain wished to help France in case of a German attack, and the BEF was created in 1908 to ensure that British forces would be trained and ready to respond quickly. It consisted of six INFANTRY divisions and one CAVALRY division. Five divisions sent to France at the outbreak of World War I sustained heavy losses and were succeeded by vast British armies. Divisions sent to France early in World War II (1939) returned to England when France fell the next year.

British Guiana See GUYANA

British Honduras See BELIZE

British Invasion Musical movement of the mid-1960s composed of British rock-and-roll ("beat") groups whose popularity spread rapidly to the United States, beginning with the triumphant arrival of Liverpool's BEATLES in New York in 1964 and continuing with the ROLLING STONES, the Animals, and others. Building on 1950s American models, these groups incorporated such local musical traditions as skiffle (acoustic drummerless ensembles), dancehall, and Celtic folk.

British Library National library of Great Britain, formed by the British Library Act (1972) and organized July 1, 1973. It consists of the former BRITISH MUSEUM library, National Central Library, National Lending Library for Science and Technology, and the British National Bibliography. The British Museum library, founded in 1753 based on earlier collections and later increased by the addition of royal libraries, had the right to a free copy of all books published in the United Kingdom. Its collection included a rich series of charters (including those of the Anglo-Saxon kings), codices, psalters, and other papers ranging from the 3rd century BC to modern times.

British Museum Britain's national museum of archaeology and antiquities, established in London in 1753 when the government purchased three large private collections consisting of books, manuscripts, prints, drawings, paintings, medals, coins, seals, cameos, and natural curiosities. In 1881 the natural-history collections were transferred to another building to form the Natural History Museum, and in 1973 the library collections were consolidated to form the BRITISH LIBRARY. Among the museum's most famous holdings are the ELGIN MARBLES, the ROSETTA STONE, the PORTLAND VASE, and Chinese ceramics. In 1808 the department of prints and drawings opened with over 2,000 drawings. It is now one of the world's largest and most comprehensive collections.

British North America Act (1867) Act of the British Parliament by which three British colonies—Nova Scotia, New Brunswick, and Canada—were united as "one Dominion under the name of Canada." The act also divided the province of Canada into the provinces of Quebec and Ontario. It served as Canada's "constitution" until 1982, when it became the basis of the CANADA ACT.

British Petroleum Co. PLC (BP) British petrochemical corporation. Formed in 1909 as the Anglo-Persian Oil Co., Ltd., to finance an oil-field concession granted by the Iranian government to WILLIAM KNOX D'ARCY, it became one of the largest oil companies in the world, with oil fields and refineries in Alaska and the North Sea. The British government was for many years BP's largest single stockholder, but by the late 1980s it had turned over the company to private ownership. In 1987 BP consolidated its U.S. interests by acquiring the STANDARD OIL CO. In 1998 it merged with Amoco (formerly Standard Oil of Indiana) to form BP–Amoco. In addition to oil and natural gas, it produces chemicals, plastics, and synthetic fibers. Its headquarters are in London.

British Somaliland Former British protectorate, southern shore of the Gulf of ADEN, eastern Africa. It occupied 67,936 sq mi (175,954 sq km). In the Middle Ages it was a powerful Arab sultanate; it was broken up in the 17th century. Its coast came under British influence in the early 19th century, but formal control was not acquired until it was taken from Egypt in 1884. It fell under Italian control in World War II. In 1960 it was united with the former ITALIAN SOMALILAND to form Somalia. See also SOMALILAND.

British Virgin Islands See British VIRGIN ISLANDS

Brittany *French* **Bretagne** \'brə-'tänʸ\ Historical peninsular region, northwestern France. Known in ancient times as Armorica, it comprised the coastal area between the SEINE and LOIRE rivers. Inhabited by Cymric Celts, it was conquered by JULIUS CAESAR and organized as the Roman province of Lugdunensis. Invaded in the 5th century AD by Britons (Celtic people from Britain), the extreme northwestern part was thereafter called Brittany. Subdued by CLOVIS I, it was never effectively part of the MEROVINGIAN or CAROLINGIAN kingdoms. Claimed by France in the 13th century, it remained a separate state until the 15th century. It was incorporated into France in 1532 and had province status until the FRENCH REVOLUTION.

Britten, (Edward) Benjamin *later* **Baron Britten of Aldeburgh** (1913–1976) British composer. He studied at the Royal College of Music, where he met the tenor Peter Pears (1910–1986), who would become his lifelong companion. His auspicious *Variations on a Theme of Frank Bridge* (1937) was followed by his *Sinfonia da Requiem* (1940) and *Serenade* (1943). In 1945 the opera *Peter Grimes* established him as a leading opera composer. In 1948 he cofounded the Aldeburgh Festival in the small town where he had settled; for the rest of his life his energies would principally be directed toward the festival, for which he often conducted and performed as pianist. His operas include *The Rape of Lucretia* (1946), *Albert Herring* (1947), *Billy Budd* (1951), *The Turn of the Screw* (1954), *A Midsummer Night's Dream* (1960), and *Death in Venice* (1973). His *War Requiem* (1961) was greatly acclaimed. Other vocal works include *A Ceremony of Carols* (1942) and *Spring Symphony* (1949); his best-known orchestral piece is *The Young Person's Guide to the Orchestra* (1946). In 1976 he became the first British composer in history to be ennobled, and he is generally regarded as Britain's greatest composer since W. BYRD and H. PURCELL.

Britten, 1960.
CAMERA PRESS

Brno \'bər-nō\ *German* **Brünn** \'brüen\ City (pop., 1996 est.: 389,000), southeastern Czech Republic. Located southeast of PRAGUE, it lies in an area that shows evidence of prehistoric inhabitance and traces of Celtic and SLAV settlements in the 5th–6th century AD. German colonization in the 13th century stimulated its growth; it received city status in 1243. In various wars it was besieged by the Swedes, Prussians, and French in the 15th–19th century. Before World War I it was the capital of the Austrian crown land of MORAVIA. The inhabitants, predominantly German before World War II, are now mainly Czech. GREGOR MENDEL worked on his theory of heredity (1865) in the monastery at Brno.

broaching machine MACHINE TOOL, usually hydraulically operated, for finishing surfaces by drawing or pushing a cutter called a broach entirely over and past the surface. A broach has a series of cutting teeth arranged in a row or rows, graduated in height from the teeth that cut first to those that cut last. Each tooth removes only a few thousandths of an inch, and the total depth of cut is distributed over all the teeth. Broaching is particularly suitable for internal surfaces such as holes and internal GEARS, but it can also shape external gears and flat surfaces.

broad jump See LONG JUMP

broadband Term describing the RADIATION from a source that produces a broad, continuous SPECTRUM of FREQUENCIES (contrasted with a LASER, which produces a single frequency or very narrow range of frequencies). A typical broadband-light source that can be used for either emission or absorption SPECTROSCOPY is a metal filament heated to a high temperature, such as a tungsten lightbulb. Sunlight is also broadband radiation. See also BROADBAND TECHNOLOGY.

broadband technology Telecommunications devices, lines, or technologies that allow communication over a wide band of frequencies, and especially over a range of frequencies divided into multiple independent channels for the simultaneous transmission of different signals. Broadband systems allow voice, data, and video to be broadcast over the same medium at the same time. They may also allow multiple data channels to be broadcast simultaneously.

broadcasting Transmission of sound or images by radio or television. After GUGLIELMO MARCONI's discovery of wireless broadcasting in 1901, radio broadcasting was undertaken by amateurs. The first U.S. commercial radio station, KDKA of Pittsburgh, began operation in 1920. The number of stations increased rapidly, as did the formation of national radio networks. To avoid radio monopolies, Congress passed the Radio Act of 1927, which created the FEDERAL COMMUNICATIONS COMMISSION to oversee broadcast operations. In the 1930s and '40s, the "golden age of radio," innovations in broadcast techniques and programming made radio the most popular entertainment medium. Television broadcasting began in Germany and Britain in the 1930s. After World War II, the U.S. took the lead, and television stations soon overshadowed radio networks. Color television broadcasts began in 1954 and became widespread in the 1960s. By the 1980s, satellite transmission of live television further expanded the field of broadcasting. See also ABC, BBC, CBS, CNN, NBC, PBS.

Broadway Theater district in New York City, named for the avenue that runs through the Times Square area in central Manhattan, where most of the larger theaters are located. Broadway attracted theater producers and impresarios from the mid-19th century. The number and size of the theaters grew with New York's increasing prosperity, and by the 1890s the brightly lighted street was called "the Great White Way." By 1925, the height of theatrical activity in New York, about 80 theaters were located on or near Broadway; by 1980 only about 40 remained. In the 1990s the revitalization of the seedy Times Square neighborhood attracted larger audiences, though high production costs limited the viability of serious plays in Broadway theaters, which often chose to mount big musicals and other crowd-pleasing commercial ventures. See also OFF-BROADWAY.

Broca \'brō-kə\, **Paul** (1824–1880) French surgeon. His study of brain lesions contributed significantly to understanding of the origins of aphasia. Much of Broca's research concerned the comparative study of the skulls of the races of humankind, work that aided the development of modern physical anthropology. He originated methods to study the brain's form, structure, and surface features and sections of prehistoric skulls. His discovery (1861) of the brain's speech center (convolution of Broca) was the first anatomical proof of localization of brain function.

Detail of handwoven Italian silk brocaded on silk with floral motif, c. 1730–50.
BY COURTESY OF SCALAMANDRE, NEW YORK CITY

brocade Woven fabric having a raised floral or figured design that is introduced during the weaving process. The design, appearing only on the fabric face, is usually made in a SATIN or TWILL weave (see WEAVING). The background may be twill, satin, or plain weave. The rich, fairly heavy fabric is frequently used for evening dresses, draperies, and upholstery.

broccoli Plant (*Brassica oleracea* 'italica') closely related to CABBAGE in the MUSTARD FAMILY. A fast-growing, upright, branched, annual plant, it bears dense green clusters of edible flower buds. Native to the eastern Mediterranean and Asia Minor, it was introduced to the U.S. probably in colonial times. Broccoli thrives in moderate to cool climates. Its flavor resembles that of cabbage but is somewhat milder. It is one of the most broadly nutritious of all common vegetables.

Broccoli (*Brassica oleracea* variety *italica*).
G.R. ROBERTS

Broch \'brōk\, **Hermann** (1886–1951) German writer. A student of physics, mathematics, and philosophy, Broch published his first major work, *The Sleepwalkers* (1931–32), when he was in his 40s. A trilogy tracing the disintegration of European society between 1888 and 1918, it exemplifies his innovative multidimensional novels in its use of many different narrative forms to present a wide range of experience. His other novels include *The Death of Virgil* (1945), which presents the last 18 hours of VIRGIL's life, and *The Spell* (1953), a portrayal of a Hitlerian stranger's domination of a village. He also wrote essays, letters, and reviews.

Brocken Highest point, HARZ MTNS., central Germany. Its granite peak reaches 3,747 ft (1,142 m). When the sun is low, shadows from the peak become magnified, casting gigantic silhouettes on the upper surfaces of low-lying clouds or fog below the mountain. This effect, known as the Brocken bow or Brocken specter, has mystical significance in the mountain's folklore. Traditional rites enacted there on WALPURGIS NIGHT became connected with the legend of FAUST.

Brodsky, Joseph *orig.* **Iosip Aleksandrovich Brodsky** (1940–1996) Russian-U.S. poet. In the Soviet Union his independent spirit and irregular work record led to a five-year sentence to hard labor. Exiled in 1972, he settled in New York. He was poet laureate of the U.S. 1991–92. His lyric and elegiac poems ponder the universal concerns of life, death, and the meaning of existence. His poetry collections include *A Part of Speech* (1980), *History of the Twentieth Century* (1986), and *To Urania* (1988). He was awarded the Nobel Prize in 1987.

Broglie \'brȯi\, **Louis-Victor (-Pierre-Raymond), duc (Duke) de** (1892–1987) French physicist. A descendant of the de BROGLIE FAMILY of diplomats and politicians, he was inspired to study atomic physics by the work of MAX PLANCK and ALBERT EINSTEIN. In his doctoral thesis he described his theory of electron waves, then extended the WAVE-PARTICLE DUALITY theory of light to matter. He is noted both for his discovery of the wave nature of electrons and for his research on quantum theory. Einstein built on de Broglie's idea of "matter-waves"; based on this work, ERWIN SCHRODINGER constructed the system of wave mechanics. De Broglie remained at the Sorbonne after 1924 and taught theoretical physics at the Henri Poincaré Institute 1928–62. He was awarded a Nobel Prize in 1929 and UNESCO's Kalinga Prize in 1952.

Broglie family \'brȯi\ French noble family, descended from a Piedmontese family of the 17th century, that produced many high-ranking soldiers, politicians, and diplomats. Prominent members included François-Marie, duc de Broglie (1671–1745), general and marshal of France; Victor-François, duc de Broglie (1718–1814), a soldier and marshal of France; Victor, duc de Broglie (1785–1870), a prime minister who campaigned against reactionary forces; and Albert, duc de Broglie (1821–1901), who served as premier in the early years of the French Third Republic. The family also included the physicist L.-V. de BROGLIE.

bromegrass Any of about 100 annual and perennial species of weeds and forage GRASSES that make up the genus *Bromus,* in the family Poaceae (Gramineae). Found in temperate and cool climates, bromegrasses have flat, thin leaves and open, spreading, erect or drooping flower clusters. More than 40 species are found in the U.S.; about half are native grasses. Rescue grass *(B. catharticus),* a forage and pasture grass, and smooth brome *(B. inermis),* a forage plant and soil binder, are the economically important species. Downy brome or cheatgrass *(B. tectorum),* ripgut grass *(B. diandrus),* and foxtail brome *(B. rubens)* are dangerous to grazing animals; their spines can puncture the animals' eyes, mouths, and intestines, leading to infection and possible death.

bromeliad \brō-'mē-lē-ˌad\ Any of the flowering plants of the order Bromeliales, containing a single family, Bromeliaceae, with almost 2,600 species. All but one species are native to the tropical New World and the West Indies. Bromeliad flowers have three parts like lilies, but with contrasting sepals and petals. Many bromeliads are short-stemmed EPIPHYTES. Many species bear flowers in a long spike, with colored BRACTS below or along the spike. Most have fleshy fruit, but some produce dry pods. SPANISH MOSS and the edible fruit of the PINEAPPLE are the major economic products of the family. The leaves of some species contain fibers that are made into rope, fabric, and netting. The largest known bromeliad is the giant *Puya raimondii* of Peru and Bolivia, which may grow to more than 30 ft (9 m). Some species are cultivated indoors as ornamentals for their colorful flowers and foliage.

bromine \'brō-ˌmēn\ Nonmetallic chemical ELEMENT, chemical symbol Br, atomic number 35. It is one of the HALOGENS, a deep red, fuming liquid at ordinary temperatures (freezing point 19°F, or –7.2°C; boiling point 138°F, or 59°C), containing diatomic molecules of Br_2, and does not occur free in nature. It is obtained from seawater and brines or salt beds. Extremely irritating and toxic, bromine is a strong oxidizing agent (see OXIDATION-REDUCTION). Its compounds, in which it may have VALENCE 1, 3, 5, or 7, have many uses, including as petroleum additives (ethylene dibromide), in photographic EMULSIONS (silver bromide), as sedatives, and in flour (potassium bromate).

bronchiectasis \ˌbräŋ-kē-'ek-tə-səs\ Abnormal expansion of bronchi in the LUNGS. It usually results when preexisting lung disease causes bronchial INFLAMMATION and obstruction. Bronchial wall fibers degenerate, and bronchi become dilated or paralyzed, preventing removal of secretions, which stagnate. Infection spreads and intensifies. Evidence of the disease includes presence of infective agents, excess mucous secretions, labored breathing, bluish skin tint, and, in children, fatigue and growth retardation. Complications include recurrent PNEUMONIA, lung abscesses, spitting up blood, and, in chronic cases, toe and finger clubbing. Treatment involves frequent, long-term drainage or (if the disease is on one side only) surgical removal of affected lung segments and a short course of antibiotics.

bronchitis \bräŋ-'kī-təs\ INFLAMMATION in the bronchi of the LUNGS. Microbes and foreign matter in air stimulate secretion of bronchial mucus, motion of cilia (see CILIUM) to move the foreign material up and out, and coughing; these normal responses can irritate the bronchi and can cause inflammation, particularly if the person has other lung-damaging conditions. A cold or other short-term infection or injury may lead to acute bronchitis; long-term repetitive injury, as from smoking, may lead to chronic bronchitis. Untreated acute bronchitis may become chronic bronchitis, in which severe, irreversible damage leaves the lungs open to infection, fibrosis, EMPHYSEMA, PULMONARY HEART DISEASE, and PNEUMONIA. Treatment includes drugs to dilate the bronchi and promote coughing, prevention of infection, and lifestyle adaptations (e.g., quitting smoking).

Brontë family \'brän-tē\ Family of English writers. The daughters of an Anglican clergyman, they were brought up in Haworth on the Yorkshire moors. Their mother died early. Charlotte Brontë (1816–1855) attended the Clergy Daughter's School with her sister Emily and subsequently taught school and served as a governess. She and Emily made an unsuccessful attempt to open a school. Her novel *Jane Eyre* (1847), a powerful narrative of a woman in conflict with her natural desires and social situation, which gave a new truthfulness to Victorian fiction, was an immediate success. It was followed by the novels *Shirley* (1849) and *Villette* (1853). In 1854 she married her father's curate, and she died soon after at 38. Emily (Jane) Brontë (1818–1848) was perhaps the greatest writer of the three. *Poems by Currer, Ellis and Acton Bell* (1846), published jointly by the sisters, contained 21 of her poems; many critics believe that her verse alone reveals poetic genius. Her one novel, *Wuthering Heights* (1847), is a highly imaginative story of passion and hatred set on the Yorkshire moors. Though not a success when published, it later came to be considered one of the finest novels in English. Soon after its publication, her health began to fail, and she died of tuberculosis at 30. Anne Brontë (1820–1849) contributed 21 poems to

Poems by Currer, Ellis and Acton Bell, and wrote two novels, *Agnes Grey* (1847) and *The Tenant of Wildfell Hall* (1848). She died of tuberculosis at 29.

Brontosaurus See *APATOSAURUS*

Bronx Borough (pop., 1990: 1,204,000), NEW YORK CITY. One of New York's five boroughs, it is the only mainland borough, and is connected to MANHATTAN by a dozen bridges and railroad tunnels, and to QUEENS by the Triborough, Bronx-Whitestone, and Throgs Neck bridges. The site was called Keskesbeck by the Indians who sold it in 1639 to the Dutch West India Co. The borough was a part of Westchester Co. until 1898, when it was incorporated into the city of New York. Though primarily residential, much of its more than 80 mi (130 km) of waterfront is used for shipping, warehouses, and industry. It is home to baseball's Yankee Stadium. It has an extensive park system and includes the BRONX ZOO and the New York Botanical Gardens.

Bronx Zoo *formally* **New York Zoological Park** ZOO in New York City. It opened in 1899 on 265 acres (107 hectares) in the northwestern area of the Bronx. In 1941 it added the 4-acre (1.6-hectare) African Plains, which features large groups of animals in natural surroundings. The zoo also includes the World of Darkness (the world's first major exhibit of nocturnal animals, added in the 1960s), the World of Birds (a huge, indoor free-flight exhibit), the Rare Animal Range (near-extinct species in natural settings), a Children's Zoo, Wild Asia (Asian mammals and birds), and the Congo Gorilla Forest. Managed by the New York Zoological Society and financed by the society and the city, it supports much research and oversees the Wildlife Survival Center on St. Catherine's Island, Georgia.

bronze ALLOY traditionally composed of COPPER and TIN. Bronze was first made before 3000 BC (see BRONZE AGE) and is still widely used, though iron often replaced bronze in tools and weapons after about 1000 BC because of iron's abundance compared to copper and tin. Bronze is harder than copper, more readily melted, and easier to cast. It is also harder than iron and far more resistant to corrosion. Bell metal (which produces pleasing sounds when struck) is bronze with 20–25% tin content. Statuary bronze, with less than 10% tin and an admixture of zinc and lead, is technically a BRASS. The addition of less than 1% phosphorus improves the hardness and strength of bronze; that formulation is used for pump plungers, valves, and bushings. Also useful in mechanical engineering are manganese bronzes, with little or no tin but considerable amounts of zinc and up to 4.5% manganese. Aluminum bronzes, containing up to 16% aluminum and small amounts of other metals such as iron or nickel, are especially strong and corrosion-resistant; they are cast or wrought into pipe fittings, pumps, gears, ship propellers, and turbine blades. Most "copper" coins are actually bronze, typically with about 4% tin and 1% zinc.

Bronze Age Third phase in the development of material culture among the ancient peoples of Europe, Asia, and the Middle East, following the PALEOLITHIC and NEOLITHIC periods and preceding the IRON AGE. The term also denotes the first period in which metal was used. The date at which the age began varied by region; in Greece and China it began before 3000 BC, in Britain not until c. 1900 BC. The beginning of the period is sometimes called the Chalcolithic (Copper-Stone) Age, referring to the initial use of pure copper (along with its predecessor, stone). By 3000 BC the use of copper was well known in the Middle East, had extended westward into the Mediterranean area, and was beginning to infiltrate Europe. Only in the 2nd millennium BC did true BRONZE come to be widely used. The age was marked by increased specialization and the invention of the wheel and the ox-drawn plow. From c. 1000 BC the ability to heat and forge iron brought the Bronze Age to an end.

Bronzino \brȯn-'dzē-nō\, **Il** *orig.* **Agnolo *or* Agniolo di Cosimo** (1503–1572) Italian painter active in Florence. He was the student and adopted son of JACOPO DA PONTORMO. His work lacked the emotional intensity characteristic of contemporary religious painting, but he excelled as a portraitist and was court painter to Cosimo I de' MEDICI for most of his career. His portraits were emotionally inexpressive, but in their elegance and decorative qualities they embodied the courtly ideal under the Medici dukes. His work influenced European court portraiture for the next century, while his polished, sophisticated religious and mythological paintings epitomized the Mannerist style of his time. In 1563 he became a founding member of the Accademia del Disegno.

"Portrait of a Young Man" (possibly Guidobaldo II, duke of Urbino), oil painting by Il Bronzino; in the Metropolitan Museum of Art, New York City.

THE METROPOLITAN MUSEUM OF ART, NEW YORK CITY, BEQUEST OF MRS. H.O. HAVEMEYER, 1929, THE H.O. HAVEMEYER COLLECTION (29.100.16), COPYRIGHT © 1981

brooch Ornamental pin with a clasp to attach it to a garment. Brooches developed from the Greek and Roman fibula, which resembled a decorative safety pin and was used as a fastening for cloaks and tunics. Brooches have been made in a wide variety of shapes throughout history, the ornamentation and design varying from region to region. In the 19th century, with the expansion of wealth and the creation of a market for inexpensive jewelry, the brooch became a popular form of personal decoration.

Brook, Peter (Stephen Paul) *later* **Sir Peter** (born 1925) British director and producer. After directing plays in Stratford-upon-Avon, he became director of the Royal Opera House, COVENT GARDEN (1947–50). He directed several new Shakespearean productions that aroused controversy with their innovative approach. Appointed codirector of the ROYAL SHAKESPEARE CO. in 1962, he directed critically acclaimed productions of *King Lear* (1962) and *A Midsummer Night's Dream* (1970). He won international fame with his avant-garde direction of PETER WEISS's *Marat/Sade* (1964). His films include *Lord of the Flies* (1962), *King Lear* (1969), and the six-hour *Mahabharata* (1989). In 1970 he cofounded, with J.-L. BARRAULT, the International Centre for Theatre Research.

Brook Farm (Institute of Agriculture and Education) Utopian experiment in communal living in West Roxbury, Mass. (near Boston), 1841–47, founded by GEORGE RIPLEY. The best known of the many utopian communities organized in the U.S. in the mid-19th century, Brook Farm is remembered for the distinguished literary figures and intellectual leaders associated with it, including CHARLES A. DANA, NATHANIEL HAWTHORNE, MARGARET FULLER, HORACE GREELEY, JAMES RUSSELL LOWELL, JOHN GREENLEAF WHITTIER, and RALPH WALDO EMERSON (not all of them actual members), and for the modern educational theory of its excellent school. See also ONEIDA COMMUNITY.

brook trout *or* **speckled trout** Popular freshwater game fish *(Salvelinus fontinalis)*, a variety of CHAR, valued for its flavor and its fighting qualities when hooked. The brook trout is a native of the northeastern U.S. and Canada and has been transplanted to many parts of the world. It lives in cold, clean freshwater and carries dark, wormlike markings on the back and red and whitish spots on the body. The brook trout may weigh up to 6 lbs (3 kg). Some individuals migrate to large lakes or the sea and grow much larger and more silvery.

Brooke, Alan Francis *later* **Viscount Alanbrooke (of Brookeborough)** (1883–1963) British military leader. He served in World War I and became director of military training (1936–37) and an expert on gunnery. He began World War II as commander of a corps in France and covered the Dunkirk Evacuation. After serving as commander of the British home forces (1940–41), he was promoted to chief of staff (1941–46). He established good relations with the U.S. forces and exercised a strong influence on Allied strategy. He was promoted to field marshal in 1944 and created a viscount in 1946.

Rupert Brooke, posthumous portrait drawing by J.H. Thomas; in the National Portrait Gallery, London.

BY COURTESY OF THE NATIONAL PORTRAIT GALLERY, LONDON

Brooke, Rupert (1887–1915) English poet. His best-known work, the sonnet sequence *1914* (1915), which includes the popular poem "The Soldier," expresses an idealism in the face of death that is in strong contrast to later poetry of trench warfare. His death at 27 in World War I contributed to his idealized image in the interwar period.

Brooke Raj (1841–1946) Dynasty of British rajas that ruled Sarawak (now a state in Malaysia) for a century. Sir James Brooke (1803–1868) served with the British EAST INDIA CO. and fought in the first ANGLO–BURMESE WAR before using his family fortune to outfit a schooner and sale for the Indies (1838). He was awarded the title of raja of Sarawak by the sultan of Brunei for helping suppress a rebellion. Brooke established a secure government on Sarawak and was succeeded by his nephew, Sir Charles Anthony Johnson Brooke (1829–1917), who had spent much of his life on Sarawak, knew the local language, and respected local beliefs and customs. Under him, social and economic changes were limited. His eldest son, Sir Charles Vyner de Windt Brooke (1874–1963), succeeded him and embarked on modernization in the aftermath of World War I. He terminated Brooke rule in 1946, ceding Sarawak to Britain.

Brookings Institution Nonprofit public-policy THINK TANK based in Washington, D.C. It was formed in 1927 through the merger of the Institute for Government Research (founded 1916), the Institute of Economics (1922), and the Robert Brookings Graduate School of Economics and Government (1924). Robert Brookings (1850–1932), a St. Louis businessman, was influential in the formation of the first two organizations. The institution is funded by an endowment as well as philanthropic foundations, corporations, and private individuals. Its chief activity is public-policy analysis, which it disseminates through conferences and publications. It also conducts government studies under contract, reserving the right to publish its findings.

Brooklyn Borough (pop., 1990: 2,301,000), NEW YORK CITY. Separated from MANHATTAN by the EAST RIVER, it is bordered to the south by the Atlantic Ocean. Brooklyn is connected to Manhattan by bridges (including the BROOKLYN BRIDGE), a vehicular tunnel, and rapid transit services. The first settlement in the area by Dutch farmers in 1636 was soon followed by other villages, including Breuckelen (1645). The Battle of Long Island was fought in Brooklyn in 1776. It became a borough of New York City in 1898. Brooklyn is both residential and industrial, and also handles considerable oceangoing traffic. Among its educational institutions is PRATT INSTITUTE. CONEY ISLAND is located there.

Brooklyn Bridge Suspension bridge built (1869–83) over the East River to link Brooklyn to Manhattan island. It was designed by the cable manufacturer JOHN A. ROEBLING and his son Washington. A brilliant feat of 19th-century engineering, the bridge was the first to use steel for cable wire and the first in which explosives were used inside a pneumatic CAISSON during construction. In 1869 John was killed in one of at least 27 fatal construction accidents; his son saw the project to completion. The bridge's main span of 1,595 ft (486 m) was the longest in the world to date. It opened to such fanfare that within 24 hours an estimated quarter-million people crossed over it, using an elevated walkway designed to give pedestrians a dramatic view of the city.

Brooks, Gwendolyn (Elizabeth) (1917–2000) U.S. poet. Born in Topeka, Kan., and reared in the Chicago slums, she published her first poem at 13. With *Annie Allen* (1949), a loosely connected series of poems about growing up in Chicago, she became the first black poet to win the Pulitzer Prize. *The Bean Eaters* (1960) contains some of her best verse. Among her other books are *In the Mecca* (1968), the autobiographical *Report from Part One* (1972), *Primer for Blacks* (1980), *Young Poets' Primer* (1981), and *Children Coming Home* (1991).

Brooks, James L. (born 1940) U.S. screenwriter, director, and producer. Born in Brooklyn, N.Y., he worked in television from 1964. He cocreated and produced the hit *Mary Tyler Moore Show* (1970–77) and several other TV programs and series, including *The Tracey Ullman Show* (1986–90) and *The Simpsons* (from 1989). As writer, producer, and director of the film *Terms of Endearment* (1983), he won three Academy Awards; he also wrote, directed, and produced *Broadcast News* (1987), *I'll Do Anything* (1994), and *As Good as It Gets* (1997).

Brooks, Louise (1906–1985) U.S. film actress. Born in Cherryvale, Kan., she danced in FLORENZ ZIEGFELD's *Follies* (1925) and soon gained a Hollywood contract. Noted for her magnetic screen presence and dark bobbed hair, she personified the 1920s flapper in the silent films *A Girl in Every Port* (1928) and *Beggars of Life* (1928). In Germany she gave legendary performances in G. W. PABST's *Pandora's Box* (1928) and *Diary of a Lost Girl* (1929). Back in Hollywood (1930), however, she was offered only minor roles, and she retired in 1938 with little fame and no fortune. Her films were rediscovered in the 1950s, and her book *Lulu in Hollywood* (1982) won critical praise.

Brooks, Mel *orig.* **Melvin Kaminsky** (born 1926) U.S. director, producer, and actor. Born in New York City, he worked as a comic in Catskills resorts after World War II, wrote comedy routines for SID CAESAR's television shows (1949–59), and cocreated the TV series *Get Smart* (1965). He wrote and directed his first feature film, *The Producers* (1968, Academy Award), which exploded cliches to hilarious effect with its portrait of two producers who hope to get rich off their play's failure. He directed, produced, and cowrote (and sometimes acted in) such film comedies as *Blazing Saddles* (1974), *Young Frankenstein* (1974), *High Anxiety* (1977), *History of the World Part One* (1981), *Spaceballs* (1987), and *Robin Hood: Men in Tights* (1993).

Brooks, Rodney Allen (born 1954), Australian computer scientist. By the time he finished his doctorate (1981) at Stanford University, Cal., Brooks was disillusioned by the traditional "model-based" approach to ARTIFICIAL INTELLIGENCE (AI). After moving to the Mobile Robotics Laboratory at the MASSACHUSETTS INSTITUTE OF TECHNOLOGY (MIT) in 1984, he built simple robots that could perform "insectlike" actions on the premise that learning comes from real-world interactions. In 1997 Brooks became director of the MIT AI Research Laboratory.

Brooks, Romaine (Goddard) *orig.* **Beatrice Romaine Goddard** (1874–1970) U.S. painter. Born in Rome to wealthy American parents, she studied painting in Italy. After a brief marriage, she moved to Paris in 1905, where she established herself in literary, artistic, and homosexual circles. Her reputation reached its height in 1925 with several important exhibitions. Her gray-shaded portraits, touched by occasional color, distilled their subjects' personalities to a disturbing degree. *L'Amazone,* Brooks's portrait of her long-time lover Natalie Clifford Barney (1876–1972), is among her finest works.

Brooks Islands See MIDWAY

Brooks Range Mountain range, northern Alaska. It extends about 600 mi (1,000 km) from Kotzebue Sound to the Canadian border. Its highest peak is Mount Isto, at 9,060 ft (2,760 m). Forming the northwestern end of the ROCKY MTNS., it lies within GATES OF THE ARCTIC NATIONAL PARK. Huge reserves of oil were discovered at PRUDHOE BAY, and the range is crossed at Atigon Pass by the TRANS-ALASKA PIPELINE.

broom In botany, any of several leguminous shrubs or small trees of the genus *Cytisus,* native to temperate regions of Europe and western Asia. They are cultivated widely, chiefly for their attractive flowers. The compound leaves have three leaflets. The solitary or clustered yellow, purple, or white flowers resemble pea flowers. The fruit is a flat pod. A common, almost leafless species is *C. scoparius,* a shrub with bright yellow flowers often grown for erosion control in warm climates. Butcher's broom *(Ruscus aculeatus)* is a shrub of the LILY FAMILY with small whitish flowers and red berries.

Broom (*Cytisus beanii*).

VALERIE FINNIS

Brouwer \'braů-ər\, **Adriaen** (1605/6–1638) Flemish painter. After studying with FRANS HALS in Haarlem c. 1623, he returned to Flanders and settled in Antwerp by 1631. His pictures, mostly small and painted on panels, typically depict peasants drinking and brawling in taverns. The coarseness of his subjects was in direct contrast to his delicate technique; his virtuoso brushwork and sparkling tonal values were unsurpassed. Brouwer popularized genre painting in both countries. ADRIAEN VAN OSTADE and DAVID TENIERS were among his many followers.

Browder, Earl (Russell) (1891–1973) U.S. Communist Party leader (1930–44). Born in Wichita, Kan., he was imprisoned in 1919–20 for his opposition to U.S. participation in World War I. In 1921 he joined the U.S. Communist Party; he served as the party's general secretary 1930–44 and was its presidential candidate in 1936 and 1940. In 1944 he was removed from his position for declaring that capitalism and socialism could coexist, and in 1946 he was expelled from the party.

Brown, Capability *orig.* **Lancelot** (1715–1783) British master of naturalistic garden design. He worked for years at Stowe, Buckinghamshire, one of the most talked-of gardens of the day, under William Kent (1685–1748). By 1753 he was the leading "improver of grounds" in England. At BLENHEIM PALACE he created masterly lakes and almost totally erased the earlier formal scheme. His landscapes consisted of expanses of grass, irregularly shaped bodies of water, and trees placed singly and in clumps. His style is often thought of as the antithesis of that of ANDRE LE NOTRE, designer of the formal VERSAILLES gardens. Brown's nickname arose from his habit of saying that a place had "capabilities."

Brown, Charles Brockden (1771–1810) U.S. writer. Born in Philadelphia, he left the law to devote himself to writing. His gothic novels in American settings were the first in a tradition later adapted by EDGAR ALLAN POE and NATHANIEL HAWTHORNE. *Wieland* (1798), his best-known work, shows the ease with which mental balance is lost when common sense is confronted with the uncanny. His writings reflect a thoughtful liberalism while exploiting horror and terror. He has been called the "father of the American novel."

Brown, Clifford (1930–1956) U.S. jazz trumpeter and principal figure in the hard-bop idiom (see BEBOP). Born in Wilmington, Del., he became the most influential trumpeter of his generation, inspired by FATS NAVARRO to combine technical brilliance with lyrical grace in his playing. After touring with LIONEL HAMPTON's big band in 1953, he worked with ART BLAKEY; in 1954 he and drummer MAX ROACH formed a quintet that became one of the outstanding groups in modern jazz. He died in a car crash at age 25.

Brown, Ford Madox (1821–1893) British painter. He studied in Bruges, Antwerp, Paris, and Rome. In Italy (1845) he met Peter von Cornelius, a member of the NAZARENES, who influenced his palette and style. His use of brilliant color, meticulous handling, and taste for literary subjects had a strong effect on the PRE-RAPHAELITES, most notably DANTE GABRIEL ROSSETTI. His most famous paintings are *The Last of England* (1852–55), a poignant tribute to emigration, and *Work* (1852–63), a Victorian social commentary. In 1861 he became a founding member of WILLIAM MORRIS's company, for which he designed stained glass and furniture.

Brown, George (1818–1880) Canadian (Scottish-born) journalist and politician. He emigrated to New York in 1837 and moved to Toronto in 1843, where he founded *The Globe* (1844), a reform political newspaper. As a member of the Canadian assembly (1857–65), he advocated proportional representation, the confederation of British North America, acquisition of the Northwest Territories, and separation of church and state. He later became a leader of the CLEAR GRITS movement. In 1873 he was appointed to the Canadian Senate, while continuing to manage his influential and popular newspaper (later *The* GLOBE AND MAIL).

Brown, James (born 1928) U.S. singer and songwriter. Growing up in Georgia during the Depression, Brown first sang and danced on street corners for money. He later formed a trio, appearing at small clubs throughout the South. He gradually evolved a highly personal style, combining BLUES and GOSPEL-MUSIC elements with his own emotionally charged and highly rhythmic delivery, accented by a strong sense of showmanship. His first hit, "Please, Please, Please" (1956), was followed by other million-selling singles, including "Papa's Got a Brand New Bag"; his style, marked by strong dance-oriented rhythms and heavy syncopation, became known as funk. His checkered personal life was highlighted in 1988 when he received a three-year jail sentence on a variety of charges.

Brown, Jim *orig.* **James Nathaniel** (born 1936) U.S. football player, often considered the greatest running back of all time. Born in St. Simons, Ga., he was an All-American at Syracuse University. In his nine seasons with the Cleveland Browns (1957–65), he set overall rushing and combined yardage records that stood until 1984. He holds records for highest career rushing average (5.22 yards) and for most seasons leading the league in rushing touchdowns (1957–59, 1963, 1965). He led the NFL in rushing in eight of the nine years he played, a record no one has yet approached. After retiring from football, Brown became a movie actor.

Brown, John (1735–1788) British physician. He propounded the "excitability" theory published in *Elementa medicinae* (1780), which classified diseases as over- or understimulating and held that internal and external "exciting powers," or stimuli, operate on living tissues. Brown viewed diseases as states of decreased excitability, requiring stimulants, or increased excitability, requiring sedatives. HERMANN VON HELMHOLTZ discredited the theory.

Brown, John (1800–1859) U.S. abolitionist. Born in Torrington, Conn., he grew up in Ohio, where his mother died insane when he was 8. He moved around the country working in various trades, and fathered 20 children. An ardent advocate for overt action to end slavery, he traveled to Kansas in 1855 with his five sons to retaliate against proslavery actions in Lawrence. He and his group murdered five proslavery settlers (see BLEEDING KANSAS). In 1858 he proposed to establish a mountain stronghold in Maryland for escaping slaves, to be financed by abolitionists. He hoped that taking the federal arsenal at Harpers Ferry, W.V., would inspire slaves to join his "army of emancipation." In 1859 his small force overpowered the arsenal's guard; after two days it was in turn overpowered by federal forces led by Col. ROBERT E. LEE. Brown was tried for treason, convicted, and hanged. His raid made him a martyr to northern abolitionists and heightened sectional animosities that led to the Civil War.

Brown, Joseph (Rogers) (1810–1876) U.S. inventor and manufacturer. Born in Warren, R.I., he perfected and produced a highly accurate linear dividing engine in 1850, and then developed a VERNIER caliper and also applied vernier methods to the PROTRACTOR. With Lucian Sharpe he founded the Brown and Sharpe Manufacturing Co. His MICROMETER caliper appeared in 1867. He invented a precision gear cutter to produce clock gears, a universal milling machine, and (perhaps his finest innovation) a universal grinding machine, in which articles were hardened first and then ground, thereby increasing accuracy and eliminating waste.

Brown, Molly *orig.* **Margaret Tobin** (1867–1932) U.S. social figure. Born in Hannibal, Mo., she followed her brother c. 1884 to Colorado, where she met and married James Brown, a miner. After he found gold in 1894, they moved to Denver, where she tried unsuccessfully to enter society. Her husband left her, and she traveled to New York and Newport, where her gifts as a raconteur earned her social success. As a passenger on the disastrous maiden voyage of the *TITANIC* (1912), she helped command a lifeboat, and was celebrated by the U.S. press as "the Unsinkable Mrs. Brown." Her life, in the semilegendary form she herself recounted it, was popularized in a stage musical and movie.

Brown, Robert (1773–1858) Scottish botanist. The son of a clergyman, he studied medicine in Aberdeen and Edinburgh before entering the British army as an ensign and assistant surgeon (1795). He obtained the post of naturalist aboard a ship bound to survey the coasts of Australia (1801), and on the journey he gathered some 3,900 plant species. He published some of the results of his trip in 1810 in his classic *Prodromus Florae Novae Hollandiae . . .*, laying the foundations of Australian botany and refining prevailing plant classification systems. In 1827 he transferred JOSEPH BANKS's botanical collection to the British Museum and became keeper of the museum's newly formed botanical department. The following year he published his observation of the phenomenon that came to be called BROWNIAN MOTION. In 1831 he noted the existence in plant cells of what he called the NUCLEUS. He was the first to recognize the distinction between GYMNOSPERMS and angiosperms (FLOWERING PLANTS).

Brown, William Wells (1814?–1884) U.S. writer. Born into slavery near Lexington, Ky., he escaped and educated himself, settling in the Boston area. He wrote a popular autobiography, *Narrative of William W. Brown, A Fugitive Slave* (1847), and lectured on abolitionism and temperance reform. *Clotel* (1853), his only novel, concerning the descendants of THOMAS JEFFERSON and a slave, was the first novel ever published by an African-American. His only play, *The Escape* (1858), is about two slaves who secretly marry.

brown bear Shaggy-haired, characteristically brown species *(Ursus arctos)* of BEAR with numerous races native to Eurasia and to northwestern North America. North American brown bears are usually called GRIZZLY BEARS. Eurasian brown bears are generally solitary animals, able to run and swim well, and usually 48–84 in. (120–210 cm) long and 300–550 lbs (135–250 kg). They feed on mammals, fish, vegetable materials, and honey. The exceptionally large Siberian brown bear is similar in size to the grizzly.

brown dwarf Astronomical object intermediate in mass between a planet and a star. Sometimes described as failed stars, brown dwarfs are believed to form in the same way as stars, from fragments of an interstellar cloud that contract into gravitationally bound objects. However, they do not have enough mass to produce the internal heat that in stars ignites hydrogen and establishes nuclear fusion. Though they generate some heat and light, they also cool rapidly and shrink; they may differ from high-mass planets only in how they form.

brown lung disease *or* **byssinosis** \ˌbi-sə-ˈnō-səs\ Respiratory disorder caused by dust from cotton and other fibers, common among textile workers. When inhaled, the dust stimulates histamine release; air passages constrict, making breathing difficult. Over time the dust accumulates in the lung, producing a typical brown discoloration. First recognized in the 17th century, byssinosis today is seen in most cotton-producing regions of the world. Several years of exposure to cotton dust are needed before byssinosis develops. In advanced stages, it causes chronic, irreversible obstructive lung disease. Though cotton is by far the most common cause, flax, hemp, and other organic fibers can also produce byssinosis.

brown recluse spider Venomous species *(Loxosceles reclusa)* of brown spider, most common in the western and southern U.S. The brown recluse is light-colored, with a dark violin-shaped design on its back, for which it is sometimes called the violin spider. About 0.25 in. (7 mm) long, it has a leg span of about 1 in. (2.5 cm). It has extended its range into parts of the northern U.S. and is often found under stones or in dark corners inside buildings. The venom of the brown recluse destroys the walls of blood vessels near the site of the bite, sometimes causing a skin ulcer; the slow-healing wound is occasionally fatal.

brown snake Any of several species of snake named for their usual predominant color. In New Guinea and eastern Australia, the brown snake *(Demansia textilis)* is a slender, small-headed elapid. Up to 7 ft (over 2 m) long, it is bad-tempered and highly venomous. New World brown snakes, sometimes called grass snakes, are the two species of the genus *Storeria* (family Colubridae) found from eastern Canada to Honduras. They are small (mostly less than 1 ft, or 30 cm, long), shy, and harmless. The northern brown snake *(S. dekayi)* is the only North American snake to survive in abundance in densely populated areas. See also indigo snake.

brown trout Prized and wary European game fish (*Salmo trutta*, family Salmonidae), favored for food. The species includes several varieties (e.g., the Loch Leven trout of Britain). The brown trout is recognized by the light-ringed black spots on its brown body. It has been transplanted to many areas of the world because it can thrive in warmer waters than most other trout. It grows to about 8 lbs (3.6 kg). Oceangoing individuals, called sea trout, are larger than freshwater forms and provide good sport, as do those that enter large lakes.

Brown trout (*Salmo trutta*).

TREAT DAVIDSON—THE NATIONAL AUDUBON SOCIETY COLLECTION/PHOTO RESEARCHERS

Brown University Private university in Providence, R.I., a traditional member of the Ivy League. It was founded in 1764 as Rhode Island College and renamed in 1804 for a benefactor, Nicholas Brown. It became coeducational in 1971 when it merged with Pembroke, a women's college founded in 1891. Today it offers undergraduate and graduate degrees in all major academic fields; its school of medicine awards the MD. Research facilities include centers for geological, astronomical, and educational research. Total enrollment is about 7,600.

Brown v. Board of Education (of Topeka) 1954 case in which the U.S. Supreme Court ruled unanimously that racial segregation in public schools violated the 14th Amendment to the U.S. Constitution, which says that no state may deny equal protection of the laws to any person within its jurisdiction. The Court declared separate educational facilities to be inherently unequal, thus reversing its 1896 ruling in *Plessy vs. Ferguson*. The *Brown* decision was limited to the public schools, but it was believed to imply that segregation is not permissible in other public facilities. Guidelines for ending segregation were presented and school boards were advised to proceed "with all deliberate speed." See also Thurgood Marshall.

Browne, Thomas *later* **Sir Thomas** (1605–1682) British physician and author. While practicing medicine, he began a parallel career as a writer. His best-known work, *Religio Medici* (1642), is a journal of reflections on the mysteries of God, nature, and man. A larger work commonly known as *Browne's Vulgar Errors* (1646) attempted to correct popular beliefs and superstitions. He also wrote treatises on antiquarian subjects and the beautiful and subtle *A Letter to a Friend* (1690).

Brownian motion Any of various physical phenomena in which some quantity is constantly undergoing small, random fluctuations. It was named for Robert Brown, who was investigating the fertilization process of flowers in 1827 when he noticed a "rapid oscillatory motion" of pollen grains suspended in water. He later discovered that similar motions could be seen in smoke or dust particles suspended in air and other fluids. The idea that molecules of a fluid are constantly in motion is a key part of the kinetic theory of gases, developed by James Clerk Maxwell, Ludwig Boltzmann, and Rudolf Clausius (1822–1888) to explain heat phenomena.

Browning, Elizabeth Barrett *orig.* **Elizabeth Barrett** (1806–1861) British poet. Though she was an invalid who was afraid to meet strangers, her poetry became well known in literary circles with the publication of volumes of verse in 1838 and 1844. She met Robert Browning in 1845, and after a courtship kept secret from her despotic father, they married and settled in Florence. Her reputation rests chiefly on the love poems written during their courtship, *Sonnets from the Portuguese* (1850). Her most ambitious work, the blank-verse novel *Aurora Leigh* (1857), was a huge popular success.

Elizabeth Barrett Browning, detail of an oil painting by Michele Gordigiani, 1858; in the National Portrait Gallery, London.

BY COURTESY OF THE NATIONAL PORTRAIT GALLERY, LONDON

Browning, Robert (1812–1889) British poet. His early works include verse dramas, notably *Pippa Passes* (1841), and long poems, including *Sordello* (1840). In the years of his marriage (1846–61) to Elizabeth Barrett Browning, spent in Italy, he produced little other than *Men and Women* (1855), which contains dramatic lyrics such as "Love Among the Ruins" and the great monologues "Fra Lippo Lippi" and "Bishop Blougram's Apology." *Dramatis Personae* (1864), including "Rabbi Ben Ezra" and "Caliban upon Setebos," finally won him popular recognition. *The Ring and the Book* (1868–69), a book-length poem, is based on a 1698 murder trial in Rome. He influenced many modern poets through his development of the dramatic monologue (with its emphasis on individual psychology) and through his success in writing about the variety of modern life in language his contemporaries found often difficult as well as original.

Browning, Tod (1882–1962) U.S. film director. Born in Louisville, Ky., he was a circus performer and vaudeville comic before joining the Biograph film studio in 1915. He wrote several screenplays, then directed melodramas and adventure films (1917–25). He directed the macabre film *The Unholy Three* (1925), starring Lon Chaney, followed by *Dracula* (1931) and *Freaks* (1932), which established his reputation for films of horror and the grotesque. He retired in 1939.

Brownshirts See SA

Brownsville Affair Racial incident in 1906 involving whites in Brownsville, Texas, and black soldiers stationed at nearby Fort Brown. On an August night, rifle shots killed one white and wounded another. The mayor and other whites accused black soldiers of the crime. Though their white officers stated the soldiers were in their barracks, investigators accepted the mayor's version, and Pres. Theodore Roosevelt ordered dishonorable discharges for 167 black soldiers. A 1972 congressional investigation cleared them of guilt.

browser SOFTWARE that allows a computer user to find and view information on the INTERNET. The first text-based browser for the WORLD WIDE WEB became available in 1991; Web use expanded rapidly after the release in 1993 of a browser called Mosaic, which used "point-and-click" graphical manipulations. Such Web browsers interpret the HTML tags in downloaded documents and format the displayed data according to a set of standard style rules. Netscape Navigator became the dominant Web browser soon after its release in 1994; Microsoft's Internet Explorer was introduced a year later and has become widespread.

Brubeck, Dave *orig.* **David Warren** (born 1920) U.S. pianist and composer, leader of one of the most popular groups in jazz history. Born in Concord, Cal., Brubeck studied composition with D. MILHAUD before working as a jazz pianist. He formed a quartet with saxophonist Paul Desmond in 1951. His use of unconventional meters contributed to his immense appeal: the recording of Desmond's "Take Five" became the first jazz instrumental to sell over a million copies. This exposure brought many new listeners to jazz, particularly on college campuses during the 1950s and '60s.

Bruce, Blanche K(elso) (1841–1898) U.S. senator from Mississippi during RECONSTRUCTION. Born in Prince Edward Co., Va., to a slave mother and a white father, he was educated by his father. He moved to Mississippi, where he served in political positions and purchased a plantation. In the U.S. Senate (1875–81), he advocated just treatment of blacks and Indians. He later served as register of the U.S. treasury (1881–85, 1895–98) and District of Columbia recorder of deeds (1889–95), and was a trustee of Howard Univ.

Bruce, Lenny *orig.* **Leonard Alfred Schneider** (1925–1966) U.S. stand-up comedian. Born in New York City, he studied acting and began performing stand-up routines in nightclubs in the 1950s, soon developing a style marked by black humor and punctuated with obscenity. As he gained notoriety, he focused his material on criticisms of the social and legal establishments, organized religion, and other controversial subjects. He was banned from performing in England in 1963, the same year he was first arrested for possession of narcotics. After dying from a drug overdose three years later, he acquired iconic status as a folk hero or martyr. His confrontational performance style and uncensored material have greatly influenced generations of stand-up comedians.

brucellosis \ˌbrü-sə-ˈlō-səs\ *or* **Malta fever** *or* **Mediterranean fever** *or* **undulant fever** Infectious disease of humans and domestic animals characterized by gradual onset of fever, chills, sweats, weakness, and aches, usually ending within six months. It is named after the British doctor David Bruce (1855–1931), who first identified (1887) the causative bacteria. Three main species in the genus *Brucella* commonly cause the disease in humans, who contract it from infected animals (goats, sheep, pigs, cattle). Brucellosis is rarely transmitted between humans but spreads rapidly in animals, causing severe economic losses. Drug therapy is not practical for animal brucellosis, but vaccination of young animals is useful. Infected animals must be removed from herds. ANTIBIOTICS are effective against acute disease in humans, in whom it can cause liver and heart problems if untreated.

Bruch \ˈbrük\, **Max (Karl August)** (1838–1920) German composer. He held many conducting positions and taught 20 years at the Berlin Academy. He was known in his lifetime principally for his many sacred and secular choral pieces, including *Odysseus* (1872) and *Das Lied von der Glocke* (1879). Today he is remembered especially for his first violin concerto (1868); his other works include two further violin concertos (1878, 1891), three operas, three symphonies (1870, 1870, 1887), and the *Kol Nidre* (1881).

Brücke \ˈbrü̅-kə\, **Die** (German: "The Bridge") Organization of German Expressionist artists. It was founded in 1905 by four architectural students at the Dresden Technical School, including ERNST LUDWIG KIRCHNER and KARL SCHMIDT-ROTTLUFF, who were soon joined by other German and European artists. Its name reflects their hope that their work would be a bridge to the art of the future. Strongly influenced by primitive art, German Gothic woodcuts, and the prints of EDVARD MUNCH, they produced figure paintings and portraits depicting human suffering and anxiety, as well as still lifes and landscapes characterized by harshly distorted shapes and violent colors. They contributed to the 20th-century revival of the woodcut. The group disbanded in 1913. See photograph opposite.

Bruckner \ˈbrůk-nər\, **(Joseph) Anton** (1824–1896) Austrian composer. Son of a rural schoolmaster who died in Anton's youth, he was taken into a monastery as a choirboy and there learned to play the organ. Greatly gifted, he became organist at Linz Cathedral in 1855; throughout his composing career, his orchestrations would be compared to organ sonorities. In 1865 he heard *Tristan und Isolde* in Munich and thereafter idolized RICHARD WAGNER, though his own works remained indebted to LUDWIG VAN BEETHOVEN. In 1868 he was appointed professor at the Vienna Conservatory and settled in Vienna for the rest of his life. He was 60 before he achieved fame with his Symphony No. 7. He was socially awkward and eccentric, and he remained a deeply devout Christian to his death. His reputation rests on his nine mature symphonies (1866–96), his three masses (1864, 1866, 1868), and his *Te Deum* (1884).

Bruegel \ˈbrȯi-gəl\, **Pieter, the Elder** (c. 1525–1569) Greatest Netherlandish painter of the 16th century. Not much is known of his early life, but in 1551 he set off for Italy, where he produced his earliest signed painting, *Landscape with Christ and the Apostles at the Sea of Tiberias* (c. 1553). Returning to Flanders in 1555, he achieved some fame with a series of satirical, moralizing prints in the style of HIERONYMUS BOSCH, commissioned by an Antwerp engraver. He is best known for his paintings of Netherlandish proverbs, seasonal landscapes, and realistic views of peasant life and folklore, but he also took a novel approach to religious subject matter, portraying biblical events in panoramic scenes, often viewed from above. He had many important patrons; most of his paintings were commissioned by collectors. In addition to many drawings and engravings, about 40 authenticated paintings from his enormous output have survived. His sons, Peter Brueghel the Younger (1564–1638) and JAN, THE ELDER BRUEGHEL (both of whom restored to the name the *h* their father had abandoned), as well as later imitators carried his style into the 18th century.

Brueghel \ˈbrȯi-gəl\, **Jan, the Elder** (1568–1625) Flemish painter and draftsman, second son of PIETER, THE ELDER BRUEGEL the Elder. Early in his career he went to Italy, where he painted under the patronage of Cardinal Federigo Borromeo. After returning to Antwerp in 1596, he enjoyed a highly successful and prestigious career. In 1608 he was appointed court painter to the archdukes of Habsburg, regents of the southern Netherlands. He is known for his small-scale landscapes and exquisite flower paintings, all painted in a miniaturistic style on copper or panel. His skill at depicting delicate textures earned him the nickname "Velvet." He often collaborated with other artists, including his friend PETER PAUL RUBENS. His sons, Jan the Younger and Ambrosius, were also painters.

"Dodo and Her Brother," oil painting by Die Brücke artist Ernst Ludwig Kirchner, c. 1908; in the Smith College Museum of Art, Northampton, Mass.

Brugge \ˈbrü̅-kə, *Engl* ˈbrů-gə\ *or* **Bruges** \ˈbrü̅zh\ City (pop., 1996 est.: 116,000), northwestern Belgium. First mentioned in 7th-century records, it was the site of a castle built in the 9th century by the first counts of FLANDERS against Norman invaders. It joined the HANSEATIC LEAGUE and was a major marketplace in the 13th century. As the center of the Flemish cloth industry, it was the commercial hub of northern Europe. In the 15th century it was home to JAN VAN EYCK and other painters of the Flemish school (see FLEMISH ART). It declined as a port and textile center but later revived with the construction of canals linking it with the North Sea. Shipbuilding, food processing, chemicals, electronics, and tourism are the main industries.

Brugghen, Hendrik ter See Hendrik TERBRUGGHEN

Brugmann \ˈbrůg-ˌmän\, **(Friedrich) Karl** (1849–1919) German linguist. A professor of Sanskrit and comparative linguistics, he belonged to the Neogrammarian school, which asserted the inviolability of phonetic laws and adhered to strict research methodology. Among the best-known of his 400 publications are the two volumes on sounds and forms that he contributed to the *Outline of the Comparative Grammar of the Indo-Germanic Languages* (1886–93).

Bruhn \'brün\, **Erik** *orig.* **Belton Evers** (1928–1986) Danish ballet dancer admired for his classical technique. From 1937 he studied at the Royal Danish Ballet training school, joining the company in 1947. He performed as guest soloist with many other companies, including the American Ballet Theatre in the 1950s and '60s, dancing leading roles in such ballets as *La sylphide, Swan Lake,* and *Carmen.* He later served as director of the Royal Swedish Opera House (1967–72), and assistant director (1973–81) and director (1983–86) of Canada's National Ballet.

Bruhn as Romeo, 1967.
FRED FEHL

bruise *or* **contusion** Visible bluish or purplish mark beneath the surface of unbroken skin, resulting from the bursting of blood vessels in deeper tissue layers. Usually caused by a blow or pressure, bruises may occur spontaneously in aged persons. The yellowish hue that becomes visible as a bruise heals comes from the formation of Bile pigments and the disintegration and gradual absorption of blood. In untreated Hemophilia, bruises of the skin and soft tissue may almost always be present.

Brumaire \brūe-'mer\, **Coup of 18–19** (1799) French coup d'état that overthrew the Directory and substituted the Consulate, making way for the despotism of Napoleon. Planned by Emmanuel Joseph Sieyes and Charles Maurice de Talleyrand with the aid of Napoleon, the coup took place on November 9–10 (18–19 Brumaire in the French republican calendar). It is often considered the effective end of the French Revolution.

Brummell, Beau *orig.* **George Bryan** (1778–1840) English dandy. Son of Lord North's private secretary, he attended Oxford and became famous for his dress and wit as well as for his friendship with George, Prince of Wales (later King George IV). The leader of English fashion of his time, by 1816 he had exhausted his inherited fortune on gambling and extravagance and his sharp tongue had alienated his patron. He fled to Calais to avoid his creditors and struggled for 14 years before becoming British consul at Caen (1830–32). In 1835 his friends rescued him from debtor's prison, but he soon lost all interest in his personal appearance, and he spent his final years in a charitable asylum.

Brummell, engraving by John Cooke after a portrait miniature, 1844.
BY COURTESY OF THE TRUSTEES OF THE BRITISH MUSEUM; PHOTOGRAPH, J.R. FREEMAN & CO. LTD.

Brun, Charles Le See Charles Le Brun

Brundage, Avery (1887–1975) U.S. sports administrator. Born in Detroit, he competed in the 1912 Olympic Games, and was U.S. champion in the "all-around" in 1914, 1916, and 1918. He founded a construction company in 1915 and eventually became a multimillionaire. He served as president of the U.S. Olympic Association and Committee 1929–53, and as vice president (1945–52) and president (1952–72) of the International Olympic Committee. Controversial and domineering, he demanded strict adherence to the rules of amateur competition, and he often dismissed political events as unrelated to Olympic competition. He was unable to stop the Games' growth and commercialism, caused partly by worldwide television coverage.

Brundtland \'brůnt-land\, **Gro Harlem** *orig.* **Gro Harlem** (born 1939) Norwegian politician, first woman prime minister of Norway (1981, 1986–89, 1990–96). Trained as a physician, she worked with various government health services, then served as minister of the environment 1974–79. She served in the Norwegian parliament 1977–97. As leader of the Labor Party group, she served as premier three times. In 1987 she chaired the U.N. World Commission on Environment and Development, and in 1998 she was elected director-general of the World Health Organization.

Brunei \brů-'nī\ *officially* **State of Brunei Darussalam** \ˌdär-ə-sə-'läm\ Independent sultanate, northeastern Borneo. The country is divided into two parts, each surrounded by the Malaysian state of Sarawak; they both have coastlines on the China Sea and Brunei Bay. Area: 2,226 sq mi (5,765 sq km). Population (1997 est.): 308,000. Capital: Bandar Seri Begawan. Brunei has a mixture of S.East Asian ethnic groups: about two-thirds is Malay, one-fifth Chinese, and the remainder indigenous peoples and Indians. Languages: Malay (official); English is widely understood. Religions: Islam (official), Buddhism, Christianity, and animism. Currency: Brunei dollar or ringgit. The narrow northern coastal plain gives way to rugged hills in the south. Brunei's western enclave consists of the valleys of the Belait, Tutong, and Brunei rivers; it is mainly hilly, rising more than 1,640 ft (500 m). The eastern enclave contains the Pandaruan and Temburong river basins, and the country's highest point, Pagan Peak (6,070 ft, or 1,850 m). Much of Brunei is covered by dense tropical rain forest; very little land is arable. Its economy is dominated by production from major oil and natural-gas fields. It has one of the highest per-capita incomes in Asia. It is a monarchy; the head of state and government is the sultan. Brunei traded with China in the 6th century AD Through allegiance to the Javanese Majapahit kingdom (13th–15th century), it came under Hindu influence. In the early 15th century, with the decline of the Majapahit kingdom, many converted to Islam, and Brunei became an independent sultanate. When Ferdinand Magellan's ships visited in 1521, the sultan of Brunei controlled almost all of Borneo and its neighboring islands. In the late 16th century, Brunei lost power because of the Portuguese and Dutch activities in the region; they were soon joined by the British. By the 19th century, the sultanate of Brunei included Sarawak, present-day Brunei, and part of North Borneo (now part of Sabah). In 1841 a revolt took place against the sultan, and a British soldier, James Brooke, helped put it down; he was later proclaimed governor (see Brooke Raj). In 1847 the sultanate entered into a treaty with Great Britain, and by 1906 had yielded all administration to a British Resident. Brunei reject-

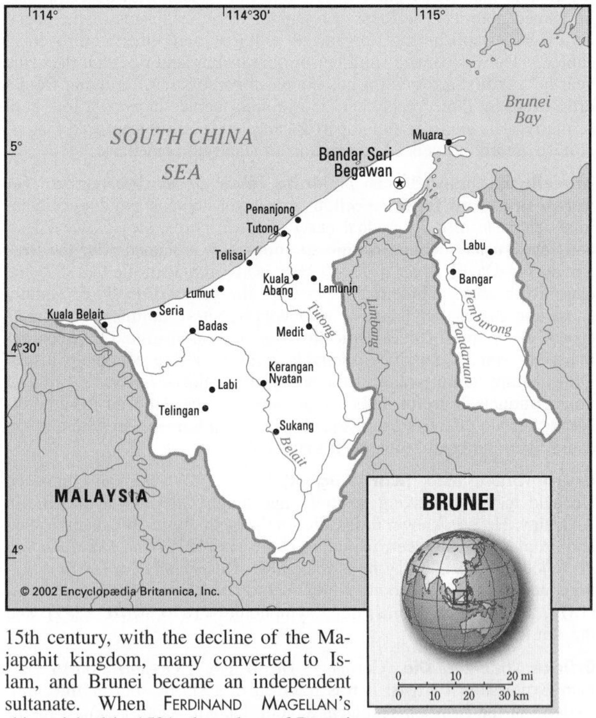

ed membership in the federation of Malaysia in 1963, negotiated a new treaty with Britain in 1979, and achieved independence in 1984, with membership in the Commonwealth. Today Brunei is considering ways to diversify the economy and to encourage tourism.

Brunei See Bandar Seri Begawan

Brunel \brü-'nel\, **Isambard Kingdom** (1806–1859) British civil and mechanical engineer. He was the son of Marc Brunel. His introduction of the broad-gauge railway, with rails 7 ft (2 m) apart, made possible high speeds and provided a great stimulus to railroad progress. He was responsible for building more than 1,000 mi (1,600 km) of railway in Britain, and also oversaw construction of railway lines in Italy, Australia, and India. His use of a compressed-air caisson to sink bridge pier foundations helped gain acceptance of compressed-air techniques in underwater and underground construction. Brunel made outstanding contributions to marine engineering with three steamships—the *Great Western,* the *Great Britain*, and the *Great Eastern*—each the largest in the world at date of launching. The *Great Western* instituted the first regular transatlantic service, and *Great Eastern* laid the first successful transatlantic cable.

Brunel, Marc (Isambard) *later* **Sir Marc** (1769–1849) French-British engineer and inventor. He perfected a method for making ships' blocks (pulleys) by mechanical means rather than by hand; the system of 43 machines, run by 10 men, produced blocks superior in quality and consistency to those previously handmade by more than 100 men. This installation was an early example of completely mechanized production (see mechanization). In 1818 he patented the tunneling shield, a device that made safe tunneling through waterbearing strata possible. In 1825 operations began for building the Brunel-designed tunnel under the Thames River, an unprecedented feat completed in 1842. He was the father of I. K. Brunel.

Brunelleschi \,brü-nᵊl-'es-kē\, **Filippo** (1377–1446) Florentine architect and engineer. Trained as a sculptor and goldsmith, he turned his attention to architecture after failing to win a competition for the bronze doors of the Baptistery of Florence, having tied with Lorenzo Ghiberti. He worked out the laws of linear perspective (later codified by Leon Battista Alberti). By the early 1420s Brunelleschi was Florence's most prominent architect. His major work, the octagonal dome of the Florence Cathedral (1420–36), was constructed with the aid of machines of his own invention. The Medici family commissioned him to design the (old) sacristy and basilica of San Lorenzo (begun 1421), considered keystones of the early Renaissance; he adhered to the conventional format while adding his own interpretation of antique designs for capitals, friezes, pilasters, and columns. His later monumental works foreshadowed the strong profiles and massive grandeur of the work of Leon Battista Alberti and Donato Bramante.

Interior of Santo Spirito, Florence, designed by Filippo Brunelleschi, begun 1436.

ALINARI—ART RESOURCE

Brunhild \'brün-,hild\ (534?–613) Queen of the Frankish kingdom of Austrasia. Daughter of a king of the Visigoths, she married the Austrasian king Sigebert I in 567. One of the most forceful monarchs of the Merovingians, she urged Sigebert to reclaim her murdered sister's lands from Chilperic I. When her husband was assassinated in 575, Brunhild was imprisoned at Rouen. She later took refuge at Metz, where her son Childebert II had been proclaimed king, and she opposed the Austrasian magnates for the next 30 years. After Childebert's death she fell into the hands of her enemies; she was tortured and then dragged to death by a horse.

Brunhild *or* **Brunhilda** *or* **Brynhild** Beautiful Amazon-like heroine of ancient Germanic literature. She is known from Old Norse sources, notably the Eddas and the Völsunga saga, and from the German *Nibelungenlied.* She also appears in the operas of Richard Wagner's *Ring* cycle. She vowed to wed only a man of the most outstanding qualities who could surpass her in strength. She was successfully wooed by Siegfried, but when she discovered that he was acting on behalf of another, she exacted vengeance and Siegfried was killed. In some Norse sources, Brunhild has supernatural qualities and is described as a Valkyrie.

Brüning \'brue-niŋ\, **Heinrich** (1885–1970) German politician. Elected to the Reichstag in 1924, he became noted as a financial expert. Leader of the Catholic Center Party from 1929, he became chancellor of Germany in 1930. In response to the Great Depression, he instituted harsh austerity measures that paralyzed the German economy. He ignored the Reichstag and governed by presidential decree, which hastened the drift toward rightist dictatorship and Adolf Hitler's rise to power. Forced to resign in 1932, he left Germany in 1934 and eventually moved to the U.S., where he taught at Harvard University 1937–52.

Brünn See Brno

Brunner \'brün-ər\, **(Heinrich) Emil** (1889–1966) Swiss Reformed theologian. After serving as a pastor at Obstalden (1916–24), he taught many years at the University of Zurich (1924–53), during which he lectured widely and was a delegate to the founding session of the World Council of Churches in 1948. His theology was influenced by Martin Buber's view of the relationship between God and man. Like Karl Barth, he rejected 19th–century liberal theology in favor of reaffirming the central tenets of the Reformation, but his assertion that God was revealed in creation led to a dispute with Barth. His works include *The Theology of Crisis* (1929), *Man in Revolt* (1937), and *Justice and the Social Order* (1945).

Bruno, Giordano *orig.* **Filippo** (1548–1600) Italian philosopher, astronomer, mathematician, and occultist. Though initially a Dominican friar, he was forced out of the order c. 1576 because of his freethinking. He moved to Geneva in 1578 and thereafter traveled Europe as a lecturer and teacher. He hypothesized an infinite universe and multiple worlds, rejecting the traditional geocentric astronomy for a theory even more radical than that of Copernicus. His theories anticipated elements in modern science and led to his excommunication by the Roman Catholic, Calvinist, and Lutheran churches. After an eight-year trial by the Inquisition, he was burned at the stake. His ethical ideas have appealed to modern humanistic activists, as has his ideal of religious and philosophical tolerance. His most important works are *On the Infinite Universe and Worlds* (1584) and *The Expulsion of the Triumphant Beast* (1584).

Bruno of Querfurt, St. *or* **St. Boniface of Querfurt** \'kfer-,fürt\ (974?–1009) Missionary and martyr. A member of a noble family, he was attached to the clerical household of the emperor Otto III. After the martyrdom of St. Adalbert (997), Bruno entered a monastery, taking the name Boniface, and continued Adalbert's work in Christianizing the pagan Prussians. The members of a mission he sent to Poland, including Sts. Benedict and John, were killed en route; Bruno wrote biographies of both saints, as well as an acclaimed biography of Adalbert. As archbishop, he visited the rulers of Germany, Hungary, and Ukraine seeking aid. He temporarily converted the pagan Pechenegs. He was killed on his way to his Prussian mission.

Brunswick *German* **Braunschweig** \'braun-,shfīk\ Former duchy, central Germany. A possession of the Welf family, the duchy of Brunswick-Lüneberg was created by emperor Frederick II and included the lands surrounding the town of Brunswick (founded late 9th century). The electorate of Hanover was included in 1692; its rulers established the English royal house of Hanover. The duchy became part of the German empire in 1871 and a German state after 1919. After World War II the region was incorporated into the state of Lower Saxony. The city of Brunswick (pop., 1992 est.: 259,000) is today an important industrial center.

Brusa See Bursa

Brusilov \brü-'syē-lóf\, **Aleksey (Alekseyevich)** (1853–1926) Russian general. He distinguished himself in the Russo–Turkish War (1877–78) and was promoted to general in 1906. In World War I he led the Russian campaign in Galicia (1914) and was most famous as commander of the "Brusilov breakthrough" on the Eastern Front against Austria-Hungary (1916), inflicting losses that forced Germany to divert troops from the Battle of Verdun against France on the Western Front. He later served in the Bolshevik government as a military consultant (1920–24).

Brussels *French* **Bruxelles** \brue̅-'sel, brue̅k-'sel\ *Flemish* **Brussel** \'brue̅-səl\ City (pop., 1996: 136,000), capital of Belgium. Part of the Brussels Capital Region (pop., 1996 est.: 948,000), one of the three regions into which Belgium is divided, it lies on the Senne River, a tributary of the SCHELDE. The village began on an island in the Senne and ultimately became a holding of the dukes of BRABANT. In 1530 it became the capital of the Netherlands, which was then under HABSBURG control. Part of the Kingdom of the Netherlands from 1815, it became a center of Belgian rebellion in 1830 and then the capital of Belgium. An important industrial and commercial center, it is the headquarters of both NATO and the EUROPEAN UNION.

Brussels sprout Small CABBAGE-related plant *(Brassica oleracea* 'gemmifera') of the MUSTARD FAMILY, widely grown in Europe and the U.S. In early stages, the plant closely resembles the common cabbage, but the main stem grows to a height of 2–3 ft (60–90 cm) and the axillary buds along the stem develop into small heads (sprouts) similar to heads of cabbage but measuring only 1–1.6 in. (25–40 mm) in diameter. The plant requires a mild, cool climate and is harmed by hot weather. Highly nutritious, brussels sprouts are a particularly good source of vitamins A and C.

Brussels Treaty (1948) Agreement signed by Britain, France, Belgium, the Netherlands, and Luxembourg, creating a collective-defense alliance. It led to the formation of NATO and the WESTERN EUROPEAN UNION. A goal of the treaty was to show that Western European states could cooperate, thus encouraging the U.S. to play a role in the security of Western Europe.

Brutalism *or* **New Brutalism** Term coined (1953) to describe LE CORBUSIER'S use of monumental, sculptural shapes and raw, unfinished molded concrete, an approach that represented a departure from INTERNATIONAL STYLE. New Brutalist architects displayed a willful avoidance of polish and elegance in their buildings, exposing such structural elements as steel beams and precast concrete slabs to convey a stark, austere rectilinearity. See also LOUIS KAHN, JAMES STIRLING.

Marcus Brutus, marble bust; in the Capitoline Museum, Rome.
ALINARI—ART RESOURCE

Brutus, Marcus Junius *or* **Quintus Caepio Brutus** (85–42 BC) Roman politician, leader of the conspirators who assassinated Julius CAESAR in 44 BC. He joined POMPEY'S army against Caesar in the civil war (49), but was pardoned by Caesar after Pompey's death. He joined the plot to murder Caesar out of his desire to restore the Roman republic. After Caesar's death, he and GAIUS CASSIUS formed an army in Macedonia; Brutus defeated the Caesarians under Octavian (AUGUSTUS) in the first engagement of the Battle of PHILIPPI, but Mark ANTONY and Octavian crushed his army in a second encounter. Realizing the republican cause was lost, he committed suicide.

Bruyère, Jean de La See Jean de LA BRUYERE

Bryan, William Jennings (1860–1925) Democratic leader and orator. Born in Salem, Ill., he practiced law in Nebraska. In the U.S. House of Representatives (1891–95), he became the national leader of the FREE SILVER MOVEMENT; he advocated its aims in his "Cross of Gold" speech, which won him the Democratic nomination for president in 1896; he would receive the Democratic nomination twice more, in 1900 and 1908. He founded *The Commoner* newspaper (1901) and lectured widely to audiences who admired his oratorical style; he was called "the Great Commoner." He helped secure the presidential nomination for WOODROW WILSON in 1912 and served as his secretary of state (1913–15), contributing to world law by espousing arbitration to prevent war. A believer in a literal interpretation of the Bible, he was a prosecuting attorney in the SCOPES TRIAL (1925), in which he debated CLARENCE DARROW on the issue of evolution; the trial took a heavy toll, and he died soon after it ended.

Bryan, c. 1908.
BY COURTESY OF THE LIBRARY OF CONGRESS, WASHINGTON, D.C.

Bryant, Bear *orig.* **Paul William** (1913–1983) U.S. collegiate football coach. Born in Kingsland, Ark., he was an all-state tackle in high school and went on to play blocking end at the University of Alabama (1932–36). As head coach at the University of Kentucky (1946–53), his team won 60 games, lost 23, and tied five. After coaching at Texas A&M University (1954–57), he returned to Alabama (1957–82). His Alabama coaching record of 323 wins, 85 losses, and 17 ties broke AMOS ALONZO STAGG'S long-standing coaching record for games won; in 1985 it was broken by Eddie Robinson of Grambling State. In all, he took Alabama to 28 bowl games and six national championships.

Bryant, William Cullen (1794–1878) U.S. poet. Born in Cummington, Mass., at 17 he wrote "Thanatopsis," a meditation on nature and death that remains his best-known poem; influenced by deism, it in turn influenced RALPH WALDO EMERSON and HENRY DAVID THOREAU. Admitted to the bar at 21, he spent nearly 10 years as an attorney, a profession he hated. His *Poems* (1821), including "To a Waterfowl," secured his reputation. In 1825 he moved to New York City, where for almost 50 years (1829–1878) he was editor in chief of the *Evening Post*, which he transformed into an organ of progressive thought.

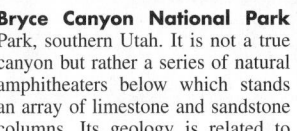

William Cullen Bryant, detail of an oil painting by Daniel Huntington, 1866; in the Brooklyn Museum collection.
BY COURTESY OF THE BROOKLYN MUSEUM, NEW YORK

Bryce Canyon National Park Park, southern Utah. It is not a true canyon but rather a series of natural amphitheaters below which stands an array of limestone and sandstone columns. Its geology is related to that of GRAND CANYON and ZION national parks, since the stone of all three was formed while the entire region was under a shallow sea. The park, established in 1928, covers 35,835 acres (14,513 hectares).

Bryn Mawr College \'brin-'mȯr\ Private women's liberal-arts college in Bryn Mawr, Pa., near Philadelphia. Though founded in 1885 by a group of Quakers, it has long operated on a nondenominational basis. A liberal-arts college, it offers a range of undergraduate and graduate programs in the arts and sciences and a doctoral program in social work. It enjoys an academic exchange with nearby HAVERFORD and SWARTHMORE colleges and the University of PENNSYLVANIA. Enrollment is about 1,900.

Brynhild See BRUNHILD

bryophyte \'brī-ə-ˌfīt\ Any of the green, seedless land plants that make up the division Bryophyta, numbering at least 18,000 species and divided into three classes: MOSSES, LIVERWORTS, and HORNWORTS. They are distinguished from VASCULAR PLANTS and SEED PLANTS by the production of only one SPORE-containing organ in their spore-producing stage. Most bryophytes are 0.8–2 in. (2–5 cm) tall; a few are more than 12 in. (30 cm) long. Found throughout the world, from polar regions to the tropics, they are most abundant in humid environments, though none is marine. Bryophytes are extremely tolerant of dry and freezing conditions. PEAT MOSS is economically important to humans in horticulture and as an energy source. Some bryophytes are used ornamentally, as in moss gardens. In nature, bryophytes initiate soil formation on barren terrain and maintain soil moisture, and they recycle nutrients in forest vegetation. They are found on rocks, logs, and forest litter.

bryozoan \ˌbrī-ə-'zō-ən\ Aquatic INVERTEBRATE of the phylum Bryozoa ("moss animals"), members (called zooids) of which form colonies.

Each zooid is a complete and fully organized animal. Species range in size from a one-zooid "colony" small enough (less than 0.04 in., or 1 mm, long) to live between sand particles to colonies that hang in clumps or chains as much as a 1.6 ft (0.5 m) across. The texture of colonies varies from soft and gelatinous to hard with calcium-containing skeletons. Freshwater bryozoans attach primarily to leaves, stems, and tree roots in shallow water. Marine bryozoans have a wide range of habitats, from coastal areas to great ocean depths, but are most common just below the tidemarks. Bryozoans feed by capturing plankton with their tentacles.

brytenwalda See BRETWALDA

BSE See MAD COW DISEASE

bubble chamber SUBATOMIC-PARTICLE detector that uses a superheated liquid which boils into tiny bubbles of vapor around IONS produced along the tracks of particles. As charged particles move through the liquid, they knock electrons from the atoms of the liquid, creating ions. If the liquid is close to its boiling point, the first bubbles form around these ions. The observable tracks of bubbles trace the path of the charged particles. Developed in 1952 by DONALD GLASER, the bubble chamber allows the observation of many nuclear reactions and was used in the 1960s and '70s to study the behavior of unstable particles of matter.

Buber \'bü-bər\, **Martin** (1878–1965) German Jewish religious philosopher and biblical translator. Brought up in Lemberg (now Lviv, Ukraine), he studied in Vienna, Berlin, Leipzig, and Zurich. FRIEDRICH NIETZSCHE's heroic nihilism led Buber, a nonobservant Jew, to Zionism. He advocated Jewish-Arab cooperation in Palestine and saw Hasidism as a healing power for the malaise of modern Judaism. Under Nazi pressure, he emigrated to Palestine in 1938, and he taught at Hebrew University until 1951. *I and Thou* (1923) expresses Buber's belief that the human (I) encounters God (Thou) as a distinct being, rather than merging in mystical union. The Bible was for Buber derived from the encounter between God and his people, but he rejected many of the Talmud's laws as emerging from a relationship in which God was objectified rather than truly addressed.

Buber.

BY COURTESY OF ISRAEL INFORMATION SERVICES

Bubka \'bu̇b-kə\, **Sergey** (born 1963) Ukrainian pole vaulter. Born in Voroshilovgrad (now Luhansk), he began vaulting at 9. He first cleared 6 m (19 ft 8 in.), long considered impossible, in Paris in 1985. In 1991 he cleared 6.1 m (20 ft), and remains the only pole vaulter to have done so. He won an Olympic gold medal in 1988, but failed to place at the 1992 Olympic Games. In 1994, at Sestriere, Italy, he vaulted a record 6.14 m (20 ft 1¾ in.) for his 17th outdoor record and his 35th overall.

buccal cavity See MOUTH

buccaneer Any of the British, French, or Dutch sea adventurers who chiefly haunted the Caribbean and the Pacific seaboard of South America during the later 17th century, preying on Spanish settlements and shipping. Though inspired by such PRIVATEERS as FRANCIS DRAKE, the buccaneers were not legitimate privateers, nor were they the outlawed pirates of the 18th century. Usually escaped servants, former soldiers, or loggers, they ran their ships democratically, divided plunder equitably, and even provided a form of accident insurance. They influenced the founding of the South Sea Co., and stories of their adventures inspired more serious voyages of exploration as well as the tales of JONATHAN SWIFT, DANIEL DEFOE, and ROBERT LOUIS STEVENSON.

Buchanan \byü-'ka-nən\, **George** (1506–1582) Scottish humanist, scholar, and educator. As a teacher of Latin in Paris, Buchanan wrote bitter attacks on the Franciscans that landed him in jail for heresy. He escaped and became a teacher in Bordeaux, where MICHEL DE MONTAIGNE was one of his pupils. There he translated two of EURIPIDES' plays into Latin and wrote original dramas. His paraphrase of the Psalms was long used for Latin instruction. At first a supporter of MARY, QUEEN OF SCOTS, he later helped prepare the case that led to her execution. In *De jure regni apud Scotos* (1579), he argued for limited monarchy; *Rerum Scoticarum historia* (1582) traces Scotland's history.

Buchanan \byü-'ka-nən\, **James** (1791–1868) 15th president of the U.S. (1857–61). Born in Mercersburg, Pa., he became a lawyer and member of the Pennsylvania legislature before serving in the U.S. House of Representatives (1821–31), as minister to Russia (1832–34), and in the U.S. Senate (1834–45). He was secretary of state in Pres. JAMES POLK's cabinet (1845–49). As minister to Britain (1853–56), he helped draft the OSTEND MANIFESTO. In 1856 he secured the Democratic nomination and election as U.S. president, defeating JOHN C. FREMONT. Though experienced in government and law, he lacked the moral courage to deal effectively with the slavery crisis and equivocated on the question of Kansas's status as a slaveholding state. The ensuing split within his party allowed ABRAHAM LINCOLN to win the election of 1860. He denounced the secession of South Carolina following the election and sent reinforcements to Fort Sumter, but failed to respond further to the mounting crisis.

James Buchanan, photograph by Mathew Brady.

BY COURTESY OF THE LIBRARY OF CONGRESS, WASHINGTON, D.C.

Bucharest \'bü-kə-ˌrest\ *Romanian* **Bucuresti** \ˌbü-kü-'reshtʸ\ City (pop., 1994 2,080,000), capital of Romania. Excavations have revealed evidence of prehistoric settlement. It gained in importance when the rulers of WALACHIA moved there in the 14th century. VLAD III built its fortress in the 15th century to ward off invading Turks; they eventually took it and made it their Ottoman Walachian capital in 1659. In the 19th century civic unrest helped force the union of Walachia and MOLDAVIA, and Bucharest became the capital of the new Romanian state in 1862. Occupied by the Soviet army after World War II, it along with the nation came under communist control. During the 1980s uprisings in eastern Europe, it was the scene of political demonstrations against the government of NICOLAE CEAUSESCU that resulted in his overthrow and execution.

Bucharest, Treaty of (May 7, 1918) Settlement forced on Romania after it had been defeated by the CENTRAL POWERS in World War I. Romania was required to return southern Dobruja to Bulgaria, give Austria-Hungary control of the passes in the Carpathian Mtns., and lease its oil wells to Germany for 90 years. When the Central Powers collapsed in November 1918, the treaty was nullified.

Buchenwald \'bü-k̲ən-ˌvält\ One of the first and biggest of the German Nazi concentration camps, established in 1937 near Weimar. In World War II it held about 20,000 prisoners, most of whom worked as slave laborers in nearby factories. Though there were no gas chambers, many perished through disease, malnutrition, exhaustion, beatings, and executions. Inmates were used to test the effects of viral infections and vaccines. The commandant's wife was the infamously sadistic Ilsa Koch (1906?–1967), the "Witch of Buchenwald." See also HOLOCAUST.

Büchner \'bu̅e̅k̲-nər\, **Georg** (1813–1837) German dramatist. As a medical student, he became involved in revolutionary politics and was forced to flee to Zürich. There he wrote plays marked by vivid imagination and unconventional structure, combining extreme naturalism with visionary power; he is regarded as a forerunner of the Expressionist movement. His first play, *Danton's Death* (1835), a drama of the French Revolution, was followed by *Leonce and Lena* (1836), a satire on the illusions of Romanticism. His last play, *Woyzeck* (1836), anticipated the social drama of the 1890s with its compassion for the poor and oppressed; it became the basis of a famous opera by A. BERG. He died of typhoid at 24.

Buchner \'bük̲-nər\, **Hans** (1850–1902) German bacteriologist. He served as physician in the Bavarian army in the 1870s and taught at the University of Munich from 1880 until his death. Buchner was one of the first to note that a substance in blood serum could destroy bacteria. He named the substance alexin; now known as complement, it consists of proteins called gamma globulins and is of great importance in immunology.

Buchwald \'bu̇k-ˌwȯld\, **Art(hur)** (born 1925) U.S. humor writer and columnist. Born in Mount Vernon, N.Y., he moved to Paris in 1948. His popular original column—reviews of the city's nightlife for the *International Herald Tribune*—increasingly included offbeat spoofs and candid comments from celebrities. After moving in 1961 to Washington, D.C., he began poking fun at issues in the news, soon becoming established as one of the sharpest satirists of American politics and modern life. His widely syndicated work won a Pulitzer Prize in 1982. His books include numerous collections of columns and the memoir *I'll Always Have Paris* (1996).

Buck, Pearl *orig.* **Pearl Sydenstricker** (1892–1973) U.S. author. Born in Hillsboro, W.V., she was reared in China by her missionary parents, and later taught in a Chinese university. Her first book to reach a wide audience was *The Good Earth* (1931, Pulitzer Prize), describing the struggles of a Chinese peasant and his slave wife. *Sons* (1932) and *A House Divided* (1935) followed; the trilogy was published as *The House of Earth* (1935). Among her later works are short stories, novels (including five under the pseudonym John Sedges), and an autobiography. She received the Nobel Prize in 1938.

buckeye Any of about 13 trees and shrubs of the genus *Aesculus* (family Hippocastanaceae), native to North America, southeastern Europe, and eastern Asia. The name refers to the resemblance of the nut, which has a pale patch on a shiny red ground, to the eye of a deer. Buckeyes are valued as ornamental trees for their handsome candelabra-like flower clusters. Both the young foliage and the nuts are poisonous. Among the most notable is the Ohio buckeye *(A. glabra),* also called fetid buckeye and American horse chestnut, with twigs and leaves that yield an unpleasant odor when crushed. The sweet, or yellow, buckeye *(A. flava,* or *A. octandra)* is the largest buckeye, up to 89 ft (27 m) tall, and is naturally abundant in Great Smoky Mountains National Park.

Buckingham \'bək-iŋ-əm\, **1st Duke of** *orig.* **George Villiers** (1592–1628) English courtier and politician. Charming and handsome, he quickly became a royal favorite of JAMES I and the future CHARLES I. He became lord high admiral in 1619 and was created a duke in 1623, but his arrogance and abuse of power made him highly unpopular. His erratic foreign policy led to a series of disasters, including failed military expeditions to Spain and France. A bill to impeach him was introduced in Parliament in 1626, prompting Charles to dissolve Parliament. When Buckingham was assassinated by a naval lieutenant, the populace of London rejoiced.

Buckingham, 2nd Duke of *orig.* **George Villiers** (1628–1687) English politician. Born eight months before the assassination of his father, the 1st duke of BUCKINGHAM, he was brought up with the family of CHARLES I. He fought for CHARLES II in the ENGLISH CIVIL WARS, and after the Restoration in 1660 Buckingham became a leading member of the king's inner circle of ministers, known as the Cabal. Parliament had him dismissed from his posts for alleged Catholic sympathies in 1674.

Buckingham Palace London residence of the British sovereign. It takes its name from the house built there early in the 18th century for the dukes of Buckingham. VICTORIA was the first sovereign to live there. JOHN NASH began the reconstruction of Buckingham House as a Neoclassical palace in 1821, but was not allowed to finish. His garden front remains virtually unchanged, but the Mall front was redesigned in 1913 by Sir Aston Webb (1849–1930) as a background for the Queen Victoria Memorial statue.

Buckinghamshire \'bə-kiŋ-əm-ˌshir\ County (population 1995 est.: 473,000), southern England. It is bordered by the THAMES RIVER, London, and the Great Oise River valley in the north; its county seat is at AYLESBURY. It was affected by each phase of English settlement, from the Neolithic to the Saxon. Under Saxon rule, as part of the kingdom of MERCIA, it resisted Danish invasion and became prosperous. Before the 20th century it was a rural area, but the modern growth of London and the expansion of transportation links with it has brought population growth.

Buckley, William F(rank), Jr. (born 1925) U.S. writer and editor. Born in New York City, he attended Yale University and in 1955 founded the journal *National Review.* As editor-in-chief he used the magazine as a forum for his conservative views. His column "On the Right" was syndicated in 1962 and eventually appeared in over 200 newspapers. From 1966 he hosted *Firing Line*, a weekly television interview program in which he often employed his wit and debating talents against ideological opponents. His books include *God and Man at Yale* (1951), *Rumbles Left and Right* (1963), and a series of spy novels.

buckling Mode of failure under compression of a structural component that is thin (see SHELL STRUCTURE) or much longer than wide (e.g., post, COLUMN, leg bone). LEONHARD EULER first worked out in 1757 the theory of why such members buckle. The definition by THOMAS YOUNG of the ELASTIC MODULUS significantly propelled building construction science forward. The elastic theory formed the basis of structural analysis until World War II, when the behavior of bomb-damaged buildings forced the modification of some of the theory's underlying assumptions. See also POST-AND-BEAM SYSTEM.

buckminsterfullerene See FULLERENE

Bucknell University \ˌbək-'nel\ Private university in Lewisburg, Pa. It was founded in 1846, first admitted women in 1883, and acquired its current name in 1886 to honor longtime trustee William Bucknell. It offers bachelor's and master's degree programs in the sciences, arts, business, and education. Research facilities include an observatory and an environmental preserve. Enrollment is about 3,600.

Buckner, Simon Bolivar (1823–1914) U.S. and Confederate military leader. Born near Munfordville, Ky., he graduated from West Point and served in the Mexican War. In the Civil War he established the Kentucky militia and became a Confederate general. Ordered to reinforce Fort Donelson, Tenn. (1862), he found the situation hopeless and unconditionally surrendered to ULYSSES S. GRANT. After a prisoner exchange, he served the Confederacy in many capacities. After the war he returned to Kentucky, where he later became governor (1887–91).

buckwheat Either of two species *(Fagopyrum esculentum,* or *sagittatum,* and *F. tataricum)* of herbaceous plants and their edible, triangular seeds, used as a CEREAL grain though the plant is not a cereal GRASS. It is less productive than other grain crops on good soils but is particularly adapted to arid, hilly land and cool climates. Because it matures quickly, it can be grown as a late-season crop. It improves conditions for the cultivation of other crops by smothering weeds and may be planted as a GREEN-MANURE crop. Buckwheat is often used as a feed for poultry and other livestock. It is high in carbohydrates and is about 11% protein and 2% fat. The hulled kernels, or groats, can be cooked and served much like rice. Buckwheat flour is unsatisfactory for bread but is used to make pancakes ("buckwheat cakes").

buckyball See FULLERENE

bud Small lateral or terminal protuberance on the stem of a VASCULAR PLANT that may develop into a flower, leaf, or shoot. Buds arise from MERISTEM tissue. In temperate climates, trees form resting buds that are resistant to frost in preparation for winter. Flower buds are modified leaves.

Budapest \'bü-də-ˌpest\ City (pop., 1997: 1,885,000), capital of Hungary. Situated on the DANUBE RIVER, it acquired its name in 1873 when the towns of Buda and Obuda on the river's right bank and the town of Pest on its left bank amalgamated. Inhabited from Neolithic times, Buda was the site of a Roman camp in the AD 2nd century. By the 13th century both Buda and Pest had German inhabitants. Buda was fortified by MATTHIAS I Corvinus in the 15th century and became the capital of Hungary. It was taken and held by the Turks 1541–1686, then retaken by Charles V, duke of Lorraine. In 1848–49 both towns experienced nationalistic revolt, and Pest became the capital of LAJOS KOSSUTH's revolutionary government. It became the center of revolt for Hungarian independence in 1918. After World War II, it, along with Hungary, came under communist control. It was the center of an unsuccessful anticommunist uprising in 1956 (see HUNGARIAN REVOLUTION). Anticommunist unrest there in the 1980s led to the declaration of the Hungarian republic in 1989. Budapest is a vital Hungarian transport center; its economy includes heavy industry and manufactures from telecommunications and electronics.

Buddha \'bü-də\ *orig.* **Siddhartha Gautama** (fl. c. 6th–4th century BC) Indian spiritual leader and founder of BUDDHISM. The term Buddha (Sanskrit: "Enlightened One") is a title rather than a name, and Buddhists believe that there are an infinite number of past and future buddhas. The historical Buddha, referred to as the Buddha Gautama or simply as the Buddha, was born a prince of the Sakyas, on the India-Nepal border. He is said to have lived a sheltered life of luxury that was interrupted when he left the palace and encountered an old man, a sick man, and a corpse. Renouncing his princely life, he spent seven years seeking out teachers and trying various ascetic practices, including fasting, to gain enlightenment. Unsatisfied with the results, he meditated beneath the BODHI TREE, where, after temptations by MARA, he realized the FOUR NOBLE TRUTHS and achieved enlightenment. At Sarnath he preached his first sermon to his companions, outlining the EIGHTFOLD PATH, which offered a middle way between self-indulgence and self-mortification and led to the liberation of NIRVANA. The five ascetics who heard this sermon became his first disciples and were admitted as BHIKSUS (monks) into the SANGHA or Buddhist order. His mission fulfilled, the Buddha died at Kusinara (present-day Kasia), after eating poisonous mushrooms served him by accident, and escaped the cycle of rebirth; his body was cremated, and stupas were built over his relics.

Buddhism Religion and philosophy founded in northeastern India in the 5th century BC based on the teachings of Siddhartha Gautama, called the BUDDHA. One of the major world religions, Buddhism takes as its goal the escape from suffering and the cycle of rebirth and the attainment of NIRVANA, and it emphasizes MEDITATION and the observance of moral precepts. The Buddha's teachings were transmitted orally by his disciples; during his lifetime he established the Buddhist monastic order (SANGHA). He adopted some ideas from the HINDUISM of his time, notably the doctrine of KARMA, but also rejected many of its doctrines and all of its gods. Buddhism's main teachings are summarized in the FOUR NOBLE TRUTHS, of which the fourth is the EIGHTFOLD PATH. Buddhism's two major branches, MAHAYANA and THERAVADA, have developed distinctive practices. In India, the emperor ASHOKA promoted Buddhism during the 3rd century BC, but it declined in succeeding centuries and was nearly extinct there by the 13th century. It spread south and flourished in Sri Lanka and S.East Asia, as well as moving through Central Asia and Tibet (see TIBETAN BUDDHISM) to China, Korea, and Japan (see PURE LAND BUDDHISM and ZEN). Today the various traditions of Buddhism together have about 400 million followers.

Buddhist councils In most Buddhist traditions, two early councils on doctrine and practice. The first, which most modern scholars do not accept as historical, was reputedly held at Rajagrha (modern Rajgir), India, during the first rainy season after the BUDDHA's death, to compile his remembered words, including the SUTRAS and monastic rules. The second, which is accepted as historical, met more than a century later at Vaisali, India, to resolve disputes within the monastic community. Theravada Buddhism recognizes subsequent councils: a third, called by ASHOKA c. AD 247, at which the doctrinal disputes were resolved in its favor, and others continuing up to the mid-20th century. Other Buddhist traditions recognize other important councils at which their respective canons were established or edited.

budding bacteria Group of bacteria that reproduce by budding. Each bacterium divides following unequal cell growth; the mother cell is retained, and a new daughter cell forms. In budding, the cell wall grows from one point on the cell rather than throughout the cell; this type of growth permits the development of more complex structures and processes. Most budding bacteria are aquatic and can attach to surfaces by their stalks; some are free-floating.

buddleia \'bəd-lē-ə\ *or* **butterfly bush** Any of more than 100 species of plants constituting the genus *Buddleia*, native to tropical and subtropical areas of the world. The genus was formerly included in the family Loganiaceae (order Gentianales) but is now placed in the family Buddlejaceae (order Scrophulariales), which includes about 10 genera and more than 150 species. Most species of *Buddleia* have hairy or scaly leaves and clusters of purple, white, yellow, or orange flowers. Several species are cultivated as garden ornamentals.

Budenny \bü-'dyȯ-nē\, **Semyon (Mikhaylovich)** (1883–1973) Russian army officer. In 1919 he joined the Communist Party and, as commander of the 1st Cavalry Army in the RUSSIAN CIVIL WAR, he played a crucial role in defeating the White (anti-Bolshevik) generals ANTON DENIKIN and PYOTR WRANGEL and in fighting the Poles (1920). He later became a marshal of the Soviet Union and was commander of Moscow's military district.

Budge, (John) Don(ald) (1915–2000) U.S. tennis player. Born in Oakland, Cal., he won his very first tournament, the California Boys State Singles title (1930). In 1936 he became the first lawn-tennis player to win the Grand Slam (the Australian, French, British, and U.S. singles championships). At Wimbledon in both 1937 and 1938, he won not only the singles but also the men's doubles and mixed doubles. Representing the U.S. four times in the DAVIS CUP competition (1935–38), he won 25 of 29 matches. He turned professional in 1939. He is noted for having developed the backhand into an offensive stroke.

Buell \'byül\, **Don Carlos** (1818–1898) U.S. general. Born near Marietta, Ohio, he graduated from West Point. He was appointed general of volunteers at the start of the Civil War, and helped organize the Union's Army of the Potomac. He was sent to Kentucky to succeed WILLIAM T. SHERMAN and to organize the Army of the Ohio. In 1862 he commanded in the Kentucky campaign against Confederate forces under BRAXTON BRAGG. Following the battle at Perryville, he was removed from command for failing to pursue Confederate forces.

Buena Vista \,bwā-nä-'vēs-tä\, **Battle of** Battle fought in 1847 near Monterrey, Mexico, in the MEXICAN WAR. A U.S. force of 5,000 commanded by Gen. ZACHARY TAYLOR and assisted by JEFFERSON DAVIS invaded northern Mexico and engaged a Mexican force of 14,000 under Gen. ANTONIO SANTA ANNA. The U.S. forces repulsed the Mexican attack, and the Mexicans retreated with 1,500 casualties. Taylor's victory helped him win the 1848 U.S. presidential election.

Buenos Aires \,bwā-nəs-'ar-ēz, *Span* ,bwā-nōs-'ī-rās\ City (pop., 1995 est.: 2,988,000), capital of Argentina. Located on an estuary of the Río de la PLATA in eastern central Argentina about 130 mi (210 km) from the sea, it is nevertheless a major port. First colonized by the Spanish in 1536, it was not permanently settled until 1580. It became the seat of the viceroyalty of la PLATA in 1776. In 1854 it drew up a constitution separate from those of the provinces and began intermittent conflict with them over control of the Argentine government. Upon being made a Federal District and Argentina's capital, it settled its wars with the provinces in 1880, and by World War I it had become a thriving port. The country's largest and most influential city, it is an important industrial and transportation center.

buffalo Any member of several BOVID species, including the massive WATER BUFFALO and CAPE BUFFALO. The name is often applied to the American BISON. The anoa *(Anoa depressicornis)* is a tiny, dark-brown buffalo of the dense, mature forests of Sulawesi. A shy animal, it stands 2.5–3 ft (0.75–1 m) at the shoulder and has straight, sharp-tipped horns. It is hunted for food, hides, and horns. A slightly larger species, the tamarau *(A. mindorensis)*, inhabits the Philippine island of Mindoro. Exceedingly shy and wild, its numbers have been greatly reduced.

Cape, or African, buffalo (*Syncerus caffer*).
MARK BOULTON FROM THE NATIONAL AUDUBON SOCIETY COLLECTION—PHOTO RESEARCHERS/EB INC.

Buffalo City (pop., 1996 est.: 310,000), western New York. Located at the northeastern point of Lake ERIE on the NIAGARA RIVER, it is the terminus of the New York State Barge Canal. Settled by American Indians in 1780, the site was platted at the beginning of the 19th century. It was a military post in the WAR OF 1812 and was burned by the British. Rebuilt in 1814–15, it became the western terminus of the ERIE CANAL, which brought an economic boom to the community. A major port on the ST. LAWRENCE SEAWAY and the main U.S. gateway to Ontario's Toronto–Hamilton industrial region, it processes much of U.S.-Canadian trade. It is also an educational and medical research center.

Buffalo Bill See William F. CODY

buffalo soldier Member of black cavalry regiments of the U.S. Army who served in the western U.S. 1867–96. An 1866 law authorized the Army to form cavalry and infantry regiments of black men, under the command of white officers. Their primary charge was controlling Indians in the western frontier (the nickname "buffalo" was given by the Indians). The soldiers took part in almost 200 engagements. Noted for their courage and discipline, they had the Army's lowest desertion and court-martial rates. One of the 10th Cavalry's officers was JOHN PERSHING, whose nickname Black Jack reflected his advocacy of black troops.

buffer Solution usually containing a weak ACID and its conjugate weak BASE, or a SALT, of such a composition that the PH is held constant within a certain range. An example is a solution containing acetic acid (CH_3COOH) and the acetate ION (CH_3COO^-). The pH depends on their relative concentration and can be found with a simple formula involving their ratio. Relatively small additions of acid or base will change the concentration of the two species, but their ratio, and hence the pH, will not change much. Different buffers are useful in different pH ranges; they include phosphoric acid, citric acid, and boric acid, each with their salts. Biological fluids such as blood, tears, and semen have natural buffers to maintain them at the pH required for their proper function. See also law of MASS ACTION.

Buffett, Warren (born 1930) U.S. businessman and investor. Born in Omaha, he attended the University of Nebraska and Columbia Univ., where he learned to invest in companies selling stock below their intrinsic value. Returning to Omaha, he turned $105,000 of initial investment in his Buffett Partnership (1956–69) into $105 million by the time of its dissolution. He began investing in businesses, bought under the umbrella of the textile manufacturer Berkshire Hathaway. He is said to be the first person to have made $1 billion in the stock market. His financial reports are read eagerly by stock-market novices and experts alike for their pithy wisdom.

Buffon \bū̄-'fōⁿ\, **G(eorges)-L(ouis) Leclerc** *later* **comte (Count) de Buffon** (1707–1788) French naturalist. He studied mathematics, medicine, and botany until a duel forced him to cut short his studies. He settled on his family's estate, where he researched the calculus of probability, the physical sciences, and forest management. Appointed keeper of the royal botanical garden (Jardin du Roi) in 1739, he was also assigned the cataloging of the royal natural-history collections, an undertaking that grew into his comprehensive work *Histoire naturelle, generale et particuliere* (1749–1804), an attempt to account for all known flora and fauna, of which he published 36 of the proposed 50 volumes before his death. He was ennobled in 1773.

bug Coding error in a computer program that prevents it from functioning as designed. Most software companies have a quality-assurance department which is charged with finding program bugs while the program is in development (debugging); bugs are also often detected by means of beta testing (testing of a product, often by potential consumers, before it is placed on the market). The term originated in a computer context in 1945 when a moth flew into and jammed an electrical relay of the Harvard Mark II computer; it was extracted and taped into the log book with the inscription "First actual case of bug being found" (the term having previously been used for other kinds of mechanical defects).

bug Commonly, any INSECT; scientifically, any member of the insect order Heteroptera. In scientific usage, when the word "bug" is part of the common name for a member of the order Heteroptera, it is a separate word (e.g., "chinch bug"); when used as part of the common name for an organism that is not a heteropteran, it is not separated (e.g., the ladybug, in the order Coleoptera). In common usage, there are many exceptions to this convention (e.g., BEDBUGS are heteropterans).

Bug River *or* **Western Bug River** \'büg\ River, eastern central Poland. Rising in western Ukraine, it flows north along the Poland-Ukraine and Poland-Belarus borders to Brest, and turns west into Poland to the VISTULA RIVER north of WARSAW, running a total of 481 mi (774 km). It is navigable below Brest. In World War I several battles were fought along its course in 1915. About 200 mi (322 km) of its central course formed part of the CURZON LINE. This same section was included in the 1939 Russo-German boundary, and largely retained after World War II in the boundary between the U.S.S.R. and Poland.

bugaku \bü-'gä-kü\ Repertoire of stylized dances of the Japanese imperial court, derived from dance forms imported mainly from China and Korea. The dances are divided into two basic forms: "dances of the left" *(saho no mai)*, accompanied by music derived from China, with dancers wearing red costumes; and "dances of the right" *(uho samai no mai)*, accompanied by music introduced from Korea, with dancers wearing costumes of blue or green. The dancers wear elaborate masks of painted wood to portray fictional characters.

Buganda \bü-'gän-də\ Former kingdom, East Africa. Located along the northern shore of Lake VICTORIA in present-day Uganda, the area, by the 19th century, was inhabited by the GANDA people and Buganda had come under the Ganda ruler. In 1900 it became a British protectorate. The Ganda subsequently played a major role in assisting British administration in East Africa. When Uganda became independent in 1962, Buganda was accorded special federal status within the state. Ensuing tensions with the central government led in 1967 to the kingdom's abolition and the area's integration into Uganda.

Bugatti \bü-'gät-tē\, **Ettore (Arco Isidoro)** (1881–1947) Italian builder of racing and luxury automobiles. His factory at Mosheim, Alsace (founded 1909), produced a highly successful low-powered racer for LE MANS. His luxurious Type 41 ("Golden Bugatti" or "La Royale"), produced in the 1920s, was probably the most meticulously built of all cars; no more than eight were constructed. His firm did not survive long after his death.

Buginese \ˌbəg-ə-'nēz\ Culturally dominant ethnic group of Celebes (SULAWESI), Indonesia. Their trading-port city Makasar (UJUNG PANDANG) fell to the Dutch in 1667, and they emigrated to other parts of the Malay Peninsula, establishing Buginese states in Selangor and Riau. They continued to harry the Dutch and also fought with the Malays. Their conflicts with the latter cost them their supremacy in the region by 1800. Early converts to Buddhism, the Buginese were converted to Islam in the 17th century. Today they number about 3.3 million. Their village economy is based on rice cultivation and some trade between islands.

bugle Soprano BRASS INSTRUMENT historically used for hunting and military signaling. It developed from an 18th-century semicircular German hunting horn with widely expanding bore. In the 19th century the semicircle was reshaped into an oblong double loop. Natural bugles use only harmonics 2–6 (producing tones of the C triad) in their calls ("Reveille," "Taps," etc.). The keyed bugle, patented in 1810, has six sideholes and keys which give it a complete chromatic scale. In the 1820s valves were added to produce the FLUGELHORN and, in lower ranges, the baritone, EUPHONIUM, and saxhorns.

building code Systematic statement of a body of rules that govern and constrain the design, construction, alteration, and repair of buildings. Such codes are based on requirements for the safety, health, and quality of life of building users and neighbors, and vary from city to city. Model codes developed by states, professional societies, and trade associations—including the BOCA (Building Officials and Code Administrators) coda, National Building Code, Uniform Building Code, and Standard Building Code—are typically adopted by local communities, with amendments. New York City's code is the oldest (1916) and, because of the city's population density and such concerns as fire prevention, adequate light, and ventilation, the most stringent.

building construction Techniques and industry involved in the assembly and erection of structures. Early humans built primarily for shelter, using simple methods. Building materials came from the land, and fabrication was dictated by the limits of the materials and the builder's hands. The erection sequence involved, as now, first placing a FOUNDATION (or using the ground). The builder erected the structural system; the structural material (masonry, mud, or logs) served as both skeleton and enclosure. Traditional bearing-wall and POST-AND-BEAM SYSTEMS eventually gave way to FRAMED STRUCTURES, and builders became adept at sealing and FIREPROOFING with a variety of claddings (exterior coverings) and finishes. Steel-framed buildings are usually enclosed by CURTAIN WALLS. In modern-day construction, sheathing the skeleton of the building is only the beginning; specialists then begin the bulk of the work inside, installing PLUMBING, electrical wiring, HVAC (HEATING, VENTILATING, and AIR-CONDITIONING), WINDOWS, FLOOR COVERINGS, plasterwork, MOLDINGS, ceramic TILE, cabinets, and other features. See also ARCHITECTURE.

building stone See building STONE

Bujumbura \ˌbü-jəm-ˈbu̇r-ə\ *formerly* **Usumbura** City (pop., 1994: 300,000), capital of Burundi. Lying on the northern end of Lake TANGANYIKA, it is the country's chief port and largest urban center. Known as Usumbura in the 1890s when German troops occupied the area and incorporated it into GERMAN EAST AFRICA, it was included in a TUTSI kingdom. When Burundi achieved independence in 1962, the city's name was changed to Bujumbura. Its industry specializes in textiles and agricultural products; most of Burundi's foreign trade is shipped between the capital and Kigoma, Tanzania.

Bukhara *or* **Bokhara** *or* **Boukhara** \bo̊-ˈk̲ä-rä, bü-ˈkär-ə\ City (pop., 1993 est.: 238,000), western Uzbekistan. Lying east of the AMU DARYA, it was founded in the 1st century AD and was a major trade center when the Arabs captured it in 710. Built up by the Samanid dynasty, it became the capital of their realm, which stretched from BAGHDAD to India and from Bukhara to the PERSIAN GULF. Falling to GENGHIS KHAN in 1220 and to TIMUR in 1370, it was taken by the Uzbeks, who in the 16th century made it the capital of the khanate of Bukhara. In 1868 the khanate was made a Russian protectorate, and in 1920 a Soviet republic. Bukhara was the capital until the republic was absorbed into the Uzbek S.S.R. in 1924. It became part of Uzbekistan on that country's independence in 1991.

Bukhari \bü-ˈk̲är-ē\, **(Abu Abd Allah Muhammad ibn Ismail) al-** (810–870) Muslim compiler and scholar of HADITH. He began his study as a child in Central Asia and traveled as far as Mecca and Cairo to learn about MUHAMMAD and his utterances. Of the 600,000 traditions he collected, he deemed 7,275 authentic and included them in *Kitab al-Jami al-sahih* ("Entirety of the Genuine"). His *Kitab al-Tarikh al-kabir* ("The Great History") contains biographies of those who passed on the oral traditions from the days of the Prophet to Bukhari's own era.

Bukharin \bü-ˈk̲är-ən\, **Nikolay (Ivanovich)** (1888–1938) Russian communist leader and economist. After the Bolsheviks seized power, he became the editor of the party newspaper *Pravda* (1917–29). A member of the Politburo and a prominent leader of the Comintern, he also wrote several theoretical economic works. In 1938, he was a defendant in the last of the public PURGE TRIALS. Falsely accused of counterrevolutionary activities and espionage, he was found guilty and executed.

Bukovina \ˌbü-kō-ˈvē-nä\ Region, eastern central Europe. It consists of part of the northeastern CARPATHIAN MTNS. and the adjoining plain. Settled by both Ukrainians and Romanians, it became an integral part of MOLDAVIA in the 14th century. It acquired its own name in 1775, when it was ceded to Austria by the Turks. Romania occupied it when AUSTRIA-HUNGARY collapsed in 1918, and was granted it through treaty in 1919. In 1944 the Soviet Union took the northern region, which became part of the Ukrainian S.S.R. (now Ukraine), while the rest became part of the Romanian People's Republic (now Romania).

Bukowski, Charles (1920–1994) U.S. (German-born) poet, short-story writer, and novelist. His family emigrated to Los Angeles in 1922, and he attended Los Angeles City College. He began publishing short stories in the mid-1940s. His first poetry collection, *Flower, Fist and Bestial Wail,* appeared in 1959, and the poetry volumes he published regularly for the next few years earned a devoted cult following. His novels include *Post Office* (1971) and *Factotum* (1975); he also wrote the screenplay for the film *Barfly* (1987), a semiautobiographical comedy about alcoholic lovers. The novel *Hollywood* (1989) dealt with its filming. His writing, often scurrilous but humorous, frequently reflected his perpetually down-and-out mode of existence.

Bulawayo \ˌbü-lä-ˈwä-yō\ City (pop., 1992: 621,000), southwestern Zimbabwe. The country's second-largest city, it lies 4,400 ft (1,340 m) above sea level. Originally the headquarters of the king of the NDEBELE, it was occupied in 1893 by the British. It is Zimbabwe's principal industrial center and, as headquarters for the country's railroads, its main transshipment point for goods to and from South Africa.

bulb In botany, the resting stage of certain SEED PLANTS, particularly PERENNIAL monocotyledons (see COTYLEDON), consisting of a relatively large, usually globe-shaped, underground BUD with membranous or fleshy overlapping leaves arising from a short stem. The fleshy leaves function as food reserves that enable a plant to lie dormant when water is unavailable (during winter or drought) and to resume active growth when favorable conditions again prevail. There are two main types. One, typified by the ONION, has a thin papery covering protecting its fleshy leaves. The other, the scaly bulb, as seen in true lilies, has naked storage leaves, with no papery covering, making the bulb appear to consist of angular scales. Bulbs enable many common ornamentals, such as NARCISSUS, TULIP, and HYACINTH, to flower rapidly in early spring when growing conditions are favorable. Other bulb-producing plants bloom in the summer (e.g., lilies) or fall (e.g., the AUTUMN CROCUS). The solid CORMS of the CROCUS and GLADIOLUS, and the elongated RHIZOMES of some irises are not bulbs.

Bulfinch, Charles (1763–1844) First professional U.S. architect. Born in Boston, he studied at Harvard Univ., then toured Europe, visiting major architectural sites in France and Italy. Most of his works incorporate Classical orders and show a mastery of proportion. Chiefly a designer of government buildings, he served as architect of the U.S. CAPITOL 1817–30. He used the plans of his immediate predecessor, BENJAMIN H. LATROBE, for the wings, but prepared a new design for the ROTUNDA. His son Thomas Bulfinch (1796–1867) wrote the famous *Bulfinch's Mythology.*

Bulgakov \bu̇l-ˈgá-kəf\, **Mikhail (Afanasyevich)** (1891–1940) Russian playwright, novelist, and short-story writer. He wrote and staged many popular plays in the years 1925–29, including dramatizations of his own novels, but by 1930 his trenchant criticism of Soviet mores had caused him to be effectively prohibited from publishing. His works, known for their scathing humor, include the novella *The Heart of a Dog* (written 1925), a satire on pseudoscience that did not appear openly in the Soviet Union until 1987, and the dazzling fantasy *The Master and Margarita*, not published in unexpurgated form until 1973.

Bulganin \bu̇l-ˈgä-nyin\, **Nikolay (Aleksandrovich)** (1895–1975) Soviet statesman and industrial and economic administrator. After supporting NIKITA KHRUSHCHEV in the latter's power struggle with GEORGY MALENKOV, Bulganin was made premier of the Soviet Union (1955–58). Though closely identified with Khrushchev, he joined an "antiparty group" that tried to oust Khruschev in 1957, a move that led to his own downfall.

Bulgaria *officially* **Republic of Bulgaria** Nation, southeastern Europe. Area: 42,823 sq mi (110,912 sq km). Population (1997 est.): 8,329,000. Capital: SOFIA. Bulgarians make up about 85% of the population; smaller groups include Turks, Gypsies, and Macedonians. Languages: Bulgarian (official), regional dialects. Religions: Eastern Orthodoxy; also Roman Catholicism, Protestantism, and Islam. Currency: lev. Three major regions define the landscape. The northernmost is the Danubian Plain, a fertile area occupying a third of the country. Immediately south lie the BALKAN MTNS. (Stara Planina), which rise 3,500–7,800 ft (1,050–2,375 m). In the southwest and south lies the Rhodope Range, with the country's highest point, Musala Peak, at 9,596 ft (2,925 m). Smaller than the three major regions, Bulgaria's Black Sea coast, including its cities of VARNA and BURGAS, is a popular eastern Europe resort area. Its major drainage systems include the Black and AEGEAN seas. It had a planned economy modeled on the Soviet system 1946–89. Since 1991 the noncommunist government has been moving to privatize some sectors of the economy, including agriculture. It is a republic with one legislative body; its chief of state is the president and its head of government, the prime minister. Evidence of human habitation dates from prehistoric times. Thracians were its first recorded inhabitants, dating from c. 3500 BC, and their first state dates from about the 5th century BC; the area was subdued by the Romans, who divided it into the provinces of MOESIA and THRACE. In the 7th century AD the Bulgars took the region to the south of the Danube. The Byzantine empire in 681 formally recognized Bulgar control over the area between the BALKANS and the Danube. In 1185 Bulgaria fell to the Turks and ultimately lost its independence. At the end of the RUSSO-TURKISH WAR (1877–78), Bulgaria rebelled. The ensuing Treaty of SAN STEFANO was unacceptable to the Great Powers, and the Congress of BERLIN (1878) resulted. In 1908 the Bulgarian ruler, FERDINAND, declared Bulgaria's independence. After its involvement in the BALKAN WARS (1912–13, 1913), Bulgaria lost territory. It sided with the Central Powers in World War I and with Germany in

A
B

World War II. A communist coalition seized power in 1944, and in 1946 a people's republic was declared. With other eastern European countries in the late 1980s, Bulgaria experienced political unrest; its communist leader resigned in 1989. A new constitution proclaiming a republic was implemented in 1991. The rest of the decade brought economic turmoil.

Bulgarian Horrors Atrocities committed by the Ottoman empire in subduing the Bulgarian rebellion of 1876. The name was used by WILLIAM E. GLADSTONE in his pamphlet publicizing the incident. About 15,000 persons were reportedly massacred at Philippopolis (now Plovdiv), and villages and monasteries were destroyed. Despite widespread public indignation, the European powers did little in response. The crisis ended with the Congress of BERLIN, which created a small, autonomous principality of Bulgaria.

Bulgarian language South SLAVIC LANGUAGE spoken by about 9 million people in Bulgaria and enclaves in Romania, Moldova, Ukraine, and Turkey. Closely related is Macedonian, spoken by 2–2.5 million people in the Republic of Macedonia, adjacent parts of Albania and Greece, and enclaves elsewhere. Both languages differ from other major Slavic languages in their complete loss of a case system for nouns, use of a postposed definite article, and preservation and elaboration of the Common Slavic system of aorist, imperfect, and perfect tenses. Both are direct descendants of OLD CHURCH SLAVIC. Under Ottoman rule, literary production was solely in Church Slavic. The Bulgarian vernacular became a literary language only in the mid-19th century; it was codified on the basis of northeastern Bulgarian dialects in 1899. Though efforts to create a literary Macedonian were underway before the BALKAN WARS (1912–13), it was not formally recognized as a distinct language until the declaration of a Macedonian Republic within nascent Communist Yugoslavia (1944).

Bulge, Battle of the (December 16, 1944–January 16, 1945) In WORLD WAR II, the last German offensive on the Western Front, an unsuccessful attempt to divide the Allied forces and prevent an invasion of Germany. The "bulge" refers to the wedge that the Germans drove into the Allied lines. In December 1944, Allied forces were caught unprepared by a German counterthrust in the wooded Ardennes region of southern Belgium. The German drive, led by GERD VON RUNDSTEDT'S PANZER army, was initially successful but was halted by Allied resistance and reinforcements led by GEORGE PATTON. The Germans withdrew in January 1945, but both sides suffered heavy losses.

Buli style \'bü-lē\ African wood sculpture made by the Luba people in the village of Buli, Congo (Zaire). The most typical examples are statues of ancestor figures and stools with seats supported on the heads and fingertips of figures. Because the carvings are almost identical and differ from other Luba carvings, they were once thought to be the work of a single artist, known as the Master of Buli, but it was later determined that they were actually produced in a workshop.

bulimia \bü-'lē-mē-ə\ Eating disorder, mostly in females, in which excessive concern with weight and body shape leads to binge eating followed by induced vomiting. It usually begins in adolescence or early adulthood, and is associated with depression, anxiety, and low self-esteem. Bulimia can have serious medical complications, such as dental decay, stomach rupture, or dehydration, and can be fatal. Treatment may include psychotherapy. Unlike those with ANOREXIA NERVOSA, most bulimics remain close to their proper weight.

bulk modulus \'mä-jə-ləs\ Numerical constant that describes the elastic properties of a solid or fluid under PRESSURE from all sides. It is the ratio of the TENSILE STRENGTH or compressive force per unit surface area to the change in volume per unit volume of the solid or fluid, and thus is a measure of a substance's ability to resist DEFORMATION. Its units are newtons per square meter (N/m^2). Matter that is difficult to compress has a large bulk modulus; for example, steel has a bulk modulus of $1.6 \times 10^{11} N/m^2$, three times that of glass (i.e., glass is three times more compressible than steel).

Bull, John (1562/63–1628) British composer. He became organist of Hereford Cathedral in 1582, then organist at the Chapel Royal in 1591. In 1613 he departed for the continent to escape punishment for adultery; he held important organist positions in Brussels and Antwerp until his death. He wrote many verse anthems, but is remembered for his keyboard works. In an era of remarkable English virginal music, he produced works that, reflecting his own brilliant keyboard technique, outdazzle those of contemporaries such as W. BYRD and O. GIBBONS.

Bull \'bül\, **Ole (Bornemann)** (1810–1880) Norwegian violinist. After training in his native Bergen, he freelanced in Christiania (now Oslo) 1828–31. His Paris concerts, which featured Norwegian songs played on a folk violin, won much attention, and he toured Europe and the U.S. for two decades, greatly celebrated. A longtime nationalist, he was brought back home by the revolution of 1848. He helped found the Norwegian Theater in Bergen, and in 1852–53 he established the socialist colony Oleona in Pennsylvania; debts from the failed experiment kept him touring the rest of his life. Much of the music he composed is lost.

bull market In securities and commodities trading, a rising market. A bull is an investor who expects prices to rise and, on this assumption, buys a SECURITY or commodity in hopes of reselling it later for a profit. A bullish market is one in which prices are expected to rise. See also BEAR MARKET.

Bull Moose Party U.S. dissident political faction that nominated former president THEODORE ROOSEVELT for the presidency in 1912. It was formed by Sen. ROBERT LA FOLLETTE in 1911 as the National Republican Progressive League, in opposition to the conservatism of the REPUBLICAN PARTY controlled by Pres. WILLIAM H. TAFT. The party derived its name from the characteristics of strength and vigor that Roosevelt used to describe himself. In 1912 Roosevelt won 25% of the popular vote, but this allowed the Democrat, WOODROW WILSON, to win the election. The party gradually dissolved, and the Republicans were reunited in 1916. See also PROGRESSIVE PARTY.

bull-roarer Flat piece of wood, several inches to a foot in length, fastened at one end to a string, by which it is swung around in the air to produce a whirring or howling sound likened to those of animals or spirits. It has been observed in Australia, the Americas, and other areas where indigenous societies survive. It may symbolize totemic ancestors, or it may be believed to cause or cure sickness, warn women and children away from men's sacred ceremonies, control the weather, or promote fertility in animals and crops.

Bull Run, Battles of Two engagements in the AMERICAN CIVIL WAR fought at a stream near Manassas, Va. The first battle (also called First Manassas) was fought on July 21, 1861, between 37,000 Union troops under Gen. Irvin McDowell (1818–1885) and 35,000 Confederate troops under P.G.T. BEAUREGARD and JOSEPH JOHNSTON. In this first major encounter of the war, the Union assault was beaten back and the army retreated to Washington, D.C. The second battle took place on August 29–30, 1862, between a Confederate force of over 56,000 under ROBERT E. LEE and a Union army of over 70,000 under JOHN POPE. To prevent the Union force from being joined by the Army of the Potomac, Lee sent troops under STONEWALL JACKSON to outflank the Union army. Lee's attack forced the Union troops to withdraw as far as Washington, D.C. Casualties numbered 15,000 for the North and 9,000 for the South. Both battles strengthened the South's resolve and caused the North to review its military leadership and strategy.

bull terrier Breed of dog developed in 19th-century England from the BULLDOG and the now-extinct white English TERRIER. The Spanish POINTER was later bred into the line to increase its size. The bull terrier was developed as a courageous fighting dog but not an aggressive fight provoker, and it is generally friendly. A muscular dog, it is considered, for its weight, the strongest of all dogs. It has a short coat, tapering tail, erect ears, and deep-set eyes. It stands 19–22 in. (48–56 cm) high and weighs 50–60 lbs (23–27 kg). There are two varieties, colored and white.

bulldog *or* **English bulldog** Centuries-old breed of dog developed in Britain to fight bulls. Powerful and courageous, often vicious, and largely unaware of pain, the bulldog nearly disappeared when dogfighting was outlawed in 1835. Fanciers of the breed saved it and bred out its ferocity. It is now considered gentle and reliable. It has a large head, folded ears, a short muzzle, a protruding lower jaw, and loose skin that forms wrinkles on the head and face. Its short, fine coat is tan, white, reddish brown, brindle, or piebald. It stands 13–15 in. (34–38 cm) high and weighs 40–50 lbs (18–23 kg).

Buller River River, South Island, New Zealand. It was named for Charles Buller, founder of the New Zealand Co. It is the major river of the island's west coast. Rising in the central highlands, it flows west 110 mi (177 km) into the TASMAN SEA. Its gorge, which is most scenic at Inangahua Junction, is an important tourist attraction.

bulletin-board system (BBS) Computerized system used to exchange public messages or files. A BBS is typically reached by using a dial-up modem. Most are dedicated to a special interest, which may be an extremely narrow topic. Any user may "post" his or her own message (so that they appear on the site for all to read). Bulletin boards produce "conversations" between interested participants, who may download or print out messages they desire to keep or pass on to others. BBS sites today number in the tens of thousands. See also NEWSGROUP.

bullfighting Spectacle popular in Spain, Portugal, and Latin America, in which MATADORS ceremonially taunt, and usually kill, bulls in an arena. Spectacles with bulls were common in ancient Crete, Thessaly, and Rome. In the modern era, Roman amphitheaters were rebuilt and embellished for use as bullrings. The largest are in Madrid, Barcelona, and Mexico City. The corrida, which usually involves six individual fights, begins with a procession of matadors and their entourages. At the beginning of each fight an assistant (banderillero) performs a preliminary maneuver to allow the matador to assess the animal's behavior. The matador then performs his capework, drawing the bull as close to him as possible without being gored. This is followed by the entrance of the picadors, horsemen who jab the bull with lances to weaken its neck and shoulder muscles. The matador then ritually slays the bull using a sword. In the Portuguese version of the ritual, the bull is fought from horseback and is not killed. Bullfighting has been banned in many countries.

Manolete executing a natural, a close *pase* with his left hand.
BARNABY CONRAD

bullfinch Any of several species of stocky, stout-billed songbird (family Fringillidae). Eurasia has six species of the genus *Pyrrhula,* all boldly marked. The common bullfinch *(P. pyrrhula),* 6 in. (15 cm) long, is black and white; the male has a pinkish orange underside. It has a soft warbling call and is a popular cage bird. Usually found in evergreen groves and hedgerows, it is notorious for eating the buds of fruit trees. The trumpeter bullfinch *(Rhodopechys githaginea),* of arid localities from the Canary Islands to India, is a pale bird with a blaring buzzy note.

Common bullfinch (*Pyrrhula pyrrhula*).
H.M. BARNFATHER–BRUCE COLEMAN LTD.

bullfrog Solitary aquatic FROG *(Rana catesbeiana)* named for its loud call. The largest U.S. frog, native to the eastern states, the bullfrog has been introduced into the western states and into other countries. The bullfrog is green or brown with a white to yellowish belly and dark-barred legs. Its body is about 8 in. (20 cm) long, and its hindlegs may be 10 in. (25 cm) long. Large adults weigh 1 lb (0.5 kg) or more. Bullfrogs usually live in or near a body of still water. They are used for food and as laboratory animals. The name is sometimes applied to other large frogs.

Bullfrog (*Rana catesbeiana*).
RICHARD PARKER

bullhead Any of several species of North American freshwater CATFISH in the genus *Ictalurus,* valued as food and sport fishes. Bullheads are related to the channel catfish *(I. punctatus)* and other large North American species, but their tail is squared, rather than forked, and they are generally less than 12 in. (30 cm) long. The black bullhead *(I. melas)* is found in the Mississippi Valley, the yellow and brown bullheads *(I. natalis* and *I. nebulosus)* east of the Rocky Mtns., and the flat bullhead *(I. platycephalus)* in coastal streams between North Carolina and Florida. The name is sometimes applied to SCULPINS.

bullionism Monetary policy of MERCANTILISM, which called for national regulation of transactions in foreign currency and precious metals (bullion) in order to maintain a favorable balance in the home country. Bullionism is most closely associated with 16th- and 17th-century Spain, which was thought to owe its prosperity and military might to the gold and silver of its New World colonies. This view gave rise to the theory that a favorable BALANCE OF TRADE would increase the nation's supply of precious metals. Spain's abundant treasure led it to buy goods and services abroad and to neglect domestic industry, and it later became one of the most impoverished European states.

Bullock, Wynn (1902–1975) U.S. photographer. Born in Chicago, he was strongly influenced in his early work—mainly "solarizations," in which the image is partly negative and partly positive—by the avant-garde experiments of LASZLO MOHOLY-NAGY. In 1948 EDWARD WESTON persuaded him to focus on realism and tonal beauty, and Bullock followed his advice so closely that his images often resembled Weston's. He is best known for realistic images that are meant to be viewed as "equivalents," or visual metaphors (e.g., the passing of time, the inevitability of death).

Bülow \'bü̅-lō\, **Bernhard (Heinrich Martin Karl), Fürst (Prince) von** (1849–1929) German imperial chancellor and Prussian prime minister (1900–1909). After holding a number of diplomatic posts, he was appointed state secretary for the foreign department in 1897. He quickly became a potent force and succeeded to the chancellorship in 1900. In cooperation with WILLIAM II, he pursued a policy of German aggrandizement in the years preceding World War I. He was unable to prevent the formation of the English-French-Russian alliance against Germany (see ENTENTE CORDIALE, TRIPLE ENTENTE) and increased international tension with the first of the MOROCCAN CRISES.

Bülow \'bü̅-lō\, **Hans (Guido), Freiherr (Baron) von** (1830–1894) German conductor and pianist. He studied piano with C. SCHUMANN's father. His meetings with F. LISZT (1849) and RICHARD WAGNER (1850) led to his decision to give up law for music, and with their help he launched a renowned career as conductor and pianist, studying with Liszt from

1851 and marrying his daughter Cosima in 1857. He was appointed court conductor to LUDWIG II and later director of the Munich Conservatory. He conducted the premieres of Wagner's *Tristan und Isolde* (1859) and *Die Meistersinger* (1868). Cosima left him for Wagner in 1869 in the middle of their collaboration, but he remained friendly with both.

bulrush Any of the annual or perennial grasslike plants constituting the genus *Scirpus,* especially *S. lacustris,* in the SEDGE FAMILY, that bear solitary or much-clustered spikelets. Bulrushes grow in wet locations, including ponds, marshes, and lakes. Their stems are often used to weave strong mats, baskets, and chair seats. Bulrushes may act as a filter, absorbing poisonous metals and toxic microorganisms, thus helping to reduce water pollution. In Britain, the term bulrush refers to either of two CATTAILS *(Typha latifolia* and *T. angustifolia).*

Bultmann \'bu̇lt-ˌmän\, **Rudolf (Karl)** (1884–1976) German Protestant theologian and New Testament scholar. Son of a Lutheran pastor, he studied at the University of Tübingen and later taught many years at Marburg (1921–51). He established his reputation with his analysis of the Gospels in *History of the Synoptic Tradition* (1921). Influenced by his colleague MARTIN HEIDEGGER, he held that Christian faith should focus less on the historical Jesus and more on the transcendent Christ, and he examined the New Testament in mythical terms. During the Nazi era he supported the anti-Nazi CONFESSING CHURCH. His postwar books included *Kerygma and Myth* (1953), *History and Eschatology* (1957), and *Jesus Christ and Mythology* (1960).

Bulwer, (William) Henry Lytton (Earle) *later* **Baron Dalling and Bulwer (of Dalling)** *known as* **Sir Henry Bulwer** (1801–1872) British diplomat. In the diplomatic service from 1829, he negotiated the Ponsonby Treaty (1838), which was advantageous to British trade with the Ottoman empire. As ambassador to the U.S. (1849–52), he negotiated the controversial CLAYTON-BULWER TREATY, which was intended to resolve (but in fact aggravated) Anglo-American disputes in Latin America. In 1856 he played a major part in the negotiations following the CRIMEAN WAR. His brother was the novelist EDWARD BULWER-LYTTON.

Bulwer-Lytton, Edward (George Earl) *later* **Baron Lytton of Knebworth** (1803–1873) British politician, novelist, and poet. His first novel, *Pelham,* was published in 1828. He entered Parliament as a Liberal in 1831, retired in 1841, and returned in 1852 as a Tory. In the interim he wrote his long historical novels, including *The Last Days of Pompeii* (3 vols., 1834) and *Harold, the Last of the Saxon Kings* (1848). He was created a peer in 1866. The opening to his 1830 novel *Paul Clifford* ("It was a dark and stormy night . . .") led to an annual Bulwer-Lytton Fiction Prize, in which entrants vie to create the most overwritten first sentence to a hypothetical novel.

bumblebee Any member of two genera constituting the insect tribe Bombini (family Apidae, order Hymenoptera), found almost worldwide but most common in temperate climates. Bumblebees are robust and hairy, average about 0.6–1 in. (1.5–2.5 cm) in length, and are usually black with broad yellow or orange bands. *Bombus* species are nest builders, often nesting in the ground, commonly in deserted bird or mouse nests. They live in organized groups, with a queen, drones, and workers (see CASTE). *Psithyrus* species are social parasites (see PARASITISM); they lay their eggs in *Bombus* nests, where the eggs and larvae are cared for by *Bombus* workers.

Bunau-Varilla \bü̅-nō-vȧ-rē-'yȧ\, **Philippe (-Jean)** (1859–1940) French engineer. He worked for the French Panama Canal Co. (1884–89) until the French project failed. He helped to instigate the revolution that resulted in Panamanian independence and was appointed by the provisional government to negotiate a treaty with the U.S. for the construction of a canal. In 1903 he signed a treaty with U.S. Secretary of State JOHN HAY, assuring the construction of the PANAMA CANAL under U.S. control.

bunchberry Creeping perennial herbaceous plant *(Cornus canadensis),* also called dwarf cornel, of the DOGWOOD family. The small and inconspicuous yellowish flowers, grouped in heads surrounded by four large and showy white (rarely pink) petal-like bracts, give rise to clusters of red fruits. Bunchberry is found in acid soils, bogs, and upland slopes in Asia and from Greenland to Alaska, and south as far as Maryland, New Mexico, and California.

Bunche \'bənch\, **Ralph (Johnson)** (1904–1971) U.S. diplomat. Born in Detroit, he earned graduate degrees at Harvard University and taught at Howard University from 1928. After studying colonial policy in Africa, he collaborated with GUNNAR MYRDAL in the study of U.S. race relations *An American Dilemma* (1944). He worked in the U.S. war and state departments during World War II. In 1947 he became director of the trusteeship department of the U.N. Secretariat. His work in forging a truce between Palestinian Arabs and Jews earned him the 1950 Nobel Peace Prize. As U.N. undersecretary for political affairs, he oversaw U.N. peacekeeping forces around the Suez Canal (1956), in the Congo (1960), and in Cyprus (1964). He also served on the board of the NAACP for 22 years.

Bunche.
H. ROGER-VIOLLET

Bundelkhand \'bu̇n-dəl-ˌkənd\ Historic region, central India. Long inhabited by various dynasties, it was finally settled by the Bundela Rajputs in the 14th century. For centuries afterward they engaged in warfare with the Muslim power of DELHI. After a period of MUGHAL rule, the Marathas extended their influence, but by 1817 the British government had acquired all territorial rights over the region. After Indian independence was achieved, Bundelkhand in 1948 merged into Vindhya Pradesh, which in turn merged with MADHYA PRADESH in 1956.

Bundestag \'bu̇n-dəs-ˌtäk\ Lower house of the German bicameral legislature. It represents the nation as a whole and is elected by universal suffrage under a system of mixed direct and proportional representation. Members serve four-year terms. The Bundestag in turn elects the chancellor. The term was formerly used to refer to the federal Diet of the German Confederation (1815–66), known as the Reichstag under the WEIMAR REPUBLIC (1919–34). Its building burned down in 1933 (see REICHSTAG FIRE), and its members were not allowed to meet again for the duration of the Nazi regime (1933–45). The Reichstag was reconstituted as the Bundestag in the governmental reorganization of 1949. Its membership was again reorganized after German unification in 1990.

bundle theory Theory advanced by DAVID HUME to the effect that the mind is merely a bundle of perceptions without deeper unity or cohesion, related only by resemblance, succession, and CAUSATION. Hume's well-argued denial of a substantial or unified self precipitated a philosophical crisis from which IMMANUEL KANT sought to rescue Western philosophy.

Bundy, McGeorge (1919–1996) U.S. public official and educator. Born in Boston, he served in World War II as an intelligence officer. In 1949 he joined the Harvard University faculty and became dean of arts and sciences in 1953. He served as special assistant for national security to presidents JOHN F. KENNEDY and LYNDON B. JOHNSON and was a forceful advocate of expanding U.S. involvement in the Vietnam War. He resigned to become president of the Ford Foundation (1966–79) and later taught at NYU (1979–89).

bungee jumping \'bən-jē\ Sport in which the jumper falls from a high place with a rubber ("bungee") cord attached both to his or her feet and to the jump site, and, after a period of headfirst free fall, is bounced partway back when the cord rebounds from its maximum stretch. It traces its roots to the "land diving" practiced on Pentecost Island, Vanuatu, in which divers jump off a high tower, their feet connected to it by a vine whose length is calculated to allow the jumper to fall until his hair just brushes the ground below. The Oxford Dangerous Sports Club, inspired by reports of the Pentecost Island divers, made the first Western bungee jumps, and bungee jumping was first offered commercially to the public in New Zealand in 1988.

Bunin \'bü-nʸin\, **Ivan (Alekseyevich)** (1870–1953) Russian poet and novelist. He worked as a journalist and clerk while writing and translating poetry, and made his name as a short-story writer with such masterpieces as the title story of *The Gentleman from San Francisco* (1916). His other works include the novel *Mitya's Love* (1925), the story collection *Dark Avenues* (1943), fictional autobiography, memoirs, and books on LEO TOLSTOY and ANTON CHEKHOV. The first Russian awarded the Nobel Prize for Literature (1933), he is among the best stylists in the language.

Bunker Hill, Battle of Important colonial victory early in the American Revolution. Two months after the battles of Lexington and Concord, over 15,000 colonial troops assembled near Boston to stop the British army from occupying several hills around the city. The colonists fortified Bunker Hill (originally Breed's Hill) across the Charles River from Boston; they withstood a cannonade from British ships in Boston Harbor on June 17, 1775, and also fought off assaults by 2,300 British troops, but were eventually forced to retreat. British casualties (about 1,000) and the colonists' fierce resistance convinced the British that subduing the rebels would be difficult.

bunraku \'bu̇n-rä-ku̇\ Japanese traditional puppet theater, in which nearly life-size dolls act out a chanted dramatic narrative, called *joruri*, to the accompaniment of a small shamisen. Puppet theater reached its height in the 18th century with the plays of Chikamatsu Monzaemon, and declined later because of a lack of excellent *joruri* writers.

Bunsen, Robert (Wilhelm) (1811–1899) German chemist. With Gustav Kirchhoff, he observed (c. 1859) that each element emits light of a characteristic wavelength, opening the field of spectrochemical analysis. They discovered several new elements (including helium, cesium, and rubidium) by spectroscopy. His only book discussed methods of measuring volumes of gases. He invented the carbon-zinc battery, grease-spot photometer (see photometry), filter pump, ice calorimeter, and vapor calorimeter. Though often credited with inventing the Bunsen burner, he seems to have made only a minor contribution to its development.

bunting Any of about 37 species of seed-eating finch in the Old World genus *Emberiza* (subfamily Emberizinae, family Fringillidae), recognizable by their strong head pattern, and similar-appearing species. *Emberiza* species commonly breed in temperate Eurasia and from northern Africa to India. The snow bunting (*Plectrophenax nivalis,* subfamily Emberizinae) breeds in the far north, and the lark bunting (*Calamospiza melanocorys,* Emberizinae) inhabits the U.S. Great Plains. In the U.S., buntings in the subfamily Cardinalinae (family Fringillidae) include the indigo bunting *(Passerina cyanea)* and the painted bunting *(P. ciris)*. The male painted bunting, with red, green, and blue feathers, is the gaudiest bird that breeds in the U.S.

Painted bunting (*Passerina ciris*).
DONALD D. BURGESS FROM E.R. DEGGINGER–EB INC.

Buñuel \ˌbu̇n-yu̇-'wel\, **Luis** (1900–1983) Spanish film director. As a student at the University of Madrid he met Salvador Dali and founded a cinema club. He went to Paris in 1925 and worked in the French film industry. He made the surrealist film *Un chien andalou* (1928) with Dalí, then directed the anticlerical *Golden Age* (1930) and the documentary *Land Without Bread* (1932). After working as a commercial producer in Spain and a technical adviser in Hollywood, he moved to Mexico, where he directed *Los olvidados* (1950) and *Nazarín* (1958). He returned to Spain to make *Viridiana* (1961), suppressed there as anticlerical but internationally acclaimed. He attacked conventional morality in such later films as *Belle de jour* (1967), *Tristana* (1970), *The Discreet Charm of the Bourgeoisie* (1972), and *That Obscure Object of Desire* (1977).

Buñuel.
CAMERA PRESS

Bunyan, John (1628–1688) English minister and author. Of humble rural origins, Bunyan encountered the seething religious life of various left-wing sects while serving in Oliver Cromwell's army in the English Civil Wars. He underwent a period of spiritual crisis, converted to Puritanism, and become a preacher. After the Restoration, he was jailed as a Nonconformist for 12 years, during which he wrote his spiritual autobiography, *Grace Abounding* (1666). He is best known for *The Pilgrim's Progress* (1678–84), a religious allegory expressing the Puritan religious outlook. A symbolic vision of the character Christian's pilgrimage through life, it was at one time second only to the Bible in popularity among ordinary readers. Despite his ministerial responsibilities, he published numerous works in his last 10 years.

John Bunyan, pencil drawing on vellum by Robert White; in the British Museum.
BY COURTESY OF THE TRUSTEES OF THE BRITISH MUSEUM

Bunyan, Paul Legendary giant lumberjack of the U.S. frontier. A symbol of strength and vitality, he is accompanied by a giant blue ox, Babe. He was credited with creating Puget Sound, digging the Grand Canyon, and building the Black Hills, and was known for his prodigious appetite, eating hotcakes off a griddle so large it was greased by men using sides of bacon as skates. Tales of his exploits probably originated in lumber camps, and were first published by James MacGillivray in "The Round River Drive" (1910), which soon led to a national myth.

Bunyoro See Nyoro

Buonarroti, Michelangelo See Michelangelo

buoyancy See Archimedes' principle

burakumin \bu̇-'rä-ku̇-min\ Japanese minority group that suffers discrimination based on its historical outcaste status. In the late 16th century, when Toyotomi Hideyoshi divided the populace into four social classes, one group remained outside and beneath the system: those whose occupation involved the taking of life (such as butchers or executioners) or the handling of flesh or dead bodies (such as leatherworkers or gravediggers). Buddhist and Shinto beliefs in the polluting nature of these occupations have long stigmatized those who held them. Though their outcaste status was removed by law in 1871, prejudice remains, and burakumin heritage often stands in the way of marriages and employment opportunities. Burakumin are estimated to number 1–3 million.

Burbage \'bər-bij\, **Richard** (1567?–1619) British actor. A popular actor by age 20, he was a member of the Earl of Leicester's company and the Chamberlain's (later King's) Men. Closely associated with William Shakespeare, he was the first to play such roles as Richard III, Romeo, Henry V, Hamlet, Macbeth, Othello, and King Lear. He also performed in plays by Thomas Kyd, Ben Jonson, and John Webster. He was a major shareholder of the Globe and Blackfriars theaters, built by his father, the actor-manager James Burbage, and managed by his brother.

Burbank, Luther (1849–1926) U.S. plant breeder. Reared on a farm in Lancaster, Mass., he never obtained a college education. Influenced by Charles Darwin's writings on domesticated plants, he began a plant-breeding career at 21. On the proceeds of his rapid development of the hugely successful Burbank potato, he set up a nursery garden, greenhouse, and experimental farms in Santa Rosa, Cal. There he developed more than 800 new and useful strains and varieties of fruits, flowers, vegetables, grains, and grasses, many of which are still commercially important. His laboratory became world-famous, and he helped make plant breeding a modern science. He published two multivolume works and a series of descriptive catalogs.

Burbank.
COURTESY OF HUNT INSTITUTE FOR BOTANICAL DOCUMENTATION, CARNEGIE MELLON UNIVERSITY, PITTSBURGH, PA.

Burbidge, (Eleanor) Margaret *orig.* **Eleanor Margaret Peachey** (born 1923) English astronomer. She served as acting director (1950–51) of the Observatory of the University of London. In 1955 her husband, Geoffrey Burbidge (born 1925), became a researcher at the Mount Wilson Observatory, and she accepted a research post at Caltech. She later joined the faculty at UC–San Diego, briefly serving as director of the Royal Greenwich Observatory (1972–73). Jointly with her husband, she made notable contributions to the theory of quasars and to the understanding of how the elements are formed in the depths of stars through nuclear fusion (nucleosynthesis).

burbot \'bər-bət\ Elongated fish *(Lota lota),* the only freshwater member of the COD family. It lives in cold rivers and lakes of Europe, Asia, and North America. A mottled, greenish or brown bottom-dweller, it descends as deep as 700 ft (200 m). It may grow about 3.6 ft (1.1 m) long. It has very small, embedded scales, a long anal fin, and two dorsal fins. The burbot is valued as food in some areas.

Burchfield, Charles (Ephraim) (1893–1967) U.S. painter. Born in Ashtabula Harbor, Ohio, he attended the Cleveland School of Art and, after service in World War I, worked as a wallpaper designer in Buffalo, N.Y. In the 1920s and '30s he was one of the leading U.S. scene painters; his work was associated with EDWARD HOPPER in its portrayal of the loneliness and bleakness of small-town life (e.g., *November Evening*, 1934). In the 1940s he abandoned realism for a more personal interpretation of nature, emphasizing its mystery, movement, and color from season to season (e.g., *The Sphinx and the Milky Way*, 1946).

Burckhardt \'bu̇rk-ˌhärt\, **Jacob (Christopher)** (1818–1897). Swiss historian of art and culture. After abandoning his study of theology, Burckhardt studied art history, then a new field, at the University of Berlin (1839–43). As he matured he became a cultural conservative, alienated from the contemporary world and preoccupied with reclaiming the past. From 1843 he taught primarily at the University of Basel; from 1886 until his retirement (1893) he taught art history exclusively. He is famous for *The Civilization of the Renaissance in Italy* (1860), which examines daily life in the Renaissance in terms of such phenomena as the development of individuality and the modern sense of humor; it became a model for cultural historians. He died while working on a four-volume survey of Greek civilization.

Burden, Henry (1791–1835) Scottish-U.S. ironmaster and inventor. He invented labor-saving machines, including a threshing machine, an improved PLOW, the first cultivator made in the U.S., a machine for making WROUGHT-IRON spikes, and the first patented horseshoe machine.

burdock Any plant of the genus *Arctium,* in the COMPOSITE FAMILY, bearing globular flower heads with prickly BRACTS. Native to Europe and Asia, burdock species have been naturalized throughout North America. Regarded as weeds in the U.S., they are cultivated for their edible root in Asia. Their fruits are round burrs that stick to clothing and fur.

Bureau of Standards *since 1988* **U.S. National Institute of Standards and Technology (NIST)** Agency of the U.S. Department of Commerce responsible for the standardization of weights and measures, timekeeping, and navigation. Active since at least the mid-19th century, the agency works closely with the U.S. Naval Observatory and the Bureau International de l'Heure in Paris to ensure global standardized time.

bureaucracy Professional corps of officials organized in a pyramidal hierarchy and functioning under impersonal, uniform rules and procedures. Its characteristics were first formulated systematically by MAX WEBER, who saw in the bureaucratic organization a highly developed DIVISION OF LABOR, authority based on administrative rules rather than personal allegiance or social custom, and a "rational" and impersonal institution whose members function more as "offices" than as individuals. For Weber, bureaucracy was a form of legalistic "domination" inevitable under CAPITALISM. Later writers saw in bureaucracy a tendency to concentrate power at the top and become dictatorial, as occurred in the Soviet Union. ROBERT K. MERTON emphasized its red tape and inefficiency due to blind conformity to procedures. Recent theories have stressed the role of managerial cliques, occupational interest groups, or individual power-seekers in creating politicized organizations characterized by internal conflict.

Burgas \bu̇r-'gäs\ City (pop., 1996: 199,000), eastern Bulgaria. Located on an inlet of the BLACK SEA, it is one of Bulgaria's chief ports. It was founded in the 17th century; its development received impetus with the coming of the railroad in the late 19th century. It claims much of Bulgaria's Black Sea trade and handles most of its fish catch. With several neighboring towns, Burgas is part of the developing Black Sea Riviera.

Bürger \'bu̅e̅r-gər\, **Gottfried August** (1747–1794) German poet. He was associated with the Göttinger Hain, a circle of STURM UND DRANG poets who reawakened interest in folk and nature themes. His bizarre ballad "Lenore" (1773) had a profound effect on the subsequent development of literary Romanticism throughout Europe, and he is remembered as a founder of German Romantic BALLAD literature. He is also noted for his Petrarchan sonnets and translations from English, especially Thomas Percy's *Reliques of Ancient English Poetry*.

Burger, Warren E(arl) (1907–1995) U.S. jurist. Born in St. Paul, Minn., he graduated from law school there, joined a prominent law firm, and became active in the Republican Party. He was appointed an assistant U.S. attorney general (1953) and named to the U.S. Court of Appeals for the District of Columbia (1955), where his conservative approach commended him to Pres. R. Nixon, who nominated him for chief justice of the U.S. Supreme Court in 1969. Contrary to the expectations of some, he did not try to reverse the tide of activist decisions on civil-rights issues and criminal law made during the tenure of his predecessor, EARL WARREN. The Burger Court upheld the 1966 *MIRANDA VS. ARIZONA* decision, busing as a permissible means of racially desegregating public schools, and the use of racial quotas in the distribution of federal grants and contracts to minorities. Burger voted with the majority in *ROE VS. WADE* (1973). Actively interested in judicial administration, he became deeply involved in efforts to improve the judiciary's efficiency. He retired in 1986 and was awarded the Presidential Medal of Freedom in 1988.

Burgess \'bər-jəs\, **Anthony** *orig.* **John Anthony Burgess Wilson** (1917–1993) English novelist, critic, and composer. His experiences in S.East Asia produced the novel trilogy *The Long Day Wanes* (1956–59). *A Clockwork Orange* (1962; film, 1971), his most original work, is a satire on extreme political systems. His other novels, which combine mordant wit, moral seriousness, verbal dexterity, and the bizarre, include *The Wanting Seed* (1962), *Inside Mr. Enderby* (1963), and *Earthly Powers* (1980). In addition to his extensive literary criticism, biographies, and works on linguistics and music, he composed over 65 musical works.

Burgess \'bər-jəs\, **Guy (Francis de Moncy)** (1911–1963) British diplomat and Soviet spy. At Cambridge University in the 1930s, he became part of a group of young men, including Donald Maclean (1913–1983), who disdained capitalist democracy. They were recruited by Soviet intelligence operatives and supplied information from their positions, mainly in the British foreign office (Maclean from 1934, Burgess from 1944). Maclean's post with the British embassy in Washington, D.C., enabled him to pass secret information about NATO to the Soviets; Burgess also served in Washington. In 1951 both men were warned by their colleague KIM PHILBY that an investigation was closing in on Maclean. With the aid of ANTHONY BLUNT, they fled England and vanished, then surfaced in Moscow in 1956.

Burgess \'bər-jəs\, **Thornton W(aldo)** (1874–1965) U.S. children's author and naturalist. Born in Sandwich, Mass., he loved nature as a child. His first book, *Old Mother West Wind* (1910), introduced the animal characters that were to populate his subsequent stories, which were published in many languages. He promoted conservationism through his "Wildlife Protection Program," his "Radio Nature League," and other organizations. He wrote more than 170 books and 15,000 stories for newspaper columns.

Burgess Shale \'bər-jəs\ Fossil formation containing remarkably detailed traces of soft-bodied marine organisms of the middle of the Cambrian epoch (520–512 million years ago). Collected from a fossil bed in the Burgess Pass of the Canadian Rockies, the Burgess Shale is one of the best preserved and most important fossil formations in the world. Since it was discovered in 1909, over 60,000 specimens have been retrieved from the bed.

Burgesses \'bər-jəs-əz\, **House of** Representative assembly in colonial Virginia, the first elective governing body in a British colony. It was a division of the legislature established by the colonial governor at Jamestown in 1619, to which each Virginia settlement was entitled to elect two delegates, or burgesses (citizens of a borough in England). See also LONDON CO.

Burghley, Baron See William CECIL

burglary Crime of breaking into and entering a structure with the intent to commit a FELONY within. It is one of several crimes in the general category of theft. Some state statutes specify degrees of burglary based on when and where the crime occurred, the presence of people, and the use (or non-use) of a deadly weapon.

Burgoyne \bər-ˈgȯin\, **John** (1722–1792) British general. After serving in the Seven Years' War he was elected to the British House of Commons in 1761 and 1768. Assigned to Canada in 1776, he began a campaign to join British forces from the north, south, and west to isolate the rebellious New England colonies. In 1777 his army captured Fort TICONDEROGA, N.Y., but was stopped at the Hudson River by a larger army of colonists under HORATIO GATES and BENEDICT ARNOLD. After several months of fighting, he surrendered to Gates at Saratoga Springs, N.Y.; he returned to England to face criticism for his defeat.

Burgundian school Group of 15th-century French composers, most of whom were associated with courts of various dukes of BURGUNDY. They are best known for their three-part CHANSONS in rondeau form (see FORMES FIXES), usually with text only in the highest part—perhaps implying a solo voice accompanied by instruments, written in full triadic harmony. The most important Burgundian composers were G. DUFAY, Gilles Binchois (c. 1400–1460), and Antoine Busnois (c. 1430–1492).

Burgundy *French* **Bourgogne** \bür-ˈgōn^{y}\ Historical region, France. The name was originally applied to a kingdom in the RHONE valley and western Switzerland founded by the Burgundians, a Germanic people who fled Germany in the 5th century. Conquered by the MEROVINGIANS c. 534, it was incorporated into the Frankish empire. By the 843 Treaty of VERDUN, it was included in the Middle Kingdom of LOTHAIR I's HOLY ROMAN EMPIRE. It was later divided into Cisjurane (Lower) Burgundy, or PROVENCE (founded 879), and Transjurane (Upper) Burgundy (founded 888); they united in 933 to form the kingdom of Burgundy. After the 13th century, it was known as the kingdom of ARLES; the name Burgundy was applied to the duchy of Burgundy, formed in the 9th century from lands in the northwestern part of the original kingdom. On the death of Burgundy's duke in 1361, the duchy reverted to the French crown. Given to PHILIP II, by 1477 its lands extended into the LOW COUNTRIES. It was seized by LOUIS XI, annexed to the French crown, and was a province until the FRENCH REVOLUTION. Today the area forms a governmental region with its capital at DIJON. Winemaking is an important part of the economy.

burial Ritual disposal of human remains, often intended to facilitating the deceased's entry into the afterworld. Grave burial dates back at least 125,000 years. Types of grave range from trenches to large burial mounds to great stone tombs such as PYRAMIDS. Caves have also long been used for the dead, as in the case of the ancient Hebrews or the thousands of sepulchral caves (rock temples) of western India and Sri Lanka. Water burial, such as occurred among the Vikings, has also been common. Cremation and the scattering of ashes on water is widely practiced, especially in Asia; in India the remains of the deceased are thrown into the sacred GANGES RIVER. Some peoples (American Indian groups, Parsis, etc.) employ exposure to the elements to dispose of their dead. Among many peoples, the first burial is followed by a second, after an interval that often coincides with the duration of bodily decomposition. This reflects a concept of death as slow passage from the society of the living to that of the dead. Jewish custom requires speedy burial; a prayer known as the Kaddish is recited at the graveside, and a gravestone is normally erected a year after burial. Christian burials are often preceded by a wake, a "watch" held over the deceased's body sometimes accompanied by festivity. Under Islam, the head of the dead must face Mecca.

Buridan \bü̅-rē-ˈdä^{n}, *Engl* ˈbyu̇r-əd-ᵊn\, **Jean** (1300–1358) French philosopher, logician, and scientific theorist. He studied under William of OCKHAM at the University of Paris and later taught there. He asserted a modified version of DETERMINISM. Among his achievements in mechanics was his revision of ARISTOTLE's theory of motion; he developed a theory of impetus by which the mover imparts to the moved a power, proportional to the former's speed and mass, which keeps it moving. His studies of optical images prefigured modern developments in cinematics. In logic he explicated doctrines of Aristotle and Peter of Spain (c. 1210–1277). His works include *Summula de dialecta* (1487) and *Consequentie* (1493).

Burke, Edmund (1729–1797) British (Irish) parliamentarian, orator, and political philosopher. The son of a lawyer, he began legal studies but lost interest. Essays he published in 1757–58 gained the attention of DENIS DIDEROT, IMMANUEL KANT, and GOTTHOLD LESSING, and he was hired to edit a yearly survey of world affairs (1758–88). He entered politics (1765) as secretary to a Whig leader and soon became involved in the controversy over whether Parliament or the monarch controlled the executive. He argued (1770) that GEORGE III's efforts to reassert a more active role for the crown violated the constitution's spirit. Elected to Parliament (1774–80), he contended that its members should exercise judgment rather than merely follow their constituents' desires. Though a strong constitutionalist, he was not a supporter of pure democracy. Though a conservative, he eloquently championed the cause of the American colonists, whom he regarded as badly governed, and he supported the abolition of the international slave trade. He tried unsuccessfully to legislate relief for Ireland and to reform the governance of India. He disapproved of the French Revolution for its leaders' precipitous actions and its anti-aristocratic bloodshed. He is often regarded as the founder of modern CONSERVATISM.

Burkina Faso \bu̇r-ˈkē-nə-ˈfä-sō\ *formerly* **Upper Volta** Republic, West Africa. A landlocked country, it lies south of the SAHARA Desert. Area: 105,869 sq mi (274,201 sq km). Population (1997 est.): 10,891,000. Capital: OUAGADOUGOU. Its two principal ethnic groups are the Voltaic (Gur), and the MOSSI; there are also HAUSA and FULANI. Languages: French (official), Moré, Dyula. Religions: About one-fifth of the population practice traditional religions; another one-fifth are Muslims; a small number are Christian. Currency: CFA franc. Burkina Faso consists of an extensive plateau, characterized by a savanna, grassy in the north and sparsely forested in the south. The plateau is notched by the valleys of the Mouhoun (Black Volta), Nazion (Red Volta), and Nakanbe rivers, which flow south into Ghana. Its economy is largely agricultural. It is a republic with one advisory body and one legislative body; its chief of state is the president and its head of government, the prime minister. Probably in the 14th century, the Mossi and Gurma peoples established themselves in eastern and central areas. The Mossi kingdoms of Yatenga and Ouagadougou existed into the early 20th century. A French protectorate was established over the region 1895–97, and its southern boundary was demarcated through an Anglo-French agreement. It was part of the Upper-Senegal-Niger (see MALI) colony, then became a separate colony in 1919. It was constituted an overseas territory within the FRENCH UNION in 1947, became an autonomous republic within the FRENCH COMMUNITY in 1958, and achieved total indepen-

dence in 1960. Since then, it has been ruled primarily by the military and has experienced several coups; following one in 1984, the country received its present name. A new constitution, adopted in 1991, restored multiparty rule.

Burkitt, Denis P(arsons) (1911–1993) British surgeon and medical researcher. He discovered Burkitt's LYMPHOMA, a lethal cancer of the lymphatic system with a high incidence among children. He showed that it was common in equatorial African regions where malaria and yellow fever are endemic and linked it to Epstein-Barr virus in children with immune systems depressed by chronic malaria. He later helped develop an effective chemotherapy treatment. Burkitt was also known for his theory that a high-fiber diet protects against colon cancer, publicized in his book *Don't Forget Fibre in Your Diet* (1979).

burlesque In literature, comic imitation of a serious literary or artistic form that relies on an extravagant incongruity between a subject and its treatment. It is closely related to PARODY, though burlesque is generally broader and coarser. Early examples include the comedies of ARISTOPHANES. English burlesque is chiefly drama. JOHN GAY's *The Beggar's Opera* (1728), HENRY FIELDING's *Tom Thumb* (1730), and RICHARD BRINSLEY SHERIDAN's *The Critic* (1779) are parodies of popular dramatic forms of the period. Victorian burlesque, usually light entertainment with music, was eclipsed by other popular forms by the late 19th cent, and burlesque eventually came to incorporate and be identified with striptease acts (see BURLESQUE SHOW).

burlesque show Stage entertainment designed for male amusement. Introduced in the U.S. by a company of English chorus girls in 1868, it developed as a version of the MINSTREL SHOW, divided into three parts: (1) a series of coarse humorous songs, SLAPSTICK sketches, and comic monologues; (2) the olio, or mixture of variety acts (e.g., acrobats, magicians, singers); and (3) chorus numbers and occasionally a takeoff, or burlesque, on politics or a current play. The show ended with an exotic dancer or a boxing match. In the early 20th century, such performers as FANNY BRICE, A. JOLSON, and W. C. FIELDS began their careers in burlesque. The addition of the striptease in the 1920s made a star of Gypsy Rose LEE, but censorship and competition from motion pictures soon led to burlesque's decline.

Burlingame, Anson (1820–1870) U.S. diplomat. Born in New Berlin, N.Y., he served in the U.S. House of Representatives as a candidate of the KNOW-NOTHING PARTY (1855–61) and helped found the REPUBLICAN PARTY. As U.S. minister to China (1861–67), he implemented a policy of cooperation between the Western powers and China. In 1861 the Chinese government appointed him imperial envoy to conduct China's international relations. He concluded the Burlingame Treaty, which established reciprocal rights of Chinese and U.S. citizens.

Burlingame, detail of an engraving by Perine & Giles, late 19th century.

BY COURTESY OF THE LIBRARY OF CONGRESS, WASHINGTON, D.C.

Burlington City (pop., 1996 est.: 39,000), northwestern Vermont. Lying on a hillside sloping toward Lake CHAMPLAIN, it is the largest city in the state and a port of entry. Chartered by Gov. Benning Wentworth of New Hampshire in 1763, it was named for the Burling family, who were pioneer landowners. Settlement began in 1773. Later it was a military post; in the WAR OF 1812 it saw several engagements between land batteries and British warships on the lake. It was the home of ETHAN ALLEN. It is the seat of the University of VERMONT. Shelburne Museum, a reconstruction of early American life, is nearby.

Burma See MYANMAR

Burma Road Former highway, South Asia. It ran 681 mi (1,096 km) from Lashio (in eastern Burma, now Myanmar) northeast to Kunming (in YUNNAN, China). An extension ran east from Kunming, then north to CHONGQING. Completed in 1939, it functioned as a supply route to the interior of China, carrying war goods. It was seized by the Japanese in 1942. It was reopened when it was connected to the STILWELL ROAD from India in 1945. Its importance diminished after World War II, but it remains a link in a 2,100-mi (3,400-km) road system from YANGON, Myanmar, to Chongqing, China.

Burmese cat Breed of DOMESTIC CAT, presumably of Asian origin. Compactly built, it has a small, rounded head and wide-set, round, yellow eyes. The short, finely textured, glossy coat darkens as it matures from milk-chocolate to a rich sable brown and is paler on the underside; the ears, face, legs, and tail may be darker. The tapered tail may be kinked near the tip.

burn Damage caused to the body by contact with flames, hot substances, some chemicals, radiation (including sunlight), or electricity. Burns are classified by depth of SKIN damage and by percentage of skin damaged. First-degree burns injure only the epidermis (top layer), with redness, pain, and minimal EDEMA. In a second-degree burn, damage extends into the dermis (inner layer), with redness and blisters. Third-degree burns destroy the entire thickness of the skin. There is no pain, because the skin's pain receptors are destroyed. Burns deeper than the skin can release toxic materials into the bloodstream and may require amputation. Secondary SHOCK follows severe burns, caused by loss of fluid both in the destroyed tissue and in leaks from the damaged area. Treatment depends on severity; first-degree burns need only first aid; third-degree burns require long-term hospitalization. Depending on the type, extent, and site of the burn, it may be left exposed, covered with a bandage, or excised to remove dead tissue in preparation for skin grafts. Complications of burns include respiratory problems, infection, ULCERS in the stomach or duodenum, and, especially in brown skin, thick scarring. Seizures and hypertension after burns occur almost entirely in children. Survivors usually require plastic surgery, long-term physical therapy, and psychotherapy.

Burnaby District municipality (pop., 1991: 159,000), southwestern British Columbia. The settlement developed along with VANCOUVER in the late 19th century and is now an eastern suburb of that city. It is one of the province's chief commercial and industrial centers, with important trucking, warehousing, and petroleum-distribution facilities.

Burne-Jones \'bərn-'jōnz\, **Edward (Coley)** *later* **Sir Edward** (1833–1898) British painter, illustrator, and designer. At Oxford he met his future collaborator WILLIAM MORRIS. In 1856 he became apprenticed to DANTE GABRIEL ROSSETTI. His paintings portray the romantic medieval imagery favored by the PRE-RAPHAELITES, and he drew inspiration from the elongated, melancholy figures of FRA FILIPPO LIPPI and SANDRO BOTTICELLI. He first achieved great success in 1877 with an exhibition of paintings including *The Beguiling of Merlin* (1873–77). He was a founding member of Morris & Co. (1861), notably as a designer of stained glass and tapestry, and he executed 87 designs for the Kelmscott Press edition of GEOFFREY CHAUCER (1896), considered one the world's finest printed books. His work had great influence on the French Symbolist movement, and his revival of the ideal of the artist-craftsman influenced the development of 20th-century industrial design.

Burnet \bər-'net\, **(Frank) Macfarlane** *later* **Sir Macfarlane** (1899–1985) Australian physician and virologist. Burnet received his medical degree from the University of Melbourne. He later discovered a method for identifying bacteria by the viruses (bacteriophages) that attack them, and shared a 1960 Nobel Prize with PETER MEDAWAR for the discovery of acquired immunological tolerance to tissue transplants. He was knighted in 1951.

Burnett, Carol (born 1933) U.S. comedian, actress, and singer. Born in San Antonio, Tex., she made her Broadway debut in *Once upon a Mattress* (1959), then appeared regularly on television in *The Garry Moore Show* (1959–62). Her gift for parody and her knock-kneed comic grace gained her a wide following. The weekly *Carol Burnett Show* (1966–77) became one of television's most popular programs and won her five Emmy awards. She acted in several films, including *Pete 'n' Tillie* (1972), *Four Seasons* (1981), and *Annie* (1982), and returned to Broadway in *Moon over Buffalo* (1995).

Burnett, Frances (Eliza) *orig.* **Frances Eliza Hodgson** (1849–1924) British-U.S. playwright and author. She is best remembered for the popular children's novel *Little Lord Fauntleroy* (1886), about an American boy who inherits an English earldom. *The Secret Garden* (1911), considered her best work, is a classic of children's literature.

Other works include the novel *Through One Administration* (1883), about corruption in Washington, D.C., and the play *A Lady of Quality* (1896).

Burney, Charles (1726–1814) British music historian. After being apprenticed to T. Arne, he taught music and played the organ. In 1770 he set off on European travels, undertaken to research his seminal *General History of Music* (4 vols., 1776–89). His accounts of the many famous musicians and others he met, including C.W. Gluck, C.P.E. Bach, Farinelli, P. Metastasio, Denis Diderot, and J.-J. Rousseau, provide an entertaining and invaluable snapshot of 18th-century European musical life and intellectual life in general. Fanny Burney was his daughter.

Burney (d'Arblay), Fanny *orig.* **Frances** (1752–1840) English novelist. The self-educated daughter of C. Burney, she wrote lively accounts of his social musical evenings. Her habit of recording observations of society led to *Evelina* (1778), an epistolary novel about an unsure young girl's social development; a landmark in the evolution of the novel of manners, it pointed the way to Jane Austen's novels. Her later novels include *Cecilia* (1782) and the potboiler *Camilla* (1796).

Fanny Burney, detail of an oil painting by her brother, E.F. Burney; in the National Portrait Gallery, London.

BY COURTESY OF THE NATIONAL PORTRAIT GALLERY, LONDON

Burnham, Daniel H(udson) (1846–1912) U.S. architect and city planner. Born in Henderson, N.Y., he pioneered the development of Chicago commercial architecture with his partner, John Wellborn Root (1850–1891). Three of the firm's Chicago buildings were designated landmarks in 1962: the Rookery (1886), the Reliance Building (1890), and the Monadnock Building (1891), the last and tallest (16-story) U.S. masonry skyscraper. As chief consulting architect for Chicago's World's Columbian Exposition (1893), Burnham chose firms working in academic eclecticism, the antithesis of the Chicago school. The resulting "White City," with its boulevards, gardens, and Classical facades, influenced planning in the U.S. Burnham's plan for Chicago (1907–9) is a classic example of U.S. city planning.

Burns, George *orig.* **Nathan Birnbaum** (1896–1996) U.S. comedian best known for his collaboration with Gracie Allen (1902–1964). Both were born in New York City to theatrical families and were vaudeville performers from childhood. They formed a comedy team in 1925 and were married in 1926. They performed on radio in *The George Burns and Gracie Allen Show* (1932–50), with Burns playing the straight man to Allen's malaprop-prone chatterbox, before their show moved to television (1950–58). They made 13 films together, including *The Big Broadcast* films of 1932, 1936, and 1937. Burns returned to the screen in such films as *The Sunshine Boys* (1975, Academy Award), *Oh, God!* (1977) and its sequels, and *Going in Style* (1979). Famous for his wry humor and his cigars, he continued performing into his late nineties.

Burns, Ken(neth Lauren) (born 1953) U.S. documentary filmmaker. Born in Brooklyn, N.Y., he founded his own production company in 1975 and made such documentary films as *Brooklyn Bridge* (1981), *The Shakers* (1984), *The Statue of Liberty* (1985), and *The Congress* (1988). His acclaimed series *The Civil War* (1990), televised on PBS, won numerous filmmaking and history awards. His later television documentaries include *Baseball* (1994), *Lewis and Clark* (1997), *Frank Lloyd Wright* (1998), and *Jazz* (2001).

Burns, Robert (1759–1796) National poet of Scotland. Son of a poor farmer, he became familiar early with orally transmitted folk song and tales. His father's farm failed, and a farm he started himself quickly went bankrupt. Handsome and high-spirited, he engaged in a series of love affairs, some of which produced illegitimate children, and celebrated his lovers in his poems. His *Poems, Chiefly in the Scottish Dialect* (1786) brought acclaim but no financial security, and he eventually took a job as an exciseman. He later began collecting and editing hundreds of traditional airs for James Johnson's *Scots Musical Museum* (1787–1803) and George Thomson's *Select Collection of Original Scotish Airs* (1793–1818); he substantially wrote many of these songs, though he did not claim them or receive payment for them. Among his best-known songs are "Auld Lang Syne," "Green Grow the Rashes, O," "John Anderson My Jo," "A Red, Red Rose," and "Ye Banks and Braes o' Bonnie Doon." He freely proclaimed his radical opinions, his sympathies with the common people, and his rebellion against orthodox religion and morality. His death at 37 resulted from endocarditis.

Robert Burns, detail of an oil painting by Alexander Nasmyth; in the National Portrait Gallery, London.

BY COURTESY OF THE NATIONAL PORTRAIT GALLERY, LONDON

Burnside, Ambrose (Everett) (1824–1881) Union general in the American Civil War. Born in Liberty, Ind., he graduated from West Point. In the Civil War, he was promoted to major general in 1862. He replaced George B. McClellan as commander of the Army of the Potomac, but was himself replaced after the Union loss at the Battle of Fredericksburg. He resigned in 1864 after the "Burnside mine" fiasco in the Petersburg Campaign, when a mine explosion intended to damage Confederate troops resulted in heavy Union losses. He was governor of Rhode Island 1866–69, and a U.S. senator 1875–81. He originated the fashion of side whiskers, later known as "sideburns."

Burnt Njáll See Njáls saga

Burr, Aaron (1756–1836) U.S. politician, third vice president of the U.S. (1801–5). Born in Newark, N.J., he served in the American Revolution on George Washington's staff until 1779. He had a successful law practice in New York from 1782 and served as state attorney general 1789–91 and in the U.S. Senate 1791–97. He ran for president in 1800. The electoral-vote tie between Burr and Thomas Jefferson sent the election to the House of Representatives; Jefferson was chosen after Alexander Hamilton endorsed him; Burr became vice president. Resentful of Hamilton's action and his later effort to block Burr's nomination for governor of New York in 1804, he challenged Hamilton to a duel following some remarks about Burr's character. He mortally wounded Hamilton and fled to Philadelphia. There he contacted Gen. James Wilkinson, with whom he planned an invasion of Mexico. He was tried for treason in 1807 before John Marshall, whose narrow interpretation of the constitutional charge led to acquittal. Under a cloud, Burr left for Europe, where he tried in vain to interest English and French authorities in his scheme to conquer Florida. In 1812 he returned to New York to resume his law practice.

burro See donkey

Burroughs, Edgar Rice (1875–1950) U.S. novelist. Born in Chicago, he worked as an advertising copywriter before trying fiction. His jungle adventure novel *Tarzan of the Apes* (1914) became the first of 25 books featuring Tarzan, the son of an English nobleman abandoned in Africa and raised by apes. He wrote 43 other novels.

Burroughs, John (1837–1921) U.S. essayist and naturalist. Born near Roxbury, N.Y., he worked in his early years as a teacher, farmer, and U.S. Treasury Department clerk, and in 1873 moved to a farm in the Hudson River valley. He often traveled and camped out with such friends as John Muir and Theodore Roosevelt. His many books, which helped establish the genre of the nature essay, include *Wake-Robin* (1871), *Birds and Poets* (1877), *Locusts and Wild Honey* (1879), *Ways of Nature* (1905), and *Field and Study* (1919).

Burroughs, William S(eward) (1855–1898) U.S. inventor. Born in Auburn, N.Y., he was self-supporting from age 15. In 1885 he constructed his first calculating machine; though it proved commercially impractical, he patented a practical model in 1892. This machine was a commercial success, but he died at 43 before he could earn much money from it. A year before his death he received the Franklin Institute's John Scott Medal. In 1905 the Burroughs Adding Machine Co. was organized as successor to the company he had started. William S. Burroughs was his grandson.

A
B

Burroughs, William S(eward) (1914–1997) U.S. novelist. The grandson of WILLIAM S. BURROUGHS, he attended Harvard University and later became a member of the central group of the BEAT MOVEMENT. His experimental novels evoke, in deliberately erratic prose, a nightmarish, sometimes wildly humorous world. His early *Junkie* (1953) frankly describes his experiences as a heroin addict. *The Naked Lunch* (1959; film, 1991), his best-known work, is preoccupied with homosexuality and police persecution and vividly satirizes the grotesque world of the addict. In his later novels, including *The Soft Machine* (1961), *Nova Express* (1964), *The Wild Boys* (1971), *Cities of the Red Night* (1981), and *The Western Lands* (1987), he further experimented with dystopian visions and radical technical devices.

Bursa *formerly* **Brusa** *ancient* **Prusa** City (pop., 1990: 835,000), northwestern Turkey. It was founded in the 3rd century BC, at the foot of the Mysian Mount Olympus near the southeastern shore of the Sea of MARMARA, as the seat of the kings of BITHYNIA. It flourished under Roman and later Byzantine emperors. After the Crusaders took CONSTANTINOPLE in 1204, it was a seat of Byzantine resistance. The Ottoman empire took it in the early 14th century and made it their first great capital. Conquered by TIMUR in the early 15th century, it was recovered by the Ottomans. Though the Ottoman capital was later moved to Constantinople, Bursa continued to prosper. Today it is a center for an agricultural area, and is noted for its carpets and its many 15th-century mosques.

Burschenschaft \'bu̇r-shən-ˌshäft\ (German: "youth association") German student organization that started as an expression of the nationalism prevalent in post-Napoleonic Europe. First appearing in 1815, the early groups were liberal and egalitarian and favored the political unification of Germany. The groups were suppressed under the CARLSBAD DECREES and went underground until 1848, when they participated in the German revolution (see REVOLUTIONS OF 1848). After German unification, they adopted a new and aggressive nationalism.

bursitis \bər-'sī-təs\ INFLAMMATION of the lubricating sac (bursa) over a JOINT or extension of a joint, or between TENDONS and muscles or bones, caused by infection, injury, arthritis or gout, calcium deposits along a tendon or joint, or repetitive minor irritation. Common types are "housemaid's knee," "soldier's heel," "tennis elbow," and "weaver's bottom." Bursitis in the shoulder is the most common form. Usually occurring in people unused to physical labor, it may be so painful that the affected arm cannot be raised. Treatment includes rest, heat, mild exercise, and medication to relieve inflammation and remove calcium deposits.

Burt, Cyril (Lodowic) *later* **Sir Cyril** (1883–1971) British psychologist. He taught at the University of London 1924–50, becoming known for his pioneering work in educational psychology, especially mental testing and statistical analysis. His studies of human intelligence convinced him that intelligence was primarily inherited. Subsequent examination indicated that he had fabricated some of the data, though some of his earlier work remained unaffected by this revelation. His books, which were very popular in England and went through many editions, include *The Factors of the Mind* (1940), *The Backward Child* (1961), *The Young Delinquent* (1965), and *The Gifted Child* (1975).

Burton, James H. (1823–1894) U.S. inventor and manufacturer. He served as master armorer at the Harpers Ferry armory (from 1849) and later as chief engineer at the Enfield Armory in England (1855–60), where he supervised installation of production machinery that brought the AMERICAN SYSTEM OF MANUFACTURE to England. In the American Civil War he oversaw all the armories of the Confederacy. After the war he brought modern manufacturing techniques to the Tula armory in Russia.

Burton, Richard *orig.* **Richard Walter Jenkins, Jr.** (1925–1984) British-U.S. actor. He first won success on the stage in *The Lady's Not for Burning* in London (1949) and on Broadway (1950). After his U.S. film debut in *My Cousin Rachel* (1952), he starred in such films as *The Robe* (1953) and *Alexander the Great* (1956). During the filming of *Cleopatra* (1963) he had a highly publicized love affair with ELIZABETH TAYLOR, whom he later twice married. Known for his resonant voice and his Welsh mournfulness, he starred again on Broadway in *Camelot* (1960) and an acclaimed *Hamlet* (1964). Among his other films are *The Night of the Iguana* (1964), *The Spy Who Came in from the Cold* (1965), *Who's Afraid of Virginia Woolf?* (1966), and *Equus* (1977).

Burton, Richard F(rancis) *later* **Sir Richard** (1821–1890) British scholar-explorer and Orientalist. Expelled from Oxford in 1842, Burton went to India as a subaltern officer. There he disguised himself as a Muslim and wrote detailed reports of merchant bazaars and urban brothels. He then traveled to Arabia, again disguised as a Muslim, and became the first non-Muslim European to penetrate the forbidden holy cities; he recounted his adventures in *Pilgrimage to El-Medinah and Mecca* (1855–56), a classic account of Muslim life. In 1857–58 he led an expedition with JOHN HANNING SPEKE in search of the source of the NILE RIVER; stricken with malaria, he turned back after becoming the first European to reach Lake TANGANYIKA. His travels resulted in a total of 43 accounts of such subjects as Mormons, West African peoples, Brazilian devil cults, Iceland, and Etruscan Bologna. He learned 25 languages and numerous dialects; among his 30 volumes of translations were ancient Eastern manuals on the art of love, and he larded his famous *Arabian Nights* translation with ethnological footnotes and daring essays that won him many enemies in Victorian society. After his death his wife, Isabel, burned his 40 years of diaries and journals.

Burton, Robert (1577–1640) British scholar and writer. He spent most of his life as a vicar at Oxford. His great *Anatomy of Melancholy* (1621) describes the kinds, causes, symptoms, and cures of melancholy in a lively, elegant, and sometimes humorous style; a mine of classical erudition and curious information, it is an index to the philosophical and psychological ideas of its time. His Latin comedy *Philosophaster* (1606) is a vivacious exposure of charlatanism.

Burton, Tim (born 1958) U.S. film director. Born in Burbank, Cal., he worked as an animator with Disney Productions before making his first short film in 1982. He directed the hit *Pee-Wee's Big Adventure* (1985), followed by *Beetlejuice* (1988), establishing an original, quirky style, and later the successful *Batman* (1989) and its sequel (1992), *Edward Scissorhands* (1990), *Ed Wood* (1994), *Mars Attacks!* (1996), and *Sleepy Hollow* (1999).

Buru *Dutch* **Boeroe** \'bü-rü\ Island, Indonesia. Located west of CERAM in the western MOLUCCAS, it measures 90 mi (145 km) long by 50 mi (81 km) wide. Namlea, the chief town, lies on the narrow coastal plain. It was taken by the Dutch in the mid-17th century. It became part of Indonesia after World War II. Indonesia used Buru for a prison camp following the 1965 attempted coup; most of the prisoners had been freed by 1981.

Burundi \bu̇-'rün-dē\ *officially* **Republic of Burundi** Country, central Africa. Area: 10,759 sq mi (27,866 sq km). Population (1997 est.):

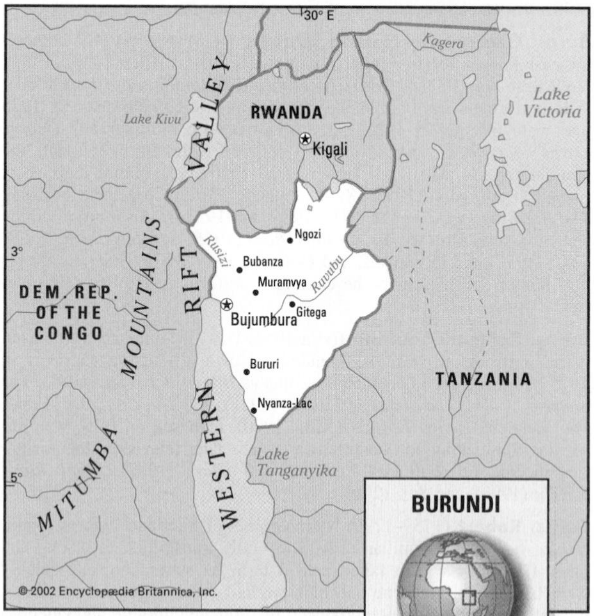

6,053,000 (not adjusted for casualties or refugees of recent war). Capital: BUJUMBURA. The population is divided primarily between the four-fifths who are HUTU and the one-fifth who are Tutsi. Its first inhabitants, the Twa Pygmies, make up about 1% of the population. Languages: Rundi (Kirundi), French (both official), Swahili, English. Religions: Roman Catholicism, local traditional religions. Currency: Burundi franc. Burundi occupies a high plateau, straddling the divide of the Nile and Congo (Zaire) rivers. The divide runs north to south, rising to 9,055 ft (2,760 m) at its highest point. The plateau contains the Ruvubu River basin, the southernmost extension of the Nile basin. In the west, the Rusizi River connects Lake Kivu in the north with Lake Tanganyika to the south. It has a developing economy, based primarily on agriculture. It is under a military regime. Normally, it has one legislative house, and its head of state and government is the president assisted by the prime minister. Original settlement by the Twa was followed by Hutu settlement, which occurred gradually and was completed by the 11th century. The Tutsi arrived 300–400 years later; though a minority, they established the kingdom of Burundi in the 16th century. In the 19th century, the area came within the German sphere of influence, but the Tutsi remained in power. Following World War I the Belgians took control of the area, then known as the mandate of Ruanda-Urundi. This was replaced by a U.N. trusteeship after World War II. Colonial-period conditions had intensified Hutu-Tutsi ethnic animosities, and as independence neared, hostilities flared. Independence was granted in 1962 in the form of a kingdom ruled by the Tutsi. In 1965 the Hutu rebelled but were brutally repressed. The rest of the 20th century saw violent clashes between the two groups, leading to charges of genocide in the 1990s. The very unstable government was overthrown by the military in 1996.

bus Device on a computer's motherboard that provides a data path between the CPU and attached devices (keyboard, mouse, disk drives, video cards, etc.). Like a vehicular bus that stops at designated stations to pick up or drop off riders, a computer bus receives a data signal from the CPU and drops it off at the appropriate device (for example, the contents of a file in RAM are sent, via the bus, to a disk drive to be stored permanently). Conversely, data signals from devices are sent back to the CPU. On a network, a bus provides the data path between the various computers and devices. See also USB.

bus Large motor vehicle designed to carry passengers usually along a fixed route according to a schedule. The first gasoline-powered bus was built in Germany in 1895 and carried eight passengers. The first integral-frame bus was constructed in the early 1920s in the U.S. In the 1930s diesel engines were introduced, providing greater power and fuel efficiency to larger buses. With the development of highway systems, transcontinental bus lines became common in North America. Double-decked buses are used in some European cities; articulated buses pull trailers with flexible joints. Trolley buses, whose electric motors draw power from overhead wires, are now used mostly in European cities.

Bush, George (Herbert Walker) (born 1924) 41st president of the U.S. (1989–93). Born in Milton, Massachusetts, the son of Prescott Bush, later U.S. senator from Connecticut, he served in World War II, graduated from Yale University, and started an oil business in Texas. He served in the U.S. House of Representatives 1966–70 as a Republican. He then served as ambassador to the U.N. (1971–72), chief of liaison to China (1974–76), and head of the CIA (1976–77). In 1980 he ran for president but lost the nomination to Ronald Reagan. He served as vice president with Reagan (1981–88), whom he succeeded as president, defeating Michael Dukakis. He made no dramatic departures from Reagan's policies. In 1989 he ordered a brief military invasion of Panama, which toppled that country's leader, General Manuel Noriega. He helped impose a U.N.-approved embargo against Iraq in 1990 to force its withdrawal from Kuwait. When Iraq refused, he authorized a U.S.-led air offensive that began the Persian Gulf War. Despite general approval of his foreign policy, an economic recession led to his defeat by William Jefferson Clinton in 1992. His son George W. Bush was elected governor of Texas in 1994 and president of the U.S. in 2000. Another son, Jeb Bush, was elected governor of Florida in 1998.

Bush, George W(alker) (born 1946) Governor of Texas (1995–2000) and 43rd president of the U.S. (from 2001). The eldest child of George Bush, the 41st president of the U.S. (1989–1993), he attended Yale University and Harvard Business School. After spending a decade in the oil business with mixed success, he served as managing general partner of the Texas Rangers baseball franchise. In 1994 he was elected governor of Texas. Popular for his genial style and his support of education reform, he was reelected by a landslide in 1998. In 1999 he launched his presidential campaign and quickly raised the largest presidential war chest in U.S. history. Despite losing the national popular vote to Al Gore by more than 500,000 votes, he gained the presidency when a U.S. Supreme Court ruling effectively ended a statewide recount of ballots in Florida, whose 25 electoral votes were needed by both candidates to secure a narrow majority in the electoral college. In June 2001 Bush signed into law a $1.35 trillion tax-cut bill. In foreign affairs, he faced worldwide criticism for his administration's abrogation of the Kyoto Protocol on reducing the emission of gases responsible for the greenhouse effect, its withdrawal from the Treaty on Antiballistic Missiles, and its attempts to remove American citizens from the jurisdiction of the new International Criminal Court. Following the terrorist attacks on the World Trade Center in New York City and the Pentagon building near Washington, D.C., in September 2001 (see September 11 attacks), the Bush administration's main priorities shifted to domestic security and counterterrorism. Identifying Osama bin Laden and his Al-Qaeda network as responsible for the attacks and charging the Taliban government of Afghanistan with harboring bin Laden and his followers, Bush ordered a massive bombing campaign in Afghanistan beginning in October that routed Al-Qaeda and forced the Taliban from power. Bush subsequently attempted to build international support for the overthrow of Iraqi leader Saddam Hussein.

George W. Bush.

ERIC DRAPER—WHITE HOUSE PHOTO

Bush, Vannevar (1890–1974) U.S. electrical engineer and administrator. Born in Everett, Mass., he taught principally at MIT (1919–38, 1955–71). In the late 1920s and '30s, Bush and his students built several electronic analog computers to solve differential equations. He helped found Raytheon Co., and he served as president of the Carnegie Institute 1939–55. In 1941, as director of the U.S. Office of Scientific Research and Development, he helped organize the Manhattan Project. By providing government support for university-based scientific research, the agency paved the way for postwar federal support of basic scientific research. As adviser to Pres. Franklin Roosevelt, he laid the groundwork for the establishment of the National Science Foundation (1950). An information retrieval and annotation system he described became the theoretical prototype of hypertext, the basis of the World Wide Web.

bushido \'bu̇-shi-dō\ (Japanese: "Way of the Warrior") Code of conduct of the samurai class of Japan, first formulated in the 17th century. Its precise content varied over time, taking on overtones of Zen Buddhism and Confucianism. Along with self-discipline, honor, and austerity, one constant feature was the samurai's obligation to his lord, which superseded even familial ties. This obligation of loyalty and sacrifice was transferred to the emperor with the Meiji Restoration and was a salient feature of the Japanese national mindset during World War II.

bushmaster Species *(Lachesis muta)* of pit viper, found in scrublands and forests from Costa Rica south to the Amazon River basin. It is normally about 6 ft (1.8 m) long but reportedly may grow to twice this length. It is pinkish or tan, marked with large, dark, diamond-shaped blotches. Though seldom encountered, it is potentially lethal.

Bushmen See San

business cycle Periodic fluctuation in the rate of economic activity, as measured by levels of employment, prices, and production. Economists have long debated why periods of prosperity are eventually followed by economic crises (stock-market crashes, bankruptcies, unemployment, etc.). Some have identified recurring eight-to-ten-year cycles in market economies; longer cycles have also been proposed, notably by Nikolay Kondratev. Apart from random shocks to the economy, such as wars and technological changes, the main influences on the level of economic activity are investment and consumption. An increase in investment, as when a factory is built, leads to consumption because the workers employed to build the factory have wages to spend. Conversely, increases in consumer demand cause new factories to be built to satisfy the demand. Eventually the economy reaches its full capacity, and, with little free capital and no new demand, the process reverses itself and contraction ensues. Natural fluctuations in agricultural markets, psychological factors such as a bandwagon mentality, and changes in the MONEY SUPPLY have all been proposed as explanations for initial changes in investment and consumption. Since World War II, government MONETARY POLICY has aimed at moderating the business cycle, preventing the extremes of INFLATION and DEPRESSION by stimulating the economy in slack times and restraining it during expansions.

business finance Raising and managing of funds by business organizations. Such activities are usually the concern of senior managers, who must use financial forecasting to develop a long-term plan for the firm. Shorter-term budgets are then devised to fit this scheme. When a company plans to expand, it may rely on cash reserves, expected increases in sales, or bank loans and trade credits extended by suppliers. Managers may also decide to raise long-term capital in the form of either DEBT (BONDS) or EQUITY (STOCK). The value of the company's stock is a constant concern, and managers must decide whether to reinvest PROFITS or to pay DIVIDENDS. Other duties of financial managers include managing ACCOUNTS RECEIVABLE and fixing the optimum level of INVENTORIES. When deciding how to deploy corporate assets to increase growth, financial managers must also consider the benefits of mergers and acquisitions, analyzing economies of scale and the ability of businesses to complement each other.

business law *or* **commercial law** *or* **mercantile law** Legal rules and principles bearing on business organizations and commercial matters. It regulates various forms of legal business entities, including sole proprietors, partnerships, registered companies with limited liability, agents, and multinational corporations. Nearly all statutory rules governing business organizations are intended to protect creditors or investors. In addition, specific bodies of law regulate commercial transactions, including the sale and carriage of goods (terms and conditions, specific performance, breach of contract, insurance, bills of lading), consumer credit agreements (letters of credit, loans, security, bankruptcy), and relations between employers and employees (wages, conditions of work, health and safety, fringe benefits, and trade unions). It is a broad and continually evolving field. See also AGENCY, CORPORATION, DEBTOR AND CREDITOR, INTELLECTUAL PROPERTY, LABOR LAW, NEGOTIABLE INSTRUMENTS.

Busoni \bü-'sō-nē\, **Ferruccio (Dante Michelangiolo Benvenuto)** (1866–1924) Italian-German composer and pianist. He first performed in public at 7, and at 12 he conducted his own *Stabat Mater*. He taught in Helsinki, Moscow, and Boston before settling permanently in Berlin in 1894. He won fame as a virtuoso pianist and gave premieres of the works of major composers. His most celebrated work in his lifetime, the opera *Die Brautwahl* (1910), was followed by the operas *Arlecchino* (1916) and *Turandot* (1917), but the posthumously produced *Doktor Faust* is regarded as his masterpiece. Of his many orchestral works, his piano concerto (1904) is most widely performed. His many piano pieces include the *Fantasia contrappuntistica* (1910), six sonatinas (1910–20), and arrangements of many organ works by J.S. BACH.

Busra \'bùs-rə\ *or* **Bosra** \'bäs-rə\ Ruined city, southwestern Syria. Lying south of DAMASCUS, it was first a Nabataean city, and was later conquered by TRAJAN. As Bostra, it was the capital of the Roman province of Arabia, and served as a fortress east of the JORDAN RIVER. It became the see of a bishop early in the 4th century AD, but fell to the Muslims in the 7th century. The Crusaders captured it in the 12th century but failed to hold it, and it quickly fell into decline. It is the site of monumental remains of temples, triumphal arches, aqueducts, churches, and mosques.

bustard Any of about 23 species of medium-sized to large game birds in the family Otididae, related to the CRANES and RAILS in the order Gruiformes. Bustards are found in Africa, southern Europe, Asia, Australia, and New Guinea. A tall running bird, they have long legs, a compact body carried in a horizontal position, and an erect neck placed forward of the legs. The best-known species is the great bustard *(Otis tarda)*, the largest European land bird. Males of this species weigh as much as 31 lbs (14 kg) and reach lengths of 4 ft (1.2 m), with 8-ft (2.4-m) wingspreads.

Bute, Earl of *orig.* **John Stuart** (1713–1792) Scottish-born British statesman. He was the tutor and constant companion of the future GEORGE III; when the latter ascended to the throne, he named Bute secretary of state (1761). As prime minister (1762–63), Bute negotiated the peace ending the SEVEN YEARS' WAR, but, having failed to create a stable administration, he resigned in 1763.

Buthelezi \ˌbüt-ᵊl-'ā-zē\, **Mangosuthu G(atsha)** (born 1928) ZULU chief and leader of the INKATHA FREEDOM PARTY. Descended from CETSHWAYO, he assumed leadership of the Buthelezi clan in 1953. He was elected head of the nonindependent black state of KwaZulu in 1972, and revived Inkatha in 1974 after breaking with the AFRICAN NATIONAL CONGRESS (ANC). Rejecting full independence for KwaZulu, he worked within the white establishment to end APARTHEID. In 1990–94 he engaged in a fierce struggle for leadership with the ANC; thousands were killed in Inkatha–ANC clashes. Following the 1994 national elections, he was appointed minister of home affairs by NELSON MANDELA.

Butkus \'bət-kəs\, **Dick** *orig.* **Richard J.** (born 1942) U.S. football player. Born in Chicago, he played for Chicago Vocational High School and the University of Illinois before joining the Chicago Bears (1965–73). He became known for his ability to break up plays, sack the quarterback, and intercept passes. His career was shortened by injuries; after retirement he became active in television and sports promotion. Butkus is often considered the best middle linebacker of all time.

Butler, Benjamin F(ranklin) (1818–1893) U.S. army officer. Born in Deerfield, N.H., he became a lawyer and legislator in Massachusetts. In the Civil War he commanded Fort Monroe, Va., where he refused to return fugitive slaves to the Confederacy, calling them "contraband of war," an interpretation later upheld by the government. He oversaw the occupation of New Orleans in 1862, but was recalled because of his harsh rule. He led the Union army in Virginia, but after several defeats was relieved of command in 1865. In the U.S. House of Representatives (1867–75, 1877–79), he was a Radical Republican prominent in the impeachment trial of Pres. ANDREW JOHNSON. He switched parties in 1878 to support the Greenback movement, and served as governor of Massachusetts 1882–84.

Butler, Joseph (1692–1752) British bishop and moral philosopher. He became dean of St. Paul's Cathedral in 1740 and bishop of Durham in 1750. He attempted to reconcile enlightened self-interest and the pursuit of happiness with morality, in part by way of the idea of conscience. His most important book was *The Analogy of Religion* (1736).

Butler, Nicholas M(urray) (1862–1947) U.S. educator. Born in Elizabeth, N.J., he received his PhD from Columbia University. He was the founding president of what is today Columbia's Teachers College (1886–91). As president of Columbia University. itself (1901–45), he led the institution to world renown. Early in his career he criticized prevailing pedagogical methods, but later he turned on pedagogical reform itself, decrying vocationalism in education and behaviorism in psychology. A champion of international understanding, he helped establish the Carnegie Endowment for International Peace in 1910 and served as its president 1925–45. In 1931 he shared the Nobel Peace Prize with JANE ADDAMS.

Butler, R(ichard) A(usten) *later* **Baron Butler (of Saffron Walden)** (1902–1982) British politician. Known as "Rab" Butler, he was elected to Parliament in 1929 and served in various Conservative governments in the 1930s. As minister of education, he was responsible for the 1944 Education Act, which established free secondary education. After the Tories' electoral losses in 1945, he helped remold the Conservative Party, serving as its leader 1955–61. He served as chancellor of the exchequer 1951–55, home secretary 1957–62, and foreign secretary 1963–64.

Butler, Samuel (1612–1680) British poet and satirist. He held several clerical positions, where he could observe cranks and scoundrels like those whose antics he targeted. He is famous for *Hudibras* (1663–78), a mock-heroic poem skewering the fanaticism, pretentiousness, pedantry, and hypocrisy he saw in militant PURITANISM. It is the most memorable BURLESQUE poem in English and the first English satire to successfully attack ideas rather than personalities.

Butler, Samuel (1835–1902) British novelist, essayist, and critic. Descended from distinguished clergymen, he grappled for many years with Christianity and evolution, first embracing, then rejecting, CHARLES DAR-

WIN's theories in his writings. He is best known for *The Way of All Flesh* (1903), his autobiographical novel that tells, with ruthless wit and lack of sentiment, the story of his escape from the suffocating moral atmosphere of his home circle. In his lifetime his reputation rested on the utopian satire *Erewhon* (1872), which foreshadowed the end of the Victorian illusion of eternal progress.

Samuel Butler, detail of an oil painting by Charles Gogin, 1896; in the National Portrait Gallery, London.
BY COURTESY OF THE NATIONAL PORTRAIT GALLERY, LONDON

Buto \'byü-tō\ In ancient EGYPTIAN RELIGION, the cobra goddess who was tutelary goddess of Lower Egypt and, with the vulture-goddess Nekhbet of Upper Egypt, protector of the king. She was nurse to the infant god HORUS and helped his mother, ISIS, protect him from his uncle SETH. She was later identified with LETO. She is depicted as a cobra twined around a papyrus stem.

Buton \'bü-ˌtȯn\ *or* **Butung** \'bü-ˌtu̇ŋ\ Island (pop., 1980: 317,000), Indonesia. Lying off the southeast coast of SULAWESI, it is about 100 mi (160 km) long and has an area of about 2,000 sq mi (5,200 sq km). Its chief town is Baubau, on the southwestern coast. The coastal people are chiefly trading sailors and fishermen.

butte \'byüt\ (French: "hillock" or "rising ground") Flat-topped hill surrounded by a steep cliff, from the bottom of which a slope descends to the plain. The term is sometimes used for an elevation higher than a hill but not high enough to be a mountain. Buttes topped by horizontal platforms of hard rock are characteristic of the arid plateau region of the western U.S. A butte is similar to a MESA but generally smaller; both are created by erosional processes.

butter Solid emulsion of FAT globules, water, and salt made by churning CREAM, used as a food. Presumably known since the advent of animal husbandry, butter has long been used as a cooking fat and as a spread. It was traditionally a farm product, but with the advent of the cream separator in the late 19th century it began to be mass-produced. It is a high-energy food, containing about 715 calories per 100 grams. It is high in butterfat (80–85%) and low in protein. In the U.S., coloring is often added to enhance its natural yellow color (from CAROTENE).

butter-and-eggs *or* **toadflax** Common perennial herbaceous plant *(Linaria vulgaris)* of the SNAPDRAGON FAMILY, native to Eurasia and widely naturalized in North America. The plant bears flaxlike leaves and showy yellow and orange flowers that are two-lipped and spurred like snapdragons.

buttercup Any of about 250 species of herbaceous flowering plants constituting the genus *Ranunculus* of the family Ranunculaceae. Buttercups are especially common in the woods and fields of the northern temperate zone. The turban, or Persian buttercup *(R. asiaticus),* is the florist's ranunculus. Among the many wild species are the tall meadow buttercup *(R. acris)* and common water crowfoot *(R. aquatilis).* Other members of the family Ranunculaceae are widely distributed in all temperate and subtropical regions. In the tropics they occur mostly at high elevations. Their leaves are usually alternate and stalkless and may be simple or much divided. The flowers may be radially symmetrical or irregular. The family includes such flowers as ANEMONE, LARKSPUR, MARSH MARIGOLD, CLEMATIS, and hepatica (genus *Hepatica*).

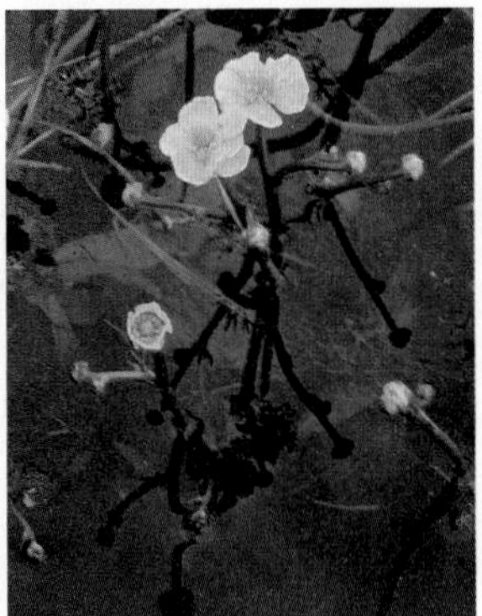
Aquatic buttercup (*Ranunculus flabellaris*).
KITTY KOHOUT FROM ROOT RESOURCES

butterfly Any of several thousand LEPIDOPTERAN species belonging to about six families and found worldwide. Unlike MOTHS, butterflies are usually bright or strikingly colored and are active during the day. Distinctive features are its club-tipped antennae and its habit of holding its wings vertically over its back when at rest. The larvae and adults of most species are plant eaters. The metalmarks (family Riodinidae) are found chiefly in the New World tropics; members of the family Libytheidae are called snout butterflies. Other species (with their families) include the WHITE and SULPHUR butterflies (Pieridae), the SWALLOWTAIL BUTTERFLY (Papilionidae), the BLUE, COPPER, and HAIRSTREAK butterflies (Lycaenidae), and the ADMIRAL, MONARCH, and PAINTED LADY (Nymphalidae).

butterfly bush See BUDDLEIA

butterfly effect See CHAOTIC BEHAVIOR

butterfly weed North American plant *(Asclepias tuberosa)* of the MILKWEED FAMILY, a stout, rough-haired perennial with long horizontal roots. The leafy, erect, somewhat branching stem is about 1–3 ft (0.3–0.9 m) tall. In midsummer it bears numerous clusters of bright-orange flowers. Unlike most milkweeds, it has a scanty milky juice. It is native to dry fields and is often planted in wild gardens or grown as a border plant.

butternut Deciduous NUT-producing tree *(Juglans cinerea)* of the WALNUT family, native to eastern North America. A mature tree has gray, deeply furrowed bark. Each leaf has 11–17 yellowish-green leaflets that are hairy underneath. Chocolate-colored partitions divide the pith of the twig into many chambers. The egg-shaped fruit has a sticky, greenish-brown husk. The hard, woody nut bears many ridges and contains a sweet, oily seed. The tree is economically important for its edible nuts and for a yellow or orange dye obtained from the fruit husks. Some substances in the inner bark of the roots are used in medicines.

button Small disk or knob used as a fastener or ornament. It usually has holes or a shank through which it is sewn to one side of a garment. It is used to fasten or close the garment when it is passed through a loop or hole in the other side. The ancient Greeks fastened their tunics with buttons and loops. In medieval Europe, garments were laced or fastened together with brooches or clasps until the buttonhole was invented in the 13th century. Throughout history, buttons have been made in a range of sizes and materials. In the 20th century, buttons were replaced by the zipper on some garments.

buttress Exterior support, usually of masonry, projecting from the face of a wall and serving to strengthen it or resist outward thrust from an arch or roof. Buttresses also have a decorative function. Though used since ancient times (Mesopotamian temples featured decorative buttresses, as did Roman and Byzantine structures), they are especially associated with GOTHIC ARCHITECTURE. See also FLYING BUTTRESS.

Butung See BUTON

Buxtehude \ˌbu̇k-stə-'hü-də\, **Dietrich** (1637?–1707) Danish-German composer. He held two organist positions before being appointed organist at Lübeck's important Marienkirche, where he remained almost 40 years. There he reinstated the tradition of the Abendmusik, an annual series of church concerts. His reputation was such that in 1705 J.S. BACH traveled 200 miles there to hear him play and ended up staying three months. Buxtehude's approximately 130 surviving vocal works, usually called cantatas, can instead be classified as concertos, chorale settings, and arias. He left almost 100 works for organ, some 20 keyboard suites, and over 20 chamber sonatas.

Buyid dynasty \'bü-yid\ *or* **Buwayhid dynasty** \bü-'wī-hid\ (945–1055) Shiite dynasty founded by three sons of Buyeh, a Daylamite (N Persian) fisherman. They captured Baghdad in 945, restoring native control to their homeland. Each brother took a portion of territory, and after they died, one son, Adud al-Dawlah, consolidated control (977) and enlarged the Buyid domain. After 983 the territories were split among family members. The dynasty ended when the Seljuq Turks (see SELJUQ DYNASTY) took Baghdad in 1055. Buyid art maintained its influence throughout the Seljuq reign; Buyid silverwork is notable.

buzz bomb See V-1 MISSILE

buzzard Chiefly British term for any of several BIRDS OF PREY of the HAWK genus *Buteo* (family Accipitridae) and, in North America, various New World VULTURES, especially the TURKEY VULTURE. In Australia, a large hawk of the genus *Hamirostra* is called a black-breasted buzzard. The buteos, also called buzzard hawks, can usually be distinguished when soaring by their broad wings and expansive rounded tail. The plumage of most species is dark brown above and white or mottled brown below; the tail and underside of the wings are usually barred. Buteos customarily prey on insects, small mammals, and occasionally birds. They nest in trees or on cliffs. Species range over much of the New World, Eurasia, and Africa. The red-tailed hawk, the most common North American buteo, is about 2 ft (60 cm) long.

Buzzards Bay Inlet of the Atlantic Ocean, southeastern Massachusetts. Connected to Cape Cod Bay by the Cape Cod Canal on the northeast and bordered on the southeast by the Elizabeth Islands, it is 30 mi (48 km) long and 5–10 mi (8–16 km) wide. Its coastline is dotted with fishing villages and summer resorts. Buzzards Bay town (pop., 1990: 3,300), is the site of Mass. Maritime Academy.

Byatt, A(ntonia) S(usan) *orig.* **Antonia Susan Drabble** (born 1936) British novelist and scholar. Sister of MARGARET DRABBLE, she was educated at Cambridge and taught at University College London. Her third novel, *The Virgin in the Garden* (1978), won high acclaim; the sequel *Still Life* (1985) followed. *Possession* (1990), a virtuoso double narrative, won the 1990 Booker Prize, and *Angels and Insects* (1991) became a film. Her story collections include *The Djinn in the Nightingale's Eye* (1995) and *Elementals* (1998). *Degrees of Freedom* (1965) was the first major study of IRIS MURDOCH.

Byblos \'bi-bləs\ *modern* **Jubayl** \jü-'bāl\ Ancient city, eastern Mediterranean coast. Located north of modern BEIRUT, it was occupied at least by the NEOLITHIC PERIOD; extensive settlement developed during the 4th millennium BC. As the chief harbor for the export of cedar to Egypt, it was a great trading center. Papyrus received its early Greek name, *byblos,* from its export to the Aegean through Byblos; *Bible* means essentially "the (papyrus) book." Byblos has yielded almost all the known early Phoenician inscriptions, most from the 10th century BC. By that time TYRE had become predominant in Phoenicia, and Byblos, though it flourished into Roman times, never recovered its former supremacy.

Bydgoszcz \'bid-ˌgȯshch\ City (pop., 1996 est.: 386,000), northern Poland. Originally a commercial city of the TEUTONIC ORDER, it received town rights in 1346. It prospered as a grain and timber center until it was devastated in the 17th-century Swedish wars. In the 18th century the Bydgoszcz Canal, which linked the basins of the VISTULA and ODER rivers, made the city a major inland port. It was under Prussian rule 1772–1919. The Germans held it throughout World War II, but it was noted for its staunch resistance to the Nazi attack of 1939. It remains important as a water transport route, connecting Upper Silesia with the Baltic ports.

Byelarus See BELARUS

Byelorussian language See BELARUSIAN LANGUAGE

bylina \bə-'lē-nə\ Traditional form of orally transmitted Old Russian and Russian heroic narrative poetry. Though byliny originated about the 10th century, or possibly earlier, they were first written down around the 17th century. They have been classified into several groupings, the largest of which deal with the golden age of Kiev in the 10th–12th century. Taken together, they constitute a folk history often at variance with official history.

bypass surgery See CORONARY BYPASS

Byrd, Richard E(velyn) (1888–1957) U.S. naval officer, aviator, and polar explorer. He was born in Winchester, Va. After serving in World War I, he worked developing navigational aids for aircraft. In 1926 he and Floyd Bennett claimed to have reached the North Pole by airplane, becoming the first to do so. In 1928 Byrd began his explorations of Antarctica with the first expedition to his "Little America" base, which was followed in 1929 by a flight with three companions over the South Pole, again the first such flight. He led subsequent expeditions that discovered and mapped large areas of Antarctica. His several books include *Discovery* (1935) and *Alone* (1938), which chronicled his months spent alone in a camp near the South Pole. His brother Harry F. Byrd (1887–1966) served as senator from Virginia 1933–65.

Byrd, William (1543–1623) British composer. He studied under T. TALLIS, and was appointed organist of Lincoln Cathedral at 20. In 1572 he became organist of the Chapel Royal jointly with Tallis. In 1575 the two men received from ELIZABETH I the exclusive license for the printing and selling of music in Britain. Though repeatedly prosecuted as a Roman Catholic, Byrd remained in favor with the queen. He apparently taught most of the important composers of the next generation. He is renowned as Britain's finest composer of sacred choral works, as well as for his keyboard music and songs. His works include three masses (for three, four, and five voices), some 220 Latin motets, four important Anglican services, and some 60 anthems, as well as some 100 virginal pieces (many preserved in the collections *Parthenia* and *The Fitzwilliam Virginal Book*). He is regarded as the greatest British composer up to his time.

Byrne, David (born 1952) Scottish-U.S. singer and songwriter. At the Rhode Island School of Design in the mid-1970s, he cofounded the rock group Talking Heads as singer and guitarist. Identified with the new-wave movement (see PUNK ROCK), the band's debut album *Talking Heads '77* (1977) was followed by releases that reflected Byrne's interest in experimental pop and African rhythms, including *Speaking in Tongues* (1983), the album and film *Stop Making Sense* (1984), and such solo albums as *Rei Momo* (1989). An ethnomusicologist and producer, Byrne also wrote the score for TWYLA THARP's *The Catherine Wheel* (1980) and directed the film *True Stories* (1986).

Byron, George (Gordon), Baron *known as* **Lord Byron** (1788–1824) British Romantic poet and satirist. Born with a clubfoot and extremely sensitive about it, he was 10 when he unexpectedly inherited his title and estates. Educated at Cambridge, he gained recognition with *English Bards and Scotch Reviewers* (1809), a satire responding to a critical review of his first published volume, *Hours of Idleness* (1807). At 21 he embarked on a European grand tour. *Childe Harold's Pilgrimage* (1812–18), a poetic travelogue expressing melancholy and disillusionment, brought him fame, while his complex personality, dashing good looks, and many scandalous love affairs captured the imagination of Europe. Settling near Geneva, he wrote the verse tale *The Prisoner of Chillon* (1816), a hymn to liberty and an indictment of tyranny, and *Manfred* (1817), a poetic drama whose hero reflected Byron's own guilt and frustration. His greatest poem, *Don Juan* (1819–24), is an unfinished epic picaresque satire in OTTAVA RIMA. Among his numerous other works are verse tales and poetic dramas. He died of fever in Greece while aiding the struggle for independence, making him a Greek national hero.

byssinosis See BROWN LUNG DISEASE

byte See BIT

Byzantine architecture \'bi-zən-ˌtēn\ Building style of Constantinople (now Istanbul, formerly ancient Byzantium) after AD 330. Byzantine architects were eclectic, at first drawing heavily on Roman temple features. Their combination of the BASILICA and symmetrical central-plan (circular or polygonal) religious structures resulted in the characteristic Byzantine Greek-cross-plan church, with a square central mass and four arms of equal length. The most distinctive feature was the domed roof. To allow a dome to rest above a square base, either of two devices was used: the squinch (an arch in each of the corners of a square base that transforms it into an octagon) or the PENDENTIVE. Byzantine structures featured soaring spaces and sumptuous decoration: marble columns and inlay, mosaics on the vaults, inlaid-stone pavements, and sometimes gold coffered ceilings. The architecture of Constantinople extended throughout the Christian East and in some places, notably Russia, remained in use after the fall of Constantinople (1453). See also HAGIA SOPHIA.

Byzantine art Art associated with the BYZANTINE EMPIRE. Its characteristic styles were first codified in the 6th century and persisted with remarkable homogeneity until the capture of Constantinople by the Turks in 1453. Concerned almost exclusively with religious expression, it tends to reflect an intensely hierarchical view of the universe. It relies on vigor of line and brilliance of color; individual features are absent, forms are flattened, and perspective is absent. Walls, vaults, and domes were covered in mosaic and fresco decoration in a total fusion of architectural and pictorial expression. Byzantine sculpture was largely limited to small ivory reliefs. The importance of Byzantine art to European religious art was immense; the style was spread by trade and expansion to the Mediterranean basin, eastern European centers, and especially Russia. See also BYZANTINE ARCHITECTURE.

Byzantine chant Unison liturgical chant of the GREEK ORTHODOX CHURCH from the era of the BYZANTINE EMPIRE to the 16th century. It probably derived principally from Hebrew and Syrian Christian liturgies. Until the 10th century it lacked any notation except vague ecphonetic accent marks above the text that served as memory aids; thereafter it employed more precise neumes, which by the 13th century are precise enough to be accurately and completely transcribed. A system of eight MODES, very similar to the eight Greek modes, was used for psalms and hymns, each mode (or *echos*) consisting primarily of a few melodic formulas. The principal hymn genres were the *troparion* (one or more stanzas of poetic prose), the *kontakion* (a metrical sermon), and the *kanon* (a complexly ordered set of hymn types). See also GREGORIAN CHANT.

Byzantine empire Empire, southeastern and southern Europe and western Asia. It began as the city of Byzantium, which had grown from an ancient Greek colony founded on the European side of the BOSPORUS. The city was taken in AD 330 by CONSTANTINE I, who refounded it as CONSTANTINOPLE. The area at this time was generally termed the Eastern Roman empire. On the death of Constantine in 395, THEODOSIUS I divided the empire between his two sons. The fall of Rome in 476 ended the western half of the Roman empire; the eastern half continued as the Byzantine empire, with Constantinople as its capital. The eastern realm differed from the west in many respects: heir to the civilization of the HELLENISTIC era, it was more commercial and more urban. Its greatest emperor, JUSTINIAN (r.527–565), reconquered some of western Europe, built the HAGIA SOPHIA, and issued the basic codification of Roman law. After his death, the empire weakened. Though its rulers continued to style themselves "Roman" long after Justinian's death, the term "Byzantine" more accurately describes the medieval empire. The long controversy over ICONOCLASM within the Eastern Church prepared it for the break with the Roman Church (see SCHISM OF 1054). During the controversy, Arabs and Seljuq Turks increased their power in the area. In the late 11th century, ALEXIUS I COMNENUS sought help from Venice and the Pope; these allies turned the ensuing CRUSADES into plundering expeditions. In the Fourth Crusade the Venetians took over Constantinople and established a line of Latin emperors. Recaptured by Byzantine exiles in 1261, the empire was now little more than a large city-state. In the 14th century the Ottoman Turks began to encroach; their extended siege of Constantinople ended in 1453, when the last emperor died fighting on the city walls and the area came under Ottoman control.

Byzantium See ISTANBUL

Byzantine Emperors

Zeno	474–491	Theodora (*empress*)	1055–56
Anastasius I	491–518	Michael VI Stratioticus	1056–57
Justin I	518–527	Isaac I Comnenus	1057–59
Justinian I	527–565	Constantine X Ducas	1059–67
Justin II	565–578	Romanus IV Diogenes	1067–71
Tiberius II Constantine	578–582	Michael VII Ducas	1071–78
Maurice Tiberius	582–602	Nicephorus III Botaniates	1078–81
Phocas	602–610	Alexius I Comnenus	1081–1118
Heraclius	610–641	John II Comnenus	1118–43
Heraclius Constantine	641	Manuel I Comnenus	1143–80
Heraclonas (or Heraclius)	641	Alexius II Comnenus	1180–83
Constans II (Constantine Pogonatus)	641–668	Andronicus I Comnenus	1183–85
		Isaac II Angelus	1185–95
Constantine IV	668–685	Alexius III Angelus	1195–1203
Justinian II Rhinotmetus	685–695	Isaac II Angelus (*restored*) & Alexius IV Angelus	1203–4
Leontius	695–698		
Tiberius III	698–705	Alexius V Ducas Murtzuphlus	1204
Justinian II Rhinotmetus (*restored*)	705–711	**Latin emperors**	
Philippicus	711–713	Baldwin I	1204–5
Anastasius II	713–715	Henry	1206–16
Theodosius III	715–717	Peter	1217
Leo III	717–741	Yolande (*empress*)	1217–19
Constantine V Copronymus	741–775	Robert	1221–28
		Baldwin II	1228–61
Leo IV	775–780	John	1231–37
Constantine VI	780–797	**Nicaean emperors**	
Irene (*empress*)	797–802	Constantine (XI)	1204–5?
Nicephorus I	802–811	Theodore I Lascaris	1205?–22
Stauracius	811	John III Ducas Vatatzes	1222–54
Michael I Rhangabe	811–813	Theodore II Lascaris	1254–58
Leo V	813–820	John IV Lascaris	1258–61
Michael II Balbus	820–829	**Greek emperors restored**	
Theophilus	829–842	Michael VIII Palaeologus	1261–82
Michael III	842–867		
Basil I	867–886	Andronicus II Palaeologus	1282–1328
Leo VI	886–912		
Alexander	912–913	Andronicus III Palaeologus	1328–41
Constantine VII Porphyrogenitus	913–959		
		John V Palaeologus	1341–76
Romanus I Lecapenus	920–944	John VI Cantacuzenus	1347–54
Romanus II	959–963	Andronicus IV Palaeologus	1376–79
Nicephorus II Phocas	963–969		
John I Tzimisces	969–976	John V Palaeologus (*restored*)	1379–90
Basil II Bulgaroctonus	976–1025		
Constantine VIII	1025–28	John VII Palaeologus	1390
Romanus III Argyrus	1028–34	John V Palaeologus (*restored*)	1390–91
Michael IV	1034–41		
Michael V Calaphates	1041–42	Manuel II Palaeologus	1391–1425
Zoe (*empress*)	1042–50	John VIII Palaeologus	1421–48
Constantine IX Monomachus	1042–55	Constantine XI Palaeologus	1449–53

*For emperors of the Eastern Roman Empire (at Constantinople) before the fall of Rome, see ROMAN REPUBLIC AND EMPIRE.

C High-level procedural computer PROGRAMMING LANGUAGE with many low-level features, including the ability to handle memory addresses and bits. It is highly portable among platforms and therefore widely used in industry and among computer professionals. C was developed by Dennis M. Ritchie (born 1941) of Bell Laboratories in 1972. The OPERATING SYSTEM UNIX was written almost exclusively in C, and C has been standardized as part of POSIX (Portable Operating System Interface for UNIX).

C++ \'sē-'pləs-'pləs\ Object-oriented version (see OBJECT-ORIENTED PROGRAMMING) of the computer PROGRAMMING LANGUAGE C. Developed by Bjarne Stroustrup of Bell Laboratories in the early 1980s, it is traditional C language with added object-oriented capabilities. C++, along with JAVA, has become popular for developing commercial software packages that incorporate multiple interrelated applications.

C-section See CESAREAN SECTION

Cabala See KABBALA

Caballero, Francisco Largo See Francisco LARGO CABALLERO

cabaret \ˌka-bə-'rā\ Restaurant that serves liquor and offers light musical entertainment. The cabaret originated in France in the 1880s as a small club that presented amateur acts and satiric skits lampooning bourgeois conventions. The first German *Kabarett* was opened in Berlin c. 1900 by Baron Ernst von Wolzogen and accompanied its musical acts with biting political satire. It became the center for underground political and literary expression and a showcase for the works of such social critics as BERTOLT BRECHT and K. WEILL, a decadent but fertile artistic milieu later portrayed in the musical *Cabaret* (1966). The English cabaret derived from concerts given in city taverns in the 18th–19th century and evolved into the MUSIC HALL. In the U.S., the cabaret developed into the nightclub, where comedians, singers, or musicians performed. Small jazz and folk clubs and, later, comedy clubs evolved from the original cabaret.

cabbage Leafy garden plant (*Brassica oleracea* 'capitata') of European origin, with a short stem and a globular head of usually green leaves. A member of the MUSTARD FAMILY, it is a major table VEGETABLE in most countries of the temperate zone. The term cabbage also refers more generally to a vegetable and fodder plant of various horticultural forms developed by long cultivation from the wild, or sea, cabbage *(Brassica oleracea)* found near the seacoast in England and continental Europe. The common forms may be classified by the plant parts used for food: leaves (e.g., KALE, COLLARD, common cabbage, BRUSSELS SPROUT); flowers and flower stalks (e.g., BROCCOLI, CAULIFLOWER); and stems (e.g., KOHLRABI). Cabbages grow best in mild to cool climates and tolerate frost. Edible portions are low in caloric value and are an excellent source of ascorbic acid, minerals, and bulk. See also CHINESE CABBAGE.

cabbage looper Distinctive green, white-lined LARVA, or CATERPILLAR *(Trichoplusia ni),* of the owlet MOTH family (Noctuidae). Like other LOOPERS, it moves in an "inching" motion. It is an economic pest of cabbages and associated crops, particularly in the U.S. and Europe. The adults, known as Ni moths, migrate considerable distances. They are mottled brown with a pale Y-shaped mark on each forewing. The typical adult wingspan is about 1 in. (25 mm).

cabbage palmetto See PALMETTO

cabbage white *or* **cabbage butterfly** European cabbage BUTTERFLY *(Pieris rapae).* Its LARVA is a major economic pest, attacking cabbage and related plants. Introduced into North America c. 1860, the cabbage white is today one of the most common North American WHITE BUTTERFLY species.

Cabbala See KABBALA

Cabeiri *or* **Cabiri** \kə-'bī-ˌrī\ Important group of deities, probably of Phrygian origin, worshiped in Asia Minor and in Macedonia and northern and central Greece. In classical times there were two males, Axiocersus and his son Cadmilus, and two females, Axierus and Axiocersa. They were promoters of fertility and protectors of seafarers. The male pair, the more important, was often confused with the DIOSCURI. The Cabeiri were also identified with the Great Gods of Samothrace, and their cult reached its height in the 4th century BC.

Cabell \'kab-əl\, **James Branch** (1879–1958) U.S. writer. Born in Richmond, Va. to a distinguished family, he attacked American orthodoxies and institutions in his best-known novel, *Jurgen* (1919), a story replete with sexual symbolism. His other works, many of them allegories set in an imaginary medieval province, include *The Cream of the Jest* (1917), *Beyond Life* (1919), and *The High Place* (1923). Though much praised in the 1920s, his mannered style and skeptical view of human experience soon lost favor.

Cabeza de Vaca \kə-'bā-zə-də-'vä-kə\, **Álvar Núñez** (c. 1490–c. 1560) Spanish explorer. He took part in an expedition that reached what is now Tampa Bay, Fla., in 1528. One of only four members of the expedition to survive, he spent eight years in the Gulf region of modern Texas. His accounts of the legendary Seven Cities of CÍBOLA probably inspired the extensive explorations of North America by HERNANDO DE SOTO and FRANCISCO VAZQUEZ DE CORONADO.

Cabezón \ˌkä-bā-'thōn\, **Antonio de** (1510–1566) Spanish composer and organist. Of noble birth, he was blind from early childhood. In 1526 he became organist to Isabella, wife of CHARLES V. He remained a royal favorite, especially to Philip II, whom he accompanied on his travels. His works, which influenced the English virginalists and J.P. SWEELINCK, are almost entirely for keyboard; they include numerous *tientos* (ricercars or fantasias) and *diferencias* (variations), a genre of which he was one of the first masters.

cabildo (Spanish: "municipal council") Fundamental unit of local government in colonial Latin America. It was in charge of all ordinary aspects of municipal government, including policing, sanitation, taxation, price and wage regulation, and the administration of justice. Its jurisdiction extended beyond the city to the surrounding hamlets and countryside. By the mid-16th century appointments to cabildos were usually made by the Spanish crown and could be sold or inherited. Cabildos were often corrupt, but *cabildos abiertos* (open town meetings) were important to the Latin American independence movement of the early 19th century.

cabinet Body of senior ministers or, in the U.S., advisers to a chief executive, whose members also serve as the heads of government departments. The cabinet has become an integral part of parliamentary government in many countries, though its form varies. It developed from the British PRIVY COUNCIL, when King CHARLES II and Queen ANNE regularly consulted the council's leading members to reach decisions before meeting with the unwieldy full council. The modern British cabinet consists of departmental ministers, drawn from the members of Parliament and appointed by the prime minister. In the U.S., the cabinet serves as an advisory group to the PRESIDENT without the sanction of law. Members' appointments are subject to Senate approval, and the U.S. Constitution sets cabinet members' order of succession to the presidency. The cabinet includes the secretaries of State, Treasury, Defense, Interior, Agriculture, Commerce, Labor, Health and Human Services, Housing and Urban Development, Transportation, Education, Energy, and Veterans Affairs and the attorney general.

cable car See STREETCAR

cable modem MODEM used to convert analog data signals to digital form and vise versa, for transmission or receipt over cable television lines, especially for connecting to the INTERNET. A cable modem modulates and demodulates signals like a telephone modem, but is a much more complex device. Data can be transferred over cable lines much more quickly than over traditional phone lines. Transmission rates are typically around 1.5 megabits per second. Faster transmission is actually possible, but speed is usually restricted by the cable company's (typically slower) connection to the Internet. Cable Internet access is regarded as a replacement for slower dial-up and ISDN services, and is competitive with other broadband modes of delivery (e.g., DSL connections). See also BROADBAND TECHNOLOGY.

Cable News Network See CNN

cable structure Form of long-span structure that is subject to tension and uses suspension cables for support. Highly efficient, cable structures include the suspension bridge, the cable-stayed roof, and the bicycle-wheel roof. The graceful curve of the huge main cables of a suspension bridge is almost a catenary, the shape assumed by any string or cable suspended freely between two points. The cable-stayed roof is supported from above by steel cables radiating downward from masts that rise above roof level. The bicycle-wheel roof involves two layers of tension cables radiating from an inner tension ring and an outer compression ring, which in turn is supported by columns.

cable television System that distributes TELEVISION signals by means of COAXIAL or FIBER-OPTIC cables. Cable television systems originated in the U.S. in the early 1950s to improve reception in remote and hilly areas, where broadcast signals were weak. In the 1960s they were introduced in large metropolitan areas where reception is sometimes degraded by reflection of signals from tall buildings. Since the mid-1970s there has been a proliferation of cable systems offering special services, which generally charge a monthly fee. Besides providing high-quality signals, some systems can deliver hundreds of channels. Another feature increasingly offered by cable operators is two-way, interactive communication by which viewers can, for example, participate in public-opinion polls as well as connect to the INTERNET. Cable operators are also involved in the development of video compression, digital transmission, and HIGH-DEFINITION TELEVISION.

Cabot, George (1752–1823) U.S. Federalist Party leader. Born in Salem, Mass., he became a shipowner and merchant, retiring from business in 1794. Elected to the U.S. Senate (1791–96), he supported ALEXANDER HAMILTON's fiscal policies and was appointed a director of the BANK OF THE U.S. As a leading Federalist, he was a member of the ESSEX JUNTO. In 1814 he presided at the HARTFORD CONVENTION.

Cabot, John *orig.* **Giovanni Caboto** (c. 1450–1499?) Italian navigator and explorer. In the 1470s, he became a skilled navigator in travels to the eastern Mediterranean for a Venetian mercantile firm. In the 1490s he moved to Bristol, England, and with support from city merchants, he led an expedition in 1497 to find trade routes to Asia. After landing somewhere in North America, possibly southern Labrador or Cape Breton Island, he took possession of the land for HENRY VII and conducted explorations along the coastline. On a second expedition in 1498, he may have reached America but probably was lost at sea. His two voyages for England helped lay the groundwork for the later British claim to Canada. SEBASTIAN CABOT was his son.

Cabot, Sebastian (1476?–1557) English navigator, explorer, and cartographer. The son of JOHN CABOT, he served at various times both the English and Spanish crowns. In 1525 he took charge of a Spanish expedition, abandoning the original goal of developing trade with the Orient and instead embarking on a fruitless expedition to South America. Later he served in England as governor of the Merchant Adventurers, organizing an expedition to search for a northeast passage from Europe to the Orient.

Cabral \kə-'bräl\, **Amílcar** (1921–1973) Guinean nationalist politician. In 1956 he founded the Partido Africano da Independência da Guiné e Cabo Verde (PAIGC), which in 1962 began a war of liberation against Portuguese forces. By the late 1960s Cabral controlled much of Portuguese Guinea. He was assassinated in 1973. His half-brother, Luís de Almeida Cabral, became the first president of independent Guinea-Bissau in 1974.

Cabral, Pedro Álvares (1467?–1520) Portuguese navigator credited with the discovery of Brazil. A nobleman, Cabral long enjoyed the favor of MANUEL I of Portugal, who in 1500 sent him and 13 ships on the second Portuguese voyage to India, following the route taken by VASCO DA GAMA, to strengthen commercial ties and further Portugal's conquests. Cabral sailed southwest on a route that took him close to lands that had previously been sighted and claimed by the Portuguese. On April 22, 1500, he landed on the coast of what is now Brazil and formally took possession of the country for Portugal. The rest of his journey to India and back was beset by misfortune; only four ships returned to Portugal.

Cabrillo \kə-'bri-lō\, **Juan Rodríguez** (died 1543?) Explorer in the service of Spain and discoverer of California. Little is known of his early life, though he may have been born in Portugal. In 1520 he accompanied Spanish explorers to Mexico. He was one of the conquerors of present-day Guatemala, where he may have served as governor. In 1542 he left Mexico and sailed along the California coast, entering San Diego and Monterey bays. He landed on several islands off the coast, and apparently died of complications from a broken leg suffered on one such landing.

Cabrini, St. Frances Xavier *known as* **Mother Cabrini** (1850–1917) Italian-U.S. missionary, the first U.S. citizen to be canonized by the Roman Catholic church. Born at Sant' Angelo Lodigiano, she was determined from childhood to become a missionary, and she took her vows in 1877. She founded the Missionary Sisters of the Sacred Heart in 1880, and in 1889 Pope LEO XIII sent her to the U.S. to work among Italian immigrants. She lived in New York and Chicago but traveled in the Americas and Europe to found 67 houses of her order. She was canonized in 1946.

cacao \kə-'kau̇\ Tropical New World tree *(Theobroma cacao)* of the chocolate family (Sterculiaceae, or Byttneriaceae). Its seeds, after fermentation and roasting, yield cocoa and CHOCOLATE. Cocoa butter is extracted from the seed. The tree is grown throughout the wet lowland tropics, often in the shade of taller trees. Its thick trunk supports a canopy of large, leathery, oblong leaves. The small, foul-smelling, pinkish flowers are borne directly on the branches and trunk; they are followed by the fruit, or pods, each yielding 20–40 seeds, or cocoa beans.

Caccini \kät-'chē-nē\, **Giulio** *or* **Giulio Romano** (c. 1545–1618) Italian composer and singer. He accompanied his patron, Cosimo I de MEDICI, to Florence in the 1570s; there he became associated with the Camerata, an academy that dedicated much attention to producing an equivalent of ancient Greek drama. His *Euridice* (1600), embodying the Camerata's ideals, was the first opera to be published, and one of the first two surviving operas; the other, also titled *Euridice*, is largely by Jacopo Peri (1561–1633), whose lost *Dafne* (1598) was the first opera of all. Caccini's *Le nuove musiche* (1602), a collection of songs with basso continuo, was of landmark importance, centrally important in establishing the new monodic style.

cachalot See SPERM WHALE

cache \'kash\ Temporary computer storage used for quick retrieval of data in order to increase processing speed. The cached data can be stored in a reserved area of RAM, a special cache chip (separate from the CPU) that provides faster access than RAM, or on the disk drive. By keeping frequently accessed data in a rapidly accessible place, the computer can respond quickly to requests for those data without having to perform time-consuming searches of RAM or hard drives. Since a "stale" cache will contain data that have been superseded by later information, the cached data must be refreshed periodically.

cachet, lettre de See LETTRE DE CACHET

cactus Any of the flowering plants that make up the family Cactaceae, containing about 1,650 species, native through most of North and South America, with the greatest number and variety in Mexico. Cacti are SUCCULENT perennials. Most live in and are well adapted to dry regions. Cacti generally have thick herbaceous or woody stems containing chlorophyll. Leaves usually are absent or greatly reduced, minimizing the surface area from which water can be lost; the stem is the site of photosynthesis. The generally thin, fibrous, shallow root systems range widely in area to absorb superficial moisture. Cacti vary greatly in size and appearance, from buttonlike PEYOTE and low clumps of PRICKLY PEAR and hedgehog cactus *(Echinocereus)* to the upright columns of barrel cacti *(Ferocactus* and *Echinocactus)* and the imposing SAGUARO. Cacti can be distinguished from other succulent plants by the presence of small cushion-like structures (areoles) from which, in almost all species, spines arise,

Golden rainbow cactus (*Echinocereus dasyacanthus*), a hedgehog cactus, growing in the desert of southwestern Texas.

©ROBERT AND LINDA MITCHELL

as do flowers, branches, and leaves (when present). Flowers, often large and colorful, are usually solitary. Cacti are widely cultivated as ornamentals. Various species, notably prickly pears and CHOLLAS, are cultivated as food. Barrel cacti are an emergency source of water for humans.

Cacus and Caca \'kā-kəs...'kā-kə\ In ROMAN RELIGION, brother and sister fire deities of the early Roman settlement on the Palatine Hill. VIRGIL described Cacus as the son of VULCAN and as a fire-breathing brigand who terrorized the countryside. He stole some of the giant Geryon's cattle from HERACLES and hid them in his lair, but Heracles discovered Cacus's hiding place and killed him. The story is traditionally connected with the establishment of Heracles' oldest Roman place of worship, the Ara Maxima, in the Forum Boarium (cattle market).

Cadbury, George (1839–1922) British businessman and social reformer. In 1861 he and his brother Richard took over their father's failing business and built it into the highly prosperous Cadbury Brothers cocoa- and chocolate-manufacturing firm. They improved working conditions and introduced a private social-security program for employees. George was also noted for his successful experiments in housing and town planning in Bournville, where he built affordable working-class homes with large gardens.

CAD/CAM \'kad-ˌkam, ˌkad-'kam\ *in full* **computer-aided design/computer-aided manufacturing.** Integration of design and manufacturing into a system under direct control of DIGITAL COMPUTERS. CAD systems use a computer with terminals featuring video monitors and interactive graphics-input devices to design such things as machine parts, patterns for clothing, or INTEGRATED CIRCUITS. CAM systems use numerically controlled (see NUMERICAL CONTROL) machine tools and high-performance programmable industrial ROBOTS. Drawings developed during the design process are converted directly into instructions for the production machines, thus optimizing consistency between design and finished product, and providing flexibility in altering machine operations. These two processes are sometimes grouped as CAE (computer-aided engineering).

caddis fly Any member of about 7,000 species of mothlike aquatic insects (order Trichoptera) found worldwide, usually in freshwater habitats but sometimes in brackish and tidal waters. Generally dull brownish, caddis flies have long antennae and hairy wings that fold rooflike over the abdomen. They feed primarily on plant juices and flower nectar, though a few are predaceous. Many caddis-fly larvae construct a portable case from grains of sand, bits of shells, and plant debris glued together by a sticky substance they secrete. This case surrounds the larva's abdomen while it matures. Caddis flies are important to freshwater ecosystems because they clean the water by consuming plant and animal debris and serve, as larvae and adults, as an important food for fish, particularly TROUT.

Caddo One of a group of North American Indian peoples of the Caddoan linguistic family that originally occupied the lower Red River area in Louisiana and Arkansas. The Caddo occupied the land from ancient times, and many striking examples of prehistoric pottery and basketry have been found. They were a semisedentary agricultural people who lived in conical pole-and-thatch dwellings. In the 18th century pressures from white settlers pushed many Caddo off their lands, a process that intensified with the LOUISIANA PURCHASE in 1803. By 1835 the Caddo had ceded all their land to the U.S., and by 1859 most were living on reservations in Oklahoma. Today they number about 3,000.

Incised redware cat effigy bowl, Caddoan from Louisiana; in the Museum of the American Indian, Heye Foundation, New York City.

BY COURTESY OF THE MUSEUM OF THE AMERICAN INDIAN, NEW YORK

Cade's Rebellion (1450) Uprising against the government of HENRY VI of England. Jack Cade, an Irishman of uncertain occupation living in Kent, organized a rebellion among local small property holders angered by high taxes and prices. He took the name John Mortimer, identifying himself with the family of Henry's rival, the duke of York. Cade and his followers defeated a royal army in Kent and entered London, where they executed the lord treasurer. They were soon driven out of the city; Cade's followers dispersed on being offered a pardon, and Cade was mortally wounded in Sussex. His rebellion contributed to the breakdown of royal authority that led to the Wars of the ROSES.

Cádiz \kə-'diz, *Span* 'kä-t͟hēs\ City (pop., 1995 est.: 155,000), southwestern Spain. Located on a peninsula in the Bay of CÁDIZ northwest of GIBRALTAR, it is the main seaport of Cádiz province in ANDALUSIA. Founded as Gadir by PHOENICIANS from TYRE c. 1100 BC, it was later ruled by CARTHAGE, Rome (as Gades), and the VISIGOTHS. It was held by the MOORS from AD 711. It was captured in 1262 by Alfonso X of CASTILLA Y LEÓN. It enjoyed great prosperity as a center for Spanish trade with the American colonies in the 16th–18th century (see SEVILLE). It now has naval and mercantile shipbuilding yards.

Cádiz, Bay of Inlet of the Gulf of Cádiz, southwestern Spain. An inlet indenting the coast of Cádiz province, it receives the Guadalete River and is partially protected by the Isle of Léon, on which the port of CÁDIZ is located. The Spanish-U.S. air and naval base at Rota is situated on the bay.

cadmium Metallic chemical ELEMENT, chemical symbol Cd, atomic number 48. It normally occurs along with other metals, especially ZINC, in ORES. A silvery-white METAL, capable of taking a high polish, cadmium does not corrode under alkaline (see ALKALI) conditions; one of its major uses is in ELECTROPLATING other metals and ALLOYS to protect them. Because it absorbs NEUTRONS effectively, it is used in control rods in some nuclear reactors. Its compounds, in which it has VALENCE 2, are very toxic. They are used as pigments, as phosphors in TELEVISIONS or computer monitors, as pesticides, and in photographic applications and analytical chemistry.

Cadmus In GREEK MYTHOLOGY, the son of the king of Phoenicia, brother of EUROPA, and founder of THEBES. When ZEUS carried off Europa, Cadmus was sent to find her. The Delphic ORACLE ordered him to end his search, follow a cow, and build a town where it lay down. That town became Thebes. He built the citadel of Thebes with the help of fierce armed men who sprang up where he sowed the teeth of a dragon he had slain. He married Harmonia, daughter of ARES and APHRODITE, and their five children included SEMELE. Cadmus was said to have brought the alphabet to Greece.

Cadogan \kə-'dəg-ən\, **William** *later* **Earl Cadogan** (1672–1726) British soldier. He served as a trusted colleague with the duke of MARLBOROUGH in the War of the SPANISH SUCCESSION. Later he became involved in intrigues to secure the succession for the Hanoverian GEORGE I (1714). He crushed a JACOBITE rebellion in 1716, was granted an earldom in 1718, and was promoted to commander in chief in 1722.

caduceus \kə-'dü-sē-əs\ Staff carried by HERMES as a symbol of peace. It served as a badge of protection for ancient Greek and Roman heralds and ambassadors. It was originally depicted as a rod or olive branch ending in two shoots and decorated with garlands or ribbons; in later iconography the garlands became two snakes and a pair of wings was attached to the staff to represent Hermes' speed. The caduceus was adopted as a symbol of physicians because of its similarity to the staff of ASCLEPIUS.

caecilian \si-'sil-yən\ Any of 155 species of wormlike AMPHIBIANS found in humid regions from Mexico to northern Argentina and in Africa, S.East Asia, and the Seychelles. The elongate, ringed, limbless body is 4–60 in. (10–150 cm) long. Color ranges from blackish to pinkish tan. The tiny eyes are covered by skin and often by bone. A chemosensory tentacle lies between the eye and nostril. Some species lay eggs, which are guarded by the female and hatch into free-living larvae; other species bear live young. Caecilians spend their lives underground and eat worms and insects.

Caecus, Appius Claudius See Appius CLAUDIUS CAECUS

Caedmon \'kad-mən\ (fl. 658–680) Earliest known Old English Christian poet. According to BEDE, he was a herdsman who received a divine call in a dream to sing of "the beginning of things," and began to utter "verses which he had never heard." He entered a monastery, where he produced vernacular poetry on sacred themes expounded to him by more learned brethren. Only the nine-line original dream hymn can be confidently attributed to him, but it set the pattern for almost all of Anglo-Saxon religious verse.

Caen \'kä^{n}\ City (pop., 1990: 116,000), northwestern France. Situated on the ORNE RIVER, it was the capital of lower NORMANDY in the 11th century. The English took it in 1346 and 1417 and held it until 1450. It suffered in the Wars of RELIGION and fell to the Protestants in 1562. During the FRENCH REVOLUTION, it was a center for the GIRONDIN movement. The city was severely damaged in the Allied NORMANDY CAMPAIGN (1944), but it was rebuilt. Notable structures include the 11th-century abbey and the university. It is a transportation center and manufactures automobiles and electrical equipment.

Caere \'kī-rā\ Ancient city, ETRURIA. Located northwest of Rome near the modern city of Ceveteri, it was an important trading center. Brought under the Romans in 253 BC, it prospered under the empire but declined in later centuries. The derived Latin word *caeremonium* (source of English *ceremony*) reflects the Etruscan fascination with divination and prophecy. Tomb chambers have yielded gold and silver objects, which show an orientalizing tendency in the Etruscan art of the 7th century BC.

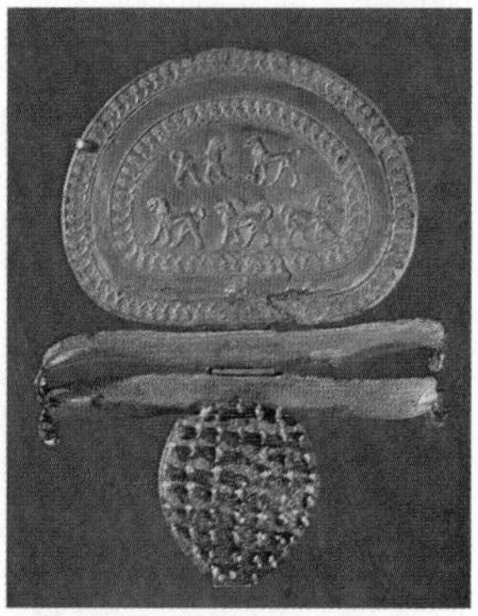

Gold fibula from the Regolini-Galassi tomb, Caere, 7th century BC; in the Vatican Museum.
SCALA–ART RESOURCE

Caernarvon \kīr-'när-vȯn, kär-'när-vȯn\ Town (pop., 1995 est.: 10,000), seat of Gwynedd county, Wales. Located near the west end of the MENAI STRAIT, it was the site of a Roman fort, Segontium, built c. AD 75. After the Roman withdrawal (c. 380–390), it was the seat of local chieftains. The township was completely transformed by EDWARD I after his conquest of Wales in 1282. The imposing castle he built (birthplace of his son EDWARD II) has been preserved, and since 1911 it has been the site of the investiture of the Prince of Wales.

Caesar, Irving *orig.* **Isidor** (1895–1996) U.S. lyricist. Born in New York City, Caesar worked with HENRY FORD during World War I before turning to songwriting. Working with various collaborators, he provided the lyrics for such standards as "Swanee," "Sometimes I'm Happy," "Crazy Rhythm," and "Tea for Two," one of the most frequently recorded tunes ever written. He died at the age of 101.

Caesar, (Gaius) Julius (100?–44 BC) Celebrated Roman general, statesman, and DICTATOR. A PATRICIAN by birth, he held the prominent posts of QUAESTOR and PRAETOR before becoming governor of Farther Spain 61–60. He formed the First TRIUMVIRATE with POMPEY and MARCUS LICINIUS CRASSUS in 60 and was elected CONSUL in 59 and PROCONSUL in Gaul and Illyria in 58. After conducting the GALLIC WARS, during which he invaded Britain (55, 54) and crossed the Rhine (55, 53), he was instructed by the Senate to lay down his command, Senate conservatives having grown wary of his increasing power, as had a suspicious Pompey. When the Senate would not command Pompey to give up his command simultaneously, Caesar, against regulations, led his forces across the Rubicon River (49) between Gaul and Italy, precipitating the Roman Civil War. Pompey fled from Italy, but was pursued and defeated by Caesar in 48, then fled to Egypt, where he was murdered. Having followed Pompey to Egypt, Caesar became lover to CLEOPATRA and supported her militarily. He defeated Pompey's last supporters in 46–45. He was named dictator for life by the Romans. He was offered the crown (44) but refused it, knowing the Romans' dislike for kings. He was in the midst of launching a series of political and social reforms when he was assassinated in the Senate House on the ides of March by conspirators led by CASSIUS and BRUTUS. His writings on the Gallic and Civil wars are considered models of classical historiography.

Caesar, Sid (born 1922) U.S. comedian. Born in Yonkers, N.Y., he began his career as a band musician but switched to comedy. He starred in the Coast Guard service show *Tars and Spars* and its film version (1946). Noted for his pantomime skills and his ability to mimic foreign languages at high speed, he performed comic routines in live television shows and costarred with Imogene Coca (1908–2001) and CARL REINER in the popular comedy variety program *Your Show of Shows* (1950–54), created his own *Caesar's Hour* (1954–57), and later appeared in television specials.

Caesar Augustus See Caesar AUGUSTUS

Caesarea \ˌsē-zə-'rē-ə\ *modern* **Horbat Qesari** \'k̲ȯr-bȧt-'kā-sȧ-rē\ Ancient seaport, PALESTINE. Located on the coast of present-day Israel south of HAIFA, it was originally a PHOENICIAN settlement. Taken by the Romans and rebuilt in the 1st cent BC by HEROD THE GREAT, it was renamed for his patron AUGUSTUS. The capital of the Roman province of JUDAEA in AD 6, it was the site of an early Christian church and often visited by St. PAUL. It later declined under Byzantine and Arab rule, and was destroyed by the sultan BAYBARS in the 13th century.

caesaropapism \ˌsē-zə-rō-'pā-ˌpi-zəm\ Political system in which the head of the state is also the head of the church and supreme judge in religious matters. It is often associated with the Byzantine Empire, where emperors presided over church councils and appointed patriarchs. The term has also been applied to other historical eras, including the rule of Czar PETER I, who made the Russian Orthodox Church a department of the state, and the reign of HENRY VIII in England.

caffeine HETEROCYCLIC COMPOUND that, like other ALKALOIDS, has marked physiological effects. It occurs in COFFEE beans, TEA leaves, KOLA NUTS, CACAO, maté, and guarana, and in the products made from them. Its stimulating effect on the central NERVOUS SYSTEM, HEART, CARDIOVASCULAR SYSTEM, and KIDNEYS makes it medically useful in treating respiratory depression caused by overdose of BARBITURATES, MORPHINE, or HEROIN. Its positive effects can include improved motor performance, decreased fatigue, increased alertness, and enhanced sensory activity. Excessive caffeine can produce irritability, anxiety, insomnia, and potentially serious symptoms such as heart irregularities and delirium. Much of the caffeine included in products such as NoDoz and in many over-the-counter cold remedies and painkillers has been removed from decaffeinated coffee and tea.

Cagayan de Oro \ˌkä-gä-'yän-dā-'ō-rō\ City (pop., 1994 est.: 414,000), northern MINDANAO, Philippines. Located along the CAGAYAN RIVER near the head of Macajalar Bay, it was established as a mission station in the 17th century and fortified by the Spaniards. Chartered as a city in 1950, it has become northern Mindanao's transportation and commercial hub.

Cagayan River *or* **Río Grande de Cagayan** River, northeastern LUZON, Philippines. Flowing north 220 mi (354 km) to the port of Aparri on the Babuyan Channel, it is the longest river in Luzon and is navigable for much of its course. Its chief tributary is the Chico. Its valley, 50 mi (80 km) wide, is agriculturally important.

Cage, John (Milton) (1912–1992) U.S. avant-garde composer and writer. Born in Los Angeles, the son of an inventor, he studied with A. SCHOENBERG and H. COWELL. From the early 1940s he was closely associated with the choreographer MERCE CUNNINGHAM. Though he began as a twelve-tone composer, by 1943 his sonic experiments had marked him as notably original. He soon turned to Zen Buddhism and concluded that all activities that make up music are part of a single natural process and that all sounds are potentially musical; thenceforth he advocated indeterminism and endeavored to ensure randomness in his works, which called for increasingly inventive notation and often relied on the Taoist *Yi jing (I ching)*. By the 1960s he had expanded into the realm of multimedia. His disparate works include *Bacchanale* for prepared piano (1938), *Imaginary Landscape No. 4* for 12 radios (1951), *Fontana Mix* for tape (1958), *HPSCHD* for seven harpsichords, 51 tapes, and nonmusical media (1969), and *Roaratorio* (1979). His widely read books include *Silence* (1961), *A Year from Monday* (1967), *Notations* (1969), and *M* (1973). His international influence was far greater than that of any previous American composer.

Cage, Nicolas *orig.* **Nicholas Coppola** (born 1964) U.S. actor. Born in Long Beach, Cal., a nephew of FRANCIS FORD COPPOLA, he made his television debut in 1981. After his first film, *Valley Girl* (1983), he won fame with his intense performances in such popular films as *Peggy Sue Got Married* (1986), *Raising Arizona* (1987), *Moonstruck* (1987), *Wild at Heart* (1990), *Leaving Las Vegas* (1995, Academy Award), and *Bringing Out the Dead* (1999).

Cagliari \'käl-yä-rē\ *ancient* **Caralis.** City (pop., 1996 est.: 174,000), and capital of SARDINIA region, Italy. Located on the island's southern coast, it was founded by the PHOENICIANS. Held successively by Rome, the SARACENS, PISA, Spain, and Austria, it passed with the rest of Sardinia to the House of SAVOY in 1718. Long the military headquarters of the island, Cagliari was bombed heavily in World War II. The rebuilt harbor is Sardinia's principal port.

Cagney, James (1899–1986) U.S. actor. Born in New York City, he toured in vaudeville as a song-and-dance man before starring in the successful Broadway musical *Penny Arcade* (1929) and its film version, *Sinner's Holiday* (1930). He played the first of a series of gangster roles in the film *Public Enemy* (1931), followed by *Angels with Dirty Faces* (1938) and *White Heat* (1949). As GEORGE M. COHAN in *Yankee Doodle Dandy* (1942, Academy Award) he showed off his dance skills and streetwise charm. Later films include *Mister Roberts* (1955), *Man of a Thousand Faces* (1957), *One, Two, Three* (1961), and *Ragtime* (1981).

Cahn, Sammy *orig.* **Samuel Cohen** (1913–1993) U.S. song lyricist. Born in New York City, he became a professional songwriter while still a teenager. He later formed a songwriting team with Saul Chaplin; their first hit was "Rhythm Is Our Business" (1935). With JULE STYNE he collaborated on songs for many films and musicals, including "Three Coins in the Fountain" (Academy Award). In 1955 Cahn and JIMMY VAN HEUSEN formed a partnership and wrote dozens of songs for FRANK SINATRA, whose recordings won them Academy Awards for "All the Way," "High Hopes," and "Call Me Irresponsible."

Caicos Islands See TURKS AND CAICOS ISLANDS

Caillaux \kà-'yō\, **Joseph (-Marie-Auguste)** (1863–1944) French politician. Serving several times as minister of finance, he was an early but unsuccessful advocate of a national income tax. He was named premier in 1911 but was forced to resign after negotiating a controversial treaty with Germany over the second of the MOROCCAN CRISES. Later, his opposition to World War I and friendship with German agents led to conviction on charges of corresponding with the enemy. Granted amnesty in 1924, he was later elected to the Senate and became head of the Commission of Finance (1927–40).

Caillebotte \kà-yə-'bȯt\, **Gustave** (1848–1894) French painter and art collector. Born to a wealthy family, he was a naval architect by profession. He pursued his interest in painting at the École des Beaux-Arts and became a prolific painter of contemporary subjects, town and country views, still lifes, and boating scenes. He was the chief organizer, promoter, and financial backer of the Impressionist exhibitions, and he purchased works by EDOUARD MANET, EDGAR DEGAS, CLAUDE MONET, PAUL CÉZANNE, and others. He bequeathed his collection to the state, and in 1897 it formed the basis of the first Impressionist exhibition in a French museum.

caiman \'kā-mən\ Any member of several species of Central and South American reptiles of the ALLIGATOR family. Like the rest of the CROCODILE order, caimans are amphibious, lizardlike carnivores. They live along the edges of rivers and other bodies of water, and reproduce by laying hard-shelled eggs in nests built and guarded by the female. The largest species is the black caiman *(Melanosuchus niger)*, a potentially dangerous animal with a maximum length of about 15 ft (4.5 m). Average lengths for the other species (genera *Caiman* and *Paleosuchus*) are 4–7 ft (1.2–2.1 m).

Cain and Abel In the Old Testament, the sons of ADAM AND EVE. According to GENESIS, Cain, the first-born, was a farmer, and his brother Abel was a shepherd. Cain was enraged when God preferred his brother's sacrifice of sheep to his own offering of grain, and he murdered Abel. When God asked where Abel was, Cain pretended ignorance, saying, "Am I my brother's keeper?" God punished Cain by sending him into exile but marked him with a sign as a warning to others, promising that he would be avenged if he were killed.

cairn terrier Breed of TERRIER developed in Scotland to rout animals that prey on game. The modern breed's characteristics are carefully patterned on those of the dog's ancestor, a 17th-century terrier of the Isle of Skye. This short-legged dog has a short, broad face. Its coarse coat is usually bluish gray, tan, or pale yellowish brown. Generally active, hardy, alert, and spirited, it is valued as a pet and watchdog. It stands 9–10 in. (23–25.5 cm) high and weighs about 13–14 lbs (6–6.5 kg).

Cairngorm Mountains \'karn-ˌgȯrm\ Mountain range, northeastern SCOTLAND. It is located in the Highlands between the SPEY and Dee river valleys; its highest peak is Ben Macdui, at 4,296 ft (1,309 m) the second-highest (after BEN NEVIS) in the British Isles. Since World War II winter sports have developed in the area. It is a chief source of the cairngorm variety of quartz.

Cairo \'kī-rō\ *Arabic* **Al-Qahirah** \àl-'kä-hē-rə\ City (pop., 1996: 6,789,479; metro. area pop., 1999 est.: 10,345,000), capital of Egypt. Located on the banks of the NILE near the site of a Roman city captured by the Arabs in 641, Old Cairo (Al-Fustat) was then built by the Arabs as a military camp. Cairo's newer section (Al-Qahirah) was built by the FATIMID DYNASTY c. 968 and was made the capital in 973. From the 13th century, as the capital of the MAMLUK sultans, it reached its greatest prosperity as a trade and cultural center. Invaded by NAPOLEON in 1798, it was held by the French for three years. In World War II it was a British and U.S. base and was also the site of two Allied conferences (see CAIRO CONFERENCES). The ancient metropolis is a blend of old and new, East and West. It is the largest city of the Middle East and of Africa, and the chief cultural center of the Arab world. The Pyramids of GIZA are at the southwestern edge of the city. A manufacturing center, it is also the site of several universities and colleges.

Cairo conferences (November–December 1943) Two meetings held in Cairo during WORLD WAR II. At the first, WINSTON CHURCHILL and FRANKLIN ROOSEVELT discussed plans for the Normandy invasion (see NORMANDY CAMPAIGN). With CHIANG KAI-SHEK, they announced their goal of stripping Japan of all the territories it had seized since 1914 and restoring Korea to independence. At the second conference, Churchill and Roosevelt tried unsuccessfully to persuade Turkey's Pres. Ismet Inönü to bring his country into the war on the side of the Allies.

Caishen *or* **Ts'ai-shen** \'tsī-'shən\ Chinese god of wealth, believed to bestow on his devotees the riches carried about by his attendants. A Ming-dynasty novel relates that a hermit, Zhao Gongming, employed magic to support the collapsing SHANG DYNASTY. He was killed by Jiang Ziya, a supporter of the ZHOU DYNASTY. Rebuked for causing the death of a virtuous man, Jiang apologized in a temple, extolled Zhao's virtues, and canonized him as the god of wealth. During Chinese New Year, incense is burned in Caishen's temple and the greeting "May you become rich" is exchanged.

caisson \'kä-ˌsän\ In engineering, a type of FOUNDATION most commonly used underwater for a bridge, but sometimes used in building construction. It is a large hollow structure that is sunk down through the earth by workers excavating from inside it; ultimately it becomes a permanent part of the PIER. There are three types: the open caisson, open at both top and bottom; the box caisson, closed at the bottom; and the pneumatic caisson, with an airtight chamber to accommodate submerged workers. Caisson columns, typically 2 ft (0.6 m) or more in diameter, may be used as an alternative to bearing PILES. A round hole is dug or bored to a stable layer of earth and temporarily supported by a steel shell, then filled with concrete poured around a cage of reinforcing bars.

caisson disease See DECOMPRESSION SICKNESS

Caitanya \kī-'tän-yə\, **Sri Krishna** *orig.* **Vishvambhara Mishra** (1485–1533) Indian Hindu mystic. Born into a Brahman family in Bengal, he became a teacher. While on a pilgrimage to perform his father's death-anniversary ceremony, he had a profound religious experience, and he returned home indifferent to worldly matters. Disciples joined him in worship that consisted of choral singing of the name of God, often accompanied by dance movements and ending in trance states. He took his new name on initiation as an ascetic in 1510. In his lifetime his following came to constitute a major sect of VAISHNAVISM (see CAITANYA MOVEMENT). According to tradition, he died when he left his body by walking into the ocean at Puri while lost in a devotional trance.

Caitanya movement Emotional form of HINDUISM that developed in the 16th century, inspired by the mode of worship originated by CAITANYA. Centered in Bengal, the movement was organized by Caitanya's followers Nityananda and Advaita. BHAKTI (devotion) is central and takes the form of singing for hours, with accompaniment, hymns that repeat God's name. Caitanya himself came to be worshiped as an incarnation of both KRISHNA and his beloved, Radha. Caitanya, Nityananda, and Advaita are regarded as the movement's three masters. A group of six of Caitanya's disciples developed its theology and devotional literature. Its present leaders are mostly lineal descendants of the early disciples. See also HARE KRISHNA MOVEMENT.

Cajun Any descendant of French Canadians driven by the British in the 18th century from the captured French colony of Acadia (now Nova Scotia and adjacent areas) who settled in the fertile bayou lands of southern Louisiana. Many Cajuns speak a dialect of North American French. In recent decades Cajun cuisine, noted for its use of hot seasonings, and ZYDECO music have become popular among non-Cajuns.

cakravartin See CHAKRAVARTIN

Calabar \'ka-lə-ˌbar\ City (pop., 1993 est.: 162,000), southeastern Nigeria. Lying along the Calabar River above its confluence with the CROSS RIVER, it was settled in the 17th century by the Efik, and became an important trading center for Europeans arriving on the African coast. After accepting British protection in 1884, it served as capital of a British protectorate until British administrative headquarters were moved to LAGOS in 1906. With its natural harbor, it remains an important port.

calabash Tree *(Crescentia cujete)* of the trumpet-creeper family (Bignoniaceae) that grows in Central and South America, the West Indies, and extreme southern Florida. It is often grown as an ornamental. It produces large spherical fruits, the hard shells of which are useful as bowls, cups, and other water containers when hollowed out. The fruit's shell encloses a whitish pulp and thin, dark brown seeds. The tree bears funnel-shaped, light green and purple-streaked flowers and evergreen leaves. Fruits of the unrelated bottle gourd *(Lagenaria siceraria)* are also known as calabashes.

Calabria \kä-'lä-brē-ä\ Autonomous region (pop., 1996 est.: 2,076,000), southern Italy. Forming the "toe" of the Italian "boot," it is a peninsula that separates the TYRRHENIAN and Ionian seas. A mountainous area, it has been subject to earthquakes. Its capital is CATANZARO. Founded as a Greek colony and known in ancient times as Bruttium, it was taken by the Romans in the 3rd century BC; it gradually went into decline. It eventually passed to the Byzantines, who renamed it Calabria. Conquered by the Normans, it was united to the Kingdom of NAPLES in the 11th century. A stronghold of Italian republicanism until the RISORGIMENTO, it became part of Italy after the 1860 expedition of GIUSEPPE DE GARIBALDI. Long a poor area dependent on farming, it underwent a land reform system in the mid-20th century that promoted more diverse profitable crops.

caladium \kə-'lā-dē-əm\ Any of the tropical New World tuberous herbaceous plants that make up the genus *Caladium,* in the ARUM FAMILY, widely cultivated for their showy, fragile-looking, variably colored leaves. Caladiums are nonhardy BULBS used as potted plants indoors and in summer outdoor plantings. They keep surprisingly well if protected from chills and wintry drafts.

Calah \'kā-lə\ *modern* **Nimrud** \'nim-ˌrüd\ Ancient city, ASSYRIA. Lying south of modern MOSUL, Iraq, it was founded in the 13th century BC by Shalmaneser I. It remained unimportant until Ashurnasirpal II chose it in the 9th century BC as the capital of Assyria and his royal seat. It was the site of a religious building founded in 798 BC by Queen Sammu-remat (Semiramis of Greek legend). Excavations there have yielded thousands of carved ivories from the 9th–8th century BC.

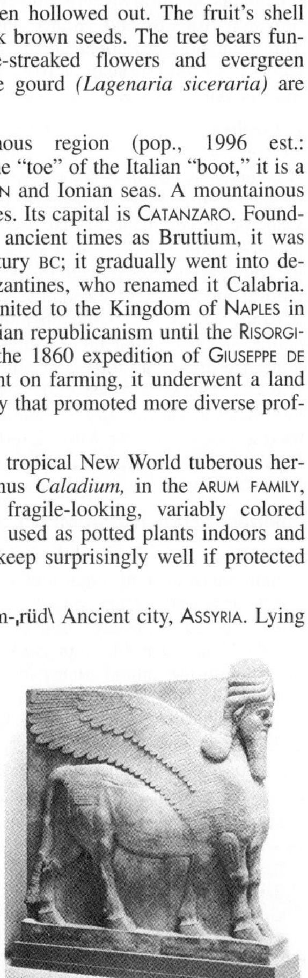

Winged bull of alabaster, guardian of a gate of the palace of Ashurnasirpal II at Nimrud; in the Metropolitan Museum of Art, New York City.

BY COURTESY OF THE METROPOLITAN MUSEUM OF ART, NEW YORK, GIFT OF JOHN D. ROCKEFELLER, JR., 1932

Calais \kȧ-'le, ka-'lā\ Seaport (pop., 1990: 76,000), northern France, located on the Strait of DOVER. Originally a fishing village built on an island, it was improved by the count of Flanders in 997 and fortified by the count of Boulogne in 1224. It was taken in 1347 by EDWARD III of England, and after 1450 was the only remaining English possession in France. The 2d duc de GUISE, took Calais from the English in 1558. In WORLD WAR II it was a main objective in the German drive to the sea in 1940. It is an important passenger port and is near the French terminus of the CHANNEL TUNNEL. The city is famous for its lace and embroideries.

Calamity Jane *orig.* **Martha Jane Cannary** (1852?–1903) U.S. frontierswoman. Born in Princeton, Mo., she grew up in Montana and worked in mining camps, acquiring riding and shooting skills. In 1876 she settled in Deadwood, S.D., site of new gold strikes, and hauled goods and machinery to the outlying camps. There she probably first met Wild Bill HICKOK, who would become her companion. In 1891 she married Charley Burke, and from 1895 she toured with Wild West Shows in the Midwest. Facts about her life were embellished by contemporary feature-magazine writers.

Calamity Jane.

THE BETTMANN ARCHIVE

Calatrava \ˌkä-lä-'trä-vä\, **Order of** Oldest military and religious order in Spain. It was founded in 1158 by two Cistercian monks who proclaimed a holy crusade to defend the city of Calatrava against the MOORS. The order had 200,000 members by 1493, when it was incorporated into the crown by FERDINAND V and ISABELLA I, who deemed that all private armies had outserved their usefulness.

calcedony See CHALCEDONY

calcite \'kal-ˌsīt\ Most common form of natural calcium carbonate ($CaCO_3$), a widely distributed mineral known for the beautiful development and great variety of its crystals. It occurs in stalagmites and stalactites and forms the structure of coral reefs. Calcite is the most important mineral in limestones and marbles used in the building, steel, chemical, and glass industries. Transparent crystals are called Iceland spar.

calcium Chemical ELEMENT, one of the ALKALINE EARTH METALS, chemical symbol Ca, atomic number 20. The most abundant metallic element in the human body, it is stored in BONES and teeth and has many functions (see CALCIUM DEFICIENCY). It is the fifth most abundant element in the earth's crust but does not occur naturally in the free state. Its compounds, in which it has VALENCE 2, include LIMESTONE, CHALK, MARBLE, and DOLOMITE. It occurs in eggshells, pearls, coral, and many marine shells as calcium carbonate, or CALCITE, in APATITE (as calcium phosphate), in GYPSUM (as calcium sulfate), and in many other minerals. It is used as an alloying agent and in other metallurgical applications; its ALLOY with lead is used as cable sheathing and grids for BATTERIES. Calcite is used as a lime source, filler, neutralizer, and extender; in pure form it is used as an antacid and calcium supplement and in baking powder. Calcium oxide (lime) and its product after water addition, calcium hydroxide (slaked lime), are important industrially. Other important compounds are the chloride (a drying agent), the hypochlorite (a BLEACH), the sulfate (GYPSUM and PLASTER OF PARIS), and the phosphate (a plant food and stabilizer for plastics).

calcium deficiency Inadequate supply or METABOLISM of CALCIUM, the main structural element of bones and teeth. Its metabolism is regulated by VITAMIN D, PHOSPHORUS, and HORMONES (see PARATHYROID GLAND). Calcium in the blood has roles in muscle contraction, nerve-impulse transmission, blood clotting, milk production, hormone secretion, and enzyme function, for which calcium is pulled from the bones if deficiency develops. Chronic deficiency may cause OSTEOPOROSIS or osteomalacia (softening of bone) and may contribute to HYPERTENSION and colon cancer. Acute calcium deficiency (hypocalcemia), usually the result of a metabolic problem rather than a dietary deficiency, causes numbness, tingling, and painful muscle aches and spasms.

calculator Machine for performing arithmetic operations and certain mathematical functions automatically. BLAISE PASCAL devised a digital arithmetic machine in 1642. By the late 19th century, such machines had become smaller and easier to use, and desktop machines appeared in the early 20th century. Electronic DATA-PROCESSING systems in the mid-1950s led to the obsolescence of mechanical calculators. Miniature SOLID-STATE DEVICES ushered in calculators that could perform mathematical functions in addition to basic arithmetic, and also store data and instructions in memory registers, providing programming capabilities similar to those of small computers.

calculus Field of mathematics that analyzes aspects of change in processes or systems that can be modeled by FUNCTIONS. Through its two primary tools the DERIVATIVE and the INTEGRAL—it allows precise calculation of rates of change and of the total amount of change in such a system. The derivative and the integral grew out of the idea of a LIMIT, the logical extension of the concept of a function over smaller and smaller intervals. Discovered in the late 17th century independently by ISAAC NEWTON (see DIFFERENTIAL CALCULUS) and G. W. LEIBNIZ (see INTEGRAL CALCULUS), calculus was one of the major scientific breakthroughs of the modern era. See also fundamental theorem of CALCULUS.

calculus, fundamental theorem of Basic principle of calculus. It relates the DERIVATIVE to the INTEGRAL and provides the principal method for evaluating definite integrals (see DIFFERENTIAL CALCULUS and INTEGRAL CALCULUS). In brief, it states that any FUNCTION that is continuous (see CONTINUITY) over an interval has an antiderivative (indefinite integral) on that interval. Further, the definite integral of such a function over an interval $a < x < b$ is the difference $f(b) - f(a)$, where f is an antiderivative (indefinite integral) of the function. This particularly elegant theorem shows the inverse relationship of the derivative and the integral and serves as the backbone of the physical sciences. It was articulated independently by ISAAC NEWTON and G. W. LEIBNIZ.

Calcutta See KOLKATA

Caldecott \'kȯl-də-kət\, **Randolph** (1846–1886) British graphic artist and watercolorist. While working as a bank clerk, he began drawing for periodicals such as *London Society,* and, after moving to London, *Punch* and *Graphic*. He developed a gently satirical style and achieved success with illustrations for WASHINGTON IRVING's *Sketch Book* (1875) and *Bracebridge Hall* (1876). He is best known as an illustrator of children's books, including WILLIAM COWPER's *John Gilpin* (1878) and OLIVER GOLDSMITH's *Elegy on a Mad Dog* (1879). Always frail in health, he died at 39 in Florida, where he had gone to improve his condition. Since 1938 the Caldecott Medal has been awarded annually to the illustrator of the most distinguished U.S. picture book for children.

Calder \'kȯl-dər\, **Alexander (Stirling)** (1898–1976) U.S. sculptor. Born in Philadelphia, he was the son and grandson of sculptors, and his mother was a painter. He studied mechanical engineering, and in 1923 attended the Art Students League, where he was influenced by artists of the ASH CAN SCHOOL. In 1924 he contributed illustrations to the *National Police Gazette*. In 1926 he moved to Paris and began making toylike animals and circus figures of wood and wire; from these he developed his famous miniature circus, which led to his later monumental wire sculptures. In the 1930s he became well known in Paris and the U.S., not only for his sculptures but for portraits, continuous line drawings, and abstract, motor-driven constructions. He is best known as the inventor of the MOBILE, a forerunner of KINETIC SCULPTURE. He also constructed nonmovable works known as stabiles, and designed rugs, tapestries, jewelry, and book illustrations. His career was long and successful.

Calder, photograph by Yousuf Karsh, 1966.

caldera \kal-'der-ə\ Large, bowl-shaped volcanic depression that forms when the top of a volcanic cone collapses into the space left after MAGMA is ejected during a violent volcanic eruption. The term is Spanish for "caldron." Subsequent minor eruptions may build small cones on the floor of the caldera which may still later fill up with water; an example is Crater Lake in Oregon.

Calderón de la Barca \ˌkäl-də-'rōn-dā-lə-'bär-kə\, **Pedro** (1600–1681) Spanish playwright. He abandoned religious studies in 1623 to write plays for the court of PHILIP IV of Spain. His secular plays included *The Surgeon of His Honor* (1635), *Life Is a Dream* (1638), and his masterpiece, *The Daughter of the Air* (1653). His many plays on religious themes include *The Constant Prince* (1629) and *The Wonder-Working Magician* (1637). He also created 76 one-act religious dramas, notably *The Great Theater of the World* (1635) and *The Faithful Shepherd* (1678). Considered the successor to LOPE DE VEGA, he was noted for his well-constructed plots and his preoccupation with the vanity of human existence.

Caldwell, Erskine (1903–1987) U.S. author. Born in Coweta Co., Ga., he became familiar with poor sharecroppers through his father's missionary work. Fame arrived with *Tobacco Road* (1932), a controversial novel whose title became a byword for rural squalor; adapted as a play, it ran over seven years on Broadway. *God's Little Acre* (1933), also a best-seller, featured a cast of hopelessly poor degenerates. Like his other novels and stories about the rural southern poor, they mix violence and sex in grotesque tragicomedy. He also wrote the text for documentary books with photographs by MARGARET BOURKE-WHITE, whom he married.

Caledonian orogenic belt \ˌkal-ə-'dō-nē-ən-ˌȯr-ə-'je-nik\ Range of mountains in northwestern Europe, extending in a southwest-northeast direction from Ireland, Wales, and northern England through Norway. The mountains developed in the period from the start of the CAMBRIAN PERIOD (543 million years ago) to the end of the Silurian period (c. 417 million years ago). Remnants also exist in eastern Greenland.

calendar System for dividing time over extended periods, such as days, months, or years, and arranging these divisions in a definite order. A calendar is essential for the study of chronology, which reckons time by regular divisions, or periods, and uses these to date events. It is also vital for any civilization that needs to measure periods for agricultural, business, domestic, or other reasons. The lunation, or period in which the moon completes a cycle of its phases (29½ days), is the basis for the month; most ancient calendars were collections of months. Days and seasons, which are a solar phenomena, do not have periods that evenly divide, so ancient calendars employed various means, such as the periodic insertion of an intercalary month, to reconcile the months with the seasons. The GREGORIAN CALENDAR used almost universally today is a modification of the Julian calendar adopted by Julius Caesar, which used a 365¼-day year with 12 months that came to have the number of days we know today. See also Jewish CALENDAR, Muslim CALENDAR, SIDEREAL PERIOD.

calendar, French republican See FRENCH REPUBLICAN CALENDAR

calendar, Jewish *or* **Hebrew calendar** Religious and civil dating system based on both lunar and solar cycles. In the calendar used today, a day is counted from sunset to sunset, a week comprises 7 days, a month has 29 or 30 days, and a year has 12 lunar months plus approximately 11 days (or 353, 354, or 355 days). In order to bring the calendar in line with the annual solar cycle, a 13th month of 30 days is added in the 3rd, 6th, 8th, 11th, 14th, 17th, and 19th years of a 19-year cycle. Therefore, a leap year may have from 383 to 385 days. The Jewish calendar in use today was popularly accepted around the 4th century AD and is based on Biblical calculations placing the creation in 3761 BC.

Month	Days	Month	Days
Tishri (Sept.–Oct.)	30	Nisan (Mar.–Apr.)	30
Heshvan (Oct.–Nov.)	29 or 30	Iyar (Apr.–May)	29
Kislev (Nov.–Dec.)	29 or 30	Sivan (May–June)	30
Tebet (Dec.–Jan.)	29	Tammuz (June–July)	29
Shebat (Jan.–Feb.)	30	Ab (July–Aug.)	30
Adar (Feb.–Mar.)	29 or 30	Elul (Aug.–Sept.)	29

calendar, Muslim *or* **Islamic calendar** Dating system used in the Muslim world and based on a year of 12 months, each month beginning approximately at the time of the new moon. The months are alternately 30 and 29 days long except for the 12th, Dhu al-Hijjah, the length of which is varied in a 30-year cycle intended to keep the calendar in step with the true phases of the moon. In 11 years of this cycle, Dhu al-Hijjah has 30 days, and in the other 19 years it has 29. Thus the year has either 354 or 355 days. No months are added as in leap years, so the named months do not remain in the same seasons but retrogress through the entire solar, or seasonal, year (of about 365¼ days) every 32½ solar years. See table on following page.

Month	Days	Month	Days
Muharram	30	Rajab	30
Safar	29	Shaban	29
Rabi I	30	Ramadan	30
Rabi II	29	Shawwal	29
Jumada I	30	Dhu al-Qadah	30
Jumada II	29	Dhu al-Hijjah	29
		in leap years	30

calendering Process of smoothing and compressing a material (notably PAPER) during production by passing a continuous sheet through a number of pairs of heated rolls. The rolls in combination are called calenders; they are made of hardened steel or steel covered with fiber. In paper production, they typically exert a pressure of 500 lbs per linear in. (89 kg per cm). Coated papers are calendered to obtain a smooth, glossy finish. Calendering is also widely used in the manufacture of TEXTILES, coated fabrics, and plastic sheeting.

calendula \kə-'len-jə-lə\ Any herbaceous plant of the small genus *Calendula,* in the COMPOSITE FAMILY, found in temperate regions. Calendulas produce yellow-rayed flowers. The pot marigold *(C. officinalis)* is grown especially for ornamental purposes.

Calgary \'kal-gə-rē\ City (metro. area pop., 1996: 822,000), southern Alberta, Canada. It was founded in 1875 as a fort on the BOW RIVER for the Northwest Mounted Police. The arrival of the Canadian Pacific Railway in 1883 aided its growth, as did the discovery of nearby oil and gas fields in 1914 and 1947. Its major industries are petroleum refining, meat packing, and lumbering. The annual Calgary Stampede, founded in 1912, is a world-famous rodeo and celebration of the Old West.

Calgary, University of Public university in Calgary, Alberta. It was founded in 1945 as part of the University of ALBERTA and gained full autonomy in 1966. It has faculties of education, engineering, environmental design, fine arts, graduate studies, humanities, law, management, medicine, nursing, physical education, science, social sciences, and social work. It has special programs devoted to space research, international development, gifted education, and world tourism. Total enrollment is about 24,000.

Calhoun \kal-'hün\, **John C(aldwell)** (1782–1850) U.S. politician. Born in Abbeville district, S.C., he became an ardent Jeffersonian Republican and was elected to the U.S. House of Representatives (1811–17), where as leader of the WAR HAWKS he introduced the declaration of war against Britain in June 1812. He served as U.S. secretary of war 1817–25. He was elected vice president (under JOHN QUINCY ADAMS) in 1824, and would be elected again (under ANDREW JACKSON) in 1828. In the 1830s he became extreme in his devotion to strict construction of the U.S. Constitution, a champion of states' rights and slavery, and a supporter of NULLIFICATION. He resigned the vice presidency in 1832 and was elected to the U.S. Senate, where he served 1832–50, interrupted only by brief service as secretary of state (1843–45). His exuberant defense of slavery as a "positive good" aroused strong anti-Southern feeling in the free states.

John Calhoun, detail of a daguerreotype by Mathew Brady, c. 1849.

BY COURTESY OF THE LIBRARY OF CONGRESS, WASHINGTON, D.C.

Cali \'kä-lē\ City (pop., 1992 est.: 1,624,000), western Colombia. Lying on both sides of the Cali River, it was founded in 1536. Located far from the coast, it did not develop economically until the 20th century, when the upper CAUCA RIVER was drained to generate electrical power and prevent flooding. It is a major service center for area products and rivals BOGOTÁ, BARRANQUILLA, and MEDELLÍN as an industrial center. In the late 20th century Cali was notorious for its drug operations.

calico cat In North America, a blotched or spotted DOMESTIC CAT, usually predominantly white with red and black patches (a pattern also called tortoiseshell-and-white). Because genetic determination of some coat colors in cats is linked to the sex chromosome, calicoes are almost always female.

California State (pop., 1997 est.: 32,268,000), western U.S. Lying on the Pacific Ocean, it is the largest state in population and the third-largest in area, extending about 800 mi (1,300 km) north to south and 250 mi (400 km) east to west. The capital is SACRAMENTO. Within 85 mi (137 km) of each other lie Mount WHITNEY and DEATH VALLEY, the highest and lowest points in the 48 contiguous states. It was inhabited originally by American Indians. The first European coastal expansion took place in 1542–43 when JUAN CABRILLO established a Spanish claim to the area. The first mission was established by JUNIPERO SERRA at SAN DIEGO in 1769. The region remained under Spanish, and after the 1820s, Mexican, control until it was taken by U.S. forces in the MEXICAN WAR, and ceded to the U.S. by the Treaty of GUADALUPE HIDALGO in 1848. Though settlement had begun by the U.S. in 1841, it was greatly accelerated by the 1848 GOLD RUSH. California was admitted to the Union in 1850 as a slavery-free state under the COMPROMISE OF 1850. Its already expanding population grew immensely in the 20th century. It has the largest economy of any state. It has suffered severe earthquakes, most destructively those of SAN FRANCISCO in 1906 and 1989 and LOS ANGELES in 1994.

California, Gulf of *or* **Sea of Cortés** Gulf separating BAJA CALIFORNIA from the rest of Mexico. Its area is about 59,000 sq mi (153,000 sq km). Its waters were colored by red plankton when 16th-century Spanish explorers named it Mar Bermejo ("Vermilion Sea"). Some geologists hold that the gulf is structurally part of the Pacific; others claim Baja California is pulling away from the continent as it moves north along the SAN ANDREAS FAULT, allowing the gulf to form.

California, Lower See BAJA CALIFORNIA

California, University of Public university with campuses at Berkeley (main campus), Davis, Irvine, Los Angeles, Riverside, San Diego (La Jolla), San Francisco, Santa Barbara, and Santa Cruz. It is the third-largest university system in the U.S. (total enrollment 152,000). It was established in 1868 in Oakland. In the 1930s research at the Berkeley campus produced the first CYCLOTRON, the isolation of the human polio virus, and the discovery of several new chemical elements. Today the Berkeley campus remains a leader in scientific fields as well as in many other academic areas. Its 130 departments and programs are organized into 14 colleges and schools. The Los Angeles branch (UCLA), founded in 1919, includes schools of law, medicine, and engineering. The San Francisco campus, originally the university's Medical Center (1873), has schools of medicine, nursing, dentistry, and pharmacy. The San Diego campus, founded as a marine station, became part of the university in 1912; it includes the Scripps Institution of Oceanography. The Davis and Riverside campuses grew out of agricultural institutes and were both added in 1959. The Santa Barbara campus was granted university status in 1944, and those at Santa Cruz and Irvine in 1965. The university operates the Lawrence Berkeley Laboratory, the Lawrence Livermore National Laboratory (both nuclear-science research centers) and the LOS ALAMOS National Laboratory.

California Institute of Technology *known as* **Caltech** Highly select private university and research institute in Pasadena offering graduate and undergraduate instruction and research in pure and applied science and engineering. Established in 1891, it is today considered one of the world's premier scientific research centers. In 1958 its Jet Propulsion Laboratory, in conjunction with NASA, launched Explorer I, the first U.S. satellite. The astronomical observatories at Palomar Mtn., Mount Wilson, Big Bear Lake, and Las Campanas (Chile) are jointly operated by Caltech and the Carnegie Institution of Washington. Other institute facilities include a seismology laboratory, a marine-biology laboratory, and a center for the study of radio astronomy. Total enrollment is about 1,900.

California Institute of the Arts *known as* **Calarts** Private institution of higher learning in Valencia. It was created in 1961 through the merger of two other art institutes. It consists of five schools—of art, dance, film and video, music, and theater—and a division of critical studies, all of which enjoy high reputations in their fields. All schools award BFA and MFA degrees. A community arts program teaches young students in disadvantaged areas of Los Angeles. Enrollment is about 1,000.

California poppy Annual garden plant *(Eschscholzia californica)* in the POPPY FAMILY, native to the western coast of North America and naturalized in parts of southern Europe, Asia, and Australia. The flowers are usually pale yellow, orange, or cream in the wild, but whites and shades of red and pink have been developed in cultivation. The foliage is gray-green and feathery. The flowers open only in sunlight. They blossom all summer in northern climates and into the winter in areas with mild winters.

California poppy (*Eschscholzia californica*).
GRANT HEILMAN

Californian Indians American Indian peoples originally living in and around present-day California. Of the many Californian groups, most were composed of independent territorial and political units that were smaller than the average groupings of other North American Indians. Food varied with the region inhabited (coastal peoples fished, desert peoples hunted and practiced marginal agriculture, etc.), as did style of housing. Shamanism was common to all groups, and magic was used in attempts to control events or transform reality (e.g., heal illness or increase the harvest). Goods and foodstuffs were distributed through reciprocal trade between kin and through "trade fairs"; professional traders linked coastal peoples with peoples of Arizona and New Mexico. Californian Indians had a renowned oral literature, and Californian basketwork is considered exquisite. See also MODOC, NORTHWEST COAST INDIANS, POMO, SHAMAN, YUMAN.

Caligula \kə-ˈli-gyə-lə\ *officially* **Gaius Caesar** (Germanicus) (AD 12–41) Roman emperor (37–41). Known by his childhood nickname, Caligula ("Little Boots") was declared heir to the throne by TIBERIUS following the suspicious deaths of Caligula's parents and brothers, and probably connived in Tiberius' death. He suffered a severe illness seven months into his rule and began displaying mental instability, engaging in despotic caprice and cruelty. Restoring treason trials (38), he executed former supporters and extorted money from the citizens. He plundered Gaul in 40 and began planning to invade Britain. He made pretensions to divinity and declared his sister Drusilla a goddess on her death. Weary of his tyranny, a group of conspirators assassinated him.

caliper Instrument that consists of two adjustable legs or jaws for measuring the dimensions of material parts. Spring calipers have an adjusting screw and nut; firm-joint calipers use friction at the joint to hold the legs unmoving. Outside calipers measure thicknesses and outside diameters of objects; inside calipers measure hole diameters and distances between surfaces. Hermaphrodite calipers, which have one leg bent inward and one straight leg ending in a sharp point, are used for scribing lines at a specified distance from a flat or curved surface. See also MICROMETER.

caliph \ˈkā-ləf, ˈka-ləf\ (from Arabic *khalifah:* "deputy, successor") Title given to those who succeeded the prophet Muhammad as real or nominal ruler of the Muslim world, with all his powers except that of prophecy. Controversy over the selection of the fourth caliph, ALI, split Islam into the SUNNI and SHIITE sects. Ali's rival, al-MUAWIYAH I, established the Umayyad caliphate (see UMAYYAD DYNASTY), which produced 14 caliphs (661–750). The ABBASID DYNASTY (750–945), the most widely observed caliphate, associated with 38 caliphs, moved the capital from DAMASCUS to BAGHDAD. The MONGOL conquest of Baghdad in 1258 effectively ended their political power. Other Muslim leaders created caliphates with limited success. The FATIMID DYNASTY proclaimed a new caliphate in 920; ABD AL-RAHMAN III announced one in opposition to both the Abbasids and the Fatimids in 928. Mamluks (see MAMLUK REGIME) were caliphs from 1258 until the Ottomans took over the title in 1517 (see OTTOMAN EMPIRE). The Turkish republic abolished it in 1924.

calisthenics Systematic rhythmic bodily exercises (e.g., jumping jacks, push-ups), usually performed without apparatus. Calisthenics promote strength, endurance, flexibility, and general well-being by placing regular demands on the cardiovascular system. The exercises, initially conceived as primarily for women, arose in the 19th century in Germany and Sweden. CATHARINE ESTHER BEECHER in the U.S. advocated women's calisthenics. As their health benefits became known, they became an activity for both sexes.

Calixtus II \kə-ˈlik-stəs\ *orig.* **Guido of Burgundy** (died 1124) Pope (1119–24). As archbishop of Vienne in Lower Burgundy, he became known as an advocate of reform and an opponent of Holy Roman emperor Henry V. Elected pope in 1119, he condemned lay investiture and excommunicated Henry. They were later reconciled, and the Concordat of Worms (1122) ended the INVESTITURE CONTROVERSY. Calixtus called the first LATERAN COUNCIL (1123), which secured peace between church and empire for the next 35 years. His bull *Etsi Judaeis* (1120) protected Roman Jews.

calla Either of two distinct kinds of plants of the ARUM FAMILY. *Calla palustris* is known as the arum lily, water arum, or wild calla. The common name calla is also generally given to several species of *Zantedeschia,* often called calla lilies. The handsome *C. palustris* occurs widely in wet places in cool, northern temperate and subarctic regions. It has heart-shaped leaves, showy white floral leaves, and clusters of brilliant red berries. Its juice is violently poisonous. The most important of the calla lilies, all native to South Africa, is the common florist's calla *(Z. aethiopica),* a stout herb with a fragrant white spathe and arrow-shaped leaves; a popular indoor plant, it is grown commercially for cut flowers.

Arum lily (*Calla palustris*).
INGMAR HOLMASEN

Callaghan \ˈka-lə-ˌhan\, **(Leonard) James** (born 1912) British politician. A trade-union official, he entered Parliament as a Labour Party member in 1945. He served in Labour governments as chancellor of the exchequer (1964–67), home secretary (1967–70), and foreign secretary (1974–76) before becoming prime minister (1976–79). A moderate within his party, he tried to stem the vociferous demands of the trade unions. After a series of paralyzing labor strikes in 1978–79, his government was brought down by a parliamentary vote of no confidence.

Callaghan \ˈka-lə-ˌhan\, **Morley (Edward)** (1903–1990) Canadian novelist and short-story writer. A native of Toronto, he received a law degree in 1928 but never practiced. He won acclaim for the short-story collection *A Native Argosy* (1929). His first novel, *Strange Fugitive* (1928), describes the destruction of a social misfit, a type that recurs in his fiction. Later novels, including *They Shall Inherit the Earth* (1935) and *The Loved and the Lost* (1951, Governor General's Award), emphasize Christian love as an answer to social injustice. *That Summer in Paris* (1963) describes Callaghan's friendship with F. SCOTT FITZGERALD and ERNEST HEMINGWAY. Later works include *A Fine and Private Place* (1975) and *A Time for Judas* (1983).

Callahan, Harry (Morey) (1912–1999) U.S. photographer. Born in Detroit, he had no formal training in photography and first developed an interest in it in 1938. In 1941 ANSEL ADAMS's photographs inspired him to develop his own style. His subjects included landscapes, cityscapes, and unconventional portraits of his wife and daughter. He was best known as a teacher; he was head of the photography department at the Chicago Institute of Design (1949–61) and developed the photography department at RISD (1961–76). In 1980 two collections of his works were published, *Water's Edge* and *Harry Callahan: Color, 1945–1980.*

Callao \kä-ˈyä-ō\ City (pop., 1993: 615,000), chief seaport, Peru. It was founded in 1537 by FRANCISCO PIZARRO on Callao Bay west of LIMA. As the leading shipping point for gold and silver taken by Spanish conquerors from the INCAS, it was frequently assaulted by pirates and Spain's European rivals. It was destroyed by a tidal wave in 1746, then rebuilt near its original site. It withstood several sieges by Spanish forces during the wars for independence. SIMON BOLIVAR landed here in 1823, and three years later it was the scene of the final Spanish surrender. It suffered heavy earthquake damage in 1940, but has since expanded and modernized.

Callas \ˈka-ləs\, **Maria** *orig.* **Cecilia Sophia Anna Maria Kalogeropoulos** (1923–1977) U.S. soprano. Born in New York City, she moved to Greece as a teenager and made her debut there in 1939. She became an international star in *La Gioconda* at the 1947 Verona Festival. She continued to sing heavy dramatic roles, including G. Puccini's Turandot and Richard Wagner's Kundry, until the conductor Tullio Serafin (1878–1968) convinced her to shift to the bel canto repertoire, in which she became immortal. Her acclaimed roles included V. Bellini's Norma, L. Cherubini's Medea, and G. Donizetti's Lucia and Anna Bolena. Though her voice lacked great beauty, her artistic integrity, vivid stage presence, striking features, and fiery temperament made her the most famous opera star in the world.

calligraphy \kə-'lig-rə-fē\ Art of beautiful, stylized, or elegant handwriting or lettering with pen or brush and ink. It involves the correct formation of characters, the ordering of the various parts, and the harmony of proportions. In the Islamic and Chinese cultures, calligraphy is as highly revered as painting. In Europe in the 14th–16th century, two scripts developed that influenced all subsequent handwriting and printing: the roman and italic styles. With the invention of modern printing (1450), calligraphy became increasingly bold and ornamental.

Callimachus (fl. 5th century BC) Greek sculptor. Though little is known of his life, he reputedly invented the Corinthian capital after seeing leaves growing around a basket placed on a girl's tomb. He was noted for the eleborate carving and detailed draperies of his sculptures, which survive only as Roman copies.

Callimachus \kə-'lim-ə-kəs\ (c.305–c.240 BC) Greek poet and scholar. He migrated to Egypt, where he worked at the Library of Alexandria. Of his voluminous writings, only fragments survive. His best-known poetical work is the *Causes* (c. 270 BC), a medley of obscure tales explaining the origins of customs, festivals, and names. He is the most representative poet of the erudite and sophisticated Alexandrian school. His most famous prose work is the *Pinakes* ("Tablets") in 120 books, a catalog of the authors whose works were held in the library.

Calliope *or* **Kalliope** \kə-'lī-ə-pē\ In Greek mythology, the foremost of the nine Muses and the patron of epic poetry. She and King Oeagrus of Thrace were the parents of Orpheus. She also bore Apollo two sons, Hymen and Ialemus. Other versions of the myth say she was the mother of Rhesus, king of Thrace, or the mother of Linus, inventor of melody and rhythm.

Callisto \kə-'lis-tō\ In Greek mythology, a nymph and a hunting companion of Artemis. Though she vowed never to wed, she was seduced by Zeus, who turned her into a she-bear to conceal his infidelity from the jealous Hera. She was then killed by Artemis during a hunt. Other versions hold that it was Artemis or Hera, enraged at her unchastity, who turned her into a bear. After her death Zeus placed her in the heavens as the constellation Ursa Major (Great Bear).

Callot \kȧ-'lō\, **Jacques** (1592–1635) French etcher, engraver, and draftsman. He learned the technique of engraving in Rome. In 1612, at the court of the Medici family in Florence, he was employed to make pictorial records of pageants and feasts. He had a genius for caricature and the grotesque; his series of etchings *The Miseries of War* (1633), documenting the atrocities of the Thirty Years' War, was used as a source by Francisco Goya. His output was prodigious; over 1,400 etchings and 2,000 drawings survive. One of the greatest of all etchers, he was also one of the first major artists to practice the graphic arts exclusively.

Cab Calloway.
SCHOMBURG CENTER FOR RESEARCH IN BLACK CULTURE; THE NEW YORK PUBLIC LIBRARY; ASTOR, LENOX AND TILDEN FOUNDATIONS

Calloway, Cab(ell) (1907–1994) U.S. singer and big-band leader who combined audacious showmanship with prodigious vocal range and imagination. Born in Rochester, N.Y., he fronted his first group in 1928; it became the house band at Harlem's Cotton Club, in 1931. An accomplished scat singer, he became most identified with his 1931 hit "Minnie the Moocher." Exposure with his band launched the careers of many important jazz soloists. George Gershwin modeled the character Sportin' Life in *Porgy and Bess* on Calloway, who later performed the role himself.

callus In botany, soft tissue that forms over a wounded or cut plant surface, leading to healing. A callus arises from cells of the cambium. When a callus forms, some of its cells may organize into growing points, some of which in turn give rise to roots while others produce stems and leaves. Thus a callus may be capable of regenerating an entire plant.

Calmette \kȧl-'met\, **Albert (Léon Charles)** (1863–1933) French bacteriologist. In the 1890s he founded the Pasteur bacteriological institutes in Saigon and later Lille. He discovered in 1908 that tuberculosis bacteria from cattle were weakened when cultured with bile, producing a strain of bacteria that provoked a protective immune reaction without causing disease. That discovery led him to develop, with Camille Guérin, a tuberculosis vaccine. He also described a test (Calmette's reaction) for tuberculosis and discovered an antivenin for snakebite.

Calmette.
HARLINGUE–H. ROGER-VIOLLET

Calonne \kȧ-'lȯn\, **Charles-Alexandre de** (1734–1802) French politician. He served as intendant of Metz (1768) and Lille (1774), and his financial genius led to his appointment as controller general of finance (1783). He soon discovered that major reforms were necessary to save France from bankruptcy. His efforts precipitated the governmental crisis that led to the French Revolution. After the Revolution began, he devoted himself to the cause of counterrevolution from his exile in England.

calorie Unit of energy or heat. Various precise definitions are used for different purposes (physical-chemistry measurements, engineering steam tables, and thermochemistry), but in all cases the calorie is about 4.2 joules, the amount of heat needed to raise the temperature of 1 g of water by 1°C. The calorie used by dietitians and food scientists and found on food labels is actually the kilocalorie (also called Calorie by scientists and abbreviated kcal or Cal), or 1,000 calories. It measures the amount of heat energy or metabolic energy contained in the chemical bonds (see bonding) of a food.

calorimeter \ˌka-lə-'ri-mə-tər\ Device for measuring heat produced during a mechanical, electrical, or chemical reaction and for calculating the heat capacity of materials. A common design, known as a bomb calorimeter, consists of a reaction chamber surrounded by a liquid that absorbs the heat produced by the reaction. The amount of heat can be determined from the increase in temperature, taking into account the properties of the container and the liquid.

Caltech See California Institute of Technology

Calukya dynasty \'kä-lək-yə\ Either of two ancient Indian dynasties. The Western Calukyas ruled as emperors in the Deccan AD 543–757 and again c. 975–c. 1189. The Eastern Calukyas ruled in Vengi (in eastern Andhra Pradesh) c. 624–c. 1070. The most significant ruling family of the Deccan in the 5th–6th century, they controlled both coasts and the major river valleys.

calumet \'kal-yə-ˌmet\ *or* **sacred pipe** *or* **peace pipe** One of the central ceremonial objects of many American Indian groups. It was considered a microcosm, its parts and its decorative colors and motifs being believed to correspond to the essential parts of the universe. It was smoked in personal prayer as well as at collective rites. Because of the narcotic effect of the tobacco and the symbolism of the indrawn and ascending smoke, it was employed as a means of communication between the spiritual world and humankind.

Calvary *or* **Golgotha** Hill in Jerusalem. The site of Jesus' crucifixion, the hill of execution was outside the city walls of Jerusalem and near the sepulchre where Jesus was buried. Its exact location is uncertain, but most scholars prefer either the spot now covered by the Church of the Holy Sepulchre or a hillock called Gordon's Calvary north of the Damascus Gate.

Calvert, George, Baron Baltimore (c. 1580–1632) English colonialist. He served in the House of Commons from 1621; charged with communicating James I's policy, he was distrusted by Parliament. After he had declared himself a Roman Catholic (1625), he gave up his office and was created Baron Baltimore, receiving land grants in Ireland. To assure the prosperity of his New World holdings, he took his family to his Newfoundland colony in 1627. When conflict arose over his Catholicism and the climate proved too severe, he petitioned Charles I for a land grant in the Chesapeake Bay area. He died before the charter was granted, and his son Cecil became proprietor of the colony of Maryland.

Calvert, Leonard (1606?–1647) First governor of the Maryland colony. The younger brother of George Calvert, the colony's proprietor, he was sent in 1633 from England to establish a settlement at St. Mary's. He gradually allowed limited legislative initiative in the colony's assembly. He lost a land conflict with William Claiborne and was forced to leave Maryland (1644–46); aided by colonists, including Margaret Brent, he returned to reinstate his proprietorial rule.

Calvin, John *French* **Jean Cauvin** \kō-'va^{n}\ (1509–1564) French Protestant theologian and major figure of the Reformation. Born in Noyon, Picardy, he studied religion at the University of Paris and law in Orléans and Bourges. When he returned to Paris in 1531 he studied the Bible and became part of a movement that emphasized salvation by grace rather than by works. Government intolerance prompted him to move to Basel, Switzerland, where he wrote the first edition of *Institutes of the Christian Religion* (1536). Gaining a reputation among Protestant leaders, he went to Geneva to help establish Protestantism in that city. He was expelled by city fathers in 1538, and returned in 1541, when the town council instituted the church order outlined in his Ecclesiastical Ordinances, including the enforcement of sexual morality and abolition of Catholic "superstition." He approved the arrest and conviction for heresy of Michael Servetus. By 1555 Calvin had succeeded in establishing a theocracy in Geneva, where he served as pastor and head of the Genevan Academy and wrote the sermons, biblical commentaries, and letters that form the basis of Calvinism.

Calvin, Melvin (1911–1997) U.S. biochemist. Born in St. Paul, Minn., he received his PhD from the University of Minnesota. He developed a system of using the radioactive isotope carbon-14 as a tracer element in his studies of the green alga chlorella. By halting the plant's growth at various stages and measuring tiny amounts of radioactive compounds present, Calvin was able to identify most of the reactions involved in the intermediate steps of photosynthesis, for which he was awarded a 1961 Nobel Prize. His research also included work in radiation chemistry and the processes leading to the origin of life.

Calvinism In Protestantism, the theology developed and advanced by John Calvin. It was further developed by his followers and became the foundation of the Reformed church and Presbyterianism. As shaped by Calvin's successor at Geneva, Theodore Beza (1519–1605), Calvinism emphasizes the doctrine of predestination, holding that God extends grace and grants salvation only to the chosen, or elect. It stresses the literal truth of the Bible, and it views the church as a Christian community in which Christ is head and all members are equal under him. It therefore rejects the episcopal form of church government in favor of an organization in which church officers are elected. Calvinism was the basis of theocracies in Geneva and Puritan New England (see Puritanism), and it strongly influenced the Presbyterian church in Scotland.

Calvino \käl-'vē-nō\, **Italo** (1923–1985) Italian writer. After early works inspired by his involvement with the Italian Resistance in World War II, he turned decisively to fantasy and allegory in the 1950s. *Cosmicomics* (1965) is a collection of whimsical narratives about the creation and evolution of the universe. The novels *Invisible Cities* (1972), *The Castle of Crossed Destinies* (1973), and *If on a Winter's Night a Traveler* (1979) use playfully innovative structures and shifting viewpoints. *The Uses of Literature* (1980) is a collection of essays he wrote for a left-wing journal he edited 1959–66.

calypso \kə-'lip-sō\ Type of folk song originally from Trinidad but sung elsewhere in the Caribbean. The calypso tradition dates to the early 19th century. The subject of a calypso text, usually witty and satiric, is an event of political or social import. The lyric often incorporates Spanish, Creole, and African phrases, employing newly invented expressions such as *bobol* (graft) and *pakoti* (unfaithfulness). The exaggeration of local speech patterns is matched by an offbeat rhythm. Favorite accompanying instruments are the shak-shak (maraca), cuatro (a string instrument), and tamboo-bamboo (bamboo poles of various lengths struck on the ground). Shaped and tuned oil drums, played together in orchestras called steel bands, have also been popular.

cam Machine component that either rotates or reciprocates (moves back and forth) to create a prescribed motion in a contacting element (the follower). Since the shape of the contacting surface of the cam is determined by the prescribed motion and the profile of the follower, cams take various forms. Cam-follower mechanisms are particularly useful when a simple motion of one part of a machine is to be converted to a more complicated prescribed motion of another part, one that must be accurately timed with respect to the simple motion and may include periods of rest (dwells). Cams are essential elements in automatic machine tools, printing machines, sewing machines, and textile machinery.

Cam Ranh \'käm-'rän\, **Vinh** *or* **Cam Ranh Bay** Inlet of the South China Sea, South Vietnam. Located between Phan Rang and Nha Trang, it was a French colonial naval base. It was used by the Japanese in World War II. From 1965 it was a major U.S. base in the Vietnam War. It later was a major Soviet naval base.

Camagüey \,kä-mä-'gwā\ City (pop., 1994 est.: 294,000), capital of Camagüey province, Cuba. Founded at the site of the present-day port of Nuevitas, it was moved inland in 1528. Because of the province's great production of livestock and agricultural products, it is now Cuba's largest interior city and an important communications, trading, and industrial center.

Camargo \kå-mår-'gō\, **Marie (-Anne de Cupis de)** (1710–1770) French ballerina noted for her technical innovations. She made her Paris Opera debut in 1726, going on to dance in 78 ballets and operas before her retirement in 1751. Admired for her speed and agility, she executed jumping steps previously performed only by male dancers, shortening her skirts and removing the heels from her slippers to do so. Her name was adopted in 1930 by a British ballet group, the Camargo Society.

Camargue \kä-'märg\ Marshy island in the delta of the Rhone River, southern France. Occupying an area of 300 sq mi (780 sq km), it is sparsely populated (about 10,000). The region was once entirely wild, with free-roaming herds of cattle and wild horses; such herds still can be found in the regional park. Vineyards, forage crops, and grains began to be planted in the late 19th century; rice growing developed after 1945. A nature reserve at the Vaccarès Lagoon protects waterbirds such as flamingos and egrets.

Cambay, Gulf of See Gulf of Khambhat

Cambio, Arnolfo di See Arnolfo di Cambio

cambium In plants, a layer of actively dividing cells between xylem (fluid-conducting) and phloem (food-conducting) tissues that is responsible for the secondary growth of stems and roots, resulting in an increase in thickness. A cambium may also form within callus tissues. See also bark, wood.

Cambodia *or* **Kampuchea** Monarchy, South Asia. Area: 69,898 sq mi (181,036 sq km). Population (1997 est.): 10,385,000. Capital: Phnom Penh. The vast majority of the population belongs to the Mon-Khmer ethnic group. Language: Khmer (official). Religion: Buddhism (official). Currency: riel. It is dominated by large central plains; the Dangrek Mountains lie along its northern border. It lies largely in the basin of the Mekong River; the large lake Tonle Sap is in its western part. Much of the country is jungle. It is one of the world's poorest countries. Agriculture employs three-fourths of the workforce. It is a constitutional monarchy with one legislative house; its chief of state is the king, and its heads of government are co-premiers. In the early Christian era, the area was under Hindu and to a lesser extent Buddhist influence. The Khmer state gradually spread in the early 7th century, and reached its height under Jayavarman II and his successors in the 9th–12th century, when it ruled the Mekong Valley and the tributary Shan states and built Angkor. Widespread adoption of Buddhism occurred in the 13th century, resulting in a script change from Sanskrit to Pali. From the 13th century it

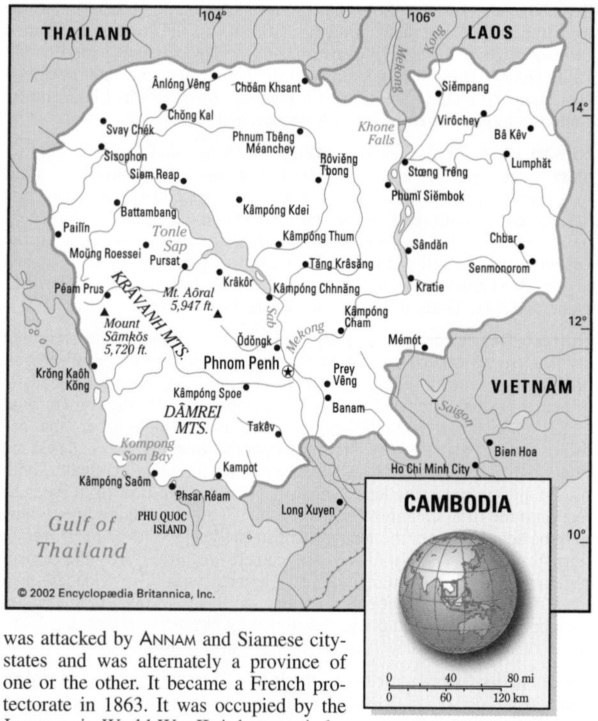

was attacked by ANNAM and Siamese city-states and was alternately a province of one or the other. It became a French protectorate in 1863. It was occupied by the Japanese in World War II; it became independent in 1954. Its borders were the scene of fighting in the VIETNAM WAR from 1961, and in 1970 its northeastern and eastern areas were occupied by the North Vietnamese and penetrated by U.S. and South Vietnamese forces. An indiscriminate U.S. bombing campaign alienated much of the population, enabling the communist KHMER ROUGE under POL POT to seize power in 1975. Their regime of terror resulted in the deaths of over 1 million Cambodians. Vietnam invaded in 1979 and drove the Khmer Rouge into the western hinterlands, but it was unable to effect reconstruction of the country and Cambodian infighting continued. A peace accord was reached by most Cambodian factions under U.N. auspices in 1991, and elections were held in 1993. Civil and military unrest continued. In 1997 King NORODOM SIHANOUK left the country, which was on the verge of civil war.

Cambodian See KHMER

Cambodian language See KHMER LANGUAGE

Cambon \kän-'bōn\, **(Pierre-) Paul** (1843–1924) French diplomat. He worked in the civil service (1870–82) before entering the diplomatic service, in which he served as ambassador to Spain and Turkey. Appointed ambassador to Britain (1898–1920), he spent his first years in smoothing over Anglo-French relations. His efforts were crowned by the signing of the ENTENTE CORDIALE in 1904. During World War I he continued to play a vital role in cooperation between the two allies.

Cambrai \kam-'brā\, **League of** (1508–10) Alliance of Pope JULIUS II, Emperor MAXIMILIAN I, King LOUIS XII, and King FERDINAND V, formed in 1508. Ostensibly directed against the Turks, its actual aim was to attack the Republic of Venice and divide its possessions among the allies. The allies were unable to act together because of their individual ambitions, and the league collapsed in 1510, when the pope joined with Venice, while Ferdinand became neutral.

Cambrai \kam-'brā\, **Treaty of** *or* **Paix des Dames** \'pe-dā-'däm\ (French: "Peace of the Ladies") (August 3, 1529) Agreement ending one phase of the wars between FRANCIS I of France and Emperor CHARLES V, temporarily confirming Spanish (Habsburg) control in Italy. It was called the Paix des Dames because it was negotiated by Louise of Savoy (1476–1531), mother of King Francis and regent in his absence, and MARGARET OF AUSTRIA, aunt of Charles and regent of the Netherlands. See also Treaty of CATEAU-CAMBRÉSIS.

Cambrian period Oldest time division of the PALEOZOIC ERA. During the Cambrian, 543–490 million years ago, there were widespread seas and several scattered landmasses. The largest continent was GONDWANA. The average climate was probably warmer than today, with less variation between regions. There were no land plants or animals, but there were marine organisms with either shells or skeletons. Because the dominant animals were TRILOBITES, the Cambrian is sometimes referred to as the Age of Trilobites.

Cambridge City (pop., 1994 est: 113,000), eastern England. The seat of CAMBRIDGESHIRE, it lies on the Cam River, a tributary of the OISE, north of London. Originally a fording site, it possesses earthworks and Roman remains. Two monastic foundations date from the 11th–12th century; it received its first charter in 1207. It is best known as the site of the University of CAMBRIDGE, noted for its educational excellence and its outstanding architecture. The city's economy is linked to the university and its research and development services.

Corpus Christi College, University of Cambridge, Cambridge.
SHOSTAL

Cambridge City (pop., 1996 est.: 94,000), northeastern Massachusetts. Adjacent to Boston, it was founded in 1630 as one of the MASSACHUSETTS BAY COLONY settlements. The first American institution of higher learning, HARVARD COLLEGE (NOW UNIV.), was founded here in 1636. GEORGE WASHINGTON took command of the Continental Forces at what is now Cambridge Common in 1775. In the 19th century it was the home of such literary leaders as HENRY W. LONGFELLOW, JAMES RUSSELL LOWELL, and OLIVER WENDELL HOLMES. The MASSACHUSETTS INSTITUTE OF TECHNOLOGY moved to Cambridge from Boston in 1916.

Cambridge, University of English autonomous institution of higher learning at Cambridge, England. Its beginnings lie in an exodus of scholars from OXFORD UNIV. in 1209; the first college was built in 1284 and the university was officially recognized by the pope in 1318. From 1511 DESIDERIUS ERASMUS did much to inculcate the new learning of the Renaissance at Cambridge. In 1546 Henry VIII founded Trinity College, which remains the largest of Cambridge's 31 colleges. From 1669 ISAAC NEWTON taught mathematics, giving this field a unique position there. In 1871 JAMES CLERK MAXWELL accepted the chair of experimental physics, beginning a leadership in physics that would continue into the next century. A host of world-renowned scholars in other fields have also taught at Cambridge. Many of its buildings, including the famous King's College Chapel and two chapels designed by CHRISTOPHER WREN, are rich in history and tradition. The library houses numerous important collections, and the Fitzwilliam Museum contains noteworthy collections of antiquities. Total enrollment is about 15,000.

Cambridge Agreement Pledge made in Cambridge, England, in 1629 by Puritan stockholders of the Massachusetts Bay Co. to emigrate to New England if the colony's government could be transferred there. The company agreed and shifted control of the corporation to the signers of the agreement. JOHN WINTHROP was elected governor, and he set sail in 1630 with a large group of Puritan followers to settle in the Boston area (see MASSACHUSETTS BAY COLONY).

Cambridge Platonists \'plā-tᵊn-ists\ Group of 17th-century British philosophic and religious thinkers. Led by Benjamin Whichcote (1609–1683), it included RALPH CUDWORTH and Henry More (1614–1687) at Cambridge and Joseph Glanvill (1636–1680) at Oxford. Educated as Puritans, they reacted against the Calvinist emphasis on the arbitrariness of divine sovereignty. In their eyes, THOMAS HOBBES and the Calvinists erred in making the voluntarist assumption (see VOLUNTARISM) that morality consists in obeying the will of a sovereign. Morality, they asserted, is essentially rational, and the good person's virtue is grounded in an understanding of the eternal and immutable nature of goodness, which not even God can alter through sovereign power.

Cambridgeshire \'kām-brij-ˌshir\ County (pop., 1995 est.: 694,000), eastern England. Greatly enlarged in the 1974 government reorganization, it now includes part of the former county of Huntingdonshire and the Isle of Ely; the county seat is CAMBRIDGE. Prehistoric tracks ring the county's fens, where drainage was begun by the Romans. Major structures include Ely Cathedral, 15th-century churches, and the buildings of the University of CAMBRIDGE. It is crossed by two major rivers, the Nen and the Great OISE, with its tributary the Cam.

Camden Town group Group of English painters formed in 1911. The artists met weekly in the studio of Walter Sickert (1860–1942), the group's prime inspiration, in a working-class area of London. They rejected the Romantic academy tradition and painted realistic aspects of urban life, as well as portraits, landscapes, and still lifes, in an Impressionist fashion. In 1913, after three exhibitions that resulted in large losses to the gallery where they were held, they merged with another group to form the London group. The name is sometimes extended to designate a distinctive lineage of early-20th-century British painting.

camel Either of two species of large, hump-backed RUMINANTS (family Camelidae) used as draft and saddle animals in desert regions, especially in Africa and Asia. Adaptations to windblown deserts include double rows of eyelashes, the ability to close the nostrils, and wide-spreading soft feet. Though docile when properly trained, camels can be dangerous. The Bactrian camel *(C. bactrianus)* is about 7 ft (2 m) tall at the top of the two humps; the Arabian camel *(Camelus dromedarius),* or dromedary, has one hump and is 7 ft (2 m) high at the shoulder. When food is available, camels store fat in their humps to be used later for sustenance and to manufacture water. They are thus able to go several days without drinking water.

Bactrian camel (*Camelus bactrianus*).

© GEORGE HOLTON, THE NATIONAL AUDUBON SOCIETY COLLECTION/PHOTO RESEARCHERS

camellia \kə-'mēl-yə\ Any of the East Asian evergreen shrubs and trees that make up the genus *Camellia* in the TEA family (Theaceae), most notable for three ornamental flowering species and for *C. sinensis* (sometimes called *Thea sinensis*), the source of tea. The common camellia *(C. japonica)* is the best known, particularly for its double (many-petaled) cultivated varieties. The tea plant *(C. sinensis),* reaching 30 ft (9 m) in the wild but in cultivation kept to a low, mounded shrub, bears fragrant white, yellow-centered flowers.

Camelot In ARTHURIAN LEGEND, the seat of King Arthur's court. It has been variously identified with Caerleon in Wales, Queen Camel in Somerset, Camelford in Cornwall, Winchester in Hampshire, and Cadbury Castle in Somerset. Camelot has come to symbolize a short-lived golden era under a beloved leader.

"The Rape of Europa," cameo in gold and enamel frame, 16th–17th century; in the Kunsthistorisches Museum, Vienna.

BY COURTESY OF THE KUNSTHISTORISCHES MUSEUM, VIENNA

cameo Hard or precious stone, glass, ceramic, or shell carved in relief above the surface. It is the opposite of INTAGLIO. Cameos survive from the early Sumerian period (c. 3100 BC) to the decline of Roman civilization, and from the Renaissance to the Neoclassical period of the 18th century. They were carved with mythological scenes and portraits, and many commemorated specific persons. In the 18th–19th century, cameos adorned diadems, belts, brooches, and bracelets.

cameo glass Glassware decorated with figures and forms in colored glass carved in relief against a glass background of a contrasting color. It is produced by blowing two layers of glass together. When the glass has cooled, an outline of the design is drawn on the surface and covered with wax. The glass is then etched down to the inner layer, leaving the design outline in relief. Fine cameo glass was produced by the Romans in the 1st century AD. The art was revived by John Northwood in England and EMILE GALLE in France in the late 19th century.

camera Device for recording an image of an object on a light-sensitive surface (see PHOTOGRAPHY). It is essentially a light-tight box with an opening (aperture) to admit light focused onto a sensitized film or plate. All cameras have included five crucial components: (1) the camera box, which holds and protects the sensitive film from all light except that entering through the LENS; (2) film, on which the image is recorded; (3) the light control, consisting of an aperture or diaphragm and a shutter, both often adjustable; (4) the lens, which focuses the light rays from the subject onto the film, creating the image; and (5) the viewing system, which may be separate from the lens system (usually above it) or may operate through it by means of a mirror. The camera was inspired by the camera obscura—a dark enclosure with an aperture (usually provided with a lens) through which light enters to form an image of outside objects on the opposite surface—and was developed by NICEPHORE NIEPCE and L.-J.-M. DAGUERRE in the early 19th century. See also DIGITAL CAMERA.

Camerarius \ˌkam-ə-'rar-ē-əs\, **Rudolph (Jacob)** *German* **Rudolph Camerer** (1665–1721) German botanist. One of the first to perform experiments in heredity, Camerarius demonstrated sexuality in plants by identifying and defining the male and female reproductive parts of the plant and by describing their function in fertilization, showing that pollen is required for the process.

Cameron, James (born 1954) Canadian-U.S. filmmaker. Born in Kapuskasing, Ontario, he later moved to California. His first successful film, *Terminator* (1984), established his reputation. Thereafter he made a series of pictures relying heavily on visual effects, including *Aliens* (1986) and *The Abyss* (1989). His 1998 *Titanic*, which he wrote and directed, won 11 Academy Awards and became the highest-grossing movie in U.S. history.

Cameron, Julia Margaret (1815–1879) British portrait photographer. In 1864, after receiving a camera as a gift, she set up a studio and darkroom and began taking portraits. Her sitters were such friends as ALFRED TENNYSON, HENRY W. LONGFELLOW, and CHARLES DARWIN. Her sensitive portraits of women, such as ELLEN TERRY, are especially noteworthy. Like many Victorian photographers, she made allegorical photographs in imitation of the Pre-Raphaelite paintings of the day. Her technical ability was criticized, but she was more interested in spiritual depth than in technical perfection, and her portraits are considered exceptionally fine.

Cameron, Simon (1799–1889) U.S. politician. Born in Maytown, Pa., he was successful in several businesses before entering the U.S. Senate, where he would serve 1845–49, 1857–61, and 1867–77. As leader of Pennsylvania's Republican Party, he helped secure the nomination of ABRAHAM LINCOLN in 1860. Appointed secretary of war in 1861, he was soon dismissed for showing favoritism in awarding army contracts.

Cameroon *French* **Cameroun** \kȧm-'rün\ *officially* **Republic of Cameroon** Republic, West Africa. Area: 183,591 sq mi (475,501 sq km). Population (1997 est.): 14,678,000. Capital: YAOUNDÉ. The country has more than 200 different ethnic groups, including the FANG (one-fifth of the population), Bamileke (one-fifth), Duala, FULANI, and other smaller groups. Pygmies (locally known as Baguielli and Babinga) live in the southern forests. Languages: French and English (official), local languages. Religions: indigenous religions, Christianity, Islam (predominant in the north). Currency: CFA franc. Cameroon has four geographic regions. The southern area consists of coastal plains and a densely forested plateau. The central region rises progressively to the north and includes the Adamawa Plateau. In the north a savanna plain slopes downward toward the Lake CHAD basin. To the west and north along the

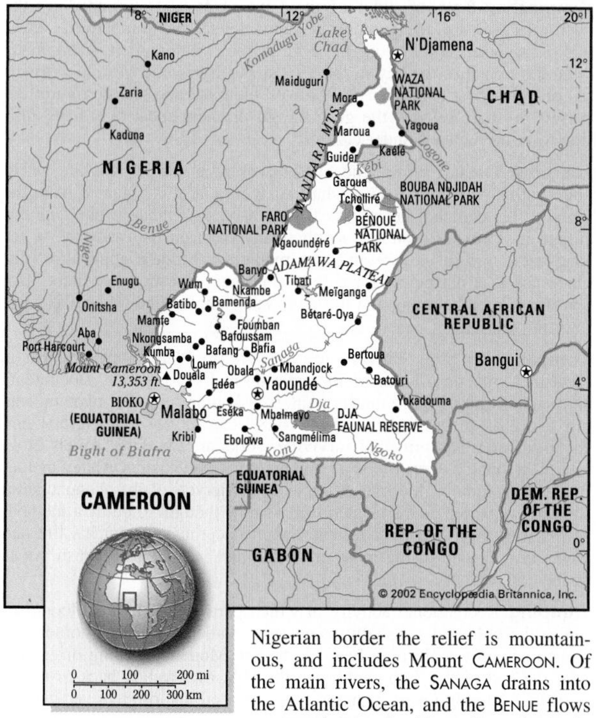

0 100 200 mi
0 100 200 300 km

Nigerian border the relief is mountainous, and includes Mount CAMEROON. Of the main rivers, the SANAGA drains into the Atlantic Ocean, and the BENUE flows westward into the NIGER RIVER basin in Nigeria. Cameroon has a developing market economy based largely on agriculture. It is a republic with one legislative house; its head of state is the president and its head of government, the prime minister. Long inhabited before European colonization, it had BANTU LANGUAGE speakers coming from equatorial Africa to settle in the south. They were followed by Muslim Fulani from the Niger River basin, who settled in the north. Portuguese explorers visited in the late 15th century and established a foothold, but they lost control to the Dutch in the 17th century. In 1884 the Germans took control and extended their protectorate over Cameroon. In World War I joint French-British action forced the Germans to retreat, and after the war the region was divided into French and British administrative zones. After World War II the two areas became U.N. trusteeships. In 1960 the French trust territory became an independent republic. In 1961 the southern part of the British trust territory voted for union with the new republic of Cameroon, and the northern part for union with Nigeria. In recent decades economic problems have produced unrest in the country.

Cameroon, Mt. Volcanic massif, Cameroon. Rising to 13,353 ft (4,070 m), it is the highest peak in West Africa. Extending 14 mi (23 km) inland from the Gulf of GUINEA, it is the westernmost extension of a series of mountains that form a natural boundary between Cameroon and Nigeria. RICHARD BURTON climbed its summit in 1861. The volcano last erupted in 1959.

Camilla In ROMAN MYTHOLOGY, a legendary warrior maiden and favorite of DIANA. According to VIRGIL, her father dedicated her to Diana and trained her as a hunter and warrior, and she led a band of warriors that included women. She fought against AENEAS and was killed as she chased a retreating soldier.

Camillus \kə-'mil-əs\, **Marcus Furius** (died 365 BC) Roman soldier and statesman. He allegedly defeated the Gauls after their sack of Rome (c. 390), for which he was honored as the city's second founder. Awarded four TRIUMPHS and made DICTATOR five times, he enjoyed his greatest victory in 396 over the Etruscans at Veii. Though a PATRICIAN, he adopted reforms beneficial to the army and the PLEBEIANS (367).

Camisards \'kam-ə-ˌzärdz\ Protestant militants in southern France who opposed LOUIS XIV's persecution of Protestantism. The armed insurrection, which began in 1702, came in response to Louis's revocation of the Edict of NANTES, ending religious toleration. The well-organized Camisards, so named for their white shirts (in French dialect, *camisa*), fought successfully and even held royal armies in check. In response, the government burned hundreds of villages and massacred their populations. By 1705, with many of the Camisard leaders captured and executed, the revolt had lost its force.

Camões \kə-'mōiⁿsh\, **Luís (Vaz) de** (1524/25–1580) Portuguese poet. A member of the impoverished aristocracy, he may have spent about 17 years in India. His masterpiece, the epic *The Lusiads* (1572), extols glorious deeds in Portuguese history as it recounts VASCO DA GAMA's discovery of the sea route to India. His numerous lyric pieces (together with many apocryphal poems) appeared posthumously in editions of *Rimas* (from 1595). He also wrote dramatic works, including *Filodemo* (1587), in which he developed the *auto,* a kind of morality play, and the comedy *The Two Amphitryons* (1587). He had an unparalleled impact on Portuguese and Brazilian literature, and is regarded as Portugal's national poet.

camouflage \'ka-mə-ˌfläzh\ Art and practice of concealment and visual deception in war. Its goal is to prevent enemy observation of installations, personnel, equipment, and activities. Camouflage came into wide use in World War I in response to air warfare. Aerial reconnaissance (and later aerial bombardment) required concealment of troops and equipment. By World War II, long-range bombing threatened warring countries in their entirety, and almost everything of military significance was hidden to some degree, using mottled, dull-colored paint patterns (green, gray, or brown), cloth garnishing, netting, and natural foliage. Dummies and decoys, including fake cities and airfields, tricked enemy planes into bombing harmless targets. It remained an important technique after World War II, used with notable success by Communist guerrilla units in the Vietnam War.

Campania \käm-'pä-nyä\ Autonomous region (pop., 1996 est.: 5,763,000), southern Italy. Located on the TYRRHENIAN SEA, its capital is NAPLES. Occupied successively by Greeks, Etruscans, and SAMNITES, it became an ally of Rome from c. 350 BC. It was a favorite resort of the Romans, and is noted for its natural beauty and famous old towns, including CUMAE, POMPEII, Capua, Salernum, and Neapolis (Naples). After the fall of Rome, it was ruled by Gaul, Byzantium, and the Normans, becoming part of the kingdom of Naples in 1282. It was united with Italy in 1861. Its economy is bolstered by agriculture, the industrial area around Naples, and tourism.

campanile \ˌkam-pə-'nē-lē\ Italian belltower, originally built beside or attached to a church. The earliest campaniles (7th–10th century) were plain round towers with a few small arched openings near the top; the LEANING TOWER OF PISA is an elaborate version of this type. The Venetian form of campanile consisted of a tall, square, slim shaft, frequently tapered, with a BELFRY at the top, above which rose the SPIRE, sometimes square as in the famous campanile of ST. MARK'S BASILICA (10th–12th century, belfry story 1510). After falling out of favor during the Renaissance, the Venetian type was revived in the 19th century, often in connection with factories, housing, or collegiate buildings.

campanula See BELLFLOWER

Campbell, John Archibald (1811–1889) U.S. jurist. Born in Washington, Ga., he became a lawyer at age 18 and moved to Alabama, where he gained a large private practice and served in the state legislature. Appointed to the U.S. Supreme Court in 1853, he became known as a strict constructionist and concurred in the DRED SCOTT DECISION. Though he opposed secession as imprudent, he resigned from the Court in 1861 and cast his lot with the South in the American Civil War, serving as assistant secretary of war for the Confederacy. Imprisoned for four months on false charges after Appomattox, he moved to New Orleans on his release and established a law practice there.

Campbell, Joseph (1904–1987) U.S. author of works on comparative mythology. Born in New York City, he studied English literature and taught at Sarah Lawrence College. He explored the common functions of myths in human cultures, examining mythic archetypes in folklore and literature from around the world. His views, strongly influenced by CARL GUSTAV JUNG, were popularized through a public-television series in the 1980s. His books include *The Hero with a Thousand Faces* (1949) and *The Masks of God* (4 vols., 1959–67).

Campbell, Kim *orig.* **Avril Phaedra** (born 1947) Prime minister of Canada (1993). Born in Port Alberni, British Columbia, she practiced law and in 1988 was elected to the federal parliament as a Progressive Conservative. In BRIAN MULRONEY's administration, she became minister for Indian affairs (1989), attorney general (1990), and defense minister (1993). On Mulroney's retirement, she became Canada's first female and first West Coast prime minister in June 1993. Her tenure was brief; her party was defeated in November, and she resigned as party leader.

Campbell, Mrs. Patrick *orig.* **Beatrice Stella Tanner** (1865–1940) British actress. She married at age 19 and made her stage debut in 1888, winning fame as Paula in *The Second Mrs. Tanqueray* in 1893. She originated the role of Eliza Doolittle in GEORGE BERNARD SHAW's *Pygmalion* (1914), and she and Shaw conducted a famous correspondence for many years. She also achieved great success in MAURICE MAETERLINCK's *Pelléas and Mélisande,* HENRIK IBSEN's *Ghosts,* and SOPHOCLES' *Electra.* She made her film debut in *Riptide* (1933) at 68 and later appeared in several more films.

Campbell-Bannerman, Henry *later* **Sir Henry** *orig.* **Henry Campbell** (1836–1908) British politician. A member of the House of Commons from 1868, he was elected leader of the Liberal Party in 1899 and served as prime minister 1905–8. His popularity unified his badly divided party. Though much of his legislative program was nullified by the House of Lords, he obtained approval of the Trades Disputes Act of 1906. He took the lead in granting self-government to the Transvaal and the Orange River Colony, thereby securing the Boers' loyalty to the British empire.

Campbell family \'kam-bəl\ *or* **Campbells of Argyll** \är-'gīl\ Scottish noble family. The Campbells of Lochow gained prominence in the later Middle Ages. In 1457 Colin Campbell, Baron Campbell (died 1493), was created 1st earl of Argyll. Archibald (died 1558), 4th earl, was a leading Protestant. Archibald (1532?–1573), 5th earl, was also a Protestant but supported the Catholic MARY, QUEEN OF SCOTS. Archibald (1607?–1661), 8th earl, was the leader of Scotland's anti-Royalist party in the ENGLISH CIVIL WARS. His son Archibald (1629–1685), 9th earl, was a Protestant leader executed for his opposition to the Roman Catholic king JAMES II. Archibald (1651?–1703), 10th earl, regained the family estates and was created 1st duke of Argyll; he organized the massacre of the Macdonalds of Glencoe. John Campbell (1678–1743), 2nd duke, supported union with England and was commander of the British forces in the JACOBITE rebellion of 1715. Archibald (1682–1761), 3rd duke, was a prominent politician during the early Hanoverian period in Britain. After he died without a legitimate heir, the succession passed to the Campbells of Mamore.

Camp David Rural retreat of U.S. presidents, northern Maryland. The scenic mountainous area (200 acres, or 81 hectares) was established as "Shangri-La" in 1942 by Pres. FRANKLIN ROOSEVELT and made an official presidential retreat by HARRY TRUMAN in 1945. In 1953 DWIGHT D. EISENHOWER renamed it Camp David for his grandson. It has been the scene of a number of high-level presidential conferences with foreign heads of state. See also CAMP DAVID ACCORDS.

Camp David Accords (1978) Two agreements reached between MENACHEM BEGIN of Israel and ANWAR AL-SADAT of Egypt with the help of U.S. Pres. JIMMY CARTER at Camp David, Md. One agreement created a framework for negotiations to arrive at a peace treaty between Egypt and Israel, formally ending some 30 years of war. This treaty, normalizing relations, was signed in 1979. The other agreement created a framework for a broader peace in the region that included a plan for Palestinian self-rule in the WEST BANK and GAZA STRIP. These provisions were not implemented. See also MOSHE DAYAN.

Campeche \käm-'pā-chā\ State (pop., 1995 est.: 643,000), southeastern Mexico. Located on the YUCATÁN PENINSULA, it is bounded by the Gulf of MEXICO, and covers an area of 21,666 sq mi (56,115 sq km); its capital is CAMPECHE. Named after the ancient Mayan province of Kimpech (Campech), it comprises much of the western part of the peninsula. Rivers in the southern part drain into Términos Lagoon, at whose gulf entrance is the area's chief depot, Ciudad del Carmen. Forest products are important to the economy, as is commercial fishing.

Campeche City (pop., 1990: 172,000), capital of CAMPECHE state, Mexico. The Spanish town was founded in 1540 on the site of a MAYAN village, the remains of which are still visible. It became the capital of the newly created Campeche state in 1863. It is a service center for offshore oil facilities.

Campeche, Bay of Inlet of the Gulf of MEXICO. Bounded by the YUCATÁN PENINSULA, the Isthmus of Tehuantepec, and southern VERACRUZ, it covers about 6,000 sq mi (15,500 sq km). Major offshore oil fields were developed in the bay in the 1970s, and it became Mexico's principal oil-producing region. In 1979 a well blew out and released 3 million barrels of crude oil into the gulf; the government spent over $100 million to bring the spill under control.

camphor Organic compound of the ISOPRENOID family. A white, waxy solid with a penetrating, somewhat musty aroma, it is obtained from the wood of the camphor laurel (see LAUREL FAMILY), *Cinnamomum camphora* (found in Asia), or produced synthetically from oil of TURPENTINE. It has long been used in incense and as a medicinal. Modern applications include use as a plasticizer for cellulose nitrate, as a moth repellent, as a flavoring, in embalming, and in fireworks. Camphorated oil is 20% camphor in olive oil.

Campin \'käm-pin\, **Robert** (c. 1375–1444) Flemish painter. He is identified with the Master of Flémalle on stylistic grounds. Documents show that Campin was a master painter in Tournai in 1406; two students are listed as in his studio in 1427–28: ROGIER VAN DER WEYDEN and Jacques Daret. His principal surviving works are two large panels of an altarpiece once believed to have come from a nonexistent Abbey of Flémalle. The famous Mérode Altarpiece, a triptych of the Annunciation formerly regarded as his masterpiece, is now thought to be by a member of his workshop or circle. Despite much uncertainty about his life and work, he was one of the most important and influential Flemish artists of the 15th century.

camping Recreational activity in which participants live outdoors, often in the wilderness, usually using tents, trailers, or motor homes, but sometimes only a sleeping bag, for shelter. Modern camping originated near the end of the 19th century in the U.S. as a rough, back-to-nature pastime for hardy lovers of nature. Canoes were the original vehicle; bicycle camping soon followed. Camping was a major part of the programs of the Boy Scouts and Girl Guides (see SCOUTING). It gained greatly in popularity after World War II. As the number of campgrounds with greater amenities grew, it became the standard holiday for many ordinary families. Recent decades have seen its continued growth, to the point of placing a serious strain on the resources of state and federal outdoor-recreation areas. See also BACKPACKING.

campion Any of the ornamental rock-garden or border plants that make up the genus *Silene,* of the PINK FAMILY, consisting of about 500 species of herbaceous plants found throughout the world. The name is also applied to members of the genus *Lychnis* of the same family. Some species of *Silene* stand erect; others are spreading plants. The stems often are covered with a sticky material. Some species have solitary flowers; others have branched clusters of red, white, or pink flowers. The fruit is a CAPSULE.

Bladder campion (*Silene vulgaris*).

JEWEL CRAIG—THE NATIONAL AUDUBON SOCIETY COLLECTION/PHOTO RESEARCHERS

Campion, Jane (born 1954) New Zealand film director. After training as a painter in Australia, she began studying filmmaking and made several notable short films. Her first feature, *Sweetie* (1989), was followed by the successful *An Angel at My Table* (1990). She wrote and directed the internationally acclaimed *The Piano* (1993) and directed *The Portrait of a Lady* (1996), and *Holy Smoke* (1999).

Campo Formio \,käm-pō-'fȯr-mē-ō\, **Treaty of** (1797) Peace settlement between France and Austria, signed at Campo Formio (now Campoformido, Italy), following Austria's defeat in NAPOLEON's first Italian campaign. The treaty preserved most of the French conquests and completed Napoleon's victory over the First Coalition, the group of European nations opposing him. See also FRENCH REVOLUTIONARY WARS.

Campobasso \,käm-pō-'bä-sō\ City (pop., 1991: 50,000), Italy. Located northeast of NAPLES, it is the capital of MOLISE autonomous region. The old hill town was abandoned in 1732 when its inhabitants built a new town on a lower fertile plain. The old town still has a medieval castle and Romanesque churches; the new town has an archaeological museum.

Campylobacter \'kam-pi-lō-ˌbak-tər\ Genus of gram-negative spiral-shaped BACTERIA infecting mammals. Many species, especially *C. fetus,* cause miscarriage in sheep and cattle. *C. jejuni* is a common cause of FOOD POISONING; perhaps 90% of U.S. chickens are contaminated. Sources also include other meats and unpasteurized milk. Infection causes acute GASTROENTERITIS, fever, headache, and joint and muscle pain; nerve damage and death may occur in severe cases.

Camus \kà-'mǖ\, **Albert** (1913–1960) Algerian-French novelist, essayist, and playwright. Born into a working-class family in Algiers, he worked with a theatrical company after graduating from its university, becoming associated with leftist causes. He spent the war years in Paris, and the French Resistance brought him into the circle of J.-P. SARTRE and EXISTENTIALISM. He became a leading literary figure with his enigmatic first novel, *The Stranger* (1942), a study of 20th-century alienation, and the philosophical essay *The Myth of Sisyphus* (1942), an analysis of contemporary nihilism and the concept of the absurd. *The Plague* (1947), his allegorical second novel, and *The Rebel* (1951), another long essay, developed related issues. Other major works include the novel *The Fall* (1956) and the short-story collection *Exile and the Kingdom* (1957). His plays include *Le malentendu* (1944) and *Caligula* (1944). He won the Nobel Prize in 1957. He died in a car accident.

Canaan \'kā-nən\ Ancient name for an area of shifting boundaries but centered on PALESTINE. Coastal Canaanite civilization dates to the Paleolithic era; towns developed in Neolithic times (c. 7000–4000 BC). The name appears in writings from the 15th century BC. Invaded by the Hebrews (JEWS) c. 1200 BC, who settled in southern areas, it was later invaded by the PHILISTINES. In the 10th century BC the Israelites, under King DAVID, broke the Philistine power, and Canaan became the Land of Israel, the "Promised Land" of the biblical book of EXODUS.

Canada Nation, North America. Area: 3,851,808 sq mi (9,976,185 sq km). Population (2002 est.): 31,244,000. Capital: OTTAWA. People of British and French descent compose more than half the population; there are significant minorities of German, Italian, Ukrainian, Chinese, Dutch, American Indian, and ESKIMO (Inuit) origin. Languages: English, French (both official). Religions: Roman Catholicism, Protestantism (United Church of Canada, Anglican Church of Canada). Currency: Canadian dollar. Canada may be divided into several physiographic regions. A large interior basin centered on HUDSON BAY and covering nearly four-fifths of the country is composed of the CANADIAN (LAURENTIAN) SHIELD, the interior plains, and the Great Lakes-St. Lawrence lowlands. Rimming the basin are highland regions, including the ARCTIC ARCHIPELAGO. Its mountains include the ROCKY MTNS., Coast Mtns., and Laurentian Mountains. Its highest peak is Mount LOGAN in YUKON TERRITORY. Five of Canada's rivers—the ST. LAWRENCE, MACKENZIE, YUKON, FRASER, and NELSON—rank among the world's 40 largest. In addition to Lakes SUPERIOR and HURON, both shared with the U.S., Canada's GREAT BEAR and GREAT SLAVE lakes are among the world's 11 largest lakes. The country also includes several major islands, including BAFFIN, ELLESMERE, VICTORIA, NEWFOUNDLAND, and MELVILLE, and many small ones. Its border with the U.S., the longest unguarded border in the world, extends 3,987 mi (6,415 km). With a developed market economy that is export-directed and closely linked with that of the U.S., Canada is one of the world's most prosperous nations. It is a parliamentary state with two legislative houses; its chief of state is the British monarch, whose representative is Canada's governor-general, and the head of government is the prime minister. Originally inhabited by American Indians and Inuit, Canada was visited c. AD 1000 by Scandinavian explorers, whose discovery is confirmed by archaeological evidence from Newfoundland. Fishing expeditions off Newfoundland by the English, French, Spanish, and Portuguese began as early as 1500. The French claim to Canada was made in 1534 when JACQUES CARTIER entered the Gulf of ST. LAWRENCE. A small settlement was made in NOVA SCOTIA (Arcadia) in 1605, and by 1608 SAMUEL DE CHAMPLAIN had reached Quebec. Fur trading was the impetus behind the early colonizing efforts. In response to French activity, the English in 1670 formed the HUDSON'S BAY CO. The British–French rivalry for the interior of upper North America lasted almost a century. The first French loss occurred in 1713 at the conclusion of QUEEN ANNE'S WAR (War of the SPANISH SUCCESSION) when Nova Scotia and Newfoundland were ceded to the British. The SEVEN YEARS' WAR (FRENCH AND INDIAN WAR) resulted in France's expulsion from continental North America in 1763. After the AMERICAN REVOLUTION the population was augmented by LOYALISTS fleeing the U.S., and the increasing number arriving in Quebec led the British to divide the colony into Upper and Lower Canada in 1791. The British reunited the two provinces in 1841. Canadian expansionism resulted in the confederation movement of the mid-19th century, and in 1867 the Dominion of Canada, comprising Nova Scotia, New Brunswick, Quebec, and Ontario, came into existence. After confederation, Canada entered a period of westward expansion. The prosperity that accompanied Canada into the 20th century was marred by continuing conflict between the English and French communities. Through the Statute of WESTMINSTER (1931), Canada was recognized as an equal partner of Great Britain. With the CANADA ACT of 1982, the British gave Canada total control over its constitution and severed the remaining legal connections between the two countries. French-Canadian unrest continued to be a major concern, with a movement growing for Quebec separatism in the late 20th century. Referendums for more political autonomy for Quebec were rejected in 1992 and 1995, but the issue remained unresolved. In 1999 Canada formed the new territory of NUNAVUT. See map on following page.

Canadian Prime Ministers

John A. Macdonald	1867–73	Richard Bedford Bennett	1930–35
Alexander Mackenzie	1873–78	W. L. Mackenzie King	1935–48
John A. Macdonald	1878–91	Louis St. Laurent	1948–57
John Abbott	1891–92	John G. Diefenbaker	1957–63
John Thompson	1892–94	Lester B. Pearson	1963–68
Mackenzie Bowell	1894–96	Pierre Elliott Trudeau	1968–79
Charles Tupper	1896	Joseph Clark	1979–80
Wilfred Laurier	1896–1911	Pierre Elliott Trudeau	1980–84
Robert Laird Borden	1911–20	John N. Turner	1984
Arthur Meighen	1920–21	Brian Mulroney	1984–93
W. L. Mackenzie King	1921–26	Kim Campbell	1993
Arthur Meighen	1926	Jean Chrétien	1993–
W. L. Mackenzie King	1926–30		

Canada, Bank of Canadian financial institution established under the Bank of Canada Act (1934). It was founded during the Great Depression to regulate CREDIT and CURRENCY. The Bank acts as the Canadian government's fiscal agent and has the sole right to issue paper money. It is directed by the Canadian Ministry of Finance; all profits go to the Receiver General of Canada.

Canada Act *or* **Constitution Act** Measure formally ending British power to legislate for Canada,. approved by the British Parliament on March 25, 1982, and proclaimed by Queen ELIZABETH II on April 17, 1982. The document contains the BRITISH NORTH AMERICA ACT and was approved by all the Canadian provinces except Quebec, which was denied its claim for a constitutional veto by Canada's Supreme Court.

Canada Bill See CONSTITUTIONAL ACT (1791)

Canada Company Organization instrumental in colonizing much of the western part of Upper Canada (now Ontario). The company was formed in 1824 to bring settlers to the region. It was directed until 1829 by John Galt (1779–1839), founder of Guelph and father of ALEXANDER GALT. Though the company, chartered with 2.5 million acres, was criticized as a monopoly, it continued to exist until the 1950s.

Canada Day *formerly* **Dominion Day** Annual Canadian holiday. Observed on July 1, it commemorates the formation of the Dominion of Canada on July 1, 1867. With the 1982 passage of the CANADA ACT, its name was officially changed to Canada Day. It is celebrated with parades, fireworks, flag display, and the singing of the national anthem, "O Canada."

Canada East *or* **Lower Canada** Region of Canada now known as QUEBEC. In 1791–1841 it was known as Lower Canada and in 1841–67 as Canada East. Populated mainly by French settlers who wanted to preserve their distinctive identity and cultural traditions, it was reluctant to join the proposed confederation with CANADA WEST. It finally agreed to confederation in 1867, providing that it would remain a territorial and governmental unit in which French Canadians would have an electoral majority.

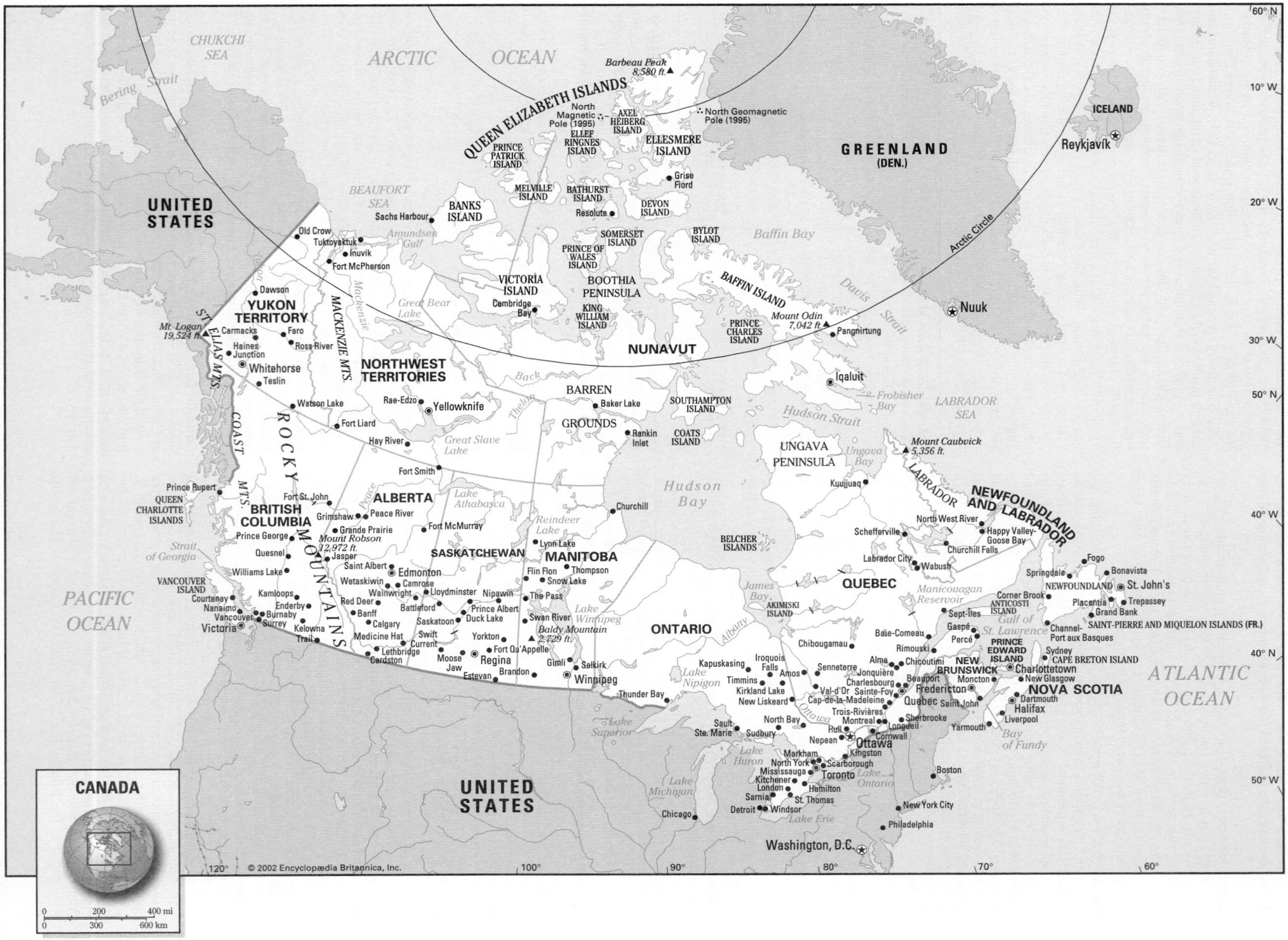
CANADA
0 200 400 mi
0 300 600 km
ARCTIC OCEAN
CHUKCHI SEA
Bering Strait
BEAUFORT SEA
Amundsen Gulf
UNITED STATES
QUEEN ELIZABETH ISLANDS
Barbeau Peak 8,580 ft.
North Magnetic Pole (1995)
North Geomagnetic Pole (1995)
AXEL HEIBERG ISLAND
ELLEF RINGNES ISLAND
ELLESMERE ISLAND
PRINCE PATRICK ISLAND
MELVILLE ISLAND
BATHURST ISLAND
Grise Fiord
DEVON ISLAND
Resolute
BANKS ISLAND
Sachs Harbour
SOMERSET ISLAND
BYLOT ISLAND
PRINCE OF WALES ISLAND
VICTORIA ISLAND
Cambridge Bay
BOOTHIA PENINSULA
KING WILLIAM ISLAND
BAFFIN ISLAND
Mount Odin 7,042 ft.
Pangnirtung
PRINCE CHARLES ISLAND
Baffin Bay
Davis Strait
GREENLAND (DEN.)
Nuuk
Arctic Circle
ICELAND
Reykjavík
NUNAVUT
Iqaluit
Frobisher Bay
LABRADOR SEA
Hudson Strait
SOUTHAMPTON ISLAND
COATS ISLAND
Rankin Inlet
Baker Lake
BARREN GROUNDS
Back
Thelon
Old Crow
Tuktoyaktuk
Inuvik
Fort McPherson
Mackenzie
MACKENZIE MTS.
Great Bear Lake
Dawson
Yukon
YUKON TERRITORY
Mt. Logan 19,524 ft.
ST. ELIAS MTS.
Carmacks
Faro
Ross River
Haines Junction
Whitehorse
Teslin
NORTHWEST TERRITORIES
Rae-Edzo
Yellowknife
Watson Lake
Fort Liard
Hay River
Great Slave Lake
Fort Smith
COAST MTS.
ROCKY MOUNTAINS
Prince Rupert
QUEEN CHARLOTTE ISLANDS
BRITISH COLUMBIA
Fort St. John
Peace
ALBERTA
Grimshaw
Peace River
Grande Prairie
Mount Robson 12,972 ft.
Jasper
Prince George
Quesnel
Williams Lake
Strait of Georgia
VANCOUVER ISLAND
Courtenay
Nanaimo
Vancouver
Burnaby
Surrey
Victoria
Kamloops
Enderby
Kelowna
Trail
PACIFIC OCEAN
Lake Athabasca
Fort McMurray
Saint Albert
Edmonton
Wetaskiwin
Camrose
Wainwright
Lloydminster
Red Deer
Banff
Calgary
Battleford
Medicine Hat
Lethbridge
Cardston
Swift Current
SASKATCHEWAN
Saskatoon
Nipawin
Prince Albert
Duck Lake
Yorkton
Moose Jaw
Regina
Fort Qu'Appelle
Estevan
Brandon
Reindeer Lake
Lynn Lake
MANITOBA
Flin Flon
Thompson
Snow Lake
The Pass
Swan River
Lake Winnipeg
Baldy Mountain 2,729 ft.
Gimli
Selkirk
Winnipeg
Churchill
Hudson Bay
UNGAVA PENINSULA
Ungava Bay
Kuujjuaq
Mount Caubvick 5,356 ft.
LABRADOR
NEWFOUNDLAND AND LABRADOR
North West River
Happy Valley-Goose Bay
Churchill Falls
Schefferville
Labrador City
Wabush
BELCHER ISLANDS
James Bay
AKIMISKI ISLAND
Albany
ONTARIO
QUEBEC
Manicouagan Reservoir
Thunder Bay
Lake Nipigon
Kapuskasing
Iroquois Falls
Timmins
Kirkland Lake
New Liskeard
Amos
Chibougamau
Senneterre
Val-d'Or
Lake Superior
Sault Ste. Marie
Sudbury
North Bay
Ottawa
Lake Huron
Lake Michigan
Chicago
Nepean
Hull
Ottawa
Markham
North York
Mississauga
Kitchener
London
Sarnia
Detroit
Windsor
Scarborough
Toronto
Hamilton
St. Thomas
Kingston
Cornwall
Lake Ontario
Lake Erie
Montreal
Longueuil
Trois-Rivières
Cap-de-la-Madeleine
Sainte-Foy
Charlesbourg
Jonquière
Alma
Chicoutimi
Beauport
Quebec
Sherbrooke
Baie-Comeau
Rimouski
Sept-Îles
Gaspé
Percé
Gulf of St. Lawrence
ANTICOSTI ISLAND
NEW BRUNSWICK
Fredericton
Saint John
Moncton
PRINCE EDWARD ISLAND
Charlottetown
NOVA SCOTIA
New Glasgow
Dartmouth
Halifax
Liverpool
Yarmouth
Bay of Fundy
Sydney
CAPE BRETON ISLAND
Channel-Port aux Basques
SAINT-PIERRE AND MIQUELON ISLANDS (FR.)
NEWFOUNDLAND
Corner Brook
Springdale
Fogo
Bonavista
St. John's
Placentia
Trepassey
Grand Bank
ATLANTIC OCEAN
Boston
New York City
Philadelphia
Washington, D.C.
60° N
50° N
40° N
10° W
20° W
30° W
40° W
50° W
120°
100°
90°
80°
70°
60°
© 2002 Encyclopædia Britannica, Inc.

Canada goose Brown-backed, light-breasted GOOSE *(Branta canadensis)* with black head and neck and white cheeks. Subspecies vary in size, from the 3-lb (1.4-kg) cackling goose to the 20-lb (8-kg) giant Canada goose, which has a wingspread of up to 6.5 ft (2 m). Canada geese breed across Canada and Alaska and winter mainly in the southern U.S. and Mexico; they have been introduced into England and other countries. They are an important game bird. Their almost incessant honking draws attention to their V-formations during migrations. In recent years their population in North America has greatly increased.

Canada goose (*Branta canadensis*).
LEONARD LEE RUE III

Canada West *or* **Upper Canada** Region of Canada now known as ONTARIO. In 1791–1841 it was known as Upper Canada and in 1841–67 as Canada West. Settled primarily by English-speaking immigrants, it sought confederation with CANADA EAST in order to secure the unified government needed for effective administration and the construction of intercolonial railways. The unified Dominion of Canada was made official by the BRITISH NORTH AMERICA ACT of 1867.

Canadian Alliance *French* **Alliance Canadienne** Conservative Canadian political party. The Canadian Alliance was created in 2000 from the merger of the former Reform Party of Canada with other conservative groups in an effort to mount a united challenge to the ruling LIBERAL PARTY OF CANADA. By 1997 the Reform Party, whose support had been concentrated in the western Canadian provinces, held 60 seats in the Canadian House of Commons and had become the official opposition party. The new Canadian Alliance gained 66 seats in the 2000 election and remained the official opposition, though it was unable to make significant inroads in eastern Canada. The party's platform generally favors a reduction in the size of government, lower taxes, and conservative positions on social issues.

Canadian Broadcasting Corp. (CBC) Canadian public broadcasting service, created in 1936 to promote Canadian culture and serve as an instrument of national unity. It offers French- and English-language programs over AM and FM radio networks, television networks, cable television channels, and shortwave radio. Noted for its news and public-affairs programs, the CBC also presents documentaries, dramas, classical music, entertainment, and educational programs as well as sports programs.

Canadian Football League Major Canadian professional FOOTBALL organization, formed in 1958. The league's Western Conference includes teams from Edmonton, Calgary, British Columbia, Saskatchewan, and Winnipeg; its Eastern Conference comprises teams from Hamilton, Montreal, Toronto, and Ottawa. The conference winners compete for the Grey Cup.

Canadian Labor Congress (CLC) Nationwide association of labor unions in Canada, formed in 1956 by the merger of the Canadian counterparts to the American Federation of Labor and the Congress of Industrial Organizations, which merged the same year (see AFL-CIO). Today, most of the 4 million unionized workers in English-speaking Canada are members of CLC-affiliated unions.

Canadian National Railway Co. Corporation created by the Canadian government in 1918 to operate a number of nationalized railroads (including the old Grand Trunk lines, Intercolonial Railway, National Transcontinental Railway, and Canadian Northern Railway) as one of Canada's two transcontinental railroad systems. Its passenger services were taken over by VIA Rail Canada in 1978, and the company was privatized in 1995. The Canadian National Railway stretches across Canada from Nova Scotia to Vancouver. It bought the Illinois Central Corp. in 1998, thus acquiring a railroad network that links Canada to the Gulf of Mexico.

Canadian Pacific Ltd. Privately owned company that operates one of Canada's two transcontinental railroad systems. The company was created in 1881 to complete a railroad from Montreal to Port Moody in British Columbia. Its passenger services were taken over by VIA Rail Canada in 1978. It now owns subsidiaries in such industries as oil and gas, minerals, forest products, and real estate; railroads account for only a small part of its earnings.

Canadian River River, southwestern U.S. Flowing across northeastern New Mexico, it cuts a gorge nearly 1,500 ft (450 m) deep before turning eastward to continue across northwestern Texas and through central Oklahoma to the ARKANSAS RIVER in Oklahoma. It is 906 mi (1,458 km) long. Its course is punctuated by flood-control and irrigation units.

Canadian Shield One of the world's largest geologic CONTINENTAL SHIELDS, centered on Hudson Bay and extending for 3 million sq mi (8 million sq km) over Canada from the Great Lakes to the Canadian Arctic and into Greenland, with small extensions into northern Minnesota, Wisconsin, Michigan, and New York. It is the largest mass of exposed PRECAMBRIAN rock on earth. The region as a whole is composed of ancient crystalline rocks whose complex structure attests to a long history of uplift and depression, mountain building, and erosion.

canal Artificial waterway built for transportation, irrigation, water supply, or drainage. The early Middle Eastern civilizations probably first built canals to supply drinking and irrigation water. The most ambitious navigation canal was a 200-mi (320-km) construction in what is now Iraq. Roman canal systems for military transport extended throughout northern Europe and Britain. The most significant canal innovation was the pound lock, developed by the Dutch c. 1373. The closed chamber, or pound, of a lock is flooded or drained of water so that a vessel within it is raised or lowered in order to pass between bodies of water at different elevations. Canals were extremely important before the coming of the railroad in the mid-19th century. Among the significant waterways in the U.S. were the ERIE CANAL, several canals linking the Great Lakes, and one connecting the Great Lakes to the Mississippi River. Modern waterway engineering enables larger vessels to travel faster by reducing delays at locks. See also GRAND CANAL, PANAMA CANAL, SUEZ CANAL.

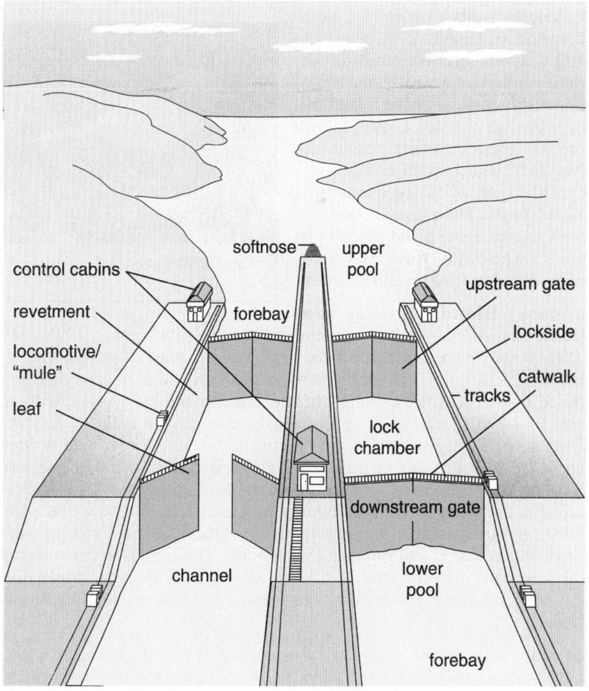

Canal with a basic lock arrangement. Boats traveling upstream pass from the lower to the upper pool through the chamber (or pound) on the left; downstream traffic uses the pound on the right.

Canal Zone *or* **Panama Canal Zone** Strip of territory, Panama, a historic administrative entity in Panama over which the U.S. exercised jurisdictional rights 1903–79. The zone came into being in 1904 when

Panama granted to the U.S., in return for annual payments, the sole right to operate and control the PANAMA CANAL, including a strip of land 10 mi (16 km) wide along the canal extending from the Atlantic to the Pacific Ocean and bisecting the Isthmus of Panama. The zone was abolished by treaty in 1979, with the return to Panama of civil control. By the same treaty a commission under joint American–Panamanian ownership was established to operate the canal until the year 2000, when Panama assumed full control.

Canaletto \ˌka-nᵊl-ˈe-tō\ *orig.* **Giovanni Antonio Canal** (1697–1768) Italian painter and etcher active in Venice. He was trained in the studio of his father, a theatrical scene painter. From 1719 to 1720 he worked in Rome, painting scenes for operas, until he turned to painting topographical images. After his return to Venice, he produced the picturesque views *(vedute)* that would bring him international fame. His pictures provide dramatic views of Venetian architecture and demonstrate skill in rendering sunlight and shadow. In the 1730s he was kept busy meeting foreign visitors' demand for souvenir views of Venice. When the War of the AUSTRIAN SUCCESSION made foreign visitors scarce, he expanded his output to include imaginative views of Roman ruins, and in 1746 he went to England to paint views of London and the great English country houses. In 1763 he was elected to the Venetian Academy. The most famous topographical painter of the 18th century, he influenced succeeding generations of landscape artists. He is not to be confused with his nephew BERNARDO BELLOTTO, also known as Canaletto.

Canaris \kä-ˈnä-rəs\, **Wilhelm (Franz)** (1887–1945) German naval officer. Under ADOLF HITLER, Canaris became head of military intelligence (Abwehr) in 1935. Believing that the Nazi regime would destroy traditional conservative values and that its foreign ambitions were dangerous to Germany, he enlisted some of the anti-Hitler conspirators into the Abwehr and shielded their activities. After the abortive JULY PLOT against Hitler in 1944, Canaris was arrested and executed.

canary Popular cage bird (*Serinus canaria;* in the GOLDFINCH family, Carduelidae) that owes its coloration and sustained vocal powers to 400 years of selective breeding. Varieties called rollers trill almost continuously; choppers have a loud trill of distinct notes. Well-known breeds include Hartz Mountain, Norwich, and Yorkshire. The average life span of a caged canary is 10–15 years. The canary is native to the Canary, Azores, and Madeira islands. The wild form is streak-backed and mostly greenish brown.

Canary (*Serinus canaria*).
ERIC HOSKING

Canary Islands *Spanish* **Islas Canarias** Island group, autonomous community (pop., 1996 est.: 1,607,000), Spain. Located off the northwestern coast of Africa, the islands lie 823 mi (1,324 km) southwest of the Spanish mainland. Composed of two provinces, Santa Cruz de Tenerife and LAS PALMAS, with an area of 2,796 sq mi (7,242 sq km), the islands' capital is SANTA CRUZ DE TENERIFE. Anciently known as the "Fortunate Islands," they were written about by both PLUTARCH and PLINY THE ELDER. Believed to be the western limit of the world, they were visited in the Middle Ages by Arabs, Portuguese, and French. They were taken by Castile (see CASTILLA Y LEÓN) in 1402, and their indigenous inhabitants, the Guanche and Canario, were gradually conquered during the 15th century. The islands became a stop on the usual route for Spanish trading vessels with the New World. Today agriculture is an economic mainstay, as is an expanding tourist trade.

canasta \kə-ˈnas-tə\ Form of RUMMY, using two full decks, in which players or partnerships try to meld groups of three or more cards of the same rank and score bonuses for seven-card melds. Eleven cards are dealt to each player, the undealt portion of the pack is placed on the table, and the top card is turned up to start the discard pile. Each player in turn must draw, may meld, and must discard one card. A hand ends when a player melds his last card (goes out). Canasta originated in Uruguay in the late 1940s; its name (meaning "basket") is probably a reference to the tray for holding discards.

Canaveral \kə-ˈna-və-rəl\, **Cape** Cape, eastern Florida. It is the location of NASA's John F. Kennedy Space Center and the launch site of U.S. space flights, including the first U.S. manned space flight in 1961 and the first lunar-landing flight in 1969, as well as the explosion of the space shuttle *CHALLENGER* in 1986. After the death of Pres. JOHN F. KENNEDY in 1963, it was renamed Cape Kennedy; it reverted to its original name in 1973.

Canberra \ˈkan-ber-ə\ City (pop., 1995: 332,000), capital of Australia. Located in the AUSTRALIAN CAPITAL TERRITORY, on the Molonglo River, it was chosen in 1908 as the site of the capital. An international competition held in 1912 chose the U.S. architect Walter B. Griffin (1876–1937) to design the city, and construction began in 1913. The transfer of Parliament from MELBOURNE took place in 1927. The city continues to expand, with residential development taking place in satellite towns. There is light industry and a growing tourist trade, though government functions dominate.

A statue by Henry Moore sits on the grounds of the National Library of Australia in Canberra.
ROBIN SMITH PHOTOGRAPHY, NEW SOUTH WALES

Cancer (Latin: "Crab") In astronomy, the constellation lying between Leo and Gemini; in ASTROLOGY, the fourth sign of the ZODIAC, governing approximately the period June 22–July 22. It is represented as a crab (or crayfish), a reference to the crab in Greek mythology that pinched HERACLES while he was fighting the Lernaean hydra. Heracles crushed the crab, but his enemy Hera rewarded it by placing it in the sky as a constellation.

cancer Uncontrolled multiplication of abnormal cells. Cancerous cells and tissues have abnormal growth rates, shapes and sizes, and functioning. Cancer may progress from a localized TUMOR (confined to the site of origin) to direct extension (spread into nearby tissue or lymph nodes) and metastasis (spread to more distant sites via the blood or lymphatic system). This malignant growth pattern distinguishes cancerous tumors from benign ones. Cancer is also classified by grade, the extent to which cell characteristics remain specific to their tissue of origin. Both stage and grade affect the chances of survival. Genetic factors and immune status affect susceptibility. Triggers include hormones, viruses, smoking, diet, and radiation. Cancer can begin in almost any tissue, including blood (see LEUKEMIA) and lymph (see LYMPHOMA). When it metastasizes, it remains a cancer of its tissue of origin. Early diagnosis and treatment increase the chance of cure. Treatment may include CHEMOTHERAPY, surgery, and RADIATION THERAPY. See also BREAST CANCER, CARCINOGEN, KAPOSI'S SARCOMA, LARYNGEAL CANCER, LUNG CANCER, SKIN CANCER.

Cancer, Tropic of See TROPIC OF CANCER

Cancún \kan-ˈkün\ City (pop., 1990: 168,000) and island resort, southeastern Mexico. The city, on the northeastern coast of the YUCATÁN PENINSULA, is a service town for the resort on Cancún Island (13 mi, or 21 km, long), which is connected by a causeway to the city. Originally settled by MAYA Indians, the area was first described by JOHN LLOYD STEPHENS in his *Incidents of Travel in Yucatán* (1843). Cancún remained a fishing village until in 1970 the area was selected as a suitable site for a resort. The plan proved hugely successful; today Cancún is Mexico's busiest resort.

Candela \kän-'dā-lə\, **Felix** (1910–1997) Spanish-Mexican engineer and architect. He emigrated to Mexico in 1939 and began to design and construct buildings there. His ferroconcrete structures are distinguished by thin, curved shells that are extremely strong and economical; his imaginative use of paraboloid barrel-vaulting helped dispel mistaken notions of the limits of this material. Notable works include the expressionistic church of Nuestra Señora de los Milagros in Mexico City (1955), with a hyperbolic paraboloid roof of ferroconcrete only 1.5 in. (3.8 cm) thick.

candida \'kan-də-də\ Any of the parasitic imperfect fungi (see FUNGUS) that make up the genus *Candida,* which resemble YEASTS and occur especially in the mouth, vagina, and intestinal tract. Though usually benign, candidas can become pathogenic, causing diseases including candidiasis and thrush.

Candlemas (February 2) In the Christian church, the celebration of the presentation of the infant JESUS and the post-childbirth purification of MARY in the Temple, in accordance with Jewish law. The Greek church calls it Hypapante ("Meeting") in reference to Jesus' meeting there with Simeon, to whom it had been revealed that he would not die before meeting the Messiah. The festival is first documented in Jerusalem in the late 4th century; the custom of observing it with lighted candles (the source of its name) dates to at least the mid-5th century. See also GROUNDHOG DAY.

Candolle \kä^n-'dȯl\, **Augustin (Pyrame de)** (1778–1841) Swiss botanist. In Paris (from 1796) he became an assistant to GEORGES CUVIER and worked with J.-B. LAMARCK on revising his botanical works. He carried out a government-commissioned botanical and agricultural survey of France (1806–12). In 1813 he published his most important work, *Théorie élémentaire de la botanique*, in which he contended that plant ANATOMY, not PHYSIOLOGY, must be the basis of classification, for which he coined the term TAXONOMY. He introduced the concept of homologous parts for plants (following Cuvier's work on animals). From 1817 until his death he taught at the University of Geneva. He outlined systematic laws of botanical nomenclature (1818–21); his taxonomy suffered from certain weaknesses, but he achieved extensive subdivision of FLOWERING PLANTS, describing 161 families of dicotyledons, and his system supplanted that of CAROLUS LINNAEUS. He completed seven volumes of a descriptive classification of all known seed plants (from 1824).

Candomblé \ˌkan-dōm-'blā\ Major expression of Afro-Brazilian religion. Most prominent in the Brazilian state of Bahia, Candomblé is the most African of the Afro-Brazilian sects. Its deities, called *orixás,* have personalities (often capricious) and are associated with occupations, colors, days of the week, and natural phenomena. Rituals include the sacrifice of animals (such as cocks), spirit offerings (such as flowers), and dances. See also MACUMBA, VODUN.

Candra Gupta \'kən-drə-'gu̇p-tə\ *or* **Maurya** (r.321?–297? BC) Founder of the Maurya dynasty and the first emperor to unify most of India under one administration (see MAURYAN EMPIRE). Born to a destitute migrant Mauryan family, he was sold into slavery and eventually purchased by a Brahman politician, who gave him an education in military tactics and the arts. Candra Gupta gathered mercenary soldiers, secured public support, overthrew the NANDA DYNASTY, and established his own in modern-day Bihar. On the death of ALEXANDER THE GREAT (323 BC), he won control of the Punjab (c. 322). He expanded his empire east to borders of Persia, south to India's tip, and north to the Himalayas and the Kabul valley. His administration was patterned on that of the Persian ACHAEMENIAN DYNASTY (559–330 BC). He died fasting in sympathy for his people during a time of famine.

Candra Gupta II *or* **Vikramaditya** (r.380?–415?) Powerful emperor of the GUPTA DYNASTY (4th–6th century) of northern India and grandson of Candra Gupta I (r.320–c. 330). He is thought to have achieved power by assassinating a weak elder brother. He inherited a large empire and extended control over neighboring territories through battle and marriage alliances. Under him, India enjoyed peace and relative prosperity. His system of government and his charity were admired by the Chinese pilgrim FAXIAN. He was a patron of the poet KALIDASA. Though a devout Hindu, he tolerated the Buddhist and Jain religions.

candy Sweet SUGAR- or CACAO-based confection. The Egyptians made candy from HONEY (combined with figs, dates, nuts, and spices), sugar being unknown. With the spread of SUGARCANE cultivation in the 15th century, the industry began to grow. In the late 18th century the first candy manufacturing machinery was produced. The main ingredients are cane and beet sugars combined with other carbohydrate foods such as CORN SYRUP, cornstarch, honey, molasses, and maple sugar. To the sweet base are added CHOCOLATE, fruits, nuts, peanuts, eggs, milk, flavors, and colors. Common varieties include hard candy (crystallized sugar), caramels and toffee, nougats, jellies, marshmallows, marzipan, truffles, cotton candy, licorice, and chewing gum.

cane Hollow or pithy and usually slender and flexible jointed stem (as of a REED). Also, any of various slender woody stems, especially an elongated flowering or fruiting stem (as of a rose) usually arising directly from the ground. The term is also applied to any of various tall woody GRASSES or reeds, including the coarse grasses of the genus *Arundinaria* (see BAMBOO), SUGARCANE, and SORGHUM.

Canetti, Elias (1905–1994) Bulgarian-British novelist and playwright. From a Spanish-speaking Jewish family, his early life was highly cosmopolitan. His best-known work, the novel *Auto-da-Fé* (1935), deals with the dangers in believing that detached intellectualism can prevail over evil and chaos. He settled in Britain in 1938. Later works that reflect his interest in the psychopathology of power include *Crowds and Power* (1960), the plays *The Wedding* (1932), *Comedy of Vanity* (1950), and *Life-Terms* (1964), and his series of autobiographies beginning with *The Tongue Set Free* (1977). He was awarded the Nobel Prize in 1981.

Canetti.
HORST TAPPE/CAMERA PRESS/GLOBE PHOTOS

Cange, Charles du Fresne, seigneur du See Charles du Fresne, seigneur DU CANGE

canine *or* **canid** \'kā-nəd, 'kā-nəd\ Any domestic or wild DOG or doglike mammal (e.g., WOLF, JACKAL, FOX) in the family Canidae, found throughout the world except in Antarctica and on most ocean islands. Canines tend to be slender and long-legged, with a long muzzle, bushy tail, erect pointed ears, and well-developed canine and cheek teeth. They prey on all types of animals; some also eat carrion and vegetable matter. They probably were the first animals to be domesticated. Though helpful in controlling rodent and rabbit populations, canines have been hunted for their pelts and slaughtered to prevent their reputed (and sometimes real) destruction of livestock and large game.

cankerworm See LOOPER

canna Any of the tropical herbaceous plants that make up the family Cannaceae, of the GINGER order (Zingiberales), containing a single genus with about 55 species, found from southeastern North America through South America. Cannas have RHIZOMES with erect stems growing to 10 ft (3 m) high. The green or bronze leaves are spirally arranged. The flowers are asymmetrical. Spotted variations of the scarlet, red-orange, or yellow flowers sometimes occur. The genus *Canna* is widely grown for ornamental use. *C. edulis,* from Peru, has edible, starchy rhizomes.

cannabis \'ka-nə-bəs\ Any plant of the genus *Cannabis,* which contains a single species, *C. sativa.* It is widely cultivated throughout the northern temperate zone. HEMP fiber is obtained from a tall, canelike variety, while MARIJUANA is obtained from the female plant of a smaller variety.

Cannae \'ka-nē\, **Battle of** (216 BC) Major battle near the ancient village of Cannae, in Apulia, southeastern Italy, during the Second PUNIC WAR. The Romans, with 80,000 men to the Carthaginians' 50,000, were crushed by HANNIBAL's Carthaginians and allied Africans, Gauls, and Spaniards. Hannibal's troops gradually surrounded their foe and annihilated them in a classic example of the "double envelopment" maneuver.

C D

Roman losses exceeded 65,000 men, while the Carthaginians lost only about 6,000.

Cannes \'kån\ City (pop., 1990: 69,000), southeastern France. Located on the Mediterranean Sea southwest of NICE, it is an international resort. Probably settled by Ligurians, it was occupied successively by Phocaeans, Celts, and Romans. In the 10th century the monks of Lérins built fortifications to guard against Muslim sea raiders. NAPOLEON, on his return from ELBA in 1815, camped nearby. A resort since the 19th century, the city is home to the CANNES FILM FESTIVAL.

Cannes Film Festival \'kån\ Film festival held annually in Cannes, France. First held in 1946 for the recognition of artistic achievement, the festival came to provide a rendezvous for those interested in the art and influence of the movies. Like other film festivals, it became an international marketplace where producers and distributors could exchange ideas, view films, and sign contracts. The phenomenon of international coproduction arose at Cannes in the late 1940s. The festival was at times the site of artistic contention as well, as in 1958–59, when advocates and opponents of the French NEW WAVE exchanged diatribes and manifestos.

cannibalism Eating of human flesh by humans. The term derives from the Spanish name (*Caríbales,* or *Caníbales*) for the Carib people, first encountered by Columbus. Reliable firsthand accounts of the practice are comparatively rare, causing some to question whether full-blown cannibalism has ever existed. Most agree that the consumption of particular portions or organs was a ritual means by which certain qualities of the person eaten might be obtained or by which powers of WITCHCRAFT OR SORCERY might be exercised. In some cases, a small portion of the dead person was ritually eaten by relatives. Headhunters (see HEADHUNTING) sometimes consumed bits of the bodies or heads of deceased enemies. The AZTECS apparently practiced cannibalism on a large scale as part of the ritual of HUMAN SACRIFICE.

cannibalism In zoology, the eating of any animal by another member of the same species. Certain ANTS regularly consume injured immatures and, when food is scarce, eat healthy immatures; this practice allows the adults to survive the food shortage and live to breed again. Male LIONS taking over a pride may kill and eat the existing young. After losing her cubs the mother will become impregnated by the new dominant male, thereby ensuring his genetic contribution. Aquarium GUPPIES sometimes regulate their population size by eating most of their young.

canning Method of preserving food from spoilage by storing it in containers that are hermetically sealed and then sterilized by heat. The process was invented in 1809 by Nicolas Appert (c. 1750–1841) of France, who used glass bottles. In the 19th century tin-coated iron cans with soldered tops, bottoms, and seams were used, but in the early 20th century these were replaced by tin-plated steel containers with interlocking seams and polymer seals. In the later 20th century seamless aluminum cans (punched out from a single sheet) capped with a steel or aluminum lid became common, particularly in the beverage industry. In modern canning, food is passed under hot water or steam, transferred to a sterile container, sealed inside, and subjected to heat sufficient to kill any remaining microorganisms. The process preserves most nutrients but often affects consistency and taste.

George Canning, painting by Sir Thomas Lawrence and R. Evans; in the National Portrait Gallery, London.

BY COURTESY OF THE NATIONAL PORTRAIT GALLERY, LONDON

Canning, George (1770–1827) British politician. As a young man he came under the influence of WILLIAM PITT, who helped him win a seat in Parliament (1793) and a post as undersecretary for foreign affairs (1796–99). Canning served twice as foreign secretary (1807–9, 1822–27); his policies included cutting England adrift from the HOLY ALLIANCE and recognizing the independence of the Spanish-American colonies. He became prime minister in 1827 but died a few months later. He helped the Tory Party take a more liberal view on many questions of domestic, colonial, and foreign policy.

Canning, Stratford *later* **Viscount Stratford (of Redcliffe)** (1786–1880) British diplomat. A cousin of GEORGE CANNING, he served as minister to Switzerland (1814–18) and later to the U.S. (1820–23). As ambassador to Constantinople intermittently for almost 20 years, he exerted a strong influence on Turkish policy. He was involved with the movement for Greek independence from Turkey. He later became friends with the Ottoman sultan and encouraged the TANZIMAT program of reforms. He supported Turkish resistance to Russian attempts to influence Ottoman affairs and tried in vain to prevent the CRIMEAN WAR. He retired after leaving Turkey in 1858.

cannon Big GUN, howitzer, or MORTAR, as distinguished from a MUSKET, RIFLE, or other small arms. Huge ARTILLERY first appeared in Europe in the 15th century. These early cannons, smooth-bored and forged of iron, weighed 6,000–8,000 lbs (2,800–3,600 kg) and were loaded through the muzzle. They were mounted on wheeled carriages, which were thrown backward when the cannon was fired. Rifled bores and breechloading were adopted in the later 19th century, and new mechanisms such as the hydraulic buffer absorbed the recoil. Before 1850 ammunition was either cannister, grapeshot, or round, solid cannonballs and black powder, but rifled bores made possible the use of elongated projectiles, which had a longer range. The SHRAPNEL shell was widely used in the 19th–20th century. Modern cannons, of high-grade steel, are mounted on wheeled carriages or on tanks and aircraft. In 1953 the U.S. Army introduced a 280-mm gun called an atomic cannon, the first to fire atomic-explosive shells.

Cannon, Joseph (Gurney) (1836–1926) U.S. politician. Born in Guilford Co., N.C., he practiced law in Illinois from 1859 and was elected to the U.S. House of Representatives, where he would serve 46 years (1873–91, 1893–1913, 1915–23). A staunchly conservative Republican, he used his power as speaker (1903–11) in a partisan manner. In 1910 a coalition of Democrats and insurgent Republicans passed a resolution that made the speaker ineligible for membership on the rules committee, the main source of his power. Personally well liked, he was popularly known as "Uncle Joe."

Cannon, Walter B(radford) (1871–1945) U.S. neurologist and physiologist. Born in Prairie du Chien, Wis., he was the first to use X rays in physiological studies. He also investigated hemorrhagic and traumatic SHOCK during World War I and worked on methods of blood storage. He researched the emergency functions of the sympathetic nervous system and homeostasis and sympathin, an epinephrine-like substance released by certain neurons. With Philip Bard he developed the Cannon-Bard theory, which proposed that emotional and physiological responses to external situations arise simultaneously and that both prepare the body to deal with the situation.

Cano \'kä-nō\, **Alonso** (1601–1667) Spanish painter, sculptor, and architect. He studied in Seville with Francisco Pacheco and was active as court painter in Madrid (1638–44). Despite a violent temperament, he produced serene and elegant religious paintings and sculpture. He worked for much of his career in Granada, where he designed the facade of the Granada Cathedral (1667), one of the masterpieces of Spanish baroque architecture. He is often called the Spanish Michelangelo for the diversity of his talents.

canoe Lightweight boat pointed at both ends and propelled by one or more paddles. The earliest canoes had light frames of wood covered by tightly stretched tree bark. The birchbark canoe was first used by the Algonquian Indians in what is now the northeastern U.S. and Canada, and its use passed westward. Canoes were often about 20 ft (6 m) in length, though war canoes might be as long as 100 ft (30 m). The dugout canoe, made from a hollowed-out log, was used by Indians in what is now the southeastern U.S. and along the Pacific coast as far north as Canada, as well as by peoples in Africa and New Zealand. Modern canoes are made of wood, canvas over wood frames, aluminum, and molded plastic or fiberglass. Most are open from end to end, but the KAYAK is also considered a canoe. See also CANOEING.

canoeing Use of a CANOE or KAYAK for recreation or competition. Both types of boat are used in water touring, in speed competitions, and in white-water sport, or navigation through rapids (which includes, in the case of kayaks, ocean surf). The Scottish philanthropist John MacGregor (1825–1892) is traditionally credited with establishing the modern outdoor activity of canoeing in the 1860s. Canoeing events became part of the Olympic Games in 1936 (1948 for women). In addition to various singles, pairs, and team still-water events for distance and speed, there are white-water racing competitions and, for kayaks, slalom events involving the use of gates similar to those of slalom skiing.

canon Musical form and compositional technique in which an melody is imitated at a specified time interval by one or more parts, either at the same pitch or at some other pitch. Imitation may occur in the same note values, in augmentation (longer notes), or in diminution (shorter notes); in retrograde order (beginning at its end), mirror inversion (each ascending melodic interval becoming a descending interval, and vice versa), or retrograde mirror inversion; and so on. Canons range from folk rounds such as "Three Blind Mice" and "Frère Jacques" to the massively complex canons of J.S. BACH.

canon law Body of laws established within Roman Catholicism, Eastern Orthodoxy, independent churches of Eastern Christianity, and the Anglican Communion for church governance. Canon law concerns the constitution of the church, relations between it and other bodies, and matters of internal discipline. GRATIAN published the first definitive collection of Roman Catholic canon law between 1139 and 1150; the *Decretum Gratiani* drew on older local collections, councils, Roman law, and church fathers. The enlarged *Corpus juris canonici* ("Corpus of Canon Law") was published in 1500. A commission of cardinals issued the new *Codex juris canonici* ("Code of Canon Law") in 1917 and a revised version in 1983 after the Second VATICAN COUNCIL. Following the Schism of 1054, the Eastern Orthodox Church developed its own canon law under the patriarch of Constantinople. The Anglican, Coptic, and Ethiopian Orthodox churches also formulated their own collections.

canonization Official act of a Christian church declaring a deceased member worthy of veneration and entering his or her name in the canon (authorized list) of SAINTS. The cult of local martyrs was widespread in the early church, and by the 10th century church authorities were considering the need for formal recognition of saints by Rome, a change that was formalized by GREGORY IX in the 13th century. Responsibility for beatification (declaring a person worthy of limited veneration) was assigned to the ROMAN CURIA under SIXTUS V (r.1585–90). A candidate's writings, miracles, and reputation for sanctity are investigated: one official gathers evidence in favor of beatification; another (the "devil's advocate") is charged with seeing that the entire truth is made known about the candidate. Canonization requires proof of two miracles subsequent to beatification. The process in the Eastern Orthodox Church is less formal; popular devotion by the faithful serving as the usual basis for sainthood.

canopic jar In ancient Egyptian funerary ritual, a covered vessel of wood, stone, pottery, or faience containing the embalmed viscera removed from a body during mummification. First used during the Old Kingdom (c. 2575–c. 2130 BC), the jars became more elaborate during the Middle Kingdom (c. 1938–c. 1600 BC), when their lids were decorated with sculpted human heads (probably representations of the deceased). From the 19th dynasty until the end of the New Kingdom (1539–1075 BC), the heads represented the four sons of HORUS. During the 20th dynasty (1190–1075 BC), the practice began of returning the viscera to the body, and the art of canopic jars declined.

Canova, Antonio (1757–1822) Italian sculptor. Apprenticed to a sculptor at an early age, he opened his own studio in Venice by 1775. In 1778–79 he produced his first important sculpture, *Daedalus and Icarus;* the figures were so realistic that he was accused of making plaster casts from live models. In 1779 he settled in Rome and became strongly influenced by classical antiquity. Among his most important commissions were the tombs of two popes, Clement XIII and Clement XIV. In 1802 he became court sculptor to NAPOLEON I in Paris. In 1816 Pope Pius VII awarded him the title of marquis of Ischia for arranging the return of Italian art looted by the French. He also painted portraits and re-creations of paintings discovered at POMPEII and HERCULANEUM. Canova dominated European sculpture around the turn of the century and was of primary importance in the development of the Neoclassical style in sculpture.

Canso, Strait of *or* **Gut of Canso** Channel, NOVA SCOTIA. Separating Nova Scotia and CAPE BRETON ISLANDS, it is 4.5 mi (23 km) long and 1 mi (2 km) wide, with depths of 200 ft (60 m). Since 1955 the 7,000-ft (2,100-m) Canso Causeway has linked Cape Breton with the mainland. A navigation lock can handle most oceangoing vessels.

Cantabria \kän-'tä-brē-ə\ Historical region, autonomous community (pop., 1996 est.: 527,000), and province, northern Spain. It borders the Bay of BISCAY and covers an area of 2,042 sq mi (5,289 sq km); its coastal hills rise gradually into the CANTABRIAN MTNS. Its capital is SANTANDER. The Cantabri, an Iberian tribe, dominated the region until 19 BC when they were subdued by the Romans. Because of its isolation, the area was little affected by the Iberian Moorish invasions c. 8th–11th century. In the Middle Ages, Cantabria came under Castilian influence. Formerly known itself as Santander, much of the region's population is centered on the city of Santander. Mining is an important part of the economy.

Cantabrian Mountains \kan-'tā-brē-ən\ Mountain range, northern Spain. The mountains, which extend about 180 mi (300 km), are geologically of similar origin to the PYRENEES, though classified as a separate formation. They include many tall peaks, the highest being Torre de Cerredo (8,787 ft, or 2,678 m), and thus form a more formidable barrier than the Pyrenees. The region is economically important for its coal and iron.

cantata Work for voice or voices and instruments of the baroque era. From its beginnings in early-17th-century Italy, both secular and religious cantatas were written. The earliest cantatas were generally for solo voice and minimal instrumental accompaniment. Cantatas soon developed a dramatic character and alternating sections of RECITATIVE and ARIA, paralleling the simultaneous development of OPERA, and came to resemble unstaged operatic scenes or acts. In Germany the Lutheran cantata developed more directly out of the expanding choral MOTET, and almost always involved a chorus. A single chorale (HYMN) often served as the basis for an entire cantata, which might have up to 10 diverse numbers, including duets, recitatives, and choral fugues. The most celebrated are the approximately 200 written by J.S. BACH. After c. 1750 the cantata gradually declined.

Canterbury Cathedral town (pop., 1995 est.: 43,000), southeastern England. Located on the Great STOUR RIVER, the site has been occupied since pre-Roman times; the Roman town of Durovernum Cantiacorum was established after the invasion of CLAUDIUS in AD 43. It has been an ecclesiastical metropolis of England since St. AUGUSTINE OF CANTERBURY founded a monastery there in 602 and later established a cathedral. The cathedral was the scene of the murder of Archbishop ST. THOMAS BECKET in 1170. After his canonization in 1172 it became a pilgrimage shrine; it is the destination of the pilgrims in GEOFFREY CHAUCER's *Canterbury Tales.* The town was heavily bombed in World War II, but the cathedral largely escaped damage.

cantilever \'kan-tə-,lē-vər\ Projecting beam or other horizontal member supported at one or more points but not at both ends. Some engineers distinguish between a cantilever, supported at only one fixed end, and an overhanging beam that projects beyond one of its end supports. The free, unsupported end is capable of supporting a weight or surface, such as a concrete slab. Any beam built into a wall with a projecting free end forms a cantilever, which may carry a balcony, canopy, roof, or part of a building above. Cantilevering can be used for constructions as simple as bookshelves or as complicated as bridges.

Canton See GUANGZHOU

canton Political subdivision of Switzerland, France, and some other European countries. Each of Switzerland's 26 cantons and half-cantons has its own constitution, legislature, executive, and judiciary. Five preserve the ancient democratic assembly, in which all citizens meet; the remaining 21 have a cantonal legislature with elective representatives and usually proportional representation. In France, the canton is a territorial and administrative subdivision of an arrondissement but not an actual unit of local government.

Canton system System of trade that developed between Chinese and foreign merchants in the southern China city of GUANGZHOU (Canton). From 1759 to 1842, all foreign trade coming into China was confined to Guangzhou and had to be conducted with authorized Chinese merchants. Foreign merchants were confined to a small area outside the city wall and were subject to Chinese law and other restrictions. British merchants' complaints grew during the early 19th century, and with Britain's victory in the first OPIUM WAR (1839–42) China was forced to abolish the system. See also British EAST INDIA CO., Treaty of NANJING.

cantor In Judaism and Christianity, an ecclesiastical official in charge of music or chants. In Judaism, the hazan (cantor) leads liturgical prayer and chanting. In medieval Christianity, the cantor had charge of a cathedral's music—specifically, of supervising the choir's singing. The term also designated the head of a college of church music.

Cantor, Eddie *orig.* **Edward Israel Iskowitz** (1892–1964) U.S. comedian and singer. As a child, Cantor clowned and sang for coins on street corners in his native New York City. He dropped out of elementary school, could not keep a job because of his irrepressible clowning, and soon went into VAUDEVILLE as a blackface song-and-dance man. He toured with FLORENZ ZIEGFELD's Follies and the Shuberts. He appeared in several Broadway reviews, and from 1923 to 1926 he was a star in *Kid Boots.* From 1931 Cantor performed for 18 years on "The Chase and Sanborn Hour" as a standup comedian. His films included *Roman Scandals* (1933) and *Strike Me Pink* (1936). In the 1950s he hosted a television show.

C D

Cantor \'kän-tōr\, **Georg** (1845–1918) German mathematician, founder of SET THEORY. A student of KARL WEIERSTRASS in Berlin, he wrote his doctoral thesis at age 22. His work in NUMBER THEORY built on that of CARL FRIEDRICH GAUSS. Set theory and transfinite numbers were his major life's work. One of his most important discoveries was a way to list the RATIONAL NUMBERS so as to prove them countable. His investigations into such listings led him to the classification of transfinite numbers, which are, informally speaking, degrees of INFINITY. Cantor's work was fundamental to the development of FUNCTIONAL ANALYSIS and TOPOLOGY, as well as to the philosophy of mathematics, in particular regarding the question "What is a number?"

cantus firmus (Latin: "fixed chant"). Plainchant of the Catholic church (see GREGORIAN CHANT) used as the basis of counterpoint in musical compositions, starting in the 10th century. In melismatic ORGANUM, the tones of the plainchant melody for such words as "alleluia" and "amen" were held by one voice (the tenor), while another, more active, improvised line was added. Developments introduced by the NOTRE-DAME SCHOOL included rhythmic patterning of the added voice and the addition of two or three voices. The composition of nonliturgical words for the added voice or voices in the 13th century resulted in the independent MOTET. Cantus-firmus technique remained the basis of most composition of the 14th–15th century (though the "chant" was now often a secular melody) and remained important in the 16th-century MASS. It was later codified in the pedagogical method called species COUNTERPOINT.

Canute the Great *Danish* **Knut** \kə-'nüt\ (died 1035) Danish king of England (1016–35), Denmark (1019–35), and Norway (1028–35). He helped his father, SWEYN FORKBEARD, invade England in 1013. Sweyn was accepted as king of England but died in 1014; Canute returned and defeated rivals to win the English throne. At first he ruled ruthlessly, killing English opponents and appointing Danes in their places, but within a few years he was granting earldoms to Englishmen. Canute proved an effective ruler who brought peace and prosperity to England, and he became a strong supporter of the church. With English help he secured the throne of Denmark on his brother's death.

canvas Stout cloth. Canvas (probably named for cannabis, or HEMP), has been made from hemp- and FLAX-FAMILY fibers since ancient times to produce cloth for sails. More recently, it has also been made from tow, JUTE, COTTON, and mixtures of such fibers. Flax canvas is essentially of double warp (see WEAVING), being invariably intended to withstand pressure or rough usage. Articles made from canvas include camera and golf bags, running shoes, tents, and mailbags. Tarred canvas is used for tarpaulins to cover goods. Artists' canvas for painting is much lighter than sail canvas; the best qualities are made of cream or bleached flax fiber.

canvasback DIVING DUCK *(Aythya valisineria),* one of the most popular game birds. The male weighs about 3 lbs (1.4 kg). During the breeding season he has a red head and neck and a black breast, with white back and sides finely lined in gray. In eclipse (nonbreeding) plumage, he resembles the female, with tan head and gray-brown back. Canvasbacks breed in northwestern North America and winter along the coasts from British Columbia and Massachusetts south to central Mexico. They prefer the roots of wild celery (eelgrass) but will eat many other plants and even some animal foods.

canyon Very narrow, deep valley cut by a river through resistant rock and having steep, almost vertical sides. Canyons occur most often in arid or semiarid regions. Some canyons (e.g., the GRAND CANYON) are spectacular natural features. See also SUBMARINE CANYON.

Canyon de Chelly National Monument \də-'shā\ Preserve, northeastern Arizona. Located on the NAVAJO Indian reservation immediately east of Chinle, the preserve was established in 1931 and occupies 131 sq mi (339 sq km). It includes several hundred pre-Columbian cliff dwellings, some of them built in caves on the canyon walls. They represent a broader time span than any other ruins in the Southwest, with many dating from the 11th century. Modern Navajo homes and farms occupy the canyon floor.

Canyonlands National Park Park, southeastern Utah. The park, established in 1964, occupies a wilderness of water-eroded sandstone spires, canyons, and mesas extending over 527 sq mi (1,366 sq km). Some of its rock walls display Indian petroglyphs. The Needles section in its southern part contains the Angel and Druid arches, gigantic balanced rock formations.

Cao Cao *or* **Ts'ao Ts'ao** \'tsau̇-'tsau̇\ (AD 155–220) Chinese general who, at the end of the HAN DYNASTY, assumed imperial prerogatives. Cao Cao rose to prominence when he suppressed the YELLOW TURBAN rebellion in the last years of the Han. Though the rebellion was suppressed, the dynasty was irreparably weakened, and in the ensuing chaos Cao Cao occupied the strategic northern section of China around the capital of Luoyang. His domain was known as the kingdom of Wei (see THREE KINGDOMS). Confucian historians and popular legends alike describe him as the archetypal unscrupulous villain; he is portrayed as such in the famous 14th-century novel *Sanguozhi yanyi* ("Romance of the Three Kingdoms"). His son, Cao Pei, founded the Wei dynasty (220–265/6).

Cao Dai \'kau̇-'dī\ Syncretist modern Vietnamese religious movement with a strongly nationalist political character. Cao Dai draws upon ethical precepts from CONFUCIANISM, occult practices from TAOISM, theories of karma and rebirth from BUDDHISM, and hierarchical organization (including a pope) from ROMAN CATHOLICISM. It was formally established in 1926 by Ngo Van Chieu (1878–1926?), an administrator for the French in Indochina who had had a communication from the supreme deity. The movement met with resistance from the Vietnamese government both before and after the communist takeover in 1975. It was reported to have some 3 million adherents in Vietnam and abroad in the early 21st century.

Cao Zhan *or* **Ts'ao Chan** \'tsau̇-'jän\ (1715?–1763) Chinese novelist. He is the author of *Dream of the Red Chamber* (1791), generally considered China's greatest novel. A partly autobiographical work written in the vernacular, it describes in lingering detail the decline of a powerful family and an ill-fated love between cousins. Cao finished at least 80 of its 120 chapters; it was completed after his death, probably by Gao E, about whom little is known.

Capa, Robert *orig.* **Andrei Friedmann** (1913–1954) Hungarian-U.S. photojournalist. In Paris he represented his photographs as the work of a fictitious rich American, Robert Capa; the deception was soon discovered but he kept the name. He first achieved fame as a war correspondent in the Spanish Civil War (1936). In World War II he covered the fighting in Africa, Sicily, and Italy for *Life* magazine; images of the Normandy invasion are among his most memorable works. In 1947 he founded Magnum Photos with HENRI CARTIER-BRESSON and David Seymour. He was killed by a land mine while photographing the French Indochina war for *Life.*

Capablanca, José (Raúl) (1888–1942) Cuban chess master. He learned chess from his father at 4 and beat Cuba's best player at 12. He defeated EMANUEL LASKER to become world champion in 1921; in 1927 he was defeated by Alexander Alekhine (1892–1946). From 1916 to 1924 he did not lose a game. In 1921 he published an instruction manual, *Chess Fundamentals.*

capacitance \kə-'pa-sə-təns\ Property of a pair of electric CONDUCTORS separated by a nonconducting material (such as air) that permits storage of electric energy by the separation of ELECTRIC CHARGE, and that is measured by the amount of separated charge that can be stored per unit of ELECTRIC POTENTIAL between the conductors. If electric charge is transferred between two initially uncharged conductors, they become equally (but oppositely) charged. A potential difference is set up between them and some of the electricity can be stored. Capacitance C is the ratio of the amount of charge q on one of the conductors to the potential difference V between the conductors, or $C = q/V$. The unit of capacitance is coulombs per volt (C/V), or farads (F).

Cape Agulhas See Cape AGULHAS

Cape Ann See Cape ANN

Cape Bojador See Cape BOJADOR

Cape Bon See Cape BON

Cape Breton Island \'bret-ᵊn\ Island, (pop., 2001: 109,330), eastern part of NOVA SCOTIA. Separated from the mainland by the Strait of CANSO, it is 110 mi (175 km) long and up to 75 mi (120 km) wide, with an area of 3,981 sq mi (10,311 sq km). It contains the BRAS D'OR salt lakes. Originally called Île Royale as a French colony, it later took the name of its eastern cape, probably the first land visited by JOHN CABOT on his 1497–98 voyage and probably named by Basque fishermen from Cap Breton, France. It was ceded to the British by the 1763 Treaty of PARIS and joined to Nova Scotia. In 1784 it became a separate British crown colony, but was rejoined to Nova Scotia in 1820. In 1955 the island was linked to the mainland by a causeway. Cape Breton Highlands National Park was established in 1936. Tourism is an important industry on the island.

Cape buffalo Massive, black, horned BUFFALO *(Syncerus caffer)* formerly found throughout sub-Saharan Africa but now greatly reduced by disease and hunting. It is a gregarious animal of open or scrub-covered plains and open forests. When wounded, it is regarded as one of the most dangerous animals to humans. It stands up to 5 ft (1.5 m) tall at the shoulder, and bulls can weigh almost a ton (about 900 kg). Its heavy horns typically curve downward, then up and inward. A smaller subspecies is found in dense West African forests.

Cape Canaveral See Cape CANAVERAL

Cape Cod Peninsula, eastern Massachusetts. Some 65 mi (105 km) long and 1–20 mi (2–32 km) wide, it extends into the Atlantic Ocean in a wide curve enclosing Cape Cod Bay, and touches BUZZARDS BAY. The Cape Cod Canal, cutting across the base of the peninsula, forms part of the ATLANTIC INTRACOASTAL WATERWAY. Named by an English explorer who visited its shores in 1602 and took aboard a "great store of codfish," it was the site, near PROVINCETOWN, of the PILGRIMS' landing in 1620. Extending into the warm GULF STREAM, its coastal towns and villages have become densely populated resorts in summer. In the 19th century, Provincetown was an active whaling port. The cape's northern hook was designated the Cape Cod National Seashore in 1961.

Cape Dezhnev See Cape DEZHNEV

Cape Fear River River, central and southeastern North Carolina. Formed by the confluence of the Deep and Haw rivers, it flows southeast about 200 mi (320 km) to enter the Atlantic Ocean near Southport at Cape Fear. The southern estuary forms part of the ATLANTIC INTRACOASTAL WATERWAY. A series of locks and dams makes the river navigable from Wilmington to Fayetteville.

Cape Horn See Cape HORN

Cape Krusenstern National Monument \'krü-zən-ˌstern\ National preserve, northwestern Alaska, on the coast of the Chukchi Sea. Established in 1978, it was enlarged in 1980 to 1,031 sq mi (2,670 sq km). Its remarkable archaeological sites illustrate the cultural evolution of the Arctic peoples over some 4,000 years.

Cape of Good Hope See Cape of GOOD HOPE

Cape Province *or* **Cape of Good Hope** *formerly (1826–1910)* **Cape Colony** Former province, South Africa. Occupying the southern extremity of the African continent, it comprised the southern and western portions of South Africa; its capital was CAPE TOWN. The black state of CISKEI and parts of two others, TRANSKEI and BOPHUTHATSWANA, lay within its boundaries. Its name refers to the Cape of GOOD HOPE, 30 mi (50 km) south of Cape Town. The original inhabitants included BANTU, SAN, and KHOIKHOI peoples. BARTOLEMEU DIAS, en route to India in 1488, became the first European to visit the area. A colony was founded by the Dutch at TABLE BAY in 1652; it was ceded to the British in 1814. It joined the Union of South Africa in 1910 and the Rep. of South Africa in 1961. The province ceased to exist in 1994, when it was split roughly into Eastern Cape, Northern Cape, and Western Cape provinces.

Cape Town *Afrikaans* **Kaapstad** \'käp-ˌstät\ City (pop., 1996 est.: metro. area pop.: 2,415,408), legislative capital, South Africa. Located on TABLE BAY, it was formerly the capital of CAPE PROVINCE. Long the country's major seaport, it was surpassed in the 1980s by DURBAN. The first settlement at Table Bay, it was founded by the Dutch navigator Jan van Riebeeck for the Dutch EAST INDIA CO., and it soon served as a stopover for ships plying the Europe-to-India route. It was under Dutch rule intermittently until finally being taken by the British in 1806. Today it is a commercial and cultural center. See also PRETORIA, BLOEMFONTEIN.

Cape Verde \'vərd\ *officially* **Republic of Cape Verde** Island republic, central Atlantic Ocean. Lying 385 mi (620 km) off the western coast of Senegal, it consists of 10 islands and five islets. Area: 1,557 sq mi (4,033 sq km). Population (2000): 434,812. Capital: PRAIA. More than two-thirds of its population is Creole (mulatto); the remainder are European and black African. Languages: Portuguese (official), Crioulo (a Portuguese dialect). Religions: Roman Catholicism (official), Protestantism. Currency: Cape Verde escudo. The mountainous windward islands are craggy and furrowed by erosion; the flat leeward islands are largely plains and lowlands. The islands are volcanic in origin. Fogo Island has an active volcano that erupted in 1951; it is also the location of the highest peak, which rises 9,281 ft (2,829 m). The largest of the other islands are Santo Antão, São Vincente, and São Nicolau. Cape Verde has a developing mixed economy based largely on agriculture, though tourism has been promoted. It is a republic with one legislative house; its chief of state is the president and its head of government, the prime minister. When visited by the Portuguese 1456–60, the islands were uninhabited. In 1460 Diogo Gomes sighted and named Maio and São Tiago, and in 1462 the first settlers landed on São Tiago, founding the city of Ribeira Grande. The city's importance grew with the development of the slave trade, and its wealth attracted pirates so often that it was abandoned after 1712. The prosperity of the Portuguese-controlled islands vanished with the decline of the slave trade in the 19th century, but later improved because of their position on the great trade routes between Europe, South America, and South Africa. In 1951 the colony became an overseas province of Portugal. Many islanders preferred outright independence, and it was finally granted in 1975. Once associated politically with Guinea-Bissau, Cape Verde split from it in 1981.

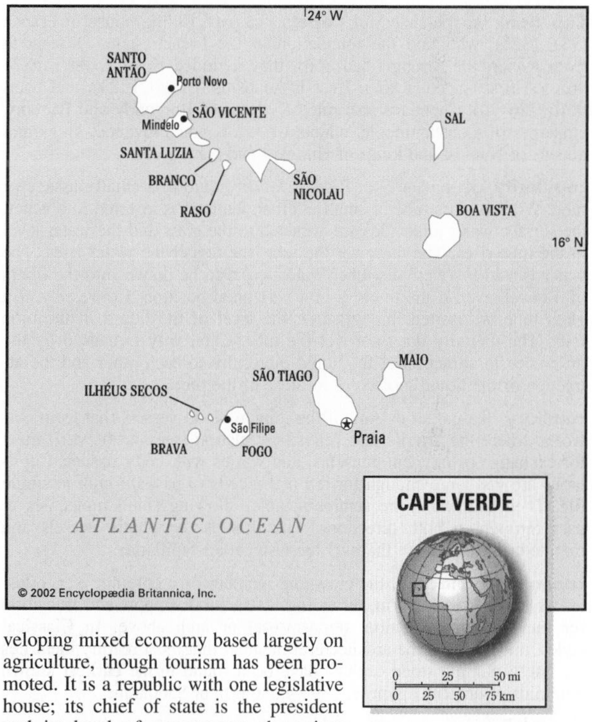

Capek \'chä-pek\, **Karel** (1890–1938) Czech novelist, short-story writer, and playwright. Born in Bohemia, he was educated abroad. His "black utopias," works showing the dangers of technological progress, include the cautionary play *R.U.R.: Rossum's Universal Robots* (1920), a depiction of a society dependent on mechanical workers called "robots" (a term he coined from a Czech word for forced labor). The comic fantasy *The Insect Play* (1921; with his brother Josef) satirizes human greed. *The Makropoulos Affair* (1922) was made into an opera by L. JANACEK. He explored aspects of knowledge in the novel trilogy *Hordubal* (1933), *Meteor* (1934), and *An Ordinary Life* (1934).

caper Any of the low prickly shrubs that make up the genus *Capparis* (family Capparaceae), of the Mediterranean region. The European caperbush *(C. spinosa)* is known for its flower buds, which are pickled in vinegar and used as a spicy condiment. The term caper also refers to one of the pickled flower buds or young berries. Buds of *C. decidua* are eaten as potherbs, and CURRIES are prepared from seeds and fruits of *C. zeylandica.*

Capernaum \kə-ˈpər-nā-əm\ Ancient city, PALESTINE. Located on the northwestern shore of the Sea of GALILEE, it was the home of JESUS for much of his ministry. His disciples Peter, Andrew, and Matthew were from Capernaum, and he performed many of his miracles there. The long dispute over nearby modern Kefer Nahum's identification with Capernaum was settled in its favor by excavations begun in 1905. Among the remains discovered was a synagogue dating from the 2nd–3rd century AD; an older synagogue may be buried beneath it.

Capet, Hugh See HUGH CAPET

Capetians \kə-ˈpē-shənz\ *or* **Capets** \ˈkā-pəts\ Ruling house of France (987–1328), who laid the foundation of the French state. Descended from Robert the Strong (died 866), they included HUGH CAPET (r.987–96), the first Capetian king; PHILIP II AUGUSTUS (r.1180–1223); and LOUIS IX (r.1226–70). Capetians also ruled as dukes of Burgundy and Brittany, emperors of Constantinople, counts of Artois and Provence, kings and queens of Naples, and kings of Hungary and Navarre.

capillarity \ˌka-pə-ˈlar-ə-tē\ Rise or fall of liquid in a small passage or tube. When a glass tube of small internal diameter is inserted into water, the surface water molecules are attracted to the glass and the water level in the tube rises. The narrower the tube, the higher the water rises. The water is said to "wet" the tube. Water will also be drawn into the fibers of a towel, even if the towel is in a horizontal position. Conversely, if a glass tube is inserted into MERCURY, the level of the liquid in the tube falls. The mercury does not wet the tube. Capillarity is caused by the difference in attraction of the liquid molecules to each other and the attraction of the liquid molecules to those of the tube.

capillary \ˈka-pə-ˌler-ē\ Any of the minute blood vessels that form networks where the arterial and venous circulation (see ARTERY, VEIN) meet for exchange of oxygen, nutrients, and wastes with body tissues. Capillaries are just large enough for red blood cells to pass through in single file. Their thin walls are semipermeable, allowing small molecules to pass through in both directions. The smallest lymphatic vessels and minute bile channels in the liver are also called capillaries.

capital In architecture, the crowning member of a column, pier, pilaster, or other vertical form, providing a structural support and transition for the horizontal member (ENTABLATURE) or arch above. In Classical styles, the capital is the architectural member that most readily identifies the ORDER. Simple stone capitals have been found in the earliest known pyramids of ancient Egypt (c. 2890–2686 BC), at Saqqarah.

capital In economics, the stock of resources that are used to produce other goods now and in the future. In CLASSICAL ECONOMICS the three factors of production are capital, LABOR, and land. Capital embodies the man-made resources. It is defined to include the buildings, plant, equipment, and inventories created by all three factors. In this sense, capital goods may be contrasted with CONSUMER GOODS. The creation of capital goods means that consumption must be forgone, that there is saving. The flow of saving becomes a flow of INVESTMENT. Expenditures on education and training are often referred to as investment in human capital (see GARY S. BECKER). Financial capital is the term given to the STOCKS and BONDS issued in order to finance the acquisition of capital goods.

capital-gains tax Tax levied on gains realized from the sale or exchange of capital assets. Though capital gains have been taxed in the U.S. since the advent of the federal INCOME TAX, certain capital gains are taxed less heavily than regular income or are exempted from taxation. This preferential treatment is intended to encourage INVESTMENT and so stimulate economic growth. In theory, the tax break encourages investors to risk their capital in new ventures. Critics argue that preferential treatment results in distorted patterns of investment because regular income is converted into capital gains in order to avoid paying tax. See also CORPORATE INCOME TAX.

capital goods See PRODUCER GOODS

capital levy Direct tax assessed simultaneously on the capital resources of all persons possessing taxable wealth in excess of a minimum value and paid at least partly out of capital resources. It aims at capturing a substantial portion of the taxpayers' wealth to enable the government to cope with a major emergency or to redistribute wealth. Capital levies were adopted in many European nations after World Wars I and II.

capital punishment *or* **death penalty** Penalty of death imposed on a criminal convicted of a serious crime. In 18th-century England, hundreds of specific offenses, including many against property, carried a sentence of death. The writings of ENLIGHTENMENT thinkers, the rise of the industrial working class, and humanitarian movements stimulated reform. By the 1970s many countries had eliminated capital punishment. In 1972 the U.S. Supreme Court ruled capital-punishment laws, as then enforced, unconstitutional, but a later ruling found the death penalty per se to be constitutional. Today the U.S. is the only Western industrialized nation that permits capital punishment, but twelve states and the District of Columbia bar it. Advocates maintain that it deters crime. They claim that life imprisonment is not as effective and exposes other prisoners and (in the event of escape or parole) members of society at large to dangerous criminals. Opponents maintain that the death penalty has never been proved to be an effective deterrent, that errors sometimes lead to the execution of innocent persons, and that capital punishment is applied unequally, mostly to the poor and members of racial minorities.

capitalism *or* **free-market economy** *or* **free-enterprise system** Economic system in which most of the means of production are privately owned, and production is guided and income distributed largely through the operation of markets. Capitalism has been dominant in the Western world since the end of MERCANTILISM. It was fostered by the REFORMATION, which sanctioned hard work and frugality, and by the rise of industry during the INDUSTRIAL REVOLUTION, especially the English textile industry (16th–18th cent). Unlike earlier systems, capitalism used the excess of production over consumption to enlarge productive capacity rather than investing it in economically unproductive enterprises such as cathedrals. The strong national states of the mercantilist era provided the social conditions, such as uniform monetary systems and legal codes, necessary for the rise of capitalism. The ideology of classical capitalism was expressed in ADAM SMITH'S *Wealth of Nations* (1776), and Smith's free-market theories were widely adopted in the 19th century. In the 20th century the GREAT DEPRESSION effectively ended LAISSEZ-FAIRE economics in most countries, but the demise of the state-run COMMAND ECONOMIES of Eastern Europe and the former Soviet Union (see COMMUNISM) and the adoption of some free-market principles in China left capitalism unrivaled (if not untroubled) at the end of the 20th century.

Capitol, United States Meeting place of the U.S. Congress. In 1792 a competition for its design was won by William Thornton (1759–1828); his revised FEDERAL-STYLE design of 1795 was executed as the exterior of the wings adjacent to the central ROTUNDA. BENJAMIN H. LATROBE, as Surveyor of Public Buildings (1803), followed Thornton's conception of the exterior but used his own interior designs; perhaps his best-known contribution was his invention of tobacco-leaf and corn-cob CAPITALS. After the British set fire to the Capitol in 1814, Latrobe began its reconstruction, but resigned in 1817. By 1827 his successor, CHARLES BULFINCH, had joined the two wings and built the first dome and the rotunda. In 1850 Thomas Ustick Walter (1804–1887) won a competition to expand the wings; he also designed the 287-ft- (87-m-) high cast-iron dome (1855–66), which was based on Michelangelo's dome for ST. PETER'S BASILICA. The marble and sandstone building contains about 540 rooms and stands in a 131-acre (53-hectare) park.

Capitol Reef National Park Park, southern Utah. A 20-mi (32-km) buttressed cliff of colored sandstone, it occupies 379 sq mi (982 sq km). Established as a national monument in 1937, it became a national park in 1971. It is so-named because its rock towers reminded geologists of coral reefs, while its dome-shaped formations suggest capitol architecture. The cliff walls are covered with pre-Columbian petroglyphs.

Capone, Al(phonse) (1899–1947) U.S. gangster. Quitting school after the sixth grade, he joined gangs in his native Brooklyn and earned the nickname "Scarface" after a knife fight. He joined Johnny Torrio in Chicago and became crime czar there on Torrio's retirement (1925), running gambling, prostitution, and bootlegging rackets. He expanded his territory by killing his rivals, most famously in the St. Valentine's Day Massacre, in which members of the gang of Bugs Moran were machine-gunned in a garage on February 14, 1929. In 1931 Capone was convicted for income-tax evasion and sentenced to 11 years in prison. Suffering from paresis, he was released in 1939 and later retired to Florida, where he died in 1947.

Caporetto, Battle of (October 24, 1917) Italian military disaster in WORLD WAR I in which Italian troops retreated before an Austro-German offensive near Trieste on the Isonzo front (see Battles of the ISONZO). More than 600,000 Italian soldiers either deserted or surrendered. The defeat prompted Italy's allies, France and Britain, to send reinforcements and eventually to establish the Supreme War Council to unify the Allied war effort.

Capote \kə-'pō-tē\, **Truman** *orig.* **Truman Streckfus Persons** (1924–1984) U.S. novelist, short-story writer, and playwright. Born in New Orleans, he spent much of his youth in small towns in Louisiana and Alabama. His early works, in the Southern gothic tradition, include the novels *Other Voices, Other Rooms* (1948) and *The Grass Harp* (1951) and the story collection *A Tree of Night* (1949). His later journalistic style was exemplified in the highly successful "nonfiction novel" *In Cold Blood* (1966), an account of a multiple murder. Other works include the novella *Breakfast at Tiffany's* (1958; film, 1961), the musical *House of Flowers* (1954; with H. ARLEN), and the collections *The Dogs Bark* (1973) and *Music for Chameleons* (1980).

Capp, Al *orig.* **Alfred Gerald Caplin** (1909–1979) U.S. cartoonist. Born in New Haven, Conn., he studied landscape architecture before turning to cartooning. His comic strip *Li'l Abner* first appeared in the *New York Mirror* in 1934 and was soon being syndicated throughout the country. Set in the backwoods community of Dogpatch, U.S.A., it featured Li'l Abner, a shy, awkward woodsman; Daisy Mae, a persistent maiden who succeeded in catching Abner after a 17-year pursuit; and a host of colorful characters.

Cappadocia \ˌka-pə-'dō-shə\ Ancient district, eastern Asia Minor. It is a mountainous area located in modern-day central Turkey; its earliest records date from the 6th century BC, when it was a Persian satrapy. It became a semi-independent kingdom under Ariarathes I, a contemporary of ALEXANDER THE GREAT. Important as a Roman ally and client, it was annexed by TIBERIUS in AD 17 and made a Roman province. With its command over strategic passes in the TAURUS MTNS., it went on to become a bulwark of the BYZANTINE EMPIRE until the 11th century.

Capra, Frank (1897–1991) U.S. (Italian-born) film director. At age 6 he emigrated with his family to the U.S. After holding various jobs in the film industry, he emerged as a major director with *That Certain Thing* (1928), *Platinum Blonde* (1931), and *Lady for a Day* (1933). He won Academy Awards for *It Happened One Night* (1934) and *Mr. Deeds Goes to Town* (1936), portraying naive idealists who triumph over more worldly types, as well as for *You Can't Take It with You* (1938). He chose the same theme for his next film, *Mr. Smith Goes to Washington* (1939), but departed from his usual style in *Lost Horizon* (1937) and *Meet John Doe* (1941). He made the wartime documentary series *Why We Fight*, then won wide audiences with *Arsenic and Old Lace* (1944) and *It's a Wonderful Life* (1946).

Capri \'kä-prē, kə-'prē\ Island, southern Italy. Located at the southern entrance to the Bay of NAPLES, it has an area of 4 sq mi (10 sq km). Cliffs on the eastern side rise 900 ft (275 m); its highest point is 1,923 ft (586 m). It was a colony of ancient Greece; later it became a favorite resort of Roman emperors. In the Middle Ages it belonged to the abbey of Montecassino and to the republic of AMALFI before passing to the kingdom of NAPLES. Its rocky shores abound with caves, notably the famous Blue Grotto. Capri is one of Italy's most popular resorts.

Capricorn *or* **Capricornus** (Latin: "Goat horn") In astronomy, the constellation lying between Aquarius and Sagittarius; in ASTROLOGY, the tenth sign of the ZODIAC, governing approximately the period December 22–January 19. It is represented as a goat with what appears to be a fishtail. One explanation for this odd depiction is that it derives from the Greek myth of PAN. To avoid the monster Typhon, Pan jumped into the water just as he was changing into animal shape. The half of his body above water became a goat, while the submerged half took the shape of a fish. Another relates the form to the Mesopotamian deity Enki (see EA).

Capricorn, Tropic of See TROPIC OF CAPRICORN

Caprivi \kä-'prē-vē\, **(Georg) Leo, Graf (Count) von** (1831–1899) German soldier and politician. A distinguished soldier, he served as chief of the admiralty 1883–88. He succeeded OTTO VON BISMARCK as Germany's imperial chancellor (1890–94) and Prussian minister president (1890–92). His achievements included an Anglo-German agreement concerning spheres of influence in Africa, commercial treaties with Austria, Romania, and other states, and the reorganization of the German army.

capsicum See PEPPER

capstan Mechanical device used chiefly on board ships or in shipyards for moving heavy weights by means of ropes, cables, or chains. A capstan consists of a drum, driven either manually or by steam or electricity, that rotates about a vertical axis to wind in a line wrapped around it. The grip between the line and the drum depends on friction and on the number of times the line is wrapped around the drum. A notched track (RATCHET) on the base plate and pawls attached to the drum prevent backward rotation.

capsule In botany, a dry fruit that opens when ripe. It splits from top to bottom into separate segments known as valves, as in the IRIS, or forms pores at the top (e.g., POPPY), or splits around the circumference, with the top falling off (e.g., pigweed and PLANTAIN). The spore-forming organ (see SPOROPHYTE) of LIVERWORTS and MOSSES is also called a capsule.

Capuchin \'ka-pyə-shən\ Member of the Order of Friars Minor Capuchin, an autonomous branch of the FRANCISCANS. It began in 1525 as a reform movement led by Matteo da Bascio (c. 1495–1552), who wanted the Franciscans to return to strict observance of the Rule of St. Francis. He and his followers wore robes with pointed hoods (Italian, *cappuccino*), went barefoot, and lived in extreme poverty. Other Franciscans harassed them, and the pope forbade them to extend their membership outside Italy. The new order was nearly ruined by the defection of their vicar-general, Bernardino Ochino, to Protestantism in 1542, but it later grew quickly, reaching a membership of 17,000 by 1571. It was active in the COUNTER-REFORMATION in keeping the common people loyal to Catholicism. An independent order since 1619, they are known for their missionary and social work.

capuchin (monkey) \'ka-pyə-shən, kə-'pyü-shən\ Any of four species of tropical monkeys (genus *Cebus*) found from Nicaragua to Paraguay. Considered among the most intelligent New World monkeys, capuchins are named for their cap of crown hair, which resembles the cowl of Capuchin monks. These stocky, round-headed monkeys are 12–22 in. (30–55 cm) long, with a hairy, prehensile tail of about the same length, and are brown or black, sometimes with white markings. Capuchins live in troops, often in the treetops. They eat fruit and small animals and sometimes raid plantations for oranges and other food. Easily trained, they are valued as gentle pets.

capybara \ka-pi-'bar-ə\ Either of two species (genus *Hydrochoerus*) of semiaquatic Central and South American rodents sometimes classified with the CAVY and GUINEA PIG. Capybaras are the largest living rodents, growing as large as 50 in. (1.25 m) long and weighing 110 lbs (50 kg) or more. They are sparsely haired and brownish, with a blunt snout, short legs, small ears, and almost no tail. Capybaras are shy and associate in groups along the banks of lakes and rivers. Herbivores, they can become pests when they eat cultivated melons, grain, and squash. They swim and dive readily and commonly enter water to elude predators.

caracal \'kar-ə-ˌkal\ Short-tailed CAT *(Felis caracal)* found in hills, deserts, and plains of Africa, the Middle East, and central and South Asia. It is sleek and short-haired, with a reddish brown coat and long tufts of black hairs on its pointed ears. Long-legged and short-tailed, it stands 16–18 in. (40–45 cm) and is 26–30 in. (66–76 cm) long, excluding its tail. Generally solitary and nocturnal, it preys on birds and mammals, including peafowl, gazelles, and hares. In Asia, where it has become rare, it has been trained as a hunting animal.

Caracalla \ˌkar-ə-ˈka-lə\ *officially* **Marcus Aurelius Severus Antoninus Augustus** *orig.* **Septimius Bassianus** (AD 188–217) Roman emperor (198–217). He was nicknamed Caracalla for a Gallic cloak he allegedly introduced. Until 211 he ruled with his father, SEPTIMIUS SEVERUS, a North African who became emperor in 193. To assure his undisputed rule, he killed his brother Geta and many of his friends. He built colossal baths in Rome, which still stand. He gave Roman citizenship to all free inhabitants of the empire (212), but showed extreme cruelty toward all who opposed him, and he massacred Germans, Parthians, and Alexandrians. He was murdered by the praetorian PREFECT. He is regarded as one of Rome's most bloodthirsty tyrants, and his reign contributed to the empire's decay.

Caracas \kä-ˈrä-käs, kə-ˈra-kəs\ City (population 1992: 1,965,000; metro. area pop.: 2,784,000), capital of Venezuela. Its Caribbean port is La Guaira. Lying at an altitude of about 3,000 ft (9,000 m), it is one of the most developed cities in Latin America. It was founded in 1567 by Diego de Losada; in 1595 it was sacked by the English. It was the birthplace of SIMON BOLIVAR (1783), under whose leadership it became the first colony to revolt from Spain (c. 1810). Caracas has become the country's primary center of industry, commerce, education, and culture.

Caramanlis, Constantine See Konstantinos KARAMANLIS

Caravaggio \ˌkar-ə-ˈvä-jō\ *orig.* **Michelangelo Merisi** (1571–1610) Italian painter. Born in Caravaggio, he was orphaned at 11. After an apprenticeship in Milan, he went to Rome in 1590, where he won the patronage of a cardinal. A series of large paintings of the life of St. Matthew (1599–1603) established him as the most renowned and controversial painter in Rome. Breaking with conventional formulas used in depicting saints, he used ordinary people as models and painted them with unforgiving realism; his inclination against tradition gave new meaning to the interpretation of traditional themes in religious painting. His use of tenebrism—dramatic, selective illumination of form out of deep shadow to heighten the emotional tension, focus the details, and isolate the figures—became the most outstanding feature of his style and a hallmark of the baroque period. After c. 1600 he received many commissions, including the monumental *Entombment of Christ* (1602–4) and *Death of the Virgin* (1601–3), refused by the Carmelites because of the Virgin's plebeian features, bared legs, and swollen belly. His reputation and income increased despite harsh criticism and a turbulent lifestyle. After killing a man in a brawl in 1606, he fled Rome, first to Naples, then to Malta, then to Sicily, always painting. In Naples again, he was attacked and badly wounded at an inn. He died of fever on his way back to Rome, where a papal pardon awaited him. He had an enormous impact on painting throughout Europe; his many followers include JOSE DE RIBERA, HENDRIK TERBRUGGHEN, GERRIT VAN HONTHORST, ARTEMISIA GENTILESCHI, SIMON VOUET, and GEORGES DE LA TOUR.

"The Deposition of Christ," oil on canvas by Caravaggio, 1602–04; in the Vatican Museum.

SCALA/ART RESOURCE, NEW YORK CITY

caravan Group of merchants, pilgrims, or travelers journeying together, usually for mutual protection, in deserts or other hostile regions. The CAMEL was the most common means of transport. Caravans have been described since the beginning of recorded history, and they were a major factor in the growth of settlements along their routes. One caravan trail developed into the SILK ROAD. During the height of caravan travel, which lasted until the 19th century, a single caravan of Muslim pilgrims journeying from Cairo and Damascus to Mecca might employ as many as 10,000 camels.

caravansary \ˌkar-ə-ˈvan-sə-rē\ *or* **caravanserai** \ˌkar-ə-ˈvan-sə-ˌrī\ Public building used for sheltering caravans and other travelers in the Middle East. The structure is quadrangular in form and enclosed by a massive wall that has small windows near the top and a few narrow air holes near the bottom. The central court, surrounded by an ARCADE and storerooms, is usually large enough to contain 300–400 camels. It is open to the sky and has a well with a fountain basin in its center. There are rooms upstairs for lodging.

caraway Dried fruit, commonly called the seed, of *Carum carvi,* a biennial herb of the PARSLEY family. Native to Europe and western Asia. it has been cultivated since ancient times. It has a distinctive aroma and a warm, slightly sharp taste. It is used as a seasoning, and the oil is used to flavor alcoholic beverages and as a medicine.

carbamide See UREA

carbide Inorganic compound, any of a class of chemical compounds in which CARBON is combined with a METAL or semimetallic element. The nature of the second element (its position in the PERIODIC TABLE) determines the carbide's type of BONDING and its properties. Calcium carbide is useful as a source of ACETYLENE. Carbides of tungsten, silicon (see CARBORUNDUM), and boron, called refractory carbides, are extremely hard, remain stable when heated, and have a high melting point and chemical resistance. They are used as abrasives and in cutting tools, as furnace linings, and in other high-temperature applications. Iron carbide (cementite) is an important constituent of STEEL and CAST IRON.

carbine Light, short-barreled MUSKET or RIFLE. First used in the 16th century, it was chiefly a CAVALRY weapon until the 18th century. It was later carried by some unmounted officers, artillerymen, and other specialists. By the end of the 20th century, light assault rifles (such as the Soviet AK-47 or the U.S. M16 RIFLE) had made the carbine obsolete as a military weapon, but it remained popular as a recreational weapon for hunting in heavy brush or on horseback.

carbohydrate Any member of a very abundant and widespread class of natural organic compounds that includes SUGARS, STARCH, and CELLULOSE. They are commonly classified as MONOSACCHARIDES (simple sugars, e.g., GLUCOSE, FRUCTOSE), disaccharides (2-unit sugars, e.g., SUCROSE, LACTOSE), OLIGOSACCHARIDES (3–10 or so sugars), and POLYSACCHARIDES (large molecules with up to 10,000 monosaccharide units, including cellulose, starch, and GLYCOGEN). Green plants produce carbohydrates by PHOTOSYNTHESIS. In most animals, carbohydrates are the quickly accessible reservoir of energy, and oxidation (see OXIDATION-REDUCTION) of glucose in tissues supplies energy for METABOLISM. Many (but by no means all) carbohydrates have the general chemical formula $C_n(H_2O)_n$. The carbon (C) atoms are bonded to hydrogen atoms (—H), hydroxyl groups (—OH; see FUNCTIONAL GROUP), and carbonyl groups (—C=O), whose combinations, order, and geometrical arrangement lead to a large number of ISOMERS with the same chemical formula but different properties. The class is further enlarged because each isomer has various derivatives: uronic acids, sugars with an oxidized group; sugar alcohols, sugars with a reduced group; GLYCOSIDES, compounds of sugars with other hydroxyl-group-containing molecules, and amino sugars, sugars with an amino group (see AMINO ACID).

carbolic acid \kär-ˈbä-lik\ *or* **phenol** \ˈfē-ˌnōl, ˈfē-ˌnȯl\ Organic compound, simplest member of the class of PHENOLS. A colorless liquid with a bland, sweetish odor, it is toxic and caustic. It is a high-volume industrial chemical, used chiefly in the manufacture of phenol-formaldehyde RESINS (see FORMALDEHYDE, PLASTICS), EPOXY resins, nylon, herbicides, biocides, other synthetic chemicals and pharmaceuticals, and DYES. It is also a SOLVENT and general disinfectant. The "phenol coefficient" is a number that expresses the germicidal action of a chemical compared to that of phenol.

carbon Nonmetallic chemical ELEMENT, chemical symbol C, atomic number 6. The usual stable ISOTOPE is carbon-12; carbon-13, another stable isotope, is 1% of natural carbon. Carbon-14 is the most stable and best known of five radioactive isotopes (see RADIOACTIVITY); its HALF-LIFE of approximately 5,730 years makes it useful in CARBON-14 DATING and radiolabeling of research compounds. Carbon occurs in three ALLOTROPES: DIAMOND, GRAPHITE, and carbon black (amorphous carbon), including COAL, COKE, and CHARCOAL. Carbon forms more compounds than all other elements combined; several million are known. Each carbon atom forms four bonds (four single bonds, two single and one double bond, two double bonds, or one single and one triple bond) with up to four other atoms. Multitudes of chain, branched, ring, and three-dimensional structures can occur. The study of these carbon compounds and their properties and reactions is organic chemistry. With hydrogen, oxygen, nitrogen, and a few other elements whose small amounts belie their important roles, carbon forms the compounds that make up all living things: PROTEINS, CARBOHYDRATES, LIPIDS, and NUCLEIC ACIDS. BIOCHEMISTRY is the study of how those compounds are synthesized and broken down and how they associate with each other in living organisms. Organisms consume carbon and return it to the environment in the CARBON CYCLE. CARBON DIOXIDE, produced when carbon is burned, is about 0.03% of air, and carbon occurs in the earth's crust as CARBONATE rocks and the HYDROCARBONS in coal, PETROLEUM, and NATURAL GAS. The oceans contain large amounts of dissolved carbon dioxide and carbonates.

carbon-14 dating *or* **radiocarbon dating** Method of determining the age of once-living material, developed by U.S. physicist WILLARD LIBBY c. 1946. It depends on the decay of the radioactive isotope carbon-14 (radiocarbon) to nitrogen. All living plants and animals continually take in carbon: green plants absorb it in the form of carbon dioxide from the atmosphere, and it is passed to animals through the food chain. Some of this carbon is radioactive carbon-14, which slowly decays to the stable isotope nitrogen-14. When an organism dies it stops taking in carbon, so the amount of carbon-14 in its tissues steadily decreases. Because carbon-14 decays at a constant rate, the time since an organism died can be estimated by measuring the amount of radiocarbon in its remains. The method is a useful technique for dating fossils and archaeological specimens from 500 to 50,000 years old and is widely used by geologists, anthropologists, and archaeologists.

carbon cycle Circulation of CARBON in the form of the simple ELEMENT and its compounds through nature. The source of carbon in living things is CARBON DIOXIDE (CO_2), from air or dissolved in water. ALGAE and green PLANTS (producers) use CO_2 in PHOTOSYNTHESIS to make CARBOHYDRATES, used in the processes of METABOLISM to make all other compounds in their tissues and those of animals that consume them (HERBIVORES). The carbon may pass through several levels of herbivores and CARNIVORES (consumers). Animals and (at night) plants return the CO_2 to the atmosphere as a byproduct of RESPIRATION. The carbon in animal wastes and the bodies of organisms is released as CO_2, in a series of steps, by decay organisms (decomposers), chiefly BACTERIA and fungi (see FUNGUS). Some organic carbon (the remains of organisms) has accumulated in the earth's crust in FOSSIL FUELS, LIMESTONE, and CORAL. The carbon of fossil fuels, removed from the cycle in prehistoric times, is being returned in vast quantities as CO_2 via industrial and agricultural processes, some accumulating in the oceans as dissolved CARBONATES and some staying in the atmosphere (see GREENHOUSE EFFECT).

carbon dioxide Inorganic compound, a colorless gas with a faint, sharp odor and a sour taste when dissolved in water, chemical formula CO_2. About 0.03% of air by volume, it is produced when carbon-containing materials burn completely and from FERMENTATION and animal RESPIRATION. Plants use CO_2 in PHOTOSYNTHESIS to make CARBOHYDRATES. In the atmosphere, CO_2 keeps some of the sun's energy received by the earth from radiating into space (see GREENHOUSE EFFECT). In water, it forms a solution of a weak ACID, carbonic acid (H_2CO_3). Its reaction with AMMONIA is the first step in synthesizing UREA. An important industrial material, CO_2 is recovered from sources including flue gases, the process that produces HYDROGEN, and limekilns. It is used as a refrigerant, chemical intermediate, and inert atmosphere; in fire extinguishers, foaming rubber and plastics, carbonated beverages (see CARBONATION), and aerosol sprays; in water treatment, welding, and cloud seeding; and for promoting plant growth in greenhouses. Under pressure it becomes a liquid, the form most used in industry. If the liquid is allowed to expand, it cools and partially freezes to the solid form, DRY ICE.

carbon monoxide Inorganic compound, a highly toxic, colorless, odorless, flammable gas, chemical formula CO. It is produced when CARBON (including COAL and COKE) or carbon-containing fuels (including PETROLEUM HYDROCARBONS, e.g., GASOLINE, fuel oil) do not burn completely to CARBON DIOXIDE, because of insufficient OXYGEN. It is present in the exhaust gases of internal combustion engines and furnaces. CO is toxic because it binds to HEMOGLOBIN much more strongly than oxygen, interfering with transport of oxygen from the lungs to the tissues (see HYPOXIA, RESPIRATION). Symptoms of CO poisoning include headache, nausea, syncope, and on to coma, weak pulse, respiratory failure, and death. CO is used industrially as a fuel and in synthesis of numerous organic compounds, including methanol, ethylene, and aldehydes.

carbon steel ALLOY of IRON and CARBON in which the carbon content may range from less than 0.015% to slightly more than 2%. Adding this tiny amount of carbon produces a material that exhibits great strength, hardness, and other valuable mechanical properties. Carbon steels account for about 90% of the world's STEEL production. They are used extensively for automobile bodies, appliances, machinery, ships, containers, and the structures of buildings. Carbon steel, formerly made by the BESSEMER, CRUCIBLE, or OPEN-HEARTH PROCESS, is now made by the BASIC OXYGEN PROCESS, or by an ARC FURNACE.

Carbonari \\ˌkär-bə-ˈnä-rē\\ (Italian dialect: "Charcoal Burners") Members of a secret society (the Carbonaria) in early-19th-century Italy. Advocating liberal and patriotic ideas, the Carbonari favored constitutional and representative government and aimed to protect Italian interests against foreigners. They helped lead the unsuccessful revolts of 1820 and 1831 and were gradually absorbed into the YOUNG ITALY movement. Their influence prepared the way for the RISORGIMENTO.

carbonate Any member of two classes of chemical compounds derived from carbonic acid (H_2CO_3) or CARBON DIOXIDE (CO_2). Inorganic carbonates (MCO_3 or M_2CO_3, where M is any METAL) are SALTS of carbonic acid. The shells and other hard parts of shellfish are calcium carbonate, as is the LIMESTONE they turn into. Many other minerals, including CALCITE, DOLOMITE, and ARAGONITE, consist of or contain carbonates. Sodium carbonate is one of the four most important basic chemical commodities. Organic carbonates are ESTERS of carbonic acid and various ALCOHOL groups (methyl, ethyl, or phenyl). These are liquids used as SOLVENTS and to synthesize plastics and other compounds.

carbonate mineral Any member of a family of minerals that contains the carbonate ion, CO_3^{2-}, as the basic structural unit. The carbonates are among the most widely distributed minerals in the earth's CRUST; the most common are CALCITE, DOLOMITE, and ARAGONITE. Dolomite replaces calcite in limestones; when this replacement is extensive, the rock is called dolomite. Other relatively common carbonate minerals are SIDERITE, RHODOCHROSITE, strontianite (strontium-rich); smithsonite (zinc-rich); witherite (barium-rich); and cerussite (lead-rich).

carbonation Addition of CARBON DIOXIDE gas to a beverage, imparting sparkle and a tangy taste and preventing spoilage. The liquid is chilled and cascaded down in an enclosure containing carbon dioxide (either dry ice or pressurized liquid) under pressure. Increasing pressure and lowering temperature maximize gas absorption. Carbonated beverages do not require PASTEURIZATION. The carbonation in sparkling wine comes from FERMENTATION of sugar added to the initial wine.

Carboniferous period Interval of geologic time 354–290 million years ago, marked by great changes in world geography. All the landmasses drew closer together as a result of tectonic plate movements. The supercontinent GONDWANA occupied much of the Southern Hemisphere. By the end of the period, present-day North America, Greenland, and northern Europe were also part of Gondwana. Siberia and China (including Southeast Asia) remained individual continents located at high latitudes in the Northern Hemisphere. During this period, swamp forests became widespread, and enormous coal deposits formed. Plants made great advances in the complex forests, and vertebrates were undergoing extensive evolution. Amphibians became widespread and diverse, and reptiles appeared for the first time and rapidly adapted to many habitats.

carbonyl chloride See PHOSGENE

Carborundum \\ˌkär-bə-ˈrən-dəm\\ Trademark name of silicon CARBIDE, an inorganic compound discovered in the 1880s by E.G. ACHESON. Carborundum has a crystal structure like that of DIAMOND and is almost as hard. It is used as an abrasive for cutting, grinding, and polishing, as an antislip additive, and as a REFRACTORY.

carboxylic acid \\ˌkär-bäk-ˈsi-lik\\ Any organic compound with the general chemical formula —COOH in which a carbon (C) atom is bonded to an oxygen (O) atom by a double bond to make a carbonyl group (—C=O; see FUNCTIONAL GROUP) and to a hydroxyl group (—OH) by a single bond (see BONDING). The fourth bond on the carbon links it to a hydrogen (H) atom (for FORMIC ACID), a methyl (—CH_3) group (for ACETIC ACID), or another natural or synthetic monovalent group. Carboxylic acids occur widely in nature. In FATTY ACIDS, the fourth group is a HYDROCARBON chain. In aromatic acids (see AROMATIC COMPOUND), it is a ring-structured hydrocarbon. In AMINO ACIDS, it contains a nitrogen atom.

Carboxylic acids participate in chemical reactions as ACIDS, usually fairly weak. Many carboxylic acids (acetic acid, CITRIC ACID, LACTIC ACID) are intermediates in METABOLISM and can be found in natural products; others (e.g., SALICYLIC ACID) are used as SOLVENTS and to prepare many chemical compounds. Important carboxylic-acid derivatives include ESTERS, ANHYDRIDES, AMIDES, halides (see HALOGEN), and SALTS (see SOAP).

carburetor \'kär-bə-ˌrā-tər\ Device for supplying a spark-ignition ENGINE with a mixture of fuel and air. Carburetors for automobile engines usually contain a storage chamber for liquid fuel, a choke, an idling jet, a main jet, an air-flow restriction, and an accelerator pump. The quantity of fuel in the storage chamber is controlled by a valve actuated by a float. The choke, a butterfly VALVE, reduces the intake of air so that a fuel-rich charge is drawn into the cylinders when a cold engine is started. As the engine warms up, the choke is gradually opened. Reduced pressure near the partially closed throttle valve causes the fuel to flow from the idling jet into the intake air. Further opening the throttle valve activates the main fuel jet. Then the venturi-shaped air-flow restriction creates reduced pressure, drawing fuel from the main jet into the air stream at a rate related to the air flow so that a nearly constant fuel-air ratio is obtained. The accelerator pump injects fuel into the inlet air when the throttle is opened suddenly. See also GASOLINE ENGINE, VENTURI TUBE.

carburizing Oldest method for surface-hardening STEEL, by heat or mechanical means to increase the hardness of the outer surface while leaving the core relatively soft. The combination of hard surface and soft interior withstands very high STRESS and FATIGUE, and also offers low cost and superior flexibility in manufacturing. To carburize, the steel parts are placed in a carbonaceous environment (with charcoal, coke, and carbonates, or with carbon dioxide, carbon monoxide, methane, or propane) at a high temperature for several hours. The CARBON diffuses into the surface of the steel, altering the crystal structure of the metal. Gears, ball and roller bearings, and piston pins are often carburized.

Carcassonne \ˌkär-kä-'sȯn\ *ancient* **Carcaso.** City (pop., 1990: 45,000), southwestern France. Situated on the Aude River, it was occupied by the IBERIANS in the 5th century BC and later by Gallo-Romans. Muslims took it in AD 728. The English soldier SIMON DE MONTFORT captured it c. 1209, and in 1247 it was united with the French crown. It was burned by EDWARD THE BLACK PRINCE in 1355 when he failed to take the citadel. A 13th-century church and cathedral survive, as do remains of medieval fortifications. The modern city's main economic activity is tourism.

Carchemish \'kär-kə-ˌmish\ Ancient city-state, western bank of the EUPHRATES RIVER. It lay southeast of GAZIANTEP, on the modern-day Syria-Turkey border. It was a city of the MITANNI kingdom in the 2nd millennium BC, and later a chief HITTITE city. Captured by the Egyptians under THUTMOSE III in the 15th century BC, it came under Assyrian rule in 717 BC. In a battle at Carchemish in 605 BC, NEBUCHADNEZZAR II expelled the Egyptians from Syria.

carcinogen \kär-'si-nə-jən\ Agent that can cause CANCER. Exposure to one or more carcinogens, including certain chemicals, radiation, and certain viruses, can initiate cancer under conditions not completely understood. Some people have a genetic tendency to develop cancer when exposed to a specific carcinogen or combination of carcinogens. Repeated local injury or irritation to a part of the body can be carcinogenic. Identifying and eliminating carcinogens in time can reduce the incidence of cancer.

cardamom \'kär-də-məm\ Spice consisting of whole or ground dried fruit, or seeds, of *Elettaria cardamomum,* a perennial herb of the GINGER family. The flavor is warm, slightly pungent, and highly aromatic. Cardamom is a popular seasoning. Native to moist forests of southern India, the fruit may be collected from wild plants, but most is cultivated. The whole fruit is a green, three-sided oval CAPSULE containing 15–20 dark, hard, angular seeds.

Cárdenas, Bartolomé de See Bartolome BERMEJO

Cárdenas (del Río) \'kär-dᵊn-ˌäs\, **Lázaro** (1895–1970) President of Mexico (1934–40). Of Indian descent, he joined the armed struggle against the dictatorial VICTORIANO HUERTA, rising through the ranks of the revolutionary forces. His faction triumphed, and Cárdenas was made a general in the Mexican Army in 1920. In 1928 he became governor of Michoacán, and in 1934 he became president. Noted for his efforts to carry out the social and economic aims of the revolution, he distributed a record amount of land to peasants, made loans available to them, organized workers' and peasants' confederations, and nationalized the oil industry, the principal railways, and other foreign-owned industries. He opposed U.S. influence in Mexico and later supported FIDEL CASTRO. For many Mexicans he remains the principal symbol of the political left. His son Cuauhtémoc, a prominent leader of the opposition to Mexico's ruling party, is widely believed to have been denied victory in the 1988 presidential elections by fraud; he has since served as mayor of Mexico City. See also INDIGENISMO.

cardiac arrhythmia \ā-'rit͟h-mē-ə\ Variation from the heartbeat's normal rate or rhythm, caused by problems in the HEART'S PACEMAKER or in nerves conducting its signals. Occasional arrhythmias are normal. TACHYCARDIA is a fast regular rhythm; bradycardia is a slow rhythm. Premature atrial or ventricular beats are extra contractions in normal rhythm. Ongoing arrhythmia in some heart diseases can reduce the heart's ability to supply the body with blood and lead to HEART FAILURE. Severe arrhythmias can trigger ATRIAL or VENTRICULAR fibrillation. Arrhythmias are detected by ELECTROCARDIOGRAPHY and treated by electric shock (often with an implanted pacemaker) or by drugs such as quinidine and DIGITALIS.

cardiac output Volume of blood expelled by the HEART, usually expressed in liters of blood per minute, calculated by multiplying output per heartbeat and beats per minute. It varies slightly with position and emotional states, and more with exercise and cardiac health. Cardiac output helps estimate how much oxygen is delivered to the tissues by circulation.

Cardiff City (pop., 1998 est.: 320,900), capital of Wales, located on the BRISTOL CHANNEL in southeastern Wales. The Romans built a fort there c. AD 75, but the town itself was only established with the arrival of the Normans in the 11th century. Its population was small into the early 19th century, but by the early 20th century Cardiff had become the largest coal-exporting port in the world. The coal trade ceased in the 1960s, but the city remains the largest in Wales and its principal commercial center.

Cardigan, Earl of *orig.* **James Thomas Brudenell** (1797–1868) British general. After entering the army (1824), he purchased promotions to become a lieutenant colonel (1832) and gained a reputation as a martinet. He spent his inherited wealth to make his regiment the best dressed in the service (introducing the later-named cardigan jacket). At the outbreak of the CRIMEAN WAR (1853), he was appointed commander of the Light Brigade of British cavalry, which he led in the ill-fated charge at the Battle of BALAKLAVA. Despite the disaster, Cardigan was lionized on his return to England and appointed inspector general of cavalry.

Cardigan Bay Bay, western WALES. A widemouthed inlet of ST. GEORGE'S CHANNEL, it is about 65 mi (105 km) long. Two national parks, Snowdonia and Pembrokeshire Coast, incorporate substantial stretches of shoreline. Many resort towns line the bay, including ABERYSTWYTH and Fishguard, a base for ferry service between Wales and Ireland.

Cardin \kär-'daⁿ\, **Pierre** (born 1922) French fashion designer. At 17 he went to Vichy to become a tailor at a men's shop. After World War II he joined the Parisian fashion house of Paquin and designed the costumes for JEAN COCTEAU's film *Beauty and the Beast* (1945). In the 1950s he opened his own shop, designing gowns for costume balls and ready-to-wear collections for men and women. He was a master of the bias cut. His men's clothing has influenced other designers, including Bill Blass.

cardinal Member of the Sacred College of Cardinals. Their duties include electing the POPE, acting as his principal counselors, and aiding in governing the Roman Catholic church. Cardinals serve as officers of the ROMAN CURIA, BISHOPS of major dioceses, and papal envoys. Since 769 only cardinals have been eligible to become pope, and since 1059 cardinals have elected the pope. The first cardinals were the deacons of the seven regions of Rome. Their successors are today's cardinal deacons. Cardinal bishops are successors of the bishops of the sees just outside Rome and of the patriarchal sees of the Eastern Catholic Church. Cardinal priests are the bishops of important sees around the world and are the most numerous order of cardinals. For 400 years, the number of cardinals was limited to 70, but JOHN XXIII removed the limit and there are now more than 100. A red biretta and ring are symbolic of the office.

cardinal *or* **redbird** Songbird (*Cardinalis,* formerly *Richmondena, cardinalis,* family Fringillidae, or Emberizidae) of North America east of the Rocky Mtns. It is 8 in. (20 cm) long and has a pointed crest. The male is bright red, the female a duller red or olive brown. Pairs of cardinals utter loud, clear whistling notes year-round in gardens and open woodlands. They feed on insects, wild seeds, and fruits. Cardinals are especially abundant in the southeastern U.S. and have been introduced into Hawaii, southern California, and Bermuda. This species is also sometimes called the cardinal GROSBEAK.

Cardinal (*Cardinalis cardinalis*).
STEPHEN COLLINS

cardinal flower Any of several closely related species of the genus *Lobelia,* perennial plants of the LOBELIA FAMILY, native to North and Central America. All bear spikes of scarlet, lipped flowers on leafy stems up to 5 ft (1.5 m) tall. *L. cardinalis* and *L. splendens,* considered to be one species by some authorities, are taller than *L. fulgens,* the Central American parent species of the garden cardinal flower. The blue cardinal *(L. siphilitica)* is smaller than the others and has blue or whitish flowers.

carding In YARN production, a process of separating individual fibers and causing many of them to lie parallel, and also removing most of the remaining impurities. COTTON, WOOL, waste SILK, and man-made staple are subjected to carding. Carding produces a thin sheet of uniform thickness that is then condensed to form a thick, continuous, untwisted strand called sliver. When very fine yarns are desired, carding is followed by combing, a process that removes short fibers, leaving a sliver composed entirely of long fibers, all laid parallel, and both smoother and more lustrous than uncombed types. Carded and combed sliver is then spun.

carding machine Machine for CARDING TEXTILE fibers. In the 18th century, hand carding was laborious and constituted a bottleneck in the newly mechanized production of textiles. Several inventors worked to develop machines to perform the task, notably JOHN KAY, OLIVER EVANS, LEWIS PAUL, R. ARKWRIGHT, and JOHANN BODMER.

cardiology Medical specialty dealing with HEART DISEASES and disorders. It began with the 1749 publication by Jean Baptiste de Sénac of contemporary knowledge of the heart. Diagnostic methods improved in the 19th century, and in 1905 the electrocardiograph was invented. The 20th century saw many surgical advances in cardiology, including heart transplants and the use of ARTIFICIAL HEARTS. Current diagnostic methods include chest percussion (tapping) and AUSCULTATION, ELECTROCARDIOGRAPHY, and echocardiography (see ULTRASOUND). Cardiologists provide continuing care of heart patients, doing basic heart-function studies, supervising therapy, including drug therapy, and working closely with heart surgeons.

cardiopulmonary resuscitation (CPR) Emergency procedure to restore breathing and circulation in an unconscious person. A trained rescuer opens the airway and confirms the absence of breathing and PULSE. Resuscitation itself consists of alternating mouth-to-mouth breathing (see ARTIFICIAL RESPIRATION) and repeated pressure on the chest to circulate the blood.

cardiovascular system System of vessels that convey BLOOD to and from tissues throughout the body, bringing nutrients and oxygen and removing wastes and carbon dioxide. It is essentially a long, closed tube through which blood moves in a double circuit—one through the lungs (PULMONARY CIRCULATION) and one through the rest of the body (SYSTEMIC CIRCULATION). The HEART pumps blood through the ARTERIES, which branch into smaller arterioles, which feed into microscopic CAPILLARIES. These converge to form small venules, which join to become larger VEINS, generally following the same path as the arteries back to the heart. Cardiovascular diseases include ARTERIOSCLEROSIS, congenital and rheumatic heart disease, and vascular inflammation.

Cardoso, Fernando Henrique (born 1931) President of Brazil (from 1994). Born into a wealthy military family, he taught sociology at the University of São Paulo and was a prominent member of the left-wing intellectual opposition when Brazil was under military rule, though he turned more centrist after civilian rule was restored. In 1993 he became finance minister and supervised the creation of the Real Plan, an effective anti-inflation package that helped him gain the presidency in 1994. He has worked for privatization of state-owned companies and increased foreign investment. In 1998 he became the first president in Brazilian history to be reelected. A foreign-exchange crisis in 1999 damaged Brazil's growth prospects. See also LUIS SILVA.

Cardozo, Benjamin (Nathan) (1870–1938) U.S. jurist. Born in New York City into a distinguished Jewish family, he was admitted to the New York bar in 1891 and became a successful courtroom lawyer. Elected to the state Supreme Court as a reform candidate (1913), he was quickly promoted to the Court of Appeals. During his tenure many thought the quality of the appellate bench exceeded that of the U.S. Supreme Court. He influenced the trend in U.S. appellate judging toward greater involvement in public policy and consequent modernization of legal principles. He was both a creative COMMON-LAW judge and a notable legal essayist. Appointed to the U.S. Supreme Court in 1932, he usually voted with liberals LOUIS BRANDEIS and HARLAN FISKE STONE. He wrote the majority opinion upholding the SOCIAL SECURITY program (1937). In a 1937 case on DOUBLE JEOPARDY, he held that the states were not required to implement all the provisions of the BILL OF RIGHTS, a position that became known as "selective incorporation." He served on the Court until 1938. The law school at YESHIVA UNIV. is named for him.

Cardozo.
BY COURTESY OF THE LIBRARY OF CONGRESS, WASHINGTON, D.C.

cards, playing See PLAYING CARDS

Carducci \kär-'dü-chē\, **Giosuè** (1835–1907) Italian poet. He taught literary history in Bologna for 40 years, and in later years served as a senator. He opposed the prevailing Romanticism and advocated a return to classical models of prosody, but his rhetorical tirades provoked resistance to reform. His best volumes of verse, *The New Lyrics* and *The Barbarian Odes* (1887), contain evocations of landscape, memories of childhood, and representations of the glory of ancient Rome. Regarded in his time as Italy's national poet, he won the Nobel Prize in 1906.

Carême \kå-'rem\, **Marie-Antoine** (1784–1833) French chef. Born into a poor family, he attained employment in a pastry shop frequented by CHARLES MAURICE DE TALLEYRAND. He served as Talleyrand's chef for 12 years, and subsequently created grandiose dishes and elaborately sculpted confections for the most splendid households of Europe, including those of the young GEORGE IV, Czar ALEXANDER I, and the Baron de ROTHSCHILD. He wrote several classics of *grande cuisine.*

Carew, Rod *orig.* **Rodney Cline** (born 1945) U.S. baseball player. Born in Gatún, Panama, he moved to New York City in 1962, where he learned sandlot ball. Playing for the Minnesota Twins (1967–78), he became one of the great hitters of the modern era, leading the American League in batting seven times between 1969 and 1978. His highest average was .388, in 1977. He was traded in 1979 to the California (later Anaheim) Angels, and retired in 1986 with a lifetime batting average of .328.

Carey, Peter (Philip) (born 1943) Australian writer. He worked as an advertising copywriter and at other odd jobs until 1988, when he became a full-time writer. His short-story collection *The Fat Man in History* (1974) contains macabre elements. His novels, more realistic but laced with black humor, include *Bliss* (1981), *Illywhacker* (1985), *Oscar and Lucinda* (1988, Booker Prize), *The Unusual Life of Tristan Smith* (1994), and *Jack Maggs* (1998).

cargo cult Any of the religious movements, chiefly in Melanesia in the late 19th and early 20th century, based on the observation by local residents of the delivery of exotic supplies by ship and aircraft to colonial officials. The cults exhibited the expectation of a new age of blessing and prosperity to be initiated by the arrival of a special "cargo" of goods

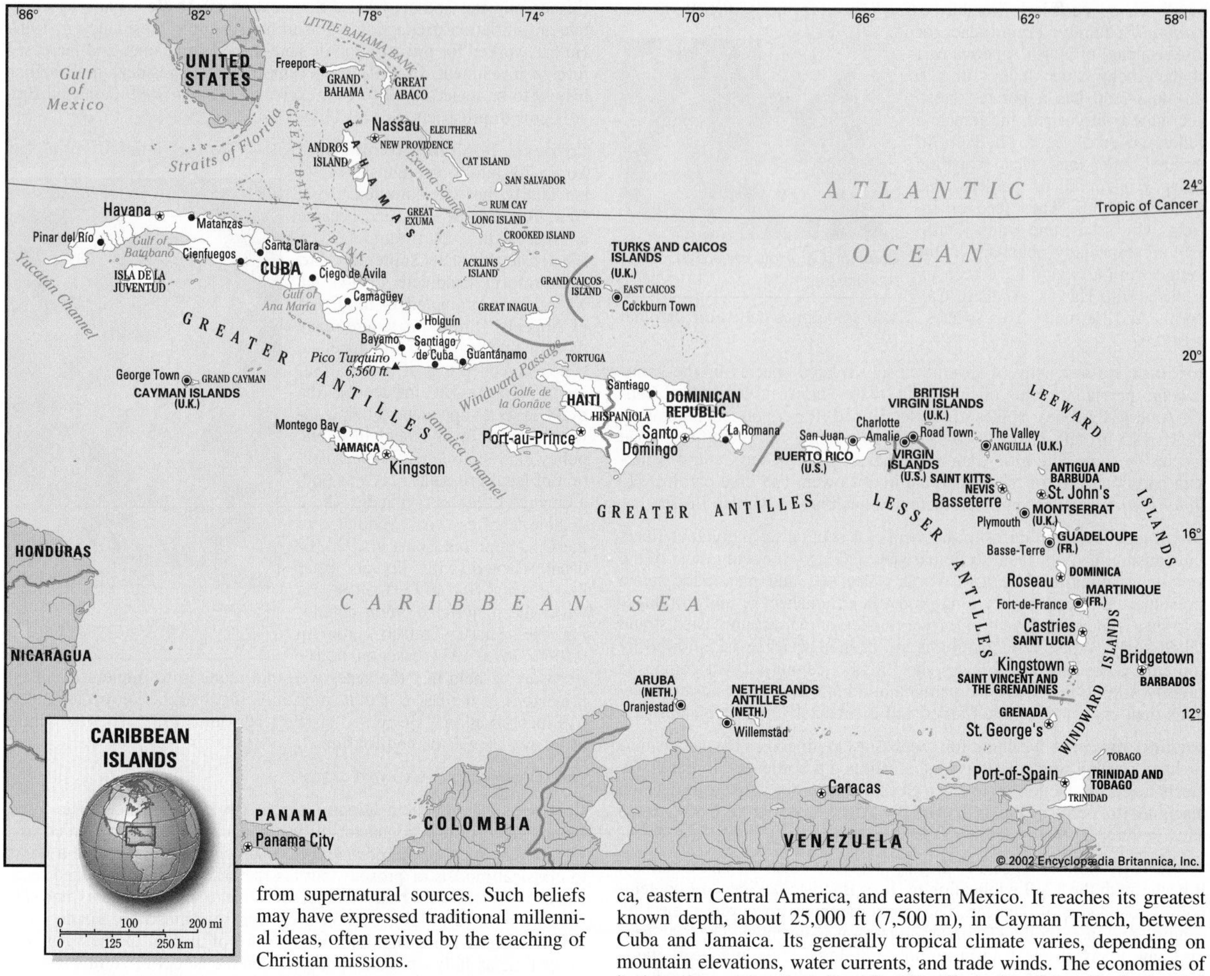

from supernatural sources. Such beliefs may have expressed traditional millennial ideas, often revived by the teaching of Christian missions.

Caria \'kar-ē-ə\ Ancient district, South Asia Minor. It was one of the most thoroughly Hellenized districts; its territory included Greek cities along its Aegean shore and a mountainous interior bounded by LYDIA, PHRYGIA, and LYCIA. Absorbed by Lydia, it later was joined to Persia's empire in the 4th century BC. MAUSOLUS transferred the capital from Mylasa to HALICARNASSUS in Caria. Taken from Persia in 334 BC by ALEXANDER THE GREAT, it was incorporated into the Roman province of Asia in 129 BC.

Carib \'kar-əb\ American Indian people who inhabited the Lesser Antilles and parts of the South American coast at the time of the Spanish conquest. The Island Carib (now extinct) were a warlike, individualistic people who reportedly practiced CANNIBALISM (the term derives from their name). Carib groups on the mainland, some of whom still survive, lived in the Guianas and south to the Amazon River; they subsisted by hunting and growing crops and were less aggressive than their island relatives.

Cariban languages \'kar-e-bən\ Large family of South American Indian languages. It has an estimated 43 members; nearly half are now extinct, and most of the remainder have very few speakers. Most Cariban languages are spoken in southern Venezuela, the Guianas, and Brazil north of the Amazon, though several have strayed far from this area. Cariban incursions into the mainly ARAWAKAN-SPEAKING Antilles at the time of Columbus provided European languages with the names "Carib" (hence, "Caribbean") and "cannibal," both perhaps from a proto-Cariban form meaning "Indian, person."

Caribbean Sea Arm of the Atlantic Ocean. It covers about 1,049,500 sq mi (2,718,200 sq km) and washes the northern coast of South America, eastern Central America, and eastern Mexico. It reaches its greatest known depth, about 25,000 ft (7,500 m), in Cayman Trench, between Cuba and Jamaica. Its generally tropical climate varies, depending on mountain elevations, water currents, and trade winds. The economies of its island countries, including St. Kitts-Nevis, Dominica, St. Lucia, and Barbados, are greatly dependent on tourism; the region is one of the world's principal winter resort areas.

caribe See PIRANHA

caribou \'kar-ə-ˌbü\ Arctic DEER *(Rangifer tarandus)* of the tundra, taiga, and forests, native to North America and, until recently, ranging from Scandinavia to eastern Siberia. Both sexes have antlers. Caribou stand 2.3–4.6 ft (0.7–1.4 m) tall at the shoulder and weigh up to 660 lbs (300 kg); domesticated races are about the size of donkeys. They are usually grayish or brownish with lighter underparts, but may be whitish or nearly black. Their herds are famous for their seasonal migration between summer and winter ranges. Their staple winter food is a lichen, popularly called reindeer moss, which they reach by scraping the snow away with their feet. In summer, they also eat grasses and saplings. See also REINDEER.

caricature \'kar-i-kə-ˌchu̇r\ Comically distorted drawing or likeness intended to satirize or ridicule its subject. The word, derived from the Italian *caricare* ("to load or charge"), was probably coined by CARRACCI FAMILY, who defended the practice as a counterpart to idealization. In the 18th century, the caricature became connected with journalism and was put to virulent use by political commentators. In the 1880s, photo-process engraving made it possible to produce and illustrate daily newpapers cheaply, bringing caricatures to the general public. Important caricaturists include JACQUES CALLOT, GEORGE CRUIKSHANK, HONORE DAUMIER, and GUSTAVE DORE.

caries \'kar-ēz\ *or* **tooth decay** Localized disease that causes decay and cavities in teeth. It begins at the TOOTH's surface and may penetrate the dentin and the pulp cavity. Microorganisms in the mouth are believed to consume sugars and produce acids that eat away at tooth enamel. The dentin's protein structure is then destroyed by enzymes. Diet, general health, structural tooth defects, and heredity affect the risk of having caries. Prevention involves avoiding excessive sweets, brushing and flossing the teeth, and having regular dental care. Treatment includes restoration of teeth with cavities. FLUORIDATION OF WATER can reduce the occurrence of caries by as much as 65%.

carillon \'kar-ə-ˌlän\ Musical instrument consisting of at least 23 cast bronze bells tuned in chromatic order. Usually located in a tower, it is played from a keyboard. Most carillons encompass three to four octaves. The carillon originated in Flanders c. 1480, and the art of carillon building reached its height in the Netherlands in the 17th century, when the tuning of the bells became highly refined.

Carillon clavier.
GILLETT & JOHNSTON (CROYDON) LIMITED

Carinthia *German* **Kärnten** \'kernt-ᵊn\ State (pop., 1995 est.: 561,000), southern Austria. Bordered by Italy and Slovenia, it occupies an area of 3,681 sq mi (9,534 sq km) and has its capital at Klagenfurt. Originally inhabited by Celts, it became part of the Roman province of NORICUM. Made a separate duchy in 976, it came under the HABSBURGS in 1335, and became an Austrian crown land in 1849. In 1918 parts were claimed by Yugoslavia and Italy. Yugoslavia's possession of the southern part was confirmed in 1920, but the Klagenfurt area was retained by Austria.

Carissimi \kä-'rēs-sē-mē\, **Giacomo** (1605–1674) Italian composer. He worked as *maestro di cappella* at the Collegio Germanico in Rome, a musically important post at a notable Jesuit institution, from 1629 until his death. His approximately 15 oratorios (performed in place of operas during Lent), including *Baltazar, Ezechia, Jephte, Jonas,* and *Judicium extremum,* made him the principal oratorio composer of the mid-17th century. He also wrote some 150 cantatas and nearly 100 motets.

Carl XVI Gustaf *Swedish* **Carl Gustaf Folke Hubertus** (born 1946) King of Sweden from 1973. Grandson of King Gustav VI Adolf (1882–1973), he became crown prince in 1950, his father having died in 1947. After studying at military schools, he became a naval officer. His accession occurred at a time when the role of the Swedish monarchy was being radically altered; the new constitutional laws of 1973 left the king with a solely symbolic function rather than a formal role in the country's administration.

Carleton, Guy *later* **Baron Dorchester (of Dorchester)** (1724–1808) Irish soldier-statesman. In 1759 he was sent to Canada and fought in the Battle of Quebec. He served as lieutenant governor (1766–68) and governor (1768–78) of Quebec province. His conciliatory policies toward the French Canadians led to passage of the QUEBEC ACT of 1774. He helped repel the attack on Quebec by American Revolutionary forces in 1775. He was appointed commander of British forces in North America in 1782 and then governor in chief of British North America (1786–96).

Carleton College \'kär-əl-tən\ Private liberal-arts college in Northfield, Minn., founded in 1866. It offers a variety of undergraduate majors. Small classes and opportunities to participate in faculty research projects attract a select student body, most from out of state. Enrollment is about 1,700.

Carlisle \kär-'līl\ City (metro area pop., 1995 est: 103,000), and seat of CUMBRIA county, northwestern England. It was founded as Luguvallium by the Romans on the EDEN RIVER opposite a fortified camp on the line of HADRIAN'S WALL. Destroyed by Norse invaders c. 875, it was restored when claimed from the Scots by WILLIAM II in 1092. MARY, QUEEN OF SCOTS, was imprisoned there in 1568. It was besieged during the ENGLISH CIVIL WARS, and its Royalist defenders eventually surrendered to Parliamentary forces in 1645. Its cotton-textile industry grew in the 18th–19th century, and it has remained the center of the northern England cotton industry.

Carlism Spanish political movement of traditionalist character that originated in the 1820s. Carlists supported the claims of FERDINAND VII's brother Don Carlos (1788–1855) and his descendants to the throne, rejecting the succession of Ferdinand's daughter ISABELLA II by invoking the Salic Law (introduced into Spain in 1713), which excluded females from the royal succession. The disputed succession led to several unsuccessful civil rebellions, known as the Carlist Wars (1833–39, 1872–76). Later adherents of Carlism formed the Traditionalist Party (1918), which merged with the FALANGE in 1937.

Carlsbad See KARLOVY VARY

Carlsbad Caverns National Park Preserve, southeastern New Mexico. Established as a national monument in 1923 and as a national park in 1930, it covers 73 sq mi (189 sq km). Beneath the surface winds a maze of underground chambers; one of the largest caverns ever discovered, the Big Room, is about 2,000 ft (600 m) long and 1,100 ft (330 m) wide, and its ceiling arches 255 ft (78 m) above the floor. In the summer a colony of bats inhabits a part of the caverns known as Bat Cave.

Carlsbad Decrees (1819) Resolutions issued by German leaders to suppress liberal and nationalistic tendencies. Meeting at Carlsbad (now Karlovy Vary, Czech Republic), the conference of ministers from the major German states agreed to KLEMENS, FURST VON METTERNICH's proposals advocating censorship, the disbanding of the BURSCHENSCHAFT groups, and the creation of a commission to ferret out conspiratorial organizations. In the long run, the repressive decrees failed to stifle German nationalism or liberal developments.

Carlsson, Arvid (born 1923) Swedish pharmacologist. He received his MD from the University of Lund. Carlsson established that DOPAMINE is an important neurotransmitter, showing that high levels of dopamine are found in areas of the brain that control walking and other voluntary movements. He determined that l-dopa, a substance that the brain uses to make dopamine, could be employed as a treatment for PARKINSONISM. His work also contributed to an understanding of the relationship between neurotransmitters and mental states such as clinical DEPRESSION, which led to new antidepressant drugs, including PROZAC. Along with ERIC KANDEL and PAUL GREENGARD, Carlsson was awarded the Nobel Prize in 2000.

Carlton, Steve(n Norman) (born 1944) U.S. baseball pitcher. Born in Miami, he pitched in junior college before signing with the St. Louis Cardinals in 1965. A left-handed pitcher, he won 20 or more games in a single season six times and was a four-time Cy Young award winner for best pitcher. He played for the Cardinals (1966–70), the Philadelphia Phillies (1971–83), and several other teams. His career total of 4,136 strikeouts is second only to that of NOLAN RYAN.

Carlyle, Thomas (1795–1881) Scottish historian and essayist. The son of a mason, he was reared in a strict Calvinist household and educated at the University of Edinburgh. He moved to London in 1834. An energetic, irritable, fiercely independent idealist, he became a leading moral force in Victorian literature. His humorous essay *Sartor Resartus* (1836) is a fantastic hodgepodge of autobiography and German philosophy. *The French Revolution* (3 vols., 1837), perhaps his greatest achievement, contains outstanding set pieces and character studies. *On Heroes, Hero-Worship, and the Heroic in History* (1841) showed his reverence for strength, particularly when combined with the conviction of a God-given mission. He later published a study of OLIVER CROMWELL (1845) and a huge biography of FREDERICK II THE GREAT (6 vols., 1858–65).

Carlyle, detail of an oil painting by G.F. Watts, 1877; in the National Portrait Gallery, London.

BY COURTESY OF THE NATIONAL PORTRAIT GALLERY, LONDON

Carmarthen \kər-ˈmär-t͟hən\ Town (pop., 1991: 13,524), seat of Dyfed county, southern Wales. It lies on the River Towy above the mouth of the BRISTOL CHANNEL. Both the Romans and Normans built strongholds there. An Augustinian priory, dating from the Norman period, housed the oldest extant Welsh manuscript, the *Black Book of Carmarthen* (c. 1170–1230).

Carmelite Mendicant order of the Roman Catholic church. It originated c. 1155 on Mount Carmel in Palestine, where a number of former pilgrims and crusaders began to live as hermits. Their rule was written by St. Albert, Latin patriarch of Jerusalem, and approved by Pope HONORIUS III in 1226. As Muslim incursions made Palestine increasingly unsafe, the Carmelites scattered to Cyprus, Sicily, France, and England. In England and Western Europe the order transformed itself from a group of hermits into one of mendicant friars. The first institution of Carmelite nuns was founded in 1452. St. TERESA OF ÁVILA and St. JOHN OF THE CROSS reemphasized the strictness and austerity of Carmelite traditions, establishing Discalced (barefoot) Carmelite orders in 1562 and 1569, which gave rise to an independent order in 1593. Both the reformed and the original orders suffered greatly during the French Revolution and the Napoleonic era, but they were later restored in most of Western Europe as well as in the Middle East, Latin America, and the U.S.

Carmichael, Hoagy *orig.* **Hoagland Howard** (1899–1981) U.S. songwriter. Born in Indiana, Carmichael met many jazz musicians while studying law there, including BIX BEIDERBECKE, who recorded his first composition, "Riverboat Shuffle" (1924). The relaxed tunefulness of such later songs as "Georgia (Georgia on My Mind)," "Rockin' Chair," and "Lazy River" made them universally attractive. For Hollywood films he wrote "Two Sleepy People," "Heart and Soul," and "In the Cool, Cool, Cool of the Evening" (Academy Award). His "Stardust" is reputedly the most recorded popular song of all time. He acted in several films, including *To Have and Have Not* (1944) and *Young Man with a Horn* (1950), and wrote the memoirs *The Stardust Road* (1946) and *Sometimes I Wonder* (1965).

Carmona \kär-ˈmō-nə\, **António Oscar de Fragoso** (1869–1951) Portuguese general and politician. A career officer, he rose to the rank of general by 1922. He took part in the army coup of May 1926 and became premier later that year. He ruled as a virtual dictator before calling for a plebiscite; elected president, he served from 1928 to 1951, acting as a symbol of political continuity after he named ANTONIO DE OLIVEIRA SALAZAR premier in 1932.

Carnap, Rudolf (1891–1970) German-U.S. philosopher. A student of GOTTLOB FREGE, he was a member of the VIENNA CIRCLE and a proponent of UNIFIED SCIENCE. He fled to the U.S. in 1935, where he taught at the Univs. of Chicago (1936–52) and California (1954–70), continuing to contribute to logic, epistemology, the philosophy of language, probability theory, and the philosophy of science. His epistemology systematically analyzes the logic of knowledge, instead of taking a psychological approach as earlier empiricists had. His works include *The Logical Structure of the World* (1928), *The Logical Syntax of Language* (1934), *Introduction to Semantics* (1942), *Meaning and Necessity* (1947), and *The Logical Foundations of Probability* (1950).

carnation Herbaceous plant *(Dianthus caryophyllus)* of the PINK FAMILY, native to the Mediterranean, widely cultivated for its fringe-petaled, often spicy-smelling flowers. Border, or garden, carnations include a range of varieties and hybrids. The perpetual flowering carnation, taller and stouter, produces larger flowers and blooms almost continuously in the greenhouse; miniature (baby) and spray varieties are also grown for the florist trade. Carnations are among the most popular cut flowers, used in floral arrangements, corsages, and boutonnieres.

carnauba wax Very hard wax obtained from fronds of the carnauba tree, *Copernicia cerifera,* a fan PALM of Brazil. During the regular dry seasons in Brazil, where it is called the tree of life, the carnauba palm protects its fanlike fronds from loss of moisture by secreting a coat of carnauba wax. Carnauba has been used in high-gloss polishes, phonograph records, and explosives. Synthetics have replaced it for many applications.

Carné \kår-ˈnā\, **Marcel** (1909–1996) French film director. Son of a cabinetmaker, he worked as an assistant director before directing his first feature, *Jenny* (1936). This success was followed by *Bizarre, Bizarre* (1937), *Port of Shadows* (1938), and *Daybreak* (1939), works of poetic realism that were the fruit of his collaboration with screenwriter JACQUES PREVERT. During the Nazi occupation he made *The Devil's Envoys* (1942), and later his masterpiece, *The Children of Paradise* (1945), which chronicled life in the theater and celebrated the French spirit. His work declined after his breakup with Prévert in 1948.

Carnegie \kär-ˈne-gē, ˈkär-nə-gē\, **Andrew** (1835–1919) U.S. industrialist and philanthropist. The son of a Scottish weaver, he emigrated to the U.S. with his family in 1848. A job in a telegraph office led to his early career with the PENNSYLVANIA RAILROAD CO., and his canny investments made him wealthy by age 30. In 1872–73 he founded the steelworks near Pittsburgh that evolved into the Carnegie Steel Co. in 1889. By adopting technological innovations such as the open-hearth furnace and by increasing efficiency through VERTICAL INTEGRATION, Carnegie built a vast enterprise that dominated the U.S. steel industry. In 1901 he sold his company to J. P. MORGAN, and it became part of U.S. STEEL. Believing that rich men were obliged to use their surplus wealth for the improvement of mankind, Carnegie retired to devote himself to philanthropy, giving hundreds of millions of dollars to libraries and universities, including CARNEGIE-MELLON UNIV., and endowing such organizations as the Carnegie Institute of Pittsburgh and the Carnegie Corp. of New York, the largest of all his foundations.

Andrew Carnegie.

BROWN BROTHERS

Carnegie, Dale *orig.* **Dale Carnegey** (1888–1955) U.S. lecturer and author. Born into poverty in Maryville, Mo., he worked as a traveling salesman 1908–12, and began lecturing on public speaking at a New York City YMCA in 1912. After publishing *The Art of Public Speaking* (1915) and other books, he began to focus on the importance of an individual's attitude in achieving financial success. His *How to Win Friends and Influence People* (1936) became one of the best-selling books of all time, and the Dale Carnegie Institute subsequently established hundreds of chapters throughout the country.

Carnegie Hall Concert hall in New York City. Endowed by ANDREW CARNEGIE at the insistence of Walter Damrosch (1862–1950) and designed by William Burnet Tuthill, it opened in 1891, with P. TCHAIKOVSKY as guest of honor. Threatened by destruction in the late 1950s, it was saved by a public outcry and purchased by the city. It was extensively renovated in 1982–86. Admired for its beauty and its superb acoustics, it seats almost 2,800 people and has long been the most famous concert hall in the U.S.

Carnegie Mellon University Private university in Pittsburgh, Pa. It was formed in 1967 through the merger of the Carnegie Institute of Technology (created in 1900 through a gift from Andrew Carnegie) and the Mellon Institute of Industrial Research (founded in 1913 through a gift from Andrew W. Mellon). It comprises schools of technology, science, computer science, humanities and social sciences, fine arts, public policy, and industrial administration. It has built a reputation as an arts center, operating three galleries, two concert halls, and two theaters. Total enrollment is about 7,800.

carnelian \kär-ˈnē-lē-ən\ *or* **cornelian** Translucent, semiprecious variety of the silica mineral chalcedony that owes its red to reddish brown color to the incorporation of small amounts of iron oxide. A closely related variety of chalcedony, sard, differs only in the shade of red. Carnelian was highly valued and used in rings and signets by the Greeks and Romans, some of whose intaglios have retained their high polish better than those made from harder stones. Carnelian is mined principally in India, Brazil, and Australia. Its physical properties are those of quartz.

Carney, Art(hur William Matthew) (born 1918) U.S. actor. Born in Mount Vernon, N.Y., he appeared in comedy acts, on radio, and in several Broadway plays before winning national fame as Ed Norton in the television comedy series *The Jackie Gleason Show* (1952–57) and in the spin-off series *The Honeymooners.* He appeared in several films in the 1970s and '80s, including *Harry and Tonto* (1974, Academy Award). He won six Emmy awards for his work in television.

Carniola Region, southern Europe. Located northeast of the head of the Adriatic Sea, it includes a mountainous area. Its chief town is Ljubljana, Slovenia. It was part of the Roman province of Pannonia in ancient times and was occupied by the Slovenes in the 6th century AD. In the 13th century it became part of the Holy Roman Empire. In 1335 it became a possession of the Austrian Habsburgs, who held it as a duchy until 1849, when it was recognized as an Austrian crown land (1849–1918). After World War I it was divided between Italy and the new Kingdom of Serbs, Croats, and Slovenes (later Yugoslavia); it was incorporated entirely into Yugoslavia by a 1947 treaty. When Yugoslavia was fragmented in the 1990s, it was included in Slovenia.

carnival Final celebration before the fasting and austerity of Lent in some Roman Catholic regions. The most famous and probably most exuberant carnival is that of Rio de Janeiro, which is celebrated with masked balls, costumes, and parades; the best-known U.S. celebration is Mardi Gras in New Orleans. The first day of carnival season varies with local traditions, but carnival usually ends on Shrove Tuesday, the day before the start of Lent.

carnivore Any meat-eating animal, but especially any member of the order Carnivora, consisting of 10 families of primarily predatory mammals: Canidae (e.g., dogs), Ursidae (bears), Procyonidae (raccoons), Mustelidae (weasels), Viverridae (civets), Hyaenidae (hyenas), Felidae (cats), Otariidae and Phocidae (seals), and Odobenidae (walrus). Though most carnivores eat only meat, some rely heavily on vegetation (e.g., the panda). Most have a complex tooth structure and a lower jaw that can move only vertically but can exert great power. The earliest carnivores, which probably evolved from an insectivorous ancestor, appeared during the Paleocene epoch (about 65–55 million years ago). Carnivores are highly intelligent.

carnivorous plant Any of about 400 diverse species of plants specially adapted for capturing insects and other tiny animals by ingenious pitfalls and traps and for digesting the nitrogen-rich animal proteins to obtain nutrients. These adaptations are thought to enable such plants to survive under otherwise marginal or hostile environmental conditions. The conspicuous trapping mechanism (a leaf modification) draws the prey's attention to the plant. More than half the species belong to the family Lentibulariaceae, most being bladderworts. The remainder belong to several families composed of the pitcher plants, sundews, and flytraps (see Venus's-flytrap). Most are found in damp heaths, bogs, swamps, and muddy or sandy shores where water is abundant and where nitrogenous materials are often scarce or unavailable because of acid or other unfavorable soil conditions. The smallest *Drosera* species are often hidden among the moss of a sphagnum bog; most carnivorous plants are small herbaceous perennials. Some become large shrubby vines.

carnosaur Any of the large carnivorous dinosaurs, a branch of theropod dinosaurs that evolved into predators of large herbivorous dinosaurs. Carnosaurs were massive animals with short necks, large skulls, and wide, gaping mouths equipped with formidable teeth. They walked on two legs. Tyrannosaurs were the largest of all carnosaurs. The carnosaurs became extinct at the end of the Cretaceous period (65 million years ago).

Carnot \kär-ˈnō\, **Lazare (-Nicolas-Marguerite)** (1753–1823) French statesman and administrator in successive governments of the French Revolution. He entered the army as an engineer (1773) and was elected to the Legislative Assembly in 1791. As a leading member of the Committee of Public Safety, and the Directory, he helped mobilize the Revolutionary armed forces and matériel, and he was lauded as the "Organizer of Victory." During the Coup of 18 Fructidor he fled France to escape arrest. He returned after Napoleon rose to power and served him in various offices, including minister of the interior during the Hundred Days.

Carnot \kär-ˈnō\, **(Nicolas-Léonard-) Sadi** (1796–1832) French scientist, known for describing the Carnot cycle. Son of Lazare Carnot, he was an army officer most of his life. Convinced that Britain's advanced steam engines and France's inadequate use of steam were factors in Napoleon's downfall, he wrote a nontechnical essay on steam engines (1824). He subsequently developed a theory of heat engines predicting that efficiency depends only on the temperature of the hottest and coldest parts and not on the substance (steam or any other fluid) that drives the mechanism. Though adopted only slowly, his theory was eventually incorporated into the general theory of thermodynamics.

Carnot, (Marie-François-) Sadi (1837–1894) French politician. Grandson of Lazare Carnot and son of Sadi Carnot, he worked as a government engineer before turning to politics. After serving as minister of public works (1880–81) and finance (1885–87), he was elected in 1887 as fourth president of the Third Republic. He competently handled the plots by Georges Boulanger, anarchist agitation, and the Panama Canal scandals, and retained his popularity through 10 different governments, but was assassinated in 1894 by an Italian anarchist.

Carnot cycle In heat engines, the ideal cycle of changes of pressures and temperatures of a working fluid, such as steam or ammonia, conceived by Sadi Carnot. It is the standard of performance of all heat engines operating between a high and a low temperature. In the cycle, the working fluid undergoes four successive changes: (1) the fluid receives heat, expanding at high temperature; (2) it delivers work during the reversible adiabatic expansion (it changes in volume or pressure without losing or gaining heat); (3) it rejects heat (to the heat sink) during compression at low temperature; and (4) it receives work during the reversible adiabatic compression. The efficiency is determined by the difference between the temperatures of the heat source and the heat sink divided by the temperature of the heat source. See also Rankine cycle.

Carnuntum Ancient town, Roman empire. Located in northern Pannonia on the Danube River, it was an important Roman post from the time of Augustus. It was used as a base by Marcus Aurelius in his campaign against the Marcommani (AD 171–73); there he wrote the second book of his *Meditations.* The camp was finally destroyed by Germans in the 4th century.

carob Leguminous evergreen tree *(Ceratonia siliqua)* native to the eastern Mediterranean region and cultivated elsewhere. It is sometimes known as locust, or St. John's bread, in the belief that the "locusts" on which John the Baptist fed were carob pods. The tree, about 50 ft (15 m) tall, bears compound, glossy leaves with thick leaflets. Its red flowers are followed by flat, leathery pods that contain 5–15 hard brown seeds embedded in a sweet, edible pulp that tastes similar to chocolate.

carol Popular religious song, usually joyful, associated with a season such as Christmas. It typically alternates verses with a repeated refrain or burden. The carol originated in medieval England, with texts in English or Latin or both, and was often associated with dancing and processions. The French *noël,* the German *Weihnachtslied,* and the Spanish *villancico* can also be regarded as carols.

Carol I \ˈkä-ròl, *Engl* ˈkar-əl\ *orig.* **Karl Eitel Friedrich, Prinz (Prince) von Hohenzollern-Sigmaringen** (1839–1914) King of Romania (1881–1914). Originally a German prince, he became Prince of Romania in 1866, and when Romania gained full independence from the Ottoman empire he was crowned king. He brought notable military and economic development along Western lines but his neglect of festering rural problems led to the bloody peasant rebellion of 1907.

Carol II (1893–1953) King of Romania (1930–40). He became crown prince on the death of his great uncle, Carol I, in 1914. Because of his scandalous affair with Magda Lupescu (1896?–1977), he was obliged to renounce his rights to the throne and go into exile in 1925, but he returned in 1930 and became king. He gradually undermined Romanian democracy and in 1938 proclaimed a corporatist dictatorship, but in 1940 he was forced to abdicate in favor of his son Michael.

Caroline Islands Archipelago (pop., 2000 est.: 137,200), western Pacific Ocean. Lying south of the Philippines, the islands and their lagoons comprise an area of 3,740 sq mi (9,687 sq km). Formerly part of the U.S. Trust Territory of the Pacific Islands, the group consists of more than 550 islands, as well as many coral islets and reefs. Though explored by the Spanish in the 17th century, they were rarely visited until Germany took them in 1899. Granted as a mandate to Japan after World War I, they were placed under U.S. trusteeship in 1947. With the exception of Palau, the islands became the Federated States of Micronesia in 1979. Palau became independent in 1994.

Carolingian art \,kar-ə-'lin-jən\ Art produced in Europe during the reign of Charlemagne and his successors until c. 900. The outstanding characteristic of the period was a revival of interest in Roman antiquity. Works of Byzantine art and architecture served as models. Illuminated manuscripts and relief scenes in ivory and metalwork reflected classical motifs; mosaics and murals were also produced, but few have survived.

Ivory book cover from the Lorsch Gospels, early 9th century; in the Victoria and Albert Museum, London.

Carolingian dynasty Family of Frankish aristocrats that ruled Western Europe 751–887. Pepin I (died 640), the dynasty's founder, came to power in the office of mayor of the palace under the Merovingian king Dagobert I, with authority over Austrasia. From this post, his descendants, including Charles Martel, continued to usurp authority from the Merovingians, who remained on the throne as figureheads until 751, when Charles's son Pepin III deposed Childeric III and formally took the title of King of the Franks. Under Pepin's son Charlemagne (Carolus Magnus—the source of the dynasty's name), the Carolingian realm was extended over Gaul and into Germany and Italy. On his death his three sons divided the realm, and by 887 Carolingian power had dissipated, though there were resurgences in France in the years c. 895–923 and 936–87.

carotene \'kar-ə-,tēn\ Any of several organic compounds widely distributed in plants and animals. They are pigments that give orange, yellow, or sometimes red colors to dandelions, apricots, carrots, sweet potatoes, butter, egg yolks, canary feathers, and lobster shells. Carotenes are converted in the body into vitamin A but unlike the vitamin are not toxic even at high doses. Carotene has an antioxidant effect and is therefore used in pharmaceuticals and as a food and feed additive.

Carothers \kə-'rət͟h-ərz\, **W(allace) H(ume)** (1896–1937) U.S. chemist. Born in Burlington, Iowa, he became director of organic chemical research at Du Pont in 1928. There he first worked on polymerization of acetylene and derivatives, leading to the development of neoprene. His outstanding achievement involved the theory of linear polymerization; he tested it by synthesizing polymers structurally resembling cellulose and silk, culminating in the production of nylon. The first synthetic polymer fiber to be produced commercially (1938), it laid the foundation of the synthetic fiber industry.

carp Hardy, greenish brown fish (*Cyprinus carpio,* family Cyprinidae) native to Asia but introduced into Europe, North America, and elsewhere. Large-scaled, with two barbels (fleshy, whiskerlike feelers) on each side of its upper jaw, the carp lives alone or in small schools in quiet, weedy, mud-bottomed ponds, lakes, and rivers. An omnivore, it often stirs up sediment while rooting about for food, adversely affecting many plants and animals. Carp grow to an average length of about 14 in. (35 cm); some grow to 40 in. (100 cm) and 49 lbs (22 kg). In captivity they may live more than 40 years.

Carpaccio \kär-'pät-chō\, **Vittore** (c. 1460–1525/26) Italian painter active in Venice. The dominant influences on his work were the Bellini family and Antonello da Messina. In the 1490s he began the first of four cycles of paintings that are his greatest achievement: scenes from the *Life of St. Ursula*, now in the Accademia, Venice; scenes from the *Lives of St. George, St. Jerome, and St. Tryphon* (1502–7) for the Scuola di San Giorgio degli Schiavoni, Venice; and scenes from the *Life of the Virgin* (c. 1500–10) and the *Life of St. Stephen* (1511–20). He was one of the great narrative painters of the Venetian school.

carpal tunnel syndrome \'kär-pəl\ (CTS) Painful condition caused by repetitive stress to the wrist. The median nerve and the tendons that bend the fingers pass through the carpal tunnel on the inner side of the wrist, between the wrist (carpal) bones on three sides and a ligament on the fourth. Repetitive finger and wrist movements rub the tendons against the walls of the carpal tunnel and may make the tendons swell, squeezing the nerve. Numbness, tingling, and pain in the wrist and hand may progress to loss of muscle control. CTS is most common in assembly-line workers and computer keyboard users. Treatment may include anti-inflammatory drugs, brace or splint use, and surgery.

Carpathian Mountains \kär-'pā-thē-ən\ Mountain system, eastern Europe. It extends along the Slovakia–Poland border and southward through Ukraine and eastern Romania about 900 mi (1,450 km). Its highest peak, Gerlachovka (in Slovakia), rises 8,711 ft (2,655 m). The Little Carpathians and White Carpathians are its southwestern extensions; the Transylvanian Alps are sometimes called the South Carpathians. The mountains are the source for the Vistula, Dniester, and Tisza rivers. Agriculture, forestry, and tourism are economically important.

carpel One of the leaflike, seed-bearing structures that constitute the innermost whorl of a flower. One or more carpels make up the pistil. Fertilization of an egg within a carpel by a pollen grain from another flower results in seed development within the carpel.

Carpentaria \,kär-pen-'tär-ē-ə\, **Gulf of** Gulf, northeastern Australia. An inlet of the Arafura Sea, it is bordered by the Northern Territory and by Cape York Peninsula and extends north-south about 480 mi (770 km) and east-west 400 mi (645 km). It was explored by the Dutch 1605–28; its western coasts were discovered by Abel Janszoon Tasman in 1644. Neglected for centuries, it became internationally significant in the late 20th century for its bauxite and manganese deposits and for its prawn-rich waters.

Carpenter Gothic U.S. domestic architecture style of the 19th century. The houses executed in this phase of the Gothic Revival style display little awareness of the original Gothic approach, but rather an eclectic and naive use of superficial Gothic decorative motifs. Turrets, spires, and pointed arches were liberally applied, as was much decorative gingerbread, made possible by the invention of the scroll saw.

Carpentier, Alejo (1904–1980). Latin American novelist, essayist, and playwright, a leading literary figure. Born in Lausanne, Switzerland, to a French father and a Russian mother, Carpentier spoke French before he learned Spanish, although he was taken to Havana, Cuba, as an infant. Educated in Havana, he helped found the Afro-Cuban movement that sought to incorporate African forms into the arts. He initiated the use of magic realism, readily apparent in his story collection *Guerra del tiempo* (1958; *War of Time*). His best-known novel, *Los pasos perdidos* (1953; *The Lost Steps*), portrays a character who travels to the Orinoco jungle in search of the origins of time. His historical novel *El siglo de las luces* (1962; *Explosion in a Cathedral*) chronicles the French Revolution's effect on Caribbean countries. Carpentier fled Cuba in 1928 and settled in Paris. In 1945 he went to Venezuela, but in 1959 he returned to Cuba and became a diplomat in Fidel Castro's regime.

carpet See rug and carpet

carpetbagger Epithet used during the Reconstruction period (1865–77) to describe a Northerner in the South seeking private gain. The word referred to an unwelcome outsider arriving with nothing more than his belongings packed in a satchel or carpetbag. Many carpetbaggers were involved in corrupt financial schemes, but others helped rebuild the economy in the South and participated in educational and social reform.

Carpocratian \ˌkär-pə-ˈkrā-shən\ Follower of the 2nd-century Christian Gnostic Carpocrates, whose sect flourished in Alexandria. Carpocratians revered Jesus as an ordinary man whose soul had not forgotten that its origin and true home was within the sphere of the unknown perfect God. They rejected the created world, claimed superiority due to their ability to communicate with demons, and subverted biblical law as the work of the evil angels who created the world. Their goal of transcendent freedom required having every possible experience, which required several lifetimes. The first sect known to have used pictures of Christ, they also made images of PLATO, PYTHAGORAS, and ARISTOTLE. See also GNOSTICISM.

Carracci family \kä-ˈrät-chē\ Family of Italian painters. Annibale Carracci (1560–1609) was prominent in Bologna and Rome in the movement against MANNERISM. In the 1580s, with his brother and cousin, he founded a teaching academy in Bologna, the Accademia degli Incamminati ("Academy of the Progressives"). He specialized in fresco painting and monumental religious altarpieces, but was also a pioneer in the development of ideal landscapes, genre subjects, and caricature. The fresco decoration of the Gallery of the Farnese Palace in Rome (1597–1601), comprising scenes from the loves of the gods, remains his masterpiece; it was indispensable as a source of figure design and technical procedure for young painters into the 18th century. His elder brother, Agostino (1557–1602), assisted him in decorating the Farnese Gallery but was known primarily as a teacher and engraver; his anatomical studies were used as teaching aids for nearly two centuries. His cousin Lodovico (or Ludovico) Carracci (1555–1619) collaborated with them on various fresco commissions. He directed the academy in Bologna after his cousins had gone to Rome, produced works of a passionate and poetic quality, and trained some of the major Bolognese artists of the next generation, including DOMENICHINO, GUIDO RENI, and ALESSANDRO ALGARDI. See also BOLOGNESE SCHOOL.

Carranza \kär-ˈrän-sä\, **Venustiano** (1859–1920) First president of the post-P. DÍAZ Mexican Republic (1917–20). The son of a landowner, he was active in politics from 1877. In 1910 he joined the struggle of FRANCISCO MADERO against Díaz. A moderate and a nationalist, he favored political but not social reform. Because he did little to implement the far-reaching reforms called for in the Constitution of 1917, his presidency was plagued by social unrest and clashes with the more radical leaders PANCHO VILLA and EMILIANO ZAPATA, as well as by serious financial problems. His nationalism led him to oppose U.S. intervention in Mexican affairs, even when he stood to benefit from it. He is held responsible for Zapata's assassination, and was himself murdered while fleeing an armed rebellion. See also MEXICAN REVOLUTION.

Venustiano Carranza, c. 1910.
ARCHIVO CASASOLA

Carré, John Le See John LE CARRE

Carrel \kə-ˈrel\, **Alexis** (1873–1944) French surgeon, sociologist, and biologist. He received a 1912 Nobel Prize for developing a way to suture (stitch) blood vessels and laid the groundwork for further studies of blood-vessel and organ transplantation. He also researched preservation of tissues outside the body and the application of the process to surgery, and helped develop the Carrel-Dakin method of flushing wounds with an antiseptic. His writings include *Man, the Unknown* (1935), *The Culture of Organs* (with CHARLES A. LINDBERGH, 1938), and *Reflections on Life* (1952).

Carrhae \ˈkar-ē\, **Battle of** (53 BC) Battle that stopped the Roman invasion of Parthian Mesopotamia (see PARTHIA). The Romans were led by CRASSUS, who wanted a victory to balance those of his fellow triumvirs POMPEY and Julius CAESAR. With seven legions (about 44,000 men) but little cavalry, he was defeated in the desert by 10,000 mounted Parthian archers and was killed while trying to negotiate. His defeat damaged Roman prestige, and his death gave impetus to Caesar's quest for power.

carriage Four-wheeled, horse-drawn vehicle, mainly for private passenger use. It was the final refinement of the horse-drawn passenger conveyance, having developed from the WAGON, CHARIOT, and COACH. Light carriages with enhanced suspension for added comfort had been developed by the 17th century. A variety of carriages were common in the 19th century, including the brougham and the buggy. Carriage manufacturers provided the very similar early designs for automobile bodies (see FREDERICK FISHER).

Carrickfergus \ˌkar-ik-ˈfər-gəs\ District (pop., 1995 est. : 35,000), northeastern Northern Ireland. Established in 1974, it lies on Belfast Lough. The name, meaning "rock of Fergus," commemorates King Fergus, shipwrecked off the coast c. AD 320. Carrickfergus town (pop., 1981: 18,000), is the district seat. Carrickfergus Castle, a relic of the Norman period, sits on a crag above the town; it was a refuge for the Protestants of ANTRIM in the ENGLISH CIVIL WAR.

Carrier, Willis Haviland (1876–1950) U.S. inventor and industrialist. Born in Angola, N.Y., Carrier designed the first system to control temperature and humidity in 1902. His "Rational Psychrometric Formulae," introduced in 1911, initiated scientific AIR-CONDITIONING design. In 1915 he cofounded the Carrier Corp. to manufacture air-conditioning equipment.

Carriera \ˌkä-rē-ˈā-rə\, **Rosalba** (1675–1757) Venetian pastel portraitist and miniaturist. She became known for her miniature portraits on snuffboxes and was the first artist to use ivory rather than vellum as a support for miniatures. She achieved spectacular success throughout Europe with her fashionable pastel portraits of notables. On a trip to Paris (1720–21) she received commissions for numerous portraits, including one of LOUIS XV as a child. In 1721 she was elected to the French Royal Academy.

Carroll, Charles (1737–1832) American patriot leader. Born in Annapolis, Md., he attended Jesuit colleges in Maryland and studied law in France and England. He served on Committees of Correspondence, signed the Declaration of Independence, and served in the Continental Congress (1776–78). He was a U.S. senator 1789–92.

Carroll, Lewis *orig.* **Charles Lutwidge Dodgson** (1832–1898) British logician, mathematician, and novelist. An unmarried deacon and a lecturer in mathematics at Oxford, he enjoyed the company of young girls. His novel *Alice's Adventures in Wonderland* (1865; illustrated by JOHN TENNIEL) is based on stories he told to amuse young friends, especially Alice Liddell. Its sequel, *Through the Looking-Glass* (1871), describes Alice's further adventures. The two books, full of whimsy but also of sophisticated wit and puzzles, became perhaps the most famous and admired children's books in the world. His other works include the narrative nonsense poem *The Hunting of the Snark* (1876) and the children's novels *Sylvie and Bruno* (1889) and *Sylvie and Bruno Concluded* (1893). He was also an important early portrait photographer.

carrot Herbaceous, generally biennial plant *(Daucus carota)* of the PARSLEY family, that produces an edible globular or long TAPROOT in the first growing season. Native to Afghanistan and neighboring lands, it is grown extensively in temperate zones. It is a rich source of carotene. An erect rosette of feathery leaves develops above ground in the first season; the edible carrot is below. After a rest period at temperatures near freezing, large flower stalks arise, bearing large compound umbels.

Carrot (*Daucus carota*).
KENNETH AND BRENDA FORMANEK

Carson, Edward Henry *later* **Baron Carson (of Duncairn)** (1854–1935) Irish lawyer and politician. He was elected to the British House of Commons in 1892 and later served as Irish solicitor general (1892), British solicitor general (1900–1905), attorney general (1915), first lord of the Admiralty (1916–17), and lord of appeal (1921–29). Known as the "uncrowned king of

Ulster," he successfully led Northern Irish resistance to the British government's attempts to introduce HOME RULE for all of Ireland.

Carson, Johnny *orig.* **John William** (born 1925) U.S. television personality. Born in Corning, Iowa, he worked as a radio announcer and television comedy writer before hosting several TV quiz shows (1955–62). As the long-standing host of *The Tonight Show* (1962–92), he was noted for his wry monologues, comedy sketches, and genial banter, and the program became a staple for a large and faithful late-night audience.

Carson, Kit *orig.* **Christopher** (1809–1868) U.S. frontiersman, scout, and Indian agent. Born in Madison Co., Ky., and raised in Missouri, he ran away from home at 15 to become a trapper and trader in the Southwest. In the early 1840s he served as a guide to JOHN C. FREMONT's explorations of the West. He guided Gen. STEPHEN KEARNY's expedition to California during the Mexican War, often carrying war dispatches to Washington, D.C. In 1854 he was appointed Indian agent at Taos, N.M. During the Civil War he commanded the 1st New Mexico Volunteers. In 1868 he was appointed superintendent of Indian affairs for the Colorado Territory. His contributions to westward expansion made him a folk hero.

Kit Carson.

BY COURTESY OF THE LIBRARY OF CONGRESS, WASHINGTON, D.C.

Carson, Rachel (Louise) (1907–1964) U.S. biologist and science writer. Born in Springdale, Pa., Carson trained as a marine biologist and had a long career at the U.S. Fish and Wildlife Service. *The Sea Around Us* (1951) won the National Book Award. Her prophetic *Silent Spring* (1962), about the dangers of pesticides in the food chain, is regarded as the seminal work in the history of the environmental movement, which in some respects can be seen to date from its publication.

Carson City City (pop., 1995 est.: 47,000), capital of Nevada. Located east of Lake TAHOE and south of RENO, it was settled in 1858, and later renamed for KIT CARSON. The discovery of silver in 1859 in the nearby Virginia City area stimulated Carson City's economy. The federal government established a mint at Carson City, which later became the Nevada State Museum. It became the state capital in 1864 when Nevada gained statehood.

State Capitol, Carson City, Nev.

DONALD DONDERO

cart Two-wheeled vehicle drawn by a draft animal, used throughout recorded history for transporting freight and people. The simplest of vehicles, its frame consists merely of crossed wooden stakes or a box with shafts as an extension of the frame. Carts are known to have been used by the Greeks and Assyrians by 1800 BC, though earlier use (c. 3500 BC) can be assumed.

Cartagena \ˌkär-tä-ˈhā-nä\ City (pop., 1997 est.: 812,000), Colombia. Located on the northwestern coast, it has a good harbor and is Colombia's principal oil port. Founded in 1533, it became one of Spanish America's chief cities. It was strongly fortified and often attacked, notably by British forces under FRANCIS DRAKE (1585) and Edward Vernon (1741). It remained under Spanish control until 1815, when it was taken by SIMON BOLIVAR. Though soon lost, it was retaken by independence forces in 1821. It declined in the 19th century, but regained prominence in the 20th century as an oil-processing center.

Cartagena Port city (pop., 1991: 167,000), southeastern Spain. Founded by the Carthaginians under Hasdrubal in 227 BC, it was captured by SCIPIO AFRICANUS THE ELDER in 209 BC and made a Roman colony. It was sacked by the GOTHS in AD 425. It was held by the MOORS from 711 until it was taken by JAMES I of Aragon in 1269. In the 16th century PHILIP II made it a great naval port; it remains Spain's chief Mediterranean naval base as well as a commercial port.

cartel \ˌkär-ˈtel\ Organization of a few, independent producers for the purpose of improving the profitability of the firms involved (see OLIGOPOLY). This usually involves some restriction of output, control of price, and allocation of market shares. Members of a cartel generally maintain their separate identities and financial independence while engaging in cooperative policies. Cartels can either be domestic (e.g., IG FARBEN) or international (e.g., OPEC). Because cartels restrict competition and result in higher prices for consumers, they are outlawed in some countries. The only industry operating in the U.S. with a blanket exemption from the ANTITRUST LAWS is major-league baseball, but several U.S. firms have been given permission to participate in international cartels.

Cartel des Gauches \kär-ˈtel-dā-ˈgōsh\ (French: "Coalition of the Left") In the French THIRD REPUBLIC, a coalition of left-wing parties (the Socialists and the Radicals) in the Chamber of Deputies. They formed the Cartel in opposition to the right-wing BLOC NATIONAL, which they defeated in the elections of 1924. Led by EDOUARD HERRIOT and later ARISTIDE BRIAND, the Cartel was defeated in 1926 by a financial crisis brought about by continuing inflation.

Carter, Benny *orig.* **Bennett Lester** (born 1907) U.S. jazz musician. Known as one of the primary stylists of the alto saxophone, he was also an accomplished arranger, composer, clarinetist, trumpeter, and bandleader. Born in New York, City, he played in the big bands of Chick Webb and FLETCHER HENDERSON before assuming leadership of McKinney's Cotton Pickers (1931–32). Carter worked in Europe 1935–38, and moved to California in 1945 to write music for film and television. His best-known composition is "When Lights Are Low."

Carter, Elliott Cook, Jr. (born 1908) U.S. composer. Born to a wealthy family, he studied English and music at Harvard University and later studied in Paris with N. BOULANGER. He taught at many institutions, after 1972 primarily at the Juilliard School. He absorbed a range of influences, including I. STRAVINSKY and C. IVES. His style evolved into a densely contrapuntal, dissonant, and rhythmically complex texture in which the various instrumental parts frequently suggest conversation and combat. His principal works include a sonata for flute, oboe, cello, and harpsichord (1952), *Variations for Orchestra* (1955), a double concerto for piano and harpsichord (1961), a piano concerto (1965), *Concerto for Orchestra* (1969), *A Symphony of Three Orchestras* (1977), *Night Fantasies* for piano (1980), and four string quartets (1951, 1959, 1971, 1986), two of which received the Pulitzer Prize. He is often called the greatest American composer of the late 20th century.

Carter, Jimmy *orig.* **James Earl** (born 1924) 39th president of the U.S. (1977–81). Born in Plains, Ga., he graduated from Annapolis and served in the U.S. Navy until 1953, when he left to manage the family peanut business. He served in the state senate 1962–66. Elected governor (1971–75), he opened Georgia's government offices to blacks and women and introduced stricter budgeting procedures for state agencies. In 1976, though lacking a national political base or major backing, he won the Democratic nomination and the presidency, defeating the sitting president, GERALD FORD. As president, he helped negotiate a peace treaty between Egypt and Israel, signed a treaty with Panama to make the PANAMA CANAL a neutral zone after 1999, and established full diplomatic relations with China. In 1979–80 the IRAN HOSTAGE CRISIS became a major political liability. He responded more forcefully to the Soviet Union's invasion of Afghanistan in 1979, embargoing the shipment of U.S. grain to that country and pressing for a U.S. boycott of the 1980 Summer Olympics in Moscow. Hampered by high inflation and a recession engineered to tame it, he lost his bid for reelection to RONALD REAGAN. He subsequently became involved in nu-

Jimmy Carter, 1979.

UPI/BETTMANN NEWSPHOTOS

merous international diplomatic negotiations and helped oversee elections in countries with insecure democratic traditions.

Carter family U.S. singing group, consisting of Alvin Pleasant Carter (1891–1960), his wife Sara (1898–1979), and his sister-in-law Maybelle (1909–1978), that helped popularize Appalachian folk songs. Natives of Virginia, their career began in 1927 in response to an advertisement placed by a talent scout. Over 14 years, with two of Sara's children and three of Maybelle's (Helen, June, and Anita), they recorded over 300 songs from the 19th and early 20th century, including "Wabash Cannonball," "It Takes a Worried Man to Sing a Worried Song," and "Wildwood Flower." After the original group broke up in 1941, members continued to perform under the Carter family name, and "Mother" Maybelle Carter performed with her son-in-law J. CASH. The original Carter family was the first group admitted to the Country Music Hall of Fame.

Carteret \'kärt-ə-ˌret\, **George** *later* **Sir George** (1610?–1680) British politician and colonial proprietor. His naval exploits and service as lieutenant governor of the Channel Island of Jersey won him a knighthood (1644) and baronetcy (1645). After the 1660 Restoration he became a powerful administrator and legislator. In 1663 he became one of eight original proprietors granted the area of Carolina; in 1664 he received half of New Jersey, named for his birthplace. The other owner sold out to the Quakers in 1674. With the Quakers Carteret agreed to divide the colony; after his death his heirs sold his portion to them.

Cartesian circle \ˌkär-'tē-zhən\ Allegedly circular reasoning used by RENE DESCARTES. Since he clearly and distinctly understands God to be the wholly perfect being, Descartes infers that God exists and could not deceive him. If a clearly and distinctly perceived idea could be false, then since God endowed him with the tendency to affirm any idea that he clearly and distinctly perceives, the conclusion would follow that God was capable of deceiving him. Therefore, a clearly and distinctly perceived idea cannot be false. The argument is circular because, unless it is already assumed that clear and distinct ideas must be true, there is no sufficient reason to accept the first step.

Cartesianism Philosophical tradition derived from the philosophy of RENE DESCARTES. A form of RATIONALISM, Cartesianism also upholds a metaphysical DUALISM of two finite substances, mind and matter. The essence of mind is thinking; the essence of matter is extension in three dimensions. God is a third, infinite substance, whose essence is necessary existence. God unites minds with bodies to create a fourth, compound substance, homo sapiens. Mind-body dualism generates problems concerning causal interaction and knowledge (see MIND-BODY PROBLEM), and various lines of Cartesianism developed from proposing different solutions to these problems. An influential Cartesian theory holds that animals are essentially machines, lacking even the ability to feel pain. See also ARNOLD GEULINCX, NICOLAS DE MALEBRANCHE, OCCASIONALISM.

Carthage Ancient city and state, northern Africa. Located near modern TUNIS, it was built around a citadel called the Byrsa. Founded by colonists from TYRE, probably in the 8th century BC, it undertook conquests in western Africa, SICILY, and SARDINIA in the 6th century BC. Under the descendants of Hamilcar, it came to dominate the western Mediterranean. In the 3rd century BC it fought the PUNIC WARS with Rome. Destroyed by the younger SCIPIO AFRICANUS, it was later the site of a colony founded by JULIUS CAESAR in 44 BC; in 29 BC AUGUSTUS made it the administrative center of the province of Africa. Among the Christian bishops who served there were TERTULLIAN and St. CYPRIAN. Captured by the VANDALS in 439 and Byzantium in the 6th century, it was taken by the Arabs in the 7th century, and was eclipsed by their emphasis on Tunis.

Carthaginian Wars See PUNIC WARS

Carthusian \kär-'thü-zhən\ Member of a Roman Catholic monastic order founded by St. Bruno of Cologne (c. 1030–1101) in 1084 in the Chartreuse valley of southeastern France. Members of the Order of Carthusians pray, study, eat, and sleep alone but gather in church for morning mass, vespers, and the night office. They dine together on Sundays and major holidays and walk together once a week. They wear hair shirts, abstain from eating meat, and consume only bread and water on Fridays and fast days. At the motherhouse, or Grande Chartreuse (today in Voiron, Isère), the monks distill the liqueur that bears the house's name. Carthusian nuns are also strictly cloistered and contemplative.

Cartier \kär-'tyā\, **George Étienne** *later* **Sir George** (1814–1873) Canadian prime minister jointly with JOHN MACDONALD (1858–62). Born in St. Antoine, Lower Canada (now Quebec), he was elected as a Liberal to the Canadian legislative assembly (1848) and was later appointed provincial secretary (1855) and attorney general for Canada East (1857). In 1858 he represented Canada East in the alliance with Macdonald and promoted the improvement of Anglo-French relations in Canada. He was a proponent of the GRAND TRUNK RAILWAY. In 1867, despite great opposition, he carried his native province into confederation. He then served as minister of militia and defense in Macdonald's first Confederation cabinet (1867–72).

Cartier \kär-'tyā\, **Jacques** (1491–1557) French sailor and explorer. He was commissioned by FRANCIS I to explore North America in the hope of discovering gold, spices, and a passage to Asia. Cartier's explorations of the North American coast and the St. Lawrence River (1534, 1535, 1541–42) did not produce the desired results, but they did lay the basis for later French claims to Canada.

Cartier-Bresson \kȧr-tyā-brə-'sōⁿ\, **Henri** (born 1908) French photographer. He studied art in Paris and literature and painting at Cambridge University. His interest in photography developed c. 1930 when he encountered the works of EUGENE ATGET and MAN RAY. He is known for spontaneous, sequential images in still photography, a technique inspired by his enthusiasm for filmmaking. He helped establish photojournalism as an art form, and with ROBERT CAPA and David Seymour founded the cooperative Magnum Photos (1947). The best known of his many collections is *The Decisive Moment* (1952).

cartilage \'kär-tᵊl-ij\ Dense CONNECTIVE TISSUE in parts of the human skeleton. A network of COLLAGEN fibers in a firm, gelatinous base, it contains no blood vessels. Different types of cartilage are found at the ends of some bones and in nasal and respiratory structures; in the spinal disks; and in the ear and epiglottis (back of the throat). Most of the skeleton of an embryo is made of cartilage, which is later replaced by bone.

Cartland, (Mary) Barbara (Hamilton) *later* **Dame Barbara** (1901–2000) English author. Her first novel, *Jigsaw* (1925), was a popular success. She wrote two more novels and a play during the 1920s; thereafter her output grew steadily, and by the 1970s she was averaging 23 books a year, all of which she dictated. Her approximately 600 books, mostly formulaic romance novels, have sold more than 600 million copies. Her nonfiction includes autobiographies and books on health food, vitamins, and beauty. She was the step-grandmother of DIANA, PRINCESS OF WALES.

cartography \kär-'tä-grə-fē\ *or* **mapmaking** Art and science of representing a geographic area graphically, usually by means of a map or chart. Political, cultural, or other nongeographic features may be superimposed. PTOLEMY's eight-volume *Geography* showed a spherical earth. Medieval European maps followed Ptolemy's guide but placed east at the top of the map. The 14th century saw the development of more accurate maps for use in navigation. The first surviving globe dates from 1492. Discovery of the New World led to new techniques in cartography, notably projection of a curved surface onto a flat surface. GERARDUS MERCATOR used a cylindrical projection; which treats the earth as a cylinder. Cylindrical projections have many advantages, though they cause distortions at high latitudes. Contour maps show relief by connecting points of equal elevation with lines, mean sea level being the reference point. Modern cartography uses aerial photography and satellite radar for a degree of accuracy previously unattainable. Satellites have also made possible the mapping of features of the moon and of several planets and their moons. See also GEOGRAPHIC INFORMATION SYSTEM, GLOBAL POSITIONING SYSTEM.

cartoon Originally, a full-size drawing used for transferring a design to a painting, tapestry, or other large work. Cartoons were used from the 15th century by fresco painters and stained-glass artists. In the 19th century the term acquired its popular meaning of a humorous drawing or parody. Cartoons in that sense are used today to convey political commentary, editorial opinion, and social comedy in newspapers and magazines. The greatest early figure is WILLIAM HOGARTH, in 18th-century Britain. In 19th-century France, HONORE DAUMIER introduced accompanying text that conveyed his characters' unspoken thoughts. Britain's *PUNCH* became the foremost 19th-century venue for cartoons; in the 20th century *The* NEW YORKER set the American standard. A Pulitzer Prize for editorial cartooning was established in 1922. See also CARICATURE, COMIC STRIP.

Cartwright, Alexander (Joy) (1820–1892) U.S. surveyor and BASEBALL enthusiast. Born in New York City, he was a founder of the amateur New York Knickerbocker Base Ball Club and chaired the commission that established baseball's official rules. These included the requirement of tagging out a base runner rather than hitting him with a thrown ball, and fixing the distance between bases at 90 ft (27.4 m). The first game under the newly codified rules was apparently played in Hoboken, N.J., in 1846. See also ABNER DOUBLEDAY.

Cartwright, Edmund (1743–1823) British inventor. On visiting R. ARKWRIGHT's cotton-spinning mills, he was inspired to construct a power-driven machine for weaving. He invented a power LOOM and set up a weaving and spinning factory in Yorkshire. In 1789 he patented a wool-combing machine. In 1809 the House of Commons voted to reward him for the benefits his loom had conferred on the nation. His other inventions included a cordelier (machine for making rope) and a steam engine that used alcohol instead of water.

Caruso \kə-'rü-sō\, **Enrico** (1873–1921) Italian tenor. Born in Naples and apprenticed to a mechanical engineer at 10, at 18 he began to sing in public in his free time. He attracted the notice of a teacher, and made his professional debut in 1894. He sang his best-known role, Canio in RUGGIERO LEONCAVALLO's *Pagliacci*, for the first time in 1896. He recovered from a disastrous La Scala debut in 1900 and within two years had gained the high notes that made him an international star and a legend. He sang at the Metropolitan Opera 1903–20 in almost 60 roles, becoming the most famous male opera star of his time. His warm, appealing tenor voice of great emotive power made his recordings (which include some of the first vocal recordings ever made) best-sellers for decades after his death at 48.

Carver, George Washington (1861?–1943) U.S. agricultural chemist and agronomist. Born a slave near Diamond Grove, Mo., Carver lived until age 10 or 12 on his former owner's plantation, then left and worked at a variety of menial jobs. He did not obtain a high-school education until his late twenties; he then obtained bachelor's and master's degrees from Iowa State Agricultural College. In 1896 he joined BOOKER T. WASHINGTON at the Tuskegee Institute (now TUSKEGEE UNIV.) in Alabama, where he became director of agricultural research. He was soon promoting the planting of PEANUTS and SOYBEANS, legumes that he knew would help restore the fertility of southern U.S. soil depleted from cotton cropping. To make such crops profitable, he worked intensively with the SWEET POTATO and the peanut (then not even recognized as a crop), ultimately developing 118 derivative products from sweet potatoes and 300 from peanuts. His efforts helped liberate the South from its untenable cotton dependency; by 1940 the peanut was the South's second largest cash crop. During World War II he devised 500 dyes to replace those no longer available from Europe. Despite international acclaim and extraordinary job offers, he remained at Tuskegee throughout his life, donating his life's savings in 1940 to establish the Carver Research Foundation at Tuskegee.

George Washington Carver.

BY COURTESY OF THE TUSKEGEE INSTITUTE, ALABAMA; PHOTOGRAPH, P.H. POLK

Carver, Jonathan (1710–1780) American explorer. Born in Weymouth, Mass., he served in the French and Indian War. In 1766 he was sent by Maj. ROBERT ROGERS to explore an area west of northern Michigan. He traveled through the Great Lakes and up the Mississippi River, wintering in a Sioux village. His travel journal (published 1778) was a huge success, but he died penniless.

Cary, (Arthur) Joyce (Lunel) (1888–1957) British novelist. Born in Northern Ireland, he studied art in Edinburgh and Paris before graduating from Oxford. After serving in West Africa in World War I, he began publishing short stories, then novels, some set in Africa, including *An American Visitor* (1933) and *Mister Johnson* (1939). *The Horse's Mouth* (1944), his best-known novel, was the third in a trilogy in which each volume is narrated by one of three protagonists. Other works include a second trilogy, *A Prisoner of Grace* (1952), *Except the Lord* (1953), and *Not Honour More* (1955).

caryatid \,kar-ē-'a-təd\ Supporting column sculpted in the form of a draped female figure. Caryatids first appeared in three small buildings (treasuries) at Delphi (550–530 BC). The most celebrated example is the caryatid porch of the Erechtheum (421–406 BC), with six figures, on the Acropolis (see ACROPOLIS) of Athens. Caryatids are sometimes called *korai* ("maidens"). Their male counterpart is the ATLAS.

Casa Grande Ruins National Monument \'kä-sə-'grän-dā\ Preserve, southern Arizona. Established in 1918, it occupies 472 acres (191 hectares). The site's pre-Columbian ruins are dominated by the Casa Grande ("Big House"), a multistory building topped by a watchtower built by Salado Indians in the 14th century, and the only surviving building of its type. Nearby are partially excavated village sites established much earlier by Hohokam Indians (see HOHOKAM CULTURE).

Casablanca Coastal city (metro area pop., 1994: 2,941,000), western Morocco. It occupies the site of the ancient city of Anfa, destroyed by the Portuguese in 1468. The Portuguese returned in 1515 and built a new town, Casa Branca ("White House"). Abandoned after an earthquake, it was occupied by a Moroccan sultan in 1757. European traders, including the French, began to settle there. In 1907, provoked by the murder of French citizens, French forces occupied the town. During the French protectorate, it became Morocco's chief port. Since then, its growth and development have been continuous. In World War II it surrendered to the Allies in 1942, and in 1943 the CASABLANCA CONFERENCE was held there.

Casablanca Conference (1943) Meeting during WORLD WAR II at Casablanca, Morocco, between FRANKLIN ROOSEVELT and WINSTON CHURCHILL. They planned future global military strategy for the Western allies, reaching agreement on such issues as the invasion of Sicily, operations in the Pacific theater, and the concentrated bombing of Germany. Most importantly, they issued a demand for an "unconditional surrender" from Germany, Italy, and Japan.

Casals \kə-'sälz\, **Pablo (Carlos Salvador Defilló)** *orig.* **Pau** (1876–1973) Spanish (Catalan)-U.S. cellist and conductor. He received early instruction from his organist father, and took up the cello and composition in his teens. Sent by royal sponsors to the Brussels Conservatory in 1895, he was told they could teach him nothing. An audition with the conductor Charles Lamoureux (1850–1899) in 1899 led to recognition as a supreme musician. He performed internationally as soloist, in a trio with Alfred Cortot (1877–1962) and Jacques Thibaud (1880–1953), and from the 1920s as a conductor. Refusing to return to Spain after FRANCISCO FRANCO took power, he ultimately made his home in Puerto Rico.

Casamance River \,kä-zä-'mä^{n}s\ River, Senegal. Rising in southern Senegal, it flows west between Gambia and Guinea-Bissau, and empties into the Atlantic Ocean after a course of about 200 mi (322 km). Only some 80 mi (130 km) of the river are navigable.

Casanova \,ka-sə-'nō-və\, **Giovanni Giacomo** (1725–1798) Italian ecclesiastic, writer, soldier, spy, and diplomatist. Expelled from a seminary for scandalous conduct, he launched a dissolute career that took him throughout Europe. In Venice in 1755 he was denounced as a magician and imprisoned; he escaped and fled to Paris, where he mingled with the aristocracy. Fleeing from creditors, he took the name Chevalier de Seingalt and traveled again before returning to Venice in 1774 to become a spy for the Venetian inquisitors of state. He spent his late years (1785–98) as librarian to the Count von Waldstein in Bohemia. His huge autobiography, first published in 12 volumes in 1825–38, gives a splendid picture of 18th-century Europe and established his reputation as an extraordinary seducer of women.

Casas, Bartolomé de las See Bartolome de LAS CASAS

Cascade Range Mountain range, western U.S. A continuation of the SIERRA NEVADA, it extends north from Mount LASSEN in northeastern California across Oregon and Washington for 700 mi (1,100 km). Its highest elevation is Mount RAINIER. Some of the summits, including Mount ST. HELENS, have erupted in the recent past. The LEWIS AND CLARK EXPEDITION passed through the range in the Columbia River Gorge. Its northern continuation in British Columbia is known as the Coast Mountains. See also North Cascades National Park.

CASE *in full* **computer-aided software engineering** Use of computers in designing sophisticated tools to aid the software engineer and to automate the software development process as much as possible. It is particularly useful where major software products are designed by teams of engineers who may not share the same physical space. CASE tools can be used for simple operations such as routine coding from an appropriately detailed design in a specific programming language, or for more complex tasks such as incorporating an expert system to enforce design rules and eliminate software defects and redundancies before the coding phase.

Case, Stephen M(aul) (born 1955) U.S. businessman. Born in Hawaii, he graduated from Williams College (1980), then held management positions at Proctor & Gamble, Pizza Hut, and Control Video. In 1985 he cofounded Quantum Computer Services, whose name was changed in 1991 to America Online. As chairman and CEO of the company, he developed it into the world's leading interactive services company, and helped turn the Internet into a mass medium.

Case Western Reserve University Independent research university in Cleveland, Ohio. It was created in 1967 through the merger of Western Reserve University (founded 1826) and Case Institute of Technology (1880). It operates professional schools of law, medicine, dentistry, and nursing, a college of arts and sciences, and schools of engineering, social sciences, management, and graduate studies. Research facilities include a biological field station and two astronomical observatories. Total enrollment is about 10,000.

Casement, Roger (David) *later* **Sir Roger** (1864–1916) British civil servant and Irish rebel. As British consul in Africa (1895–1904) and Brazil (1906–11), he became famous for his reports revealing white traders' cruel exploitation of native labor in the Congo and in the Putumayo River region of Peru. Ill health forced his retirement to Ireland (1912), where he joined the Irish nationalists and helped form the Irish National Volunteers. After World War I broke out, he sought German support for the Irish independence movement. For his additional intrigue in the Easter Rising, he was convicted of treason and hanged. His execution made him an Irish martyr in the revolt against British rule in Ireland.

Cash, Johnny *orig.* **John R.** (born 1932) U.S. singer and songwriter. Born in Kingsland, Ark., he learned guitar and began writing songs in the military. Settling in Memphis, he earned regular appearances on "Louisiana Hayride" and the Grand Ole Opry with such hits as "Hey, Porter," "Folsom Prison Blues," and "I Walk the Line." By 1957 Cash was acknowledged the top country-music artist. His popularity waned for a time because of health and drug-addiction problems, but in the late 1960s his *Johnny Cash at Folsom Prison* album led to his rediscovery by a wider audience. In 1968 he married June Carter of the Carter Family, with whom he had appeared since 1961. His autobiography, *Man in Black,* appeared in 1975. His later albums include *Unchained* (1998).

cash flow Financial and accounting concept. Cash flow results from three major groups of activities: operating activities, investing activities, and financing activities. A cash-flow statement differs from an income statement in reflecting actual cash on hand rather than money owed (accounts receivable). Its purpose is to throw light on management's use of its available financial resources and to help in evaluating a company's liquidity.

cashew Edible seed or nut of *Anacardium occidentale,* a tropical and subtropical evergreen shrub or tree in the sumac family, native to tropical Central and South America. Important chiefly for its nuts, the tree also produces wood used for shipping crates, boats, and charcoal, and a gum similar to gum arabic. Related to poison ivy and poison sumac, it must be handled with care. The two-shelled nut is shaped like a large, thick bean. A brown oil between the two shells blisters human skin and is used as a lubricant and an insecticide and in the production of plastics. The nut is rich and distinctively flavored.

Cashew apples (hypocarp) and nuts of the domesticated cashew tree (*Anacardium occidentale*).
W.H. HODGE

cashmere Animal-hair fiber forming the downy undercoat of the Kashmir goat. The fiber became known for its use in beautiful shawls and other handmade items produced in Kashmir, India. The fibers have diameters finer than those of the best wools. Natural color, usually gray or tan, ranges from white to black. Cashmere fabric is warm and comfortable and has excellent draping qualities and soft texture; it is used mainly for fine coat, dress, and suit fabrics and for high-quality knitwear and hosiery. A sweater requires the fleece of four to six goats; an overcoat uses that of 30–40. Because world production is small and gathering and processing are costly, cashmere is a luxury fiber.

Casimir III \'kä-zə-ˌmir\ *Polish* **Kazimierz** *known as* **Casimir the Great** (1310–1370) King of Poland (1333–70). He was the son of Wladyslaw I, who revived the Polish kingship, and he continued his father's quest to make Poland a power in central Europe. He crafted treaties with Hungary, Bohemia, and the Teutonic Order and acquired Red Russia and Masovia by diplomacy. Casimir also arranged a series of dynastic alliances that tied Poland to many royal European families. He codified Teutonic law, gave new towns self-government under the Magdeburg Law, and founded the University of Kraków.

Casimir IV *Polish* **Kazimierz** *known as* **Casimir Jagiellonian** \yäg-yel-'lō-nē-ən\ (1427–1492) Grand duke of Lithuania (1440–92) and king of Poland (1447–92). He became ruler of Lithuania by will of the boyars and king of Poland on his brother's death. He sought to preserve the political union between Poland and Lithuania and to recover the lost lands of old Poland. Through his own marriage to Elizabeth of Habsburg and the marriages of his children, he formed alliances with various European royal houses and built the Jagiellon dynasty. The great triumph of his reign was the effective destruction of the Teutonic Order (1466), which brought Prussia under Polish rule.

casino Building or room used for gambling. The term originally referred to a public hall for music and dancing, but by the later 19th century it had come to denote a gaming house, particularly one in which card and dice games were played. Today casinos are places where gamblers can risk their money against a common gambler (called the banker or house), and they have an almost uniform character throughout the world. One of the oldest and best-known casinos is that at Monte Carlo, founded in 1861. Others include those at Cannes and Nice (France), Corfu (Greece), Baden-Baden (Germany), Rio de Janeiro (Brazil), and Las Vegas and Reno. The casino in Havana was closed after the 1959 revolution. Casino gambling was introduced in Atlantic City, N.J., in 1978, and from the 1980s casinos began appearing on American Indian reservations, which are not subject to state anti-gambling statutes. U.S. casino gambling has expanded vastly in recent decades as gambling has become legal in more states, particularly as a riverboat operation.

Casper City (pop., 1996 est.: 49,000), eastern central Wyoming, on the North Platte River. Founded in 1888, it was located on the Oregon Trail and the Pony Express route. The discovery of oil in the 1890s began an oil boom, and the oilfields of the Teapot Dome scandal were located nearby. Casper's economy is based on the production of oil and natural gas and the manufacture of oilfield equipment. Mining (uranium, coal, bentonite) and cattle and sheep raising also are important.

Caspersson \kȧs-'per-ˌsōn\, **Torbörn Oskar** (born 1910) Swedish cell biologist and geneticist. After receiving his medical degree from the University of Stockholm in 1936, he initiated the use of the ultraviolet microscope to determine the nucleic-acid content of cellular structures such as the nucleus and nucleolus. He theorized that nucleic acids must be present for protein synthesis to occur. He was the first to perform cellular chemical studies on the giant chromosomes found in insect larvae. He also investigated the role of the nucleolus in protein synthesis.

Caspian Sea Inland salt lake between Europe and Asia, bordering Azerbaijan, Russia, Kazakhstan, and Iran. With a basin 750 mi (1,200 km) long and 270 mi (434 km) wide and an area of 143,550 sq mi (371,795 sq km), it is the largest inland body of water in the world. Though it receives many rivers, including the Volga, Ural, and Kura, the sea itself has no outlet. It was important as a commercial route in the Middle Ages, when it formed part of the Mongol–Baltic trade route for goods from Asia. Today it is a source of caviar and oil. Its numerous ports include BAKU in Azerbaijan and Enzeli and Bander-e Torkeman in Iran.

Cass, Lewis (1782–1866) U.S. politician. Born in Exeter, N.H., he fought in the War of 1812 and served as governor of Michigan Territory 1813–31. As secretary of war (1831–36) under Pres. ANDREW JACKSON, he directed the conduct of the Black Hawk and Seminole wars. He served as U.S. minister to France 1836–42. In the U.S. Senate (1845–48, 1849–57), he supported westward expansion and the Compromise of 1850. As the Democratic presidential nominee in 1848, he lost to ZACHARY TAYLOR. He later served as secretary of state (1857–60), but resigned when Pres. JAMES BUCHANAN took no action to counter the secession of the Southern states.

Cassandra In GREEK MYTHOLOGY, the daughter of King PRIAM of Troy. APOLLO promised her the gift of prophecy if she would grant his desires; she accepted the gift but rebuffed the god, who took his revenge by ordaining that her prophecies should never be believed. She predicted the fall of Troy and the death of Agamemnon, but her warnings went unheeded. Given as part of the war spoils to Agamemnon, she was murdered with him.

Cassatt \kə-'sat\, **Mary** (1844–1926) U.S. painter and printmaker, active in Paris. Born in Allegheny City, Pa., she spent her early years traveling in Europe with her wealthy family. She attended the Pennsylvania Academy of Fine Arts (1860–65) and later studied in Paris, copying old masters. She became a close friend of EDGAR DEGAS, who influenced her style and encouraged her to exhibit with the Impressionists, of whose work she became a tireless champion. She portrayed scenes of everyday life, particularly images of mothers and children, and was skilled at drawing and printmaking. Some of her best works were executed in pastel. Through her social contacts with wealthy private collectors, she promoted IMPRESSIONISM in the U.S. and exerted a lasting influence on U.S. taste.

cassava \kə-'sä-və\ *or* **manioc** *or* **yuca** Tuberous edible perennial plant *(Manihot esculenta)* of the SPURGE family, from the New World tropics. It is cultivated for its tuberous roots, from which cassava flour, breads, tapioca, a laundry starch, and an alcoholic beverage are derived. It has conspicuous, almost palmate (fan-shaped) leaves and fleshy roots. Different varieties range from low herbs through many-branched shrubs to slender, unbranched trees adapted to diverse habitats.

Cassavetes \ˌka-sə-'vē-tēz\, **John** (1929–1989) U.S. film director and actor. Born in New York City, he acted in films and television dramas before making his directorial debut with the critically praised *Shadows* (1961), a low-budget independent film in the CINÉMA VERITÉ style. He played featured roles in such films as *The Dirty Dozen* (1967) and *Rosemary's Baby* (1968), and returned to directing independent films with *Faces* (1968), *Husbands* (1970), and *A Woman under the Influence* (1974), which dramatized marital problems. His later films include *Gloria* (1980) and *Love Streams* (1984).

cassia \'ka-shə\ Spice, also called Chinese cinnamon, consisting of the aromatic bark of the *Cinnamomum cassia* plant, of the LAUREL FAMILY. Similar to true CINNAMON bark, cassia bark has a more pungent, less delicate flavor and is thicker. It is used as a flavoring in cooking. Whole buds, the dried, unripe fruits of *C. cassia* and *C. loureirii,* taste like the bark and are added to foods for flavoring. Confusion sometimes arises with another group of plants because *Cassia* is the name of an extensive genus of legumes, the source of various medicinal products and of SENNA leaves.

Cassidy, Butch *orig.* **Robert Leroy Parker** (1866–1909?) U.S. outlaw. Born in Beaver, Utah, he became a cattle rustler and later a robber, taking his name from an older outlaw mentor. In 1900 he joined Harry Longabaugh, the Sundance Kid (1870–1909?), whose nickname derived from a town where he had once been imprisoned. They became the foremost members of the Wild Bunch, a collection of bank and train robbers. The two eluded Pinkerton detectives by escaping to South America in 1901. They bought a ranch in Argentina but returned to a life of outlawry in 1906. In 1909, trapped by soldiers in Bolivia, Sundance was mortally wounded and Cassidy shot himself. The time, place, and circumstances of their deaths vary widely in different accounts.

Cassini, Gian Domenico (1625–1712) Italian-French astronomer. His early studies were mainly observations of the sun, but after obtaining more powerful telescopes he turned his attention to the planets. He calculated Jupiter's and Mars's rotational periods and compiled a table of the positions of Jupiter's satellites. His observations of the moon (1671–79) led to his compiling a large map. In 1683, after a study of the ZODIACAL LIGHT, he concluded it was of cosmic origin. He discovered four of Saturn's moons: Iapetus (1671), Rhea (1672), Tethys (1684), and Dione (1684). The dark gap between the two main rings of Saturn (Cassini's division) is named for him.

Cassiodorus \ˌka-sē-ə-'dōr-əs\ *in full* **Flavius Magnus Aurelius Cassiodorus** (c. 490–c. 585) Historian, statesman, and monk who helped preserve Roman culture after the collapse of the Roman Empire. He was secretary to THEODORIC and later held other high imperial offices. Soon after 540 he founded a monastery to perpetuate the culture of Rome. He collected pagan and Christian manuscripts and had the monks copy them, establishing a practice continued in later centuries. His own works included the *Chronicon*, a history of mankind to 519; *De anima*, on the soul after death; and *Institutiones divinarum et saecularium litterarum*, on the study of scripture and the seven liberal arts.

Cassirer \kä-'sir-ər\, **Ernst** (1874–1945) German philosopher. He taught at the Univs. of Berlin (1905–19) and Hamburg (1919–33) before being forced to flee to Sweden and the U.S. A Neo-Kantian, he believed that human beings have innately determined ways of structuring experiences—myth, language, science—that shape their understanding of themselves and of nature. His most important original work was *The Philosophy of Symbolic Forms* (1923–29), but he also wrote about the history of philosophy, including works on IMMANUEL KANT, G. W. LEIBNIZ, Renaissance cosmology, and the Cambridge Platonists.

Cassius (Longinus) \'kash-əs\, **Gaius** (died 42 BC) Roman general and administrator. He fought alongside POMPEY against Julius CAESAR, but was reconciled with Caesar after Pompey's defeat. Motivated by jealousy and bitterness, he joined BRUTUS in the successful conspiracy to assassinate Caesar (44 BC). Forced to leave Rome after the assassination, he went to Syria, where he ousted the governor (43). With Brutus he raised an army in Macedonia to challenge the Second TRIUMVIRATE. Defeated at the Battle of PHILIPPI by Mark ANTONY, he had his freedmen slay him. He was lamented by Brutus as "the last of the Romans."

cassone \kə-'sō-nā\ *or* **marriage chest** Chest, usually of wood, intended to contain a bride's dowry or to be given as a wedding present. It was the most elaborately decorated piece of furniture in Renaissance Italy. In the 15th century, wealthy Florentine families employed artists such as SANDRO BOTTICELLI and PAOLO UCCELLO to decorate *cassoni* with paintings. They were often made in pairs, bearing the respective coats of arms of the bride and groom. Though *cassoni* were made in many countries, the finest come from Italy.

cassowary \'ka-sə-ˌwer-ē\ Any of several species of RATITE (family Casuariidae) of the Australo-Papuan region. Related to the EMU, it has been known to kill humans with slashing blows of its feet, which have long, daggerlike nails on the innermost toe. It has a naked blue head protected by a bony helmet and a black body (immature birds are brownish). It moves rapidly along narrow tracks in the bush. Cassowaries eat fruits and small animals. The largest species (the common, or Australian, cassowary; *Casuarius casuarius*) is almost 5 ft (1.5 m) tall.

Common, or southern, cassowary (*Casuarius casuarius*).
ANTHONY MERCIECA FROM ROOT RESOURCES

cast iron ALLOY of IRON that contains 2–4% CARBON, along with SILICON, MANGANESE, and impurities. It is made by reducing iron ORE in a BLAST FURNACE (cast iron is chemically the same as blast-furnace iron) and CASTING the liquid iron into INGOTS called pigs. PIG IRON is remelted, along with scrap and alloying elements, in cupola furnaces and recast into molds for a variety of products. In the 18th–19th century, cast iron was a cheaper engineering material than WROUGHT IRON (not requiring intensive refining and hammering). It is more brittle and lacks tensile strength. Its compressive (load-bearing) strength made it the first important structural metal. In the 20th century, STEEL replaced it as a construction material, but cast iron still has industrial applications in automobile engine blocks, agricultural and machine parts, pipes, hollowware, stoves, and furnaces. Most cast iron is either so-called gray iron or white iron, the colors shown by fracture; gray iron contains more silicon and is less hard and more machinable than white iron. Both are brittle, but malleable cast iron (produced by prolonged HEAT TREATING), first made in 18th-century France, was developed into an industrial product in the U.S. (see SETH BOYDEN). Cast iron that is ductile as cast was invented in 1948. The latter now constitutes a major family of metals, widely used for gears, dies, automobile crankshafts, and many other machine parts.

Castagno \kä-'stä-nyō\, **Andrea del** *orig.* **Andrea di Bartolo** (1419?–1457) Italian painter active in Florence. Little is known of his early life, and many of his paintings have been lost. His earliest dated works are frescoes in the church of San Zaccaria in Venice (1442). In 1447 he began his greatest work, a series of monumental frescoes depicting the Last Supper and other scenes of Christ's Passion for the convent of Sant' Apollonia in Florence (now a museum). His use of pictorial illusionism and scientific perspective, as well as the powerful, sculptural form of his figures, established him as one of the most influential Renaissance painters of the 15th century.

caste Group of people having a specific social rank, defined largely by DESCENT, MARRIAGE, and occupation. Widespread in India, caste is rooted in antiquity and specifies the rules and restrictions governing social intercourse and activity. Each caste has its own customs that restrict the occupations and dietary habits of its members and their social contact with other castes. There are about 3,000 castes, or *jatis* (broadly, "form of existence fixed by birth"), and more than 25,000 subcastes in India. They are traditionally grouped into four major classes, or *VARNAS* ("colors"). At the top are the BRAHMANS, followed by the KSHATRIYAS, VAISHYAS, and SUDRAS. Those with the most defiling jobs are ranked beneath the Sudras. Considered untouchable, they were simply dubbed as "the fifth" (*panchama*) category. Although a great many spheres of life in modern India are little influenced by caste, most marriages are nevertheless arranged within the caste. This is in part because most people live in rural communities, and because the arrangement of marriages is a family activity carried out through existing networks of kinship and caste.

caste \'kast\ In biology, a subset of individuals within a colony of social animals (chiefly ANTS, BEES, TERMITES, and WASPS) that has a specialized function and is distinguished from other subsets by morphological and anatomical differences. Typical insect castes are the queen (the female responsible for reproduction), workers (the usually sterile female caretakers of the queen, eggs, and larvae), soldiers (defenders of the colony; also sterile females), and sometimes drones (short-lived males). The differentiation of larvae into various castes is often determined by diet, though hormonal and environmental factors can also play a role.

Castelo Branco \kȧsh-'tel-ü-'brä^{n}ŋ-kü\, **Camilo** *later* **visconde (viscount) de Correia Botelho** (1825–1890) Portuguese novelist. An orphan from a family with a tendency to insanity, he studied medicine and theology before beginning to write. While imprisoned for eloping with another man's wife, he wrote his best-known work, *Amor de perdição* (1862; "Fatal Love"), about a thwarted love that leads to crime and exile. His 58 novels, many mirroring his passionate life, range from Romantic melodrama to realism. His best works include *O romance d'um homem rico* (1861; "The Love Story of a Rich Man") and *O retrato de Ricardina* (1868; "Portrait of Ricardina"). Ennobled in 1885, he committed suicide five years later.

Castiglione \ˌkäs-tēl-'yō-nä\, **Baldassare** (1478–1529) Italian diplomat, courtier, and writer. Born into a noble family, he was attached to the courts of Mantua and Urbino and later entered papal service. He is remembered for *The Book of the Courtier* (1528). Written in the form of a philosophical dialogue, it describes the conduct of the perfect courtier, the qualities of a noble lady, and the ideal relationships between the courtier and his prince. Immediately successful in Italy and beyond, it became a manual for those aspiring to aristocratic manners during the Renaissance. See photograph opposite.

Castile \ka-'stēl\ *Spanish* **Castilla** \kä-'stē-lyä\ Traditional region, peninsular Spain. Comprised of several modern provinces, its northern part is called Old Castile and its southern part New Castile. Castilian territory was united under LEÓN by Fernán González in the 10th century. Though it separated from León in the 12th century, it was reunited with it by Ferdinand III in 1230. The Spanish part of the kingdom of NAVARRE was annexed by Castile in 1512, thus completing the formation of modern Spain. It remains Spain's center of political and administrative power. See also CASTILLA Y LEÓN, CASTILLA-LA MANCHA.

Castilho \kȧsh-'tel-yü\, **António Feliciano de** (1800–1875) Portuguese poet. Though blind from childhood, he became a classical scholar and by age 16 was publishing poems, translations, and pedagogical works. With his *Obras completas* (1837; "Complete Works"), he became a literary figure in Lisbon. As director of the important journal *O panorama* and later of the major cultural review *Revista universal Lisbonense*, he became a central figure in the Portuguese Romantic movement. After 1850 he gradually returned to a genteel traditionalism. His lifeless style so dominated literary taste that it provoked a rebellion by younger writers, and he was dethroned as literary arbiter.

Castilla-La Mancha \kä-'stē-lyä-lä-'män-chä\ Autonomous community (pop., 1996 est.: 1,713,000) and historic region, central Spain. Established in 1982, it encompasses the provinces of Toledo, Ciudad Real, Cuenca, Guadalajara, and Albacete, and covers an area of 30,591 sq mi (79,231 sq km); its capital is TOLEDO. The watershed of the low-lying Toledo Mountains bisects the region; land to their north is drained by the TAGUS RIVER, and the plains of La Mancha to the south are drained by the GUADIANA. Emigration to Madrid has depleted the population; for those who remain, agriculture dominates the economy. See CASTILE, MIGUEL DE CERVANTES.

Castilla y León \kä-'stē-lyä-ē-lā-'ōn\ Autonomous community (pop., 1996 est.: 2,508,000) and historic region, northern Spain. Established in 1983, it encompasses the provinces of Valladolid, Burgos, León, Salamanca, Zamora, Polencia, and Segovia, and covers an area of 36, 368 sq mi (94,193 sq km); its capital is VALLADOLID. It occupies the elevated Central Plateau, and is drained by the DOURO RIVER, which bisects the region. The CANTABRIAN MTNS. rise to the north. The area's population has declined since 1900, with notable emigration from the countryside to the provincial capitals. Its economy is largely agricultural. See also CASTILE

Castillo de San Marcos National Monument \ka-'stē-yō-dā-san-'mär-kōs\ Preserve, northeastern Florida. Established in 1924, it is the 20-acre (8-hectare) site of the oldest masonry fort in the U.S., built by the Spanish 1672–96 to protect ST. AUGUSTINE. The fort played an important role in the Spanish-English struggle for the Southeast (1650–1750). In the 19th century it served as a U.S. military prison.

casting Pouring of molten METAL into a MOLD, where it solidifies into the shape of the mold. The process was well established in the BRONZE AGE, when it was used to form BRONZE pieces now found in museums. It is particularly valuable for the economical production of complex shapes, ranging from mass-produced parts for automobiles to one-of-a-kind production of statues, jewelry, or massive machinery. Most steel and iron castings (see CAST IRON) are poured into silica sand. For metals of lower melting point, such as aluminum or zinc, molds can be made of another metal or of sand. See also DIE CASTING, FOUNDING, INVESTMENT CASTING, LOST-WAX CASTING, PATTERNMAKING.

Baldassare Castiglione, detail of a portrait by Raphael, 1516; in the Louvre, Paris.

GIRAUDON—ART RESOURCE

castle Medieval European stronghold, generally the fortified dwelling of the king or lord of the territory in which it stood. The castle developed rapidly in Western Europe from the 9th century. In form it was somewhat sprawling compared to later fortified buildings. The castle's enceinte (outer wall) was surrounded by one or more moats, these being crossed by drawbridges that could be raised from the inner side. The gateway itself was heavily protected and often defended by a barbican, or watchtower. One or more baileys, or walled courtyards, surrounded the DONJON.

The age of the medieval castle came to an end with the increasing use of firearms in the 15th–16th century.

Castle, Vernon and Irene *orig.* **Vernon Blythe and Irene Foote** (1887–1918, 1893–1969) British-U.S. husband-and-wife BALLROOM DANCE team. Irene was born in New Rochelle, N.Y. Vernon moved to the U.S. in 1906 and married Irene in 1911. They gained worldwide popularity for their graceful style, and introduced such dances as the one-step, fox-trot, turkey trot, castle polka, castle walk, and hesitation waltz, and popularized several others. Irene is credited with creating the fashion for bobbed hair. Following Vernon's death in an airplane crash, Irene retired from dancing. A biographical movie starring FRED ASTAIRE and Ginger Rogers appeared in 1939.

Castlereagh \'ka-səl-ˌrā\ District (pop., 1995 est.: 63,000), Northern IRELAND. Located southeast of BELFAST, it was established in 1973. The area was settled in the 14th century by the O'Neill clan of Ulster, from whose main stronghold, Grey Castle (no longer extant), it takes its name. It is closely linked to eastern Belfast, the district seat, where many of its residents are employed.

Castlereagh, Viscount *orig.* **Robert Stewart** (1769–1822) British politician. Born in Ireland, he was elected to the Irish Parliament in 1790 and later served in the English Parliament (1794–1805, 1806–22). As chief secretary for Ireland (1798–1801), Castlereagh singlehandedly forced the Act of UNION through the Irish Parliament in 1800. He served as Britain's secretary for war (1805–6, 1807–9) and as secretary for foreign affairs and leader of the House of Commons (1812–22). Considered one of the most distinguished foreign secretaries in British history, he played a leading role in bringing together the Grand Alliance that overthrew NAPOLEON and in deciding the form of the peace settlements at the Congress of VIENNA. Beset with paranoia and believing that he was being blackmailed, he eventually committed suicide.

Castor and Pollux See DIOSCURI

castor-oil plant Large plant *(Ricinus communis)* of the SPURGE family, probably native to Africa and naturalized throughout the tropics. It is grown commercially for the pharmaceutical and industrial uses of its oil and for use in landscape gardening because of its handsome, giant, fanlike leaves. The bristly, spined, bronze-to-red clusters of fruits are attractive but are often removed before they mature because of the poison concentrated in their mottled, beanlike seeds. There are hundreds of natural forms and many horticultural varieties of this species.

Castor-oil plant (*Ricinus communis*).
KENNETH AND BRENDA FORMANEK

castration *or* **neutering** Removal of the TESTES. The procedure stops most production of the hormone TESTOSTERONE. If done before PUBERTY, it prevents the development of functioning adult sex organs. Castration after sexual maturity makes the sex organs shrink and stop functioning, ending sperm formation and sexual interest and behavior. Livestock and pets are castrated to keep them from reproducing (see STERILIZATION) or to create a more docile animal. In humans, castration has been used for both cultural (see EUNUCH, CASTRATO) and medical (e.g., for testicular cancer) reasons.

castrato \ka-'strä-ˌtō\ Male soprano or alto voice produced as a result of CASTRATION before puberty. The castrato voice was introduced in the Vatican's Sistine Chapel in the 16th century, when women were still banned from church choirs as well as the stage. It reached its greatest prominence in 17th- and 18th-century opera. The illegal and inhumane practice of castration, largely practiced in Italy, could produce a treble voice of extraordinary power, attributable to the lung capacity and physical bulk of the adult male. The unique tone quality and the ability of intensively trained singers to execute virtuosic passagework made castrati the rage among opera audiences and contributed to the spread of Italian opera. Most male singers in 18th-century opera were castrati; the most famous bore the stage names Senesino (Francesco Bernardi; died c. 1750), Caffarelli (Gaetano Majorano; 1710–1783), and FARINELLI. Castrati sang in the Sistine Chapel choir until 1903.

Castries \kȧ-'strē, 'käs-ˌtrē\ Seaport (pop., 1991: 11,000), capital of ST. LUCIA. Located on the island's northwestern coast, its fine harbor is St. Lucia's chief port. A fortress on Mount Fortune (852 ft, or 260 m) overlooks the town. It is a gateway for tourists visiting the island.

Castro (Ruz), Fidel (born 1926/27) Political leader of Cuba (from 1959). Son of a prosperous sugar planter, he became a lawyer, and worked on behalf of the poor in Havana. He was a candidate for Cuba's legislature when Gen. FULGENCIO BATISTA overthrew the government in 1952. He organized a rebellion against Batista in 1953, but it failed; captured, he served time in prison, then went to Mexico, where he and others, including CHE GUEVARA, continued to plot Batista's overthrow. He led an armed expedition back to Cuba in 1956; most of his men were killed, but a dozen survivors took refuge in the mountains, where they gradually managed to organize guerrillas throughout the island. On January 1, 1959, Batista was forced to flee the country. Castro nationalized private commerce and industry and expropriated U.S.-owned land and businesses, vastly expanded health services and eliminated illiteracy, and ruthlessly suppressed all opposition, outlawing all political groups but the Communist Party. The U.S. attempted to bring about his overthrow and failed (see BAY OF PIGS), precipitating the CUBAN MISSILE CRISIS. Castro exercised total control of the government and economy, which was increasingly dependent on subsidies from the Soviet Union. The Soviet Union's collapse (1991) devastated Cuba's economy, and Castro has attempted to replace its former revenues by encouraging tourism.

Castro y Bellvís \'käs-trō-ē-belʸ-'vēs\, **Guillén de** (1569–1631) Spanish playwright. Of his 50-odd plays, the best remembered is *Las mocedades del Cid* ("The Youth of the Cid"; c. 1599), on which PIERRE CORNEILLE based his *Le Cid* (1637). Castro's play is notable for its naturalistic dialogue. He was one of the earliest playwrights to deal with the difficulties of marriage, as in *Los mal casadas de Valencia* ("The Unhappy Marriages of Valencia"). He drew heavily on traditional Castilian ballads and based three of his plays on novels by MIGUEL DE CERVANTES.

casualty insurance Provision against loss to persons and property, covering legal hazards as well as those of accident and sickness. Major classes include LIABILITY, theft, aviation, WORKERS' COMPENSATION, CREDIT, and title. Liability insurance contracts may cover liability arising from use of an automobile, operation of a business, professional negligence (MALPRACTICE insurance), or property ownership. Credit insurance may cover the risk of bad debts from insolvency, death, and disability, the risk of loss of savings from bank failure, and the risk of loss of export credit due to commercial or political changes.

casuarina \ˌkazh-yə-'rē-nə\ Any of the chiefly Australian trees that make up the genus *Casuarina* (family Casuarinaceae), which have whorls of scalelike leaves and jointed stems resembling HORSETAILS. Several species, especially *C. equisetifolia,* are valued for their hard, dense, yellowish- to reddish-brown wood, which is strong and reputed to be resistant to termite attack. Beefwood and ironwood are common names that reflect the wood's color and hardness.

cat Any member of the most highly specialized CARNIVORE family, Felidae, which consists of the true cats (genera *Panthera* and *Felis*) and the CHEETAH *(Acinonyx)*. Modern-type cats appeared in the fossil record about 10 million years ago. Cats in the genus *Panthera* (sometimes *Leo*) (e.g., TIGER and LION) roar but cannot purr, and their pupils are round. Cats in the genus *Felis* (e.g., COUGAR) can purr but do not roar; the pupil is usually vertical. Cats have sharp, retractable claws, and their teeth are adapted for stabbing, anchoring, and cutting. They almost always land on their feet when they fall from a height. Most species are nocturnal, and their eyes are adapted for seeing in low light. Cats are known for their habit of grooming themselves with their rasplike tongue. Small cats have been domesticated for some 3,500 years (see DOMESTIC CAT). The wild cats include the BOBCAT, CARACAL, JAGUAR, LEOPARD, LYNX, OCELOT, SERVAL, SNOW LEOPARD, and WILDCAT.

CAT See COMPUTED AXIAL TOMOGRAPHY

cat bear See lesser PANDA

catacomb Subterranean cemetery of galleries with recesses for tombs. The term was probably first applied to the cemetery under St. Sebastian's Basilica that was a temporary resting place for the bodies of Sts.

Arched niche of a tomb with early Christian paintings of scenes from the Old and New Testaments, in the catacomb on Via Latina, Rome.
PONT. COMM. DI ARCH. SACRA/M. GRIMOLDI

Peter and Paul in the late 3rd century AD, but it came to refer to all the subterranean cemeteries around Rome. In addition to serving as burial sites, catacombs in early Christian Rome were the sites of funeral feasts celebrated in family vaults on the day of burial and on anniversaries. They were used as hiding places during times of persecution; Pope Sixtus II was supposedly captured and killed (AD 258) while hiding in the St. Sebastian's catacomb during Valerian's persecution. Catacombs are also found in Sicily and other parts of Italy, in Egypt, and in Lebanon.

Catalan language \'ka-tə-ˌlan\ Romance language spoken in eastern and northeastern Spain, chiefly Catalonia and Valencia, and in Andorra, the Balearic Isles, and the Roussillon region of France. Its literary tradition dates from the 12th century, when it was the official language of the kingdom of Aragon. As Catalonia achieved greater autonomy in the late 20th century, Catalan revived as the language of politics and education there. Its dialects, divided into an Occidental and an Oriental group, remain mutually intelligible. Catalan is related to the Occitan language of southern France and to Spanish.

Catalhüyük \chä-ˌtäl-hue-'yuek, *Engl* chä-ˌtäl-hü-'yük\ Neolithic site, Middle East. Located near Konya in southern Turkey, it was in Neolithic times the center of an advanced culture. The earliest period is tentatively dated to c. 6700 BC and the latest to c. 5650 BC. Excavation of the religious quarter produced a series of shrines; the wall paintings have been linked with Upper Paleolithic art.

Catalonia Autonomous community (pop., 1996 est.: 6,090,000) and historic region, northeastern Spain. It encompasses the provinces of Gerona, Barcelona, Tarragona, and Lérida, and covers an area of 12,328 sq mi (31,930 sq km); its capital is Barcelona. The Pyrenees separate Catalonia from France; the Mediterranean Sea lies to the east. Its principal rivers, the Ter, Llobrégat, and Ebro, all run into the Mediterranean. Catalonia was one of Rome's first Spanish possessions. Occupied in the 5th century AD by the Goths, it was taken by the Moors in 712 and by Charlemagne in 795. After the unification of Spain (1469), Catalonia lost its centrality in Spanish affairs, and by the 17th century its conflict of interest with Castilla y León led to the first of a series of separatist movements. Catalan nationalism became a serious force after 1876. In 1932 a compromise with the central government granted Catalonia autonomy; this was revoked with the 1939 Nationalist victory, and Francisco Franco's government adopted a repressive policy toward Catalan nationalism. The reestablishment of democratic rule after Franco's death again led to autonomy in 1979. Today Catalonia is the richest and most industrialized part of Spain.

catalpa \kə-'tal-pə\ Any of 11 species of trees in the genus *Catalpa* (family Bignoniaceae), native to eastern Asia, eastern North America, and the West Indies. Catalpas have large, attractive leaves and showy white, yellowish, or purplish flowers. The catalpa fruit is a long cylindrical pod bearing numerous seeds with white tufts of hair at each end. The common catalpa, *C. bignonioides,* yields a durable timber and is one of the most widely planted ornamental species.

catalysis \kə-'ta-lə-səs\ Modification (usually acceleration) of a chemical reaction rate by addition of a catalyst, which combines with the reactants but is ultimately regenerated so that its amount remains unchanged and the chemical equilibrium of the conditions of the reaction is not altered. Catalysts reduce the activation energy barrier between reactants and products. When more than one reaction is possible, a catalyst that accelerates only one reaction pathway selectively enhances the creation of its product. Catalysis is inhibited if the reactant or the catalyst is removed or altered by any of several types of agents (inhibitors). Catalysis in a single phase (e.g., in a liquid solution or gaseous mixture) is homogeneous; that in more than one phase (e.g., in a liquid and a solid) is heterogeneous. Chemisorption, a type of heterogeneous catalysis, often involves bonding between the catalyst's solid surface and the reactant, changing the nature of the chemisorbed molecules. To make the accessible surface area as large as possible, such catalysts are finely powdered or highly porous solids. Catalysis is essential to the modern chemical industry. See also enzyme.

catalyst \'ka-tᵊl-əst\ Any substance of which a small proportion notably affects the reaction rate of a chemical reaction without itself being changed or consumed (see catalysis). One molecule may transform several million reactant molecules a minute. Gaseous, liquid, or solid, catalysts may be inorganic compounds, organic compounds, or complex combinations. They tend to be highly specific, reacting with only one substance or a small set of substances. Substances that alter them or block reactants' access to them may inhibit (poison) them. Catalysts are essential to virtually all industrial chemical reactions, especially in petroleum refining and synthetic organic chemical manufacturing. Most solid catalysts are fine-grained transition elements (metals) or their oxides. In a car's catalytic converter, the platinum catalyst converts unburned hydrocarbons and nitrogen compounds to products harmless to the environment. Water, especially salt water, catalyzes oxidation (see oxidation-reduction) and corrosion. Enzymes are among the most active and selective catalysts known.

catalytic converter In automobiles, a component of emission control systems used to reduce the discharge of noxious gases from the internal-combustion engine. The catalytic converter consists of an insulated chamber containing pellets of catalyst through which the exhaust gases are passed. The exhaust's hydrocarbons and carbon monoxide are converted to water vapor and carbon dioxide.

catamaran \'ka-tə-mə-ˌran\ Twin-hulled sailing and engine-powered boat. Its design was based on a raft of two logs bridged by planks used by peoples in the Indonesian archipelago, Polynesia, and Micronesia. Up to 70 ft (21 m) long, early catamarans were paddled by many men and used for travel, in war, and in recreation. Especially after the sail was added, voyages as long as 2,000 mi (3,700 km) were made. In the 1870s they sailed so successfully against monohulled boats that they were barred from racing. The modern catamaran, which averages about 40 ft (12 m) in length, has been produced since 1950. They are very fast craft, achieving speeds of 20 mph (32 kph).

Catania \kä-'tä-nyä\ City (pop., 1996: 342,000), Sicily. It was founded by Greeks in 729 BC at the foot of Mount Etna on the Gulf of Catania. Taken by the Romans in the First Punic War (263 BC), it was made a Roman colony by Octavian (later Augustus). Catanian Christians suffered under the emperors Decius and Diocletian; their martyrs included St. Agatha, patron saint of the city. Catania fell successively to the Byzantines, Arabs, and Normans, and suffered devastation by earthquakes especially in 1169 and 1693. In World War II the city was severely damaged by bombing. Rebuilt, it is Sicily's second-largest city, and is an industrial and transportation center.

Catanzaro \ˌkä-tänd-'zä-rō\ City (pop., 1991: 93,000), capital of Calabria, southern Italy. It lies near the Gulf of Squillace. It was probably founded in the 10th century by Byzantines, but was taken in 1059 by the Normans under Robert Guiscard. It played an important part in the Napoleonic Wars and in the movement for Italian unity. Catanzaro suffered severely from earthquakes in 1905 and 1907, and from bombing in World War II. It is an agricultural center.

catapult Mechanism for forcefully propelling stones, spears, or other projectiles, in use since ancient times. Nearly all catapults employed in ancient and medieval ARTILLERY operated by a sudden release of tension on wooden beams or twisted cords of horsehair, gut, sinew, or other fibers. An exception was the medieval trebuchet, powered by a counterweight. Modern mechanisms using steam, hydraulic pressure, tension, or other force to launch gliders, aircraft, or missiles are also called catapults.

cataract Opacity of the EYE's crystalline lens. Cataracts causing central VISUAL-FIELD DEFECTS are most likely to affect vision. Cataracts may occur in newborns and infants. Diabetes mellitus, prolonged exposure to ultraviolet rays, or trauma can cause them in adults, but they most often occur with age, resulting from gradual loss of transparency of the lens. Treatment is a surgical procedure to replace the lens with an artificial one.

catastrophe theory Branch of mathematics (considered a branch of geometry) that explores how gradual changes to a system produce sudden, drastic results (though usually not as dire as the name suggests). A simple example is how a plastic coffee stirrer subjected to gradually increasing pressure from both ends will suddenly buckle in one direction or another. Other "catastrophes" include optical phenomena such as reflection or refraction of light through moving water. More speculatively, ideas from catastrophe theory have been applied by social scientists to such situations as the sudden eruption of mob violence.

Catatumbo River \ˌkä-tä-ˈtüm-bō\ River, northern South America. Rising in northern Colombia, it flows northeast across the Venezuelan border and the oil-rich Maracaibo Lowland to empty into Lake MARACAIBO after a course of 210 mi (338 km).

Catawba \kə-ˈtȯ-bə\ North American Indian people who inhabited the Catawba River area in the Carolinas. They subsisted principally by farming, harvesting corn, beans, squash, and gourds. Fish and birds were also staples of their diet. Bowls, baskets, and mats were traded to other Indian groups and white colonists. Each village was governed by a council presided over by a chief. After contact with European settlers, disease and other factors diminished their numbers rapidly. Today about 1,200 Catawba live around Rock Hill in South Carolina.

Catawba River River, southeastern U.S. Rising in North Carolina's BLUE RIDGE MTNS., it flows south into South Carolina, where it becomes the WATEREE RIVER. It is 220 mi (350 km) long. With the Wateree, it forms an important source of hydroelectric power for South Carolina.

catbird Any of several PASSERINE species (family Mimidae) named for their mewing calls, which they use in addition to song. The North American catbird *(Dumetella carolinensis)* is 9 in. (23 cm) long and gray with a black cap. It is found in gardens and thickets. The black catbird *(Melanoptila glabrirostris)* is found in coastal Yucatán. Three species of the BOWERBIRD family are also called catbirds; they are found in Australia, New Guinea, and nearby islands and do not build bowers but hold territories in the forest by loud singing.

catch English round, or simple vocal CANON, for three or more unaccompanied voices. Catches were sung by men as a popular pastime in the 16th–19th century. The increasingly intricate and clever interaction of the voices often produced comic and off-color verbal effects, especially in the late-17th-century RESTORATION period.

Cateau-Cambrésis \kȧ-tō-kä^n-brā-ˈzē\, **Treaty of** (1559) Agreement marking the end of the 65-year struggle (1494–1559) between France and Spain for the control of Italy. France gave up its claims to Italian territory, leaving Habsburg Spain the dominant power there. France returned Savoy and Piedmont to Spain's ally Emmanuel-Philibert of Savoy (1528–1580) and restored Corsica to Genoa. Elsewhere, France retained Calais, which it had seized from England in 1558, and the bishoprics of Toul, Metz, and Verdun, taken from Emperor CHARLES V.

catechesis See KERYGMA AND CATECHESIS

catechism Manual of religious instruction usually arranged in the form of questions and answers and used to instruct the young, win converts, and testify to the faith. The medieval catechism concentrated on the meaning of faith, hope, and charity. Later catechisms added other subjects and became more important following the REFORMATION and the invention of the printing press. MARTIN LUTHER's Small Catechism (1529) added discussions of baptism and the EUCHARIST. JOHN CALVIN published a children's catechism in 1542. The Anglican catechism is included in the Book of COMMON PRAYER. The Baltimore Catechism (1885) is the Catholic catechism best known in the U.S. In 1992 the Vatican issued a new universal *Catechism of the Catholic Church.*

catecholamine \ˌka-tə-ˈkō-lə-ˌmēn\ Any naturally occurring AMINE functioning as a NEUROTRANSMITTER or HORMONE, including DOPAMINE, NOREPINEPHRINE, and EPINEPHRINE. All are derived from TYROSINE, and have a catechol group (BENZENE ring with two hydroxyl groups) with an attached amine group. Neurons in the brain, in the adrenal gland, and in some sympathetic nerve fibers produce different catecholamines.

categorical imperative In IMMANUEL KANT's moral philosophy, an imperative that presents an action as unconditionally necessary (e.g., "Thou shalt not kill"), as opposed to an imperative that presents an action as necessary only on condition that the agent wills something else (e.g., "Pay your debts on time, if you want to be able to obtain a mortgage"). Kant held that there was only one formally categorical imperative, from which all specific moral imperatives could be derived. In one famous formulation, it is: "Act only according to that maxim by which you can at the same time will that it should become a universal law." See also DEONTOLOGICAL ETHICS.

categorical proposition In SYLLOGISTIC, a proposition in which the predicate is affirmed or denied of all or part of the subject. Thus, categorical propositions are of four basic forms: "Every S is P," "No S is P," "Some S is P," and "Some S is not P." These are designated by the letters A, E, I, and O, respectively; thus, "Every man is mortal" is an A-proposition. Categorical propositions are to be distinguished from compound and complex propositions, into which they can enter as integral terms. In particular, they contrast especially with hypothetical propositions, such as "If every man is mortal, then Socrates is mortal."

caterpillar LARVA of a BUTTERFLY or MOTH. Caterpillars have a cylindrical body consisting of 13 segments, with three pairs of legs on the thorax and "prolegs" on the abdomen. The head has six eyes on each side, short antennae, and strong jaws. Though not true WORMS, many caterpillars are called worms (e.g., the inchworm, or LOOPER, and the CUTWORM). Caterpillar-like larvae are also found in other insect groups (e.g., SAWFLIES and scorpionflies).

catfish Any of about 2,500 species of scale-less, mostly freshwater, fishes (order Siluriformes) related to CARP and MINNOWS and named for their whiskerlike barbels (fleshy feelers). All species have at least one pair of barbels on the upper jaw, and some have a pair on the snout and additional pairs on the chin. Many species possess spines that may be associated with venom glands. Found almost worldwide, they are generally bottom-dwelling scavengers that feed on almost any kind of plant or animal matter. Species vary from 1.5 in. to 15 ft (4 cm–4.5 m) long and may weigh up to 660 lbs (300 kg). Many small species are popular aquarium fishes; many large species are used for food.

Cathari \ˈka-thə-ˌrī\ *or* **Albigensians** \al-bə-ˈjen-sē-ənz\ Heretical Christian sect that flourished in Western Europe in the 12th–13th century. The Cathari adhered to the dualist belief that the material world is evil and that humans must renounce the world to free their spirits, which are good and long for communion with God. Jesus was seen as an angel whose human suffering and death were an illusion. Followers divided themselves into the "perfect," who had to maintain the highest moral standards, and ordinary "believers," of whom less was expected. By 1200 they had established 11 bishoprics in France and Italy. In an effort to stamp out their HERESY, Pope INNOCENT III declared the ALBIGENSIAN CRUSADE, in which the populace in Cathar regions was indiscriminately massacred. Persecution through the INQUISITION, sanctioned by St. LOUIS IX, was even more effective, and when the Cathar stronghold of Montségur fell in 1244, most Cathari fled to Italy. The movement disappeared in the 15th century.

catharsis \kə-ˈthär-səs\ Purging or purification of emotions through art. The term is derived from the Greek *katharsis* (purgation, cleansing), a medical term used by ARISTOTLE as a metaphor to describe the effects of dramatic tragedy on the spectator: By arousing vicarious pity and terror, tragedy directs the spectator's own anxieties outward and, through sympathetic identification with the tragic protagonist, purges them.

Cathay \ka-ˈthā\ Former name for China, especially northern China. The word is derived from Khitay, the name of a seminomadic people who dominated northern China in the 10th–12th century. By the time of GENGHIS KHAN, the MONGOLS had begun referring to northern China as Kitai (still the Russian word for China). The name may have been introduced to Europe by returning Franciscan friars c. 1254, but it was MARCO POLO's *Travels* 50 years later that put Cathay's image before the European public.

cathedral Church, often large and magnificent, in which a residential bishop has his official seat. Cathedrals are usually embellished versions of early Christian BASILICAS; their construction, on an ever-larger scale, was a major preoccupation throughout Europe in the Middle Ages. Masonry vaulting replaced the earlier timber roofs, and the basilican plan grew more complex. Above the arches of the NAVE, and below the CLERESTORY, was the triforium, an arcaded upper story that often contained vaulted tribune GALLERIES open to the nave. The portion containing seats for the choir, usually east of the TRANSEPT, was called the chancel. Between the chancel and the sanctuary (high altar) was the presbytery, a raised area occupied only by clergy. The chapter house, a popular feature of English cathedrals, was a chamber, typically octagonal, in which business was transacted. Small chapels, including the founder's chantry and the Lady Chapel (dedicated to the Virgin Mary) were often added. Many cathedrals of the Île-de-France region were remodeled to embody a chevet, or arc of radiating chapels, on the eastern wall, a feature reflected in England in WESTMINSTER ABBEY and Canterbury Cathedral.

Cather \'ka-t͟hər\, **Willa** *orig.* **Wilella Sibert Cather** (1873–1947) U.S. novelist. Born in Winchester, Va., she moved with her family to Nebraska at age 9; she returned east 12 years later, eventually settling in New York. *The Troll Garden* (1905), her first short-story collection, contains some of her best-known work. The novels *O Pioneers!* (1913) and *My Ántonia* (1918), often judged her finest achievement, celebrate frontier spirit and courage. *Song of the Lark* (1915), *Youth and the Bright Medusa* (1920), and other works reflect the struggle of a talent to emerge from small-town provincialism. *One of Ours* (1922, Pulitzer Prize) and *A Lost Lady* (1923) mourn the loss of the pioneer spirit. Pioneers of earlier eras also inspired *Death Comes for the Archbishop* (1927) and *Shadows on the Rock* (1931).

Catherine I *Russian* **Yekaterina Alekseyevna** *orig.* **Marta Skowronska** (1684–1727) Second wife of PETER I and empress of Russia (1725–27). A peasant woman of Baltic origin, she became Peter's mistress in 1702. In 1703, after the birth of their first child, she was received into the Russian Orthodox church and rechristened. She married Peter in 1712, and in 1724 was crowned empress-consort. After Peter's death (1725), she served two years as empress of Russia.

Catherine II *Russian* **Yekaterina Alekseyevna** *orig.* **Sophie Friederike Auguste, Prinzessin (Princess) von Anhalt-Zerbst,** *known as* **Catherine the Great** (1729–1796) German-born empress of Russia (1762–96). The daughter of an obscure German prince, she was chosen at 14 to be the wife of the future PETER III. The marriage was a complete failure. Because her neurotic husband was incapable of ruling, the ambitious Catherine saw the possibility of eliminating him and governing Russia herself. After Peter became emperor in 1762, she conspired with her lover, GRIGORY G., COUNT ORLOV, to force Peter to abdicate (he was murdered soon after) and have herself proclaimed empress. In her 34-year reign, she led Russia into full participation in European political and cultural life. With her ministers she reorganized the administration and law of the Russian empire and extended Russian territory, adding the Crimea and much of Poland. Though she had once intended to emancipate the serfs, she instead strengthened the system she had once condemned as inhuman. She had great energy and wide interests, and her personal life was notable for her many lovers, including GRIGORY POTEMKIN.

Catherine de Médicis \kä-trēn-də-mā-dē-'sēs\ *orig.* **Caterina de' Medici** (1519–1589) Queen consort of HENRY II (1547–59), mother of FRANCIS II, CHARLES IX, and HENRY III, and regent of France (1560–74). A member of the MEDICI FAMILY, she married Henry in 1533 and bore him 10 children. She became queen when Henry inherited the crown in 1547 and greatly mourned his accidental death in 1559. After their son Francis became king, she began a long struggle with members of the GUISE family, extremists who sought to dominate the crown. After Francis's premature death in 1560, she became regent for Charles IX until 1563 and dominated the rest of his reign until 1574. She attempted to settle the Wars of RELIGION between Catholics and HUGUENOTS. She has traditionally been blamed for the ST. BARTHOLOMEW'S DAY MASSACRE, but though she authorized the assassination of GASPARD II DE COLIGNY and his principal followers, it appears that she did not authorize the massacre that followed.

Catherine of Alexandria, St. (fl. early 4th century AD) Early Christian martyr. According to tradition, she was a learned girl of noble birth who protested the persecution of Christians during the reign of the Roman emperor Maxentius. She converted the emperor's wife and defeated in debate the best scholars he sent to oppose her. She was sentenced to be killed with a spiked wheel (the catherine wheel), but when it broke she was beheaded. Her body was transported by angels to the top of Mount Sinai. One of the most popular saints of the Middle Ages, she was patron of philosophers and scholars. Her historicity is doubtful.

Catherine of Aragon (1485–1536) First wife of HENRY VIII. The daughter of FERDINAND II and ISABELLA I, she married Henry in 1509. She gave birth to six children, but only one daughter (later MARY I) survived infancy. Henry's desire for a legitimate male heir prompted him in 1527 to appeal to Rome for an annulment, but Pope CLEMENT VII refused, triggering the break between Henry and Rome and leading to the English Reformation. In 1533 Henry had his own archbishop of Canterbury, THOMAS CRANMER, annul the marriage, and Catherine spent her last years isolated from public life.

Catherine of Aragon, detail of an oil painting by an unknown artist; in the National Portrait Gallery, London.
BY COURTESY OF THE NATIONAL PORTRAIT GALLERY, LONDON

Catherine of Braganza (1638–1705) Portuguese wife of CHARLES II of England. She was married to Charles in 1662 as part of an alliance between England and Portugal, bringing England trading privileges and the port cities of Tangier and Bombay (now Mumbai). She produced no heir. Though not a faithful husband, Charles defended her against accusations of scheming to poison him. She helped convert him to Catholicism shortly before his death. In 1692 she returned to Portugal, and in 1704 she governed the country as regent for her ailing brother, Pedro II.

Catherine of Siena, St. *orig.* **Caterina Benincasa** (1347–1380) Dominican mystic and patron saint of Italy. She joined the Dominican third order in Siena in 1363 and soon became known for her holiness and severe asceticism. Catherine called for a crusade against the Muslims as a means of calming domestic conflict in Italy. She also played a major role in returning the papacy from Avignon to Rome (see AVIGNON PAPACY). Her writings include four treatises on religious mysticism known as *The Dialogue of St. Catherine*.

catheterization \ˌka-thə-tə-rə-'zā-shən\ Threading of a flexible tube (catheter) through a channel in the body to inject drugs or a CONTRAST MEDIUM, measure and record flow and pressures, inspect structures, take samples, diagnose disorders, or clear blockages. A cardiac catheter, passed into the heart through an artery or vein (the incision is often in the groin), can also carry pacemaker electrodes. A bladder catheter goes through the urethra into the bladder.

cathode Terminal or ELECTRODE at which electrons enter a system, such as an electrolytic cell or an electron tube. In a BATTERY or other source of DIRECT CURRENT, the cathode is the positive terminal. In a passive load it is the negative terminal. In an electron tube, such as a CATHODE-RAY TUBE, electrons stream off the cathode and travel through the tube toward the ANODE.

cathode ray Stream of ELECTRONS leaving the negative ELECTRODE, or CATHODE, in a discharge tube (an electron tube that contains gas or vapor at low pressure), or emitted by a heated filament in certain electron tubes. Cathode rays cause fluorescent materials to luminesce and are utilized in cathode-ray oscilloscopes and television tubes (see CATHODE-RAY TUBE).

cathode-ray tube (CRT) Vacuum tube that produces images when its phosphorescent surface is struck by electron beams. CRTs can be monochrome (using one electron gun) or color (typically using three electron

C
D

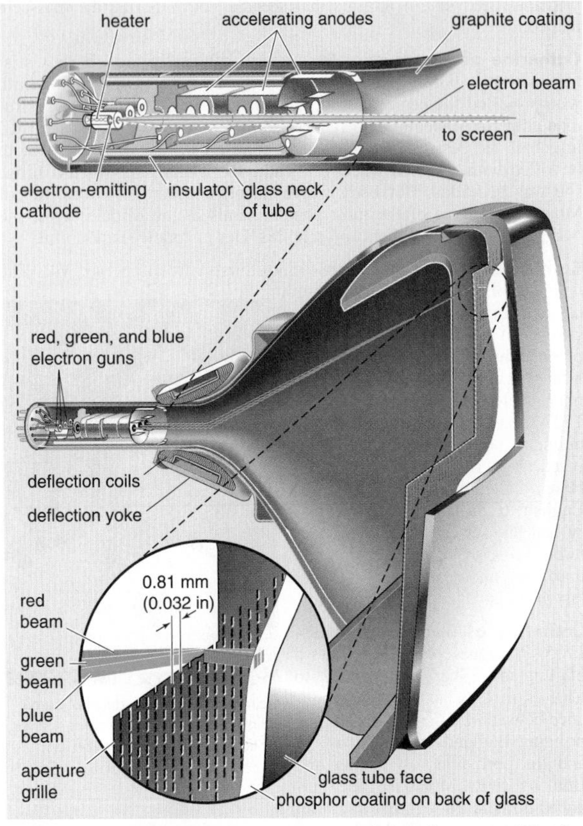

In a color-television tube, three electron guns (one each for red, green, and blue) fire electrons toward the phosphor-coated screen. The electrons are directed to a specific spot (pixel) on the screen by magnetic fields, induced by the deflection coils. To prevent "spillage" to adjacent pixels, a grille or shadow mask is used. When the electrons strike the phosphor screen, the pixel glows. Every pixel is scanned about 30 times per second.

guns to produce red, green, and blue images that, when combined, render a multicolor image). They come in a variety of display modes, including CGA (Color Graphics Adapter), VGA (Video Graphics Array), XGA (Extended Graphics Array), and the high-definition SVGA (Super Video Graphics Array).

Catholic church, Old See OLD CATHOLIC CHURCH

Catholic Emancipation Freedom from discrimination and civil disabilities granted to the Roman Catholics of Britain and Ireland in the late 18th and early 19th century. After the REFORMATION, Roman Catholics in Britain could not purchase land, hold offices or seats in Parliament, inherit property, or practice their religion without incurring civil penalties. Irish Catholics faced similar limitations. By the late 18th century, Catholicism no longer seemed so great a danger, and a series of laws, culminating in the Emancipation Act of 1829, eased the restrictions. A major figure in the struggle for emancipation was DANIEL O'CONNELL.

Catholic League (1609–35) Military alliance of the Catholic powers of Germany, led by MAXIMILIAN I, duke of Bavaria, and designed to stem the growth of Protestantism in Germany. Plans for a league had long been discussed, but the formation of the Protestant Union in 1608 finally caused the Catholics to unite. In alliance with the Habsburg emperors, the League's forces, led by Graf von TILLY, played a key role in the THIRTY YEARS' WAR. The league was abolished by the Peace of Prague (1635).

Catholic Reformation See COUNTER-REFORMATION

Catiline \'kat-ᵊl-ˌīn\ *Latin in full* **Lucius Sergius Catilina** (108?–62 BC) Roman aristocrat turned demagogue who sought to overthrow the republic. He was first suspected of conspiracy in 65, after which he sought to be elected CONSUL. Failing twice, he planned a coup, known as Catiline's conspiracy (63), assembling an army outside Rome from his supporters among the alienated and discontented elements of society. CICERO, then consul, learned of the conspiracy; with Senate approval, he caught and executed a group of the plotters in Rome, and later sent the army to defeat and kill Catiline in northern Italy (62).

cation \'kat-ˌī-ən\ ATOM or group of atoms carrying a positive ELECTRIC CHARGE, indicated by a superscript plus sign after the chemical symbol. Cations in a liquid subjected to an ELECTRIC FIELD collect at the negative pole (CATHODE). Examples include SODIUM (Na^+), CALCIUM (Ca^{2+}), and ammonium (NH_4^+; see AMMONIA). See also ION.

catkin Elongated cluster of single-sex flowers bearing scaly BRACTS and usually lacking petals. Many trees bear catkins, including WILLOWS, BIRCHES, and OAKS. Wind carries pollen from male to female catkins or from male catkins to female flowers that take a different form (e.g., spikes).

Catlett, Elizabeth (born 1919) Expatriate American sculptor and printmaker. Catlett was born into a middle-class Washington family. After studying sculpture, she went to Mexico City in 1946 to work at the Taller de Gráfica Popular, an artists' collective, where she created prints depicting Mexican life. About 1962 she took Mexican citizenship. In her sculptures and prints, Catlett focused on mother-child pairings, famous subjects such as Harriet Tubman and Malcolm X, and anonymous workers—notably strong, solitary black women.

Catlin, George (1796–1872) U.S. painter and author. Born in Wilkes-Barre, Pa., he practiced law briefly before becoming a self-taught portrait painter in Philadelphia (1823). Long interested in Native American life, in 1830 he began a series of visits to various tribes on the Great Plains. He produced some 500 paintings and sketches based on his travels and exhibited them in the U.S. and Europe. He published several illustrated books on Native American life.

catnip *or* **catmint** Aromatic herb *(Nepeta cataria)* of the MINT family. Catnip has spikes of small, purple-dotted flowers. It has been used as a seasoning and as a medicinal tea. Because its mintlike flavor and aroma are particularly exciting to domestic cats, it is often used as a stuffing for cat playthings.

Catnip (*Nepeta cataria*).

WALTER CHANDOHA

Cato \'kā-tō\, **Marcus Porcius** *known as* **Cato the Censor** *or* **Cato the Elder** (234–149 BC) Roman statesman and orator, the first important Latin prose writer. Born of yeoman stock, he fought in the Second PUNIC WAR. His oratorical skills paved the way for his political career. He held conservative anti-Hellenic views and opposed the pro-Hellenic Scipio family, whose power he broke. Elected censor (magistrate in charge of censuses, taxes, and the public good) in 184, he tried to restore the *mos majorum* ("ancestral custom") and combat Greek influence, which he believed undermined Roman morality. He crafted laws against luxury and the financial freedom of women and never ceased to demand the destruction of Carthage. His writings include works on history, medicine, law, military science, and agriculture.

Cats \'käts\, **Jacob(us)** *known as* **Father Cats** (1577–1660) Dutch poet. A magistrate and high official, he was enormously popular as a writer of emblem books, consisting of woodcuts or engravings with verses pointing to a moral. His *Mirror of Old and New Times* (1632) contains many quotations that have become household sayings in Holland, and he used it to express the ethical concerns of Dutch Calvinists, especially about love and marriage.

cat's-eye Any of several gemstones that display a luminous band reminiscent of the eye of a cat. Grayish green or greenish quartz cat's-eye is the most common type; although it comes from the Orient, it is often called occidental cat's-eye to differentiate it from the rarer, and more valuable, precious or oriental cat's-eye, which is a greenish variety of chrysoberyl. Crocidolite cat's-eye (African cat's-eye) is more commonly known as TIGEREYE. Corundum cat's-eye is an imperfect star sapphire or ruby in which the star is reduced to a luminous zone.

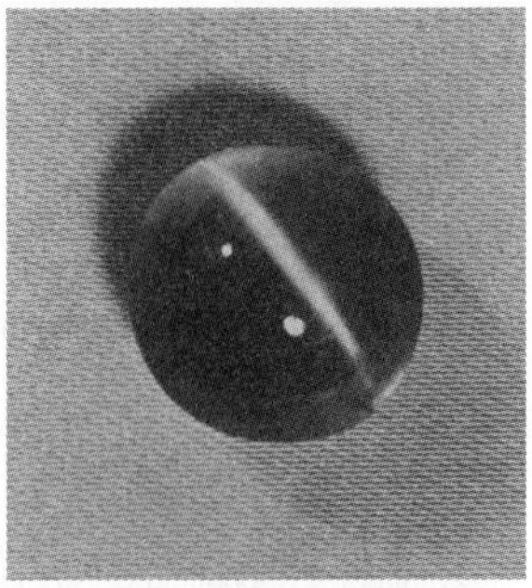

Chrysoberyl cat's-eye with yellow banding on a brown stone.
JOHN H. GERARD

Catskill Mountains Mountain group of the APPALACHIAN MTN. system, southeastern New York. It is bounded by the MOHAWK and HUDSON rivers. Many of its peaks reach 3,000 ft (900 m); the highest, Slide Mtn., reaches 4,204 ft (1,281 m). The area has many resorts, and its lakes supply New York City with water. The mountains were made famous through WASHINGTON IRVING's stories of Rip Van Winkle, who supposedly took his long nap near the town of Catskill.

Catt, Carrie Chapman *orig.* **Carrie Lane** (1859–1947) U.S. women's-suffrage advocate. Born in Ripon, Wis., she became a high-school principal in Mason City, Iowa, in 1881, and in 1883 one of the nation's first female school superintendents. She married Leo Chapman in 1884. After his untimely death in 1886 she devoted herself to organizing the Iowa Woman Suffrage Association (1887–90). After marrying George Catt in 1890, she reorganized the National American Woman Suffrage Association along political-district lines; she served as its president from 1915. After the 19th Amendment granted voting rights to women, she reorganized the 2-million-member association as the League of Women Voters to work for progressive legislation, including the cause of world peace. See also WOMEN'S SUFFRAGE MOVEMENT.

Carrie Chapman Catt.
BY COURTESY OF THE LEAGUE OF WOMEN VOTERS OF ILLINOIS

cattail Any of the tall reedy marsh plants (see REED) that bear brown, furry fruiting spikes and make up the genus *Typha* (family Typhaceae), particularly *T. latifolia,* the long flat leaves of which are used especially for making mats and chair seats. Cattails are found mainly in temperate and cold regions of the Northern and Southern hemispheres. Important to wildlife, they are also often cultivated ornamentally as pond plants and for dried-flower arrangements. The leaves, which swell when wet, are used for caulking cracks in barrels and boats.

Cattell \kə-ˈtel\, **James McKeen** (1860–1944) U.S. psychologist. Born in Easton, Pa., he studied with WILHELM WUNDT in Leipzig and later assisted FRANCIS GALTON in London. Teaching at the University of Pennsylvania (1888–91) and Columbia University (1891–1917), where EDWARD L. THORNDIKE was his student, he oriented U.S. psychology toward use of objective experimental methods, mental testing, and applied psychology. Much of his career was devoted to editing and publishing scientific periodicals; he was a founder of *Psychological Review* (1894), edited *Science* for 50 years (from 1894), and founded the directory *American Men of Science* (1906).

cattle Domesticated BOVIDS that are raised for meat, milk, or hides or for draft purposes. Depending on the breed, mature bulls (fertile males) weigh 1,000–4,000 lbs (450–1,800 kg); cows (fertile females) weigh 800–2,400 lbs (360–1,080 kg). All modern cattle are believed to belong to either of two species (*Bos indicus* or *B. taurus*) or to be crosses of the two. About 277 identifiable breeds include those prominent in beef production (e.g., ANGUS, HEREFORD, and SHORTHORN) and DAIRY FARMING. Cattle feed primarily by grazing on pasture, but in modern farming their diet is ordinarily supplemented with prepared animal FEEDS. See also AUROCHS, BRAHMAN, OX.

Cattle Raid of Cooley, The See TÁIN BÓ CÚAILGNE

Catullus \kə-ˈtəl-əs\, **Gaius Valerius** (84?–54? BC) Roman poet. Few facts about his life are certain. Of 116 extant poems, 25 portray an intense and unhappy affair with a married woman ("Lesbia"); others reflect an affair with the youth Juventius; still others are outbursts of contempt for Julius CAESAR and other personages. He displayed remarkable versatility in assorted poetic forms, and his conversational rhythms carry an immediacy unrivaled by any other classic poet. His expressions of love and hatred represent perhaps the finest lyric poetry of ancient Rome.

Cauca River \ˈkau̇-kä\ River, western Colombia. It rises in the ANDES and flows northward between the Cordilleras Occidental and Oriental 838 mi (1,348 km) to join the MAGDALENA RIVER north of Mompós. In its middle reaches it flows through the Valle del Cauca, important for its agriculture and cattle raising. Two-thirds of Colombia's coffee is produced in the adjacent uplands.

Caucasia \kȯ-ˈkā-zhə\ *or* **Caucasus** \ˈkȯ-kə-səs\ *Russian* **Kavkaz** \kåf-ˈkås\ Mountainous region, between the BLACK and CASPIAN seas. Occupying 154,250 sq mi (399,510 sq km), it is divided among Russia, Georgia, Azerbaijan, and Armenia and forms part of the traditional dividing line between Europe and Asia. It is bisected by the CAUCASUS MTNS.; the area north of the Greater Caucasus range is called Ciscaucasia, and the region to the south Transcaucasia. Inhabited from ancient times, it was under nominal Persian and Turkish suzerainty until conquered by Russia in the 18th–19th century.

Caucasian languages \kȯ-ˈkā-zhən\ Group of languages spoken in the Caucasus region that are not members of any language families spoken elsewhere in the world. Caucasian languages, spoken by perhaps close to 9 million people, are divided into three subgroups: the South Caucasian, or Kartvelian family; the Northwest Caucasian, or Abkhaz-Adyghe languages; and the Northeast Caucasian, or Nakh-Dagestanian languages. Kartvelian, with over 4.5 million speakers, comprises four relatively closely related languages, including GEORGIAN. Northwest Caucasian languages include Abkhaz and a chain of dialects called collectively CIRCASSIAN. The Northeast Caucasian languages are further divided into two groups, Nakh and Daghestanian. The Nakh languages include Chechen and Ingush, spoken by over a million people mainly in CHECHNYA and Ingushetia. Daghestanian is an extraordinarily diversified group of 25–30 languages spoken by some 1.7 million people mainly in northern Azerbaijan and the Republic of Dagestan. Several Daghestanian languages, including Avar, Lak, Dargva, and Lezgi, number their speakers in the hundreds of thousands; others are spoken in only a few villages. In spite of their great diversity, most Caucasian languages have in common large consonant inventories and a tendency toward ERGATIVITY in case marking, verb indexing, or syntax. Those Caucasian languages with standard written forms employ the CYRILLIC ALPHABET, with the prominent exception of Georgian. An effort is being made to introduce the LATIN ALPHABET for Chechen in Chechnya.

Caucasoid See RACE

Caucasus Mountains \ˈkȯ-kə-səs\ *Russian* **Kavkazskiy Khrebet** \kəf-ˈkä-skē-k̲ryi-ˈbyet\ Mountain range between the BLACK and CASPIAN seas, often considered the southeastern limit of Europe. It extends about 700 mi (1,125 km) across southern Russia, Georgia, Azerbaijan, and Armenia, and is of volcanic origin. Many peaks rise above 15,000 ft (4,575 m); the highest is Mount ELBRUS. It is crossed by several high passes, including the Daryal and Mamison. It possesses considerable water-power resources, including those of the KURA RIVER, and valuable petroleum and natural gas reserves.

Cauchy \kō-ˈshē\, **Augustin-Louis** (1789–1857) French mathematician, pioneer of ANALYSIS and GROUP THEORY. After a career as a military engineer in Napoleon's navy, he wrote a treatise in 1813 that became the basis of the theory of COMPLEX VARIABLES. He also clarified the theory of CALCULUS by developing the concepts of LIMITS and CONTINUITY, laid the foundations for the mathematical theory of elasticity, and made important contributions to NUMBER THEORY. He is considered one of the greatest mathematicians of the modern era.

caudillo \kau̇-ˈdē-yō\ Latin American military dictator. In the wake of the Latin American independence movement in the early 19th cent, politically unstable conditions and the long experience of armed conflict led to the emergence in many of the new countries of strongmen who were often charismatic and whose hold on power depended on control over armed followers, patronage, and vigilance. Because their power was based on violence and personal relations, the legitimacy of the caudillos' rule was always in doubt, and few could withstand the challenges of new leaders who emerged among their own followers and wealthy patrons. See also MACHISMO, PERSONALISMO.

Caulaincourt \ˌkō-ˌla^{n}-ˈku̇r\, **Armand (-Augustin-Louis), marquis de** (1773–1827) French general and diplomat. He became aide-de-camp to NAPOLEON (1802) and was the emperor's loyal master of horse from 1804. He later served as ambassador to Russia (1807–11) and foreign minister (1813–14, 1815). Created duc de Vicence (1808), he was at Napoleon's side in his great battles. His *Mémoires* provide an important source for the period 1812–14.

cauliflower Form of CABBAGE (*Brassica oleracea,* Botrytis group) of the MUSTARD FAMILY, consisting of a compact terminal mass of greatly thickened, modified, and partially developed flower structures, together with their embracing fleshy stalks. This terminal cluster forms a firm, white, succulent "curd" that is served as a cooked vegetable and is highly nutritious. The separated flower structures are also eaten raw.

Cauliflower (*Brassica oleracea,* Botrytis group).
DEREK FELL

Caulkins, Tracy (born 1963) U.S. swimmer. Born in Winona, Minn., in 1978 she became (at age 15) the first woman to swim the 200-yard medley in under two minutes. By 1982 she had surpassed JOHNNY WEISSMULLER's record of 36 U.S. national titles and had won more titles than any other U.S. amateur athlete. By the time she retired after the 1984 Olympic Games, where she won three gold medals, she had won 48 national titles and set 66 world or U.S. records, and was the only swimmer who had set U.S. records in every stroke.

causation RELATION that holds between two temporally simultaneous or successive events when the first event (the cause) brings about the other (the effect). DAVID HUME held that the idea of necessary connection that is part of the common conception of causation is subjective. According to Hume, the objective content of an assertion that events of type A cause events of type B is merely that we have found through experience that events of type A are invariably followed by events of type B. Some philosophers recognize a distinction between agent (or substance, or immanent) causation ("An arsonist started the fire") and event (or transeunt) causation ("A short circuit caused the fire").

caustic soda SODIUM HYDROXIDE (NaOH), an inorganic compound. The ALKALIES called caustic soda and caustic potash (POTASSIUM hydroxide) are very important industrial chemicals, with uses in the manufacture of soaps, glass, and numerous other products. They have been easily extracted since ancient times by soaking wood ashes in water (see LYE). Industrial methods of caustic-soda production developed in the 18th century (the Leblanc process) and 19th century (the Solvay, or ammonia-soda, process) have been largely displaced by ELECTROLYSIS.

Cauvery River See KAVERI RIVER

Cavafy \kə-ˈväf-ē\, **Constantine** *orig.* **Konstantínos Pétrou Kaváfis** (1863–1933) Egyptian poet who wrote in Greek. Born to Greek parents in Alexandria, he worked as an obscure civil servant there his entire adult life. His small body of work, some 200 poems in an intimate, realistic, lyrical style, is written in a strange combination of classically-based and modern Greek. Many deal with history, principally the Hellenistic era; many others reflect Cavafy's homosexual life. His poems became popular and influential after his death, and he is now widely regarded as one of the greatest of modern Greek poets.

Cavafy.
DIMITRI PAPADIMOS

Cavaignac \kȧ-ven-ˈyȧk\, **Louis-Eugène** (1802–1857) French general. He served with distinction in the French conquest of Algeria in the 1840s. In the REVOLUTIONS OF 1848 he was appointed minister of war. In June he suppressed a workers' revolt, becoming known as "the butcher of June" (see JUNE DAYS). That month he was named chief executive of France. In December he lost the presidential election to Louis-Napoléon Bonaparte (later NAPOLEON III), but remained a leader of the opposition.

Cavaillé-Coll \kə-vī-yā-ˈkȯl\, **Aristide** (1811–1899) French organ builder. He settled in Paris in 1833 at G. ROSSINI's suggestion, and with his brother and father built almost 500 organs in France, Belgium, the Netherlands, and elsewhere, including those in the Paris churches of Notre-Dame, La Madeleine, Ste Clotilde, and La Trinité. With the goal of achieving an orchestral richness and variety of timbre, he introduced countless innovations; he is regarded as the creator of the French Romantic organ (which had great influence elsewhere as well), and his instruments inspired the works of such composers as C. FRANCK and O. MESSIAEN.

Cavalcanti \ˌkä-väl-ˈkän-tē\, **Guido** (1255?–1300) Italian poet. Born into an influential Florentine family, he studied with the philosopher and scholar Brunetto Latini, who had earlier taught DANTE, Cavalcanti's close friend. After Dante, he is considered the greatest Italian poet and personality in 13th-century Italian literature. He left about 50 poems, many addressed to two women and on the theme of love. His language demonstrates the grace and directness of the *dolce stil nuovo* ("sweet new style"). DANTE GABRIEL ROSSETTI and EZRA POUND translated his poems.

Cavalier \ˌkav-ə-ˈlir\ In the ENGLISH CIVIL WARS, the name adopted by CHARLES I's supporters, who contemptuously called their opponents Roundheads (a reference to the short-haired apprentices who had formed part of an anti-Cavalier mob). The term (similar to the French *chevalier*) originally meant a rider or cavalryman. At the RESTORATION, the court party preserved the name Cavalier, which survived until the rise of the term TORY. See also CAVALIER POET.

Cavalier poets \ˌkav-ə-ˈlir\ Group of English gentlemen poets who were Cavaliers (supporters of CHARLES I during the ENGLISH CIVIL WARS). The term embraces SIR JOHN SUCKLING, EDMUND WALLER, ROBERT HERRICK, Thomas Carew (1594?–1640?), and Richard Lovelace (1618–1657). Accomplished as soldiers, courtiers, gallants, and wits, they wrote polished and elegant lyrics, typically on love and dalliance, and sometimes on war, honor, and their duty to the king.

Cavalli \kä-ˈväl-lē\, **(Pier) Francesco** *orig.* **Pietro Francesco Caletti-Bruni** (1602–1676) Italian opera composer. In his teens he was a singer under C. MONTEVERDI at ST. MARK'S BASILICA, Venice. Also an organist, he would rise to the post of *maestro di cappella* there in 1668. He wrote some 30 operas for Venice's public opera houses. The most popular opera composer of the decades following Monteverdi's death, he was the latter's leading successor, his chief rival for that status being Antonio Cesti (1623–1669). His most celebrated operas were *Egisto* (1643), *Giasone* (1649), *Xerse* (1654), and *Erismena* (1655).

Cavallini \ˌkä-väl-ˈlē-nē\, **Pietro** (c. 1250–c. 1330) Italian painter and mosaicist, active mainly in Rome. His major surviving works are mosaics of *The Life of the Virgin* for the Roman church of Santa Maria in Trastevere (1290s) and fragments of a fresco cycle, including a *Last Judgment*, for the church of Santa Cecilia in Trastevere (c. 1293). He was the first to make a break with the stylizations of Byzantine art; his figures have a real sense of weight and three-dimensionality. He had many students and his work was an important influence on his great contemporary GIOTTO.

cavalry \ˈka-vəl-rē\ Military force mounted on horseback, formerly an important element in the armies of all major powers. When used in combination with other military forces, its main duties included gathering information about the enemy, screening movements of its own army, pursuing a defeated enemy, striking suddenly at detected weak points, turning exposed flanks, and exploiting a penetration or breakthrough. In the late 19th century, largely because of the introduction of repeating rifles and machine guns, cavalry lost much of its former value. By World War I, a cavalry charge against a line of entrenched troops with rapid-firing small arms was suicidal. ARMORED VEHICLES soon replaced horses, and by the 1950s neither the U.S. nor the British army had horse-mounted cavalry units. Today's units designated "cavalry" have helicopters and light armored vehicles that are used in ways analogous to horse cavalry.

cave Naturally formed underground cavity. A cave often consists of a number of underground chambers, constituting a series of caverns. An assemblage of such caverns interconnected by smaller passageways makes up a cave system. Primary caves, such as lava tubes and coral caves, develop during the time when the host matrix is solidifying or being deposited. Secondary caves, such as marine grottoes, originate after the host matrix has been deposited or consolidated. Most caves are of the latter type, including solution caves formed by the chemical dissolution of a soluble host rock that has been weakened by fracturing and mechanical erosion; MAMMOTH CAVE and CARLSBAD CAVERNS are examples of solution caves.

Cavell \'ka-vəl\, **Edith (Louisa)** (1865–1915) English nurse and heroine of World War I. She began her nursing career in 1895, and in 1907 became first matron of a hospital in Brussels, where she greatly improved the standard of nursing. After the German occupation of Belgium (1914), she became involved in an underground group that helped about 200 Allied soldiers escape to the Netherlands. She was subsequently arrested and executed by the Germans.

Edith Cavell.
SYNDICATION INTERNATIONAL LTD.

Cavendish \'kav-ən-dish\, **Henry** (1731–1810) English physicist and chemist. A millionaire by inheritance, he lived as a recluse most of his life. He discovered the nature and properties of hydrogen, the specific heat of certain substances, and various properties of electricity. He measured the density and mass of the earth by the method now known as the CAVENDISH EXPERIMENT. He discovered the composition of air, work that led to the discovery that water is a compound rather than an element, and to the discovery of nitric acid. He anticipated Ohm's law, and independently discovered Coulomb's law of electrostatic attraction. He left his fortune to relatives who later endowed the Cavendish Laboratory at Cambridge University (1871).

Cavendish experiment \'kav-ən-ˌdish\ Measurement of the force of gravitational attraction between pairs of lead spheres, which allowed the first calculation of the value of the universal gravitational constant, *G*. Performed in 1797–98 by the British scientist HENRY CAVENDISH (1731–1810) using a TORSION BALANCE, the experiment was popularly known as "weighing earth," because determination of *G* permitted calculation of earth's mass.

caviar Eggs, or roe, of STURGEON preserved with salt. Most true caviar is produced in Russia and Iran, from fish taken from the Caspian and Black seas. The best grade, beluga, is prepared from large black or gray eggs; fresh beluga is relatively scarce and thus expensive. Lesser grades are from smaller, denser eggs. In the U.S., the roe of salmon, whitefish, lumpfish, and paddlefish is sometimes sold under the name caviar.

cavitation Formation of vapor bubbles within a liquid at low-pressure regions that occur in places where the liquid has been accelerated to high velocities, as in the operation of CENTRIFUGAL PUMPS, water TURBINES, and marine PROPELLERS. Cavitation is undesirable because it produces extensive erosion of the rotating blades, additional noise from the resultant knocking and vibrations, and a significant reduction of efficiency because it distorts the flow pattern. The cavities form when the pressure of the liquid has been reduced to its vapor pressure; they expand as the pressure is further reduced along with the flow, and they suddenly collapse when they reach regions of higher pressure.

cavity wall In architecture, a double wall consisting of two wythes (vertical layers) of masonry separated by an air space and joined together by metal ties. The cavity allows moisture that penetrates the exterior wythe to drain. Cavity walling is used as both non-load-bearing infill for framed buildings and for BEARING-WALL construction.

Cavour \kə-'vu̇r\, **Camillo Benso, conte (Count) di** (1810–1861) Italian statesman, leading figure of the RISORGIMENTO. Born in Turin, Piedmont, he was influenced by revolutionary ideas from an early age. After travels to Paris and London, in 1847 he founded the liberal newspaper *Il Risorgimento*, and he helped persuade CHARLES ALBERT to grant a liberal constitution. Elected to Parliament in 1848, Cavour held several cabinet posts before becoming prime minister of Piedmont (1852–59, 1860–61). His exploitation of international rivalries and of revolutionary movements brought about the unification of Italy under the House of SAVOY, with himself as the first prime minister of the new kingdom (1861).

cavy \'kā-vē\ Any of several species of South American RODENTS constituting the family Caviidae. Species in the genera *Cavia, Kerodon, Galea,* and *Microcavia* resemble the GUINEA PIG. They are stout, gray or brown, and 10–12 in. (25–30 cm) long, with short ears and legs and no visible tail. The Patagonian and salt desert cavies *(Dolichotis)* are more long-legged and rabbitlike. Cavies are social animals found in various habitats, including plains, marshes, and rocky areas. They live in burrows (which sometimes weaken the ground above so much that it collapses when walked on), and they feed on grass, leaves, and other vegetation.

Patagonian cavy (*Dolichotis patagona*).
GEORGE HOLTON—PHOTO RESEARCHERS

Cawnpore See KANPUR

Caxton, William (1422?–1491) First British printer. He was a prosperous mercer when he began to translate French literature and learn printing. He set up a press in Belgium and published his translation *The Recuyell of the Historyes of Troye* (1475), the first book printed in English. Returning to England, he set up another press and produced the first dated book printed in English, *Dictes and Sayenges of the Phylosophers* (1477). His varied output—about 100 items, including books on chivalric romance, morality, and history, and an encyclopedia that was the first illustrated English book (1481)—shows that he catered to a general public as well as wealthy patrons.

Cayce \'kā-sē\, **Edgar** (1877–1945) U.S. faith healer. Born in Hopkinsville, Ky., he received little formal education. He began his cures in the 1920s, often accomplishing them long-distance. In 1925 he settled in Virginia Beach, Va., where he established a hospital (1928) and the Association for Research and Enlightenment (1931). He also made prophecies (including of the destruction of New York City and California) and claimed to be able to recall past lives. He believed in the existence of a great civilization in ATLANTIS some 12,000 years ago.

Cayenne \kī-'en\ Seaport (pop., 1990: 37,000), capital of FRENCH GUIANA. The city was founded by the French in 1643 on northwestern Cayenne Island, which is formed by the estuaries of the Cayenne and Mahury rivers. In the mid-19th century it became a center of French penal settlements in Guiana and was known as the "city of the condemned." (See DEVIL'S ISLAND) The prisons were closed in 1945.

Cayley, George *later* **Sir George** (1773–1857) British pioneer of aerial NAVIGATION and founder of the science of AERODYNAMICS. By 1799 he had established the basic configuration of the modern AIRPLANE. He built his first model GLIDER in 1804, and in 1809 he published his groundbreaking aerodynamic research. Further research into the effects of streamlining, stability, and wing design led to his construction of the first full-size glider, which flew briefly in 1853. Cayley also invented the caterpillar TRACTOR (1825) and founded a polytechnic school in London (1839).

Cayman Islands British colony (pop., 1990: 25,000), Caribbean Sea. Located about 200 mi (320 km) northwest of Jamaica, it has a total land area of 118 sq mi (306 sq km). The group includes Grand Cayman (the largest island and the location of the capital, George Town), Little Cayman, and Cayman Brac. Though discovered by CHRISTOPHER COLUMBUS in 1503, the islands were never occupied by the Spanish. Ceded to the British in 1670, they were subsequently settled by the English arriving from Jamaica. The islands were administered as a dependency of Jamaica until Jamaican independence in 1962; a constitution providing for an elected governor was enacted in 1972. A popular tourist area, it is also a financial center.

CBS Inc. Major U.S. broadcasting company and network. It began in 1928 as the Columbia Broadcasting System, a small radio network directed by WILLIAM S. PALEY. By offering programming free to affiliated stations in return for their agreement to broadcast sponsored shows, Paley built the network from 22 stations to 114 in 10 years. Such stars as FRED ALLEN, BING CROSBY, and KATE SMITH increased audience ratings into the 1940s. JACK BENNY, ED SULLIVAN, LUCILLE BALL, MARY TYLER MOORE, and WALTER CRONKITE made CBS the dominant television network into the 1970s. The company diversified into several other fields, but only Columbia Records was successful, and the corporation sold all its other divisions in 1985 to concentrate on broadcasting. A decline in ratings and in the number of affiliated stations led to its sale to WESTINGHOUSE ELECTRIC CORP. in 1995. CBS Corp. and Viacom Inc. merged in 2000.

CCC See CIVILIAN CONSERVATION CORPS

CCD *in full* **charge-coupled device** SEMICONDUCTOR device in which the individual semiconductor components are connected so that the electrical charge at the output of one device provides the input to the next device. Because they can store electrical charges, CCDs can be used as memory devices, but they are slower than RAMs. CCDs are sensitive to light, and are therefore used as the light-detecting components in video and digital cameras and in optical scanners.

CCNY See CITY UNIVERSITY OF NEW YORK

CD See CERTIFICATE OF DEPOSIT

CD See COMPACT DISC

CD-ROM *in full* **compact disc read-only memory** Type of computer storage medium that is read optically (e.g., by a LASER). A CD-ROM drive uses a low-power laser beam to read digitized (binary) data that have been encoded onto an optical disc in the form of tiny pits, then feeds the data to a computer for processing. Because it uses digital data, a CD-ROM can store images and sound in addition to text and is thus used in video and audio devices to store music, graphics, and movies (see COMPACT DISC). Unlike conventional magnetic-storage technologies (e.g., HARD DISKS), CD-ROM drives cannot write information (that is, accept the input of new data), hence the tag "read-only." Recordable compact discs (called CD-R) must be written on a CD-R recorder and can be played on any CD-ROM drive.

CDC See CENTERS FOR DISEASE CONTROL AND PREVENTION

Ceausescu \chau̇-'shes-kü\, **Nicolae** (1918–1989) Romanian politician. Prominent in the Romanian Communist Party, in 1965 he succeeded GHEORGHE GHEORGHIU-DEJ as the party's leader. In 1967 he became head of state and in 1974 president of Romania. He charted an independent, nationalistic course, but also maintained rigidly repressive controls over free speech and internal dissent. His harsh economic policies and grand building projects reduced Romania from relative prosperity to near starvation. He was overthrown in a revolution in 1989, and after a hasty trial, he and his wife were executed by firing squad.

Ceausescu.
PICTORIAL PARADE—EB INC.

Cebu \sā-'bü\ Island (pop., 1990 : 2,646,000) and (with adjacent islets) province, central Philippines. It is 139 mi (224 km) long and about 20 mi (32 km) wide, with an area of 1,707 sq mi (4,421 sq km). Its chief city is CEBU. A mountain chain extends its entire length. It is separated from BOHOL Island by Bohol Strait, and from NEGROS Island by Tanon Strait. Visited by FERDINAND MAGELLAN in 1521, it was occupied by the Spanish in 1565. It is one of the Philippines' most densely populated islands; it produces coal and copper.

Cebu *officially* **City of Cebu** City (pop., 1994: 688,000), capital of CEBU province, Philippine Islands. Located on the eastern coast of Cebu Island, it is the oldest Spanish city in the Philippines. It possesses an excellent harbor, sheltered by Mactan Island. Attracted by Cebu's focal position, FERDINAND MAGELLAN landed there in 1521 and converted the ruler to Christianity; in a later war expedition on the ruler's behalf, Magellan was killed on Mactan Island. Occupied by Miguel López de Legazpi in 1565, it was until 1571 the capital of Spanish possessions in the Philippines. It remained the primary Spanish bastion in the south, and had prominent roles in insurrections against both Spain and the U.S. Having recovered from heavy damage sustained in World War II, Cebu is now a cultural and commercial center.

Cech \'chek\, **Thomas (Robert)** (born 1947) U.S. biochemist, molecular biologist, and Nobel laureate. Born in Chicago, he received his PhD from UC–Berkeley in 1975. In 1982 he became the first to show that an RNA molecule could catalyze a chemical reaction. He and SIDNEY ALTMAN were awarded a 1989 Nobel Prize for their independent discoveries that RNA, previously thought to be only a messenger of genetic information, can also catalyze cellular chemical reactions essential to life.

Cecil \'se-səl\, **Robert** *later* **Earl of Salisbury** (1563–1612) English statesman. Trained in statesmanship by his father, WILLIAM CECIL, Robert entered the House of Commons in 1584. He became acting secretary of state in 1590 and was formally appointed to the post by ELIZABETH I in 1596. He succeeded his father as chief minister in 1598 and guided the peaceful succession of Elizabeth by JAMES I, for whom he continued as chief minister from 1603 and lord treasurer from 1608. He negotiated the end of the war with Spain in 1604 and allied England with France.

Cecil (of Chelwood), Viscount *orig.* **(Edgar Algernon) Robert Gascoyne-Cecil** *known as* **Lord Robert Cecil** (1864–1958) British statesman. The son of the marquess of SALISBURY, he served during World War I as minister of blockade and as assistant secretary of state for foreign affairs. He was one of the principal draftsmen of the LEAGUE OF NATIONS covenant in 1919 and, as president of the League of Nations Union (1923–45), one of the League's most loyal workers until it was superseded by the UNITED NATIONS. In 1937 he was awarded the Nobel Peace Prize.

Cecil, William *later* **Baron Burghley** \'bər-lē\ (1520–1598) English statesman, principal adviser to ELIZABETH I through most of her reign and a master of Renaissance statecraft. Having served as a councillor and cosecretary to EDWARD VI, he was appointed Elizabeth's sole secretary when she became queen in 1558. A dedicated and skillful adviser to the queen, Cecil was created Baron Burghley in 1571 and appointed lord high treasurer (1572–98). He obtained the trial and execution of MARY, QUEEN OF SCOTS, thus securing the Protestant succession, and his preparations enabled England to survive the Spanish ARMADA. But he failed to induce Elizabeth to marry or to reform her church along more Protestant lines.

Cecilia, St. (fl. 2nd–3rd century AD) Early Christian martyr and patron saint of music. A noble Roman who had dedicated her virginity to God as a child, she was married against her will to a pagan named Valerian. She told him of her vow, and he promised he would let her keep it if he could see the angel with whom she conversed. After being baptized, Valerian saw Cecilia talking to the angel. Valerian's brother also converted, and both were eventually martyred. Cecilia's good works infuriated the Roman prefect, who ordered her burned at the stake; when the flames did not harm her, she was beheaded.

cedar Any of four species of tall ornamental and timber evergreen coniferous trees of the genus *Cedrus,* in the PINE family. Three cedars are native to mountainous areas of the Mediterranean region and one to the western Himalayas. These "true" cedars are the Atlas cedar *(C. atlantica),* the Cyprus cedar *(C. brevifolia),* the deodar *(C. deodara),* and the cedar of Lebanon *(C. libani).* Cedarwood is light, soft, resinous, and durable, even when in contact with soil or moisture. Many

Cedar of Lebanon (*Cedrus libani*).
G.E. HYDE FROM THE NATURAL HISTORY PHOTOGRAPHIC AGENCY

other conifers known as cedars resemble true cedars in being evergreen and in having aromatic, often red or red-tinged wood that in many cases is decay-resistant and insect-repellent. The giant ARBORVITAE, incense cedar, and some JUNIPERS (red cedar) provide the familiar "cedarwood" of pencils, chests, closet linings, and fence posts. See also WHITE CEDAR.

Cedar Breaks National Monument Preserve, southwestern Utah. Established as a national monument in 1933, it consists of a vast natural amphitheater (10 sq mi [26 sq km]) eroded in a limestone escarpment. Iron and manganese oxide impurities in the cliff produce an amazing variety of colors that change constantly.

Cedar Rapids City (pop., 2000: 120,758), eastern Iowa. It was settled in the 1830s next to rapids of the CEDAR RIVER, used as a source of water power; its original name was Rapids City. With the coming of the railroads, it developed as a grain and livestock market. Neighboring Kingston was annexed in 1870, and Kenwood Park in 1926. Its manufactures include electronic equipment and farm machinery. It was the home of the artist GRANT WOOD.

Cedar River River, northern central U.S. Flowing from southeastern Minnesota southeasterly across Iowa, it joins the Iowa River about 20 mi (32 km) from the MISSISSIPPI RIVER. Over its 329-mi (529-km) course it passes through many cities, including CEDAR RAPIDS. The river is named for the stands of red cedar along its lower course.

ceiling Overhead surface of a room, and the underside of a floor or roof. Suspended ceilings, which hang from the beams above, are used to conceal construction, mechanical equipment, wiring, and light fixtures. During the Renaissance, ceilings were often coffered (see COFFER), vaulted (see VAULT), or transformed into one large framed painting.

Cela (Trulock) \'thā-lä\, **Camilo José** (1916–2002) Spanish writer. As a young man he served with FRANCISCO FRANCO's forces in the Spanish Civil War; his literary works, however, represent a renunciation of his former Falangist sympathies. Primarily novels, short narratives, and travel diaries of Spain and Latin America, they are characteristically experimental and innovative in form and content. He is sometimes credited with establishing *tremendismo*, a narrative style tending to emphasize violence and grotesque imagery. He is perhaps best known for his first novel, *The Family of Pascual Duarte* (1942); other works include *The Hive* (1951) and the avant-garde *San Camilo, 1936* (1969). He was awarded the Nobel Prize in 1989.

celadon Chinese, Korean, Siamese, and Japanese stoneware decorated with glazes the color range of which includes greens of various shades, olive, blue, and gray. The colors are the result of a wash of slip (liquefied clay) containing a high proportion of iron that is applied to the body before glazing. The iron interacts with the glaze during the firing and colors it. Celadons were prized in the Eastern world long before their comparatively late introduction to the West. A wide demand led to their export to India, Persia, and Egypt in the TANG DYNASTY (618–907) and to most of Asia in the SONG (960–1279) and MING (1368–1644) dynasties. The ware was popular because of its beauty, because of a superstition that a celadon dish would break or change color if poisoned food were put into it, and because, to the Chinese, it resembled jade. Yüeh ware, first made in the HAN DYNASTY (206 BC–AD 220), is the earliest celadon.

Celan \'tsā-ˌlän\, **Paul** *orig.* **Paul Antschel** (1920–1970) Romanian poet who wrote in German. When Romania came under Nazi control during World War II, Celan, a Jew, was sent to a forced-labor camp; his parents were murdered. He moved to Vienna in 1947 and published his first volume of poetry, *The Sand from the Urns*, in 1948. His second volume, *Poppy and Memory* (1952), established his reputation in West Germany. He produced seven more volumes before taking his own life by drowning in the Seine. His dense and complex verse is marked by his experience of World War II; his early poem "Todesfuge" is probably the most famous poetic expression of the Holocaust.

Celebes See SULAWESI

Celebes black ape *or* **Celebes crested macaque** \mə-'kak\ Stump-tailed, arboreal MACAQUE *(Cynopithecus niger)* found on Sulawesi (Celebes), Bacan, and nearby islands. It has overhanging brows, a hairless black face, and a long, flat muzzle. It is 22–26 in. (55–65 cm) long, without the 0.4–0.8-in. (1–2-cm) tail, and has dark brown or black fur. The male, especially, bears a longitudinal crest of crown hair. It is diurnal, feeds on fruit, and lives in rain forests. Certain peoples look on it as their ancestor.

Celebes Sea \'se-lə-ˌbēz\ Part of the western Pacific Ocean. It is bordered by the SULU ARCHIPELAGO, MINDANAO, the Sangihe Islands, SULAWESI, and BORNEO. It extends 420 mi (675 km) north-south and 520 mi (837 km) east-west, occupying about 110,000 sq mi (280,000 sq km). It is connected with the Java Sea by the MAKASSAR STRAIT. Over half of it is more than 13,000 ft (4,000 m) deep, and its maximum depth is 20,406 ft (6,220 m). Traders and pirates from Borneo and nearby islands ruled the sea until it came under colonial control in the late 19th century.

celeriac \sə-'ler-ē-ˌak\ *or* **celery root** Type of CELERY *(Apium graveolens* 'rapaceum') grown for its knobby edible root, which is used as a raw or cooked vegetable. Originally cultivated in the Mediterranean and in northern Europe, it was introduced into Britain in the 18th century.

celery Herb *(Apium graveolens)* of the PARSLEY family, native to the Mediterranean and the Middle East. The varieties with large, fleshy, succulent, upright leafstalks were developed in the late 18th century. Celery is usually eaten cooked in Europe but raw in the U.S. The tiny fruit, or seed, of the celery resembles the plant itself in taste and aroma and is used as a seasoning.

celestial coordinates Set of numbers used to pinpoint the position in space of a celestial object. COORDINATE SYSTEMS used include the horizon system (ALTITUDE AND AZIMUTH), GALACTIC COORDINATES, the ecliptic system (measured relative to the orbital plane of the earth), and the equatorial system (right ascension and declination, directly analogous to terrestrial longitude and latitude).

celestial mechanics Branch of ASTRONOMY that deals with the mathematical theory of the motions of celestial bodies. KEPLER's laws of planetary motion (1609–19) and NEWTON'S LAWS OF MOTION (1687) are fundamental to it. In the 18th century, powerful methods of mathematical analysis were generally successful in accounting for the observed motions of bodies in the solar system. One branch of celestial mechanics deals with the effect of GRAVITATION on rotating bodies, with applications to earth and the gas giants (see TIDE).

celestial sphere Apparent surface of the heavens, on which the stars seem to be fixed. For the purpose of establishing CELESTIAL COORDINATE systems to mark the positions of heavenly bodies, it can be thought of as a real sphere at an infinite distance from earth. Earth's axis, extended to infinity, touches this sphere at the northern and southern celestial poles, around which the heavens seem to turn. The intersection of the plane of earth's EQUATOR with the sphere marks the celestial equator.

celiac disease \'sē-lē-ˌak\ *or* **nontropical sprue** Relatively rare syndrome of unknown cause. Poor nutrient absorption causes foul, bulky, fatty stools, malnutrition, slow growth, and anemia similar to pernicious anemia. It can run in families. Children begin having intermittent intestinal upset, diarrhea, and wasting at 6–21 months. In adults it usually begins after 30, with appetite loss, depression, irritability, and alternating constipation and diarrhea. Symptoms in advanced cases stem from nutritional deficiencies and may require supportive measures. A high-protein diet low in glutens and saturated fats usually relieves symptoms, suggesting a deficiency of gluten-digesting enzymes.

celibacy \'se-lə-bə-sē\ State of being unmarried, usually in connection with a religious role or practice. It has existed in some form in most world religions. It may indicate a person's ritual purity (sexual relations being viewed as polluting) or may be adopted to facilitate spiritual advancement (family being seen as an entangling distraction). In shamanistic religions, shamans are often celibate. In Hinduism, "holy men" (or women) who have left ordinary secular life to seek final liberation are celibate. Buddhism began as a celibate order, though many sects have since given up celibacy. Chinese Taoism has monastics and independent celibate adepts. Islam has no institutional celibacy, but individuals may embrace it for personal spiritual advancement. Judaism has prescribed periods of abstinence, but long-term celibacy has not played a large role. The early Christian church tended to regard celibacy as superior to marriage. Since the 12th century it has been the rule for Roman Catholic clergy, though clerical celibacy was never adopted by Protestantism.

Céline \sā-'lēn\, **Louis-Ferdinand** *orig.* **Louis-Ferdinand Destouches** (1894–1961) French writer. Born into poverty, in World War I he suffered wounds and shell shock whose mental and physical effects lingered throughout his life. From 1924 he practiced medicine. His *Journey to the End of Night* (1932), about a man's tortured search for meaning, is written in a vehement and disjointed style that marked him as a major innovator. *Death on the Installment Plan* (1936) is a bleak portrayal of a world bereft of value, beauty, and decency. He thereafter became increasingly conservative, anti-Semitic, and misanthropic. After World War II he fled to Denmark as a suspected Nazi collaborator, but was later exonerated. His later works include the trilogy *Castle to Castle* (1957), *North* (1960), and *Rigadoon* (1969).

cell In biology, the basic unit of which all living things are composed; the smallest structural unit of living matter that is able to function independently. A single cell can be a complete organism in itself, as in BACTERIA and PROTOZOANS. Groups of specialized cells are organized into tissues and organs in multicellular organisms such as higher plants and animals. There are two distinct types of cells: prokaryotic cells, found only in bacteria (including blue-green algae, or CYANOBACTERIA), and eukaryotic cells, composing all other life-forms. Though the structures of prokaryotic and eukaryotic cells differ (see PROKARYOTE, EUKARYOTE), their molecular compositions and activities are very similar. The chief molecules in cells are NUCLEIC ACIDS, PROTEINS, and POLYSACCHARIDES. A cell is bounded by a MEMBRANE that enables it to exchange certain materials with its surroundings. In plant cells, a rigid cell wall encloses this membrane.

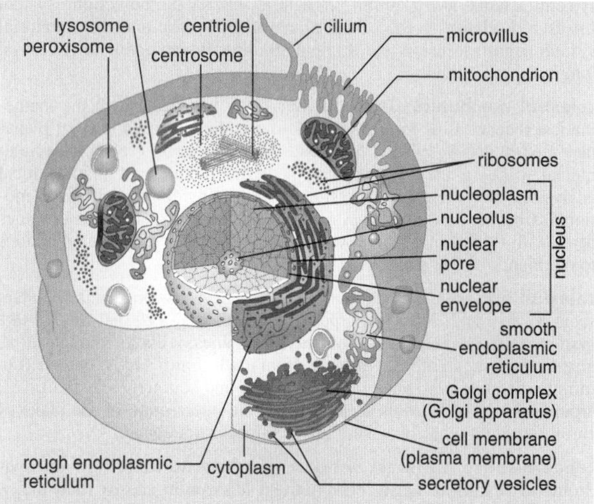

Principal structures of an animal cell. Cytoplasm surrounds the cell's specialized structures, or organelles. Ribosomes, the sites of protein synthesis, are found free in the cytoplasm or attached to the endoplasmic reticulum, through which materials are transported throughout the cell. Energy needed by the cell is released by the mitochondria. The Golgi complex, stacks of flattened sacs, processes and packages materials to be released from the cell in secretory vesicles. Digestive enzymes are contained in lysosomes. Peroxisomes contain enzymes that detoxify dangerous substances. The centrosome contains the centrioles, which play a role in cell division. The microvilli are fingerlike extensions found on certain cells. Cilia, hairlike structures that extend from the surface of many cells, can create movement of surrounding fluid. The nuclear envelope, a double membrane surrounding the nucleus, contains pores that control the movement of substances into and out of the nucleoplasm. Chromatin, a combination of DNA and proteins that coil into chromosomes, makes up much of the nucleoplasm. The dense nucleolus is the site of ribosome production.

© 2002 MERRIAM-WEBSTER INC.

cell division See MEIOSIS, MITOSIS

cell(ular) phone Wireless telephone that permits telecommunication within a defined area that may include hundreds of square miles, using radio waves in the 800–900 megahertz (MHz) band. To implement a cell-phone system, a geographic area is broken into smaller areas, or cells, usually mapped as uniform hexagrams but in fact overlapping and irregularly shaped. Each cell is equipped with a low-powered radio transmitter and receiver that permit propagation of signals among cell-phone users.

cella \'se-lə\ *or* **naos** \'nā-ˌäs\ Enclosed body of a TEMPLE (as distinct from the PORTICO), in which the image of the deity was housed. In early Greek and Roman architecture it was usually rectangular, with an entrance at one end; the side walls were often extended to form a porch. In larger temples the cella was sometimes open to the sky. In the Byzantine architectural tradition, the naos is the area of a central-plan church where the liturgy is performed.

cellar Portion of a building beneath ground level, used for utilitarian and storage purposes. It is often called a basement, especially when constructed as part of a foundation. A cellar used for food storage (e.g., a root cellar) may be beneath a house or located outdoors, partly underground, with the upper part mounded over with earth to maintain fairly constant temperature and humidity; the entire enclosure may be concrete, or the floor may be of dirt and the ceiling of timber.

Cellini \chə-'lē-nē\, **Benvenuto** (1500–1571) Italian sculptor and goldsmith active principally in Florence. Early in his career he worked in Rome, producing coins, medallions, seals, vessels, and a variety of other objects in precious and semiprecious metals. In 1540 he began his most famous work of this type, a gold saltcellar encrusted with enamel, for FRANCIS I at Fontainebleau. Other royal commissions followed. For Cosimo I de' MEDICI he produced large-scale sculpture in the round; the bronze *Perseus* (1545–53) in the Loggia dei Lanzi in Florence is his masterpiece. His fame owes as much to his autobiography as to his work as an artist; it achieved immediate popularity for its lively account of his tumultuous life and its vivid picture of Renaissance Italy.

Saltcellar of Francis I, encrusted enamel and gold, by Benvenuto Cellini, 1540; in the Kunsthistorisches Museum, Vienna.

BY COURTESY OF THE KUNSTHISTORISCHES MUSEUM, VIENNA

cello \'che-ˌlō\ *or* **violoncello** Bowed STRINGED INSTRUMENT, the bass member of the VIOLIN family (its full name means "little violone"—i.e., "little big viol"). Its proportions resemble those of the violin. It is played between the legs, its weight supported by a metal spike that touches the floor. It has four strings, tuned an octave below those of the viola. The cello developed in the early 16th century along with the violin and viola; later innovations increased its power. It gradually displaced the bass viola da gamba in the 18th century, especially as a CONTINUO instrument. It has been essential to chamber-music ensembles for 250 years. The modern orchestra includes six to 12 cellos. In the 19th–20th century it was increasingly used as a solo instrument.

cellular automaton Simplest model of a spatially distributed process that can be used to simulate various real-world processes. Cellular automata were invented in the 1940s by JOHN VON NEUMANN and STANISLAW ULAM at Los Alamos National Laboratory. They consist of a two-dimensional array of cells, each of which can be in a number of different states that are determined by rules and by the states of neighboring cells. Though apparently simple, such a system is actually highly complex. The best-known cellular automaton, John Conway's "Game of Life" (1970), simulates the processes of life, death, and population dynamics.

celluloid \'sel-yə-ˌlȯid\ Name for the first synthetic PLASTIC material, developed in 1869. Made of a colloid of CELLULOSE NITRATE (nitrocellulose) plasticized with CAMPHOR, it is tough, cheap to produce, and resistant to water, oils, and dilute acids. It found a great variety of uses in combs, films, toys, and many other mass-produced consumer goods. Though it has been replaced in many uses by nonflammable synthetic POLYMERS (originally cellulose acetate and Bakelite, then a host of others), it is still manufactured and used.

cellulose Complex CARBOHYDRATE (POLYSACCHARIDE) consisting of 1,000–3,000 or more GLUCOSE units in a linear chain structure that can pack into fibers of great TENSILE STRENGTH. The basic structural component of plant cell walls, cellulose is the most abundant of all naturally occurring organic compounds (90% of cotton and 50% of wood). Mammals (including humans) cannot digest cellulose, but BACTERIA in the rumens of cattle and other RUMINANTS and PROTOZOANS in the gut of TERMITES produce ENZYMES that can break it down. Soil fungi can also break it down. The most important uses of cellulose are in wood, paper, and fiber products, as an ethanol and methanol source, and specialized uses. Cellulose derivatives are used in plastics, photographic films, rayon fibers, cellophane, coatings, explosives (nitrocellulose), and foods (carboxymethylcellulose).

Celsius \'sel-sē-əs\, **Anders** (1701–1744) Swedish astronomer. He taught at the University of Uppsala from 1730 to his death. In 1733 he published a collection of 316 observations of the aurora borealis. In 1744 he built the Uppsala Observatory. He is best known for his invention of the Celsius (often called centigrade) thermometer scale (1742), which set the freezing point of water at 0° and the boiling point of water at 100°.

Celsus \'sel-səs\, **Aulus Cornelius** (fl. 1st century AD) Roman medical writer. His famous treatise *De medicina,* a major source of knowledge of early medicine, shows that it was remarkably advanced, urging cleanliness and use of antiseptics, describing facial skin grafting, and stating the four cardinal signs of inflammation. The book's three parts discuss diseases requiring diet, drug, or surgical therapy.

Celtiberia \ˌsel-tə-'bir-ē-ə\ Mountainous district, ancient Spain. Located in northeastern Spain between the EBRO and TAGUS rivers, it had long been inhabited before it was occupied in the 3d century BC by tribes of mixed Iberian and Celtic stock. The Celtiberians first submitted to Rome in the early 2nd century BC but were not completely dominated until 133 BC. Excavated horse bits, daggers, and shield fittings attest to their warlike nature.

Celtic languages \'kel-tik\ Branch of the INDO-EUROPEAN LANGUAGE family spoken across a broad area of western and central Europe by the CELTS in pre-Roman and Roman times, now confined to small coastal areas of northwestern Europe. Celtic can be divided into a continental group of languages (all extinct) and an insular group. Attestation of Insular Celtic begins around the time Continental Celtic fades from the scene as Celtic tongues gave way to Latin and other languages on the European continent. The Insular Celtic languages are conventionally divided into Goidelic (IRISH, Manx, and SCOTTISH GAELIC) and Brythonic (WELSH, Cornish, and BRETON). Traditional Cornish was supplanted by English at the end of the 18th century. Manx, spoken on the Isle of MAN, expired in the 20th century with the death of the last reputed native speaker in 1974. Both Manx and Cornish have been revived by enthusiasts recently, though neither can be considered community languages.

Celtic religion Beliefs and practices of the ancient Celts of Gaul and the British Isles. Celtic worship centered on the interplay of the divine element with the natural world. Springs, rivers, and hills were thought to be inhabited by guardian spirits, usually female. Some gods were widely worshiped; lesser deities were associated with particular tribes or places. The most honored god was LUGUS, who was skilled in all the arts. CERNUNNOS was lord of the animals; the goddess of mares and fertility was called EPONA (Gaul), Macha (Ireland), or RHIANNON (Britain). Goddesses often came in groups of three. The priests of Celtic religion were the DRUIDS; they maintained an oral tradition and left no writings. Seasonal festivals included Samhain (November 1), which marked summer's end and served as a feast of the dead, and BELTANE (May 1). Oak trees, holly, and mistletoe were considered sacred. The Celts believed in life after death as well as transmigration of souls. See also BRÂN, BRIGIT.

Celts \'kelts, 'selts\ Early Indo-European people who from the 2nd millennium BC to the 1st century BC spread over much of Europe. They were absorbed into the Roman empire as Britons, GAULS, Boii, Galatians, and Celtiberians. Early archaeological evidence (c. 700 BC) comes from the HALLSTATT site in Austria. People of this IRON AGE culture controlled trade routes along the Rhône, Seine, Rhine, and Danube rivers. As they moved west, Hallstatt warriors introduced the use of iron, which helped them dominate other Celtic tribes. By the mid-5th century BC, the LA TÈNE culture emerged along the Rhine and moved into eastern Europe and the British Isles. Celts sacked Rome c. 390 BC and raided the whole peninsula, then settled south of the Alps (Cisalpine GAUL) and menaced Rome until they were defeated in 225 BC. In the Balkans, they sacked Delphi in 279 BC but were defeated by the Aetolians. They crossed to Anatolia and looted until they were subdued by ATTALUS I c. 230 BC. Rome controlled Cisalpine Gaul by 192, and in 124 took territory beyond the Alps. In Transalpine Gaul, from the Rhine and the Alps west, the Celts were pressed by Germanic tribes from the west and Romans from the south. By 58 Julius CAESAR had begun campaigns to annex all of Gaul. Celtic settlement of Britain and Ireland is deduced from archaeological and linguistic evidence. The Celtic social system comprised a warrior aristocracy and freemen farmers; DRUIDS, with magico-religious duties, ranked higher than warriors. They had a mixed farming economy. Their oral literary composition was highly developed, as was their art; they manufactured gold and silver jewelry, swords and scabbards, and shields inlaid with enamel.

cement Agent that binds CONCRETE and MORTAR. Cements are finely ground powders that, when mixed with water, set to a hard mass. The cement of 2,000 years ago was a mixture of ash and lime. Volcanic ash mined near the city of Puteoli (now Pozzuoli), near Naples, was particularly rich in essential aluminosilicate minerals, giving rise to the pozzolana cement of the Roman era. See also PORTLAND CEMENT.

cementation In geology, the hardening and welding of clastic sediments (those formed from preexisting rock fragments) by the precipitation of mineral matter in the pore spaces. It is the last stage in the formation of sedimentary rock. Many minerals may act as cements; the most common is silica (generally quartz), but calcite and other carbonates also occur, as do iron oxides, barite, anhydrite, zeolites, and clay minerals.

Cenis \sə-'nē\, **Mont** *Italian* **Monte Cenisio** \'mòn-tā-chā-'nē-zyō\ Massif and pass, ALPS. Located in southeastern France west of TURIN, Italy, the pass was an invasion route from earliest times and is traversed by a road 24 mi (38 km) long, built by NAPOLEON in 1803–10. The road climbs to Mount Cenis Pass (elevation 6,834 ft, or 2,083 m) and passes between two peaks more than 8,000 ft (2,500 m) high. The Mount Cenis railway tunnel, 8.5 mi (14 km) long, was the first great tunnel through the Alps (opened 1871). The road tunnel, 10 mi (16 km) long, opened in 1980.

Cennini \chān-'nē-nē\, **Cennino (d'Andrea)** (c. 1370–c. 1440) Italian painter and writer active in Florence. A few surviving paintings are attributed to him, but he is best known as the author of *Il libro dell'arte* (*The Craftsman's Handbook,* c. 1390), the most important sourcebook on artistic practice in the late Middle Ages. His detailed descriptions of tempera and fresco painting reflect the technical procedures of the great Florentine painting tradition. He believed that painting held a high place among occupations because it combined theory or imagination with the skill of the hand.

cenotaph \'se-nə-ˌtaf\ (Greek: "empty tomb") Monument, sometimes in the form of a tomb, to a person buried elsewhere. Ancient Greek writings tell of many cenotaphs, none of which survives. Existing cenotaphs of this type are found in churches (e.g., in Santa Croce, Florence, where there are memorials to DANTE, NICCOLO MACHIAVELLI, and GALILEO). The term is now applied to national war memorials.

Cenozoic era \ˌsē-nə-'zō-ik\ Third of the major eras of earth history and the interval of time during which the continents assumed their modern configurations and geographic positions. It was also the time when the earth's flora and fauna evolved toward those of the present. The Cenozoic, from the Greek for "recent life," began c. 65 million years ago and is divided into two periods, the TERTIARY (65–1.8 million years ago) and the QUATERNARY (1.8 million years ago to the present).

censor In ancient eastern Asia, a government official whose primary duty was to scrutinize the conduct of officials and rulers. During the QIN (221–206 BC) and HAN (206 BC–AD 220) dynasties, the censor's function was to criticize the emperor's acts, but in later periods the censorate was expanded and became an instrument for imperial control of the bureaucracy. Censors checked important documents, supervised construction projects, reviewed judicial proceedings, kept watch over state property, and looked for cases of subversion and corruption.

censorship Act of changing or suppressing speech or writing that is condemned as subversive of the common good. In the past, most governments believed it their duty to regulate the morals of their people; only with the rise in the status of the individual and individual rights did censorship come to seem objectionable. Censorship may be preemptive (preventing the publication or broadcast of undesirable information) or punitive (punishing those who publish or broadcast offending material). In Europe, both the Roman Catholic and Protestant churches practiced censorship, as did the absolute monarchies of the 17th–18th century. Authoritarian governments such as those in China and the former Soviet

Union have employed pervasive censorship, which is generally opposed by underground movements engaged in actions such as SAMIZDAT publication. In the U.S. in the 20th century, censorship focused largely on works of literature deemed guilty of OBSCENITY (e.g., JAMES JOYCE's *Ulysses* and D. H. LAWRENCE's *Lady Chatterley's Lover*), though periodic attempts at political censorship also occurred (e.g., the effort to purge school textbooks of possible left-wing content in the 1950s). Recently some have called for censorship of so-called hate speech, language deemed threatening (or sometimes merely offensive) to various subsections of the population. Any censorship is usually opposed by the AMERICAN CIVIL LIBERTIES UNION. See also PENTAGON PAPERS.

census Enumeration of people, houses, firms, or other important items in a country or region at a particular time. The first U.S. population census was taken in 1790 to establish a basis for representation in Congress. Censuses were taken in England, France, and Canada in 1801, 1836, and 1871, respectively. China was the last major country to report a census, in 1953. Census information is obtained by using a fixed questionnaire covering such topics as place of residence, sex, age, marital status, occupation, citizenship, language, ethnicity, religious affiliation, and education. From the responses demographers derive data on population distribution, household and family composition, internal migration, labor-force participation, and other topics. See also DEMOGRAPHY.

centaur \'sen-ˌtȯr\ In GREEK MYTHOLOGY, one of a race of creatures, part horse and part man, living in the mountains of Thessaly and Arcadia. They were best known for their battle with the Lapiths, occasioned by their attempt to carry off the bride of a Lapith prince. Centaurs were often depicted drawing DIONYSUS' chariot or ridden by EROS, in reference to their drunken and amorous habits. Their king CHIRON, however, was notable for being civilized, gentle, and the tutor of heroes.

Centaur object Icy body, similar to an ASTEROID in size but to a COMET in composition, that orbits the sun mainly between the orbits of Jupiter and Neptune. The first known Centaur object, CHIRON, was found in 1977, but its affinity with comets was not recognized until more than a decade later. Subsequently, dozens of Centaur objects have been reported. They are thought to have originated in the KUIPER BELT, the vast reservoir of comet nuclei beyond Neptune's orbit.

centering See FALSEWORK

Centers for Disease Control and Prevention (CDC) Agency of the U.S. Department of HEALTH AND HUMAN SERVICES, headquartered in Atlanta, whose mission is "to promote health and quality of life by preventing and controlling disease, injury, and disability." Part of the Public Health Service, it was founded in 1946 as the Communicable Disease Center to fight malaria and other contagious diseases. As its scope widened to polio, smallpox, and disease surveillance, the name was changed to the Center for Disease Control and later pluralized. It now subsumes health statistics, infectious diseases, and environmental health; a National Immunization Program; and an Office on Smoking and Health. It consolidates disease control data, health promotion, and public-health programs, and it provides grants for studies and programs, health information to health care professionals and the public, and publications on epidemiology. Today it is regarded as perhaps the world's foremost epidemiological center.

centipede Any of about 2,800 species (class Chilopoda) of long, flattened, many-segmented ARTHROPODS having one pair of legs on each segment except the hindmost. Centipedes remain under stones, bark, and ground litter by day; at night they prey on other small invertebrates. They move rapidly on 14–177 pairs of legs and have one pair of long, many-jointed antennae and a pair of jawlike, venomous claws just behind the head. The 1-in. (2.5-cm) house centipede of Europe and North America is the only species common in dwellings. The largest centipedes, found in the tropics, may grow as long as 11 in. (28 cm) and can inflict severe bites.

Centipede (genus *Scolopendra*).
E.S. ROSS

CENTO *in full* **Central Treaty Organization** *originally* **Middle East Treaty Organization** *or* **Baghdad Pact Organization** A mutual-security organization, originally composed of Turkey, Iran, Iraq, Pakistan, and Britain, it was formed, at the urging of the U.S. and Britain, to counter the threat of Soviet expansion into Middle East oil fields. Its internal cohesion was never strong. Iraq withdrew after its anti-Soviet monarchy was overthrown in 1959. That same year the U.S. became an associate member, and its headquarters were moved to Ankara, Turkey. After the fall of MOHAMMAD REZA SHAH PAHLAVI in 1979, Iran withdrew and CENTO was dissolved.

Central African Republic *French* **République Centrafricaine** \ˌrā-pɯ̄-'blek-ˌsäⁿ-trȧ-frē-'ken\ *formerly* **Ubangi-Shari** \ü-ˌbäŋ-gē-'shär-ē\ Republic, central Africa. Area: 240,376 sq mi (622,374 sq km). Population (2001): 3,577,000. Capital: BANGUI. Almost all the inhabitants trace their origin to communities founded in the 18th–19th century when various African peoples fled into the interior to escape slave traders. They now form heterogeneous ethnic groups, with the Banda, Baya (Gbaya), Ngbandi, and AZANDE almost three-quarters of its inhabitants. Languages: French, Sango (both official), Zande. Religions: animism, Christianity. Currency: CFA franc. A landlocked country, it consists of a plateau with an average altitude of about 2,200 ft (670 m). The northern half is characterized by savanna and is drained by tributaries of the CHARI RIVER. The southern half is densely forested. The country has a developing free-enterprise economy of mixed state and private structure; agriculture is its main component. It is a republic with one legislative body; its chief of state is the president and its head of government, the prime minister. Though seemingly inhabited for a long time, the area has yielded few archaeological remains. For several centuries before the arrival of Europeans, the territory was subjected to slave traders. The French explored and claimed central Africa and in 1889 established a post at Bangui. In 1898 they partitioned the colony among commercial concessionaires. United with Chad in 1906 to form the French colony of Ubangi-Shari-Chad, it later became part of FRENCH EQUATORIAL AFRICA. It was separated from Chad in 1920 and became an overseas territory in 1946. An autonomous republic within the FRENCH COMMUNITY in 1958, it achieved independence in 1960. In 1966 the military overthrew a civilian government and installed J.-B. BOKASSA, who in 1976 renamed the country the Central African Empire. He was overthrown in 1979, but the military again seized power in the 1980s. Elections in 1993 led to installation of a civilian government.

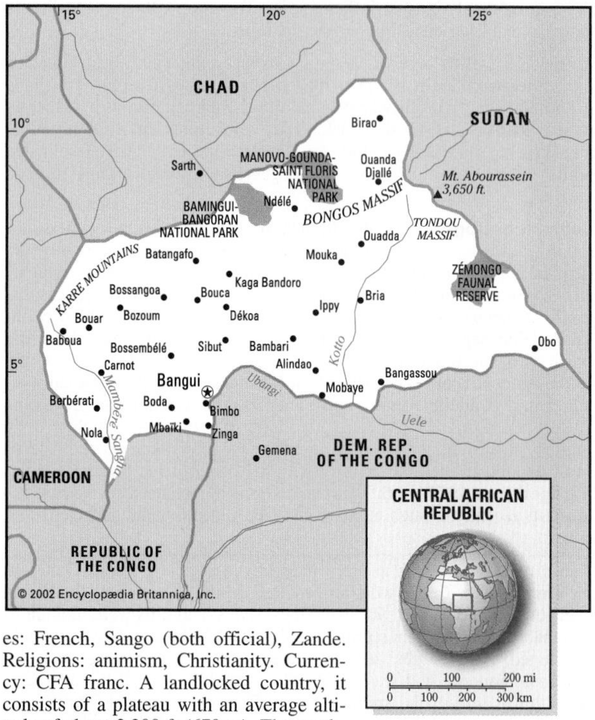

Central America Southern portion of North America (pop., 1993 est.: 30,610,000). It extends from the southern border of Mexico to the northwestern border of Colombia and from the Pacific Ocean to the Caribbean Sea. It includes Guatemala, Belize, Honduras, El Salvador, Nicaragua, Costa Rica, and Panama. Some geographers also include five states of Mexico: QUINTANA ROO, YUCATAN, CAMPECHE, TABASCO, and CHIAPAS. Area: 202,000 sq mi (523,000 sq km). Two-thirds of the population is of mixed American Indian and Spanish ancestry. Language: Spanish (official), except Belize (English, official); also American Indian languages. Religion: chiefly Roman Catholicism. The region is largely hilly or mountainous, with humid swamps and lowlands extending along both coasts. TAJUMULCO VOLCANO, western Guatemala, is the highest point. The region has some 40 volcanoes, many of them active, and it has frequent earthquakes. The volcanic zones have fertile soil and are productive agricultural areas. The area was long inhabited by indigenous peoples, including the MAYA, before the Spanish arrived and conquered the region in the early 16th century; they continued to rule for about 300 years. CHRISTOPHER COLUMBUS skirted the Atlantic coast from Honduras to the Gulf of Darien in 1502; the first European settlement (1510) was on the gulf. Spain organized the region (except Chiapas and Panama) into the captaincy general of Guatemala c. 1560. The English arrived in the 17th century, settling what became British Honduras (Belize). Independence from Spanish rule came in 1821, and in 1823 the United Provinces of Central America was formed (Guatemala, El Salvador, Honduras, Nicaragua, and Costa Rica). British Honduras, still a colony, did not join the federation, and Panama remained part of Colombia. In 1824 the federation adopted a constitution, but in 1838 Costa Rica, Honduras, and Nicaragua seceded, thus effectively terminating the federation. Treaties of amity were drawn up by a Washington conference of Central American states in 1923. The Central American Common Market was established in 1960 to create a customs union and promote economic cooperation. For further information, see individual countries.

Central Asian arts Arts of Afghanistan, Azerbaijan, Kazakhstan, Kyrgyzstan, Mongolia, Nepal, Tibet, Turkmenistan, Uzbekistan, and parts of China and Russia. The term usually denotes only those traditions not influenced by the ISLAMIC ARTS. The most important pre-Islamic influence was BUDDHISM. From the 7th century, written literatures developed in Tibet and Mongolia as a result of contact with Buddhist cultures on the Indian subcontinent. Musical styles range from the classical (Turkic) to religious chants (Buddhist) to folk song. Traditions in architecture and painting, introduced in Nepal and Tibet from the 8th century, were adaptations of those of India, both Hindu and Buddhist.

central bank Institution, such as the U.S. FEDERAL RESERVE SYSTEM, charged with regulating the size of a nation's MONEY SUPPLY, the availability and cost of CREDIT, and the foreign-exchange value of its CURRENCY (see FOREIGN EXCHANGE). Central banks act as the fiscal agent of the government, issuing notes to be used as legal tender, supervising the operations of the commercial banking system, and implementing MONETARY POLICY. By increasing or decreasing the supply of money and credit, they affect interest rates, thereby influencing the economy. Modern central banks regulate the money supply by buying and selling assets (e.g., through the purchase or sale of government securities). They may also raise or lower the DISCOUNT RATE to discourage or encourage borrowing by COMMERCIAL BANKS. By adjusting the reserve requirement (the minimum cash reserves that banks must hold against their deposit liabilities), central banks contract or expand the money supply (see FRACTIONAL RESERVE SYSTEM). Their aim is to maintain conditions that support a high level of employment and production and stable domestic prices. Central banks also take part in cooperative international currency arrangements designed to help stabilize or regulate the foreign-exchange rates of participating countries. Central banks have become varied in authority, autonomy, functions, and instruments of action, but there has been consistent increased emphasis on the interdependence of monetary and other national economic policies, especially FISCAL POLICIES and debt-management policies. See also BANK, INVESTMENT BANK, SAVINGS BANK.

Central Intelligence Agency (CIA) Principal intelligence and counterintelligence agency of the U.S., established in 1947 as a successor to the World War II-era OFFICE OF STRATEGIC SERVICES. The law limits its activities to foreign countries; it is prohibited from gathering intelligence on U.S. soil, which is a responsibility of the FEDERAL BUREAU OF INVESTIGATION. Officially a part of the U.S. Defense Department, it is responsible for preparing analyses for the NATIONAL SECURITY COUNCIL. Its budget is kept secret. Though intelligence gathering is its chief occupation, the CIA has also been involved in many covert operations, including the expulsion of MUHAMMAD MOSADDEQ from Iran (1953), the attempted BAY OF PIGS INVASION of Cuba, and support of the Nicaraguan CONTRAS in the 1980s.

central limit theorem In statistics, any of several fundamental theorems in PROBABILITY. Originally known as the law of errors, in its classic form it states that the sum of a set of independent RANDOM VARIABLES will approach a NORMAL DISTRIBUTION regardless of the distribution of the individual variables themselves, given certain general conditions. Further, the mean (see MEAN, MEDIAN, AND MODE) of the normal distribution will coincide with the (arithmetic) mean of the (statistical) means of each random variable.

central nervous system See NERVOUS SYSTEM

Central Pacific Railroad U.S. railroad company founded in 1861 by a group of California merchants including MARK HOPKINS and LELAND STANFORD. It was built with land grants and subsidies from the Pacific Railway Act (1862); thousands of Chinese laborers were hired to build it. Its tracks joined up with those of the UNION PACIFIC on May 10, 1869, in Promontory, Utah. From 1884 it was leased to the Southern Pacific Co., with which it merged in 1959.

Central Park Public park, NEW YORK CITY. Located in MANHATTAN, it occupies an area of 840 acres (340 hectares). It was designed by FREDERICK LAW OLMSTED and opened in 1876; it was artificially landscaped to create an impression of wild and varied terrain. It includes footpaths and bicycle paths, athletic fields, boating lakes, and a zoo. Free public concerts and performances are frequent, notably the Shakespeare in the Park series at an open-air theater. The METROPOLITAN MUSEUM OF ART adjoins the park.

Central Powers WORLD WAR I coalition that was defeated by the ALLIED POWERS. Its primary members were the German empire and Austria-Hungary, the "central" European states that were at war from August 1914 against France, Britain, and Russia. The Ottoman empire entered the war on the side of the Central Powers in October 1914, followed by Bulgaria in October 1915.

central processing unit See CPU

Central Treaty Organization See CENTO

Central Valley *Spanish* **Valle Central** \'bä-yā-sen-'träl\ Valley, Chile. Located in central Chile between the Western Cordillera of the ANDES and the coastal range, it extends about 400 mi (650 km) from the Chacabuco Range in the north to the BÍO-BÍO RIVER in the south. The agricultural heartland of Chile, it was the original center of European colonization beginning in the mid-1500s, and it continues to be home to most Chileans. SANTIAGO is at its northern end.

Central Valley Valley, California. Located between the SIERRA NEVADA and COAST RANGES, it is over 400 mi (640 km) long and 20–50 mi (32–80 km) wide. The SACRAMENTO and SAN JOAQUIN rivers, which run through the valley, are fed by abundant rains and melting snows of the Sierras. Because of the irrigation made possible by numerous dams and canals, the area now contains some of the richest farmland in the U.S.

centrifugal force \sen-'trif-yə-gəl\ Fictitious force, peculiar to circular motion, that is equal but opposite to the centripetal force that keeps a particle on a circular path (see CENTRIPETAL ACCELERATION). For example, a stone attached to a string and whirling in a horizontal circular path is accelerated toward the center of its path by the tension in the string, the only force acting on the string. However, in a reference frame at rest with the stone, another force—the centrifugal force—must be introduced for NEWTON'S LAWS OF MOTION to apply. Centrifugal force is a useful concept in analyzing behavior in rotating systems.

centrifugal pump \sen-'trif-yə-gəl\ Machine for moving liquids and gases. Its two major parts are the impeller (a WHEEL with vanes) and the circular pump casing around it. In the most common type, called the volute centrifugal pump, fluid enters the PUMP at high speed near the center of the rotating impeller and is thrown against the casing by the vanes. The centrifugal pressure forces the fluid through an opening in the casing; this outlet widens progressively in a spiral fashion, which reduces the speed of the fluid and thereby increases pressure. Centrifugal pumps are used for many purposes, such as pumping liquids for water supply, irrigation, and sewage disposal systems. They are also used as gas COMPRESSORS.

centrifuge \'sen-trə-ˌfyüj\ Machine that applies a sustained CENTRIFUGAL FORCE. Effectively, the centrifuge substitutes a similar, stronger force for that of gravity. Every centrifuge contains a spinning vessel; there are many configurations, depending on use. A revolving object exerts a force away from the center of rotation (see NEWTON'S LAWS OF MOTION), called the centrifugal force; it is usually stated as so many "times gravity" or so many "G," and may range from a few G for the basket in a home washing machine or an industrial separator to hundreds of thousands of G for centrifuges to separate isotopes of uranium or to purify vaccines.

centripetal acceleration \sen-'trip-ə-təl\ Property of the motion of an object traveling in a circular path. Centripetal describes the FORCE on the object, directed toward the center of the circle, which causes a constant change in the object's direction, thus its ACCELERATION. The magnitude of centripetal acceleration a is equal to the square of the object's speed v along the curved path divided by the object's distance r from the center of the circle, or $a = v^2/r$.

centroid In geometry, the center of mass of a two-dimensional figure or three-dimensional solid. Thus the centroid of a two-dimensional figure represents the point at which it could be balanced if it were cut out of, for example, sheet metal. The centroid of a circle or sphere is its center. More generally, the centroid represents the point designated by the mean (see MEAN, MEDIAN, AND MODE) of the coordinates of all the points in a set. If the boundary is irregular, finding the mean requires using CALCULUS (the most general formula for the centroid involves an INTEGRAL).

centromere \'sen-trə-ˌmir\ Structure in a CHROMOSOME that holds together the two chromatids. It is the point of attachment to the structure that pulls the chromatids to opposite ends of the cell during cell division (see MITOSIS). During the middle stage of mitosis, the centromere duplicates and the chromatid pair separates, each chromatid becoming a separate chromosome. Thus, when the cell divides, both daughter cells have complete sets of chromosomes.

century plant *or* **American aloe** *or* **maguey** \mə-'gā\ Species of AGAVE *(Agave americana),* of Mexico and the southwestern U.S. It takes many years (from five to 100) to mature, flowers only once, and then dies. It is widely cultivated for its large spiny leaves and enormous flower cluster, and may reach 20 ft (6 m) in height. Century plants provide the distinctive ingredient for the alcoholic drinks pulque and mescal.

Cephalonia Largest of the IONIAN ISLANDS, western Greece. With Ithaca and smaller nearby islands, it forms the Kefallinia department (pop., 1991: 32,000). The mountainous island occupies 302 sq mi (781 sq km) and rises to 5,341 ft (1,628 m) at Mount Ainos. Argostolion, the chief town and a port on the southwestern coast, is the department capital. It was an important MYCENAEAN center, which the Romans seized in 189 BC. In the Middle Ages it was captured by ROBERT GUISCARD. Later, it was ruled by various Neapolitan and Venetian families. In 1809 it was taken by the British, then ceded to Greece in 1864. It experienced a devastating earthquake in 1953.

cephalopod \'se-fə-lə-ˌpäd\ Any marine MOLLUSK of the class Cephalopoda (e.g., CUTTLEFISH, NAUTILUS, OCTOPUS, and SQUID), which includes the most active and largest living INVERTEBRATES. Cephalopods are bilaterally symmetrical and typically have a highly developed centralized nervous system. Their image-forming eyes are similar in structure to VERTEBRATE eyes, and their heads are armed with tentacles that have rows of round suction disks. Most cephalopods can change skin color to blend in with their surroundings. All can swim by propelling themselves backward by expelling water forcefully. Most are carnivores that feed on fish, crustaceans, and other mollusks.

Cepheid variable \'sef-ē-əd\ One of a class of VARIABLE STARS whose period of variation is proportional to its luminosity and is therefore useful in measuring the distances to clusters of stars and galaxies. Named for the prototype of this class found in the constellation Cepheus, classical Cepheids have a dependable period-luminosity relationship, with periods from about 1.5 days to over 50 days, and are Population I stars (see POPULATIONS I AND II). The longer a star's period, the greater its natural brightness; this relationship, discovered in 1912 by Henrietta Leavitt (1868–1921), has been used to establish the distance of remote star systems.

Ceram *or* **Seram** \'sā-ˌräm\ Island of the central MOLUCCAS, Indonesia. It has an area of 6,621 sq mi (17,148 sq km). The terrain is mountainous and covered with tropical forests; seismic activity is common. Portuguese missionaries arriving in the 15th century found Hindu and Islamic influences present; it came under nominal Dutch control c. 1650. During World War II the Japanese occupied it; after the war it became part of Indonesia.

ceramics Traditionally, objects created from such naturally occurring raw materials as clay minerals and quartz sand, by shaping the material and then hardening it by firing at high temperatures to make the object stronger, harder, and less permeable to fluids. The principal ceramic products are containers, tableware, bricks, and tiles. See also EARTHENWARE, PORCELAIN, POTTERY, STONEWARE, TERRA-COTTA.

Ceratium \sə-'rā-shē-əm\ Genus of one-celled aquatic PROTISTS. Members are DINOFLAGELLATES with both plant and animal characteristics. The cell is flattened horizontally and contains yellow, brown, or green pigments. *Ceratium* species are covered by a theca, or armor, composed of many textured plates that form one horn in the front and usually two in the back; these horns slow the sinking of the organism. The body form varies according to the salt content and temperature of the surrounding water: the spines tend to be short and thick in cold, salty water and long and thin in less salty, warmer water. Members form an important part of the PLANKTON found in northern seas.

Cerberus \'sər-bə-rəs\ In GREEK MYTHOLOGY, the monstrous watchdog of the underworld. He was usually said to have three heads, though HESIOD says he had 50. Heads of snakes grew from his back, and he had a serpent's tail. He devoured anyone who tried to escape HADES' kingdom, and he refused entrance to living humans, though ORPHEUS gained passage by charming him with music. One of the labors of HERACLES was to bring Cerberus up to the land of the living; after succeeding, he returned the creature to Hades.

cereal *or* **grain** Any GRASS yielding starchy seeds suitable for food. The most commonly cultivated cereals are WHEAT, RICE, RYE, OAT, BARLEY, CORN, and SORGHUM. As human food, cereals are usually marketed in raw grain form or as ingredients of food products. As animal feed, they are consumed mainly by livestock and poultry, which are eventually rendered as meat, dairy, and poultry products for human consumption. They also are used industrially in the production of a wide range of substances, such as GLUCOSE, adhesives, oils, and alcohols. Wheat is the world's most widely grown cereal crop; rice is the second. Grains are generally rich in carbohydrates and energy value but comparatively low in protein and naturally deficient in calcium and vitamin A. Breads are usually enriched to compensate for any nutritional deficiencies in the cereal used. Though often consumed in the areas where grown, cereal and cereal by-products are also major commodities in international trade.

cereal Prepared foodstuff of CEREAL grain. Cereals are used for both human and animal food. The first step in making cereal is milling, grinding the grain so that it can be easily processed. Modern automated systems employ steel cylinders, followed by air purification and numerous sievings to separate the endosperm from the outer coverings and the germ; corn is milled by wet processes. Cereal products include FLOUR, RICE, meal (coarsely ground and unsifted grain), cornstarch, and PASTA. Breakfast cereals include raw cereals such as oatmeal and farina (which must be boiled), shredded cereals (usually whole wheat that is boiled, dried, and cut), flaked cereals (usually corn that is broken down into grits and cooked under pressure with flavoring syrup before being pressed and toasted), puffed cereals (grains heated in a pressure chamber and then released to cause expansion), and granular cereals (flour-based cereals made from dough that is cooked and ground into small bits). All cereals are high in STARCH.

cerebellum \ˌser-ə-'bel-əm\ Part of the BRAIN that integrates sensory input from the inner ear and from proprioceptors (see PROPRIOCEPTION) in muscle with nerve impulses from the cerebrum (see CEREBRAL CORTEX), coordinating muscle responses to maintain balance and produce smooth, coordinated movements. Located below the cerebral hemispheres and behind the upper medulla oblongata and pons, each of its two connected hemispheres has a core of white matter within a cortex of gray matter. Disorders usually produce neuromuscular disturbances, in particular ATAXIA.

cerebral cortex \sə-ˈrē-brəl, ˈser-ə-brəl\ Layer of gray matter that constitutes the outer layer of the CEREBRUM and is responsible for integrating sensory impulses and for higher intellectual functions. It is divided into four lobes, roughly defined by major surface folds; sometimes the limbic system, or limbic lobe, is considered to be a fifth lobe. The frontal lobe controls motor activity and speech, the parietal controls touch and position, and the temporal lobe handles auditory reception and memory. The occipital lobe at the back of the brain holds the brain's major visual-reception area. The limbic lobe controls smell, taste, and emotional responses.

cerebral palsy Paralysis resulting from abnormal development or damage to the brain before or soon after birth. Cases are of four main types: spastic, with spasms contracting the extremities, and often mental retardation and epilepsy; athetoid, with slow, changing spasms in the face, neck, and extremities, grimacing, and inarticulate speech (dysarthria); ataxic, with poor coordination, muscle weakness, an unsteady gait, and difficulty performing rapid or fine movements; and mixed, in which symptoms of two or more types are present.

cerebral seizures See EPILEPSY

cerebrospinal fluid \sə-ˌrē-brō-ˈspī-nᵊl\ (CSF) Clear, colorless liquid that surrounds the BRAIN and SPINAL CORD and fills the spaces in them, helps support the brain, acts as a lubricant, maintains pressure in the skull, and cushions shocks. Analysis of CSF obtained by a spinal tap (lumbar puncture) helps diagnose a number of disorders, including MENINGITIS and hemorrhage in the central nervous system.

cerebrum \sə-ˈrē-brəm, ˈser-ə-brəm\ Largest part of the BRAIN. The two cerebral hemispheres consist of an inner core of myelinated nerve fibers, the white matter, and a heavily convoluted outer cortex of gray matter (see CEREBRAL CORTEX). Nerve fibers in the white matter connect functional areas of the cortex in the same hemispheres, connect functional areas of the cortex in opposite hemispheres, and connect the cerebral cortex to lower centers (e.g., the spinal cord). A front-to-back fissure divides the cerebrum's two hemispheres. One is dominant, holding speech and thought centers and determining right- or left-handedness. The other handles more complex perceptions, such as face recognition. Each controls the opposite side of the body. The corpus callosum, a thick band of white matter, connects them, allowing integration of sensory data and responses from both sides of the body. Other important cerebral structures include the HYPOTHALAMUS and the thalamus, a sensory relay center involved with emotions and instincts.

Ceres \ˈsir-ēz\ In ROMAN RELIGION, the goddess of the growth of food plants, sometimes worshiped in association with the earth goddess Tellus. Her cult was overlaid by that of DEMETER, who was worshiped in Greece and Sicily. According to tradition, her cult was introduced into Rome in 496 BC to check a famine. Her temple on Aventine Hill was known as a center of plebeian religious and political activities.

Ceres, classical sculpture; in the Vatican Museum.

ALINARI—ART RESOURCE

Ceres \ˈsir-ˌez\ Largest known ASTEROID in the solar system and the first discovered, in 1801. Named after the goddess CERES, it revolves around the sun in 4.6 terrestrial years and is about 580 mi (930 km) across.

cereus Any of various large cacti (genus *Cereus* and related genera) of the western U.S. and tropical New World, including the SAGUARO and the organ-pipe cactus *(Lemairocereus thurberi,* also *L. marginatus* or *C. thurberi).* The genus *Selenicereus* (night-blooming cereus, or moon cactus), containing about 20 species, is known for its large, usually fragrant, night-blooming white flowers, among the largest in the CACTUS family. The queen-of-the-night *(S. grandiflorus),* the best-known night-blooming cereus, is often grown indoors.

Cerf \ˈsərf\, **Bennett (Alfred)** (1898–1971) U.S. publisher and editor. With Donald S. Klopfer, in 1925 Cerf acquired the Modern Library imprint, which subsequently became a highly profitable series of reprints of classic books. In 1927 they began publishing books other than Modern Library titles as RANDOM HOUSE, of which Cerf served as president 1927–65 and chairman 1965–70. He became known as an opponent of censorship and as the publisher of many eminent authors. He was an inveterate punster and raconteur.

cerium \ˈsir-ē-əm\ Chemical ELEMENT, a RARE EARTH METAL of the LANTHANIDE series (hence having many properties of the TRANSITION ELEMENTS), chemical symbol Ce, atomic number 58. It is iron-gray and fairly soft and ductile. Found in many ORES, it is about as abundant as copper and three times as abundant as lead. The metal is used in ALLOYS and other metallurgical applications and (because it oxidizes strongly and rapidly) in illumination, ignition and signaling devices, and propellants. Misch metal, used in lighter flints, is 50% cerium. Cerium compounds (in which it has VALENCE 3 or 4) are used in lantern mantles, in the ceramic, photographic, and textile industries, and in analytical chemistry.

CERN *in full* **Organisation Européenne pour la Recherche Nucléaire** *formerly* **Conseil Européen pour la Recherche Nucléaire** International scientific organization established for collaborative research into subnuclear physics. Headquartered in Geneva, CERN includes extensive facilities at sites on both sides of the Swiss–French border. The results of its experimental and theoretical work are made generally available. It was established in part in order to reclaim European physicists who had emigrated to the U.S. as a result of World War II. In 2000 it had 20 European member nations and several nations with observer status.

Cernunnos \ker-ˈnü-nōs\ In CELTIC RELIGION, a deity worshiped as "lord of wild things." He wore stag antlers and sometimes carried a torque (sacred neck ornament). He was worshiped primarily in Britain, but there are also traces of his cult in Ireland. He is probably the source for the horned god that appears in Christian medieval manuscripts as a symbol of the ANTICHRIST.

Cerrito, Fanny *orig.* **Francesca Teresa Giuseppa Raffaela** (1817–1909) Italian ballerina and choreographer. She made her debut in Naples (1832) and gained international fame in London (1840–48). She was known for the brilliance, strength, and vivacity of her dancing. Her greatest role was in *Ondine* (1843), created for her by JULES PERROT. Cerrito married her regular partner, ARTHUR SAINT-LÉON, in 1845. In 1854 she both choreographed and danced in *Gemma* at the Paris Opéra. She retired in 1857. She was one of the few women in the 19th century to achieve distinction as a choreographer.

Cerro Gordo \ˈser-ō-ˈgȯr-dō\, **Battle of** Confrontation between U.S. and Mexican troops in April 1847 when U.S. forces under WINFIELD SCOTT first met serious resistance in the MEXICAN WAR. As Scott's army marched from Veracruz to Mexico City, it attacked an entrenched Mexican force of 12,000 under ANTONIO SANTA ANNA at a mountain pass near Cerro Gordo. Scott's troops routed the Mexicans, who left 1,130 casualties; the U.S. lost 63 men.

certificate, digital See DIGITAL CERTIFICATE

certificate of deposit (CD) Receipt from a bank acknowledging the deposit of a sum of money. The most common type, the time certificate of deposit, is for a fixed-term interest-bearing deposit in a large denomination. It consequently pays higher interest than a savings account, though the investor who withdraws money before its maturity date is subject to a penalty. Introduced in the early 1960s, CDs have become a popular method of saving.

certiorari \ˌsər-shə-ˈrar-ē\ In law, a WRIT issued by a superior court for the reexamination of an action of a lower court. The writ of certiorari was originally a writ from England's Court of Queen's (King's) Bench to the judges of an inferior court; it was later expanded to include the EQUITY (chancery) courts. In the U.S., certiorari is the most common way to have a case from the U.S. COURTS OF APPEALS reviewed by the U.S. SUPREME COURT.

Cervantes (Saavedra) \sər-ˈvän-ˌtēz\, **Miguel de** (1547–1616) Spanish novelist, playwright, and poet, the most celebrated figure in

Spanish literature. After studying in Madrid, he joined the Italian infantry, fought the Turks at Lepanto, and was captured with his brother and sold into slavery in Algiers for five years. Back in Spain, his chronic financial problems and tangled affairs led to brushes with the law and brief imprisonment. While in tedious civil-service employment, he wrote the pastoral romance *La galatea* (1585) and plays, poetry, and short stories, to small success. His great creation *Don Quixote* (1605, 1615), brought immediate success and literary eminence, if not riches. It parodies chivalric romances of the day with the comic adventures of a bemused elderly knight who sets out on his old horse, Rosinante, with his pragmatic squire, Sancho Panza. Considered the first and one of the greatest of all novels, it has influenced many writers and inspired numerous creations in other genres and media. He also published a large set of eight comedies and eight interludes for the stage (1615) and the romance *The Labors of Persiles and Sigismunda* (1617).

cervical erosion Ulceration of the lining of the cervix of the uterus. Caused by infection and discharge, it heals once these are cured. It may precede cervical cancer. Erosions tend to occur in the years of menstruation, in mothers, and during cervical or vaginal infections. Cancerous erosions are removed surgically, which does not cause infertility.

cervical spondylosis \ˌspän-də-ˈlō-səs\ Degenerative disease of the neck vertebrae. Compression of the spinal cord and cervical nerves by narrowing of spaces between vertebrae causes radiating neck or arm pain and stiffness, restricted head movement, headaches, spastic paralysis, and arm and leg weakness. Cervical spondylosis can resemble neurological disease with unrelated arthritis. It is treated with rest, traction, and possibly a cervical collar. Removal of herniated disks or fusion of vertebrae may be necessary.

cervicitis \ˌsər-və-ˈsī-təs\ Inflammation of the cervix of the uterus, caused by infection or irritation. It is most common during the years of menstruation. Cervicitis can be acute or chronic and may worsen during pregnancy. It does not cause pain but may lead to polyps. The major symptom is an abundant discharge, which can impair fertility. Treatment may include cauterization or surgery to repair or remove the cervix; this does not affect fertility.

Césaire \sā-ˈzer\, **Aimé (-Fernand)** (born 1913) French (Martinican) poet and playwright. Educated in Paris, he returned to Martinique to be elected to the National Assembly as a Communist. A cofounder with Leopold Senghor of the Negritude movement, he ardently supported the decolonization of French colonies of Africa, a view expressed in the fiery poems of *Return to My Native Land* (1939) and *Soleil cou-coupé* (1948, "Sun's Slashed Throat"). Discarding Negritude for black militancy, he turned to the theater and wrote the political dramas *The Tragedy of King Christophe* (1963) and *A Season in the Congo* (1966).

cesarean section \si-ˈzar-ē-ən\ *or* **C-section** Surgical removal of a fetus from the uterus through an abdominal incision at or before full term. It is usually performed when vaginal delivery would endanger the life or health of the mother or the child. Vaginal delivery is often possible in subsequent pregnancies. Cesarean section carries the usual risks of major surgery. Once overused, largely for fear of malpractice suits, its use has been greatly reduced by the natural childbirth movement.

cesium \ˈsē-zē-əm\ Chemical element, one of the alkali metals, chemical symbol Cs, atomic number 55. The first element discovered by spectroscopy (1860), it is silvery white, liquid at warm room temperature (melting at 83°F, or 28.4°C), and very soft when solid. About half as abundant as lead, it occurs in minute quantities as ores. It reacts explosively with cold water and is used to scavenge traces of oxygen and other gases in electron tubes. Other uses are as a catalyst and in photoelectric cells, ion propulsion systems, atomic clocks, and plasma for thermoelectric conversion. Cesium salts have various specialty applications, including in mineral waters.

Céspedes (y Borja del Castillo) \ˈsās-pā-ˌthās\, **Carlos Manuel de** (1819–1874) Cuban revolutionary hero. Born to a prominent plantation family, he studied law in Spain. On returning to Cuba, he opened a law practice and secretly organized an independence movement. He launched his insurrection in 1868. Thousands flocked to his rebel army, which scored some stunning victories. He led a revolutionary government, which actively sought annexation by the U.S. He was deposed in 1873 and went into hiding, but was discovered and shot by Spanish troops.

cetacean \si-ˈtā-shən\ Any of several species of exclusively aquatic placental mammals constituting the order Cetacea, found in oceans worldwide and in some freshwater environments. Modern cetaceans are grouped in two suborders: about 70 species of toothed whales (Odontoceti) and 13 species of toothless baleen whales (Mysticeti). They have a tapered body, no external hind limbs, and a tail ending in a horizontal blade of two lobes, or flukes. Cetaceans must come to the water's surface to breathe through blowholes located on top of their head. See also whale.

Cétsamain See Beltane

Cetshwayo \kech-ˈwä-yō\ (1826?–1884) Last great king of the Zulus (r.1872–79). Nephew of the great Shaka, Cetshwayo commanded a disciplined army of 40,000. Attacked by the British in 1879, he defeated them at Isandhlwana but lost at Ulundi. Part of his kingdom was returned in 1883, but his subjects drove him out of power.

Ceuta \ˈthā-ü-tä, ˈsyü-tä\ *Arabic* **Sebta** \ˌseb-tə\ Spanish enclave (pop., 1996 est.: 69,000), North Africa. A military station and seaport, it constitutes with Melilla an autonomous community of Spain. The city is on a narrow isthmus that connects Jebel Musa (one of the Pillars of Hercules) to the mainland. Located in northern Morocco at the eastern end of the Strait of Gibraltar, it was successively colonized by Carthaginians, Greeks, and Romans. Long a flourishing trading town, it was taken by the Portuguese in 1415, and it passed to Spain in 1580. In 1995 the Spanish government approved statutes of autonomy for Ceuta.

Ceylon See Sri Lanka

Cézanne \sā-ˈzän\, **Paul** (1839–1906) French painter, one of the fathers of modern painting. In 1859 he entered law school; in 1861 he left to study art in Paris. Works he exhibited at the Salon des Refusés (1863) were denounced, but he persevered. He became associated with the Impressionists Claude Monet, Camille Pissarro, Edouard Manet, Edgar Degas, and Auguste Renoir; in 1874 and 1877 he exhibited with them. Unlike the Impressionists, he emphasized the structure of objects rather than the vision presented by the light that emanated from them, composing with cubic masses, patches of color, and architectonic lines. From the 1870s he developed a radically new way of simultaneously depicting deep space and flat design; great works of the period include the series of monumental landscapes of Mont Ste.-Victoire. He used the same approach in portraiture and everyday scenes, most notably in *Madame Cézanne in a Yellow Armchair* (1890) and *The Card Players* (1890–92). He painted more than 200 still lifes. Public reception of his first one-man exhibition (1895) was cool, but after he exhibited at the Salon des Indépendants (1899, 1901, 1902) and the Exposition Universelle (1900), the galleries finally began seeking his works. The year after his death, a retrospective showing of 56 paintings won critical acclaim. His work was a major source of inspiration for the Cubists Georges Braque, Pablo Picasso, and Juan Gris. See also Cubism, Impressionism, Postimpressionism.

Self-portrait by Paul Cézanne, oil on canvas, c. 1878–80; in the Phillips Collection, Washington, D.C.
PHILLIPS COLLECTION, WASHINGTON, D.C.

CFC See chlorofluorocarbon

CGI *in full* **Common Gateway Interface** Specification by which a Web server passes data between itself and an application program. Typically, a Web user will make a request of the Web server, which in turn passes the request to a CGI application program. The program processes the request and passes the answer to the server, which in turn sends it to the user. The entire interchange follows the rules of the CGI specification, which is actually part of the HTTP protocol. CGI application programs can be written in such programming languages as C++ and Visual Basic, but are usually written in Perl.

Chaadayev \ˌchə-ˌə-ˈdá-yəf\, **Pyotr (Yakovlevich)** (1794–1856) Russian writer. In 1827–31 he wrote in French his *Lettres philosophiques*

("Philosophical Letters"), which explored among other issues Russia's relation to the West; he urged a Western path of development for Russia. After a Russian translation of the first letter appeared, it was banned, and Chaadayev was declared insane. He continued to live in Moscow, however, where he was venerated by young Westernizers, whose ideas of Russian history precipitated the debate between SLAVOPHILES AND WESTERNIZERS.

Chabrier \ˌshä-brē-ˈā\, **(Alexis-) Emmanuel** (1841–1894) French composer. Though he was a piano prodigy, his parents obliged him to obtain a law degree and take a government job, but he relinquished the latter in 1880 to pursue composition full-time. His opera *Gwendoline* enjoyed several productions in his lifetime, but he never achieved significant success. His other works include nine other operas and operettas, including *Le roi malgré lui* (1887), and the orchestral rhapsody *España* (1883).

Chabrol \shä-ˈbrȯl\, **Claude** (born 1930) French film director, screenwriter, and producer. After working in public relations in 20th Century-Fox's Paris office, he wrote and produced *Bitter Reunion* (1958) and directed *The Cousins* (1959) and *The Good Women* (1960), all representative of the NEW WAVE movement. Among his many other films are *Landru* (1962), *Les biches* (1968), *Violette* (1978), *The Story of Women* (1988), and *Madame Bovary* (1991). He admired ALFRED HITCHCOCK and used a similar style in several mystery thrillers, including *This Man Must Die* (1969).

Chaco See GRAN CHACO

Chaco Culture National Historical Park \ˈchä-kō\ National preserve, northwestern New Mexico. Established as a national monument in 1907, it was redesignated and renamed in 1980. Occupying 53 sq mi (137 sq km), it contains 13 major pre-Columbian ruins and more than 300 smaller archaeological sites representing PUEBLO cultures. Pueblo Bonito, built in the 10th century, is the largest Pueblo excavated site; it contained some 800 rooms.

Chaco War \ˈchä-kō\ (1932–35) Costly conflict between Bolivia and Paraguay over possession of the Chaco, a wilderness region thought to contain oil reserves. Bolivia, landlocked since the War of the PACIFIC, was motivated as well by the need to gain access to the Atlantic coast through the Río de la Plata system. The war cost about 100,000 lives and so seriously disrupted Bolivia's economy that its deprived masses demanded reform. In a treaty arranged by neighboring countries and the U.S., Bolivia was given a corridor to the Paraguay River and a port, but Paraguay gained clear title to most of the disputed region.

Chad *French* **Tchad** \ˈchad\ Republic, northern central Africa. Area: 495,752 sq mi (1,283,998 sq km). Population (1997 est.): 7,166,000. Capital: N'DJAMENA. The Sara is the largest ethnic group, at about one-quarter of the total population; other groups include the Bagirmi and Bongo, the Lake and Mbum, the Tangale, and the Buduma, Kuri, and Kanemba. Arabs, composed of a multitude of tribes, represent a single ethnic group. Languages: French, Arabic (both official), and more than 100 dialects and languages. Religions: Islam, animism, Roman Catholicism, Protestantism. Currency: CFA franc. The landlocked country's terrain is a shallow basin that rises gradually from 750 ft (228 m) above sea level at Lake CHAD. The basin is rimmed by mountains, including the volcanic Tibesti Massif to the north, rising to 11,204 ft (3,415 m) at Mount Koussi. Its lowest elevation is the Djourab Depression, at 573 ft (175 m). Chad's river network is limited to the CHARI and LOGONE rivers and their tributaries, which flow from the southeast into Lake Chad. It has an agricultural economy. It is a republic with one legislative body; its chief of state is the president and its head of government, the prime minister. Around AD 800 the kingdom of Kanem was founded, and by the early 1200s its borders had expanded to form a new kingdom, KANEM-BORNU, in the northern regions of the area. Its power peaked in the 16th century with its command of the northern terminus of the trans-Sahara trade route to TRIPOLI. Around this time the rival kingdoms of Baguirmi and Wadai evolved in the south. In the years 1883–93 all three kingdoms fell to the Sudanese adventurer Rabih az-Zubayr, who was in turn pushed out by the French in 1891. Extending their power, the French in 1910 made Chad a part of FRENCH EQUATORIAL AFRICA. Chad became a separate colony in 1920 and was made an overseas territory in 1946. The country achieved independence in 1960. This was followed by decades of civil war, and frequent intervention by France and Libya.

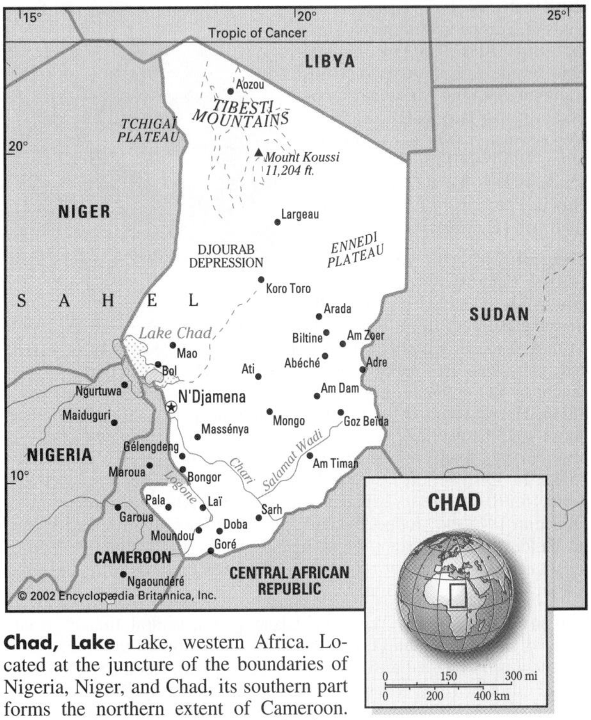

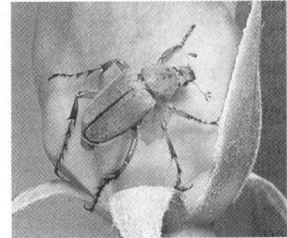

Chad, Lake Lake, western Africa. Located at the juncture of the boundaries of Nigeria, Niger, and Chad, its southern part forms the northern extent of Cameroon. Fed by the CHARI RIVER, its area varies from year to year, usually ranging between 3,800 and 9,900 sq mi (9,850–25,600 sq km). In the 1970s and '80s it dropped to about 1,500 sq mi (3,900 sq km), a change apparently related to the desertification of the surrounding SAHEL region. The lake was first explored by Europeans in 1823.

Chaeronea \ˌker-ə-ˈnē-ə\ Ancient city, eastern Greece. Its ruins are located in western BOEOTIA southeast of Mount PARNASSUS, near ORCHOMENUS. PHILIP II of Macedon won the Battle of CHAERONEA there in 338 BC. In 86 BC it was the scene of a victory of SULLA over MITHRADATES VI of PONTUS. PLUTARCH was born there c. AD 46.

Chaeronea, Battle of (338 BC) Battle in Boeotia, central Greece, in which PHILIP II of Macedonia defeated THEBES and ATHENS. The victory, partly credited to Philip's young son ALEXANDER THE GREAT, gave Macedonia a foothold in Greece and represented a start toward Alexander's eventual empire.

Chafee \ˈchā-fē\, **Zechariah, Jr.** (1885–1957) U.S. legal scholar. Born in Providence, R.I., he graduated from Harvard Law School and joined its faculty in 1916. Concerned about the restrictions on FREEDOM OF SPEECH imposed in World War I, he wrote *Freedom of Speech* (1920), which became a leading text of U.S. libertarian thought. Chafee became recognized as an expert on CIVIL LIBERTIES, influencing LOUIS BRANDEIS and OLIVER WENDELL, JR. HOLMES He was also an authority on EQUITY, NEGOTIABLE INSTRUMENTS, and ANTITRUST LAW.

chafer Any of several species of SCARAB BEETLE (most in the subfamily Melolonthinae). Adult leaf chafers (genus *Macrodactylus*) eat foliage; the female deposits her eggs in the soil, and the larvae live underground for years, feeding on plant roots. The well-known rose chafer, a tan, long-legged beetle, feeds on the flowers and foliage of grapes, roses, and other plants. Poultry that eat rose-chafer grubs may be poisoned.

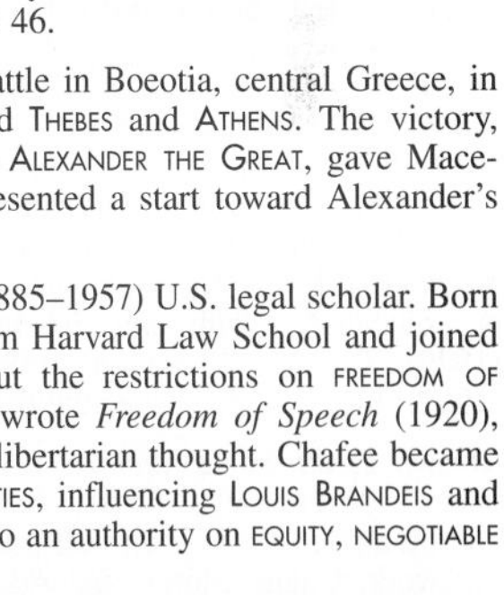

Rose chafer (*Macrodactylus subspinosus*).
GRANT HEILMAN

C
D

chaffinch Songbird *(Fringilla coelebs)* that breeds in gardens and farmlands of Europe and northern Africa to central Asia (and, by introduction, South Africa). It is the most common FINCH in western Europe. The 6-in. (15-cm) male has a bluish crown, rust-brown back, greenish rump, and pinkish to rust face and breast; the female is greenish brown. The Canary Islands, or blue, chaffinch *(F. teydea)* is similar.

Chaffinch (*Fringilla coelebs*).
H. SCHUNEMANN–BAVARIA-VERLAG

Chagall \shä-ˈgäl\, **Marc** (1887–1985) Belarusan-French painter, printmaker, and designer. After studying painting in St. Petersburg, he moved to Paris in 1910. He exhibited at the SALON DES INDÉPENDANTS and had a one-man show in Berlin in 1914. On a visit home he was caught by the outbreak of World War I and then by the Bolshevik revolution. He was named head of the revolutionary art school in Vitebsk, but in 1923 he was able to return to Paris. There he launched a career in printmaking, producing hundreds of etchings for special editions of books. In 1941 he left for New York, where he designed sets and costumes for I. STRAVINSKY's ballet *The Firebird.* After settling again in France in 1948, he produced stained-glass windows and murals for public buildings in Jerusalem, Paris, and the U.S. His distinctive style of fairy-tale fantasy drew principally on memories of Jewish life and folklore in Belarus and the Bible.

Chagos Archipelago \ˈchä-gəs\ Island group, central Indian Ocean. Located about 1,000 mi (1,600 km) south of the tip of the Indian subcontinent, it has a total area of 23 sq mi (60 sq km). Acquired by Britain from France in 1814, it was originally administered by Britain as a dependency of Mauritius; since 1976 it has been the sole member of the British Indian Ocean Territory. Strategically situated at the center of the Indian Ocean, its chief island, Diego Garcia, was developed as an air and naval refueling station by the U.S. and Great Britain in the mid-20th century, causing strong opposition from the region's coastal and island states.

Chagres River \ˈchä-grəs\ River, Panama. Rising in central Panama, and part of the PANAMA CANAL system, it flows southwest where it is dammed to form GATUN LAKE. It drains northwest out of the lake and into the Caribbean Sea.

Chaikin \ˈchā-kən\, **Joseph** (born 1935) U.S. stage director, actor, and writer. Born in Brooklyn, N.Y., he joined the LIVING THEATER, winning praise for his performances in *Dark of the Moon* (1958), *The Connection* (1959), and *Man is Man* (1962). In 1963 he founded the Open Theater and became a central figure in experimental theater. His celebrated productions, the results of intense collaboration between writer, director, and actors, included *America Hurrah* (1966), *The Serpent* (1969), *Terminal* (1970), *The Mutation Show* (1971), and *Nightwalk* (1973). He later collaborated with SAM SHEPARD on *Tongues* (1978), *Savage/Love* (1979), *The War in Heaven* (1984), and *When the World Was Green* (1996). In 1977 he received the first lifetime-achievement Obie Award.

Chain, Ernst Boris *later* **Sir Ernst** (1906–1979) German-British biochemist. With HOWARD WALTER FLOREY he isolated and purified penicillin and performed the first clinical trials of the antibiotic. For their pioneering work, Chain, Florey, and ALEXANDER FLEMING shared a 1945 Nobel Prize. In addition to his work on antibiotics, Chain studied snake venoms, the spreading factor (an enzyme that aids the dispersal of fluids in tissue), and insulin. He was knighted in 1969.

chain drive Device widely used for the transmission of power where shafts are separated at distances greater than that for which gears are practical. In such cases, sprockets (wheels with teeth shaped to mesh with a chain) take the place of gears and drive one another by means of a chain passing over the sprocket teeth. The chains used in conveyor belts are commonly block chains, and consist of solid or laminated blocks connected by side plates and pins. The blocks engage with teeth on sprocket wheels. Depending on the material being moved, buckets, hooks, or other devices are connected to the blocks.

chain mail *or* **mail** Form of body ARMOR worn by European knights and other medieval warriors. An early form, made by sewing iron rings to fabric or leather, was worn in late Roman times and may have originated in Asia. Medieval armorers interlaced the rings, which were closed by welding or riveting. In the 8th century, mail was a short coat with a separate sleeve for the sword arm. By the Norman Conquest (1066), the coat was long and fully sleeved; a hood, usually fitting under a helmet, covered the head and neck. By the 12th century, mail was fitted to hands, feet, and legs. The addition of plates to increase chest and back protection gradually evolved in the 14th century into complete plate armor, displacing mail.

Turkish coat of chain mail, 16th century.
BY COURTESY OF THE JOHN WOODMAN HIGGINS ARMOURY MUSEUM

chain reaction Process yielding products that initiate further processes of the same kind. Nuclear chain reactions are a series of NUCLEAR FISSIONS initiated by NEUTRONS produced in a preceding fission. A CRITICAL MASS, large enough to allow more than one fission-produced neutron to be captured, is necessary for the chain reaction to be self-sustaining. Uncontrolled chain reactions, as in an ATOMIC BOMB, occur when large numbers of neutrons are present and the reactions multiply very quickly. Nuclear reactors control their reactions through the careful distribution of the fissionable material and insertion of neutron-absorbing materials.

chain silicate See INOSILICATE

chair Seat, usually with four legs and a back, intended for one person. It is one of the most ancient forms of furniture, dating to the 3rd Egyptian dynasty (c. 2650–2575 BC). Various styles were developed throughout Europe. In the 16th century, many chairs began to be covered with upholstery over padding and decorated with elaborate wood carving. U.S. chairs adapted versions of English styles from the late 17th century.

Chajang Yulsa \ˈjä-ˈyäŋ-ˈyu̇l-ˈsä\ (7th century) Korean Buddhist monk who attempted to make BUDDHISM the state religion. He went to Tang-dynasty China in 636 for seven years of study and practice and returned with some of the supposed remains of the historical BUDDHA. Appointed to the highest Buddhist post in SILLA, he erected a tower to house the remains and asserted Silla's leadership over the other kingdoms of Korea. He sought China's aid in wars against them. He built the Tongdo Temple to uphold monastic austerity as a model for the nation and sought to make Buddhism a unifying force in Korean society.

chakra \ˈchä-krə\ In HINDUISM and Tantra, any of 88,000 focal points in the human body where psychic forces and bodily functions can merge and interact. In Hinduism there are seven and in Tantra four major chakras, each associated with a color, shape, sense organ, natural element, deity, and MANTRA. The most important are the heart chakra, the chakra at the base of the spine, and the chakra at the top of the head.

chakravartin *or* **cakravartin** \ˌchə-krə-ˈvär-tᵊn\ Ancient Indian conception of the world ruler. Buddhist and Jain sources distinguish three types of secular chakravartins: *cakravala cakravartin*, ruler over all four of the continents of Indian cosmography; *dvipa cakravartin*, ruler of one continent; and *pradesa cakravartin*, a ruler of part of a continent. The chakravartin was considered a secular counterpart to a buddha.

Chakri dynasty Thailand's ruling family. Phraphutthayotfa Chulalok (1737–1809) founded the dynasty and ruled as Rama I (r.1782–1809). He reorganized Siam's defenses to successfully repel numerous Burmese attacks. His descendants have reigned in an unbroken line ever since. Rama III (r.1824–51) increased trade with Europe and negotiated a treaty with the British EAST INDIA CO.; King MONGKUT (Rama IV; r.1851–68) and King CHULALONGKORN (Rama V; r.1868–1910) helped modernize the government along Western lines and thereby avoided colonial rule. King VAJIRAVUDH (Rama VI; r.1910–25) instituted social reforms and restored the nation's fiscal autonomy (lost to the West under Rama IV). BHUMIBOL ADULYADEJ (Rama IX) has reigned since 1946 as Thailand's ceremonial head of state.

Chalcedon \'kal-sə-ˌdän\, **Council of** (451) Fourth ecumenical council of the Christian Church, held in Chalcedon (modern Kadiköy, Turkey). Called by the emperor Marcian, it approved the creeds of Nicaea (325) and Constantinople (381, later known as the NICENE CREED) and rejected the MONOPHYSITE HERESY. The council disciplined clergy and declared Jerusalem and Constantinople patriarchates.

chalcedony *or* **calcedony** \kal-'se-d^{ə}n-ē\ Very fine-grained variety of the silica mineral QUARTZ. A form of CHERT, it occurs in a great variety of colors, usually bluish white, gray, yellow, or brown. Other physical properties are those of quartz. For centuries, chalcedony has been the stone most used by gem engravers, and many varieties are still cut and polished as ornamental stones. See also AGATE, CARNELIAN, ONYX.

Chalcis See KHALKÍS

chalcocite \'kal-kə-ˌsīt\ SULFIDE MINERAL, Cu_2S, that may be an important ore of copper. It belongs to a group of sulfide minerals formed at relatively low temperatures. Chalcocite alters to native copper and other copper minerals. Valuable deposits occur in Nevada and Arizona, where other components of the original rock have been dissolved away; chalcocite is also found with bornite in sulfide veins in Montana and Namibia.

Chalcocite from Bristol, Conn.

EMIL JAVORSKY

chalcopyrite \ˌkal-kə-'pī-ˌrīt\ Most common copper mineral, a copper and iron sulfide ($CuFeS_2$), and a very important copper ore. It typically occurs in ore veins deposited at medium and high temperatures, as in parts of Spain, Japan, Montana, and Missouri. Chalcopyrite is a member of a group of SULFIDE MINERALS, and it crystallizes in the tetragonal CRYSTAL system. Its atomic structure is related to that of SPHALERITE.

Chaldea \kal-'dē-ə\ Ancient region, on the EUPHRATES RIVER and the PERSIAN GULF. It was originally the southern part of BABYLONIA; the name Chaldea has been used (especially in the Bible) as equivalent to all of Babylonia after it was occupied by the Chaldeans, a Semitic people who had attacked the region from the 11th century BC. Securing the throne, they established a Chaldean (or neo-Babylonian) dynasty c. 625 BC. Under NEBUCHADNEZZAR II the empire expanded, subduing JUDAEA and capturing JERUSALEM. It fell to PERSIA in 539 BC.

Chaleur Bay \shä-'lœr\ Inlet of the Gulf of ST. LAWRENCE, southeastern Canada. It extends about 85 mi (137 km) between northern NEW BRUNSWICK and the GASPÉ PENINSULA. It receives many rivers, including the Restigouche. The bay is famous as a fishing ground, especially for salmon. It was navigated and named c. 1535 by JACQUES CARTIER.

Chalgrin \shäl-'gra^{n}\, **Jean-François-Thérèse** (1737–1811) French architect. He was trained by E.-L. BOULLÉE and won the Academy of Architecture's Grand Prix de Rome at 19. His Saint-Philippe-du-Roule, Paris (1764), was influential in reviving the BASILICA plan as a standard for European churches; it is characterized by a simplicity of design in stark contrast to the complex interiors of existing Gothic and Renaissance churches of the time. Chalgrin died before finishing his masterpiece, the ARC DE TRIOMPHE.

Chaliapin \shə-'lyä-pin\, **Feodor (Ivanovich)** (1873–1938) Russian singer. Born a peasant, he received little early musical training, but his talent led to his taking leading roles with a touring opera company in his teens. Coached by Dimitri Usatov (1847–1913), he had debuts in St. Petersburg (1894) and Moscow (1896), where he played Boris Godunov, the role he would be most associated with. These led to his triumphant 1901 La Scala debut as Mefistofele. His imposing stage presence and fine acting gave him a popularity among male singers second only to E. CARUSO.

chalk Soft, fine-grained, easily pulverized, white-to-grayish variety of LIMESTONE, composed of the shells of minute marine organisms. The purest varieties contain up to 99% calcium carbonate in the form of the mineral calcite. Extensive deposits occur in western Europe south of Sweden and in England, notably in the chalk cliffs of Dover along the English Channel. Other extensive deposits occur in the U.S. from South Dakota to Texas and eastward to Alabama. Chalk is used for making lime and portland cement and as a soil additive. Finely ground and purified chalk is known as whiting and is used as a filler, extender, or pigment in a wide variety of materials, including ceramics, putty, cosmetics, crayons, plastics, rubber, paper, paints, and linoleum. The chalk commonly used in classrooms is a manufactured substance rather than natural chalk.

Challenger One of the first four U.S. SPACE SHUTTLES. It made its first flight in 1983. At the launch for its tenth mission in January 1986, faulty O-rings in the seams of its solid rocket booster failed and the booster exploded, destroying the *Challenger* and killing its seven-member crew.

chalybite See SIDERITE

Chambal River \'chəm-bəl\ River, central India. Rising in the western Vindhya Mountains near INDORE, it flows easterly 550 mi (900 km) before emptying into the YAMUNA RIVER, of which it is the chief tributary, west of Kranpur.

chamber music Music composed for small instrumental ensembles and performed without a conductor. Traditionally intended for performance in a room or reception hall, often solely for the performers' own pleasure, chamber music is now often heard in concert halls. It began with the 16th-century instrumental consort, and long continued to be associated with aristocratic households. The duo sonata (usually for violin and CONTINUO) and TRIO SONATA appeared in early-17th-century Italy. The STRING QUARTET arose in the 1750s and remains the best-known chamber genre and ensemble. The serenade, nocturne, and DIVERTIMENTO were Classical genres for varying instrumental forces, often intended to accompany meals and other activities. Standard ensembles include the string trio (violin, viola, cello), string quintet (two violins, two violas, cello), and piano trio (piano, violin, cello). The chamber orchestra, usually with fewer than 25 musicians, is often used for 18th-century music and usually requires a conductor. See also SONATA.

chamber of commerce *or* **commercial association** Any of various voluntary organizations of business firms, public officials, professional people, and public-spirited citizens whose primary interest is in publicizing, promoting, and developing commercial and industrial opportunities in their local area, and usually also community schools, streets, housing, and public works. The International Chamber of Commerce (founded 1920) acts as the voice of the business community in the international field and runs a court of arbitration for settling commercial disputes. National chambers of commerce exist in most industrialized, free-enterprise countries. The first to use the name was founded in Paris in 1601; the first U.S. chamber of commerce was that of the state of New York, founded in 1768.

Chamberlain \'chām-bər-lən\, **(Joseph) Austen** *later* **Sir Austen** (1863–1937) British statesman. Son of JOSEPH CHAMBERLAIN and half brother of NEVILLE CHAMBERLAIN, he entered the House of Commons in 1892. He held a variety of posts, including chancellor of the exchequer (1903–5, 1919–21) and secretary of state for India (1915–17) As foreign secretary (1924–29), he helped bring about the LOCARNO PACT, intended to secure peace in Western Europe. For that accomplishment, he shared the 1925 Nobel Peace Prize with CHARLES DAWES.

Chamberlain, Charles Joseph (1863–1943) U.S. botanist. He was born near Sullivan, Ohio. His research into the structure and life cycles of primitive plants (cycads) enabled him to suggest a course of evolutionary development for the egg and embryo of seed plants (spermatophytes) and to speculate about a cycad origin for flowering plants (angiosperms). He organized

Charles Chamberlain, 1925.

BY COURTESY OF THE HARSHBERGER COLLECTION, UNIVERSITY OF PENNSYLVANIA, PHILADELPHIA, AND THE HUNT INSTITUTE, PITTSBURGH

and directed the botanical laboratories at the University of Chicago (1897–1931), where, with plants collected in Mexico, Australia, New Zealand, South Africa, and Cuba, he created the world's foremost collection of living cycads.

Chamberlain, Houston Stewart (1855–1927) British-born Germanophile writer. An admirer of RICHARD WAGNER, he wrote a biography of the composer and several books on his works (1892–95) and later married Wagner's daughter. In his *Foundations of the Nineteenth Century* (2 vols., 1899), he presented a broad but biased analysis of European culture and proclaimed the racial and cultural superiority of the so-called Aryan element in European culture. His theories, which owed much to the writings of JOSEPH ARTHUR, COMTE DE GOBINEAU, influenced German nationalist thought, particularly ADOLF HITLER's National Socialist movement.

Chamberlain \'chām-bər-lin\, **John (Angus)** (born 1927) U.S. sculptor. Born in Rochester, Ind., he studied at the Art Institute of Chicago and at Black Mountain College. In 1957 he had his first one-man exhibition in Chicago. His Abstract Expressionist sculptures are constructed of fragments of automobiles, crushed and jammed together, producing an effect of isolated, frozen movement, often painted in bright, industrial colors.

Chamberlain, Joseph (1836–1914) British politician and reformer. Early success in business enabled him to retire at 38 with a substantial fortune. He was elected to Parliament (1876–1906), where he became a leader of the left wing of the Liberal Party. In 1886 in opposition to Irish HOME RULE, he joined other dissident Liberals (Liberal Unionists) to defeat the Liberal government. He used his control of the Liberal Unionists to pressure the subsequent Conservative government to adopt a more progressive social policy. As colonial secretary (1895–1903), he advocated tax reform and a federated empire of self-governing colonies, helping pass the Commonwealth of Australia bill (1900). He resigned when his proposals for a tariff giving preference to imperial products were rebuffed by the government.

Joseph Chamberlain, detail of an oil painting by Frank Holl, 1886; in the National Portrait Gallery, London.

BY COURTESY OF THE NATIONAL PORTRAIT GALLERY, LONDON

Chamberlain, (Arthur) Neville (1869–1940) British prime minister (1937–40). Son of JOSEPH CHAMBERLAIN and half brother of AUSTEN CHAMBERLAIN, he prospered in the metal-working industry in Birmingham; as the city's lord mayor (1915–16) he organized England's first municipal bank. He served in the House of Commons 1918–40, and served in Conservative governments as minister of health and chancellor of the exchequer. As prime minister (1937–40), he sought to prevent the outbreak of a general European war over ADOLF HITLER's demand that Czechoslovakia cede the Sudetenland to Germany. In 1938 he and France's EDOUARD DALADIER granted most of Hitler's demands in the MUNICH AGREEMENT, after which he returned to England a popular hero, speaking of "peace in our time." He repudiated APPEASEMENT after Hitler seized the rest of Czechoslovakia, and when Germany attacked Poland, he declared war. He lost the support of many Conservatives after the failure of a British expedition to Norway and resigned in 1940.

Chamberlain, Wilt(on Norman) (1936–1999) U.S. basketball player, one of the greatest offensive players in basketball history. Born in Philadelphia, the 7-ft 1-in. (2-m 16-cm) Chamberlain played two years (1956–58) for the University of Kansas. "Wilt the Stilt" later played center for the Philadelphia (later Golden State) Warriors (1959–65), the Philadelphia 76ers (1965–68), and the Los Angeles Lakers (1968–73). In the 1961–62 season he became the first player to score more than 4,000 points in regular-season NBA games, including a record 100 points in a single game (1962). He led the NBA in scoring seven consecutive years (1959–65) and in rebounding 11 times. He is one of only three players (with KAREEM ABDUL-JABBAR and JULIUS ERVING) to have scored more than 30,000 points in a professional career (31,419), and ranks first in career rebounds (23,924), second in scoring average (30.1), and second in field goals (12,681).

Chamberlain's Men *or* **Lord Chamberlain's Men** English theatrical company, the most important in Elizabethan and Jacobean England. It was based at the GLOBE THEATRE 1599–1608. In 1603 it was taken under royal patronage as the King's Men. WILLIAM SHAKESPEARE was connected with it for most of his career; it also presented works by BEN JONSON, Thomas Dekker, and FRANCIS BEAUMONT and John Fletcher. It ceased to exist when the theaters were closed at the outbreak of the ENGLISH CIVIL WARS in 1642.

Chamberlen, Hugh (1630–c. 1720) British midwife. He was grandnephew of Peter Chamberlen the Elder (1560–1631), who invented the obstetrical forceps. A midwife to Catherine, queen of Charles II of England, Chamberlen used his position to exploit his use of the forceps, previously a family secret, and referred to them in the preface to his translation of a French treatise on midwifery, a standard in obstetrics for 75 years. Near the end of his life, he sold his secret to a Dutch surgeon.

Chambers, Robert and William (1802–1871, 1800–1883) Scottish publishers. Robert, who began business as a bookstall keeper in Edinburgh, wrote historical, literary, and geological works. In 1832 the brothers started *Chambers's Edinburgh Journal*, which led to the establishment of the publishing firm of W. & R. Chambers, Ltd. Their *Chambers's Encyclopaedia* (1859–68) was based on a translation of the German *Konversations-Lexikon*. Considered scholarly and reliable on historical subjects, the encyclopedia has gone through several editions, but the lack of a continuous revision system has led to the dating of much of its material.

Chambers, (David) Whittaker *orig.* **Jay Vivian Chambers** (1901–1961) U.S. journalist. Born in Philadelphia, he joined the Communist Party in 1923 and worked at various times as an editor at *New Masses, The Daily Worker,* and *Time* magazine. In August 1948, before the House Un-American Activities Committee, he named ALGER HISS as a fellow member of a 1930s Communist spy ring. Hiss denied the charges and sued Chambers for slander. In the trials that followed, Chambers produced material he claimed Hiss had given him to pass along to Soviet agents. His autobiography, *Witness,* was published in 1952.

Chambord \shäⁿ-'bȯr\, **Henri Dieudonné d'Artois, comte (Count) de** (1820–1883) French nobleman, last heir of the elder branch of the House of BOURBON and, as Henry V, pretender to the French throne from 1830. Son of the duc de BERRY, he was forced to flee France in 1830 when his grandfather, CHARLES X, abdicated and LOUIS-PHILIPPE seized the throne. In 1870, after the fall of NAPOLEON III, Chambord invited France to reunite under the Bourbons. For a time the restoration of the monarchy seemed possible, but Chambord's hostility toward the principles of the FRENCH REVOLUTION undermined his support.

chameleon Any member of a group of Old World, primarily tree-dwelling, LIZARDS (family Chamaeleontidae) characterized chiefly by their ability to change body color. Other traits include toes fused into opposite bundles of two and three, teeth attached to the jaw edge, and a long, slender, extensile tongue. About half of the 89 species are found only in Madagascar; the others live mostly in sub-Saharan Africa. A few are found elsewhere. Most are 7–10 in. (17–25 cm) long, with a body flattened from side to side. The bulged eyes move independently. Each species can undergo a particular range of color change. Insects are the main diet, but larger species also eat birds.

chamomile \'ka-mə-ˌmīl\ Any of the more than 100 species of Eurasian herbs that make up the genus *Anthemis,* in the COMPOSITE FAMILY; also, a similar plant in the genus *Chamaemelum* of the same family. Both genera have yellow or white ray flowers and yellow disk flowers. Several *Anthemis* species are cultivated as ornamentals, especially golden marguerite, or yellow cham-

Chamomile (*Anthemis tomentosa*).

ANTHONY J. HUXLEY–EB INC.

omile *(A. tinctoria)*. The strong-smelling mayweed *(A. cotula)* has been used in medicines and insecticides. Chamomile tea, used as a tonic and an antiseptic as well as in herbal remedies, is made from *C. nobile*, or *A. nobilis*.

Chamorro \chä-'mȯr-rō\, **Violeta (Barrios de)** (born 1929) President of Nicaragua (1990–96). Born into a wealthy family, she married the publisher of *La Prensa*, a newspaper that opposed the Anastasio Somoza dictatorship (see SOMOZA FAMILY). After her husband was assassinated in 1978, she took his place as publisher. When the SANDINISTAS overthrew Somoza, she served briefly on a ruling civilian junta, but her newspaper soon became critical of DANIEL ORTEGA and supportive of U.S. policies, which included extensive support for the anti-Sandinista CONTRAS. Advocating an end to military and economic conflicts with the U.S., she was elected president in 1990. Her presidency was troubled by continuing deep political divisions and the significant power still held by the Sandinistas.

Chamoun \shȧm-'ün\, **Camille (Nimer)** *or* **Camille (Nimer) Shamun** (1900–1987) President of Lebanon (1952–58). He reorganized government departments to increase efficiency and allowed the press and opposition considerable freedom. International tensions rose in 1956 when he refused to break relations with Britain and France over the SUEZ CRISIS. In 1958, when Syria and Egypt formed the short-lived United Arab Republic, he refused pleas from Lebanon's Muslims to join. Armed rebellion broke out, and Chamoun did not seek a second presidential term. He held ministerial posts during the LEBANESE CIVIL WAR (1975–91).

Champa Ancient kingdom, INDOCHINA. Occupying a region now part of central Vietnam, it was formed in the 2nd century AD during the breakup of China's HAN DYNASTY when the Han official in charge of the region established his own kingdom around present-day HUE. Coming under Indian cultural influence, it withstood over the next several centuries attacks from China, JAVA, Vietnam, and the KHMER empire. By the late 14th century, incessant wars had led to its demise.

Champagne \sham-'pān\ Historical and cultural region, northeastern France. The terrain is interrupted by low hills and by the MARNE RIVER valley. It was an important medieval French county, held by the houses of Vernandois, Blois, and NAVARRE. In the 12th and 13th century, it was the site of six great trade fairs and was a banking center for all Europe. Conflicts between the counts of Champagne and the kings of France ended with the marriage (1284) of Joan of Navarre to the future king PHILIP IV of France, and it was united to the crown in 1314. As a frontier region it has been frequently invaded; it was the site of fierce battles in World Wars I and II. The region is famous for its wines.

champagne Sparkling WINE named for the site of its origin, the Champagne region of northeastern France. Champagne is made from only three grapes: pinot and meunier (both black) and chardonnay (white). It is initially fermented in stainless-steel vats. A mixture of wine, sugar, and yeast is added, and it is then transferred to pressure tanks for a second FERMENTATION that yields carbon dioxide and effervescence. It is chilled, sweetened, bottled, and left to mature. It generally has a crisp, flinty taste that varies in degree of sweetness, depending on the type.

Champaigne \shä^{n}-'pän^{y}\, **Philippe de** (1602–1674) Flemish-French painter. Trained in Brussels, he arrived in Paris in 1621. His patrons included LOUIS XIII, MARIE DE MÉDICIS, and Cardinal RICHELIEU, and he became the outstanding French portraitist of the baroque period. He became a professor at the Royal Academy (1653) and produced many pieces for the palaces and churches of Paris. His finest work includes two portraits of Richelieu and various paintings for the Jansenist Convent of Port-Royal, especially the austere *Ex-voto: Mother Agnès and Sister Catherine* (1662), commemorating his daughter Catherine's miraculous cure through Mother Agnès's prayers.

Champlain \sham-'plān\, **Lake** Lake between Vermont and New York. Located on the states' northern boundaries and extending into Canada about 6 mi (10 km), it is about 125 mi (200 km) long and has an area of 430 sq mi (1,115 sq km). It was visited in 1609 by SAMUEL DE CHAMPLAIN. In 1776 it was the scene of the first British–American naval battle, and in 1814 of a U.S. naval victory over the British. A link in the waterway between New York City's harbor and the lower ST. LAWRENCE RIVER, it is used extensively for commercial and pleasure-boat navigation.

Champlain, Samuel de (1567–1635) French explorer. He made several expeditions to North America before founding Quebec in 1608 with 32 colonists, most of whom did not survive the first winter. He joined with the northern Indian tribes to defeat Iroquois marauders and promoted the fur trade with the Indians. He discovered Lake Champlain in 1609 and made other explorations of what are now northern New York, the Ottawa River, and the eastern Great Lakes. English privateers besieged Quebec in 1628, when England and France were at war, and he was taken prisoner. In 1632 the colony was restored to France, and in 1633 Champlain made his last voyage to Quebec, where he lived until his death.

champlevé \shäü-lə-'vā\ Decorative enameling technique. The process consists of cutting away cells or troughs in a metal plate and filling the depressions with pulverized vitreous enamel. The raised metal lines between the cut-out areas form the design outline. Champlevé was practiced in the Celtic areas of western Europe in the Roman period. It flourished in the Rhine Valley near Cologne and in Belgium in the 11th–12th century. The most notable enamelers were Nicholas of Verdun and Godefroid de Claire.

Detail of a champlevé crucifix by Godefroid de Claire, 12th century; in the British Museum.
BY COURTESY OF THE TRUSTEES OF THE BRITISH MUSEUM

Champollion \shä^{n}-pȯl-'yō^{n}\, **Jean-François** (1790–1832) French scholar who played a major role in the deciphering of Egyptian HIEROGLYPHS. Champollion was a linguistic prodigy who had immersed himself in Hebrew, Arabic, Syriac, and Coptic as well as Greek and Latin by the age of 19. After study of the ROSETTA STONE and other texts, Champollion demonstrated decisively in *Summary of the Hieroglyphic System of the Ancient Egyptians* (1825) that a phonetic value could be assigned to some hieroglyphs. He became curator of the Louvre's Egyptian collection (1826) and conducted an archaeological expedition to Egypt (1828–30). See also EGYPTIAN LANGUAGE.

Champs-Élysées \'shäü-zā-lē-'zā\ (French: "Elysian Fields") One of the world's most remarkable avenues, stretching 1.17 mi (1.88 km) from the ARC DE TRIOMPHE to the Place de la Concorde, in Paris. It is divided into two parts by the Rond-Point des Champs-Élysées. The lower part, toward the Place de la Concorde, is surrounded by gardens, museums, theaters, and restaurants. The upper part, toward the Arc de Triomphe, was traditionally a luxury commercial district. Twelve imposing avenues radiate to form a star *(étoile)* at the avenue's upper end, with the Arc de Triomphe at its center; it was called Place de l'Étoile from 1753 until 1970, when it was renamed Place Charles de Gaulle.

Chan Chan \'chän-'chän\ Ancient city, northern Peru. Located 300 mi (480 km) north of modern-day Lima, it was the capital of the Chimí, a pre-Incan civilization that flourished c. AD 1200–1400. The ruins, which cover nearly 14 sq mi (36 sq km), consist of walled citadels containing temples, cemeteries, and gardens. The successors of the MOCHE civilization, the Chimí came under INCA rule c. 1465–70.

Death mask of gold and silver alloy with copper eyes and ears, Chimú culture, c. 1000–c. 1465, centred at Chan Chan; in a private collection.
FERDINAND ANTON

chancellor In Western Europe, the title of holders of numerous offices of varying importance, ultimately political in nature. The PRIME MINISTERS of Germany and Austria are called chancellors. In Britain, the chancellor of the exchequer is the cabinet member in charge of finance. In the U.S., the title is found mostly among the chief administrators of universities.

Chancellorsville, Battle of Assault in May 1863 near Chancellorsville, Va., in the AMERICAN CIVIL WAR that ended in a Confederate victory. The Union army under JOSEPH HOOKER attempted to encircle the Confederate army under ROBERT E. LEE, but was surprised by a flanking force led by STONEWALL JACKSON and forced to withdraw. Three days of fighting resulted in a Union retreat north of the Rappahannock River. The Union army lost over 17,000 men out of a force of 130,000; the Confederate army lost over 12,000, including Jackson, out of 60,000.

chancery \'chan-sə-rē\ Court of public record and archive of state documents. The chancery system of the Roman Empire served as the model for the royal chanceries of medieval France and Germany. Medieval royal chanceries were headed by archchancellors and chancellors, who oversaw the work of scribes and notaries and sometimes served as advisers to the monarch.

Chancery, Court of See EQUITY, CHANCELLOR

chancre \'shaŋ-kər\ Primary sore or ulcer at the site of entry of a pathogen; specifically, the typical skin lesion of primary infectious SYPHILIS. In women, it is often internal and may go unnoticed. This single red papule (bump), usually occurring about three weeks after infection, and painless regional lymph-node swelling are the major signs of early-stage syphilis. Identification of *Treponema pallidum* in its fluid makes the diagnosis. The chancre heals in two to six weeks, but syphilis progresses unless treated with PENICILLIN.

Chandigarh \'chən-dē-gər\ City (pop., 1991: 511,000), and union territory (pop., 1994 est.: 725,000), joint capital of HARYANA and PUNJAB states, northern India. Located just south of the Shiwalik Hills, the site was selected to replace the former capital of LAHORE, lost to Pakistan at partition in 1947. The city was laid out in the 1950s by LE CORBUSIER in collaboration with Indian architects. Today it is a major communications junction.

Chandler, Raymond (Thornton) (1888–1959) U.S. writer of detective fiction. Born in Chicago, he worked as an oil-company executive in California before turning to writing in the Depression. Early short stories were followed by screenplays, including *Double Indemnity* (1944), *The Blue Dahlia* (1946), and *Strangers on a Train* (1951). His character Philip Marlowe, a hard-boiled private detective working in the Los Angeles underworld, appears in all seven of his novels, including *The Big Sleep* (1939; film, 1946), *Farewell, My Lovely* (1940; film *Murder, My Sweet,* 1944), and *The Long Good-Bye* (1953; film, 1973). Chandler and DASHIELL HAMMETT are regarded as the classic authors of the hard-boiled genre.

Chandrasekhar \,chən-drə-'shā-kär\, **Subrahmanyan** (1910–1995) Indian-U.S. astrophysicist. He left Cambridge University to join the staff of the University of Chicago in 1938. He determined that, following its red-giant phase, a star with a remaining mass greater than 1.4 times that of the sun (the Chandrasekhar limit) collapses and becomes a neutron star during a supernova explosion. Stellar remnants more massive than about three solar masses collapse even further to become BLACK HOLES. He shared a 1983 Nobel Prize with WILLIAM A. FOWLER.

Chanel \shȧ-'nel\, **Gabrielle** *known as* **Coco Chanel** (1883–1971) French fashion designer. Little is known of her early life. In 1913 she opened a millinery shop in Deauville, and within five years her innovative use of jersey fabric and accessories was attracting wealthy patrons. Her nonconformist designs, stressing simplicity and comfort, revolutionized the fashion industry for the next 30 years. She popularized turtleneck sweaters, the "little black dress," and the much-copied "Chanel suit." Chanel industries included a Parisian fashion house, a textile business, perfume laboratories, and a workshop for costume jewelry. The financial basis of her empire was Chanel No. 5 perfume, introduced in 1922 and still popular.

Lon Chaney.
BROWN BROTHERS

Chaney, Lon *orig.* **Alonso** (1883–1930) U.S. film actor. Born in Colorado Springs, Col., to deaf-mute parents, he learned pantomime and became an actor at 17. He moved to Hollywood in 1912 and played supporting roles until *The Miracle Man* (1919) made him a star. Known as "the man of a thousand faces," he was famous for his ability to transform himself through makeup. He often played grotesque or dual characters in films directed by TOD BROWNING, including *The Unholy Three* (1925). His other silent films include *The Hunchback of Notre Dame* (1923), *The Phantom of the Opera* (1925), and *London after Midnight* (1927). His son Lon Chaney, Jr. (1905–1973), appeared in numerous horror films in such repeated roles as the Wolf Man and the Mummy, and notably in *Of Mice and Men* (1939).

Chang Chih-tung See ZHANG ZHIDONG

Chang Chü-cheng See ZHANG JUZHENG

Chang Heng See ZHANG HENG

Chang Jiang See YANGTZE RIVER

Chang Tao-Ling See ZHANG DAOLING

Chang Tsai See ZHANG ZAI

Chang Tso-lin See ZHANG ZUOLIN

Changan *or* **Ch'ang-an** \'chäŋ-'än\ Ancient capital of China during the HAN, SUI, and TANG dynasties, near present-day Xi'an. From the mid-4th century it was a center of Buddhist studies. WENDI, first emperor of the Sui, expanded Changan: its outer walls were 6 mi (9.7 km) by 5 mi (8.2 km), with 14 avenues running north-south and 11 running east-west. The center of the northern boundary was the site of the imperial palace; in front of it was an administrative compound 3 mi (4.5 km) square. Until the proscription of foreign religions in the 840s, Changan contained numerous Buddhist temples, along with Nestorian, Manichaean, and Zoroastrian churches and many Taoist monasteries. It was reduced to ruins in the 880s by the rebel Huang Zhao, and future dynasties established their capitals elsewhere.

Changchun See QIU CHUJI

Changchun *or* **Ch'ang-ch'un** \'chäŋ-'chu̇n\ City (pop., 1990: 1,679,000), capital of JILIN province, northeastern China. It was a small village until the end of the 18th century, when farmers from SHANDONG began to settle near the SONGHUA RIVER. It gained in importance after the completion of the Chinese Eastern Railway. It came under Japanese control following the SINO-JAPANESE WAR of 1894–95. At the time of the Japanese seizure of Manchuria in 1931, the capital of the Japanese puppet state of MANCHUGUO was moved from Mukden (SHENYANG) to Changchun. Following World War II, the city suffered severely in the fighting between Communist and Nationalist forces. Having experienced phenomenal growth under Chinese communist rule, it is now a center for industrial expansion, as well as the cultural and educational center of the province.

change ringing Custom of ringing tower or hand bells in a succession of different orders, dating to the 10th century. Control of bell ringing was much enhanced with the invention of the bell wheel in the 14th century; further improvements in bearings and fittings allowed the bells to swing at the same speed, and led to recognizably modern change ringing by the 17th century. A "ring" (set) of six bells can be tolled in 720 different "changes" (orders); eight bells allow 40,320 different changes, and 10 bells allow over 3 million. In practice, only a selection of the possible changes is rung, derived by a "method" (a shuffling algorithm), usually involving switching pairs of bells in a certain order (e.g., 123456 becomes 214365, which can then become 241635, etc.). "Rounds"—all the bells in order from highest to lowest—is rung before and after a method is completed.

Changsha *or* **Ch'ang-sha** \'chäŋ-'shä\ City (pop., 1990: 1,113,000), capital of HUNAN province, China. Located in southeastern central China, it was (according to tradition) formerly enclosed by a wall built in 202 BC. In AD 750–1100 Changsha was an important commercial city, and its population increased greatly. Under the QING DYNASTY, from 1664, it was the capital of Hunan province, and a major rice market. It was besieged during the TAIPING REBELLION but never fell. It was the site of MAO ZEDONG's conversion to Communism. It was the scene of major battles in the SINO-JAPANESE WAR, and briefly occupied by the Japanese. Rebuilt since 1949, the city is now a major port and a commercial and industrial center.

Channel, The See ENGLISH CHANNEL

Channel Islands Group of islands (pop., 1990 est.: 144,000), United Kingdom. Located in the ENGLISH CHANNEL, 10–30 mi (16–48 km) off the western coast of France, the islands cover an area of 75 sq mi (194 sq km). Made up of the islands of Jersey, Guernsey, Alderney, Sark, and several islets, they are domestically independent of the British government. Structures, including MENHIRS, are evidence of prehistoric occupation. A part of NORMANDY in the 10th century AD, the islands came under the British at the time of the NORMAN CONQUEST in 1066. The islets of Ecrehous and Les Minquiers were disputed between England and France until 1953, when the International Court of Justice confirmed British sovereignty. The dispute revived in the late 20th century, because sovereignty determines the rights to the continental shelf's economic development (especially petroleum). It was the only British territory occupied by Germany in World War II. The islands are famous for their cattle breeds, including the JERSEY and GUERNSEY.

Channel Islands *or* **Santa Barbara Islands** Chain of islands, southern California. Extending 150 mi (240 km) along and 25–90 mi (40–145 km) off the coast, it is divided into the Santa Barbara group (San Miguel, Santa Rosa, Santa Cruz, and Anacapa) and the Santa Catalina group (Santa Barbara, San Nicolas, Santa Catalina, and San Clemente). The islands range in size from Santa Cruz (98 sq mi, or 254 sq km) to the small Anacapa islets. Rugged and mountainous, they are frequented by colonies of sea lions, seals, and birds, and are noted for their distinctive plant life (about 830 varieties). The larger islands support sheep and cattle ranches, and Santa Catalina is a noted resort. Channel Islands National Park (established as a national monument in 1938) embraces Anacapa, San Miguel, Santa Barbara, Santa Cruz, and Santa Rosa.

Channel Tunnel *or* **Eurotunnel** Rail tunnel that runs beneath the English Channel between Folkestone, England, and Sangatte (near Calais), France. A rail tunnel was chosen over proposals for a very long suspension bridge, a bridge-and-tunnel link, and a combined rail-and-road link. The 31-mi (50-km) tunnel, which opened in 1994, consists of three separate tunnels, two for rail traffic and a central tunnel for services and security. Trains, which carry motor vehicles as well as passengers, can travel through the tunnel at speeds as high as 100 mph (160 kph).

Channing, William Ellery (1780–1842) U.S. Unitarian clergyman. Born in Newport, R.I., he studied theology at Harvard University and became a successful preacher. From 1803 until his death he was pastor of Boston's Federal Street Church. He began his career as a Congregationalist but gradually adopted liberal and rationalist views that came to be labeled Unitarian. In 1820 he established a conference of liberal Congregationalist clergy, later reorganized as the American Unitarian Association Known as the "apostle of UNITARIANISM," he also became a leading figure in New England TRANSCENDENTALISM, and his lectures and essays on slavery, war, and poverty made him one of the most influential clergymen of his day.

chanson \shä^n-'sō^n\ French art song. The unaccompanied chanson for a single voice part, composed by the TROUBADOURS and later the TROUVÈRES, first appeared in the 12th century. Accompanied chansons, with parts for one or more instruments, were written in the 14th–15th century by G. DE MACHAUT and others in the strict FORMES FIXES. Around 1500 chansons for several voices began to be written by JOSQUIN DES PREZ and his contemporaries. In recent centuries the term has often been used for any piano-accompanied French art song.

chanson de geste \shä^n-'sō^n-də-'zhest\ Any of several Old French epic poems that form the core of the CHARLEMAGNE legends. More than 80 chansons de geste have survived in 12th–15th-century manuscripts. Dealing chiefly with events of the 8th–9th century, they contain a core of historical truth overlain with legend. Most are anonymous. The *CHANSON DE ROLAND* was the formative influence on later chansons de geste, which in turn influenced literature throughout Europe.

Chanson de Roland \shä^n-'sō^n-də-rȯ-'lä^n\ *English* **Song of Roland** Old French epic poem written c. 1100, the masterpiece and probably the earliest of the CHANSON DE GESTE form. Its probable author was a Norman, Turold (Turoldus), whose name is introduced in its last line. It deals with the Battle of RONCESVALLES (778), a skirmish against the Basques that the poem portrays as a heroic battle against the Saracens. Direct and sober in style, it highlights a clash between the recklessly courageous Roland and his prudent friend Oliver, which is also a conflict between divergent conceptions of feudal loyalty.

chant See BYZANTINE CHANT, GREGORIAN CHANT

chanterelle \ˌshan-tə-'rel\ Highly prized, fragrant edible MUSHROOM (*Cantharellus cibarius,* order Polyporales), rich yellow in color, found in woods in summer and autumn. Its similarity to the poisonous jack-o-lantern (*Clitocybe illudens,* order Agaricales), an orange-yellow FUNGUS of woods and stumps that glows in the dark, emphasizes the need for careful identification by the mushroom gatherer.

Chantilly lace \shan-'ti-lē\ Lace made at Chantilly, north of Paris, from the 17th century. The silk laces that made the town famous date from the 18th century. Black, white, and blond lace (derived from natural silk) were made in the 19th century, and by 1840 machine-made imitations were available. The designs are characterized by naturalistic flowers and ribbons on a spotted background.

Chantilly lace from France, c. 1870; in the Institut Royal du Patrimoine Artistique, Brussels.

BY COURTESY OF THE INSTITUT ROYAL DU PATRIMOINE ARTISTIQUE, BRUSSELS; PHOTOGRAPH, © A.C.L., BRUSSELS

Chantilly porcelain Either of two types of soft-paste porcelain produced from c. 1725 to c. 1800 at Chantilly, France. In the first type, made until c. 1750, an opaque, milk-white tin glaze was applied to a yellowish ground; the designs were simplified Japanese patterns. In the second type (c. 1750–1800), a traditional transparent lead glaze was applied over a colored ground; the designs were influenced by MEISSEN and SÈVRES porcelain. Production consisted primarily of domestic ware (plates, basins, jugs) with painted decoration in a limited palette. The motifs were often small flower bouquets, known as Chantilly sprigs, or scrolls and plaits.

Chantilly porcelain plate decorated with dragons, c. 1725; in the Victoria and Albert Museum, London.

BY COURTESY OF THE VICTORIA AND ALBERT MUSEUM, LONDON

Chao Phraya River \chau̇-'prī-ə\ *or* **Me Nam River** \mā-'näm\ River, Thailand. Flowing south from the highlands on the country's northern border to the head of the Gulf of Thailand near BANGKOK, it is 227 mi (365 km) long and is Thailand's principal river. It is important for the transport of the country's exports. It also forms a highly productive agricultural valley. The name strictly applies only to the river's lower course, which begins at the confluence of the Nan and Ping rivers and is 160 mi (257 km) long.

Chaos \'kā-ˌäs\ In Greek cosmology, either the primeval emptiness before things came into being or the abyss of Tartarus, the underworld. In HESIOD's *Theogony*, there was first Chaos, then GAEA and EROS. The offspring of Chaos were Erebus (Darkness) and Nyx (Night). OVID gave Chaos its modern meaning: the original formless and disordered mass from which the ordered universe is created. The early church fathers applied this interpretation to the creation story in GENESIS.

chaos theory \'kā-ˌäs\ Mathematical theory that describes CHAOTIC BEHAVIOR in a complex system. Applications include the study of TURBULENT FLOW in fluids, irregularities in biological systems, population dynamics, chemical reactions, PLASMA physics, meteorology, the motions of groups and clusters of stars, transportation dynamics, and many other fields.

chaotic behavior Behavior in a complex system that appears irregular or unpredictable, but is actually determinate. The apparently random or unpredictable behavior in systems governed by complicated (nonlinear) deterministic laws is the result of high sensitivity to initial conditions.

For example, EDWARD LORENZ discovered that a simple model of heat CONVECTION exhibits chaotic behavior. In the now-classic example of such sensitivity to initial conditions, he suggested that the mere flapping of a butterfly's wings could eventually result in large-scale changes in the weather (the "butterfly effect").

Chapala \chä-'pä-lä\, **Lake** Lake, JALISCO state, Mexico. Mexico's largest lake, it is 50 mi (81 km) long and has an area of 651 sq mi (1,686 sq km). A popular resort area, it is traversed by the Río Santiago, which enters the lake as the Río Lerma.

chaparral \ˌsha-pə-'ral\ Vegetation composed of broad-leaved evergreen shrubs, bushes, and small trees, often forming dense thickets. Chaparral is found in regions with a Mediterranean climate, characterized by hot, dry summers and mild, wet winters. The name is applied mainly to the coastal and inland mountain vegetation of southwestern North America. Chaparral vegetation becomes extremely dry by late summer. The fires that commonly occur during this period are necessary for the germination of many shrub seeds, and they clear away dense ground cover, thus maintaining the shrubby growth form of the vegetation by preventing the spread of trees. New chaparral growth provides good grazing for domestic livestock, and chaparral vegetation also is valuable for watershed protection in areas with steep, easily eroded slopes.

chaparral cock See ROADRUNNER

Chaplin, Charlie *orig.* **Charles Spencer** *later* **Sir Charles** (1889–1977) British-U.S. actor and director. The son of poverty-stricken music-hall entertainers, he became a vaudeville performer at 8. On tour in New York (1913), he caught the eye of MACK SENNETT, who signed him to a film contract. While making his second film, *Kid Auto Races at Venice* (1914), Chaplin developed the costume—baggy pants, derby hat, oversized shoes, and cane—that was to become the hallmark of his famous "little tramp" character. He was soon directing his own films, and he became an instant star in *The Tramp* (1915). After cofounding UNITED ARTISTS in 1919, he produced, directed, and starred in such classics as *The Gold Rush* (1925), *City Lights* (1931), *Modern Times* (1936), *The Great Dictator* (1940), *Monsieur Verdoux* (1947), and *Limelight* (1952). Harassed for his leftist political views, he moved to Switzerland in 1952. In 1972 he returned to accept a special Academy Award.

Chapman, Frank M(ichler) (1864–1945) U.S. ornithologist. Born in Englewood, N.J., the self-taught Chapman worked from 1888 at the American Museum of Natural History, principally as curator of ornithology (1908–42). He founded and edited (1899–1935) the magazine *Bird-Lore.* Among his many important works are *Handbook of Birds of Eastern North America* (1895) and several on South American birds.

Chapman, Maria Weston *orig.* **Maria Weston** (1806–1885) U.S. abolitionist. Born in Weymouth, Mass., in 1830 she married Henry Chapman, a Boston merchant. In 1832 she helped found the Boston Female Anti-Slavery Society. She soon became chief assistant to WILLIAM LLOYD GARRISON in the Massachusetts Anti-Slavery Society. In 1839 she published a pamphlet arguing that the divisions among abolitionists stemmed from their disagreements over women's rights.

Chapultepec \chä-'pül-tā-ˌpek\ Rocky hill, southwest of MEXICO CITY, Mexico. The AZTECS fortified it and built a religious center and a residence for their rulers in the early 14th century. The Spanish CONQUISTADORS built a chapel in 1554, and in the 1780s the Spanish viceroys constructed a summer palace there, which became the home of the National Military Academy in 1841. The hill was captured by a U.S. assault (1847) in the MEXICAN WAR. In the 1860s Mexico's emperor MAXIMILIAN rebuilt the castle; it remained the official residence of Mexican presidents until 1940, when it was converted into a museum.

char Any of several freshwater food and game fishes (genus *Salvelinus*) of the SALMON family, distinguished from the similar TROUT by light, rather than black, spots; by a boat-shaped, rather than flat, vomer (bone) on the roof of the mouth; and by having teeth on the front of the vomer rather than on the shaft. Char often have smaller scales than their relatives. The Arctic char, of North America and Europe, inhabits the Arctic and adjacent oceans and enters rivers and lakes to breed. It may weigh 15 lbs (7 kg) or more. The BROOK TROUT, Dolly Varden trout, and LAKE TROUT are native North American char.

charcoal Impure form of CARBON, obtained as a residue when material containing carbon is partially burned or heated with limited access to air. COKE, carbon black, and soot are forms of charcoal; other forms are named for their source material, such as wood, blood, or bone. Largely replaced by coke in blast furnaces and by NATURAL GAS as a raw material, charcoal is still used to make black GUNPOWDER and in case-hardening metals. Activated charcoal is a finely powdered or highly porous form whose surface area is hundreds or thousands of square meters per gram. It has many uses as an adsorbent (see ADSORPTION), including for poison treatment, and as a catalyst or catalyst carrier.

Charcot \shär-'kō\, **Jean-Martin** (1825–1893) French medical teacher and clinician. With Guillaume Duchenne (1806–1875) he is considered the founder of modern neurology. In 1882 he opened Europe's greatest neurological clinic of the day. An extraordinary teacher, he was known for his work with hysteria and hypnosis, which influenced many students, including SIGMUND FREUD. He described the symptoms of locomotor ataxia and the disintegration of ligaments and joint surfaces it causes (Charcot's disease or Charcot's joint), pioneered the linking of brain sites with specific functions, and discovered miliary aneurysms in the brain.

chard *or* **Swiss chard** Edible leaf BEET (*Beta vulgaris* 'cicla'), a variety of beet in which the tender leaves and leafstalks have become greatly developed. They are a good source of vitamins A, B, and C. Chard is popular as a home-garden potherb because it is easy to grow, productive, and tolerant of moderate heat. Highly perishable, it is difficult to ship to distant markets.

Chard (*Beta vulgaris* variety *cicla*).
W.H. HODGE

chardin \shär-'daⁿ\, **Jean-Baptiste-Siméon** (1699–1779) French painter. He first received acclaim in 1728, when he became a member of the Royal Academy of Painting in Paris. He became a successful painter of small canvases depicting domestic scenes and objects from everyday middle-class life, somewhat reminiscent of the works of JOHANNES VERMEER. In his later years he produced stunning pastel portraits. He was the greatest still-life painter of the 18th century, well known in his lifetime through engravings of his work. Many 20th-century artists have been inspired by the abstract qualities of his compositions.

Charente River \shä-'räüt\ River, western France. Rising in the department of Haute-Vienne, it flows generally westward 226 mi (360 km) to the Bay of BISCAY. It receives its chief tributary, the Boutonne, from the plain of Poitou to the north. It is navigable for small craft as far as ANGOULÊME.

charge-coupled device See CCD

Chargoggagoggmanchauggauggagoggchaubunagungamaugg \chär-ˌgò-gə-ˌgòg-man-ˌchò-ˌgò-gə-ˌgòg-chò-ˌbə-nə-'gəŋ-gə-ˌmòg\, **Lake** *or* **Lake Webster** Lake, central Massachusetts. Located in southern Worcester county, near the town of Webster, the lake's Indian name means "You fish on your side; I fish on my side; nobody fishes in the middle."

Chari River *or* **Shari River** \'shä-rē\ River, northern central Africa. It flows about 590 mi (949 km) from the Central African Republic northwest into Lake CHAD; it has many tributaries in the Central African Republic. N'DJAMENA is at the head of the river's delta.

chariot Open two- or four-wheeled vehicle of ancient origin. The chariot probably originated in Mesopotamia about 3000 BC; early monuments show heavy vehicles with solid wheels. Chariots were probably first used in royal funeral processions. Two-wheeled horse-drawn versions evolved for speed in battle c. 2000 BC, appearing first in Greece and later in Egypt and the eastern Mediterranean. Chariot racing was popular in Greece at the Olympic Games; in Rome it was the main event in the circus games, where two to four horses drew each lightweight chariot in a competition of four or six vehicles; and in Byzantium such races became the dominant events of civic life.

charismatic movement See PENTECOSTALISM

Charlemagne \'shär-lə-ˌmān\ *or* **Carolus Magnus ("Charles the Great")** (742?–814) King of the Franks (768–814) and Holy Roman Emperor (800–14). The elder son of the Frankish king PEPIN III the Short, he ruled the Frankish kingdom jointly with his brother Carloman until the latter's death in 771. He then became sole king of the Franks, and began a series of campaigns to conquer and Christianize neighboring kingdoms, defeating and becoming king of the Lombards in northern Italy (774). His expedition against the Moors in Spain failed (778), but he successfully annexed Bavaria (788). Charlemagne fought against the Saxons for many years, finally defeating and Christianizing them in 804. He subdued the AVARS of the Danube and gained control of many of the Slav states. With the exception of the British Isles, southern Italy, and part of Spain, he united in one vast state almost all the Christian lands of Western Europe. His coronation as emperor at Rome on Christmas Day, 800, after restoring Leo III to the papacy, marks the inception of the HOLY ROMAN EMPIRE. He established his capital at Aachen (Aix-la-Chapelle), where he built a magnificent palace and invited many scholars and poets; he codified the laws and promoted a cultural revival known as the Carolingian renaissance. See also CAROLINGIAN DYNASTY.

Charleroi \shär-lə-'rwä\ City (pop., 1992 est.: 207,000), southwestern Belgium. Following the Treaty of the Pyrenees (1659), in which Spain was ceded French territory, Spain in 1666 decreed that a new fortress, named for Charles II of Spain, be built there, at the site of a medieval village. It was strategically important in the 17th–19th century and held variously by France, Spain, Austria, and Holland. Though the fortress was dismantled in the late 19th century, the area retained its strategic importance; it was the scene of one of the first battles of World War I.

Charles (Philip Arthur George), Prince of Wales (born 1948) Heir apparent to the British throne, son of ELIZABETH II and PHILIP, DUKE OF EDINBURGH. In 1971 he studied at Cambridge Univ., becoming the first heir to the throne to obtain a university degree, and later attended the Royal Air Force College and the Royal Naval College, Dartmouth. He took a tour of duty with the Royal Navy (1971–76). In 1981 he married Lady Diana Spencer (see DIANA, PRINCESS OF WALES), and they had two sons. Their marriage grew strained amid intense scrutiny from the press and rumors of infidelity; they divorced in 1996. He subsequently began keeping company publicly with Camilla Parker Bowles (born 1947). He has been known for his advocacy of excellence in architecture and other causes.

Charles, Ray *orig.* **Ray Charles Robinson** (born 1930) U.S. pianist, singer, and songwriter. He was born in Georgia, but his family soon moved to Greenville, Fla., where he began his career at age 5 in a neighborhood café. By 7 he had completely lost his sight. He learned to write scores in braille. Orphaned at 15, he left school to play professionally. He recorded "Mess Around" and "It Should've Been Me" in 1952–53, and his arrangement for Guitar Slim's "The Things That I Used to Do" became a million-seller. Combining BLUES and GOSPEL-MUSIC influences, Charles later had hits with "What'd I Say," "Georgia on My Mind," and "Hit the Road, Jack." His *Modern Sounds in Country and Western Music* (1962), marking unusual territory for a black performer, sold over a million copies. He has received 10 Grammy Awards.

Charles I *German* **Karl Franz Josef** (1887–1922) Emperor of Austria (1916–18) and king of Hungary (as Charles IV), last ruler of the Austro-Hungarian monarchy. He became heir presumptive to the Habsburg throne on the assassination of his uncle, FRANCIS FERDINAND. After he succeeded FRANCIS JOSEPH in 1916, he made several abortive attempts to take Austria-Hungary out of World War I. He renounced participation in affairs of state in 1918 and was deposed in 1919. After two failed attempts to regain his Hungarian throne in 1921, he was sent into exile in Madeira, where he died.

Charles I (1600–1649) King of Great Britain and Ireland (1625–49). Son of JAMES I, he acquired from his father a belief in the divine right of kings, and his earliest surviving letters reveal a distrust of the House of Commons. He became king in 1625 and soon after married HENRIETTA MARIA. He came into conflict with his first Parliament because of religious issues, his war against Spain, and the general distrust of his adviser the 1st duke of BUCKINGHAM. After dissolving several successive Parliaments, Charles ruled his kingdom for 11 years without calling a Parliament. Among the measures he took to be independent of parliamentary grants was the levying of SHIP MONEY. In 1639 he went to war against Scotland, and the need to raise money prompted him to summon what came to be known as the Short Parliament and the LONG PARLIAMENT. Eventually his authoritarian rule and quarrels with Parliament provoked the ENGLISH CIVIL WARS. After his forces were defeated in the second of these wars, the army demanded that he stand trial for treason as "the grand author of our troubles." In 1649 he was convicted and executed, and OLIVER CROMWELL proclaimed the Commonwealth.

Charles I *Hungarian* **Karoly** *known as* **Charles Robert of Anjou** \'an-jü\ (1288–1342) King of Hungary (1301, 1308–42). He claimed the Hungarian throne with papal approval and was crowned in 1301, but his claim was disputed, and he was not recognized as king until 1308. A courtly and pious ruler, Charles restored Hungary to the status of a great power. An alliance with Poland enabled him to defeat the Holy Roman Emperor and the Austrians. He failed to unite Hungary and Naples but negotiated a pact providing that his eldest son would become king of Poland.

Charles I *known as* **Charles of Anjou** \'an-jü\ (1226–1285) King of Naples and Sicily (1266–85), the first of the ANGEVIN DYNASTY. The younger brother of Louis IX of France, Charles allied with the papacy and conquered Naples and Sicily in the 1260s. He created a great but short-lived Mediterranean empire, expanding into the Balkans and becoming heir to the kingdom of Jerusalem (1277). The Sicilians rebelled and drove out the Angevins in 1284; Charles died while preparing a counteroffensive.

Charles II (1630–1685) King of Great Britain and Ireland (1660–85). Son of CHARLES I and HENRIETTA MARIA, he supported his father in the ENGLISH CIVIL WARS. After his father's execution, he invaded England in 1651 but was defeated at Worcester. He then spent years in exile until OLIVER CROMWELL died and conditions favored a return to the monarchy. His Declaration of BREDA paved the way for him to be proclaimed king in May 1660 (see RESTORATION). He became known as "the Merry Monarch" for his lifting of Puritan restrictions on entertainment and his own love of pleasure; his best-known mistress was the actress NELL GWYN. Important events of his reign included the controversial Treaty of DOVER and two wars with the Dutch (see ANGLO-DUTCH WARS). By the 1670s the miscarriages of his queen, CATHERINE OF BRAGANZA, had reduced hopes that he would have a legitimate heir (though he left at least 14 illegitimate offspring). He almost lost control of his government when hysteria arose over the so-called POPISH PLOT to replace him with his Roman Catholic brother James (the future JAMES II). Charles kept his nerve, reestablished his political control, and eventually enjoyed a resurgence in loyalty. His political adaptability and acumen enabled him to steer his country through the struggle between Anglicans, Catholics, and dissenters that marked his reign.

Charles II *known as* **Charles of Anjou** \'an-jü\ *or* **Charles the Lame** (1254?–1309) King of Naples and ruler of several other European territories. He guarded Naples while his father, CHARLES I, launched a campaign to regain Sicily from the Aragonese. He was captured and imprisoned (1284–88); on being freed he promised to give up his claim to Sicily, but the pope released him from the vow, and he fought unsuccessfully for Sicily until 1302. He built alliances through the marriages of his children and extended his control over Piedmont, Provence, Hungary, Athens, and Albania.

Charles II *Spanish* **Carlos** (1661–1700) King of Spain (1665–1700), the last monarch of the Spanish HABSBURG DYNASTY. Son of PHILIP IV and Maria Anna of Austria, he was slow-witted and became known as Charles the Mad. His reign opened with a 10-year regency under the queen mother. The first phase of his personal government was concerned with resistance to the French imperialism of LOUIS XIV, and the second was dominated by the succession problem, for it was clear that he would father no children. His death led to the War of the SPANISH SUCCESSION.

Charles II *known as* **Charles the Bad** (1332–1387) King of Navarre (1349–87). He acquired Normandy from JOHN II of France by threatening an English alliance. Arrested for his treachery in 1356, he escaped a year later and regained Normandy. He pursued shifting alliances in Spain in an effort to expand Navarrese power. CHARLES V voided his claims in France, and the discovery of his plot to poison the French king cost him all of Normandy except Cherbourg.

Charles II *known as* **Charles the Bald** (823–877) King of France (843–77) and Holy Roman emperor (875–77). The son of the emperor Louis I, he fought his half brothers in a series of civil wars (829–43) until the Treaty of Verdun settled the terms of succession. Charles was granted the kingdom of the West Franks, which he ruled despite the wavering loyalties of his vassals and the attacks of Norsemen, Bretons, and Germans. In 864 he won control of Aquitaine, and in 870 he gained western Lorraine. He was crowned emperor in 875 but died two years later in the midst of invasion and internal revolt.

Charles III *known as* **Charles the Simple** (879–929) King of France (893–922). In 911 he ceded territory by treaty, in the area later known as Normandy, to the Vikings, to end their raids; their descendants became the Normans. The magnates of Lorraine (Lotharingia) accepted Charles's authority on the death of their last Carolingian king. His preoccupation with Lotharingian affairs alienated the French nobles, and in 922 they elected Robert I king in his stead.

Charles III *Spanish* **Carlos** (1716–1788) King of Spain (1759–88). Son of Philip V and Isabella of Parma, he was duke of Parma (1732–34) and king of Naples (as Charles VII, 1734–59) before becoming king of Spain. He was convinced of his mission to reform Spain and make it once more a first-rate power, but his foreign policy was not successful; Spain's losses in the Seven Years' War revealed naval and military weakness. He was more successful in strengthening his own empire; during his reign Spain undertook commercial reforms, made territorial adjustments in the interest of defense, and introduced a modern administrative system. One of the enlightened despots of the 18th century, he helped lead Spain to a brief cultural and economic revival.

Charles III *known as* **Charles the Fat** (839–888) Frankish king and Holy Roman emperor (881–87). The great-grandson of Charlemagne, he inherited the kingdoms of Swabia (876) and Italy (879). Charles was crowned emperor by the pope in 881. He gained control of the East and West Frankish kingdoms on the deaths of their rulers, and by 885 he had reunited all of Charlemagne's empire except Provence. Chronically ill, he failed to attack the Saracens and used tribute to buy off Viking invaders. His nephew Arnulf led an uprising against him in 887, and his fall marked the final disintegration of the empire of Charlemagne.

Charles IV *known as* **Charles the Fair** (1294–1328) King of France and of Navarre (as Charles I) 1322–28. The last of the direct line of the Capetian dynasty, he took the throne on the death of his brother Philip V. His intrigues aimed at gaining the German throne and annexing Flanders were unsuccessful. He renewed war with England by invading Aquitaine and won a generous settlement in the peace of 1327.

Charles IV *orig.* **Wenceslas** *known as* **Charles of Luxembourg** (1316–1378) King of the Germans and of Bohemia (1346–78) and Holy Roman emperor (1355–78). Charles was elected German king in place of Louis IV in 1346. That year his father died in a war, and Charles became king of Bohemia. He invaded Italy and won the crown of Lombardy as well as the imperial crown at Rome. Charles enlarged his power through skillful diplomacy and made Prague the political and cultural center of the empire. He issued the Golden Bull of 1356 and won the right of succession to the German throne for his son Wenceslas.

Charles IV *Spanish* **Carlos** (1748–1819) King of Spain (1788–1808) during the turbulent period of the French Revolution. Son of Charles III, he lacked leadership qualities and entrusted the government to Manuel de Godoy. After a French invasion in 1794, Spain was reduced to the status of a French satellite. When Napoleon again occupied northern Spain in 1807, Charles was forced to abdicate (1808) and go into exile.

Charles V *known as* **Charles the Wise** (1338–1380) King of France (1364–80). He raised money to ransom his father, John II, from the English, under the terms of the Treaty of Brétigny. Crowned king on his father's death in 1364, Charles helped the country recover its losses in the first phase of the Hundred Years' War. When war with England broke out again (1369), he won a series of victories for the French that nullified the damaging treaties of 1360. The plots of his enemy Charles II (of Navarre) prompted him to seize most of the king's French lands. His support of Pope Clement VII helped cause the Western Schism.

Charles V *German* **Karl** (1500–1558) Holy Roman emperor (1519–56) and king of Spain (as Charles I, 1516–56). Son of Philip I of Castile and grandson of Ferdinand V and Isabella I and of Emperor Maximilian I, he succeeded to his grandfathers' kingdoms on their deaths in 1516 and 1519, respectively. Important events of his reign include the Diet of Worms and the beginning of the Reformation; his defeat of Francis I, which assured Spanish supremacy in Italy (see Italian Wars); wars against Turkey under Süleyman I the Magnificent; the formation of the Schmalkaldic League; the Council of Trent; and the Peace of Augsburg. He struggled to hold his vast Spanish and Habsburg empire together against the growing forces of Protestantism, Turkish and French pressure, and even hostility from Pope Adrian VI. In 1555–56 Charles abdicated his claims to the Netherlands and Spain in favor of his son Philip II and the title of emperor to his brother Ferdinand I, and in 1557 he retired to a monastery in Spain.

Charles VI *known as* **Charles the Well-Beloved** *or* **Charles the Mad** (1368–1422) King of France (1380–1422). Crowned at age 11, he allowed his uncles and advisers to rule France until 1388. He suffered fits of madness from 1392, and royal power waned as the dukes of Burgundy and Orléans grew stronger. The English invasion and victory at the Battle of Agincourt (1415) obliged Charles to sign the Treaty of Troyes (1420), which provided for the marriage of his daughter Catherine of Valois to Henry V of England, who was declared regent of France and heir to the French throne.

Charles VI *German* **Karl** (1685–1740) Holy Roman emperor (1711–40) and king of Hungary (as Charles III). Son of Emperor Leopold I, he tried unsuccessfully to claim the Spanish throne (as the pretender Charles III), which caused the War of the Spanish Succession. He conducted a successful war against the Ottoman empire (1716–18) but lost the War of the Polish Succession (1733–38), and a new conflict with Turkey (1736–39) resulted in the loss of most of the territories gained in 1718. He promulgated the Pragmatic Sanction in an attempt to ensure that his daughter Maria Theresa would succeed him, which led to the War of the Austrian Succession.

Charles VII *known as* **Charles the Well-Served** (1403–1461) King of France (1422-61). Despite the treaty signed by his father, Charles VI, which excluded his succession, Charles assumed the title of king on his father's death. In 1429, with the aid of Joan of Arc, he raised the siege of Orléans. He drove the English from France (1436) and gradually recovered French lands, ending the Hundred Years' War. His financial and military reforms increased the power of the monarchy.

Charles VIII (1470–1498) King of France (1483–98). He abandoned claims to parts of present-day France and Spain, and consolidated French ownership of Brittany, in preparation for his grand enterprise, an expedition to Italy to assert his inherited right to the kingdom of Naples. This inaugurated wars with Italy that lasted more than 50 years and gained little in return for vast outlays. Charles was crowned in Naples, but his opponents rallied; he escaped with difficulty and lost his conquests. He died while preparing another expedition.

Charles IX (1550–1574) King of France (1560–74). Son of Catherine de Médicis, he became king on the death of his brother Francis II, under his mother's regency. Though he was proclaimed of age in 1563, he remained under his mother's domination. His reign was marked by conflicts between Catholics and Huguenots, and he was remembered for authorizing the Saint Bartholomew's Day Massacre (1572) at his mother's instigation, an event that apparently haunted him the rest of his life. He died of tuberculosis at 23.

Charles IX *Swedish* **Karl** (1550–1611) King of Sweden (1604–11). Third son of Gustav I Vasa, he helped lead a rebellion against the rule of his half brother Erik XIV that placed his other brother on the throne as John III. After the accession (1592) of his devoutly Catholic nephew, Sigismund III, Charles called the Convention of Uppsala, which demanded that Lutheranism be retained as the national religion. He opposed Sigismund in a civil war, and after the latter was deposed Charles became the virtual ruler of Sweden (1599–1604). Declared king in 1604, he pursued an aggressive foreign policy that led to war with Poland (1605) and Denmark (the Kalmar War, 1611–13).

Charles X (1757–1836) King of France (1824–30). Fifth son of the dauphin Louis, and grandson of Louis XV, until 1824 he was known as Charles-Philippe, comte d'Artois. During the French Revolution, he went into exile and became the leader of the ÉMIGRÉ NOBILITY. Returning to France in 1814, he led the ULTRAS during the BOURBON RESTORATION. On the death of his brother LOUIS XVIII, Charles became king. His popularity waned as his reign became increasingly reactionary. After the JULY REVOLUTION he was forced to abdicate in favor of LOUIS-PHILIPPE. His reign dramatized the failure of the Bourbons to reconcile the tradition of the monarchy by divine right with the democratic spirit produced in the wake of the Revolution.

Charles X Gustav *Swedish* **Karl Gustav** (1622–1660) King of Sweden (1654–60). Nephew of GUSTAV II ADOLF, he failed in his efforts to marry the Swedish queen CHRISTINA, but she named him to succeed her. As king he attempted to restore the public finances but was forced to devote most of his attention to military matters. He conducted the First NORTHERN WAR (1655–60) against a coalition that eventually included Poland, Russia, Brandenburg, the Netherlands, and Denmark, with the aim of establishing a unified northern state. After conquering Poland (1655–56), he won back lands in southern Sweden from Denmark by the Treaty of Roskilde (1658).

Charles XI *Swedish* **Karl** (1655–1697) King of Sweden (1660–97). He was 5 when he succeeded his father, CHARLES X GUSTAV, and the kingdom was ruled under a regency of aristocrats until Charles came of age in 1672. The regents drew Sweden into the Dutch War (1672–78), but Charles took control of the armies and won favorable results for Sweden by the Treaties of NIJMEGEN, after which he maintained a foreign policy of neutrality. Within Sweden, Charles expanded royal power at the expense of the higher nobility and established an absolutist monarchy.

Charles XII *Swedish* **Karl** (1682–1718) King of Sweden (1697–1718). Son of CHARLES XI, he became absolute monarch at 15. He defended his country for 18 years in the Second NORTHERN WAR, gradually taking increased responsibility for planning and executing armed operations. He launched a disastrous invasion of Russia (1707–9) that resulted in the collapse of the Swedish armies and the loss of Sweden's status as a great power. A ruler of the early Enlightenment era, he promoted significant domestic reforms. He was killed during an invasion of Norway.

Charles XIII *Swedish* **Karl** (1748–1818) King of Sweden (1809–18) and first king of the union of Sweden and Norway (1814–18). Second son of King Adolf Frederick (1710–1771), he served as admiral of the fleet in the Russo-Swedish war. On the death of his brother GUSTAV III (1792), Charles became regent for his nephew GUSTAV IV. After the latter's deposition in 1809, Charles was elected king. He was prematurely aged and childless. In 1810 Jean-Baptiste Bernadotte (later CHARLES XIV JOHN) was named heir apparent; from then on, Charles was eclipsed by the crown prince.

Charles XIV John *Swedish* **Karl Johan** ***orig.*** **Jean-Baptiste Bernadotte** (1763–1844) King of Sweden and Norway (1818–44). Born in France, he became an ardent supporter of the French Revolution and rose rapidly in the army ranks to brigadier general (1794). Named marshal of France in 1804, he supported NAPOLEON in several campaigns (1805–9) but subsequently shifted his allegiance. In 1810 he was invited to become crown prince of Sweden; taking the name of Charles John, he assumed control of the government. He helped defeat Napoleon at the Battle of LEIPZIG, then defeated France's ally Denmark, forcing that country to transfer Norway to the Swedish crown. On the death of CHARLES XIII in 1818, he became king of Sweden and Norway. His foreign policy led to a long and favorable period of peace.

Charles Albert *Italian* **Carlo Alberto** (1798–1849) King of Sardinia-Piedmont (1831–49). A member of the House of SAVOY, he ascended the throne after the death of Charles Felix in 1831. He mitigated the harsh administration of his country and accelerated its economic and social development. The spread of revolutionary ideas forced him to grant a statute for representative government in 1848. After the election of PIUS IX as pope and the Austrian occupation of Ferrara, he sought to lead the liberation of Italy. He went to war against Austria in 1848 and again in 1849, but after his defeat in the Battle of NOVARA he abdicated in favor of his son, VICTOR EMMANUEL II.

Charles Martel \mär-'tel\ *Latin* **Carolus Martellus ("Charles the Hammer")** (688?–741) Mayor of the palace of AUSTRASIA (715–41). He was the illegitimate son of Pepin of Herstal, a mayor of the palace who governed parts of the Frankish realm at a time when the MEROVINGIAN kings ruled in name only. On his father's death he overcame family opposition and rivals among the nobility to reunite and rule the entire Frankish realm. He subdued Neustria (724), attacked Aquitaine, and fought against the Frisians, Saxons, and Bavarians. His victory at the Battle of TOURS/POITIERS (732) stemmed the Muslim invasion, and he controlled Burgundy by 739. His sons divided the kingdom; his grandson was CHARLEMAGNE.

Charles of Anjou See CHARLES I (Naples)

Charles of Luxembourg See CHARLES IV (Holy Roman Empire)

Charles River River, eastern Massachusetts. The longest river wholly in the state, it flows into Boston Bay after a course of about 80 mi (130 km). Navigable for about 7 mi (11 km), its estuary separates the cities of BOSTON and CAMBRIDGE.

Charles River Bridge v. Warren Bridge (1837) U.S. Supreme Court decision holding that rights not specifically conferred by a charter cannot be inferred from the language of the document. Chief Justice ROGER B. TANEY rejected the claim of a bridge company (Charles River) that the state legislature's subsequent grant of a charter to another bridge company (Warren) impaired the charter to the first company. His opinion in this case represented a departure from the Supreme Court's construction of the U.S. Constitution's Contract Clause under JOHN MARSHALL.

Charles Robert of Anjou See CHARLES I (Hungary)

Charles the Bad See CHARLES II (Navarre)

Charles the Bald See CHARLES II (France)

Charles the Bold (1433–1477) Last of the great dukes of BURGUNDY (1467–77). An opponent of LOUIS XI of France, Charles tried to make Burgundy an independent kingdom. He had great success until 1474, casting off French rule, extending Burgundy's possessions, and building a centralized government. Charles brutally quelled a revolt in Liège (1468) and invaded Normandy (1471). Through negotiation, warfare, and purchases he sought to extend his territory as far as the Rhine, but a coalition of Swiss, Austrians, and towns on the upper Rhine resisted him. He suffered defeats by the Swiss in 1476 and was killed in battle near Nancy.

Charles the Fair See CHARLES IV (France)

Charles the Fat See CHARLES III (Holy Roman Empire)

Charles the Well-Beloved See CHARLES VI (France)

Charles the Wise See CHARLES V (France)

Charleston Seaport city (pop., 1996 est.: 71,000), southeastern South Carolina. Originally called Charles Towne, it was founded by English colonists in 1670. During the AMERICAN REVOLUTION it was held by the British 1780–82. Known as Charleston from 1783, it was the chief winter port of the U.S. until the WAR OF 1812. In 1861 the Confederate capture of FORT SUMTER in Charleston Harbor precipitated the AMERICAN CIVIL WAR. Blockaded by Union forces, it was under siege 1863–65, then evacuated by Gen. WILLIAM T. SHERMAN's forces. It was seriously damaged by an earthquake in 1886 and a hurricane in 1989. It is the site of the College of Charleston (1770), The CITADEL (1842), and the Charleston Museum (1773), the oldest museum in the U.S.

Charleston City (pop., 1996 est.: 58,000), capital of West Virginia. Situated in the ALLEGHENY MTNS. at the confluence of the Elk and KANAWHA rivers, it was settled around Fort Lee shortly after the AMERICAN REVOLUTION. It was the home for a time of DANIEL BOONE. Divided in allegiance during the AMERICAN CIVIL WAR, it was occupied by Union troops in 1862. It was named the state capital in 1870; the capital was briefly transferred to Wheeling but returned to Charleston in 1885. It is a distribution center for coal, oil, and gas, and its manufactures include chemicals. Its capitol building (completed 1932) was designed by CASS GILBERT.

Charleston Social jazz dance popular in the 1920s and later, characterized by its toes-in, heels-out twisting steps. Originally a Southern black folk dance, it had parallels in dances of Trinidad, Nigeria, and Ghana. It was popularized by its appearance in the black musical *Runnin' Wild* in 1923 and took its name from one of the show's songs.

Charlotte *orig.* **Charlotte Sophia of Mecklenburg-Strelitz** (1744–1818) Queen consort of GEORGE III of England. In 1761 she was selected unseen after the British king asked for a review of all eligible German

Protestant princesses. The marriage was a success, and the couple had 15 children, including GEORGE IV. After the king was declared insane (1811), Charlotte was given custody of him by Parliament.

Charlotte City (pop., 1996 est.: 441,000), North Carolina. The Carolinas' biggest metropolis, it lies near the CATAWBA RIVER, 15 mi (24 km) north of South Carolina. It was settled c. 1748 and named for Charlotte Sophia of Mecklenburg-Streliz (later the wife of GEORGE III). In the AMERICAN REVOLUTION it was occupied by Lord CORNWALLIS, who dubbed it "the hornet's nest." Until the 1849 GOLD RUSH, it was the center of U.S. gold production. In the American Civil War it was the site of a Confederate naval yard. Presidents ANDREW JACKSON and JAMES POLK were born nearby and received their early schooling there. Its industry includes textiles, machinery, and chemical production, and it is the site of several institutions of higher education.

C–D

Charlotte Amalie \'shär-lət-ə-'mäl-yə\ City (pop., 1990: 12,000), capital of the island of ST. THOMAS and of the U.S. VIRGIN ISLANDS. Lying on St. Thomas harbor, it was established as a Danish colony in 1672 and named for the Danish queen (its name was St. Thomas 1921–36). The largest city in the Virgin Islands, it is built on three low volcanic spurs. Two castles, attributed to the pirates BLACKBEARD and Bluebeard, overlook the harbor. Tourism is economically important.

Charlotte Harbor Inlet of the Gulf of MEXICO, western coast of Florida. It is about 25 mi (40 km) long and 5 mi (8 km) wide. It receives the PEACE RIVER in the northeast, and a dredged channel serves the port of Punta Gorda. In 1521 JUAN PONCE DE LEON tried to establish a colony in the area but was driven away by hostile Indians.

Charlottesville City (pop., 1994 est.: 41,000), central Virginia. Located in the foothills of the BLUE RIDGE MTNS. and settled in the 1730s, it grew as a tobacco-trading center and later was noted as the home of presidents THOMAS JEFFERSON and JAMES MONROE. In 1781 the British raided Charlottesville in hopes of capturing Jefferson and other leaders of the AMERICAN REVOLUTION. Sites of interest include Jefferson's home, MONTICELLO; Monroe's home, Ash Lawn; and the University of VIRGINIA.

Charlottetown City (pop., 1991: 15,000), capital of PRINCE EDWARD ISLAND. Lying on Hillsborough Bay, it originated in the 1720s as the French settlement Port la Joie. Renamed in honor of the wife of GEORGE III after the island passed to Britain in 1763, it became the capital in 1765. Its economy centers on tourism and government business, and with its excellent harbor, it is the province's commercial center. It is the site of Province House, where in 1864 Canada's unification was first discussed, and the Confederation Center of the Arts, a national memorial to the Fathers of Confederation.

Charlottetown Conference First in a series of meetings in 1864 that led to the formation of the Dominion of Canada in 1867. The conference, held at Charlottetown, Prince Edward Island, was originally called to discuss a union of the three Maritime Provinces. The gathering failed to reach agreement but reconvened in Halifax and later in Quebec, where a constitution for a federal union was drafted, resulting in the BRITISH NORTH AMERICA ACT.

charm In PARTICLE PHYSICS, the property or internal QUANTUM number that is conserved in strong and electromagnetic interactions, but not in weak interactions (see STRONG FORCE, ELECTROMAGNETIC FORCE, WEAK FORCE). Charmed particles contain at least one charmed QUARK; the charm number of these quarks is +1. Charmed antiquarks (see ANTIMATTER) have a charm number of –1. The first charmed particle was discovered in 1974.

Charolais \,shar-ə-'lā\ Breed of large, light-colored CATTLE developed in France for draft purposes but now kept for beef production and used for crossbreeding. White cattle had long been characteristic of the Charolais region, but the breed was first recognized c. 1775. A typical Charolais is massive, horned, and cream-colored or slightly darker. The breed was first imported into the U.S. from a Mexican herd in 1936, but because of problems with disease in the French herds, few were later imported. It is crossbred with beef breeds and dairy cows.

Charon \'kar-ən\ In GREEK MYTHOLOGY, the son of Erebus (Darkness) and Nyx (Night), whose duty it was to ferry the souls of the dead across the Rivers STYX and Acheron, his payment being the coin placed in the mouth of the corpse before burial. He continues in modern Greek folklore as Charos, or Charontas, the angel of death.

Charophyceae \,kar-ə-'fī-sē-ē\ Class of ALGAE, certain members of which are commonly known as stoneworts. Stoneworts contain calcium carbonate deposits so extensive that they may form the major part of lake bottoms. Superficially resembling higher plants, stoneworts have rootlike and stemlike structures, as well as whorls of branches at regular intervals. They grow underwater, attached to the muddy bottoms of fresh or brackish rivers and lakes. Except for one form that is sometimes destructive in fish hatcheries, they are of little importance to humans.

Charpentier \shär-pän-'tyā\, **Marc-Antoine** (c. 1645–1704) French composer. He was a student of G. CARISSIMI in Rome in the 1660s. Back in Paris, he succeeded J.-B. LULLY as music director with MOLIÈRE's acting troupe (later the COMÉDIE-FRANÇAISE). He became music director at the principal Jesuit church in Paris, and for his last six years held the prestigious post of *maître de chapelle* at the Sainte-Chapelle. Enormously prolific, he was the most important French composer of his generation. He wrote 11 masses, 84 psalm settings, and 207 motets, including some 35 dramatic motets or Latin oratorios, a genre he introduced into France. His works include the oratorio *Judicium Salomonis* (1702), the mass *Assumpta est Maria,* and the operas *Médée* (1693) and *David et Jonathas* (1688).

charter Document granting certain specified rights, powers, privileges, or functions from the sovereign power of a state to a person, corporation, city, or other unit of local organization. In the MAGNA CARTA, King John granted certain liberties to the English people. Elsewhere in medieval Europe, monarchs issued charters to towns, guilds, universities, and other institutions, granting the institution certain privileges and sometimes specifying how they should conduct their internal affairs. Later, charters were granted to overseas trading companies (e.g., the British EAST INDIA CO.), granting them monopolies in certain areas. Britain's colonies in North America were established by charter. Modern charters may be corporate or municipal. A corporate charter, issued by a governmental body, grants individuals the power to form a corporation, or LIMITED-LIABILITY company. A municipal charter is a law that creates a new political subdivision and allows the people within it to organize themselves into a municipal corporation, in effect delegating to the people the powers of local self-government.

Charter Oath *or* **Five Articles Oath** Oath issued in 1868 by Japan's MEIJI EMPEROR. One article, important in spurring the creation of a new legislative body, promised that assemblies would be widely established and that all matters would be "decided by public discussion." Two articles promised an end to feudal class restrictions and "evil customs of the past," and another stated that all classes should work together to "carry out the plan of government." Lastly, it was declared that "knowledge shall be sought throughout the world to promote the welfare of the empire." The Charter Oath set the progressive tone of the MEIJI PERIOD. See also MEIJI RESTORATION.

Charter of 1814 *or* **Charte Constitutionnelle** \'shärt-,kōn-stē-tūē-syō-'nel\ French constitution issued by LOUIS XVIII after he became king (see BOURBON RESTORATION). The charter, which was revised in 1830 and remained in effect until 1848, preserved many liberties won by the FRENCH REVOLUTION. It established a constitutional monarchy with a bicameral parliament, guaranteed civil liberties, proclaimed religious toleration, and acknowledged Catholicism as the state religion.

chartered company Type of corporation that evolved in the 16th century in Europe. Under a charter granted by the state's sovereign authority, the company had certain rights and obligations which usually gave it a trading monopoly in a specific geographic area or for a specific type of trade item. In the 17th century, chartered companies were encouraged by the English, French, and Dutch governments to assist trade and encourage overseas exploration. Those companies formed for trade with the Indies (see English EAST INDIA COMPANY, Dutch EAST INDIA COMPANY, French EAST INDIA COMPANY) and the New World (see HUDSON'S BAY CO.) had the most wide-reaching influence. Some chartered companies were also involved in the settlement of colonists (see LONDON CO., PLYMOUTH CO.). Eventually the development of the modern LIMITED-LIABILITY company or corporation led to a decline in the importance of chartered companies.

Chartism British working-class movement for parliamentary reform. It was named after the People's Charter, a bill drafted by William Lovett (1800–1877) in 1838 that demanded universal manhood suffrage, equal electoral districts, vote by ballot, annually elected Parliaments, payment of members of Parliament, and abolition of property qualifications for membership. Born amid an economic depression, the movement rose to national importance under the leadership of FEARGUS O'CONNOR. Parliament refused to take action on three Chartist petitions presented to it, and the movement declined after 1848.

Chartres \'shärt, 'shärtr^{ə}\ City (pop., 1999: 40,361), northwestern France. Situated on the EURE RIVER southwest of PARIS, it was the capital and center of Druidic worship for the Carnutes, a Celtic tribe. The Normans burned the city in 858. In the Middle Ages it was held by the counts of Blois and CHAMPAGNE. The city was sold to France in 1286 and was occupied by the English in 1417–32. HENRY IV was crowned there in 1594. The Germans held it in 1870, and it was severely damaged in World War II. Landmarks include the Gothic CHARTRES CATHEDRAL.

Chartres Cathedral \'shärtr^{ə}\ Cathedral of Notre-Dame at Chartres, one of the most influential examples of High GOTHIC ARCHITECTURE. The main part of this great cathedral was built between 1194 and 1220. It replaced a 12th-century church of which only the CRYPT, the base of the towers, and the western facade remain. Abandonment of the traditional tribune GALLERIES and the use of a unique type of FLYING BUTTRESS allowed for a larger CLERESTORY. Remarkable stained-glass windows and a Renaissance choir screen add to its beauty.

The cathedral at Chartres, Fr.

EVERETT C. JOHNSON—DEWYS INC.

Chase, Salmon P(ortland) (1808–1873) U.S. antislavery leader and sixth chief justice of the U.S. (1864–73). Born in Cornish Township, N.H., he practiced law in Cincinnati from 1830 and defended runaway slaves and white abolitionists. He led the LIBERTY PARTY in Ohio from 1841 and helped found the FREE SOIL PARTY (1848) and the REPUBLICAN PARTY (1854). He served in the U.S. Senate (1849–55, 1860–61) and was the first Republican governor of Ohio (1855–59). He served as secretary of the treasury under Pres. ABRAHAM LINCOLN (1861–64). He was appointed chief justice by Lincoln, in which post he presided over the impeachment trial of Pres. ANDREW JOHNSON and tried to protect the rights of blacks from infringement by state action.

Chase, Samuel (1741–1811) U.S. jurist. Born in Princess Anne, Md., he became a lawyer and served 20 years in the state legislature. An ardent patriot, he helped lead the Sons of LIBERTY in violent resistance to the STAMP ACT. He served on the state COMMITTEE OF CORRESPONDENCE (1774), was elected to the CONTINENTAL CONGRESS, and signed the DECLARATION OF INDEPENDENCE. When ALEXANDER HAMILTON exposed his attempt to corner the flour market (1778), Chase retired from Congress, only to return in 1784. He was appointed to the U.S. Supreme Court in 1796 by Pres. GEORGE WASHINGTON. Chase upheld the primacy of U.S. treaties over state statutes in *Ware vs. Hylton*. In *Calder vs. Bull* (1798) he contributed to the definition of DUE PROCESS. At THOMAS JEFFERSON's instigation, Chase was impeached for partisan conduct in 1804. His acquittal established the principle that federal judges can be removed only for indictable criminal acts, thus strengthening the independence of the judiciary. Chase served until 1811.

Chase, William Merritt (1849–1916) U.S. painter and teacher. Born in Williamsburg (now Nineveh), Ind., he studied in New York and for six years in Munich. He became the most important U.S. teacher of his generation, first at New York's Art Students League and later at his own school, founded in 1896, greatly influencing the course of early-20th-century U.S. painting.; among his students were GEORGIA O'KEEFFE and CHARLES DEMUTH. As a painter he was very prolific; his 2,000 paintings include portraits, interiors (e.g., *In the Studio*, 1880–83), figure studies, still lifes, and landscapes characterized by bold, spontaneous brushwork.

Chase Manhattan Corp. U.S. HOLDING COMPANY incorporated in 1969 with the Chase Manhattan Bank as its main subsidiary. The bank itself was created in 1955 by the merger of the Bank of Manhattan Co. (founded 1799) and the Chase National Bank (founded 1877). The creation of Chase Manhattan was part of a general movement in U.S. banking to establish holding companies that could bring together banks and financial institutions ordinarily excluded by law from the field of banking. In 1996 it merged with CHEMICAL BANKING CORP. (which then owned the nation's second-largest bank) but kept the Chase Manhattan name. A merger with investment bank J.P. Morgan & Co. in 2000 created J.P. Morgan Chase & Co. See also DAVID ROCKEFELLER.

chat Real-time conversation among computer users in a networked environment such as the INTERNET. After a user types a text message and presses the Enter key, the text immediately appears on the other users' computers, permitting typed conversations that are often only somewhat slower than normal conversation. A chat can be private (between two users) or public (where other users can see the messages and participate if they wish). Public chatting is conducted in "chat rooms," Web sites devoted to chat, usually about a specific topic. The thousands of chat rooms now available typically use the IRC (Internet Relay Chat) PROTOCOL, developed in 1988 by Jarkko Oikarinen of Finland. See also BULLETIN-BOARD SYSTEM.

chat Any of several species of songbird named for their harsh, chattering notes. True chats (chat-thrushes) make up a major division of the THRUSH family (Turdidae). Australian chats (usually placed in the family Maluridae), which inhabit scrubby open lands, are about 5 in. (13 cm) long. The yellow-breasted chat (*Icteria virens,* family Parulidae) of North America is the largest WOOD WARBLER (7.5 in., or 19 cm, long). Greenish gray above and bright yellow below, with white "spectacles," it hides in thickets but may perch in the open to utter its mewing, churring, and whistling sounds. See also REDSTART.

Yellow-breasted chat (*Icteria virens*).

RON AUSTING—BRUCE COLEMAN INC.

Chateaubriand \shä-tō-brē-'ä^{n}\, **(François-Auguste-) René** *later* **vicomte (viscount) de Chateaubriand** (1768–1848) French author and statesman. A cavalry officer at the start of the Revolution, he refused to join the Royalists and instead sailed to the U.S., where he traveled with fur traders. On Louis XVI's fall he returned to join the Royalist army. *Atala* (1801), part of an unfinished epic, drew on his travels in the U.S. *The Genius of Christianity* (1802), which asserted the value of Christianity based on its poetic and artistic appeal, influenced many Romantic writers and brought him briefly into favor with Napoleon. With the 1814 Restoration he became a major political figure. Other works include the novel *René* (1805) and his memoirs (6 vols., 1849–50), perhaps his most lasting monument. He was the preeminent French writer of his day.

Viscount de Chateaubriand, detail of an oil painting by Girodet-Trioson; in the National Museum of Versailles and the Trianons, France.

CLICHE MUSEES NATIONAUX

Châteauguay \'sha-tə-gē\, **Battle of** (October 26, 1813) Engagement in the WAR OF 1812 in which the British compelled U.S. forces to abandon an attack on Montreal. An advance unit of 1,500 men from the invading U.S. troops under WADE HAMPTON was stopped at Châteauguay, Quebec, by British troops (most of them French Canadians), who occupied the woods along the riverbank. The battle was followed by the U.S. troops' withdrawal from Canada.

Chatham, Earl of See William PITT, the Elder

Chatham Strait \'chat-^{ə}m\ Narrow passage, North Pacific Ocean. Extending off southeastern Alaska 150 mi (240 km) between the ADMIRALTY and Kuiu islands on the east and the Chicagof and Baranof islands on the west, it is 3–10 mi (5–16 km) wide. It forms part of the INSIDE PASSAGE between Alaska and Washington state.

Chattahoochee River \ˌcha-tə-ˈhü-chē\ River, southeastern U.S. Rising in northeastern Georgia, it flows southwest to the Alabama border and then south, forming a section of the Alabama–Georgia and Georgia–Florida boundaries, to join the Flint River at Chattahoochee, Fla., after a course of about 436 mi (702 km). Dammed at the Georgia–Florida border, it forms Lake Seminole, below which the river is known as the Apalachicola River.

Chattanooga City (pop., 1996 est.: 151,000) and port of entry, southeastern Tennessee. Lying on the TENNESSEE RIVER, between Missionary Ridge to the east and Lookout Mountain to the southwest, it was established as a trading post (Ross' Landing) in 1815. Renamed Chattanooga in 1838, it developed as a river port. A strategic Confederate communications point in the AmericanCivil War, it was a major objective of the Union armies, with fighting culminating in the battles of CHICKAMAUGA and CHATTANOOGA (1863). The city is the headquarters for the TENNESSEE VALLEY AUTHORITY.

Chattanooga, Battle of (November 23–25, 1863) Decisive engagement in the AMERICAN CIVIL WAR at Chattanooga, Tenn., a vital railroad junction. A Confederate army under BRAXTON BRAGG besieged a Union army in September 1863, and to lift the siege, Union troops under ULYSSES S. GRANT marched on Bragg's troops. At battles on Lookout Mountain and Missionary Ridge, the Union troops forced the Confederate army to retreat. With this victory, the North was poised to split the South horizontally by marching across Georgia to the sea. See also Battle of CHICKAMAUGA.

Chatterjee \ˈchät-ər-jē\, **Bankim Chandra** *orig.* **Bankim Chandra Cattopadhyay** (1838–1894) Indian novelist. Born in Bengal, he was educated in Calcutta (now Kolkata) and served as a deputy magistrate in civil service for many years. His first notable Bengali work was *Daughter of the Lord of the Fort* (1865). His epoch-making newspaper, *Bangadarsan*, serialized some of his later works. Though his novels were considered structurally faulty, his contemporaries saw him as a prophet, and his valiant Hindu heroes aroused great pride and patriotism. He helped create the Indian school of fiction and established Bengali prose as a literary language. Chatterjee is considered the greatest Bengali novelist.

Chatterton, Thomas (1752–1770) English poet. At age 11 Chatterton wrote a pastoral eclogue on an old parchment and passed it off successfully as a 15th-century work. Thereafter he created more poems in a similar vein, attributing them to a fictitious monk he called Thomas Rowley. After a mock suicide threat freed him from an apprenticeship to an attorney, he set out for London. There he had some success with a comic opera, *The Revenge,* but when a prospective patron died, he found himself penniless and without prospects and committed suicide at 17. Considered a precursor of ROMANTICISM, he was praised by such poets as SAMUEL TAYLOR COLERIDGE, JOHN KEATS, Lord BYRON, and WILLIAM WORDSWORTH.

Chaucer \ˈchȯ-sər\, **Geoffrey** (1342/43–1400) English poet. Of middle-class birth, he was a courtier, diplomat, and civil servant trusted by three kings in his active and varied career, and a poet only by avocation. His first important poem, *Book of the Duchesse* (1369/70), was a dream-vision elegy for the Duchess of Lancaster. In the 1380s he produced mature works including *The Parliament of Fowls,* a dream-vision for St. Valentine's Day about a conference of birds choosing their mates; the fine tragic verse romance *Troilus and Criseyde*; and the unfinished dream-vision *Legend of Good Women.* His best-known work, the unfinished *Canterbury Tales* (written 1387–1400), is an intricate dramatic narrative that employs a pilgrimage to the shrine of Thomas BECKET in Canterbury as a framing device for a highly varied collection of stories; not only the most famous literary work in Middle English, it is one of the greatest works of English literature. In this and other works Chaucer established the southern English dialect as England's literary language, and he is regarded as the first great English poet.

Chaumette \shō-ˈmet\, **Pierre-Gaspard** (1763–1794) French Revolutionary leader. In 1791 he signed the petition that demanded the abdication of LOUIS XVI. As procurator-general of the Paris commune from 1792, he instituted such social reforms as improved hospital conditions. Strenuously anti-Catholic, he promoted the anti-Christian cult of the goddess Reason. He was executed during the REIGN OF TERROR because of his democratic extremism.

Chaumont \shō-ˈmōⁿ\, **Treaty of** (1814) Treaty signed by Austria, Prussia, Russia, and Britain binding them to defeat NAPOLEON. The British foreign secretary Viscount CASTLEREAGH played a leading part in negotiating the treaty, by which the signatories undertook not to negotiate separately, and promised to continue the struggle until Napoleon was overthrown. The treaty tightened allied unity and made provision for a durable European settlement.

Chauncy, Charles (1705–1787) American clergyman. Born in Boston, he served as minister of the First Church of Boston from 1727 until his death. He opposed the establishment of an Anglican bishopric in the American colonies. He is best known as a leading critic of the GREAT AWAKENING. He also wrote books, pamphlets, and sermons espousing the cause of the AMERICAN REVOLUTION.

Chausson \shō-ˈsōⁿ\, **(Amédée-) Ernest** (1855–1899) French composer. He studied with J. MASSENET and C. FRANCK. Having a comfortable income, he kept a notable artistic salon in Paris and had no need for regular employment. His most important works are the orchestral song cycle *Poème de l'amour et de la mer* (1893), the incidental music to *La légende de Sainte Cécile* (1891), a symphony (1890), the opera *Le roi Arthus* (1895), and *Poème* for violin and orchestra (1896). He died in a cycling accident.

chautauqua movement \shə-ˈtȯ-kwə\ Popular U.S. movement in adult education founded in 1874. It began as a Sunday-school teacher training assembly at Chautauqua Lake, N.Y., but gradually spread to various circuit "chautauquas" and broadened in scope to include general education and popular entertainments. Outstanding speakers were brought in for summer lectures and classes. The movement has declined after reaching a peak in 1924 (though the organization still holds meetings), but its legacy contributed to the growth of COMMUNITY COLLEGES and CONTINUING EDUCATION programs. See also LYCEUM MOVEMENT.

Chautemps \shō-ˈtäⁿ\, **Camille** (1885–1963) French politician. A Radical Socialist, he was elected to the Chamber of Deputies in 1919. He served in several cabinet posts and as premier of France in 1930, 1933–34, and 1937–38. As a cabinet member in 1940, he was among the first to suggest the surrender of France to Nazi Germany. He held a ministry in the Vichy government (see VICHY FRANCE) but broke with PHILIPPE PETAIN's government after arriving in the U.S. on an official mission. He lived in the U.S. for much of the rest of his life. After World War II a French court convicted him in absentia for collaborating with the enemy.

Chavannes, Pierre Puvis de See Pierre PUVIS DE CHAVANNES

Chávez (y Ramírez) \ˈchä-ˌvez\, **Carlos (Antonio de Padua)** (1899–1978) Mexican composer and conductor. Trained as a pianist, he was largely self-taught as a composer. When Mexico's first permanent symphony orchestra was formed in 1928, he became its director; he held the post for 20 years, touring widely and conducting many premiere performances. As director of the National Conservatory 1928–34, he reformed the curriculum and organized several concert series. He was Mexico's most prominent and honored musician of the 20th century; his works, notable for their rhythmic vitality and orchestral color, include seven numbered symphonies, including *Sinfonía de Antígona* (1933) and *Sinfonía india* (1936); five ballets, including *Caballos de vapor* (1927) and *La hija de Cólquide* (1943); a piano concerto (1940); a violin concerto (1950); and the opera *The Visitors* (1956).

Chavez \ˈchä-väs, *Engl* ˈchäv-ˌez\, **Cesar (Estrada)** (1927–1993) U.S. organizer and leader of migrant farm workers. Born into a family of Mexican-American migrant laborers, he spent his early years in a succession of migrant camps, attending school only sporadically. After two years in the Navy, he returned to migrant farmwork. He began organizing the largely Hispanic farmworkers of Arizona and California in 1962. A charismatic figure, he used strikes and nationwide boycotts to win union recognition and contracts from California grape and lettuce growers. He brought his union into the AFL-CIO, and in 1971 it became the United Farm Workers of America (UFW). He successfully battled the Teamsters Union for the right to organize field hands in the 1970s, but in later years his leadership faltered and the UFW declined.

Chavín de Huántar \chä-ˈvēn-thä-ˈwän-tär\ Site of temple ruins, western central Peru. The ruins belong to the Chavín pre-Columbian culture, which flourished c. 900–200 BC. The central building is a massive temple complex constructed of rectangular stone blocks; it contains interior galleries and incorporates bas-relief carvings on pillars and lintels.

Chayefsky \chä-'yef-skē\, **Paddy** *orig.* **Sidney** (1923–1981) U.S. playwright. Born in New York City, he wrote his first full-length television play in 1952, and his work became prominent in the early flowering of television drama. Known for chronicling the lives of ordinary people, his greatest television and film success was *Marty* (1955, Academy Award). *The Catered Affair* (1956) and *The Bachelor Party* (1957) were also well received. His stage plays include *The Tenth Man* (1959), *Gideon* (1961), and *The Latent Heterosexual* (1968). He returned to screenwriting with *The Hospital* (1971, Academy Award) and *Network* (1976, Academy Award).

chayote \chī-'yō-tē\ Tendril-bearing perennial vine *(Sechium edule)* of the GOURD family, native to the New World tropics, where it is widely cultivated for its edible fruits. Chayote also is grown as an annual plant in temperate climates. The fast-growing vine bears small, white flowers and green or white pear-shaped fruits with furrows. Each fruit contains one seed. The fruits are eaten cooked or raw, and the young root tubers are prepared like potatoes.

Chayote (*Sechium edule*).
EUGENE BELT—SHOSTAL

Chechnya \chech-'nyä, 'chech-nyə\ Subdivision, Russian Federation. Part of the Checheno-Ingush autonomous republic of the former U.S.S.R., it became a republic within Russia in 1992, as did Ingushetia. It is populated mainly by Chechens, a Muslim ethnolinguistic group. Chechnya's demand for independence from Russia in 1992 led to an invasion by Russian troops in 1993–94. Fighting led to severe devastation of the area. A cease-fire agreement was reached in 1996, but fighting resumed in 1999. The capital, Grozny (pop., 1992 est.: 388,000), a major oil center with pipelines to the Caspian and Black seas, received heavy damage in both periods of fighting.

check Bill of exchange drawn on a bank and payable on demand. Checks have become the chief form of MONEY in the domestic commerce of developed countries. As a written order to pay money, a check may be transferred from one person to another by endorsement. Most checks are not paid in currency but by the debiting and crediting of bank deposits. There are several special forms of checks. A cashier's check is issued by a bank and has unquestioned acceptability, as does a certified check, which is a depositor's check that has been guaranteed by a bank. Traveler's checks are cashier's checks sold to travelers, which must be signed twice by the payee, once when the check is issued and once when it is cashed; reimbursement is guaranteed if they are lost or stolen.

checkers Board game for two players, each with 12 pieces positioned on (usually) the black squares of a 64-square checkerboard. Play consists of advancing a piece diagonally forward to an adjoining square, the goal being to jump and thus capture each of an opponent's pieces until all are removed and victory is declared. When a piece reaches the final (king) row, it is crowned with a piece of the same color and can begin to move in any direction. Similar games have been played in various cultures and in times extending back to antiquity.

checks and balances Principle of government under which separate branches are empowered to prevent actions by other branches. This keeps any one branch from gaining too much power over the others or over the people it governs. Most multibranch constitutional governments have checks and balances. In one-party political systems, informal checks and balances may operate when organs of an authoritarian or totalitarian regime compete for power. See also *The* FEDERALIST, JUDICIAL REVIEW, SEPARATION OF POWERS.

cheese Food consisting of the coagulated, compressed, and usually ripened curd of MILK separated from the whey. When milk sours, it forms both a protein-rich gel, or curd, and a lactose-rich fluid, or whey. Coagulation is often facilitated by adding rennin, an enzyme that acts on the milk's chief protein, casein. The resulting curd is then cut or broken to release most of the whey. Ripening and curing are affected by moisture content, acidity, presence of microorganisms, and other factors. Cheese is made from the milk of cows, goats, sheep, water buffalo, llamas, yaks, and other animals; in the West, cow's milk is most common. Products vary according to fat content of the milk, heating or PASTEURIZATION, and addition of enzymes or cultures of BACTERIA, MOLDS, or YEASTS. Cheese varieties include hard cheeses (e.g., cheddar, Edam, Emmental, Gouda, Provolone, Romano, Swiss), semisoft cheeses (Gorgonzola, Limburger, Muenster, Roquefort), and soft cheeses (Brie, Camembert, cottage, Neufchâtel, and ricotta). Cheese is a source of protein, fat, minerals (calcium, phosphorus, sulfur, iron), and vitamin A.

cheetah Slender, long-legged CAT *(Acinonyx jubatus)* that lives on open plains of southern, central, and eastern Africa, and in the Middle East, where it is all but extinct. The fastest land animal in the world over short distances, it can reach a speed as great as 71 mph (114 kph). Its claws differ from those of other cats in being only partly retractable and in lacking protective sheaths. Like cats in the genus *Felis,* cheetahs purr rather than roar. The cheetah grows to about 55 in. (140 cm) long, excluding the 29–31-in. (75–80-cm) tail, and weighs 75–119 lbs (34–54 kg). The adult's coarse fur is sandy yellow above, white below, and covered with small black spots; a black streak runs down the face from the corner of each eye. The cheetah hunts by day, alone or in small groups.

Cheever, John (1912–1982) U.S. short-story writer and novelist. Born in Quincy, Mass., he lived principally in southern Connecticut. His stories appeared notably in the *New Yorker,* his clear and elegant prose delineating the drama and sadness of life in comfortable suburban America, often through fantasy and ironic comedy. His collections included *The Enormous Radio* (1953), *The Brigadier and the Golf Widow* (1964), and *The Stories of John Cheever* (1978, Pulitzer Prize). Among his novels are *The Wapshot Chronicle* (1957), *The Wapshot Scandal* (1964), and *Falconer* (1977). His revealing journals were published in 1991.

Cheke \'chēk\, **John** *later* **Sir John** (1514–1557) English humanist. A supporter of the REFORMATION, he was named professor of Greek at Cambridge University by Henry VIII and knighted by Edward VI. With his friend, the statesman Thomas Smith (1513–1577), he ably defended the historical pronunciation of Attic Greek, introduced by ERASMUS, in opposition to the post-classical pronunciation that was then the norm. Cheke was imprisoned briefly on the accession of Mary I; he fled abroad, but was captured in the Netherlands in 1556 and confined to the Tower of London. He recanted Protestantism to avoid execution and died the following year, allegedly depressed by his forced abjuration.

Chekhov \'chek-əf, *Engl* 'chek-ȯf\, **Anton (Pavlovich)** (1860–1904) Russian playwright and short-story writer. The son of a former serf, he supported his family by writing popular comic sketches while studying medicine in Moscow. While practicing as a doctor, he had his first full-length play, *Ivanov* (1887), produced, to a disappointing reception. He took up serious themes with such stories as "The Steppe" (1888) and "A Dreary Story" (1889); later stories include "The Black Monk" (1894) and "Peasants" (1897). He converted his second long play, *The Wood Demon* (1889), into the masterpiece *Uncle Vanya* (1897). His play *The Seagull* (1896) was badly received until its successful revival in 1899 by KONSTANTIN STANISLAVSKY and the MOSCOW ART THEATRE. He moved to the Crimea to nurse his eventually fatal tuberculosis, and there he wrote his great last plays, *Three Sisters* (1901) and *The Cherry Orchard* (1904), for the Moscow Art Theatre. Chekhov's plays, which take a tragicomic view of the staleness of provincial life and the passing of the Russian gentry, received international acclaim after their translation into English and other languages, and as a short-story writer he is still regarded as virtually unmatched.

Chekhov, 1902.
DAVID MAGARSHACK

Chekiang See ZHEJIANG

chelate \'kē-ˌlāt\ Any of a class of coordination or complex compounds consisting of a central ATOM of a METAL (usually a TRANSITION ELEMENT) attached to a large MOLECULE (LIGAND). Any ligand that can bind to the metal at two or more points to form a ring structure, more stable than a nonchelated compound of the same general CHEMICAL FORMULA, is a chelating agent. The process of binding to the metal is called chelation. Chelating agents such as EDTA salts are used in medicine to remove toxic metals (e.g., LEAD, CADMIUM) from the body. Others are used in ANALYSIS as indicators and in industry to extract metals. The iron-binding group of PORPHYRIN in HEMOGLOBIN, the magnesium-binding CHLOROPHYLL, and the cobalt-binding vitamin B_{12} are natural chelators.

Chelif River \shā-'lēf\ River, Algeria. Rising in the ATLAS MTNS., it flows north and west into the Mediterranean Sea east of ORAN. At 422 mi (679 km) long, it is Algeria's longest river, though it is mostly unnavigable and has an irregular flow.

Chelmsford \'chelmz-fərd\ Town (pop., 1998 est.: 154,600), county seat of ESSEX, southeastern England, on the northeastern periphery of Greater LONDON. It has remains of the Roman settlement of Caesaromagus. In 1227 it became the regular seat of the county judicial gatherings known as assizes. The world's first wireless telegraph service was transmitted in 1920 from the local premises of GUGLIELMO MARCONI'S company. Light engineering, especially electronics, is important to the economy.

Cathedral of Saint Mary, Chelmsford, England.

THE J. ALLAN CASH PHOTOLIBRARY

Chelmsford (of Chelmsford), Viscount *orig.* **Frederic John Napier Thesiger** (1868–1933) English colonial administrator. In 1905 he was appointed governor of Queensland, Australia, and in 1909 of New South Wales. He left Australia in 1913 to serve in India as a captain in the Dorsetshire regiment. As viceroy of India in a time of surging Indian nationalism (1916–21), he helped to institute reforms increasing Indian representation in government but provoked opposition by his severe measures against nationalists.

Chelsea porcelain Soft-paste PORCELAIN made in the London borough of Chelsea. The factory, established c. 1743, produced its greatest wares—tableware and bird figures, with designs inspired by MEISSEN PORCELAIN and marked with a raised anchor on an oval medallion—from 1750 to 1752. Later marks used were the red anchor (1752–58) and the gold anchor (1758–70). Production from 1770 to 1784, when the factory was maintained by William Duesbury of Derby, is known as Chelsea-Derbyware. Reproductions and forgeries are numerous.

Chelsea soft-paste porcelain vase in the French Rococo style of Sèvres ware with "mazarin blue" ground and a "reserve" panel painting by John Donaldson (after François Boucher), gold anchor mark, c. 1763; in the Victoria and Albert Museum, London.

BY COURTESY OF THE VICTORIA AND ALBERT MUSEUM, LONDON

Chelyabinsk \chel-'yä-bənsk\ City (pop., 2000 est.: 1,083,000), western Russia. Located 125 mi (200 km) south of YEKATERINBURG on the Trans-Siberian railroad, it is the capital of Chelyabinsk Oblast (pop., 2000 est.: 3,672,000). Founded as a frontier outpost on the site of a Bashkir village in 1736, its growth was greatly stimulated by the eastward evacuation of Russian industry in World War II. It is now the principal city of the southern Urals industrial region.

Chemical Banking Corp. Former U.S. bank HOLDING COMPANY that merged with the CHASE MANHATTAN CORP. in 1996. Its principal subsidiary was Chemical Bank, which was chartered in 1824 as a division of a New York chemical manufacturing company. The 1996 merger made the resulting firm (the Chase Manhattan Corp.) briefly the largest bank in the U.S. Another merger in 2000 created J.P. Morgan Chase & Co.

chemical dependency See DRUG ADDICTION

chemical element See chemical ELEMENT

chemical energy Energy stored in the bonds of chemical compounds. Chemical energy may be released during a chemical reaction, often in the form of heat; such reactions are called exothermic. Reactions that require an input of heat to proceed may store some of that energy as chemical energy in newly formed bonds. The chemical energy in food is converted by the body into mechanical energy and heat. The chemical energy in coal is converted into electrical energy at a power plant. The chemical energy in a battery can also supply electrical power by means of electrolysis.

chemical engineering Academic discipline and industrial activity concerned with developing processes and designing and operating plants to change materials' physical or chemical states. With roots in the inorganic and coal-based chemical industries of western Europe and the oil-refining industry in North America, it was spurred by the need to supply chemicals and products during the two World Wars. The field includes research, design, construction, operation, sales, and management activities. Chemical engineers must master chemistry (including the nature of CHEMICAL REACTIONS, the effects of TEMPERATURE and PRESSURE on EQUILIBRIUM, and the effects of CATALYSTS on REACTION RATES), physics, and mathematics. The engineering aspect, involving fluid flow (see DEFORMATION AND FLOW) and HEAT and MASS transfer, is broken down into "unit operations," including VAPORIZATION, DISTILLATION, ABSORPTION, filtration, extraction, crystallization, agitation and mixing, drying, and size reduction; each is described mathematically, and its principles apply to any material. Chemical engineers work not only in the chemical and oil industries but also in such processing industries as foods, paper, textiles, plastics, nuclear, and biotechnology.

chemical equation Method of writing the essential features of a CHEMICAL REACTION using CHEMICAL SYMBOLS (or other agreed-upon abbreviations). By convention, reactants (present at the start) are on the left, products (present at the end) on the right. A single arrow between them denotes an irreversible reaction, a double arrow a reversible reaction. The law of conservation of MATTER (see CONSERVATION LAW) requires that every ATOM on the left appear on the right (the equation must balance); only their arrangements and combinations change. For example, one OXYGEN MOLECULE combining with two HYDROGEN molecules to form two water molecules is written $2H_2 + O_2 \rightarrow 2H_2O$. The DISSOCIATION of salt into sodium and chloride IONS is written $NaCl \rightarrow Na^+ + Cl^-$. See also STOICHIOMETRY.

chemical formula Expression of the composition or structure of a chemical COMPOUND. Formulas for MOLECULES use CHEMICAL SYMBOLS with subscript numbers to show the number of ATOMS of each ELEMENT: O_2 for oxygen, O_3 for ozone, CH_4 for methane, C_6H_6 for benzene. Parentheses may enclose ATOMS that act as a group. General formulas show the proportions of atoms in members of a class (e.g., C_nH_{2n+2} for ALKANES). If the substance does not exist as molecules (see IONIC BOND), empirical formulas show the relative proportions of the constituents (e.g., NaCl for sodium chloride). Structural formulas show bonds (see BONDING) between atoms in a molecule as short lines between symbols; they are particularly useful for showing how ISOMERS differ. A projection formula also indicates the three-dimensional arrangement of the atoms (see FISCHER PROJECTION, STEREOCHEMISTRY).

chemical hydrology *or* **hydrochemistry** Subdivision of HYDROLOGY that deals with the chemical characteristics of the water on and beneath the surface of the earth. Water in all forms is affected chemically by the materials with which it comes into contact, and it can dissolve many elements in significant quantities. Chemical hydrology is concerned with the processes involved and thus includes study of phenomena such as the transport of salts from land to sea (by erosion of rocks and surface runoff) and from sea to land (by evaporation, cloud formation, and precipitation) and the age and origin of groundwater in desert regions and of ice sheets and glaciers.

chemical reaction Any chemical process in which substances are changed into different ones, with different properties, as distinct from changing position or form (PHASE). Chemical reactions involve the rupture or rearrangement of the bonds holding ATOMS together (see BONDING), never atomic nuclei. The total MASS and number of atoms of all reactants equals those of all products, and ENERGY is almost always consumed or liberated (see heat of REACTION). The speed of reactions varies (see REACTION RATE). Understanding their mechanisms lets chemists alter reaction conditions to optimize the rate or the amount of a given product; the reversibility of the reaction and the presence of competing reactions and intermediate products complicate these studies. Reactions can be syntheses, decompositions, or rearrangements, or additions, eliminations, or substitutions. Examples include OXIDATION-REDUCTION, POLYMERIZATION, ionization (see ION), combustion (burning), HYDROLYSIS, and ACID-BASE reactions.

chemical symbol One- or two-letter notation derived from the scientific names of the chemical ELEMENTS (e.g., S for sulfur, Cl for chlorine, Zn for zinc). Some hark back to Latin names: Au (aurum) for gold, Pb (plumbum) for lead. Others are named for people or places (e.g. einsteinium, Es, for Einstein). The present symbols express the system set out by the atomic theory of matter. JOHN DALTON first used symbols to designate single atoms of elements, not indefinite amounts, and JONS JACOB BERZELIUS gave many of the current names. Chemical formulas of COMPOUNDS are written as combinations of the elements' symbols, with numbers indicating their atomic proportions, using various conventions for ordering and grouping. Thus, sodium chloride is written as NaCl and sulfuric acid as H_2SO_4.

chemical warfare Use of chemical compounds, usually toxic agents, in warfare, and the methods of combating such agents. The compounds involved may be lethal or nonlethal. In humans, they generally paralyze the nervous system (NERVE GASES, such as sarin and VX); induce temporary blindness, deafness, nausea, or vomiting; cause severe burns to skin, eyes, or lungs; or stifle respiration. Also included are chemical DEFOLIANTS and HERBICIDES used for military purposes, such as AGENT ORANGE. World War I saw the first significant use of chemical warfare. From 1915 to 1918 the Germans introduced—and the Allies duplicated—a succession of poison gases: CHLORINE, PHOSGENE, and mustard gas. The Allies also developed gas masks to protect soldiers. In the war's final year both sides used mustard gas extensively. Universal revulsion led to a 1925 Geneva protocol banning chemical warfare, which generally held through World War II, though the Germans developed highly toxic nerve gases and both Italy and Japan used gas against some of their enemies. Both Iran and Iraq used chemical weapons in the Iran-Iraq War in the 1980s, and Iraq threatened to use them in the Persian Gulf War in 1991. See also BIOLOGICAL WARFARE.

chemin de fer \shə-ˌman-də-'fer\ *or* **shimmy** Card game in which two or three cards are dealt to up to 12 players, who bet one at a time against each other rather than against the house. The winning hand is the one that comes closer to but does not exceed a count of 9. The game (whose French name means "railroad") derives from BACCARAT and has similar rules.

chemistry Science that deals with the properties, composition, and structure of substances (ELEMENTS and COMPOUNDS), the reactions and transformations they undergo, and the ENERGY released or absorbed during those processes. Often called the "central science," chemistry is concerned with ATOMS as building blocks (rather than with the subatomic domain; see QUANTUM MECHANICS), with everything in the material world, and with all living things. Branches of chemistry include inorganic (see INORGANIC COMPOUND), organic (see ORGANIC COMPOUND), PHYSICAL, and analytical (see ANALYSIS) chemistry; BIOCHEMISTRY; ELECTROCHEMISTRY; and GEOCHEMISTRY. CHEMICAL ENGINEERING (applied chemistry) uses the theoretical and experimental information obtained in chemistry to build chemical plants and make useful products.

Chemnitz \'kem-nits\ *formerly (1953-90)* **Karl-Marx-Stadt** \ˌkärl-'märks-ˌshtät\ City (pop., 1999 est.: 266,000), eastern Germany. It lies along the Chemnitz River southeast of Leipzig. It began as a trading place on a salt route to Prague and was chartered in 1143. Germany's first spinning mill was operating there in 1800, and the first German locomotive was built there. The city remains an industrial center.

chemoreception \ˌkē-mō-ri-'sep-shən\ Sensory process by which organisms respond to external chemical stimuli, by employing specialized cells (chemoreceptors) that convert the stimuli directly or indirectly into nerve impulses. Chemoreceptors that are components of sensory neurons that directly convert chemical stimuli are termed primary receptors. So-called secondary receptors are not part of neurons but respond to stimulation by inducing activity in an adjacent neuron. Most mammals possess two classes of chemoreceptors: the primary receptors involved in smell and located in the epithelium of the nasal cavity, and the secondary receptors involved in taste and located in the tongue's taste buds. Aquatic animals and terrestrial species with mucus-secreting skins typically possess chemoreceptors all over the body. For many animals, chemoreception is the most important means of receiving information about their surrounding environment. Chemoreception plays roles in finding appropriate food and in reproductive behavior (see PHEROMONES). It serves additional purposes in some animals, such as distinguishing members of the same community from outsiders.

chemotaxonomy \ˌkē-mō-tak-'sä-nə-mē\ Method of biological classification based on similarities in the structure of certain compounds among the organisms being classified. Advocates argue that, because proteins are more closely controlled by GENES and less subject to NATURAL SELECTION than are anatomical features, they are more reliable indicators of genetic relationships.

chemotherapy \ˌkē-mō-'ther-ə-pē\ Treatment of diseases, including CANCER, with chemicals. Some cancer drugs interfere with cancer-cell division or enzyme processes. However, they have serious side effects, attacking some healthy cells and reducing resistance to infection. Certain STEROIDS are used to treat breast and prostatic cancers, LEUKEMIA, and LYMPHOMAS. Derivatives of plants such as periwinkle (vincristine, vinblastine) and yew (TAXOL) have been found effective against HODGKIN'S DISEASE, leukemia, and BREAST CANCER.

Chen Duxiu *or* **Ch'en Tu-hsiu** \'chən-'dü-shē-'ü\ (1879–1942) Chinese political and intellectual leader, cofounder of the CHINESE COMMUNIST PARTY. As a young man, Chen studied in Japan. In China, he started subversive periodicals that were quickly suppressed by the government. In 1915, after the establishment of the Chinese Republic, he created the monthly *Qingnian zazhi* ("Youth Magazine"), renamed *Xin qingnian* ("New Youth"), in which he proposed that the youth of China rejuvenate the nation intellectually and culturally; LU XUN, HU SHI, and MAO ZEDONG were all contributors. In 1917 Chen was appointed dean of the School of Letters at Beijing University. In 1919 he was imprisoned briefly for his role in the MAY FOURTH MOVEMENT; on his release he became a Marxist. With LI DAZHAO he founded the CHINESE COMMUNIST PARTY in 1920; he is regarded as "China's Lenin." The Communist International had him removed as party leader when the party's alliance with the Nationalists (GUOMINDANG) fell apart, and he was expelled from the party in 1929. Arrested in 1932, he spent five years in prison.

Chenab River \chə-'näb\ *ancient* **Acesines** River, India and Pakistan. Rising in HIMACHAL PRADESH in the Indian HIMALAYAS, it flows west through JAMMU, Kashmir, and the central PUNJAB, Pakistan, to unite with the SUTLEJ to form the Panjnad. Joined by the JHELUM in the western Punjab, it is 599 mi (964 km) long. One of the "five rivers" of the Punjab, it is the source of an extensive canal and irrigation system.

Cheney, Richard B. (born 1941) U.S. Republican politician and vice president of the U.S. from 2001. Born in Lincoln, Nebraska, he grew up in Casper, Wyoming. He became a deputy assistant to President GERALD FORD in 1974 and his chief of staff from 1975 to 1977. In 1978 he was elected from Wyoming to the first of six terms in the U.S. House of Representatives. From 1989 to 1993 he served as secretary of defense in the administration of President GEORGE BUSH, presiding over reductions in the military following the breakup of the Soviet Union. He left government service and spent several years in the private sector before being elected vice president on a ticket with GEORGE W. BUSH in 2000.

Cheng Ch'eng-kung See ZHENG CHENGGONG

Cheng-chou See ZHENGZHOU

Cheng Hao and Cheng Yi *or* **Ch'eng Hao and Ch'eng I** \'chəŋ-'hau̇...'chəŋ-'ē\ (1032–1085, 1033–1107) Brothers who developed NEO-

CONFUCIANISM into an organized philosophical school. Cheng Hao studied Buddhism, Taoism, and then Confucianism. He was dismissed from Chinese government service for opposing the reforms of WANG ANSHI, and he joined his brother in Honan, where they gathered a circle of disciples. Cheng Yi's stern morality led him to decline high office and criticize those in power. He was twice censured and pardoned. The brothers built their philosophies on the concept of *li* (basic truths), but Cheng Hao stressed calm introspection while Cheng Yi stressed investigation of the myriad things of the universe and participation in human affairs. Cheng Hao's idealism was continued by LU XIANGSHAN and WANG YANGMING, and Cheng Yi's realism was developed by ZHU XI.

Cheng Ho See ZHENG HE

Cheng-hsien See ZHENGZHOU

Ch'eng-tsung See DORGON

Cheng-Zhu school *or* **Ch'eng-Chu school** \'chəŋ-'jü\ Chinese school of NEO-CONFUCIANISM. Its leading philosophers were Cheng Yi (see CHENG HAO AND CHENG YI) and ZHU XI, for whom the school is named. Cheng Yi taught that to understand *li* (basic truths), one should investigate all things in the world through induction, deduction, historical study, or political activity. Zhu Xi maintained that rational investigation was central to moral cultivation. The school dominated Chinese philosophy until the Republican Revolution (1911).

Chengdu *or* **Ch'eng-tu** \'chəŋ-'dü\ City (pop., 1990: 1,713,000), capital of SICHUAN province, China. It lies in the fertile Chengdu plain, the site of one of China's most ancient and successful irrigation systems, watered by the MIN RIVER. First set up in the late 3rd century BC, the system has survived, and it enables the area to support what has been called the densest agrarian population in the world. Chengdu was the capital of various dynasties, and in the 10th century AD it was immensely prosperous; its merchants introduced the use of paper money, which spread throughout China under the SONG DYNASTIES. In medieval times it was famous for its brocades and satins. The capital of Sichuan since 1368, it has remained a major administrative center. Today it is a transportation and industrial hub, as well as an educational center.

Chengzong See DORGON

Chennai \ˌchen-'nī\ *formerly* **Madras** \mə-'dräs\ City (metro. area pop., 2001 prelim.: 6,424,624), capital of TAMIL NADU state, India, on the Coromandel Coast of the Bay of BENGAL. Founded in 1639 by the British EAST INDIA CO. as a fort and trading post, it was known as Fort St. George and was used as a base for the company's expansion in southern India. The city of St. Thomé, established by the Portuguese in the 16th century, was ceded to the British in 1749 and incorporated into it. The English made Chennai their administrative and commercial capital c. 1800. It is an industrial center, and the site of numerous educational and cultural institutions. It is traditionally considered the burial place of St. THOMAS the apostle.

Chennault \shə-'nȯlt\, **Claire L(ee)** (1890–1958) U.S. brigadier general. He served in the army air corps for 20 years before he was retired in 1937 because of increasing deafness. He became an air adviser to CHIANG KAI-SHEK , and he formed the group of U.S. volunteer aviators called the FLYING TIGERS to combat the Japanese. Recalled to active duty in World War II, he commanded U.S. Army Air Forces in China 1942–45. He and his Chinese wife, Anna, remained influential supporters of Chiang Kai-shek.

Cher River \'sher\ River, central France. Rising in the northwest of the MASSIF CENTRAL, it flows northwest, passing through Chenonceaux, where it is bridged by a historic chateau, then passes south of TOURS to join the LOIRE RIVER after a course of 217 mi (349 km).

Cherbourg \sher-'bür, *Engl* 'sher-ˌbu̇rg\ Seaport (pop., 1990: 29,000) and naval station, northwestern France. Located on the ENGLISH CHANNEL, it is believed to occupy the site of an ancient Roman station. The French and English fought over the site in the Middle Ages. It was taken by the English in 1758, then passed to France and was extensively fortified by LOUIS XVI. In World War II the Germans held it until the Allies captured it in 1944; it became an important Allied supply port. Industries include transatlantic shipping, shipbuilding and the manufacture of electronics and telephone equipment. Yachting and commercial fishing are also important.

Cherenkov radiation \chə-'reŋ-kȯf\ Light produced by charged particles when they pass through an optically transparent medium at speeds greater than the speed of light in that medium. For example, when ELECTRONS from a nuclear reactor travel through shielding water, they do so at a speed greater than that of light through water and they displace some electrons from the atoms in their path. This causes emission of ELECTROMAGNETIC RADIATION that appears as a weak bluish-white glow. The phenomenon is named for Pavel A. Cherenkov (1904–1990), who discovered it; he shared a 1958 Nobel Prize with Igor Y. Tamm (1895–1971) and Ilya M. Frank (1908–1990), who interpreted the effect.

Chernenko \cher-'nʸeŋ-kō\, **Konstantin (Ustinovich)** (1911–1985) Soviet leader. He joined the Communist Party in 1931 and rose through the ranks to become LEONID BREZHNEV's chief of staff (1964). He was a full member of the Central Committee from 1971 and of the Politburo from 1977. An old-line conservative, he was considered by some to be Brezhnev's heir apparent, but failed in a bid to succeed Brezhnev as party leader in 1982. When YURI ANDROPOV died, Chernenko succeeded him in 1984. His physical frailty soon became apparent, suggesting that his election had been intended as an interim measure; he died the next year.

Chernigov \chir-'nē-gəf\ City (pop., 1991 est.: 306,000), Ukraine. Capital of Chernigov Oblast, it lies northeast of KIEV on the Desna River. Mentioned as early as AD 907, it became the capital of Chernigov principality in the 11th century, when its cathedral was built. Chernigov lost importance after the TATAR invasion (1239–40) and remained a minor provincial center until modern times, when it developed as a railway junction.

Chernobyl accident \chər-'nō-bəl\ Accident at the Chernobyl (Ukraine) nuclear power station in the Soviet Union, the worst in the history of nuclear power generation. On April 25–26, 1986, technicians attempted a poorly designed experiment, causing the chain reaction in the core to go out of control. The reactor's lid was blown off, and large amounts of radioactive material were released into the atmosphere. A partial meltdown of the core also occurred. A cover-up was attempted, but after Swedish monitoring stations reported abnormally high levels of wind-transported radioactivity, the Soviet government admitted the truth. Beyond 32 immediate deaths, several thousand radiation-induced illnesses and cancer deaths were expected in the long term. The incident set off an international outcry over the dangers posed by radioactive emissions.

Chernov \chər-'nȯf\, **Viktor (Mikhaylovich)** (1873–1952) Russian revolutionary, cofounder of the Russian SOCIALIST REVOLUTIONARY PARTY. A revolutionist from 1893, he became a member of his party's central committee in 1902 and wrote the party's platform. In 1917 he served briefly as minister of agriculture. He was elected president of the constituent assembly that opened in Petrograd on January 18, 1918, but was dispersed the next day by the Bolsheviks. He emigrated in 1920, wrote (sometimes as Boris Olenin) and lived in Paris until 1940, then went to the U.S., where he wrote for anticommunist periodicals.

Chernyshevsky \chər-ni-'shef-skē\, **N(ikolay) G(avrilovich)** (1828–1889) Russian radical journalist and politician. In 1854 he joined the staff of the review *Sovremennik* ("Contemporary"), where he focused on social and economic evils. Arrested on charges of subversion, he was imprisoned in 1862 and then exiled to Siberia, where he remained until 1883. While in prison he wrote the classic novel *What Is to be Done?* (1863), which greatly influenced future Russian revolutionaries.

Cherokee American Indian people of Iroquoian lineage who inhabited eastern Tennessee and the western Carolinas. Cherokee culture resembled that of the CREEK and other SOUTHEASTERN INDIANS. They possessed stone implements, wove baskets, made pottery, cultivated corn, beans, and squash, and hunted deer, bear, and elk. Wars and treaties in the late 18th century severely reduced Cherokee power and landholdings. After a series of failed raids against U.S. troops and civilian settlements, land was ceded to attain peace and to pay debts. After 1800 the Cherokee were remarkable for their assimilation of white culture, forming a government modeled on that of the U.S. and adopting European methods of farming and homemaking. Most became literate following the development of a syllabary by SEQUOYAH. Beginning c. 1835, when gold was discovered on Cherokee land in Georgia, agitation increased for their removal to the West. The ensuing events, culminating in the TRAIL OF TEARS, left many Cherokee dead and most of their descendants (today numbering about 200,000) living in Oklahoma.

cherry Any of various trees of the genus *Prunus,* and their edible fruits. Most are native to the Northern Hemisphere, where they are widely grown. Three types are grown mainly for their fruit: sweet cherries *(P. avium);* sour, or tart, cherries *(P. cerasus);* and, to a much lesser extent, dukes (crosses of sweet and sour cherries). Sweet-cherry trees are large and bear fruit that is generally heart-shaped to nearly globular, varies in color from yellow through red to nearly black, and has a low acid content. Sour-cherry trees are smaller and bear fruit that is round to oblate, generally dark red, and too acidic to eat fresh. Dukes are intermediate in both tree and fruit characteristics. The wood of some cherry species is especially esteemed for the manufacture of fine furniture. Ornamental varieties selected for the beauty of their flowers are a common feature of gardens.

Cherry (*Prunus cerasus*).
GRANT HEILMAN

Cherry Valley Raid (November 11, 1778) Attack during the AMERICAN REVOLUTION by IROQUOIS on a New York frontier settlement. In retaliation for earlier assaults on two Indian villages, the Iroquois chief JOSEPH BRANT joined with British loyalists to lead the attack on the fortified village at Cherry Valley, in which 30 militiamen and settlers were killed.

Chersonese \'kər-sə-ˌnēz\ In ancient geography, any of several peninsulas in Europe and Asia (the term means "peninsula"). Tauric Chersonese comprised the CRIMEA and often the city of Chersonese, near modern SEVASTOPOL. The city, founded by Ionian Greeks in the 6th century BC, later traded with Athens, Delos, and Rhodes and flourished under the Romans and Byzantines. Thracian Chersonese constituted the modern GALLIPOLI Peninsula. On the main trade route between Europe and Asia, it was the site of several cities founded by Aeolians and Ionians in the 7th century BC. Abandoned to DARIUS I in 493 BC, it came under Athenian control and was later dominated by AUGUSTUS.

chert and flint Very fine-grained QUARTZ, a silica mineral with minor impurities. Flint is gray to black and nearly opaque (translucent brown in thin splinters). Opaque, dull, whitish to pale-brown or gray specimens are called simply chert. Chert and flint provided the main source of tools and weapons for STONE AGE people. Flint is used today as an abrasive agent on sandpapers and in mills that grind raw materials for the ceramic and paint industries. Considerable amounts of chert are also used in road construction and as concrete aggregate. Some chert takes an excellent polish and is used as semiprecious jewelry. See also SILICEOUS ROCK.

cherub In Jewish, Christian, and Islamic literature, a celestial winged being with human, animal, or birdlike characteristics. They are included among the ANGELS, and in the Old Testament they are described as the throne-bearers of God. In Christianity and Islam, they are celestial attendants of God and praise him continually. Known as *karubiyun* in Islam, they repeat "Glory to Allah" ceaselessly, and they dwell in a section of heaven inaccessible to attacks by the devil. In art they are often depicted as winged infants. See also SERAPH.

Cherubini \ˌkā-rü-'bē-nē\, **Luigi (Carlo Zanobi Salvadore Maria)** (1760–1842) Italian-French composer. Born into a musical family, the precociously gifted youth had written dozens of works before he was 20, and he produced his first opera that year. In 1788 he settled permanently in Paris. He enjoyed operatic successes in the 1790s, and NAPOLEON expressed his particular admiration. He became co-superintendent of the royal chapel in 1816, and in 1822 director of the Paris Conservatoire, where he would remain the rest of his life. LUDWIG VAN BEETHOVEN called Cherubini his greatest contemporary. His counterpoint text (1835) was used widely for a century. Of his nearly 40 operas, the most popular were *Lodoïska* (1791), *Médée* (1797), and *Les deux journées* (1800). His other important works include a symphony (1815), six string quartets, Requiems in C minor and D minor (1816, 1836) and nine surviving masses.

Chesapeake \'che-sə-ˌpēk\ City (pop., 1996 est.: 192,000), southeastern Virginia. Located south of NORFOLK, it was formed as an independent city in 1963 by the merger of Norfolk Co. and the city of South Norfolk. At 341 sq mi (883 sq km), it is one of the largest cities in area in the U.S. The area, encompassing part of DISMAL SWAMP, was once the home of the Chesapeake Indians and was settled by colonists in the 1630s.

Chesapeake and Ohio Canal National Historical Park Park, eastern U.S. It consists of the former Chesapeake and Ohio Canal, a waterway running along the POTOMAC RIVER between WASHINGTON, D.C., and Cumberland, Md. The canal, which extends 185 mi (297 km), was built beginning in the 1820s. Competition from the railroads later caused its economic decline. The canal was purchased in 1938 by the U.S. government; it was restored and established as a historical park in 1971.

Chesapeake and Ohio Railway Co. (C&O) U.S. railroad company established in 1868 with the consolidation of two smaller lines, the Virginia Central and the Covington and Ohio. The railroad later acquired several other lines, mainly in the upper South and the Midwest, which together became known as the Chessie System. In 1972 its passenger services were taken over by AMTRAK, and in 1980 it merged with Seaboard Coast Line Industries, Inc., to form the CSX Corp.

Chesapeake Bay Inlet of the Atlantic Ocean, eastern U.S. With its lower section in Virginia and its upper section in Maryland, it is 193 mi (311 km) long and 3–25 mi (5–40 km) wide and has an area of about 3,230 sq mi (8,365 sq km). It receives many rivers, including the SUSQUEHANNA, Patuxent, POTOMAC, and JAMES. JAMESTOWN, the area's first European settlement, was founded in 1607; a year later, Capt. JOHN SMITH explored and mapped the bay. The bay's waters had supported vast amounts of marine life, but by the 1970s development of the surrounding area led to alarming pollution of the bay; fishing dropped off sharply. Efforts have since been made to reverse the damage.

Cheselden \'chez-əl-dən\, **William** (1688–1752) British surgeon and teacher. His *Anatomy of the Human Body* (1713) and *Osteographia* (1733) were both used by anatomy students for nearly a century. His technique for extracting bladder stones through an incision in the side rather than the front (1727) was soon used by surgeons throughout Europe. He also devised a way to surgically create an "artificial pupil" to treat some forms of blindness.

Cheshire \'che-shər\ County (population 1995 est.: 978,000), western ENGLAND. Established in 1974, it includes most of the former county that was Cheshire except for parts now in MERSEYSIDE and GREATER MANCHESTER; the county seat is CHESTER. Bordering WALES and fronting the Dee and MERSEY river estuaries to the north, it lies partly within the Peak District National Park. Evidence of hill forts from the Bronze and Iron ages have been found, as well as ruins of structures from the Roman occupation. The county is largely agricultural, with dairy farming predominant.

Chesnut, Mary *orig.* **Mary Boykin Miller** (1823–1886) U.S. writer. Born in Pleasant Hill, S.C., she married James Chesnut, Jr., who would play an important role in the secession movement and the Confederacy. She accompanied him on his military missions as a staff officer and recorded her views and observations in her journal. Her *Diary from Dixie*, a perceptive view of Southern life during the Civil War, was first published in 1905.

Chesnutt, Charles (Waddell) (1858–1932) U.S. writer, the first important African-American novelist. As a young school principal in North Carolina, he was so distressed by the treatment of blacks that he moved his family to Cleveland, where he became an attorney and began writing in his spare time. He published numerous tales and essays, two collections of short stories, a biography of FREDERICK DOUGLASS, and three novels, including *The Colonel's Dream* (1905). A psychological realist, he used familiar scenes of folk life to protest social injustice.

chess Checkerboard game for two players, each of whom moves 16 pieces according to fixed rules across the board and tries to capture or immobilize (checkmate) the opponent's king. The game may have originated in Asia around the 6th century, though it continued to evolve as it spread into Europe in Byzantine times; its now-standard rules first became generally accepted in Europe in the 16th century. Each opponent,

Chess pieces located at their starting positions on the chessboard.

designated white and black, start with their pieces and pawns as shown in the diagram. Kings move one square in any direction—but not into attack (check). Bishops move diagonally, and rooks horizontally or vertically, any number of unobstructed squares. Queens move like either a bishop or a rook. Knights move to the nearest nonadjacent square of the opposite color (an "L" shape) and ignore intervening chessmen. Pieces capture by moving to an (enemy) occupied square. Pawns move forward one square (one or two on their first move) and are promoted to any non-king piece if they reach the last row. Pawns only capture one diagonal square forward of them. For one turn, a pawn has the option, known as *en passant,* of capturing a pawn that has just moved two squares and landed beside it; the capture occurs as though the pawn had moved only one square. When the first row between a king and either rook is clear, and as long as the king and that rook have not moved, a maneuver known as castling can be done in which the king is shifted two squares toward that rook and the rook is placed directly on the other side of the king. Kings cannot castle when in check or through any square in which they would be in check. A draw known as stalemate occurs if a player to move is not in check and any move would place him in check. A draw also occurs if the same position occurs three times (such as through "perpetual check").

Chess, Leonard *orig.* **Leonard Czyz** (1917–1969) U.S. (Polish-born) record producer. He emigrated to the U.S in 1928 with his brother, Phil (born c. 1920), and settled in Chicago, where they opened a lounge. In the late 1940s, Leonard joined the Aristocrat record company; in 1950 he bought the company and, with Phil as partner, renamed it Chess. Fans of the electric blues that were being heard in the city after World War II, they signed such artists as M. WATERS, WILLIE DIXON, C. BERRY, Howlin' Wolf (1910–1976), and Bo Diddley (born 1928), and played a major role in introducing black music to a wider white audience.

Chester *ancient* **Deva** *or* **Devana Castra.** City (pop., 1999 est: 115,971), county seat of CHESHIRE, England. Located on the Dee River south of LIVERPOOL, it is an active port and railroad center. For several centuries after AD 60, it was the Roman "camp on the Dee," headquarters of the 20th Legion; well-preserved Roman walls remain. It was the last place in England to surrender to WILLIAM THE CONQUEROR (1070). It became an important port in the 13th–14th century, trading especially with Ireland. From about the 14th century, it was the scene of the presentation of the MYSTERY PLAYS of the Chester Cycle. The gradual silting of the Dee led to the city's decline, but in the 19th century railroad traffic renewed its prosperity.

Chesterton, G(ilbert) K(eith) (1874–1936) British man of letters. Though he studied art, he never practiced it professionally but instead went into journalistic writing. His works of social and literary criticism include *Robert Browning* (1903), *Charles Dickens* (1906), and *The Victorian Age in Literature* (1913). Even before his conversion to Roman Catholicism in 1922, he was interested in theology and religious argument. His fiction includes *The Napoleon of Notting Hill* (1904), the popular allegorical novel *The Man Who Was Thursday* (1908), and his most successful creation, the series of detective novels featuring the priest-sleuth Father Brown.

Chesterton, chalk drawing by James Gunn, 1932; in the National Portrait Gallery, London.

chestnut Any of four species of deciduous ornamental and timber trees of the genus *Castanea,* in the BEECH family, native to temperate regions of the Northern Hemisphere, with burlike fruits that contain two or three edible NUTS. The usually tall trees have furrowed bark and lance-shaped leaves. The American chestnut *(C. dentata),* which once extended over a large area of eastern North America, has been almost eliminated by CHESTNUT BLIGHT. The other three species are the European chestnut *(C. sativa),* the Chinese chestnut *(C. mollissima),* and the Japanese chestnut *(C. crenata).*

chestnut blight Plant disease caused by the FUNGUS *Endothia parasitica.* Accidentally imported from the Orient and first observed in 1904 in New York, it has killed almost all native American CHESTNUTS *(Castanea dentata)* in the U.S. and Canada and is destructive in other countries. Other blight-susceptible species include the European chestnut *(C. sativa),* the post oak *(Quercus stellata),* and the LIVE OAK. Symptoms include reddish-brown bark patches that develop into sunken or swollen and cracked cankers that kill twigs and limbs. Leaves on such branches turn brown and wither but remain attached for months. Gradually the entire tree dies. The fungus persists for years in short-lived sprouts from old chestnut roots and in less susceptible hosts. It is spread locally by splashing rain, wind, and insects, and over long distances by birds. Chinese *(C. mollissima)* and Japanese *(C. crenata)* chestnuts are resistant.

Chetumal \ˌchā-tü-ˈmäl\ City (pop., 2000 est.: 118,000), capital of QUINTANA ROO state, Mexico. Located on the eastern coast of the YUCATÁN PENINSULA just north of Belize, it lies only 20 ft (6 m) above sea level. Founded in 1899, it became the territorial capital when Quintana Roo was separated from YUCATÁN state in 1902. It is set in tropical rain forests and depends on forest products for its income.

chevalier See KNIGHT

Chevalier \shə-väl-ˈyā\, **Maurice** (1888–1972) French singer and actor. He first appeared as a singer

Maurice Chevalier.

and comedian at the FOLIES BERGÈRE in 1909. He spent two years in a German prison camp during World War I. Known for his jaunty straw hat and bow tie and his lively, roguish manner, he went to Hollywood in 1929, where he appeared in movies that helped establish the musical as a film genre, including *The Love Parade* (1929) and *The Merry Widow* (1934). He was criticized for entertaining the Germans during the wartime occupation of France. His later films include *Gigi* (1958) and *Fanny* (1961). In 1958 he was awarded an honorary Academy Award.

Cheviot Hills \'shi-vē-ət\ Range of hills along the England–Scotland border. Extending northeast-southwest by the two countries' boundary, its highest elevation is Cheviot, at 2,676 ft (816 m). Evidence of prehistoric occupation is widespread. The land controlled by the Forestry Commission became a National Forest Park in 1955, and an even larger area was designated as Northumberland National Park.

Chevreuse \shəv-'rœz\, **duchesse de** *orig.* **Marie de Rohan-Montbazon** *known as* **Madame de Chevreuse** (1600–1679) French princess. She participated in several conspiracies against the ministerial government in LOUIS XIII's reign and the regency for LOUIS XIV. She was exiled several times for her activities, including participating in a plot against Cardinal de RICHELIEU, betraying state secrets to Spain, and plotting to assassinate JULES MAZARIN.

chevrotain \'shev-rə-ˌtān\ *or* **mouse deer** Any of several species (family Tragulidae) of small, delicately built RUMINANTS of Asia and Africa. Resembling tiny deer, chevrotains stand about 12 in. (30 cm) at the shoulder and seem to walk on their hooftips. Their fur is reddish brown with spots and pale stripes. Males have small, curved tusks protruding downward from the upper jaw. Shy and solitary, they are active at night. Asiatic chevrotains are found in forests from India to the Philippines. The water chevrotain of western equatorial Africa inhabits thick cover on the banks of rivers and seeks escape in the water when disturbed.

Chewa Bantu-speaking people living in eastern Zambia, northwestern Zimbabwe, and Malawi. They practice slash-and-burn agriculture, hunt, and fish. Slavery was formerly standard among the Chewa. Descent, inheritance, and succession are matrilineal and polygyny is general. Chewa settlements are governed by a hereditary headman and a council of elders.

chewing *or* **mastication** Up-and-down and side-to-side movements of the lower jaw, using the teeth to grind food for easier swallowing. During chewing, the tongue shapes food into a lump and saliva lubricates it for swallowing. Chewing softens tough meat or vegetable fibers and exposes them to digestive enzymes.

chewing gum Sweetened product made from chicle and similar resilient substances and chewed for its flavor. Tree resins have been chewed by peoples around the world as teeth cleaners and breath fresheners since ancient times. The latex (called chicle) of the Central American sapodilla tree was first used to mass-produce chewing gum in the 19th century; its plasticity, insolubility in water, and ability to hold a flavor made it an ideal chewing-gum base. After World War II other gums and synthetic rubbers came to replace chicle.

Cheyenne PLAINS INDIAN people of Algonquian stock (see ALGONQUIAN LANGUAGES) who inhabited the regions around the Platte and Arkansas rivers in the 19th century. Originally farmers, hunters, and gatherers, they became more dependent on the buffalo for food after acquiring horses and developed a tepee-dwelling nomadic mode of life. They performed the SUN DANCE and placed heavy emphasis on visions in which an animal spirit adopted the individual and bestowed special powers on him. They had well-organized military societies, and fought constantly with the KIOWA until c. 1840. In the 1870s they participated in various Indian uprisings, joining the SIOUX at LITTLE BIGHORN in 1876. Today there are about 5,000 Cheyenne living in southeastern Montana and 5,000 Cheyenne-Arapaho in Oklahoma.

Cheyenne \shī-'an\ City (pop., 2000: 53,011), capital of Wyoming. It is the state's largest city, and its capital since 1869. It became an outfitting point for the BLACK HILLS goldfields to the northeast and a major shipping point for cattle from Texas. Its own grazing lands became famed for their herds and cattle barons. In July it celebrates Frontier Days, which includes one of America's oldest and largest rodeos. Nearby Fort Francis E. Warren was the site of the nation's first intercontinental ballistic missile base (1957).

Cheyenne River River, northern central U.S. Rising in eastern Wyoming, it flows northeast 527 mi (850 km) to join the MISSOURI RIVER in central South Dakota. Angostura Dam, part of the Missouri River basin irrigation project, is on the river near Hot Springs, S.D.

Cheyne \'chān\, **William Watson** *later* **Sir William** (1852–1932) English surgeon and bacteriologist. His early work on preventive medicine and bacterial causes of disease was strongly influenced by that of ROBERT KOCH. He became a devoted follower of JOSEPH LISTER and was a pioneer of antiseptic surgical methods in Britain. He published the important works *Antiseptic Surgery* (1882) and *Lister and His Achievements* (1885).

Chhattisgarh State (pop., 2001 prelim.: 20,795,956), central India. It occupies 52,199 sq mi (135,194 sq km); its capital is Raipur. The Chhattisgarh Plain covers much of the state, with the land becoming more hilly to the north and west. The area now comprising Chhattisgarh was the eastern portion of MADHYA PRADESH state before it was made into a separate state in 2000. It is rich in minerals, but the population is mainly engaged in agriculture.

Ch'i See QI

ch'i See QI

ch'i-lin See QILIN

Chian-ning See NANJING

Chiang Ching-kuo *or (pinyin)* **Jiang Jinguo** \jē-'äŋ-'jiŋ-'gwō\ (1910–1988) Son of CHIANG KAI-SHEK, and his successor as leader of the Republic of China. He was formally elected by the National Assembly to a six-year presidential term in 1978 and reelected in 1984. He tried to maintain Taiwan's foreign-trade relationships and political independence as other countries began to break off diplomatic relations in order to establish ties with mainland China. Throughout his presidency Chiang opposed Taiwanese recognition of the Chinese Communist regime and negotiations for reunification with the mainland.

Chiang Kai-shek \jē-'äŋ-'kī-'shek, *Engl.* chaŋ-kī-'shek\ *or* **Chiang Chieh-shih** *or* **Jiang Jieshi** \jē-'äŋ-jē-'esh-'ē\ (1887–1975) Head of the Nationalist government in China (1928–49) and later in Taiwan (1949–75). After receiving military training in Tokyo, in 1918 he joined SUN YAT-SEN, leader of the NATIONALIST PARTY, which was trying to consolidate control over a nation in chaos. In the 1920s Chiang became commander in chief of the revolutionary army, which he sent to crush warlords active in the north (see NORTHERN EXPEDITION). In the 1930s he and WANG JINGWEI vied for control of a new central government with its capital at NANJING. Faced with Japanese aggression in Manchuria and communist opposition led by MAO ZEDONG in the hinterland, Chiang decided to crush the communists first. This proved to be a mistake, and Chiang was forced into a temporary alliance with the communists when war broke out with Japan in 1937. After the war China's civil war resumed, culminating in the Nationalists' flight to Taiwan in 1949, where Chiang ruled, supported by U.S. economic and military aid, until his death, when his son, CHIANG CHING-KUO, took up the reins of government. His years ruling Taiwan, though dictatorial, oversaw the island's economic development and increasing prosperity even in the face of its precarious geopolitical position. His failure to keep control of mainland China has been attributed to poor morale among his troops, lack of responsiveness to popular sentiment, and lack of a coherent plan for making the deep social and economic changes China required.

Chiang Kai-shek.
CAMERA PRESS

Chiang Mai \'jyäŋ-'mī\ City (pop., 1991 est.: 162,000), northwestern Thailand. Located on the Ping River about 80 mi (130 km) east of Myanmar, it was founded in the late 13th century as the capital of the independent LAN NA kingdom. Later subject to Myanmar, it was taken by the

Siamese in 1774, but retained a degree of independence from BANGKOK until the late 19th century. It is now northern Thailand's religious, economic, and cultural center. Nearby is the temple complex of Wat Phra That Doi Suthop, whose monastery was built in the 14th century.

Chiapas \chē-'ä-päs\ State (pop., 2000: 3,920,892), southeastern Mexico. Bounded by Guatemala and the Pacific Ocean, it is mountainous and forested and covers 28,653 sq mi (74,211 sq km). The capital is TUXTLA GUTIÉRREZ. It is inhabited mainly by Indian peoples. The extraordinary MAYA ruins of PALENQUE are in the northeastern rainforests. Bonhampak, with its famous Mayan murals, can be reached from Tuxtla. Linked with Guatemala in colonial days, Chiapas became a Mexican state in 1824; its boundaries were fixed in 1882. In 1994 impoverished Indians and middle-class residents, protesting economic and social inequalities, created the Zapatista National Liberation Army and launched an armed uprising that continued into the 21st century.

chiaroscuro \kē-,är-ə-'skyůr-ō\ (Italian: "light-dark") Contrasting effects of light and shade in a work of art. LEONARDO DA VINCI brought the technique to its full potential, but it is usually associated with such 17th-century artists as CARAVAGGIO and REMBRANDT, who used it to outstanding effect. The chiaroscuro woodcut, produced by printing different tones of a color from separate woodblocks on a single sheet of paper, was first produced in 16th-century Italy.

Chibcha \'chib-,chä\ *or* **Muisca** \'mwēskə\ Group of South American Indians who at the time of the Spanish conquest occupied the high valleys surrounding what are now Bogotá and Tunja in Colombia. They had a population of over 500,000 and were more centralized politically than any other South American people outside the INCA empire. Their economy was based on intensive agriculture, a variety of crafts, and extensive trade. Society was highly stratified. The Chibchas' political structure was crushed by Spanish invaders in the 16th century, and by the 18th century they had been assimilated into the rest of the population. See also ANDEAN CIVILIZATION.

Chicago City (pop., 2000: 2,896,016), northeastern Illinois. Located on Lake MICHIGAN, with the CHICAGO RIVER flowing through it, Chicago has extensive port facilities. In the 17th century the name was associated with a portage between the DES PLAINES and Chicago rivers connecting the ST. LAWRENCE RIVER and the GREAT LAKES with the MISSISSIPPI RIVER. Fort Dearborn was built in 1803 on a tract acquired from Indians. It expanded rapidly after the completion of the Illinois and Michigan Canal (1848), which connected the Chicago and Mississippi rivers, and also became the nation's chief rail center. Rebuilt quickly after a hugely destructive fire in 1871, it was the site of the World's Columbian Exposition in 1893. It was the birthplace of the steel-frame skyscraper in the late 19th century, and it boasts designs by eminent architects, including LOUIS SULLIVAN, FRANK LLOYD WRIGHT, and LUDWIG MIES VAN DER ROHE. Nuclear scientists produced the first nuclear chain reaction at the University of CHICAGO in 1942. After World War II the city underwent another building boom, but as in other large cities its population subsequently dropped as its suburbs grew. The 3d largest U.S. city, it is a major industrial, commercial, and transportation center and is the site of the Chicago Mercantile Exchange and the Chicago Board of Trade. Several museums and the ART INSTITUTE OF CHICAGO are located there.

Chicago, Judy *orig.* **Judy Cohen** (born 1939) U.S. multimedia artist. She studied at UCLA, and in 1970 she adopted the name of her hometown. Motivated by perceived discrimination in the art world and alienation from Western art traditions, she developed the concepts of "vaginal iconography" and "central core" imagery. Her most notable work, *The Dinner Party* (1974–79), is a triangular table with place settings for 39 important women represented by ceramic plates with feminine imagery and table runners embellished with embroidery styles typical of their eras. In 1973 she cofounded the Feminist Studio Workshop and Woman's Building in Los Angeles.

Chicago, University of Independent university in Chicago, founded in 1891 with an endowment from DAVID ROCKEFELLER. William Rainey Harper, its first president (1891–1906), did much to establish its reputation, and under ROBERT M. HUTCHINS (1929–51) it came to be recognized for its broad liberal-arts curriculum. The world's first department of sociology was established there in 1892 under ROBERT E. PARK. In 1942 it was the site of the first controlled self-sustaining nuclear chain reaction, under the direction of ENRICO FERMI. Other notable achievements include the development of CARBON-14 DATING and the isolation of PLUTONIUM. The university comprises an undergraduate college, several professional schools, and centers for advanced research, including the Oriental Institute (Middle Eastern studies), Yerkes Observatory, the Enrico Fermi Institute, and the Center for Policy Study. The university operates the Argonne National Laboratory. Total enrollment is about 13,000.

Chicago and North Western Transportation Co. U.S. railroad company. It was formed when employees of the financially troubled Chicago and North Western Railway Co. purchased its assets in 1972. The initial company, created in 1859, evolved from the Galena and Chicago Union Railroad, which had been the first railroad to enter Chicago (1848). Employees ceased to hold a majority of the company's stock in 1983. The system served an 11-state region west of Lake Michigan, with principal routes in Wisconsin, Minnesota, Iowa, and Nebraska. It was purchased by UNION PACIFIC in 1995.

Chicago literary renaissance Flourishing of literary activity in Chicago c. 1912–25. Its leading writers—T. DREISER, SHERWOOD ANDERSON, EDGAR LEE MASTERS, and CARL SANDBURG—realistically depicted the contemporary urban environment, condemning the loss of traditional rural values in the increasingly industrialized and materialistic American society. Associated with the period were The Little Theatre, an outlet for young playwrights; The Little Room, a literary group; and magazines including *The Dial*, *Poetry*, and *The Little Review*. The renaissance also encompassed a revitalization of newspaper journalism as a literary medium.

Chicago Race Riot of 1919 Most severe of about 25 race riots throughout the U.S. in the summer after World War I. Racial friction was intensified by the migration of blacks to the North. In Chicago's South Side, the black population had increased in 10 years from 44,000 to 109,000. The riot was triggered by the stoning death of a black youth swimming in Lake Michigan near a white beach. When police refused to arrest the white man allegedly responsible, fighting broke out between gangs of both races. Violence spread throughout the city, undeterred by the state militia. After 13 days, 38 were dead (23 blacks, 15 whites), 537 injured, and 1,000 black families made homeless.

Chicago River River, CHICAGO, Illinois. A small river, consisting of a northern and southern branch, it originally flowed into Lake MICHIGAN. After a severe storm in 1885 caused the river to empty large amounts of polluted water into the lake, its flow was reversed by constructing a canal in 1900, the building of which was considered a significant engineering feat. Now flowing inland, it is connected with the DES PLAINES RIVER by the Chicago Sanitary and Ship Canal.

Chicago school Group of architects and engineers who in the 1890s exploited the twin developments of structural steel framing and the electrified elevator, paving the way for the ubiquitous modern-day skyscraper. Their work earned for Chicago the title "birthplace of modern architecture." Among the school's members were LOUIS SULLIVAN, DANIEL BURNHAM, and John Wellborn Root (1850–1891).

Chicago Tribune Daily newspaper published in Chicago, one of the leading U.S. newspapers and long the dominant voice of the Midwest. Founded in 1847, it was bought in 1855 by six partners, including Joseph Medill (1823–99), who made the paper successful and increased its stature while promulgating his generally liberal views. He bought a controlling interest in 1874 and was publisher until his death. During ROBERT McCORMICK's tenure (1914–55), the paper reflected his nationalist-isolationist views, but after his death it relaxed its jingoism and political conservatism. It subsequently became the flagship of the Tribune Company, which has holdings in broadcast, cable, publishing, and other media.

Chichén Itzá \chē-'chen-ēt-'sä\ Ancient ruined Mayan city in Mexico's Yucatán state. Chichén Itzá was founded by MAYAS around the 6th century AD in an arid region where water was obtained from natural wells called cenotes. The city was invaded in the 10th century—probably by a Mayan-speaking group under strong TOLTEC influence—and the invaders constructed another series of buildings, including the famous stepped pyramid known as El Castillo and a ball court. The site had been largely abandoned by the time the Spanish arrived in the 16th century, but remained sacred to Mayan Indians. See photograph opposite on following page.

Chicherin \chi-'cher-yin\, **Georgy (Vasilyevich)** (1872–1936) Russian diplomat. An aristocrat by birth, he entered the imperial diplomatic service in 1897 but resigned to join the revolutionary movement and the

MENSHEVIK faction (1905). In 1918 he joined the BOLSHEVIKS and resumed his diplomatic career, helping negotiate the Treaty of BREST-LITOVSK. As people's commissar for foreign affairs (1918–28), he led the Soviet delegation to the Conference of GENOA and later secretly negotiated the Treaty of RAPALLO with Germany.

Chichester Town (pop., 1995 est: 28,000; metro area pop.: 103,000), England. Located northeast of PORTSMOUTH, it is the county seat of WEST SUSSEX. The basic plan of the Roman town is preserved in the modern city. The area is mainly residential and agricultural. Chichester is noted for its early Norman cathedral, begun in the late 11th century, and for its pastoral landscapes.

chickadee Any of several North American songbird species in the genus *Parus* (family Paridae), whose name imitates their call notes. They are friendly and easily attracted to feeders. The black-capped chickadee (*P. atricapillus),* found across North America, is 5 in. (13 cm) long and has a dark cap and bib. Old World members of the genus and some New World members are called TITS or titmice.

Black-capped chickadee (*Parus atricapillus*).
WILLIAM D. GRIFFIN

Chickamauga, Battle of (September 19–20, 1863) Engagement in the AMERICAN CIVIL WAR to control the railroad center of nearby Chattanooga, Tenn. Confederate forces under BRAXTON BRAGG and JAMES LONGSTREET attacked Union forces under WILLIAM ROSECRANS. After two days of fierce battle, most of the Union army withdrew in disorder, but troops under GEORGE H. THOMAS withstood the assault until he could organize an orderly withdrawal to Chattanooga. Casualties numbering 16,000 Union and 18,000 Confederate troops made this one of the bloodiest battles of the war. Bragg and the Confederate force did not follow up their victory, and the subsequent Battle of CHATTANOOGA reversed the results.

Chickasaw North American Indian people of MUSKOGEAN LANGUAGE stock who formerly inhabited northern Mississippi and Alabama. The Chickasaw were a seminomadic people whose dwellings were loosely scattered along rivers rather than clustered in villages. They traced descent through the maternal line. The supreme deity was associated with the sky, sun, and fire. They frequently raided and intermarried with other tribes, and were known to white traders as "mixed-bloods" or "breeds." In the 1830s they were forcibly removed to Indian Territory (Oklahoma), where today some 20,000 live.

The Castillo (background) and a portion of the Colonnade, Chichén Itzá.
JOSEF MUENCH

chicken One of the most widely domesticated poultry species *(Gallus gallus),* raised worldwide for its meat and eggs. Descended from the wild red JUNGLE FOWL of India, chickens have been domesticated for at least 4,000 years. Not until the 19th century did chicken meat and eggs become mass-production commodities. Modern high-volume poultry farms, with rows of cages stacked indoors for control of heat, light, and humidity, began to proliferate in Britain c. 1920 and in the U.S. after World War II (see FACTORY FARMING). Females are raised for meat and eggs; immature males are castrated to become meat birds called capons. See also PRAIRIE CHICKEN.

chickenpox *or* **varicella** \ˌvar-ə-ˈse-lə\ Contagious VIRAL DISEASE producing itchy blisters. It usually occurs in epidemics among young children, causes a low fever, and runs a mild course, leaving patients immune. The blisters can scar if scratched. The virus that causes chickenpox (varicella-zoster-virus) can reactivate years later, causing SHINGLES. Zoster immune globulin (ZIG) can prevent chickenpox in children with leukemia or immunodeficiency disorders who are exposed to the virus. A vaccine has also been developed.

chickpea *or* **garbanzo** Annual legume *(Cicer arietinum)* widely grown for its nutritious seeds. The bushy 2-ft (60-cm) plants bear pinnate leaves and small white or reddish flowers. The yellow-brown peas are borne one or two to a pod. Chickpeas are an important food plant in India, Africa, and Central and South America. They are the main ingredient of hummus, a sauce originating in the Middle East. In southern Europe, chickpeas are a common ingredient in soups, salads, and stews. A kind of meal or flour is also made from chickpeas.

chickweed Either of two species of small-leaved weeds, in the PINK FAMILY. Common chickweed, or stitchwort *(Stellaria media),* is native to Europe but widely naturalized. It usually grows to 18 in. (45 cm) but is a low-growing and spreading annual weed in mowed lawns. Mouse-ear chickweed *(Cerastium vulgatum),* also from Europe, is a usually shorter, mat-forming, spreading perennial with many upright stems. It grows in lawns, pastures, and cultivated fields throughout temperate regions. Both species have inconspicuous but delicate white, star-shaped flowers.

chicory Blue-flowered perennial plant *(Cichorium intybus)* of the COMPOSITE FAMILY. Native to Europe, it was introduced to the U.S. late in the 19th century. Chicory has a long, fleshy taproot; a rigid, branching, hairy stem; and lobed, toothed leaves, similar in appearance to dandelion leaves, around the base. Both roots and leaves are edible. The roots are also used as a flavoring in or substitute for coffee. The plant is also grown as a fodder or herbage crop for cattle.

chief justice Presiding judicial officer within any multijudge court. It is the title of the highest judicial officer in any U.S. state, and of the leader of the U.S. SUPREME COURT. The U.S. chief justice, like the associate justices, is nominated by the president and confirmed by the Senate for a lifetime tenure. The chief justices of some state supreme courts are subject to popular election and mandatory retirement ages. Chief justices are normally responsible for the administration of their own court and the preparation of the judiciary's budget.

chiefdom Type of sociopolitical organization in which political and economic POWER is exercised by a single person (or group) over many communities. It represents the centralization of power and authority at the expense of local and autonomous groupings. Political authority in chiefdoms, such as those found in western Africa or Polynesia, is inseparable from economic power, including the right by rulers to exact tribute and taxation. A principal economic activity of the heads of chiefdoms is to stimulate the production of economic surpluses, which they then redistribute among their subjects on various occasions. See also SOCIOCULTURAL EVOLUTION.

Chiem \ˈkēm\, **Lake** *German* **Chiemsee** \ˈkēm-ˌzā\ Lake, southern Germany. Located southeast of MUNICH, it lies 1,699 ft (518 m) above sea level, and drains through the Alz River into the INN RIVER. At 9 mi (15 km) long and 5 mi (8 km) wide, it is BAVARIA's largest lake. One of its three islands has a Benedictine monastery and a royal castle modeled on the palace at VERSAILLES.

Ch'ien-lung emperor See QIANLONG EMPEROR

C
D

chigger LARVA of some 10,000 MITE species, ranging in length from 0.004 to 0.6 in. (0.1–16 mm). Some are terrestrial; others live in freshwater or salt water. They may be predators, scavengers, or plant feeders, and some are pests of humans, either as parasites or as carriers of disease. In North America, the common chigger that attacks humans is found from the Atlantic coast to the Midwest and Mexico. The larva penetrates clothing and, once attached to the skin, injects a fluid that digests tissue and causes severe itching. After feeding, the larva drops to the ground and begins to mature.

Chih-i See ZHIYI

Chihli See HEBEI

Chihli, Gulf of See BO HAI

Chihuahua \chē-'wä-wä\ State (pop., 2000 est.: 3,047,867), northern Mexico. The country's largest state, it covers 94,571 sq mi (244,938 sq km) and borders the U.S. states of New Mexico and Texas. Its capital is CHIHUAHUA city. It consists largely of an elevated plain sloping toward the RÍO GRANDE. Its western area is broken by the SIERRA MADRE Occidental. Chihuahua's Barranca del Cobre (Copper Canyon) resembles the GRAND CANYON in scale. In Spanish colonial times it was ruled with DURANGO, but was made a separate state in 1823. The state's principal industry is mining; livestock raising is also important.

Chihuahua City (pop., 2000 est.: 650,000), capital of CHIHUAHUA state, Mexico. Founded in 1709, it was a prosperous mining center during the colonial era. It was twice captured by U.S. forces during the MEXICAN WAR. Now the center of a cattle-raising area, it has many noteworthy buildings, including the Church of San Francisco, one of Mexico's best 18th-century architectural specimens.

Chihuahua Smallest recognized dog breed, named for the Mexican state where it was first noted in the mid-19th century. It probably derived from the Techichi, a small, mute dog kept by the TOLTEC people as long ago as the 9th century. Typically a feisty-looking, alert dog, sturdier than its small build would suggest, it stands about 5 in. (13 cm) high and weighs 1–6 lbs (0.5–2.7 kg). It has a rounded head, large, erect ears, prominent eyes, and a compact body. The coat varies in color and may be either smooth and glossy or long and soft.

Chikamatsu Monzaemon \chē-'kä-mät-sü-mōn-'zä-ā-mōn\ *orig.* **Sugimori Nobumori** (1653–1725) Japanese playwright. Born into a samurai family, he was attached to the court aristocracy at Kyoto before moving to Osaka to be near its puppet theater. He is credited with more than 100 plays, mainly historical romances and domestic tragedies, many based on actual incidents. Most were written for the BUNRAKU, which he raised to artistic heights. His most popular work was *The Battles of Coxinga* (1715), a historical melodrama based on the life of ZHENG CHENGGONG. Also famous is *Double Suicide at Amijima* (1720). He is widely regarded as the greatest of Japanese dramatists.

Child, Julia *orig.* **Julia McWilliams** (born 1912) U.S. cooking expert and television personality. Born in Pasadena, Cal., she lived in Paris after her marriage in 1945, studying at the Cordon Bleu and with a master chef. After cowriting the best-seller *Mastering the Art of French Cooking* (1961) and moving to Boston, she created the popular PBS cooking series *The French Chef* (1962–73), and later other cooking shows. Through her programs and books, she helped educate the U.S. public about traditional French cuisine and sparked interest in the culinary arts.

Child, Lydia Maria *orig.* **Lydia Maria Francis** (1802–1880) U.S. abolitionist. Born in Medford, Mass., she wrote historical novels and a popular manual, *The Frugal Housewife* (1829), and founded the first children's periodical, *Juvenile Miscellany.* After meeting WILLIAM LLOYD GARRISON in 1831, she became active in abolitionist work. Her *Appeal in Favor of That Class of Americans Called Africans* (1833) was widely read and induced many to join the abolitionist cause. She edited the *National Anti-Slavery Standard* (1841–43) and made her home a stage on the UNDERGROUND RAILROAD.

child abuse Crime of inflicting physical or emotional injury on a child. The term can denote the use of inordinate physical violence or verbal abuse; the failure to furnish proper shelter, nourishment, medical treatment, or emotional support; INCEST, RAPE, or other instances of sexual molestation; and the making of child PORNOGRAPHY. It can have serious consequences for the victim and is a widespread but underreported phenomenon. At least 500,000 children are physically abused in the U.S. each year; many more are emotionally abused and neglected. In many cases, the abuser suffered abuse as a child. When abuse results in death, evidence of child abuse or battered-child syndrome (e.g., broken bones and lesions, either healed or active) is often used to establish that death was not accidental.

child development Growth of perceptual, emotional, intellectual, and behavioral capabilities and functioning during childhood (prior to puberty). It includes development of language, symbolic thought, logic, memory, emotional awareness, empathy, a moral sense, and a sense of identity, including sex-role identity.

child labor Employment of children in nonfarm occupations. Such labor is strictly controlled in Europe, North America, Australia, and New Zealand as a result of the effective enforcement of laws passed in the first half of the 20th century. In developing nations, the use of child labor is still common. Restrictive legislation has proved ineffective in impoverished societies with few schools.

child psychiatry Branch of medicine concerned with mental, emotional, and behavioral disorders of childhood. It arose as a separate field in the 1920s, largely because of the pioneering work of ANNA FREUD. Therapy usually involves the family, whose behavior powerfully affects children's emotional health. Parental death or divorce may affect a child's emotional growth. CHILD ABUSE and neglect have also been recognized as significant in childhood disorders. LEARNING DISABILITIES need to be distinguished from emotional problems—which they can also cause if not diagnosed in time.

child psychology Study of the psychological processes of children. The field is sometimes subsumed under DEVELOPMENTAL PSYCHOLOGY. Data are gathered through observation, interviews, tests, and experimental methods. Principal topics include language acquisition and development, motor skills, personality development, and social, emotional, and intellectual growth. The field began to emerge in the late 19th century through the work of G. STANLEY HALL and others. In the 20th century, the psychoanalysts ANNA FREUD and MELANIE KLEIN devoted themselves to child psychology, but its most influential figure was JEAN PIAGET, who described the various stages of childhood learning and characterized the child's perception of him- or herself and the world at each stage. See also SCHOOL PSYCHOLOGY.

childbed fever See PUERPERAL FEVER

childbirth See PARTURITION

Childe, V(ere) Gordon (1892–1957) Australian-British archaeologist. He taught at the University of Edinburgh (1927–46) and later directed the Institute of Archaeology at the University of London (1946–56). His study of European prehistory, especially in *The Dawn of European Civilization* (1925), sought to evaluate the relationship between Europe and the Middle East and to examine the structure and character of ancient cultures of the Western world. His later books included *The Most Ancient Near East* (1928) and *The Danube in Prehistory* (1929). His approach established a tradition of prehistoric studies.

Childebert II \'chil-də-,bərt\ (570–595) MEROVINGIAN king of AUSTRASIA (575–95) and king of BURGUNDY (592–95). He inherited the East Frankish kingdom of Austrasia on the death of his father, SIGEBERT I, and was dominated by his mother in the early years of his reign. His uncle, Guntram of Burgundy, adopted Childebert as his heir in 577. When he came of age he purged the Austrasian nobility (584) and launched a series of unsuccessful campaigns against the Lombards of Italy. He became ruler of Burgundy on his uncle's death in 592.

childhood diseases Illnesses that strike primarily during childhood, including CHICKEN POX, MEASLES, MUMPS, and RUBELLA, and impart long-term IMMUNITY to survivors. They remain a leading cause of mortality in developing countries. Respiratory diseases of childhood include CROUP, WHOOPING COUGH, and RESPIRATORY DISTRESS SYNDROME. The special nutritional needs of growing children also make them susceptible to dietary deficiencies. See also CONGENITAL DISORDERS.

Children's Crusade (1212) Religious movement in Europe in which thousands, including many children and young people, set out to take the Holy Land from the Muslims by love instead of by force. The events of the crusade are disputed. According to one version, only partially accurate, the first group of c. 30,000 was led by a French shepherd boy,

Stephen of Cloyes, who had seen a vision of Jesus; at Marseille they were shipped to slave markets in North Africa. A German boy led the second group across the Alps; a few survived to reach Rome, where Innocent III released them from their vows. Though the movement ended in disaster, it excited religious fervor that helped initiate the Fifth Crusade (1217–21).

children's literature Body of written works and accompanying illustrations produced to entertain or instruct young people. The genre encompasses a wide range of works, including acknowledged classics of world literature, picture books and easy-to-read stories, and fairy tales, lullabies, fables, folk songs, and other primarily orally transmitted materials. It emerged as a distinct and independent form only in the second half of the 18th century and blossomed in the 19th century. In the 20th century, with the attainment of near-universal literacy in the developed nations, children's books came almost to rival the diversity of adult popular literature.

Childress \'chil-drəs\, **Alice** (1916–1994) U.S. playwright, novelist, and actress. She grew up in Harlem and studied drama with the American Negro Theatre, where she wrote, directed, and starred in her first play, *Florence* (produced 1949). Her other plays, some featuring music, include *Trouble in Mind* (produced 1955), *String* (1969), *The African Garden* (1971), and *Gullah* (1984). She was also a successful writer of children's books, including *A Hero Ain't Nothing But a Sandwich* (1973).

Chile \'chē-lā, *Engl* 'chi-lē\ *officially* **Republic of Chile** Country, southwestern South America, bounded by Peru, Bolivia, Argentina, the Drake Passage, and the Pacific Ocean. Area: 292,257 sq mi (756,946 sq km). Population (1997 est.): 14,583,000. Capital: Santiago. The indigenous peoples before Spanish colonization included the Diaguita, Picunche, Mapuche, Araucanian, Huilliche, Pehunche, and Cunco Indians. Spanish colonists arrived during the 16th–17th century, followed by Basques in the 18th century. A relatively homogeneous, primarily mestizo population has developed. Language: Spanish (official). Religion: Roman Catholicism. Currency: Chilean peso. Chile is a long narrow country lying between the Andes and the Pacific Ocean. From north to south, it is 2,650 mi (4,265 km) long, and nowhere more than 221 mi (356 km) wide. The north has an arid plateau, the Atacama Desert, and contains several peaks above 1,900 ft (5,790 m), but most of the highest peaks are on the boundaries with Bolivia and Argentina. Its rivers, including the Bío-Bío, are limited in size. There are many lakes, including the Llanquihue. The extreme southern coast is marked by many inlets, islands, and archipelagos; the western half of Tierra del Fuego and the island on which Cape Horn is located are Chilean, as are small islets of Juan Fernández and Easter Island. Chile has a partially developed free-market economy based mainly on mining and manufacturing. It is a republic with two legislative houses; its head of state and government is the president. Originally inhabited by native peoples, including the Mapuche, the area was invaded by the Spanish in 1536. A settlement begun at Santiago in 1541 was governed under the viceroyalty of Peru, but became a separate captaincy general in 1778. It revolted against Spanish rule in 1810; its independence was finally assured by the victory of Jose de San Martin in 1818, and the area was then governed by Bernardo O'Higgins to 1823. In the War of the Pacific against Peru and Bolivia, it won the rich nitrate fields on the coast of Bolivia, effectively forcing that country into a landlocked position. Chile remained neutral in World War I; it entered World War II on the side of the Axis, but severed ties with them in 1943. In 1970 Salvador Allende was elected president, becoming the first avowed Marxist to be elected chief of state in Latin America. Following economic upheaval, he was ousted in 1973 in a coup led by Augusto Pinochet, whose military junta for many years harshly suppressed all internal opposition. A national referendum in 1988 rejected Pinochet, and elections held in 1989 returned the country to civilian rule.

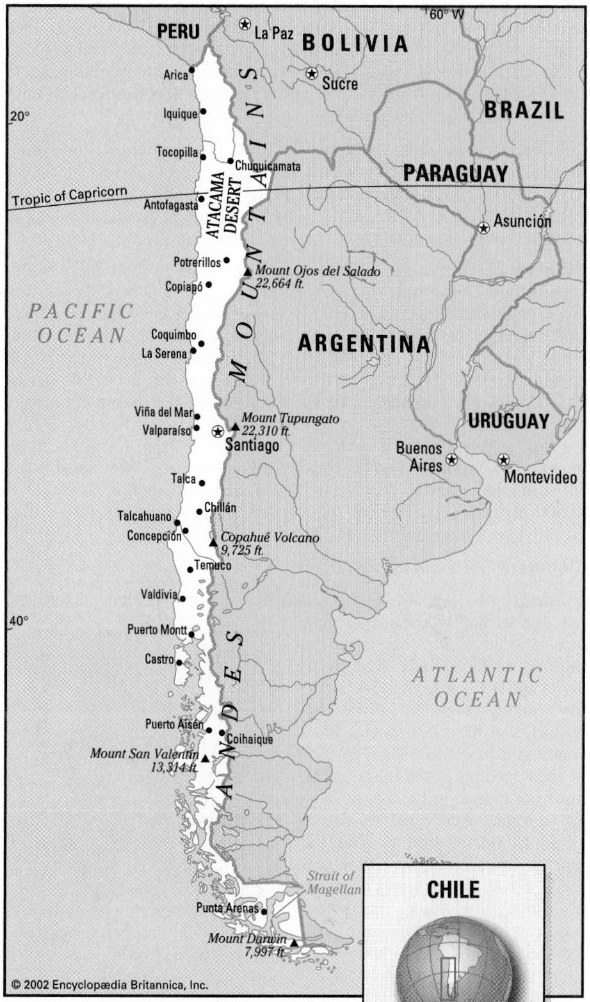

Chilia rug See Baku rug

Chilka Lake Lake, eastern India. Located in Orissa state, and separated from the Bay of Bengal by a narrow spit, it is one of India's largest lakes, at 40 mi (65 km) long and 5–13 mi (8–20 km) wide. It was once a bay of the ocean until it was silted up by monsoon tides. Dotted with islands, it offers good hunting, boating, and fishing.

Chiloé \,chē-lō-'ā\ Island (pop., 1982: 68,000), southwestern Chile. Lying 30 mi (48 km) off the mainland, it has an area of 3,241 sq mi (8,394 sq km). Spaniards captured it from Indians in 1567 and controlled it until 1826, making it a last foothold in Chile of royalist forces during the wars for independence. Heavily forested, the island is little developed.

Chilpancingo (de los Bravos) \,chēl-pän-'sēŋ-gō\ City (pop., 1990: 136,000), capital of Guerrero state, southern Mexico. Located in the Sierra Madre del Sur, it was founded in 1591 and gained prominence as the site of the first Mexican congress, convoked in 1813. Battles were fought there in both the wars for independence from Spain and in the Mexican Revolution. It is the center for an agricultural region.

Chilperic I \'chil-pə-rik\ (539?–584) Merovingian king of Soissons. On the death of his father, Chlotar I, he and his three half brothers divided the kingdom. Chilperic received Soissons, the poorest share, but he gained more land when one of his brothers died, ruling most of the kingdom later known as Neustria. Ambitious, brutal, and debauched, Chilperic murdered his own wife, an action that led to years of intrigue by family members seeking revenge. He was finally killed by an unknown assassin, leaving an infant son.

Chilwa \'chil-wä\, **Lake** Lake, southeastern Malawi. It lies in a depression southeast of Lake Malawi between the Shire Highlands and the Mozambique border. Today it covers about 1,000 sq mi (2,600 sq km); it was much larger when David Livingstone arrived there in 1859, and originally it filled the entire depression.

Chimborazo \ˌchēm-bō-ˈrä-zō\ Mountain peak, Ecuador. The highest peak in the Andean Cordillera Real, at 20,561 ft (6,267 m), it was once thought to be the highest mountain in the ANDES (see Mount ACONCAGUA). An active volcano, it is heavily glaciated. Many attempted to climb it in the 18th–19th century, but the summit was not reached until 1880, by the Briton Edward Whymper.

Chimera \kī-ˈmir-ə\ In GREEK MYTHOLOGY, a fire-breathing female monster. Its foreparts resembled a lion, its middle a goat, and its hindquarters a dragon. It devastated the land around Caria and Lycia until it was killed by BELLEROPHON. The word is now often used to denote a fantasy or a figment of the imagination.

chimera *or* **chimaera** \kī-ˈmir-ə\ Any of the 28 species of cartilaginous fishes constituting the subclass Holocephali (class Chondrichthyes), found in temperate to cold waters of all oceans. Like SHARKS and RAYS, chimeras have a cartilaginous skeleton, and the males possess external reproductive organs (claspers). They have a single external gill opening, covered by a flap as in the bony fishes, on each side of the body. Males have a supplemental clasping organ that is unique among fishes. Chimeras have large pectoral and pelvic fins and two dorsal fins, the first preceded by a sharp spine. They range in length from 24 to 80 in. (60–200 cm) and in color from silvery to blackish. They inhabit rivers, estuaries, coastal waters, and open ocean to depths of 8,000 ft (2,500 m) or more. They eat small fishes and invertebrates. Their liver oil provides a lubricant for guns and fine instruments.

Chimkent See SHYMKENT

chimpanzee Species *(Pan troglodytes)* of great APE that inhabits the rain forests and woodland savannas of equatorial Africa, the closest living relative to humans. Chimps are 3–5.5 ft (1–1.7 m) tall when standing upright, weigh 70–130 lbs (32–60 kg), and have a brown or black coat and a bare face. They do most of their feeding in the trees, swinging from branch to branch; to move any distance they walk, usually on all fours, on the ground. They eat mostly fruits, berries, leaves, and seeds, some termites and ants, and occasionally a young baboon or bush pig. They are capable of problem solving, tool use, and deceit. Chimpanzees are highly social and live in flexible groups (15–100 or more members) known as communities. In the wild they live about 45 years, in captivity more than 50. See also BONOBO.

West African, or masked, chimpanzee (*Pan troglodytes verus*).
HELMUT ALBRECHT—BRUCE COLEMAN LTD.

Chimu \chē-ˈmü\ South American Indians who maintained the largest and most important political system in Peru before the advent of the INCAS. The Chimu state took shape in the early 14th century. It was a highly stratified society, with a mass of peasants laboring under the ruling nobility. Its capital, CHAN CHAN, on the northern seacoast of present-day Peru, is now a major archaeological site. The Chimu produced fine textiles and gold, silver, and copper objects. In the 15th century they were conquered by the Incas, who absorbed much of Chimu high culture into their own imperial organization.

Chin dynasty See JIN dynasty, JUCHEN DYNASTY

Ch'in dynasty See QIN DYNASTY

Chin Hills Mountainous region, northwestern Myanmar. Extending along the India border, it forms the central part of an arc that stretches from the Arakan Mountains to the Patkai Range. Varying from 7,000 to 10,000 ft (2,000–3,000 m) high, these elevations and the arc are part of the north-south trend line of INDOCHINA, which has hindered east-west movement while facilitating the populating of the region by the Chin peoples from the north. The region is a frontier zone between Myanmar and Indian cultures.

Ch'in Kuei See QIN GUI

Chin-sha River See JINSHA RIVER

Ch'in tomb See QIN TOMB

China *officially* **People's Republic of China** *formerly (until 1912)* **Chinese Empire** Country, eastern Asia. Area: 3,696,100 sq mi (9,572,900 sq km). Population (1997 est.): 1,227,740,000. Capital: BEIJING. The Han, or ethnic Chinese, form more than nine-tenths of the population. Languages: dialects of Han Chinese, most importantly MANDARIN. Religions: Buddhism, Islam, Protestantism, Roman Catholicism, Taoism (all legally sanctioned). Currency: renminbi (of which the unit is the yuan). China has several topographic regions. The southwestern area contains the Plateau of Tibet, which averages over 13,000 ft (4,100 m) above sea level; its central area, averaging more than 16,000 ft (5,000 m), is called "the Roof of the World." Higher yet are the border ranges, the KUNLUN MOUNTAINS to the north and the HIMALAYAS to the south. China's northwestern region stretches from Afghanistan to the northeastern Manchurian Plain. The TIAN SHAN mountains separate China's two major interior basins, the Tarim Basin (containing the TAKLIMAKAN desert) and the Dzungarian Basin. The Mongolian Plateau contains the southernmost part of the GOBI DESERT. The lowlands of the eastern region include the Sichuan Basin, which runs along the YANGTZE RIVER (CHANG JIANG). The eastern region is divided into northern and southern parts by the Yangtze. The TARIM is the major river in the northwest. China's smallest watershed, in the southwest, provides headwaters for the BRAHMAPUTRA, SALWEEN, and IRRAWADDY rivers. Its many other rivers include the XI, SONGHUA, Zhu (Pearl), and Lancang, which becomes the MEKONG in Southeast Asia. The discovery of Peking man in 1927 (see ZHOUKOUDIAN) dates the advent of early hominids to the PALEOLITHIC PERIOD. Chinese civilization probably spread from the Huang He (Yellow River) valley, where it existed c. 3000 BC. The first dynasty for which there is definite historical material is the SHANG (c. 17th century BC), which had a writing system and a calendar. The ZHOU, a subject state of the Shang, overthrew its Shang rulers in the 11th century BC and ruled until the 3rd century BC. TAOISM and CONFUCIANISM were founded in this era. A time of conflict, called the Warring States Period, lasted from the 5th century BC until in 221 BC the QIN (CH'IN) DYNASTY (from whose name China is derived) was established after its rulers had conquered rival states and created a unified empire. The HAN DYNASTY was established in 206 BC and ruled until AD 220. A time of turbulence followed, and Chinese reunification was not achieved until the SUI DYNASTY was established in 581. After the founding of the SONG DYNASTY in 960, the capital was moved to the south because of northern invasions. In 1279 this dynasty was overthrown and Mongol (YUAN) domination began. During this time, MARCO POLO visited KUBLAI KHAN. The MING DYNASTY followed the period of Mongol rule and lasted from 1368 to 1644, cultivating antiforeign feelings to the point that China closed itself off from the rest of the world. Peoples from MANCHURIA overran China in 1644 and established the QING (MANCHU) DYNASTY. Ever-increasing incursions by Western and Japanese interests led in the 19th century to the OPIUM WARS, the TAIPING REBELLION, and the SINO-JAPANESE WAR, all of which weakened the Manchus. The dynasty fell in 1911 and a republic was proclaimed in 1912 by SUN YAT-SEN. The power struggles of warlords weakened the republic. Under Sun's successor, CHIANG KAI-SHEK, some national unification was achieved in the 1920s, but Chiang soon broke with the Communists, who then formed their own armies. Japan invaded northern China in 1937; its occupation lasted until 1945 (see MANCHUGUO). The Communists gained support after the LONG MARCH (1934–35), in which MAO ZEDONG emerged as their leader. Upon Japan's surrender at the end of World War II, a fierce civil war began; in 1949 the Nationalists fled to Taiwan and the Communists proclaimed the People's Republic of China. The Communists undertook extensive reforms, but pragmatic policies alternated with periods of revolutionary upheaval, most notably in the GREAT LEAP FORWARD and the CULTURAL REVOLUTION. The chaos of the latter led, after Mao's death in 1976, to a turn to moderation under DENG XIAOPING, who undertook economic reforms and renewed China's ties to the West. The government established diplomatic ties with the U.S. in 1979. It suppressed the TIANANMEN SQUARE student demonstration in 1989. The economy has been in transition since the late 1970s, moving from central planning and state-run industries to a mixture of state-owned and private enterprises in manufacturing and services. The death of Deng in 1997 marked the end of a political era, but power passed peacefully to JIANG ZEMIN. In 1997 HONG KONG reverted to Chinese rule, as did MACAO in 1999. See map on following page.

china, bone See BONE CHINA

China Sea Part of the Pacific Ocean. Reaching from Japan to the southern end of the MALAY PENINSULA, it is divided by Taiwan into two

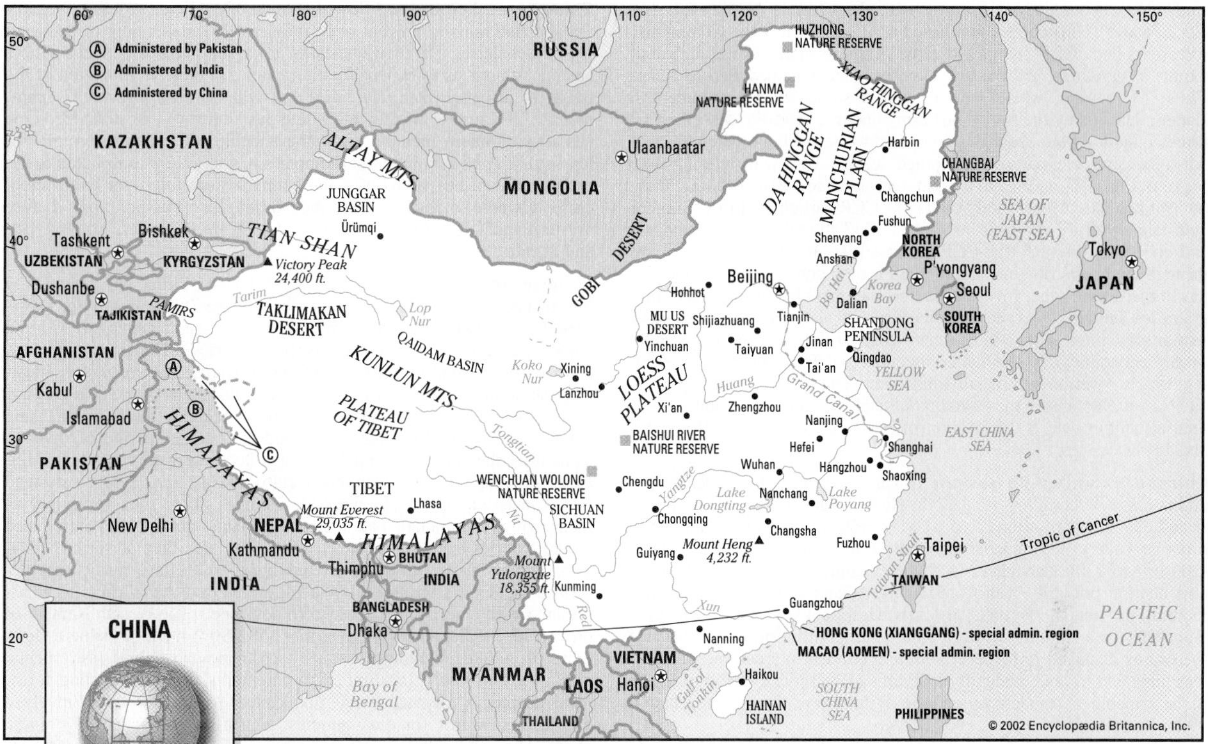

sections. The northern section is the East China Sea, or Eastern Sea, which covers an area of 482,300 sq mi (1,249,157 sq km), has a maximum depth of 9,126 ft (2,782 m), and is enclosed by eastern China, South Korea, KYUSHU island, RYUKYU ISLANDS, and Taiwan. The southern section is the South China Sea, often called simply the China Sea, which covers an area of 895,400 sq mi (2,319,086 sq km), has a maximum depth of about 15,000 ft (4,600 m), and is enclosed by southeastern China, Indochina, the Malay Peninsula, Borneo, the Philippines, and Taiwan.

chinchilla \chin-'chi-lə\ Small South American RODENT (genus *Chinchilla,* family Chinchillidae) long valued for its extremely fine-textured fur. Chinchillas look like long-tailed, small-eared rabbits. They are about 14 in. (35 cm) long, including the tufted tail. The soft fur is gray with dusky overtones; a black streak runs the length of the tail, above and below. Chinchillas live in loose communities in arid, rocky regions of the Chilean and Bolivian Andes, in burrows or rock crevices. They eat seeds, fruit, grain, herbs, and moss. Once hunted almost to extinction, they are still scarce in the wild. They are raised commercially; almost all animals in captivity have descended from a few animals introduced into the U.S. in 1923.

Chinchilla (*Chinchilla laniger*).
JANE BURTON—BRUCE COLEMAN LTD.

Chindwin River River, western Myanmar. Rising in the northern mountains, it flows 720 mi (1,158 km) northwest through the Hukawng Valley and then south along the Indian border to join the IRRAWADDY at Myingyan. It is generally navigable below its confluence with the Uyu River. It was the scene of heavy fighting during World War II.

Chinese architecture Building styles and methods of China. Though masonry was used for tombs, PAGODAS, and defensive walls (see GREAT WALL of China), traditional construction is chiefly in timber, and little from ancient times has survived. The oldest datable timber building is the small main hall of the Nanchan Temple, on Mount Wutai in Shanxi province, restored in 782. The basic elements in a Chinese timber building are its platform of stone or tile, post-and-beam frame, system of often elaborate roof-supporting brackets, and heavy tiled roof. Beams are used as tensile elements to define the distinctive curving GABLE shape of the overhanging roof with upturned eaves. Flexibility in overall design is achieved by using multiples of a basic rectilinear unit; these are arranged along a central axis with open, connecting GALLERIES around courtyards. The traditional building system is hierarchical, modular, and highly standardized. See also FORBIDDEN CITY, TEMPLE OF HEAVEN.

Chinese art Painting, calligraphy, pottery, sculpture, bronzes, and other fine or decorative artwork produced in China over the centuries. China's is the oldest continuous art tradition in the world, dating back some 7,000 years in some media. Pottery and jade carvings can be traced back to c. 3000–1500 BC. By 1000 BC bronze casting had reached a perfection not matched in the ancient Western world. Chinese writing developed in the 18th–12th century BC. Calligraphy, one of the oldest and most fundamental Chinese arts, has a close relation to Chinese painting, which uses essentially the same materials and is judged by the same criteria. The earliest extant paintings and calligraphy date from the 11th–3rd century BC. True pottery glazes were developed in China before the end of the 2nd millennium BC, and porcelain was developed by the 6th century AD, more than 1,000 years before its discovery in Europe. The other principal Chinese decorative arts are lacquerware, furniture design, and textiles. See also CHINESE ARCHITECTURE.

Chinese cabbage Either of two widely cultivated members of the MUSTARD FAMILY, BOK CHOY and *Brassica pekinensis.* The latter vegetable, also called celery cabbage, forms a tight head of crinkled light green leaves. It has long been grown in the U.S. as a salad vegetable. All Chinese cabbages are delicate and crisp, qualities that enable them to combine with a wide variety of foods. Kimchi, the universal Korean pickle, is often made with Chinese cabbage.

Chinese Communist Party (CCP) Political party founded in China in 1921 by CHEN DUXIU and LI DAZHAO. It grew directly from the reform-oriented MAY FOURTH MOVEMENT and was aided from the start by Russian organizers. Under Russian guidance, the CCP held its First Congress in 1921; the Russians also invited many members to the Soviet Union for study and encouraged cooperation with the Chinese Nationalists (see GUOMINDANG). This cooperation lasted until 1927, when the Communists were expelled. CCP fortunes declined rapidly after several failed attempts at uprisings, and the few members that remained fled to central China to regroup, where they formed a soviet-style government in Jiangxi. Harried by the Nationalist army under CHIANG KAI-SHEK, the CCP forces undertook the LONG MARCH to northwestern China, when MAO ZEDONG became the party's undisputed leader. War with the Japanese broke out in 1937 and led to a temporary alliance between the CCP and the Nationalists. After World War II, the CCP participated in U.S.-mediated talks with the Nationalists, but in 1947 the talks were abandoned and civil war resumed. The CCP increased its already strong rural base through land redistribution, and in 1949 it took control of mainland China. In the decades that followed, radical members led by Mao and moderates led initially by LIU SHAOQI vied for control of the party and the direction of China. After Mao's death in 1976 the party moved steadily toward economic, if not political, liberalization. Today the CCP sets policy, which government officials implement. The organs at the top of the CCP are the Politburo, the Politburo's Standing Committee, and the Secretariat, among which the division of power is constantly shifting. See also LIN BIAO.

Chinese examination system In China, system of competitive examinations for recruiting officials that linked state and society and dominated education from the SONG DYNASTY (960–1279) onward, though its roots go back to the imperial university established in the HAN DYNASTY (206 BC–AD 220). Candidates faced fierce competition in a series of exams dealing primarily with Confucian texts and conducted on the prefectural, provincial, and national levels. Despite a persistent tendency to emphasize rote learning over original thinking and form over substance, the exams managed to produce an elite grounded in a common body of teachings and to lend credibility to claims of meritocracy. Too inflexible to be capable of modernization, the system was finally abolished in 1905. See also FIVE CLASSICS, FOUR BOOKS.

Chinese languages *or* **Sinitic languages** Family of languages comprising one of the two branches of SINO-TIBETAN. They are spoken by about 95% of the inhabitants of China and by many communities of Chinese immigrants elsewhere. Linguists regard the major dialect groups of Chinese as distinct languages, though because all Chinese write with a common system of logographic characters (see CHINESE WRITING SYSTEM) and share Classical Chinese as a heritage, traditionally all varieties of Chinese are regarded as dialects. There is a primary division in Chinese languages between the so-called Mandarin dialects—which have a high degree of mutual intelligibility and cover all of the Chinese speech area north of the Yangtze River and west of Hunan and Guangdong—and a number of other dialect groups concentrated in southeastern China. Far more people—over 885 million—speak a variety of Mandarin Chinese as a first language than any other language in the world. The northern Mandarin dialect of Beijing is the basis for Modern Standard Chinese, a spoken norm that serves as a supradialectal LINGUA FRANCA. Important dialect groups other than Mandarin are Wu (spoken in Shanghai), Gan, Xiang, Min (spoken in Fujian and Taiwan), Yue (including Cantonese, spoken in Guangzhou and Hong Kong), and Kejia (Hakka), spoken by the HAKKA. The modern Chinese languages are TONE languages, the number of tones varying from four in Modern Standard Chinese to nine in dialects.

Chinese law Law that evolved in China, from the earliest times until the 20th century, when Western socialist law (see SOVIET LAW) was introduced. The oldest complete Chinese law code extant was compiled in AD 653 during the TANG DYNASTY. Traditional Chinese law was influenced both by CONFUCIANISM, which allowed variability in moral conduct according to status and circumstances, and by Legalist, or Fajia, principles, which stressed reliance on uniform objective standards. The emperor's divine role in the universe also affected law. The emperor was considered responsible to Heaven for any disturbance in the earthly sphere; whenever a disturbance occurred, punishment was considered a means of restoring the cosmic equilibrium. All citizens had an obligation to denounce wrongdoers to the local magistrate's office. The magistrate studied the facts of a case and, using the penal code, determined punishments, including beatings and torture. A profession of advocates, or lawyers, never developed in China. Traditional law continued to exert an influence even under the Communists in the 20th century.

Chinese medicine, traditional System of medicine at least 23 centuries old that aims to prevent or heal disease by maintaining or restoring YIN-YANG balance. Detailed questions are asked about a patient's illness and such things as taste, smell, and dreams, but close examination of the pulse, at different sites and times and with varying pressure, is paramount. Of Chinese medicine's numerous remedies, Western medicine has adopted many, including iron (for anemia) and chaulmoogra oil (for leprosy). Use of certain animal remedies has seriously contributed to the endangered-species status of some animals (including tiger and rhinoceros). Chinese medicine used inoculation for smallpox long before Western medicine. Other practices include HYDROTHERAPY, ACUPUNCTURE, and ACUPRESSURE.

Chinese music Traditional music of China. China has historically looked back to its "golden age," especially the ZHOU DYNASTY (c. 1050–256/255 BC), when the basic division between "art" music *(yayue)* and "folk" music *(suyue)* was established. A period of disunity followed, and one of the philosophical traditions that arose, CONFUCIANISM, idealized Zhou musical practices. With the establishment of the HAN DYNASTY (206 BC–AD 220), an attempt was made to recreate the tradition using the few surviving Zhou pieces as models. Another period of division came after the Han, and both TAOISM and BUDDHISM were important influences on music: Taoist gentlemen cultivated the *qin*, a seven-stringed lute, concentrating on its expressive qualities rather than self-improvement, which Confucians had stressed. Buddhist missionaries introduced modal theories from INDIAN MUSIC; somewhat later, they performed *bianwen,* a popular narrative form combining words and music that described incidents from the Buddha's life. The PIPA, which came to be associated with entertainment, was also developed. The reestablishment of order with the SUI and TANG dynasties (581–907) made possible a flowering of culture, including *yenyue,* a cosmopolitan hybrid instrumental music (*yayue* now being limited to ceremonial uses). Folk-song forms were adapted for lyrical expression called *quzi,* which often involved writing new words for old melodies, later a basic practice of Chinese opera. The SONG (960–1279) and MING (1368–1644) dynasties saw increased urbanization, and with it the rise of theatrical forms, only for the masses at first but later for the elite as well. With the Nationalist Revolution of 1911, musical experimentation became far more common. After 1949 the communist regime encouraged preservation of folk traditions and sought to create a hybrid modern Chinese music (including orchestras that include both Western and Chinese instruments). The "black-key" pentatonic scale is only one of several five-tone scales used in Chinese music; seven-tone scales were also common, and there is even evidence that a twelve-tone scale was derived as early as the 3rd century BC.

Chinese mustard See BOK CHOY

Chinese Nationalists See GUOMINDANG

Chinese New Year See NEW YEAR'S DAY

Chinese writing system System of symbols used to write the CHINESE LANGUAGE. Chinese writing is fundamentally logographic: there is an exact correspondence between a single symbol, or character, in the script and a MORPHEME. Each character, no matter how complex, is fit into a hypothetical rectangle of the same size. The Chinese script is first attested in divinatory inscriptions incised on bone or tortoise shells dating from the SHANG DYNASTY. Early forms of characters were often clearly pictorial or iconic. Shared elements of characters, called radicals, provide a means of classifying Chinese writing. It is thought that an ordinary literate Chinese person can recognize 3,000–4,000 characters. Efforts have been made to reduce the number of characters and to simplify their form, though the fact that they can be read by a speaker of any Chinese language and their inextricable link with China's 3,000-year-old culture makes abandonment of the system unlikely. Chinese characters have also been adapted to write Japanese, Korean, and Vietnamese.

Ch'ing dynasty See QING DYNASTY

Ch'ing-hai See QINGHAI

Chinggis Khan See GENGHIS KHAN

chinoiserie \shēn-ˈwäz-rē\ Fanciful European interpretations of Chinese styles in the design of interiors, furniture, pottery, textiles, and gardens. The expansion of trade with the Far East produced a lively vogue for Chinese fashions in the 17th–18th century. The most outstanding chinoiserie interior was the Trianon de Porcelaine (1670–71), built for LOUIS XIV at Versailles. The style featured lavish gilding and lacquering, the use of blue and white (as in DELFTWARE), asymmetrical forms, unorthodox perspective, and Oriental motifs. In the 19th century, the fashion gave way to Turkish and other styles considered exotic.

Chinook \shə-ˈnu̇k\ NORTHWEST COAST INDIAN people who lived along the lower Columbia River and spoke Chinookan languages. They were famous as traders, with connections stretching as far as the Great Plains. They traded dried salmon, canoes, shells, and slaves. Chinook Jargon, the trade language of the Northwest Coast, was a combination of Chinook with Nootka and other Indian, English, and French terms. The Chinook were first described by the explorers Lewis and Clark, who contacted them in 1805. The basic social unit was the CLAN. Chinook religion focused on salmon rites and guardian spirits, and the POTLATCH was an important social ceremony. Following a smallpox epidemic in the early 19th century, the remaining Chinook were absorbed into other Northwest Coast groups.

chinook salmon *or* **king salmon** Prized North Pacific food and sport fish *(Oncorhynchus tshawytscha)* of the SALMON family. The average weight is about 22 lbs (10 kg), but individuals of 50–80 lbs (22–36 kg) are not unusual. Chinook salmon are silvery, with round black spots, and range from the Yukon River to China and the Sacramento River. During spring spawning runs, adults swim as far as 2,000 mi (3,200 km) up the Yukon, spawn, and then die. Young chinook salmon enter the sea at one to three years old. They were successfully introduced into Lake Michigan, creating a new sport fishery after the virtual elimination of lake trout by sea lampreys in the mid-20th century.

Chios \ˈkī-ˌäs\ *or* **Khíos** \ˈk̲ē-ȯs\ Island (pop., 1991: 53,000), AEGEAN SEA. Lying 5 mi (8 km) west of Turkey, it comprises, with some adjacent islands, a department of Greece. Of volcanic origin, it is 30 mi (48 km) long and 8–15 mi (13–24 km) wide, with an area of 325 sq mi (842 sq km). It was noted in antiquity as HOMER's birthplace and the home of a school of sculptors. It was colonized by IONIANS but became subject to PERSIA in 546 BC. Though later a member of the DELIAN LEAGUE, it revolted several times against Athens. It prospered successively under Rome, VENICE, GENOA, and the Ottoman empire; it passed to Greece after the BALKAN WARS (1912–13). The city of Chios is the department's capital.

chip, computer See COMPUTER CHIP, INTEGRATED CIRCUIT

chipmunk Any of 17 species of terrestrial RODENTS in the SQUIRREL family. The eastern chipmunk *(Tamias striatus),* found in eastern North America, is 5.5–7.5 in. (14–19 cm) long, excluding a bushy, 3–4-in. (8–10-cm) tail. It is reddish brown with five black stripes alternating with two brown and two white stripes. The other species (all in the genus *Eutamia)* are found in western North America and Central and eastern Asia; they are smaller and have different stripe patterns. Chipmunks are active burrow dwellers that eat seeds, berries, tender plants, and sometimes flesh. They store seeds underground, carrying them in roomy cheek pockets. Their call is a shrill chirring or chipping sound.

Eastern chipmunk (*Tamias striatus*).
KEN BRATE—PHOTO RESEARCHERS

Chippendale, Thomas (1718–1779) English cabinetmaker. Little is known of his life before 1753, when he opened a showroom and workshop in London. In 1754 he published *The Gentleman and Cabinet-Maker's Director*, a popular collection of designs illustrating almost every type of domestic furniture. The designs were mostly his improvements on already existing styles. Though much 18th-century furniture is attributed to him, only a few pieces can be assigned with certainty to his workshop. See also CHIPPENDALE STYLE.

Chippendale style Style of furniture derived from designs by THOMAS CHIPPENDALE. The term specifically refers to English furniture made in a modified ROCOCO STYLE in the 1750s and '60s, though Chippendale also designed furniture in Gothic and Chinese styles. Some of his designs are adapted from the LOUIS XV STYLE. Furniture based on his designs was also made in Europe and the American colonies.

Chippewa See OJIBWA

Chippewa \ˈchi-pə-ˌwȯ\, **Battle of** (July 5, 1814) Engagement in the WAR OF 1812 that restored U.S. military morale. After U.S. troops under WINFIELD SCOTT captured Fort Erie, N.Y., they began to push north into Canada. A British force marched south from Fort George and attacked them at Chippewa. The British were defeated, suffering 604 casualties to 335 of the U.S.

Chiquita Brands International, Inc. *formerly (1970–90)* **United Brands Co.** Diversified U.S. corporation. It was formed in 1970 by the merger of UNITED FRUIT CO., a grower and marketer of bananas, and AMK Corp., the HOLDING COMPANY for the meatpacker John Morrell and Co. Chiquita owns and leases extensive plantations in Central America, northern South America, and the Caribbean. It grows bananas, sugar, cocoa, and abaca and harvests tropical woods, essential oils, and rubber; bananas account for more than half its income. It also processes and distributes packaged foods. Its headquarters are in New York City. "Miss Chiquita," its well-known trademark, was introduced in 1944.

Chirac \shē-ˈrȧk\, **Jacques (René)** (born 1932) President of France (from 1995). In 1967 he was elected to the National Assembly as a Gaullist. As prime minister (1974–76), he resigned over differences with VALERY GISCARD D'ESTAING and formed a neo-Gaullist group, RALLY FOR THE REPUBLIC. As mayor of Paris (1977–95), he continued to build a conservative political base. His campaign for the presidency in 1981 split the conservative vote and allowed FRANCOIS MITTERRAND to win. Mitterrand later appointed Chirac prime minister (1986–88) in an unusual power-sharing arrangement. Though defeated again in presidential elections in 1988, Chirac won the presidency on his third try, in 1995. He was reelected in 2002 in a landslide victory.

Chiricahua National Monument \ˌchir-i-ˈkä-wə\ Preserve, southeastern Arizona, characterized by tall volcanic-rock formations that lie to the west of the Chiricahua Mountains. Established in 1924, the 19-sq-mi (48.5-sq-km) park unfolds a geologic story of nearly 1 billion years. The region was once a stronghold of APACHE Indians under COCHISE and GERONIMO.

Chirico \ˈkē-rē-ˌkō\, **Giorgio de** (1888–1978) Italian (Greek-born) painter. Born to Italian parents in Greece, he studied art in Munich and began painting images juxtaposing the fantastic with the commonplace. He moved to Paris in 1911, where he produced ominous scenes of deserted piazzas with classical statues, isolated figures, and oppressive architecture. The element of mystery in his work exerted a great influence on SURREALISM in the 1920s. He is known as the founder, with Carlo Carrà and GIORGIO MORANDI, of METAPHYSICAL PAINTING.

Chiron \ˈkī-ˌrän\ In GREEK MYTHOLOGY, one of the CENTAURS. The son of CRONUS and the sea nymph Philyra, he lived at the foot of Mount Pelion in Thessaly and was renowned for his wisdom and his knowledge of medicine. He was the teacher of many Greek heroes, including ACHILLES, HERACLES, JASON, and ASCLEPIUS. Wounded accidentally by a poisoned arrow shot by Heracles, he was in such agony that he surrendered his immortality in order to die. Zeus placed him among the stars as the constellation SAGITTARIUS.

Chiron COMET once thought to be the most distant known ASTEROID. Discovered in 1977, it travels in an unstable, eccentric orbit between those of Saturn and Uranus. In 1989 astronomers detected a fuzzy cloud (coma) around Chiron. Because such a cloud is a defining feature of comets, Chiron was reclassified as a comet. See also CENTAUR OBJECT.

chiropody See PODIATRY

chiropractic \ˈkī-rə-ˌprak-tik\ System of healing based on the theory that disease results from lack of normal nerve function, often caused by displaced vertebrae putting pressure on nerve roots. Treatment involves manipulations of body structures, primarily the spinal column, and use of other techniques when necessary. It concerns the relationship between musculoskeletal structures and functions of the body and the NERVOUS SYSTEM. The chiropractic method was propounded in 1895 by Daniel David Palmer (1845–1913). Practitioners are trained at accredited chiropractic colleges.

chisel Cutting tool with a sharpened edge at the end of a metal blade, used (often by driving with a mallet or hammer) in dressing, shaping, or working a solid material such as wood, stone, or metal. Flint ancestors of the chisel existed by 8000 BC; the ancient Egyptians used copper and later bronze chisels to work both wood and soft stone. Chisels today are made of steel, in various sizes and degrees of hardness, depending on use.

Chisholm, Shirley *orig.* **Shirley Anita St. Hill** (born 1924) U.S. politician. Born in Brooklyn, N.Y., she was a schoolteacher before becoming active in local politics. In 1968 she became the first black woman to be elected to the U.S. Congress, where she served until 1983, becoming known as a strong liberal who opposed the Vietnam War and favored full-employment proposals. She cofounded the National Women's Political Caucus. A candidate for the 1972 Democratic presidential nomination, she won 152 delegates before withdrawing from the race.

Chisholm Trail \'chiz-əm\ 19th-century route for cattle drives from Texas to Kansas, probably named for the trader Jesse Chisholm (1806?–1868?). The trail ran from south of San Antonio, across Oklahoma to Abilene, Kan., where a railhead was established in 1867. Between 1867 and 1871 1.5 million head of cattle were driven north over the trail to be shipped to markets in the East. After the 1880s the trail's importance declined as other railheads were established.

Chisinau \ˌkē-shē-'naù\ *formerly (1812–1918, 1940–91)* **Kishinev** \'ki-shi-ˌnef\ City (pop., 1993: 658,000), capital of Moldova. It lies on a tributary of the DNIESTER RIVER. Ruled by Moldavia in the 15th century and taken by the Ottoman Turks in the 16th century, it was ceded to Russia in 1812. From 1918 the city was controlled by Romania; it was ceded back to the Soviet Union in 1940 and became the capital of the newly formed Moldavian S.S.R. The city is a commercial center and the site of a university.

chitin \'kī-tᵊn\ White, horny substance found in the external skeleton of CRABS, LOBSTERS, and many insects; in internal structures of some other invertebrates; and in some fungi, algae, and yeasts. It is a POLYSACCHARIDE, the MONOMER unit being glucosamine. It is used industrially in purifying wastewater, thickening and stabilizing foods and pharmaceuticals, and sizing and strengthening paper, and as a wound-healing agent, an ION-EXCHANGE RESIN, a membrane for industrial separations, and a binder for dyes, fabrics, and adhesives.

Chittagong \'chi-tə-ˌgäŋ\ City (pop., 1991: 1,570,000; metro. area pop.: 2,040,000), chief Indian Ocean port, Bangladesh. It is the country's second most important industrial city, with jute mills, engineering works, and a large oil refinery. Known to Arab sailors by the 10th century AD, it was conquered by Muslims in the 14th century and occupied by the governor of BENGAL in the 17th century. Ceded to the British EAST INDIA CO. in 1760, it was constituted a municipality in 1864. Damaged in the conflict between India and Pakistan in 1971, its port facilities have been rebuilt. It is the site of the University of Chittagong (founded 1966).

Ch'iu Ch'u-chi See QIU CHUJI

chivalry \'shi-vəl-rē\ Knightly class of feudal Europe, and especially the gallantry and honor expected of medieval knights. The ideal of courteous knightly conduct developed in the 12th–13th century. It arose out of feudal obligation (see FEUDALISM) and stressed loyalty and obeisance by a knight to his God, his lord, and his lady, thus melding Christian and military virtues. Chivalry was greatly strengthened by the CRUSADES, a military endeavor on behalf of Christianity, which led to the founding of the earliest orders of chivalry, the KNIGHTS OF MALTA and the TEMPLARS. In addition to loyalty and honor, the chivalric virtues included valor, piety, courtesy, and chastity. Questions of love and honor were combined in the ethos of COURTLY LOVE. The knight's lady was meant to be unobtainable, ensuring chastity; the feminine ideal thus became melded with the Virgin Mary. In the 14th–15th century, chivalry came to be associated increasingly with aristocratic display and public ceremony, particularly in JOUSTING tournaments, rather than with service in the field.

chive Small, hardy perennial plant *(Allium schoenoprasum)* of the LILY FAMILY, related to the ONION. Its small, white, elongated BULBS and thin, tubular leaves grow in clumps. Dense, attractive, spherical umbels of bluish or lilac flowers rise above the foliage. Chive leaves may be cut off at earth level and used for seasoning foods.

Wild chives (*Allium schoenoprasum*).
INGMAR HOLMASEN

Chivington Massacre See SAND CREEK MASSACRE

chlamydia \klə-'mi-dē-ə\ Any of the bacterial parasites that make up the genus *Chlamydia,* which cause several diseases in humans, including CONJUNCTIVITIS and chlamydial PNEUMONIA. One form causes a variety of sexually transmitted diseases. In men, symptoms are similar to those of GONORRHEA. In women, chlamydial infection ordinarily produces few if any symptoms, and most infected women thus are ignorant of their condition. However, untreated infections in women can lead to sterility, a higher risk of premature births, and ECTOPIC PREGNANCIES. Chlamydia frequently causes conjunctivitis or pneumonia in the newborn infant. The preferred treatment is TETRACYCLINE; other antibiotics are also effective. In the 1990s chlamydia was discovered to be the most common sexually transmitted disease in the U.S.

Chlamydomonas \ˌkla-mə-'dä-mə-nəs\ Genus of single-celled green ALGAE considered to be primitive life-forms of evolutionary significance. The cell has a spherical cellulose MEMBRANE, an eyespot, and a cup-shaped, pigment-containing CHLOROPLAST. Though capable of PHOTOSYNTHESIS, *Chlamydomonas* may also absorb nutrients through the cell surface. It is found in soil, ponds, and ditches polluted by manure. It may color water green. A red-pigmented species turns melting snow red.

chlorella \klə-'re-lə\ Any green ALGAE of the genus *Chlorella,* found in fresh or salt water and in soil. They have a cup-shaped CHLOROPLAST. Chlorellas are used often in studies of PHOTOSYNTHESIS, in mass cultivation experiments, and for purifying sewage wastes. Because they multiply rapidly and are rich in proteins and in B-complex vitamins, they have been studied as a potential food product for humans both on earth and in outer space. Chlorella farms, closed systems that provide humans with food, water, and oxygen, have been established in the U.S., Japan, The Netherlands, Germany, and Israel.

chlorine Nonmetallic chemical ELEMENT, chemical symbol Cl, atomic number 17. It is a toxic, corrosive, greenish yellow GAS (Cl_2 as the diatomic molecule) that severely irritates the eyes and respiratory system (and was used for that purpose as a CHEMICAL-WARFARE agent in World War I). Its best-known VALENCE is 1, as the chloride ION, but it has other valences in hypochlorites, chlorites, chlorates, and perchlorates. Chlorine and its compounds are important industrial materials with myriad uses in the manufacture of other chlorinated compounds (e.g., PVC, HYDROCHLORIC ACID, ethylene dichloride, trichloroethylene, PCBs), in water purification (municipal systems, swimming pools), in textile industries, in flame retardants, in special BATTERIES, and in food processing. SODIUM CHLORIDE (table salt) is by far the most familiar of its compounds. See also BLEACH.

chlorite Widespread group of layer silicate minerals composed of hydrous aluminum silicates, usually of magnesium and iron. The name, from the Greek for "green," refers to chlorite's typical color. Chlorites have a silicate layer structure similar to that in micas. They characteristically occur as alteration products of other higher temperature minerals and are most common in sedimentary and igneous rocksand in some metamorphic rocks.

chloroethylene See VINYL CHLORIDE

chlorofluorocarbon (CFC) Any of several organic compounds containing CARBON, FLUORINE, CHLORINE, and HYDROGEN. CFCs are one class of FREONS. Developed in the 1930s, these halogenated HYDROCARBONS were widely used because they are nontoxic, nonflammable, and readily evaporated and condensed. However, CFCs released into the atmosphere rise into the stratosphere, where solar radiation breaks them down; the chlorine released reacts with OZONE, depleting the OZONE LAYER. In 1992 most developed countries agreed to end CFC production by 1996; 1997 production, weighted according to the ozone depletion potential of each CFC, was 10% of peak (1988) production.

chloroform Clear, colorless, heavy, nonflammable liquid organic compound with a pleasant etherlike odor, chemical formula $CHCl_3$. It was the first substance successfully used as a surgical ANESTHETIC (1847); being somewhat toxic, it has been increasingly displaced by other substances for this purpose. It has some industrial uses, primarily as a solvent.

chlorophyll Any member of one of the most important classes of PIGMENT molecules involved in PHOTOSYNTHESIS. Found in almost all photosynthetic organisms, it consists of a central magnesium atom surrounded by a nitrogen-containing structure called a PORPHYRIN ring, to which is attached a long carbon-hydrogen side chain, known as a phytol chain. In structure it is remarkably similar to HEMOGLOBIN. Chlorophyll uses energy that it absorbs from light to convert carbon dioxide to carbohydrates. In higher plants it is found in CHLOROPLASTS.

chloroplast Microscopic, ellipsoidal organelle in a green plant cell. It is the site of PHOTOSYNTHESIS. It is distinguished by its green color, caused by the presence of CHLOROPHYLL. It contains disk-shaped structures called thylakoids that make possible the formation of ATP, an energy-rich storage compound.

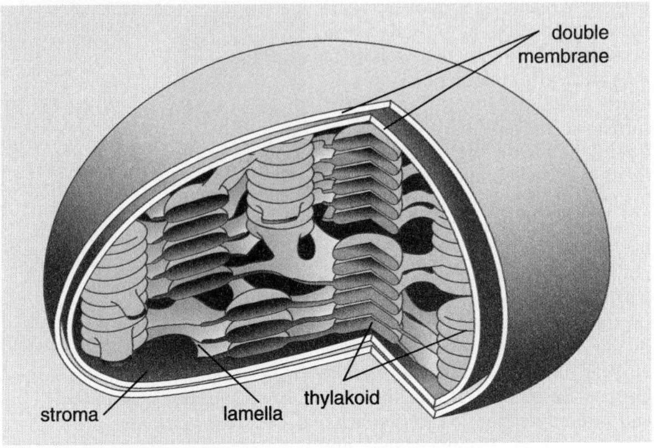

Internal structures of the chloroplast. The interior contains flattened sacs of photosynthetic membranes (thylakoids) formed by the invagination and fusion of the inner membrane. Thylakoids are usually arranged in stacks (grana) and contain the photosynthetic pigment (chlorophyll). The grana are connected to other stacks by simple membranes (lamellae) within the stroma, the fluid proteinaceous portion containing the enzymes essential for the photosynthetic dark reaction, or Calvin cycle.

Chlotar I \'klō-ˌtär\ (c. 500–561) MEROVINGIAN king of Soissons from 511 and of the whole Frankish kingdom from 558. The youngest of CLOVIS I's sons, he shared in the partition of his father's kingdom in 511 and extended his lands by murder and intrigue. He launched campaigns against the Burgundians (523, 532–34), the Visigoths (532, 542), and the Thuringians (c. 531). A ruthless and brutal ruler, Chlotar put to death his rebellious son Chram with his family (560).

Chobe National Park \'chō-bā\ National preserve, northern Botswana. The preserve, which acquired national-park status in 1968, borders Namibia and touches Zimbabwe and Zambia, and covers 4,500 sq mi (11,700 sq km). It is noted for its wildlife, particularly its large elephant population.

chocolate Food prepared from ground roasted CACAO beans. It is consumed as CANDY, used to make beverages, and added as a flavoring or coating for confections and baked products. It was introduced in Europe by HERNAN CORTES following his visit in 1519 to the court of MONTEZUMA II, who served the conquistador a bitter cacao-bean drink, *xocoatl.* In making chocolate, the kernels of fermented and roasted cacao beans are ground into a paste called chocolate liquor, which may be hardened in molds to form baking (bitter) chocolate, pressed to reduce the cocoa-butter (vegetable-fat) content, and then pulverized to make cocoa powder or mixed with sugar and additional cocoa butter to make sweet (eating) chocolate. The addition of concentrated milk to sweet chocolate produces milk chocolate or white chocolate. Rich in CARBOHYDRATES and FAT and containing small amounts of CAFFEINE, chocolate is an excellent source of quick energy.

Brazilian cocoa pods.
CARL FRANK—PHOTO RESEARCHERS

Choctaw North American Indian people of MUSKOGEAN LANGUAGE stock that lived in what is now southeastern Mississippi. They are closely related to the CHICKASAW. The Choctaw were the most skillful of the southeastern farmers, usually having surplus produce to sell or trade. They fished, gathered nuts and wild fruits, hunted deer and bear, and planted corn, beans, and pumpkins. Their principal religious ceremony was the Busk (Green Corn) festival, a first-fruits and new-fire rite celebrated at midsummer. In the 19th century, pressure by white cotton-growers resulted in 5 million acres being ceded and most Choctaws being removed to Oklahoma. Today Choctaw descendants number about 17,500.

Ch'oe Si-hyong \'chœ-'sē-'yȯŋ\ (1827–1898) Second leader of the Korean Tonghak (now CH'ONDOGYO) religion. He organized the underground network that spread the apocalyptic, antiforeign Tonghak sect following the execution of its founder, Ch'oe Che-u (1824–1864). He published the first two Tonghak scriptures in 1880 and 1881, adding public service to the founder's principle of human equality and obligation to serve heaven. Preaching the need for Korea to become as strong as Western imperialist powers, in 1894 he led the TONGHAK UPRISING, which was viciously suppressed. He was arrested and executed in 1898, by which time Tonghak had spread throughout Korea.

choir Body of singers with more than one voice to a part. For many centuries, church choirs sang only plainsong (see GREGORIAN CHANT). The relative complexity of early polyphony required solo voices rather than choral performance, but by the 15th century polyphony was being performed chorally. The growth of the secular choir (or chorus) coincided with the beginnings of OPERA, which has generally called for professional choruses, ORATORIOS, by contrast, being traditionally sung by amateurs.

Choiseul \shwä-'zəl\, **Étienne-François, duc (Duke) de** (1719–1785) French foreign minister. He served with distinction in the War of the AUSTRIAN SUCCESSION. After serving as ambassador to the Vatican (1753–57) and to the Austrian court, he was made a duke and named minister of foreign affairs (1758), in which position he came to dominate the government of LOUIS XV. In 1761 he concluded a military alliance with Spain (the "Family Compact"), and at the end of the Seven Years' War he negotiated the best terms for a defeated France. He rebuilt France's military strength, but was dismissed from office in 1770 for advocating war against Britain.

chokecherry One of several varieties of shrub or small tree *(Prunus virginiana)* of the ROSE family, native to North America. Though it is aptly named for the astringent, acidic taste of its reddish cherries, its fruit may be made into jelly and preserves. The stones and wilted foliage are poisonous. The trees often form dense thickets on moist soils. They are frequently attacked and defoliated by eastern TENT CATERPILLARS. Foul-scented white flowers are produced in hanging spikes, and the slender brown twigs also have an unpleasant odor and a bitter taste.

cholera \'kä-lə-rə\ Acute BACTERIAL infection with *Vibrio cholerae,* causing massive DIARRHEA with severe depletion of body fluids and salts. It often occurs in epidemics, spreading in contaminated water or food. The bacteria secrete a toxin that causes the diarrhea, which along with vomiting leads to DEHYDRATION, with severe muscle cramps and intense thirst. Stupor and coma may precede death by SHOCK. With fluid and salt replacement, the disease passes in two to seven days, less if antibiotics are taken the first day. Prevention requires good sanitation, especially clean drinking water.

cholesterol Waxy organic compound found in BLOOD and all animal tissues. It is a STEROID, with molecular formula $C_{27}H_{46}O$, containing four rings in its structure. Cholesterol is essential to life; it is a primary component of CELL MEMBRANES and a starting or intermediate material from which the body makes BILE acids, other steroid HORMONES, and VITAMIN D. It is made in the LIVER and some other organs, in greater or lesser amounts depending on the amount recently consumed in the diet. It circulates in the blood in compounds called LIPOPROTEINS, since it is not water-soluble alone. Excess cholesterol in the blood forms deposits in arteries (see ARTERIOSCLEROSIS), which can lead to CORONARY HEART DISEASE.

Michael Brown (born 1941) and Joseph Goldstein (born 1940) won a Nobel Prize in 1985 for their work in discovering this process. Since the body makes cholesterol from FATS, blood cholesterol cannot be reduced by limiting only the amount of cholesterol in the diet; the amount of fat, especially saturated fat (see SATURATION, FATTY ACID) must also be reduced. See also TRIGLYCERIDE.

choline \'kō-ˌlēn\ Organic compound related to VITAMINS in its activity. It is important in METABOLISM as a component of the LIPIDS that make up cell MEMBRANES and of ACETYLCHOLINE. It is also important as a source of chemical raw materials for CELLS and in transport of FATS from the LIVER. It is usually classified with the B vitamins (see VITAMIN B COMPLEX) because it resembles them in function and in its distribution in foods. In humans it is interconvertible with certain other compounds, such as METHIONINE, so deficiency does not lead to disease, but some other animals and birds need it in their diet. Choline has various uses in medicine, nutrition, and the processing of foods and feeds.

cholla \'chȯi-yə\ Any CACTUS of the genus *Opuntia,* native to North and South America, having needlelike spines partly enclosed in a papery sheath. Chollas vary greatly in size and have small flowers, sometimes chartreuse and inconspicuous, but usually of more striking colors. *O. leptocaulis,* the desert Christmas cactus, bears bright red fruits through the winter. Living plants serve as food for desert animals. Cholla wood, a hollow cylinder with regularly spaced holes, is used for fuel and novelties. Some cholla fruit is edible.

Jumping cholla (*Opuntia bigelovii*).
GRANT HEILMAN

Chomsky, (Avram) Noam (born 1928) U.S. linguist and political activist. He was born in Philadelphia and received his PhD from the University of Pennsylvania. He joined the faculty at MIT in 1955. Through a long series of books and articles beginning with *Syntactic Structures* (1957), Chomsky has maintained as his goal the articulation of a theory of universal grammar, that is, a framework of principles that would account for all language-specific rules. His work has had two decisive effects. One was to focus new emphasis on SYNTAX, previously a relatively unexplored area of language. The other was to make theories of language and linguistic competence independent of any particular language corpus, so that linguists tended to develop models of syntax or PHONOLOGY and test them against real-language "facts," rather than draw theoretical generalizations from a collection of data. Chomsky has also been well-known for his long career of protest against U.S. government foreign policy, from the Vietnam War in the 1960s to the bombing of Yugoslavia in 1999. His political views have been expounded in many books and articles, including *On Power and Ideology* (1987) and *World Orders, Old and New* (1994).

Ch'ondogyo \'chən-'dȯ-'gyō\ **(Korean: "Religion of the Heavenly Way")** *formerly* **Tonghak** ("Eastern Learning") Korean religion combining elements of Confucianism, Buddhism, Taoism, shamanism, and Roman Catholicism. Its basic principle that "Man and God are one" is realized through faith in the unity of one's body and spirit and in the universality of God. Converts are instructed to meditate on God, pray upon leaving and entering home, dispel harmful thoughts, and worship God in church on Sundays. Ch'oe Che-u (1824–1864) established the religion in 1860 after receiving inspiration from the Heavenly Emperor. His efforts at social change led to his execution. His successor, CH'OE SI-HYONG, was executed following the TONGHAK UPRISING. Today Ch'ondogyo has about 3 million adherents.

Chongqing *or* **Ch'ung-ch'ing** \'chu̇ŋ-'chiŋ\ *or* **Chungking** \'chəŋ-'kiŋ\ City and municipality with provincial status (pop., 1999 est.: city, 3,193,889; municipality, 30,750,000). The leading river port and industrial center of southwestern China, Chongqing ("Double-Blessed") lies at the confluence of the Yangtze River (Chang Jiang) and Jialing River. In the 11th century BC, it was a feudal state under the western Chou dynasty. Over the next several centuries, its status alternated from being ruled by an empire in northern China to being an independent state. It finally came under Chinese rule in the MING DYNASTY, continuing under the MANCHU DYNASTY. It was opened to foreign trade in 1890. It played a large role in the Revolution of 1911. Once a city of narrow and irregular streets, Chongqing changed greatly as a result of a modernization program introduced during World War II, when it became the GUOMINDANG capital. Since the war it has become an important industrial center. It is home to Chongqing University (founded 1929).

Chons See KHONS

Chopin \shō-'pan\, *Engl* 'shō-ˌpan\, **Frédéric (François)** *orig.* **Fryderyk Franciszek** (1810–1849) Polish-French composer. He was born to middle-class French parents in Poland. He published his first composition at 7 and began performing in aristocratic salons at 8. A successful international concert tour was followed by a Warsaw performance in 1830 that virtually endowed him with the status of Poland's national composer. He moved to Paris in 1831, and his first Paris concert the next year thrust him into the highest realm of celebrity. Renowned as a piano teacher, he spent his time in the highest society. He contracted tuberculosis apparently in the 1830s. In 1837 he began a 10-year liaison with the writer GEORGE SAND; she left him in 1847, and a rapid decline led to his death two years later. Chopin stands not only as Poland's greatest composer but perhaps as the most significant composer in the history of the piano, whose capacities for charm, excitement, variety, and timbral beauty he exhaustively exploited. Apart from two piano concertos (both 1830) and four other works for piano and orchestra, virtually all his compositions are for solo piano; they include some 60 mazurkas, 27 études, 26 preludes, 21 nocturnes, some 20 waltzes, 16 polonaises, four ballades, four scherzos, and three sonatas.

Frédéric Chopin, detail of a portrait by Eugène Delacroix; in the Louvre.
GIRAUDON—ART RESOURCE

Chopin \shō-'pan\, **Kate** *orig.* **Katherine O'Flaherty** (1851–1904) U.S. writer. Born in St. Louis, she lived in Louisiana during her marriage and began to write after her husband's death. A local colorist and interpreter of New Orleans culture, she foreshadowed later feminist themes. Among her more than 100 short stories are "Désirée's Baby" and "Madame Celestin's Divorce." *The Awakening* (1899), a realistic novel about the sexual and artistic awakening of a young mother who abandons her family, was initially condemned for its sexual frankness but later acclaimed.

chorale prelude Organ prelude based on a Protestant HYMN, or chorale, originally intended to precede the congregational singing of the hymn. Each line of the hymn tune was generally preceded by an improvisational treatment of its motifs. The form reflects the convention of improvised introductions to sung chorales. Many examples were composed by such 17th–18th-century Lutheran composers as J. PACHELBEL, J.S. BACH, and G.P. TELEMANN. Related genres include the chorale motet, chorale variations, chorale fantasia, and chorale fugue.

chord Grouping of three or more musical tones, especially as sounded simultaneously. The tones C-E-G constitute a "C major chord," or "C major triad." Chords may comprise any number of separate tones, and may be highly dissonant (see CONSONANCE AND DISSONANCE). The term HARMONY is often used loosely as a synonym.

chordate \'kȯr-ˌdāt\ Any member of the phylum Chordata, which includes the most highly evolved animals, the VERTEBRATES, as well as the marine invertebrate cephalochordates (see AMPHIOXUS) and TUNICATES. All chordates, at some time in their life cycle, possess a dorsal supporting rod (notochord), gill slits, and a dorsal nerve cord. Unlike vertebrates, tunicates and cephalochordates lack any kind of brain or skeleton. Chordate bodies consist of a body wall encasing a gut, with a space between called the coelom. The body is usually long and bilaterally symmetrical, with the mouth and sense organs at the front end.

chorea \kə-'rē-ə\ Neurological disorder causing irregular, involuntary, purposeless movements, believed to be caused by degeneration of the basal ganglia in the CEREBRAL CORTEX. Sydenham's chorea (St. Vitus' dance) is usually associated with RHEUMATIC FEVER. It usually occurs between ages 5 and 15, more often in girls; typical jerking movements, mostly in the extremities and face, may affect speech and swallowing and range from mild to incapacitating; attacks last several weeks and recur frequently. Senile chorea, a progressive disease resembling Sydenham's chorea, usually occurs late in life. Huntington's chorea is rare, hereditary, and fatal; it usually begins between ages 35 and 50, progressing to random, often violent, and eventually totally incapacitating spasms, absent only during sleep. Mental deterioration begins later and death occurs in 10–20 years. There is no effective therapy. Children of those afflicted have a 50% chance of developing the illness.

choreography Art of creating and arranging dances. The word is derived from the Greek for "dance" and "write," reflecting its early meaning as a written record of dances. By the 19th century the term was used mainly for the creation of dances, and the written record became known as DANCE NOTATION. In the 16th century dance masters at the French court arranged their social dances into specific patterns. In the 17th century such dances became more complex and were performed as theatrical BALLETS by trained professionals. In the late 18th century J.-G. NOVERRE and GASPARO ANGIOLINI introduced choreography that combined expressive mime and dance steps to produce the dramatic ballet. This was further developed in 19th-century Romantic ballets by MARIUS PETIPA, JULES PERROT, and AUGUST BOURNONVILLE. Radical change in the 20th century began with choreographers of the BALLETS RUSSES, including MICHEL FOKINE and LEONID MASSINE, and continued with GEORGE BALANCHINE, MARTHA GRAHAM, FREDERICK ASHTON, JEROME ROBBINS, MERCE CUNNINGHAM, and TWYLA THARP. See also ALVIN AILEY, AGNES DE MILLE, SERGE LIFAR, BRONISLAVA NIJINSKA, S. VIGANO.

chorus Group of actors who performed as an ensemble in Greek drama to describe and comment on the play's action with song, dance, and recitation. Choral performances, which originated in the singing of DITHYRAMBS in honor of DIONYSUS, dominated Greek drama until the mid-5th century BC, when AESCHYLUS added a second actor and reduced the chorus from 50 to 12 performers. As the importance of individual actors increased, the chorus gradually disappeared. It was revived in such modern plays as EUGENE O'NEILL's *Mourning Becomes Electra* (1931) and T. S. ELIOT's *Murder in the Cathedral* (1935). Choruses of singers and dancers came to be featured in musical comedies, especially in the 20th century, first as entertainment and later to help develop the plot.

Choshu \'chō-ˌshü\ Japanese HAN (domain) that, along with the han of SATSUMA, supported the overthrow of the TOKUGAWA SHOGUNATE and the creation of a new government headed by the emperor. With their superior familiarity with Western weapons, the Satsuma-Choshu alliance was able to defeat the shogunal forces, bringing the emperor to power in the MEIJI RESTORATION of 1868.

Choson dynasty \'chō-ˌsȯn\ *or* **Yi dynasty** (1392–1910) Last and longest-lived of Korea's dynasties. Chinese cultural influences were very strong in this period, when NEO-CONFUCIANISM was adopted as the ideology of the state and society. In the late 16th and early 17th century, Korea suffered invasions at the hands of the Japanese and MANCHUS. Many cultural assets were lost, and it took the nation nearly a century to recover. At the end of the 19th century foreign powers once again threatened Korea; it was annexed by Japan in 1910. The Choson dynasty witnessed the creation of the Korean alphabetic script (see KOREAN LANGUAGE), and the establishment of the YANGBAN, a new aristocracy. See also YI SONG-GYE.

Chott el Hodna See Chott el HODNA

Chou dynasty See ZHOU DYNASTY

Chou En-lai See ZHOU ENLAI

Chou-kung See ZHOUGONG

Chouteau \shü-'tō\, **(René) Auguste** (1749–1829) American fur trader and cofounder of ST. LOUIS. Born in New Orleans, he moved to Missouri Territory with his mother and Pierre Liguest (1724?–1778), with whom he later cofounded St. Louis in 1764. The two men built a prosperous fur trade, which Chouteau later expanded. By 1794 he had a monopoly on the trade with the Osage and helped finance most of the fur-trading companies in Louisiana Territory. He became the unofficial banker to the St. Louis community and its largest landowner.

chow chow *or* **chow** Breed of dog that shares with the SHAR-PEI an unusual blue-black tongue. The chow chow originated in China and dates to the Han dynasty (206 BC–AD 220); it may be one of the oldest of all breeds. It is compact and has a large head and a thick coat that forms a dense ruff about the neck. The coat is evenly colored, either reddish brown, black, or blue-gray. The adult stands about 18–20 in. (46–51 cm) high and weighs 45–70 lbs (20–32 kg). The breed is usually loyal to owners but aloof with strangers.

Chow chow.
SALLY ANNE THOMPSON—EB INC.

Chrétien \krā-'tyaü\, **(Joseph-Jacques) Jean** (born 1934) Canadian prime minister (from 1993). Born the 18th of 19 children in a working-class family in Shawinigan, Quebec, he studied law at Laval University and began to practice in Quebec in 1958. He served in the Canadian House of Commons (1963–86) and held various posts in the administrations of LESTER PEARSON and PIERRE TRUDEAU, including minister of finance (1977), the first French Canadian to hold the office. In 1990 he was reelected to the House of Commons and became leader of the LIBERAL PARTY OF CANADA. Advocating a united Canada, he won a landslide victory to become prime minister. He later led the Liberal Party to successive victories in 1997 and 2000.

Chrétien de Troyes \krā-'tya^{n}-də-'trwä\ (fl. 1165–1180) French poet. Little is known of his life. He is the author of the five Arthurian ROMANCES *Erec*, *Cligès*, *Lancelot*, *Yvain*, and *Perceval*, and possibly a non-Arthurian tale. Written in the vernacular, his romances were derived from the writings of GEOFFREY OF MONMOUTH and combine separate adventures into well-knit stories. They were imitated almost immediately by other French poets and were translated and adapted frequently as the romance continued to develop as a narrative form. See also ARTHURIAN LEGEND.

Christ, Church of Any of various conservative Protestant churches found mainly in the U.S. Each congregation is autonomous in government, with elders, deacons, and a minister or ministers; there is no national administrative organization. These churches originated in the early 19th century with the DISCIPLES OF CHRIST movement, which relied on the Bible as the only standard of Christian faith and worship. Controversies split the movement, and the Churches of Christ designated those congregations that opposed organized mission societies and the use of instrumental music in worship. After their separation from the Disciples, the Churches of Christ continued to grow. Worship services consist of prayer, preaching, unaccompanied singing, and the Lord's Supper.

Christchurch City (pop., 1996: 314,000), South Island, New Zealand. Founded in 1850 as a model Church of England settlement, it was the last and most successful colonizing project inspired by EDWARD GIBBON WAKEFIELD and his New Zealand Co. It is the country's second-largest city and an important industrial center; its port is Lyttelton. Called the "Garden City of the Plains" for its numerous parks and gardens, it is home to the University of Canterbury (founded 1873), Christ's College, and Lincoln University (1990).

Christian, Charlie *orig.* **Charles** (1916–1942) U.S. guitarist, the first great electric guitarist in jazz. Christian grew up in Oklahoma City and joined BENNY GOODMAN to perform in both big-band and small-group settings in 1939. He created a sensation through his technically adept and innovative use of amplification, thus changing the guitar's primary role from accompanist to soloist. One of the most advanced and influential jazz soloists of the SWING era, Christian participated in the jam sessions at Minton's Playhouse in Harlem with THELONIOUS MONK and DIZZY GILLESPIE that pioneered the harmonic advances of BEBOP. He died of tuberculosis at age 25.

Christian II (1481–1559) King of Denmark and Norway (1513–23) and of Sweden (1520–23). He succeeded his father, John, king of Denmark and Norway. In 1517 he decided to conquer Sweden, defeating the forces of the Swedish regent, and was crowned Sweden's king in 1520. However, he ordered a massacre of Swedish nobles (the Stockholm Bloodbath) that helped incite a successful Swedish war for independence, marking the end of the KALMAR UNION in 1523. That year a revolt in Denmark forced Christian to flee to the Netherlands. After attempting to regain his kingdom, he was arrested by Danish forces in 1532 and spent the rest of his life imprisoned in Danish castles.

Christian III (1503–1559) King of Denmark and Norway (1534–59). Son of King Frederick I, he assumed control of the kingdom after winning a civil war known as the Count's War. He arrested the Catholic bishops who had opposed him and organized the Diet of Copenhagen (1536), which confiscated episcopal property and established the state Lutheran Church. By forming close ties between the church and the crown, he laid the foundation for the absolutist Danish monarchy of the 17th century.

Christian IV (1577–1648) King of Denmark and Norway (1588–1648). He succeeded to the throne on the death of his father, Frederick II, but a regency ruled until 1596. After his coronation he succeeded in limiting the powers of the Rigsråd (state council). He led two unsuccessful wars against Sweden and brought disaster to his country by leading it into the THIRTY YEARS' WAR. He was eventually forced to accept the increased power of the nobility, which had long opposed his warlike policies. However, he energetically promoted trade and shipping, was a great builder and founder of cities, left a national heritage of fine buildings, and was considered one of the most popular of Danish kings.

Christian IV, detail of an oil painting by Pieter Isaacsz, 1612; in Frederiksborg Castle, Denmark.

BY COURTESY OF DET NATIONALHISTORISKE MUSEUM PAA FREDERIKSBORG, DENMARK

Christian IX (1818–1906) King of Denmark (1863–1906). He succeeded the childless FREDERICK VII, whose cousin he had married. When he became king, he was forced by popular feeling to sign the November Constitution, which incorporated Schleswig into the state (see SCHLESWIG-HOLSTEIN QUESTION). This led to the disastrous war of 1864 against Prussia and Austria. After the war, he unsuccessfully resisted the advance of full parliamentary government in Denmark.

Christian X (1870–1947) King of Denmark (1912–47) who symbolized his nation's resistance to the German occupation in World War II. He assumed the throne on the death of his father, Frederick VIII (1843–1912). In 1915 Christian signed a constitution granting equal suffrage to men and women. After the German occupation began in 1940, he rode frequently on horseback through the streets of Copenhagen, showing that he had not abandoned his claim to national sovereignty, and he opposed Nazi demands for anti-Jewish legislation. His speech against the occupation forces in 1943 led to his imprisonment until the end of the war.

Christian caste In India, social stratification among Christians based on CASTE membership at the time of an individual's or an ancestor's conversion. Indian Christians are grouped by denomination, geography, and caste. The Syrian Christians along the Malabar coast, descended from 1st-century converts of high birth, retain mid-rank status in Hindu society. Portuguese missionaries of the 16th century converted lower-caste fisherfolk. Missionaries in the 19th century insisted on social reform and tended to draw from the lowest classes. Caste distinctions are breaking down at about the same rate among contemporary Indian Christians and other Indians.

Christian Democracy Political movement that has a close association with ROMAN CATHOLICISM and its philosophy of social and economic justice. It incorporates both traditional church and family values and progressive values such as social welfare. After World War II, a number of Christian Democrat parties appeared in Europe, including the Italian CHRISTIAN DEMOCRATIC PARTY, the French POPULAR REPUBLICAN MOVEMENT, and the most successful, the German CHRISTIAN DEMOCRATIC UNION. The same period also saw the appearance of Christian Democrat parties in Latin America. Though most were small splinter groups, Christian Democrats eventually achieved power in Venezuela, El Salvador, and Chile.

Christian Democratic Party (1943–93) Centrist Italian political party whose factions were united by Roman Catholicism and anticommunism. The ITALIAN POPULAR PARTY (founded 1919) was the predecessor of the Christian Democratic Party, which was formed in 1943. The party largely dominated Italian politics from World War II until the mid-1990s. After some of its leading members were implicated in financial scandals and political corruption, the struggling party reverted to its original name in 1993. In parliamentary elections the next year, the Italian Popular Party fell from power. See also CHRISTIAN DEMOCRACY.

Christian Democratic Union (CDU) German political party advocating regulated economic competition and close cooperation with the U.S. in foreign policy. It held power from the establishment of the West German republic in 1948 until 1969, and again in the years 1982–98. In 1990, with HELMUT KOHL as chancellor, it oversaw the reunification of Germany. In the following years it and its coalition partners faced discontent over the economic burden of reunification, but the coalition retained a reduced power. Revelations of financial corruption in 1999 severely damaged the reputation of the party and of former chancellor Kohl. See also KONRAD ADENAUER, CHRISTIAN DEMOCRACY.

Christian Science *officially* **Church of Christ, Scientist** Religious denomination founded in the U.S. in 1879 by MARY BAKER EDDY. Like other Christian sects, Christian Science subscribes to an omnipotent God and the authority (but not inerrancy) of the Bible, and takes the crucifixion and resurrection of JESUS as essential to human redemption. It departs from traditional Christianity in considering Jesus divine but not a deity and in regarding creation as wholly spiritual. Sin denies God's sovereignty by claiming that life derives from matter. Spiritual cure of disease is a necessary element of redemption from the flesh. Most members refuse medical help for disease, and members engaged in the full-time healing ministry are called Christian Science practitioners. Elected readers lead Sunday services based on readings from the Bible and Eddy's *Science and Health.* See also NEW THOUGHT.

Christian Science Monitor, The Daily newspaper of national and international news and features, published Monday through Friday in Boston under the auspices of the Church of Christ, Scientist (see CHRISTIAN SCIENCE). Established in 1908 at the urging of MARY BAKER EDDY as a protest against the sensationalism of the popular press, it became one of the most respected U.S. newspapers, famous for its thoughtful treatment of the news and for the quality of its assessments of political, social, and economic developments. It strictly limits the kinds of advertising it accepts. It maintains its own bureaus to gather news abroad and publishes a weekly world edition.

Christian Social Union (CSU) Conservative German political party that was founded in Bavaria, West Germany, in 1946 by Roman Catholic and Protestant groups. It was committed to free enterprise, federalism, and a united Europe that would operate under Christian principles. From 1946 it held the government of Bavaria continuously, except in 1954–57. In national elections it usually cooperated with the CHRISTIAN DEMOCRATIC UNION.

Christian Socialism Mid-19th-century social movement of European Christian activists who attempted to combine the fundamental aims of SOCIALISM with the religious and ethical convictions of CHRISTIANITY, promoting cooperativism over competition as a means to help the poor. The term was devised in Britain in 1848 after the failure of CHARTISM. The movement found followers in France and Germany; the German group combined its activities with ANTI-SEMITISM. In the U.S., the movement died out in the early 20th century, but it retains an important following in Europe.

Christiania See OSLO

Christianity Religion stemming from the teachings of JESUS in the 1st century AD. Its sacred scripture is the BIBLE, particularly the NEW TESTAMENT. Its principal tenets are that Jesus is the son of God (the second person of the Holy TRINITY), that God's love for the world is the essential component of his being, and that Jesus died to redeem humankind. Christianity was originally a movement of Jews who accepted Jesus as the MESSIAH, but the movement quickly became predominantly gentile. The early church was shaped by St. PAUL and other early Christian missionaries and theologians; it was persecuted under the Roman empire but supported by CONSTANTINE I, the first Christian emperor. During the two millennia since Jesus' death, Christianity has subdivided into numerous churches that continue to proliferate; the major divisions are ROMAN CATHOLICISM, EASTERN ORTHODOXY, and PROTESTANTISM. Nearly all Christian churches have an ordained clergy, members of which are typically though not universally male. Members of the clergy lead group worship services and are viewed as intermediaries between the laity and the divine in some churches. Most Christian churches administer two sacraments, baptism and the Lord's Supper. There are now nearly 2 billion adherents of Christianity throughout the world, found on all continents.

Christie, Agatha (Mary Clarissa) *later* **Dame Agatha** (1890–1976) British detective novelist and playwright. Her first novel, *The Mysterious Affair at Styles* (1920), introduced Hercule Poirot, the eccentric Belgian detective who would appear in about 25 novels. The elderly spinster Miss Jane Marple, her other principal detective figure, first appeared in *Murder at the Vicarage* (1930). Most of her approximately 75 novels were bestsellers; translated into 100 languages, they have sold over 100 million copies. Her plays include *The Mousetrap* (1952), which set a world record for longest continuous run, and *Witness for the Prosecution* (1953; film, 1958). She was married to the eminent archaeologist Sir Max Mallowan (1904–1978).

Agatha Christie, 1946.
UPI/CORBIS-BETTMANN

Christie's Popular name for the London firm of Christie, Manson & Woods, the oldest fine-arts auctioneers in the world. It was founded by James Christie (1730–1803), who opened his salesrooms in 1766. He became friends with JOSHUA REYNOLDS and THOMAS GAINSBOROUGH, among others, and developed a tradition of holding studio sales for prominent artists. Christie's has handled some of the most important art sales in history, including the sale of paintings to CATHERINE II the Great of Russia. The firm, which became a public company in 1973, now has branches all over the world.

Christina *Swedish* **Kristina** (1626–1689) Queen of Sweden (1644–54). The successor to her father, GUSTAV II ADOLF, she was a prime mover in concluding the Peace of WESTPHALIA and ending the THIRTY YEARS' WAR. After 10 years of rule she stunned Europe by abdicating the throne, claiming that she was ill and that the burden of ruling was too heavy for a woman. Her real reasons were her aversion to marriage and her secret conversion to Roman Catholicism, which was proscribed in Sweden. She moved to Rome and subsequently attempted, without success, to gain the crowns of Naples and Poland. One of the wittiest and most learned women of her age, she was a lavish patroness of the arts and an influence on European culture.

Christina, engraving by Cornelis Visscher published byP. Soutman, 1650.
BY COURTESY OF THE SVENSKA PORTRATTARKIVET, STOCKHOLM

Christine de Pisan *or* **Christine de Pizan** \krēs-'tēn-də-pē-'zäⁿ\ (1365?–1431?) French writer. Daughter of an astrologer to CHARLES V and wife of a court secretary, she took up writing to support her children when she was widowed, producing 10 volumes of graceful verse, including ballads, rondeaux, lays, and complaints, many in the COURTLY-LOVE tradition. Some works, both poetry and prose, champion women, notably *The Book of the City of Ladies* (1405). She also wrote a life of Charles V and *Le Ditié de Jehanne d'Arc* (1429), inspired by JOAN OF ARC's early victories.

Christmas Christian festival celebrated on December 25, commemorating the birth of JESUS. December 25 had already been identified by Sextus Julius Africanus in 221 as the day on which Christmas would be celebrated, and it was celebrated in Rome by AD 336. During the Middle Ages Christmas became extremely popular, and various liturgical celebrations of the holiday were established. The practice of exchanging gifts began by the 15th century. The Yule log, cakes, and fir trees derive from German and Celtic customs. Christmas today is regarded as a family festival with gifts brought by Santa Claus (see St. NICHOLAS). As an increasingly secular festival, it has come to be celebrated by many non-Christians.

Christmas tree Evergreen tree, usually decorated with lights and ornaments, to celebrate the Christmas season. The use of evergreen trees, wreaths, and garlands as symbols of eternal life was common among the ancient Egyptians, Chinese, and Hebrews. The Christian symbol can be traced to a German medieval play about Adam and Eve, which included the "paradise tree," hung with apples. The modern, decorated version was widespread among German Lutherans by the 18th century. Brought to North America by German settlers in the 17th century, it had become widespread there by the mid-19th century. It was popularized in 19th-century England by VICTORIA's consort, the German Prince ALBERT of Saxe-Coburg.

Christo *orig.* **Christo Javacheff** (born 1935) Bulgarian-U.S. environmental artist. After attending Sofia's Fine Arts Academy, he moved to Paris in 1958, where he invented *empaquetage,* the wrapping of objects in various materials as art. He began with cans and bottles, and eventually his projects expanded to buildings and landscapes. In 1964 he moved to New York. He is noted for such monumental outdoor projects as *Valley Curtain* (1970–72) in Rifle Gap, Col., and *Running Fence* (1972–76) in Marin and Sonoma cos., Cal. In 1995 he wrapped the Berlin Reichstag in metallic silver fabric. Though his displays, which are temporary and involve hundreds of workers, are controversial among environmentalists, they have been critically well received. Since 1961, most have been collaborative efforts with his wife, Jeanne-Claude (born 1935).

Christopher, St. (fl. 3rd century) Patron saint of travelers and motorists. He is said to have been martyred in Lycia under the Roman emperor Decius (c. 250). Legends depict him as a giant who devoted his life to carrying travelers across a river. One day a small child asked to be transported, and in the middle of the river the child became so heavy that he staggered under the burden. The child revealed to the saint that he had been carrying Christ and the sins of the world, thus giving rise to Christopher's name (Greek: "Christ-bearer"). His historicity is doubtful.

Christus \'kris-tüs\, **Petrus** (c. 1410–1475/76) Flemish painter. He is documented as working in Bruges in 1444, where he was influenced by the work of JAN VAN EYCK. He was known for his sensitive portraits, but his most important contributions were the introduction of geometric perspective to Netherlandish painting, and his genrelike treatment of religious subjects, seen in such works as *St. Eligius as a Goldsmith* (1449) and *Virgin and Child in a Domestic Interior* (c. 1450–60).

chromaticism \krō-'ma-tə-ˌsi-zəm\ In music, the use of all twelve tones, especially for heightened expressivity. A standard KEY or MODE principally employs seven tones, leaving five tones for discretionary use. Use of all twelve tones in a given piece increased in the 18th and 19th century. Strictly controlled chromaticism, as in the ornamentation of F. CHOPIN, did not threaten the perception of TONALITY. However, from the mid-19th century on, complaints were heard with ever greater frequency that it was difficult to perceive what a given piece's tonal center was, the chromaticism in the works of RICHARD WAGNER being the most notorious. The virtual breakdown in tonality in the works of advanced composers led to the free ATONALITY of A. SCHOENBERG and his followers in the early 20th century.

chromatography \ˌkrō-mə-'tä-grə-fē\ Method first described in 1903 by MIKHAIL S. TSVET for separating mixed chemical substances. Tsvet's neglected work, rediscovered in the 1930s, uses the different affinities of substances in a solution in a mobile PHASE (a moving stream of gas or liquid) for adsorbtion onto a stationary phase (a fine-grained solid, a sheet of filtering material, or a thin film of a liquid on a solid surface).

Choices of materials for these phases allow enormous versatility for separating substances including biological fluids (e.g., AMINO ACIDS, STEROIDS, CARBOHYDRATES, PIGMENTS), chemical mixtures, and forensic samples. In the original technique, an organic SOLVENT flowed through a column of powdered alumina (see ALUMINUM), sodium carbonate, or even powdered sugar to separate mixed plant pigments. Among current adaptations are PAPER CHROMATOGRAPHY (PC), THIN-LAYER CHROMATOGRAPHY (TLC), liquid chromatography (LC, including high-performance liquid chromatography, or HPLC), and GAS CHROMATOGRAPHY (GC). Some remain LABORATORY techniques, but some (especially HPLC) can be used on an industrial scale. They require different methods for detecting and identifying the separated components, including COLORIMETRY, SPECTROPHOTOMETRY, MASS SPECTROMETRY, and measurement of fluorescence, ionization potential, or thermal conductivity. A. J. P. Martin shared a 1952 Nobel Prize for developing LC and PC, and in his Nobel lecture announced the development (with his cowinner R. L. M. Synge and other colleagues) of GC.

chromite Relatively hard, metallic, black OXIDE MINERAL of chromium and iron ($FeCr_2O_4$) that is the chief commercial source of chromium. Chromite is commonly found as brittle masses in peridotites, serpentines, and other basic igneous and metamorphic rocks. The principal producing areas are South Africa, Russia, Albania, the Philippines, Zimbabwe, Turkey, Brazil, India, and Finland.

chromium Metallic chemical ELEMENT, one of the TRANSITION ELEMENTS, chemical symbol Cr, atomic number 24. A hard, steel-gray METAL that takes a high polish, it is used in ALLOYS (e.g., ferrochromium, steel, stainless steel) to increase strength and corrosion resistance. It usually has VALENCE 2, 3, or 6 and always occurs combined with other elements, especially oxygen; CHROMITE is its only commercial source. Various colored gemstones (e.g., ruby, emerald, serpentine) owe their color to chromium. Sodium chromate and dichromate are used in leather tanning, in metal surface treatment, and as catalysts. Chromium trioxide is used in chrome plating and as a colorant for ceramics. Chromium oxide, lead chromate, and various other chromium compounds are used as pigments. Chromium dioxide, strongly magnetic, is used in recording tapes and as a catalyst.

chromodynamics See QUANTUM CHROMODYNAMICS

chromosomal disorder Syndrome caused by CHROMOSOME abnormality. Normally, humans have 23 pairs of chromosomes, including one pair of SEX CHROMOSOMES. Any variation from this pattern causes abnormalities. A chromosome may be duplicated (trisomy) or absent (monosomy); one or more extra full sets of chromosomes can be present (see PLOIDY); or part of a chromosome may be missing (deletion) or transferred to another (translocation). Resulting disorders include DOWN'S SYNDROME, mental retardation, heart malformation, abnormal sexual development, malignancies, and sex-chromosome disorders (e.g., TURNER'S SYNDROME, KLINEFELTER'S SYNDROME). Chromosomal disorders occur in 0.5% of births; many can now be diagnosed before birth by AMNIOCENTESIS.

chromosome Microscopic, threadlike part of a CELL that carries hereditary information in the form of GENES. The structure and location of chromosomes differentiate prokaryotic cells from eukaryotic cells (see PROKARYOTE, EUKARYOTE). Every species has a characteristic number of chromosomes; humans have 23 pairs (22 pairs of autosomal, or nonsex, chromosomes and one pair of sex chromosomes). Human chromosomes consist primarily of DNA. During cell division (see MEIOSIS, MITOSIS), chromosomes are distributed evenly among daughter cells. In sexually reproducing organisms, the number of chromosomes in somatic (nonsex) cells is diploid, while gametes or sex cells (egg and sperm) produced by meiosis are haploid (see PLOIDY). FERTILIZATION restores the diploid set of chromosomes in the zygote. See illustration opposite.

chromosphere Layer of the SUN's atmosphere, several thousand miles thick, above the PHOTOSPHERE and below the CORONA. The chromosphere (literally "color sphere") is briefly visible as a thin ring, red from hydrogen's emission spectrum, during solar eclipses when the photosphere is obscured by the moon. At other times it can be observed only with special instruments. Its temperatures range from about 7,000°F (4,000°C) about 700 mi (1,100 km) above the photosphere, increasing with altitude to several hundred thousand degrees. SOLAR FLARES and SOLAR PROMINENCES are mainly chromospheric phenomena.

chronic fatigue syndrome (CFS) Sudden debilitating fatigue of unknown cause, usually with mild fever, tender lymph nodes, sore throat, headaches, weakness, muscle and joint pain, and confusion or difficulty in concentrating. To meet the criteria of CFS, the syndrome must be new, with a definite point of onset, and must persist more than six months. Once dismissed as imaginary, CFS has now been recognized by the Centers for Disease Control and Prevention, which estimates that it affects three out of every thousand individuals, mostly women. It may have existed for many years; and may be similar to the condition known in the 19th century as neurasthenia, though it is also conjectured to result from a variety of factors, including some environmental factors that have arisen more recently. Skeptics continue to dispute that it represents a discrete disease. No diagnostic test yet exists to distinguish it from similar illnesses. No effective treatment has been found, but most patients improve gradually.

chronicle play *or* **history play** Play with a theme from history, which often holds up the past as a lesson for the present. Chronicle plays developed from medieval MORALITY PLAYS and flourished in times of nationalistic fervor, as in England from the 1580s to the 1630s. They included such plays as *The Victories of Henry the Fifth* and *The True Tragedie of Richard III* and reached maturity with CHRISTOPHER MARLOWE's *Edward II* and WILLIAM SHAKESPEARE's *Henry VI*.

chronometer \krə-ˈnä-mə-tər\ Mechanical timekeeping device of great accuracy, particularly one used for determining longitude (see LATITUDE AND LONGITUDE) at sea. Early weight- and pendulum-driven CLOCKS were inaccurate because of friction and temperature changes and could not be used at sea because of the ship's motion. In 1735 JOHN HARRISON invented and constructed the first of four practical marine timekeepers. The modern marine chronometer is suspended to remain horizontal whatever the inclination of the ship and differs in parts of its mechanism from the ordinary watch. A chronometer may provide timekeeping accurate to within 0.1 second per day. See also FERDINAND BERTHOUD.

Chrysander \k̲rē-ˈzän-dər\, **(Karl Franz) Friedrich** (1826–1901) German musicologist. Trained as a schoolteacher, he soon became involved in music scholarship and published studies of folk song (1853). One of the founders of the discipline of musicology (with Philipp Spitta

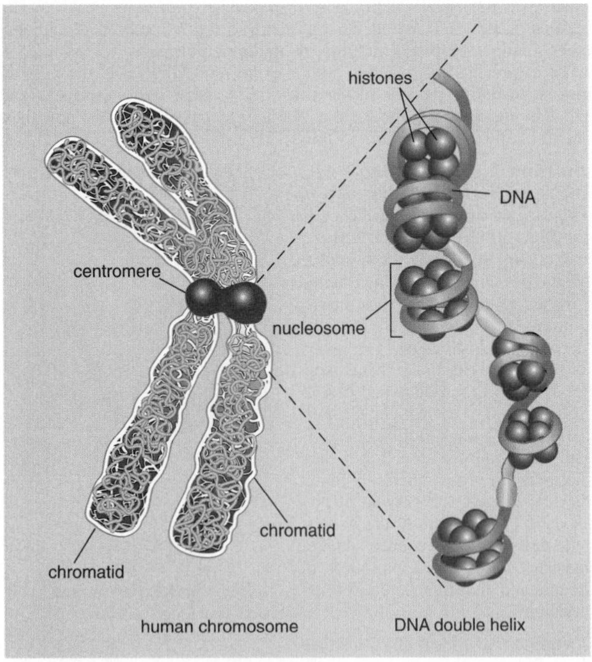

Human chromosome with close-up of coiled DNA. Immediately before cell division, DNA, existing as thin uncoiled strands, duplicates to form two daughter strands (chromatids) joined at a centromere. During the first stages of cell division, DNA wraps around binding proteins (histones) to become a highly coiled dense structure recognizable as the rod-shaped chromosome. Following cell division, the DNA uncoils; the uncoiled DNA with its associated proteins is termed chromatin.

and G. ADLER), he wrote on a wide range of subjects, but his great project was the first edition of the complete works of G.F. HANDEL, to which he devoted the years 1858–94.

chrysanthemum \kri-'san-thə-ˌməm\ Any of the ornamental plants that make up the genus *Chrysanthemum,* in the COMPOSITE FAMILY. The genus includes about 100 species native primarily to subtropical and temperate areas of the Old World. Cultivated species, often called mums, have large flower heads; those of wild species are much smaller. Most species have aromatic, alternate leaves. Some have both disk and ray flowers in the heads; others lack ray flowers. Costmary *(C. balsamita),* PYRETHRUM, MARGUERITE, Shasta daisy (hybrid forms of *C. maximum*), florists' chrysanthemum *(C. morifolium),* feverfew *(C. parthenium),* corn marigold *(C. segetum),* and TANSY are popular garden plants. Feverfew and pyrethrum are used in insecticides.

Chrysler Building Office building in New York City (1928–30), designed by William Van Alen (1883–1954). It is the epitome of sleek ART DECO. Its tapering sunburst-patterned stainless-steel spire remains a striking feature of the Manhattan skyline. Much of its futuristic automotive ornamentation was specified by its owner, Walter P. Chrysler (see CHRYSLER CORP.). It was briefly the tallest in the world (1,048 ft, or 319.4 m) until the EMPIRE STATE BUILDING opened in 1931.

Chrysler Corp. U.S. automotive company first incorporated in 1925 and reorganized and newly incorporated in 1986. It was founded by Walter P. Chrysler (1875–1940), who built it into the country's second-largest automobile manufacturer, noted for its Plymouth, Dodge, and Chrysler cars. In 1980 the corporation was rescued from the verge of bankruptcy by a government bailout organized by LEE IACOCCA. In 1998 Chrysler Corp. merged with the German automaker Daimler-Benz to become DAIMLER CHRYSLER AG.

Chrysostom \'kris-əs-təm\, **St. John** (c. 347–407) Early church father, biblical interpreter, and archbishop of Constantinople. Born in Syria and raised a Christian, he lived as a hermit until his health gave way, after which he returned to Antioch and was ordained a priest. He earned a reputation as a great preacher (Chrysostom means "golden-mouthed"). Against his wishes, he was appointed archbishop of Constantinople in 398. He angered the wealthy with his concern for the poor and criticisms of the misuse of riches. A synod convened in 403 by Theophilus of Alexandria condemned him on 29 charges and banished him to Armenia. He died en route to a more distant exile on the Black Sea. In 438 his relics were brought to Constantinople, and he was rehabilitated by the church.

St. John Chrysostom, detail of a 12th-century mosaic; in the Palatine Chapel, Palermo.

ANDERSON—ALINARI FROM ART RESOURCE

chrysotile \'kri-sə-ˌtīl\ Fibrous variety of the magnesium silicate mineral SERPENTINE; it is the most important ASBESTOS mineral. Individual fibers are white and silky, but the aggregate in veins is usually green or yellowish. Chrysotile fibers have a high tensile strength, similar to that of other asbestos minerals (see AMPHIBOLE ASBESTOS). The largest deposits of chrysotile are in Quebec and in the Ural Mtns.

Chu *or* **Ch'u** One of the states contending for power in China, 770–221 BC. Chu emerged in the 8th century BC in the Chang (Yangtze) River valley, then not a part of China. It struggled with other states for supreme control over China in the 3rd century BC but lost out to QIN, which formed the first great Chinese empire.

Chu Hsi See ZHU XI

Chu-ko Liang See ZHUGE LIANG

Chu Teh See ZHU DE

Ch'ü Yüan See QU YUAN

Chu Yüan-chang See HONGWU EMPEROR

Chuan Leekpai (born 1938) Prime minister of Thailand (1992–95, 1997–2001). Son of a schoolteacher, he became a lawyer and was first elected a member of Parliament in 1969. He served in various capacities in the government and was first made prime minister in 1992 after his predecessor resigned in the wake of street violence brought on by Thailand's worsening economic crisis. He lost elections in 1995 largely because his government was seen as plodding and slow, but he was returned to power in 1997. He was Thailand's first prime minister to come to power without either aristocratic or military backing.

Chuang-tzu See ZHUANGZI

chub Any of several freshwater fishes of the CARP family that are commonly caught for bait, sport, and food. Popular species include the European chub *(Leuciscus cephalus)* of Europe and Britain, a voracious predator of insects and other fish, and in North America, the creek chub, or horned DACE *(Semotilus atromaculatus),* and the hornyhead chub *(Nocomis,* or *Hybopsis, biguttata).* These species range in length from 6 in. to 2 ft (15–60 cm). Their colors vary, tending toward bluish or greenish above, with a lighter or silvery belly. In North America the name is applied to many cyprinids and elsewhere to other, unrelated, fishes.

European chub (*Leuciscus cephalus*).

W.S. PITT—ERIC HOSKING

Chubut River \chü-'büt\ River, southern Argentina. Rising in the ANDES, it flows eastward across Chubut province 500 mi (800 km) before emptying into the Atlantic Ocean at Punta Castro. It is unnavigable, but its lower course irrigates the adjacent valley.

Chuckchi See SIBERIAN PEOPLES

Chughtai, Abdur Rahman (1894–1975) Pakistani artist. In the 1920s he created large watercolors in a modified Bengal-school style. By the 1940s his painting style was influenced by Mughal architecture, Islamic calligraphy, miniature painting, and Art Nouveau, and his diverse subject matter included heroes and heroines from Islamic history, Mughal kings and queens, and episodes from Punjabi, Persian, and Indo-Islamic legends and folktales. After the partition of the subcontinent in 1947, he came to be known as the national artist of Pakistan.

Chuikov \'chü-i-ˌkȯf\, **Vasily (Ivanovich)** (1900–1982) Soviet general. In World War II he commanded the defense at the Battle of STALINGRAD, joined in turning ADOLF HITLER's armies back, and led the Soviet drive to Berlin. He personally accepted the German surrender of Berlin in 1945. After the war he commanded the Soviet occupation forces in Germany (1949–53). He headed the Kiev military district 1953–60, and thereafter held a variety of military assignments in Moscow.

Chula Vista \ˌchü-lə-'vis-tə\ City (pop., 2000: 173,556), southwestern California. It lies on the eastern shore of San Diego Bay south of SAN DIEGO. Laid out in 1888 by the Santa Fe Railway and named for its "pretty view," it developed as a citrus center, later turned to truck gardening, and is now primarily residential.

Chulalongkorn \'chü-'lä-'lȯŋ-'kȯn\ *or* **Phrachunlachomklao** \ˌprä-chün-ˌlä-ˌkȯm-'klaù\ *or* **Rama V** (1853–1910) King of Siam (r.1868–1910). He succeeded to the throne at 15 but did not assume his duties until he was 20. He enacted ambitious reforms patterned on Western models, abolishing slavery, instituting the rule of impersonal law, and overhauling his antiquated administration. By persuading Western colonial powers that Siam was a modern state and playing their interests against one another, he preserved

Chulalongkorn.

BBC HULTON PICTURE LIBRARY

Siam from colonization for decades, but in 1907 Siam was forced to give up its rights in Laos and western Cambodia to the French, and in 1909 it ceded four Malay states to Britain.

chum salmon *or* **dog salmon** Lightly speckled North Pacific fish *(Oncorhynchus keta)* of the SALMON family. The chum salmon ranges from the Mackenzie and Lena rivers in the southern Arctic southward to Japan and the Rogue River. Its weight averages about 10–12 lbs (4.5–5.5 kg). During the autumn spawning season it swims more than 2,000 mi (3,200 km) up the Yukon River.

Ch'ung-ch'ing See CHONGQING

Chung Yung See ZHONG YONG

Chungking See CHONGQING

Chunqiu *or* ***Ch'un-ch'iu*** \'chün-'chyü\ (Chinese: "Spring and Autumn Annals") First Chinese chronological history, the traditional history of LU, as revised by CONFUCIUS. One of the FIVE CLASSICS of CONFUCIANISM, it recounts events during the reign of 12 rulers of Lu from 722 BC to just before Confucius's death in 479 BC. The Confucian DONG ZHONGSHU claimed that the natural phenomena recorded (e.g., drought, eclipse) were intended to warn future rulers of what happens when leaders prove unworthy. Since Confucian scholars were official interpreters of the classics, the book was a means for imposing Confucian ideals. The commentary called *ZUO ZHUAN* is significant.

church Building for Christian worship. The earliest Western churches were based on the plan of the Roman BASILICA. In Constantinople, Anatolia, and Eastern Europe, the Orthodox church adopted the symmetrical Greek-cross plan, which had four wings of equal size projecting from a central, square, domed area (see BYZANTINE ARCHITECTURE). The late 11th century saw increased complexity in CATHEDRALS, but the innovative HALL CHURCH did not establish itself until the 14th century. The basilica and hall church dominated Western church design until the mid-20th century. Modernization of rituals and an innovative spirit have resulted in architectural experimentation that sometimes departs completely from traditional forms.

church In Christian doctrine, the religious community as a whole, or an organized body of believers adhering to one sect's teachings. The word church translates the Greek *ekklesia,* used in the New Testament for the body of faithful and the local congregation. Christians established congregations modeled on the SYNAGOGUE and a system of governance centered on the BISHOP. The NICENE CREED characterized the church as one (unified), holy (created by the HOLY SPIRIT), catholic (universal), and apostolic (historically continuous with the APOSTLES). The schism of Eastern and Western churches (1054) and the REFORMATION (16th century) ended institutional unity and universality. St. AUGUSTINE stated that the real church is known only to God, and MARTIN LUTHER held that the true church had members in many Christian bodies and was independent of any organization.

Church, Alonzo (1903–1995) U.S. mathematician. Born in Washington, D.C., he earned a PhD from Princeton University. His contributions to number theory and the theories of algorithms and computability laid the foundations of computer science. The rule known as Church's theorem or Church's thesis (proposed independently by ALAN M. TURING) states that only recursive functions can be calculated mechanically and implies that arithmetic procedures cannot be used to decide the consistency of statements formulated in accordance with the laws of arithmetic. He wrote the standard textbook *Introduction to Mathematical Logic* (1956) and helped found the *Journal of Symbolic Logic,* which he edited until 1979.

Church, Frederic Edwin (1826–1900) U.S. landscape painter. Born in Hartford, Conn., he studied with THOMAS COLE in Catskill, N.Y., and soon became one of the most prominent members of the HUDSON RIVER SCHOOL. He traveled widely, seeking out spectacular scenery and marvels of nature such as Niagara Falls, volcanoes, icebergs, and the tropical forests of South America, and achieved fame and success at home and in Europe. His house, Olana, on the Hudson River, is now a museum.

church and state Relationship between religious and secular authority in society. The idea that the two should be separate is largely Christian in origin; before Christianity, religious and political authority were generally vested in the same individuals. Following the collapse of the western Roman empire (c. 410), the Church became the seat of temporal as well as spiritual power. The REFORMATION greatly undermined Church authority, and the pendulum swung toward state authority, with many rulers claiming divine right for their positions as head of church and state. The concept of secular government, as evinced in the U.S. and postrevolutionary France, was influenced by ENLIGHTENMENT thinkers. In Western Europe today, all states protect freedom of worship and a distinction between civil and religious authority. In some modern Muslim nations, Islamic SHARIA law is the law of the land. In the U.S., the separation of church and state is tested in the arena of public education, with such issues as school prayer, public funding of parochial schools, and the teaching of creationism.

church modes MODES employed for medieval liturgical melodies. The modal system was conceived for the purpose of codifying plainchant (see GREGORIAN CHANT); their names were borrowed from the system used by the ancient Greeks, though the Greek system was inadequately understood and the connection between the two is illusory. The modes are distinguished according to the note used as the final (last note) and the emphasis placed on another note, called the dominant. The Dorian mode's final is D, the Phrygian mode's is E, the Lydian mode's is F, and the Mixolydian's is G. Each of these four original modes had a parallel mode (Hypodorian, Hypophrygian, Hypolydian, and Hypomixolydian) with a lower range. Though they principally employ the tones A-B-C-D-E-F-G, some replace B with B-flat. In the 16th century, further modes were identified—the Aeolian, on A, and the Ionian, on C (corresponding to modern minor and major). The mode on B was ignored because of B's problematic tonal relationship within the scale.

Church of Christ See Church of CHRIST

Church of England See Church of ENGLAND

Churchill, Randolph (Henry Spencer), Lord (1849–1895) British politician. Third son of the 7th duke of Marlborough, he entered the House of Commons in 1874. In the early 1880s he joined other Conservatives in forming the Fourth Party, which advocated a "Tory democracy" of progressive conservatism. In 1886, at 37, he became leader of the House of Commons and chancellor of the exchequer, but he resigned after his first budget was rejected. Though he had seemed destined to be prime minister, this miscalculation effectively ended his political career. He remained in the Commons until his death, but lost interest in politics and devoted much time to horse racing. WINSTON CHURCHILL was his son.

Churchill, Winston (Leonard Spencer) *later* **Sir Winston** (1874–1965) British statesman and author. Son of Lord RANDOLPH CHURCHILL and the American Jennie Jerome, he had an unhappy childhood and was an unpromising student. After joining the 4th Hussars in 1895, he saw service as both soldier and journalist, and his dispatches from India and South Africa attracted wide attention. Fame as a military hero helped him win election to the House of Commons in 1900. He quickly rose to prominence and served in several cabinet posts, including first lord of the admiralty (1911–15), though in World War I and during the following decade he acquired a reputation for erratic judgment. In the years before World War II, his warnings of the threat posed by ADOLF HITLER's Germany were repeatedly ignored. When war broke out, he was appointed to his old post as head of the admiralty. After NEVILLE CHAMBERLAIN resigned, Churchill headed a coalition government as prime minister (1940–45). He committed himself and the nation to all-out war until victory was achieved, and his great eloquence, energy, and indomitable fortitude made him an inspiration to his countrymen, especially in the Battle of BRITAIN. With FRANKLIN ROOSEVELT and JOSEPH STALIN, he shaped Allied strategy through the ATLANTIC CHARTER and at the CAIRO, CASABLANCA, and TEHRAN conferences. Though he was the architect of victory, his government was defeated in the 1945 elections. After the war he alerted the West to the expansionist threat of the Soviet Union. He led the Conservative Party back into power in 1951 and remained prime minister until 1955, when ill health forced his resignation. For his many writings, including *The Second World War* (6 vols., 1948–53) he was awarded the Nobel Prize for Literature in 1953; his later works include his *History of the English-Speaking Peoples* (4 vols., 1956–58). He was knighted in 1953; he later refused the offer of a peerage. He was made an honorary U.S. citizen in 1963. In his late years he attained heroic status as one of the titans of the 20th century.

Churchill Falls *formerly* **Grand Falls** Part of a series of cataracts and rapids on the CHURCHILL RIVER, Newfoundland. The falls drop 245 ft (75 m) and are 200 ft (60 m) wide. They power one of Canada's largest hydroelectric stations. Visited in 1839 by John McLean of the HUDSON'S BAY CO., the cataracts were called Grand Falls until 1965, when both falls and river were renamed for WINSTON CHURCHILL, who died that year.

Churchill River River, central Canada. Rising in southwestern Saskatchewan, it flows east across Saskatchewan and northern Manitoba and turns northeast into Hudson Bay at Churchill. At 1,000 m (1,609 km) long, it has many rapids and passes through several lakes, including Churchill Lake (213 sq mi, or 552 sq km) in Saskatchewan, and Granville in Manitoba.

churinga See TJURUNGA

Churrigueresque \ˌchu̇r-i-gə-ˈresk\ Spanish ROCOCO architectural style named after the architect José Churriguera (1665–1725). Visually frenetic, it featured a plethora of extravagant ornament and surfaces bristling with broken pediments, undulating cornices, spirals, balustrades, stucco shells, and garlands. In Spanish America, tendencies from both Native American and Mudéjar (Spanish-Moorish) art were incorporated, and the Churrigueresque column, an inverted cone, became the most common motif.

Chuzenji \chü-ˈzen-jē\, **Lake** Lake, HONSHU, Japan. Situated at an altitude of 4,375 ft (1,334 m), it is a resort site noted for its shrines, yachting, trout fishing, and skiing. Volcanic Mount Nantai towers to 8,169 ft (2,490 m) above the lake's northern shore; lower mountains surround most of the irregular 15 mi (24 km) shoreline.

chyme \ˈkīm\ Thick semifluid mass of partly digested food and secretions, formed in the stomach and intestines during DIGESTION. Its composition changes as various digestive juices and cellular debris and other waste products are added, and water and nutrients are absorbed from it during its passage through the digestive tract, at the end of which it is stored for excretion.

CIA See CENTRAL INTELLIGENCE AGENCY

Ciano \ˈchä-nō\, **Galeazzo, Conte (Count) di Cortellazzo** (1903–1944) Italian politician. He took part in the Fascist March on ROME and later entered the diplomatic corps. After marrying BENITO MUSSOLINI's daughter Edda in 1930, he became minister of foreign affairs (1936) and initiated the ROME–BERLIN AXIS that helped bring Italy into World War II. After several Axis defeats in 1942, he advocated a separate peace with the Allies. Mussolini dismissed his cabinet (1943), but Ciano and other leading Fascists forced Mussolini's resignation. Later, on Mussolini's orders, Ciano was tried for treason and executed.

Ciaran of Clonmacnoise \ˈkir-ən...ˌklan-mək-ˈnȯiz\, **St.** *or* **Kieran the Younger** (516?–549?) Irish abbot, one of the founders of monasticism in Ireland. Ciaran was educated with St. COLUMBA at the monastery of Clonard and then lived on the island of Aranmore as a disciple of St. Enda. He traveled to central Ireland and settled with eight companions at Clonmacnoise, where he founded an abbey (548) that later won renown as a center of medieval learning. Ciaran's abbey was so influential that more than half the monasteries in Ireland followed its severely ascetic rule. There is an annual pilgrimage to Clonmacnoise on his feast day, September 9.

Ciba-Geigy AG \ˌsē-bə-ˈgī-gē\ Swiss pharmaceutical company formed in 1970 from the merger of Ciba AG and J. R. Geigy SA. Ciba started out in the 1850s as a silk-dyeing business and branched out into pharmaceuticals in 1900, by which time it was the largest chemical company in Switzerland. J. R. Geigy dates to 1758, when Johann Rudolf Geigy set up a chemist's shop in Basel. The company soon began manufacturing dyes for the textile industry. It entered the pharmaceutical market in the 1930s. In 1997 Ciba-Geigy merged with the Swiss company Sandoz to form Novartis AG, one of the world's largest pharmaceutical companies.

Cibber \ˈsib-ər\, **Colley** (1671–1757) British actor-manager, playwright, and poet. He began his career as an actor in 1690. His *Love's Last Shift* (1696) is considered the first sentimental comedy. Cibber and two other actor-managers, called the "triumvirate," comanaged the DRURY LANE THEATRE (1710–33). He wrote and adapted such plays as *The Non-Juror* (1717) and *The Provok'd Husband* (1728). He was appointed POET LAUREATE in 1730 and retired from acting in 1745. He was mocked as king of the Dunces in ALEXANDER POPE's satire *The Dunciad*. See also ACTOR-MANAGER SYSTEM.

Cíbola \ˈsē-bō-lä\, **Seven Cities of** Legendary pueblos of splendor and riches sought by Spanish CONQUISTADORS in North America during the 16th century. They were first reported by ALVAR NUNEZ CABEZA DE VACA, who was shipwrecked off Florida in 1528 and who wandered through what later became Texas and northern Mexico before his rescue in 1536. Expeditions sent to search for the cities were unsuccessful; one led by FRANCISCO VAZQUEZ DE CORONADO in 1540 located a group of pueblos but failed to find vast treasures.

Ciboney \si-ˈbō-nā\ Extinct group of Indian people who inhabited the Greater Antilles in the Caribbean Sea. By the time the Spanish arrived in the 16th century, they had been driven by their more powerful TAINO neighbors to a few isolated locations in present-day Cuba and Haiti. They lived in settlements of one or two families and apparently subsisted largely on seafood. The tool technology of the Cuban Ciboney was based on shell, that of the Haitian Ciboney on stone. Within a century after the first European contact, the Ciboney were extinct.

cicada \sə-ˈkā-də\ Any insect in the order Homoptera having two pairs of membranous wings, prominent compound eyes, and three simple eyes (ocelli). Most of the 1,500 known species are in the family Cicadidae and are found in tropical deserts, grasslands, and forests. Males produce loud noises by vibrating membranes near the base of the abdomen. Most North American cicadas produce rhythmical ticks, buzzes, or whines, though the "song" of some species is musical. The species are easily distinguishable by song, behavior, and appearance. Periodic cicadas (species that occur in large numbers in chronologically and geographically isolated broods) appear in regular cycles, including the well-known 17-year cicada (often erroneously called the 17-year LOCUST) and 13-year cicada. The larvae (nymphs) burrow into the ground, where they remain for 13 or 17 years, feeding on juices sucked from roots; they then emerge in large numbers to live aboveground as adults for a single week.

Newly emerged adult cicada (*Tibicen pruinosa*).
RICHARD PARKER

Cicero \ˈsi-sə-ˌrō\, **Marcus Tullius** (106–43 BC) Roman statesman, lawyer, scholar, and writer. Born to a wealthy family, he quickly established a brilliant career in law and plunged into politics, then rife with factionalism and conspiracy. He was elected consul in 63 BC. Of his speeches, perhaps the best known are those he made against CATILINE, whose uprising he foiled. He vainly tried to uphold republican principles in the civil wars that destroyed the Roman republic. After the death of Julius CAESAR he delivered his 14 Philippic orations against Mark ANTONY. When the triumvirate of Antony, Octavian (later AUGUSTUS), and Marcus LEPIDUS was formed, he was executed. His extant works include 58 orations and over 900 letters, as well as many poems, philosophical and political treatises, and books of rhetoric. He is remembered as the greatest Roman orator and the innovator of what became known as Ciceronian rhetoric, which remained the foremost rhetorical model for many centuries.

cichlid \ˈsi-kləd\ Any of more than 600 primarily freshwater fish species (family Cichlidae), including many popular aquarium species. Cichlids are found in the New World tropics, Africa and Madagascar, and southern Asia. Most species are African, appearing in great diversity in the major African lakes. Cichlids are deep-bodied and have a rounded tail. They usually grow no longer than about 12 in. (30 cm). Species may be omnivores, herbivores, or carnivores. Cichlids are noted for their complex mating and breeding behavior. Certain species (e.g., TILAPIA), known as mouthbreeders, carry their eggs in the mouth until hatched. See also ANGELFISH.

Cid \ˈsid\, **the** *Spanish* **El Cid ("the Lord")** *orig.* **Rodrigo Díaz de Vivar** (1043–1099) Castilian military hero. Brought up at the court of Ferdinand I, he served the king's eldest son, Sancho II, in his campaign to gain control of León. On Sancho's death he shifted to the service of

C
D

ALFONSO VI. His unauthorized raid on the Moorish kingdom of Toledo (1081) prompted Alfonso to send him into exile. He then entered the service of the Muslim rulers of Saragossa, becoming known as a general who was never defeated in battle. Alfonso tried unsuccessfully to win him back during the ALMORAVID invasion of Spain. The Cid maneuvered to gain control of the Moorish kingdom of Valencia, finally succeeding in 1094. He is the national hero of Castile, celebrated in a famous 12th-century epic poem.

cider Expressed juice of APPLES. Apples are ground into a fine pulp and then pressed. Hard (alcoholic) cider is fermented in vats for up to three months before being filtered, aged in containers, and served (see FERMENTATION). Sweet cider is unfermented and either served directly (as in the U.S.) or mellowed in pressurized tanks first (particularly in Europe). Most cider in the U.S. is now pasteurized. Juice that is pasteurized, treated with a preservative, and often clarified before being hermetically sealed in cans or bottles is marketed as apple juice.

científicos \sē-en-'tē-fi-kōs\ (Spanish: "scientists") Group of officials who served in the government of PORFIRIO DIAZ (1877–1911) in Mexico. Influenced by POSITIVISM and rejecting metaphysics, theology, and idealism as inadequate to solve Mexico's problems, they advocated applying what they considered to be the scientific methods of the social sciences to the problems of finance, education, and industrialization. They had little influence on Díaz, but the movement took root in other parts of Latin America in the late 19th and early 20th century.

cigar Cylindrical roll of TOBACCO for smoking, consisting of cut tobacco filler formed in a binder leaf and with a wrapper leaf rolled spirally around the bunch. Wrapper leaf, the most expensive leaf used in cigars, must be strong, elastic, silky in texture, and even in color; it must have a pleasant flavor and good burning properties. Cigars are bigger than CIGARETTES, and the odor and smoke they produce are stronger. Cigars were being smoked by Maya Indians by the 10th century; they were reported back to Spain by CHRISTOPHER COLUMBUS and other explorers and became popular there long before they spread to other European countries.

cigarette Paper-wrapped roll of finely cut TOBACCO for smoking. Cigarette tobacco is usually milder than CIGAR tobacco. The Aztecs and other New World peoples smoked tobacco in hollow reeds, canes, or wrapped in leaves, but it was in pipes and as cigars (cut tobacco wrapped in a tobacco leaf) that the Europeans first smoked tobacco. Early in the 16th century, beggars in Seville began picking up discarded cigar butts and wrapping them in scraps of paper to smoke, creating the first European cigarettes. In the late 18th century cigarettes acquired respectability, and in the 19th century their use spread throughout Europe. After World War I smoking cigarettes became generally respectable for women and consequently increased markedly. In the 1950s and '60s the health hazards associated with smoking (including LUNG CANCER) became widely known, and some countries launched campaigns against smoking. Declines in smoking in those countries have been offset by vastly increased numbers of smokers in developing nations.

cilantro See CORIANDER

Cilicia \sə-'li-shə\ Ancient district, southern ASIA MINOR. Located along the Mediterranean coast south of the TAURUS MTNS., in ancient times it controlled the only route from Asia Minor to Syria, making it a prized territory. Controlled by the Hittites in the 14th–13th century BC, the Assyrians in the 8th century BC, and the Persians in the 6th–4th cent BC, it later came under Macedonian and Seleucid rule. In the 1st century BC it was a Roman province. St. PAUL visited the district, which has early Christian monuments. Muslim Arabs occupied it in the 7th–10th century AD, when it was reconquered for Byzantium. Ruled by the Ottoman Turks from 1515, it has belonged to Turkey since 1921.

Cilician Gates See TAURUS MTNS.

cilium \'si-lē-əm\ Short, eyelashlike filament that is numerous on tissue cells of most animals. Capable of beating in unison, cilia perform a variety of functions, including providing the means of locomotion for some protozoans, moving mammalian ova (eggs) through oviducts, generating water currents to carry food and oxygen past the gills of clams, and cleaning debris from mammalian respiratory systems. Like a FLAGELLUM, a cilium has a central core consisting of two central fibers surrounded by an outer ring of nine double fibers. Movement is controlled by the basal body, located just inside the cell surface at the base of the cilium. Beneath the surface of some cells is a network of MICROTUBULES that may coordinate ciliary beating.

Cimabue \ˌchē-mə-'bü-ā\ *orig.* **Benciviene di Pepo** (c. 1240–1302) Florentine painter and mosaicist. He is documented as a master painter in Rome in 1272. It is assumed that he was apprenticed to an Italo-Byzantine painter, as he was strongly influenced by the Greek Byzantine style. Though a number of works are attributed to him, the only one dated is the mosaic of *St. John the Evangelist* (1301–2) in Pisa Cathedral. He was the outstanding master of his generation and began the movement toward greater realism that culminated in the Renaissance. His style influenced GIOTTO and DUCCIO. Cimabue ("Bull-headed") was a nickname.

Cimarosa \ˌchē-mä-'rò-zä\, **Domenico** (1749–1801) Italian opera composer. Son of a stonemason, he studied at the Naples Conservatory. His first opera was produced in 1772, and by the mid-1780s he was internationally known. A short engagement as kapellmeister at the Viennese court resulted in the famous comic opera *Il matrimonio segreto* (1792). In 1796 he became organist in the royal chapel of Naples. He wrote some 75 operas, several oratorios, over 15 masses, and some 80 piano sonatas. His reputation as a composer of Italian opera remained close to that of W.A. MOZART long after his death.

Cimarron River \'si-mə-ˌrōn, 'si-mə-ˌrän\ River, southwestern U.S. Rising in northeastern New Mexico it flows about 500 mi (800 km) to enter the ARKANSAS RIVER near TULSA, Okla. Traversing the northern Oklahoma Panhandle, southeastern Colorado, and southwestern Kansas, the riverbed in this area is often dry and is known as the Dry Cimarron. The SANTA FE TRAIL crossed its valley for 100 mi (160 km), and travelers knew the Oklahoma Panhandle as the "Cimarron Cutoff."

Cimmerian Bosporus Ancient Greek kingdom, in modern southern Ukraine. It was first settled by Milesians (6th century BC) at Panticapaeum, which later became the capital. Gradually the kingdom grew to include all of the CRIMEA. It maintained close ties with Athens in 5th–3rd century BC, reaching the peak of its power in the 4th century BC. It came under the rule of Mithradates VI of Pontus c. 100 BC. For 300 years it belonged to the Roman empire, and after AD 342 it was alternately under barbarian and Byzantine control.

Cimmerians \sə-'mir-ē-ənz\ Ancient people living north of the Caucasus and the Sea of Azov. Their origins are obscure; linguistically they are usually regarded as Thracian or Iranian. Driven by the SCYTHIANS out of southern Russia and over the Caucasus, they entered Anatolia toward the end of the 8th century BC. In 696–695 BC they conquered Phrygia. They reached the summit of their power in 652 after taking Sardis, capital of Lydia. Their decline soon began, and their final defeat may be dated from 637 or 626, when they were routed by Alyattes of Lydia.

Cimon \'sī-mən\ (c. 510–451? BC) Athenian statesman and general who laid the groundwork for the Athenian empire. He was the son of MILTIADES. A conservative, he promoted SPARTA and opposed PERICLES. After helping defeat the Persians at the Battle of SALAMIS (480), he was elected STRATEGUS every year until 461. As commander of the DELIAN LEAGUE, he cleared the Persians from the eastern Mediterranean. In 461 he was accused by Pericles of collaborating with Macedonia and Sparta and was exiled for 10 years. He died leading a naval expedition against Persia.

cinchona \siŋ-'kō-nə, sin-'chō-nə\ Any of about 40 species, mostly trees, that make up the genus *Cinchona,* in the MADDER FAMILY, native to the Andes Mtns. The bark of four species, cultivated for many years mostly in Java, was processed to obtain QUININE, used to treat MALARIA and fever and pain, and quinidine, used mainly for cardiac rhythmic disorders. High demand for quinine among Europeans living in the tropics led naturalists to smuggle *Cinchona* seeds from South America to plantations in Asia in the mid-1800s and to conduct intensive research leading to new high-yield strains and improved processing methods.

Cincinnati City (pop., 1996 est.: 346,000), Ohio. Situated on the Ohio River across from Kentucky, it was first settled in 1788; the area was renamed in 1790 to honor the Society of the CINCINNATI. A river port after 1811, it grew in importance with the opening of the Miami and Erie Canal in 1832. Its manufactures include transportation equipment and building materials, and it is a major inland coal port. A cultural center, it has an orchestra, opera and ballet companies, and a museum. It is the seat of the University of Cincinnati (1819), the birthplace of WILLIAM H.

TAFT (now a national historical site), and the site of HARRIET BEECHER STOWE house, where she lived 1832–50.

Cincinnati, Society of the Hereditary, military, and patriotic organization formed in 1783 by officers who had served in the AMERICAN REVOLUTION. The group's aims were to promote union, maintain war-forged friendships, and help members in need. Membership was offered to all officers and their eldest male descendants. GEORGE WASHINGTON was its first president. The group took its name from the Roman citizen-soldier Cincinnatus, and the city of Cincinnati was named in its honor in 1790.

Cinco de Mayo \'sēŋ-kō-t͟hā-'mī-ō\ (Spanish: "Fifth of May") Mexican holiday commemorating the Mexican victory over the French at PUEBLA in 1862. The French army, better equipped and far larger than the Mexican army, had been sent by NAPOLEON III to conquer Mexico. The Mexicans, under Gen. Ignacio Zaragoza, defeated the French at Puebla, inflicting serious losses. The French withdrew to the coast, but returned the next year to take Puebla; they would control most of Mexico for the next four years. Cinco de Mayo celebrations often include music, dancing, and parades.

cinder cone *or* **ash cone** Deposit around a volcanic vent, formed by rock fragments or cinders that accumulate and gradually build a conical hill with a bowl-shaped crater at the top. Cinder cones develop from explosive eruptions of lavas and are often found along the flanks of shield (gently sloping) volcanoes. Lava flows may break out of the cone, or they may flow from under the cone through tunnels. Cinder cones are common in nearly all volcanic areas. Although they are composed of loose or only moderately consolidated cinder, many are surprisingly long-lasting, because rain falling on them sinks into the highly permeable cinders instead of running off down their slopes and eroding them.

cinéma vérité \'si-nə-mə-ˌver-i-'tā\ (French: "truth cinema") French film movement of the 1960s that strove for candid realism by showing people in everyday situations with authentic dialogue. Influenced by DOCUMENTARY filmmaking and Italian NEOREALISM, the method produced such outstanding examples as Jean Rouch's *Chronicle of a Summer* (1961) and Chris Marker's *Joli Mai* (1962). A similar movement in the U.S., where it was called "direct cinema," captured the reality of a person or an event by using a handheld camera to record action without narration, as in Frederick Wiseman's *Titicut Follies* (1967) and the MAYSLES brothers' *Salesman* (1969).

cinematography Art and technology of motion-picture photography. It involves the composition of a scene, lighting of the set and actors, choice of cameras, camera angle, and integration of special effects to achieve the photographic images desired by the director. Cinematography focuses on relations between the individual shots and groups of shots that make up a scene to produce a film's effect. Well-known cinematographers include NESTOR ALMENDROS, GREGG TOLAND, and SVEN NYKVIST.

cinnabar Mercury SULFIDE (HgS), the chief ORE mineral of MERCURY. It is commonly encountered with PYRITE, MARCASITE, and STIBNITE in veins near recent volcanic rocks and in hot-springs deposits. It has been used as a bright orange-red pigment in stage makeup (now known to be toxic), painting, and Chinese lacquerwork.

Cinnabar from Red Devil Mine, north of Homer, Alaska.
BY COURTESY OF THE MACFALL COLLECTION; PHOTOGRAPH, MARY A. ROOT

cinnamon Bushy evergreen tree *(Cinnamomum zeylanicum)* of the LAUREL FAMILY, native to Sri Lanka, India, and Burma, and cultivated in South America and the West Indies for the spice consisting of its dried inner bark. The light-brown spice has a delicately fragrant aroma and warm, sweet flavor. It was once more valuable than gold. Today cinnamon is used to flavor various foods; in Europe and the U.S. it is especially popular in bakery goods. The oil is distilled from bark fragments for use in food, liqueur, perfume, and drugs.

Cinque Ports \'siŋk\ Medieval confederation of English Channel ports, southeastern England. To the original "five ports"—Hastings, New Romney, Hythe, DOVER, and Sandwich—were later added Winchelsea and Rye. Probably first associated in the reign of EDWARD THE CONFESSOR (r.1042–66) to defend the coast and cross-channel traffic, they were granted special privileges by the crown and in exchange provided the permanent nucleus of ships and men for the royal fleet. They declined in importance after the 14th century.

cinquefoil \'siŋk-ˌfȯil\ Any of the approximately 500 species of shrubs and herbaceous plants in the genus *Potentilla* (ROSE family). The common name, meaning "five-leaved," refers to the number of leaflets in the compound leaf of most species. Most species are native to the northern temperate zone and the Arctic and are chiefly perennial. The stems are creeping or erect. The solitary, five-petaled flowers are usually yellow, sometimes white or red in horticultural varieties. *P. fruticosa* includes many dwarf shrubs used in landscaping (see LANDSCAPE GARDENING).

Common cinquefoil (*Potentilla simplex*).
ARTHUR W. AMBLER FROM THE NATIONAL AUDUBON SOCIETY COLLECTION/PHOTO RESEARCHERS—EB INC.

Ciompi \'chäm-pē\, **Revolt of the** (1378) Uprising of cloth workers and other craftsmen in Florence that brought a democratic government to power. A struggle between ruling factions triggered the rebellion, which was led by the *ciompi* (wool carders). The rebels demanded a more equitable fiscal policy and the right to establish GUILDS for those groups not already organized. They took over the government briefly, but worsening economic conditions and the combined efforts of the established guilds soon led to their ouster.

circadian rhythm \sər-'kā-dē-ən\ Inherent cycle of approximately 24 hours in length that appears to control or initiate various biological processes, including sleep, wakefulness, and digestive and hormonal activity. The natural signal for the circadian pattern is the change from darkness to light. The controlling mechanism for these cyclic processes within the body is thought to be the HYPOTHALAMUS. Any change in the circadian cycle (such as JET LAG and other conditions associated with travel) requires a certain period for readjustment.

Circassian language \sər-'ka-shən\ NW CAUCASIAN LANGUAGE, with major eastern and western dialect groups. Until the 1860s Circassian-speaking tribes inhabited the entire northwestern Caucasus region, including the Black Sea coast. After the Russian conquest of the northwestern Caucasus in 1864, most Circassian-speakers emigrated to the Ottoman Empire and were eventually settled in present-day Turkey, Syria, Jordan, and Israel. Only scattered enclaves of Western Circassian-speakers stayed in Russia. A greater number of Eastern Circassians remained; most now live in Russia's northern Caucasus republics. Russian Circassian-speakers now number about 550,000; the number outside Russia is indeterminable, because many ethnic Circassians have switched to other languages. Circassian, like other northwestern Caucasian languages, has a very large inventory of consonant phonemes and few phonemic vowels. Nouns have few case distinctions, and grammatical relations are expressed by pronominal elements prefixed to the verb stem.

Circe \'sər-sē\ In Greek legend, a sorceress, the daughter of the sun god HELIOS and the ocean nymph Perse. By means of drugs and incantations she turned humans into lions, wolves, or swine. ODYSSEUS visited her on his return from the Trojan War, and she changed his companions into swine. Odysseus himself was protected by an herb given him by Hermes, and he compelled the sorceress to restore his companions. He and Circe became lovers, but after a yearlong stay he resumed his journey homeward.

Circeo \chir-'chā-ō\, **Mt.** *ancient* **Circaeum Promontorium.** Mountain, southwestern coast of Italy. The promontory, on the TYRRHENIAN SEA, rises 1,775 ft (541 m), and is connected with the mainland by a low saddle. About 33 sq mi (86 sq km) are preserved as a national park. From the sea it resembles an island, and it has been associated with the legend of CIRCE since classical times. Its coastal grottoes have yielded traces of Stone Age settlement, and there are remains of a Roman acropolis.

circle Geometrical curve, one of the CONIC SECTIONS, consisting of the set of all points the same distance (the radius) from a given point (the center). A line connecting any two points on a circle is called a chord, and a chord passing through the center is called a diameter. The distance around a circle (the circumference) equals the length of a diameter multiplied by π (see PI). The area of a circle is the square of the radius multiplied by π. An arc consists of any part of a circle encompassed by an angle with its vertex at the center (central angle). Its length is in the same proportion to the circumference as the central angle is to a full revolution.

circuit *or* **electric circuit** Path that transmits ELECTRIC CURRENT. A circuit includes a battery or a generator that gives energy to the charged particles; devices that use current, such as lamps, motors, or electronic computers; and connecting wires or transmission lines. Circuits can be classified according to the type of current they carry (see ALTERNATING CURRENT, DIRECT CURRENT) or according to whether the current remains whole (series) or divides to flow through several branches simultaneously (parallel). Two basic laws that describe the performance of electric circuits are OHM'S LAW and KIRCHHOFF'S CIRCUIT RULES. See also TUNED CIRCUIT.

circuit, printed See PRINTED CIRCUIT

circuit riding In the U.S., the act, once undertaken by a judge, of traveling within a judicial district (or circuit) to facilitate the hearing of cases. The practice was largely abandoned with the establishment of permanent courthouses and laws requiring parties to appear before a sitting judge.

circuitry, computer See COMPUTER CIRCUITRY

circulation Process by which nutrients, respiratory gases, and metabolic products are transported throughout the body. In humans, BLOOD remains within a closed CARDIOVASCULAR SYSTEM composed of the HEART, blood vessels, and blood. ARTERIES carry blood away from the heart under high pressure exerted by the heart's pumping action. Arteries divide into smaller arterioles, which branch into a network of tiny capillaries with thin walls across which gases and nutrients diffuse. CAPILLARIES rejoin into larger venules, which unite to form VEINS, which carry blood back to the heart. The right and left heart chambers send blood into separate PULMONARY and SYSTEMIC circulations. In the first, blood is carried from the heart to the lungs, where it picks up oxygen and releases carbon dioxide; in the second, blood is carried between the heart and the rest of the body, where it carries oxygen, nutrients, metabolic products, and wastes. See illustration opposite.

circumcision Cutting away of all or part of the foreskin (prepuce) of the PENIS. The practice is known in many cultures. It is performed either shortly after birth (e.g., among Muslims and Jews), within a few years of birth, or at PUBERTY. For Jews it represents the fulfillment of the covenant between God and Abraham (Genesis 17:10–14). That Christians were not obliged to be circumcised was first recorded biblically in Acts 15. Evidence regarding the purported medical benefits of circumcision (e.g., reduced risk of cancer) is inconclusive, and the practice persists mainly for cultural reasons. See also CLITORIDECTOMY.

circumstantial evidence In law, evidence that is drawn not from direct observation of a fact at issue but from events or circumstances that surround it. If a witness arrives at a crime scene seconds after hearing a gunshot to find someone standing over a corpse and holding a smoking pistol, the evidence is circumstantial, since the person may merely be a bystander who picked up the weapon after the killer dropped it. The popular notion that one cannot be convicted on circumstantial evidence is false. Most criminal convictions are based, at least in part, on circumstantial evidence that sufficiently links criminal and crime.

circus Entertainment or spectacle featuring animal acts and human feats of daring. The modern circus was founded in England in 1768 by the bareback rider Philip Astley (1742–1814), who built stands around his performance ring and opened Astley's Amphitheatre. One of his riders later established the Royal Circus (1782), the first modern use of the term. The first U.S. circus opened in Philadelphia in 1793. Horse acts were later joined by wild-animal acts. After the invention of the flying trapeze by Jules Léotard (1859), aerial acts were featured. P. T. BARNUM expanded the traditional circus by adding two rings to create the three-ring circus (1881) and augmented it with sideshow performers. Circuses traveled throughout the U.S., Europe, and Latin America, performing in a tent (the Big Top) into the 1950s. Today circuses usually perform in permanent buildings, though small troupes still travel with tents in some regions.

Cirenaica See CYRENAICA

cirrhosis \sə-'rō-səs\ Degeneration of functioning LIVER cells and their replacement with fibrous CONNECTIVE TISSUE, leading to scarring. The most common cause is alcohol abuse with malnutrition. Others include bile duct obstruction, viral infection, toxins, iron or copper accumulation in liver cells, and syphilis. JAUNDICE, EDEMA, and great abdominal swelling are common in all. Death usually results from internal bleeding or hepatic coma due to blood chemical imbalance.

Cisalpine Republic \sis-'al-pīn\ Former republic, northern Italy. Created by NAPOLEON in 1797 from conquered territories, it was centered in the PO RIVER valley and included the lands around MILAN and BOLOGNA. It was incorporated into the kingdom of Italy in 1805.

Ciskei \'sis-ˌkī\ Former black enclave, South Africa. Inhabited principally by Xhosa-speaking peoples, it bordered the Indian Ocean and South Africa. In the late 18th century the XHOSA peoples living in the area came into conflict with European settlers; the ensuing wars resulted in the region's incorporation into the Cape Colony by the end of the 19th century Ciskei became an administratively distinct territory within South Africa in 1961. In 1972 it was declared a self-governing black state, with its capital at Bisho. In 1981 it became nominally independent. Under the new South African constitution, it was reincorporated (1994) into South Africa as part of the new Eastern Cape province.

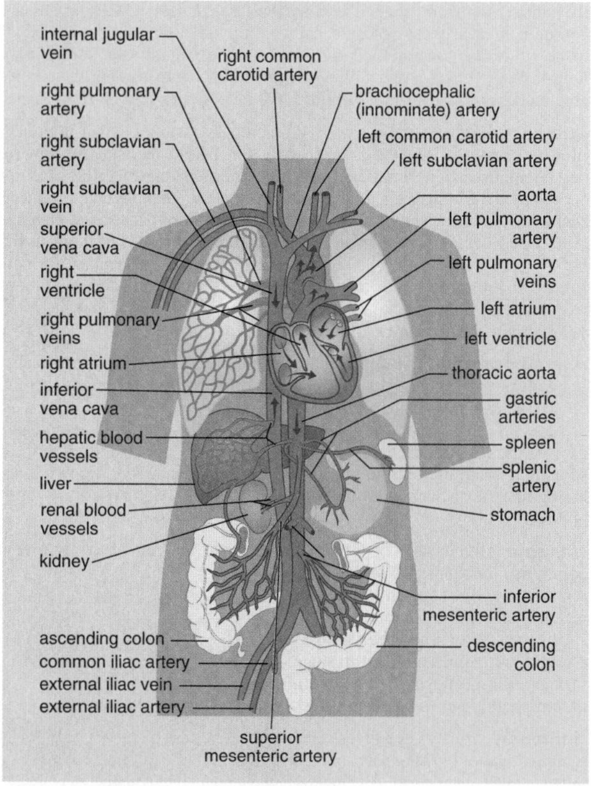

Human circulatory system. Oxygen-rich blood is shown in red, oxygen-poor blood in blue. The pulmonary circulation consists of the right ventricle and the exiting pulmonary artery and its branches, the arterioles, capillaries, and venules of the lung, and the pulmonary vein. Unlike the other arteries and veins, the pulmonary arteries carry deoxygenated blood and the pulmonary veins carry oxygenated blood. The aorta arises from the left ventricle. The brachiocephalic artery arises from the aorta and divides into the right common carotid and right subclavian arteries. The left and right common carotids extend on either side of the neck and supply much of the head and neck. The left subclavian artery (arising from the aorta) and the right subclavian artery supply the arms. In the lower abdomen, the aorta divides into the common iliac arteries, which give rise to external and internal branches supplying the legs.

Cistercian \sis-'tər-shən\ *or* **White Monk** *or* **Bernardine** Member of a Roman Catholic monastic order founded by St. Stephen Harding (1098) at Cîteaux (Latin, Cistercium), Burgundy, by BENEDICTINES dissatisfied with their abbey's laxity. Cistercians were severely ascetic, rejected feudal revenues, and engaged in manual labor. Uniform rules applied to all houses, and all abbots were to meet annually at Cîteaux. St. BERNARD DE CLAIRVAUX founded 68 abbeys in his lifetime. Discipline declined as the order grew, and Cistercians disappeared from northern Europe after the REFORMATION. The order underwent reforms in the 16th–17th century; members of the reformed order are popularly known as Trappists after the abbey of La Trapp. Until the 1960s, they slept, ate, and worked in perpetual silence. The original order, which underwent more moderate reforms, also survives.

Citadel, The Public military college in Charleston, S.C., founded in 1842. Though it lacks a direct affiliation with the U.S. military, it has long been an important source of trained officers. Citadel cadets fired the shots at FORT SUMTER that began the American Civil War; the college was occupied by federal forces 1865–79. A court decision in 1995 opened its admissions to women cadets. Total enrollment is about 3,700.

Citation (foaled 1945) U.S. Thoroughbred racehorse. In four seasons he won 32 of 45 races, finished second in ten, and third in two. He won the 1948 TRIPLE CROWN, and became the first horse to win $1 million. He set a world record in 1950 by running a mile in 1:33 3/5.

Citigroup U.S. HOLDING COMPANY formed in 1998 from the merger of Citicorp (itself a holding company incorporated in 1967) and Travelers Group, Inc. (see TRAVELERS INC.). The $70 billion merger included one of the largest U.S. investment banks, Salomon Smith Barney Inc., and aimed at creating a global retail financial-services business. Citicorp, whose lineage can be traced to the First Bank of the United States, was noteworthy for its pioneering installation of automated teller machines throughout its branch offices in the 1970s. Before its merger with Travelers Group, Inc., Citicorp was the largest U.S. bank and one of the largest financial companies in the world, with about 3,000 branch offices worldwide.

Citizen Genêt Affair \zhə-'ne\ Incident precipitated by the French diplomat Citizen Edmond C. Genêt (1763–1834), who was sent to the U.S. in 1793 by the French government to gain support for France's war with Britain and Spain. In South Carolina Genêt organized privateers to prey on British commerce and expeditions to attack Spanish and British territories. Pres. GEORGE WASHINGTON considered Genêt's activities a violation of U.S. neutrality and demanded his recall. Facing possible death at the hands of the new regime in France, he was allowed to remain in the U.S.

citizenship Relationship between an individual and a state in which an individual owes allegiance to that state and in turn is entitled to its protection. In general, full political rights, including the right to vote and to hold public office, are predicated on citizenship. The usual responsibilities of citizenship are allegiance, payment of taxes, and military service. The concept first arose in ancient Greece, where it was granted only to property owners. The Romans initially used it as a privilege that could be conferred on or withheld from conquered peoples, but granted it to all the empire's free inhabitants in AD 212. The concept disappeared in Europe during the feudal era, but was revived in the Renaissance. Citizenship may normally be gained by birth within a certain territory, descent from a citizen parent, marriage to a citizen, or NATURALIZATION. See also NATIONALITY.

Citlaltépetl \sē-ˌtläl-'tā-ˌpe-tᵊl\ *or* **Orizaba** \ˌō-rē-'sä-bä\ Volcano, southern central Mexico. At 18,700 ft (5,700 m), its symmetrical, snow-capped cone is the highest point in Mexico and the third-highest peak in North America. The volcano has been dormant since 1687.

citric acid Colorless, crystalline organic compound ($C_6H_8O_7$), one of the CARBOXYLIC ACIDS. It is present in almost all plants (especially CITRUS fruits) and in many animal tissues and fluids. It is one of a series of compounds involved in the physiological oxidation (see OXIDATION-REDUCTION) of FATS, PROTEINS, and CARBOHYDRATES to carbon dioxide and water (see TRICARBOXYLIC ACID CYCLE). It has a characteristic sharply sour taste and is used in many foods, confections, and soft drinks. It is added to certain foods to improve their stability in metal containers. Industrially, it is used as a water conditioner, cleaning and polishing agent, and chemical intermediate.

citric-acid cycle See TRICARBOXYLIC ACID CYCLE

citrine \si-'trēn\ Transparent, coarse-grained variety of the silica mineral QUARTZ. Citrine is a semiprecious gem that is valued for its yellow to brownish color and its resemblance to the rarer TOPAZ. Natural citrine is rarer than amethyst or smoky quartz, both of which are often heated to change their natural color to that of citrine. Citrine is often marketed under various names that confuse it with topaz to inflate its price; it may be distinguished from topaz by its inferior hardness. It occurs mainly in Brazil, Uruguay, the Ural Mtns., Scotland, and North Carolina.

Citroën \si-trō-'en\ Major French automobile manufacturer. It was founded by André-Gustave Citroën (1878–1935), an engineer and industrialist who initially prospered selling munitions in World War I. He converted his arms factory to produce small, inexpensive automobiles, introducing mass-production methods to the French auto industry, and the first Citroën car appeared in 1919. The firm is now a unit of Peugeot SA, France's largest automaker.

citron Small evergreen tree or shrub *(Citrus medica)* in the RUE FAMILY, cultivated in Mediterranean countries and the West Indies. It has irregular, spreading, spiny branches and large, pale green, broadly oblong leaves. The flowers of the acidic varieties (e.g., the Diamante) are purple on the outside and white on the inside; those of sweet varieties (e.g., the Corsican) are creamy white. The oval or oblong fruit yields firm pulp, either acidic or sweet, that is used only for by-products. The thick peel is cured in brine, candied, and sold as a confection. The fruit of the Etrog variety is used in Jewish religious rites.

citrus Any of the plants that make up the genus *Citrus,* in the RUE FAMILY, that yield pulpy fruits covered with fairly thick skins. The genus includes the LEMON, LIME, sweet and sour ORANGES, TANGERINE, GRAPEFRUIT, CITRON, and shaddock (*C. maxima,* or *C. grandis;* also called pomelo).

citrus family See RUE FAMILY

city Relatively permanent and highly organized center of population, of greater size or importance than a town or village. The first cities appeared in NEOLITHIC times when the development of agricultural techniques assured surplus crop yields large enough to sustain a permanent population. The Hellenistic period saw the creation of the CITY-STATE, a form also important in the emergence of the ROMAN EMPIRE as well as the medieval Italian trading centers of VENICE, GENOA, and FLORENCE. After the Middle Ages, cities came increasingly under the political control of centralized government and served the interests of the nation-state. The INDUSTRIAL REVOLUTION further transformed city life, as factory cities blossomed rapidly in England, northwestern Europe, and the northeastern U.S. By the mid-20th century, 30–60% of a country's population might be living in its major urban centers. With the rise of the automobile came the growth of suburbs and urban sprawl, as factories, offices, and residences erected in earlier periods became aged and obsolete. Today many cities suffer from lack of adequate housing, sanitation, recreational space, and transportation facilities, and face problems of inner-city decay or burgeoning shantytowns. Local governments have sought to alleviate these problems through URBAN PLANNING.

city government Set of governmental institutions that serve an urban area or urban municipality. All cities derive their existence from a larger political entity, either a state or national government. City government generally includes an EXECUTIVE (a MAYOR or manager) and a legislature (a council or commission), both of which may be subject to popular election. Their most important functions are the provision of services, including public safety, health care, education, recreation, housing, utilities, transportation, and cultural facilities. Revenues come from local taxes and fees as well as grants and subsidies from its state or national government.

city-state Political system consisting of an independent city with SOVEREIGNTY over a fixed surrounding area for which it served as leader of religious, political, economic, and cultural life. The term was coined in the 19th century to describe ancient Greek and Phoenician settlements that differed from tribal or national systems in size, exclusivity, patriotism, and ability to resist incorporation by other communities. They may have developed when earlier tribal systems broke down and splintered groups established themselves as independent nuclei c. 1000–800 BC; by the 5th century BC they numbered in the hundreds, with ATHENS, SPARTA, and THEBES among the most important. Incapable of forming any lasting union or federation, they eventually fell victim to the Macedonians, the

Carthaginians, and the Roman empire. In the 11th century the city-state revived in Italy; the success of medieval Italy's city-states, including Pisa, Florence, Venice, and Genoa, was due to growing prosperity from trade with the East, and several survived into the 19th century. Germany's medieval city-states included Hamburg, Bremen, and Lübeck. The only city-state extant today is Vatican City.

City University of New York (CUNY) Institution created in 1961 to combine New York City's 17 municipally supported colleges. It is the second-largest university system in the U.S. (total enrollment about 200,000). It includes a Graduate Center, New York's four original liberal-arts colleges (City College of New York, Hunter College, Brooklyn College, and Queens College), six other four-year colleges (including Staten Island College, Lehman College, Baruch College, John Jay College of Criminal Justice, and Medgar Evers College), and seven two-year community colleges. The Mount Sinai School of Medicine is affiliated with CUNY. In 1970 CUNY instituted a controversial open-admissions policy at some campuses.

Ciudad Guayana \\ˌsyü-ˈt͟häth-gä-ˈyä-nä\\ *formerly* **Santo Tomé de Guayana** City (pop., 1992 est.: 524,500), Venezuela. Located at the confluence of the Caroní and Orinoco rivers in the Guiana Highlands, it was first settled in 1576. An amalgamation of several cities, it is a planned community founded by the state assembly in 1961. It has forestry, diamond mining, and paper and pulp enterprises.

Ciudad Juárez See Juárez

Ciudad Victoria \\ˌsyü-ˈt͟häth-vēk-ˈtōr-yä\\ City (pop., 1990: 195,000), capital of Tamaulipas state, northeastern Mexico. Founded in 1750, the settlement was renamed in 1825 for Mexico's first president, Guadalupe Victoria. In addition to being a distribution point in an agricultural region, it is a tourist destination and a center for hunting, fishing, and swimming. The University of Tamaulipas was established in 1956.

civet \\ˈsi-vət\\ Any of 15–20 species of long-bodied, short-legged carnivores (family Viverridae) found in Africa, southern Europe, and Asia. Catlike in appearance, civets have a thickly furred tail, small ears, and pointed snout. Civets are commonly buff or grayish, with black spots or stripes or both. They range in length from 16 to 34 in. (40–85 cm), excluding the 5–26-in. (13–66-cm) tail, and in weight from 3.3 to 24 lbs (1.5–11 kg). Civets mark territories with a greasy, musklike secretion (called civet) stored in a pouch under the tail; civet is sometimes used in the manufacture of perfumes. Usually solitary, civets feed on small animals and on vegetable matter. Five species are considered in possible danger of extinction.

African palm civet (*Nandinia binotata*).
ROBERT C. HERMES FROM THE NATIONAL AUDUBON SOCIETY COLLECTION/PHOTO RESEARCHERS—EB INC.

civic center Grouping of municipal facilities in a limited precinct often adjacent to the central business district of a city. The civic center is based on both the Greek acropolis and the Roman forum. The plan includes the city hall and adjoining park or plaza, headquarters for city departments, courthouses, and often a post office, public-utility offices, public health facilities, and government offices.

civic theater Theater wholly or party subsidized by the city in which it operates. The term is also used for a noncommercial community theater. Most civic theaters in Europe are professional organizations; in the U.S. they are often run by amateur groups, which may then become resident professional theaters. The first major U.S. civic theater was established in New Orleans in 1919.

Civil Constitution of the Clergy (1790) Act passed by the National Assembly in the French Revolution that subordinated the Roman Catholic Church in France to the state. Under its provisions, enfranchised citizens would elect bishops and parish priests and the state would pay the clergy's wages. The act soon provoked opposition, and when the National Assembly ordered the clergy to take an oath supporting the Civil Constitution, many refused. The resulting schism within the French church caused many devout Catholics to turn against the Revolution.

civil defense All nonmilitary actions taken to reduce loss of life and property resulting from enemy action. The threat of aerial attack on cities led to organized civil-defense planning in World War II. The British government provided its people with gas masks, and nearly all countries trained citizens in fire fighting, rescue, and first aid. Blackouts reduced the glow from city lights that could guide enemy pilots; sirens warned of bombing attacks, and citizens took cover in air-raid shelters, basements, and subways. The postwar threat of nuclear attack prompted civil authorities to mark buildings that offered the best shelter from fallout. By the 1970s the West had largely abandoned civil-defense preparations as it became clear that surviving a direct nuclear attack was unlikely.

civil disobedience *or* **passive resistance** Refusal to obey government demands or commands and nonresistance to consequent arrest and punishment. It is used especially as a nonviolent and usually collective means of forcing government concessions and has been a major tactic of nationalist movements in Africa and India, of the U.S. civil-rights movement, and of labor and antiwar movements in many countries. Those who engage in it feel obligated by a higher principle to break a given law. Its philosophical roots can be traced back to Cicero, Thomas Aquinas, and Henry David Thoreau; Mohandas K. Gandhi most clearly formulated the concept of civil disobedience for the modern world. In the U.S., it was most fully articulated and employed by Martin Luther King, Jr.

civil engineering Profession of designing and executing structural works that serve the general public, including bridges, canals, dams, harbors, lighthouses, roads, tunnels, and environmental works (e.g., water-supply systems). The modern field includes power plants, aircraft and airports, chemical-processing plants, and water-treatment facilities. Civil engineering today involves site investigations and feasibility studies, structural design and analysis, construction, and facilities maintenance. The design of engineering works requires the application of design theory from many fields (e.g., hydraulics, thermodynamics, nuclear physics). Research in structural analysis and the technology of materials such as steel and concrete has opened the way for new concepts and greater economy of materials. The engineer's analysis of a building problem determines the structural system to be used. Structural designs are rigorously analyzed by computers to determine if they will withstand loads and natural forces.

civil law Body of law developed from Roman law and used in continental Europe and most former colonies of European nations, including the province of Quebec and the state of Louisiana. The most significant codifications of modern civil law were the French (Napoleonic Code, 1804) and the German. The basis of law in civil-law jurisdictions is statute, not custom; civil law is thus to be distinguished from common law. In civil law, judges apply principles embodied in statutes, or law codes, rather than turning to case precedent. French civil law formed the basis of the legal systems of The Netherlands, Belgium, Luxembourg, Italy, Spain, most of France's former possessions overseas, and many Latin-American countries. German civil law prevailed in Austria, Switzerland, the Scandinavian countries, and certain countries outside Europe, such as Japan, that westernized their legal systems. The term is also used to distinguish the law that applies to private rights from the law that applies to criminal matters. See also criminal law, tort.

civil liberty In U.S. law, freedom from arbitrary interference in one's pursuits by individuals or by the government as guaranteed by the Bill of Rights and the 13th, 14th, and 15th Amendments to the U.S. Constitution. The term is usually used in the plural. The 13th Amendment prohibits slavery and involuntary servitude; the 14th bars the application of any law that would abridge the "privileges and immunities" of U.S. citizens or deprive any person of "life, liberty, or property . . . without due process of law" or deny any person equal protection under the law; and the 15th guarantees the right of all U.S. citizens to vote. The related term civil right(s) often refers to one or more of these liberties as well as to those guaranteed by the Civil Rights Act of 1964. See also American Civil Liberties Union.

civil religion Set of quasi-religious attitudes, beliefs, rituals, and symbols that tie members of a political community together. As originally formulated by J.-J. Rousseau, the concept referred to the virtues that citizens need to properly serve the state. The concept was later elaborated by the American sociologist Robert N. Bellah (born 1927), who found in the U.S. a strong sense of American "exceptionalism" and reverence for such secular elements as the national flag, the Constitution, the Founding Fathers, the annual holiday calendar, and the concepts of individualism and self-reliance. Another form of civil religion is presented by the example of CONFUCIANISM, where the nation is subordinated to a moral order.

Civil Rights Act of 1964 Comprehensive U.S. law intended to end discrimination based on race, color, religion, or national origin. It is generally considered the most important U.S. law on civil rights since RECONSTRUCTION (1865–77). It guarantees equal voting rights (Title I); prohibits segregation or discrimination in places of public accommodation (Title II); bans discrimination, including sex-based discrimination, by trade unions, schools, or employers that are involved in interstate commerce or do business with the federal government (Title VII); calls for the desegregation of public schools (Title IV); and assures nondiscrimination in the distribution of funds under federally assisted programs (Title VI). A 1972 amendment, the Equal Employment Opportunity Act, extended Title VII coverage to employees of state and local governments and increased the authority of the Equal Employment Opportunity Commission, which was created in 1964 to enforce Title VII provisions. The act was proposed by Pres. JOHN F. KENNEDY in 1963 and strengthened and passed into law under Pres. LYNDON B. JOHNSON. See also CIVIL-RIGHTS MOVEMENT.

civil rights movement Movement for racial equality in the U.S. that, through nonviolent protest, broke the pattern of racial segregation in the South and achieved equal-rights legislation for blacks. Following the U.S. Supreme Court decision in *BROWN VS. BOARD OF EDUCATION* (1954), blacks and white supporters attempted to end entrenched segregationist practices. When ROSA PARKS was arrested in 1955 in Montgomery, Ala., a black boycott of the bus system was led by MARTIN LUTHER KING and RALPH ABERNATHY. In the early 1960s the Student Nonviolent Coordinating Committee led boycotts and sit-ins to desegregate many public facilities. Using the nonviolent methods of MOHANDAS K. GANDHI, the movement spread, forcing the desegregation of department stores, supermarkets, libraries, and movie theaters. The Deep South remained adamant in its opposition to most desegregation measures, often violently; protesters were attacked and occasionally killed. Their efforts culminated in a march on Washington, D.C., in 1963 to support legislation. Following the assassination of JOHN F. KENNEDY, Pres. LYNDON B. JOHNSON persuaded Congress to pass the CIVIL RIGHTS ACT IN 1964, a victory that was followed by the VOTING RIGHTS ACT in 1965. After 1965, militant groups such as the BLACK PANTHER PARTY split off from the movement, and riots in black ghettos and King's assassination caused many supporters to withdraw. In the succeeding decades, leaders sought power through elective office and substantive economic and educational gains through AFFIRMATIVE ACTION.

civil service Body of government officials employed in civil occupations that are neither political nor judicial. In well-ordered societies, they are usually recruited and promoted on the basis of a merit-and-seniority system, which may include examinations; elsewhere, corruption and patronage are rampant. They often serve as neutral advisers to elected officials and political appointees. While not responsible for making policy, they are charged with its execution. The civil service originated in the earliest known Middle Eastern societies; the modern European civil services date back to 17th–18th-century Prussia and the electors of Brandenburg. In the U.S., senior officials change with each new administration; in Europe, regulations were established in the 19th century to minimize favoritism and ensure a wide range of knowledge and skills. See also CHINESE EXAMINATION SYSTEM, SPOILS SYSTEM.

Civil Service Act, Pendleton See PENDLETON CIVIL SERVICE ACT

Civil War See AMERICAN CIVIL WAR

Civil Wars, English See ENGLISH CIVIL WARS

Civilian Conservation Corps (CCC) (1933–42) U.S. unemployment program. One of the earliest NEW DEAL programs, it was established to relieve unemployment during the GREAT DEPRESSION by providing national conservation work primarily for young unmarried men. Recruits lived in semimilitary work camps and received $30 a month as well as food and medical care. Projects included planting trees, building flood barriers, fighting forest fires, and maintaining forest roads and trails. It employed a total of 3 million men during its existence.

Cixi *or* **Tz'u-hsi** \'tsə-'shē\ *known as* **the Empress Dowager** (1835–1908) Imperial consort who controlled the Chinese QING DYNASTY for almost half a century. A low-ranking concubine of the Xianfeng emperor (r.1850–61), Cixi bore his only son, the future Tongzhi emperor, in 1856. After the emperor's death, Cixi joined a triumviral regency that governed in the name of her son, who was only 6 at his accession. During this period the TAIPING and NIAN Rebellions were put down and the government was briefly revitalized. When Cixi's son died in 1875, Cixi violated the laws of succession and had her adoptive nephew enthroned. The regency thus continued, with Cixi becoming sole regent in 1884. In 1889 she nominally relinquished control, but returned in 1898 to undo a set of radical reforms and had her nephew imprisoned in his palace. She supported the unsuccessful BOXER REBELLION, with bad consequences for China. In 1902 she began to implement the reforms she had earlier reversed. Before she died, she ordered her nephew poisoned. See also ZENG GUOFAN, ZHANG ZHIDONG.

Cixous \sēk-'züs\, **Hélène** (born 1937) French feminist critic, novelist, and playwright. Reared in Algiers, she has taught principally at the University of Paris. Her essays, in collections such as *The Newly Born Woman* (1975; with Catherine Clément), explore issues of sexual difference and female experience in writing. *The Book of Promethea* (1983) and other works reinterpret myths and the mythic past and analyze Western representations of women. Her novels include *Inside* (1969) and *Reading with Clarice Lispector* (1989).

Cizin \kē-'sēn\ Mayan god of earthquakes and death. He may have represented one aspect of a malevolent underworld deity known by various names and in various guises. In Mayan manuscripts, he was depicted with the god of war in scenes of human sacrifice; he was also depicted as a dancing skeleton. His death collar was adorned with eyeballs dangling by their nerve cords. After the Spanish Conquest, he merged with the Christian devil, Satan.

Claiborne, William (1587?–1677?) British-American colonial trader and public official. He emigrated to Virginia in 1621 and was appointed secretary for the colony. He traded with the Indians of Chesapeake Bay and in 1631 established a settlement on Kent Island. Denied his claim for the island, in 1644 he incited a revolt that ousted the Maryland governor and left Claiborne in charge of the colony until 1646. He was a member of the commission that governed Maryland 1652–57.

Clair, photograph by Yousuf Karsh.

Clair, René *orig.* **René-Lucien Chomette** (1898–1981) French film director. He acted in silent films from 1920 until 1923, when he wrote and directed *Paris qui dort.* That film, *Entr'acte* (1924), and the satiric farce *The Italian Straw Hat* (1927) established his reputation as a leader of the avant-garde. He used sound creatively in early talkies such as *Sous les toits de Paris* (1930) and *A nous la liberté!* (1931). *The Ghost Goes West* (1935), made in England, was an international success. During World War II he directed several Hollywood films, including *And Then There Were None* (1945), then returned to France to make *Le silence est d'or* (1947) and *Les belles de nuit* (1952).

(Left) Quahog (*Mercenaria*); (right) soft-shell clam (*Mya*).

clam In general, any BIVALVE MOLLUSK. True clams, in the strict sense, have equal shells, closed by two opposing muscles, and a powerful, muscular, burrowing foot. They usually lie buried in the sand in shallow marine waters. Clams draw in and expel water for respiration and feeding through two tubes, the siphons. Species range in size from 0.004 in. to 4 ft (0.1 mm–1.2 m) across. Many species are edible, including the COQUINA CLAM, GEODUCK, QUAHOG, and soft-shell clam.

clan Kinship group based on actual or purported DESCENT from a common ancestor, as traced through the male (patriclan) or the female (matriclan) line. Clans are normally exogamous, marriage within the clan being regarded as INCEST. Clans may segment into subclans or lineages, and genealogical records and myths may be altered to incorporate new members who lack KINSHIP ties with the clan. Clan membership may be useful in ensuring mutual support and defense as well as in the mediation of disputes over property rights and the mode of residence after MARRIAGE. Some clans express their unity by means of a common emblem. See also EXOGAMY AND ENDOGAMY.

Clancy, Tom *orig.* **Thomas** (born 1947) U.S. novelist. A native of Maryland, he worked as an insurance agent before beginning his writing career. His first novel was the surprise best-seller *The Hunt for Red October* (1984; film, 1990), which virtually created the "technothriller" genre, suspenseful novels that rely on extensive knowledge of military technology and espionage. Later successes include *Red Storm Rising* (1986), *Patriot Games* (1987; film, 1992), *Clear and Present Danger* (1989; film, 1994), and *Sum of All Fears* (1991; film, 2000).

clapboard \'kla-bərd\ Narrow board tapered toward one edge, used as SIDING to cover the exterior of a framed building. Clapboards are attached horizontally, each overlapping the next one down. Cleft oak clapboard was introduced to New England in the 17th century; later materials included pine, cypress, and cedar.

claque \'klak\ Group of people hired to clap (French, *claquer*) and show approval in order to influence a theater audience. The claque dates from ancient times. Comedy competitions in Athens were often won by contestants who infiltrated audiences with paid supporters. The practice was widespread in Rome, where NERO established a school of applause. In 19th-century France, most theaters had specialized claques: *rieurs* laughed loudly at comedies, *pleureuses* wept at melodramas, and *bisseurs* shouted for encores. The practice persists today in the operatic world.

Clare County (pop., 1996: 94,000), western Ireland. Bordered by the SHANNON RIVER and the Atlantic Ocean, it has an area of 1,231 sq mi (3,188 sq km); its county seat is Ennis. It has peat- and bog-covered hills, plateaus, lowlands, and limestone areas. Chief crops are oats and potatoes; livestock raising and fishing also are important. Evidence of prehistoric settlement includes many megaliths and some 2,000 fortified enclosures. There are numerous early Christian sites. The region remained under the lordship of the O'Briens until the 16th century despite Anglo-Norman colonization in the 12th century. It was made a shire in the reign of ELIZABETH I. In 1828 DANIEL O'CONNELL won the election in Clare that led to the emancipation of Catholics in Ireland.

Clare, John (1793–1864) British poet. He grew up in Northamptonshire in extreme rural poverty, with little access to books, but he had a prodigious memory and absorbed folk ballads. His *Poems Descriptive of Rural Life and Scenery* (1820) brought a short period of celebrity, but later volumes, including *The Shepherd's Calendar* (1827) and *The Rural Muse* (1835), sold poorly. Suffering from penury and poor health, he fell prey to delusions and was placed in an asylum in 1837. After four years he briefly escaped; certified insane, he spent his final 23 years in another asylum, where he wrote some of his most lucid, lyrical poetry.

Clare of Assisi, St. (1194–1253) Founder of the order of Poor Clares (Clarissines). Born in Assisi to a noble family, she became devoted to her fellow Assisian St. FRANCIS. She refused to marry, and at 18 she fled to a chapel. He received her vows; she was soon joined by her sister, St. AGNES, and her mother, and St. Francis set them up as the nucleus of a female community that would become its own order as the counterpart of the FRANCISCANS. Still allied with the Franciscans, the Poor Clares are noted for their perfect poverty and their life of penitential prayer led for the good of church and society.

Claremont Colleges Consortium of private colleges in Claremont, Cal. It comprises Pomona College (founded 1887), the Claremont Graduate School (1925), Scripps College (1926), Claremont McKenna College (1946), Harvey Mudd College (1955), and Pitzer College (1963). Each offers a broad range of degree programs, and they share a high academic reputation. The campuses are adjacent to one another and many facilities are shared. Total enrollment is about 7,000.

Clarendon, Constitutions of (1164) Sixteen articles issued by King HENRY II defining church-state relations in England. Designed to restrict ecclesiastical privileges and curb the power of the church courts, the constitutions provoked the famous quarrel between Henry and ST. THOMAS BECKET. Among their controversial measures were the provisions that all revenues from vacant sees and monasteries reverted to the king, who had discretion in filling the vacant offices, and that clerics charged with serious crimes were to be tried in secular courts. Becket's martyrdom in 1170 forced Henry to moderate his attack on the clergy, but he did not repudiate the constitutions.

Clarendon, Earl of *orig.* **Edward Hyde** (1609–1674) English statesman and historian. A successful lawyer, he was also well known in literary circles. As a member of Parliament, he became an adviser to CHARLES I, recommending moderate policies, but was unable to prevent the ENGLISH CIVIL WARS. He helped bring about the RESTORATION of CHARLES II, and was created earl of Clarendon in 1661. As lord chancellor (1660–67) he dominated most aspects of the administration. His criticism of the king's immorality eventually destroyed their friendship, and Parliament made him a scapegoat for the disasters of the ANGLO-DUTCH WAR of 1665. Dismissed as lord chancellor in 1667, he spent the rest of his life in exile in France, where he completed his *History of the Rebellion and Civil Wars in England.*

Clarendon, 4th Earl of *orig.* **George William Frederick Villiers** (1800–1870) British statesman. After serving as British ambassador to Spain (1833–39), he held various cabinet posts until Lord ABERDEEN named him secretary of state for foreign affairs in 1853. He failed to prevent the outbreak of the CRIMEAN WAR and his performance during it was undistinguished, but he secured favorable terms for Britain at the Congress of PARIS (1856). He continued in office under Lord PALMERSTON until 1858 and also served as foreign secretary under EARL RUSSELL (1865–66) and WILLIAM E. GLADSTONE (1868–70).

Clarendon Code (1661–65) Four acts passed in England during the ministry of the Earl of CLARENDON, designed to cripple the power of the NONCONFORMISTS, or Dissenters. The Corporation Act forbade municipal office to those not taking the sacraments at a parish church, the Act of Conformity excluded them from church offices, the Conventicle Act made meetings for Nonconformist worship illegal, and the Five-Mile Act forbade Nonconformist ministers to live or visit within five miles of any place where they had ministered.

clarinet Single-reed WOODWIND INSTRUMENT. It is a standard member of both orchestras and bands. It has a cylindrical bore and a flared bell, and is usually made of African blackwood (grenadilla). It has a 3½-octave range; its lower register is rich and its top register is brilliant. It developed from the slightly older two-key chalumeau; the German flutemaker Johann Christoff Denner (1655–1707) is said to have invented it at the beginning of the 18th century. The B-flat clarinet is the standard instrument today; the A clarinet often replaces it in sharp keys. Clarinets with the fingering system devised by T. BOEHM are standard in America, Britain, and France; those employing an older fingering style are used in Germany and Russia. The B-flat bass clarinet, with its rich timbre, is the next most frequently employed member of the clarinet family. The basset horn is an angled clarinet pitched a 4th lower than the standard B-flat clarinet; probably invented in Bavaria c. 1770, it had largely fallen out of use by 1850.

Clark, Champ *orig.* **James Beauchamp** (1850–1921) U.S. politician. Born near Lawrenceburg, Ky., he moved to Missouri in 1876. He was a newspaper editor, prosecuting attorney, and state legislator, then was elected to the U.S. House for 13 terms (1893–95, 1897–1921). A follower of WILLIAM JENNINGS BRYAN, he supported agrarian measures. As a member of the House rules committee in 1910, he led the revolt against JOSEPH C. CANNON and succeeded him as speaker (1911–19). At the 1912 Democratic Party convention, Clark was a leading contender for the presidential nomination until Bryan switched his support to Wilson.

Clark, Dick (born 1929) U.S. television personality. Born in Mount Vernon, N.Y., he worked as a radio and television announcer before beginning his long engagement as host of the TV show *American Bandstand* (1956–89), a showcase for popular music. He formed his own production company in 1956 and produced over 30 series, 250 specials, and 20 TV movies.

Clark, Helen (born 1950) New Zealand politician who became prime minister in 1999. She was the first woman in New Zealand to hold the office of prime minister immediately following an election. Raised on a sheep and cattle farm in Te Pahu, west of Hamilton, Clark attended grammar school in Aukland. She received bachelor's (1971) and master's (1974) degrees in political science at the University of Auckland, where she taught from 1973 to 1981. She joined the Labour Party in 1971 and served in a variety of party positions during the next decade. Elected to Parliament in 1981, she held various cabinet portfolios beginning in 1987. In 1989–90 she served as deputy prime minister and in 1990 was appointed to the Privy Council, both firsts for a woman in New Zealand. In 1993 she was elected head of the Labour Party, becoming the first woman in New Zealand to head a major party. In 1999, when the Labour Party was able to form a governing coalition, Clark was elected prime minister. She was awarded the prestigious Peace Prize from the Danish Peace Foundation in 1986.

Clark, James H. (born 1944) U.S. businessman. Born in Plainview, Texas, he dropped out of high school to join the Navy. He received his PhD in computer science from the University of Utah and taught at UC–Santa Cruz (1974–78) and Stanford (1979–82). He founded Silicon Graphics in 1981 and served as its chairman 1982–94, building it into a billion-dollar company that produced workstations for graphics-intensive applications. In 1994 he cofounded Netscape Communications, whose graphical interface Web browser revolutionized the Internet by making it easy to access Internet documents.

Clark, Kenneth (Mackenzie) *later* **Baron Clark** (of Saltwood) (1903–1983) British art historian and administrator. Born to a wealthy family, he studied at Oxford University. After two years of study with BERNARD BERENSON in Florence, he served as keeper of fine art at Oxford's Ashmolean Museum (1931–34) and director of London's National Gallery (1934–39). He was involved in academic research and public service for most of his life. He published widely and became internationally known in 1969 as the writer and host of the BBC series *Civilisation*, a survey of European art from the Dark Ages to the 20th century.

Clark, Mark (Wayne) (1896–1984) U.S. army officer. Born in Madison Barracks, N.Y., he graduated from West Point and rose through the ranks to become chief of staff of army ground forces in 1942. He commanded the U.S. landing at Salerno, Italy, in September 1943 and received the surrender of the government of PIETRO BADOGLIO. He then directed the hard-fought campaign to wrest the Italian peninsula from Axis control, taking Rome in June 1944, and receiving the surrender of the last German forces in northern Italy in May 1945. In the Korean War he commanded all U.N. troops 1952–53. After his retirement, he served as president of The Citadel 1954–66.

Clark, Tom *orig.* **Thomas Campbell** (1899–1977) U.S. jurist. Born in Dallas, he studied law at the University of Texas and entered private practice. As a civil district attorney he became involved in Democratic politics. At the U.S. Justice Department (1937–45), he worked primarily on ANTITRUST and war-fraud cases. As U.S. attorney general (1945) he gained a reputation for vigorous antisubversive programs and the broadening of FBI powers. Appointed to the U.S. Supreme Court (1949), he remained vigorously opposed to subversive activities yet was a frequent supporter of CIVIL LIBERTIES. He resigned in 1967 when his son, Ramsey Clark (born 1927), was appointed U.S. attorney general.

Clark, William (1770–1838) U.S. explorer and soldier. Born in Caroline Co., Va., the brother of GEORGE ROGERS CLARK, he joined the army and participated in Indian campaigns under ANTHONY WAYNE. After resigning his commission, he was recruited by his former army friend MERIWETHER LEWIS to help lead the first overland expedition to the Pacific coast. On the famed LEWIS AND CLARK EXPEDITION (1804–6) he proved an able leader, with valuable wilderness and mapmaking skills. Later, as governor of the Missouri Territory (1813–21), he was known for the effectiveness of his diplomacy with Native Americans.

Clarke, Arthur C(harles) (born 1917) British-Sri Lankan science-fiction writer. He first published stories while in the Royal Air Force and, after earning a degree in physics and mathematics, wrote such novels as *Childhood's End* (1953), *Earthlight* (1955), *Rendezvous with Rama* (1973), and *The Fountains of Paradise* (1979). He collaborated with STANLEY KUBRICK in making *2001: A Space Odyssey* (1968, film and novel), which was followed by two sequels. Some of Clarke's ideas have proved remarkably prescient. Since the 1950s he has lived in Sri Lanka.

class, social Group of people within a society who possess the same socioeconomic status. The term was first widely used in the early 19th century, following the industrial and political revolutions of the late 18th century. The most influential early theory of class was that of KARL MARX, who focused on how one class controls and directs the process of production while other classes are the direct producers and the providers of services to the dominant class. The relations between the classes were thus seen as antagonistic. MAX WEBER emphasized the importance of political power and SOCIAL STATUS or prestige in maintaining class distinctions. Despite controversies over the theory of class, there is general agreement on the characteristics of the classes in modern capitalist societies. The upper class is distinguished above all by the possession of largely inherited wealth (in the U.S., more than 30% of all wealth is concentrated in the hands of the top 1% of property owners, and nearly two-thirds in the top 5%). The working class consists mostly of manual laborers and food- and service-industry workers who earn moderate or low wages and have little or no access to inherited wealth. The middle class includes the middle and upper levels of clerical workers, those engaged in technical and professional occupations, supervisors and managers, and such self-employed workers as small-scale shopkeepers, businesspeople, and farmers. There is also often an urban substratum of permanently jobless and underemployed workers termed the underclass. See also BOURGEOISIE.

class action In law, an action in which a representative plaintiff sues or a representative defendant is sued on behalf of a class of plaintiffs or defendants who have the same interests in the litigation as their representative and whose rights or liabilities can be better determined as a group than in a series of individual suits. Class-action suits that received national attention in the U.S. include a suit brought against manufacturers of AGENT ORANGE by Vietnam veterans exposed to the herbicide (settled in 1984) and a suit concerning the effects of passive smoking brought against tobacco firms (settled in 1997).

Classical architecture Architecture of ancient Greece and Rome, especially from the 5th century BC in Greece to the 3rd century AD in Rome, that emphasized the COLUMN and PEDIMENT. Greek architecture was based chiefly on the POST-AND-BEAM SYSTEM, with columns carrying the load. Timber construction was superseded by construction in marble and stone. The column, a unit human in scale, was used as a MODULE for all of a temple's proportions. The Doric ORDER, probably the earliest, remained the favorite of the Greek mainland and western colonies. The Ionic order developed in eastern Greece; on the mainland, it was used chiefly for smaller temples and interiors. The greatest Greek architectural achievement was the Athens ACROPOLIS. By the late 5th century BC, the orders were applied to such structures as STOAS and theaters. The HELLENISTIC AGE produced more elaborate and richly decorated architecture, with often colossal buildings. Many of the great buildings were secular rather than religious, and the Ionic and especially the newer Corinthian orders were widely used. The Romans used the Greek orders and added two new ones (Tuscan and Composite); the Corinthian was by far the most popular. Roman architects used columns not only as functional bearing elements, but also as applied (engaged) decoration. Though rigidly adhering to symmetry, the Romans used a variety of spatial forms. Whereas Greek temples were isolated and almost always faced east-west, Roman temples were oriented with respect to other buildings. Roman columns carried ARCHES as well as ENTABLATURES, permitting greater spatial freedom. The discovery of concrete enormously facilitated construction using the arch, VAULT, and DOME, as in the PANTHEON. Other public buildings included BASILICAS, baths (see THERMAE), AMPHITHEATERS, and TRIUMPHAL ARCHES. Classical architecture may also refer to architecture of later periods that employs Greek or Roman forms.

classical economics School of economic thought largely centered in Britain that originated with ADAM SMITH and reached maturity in the works of DAVID RICARDO and JOHN STUART MILL. The theories of the classical school were mainly concerned with the dynamics of economic growth. Reacting against MERCANTILISM, classical economics emphasized economic freedom. It stressed ideas such as LAISSEZ-FAIRE and free competition. Many of the fundamental principles of classical economics were set forth in Smith's *Wealth of Nations* (1776), in which he argued that a nation's wealth was greatest when its citizens followed their own self-interest. Neoclassical economists such as ALFRED MARSHALL showed that the forces of SUPPLY AND DEMAND would ration economic resources to their most effective uses. Smith's ideas were elaborated and refined by

Ricardo, who formulated the principle that the price of goods produced and sold under competitive conditions tends to be proportionate to the labor costs incurred in producing them. Mill's *Principles of Political Economy* (1848) gave the ideas greater currency by relating them to contemporary social conditions. Among those who have modified classical economics to reach very different conclusions are KARL MARX and JOHN MAYNARD KEYNES.

classicism In the arts, the principles, historical tradition, aesthetic attitudes, or style of the art of ancient Greece and Rome. The term may refer either to work produced in antiquity or to later works inspired by those of antiquity; the term neoclassicism usually refers to art produced later but inspired by antiquity. More broadly, classicism refers to the adherence to virtues regarded as characteristic of classicism or as universally and enduringly valid, including formal elegance and correctness, simplicity, dignity, restraint, order, and proportion. Classicism is often opposed to ROMANTICISM. Periods of classicism in literature, music, and the visual arts have generally coincided.

Classicism and Neoclassicism Art-historical tradition or aesthetic attitudes based on the art of ancient Greece and Rome. "Classicism" refers to the art produced in antiquity or to later art inspired by that of antiquity; "Neoclassicism" refers to art inspired by that of antiquity, and thus is contained within the broader meaning of "Classicism." Classicism is traditionally characterized by harmony, clarity, restraint, universality, and idealism. In the visual arts, Classicism has generally denoted a preference for line over color, straight lines over curves, and the general over the particular. The Italian RENAISSANCE was the first period of thorough Classicism after antiquity. Neoclassicism became the dominant aesthetic movement in Europe in the late 18th and early 19th century, as practiced by ANTONIO CANOVA and J.-L. DAVID. It bred a reaction in favor of subjective feeling, longing for the sublime, and a taste for the bizarre that came to be termed ROMANTICISM. Recurring alternations between Classical and non-Classical ideals have often been seen to characterize Western aesthetics. See also CLASSICAL ARCHITECTURE.

Claude Lorrain \'klōd-lō-'raⁿ\ *orig.* **Claude Gellée** (c. 1600–1682) French painter. Born in the duchy of Lorraine, he went to Rome as a youth, and there trained with the landscape and fresco painter Agostino Tassi and encountered the work of NICOLAS POUSSIN. He became known as the master of the ideal landscape, a view of nature more beautiful and harmonious than nature itself; his landscapes and coastal scenes contain architectural fragments and figures. His reputation is based particularly on his sensitivity to the tonal values of light and atmosphere. By the 1630s he was well known and successful, with illustrious patrons among the French and Italian aristocracy. His work influenced the Dutch painters in Rome in the 1630s and '40s, as well as the entire course of European landscape painting. Some 250 paintings and over 1,000 drawings survive.

Claudel \klō-'del\, **Camille (-Rosalie)** (1864–1943) French sculptor. She was educated with her brother, PAUL CLAUDEL, and by her teens she was a skilled sculptor. In 1881 she moved with her family to Paris and entered the Colarossi Academy. In 1882 she met AUGUSTE RODIN. She is best known today as his student, collaborator, model, and mistress. She contributed whole figures and parts of figures to Rodin's projects, particularly *The Gates of Hell* (1880–1900). She exhibited her own work successfully at the official salons and in galleries, but also destroyed many pieces. In 1913, still distraught from her break with Rodin in 1898, she was committed to a mental institution, and from 1914 until her death she lived in a rest home.

Claudel \klō-'del\, **Paul (-Louis-Charles-Marie)** (1868–1955) French poet, playwright, and diplomat. He converted to Catholicism at 18. His brilliant diplomatic career began in 1892, and he eventually served as ambassador to Japan (1921–27) and the U.S. (1927–33). At the same time he pursued a literary career, expressing in poetry and drama his conception of the grand design of creation. He reached his largest audience through such plays as *Break of Noon* (1906), *The Hostage* (1911), *Tidings Brought to Mary* (1912), and his masterpiece, *The Satin Slipper* (1929), which explore the struggle between good and evil and the search for salvation. He wrote the librettos for D. MILHAUD's opera *Christopher Columbus* (1930) and A. HONEGGER's oratorio *Joan of Arc* (1938). His best-known poetic work is the *Cinq grandes odes* (1910).

Claudius *in full* **Tiberius Claudius Caesar Augustus Germanicus** ***orig.*** **Tiberius Claudius Nero Germanicus** (10 BC–AD 54) Roman emperor (AD 41–54). Nephew of TIBERIUS, Claudius became emperor unexpectedly after CALIGULA's murder. Sickly, clumsy, unattractive, and scholarly, he wrote several histories, none of which survive. He was ruthless toward individual senators and the equites (see EQUES) and tended to disfavor the upper classes, but catered to the freedmen. The invasion of Britain in 43 was part of his general expansion of frontiers; he also annexed Mauretania in northern Africa, Lycia in Asia Minor, and Thrace, and made Judaea a province. He encouraged urbanization, spent lavishly on public works, and extended Roman citizenship throughout the empire. Having executed his scheming third wife, Valeria Messaline, in 48, he married his niece AGRIPPINA THE YOUNGER. She pressured Claudius into naming her son Lucius (later NERO) heir instead of his own son Britannicus. Claudius may have been poisoned by Agrippina.

Claudius I, detail of a bust found near Priverno; in the Vatican Museum.
ALINARI—ART RESOURCE/EB INC.

Claudius Caecus \'sē-kəs\, **Appius** (late 4th-early 3rd century BC) Roman statesman and legal reformer. Elected censor, Appius extended the rights of the sons of freedmen and the landless. He completed the Aqua Appia, Rome's first AQUEDUCT, and began the APPIAN WAY. He was CONSUL in 307, censor a second time in 296, and PRAETOR in 295. By publishing the *legis actiones* ("methods of legal practice") and lists of court days, he provided greater public access to the legal system. In his old age he convinced the Senate to drive PYRRHUS from southern Italy.

Clausewitz \'klaů-zə-,vits\, **Carl (Philipp Gottlieb) von** (1780–1831) Prussian general and author. Born near Magdeburg to a poor middle-class professional family, he joined the Prussian army at 12 and entered the War College in Berlin in 1801. After serving with distinction in the NAPOLEONIC WARS, he became a general and was appointed director of the War College (1818). His major work on STRATEGY, *On War* (1832–37), analyzed the workings of military genius by isolating the factors that decide success in war. Rather than producing a rigid system of strategy, he emphasized the necessity of a critical approach to strategic problems. He asserted that war is a tool for achieving political aims rather than an end in itself ("merely the continuation of policy by other means"), and argued that defensive warfare is both militarily and politically the stronger position. He also advocated the concept of TOTAL WAR. Published posthumously, *On War* had a profound influence on modern military strategy.

Clausewitz, lithograph by Franz Michelis after an oil painting by Wilhelm Wach, 1830.
BY COURTESY OF THE STAATSBIBLIOTHEK, WEST BERLIN

clavichord Early keyboard instrument, an important forerunner of the PIANO. It flourished c. 1400–1800, especially in Germany. It is usually rectangular, with the keyboard inset. The strings are struck by metal tangents, rather than plucked as on the HARPSICHORD. The tangent becomes the endpoint of the vibrating string; thus the point where it strikes determines the pitch. So-called fretted clavichords permit more than one tangent to strike a single pair of strings (which somewhat limits the notes that can be sounded simultaneously); unfretted clavichords use only one tangent per pair of strings. Its sound is generally so soft as to be nearly inaudible, and it is thus suited only to solo performance, usually without an audience. The player's touch can produce dynamic variation; variation in finger pressure can even produce vibrato.

clay SOIL particles with diameters are less than 0.005 mm; also a material composed essentially of clay particles (see CLAY MINERAL). In soils, clays provide the environment for almost all plant growth. The use of clay in POTTERY making predates recorded human history. As building materials, clay BRICKS (baked and as ADOBE) have been used in construction since the earliest times. Kaolin, or china clay, is required for the finer grades of CERAMIC materials; used for paper coating and filler, it gives the paper a gloss, permitting high-quality reproduction, and increases paper opacity. Clay materials have many uses in engineering; earth dams are made impermeable to water by a core of clay, and water loss in canals may be reduced by lining the bottom with clay (called puddling). The essential raw materials of PORTLAND CEMENT include clays.

Clay, Cassius See Muhammad ALI

Clay, Cassius Marcellus (1810–1903) U.S. abolitionist and politician. Born in Madison Co., Ky., he was the son of a slaveholder and a relative of HENRY CLAY but was strongly influenced by the ideas of WILLIAM LLOYD GARRISON. In 1845 he founded the antislavery publication *True American,* but was forced by opponents to move it to Cincinnati and then to Louisville, Ky., where it was renamed *The Examiner.* He helped found the REPUBLICAN PARTY in 1854, and later served as U.S. minister to Russia (1861–62, 1863–69), where he helped negotiate the ALASKA PURCHASE.

Clay, Henry (1777–1852) U.S. politician. Born in Hanover Co., Va., he practiced law from 1797 in Virginia and then Kentucky, where he served in the state legislature (1803–9). He was elected to the U.S. House of Representatives (1811–14, 1815–21, 1823–25) and as speaker (1811–14), he was among those who pushed the U.S. into the WAR OF 1812. He supported a national economic policy, known as the American System, of protective tariffs, a national bank, and internal transportation improvements. His support of the MISSOURI COMPROMISE earned him the nicknames "The Great Pacificator" and "The Great Compromiser." After supporting JOHN QUINCY ADAMS in the 1824 election, he became his secretary of state (1825–29). He served in the U.S. Senate 1806–7, 1810–11, and 1831–42, where he supported the compromise tariff of 1833. He was the Whig Party candidate for president in 1832 and 1844. In his last Senate term (1849–52) he argued strongly for passage of the COMPROMISE OF 1850.

Clay, by Frederick and William Langenheim, 1850.

BY COURTESY OF THE LIBRARY OF CONGRESS, WASHINGTON, D.C.

Clay, Lucius D(uBignon) (1897–1978) U.S. army officer. Born in Marietta, Ga., he graduated from West Point and served in army engineer assignments. In World War II he directed the U.S. Army procurement program (1942–44). After the war he served as the first director of civilian affairs in defeated Germany, as military governor in the U.S. zone in Germany, and as commander in chief of U.S. forces in Europe (1947–49), conducting the successful 1948 Berlin airlift. After retiring in 1949, he entered private business and was an unofficial adviser to Pres. DWIGHT D. EISENHOWER.

clay mineral Any of a group of important hydrous aluminum silicates with a layered structure and very small (less than 0.005 mm or microscopic) particle size. They are usually the products of weathering. Clay minerals occur widely in such sedimentary rocks as mudstones and shales, in marine sediments, and in soils. Different geologic environments produce different clay minerals from the same parent rock. They are used in the petroleum industry (as drilling muds and as catalysts in refining) and in the processing of vegetable and mineral oils (as decolorizing agents).

Clayton, John Middleton (1796–1856) U.S. politician. Born in Dagsboro, Del., he served as Delaware's secretary of state (1826–28) and chief justice (1837). He served in the U.S. Senate 1829–36 and 1845–49. As U.S. secretary of state (1849–50) under Pres. ZACHARY TAYLOR, he negotiated the CLAYTON-BULWER TREATY.

Clayton-Bulwer Treaty (1850) Compromise agreement designed to harmonize contending British and U.S. interests in Central America. The treaty provided that the two countries jointly control and protect what was to become the Panama Canal. It was superseded in 1901 by the Hay-Pauncefote Treaty, under which the British government agreed to allow the U.S. to construct and control the canal.

Clazomenae \klə-'zä-mə-ˌnē\ Ancient Ionian Greek city, Asia Minor. Founded on the mainland, the city was subsequently moved to a nearby island; ALEXANDER THE GREAT later built a pier to connect the island to the mainland. During the 5th century BC it was controlled by ATHENS; it became subject to PERSIA in 387 BC. The philosopher ANAXAGORAS was born there. Part of the Ionian Dodecapolis, it was known for its painted terracotta sarcophagi (6th century BC).

clear-cell carcinoma See RENAL CARCINOMA

Clear Grits Political movement in CANADA WEST (now Ontario). It developed in 1849 within the Reform Party in opposition to the province's premier, ROBERT BALDWIN, who advocated reforms that included the use of crown lands to support the Protestant churches. It allegedly took its name from the motto "All sand and no dirt, clear grit all the way through." Its early leader was Peter Perry; after his death in 1851, control gradually passed to GEORGE BROWN. It eventually joined other groups to form the LIBERAL PARTY, and the term "Grit" denotes a member of that party.

clearinghouse Institution established by firms engaged in similar activities to enable them to offset transactions with one another in order to limit payment settlements to net balances. Clearinghouses play an important role in settling international payments and the transactions of banks, railroads, and stock and commodity exchanges. Bank clearinghouses are usually voluntary associations of local banks set up to simplify the exchange of checks, drafts, and notes, as well as to settle balances. The clearinghouse idea was applied to various forms of trade from an early time. The Amsterdam Exchange Bank, founded in 1609, became Europe's largest clearinghouse and made the city an international financial center. The first modern bank clearinghouse was established in London in 1773. The first bank clearinghouse in the U.S. was established in 1853.

cleavage Tendency of a crystalline substance to split into fragments bounded by plane surfaces. Cleavage surfaces are seldom as flat as crystal faces, but the angles between them are highly characteristic and valuable in identifying a crystalline material. Cleavage occurs on planes where the atomic bonding forces are weakest; for example, galena cleaves parallel to all faces of a cube. Cleavage is described by its direction (as cubic, prismatic, basal) and by the ease with which it is produced. A perfect cleavage produces smooth, lustrous surfaces. Other degrees include distinct, imperfect, and difficult. See also FRACTURE.

Cleese, John (Marwood) (born 1939) British actor and screenwriter. Educated at Cambridge Univ., he wrote and performed comedy material for British television in the 1960s before helping create the popular comedy show *Monty Python's Flying Circus* (1969–74), which later won a large U.S. following with its surreal yet enjoyably silly brand of humor. He cowrote and acted in the television series *Fawlty Towers* and collaborated with the rest of the MONTY PYTHON troupe on films such as *Monty Python and the Holy Grail* (1975), *The Life of Brian* (1979), and *The Meaning of Life* (1983). His other films include *A Fish Called Wanda* (1988) and *Fierce Creatures* (1997).

clef (French: "key") MUSICAL-NOTATION symbol at the beginning of a staff to indicate the PITCH of the notes on the staff. Clefs were originally letters, identifying letter-named pitches, that were affixed to one or more of the staff's lines (thus providing a "key" to their identity). Knowing the identity of a single line permitted the musician to identify all the other lines and spaces above and below. Clefs were first regularly used in the 12th century. The Gothic letter forms of G and F evolved into the modern treble and bass clefs, respectively; the letter C evolved into the rarer alto, tenor, baritone, and soprano clefs.

cleft palate Fairly common CONGENITAL DISORDER in which a fissure forms in the roof of the mouth. It may affect only the soft PALATE or extend through the hard palate, so that the nasal cavity opens into the mouth. The septum (dividing wall) between the nostrils is often absent. Cleft lip, a fissure in the lip beneath the nostril, or other abnormalities may accompany it. Cleft palate limits the ability of an infant to suck, which may lead to malnutrition, and causes speech problems in childhood. Surgical repair, usually at about 18 months of age, forms an airtight separation between nose and mouth. Speech training is still needed, and patients may have a high risk of nose, ear, and sinus infections.

Cleisthenes of Athens \'klīs-thə-ˌnēz\ (c. 570–508? BC) Athenian statesman and chief ARCHON (525–524), regarded as the founder of Athenian democracy. A member of the ALCMAEONID FAMILY, he allied himself with the ECCLESIA in 508 and imposed democratic reforms by which the basis of organization was changed from family and clan to locality. The four blood TRIBES were replaced by 10 local tribes, each with representation from city, coast, and hill areas. The BOULE grew to 500 members. He based all his reforms on *isonomia* ("equal rights for all").

Cleitias *or* **Kleitias** *or* **Clitias** \'klī-tē-əs\ (fl. c. 580–550 BC) Greek vase painter and potter. An outstanding master of the Archaic period, he executed the decorations on the François Vase (c. 570 BC), discovered in 1844 in an Etruscan tomb. Painted in the black-figure style (see BLACK-FIGURE POTTERY), the large vase, signed and decorated with more than 200 figures, is among the greatest treasures of Greek art. Other vases and fragments attributed to him are in the Acropolis Museum, Athens.

"Mask of Medusa," top view of stand made by Ergotimos and painted by Cleitias, c. 560 BC; in the Metropolitan Museum of Art, New York City.

BY COURTESY OF THE METROPOLITAN MUSEUM OF ART, NEW YORK, FLETCHER FUND, 1931

clematis \'kle-mə-təs, kli-'ma-təs\ Any of the more than 200 species of perennial, chiefly climbing shrubs of the genus *Clematis* (BUTTERCUP family), found through most of the world, especially in Asia and North America. Many species are cultivated in North America for their attractive flowers, either solitary or in large clusters. The leaves usually are compound. Common species include WOODBINE; traveler's joy, or old-man's-beard *(C. vitalba);* virgin's bower *(C. cirrhosa);* and vine bower *(C. viticella).* The most popular horticultural hybrids are of primarily three species: *C. florida, C. patens,* and *C. jackmanii.*

Clemenceau \klā-mäⁿ-'sō, *Engl* ˌkle-mən-'sō\, **Georges** (1841–1929) French statesman and journalist. A doctor before turning to politics, he served in the Chamber of Deputies 1876–93, becoming a leader of the radical republican bloc. He founded the newspapers *La Justice* (1880), *L'Aurore* (1897), and *L'Homme Libre* (1913) and came to be ranked among the foremost political writers of his time. His support for ALFRED DREYFUS brought him into favor, and he served in the Senate 1902–20. He served as interior minister in 1906 and premier 1906–9. During World War I, at 76, he became premier again (1917–20), and his steadfast pursuit of the war won him the title "Father of Victory." He also helped frame the postwar Treaty of VERSAILLES, endeavoring to reconcile French interests with those of Britain and the U.S. Defeated in a presidential election in 1920, he retired from politics.

Clemens, (William) Roger (born 1962) U.S. baseball player. Born in Dayton, Ohio, he has played for the Boston Red Sox (1984–96), Toronto Blue Jays (1997–1998), and New York Yankees (from 1999). In 1986 he became the first pitcher to strike out 20 batters in a single (nine-inning) game; he later tied his own record (1996). He won the Cy Young Award for best pitcher five times (1986, 1987, 1991, 1997, 1998).

Clement, Joseph (1779–1844) British engineer. Born into a weaver's family in Westmorland, he learned metal-working skills and was soon building power looms. He moved to London in 1813, where he held high positions at two renowned engineering firms. In 1823 he joined CHARLES BABBAGE in his difference-engine project. His machine tools, including his planing machine and screw-cutting taps, were valued for their precision.

Clement V *orig.* **Bertrand de Got** (c. 1260–1314) Pope (1305–14), the first to reside at Avignon, France. He became archbishop of Bordeaux in 1299 and was elected pope six years later. By creating a majority of French CARDINALS, he ensured the election of a line of French popes. He moved the seat of the papacy to Avignon, primarily for political reasons (see AVIGNON PAPACY). PHILIP IV of France forced him to restrict the church's role in secular affairs and to dissolve the TEMPLARS. Clement opposed Holy Roman emperor HENRY VII after 1313 and appointed the king of Naples as imperial vicar on Henry's death. His decretals, the *Clementinae,* were a notable contribution to canon law.

Clement VI *orig.* **Pierre Roger** (1291?–1352) Pope (1342–52). The archbishop of Sens and Rouen, he was made cardinal in 1338 and was consecrated pope at Avignon four years later (see AVIGNON PAPACY). He launched a crusade against Smyrna in 1344, ending the piracy of the Ottoman Turks. He also restored papal authority in the Italian region of Romagna, which was disputed by families of the Italian nobility. In exchange for his protection, JOAN I of Naples sold him Avignon. Clement opposed the Franciscan ascetics known as the Spirituals, enlarged the papal palace, and fostered art and scholarship.

Clement VII *orig.* **Giulio de' Medici** (1478–1534) Pope (1523–34). The illegitimate son of Giuliano de' Medici (see MEDICI FAMILY), he was raised by his uncle Lorenzo de' MEDICI. In 1513 he was made archbishop of Florence and cardinal by his cousin Pope LEO X. He commissioned art from RAPHAEL and MICHELANGELO. A weak and vacillating political figure mainly interested in advancing Medici interests, Clement allied with France in 1527, which led to Emperor CHARLES V's sack of Rome. Clement's indecisiveness complicated HENRY VIII's request for an annulment of his marriage to Catherine of Aragon.

Clement of Alexandria, St. *Latin* **Titus Flavius Clemens** (c. AD 150–215) Christian apologist, missionary theologian to the Hellenistic world, and leader of the catechetical school at Alexandria. Born in Athens, he was converted to Christianity by Pantaenus, a former Stoic who preceded him as head of the Alexandria school. Clement believed that philosophy was for the Greeks what the Law of Moses was for the Jews, a preparatory discipline leading to the truth. He asserted that men lived first as citizens of heaven and second as earthly citizens and defended the right of an enslaved people to rebel against its oppressors. Persecution by the emperor Severus in 201–2 obliged him to leave Alexandria and take refuge with Alexander, bishop of Jerusalem. He was revered as a saint in the Latin church until 1586, when doubts about his orthodoxy led to the removal of his name from the list of Roman saints.

Clemente \klə-'men-tā\, **Roberto** (1934–1972) U.S. baseball player. Born in San Juan, Puerto Rico, he played in the minor leagues in Puerto Rico before joining the Pittsburgh Pirates in 1955. He led the National League in hitting in 1961, 1964, 1965, and 1967, and batted .362 in two World Series (1960, 1970). He was also known for his fielding, throwing, and base-stealing. His career was cut short when he died in the crash of an airplane loaded with relief supplies he had collected for Nicaraguan earthquake victims.

Roberto Clemente.

UPI

Clementi, Muzio (1752–1832) British (Italian-born) composer, publisher, and manufacturer. Brought to England at 13 by a wealthy English traveler who had heard his organ playing, he was set to solitary music studies for seven years on a country estate. His keyboard playing and early sonatas thereafter gained him renown in London. In 1781 he and W.A. MOZART competed before the emperor, and he later toured extensively as conductor and pianist. In 1798 he restarted a successful music-publishing and piano-manufacturing firm. His piano pieces were highly influential, and he taught many leading pianists. His works include over 100 piano sonatas and *Gradus ad Parnassum* (3 vols., 1817–26), a popular pedagogical set of 100 diverse piano pieces.

Cleomenes I \klē-'ä-mə-ˌnēz\ (died 491 BC) Spartan king (519–491). An Agiad, he ruled jointly with Demaratus. In 510 he expelled the tyrant HIPPIAS from Athens, then supported the oligarchic party against the democratic CLEISTHENES and refused to help Athens combat Persia. His policies did much to solidify Sparta's position as the leading power in the Peloponnesus. He bribed the oracle at DELPHI to depose Demaratus, but was discovered and fled. Though reinstated, he went insane and committed suicide.

Cleomenes III (died 219 BC) Agiad Spartan king (235–222). Seeking to institute social reforms, in 227 he canceled debts, redistributed land, and restored the training of youth. He abolished the EPHORS and introduced the *patronomoi* (board of six elders). His early attempts to weaken the ACHAEAN LEAGUE (from 229) were successful, but in 222 his army fell at Sellasia to a Macedonian force summoned by the league. He fled to Egypt, where he was imprisoned but escaped (219); having failed to stir up revolt in Alexandria, he committed suicide.

Cleon (died 422 BC) Athenian politician. The first prominent representative of the merchant class in Athenian politics, he became leader of Athens in 429 BC after the death of his enemy PERICLES. Advocating an offensive strategy in the PELOPONNESIAN WAR, he proposed that all citizens of the rebellious Mytilene be put to death and its women and children enslaved; the measure passed but was reversed the next day. He reached the summit of his fame when he captured the Spartan island of Sphacteria, but was killed by the Spartans while trying to retake Thrace.

Cleopatra (VII) (69–30 BC) Egyptian queen (of Macedonian descent), last ruler of the Ptolemaic dynasty in Egypt. Daughter of Ptolemy XII (112?–51 BC), she ruled with her two brother-husbands, Ptolemy XIII (51–47) and Ptolemy XIV (47–44), both of whom she had killed, and with her son, Ptolemy XV or Caesarion (44–30). She claimed the latter was fathered by Julius CAESAR, who had become her lover after entering Egypt in 48 BC in pursuit of Pompey. She was with Caesar in Rome when he was assassinated (44), after which she returned to Egypt to install her son on the throne. She lured Mark ANTONY, Caesar's heir apparent, into marriage (36), inviting the wrath of Octavian (later AUGUSTUS), whose sister Antony had earlier wed. She schemed against and antagonized Antony's friend HEROD THE GREAT, thereby losing his support. At a magnificent celebration in Alexandria after Antony's Parthian campaign (36–34), he bestowed Roman lands on his foreign wife and family. Octavian declared war on Cleopatra and Antony and defeated their joint forces at the Battle of ACTIUM (31). Antony committed suicide and, after a failed attempt to beguile Octavian, so too did Cleopatra, by exposing her breast to an asp.

Cleopatra, detail of a bas relief, c. 69–30 BC; in the Temple of Hathor, Dandarah, Egypt.

BY COURTESY OF THE ORIENTAL INSTITUTE, THE UNIVERSITY OF CHICAGO

Cleophrades Painter *or* **Kleophrades Painter** \klē-'ä-frə-ˌdēz\ (fl. late 6th-early 5th century BC) Greek vase painter. Of unknown identity, he takes his name from that of the potter who signed one of his principal works; he may have been a pupil of Euthymides. He decorated large vases with popular scenes, such as athletic contests and mythological epics, mostly in the red-figure style (see RED-FIGURE POTTERY). Over 100 vessels have been attributed to him.

clepsydra See WATER CLOCK

clerestory \'klir-ˌstōr-ē\ Windowed wall of a room that rises higher than the surrounding roofs to light the interior space. In large buildings, where internal walls are far from the outermost walls, the clerestory provides daylight to spaces that otherwise would be dark and windowless. This device was used in Byzantine and early Christian architecture and most highly developed in Romanesque and Gothic cathedrals. As the NAVE rose much higher than the roofs of the side aisles, its walls could be pierced by a row of windows near the ceiling.

Clergy, Civil Constitution of the See CIVIL CONSTITUTION OF THE CLERGY

Clergy Reserves Lands set aside for the Church of England in Canada. Established by the CONSTITUTIONAL ACT of 1791 "for the support and maintenance of a Protestant clergy," they amounted to one-seventh of all land grants. They became controversial after 1815, as some denominations demanded equal reserves and others argued that the lands should serve general public purposes independent of religion. An imperial act of 1827 allowed for the sale of one-fourth of the reserved land; in 1840 another imperial act forbade the creation of any new reserves. The reserves were finally secularized in 1854.

Clermont \kler-'mō^{n}\, **Council of** (1095) Assembly for church reform called by Pope URBAN II. When the Byzantine emperor ALEXIUS I COMNENUS requested aid against the Muslim Turks, the council became the occasion for launching the First CRUSADE. Urban thus launched a movement that caught the popular imagination with the idea of retaking Jerusalem.

cleruchy \'klir-ə-kē\ In ancient Greece, a body of Athenian citizens in a dependent country holding grants of land awarded by Athens. Athens used the cleruchy to cripple dependent states; plantations took the best land, and the colonizers formed military garrisons. SALAMIS, captured in the 6th century BC, may have held the earliest cleruchy. Under the DELIAN LEAGUE and the Second Athenian League (5th–4th century BC), the cleruchy was a regular instrument of Athenian imperialism. The financial advantage of being a cleruch encouraged many citizens to leave Athens, relieving population pressures.

Cleveland Former county, northeastern England. Created in the government reorganization of 1974, it was located on the North Sea north of NORTH YORKSHIRE; the county seat was MIDDLESBROUGH. The county was reorganized in 1996. An industrial center, it has one of the country's major concentrations of steel making, heavy chemicals, and petroleum refining.

Cleveland City (pop., 1996 est.: 498,000), northeastern Ohio. Located on the southern shore of Lake ERIE, it is Ohio's second-largest city. Initially the site of French and Indian trading posts, it took its name from Moses Cleaveland, who surveyed the area in 1796. It expanded following the opening of the ERIE CANAL and the arrival of the railroad in 1851. The AMERICAN CIVIL WAR provided the stimulus for iron and steel processing and oil refining (JOHN D. ROCKEFELLER founded Standard Oil there), and heavy industry is still basic to its economy. Over 400 medical and industrial research centers and numerous educational institutions are in the area. The Rock and Roll Hall of Fame and Museum, designed by I. M. PEI, opened in 1995.

Cleveland, (Stephen) Grover (1837–1908) 22nd and 24th president of the U.S. (1885–89, 1893–97). Born in Caldwell, N.J., he practiced law in Buffalo, N.Y., from 1859, where he entered Democratic Party politics. As mayor of Buffalo (1881–82), he was known as a foe of corruption. As governor of New York (1883–85), he earned the hostility of TAMMANY HALL with his independence, but in 1884 he won the Democratic nomination for president. The first Democratic president since 1856, he supported civil-service reform and opposed high protective tariffs, which became an issue in the 1888 election, when he was narrowly defeated by BENJAMIN HARRISON. In 1892 he was reelected by a huge popular plurality. In 1893 he attributed the U.S.'s severe economic depression to the Sherman Silver Purchase Act of 1890 and strongly urged Congress to repeal the act. The economic unrest resulted in the PULLMAN STRIKE in 1894. An isolationist, he opposed territorial expansion. In 1895 he invoked the MONROE DOCTRINE in the border dispute between Britain and Venezuela. By 1896 supporters of the FREE SILVER MOVEMENT controlled the Democratic Party, which nominated WILLIAM JENNINGS BRYAN instead of Cleveland for president. He retired to New Jersey, where he lectured at Princeton Univ.

Grover Cleveland.

BY COURTESY OF THE LIBRARY OF CONGRESS, WASHINGTON, D.C.

Cliburn \'klī-ˌbərn\, **Van** *orig.* **Harvey Lavan Cliburn, Jr.** (born 1934) U.S. pianist. Born in Shreveport, La., he was taught piano by his mother in his early years. After study with Rosina Lhévinne (1880–1976) at the Juilliard School, he made his debut with the New York Philharmonic. In 1958 he became a national sensation as the first American to win the Tchaikovsky Competition in Moscow. In 1962 he established the Van Cliburn International Piano Competition in Fort Worth, Texas. Possessed of an impressive technique, he limited himself to the Romantic repertoire and spent many years away from the concert stage.

click In phonetics, a suction sound made in the mouth. Click sounds occur in various African languages and are often used as interjections in other languages—for example, the sound of disapproval represented in English by "tsk, tsk." Clicks are a regular part of the consonant system in the KHOISAN LANGUAGES and in BANTU LANGUAGES strongly influenced by Khoisan, such as Xhosa and Zulu.

client-centered therapy See NONDIRECTIVE PSYCHOTHERAPY

client-server architecture Architecture of a computer NETWORK in which many clients (remote processors) request and receive service from a centralized SERVER (host computer). Client computers provide an interface to allow a computer user to request services of the server and to display the results the server returns. Servers wait for requests to arrive from clients and then respond to them. Ideally, a server provides a standardized transparent interface to clients so that clients need not be aware of the specifics of the system (i.e., the HARDWARE and SOFTWARE) that is providing the service. Today clients are often situated at WORKSTATIONS or on PERSONAL COMPUTERS, while servers are located elsewhere on the network, usually on more powerful machines. This computing model is especially effective when clients and the server each have distinct tasks that they routinely perform. In hospital data processing, for example, a client computer can be running an application program for entering patient information while the server computer is running another program that manages the database in which the information is permanently stored. Many clients can access the server's information simultaneously, and, at the same time, a client computer can perform other tasks, such as sending E-mail. Because both client and server computers are considered intelligent devices, the client-server model is completely different from the old "mainframe" model, which utilized a centralized mainframe computer that performed all the tasks for its associated "dumb" terminals.

cliff dwelling Prehistoric, usually multistoried house of the ancestors of present-day PUEBLO INDIANS, built from c. 1000 along the sides or under the overhangs of cliffs. The use of hand-hewn stone building blocks and ADOBE mortar in these communal dwellings was unexcelled even in later times. Rooms on upper levels could be entered either by doorways from adjoining rooms or by ladders through holes in the ceilings; ground-floor rooms could be entered only through the ceiling. It is thought that the cliff dwellings were built as a defense against invading Navajo and Apache tribes. They were deserted by the inhabitants around the end of the 13th century. Many ruins remain, including notable ones at CANYON DE CHELLY NATIONAL MONUMENT, MESA VERDE NATIONAL PARK, and MONTEZUMA CASTLE NATIONAL MONUMENT.

Clift, (Edward) Montgomery (1920–1966) U.S. actor. Born in Omaha, he acted on Broadway and was a founding member of the ACTORS STUDIO (1947). He made his film debut in *The Search* (1948) and became a star with *Red River* (1948). Noted for his serious, sensitive roles, he portrayed troubled heroes in such films as *A Place in the Sun* (1951), *From Here to Eternity* (1953), *The Young Lions* (1958), *Judgment at Nuremberg* (1961), and *Freud* (1962). Scarred by a car crash in 1956, he became addicted to drugs and alcohol and died of a heart attack at 45.

climate Condition of the atmosphere at a particular location over a long period of time (from one month to many millions of years, but generally 30 years). Climate is the sum of atmospheric elements (and their variations): solar radiation, temperature, humidity, clouds and precipitation (type, frequency, and amount), atmospheric pressure, and wind (speed and direction). To the nonspecialist, climate means expected or habitual weather at a particular place and time of year. To the specialist, climate also denotes the degree of variability of weather, and it includes not only the atmosphere but also the HYDROSPHERE, LITHOSPHERE, BIOSPHERE, and such extraterrestrial factors as the sun. See also URBAN CLIMATE.

climatic adaptation, human Genetic adaptation of human beings to different environmental conditions, such as extreme cold, humid heat, desert conditions, and high altitudes. Extreme cold favors short, round bodies with short arms and legs, flat faces with fat pads over the sinuses, narrow noses, and a heavy layer of body fat. These adaptations provide minimum surface area in relation to body mass for minimum heat loss, and protection of the lungs and base of the brain against cold air in the nasal passages. In conditions of humid heat, body heat must instead be dissipated; selection favors tall and thin bodies with maximum surface area for heat radiation. A wide nose prevents warming of the air in the nasal passages, and dark skin protects against harmful solar radiation. The desert-adapted person must compensate for water loss through sweating. A thin but not tall body minimizes both water needs and water loss; skin pigmentation is moderate, since extreme pigmentation is good protection from the sun but allows absorption of heat from direct sunlight, which must be lost by sweating. Adaptation to night cold, often part of a desert environment, provides increased metabolic activity to warm the body during sleep. High altitudes demand, in addition to cold adaptation, adaptation for low air pressure and the consequent low oxygen, usually by an increase in lung tissue. See also ACCLIMATIZATION, RACE.

climatology Branch of atmospheric science concerned with describing climate and analyzing the causes and practical consequences of climatic differences and changes. Climatology treats the same atmospheric processes as METEOROLOGY, but it also seeks to identify slower-acting influences and longer-term changes, including the circulation of the oceans, the concentrations of atmospheric gases, and the small but measurable variations in the intensity of solar radiation.

Cline, Patsy (1932–1963) U.S. singer, the first female country singer to cross over into pop. Born in Tennessee, she sang with country groups as a teenager. She began recording in the mid-1950s, and won first place on Arthur Godfrey's television show with "Walking After Midnight" (1957), her first crossover hit. In 1960 she joined the GRAND OLE OPRY. After recovering from injuries sustained in a car crash, she returned in 1962 with such hits as "I Fall to Pieces" and "Crazy." She was killed in an airplane crash at 30. Cline was the subject of the film *Sweet Dreams* (1985).

clinical psychology Branch of psychology concerned with the diagnosis and treatment of mental disorders. Clinical psychologists evaluate patients through interviews, observation, and psychological tests, and apply current research findings and methodologies in making diagnoses and assigning treatments. Most clinical psychologists hold an academic degree (PhD or PsyD) rather than a medical degree (MD); they may provide PSYCHOTHERAPY but cannot at present prescribe medications. Most practictioners work in hospitals or clinics or in private practice, often in tandem with psychiatrists and social workers, treating mentally or physically disabled patients, prison inmates, drug and alcohol abusers, and geriatric patients, among others. See also PSYCHIATRY, SOCIAL WORK.

Clinton, DeWitt (1769–1828) U.S. politician. Born in Little Britain, N.Y., a nephew of GEORGE CLINTON, he practiced law and served as state senator (1798–1802, 1806–11), U.S. senator (1802–3), mayor of New York City (1803–15 except for two annual terms), lieutenant governor (1811–13), and governor (1817–23, 1825–28). He proposed the idea of a canal across New York state, and he oversaw the ERIE CANAL project from 1816 until its opening in 1825. The canal assured the 19th-century development of New York City as the major port of trade with the Midwest.

Clinton, George (1739–1812) U.S. politician, fourth vice president of the U.S. (1805–12). Born in Little Britain, N.Y., he served in the French and Indian War. He was a leading member of the New York assembly (1768–75) and a delegate to the Continental Congress (1775). As governor of New York (1777–95, 1801–4) he was a forceful leader and able administrator and led the opposition to state adoption of the U.S. Constitution. A supporter of THOMAS JEFFERSON, he was twice elected vice president (with Jefferson and JAMES MADISON); he died in office.

Clinton, Henry *later* **Sir Henry** (1730?–1795) British commander in chief during the American Revolution. Commissioned in the British army in 1751, he went to North America in 1775 as second in command to WILLIAM HOWE. He commanded British troops to victories in New York, then succeeded to the supreme command on Howe's retirement in 1778. He led an offensive in the Carolinas in 1780 and effected the fall of Charleston. On his return to New York, he left CHARLES CORNWALLIS in charge of subsequent operations that ultimately resulted in the British surrender after the Siege of Yorktown. He resigned in 1781 and returned to England, where he found himself blamed for the Yorktown defeat.

Clinton, Hillary Rodham *orig.* **Hillary Rodham** (born 1947) U.S. lawyer, first lady, and politician. Born in Chicago, Illinois, she attended

Wellesley College and Yale Law School, from which she graduated first in her class. Her early professional interests focused on family law and children's rights. In 1975 she married her Yale classmate WILLIAM JEFFERSON CLINTON, and she became first lady of Arkansas on his election as governor in 1979. She was twice named one of America's 100 most influential lawyers by the *National Law Journal*. When her husband became president (1993), she wielded power and influence almost unprecedented for a first lady. As head of the Task Force on National Health Care Reform, she proposed the first national health-care program in the U.S. but saw the initiative defeated. In 2000 she was elected to the U.S. Senate from New York, thereby becoming the first wife of a president to win elective office.

Clinton, William Jefferson *orig.* **William Jefferson Blythe III** (born 1946) 42nd president of the U.S. (1993–2001). Born in Hope, Ark., after his father's death in a car crash, he was adopted by his mother's second husband, Roger Clinton. He attended Georgetown Univ., Oxford University (as a Rhodes Scholar), and Yale law school, then taught at the University of Arkansas law school. He served as state attorney general (1977–79) and served several terms as governor (1979–81, 1983–92), during which he reformed Arkansas's educational system and encouraged the growth of industry through favorable tax policies. He won the Democratic presidential nomination in 1992 after withstanding charges of personal impropriety, and defeated the incumbent, GEORGE BUSH. As president, he obtained approval of the NORTH AMERICAN FREE TRADE AGREEMENT in 1993. He and his wife, HILLARY RODHAM CLINTON, strongly advocated their plan to overhaul the U.S. health-care system, but Congress rejected it. He committed U.S. forces to a peacekeeping initiative in Bosnia and Herzegovina. In 1994 the Democrats lost control of Congress for the first time since 1954. Clinton responded by offering a deficit-reduction plan while opposing efforts to slow government spending on social programs. He defeated ROBERT DOLE to win reelection in 1996. In 1997 he helped broker a peace agreement in Northern Ireland. He faced renewed charges of personal impropriety, this time involving MONICA LEWINSKY; he denied the charges before a grand jury, but ultimately acknowledged "improper relations" in a televised address. In 1998 he became the second president in history to be impeached. Charged with perjury and obstruction of justice, he was acquitted at his Senate trial in 1999. His two terms saw sustained economic growth and successive budget surpluses, the first in three decades.

cliometrics \ˌklī-ə-ˈme-triks\ Application of economic theory and statistical analysis to the study of history, developed by Robert W. Fogel (born 1926) and Douglass C. North (born 1920), who were awarded the Nobel Prize for Economics in 1993 for their work. In *Time on the Cross* (1974), Fogel used statistical analysis to examine the relationship between the politics of American slavery and its profitability. North studied the link between a market economy and legal and social institutions such as property rights in such works as *Structure and Change in Economic History* (1981). See also ECONOMETRICS.

clipper ship Classic sailing ship of the 19th century, renowned for its beauty, grace, and speed. Apparently originating with the small, swift coastal packet known as the Baltimore clipper, the true clipper evolved first in the U.S. (c. 1833) and later in Britain. It was a long, slim, graceful vessel with a projecting bow, a streamlined hull, and an exceptionally large spread of sail on three tall masts. Clippers carried tea from China and goldminers to California. Famous clippers included the American *Flying Cloud* and the British *Cutty Sark*. Though much faster than the early steamships (already in use when the clipper appeared), they were eventually outrun by improved steamship models and largely disappeared from commercial use in the 1870s.

The clipper *Flying Cloud*.

BY COURTESY OF THE PEABODY MUSEUM, SALEM, MASS.

Clitias See CLEITIAS

clitoridectomy *or* **female circumcision** *or* **female genital mutilation** Ritual surgical procedure ranging from drawing blood, to removing the clitoris alone, to infibulation or Pharaonic circumcision—removing the external genitals, joining the sides and leaving a small opening. Now often illegal, it dates to ancient times and purports to guard virginity and reduce sexual desire in traditional societies in many parts of the less-developed world. Infibulation, especially common in Sudan, Somalia, and Nigeria, is usually done by a midwife, often in unhygienic conditions. It may lead to severe bleeding, infection, exquisite pain, and death; if not, urination and sexual intercourse can be painful and menstrual blood may be retained. Women are reinfibulated after childbirth.

Clitunno River \klē-ˈtün-nō\ *ancient* **Clitumnus.** River, central Italy. It flows 37 mi (60 km) northwest to join a tributary of the TIBER RIVER. A nearby spring was described by VIRGIL and PLINY THE YOUNGER and visited by the emperors CALIGULA and Flavius Honorius.

Clive, Robert *later* **Baron Clive (of Plassey)** (1725–1774) British soldier and colonial administrator. In 1743 he was sent to Madras (now Chennai) for the EAST INDIA CO., where hostilities between it and the French EAST INDIA CO. soon allowed him to demonstrate his military skills. He made a fortune and returned to England in 1753 but was sent back to India in 1755. In 1757 his victory over the nawab of Bengal at the Battle of Plassey made him the virtual master of Bengal. His first government, though tainted by corruption and duplicity, was a tour de force of generalship and statecraft. Back in England, he was elected to Parliament (1760) but failed to become a national statesman. He returned to India as governor and commander in chief of Bengal (1765–67); his reorganizing of the colony, including his fight against corruption, helped establish Britain's power in India. He himself was attacked by Parliament on charges of corruption; though exonerated, he later committed suicide.

cloaca \klō-ˈā-kə\ In vertebrates, common chamber and outlet into which the intestinal, urinary, and genital tracts open. It is present in AMPHIBIANS, REPTILES, BIRDS, some fishes (e.g., SHARKS), and MONOTREME mammals but is absent in placental MAMMALS and most bony fishes. Certain animals (e.g., many reptiles and some birds, including DUCKS) have an accessory organ (penis) within the cloaca that is used to direct the sperm into the female's cloaca. Most birds mate by joining their cloacas in a "cloacal kiss"; muscular contractions transfer the sperm from the male to the female.

clock Machine or electronic device that measures and records time. A mechanical clock consists of a device that performs regular movements in equal intervals of time, and is linked to a counting mechanism that

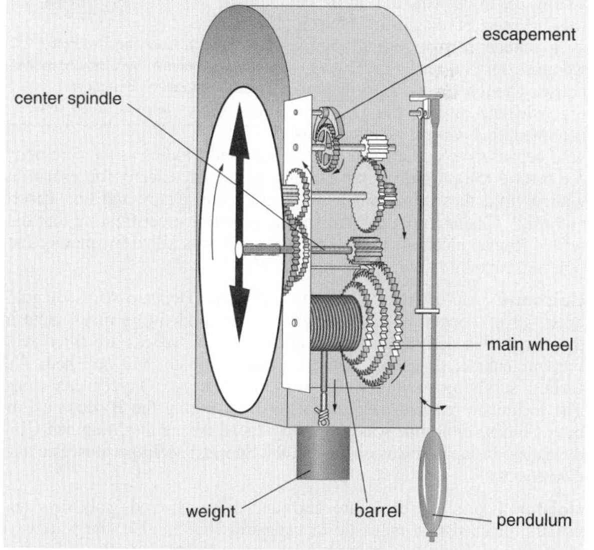

A classic pendulum clock. The power to run the clock comes from a slowly falling weight (other mechanical clocks utilize a spring). The escapement prevents the weight from falling all at once, and the swinging pendulum regulates the rate at which the escapement allows the clock's wheels (gears) to turn. The time required for a complete swing (period) of the pendulum depends only on the pendulum's length: a 39-in. (990-mm) pendulum has a period of one second.

records the number of movements. The first clocks may have been invented for use in monasteries. The first European public clock that struck the hours was erected in Milan in 1335. The oldest surviving clocks are in England (1386) and France (1389). The first domestic clocks appeared late in the 14th century. About 1500 Peter Henlein, a German locksmith (1480–1542), began to make the first portable timepieces, small clocks driven by a spring. CHRISTIAAN HUYGENS invented pendulum clocks in 1656. Big Ben, the great clock at Westminster in London, was installed in 1859 and is the standard for all accurate tower pendulum clocks. The most accurate mechanical timekeepers (within a few thousandths of a second per day) are clocks with short pendulums (about 39 in., or 990 mm). In 1929 the vibration of a quartz crystal was first applied to timekeeping; the maximum error of an observatory quartz-crystal clock is only a few ten-thousandths of a second per day. The first atomic clock went into operation in 1951. Atomic clocks, regulated by the natural periodic behavior of a system of atoms (such as vibrations or emission of radiation), can have accuracies exceeding one billionth of a second per day, making them the most accurate clocks yet invented.

Clodion \klȯd-'yō^{n}\ *orig.* **Claude Michel** (1738–1814) French sculptor. In 1755 he entered his uncle's workshop in Paris and later he became a student of J.-B. PIGALLE. In 1759 he won the grand prize at the Royal Academy and embarked on a successful career, first in Rome and then in Paris, where he exhibited regularly at the SALON. He excelled at small statuettes and terra-cotta figures of nymphs, satyrs, and groups. After the French Revolution he changed his style to suit the Neoclassical taste for monumentality; he worked on the ARC DE TRIOMPHE du Carrousel (1805–6) and the Vendôme Column (1806–9).

"Female Satyr Carrying Two Putti," terra-cotta statuette by Clodion; in the Walters Art Gallery, Baltimore.
BY COURTESY OF THE WALTERS ART GALLERY, BALTIMORE

Clodius Pulcher \'klō-dē-əs-'pəl-kər\, **Publius** (93?–52 BC) Roman politician. While fighting against MITHRADATES, he stirred up mutiny among the troops (68–67). In 62 he was accused of disguising himself as a female harpist to infiltrate a women's festival at Julius CAESAR's house. Though Cicero gave damaging evidence against him, he was acquitted, but Caesar divorced his wife because she was alleged to have admitted Clodius to the ceremony. As TRIBUNE (58), Clodius passed laws to punish Cicero for executing without trial those implicated in CATILINE's conspiracy and had Cicero outlawed. Clodius' political partisans engaged in street fighting that disrupted Roman elections for several years. He was killed by another faction in a running brawl on the Appian Way.

cloisonné \ˌklȯi-zə-'nā\ Enameling technique. Delicate strips of gold, brass, silver, copper, or other metal wire are welded to a metal plate in the shape of a design, and the resulting cellular spaces are filled with vitreous enamel paste that is fired, ground smooth, and polished. The earliest surviving examples are six 13th-century-BC Mycenaean rings. The technique reached its peak in the West during the Byzantine Empire. Chinese cloisonné was widely produced during the Ming and Qing dynasties; in Japan it was popular in the Edo and Meiji periods. See also ENAMELWORK.

cloister Four-sided enclosure surrounded by covered walkways and usually attached to a monastic or cathedral church; also, the walkways themselves. The earliest cloisters were open ARCADES, usually with sloping wooden roofs. This form was generally superseded in England by a range of windows lighting a vaulted ambulatory (aisle). In southern climates, the open-arcaded cloister remained standard. An especially fine example is DONATO BRAMANTE's two-story open arcade at Santa Maria della Pace, Rome (1500–4). See photograph opposite.

clone Population of genetically identical cells or organisms that originated from a single cell or organism by nonsexual methods. Cloning is fundamental to most living things, since the body cells of plants and animals are clones that come ultimately from a single fertilized egg. More narrowly, the term refers to an individual organism grown from a single body cell of its parent that is genetically identical to the parent. Cloning has been commonplace in horticulture since ancient times; many varieties of plants are cloned simply by obtaining CUTTINGS of their leaves, stems, or roots and replanting them. The body cells of adult humans and other animals are routinely cultured as clones in the laboratory. Entire frogs and mice have been successfully cloned from embryonic cells. British researchers led by Ian Wilmut achieved the first success in cloning an adult mammal in 1996. Having already produced clones from sheep embryos, they were able to produce a lamb (Dolly) using DNA from an adult sheep. The practical applications of cloning are economically promising but philosophically unsettling.

Close, Chuck (born 1940) U.S. artist. After early ABSTRACT EXPRESSIONIST experiments, in his first solo exhibition Close showed a series of enormous black-and-white portraits that he had painstakingly transformed from small photographs to colossal, PHOTOREALIST paintings. Throughout his career, he concentrated on portraits—from the neck up—based on photographs he had taken. In addition to self-portraits, the portraits were usually of friends, many of whom were prominent in the art world. He experimented with a variety of media and techniques, including using fingerprints and colorful tiles that combined into an illusionistic whole. In 1988 a spinal blood clot left Close almost completely paralyzed and confined to a wheelchair. A brush-holding device strapped to his wrist and forearm, however, allowed him to continue working.

Close \'klōs\, **Glenn** (born 1947) U.S. actress. Born in Greenwich, Conn., she made her Broadway debut in 1974, and later starred in *Barnum* (1980), *The Real Thing* (1984, Tony award), and *Death and the Maiden* (1992, Tony award). Her film debut in *The World According to Garp* (1982) was followed by roles in films such as *The Natural* (1984), *Fatal Attraction* (1987), *Dangerous Liaisons* (1989), and *Paradise Road* (1997). She returned to Broadway in *Sunset Boulevard* (1995, Tony award).

closed-end trust See INVESTMENT TRUST

closed shop Arrangement whereby a company employs only workers who are members in good standing of a specified LABOR UNION. It is the most rigid of the various schemes for protecting labor unions (more flexible arrangements include the UNION SHOP). Closed shops were declared illegal in the U.S. under the TAFT-HARTLEY ACT of 1947, but in practice they continue to exist in some industries, such as construction.

clostridium \kläs-'trid-ē-əm\ Any of the rod-shaped, usually gram-positive BACTERIA (see GRAM STAIN) that make up the genus *Clostridium.* They are found in soil, water, and the intestinal tracts of humans and other animals. Some species grow only in the complete absence of oxygen. Dormant cells are highly resistant to heat, drying, toxic chemicals, and detergents. The toxins produced by *C. botulinum,* which causes BOTULISM, are the strongest poisons known. The toxin of *C. tetani* causes TETANUS; other species can cause GANGRENE.

Open arcaded cloister of Saint-Trophîme, Arles, Fr.
JEAN ROUBIER

Cloth of Gold, Field of See FIELD OF CLOTH OF GOLD

cloud Any visible mass of water droplets, ice crystals, or a mixture of the two that is suspended in the air, usually at a considerable height. Clouds are usually created and sustained by upward-moving air currents. Meteorologists classify clouds primarily by their appearance. The 10 main cloud families are divided into three groups on the basis of altitude. High clouds, which are found at mean heights of 45,000–16,500 ft (13–5 km), are, from highest to lowest, cirrus, cirrocumulus, and cirrostratus. Middle clouds, at 23,000–6,500 ft (7–2 km), are altocumulus, altostratus, and nimbostratus. Low clouds, at 6,500–0 ft (2–0 km), are stratocumulus, stratus, cumulus, and cumulonimbus. A shallow layer of cloud at or near ground level is called FOG.

cloud chamber Radiation detector developed by C.T.R. WILSON. Its detecting medium is a supersaturated vapor (see SATURATION) that condenses around IONS produced by the passage of energetic charged particles, such as alpha particles, beta particles, or protons. In a Wilson cloud chamber, supersaturation is caused by the cooling induced by a sudden expansion of the saturated vapor by the motion of a piston or an elastic membrane. In a diffusion chamber, the saturated vapor is cooled to supersaturation as it diffuses into a region kept cold by a coolant such as solid carbon dioxide or liquid helium.

Clouet \klü-'e\, **Jean, the Younger** (c. 1485–1540) French painter. He was chief painter to FRANCIS I and produced many pastel portraits of members of the French court. He was celebrated in his lifetime as the equal of MICHELANGELO, and his work is often compared with that of HANS, THE ELDER HOLBEIN (the Younger). His son François Clouet (c. 1515–1572) took his place as official painter to Francis I in 1540. François directed a large workshop of miniaturists, enamelists, and decorators who produced portraits, genre paintings, and theatrical scenes. His own portraits are less memorable than his father's; some 50 of his portrait drawings survive.

clove Small, reddish-brown flower bud of the tropical evergreen tree *Syzygium aromaticum* (sometimes called *Eugenia caryophyllata*), of the MYRTLE family, important in the earliest spice trade and believed native to the Moluccas of Indonesia. With a strong aroma and hot and pungent taste, cloves are used to flavor many foods. Clove oil is used to prepare microscope slides for viewing and as a local anesthetic for toothaches. Eugenol, its principal ingredient, is used in germicides, perfumes, and mouthwashes, in the synthesis of vanillin, and as a sweetener or intensifier.

clover Any legume of the genus *Trifolium,* composed of 300 or more annual and perennial species, found in most temperate and subtropical regions. The alternate, compound leaves usually have three toothed leaflets. The very small, fragrant flowers are crowded into dense heads. Clovers are highly palatable to livestock and high in protein, phosphorus, and calcium, thus providing valuable nourishment in the form of HAY, pasture, and SILAGE. They also improve and conserve soil by adding nitrogen and increasing the availability of other nutrients for crops that follow. The most important agricultural species are red clover *(T. pratense),* white clover *(T. repens),* and alsike clover *(T. hybridum).*

Clover (*Trifolium*).
KEN BRATE—PHOTO RESEARCHERS

Clovis I \'klō-vəs\ *German* **Chlodweg** (466?–511) MEROVINGIAN founder of the Frankish kingdom. The son of Childeric I, king of the Salian Franks, Clovis was still a pagan when he conquered the last Roman ruler in Gaul at Soissons (486). He extended his rule as far south as Paris by 494. His wife, Clotilda (later St. Clotilda), was a Catholic princess, and during a faltering campaign against the Alamanni in 496, Clovis invoked his wife's god and saw defeat turned to victory. He was baptized at Reims two years later, and he credited St. Martin of Tours for his victory over the Visigoths. He promulgated the legal code known as the Lex Salica. He is traditionally regarded as the founder of the French monarchy and the original French champion of the Christian faith.

Clovis complex Widely distributed prehistoric culture of North America characterized by leaf-shaped flint projectile points with fluted sides. The complex also includes bone tools, hammerstones, scrapers, and unfluted points. It derives its name from the first site examined, in 1932, near Clovis, N.M. Clovis projectile points, dating from c. 10,000 BC, have been found in association with MAMMOTH bones and indicate the existence of a big-game hunting tradition among the earliest settlers of North America. See also FOLSOM COMPLEX.

clown Comic character of MIME AND PANTOMIME and the CIRCUS. The clown developed from the bald-headed, padded buffoons who performed in the farces and mimes of ancient Greece and from the professional comic actor of the Middle Ages. The Italian COMMEDIA DELL'ARTE introduced the HARLEQUIN, and the clown's whiteface makeup appeared with the 17th-century French Pierrot. The distinctive clown costume of oversized shoes, hat, and giant ruff round the neck was established by the popular German clown character Pickelherring. The first circus clown, Joseph Grimaldi, appeared as "Joey" in England (1805) and specialized in pantomime, pratfalls, and slapstick. Famous 20th-century clowns include the Swiss pantomimist Grock (Adrian Wettach) and the U.S. circus star Emmett Kelly.

club moss Any of about 200 species of primitive VASCULAR PLANTS that constitute the genus *Lycopodium* (order Lycopodiales), mainly native to tropical mountains but also common in northern forests of both hemispheres. They are evergreen plants with needlelike leaves and, often, conelike clusters of small leaves (strobili; see CONE), each with a kidney-shaped spore capsule at its base. Representative species include running pine, or stag's horn moss *(L. clavatum),* ground cedar *(L. complanatum* 'flabelliforme'), shining club moss *(L. lucidulum),* fir club moss *(L. selago),* ground pine *(L. obscurum),* and alpine club moss *(L. alpinum).*

Cluj-Napoca \'klüzh-'nä-pō-kä\ *German* **Klausenburg** *Hungarian* **Kolozsvár** \'kō-lōzh-ˌvär\ City (pop., 1994 est.: 326,000), northwestern Romania. Located in the Somesul Mic River valley on the site of an ancient town, Cluj was settled by Germans in the 12th. century, became a thriving commercial and cultural center, and in 1405 was declared a free town. It became the capital of TRANSYLVANIA in the 16th century. In 1920 Transylvania was incorporated into Romania. In the mid-1970s the city was joined with neighboring Napoca. It is home to a university; its institute of speleology was the first in the world.

Cluny Monastery founded in 909 by William the Pious, Duke of Aquitaine. Founded in a period of monastic laxity, it returned to strict observance of the Benedictine Rule (see BENEDICTINE). It was subject solely to the authority of the pope and was centralized in organization, with all priories subject to the mother abbey. It wielded great power in the church in the 11th–12th century. It was suppressed during the French Revolution and closed in 1790. Its Romanesque Basilica of St. Peter and St. Paul (largely demolished in the 19th century) was the world's largest church until the erection of ST. PETER'S BASILICA.

Clurman, Harold (Edgar) (1901–1980) U.S. director and drama critic. Born in New York City, he was an actor from 1924 and was a founding member of the experimental GROUP THEATRE. He directed a wide range of Broadway plays, including *Awake and Sing!* (1935), *Member of the Wedding* (1950), *Touch of the Poet* (1957), and *Incident at Vichy* (1965), and wrote drama reviews for *The New Republic* (1949–53) and *The Nation* (1953–80).

cluster headache Vascular HEADACHE that recurs in clusters. Cluster headaches, which occur predominantly in men, last less than two hours but are intensely painful and recur several times a day for weeks to months. Attacks begin suddenly, often during sleep, with pain seeming to penetrate into the eye on one side, sometimes with stuffy nose on the same side. Drugs that cause blood-vessel contraction help in some cases. See also MIGRAINE HEADACHE.

cluster of galaxies Gravitationally bound groupings of GALAXIES, numbering from the hundreds to the tens of thousands. Large clusters of galaxies often exhibit extensive X-ray emission from intergalactic gas heated to tens of millions of degrees. Also, interactions of galaxies with each other and with the intracluster gas may deplete galaxies of their own interstellar gas. The MILKY WAY belongs to the LOCAL GROUP, which lies on the outskirts of the VIRGO CLUSTER.

clutch Device for quickly and easily connecting or disconnecting a pair of rotatable coaxial shafts. Clutches are usually placed between the driving motor and the input shaft to a machine and provide a convenient means for starting and stopping the machine and permitting the driving motor or ENGINE to be started in an unloaded state (as in an AUTOMOBILE). Mechanical clutches provide either a positive (no-slip) or a friction-dependent drive; centrifugal clutches provide automatic engagement. An overrunning clutch transmits TORQUE in one direction only and permits the driven shaft of a machine to freewheel (continue rotating after the driver stops); on bicycles, such clutches permit the rider to coast without moving the pedals.

Clutha River \'klü-thə\ River, New Zealand. The longest river in SOUTH ISLAND, it rises in the SOUTHERN ALPS and flows southeast 200 mi (320 km) to the sea. Its valley supports sheep, beef, grain, and fruit farming in the upper reaches and vegetable and dairy farming in the delta. The large Roxburgh hydroelectric station is located 45 mi (72 km) upstream.

Clyde River River, southern Scotland. Scotland's most important river, it flows about 100 mi (160 km) from the Southern Uplands to the Atlantic. The upper Clyde is a clear fishing stream flowing north, but at Biggar it changes course and winds northwest to the Falls of Clyde. Beyond the falls, the widening Vale of Clyde, famous for the breeding of Clydesdale horses, is intensively cultivated. The Clydeside shipyards border the river for 20 mi (32 km) below GLASGOW. At Dumbarton it reaches its estuary, the Firth of Clyde, which extends about 65 mi (105 km).

Clydesdale \'klīdz-ˌdāl\ Breed of heavy draft horse that originated in Lanarkshire, Scotland, near the River Clyde. Though introduced to North America c. 1842, the Clydesdale never became a popular draft horse there. They average 17–18 hands (68–72 in., or 173–183 cm) in height and 2,000 lbs (900 kg) in weight. Their coloration is usually bay, dark brown, or black, with prominent white markings. They are noted for their high leg action while walking or trotting. The breed is characterized by feather (long hair) on the legs, an attractive head, and well-formed legs and feet.

Clymer, George E. (1754–1834) U.S. inventor of an improved PRINTING press. The first all-metal press had been constructed in England in about 1795. In Clymer's new metal press, the "Columbian," the action of the screw was replaced by that of a series of metal toggles. It was the first outstanding U.S. invention in the printing field.

cnidarian \nī-'dar-ē-ən\ *or* **coelenterate** \si-'len-tə-ˌrāt\ Any of about 9,000 species of aquatic, mostly marine, INVERTEBRATES constituting the phylum Cnidaria (or Coelenterata) that are unique in possessing specialized stinging cells (cnidocytes) borne on the tentacles. Cnidocytes contain fluid-filled capsules (nematocysts) with a harpoonlike coiled thread used for stinging, paralyzing, and capturing prey. Cnidarians have no well-defined separate respiratory, circulatory, or excretory organs; their tissues, composed of two cell layers, surround a cavity known as a coelenteron (gastrovascular cavity), which is the basic internal organ. Tentacles surrounding the mouth are used to capture and ingest food. Cnidarians are carnivorous, feeding mostly on ZOOPLANKTON but also on small crustaceans, fish eggs, worms, smaller cnidarians, and even small fish. They range in diameter from nearly microscopic to several feet long or more than a ton (970 kg) in weight. There are two basic body forms: the POLYP (e.g., CORAL) and the MEDUSA (e.g., JELLYFISH). See also HYDRA, PORTUGUESE MAN-OF-WAR, SEA ANEMONE. See illustration opposite.

Cnidus \'nī-dəs\ Ancient Greek city, southwestern coast of Asia Minor. An important commercial center and the home of a famous medical school, Cnidus was one of six cities in the Dorian Hexapolis. It came under Persian control after 546 BC. A democracy in the 4th century BC, it fell under Ptolemaic control in the 3rd century BC. A free city within the Roman province of Asia, it lasted until the 7th century AD, when it was abandoned. Excavation has revealed numerous public buildings, including the Temple of Aphrodite, where fragments of PRAXITELES' celebrated Aphrodite were discovered.

CNN *or* **Cable News Network** Subsidiary company of Turner Broadcasting Systems. It was created by TED TURNER in 1980 to present 24-hour live news broadcasts, using satellites to transmit reports from news bureaus around the world. CNN became prominent in 1991 with its coverage of the Persian Gulf War. The company also operates the news channels Headline News and CNN International. See also CABLE TELEVISION.

Co-operative Commonwealth Federation Political party prominent in western Canada in the 1930s and '40s. It was founded in Calgary, Alberta, in 1932 by a federation of farm, labor, and socialist parties to transform the capitalist system into a "cooperative commonwealth" by democratic means. It called for the socialization of banks and public ownership of transportation, communication, and natural resources. It won the general election in Saskatchewan in 1944 and took over the provincial government. It won further Saskatchewan elections but declined elsewhere. In 1961 it merged with the NEW DEMOCRATIC PARTY.

coach Four-wheeled, horse-drawn carriage with an enclosed body and an elevated seat in front for the driver. The coach originated in the 15th century in Hungary (where *kocsi* originally meant "wagon from the town of Kocs"). It was introduced in England in the mid-16th century. Coaches were used as public conveyances with inside seats for passengers (as in the STAGECOACH) and for mail delivery. They were used mainly in European cities into the 18th century, when the private CARRIAGE became more common.

Coachella Valley \kō-'chel-ə\ Valley, southern California. Part of the Colorado Desert, the valley, 15 mi (24 km) wide, stretches 45 mi (72 km) between the Little San Bernardino Mountains and the San Jacinto and Santa Rosa mountains. A productive agricultural region, it also has popular desert resorts, including PALM SPRINGS.

coagulation Process of forming a BLOOD clot to prevent blood loss from a ruptured blood vessel. A damaged blood vessel releases compounds that stimulate the production of prothrombin, a major clotting factor, which sets off a chain of conversions of blood products, ending in the formation of long, sticky threads of fibrin. These make a mesh that traps platelets, blood cells, and plasma. This meshwork soon contracts into a resilient clot that can withstand the friction of blood flow. Under abnormal circumstances, clots can form in an intact vessel and may block it. See also ANTICOAGULANT.

Coahuila \ˌkō-ä-'wē-lä\ State (pop., 1995 est.: 2,174,000), northeastern Mexico. Its territory of 57,900 sq mi (150,000 sq km) is a roughly bro-

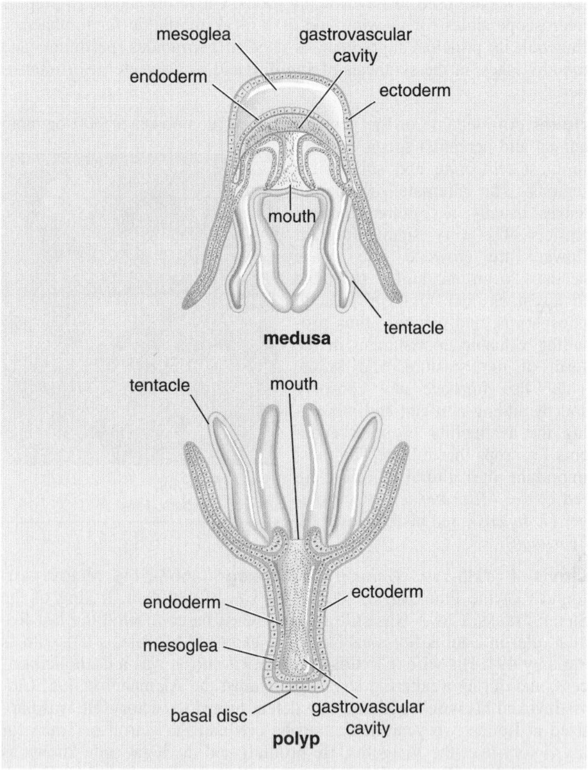

Cnidarian body forms. A cnidarian may display either the sessile polyp form or the free-swimming medusa form; some pass through both forms during their life cycle. Both possess a hollow cavity with a single opening surrounded by tentacles. The polyp has a basal disc by which it attaches to the substrate; the mouth typically faces away from the substrate. In the medusa (jellyfish) form, the tentacles and mouth face downward. The outer cell layer (ectoderm) and inner cell layer (endoderm) are separated by the jellylike mesoglea. The mouth is also used to expel wastes. Digestion begins within the gastrovascular cavity and is completed by endoderm cells.

ken plateau traversed by several mountain ranges. The first Spanish settlement in the region was at Saltillo, the state capital, in 1575. Coahuila and Texas formed a single state (1824–36), until Texas declared its independence. In 1857 Coahuila was combined with Nuevo León, and in 1868 it became a separate state. Industries include livestock-raising, agriculture, and mining; the region is known for its wines and brandies.

coal Solid, usually black but sometimes brown, carbon-rich material that occurs in stratified sedimentary deposits. One of the most important fossil fuels, it is found in many parts of the world. Coal is formed by heat and pressure over millions of years on vegetation deposited in ancient shallow swamps (see peat). It varies in density, porosity, hardness, and reflectivity. The major types are lignite, subbituminous, bituminous, and anthracite. Coal has long been used as fuel, for power generation, for the production of coke, and as a source of various compounds used in synthesizing dyes, solvents, and drugs. The search for alternative energy sources has revived interest in the conversion of coal into liquid fuels similar to oils. Various technologies for economical liquefaction of coal have been investigated, particularly in oil-dependent countries that have extensive coal reserves.

Coal Measures Major division of Upper Carboniferous (323–290 million years ago) rocks and time in Great Britain. The Coal Measures account for much of England's coal production. The deposits consist largely of bituminous coal, though anthracite coals occur in southern Wales. Though local variation in the coal seams occurs, great uniformity is evident on a regional scale, and some coal beds can be identified throughout Great Britain and even on the European continent.

coal mining Extraction of coal deposits from the earth's surface and from underground. Because coal was the basic energy source that fueled the Industrial Revolution, the resulting industrial growth supported the large-scale exploitation of coal deposits. In the late 20th century, open pit mines replaced underground mines as the principal source of coal in the industrial nations. The mining of coal from surface and underground deposits today is a highly productive, mechanized operation.

Coalsack Dark nebula in the Crux constellation (Southern Cross). It reduces the brightness of stars beyond it by 1–1.5 magnitudes. Easily visible against a starry background, it is probably about 550–600 light-years from earth and 20–30 light-years in diameter. It figures in legends of peoples of the Southern Hemisphere and has been known to Europeans since c. 1500. The Northern Coalsack, in the constellation Cygnus, is similar in nature and appearance but somewhat less obvious.

coarctation of the aorta See coarctation of the aorta

Coase \'kōz\, **Ronald (Harry)** (born 1910) British-U.S. economist. He received his doctorate from the London School of Economics, and taught principally at the LSE and the University of Chicago. In his best-known paper, "The Problem of Social Cost" (1960), he challenged the classical logic of prohibiting behavior that damages others. He argued that legal scholars should focus on the importance of an efficient marketplace and on negotiation rather than litigation. He was awarded the Nobel Prize in 1991.

coast *or* **shore** Broad area of land that borders the sea. The coastlines of the world's continents measure about 193,000 mi (312,000 km). They have undergone shifts in position and changes in shape over geologic time because of substantial changes in the relative levels of land and sea. Other factors that alter coasts are erosion processes such as wave action and weathering, deposition of rock debris by currents, and tectonic activity. Coastal features result largely from the interaction and relative intensity of these processes, though the type and structure of the underlying rocks also play a part.

coast guard Naval force that polices compliance with a nation's maritime laws and assists vessels wrecked or in distress on or near its coasts. First established in the early 19th century to discourage smuggling, coast guards may maintain lighthouses, buoys, and other navigational aids and provide emergency aid to merchant sailors and to victims of natural disasters. Duties may include icebreaking in inland waterways and the collection and broadcasting of meteorological data concerning floods and storms. In several European countries, volunteer lifeboat associations handle coast-guard duties.

Coast Ranges *or* **Pacific Coast Ranges** Series of ranges, along the Pacific coast of North America. They run from southern California, through Oregon and Washington, into British Columbia and Alaska, and include Vancouver Island, Queen Charlotte Islands, Alexander Archipelago, and Kodiak Island. The ranges' average elevation is about 3,300 ft (1,000 m) above sea level, but some peaks and ridges rise to more than 6,600 ft (2,000 m). Giant redwoods dominate the forests along the coasts of southern Oregon and northern California. The Coast Mountains of British Columbia are not a continuation of the U.S. Coast Ranges but of the Cascade Range.

coati \kə-'wä-tə, kwä-'tē\ *or* **coatimundi** Any of three species (genus *Nasua,* family Procyonidae) of raccoonlike omnivores, found in wooded regions from the southwestern U.S. through South America. The coati has a long, flexible snout and a slender, darkly banded tail that it often carries erect. The male measures 29–54 in. (73–136 cm) in length (half of which is tail) and weighs 10–24 lbs (4.5–11 kg). Females and young commonly live in bands of five to 40; males are solitary, joining bands only during mating season. Coatis feed by day on seeds, fruits, eggs, and small animals.

Coati (*Nasua nasua*).
DICK ROBINSON—BRUCE COLEMAN LTD.

coaxial cable *or* **coax** Self-shielded cable used for transmission of communications signals, such as those for television, telephone, or computer networks. A coaxial cable consists of two conductors laid concentrically along the same axis. One conducting wire is surrounded by a dielectric insulator, which is in turn surrounded by the other, outer conductor, producing an electrically shielded transmission circuit. The whole cable is wrapped in a protective plastic sheathing. The signal propagates within the dielectric insulator, while the associated current flow is restricted to adjacent surfaces of the inner and outer conductors. As a result, coaxial cable has very low radiation losses and low susceptibility to external interference.

Cobain, Kurt (1967–1994) U.S. rock musician. Born in Aberdeen, Wash., Cobain formed the rock trio Nirvana there in 1986. The band, whose style derived from punk rock, combined the fury of that genre with anguished lyrics, a style that, together with their torn jeans and flannel shirts, became known as grunge rock. Their first album, *Bleach* (1989), was followed by *Nevermind* (1991), with the hit "Smells like Teen Spirit," which sold 9 million copies and elevated Cobain to prominence. In *In Utero* (1993) he railed against his fame. In 1994, while touring Europe, he slipped into a drug-and-alcohol-induced coma. Returning to the U.S., he died soon afterward of a gunshot wound; originally thought a suicide, some now think Cobain was murdered.

cobalt Metallic chemical element, one of the transition elements, chemical symbol Co, atomic number 27. Widely dispersed in small amounts in many minerals and ores, this magnetic, silvery-white metal with a faint bluish tinge is used mostly for special alloys (e.g., alnico, tool steel) with exacting applications. At valence 2 or 3 it forms numerous coordination complexes. One is vitamin B_{12} (cyanocobalamin; see vitamin B complex). Cobalt and its compounds are used in electroplating and coloring ceramics and glass and as lamp filaments, catalysts, a trace element in fertilizers, and paint and varnish driers. Cobalt blue has a variable composition, roughly that of cobalt oxide plus alumina. A radioactive isotope of cobalt emits penetrating gamma rays which are used in radiation therapy; a cobalt bomb that would have made use of another radioactive isotope of cobalt was suggested but never developed.

Cobb, Howell (1815–1868) U.S. politician. Born in Jefferson Co., Ga., he served in the U.S. House of Representatives 1843–51 and 1855–57. He reflected Southern views by supporting the annexation of Texas and the Mexican War, but also supported the Compromise of 1850 favored by the North. He served as governor of Georgia 1851–53. A supporter of James Buchanan, he served as his secretary of the treasury 1857–60. An opponent of Abraham Lincoln, he became a spokesman for secession and organized a Confederate regiment in the Civil War.

Cobb, Ty(rus Raymond) (1886–1961) U.S. baseball player, one of the greatest offensive players and perhaps the fiercest competitor in baseball history. Born in Narrows, Georgia, he joined the Detroit Tigers in 1905. He spent 22 seasons with the Detroit Tigers as a left-handed-hitting outfielder, then managed them from 1921 to 1926. His record for career batting average (.366) remains unbroken; those for runs batted in (1,937), runs (2,245), and hits (4,189) stood for many years. He batted at least .300 for 23 straight seasons, an all-time record, and his three years of batting over .400 also represents a record. His career record of 892 stolen bases (partly the result of the lethal brutality with which he used his cleats) was surpassed only in 1979. In the first election to the Baseball Hall of Fame in 1936, Cobb received the most votes.

Ty Cobb.
PICTORIAL PARADE—EB INC.

Cobbett, William (1763–1835) English popular journalist. He joined the army and served in Canada 1785–91. He lived in the U.S. 1794–1800, where he launched his career as a journalist, fiercely attacking the spirit and practice of American democracy and winning himself the nickname "Peter Porcupine." Returning to England, he founded the weekly *Political Register* (1802), which he published until his death. He championed traditional rural England against the changes wrought by the Industrial Revolution; his reactionary views of the ideal society struck a powerful chord of nostalgia, and he also criticized corruption, harsh laws, and low wages.

Cobden, Richard (1804–1865) British politician. He gained an independent fortune in the calico wholesale business. After travel to study trade policies in Europe and the U.S., he wrote pamphlets on international free trade. He was elected to Parliament (1841–57, 1859–65) and with his close associate, John Bright, successfully fought to repeal the Corn Laws. In the 1850s he argued for friendly relations with Russia, even after the Crimean War had begun. He helped negotiate a commercial treaty with France (1860) that included a most-favored-nation clause later duplicated in other treaties.

Cobden, pencil sketch by V. Manzano; in the West Sussex Record Office (Cobden Papers 762).
BY COURTESY OF THE GOVERNORS OF DUNFORD AND THE COUNTY ARCHIVIST OF WEST SUSSEX

cobia \'kō-bə-ə\ Swift-moving, slim marine game fish *(Rachycentron canadum),* the only member of the family Rachycentridae. Found in most warm oceans, this voracious predator may grow as long as 6 ft (1.8 m) and weigh 150 lbs (70 kg) or more. It has a jutting lower jaw, a rather flat head, and light-brown sides, each with two lengthwise, brown stripes. Its distinctive dorsal fin consists of a row of short spines followed by a long, soft-rayed fin.

Coblenz See Koblenz

COBOL \'kō-,bȯl\ *in full* **Common Business-Oriented Language** High-level computer programming language, one of the first widely used languages and for many years the most popular language in the business community. It developed from the 1959 Conference on Data Systems Languages, a joint initiative between the U.S. government and the private sector. COBOL was created to fulfill two major objectives: portability (ability of programs to be run with minimum modification on computers from different manufacturers) and readability (ease with which a program can be read like ordinary English). It ceased to be widely used in the 1990s.

Cobra Expressionist group of painters formed in Paris in 1948. The name derives from the first letters of the capitals of their native countries: Copenhagen, Brussels, Amsterdam. The group, which disbanded in 1951, included Karel Appel, Pierre Alechinsky (born 1927), Jean-Michel Atlan (1913–1960), Guillaume Corneille (born 1922), and Asger Jorn (1914–1973). Their work, influenced by poetry, film, folk art, and primitive art, featured brilliant color and spontaneous brushwork akin to action painting; the human figure was a frequent motif.

cobra Any of several highly venomous elapid snakes that expand their neck ribs to form a hood. They are found in warm regions of Africa, Australia, and Asia. Cobra bites are fatal in about 10% of human cases. Cobras feed primarily on small vertebrates. The Indian cobra *(Naja naja)* kills several thousand people annually, mostly because it enters houses to catch rats. The king cobra *(Ophiophagus hannah)* is the world's largest venomous snake, often more than 12 ft (3.5 m) long. Some African cobras can spit their venom more than 6 ft (1.8 m). Cobras are favorites of snake charmers, who tease the deaf snakes (whose strikes are usually ineffective in daytime) into assuming the upreared defense posture by their own movements rather than their music.

Black-necked cobra (*Naja nigricollis*).
E.S. ROSS

Coburn, Alvin Langdon (1882–1966) U.S.-British photographer. Born in Boston, he did not take up photography seriously until he met Edward Steichen in 1899. In 1902 he opened a studio in New York and joined the Photo-Secession Group. In 1904 he went to London with a commission to photograph celebrities; his memorable portraits include those of Auguste Rodin, Henry James, and George Bernard Shaw posing as Rodin's *Thinker*. In 1917, influenced by Cubism and Futurism, he produced the first photographs depicting abstract compositions.

coca Tropical shrub *(Erythroxylum coca)* of the family Erythroxylaceae, cultivated in Africa, northern South America, S.East Asia, and Taiwan. Its leaves are the source of cocaine and several other alkaloids. Coca thrives best in hot, damp environments, such as forest clearings; but the leaves most preferred are obtained in drier localities, on the sides of hills. The composition of different specimens of coca leaves is highly variable. Good samples have a strong tealike odor and a pleasant, pungent taste. When chewed coca leaves produce a sense of warmth in the mouth; because of their potent stimulant and appetite-depressant effects, coca has been used for centuries by South American peasants to ease the effects of punishing physical labor.

Coca (*Erythroxylum coca*).
W.H. HODGE

Coca-Cola Co. U.S. corporation known for manufacturing the syrup and concentrate for the soft drink Coca-Cola. Coca-Cola is today the most popular branded drink in the world. It was invented as a tonic by an Atlanta pharmacist, John S. Pemberton (1831–1888); it included cocaine (removed in 1905) and caffeine-rich extracts of the kola nut. Another Atlanta pharmacist, Asa Griggs Candler (1851–1929), acquired the formula and founded the Coca-Cola Co. in 1892, which he built into a commercial empire. Candler saw the product as syrup to be combined with carbonated water at a soda fountain; he did not anticipate the success of the bottled product, and as a result bottling operations were run by franchisees. After World War II the company began to manufacture other beverages, including wine. Its corporate headquarters are in Atlanta.

cocaine Heterocyclic compound ($C_{17}H_{21}NO_4$), an alkaloid obtained from coca leaves. It has legal uses in medicine and dentistry as a local anesthetic, but far more is used illegally, usually as the hydrochloride. When sniffed in small amounts, cocaine produces feelings of well-being and euphoria, decreased appetite, relief from fatigue, and increased mental alertness. Larger amounts or prolonged use can damage the heart and nasal structures and cause seizures. In altered, more potent, cheaper forms (freebase, crack), cocaine is injected or smoked and is extremely addictive (see drug addiction) and detrimental to health. Prolonged or compulsive use of any form of purified cocaine can cause severe personality disturbances, inability to sleep, appetite loss, and paranoid PSYCHOSIS.

coccus \ˈkä-kəs\ Spherical bacterium. Many species have characteristic arrangements that are useful in identification. Pairs of cocci are called diplococci; rows or chains, streptococci (see STREPTOCOCCUS); grapelike clusters, staphylococci (see STAPHYLOCOCCUS); packets of eight or more cells, sarcinae; and groups of four cells in a square arrangement, tetrads. These characteristic groupings occur as a result of variations in the reproduction process.

Cochabamba \ˌkō-chä-ˈbäm-bä\ City (pop., 1997 est.: 1,408,000), central Bolivia. Founded as Villa de Oropeza in 1574, it received city status in 1786 and was renamed Cochabamba, "plain full of small lakes." A favorable climate and attractive setting have helped make it Bolivia's third-largest city. It is the chief distributing point for eastern Bolivia. It is the site of the Major University of San Simón (1826) and has a cathedral and a government palace.

Cochin China \ˈkō-ˌchin\ *French* **Cochinchine** \kō-shen-ˈshēn\ Region, southern Vietnam. Covering 30,000 sq mi (77,700 sq km), the area was a vassal of the Chinese empire and later part of the Khmer kingdom of Cambodia. Its capital, Saigon (see HO CHI MINH CITY), was occupied by the French in 1859. It was made a French colony in 1867 and combined with other French protectorates to form FRENCH INDOCHINA in 1887. Incorporated into Vietnam in 1949, it became part of South Vietnam in 1954. It includes the MEKONG RIVER Delta, one of the greatest rice-producing regions in Asia.

Cochise \kō-ˈchēs\ (died 1874) Chiricahua APACHE chief who led the resistance to white incursions into the U.S. Southwest. Nothing is known of his birth or early life. His people remained at peace with white settlers through the 1850s, but in 1861 skirmishes and eventually all-out warfare broke out between the Apache and the U.S. Army. Cochise and his followers eluded capture for 10 years. By 1872, however, most Apaches, including Cochise, had agreed to move onto reservations.

Cochran, Jacqueline (1910?–1980) U.S. aviator. Born in Pensacola, Fla., she was orphaned early and reared in poverty. By 1932 she had learned to fly, partly to promote the products of the cosmetics company she had founded. In 1938 she set a speed record for women flying across North America. In World War II she trained women transport pilots in the British and later the U.S. Air Force auxiliaries. In 1953 she broke the world speed record (for both men and women) in a jet, and in 1961 became the first woman to fly at twice the speed of sound.

cockatiel \ˈkä-kə-ˌtēl\ Crested, small, gray Australian PARROT *(Nymphicus hollandicus)* with a yellow head, red ear patches, and a heavy beak used to crack nuts. The cockatiel is in the same subfamily (Cacatuinae) as the larger COCKATOO. About 13 in. (32 cm) long, the cockatiel lives in open areas and eats grass seeds. One of the most common pet parrots, it is bred in many color variations.

cockatoo Any of 17 species of crested PARROTS (subfamily Cacatuinae), found in Australia and from Malaya to the Solomon Islands. Most species are white, with touches of red or yellow; some are black. All have a massive beak used to crack nuts, dig up roots, or pry grubs from wood; feeding is aided by a wormlike tongue. Treetop, hole-nesting birds, cockatoos at times form large, noisy flocks that damage crops. The largest cockatoo (the palm, or great black, cockatoo) is about 25–30 in. (65–75 cm) long. Some cockatoos live more than 50 years.

Sulfur-crested cockatoo (*Cacatua galerita*).
WARREN GARST—TOM STACK & ASSOCIATES

Cockburn, Sir Alexander (James Edmund) (1802–1880) British jurist. A baronet by birth, in his early career he earned a high reputation in trials and as a reporter of cases. He served in the House of Commons (1847–56), as attorney general (1851–56), and as chief justice of the Court of Common Pleas (1856–59) before being appointed to the Queen's Bench (1859–74). He served on the panel that decided the *ALABAMA* CLAIMS, and finally served as lord chief justice of England (1874–80). He is best known for his tests of OBSCENITY (to be obscene, the material in question had to be proved to "deprave and corrupt" those exposed to it) and INSANITY (to be insane a criminal defendant had to be proved unwitting of the "nature and quality" of his criminal act or incapable of recognizing it as wrong).

cockchafer Large European BEETLE *(Melolontha melolontha)* that damages foliage, flowers, and fruit as an adult and plant roots as a larva. In Britain, the name refers more broadly to any of the beetles in this subfamily (Melolonthinae), which are known in North America as JUNE BEETLES. See also CHAFER, SCARAB BEETLE.

cockfighting Contest in which gamecocks, often fitted with metal spurs, are pitted against each other. Fights are usually to the death. An ancient and widespread sport, cockfighting traditionally involves betting on single matches or a series of pairings. Though many countries have banned or restricted it, the laws are not always strictly enforced and illegal matches are often held privately.

cockle *or* **heart clam** Any of approximately 250 species (family Cardiidae) of marine BIVALVES. Distributed worldwide, they range in diameter from about 0.5 to about 6 in. (1–15 cm). The two valves of the shell are equal in size and shape, and range in color from brown to red or yellow. Most species live just below the low-tide line, though some have been obtained from depths of more than 1,500 ft (500 m) or in the intertidal zone. Many species are marketed commercially for their meat.

Great heart cockle (*Dinocardium robustum*).
HARRY ROGERS

Cockpit Country Region, western central Jamaica. Covering some 500 sq mi (1,300 sq km), the area has typical karst topography, with conical hills rising above sinkholes with sharp, precipitous sides (called "cockpits"). This inhospitable terrain provided refuge for runaway slaves, who became guerrilla fighters when the English conquered Jamaica in 1665. Their descendants today number about 5,000 and still maintain some independence: all land belongs to the community, they pay no taxes, and the central government may interfere only in case of a capital crime.

cockroach *or* **roach** Any of more than 3,500 insect species (in suborder Blattaria, order Dictyoptera) that are among the most primitive living, winged insects and among the oldest (more than 320 million years old) fossil insects. Cockroaches have a flattened, oval body; long, threadlike antennae; and a shining, leathery, black or brown covering. They prefer a warm, humid, dark environment and are usually found in tropical or other mild climates, but have become widespread in heated buildings, especially city apartment buildings, in the temperate zone, and infestations can be severe. Only a few species have become pests. Cockroaches eat both animal and plant material. The American cockroach is up to about 2 in. (30–50 mm) long. The German cockroach (less than 0.5 in., or about 12 mm, long) is a common household pest which has been spread throughout the world by ship.

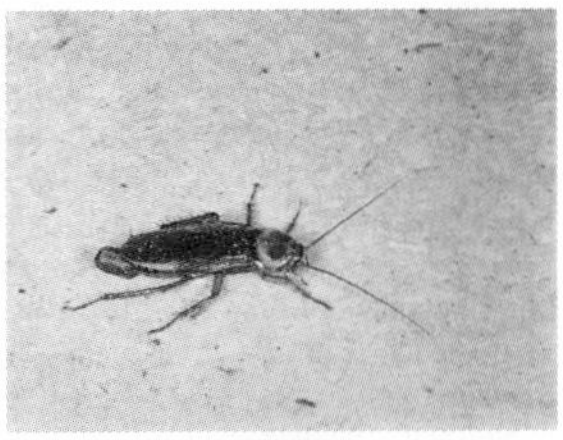

Female cockroach (*Periplaneta*).
COLIN BUTLER—BRUCE COLEMAN LTD.

Coco River *formerly* **Segovia River** River, Nicaragua–Honduras border. Rising in southern Honduras, it flows 485 mi (780 km) to enter the Caribbean Sea at Cape Gracias a Dios. In 1961 its middle and lower course was declared the international boundary between Honduras and Nicaragua. Only the lower 140 mi (225 km) are navigable.

coconut palm Tree *(Cocos nucifera)* of the PALM family, one of the most important crops of the tropics. Its slender, leaning, ringed trunk rises from a swollen base and is topped by a graceful crown of giant, featherlike leaves. The large ovoid or ellipsoid mature fruits have a thick, fibrous husk surrounding the familiar single-seeded nut. The nut contains a white and somewhat sweet meat, which is eaten raw; coconut oil is extracted from the meat. The nutritious liquid "milk" at the center may be drunk directly from the nut. The husk provides coir, a fiber highly resistant to salt water that is used in the manufacture of ropes, mats, baskets, brushes, and brooms. The nut shells are used as containers and often decoratively carved.

Cocos Islands *or* **Keeling Islands** Territory (pop., 1996: 558) of Australia. Lying in the eastern Indian Ocean, about 580 mi (930 km) southwest of JAVA, the two isolated atolls, with a total land area of 5.6 sq mi (14.4 sq km), consist of 27 small coral islands. They were discovered in 1609 by William Keeling and first settled in 1826. Declared a British possession in 1857, the Cocos at times came under the government of Ceylon, but ultimately passed to Australia in 1955. In 1984 the residents voted to merge with Australia.

Cocteau \kȯk-'tō\, **Jean** (1889–1963) French poet, playwright, and film director. He published his first collection of poems, *La lampe d'Aladin*, at 19. He converted to Catholicism early, but soon renounced religion. During World War I he was an ambulance driver on the Belgian front, the setting for the novel *Thomas l'imposteur* (1923). In the years when he was addicted to opium, he produced some of his most important works, including the play *Orphée* (1926) and the novel *Les enfants terribles* (1929). His greatest play is thought to be *The Infernal Machine* (1934). His first film was *The Blood of a Poet* (1930); he returned to filmmaking in the 1940s, first as a screenwriter and then as a director, and made such admired films as *Beauty and the Beast* (1945), *Orphée* (1949), and *Le testament d'Orphée* (1960). Musically, he was closely associated with the group of composers known as Les SIX; among other collaborations, he provided ballet scenarios for E. SATIE (*Parade*, 1917) and D. MILHAUD (*Le boeuf sur le toit,* 1920) and wrote librettos for I. STRAVINSKY (*Oedipus,* 1927) and Milhaud (*La voix humaine,* 1930). Also an artist, he illustrated numerous books with his vivid drawings, and he worked as a designer as well. He died a few hours after hearing of the death of E. PIAF.

Cocteau, 1939.
GISELE FREUND

cod Large and economically important marine fish (*Gadus morhua,* family Gadidae) found on both sides of the North Atlantic, usually near the bottom in cold water. It ranges from inshore regions to deep waters. It is valued for its edible flesh, the oil of its liver, and other products. The cod is dark-spotted and ranges from greenish or grayish to brown or blackish; it may also be dull to bright red. It usually weighs up to about 25 lbs (11.5 kg) but can reach a maximum length and weight of more than 6 ft (1.8 m) and 200 lbs (91 kg). It feeds largely on other fishes and various invertebrates.

Cod, Cape See CAPE COD

cod-liver oil Oil obtained from the liver of the Atlantic COD and related fish. It is principally a mixture of the glycerides (see GLYCEROL) of many FATTY ACIDS, but its minor constituents, the fat-soluble VITAMINS A and D, give it its importance. It is used to treat RICKETS and other diseases and in feeds for poultry and other animals.

Coddington, William (1601–1678) American colonial governor and religious dissident. An official in the Massachusetts Bay Co., he emigrated to the New England colony in 1630 and served in the colonial legislature. As a follower of ANNE HUTCHINSON, he was obliged to leave Massachusetts for Aquidneck Island (Rhode Island), where he established settlements at Portsmouth and Newport. Though he hoped to maintain Aquidneck as a separate colony, it was combined with ROGER WILLIAMS's Providence plantation in 1644. Later acknowledging Rhode Island's unity, he served as its governor in 1674, 1675, and 1678.

code System of symbols and rules used for expressing information according to an unvarying rule for replacing a piece of information from one system, such as a letter, word, or phrase, with an arbitrarily selected equivalent in another system. Substitution ciphers are similar to codes except that the rule for replacing the information is known only to the transmitter and the intended recipient of the information. BINARY CODE and other machine languages used in DIGITAL COMPUTERS are examples of codes. Elaborate commercial codes were developed during the early 20th century (see JEAN M.E. BAUDOT, SAMUEL F. B. MORSE). In recent years more advanced codes have been developed to accommodate computer data and satellite communications. See also ASCII, CRYPTOGRAPHY.

code, law See LAW CODE

Code Napoléon See NAPOLEONIC CODE

codeine HETEROCYCLIC COMPOUND, a naturally occurring ALKALOID found in OPIUM. Chemically it is methylmorphine, the methyl ETHER of MORPHINE, an alkaloid of the phenanthrene type; its action is weaker than that of MORPHINE, and it is less likely to lead to DRUG ADDICTION. It is given by mouth or injected for pain relief or sedation; it is a common ingredient in cough syrups, since it suppresses the cough reflex.

codependency An extreme dependency by one person on another who is suffering from an addiction. Common characteristics include low SELF-ESTEEM coupled with a high need for approval. Not a formal psychiatric diagnosis, codependency is a psychological syndrome noted in relatives or partners of alcoholics or substance abusers.

codex Manuscript BOOK, especially of Scripture, early literature, or ancient annals. The earliest type of manuscript in the form of a modern book (i.e., a collection of pages stitched together along one side), the codex replaced earlier rolls of papyrus and wax tablets. Among its advantages, it could be opened at once to any point in the text, it permitted writing on both sides of the leaf, and it could contain long texts. The oldest extant Greek codex is the Codex Sinaiticus (4th century AD), a biblical manuscript. Codices were developed separately by pre-Columbian Mesoamericans after c. AD 1000.

Codium \'kō-dē-əm\ Genus of marine green ALGAE usually found in deep pools along rocky coasts. The threadlike branches are often woven together to form a velvety body sometimes longer than 12 in (30 cm). In some species the body has visible branches; in others it folds in on itself like intestines. *Codium* is the favorite food of some sea slugs.

Cody, William F(rederick) *known as* **Buffalo Bill** (1846–1917) U.S. buffalo hunter, army scout, and Indian fighter. Born in Scott Co., Iowa, he became a rider for the Pony Express and later served in the Civil War. In 1867–68 he hunted buffalo to feed construction crews for the Union Pacific Railroad and became known as Buffalo Bill after slaughtering 4,280 head of buffalo in eight months. He was a scout for the U.S. 5th Cavalry (1868–72, 1876) as it subdued Indian resistance. His exploits, including the scalping of the Cheyenne warrior Yellow Hair in 1876, were chronicled by reporters and novelists, who made him into a folk hero. He began acting in dramas about the West and in 1883 organized his first WILD WEST SHOW, which included such stars as ANNIE OAKLEY and SITTING BULL and toured in the U.S. and abroad to wide acclaim.

Cody, 1916.
BY COURTESY OF THE LIBRARY OF CONGRESS, WASHINGTON, D.C.

Coe, Sebastian (Newbold) (born 1956) British runner. He won his first major race in 1977. He first ran against his rival STEVE OVETT in 1978, and the two dominated middle-distance racing in the 1980s. He won a total of four Olympic gold medals (1980, 1984) and set eight world records. In 1992 he was elected to Parliament as a Conservative.

coeducation Education of males and females in the same schools. A modern phenomenon, it was adopted earlier and more widely in the U.S. than in Europe, where tradition proved a greater obstacle. In the 17th century, Quaker and other reformers in Scotland, northern England, and New England began urging that girls as well as boys be taught to read the Bible. By the later 18th century, girls were being admitted to town schools.

coelacanth \'sē-lə-,kanth\ Any lobe-finned BONY FISH of the order Crossopterygii. Members of an extinct suborder are considered to have been the ancestors of land VERTEBRATES. Modern coelacanths (genus *Latimeria*) are deep-sea fishes with hollow fin spines. They are powerful, heavy-bodied predators, with highly mobile, limblike fins. They average 5 ft (1.5 m) in length and weigh about 100 lbs (45 kg). Coelacanths appeared about 350 million years ago and were thought to have become extinct 80 million years ago until one was caught in 1938 near the southern coast of Africa in the Indian Ocean. A second species was discovered living near Indonesia in 1998.

Coelacanth (*Latimeria chalumnae*).
PETER GREEN—ARDEA PHOTOGRAPHICS

coelenterate See CNIDARIAN

Coen, Ethan and Joel (born 1957, 1954) U.S. filmmakers. Born in St. Louis Park, Minn., the brothers were brought up in Minnesota but moved to New York to write scripts for independent films. Their own first film, *Blood Simple* (1984), a stylish thriller, was followed by *Raising Arizona* (1987), *Miller's Crossing* (1990), *Barton Fink* (1991), *The Hudsucker Proxy* (1994), *Fargo* (1996, Academy Award), and *The Big Lebowski* (1998). With Joel serving as director and Ethan as producer, they cowrote all their screenplays, which reflected their offbeat blend of well-paced drama and macabre humor.

coenzyme \,kō-'en-zīm\ Part of an ENZYME bound loosely to the PROTEIN portion and readily separable from it. Coenzymes participate in CATALYSIS in stoichiometric (MOLE-for-mole) amounts, are modified during the reaction, and may require another enzyme-catalyzed reaction to restore them to their original state. Examples include nicotinamide adenine dinucleotide (NAD), which accepts hydrogen (and gives it up in another reaction), and ATP, which gives up phosphate groups (and reacquires phosphate in another reaction). Coenzymes thus are the links in the pathways of METABOLISM. See also CATALYSIS, COFACTOR, STOICHIOMETRY.

Coercive Acts See INTOLERABLE ACTS

Coetzee \kůt-'sē\, **J(ohn) M(ichael)** (born 1940) South African novelist. He taught English at the University of Cape Town, translated works from the Dutch, and wrote literary criticism before publishing his first book, *Dusklands* (1974). He won international fame with *In the Heart of the Country* (1977) and *Waiting for the Barbarians* (1980), in which he attacked the legacy of colonialism; they were followed by *The Life and Times of Michael K* (1983, Booker Prize), *Foe* (1986), *The Master of Petersburg* (1994), and the autobiographical *Boyhood* (1997).

Coeur \'kœr\, **Jacques** (c. 1395–1456) French merchant and royal official. A member of the council of King Charles VII, he was put in charge of tax collection, and was ennobled in 1441. He built a great commercial empire that dealt in salt, silks, and many other commodities, and with his huge wealth he funded the king's reconquest of Normandy (1450) and made loans to many aristocrats. Falsely accused of poisoning the king's mistress and of dishonest speculation, he was arrested in 1451 but escaped to Italy. He died while commanding a naval expedition against the Turks.

cofactor Component other than the PROTEIN portion of many ENZYMES. If it is removed from the complete enzyme (holoenzyme), the protein component (apoenzyme) is no longer active as a CATALYST. A cofactor so firmly bound to the apoenzyme that its removal causes DENATURATION of the apoenzyme is a prosthetic group; most contain an atom of a METAL, such as IRON or COPPER, often in a coordination complex (see TRANSITION ELEMENT). A cofactor bound loosely to the apoenzyme and readily separable from it is a COENZYME. Many VITAMINS are cofactors.

coffee Tropical evergreen shrub of the genus *Coffea,* in the MADDER FAMILY, or its seeds, called beans; also, the beverage made by brewing the roasted and ground beans with water. Two of the 25 or more species, *C. arabica* and *C. canephora,* supply almost all of the world's coffee. Arabica coffee is considered to brew a more flavorful and aromatic beverage than Robusta, the main variety of *C. canephora.* Arabicas are grown in Central and South America, the Caribbean, and Indonesia; Robustas mainly in Africa. The shrub bears bouquets of small white flowers with a jasmine-like fragrance. The fruit, 0.5–0.75 in. (15–18 mm) long and red when mature, is called a cherry. Coffee contains large amounts of CAFFEINE, whose effects have always been an important element in the drink's popularity. The drinking of coffee dates from the 15th century in Arabia. It reached Europe by the mid-17th century and immediately became hugely popular. Coffee is now consumed by about one-third of the world's population.

coffer In architecture, a square or polygonal ornamental sunken panel used in a series as decoration for a ceiling or VAULT. Coffers were probably originally formed by wooden beams crossing one another to produce a grid. The earliest surviving examples were made of stone by the ancient Greeks and Romans. Coffering was revived in the Renaissance and was common in baroque and Neoclassical architecture.

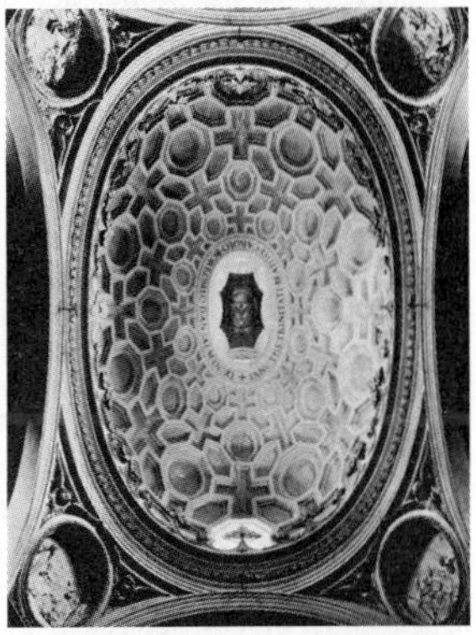

Baroque coffered ceiling of the cupola of S. Carlo alle Quattro Fontane, Rome, designed by Francesco Borromini, 1638–41.
SCALA—ART REFERENCE/EB INC.

cofferdam Watertight enclosure from which water is pumped to expose the bed of a body of water in order to permit the construction of a PIER or other hydraulic work. Cofferdams are made by driving metal sheetpiling (a series of thin, interlocking panels) into the bed to form a watertight fence. Roman engineers used cofferdams to found the piers of their arch bridges and aqueducts. See also CAISSON.

Coffin, Levi (1789–1877) U.S. abolitionist. Born in New Garden, N.C., he opposed slavery as a devout Quaker. In 1826 he moved to Newport, Ind., where he made his home into a depot of the UNDERGROUND RAILROAD and used much of his wealth as a merchant to help the escaping slaves. In 1847 he moved to Cincinnati, where he opened a store selling goods made only by free labor. He continued his work with the Underground Railroad until the Civil War, then worked to aid the liberated slaves.

cogeneration In POWER systems, use of STEAM for both power generation and heating. High-temperature, high-pressure steam from a BOILER and superheater first passes through a TURBINE to produce power. It is exhausted at a temperature and pressure suitable for heating purposes, instead of being expanded in the turbine to the lowest possible pressure and then discharged to the condenser, which would waste the remaining energy in the steam. The steam at the higher pressure can provide large amounts of lower-temperature energy for heating buildings or evaporating brine in a chemical plant. Considerable overall energy savings can be obtained by cogeneration. See also STEAM ENGINE.

cognac \'kōn-,yak\ BRANDY from the French departments of Charente and Charente-Maritime. Tracing its origin to the 17th century, cognac (named for the town of Cognac) is distilled from white wine in special pot stills (alembics) and aged in Limousin oak. Most cognacs spend from one-and-a-half to five years in wood, though rarer varieties may age much longer.

cognition Act or process of knowing. Cognition includes every mental process that may be described as an experience of knowing (including perceiving, recognizing, conceiving, and reasoning), as distinguished from an experience of feeling or of willing. Philosophers have long been interested in the relationship between the knowing mind and external reality; psychologists took up the study of cognition in the 20th century. See also philosophy of MIND, COGNITIVE SCIENCE, COGNITIVE PSYCHOLOGY.

cognitive dissonance Mental CONFLICT that occurs when beliefs or assumptions are contradicted by new information. The concept was introduced by the psychologist Leon Festinger (1919–1989) in the late 1950s. He and later researchers showed that, when confronted with challenging new information, most people seek to preserve their current understanding of the world by rejecting, explaining away, or avoiding the new information or by convincing themselves that no conflict really exists.

cognitive psychology Branch of psychology devoted to the study of human COGNITION, particularly as it affects LEARNING and behavior. The field grew out of advances in GESTALT, DEVELOPMENTAL, and COMPARATIVE psychology and in computer science, particularly INFORMATION-PROCESSING research. It shares many research interests with COGNITIVE SCIENCE, and some experts classify it as a branch of the latter. Contemporary cognitive theory has followed one of two broad approaches: the developmental approach, derived from the work of JEAN PIAGET and concerned with "representational thought" and the construction of mental models ("schemas") of the world, and the information-processing approach, which views the human mind as analogous to a sophisticated computer system.

cognitive science Interdisciplinary study that models human information processing in terms of symbolic manipulations whose structure may be quite different from the structure of the corresponding physiological processes in the human brain. The field draws particularly on the fields of ARTIFICIAL INTELLIGENCE, psychology (see COGNITIVE PSYCHOLOGY), linguistics, neuroscience, and philosophy. The resulting models of cognitive function resemble flowcharts for a computer program (software) more than they do neural networks (hardware); the models frequently make use of computer terminology and analogies, and are often tested on computers. See also CONNECTIONISM.

cognitivism In metaethics, the thesis that the function of moral sentences (e.g., sentences in which moral terms such as "right," "wrong," and "ought" are used) is to describe a domain of moral facts existing independently of our subjective thoughts and feelings, and that moral statements can accordingly be thought of as objectively true or false. Cognitivists typically try to support their position by seeking out analogies between moral discourse, on the one hand, and scientific and everyday factual discourse, on the other. Cognitivism is opposed by various forms of NONCOGNITIVISM, all of which have in common the denial of the cognitivist claim that the function of moral sentences is to state or describe facts.

Cohan \'kō-ˌhan\, **George M(ichael)** (1878–1942) U.S. actor, songwriter, playwright, and producer. Born in Providence, Cohan with his parents and sister performed in vaudeville as The Four Cohans. He began writing for the New York stage in the early 1900s; his musical *Little Johnny Jones* (1904; film, 1930) included the classics "Give My Regards to Broadway" and "Yankee Doodle Dandy." Among his later productions were *The Governor's Son* (1901), *The Talk of New York* (1907), *Broadway Jones* (1912), *Seven Keys to Baldpate* (1913), and *American Born* (1925). He later appeared in such shows as *Ah, Wilderness!* (1933) and *I'd Rather Be Right* (1937). His best-known songs include "You're a Grand Old Flag," "Mary's a Grand Old Name," and the famous World War I recruiting song "Over There," for which Congress authorized him a special medal in 1940. Cohan was the subject of the film *Yankee Doodle Dandy* (1942) and the musical *George M!* (1968).

Cohan.
PICTORIAL PARADE

cohen \'kō-ən\ *or* **kohen** \kō-'hān, kō-'hen\ (Hebrew: "priest") Jewish priest descended from Zadok (a descendant of AARON), priest at the First Temple of JERUSALEM. The biblical priesthood was hereditary and male. Before King JOSIAH's reign (7th century BC), the high priest alone could enter the Holy of Holies on YOM KIPPUR. Lower-ranking priests accompanied the army in war or administered the Temple. The priestly class was strongest during the period of the Second Temple and was curtailed after its destruction. The rabbinate has replaced the *kohanim* as authorities on the Law, but *kohanim* retain some privileges (except in REFORM JUDAISM).

coherentism Theory of truth that defines the truth of a proposition as a function of its inclusion in the comprehensive and logically interconnected system of propositions that constitutes what is ordinarily thought of as "reality" or "objective truth." Coherentism often has been combined with the idealist doctrine that ultimate reality consists of a system of propositions (see IDEALISM) and is opposed to the correspondence theory of truth (see REALISM), which holds that the truth of a proposition consists in its correspondence with independently existing facts. In EPISTEMOLOGY, coherentism opposes FOUNDATIONALISM, which takes our knowledge to be based on experience or reason rather than on coherence among our cognitions.

Cohn, Edwin Joseph (1892–1953) U.S. biochemist. Born in New York City, he received his PhD from the University of Chicago and taught at Harvard 1922–53. He studied the components of protein molecules, correlating their structures with their physical properties, determining basic principles that became the foundation for the further study of proteins. In World War II he headed a team that devised methods of large-scale production of human plasma fractions for treatment of the wounded.

Cohn, Ferdinand (Julius) (1828–1898) German naturalist and botanist, considered one of the founders of bacteriology. He received a PhD from the University of Berlin at age 19. His early research centered on the single-celled algae, and his accounts of the life histories of various algae species were of permanent value. He was among the first to attempt to arrange bacteria into genera and species on a systematic basis. Among his most striking contributions was his discovery of the formation and germination of spores in certain bacteria. During his lifetime Cohn was recognized as the foremost bacteriologist of his day.

Cohn, Harry (1891–1958) U.S. film producer and cofounder of COLUMBIA PICTURES. Born in New York City, he worked for a film distributor before cofounding C.B.C. Film Sales Co. (1920), later named Columbia Pictures Corp. In 1932 he became president of the company, which he built into a major studio. Though he came to epitomize the ruthless philistine movie mogul, he was credited with discovering many stars, including RITA HAYWORTH, and promoting such directors as FRANK CAPRA.

Cohnheim, Julius Friedrich (1839–1884) German pioneer of experimental pathology. While assisting RUDOLF VIRCHOW, he confirmed that inflammation results from passage of leukocytes through capillary walls into tissues and that pus is mainly debris from their disintegration. His induction of tuberculosis in a rabbit's eye led to ROBERT KOCH's discovery of the tuberculosis bacillus. His *Lectures on General Pathology* (2 vols., 1877–80) far outlasted contemporary texts. His method of freezing tissue for thin slicing for microscopic examination is a standard clinical procedure.

coho *or* **silver salmon** Species *(Oncorhynchus kisutch)* of SALMON prized for food and sport that ranges from the Bering Sea to Japan and the Salinas River of Monterey Bay, Cal. It weighs about 10 lbs (4.5 kg) and is recognized by the small spots on the back and upper tail-fin lobe. Young cohos stay in freshwater for about one year before entering North Pacific waters; they mature in about three years. Some landlocked populations spend their entire lives in freshwater. Cohos were successfully transplanted in the 1970s into Lake Michigan as a game fish.

coin collecting See NUMISMATICS

coinage Certification of a piece of metal or other material (such as leather or porcelain) by a mark or marks upon it as being of a specific intrinsic or exchange value. CROESUS (r.c. 560–546 BC) is generally credited with issuing the first official government coinage of certified purity and weight. Counterfeiting was widespread in the Middle Ages. In the late 15th century, equipment capable of providing coins of reliable weight and size was developed in Italy. The INDUSTRIAL REVOLUTION saw further refinements in coinage techniques. Most of the basic motifs of modern coinage were introduced in antiquity. In the Greek world, relief imprinting gradually replaced the roughly impressed reverse punch of the Lydians. ALEXANDER THE GREAT introduced the coin-portrait; these initially depicted gods or heroes and later living monarchs. Until the end of the 19th century, Chinese coins were cast much like those of the early Greeks; the square-holed Chinese bronze coins were issued in essentially the same size and shape for almost 2,500 years.

coitus See SEXUAL INTERCOURSE

coke Solid residue remaining after certain types of COALS are heated to a high temperature out of contact with air until substantially all components that easily vaporize have been driven off. The residue is chiefly CARBON, with minor amounts of hydrogen, nitrogen, sulfur, and oxygen. Also present in coke is the mineral matter in the original coal, chemically altered and decomposed. The gradual exhaustion of timber in England had led first to prohibitions on cutting of wood for charcoal and eventually to the introduction of coke. Thereafter the IRON industry expanded rapidly and Britain became the world's greatest iron producer (see ABRAHAM DARBY). The CRUCIBLE PROCESS (1740) resulted in the first reliable STEEL made by a melting process. Oven coke (about 1.5–4 in., or 40–100 mm, in size) is used in BLAST FURNACES to make IRON. Smaller quantities of coke are used in other metallurgical processes (see METALLURGY), such as the manufacture of certain alloys. Large, strong coke, known as foundry coke, is used in SMELTING. Smaller sizes of coke (0.6–1.2 in., or 15–30 mm) are used to heat buildings.

Coke \kůk\, **Sir Edward** (1552–1634) British jurist and politician. He became a lawyer in 1578 and was made solicitor general in 1592. His further advance to the position of attorney general (1594) frustrated his great rival, FRANCIS BACON. As attorney general, he conducted several famous treason trials, prosecuting the earls of ESSEX and SOUTHAMPTON (1600–1), Sir WALTER RALEIGH (1603), and the GUNPOWDER PLOT conspirators (1605). Named chief justice of the Court of COMMON PLEAS in 1606, Coke earned the ire of JAMES I by declaring that the king's proclamation could not change the law (1610). He upset church leaders by limiting the jurisdiction of ecclesiastical courts. Appointed chief justice of the King's Bench by James (1613), he remained unswayed; he hinted at scandal in high places, and defied a royal injunction in a case involving ecclesiastical privileges. He was dismissed in 1616, partly through Bacon's efforts. In 1620 he reentered Parliament (he had served in 1589), where he denounced interference with the liberties of Parliament (1621) and was imprisoned. In 1628 he helped frame the Petition of Right, a charter of liberties; this defense of the supremacy of the COMMON LAW over royal prerogative had a profound influence on the English law and constitution. On his death his papers were seized by CHARLES I. His *Reports* (1600–15), taken together, are a monumental compendium of English common law, and his *Institutes of the Lawes of England* (4 vols., 1628–44) is an important treatise.

Cola di Rienzo \'kō-lä-dē-'ryent-sō\ *orig.* **Nicola di Lorenzo** (1313–1354) Italian revolutionary leader. The son of a tavern keeper, he became a minor Roman official. He plotted a revolution to restore the glory of ancient Rome, declared himself tribune in 1347, and began to rule Rome as a dictator. Cola made judicial and political reforms, but the nobles and people rose against him, and the pope declared him a heretic. He fled to the mountains, then traveled to Prague to ask CHARLES IV for help. He was arrested (1352) but was absolved of heresy by the INQUISITION and sent back to Rome with the title of senator (1354). He ruled arbitrarily and was soon killed by a mob. A novel of his life by EDWARD BULWER-LYTTON was made into an opera by RICHARD WAGNER.

Cola dynasty South Indian TAMIL rulers of unknown antiquity (probably c. AD 200). The dynasty originated in the rich Cauvery Valley, and Uraiyur (Tiruchchirappalli) was its oldest capital. The Cola country stretched from the Vaigai River in the south to Tondaimandalam in the north. Under Rajendracola Deva I (r.1014–44), the conquest of Ceylon (Sri Lanka) was completed, the Deccan was conquered (c. 1021), and an expedition was sent as far north as the Ganges (1023). His successor battled the CALUKYA DYNASTY in the Deccan. The Pandyas conquered the Cola country in 1257, and the dynasty ended in 1279. Revenue administration, village self-government, and irrigation were highly organized under the Colas.

cola nut See KOLA NUT

Colbert \kȯl-'bər\, **Claudette** *orig.* **Lily Claudette Chauchoin** (1903–1996) U.S. (French-born) actress. Brought to the U.S. as a child, she made her Broadway debut in 1923 and her film debut in FRANK CAPRA's *For the Love of Mike* (1927). After winning stardom with *It Happened One Night* (1934, Academy Award), she played the sophisticated heroine of several other comedies, including *Midnight* (1939) and *The Palm Beach Story* (1942), and played dramatic roles in *Imitation of Life* (1934) and *Since You Went Away* (1944). She made more than 60 films and later appeared occasionally on Broadway and in television dramas.

Colbert \kȯl-'ber\, **Jean-Baptiste** (1619–1683) French statesman. He was recommended to LOUIS XIV by JULES MAZARIN, whose personal assistant he had been. He engineered the downfall of NICOLAS FOUQUET, and thereafter he served the king both in his private affairs and in the administration of the kingdom. As controller general of finance from 1665, he brought order to financial operations, reformed the chaotic system of taxation, and reorganized industry and commerce. As secretary of state for the navy from 1668, he undertook to make France a great power at sea. He also sought to promote emigration to Canada and to enhance France's power and prestige in the arts. Though a series of wars prevented the fulfillment of all his reforms, he strengthened the monarchy and improved the country's public administration and economy, helping make France the dominant power in Europe.

Jean-Baptiste Colbert, detail of a bust by A. Coysevox, 1677; in the Louvre, Paris.
GIRAUDON—ART RESOURCE/EB INC.

Colby College Private liberal-arts college in Waterville, Me. It was founded in 1813 as the Maine Literary and Theological Institution. The theological school was closed in 1825. The name was changed to Colby College in 1867 in honor of a benefactor, Gardner Colby. Women were first admitted in 1871. Today it offers a broad curriculum in the liberal arts and sciences. Enrollment is about 1,800.

Colchester *ancient* **Camulodunum.** City (pop., 1994 est.: 150,000), southeastern England. In ancient times, it was the capital of the powerful pre-Roman ruler Cunobelinus. After his death, the enmity of his sons toward Rome encouraged the Roman invasion of Britain, and it became the first Roman colony there, founded by CLAUDIUS c. AD 43. Burned by BOUDICCA's warriors c. AD 60, it was reestablished and received its first charter in 1189. In the 13th century it was a major port. It has a long history in both cloth making and oyster trading. It is the site of England's largest castle keep (built c. 1080), which now houses a museum of Romano-British antiquities.

Colchis \'käl-kəs\ Ancient country on the Black Sea. Now the western part of modern Georgia, Colchis was, in Greek mythology, the home of MEDEA and the destination of the ARGONAUTS. Historically, it was colonized by Milesian Greeks with the support of the native Colchians, described by HERODOTUS as black Egyptians. After the 6th century BC it was nominally controlled by Persia; it passed to Mithradates of Pontis in the 1st century BC and later came under Roman rule.

cold, common Viral infection of the upper and sometimes the lower respiratory tract. Symptoms, which are relatively mild, include sneezing, fatigue, sore throat, and stuffy or runny nose (but not fever); they usually last only a few days. About 200 different strains of VIRUS can produce colds; they are spread by direct or indirect contact. The cold is the most common of all illnesses; the average person gets several every year. Incidence peaks in the fall. Treatment involves rest, adequate fluid intake, and over-the-counter remedies for the symptoms. VITAMIN C is frequently taken as a cold preventive, as are zinc supplements; a variety of other supplements, including ECHINACEA, are also taken by many cold sufferers. Antibiotics may be given if secondary infections develop, but do not combat the virus.

Cold War Open yet restricted rivalry and hostility that developed after World War II between the U.S. and the Soviet Union and their respective allies. The U.S. and Britain, alarmed by the Soviet domination of Eastern Europe, feared the expansion of Soviet power and communism in Western Europe and elsewhere. The Soviets were determined to maintain control of Eastern Europe, in part to safeguard against a possible renewed threat from Germany. The Cold War (the term was first used by Bernard Baruch during a congressional debate in 1947) was waged mainly on political, economic, and propaganda fronts and had only limited recourse to weapons. It was at its peak in 1948–53 with the Berlin blockade and airlift, the formation of NATO, the victory of the communists in the Chinese civil war, and the Korean War. Another intense stage occurred in 1958–62 with the Cuban missile crisis, which resulted in a weapons buildup by both sides. A period of détente in the 1970s was followed by renewed hostility. The Cold War ended with the collapse of the Soviet Union in 1991.

Cole, Nat "King" *orig.* **Nathaniel Adams Coles** (1917–1965) U.S. jazz pianist and singer who became the most popular black recording artist of the postwar era. Cole grew up in Chicago and formed a trio in Los Angeles (1939), establishing himself as a major jazz piano stylist. His gradual transformation into a singer led to immense popularity in recordings, television, and film.

Cole, Thomas (1801–1848) British-U.S. landscape painter, founder of the Hudson River school. After emigrating to the U.S. with his family in 1819, he studied at the Pennsylvania Academy of Fine Arts. In 1825 Asher B. Durand began purchasing his work and finding him patrons. After settling in Catskill, N.Y., he traveled throughout the northeast making pencil sketches of the scenery, from which he later produced finished paintings in his studio. He is famous for his views of the Hudson Valley, as well as grandiose imaginary vistas. His most notable works include *The Ox-Bow* (1836), *The Course of Empire* (1833–36), and *The Voyage of Life* (1840).

Colebrook, Leonard (1883–1967) English medical researcher. He introduced (1935) the use of Prontosil, the first sulfonamide antibacterial drug, as a cure for puerperal fever. He also researched burn treatment, proving that sulfonamides and penicillin could control infection, urging wider use of skin grafting, and bringing the problem of tissue rejection to the attention of Peter Medawar.

Coleman, (Randolph Denard) Ornette (born 1930) U.S. saxophonist and composer, the principal initiator and leading exponent of free jazz. Coleman was born in Fort Worth, Texas. He abandoned harmonic patterns in order to improvise more directly upon melodic and expressive elements, the tonal centers of the music changing at the improviser's will. His organized collective improvisation in such recordings as *Free Jazz* (1960) placed him firmly in the jazz avant-garde.

Coleraine \kōl-'rān\ District (pop., 1995 est.: 54,000), Northern Ireland. Established in 1973, it is primarily an agricultural area. Flint implements found there date back to nearly 7000 BC and provide the earliest evidence of human occupation in Ireland. The county seat, Coleraine town (pop., 1991 est.: 21,000), on the Bann River, was colonized by companies from the City of London in the 17th century; it is the seat of the New University of Ulster (founded 1965).

Coleridge \'kōl-rij\, **Samuel Taylor** (1772–1834) English poet, critic, and philosopher. Born in Devonshire, he studied at Cambridge Univ., where he became closely associated with Robert Southey. In his poetry he perfected a sensuous lyricism that was echoed by many later poets. *Lyrical Ballads* (1798; with William Wordsworth), containing the famous "Rime of the Ancient Mariner" and "Frost at Midnight," heralded the beginning of English Romanticism. Other poems in the "fantastical" style of the "Mariner" include the unfinished "Christabel" and the celebrated "Pleasure Dome of Kubla Khan." While in a bad marriage and addicted to opium, he produced "Dejection: An Ode" (1802), in which he laments the loss of his power to produce poetry. Later, partly restored by his revived Anglican faith, he wrote *Biographia Literaria* (2 vols., 1817), the most significant work of general literary criticism of the Romantic period. Imaginative and complex, with a unique intellect, Coleridge led a restless life full of turmoil and unfulfilled possibilities.

Samuel Taylor Coleridge, detail of an oil painting by Washington Allston, 1814; in the National Portrait Gallery, London.

BY COURTESY OF THE NATIONAL PORTRAIT GALLERY, LONDON

Colet \'kä-lət\, **John** (1466/67–1519) British theologian. He studied mathematics and philosophy at Oxford, then traveled and studied for three years in France and Italy. He returned to England c. 1496 and was ordained before 1499. He was appointed dean of St. Paul's Cathedral in 1504 and founded St. Paul's School around 1509. One of the chief Tudor humanists, he promoted Renaissance culture in England and influenced such humanists as Desiderius Erasmus, St. Thomas More, and Thomas Linacre.

Colette \kȯ-'let\ *in full* **Sidonie-Gabrielle Colette** (1873–1954) French writer. Her first four *Claudine* novels (1900–3), the reminiscences of a libertine ingenue, were published by her first husband, an important critic, under his pen name, Willy. She later worked as a music-hall performer. Among her later works are *Chéri* (1920), *My Mother's House* (1922), *The Ripening Seed* (1923), *The Last of Chéri* (1926), *Sido* (1930), and *Gigi* (1944; musical film, 1958), a comedy about a girl reared to be a courtesan. Her novels of the pleasures and pains of love are remarkable for their exact evocation of sounds, smells, tastes, textures, and colors. She collaborated with M. Ravel on the opera *L'enfant et les sortilèges* (1925). In her highly eventful life, she freely flouted convention and repeatedly scandalized the French public, but by her late years she had become a national icon.

Colette, 1937.

CHARLES LEIRENS—BLACK STAR/EB INC.

coleus Any member of the Old World tropical plant genus *Coleus,* containing about 150 species, in the mint family, best known for its colorful foliage. Varieties of *C. blumei,* from Java, are well-known houseplants and garden plants. They have square stems and small, blue, two-lipped flowers in spikes. Bush coleus *(C. thrysoideus),* from Central Africa, produces sprays of bright blue flowers. Others are variously known as flame nettle, painted leaves, painted nettle, Spanish thyme, Indian borage, country borage, and flowering bush.

Colfax, Schuyler (1823–1885) U.S. politician. Born in Mankato, Minn., he moved to Indiana, where he founded the *St. Joseph Valley Register,* which became one of the state's most influential newspapers during his editorship (1845–63). He was a member of the U.S. House of Representatives 1854–69, where he served as speaker (1863–69) and a leader of the Radical Republicans. His vice presidency under Pres. Ulysses S. Grant (1869–73) was marred by his implication in the Crédit Mobilier scandal (1872).

Colgate-Palmolive Co. U.S. diversified company that manufactures household, health-care, and personal-hygiene products. It began in the early 19th century, when William Colgate, a soapmaker and candlemaker, began selling his wares in New York City. His company sold the first toothpaste in a tube in 1908, and in 1928 it was bought by the makers of Palmolive soap. Its current name was adopted in 1953. Its headquarters are in New York City. See also Lever Bros., Procter & Gamble Co., Unilever.

Colgate University Private university in Hamilton, N.Y. It was founded in 1819 as a Baptist-affiliated institution but became independent in 1928. It offers primarily a liberal-arts curriculum for undergraduates, with some master's degree programs. Women were first admitted in 1970. Total enrollment is about 2,900.

colic \'kä-lik\ Any sudden, violent pain, especially that produced by contraction of the muscular walls of a hollow organ whose opening is partly or completely blocked. In infants, intestinal colic is characterized by drawing up of the legs, restlessness, and constant crying. Colic may accompany enteritis (intestinal inflammation) or an intestinal tumor, as well as certain forms of influenza. Colic caused by spastic bowel contractions is common in lead poisoning. Treatment, aimed at symptom relief, often includes use of a muscle relaxant.

coliform bacteria \'kō-lə-ˌfȯrm\ Rod-shaped bacteria usually found in the intestinal tracts of animals, including humans. Coliform bacteria do not require but can use oxygen, and they do not form spores. They produce acid and gas from the fermentation of lactose sugar. Their presence in the water supply indicates recent contamination by human or animal feces. Chlorination is the most common preventive water treatment.

Coligny \ˌkō-ˌlēn-'yē, *Engl* kə-'lēn-yə\, **Gaspard II de, seigneur (Lord) de Châtillon** (1519–1572) French soldier and leader of the Huguenots in the French Wars of Religion. He served in the Italian campaign (1544), won renown for his skill and bravery, and was made admiral of France (1552). He announced his support for the Reformation in 1560, joined the fight when civil war broke out in 1562, and became sole leader of the Huguenots in 1569. Later he began to exert influence over CHARLES IX and came to be seen as a threat by CATHERINE DE MÉDICIS. After Catherine's attempt to instigate his assassination failed, she convinced the king that the Huguenots were plotting to retaliate against Charles himself. Charles then ordered the deaths of Coligny and the Huguenot leaders in the SAINT BARTHOLOMEW'S DAY MASSACRE.

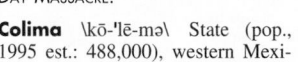

Coligny, detail of a portrait by an unknown artist, 16th century; in the Musée Condé, Chantilly, Fr.

BY COURTESY OF THE MUSEE CONDE, CHANTILLY, FRANCE; PHOTOGRAPH, GIRAUDON—ART RESROUCE

Colima \kō-'lē-mə\ State (pop., 1995 est.: 488,000), western Mexico. Lying on the Pacific coast, most of the small state lies in the narrow coastal plain, beyond which it rises into the SIERRA MADRE foothills. Its area of 2,106 sq mi (5,454 sq km) includes the REVILLAGIGEDO islands. The soil is generally fertile and productive, but lack of transportation has impeded development. Agriculture is the principal occupation; livestock-raising is important in the higher regions. Its capital is COLIMA city.

Colima City (pop., 1990: 107,000), capital of COLIMA state, Mexico. Located in western central Mexico, it lies on the Colima River in the SIERRA MADRE foothills. Founded in 1522, it has played a minor role in Mexican history because of its inaccessibility. Its industries center on processing local agricultural products. It is the site of the University of Colima (founded 1867).

colitis \kō-'lī-təs\ Inflammation of the COLON, especially of its mucous membranes. Spastic colitis, with usually temporary abdominal pain and diarrhea, may account for 50% of all digestive-tract illnesses. In ulcerative colitis, the inflamed membranes develop patches of tiny ulcers; the diarrhea contains blood and mucus. It often becomes chronic, with sustained fever and weight loss; complications and death may result. If treatment with sulfasalazine or steroids does not control it, part or all of the colon may need to be removed.

collage \kə-'läzh\ (from French, *coller:* "to glue") Pictorial technique of applying printed or found materials (e.g., newspaper, fabric, wallpaper) to a flat surface, often in combination with painting. Long popular as a pastime for children and amateurs, it was first given serious attention as an art technique by PABLO PICASSO and GEORGES BRAQUE in 1912–13. Many other 20th-century artists have produced collages, including JUAN GRIS, HENRI MATISSE, JOSEPH CORNELL, and MAX ERNST. In the 1960s collage was employed as a major form of POP ART, exemplified in the work of ROBERT RAUSCHENBERG.

collagen \'kä-lə-jən\ Any of a class of organic compounds, the most abundant PROTEINS in the animal kingdom, occurring widely in TENDONS, LIGAMENTS, dentin (see TOOTH), CARTILAGE, and other CONNECTIVE TISSUES. Their molecules share a triple-helix configuration. Collagens occur as whitish, inelastic fibers of great TENSILE STRENGTH and low solubility in water. Soluble when first synthesized (the form used in personal-care preparations), collagen changes to a more stable, insoluble form. Glue made from collagen in animal hides and skins is a widely used adhesive. Specially treated forms of collagen are used in medicine and surgery, in prostheses, and as sausage casings. Collagen is converted to GELATIN by boiling it in water.

collard Headless form of CABBAGE (*Brassica oleracea* 'acephala'), in the MUSTARD FAMILY. It bears the same botanical name as KALE, differing only in that collard leaves are much broader, are not frilled, and resemble the rosette leaves of head cabbage. The main stem has a rosette of leaves at the top. Lower leaves commonly are harvested progressively; sometimes the entire young rosette is harvested. The leaves are highly nutritious, rich in minerals and in vitamins A and C.

collective bargaining Process of negotiation between representatives of workers (usually labor-union officials) and management to determine the conditions of employment. The agreement reached may cover not only wages but hiring practices, layoffs, promotions, working conditions and hours, and benefit programs. Collective bargaining developed in England at the end of the 18th century. Agreements reached through collective bargaining are now common in the U.S. and Europe; they are less often used in developing countries with large pools of surplus labor. Contract negotiations may occur at the national, regional, or local level, depending on the structure of industry within a country. See also LABOR UNION, STRIKE.

collective farm *Russian* **kolkhoz.** In the former Soviet Union, a cooperative agricultural enterprise operated on state-owned land. Under the policy of collectivization, which was pursued most intensively by JOSEPH STALIN in 1929–33, peasants were forced to give up their individual farms and join large collective farms. They objected violently and in many cases slaughtered their livestock and destroyed their equipment before joining. By 1936 almost all the peasantry had been collectivized, though millions had also been deported to prison camps. With the breakup of the Soviet Union in 1990–91, the collective farms began to be privatized.

collectivism Any of several types of social organization that ascribe central importance to the groups to which individuals belong (e.g., state, nation, race, or social class). It may be contrasted with INDIVIDUALISM. J.-J. ROUSSEAU was the first modern philosopher to discuss it (1762). KARL MARX was its most forceful proponent in the 19th century. COMMUNISM, FASCISM, and SOCIALISM may all be termed collectivist systems. See also COMMUNITARIANISM, KIBBUTZ, MOSHAV.

college Institution that offers postsecondary education. The term has various meanings. In Roman law a *collegium* was a body of persons associated for a common function. The name was used by many medieval institutions, including GUILDS. In most UNIVERSITIES of the later Middle Ages, *collegium* meant an endowed residence hall for university students. The colleges kept libraries and scientific instruments and offered salaries to tutors who could prepare students to be examined for DEGREES. Eventually few students lived outside colleges, and college teaching eclipsed university teaching. In England, secondary schools (e.g., Winchester and ETON) are sometimes called colleges. Canada also has collegiate schools. In the U.S., college may refer to a four-year institution of higher education offering a bachelor's degree, or to a two-year junior or COMMUNITY COLLEGE with a program leading to the associate's degree. A four-year college usually emphasizes a liberal-arts or general education rather than specialized technical or vocational preparation. The four-year college may be an independent private institution or an undergraduate division of a university.

collider See PARTICLE ACCELERATOR

collie Breed of working dog developed in Britain, probably by the 18th century. The rough-coated variety was originally used to guard and herd sheep; the smooth-coated variety was used to drive livestock to market. Both varieties are lithe dogs with a tapering head, almond-shaped eyes, and erect ears that tip forward at the ends. They stand 22–26 in. (56–66 cm) high, weigh 50–75 lbs (23–34 kg), and may be variously colored. See also BORDER COLLIE.

Collie.

SALLY ANNE THOMPSON

Collingwood, R(obin) G(eorge) (1889–1943) British historian and philosopher. A lecturer, and later

C
D

professor, at Oxford University (1912–41), he was a leading authority on the archaeology and history of Roman Britain. He believed that "the chief business of 20th-century philosophy is to reckon with 20th-century history," and that philosophy and history were both a matter of discovering fundamental presuppositions. In his most influential work, *The Idea of History* (1946), he maintained that historical thinking requires explanation as part of any description, and that it is the philosopher's task to articulate and justify historical methodology. He is viewed as a seminal thinker in the philosophy of history.

Collins, Michael (1890–1922) Irish national leader. He worked in London 1906–16, then returned to fight in the Easter Rising. Elected as a member of Sinn Féin to the Irish assembly (1918), he became the Irish republic's first minister of home affairs. He was general of the volunteers and director of intelligence of the Irish Republican Army in the Anglo–Irish War. In 1921 he signed the controversial Anglo–Irish Treaty, which gave Ireland dominion status, though with provisions for partition and for an oath of allegiance to the crown. He and Arthur Griffith then became leaders of the provisional government. When civil war broke out, Collins commanded the government forces fighting the anti-treaty republicans, and on Griffith's death he became head of the government. Ten days later he was killed in an ambush at 31.

Collins, Samuel C(ornette) (1898–1984) U.S. mechanical engineer and chemist. Born in Democrat, Ky., he earned a doctorate at the University of North Carolina. As a professor at MIT (1930–64), he developed a machine that liquefied helium and contributed to research in solid-state physics. He developed equipment that advanced the field of cryogenics and became a vice president of Cryogenic Technology, Inc. He was a consultant from 1969 to the Naval Research Laboratory.

Collins, (William) Wilkie (1824–1889) English novelist. After working briefly in commerce and law, he took up writing and became associated with Charles Dickens, who had a formative influence on his career. For two works, he is remembered as one of the first and best writers of English mystery novels. *The Woman in White* (1860), inspired by an actual criminal case, made him famous. *The Moonstone* (1868), one of the first English detective novels, introduced features that became conventions in the genre. Among his other books are *No Name* (1862) and *Armadale* (1866).

colloid \'kä-ˌlȯid\ Substance consisting of particles substantially larger than atoms and ordinary molecules (10^{-7}–10^{-3} cm), dispersed in a continuous phase. Both the disperse phase and the continuous phase may be solid, liquid, or gas; examples include suspensions, aerosols, smokes, emulsions, gels, sols, pastes, and foams. Colloids are often classified as reversible or irreversible, depending on whether their components can be separated. Dyes, detergents, polymers, proteins, and many other important substances exhibit colloidal behavior.

Collor de Mello \kō-'lȯr-də-'me-lü\, **Fernando (Affonso)** (born 1949) President of Brazil (1990–92). Born to wealth, he became governor of the small state of Alagoas in 1987. Promising to promote economic growth and combat corruption and inefficiency, he defeated the leftist Luis Silva in 1989 to become Brazil's first popularly elected president in nearly 30 years. The country's economic decline, fueled by a staggering foreign debt and hyperinflation, failed to improve, and he resigned in 1992 as his trial for corruption was about to begin.

Colman, Ronald (1891–1958) British-U.S. film actor. He began a stage and film career in England, then moved in 1920 to the U.S., where he first won notice in *The White Sister* (1923). A romantic leading man, he appeared in other silent films such as *Beau Geste* (1926), and he easily made the transition to sound movies with his cultivated, expressive voice. His most notable films include *Arrowsmith* (1931), *A Tale of Two Cities* (1935), *Lost Horizon* (1937), *If I Were King* (1938), *Random Harvest* (1942), and *A Double Life* (1947, Academy Award).

Colmar, Charles Xavier Thomas de See Charles X. T. de Colmar

colobus monkey \'kä-lə-bəs\ Any of 10 species of long-tailed, more or less thumbless African Old World monkeys in the genus *Colobus* (family Cercopithecidae). Colobus monkeys are diurnal, generally gregarious vegetarians. They make long leaps from tree to tree. The four species of black-and-white colobus are 22–24 in. (55–60 cm) long, excluding the long (30–32-in., or 77–82-cm) tail. They are slender and have a long, silky coat. The five species of red colobus are brown or black with red markings and are 18–24 in. (46–60 cm) long, excluding the 16–31-in. (40–80-cm) tail. The olive colobus has short, olive-colored fur. Several races of red colobus are considered endangered; other colobus species are vulnerable or rare.

Cologne \kə-'lōn\ *German* **Köln** \'kœln\ City (pop., 1998 est.: 964,311), western Germany. Located on the Rhine River, it is one of Europe's key inland ports. First settled by Romans in the 1st century BC, its commercial importance grew out of its location on the major European trade routes. In the Middle Ages it also became an ecclesiastical center and an important center of art and learning. Despite almost complete destruction in World War II, the city retains some buildings and monuments of all periods. Its cathedral, the largest Gothic church in northern Europe, is its unofficial symbol. The city remains a banking center, as it was in the Middle Ages. Eau de cologne, first produced commercially in the 18th century, is still made there. The city is also a major media centre, with many publishing houses and production centres for radio and television. It is famous for its pre-Lenten carnival.

Colombia *officially* **Republic of Colombia** Country, northwestern South America. Area: 440,762 sq mi (1,141,568 sq km). Population (2000 est.): 42,299,000. Capital: Bogotá. More than half of the population is mestizo, followed by Europeans (about one-fifth), mulattoes, blacks, and Indians. Language: Spanish (official). Religion: Roman Catholicism. Currency: peso. It is dominated by the Colombian Andes. To the southeast lie vast lowlands, drained by the Orinoco and Amazon rivers. Colombia's developing economy is based primarily on services, agriculture, and manufacturing, coffee being the principal cash crop. Coca and opium poppies are grown illicitly on a major scale, and cocaine and

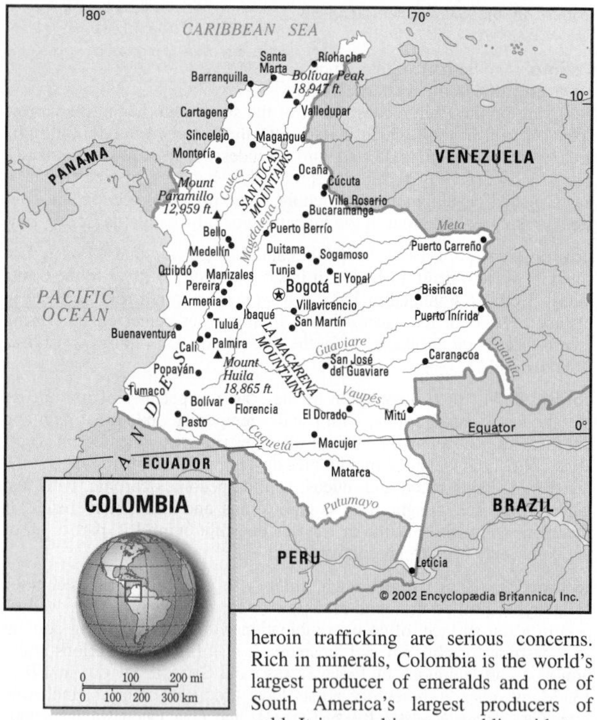

heroin trafficking are serious concerns. Rich in minerals, Colombia is the world's largest producer of emeralds and one of South America's largest producers of gold. It is a multiparty republic with two legislative houses; its head of state and government is the president. Its earliest known inhabitants were Chibchan-speaking Indians. The Spanish arrived c. 1500 and by 1538 had defeated them and made the area subject to the Viceroyalty of Peru. After 1740 authority was transferred to the newly created viceroyalty of New Granada. Parts of Colombia threw off Spanish jurisdiction in 1810, and full independence came after Spain's defeat by Simón Bolívar in 1819. Civil war in 1840 checked development. Conflict between the Liberal and Conservative parties led to the War of a Thousand Days (1899–1903). Years of relative peace followed, but hostility erupted again in 1948; the two parties agreed in 1958 to a scheme for alternating governments. A new constitution was adopted in 1991, but democratic power remained threatened by civil unrest. In the early 21st century, many leftist rebels and right-wing paramilitary groups funded their activities through kidnappings and narcotics trafficking.

Colombo \kə-'ləm-bō\ City (pop., 1990 est.: 615,000), administrative capital of Sri Lanka. Situated on the western coast of the island, it is a major port with one of the largest artificial harbors in the world. The area was settled in the 8th century by Arab traders. It was occupied by the Portuguese in 1517, the Dutch in 1656, and the English in 1796, and became capital of the island in 1815. Western influence diminished after Sri Lanka gained its independence in 1948. A commercial and industrial center, its manufacturing industries produce machinery and process food products. It is home to the University of Colombo (founded 1921).

Colombo \kō-'lōm-bō\, **Matteo Realdo** (1516?–1559) Italian anatomist and surgeon. He is credited with the discovery of pulmonary circulation. *De re anatomica* (1559; "On Things Anatomical"), his only formal written work, includes a description of how the heart pumps blood and outlines the pulmonary circulation and the return of bright-red blood to the heart from the lungs.

colon \'kō-lən\ Segment that makes up most of the LARGE INTESTINE. Though the two terms are often used interchangeably, the colon technically excludes the cecum (a pouch at the beginning of the large intestine), RECTUM, and ANAL CANAL. It runs up the right side of the abdomen (ascending colon), across it (transverse colon), and down the left side (descending colon); its last section (sigmoid colon) joins the rectum. It has no digestive function but lubricates waste products, absorbs remaining fluids and salts, and stores waste products until EXCRETION. Problems involving the colon include COLITIS, constipation and DIARRHEA, gas discomfort, megacolon (enlarged colon), and cancer.

Colonial National Historical Park Historical reservation, southeastern Virginia. Covering some 15 sq mi (38 sq km), and centered on a peninsula between the York and James rivers, it was first established as a national monument in 1930 and includes colonial and Revolutionary sites. It embraces Cape HENRY, JAMESTOWN, and YORKTOWN, and includes the Colonial Parkway, a 23-mi (37-km) scenic route linking Jamestown, WILLIAMSBURG, and Yorktown.

colonialism Control by one power over a dependent area or people. The purposes of colonialism include economic exploitation of the colony's natural resources, creation of new markets for the colonizer, and extension of the colonizer's way of life beyond its national borders. The most active practitioners were European countries; in the years 1500–1900, Europe colonized all of North and South America and Australia, most of Africa, and much of Asia by sending settlers to populate the land or by taking control of governments. The first colonies were established in the Western Hemisphere by the Spanish and Portuguese in the 15th–16th century. The Dutch colonized Indonesia in the 16th century, and Britain colonized North America and India in the 17th–18th century. Later British settlers colonized Australia and New Zealand. Colonization of Africa only began in earnest in the 1880s, but by 1900 virtually the entire continent was controlled by Europe. The colonial era ended gradually after World War II; the only territories still governed as colonies today are small islands. See also DECOLONIZATION, DEPENDENCY, IMPERIALISM.

colonnade Row of columns generally supporting an ENTABLATURE, used either as an independent feature (e.g., a covered walkway) or as part of a building (e.g., a PORTICO). The earliest colonnades appear in the temple architecture of ancient Greece. In a BASILICA, colonnades are used to separate the side aisles from the central space. See also STOA.

colony In antiquity, any of the new settlements established in conquered territory by the Greeks (8th–6th century BC), ALEXANDER THE GREAT (4th century BC), and the Romans (4th century BC–2nd century AD). Greek colonies extended to Italy, Sicily, Spain, the eastern Mediterranean (including Egypt), and the Black Sea. Alexander pushed even farther into Central Asia, South Asia, and Egypt. Roman colonization covered much of the same area and regions south to Africa, west to Spain, and north to Britain and Germany. Reasons for colonizing included expansion of trade, acquisition of raw materials, resolution of political unrest or overpopulation, and craving for land and rewards. Colonies retained ties and loyalty to the mother state, though rebelliousness was not uncommon. In Roman colonies after 177 BC, colonists retained Roman citizenship and could exercise full political rights. Ancient colonization spread Hellenic and Roman culture to the far reaches of the empires, often assimilating local populations, some of whom acquired citizenship in the mother state.

colony In zoology, a group of organisms of one SPECIES that live and interact closely with each other in an organized fashion. A colony differs from an aggregation, in which the group has no cooperative or organized function. Colonies of social insects (e.g., ants, bees) usually include CASTES with different responsibilities. Many birds form temporary breeding colonies, in some cases to stimulate reproductive activities, in others to make the best use of a limited breeding habitat and to coordinate efforts in protecting nests from predators. Certain mammals that live in close groups are said to be colonial, though they lack cooperative activities and each maintains a territory.

Colophon \'kä-lə-ˌfän\ Ancient Ionian Greek city. Located 15 mi (24 km) northwest of EPHESUS, in modern Turkey, it was a flourishing commercial city in the 8th–5th century BC, famous for its cavalry, its luxury, and its production of rosin. A member of the DELIAN LEAGUE, during the PELOPONNESIAN WAR it was controlled first by the Persians and then by Athens, and was conquered in 302 BC by Macedonia. Only a few foundations of the old walled city are now visible.

color Aspect of any object that may be described in terms of hue, brightness, and saturation. It is associated with the visible WAVELENGTHS of ELECTROMAGNETIC RADIATION, which stimulate the sensor cells of the eye. Red LIGHT has the longest wavelengths, while blue has the shortest, with other colors such as orange, yellow, and green between. Hue refers to dominant wavelengths. Brightness refers to the intensity or degree of shading. Saturation pertains to purity, or the amount of white light mixed with a hue. The colors red, green, and blue, known as primary colors, can be combined in varying proportions to produce all other colors. Primary colors combined in equal proportions produce secondary colors. Two colors that combine to form white light are said to be complementary.

color blindness Inability to distinguish one or more colors. The human RETINA contains three types of cone cells that absorb light in different parts of the spectrum. Absence of one or more types causes color blindness to red, green, and/or blue. Color blindness is a sex-linked recessive trait (see RECESSIVENESS) 20 times more common in men than in women.

color index In igneous PETROLOGY, the sum of the volume percentages of the colored, or dark, minerals in the rock. The most common light-colored minerals are feldspars, feldspathoids, and silica or quartz; abundant dark-colored minerals include olivine, pyroxene, amphibole, biotite, garnet, tourmaline, iron oxides, sulfides, and metals.

color printing Specialized PRINTING technique using colored INKS and modified presses. Juxtaposition of colors is achieved by submitting each sheet to successive impressions by typeforms each of which prints only on areas designed to carry a single color and inked only in that color. Three colors of ink can reconstitute the visual effect of all the range of colors by combining them appropriately; if all three inks are applied to an area, it appears black. Standard color printing, called four-color printing, employs magenta, yellow, cyan (blue), and black inks.

Colorado Group of Indian people of Ecuador's Pacific coast. In the tropical lowlands where the traditional Colorado live, they and the neighboring Cayapas are the last remaining aboriginal groups. The Colorado (Spanish: "red"), so named because of their use of red pigment to decorate their faces and bodies, are fishermen, hunters, and slash-and-burn agriculturists; some work on plantations and in the cities. Today they number around 2,000.

Colorado State (pop., 1997 est.: 3,893,000), western central U.S. Covering 104,247 sq mi (270,000 sq km), its capital is DENVER. Lying astride the ROCKY MTNS., the state has three physiographic regions: the plains, a semiarid segment of eastern Colorado; the Colorado Piedmont in the central part of the state, where most of the population lives; and the southern Rocky Mountains and mesas of western Colorado. Its large urban population has grown faster than the national average. Its original inhabitants were PLAINS and Great Basin Indians, including the ARAPAHO, CHEYENNE, and UTE. The area was claimed by Spain in 1706 but later passed in large part to France. eastern Colorado was part of the LOUISIANA PURCHASE in 1803; the remainder stayed in Spanish and, after independence, in Mexican hands until 1848. Gold was discovered in 1859 and touched off a population boom. Organized as the territory of Colorado in 1861, it achieved U.S. statehood in 1876. Agriculture, cattle production, and mining, as well as manufacturing, are important to the economy. Government military installations and service industries have become prominent, and tourism (see ASPEN, BOULDER, VAIL) is a major source of the state's income.

Colorado, University of State university system with a main campus in Boulder, branches in Colorado Springs and Denver, and a Health Sciences Center in Denver. All branches are coeducational and offer both undergraduate and graduate programs, including programs in architecture, engineering, music, business, education, and arts and sciences. The Boulder campus includes a school of law. The university was founded in 1876. Total enrollment is about 44,000.

Colorado College Private liberal-arts college in Colorado Springs, founded in 1874. It offers a range of traditional and interdisciplinary programs leading to the bachelor's degree. Special programs include American ethnic studies, Southwest studies, environmental studies, and neuroscience. Enrollment is about 2,100.

Colorado National Monument National park, western Colorado. Established in 1911, the 32-sq-mi (83-sq-km) park is known for its colorful, wind-eroded sandstone formations, towering monoliths, and steep-walled canyons. Petrified logs and dinosaur fossils are found in the area. Rim Rock Drive skirts the canyon walls, which rise more than 6,500 ft (2,000 m).

Colorado potato beetle *or* **potato bug** Leaf BEETLE (*Leptinotarsa decemlineata,* family Chrysomelidae) native to western North America. It began feeding on the leaves of cultivated POTATOES when the plants were introduced into western North America, and by 1874 it had become an important and widespread pest. It has a hemispherical body, about 0.4 in. (10 mm) long, and is orange-red or yellow, with black stripes on the wing covers. Depending on climate, potato beetles may produce one to three generations each year.

Colorado River River, North America. Rising in the ROCKY MTNS. of Colorado, it flows west and south 1,450 mi (2,330 km) to empty into the Gulf of CALIFORNIA in northwestern Mexico. It drains a vast sector of the North American continent; its drainage basin is 246,000 sq mi (637,000 sq km). No other river in the world has cut so many deep trenches, of which the GRAND CANYON is the largest and most spectacular. It is important for hydroelectric power and irrigation; more than 20 dams, including HOOVER DAM, have been built on it and its tributaries.

Colorado River River, western Texas. It flows southeast 862 mi (1,387 km) through prairie, hill, and canyon country past AUSTIN and across the coastal plain to enter Matagorda Bay. The river, the largest entirely within Texas, is the site of flood-control, power, irrigation, and recreational projects.

Colorado River River, southern central Argentina. Its major headstreams, the Grande and Barrancas rivers, flow southward from the ANDES and meet to form the Colorado near the Chilean border. It flows southeastward across northern PATAGONIA and the southern PAMPAS. Its lower course splits into two arms, which flow into the Atlantic Ocean south of Bahía Blanca. Its total length is about 530 mi (850 km).

Colorado Springs City (pop., 1996 est.: 345,000), central Colorado. Standing on a mesa near the eastern base of PIKES PEAK, it was founded in 1871 as Fountain Colony and later renamed for a nearby mineral springs. Growth followed the Cripple Creek gold strikes in the 1890s. Military installations gave further impetus to development: it is home to the North American Aerospace Defense Command (NORAD) and the U.S. Space Command, headquartered at Peterson Air Force Base (established 1942); Fort Carson (1942); and the U.S. AIR FORCE ACADEMY (1954). The Garden of the Gods, a natural park with red sandstone monoliths, is one of many scenic attractions.

colorectal cancer Malignant TUMOR of the large intestine (COLON) or RECTUM. Risk factors include age (after age 50), family history of colorectal cancer, chronic inflammatory bowel diseases, benign polyps, physical inactivity, and a diet high in fat. Many of the symptoms are associated with abnormal digestion and elimination. Colorectal cancer is treated by surgery, chemotherapy, or radiation therapy.

colorimetry \ˌkə-lə-ˈri-mə-trē\ Measurement of the intensity of ELECTROMAGNETIC RADIATION in the visible SPECTRUM transmitted through a solution or transparent solid. It is used to identify and determine the concentrations of substances that absorb LIGHT of a specific wavelength or color according to Lambert's law, which relates the amount of light absorbed to the distance traveled through the absorbing medium, and Beer's law, relating it to the concentration of absorbing substance in the colored solution. A PHOTOCELL is often used to measure the amount of light transmitted through a glass tube containing the solution to be analyzed; the result is compared with results from a similar tube containing solvent alone. Most ELEMENTS and many COMPOUNDS, in appropriately treated samples, may be identified by colorimetry or SPECTROPHOTOMETRY, a closely related technique.

colossal order *or* **giant order** Architectural ORDER in which the columns extend beyond one interior story, often through several stories. Though giant columns were used in antiquity, they were first applied to building facades in Renaissance Italy. Any of the orders might be treated in this manner. The colossal order was revived in 18th-century Europe.

Colossal order, court facade of Blenheim Palace, Oxfordshire, England, by Sir John Vanbrugh, begun 1705.

A.F. KERSTING

Colosseum Flavian Amphitheater in Rome, erected c. AD 70–82 under the emperors VESPASIAN and TITUS. The name Colosseum was applied some time after the 8th century because of its immense size and capacity, holding some 50,000 people. Unlike earlier amphitheaters, which were nearly all dug into hillsides for extra support, the Colosseum is a freestanding oval colonnaded structure of stone and concrete. It was the scene of combats between gladiators, contests of men with animals, and even mock naval engagements. The Colosseum was damaged by lightning and earthquakes in medieval times and, even more severely, by vandals. A restoration project was undertaken in the 1990s, and in 2000 the Colosseum staged a series of plays that marked the first time in more than 1,500 years that live performances had been held there.

Colossus of Rhodes See Colossus of RHODES

colostomy \kə-ˈläs-tə-mē\ Surgical formation of an artificial anus by making an opening from the COLON through the abdominal wall. It may be done to decompress an obstructed colon, to allow EXCRETION when part of the colon must be removed, or to permit healing of the colon. Colostomy may be temporary or permanent. A sigmoid colostomy, the most common type of permanent colostomy, requires no appliances (though a light pouch is sometimes worn for reassurance) and allows a normal life except for the route of fecal excretion. See also OSTOMY.

Colt, Samuel (1814–1862) U.S. inventor. Born in Hartford, Conn., he worked in his father's textile factory before going to sea in 1830. On a voyage to India he conceived the idea for his first REVOLVER, which he later patented (1835–36). Colt's six-shooters were slow to gain acceptance, and his company in Paterson, N.J., failed in 1842. He invented a naval mine with the first remotely controlled explosive in 1843 and conducted a telegraph business that used the first underwater cable. Soldiers' favorable reports prompted an order for 1,000 pistols during the Mexican War, and Colt resumed manufacture in 1847. Assisted by Eli Whitney, Jr., he advanced the development of INTERCHANGEABLE PARTS and the ASSEMBLY LINE. His firm, based in Hartford, produced the revolvers most widely used in the American Civil War and in the settlement of the West, including the famous Colt .45.

Colter, John (1775?–1813) U.S. explorer. Born near Staunton, Va., he was a member of the LEWIS AND CLARK EXPEDITION (1803–6). In 1807 he was sent to contact Indian tribes in the Yellowstone River area and became the first white man to see and describe the region. In three expeditions to the head of the Missouri River (1808–10), he narrowly escaped death during Indian battles. He retired to a farm on the Missouri.

Colton, Gardner (Quincy) (1814–1898) U.S. anesthetist and inventor. Born in Georgia, Vt., he was among the first to use nitrous oxide as an anesthetic in dentistry; after a dentist suggested its use, he safely used it in extracting thousands of teeth. He also invented an electric motor, exhibited in 1847.

Coltrane, John (William) (1926–1967) U.S. saxophonist and composer, the most influential JAZZ musician of the 1960s. Born in Hamlet, N.C., he moved to Philadelphia as a youth. He gained early experience in the bands of DIZZY GILLESPIE and JOHNNY HODGES. Associations with MILES DAVIS and THELONIOUS MONK in the 1950s established his place in the vanguard of modern jazz, and his quartet of the early 1960s is one of the outstanding groups in jazz history. His style encompassed the modal jazz first explored with Davis, the complex chord structures of his own compositions, and ultimately the extremes of timbre, dynamics, and register associated with free jazz. Coltrane's total mastery of the tenor and soprano saxophones, the rich harmonic density of his compositions, and his clear projection of emotion enabled him to reconcile technical virtuosity with an often spiritual profundity.

John Coltrane, 1966.

REPRINTED WITH PERMISSION OF DOWN BEAT MAGAZINE

Columba, St. *or* **Colum** *or* **Columcille** \'kəl-əm-ˌkil\ (521?–597) Irish abbot and missionary. A member of the warrior aristocracy, he was excommunicated for his part in a bloody battle. Exiled, he set out to do penance as a missionary. He founded two famous monasteries in Ireland before taking 12 disciples to the Scottish island of Iona (c. 563), where they built a church and monastery that served as a base for the conversion of the Scottish PICTS, and thereby Scotland, to Christianity.

Columban, St. (543?–615) Irish abbot and missionary. One of the greatest missionaries of the Celtic church, he initiated a revival of spirituality on the European continent. He left Ireland c. 590 with 12 monks and settled in the Vosges Mountains in Gaul, building the nearby monasteries of Luxovium and Fontaines. He was disciplined for keeping Easter according to the Celtic usage, and for his criticism of the sins of the Burgundian court he was forced out of France into Switzerland, where he preached to the Alemanni. He later settled in Italy and founded the monastery of Bobbio (c. 612).

Columbia City (pop., 1996 est.: 113,000), capital of South Carolina. Located in the center of the state on the Congaree River, it dates from 1786, when a town was laid out to replace CHARLESTON as the state capital. During the AMERICAN CIVIL WAR, it was a transportation center and the seat of many Confederate agencies; in 1865 it was occupied by Union troops and virtually destroyed by fire. Rebuilt after the war, it developed a diversified economy based on government, industry, and agriculture. Cotton, peaches, and tobacco are important crops in the surrounding area. It is the seat of the University of SOUTH CAROLINA.

Columbia Broadcasting System See CBS

Columbia Pictures Entertainment, Inc. Major U.S. film studio. It originated in 1920 when the brothers Jack and HARRY COHN formed a company with Joe Brandt to produce short films and low-budget westerns. It became Columbia Pictures in 1924. Harry Cohn, who served as president and head of production from 1932 till his death, was the driving force behind its success. The studio produced the 1930s films of FRANK CAPRA and many other successful films, including *All the King's Men* (1949), *From Here to Eternity* (1953), *The Caine Mutiny* (1954), *Lawrence of Arabia* (1962), *Five Easy Pieces* (1970), *Close Encounters of the Third Kind* (1977), *Tootsie* (1982), and *The Last Emperor* (1987). After Columbia was purchased by the COCA-COLA CO. in 1982, it helped launch Tri-Star Pictures. The two studios merged in 1987 as Columbia Pictures Entertainment, which was bought by SONY CORP. in 1989.

Columbia River River, southwestern Canada and northwestern U.S. Rising in the Canadian Rockies, it flows through Washington state, entering the Pacific Ocean at Astoria, Ore.; it has a total length of 1,240 mi (2,000 km). It was a major transportation artery in the Pacific Northwest until the coming of the railroads. Development of the river began in the 1930s with construction of the Grand Coulee and Bonneville dams, and within 50 years the entire river within the U.S. had been converted into a series of "stair steps" by a total of 11 dams. Its many hydroelectric power plants are basic to the power-generating network of the Pacific Northwest.

Columbia University Private university in New York City, a traditional member of the IVY LEAGUE. Founded in 1754 as King's College, it was renamed Columbia College when it reopened in 1784 after the American Revolution. It became Columbia University in 1912. Its liberal-arts college began admitting women in 1983. Neighboring Barnard College, founded in 1889 and part of the university since 1900, remains a women's liberal-arts school; most courses are open to students of both colleges. From the outset Columbia differed from other private Eastern universities in its emphasis on such subjects as nature study, commerce, history, and government. It has strong graduate programs in the arts and sciences and several notable research institutes. Among its professional schools are those of medicine (including a center at Columbia-Presbyterian Hospital), law, education (Columbia Teachers College), architecture, engineering, journalism, business, public health, nursing, social work, and international and public affairs. Total enrollment is about 20,000 (with affiliates, 27,000).

columbine Any of approximately 70 species of perennial herbaceous plants constituting the genus *Aquilegia,* in the BUTTERCUP family, native to Europe and North America. They are distinctive for their five-petaled flowers with long, backward-extending spurs. Sepals and petals are brightly colored. *A. caerulea* and *A. chysantha* are native to the Rocky Mountains. The wild columbine of North America *(A. canadensis),* bearing red flowers with touches of yellow, grows in woods and on rocky ledges from southern Canada southward. Many garden hybrids are cultivated for their showy flowers.

Columbus City (pop., 1996 est.: 183,000), western Georgia. Located on the CHATTAHOOCHEE RIVER, it was founded in 1827 and by 1840 had become a leading inland cotton port with a thriving textile industry. During the AMERICAN CIVIL WAR it was a major supply city for the Confederacy and the site of the last battle east of the Mississippi. Now highly industrialized, Columbus is one of the South's largest textile centers. It is home to the Confederate Naval Museum. Fort Benning (established 1918) is nearby.

Columbus City (pop., 1996 est.: 657,000), capital of Ohio. Located at the junction of the Scioto and Olentangy rivers, the city was planned in 1812 as a political center and sited opposite the original 1797 settlement of Franklinton; the state government moved to the city in 1816. The arrival of roads, canals, and rail in the mid-19th century led to significant growth, and by 1900 Columbus had emerged as an important transportation and commercial center. Ohio's largest city, its economy is supported by industry, governmental agencies, and numerous educational and research institutions, including OHIO STATE UNIV.

Columbus, Christopher *Italian* **Cristoforo Colombo** *Spanish* **Cristóbal Colón** (1451–1506) Genoese navigator and explorer whose transatlantic voyages opened the way for European exploration, exploitation, and colonization of the Americas. Born in Genoa (now in Italy), he began his career as a young seaman in the Portuguese merchant marine. In 1492 he obtained the sponsorship of the Spanish monarchs FERDINAND V and ISABELLA I for an attempt to reach Asia by sailing westward over what was presumed to be open sea. On his first voyage, he set sail in August 1492 with three ships—the *Santa María,* the *Niña,* and the *Pinta*—and land was sighted in the Bahamas on October 12. He sailed along the northern coast of Hispaniola and returned to Spain in 1493. He made a second voyage (1493–96) with at least 17 ships, and founded La Isabela (in modern Dominican Republic), the first European town in the New World. This voyage also began Spain's effort to promote Christian evangelization. On his third voyage (1498–1500), he reached South America and the Orinoco River delta. Allegations of his poor administration led to his being returned to Spain in chains. On his fourth voyage (1502–4), he returned to South America and sailed along the coasts of modern Honduras and Panama. He was unable to attain his goals of nobility and great wealth. His character and achievements have long been debated, but scholars generally agree that he was an intrepid and brilliant navigator.

Columbus Platform In REFORM JUDAISM, a declaration issued by a conference of U.S. Reform rabbis meeting in Columbus, Ohio, in 1937. It supported the use of traditional ceremonies and Hebrew in the liturgy and reemphasized the idea of the Jewish people, a dramatic revision of the Reform principles stated in the PITTSBURGH PLATFORM (1885).

Columcille See St. COLUMBA

column In architecture, a vertical element, usually a slender shaft, that provides structural support by carrying axial loads in compression; columns are also subject to buckling. Columns may be exposed or hidden in walls; constructed of precast concrete, masonry, stone, or wood or of steel wide-flange, pipe, or tubular sections; they may be plain, fluted, or sculpted, with or without a CAPITAL and base. Columns may also be nonstructural, used for decorative or monumental purposes. See also INTERCOLUMNIATION, ORDER.

Doric columns on the Greek temple at Segesta, Sicily, c. 424–416 BC.

SCALA/ART RESOURCE, NY

Colville, Alex(ander) (born 1920) Canadian painter. Born in Toronto, he studied and taught at Mount Allison Univ.; his mural *History of Mount Allison* (1948) still survives there. His work employs images of human figures juxtaposed with inanimate objects, animals, or other humans (e.g., *Nude and Dummy*, 1950); he is the leading Canadian exponent of magic realism. An official war artist, he is well represented in the Canadian War Museum, Ottawa. Other works include designs for special issues of Canadian coins commemorating the centenary of Confederation (1967).

coma Complete lack of consciousness, with loss of reaction to stimulus and of spontaneous nervous activity, usually associated with cerebral injury of metabolic or physical origin. Simple CONCUSSIONS cause short losses of consciousness. Coma from lack of oxygen may last several weeks and is often fatal. Coma caused by STROKE can be sudden, while that caused by metabolic abnormalities (as in DIABETES MELLITUS) or cerebral TUMORS comes on gradually. Treatment depends on the cause.

Comana \kə-'mā-nə\ Ancient city, CAPPADOCIA. Located on the Seyhan River in the TAURUS MTNS., it was the center of the cult of the mother goddess Ma-Enyo and the site of lavish celebrations. It was governed by the chief priest, usually a member of the reigning Cappadocian family, who ranked next to the king. A Roman colony in the 3rd century AD, it lay on the chief military road to the empire's eastern frontier.

Comanche \kə-'man-chē\ Nomadic North American Indian group that roved the southern Great Plains in the 18th and 19th century. An offshoot of the SHOSHONE, their language was of UTO-AZTECAN stock. They were organized into about 12 autonomous bands, local groups that lacked the lineages, clans, military societies, and tribal government of most other PLAINS INDIANS. Their staple food was buffalo meat. Their highly skilled horsemen set the pattern of equestrian nomadism on the Plains. In 1864 Col. KIT CARSON led U.S. forces in an unsuccessful campaign against them. Treaties were signed in 1865 and 1867, but the federal government failed to keep whites off the land promised to them, which led to violent conflicts. Today about 4,000 Comanche live in and around Lawton, Okla.

Comaneci \ˌkō-mə-'nē-chē\, **Nadia** (born 1961) Romanian-U.S. gymnast. She entered her first international competition in 1972 and won three gold medals. Her performance in the 1976 Olympic Games may never be matched. In that competition, the first in which a perfect score of 10 was ever awarded in an Olympic gymnastic event, she received an astounding seven perfect scores and won the gold medals for the balance beam, uneven parallel bars, and all-around competitions. In the 1980 Olympics she won gold medals for the beam and the floor exercises. She retired from competition in 1984, and defected to the U.S. in 1989.

comb jelly See CTENOPHORE

Combes \kōⁿb\, **(Justin-Louis-) Émile** (1835–1921) French politician. He became mayor of Pons in 1875 and was elected to the Senate in 1885 as a member of the anticlerical Radical Party. As premier (1902–5), he presided over the separation of church and state in the wake of the ALFRED DREYFUS affair. He agreed to laws exiling almost all religious orders from France and dismantling major aspects of the church's public functions, especially in education. Admired by many republicans, he later served as minister without portfolio (1915), despite his advanced age.

combination See PERMUTATIONS AND COMBINATIONS

Combination Acts British acts of 1799 and 1800 that outlawed trade unions. The laws made it illegal for any workingman to combine with another to gain an increase in wages or a decrease in hours, to solicit anyone else to leave work, or to object to working with any other workman. They were repealed in 1824 through the efforts of the radical reformer Francis Place (1771–1854).

combinatorics \ˌkäm-bə-nə-'tȯr-iks\ Branch of mathematics concerned with the selection, arrangement, and combination of objects chosen from a finite set. The number of possible bridge hands is a simple example; more complex problems include scheduling classes in classrooms at a large university and designing a routing system for telephone signals. No standard algebraic procedures apply to all combinatorial problems; a separate logical analysis may be required for each problem. Combinatorics has its roots in antiquity, but new uses in COMPUTER SCIENCE and systems management have increased its importance in recent years. See also PERMUTATIONS AND COMBINATIONS.

combine harvester Farm machine used, mainly in developed countries, to harvest wheat and often other cereals. The mechanical ancestor of today's large combines was CYRUS H. MCCORMICK'S REAPER, introduced in 1831. Threshing machines were powered first by men or animals, often using treadmills, later by STEAM ENGINES and INTERNAL-COMBUSTION ENGINES. The modern combine harvester, originally introduced in California c. 1875, came into wide use in the U.S. in the 1920s and '30s and in Britain in the 1940s. The self-propelled combine was introduced in 1940. The combine cuts the standing grain, threshes out the grain from the straw and chaff, cleans the grain, and empties it into bags or grain-storage facilities. It has greatly reduced harvesting time and labor; whereas in 1829 harvesting an acre of wheat required 14 man-hours, the modern combine requires less than 30 minutes.

combining weight See EQUIVALENT WEIGHT

Comden, Betty *orig.* **Elizabeth Cohen** (born 1919) U.S. musical-comedy writer and lyricist. Born in New York, Comden formed a nightclub act in 1938 with Adolph Green (born 1915), Judy Holliday (1922–1965), and others. In 1944 Comden and Green wrote the book and lyrics for LEONARD BERNSTEIN'S *On the Town*. They later collaborated with J. STYNE on such musicals as *Peter Pan* (1954), *Bells Are Ringing* (1956), and *Hallelujah, Baby!* (1967, Tony award). Their lyrics for *Wonderful Town* (1953), *Applause* (1970), and *On the 20th Century* (1978) won them three more Tonys. Their screenplays include *Singin' in the Rain* (1952) and *Auntie Mame* (1958). "Just in Time" and "The Party's Over" are two of their best-known songs.

Comecon See COUNCIL FOR MUTUAL ECONOMIC ASSISTANCE

Comédie-Française \kȯ-mā-'dē-fräü-'sez\ National theater of France. The world's longest-established national theater, it was founded in 1680 by the merger of two theatrical companies in Paris, one of them the troupe that had worked under MOLIÈRE. The French Revolution divided the company's loyalties, and the revolution's supporters, led by FRANÇOIS-JOSEPH TALMA, moved to the theater's present home in 1791. The company was reconstituted in 1803. Under its rules of organization, established by NAPOLEON in 1812, its members share responsibilities and profits. Its illustrious actors have included SARAH BERNHARDT and J.-L. BARRAULT. The theater is known for productions of the French classics, though it also performs contemporary plays.

comedy Genre of dramatic literature that deals with the light and amusing, or with the serious and profound in a light, familiar, or satirical manner. Comedy can be traced to revels associated with worship in Greece in the 5th century BC. ARISTOPHANES, MENANDER, TERENCE, and PLAUTUS produced comedies in classical literature. It reappeared in the late Middle Ages, when the term was used to mean simply a story with a happy ending (e.g., Dante's *Divine Comedy*), the same meaning it has in novels of the last three centuries (e.g., the fiction of JANE AUSTEN). See also TRAGEDY.

comedy of manners Witty, ironic form of drama that satirizes the manners and fashions of a particular social class or set. It is concerned with social usage and the ability or inability of certain characters to meet social standards, which are often exacting but morally trivial. The plot, usually concerning an illicit love affair or other scandalous matter, is subordinate to the play's brittle atmosphere, witty dialogue, and pungent commentary on human foibles. Its notable exponents include WILLIAM CONGREVE, OLIVER GOLDSMITH, RICHARD BRINSLEY SHERIDAN, OSCAR WILDE, and NOEL COWARD.

Comenius \kə-ˈmē-nē-əs\, **John Amos** *Czech* **Jan Amos Komenský** (1592–1670) Czech educational reformer and religious leader. He favored the learning of Latin to facilitate the study of European culture, but emphasized learning about things rather than about grammar per se. His *Janua Linguarum Reserata* (1631), a textbook that described useful facts about the world in both Latin and Czech, revolutionized Latin teaching and was translated into 16 languages. He also produced one of the first illustrated schoolbooks, *Orbis Sensualium Pictus* (1658).

comet Any of a class of small celestial objects orbiting the sun that develop diffuse gaseous envelopes and often long glowing tails when near the sun. They are distinguished from other objects in the solar system by their composition, hazy appearance, and elongated orbits. Many comets originate in the OORT CLOUD or in the closer KUIPER BELT. Other bodies' gravity can alter their orbits, causing them to pass close to the sun. Short-period comets return in 200 years or less, others in thousands of years or not at all. Comets usually consist of a small, irregular nucleus, often described as a "dirty snowball," with dust and other materials frozen in water mixed with volatile compounds. When one nears the sun, the heat melts its surface, releasing gases and dust particles, which form a cloud (coma) around its core; some comets are later pushed away from the sun by its radiation and the SOLAR WIND, forming tails that scatter sunlight. METEOR SHOWERS occur when earth passes through dust left by the passage of a comet.

comfrey \ˈkəm-frē\ Any herb of the Eurasian genus *Symphytum* (BORAGE family). Best known is the medicinal common comfrey *(S. officinale),* used to treat wounds and as a source of a GUM used to treat wool. Traditionally it was also taken internally for various complaints. Organic farmers use it to deter slugs and as a GREEN MANURE. The coiled sprays of bell-like, hanging comfrey blooms are usually pollinated by bees. Common comfrey is about 3 ft (90 cm) tall, with winged, hairy stems and blue, purplish, or yellow flowers.

comic book Bound collection of COMIC STRIPS, usually in chronological sequence, typically telling a single story or a series of different stories. The first true comic books were marketed in 1933 as giveaway advertising premiums. By 1935 reprints of newspaper strips and books with original stories were selling in large quantities. During World War II comics dealing with war and crime found many readers among soldiers stationed abroad, and in the 1950s comic books were blamed for juvenile delinquency. Though the industry responded with self-censorship, some adventure strips continued to be criticized. In the 1960s comic books satirizing the cultural underworld became popular, especially among college students, and comic books have been used to deal with serious subjects (e.g., Art Spiegelman's *Maus* books, about the Holocaust). Today comic "'zines" represent a thriving subculture.

comic strip Series of drawings that read as a narrative, arranged together on the page of a newspaper, magazine, or book. In the 1890s several U.S. newspapers featured weekly drawings that were funny, but without indicated speech. In 1897 RUDOLPH DIRKS's *Katzenjammer Kids,* in the *New York Journal,* featured humorous strips containing words presumably spoken by the characters. Soon speeches in balloons appeared in other CARTOONS, arranged in a series to form a strip. The comic strip arrived at its maturity in 1907 with Bud Fisher's *Mutt and Jeff,* which appeared daily in the *San Francisco Chronicle*. Important later comic-strip artists include GEORGE HERRIMAN, AL CAPP, WALT KELLY, CHARLES SCHULZ, and GARRY TRUDEAU.

Cominform *in full* **Communist Information Bureau** Agency of international communism founded under Soviet auspices in 1947. Its original members were the Communist Parties of the Soviet Union, Bulgaria, Czechoslovakia, Hungary, Poland, Romania, Yugoslavia, France, and Italy, but Yugoslavia was expelled in 1948. The Cominform's activities consisted mainly of publishing propaganda to encourage international communist solidarity. It was dissolved by Soviet initiative in 1956 as part of a Soviet program of reconciliation with Yugoslavia.

Comintern *or* **Communist International** *or* **Third International** Association of national communist parties founded in 1919. VLADIMIR ILICH LENIN called the first congress of the Comintern to undermine efforts to revive the SECOND INTERNATIONAL. To join, parties were required to model their structure in conformity with the Soviet pattern and to expel moderate socialists and pacifists. Though the Comintern's stated purpose was the promotion of world revolution, it functioned chiefly as an organ of Soviet control over the international communist movement. In 1943, during World War II, JOSEPH STALIN dissolved the Comintern to allay fears of communist subversion among his allies.

Comitia Centuriata \kə-ˈmish-ə-ˌsen-ˌtu̇r-ē-ˈä-tə\ Ancient Roman military assembly, instituted c. 450 BC. It decided on war and peace, passed laws, elected CONSULS, PRAETORS, and CENSORS, and considered appeals of capital convictions. Unlike the older patrician Comitia Curiata, it included PLEBEIANS as well as PATRICIANS, assigned to classes and centuriae (centuries, or groups of 100) by wealth and the equipment they could provide for military duty. Voting started with the wealthier centuries, whose votes outweighed those of the poorer.

command economy Economic system in which the means of production are publicly owned and economic activity is controlled by a central authority. Central planners determine the assortment of goods to be produced, allocate raw materials, fix quotas for each enterprise, and set prices. Most communist countries have had command economies; capitalist countries may also adopt such a system during national emergencies (e.g., wartime) in order to mobilize resources quickly. See also CAPITALISM, COMMUNISM.

commando Military unit consisting of soldiers trained to use GUERRILLA-like tactics ranging from hand-to-hand combat to hit-and-run raids. It is roughly equivalent to an infantry BATTALION. A member of such a unit is also called a commando. In common usage, the term may refer to irregular or guerrilla tactics carried out by small regular units.

commedia dell'arte \kōm-ˈmād-yä-del-ˈlär-tā\ Italian theatrical form that flourished throughout Europe in the 16th–18th century. The characters, many portrayed by actors wearing masks (including the witty gentleman's valet HARLEQUIN, the Venetian merchant Pantelone, the honest and simpleminded servant Pierrot, the maidservant Columbina, the unscrupulous servant Scaramouche, and the braggart captain or Capitano), were derived from the exaggeration or parody of regional or stock fictional types. The style emphasized improvisation within a framework of conventionalized masks and stock situations. It was acted by professional companies using vernacular dialects and plenty of comic action; the first known commedia dell'arte troupe was formed in 1545. Outside Italy, it had its greatest success in France as the Comédie-Italienne; in England, it was adapted in the harlequinade and the Punch-and-Judy show (see PUNCH). See also ANDREINI FAMILY.

Commerce, U.S. Department of (DOC) Federal executive division responsible for programs and policies relating to international trade, national economic growth, and technological advancement. Established in 1913, it administers the Bureau of the Census, the National Oceanic and Atmospheric Administration (NOAA), the Patent and Trademark Office, and U.S. Travel and Tourism Administration (USTTA).

commerce clause In the U.S. CONSTITUTION (Art. I, sec. 8), the authorization for Congress "To regulate Commerce with foreign Nations, and among the several States, and with Indian Tribes." It is the legal foundation of much of the U.S. government's regulatory authority. See also INTERSTATE COMMERCE.

commercial bank Bank that makes loans to businesses, consumers, and nonbusiness institutions. Early commercial banks were limited to accepting deposits of money or valuables for safekeeping and verifying coinage or exchanging one jurisdiction's coins for another's. By the 17th century most of the essentials of modern banking, including FOREIGN EXCHANGE, the payment of INTEREST, and the granting of loans, were in place. It became common for individuals and firms to exchange funds through bankers with a written draft, the precursor to the modern CHECK. Because a commercial bank is required to hold only a fraction of its deposits as cash reserves (see FRACTIONAL RESERVE SYSTEM), it can use some of the money deposited by its customers to extend loans. When a borrower receives a loan, his or her checking account is credited with the amount of the loan, and total demand deposits are thus increased until the loan is repaid. Commercial banks also offer a range of other services, including savings accounts, safe-deposit boxes, and trust services. See also BANK, CENTRAL BANK, INVESTMENT BANK, SAVINGS BANK.

commercial law See BUSINESS LAW

Commercial Revolution Great increase in commerce in Europe that began in the late Middle Ages. It received stimulus from the voyages of exploration undertaken by England, Spain, and other nations to Africa, Asia, and the New World. Among the features associated with it were a surge in overseas trade, the appearance of the CHARTERED COMPANY, acceptance of the principles of MERCANTILISM, the creation of a money economy, increased economic specialization, and the establishment of such new institutions as the state bank, the bourse, and the futures market. The Commercial Revolution helped set the stage for the INDUSTRIAL REVOLUTION.

Committee for the Defense of Legitimate Rights Saudi Arabian opposition group founded in 1992 and composed of Sunni Muslim academics and religious leaders. It considers itself a pressure group for peaceful reform and the improvement of human rights in Saudi Arabia. Its leader is a former physics professor, Muhammad ibn al-Masaari. In 1994, after experiencing government repression, the group moved its headquarters to London; it is consequently no longer considered a serious threat to the ruling family.

Committee of Public Safety Political body of the FRENCH REVOLUTION that controlled France during the REIGN OF TERROR. It was set up in April 1793 to defend France against its enemies, foreign and domestic. At first it was dominated by GEORGES J. DANTON and his followers, but they were soon replaced by the radical JACOBINS, including MAXIMILIEN ROBESPIERRE. Harsh measures were taken against alleged enemies of the Revolution, the economy was placed on a wartime basis, and mass conscription was undertaken. Dissension within the committee contributed to the downfall of Robespierre in 1794, after which it declined in importance.

Committees of Correspondence Groups appointed by the legislatures of all 13 American colonies to provide a means of intercolonial communication. The first standing group was formed by SAMUEL ADAMS in Boston (1772), and within three months 80 others were formed in Massachusetts. In 1773 Virginia organized a committee with 11 members, including THOMAS JEFFERSON and PATRICK HENRY. The committees were instrumental in promoting colonial unity and in summoning the First CONTINENTAL CONGRESS in 1774.

commode Piece of furniture resembling the English chest of drawers, used in France from the late 17th century. Most had marble tops, and some were fitted with pairs of doors. A.-C. BOULLE was among the first to make commodes, which were heavy in form and elaborately decorated in marquetry veneers and ormolu. In the Louis XV period (1715–74), extravagant curves and flamboyant surface ornament became fashionable. The 19th-century commode lost its decorative features and became purely functional.

commodity exchange Organized market for the purchase and sale of enforceable contracts to deliver a commodity (such as wheat, gold, or cotton) or a financial instrument (such as U.S. TREASURY BILLS) at some future date. Such contracts are known as FUTURES and are bought and sold in a competitive auction process on commodity exchanges (also called futures markets). The largest commodity exchange is the Chicago Board of TRADE.

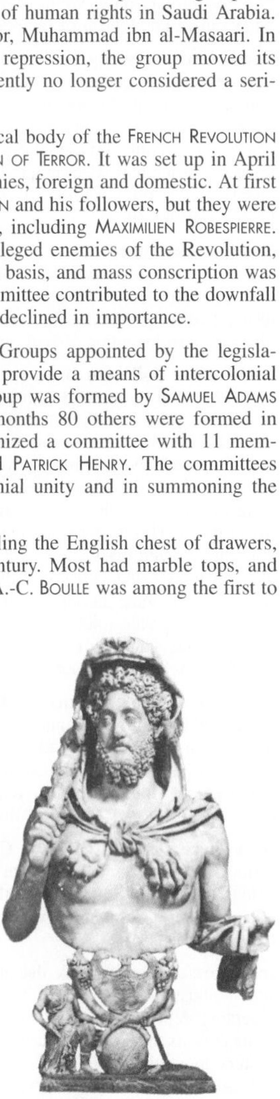

Commodus as Hercules, marble bust; in the Capitoline Museum, Rome.
ANDERSON–ALINARI FROM ART RESOURCE/EB INC.

Commodus *in full* **Caesar Marcus Aurelius Commodus Antoninus Augustus** *orig.* **Lucius Aelius Aurelius Commodus** (AD 161–192) Roman emperor (AD 177–92). He ruled with his father, MARCUS AURELIUS, until the latter's death in 180; recalled from the frontier, he plunged into a life of dissipation in Rome. After his sister tried to have him killed (182), he executed the senators involved and began ruling capriciously. His brutality stirred unrest that ended years of Roman stability and prosperity. He renamed Rome Colonia Commodiana. Physically impressive, he claimed he was Hercules and performed as a gladiator. His mistress and advisers had him strangled, ending the Antonine dynasty.

common cold See common COLD

common fox See RED FOX

common gallinule See MOORHEN

common law Body of law based on custom and general principles and that, embodied in case law, serves as precedent or is applied to situations not covered by statute. Under the common-law system, when a court decides and reports its decision concerning a particular case, the case becomes part of the body of law and can be used in later cases involving similar matters. This use of precedents is known as STARE DECISIS. Common law has been administered in the courts of England since the Middle Ages; it is also found in the U.S. and in most of the British Commonwealth. It is distinguished from CIVIL LAW.

common-law marriage Marriage that is without a civil or religious ceremony and is based on the parties' agreement to consider themselves married and usually also on their cohabitation for a period of time. Most jurisdictions no longer allow this type of marriage to be formed, though they may recognize such marriages formed before a certain date or formed in a jurisdiction that permits such marriages.

common-lead dating See URANIUM-THORIUM-LEAD DATING

Common Market See EUROPEAN ECONOMIC COMMUNITY

Common Pleas, Court of English court of law founded in 1178 to hear civil disputes. Under the MAGNA CARTA (1215), it attained jurisdiction separate from the King's (Queen's) Court, though its decisions were subject to review by the latter. Beginning in the 15th century, it competed with the King's (Queen's) Court and the Court of EXCHEQUER for COMMON-LAW business. By the 19th century, the complexity of overlapping jurisdictional rules had become unbearable, and all three courts were replaced (under the Judicature Act of 1873) by the Supreme Court of Judicature, which remains the court of general jurisdiction in England and Wales.

Common Prayer, Book of Liturgical book used by the churches of the Anglican Communion. First authorized for the Church of England in 1549, it went through several versions; the 1662 revision has remained the standard (with minor changes) throughout the Commonwealth of Nations. The Church of ENGLAND and the Protestant EPISCOPAL CHURCH in the U.S. adopted a liturgy in contemporary language in the 1970s.

common rorqual See FIN WHALE

Commoner, Barry (born 1917) U.S. biologist and educator. Born in Brooklyn, N.Y., he studied at Harvard University and taught at Washington University and Queens College. His warnings, since the 1950s, of the environmental threats posed by modern technology (including nuclear weapons, use of pesticides and other toxic chemicals, and ineffective waste management) in such works as his classic *Science and Survival* (1966) made him one of the foremost environmentalist spokesmen of his time. He was a third-party candidate for U.S. president in 1980.

Commons, House of Popularly elected lower house of the bicameral British PARLIAMENT. Since it alone has the power to levy taxes and allocate expenditures, it is Britain's chief legislative authority. It originated in the late 13th century, when property owners (commoners rather than nobility) first gained the right to commit their constituents to the payment of taxes and present their grievances to the king. For centuries it was the less powerful house, but in 1911 the Reform Bill gave it the power to override the House of LORDS. The party with the greatest representation in the Commons forms the government, and the PRIME MINISTER chooses the CABINET from the party's members. In 1999 there were 659 members, elected from single-member districts. See also Canadian PARLIAMENT, PARLIAMENTARY DEMOCRACY.

Commons, John R(ogers) (1862–1945) U.S. economist. Born in Hollandsburg, Ohio, he taught at the University of Wisconsin (1904–32) and published such works as *A Documentary History of American Industrial Society* (10 vols., 1910–11) and *A History of Labor in the United States* (4 vols., 1918–35), in which he linked the evolution of the U.S. labor movement to changes in the market structure. He drafted reform legislation for Wisconsin and worked for the federal government in areas including civil service and worker's compensation.

Commonwealth *or* **Commonwealth of Nations** Free association of sovereign states consisting of Britain and many of its former dependencies who have chosen to maintain ties of friendship and cooperation. It was established in 1931 by the Statute of WESTMINSTER as the British Commonwealth of Nations. Later its name was changed and it was redefined to include independent nations. Most of the dependent states that gained independence after 1947 chose Commonwealth membership. The British monarch serves as its symbolic head, and meetings of the more than 50 Commonwealth heads of government take place every two years. See also BRITISH EMPIRE.

commonwealth Body politic founded on law for the common "weal," or good. The term was often used by 17th-century writers to signify an organized political community, its meaning thus being similar to the modern meaning of state or nation. Today it primarily refers to the COMMONWEALTH. Four U.S. states (Kentucky, Massachusetts, Pennsylvania, and Virginia) call themselves commonwealths, a distinction in name only. Puerto Rico has been a commonwealth rather than a state since 1952; its residents, though U.S. citizens, have only a nonvoting representative in Congress and pay no federal taxes.

Commonwealth Games sports competition for Commonwealth countries, founded in 1891. It includes athletics (TRACK AND FIELD) GYMNASTICS, BOWLS, and SWIMMING events for both men and women, and BOXING, CYCLING, SHOOTING, WEIGHT LIFTING, and WRESTLING for men only. ROWING, BADMINTON, and FENCING have also occasionally been included.

Commonwealth of Independent States Free association of sovereign states formed in 1991, comprising Russia and 11 other republics that were formerly part of the Soviet Union. Members are Russia, Ukraine, Belarus, Kazakhstan, Kyrgyzstan, Tajikistan, Turkmenistan, Uzbekistan, Armenia, Azerbaijan, Georgia, and Moldova. Its administrative center is in Minsk, Belarus. The Commonwealth's functions are to coordinate its members' policies regarding their economies, foreign relations, defense, immigration policies, environmental protection, and law enforcement.

commune \ˌkäm-ˌyün, kə-ˈmyün\ Group of people living together who hold property in common and live according to a set of principles usually arrived at or endorsed by the group. The UTOPIAN SOCIALISM of ROBERT DALE OWEN and others led to experimental communities of this sort in the early 19th century in Britain and the U.S., including New Harmony, BROOK FARM, and the ONEIDA COMMUNITY. Many communes are inspired by religious principles; monastic life is essentially communal (see MONASTICISM). B. F. SKINNER's *Walden Two* (1948) inspired many American attempts at communal living, especially in the late 1960s and early 1970s. See also COLLECTIVE FARM, COMMUNITARIANISM, KIBBUTZ, MOSHAV.

commune \ˈkäm-ˌyün, kə-ˈmyün\ In medieval European history, a town that acquired self-governing municipal institutions. Most such towns were defined by an oath binding the citizens or burghers of the town to mutual protection and assistance. The group became an association able to own property, make agreements, exercise jurisdiction over members, and exercise governmental powers. Communes were particularly strong in northern and central Italy, where the lack of a powerful central government allowed them to develop into independent city-states. Those of France and Germany were more often limited to local government.

Commune of Paris See PARIS COMMUNE

communication theory *or* **information theory** Field of mathematics that studies the problems of signal transmission, reception, and processing. It stems from CLAUDE E. SHANNON's mathematical methods for measuring the degree of order (nonrandomness) in a signal, which drew largely on PROBABILITY THEORY and STOCHASTIC PROCESSES and led to techniques for determining a source's rate of information production, a channel's capacity to handle information, and the average amount of information in a given type of message. Crucial to the design of communications systems, these techniques have important applications in LINGUISTICS, PSYCHOLOGY, and even literary theory.

communications satellite Earth-orbiting system capable of receiving a signal (e.g., data, voice, TV) and relaying it back to the ground. Communications satellites have been a significant part of domestic and global communications since the 1970s. Typically they move in geosynchronous orbits about 22,300 mi (35,900 km) above the earth and operate at frequencies near 4 gigahertz (GHz) for downlinking and 6 GHz for uplinking.

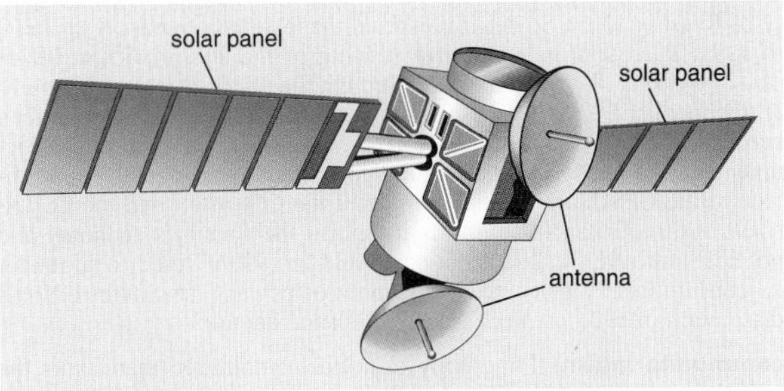

The satellite's solar panels are arrays of solar cells that provide the electrical energy needed for its functions, the power being stored in batteries. Its antennas may be 8 ft (2.5 m) in diameter and may transmit wide-area-of-coverage beams or narrowly focused "spot" beams.

communism Political theory advocating community ownership of all property, the benefits of which are to be shared by all according to the needs of each. The theory was principally the work of KARL MARX and FRIEDRICH ENGELS. Their *COMMUNIST MANIFESTO* (1848) further specified a "dictatorship of the PROLETARIAT," a transitional stage Marx called SOCIALISM; communism was the final stage in which not only class division but even the organized state—seen by Marx as inevitably an instrument of oppression—would be transcended (see MARXISM). That distinction was soon lost, and "communist" began to apply to a specific party rather than a final goal. VLADIMIR ILICH LENIN maintained that the proletariat needed professional revolutionaries to guide it (see LENINISM). JOSEPH STALIN's version of communism (see STALINISM) was synonymous to many with TOTALITARIANISM. MAO ZEDONG mobilized peasants rather than an urban proletariat in China's Communist revolution (see MAOISM). European communism (see EUROCOMMUNISM) lost most of its following with the collapse of the Soviet Union (1991). See also COMMUNIST PARTY, DIALECTICAL MATERIALISM, FIRST INTERNATIONAL, SECOND INTERNATIONAL.

Communism Peak *formerly* **Stalin Peak** *or* **Garmo Peak** Peak, western PAMIRS, northeastern Tajikistan. Located in the Academy of Sciences Range, it rises to 24,590 ft (7,495 m), and is the highest point in Tajikistan and in the system. It was first climbed by a Russian team in 1933.

Communist Information Bureau See COMINFORM

Communist International See COMINTERN

Communist Manifesto Pamphlet published in 1848 by KARL MARX and FRIEDRICH ENGELS, reflecting their analysis of history as the story of class struggle and the direction they believed society would take. It asserted that industrialization had exacerbated the divide between the capitalist ruling class and the PROLETARIAT, which was seen as increasingly impoverished, and called on the proletariat to overthrow the capitalists, abolish private property, and take over the means of production, efforts which would lead eventually to a classless society and a gradual diminution of the need for a state.

Communist Party Political party organized to facilitate the transition of society from CAPITALISM through SOCIALISM to COMMUNISM. Russia was the first country in which communists came to power (1917). In 1918 the BOLSHEVIK party was renamed the All-Russian Communist Party; the name was taken to distinguish its members from the socialists of the SECOND INTERNATIONAL who had supported capitalist governments during World War I. Its basic unit was the workers' council (SOVIET), above which were district, city, regional, and republic committees. At the top was the party congress, which met only every few years; the delegates elected the members of the Central Committee, who in turn elected the members of the POLITBURO and the SECRETARIAT, though those organizations were actually largely self-perpetuating. The Soviet Union dominated communist parties worldwide through World War II. Yugoslavia challenged that hegemony in 1948 and China went its own way in the 1950s and '60s. Communist parties have survived the demise of the Soviet Union (1991), but with reduced political influence. Cuba's party remains in control, as does a hereditary communist party in North Korea.

Communist Party of the Soviet Union (CPSU) Major political party of Russia and the Soviet Union from the RUSSIAN REVOLUTION OF 1917 to 1991. It arose from the BOLSHEVIK wing of the RUSSIAN SOCIAL-DEMOCRATIC WORKERS' PARTY. From 1918 through the 1980s it was a monolithic, monopolistic ruling party that dominated the Soviet Union's political, economic, social, and cultural life. The constitution and other legal documents that supposedly regulated the government were actually subordinate to the CPSU, which also dominated the COMINTERN and the COMINFORM. MIKHAIL GORBACHEV's efforts to reform the country's economy and political structure weakened the party, and in 1990 it voted to surrender its constitutionally guaranteed monopoly of power. The Soviet Union's dissolution in 1991 marked the party's formal demise.

communitarianism Philosophy of social organization that favors the interaction of participants in community who come together to identify common goals and agree to rules governing the communal order. Adherents believe that harmony is created in part by recognizing community policies (laws) as fulfilling legitimate needs rather than having been arbitrarily imposed. Members of the community (neighborhood, city, or nation) accept responsibilities to achieve common goals. It found expression in the 1990s in the work of Amitai Etzioni and other U.S. academics. See also COLLECTIVISM, COMMUNISM, LIBERALISM, SOCIAL DEMOCRACY, SOCIALISM.

community center See SETTLEMENT HOUSE

community college *or* **junior college** Educational institution that provides up to two years of COLLEGE-level academic instruction as well as technical and vocational training to prepare graduates for careers. There are over 1,000 community colleges in the U.S. and over 100 in Canada. Roots of the community college may be traced to the CHAUTAUQUA MOVEMENT and other adult-education programs created after the American Civil War. The first junior college opened in Joliet, Ill., in 1901. Usually publicly supported, community colleges offer a variety of flexible programs that are often nontraditional in style and content. They have pioneered in offering part-time study, evening sessions, instruction by television, weekend workshops, and other services for members of their communities. Students rarely live on campus. Graduates of community colleges ordinarily earn an associate's degree. They may transfer to a four-year college or enter the workforce. See also CONTINUING EDUCATION.

community property PROPERTY held jointly by husband and wife. Property acquired by either spouse after marriage may be deemed, in states having a community-property system, to belong to each spouse as an undivided one-half interest. Some property (e.g., gifts to one spouse) may be classified as separate, but in lawsuits over the classification of property the presumption is in favor of the community category.

commutative law Two closely related laws of number operations. In symbols, they are stated: $a + b = b + a$ and $ab = ba$. Stated in words: Quantities to be added or multiplied can be combined in any order. More generally, if two procedures give the same result when carried out in arbitrary order, they are commutative. Exceptions occur (e.g., in vector multiplication). See also ASSOCIATIVE LAW, DISTRIBUTIVE LAW.

Commynes \kȯ-'mēn\, **Philippe de** (1447?–1511) Statesman and chronicler. Brought up in the Burgundian court, he was counselor to CHARLES THE BOLD (1467–72) and then to Charles's former enemy LOUIS XI. He was implicated in the "Mad War" between Anne of Beaujeu, regent of France, and the duc d'Orleans (later LOUIS XII). He was briefly imprisoned but restored to favor in 1489 by Charles VIII and later helped formulate Louis's Italian policy. His *Mémoires* (1524) reveal much about the era.

Como, Lake *ancient* **Lacus Larius** Lake, LOMBARDY, northern Italy. It lies at an elevation of 653 ft (199 m) in a depression surrounded by limestone and granite mountains. It is 29 mi (47 km) long and up to 2.5 mi (4 km) wide, with an area of 56 sq mi (146 sq km) and a maximum depth of 1,358 ft (414 m). Famous for its natural beauty, its shores have many resorts.

Comoros \'kä-mə-ˌrōz\ *officially* **Federal Islamic Republic of the Comoros** Islamic republic off the eastern coast of Africa. Area: 719 sq mi (1,862 sq km). Population (2000 est.): 509,200. Capital: MORONI. The people are a mixture of Malay immigrants, Arab traders, and peoples from Madagascar and continental Africa. Languages: Comorian (a Bantu language), Arabic, French (all official). Religion: Islam (official). Currency: Comorian franc. Comoros comprises a group of islands between Madagascar and the mainland that includes Grande Comore (Njazidja), Mohéli (Mwali), and Anjouan (Nzwani) but excludes MAYOTTE. They are generally rocky, with shallow soils and poor harbors, though Mohéli, the smallest, has fertile valleys and forested hillsides.

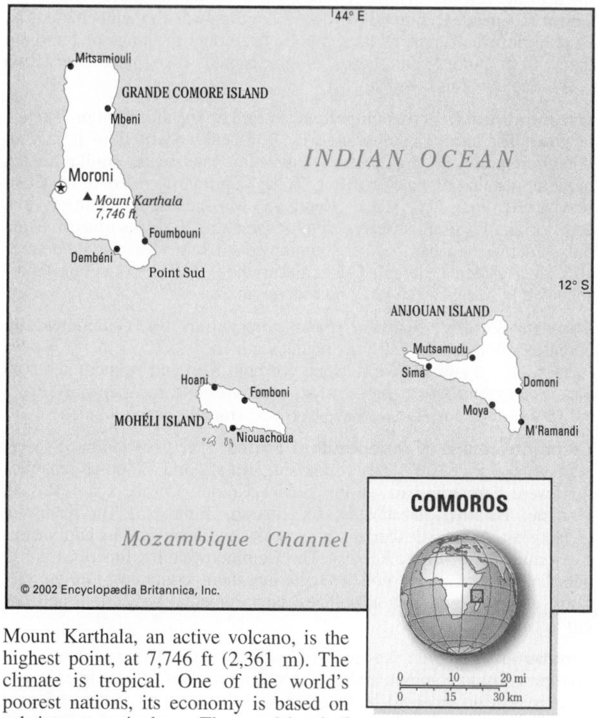

Mount Karthala, an active volcano, is the highest point, at 7,746 ft (2,361 m). The climate is tropical. One of the world's poorest nations, its economy is based on subsistence agriculture. The usual head of state and government is the president. Known to European navigators since the 16th century, the dominant influence on the islands was then and for long afterward Arab. In 1843 France officially took possession of Mayotte and in 1886 placed the other three islands under protection. Subordinated to Madagascar in 1914, the Comoros became an overseas territory of France in 1947. In 1961 they were granted autonomy. In 1974 majorities on three of the islands voted for independence, which was granted in 1975. The following decade saw several coup attempts, culminating in the assassination of the president in 1989. French intervention permitted multiparty elections in 1990, but the country remained in a state of chronic instability. In 1999 the army took control of the government.

compact disc (CD) Molded plastic disc containing digital data that is scanned by a laser beam for the reproduction of recorded sound or other information. Since its commercial introduction in 1982, the audio CD has become the dominant format for high-fidelity recorded music. Digital audio data can be converted to analog form to reproduce the original audio signal (see DIGITAL-TO-ANALOG CONVERSION). Coinvented by Philips Electronics and Sony Corp. in 1980, the compact disc has expanded beyond audio recordings into other storage-and-distribution uses, notably for computers (CD-ROM) and entertainment systems (VIDEODISC and DVD). An audio CD can store just over an hour of music. A CD-ROM can contain up to 680 megabytes of computer data. A DVD, the same size as traditional CDs, is able to store up to 17 gigabytes of data, such as high-definition digital video files.

Companions of the Prophet *Arabic* **Sahaba** *or* **Ashab.** Followers of MUHAMMAD who had personal contact with him, including any Muslim contemporary who saw him. As eyewitnesses, they are the most important sources of HADITH. SUNNI Muslims regard the first four CALIPHS (among the ten Companions to whom Muhammad promised paradise) as the most important. SHIITE Muslims disregard the Companions, whom they consider responsible for the loss of the caliphate by the family of ALI.

comparative advantage Economic theory first developed by DAVID RICARDO that analyzes international trade in terms of differences in relative OPPORTUNITY COSTS. The theory suggests that countries should specialize in the goods they can produce most efficiently rather than trying for self-sufficiency and argues strongly in favor of free international trade.

comparative psychology Study of similarities and differences in behavioral organization among living beings. The discipline pays particular attention to the psychological nature of humans in comparison with other animals. It began to emerge in the late 19th century and grew rapidly in the 20th century, involving experimental studies on human and animal brain function, LEARNING, and motivation. Well-known studies have included those of IVAN PAVLOV on CONDITIONING in laboratory dogs, those of Harry Harlow (1905–1981) on the effects of social deprivation in monkeys, and those of various researchers on language abilities in apes.

comparator \kəm-'par-ə-tər\ Instrument for comparing something with a similar thing or with a standard measure, in particular to measure small displacements in mechanical devices. In astronomy, the blink comparator is used to examine photographic plates for signs of moving bodies. Machinists use comparators or visual gauges to center or align work in MACHINE TOOLS.

compass In NAVIGATION or SURVEYING, the chief device for direction-finding on the earth's surface. Compasses may operate on magnetic or gyroscopic (see GYROSCOPE) principles or by determining the direction of the sun or a star. The oldest and most familiar type is the magnetic compass, used in different forms in aircraft, ships, and land vehicles and by surveyors. Magnetic compasses work as they do because earth itself acts as a MAGNET with a north-south field (see GEOMAGNETIC FIELD) that causes freely moving magnets to align themselves with the field.

compatibilism Thesis that free will, in the sense required for moral responsibility, is consistent with universal causal DETERMINISM. It is important to distinguish the question of the logical consistency of belief in universal causal determinism with belief in free will from the question whether the thesis of free will (or that of causal determinism) is true. Compatibilists need not assert (though many have) the reality both of free will and of causal determinism. Among incompatibilists, some maintain the existence of free will and accordingly deny universal causal determinism, while others uphold universal causal determinism and deny the existence of free will. See also FREE WILL PROBLEM.

compensation, just See JUST COMPENSATION

compiler Computer SOFTWARE that translates (compiles) source code written in a high-level language (e.g., C++) into a set of MACHINE-LANGUAGE instructions that can be understood by a DIGITAL COMPUTER's CPU. Compilers are very large programs, with error-checking and other abilities. Some compilers translate high-level language into an intermediate ASSEMBLY LANGUAGE, which is then translated (assembled) into machine code by an assembly program or assembler. Other compilers generate machine language directly.

complement In physiology, a complex system of at least 20 PROTEINS (complement components) in normal BLOOD serum. The binding of one component to an ANTIGEN-ANTIBODY complex begins a chemical chain reaction important in many immunological processes, including breakdown of foreign and infected cells, ingestion of foreign particles and cell debris, and inflammation of surrounding tissue. Complement components and antibodies are the substances in human serum responsible for killing bacteria.

complementary medicine See ALTERNATIVE MEDICINE

completeness Concept of the adequacy of a FORMAL SYSTEM that is employed both in proof theory and in model theory (see LOGIC). In proof theory, a formal system is said to be syntactically complete if and only if every closed sentence in the system is such that either it or its negation is provable in the system. In model theory, a formal system is said to be semantically complete if and only if every theorem of the system is provable in the system.

complex number Any number consisting of both REAL NUMBERS and IMAGINARY NUMBERS. It has the form $a + bi$, where a and b are real numbers and $i = \sqrt{-1}$; a is called the real part and bi the imaginary part. Because a or b can equal 0, any real or imaginary number is also a complex number. Invented as an extension of the real numbers so that certain ALGEBRAIC EQUATIONS such as $x^2 + 1 = 0$ would have solutions, the complex numbers form an algebraic field, meaning that they obey the COMMUTATIVE LAW and the ASSOCIATIVE LAW (with respect to addition and multiplication), as well as certain other rules in much the same way real numbers do (see FIELD THEORY).

complex variable In mathematics, a VARIABLE that can take on the value of a COMPLEX NUMBER. In basic algebra, the variables x and y generally stand for values of real numbers. The algebra of complex numbers (complex analysis) uses the complex variable z to represent a number of the form $a + bi$. The modulus of z is its ABSOLUTE VALUE. A complex variable may be graphed as a VECTOR from the origin to the point (a,b) in a rectangular COORDINATE SYSTEM, its modulus corresponding to the vector's length. Called an Argand diagram, this representation establishes a connection between complex analysis and vector analysis. See also EULER'S FORMULA.

composite (material) Solid material that results when two or more different substances, each with its own characteristics, are combined (physically, not chemically) to create a new substance whose properties are superior in a specific application to those of the original components. The term specifically refers to a structural material (such as plastic) within which a fibrous material (such as silicon carbide) is embedded. Glass-fiber-reinforced plastic is the best-known composite. Because of their stiffness, lightness, and heat resistance, composites are the materials of choice in numerous structural, reinforcing, and high-performance applications.

composite family Family Compositae, one of the largest plant families (also known as Asteraceae, DAISY family, and ASTER family), which contains more than 1,100 genera and almost 20,000 species of herbaceous plants, shrubs, and trees, found throughout the world. Though diverse in habit and habitat, composites tend to grow in sunlit places in temperate and subtropical regions. The family includes many garden ornamentals, including AGERATUMS, asters, CHRYSANTHEMUMS, COSMOS, DAHLIAS, MARIGOLDS, and ZINNIAS. Some genera include weeds such as DANDELION, RAGWEED, and THISTLE. ARTEMISIA, ARTICHOKE, ENDIVE, SAFFLOWER, SALSIFY, LETTUCE, and SUNFLOWER are important for the products derived from their flowers, seeds, leaves, roots, or tubers. Flower heads in this family are composed of many small flowers (florets) surrounded by BRACTS. Bell-shaped disk florets form the center of each head; strap-shaped ray florets extend out like petals from the center and are sometimes reflexed (bent back). Some species have flowers with only disk or only ray florets.

compost Mass of rotted organic matter made from decomposed plant materials or from waste-plant residues. It is used in agriculture and gardening generally to improve soil structure rather than as a fertilizer, because it is low in plant nutrients. When properly prepared, it is free of obnoxious odors. Composts commonly contain about 2% nitrogen, 0.5–1% phosphorus, and about 2% potassium. Lime and nitrogen fertilizers and manure may be added to speed decomposition. The nitrogen of compost becomes available slowly and in small amounts. Because of their low nutrient content, composts are applied in large amounts.

compound Any substance composed of identical MOLECULES consisting of ATOMS of two or more ELEMENTS. Millions are known, each unique, with unique properties. Most common materials are mixtures of compounds. Pure compounds can be obtained by physical separation methods, such as precipitation and DISTILLATION. Compounds can be broken down into their constituents to various degrees or changed into new compounds by CHEMICAL REACTIONS. Atoms always combine into molecules in fixed proportions, distinguishing compounds from SOLUTIONS and other mechanical mixtures. Compounds are often classified as INORGANIC and ORGANIC COMPOUNDS; coordination complexes, which contain METAL atoms (usually TRANSITION ELEMENTS) bonded to LIGANDS that may be organic, are somewhat in between. Compounds may also be classified by whether they have IONIC or COVALENT bonds (many include both types).

comprehension Act of or capacity for grasping with the intellect. The term is most often used in connection with tests of reading skills and language abilities, though other abilities (e.g., mathematical reasoning) may also be examined. Specialists in administering and interpreting such tests are known as psychometricians (see PSYCHOMETRICS) or differential psychologists. See also DYSLEXIA, LATERALITY, PSYCHOLOGICAL TESTING, SPEECH.

compressed air AIR reduced in volume and held under PRESSURE. FORCE from compressed air is used to operate numerous tools and instruments, including rock drills, train brake systems, riveters, forging presses, paint sprayers, and atomizers. Bellows have been used since the Early Bronze age to provide air for smelting and forging. The 20th century witnessed a large increase in the use of compressed-air devices. The introduction of jet engines for military and passenger aircraft stimulated the use and improvement of centrifugal and axial-flow compressors. Digital-logic pneumatic-control components (developed in the 1960s) can be used in power and CONTROL SYSTEMS (see PNEUMATIC DEVICE).

compression ratio Degree to which the fuel mixture in an INTERNAL-COMBUSTION ENGINE is compressed before ignition. It is defined as the volume of the combustion chamber with the piston farthest out divided by the volume with the piston in the full-compression position (see PISTON AND CYLINDER). A compression ratio of six means that the action of the piston compresses the mixture to one-sixth its original volume. A high ratio promotes efficiency but may cause engine knock.

compressor Machine for increasing the pressure of a GAS by mechanically decreasing its volume. Air is the most frequently compressed gas, but natural gas, oxygen, nitrogen, and other industrially important gases are also frequently compressed. There are three general types of compressors. Positive-displacement compressors are usually of the reciprocating piston type (see PISTON AND CYLINDER), useful for supplying small amounts of a gas at relatively high pressures. Centrifugal compressors are particularly suited for compressing large volumes of gas to moderate pressures. Axial compressors are used for jet aircraft engines and gas turbines.

Compromise of 1850 Series of measures passed by the U.S. Congress to settle slavery issues and avert SECESSION. The crisis arose in late 1849 when the territory of California asked to be admitted to the Union with a constitution prohibiting slavery. The problem was complicated by the unresolved question of slavery's extension into other areas ceded by Mexico in 1848. In an attempt to satisfy pro- and antislavery forces, Sen. HENRY CLAY offered a series of measures that admitted California as a free state, left the question of slavery in the new territories to be settled by the local residents, and provided for the enforced return of runaway slaves and the prohibition of the slave trade in the District of Columbia. Support from DANIEL WEBSTER and STEPHEN A. DOUGLAS helped ensure passage of the compromise. Moderates throughout the Union accepted the terms, which averted secession for another decade but sowed seeds of discord.

Compromise of 1867 *or* **Ausgleich** \'au̇s-ˌglīk̲\ Compact that established the dual monarchy of AUSTRIA-HUNGARY. The kingdom of Hungary desired equal status with the Austrian empire, which was weakened by its defeat in the Austro–Prussian War of 1866. The Austrian emperor FRANCIS JOSEPH gave Hungary full internal autonomy, together with a responsible ministry, and in return it agreed that the empire should still be a single great state for purposes of war and foreign affairs, thus maintaining its dynastic prestige abroad.

Compton, Arthur (Holly) (1892–1962) U.S. physicist. Born in Wooster, Ohio, he taught at the University of Chicago 1923–45, and later served as chancellor (1945–54) and professor (1953–61) at Washington University. He is best known for his discovery and explanation of the COMPTON EFFECT, for which he shared with C.T.R. WILSON a 1927 Nobel Prize. He was later instrumental in initiating the MANHATTAN PROJECT, and directed the development of the first nuclear reactors.

Compton-Burnett, Ivy *later* **Dame Ivy** (1884–1967) British novelist. She graduated from the University of London and published her first novel, *Dolores,* in 1911. Her second, *Pastors and Masters* (1925), introduced the style—employing clipped, precise dialogue to reveal her characters and advance the plot—that made her name. Her novels often dealt with struggles for power: *Men and Wives* (1931) featured a tyrannical mother, *A House and Its Head* (1935) a tyrannical father. She was created Dame of the British Empire in 1967.

Compton effect Change in WAVELENGTH of X RAYS and other energetic forms of ELECTROMAGNETIC RADIATION when they collide with ELECTRONS. It is a principal way in which radiant energy is absorbed by matter, and is caused by the transfer of energy from PHOTONS to electrons. When photons collide with electrons that are free or loosely bound in atoms, they transfer some of their energy and momentum to the electrons, which then recoil. New photons of less energy and momentum, and hence longer wavelength, are produced; these scatter at various angles, depending on the amount of energy lost to the recoiling electrons. The effect demonstrates the nature of the photon as a true particle with both energy and momentum. Its discovery in 1922 by ARTHUR COMPTON was essential to establishing the WAVE-PARTICLE DUALITY of ELECTROMAGNETIC RADIATION.

computational complexity Inherent cost of solving a problem in large-scale scientific computation, measured by the number of operations required as well as the amount of memory used and the order in which it is used. The result of a complexity analysis is an estimate of how rapidly the solution time increases as the problem size increases, which can be used to analyze problems and assist in the design of ALGORITHMS for their solution.

computational linguistics (CL) Use of digital computers in LINGUISTICS research. The simplest examples are the use of computers to scan text and produce such aids as word lists, frequency counts, and concordances. From the mid-1950s to the mid-1960s progress was made by research groups working on machine translation and INFORMATION RETRIEVAL. Theoretical CL deals with formal theories about linguistic knowledge, which today have reached a degree of complexity that can only be managed using powerful computers. Applied CL focuses on practical results of modeling human language use.

computed axial tomography (CAT) \tə-'mäg-rə-fē\ *or* **computed tomography (CT)** DIAGNOSTIC-IMAGING method using a low-dose X-RAY beam that crosses the body in a single plane at many different angles. Conceived by William Oldendorf and developed independently by Godfrey Hounsfield (born 1919) and ALLAN M. CORMACK, who shared a 1979 Nobel Prize for their inventions, this major advance in imaging technology became generally available in the early 1970s. Detectors record the strength of the exiting X rays; this information is then processed by computer to produce a detailed two-dimensional cross-sectional image of the body. A series of such images in parallel planes or around an axis can show the location of abnormalities (especially tumors and other masses) more precisely than can conventional X-ray images. See also BRAIN scanning.

computer Programmable machine that can store, retrieve, and process data. Today's computers have at least one CPU that performs all calculations and includes a main memory, a control unit, and an arithmetic logic unit. Auxiliary data storage is usually provided by an on-board HARD DISK and may be supplemented by other media such as FLOPPY DISKS or CD-ROMs. Peripheral equipment includes input devices (e.g. keyboard, mouse) and output devices (e.g. monitor, PRINTER), as well as the circuitry and cabling that connect all the components. Generations of modern computers are characterized by their technology. First-generation computers, developed mostly in the U.S. after World War II, used VACUUM TUBES and were enormous. The second generation, introduced c. 1960, used TRANSISTORS and were the first successful commercial computers. Third-generation computers (late 1960s and 1970s) were characterized by miniaturization of components and use of INTEGRATED CIRCUITS. The MICROPROCESSOR chip, first introduced in 1974, defines fourth-generation computers. The fifth generation emphasizes ARTIFICIAL INTELLIGENCE, focusing on machine reasoning and logic programming languages. Early machines were ANALOG COMPUTERS, but most today are DIGITAL COMPUTERS. In the last 50 years computers have changed the way people live and work, and their development has made the information age possible. See illustration on following page.

computer, analog See ANALOG COMPUTER

computer, digital See DIGITAL COMPUTER

computer-aided software engineering See CASE

computer animation Form of animated graphics that has replaced "stop-motion" ANIMATION of scale-model puppets or drawings. Efforts to lessen the labor and costs of animation have led to simplification and computerization. Computers can be used in every step of sophisticated animation—for example, to automate the movement of the rostrum camera or to supply the in-between drawings for full animation. When a three-dimensional figure is translated into computer terms (digitized), the computer can generate and display a sequence of images that seem to move or rotate the object through space. Hence computer animation can simulate highly complex motion for medical and other scientific researchers.

computer architecture Internal structure of a DIGITAL COMPUTER, encompassing the design and layout of its instruction set and storage registers. The architecture of a computer is chosen with regard to the types of programs that will be run on it (business, scientific, general-purpose, etc.). Its principal components or subsystems, each of which could be said to have an architecture of its own, are input/output, storage, communication, control, and processing.

computer art Manipulation of computer-generated images (pictures, designs, scenery, portraits, etc.) as part of a purposeful creative process. Specialized SOFTWARE is used together with interactive devices such as DIGITAL CAMERAS, optical SCANNERS, styli, and electronic tablets. Because graphic images require large programs, the computers used in such work are generally among the fastest and most powerful available. Computer art has wide applications in advertising, publishing, and film.

computer-assisted instruction Use of instructional material presented by a computer. Since the advent of microcomputers in the 1970s, computer use in schools has become widespread, from primary schools through the university level and in some preschool programs. Instructional computers either present information or fill a tutorial role, testing

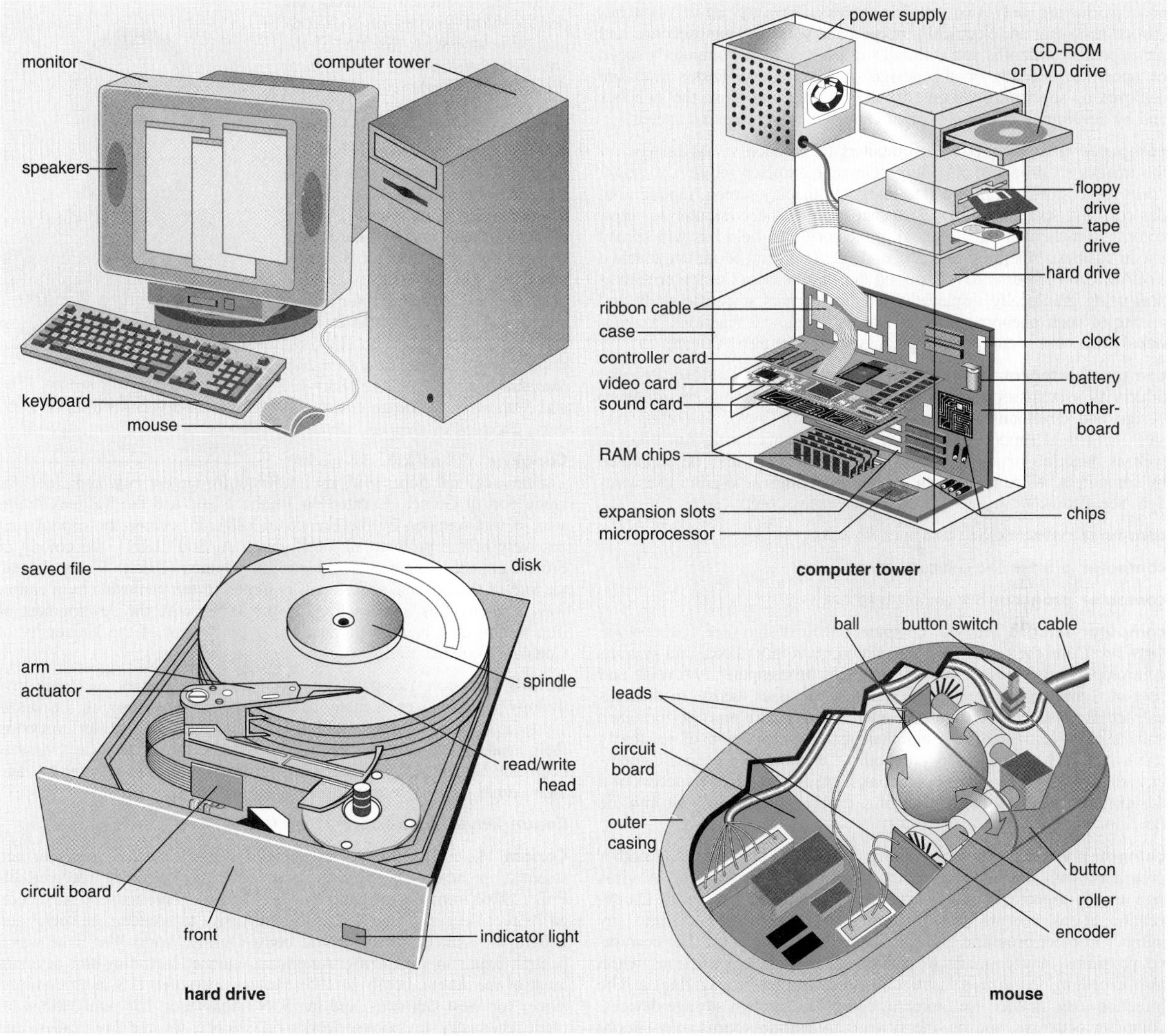

A typical personal computer system consists of the computer itself, a video monitor, a keyboard, a mouse, and speakers. Chips and circuit boards ("cards") are plugged into the motherboard; other components, such as disk drives, are housed in the computer case. The microprocessor directs the computer's activity, and data and programs in use are stored in the RAM chips. Some circuit boards, such as the sound card, are dedicated to specific functions. Additional boards, such as a modem, may be inserted into expansion slots. The power supply converts standard AC power into the voltages and currents required to operate the computer. A battery retains clock and configuration data when the AC power is turned off. The hard drive, the primary storage medium, usually contains several rigid disks attached to a rotating spindle. The disks are accessed by read/write heads attached to the ends of moving arms. The mouse is an input device used to position a pointer on the computer's screen. On-screen selections are made by "clicking" one of the mouse's buttons, sending a signal to the computer.

the student for comprehension. By providing one-on-one interaction and producing immediate responses to input answers, computers allow students to demonstrate mastery and learn new material at their own pace. A disadvantage is that computerized instruction cannot extend the lesson beyond the limits of the programming.

computer chip *or* **chip** INTEGRATED CIRCUIT or small wafer of SEMICONDUCTOR material embedded with integrated circuitry. Chips comprise the processing and memory units of the modern DIGITAL COMPUTER (see MICROPROCESSOR, RAM). Chip making is extremely precise and is usually done in a "clean room," since even microscopic contamination could render the chip defective. Computer chips have grown smaller and more powerful at a steady rate in the last years of the 20th century. Micro- and nanotechnology is expected to make them even smaller and more powerful in the 21st century.

computer circuitry Complete path or combination of interconnected paths for ELECTRON flow in a computer. Computer circuits are binary in concept, having only two possible states. They use on-off switches (TRANSISTORS) that are electrically opened and closed in nanoseconds and picoseconds (billionths and trillionths of a second). A computer's speed of operation depends on the design of its circuitry. Faster rates are achieved by shortening the time it takes to open and close the switches and by developing circuit paths that can handle the increased speeds.

computer graphics Use of computers to produce visual images, or the images so produced. Creating computer graphics requires a DIGITAL COMPUTER to store and manipulate images, a display screen, input/output devices, and specialized SOFTWARE that enables the computer to draw, color, and manipulate images held in memory. The field has widespread use in business, scientific research, and entertainment. Monitors attached to CAD/CAM systems have replaced drafting boards. Computer SIMULATION using graphically displayed quantities permits scientific study and testing of such phenomena as nuclear and chemical reactions, gravitational interactions, and physiological systems. See also COMPUTER ART.

computer-integrated manufacturing Data-driven AUTOMATION that affects all systems or subsystems within a manufacturing environment: design and development, production (see CAD/CAM), marketing and sales, and field support and service. Basic manufacturing functions as well as materials-handling and inventory control can also be simulated by computers before the system is built in an attempt to eliminate wastage. See also ARTIFICIAL INTELLIGENCE, EXPERT SYSTEMS, ROBOTICS.

computer network See computer NETWORK

computer printer See computer PRINTER

computer program See computer PROGRAM

computer science Study of computers, their design (see COMPUTER ARCHITECTURE), and their uses for computation, DATA PROCESSING, and systems control, including design and development of computer HARDWARE and SOFTWARE, and programming. The field encompasses theory, mathematical activities such as design and analysis of algorithms, performance studies of systems and their components, and estimation of reliability and availability of systems by probabilistic techniques. Because computer systems are often too large and complicated for failure or success of a design to be predicted without testing, experimentation is built into the development cycle.

computer virus Computer program designed to copy itself into other programs, with the intention of causing mischief or damage. A virus will usually execute when it is loaded into a computer's memory. On execution, it instructs its host program to copy the viral code into any number of other programs and files stored in the computer. The corrupted programs may continue to perform their intended functions while also executing the virus's instructions, thus further propagating it. The infection may transfer itself to other computers through storage devices, computer networks, and on-line systems. A harmless virus may simply cause a cryptic message to appear when the computer is turned on; a more damaging virus can destroy valuable data. Antivirus software may be used to detect and remove viruses from a computer, but the software must be updated frequently for protection against new viruses.

computer vision Field of ROBOTICS in which programs attempt to identify objects represented in digitized images provided by video cameras, thus enabling robots to "see." Much work has been done on stereo vision as an aid to object identification and location within a three-dimensional field of view. Recognition of objects in real time, as would be needed for active robots in complex environments, usually requires computing power beyond the capabilities of present-day technology. See also PATTERN RECOGNITION.

computing, quantum See QUANTUM COMPUTING

Comstock, Anthony (1844–1915) U.S. reformer. Born in New Canaan, Conn., he began early to agitate against abortion and pornography. He lobbied successfully for the enactment (1873) of a severe federal statute outlawing the transportation of obscene matter in the mails (the Comstock Law). That same year he founded the Society for the Suppression of Vice, which he directed until his death. As a special agent of the U.S. Post Office (1873–1915), he conducted spectacular raids on publishers and vendors. His books include *Traps for the Young* (1883) and *Morals Versus Art* (1888).

Comte \'kō^{n}t\, **(Isidore-) Auguste (-Marie-François-Xavier)** (1798–1857) French thinker, the philosophical founder of SOCIOLOGY and of POSITIVISM. A disciple of the comte de SAINT-SIMON, he taught at the École Polytechnique (1832–42) but gave free lectures to workingmen. He gave the science of sociology its name and established the new subject on a conceptual (though not empirical) basis, believing that social phenomena could be reduced to laws just as natural phenomena could. His ideas influenced JOHN STUART MILL (who supported him financially for many years), É. DURKHEIM, HERBERT SPENCER, and EDWARD BURNETT TYLOR. His most important works are *Cours de philosophie positive* (6 vols., 1830–42) and *Système de politique positive* (4 vols., 1851–54).

Comte, drawing by Tony Toullion, 19th century; in the Bibliothèque Nationale, Paris.

H. ROGER-VIOLLET

Conakry \'kä-nə-ˌkrē, kò-nä-'krē\ Capital (regional pop., 1995 est.: 1,508,000), largest city, and chief Atlantic port of Guinea. Located on Tombo Island and the Kaloum Peninsula, it was founded by the French in 1884. It became the capital successively of the protectorate of Rivières du Sud (1891), the colony of French Guinea (1893), and independent Guinea (1958). Tombo Island, the site of the original settlement, is linked to the peninsula by a causeway. The city was industrialized in the 1950s with the development of iron mining and bauxite production. It is the seat of the University of Conakry (founded 1962).

Conall Cernach \'kō-nəl-'k^{y}er-nək\ Legendary warrior of Celtic mythology who appears in many stories. In *Bricriu's Feast,* in the ULSTER CYCLE, he is one of three knights challenged by a giant to let him chop their heads off after they behead him; of the three, only CÚ CHULAINN keeps the bargain. Conall Cernach is probably related to CERNUNNOS, and their names may be cognates. See also GAWAIN.

Conan Doyle, Arthur See Arthur Conan DOYLE

Conant \'kō-nənt\, **James B(ryant)** (1893–1978) U.S. educator and scientist, president of HARVARD UNIV. (1933–53). Conant received his PhD (1916) from Harvard and taught chemistry there until he was elected its president in 1933. He led the university to broaden the social and geographic makeup of its student body. During World War II he was a central figure in organizing American science, including the development of the atomic bomb. In 1953 he was appointed U.S. high commissioner for West Germany, and in 1955 ambassador. His publications include chemistry textbooks, works on science for the lay reader, and books on educational policy.

concentration camp Internment center established by a government to confine political prisoners or members of national or minority groups for reasons of state security, exploitation, or punishment. The prisoners are usually selected by executive decree or military order. Camps are usually built to house many people in very crowded conditions. Nations that have used such camps include Britain during the SOUTH AFRICAN WAR, the Soviet Union (see GULAG), the U.S. (see MANZANAR RELOCATION

CENTER), and Japan, which interned Dutch civilians in the Dutch East Indies during World War II. "Reeducation camps," sometimes extremely brutal, were widely used by the communists in China during the CULTURAL REVOLUTION and in Cambodia under the KHMER ROUGE. Most notorious are the death camps of Nazi Germany, including AUSCHWITZ, BERGEN-BELSEN, BUCHENWALD, DACHAU, and TREBLINKA.

Concepción \ˌkȯn-sep-ˈsyȯn\ City (pop., 1993 est.: 318,000), capital of Bío-Bío region, southern central Chile. Chile's second-largest city, it was founded in 1550 on the Pacific coast, and was shortly afterward burned twice by ARAUCANIAN Indians. It was struck by numerous earthquakes, two of them followed by tsunamis, and in 1754 it was moved inland to its present site near the mouth of the BÍO-BÍO RIVER. Despite frequent earthquakes, it has become a major commercial and industrial center. A distribution center for southern Chile, it manufactures textiles, food products, and steel.

concept formation Process of developing abstract rules or mental constructs based on sensory experience. Concept formation figures prominently in cognitive development and was a subject of great importance to JEAN PIAGET, who argued that LEARNING entails an understanding of a phenomenon's characteristics and how they are logically linked. NOAM CHOMSKY has argued that certain cognitive structures (such as basic grammatical rules) are innate in human beings. Both men held that, as a concept emerges, it becomes subject to testing: a child's concept of "bird," for example, will be tested against specific instances of birds. The human capacity for PLAY contributes importantly to this process by allowing for consideration of a wide range of possibilities.

Conception Bay Inlet of the Atlantic Ocean, southeastern Newfoundland. Named by a Portuguese explorer who visited the coast in 1500 on the Feast of the Conception, it is about 30 mi (50 km) long and 12 mi (19 km) wide. Its shore settlements, among Newfoundland's oldest and most densely populated, support seafood canneries and beach resorts.

conceptual art Any of various art forms in which the idea for a work of art is considered more important than the finished product. The theory was explored by MARCEL DUCHAMP from c. 1910, but the term was only coined in the late 1950s by EDWARD KIENHOLZ. In the 1960s and '70s it became a major international movement; its leading exponents were Sol LeWitt (born 1928) and Joseph Kosuth (born 1945). Its adherents radically redefined art objects, materials, and techniques, and began questioning the very existence and use of art. Its claim is that the "true" work of art is not a physical object produced by the artist for exhibition or sale, but rather consists of "concepts" or "ideas." Typical conceptual works include photographs, texts, maps, graphs, and image-text combinations that are deliberately rendered visually uninteresting or trivial in order to divert attention to the "ideas" they express. Its manifestations have been extremely diverse; a well-known example is Kosuth's *One and Three Chairs* (1965), which combines a real chair, a photograph of a chair, and a dictionary definition of "chair." Conceptual art was fundamental to much of the art produced in the late 20th century.

Concert of Europe In the post-Napoleonic era, the consensus among the European monarchies favoring preservation of the territorial and political status quo. The term assumed the responsibility and the right of the great powers to intervene in states threatened by internal rebellion. The powers discussed such intervention at several congresses, including those of AIX-LA-CHAPELLE, TROPPAU, LAIBACH, and VERONA.

concertina Portable bellows-operated musical instrument. The first concertina was patented by Sir Charles Wheatstone in London in 1829, and he later produced an instrument with full chromatic capacity. Like the ACCORDION, its sound is produced by free reeds, but it uses buttons rather than keys. The very similar Argentinian bandoneon is square rather than hexagonal.

concerto \kən-ˈcher-tō\ Musical composition for solo instrument and orchestra. The solo concerto grew out of the older CONCERTO GROSSO. Giuseppe Torelli's violin concertos of 1698 are the first known solo concertos. A. VIVALDI, the first important concerto composer, wrote over 350 solo concertos, mostly for violin. J.S. BACH wrote the first keyboard concertos. From the Classical period on, most concertos have been written for piano, followed in popularity by the violin and then the cello. W.A. MOZART wrote 27 piano concertos; LUDWIG VAN BEETHOVEN wrote five; F. MENDELSSOHN, F. CHOPIN, F. LISZT, and J. BRAHMS wrote two apiece. From the outset the concerto has been almost exclusively a three-movement form, with fast tempos in the outer movements and a slow central movement. It has generally been intended to display the soloist's virtuosity, particularly in the unaccompanied and often improvised cadenzas near the ends of the outer movements. 19th- and 20th-century concertos were usually conceived as a kind of dramatic struggle between soloist and orchestra.

concerto grosso Principal orchestral form of the baroque era, characterized by contrast between a small group of soloists and a larger orchestra. The small group (concertino) usually consisted of two violins and CONTINUO, the instruments of the older TRIO SONATA, though wind instruments were also used. The larger group (ripieno) generally consisted of strings with continuo. Alessandro Stradella wrote the first known concerto grosso c. 1675. A. CORELLI's set of 12 (c. 1680–90), J.S. BACH's six Brandenburg Concertos (c. 1720), and G.F. HANDEL's 12 Op. 6 concertos (c. 1740) are the most celebrated examples. From 1750 the concerto grosso was eclipsed by the solo CONCERTO.

conch \ˈkäŋk, ˈkänch\ Marine SNAIL whose shell has a broadly triangular outer whorl and a wide lip, often jutting toward the uppermost point. True conchs (family Strombidae) feed on fine plant matter in warm waters. The queen conch *(Strombus gigas)*, found from Florida to Brazil, has an ornamental shell; the pink opening into the first whorl of the shell may be 12 in. (30 cm) long. The clam-eating fulgur conchs (family Melongenidae) include the channeled conch *(Busycon canaliculatum)* and the lightning conch *(B. contrarium)*, both about 7 in. (18 cm) long and common on the U.S. Atlantic coast. See also WHELK.

Florida horse conch (*Pleuroploca gigantea*).

© E.R. DEGGINGER, THE NATIONAL AUDUBON SOCIETY COLLECTION/PHOTO RESEARCHERS, INC.

Conchobar mac Nessa \ˈkä-nü-ər-mək-ˈne-sə, ˈkäŋ-kō-ər-mək-ˈne-sə\ *or* **Conor** \ˈkä-nər\ In ancient Irish Gaelic literature, the reputed king of the Ulaids of northeastern Ireland at the beginning of the 1st century BC. In the ULSTER CYCLE he is the ideal Irish king. In *The Book of Leinster* (c. 1160), Conor fell in love with the beauty Deirdre. Deirdre, however, was in love with Noísi, with whom she eloped and lived in Scotland; Conor's slaying of his rival caused a revolt in Ulster, and Deirdre killed herself.

Conciliar Movement \kən-ˈsi-lē-ər\ (1409–49) In Roman Catholicism, an effort to strengthen the authority of church councils over that of the papacy. Originally aimed at ending the Western SCHISM, the Conciliar Movement had its roots in legal and intellectual circles in the 13th century but emerged as a force at the Council of Pisa (1409), which elected a third pope in an unsuccessful attempt to reconcile the parties of the existing pope and ANTIPOPE. A second council, the Council of CONSTANCE (1414–18), ended the schism by voiding all papal offices and electing a new pope. Participants hoped to play an ongoing role in the church, but the popes continued to seek supremacy, and the Council of BASEL (1431–49) ended fruitlessly.

conclave In the Roman Catholic church, the assembly of CARDINALS gathered to elect a new POPE, and the system of strict seclusion to which they are submitted. From 1059 the election became the responsibility of the cardinals. When, after the death of Clement IV (1268), the cardinals dithered for two years, the local magistrate locked them in the episcopal palace and fed them only bread and water until they elected GREGORY X. The system of meeting in closed conclave was codified in 1904 by PIUS X. Today election requires a majority of two-thirds plus one. Voting by secret ballot takes place twice a day; ballots are burned after each vote. Until the needed majority is obtained, they are burned with wet straw to make black smoke; white smoke issuing from the Vatican Palace indicates that the vote has resulted in election of a new pope.

Concord \ˈkän-kərd, ˈkän-ˌkȯrd\ City (pop., 1996 est.: 115,000), western California. Located near SAN FRANCISCO, it was laid out in 1868 as Todos Santos and renamed in 1869 for Concord, Mass. Developed as an orchard and poultry center after the railroad reached it in 1912, it is now mainly residential.

Concord Town (pop., 1996 est.: 18,000), eastern Massachusetts. Founded in 1635, it was the first inland Puritan settlement. In 1775 the

British were marching to seize its storehouse of military supplies when they were checked by MINUTEMEN (see Battles of LEXINGTON AND CONCORD). In the 19th century, it was a noted cultural center and the home of writers RALPH WALDO EMERSON, HENRY DAVID THOREAU, NATHANIEL HAWTHORNE, and LOUISA MAY ALCOTT (all buried there). Several historic houses are now museums; Walden Pond, where Thoreau lived and wrote, is nearby.

Concord City (pop., 1996 est.: 37,000), capital of New Hampshire. It lies along the MERRIMACK RIVER above MANCHESTER. Settled in 1727, the community was incorporated in 1733 by Massachusetts as Rumford, but, following bitter litigation, was determined in 1762 to be within the jurisdiction of New Hampshire. Renamed Concord in 1765, it was made the capital in 1808. Printing, carriage making, and granite quarrying were important in its early development; Concord granite is still quarried.

Concord, Battles of Lexington and See Battles of LEXINGTON AND CONCORD

Concordat of 1801 Agreement between NAPOLEON and Pope Pius VII that defined the status of the Roman Catholic Church in France and ended the breach caused by the church reforms of the FRENCH REVOLUTION (see CIVIL CONSTITUTION OF THE CLERGY). The Roman Catholic faith was acknowledged as the religion of the majority of the French people but was not proclaimed as the established religion of the state. Napoleon gained the right to nominate bishops, but their offices were conferred by the pope. The government agreed to pay the clergy, but confiscated church property was not restored. The Concordat remained in effect until 1905.

Concorde First supersonic, passenger-carrying, commercial airplane. Built jointly by British and French manufacturers, it entered regular service in 1976. Its maximum cruising speed is 1,354 mph (2,179 kph), more than twice the speed of sound; the London–New York flight takes less than four hours and can cost close to $10,000.

concrete Artificial stone made of a mixture of CEMENT, aggregate (hard material), and water. In addition to its potential for immense compressive strength and its ability, when poured, to adapt to virtually any form, concrete is fire-resistant and has become one of the most common building materials in the world. The binder usually used today is PORTLAND CEMENT. The aggregate is usually sand and gravel. Additives called admixtures may be used to accelerate the curing (hardening) process in low temperature conditions. Other admixtures trap air in the concrete or slow shrinkage and increase strength. See also PRECAST CONCRETE, PRESTRESSED CONCRETE, REINFORCED CONCRETE.

concubinage \kən-'kyü-bə-nij\ Cohabitation of a man and a woman without the full sanctions of legal MARRIAGE. The Judeo-Christian term concubine has been generally applied exclusively to women; Western studies of non-Western societies use it to refer to partners who are sanctioned by law but lack the status of full wives. See also COMMON-LAW MARRIAGE, HAREM, POLYGAMY.

concurrent programming Computer programming designed for execution on multiple processors, where more than one processor is used to execute a program or complex of programs running simultaneously. It is also used for programming designed for a multitasking environment, where two or more programs share the same memory while running concurrently.

concussion Period of nervous-function impairment that results from relatively mild brain injury, often with no bleeding in the CEREBRAL CORTEX. It causes brief unconsciousness, followed by mental confusion and physical difficulties. These effects usually clear up within hours, but in some cases disturbance of consciousness continues, and there may be residual symptoms. Some level of AMNESIA often accompanies concussion. Recovery from concussion is almost always complete unless more serious injury, such as skull fracture, accompanies it.

Condé \kō^{n}-'dā\, **Louis II de Bourbon, 4th prince de** *known as* **the Great Condé** (1621–1686) French military leader. He distinguished himself in battles with Spain in the Thirty Years' War, and in 1649 he helped suppress the FRONDE uprising. After being arrested by Mazarin in 1650, he rebelled and led the second Fronde, fighting from Spain until he was defeated at the Battle of the Dunes in 1658. Pardoned the next year, he again became one of Louis XIV's greatest generals, winning numerous battles in Spain, Germany, and Flanders. He was a man of great courage, unconventional habits, and an uncommonly sound independence of mind; broadly cultivated, he counted MOLIÈRE and JEAN RACINE among his friends. See also CONDÉ FAMILY.

Condé family \kōn-'dā\ Important French branch of the House of BOURBON, whose members played a significant role in French dynastic politics. The line began with Louis I de Bourbon (1530–1569), 1st prince de Condé, a military leader of the HUGUENOTS in France's Wars of RELIGION. The family's most prominent member was the 4th prince de CONDÉ, one of LOUIS XIV's greatest generals. The princely line died out when Louis-Antoine-Henri de Bourbon-Condé (1772–1804), duc d'Enghien and sole heir of the last prince de Condé, was falsely arrested and shot for treason on NAPOLEON's orders.

condensation Formation of a liquid or solid from its vapor. Condensation usually occurs on a surface that is cooler than the adjacent gas. A substance condenses when the PRESSURE exerted by its vapor exceeds the vapor pressure of its liquid or solid phase at the temperature of the surface where the condensation is to occur. The process causes the release of THERMAL ENERGY. Condensation occurs on a glass of cold water on a warm, humid day when water vapor in the air condenses to form liquid water on the glass's colder surface. Condensation also accounts for the formation of dew, fog, rain, snow, and clouds.

condenser Device for reducing a gas or vapor to a liquid. Condensers are used in power plants to condense exhaust steam from TURBINES and in REFRIGERATION plants to condense refrigerant vapors, such as AMMONIA and FREONS. The petroleum and chemical industries use condensers for hydrocarbons and other chemical vapors. In DISTILLATION, a condenser transforms vapor to liquid. All condensers work by removing heat from the gas or vapor. In some, the gas passes through a long tube of heat-conductive metal, such as copper (usually arranged in a coil or other compact shape), and heat escapes into the surrounding air. Large industrial condensers use water or some other liquid to remove the heat. The term condenser also refers to a device attached to carding machines in textile factories to collect fibers into roving for spinning machines.

Condillac \kō^{n}-dē-'yåk\, **Étienne Bonnot de** (1715–1780) French philosopher, psychologist, and economist. He was ordained a priest in 1740. In his *Essay on the Origin of Human Knowledge* (1746), he systematically discussed the empiricism of JOHN LOCKE. In *Treatise on Sensations* (1754), he questioned Locke's doctrine that the senses provide intuitive knowledge. His economic views, presented in *Commerce and Government* (1776), were based on the notion that value depends on utility rather than labor. The need for something useful, he argued, gives rise to value, while prices result from the exchange of valued items.

conditioning Process in which the frequency or predictability of a behavioral response is increased through reinforcement (i.e., a stimulus or a reward for the desired response). Classical, or respondent, conditioning, involving stimulus substitution, is based on the work of IVAN PAVLOV, who conditioned dogs by ringing a bell each time the aroma of food was presented. Eventually the dogs salivated when the bell rang, even if no food odor was present; salivation was thus the conditioned response. In instrumental, or operant, conditioning, a spontaneous (operant) behavior is either rewarded (reinforced) or punished. When rewarded, a behavior increases in frequency; when punished, it decreases. Operant conditioning was studied in detail by B. F. SKINNER.

condominium In modern property law, individual ownership of one dwelling unit within a multidwelling building. Unit owners have undivided ownership interest in the land and those portions of the building shared in common. This type of cooperative ownership has been present in Europe since the end of the Middle Ages; in the U.S. it dates to the latter half of the 19th century and has been popular in crowded urban areas.

condor Either of two species of large New World VULTURE. Two of the largest flying birds, each is about 50 in. (130 cm) long and weighs 22 lbs (10 kg). Both feed on dead animals. The Andean condor *(Vultur gryphus)*, which ranges from the Pacific coast of South America to the high Andes, has slightly longer wings (10 ft, or 3 m) and is black with a white ruff and bare pinkish head, neck, and crop. The California condor *(Gymnogyps californianus)* is nearly black, with white wing linings, bare yellow head, and red neck and crop. It hovered on the brink of extinction in the 1980s, and every California condor was captured; careful nurturing has recently led to the release of dozens of condors into the wild.

Condorcet \kōⁿ-dȯr-'se\, **marquis de** *orig.* **Marie-Jean-Antoine-Nicolas de Caritat** (1743–1794) French mathematician, statesman, and revolutionary. He showed early promise as a mathematician and was a protégé of JEAN LE ROND D'ALEMBERT. In 1777 he became secretary of the Academy of Sciences. In sympathy with the French Revolution, he was elected to represent Paris in the Legislative Assembly (1791–92), where he called for a republic. His opposition to the arrest of the moderate GIRONDINS led to his being outlawed (1792). While in hiding he wrote his famous *Sketch for a Historical Picture of the Progress of the Human Mind*, in which he advanced the idea of the continuous progress of the human race to an ultimate perfection. He was captured and subsequently found dead in prison.

conducting Art of leading a group of musical performers. Simple coordination does not always require a conductor (members of a Renaissance choir kept together by one tapping another on the shoulder, for example, and musicians in a recording studio listen to a "click track" on headphones). Before c. 1800, the first violinist usually gave the few necessary signals with his bow; the keyboard player might also lead the orchestra, using his hands and head. The growing size of ensembles and growing complexity of the music in the 19th century, including its varying tempos and heightened expressiveness, made it necessary for a person to coordinate and interpret the music for the group. The first conductors, including F. MENDELSSOHN, H. BERLIOZ, and RICHARD WAGNER, were composers themselves. By the end of the 19th century, conducting had become a specialty and the great conductors had become musical stars.

conduction See THERMAL CONDUCTION

conductor Any of various substances that allow the flow of ELECTRIC CURRENT or THERMAL ENERGY. A conductor is a poor INSULATOR because it has a low RESISTANCE to such flow. Electrical conductors are used to conduct electric current, as in the metal wires of an electric CIRCUIT. Electrical conductors are usually metallic. Thermal conductors allow thermal energy to flow because they do not absorb radiant heat; they include materials such as metal and glass.

cone *or* **strobilus** \strō-'bī-ləs, 'strō-bə-ləs\ In botany, a mass of scales or bracts, usually ovate, containing the reproductive organs of certain non-flowering plants. A distinguishing feature of PINES and other CONIFERS, the cone is roughly analogous to the FLOWER of other plants. Cones (strobili) are also found on CLUB MOSSES and HORSETAILS.

coneflower Any of three genera (ECHINACEA, Ratibida, and *Rudbeckia*) of weedy plants in the COMPOSITE FAMILY, native to North America. Some species in each genus have reflexed ray flowers. The purple-flowered perennials *E. angustifolia* and *E. purpurea* are often cultivated as border plants; they have strong-smelling black roots and hairy stems. *Ratibida* species have yellow ray flowers and brownish disk flowers. Prairie coneflower *(Ratibida columnaris)* and *R. pinnata* are grown in wildflower gardens. *Rudbeckia* species have yellow ray flowers and brown or black disk flowers. BLACK-EYED SUSAN, thimble-flower *(R. bicolor)*, and coneflower *(R. laciniata)* are grown as border plants.

Conestoga wagon Horse-drawn covered freight wagon. It originated in the 18th century in the Conestoga Creek region of Pennsylvania. It had a flat body and low sides; with its floor curved up at each end to prevent freight from shifting, it was well suited for travel over early American roads. It became famous as later adapted by westward-traveling pioneers for hauling their possessions; with its tall white canvas top, it resembled a sailing ship from a distance, which earned it the name "prairie schooner."

coney See CONY

Coney Island Amusement area, southern BROOKLYN, New York, on the Atlantic Ocean. Formerly an island, after its creek silted up it became part of LONG ISLAND. The first pavilion and bathhouse were erected in 1844, and it gained popularity with the coming of the subway in 1920. It has a 3.5-mi (5.6-km) boardwalk, an amusement park known for its rollercoaster (the Cyclone), and freak shows (notably Coney Island U.S.A.). It is also the site of the New York Aquarium.

Confederate States of America *or* **Confederacy** Government of the 11 Southern states that seceded from the Union in 1860–61 until its defeat in the AMERICAN CIVIL WAR in 1865. In the months following ABRAHAM LINCOLN's election as president in 1860, seven states of the Deep South (Alabama, Florida, Georgia, Louisiana, Mississippi, South Carolina, and Texas) seceded. After the attack on FORT SUMTER in April 1861, Arkansas, North Carolina, Tennessee, and Virginia joined them. The government was directed by JEFFERSON DAVIS as president, with ALEXANDER H. STEPHENS as vice president. Its principal goals were the preservation of states' rights and the institution of slavery. The government's main concern was raising and maintaining an army. It counted on the influence of KING COTTON to exert financial and diplomatic pressure on the Union from sympathetic European governments. Battlefield victories for the South in 1861–62 gave the Confederacy the moral strength to continue fighting, but from 1863 dwindling finances and battlefield reverses increasingly led to demoralization. The surrender at Appomattox by Gen. ROBERT E. LEE precipitated its dissolution.

Confederation, Articles of See ARTICLES OF CONFEDERATION

Confederation of the Rhine (1806–13) Union of all the states of Germany, except Austria and Prussia, under the aegis of NAPOLEON. Napoleon's primary interest in the confederation, which enabled the French to unify and dominate the country, was as a counterweight to Austria and Prussia. The confederation was abolished after Napoleon's fall from power, but the consolidation it entailed contributed to the movement for German unification.

Confessing Church *German* **Bekennende Kirche.** Movement for revival within the German Protestant churches that developed in the 1930s in resistance to ADOLF HITLER's attempt to make the churches an instrument of Nazi propaganda and politics. The Confessing Church, whose leaders included MARTIN NIEMOLLER and DIETRICH BONHOEFFER, opposed Hitler's "German Christians" and was forced underground as Nazi pressure intensified. The movement continued in World War II, though it was hampered by the conscription of clergy and laity. In 1948 the church ceased to exist when the reorganized Evangelical Church was formed.

confession In the Judeo-Christian tradition, acknowledgment of sinfulness, in public or private, regarded as necessary for divine forgiveness. In the Temple period, YOM KIPPUR included a collective expression of sinfulness, and the day continues in JUDAISM as one of prayer, fasting, and confession. The early Christian Church followed JOHN THE BAPTIST's practice of confession before BAPTISM, but soon instituted confession and penance for the forgiveness of sins committed after baptism. The fourth LATERAN COUNCIL (1215) required annual confession. The Roman Catholic and Eastern Orthodox churches consider penance a SACRAMENT, but most Protestant churches do not.

confidential communication See PRIVILEGED COMMUNICATION

configuration In chemistry, the arrangement in space of the ATOMS in a MOLECULE. It is especially important in organic chemistry (see ORGANIC COMPOUND), because each CARBON atom is at the center of a tetrahedron, with four bonds (see BONDING), one to each corner; if three or all four atoms bonded to the carbon are different, the molecule can assume two different mirror-image (see OPTICAL ACTIVITY, ISOMER) forms. Configuration also applies to some inorganic compounds. Until late in the 20th century, it was hard to determine the true three-dimensional form of a molecule (absolute configuration) experimentally, but modern optical and chemical methods have made it much simpler. Electron configuration is used to describe the number of electrons in the various shells of an atom, which defines its chemical reactivity and the type of bonding it participates in.

confirmation Christian rite in which believers reaffirm the faith into which they were baptized as infants or young children. The rite did not exist in the early church, since those who joined did so as adults and were baptized after instruction. As BAPTISM of infants became common, some means of ascertaining their knowledge and commitment as young adults became necessary. A period of instruction was introduced, after which the candidates were examined and confirmed. In Roman Catholicism confirmation became a SACRAMENT, usually performed by a bishop. The rite is also used in the Anglican and Lutheran churches.

confiscation In law, the act of seizing property without compensation and submitting it to the public treasury. Illegal items such as narcotics or firearms, or profits from the sale of illegal items, may be confiscated by the police. Additionally, government action (e.g., ZONING or rate setting) that reduces the value of property to an owner so as to make it nearly worthless has been held to constitute confiscation. See also EMINENT DOMAIN, SEARCH AND SEIZURE.

conflict In psychology, mental struggle resulting from incompatible or opposing needs, drives, wishes, or demands. A child, for example, may be dependent on his mother but fear her because she is rejecting and punitive. Conflicts that are not readily resolved may cause the person to suffer helplessness and ANXIETY.

conformal map In mathematics, a transformation of one graph into another in such a way that the angle of intersection of any two lines or curves remains unchanged. The most common example is the Mercator MAP, a two-dimensional representation of the surface of the earth that preserves compass directions. Other conformal maps, sometimes called orthomorphic projections, preserve angles but not shapes.

Confucianism Scholarly tradition and way of life propagated by CONFUCIUS in the 6th–5th century BC and followed by the Chinese for more than two millennia. Though not organized as a religion, it has deeply influenced East Asian spiritual and political life in a comparable manner. The core idea is REN ("humaneness," "benevolence"), signifying excellent character in accord with *li* (ritual norms), *zhong* (loyalty to one's true nature), *shu* (reciprocity), and XIAO (filial piety). Together these constitute DE (virtue). MENCIUS, XUNZI, and others sustained Confucianism, but it was not influential until DONG ZHONGSHU emerged in the 2nd century BC. Confucianism was then recognized as the Han state cult, and the FIVE CLASSICS became the core of education. In spite of the influence of TAOISM and BUDDHISM, Confucian ethics have had the strongest influence on the moral fabric of Chinese society. A revival of Confucian thought in the 11th century resulted in NEO-CONFUCIANISM, a major influence in Korea during the CHOSON dynasty and in Japan during the EDO PERIOD.

Confucius *Chinese* **Kongfuzi** *or* **K'ung-fu-tzu** \'kủŋ-'fü-'dzə̇\ (551–479 BC) Ancient Chinese teacher, philosopher, and political theorist. Born into a poor family in the state of Lu, he managed stables and worked as a bookkeeper while educating himself. Mastery of the six arts—ritual, music, archery, charioteering, calligraphy, and arithmetic—and familiarity with history and poetry enabled him to begin a brilliant teaching career in his thirties. Confucius saw education as a process of constant self-improvement and held that its primary function was the training of noblemen *(junzi)*. He saw public service as the natural consequence of education and sought to revitalize Chinese social institutions, including the family, school, community, state, and kingdom. He served in government posts, eventually becoming minister of justice in Lu, but his policies attracted little interest. After a 12-year self-imposed exile during which his circle of students expanded, he returned to Lu at age 67 to teach and write. His life and thoughts are recorded in the *LUNYU (Analects)*. See also CONFUCIANISM.

Congaree Swamp National Monument \'käŋ-gə-rē\ National preserve, central South Carolina. Authorized in 1976, it covers 15,138 acres (6,126 hectares) of alluvial floodplain on the Congaree River. It contains the last significant tract of virgin Southern bottomland hardwoods in the southeastern U.S., including loblolly pine, water tupelo, hickory, and oak, some of record size.

congenital disorder Structural abnormality (e.g., ATRESIA, AGENESIS), functional problem (e.g., CYSTIC FIBROSIS, PHENYLKETONURIA), or disease present at birth. Almost all are due to genetic factors (inherited or spontaneous MUTATIONS, CHROMOSOMAL DISORDERS), environmental influences during pregnancy (RUBELLA or other maternal factors, exposure to toxins or radiation), or both. The most sensitive period is the first eight weeks after conception, during which time the human EMBRYO is essentially formed. Major congenital malformations form during this period. Some inherited disorders result from simple Mendelian DOMINANCE or RECESSIVENESS. Others may involve multiple genes. Chromosomal disorders are rare, because few affected fetuses survive to be born. Environmental influences may affect only one of a pair of identical twins. At least 30 significant defects probably occur per thousand births. Incidence of specific defects varies widely in different racial groups. See also BIRTH DEFECT, DOWN'S SYNDROME.

congenital heart disease See HEART MALFORMATION

conger eel Any of about 100 species of marine EELS (family Congridae) with no scales, a large head, large gill slits, a wide mouth, and strong teeth. Conger eels are usually grayish to blackish, with a paler belly and black-edged fins. Found in all oceans, sometimes in deep water, they may grow about 6 ft (1.8 m) long. Conger eels are carnivores. Many species, such as the European conger *(Conger conger)*, are valued as food. The American conger, or sea eel *(C. oceanicus)*, is a fierce game fish.

congestive heart failure Heart failure resulting in symptoms that are distant from the heart, related mainly to salt and water retention in the tissues rather than directly to reduced blood flow. It may vary from the most minimal symptoms to sudden pulmonary EDEMA or a rapidly lethal shocklike state (see SHOCK). Chronic states of varying severity may last years. Symptoms tend to worsen as the body's attempts to compensate for the condition create a vicious circle. The patient has trouble breathing, at first during exertion and later even at rest. Fluid accumulates at the lowest point of the body and eventually may be found in the ABDOMINAL and THORACIC cavities. Blood pools in the veins (vascular congestion) because the heart does not pump efficiently enough to allow it to return.

conglomerate \kən-'glä-mə-rət\ In petrology, lithified sedimentary rock consisting of rounded fragments larger than 0.08 in. (2 mm) in diameter. It is commonly contrasted with BRECCIA. Conglomerates are usually subdivided according to the average size of their constituent materials into pebble (fine), cobble (medium), and boulder (coarse).

conglomerate In business, a widely diversified company, especially a CORPORATION that acquires other firms whose activities are unrelated to its primary activity. Conglomerate mergers are undertaken for many reasons, including the prospect of making additional use of existing facilities, improving the corporation's overall marketing position, decreasing the risk of relying on a single type of product, and effecting corporate reorganization. The practice was widespread in the 1960s and 1980s, but in the 1990s many conglomerates began to sell off unwanted subsidiaries.

Congo, Democratic Republic of the *formerly (1971–97)* **Republic of Zaire** *(1960–71)* **Congo** *(1908–60)* **Belgian Congo** *(1885–1908)* **Congo Free State** Republic, central Africa. Area: 905,356 sq mi

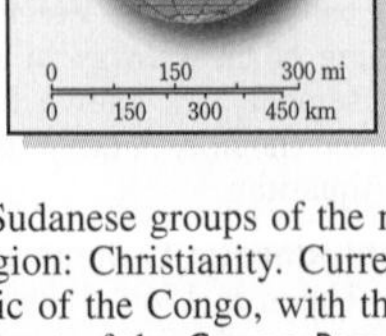

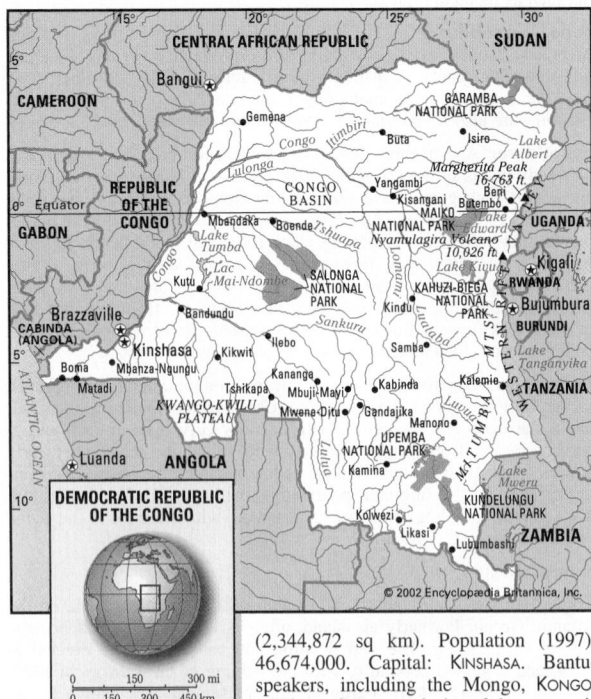

(2,344,872 sq km). Population (1997): 46,674,000. Capital: KINSHASA. Bantu-speakers, including the Mongo, KONGO, and LUBA, form a majority of the country's population; among non-Bantu speakers are Sudanese groups of the north. Languages: French, English (official). Religion: Christianity. Currency: Congolese franc. The Democratic Republic of the Congo, with the third-largest land-area in Africa, occupies the heart of the CONGO RIVER basin, from which high plateaus rise in every direction. At its narrow strip of Atlantic coast the Congo empties into the sea. The country straddles the equator; its climate is humid and tropical. It is one of the poorest countries in the world; its economy is based on mining and agriculture. Export crops include coffee, palm products, tea, cocoa, and cotton; mining products include copper, cobalt, and industrial diamonds. It is ruled by a military regime; the head of state is the president, which office was taken by the regime's leader in the late 1990s. Prior to European colonization, several native kingdoms had emerged in the region, including the 16th-century Luba kingdom and the Kuba federation, which reached its peak in the 18th century. European development began late in the 19th century when King LEOPOLD II of Belgium financed HENRY MORTON STANLEY's exploration of the Congo River. The 1884–85 Berlin West Africa Conference recognized the Congo Free State with Leopold as its sovereign. The growing demand for rubber helped finance the exploitation of the Congo, but abuses against native peoples outraged Western nations and forced Leopold to grant the Free State a colonial charter as the Belgian Congo (1908). Independence was granted in 1960, and the country's name was changed to Zaire. The post-independence period was marked by unrest, culminating in a military coup that brought Gen. MOBUTU SESE SEKO to power in 1965. Mismanagement, corruption, and increasing violence devastated the infrastructure and economy. Mobutu was deposed in 1997 by LAURENT KABILA, who restored the country's name to Congo. Instability in neighboring countries and desire for Congo's mineral wealth led to military involvement by numerous African countries. Kabila was assassinated in 2001 and succeeded by his son.

Congo, Republic of the *formerly* **Middle Congo** Republic, western central Africa. Area: 132,047 sq mi (342,000 sq km). Population (1997): 2,583,000. Capital: BRAZZAVILLE. Nearly half of the population belongs to one of the KONGO tribes. The Teki are less numerous, as are the Ubangi people. Language: French (official), various Bantu languages. Religions: Christianity, traditional religions. Currency: CFA franc. A narrow coast-

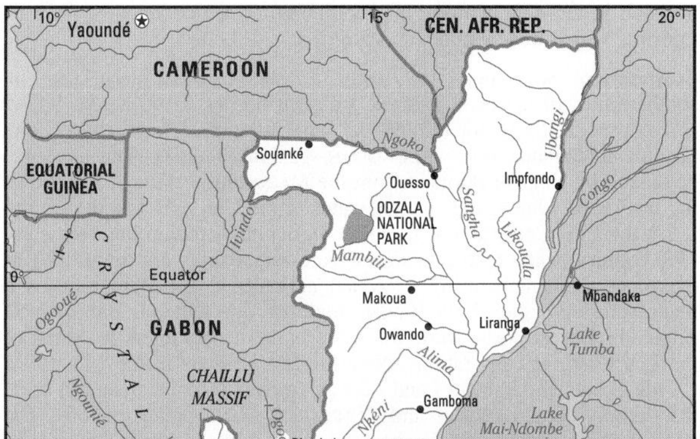

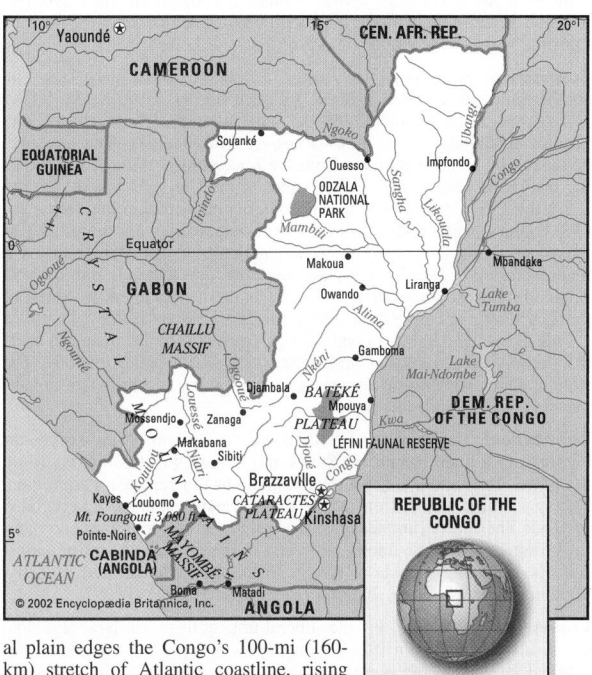

al plain edges the Congo's 100-mi (160-km) stretch of Atlantic coastline, rising into low mountains and plateaus that slope eastward in a vast plain to the CONGO RIVER. The country straddles the equator; rain forests cover nearly two-thirds of the country, and wildlife is abundant. The Congo has a centrally planned, developing economy. Mining products, crude petroleum and natural gas, account for more than 90% of the country's exports. A 1997 transitional constitution vested executive power in the president and legislative power in a national transitional council. In precolonial days the area was home to several thriving kingdoms, including the KONGO, which had its beginnings in the 1st millennium AD. The SLAVE TRADE began in the 15th century with the arrival of the Portuguese; it supported the local kingdoms and dominated the area until its suppression in the 19th. century. The French arrived in the mid-19th century and established treaties with two of the kingdoms, placing them under French protection prior to becoming part of the colony of French Congo. In 1910 it was renamed FRENCH EQUATORIAL AFRICA and the area of the Congo became known as Middle (Moyen) Congo. In 1946 Middle Congo became a French overseas territory and in 1958 voted to become an autonomous republic within the FRENCH COMMUNITY. Full independence came two years later. The area has suffered from political instability since independence. Congo's first president was ousted in 1963. A Marxist party, the Congolese Labor Party, gained strength, and in 1968 another coup, led by Major Marien Ngouabi, created the People's Republic of the Congo. Ngouabi was assassinated in 1977. A series of military rulers followed, at first militantly socialist but later oriented toward social democracy. Fighting between local militias in 1997 badly disrupted the economy; a peace process was under way in 2000.

Congo River *or* **Zaire River** \zä-'ir\ River, western central Africa. Rising in Zambia as the Chambeshi and flowing 2,900 mi (4,700 km) through the Democratic Republic of the Congo to the Atlantic Ocean, it is the second-longest river in Africa. It flows through three contrasting regions: the upper Congo, characterized by lakes, waterfalls, and rapids; the middle Congo, with seven cataracts known as Boyoma (Stanley) Falls; and the lower Congo, which divides into two branches forming a vast lake area called the Malebo (Stanley) Pool.

Congregationalism Movement that arose among English Protestant Christian churches in the late 16th and early 17th century. It developed as one branch of PURITANISM and emphasized the right and duty of each congregation to govern itself independent of higher human authority. Its greatest influence and numbers were in the U.S., where Puritans first established it at Plymouth Colony. The Half Way Covenant (1662) loosened requirements for church membership, and the GREAT AWAKENING led U.S. Congregationalism away from its Calvinist roots. Many churches defected to UNITARIANISM. In general, Congregationalists eschew creeds and emphasize preaching over sacraments, accepting only BAPTISM and the EUCHARIST. English Congregationalists are now part of the United Reform Church. Most American Congregationalists are now part of the United Church of Christ. Baptist, Disciples of Christ, and Unitarian Universalist churches also practice congregational polity.

Congress, Library of Library of the U.S., the largest and one of the greatest of what may be considered national libraries. Founded in Washington, D.C., in 1800, it was housed in the Capitol until the building was burned by British troops in 1814; it moved to permanent quarters in 1897. In addition to serving as a reference source for members of Congress and other government officers, it is outstanding among the learned institutions of the world, with magnificent collections of books, manuscripts, music, prints, and maps. It contains some 19 million books and more than 33 million manuscripts.

Congress of the United States Legislature of the U.S., established under the CONSTITUTION OF THE U.S. (1789) and separated structurally from the EXECUTIVE and judicial (see JUDICIARY) branches of government. It succeeded the unicameral congress created by the ARTICLES OF CONFEDERATION (1781). It consists of the Senate and the House of Representatives. Representation in the Senate is fixed at two senators per state. Until passage of the 17th Amendment (1913), senators were appointed by the state legislatures; since then they have been elected directly. In the House, representation is proportional to each state's population; total membership is restricted (since 1912) to 435 members. Congressional business is processed by committees: bills are debated in committees in both houses, and reconciliation of the two resulting versions takes place in a conference committee. A presidential veto can be overridden by a two-thirds majority in each house. Congress's constitutional powers include the setting and collecting of taxes, borrowing money on credit, regulating commerce, coining money, declaring war, raising and supporting armies, and making all laws necessary for the execution of its powers. All finance-related legislation must originate in the House; powers exclusive to the Senate include approval of presidential nominations, ratification of treaties, and adjudication of impeachments. See also BICAMERAL SYSTEM.

Congress Party See INDIAN NATIONAL CONGRESS

Congreve, William (1670–1729) English dramatist. He was a young protégé of JOHN DRYDEN when his first major play, *The Old Bachelour* (1693), met with great success. Later came *The Double-Dealer* (1693), *Love for Love* (1695), and *The Way of the World* (1700), his masterpiece. Other works include the once-popular tragedy *The Mourning Bride* (1697), many poems, translations, and two opera librettos. Congreve shaped the English COMEDY OF MANNERS with his brilliant comic dialogue, satirical portrayal of fashionable society, uproarious bawdiness, and ironic scrutiny of the affectations of his age. See also RESTORATION LITERATURE.

William Congreve, oil painting by Sir Godfrey Kneller, 1709; in the National Portrait Gallery, London.

BY COURTESY OF THE NATIONAL PORTRAIT GALLERY, LONDON

conic section Any two-dimensional curve traced by the intersection of a right circular cone with a plane. If the plane is perpendicular to the cone's axis, the resulting curve is a CIRCLE. Intersections at other angles result in ELLIPSES, PARABOLAS, and HYPERBOLAS. The conic sections are studied in EUCLIDEAN GEOMETRY to analyze their physical properties and in ANALYTIC GEOMETRY to derive their equations. In either context, they have useful applications to OPTICS, antenna design, structural engineering, and architecture.

conifer Any member of the order Coniferales, woody plants that bear their SEEDS and POLLEN on separate, CONE-shaped structures. They constitute the largest division of GYMNOSPERMS, with more than 550 species. Most are evergreen, upright trees and shrubs. They grow throughout the world (except in Antarctica) and prefer temperate climate zones. Conifers include the PINES *(Pinus)*, JUNIPERS *(Juniperus)*, SPRUCES *(Picea)*, HEMLOCKS *(Tsuga)*, FIRS *(Abies)*, LARCHES *(Larix)*, YEWS *(Taxus)*, CYPRESSES *(Cupressus)*, BALD CYPRESS cypresses *(Taxodium)*, DOUGLAS FIRS *(Pseudotsuga)*, ARBORVITAES *(Thuja)*, and related groups. They include the world's smallest and tallest trees. Conifers supply SOFTWOOD timber used for general construction, mine timbers, fence posts, poles, boxes and crates, and other articles, as well as pulpwood for paper. The wood is also used as fuel and in the manufacture of cellulose products, plywood, and veneers. The trees are the source of RESINS, volatile oils, TURPENTINE, tars, and pharmaceuticals. Conifer leaves vary in shape but generally have a reduced surface area to minimize water loss. Especially in the pines, firs, and spruces, the leaves are long and stiff and are commonly referred to as needles. Cypresses, CEDARS, and others have smaller, scalelike leaves. Conifers were the dominant type of vegetation just before the advent of angiosperms (see FLOWERING PLANT).

conjoined twins *or* **Siamese twins** Identical twins (see MULTIPLE BIRTH) whose EMBRYOS did not separate completely. Conjoined twins are physically joined (typically along the trunk or at the front, side, or back of the head) and often share some organs. Symmetrical conjoined twins usually have no birth anomalies except at the areas of fusion and can sometimes be separated by surgery. In asymmetrical conjoined twins, one is fairly well developed, but the other is severely underdeveloped and dependent on the larger twin for nutrition. The underdeveloped twin may have to be surgically separated to save the larger twin. The term originally referred to Chang and Eng, born in 1811 in Siam, who were joined by a ligament from breastbone to navel. Widely exhibited, they married two sisters and fathered several children.

conjugation Interaction of adjacent bonds in a chemical COMPOUND with multiple alternating single and double COVALENT BONDS; the resulting conjugated bonds are in a chemical sense intermediate between single and double bonds because of increased possible electron delocalization and sharing. One example of conjugation occurs when two double bonds originate in carbon atoms linked by a single bond; another is the carboxyl group (see CARBOXYLIC ACID, FUNCTIONAL GROUP), in which the carbonyl group (—C=O) is adjacent to a hydroxyl group (—OH). Conjugation of double bonds often gives rise to intensely colored substances.

conjunctivitis Inflammation of the conjunctiva, the delicate lining of the eyelids and the front of the white of the EYE. It may be caused by infection (when it is commonly called "pink eye"), chemical burn, physical injury, or allergy. Often the cornea is also inflamed (keratoconjunctivitis). Infectious causes include several viruses and bacteria, including those that cause trachoma and GONORRHEA, both of which can lead to blindness. Conjunctivitis from erythema multiforme, a skin eruption, can also cause blindness.

conjuring Art of entertaining by giving the illusion of performing impossible feats. The conjurer is an actor who combines psychology, manual dexterity, and mechanical aids to effect the desired illusion. The form was established by the medieval era, when traveling conjurers performed at fairs and in the homes of the nobility. In the 19th–20th century, conjuring was performed on stage by such magicians as JEAN-EUGENE ROBERT-HOUDIN, HARRY HOUDINI, and Harry Blackstone. In the late 20th century such magicians as Doug Henning and David Copperfield performed colorful spectacles on television, while the postmodern team Penn and Teller offered a quieter brand of magic that emphasized irony and illusion.

Conkling, Roscoe (1829–1888) U.S. politician. Born in Albany, N.Y., he became a lawyer, orator, and Whig Party leader. In the U.S. House of Representatives (1859–65) and Senate (1867–81), he became a leader of the Radical Republicans and advocated severe Reconstruction measures. Resisting efforts by Pres. RUTHERFORD B. HAYES to achieve civil-service reform, he retained control of New York patronage. At the 1880 Republican convention, he led the Stalwart faction in supporting former Pres. ULYSSES S. GRANT. In 1881 he resigned from the Senate in a patronage dispute with Pres. JAMES GARFIELD.

Connacht *or* **Connaught** \'kä-ˌnȯt\ Province (population 1993: 433,000), northwestern Ireland. An ancient native kingdom, it was Christianized by St. PATRICK in the 5th century. Dominated from the 11th century by the O'Connors of Roscommon, it endured an Anglo-Norman invasion in the 12th century. It is composed of the counties of Galway, Leitrim, Mayo, Roscommon, and Sligo.

Connecticut State (pop., 1997 est.: 3,270,000), northeastern U.S. The southernmost of the NEW ENGLAND states, it borders LONG ISLAND SOUND and covers 5,018 sq mi (12,997 sq km). Its capital is HARTFORD. The original inhabitants were ALGONQUIAN-speaking Indians. The area was colonized by English Puritans from the MASSACHUSETTS BAY COLONY during the 1630s. One of the original states of the Union, it was the fifth to ratify the U.S. Constitution. It was an agricultural region until the early 19th century, when textile factories were established, and by 1850 employment in manufacturing exceeded agriculture; the state remains a manufacturing center. NEW HAVEN, home of YALE UNIV., is one of New England's largest ports, while STAMFORD is the headquarters for some of the U.S.'s largest corporations. New London is home to the U.S. Coast Guard Academy. Highways and railways traverse Connecticut and serve the densely settled coastal and CONNECTICUT RIVER valley regions. The state abounds with historical sites and memorials, and there are numerous state forests and state parks.

Connecticut, University of State university system of universities incorporating a main campus in Storrs and branches in Groton, Hartford, Stamford, Torrington, and Waterbury, and a health center in Farmington. The agricultural school from which the university emerged was founded in 1881. The Storrs campus consists of colleges of agriculture and natural resources and of liberal arts and sciences and 12 professional schools, including schools of law, engineering, medicine, and dentistry. Total enrollment is about 26,000.

Connecticut College Private liberal-arts college in New London, Conn. It was founded in 1911 as a women's college, and became coeducational in 1969. It offers a range of programs leading to the bachelor's degree. It maintains centers for international studies, conservation biology, and arts and technology. Enrollment is about 1,900.

Connecticut River River, NEW ENGLAND, northeastern U.S. Rising in the Connecticut Lakes in northern New Hampshire, it flows south for a course of 407 mi (655 km) to empty into LONG ISLAND SOUND. It forms the entire boundary between Vermont and New Hampshire. The lower 60 mi (97 km) of the river are tidal. The longest river in New England, it is extensively developed for hydroelectric power.

connectionism In COGNITIVE SCIENCE, an approach that proposes to model human information processing in terms of a network of interconnected units operating in parallel. The units are typically classified as input units, hidden units, or output units. Each unit has a default activation level that can vary as a function of the strength of (1) the inputs it receives from other units, (2) the different weights associated with its connections to the other units, and (3) its own bias. Connectionism, unlike traditional computational models in cognitive science, holds that information is distributed throughout entire networks instead of being localized in functionally discrete, semantically interpretable states.

connective tissue Tissue in the body that maintains the form of the body and its organs and provides cohesion and internal support, including BONE, LIGAMENTS, TENDONS, CARTILAGE, ADIPOSE TISSUE, and aponeuroses. Its major components are different kinds of cells and extracellular fibers and the ground substance, which varies in consistency from thin gel to rigid structure. Various combinations of these elements make up the different kinds of connective tissue. Connective-tissue diseases are either genetic disorders, attacking one of its elements (e.g., MARFAN'S SYNDROME), or acquired inflammatory or immune-system diseases (e.g., RHEUMATOID ARTHRITIS, OSTEOARTHRITIS, systemic LUPUS ERYTHEMATOSUS, and RHEUMATIC FEVER).

Connelly, Marc(us Cook) (1890–1980) U.S. playwright, screenwriter, and director. Born in McKeesport, Pa., he covered theatrical news as a journalist in Pittsburgh and New York. He collaborated with GEORGE S. KAUFMAN on *Dulcy* (1921), which they followed with the comedies *To the Ladies* (1922) and *Beggar on Horseback* (1924) and the librettos for *Helen of Troy, New York* (1923), and *Be Yourself* (1924). Connelly went on to write *Green Pastures* (1930, Pulitzer Prize; film, 1936), his best-known work, and *The Farmer Takes a Wife* (1934; film, 1935). His screenplays include *Captains Courageous* (1937).

Connery, Sean *orig.* **Thomas** *later* **Sir Sean** (born 1930) Scottish actor. He worked at odd jobs and entered bodybuilding competitions before making his London stage debut in the chorus of *South Pacific* (1951). After several minor roles, he starred as James Bond in the film version of IAN FLEMING's *Dr. No* (1962) and went on to play Secret Agent 007 in six other films. A compelling character actor as well as a perennial sex symbol, he has acted in films such as *The Man Who Would Be King* (1975), *The Name of the Rose* (1986), *The Untouchables* (1987, Academy Award), *Indiana Jones and the Last Crusade* (1989), and *The Russia House* (1990).

Connolly, Maureen (Catherine) (1934–1969) U.S. tennis player. Born in San Diego, she became the youngest winner of the National Girl's Tournament at age 14. "Little Mo" won her first National Women's title in 1951. In 1953 she became the first woman to win the Grand Slam (the Wimbledon, U.S., Australian, and French singles competitions). Her career was ended in 1954 by a horseback-riding accident.

Connor, Ralph *orig.* **Charles William Gordon** (1860–1937) Canadian novelist. Ordained a Presbyterian minister in 1890, he became a missionary to mining and lumber camps in the Canadian Rocky Mtns.; this experience and memories of his childhood in Glengarry, Ontario, provided material for his novels, including *The Sky Pilot* (1899) and *The Prospector* (1904), which combining adventure with religious messages and wholesome sentiment, made him the best-selling Canadian novelist of the early 20th century. His best books are considered to be *The Man from Glengarry* (1901) and *Glengarry School Days* (1902).

Connors, Jimmy *orig.* **James Scott** (born 1952) U.S. tennis champion. Born in East St. Louis, Ill., he grew up in nearby Belleville. In 1974 he won three Grand Slam tournaments (U.S., Australian, and Wimbledon) but was barred from the French Open because he had joined World Team Tennis. He won the Wimbledon and U.S. doubles (with Ilie Nastase) in 1975, the Wimbledon singles in 1982, and the U.S. singles titles in 1976, 1978, 1982, and 1983. His famous temper tantrums ushered in an era of such displays on the championship circuit.

conodont \'kō-nə-,dänt\ Minute toothlike FOSSIL composed of the mineral apatite (calcium phosphate); conodonts are among the most frequently encountered fossils in marine sedimentary rocks of Paleozoic age. They are the remains of animals that lived 543–248 million years ago that are believed to have been small marine invertebrates living in the open oceans and coastal waters throughout the tropical and temperate zones.

Conor See CONCHOBAR MAC NESSA

conquistador \kän-'kēs-tə-,dȯr\ Any of the adventurers who took part in the Spanish conquest of the Americas in the 16th century. Under HERNAN CORTES a force of some 500 men and 16 horses conquered Mexico's AZTEC empire. A force under PEDRO DE ALVARADO went on to subdue Guatemala. FRANCISCO PIZARRO defeated the INCAS in Peru with 180 men and 37 horses; his companion DIEGO DE ALMAGRO led an expedition to Chile. Further expeditions extended Spanish rule over much of South America. Though renowned for their bravery, the conquistadores remain notorious for their avarice and the destruction they wrought on native populations and civilizations. They were soon replaced by administrators and settlers from Spain.

Conrad, Joseph *orig.* **Józef Teodor Konrad Korzeniowski** (1857–1924) Polish-British novelist and short-story writer. His father was a Polish patriot who was exiled to northern Russia, and Conrad was an orphan by 12. He managed to join the French merchant marine, and in 1878 the British merchant navy, where he pursued a career for most of the next 15 years; his naval experiences would provide the material for most of his novels. Though he knew little English before he was 20, he became one of the master English stylists. He is noted for tales in rich prose of dangerous life at sea and in exotic places, settings he used to reveal his real concern, his deeply pessimistic vision of the human struggle. Of his many novels, which include *Almayer's Folly* (1895), *An Outcast of the Islands* (1896), *The Nigger of the "Narcissus"* (1897), *Lord Jim* (1900), *Typhoon* (1902), *Nostromo* (1904), *The Secret Agent* (1907), *Under Western Eyes* (1911), *Chance* (1912), and *Victory* (1915), several are regarded as masterpieces. He also published seven story collections; the novella "Heart of Darkness" (1902) is his most famous shorter work. Conrad's influence on later novelists has been profound.

Conrad I (died 918) German king (911–18). He was duke of Franconia and a member of the powerful Franconian dynasty known as the Conradines. His reign was a bitter struggle to maintain the traditions of the Carolingian kingship against the growing power of Saxon, Bavarian, and Swabian dukes. Conrad failed to gain the support of the church, and his military campaigns were unsuccessful. Unable to establish his family as the East Frankish royal house, he proposed his opponent, Henry of Saxony, as his successor.

Conrad II (c. 990–1039) German king (1024–39) and Holy Roman Emperor (1027–39), founder of the Salian (or Franconian) dynasty. In 1016 he married a duchess to whom he was distantly related, and the emperor HENRY II used the marriage as a pretext to have him exiled. The two men were later reconciled, and Conrad was crowned king of Germany in 1024. A rebellion of German nobles and princes of Lombardy collapsed (1025), and Conrad was made successively king of Italy (1026) and emperor (1027). He instituted legislative reforms, issuing a new set of feudal constitutions for Lombardy. His son Henry was elected king in 1028 and became his chief counselor. Conrad defeated Poland (1028), regaining lands lost earlier. He inherited Burgundy (1034) and resolved dissensions among the great princes in Italy (1038).

Conrad III (1093–1152) German king (1138–52), the first of the HOHENSTAUFEN DYNASTY. Nephew of Emperor Henry V of Germany, he revolted when he was passed over as heir by the electors, and he was crowned antiking at Nuremberg (1127) and king of Italy (1128). Returning to Germany in 1132, he fought the German king Lothair II until 1135, when Conrad submitted and was pardoned. He became king when Lothair died, quelling resistance in Bavaria and Saxony. Conrad set out for Palestine on the Second CRUSADE (1147) and visited Constantinople (1148), where he cemented an alliance with MANUEL I COMNENUS. Unable to visit Rome, he never received the imperial crown.

Conrad von Hötzendorf \'kōn-,rät-fȯn-'hœt-sən-,dȯrf\, **Franz (Xaver Josef), Graf (Count)** (1852–1925) Austrian soldier. A career officer in the Austro-Hungarian army, he became chief of staff in 1906. A conservative propagandist of Austria-Hungary, he advocated preventive wars against Serbia and Italy, for which he was briefly dismissed in 1911. In World War I, he planned the successful Austro-German offensive of 1915, but was later hampered by German domination and lack of military resources. He was dismissed when CHARLES I took command in 1916.

Conrail *in full* **Consolidated Rail Corp.** U.S. railroad company created by the federal government in 1973 to take over six bankrupt northeastern railroads. Conrail began operations in 1976 with major portions of the Central Railroad Co. of New Jersey, Erie Lackawanna Railway Co., Lehigh & Hudson River Railway Co., Lehigh Valley Railroad Co., Penn Central Transportation Co., and Reading Co. Conrail's network carries freight traffic over 15 states, from the Atlantic Ocean to St. Louis and from the Ohio River north to Canada. Its passenger traffic was turned over to AMTRAK and regional transportation authorities in 1983. Its stock was put up for sale to the public in 1987.

conscientious objector One who opposes participation in military service on the basis of religious, philosophical, or political belief. A feature of Western society since the beginning of the Christian era, conscientious objection developed as a doctrine of the MENNONITES (16th century), the Society of FRIENDS (17th century), and others. Exemptions may be unconditional, conditioned on alternative civilian service, or limited to combat duty. Those who refuse CONSCRIPTION may face imprisonment. Philosophical or political reasons are acceptable grounds for exemption in many European countries, but the U.S. only recognizes membership in a religious group that endorses PACIFISM.

consciousness Quality or state of being aware. As applied to the lower animals, consciousness refers to the capacity for SENSATION and, usually, simple volition. In higher animals, this capacity may also include THINKING and EMOTION. In human beings, consciousness is understood to include "meta-awareness," an awareness that one is aware. The term also refers broadly to the upper level of mental life of which the person is aware, as contrasted with UNCONSCIOUS processes. Levels of consciousness (e.g., ATTENTION VS. SLEEP) are correlated with patterns of electrical activity in the brain (brain waves). See also philosophy of MIND.

conscription *or* **draft** Compulsory enrollment for service in a country's armed forces. It has existed at least since the Egyptian Old Kingdom in the 27th century BC. It usually takes the form of selective service rather than universal conscription. (The latter generally refers to compulsory military service by all able-bodied men between certain ages, though a few countries have also drafted women—notably Israel, which has required both men and women to serve in its armed forces since 1948.) The U.S. established a draft in the American Civil War but did not use it again until 1917. Like Britain, the U.S. abandoned conscription at the end of World War I but reverted to it when World War II threatened. The U.S. retained the draft 1948–73 but now maintains a volunteer army. See also U.S. ARMY.

consequentialism In ETHICS, the doctrine that an action is right or wrong according to whether it maximizes intrinsic value (see AXIOLOGY) in the universe. The simplest form of consequentialism is classical (or hedonistic) UTILITARIANISM, which asserts that an action is right or wrong according to whether it maximizes the net balance of pleasure over pain in the universe. Other forms differ from classical utilitarianism either in the class of things to which intrinsic value is ascribed (e.g., G. E. MOORE's ideal utilitarianism, ethical EGOISM) or in the category of things to which the test of consequences is conceived as properly applicable. See also DEONTOLOGICAL ETHICS.

conservation Planned management of a natural resource or of a particular ECOSYSTEM to prevent exploitation, pollution, destruction, or neglect and to ensure the future usability of the resource. Living resources are renewable, minerals and fossil fuels are nonrenewable. In the West, conservation efforts date to 17th-century efforts to protect European forests in the face of increasing demands for fuel and building materials. NATIONAL PARKS, first established in the 19th century, were dedicated to the preservation of uncultivated land not only to provide a safe haven to wildlife but to protect watershed areas and help ensure a clean water supply. National legislation and international treaties and regulations aim to strike a balance between the need for development and the need to conserve the environment for the future.

conservation law *or* **law of conservation** In physics, the principle that certain quantities within an isolated system do not change over time. When a substance in an isolated system changes PHASE, the total amount of MASS does not change. When ENERGY is changed from one form to another in an isolated system, there is no change in the total amount of energy. When a transfer of MOMENTUM occurs in an isolated system, the total amount of momentum is conserved. The same is true for ELECTRIC CHARGE in a system: charge lost by one particle is gained by another. Conservation laws make it possible to predict the macroscopic behavior of a system without having to consider the microscopic details of a physical process or chemical reaction.

conservation of energy See conservation of ENERGY

conservatism Political attitude or ideology denoting a preference for institutions and practices that have evolved historically and are thus manifestations of continuity and stability. It was first expressed in the modern era through the works of EDMUND BURKE in reaction to the FRENCH REVOLUTION, which he believed tarnished its ideals by its excesses. Conservatives believe that the implementation of change should be minimal and gradual. Their perspective tends to be right of center, appreciative of history, and more realistic than idealistic. Well-known conservative parties include the British Conservative Party, the Christian Democratic parties of Germany and Italy, the U.S. REPUBLICAN PARTY, and the Japanese LIBERAL-DEMOCRATIC PARTY. See also CHRISTIAN DEMOCRACY, LIBERALISM, RIGHT.

Conservative Judaism Form of Judaism that mediates between REFORM JUDAISM and ORTHODOX JUDAISM. Founded in 19th-century Germany as the Historical School, it arose among German-Jewish theologians who advocated change but found Reform positions extreme. They accepted the Reform emphasis on critical scholarship, but wished to maintain a stricter observance of Jewish law (e.g., dietary laws) and continued belief in the coming of the MESSIAH. In 1886, rabbis of this centrist persuasion founded the Jewish Theological Seminary of America (New York), leading to the development of Conservative Judaism as a religious movement.

Conservative Party *officially* **National Union of Conservative and Unionist Associations.** British political party whose guiding principles include promotion of private property and enterprise, maintenance of a strong military and foreign policy, and preservation of traditional cultural values and institutions. It is the heir of the old TORY Party, whose members began forming "conservative associations" after electoral rights were extended to the middle class in 1832. The modern party (whose members are often known as Tories) is essentially a coalition of two groups, and must balance its traditionalist and communitarian wing against its libertarian and individualist wing. It also experiences internal conflict over Britain's relationship with the EUROPEAN UNION. Its membership is heavily dependent on the landowning and middle classes, but its electoral base has extended at times to incorporate about one-third of the working class. Since World War I, it and the LABOUR PARTY have dominated British politics.

Conservative Party (Canada) See PROGRESSIVE CONSERVATIVE PARTY OF CANADA

Conservatoire des Arts et Métiers \kōü-ser-vä-'twär-dā-'zär-zā-mā-'tyā\ (French: "Conservatory of Arts and Trades") Public institution of higher learning in Paris, dedicated to applied science and technology, that grants degrees primarily in engineering. It is also a laboratory that specializes in testing, measuring, and standardization. Its third component is a national museum of technology. It was founded by JACQUES DE VAUCANSON in 1794, in the former priory of St.-Martin-des-Champs, to house his own and others' inventions; his automated LOOM, found there after his death by J.-M. JACQUARD, became the basis for Jacquard's revolutionary design. It contains numerous elaborate automatons and other mechanical devices popular in the 18th century.

conservatory In architecture, a heavily glazed structure, frequently attached to and directly entered from a dwelling, in which plants are protected and displayed. Unlike the GREENHOUSE, an informal structure situated in the working area of a garden, the conservatory became a popular 19th-century decorative architectural feature proclaiming the status of its owner. The most outstanding example is Joseph Paxton's CRYSTAL PALACE.

conservatory School devoted to musical training. Originating in the 16th-century name for Italian orphanages (from Latin, *conservare:* "to protect"), which often gave their charges musical training, the term gradually came to apply to music schools. They typically offer instruction to people of all ages, but the primary focus is on students aged 10–25. Important U.S. conservatories include the CURTIS INSTITUTE, the EASTMAN SCHOOL, the JUILLIARD SCHOOL, the Manhattan School (New York), Mannes College (New York), the New England Conservatory (Boston), the Peabody Conservatory (Baltimore), and the San Francisco Conservatory.

consonance and dissonance Perceived qualities of musical CHORDS and INTERVALS. Consonance is often described as relative "stability," dissonance as "instability." In musical contexts, certain intervals seem to call for motion by one of the tones to "resolve" perceived dissonance. The most consonant intervals are generally recognized as the unison and octave, and the next most consonant interval as the perfect 5th. Consonance tends to reflect the early intervals of the OVERTONE series (which include, in addition to the octave and perfect 5th, the major and minor 3rds and the perfect 4th), but many musical factors can affect the perception of consonance and dissonance.

consonant Any speech sound characterized by an ARTICULATION in which a closure or narrowing of the vocal tract completely or partially blocks the flow of air; also, any letter or symbol representing such a sound. Consonants are usually classified according to place of articulation (e.g., palate, teeth, lips); manner of articulation, as in stops (complete closure of the oral passage, released with a burst of air), fricatives (forcing of breath through a constricted passage), and trills (vibration of the tip of the tongue or the uvula); and presence or absence of voicing, nasalization, aspiration, and other features.

conspiracy Agreement between two or more persons to commit an unlawful act or to accomplish a lawful end by unlawful means. Some U.S. states require an overt act in addition to the agreement to constitute conspiracy. Individual conspirators need not even know of the existence or the identity of all other conspirators. In a chain conspiracy the parties act separately and successively (as in distributing narcotics). A civil conspiracy is not prosecuted as a crime but forms the grounds for a lawsuit. In ANTITRUST LAW, conspiracies in restraint of trade (e.g., price fixing) are rigorously prosecuted. In the U.S. it is common to punish a conspiracy to commit an offense more harshly than the offense itself, but there has been a growing trend to follow the European example and make the punishment for conspiracy the same as or less than that for the offense itself.

Constable, John (1776–1837) British painter. He began his career in 1799 on entering the Royal Academy Schools in London. He never went abroad; his finest works were inspired by the English countryside. In 1813–14 he filled two sketchbooks, which survive intact, with over 200 landscape drawings. He was a master of watercolor as well as oil painting on canvas. His most significant achievement was the production of many small oil sketches, painted directly from nature, depicting the atmospheric effects of changing light and moving clouds, unique at the time they were painted. In 1830 a series of mezzotints were published from his paintings. He is ranked with J.M.W. TURNER as one of the greatest 19th-century British landscape painters.

Self-portrait by John Constable, detail of a drawing in pencil and watercolor, c. 1804; in the National Portrait Gallery, London.

BY COURTESY OF THE NATIONAL PORTRAIT GALLERY, LONDON

Constance (1154–1198) Queen of Sicily (1194–98) and Holy Roman empress-consort (1191–97). The daughter of King ROGER II of Sicily, she married the future emperor HENRY VI in 1186 and was later crowned with him in Rome. Her marriage gave the HOHENSTAUFEN DYNASTY a claim to the Sicilian throne, which she asserted against the opposition of her nephew TANCRED. When Henry died (1197) she secured the protection of Pope INNOCENT III and had her son FREDERICK II crowned king in 1198.

Constance, Council of (1414–18) 16th ecumenical council of the Roman Catholic church. It was convened at the request of Emperor SIGISMUND to deal with three competing popes, examine the writings of JAN HUS and JOHN WYCLIFFE, and reform the Church. National political rivalries divided the Council of Constance. Two of the three contending popes were deposed; the third abdicated, and in 1417 the council selected a new pope, Martin V. The Council condemned propositions of Hus and Wycliffe, and Hus was burned at the stake by secular authorities.

Constance, Lake *German* **Bodensee** \'bōd-ᵊn-ˌzā\ *ancient* **Lacus Brigantinus** Lake, bordering Switzerland, Germany, and Austria. Occupying an old glacier basin at an elevation of 1,299 ft (396 m), it has an area of 209 sq mi (541 sq km) and an average depth of 295 ft (90 m). It forms part of the course of the RHINE RIVER, and by the Middle Ages was a major traffic center. With the bordering alpine scenery, the lakeshore makes a popular resort area. The remains of NEOLITHIC lake dwellings are found in the area.

Constans II Pogonatus \'kän-ˌstanz...ˌpō-gə-'nāt-əs\ (630–668) Byzantine emperor (641–68). His reign saw the loss of Byzantium's southern and eastern provinces to the Arabs. Muslim Arabs took Egypt (642), invaded Armenia (647), and defeated Constans at sea in 655. A civil war among Arabs prevented them from attacking Constantinople, and he secured a nonaggression treaty with Syria (659). Within the empire he tried to force unity on the church, forbidding debate on divisive theological questions and exiling the pope when he objected (653). He made his son co-emperor (654) and then aroused public outrage by ordering the murder of his own brother (660). He left Constantinople (663) and settled in Sicily, where he was assassinated.

Constant (de Rebecque) \kōⁿ-'stäⁿ\, **(Henri-) Benjamin** (1767–1830) French-Swiss novelist and political writer. He had a tumultuous 12-year relationship with GERMAINE DE STAEL, whose views influenced him to support the French Revolution and later to oppose Napoleon, for which he was exiled (1803–14). He later served in the Chamber of Deputies (1819–30). *Adolphe* (1816) was a forerunner of the modern psychological novel. Among his other works are the long historical analysis of religious feeling *De la Religion* (5 vols., 1824–31) and his revealing journals (first complete publication, 1952).

Constanta \kōn-'stänt-sə\ *Turkish* **Kustenja** \ˌkü-sten-'yä\ *ancient* **Constantiana** *or* **Tomis** City (pop., 1997 est.: 746,686), chief seaport, Romania. The first known settlement in the area was at the ancient city of Tomis, founded in the 7th century BC by the Greeks. Romans annexed the region in the 1st century BC; OVID was exiled there in AD 9–17. In the 4th century AD, Tomis was reconstructed by CONSTANTINE THE GREAT and renamed Constantiana. Subject to numerous invasions from the 6th century, it declined following the Turkish conquest in the early 15th century. Its modern development as an industrial, trading, and cultural center dates from its return to Romania in 1878.

Constantine \'kän-stən-ˌtēn\ *ancient* **Cirta** City (pop., 1998: 807,371), northeastern Algeria. A natural fortress, it is built on a rocky height over 800 ft (250 m) above the Rhumel River valley. By the 3rd century BC it was one of NUMIDIA's most important towns and reached its height under Micipsa in the 2nd century BC. Ruined in subsequent wars, it was restored in AD 313 and renamed for its patron, CONSTANTINE THE GREAT. Overrun by the Arabs in the 7th century and later by the Turks, it was captured by the French in 1837. Occupied in 1942 by U.S. troops, it was an important Allied campaign base in World War II. The city retains its medieval walls, and there are Roman ruins nearby. It is an agricultural market for the surrounding area.

Constantine, Donation of See DONATION OF CONSTANTINE

Constantine I *known as* **Constantine the Great** *officially* **Flavius Valerius Constantinus** (after AD 280?–337) First Roman emperor to profess Christianity. The eldest son of CONSTANTIUS I CHLORUS, he spent his youth at the court of DIOCLETIAN. Passed over as successor to the throne, he fought to make himself emperor. Victory at the Milvian Bridge outside Rome (312) made him emperor in the West; according to legend, a cross and the words *in hoc signo vinces* ("By this sign thou shalt conquer") appeared to him there and he forthwith adopted Christianity. In 313 he issued, with LICINIUS, the Edict of Milan, granting tolerance to Christians; he also gave land for churches and granted the church special privileges. He opposed heresies, notably DONATISM and ARIANISM, and convoked the important Council of NICAEA. After defeating and executing Licinius, he gained control of the East and became sole emperor. He moved the capital from Rome to the site of Byzantium, which he renamed Constantinople (324). In 326 he had his wife and eldest son killed for reasons that remain obscure. He angered the Romans by refusing to participate in a pagan rite and never entered Rome again. Under his patronage, Christianity began its growth into a world religion. Constantine is revered as a saint in the Orthodox church.

Constantine I *Greek* **Constantinos** (1868–1923) King of Greece (1913–17, 1920–22). Son of King George I of the Hellenes (1845–1913), he was educated in Germany and was commander in chief of Greek forces in the BALKAN WARS. He succeeded his father in 1913, but his neutralist, yet essentially pro-German, attitude during World War I caused the Allies and his Greek opponents to depose him in 1917. He was restored to the throne in 1920, but after a catastrophic war in Anatolia he abdicated in favor of his son, GEORGE II, in 1922.

Constantine II *Greek* **Constantinos** (born 1940) King of Greece (1964–74). Son of Paul I (1901–1964), he succeeded his father in 1964. After a military coup in 1967, he and his family fled to Rome. The military regime appointed a regent in his place and granted him a free return if he wished. In 1973 the military regime proclaimed a republic and abolished the monarchy. In 1974 a civilian referendum officially ended the monarchy.

Constantine V Copronymus \kə-'prän-ə-məs\ (718–775) Byzantine emperor (741–75). The son of LEO III, he ruled with his father from 720. He spent his life defeating Arab and Bulgar threats to the empire and was unable to prevent the Lombards from taking Ravenna (751), thus ending Byzantine influence in northern and central Italy. A strong iconoclast (see ICONOCLASM), he persecuted monks who disagreed with his position. He died in the Balkans on a military campaign against the Bulgarian kingdom.

Constantine VII Porphyrogenitus \ˌpōr-fə-rō-'jen-ət-əs\ (905–959) Byzantine emperor (913–59). Co-emperor with his father, Leo VI, from 911, he became sole ruler in 913. His father-in-law, ROMANUS I LECAPENUS, was crowned co-emperor with him in 920 and soon became the primary ruler. Shut out of government, the young emperor devoted himself to scholarship; his writings include works on the Slavic and Turkic peoples and on Byzantine ceremonies. In 944 the sons of Romanus, impatient for power, had their father deported, and the ensuing public outcry emboldened Constantine to banish them in 945; he then ruled alone until his death.

Constantine IX Monomachus \mō-'nä-mə-kəs\ (c. 980–1055) Byzantine emperor (1042–55). He gained the imperial throne by marrying ZOE, empress of the Macedonian dynasty. An opponent of the great military leaders, he neglected imperial defenses, instead spending extravagantly on luxuries and magnificent buildings. Rebellions broke out at home and abroad, and Byzantine lands were threatened by invaders in southern Italy, Thrace, Macedonia, and Armenia. Constantine tried to ally with the papacy to save southern Italy from the Normans, but growing differences between Rome and Constantinople resulted in the SCHISM OF 1054.

Constantine XI (or XII) Palaeologus \ˌpā-lē-'ä-lə-gəs\ (1404–1453) Last Byzantine emperor (1449–53). He became emperor when his brother JOHN VIII PALAEOLOGUS died childless, but he faced a losing battle against the Ottoman Turks, who were directing all their resources toward the capture of Constantinople. He acknowledged the obedience of the Greek church to Rome in order to secure help from the West, but in vain. He was killed fighting at the walls of Constantinople as the Turks broke through.

Constantine the African *Latin* **Constantinus Africanus** (c. 1020–1087) Medieval medical scholar. A native of Carthage, he was the first to translate Arabic medical works into Latin. His 37 translated books included *Pantechne* ("The Total Art"), a short version of the *Kitab al-maliki* ("The Royal Book") by the 10th-century Persian physician Ali ibn al-Abbas, introducing Islam's extensive knowledge of Greek medicine to the West. His translations of HIPPOCRATES and GALEN first gave the West a view of Greek medicine as a whole.

Constantinople See ISTANBUL

Constantinople, Council of (AD 381) Second ecumenical council of the Christian church, summoned by Emperor THEODOSIUS I. It promulgated the NICENE CREED and declared finally the Trinitarian doctrine of the equality of Father, Son, and HOLY SPIRIT. It gave the bishop of Constantinople honor second only to that of the POPE. Only Eastern bishops were summoned to the Council, but the Greeks claimed that it was ecumenical. It did come to be so regarded, though the Western Church did not accept the ranking of Constantinople as second to Rome until the 13th century. The Second Council of Constantinople, held in 553, was called by JUSTINIAN I; by endorsing an edict of Justinian's it lent support to Monophysitism and diminished the earlier Council of Chalcedon. The Third Council of Constantinople, held in 680, condemned the Monothelites, who claimed that Christ had a single will despite his two natures. The Fourth Council of Constantinople, held in 869–70 at the suggestion of BASIL I, resulted in the excommunication of St. PHOTIUS and increased the animosity between the Eastern and Western churches.

Constantius I Chlorus ("the Pale") \kən-'stan-chē-əs-'klōr-əs\ *orig.* **Flavius Valerius Constantius** (died 306) Roman emperor and father of CONSTANTINE I. A member of the tetrarchy (four-man ruling body) with his adoptive father MAXIMIAN, DIOCLETIAN, and GALERIUS, he was made caesar (subemperor) in the West (293–305) and later caesar augustus (senior emperor) (305–6). As ruler of GAUL, he subdued rebellion in Britain (296), ended piracy, restored the frontier, and largely ignored edicts against Christians.

Constantius I Chlorus, marble bust; in the Capitoline Museum, Rome.
ALINARI—ART RESOURCE

constellation Any of certain groupings of STARS that were imagined by those who named them to form images of objects, mythological figures, or creatures in the sky. They are useful in helping astronomers and navigators locate certain stars. A constellation's stars are often designated by its name and letters of the Greek alphabet in order of brightness. Of 88 named constellations in Western astronomy, about half retain the names PTOLEMY gave the 48 he identified in his *ALMAGEST*. See also ZODIAC.

constitution Set of doctrines and practices that form the fundamental organizing principle of a political state. It may be written (e.g., the CONSTITUTION OF THE U.S.) or partly written and uncodified (e.g., Britain's constitution). Its provisions usually specify how the government is to be organized, what rights it shall have, and what rights shall be retained by the people. Modern constitutional ideas developed during the ENLIGHTENMENT, when such philosophers as THOMAS HOBBES, J.-J. ROUSSEAU, and JOHN LOCKE proposed that constitutional governments should be stable, adaptable, accountable, and open, should represent the governed, and should divide power according to its purpose. The oldest constitution still in force is that of the state of Massachusetts (1780). See also SOCIAL CONTRACT.

Constitution, USS *known as* **Old Ironsides** One of the first FRIGATES built for the U.S. Navy. Launched in 1797, it was 204 ft (62 m) long and usually carried more than 50 guns and a crew of over 450. It was the successful flagship of the TRIPOLITAN WAR (1801–5), and in the WAR OF 1812 it vanquished the British frigate *Guerrière*; tradition holds that it was nicknamed by sailors who saw the British shot failing to penetrate its oak sides. It was condemned as unseaworthy in 1828, but OLIVER WENDELL HOLMES's poem "Old Ironsides" sparked a public preservation campaign. Restored in 1927–31, it is now berthed in Boston and open to the public.

Constitution Act See CANADA ACT (1982)

Constitution of 1791 French constitution created by the NATIONAL ASSEMBLY during the FRENCH REVOLUTION. It retained the monarchy, but sovereignty effectively resided in the Legislative Assembly, which was elected by a system of indirect voting. The franchise was restricted to "active" citizens who paid a minimal sum in taxes; about two-thirds of adult men had the right to vote for electors and to choose certain local officials directly. The constitution lasted less than a year.

Constitution of 1795 (Year III) French constitution established during the THERMIDORIAN REACTION in the FRENCH REVOLUTION. Prepared by the Thermidorian Convention, it was more conservative than the abortive democratic Constitution of 1793. It established a liberal republic with a franchise based on the payment of taxes similar to that of the CONSTITUTION OF 1791, a bicameral legislature to slow down the legislative process, and a five-man DIRECTORY. The central government retained great power, including emergency powers to curb freedom of the press and freedom of association.

Constitution of the United States Fundamental law of the U.S. federal system of government and a landmark document of the Western world. It is the oldest written national constitution in operation, completed in 1787 at a convention of 55 delegates who met in Philadelphia, ostensibly to amend the ARTICLES OF CONFEDERATION. Because ratification in many states hinged on the promised addition of a BILL OF RIGHTS, the Constitution was not fully certified until 1791. The framers were especially concerned with limiting the power of the government and securing the liberty of citizens. The Constitution's separation of the legislative, executive, and judicial branches of government, the CHECKS AND BALANCES of each branch against the other, and the explicit guarantees of individual liberty were all designed to strike a balance between authority and liberty. Article I vests all legislative powers in the CONGRESS—the House of Representatives and the Senate. Article II vests executive power in the PRESIDENT. Article III places judicial power in the hands of the courts. Article IV deals, in part, with relations among the states and with the privileges of the citizens, Article V with amendment procedure, and Article VI with public debts and the supremacy of the Constitution. Article VII gives ratification terms. The 10th Amendment restricted the national government's powers to those expressly listed in the Constitution; the states, unless otherwise restricted, possess all the remaining (or "residual") powers of government. Amendments to the Constitution may be proposed by a two-thirds vote of both houses of Congress or by a convention called by Congress on the application of the legislatures of two-thirds of the states. (All subsequent amendments have been initiated by Congress.) Amendments proposed by Congress must be ratified by three-fourths of the state legislatures or by conventions in as many states. Twenty-seven amendments have been added to the Constitution since 1789. In addition to the Bill of Rights, these include the 13th (1865), abolishing slavery; the 14th (1868), requiring DUE PROCESS and EQUAL PROTECTION under the law; the 15th (1870), guaranteeing the right to vote regardless of race; the 17th (1913), providing for the direct election of U.S. senators; the 19th (1920), instituting women's suffrage, and the 22nd (1951), limiting the presidency to two terms. See also CIVIL LIBERTY, COMMERCE CLAUSE, EQUAL RIGHTS AMENDMENT, ESTABLISHMENT CLAUSE, FREEDOM OF SPEECH, JUDICIARY, STATES' RIGHTS.

Constitution of the Year VIII (1799) French constitution established after the Coup of 18–19 BRUMAIRE during the FRENCH REVOLUTION. Drafted by EMMANUEL JOSEPH SIEYES, it disguised the true character of the military dictatorship created by NAPOLEON, reassuring the partisans of the Revolution by proclaiming the irrevocability of the sale of national property and by upholding the legislation against the ÉMIGRÉ NOBILITY. It created the regime known as the CONSULATE, which concentrated all real power in the hands of Napoleon. Submitted to a plebiscite, it won overwhelmingly in 1800.

Constitutional Act *or* **Canada Bill** (1791) British law repealing certain portions of the QUEBEC ACT of 1774. The new act provided a more democratic constitution for the area, establishing an elected legislature for each province, the first in that part of Canada, and a governor and an executive council appointed by the crown. Bills could originate in the legislature, but they could be disallowed by the crown.

Constitutional Convention (May–September 1787) Assembly that drafted the CONSTITUTION OF THE U.S. All states but Rhode Island sent delegates in response to a call by the ANNAPOLIS CONVENTION for a meeting in Philadelphia to amend the ARTICLES OF CONFEDERATION. The delegates decided to replace the Articles with a document that strengthened the federal government. An important issue was the apportioning of legislative representation. Two plans were presented: the Virginia plan, favored by the large states, apportioned representatives by population or wealth; the New Jersey plan, favored by the small states, provided for equal representation for each state. A compromise established the bicameral Congress to ensure both equal and proportional representation. The document was approved on September 17 and sent to the states for ratification.

Constitutional Democratic Party *or* **Kadet** Russian political party advocating a radical change in Russian government toward a constitutional monarchy like Britain's. It was founded in October 1905 by the Union of Liberation and other liberals associated with the ZEMSTVOS. Its members, called Kadets, dominated the first DUMA in 1906 but were less successful thereafter. After the Bolsheviks seized power in 1917, the party was outlawed and ceased to function.

Constitutional Laws of 1875 In France, a series of fundamental laws that, taken collectively, came to be known as the constitution of the THIRD REPUBLIC. It established a two-house legislature (with an indirectly elected Senate as a conservative check on the popularly elected Chamber of Deputies); a Council of Ministers responsible to the Chamber; and a president with powers resembling those of a constitutional monarch. It left untouched many aspects of the French governmental structure.

constitutional monarchy System of government in which a monarch (see MONARCHY) has agreed to share power with a constitutionally organized government. The monarch may remain the de facto head of state or may be a purely ceremonial head. The CONSTITUTION allocates the rest of the government's power to the legislature and judiciary. Britain became a constitutional monarchy under the Whigs; other constitutional monarchies include Belgium, Cambodia, Jordan, the Netherlands, Norway, Spain, Sweden, and Thailand.

Constitutions of Clarendon See Constitutions of CLARENDON

Constructivism Russian movement in art and architecture, initiated in 1914 by the abstract geometric constructions of VLADIMIR TATLIN. In 1920 Tatlin was joined by ANTOINE PEVSNER and NAUM GABO. Their *Realist Manifesto,* which directed their followers to "construct art," gave the movement its name. The group, soon joined by ALEKSANDR M. RODCHENKO and EL LISSITZKY, produced abstract works reflecting modern machinery and technology, using plastic, glass, and other industrial materials. Applying the same principles to architecture, they spread the movement's ideals throughout Europe and to the U.S. after Soviet opposition dispersed the group. See also BAUHAUS, DE STIJL.

constructivism Theory that interprets mathematical statements as true if and only if there is a proof of them and as false just in case there is a disproof of them. Constructivism opposes the Platonist interpretation, which construes mathematical statements as referring to a domain of timeless mathematical objects existing independently of our knowledge of them (see FORM, PLATONISM). For the constructivist, certain classically valid forms of logical inference (e.g., the law of excluded middle, the law of double negation, the postulation of infinite sets) may no longer be employed unrestrictedly in constructing mathematical proofs (see LOGIC). The constructivist therefore recognizes fewer mathematical proofs and theorems than does the Platonist. See also INTUITIONISM.

consul In the ROMAN REPUBLIC, either of two annually elected chief magistrates. The consuls had sacred rights and near-absolute authority. They were nominated by the Senate and elected by the popular assembly; each could veto the other's decisions. As heads of state, they commanded the army, presided over the Senate and assemblies and acted on their decrees, and handled foreign affairs. At the end of his one-year term, a consul was generally appointed to serve as governor of a province. The office continued in weaker form under the empire.

Consulate (1799–1804) French government established after the Coup of 18–19 BRUMAIRE. The CONSTITUTION OF THE YEAR VIII created an executive consisting of three consuls, but the First Consul, NAPOLEON, wielded all real power, while the other two, EMMANUEL JOSEPH SIEYES and Pierre-Roger Ducos (1747–1816), were figureheads. The principles of representation and legislative supremacy were discarded. The executive branch was given the power to draft new laws, and the legislative branch became little more than a rubber stamp. Elections became an elaborate charade, with voters stripped of real power. Napoleon abolished the Consulate when he declared himself emperor.

consumer credit Short- and intermediate-term loans used to finance the purchase of commodities or services for personal CONSUMPTION. The loans may be supplied by lenders in the form of cash loans or by sellers in the form of sales credit. Installment loans, such as automobile loans and credit-card purchases, are paid back in two or more payments; noninstallment loans, such as the service credit extended by utility companies, are paid back in a lump sum. Consumer loans usually carry a higher rate of interest than business loans. See also CREDIT.

consumer goods Any tangible commodity purchased by households to satisfy their wants and needs. Consumer goods may be durable or nondurable. Durable goods (e.g., autos, furniture, and appliances) have a significant life span, often defined as three years or more, and CONSUMPTION is spread over this span. Nondurable goods (e.g., food, clothing, and gasoline) are purchased for immediate or almost immediate consumption and have a life span ranging from minutes to three years. See also PRODUCER GOODS.

consumer price index Measure of living costs based on changes in retail prices. Consumer PRICE INDEXES are widely used to measure changes in the cost of maintaining a given STANDARD OF LIVING. The goods and services commonly purchased by the population covered are priced periodically, and their prices are combined in proportion to their relative importance. This set of prices is compared with the initial set of prices collected in the base year to determine the percentage increase or decrease. The population covered may be restricted to wage and salary earners or to city dwellers, and special indexes may be used for special population groups (e.g., retirees). Such indexes do not take into account shifts over time in what the population buys; when modified to take subjective preferences into account, they are called constant-utility indexes. Consumer price indexes are available for more than 100 countries.

consumer protection Legal framework promoting customer safety and education and providing protection from hazardous or substandard products and from fraud. In the U.S., the FEDERAL TRADE COMMISSION (established 1914) and the FOOD AND DRUG ADMINISTRATION (established 1927) help ensure consumer protection. Regulations address manufacture and design, advertising, labeling, and sales methods. In 1985 the U.N. produced its Guidelines for Consumer Protection (updated 1995); they cover consumer safety and product standards and education, providing a framework and a benchmark for governments (particularly of less developed countries) to establish a legal basis for consumer protection. See also CONSUMERISM, RALPH NADER.

consumer psychology Branch of SOCIAL PSYCHOLOGY concerned with the market behavior of consumers. Consumer psychologists examine the preferences, customs, and habits of various consumer groups; their research on consumer attitudes is often used to help design advertising campaigns and to formulate new products.

consumerism Movement or policies aimed at regulating the products, services, methods, and standards of manufacturers, sellers, and advertisers in the interests of the buyer. Such regulation may be institutional, statutory, or embodied in a voluntary code accepted by a particular industry, or it may result more indirectly from the influence of consumer organizations. Governments often establish formal regulatory agencies to ensure CONSUMER PROTECTION (in the U.S., e.g., the FEDERAL TRADE COMMISSION and the FOOD AND DRUG ADMINISTRATION). Some of the earliest consumer-protection laws were created to prevent the sale of tainted food and harmful drugs. The U.S. consumer protection movement gained strength in the 1960s and '70s as consumer activists led by RALPH NADER lobbied for laws setting safety standards for automobiles, toys, and numerous household products. Consumer advocates have also won passage of laws obliging advertisers to represent their goods truthfully and preventing sales representatives from using deceptive sales tactics. Consumer advocacy is carried on worldwide by the International Organization of Consumers Unions (IOCU).

consumer's surplus In economics, the difference between the total amount consumers would be willing to pay to consume the quantity of goods transacted on the market and the amount they actually have to pay for those goods. The former is generally interpreted as the monetary value of consumer satisfaction. The concept was developed in 1844 by the French civil engineer Arsène-Jules-Étienne-Juvénal Dupuit (1804–1866) and popularized by ALFRED MARSHALL. Though economists adopted a nonquantifiable approach to consumer satisfaction in the 20th century, the concept is used extensively in the fields of WELFARE ECONOMICS and taxation.

consumption In economics, the final using up of goods and services. The term excludes the use of intermediate products in the production of other goods (e.g., the purchase of buildings and machinery by a business). Economists use statistical information on income and purchases to trace trends in consumption, seeking to map consumer demand for goods and services. In CLASSICAL ECONOMICS, consumers are assumed to be rational and to allocate expenditures in such a way as to maximize total satisfaction from all purchases. Incomes and PRICES are seen as consumption's two major determinants. Critics of the model point out that there are many exceptions to rational consumer behavior—for example, the phenomenon of conspicuous consumption, in which the high price of a product increases its prestige and adds to demand.

consumption See TUBERCULOSIS

consumption tax Levy such as an excise tax, a SALES TAX, or a TARIFF paid directly or indirectly by the consumer. Consumption taxes fall more heavily on lower-income than on upper-income groups because people with less money consume a larger proportion of their income than those with more money. See also PROGRESSIVE TAX, REGRESSIVE TAX.

contact lens Thin artificial lens worn on the surface of the eye to correct refractive defects of vision. Early glass contact lenses, invented in 1887, were uncomfortable and could not be worn long. Modern plastic lenses, first developed in 1948 and made to measurements of corneal curvature taken by optical instruments, come in several types. Hard lenses are better for ASTIGMATISM but have a limited wearing time. Soft lenses are more comfortable, and some can be worn for several weeks. Contact lenses have advantages over eyeglasses for certain visual defects and may be preferred for the sake of appearance and other reasons.

containership Oceangoing vessel designed to transport large, standard-sized containers of freight. Rail-and-road containers were used early in the 20th century; in the 1960s containerization became a major element in ocean shipping as well. Containerships, which are large and fast, carry containers above deck as well as below, and their cargoes can be loaded and unloaded rapidly.

containment Strategic U.S. foreign policy of the late 1940s and early 1950s designed to check the expansionist policy of the Soviet Union through economic, military, diplomatic, and political means. It was conceived by GEORGE KENNAN soon after World War II, when the U.S. provided military and economic aid to Greece and Turkey to counter Soviet influence there.

contempt In law, willful disobedience to or open disrespect of a court, judge, or legislative body. An act of disobedience to a court order may be treated as either criminal or civil contempt; sanctions for the latter end upon compliance with the order. An act or language that consists solely of an affront to a court or interferes with the conduct of its business constitutes criminal contempt; such contempt carries sanctions designed to punish as well as to coerce compliance. In the U.S., a congressional committee can compel the attendance of witnesses. Any witness failing to appear or otherwise obstructing the committee in the course of exercising its powers may be in contempt. Witnesses are, however, protected by the 5th Amendment against forced self-incrimination. See also PERJURY.

Conti family French branch of the House of BOURBON. The title of prince of Conti, created in the 16th century, was revived in favor of Armand de Bourbon, prince de Conti (1629–1666), who was a leader in the Fronde. He was the younger brother and rival of the prince de CONDÉ ("the Great Conde"). Notable members of the Conti family include François-Louis de Bourbon, prince de Conti (1664–1709), who was a candidate for the Polish throne; and Louis-François de Bourbon, prince de Conti (1717–1776), who served in the War of the AUSTRIAN SUCCESSION. The House of Conti became extinct with the death of Louis-François-Joseph de Bourbon, prince de Conti (1734–1814), who had distinguished himself in the Seven Years' War.

continent One of seven large continuous masses of land: Asia, Africa, North America, South America, Antarctica, Europe, and Australia (listed in order of size). Europe and Asia are sometimes considered a single continent, Eurasia. The continents vary greatly in size and in ratio of coastline to total area. More than two-thirds of the world's continental land area lies north of the equator, and all the continents except Antarctica are wedge-shaped, wider in the north than in the south. See also CONTINENTAL DRIFT.

Continental Congress Body of delegates that acted for the American colonies and states during and after the AMERICAN REVOLUTION.The First Continental Congress, meeting in Philadelphia in September 1774, was called by the colonial COMMITTEES OF CORRESPONDENCE. The delegates adopted a declaration of personal rights, denounced taxation without representation, petitioned the British crown for a redress of grievances, and called for a boycott of British goods. The Second Continental Congress, meeting in May 1775, appointed GEORGE WASHINGTON commander in chief of the army. It later approved the DECLARATION OF INDEPENDENCE

(1776) and prepared the ARTICLES OF CONFEDERATION (1781), which granted certain powers to the Congress.

Continental Divide Most notable watershed of the North American continent. The mountains comprising it extend generally north- south, thus dividing the continent's principal drainage into waters flowing eastward (e.g., into HUDSON BAY in Canada or the MISSISSIPPI RIVER in the U.S.) and waters flowing westward (into the Pacific Ocean). Most of the divide runs along the crest of the ROCKY MTNS., through British Columbia in Canada and through the states of Montana, Wyoming, Colorado, and New Mexico in the U.S. Its central point is Colorado, where it has many peaks above 13,000 ft (3,962 m). It continues southward into Mexico, roughly paralleling the SIERRA MADRE, and into Central America.

continental drift Large-scale movements of CONTINENTS over the course of geologic time. The first complete theory of continental drift was proposed in 1912 by ALFRED WEGENER, who postulated that a single supercontinent, which he called PANGAEA, fragmented late in the Triassic period (248–206 million years ago) and the parts began to move away from one another. He pointed to the similarity of rock strata in the Americas and Africa as evidence to support his hypothesis. Wegener's ideas were widely rejected until they were combined with Harry H. Hess's SEAFLOOR SPREADING hypothesis in the 1960s. The modern theory states that the Americas were joined with Europe and Africa until c. 190 million years ago, when they split apart along what is now the MID-ATLANTIC RIDGE. Subsequent tectonic plate movements brought the continents to their present positions.

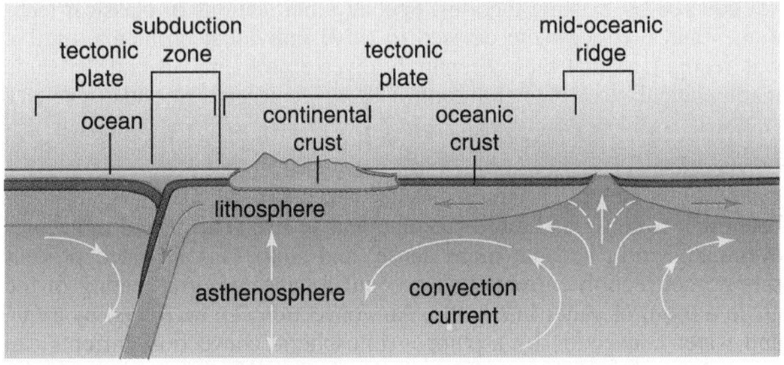

The continents are embedded in tectonic plates. As new lithosphere is created at one plate margin and subducted at another, the plate, and with it the continent, moves over the underlying mantle. The "drift" of continents amounts to only inches per year, but over hundreds of millions of years this alters their relative positions by thousands of miles.

Continental philosophy Collective term for the many distinct traditions, methods, and styles that had a significant influence on 20th-century European philosophy. Continental philosophy is usually understood in contrast to Anglo-American philosophy, or ANALYTIC PHILOSOPHY, and includes PHENOMENOLOGY and EXISTENTIALISM. Thinkers such as MARTIN HEIDEGGER, J.-P. SARTRE, and MAURICE MERLEAU-PONTY combine elements of both.

continental shelf Broad, relatively shallow submarine platform that forms a border to a continent, typically extending from the coast to depths of 330–660 ft (100–200 m). Continental shelves average about 40 mi (65 km) in width. Almost everywhere they are simply a continuation of the continental landmass: narrow, rough, and steep off mountainous coasts but broad and comparatively level offshore from plains. Continental shelves are usually covered with a layer of sand, silts, and silty muds. Their surfaces feature small hills and ridges that alternate with shallow depressions and valley-like troughs. In a few cases, steep-walled V-shaped submarine canyons cut deeply into both the shelf and the slope below. See illustration opposite.

continental shield Any of the large stable areas of low relief (little variation in elevations) in the earth's CRUST that are composed of PRECAMBRIAN crystalline rocks. These rocks are always more than 570 million years, and some are as old as 2–3 billion years. Continental shields occur on each of the continents.

continental slope Seaward border of a CONTINENTAL SHELF. The world's combined continental slope is about 200,000 mi (300,000 km) long and descends at an average angle of about 4° from the edge of the continental shelf to the beginning of the ocean basins at depths of 330–10,500 ft (100–3,200 m). The slope is most gradual off stable coasts without major rivers and is steepest off coasts with young mountain ranges and narrow continental shelves. Slopes off mountainous coastlines and narrow shelves commonly have outcrops of rock. The dominant sediments of continental slopes are muds; there are smaller amounts of sediments of sand or gravel.

Continental System In the NAPOLEONIC WARS, the blockade designed by NAPOLEON to paralyze Britain through the destruction of British commerce. In the Decrees of Berlin (1806) and MILAN (1807), France proclaimed that neutrals and French allies were not to trade with the British. England responded with a counterblockade, which led indirectly to the WAR OF 1812. Because of England's naval superiority, the contest proved disastrous to Napoleon.

continuing education *or* **adult education** Any form of learning provided for adults. In the U.S., the University of WISCONSIN was the first academic institution to offer such programs (1904). Empire College of the State University of NEW YORK was the first to be devoted exclusively to adult learning (1969). Continuing education includes such diverse methods as independent study; broadcast, videotape, on-line, and correspondence courses; group discussion and study circles; conferences, seminars, and workshops; and full- or part-time classroom study. Remedial programs, such as high-school equivalency and basic-literacy programs, are common. In recent years the variety of subject matter has expanded greatly to include such topics as auto repair, retirement planning, and computer skills. See also CHAUTAUQUA MOVEMENT.

continuity In mathematics, a property of FUNCTIONS and their GRAPHS. A continuous function is one whose graph has no breaks, gaps, or jumps. It is defined using the concept of a LIMIT. Specifically, a function is said to be continuous at a value x if the limit of the function exists there and is equal to the function's value at that point. When this condition holds true for all REAL NUMBER values of x in an interval, the result is a graph that can be drawn over that interval without lifting the pencil. Such functions are crucial to the theory of CALCULUS, not just because they model most physical systems but because the theorems that lead to the DERIVATIVE and the INTEGRAL assume the continuity of the functions involved.

continuity principle *or* **continuity equation** Principle of FLUID MECHANICS. In simple terms, it states that what flows into a defined volume in a defined time, minus what flows out of that volume in that time, must accumulate in that volume. If the sign of the accumulation is negative, then the material in that volume is being depleted. The principle is a consequence of the law of conservation of MASS. The behavior of fluids in motion is fully described by this equation, plus a second equation, based on the second of NEWTON'S LAWS OF MOTION, and a third equation, based on the conservation of ENERGY.

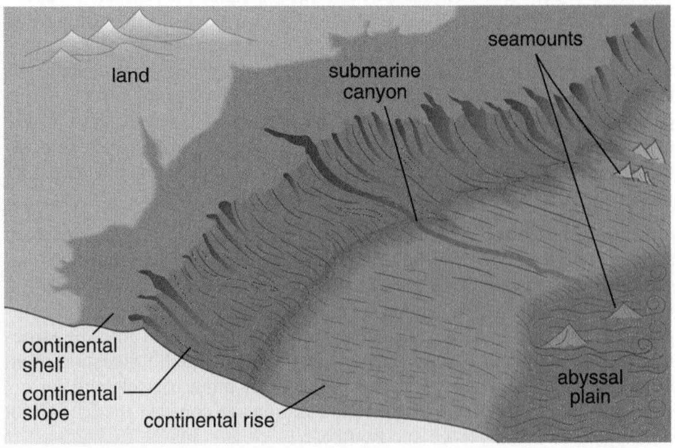

The broad, gentle pitch of the continental shelf gives way to the relatively steep continental slope. The more gradual transition to the abyssal plain is a sediment-filled region called the continental rise. The continental shelf, slope, and rise are collectively called the continental margin. Depth is exaggerated here for effect.

continuo *or* **basso continuo** In baroque music, a special subgroup of an instrumental ensemble. It consists of two instruments reading the same part: a bass instrument, such as a CELLO or BASSOON, and a chordal instrument, most often a HARPSICHORD but sometimes an ORGAN or LUTE. Its appearance in the early 17th century reflected the radically new musical texture of accompanied melody that was especially typical of the new vocal genre of OPERA. The continuo (which has a counterpart in the bass and rhythm guitar of a rock band) came to be employed in virtually all ensemble music of the baroque era. See also FIGURED BASS.

contraception Birth control by prevention of conception or impregnation. The most common method is STERILIZATION. The most effective temporary methods are nearly 99% effective if used consistently and correctly. Many methods carry health risks; barrier devices and avoidance of intercourse during the most fertile period are safest. Hormonal contraceptives use ESTROGEN and/or PROGESTERONE to inhibit ovulation. The "morning-after pill" (high-dose hormones) is effective even after intercourse. The most serious side effect of oral contraceptives is the risk of blood-clotting disorders. Intrauterine devices (IUDs) are placed inside the uterus and appear to cause a mild endometrial inflammation that either inhibits fertilization or prevent a fertilized egg from implanting. Certain types were taken off the market in the 1970s and '80s when it was found that their side effects included a high incidence of PELVIC INFLAMMATORY DISEASE, ECTOPIC PREGNANCIES, and spontaneous septic abortions. Barrier devices, such as condoms, diaphragms, cervical caps, female condoms (vaginal pouches), and vaginal sponges, prevent SPERM from entering the UTERUS. Condoms also prevent SEXUALLY TRANSMITTED DISEASES. Used with spermicides, condoms are nearly 100% effective. Fertility awareness techniques have evolved from keeping track of the menstrual cycle (the so-called "rhythm method"; see MENSTRUATION) to avoid intercourse around the time of ovulation; tracking body temperature and cervical mucus consistency can raise effectiveness to more than 80%. Experimental forms of birth control include an oral contraceptive for men.

contract Agreement between two or more parties that creates in each party a duty to do something (e.g., provide goods at a certain price according to a specified schedule); it may also create the duty not to do something (e.g., divulge an employer's trade secrets or financial status to third parties). Failure to honor a contract allows the other party to bring an action for DAMAGES in a court of law, though ARBITRATION may also be pursued in an effort to keep the matter confidential. All contracts must be entered into both willingly and freely. A contract that violates this principle, including one made with a legal minor or a person deemed mentally incompetent, may be declared unenforceable. A contract also must have a lawful objective.

contralto See ALTO

contras Counterrevolutionary force that sought to overthrow Nicaragua's SANDINISTA government. The original contras had been National Guardsmen during the regime of Anastasio Somoza (see SOMOZA FAMILY). The U.S. CENTRAL INTELLIGENCE AGENCY played a key role in training and funding the group, whose terrorist tactics were decried by the international human-rights community. In 1984 the U.S. Congress banned military aid to the contras; the RONALD REAGAN administration's efforts to circumvent the ban led to the IRAN-CONTRA AFFAIR. A general peace in the region was negotiated by OSCAR ARIAS SANCHEZ, and in 1990 Pres. VIOLETA CHAMORRO negotiated the contras' demobilization. See also DANIEL ORTEGA.

contrast medium Substance comparatively opaque to X RAYS, which appears lighter on X-ray film and allows a body structure that does not normally contrast with its background to be seen clearly on the film. Common contrast media include BARIUM sulfate and iodized organic compounds. They are given by the route that introduces them into the structure to be examined—swallowed or as an enema for the digestive tract, inhaled for the respiratory tract, or injected for blood vessels and for organs and tissues they supply. Serious reactions to contrast media are not infrequent. See also DIAGNOSTIC IMAGING.

contredanse See COUNTRY DANCE

Contreras \kōn-'trā-räs\, **Battle of** (August 19–20, 1847) Decisive engagement between U.S. and Mexican troops in the MEXICAN WAR. On its march to Mexico City, the U.S. force under WINFIELD SCOTT was blocked by a Mexican force and detoured via a difficult road across lava beds held by another Mexican force. After an engagement that lasted less than 20 minutes, Scott's troops gained control of several roads to Mexico City. They then captured the main Mexican army of ANTONIO SANTA ANNA at Churubusco.

contributory negligence In law, NEGLIGENCE on the part of a plaintiff that contributed to the injury at issue. In English law since 1945, and in many U.S. states, if a plaintiff can be shown to have contributed to the injury, the amount of damages recoverable from a defendant will usually be less than if no such negligence had occurred.

control system Means by which a set of variable quantities is held constant or caused to vary in a prescribed way. Control systems are intimately related to the concept of AUTOMATION but have an ancient history. Roman engineers maintained water levels in aqueducts by means of floating valves that opened and closed at appropriate levels. JAMES WATT's flyball governor (1769) regulated steam flow to a steam engine to maintain constant engine speed despite a changing load. In World War II, control-system theory was applied to anti-aircraft batteries and fire-control systems. The introduction of analog and digital computers opened the way for much greater complexity in automatic CONTROL THEORY. See also JACQUARD LOOM, PNEUMATIC DEVICE, SERVOMECHANISM.

control theory Field of applied mathematics relevant to the control of certain physical processes and systems. It became a field in its own right in the late 1950s and early '60s. After World War II, problems arising in engineering and economics were recognized as variants of problems in DIFFERENTIAL EQUATIONS and in the CALCULUS of variations, though they were not covered by existing theories. Special modifications of classical techniques and theories were devised to solve individual problems, until it was recognized that these seemingly diverse problems all had the same mathematical structure, and control theory emerged. See also CONTROL SYSTEM.

convection Process by which heat is transferred by movement of a heated fluid such as air or water. Most fluids expand when heated. They become less dense and more buoyant, and so rise. The heated molecules eventually cool, become more dense, and sink. This repeated process sets up convection currents that account for the uniform heating of the air in a room or water in a kettle. Air convection can be forced by a fan, and water convection by a pump. Atmospheric convection currents can be set up by local heating effects such as solar radiation or contact with cold surfaces. Such currents are usually vertical and account for atmospheric phenomena such as clouds and thunderstorms.

convection See MASS FLOW

Convention, National See NATIONAL CONVENTION

convention, political See POLITICAL CONVENTION

convergence Mathematical property of INFINITE SERIES, INTEGRALS on unbounded regions, and certain sequences of numbers. An infinite series is convergent if the sum of its terms is finite. The series $\frac{1}{2} + \frac{1}{4} + \frac{1}{8} + \frac{1}{16} + \frac{1}{32} + \ldots$ sums to 1 and thus is convergent. The harmonic series $1 + \frac{1}{2} + \frac{1}{3} + \frac{1}{4} + \frac{1}{5} + \ldots$ does not converge. An integral calculated over an interval of infinite width, called an improper integral, describes a region that is unbounded in at least one direction. If such an integral converges, the unbounded region it describes has finite area. A sequence of numbers converges to a particular number when the difference between successive terms becomes arbitrarily small. The sequence 0.9, 0.99, 0.999, etc., converges to 1.

conveyor belt One of various devices that provide mechanized movement of material, as in a FACTORY. Conveyor belts are used in industrial applications and also on large farms, in warehousing and freight-handling, and in movement of raw materials. Belt conveyors of fabric, rubber, plastic, leather, or metal are driven by a power-operated roll mounted underneath or at one end of the conveyor. The belt forms a continuous loop and is supported either on rollers (for heavy loads) or on a metal slider pan (if loads are light enough to prevent frictional drag on the belt). Motors operating through constant- or variable-speed reduction gears usually provide the power.

convolvulus See BINDWEED

convoy Vessels sailing under the protection of an armed escort, originally formed to protect merchant ships against pirates (see PIRACY). From the 17th century, neutral powers claimed the right of convoy in wartime, providing warships to escort their merchantmen and keep them secure from search or seizure. In World War I the British organized transatlantic convoys protected by a cordon of warships. The same system protected Allied shipping from German submarines in World War II.

convulsive disorder See EPILEPSY

Conway, Thomas (1735–c. 1800) Irish-French officer in the American Revolution. Sent by France to aid the Revolutionary army, he fought in the battles of Brandywine and Germantown, then was promoted to major general by Congress, against Washington's advice. He advocated that GEORGE WASHINGTON be replaced by HORATIO GATES as commander in chief; his "plot," called the Conway Cabal, was exposed, and he was forced to resign.

cony *or* **coney** Any of certain unrelated animals, including two mammals and two fishes. One mammalian cony is more commonly called a PIKA. The name cony was once applied to the RABBIT and is still sometimes used in the fur business to indicate rabbit fur. The cony of the Old World and the Bible is an unrelated mammal, the HYRAX. A variety of WHITEFISH is also called cony, as are certain varieties of SEA BASS.

Cook, James *known as* **Captain Cook** (1728–1779) British sailor and explorer. He joined the Royal Navy (1755) and in 1763–67 surveyed the St. Lawrence River and the coast of Newfoundland. In 1768 he was appointed commander of the first scientific expedition to the Pacific. Sailing on the HMS *Endeavour,* he found and charted all of New Zealand and explored the eastern coast of Australia. That voyage (1768–71) produced a wealth of scientifically collected material and was also notable for Cook's successful prevention of scurvy among crew members. Promoted to commander, he was sent with two ships to make the first circumnavigation and penetration into the Antarctic. On that expedition (1772–75), which ranks as one of the greatest of all sailing-ship voyages, he successfully completed the first west-east circumnavigation in high latitudes. On a third voyage (1776–79) in search of a Northwest Passage around Canada and Alaska, he was killed by Polynesian natives on Hawaii.

Cook, Mt. See MOUNT COOK NATIONAL PARK

Cook, Thomas (1808–1892) British innovator of the conducted tour. A Baptist missionary, in 1841 he arranged for a special train to be run to a temperance meeting; this was probably the first publicly advertised excursion train in England. He began to arrange excursions on a regular basis, and in 1856 he led his first grand tour of Europe. In the early 1860s he became an agent for the sale of travel tickets; with his son, John Mason Cook (1834–1899), he founded the Thomas Cook & Son travel agency. In the 1880s the firm also organized military transport and postal services.

Cook Inlet Inlet, Gulf of Alaska in the northern Pacific Ocean. Bounded by the Kenai Peninsula on the east, it extends northeast for 220 mi (350 km), narrowing from 80 to 9 mi (129 to 14 km). ANCHORAGE is situated near its head. It is a salmon and herring fishing ground and an oil field.

Cook Islands Island group (pop., 1990 est.: 17,000), southern Pacific. Located 2,000 mi (3,000 km) northeast of New Zealand, the fifteen islands, scattered from north to south over 900 mi (1,450 km) of ocean, are divided into a southern group of eight islands, inc. Raratonga (the seat of government), and a northern group of seven. All of the northern Cooks are true atolls; most of the southern group have volcanic interiors. They were probably settled by Polynesians from TONGA and SAMOA; there is evidence of a highly organized society c. AD 1100. Capt. JAMES COOK explored many of them during the 1770s. Established as a British protectorate in 1888, they were annexed by New Zealand in 1901. Self-government in free association with New Zealand was achieved in 1965.

Cook Strait Strait, separating North and South islands of New Zealand. Extending from the TASMAN SEA to the Pacific Ocean, it is about 14 mi (23 km) wide at its narrowest point, and averages 420 ft (128 m) in depth. Both shores are lined with steep cliffs, and that of South Island is deeply embayed. Treacherous currents and fierce storms present serious hazards to navigation. Capt. JAMES COOK explored it in 1770.

Cooke, (Alfred) Alistair (born 1908) British-U.S. journalist and commentator. Cooke settled in New York City after studies at Cambridge, Yale, and Harvard. From the late 1930s he has provided lively and insightful interpretations of American culture and history to British audiences in newspapers and radio broadcasts. His weekly radio program *Letter from America* began in 1946 and has run for more than half a century; *One Man's America* (1952) and *Talk About America* (1968) collect many of its texts. His television programs include *Omnibus* (1956–61) and the BBC-produced series *America* (1972–73). He hosted television's *Masterpiece Theatre* from the 1970s to the early 1990s.

Cooke, Jay (1821–1905) U.S. financier and fund-raiser for the federal government during the American Civil War. Born in Sandusky, Ohio, he entered a Philadelphia banking house at age 18 and opened his own in 1861. That same year, he floated a $3 million war loan for the state of Pennsylvania. During the next four years he organized the sale of hundreds of millions in BONDS for the federal government. Cooke's effort to finance construction of the NORTHERN PACIFIC RAILWAY in 1870 led to his firm's failure, but he rebuilt his fortune within a decade.

Cooke, Sam(uel) (1935–1964) U.S. singer and songwriter. The son of a Chicago Baptist minister, Cooke started his career as a GOSPEL-MUSIC singer. Switching to RHYTHM AND BLUES and SOUL MUSIC, he had a series of hits, including "You Send Me," "Wonderful World," "Cupid," "Twistin' the Night Away," and "Bring It On Home to Me." Cooke was shot to death in a Los Angeles motel room. He was inducted into the Rock and Roll Hall of Fame in 1986.

cookie File or part of a file put on a Web user's hard disk by a WEB SITE (i.e., by the server that manages the Web site) that lets a Web server store on the user's own machine information about the user, retrievable whenever the user returns to that Web site. Cookies are used to store registration data, to make it possible to customize information for visitors to a Web site, to track which Web sites a user has visited, to target Web advertising, and to keep track or the products a user wishes to order on-line. Early cookies could retrieve data from other parts of the user's hard disk; current versions prevent this and permit a site to have access only to cookies written by that site.

Cookstown District (pop., 1995 est.: 31,000), Northern Ireland. In an agricultural region, it has extensive dairy farming, and cattle-, poultry-, and sheep-raising. The town of Cookstown (pop., 1991: 10,000), the county seat, was originally a 17th-century English colonial settlement and named after its founder, Alan Cooke.

Cooley, Charles Horton (1864–1929) U.S. sociologist. Born in Ann Arbor, Mich., the son of an eminent jurist, he taught sociology at the University of Michigan from 1894. He believed that the mind is social, that society is a mental construct, and that the moral unity of society derives from face-to-face relationships in primary groups such as the family and neighborhood. His works include *Human Nature and the Social Order* (1902), *Social Organization* (1909), and *Social Process* (1918).

Coolidge, (John) Calvin (1872–1933) 30th president of the U.S. (1923–29). Born in Plymouth, Vt., he practiced law in Massachusetts from 1897 and served as lieutenant governor before being elected governor in 1918. He gained national attention by calling out the state guard during the BOSTON POLICE STRIKE in 1919. At the 1920 Republican convention, "Silent Cal" was nominated for vice president on WARREN G. HARDING's winning ticket. When Harding died in office in 1923, Coolidge became president. He restored confidence in an administration discredited by scandals and won the presidential election in 1924, defeating ROBERT LA FOLLETTE. He vetoed measures to provide farm relief and bonuses to World War I veterans. His presidency was marked by apparent prosperity. Congress maintained a high protective tariff and instituted tax reductions that favored capital. Coolidge declined to run for a second term. His conservative policies of domestic and international inaction have come to symbolize the era between World War I and the GREAT DEPRESSION.

Coolidge, William D(avid) (1873–1975) U.S. engineer and physical chemist. Born in Hudson, Mass., he taught at MIT (1897, 1901–5) before joining the General Electric Research Laboratory, where in 1908 he perfected a process to render tungsten ductile and therefore more suitable for incandescent lightbulbs. In 1916 he patented a revolutionary X-ray tube capable of producing highly predictable amounts of radiation; it was the prototype of the modern X-ray tube. With IRVING LANGMUIR, he also developed the first successful submarine-detection system.

cooling system Apparatus used to keep the temperature of a structure or device from exceeding limits imposed by needs of safety and efficiency. In a mechanical transmission, the oil loses its lubricating capacity if overheated; in a hydraulic coupling or converter, the fluid leaks under the pressure created. In an electric motor, overheating causes deterioration of the insulation. In an overheated internal-combustion engine, the pistons may seize in the cylinders. The cooling agents customarily employed are air and a liquid (usually water), either alone or in combination. In some cases, direct contact with ambient air (free convection) may be sufficient, as in cooling towers; in other cases, it may be necessary to employ forced convection, created either by a fan or by the natural motion of the hot body. Cooling systems are used in automobiles, industrial plant machinery, nuclear reactors, and many other types of machinery. See also AIR CONDITIONING, HEAT EXCHANGER.

Coomassie See KUMASI

coon cat See MAINE COON CAT

Cooney, Joan Ganz (born 1930) U.S. television producer. Born in Phoenix, she worked as a journalist before becoming a producer at a public television station in New York (1962–67). At the Children's Television Workshop from 1968, she served as president (1970–88) and chairman (from 1990), producing such educational children's programs as the influential and long-running *Sesame Street* and *The Electric Company.*

Cooper, Alfred Duff *later* **Viscount Norwich (of Aldwick)** (1890–1954) British politician. He served as a Conservative in Parliament 1924–29 and 1931–45. After a stint as secretary of state for war (1935–37), he became first lord of the admiralty (1937) but resigned to protest the Munich Agreement. Later he served as minister of information under WINSTON CHURCHILL (1940–41) and as ambassador to France (1944–47). His books include *Talleyrand, Haig,* and his autobiography, *Old Men Forget.*

Cooper, Gary *orig.* **Frank James** (1901–1961) U.S. film actor. Born in Helena, Mont., he moved to Hollywood in 1924 and played minor roles in low-budget westerns before becoming a star with *The Virginian* (1929). Lanky and handsome, he played the strong, soft-spoken man of action in such films as *A Farewell to Arms* (1932), *Mr. Deeds Goes to Town* (1936), *Beau Geste* (1939), *Meet John Doe* (1941), *Sergeant York* (1941, Academy Award), *For Whom the Bell Tolls* (1943), and *The Fountainhead* (1949). His performance in *High Noon* (1952, Academy Award) is considered his finest. Later films include *Friendly Persuasion* (1956) and *Love in the Afternoon* (1957).

Cooper, Gladys *later* **Dame Gladys** (1888–1971) British actress. After her London debut in 1906, she performed in musicals and dramas, including *The Importance of Being Earnest* (1911). She was comanager of London's Playhouse Theatre (1917–27) and then its sole manager (1927–33). She starred in *The Second Mrs. Tanqueray* (1922) and *The Letter* (1927). Her U.S. stage debut in *The Shining Hour* (1934) was followed by *Relative Values* (1951) and *The Chalk Garden* (1955), and she personified British poise in such U.S. films as *Now, Voyager* (1942), *Separate Tables* (1958), and *My Fair Lady* (1964).

Cooper, James Fenimore (1789–1851) U.S. novelist, the nation's first major novelist. He grew up in a prosperous family in the primitive settlement of Cooperstown, founded by his father, in upstate New York. *The Spy* (1821), set during the American Revolution, brought him fame. His best-known novels, the series *The Leatherstocking Tales,* feature the frontier adventures of the wilderness scout Natty Bumppo and include *The Pioneers* (1823), *The Last of the Mohicans* (1826), *The Prairie* (1827), *The Pathfinder* (1840), and *The Deerslayer* (1841). He also wrote popular sea novels, notably *The Pilot* (1823), and a history of the U.S. Navy (1839). Though internationally celebrated, he was troubled by lawsuits and political conflicts in his later years, and his popularity and income declined.

Cooper, Leon N(eil) (born 1930) U.S. physicist. Born in New York City, he taught at Ohio State University (1954–58) and Brown University (from 1958). For his role in developing the BCS THEORY of superconductivity, he shared a 1972 Nobel Prize with JOHN BARDEEN and J. Robert Schrieffer (born 1931). His principal contribution to the theory was his discovery of Cooper electron pairs (1956), electrons that under normal conditions repel each other but are attracted to each other in superconductors.

Cooper, Peter (1791–1883) U.S. inventor. Born in New York City, Cooper became involved with the Canton Iron Works, built to supply the BALTIMORE AND OHIO RAILROAD CO., for which he devised and built the diminutive but powerful *Tom Thumb* locomotive. His factory at Trenton, N.J., produced the first structural-iron beams for buildings. He supported the Atlantic-cable project of Cyrus Field (1819–1892), and became president of the North American Telegraph Co. His inventions include a washing machine, a compressed-air engine for ferry boats, and a water-power device for moving canal barges. A social idealist and reformer, he founded the COOPER UNION for the Advancement of Science and Art in 1859.

Cooper Creek *or* **Barcoo River** Intermittent stream, eastern central Australia. Rising as the Barcoo on the northern slopes of the Warrego Range in QUEENSLAND, it is joined by the Alice River, turns southwest, and receives its principal tributary, the Thomson, from which point it is known as Cooper Creek. Crossing the South Australia border, it carries water to Lake EYRE. Its total length is 880 mi (1,420 km).

Cooper Union (for the Advancement of Science and Art) Tuition-free undergraduate college located in New York City. It was endowed in 1859 by PETER COOPER, and its financial resources were later increased by the Hewitt and Carnegie families. Instruction is open to any student able to pass an entry exam. It comprises schools of art, architecture, engineering, and humanities and social sciences. Many national social-welfare agencies were founded at Cooper Union. Its library was the city's first free public reading room. Its design museum, opened in 1897, was transferred to the Smithsonian Institution in 1967 as the Cooper-Hewitt National Design Museum. Enrollment is about 1,000.

cooperative Organization owned by and operated for the benefit of those using its services. Cooperatives have been successful in such fields as the processing and marketing of farm products and the purchasing of other kinds of equipment and raw materials, and in the wholesaling, retailing, electric power, credit and banking, and housing industries. The modern consumer cooperative traces its roots to Britain's Rochdale Society of Equitable Pioneers (1844); the movement spread quickly in northern Europe. In the U.S., agricultural marketing cooperatives developed in rural areas in the 19th century, and consumer and housing cooperatives have spread in metropolitan areas in recent years. See also CREDIT UNION.

coordinate geometry See ANALYTIC GEOMETRY

coordinate system Arrangement of reference lines or curves used to identify the location of points in space. In two dimensions, the most common system is the Cartesian (after RENE DESCARTES) system. Points are designated by their distance along a horizontal (x) and vertical (y) axis from a reference point, the origin, designated (0,0). Cartesian coordinates also can be used for three (or more) dimensions. A polar coordinate system locates a point by its direction relative to a reference direction and its distance from a given point, also the origin. Such a system is used in radar or sonar tracking and is the basis of bearing-and-range navigation systems. In three dimensions, it leads to cylindrical and spherical coordinates.

coordinate system, spherical See SPHERICAL COORDINATE SYSTEM

Coos Bay \'küs\ *formerly* **Marshfield Bay** Town (pop., 1990: 15,000), southwestern Oregon. Located on Coos Bay, an inlet of the Pacific, it was settled as Marshfield in 1854, and developed early shipbuilding industries. In the early 1900s it became a major lumber-shipping port. A port of entry, it also processes seafood products and is the heart of a seaside resort area. Incorporated in 1874, it was renamed Coos Bay (for an Indian tribal name) in 1944.

Coosa River River, in Georgia and Alabama. Formed by the confluence of the Etowah and Oostanaula rivers at Rome, Ga., it flows south for 286 mi (460 km) through the Appalachian Ridge and Valley region into the Gulf coastal plain. It joins the TALLAPOOSA RIVER north of MONTGOMERY to form the ALABAMA RIVER. Locks and dams make navigation possible to Rome.

coot Any of 10 species of ducklike waterbirds (genus *Fulica*) in the RAIL family. Coots are found worldwide in larger inland waters and streams, where they swim and bob for food, mostly plants, seeds, mollusks, and worms. They have greenish or bluish gray feet, with toes fringed by a lobed membrane that helps them swim and walk over marshes. The short conical beak is topped by a flattened, fleshy shield that extends onto the forehead. The European coot is about 18 in. (45 cm) long and weighs 2 lbs (900 g). The coot of North America (mud hen) resembles the European species.

Mud hen (*Fulica americana*).
BENJAMIN GOLDSTEIN FROM ROOT RESOURCES—EB INC.

cootie See human LOUSE

Copacabana \ˌkō-pə-kə-ˈba-nə\ SE district of RIO DE JANEIRO, Brazil. Occupying a narrow strip of land between the mountains and the sea, it is a popular resort area, famous for its magnificent 2.5-mi (4-km) curved beach along the entrance to Guanabara Bay. Hotels, nightclubs, and restaurants line the waterfront.

Copán \kō-ˈpän\ Ruined ancient MAYA city, Honduras. It lies near the Guatemalan border on the bank of the Copán River, about 35 mi (56 km) from modern Santa Rosa de Copán. An important center of Mayan art and astronomy during the Classic Period (c. AD 300–900), it was at its peak in the 8th century and may have been home to as many as 20,000 people. The site consists of stone temples, two large pyramids, several stairways and plazas, and a ball court, and is particularly noted for the friezes on its buildings. The Maya had completely abandoned the site by c. 1200.

Stela with portrait sculpture, Copán, Honduras.
WALTER AGUIAR

Cope, Edward Drinker (1840–1897) U.S. paleontologist. Born in Philadelphia, he devoted 22 years to exploration and research, especially in the description of extinct fishes, reptiles, and mammals of the western U.S. He discovered about 1,000 species of extinct vertebrates, and developed the evolutionary histories of the horse and of mammalian teeth. His theory of kinetogenesis, stating that the natural movements of animals aided in the alteration and development of moving parts, led him to support J.-B. LAMARCK's theory of evolution. He engaged in a bitter, long-running feud with O. C. MARSH. Among his 1,200 books and papers are *Reptilia and Aves of North America* (1869–70) and *Relation of Man to Tertiary Mammalia* (1875).

Copenhagen \ˌkō-pən-ˈhā-gən, ˈkō-pən-ˌhä-gən\ *Danish* **København** \ˌkœ̄-bən-ˈhau̇n\ Capital and largest city (metro. area pop., 1996 est.: 1,362,000), Denmark. Located on the islands of Zealand (Sjælland) and Amager, it was a village site by the early 10th century AD; in 1167 Bishop Absalon built a castle there and fortified the town. In 1445 it was made the capital and the residence of the royal family. Its palaces include Amalienborg, home to the Danish monarchs, and Christiansborg, now housing Parliament. TIVOLI amusement park is a popular attraction. One of Europe's leading cultural and educational centers, its oldest university was founded in 1479. Historically a trade and shipping hub, it has also become an industrial city. Shipbuilding, machinery production, and canning and brewing are among the chief manufacturing activities.

Copenhagen, Battle of (April 2, 1801) British naval victory over Denmark in the NAPOLEONIC WARS. The armed-neutrality treaty of 1794 between Denmark and Sweden, to which Russia and Prussia adhered in 1800, was considered a hostile act by England. In 1801 a detachment of the British navy was sent to Copenhagen. After a fierce battle in the harbor, Adm. HORATIO NELSON, ignoring orders to withdraw from the fleet commander, Sir Hyde Parker, instead continued to destroy most of the Danish fleet. Danish losses amounted to some 6,000 dead and wounded, six times those of the British. Denmark subsequently withdrew from the neutrality treaty.

copepod \ˈkō-pə-ˌpäd\ Any of the 10,000 known species of CRUSTACEANS in the subclass Copepoda. Copepods are widely distributed and ecologically important, serving as food for many species of fish. Most species are free-living marine forms, found from the sea's surface to great depths. Some live in freshwater or in damp vegetation; others are parasites. Most species are 0.02–0.08 in. (0.5–2 mm) long. The largest species, a parasite of the FIN WHALE, grows to a length of about 13 in. (32 cm). Unlike most crustaceans, copepods have no carapace. Nonparasitic forms feed on microscopic plants or animals or even on animals as large as themselves. Members of the genus *Cyclops* (order Cyclopoida) are called water fleas. See also GUINEA WORM.

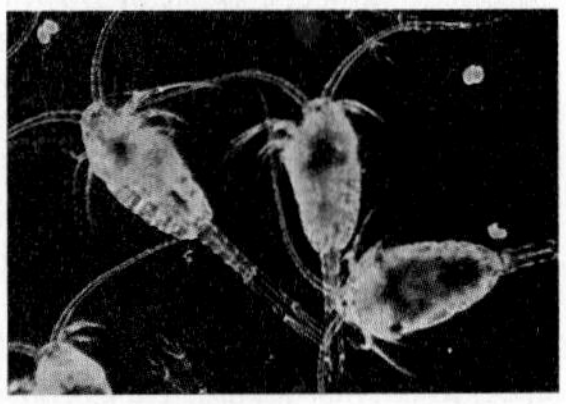
Copepods (*Temora*).
DOUGLAS P. WILSON

Copernican system \kə-ˈpər-ni-kən\ *or* **Copernican principle** Model of the SOLAR SYSTEM centered on the sun, with earth and other planets revolving around it, formulated by NICOLAUS COPERNICUS in the mid-16th century. Having the sun in this central position explained the apparent motion of PLANETS relative to the fixed stars and was truer than the earth-centered Ptolemaic system (see PTOLEMY). Scientifically, the Copernican system led to belief in a much larger universe than before (because, if the earth revolved around the sun, the stars would have to be very distant not to appear to alter their position); more broadly, the Copernican principle is invoked to argue against any theory that would give the solar system a special place in the universe. Dethronement of earth from the center of the universe caused profound shock: the Copernican system challenged the entire system of ancient authority and required a complete change in the philosophical conception of the universe.

Copernicus \kə-ˈpər-ni-kəs\, **Nicolaus** *Polish* **Mikołaj Kopernik** (1473–1543) Polish astronomer. He was educated at Kraków, Bologna, and Padua, where he mastered all the knowledge of the day in mathematics, astronomy, medicine, and theology. Elected a canon of the cathedral of Frauenburg in 1497, he took advantage of his financial security to begin his astronomical observations. His publication in 1543 of *On the Revolutions of the Celestial Spheres* marked a landmark of Western thought (see COPERNICAN SYSTEM). Copernicus had first conceived of his revolutionary model decades earlier but delayed publication because, while it explained the motion of the planets (and resolved their order), it raised new problems that had to be explained, required verification of old observations, and had to be presented in a way that would not provoke the religious authorities. The book did not see print until he was on his deathbed. By attributing to earth a daily rotation around its own axis and a yearly revolution around a stationary sun, he developed an idea that had far-reaching implications for the rise of modern science. He asserted, in contrast to Platonic instrumentalism, that astronomy must describe the real, physical system of the world. Only with JOHANNES KEPLER was Copernicus's model fully transformed into a new philosophy about the fundamental structure of the universe.

copier See PHOTOCOPIER

Copland \ˈkō-plənd\, **Aaron** (1900–1990) U.S. composer. Born to immigrant parents in Brooklyn, N.Y., he studied with Rubin Goldmark and later with N. BOULANGER at Fontainebleau. Though cosmopolitan in his tastes, he adopted notably American traits in his music, especially after c. 1930. With R. SESSIONS, he sponsored an important series of new-music concerts in New York. He cofounded the American Composers Alliance, serving as president 1937–45. For over 20 years he headed the Berkshire Music Center's faculty. Famously public-spirited and generous, he came to be unofficially regarded as the U.S.'s national composer. He is best known for his ballets, including *Billy the Kid* (1938), *Rodeo* (1942), and *Appalachian Spring* (1944, Pulitzer Prize). His influential film scores include *Of Mice and Men* (1939), *Our Town* (1940), and *The Heiress* (1948). His orchestral works include a piano concerto (1926), *El Salón México* (1936), *A Lincoln Portrait* (1942), a clarinet concerto (1948), and three symphonies (1924, 1933, 1946). His other works include the operas *The Second Hurricane* (1936) and *The Tender Land* (1954), the piano trio *Vitebsk* (1929), and the *Piano Variations* (1930).

Copley, John Singleton (1738–1815) U.S. painter of portraits and historical subjects. Born in Boston, the stepson of an engraver, he was an accomplished draftsman before age 20 and flourished as a portrait artist in his native Boston. He was famous for his *portraits d'apparat,* portrayals of his subjects with the objects associated with them in their daily lives or professions. In 1775 he settled in London and turned to the more fashionable history painting; he was elected to the Royal Academy in 1779. He revealed a gift for portraying heroic action in multifigure compositions. His first important English work, *Watson and the Shark* (1778), depicts one of the great themes of Romanticism, the struggle against nature. He is considered the greatest U.S. painter of the 18th century and the finest artist of the colonial era.

copper Metallic chemical ELEMENT, one of the TRANSITION ELEMENTS, chemical symbol Cu, atomic number 29. Sometimes found in the free state in nature, it is a reddish METAL, very ductile and an unusually good conductor of electricity and heat. Most copper is used by the electrical industries; the remainder is combined with other metals, including BRASS, BRONZE, nickel, and silver, to form ALLOYS. Copper is part of nearly all coinage metals. In compounds copper usually has VALENCE 1 (cuprous) or 2 (cupric). Cuprous compounds include cuprous oxide, a red pigment and a fungicide; cuprous chloride, a CATALYST for certain organic reactions; and cuprous sulfide, with a variety of uses. Cupric compounds include cupric oxide, a pigment, decolorizing agent, and catalyst; cupric chloride, a catalyst, wood preservative, mordant, disinfectant, feed additive, and pigment; and cupric sulfate, a pesticide, germicide, feed additive, and soil additive. Copper is a necessary trace element in the diet and essential to plant growth; in blue-blooded mollusks and crustaceans it plays the same role in hemocyanin as iron does in HEMOGLOBIN.

Crystalline copper from Michigan.

BY COURTESY OF TED BOENTE COLLECTION; PHOTOGRAPH, JOHN H. GERARD

copper (butterfly) Any member of the BUTTERFLY subfamily Lycaeninae (family Lycaenidae). Coppers are common and widely distributed. Adults, sometimes known as gossamer-winged butterflies, are delicate, with a wingspan of 0.75–1.5 in. (18–38 mm). They are rapid fliers, usually with iridescent wings. Coppers typically range from orange-red to brown, usually with a copper tinge and dark markings. Copper larvae feed on clover, dock, or sorrel.

Copper Age First part of the BRONZE AGE. The beginning of the period is sometimes called the Chalcolithic (Copper-Stone) Age, referring to the initial use of pure COPPER along with stone. By the middle of the 4th millennium BC, a rapidly developing copper metallurgy, with cast tools and weapons, was a factor leading to urbanization in Mesopotamia. By 3000 BC the use of copper was well known in the Middle East, had extended westward into the Mediterranean area, and was beginning to infiltrate the Neolithic cultures of Europe. The Copper Age began in India c. 3100 BC, in Africa c. 600 BC, and in South America c. 1200 BC.

Copperhead Term used during the AMERICAN CIVIL WAR to describe a Northerner who opposed the war policy and favored a negotiated settlement with the South. The term was first used in 1861 by the *New York Tribune,* referring to the copperhead snake that strikes without warning. Most Copperheads (also called Peace Democrats) were from the Midwest, where agrarian interests distrusted the growing federal power. The movement's leaders included CLEMENT VALLANDIGHAM. Though the movement was unable to influence the conduct of the war, Republicans used the Copperhead label to discredit the Democratic Party.

copperhead Any of several unrelated species of snake named for their reddish head color. The North American copperhead *(Agkistrodon contortrix),* also called highland moccasin, is a PIT VIPER of swampy, rocky, and wooded regions of the central and eastern U.S. It is usually less than 3 ft (1 m) long and is pinkish or reddish with a copper-colored head and reddish brown, often hourglass-shaped crossbands on its back. Its venom is relatively weak, and a bite is rarely fatal to humans. The Australian copperhead is an ELAPID, and the Indian copperhead is a RAT SNAKE.

Coppermine River River, Northwest Territories, Canada. Rising in the Barren Grounds, a subarctic prairie, it flows north for 525 mi (845 km) into Coronation Gulf, an arm of the Arctic Ocean, near the Eskimo settlement of Coppermine. Unnavigable because of numerous rapids and a short ice-free season, it is a noted Arctic char fishing stream.

Coppola \'kō-pə-lə\, **Francis Ford** (born 1939) U.S. film director, screenwriter, and producer. Born in Detroit, he worked under ROGER CORMAN before scoring his first success with the low-budget but stylish *You're a Big Boy Now* (1967). He wrote or cowrote screenplays for several films, including *Patton* (1970, Academy Award) and *The Great Gatsby* (1974). He won acclaim for writing and directing the Mafia epic *The Godfather* (1972, Academy Awards for best picture and screenplay). His other films include *The Conversation* (1974), *The Godfather, Part II* (1974, Academy Awards for best director, picture, and screenplay), *The Black Stallion* (1979), *Apocalypse Now* (1979), *The Godfather, Part III* (1990), and *The Rainmaker* (1997).

coprocessor Additional processor used in some PERSONAL COMPUTERS to perform specialized tasks such as extensive arithmetic calculations or processing of graphical displays. The coprocessor is often designed to do such tasks more efficiently than the main processor, resulting in far greater speeds for the computer as a whole.

Coptic art Liturgical art associated with the Greek- and Egyptian-speaking Christian peoples of Egypt from the 3rd to the 13th century. It includes stone reliefs, wood carvings, and wall paintings, as well as textiles. The lack of a patronage system is evident in the absence of monumental works, costly materials, and advanced training. Coptic art features flatly rendered human forms, simplified outline and detail, and a limited number of motifs.

Coptic Orthodox Church Principal Christian church in Egypt. Until the 19th century it was called simply the Egyptian Church. It agrees doctrinally with EASTERN ORTHODOXY except that it holds that Jesus has a purely divine nature and never became human, a belief the Council of CHALCEDON rejected (see MONOPHYSITE HERESY) in AD 451. After the Arab conquest (7th century), service books were written with Coptic and Arabic in parallel texts. Church government is democratic, and the patriarch, who resides in Cairo, is elected. There are congregations outside Egypt, especially in Australia and the U.S., and the church is in communion with the Ethiopian, Armenian, and Syrian Jacobite churches.

copyhold In English law, a form of landholding defined as a "holding at the will of the lord according to the custom of the manor." Its origin is found in the occupation by villeins, or nonfreemen, of portions of land belonging to the manor of the feudal lord. It was occupation at the pleasure of the lord, but in time it grew into an occupation by right, called *villenagium,* which was recognized first by custom and then by law. In 1926 all copyhold land became FREEHOLD land, though lords of manors retained mineral and sporting rights.

copyright Exclusive right to reproduce, publish, or sell an original work of authorship. It protects from unauthorized copying any published or unpublished work that is fixed in a tangible medium (including a book or manuscript, musical score or recording, script or dramatic production, painting or sculpture, or blueprint or building). It does not protect matters such as an idea, process, or system. Protection in the U.S. now extends for the life of the creator plus 70 years after his or her death. Works made for hire are now protected for a maximum of 95 years from the date of publication or 120 years from the date of the creation of the work. In 1988 the U.S. joined the BERN CONVENTION, an agreement that governs international copyright. The Digital Millennium Copyright Act, adopted in the U.S. in 1998, expanded owners' control over digital forms of their creations and penalized persons who sought to evade technological shields (such as encryption) for copyrighted material. See also INTELLECTUAL PROPERTY, PATENT, TRADEMARK.

coquina \kō-'kē-nə\ LIMESTONE formed almost entirely of sorted and cemented fossil debris, most commonly coarse shells and shell fragments. Microcoquinas are similar sedimentary rocks composed of finer material. Common among microcoquinas are those formed from the remains of crinoids (marine invertebrates, such as sea lilies, that have limy disks and a limy internal skeleton). A distinction is made between a coquina, which is a rock formed from debris, and coquinoid limestone, which is composed of coarse shelly materials with a fine-grained matrix.

coquina (clam) \kō-'kē-nə\ Any CLAM of the genus *Donax,* inhabiting sandy beaches worldwide. Coquinas are very active; they migrate up and down beaches with the tide and can reburrow between waves. They have short siphons and feed on plant material and detritus. A typical species, *D. variabilis*, is about 0.4–1 in. (10–25 mm) long. Its shell is wedge-shaped and varies in color.

coral Any of about 2,300 species of marine CNIDARIANS in the class Anthozoa that are characterized by stonelike, horny, or leathery skeletons (external or internal). The skeletons of these animals are also called coral. Corals are found in warm seas worldwide. The body is of the POLYP type. Soft, horny, and blue corals are colonial in habit (i.e., they live in large groups). Stony corals, the most familiar and widely distributed forms, are both colonial and solitary. ATOLLS and CORAL REEFS, which are composed of stony coral, grow at an average rate of 0.2–1.1 in. (0.5–2.8 cm) per year. See also SEA FAN.

Soft coral (*Sarcophyton*).

VALERIE TAYLOR—ARDEA

coral reef Ridge or hummock formed in shallow ocean areas from the external skeletons of CORALS. The skeleton consists of calcium carbonate ($CaCO_3$), or limestone. A reef may grow into a permanent coral island, or it may take one of four forms. Fringing reefs consist of a flat reef area around a nonreef island. Barrier reefs may lie a mile or more offshore, separated from the landmass by a lagoon or channel. Atolls are circular reefs without a central landmass. Patch reefs have irregular tablelike or pinnacle features.

Coral Sea Part of the South Pacific Ocean. It is located between QUEENSLAND, Australia, on the west and VANUATU and NEW CALEDONIA on the east, and bordered on the north by PAPUA NEW GUINEA and the SOLOMON ISLANDS. Occupying an area of 1,849,800 sq mi (4,791,000 sq km), it merges with the TASMAN SEA and Solomon Sea and is connected to the Arafura Sea via the TORRES STRAIT. It was named for its many coral formations, including the GREAT BARRIER REEF. During World War II it was the scene of a strategic U.S. victory over the Japanese (1942).

coral snake Any of about 65 species of strongly patterned burrowing ELAPIDS. True forms are limited to the New World, chiefly the tropics, but similar forms occur in Asia and Africa. Secretive and docile, coral snakes rarely bite when handled, but the venom of some can kill humans. Most prey on other snakes. More than 50 species in the largest genus, *Micrurus,* range from the southern U.S. to Argentina. They are ringed with red, black, and yellow or white. The eastern coral snake, or harlequin snake *(Micrurus fulvius),* of North Carolina and Missouri to northeastern Mexico is about 30 in. (76 cm) long and has wide bands of red and black separated by yellow.

Coralli, Jean *orig.* **Giovanni Coralli Peracini** (1779–1854) French dancer and choreographer. He made his debut at the Paris Opéra in 1802. His appointment as ballet master at the Opéra (1831–50) coincided with the most brilliant phase of the Romantic ballet. In 1841 Coralli began to work with the ballerina CARLOTTA GRISI in *Giselle,* now regarded as a classic. Although attributed solely to Coralli, most of its principal action was arranged by JULES PERROT. The choreography of *La Péri* (1843), however, was entirely Coralli's.

corbel \'kȯr-bəl\ Block or brick partially embedded in a wall, with one end projecting out from the face. The weight of added masonry above counterbalances the CANTILEVER and keeps the block from falling out of the wall. Corbeling often occurs over several courses, with each block or brick overhanging the one below so as to resemble a set of inverted steps. The form may be continuous, as in a corbeled arch, or a series of separate brackets, as on a medieval BATTLEMENT. Corbeling was used extensively before the development of true ARCHES and VAULTS.

Corbusier, Le See LE CORBUSIER

Corday (d'Armont) \kȯr-'de\, **(Marie-Anne-) Charlotte** (1768–1793) French patriot. A noblewoman from Caen, she moved to Paris to work for the GIRONDIN cause in the FRENCH REVOLUTION. Horrified at the excesses of the REIGN OF TERROR, she sought an interview with JEAN-PAUL MARAT, one of its leaders. On July 13, 1793, she stabbed him through the heart while he was in his bath. Arrested on the spot, she was convicted by the Revolutionary Tribunal and guillotined.

Charlotte Corday, engraving by É.-L. Baudran after a portrait by J.-J. Hauer.

BY COURTESY OF THE BIBLIOTHEQUE NATIONALE, PARIS

Cordeliers \kȯr-dəl-'yā, *Engl* ˌkȯr-də-'lērz\, **Club of the** *officially* **Society of the Friends of the Rights of Man and of the Citizen** Club founded in 1790 in the FRENCH REVOLUTION to prevent the abuse of power and "infractions of the rights of man." Popularly named for its original meeting place at the nationalized monastery of the Cordeliers (Franciscans), the club became a political force under JEAN-PAUL MARAT and GEORGES J. DANTON. Leadership later fell to JACQUES R. HEBERT and others, who helped overthrow the GIRONDINS and gave the club a more radical tone. It fell into oblivion after Hébert's execution in 1794.

Cordilleran Geosyncline \ˌkȯr-dᵊl-'yer-ən\ Linear trough in the earth's CRUST in which rocks of Late Precambrian to Mesozoic age (roughly 600–65 million years ago) were deposited along the western coast of North America. The principal mountain-building phases of the geosyncline took place during Mesozoic time. Deformation of the Cordilleran Geosyncline and the formation of the Cordilleran fold belt appear to have been related to the development of oceanic trenches along the western margins of the North American continent.

Córdoba \'kȯr-t͟hō-b͟ä\ City (metro. area pop., 1999 est.: 1,275,585), the second-largest in Argentina. It lies on the Primero River along the foothills of the Sierra de Córdoba. Founded in 1573, its location between the coast and the interior settlements favored its early development. In 1599 Jesuits settled in the city and founded the country's first university (1613). Córdoba's growth was stimulated by the completion of rail connections in 1869 and the San Roque Dam in 1866, which irrigates orchards and grain fields and provides hydroelectric power.

Córdoba *or* **Cordova** \'kȯr-də-və\ *ancient* **Corduba** City (pop., 1998 est.: 309,961), capital of Córdoba province, southern Spain. On the banks of the GUADALQUIVIR RIVER, it probably had Carthaginian origins. Occupied by the Romans in 152 BC, it became, under AUGUSTUS, the capital of the Roman province of Baetica. Declining under the Visigoths (6th–8th century AD), it was captured by the Muslims in 711. Abd al-Rahman I, of the UMAYYAD family, made it his capital in 756 and founded the Great Mosque of Córdoba, which still stands. By the 10th century it was the largest city in Europe, filled with palaces and mosques. It fell to the Castilian king Ferdinand III in 1236 and became part of Christian Spain. Modern Córdoba's streets and buildings still evoke its Moorish heritage.

Cordobés \ˌkȯr-t͟hō-'bās\, **El** *orig.* **Manuel Benítez Pérez** (born 1936?) Spanish bullfighter. He grew up an illiterate orphan in Córdoba (his nickname means "The Cordovan"), and was once imprisoned for unauthorized entry into bullrings. He began his career in 1959 and became a full matador in 1963. In the month of August 1965 alone, he killed a record 64 bulls and is believed to have been paid 35 million pesetas. The crudity of his technique was offset by his exceptional

El Cordobés.

MICHAEL KUH—BLACK STAR

reflexes and courage; handsome, dashing, and flamboyant, he became the most highly paid torero in history.

core In earth science, the part of the earth that starts about 1,800 mi (2,900 km) beneath the surface and extends downward. It consists largely of an iron-rich metallic alloy and is thought to have a two-part structure: an outer fluid region and a solid, extremely dense inner region that measures only about 1,500 mi (2,400 km) across. The alloy composition is mainly iron metal with small amounts of nickel in substitution for the iron. This composition is deduced from the chemistry of iron meteorites that presumably came from the breakup of a planetary body that also had an iron core. See also CRUST, MANTLE.

Corelli, Arcangelo (1653–1713) Italian composer and violinist. He studied in Bologna, then settled in Rome. He became widely known as a violinist, director, and teacher, and he lived with his family at the palaces of Cardinals Pamphili and Ottoboni. His many students included Francesco Geminiani (1687–1762) and Pietro Locatelli (1695–1764). As the first composer whose fame was based exclusively on his nonvocal music, his reputation rests on four sets of 12 trio sonatas each, op. 1–4 (publ. 1681–95), a set of 12 solo sonatas, op. 5 (publ. 1700), and a set of 12 concerti grossi, op. 6 (publ. 1714). Long after his death, his works were widely studied and imitated for their classic poise and serenity. In his music the ideal of full-blown TONALITY first becomes securely established.

coreopsis \ˌkōr-ē-ˈäp-səs\ Any ornamental summer-blooming plant of the genus *Coreopsis,* commonly known as tickseed, in the COMPOSITE FAMILY, consisting of about 100 species of annual and perennial herbaceous plants native to North America. Members have flower heads with yellow disk flowers and yellow, pink, white, or variegated ray flowers. The heads are solitary or in branched clusters, and some varieties have double flowers. Golden coreopsis *(C. tinctoria)* is a popular garden plant; swamp tickseed *(C. rosea)* is grown in wildflower gardens.

Corfu \kȯr-ˈfü\ *Greek* **Kérkyra** \ˈker-kē-rä\ One of the IONIAN ISLANDS, northwestern Greece. With adjacent small islands it forms the Corfu department (pop., 1995 est.: 108,000) of Greece; the town of Corfu (pop., 1995 est.: 36,000) is the capital. Occupying 229 sq mi (593 sq km), it was settled by the Corinthians c. 734 BC; off its coast the first naval battle of Greek history was fought between Corfu and CORINTH c. 664 BC. Around 435 BC it sought the aid of ATHENS against Corinth, precipitating the PELOPONNESIAN WAR. A Roman possession in 229 BC, it later passed to the Byzantines, then to the Normans. It was ruled by Venice in 1386–1797, and was under British administration from 1815 until it was ceded to Greece in 1864. Germans and Italians occupied it during World War II. Now a popular tourist spot, it also produces olive oil, figs, oranges, lemons, and wine.

Corfu incident (1923) Brief occupation of the Greek island of Corfu by Italian forces. In August 1923 Italians forming part of an international boundary delegation were murdered on Greek soil, leading BENITO MUSSOLINI to order a naval bombardment of Corfu. After the Greeks appealed to the LEAGUE OF NATIONS, the Italians were ordered to evacuate but Greece was forced to pay Italy an indemnity.

coriander *or* **cilantro** Feathery annual herb *(Coriandrum sativum)* of the PARSLEY family, and its dried fruit, native to the Mediterranean and Middle East. The seed goes by the name coriander; they have a mild, fragrant aroma and aromatic taste and are used to flavor many foods. The delicate young leaves—known in the U.S. by their Spanish name, cilantro—are widely used in Latin-American, Indian, and Chinese dishes.

Corinth \ˈkȯr-ənth\ *Greek* **Kórinthos** \ˈkȯr-ēn-thȯs\ Ancient city of the PELOPONNESE, Greece. Located on the Gulf of Corinth, the site was occupied from before 3000 BC, but it was in the 8th century BC that it developed as a commercial center. In the late 6th century BC, it was outstripped by ATHENS. Occupied in 338 BC by PHILIP II, it was destroyed in 146 BC by Rome. In 44 BC JULIUS CAESAR reestablished Corinth as a Roman colony; the New Testament includes the letters addressed to its Christian community by St. PAUL. It declined in the later Middle Ages; its ruins are near the modern city of Corinth (pop., 1991: 29,000).

Corinth, League of Alliance established at CORINTH in 337 BC. It comprised the ancient Greek states except SPARTA, and was led by PHILIP II of Macedonia. Delegates, elected in proportion to their state's military power, decided federal policies. The league declared war on Persia, but under ALEXANDER THE GREAT it contributed little to the war effort. Its major act was to condemn the Thebans to slavery and distribute their lands among other states following revolts in 336 and 335. It was disbanded after Alexander's death (323).

Corinth \kō-ˈrint\, **Lovis** (1858–1925) German painter and graphic artist. He trained in Paris with WILLIAM BOUGUEREAU. In 1902 he settled in Berlin and, with MAX LIEBERMANN, became a leading exponent of Impressionism in Germany. After recovering from a stroke in 1911, his style became much looser and more powerfully Expressionist. He was best known for his landscapes and portraits, including numerous powerfully expressive self-portraits, and produced many etchings and lithographs (e.g., *Apocalypse*, 1921).

Coriolanus \ˌkȯr-ē-ə-ˈlā-nəs\, **Gnaeus Marcius** Legendary Roman hero. He is said to have lived in the late 6th and early 5th century BC, and to have owed his surname to his courage at the siege of Corioli (493 BC) in the war against the VOLSCI. For trying to have the office of TRIBUNE abolished during a famine in Rome, he was sent into exile. Taking refuge with the King of the Volsci, he led the Volscian army against Rome, but turned back in response to pleas from his family. He is the subject of WILLIAM SHAKESPEARE's play *Coriolanus*.

Coriolis force \ˌkōr-ē-ˈō-ləs\ Apparent FORCE that must be included if NEWTON'S LAWS OF MOTION are to be used in a rotating system. First described by Gustave-Gaspard Coriolis (1792–1843) in 1835, the force acts to the right of the direction of body MOTION for counterclockwise rotation and to the left for clockwise rotation. On earth, an object that moves along a north-south path, or longitudinal line, will be apparently deflected to the right in the Northern Hemisphere and to the left in the Southern Hemisphere. The deflection is related to the motion of the object, the motion of the earth, and latitude. The Coriolis effect is important in meteorology and oceanography as well as BALLISTICS; it also has great significance in ASTROPHYSICS.

Cork Seaport city (pop., 1995 est.: 173,000), southwestern Ireland. The seat of county Cork, it is situated on Cork Harbor at the mouth of the Lee River. Founded as a monastery in the 7th century, it was often raided and was eventually settled by the Danes. It passed to HENRY II of England in 1172. The city was taken by Parliamentarian forces under OLIVER CROMWELL (1649) and by the duke of MARLBOROUGH (1690). It was heavily damaged in 1920 during the Irish uprising against England. Its industries include leatherworking, and brewing and distilling.

cork Outer bark of the EVERGREEN cork oak *(Quercus suber),* native to the Mediterranean. In its broad sense, cork consists of the irregularly shaped, thin-walled, wax-coated cells that make up the peeling BARK of many trees, but commercially only cork-oak bark is called cork. Cork is obtained from the new outer sheath of bark that forms after the original rough outer bark has been removed. This outer sheath can be stripped repeatedly without hurting the tree. Cork is unique because it is made of air-filled, watertight cells that are a remarkably effective insulating medium. The air pockets make cork very light in weight. Though specialized plastics and other artificial substances have replaced cork in some of its former uses, it has retained its traditional importance as a stopper for bottles of wine and other alcoholic beverages.

Cork oak (*Quercus suber*) with sections of cork removed.

ERIC G. CARLE—SHOSTAL/EB INC.

Corliss \ˈkȯr-ləs\, **George Henry** (1817–1888) U.S. inventor and manufacturer of the Corliss engine. He was born in Easton, N.Y. His many improvements to the STEAM ENGINE included principally the Corliss valve, which had separate inlet and exhaust ports, and he introduced springs to speed the opening and closing of valves. His Corliss Engine Co. (founded 1856) supplied the 1,400-horsepower engine that drove all the machines at the Philadelphia Centennial Exhibition (1876).

corm Vertical, fleshy, underground stem that acts as a vegetative reproductive structure in certain seed plants. It bears membranous or scaly leaves and buds. Typical corms are those of the CROCUS and GLADIOLUS.

Corms are sometimes called solid BULBS, or bulbo-tubers, but they are distinguished from true bulbs and TUBERS.

Cormack, Allan M(acLeod) (1924–1998) South African-U.S. physicist. After doing research on the interaction of subatomic particles, he became interested in the problem of X-ray imaging of soft tissues or layers of tissue of differing densities, and established the mathematical and physical foundations of computerized scanning. With Godfrey Hounsfield (born 1919), he was awarded a 1979 Nobel Prize for his work in developing COMPUTED AXIAL TOMOGRAPHY.

Corman, Roger (William) (born 1926) U.S. film director and producer. Born in Detroit, he directed his first films, *Five Guns West* and *Apache Woman,* in 1955, and by 1960 was one of the most prolific makers of low-budget "exploitation" films. His film versions of stories by EDGAR ALLAN POE, including *The House of Usher* (1960) and *The Masque of the Red Death* (1964), won him a cult following as a master of the macabre. Among his other films are *The Little Shop of Horrors* (1960), *The Wild Angels* (1966), *Bloody Mama* (1970), *Jackson County Jail* (1976), *I Never Promised You a Rose Garden* (1977), and *Frankenstein Unbound* (1990).

cormorant \'kȯr-mə-rənt\ Any of the 26–30 species of water birds, constituting the family Phalacrocoracidae, that dive for and feed on fish, mainly those of little value to humans. In the Orient and elsewhere, these glossy black underwater swimmers have been tamed for fishing. Their guano is valued as a fertilizer. Cormorants live on seacoasts, lakes, and some rivers, nesting on cliffs or in bushes or trees. They have a long, hook-tipped bill, patches of bare skin on the face, and a small throat pouch (gular sac). The most widespread species is the common, or great, cormorant *(Phalacrocorax carbo),* which grows up to 40 in. (100 cm) long and breeds from eastern Canada to Iceland, across Eurasia to Australia and New Zealand, and in parts of Africa.

corn *or* **maize** CEREAL plant *(Zea mays)* of the family Poaceae (or Gramineae), originating in the New World, from where it spread throughout the world. American Indians taught colonists to grow corn, including some varieties of yellow corn that are still popular as food, as well as varieties with red, blue, pink, and black kernels, often banded, spotted, or striped, that today are regarded as ornamental and in the U.S. are called Indian corn. The tall, annual grass has a stout, erect, solid stem and large narrow leaves with wavy margins. Corn is used as livestock feed, as human food, and as raw material in industry. Though it is a major food in many parts of the world, it is inferior to other cereals in nutritional value. Inedible parts of the plant are used in industry—stalks for paper and wallboard; husks for filling material; cobs for fuel, to make charcoal, and in the preparation of industrial solvents. Corn husks also have a long history of use in the folk arts for objects such as woven amulets and corn-husk dolls. Corn is one of the most widely distributed of the world's food plants; it is exceeded in acreage planted only by WHEAT and is the most important crop in the U.S.

Corn Belt Traditional area, midwestern U.S. Roughly covering western Ohio, Indiana, Illinois, Iowa, southern Minnesota, eastern South Dakota, Missouri, eastern Nebraska, and eastern Kansas, it is a region in which corn and soybeans are the dominant crops. Many farms are family-operated and average more than 300 acres (120 hectares). Despite the name, the region is agriculturally diverse, raising various feed-grains and livestock.

corn earworm *or* **cotton bollworm** *or* **tomato fruitworm** MOTH LARVA (*Heliothis zea,* family Noctuidae) that damages corn, tomato, cotton, and other seasonal crops. The smooth, fleshy, green or brown CATERPILLARS feed on corn kernels near the tip of the ear and burrow into tomatoes and cotton bolls. Four or five generations of the pale brown adult moths, with wingspans of 1.3 in. (3.5 cm), are produced annually.

Corn Islands *Spanish* **Islas del Maíz** \'ēs-lä-t͟hel-'mīs\ Two small islands, Caribbean Sea. Known as Great Corn and Little Corn, they lie about 40 mi (64 km) off the coast of Nicaragua, and were leased to the U.S. by Nicaragua for use as a naval base 1916–71. The islands produce copra, coconut oil, lobsters, and frozen shrimp. Tourism is important on Great Corn Island.

Corn Laws Any of the regulations governing the import and export of grain (called corn by the English) in Britain. Records mention the imposition of Corn Laws as early as the 12th century. They became politically important in the late 18th and early 19th century, during the grain shortage caused by Britain's growing population, bad harvests, and the blockades imposed in the Napoleonic Wars. When SIR ROBERT PEEL became prime minister the laws were finally repealed (1846). See also ANTI-CORN LAW LEAGUE.

corn sugar See GLUCOSE

corn syrup Viscous, sweet syrup produced by breaking down (hydrolyzing) cornstarch (a product of CORN). Corn syrup contains dextrins, maltose, and dextrose, and is used in baked goods, JELLIES AND JAMS, and CANDIES. High-fructose corn syrup is widely used in the manufacture of SOFT DRINKS and other foods because it is considerably cheaper than SUCROSE.

Corneille \kȯr-'nā\, **Pierre** (1606–1684) French poet and playwright. He studied law and was a king's counselor in Rouen (1628–50). He wrote his first comedy, *Mélite* (performed 1629), before he was 20; other comedies followed. He responded to the call for a new approach to classical tragedy by writing *Médée* (1635) and then *Le Cid* (1637), an instant success that established him as the creator of French classical tragedy; the play has come to be regarded as the most significant in the history of French drama. His next tragedies, *Horace* (1641), *Cinna* (1643), and *Polyeucte* (1643), have joined *Le Cid* as Corneille's "classical tetralogy." He returned to comedy with *Le menteur* (1644), which occupies a central place in French classical comedy. From 1660 he wrote one play a year, ending with the tragedy *Suréna* (1674).

Pierre Corneille, detail of an oil painting attributed to Charles Le Brun, 1647; in the Musée National de Versailles et des Trianons.

CLICHE MUSEES NATIONAUX, PARIS

cornelian See CARNELIAN

Cornell, Joseph (1903–1972) U.S. sculptor. Born in Nyack, N.Y., he had no formal artistic training. In the 1930s and '40s, he was associated with the Surrealists in New York (see SURREALISM). He was an originator of the ASSEMBLAGE; his most distinctive works were "boxes," usually with glass fronts, containing objects and pieces of collage arranged in elegant but enigmatic compositions. Recurrent motifs include astronomy, music, birds, seashells, glamour photographs, and souvenirs of travel. His appeal rested on the Surrealist technique of irrational juxtaposition and on nostalgia.

Cornell, Katharine (1893–1974) U.S. actress. Born in Berlin to American parents, she toured with a stock company before winning acclaim in *Little Women* in London (1919). She made her Broadway debut in 1921 and became a star in *A Bill of Divorcement* that year. She managed her own productions after 1931 and toured widely; most of her plays were directed by her husband, Guthrie McClintic (1893–1961). She starred in *Candida* (1924), *The Letter* (1925), *The Barretts of Wimpole Street* (1931, 1945), *Alien Corn* (1933), *Wingless Victory* (1936), *Three Sisters* (1942), and *Dear Liar* (1960). To a legion of supporters she vied with HELEN HAYES for the title "First Lady of the American Theater."

Cornell University Comprehensive research university in Ithaca, N.Y., a traditional member of the IVY LEAGUE. It is both publicly and privately supported. Founded as a land-grant university under the MORRILL ACT, it was privately endowed by Ezra Cornell (1807–1874), a founder of Western Union. Nonsectarian from the beginning, it offered an exceptionally broad curriculum when it opened in 1868. It was the first U.S. university to admit women, and the first to be divided into colleges offering different degrees. Agricultural science has long been important at Cornell; today the life sciences, business management, engineering, the social sciences, and the humanities are equally strong. Professional and graduate schools offer programs in law, medicine, and the arts and sciences. Total enrollment is about 19,000.

cornerstone Ceremonial building block, dated or otherwise inscribed, usually placed in an outer wall of a building to commemorate its dedication. Often the stone is hollowed out to contain newspapers, photographs, or other documents reflecting current customs, with a view to their historical use when the building is remodeled or demolished. Originally placed at a corner, the stone may today be placed elsewhere on the facade.

cornet Valved BRASS INSTRUMENT. It evolved in the 1820s from the posthorn. Like the TRUMPET, it has three valves, but its bore is somewhat more conical. It is a transposing instrument, usually in B-flat, though a higher-pitched E-flat instrument is used as well. Its range parallels that of the trumpet. Its agility made it a very popular solo instrument; it often displaced the trumpet in 19th-century orchestras, and it preceded the trumpet in modern dance and jazz bands. Recent developments have made the two instruments very similar, and the cornet's popularity has waned considerably as a result.

cornflower See BACHELOR'S BUTTON

Cornplanter *or* **John O'Bail** (1732?–1836) American Indian leader. Born to a white trader and a Seneca mother, he fought alongside the British in the American Revolution, leading attacks on white settlements in western New York and Pennsylvania. He later helped negotiate treaties that ceded large tracts of Indian land to the U.S. He earned the enmity of his tribe after advocating Indian nonresistance to white expansion and accepting a land grant from Pennsylvania.

Cornwall County (population 1995 est.: 483,000), southwestern England. Located on a peninsula jutting into the Atlantic Ocean and terminating in LAND'S END, it is the most remote of English counties; its county seat is TRURO. southern Cornwall is a popular tourist area; much of the coast is now protected by the National Trust. Tin, mined in Cornwall for at least 3,000 years, attracted prehistoric settlers, and there are stone relics in the area. Since 1337 the manors of Cornwall have belonged to the English sovereign's eldest son, who acts as duke of Cornwall. Since 1974 the county has included the offshore Isles of SCILLY.

Cornwallis, Charles *later* **Marquess Cornwallis** (1738–1805) British soldier and statesman. In 1780 he became British commander in the American South and defeated HORATIO GATES at Camden, S.C. He then marched into Virginia and encamped at YORKTOWN; trapped and besieged there, he was forced to surrender his army, a defeat that marked the end of the AMERICAN REVOLUTION. Despite his defeat, he retained esteem in England. As governor-general of India (1786–93, 1805), he introduced legal and administrative reforms; the Cornwallis Code (1793) established a tradition of incorruptible British civil servants. In the third Mysore War he defeated Tippu Sultan in 1792. As viceroy of Ireland (1798–1801), he supported the parliamentary union of Britain and Ireland. He negotiated the Anglo-French Treaty of AMIENS in 1802. Reappointed governor-general of India in 1805, he died shortly after his arrival.

Cornwallis, detail of pencil drawing by John Smart, 1792; in the National Portrait Gallery, London.

BY COURTESY OF THE NATIONAL PORTRAIT GALLERY, LONDON

corona \kə-'rō-nə\ Outermost region of the SUN's (or any STAR's) atmosphere, consisting of PLASMA. It has a temperature of about 3,600,000°F (2,000,000°C) and a very low density. Extending more than 8 million mi (13 million km) from the PHOTOSPHERE, it has no definite boundaries, continually varying in size and shape as it is affected by the sun's MAGNETIC FIELD. The SOLAR WIND is formed by expansion of coronal gases. Only about half as bright as the full moon, the corona is overwhelmed by the brilliance of the solar surface and normally not visible to the unaided eye, but a total ECLIPSE permits naked-eye observations.

Coronado, Francisco Vázquez de (1510–1554) Spanish explorer of the North American Southwest. Appointed governor of Nueva Galicia in western central Mexico, Coronado was sent north with a large force to locate and capture the legendary Seven Golden Cities of CÍBOLA, reported to be fabulously wealthy. He was disillusioned to discover instead the ZUÑI pueblos of New Mexico and a seminomadic Indian tribe in Kansas. Though the treasure he sought eluded him, his explorers were the first Europeans to view the Grand Canyon, and he extended Spanish territory over huge areas of North America. His expedition's failure led to his indictment on his return to Mexico, but he was acquitted.

coronary bypass Surgical treatment for CORONARY HEART DISEASE to relieve ANGINA PECTORIS and prevent MYOCARDIAL INFARCTION. It became widely used in the 1960s. One or more blood vessels—usually an artery in the chest or a vein from the leg—are transplanted to create new paths for blood to flow from the AORTA to the heart muscle, bypassing obstructed sections of the coronary arteries.

coronary heart disease *or* **ischemic heart disease** \is-'kē-mik\ Progressive reduction of blood supply to the heart muscle due to narrowing or blocking of a coronary artery (see ARTERIOSCLEROSIS). Short-term oxygen deprivation can cause ANGINA PECTORIS. Long-term, severe oxygen depletion causes MYOCARDIAL INFARCTION (heart attack). CORONARY BYPASS or ANGIOPLASTY is needed if medication and diet do not control the disease.

coroner Public official whose principal duty is to inquire into any death that appears to be unnatural. The name of the office as it emerged in England in the late 12th century was originally "crowner" (also called "coronator"), a reference to the coroner's principal duty of protecting the crown's property. By the late 19th century, the coroner's role had shifted to that of conducting inquests into unnatural deaths. In Canada, all coroners are appointed. In the U.S., the office is elective or appointive, depending on the jurisdiction. Coroners often possess both legal and medical qualifications, but the office is sometimes filled by laypersons, including undertakers, sheriffs, and justices of the peace. In many states the office has been replaced by that of the medical examiner, who is usually a licensed pathologist.

Corot \kȯ-'rō\, **(Jean-Baptiste-) Camille** (1796–1875) French landscape painter. Born to prosperous parents, he proved unsuited to the family business and at 25 was given a small allowance to pursue art training in Paris. He traveled frequently and painted topographical landscapes throughout his career, but preferred making small oil sketches and drawings from nature; from these he produced large finished paintings for exhibition. By the 1850s he had achieved critical success and a large income, and he was generous to less successful artists. His naturalistic oil sketches are now more highly regarded than his more self-consciously poetic finished paintings. He is often associated with the BARBIZON SCHOOL. A master of tonal gradation and soft edges, he prepared the way for the Impressionist landscape painters and had an important influence on CLAUDE MONET, CAMILLE PISSARRO, and BERTHE MORISOT.

corporal punishment Infliction of physical pain upon a person's body as punishment for a crime or infraction. Such penalties include beating, branding, mutilation, blinding, and the use of the stock and pillory. The term also denotes the physical disciplining of children in the schools and at home. From ancient times through the 18th century, corporal punishment was commonly used in instances that did not call for CAPITAL PUNISHMENT, ostracism, or exile. But the growth of humanitarian ideals during the Enlightenment and afterward led to its gradual abandonment, and today it has been almost entirely replaced in the West by imprisonment or other nonviolent penalties. Several international conventions on HUMAN RIGHTS prohibit it. Beatings and other corporeal punishments continue to be administered in the prison systems of many countries. Whipping and even amputation remain prescribed punishments in some Middle Eastern and Asian societies. Corporal punishment of schoolchildren is still sanctioned in many states.

corporate finance Acquisition and allocation of a corporation's funds or resources, with the goal of maximizing shareholder wealth (i.e., stock value). Funds are acquired from both internal and external sources at the lowest possible cost and may be obtained through EQUITY (e.g., sale of STOCK) or DEBT (e.g., BONDS, bank loans). Resource allocation is the INVESTMENT of funds; these investments fall into the categories of current assets (such as cash and INVENTORY) and fixed assets (such as real estate and machinery). Corporate finance must balance the needs of employees, customers, and suppliers against the interests of the shareholders. See also BUSINESS FINANCE.

corporate income tax Tax imposed by public authorities on the incomes of corporations. Virtually all countries assess taxes on the net profits of corporations; most are flat-rate levies rather than extensively graduated taxes. Rates on the order of 50% are common in industrialized nations, though reduced rates are sometimes granted to small corporations. A corporate income tax was adopted by the U.S. government in 1909; three-fourths of the states also levy corporate income taxes. See also CAPITAL-GAINS TAX, INCOME TAX.

corporation Specific legal form of organization of persons and material resources, chartered by the state, for the purpose of conducting business. As contrasted with the other two major forms of business ownership, the sole proprietorship and the PARTNERSHIP, the corporation has several characteristics that make it a more flexible instrument for large-scale economic activity. Chief among these are LIMITED LIABILITY, transferability of shares (rights in the enterprise may be transferred readily from one investor to another without constituting legal reorganization), juridical personality (the corporation itself as a fictive "person" has legal standing and may thus sue and be sued, make contracts, and hold property), and indefinite duration (the life of the corporation may extend beyond the participation of any of its founders). Its owners are the shareholders, who purchase with their investment a share in the proceeds of the enterprise and who are nominally entitled to a measure of control over its financial management. Direct shareholder control became increasingly impossible in the 20th century, however, as the largest corporations came to have tens of thousands of shareholders. The practice of proxy voting by management was legalized and adopted as a remedy, and today salaried managers exercise strong control over the corporation and its assets. See also MULTINATIONAL CORPORATION.

Corporation for Public Broadcasting See PBS

corporatism Theory and practice of organizing the whole of society into corporate entities subordinate to the state. According to the theory, employers and employees would be organized into industrial and professional corporations serving as organs of political representation and largely controlling the people and activities within their jurisdiction. Its chief spokesman was Adam Müller (1779–1829), court philosopher to KLEMENS, FURST VON METTERNICH, who conceived of a "class state" in which the classes operated as guilds, or corporations, each controlling a specific function of social life. This idea found favor in central Europe after the French Revolution, but was not put into practice until BENITO MUSSOLINI came to power in Italy; its implementation there had barely begun by the start of World War II, which resulted in his fall. Since the 1970s, a new variety of corporatism, democratic- or neo-corporatism, refers to a system of interest representation in which states negotiate policy with trade union and business confederations.

Corpus Christi City (pop., 1996 est.: 280,000) and port on CORPUS CHRISTI BAY, southern Texas. Founded in 1838 as a trading post, it was the scene of MEXICAN WAR operations and AMERICAN CIVIL WAR skirmishes. The arrival of the railroad in 1881 stimulated a land boom. The exploitation of gas (1923), development of a deepwater port (1926), and discovery of the Saxtet oil field (1939) laid the city's economic foundation. Resort facilities are based on the bay and the coastal barrier islands, including PADRE ISLAND. It is also the site of the Corpus Christi Naval Air Station.

Corpus Christi Bay Inlet, Gulf of MEXICO, southern Texas. Forming a deepwater harbor for the port of CORPUS CHRISTI, it is 25 mi (40 km) long and 3–10 mi (5–16 km) wide, and is sheltered on the east by Mustang Island. Its shipping serves the petroleum, chemical, and agricultural industries. The area is popular for sport fishing, waterfowl hunting, and boating. The bay was entered on the feast of Corpus Christi in 1519 by Alonso de Pineda, who claimed the region for Spain.

Correggio \kə-'re-jō\ *orig.* **Antonio Allegri** (c. 1489–1534) Italian painter. Born in Correggio, he studied the work of ANDREA MANTEGNA in Mantua and was influenced by LEONARDO DA VINCI. On a visit to Rome he was inspired by the Vatican frescoes of MICHELANGELO and RAPHAEL. By 1518 he was in Parma, the scene of his greatest activity. His first large-scale commission there was the ceiling decoration of the Camera di San Paolo, in the convent of St. Paul (c. 1518–19). His fresco in the dome of Parma Cathedral (c. 1525–30) features the dramatic illusionistic style that influenced dome painting in the baroque period. His use of bold foreshortening, his brilliant, highly original approach to color and light, and the exquisite grace of his figures established him as one of the most inventive artists of the High Renaissance.

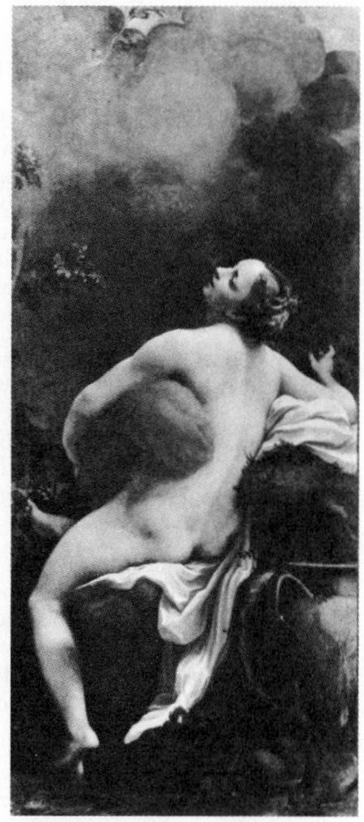
"Jupiter and Io," oil painting by Correggio, c. 1530; in the Kunsthistorisches Museum, Vienna.
BY COURTESY OF THE KUNSTHISTORISCHES MUSEUM, VIENNA

correlation In statistics, the degree of association between two RANDOM VARIABLES. The correlation between the graphs of two data sets is the degree to which they resemble each other. However, correlation is not the same as causation, and even a very close correlation may be no more than a coincidence. Mathematically, a correlation is expressed by a correlation coefficient that ranges from −1 (never occur together), through 0 (absolutely independent), to 1 (always occur together).

Correll, Charles See Freeman GOSDEN and Charles Correll

Correns \'kȯr-ens\, **Carl Erich** (1864–1933) German botanist and geneticist. In the same year as ERICH TSCHERMAK VON SEYSENEGG and HUGO DE VRIES (1900), he independently rediscovered GREGOR MENDEL's paper outlining the principles of heredity. He conducted research with garden peas, from which he drew the same conclusions Mendel had. He helped provide the overwhelming body of evidence in support of Mendel's thesis, anticipating THOMAS HUNT MORGAN's development of the concept of linkage when he developed a theory of a physical coupling of genetic factors to account for the consistent inheritance of certain traits together. See also WILLIAM BATESON.

Correspondence, Committees of See COMMITTEES OF CORRESPONDENCE

Corrigan, Dominic John *later* **Sir Dominic** (1802–1880) Irish physician. He wrote several reports on heart diseases; his paper on aortic insufficiency (1832) is the classic description; and he also produced well-known studies on cirrhosis of the lung (1838), aortitis as a cause of angina pectoris (1837), and mitral stenosis (1838). Corrigan's respiration is shallow breathing in fever; Corrigan's pulse is a jerking pulse beat.

corrosion Wearing away due to CHEMICAL REACTIONS, mainly oxidation (see OXIDATION-REDUCTION, OXIDE). It occurs whenever a gas or liquid chemically attacks an exposed surface, often a metal, and is accelerated by warm temperatures and by ACIDS and SALTS. Normally, corrosion products (e.g., rust, patina) stay on the surface and protect it. Removing these deposits reexposes the surface, and corrosion continues. Some materials resist corrosion naturally; others can be treated to protect them (e.g., by coating, painting, GALVANIZING, or ANODIZING).

corruption Improper and usually unlawful conduct intended to secure a benefit for oneself or another. Its forms include BRIBERY, EXTORTION, and the misuse of inside information. It exists where there is community indifference or a lack of enforcement policies. In societies with a culture of ritualized gift giving, the line between acceptable and unacceptable gifts is often hard to draw. See also ORGANIZED CRIME.

corset Article of clothing worn to shape or constrict the torso. It dates to at least c. 2000 BC, when it was worn as an outer garment by men as well as women in Minoan Crete. In the 16th–17th century it was worn to flatten the chest, and was reinforced with wood. Some outer corsets were jeweled and elaborately embroidered. After 1660 they were shaped to accentuate the breasts. In the 19th century the corset, now reinforced with whalebone or metal, changed with the style of dresses. It was abandoned in the 1920s, when straight clothes came into fashion, and in the 1930s it was replaced by the brassiere and girdle, made of elastic materials, and by the one-piece corselette.

Corsica \'kȯr-si-kə\ *French* **Corse** Island (pop., 1991 est.: 251,000), in the Mediterranean Sea. An administrative region of France, and the fourth-largest island in the Mediterranean, it has an area of 3,352 sq mi (8,681 sq km). While remains of human occupation date from at least the 3rd millennium BC, its recorded history begins c. 560 BC, when Greeks from Asia Minor founded a town there. Taken by the Romans in the 3rd–2nd century BC, it, together with SARDINIA, became a prosperous Roman province. Conquered later by several peoples, including the Byzantines and Arabs, it was granted to PISA in the 11th century. Later ruled mainly by GENOA through the 18th century, in 1768 it became a province of France. It was the birthplace of NAPOLEON. The island's economic life is based on tourism and agriculture.

Corso, Gregory (1930–2001) American poet. A troubled adolescent, Corso spent time in prison. In New York City he became acquainted with ALLEN GINSBERG, who became his mentor. Corso became a leading member of the Beat movement. His poetry is notable for its directness and its startling imagery. Among his poetry collections are *The Vestal Lady on Brattle* (1955), *The Mutation of the Spirit* (1964), and *Herald of the Autochthonic Spirit* (1981).

Cort, Henry (1740–1800) British inventor and industrialist. In 1783 he obtained a patent for producing iron bars quickly and economically in a rolling mill with grooved rolls. The following year he patented his PUDDLING PROCESS for converting PIG IRON into WROUGHT IRON in a REVERBERATORY FURNACE. His two inventions had a significant effect on Britain's iron-making industry, and iron production quadrupled in the next 20 years.

Cortázar \kȯr-'tä-sär\, **Julio** (1914–1984) Argentine-French novelist and short-story writer. His first story collection, *Bestiario* (1951; "Bestiary"), was published the year he moved to Paris, where he spent much of the rest of his life. His masterpiece, *Hopscotch* (1963), is an open-ended novel, or ANTINOVEL, in which the reader is invited to rearrange the chapters. One of his stories became the basis for MICHELANGELO ANTONIONI's film *Blowup* (1966).

Cortes \'kȯr-tās\ Representative assembly of the medieval Iberian kingdoms. The Cortes developed in the European Middle Ages when elected representatives of the free municipalities acquired the right to take part in the affairs of the Curia Regis ("king's court"). They were admitted because the crown was short of funds and lacked the right to raise taxes without the consent of the municipalities. Cortes were established in León and Castile by the early 13th century and soon appeared in Catalonia (1218), Aragon (1274), Valencia (1283), and Navarre (1300). Today the term refers to the national legislatures of Spain and Portugal.

Cortés \kȯr-'tez\, **Hernán** *later* **Marqués del Valle de Oaxaca** (1485–1547) Spanish CONQUISTADOR who won Mexico for Spain. Born into an old family, he left Spain for the New World at 19, joining Diego Velázquez de Cuéllar (1465–1524) in the conquest of Cuba (1511). In 1519, with 508 men and 16 horses, he burned his ships on Mexico's southeastern coast, thus committing himself to conquest. After accumulating thousands of Indian allies who resented AZTEC domination, he forged ahead to TENOCHTITLÁN, the Aztec capital (today Mexico City). The emperor MONTEZUMA II, believing Cortés to be the god QUETZALCÓATL, welcomed him, but was taken prisoner. Hearing that a Spanish force from Cuba was coming to relieve him of command, Cortés left Tenochtitlán under the command of a captain and set out to defeat his Spanish opponents. Returning with the opposition forces now under his command, he discovered that the city had revolted; he led his troops away by night in a costly retreat, but returned in 1521 to conquer the city and with it the empire. The absolute ruler of a huge territory, he was forced to retire after a disastrous expedition in 1524 to the Honduran jungles. His final years were beset by misfortune.

Cortés, Sea of See Gulf of CALIFORNIA

cortex In plants, the tissue of unspecialized cells lying between the epidermis (surface cells) and the vascular, or conducting, tissues (see PHLOEM and XYLEM) of stems and roots. Cortical cells may contain stored food or other substances, such as RESINS, LATEX, ESSENTIAL OILS, and tannins. Cortical cells in herbaceous stems, young woody stems, and stems of SUCCULENTS contain CHLOROPLASTS and can therefore make food by PHOTOSYNTHESIS. Food, usually in the form of starch, in edible roots, BULBS, and TUBERS is stored mostly in the cortex.

cortisone STEROID HORMONE produced by the cortex of the ADRENAL GLAND. It participates in the regulation of the conversion of PROTEINS to CARBOHYDRATES, and to some extent it regulates salt METABOLISM. Introduced medically in 1948 for its anti-inflammatory effect to treat ARTHRITIS, it has been largely replaced by related compounds that do not produce its undesired side effects, which include EDEMA, increased stomach acidity, and imbalances in sodium, potassium, and nitrogen metabolism. See also CUSHING'S SYNDROME.

Cortona, Luca da See Luca SIGNORELLI

Cortona, Pietro da See PIETRO DA CORTONA

corundum \kə-'rən-dəm\ Aluminum oxide mineral (Al_2O_3) that is, after diamond, the hardest known natural substance. Gem varieties are SAPPHIRE and RUBY; mixtures with iron oxides and other minerals are called EMERY. Corundum is widespread in nature, although large deposits are rare. Rich deposits occur in India, Russia, Zimbabwe, and South Africa. In addition to being a precious gem, corundum is used as an abrasive for grinding optical glass and for polishing metals and has also been made into sandpapers and grinding wheels. For most industrial applications, however, it has been replaced by synthetic materials such as alumina; synthetic corundum is also manufactured.

corvée \kȯr-'vā\ Unpaid labor that a European vassal owed a lord or that a citizen in later times owed the state, either in addition to or in lieu of taxes. The corvée was often used when money payment did not provide sufficient labor for public projects, and in wartime it was sometimes used to augment regular troops in auxiliary capacities.

corvette Fast naval vessel smaller than a FRIGATE. In the 18th–19th century corvettes were three-masted ships with square rigging and carried about 20 guns on the top deck. Often used to send dispatches within a battle fleet, they also escorted merchant ships. Early U.S. corvettes won distinction in the War of 1812. They disappeared as a class after the shift to steam power in the mid-19th century, but in World War II the term was applied to small armed vessels that served as escorts for CONVOYS. Modern corvettes, usually displacing 500–1,000 tons (454–900 metric tons) and armed with missiles, torpedoes, and machine guns, perform antisubmarine, antiaircraft, and coastal-patrol duties in small navies.

Corybant \'kȯr-ə-ˌbant\ In Oriental and Greco-Roman mythology, any of the wild, half-demonic beings who were attendants of the GREAT MOTHER OF THE GODS. Often identified or confused with the Cretan Curetes (attendants of ZEUS), they were distinctly Asian in origin and their rites were more orgiastic. Their wild dance was credited with the power of healing mental disorder.

Cosby, Bill *orig.* **William Henry** (born 1937) U.S. television actor and producer. Born in Philadelphia, he worked as a comedian in New York nightclubs and on tour in the 1960s. In the series *I Spy* (1965–68) he became the first black actor to star in a dramatic role on network television. He later frequently appeared on the children's programs *Sesame Street* and *The Electric Company.* His succession of "Cosby" shows (1969–73, 1984–92, 1994, 1996–), whose broad cross-cultural appeal rests on his relaxed, winning charm and an avoidance of racial stereotypes, has made him one of the most durable and popular stars in the history of television.

Cosgrave, William Thomas (1880–1965) Irish statesman, first president (1922–32) of the Irish Free State. Early attracted to Sinn Féin, he took part in the 1916 Easter Rising and was interned briefly by the British. As president he restored settled government in Ireland. He continued in office despite various crises until EAMON DE VALERA's victory in 1932. In 1944 he resigned as head of the United Ireland Party (FINE GAEL). His son Liam (born 1920) served as prime minister 1973–77.

Cosimo, Piero di See PIERO DI COSIMO

Cosimo the Elder See Cosimo de' MEDICI

cosine See TRIGONOMETRIC FUNCTION

cosines, law of Generalization of the PYTHAGOREAN THEOREM relating the lengths of the sides of any triangle. If *a*, *b*, and *c*> are the lengths of the sides and *C* is the angle opposite side *c*, then $c^2 = a^2 + b^2 - 2ab \cos C$.

Cosmati work \'käz-ˌmä-tē\ Type of decorative inlay or MOSAIC used by Roman decorators and architects in the 12th–13th century. Small pieces of colored stone and glass were combined with strips and disks of white marble arranged in geometric patterns. Cosmati work was used for architectural decoration and church furnishings. The term derives from craftsmen of several families named Cosmatus.

cosmetics Any of several preparations (excluding soap) applied to the human body for beautifying, preserving, or altering the appearance or for cleansing, coloring, conditioning, or protecting the skin, hair, nails, lips, eyes, or teeth. The earliest known cosmetics were in use in Egypt in the 4th millennium BC. Cosmetics were in wide use in the Roman Empire, but disappeared from much of Europe with the fall of the Roman Empire (5th century AD) and did not reappear until the Middle Ages, when crusaders returned from the Middle East with cosmetics and PERFUMES. By the 18th century they had come into use by nearly all social classes. Modern cosmetics include skin-care preparations; foundation, face powder and rouge (blusher); eye makeup; lipstick; shampoo; hair curling and straightening preparations; hair colors, dyes, and bleaches; and nail polish. Related products include antiperspirants, mouthwashes, depilatories, astringents, and bath crystals.

cosmic background radiation ELECTROMAGNETIC RADIATION, mostly in the MICROWAVE range, believed to be the highly red-shifted residual effect (see RED SHIFT) of the explosion billions of years ago from which, according to the BIG-BANG model, the universe was created. Discovered by accident in 1964 by ROBERT W. WILSON and ARNO PENZIAS, its presence supports the predictions of big-bang cosmology.

cosmic ray High-speed particle (NUCLEUS or ELECTRON) that travels through the GALAXY. Some cosmic rays originate from the sun, but most come from outside the solar system. Primary cosmic rays that reach earth's ATMOSPHERE collide with nuclei in it, creating secondaries. Because lower-energy primaries are strongly influenced by the interplanetary magnetic field and earth's magnetic field, most of those detected near earth have very high energy, corresponding to speeds about 87% that of light or more. Observations from satellites indicate that most cosmic rays come from the galaxy's disk, but the highest-energy ones are probably extragalactic. Details of their production and acceleration remain unclear, but apparently expanding shock waves from supernovas can accelerate particles. From the early 1930s to the 1950s, cosmic rays were the only source of high-energy particles used in studying the atomic nucleus and its components. Short-lived SUBATOMIC PARTICLES were discovered through cosmic-ray collisions, leading to the rise of PARTICLE PHYSICS. Even powerful PARTICLE ACCELERATORS cannot impart energy anywhere near that of the highest-energy cosmic rays. See also VICTOR FRANCIS HESS.

cosmogony See CREATION MYTH

cosmological argument Form of argument used in natural THEOLOGY to prove the existence of God. THOMAS AQUINAS, in his *Summa theologiae,* presented two versions of the cosmological argument: the first-cause argument and the argument from contingency. The first-cause argument begins with the fact that there is change in the world, and a change is always the effect of some cause or causes. Each cause is itself the effect of a further cause or set of causes; this chain moves in a series that either never ends or is completed by a first cause, which must be of a radically different nature in that it is not itself caused. Such a first cause is an important aspect, though not the entirety, of what Christianity means by God. The argument from contingency follows by another route a similar basic movement of thought from the nature of the world to its ultimate ground.

cosmological constant Term reluctantly added by ALBERT EINSTEIN to his equations of general RELATIVITY in order to obtain a solution to the equations that described a static universe, as he believed it to be at the time. The constant has the effect of a repulsive force that acts against the gravitational attraction of matter in the universe. When Einstein heard of the evidence that the universe is expanding, he called the introduction of the cosmological constant the "biggest blunder" of his life. Recent developments suggest that in the early universe there may well have been a cosmological constant with a nonzero value.

cosmology Field of study that brings together the natural sciences, especially ASTRONOMY and PHYSICS, in an effort to understand the physical UNIVERSE as a unified whole. The first great age of scientific cosmology began in Greece in the 6th century BC, when the Pythagoreans introduced the concept of a spherical earth and, unlike the Babylonians and Egyptians, hypothesized that the heavenly bodies moved according to the harmonious relations of natural laws. Their thought culminated in the Ptolemaic model (see PTOLEMY) of the universe (2nd century AD). The Copernican revolution (see COPERNICAN SYSTEM) of the 16th century ushered in the second great age. The third began in the early 20th century, with the discovery of special RELATIVITY and its development into general relativity by ALBERT EINSTEIN. The basic assumptions of modern cosmology are that the universe is homogeneous in space (on the average, all places are alike at any time) and that the laws of physics are the same everywhere.

cosmonaut See ASTRONAUT

cosmos \'käz-məs\ Any of the garden plants that make up the genus *Cosmos* (COMPOSITE FAMILY), containing about 20 species native to the tropical New World. Heads of flowers are borne along long flower stalks or together in an open cluster. The disk flowers are red or yellow; the ray flowers, sometimes notched, may be white, pink, red, purple, or other colors. Most annual ornamental varieties have been developed from the common garden cosmos *(C. bipinnatus).*

Cossacks Peoples dwelling in the northern hinterlands of the Black and Caspian seas. The term (from the Turkic *kazak,* "free person") originally referred to semi-independent Tatar groups, which formed in the Dnieper River region. Later it was also applied to peasants who had fled from serfdom in Poland, Lithuania, and Muscovy to the Dnieper and Don regions. The Cossacks had a tradition of independence and received privileges from the Russian government in return for military services. They were used as defenders of the Russian frontier and advance guards for imperial territorial expansion. Attempts in the 17th–18th century to reduce their privileges caused revolts, led by STENKA RAZIN and YEMELYAN PUGACHOV, and the Cossacks gradually lost their autonomous status.

cost Monetary value of goods and services that producers and consumers purchase. In a basic economic sense, cost is the measure of the alternative opportunities forgone in the choice of one good or activity over others (see OPPORTUNITY COST). For consumers, cost describes the PRICE paid for goods and services. For producers, cost has to do with the relationship between the value of production inputs and the level of output. Total cost refers to all the expenses incurred in reaching a particular level of output; if total cost is divided by the quantity produced, average or unit cost is obtained. A portion of the total cost known as fixed cost (e.g., the costs of building rental or of heavy machinery) does not vary with the quantity produced and, in the short run, cannot be altered by increasing or decreasing production. Variable costs, like the costs of labor or raw materials, change with the level of output. Economic decisions are based on marginal cost, the additional cost of an incremental unit of production or consumption.

cost-benefit analysis In governmental planning and budgeting, the attempt to measure the social benefits of a proposed project in monetary terms and compare them with its costs. The procedure was first proposed in 1844 by Arsène-Jules-Étienne-Juvénal Dupuit (1804–1866). It was not seriously applied until the 1936 U.S. Flood Control Act, which required that the benefits of flood-control projects exceed their costs. A cost-benefit ratio is determined by dividing the projected benefits of a program by the projected costs. A wide range of variables must be considered because the value of the benefits may be indirect or projected far into the future.

cost of living Monetary cost of maintaining a particular standard of living, usually measured by calculating the average cost of a number of goods and services. Measurement of the cost of a minimum standard of living is essential in determining relief payments, social-insurance benefits, and MINIMUM WAGES. The cost of living is customarily measured by a PRICE INDEX such as the CONSUMER PRICE INDEX. Measurements of change in the cost of living are important in wage negotiations. Cost-of-living measurements are also used to compare the cost of maintaining similar living standards in different areas. See also SOCIAL INSURANCE.

Costa-Gavras \ˌkōs-tə-'gav-rəs\, **Constantine** *orig.* **Konstantinos Gavras** (born 1933) Greek-French film director. He left Greece to study in Paris, where he became an assistant to such filmmakers as RENE CLAIR. He directed his first film, *The Sleeping Car Murders,* in 1966. His drama of political assassination, *Z* (1968, Academy Award), brought him international fame. He later directed such political thrillers as *The Confession* (1970), *State of Siege* (1972), *Missing* (1982, Academy

Award), and *Mad City* (1997). He became president of the Cinémathèque Française in 1982.

Costa Rica *officially* **República de Costa Rica** Country, Central America. Area: 19,730 sq mi (51,100 sq km). Population (1997 est.): 3,468,000. Capital: SAN JOSÉ. Most of the people are of Spanish ancestry, with Indian and black admixtures. Language: Spanish (official). Religion: Roman Catholicism (official). Currency: colón. Costa Rica's narrow Pacific coast rises abruptly into central highlands and a volcanic mountain chain that forms the backbone of the country, descending gradually to the Caribbean coastal plain. With a climate ranging from temperate to tropical, it contains a wide variety of plants and animals that include both North and South American species. It has a developing market economy largely based on coffee and banana exports. Other cash crops include beef, sugar, and cocoa. It is a multiparty republic with one legislative house; the head of state and government is the president. CHRISTOPHER COLUMBUS landed in Costa Rica in 1502 in an area inhabited by a number of small, independent Indian tribes. These peoples were not easily dominated, and it took almost 60 years for the Spaniards to establish a permanent settlement. Ignored by the Spanish crown because of its lack of mineral wealth, the colony grew slowly. Coffee exports and the construction of a rail line improved its economy in the 19th century. It joined the short-lived Mexican empire in 1821, was a member of the United Provinces of Central America 1823–38, and adopted a constitution in 1871. In 1890 Costa Ricans held what is considered to be the first free and honest election in Central America, beginning a tradition of democracy for which Costa Rica is renowned. In 1987 then president OSCAR ARIAS SANCHEZ was awarded the Nobel Peace Prize. During the 1990s Costa Rica struggled with its economic policies. It suffered severe damage from a hurricane in 1996.

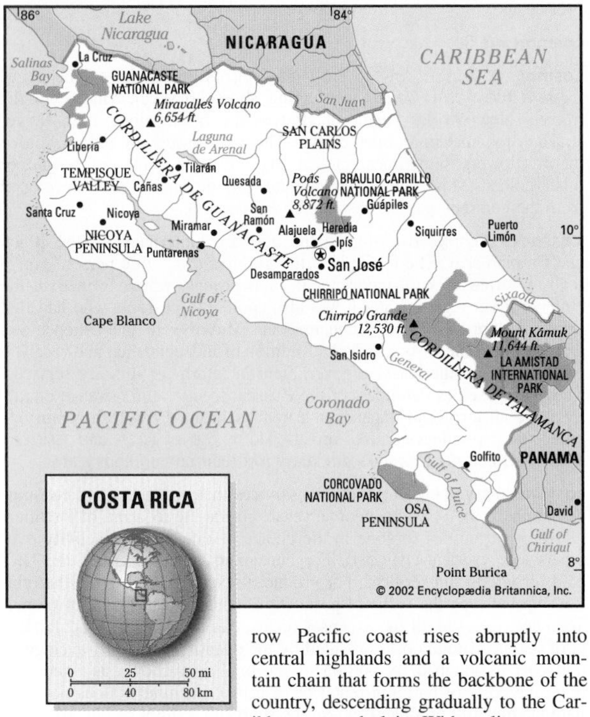

Costello, Lou See ABBOTT AND COSTELLO

Costner, Kevin (born 1955) U.S. film actor and director. Born in Compton, Cal., he first gained a starring role in *The Untouchables* (1987) as Eliot Ness. His further success in *Bull Durham* (1988) and *Field of Dreams* (1989) made him a popular leading man, and he formed his own production company in 1989. In 1990 he produced, directed, and acted in another hit, *Dances with Wolves* (Academy Awards for best director and picture). Among his later films were *JFK* (1991), *A Perfect World* (1993), *Waterworld* (1995), *Tin Cup* (1996), and *The Postman* (1997).

Cotabato River See MINDANAO RIVER

Cotán, Juan Sánchez See Juan SANCHEZ COTAN

Côte d'Azur \ˌkōt-dȧ-ˈzu̇r\ Region bordering the Mediterranean Sea, southeastern France. Encompassing the French RIVIERA between Menton and CANNES, it is noted for its scenery, and is a major tourist center. See also NICE, MONACO.

Côte d'Ivoire *or* **Ivory Coast** \ˌkōt-dē-ˈvwär\ *officially* **Republic of Côte d'Ivoire** Republic, western Africa. Area: 124,504 sq mi (322,463 sq km). Population (2001 est.): 16,393,000. Capital: YAMOUSSOUKRO, seat of government, ABIDJAN. There are about 60 independent tribes, including the Beti, Senufo, Baule, Anyi, Malinke, Dan, and Lobu. Languages: French (official), various native languages. Religions: Islam, Roman Catholicism, traditional animistic beliefs. Currency: CFA franc. Côte d'Ivoire can be divided into four major regions: a narrow coastal region, an equatorial rainforest in the west, a cultivated forest zone in the east, and a savanna region in the north. Agriculture employs more than 50% of the workforce. The country is the world's largest producer of cocoa and a major producer of coffee; other exports include bananas, cotton, rubber, timber, and diamonds. It is a republic with one legislative house; its chief of state is the president, and its head of government is the prime minister. European powers came to the area to trade in ivory and slaves beginning in the 15th century, and local kingdoms gave way to French influence in the 19th century. The French colony of Côte d'Ivoire was founded in 1893, and full French occupation took place 1908–18. In 1946 it became a territory in the FRENCH UNION; in 1947 the northern part of the country separated and became the nation of Upper Volta (now BURKINA FASO). Côte d'Ivoire peacefully achieved autonomy in 1958 and independence in 1960, when FELIX HOUPHOUET-BOIGNY was elected president. The country's first multiparty presidential elections were held in 1990.

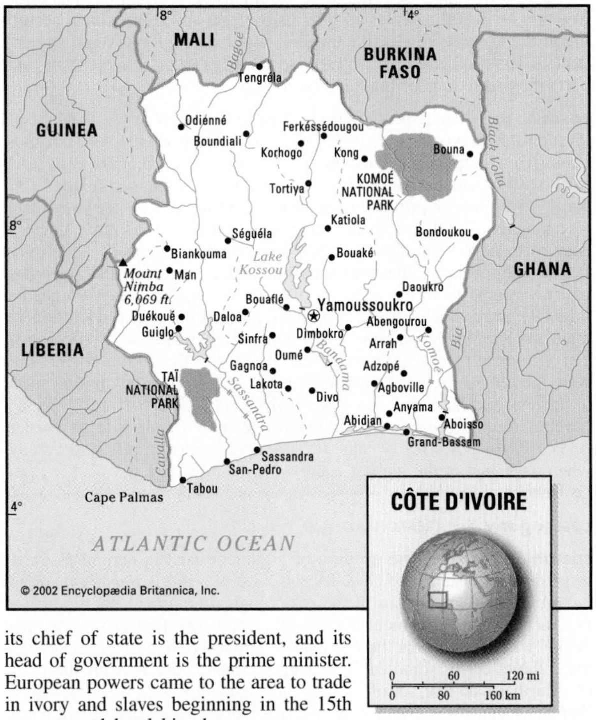

Cotonou \ˌkō-tō-ˈnü\ Port city (pop., 1994 est.: 750,000), de facto capital of Benin. Situated along the Gulf of GUINEA, it is the starting point of the Benin–Niger Railway and the site of deepwater port facilities, completed in 1965, that serve both Benin and Togo. Cotonou is the economic hub of Benin and its largest urban center. Its industries include brewing, textile production, and palm-oil processing. It is home to the National University of Benin (1970).

Cotopaxi \ˌkō-tō-ˈpäk-sē\ Volcanic peak in the ANDES, central Ecuador. Rising to 19,347 ft (5,897 m), it is the world's highest continuously active volcano. Its almost perfectly symmetrical cone is often hidden by clouds that are lit at night by the crater's fires. Its base stands on open mountain grassland; its upper part is covered with permanent snow. With a long record of violent eruption, it has seldom remained quiet for more than 15 years.

cotton Seed-hair fiber of various plants of the genus *Gossypium,* in the MALLOW FAMILY, native to most subtropical countries. The shrubby plants produce creamy-white flowers, followed by small green seedpods (cotton bolls), which contain the seeds. Fibers growing from the outer skin of the seeds become tightly packed within the boll, which bursts open at maturity, to reveal soft masses of the white to yellowish-white fibers. Cotton is harvested when the bolls open. One of the world's leading agricultural crops, cotton is plentiful and economically produced, making cotton products relatively inexpensive. The fibers can be made into a diverse array of fabrics suitable for a great variety of apparel, home furnishings, and industrial uses. Cotton fabrics can be extremely durable and are comfortable to wear. Nonwoven cotton, made by fusing or bonding the fibers, is useful for making disposable products including towels, polishing cloths, tea bags, tablecloths, bandages, and disposable uniforms and sheets for hospital and other medical uses.

Cotton (*Gossypium hirsutum*).
ROD HEINRICHS—GRANT HEILMAN

Cotton, John (1585–1652) British-American Puritan leader. He studied at Cambridge Univ., where he first encountered Puritanism. From 1612 to 1633 he served as a vicar in Lincolnshire. When English church authorities filed charges against him for his Nonconformism, he sailed for New England in 1633. As "teacher" of the First Church of Boston (1633–52), he became an influential leader of the Massachusetts Bay Colony. He wrote a widely used children's catechism and defended Puritan orthodoxy in such books as *The Way of the Churches of Christ in New England* (1645). He opposed freedom of conscience, as preached by ROGER WILLIAMS, favoring a national theocratic society.

Cotton, King See KING COTTON

Cotton, Robert Bruce *later* **Sir Robert** (1571–1631) English antiquarian. From about 1585 Cotton collected ancient records, manuscripts, books, and coins and welcomed scholars to his library. He entered Parliament in 1601 and was favored at court until c. 1615. His acquisition of so many public documents aroused misgivings, and after he wrote several works criticizing policies of CHARLES I, his library was sealed in 1629. After his death his son regained possession of the library, and his great-grandson presented it to the nation in 1700. The Cottonian Library's historical documents formed the basis of the manuscript collection of the BRITISH MUSEUM.

Cotton Belt Agricultural region of the southeastern U.S. where cotton is the main cash crop. Once confined to the pre-Civil War South, the Cotton Belt was pushed west after the war. Today it extends primarily through North and South Carolina, Georgia, Alabama, Mississippi, western Tennessee, eastern Arkansas, Louisiana, eastern Texas, and southern Oklahoma.

cotton bollworm See CORN EARWORM

Cotton Club Nightclub in New York's Harlem district in the 1920s and '30s. It opened in 1922 at 142nd Street and Lenox Avenue under the management of the reputed bootlegger Owney Madden (1892–1964). It became extremely fashionable, and featured the finest black performers in the U.S. (who would not have been allowed in as patrons), including LOUIS ARMSTRONG, CAB CALLOWAY, DUKE ELLINGTON, LENA HORNE, BILL ROBINSON, and ETHEL WATERS. It later moved downtown (1936–40). Another club with the same name opened in Harlem in the 1980s.

cotton gin Machine for cleaning COTTON of its seeds. The design that became standard was invented in the U.S. by ELI WHITNEY in 1793. The mechanization of spinning in England had created a greatly expanded market for U.S. cotton, but production was bottlenecked by the manual removal of the seeds from the raw fiber. The cotton gin pulled the cotton through a set of wire teeth mounted on a revolving cylinder, the fiber passing through narrow slots in an iron breastwork too small to permit passage of the seed. The simplicity of the invention caused it to be widely copied. It is credited with making cotton virtually the only crop of the U.S. South and so institutionalizing slavery.

cottonmouth moccasin See WATER MOCCASIN

cottonwood Any of several fast-growing trees of North America, of the genus *Populus,* in the WILLOW family, with triangular, toothed leaves and cottony seeds. The dangling leaves clatter in the wind. Eastern cottonwood *(P. deltoides)* has thick glossy leaves. Carolina poplar *(P. angulata)* and *P. eugenei* may be natural hybrids between *P. deltoides* and Eurasian black poplar *(P. nigra).* Alamo, or Fremont cottonwood *(P. fremontii),* is the tallest of the group. See also POPLAR.

Eastern cottonwood (*Populus deltoides*).
KITTY KOHOUT FROM ROOT RESOURCES—EB INC.

cottony-cushion scale SCALE INSECT (*Icerya purchasi,* order Homoptera) that is a pest especially of California CITRUS trees. The adult lays bright red eggs in a distinctive large white mass that juts out from a twig. Distributed worldwide, cottony-cushion scale is found on many other plants, including acacia, pittosporum, and willow. Australian ladybird beetles (see LADYBUG), a natural enemy, have been imported to keep it from destroying the California citrus industry.

Cottony-cushion scales (*Icerya purchasi,* magnified).
ROBERT C. HERMES—THE NATIONAL AUDUBON SOCIETY COLLECTION/PHOTO RESEARCHERS

cotyledon \,kä-tə-'lē-d^{ə}n\ Seed leaf within the embryo of a seed that provides energy and nutrients for the developing seedling. After the first true leaves have formed, they wither and fall off. FLOWERING PLANTS whose embryos have a single cotyledon are grouped as monocots, or monocotyledonous plants; embryos with two cotyledons are grouped as dicots, or dicotyledonous plants. Unlike flowering plants, GYMNOSPERMS usually have several cotyledons rather than one or two. See illustration on following page.

Coubertin \kü-ber-'ta^{n}\, **Pierre, baron de** (1863–1937) French educator, primarily responsible for the revival of the OLYMPIC GAMES in 1894. Born in Paris, he became one of the first advocates of physical education in France. His drive to restart the Olympics, after a 1,500-year suspension, was partly inspired by a visit to Greece, where excavators were uncovering the ancient Olympic site. He served as the second president (1896–1925) of the International Olympic Committee.

couch grass *or* **quack grass** Rapidly spreading GRASS *(Agropyron repens)* with flat, somewhat hairy leaves and erect flower spikes, native to Europe and introduced into other northern temperate areas for forage or EROSION control. In cultivated land, it is considered a weed because of its persistence. Its long, yellowish-white RHIZOMES must be completely dug up to eradicate the plant because broken rhizomes generate new plants. Couch grass has been used in various home remedies in Europe, and the rhizomes have been eaten during periods of famine.

Coué \'kwā\, **Émile** (1857–1926) French pharmacist and psychologist. Starting as a pharmacist at Troyes in 1882, he studied hypnosis, opened a free clinic at Nancy in 1910, and developed his own method of psychotherapy based on autosuggestion, "Couéism" which most famously required constant repetition of the formula "Every day, and in every way, I am becoming better and better."

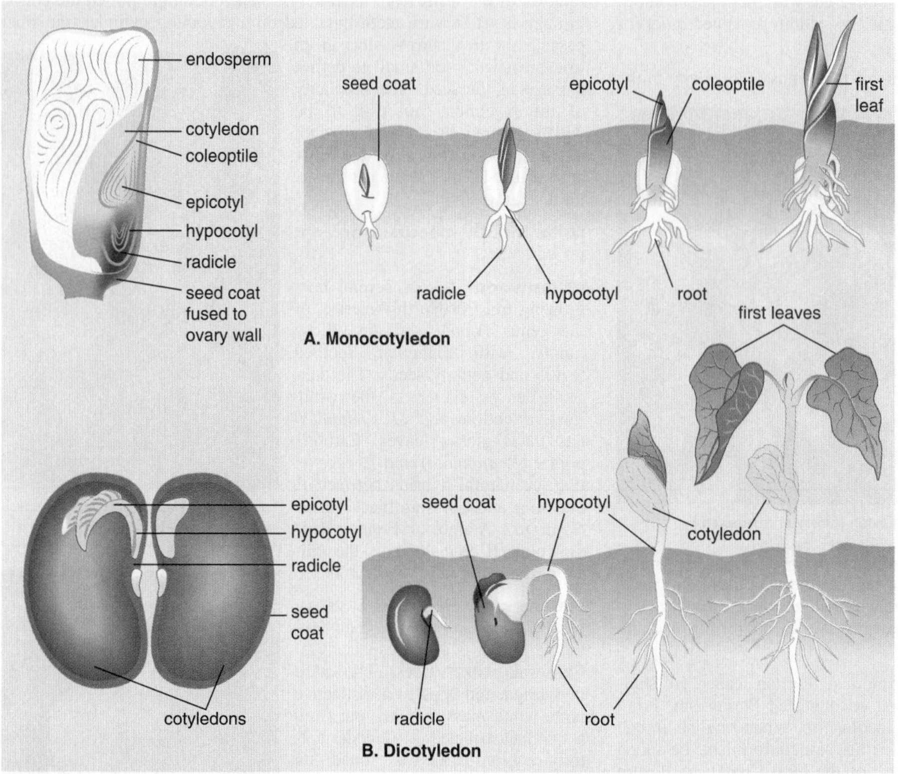

A. Monocotyledon (internal structures of a corn seed with stages of germination). Nutrients are stored in the cotyledon and endosperm tissue. The radicle and hypocotyl (region between the cotyledon and radicle) give rise to the roots. The epicotyl (region above the cotyledon) gives rise to the stem and leaves and is covered by a protective sheath (coleoptile). B. Dicotyledon (internal structures of a bean seed with stages of germination). All nutrients are stored in the enlarged cotyledons. The radicle gives rise to the roots, the hypocotyl to the lower stem, the epicotyl to the leaves and upper stem.

cougar *or* **puma** \'pü-mə, 'pyü-mə\ *or* **mountain lion** *or* **panther** Species *(Felis concolor)* of large graceful CAT that occurs from British Columbia to Patagonia in mountains, deserts, and jungles. In many regions, the species is restricted to wilderness areas, and some subspecies are considered endangered. Cougars range from pale buff to reddish brown, with dark ears and tail tip and white rump and belly. The adult weighs from 77 to more than 220 lbs (35–100 kg). A male may be about 9 ft (3 m) long, one-third of which is tail, and stand 24–30 in. (60–75 cm) tall at the shoulder. Since the cougar occasionally kills livestock, it has been intensively hunted by farmers especially in North America, and basically exterminated from the eastern U.S.. It is valuable for preventing overpopulation of prey animals (mostly deer, in North America). It rarely attacks humans.

Coughlin \'käg-lən\, **Charles E(dward)** *or* **Father Coughlin** (1891–1975) Canadian-U.S. clergyman. Born in Hamilton, Ontario, he was ordained a Catholic priest in 1923 and became pastor of a Michigan church. In 1930 he began radio broadcasts of his sermons, into which he gradually injected reactionary political views and anti-Semitic rhetoric, attracting the first mass audience in broadcast history. He attacked HERBERT HOOVER, FRANKLIN ROOSEVELT, and the NEW DEAL; Wall Street and Communism were other targets of his magazine, *Social Justice,* which was banned from the mails and ceased publication in 1942, the same year the Catholic hierarchy ordered Coughlin to stop broadcasting.

Coulomb \kü-'lōⁿ, *Engl* 'kü-ˌläm\, **Charles-Augustin de** (1736–1806) French physicist. After serving as a military engineer in the West Indies, he returned to France in the 1780s to pursue scientific research. To investigate JOSEPH PRIESTLEY's law of electrical repulsions, he invented a sensitive instrument to measure the electrical forces involved. A light rod made of an insulator, with a small conducting sphere at each end, was suspended horizontally by a fine wire so that it was free to twist when another charged sphere was brought close to it. By measuring the angle through which the rod twisted, Coulomb could measure the repulsive forces. He is best known for formulating COULOMB'S LAW. He also did research on friction of machinery, on windmills, and on the elasticity of metal and silk fibers. The coulomb, a unit of electric charge, was named in his honor.

Coulomb force See ELECTROSTATIC FORCE

Coulomb's law \'kü-ˌlämz\ Law formulated by C.-A. de COULOMB that describes the electric force between charged objects. It states that (1) like charges repel each other and unlike charges attract each other, (2) the attraction or repulsion acts along the line between the two charges, (3) the size of the force varies inversely as the square of the distance between the two charges, and (4) the size of the force is proportional to the value of each charge. See also ELECTROSTATIC FORCE.

Council for Mutual Economic Assistance *or* **Comecon** Organization founded in 1949 to facilitate and coordinate the economic development of Soviet-bloc countries. Its original members were the Soviet Union, Bulgaria, Czechoslovakia, Hungary, Poland, and Romania; other members joined later, including Albania (1949) and the German Democratic Republic (1950). Its accomplishments included the organization of Eastern Europe's railroad grid, the creation of the INTERNATIONAL BANK FOR ECONOMIC COOPERATION, and the construction of the "Friendship" oil pipeline. After the democratic revolutions of 1989, it largely lost its purpose and power. In 1991 it was renamed the Organization for International Economic Cooperation.

counseling Professional guidance of the individual by use of standard psychological methods such as collecting case-history data, using various techniques of the personal interview, and testing interests and aptitudes. The counselor's goal is generally to orient the individual toward opportunities that can best guarantee fulfillment of his or her personal needs and aspirations. The counselor usually attempts to clarify the client's own thinking rather than to solve his or her problems. Professional counselors (such as educational guidance and career counselors) and counseling psychologists (such as marriage and bereavement counselors) are found in a wide variety of institutional settings and in private practice. See also PSYCHOTHERAPY.

count *or* **earl** European title of nobility, ranking in modern times after a MARQUESS or (in countries without marquesses) a DUKE. In England, the title of earl is the equivalent of count and ranks above a VISCOUNT. The wife of a count or earl is a countess. The Roman *comes* (count) was originally a household companion of the emperor; under the Franks he was a local commander and judge. The counts were later incorporated into the feudal structure, some becoming subordinate to dukes, though a few countships were as great as duchies. As royal authority was reasserted over the feudatories, which took place at different times in the different kingdoms, the counts lost their political authority, though they retained their privileges as members of the nobility.

Counter-Reformation *or* **Catholic Reformation** In ROMAN CATHOLICISM, efforts in the 16th and early 17th century to oppose the Protestant REFORMATION and reform the Catholic Church. Early efforts grew out of criticism of the worldliness and corruption of the papacy and clergy during the Renaissance. PAUL III (r.1534–49) was the first pope to respond, convening the important Council of TRENT (1545–63), which reacted to Protestant teachings on faith, grace, and the sacraments, and attempted to reform training for the priesthood. The Roman INQUISITION was established in 1542 to control HERESY within Catholic territories, and the JESUITS under Ignatius de LOYOLA undertook educational and missionary work aimed at conversion or reconversion. Emperors CHARLES V and PHILIP II took military action against Protestant growth. Later popes of the Counter-Reformation included PIUS V, GREGORY XIII, and SIXTUS V. Sts. Charles BORROMEO, Philip NERI, JOHN OF THE CROSS, TERESA OF ÁVILA, FRANCIS DE SALES, and VINCENT DE PAUL were among the most influential reforming figures.

counterfeiting Crime of making an unauthorized imitation of a genuine article, typically money, with the intent to deceive or defraud. Because of the value conferred on money and the high level of technical skill required to imitate it, counterfeiting is singled out from other acts of FORGERY. It is generally punished as a FELONY. The international police organization INTERPOL was established primarily to organize the fight against counterfeiting. Software, credit cards, designer clothing, and watches are among nonmoney items commonly counterfeited.

counterglow See GEGENSCHEIN

counterpoint (from Latin, *punctus contra punctum:* "note against note") Combination of two or more melodic lines (also called polyphony); also, the technique of controlling the relationship between simultaneous lines. The first recorded use of two melodic lines simultaneously was in 9th-century treatises showing examples of ORGANUM, though improvised counterpoint—in which the voices probably moved mostly parallel to each other, and thus failed to convey an impression of independence—may date back to some centuries earlier. The desire to ensure pleasant consonances and avoid unpleasant dissonances when improvising (see CONSONANCE AND DISSONANCE) called for principles of simultaneous vocal motion (voice leading), and as the relative movement of voices approaching and leaving given INTERVALS was seen to produce effects that were more or less pleasing, rules came to govern such types of relative motion as parallel motion, contrary motion (one voice moving up, the other down), and oblique motion (only one voice moving). A great pedagogical advance was the invention of the systematic pedagogical method known as species counterpoint in the 18th century by Johann Joseph Fux (1660–1741). The "vertical" aspect of counterpoint came to be studied as HARMONY, especially from the 18th century. Though harmony and counterpoint are intimately intertwined, most of the multivoiced music of the Middle Ages and the Renaissance is felt to be essentially polyphonic or contrapuntal—that is, to consist of a combination of relatively independent and integral melodic lines. In the baroque era, with the invention of FIGURED BASS and the CONTINUO, the balance began to shift toward a harmonic orientation.

countertenor Adult male alto voice, either natural or falsetto. Some writers use the term only for the natural high tenor, preferring "male alto" for the falsetto voice. Like the CASTRATO tradition, the countertenor developed as a result of the prohibition on women taking part in church choirs. Since the falsetto voice lacks power, it was little used in opera. The countertenor tradition was preserved in the English cathedral choir. Today it is again being widely cultivated internationally, primarily for Renaissance and Baroque music.

country dance *or* **contredanse** \'kän-trə-ˌdans\ Type of social dance for couples, popular in the 17th century. Derived from English folk dance, the country dance is performed in one of three forms: circular or round; "longways," with rows of couples facing each other; and geometric, in squares or triangles. The main source of country-dance steps and songs is John Playford's *The English Dancing Master* (1650). The dance was the basis for the 19th-century QUADRILLE, and was brought by colonists to the U.S. as the Virginia reel and, in modified form, as the SQUARE DANCE. It has enjoyed a modest revival in recent decades.

country music *or* **country and western** Musical style that originated among whites in rural areas of the southern and western U.S. The term "country and western music" was adopted by the music industry in 1949 to replace the derogatory "hillbilly music." Its roots lie in the music of the European settlers of the Appalachians and other areas. In the early 1920s the genre began to be commercially recorded; Fiddlin' John Carson recorded its first hit. Radio programs such as Nashville's GRAND OLE OPRY and Chicago's "National Barn Dance" fueled its growth, and growing numbers of musicians such as the CARTER FAMILY and JIMMIE RODGERS began performing on radio and recording at studios. With the migration of Southern whites to industrial cities in the 1930s and '40s, country music was exposed to new influences, such as BLUES and GOSPEL MUSIC. Its nostalgic bias, with its lyrics about poverty, heartbreak, and homesickness, held special appeal during a time of great population shifts. In the 1930s such "singing cowboy" film stars as Gene Autry altered country lyrics to produce a synthetic "western" music. Other variants include western swing (see BOB WILLS) and honky-tonk (see ERNEST TUBB and H. WILLIAMS). The 1940s saw an effort to return to its root values (see BLUEGRASS), but commercialization proved a stronger influence, and in the 1950s and '60s country music became a huge commercial enterprise. Popular singers often recorded songs in a Nashville style, while many country-music recordings employed lush orchestral backgrounds. Country music has become increasingly acceptable to national urban audiences, retaining its vitality with such diverse performers as W. NELSON, Waylon Jennings, Dolly Parton, Randy Travis, Garth Brooks, Emmylou Harris, and Lyle Lovett. While embracing other styles, it has kept an unmistakable character as one of the few truly indigenous American musical styles.

coup d'état \ˌkü-dā-'tä\ *or* **coup** (French: "stroke of state") Sudden overthrow, often violent, of an existing government by a group of conspirators. Coups are most common in countries with unstable governments and in countries with little experience of successful democracy. Their success depends on surprise and speed. Coups rarely alter a nation's fundamental social and economic policies or significantly redistribute power. See also MILITARY GOVERNMENT, REVOLUTION.

Coup of 18 Fructidor See Coup of 18 FRUCTIDOR

Coup of 18–19 Brumaire See Coup of 18–19 BRUMAIRE

Couperin \küp-'raⁿ\, **François** (1668–1733) French composer, harpsichordist, and organist. He succeeded his father as organist at the important church of St. Gervais at 17 and kept the post for some 50 years. He was later also appointed organist and harpsichordist at the court of LOUIS XIV. He is best known for four books of harpsichord pieces containing some 220 elegant, vivacious, and richly ornamented works *(Pièces de clavecin,* 1713–30). His other works include a collection of over 40 organ works (*Pièces d'orgue,* 1709); much sacred vocal music (including the *Leçons de ténèbres,* c. 1715); and several sets of chamber music (including the *Concerts royaux,* 1722). His *Art of Playing the Harpsichord* (1716) is the most valuable instrumental treatise of its time. He was the foremost French composer of his generation. His uncle, Louis Couperin (1626–1661), also organist at St. Gervais, composed over 200 keyboard works.

couple In physics, a pair of equal parallel FORCES that are opposite in direction. Couples produce or prevent the turning of a body. The forces used to turn the steering wheel of a car constitute a couple; each hand exerts a force, parallel but opposite in direction, yet they work together to achieve the same goal. A couple is also used to turn a screwdriver or a doorknob, and the pair of forces acting on the opposite poles of a compass needle as it points somewhere between north and south are a couple.

couplet Two successive lines of verse marked usually by rhythmic correspondence, rhyme, or the inclusion of a self-contained utterance. Couplets may be independent poems, but they usually function as parts of other verse forms, such as the Shakespearean SONNET, which concludes with a couplet. A couplet that cannot stand alone is an open couplet; a couplet whose sense is relatively independent is a closed couplet.

courante \kü-'ränt\ (from Latin *currere,* "to run") Court dance of the 16th century, fashionable in European ballrooms into the 18th century. It was originally performed with small, back-and-forth, springing steps, which later became stately glides. Danced to music in quick triple time, the courante followed the ALLEMANDE, and later became part of the musical SUITE.

Courantyne River \'kōr-ən-ˌtīn\ *Dutch* **Corantijn** \'kōr-ən-ˌtīn\ *in Suriname* **Coeroeni** \kü-'rü-nē\ River, northern South America. Rising in the Akarai Mtns., it flows generally north for 450 mi (700 km) to the Atlantic Ocean in Suriname. It divides Suriname and Guyana; Guyana nationals have free navigation on the river but no fishing rights. It is navigable to small oceangoing vessels for 45 mi (72 km) to the first rapids at Orealla. The Courantyne basin remains largely undeveloped, with much of it unexplored forest.

Courbet \kür-'bā\, **Gustave** (1819–1877) French painter. In 1839 he went to Paris, where, after receiving some formal training, he learned by copying old masters in the Louvre. His early works were controversial but received public and critical acclaim. His images of everyday life, characterized by a powerful naturalism and boldly portrayed, cast him as a revolutionary socialist. His audacity and disrespect for authority were notorious. In 1855, refused by the jury of the Paris Universal Exposition, he opened a pavilion for his own work, calling it Le Pavillon du Réalisme. Proficient in all genres, Courbet immortalized the French countryside. In 1865 his series depicting storms at sea astounded the art world and opened the way for IMPRESSIONISM.

coureur de bois \kü-'rœr-də-'bwä\ (French: "wood runner") French-Canadian fur trader of the late 17th and early 18th century. Most of the coureurs de bois traded illicitly (i.e., without the license required by the Quebec government). They sold brandy to Indians, which created difficulties for the tribes with whom they traded. Though they defied the colonial authorities, they ultimately benefited them by exploring the frontier, developing the fur trade, and helping ally Native Americans with the French and against the English (see FRENCH AND INDIAN WAR).

Courland \'kür-ˌlänt, *Engl* 'ku̇r-lənd\ *Latvian* **Kurzeme** \'ku̇r-zə-ˌmä\ Historical region, Latvia. Located on the Baltic Sea, it was named for the Curonians, who had established a tribal kingdom there by the end of the 9th century. Conquered in the 13th century by the Livonians, in 1561 the area was incorporated into the duchy of Courland, which became a Polish fief. The duchy flourished during the 17th century with the development of industries and foreign trade. From 1737 its duke was a client of the Russian throne, and it came under Russian rule in 1795. It became part of the newly independent Latvia in 1918.

Courland Lagoon See KURSKIY ZALIV

Cournand \ku̇r-'nä^n\, **André F(rédéric)** (1895–1988) French-U.S. physician and physiologist. He shared a 1956 Nobel Prize with Dickinson W. Richards (1895–1973) and WERNER FORSSMANN for discoveries on heart catheterization and circulatory changes. Cournand and Richards perfected Forssmann's cardiac catheterization procedure for studying the functioning of diseased hearts to more accurately diagnose underlying anatomic defects. They also used the catheter in the pulmonary artery, improving diagnosis of lung diseases.

Cournot \kür-'nō\, **Antoine-Augustin** (1801–1877) French economist and mathematician. The first economist to apply mathematics effectively to the treatment of economic questions, he made important contributions with his discussion of supply-and-demand functions, the shifting of taxes, and problems of international trade, and is best remembered for his discussion of strategic behavior in a market with only two producers, a duopoly. His principal work is *Researches into the Mathematical Principles of the Theory of Wealth* (1838).

Courrèges \ku̇-'rezh\, **André** (born 1923) French fashion designer. In 1948 he went to work in a small Parisian fashion house and within a year joined the staff of CRISTOBAL BALENCIAGA. In 1961 he opened his own house and became established as one of the most original couturiers in Paris. His styles featured well-cut pants, trapezoidal lines, and miniskirts with white mid-calf boots. White became his hallmark. In the 1960s his designs were widely copied. He established control over manufacturing and distribution through licensed outlets.

court In architecture, an outdoor room surrounded by buildings or walls. Courts have existed in all civilizations from the earliest recorded times. The small garden court (ATRIUM) of a Roman house was the center of domestic activity. In medieval Europe the court was a feature of all major residential buildings, as the CLOISTER of a monastery, ward of a CASTLE, or QUADRANGLE of a college. A courtyard is often a utilitarian court (as for stables).

court Official assembly with judicial authority to hear and determine disputes in particular cases. Judicial tribunals were originally enclosures (courts in an architectural sense) where the judges sat, while lawyers and the general public had to remain outside a bar (hence the term *bar* in legal contexts). Modern British courts are divided into those trying criminal cases and those trying civil cases; a second distinction is made between inferior courts, or courts of first instance, and superior courts, or courts of appeal. In the U.S., each state has its own comprehensive system of courts, usually consisting of a superior (appellate) court, trial courts of general jurisdiction, and specialized courts (e.g., PROBATE courts). The U.S. also has a system of federal courts, established to adjudicate distinctively national questions and cases not appropriately tried in state courts. At the apex of the national system is the U.S. SUPREME COURT. The secondary level consists of the U.S. COURTS OF APPEALS. U.S. DISTRICT COURTS form the tertiary level. Crimes committed by military figures may be tried in a COURT-MARTIAL, and in the past ecclesiastical courts also had broad jurisdiction. See also INTERNATIONAL COURT OF JUSTICE, JUDICIARY.

Court, Margaret Smith *orig.* **Margaret Smith** (born 1942) Australian tennis player. She dominated women's tennis in the 1960s, winning 62 Grand Slam championships between 1960 and 1973, more than any other person. In 1970 she became the second woman (after MAUREEN CONNOLLY) to win the Grand Slam (the Wimbledon, U.S., Australian, and French singles titles). In 1963, with fellow Australian Kenneth Fletcher, she became the only player to achieve the Grand Slam in doubles as well as singles.

court-martial Military court for hearing charges brought against members of the armed forces or others within its jurisdiction; also, the legal proceeding of such a court. Most countries today have military codes of justice administered by military courts, often subject to civilian appellate review. Courts-martial are generally convened as ad hoc courts to try one or more cases referred by some high military authority. The convening officer chooses officers, and sometimes enlisted personnel, from his or her command to sit on the court, determine guilt or innocence, and hand down sentences. See also MILITARY LAW.

Court of High Commission See Court of HIGH COMMISSION

courtly love Late-medieval code that prescribed the highly conventionalized behavior and emotions of aristocratic ladies and their lovers. It was the theme of an extensive literature that began with late-11th-century TROUBADOUR poetry in France and swiftly pervaded Europe. The courtly lover, who saw himself as enslaved by passion but fired by respect, faithfully served and worshiped his lady-saint. Courtly love was invariably adulterous, given that upper-class marriage at the time was usually the result of economic interest or the seal of a power alliance. Its literary sources are believed to be found in Arabic literature, transmitted to Europe through Arab-dominated Spain; the growing religious cult of MARY was another influence. Examples of works inspired by the ideal are the *ROMAN DE LA ROSE*, PETRARCH's sonnets to Laura, DANTE's *Divine Comedy*, and the lyrics of the TROUVÈRES and MINNESINGERS. See also CHIVALRY.

Courts of Appeals, U.S. See UNITED STATES COURTS OF APPEALS

courtship behavior Animal activity that results in mating and reproduction. Courtship may simply involve a few chemical, visual, or auditory stimuli, or it may be a highly complex series of acts by two or more individuals, using several modes of communication. Females of some insect species use PHEROMONES to attract males from a distance. Painted turtles court by touch, and the courtship songs of frogs are heard on spring nights across much of the world. Certain bird species have complex courtship patterns. Courtship is important as an isolating mechanism to prevent different species from interbreeding, and elaborate courtship rituals help strengthen pair bonds that may last through raising young or longer. See also DISPLAY BEHAVIOR.

Cousteau \kü-'stō\, **Jacques-Yves** (1910–1997) French ocean explorer. A navy officer, he coinvented the Aqua-Lung, or scuba. He founded the French Office of Underseas Research (now the Center of Advanced Marine Studies) in Marseille. For decades, beginning in 1950, he traveled the world in research vessels named *Calypso*. He invented a process for using television underwater, and he hosted an internationally successful television series (1968–76). He served as director of Monaco's Oceanographic Museum (1957–88). In his later years he issued increasingly dire warnings about human destruction of the oceans. His many popular books include *The Silent World* (1953) and *The Living Sea* (1963); his films include *The Golden Fish* (1960, Academy Award).

Cousy \'kü-zē\, **Bob** *orig.* **Robert Joseph** (born 1928) U.S. basketball player and coach. Born in New York City, he played collegiate ball at Holy Cross College and joined the Boston Celtics in 1950. One of the game's great ball-handling guards and playmakers, he led the NBA in assists from 1953 to 1960. He left the Celtics in 1963 to coach at Boston College (to 1969), but eventually returned to the professional game as coach of the Cincinnati Royals (1969–73).

covalent bond \'kō-'vā-lənt\ Force holding ATOMS in a MOLECULE together as a specific, separate entity (as opposed to, e.g., colloidal aggregates; see BONDING). In covalent bonds, one or more pairs of valence ELECTRONS are shared between two atoms to give each the stability found in a NOBLE GAS. In single bonds (e.g., H—H in H_2), one electron pair is shared; in double bonds (e.g., O=O in O_2 or $H_2C{=}CH_2$ in ethylene), two; in triple bonds (e.g., HC≡CH in acetylene), three. In coordinate covalent bonds, additional electron pairs are shared with another atom, usually forming a group, like SULFATE or PHOSPHATE. The number of bonds and the atoms participating in each (including any additional paired electrons) give molecules their CONFIGURATION; the slight negative and positive charges at the opposite ends of a covalent bond are the reason most molecules have some polarity (see ELECTROPHILE, NUCLEOPHILE). Carbon in organic compounds has four single bonds, each pointing to one vertex of a tetrahedron; making certain molecules exist in mirror images (see OPTICAL ACTIVITY). Double bonds are rigid, leading to the possibility of geometric ISOMERS (see ISOMERISM). Some types of bonds, like the AMIDE linkages that join the AMINO ACIDS in PEPTIDES and PROTEINS (peptide bonds), though apparently single, have some double-bond characteristics because of the electronic structure of the participating atoms. The configurations of ENZYMES and their substrates, determined by their covalent bonds (particularly the peptide bonds) and hydrogen bonds, are crucial to the reactions they participate in, which are fundamental to all life. See also IONIC BOND.

cove See COVING

covenant \'kə-və-ˌnant\ In the OLD TESTAMENT, an agreement or treaty among peoples or nations, but most memorably the promises that God extended to humankind (e.g., the promise to NOAH never again to destroy the earth by flood, or the promise to ABRAHAM that his descendants would multiply and inherit the land of Israel). God's revelation of the law to MOSES on Mount SINAI created a pact between God and Israel known as the Sinai covenant. In Christianity, Jesus' death established a new covenant between God and humanity. Islam holds that the Last Covenant was between God and the Prophet MUHAMMAD.

Covenant, Ark of the See ARK OF THE COVENANT

covenant, restrictive See RESTRICTIVE COVENANT

Covenanters Scottish Presbyterians of the 17th century who made convenants in which they pledged to maintain specific forms of worship and church government. After the signing of the National Covenant of 1638, the Scottish Assembly abolished the episcopal system. In the Bishops' Wars of 1639–40 the Scots fought against England to maintain their religious liberty. In England the expenses of these wars were a factor in the ENGLISH CIVIL WAR, and in the Solemn League and Covenant of 1643 the Scots promised their aid to the parliamentarian faction provided that the Church of England was reformed along Presbyterian lines. Cromwell's settlement failed to satisfy the Covenanters, but their situation worsened considerably once CHARLES II came to the throne in 1660. Episcopacy was brought back, and the Covenanters endured severe persecutions. Not until the GLORIOUS REVOLUTION of 1688 was PRESBYTERIANISM reestablished in Scotland.

Covent Garden \'kə-vənt\ Square in London, now the site of the Royal Opera House, home of the British national opera and ballet companies. The land around the site, once a convent garden, was laid out as a residential square in 1630. The original Covent Garden playhouse, called the Theatre Royal, was built in 1732 and served for performances of plays, pantomimes, and opera. Twice destroyed by fire and rebuilt, the theater became the Royal Italian Opera House (1847) and was replaced by the Royal Opera Co. (1888). The square was also the site of a fruit, flower, and vegetable market from 1670 to 1974.

Coventry City (pop., 1995 est.: 302,000), central England. It was the home of Lady GODIVA who, with her husband, founded a Benedictine abbey there in 1043. It was probably the center of the presentation of the Coventry MYSTERY PLAYS in the 15th–16th century. During World War II, heavy bombing (1940–41) by the Germans left the town severely damaged. The spire of the 15th-century St. Michael's Cathedral and its ruined nave stand beside the new cathedral built in 1962. Chief industries are motor vehicle manufacturing and telecommunications.

cover crop Fast-growing CROP, such as RYE, BUCKWHEAT, COWPEA, or VETCH, planted to prevent soil EROSION, increase nutrients in the soil, and provide organic matter. Cover crops are grown either in the season during which cash crops are not grown or between the rows of some crops (e.g., fruit trees). See also GREEN MANURE.

Coverdale, Miles (1488?–1569) English bishop who issued the first printed English Bible. Ordained in 1514, he became an Augustinian friar at Cambridge, where he adopted Lutheran beliefs. By 1528 he was preaching against graven images and the mass. He lived abroad 1528–34 to escape persecution, and while in Antwerp he translated the entire Bible into English; his Bible was published in 1535. He returned to England and edited the Great Bible (1539), but was soon forced to flee by the religious policies of HENRY VIII. He returned after Henry's death and became bishop at Exeter in 1551. Under the Catholic MARY I, he lost his office but was spared execution.

covering-law model Model of explanation according to which to explain an event by reference to another event necessarily presupposes an appeal to laws or general propositions correlating events of the type to be explained (explananda) with events of the type cited as its causes or conditions (explanantia). It is rooted in DAVID HUME's doctrine that, when two events are said to be causally related, all that is meant is that they instantiate certain regularities of succession that have been repeatedly observed to hold between such events in the past. This doctrine was given more rigorous expression by the logical positivist Carl Hempel (1905–1997).

coverture \'kə-vər-ˌchu̇r\ In law, the inclusion of a woman in the legal person of her husband upon marriage. Because of coverture, married women formerly lacked the legal capacity to hold their own PROPERTY or to contract on their own behalf (see CONTRACT); similarly, a husband's tax payments or jury duty "covered" his wife as well. Aspects of coverture survived well into the 20th century; the term is still used in law when dividing jointly held property in divorce proceedings.

coving *or* **cove** Concave MOLDING or deeply arched section of a wall surface. The curve typically describes a quarter-circle and serves to connect walls and ceiling (cove ceiling). The arched sections may be used to conceal light fixtures for dramatic effect, hence the term cove lighting. Coving can also refer to the curved soffit connecting the top of an exterior wall to a projecting eave.

cow In animal husbandry, the mature female of domesticated CATTLE. The name is also applied to the mature female of various, usually large, animals (e.g., ELEPHANT, WHALE, or MOOSE), or, more broadly, to any domestic bovine animal (see BOVID) regardless of gender or age.

Coward, Noël (Peirce) *later* **Sir Noël** (1899–1973) British playwright, actor, and songwriter. An actor from age 12, he wrote light comedies between engagements, but it was a serious drama, *The Vortex* (1924), that established his reputation. His classic comedies came later: *Hay Fever* (1925), *Private Lives* (1930), *Design for Living* (1933), *Present Laughter* (1939), and *Blithe Spirit* (1941) presented sophisticated characters in a worldly milieu. He often wrote for and performed with his close friend GERTRUDE LAWRENCE. His most popular musical play was *Bitter Sweet* (1929). He wrote the poignant film *Brief Encounter* (1946), and he acted in the film versions of many of his plays. He also wrote short stories, novels, and numerous songs, including "Mad Dogs and Englishmen."

cowbird Any of six or seven PASSERINE species in the family Icteridae that are parasitic egg layers. Cowbirds lay their eggs in the nests of other birds, usually one to each host nest. Young cowbirds, which displace competing nestlings or take over their food, may grow larger than the foster parents. Some species parasitize many kinds of birds; others use the nests of only one or two kinds of ORIOLE. Cowbirds forage on the ground, often associating with cattle in order to catch insects stirred up by the cows' hooves. The male of most species is a uniform glossy black, the female grayish brown.

cowboy Horseman skilled at handling cattle in the U.S. West. From c. 1820, cowboys were employed in small numbers on Texas ranches, where they had learned the skills of the *vaquero* (Spanish: "cowboy"). After the Civil War, their numbers rapidly multiplied as cattle raising evolved into a lucrative industry throughout the western territories. Cowboys rounded up and branded the cattle, kept watch over the herd, and drove those ready for market to railroad towns. As the agricultural frontier moved west, the open range was transformed into farms, and by 1890 cowboys had been forced to settle on ranches. The romance of their image lived on in U.S. folklore and through movies and television.

Cowell, Henry (Dixon) (1897–1965) U.S. avant-garde composer. Born in Menlo Park, Cal., he began early to experiment with such techniques as tone clusters and direct manipulation of piano strings. Five tours of Europe as composer-pianist (1923–33) brought him notoriety. He coinvented the Rhythmicon, an instrument for producing several conflicting rhythms simultaneously. Immensely prolific, he wrote nearly 1,000 pieces, including 19 completed symphonies, hundreds of piano works, and many ballets. In 1927 he founded the journal *New Music*. His book *New Musical Resources* (1930) presented his compositional ideas. He was one of the most important innovators in the history of American music.

Cowley, Abraham (1618–1667) British poet and essayist. He was a fellow at Cambridge Univ., but was ejected for his political opinions during the English Civil Wars; he joined the queen's court, performing Royalist missions until 1656. In his poetic works—which include *The Mistress* (1647, 1656), the unfinished epic *Davideis* (1656), and *Pindarique Odes* (1656), in which he adapted the Pindaric ode to English verse—he used grossly elaborate, fanciful, poetic language that was more decorative than expressive. In his retirement he wrote sober, reflective essays.

Cowley, Malcolm (1898–1989) U.S. literary critic and social historian. Born in Belsano, Pa., he was educated at Harvard and in France. As literary editor of the *New Republic* (1929–44) he took part in many Depression-era literary and political battles, usually on the leftist side. He revived the reputation of WILLIAM FAULKNER with *The Portable Faulkner* (1946). His books include *Exile's Return* (1934), a history of expatriate American writers; *The Literary Situation* (1954), on the role of writers in society; and the collections *Think Back on Us* (1967) and *A Many-Windowed House* (1970).

cowpea *or* **black-eyed pea** Any of the cultivated forms of the annual legume *Vigna unguiculata*. The plants are believed to be native to India and the Middle East but in early times were cultivated in China. The compound leaves have three leaflets. The white, purple, or pale-yellow flowers usually grow in twos or threes at the ends of long stalks. The pods are long and cylindrical. In the southern U.S. the cowpea is grown extensively as a HAY crop, as a COVER or GREEN-MANURE crop, or for the edible BEANS.

Cowper \'kü-pər\, **William** (1731–1800) British poet. Throughout his life he was plagued by recurring mental instability and religious doubt. *Olney Hymns* (1779; with John Newton), a book of devotional verse, includes hymns that are still favorites in Protestant England. *The Task* (1785), a long discursive poem written "to recommend rural ease," was an immediate success. He also wrote many melodious, even humorous, shorter lyrics, and he is considered one of the best letter writers in English. His work, often about everyday rural life, brought a new directness and humanitarianism to 18th-century nature poetry, foreshadowing ROMANTICISM.

William Cowper, detail of an oil painting by Lemuel Abbott, 1792; in the National Portrait Gallery, London.
BY COURTESY OF THE NATIONAL PORTRAIT GALLERY, LONDON

Cowrie (*Cypraea*).
BUCKY REEVES FROM THE NATIONAL AUDUBON SOCIETY COLLECTION/PHOTO RESEARCHERS—EB INC.

cowrie Any of several marine SNAILS (genus *Cypraea*) found chiefly in coastal waters of the Indian and Pacific oceans. Its humped, thick shell is beautifully colored (often speckled) and glossy. That of the 4-in. (10-cm) golden cowrie was traditionally worn by royalty on Pacific Islands. The money cowrie, a 1-in. (2.5-cm) yellow species, has served as currency in Africa and elsewhere.

cowslip Any of several flowering plants, including (chiefly in British usage) the wild PRIMROSE *(Primula veris)* and (in U.S. usage) the MARSH MARIGOLD *(Caltha palustris)*. *P. veris,* once so abundant that it was used freely to make cowslip wine, is now much less common. Both *P. veris* and *C. palustris* are used in herbal remedies.

Cox, James M(iddleton) (1870–1957) U.S. politician. Born in Jacksonburg, Ohio, he worked as a reporter in Cincinnati before buying the *Dayton News* (1898) and *Springfield Daily News* (1903). A supporter of WOODROW WILSON, he served in the U.S. House of Representatives (1909–13), then was elected governor of Ohio (1913–15, 1917–21), where he introduced workers' compensation and the minimum wage. He won the Democratic presidential nomination in 1920, but was crushed by WARREN G. HARDING in a Republican landslide.

Coxey's Army Group of unemployed men who marched to Washington, D.C., in the depression year of 1894. Jacob S. Coxey (1854–1951), a businessman, led the group, which hoped to persuade Congress to authorize public-works programs to provide jobs. It left Ohio on March 25 and reached Washington on May 1 with about 500 men, the only one of several groups to reach its destination. It attracted much attention but failed to bring about any legislation.

coyote \kī-'ō-tē, 'kī-,ōt\ Species *(Canis latrans)* of wild DOG found from Alaska, throughout the entire continental U.S., south to Costa Rica. It weighs about 30–50 lbs (9–23 kg) and is about 3–4 ft (1–1.3 m) long, including its 12–16-in. (30–40-cm) tail. Its coarse fur is generally buff above and whitish below; its legs are reddish, and its tail is bushy and black-tipped. The coyote feeds mainly on rodents and hares but also eats other types of animals, vegetable matter, and carrion. Though persecuted by humans because of its potential (generally overstated) to prey on domestic or game animals, it has adapted well to human-dominated environments, including urban areas. A coyote-dog cross is called a coydog.

coypu See NUTRIA

Coysevox \kwȧz-'vȯks\, **Antoine** (1640–1720) French sculptor. In 1666 he became sculptor to LOUIS XIV and by 1678 was working at Versailles. He was known for his portrait busts, which show a naturalism and animation of expression that anticipates the Rococo style. He also executed decorative sculpture for the royal gardens and did much interior decoration. He exerted considerable influence on the development of French portrait sculpture in the 18th century.

CP violation In PARTICLE PHYSICS, the violation of the combined CONSERVATION LAWS associated with charge conjugation, C (the operation of turning a particle into its antiparticle), and PARITY, P, by the WEAK FORCE. In 1957 it was discovered that parity is violated in BETA DECAY. No fully satisfactory explanation has been devised, but CP violation does enable physicists to make an absolute distinction between MATTER and ANTIMATTER.

CPR See CARDIOPULMONARY RESUSCITATION

CPU *in full* **central processing unit** Principal component of a DIGITAL COMPUTER, composed of a control unit, an instruction-decoding unit, and an arithmetic-logic unit. The CPU is linked to main memory, peripheral equipment (including input/output devices), and storage units. The control unit integrates computer operations. It selects instructions from the main memory in proper sequence and sends them to the instruction-decoding unit, which interprets them so as to activate functions of the system at appropriate moments. Input data are transferred via the main memory to the arithmetic-logic unit for processing (i.e., addition, subtraction, multiplication, division, and certain logic operations). Larger computers may have two or more CPUs, in which case they are simply called "processors" because each is no longer a "central" unit. See also MULTIPROCESSING.

crab Any of 4,500 species of short-tailed DECAPOD, found in all oceans, in freshwater, and on land. Its carapace (upper body shield) is usually broad, and its first pair of legs is modified into pincers. Most crabs live in the sea and breathe through gills, which in land crabs are modified to serve as lungs. They walk or crawl, generally with a sideways gait; some are good swimmers. Crabs are omnivorous scavengers, but many are predatory and some are herbivorous. Two of the largest known CRUS-

TACEANS are the giant crab of Japan (13 ft, or 4 m, from claw tip to claw tip), a SPIDER CRAB; and the Tasmanian crab (up to 18 in., or 46 cm, long, and weighing more than 20 lbs, or 9 kg). Other species are less than an inch long. Well-known crabs include the HERMIT CRAB, edible crab (Britain and Europe), BLUE CRAB, DUNGENESS CRAB, FIDDLER CRAB, and KING CRAB.

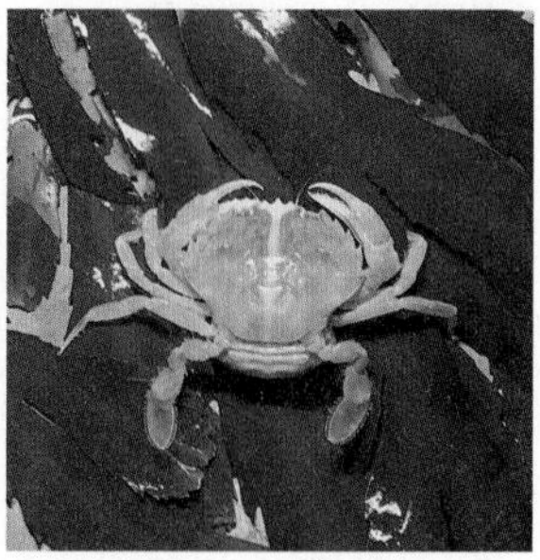
Common swimming crab (*Portunus holsatus*), showing its paddle-shaped feet.
DR. ECKART POTT–BRUCE COLEMAN LTD.

crab louse See human LOUSE

Crab Nebula Bright NEBULA in the constellation Taurus, about 5,000 light-years from earth. Roughly five to 10 light-years in diameter, it is the remnant of a SUPERNOVA, first observed by Chinese and other astronomers in 1054, that was visible in daylight for 23 days and at night for almost 2 years. Identified as a nebula c. 1731, it was named (for its form) in the mid-19th century. In 1921 it was discovered to be still expanding; the present rate is about 700 mi/second (1,100 km/second). The Crab is one of the few astronomical objects from which RADIATION has been detected over the entire measurable SPECTRUM.

Crabbe \'krab\, **George** (1754–1832) English poet. Reared in an impoverished seacoast village, Crabbe initially became a surgeon. In 1780 he left for London, where his poem *The Village* (1783) brought him fame; written partly as a protest against OLIVER GOLDSMITH's *Deserted Village* (1770), it was Crabbe's attempt to show the misery of rural poverty. *The Newspaper* followed in 1785, but he did not publish again until 1807. In "The Parish Register," he used the register of births, deaths, and marriages to depict the life of a rural community. Considered the last of the Augustan poets, he wrote in heroic couplets. His story of the isolated and violent Peter Grimes in *The Borough* became the basis of a famous opera by BENJAMIN BRITTEN.

crabgrass Any of about 300 species of GRASSES in the genus *Digitaria*, especially *D. sanguinalis* or the slightly shorter *D. ischaemum* (smooth crabgrass). *D. sanguinalis* has long hairs covering its leaves and five or six spikelets; *D. ischaemum* has no hair and only two or three spikelets. Both are natives of Europe that became widely naturalized as weeds in North America. They and a few closely related species are very troublesome in lawns and fields. One species, Arizona cottontop *(D. californica),* is a useful FORAGE grass in the American Southwest.

Crabgrass (*Digitaria sanguinalis*).
GRANT HEILMAN

Cracow See KRAKÓW

Craig, (Edward Henry) Gordon (1872–1966) British actor, stage designer, and drama theorist. The son of ELI TERRY, he acted with HENRY IRVING's company (1889–97), then turned to designing stage sets, decor, and costumes. He moved to Florence (1906), where he opened the School for the Art of the Theatre (1913). His international journal *The Mask* (1908–29) made his theatrical ideas widely known. His books *On the Art of the Theatre* (1911), *Towards a New Theatre* (1913), and *Scene* (1923) outlined innovations in STAGE DESIGN based on the use of portable screens and changing patterns of light; his theories influenced the antinaturalist trends of the modern theater.

Craig, James (Henry) *later* **Sir James** (1748–1812) British army officer and governor-general of Canada (1807–11). In the American Revolution, he was wounded at the Battle of Bunker Hill and helped repel the American army's invasion of Canada in 1776. He later served in India. As governor-general in Canada, he cooperated with the governing clique in Quebec but conducted an unpopular repressive policy toward the French Canadians. He resigned in 1811 and returned to England.

Craigavon \krā-'ga-vən\ District (pop., 1995 est.: 78,000), Northern Ireland. Established in 1973, it lies south of Lough Neagh. In the north it is flat and composed largely of peat soils; in the south it rises to lowlands. It is an important fruit-growing district and also has industries, including textiles and pharmaceutical products. Its administrative seat, Craigavon town (pop., 1991: 9,000), has light industry and is a commercial center.

Craiova \krä-'yō-vä\ City (pop., 1994 est.: 307,000), southwestern Romania. Situated near the Jiu River, the area has long been settled; the remains of a Roman fort built under TRAJAN have been excavated nearby. From the late 15th to the 18th century it was the residence of the region's military governors. It prospered as a regional trading center despite an earthquake in 1790 and a Turkish assault in 1802 during which it was burned. It has a university (1966) and cultural amenities.

cramp Painful, involuntary, sustained contraction of muscle in limbs or some internal organs. Causes may be neurological, reflex, or psychological. Common muscle cramps include swimmer's cramp from overexertion in cold water, heat cramps from loss of salt in sweat, leg cramps, and occupational (e.g., writer's) cramp. Menstrual cramps are uterine muscle contractions before or during MENSTRUATION. Cramps occur in diseases including PARKINSONISM and Huntington's CHOREA. Tetany is severe cramping noticed first in limb muscles.

Cranach \'krä-ˌnäk\, **Lucas, the Elder** *orig.* **Lucas Müller** (1472–1553) German painter and printmaker. He took his name from Kronach, the town of his birth. Little is known about his early life or training. In Vienna (c. 1501–4) he painted some notable portraits and landscapes characteristic of the DANUBE SCHOOL. From 1505 to 1550 he was court painter in Wittenberg, where he achieved great success and wealth painting portraits, mythological subjects, and altarpieces for Protestant and Catholic churches. He attracted so many young artists to Wittenberg that the town became an art center. A friend of MARTIN LUTHER, he became known as the chief pictorial propagandist of the Protestant cause in Germany. He produced numerous engravings and over 100 woodcuts, notably for the first German edition of the New Testament (1522). After his death, his style was perpetuated by his son, Lucas the Younger (1515–1586).

cranberry Fruit of any of several small creeping or trailing plants of the genus *Vaccinium* (HEATH FAMILY), related to the BLUEBERRY. The small-fruited, or northern, cranberry *(V. oxycoccus)* is found in marshy land in northern North America and Asia and in northern and central Europe. Its crimson berries, about the size of currants and often spotted, have an acid taste. The American cranberry *(V. macrocarpon),* found wild in most of the northeastern U.S. and grown extensively in Massachusetts, New Jersey, and Wisconsin and near the Pacific coast in Washington and Oregon, is more robust than *V. oxycoccus,* with larger, pink to very dark red or mottled red-and-white berries. Cranberries are used in drinks, sauces, jellies, and baked goods.

Cranberry (*Vaccinium macrocarpon*).
WALTER CHANDOHA

crane Any of a diverse group of machines that lift and move heavy objects. Cranes differ from hoists, elevators, and other devices intended for vertical lifting, and from conveyors, which continuously lift or carry bulk materials such as grain or coal. Cranes have been widely used only since the introduction of steam engines, internal-combustion engines, and electric motors in the 19th century. They range in type and function from the largest derrick cranes to small, mobile truck cranes. Most derrick cranes can lift 5–250 tons (4.5–230 metric tons). Floating cranes, built on barges for constructing bridges or salvaging sunken objects, may be able to lift 3,000 tons (2,700 metric-tons). Small truck cranes are mounted on heavy, modified trucks; they make up in mobility and ease of transport what they lack in hoisting capacity.

crane Any of 15 species (family Gruidae) of tall wading birds that resemble HERONS but are usually larger and have a partly naked head, a heavier bill, more-compact plumage, and an elevated hind toe. In flight, the long neck stretches out in front and the stiltlike legs trail behind. Cranes are found worldwide, living in marshes and on plains, except in South America. Many populations are endangered by hunting and habitat destruction. Cranes eat small animals, grain, and grass shoots. Two well-known species are the WHOOPING CRANE and the SANDHILL CRANE.

Crane, (Harold) Hart (1899–1932) U.S. poet. Born in Garrettsville, Ohio, he worked at a variety of jobs before settling in New York City. *White Buildings* (1926), his first book, includes "For the Marriage of Faustus and Helen." His desire to respond to the cultural pessimism of T. S. ELIOT's *Waste Land* resulted in the long and difficult poem *The Bridge* (1930), which attempts to create an epic myth of the American experience, celebrating the richness of modern life with visionary intensity. Alcoholic and despondent over his homosexuality, he committed suicide at 32 by jumping overboard from a ship in the Caribbean.

Crane, Stephen (1871–1900) U.S. novelist and short-story writer. Born in Newark, N.J., he briefly attended college before moving to New York City. His *Maggie: A Girl of the Streets* (1893), a sympathetic study of a slum girl's descent into prostitution, was a milestone of literary naturalism. He achieved international fame with his masterwork, *The Red Badge of Courage* (1895), depicting the psychological turmoil of a young Civil War soldier, and with his first book of poems, *The Black Riders* (1895). While traveling as a war correspondent, his ship sank and he almost drowned, resulting in his great story "The Open Boat" (1898). His story collections include *The Little Regiment* (1896), *The Monster* (1899), and *Whilomville Stories* (1900). He died at 28 of tuberculosis.

Stephen Crane, detail of a painting by C.K. Linson, 1896.

BY COURTESY OF UNIVERSITY OF VIRGINIA LIBRARY, BARRETT LIBRARY OF AMERICAN LITERATURE

Crane, Walter (1845–1915) English illustrator, painter, and designer. The son of a portrait painter, he studied Italian old masters and Japanese prints. The ideas of the PRE-RAPHAELITES and JOHN RUSKIN inspired his early paintings. He achieved international popularity designing Art Nouveau textiles and wallpapers, but is chiefly known for his illustrations of children's books. In 1894 he worked with WILLIAM MORRIS on *The Story of the Glittering Plain*, a book printed in the style of 16th-century German and Italian woodcuts. He belonged to the Art Workers' Guild, and in 1888 he founded the Arts and Crafts Exhibition Society. See also ARTS AND CRAFTS MOVEMENT.

crane flower See BIRD-OF-PARADISE

crane fly Harmless, slow-flying DIPTERAN (family Tipulidae) usually found around water or abundant vegetation. It ranges in size from tiny to slightly over 1 in. (2.5 cm) long. Larvae of the range crane fly *(Tipula simplex)* are called leatherjackets because of their tough brown skin. In northern latitudes a wingless crane-fly species is found on snow. The crane fly is also called daddy longlegs in English-speaking countries other than the U.S. (in the U.S., DADDY LONGLEGS refers to an ARACHNID).

craniosynostosis \ˌkrā-nē-ō-ˌsin-ˌäs-ˈtō-səs\ *or* **craniostosis** \ˌkrā-nē-ō-ˈstō-səs\ Cranial deformity produced when the bones of the SKULL fuse too early. Pressure from the growing brain normally causes the skull bones to grow along the seams (cranial sutures) between them. If all the sutures fuse early, the head remains abnormally small, which can cause mental retardation or blindness. If only one or some fuse early, the skull grows in other directions and becomes deformed. Surgery in the first two years to keep the sutures open longer minimizes these complications.

crank In MECHANICS, an arm secured at right angles to a shaft with which it can rotate or oscillate. Next to the wheel, the crank is the most important motion-transmitting device, because, with the connecting rod, it provides means for converting linear to rotary motion, and vice versa. The first recognizable crank is said to have appeared in China in the 1st century AD. The carpenter's brace was invented c. 1400 by a Flemish carpenter. The first mechanical connecting rods were reportedly used on a treadle-operated machine in 1430. About this time, FLYWHEELS were added to the rotating members to carry the members over the "dead" positions when the rod and the crank arm are lined up with each other.

Cranmer, Thomas (1489–1556) First Protestant archbishop of Canterbury. Educated at Cambridge Univ., he was ordained in 1523. He became involved in HENRY VIII's negotiations with the pope over divorcing CATHERINE OF ARAGON. In 1533 Henry appointed him archbishop of Canterbury, putting him in a position to help overthrow papal supremacy in England. He annulled Henry's marriage to Catherine, supported his marriage to Anne Boleyn, and later helped him divorce her. After Henry's death in 1547, he became an influential adviser to the young EDWARD VI, moving England firmly in a Protestant direction. He wrote the Forty-two Articles, from which the Thirty-nine Articles of Anglican belief were derived. When the strongly anti-Protestant MARY I became queen, Cranmer was tried, convicted of heresy, and burned at the stake.

Cranmer, detail of an oil painting by G. Fliccius, 1546; in the National Portrait Gallery, London.

BY COURTESY OF THE NATIONAL PORTRAIT GALLERY, LONDON

crannog \ˈkra-ˌnȯg, kra-ˈnōg\ In Scotland and Ireland, an artificially constructed site for a house or settlement, usually on an islet or in the shallows of a lake. Made of timber or sometimes stone, crannogs date from the Late BRONZE AGE into the Middle Ages. Usually fortified by stockades, they were among the latest prehistoric strongholds. See also LAKE DWELLINGS.

crape myrtle Shrub *(Lagerstroemia indica)* of the LOOSESTRIFE family, native to China and other tropical and subtropical countries and widely grown in warm regions for its flowers. About 25 varieties are cultivated, known primarily by the color of their clustered flowers, which range from white to pink, red, lavender, and bluish.

crappie Either of two deep-bodied freshwater North American fish species (family Centrarchidae) that are popular as food and prized by sport fishermen. Native to the eastern U.S. but introduced elsewhere, crappies may reach a length of about 12 in. (30 cm) and a weight of about 4 lbs (2 kg). The white crappie *(Pomoxis annularis)* generally inhabits warm, silty lakes and rivers. Silvery, with irregular dark markings, it is usually lighter in color than the similar black crappie, or calico bass *(P. nigromaculatus),* which typically lives in clear lakes and streams.

craps (from Louisiana French *crabs,* "losing throw") Gambling game in which each player in turn throws two dice in attempting to roll a winning combination. The player with the dice (the shooter) must first put up a stake; the other players bet against the shooter up to the amount of the stake. In some games, bettors may also bet against each other or against the house. If the shooter wins, he or she may continue to roll. A 7 or 11 on the first roll wins; a 2, 3, or 12 (craps) loses. Any other number requires the shooter to continue rolling until he or she rolls the same number again for a win or rolls a 7 (craps) and loses.

Crash of 1929, Stock Market See STOCK MARKET CRASH OF 1929

Crassus, Lucius Licinius (140–91 BC) Roman lawyer and politician. He is regarded, with Marcus Antonius (143–87), as one of the greatest Latin orators before CICERO and is portrayed in Cicero's *De oratore* (55 BC). Made CONSUL in 95, he cosponsored a law (Lex Licinia Mucia) that provided for the prosecution of anyone falsely claiming Roman citizenship, which led to the revolt of Rome's Italian allies in 90–88.

Crassus, Marcus Licinius (c. 115–53 BC) Roman financier and politician. He sided with SULLA against MARIUS in the civil war of 83–82 BC and came into conflict with POMPEY. In 72–71 he put down SPARTACUS' slave rebellion. He made loans to indebted senators, including Julius CAESAR. In 70 Crassus and Pompey were elected co-consuls. In 60 Crassus, Caesar, and Pompey formed the first TRIUMVIRATE. As governor of

Syria (54) he invaded PARTHIA; his death at the Battle of CARRHAE led to civil war between Caesar and Pompey.

crater Circular depression in the surface of a planetary body. Most craters are the result of impacts of METEORITES or of volcanic explosions. METEORITE CRATERS are more common on the moon and Mars and on other planets and natural satellites than on the earth, because most meteorites burn up in earth's atmosphere before reaching the earth and erosion hides past impacts. Craters made by exploding volcanoes (e.g., Crater Lake, Ore.) are more common on the earth than on the moon, Mars, or Jupiter's moon Io, where they have also been identified.

Crater Lake Lake, CASCADE RANGE, southwestern Oregon. The lake is in a huge volcanic caldera, whose crater is 6 mi (10 km) in diameter and 1,932 ft (589 m) deep. It is the remnant of a mountain destroyed in an eruption more than 6,000 years ago. The intensely blue lake and its surrounding region became a national park in 1902; the park covers 250 sq mi (647 sq km).

Craters of the Moon National Monument Region of volcanic cones and craters, southern central Idaho. Established in 1924, it covers an area of 53,545 acres (21,669 hectares) and has more than 35 craters, probably extinct only a few centuries. Some are nearly a half-mile across and several hundred feet deep, and reach a height of more than 6,000 ft (1,800 m). Tunnels formed by fissure eruptions feature stalactites and stalagmites in red and blue.

Crawford, Cheryl (1902–1986) U.S. actress and theater producer. Born in Akron, Ohio, she acted with the Theatre Guild from 1923 and became its casting manager (1928–30). She helped found the GROUP THEATRE in 1931. A cofounder of the ACTORS STUDIO in 1947, she went on to serve as its executive producer. Her notable Broadway productions included *Brigadoon* (1947) and TENNESSEE WILLIAMS's *The Rose Tattoo* (1951) and *Sweet Bird of Youth* (1959).

Crawford, Isabella Valancy (1850–1887) Canadian (Irish-born) poet. She emigrated to Canada with her family in 1858. From 1875 until her death, she lived with her mother in Toronto, meagerly sustained by sales of stories and poems to periodicals. The only book published during her lifetime (at her own expense) was *Old Spookses' Pass, Malcom's Katie, and Other Poems* (1884). Her work, notable for its vivid descriptions of the Canadian landscape, was rediscovered in the 1970s, and many collections have since been published.

Crawford, Joan *orig.* **Lucille Lesueur** (1908–1977) U.S. film actress. Born in San Antonio, Tex., she was a dancer in a Broadway chorus line when she won her first Hollywood contract in the mid-1920s. After portraying flappers in such films as *Our Dancing Daughters* (1928), she played girls out for the main chance in such Depression-era dramas as *Grand Hotel* (1932) and *The Women* (1939). With her dark eyebrows, padded shoulders, and hysterical intensity, she reinvented herself as a suffering heroine in *Mildred Pierce* (1945, Academy Award) and in psychological melodramas including *Possessed* (1947) and *Sudden Fear* (1952). Her later films included *Queen Bee* (1955) and *What Ever Happened to Baby Jane?* (1962).

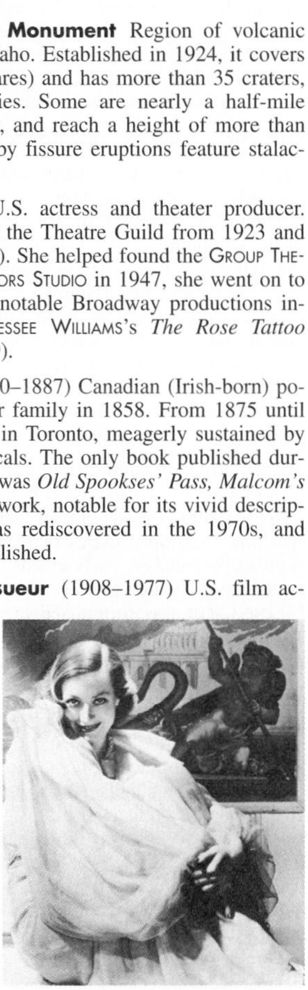

Joan Crawford, c. 1934.

BY COURTESY OF THE MUSEUM OF MODERN ART FILM STILLS ARCHIVE, NEW YORK CITY

Crawford, William H(arris) (1772–1834) U.S. political leader and presidential aspirant. Born in Amherst Co., Va., he taught school and practiced law before being elected to the Georgia legislature in 1803. He served in the U.S. Senate 1807–13, where he backed the declaration of war against Britain in 1812. He later served as minister to France (1813–15), secretary of war (1815–16), and secretary of the treasury (1816–25). He was one of four candidates in the 1824 presidential election, which was won by JOHN QUINCY ADAMS.

Crawford Seeger, Ruth *orig.* **Ruth Porter Crawford** (1901–1953) U.S. composer. Born in East Liverpool, Ohio, she studied piano as a child and was self-taught as a composer until she entered the American Conservatory. After early works modeled after DEBUSSY and SCRIABIN, she wrote several astonishing serial pieces, including her String Quartet (1931). She married the musicologist Charles Seeger (1886–1979) in 1931, becoming PETE SEEGER's stepmother, and composed little after that.

Craxi \'kräk-sē\, **Bettino** *orig.* **Benedetto** (1934–2000) Italian politician, Italy's first Socialist prime minister (1983–87). Involved initially with the Socialist youth movement, he won election to the Chamber of Deputies in 1968 and rose to become the Socialist Party's general secretary in 1976. He united the faction-ridden party, committed it to moderate social and economic policies, and tried to dissociate it from the much larger Italian Communist Party. As prime minister, he pursued anti-inflationary fiscal policies and steered a pro-U.S. course in foreign affairs. In 1993 multiple charges of political corruption forced Craxi, who denied the allegations, to resign as party leader. He moved to Tunisia, and in 1994 he was twice sentenced in absentia to prison terms.

Cray, Seymour R(oger) (1925–1996) U.S. electronics engineer. Born in Chippewa Falls, Wis., he worked in the 1950s on the UNIVAC I, a landmark first-generation digital computer that was the first commercially available computer. He led the design of the world's first transistor-based computer (the CDC 1604). In 1972 he founded Cray Research, Inc., and there built the fastest and most powerful supercomputers in the world, using his innovative design of multiprocessors for simultaneous processing. The Cray-2 (1985) could perform 1.2 billion calculations per second, an incredible pace in its day.

crayfish *or* **crawfish** *or* **crawdad** Any of more than 500 species of DECAPODS that are closely related to the LOBSTER. Nearly all the species live in freshwater, and over half are found in North America. They have a joined head and thorax (midsection) and a segmented body that is yellow, green, red, or dark brown. The head has a sharp snout, and the eyes are on movable stalks. The exoskeleton is thin but tough, and the front pair of legs have large pincers. Crayfish are usually about 3 in. (7.5 cm) long but range from 1 to 16 in. (2.5–40 cm) long.

Crazy Horse (1843?–1877) Oglala SIOUX Indian chief. Refusing to abide by an 1868 treaty granting the Sioux a large reservation in the Black Hills, Crazy Horse led his warriors in continued raids against enemy tribes as well as whites. In 1876 he joined with CHEYENNE forces in a surprise attack against Gen. George Crook in southern Montana, forcing Crook's withdrawal. He then united with Chief SITTING BULL for the Battle of the LITTLE BIGHORN, where he helped annihilate Col. GEORGE CUSTER's troops. In 1877, his tribe weakened by cold and hunger, Crazy Horse surrendered to Crook; removed to a military outpost in Nebraska, he was killed in a scuffle with soldiers.

cream Yellowish part of MILK, rich in butterfat, that rises to the surface naturally if milk is allowed to stand. In the dairy industry, cream is separated mechanically. Cream is graded by percentage of fat content. In the U.S., half-and-half, a mixture of milk and cream, contains 10.5–18% butterfat; light cream, commonly served with coffee, contains no less than 18%; and medium and heavy creams (the latter including whipped and sour cream) contain about 30% and 36% respectively. See also ICE CREAM.

creamware Cream-colored English EARTHENWARE made in the later 18th century. It was designed as a substitute for Chinese porcelain. In 1762 JOSIAH WEDGWOOD achieved commercial success with this modestly priced utilitarian ware; restrained designs and elegant transfer printing (see BATTERSEA ENAMELWARE) were compatible with his cream-glazed products. By 1790 many other factories (e.g., Liverpool, Bristol, Staffordshire) were producing creamware with success; continental imitations were generally inferior. Creamware was continually made throughout the 19th century and later.

Leeds creamware teapot decorated with green enameling and pierced work, Yorkshire, England, late 18th century; in the Victoria and Albert Museum, London.

BY COURTESY OF THE VICTORIA AND ALBERT MUSEUM, LONDON

creation myth *or* **cosmogony** \käz-'mä-gə-nē\ Symbolic narrative

C D

of the creation and organization of the world as understood in a particular tradition. Not all creation myths include a creator, though a supreme creator deity, existing from before creation, is very common. Myths in which the world emerges gradually emphasize the latent power of the earth. In other creation myths, the world is the offspring of primordial parents, derives from a cosmic egg, or is brought up from primordial waters by an animal or devil. Humans may be placed on earth by a god or rise from its depths or from a cultic rock or tree. There are often three stages of creation: that of primordial beings or gods, that of human ancestors who are often semidivine, and that of humans. Creation myths explain or validate basic beliefs, patterns of life, and culture. Rituals dramatize the myth and, particularly in initiations, validate the community's organization and rankings.

creation science *or* **creationism** Theory that matter, the various forms of life, and the world were created by God out of nothing. Creationism grew as a result of the advancement of the theory of EVOLUTION after the 1859 publication of CHARLES DARWIN's *On the Origin of Species.* Within two decades, most of the scientific community had accepted some form of organic evolution, but many religious leaders feared that the theory would result in a loss of faith. The most famous case in which the issue was argued was the SCOPES TRIAL (1925). In the U.S., creationism experienced a setback in 1987, when the Supreme Court ruled that states could not require public schools to teach it alongside evolution if the requirement was intended to promote religious belief.

creativity Ability to produce something new through imaginative skill, whether a new solution to a problem, a new method or device, or a new artistic object or form. The term generally refers to a richness of ideas and originality of thinking. Psychological studies of highly creative people have shown that many have a strong interest in apparent disorder, contradiction, and imbalance, which seem to be perceived as challenges. Such individuals may possess an exceptionally deep, broad, and flexible awareness of themselves. Studies also show that INTELLIGENCE has little correlation with creativity; thus, a highly intelligent person may not be very creative. See also GENIUS, GIFTED CHILD.

Crécy \krā-'sē\, **Battle of** (August 26, 1346) English victory in the first phase of the HUNDRED YEARS' WAR against the French. At Crécy-en-Ponthieu, EDWARD III of England defeated PHILIP VI of France, even though the English forces were greatly outnumbered. The English gained the advantage because their archers were armed with LONGBOWS and because of their strong defensive position.

credit Transaction between two parties in which one (the creditor or lender) supplies money, goods, services, or securities in return for a promised future payment by the other (the debtor or borrower). Such transactions normally include the payment of INTEREST to the lender. Credit may be extended by public or private institutions to finance business activities, agricultural operations, consumer expenditures, or government projects. Large sums of credit are usually extended through specialized financial institutions such as COMMERCIAL BANKS or through government lending programs.

credit bureau Organization that provides information to merchants or other businesses concerning the creditworthiness of their customers. Credit bureaus may be private enterprises or may be operated on a cooperative basis by the merchants in one locality. Users of the service pay a fee and receive information from various sources, including businesses that have granted the customer credit in the past, public records, newspapers, the customer's employment record, and direct investigation.

credit card Small card that authorizes the person named on it to charge goods or services to his or her account. It differs from a debit card, with which money is automatically deducted from the bank account of the cardholder to pay for the goods or services. Credit-card use originated in the U.S. in the 1920s; early credit cards were issued by various firms (e.g., oil companies and hotel chains) for use at their outlets only. The first universal credit card, usable at a variety of establishments, was issued by Diners' Club in 1950. Charge cards such as AMERICAN EXPRESS require cardholders to pay for all purchases at the end of the billing period (usually monthly). Bank cards such as MasterCard and Visa allow customers to pay only a portion of their bill; INTEREST accrues on the unpaid balance. Credit-card companies get revenue from annual fees and interest paid by cardholders and from fees paid by participating merchants. The huge increase in U.S. credit-card use in recent decades has led to unprecedented levels of consumer debt.

Crédit Mobilier scandal \'kred-it-mō-'bēl-yər, *French* krā-'dē-ˌmȯ-bēl-'yā\ (1872–73) Illegal manipulation of construction contracts for the UNION PACIFIC RAILROAD that became a symbol of corruption after the American Civil War. The railroad's major stockholders created Crédit Mobilier of America to divert its construction profits, and gave or sold stock to influential politicians in return for favors. After a newspaper exposed the scheme in 1872, a Congressional investigation led to the censure of two House members.

credit union Credit COOPERATIVE formed by a group of people with some common bond who, in effect, save their money together and make low-cost loans to each other. The loans are usually short-term consumer loans, mainly for automobiles, household needs, medical debts, and emergencies. Credit unions generally operate under government charter and supervision. They are particularly important in less developed countries, where they may be the only source of credit for their members. The first cooperative societies providing CREDIT were founded in Germany and Italy in the mid-19th century; the first North American credit unions were founded by Alphonse Desjardins in Lévis, Quebec (1900), and Manchester, N.H. (1909). The Credit Union National Association (CUNA), a federation of U.S. credit unions, was established in 1934 and became a worldwide association in 1958.

creditor See DEBTOR AND CREDITOR

Cree One of the major ALGONQUIAN-speaking Indian peoples of Canada, formerly occupying an immense area from western Quebec to eastern Alberta. They acquired firearms and engaged in the fur trade with Europeans beginning in the 17th century. There were two major divisions: the Woodland Cree, whose culture was essentially an EASTERN WOODLANDS type, and the Plains Cree, bison hunters of the northern Great Plains. Social organization in both groups was based on local BANDS. Among the Woodland Cree, rituals and taboos relating to the spirits of game animals were pervasive, as was fear of witchcraft. Among the more militant Plains Cree, rites intended to foster success in the bison hunt and warfare were common. Today over 100,000 Cree live in scattered communities in Canada.

creed Officially authorized, usually brief statement of the essential articles of faith of a religious community, often used in public worship or initiation rites. Creeds are most numerous in Western traditions. In Islam, the *shahada* declares that only God is God and MUHAMMAD is his prophet. In Judaism, early creeds are preserved in Hebrew scripture, and later creeds include the THIRTEEN PRINCIPLES OF FAITH. In Christianity, the NICENE CREED was formulated in AD 381 to exclude Arianism, and the Apostles' Creed was drafted in the 8th century from earlier baptismal creeds. Buddhism, Zoroastrianism, and modern movements of Hinduism also possess creeds; in other religions faith is confessed chiefly through liturgical expressions.

Creek MUSKOGEAN-speaking North American Indian people that originally occupied much of the Georgia and Alabama flatlands. There were two major divisions: the Muskogee (or Upper Creeks), and the Hitchiti and Alabama (or Lower Creeks). They cultivated corn, beans, and squash. Each Creek town had a plaza or community square, often with a temple, around which were built the rectangular houses. Religious observances included the Busk (Green Corn) ceremony, an annual first-fruits and new-fire rite. In the 18th century a Creek Confederacy—including the Natchez, Yuchi, SHAWNEE, and others—was organized to present a united front against both white and Indian enemies. It proved a failure, however, since at no time did all groups contribute warriors to a common battle. The Creek War against the U.S. (1813–14) ended with the defeated Creeks ceding 23 million acres and being forcibly removed to Indian

Ben Perryman, a Creek Indian, painting by George Catlin, 1836; in the National Museum of American Art, Smithsonian Institution, Washington, D.C.

NATIONAL MUSEUM OF AMERICAN ART (FORMERLY NATIONAL COLLECTION OF FINE ARTS), SMITHSONIAN INSTITUTION, WASHINGTON, D.C., GIFT OF MRS. SARAH

Territory (Oklahoma). Today about 50,000 Creeks live in Oklahoma, many of them fully assimilated into white society.

creep Slow change in the dimensions of a material from prolonged STRESS. Most common METALS exhibit creep behavior. In the creep test, loads below those that ordinarily cause plastic flow or fracture are applied to the material, and the DEFORMATION over a period of time (creep strain) under constant load is measured, usually with an extensometer or STRAIN GAUGE. Time to failure is also measured against stress. Once creep strain versus time is plotted, various mathematical techniques are available for extrapolating creep behavior beyond the test times; thus, designers can use thousand-hour test data, for example, to predict ten-thousand-hour behavior. See also TESTING MACHINE.

cremation Disposing of a corpse by burning. In the ancient world cremation took place on an open pyre. It was practiced by the Greeks (who considered it suitable for heroes and war dead) and the Romans (among whom it became a status symbol). The pagan Scandinavians also cremated their dead. In India the custom is very ancient. In some Asian countries only certain people may be cremated (e.g., high lamas in Tibet). Christianity opposed cremation and it became rare in Europe after AD 1000 except in emergencies such as the BLACK DEATH. It reemerged in the late 19th century, and was eventually accepted by both Protestant and Roman Catholics. Today most bodies in some European countries are cremated; it has remained less popular in the U.S. In modern cremation, the body is placed in a chamber and subjected to intense heat that reduces a body to ash; the ashes may be scattered or buried or kept in an urn.

Creole In the 16th–18th century, a person born in Spanish America of Spanish parents, as distinguished from one born in Spain but residing in America. Under Spanish colonial rule Creoles suffered from discrimination; it was consequently Creoles who led the 19th-century revolutions against Spain and became the new ruling class. Today Creole has widely varying meanings. In Louisiana it can mean either French-speaking white descendants of early French and Spanish settlers, or mixed-race people who speak a form of French and Spanish. In Latin America it may denote a local-born person of pure Spanish extraction or a member of the urban Europeanized classes as opposed to rural Indians. In the West Indies it refers to all people, regardless of ancestry, who are part of the Caribbean culture. See also CREOLE language.

creole Any PIDGIN language that has become established as the native language of a speech community. A creole usually arises when speakers of one language become economically or politically dominant over speakers of another. A simplified or modified form of the dominant group's language (pidgin), used for communication between the two groups, may eventually become the native language of the less powerful community. Examples include Sea Island Creole (formerly Gullah, derived from English), spoken in South Carolina's Sea Islands; Haitian Creole (derived from French); and Papiamento (derived from Spanish and Portuguese), spoken in Curaçao, Aruba, and Bonaire.

creosote \'krē-ə-ˌsōt\ Either of two entirely different substances. Coal-tar creosote, distilled from coal tar, is a complex mixture of organic compounds, largely HYDROCARBONS. It is a cheap water-insoluble wood preservative used for railroad ties, telephone poles, and marine-pier pilings and as a disinfectant, fungicide, and biocide. Wood-tar creosote consists mainly of PHENOLS and related compounds and was once widely used for pharmaceutical purposes.

Cresilas *or* **Kresilas** \'kre-si-ləs\ (fl. 5th century BC) Greek sculptor active mainly in Athens. He was a contemporary of PHIDIAS. His portrait of PERICLES (c. 445 BC) generated a type of noble, idealized portraiture. A figure of a wounded Amazon (c. 440 BC) is ascribed to him because of its resemblance to this head. Works attributed to Cresilas are known only in copies of lost bronze originals.

cress Any of several plants of the MUSTARD FAMILY, of interest for their spicy young basal leaves, which are used in salads and as seasonings and garnishes. WATERCRESS is perhaps the most popular of the edible cresses. Common garden cress, or peppergrass *(Lepidium sativum)* is widely grown, especially in its curl-leaved form, and used as a garnish. Others include weeds (e.g., *Barbarea vulgaris*), wild varieties (e.g., *Cardamine pratensis*), and ornamentals (e.g., *Arabis* species).

Cressent \kres-'äⁿ\, **Charles** (1685–1768) French cabinetmaker. He also studied sculpture and became an accomplished metalworker. In 1710 he went to Paris and worked in the studio of A.-C. BOULLE. In 1715 he was appointed official cabinetmaker to Philippe II, duc d'Orléans. In 1719 he was elected to the Academy of St.-Luc, and he consequently received important commissions from French aristocrats, including Madame de POMPADOUR. His early works were in the LOUIS XIV STYLE, but later pieces (c. 1730–50) were lighter and more curvilinear. Cressent was the leading proponent of the RÉGENCE STYLE and introduced marquetries of colored wood and ormolu to case decoration.

Creston, Paul *orig.* **Giuseppe Guttivergi** (1906–1985) U.S. composer. Born to poor immigrant parents in New York City, he was largely self-taught in music. His numerous works, many of which achieved wide performance, are highly rhythmical and tonally accessible. They include six symphonies, a Requiem and three masses, and concertos for saxophone, piano, accordion, and violin.

Cretaceous period \kri-'tā-shəs\ Interval of geologic time from c. 144 to 65 million years ago. During the Cretaceous the climate was warmer than today. In the seas, marine invertebrates flourished and bony fishes evolved. On land, flowering plants arose, and insects, bees in particular, began their thriving partnership with them. Mammals and birds remained inconspicuous throughout the Cretaceous, while the reptiles continued their dominance. The DINOSAURS reached the peak of their evolution during this period but rather suddenly became extinct at its end.

Crete *Greek* **Kríti** \'krē-tē\ *ancient* **Creta** Island (pop., 1991: 537,000), eastern Mediterranean Sea. An administrative region of Greece, it stretches for 152 mi (245 km) and varies in width from 7.5 to 35 mi (12 to 56 km). Dominated by mountains, it was home to the MINOAN civilization from c. 3000 BC, and was known for its palaces on sites that include KNOSSOS, Phaestus, and Mallia; it reached its peak in the 16th century BC. A major earthquake c. 1450 marked the end of the Minoan era. In 67 BC Rome annexed Crete; in AD 395 it passed to Byzantium. In 1204 Crusaders sold the island to Venice, from which it was wrested by the Ottoman Turks in 1669 after one of history's longest sieges. Taken by Greece in 1898, it was autonomous until its union with Greece in 1913. Agriculture is the economic mainstay of the island, and it is one of Greece's leading producers of olives, olive oil, and grapes; tourism is also important. The museum at Iráklion houses a fine collection of Minoan art.

cretinism \'krē-tᵊn-ˌi-zəm\ Endocrine disorder resulting from thyroid hormone deficiency (hypothyroidism) during fetal or early postnatal life. In the fetus, thyroid deficiency causes profound deviations from normal physical and physiological development. Metabolism is deficient. Brain growth is retarded and the anterior pituitary gland grows excessively. Visible signs of cretinism change as the child grows but generally include thick skin, sluggish movements, enlarged tongue, and broad, flat facial features. Intelligence is well below average. See also MYXEDEMA.

Creutzfeldt-Jakob disease \'krȯits-ˌfelt-'yä-ˌkōb\ *or* **CJD** Rare fatal degenerative disease of the central nervous system. It is a spreadable disease that destroys brain tissue, making it spongy and causing progressive loss of mental functioning and motor control. The disease commonly arises in adults between the ages of 40 and 70. Patients usually die within a year. There is no known cure. The disease is caused by a PRION that builds up in neurons. Inherited or random mutation accounts for 99% of cases; the rest come from prion exposure during medical procedures and possibly from eating the meat of cattle with MAD COW DISEASE.

crevasse \kri-'vas\ Fissure or crack in a GLACIER resulting from stress produced by movement. Crevasses range up to 65 ft (20 m) wide, 150 ft (45 m) deep, and several hundred yards long. Crevasses may be bridged by snow and become hidden, and they may close up as the glacier moves.

Crevasse in the Mozama Glacier on Mount Baker, Washington.

BOB AND IRA SPRING

Crèvecoeur \krev-'kœr\, **Michel-Guillaume-Saint-Jean de** *or* **J.**

Hector St. John *or* **Hector St. John de Crèvecoeur** (1735–1813) French-U.S. writer and naturalist. He came to the New World in 1755 as an officer and mapmaker and became a farmer, then served as French consul for many years. He returned to Europe in 1790. His fame rests on *Letters from an American Farmer* (1782, 1784, 1790), essays that paint a broad picture of American life. His *Travels in Upper Pennsylvania and New York* appeared in 1801. Newly discovered essays were published as *Sketches of Eighteenth Century America* in 1925. In his time he was the most widely read commentator on America.

crib death See SUDDEN INFANT DEATH SYNDROME

cribbage Card game, usually for two players, in which each tries to form various counting combinations of cards, the score being kept by moving pegs on a narrow rectangular board. Each player receives six cards. (There is also a five-card variant, as well as four-hand and three-hand variants.) Cribbage was invented by the 17th-century English poet SIR JOHN SUCKLING. The rules of play, though somewhat involved, are simple enough to make cribbage a popular pastime, particularly in Britain and the northern U.S. The game usually ends at 121 (twice around the board plus one).

C
D

Crichton \'krī-tən\, **James** (1560–1582) Scottish scholar and adventurer. After graduating from the University of St. Andrews, he publicly distinguished himself in Europe in learned activities. He entered the service of the duke of Mantua, but was slain in a street fight at 21. Reputedly a fine orator, linguist, debater, and man of letters, he was considered the model of the cultured gentleman, though admirers probably exaggerated his accomplishments. Years later he became known as "the Admirable Crichton."

Crick, Francis (Harry Compton) (born 1916) British biophysicist. Educated at University College London, he helped develop magnetic mines for naval use during World War II, but returned to biology after the war. He worked at Cambridge University with JAMES D. WATSON and MAURICE WILKINS to construct a molecular model of DNA consistent with its known physical and chemical properties, work for which the three shared a 1962 Nobel Prize. Crick also discovered that each group of three bases (a codon) on a single DNA strand designates the position of a specific amino acid on the backbone of a protein molecule, and he helped determine which codons code for each amino acid normally found in protein, thus clarifying the way the cell uses DNA to build proteins. See also ROSALIND FRANKLIN.

cricket (from Middle French *criquet,* "goal stake") Game played with a ball and bat by two sides of 11 players each on a large field centering on two wickets, each defended by a batsman. A bowler throws the ball (with a straight-arm overhand delivery), attempting to hit the wicket, which is one of several ways the batsman may be put out. Runs are scored each time the batsmen exchange positions without being put out. Cricket's origins are uncertain. It was first definitively recorded in England in the late 16th cent, and the first set of rules was written in 1744. During England's colonial history, it was exported to countries around the world. Cricket matches are divided into innings consisting of one turn at bat (approximately 10 batters) for each team; depending on pregame agreement, a match may consist of either one or two innings. International championship tournaments are under the auspices of the Test and Country Cricket Board (TCCB).

cricket Any of the approximately 2,400 species of leaping insects (family Gryllidae) known for the musical chirping of the male. Crickets vary in length from around 0.1 to 2 in. (3–50 mm) and have thin antennae, hind legs modified for jumping, and two abdominal sensory appendages (cerci). Their two forewings are stiff and leathery, and the two long, membranous hind wings are used in flying. Male crickets chirp by rubbing a scraper located on one forewing along a row of 50–250 teeth on the opposite forewing. The most common cricket songs are the calling song, which attracts the female; the courtship, or mating, song, which induces the female to copulate; and the fighting chirp, which repels other males.

crime Act, usually deemed socially harmful or dangerous, that is prohibited by public law and that carries a specific punishment (e.g., incarceration or a fine). Crimes in the COMMON-LAW tradition were originally defined primarily by judicial decision. Most common-law crimes are now codified. A general principle, *nullum crimen sine lege,* says that there can be no crime without a law. A crime generally consists of both conduct (the *actus reus*) and a concurrent state of mind (the *mens rea*). Criminal acts include ARSON, ASSAULT AND BATTERY, BRIBERY, BURGLARY, CHILD ABUSE, COUNTERFEITING, EMBEZZLEMENT, EXTORTION, FORGERY, FRAUD, HIJACKING, HOMICIDE, KIDNAPPING, PERJURY, PIRACY, RAPE, SEDITION, SMUGGLING, TREASON, THEFT, and USURY. See also rights of the ACCUSED, ARREST, CONSPIRACY, CRIMINAL LAW, CRIMINOLOGY, FELONY AND MISDEMEANOR, INDICTMENT, statute of LIMITATIONS, SELF-INCRIMINATION, SENTENCE, WAR CRIME.

Crimea \krī-'mē-ə\ Administrative subdivision (pop., 1991 est.: 2,550,000), southern UKRAINE, coextensive with the Crimean Peninsula, which extends into the BLACK SEA. It covers 10,400 sq mi (27,000 sq km); its capital is Simferopol. Early inhabitants were Cimmerians, though the area later was settled by Greeks in the 6th century BC. and ruled by the kingdom of the CIMMERIAN BOSPORUS from the 5th century BC. It became subject to Rome, and part of it later belonged to the Byzantine empire. Russia annexed Crimea in 1783. It was the scene of the CRIMEAN WAR (1853–56). In 1921 it became an autonomous republic of the Russian S.S.R. During World War II Nazi armies overran it in 1941; it was retaken in 1944. The area became an oblast of Ukraine in 1954. After the dissolution of the Soviet Union in 1991, Crimea obtained partial autonomy from Ukraine.

Crimean War (October 1853–February 1856) War fought mainly in the CRIMEA between the Russians and an alliance consisting of the Ottoman empire, Britain, France, and Sardinia-Piedmont. It arose from the conflict of great powers in the Middle East and was more directly caused by Russian demands to exercise protection over the Orthodox subjects of the Ottoman sultan. The war was managed and commanded poorly by both sides. Battles were fought at the Alma River, BALAKLAVA, and Inkerman, before the besieged SEVASTOPOL was taken by the allies. Disease accounted for many of the approximately 250,000 men lost by each side. After Austria threatened to join the allies, Russia accepted preliminary peace terms, which were formalized at the Congress of PARIS. The war did not settle the relations of the powers in Eastern Europe, but it did alert ALEXANDER II to the need to modernize Russia.

criminal law Body of law that defines criminal offenses, regulates the apprehension, charging, and trial of suspected offenders, and fixes punishment for convicted persons. Criminal offenses are those construed as being against the state. Substantive criminal law defines crimes, and PROCEDURAL LAW establishes procedure for the prosecution of crime. Today's substantive criminal law originated for the most part in COMMON LAW, which was later codified in federal and state statutes. Modern criminal law has been affected considerably by the SOCIAL SCIENCES, especially with respect to sentencing, legal research, legislation, and rehabilitation. See also CRIMINOLOGY.

criminology Scientific study of nonlegal aspects of CRIME, including its causes and prevention. Criminology originated in the 18th century when social reformers began to question the use of punishment for retribution rather than deterrence and reform. In the 19th century, scientific methods began to be applied to the study of crime. Today criminologists commonly use STATISTICS, case histories, official records, and sociological field methods to study criminals and criminal activity, including the rates and kinds of crime within geographic areas. Their findings are used by lawyers, judges, probation officers, law-enforcement and prison officials, legislators, and scholars to better understand criminals and the effects of treatment and prevention. See also DELINQUENCY, PENOLOGY.

Cripps, (Richard) Stafford *later* **Sir Stafford** (1889–1952) British statesman. A successful lawyer, he served in Parliament 1931–50. On the extreme left of the Labour Party, he helped found the Socialist League in 1932. After serving as ambassador to Moscow (1940–42), he joined the British war cabinet and conducted the Cripps Mission (1942), an unsuccessful attempt to rally Indian support against the Japanese. As chancellor of the exchequer (1947–50), he instituted a rigid austerity program to revive Britain's economy.

Crispi \'krēs-pē\, **Francesco** (1819–1901) Italian politician. A Sicilian, he was exiled for his revolutionary activities. He became an associate of GIUSEPPE MAZZINI and encouraged GIUSEPPE DE GARIBALDI to conquer Sicily in 1860. He served as a deputy from Sicily in the new Italian parliament (1861–96) and held office in several leftist governments. As premier (1887–91, 1893–96), he instituted liberal reforms and later improved the economy, but became increasingly repressive. He embarked on a disastrous foreign policy, organizing Eritrea as a colony and attempting colonial expansion in Africa. He was forced to resign after the Italian defeat at the Battle of ADOWA.

Cristofano de Giudicis, Francesco di See FRANCIABIGIO

Cristofori \krē-'stȯ-fō-ˌrē\, **Bartolomeo** (1655–1731) Italian musical-instrument maker. As custodian of musical instruments at the court of Prince Ferdinand de' Medici, he maintained a variety of instruments. His most famous experiment was the pianoforte, ancestor of the modern PIANO, which he worked on from 1698, an instrument that, unlike the harpsichord, could produce changes in volume of sound depending on the force with which the keys were struck. A diagram of its workings was published in 1711 and soon copied by others. Some of his original pianofortes survive.

critical care unit See INTENSIVE CARE UNIT

critical mass Minimum amount of a given fissionable material necessary to achieve a self-sustaining nuclear CHAIN REACTION under specified conditions. Critical mass depends on several factors, including the kind of fissionable material used, its concentration and purity, and the composition and geometry of the surrounding reaction system.

critical point In science, the set of conditions under which a liquid and its vapor become identical. The conditions are the critical TEMPERATURE, the critical PRESSURE, and the critical DENSITY. If a closed vessel is filled with a pure substance, partly liquid and partly vapor, and the average density equals the critical density, the critical conditions can be achieved. As the temperature is raised, the vapor pressure increases, and the gas PHASE becomes denser while the liquid expands and becomes less dense. At the critical point, the densities of liquid and vapor become equal, eliminating the boundary between the two.

critical theory Neo-Marxian social philosophy associated with the work of the FRANKFURT SCHOOL. Drawing particularly on the thought of KARL MARX and SIGMUND FREUD, critical theory maintains that a primary goal of philosophy is to promote emancipation by helping overcome dominating or oppressive relationships in society. Believing that science has become a mere instrument in the service of industrialized society, critical theorists caution against the faith in scientific rationality that accompanied modernizations, and maintain that scientific efficiency must not be taken as an end in itself, without reference to the goal of emancipation. Particularly since the 1970s, critical theory has become immensely influential internationally, especially in the study of the social sciences, history, and literature.

Critius and Nesiotes *or* **Kritios and Nesiotes** \'kri-shəs, 'kri-tē-əs...ˌnes-ē-'ō-ˌtēz\ (fl. early 5th century BC) Greek sculptors working in Athens. They executed the first masterpieces of free-standing sculpture of the early Classical period: the bronze figures of the *Tyrannicides* (477 BC), commissioned to replace those by ANTENOR, which were looted in the Persian sack of Athens (480 BC). Marble copies survive in the National Archaeology Museum, Naples.

Crittenden, John J(ordan) (1787–1863) U.S. politician. Born near Versailles, Ky., he served in the U.S. Senate (1817–19, 1835–40, 1842–48, 1855–61), and also served as U.S. attorney general (1840–41, 1850–53) and governor of Kentucky (1848–50). He is best known for the CRITTENDEN COMPROMISE. In 1861 he chaired the Frankfort convention of border-state leaders that asked the South to reconsider its position on secession.

Crittenden Compromise Series of compromises in 1860–61 intended to forestall the AMERICAN CIVIL WAR. Sen. JOHN J. CRITTENDEN proposed constitutional amendments that would reenact provisions of the MISSOURI COMPROMISE and extend them to the western territories, indemnify owners of fugitive slaves whose return was prevented by antislavery elements in the North, allow a form of popular sovereignty in the territories, and protect slavery in the District of Columbia. The plan was rejected by president-elect ABRAHAM LINCOLN and narrowly defeated in the Senate.

Crivelli \krē-'vel-lē\, **Carlo** (c. 1430–c. 1493) Italian painter. The son of a painter, he was born in Venice but worked mainly in the Marches, a provincial region of central Italy. All his works were of religious subjects, done in an elaborate, old-fashioned style reminiscent of the linearism of ANDREA MANTEGNA. Characterized by heavy ornamentation, sharp outlines, and exaggerated facial expressions, his paintings are closer to the religious intensity of Gothic art than to the rationalism of the Renaissance.

Cro-Magnon \krō-'mag-nən, krō-'man-yən\ Population of anatomically modern *HOMO SAPIENS* dating from the Upper PALEOLITHIC PERIOD (c. 35,000–10,000 BC). First discovered in 1868 at the Cro-Magnon cave in the Les Eyzies region in southern France, the human skeletons that came to be called Cro-Magnon are now considered representative of humans at that time. Cro-Magnon was relatively more robust and powerful than contemporary humans, with a somewhat larger brain capacity. The Cro-Magnons are generally associated with the AURIGNACIAN tool industry and artistic tradition. Cro-Magnons seem to have been a settled people, living in caves or primitive huts and lean-tos, moving only when necessary to find new hunting or because of environmental changes. It is difficult to determine how long the Cro-Magnons lasted and what happened to them; presumably they were gradually absorbed into the European populations that came later.

croaker See DRUM

Croatia \krō-'ā-shə\ *officially* **Republic of Croatia** *Serbo-Croatian* **Hrvatska** \hər-'vät-skä\ Country, western central Balkans. Area: 21,829 sq mi (56,538 sq km). Population (2000): 4,282,000. Capital: ZAGREB. The people are mainly Croats, with a large Serb minority. Language: Croatian (official). Religions: Roman Catholicism (Croats), Serbian Orthodoxy (Serbs). Currency: kuna. Croatia includes the traditional regions of DALMATIA, ISTRIA, and Croatia-Slavonia. Istria and Dalmatia, in the southwest, cover the rugged Adriatic coast. The northwest, known as the central mountain belt, contains part of the Dinaric Alps. The northeast is a fertile agricultural area; cattle breeding is also important. The central mountain belt is known for fruit, and the farms of Istria and Dalmatia

produce grapes and olives. The most important industries are food processing, wine making, textiles, chemicals, and petroleum and natural gas. It is a republic with a two-chambered legislature, its head of state is the president, and the head of government is the prime minister. The Croats, a southern Slavic people, arrived in the 7th century AD, and in the 8th century came under CHARLEMAGNE. They converted to Christianity soon afterward and formed a kingdom in the 10th century. Coming under Hungarian control in the 11th century, it remained an independent kingdom, while the union lasted some eight centuries. Most of Croatia was taken by the Turks in 1526; the rest voted to accept Austrian rule. In 1867 it became part of the Austro-Hungarian empire, with Dalmatia and Istria ruled by VIENNA and Croatia-Slavonia a Hungarian crown land. In 1918, after the defeat of AUSTRIA-HUNGARY in World War

I, it joined other south Slav territories to form the Kingdom of Serbs, Croats, and Slovenes, renamed YUGOSLAVIA in 1929. In World War II, an independent state of Croatia was established by Germany and Italy, embracing Croatia-Slavonia, part of Dalmatia, and Bosnia and Herzegovina; after the war Croatia was rejoined to Yugoslavia as a people's republic. It declared its independence in 1991, sparking insurrections by Croatian Serbs, who carved out autonomous regions with Serbian-led Yugoslav army help; Croatia had taken back most of these regions by 1995. With some stability returning, Croatia's economy began to revive in the late 1990s.

Croce \'krō-chā\, **Benedetto** (1866–1952) Italian patriot, aesthetician, critic, and cultural historian. He founded and edited (1903–37) *La Critica,* an influential journal of cultural criticism. A passionate anti-Fascist, he helped revive liberal institutions in the years following World War II, including the Liberal Party, which he led 1943–52. In 1947 he founded the Italian Institute for Historical Studies. His philosophy of the spirit, as he called it, centered on "circularity," a complex dynamic principle describing the flow between spiritual moments.

Benedetto Croce.
H. ROGER-VIOLLET

crocidolite \krō-'si-dᵊl-ˌīt\ *or* **blue asbestos** Gray-blue to green, highly fibrous (asbestiform) form of the AMPHIBOLE mineral riebeckite. It has higher tensile strength than CHRYSOTILE asbestos. The major commercial source is South Africa, where it occurs in Precambrian banded iron-formations; it is also found in Australia and Bolivia.

Crockett, Davy *orig.* **David** (1786–1836) U.S. frontiersman and politician. Born in eastern Tennessee, he fought in the Creek War (1813–15). A popular local figure, he was elected to the state legislature (1821–25) and the U.S. House of Representatives (1827–31). Attempting to offset ANDREW JACKSON, the Whig Party promoted him as a "coonskin" politician. In his third term (1833–35) the Whigs sent Crockett on a speaking tour of the East. The many stories in books and newspapers led to the legend of an eccentric but shrewd "b'ar hunter" and Indian fighter. In 1835 he went to Texas to join the war against Mexico and was killed at the ALAMO.

crocodile Any of about a dozen tropical reptile species (family Crocodilidae) found in Asia, the Australian region, Africa, Madagascar, and the Americas. Crocodiles are long-snouted, lizardlike CARNIVORES. Most feed on fishes, turtles, birds, and small mammals; large individuals may attack domestic livestock or humans. Crocodiles swim and feed in the water, floating at the surface to wait for prey, but bask in the sun and breed on land. They are reputed to be livelier than ALLIGATORS and more likely to attack humans. They have a narrower snout than alligators and a tooth on each side of the jaw that is visible when the jaw is closed.

crocus Any of about 75 species of low-growing plants, with CORMS, that make up the genus *Crocus* (IRIS FAMILY), native to the Alps, southern Europe, and the Mediterranean and widely grown for their cuplike blooms in early spring or fall. The spring-flowering sorts have a floral tube so long that the ovary is belowground, sheltered from climatic changes. SAFFRON comes from *C. sativus* of western Asia. The alpine *C. vernus* is the chief ancestor of the common garden crocus. Dutch yellow crocus *(C. flavus)* and *C. biflorus* are popular spring-flowering species.

crocus, autumn See AUTUMN CROCUS

Croesus \'krē-səs\ (died 546? BC) Last king of LYDIA, famous for his great wealth. He succeeded his father as king c. 560 BC, and after completing the conquest of mainland Ionia he faced the rising threat of the Persians under CYRUS THE GREAT. He forged an alliance with Babylon, Egypt, and Sparta to combat the Persians, but after an inconclusive effort to invade Cappadocia, he returned to his capital at SARDIS. The Persians pursued him, storming Sardis in 546 and conquering Lydia. Croesus' later fate is uncertain. HERODOTUS claims he was condemned to be burned alive but was saved by APOLLO.

Croghan \'krō-ən\, **George** (c. 1720–1782) Irish-American trader and Indian agent. He emigrated from Ireland in 1741, settling near Carlisle, Pa., where he learned Indian customs and languages to aid his trade. He was named Indian agent for Pennsylvania in the 1740s. Later, as deputy to WILLIAM JOHNSON (1756–72), he negotiated with tribes that complained of colonists' encroachments on their land. In 1765 he achieved an end to PONTIAC's War. He espoused the patriot cause in the American Revolution.

Croix de Feu \'krwä-də-'fœ\ (French: "Cross of Fire") French political movement (1927–36). Originally an organization of World War I veterans, it espoused ultranationalistic views with vaguely fascist overtones. Under François de la Rocque (1885–1946), it organized popular demonstrations in reaction to the STAVISKY AFFAIR, hoping to overthrow the government. It subsequently lost prestige and was dissolved by the Popular Front government in 1936.

Cromer, Earl of *orig.* **Evelyn Baring** (1841–1917) British administrator in Egypt. After serving as an army officer (1858–72), he became private secretary to his cousin Lord Northbrook, viceroy of India. In 1877 he went to Egypt to help resolve Egypt's financial problems. Named British agent and consul general in 1883, he instituted a form of government known as the Veiled Protectorate, whereby he ruled the Egyptian khedives. Egypt was made financially solvent by 1887, and Cromer's parsimony and encouragement of agricultural projects increased its prosperity. Until his resignation in 1907, he remained the country's real ruler, profoundly influencing Egypt's development as a modern state.

Crompton, Samuel (1753–1827) British inventor. His SPINNING MULE (probably called a mule because it was a cross between inventions of R. ARKWRIGHT and JAMES HARGREAVES) permitted large-scale manufacture of high-quality thread and yarn, by simultaneously drawing out and giving the final twisting to the cotton fibers fed into it, reproducing mechanically the actions of hand spinning.

Cromwell, Oliver (1599–1658) English soldier and statesman, lord protector of the republican Commonwealth of England, Scotland, and Ireland (1653–58). He was elected to Parliament in 1628, but CHARLES I dissolved that Parliament in 1629 and did not call another for 11 years. In 1640 Cromwell was elected to the Short and the LONG PARLIAMENT. When differences between Charles and Parliament erupted into the ENGLISH CIVIL WARS, Cromwell became one of the leading generals on the Parliamentary side, winning many notable victories, including the Battles of MARSTON MOOR and NASEBY. He was among those who brought the king to trial and signed his death warrant. After the British Isles were named the Commonwealth, he served as the first chairman of the Council of State. In the next few years he fought against the Royalists in Ireland and Scotland and suppressed a mutiny inspired by the LEVELERS. When CHARLES II advanced into England, Cromwell destroyed his army at Worcester (1651), the battle that ended the civil wars. As lord protector (1653–58), Cromwell raised his country's status once more to that of a leading European power and concluded the ANGLO-DUTCH WAR. Though a devout Calvinist, he pursued policies of religious toleration. He refused the title of king, offered to him by Parliament in 1657. After his death, he was succeeded by his son RICHARD CROMWELL.

Richard Cromwell, miniature by an unknown artist; in the National Portrait Gallery, London.
BY COURTESY OF THE NATIONAL PORTRAIT GALLERY, LONDON

Cromwell, Richard (1626–1712) Lord protector of England (September 1658–May 1659). He was the eldest surviving son of OLIVER CROMWELL, who groomed him for high office. He served in the Parliamentary army and was a member of Parliament and the council of state. After his father's death, he was proclaimed lord protector, but he soon encountered serious difficulties and was forced to abdicate. Having amassed large debts, he fled to Paris in 1660 to escape his creditors; in 1680 he returned and lived in seclusion.

Cromwell, Thomas *later* **Earl of Essex** (1485?–1540) English politician and principal adviser (1532–40) to HENRY VIII. He was a confidential adviser to THOMAS, CARDINAL WOLSEY before entering Parliament (1529), where his abilities attracted the king's notice. Entering Henry's service in 1530, he was chiefly responsible for establishing the REFORMATION in England, for the dissolution of the monasteries, and for strengthening the royal administration. He eventually came into complete control of the government, though he pretended to be acting on the king's authority. In 1539 he made the mistake of inducing Henry to marry ANNE OF CLEVES, which led to his fall. At his enemies' instigation he was arrested for heresy and treason, condemned without a hearing, and executed.

Cronenberg \ˈkrō-nən-ˌbərg\, **David** (born 1943) Canadian film director, screenwriter, and actor. Born in Toronto, he began making horror films in the 1970s. He acquired a cult following with such films as *Scanners* (1981) and *Videodrome* (1982) and a wider horror-film audience with *The Dead Zone* (1983), *The Fly* (1986), and *Dead Ringers* (1988). Later films have included *Naked Lunch* (1991), *M. Butterfly* (1993), *Crash* (1996), and *Existenz* (1999).

Cronin, A(rchibald) J(oseph) (1896–1981) Scottish novelist. Trained as a surgeon, he practiced medicine particularly in mining communities, but ceased because of ill health and used his leisure to write. His books combine sentimentality with social criticism. His first novel, *Hatter's Castle* (1931; film, 1941), was an immediate success. His classic *The Stars Look Down* (1935; film, 1939) chronicles social injustice in a mining community. Other works include *The Citadel* (1937; film, 1938), *The Keys of the Kingdom* (1942; film, 1944), *The Green Years* (1944; film, 1946), *The Judas Tree* (1961), and *A Thing of Beauty* (1956).

Cronkite, Walter (Leland, Jr.) (born 1916) U.S. journalist and television newscaster. Born in St. Joseph, Mo., he began his career as a reporter with the Houston *Post* and later worked for United Press (1939–48) and served as a war correspondent in Europe (1942–45). He joined CBS in 1950 as a news reporter and became managing editor and anchor of the widely watched *CBS Evening News* (1962–81). He hosted numerous documentaries and special reports, notably on the assassination of Pres. JOHN F. KENNEDY and the 1969 moon landing. His reassuring, avuncular manner made him one of the most beloved figures in the U.S.

Cronus *or* **Cronos** *or* **Kronos** In GREEK RELIGION, a male agricultural deity. He was the youngest of the 12 TITANS borne by URANUS and GAEA, and his castration of his father separated heaven from earth. With his sister and consort RHEA, he fathered HESTIA, DEMETER, HERA, HADES, and POSEIDON, all of whom he swallowed because he had been warned that he would be overthrown by his own child. Rhea hid his son ZEUS and tricked Cronus into swallowing a stone; Zeus later forced Cronus to disgorge the others and then vanquished him in war. He was identified with the Roman god SATURN.

Cronyn \ˈkrō-nən\, **Hume and Jessica Tandy** (born 1911, 1909–1994) U.S. actors. Cronyn, born in London, Ontario, made his Broadway debut in 1934. He was a successful character actor in many plays, including *Hamlet* (1964, Tony award), and directed such plays as *Hilda Crane* (1950) and *The Egghead* (1957). Tandy, born in London, made her Broadway debut in 1930. She was the original Blanche Du Bois in *A Streetcar Named Desire* (1947, Tony award). She and Cronyn married in 1942 and acted together in such successful plays as *The Fourposter* (1951), *A Delicate Balance* (1966), *The Gin Game* (1977), and *Foxfire* (1982), the last two of which earned Tony awards for Tandy. Cronyn's many films included *Lifeboat* (1944) and *Sunrise at Campobello* (1960), and Tandy's included *The Birds* (1963), *Driving Miss Daisy* (1989, Academy Award), and *Fried Green Tomatoes* (1991).

crop In agriculture, a plant or plant product that can be grown and harvested extensively for profit or subsistence. By use, crops fall into six categories: food crops, for human consumption (e.g., wheat, potatoes); feed crops, for livestock consumption (e.g., oats, alfalfa); fiber crops, for cordage and textiles (e.g., cotton, hemp); oil crops, for consumption or industrial uses (e.g., cottonseed, corn); ornamental crops, for landscape gardening (e.g., dogwood, azalea); and industrial and secondary crops, for various personal and industrial uses (e.g., rubber, tobacco).

crop duster Usually, an aircraft used for dusting or spraying large acreages with PESTICIDES, though other types of dusters are also employed. Aerial spraying and dusting permit prompt coverage of large areas at the moment when application of pesticide is most effective and avoid the need for wheeled vehicles that might damage crops. The technique was greatly improved in the 1960s with the development of ultra-low-volume applicators, in which concentrated pesticides are distributed in extremely small amounts. See also SPRAYING AND DUSTING.

crop rotation Successive cultivation of different CROPS in a specified order on the same fields. Some rotations are designed for high immediate returns, with little regard for basic resources. Others are planned for high continuing returns while protecting resources. A typical scheme selects rotation crops from three classifications: cultivated row crops (e.g., corn, potatoes), close-growing grains (e.g., oats, wheat) and sod-forming, or rest, crops (e.g., clover, clover-timothy). In general, cropping systems should include deep-rooting LEGUMES. In addition to the many beneficial effects on soils and crops, well-planned crop rotations make the farm a more effective year-round enterprise by providing more efficient handling of labor, power, and equipment, reduction in weather and market risks, and improved ability to meet livestock requirements.

croquet \krō-ˈkā\ (French dialect for "crook," "hockey stick") Game in which players using mallets drive wooden balls through a series of wickets, or hoops, set out on a lawn. The object is to be the first to complete the course by passing through all the wickets and hitting a goal peg. Croquet evolved from the 13th-century French game pall-mall. Championship matches are organized by governing bodies in the U.S. and Britain.

Crosby, Bing *orig.* **Harry Lillis** (1903–1977) U.S. singer and actor. Born in Tacoma, Wash., Crosby began to sing and play drums while studying law in Spokane. As a singer with the Paul Whiteman orchestra in 1927, his mellow "crooning" style and casual stage manner proved highly popular. He appeared in the early sound film *King of Jazz* (1931), and later had his own radio program. By the late 1930s his records had sold millions of copies. His recordings of "White Christmas" and "Silent Night" are among the most popular of all time. In the 1940s he starred in a popular radio variety show. His film career included the seven *Road* film comedies with BOB HOPE and Dorothy Lamour, beginning with *The Road to Singapore* (1940); *Going My Way* (1944, Academy Award); *The Bells of St. Mary's* (1945); *White Christmas* (1954); and *The Country Girl* (1954). Over 300 million of his records may have been sold, a total surpassed only by E. PRESLEY among solo artists.

Bing Crosby.
BROWN BROTHERS

cross Principal symbol of CHRISTIANITY, recalling the CRUCIFIXION of JESUS. There are four basic iconogaphic representations: the *crux quadrata,* or Greek cross, with four equal arms; the *crux immissa,* or Latin cross,

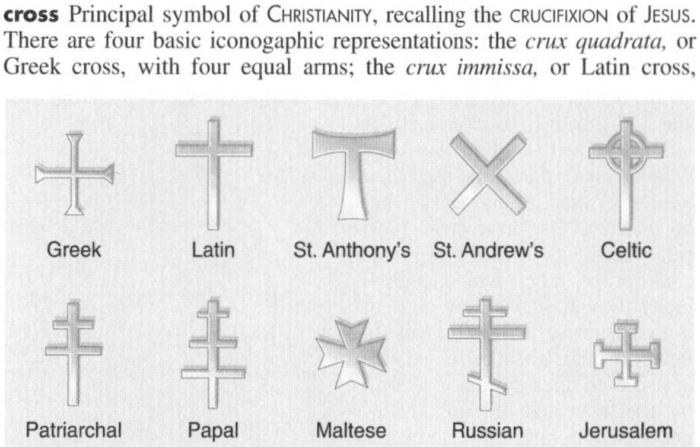

Several traditional types of crosses.

with a base stem longer than the other arms; the *crux commissa* (St. Anthony's cross), resembling the Greek letter tau (T); and the *crux decussataa* (St. Andrew's cross), resembling the Roman numeral 10 (X). Tradition holds that the *crux immissa* was used for Christ's crucifixion. Coptic Christians used the ancient Egyptian ANKH. Displaying the cross was not common before CONSTANTINE I abolished crucifixion in the 4th century. A crucifix shows Christ's figure on a cross and is typical of Roman Catholicism and Eastern Orthodoxy. Making the sign of the cross with the hand may be a profession of faith, prayer, dedication, or benediction.

cross-country running Long-distance running over open country. It developed as a competitive event in the mid-19th century. Though originally included in the revived Olympics, it was dropped after 1924 as not suitable for summer competition (most cross-country races are held in the fall or early winter). The first international women's competition was held in 1967. Standard distances are 12,000 m (7.5 mi) for men, and 2,000–5,000 m (1.25–3 mi) for women. Though rules for championship competitions have been established, world records are not kept because of the varying difficulty of courses.

cross-country skiing Skiing in open country over rolling, hilly terrain. It originated in Scandinavia as a means of travel as well as recreation. The skies used are longer, narrower, and lighter than those used in ALPINE SKIING, and bindings allow more heel movement. The standard lengths of international races range from 10 to 50 km (6.2–31 mi) for men and 5 to 30 km (3.1–18.6 mi) for women. It has been included on the Olympics program since the first Winter Olympics in 1924.

cross-fertilization Fusion of male and female sex cells from different individuals of the same species. Cross-fertilization is necessary in animal and plant species that have male and female organs on separate individuals. Methods of cross-fertilization are diverse in animals. Among most species that breed in water, the males and females shed their sex cells into the water, where FERTILIZATION takes place outside the body. Among land breeders, fertilization is internal, with the sperm being introduced into the body of the female. By recombining genetic material from two parents, cross-fertilization maintains a greater range of variability for NATURAL SELECTION to act on, thereby increasing the capacity of a species to adapt to environmental change. See also SELF-FERTILIZATION.

Cross River River, western Africa. Rising in the highlands of Cameroon, it flows west and south through Nigeria. Its course, some 300 mi (485 km) long, runs through dense tropical rain forest and mangrove swamps to the Bight of BIAFRA. It is navigable through its estuary, which it shares with the Calabar River.

cross section In nuclear physics, a measure of the probability that a given atomic NUCLEUS will exhibit a specific reaction (ABSORPTION, SCATTERING, or NUCLEAR FISSION) in relation to a particular incident particle. Cross section is expressed in terms of area, and its value is chosen so that, if the bombarding particle hits a circular target of this size perpendicular to its path and centered at the nucleus, the given reaction occurs. If it misses the area, the reaction does not occur. The unit of cross section is the barn, which equals 10^{-24} sq cm. Cross-section values for a given nucleus depend on the energy of the bombarding particle and the kind of reaction and are often different from the actual cross-sectional area of the nucleus.

crossbow Leading missile weapon of the Middle Ages, consisting of a short bow fixed transversely on a stock, with a groove to guide the missile and a trigger to release it. The missile, known as a bolt, was usually an arrow or dart. First used in antiquity, it was an important advance in warfare. Its destructive power came from its metal bow, which could propel a bolt with enough velocity to pierce CHAIN MAIL and gave it a range of up to 1,000 ft (300 m). Powerful and versatile, it remained in use even after the introduction of the LONGBOW and firearms and was not discarded until the 15th century. It has been used in modern times to hunt big game.

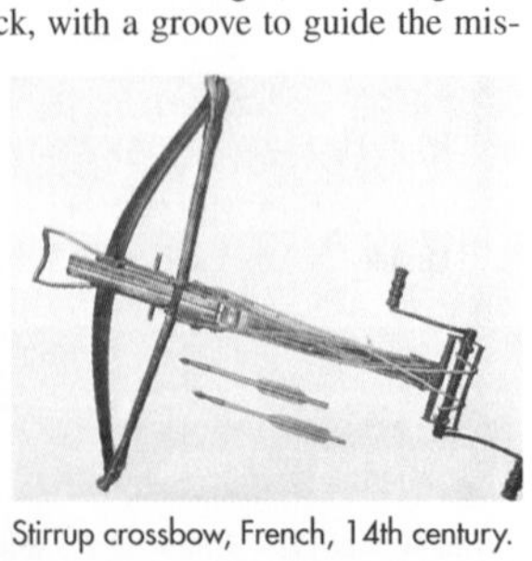

Stirrup crossbow, French, 14th century.
BY COURTESY OF THE WEST POINT MUSEUM COLLECTIONS, UNITED STATES MILITARY ACADEMY

crossword puzzle Puzzle in which words are filled into a pattern of numbered squares in answer to correspondingly numbered clues and in such a way that words can be read across and down. The first crosswords, intended primarily for children, appeared in England in the 19th century. In the U.S., the puzzle developed into a popular adult pastime. By 1923, crosswords were being published in most of the leading U.S. newspapers, and the craze soon reached England. Today crosswords in various forms are found in almost every country and language.

croton \'krō-tᵊn\ Colorful-leaved plant *(Codiaeum variegatum)* of the SPURGE family, native to Malaysia and the Pacific. Its numerous varieties of shrubs or small trees with brilliantly colored, glossy, leathery leaves are popular potted plants. Leaf colors occur solid or in combinations of green, yellow, white, orange, pink, red, crimson, and purple. Another plant of the same family but of a different genus is purging croton *(Croton tiglium)*, a small tree native to S.East Asia with seeds that yield croton oil.

croup \'krüp\ Acute laryngeal INFLAMMATION and spasms in young children, with harsh cough, hoarseness, and difficulty breathing. Causes include infection, allergy, and physical irritation of the larynx. Viral croup, the most common, usually occurs before age 3. It can usually be treated at home with a cool mist vaporizer. Bacterial croup (epiglottitis) generally strikes between ages 3 and 7. Swelling of the epiglottis rapidly causes severe breathing and swallowing difficulty, requiring antibiotics and insertion of a breathing tube.

Crow PLAINS INDIAN people of SIOUAN LANGUAGE stock, historically affiliated with the HIDATSA. They occupied the area around the Yellowstone River in northern Wyoming and southern Montana. Much of Crow life revolved around the buffalo and the horse. The Crow were prominent as middleman traders, trading horses, bows, and other items to local village Indians in return for guns and metal goods that they carried to the SHOSHONE in Idaho. The basic element in Crow religious life was the supernatural vision, induced by fasting and isolation. The Crow continually suffered losses from wars with the BLACKFOOT and SIOUX and sided with the whites in the Indian wars of the 1860s and '70s. In 1868 they accepted a reservation carved from former tribal lands in southern Montana. Today they number about 6,500.

crow Any of more than 20 species of black songbirds in the genus *Corvus* (family Corvidae) that are smaller than most RAVENS and less heavily billed. They are named for the sound of their call. Common crows are found in North America and Eurasia. They eat grain, berries, insects, carrion, and the eggs of other birds. Crows may damage grain crops, but they also eat many economically harmful insects. At times crows roost together in the tens of thousands, but most species do not nest in colonies. The crows are considered the most intelligent of all birds, and pet crows can be taught to imitate speech.

Carrion crow (*Corvus corone corone*).
ERIC HOSKING

Crowe \'krō\, **Eyre (Alexander Barby Wichart)** *later* **Sir Eyre** (1864–1925) British diplomat. In the years before World War I he strongly urged an anti-German policy, arguing in a 1907 memorandum that Germany aimed at the domination of Europe, that concessions would only increase its appetite for power, and that the entente with France must not be abandoned. On July 25, 1914, he urged a show of force by the British navy to forestall war, and when war began a few days later he induced the government to seize German vessels in British ports. He served as permanent undersecretary of state for foreign affairs 1920–25.

crowfoot See BUTTERCUP

crown gall Disease of plants caused by the bacterium *Agrobacterium tumefaciens*. Thousands of plant species are susceptible, including especially rose, grape, pome and stone fruits (e.g., apples, peaches), shade and nut trees, many shrubs and vines, and perennial garden plants. Symptoms include roundish, rough-surfaced GALLS, several inches or more in diameter. At first cream-colored or greenish, they later turn brown or black. As the disease progresses, affected plants lose vigor and may eventually die.

crown jewels Ornaments used at the coronation of a monarch and the formal ensigns of monarchy worn or carried on state occasions, as well as collections of personal jewelry consolidated by European sovereigns as valuable assets of their royal houses and the offices they filled. Most familiar are those of Britain, which include St. Edward's Crown, the Royal Sceptre (with the Star of Africa diamond), the Sceptre of Equity and Mercy, and the Sword of Offering, as well as the coronation ring, anointing spoon, ampulla (flask), and coronation bracelets. Many collections of royal jewelry have been assembled, confiscated, and dispersed over the centuries.

crown-of-thorns starfish Reddish and heavy-spined STARFISH *(Acanthaster planci)* that has 12–19 arms and is often 18 in. (45 cm) across. It feeds on CORAL POLYPS. Beginning c. 1963, its population on Australia's Great Barrier Reef exploded; it continued to multiply throughout the southern Pacific, threatening the destruction of coral reefs and islands, and intensive efforts have been made to kill it off. The explosion has been linked to the decimation of the starfish's chief predator, the Pacific triton (a marine snail), by shell collectors. Additional factors are uncertain, though runoff of nutrient-rich soil as a result of shorefront development has been implicated.

Crown-of-thorns starfish.
A. GIDDINGS—BRUCE COLEMAN INC.

crown vetch Vigorous trailing LEGUME *(Coronilla varia),* native to the Mediterranean but widely grown in temperate areas as a ground cover. It has fernlike leaves and clusters of white to pink flowers. The sturdy roots are useful in binding the soil of steep slopes and roadside embankments. As a legume, crown vetch draws nitrogen from the air, trapping it in the roots, and thus improves soil fertility. It dies back to the crown each fall in cold areas, resuming growth in spring. Cutting the plant back in the fall or early spring encourages quick growth.

crucible \'krü-sə-bəl\ Pot of CLAY or other REFRACTORY material, used from ancient times as a container for melting METALS or other materials. Modern crucibles may be small laboratory utensils for conducting high-temperature chemical reactions and analyses, or large industrial vessels for melting and calcining metal, ore, or glass, and may be made of clay, graphite, porcelain, or a relatively infusible metal.

crucible process Technique for producing cast or TOOL STEEL. It was invented in Britain c. 1740 by BENJAMIN HUNTSMAN, who heated small pieces of CARBON STEEL in a closed fireclay crucible placed in a COKE fire. This was the first process used in Europe in which the temperature (2,900°F, or 1,600°C) was high enough to melt the STEEL, producing a homogeneous metal of uniform composition. After 1870 the Siemens regenerative gas furnace replaced the coke-fired furnace. Capable of producing even higher temperatures, the Siemens furnace had a number of combustion holes, each holding several crucibles, and heated as many as 100 crucibles at a time. All high-quality tool steel and HIGH-SPEED STEEL was long made by the crucible process. In the 20th century the ELECTRIC FURNACE has replaced it in countries with inexpensive electric power. See also WOOTZ.

crucifixion Method of CAPITAL PUNISHMENT among the Persians, Seleucids, Jews, Carthaginians, and Romans from about the 6th century BC to the 4th century AD. The condemned man was usually whipped and forced to drag the crossbeam to where the upright was standing. His hands were tied or nailed to the crossbeam, which was attached to the upright 9–12 ft (2.5–3.5 m) above the ground, and his feet bound or nailed to the upright. Death was by heart failure or asphyxiation. Political or religious agitators and those without civil rights were crucified. Its overwhelming association today is with JESUS. Crucifixion was abolished by CONSTANTINE I in AD 337 after his conversion to Christianity. See also STIGMATA.

crude oil See PETROLEUM

cruelty, theater of Theory advanced by ANTONIN ARTAUD, who believed the theater's function was to rid audiences of the repressive effects of civilization and liberate their instinctual energy. He proposed to do so by shocking them with mythic spectacles that would include groans, screams, pulsating lights, and oversized stage puppets. He described the theater of cruelty in his book *The Theatre and Its Double* (1938). Though only one of his plays, *Les Cenci,* was ever produced in accordance with his theory, his ideas influenced such avant-garde movements as the LIVING THEATER and the theater of the ABSURD.

Cruikshank, George (1792–1878) English painter, illustrator, and caricaturist. His series of political caricatures for *The Scourge* (1811–16) established him as the leading political cartoonist of his generation, and he continued to satirize the policies of the Tories and Whigs in political cartoons until c. 1825. In the 1820s and '30s he produced book illustrations, notably for CHARLES DICKENS's *Sketches by "Boz"* (1836) and *Oliver Twist* (1838). In later life he embraced the cause of temperance with his series *The Bottle* (1847) and *The Drunkard's Children* (1848).

Cruikshank's "Mr. Bumble and Mrs. Corney," illustration for *Oliver Twist* by Charles Dickens, 1838.
MARY EVANS PICTURE LIBRARY

Cruise, Tom *orig.* **Thomas Cruise Mapother IV** (born 1962) U.S. actor. Born in Syracuse, N.Y., he made his screen debut in 1981 and rose to stardom in *Taps* (1981), *Risky Business* (1983), and *Top Gun* (1986). He received acclaim for his dramatic roles in *The Color of Money* (1986), *Rain Man* (1988), and *Born on the Fourth of July* (1989). His later films include *A Few Good Men* (1992), *The Firm* (1993), *Interview with the Vampire* (1994), *Mission: Impossible* (1996), *Jerry Maguire* (1996), and STANLEY KUBRICK's *Eyes Wide Shut* (1999).

cruise missile Type of low-flying strategic GUIDED MISSILE developed by the U.S. and the Soviet Union in the 1960s and '70s. The V-1 MISSILE was a precursor. Powered by JET ENGINES, cruise missiles may carry either a nuclear or a conventional warhead. They are designed to hug the ground, which makes them hard to detect by RADAR. They are launched from ships, submarines, airplanes, and the ground.

cruiser Warship built for high speed and great cruising radius, smaller than a BATTLESHIP but larger than a DESTROYER. The term originally meant FRIGATES of the sailing era, used to scout for enemy fleets and raid convoys. After 1880, it was a specific type of armored warship. By World War II, cruisers served mainly as floating bases for amphibious assaults and as protection for aircraft-carrier task forces. Today U.S. cruisers carry surface-to-air missiles vital to a fleet's air-defense screen. Nuclear propulsion has given some cruisers virtually unlimited range.

Crumb, George (Henry) (born 1929) U.S. composer. Born in Charleston, W.V., to musician parents, he studied at the University of Michigan and from 1965 taught at the University of Pennsylvania. His style is known particularly for its unusual and hauntingly evocative timbres. *Echoes of Time and the River* (1967, Pulitzer Prize) and *Ancient Voices of Children* (1970) brought him wide fame. His other works include *Madrigals, Books I–IV* (1965–70), *Night of the Four Moons* (1969), *Black Angels* (1970), *Makrokosmos I* and *II* (1972, 1973), and *Star-Child* (1977).

Crumb, R(obert) (born 1943) U.S. cartoonist. He had no formal art training, but was obsessed with drawing as a child. In 1960 he moved from his native Philadelphia to Cleveland to work for a greeting-card company. In 1967 he moved to San Francisco and became a prominent member of the hippie counterculture and a founder of the genre of underground "comix," satirical magazines that poked fun at U.S. culture. His often obscene strips with their various obsessive themes, starring such characters as Fritz the Cat, the Furry Freak Brothers, and Mr. Natural, had great influence and are still regarded as the classics of the genre.

Crusade, Children's See CHILDREN'S CRUSADE

Crusade, Stedinger See STEDINGER CRUSADE

crusader states Former territories on the Palestine coast taken by the Christian army during the first of the CRUSADES. The states were established as the kingdom of Jerusalem (1099–1187), the principality of Antioch (1098–1268), the county of Edessa (1098–1144), and the county of Tripoli (1109–1289). Threats to the states led the pope to call for future crusades.

Crusades Military expeditions beginning in the late 11th century that were organized by Western Christians in response to centuries of Muslim wars of expansion. Their objectives were to check the spread of Islam, to retake control of the Holy Land, to conquer pagan areas, and to recapture formerly Christian territories; they were seen by many of their participants as a means of redemption and expiation for sins. Between 1095, when the First Crusade was launched by Pope URBAN II at the council of CLERMONT, and 1291, when the Latin Christians were finally expelled from their kingdom in Syria, there were numerous expeditions to the Holy Land, to Spain, and even to the Baltic; the Crusades continued for several centuries after 1291, usually as military campaigns intended to halt or slow the advance of Muslim power or to conquer pagan areas. The Crusades, attempting to check this Muslim advance, initially enjoyed success, founding a Christian state in Palestine and Syria, but the continued growth of Islamic states ultimately reversed those gains. By the 14th century the Ottoman Turks had established themselves in the Balkans and would penetrate deeper into Europe despite repeated efforts to repulse them. Crusades were also called against heretics (the ALBIGENSIAN CRUSADE, 1209–29) and various rivals of the popes, and the Fourth Crusade (1202–04) was diverted against the Byzantine Empire. Crusading declined rapidly during the 16th century with the advent of the Protestant Reformation and the decline of papal authority. The Crusades constitute a controversial chapter in the history of Christianity, and their excesses have been the subject of centuries of historiography. Historians have also concentrated on the role the Crusades played in the expansion of medieval Europe and its institutions, and the notion of "crusading" has been transformed from a religio-military campaign into a modern metaphor for zealous and demanding struggles to advance the good ("crusades for") and to oppose perceived evil ("crusades against").

crush injury Effects of compression of the body (e.g., in a building collapse). Victims with severe chest and abdominal injuries usually die before help arrives. In survivors, pulse and blood pressure are usually normal at first, then blood leakage from ruptured vessels causes shock and local swelling, and blood pressure falls. Release of proteins from crushed muscles can cause kidney failure a day or two afterwards. Later, EMBOLISMS form from fat droplets that have merged after being squeezed out of fat cells and bone marrow.

crust Outermost solid part of the earth, essentially composed of a range of IGNEOUS and METAMORPHIC ROCK types. In continental regions, the crust is made up chiefly of granitic rock, whereas the composition of the ocean floor corresponds mainly to that of basalt and GABBRO. On average, the crust extends 22 mi (35 km) downward to the MANTLE, from which it is separated by the Mohorovicic discontinuity (the MOHO). The crust and top layer of the mantle together form the LITHOSPHERE.

crustacean \krəs-'tā-shən\ Any member of nearly 39,000 ARTHROPOD species (subphylum Crustacea), distributed worldwide, distinguished by having two pairs of antenna-like appendages in front of the mouth and other paired appendages near the mouth that act like jaws. Most species are marine, including SHRIMP and BARNACLES. Some, including CRAYFISH, live in freshwater habitats; others (e.g., SAND FLEAS, land CRABS, and SOW BUGS) live in moist terrestrial environments. The typical adult body is composed of a series of segments (somites) either fused or linked to each other by flexible areas that form movable joints. The carapace (shell) varies in thickness among species and must be periodically molted to allow growth. Many species of marine crustaceans are scavengers, and many (including COPEPODS and KRILL) are significant components of the diet of larger organisms. See also DECAPOD.

Cruveilhier \krūe-ve-'yā\, **Jean** (1791–1874) French pathologist and anatomist. He published a series of multivolume works on the anatomy of disease. The greatest, the beautifully illustrated *Pathological Anatomy of the Human Body* (2 vols., 1829–42) contains the first description of multiple sclerosis, depictions of gastric ulcer, and an early account of progressive muscular atrophy.

Cruz \krüs\, **Celia** (born 1924?) Cuban-U.S. singer. Cruz decided on a singing career after winning a talent show. In the early 1950s she became lead singer with the popular orchestra La Sonora Matancera, often headlining at the famous Tropicana nightclub. After Cuba's 1959 revolution the orchestra moved to Mexico, and later to the U.S. In the 1960s she released over 20 albums in the U.S., including seven with TITO PUENTE; she has since recorded dozens more. She was the subject of a 1988 BBC documentary and has appeared in films such as *The Mambo Kings* (1992).

Cruz, Sor Juana Inés de la (1651–1695) Mexican poet, dramatist, scholar, nun, and an early feminist. Born out of wedlock to a family of modest means, she was sent to relatives in Mexico City, where her great intelligence became known to the viceroy. She soon became a nun, remaining cloistered for the rest of her life. Sor Juana had one of the largest private libraries in the New World. Her most important works are the poem *Primero sueño* (1692; *Sor Juana's Dream*), which recounts the soul's quest for knowledge, and the *Respuesta* (1691; *The Answer*), her defense of women's right to knowledge.

cryogenics \,krī-ə-'je-niks\ Study and use of low-temperature phenomena. The cryogenic temperature range is from –238°F (–150°C) to ABSOLUTE ZERO. At low temperatures, matter has unusual properties. Substances that are naturally gases can be liquefied at low temperatures, and metals lose electrical RESISTANCE as they get colder (see SUPERCONDUCTIVITY). Cryogenics dates from 1877, when oxygen was first cooled to the point at which it became a liquid (–297°F, or –183°C); superconductivity was discovered in 1911. Applications of cryogenics include the storage and transport of liquefied gases, food preservation, cryosurgery, rocket fuels, and superconducting ELECTROMAGNETS.

crypt Subterranean chamber, usually under a church floor. The CATACOMBS of the early Christians were known as *cryptae,* and when churches came to be built over the tombs of saints and martyrs, subterranean chapels were built around the actual tomb. As early as the reign of CONSTANTINE I (AD 306–37), the crypt was considered a normal part of a church. Later its size was increased to include the entire space beneath the choir or chancel; the crypt of Canterbury Cathedral is an elaborate underground church with its own APSE. Many secular medieval European buildings also had richly decorated crypts.

Crypt, Canterbury cathedral (12th century), England.
A.F. KERSTING

cryptographic key See cryptographic KEY

cryptography \krip-'tä-grə-fē\ Practice of the enciphering and deciphering of messages in secret code in order to render them unintelligible to all but the intended receiver. Cryptography may also refer to the art of cryptanalysis, by which cryptographic codes are broken. Collectively, the science of secure and secret communications, involving both cryptography and cryptanalysis, is known as cryptology. The principles of cryptography are today applied to the encryption of FAX, TELEVISION, and computer NETWORK communications. In particular, the secure exchange of computer data is of great importance to banking, government, and commercial communications. See also DATA ENCRYPTION.

cryptomonad \,krip-tō-'mō-,nad\ Any small organism with two flagella that is considered both a PROTOZOAN and an alga (see ALGAE). Occurring in both fresh and salt water, cryptomonads contain pigments found only in red algae and blue-green algae (CYANOBACTERIA). They sometimes live harmlessly within other organisms. Some species conduct PHOTOSYNTHESIS. Others lack pigment-containing structures and eat organic matter, under certain conditions surviving on minerals alone.

crystal Any solid material whose ATOMS are arranged in a definite pattern and whose surface regularity reflects its internal symmetry. Each of a crystal's millions of individual structural units (unit cells) contains all the substance's atoms, molecules, or ions in the same proportions as in its chemical formula (see FORMULA WEIGHT). The cells are repeated in all directions to form a geometric pattern, manifested by the number and orientation of external planes (crystal faces). Crystals are classified into seven crystallographic systems based on their symmetry: isometric, trigonal, hexagonal, tetragonal, orthorhombic, monoclinic, and triclinic. Crystals are generally formed when a liquid solidifies or a vapor or a liquid SOLUTION can no longer retain dissolved material, which is precipitated (see PRECIPITATION). METALS, ALLOYS, MINERALS, and SEMICONDUCTORS are all crystalline, at least microscopically. (A noncrystalline solid is "amorphous.") Under special conditions, a single crystal can grow to a substantial size; examples include gemstones and some artificial crystals. Few crystals are perfect; defects affect the material's electrical behavior and may weaken or strengthen it. See also LIQUID CRYSTAL.

crystal lattice Three-dimensional configuration of points connected by lines used to describe the orderly arrangement of ATOMS in a CRYSTAL. Each point represents one or more atoms in the actual crystal. The lattice is divided into a number of identical blocks or cells that are repeated in all directions to form a geometric pattern. Lattices are classified according to their dominant symmetries: isometric, trigonal, hexagonal, tetragonal, orthorhombic, monoclinic, and triclinic. Compounds that exhibit a crystal-lattice structure include sodium chloride (table salt), cesium chloride, and boron nitride. See also SOLID-STATE PHYSICS.

Crystal Night See KRISTALLNACHT

Crystal Palace Giant glass-and-iron exhibition hall in Hyde Park, London, that housed the Great Exhibition of 1851. It was taken down and rebuilt (1852–54) at Sydenham Hill, where it survived until its destruction by fire in 1936. Designed by the greenhouse builder Sir Joseph Paxton (1801–1865), it was a remarkable assembly of prefabricated parts. Its intricate network of slender iron rods sustaining walls of clear glass established an architectural standard for later international exhibitions, likewise housed in glass CONSERVATORIES.

The rebuilt Crystal Palace at Sydenham Hill, London, designed by Sir Joseph Paxton for the Great Exhibition of 1851 (rebuilt 1852–54; destroyed 1936).
BBC HULTON PICTURE LIBRARY

crystalline rock Any rock composed entirely of crystallized minerals without glassy matter (matter without visible crystals). Intrusive igneous rocks (see INTRUSIVE ROCK) are nearly always crystalline; extrusive igneous rocks (see EXTRUSIVE ROCK) may be partly to entirely glassy. Metamorphic rocks are also always completely crystalline and are termed crystalline SCHISTS or GNEISSES. Sedimentary rocks can also be crystalline, such as crystalline limestones that precipitate directly from solution; the term is not generally applied to clastic sediments (made of fragments of preexisting rock), even though they are formed largely from the accumulation of crystalline materials.

crystallography \ˌkris-tə-ˈläg-rə-fē\ Branch of science that deals with discerning the arrangement and bonding of atoms in crystalline solids and with the geometric structure of CRYSTAL LATTICES. Classically, the optical properties of CRYSTALS were of value in mineralogy and chemistry for the identification of substances. Modern crystallography is largely based on the analysis of the DIFFRACTION of X RAYS by crystals acting as optical gratings. Chemists are able to determine the internal structures and bonding arrangements of minerals and molecules using X-ray crystallography, including the structures of large complex molecules such as proteins and DNA.

Csonka \ˈzäŋ-kə\, **Larry** *orig.* **Lawrence** (born 1946) U.S. football player. Born in Stow, Ohio, he was an All-America fullback at Syracuse Univ., noted for his straight-ahead power. As a 235-lb fullback for the Miami Dolphins (1968–74, 1979) he helped lead the team to three Super Bowls (1972–74), including two victories. In each of three consecutive years (1971–73) he rushed for over 1,000 yards. In 1972 he was a mainstay in the Dolphin's perfect 17–0–0 season. He also played for the New York Giants (1976–78).

ctenophore \ˈte-nə-ˌfōr\ *or* **comb jelly** Any of nearly 90 species (phylum Ctenophora) of usually colorless, marine invertebrates that have a series of vertical ciliary combs over their bodies. Ctenophores are sometimes mistaken for JELLYFISH. The body is round or spherical, with tentacles to capture food, and the combs beat to provide locomotion. Most species are small (not much greater than 0.1 in., or 3 mm, in diameter), but at least one species grows larger than 3 ft (1 m). Ctenophores live in almost all ocean regions, floating freely in the water. All comb jellies except one parasitic species are carnivores, consuming young mollusks and crustacean and fish larvae, COPEPODS, and other ZOOPLANKTON.

Ctesibius of Alexandria See KTESIBIOS OF ALEXANDRIA

Ctesiphon \ˈte-sə-ˌfän\ Ancient ruined city, Iraq. Located on the TIGRIS RIVER, southeast of modern BAGHDAD, it was first a Greek army camp opposite the Hellenistic city of SELEUCIA, with which it was the capital of PARTHIA in the 2nd century BC. Destroyed by the Romans in the 1st century AD, it was resettled by the Sasanian empire in the 3rd century. The Arabs conquered the city in AD 637, but abandoned it by 763 in favor of Baghdad. The site is famous for the remains of a gigantic vaulted hall, the Taq Kisra, which has one of the largest single-span brick arches in the world.

Cú Chulainn *or* **Cuchulain** \kü-ˈk̲əl-ən\ In ancient Irish Gaelic literature, a powerful warrior and the central character in the ULSTER CYCLE. The son of the god LUGUS and Dechtire, sister of CONCHOBAR MAC NESSA, he was the greatest of the warriors loyal to Conchobar. He had seven fingers on each hand, seven toes on each foot, and seven pupils in each eye. He defended Ulster single-handed at 17 against the forces of Medb, queen of Connaught. In times of rage he could become uncontrollable.

Cuauhtémoc \kwaů-ˈte-ˌmōk\ *or* **Guatimozin** \ˌgwät-ə-ˈmōt-sən\ (c. 1495–1522) Last AZTEC emperor, nephew and son-in-law of MONTEZUMA II. He became emperor on the death of Montezuma's successor in 1520, while HERNAN CORTES was marching for the second time on TENOCHTITLÁN, the Aztec capital. He defended the city during a four-month siege that left most buildings destroyed and few Indians surviving. Tortured by the Spaniards in an effort to make him reveal the location of hidden Aztec wealth, his stoicism became legendary. Later Cortés, hearing of a plot against the Spaniards, had Cuauhtémoc hanged.

Cuba *officially* **Republic of Cuba** Socialist republic, West Indies. Located 90 mi (145 km) south of Florida, it comprises the island of Cuba and surrounding small islands. Area: 42,804 sq mi (110,861 sq km). Population (1997): 11,190,000. Capital: HAVANA. The population is about one-third mulatto (black-Spanish) or black and about two-thirds white, mostly of Spanish descent. Language: Spanish (official). Religions: Roman Catholicism, Santería (both formerly discouraged). Currency: Cuban peso, U.S. dollar. The main island of Cuba is 746 mi (1,200 km) long and 25–125 mi (40–200 km) wide. About one-quarter is mountainous, with Pico Turquino at 6,476 ft (1,974 m) the highest peak; the remainder is extensive plains and basins. The climate is semitropical. Cuba was the first communist republic in the Western Hemisphere. It has a centrally planned economy that depends on the export of sugar and, to a much lesser extent, tobacco and nickel. Its cigars are considered the world's best. It is a republic with one legislative house, its head of state and government is the president. Several Indian groups, including the CIBONEY and the ARAWAK, inhabited Cuba at the time of the first Spanish contact. CHRISTOPHER COLUMBUS claimed the island for Spain in 1492, and the Spanish conquest began in 1511, when the settlement of Baracoa was founded. The native Indians were eradicated over the succeeding centuries, and African slaves, from the 18th century until slavery was abolished in 1886, were imported to work the sugar plantations. Cuba revolted unsuccessfully against Spain in the Ten Years' War (1868–78); a second war of independence began in 1895. In 1898 the U.S. entered the war (see SPANISH–AMERICAN WAR); Spain relinquished its claim to Cuba, which was occupied by the U.S. for three years before gaining its independence in 1902. The U.S. invested heavily in the Cu-

C
D

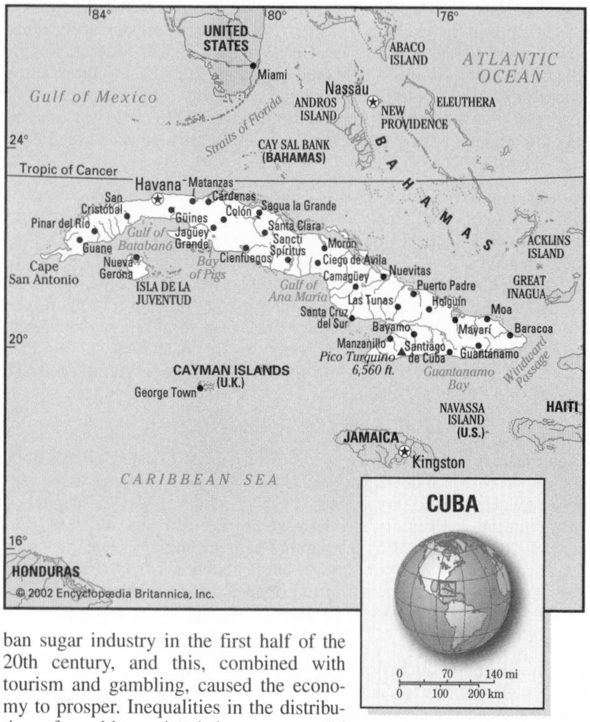

ban sugar industry in the first half of the 20th century, and this, combined with tourism and gambling, caused the economy to prosper. Inequalities in the distribution of wealth persisted, however, as did political corruption. In 1958–59 the communist revolutionary FIDEL CASTRO overthrew its longtime dictator FULGENCIO BATISTA and established a socialist state aligned with the Soviet Union, abolishing capitalism and nationalizing foreign-owned enterprises. Relations with the U.S. deteriorated, reaching a low point with the 1961 BAY OF PIGS INVASION and the 1962 CUBAN MISSILE CRISIS. In 1980 about 125,000 Cubans, including many officially labeled "undesirables," were shipped to the U.S. in the so-called Mariel Boat Lift. When communism collapsed in the U.S.S.R., Cuba lost important financial backing and its economy suffered greatly. The latter gradually improved in the 1990s with the encouragement of tourism, though diplomatic relations with the U.S. were not resumed.

Cuban missile crisis (1962) Major confrontation between the U.S. and the Soviet Union over the presence of Soviet nuclear-armed missiles in Cuba. In October 1962 a U.S. spy plane detected a ballistic missile on a launching site in Cuba. Pres. JOHN F. KENNEDY placed a naval blockade around the island, and for several days the U.S. and the Soviet Union hovered on the brink of war. NIKITA KHRUSHCHEV finally agreed to remove the missiles in return for a secret commitment from the U.S. to withdraw U.S. missiles from Turkey and never to invade Cuba. The incident fueled the nuclear arms race. See also FIDEL CASTRO.

Cubango River See OKAVANGO RIVER

Cubism Movement in the visual arts created by PABLO PICASSO and GEORGES BRAQUE in Paris between 1907 and 1914. They were later joined by JUAN GRIS, FERNAND LEGER, ROBERT DELAUNAY, and others. The name derives from a review that described Braque's work as images composed of cubes. The style was inspired by African sculpture and the later paintings of PAUL CEZANNE. A major source of ABSTRACT ART, it emphasized the flat, two-dimensional, fragmented surface of the picture plane, rejecting perspective, foreshortening, modeling, and chiaroscuro in favor of geometrical forms. Picasso's *Demoiselles d'Avignon* (1907) signaled the new style, which strongly influenced 20th-century sculpture and architecture. Cubism is recognized as a turning point in Western art.

cuckoo Any of some 60 species of tree-dwelling birds (family Cuculidae) and numerous terrestrial species found worldwide in temperate and tropical regions but most diverse in the Old World tropics. Species range from 6.5 to 36 in. (16–90 cm) long. Most are drab gray, but a few are partially or completely brightly colored or iridescent. Aside from the European cuckoo's familiar two-note call, cuckoos are best known for their habit of brood PARASITISM (see COWBIRD); their eggs resemble those of the host species (egg mimicry), and the adult cuckoo removes one or more host eggs to ensure that the substitution is indetectable (the newly hatched cuckoo may also eject eggs or nestlings).

Cuckoo (*Cuculus*).
GRAEME CHAPMAN—ARDEA, LONDON

cucumber Creeping plant *(Cucumis sativus)* of the GOURD family, probably originating in northern India and widely cultivated for its oblong fruit. It is a tender annual with a rough, succulent, trailing stem and hairy leaves with pointed lobes; the stem bears branched tendrils by which the plant can be trained to supports. Its food value is low, but its delicate flavor makes it popular for salads and relishes.

cucumber beetle Any of several leaf BEETLES (genus *Diabrotica*) that are important PESTS. They are greenish yellow, marked with black spots or stripes, and 0.1–0.5 in. (2.5–11 mm) long. The striped cucumber beetle and spotted cucumber beetle both feed on garden plants, and their larvae feed on the roots.

Cudworth, Ralph (1617–1688) English theologian and philosopher. Reared as a Puritan, he eventually adopted such Nonconformist views as the notion that church government and religious practice should be individual rather than authoritarian. He became a leader of the CAMBRIDGE PLATONISTS. In ethics, his outstanding work is *A Treatise Concerning Eternal and Immutable Morality* (1731), directed against Puritan Calvinism, RENE DESCARTES's theology, and THOMAS HOBBES's reduction of morality to civil obedience. He stressed the natural good or evil inherent in an event or act, in contrast to the Calvinist-Cartesian notion of divine law or Hobbes's concept of a secular sovereign (see INTUITIONISM, VOLUNTARISM).

Cuéllar, Javier Pérez de See Javier PEREZ DE CUELLAR

Cuernavaca \ˌkwer-nə-ˈvä-kə\ City (pop., 1990: 282,000), capital of MORELOS state, southern central Mexico. As the capital city of the Tlahuica Indians, it was known as Cuauhnáhuac. The name was changed c. 1521 when it was taken by HERNAN CORTES; it is the site of his palace, now the Morelos State House, which is decorated with murals by DIEGO RIVERA. Nearby are pre-Columbian ruins. A favorite retreat of the emperor MAXIMILIAN, the area is still popular with tourists. The University of Morelos was established there in 1953.

Cuiabá River \ˌkü-yə-ˈbä\ *formerly* **Cuyabá River** River, Brazil. Rising in central Mato Grosso state, it flows 300 mi (480 km) southwest to join the São Lourenço River. These two rivers' combined courses enter the PARAGUAY RIVER north of Corumbá. Gold deposits are found in the Cuiabá's headwaters.

Cukierman, Yizhak See Itzhak ZUCKERMAN

Cukor \ˈkyü-kər\, **George (Dewey)** (1899–1983) U.S. film director. Born in New York City, he directed plays on Broadway before going to Hollywood in 1929. His first film, *Tarnished Lady* (1931), was followed by the acclaimed *Little Women* (1933), *David Copperfield* (1935), *Camille* (1937), *The Philadelphia Story* (1940), *Gaslight* (1944), and *Born Yesterday* (1950). He directed several comedies starring KATHARINE HEPBURN and SPENCER TRACY, including *Adam's Rib* (1949) and *Pat and Mike* (1952). He was noted for his skill in working with actors, particularly women. Among his other memorable films are *Dinner at Eight* (1933), *The Women* (1939), *A Star Is Born* (1954), and *My Fair Lady* (1964, Academy Award).

Culiacán (-Rosales) \ˌkül-yə-ˈkän\ City (pop., 1990: 415,000), capital of SINALOA state, western Mexico. Located on the Culiacán River, it was founded on the site of an Indian settlement in 1531, and played an important role in early colonial days as a base for Spanish expeditions. An elaborate irrigation system in the valley provides for a variety of crops, including corn, sugarcane, tobacco, and fruits and vegetables. It is the seat of the University of Sinaloa (founded 1873).

Cullen, Countee *orig.* **Countee Porter** (1903–1946) U.S. poet of the HARLEM RENAISSANCE. Reared in New York City, he was unofficially adopted at 15 by Rev. F. A. Cullen. He won a citywide poetry contest, and later attended NYU and received an MA from Harvard, winning academic honors. His first collection of poems, *Color* (1925), received critical acclaim while he was still in college. *Copper Sun* (1927) was criticized in the black community for not giving race the attention it had in *Color.* He taught in the city's public schools from 1934 until his death.

Cullen, William (1710–1790) Scottish physician and professor. One of the first to teach in English rather than Latin, he was celebrated for his clinical lectures which he gave in the infirmary from his own notes instead of a text. He taught that life was a function of nervous energy and that muscle was a continuation of nerve. His influential classification of disease included febrile diseases, nervous diseases, diseases produced by bad bodily habits, and local diseases.

Cullinan diamond \'kə-lə-nən\ Largest gem diamond ever discovered. It weighed about 3,106 carats in rough form when it was found in 1905 at the Premier mine in Transvaal, South Africa. Named for Sir Thomas Cullinan, who had discovered the mine, the colorless stone was purchased by the Transvaal government and presented to Britain's King Edward VII. It was cut into 9 large stones and about 100 smaller ones, all flawless; they are now part of the British CROWN JEWELS.

Culloden \kə-'lä-dᵊn\, **Battle of** (April 16, 1746) Last battle of the "Forty-five Rebellion," on a moor near Inverness, Scotland. The JACOBITES, under CHARLES EDWARD STUART (the Young Pretender), were defeated by British forces under the duke of Cumberland. Some 1,000 of the Young Pretender's army of 5,000 were killed by the 9,000 Redcoats, who lost only 50 men. The battle, which lasted only 40 minutes, marked the end of any serious attempt to restore the House of STUART to the British throne.

Culpeper's Rebellion (1677–79) Popular uprising in the Albemarle section of Carolina to protest the British NAVIGATION ACTS, which denied the colonists free markets. Led by John Culpeper and George Durant, the rebels imprisoned the deputy governor (and customs collector), and other officials. They convened a legislature, chose Culpeper as governor, and ran the colony for two years. Culpeper was removed by the colony's proprietors and tried for treason but never punished.

cult Collective veneration or worship (e.g., the cult of the saints—meaning collective veneration of the saints—in Roman Catholicism). In the West, the term has come to be used for groups that are perceived to have deviated from normative religions in belief and practice. They typically have a charismatic leader and attract followers who are in some way disenfranchised from the mainstream of society. Cults as thus defined are often viewed as foreign or dangerous.

cultivar \'kəl-tə-,vär\ Any variety of a plant, originating through cloning or hybridization (see CLONE, HYBRID), known only in cultivation. In asexually propagated plants, a cultivar is a clone considered valuable enough to have its own name; in sexually propagated plants, a cultivar is a pure line (for self-pollinated plants) or, for cross-pollinated plants, a population that is genetically distinguishable.

cultivation Loosening and breaking up (tilling) of the soil. The soil around existing plants is cultivated (by hand using a hoe, or by machine using a cultivator) to destroy weeds and promote growth by increasing soil aeration and water infiltration. Soil being prepared for the planting of a crop is cultivated by a harrow or plow.

Cultivation System *or* **Culture System** Revenue system in the Dutch East Indies (Indonesia) that forced farmers to pay revenue to the Netherlands in the form of export crops or compulsory labor. The system was introduced in 1830 by governor-general Johannes van den Bosch (1780–1844). In theory, it required that a villager set aside one-fifth of his land to grow export crops (e.g., coffee, sugar) for the government and that landless peasants work for one-fifth of the year on government fields. In fact, much more land and time were required, and the system proved burdensome. Though roundly criticized in the mid-1850s, the system was not abolished until 1870.

cultural anthropology Branch of ANTHROPOLOGY that deals with the study of CULTURE and that uses the methods, concepts, and data of ARCHAEOLOGY, ETHNOGRAPHY, FOLKLORE, LINGUISTICS, and related fields in its descriptions and analyses of the diverse peoples of the world. Called social anthropology in Britain, its field of research was until the mid 20th century largely restricted to the small-scale (or "primitive"), non-Western societies that first began to be identified during the Age of Discovery. Today its field extends to all forms of human association, from village communities to corporate cultures to urban gangs. Two key perspectives used are those of holism, or understanding society as a complex, interactive whole, and cultural relativism, or the appreciation of cultural phenomena within their own context. Areas of study traditionally include social structure, law, politics, religion, magic, art, and technology. There is much debate concerning whether cultural anthropology is a science, art, or both. See also PRIMITIVE CULTURE.

Cultural Revolution *officially* **Great Proletarian Cultural Revolution** (1966–76) Upheaval launched by MAO ZEDONG to renew the spirit of the Chinese revolution. Mao feared urban social stratification in a society as traditionally elitist as China, and also believed that programs instituted to correct for the failed GREAT LEAP FORWARD showed that his colleagues lacked commitment to the revolution. He organized China's urban youths into groups called the RED GUARDS, shut down China's schools, and encouraged the Red Guards to attack all traditional values and "bourgeois things." They soon splintered into zealous rival groups, and in 1968 Mao sent millions of them to the rural hinterland, bringing some order to the cities. Within the government, a coalition of Mao's associates fought with more moderate elements, many of whom, including LIU SHAOQI and LIN BIAO, were purged and subsequently died. From 1973 to Mao's death in 1976, politics shifted between the Maoist GANG OF FOUR and the moderates headed by ZHOU ENLAI and DENG XIAOPING. After Mao's death the Cultural Revolution was brought to a close. By that time, nearly three million party members and countless wrongfully purged citizens awaited reinstatement. The post-Mao repudiation of the Cultural Revolution was profoundly disillusioning for many in China. See also JIANG QING.

cultural studies Interdisciplinary field concerned with the role of social institutions in the shaping of CULTURE. Originally identified with the Center for Contemporary Cultural Studies at the University of Birmingham (founded 1964) and with such scholars as Richard Hoggart, Stuart Hall, and Raymond Williams, today cultural studies is recognized as a discipline or area of concentration in many academic institutions and has had broad influence in SOCIOLOGY, ANTHROPOLOGY, HISTORIOGRAPHY, LITERARY CRITICISM, PHILOSOPHY, and ART CRITICISM. Among its central concerns are the place of RACE (or ethnicity), CLASS, and gender in the production of cultural knowledge.

culture Integrated pattern of human knowledge, belief, and behavior that is both a result of and integral to humankind's capacity for learning and transmitting knowledge to succeeding generations. Culture thus consists of language, ideas, beliefs, customs, taboos, codes, institutions, tools, techniques, works of art, rituals, ceremonies, and symbols. It has played a crucial role in HUMAN EVOLUTION, allowing human beings to adapt the environment to their own purposes rather than depend solely on NATURAL SELECTION to achieve adaptive success. Every human society has its own particular culture, or sociocultural system. Variation among cultures is attributable to such factors as differing physical habitats and resources; the range of possibilities inherent in areas such as language, ritual, and social organization; and historical phenomena such as the development of links to other cultures. An individual's attitudes, values, ideals, and beliefs are greatly influenced by the culture (or cultures) in which he or she lives. Culture change takes place as a result of ecological, socioeconomic, political, religious, or other fundamental changes affecting a society. See also CULTURE CONTACT, PRIMITIVE CULTURE, SOCIOCULTURAL EVOLUTION.

culture, pure See PURE CULTURE

culture contact Contact between peoples with different cultures, usually leading to change in one or both systems. Forms of culture contact traditionally include acculturation, assimilation, and amalgamation. Acculturation is the process of change in material culture, traditional practices, and beliefs that takes place when one people interferes in the cultural system of another, directly or indirectly challenging the latter to adapt to the ways of the former. Such change has characterized numerous political conquests and expansions over the centuries. Assimilation is the process whereby individuals or groups of differing ethnicity are absorbed into the dominant culture of a society—though not always completely. In the U.S., millions of European immigrants became assimilated within two or three generations owing to the upheaval of overseas relocation, the influences of the public-school system, and other forces in American life. Amalgamation (or hybridization) occurs when a society becomes ethnically mixed in a way that represents a synthesis rather than the elimination or absorption of one group by another. In Mexico, Spanish and Indian cultures became increasingly amalgamated over centuries of contact.

culture hero Mythological figure who secures for humanity the attributes of culture either in cooperation with or in opposition to the gods. The culture hero is often an animal or trickster figure, the most common motif being the animal who steals fire from the gods for the benefit of humans. In other stories the culture hero is human and must overcome the opposition of animals. In still others, the culture hero must travel to an inaccessible place to reach a life-giving or healing tree or other plant; supernatural animals may assist or obstruct him. See also PROMETHEUS.

Cumae \'kyü-mē\ Ancient city west of Naples. Probably the oldest Greek mainland colony in the west, it was home to the Cumaean SIBYL, whose cavern still exists. Founded c. 750 BC by Greeks from KHALKÍS and ERETRIA, it came to control much of the Campanian plain. Taken by the Samnites in the 5th century BC, it was subjugated by Rome in 338 BC. Under the empire it became a quiet country town. It was destroyed in AD 1205. Remains of fortifications and graves from all these periods have been found throughout the area.

Cumberland Gap National Historical Park National historical park, Tennessee. Created in 1940 to preserve the Cumberland Gap, a natural pass at 1,640 ft (500 m) through the Cumberland Plateau, it includes the Wilderness Road, blazed by DANIEL BOONE, which became the main artery that opened the Northwest Territory. The park covers 32 sq mi (83 sq km).

Cumberland Plateau Tableland that forms the western section of the APPALACHIAN MTNS. and a part of the Allegheny Plateau. It extends southwest for 450 mi (725 km) from southern West Virginia to northeastern Alabama, averages 50 mi (80 km) in width, and is 2,000–4,145 ft (600–1,263 m) high. The roughest and highest portion is a narrow ridge about 140 mi (225 km) long that forms its eastern margin in eastern Kentucky and northeastern Tennessee; the name Cumberland Mountains is generally applied to this area, which includes the CUMBERLAND GAP NATIONAL HISTORICAL PARK. The plateau has large deposits of coal, limestone, and sandstone.

Cumberland River River, Kentucky and Tennessee. It rises in southeastern Kentucky and flows west, looping through northern Tennessee before returning north to join the OHIO RIVER after a course of 687 mi (1,106 km). It drops 92 ft (28 m) at Cumberland (or Great) Falls, the site of a state park. A series of lakes on the Cumberland were developed as part of the TENNESSEE VALLEY AUTHORITY system. Wolf Creek Dam (1952) created Lake Cumberland, which extends to the base of Cumberland Falls.

Cumberland Sound Inlet of DAVIS STRAIT, Nunavut. Indenting the southeastern coast of BAFFIN ISLAND, it is 170 mi (270 km) long and 100 mi (160 km) wide. John Davis, an English navigator, sailed into the sound in 1585 in search of the NORTHWEST PASSAGE. By the late 19th century the area was noted for whaling. The Anglican church established missions early in the 20th century at settlements along its shores.

Cumbria County (pop., 1999 est.: 491,800), northwestern England. Extending along the IRISH SEA coast from Morecambe Bay to Solway Firth, it includes the famous LAKE DISTRICT. It was established in 1974, with its seat at CARLISLE. Human occupation dates from the NEOLITHIC PERIOD. The Romans constructed several roads, a series of forts, and the great complex of HADRIAN'S WALL. After the mid-10th century, northern Cumbria alternated between Scottish and English rule until it was taken by the English in 1157. Lead, silver, and iron ore have been mined in the district since the 12th century.

cumin \'kə-mən, 'kyü-mən\ Small, slender annual herb *(Cuminum cyminum)* of the carrot family, cultivated in the Mediterranean region, India, China, and Mexico. Its seeds, which are actually dried fruits, are used in many mixed spices, chutneys, and chili and curry powders; cumin is especially popular in Asian, North African, and Latin American cuisines. Its oil is used in perfumes, for flavoring liquors, and for medicinal purposes.

Cummings, E(dward) E(stlin) (1894–1962) U.S. poet and painter. Born in Cambridge, Mass., he attended Harvard University. His experience in World War I of being held in a detention camp because of a censor's error gave rise to his first prose book, *The Enormous Room* (1922). His first book of poems, *Tulips and Chimneys* (1923), was followed by 11 more. His poetry, rooted in New England traditions of dissent and self-reliance, attracted attention for its lack of capitalization, eccentric punctuation and phrasing, and often childlike playfulness, which won it a wide readership. His Norton lectures at Harvard were published as *i: six nonlectures* (1953). His paintings and drawings failed to attract as much interest as his writings.

Cuna \'kü-nə\ Chibchan-speaking Indian people who once occupied the central region of what is now Panama and the neighboring San Blas Islands and who still survive in marginal areas. In the 16th century they lived in federated villages under chiefs who wielded considerable power. They had a hierarchical society and enslaved prisoners of war. Today they live in small villages and depend on agriculture, supplemented by hunting and fishing, for subsistence.

Cunard \kyü-'närd\, **Samuel** *later* **Sir Samuel** (1787–1865) Canadian-British merchant and shipowner. Born in Halifax, Nova Scotia, he became prosperous in commerce and began laying plans in 1830 to establish mail service between England and North America. He went to England in 1838 and in 1839 cofounded the British and North American Royal Mail Steam Packet Co., known as the Cunard Line. In 1840, four Cunard liners began the first regular service across the Atlantic.

cuneiform law \ˌkyü-'nē-ə-ˌfȯrm\ Body of laws revealed by documents written in cuneiform script (see CUNEIFORM WRITING). It includes the laws of the Sumerians, Babylonians, Assyrians, Elamites, Hurrians, Kassites, and Hittites. Unlike modern legal codes, these ancient codes do not systematically treat all the rules applicable to a given area of law; rather, they treat a variety of matters but often ignore many highly important rules simply because such rules were so grounded in CUSTOM that they went unquestioned. The most important of the ancient codes is the Babylonian Code of HAMMURABI.

cuneiform writing \kyü-'nē-ə-ˌfȯrm\ System of writing employed for a number of languages of South Asia in ancient times. The original and primary writing material for cuneiform texts was a damp clay tablet, into which the scribe would press a wedge-shaped stroke with a reed stylus. A configuration of such impressions constituted a character, or sign. Proto-cuneiform signs dating from c. 3200–3000 BC were drawn rather than impressed and were largely pictographic (see PICTOGRAPHY), though these features were lost as the script evolved. A single cuneiform sign could be a logogram (an arbitrary representation of a word) or a syllabogram (a representation of the sound of a syllable). The first lan-

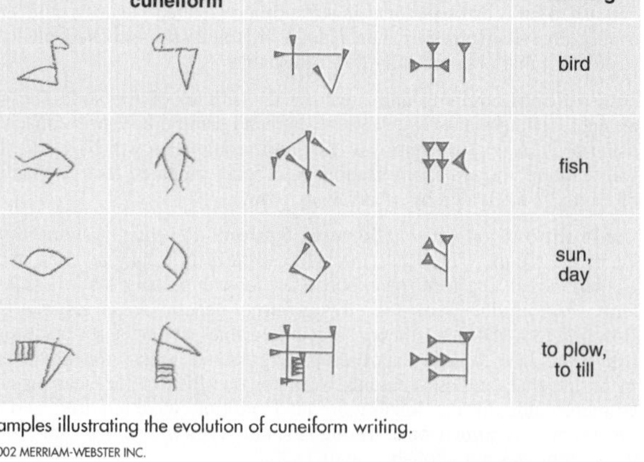

original pictograph
pictograph in position of later cuneiform
early Babylonian
Assyrian
original or derived meaning
bird
fish
sun, day
to plow, to till

Examples illustrating the evolution of cuneiform writing.

guage to be written in cuneiform was Sumerian (see SUMER). AKKADIAN began to be written in cuneiform c. 2350 BC. Later the script was adapted to other South Asian languages. Cuneiform was slowly displaced in the first millennium BC by the rise of ARAMAIC, written in an ALPHABET script of Phoenician origin. Knowledge of the value of cuneiform signs was lost until the mid-19th century, when European scholars deciphered the script.

Cunene River *or* **Kunene River** \kü-'nā-nə\ River, southwestern Angola. It flows south to enter the northern KALAHARI DESERT. Forming part of the boundary between Angola and Namibia, it passes through the NAMIB DESERT before emptying into the Atlantic Ocean after a total course of 700 mi (1,125 km).

Cunningham, Glenn (1909–1988) U.S. middle-distance runner. Born in Atlanta, Kan., he was badly burned when he was 7 and not expected to walk again. With intensive therapy and application, he overcame the odds and by high school was running competitively. He was the fastest miler in the Amateur Athletic Union in 1933 and 1935–38, and in 1934 he set a world record (4:06.7).

Cunningham, Imogen (1883–1976) U.S. photographer. Born in Portland, Ore., she began taking pictures in 1901; her earliest prints imitated contemporary academic painting. She opened a portrait studio in Seattle in 1910 and soon established a national reputation as a portrait photographer. Encouraged by EDWARD WESTON, she exhibited her plant photographs in San Francisco, where she would work for the remainder of her career. In 1932 she joined the West Coast photographers known as Group f.64. In her later years she taught at the San Francisco Art Institute.

Two Callas, by Imogen Cunningham, c. 1929.
IMOGEN CUNNINGHAM

Cunningham, Merce (born 1919) U.S. avant-garde dancer and choreographer. Born in Centralia, Wash., he joined MARTHA GRAHAM's company in 1939, where he created roles in several of her works. As an independent choreographer in 1945–52, he began his long collaboration with the composer J. CAGE. In 1952 he formed his own company, developing his interest in isolated movement and "choreography by chance." His *Suite by Chance* (1952) was the first dance performed to an electronic score. Other works include *The Seasons* (1947), *Summerspace* (1958), and *Locale* (1980).

Merce Cunningham, 1970.
JACK MITCHELL

Cuno \'kü-nō\, **Wilhelm (Carl Josef)** (1876–1933) German politician and business leader. After serving in government positions from 1907, in 1918 he became general director of the Hamburg-American Line, the largest German shipping concern. He served as chancellor of the WEIMAR REPUBLIC 1922–23, enjoying the strong support of German business and industry but failing to readjust war reparations or halt inflation. During the RUHR OCCUPATION he urged a national policy of passive resistance, which ultimately overtaxed the economy. Obliged to resign, he returned to Hamburg-American and again served as chairman 1926–33.

CUNY See CITY UNIVERSITY OF NEW YORK

cupellation \ˌkyü-pə-'lā-shən\ Separation of GOLD or SILVER from impurities by melting the impure metal in a cupel (a flat, porous dish made of a refractory material) and directing a blast of hot air on it in a special furnace. The impurities, including lead, copper, tin, and other unwanted metals, are oxidized and partly vaporized and partly absorbed into the pores of the cupel.

Cupid Ancient Roman god of love in all its varieties, identified with the Greek EROS. Cupid was the son of MERCURY and VENUS. He was usually represented as a winged infant who carried a bow and quiver of arrows, which he shot at humans to inflict wounds that inspired love or passion. He was also sometimes depicted as a beautiful youth. Though generally considered beneficent, he could be mischievous in matchmaking, often at his mother's behest.

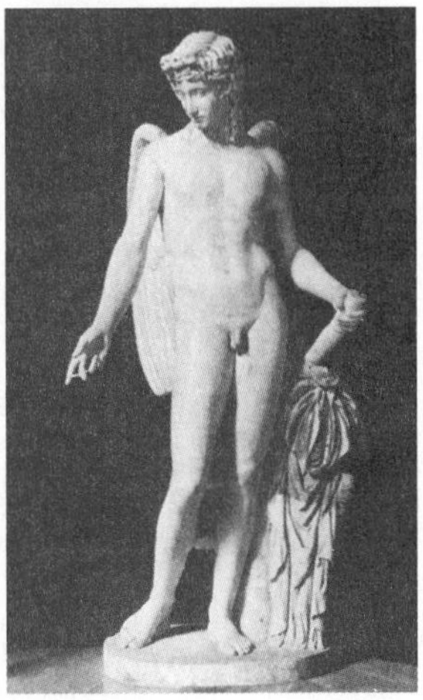

Cupid, classical statue; in the Museo Archeologico Nazionale, Naples.
ALINARI—ART RESOURCE/EB INC.

Curaçao \ˌkůr-ə-'sō, ˌkyůr-ə-'saů\ Largest island (pop., 1994 est.: 147,000) of the NETHERLANDS ANTILLES. It is located in the Caribbean Sea north of the coast of Venezuela; WILLEMSTAD is its chief town. It occupies 171 sq mi (444 sq km) and has the best natural harbor in the West Indies. First visited by Europeans in 1499, it was settled by the Spanish in 1527; Sephardic Jews from Portugal migrated there in the 1500s, originating the oldest continuously inhabited Jewish community in the Western Hemisphere. The Dutch West India Co. gained control of the island in 1634. It was awarded to the Netherlands by the 1815 Treaty of PARIS. Internal self-government was granted in 1954. Products include oranges, Curaçao liqueur, and aloes. The chief industry is the refining of oil from Venezuela; tourism is of growing importance.

curare \kyů-'rär-ē\ Organic compound, an ALKALOID that occurs in various tropical American plants (mostly of the genus *Strychnos*) and causes PARALYSIS. Crude preparations have long been used by native people as an arrow poison. It relaxes skeletal MUSCLE by competing with ACETYLCHOLINE at nerve endings. A purified form is used in ANESTHESIOLOGY to prevent any movement of patients during surgery. Small amounts bring profound relaxation, with prompt recovery and few complications. It has other medical uses as a relaxant and diagnostic aid.

curassow \'kyůr-ə-ˌsō\ Any of numerous tropical American bird species (family Cracidae); strictly defined, one of 7–12 species in which the male is glossy black and has a curled crest of feathers and a brightly colored bill ornament. The smaller female is brownish and unornamented. Curassows have delicious flesh and are hunted as game. Large species (to nearly 40 in., or 100 cm) include the great curassow *(Crax rubra)*, found from Mexico to Ecuador; the helmeted curassow *(Pauxi pauxi)* of the Venezuelan and Colombian mountains; and the razor-billed curassow *(C. mitu)* of the Amazon, which is critically endangered.

curia \'kyůr-ē-ə\ In European medieval history, a court, or group of persons who attended a ruler at any given time for social, political, or judicial purposes. The ruler and curia made policy decisions (as on war, treaties, finances, church relations), and under a powerful ruler the curia often became active as a court of law. Indeed, curiae became so loaded down with judicial work that the work gradually was delegated to special groups of judges. In England, the Curia Regis (King's Court) began at the time of the Norman Conquest (1066) and lasted to about the end of the 13th century. It was the germ from which the higher courts of law, the Privy Council, and the Cabinet were to spring. See also ROMAN CURIA.

Curia, Papal See ROMAN CURIA

Curia, Roman See ROMAN CURIA

Curie, Frédéric Joliot- See Frederic JOLIOT-CURIE

Curie \kyů-'rē\, **Marie** *orig.* **Maria Sklodowska** (1867–1934) Polish-born French physical chemist. Born in Warsaw, she studied at the Sorbonne (from 1891). Seeking for RADIOACTIVITY, recently discovered by HENRI BECQUEREL in uranium, in other matter, she found it in thorium. In

1895 she married fellow physicist Pierre Curie (1859–1906). Together they discovered the elements polonium and radium, and they distinguished alpha, beta, and gamma radiation. For their work on radioactivity (a term she coined), the Curies shared a 1903 Nobel Prize with Becquerel. After Pierre's death, Marie was appointed to his professorship and became the first woman to teach at the Sorbonne. In 1911 she won a Nobel Prize for discovering polonium and isolating pure radium, becoming the first person to win two Nobel Prizes. She died of leukemia caused by her long exposure to radioactivity. In 1995 she became the first woman whose own achievements earned her the honor of having her ashes enshrined in the Pantheon in Paris. See also FREDERIC JOLIOT-CURIE.

Marie Curie.
THE GRANGER COLLECTION, NEW YORK CITY

Curitiba \ˌku̇r-ə-ˈtē-bə\ City (metro. area pop., 1995 est.: 2,270,000), capital of Paraná state, southern Brazil. It lies about 3,050 ft (930 m) above sea level in the Brazilian Highlands near the headwaters of the IGUAZÚ RIVER. Founded in 1654 as a gold-mining camp, it became the state capital in 1854. From the early 19th century it received many European settlers, and immigration continued during the 20th century with the arrival of Syrians and Japanese. It is a modern commercial center. Its cathedral (1894) was inspired by that of BARCELONA.

curl In mathematics, a DIFFERENTIAL OPERATOR that can be applied to a vector-valued function (or vector field) in order to measure its tendency to spin. It consists of a combination of the function's first partial derivatives. One of the more common forms for expressing it is:

$$\text{curl } \mathbf{v} = i\left(\frac{\partial \mathbf{v}_3}{\partial y} - \frac{\partial \mathbf{v}_2}{\partial z}\right) + j\left(\frac{\partial \mathbf{v}_1}{\partial z} - \frac{\partial \mathbf{v}_3}{\partial x}\right) + k\left(\frac{\partial \mathbf{v}_2}{\partial x} - \frac{\partial \mathbf{v}_1}{\partial y}\right)$$

in which $\mathbf{v}$ is the vector field ($\mathbf{v}_1$, $\mathbf{v}_2$, $\mathbf{v}_3$), and $\mathbf{v}_1$, $\mathbf{v}_2$, $\mathbf{v}_3$ are functions of the variables x, y, and z, and **i, j,** and **k** are unit vectors in the positive x, y, and z directions, respectively. In fluid mechanics, the curl of the fluid velocity of the vector field (i.e., of the fluid itself) is called the vorticity or the rotation because it measures the field's tendency to rotate around a given point.

curlew Any of eight species (genus *Numenius*) of shorebirds having a sickle-shaped bill that curves downward at the tip, a streaked, gray or brown body, and a long neck and legs. Curlews breed inland in temperate and subarctic regions of the Northern Hemisphere and migrate far south. They eat insects and seeds during migration but feed on worms and fiddler crabs while wintering on marshes and coastal mudflats. The eastern curlew is the largest species (24 in., or 60 cm, long); the common, or Eurasian, curlew, almost as large, is the largest European shorebird. The Eskimo curlew is now virtually extinct.

Curley, James Michael (1874–1958) U.S. politician. Born in Boston, he served in the U.S. House of Representatives (1911–14). As mayor (1914–18, 1922–26, 1930–34, 1947–50), he dominated Boston politics for 50 years. He owed much of his success to serving the needs of Irish immigrants in exchange for votes, spending large sums on job-rich public-works projects that nearly bankrupted Boston, and continued to do so as governor of Massachusetts (1935–37). He returned to the House of Representatives (1943–47). His last mayoral term included a five-month jail term for mail fraud before Pres. HARRY TRUMAN pardoned him. Curley was among the most colorful big-city Democratic bosses; his career inspired Edwin O'Connor's 1956 novel *The Last Hurrah.*

curling Game in which two teams of four players each slide a round stone by means of a gooseneck handle on the top over a 138-ft (42-m) stretch of ice toward a target circle. The object is to deliver the stone closest to the center (called the house). Each player delivers two stones, which average 40 lbs (18.1 kg) apiece, often applying a curl to the stone's trajectory. The player's teammates use a broom to sweep the ice ahead of the oncoming stone in order to facilitate a longer slide or to adjust the arc of the curl. Blocking and knocking out an opponent's stones are important strategies of the sport. Curling originated in Scotland in the early 16th century. World championships have been held since 1959 and are usually dominated by Canadians and Scandinavians. In 1998 curling became a medal sport in the Winter Olympic Games.

Curling players sweeping vigorously as a teammate's stone nears the house.
MALAK FROM MILLER SERVICES LTD.

currant Any shrub of at least 100 species in the genus *Ribes,* in the GOOSEBERRY family, native to temperate climates of the Northern Hemisphere and western South America. The Rocky Mountains are especially rich in species. The flavorful, juicy red or black berries are used chiefly in jams and jellies. Black currants are used in lozenges and for flavoring, and are occasionally fermented. Currants are extremely high in vitamin C and also supply calcium, phosphorus, and iron. The name currant is also given to a seedless raisin frequently used in cooking.

Currant (*Ribes*).
WALTER CHANDOHA

currency In industrialized nations, the portion of the national MONEY SUPPLY (consisting of banknotes and government-issued paper money and coins) that does not require endorsement to serve as a medium of exchange. Since the abandonment of the GOLD STANDARD, governments have not been obligated to repay the holders of currency in any form of precious metal. Consequently, the volume of currency has been determined by the actions of the government or CENTRAL BANK and not by the supply of precious metals. In less developed societies, items such as livestock or tobacco may serve as currency.

current, density See DENSITY CURRENT

current, electric See ELECTRIC CURRENT

Currie, Arthur William *later* **Sir Arthur** (1875–1933) Canadian military leader. Born in Napperton, Ontario, he was a businessman in Victoria, British Columbia, before enlisting in the militia. Given command of a battalion in 1914, he won distinction in several World War I battles and succeeded a British general as commander of four divisions of the Canadian Corps. After the war he served as the first general in the Canadian army. In 1920 he became principal and vice chancellor of McGill Univ.

Currier and Ives U.S. lithographers. Nathaniel Currier (1813–1888), born in Roxbury, Mass., served apprenticeships in Boston and Philadelphia before he set up in business in New York City in 1835. He hired the New York-born James Merritt Ives (1824–1895) as a bookkeeper and made him his partner in 1857. Currier & Ives met and greatly increased the public demand for graphic images by publishing fine-quality, black-and-white and hand-colored lithographs (see LITHOGRAPHY) depicting disasters, political satire, views of city life, outdoor country scenes, and sentimental domestic scenes. They established outlets across the country and in London. Between 1840 and 1890 they published more than 7,000 titles. The firm continued under their sons until 1907.

curry (from Tamil *kari,* "sauce") Food, dish, or sauce in Indian cuisine seasoned with curry powder, a mixture of pungent spices including TURMERIC, CUMIN, CORIANDER, cayenne pepper, and FENUGREEK. Some of the curry spices are known for their antiseptic and preservative properties. Curries have been a part of South Asian cookery since antiquity. In India, such spice mixtures are known as *masala.* The primarily vegetarian curries of southern India are the most pungent, often containing hot chilies.

Those of northern India, where lamb and poultry are served, avoid hot or pungent ingredients.

curtain Panel of decorative fabric hung to regulate the admission of light at a window and to prevent drafts. Curtains made of a heavy material, arranged to fall in ornamental folds to the floor, are called draperies. Mosaics from the 2nd–6th century show curtains suspended from rods spanning arches. From the Middle Ages to the 19th century, curtains ranged in style from simple to ornamented; beds were often curtained on all sides. In the 20th century, synthetic fabrics and mechanical devices for opening and closing curtains simplified their installation and use.

curtain wall Nonbearing wall of glass, metal, or masonry attached to a building's exterior structural frame. After World War II, low energy costs gave impetus to the concept of the tall building as a glass prism, an idea originally put forth by LE CORBUSIER and LUDWIG MIES VAN DER ROHE in their visionary projects of the 1920s. The U.N.'s Secretariat Building (1949), with its green-tinted glass walls, helped set a worldwide standard for skyscrapers.

Curtis, Charles Gordon (1860–1953) U.S. inventor. Born in Boston, he became an associate of THOMAS ALVA EDISON. He patented the Curtis steam TURBINE in 1896. Its principles are still used in large ocean liners and other naval vessels; General Electric Co. has used it worldwide in its power installations. Curtis is also credited with inventing the first U.S. gas turbine, held many patents for diesel-engine improvements, and helped develop propulsion mechanisms for naval torpedoes.

Curtis, Cyrus (Herman Kotzschmar) (1850–1933) U.S. publisher. Born in Portland, Me., he began publishing a local weekly there. When fire destroyed his plant, he moved to Boston; there he published *The People's Ledger* magazine, which he continued after his move to Philadelphia in 1876. In 1879 he founded *The Tribune and Farmer,* from the women's section of which he formed the *LADIES' HOME JOURNAL*. In 1890 he organized the Curtis Publishing Co. Later acquisitions included *The Saturday Evening Post* (1897); *The Country Gentleman* (1911); the *Philadelphia Public Ledger* (1913); the *Philadelphia Press* and *The North American,* morning newspapers that he merged with the Curtis papers (1925); and the *PHILADELPHIA INQUIRER* (1930). His daughter Mary Louise (1876–1970) founded the CURTIS INSTITUTE OF MUSIC and named it for her father.

Curtis, Tony *orig.* **Bernard Schwartz** (born 1925) U.S. film actor. Born into an immigrant family in New York City, he appeared on Broadway before going to Hollywood in 1949. He acted in adventure films, becoming known for his pretty face and his Bronx accent, then earned acclaim for his roles in *Sweet Smell of Success* (1957) and *The Defiant Ones* (1958). His success in BILLY WILDER'S *Some Like It Hot* (1959) was followed by roles in other light comedies in the 1960s.

Curtis Cup Golf trophy awarded since 1932 to the winner of a biennial amateur women's match played between teams from Britain and the U.S. Teams consist of six players, two alternates, and a captain. The cup was donated by Harriot and Margaret Curtis, amateur golf champions of the early 20th century. Teams play six 18-hole foursomes and 12 18-hole singles matches.

Curtis Institute of Music Conservatory in Philadelphia, founded in 1924 by Mary Louise Curtis Bok (1876–1970), wife of EDWARD BOK, and named for her father, CHARLES G. CURTIS. Her endowment was adequate to assure scholarships for gifted students from all over the world. Many eminent musicians have served on its faculty, including W. LANDOWSKA, B. MARTINU, R. SERKIN, Leopold Auer (1845–1930), Gregor Piatigorsky (1903–1976), William Primrose (1903–1982), Leonard Rose (1918–1984), and Efrem Zimbalist (1889–1985). Graduates include S. BARBER, LEONARD BERNSTEIN, and G.C. MENOTTI.

Curtiss, Glenn (Hammond) (1878–1930) U.S. aviation pioneer. Born in Hammondsport, N.Y., he initially built engines for motorcycles. In 1904 he built a motor for a dirigible. In 1908 he flew an experimental plane to win the first public U.S. flight of 1 km (0.6 mi). In 1911 he built the first practical SEAPLANE and was awarded the first contract to build airplanes for the U.S. Navy. His factories later supplied planes to Britain and Russia as well. His best-known plane was the JN-4, or "Jenny," a trainer widely used in World War I and later by barnstormers. His company later merged with the Wright Co. to become the Curtiss-Wright Corp.

Curtiz, Michael \'kůr-tis\ *orig.* **Mihály Kertész** (1888–1962) Hungarian-U.S. film director. He directed films in Hungary and elsewhere in Europe before he was invited to Hollywood by Warner Brothers in 1926. He directed more than 100 Warner Brothers films, including adventure movies with ERROL FLYNN such as *Captain Blood* (1935), *The Adventures of Robin Hood* (1938), and *The Sea Hawk* (1940). His many other notable films include *Yankee Doodle Dandy* (1942), the hugely successful *Casablanca* (1942, Academy Award), *Mildred Pierce* (1945), *Life with Father* (1947), and *White Christmas* (1954).

curvature Measure of the rate of change of direction of a curved line or surface at any point. In general, it is the reciprocal of the radius of the circle or sphere of best fit to the curve or surface at that point. This notion of best fit derives from the principle that only one circle can be drawn though any three points not on the same line. The radius of curvature at the middle point is approximately equal to the radius of that one circle. This calculation becomes more exact the closer the points are. The precise value is found using a LIMIT. Because a straight line can be thought of as an arc of a circle of infinite radius, its curvature is zero.

curve In mathematics, an abstract term used to describe the path of a continuously moving point (see CONTINUITY). Such a path is usually generated by an equation. The word can also apply to a straight line or to a series of line segments linked end to end. A closed curve is a path that repeats itself, and thus encloses one or more regions. Simple examples include CIRCLES, ELLIPSES, and POLYGONS. Open curves such as PARABOLAS, HYPERBOLAS, and spirals have infinite length.

Curzon (of Kedleston) \'kər-zᵊn\, **Marquess** *orig.* **George Nathaniel Curzon** *known as* **Lord Curzon** (1859–1925) British viceroy of India (1898–1905) and foreign secretary (1919–24). Eldest son of a baron, he studied at Oxford and entered Parliament in 1886. A world tour left him with an infatuation for Asia, and in 1891 he became undersecretary of state for India. In 1898 he became viceroy of India. There he reduced taxes and ordered immediate punishment of any Briton who ill-treated Indian nationals. He presided over the unpopular Partition of BENGAL and resigned after a clash with Lord KITCHENER. He later served in the cabinets of H. H. ASQUITH and DAVID LLOYD GEORGE.

Curzon Line Demarcation line between Poland and Soviet Russia. The British foreign secretary, Lord CURZON, proposed it as a possible armistice line in the Russo-Polish War of 1919–20. His plan was not accepted, and the final peace treaty (1921) provided Poland with almost 52,000 sq mi (135,000 sq km) of land east of the line. With the outbreak of World War II, the Soviet Union revived the line, claiming all the territory east of it. In 1945 a Soviet–Polish treaty officially designated a line almost identical to the Curzon Line as their mutual border.

Cush *or* **Kush** Ancient country, NUBIA region of the NILE RIVER valley. In the 2nd millennium BC it was subject to Egypt. In the 8th century BC its King Piankhi invaded and conquered Egypt. It was ruled from 716 BC by Piankhi's brother Shabaka, who also invaded Egypt, and set up the 25th dynasty; he subsequently made MEMPHIS his capital. In the early 6th century BC the Cushite kingdom's capital was transferred to MEROË, where the Cushites ruled for another 900 years.

Cushing, Caleb (1800–1879) U.S. lawyer and diplomat. Born in Salisbury, Mass., he served in the U.S. House of Representatives 1835–43. As U.S. commissioner to China (1843–45), he negotiated the Treaty of Wanghia (1844), which opened five Chinese ports to U.S. trade and established the principle of extraterritoriality. He later served as U.S. attorney general (1853–57), U.S. counsel at the Geneva Conference (1871–72) to settle the *ALABAMA* CLAIMS, and minister to Spain (1874–77).

Cushing \'kůsh-iŋ\, **Harvey Williams** (1869–1939) U.S. surgeon. Born in Cleveland, he taught principally at Harvard University and became known as the leading neurosurgeon of the early 20th century, developing many procedures and techniques still basic to brain surgery and greatly reducing its mortality rate. The leading expert in the diagnosis and treatment of intracranial tumors, he was also the first to ascribe to pituitary-gland malfunction what is now known as Cushing's disease (see CUSHING'S SYNDROME). He wrote numerous scientific works, including a *Life of Sir William Osler* (1925, Pulitzer Prize).

Cushing's syndrome Metabolic disorder named for HARVEY WILLIAMS CUSHING, caused by adrenal-cortex overactivity, usually due to other diseases. If caused by a PITUITARY-GLAND tumor, it is called Cushing's disease. Symptoms include obesity of the trunk and face ("moon face"), muscle wasting, high blood pressure, easy bruising, osteoporosis, diabetes mellitus, and fat between the shoulders ("buffalo hump"). Cushing's disease also includes changes in blood vessels and endocrine glands. Excess glucocorticoid hormones, whether produced by the adrenal gland or given as drugs, cause the symptoms, which are treated by surgery, radiation, cortisol-blocking drugs, or ending of steroid treatment. Cortisol treatment may be necessary after surgery. Heart, blood-vessel, and kidney changes and osteoporosis may persist after symptoms subside.

Cushman, Charlotte (Saunders) (1816–1876) U.S. actress. She made her opera debut in her native Boston at 19, but her singing voice soon failed and she turned to the stage. In 1837 she first played her most popular role, Meg Merrilies in *Guy Mannering,* and became the first native-born U.S. star. From 1842 she managed a theater in Philadelphia, where she starred with WILLIAM MACREADY in *Macbeth.* In 1854–55 she toured England to great acclaim. Noted for her powerful emotional reach, she portrayed Lady Macbeth and such male roles as Romeo and Hamlet.

Charlotte Saunders Cushman as Meg Merrilies in *Guy Mannering.*
BY COURTESY OF THE LIBRARY OF CONGRESS, WASHINGTON, D.C.

cusk *or* **torsk** Long-bodied food fish *(Brosme brosme)* of the COD family, found along the bottom in deep, offshore waters on either side of the North Atlantic. It is a small-scaled fish with a large mouth and a barbel (fleshy feeler) on its chin. It has one dorsal and one anal fin, both long and both connected to the rounded tail. It may grow about 3–3.5 ft (90–110 cm) long. It varies from yellowish or brownish to a slaty color and when young may be vertically barred with yellow.

cusp In architecture, the intersection of lobed or scalloped forms, particularly in arches (cusped arches) and TRACERY. Thus the three lobes of a trefoil (cloverleaf form) are separated by three cusps. Cusped forms appear in early Islamic work and were especially common in the Moorish architecture of North Africa and Spain. The form was adopted wholeheartedly by European GOTHIC ARCHITECTURE.

custard apple Any of various *Annona* species of shrubs or small trees of the family Annonaceae, native to the New World tropics and Florida. The family is the largest in the magnolia order and contains approximately 1,100 species of plants in 122 genera. Many species in the family are valuable for their large, pulpy fruits. Others are valued for their timber, and still others as ornamentals. Leaves and wood are often fragrant. The fruit is a berry. The small, tropical American custard apple *(Annona reticulata)* bears fruits with reddish-yellow, sweetish, custardlike flesh. Other species include the sweetsop *(A. squamosa)* and the soursop *(A. muricata).* Bark, leaves, and roots of many species are important in folk medicine.

Custard apple (*Annona reticulata*).
WALTER DAWN

Custer, George Armstrong (1839–1876) U.S. cavalry officer. Born in New Rumley, Ohio, he graduated from West Point and at 23 became a brigadier general. His vigorous pursuit of Confederate troops under Gen. ROBERT E. LEE in retreat from Richmond hastened Lee's surrender in 1865. In 1874 he led U.S. troops to investigate rumors of gold in South Dakota's BLACK HILLS, a sacred Indian hunting ground. The resulting gold rush led to hostile encounters with the Indians. In 1876 the 36-year-old Custer commanded one of two columns of a planned attack against Indians camped near Montana's Little Bighorn River. He rashly decided to attack without the other column, and in the Battle of the LITTLE BIGHORN he and all his troops were killed.

custom In law, long-established practice common to many or to a particular place or institution and generally recognized as having the force of law. In England during the Anglo-Saxon period, local customs formed most laws affecting family rights, ownership and inheritance, contracts, and personal violence. The Norman conquerors granted the validity of customary law, adapting it to their feudal system. In the 13th–14th century, English law was given statutory authority under the crown, making the "customs of the realm" England's COMMON LAW. See also CULTURE, FOLKLORE, MYTH, TABOO.

customs duty See TARIFF

customs union Trade agreement by which a group of countries charges a common set of TARIFFS to the rest of the world while allowing free trade among themselves. It is a partial form of economic integration, intermediate between free-trade zones, which allow mutual FREE TRADE but lack a common tariff system, and common markets, which both utilize common tariffs and allow free movement of resources including capital and labor between members. Well-known customs unions include the Zollverein, a 19th-century organization formed by several German states under Prussian leadership, and the European Economic Community, which passed through a customs-union stage on the path to fuller economic integration. See also EUROPEAN COMMUNITY, GENERAL AGREEMENT ON TARIFFS AND TRADE, NORTH AMERICAN FREE TRADE AGREEMENT, WORLD TRADE ORGANIZATION.

Custoza \kü-'stōt-sə\, **Battles of** Two attempts at Custoza, Italy, to end Austrian control over northern Italy. In the first battle (July 24, 1848), an Austrian army under JOSEPH RADETZKY defeated the Sardinians, led by CHARLES ALBERT. In the second battle (June 24, 1866), as part of an Italian effort to acquire Austrian-held Venetia, a disorganized Italian army of 120,000 men, led by VICTOR EMMANUEL II, was defeated by an 80,000-man Austrian force. Despite its defeats, Italy subsequently obtained Venetia in the Treaty of Vienna (1866).

cut glass Glassware characterized by a series of facets, or patterns, cut into its surface. A marked pattern is roughed out on a glass object with a revolving abrasive wheel; the pattern is then smoothed by a sandstone wheel and polished in an acid bath. The Romans introduced a crude form of glass cutting in the 1st century AD. Modern glass cutting developed in Germany in the late 17th century with the production of a heavy, colorless crystal glass. After BOHEMIAN GLASS became popular, English and Irish glassmakers adopted the technique. The prismatic styles of their products, notably WATERFORD GLASS, became popular in the U.S. after 1780.

Cuthbert, St. (634/35–687) English saint. A shepherd, Cuthbert entered the Northumbrian monastery of Melrose in 651 after receiving a divine vision. When plague struck 10 years later, he aided the afflicted, reportedly performing miracles. In 664 he became prior of LINDISFARNE, where he instituted a severe rule. In 676 he retired to the islet of Inner Farne, where he devoted himself to prayer. His efforts to protect birds made him one of the earliest wildlife conservationists.

cutthroat trout Black-spotted game fish *(Salmo clarki)* of the SALMON family, found in western North America. The cutthroat trout is named for the bright red streak beneath its lower jaw. Considered a good table fish, it strikes at flies, baits, and lures. It reaches a weight of 4 lbs (1.8 kg). Many cutthroat trout migrate to sea when they can reach it. Like oceanic forms of other trout species, these fish are called sea trout and may not reenter freshwater for several years.

cutting In botany, a plant section originating from the STEM, LEAF, or ROOT and capable of developing into a new plant. The cutting is usually placed in warm, moist sand. Many plants, especially horticultural and garden varieties, are propagated through cuttings; by the use of new techniques, many other plants formerly not susceptible to propagation through cuttings have more successfully reproduced. The plants that develop from cuttings are CLONES. See also GRAFT, LAYERING.

cutting horse Light saddle horse trained to cut (isolate) LIVESTOCK, especially cattle, from herds. Most are QUARTER HORSES, with the intelligence, speed, and ability to make quick starts, stops, and turns. A well-trained cutting horse can maneuver an animal away from a herd and into a corner with little direction from a rider or, in some cases, without a rider.

cuttlefish Any of about 100 species of marine CEPHALOPODS in the order Sepioidea, characterized by a thick, internal calcium-containing shell called the cuttlebone. Species range between 1 and 35 in. (2.5–90 cm) in length and have a somewhat flattened body bordered by a pair of narrow fins. All have eight arms and two longer tentacles used to capture prey. Suction disks are located on the arms and at the tips of the tentacles. Cuttlefish inhabit tropical or temperate coastal waters. They feed mainly on CRUSTACEANS, small fishes, and each other. They are used by humans as food, as a source of ink, and for the cuttlebone, a dietary supplement for cage birds.

Cuttlefish (*Sepia officinalis*).
DOUGLAS P. WILSON

cutworm LARVA of certain species of owlet MOTHS (family Noctuidae). The cutworm (not a true worm) is a serious insect pest of tobacco and other crops. Some species attack such plants as corn, grasses, tomatoes, and beans at night, severing roots and stems near ground level. Other species live underground and feed on plant roots.

Cuvier \kü̅-'vyā\, **Georges (-Léopold-Chrétien-Frédéric-Dagobert)** *later* **Baron Cuvier** (1769–1832) French zoologist and statesman who established the sciences of comparative ANATOMY and PALEONTOLOGY. As a staff member at the Museum of Natural History in Paris, he published *Le règne animal distribué d'après son organisation* (1817; "The Animal Kingdom, Distributed According to Its Organization") that described his "correlation of parts" theory, in which every animal organ is functionally related to all its other organs and that an animal's functions and habits determine its anatomic form. Cuvier's classification of all animals into four completely discrete groups was a significant advance over the system of CAROLUS LINNAEUS. He applied his functional concept to the study of fossils, postulating that huge land upheavals and floods were the principal factor in the creation and destruction of species. Though the theory did not last, Cuvier's work put paleontology on a firm empirical foundation. As Napoleon's inspector of public instruction, he helped establish France's provincial universities, and he also served as chancellor of the University of Paris.

Cuyabá River See CUIABÁ RIVER

Cuyahoga River \ˌkī-ə-'hō-gə, ˌkī-ə-'hō-gə\ River, northeastern Ohio. It flows past AKRON, where it drops into a deep valley and turns north, emptying into Lake ERIE at CLEVELAND. It is navigable for lake freighters for only about 5 mi (8 km) of its total length of about 80 mi (130 km). It was at one time so severely polluted that it caught fire; by the late 1970s, antipollution measures had substantially improved its condition. The Cuyahoga Valley National Recreation Area covers about 32,000 acres (12,950 hectares) of river valley between Akron and Cleveland.

Cuyp \'kœip\, **Aelbert Jacobsz(oon)** (1620–1691) Most famous member of a family of Dutch landscape painters. He was trained by his father, Jacob Gerritsz Cuyp (1594–after 1651), and influenced by JAN VAN GOYEN. He lived most of his life in his native Dordrecht, painting animals and birds, portraits, historical pictures, and most notably river scenes and landscapes with cattle and figures bathed in a subtle glow of light and atmosphere. The Italianate style favored in Utrecht, one of Holland's artistic centers, is evident in his work. Many of his surviving paintings are signed but few are dated.

Cuyuni River \kü-'yü-nē\ River, northern South America. Rising in Venezuela and flowing through Guyana, it is about 350 mi (560 km) long. Forming the Venezuela–Guyana boundary for some 60 mi (100 km), it then flows southeast to join the Mazaruni River before entering the ESSEQUIBO RIVER. Rapids impede navigation, but the river is important for its alluvial gold and diamonds.

Cuzco \'kü-skō\ City (pop., 1993: 256,000), southern central Peru. It is located high in the ANDES at an elevation of 11,152 ft (3,399 m). Founded in the 11th century, it was once the capital of the vast INCA empire and was known as the "City of the Sun." Spanish conquistador FRANCISCO PIZARRO captured the city in 1533. It suffered major earthquake damage in 1950, though many sites have since been restored. Nearby ruins include an ancient Inca fortress, the city of MACHU PICCHU, and the Temple of the Sun. Its cathedral (1654) and university (1692) date from the colonial era.

Cwmbrân \kům-'brän\ Town (pop., 1981: 44,000), seat of GWENT county, Wales. One of 32 new towns established in Britain after World War II to relieve congestion and encourage development, Cwmbrân was designated a new town in 1949 in an area of small and decaying industrial villages. Its industries include automobile-parts production.

cyanide \'sī-ə-ˌnīd\ Any compound containing the combining group of chemical formula —CN. Ionic (see ION, IONIC BOND) and organic cyanide compounds differ in chemical properties, but both are toxic, especially the ionic ones. Cyanide poisoning inhibits cells' oxidative (see OXIDATION-REDUCTION) processes; it is extremely rapid, and an ANTIDOTE must be given promptly. Cyanides occur naturally in certain seeds (e.g., apple seeds, wild cherry pits). Cyanides, including hydrogen cyanide (HCN, or hydrocyanic acid), are used industrially in the production of acrylonitrile and acrylic fibers and synthetic rubber and other plastics as well as in electroplating, case-hardening of iron and steel, fumigation, and concentration of ORES.

cyanide process *or* **MacArthur-Forrest process** Method of extracting SILVER and GOLD from their ORES by dissolving them in a dilute solution of sodium CYANIDE or potassium cyanide. The process—invented in 1887 by the Scottish chemists John S. MacArthur, Robert W. Forrest, and William Forrest—includes contacting the finely ground ore with the cyanide solution, separating unwanted solids from the clear solution, and recovering the precious metals from the solution by precipitation with zinc dust.

cyanite See KYANITE

cyanobacteria \ˌsī-ə-ˌnō-bak-'tir-ē-ə\ *or* **blue-green algae** Any of a large group of prokaryotic, mostly photosynthetic organisms. Though classified as BACTERIA, they resemble the eukaryotic ALGAE in many ways, including some physical characteristics and ecological niches, and were at one time treated as algae. They contain certain pigments, which, with their chlorophyll, often give them a blue-green color, though many species are actually green, brown, yellow, black, or red. They are common in soil and in both salt and fresh water, and they can grow over a wide range of temperatures, from Antarctic lakes under several meters of ice to Yellowstone's hot springs. They are often among the first species to colonize bare rock and soil. Some are capable of NITROGEN FIXATION; others contain pigments that enable them to produce free oxygen as a byproduct of PHOTOSYNTHESIS. Under proper conditions (including pollution by nitrogen wastes) they can reproduce explosively, forming dense concentrations called blooms, usually colored an opaque green. Cyanobacteria played a large role in raising the level of free oxygen in the atmosphere of early earth.

Cybele See GREAT MOTHER OF THE GODS

cyberlaw Body of law bearing on the world of computer NETWORKS, especially the INTERNET. As traffic on the Internet has increased, so have the number and kind of legal issues surrounding the technology. Hotly debated issues include the OBSCENITY of some on-line sites, the right of PRIVACY, FREEDOM OF SPEECH, regulation of electronic commerce, and the applicability of COPYRIGHT laws.

cybernetics Science of regulation and control in animals (including humans), organizations, and machines when they are viewed as self-governing whole entities consisting of parts and their organization. It was conceived by NORBERT WIENER, who coined the term in 1948. Cybernetics views communication and control in all self-contained complex systems as analogous. It differs from the empirical sciences (physics, biology, etc.) in not being interested in material form but in organization, pattern, and communication in entities. Because of the increasing sophistication of computers and the efforts to make them behave in humanlike ways, cybernetics today is closely allied with ARTIFICIAL INTELLIGENCE and ROBOTICS, and it draws heavily on ideas developed in information theory.

cycad \'sī-kəd\ Any of the palmlike woody plants that constitute the order Cycadales, containing four families: Cycadaceae, Zamiaceae, Stangeriaceae, and Boweniaceae. Cycads have crowns of large, feathery compound leaves and CONES at the ends of their branches. Some have tall, unbranched, armorlike trunks; others have partially buried stems with swollen trunks. Slow-growing cycads are used as ornamental conservatory plants, but some survive outdoors in temperate regions. The stems of some cycads yield starch that is edible if thoroughly cooked. The young leaves and seeds of others also are edible.

Cyclades \'sī-klə-ˌdēz\ *Greek* **Kikládhes** \kē-'klä-t͟hēs\ Group of about 220 islands, southern Aegean Sea. They cover a land area of 976 sq mi (2,528 sq km), and constitute the Cyclades department (pop., 1991: 94,000) of Greece, which has its capital at Ermoupolis. Their name refers to the ancient tradition that they formed a circle around the sacred island of DELOS. The chief islands are ANDROS, Tinos, NAXOS, Amorgos, MELOS, Paros, Syros, Kea, Kithnos, Serifos, Ios, and THÍRA. They were the center of a Bronze Age culture, the Cycladic, noted for its white marble idols, and later belonged to the MYCENAEAN culture in the 2nd millennium BC. Colonized by Ionians in the 10th–9th century BC, they later were successively held by Persians, Athenians, Ptolemaic Egypt, and Macedonia. Ruled by Venice after the early 13th cent, the islands fell to the Turks in 1566. They became part of Greece in 1829. The economy is now based on tourism and on the export of wine, hides, pottery, and handicrafts.

cyclamen \'sī-klə-mən\ Any of about 15 species of flowering perennial herbaceous plants that make up the genus *Cyclamen,* in the PRIMROSE family (Primulaceae), native to the Middle East and southern and central Europe. The florist's cyclamen *(C. persicum),* the best-known species, is an indoor plant cultivated for its attractive white to pink to deep red flowers. Long-stalked, roundish, or kidney-shaped leaves, often variously marked, grow from the base of the plant, which has no aboveground stem. Solitary flowers grow on stalks less than 12 in. (30 cm) tall.

cycling Use of the BICYCLE in competitive sport or in recreation. The classic professional races are held mainly in Europe; the first was held in Paris in 1868. There are basically two types of race: road races and track races. The first U.S. cycling competition, a six-day race, was held in 1891. Six-day racing was reintroduced to Europe as a two-man team event in the 20th century, but it has largely died out in the U.S. The first TOUR DE FRANCE, the premier race, was held in 1903. Cycling has been part of the Olympics since the first modern games in 1896. Events include a variety of open-road and circuit races for both men and women.

cyclone Any large system of winds that rotates about a center of low atmospheric pressure in a counterclockwise direction north of the equator and in a clockwise direction south of it. Anticyclones rotate in the opposite directions: clockwise north of the equator and counterclockwise south of it. Cyclones occur chiefly in the midlatitudes, often over the oceans. Cyclones that form in the tropics are smaller than cyclones elsewhere, but they tend to be more violent and can cause considerable damage (see TROPICAL CYCLONE).

Cyclops \'sī-ˌkläps\ In GREEK MYTHOLOGY, any of several one-eyed giants. In the *Odyssey,* the Cyclopes were cannibals who lived in a faraway land (traditionally Sicily). ODYSSEUS was captured by POLYPHEMUS, but escaped being devoured by blinding the giant. According to HESIOD, there were three Cyclopes (Arges, Brontes, and Steropes) who forged thunderbolts for ZEUS. In a later tradition, they were assistants to HEPHAESTUS in this task. Apollo destroyed them after one of their thunderbolts killed ASCLEPIUS.

cyclotron \'sī-klə-ˌträn\ PARTICLE ACCELERATOR that accelerates charged atomic or SUBATOMIC PARTICLES in a constant MAGNETIC FIELD. It consists of two hollow semicircular ELECTRODES, called dees, in a large evacuated cylindrical box. An alternating ELECTRIC FIELD between the dees continuously accelerates the particles from one dee to the other, while the magnetic field guides them in a circular path. As the speed of the particles increases, so does the radius of their path, and the particles spiral outward. In this manner, a cyclotron can accelerate protons to energies of up to 25 million electron volts.

Cydones \sī-'dō-nēz\, **Demetrius** (1324?–1398?) Byzantine humanist scholar, statesman, and theologian. After studying under a Greek scholar, he made Greek translations of AUGUSTINE and THOMAS AQUINAS. He was twice prime minister of the Byzantine empire (1369–83, 1391–96). An academy of Greek culture that he established in Venice in 1390 diffused Greek thought throughout Italy, stimulating the Italian Renaissance. A convert to Latin Catholicism, he worked unsuccessfully for East–West Christian unity; in his *Symbouleutikoi* ("Exhortations") he vainly encouraged the Byzantine people to unite with the Latins against the Turks. He is considered the most brilliant Byzantine writer of the 14th century.

Cygnus A \'sig-nəs\ Brightest cosmic source of RADIO WAVES in the sky, lying in the constellation Cygnus, about 700 million light-years from earth. Because of its peculiar appearance, it was once thought to be two galaxies colliding, but this would not account for its immense energy output. Recent observations suggest that it is a relatively nearby QUASAR whose central source is heavily obscured by a surrounding dust cloud. See also ACTIVE GALACTIC NUCLEUS.

cylinder See PISTON AND CYLINDER

cylinder seal Small stone cylinder engraved in INTAGLIO on its surface to leave impressions when rolled on wet clay. It first appeared c. 3400–2900 BC and is considered to be one of the finest artistic achievements of Mesopotamia. The earliest examples used geometric or animal patterns; later seals incorporated the owner's name and depicted a variety of motifs. They were used to mark personal property and make documents legally binding. The seals were adopted in Egypt and the Indus civilization.

cymbal Percussion instrument consisting of a circular metal plate that is struck with a drumstick or two such plates that are struck together. Cymbals are of great antiquity (dating back to at least 1200 BC) and universality. They reached Europe by the 13th century AD. They were uncommon in Western orchestras until the JANISSARY music craze of the late 18th century. Though Asian cymbals are often flat, Middle Eastern and Western cymbals usually have a central concave dome, or boss, so that only the edges touch when they are clashed. The finest cymbals have long been manufactured in Turkey by means of closely guarded techniques. In popular music, cymbals are not clashed manually; instead, a cymbal suspended on a sticklike stand may be brushed or struck, and horizontal "hi-hat" cymbals are clashed lightly by use of a pedal mechanism.

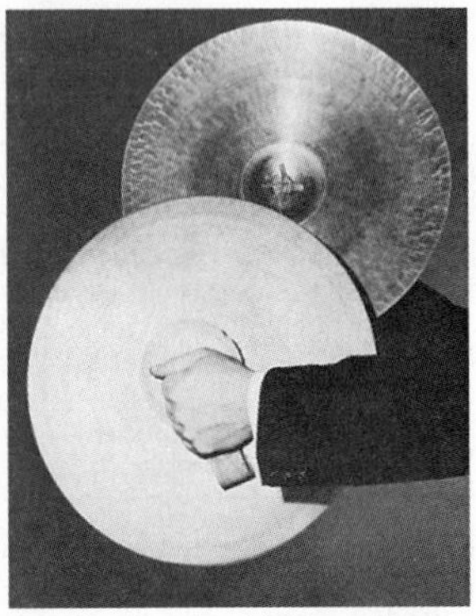

Pair of modern hand-held symphonic orchestral cymbals.
BY COURTESY OF AVEDIS ZILDJIAN COMPANY

Cynewulf *or* **Kynewulf** \'kin-ə-ˌwu̇lf\ *or* **Cynwulf** \'kin-ˌwu̇lf\ (fl. 8th or 9th century AD) Anglo-Saxon poet. He is the author of four Old English poems from late-10th-century manuscripts: *Elene,* about St. Helena; *The Fates of the Apostles,* on the mission and death of each Apostle; *The Ascension,* part of a trilogy by different authors; and *Juliana,* a life of St. Juliana. Nothing is known of the poet outside of the text; its evidence suggests he was a learned cleric of Northumbria or Mercia. Runic characters woven into the text are thought to spell his name.

Cynics \'si-niks\ Greek philosophical sect that flourished from the 4th century BC to the 6th century AD. Antisthenes (c. 445–365 BC), a disciple of SOCRATES, is considered the founder of the movement, but DIOGENES OF SINOPE was its paradigm. Named principally for their meeting place, the Cynosarges, the Cynics considered virtue—including a life of poverty and self-sufficiency and the suppression of desires—to be the sole good, but they were distinguished more for their unconventional manners and way of life than for any system of thought. The Cynics influenced the development of STOICISM.

cypress Any of about 20 species of ornamental and timber evergreen CONIFERS constituting the genus *Cupressus* of the family Cupressaceae, which includes more than 130 species found throughout the world. The leaves are usually paired or in threes and are small and scalelike. A few of the many economically important genera in the cypress family are *Cupressus, Thuja* (ARBORVITAE), *Calocedrus* (incense cedar), and *Juniperus* (JUNIPER). Arborvitae, cypress, and juniper are especially important as timber sources or ornamentals. They also contain useful oils, resins, and tannins. See photograph on following page.

Italian cypress (*Cupressus sempervirens*).
W.H. HODGE

cypress, bald See BALD CYPRESS

Cyprian \'sip-rē-ən\, **St.** *Latin* **Thascius Caecilius Cyprianus** (c. AD 200–258) Early Christian theologian and church father. Born in Carthage, he converted to Christianity c. AD 246. Within two years he was elected bishop of Carthage, and in 250 he went into hiding to escape the Decian persecution, when many Christians apostatized. The following year he returned; bishops in council supported his assertions that the church could remit the sin of apostasy, that bishops in council had final disciplinary authority, and that even unworthy laity must be accepted. In disputes with the bishop of Rome, Cyprian asserted that the people and their bishop constituted the church, that there was no "bishop of bishops" in Rome, that all bishops equally possessed the Holy Spirit, and that their consensus expressed the church's unity. He was martyred under Valerian.

Cyprus *officially* **Republic of Cyprus** *Greek* **Kypros** \'kē-pròs\ *Turkish* **Kibris** \'kē-bris\ Island nation, northeastern Mediterranean Sea. Area: 3,572 sq mi (9,251 sq km). Population (1997): 860,000 (whole island). Capital: NICOSIA (Lefkosia). Cyprus is currently divided into two de facto states. The Republic of Cyprus, the internationally recognized government, occupies the southern two-thirds of the island. Its population (1997: 662,000) is predominantly Greek. Language: Greek (official). Religion: Eastern Orthodoxy. Currency: Cyprus pound. The Turkish Republic of Northern Cyprus occupies the northern third of the country. Its population (1997: 198,000) is overwhelmingly Turkish. Language: Turkish (official), English. Religion: Islam. Currency: Turkish lira. The third-largest island in the Mediterranean, Cyprus lies about 40 mi (65 km) south of Turkey. It is largely mountainous, with a fertile heartland and coastal plains. Mount Olympus is its highest peak, at 6,401 ft (1,951 m). The climate is Mediterranean. Cyprus has a free-enterprise economy based mainly on trade and manufacturing, and it ranks high in the world in merchant shipping. The internationally recognized government is a multiparty republic with a unicameral legislature; its head of state and government is the president. Cyprus was inhabited by the early NEOLITHIC AGE; by the late BRONZE AGE it had been visited and settled by MYCENAEANS and Achaeans, who introduced Greek culture and language, and it became a trading center. By 800 BC PHOENICIANS had begun to settle there. Ruled over the centuries by the Assyrian, Persian, and Ptolemaic empires, it was annexed by Rome in 58 BC. It was part of the Byzantine empire in the 4th–11th century AD. It was conquered by RICHARD I in 1191. A part of the Venetian empire from 1489, it was taken by Ottoman Turks in 1573. In 1878 the British assumed control, and Cyprus became a British crown colony in 1924. It gained independence in 1960. Conflict between Greek and Turkish Cypriots led to the establishment of a U.N. peacekeeping mission in 1964. In 1974, fearing a movement to unite Cyprus with Greece, Turkish soldiers occupied the northern third of the country and Turkish Cypriots established a functioning government, which obtained recognition only from Turkey. Conflict has continued to the present, and the U.N. peacekeeping mission has remained in place. Reunification talks have remained deadlocked.

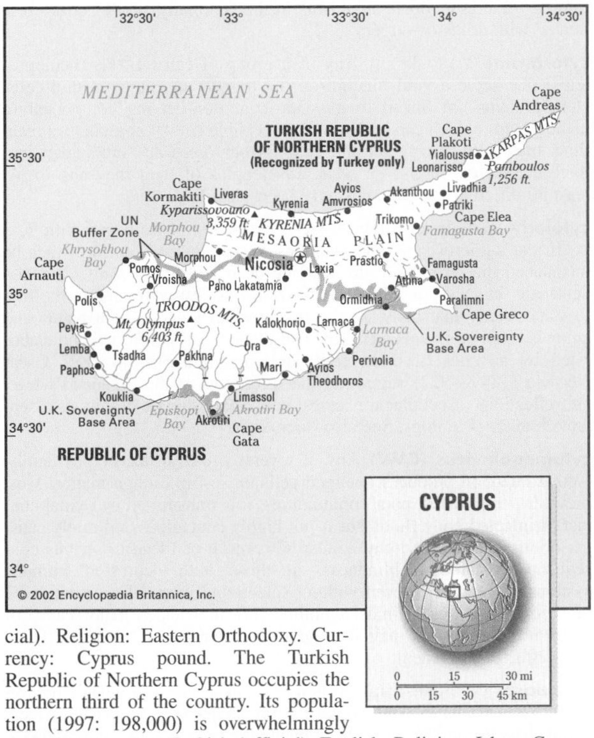

Cypselus \'sip-sə-ləs\ Tyrant of CORINTH (657?–627 BC). Though his mother belonged to the ruling Bacchiadae dynastic clan, clan members attempted to kill him at birth because his father was an outsider. When he grew up, he overthrew them and set up the first tyrant dynasty. He was encouraged in his quest for power by the oracle at DELPHI. He founded colonies in northwestern Greece, administering them through his bastard sons, including his successor, PERIANDER. Though he achieved power through demagoguery, he was reputedly so popular that he did not need a bodyguard.

Cyrano de Bergerac \'sir-ə-ˌnō-də-ˌber-zhə-'räk\, **Savinien** (1619–1655) French satirist and dramatist. He was a soldier until 1641, and studied under the philosopher Pierre Gassendi (1592–1655). He wrote plays as well as fantastical works combining science-fantasy and political satire that inspired such later writers as JONATHAN SWIFT. He became the basis of many romantic legends, including EDMOND ROSTAND's play *Cyrano de Bergerac* (1897), in which he is portrayed as a gallant and brilliant but shy and ugly lover, with a remarkably large nose (which in fact he had).

Cyrano de Bergerac, engraving after a painting.
H. ROGER-VIOLLET

Cyrenaica *or* **Cirenaica** \ˌsir-ə-'nā-ə-kə\ NE region of present-day Libya. It was colonized by the Greeks (c. 631 BC), who established five cities there. It became a Roman province in 67 BC. Arab armies conquered it in AD 642, as did the Ottomans in the 15th century. Italy colonized it in the early 20th century, but Italian forces were expelled during World War II. In 1963 it was incorporated into Libya.

Cyrenaics \ˌsir-ə-'nā-iks, ˌsī-rə-'nā-iks\ Greek school of ETHICS. CYRENE was the center of its activity and the birthplace of several of its members. Though the elder Aristippus (c. 435–366 BC), a pupil of SOCRATES, was generally recognized as its founder, the school flourished only in the late 4th century and early 3rd century BC. The Cyrenaics held that happiness consists in maximizing pleasure through rational calculation of utility. The ethical doctrines of the later Cyrenaics were eventually incorporated into EPICUREANISM.

Sanctuary of Apollo, Cyrene.
JOSEPHINE POWELL, ROME

Cyrene \sī-'rē-nē\ Ancient city, northern Africa. It was founded c. 630 BC by a group of emigrants from the island of THÍRA. Their leader, Battus, became the first king; his dynasty ruled until c. 440 BC. Under the aegis of Ptolemaic Egypt (from 323 BC), Cyrene became one of the great intellectual centers of the classical world, boasting such scholars as ERATOSTHENES and Aristippus, founder of the CYRENAICS. Taken by the Romans in 96 BC, it later declined and with the Arab conquest of AD 642 ceased to exist. Areas of the old city have been excavated, uncovering impressive ruins.

Cyril and Methodius, Sts. \'sir-əl...mi-'thō-dē-əs\ (827?–869; c. 825–884) Brothers who Christianized the Danubian Slavs. Born in Macedonia, they began missionary work among the Slavs of Moravia in 863. Gifted scholars and linguists, they translated the Holy Scriptures into the language later known as OLD CHURCH SLAVIC (or Slavonic) and are credited with inventing the Glagolithic alphabet (see CYRILLIC ALPHABET). In 868 they traveled to Rome to defend the use of a Slavic liturgy. When Cyril died, Methodius returned to Moravia as an archbishop. Known as the "apostles to the Slavs," the two brothers influenced the religious and cultural development of all Slavic peoples.

Cyril of Alexandria, St. (c. AD 375–444) Christian theologian and bishop. He became bishop of Alexandria in 412. Zealously orthodox, he closed the churches of the Novatians, a heterodox sect, and expelled the Jews from Alexandria. His greatest doctrinal conflict was with NESTORIUS over the nature of JESUS; Cyril emphasized the unity of Jesus' divine and human natures while Nestorius emphasized their distinctness. Cyril condemned Nestorius at the Council of Ephesus (431), only to be condemned himself by bishops who supported Nestorius. Eventually Nestorius was declared a heretic and a compromise on Christ's nature restored peace to the church (433).

Cyril of Jerusalem, St. (c. AD 315–386?) Early leader of the Christian church. He became bishop of Jerusalem c. 350. He was exiled three times by the Arians, but was himself suspected by the strictly orthodox many years later, at the Council of CONSTANTINOPLE (381), for his association with moderate Arians. He anticipated the doctrine of TRANSUBSTANTIATION in his writings and promoted Jerusalem as a pilgrimage center. He was named a Doctor of the Church in 1883.

Cyrillic alphabet \sə-'ril-ik\ ALPHABET used for RUSSIAN, Serbian (see SERBIAN AND CROATIAN LANGUAGE), BULGARIAN and Macedonian, BELARUSIAN, UKRAINIAN, and many non-Slavic languages of the former Soviet Union, as well as Khalka Mongolian (see MONGOLIAN LANGUAGES). The history of the Cyrillic alphabet is complex and much disputed. It is clearly derived from 9th-century Greek uncial capital letters, with the non-Greek letters probably taken from the Glagolitic alphabet, a highly original alphabet in which (along with Cyrillic) OLD CHURCH SLAVIC was written. A commonly held hypothesis is that followers of Sts. CYRIL AND METHODIUS developed Cyrillic in the southern Balkans around the end of the 9th century. The 44 original Cyrillic letters were reduced in number in most later alphabets used for vernacular languages, and some wholly original letters introduced, particularly for non-Slavic languages.

Cyrus the Great *or* **Cyrus II** (c. 585–529? BC) Conqueror and founder of the ACHAEMENIAN empire. The grandson of Cyrus I (fl. late 7th century BC), he came to power by overthrowing his maternal grandfather, the king of the Medes. The empire he developed was thenceforth centered on Persia and included Media, Ionia, Lydia, Mesopotamia, Syria, and Palestine. Cyrus conquered by diplomacy as well as by force. The subject of a rich legend in Persia and Greece (recorded by XENOPHON and others), he was called the father of his people. He appears in the Bible as the liberator of the Jews held captive in Babylon. He died battling nomads in Central Asia. His legacy is the founding not only of an empire but of a culture and civilization that continued to expand after his death and lasted for two centuries. He exerted a strong influence on the Greeks and ALEXANDER THE GREAT. Awarded heroic qualities in legend, he has long been revered by Persians almost as a religious figure. In 1971 Iran celebrated the 2,500th anniversary of his founding of the monarchy.

cyst \'sist\ Enclosed sac within body tissues. It has a distinct MEMBRANE and generally contains liquid. Most cysts are benign, but several kinds may be malignant or precancerous. Benign cysts often press on nearby organs and require removal. Formed by overproduction of epithelium (surface tissue of anatomical structures), cysts may become detached from surrounding structures and move freely. They can contain natural secretions, abnormal breakdown products, or, in infections, bacteria, larval parasites, and microbial products. Some organs, including the kidney, liver, and breast, can become filled with cysts as a result of cystic diseases that may be dangerous or may hide more serious diseases. See also TUMOR.

cysteine \'sis-tə-,ēn\ Sulfur-containing nonessential AMINO ACID. In PEPTIDES and PROTEINS, the sulfur atoms of two cysteine molecules are bonded to each other to make cystine, another amino acid. The bonded sulfur atoms form a disulfide bridge, a principal factor in the shape and function of skeletal and CONNECTIVE-TISSUE proteins and KERATIN and other structural proteins acquire their shape and are able to function.

cystic fibrosis \'sis-tik-fī-'brō-səs\ **(CF)** *or* **mucoviscidosis** \,myü-kō-,vis-ə-'dō-səs\ Inherited metabolic disorder characterized by production of thick, sticky mucus. It is recessive (see RECESSIVENESS) and the most common inherited disorder (about 1 per 2,000 live births) in those of European ancestry. Concentrated mucous secretions in the lungs plug the bronchi, making breathing difficult, promoting infections, and producing chronic cough, recurrent pneumonia, and progressive loss of lung function, the usual cause of death. The secretions interfere with digestive ENZYMES and block nutrient absorption. Abnormally salty sweat is the basis for diagnosis of cystic fibrosis. Treatment includes enzyme supplements, a diet high in calories, protein, and fat, vigorous physical therapy, and antibiotics. Persons with cystic fibrosis once seldom survived beyond childhood; now more than half reach adulthood, though males are usually sterile.

cystitis \sis-'tī-təs\ INFLAMMATION of the urinary bladder (see URINARY SYSTEM). Infections with bacteria, viruses, fungi, or parasites usually spread from nearby sites. Symptoms include burning pain during and right after urination, unusually urgent or frequent urination, and lower back pain. Women, with a shorter urethra than men, are more susceptible to cystitis, most resulting from *E. coli* bacteria from the rectum. Acute cystitis, usually bacterial, causes swelling, bleeding, small ulcers and cysts, and sometimes abscesses. Recurrent or persistent infection can lead to chronic cystitis, with bladder-wall thickening. Diagnosis is made by finding bacteria or other organisms in the (normally sterile) urine. It is treated with drugs or surgery.

cytochrome \'sī-tə-,krōm\ Any of a group of cell PROTEINS (hemoproteins) that serve a vital function in the transfer of energy within cells. Hemoproteins are linked to a nonprotein, iron-bearing component (a heme group), which can undergo the reversible OXIDATION-REDUCTION reactions that yield energy for the cell. Cytochromes are subdivided into three classes depending on what wavelengths of light they absorb. At least 30 different cytochromes have been identified.

cytology \sī-'tä-lə-jē\ Study of CELLS. Its earliest phase began with ROBERT HOOKE's microscopic investigations of cork in 1665, during which he introduced the term "cell" to describe dead cork cells. MATTHIAS JAKOB SCHLEIDEN (in 1838) and THEODOR SCHWANN (1839) were among the first to state clearly that cells are the fundamental units of both plants and animals. This pronouncement (the cell theory) was confirmed and elaborated by a series of discoveries and interpretations. In 1892 Oscar Hertwig (1849–1922) suggested that processes at the organism's level are reflections of cellular processes, thus establishing cytology as a separate branch of biology. See also PHYSIOLOGY.

cytomegalovirus (CMV) Any of several VIRUSES in the herpes family. Active infection produces enlarged cells enclosing foreign matter. Most prevalent in crowded, poor communities, it is transmitted by sexual contact or infected body fluids but is not highly contagious and rarely causes serious illness in healthy adults; however, it can lead to serious consequences, including blindness, in those with depressed immune systems. In newborns, even without spleen and liver enlargement (10% of cases), CMV is the most common infection and a major cause of congenital deafness; it may also induce retardation and blindness. There is no effective treatment.

cytoplasm \'sī-tə-,pla-zəm\ Portion of a eukaryotic cell outside the NUCLEUS. The cytoplasm contains all the organelles (see EUKARYOTE) except the nucleus itself. The organelles include the mitochondria, CHLOROPLASTS, the ENDOPLASMIC RETICULUM, the Golgi apparatus (which packages large molecules for transport), and LYSOSOMES and peroxisomes. The cytoplasm also contains the CYTOSKELETON and the cytosol (the fluid mass that surrounds the various organelles).

cytosine \'sī-tə-,sēn\ Organic compound of the PYRIMIDINE family, often called a base, consisting of a single ring, containing both nitrogen and carbon atoms, and an amino group. It occurs in combined form in NUCLEIC ACIDS and several COENZYMES. In DNA its complementary base is GUANINE. It or its corresponding NUCLEOSIDE or NUCLEOTIDE may be prepared from DNA by selective techniques of HYDROLYSIS.

cytoskeleton \'sī-tə-ˌske-lə-tᵊn\ System of microscopic filaments or fibers, present in the CYTOPLASM of eukaryotic cells (see EUKARYOTE), that organizes other cell components, maintains cell shape, and is responsible for cell locomotion and for movement of the organelles within it. Three major types of filaments make up the cytoskeleton: actin filaments, MICROTUBULES, and intermediate filaments. Actin filaments occur as constantly changing bundles of parallel fibers; they help determine cell shape, help the cell adhere to surfaces, help the cell move, and assist in cell division during MITOSIS. Intermediate filaments are very stable structures that form the cell's true skeleton; they anchor the NUCLEUS within the cell and give the cell its elastic properties.

czar *or* **tsar** \'zär, '(t)sär\ Byzantine or Russian emperor. The title, derived from "caesar," was used in the Middle Ages to refer to a supreme ruler, particularly the Byzantine emperor. With the fall of the Byzantine empire in 1453, the Russian monarch became the only remaining Orthodox monarch, and the Russian Orthodox clergy considered him a possible new supreme head of Orthodox Christianity. IVAN IV the Terrible was the first to be crowned czar, in 1547. Though theoretically wielding absolute power, he and his successors were actually limited by the power of the Orthodox Church, the Boyar Council, and the successive legal codes of 1497, 1550, and 1649. In 1721 PETER I changed his title to "emperor of all Russia," but he and his successors continued to be popularly called czars.

Czartoryski family \chär-tò-'ris-kē\ Leading noble family of Poland in the 18th century, known as the Familia. It first achieved widespread power through the efforts of Prince Michal Fryderyk Czartoryski (1696–1775) and his brother August. The Familia, which sought the enactment of constitutional reforms, attained the height of its influence in the court of AUGUSTUS III. The family estate at Pulawy was confiscated in 1794, during the third Partition of POLAND. However, the Familia continued to wield significant power, notably through the princes Adam Kazimierz Czartoryski (1734–1823), a patron of the arts, and Adam Jerzy Czartoryski (1770–1861), who worked for the restoration of Poland.

Czech language *formerly* **Bohemian language** West SLAVIC LANGUAGE spoken by close to 12 million people in the historical regions of Bohemia, Moravia, and southwestern Silesia, all now in the Czech Republic, and in emigré communities, including perhaps close to a million speakers in North America. The earliest Old Czech texts date from the late 13th century. The distinctive orthographic system of Czech, which adds diacritics to letters of the LATIN ALPHABET to denote consonants that did not exist in Latin and to mark vowel length, was introduced in the early 15th century and is associated with the religious reformer JAN HUS. The system was later adopted by other Slavic languages using the Latin alphabet, including SLOVAK, SLOVENE, and Croatian (see SERBIAN AND CROATIAN LANGUAGE). When Czech was revived as a literary language in the early 19th century, JOSEF DOBROVSKY based his codification of the language largely on the norms of 16th-century Czech, as exemplified in the Kralice Bible (1579–93), an authoritative translation. This decision has resulted in a wide gulf between Standard Czech, the literary language, and Common Czech, the spoken language, with several transitional registers bridging them.

Czech Republic *Czech* **Ceská Republika** \'ches-kä-rā-'pùb-li-kə\ *formerly (1918–92), with Slovakia,* **Czechoslovakia** Republic, central Europe. Area: 30,450 sq mi (78,866 sq km). Population (1999 est.): 10,289,621. Capital: PRAGUE. Czechs make up nine-tenths of the population; Slovaks are the largest minority. Language: Czech (official). Religion: Roman Catholicism, Protestantism. Currency: koruna. The landlocked Czech Republic is dominated by the Bohemian Massif, a ring of mountains rising to 3,000 ft (900 m) to encircle the Bohemian Plateau. The MORAVA RIVER valley, known as the Moravian Corridor, separates the Bohemian Massif from the CARPATHIAN MOUNTAINS. Woodlands are a characteristic feature of the Czech landscape; most regions have a moderate oceanic climate. The economy has been privatized since the collapse of communism and is now largely market-oriented. It is a multiparty republic with two legislative houses; its head of state is the president, and the head of government is the prime minister. Until 1918, the history of what is now the Czech Republic was largely that of BOHEMIA. In that year the independent republic of Czechoslovakia was born through the union of Bohemia and MORAVIA with SLOVAKIA. Czechoslovakia came under the domination of the Soviet Union after World War II, and from 1948 to 1989 it was ruled by a communist government. Its growing political liberalization was suppressed by a Soviet invasion in 1968 (see PRAGUE SPRING). After communist rule collapsed in 1989–90, separatist sentiments emerged among the Slovaks, and in 1992 the Czechs and Slovaks agreed to break up their federated state. On January 1, 1993, the Czechoslovakian republic was peacefully dissolved and replaced by two new countries, the Czech Republic and Slovakia, with the region of Moravia remaining in the former. In the late 1990s the Czech Republic started membership talks with the EUROPEAN UNION, and in 1999 it entered NATO.

Czerny \'cher-nē\, **Karl** (1791–1857) Austrian composer, teacher, and pianist. Son of a musician, he made his piano debut at 9 and began study with LUDWIG VAN BEETHOVEN at 10. A brilliant pianist, he later became a famous piano teacher; his students included Sigismond Thalberg (1812–1871) and F. LISZT. Though his compositions include six symphonies, six piano concertos, many piano trios and quartets, and 11 piano sonatas, he is known today almost exclusively for his hundreds of piano exercises and études.

Czestochowa \ˌchen(t)-stə-'kō-və\ City (pop., 1996 est.: 259,000), southern central Poland, situated on the WARTA RIVER. The two original settlements of Old Czestochowa (founded 13th century) and Jasna Góra (14th century) merged in 1826. Noted for its wealth by the 15th century, the city resisted sieges by the Swedes in 1655 and 1705 but was occupied by the Germans in World Wars I and II. Industries include textiles, paper, steel, iron, chemicals, and food products. The famous painting of Our Lady of Czestochowa ("The Black Madonna") is kept in an ancient monastery.

D-Day See Normandy Campaign

da Gama, Vasco See Vasco da Gama

Da Nang *formerly* **Tourane** Seaport city (pop., 1992 est.: 383,674), central Vietnam. It was first ceded to France in 1787, and after 1858 it became a French concession beyond the jurisdiction of the protectorate. It increased in importance after the partition of Vietnam in 1954, and during the Vietnam War it was the site of a U.S. military base. Its port has an excellent deepwater harbor; its manufactures include textiles and machinery.

Da Ponte \dä-'pōn-tā\, **Lorenzo** *orig.* **Emmanuele Conegliano** (1749–1838) Italian poet and librettist. When his Jewish father converted to marry a Catholic, he adopted the name of the local bishop. He took priestly orders in 1768, while teaching literature and publishing poetry. At odds with the authorities for his progressive views, he was expelled from the Venetian republic in 1779 for adultery. In 1783 he was appointed court poet for Vienna's Italian theater. There he wrote a remarkable series of over 40 opera librettos, including the masterpieces *The Marriage of Figaro* (1786), *Don Giovanni* (1787), and *Così fan tutte* (1790) for W.A. Mozart. Court intrigue forced him to leave Vienna in 1791. He settled in New York in 1805, taught at Columbia College, wrote his colorful memoirs, and helped establish Italian opera in the city.

da Sangallo the Younger \dä-säŋ-'gäl-lō\, **Antonio (Giamberti)** (1483–1546) Italian architect. He was the nephew of the architects Giuliano da Sangallo (1445?–1516) and Antonio da Sangallo the Elder (1455–1535). Throughout his career, Antonio worked on St. Peter's Basilica, first as Donato Bramante's assistant and after 1520 as chief architect. His imposing Palazzo Farnese in Rome (1534–46), a fortresslike Florentine-style palace, exercised immense influence well into the 19th century. His wooden model of St. Peter's (1539–46) still stands in the Vatican Museum.

Da xue *or* **Ta hsüeh** \'dä-'shwe\ (Chinese: "Great Learning") Short Chinese text generally attributed to Confucius and his disciple Zengzi. For centuries it existed only as a chapter of the *Li ji* (see Five Classics); it gained renown when republished as one of the Four Books. It states that world peace is impossible unless a ruler first regulates his own country, but that no ruler can do this without first setting his own household in order, which requires personal virtue. Zhu Xi's preface explains that the text is a means to personal development, instructing each individual to cultivate benevolence, righteousness, propriety, and wisdom.

Da Yu *or* **Ta Yu** \'dä-'yü\ One of China's three legendary emperors, supposed founder of the Xia dynasty. His years of strenuous labor provided outlets to the sea through dredging and made the world suitable for human habitation. See also Shun, Yao.

dabbling duck Any of about 43 species (tribe Anatini; including 38 species in genus *Anas*) of ducks found worldwide, chiefly on inland waters, and most common in temperate regions of the Northern Hemisphere. Strongly migratory, dabbling ducks include some of the world's finest game birds: the black duck, the gadwall, the garganey, the mallard, the pintail (perhaps the world's most abundant waterfowl), the shoveler, the teals, and the wigeons. They feed mainly on water plants, which they obtain by tipping-up in shallows, and infrequently by diving. They often forage near the shore for seeds and insects. They have a flat, broad bill, float high in the water, and are swift fliers. Males are slightly larger and more boldly colored than females.

Common, or northern, pintail (*Anas acuta*).

Dabrowska \dȯ^{n}m-'brȯf-skä\, **Maria** *or* **Maria Dombrowska** *orig.* **Marja Szumska** (1889–1965) Polish writer and literary critic. She lived and studied in various European countries in her early years. She is best known for her epic narrative *Nights and Days* (4 vols., 1932–34), a family saga on the theme of the human potential for development within uncertain circumstances. She also published four volumes of short stories, as well as plays, essays (including a series on Joseph Conrad), and translations (including the diary of Samuel Pepys). Long active in political and social causes, she was given a state funeral despite having protested Communist censorship.

Dacca See Dhaka

dace Any of various small, slim, active freshwater fishes of the carp family (Cyprinidae). In England and Europe, the dace *(Leuciscus leuciscus)*, a relative of the European chub, inhabits streams and rivers. It is a small-headed, silvery fish that grows to 10–12 in. (25–30 cm) long and weighs 1–1.5 lbs (0.5–0.7 kg). It lives in schools and eats plant and animal material. It is a good bait and sport fish but is not highly valued as food. In North America, the name is applied to various small cyprinids found in creeks and bogs, mostly in the central and southern U.S.

Dachau \'dä-ˌk̲au̇\ First Nazi concentration camp in Germany, established in 1933. It became the model and training center for all other SS-organized camps. In World War II the main camp was supplemented by about 150 branches in southern Germany and Austria, which were collectively called Dachau. It was the first and most important camp at which laboratories were set up to perform medical experiments on inmates. Such experiments and the harsh living conditions made Dachau one of the most notorious camps, though it was not designed as an extermination camp.

dachshund \'däks-ˌhu̇nd, 'däk-sənt\ Dog breed of hound and terrier ancestry developed in Germany to pursue badgers (German, *Dachs*) into their burrows. It is a long-bodied, lively dog with a deep chest, short legs, tapering muzzle, and long ears. Usually reddish brown, or black and tan, it is bred in two sizes (standard and miniature) and in three coat types (smooth, long, and wiry). The standard dachshund stands about 7–10 in. (18–25 cm) high and weighs 16–32 lbs (7–14.5 kg); the miniature is shorter and weighs less than 9 lbs (4 kg).

Dacia \'dā-shə\ Ancient country, central Europe. Roughly equivalent to modern Romania, the area's earliest known inhabitants were Getae and Dacian people of Thracian stock. Known for its rich silver, iron, and gold mines, the region was made a Roman province in AD 107 after two centuries of hostilities. It was abandoned to the Goths in 270 and ultimately divided into the principalities of Walachia and Moldavia.

Dada \'dä-ˌdä\ Nihilistic movement in the arts that originated in Zurich in 1916 and flourished in New York, Berlin, Cologne, Paris, and Hanover in the early 20th century. The name, French for "hobbyhorse," selected by a chance procedure, was adopted by a group of artists including Jean Arp, Marcel Duchamp, Man Ray, and Francis Picabia to symbolize their emphasis on the illogical and absurd, growing out of disgust with bourgeois values and despair over World War I. The archetypal Dada forms of expression were the nonsense poem and the readymade. Dada had far-reaching effects on the art of the 20th century; the creative techniques of accident and chance were sustained in Surrealism, Abstract Expressionism, conceptual art, and Pop art.

Daddi \'däd-dē\, **Bernardo** (fl. c. 1320–1348) Italian painter. He became one of the leading painters in Florence after the death of his teacher, Giotto. He directed a busy workshop specializing in small devotional panels and portable altarpieces. His works include a triptych for the Church of Ognissanti (1328) and the polyptych *Crucifixion with Eight Saints* (1348). His style, a fusion of Giotto's seriousness and the lightness of Sienese art, featuring smiling Madonnas and abundant flowers and draperies, remained the dominant style of Florentine painting through the 14th century.

daddy longlegs *or* **harvestman** Any of the 3,400 arachnid species constituting the order Opiliones. Daddy longlegs differ from spiders in having extremely long, thin legs and a spherical or oval body that is not divided in two. The body is approximately 0.05–1.0 in. (1–22 mm) long; the fragile legs may be 20 times the body length. Males are smaller than females. Adults have a pair of glands that secrete a foul-smelling fluid.

Daddy longlegs are very widely distributed in temperate regions and in the tropics. The U.S. and Canada have about 150 species. They feed on insects, mites, spiders, carrion, and vegetable matter. See also CRANE FLY.

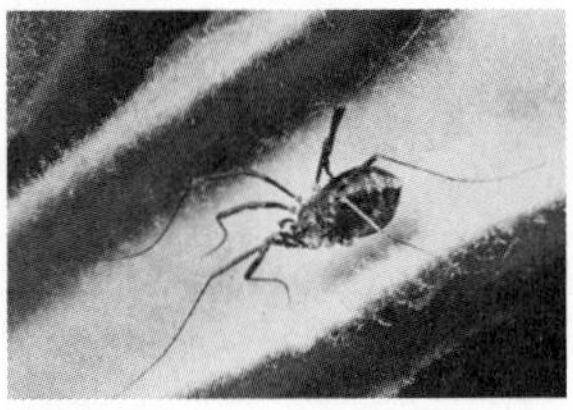

Harvestman.
E.S. ROSS

dado \'dā-dō\ In CLASSICAL ARCHITECTURE, the plain portion of the pedestal of a column, between the base and the cornice (or cap). In later architecture, a dado is a wall's paneled or decorated lower part, up to 2–3 ft (60–90 cm) above the floor and defined by a horizontal molding. Interior walls were so treated especially in the 16th–18th century. In carpentry, a dado is a rectangular groove cut across the grain of a wood member.

Dadra and Nagar Haveli \də-'drä...,nə-gər-ə-'ve-lē\ Union territory (pop., 1994 est.: 153,000), western India. It is located between GUJARAT and MAHARASHTRA states; its capital is SILVASSA. Forests cover part of the area; the rest is devoted to cultivation and grazing. Industrial development is limited. It came under Portuguese control 1783–85. In 1954 indigenous freedom movements forced the Portuguese out, and it became a union territory of India in 1961. The population is predominantly Hindu.

Daedalic sculpture *or* **Daidalic sculpture** \dē-'da-lik\ Type of figurative sculpture attributed by later Greeks to the legendary Greek artist DAEDALUS (Daidalos), associated with Bronze Age Crete and early Archaic sculpture in Greece. Daedalic sculpture displays Eastern ("Orientalizing") influences: wiglike hair, large eyes, and prominent nose; the female body is flatly geometric with a high waist and formless drapery. The style was used in figurines, on clay plaques, and in relief decoration on vases.

Daedalus \'de-də-ləs, 'dē-də-ləs\ In GREEK MYTHOLOGY, a brilliant architect, sculptor, and inventor. He was credited with building for King MINOS of Crete the Labyrinth in which the MINOTAUR was kept. When the king turned against Daedalus and imprisoned him, Daedalus secretly made wings for himself and his son Icarus, intending to escape to Sicily. Despite his father's warnings, Icarus flew too close to the sun; the wax holding the feathers to his wings melted, and he fell into the sea and drowned.

daemon See DEMON

daffodil Bulb-forming flowering plant *(Narcissus pseudonarcissus),* also called common daffodil or trumpet narcissus, native to northern Europe and widely cultivated there and in North America. It grows to about 16 in. (41 cm) and has five or six leaves about 12 in. (30 cm) long that grow from the bulb. The stem bears one large yellow trumpet-shaped blossom. The daffodil's popularity has resulted in the production of many varieties differing from the yellow parent form mainly in color.

Dafydd ap Llywelyn See DAVID AP LLYWELYN

Dagan \'dā-ˌgän\ West Semitic god of crop fertility, father of BAAL. He was the mythical inventor of the plow. He had an important temple at Ras Shamra and at sanctuaries in Palestine, where he was known as a god of the Philistines. At Ras Shamra he was second only to EL, though Baal assumed his functions as vegetation god by c. 1500 BC.

Dagda \'däg-t͟hə\ *or* **Eochaid Ollathair** \'ō-k͟ē-'ō-lə-hər\ In Irish mythology, a leader of the mythical TUATHA DÉ DANANN and father of the three BRIGITS and of MAPONOS. His name means "good god," referring to his many powers rather than to his moral character. The Dagda had an enormous appetite for food and sex and may have been associated with fertility. He possessed a cauldron that was never empty and a club that could kill men and restore them to life.

Dagobert I \'dag-ə-ˌbərt\ (605–639) Last Frankish king of the MEROVINGIAN DYNASTY to rule a politically united realm. He became king of AUSTRASIA in 623 and of the entire Frankish realm in 629. Dagobert secured a treaty with the Byzantine emperor, defeated the Gascons and Bretons, and campaigned against the Slavs in the east. In 631 he sent an army to help the Visigothic usurper in Spain. He moved his capital from Austrasia to Paris, then made his son king of Austrasia in 634. Dagobert also revised Frankish law, patronized the arts, and founded the great abbey of St.-Denis.

Daguerre \dà-'ger\, **Louis-Jacques-Mandé** (1787–1851) French inventor. Initially a scene painter for the opera, in 1822 he opened the Diorama, an exhibition of views with effects induced by changes in lighting. In 1826 J.-N. NIEPCE learned of Daguerre's experiments in obtaining permanent pictures by the action of sunlight, and the two became partners in the development of Niepce's heliographic process until Niepce's death in 1833. Continuing to experiment, Daguerre discovered that exposing an iodized silver plate in a camera would create a lasting image if the latent image on the plate was developed and fixed. In 1839 a description of his DAGUERREOTYPE process was announced at the Academy of Sciences.

daguerreotype \də-'ge-rō-ˌtīp\ First successful form of PHOTOGRAPHY. It is named for L.-J.-M. DAGUERRE, who invented the technique in collaboration with J.-N. NIEPCE. They found that if a copper plate coated with silver iodide was exposed to light in a CAMERA, then fumed with mercury vapor and fixed (made permanent) by a solution of common salt, a permanent image would be formed. The first daguerreotype image was produced in 1837, by which time Niepce had died, so the process was named for Daguerre. Many daguerreotypes, especially portraits, were made in the mid-19th century; the technique was gradually replaced by the wet collodion process, introduced in 1851.

Dahl \'däl\, **Roald** (1916–1990) British writer. A fighter pilot during World War II, he began his writing career when C.S. FORESTER encouraged him to write about his combat adventures, which were published by the *Saturday Evening Post.* The short-story collection *Someone Like You* (1953) was a best-seller; his later stories, many published in the *New Yorker,* often include bizarre or supernatural elements. His popular children's books *James and the Giant Peach* (1961) and *Charlie and the Chocolate Factory* (1964) were made into films.

Dahl, Robert A(lan) (born 1915) U.S. political scientist and educator. Born in Alaska, he obtained his PhD from Yale Univ., where he taught for 40 years (1946–86). He has written over 20 books, including *Who Governs?* (1961) and *Dilemmas of Pluralist Democracy* (1982). A leading theorist of PLURALISM, he stressed the role in politics played by associations, groups, and organizations.

dahlia \'dal-yə\ Any of the 12–20 species of tuberous-rooted herbaceous plants that make up the genus *Dahlia,* in the COMPOSITE FAMILY, native to higher elevations of Mexico and Central America. The leaves of most are segmented and toothed or cut. About six species have been bred for cultivation as ornamental flowers. Wild species have both disk and ray flowers in the flowering heads, but many varieties of ornamentals, such as the common garden dahlia *(D. bipinnata),* have shortened ray flowers. *Dahlia* flowers may be white, yellow, red, or purple.

Dahmer, Jeffrey (1960–1994) U.S. serial killer. In 1992 he confessed to killing, dismembering, and, in some cases, cannibalizing 16 young men, chiefly near his Milwaukee home, in a killing spree that started in 1978, when he murdered a young hitchhiker. The grim details, including his freezer packed with human body parts, made global news. His insanity plea was rejected by a jury, and he was sentenced to 936 years in prison. In 1994 he was bludgeoned to death by a fellow prisoner.

Dahomey See BENIN

Dahomey kingdom Western African kingdom that flourished in the 18th–19th century in what is now central Benin. Initially called Abomey, its name was changed to Dahomey after it had expanded by conquering the neighboring kingdoms of Allada (1724) and Whydah (1727). It thrived on the slave trade with Europe, reaching its high point under Gezu (1818–1858), under whom it became independent of the OYO EMPIRE. Society was rigidly stratified into royalty, commoners, and slaves; a centralized bureaucracy carried out the king's will. The nation was organized for war, both to increase its territory and to take captives for the slave market, and women served as soldiers along with men. With the end of the slave trade in the 1840s, Dahomey began exporting palm oil, which proved less profitable, and an economic decline followed. In 1892 Dahomey was defeated by a French expedition and became part of the French colony of the same name.

Dahshur \dä-'shür\ Ancient pyramid site, Egypt. It is located near MEMPHIS on the western bank of the Nile. Two of its pyramids date from the

4th dynasty and were built by Snefru (r.2575–2551 BC); the smaller is believed to be the first true pyramid. The three remaining pyramids belong to the 12th dynasty (1938–1756 BC). Nearby tombs have yielded a remarkable collection of jewelry and personal accoutrements.

The Blunted Pyramid of King Snefru at Dahshur, Egypt.
H. ROGER-VIOLLET

Daidalic sculpture See DAEDALIC SCULPTURE

Daigak Guksa \'ta-'gäk-'kük-ˌsä\ (1055–1101) Korean Buddhist priest and introducer of TIANTAI (Korean, *Ch'ont'ae*) Buddhism to Korea. He became a monk at 11 and studied in China. On his return to Korea he promoted the doctrines of TIANTAI, which attempted to reconcile the two main Korean sects, the Kyo, or Textual, School and the Son (Chinese, Chan; Japanese, ZEN) school. The introduction of Ch'ont'ae stimulated the reorganization of the Son school into the Chogye school, and these three—the Chogye, Textual, and Ch'ont'ae—became the three main divisions of Korean Buddhism. Daigak Guksa collected and published 4,750 books of Buddhist scriptures and a catalog of sectarian writings.

Daigo, Go- See GO-DAIGO

d'Ailly, Pierre See Pierre d'AILLY

Daimler \'dīm-lər\, **Gottlieb (Wilhelm)** (1834–1900) German automotive inventor. Trained as an engineer, he cofounded an engine-building company in 1882. He patented one of the first successful INTERNAL COMBUSTION ENGINES in 1885 and was the first to use a gasoline engine to power a bicycle (see MOTORCYCLE). Further innovations culminated in 1889 in a commercially feasible four-wheeled automobile. In 1890 the Daimler company was founded at Cannstadt, and in 1899 it produced the first Mercedes car. In 1926 it merged with the company founded by KARL BENZ. See also DAIMLERCHRYSLER AG.

DaimlerChrysler AG German automotive manufacturer formed through the 1998 merger of Daimler-Benz AG and American auto maker CHRYSLER CORP. Its German roots are in the auto companies founded by GOTTLIEB DAIMLER and KARL BENZ, which merged in 1926. The Mercedes-Benz luxury car, first produced by Daimler in 1901, is a basis of the company's financial success. DaimlerChrysler makes passenger cars, trucks, and commercial vehicles such as buses. Its brands include Mercedes, Dodge, Jeep, and Plymouth.

daimyo \'dī-mē-ˌō\ Any of the largest and most powerful landholding magnates in Japan (c. 10th century–19th cent). The term was originally applied to military lords who gained territorial control over the various private estates into which the country had been divided; later, in the 14th–15th century, daimyo acted as military governors for the ASHIKAGA SHOGUNATE. Though they held legal jurisdiction over areas as large as provinces, their private landholdings were relatively small. As the nation descended into internecine war, daimyo tended to hold small but consolidated domains in which all the land belonged to themselves or their vassals. Gradually, through constant battles, fewer and fewer daimyo came to hold more and more territory. When TOKUGAWA IEYASU completed unification of Japan in 1603, roughly 200 daimyo had been brought under Tokugawa hegemony. In the TOKUGAWA SHOGUNATE, the daimyo acted as local rulers in three-quarters of the country. After the MEIJI RESTORATION, the daimyo were converted into a pensioned nobility residing in Tokyo. See also HAN.

Dainan See T'AI-NAN

Dairen See DALIAN

dairy farming Form of animal husbandry that uses mammals, primarily COWS, for the production of MILK and products processed from it (including butter, cheese, and ice cream). Though CATTLE, GOATS, and SHEEP have been kept for the production of dairy products since the earliest historical times, modern dairy farming resulted from the technological advances of the past hundred years: the factory system for processing; sterile storage; refrigeration, fast vehicles and paved roads; and pasteurization and the enforcement of food-safety laws. Outstanding dairy breeds include the HOLSTEIN, GUERNSEY, JERSEY, AYRSHIRE, and Brown Swiss.

daisy Any of several species of garden plants in the COMPOSITE FAMILY, especially the oxeye daisy *(Chrysanthemum leucanthemum)* and the English, or true, daisy *(Bellis perennis)*. Both are native to Europe but have become naturalized in the U.S. These and other plants called daisies are distinguished by a flower composed of 15–30 white ray flowers surrounding a bright yellow disk flower. The cultivated Shasta daisy *(C. maximum)* resembles the oxeye daisy but has larger flower heads. The English daisy is often used as a BEDDING PLANT.

Dakar \dä-'kär, 'da-ˌkär\ City (population 1994: 785,000; 1999 est.: metro. area pop.: 1,999,000), capital of Senegal. One of the chief seaports on the western African coast, it lies midway between the mouths of the GAMBIA and SENEGAL rivers. Founded by the French in 1857, its development was spurred by the opening in 1885 of western Africa's first railway, from St.-Louis to Dakar. In 1902 it became capital of FRENCH WEST AFRICA and in 1960, of Senegal. Dakar is one of tropical Africa's leading industrial and service centers. There are museums of ethnography and archaeology there, of the sea and of history in nearby Gorée.

Dakota See SIOUX

Dakota River See JAMES RIVER

Dal River River, southern central Sweden. Formed by two forks, the Öster Dal and Vässter Dal, it flows southeast for some 325 mi (520 km) from the mountains along the Norwegian border into the Gulf of BOTHNIA.

Daladier \dȧ-lȧd-'ye\, **Édouard** (1884–1970) French politician. He was elected to the Chamber of Deputies in 1919 as a member of the Radical Party, served in several different cabinets, and formed short-lived governments in 1933 and 1934. As premier (1938–40), he sought to avoid war by signing the MUNICH AGREEMENT. Arrested after France fell to Germany in World War II, he was imprisoned by the Germans until 1945. After the war, he returned to the Chamber of Deputies (1946–58).

Dalai Lama \ˌdä-lī-'lä-mə\ Head of the dominant DGE-LUGS-PA order of TIBETAN BUDDHISM. The first of the line was Dge-'dun-grub-pa (1391–1475), founder of a monastery in central Tibet. His successors were regarded as his reincarnations and, like himself, manifestations of the BODHISATTVA AVALOKITESVARA. The second head of the order established the 'Brasspungs monastery near Lhasa as its base, and the third received the title Dalai ("Ocean") from ALTAN Khan. The fifth, Ngag-dbang-rgya-mtsho (1617–1682), established the supremacy of the Dge-lugs-pa over other orders. The 13th Dalai Lama, Thub-bstan-rgya-mtso (1875–1933), held temporal and spiritual power after the Chinese were expelled in 1912. The 14th and current Dalai Lama, Bstan-'dzin-rgya-mtsho (born 1935) was enthroned in 1940 but fled in 1959 with 100,000 followers after a failed revolt against the Chinese, who had occupied Tibet since 1950. His government-in-exile is in Dharmsala, India. A revered figure worldwide, he was awarded the 1989 Nobel Peace Prize in recognition of his nonviolent campaign to end Chinese domination of Tibet.

d'Alembert, Jean Le R. See Jean Le Rond d'ALEMBERT

Daley, Richard J(oseph) (1902–1976) U.S. politician, mayor of Chicago (1955–76). A lawyer in his native Chicago, Daley served as state director of revenue (1948–50) and clerk of Cook Co. (1950–55) before being elected mayor. He pushed urban renewal and highway construction and a sweeping reform of the police department, but was criticized for his reluctance to check racial segregation in housing and public schools, encouragement of downtown skyscraper construction, and measures taken against demonstrators at the 1968 Democratic National Convention. His tight control of city politics through job patronage won him his reputation as "the last of the big-city bosses." His last years were marred by scandals surrounding members of his administration. His son Richard M. Daley (born 1942) was first elected mayor in 1989.

Dalhousie \dal-'hau̇-zē\, **Marquess of** *orig.* **James Andrew Broun Ramsay** (1812–1860) British governor-general of India (1847–56). He entered Parliament in 1837 and later served as president of the Board of Trade, gaining a reputation for administrative efficiency. As governor-general of India he acquired territory by both peaceful and military means. Though he created the map of modern India through his annexations of independent provinces, his greatest achievement was the molding of these provinces into a modern centralized state. He developed a modern communication and transportation system and instituted social reforms. He left India in 1856, but his controversial policy of annexation was considered a contributing factor to the INDIAN MUTINY (1857).

10th Earl of Dalhousie, detail of an oil painting by Sir John Watson-Gordon, 1847; in the National Portrait Gallery, London.

BY COURTESY OF THE NATIONAL PORTRAIT GALLERY, LONDON

Dalhousie University Privately endowed university in Halifax, Nova Scotia. It was founded in 1818 as Dalhousie College by the 9th Earl of Dalhousie, then lieutenant governor of Nova Scotia, and became a university in 1863. It is organized into faculties of arts, science, management, architecture, engineering, computer science, law, medicine, dentistry, health professions, and graduate studies. Total enrollment is about 13,000.

Dalí (y Domenech) \ˈdä-lē, *Span* dä-ˈlē\, **Salvador (Felipe Jacinto)** (1904–1989) Spanish painter, sculptor, printmaker, and designer. He studied in Madrid and Barcelona before moving to Paris, where, in the late 1920s, after reading SIGMUND FREUD's writings on the erotic significance of subconscious imagery, he joined the Surrealists (see SURREALISM). His paintings depict a dream world in which commonplace objects, painted with meticulous realism, are juxtaposed, deformed, or metamorphosed in bizarre ways. In his most famous painting, *The Persistence of Memory* (1931), limp watches melt in an eerie landscape. With LUIS BUNUEL he made the Surrealist films *Un chien andalou* (1928) and *L'age d'or* (1930). Expelled from the Surrealist movement when he adopted a more academic style, he later designed stage sets, jewelry, interiors, and book illustrations. His highly accessible art—and the publicity attracted by the eccentricity, exhibitionism, and flamboyant behavior he cultivated throughout his life—made him extremely wealthy.

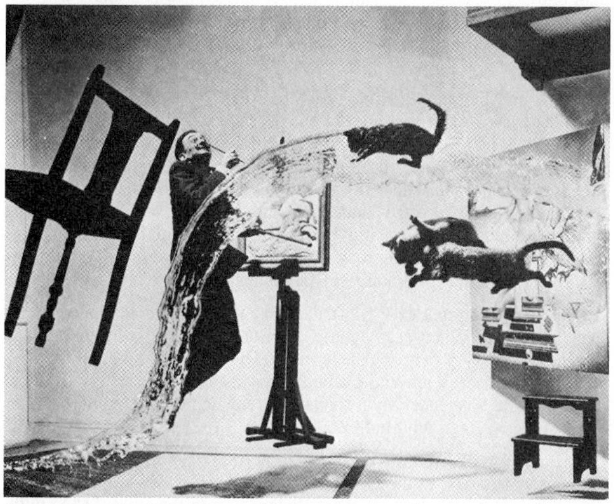
"Dali Atomicus," or Dalí with everything in suspension, photograph by Philippe Halsman, 1948.

© PHILIPPE HALSMAN

Dalian *or* **Ta-lien** \ˈdä-ˈlyen\ *formerly* **Lüda** *or* **Lü-ta** \ˈlue-ˈdä\ *Japanese and conventional* **Dairen** \ˈdī-ˈren\ City (pop., 1999 est.: 2,000,444) and deepwater port on the LIAODONG PENINSULA, LIAONING province, China. Leased to Russia in 1898, it was made a free port and terminus of the TRANS-SIBERIAN RAILROAD (1899). The Japanese occupied it during the RUSSO-JAPANESE WAR (1904), and the lease was transferred to Japan by treaty in 1905; Dalian again became a free port in 1906. Soviet troops captured the city in 1945, but by a Chinese–Soviet treaty it remained under Chinese sovereignty with preferential rights to the port for the U.S.S.R.; Soviet troops withdrew in 1955. It annexed neighboring Lüshun in 1950. Industries include fishing, shipbuilding, oil refining, and the manufacture of locomotives, machine tools, textiles, and chemicals.

Dallapiccola \ˌdäl-lä-pēk-ˈkō-lä\, **Luigi** (1904–1975) Italian composer. Originally influenced by the music of C. DEBUSSY, he later was strongly affected by that of A. SCHOENBERG, and he became the leading Italian twelve-tone composer. His *Canti di prigionia* (1941) was inspired by the experience of fascism, as was his opera *Il prigioniero* (1948). Other important works include the operas *Volo di notte* (1939), *Job* (1950), and *Ulisse* (1968); the vocal works *Tre laudi* (1937) and *Liriche greche* (1942–45); and the piano set *Quaderno musicale di Annalibera* (1952).

Dallas City (pop., 2000: 1,188,580), northern Texas. Located on the Trinity River, it was first settled in 1841, and was probably named for GEORGE DALLAS. While cotton fed the town's growth, the discovery in 1930 of the great East Texas oil field made the city a major center of the petroleum industry. It saw spectacular growth after World War II, when several large aircraft-manufacturing firms located in the area. These were followed by electronics and automobile-assembly plants. It is the headquarters of more than 100 insurance companies, and the Southwest's leading financial center, as well as a transportation hub. Its many educational institutions include Southern Methodist University (founded 1911). It is known for its cultural activities; the Dallas Theater Center is the only theater designed by FRANK LLOYD WRIGHT.

Dallas, George Mifflin (1792–1864) U.S. politician. Born in Philadelphia, he was the son of Alexander J. Dallas, secretary of the treasury 1814–16. He completed an unexpired term as U.S. senator (1831–33) and later served as minister to Russia (1835–39). He served as vice president under JAMES POLK 1845–49. As minister to Britain (1856–61), he obtained a renunciation of Britain's claimed right to search vessels on the high seas. Dallas, Texas, was named for him.

Dalmatia \dal-ˈmā-shə\ *Serbo-Croatian* **Dalmacija** \ˌdäl-ˈmät-sē-yä\ Region of Croatia. Comprising a coastal strip and islands along the Adriatic Sea, it is divided from the interior by the Dinaric Alps. Its scenic beauty has made tourism a major economic factor; DUBROVNIK and SPLIT are Mediterranean tourist attractions. Occupied by Illyrians from c. 1000 BC, it was colonized by Greeks from the 4th century BC and controlled by Rome 2nd–5th century AD. Under Venetian rule in 1420, it passed to Austria after the fall of NAPOLEON. Most of Dalmatia came under Yugoslavia in 1920. Annexed by Italy during World War II, it passed to Yugoslavia in 1947 as part of the Croatian republic.

dalmatian Breed of dog named after the Adriatic coastal region of Dalmatia, its first definite home. The time and place of the breed's origin are unknown. Though it has served as a guard dog, war dog, fire-department mascot, hunter, shepherd, and performer, it became best known as a coach or carriage dog, functioning as an escort and guard for horse-drawn vehicles. Sleek and short-haired, it is distinguished by its dark-spotted white coat. It stands 19–23 in. (48–58.5 cm) high and weighs 50–55 lbs (23–25 kg), and is generally even-tempered and friendly.

Dalriada \ˌdal-rē-ˈā-də\ Ancient kingdom, northeastern Ireland. Known from the 5th century AD, it included the northern part of the present Co. Antrim in Northern Ireland and part of the Inner HEBRIDES and Argyll in Scotland. Earlier, Argyll had received northern Irish people known as Scoti, and had become an Irish (i.e. "Scottish") area. In the late 5th century the rulers of Irish Dalriada expanded into Scottish Dalriada. Irish Dalriada gradually declined, while the Dalriada of the Scottish mainland continued to expand. In the mid-9th century the PICTS were brought permanently under Dalriadic rule, and the area was thereafter known as Scotland.

John Dalton, detail of an engraving by W. Worthington, after a portrait by William Allen, 1814.

BY COURTESY OF THE TRUSTEES OF THE BRITISH MUSEUM; PHOTOGRAPH, J.R. FREEMAN & CO. LTD.

Dalton, John (1766–1844) British chemist and physicist. He spent most of his life in private teaching and research. His work on GASES led him to state Dalton's law (see GAS LAWS). He devised a system of CHEM-

ICAL SYMBOLS, ascertained the relative weights of atoms, and arranged them into a table. His masterpiece of synthesis was the atomic theory—the theory that each element is composed of tiny, indestructible particles called ATOMS that are all alike and have the same ATOMIC WEIGHT—which elevated chemistry to a quantitative science. He was also the first to describe color blindness (1794), and his lifelong meteorological journal contains over 200,000 observations. He is remembered as one of the fathers of modern physical science.

Dalton brothers U.S. outlaws. Probably born in Cass Co., Mo., they worked as cowboys in Oklahoma but by 1889 had become horse thieves. In 1890–91 they robbed gambling houses, trains, and banks. In 1892 Bob, Grat, and Emmett Dalton and two other gang members rode into Coffeyville, Kan., to rob its banks; they were recognized, and vigilante citizens killed all but Emmett, who was wounded and sent to prison for 14 years. The fourth brother, Bill, had returned to Oklahoma before the raid; he later formed his own gang, and was shot by lawmen in 1894 while playing with his daughter.

Daly River \'dā-lē\ River, northwestern NORTHERN TERRITORY, Australia. Formed by the confluence of three smaller rivers, it flows about 200 mi (320 km) from the hills west of Arnhem Land to Anson Bay on the Timor Sea. Its basin supports cattle ranching and peanut and tobacco farming. It was first explored by Europeans in 1865. It is navigable for 70 mi (115 km) above its tidal mouth.

dam Barrier built across a stream, river, or estuary to conserve water for such uses as human consumption, irrigation, flood control, and electric-power generation. The earliest recorded dam is believed to be a masonry structure 49 ft (15 m) high built across the Nile River in Egypt c. 2900 BC. Modern dams are generally built of earth fill, rock fill, masonry, or monolithic concrete. Earth-fill (or embankment) dams, such as Egypt's ASWAN HIGH DAM, are usually used across broad rivers to retain water. The profile of an earth-fill dam is a broad-based triangle. Concrete dams may take various forms. The gravity dam uses its own dead weight to resist the horizontal force of the water. Concrete-buttress dams reduce material in the wall itself by using support buttresses around the outside base. An arch dam, such as HOOVER DAM, is built in a convex arch facing the reservoir, and owes its strength essentially to its shape, which is particularly efficient in transferring hydraulic forces to supports.

damages In law, the money awarded to a party in a civil suit as reparation for the loss or injury for which another is liable. The theory of an award of damages in a personal-injury or other TORT case is that injured parties should be placed in the position they would have been in if the injury had not occurred, so far as this can be accomplished with a monetary award. Where the legal wrong at issue is the breach of a contract, the goal of the damages remedy is to give the injured parties the benefit they would have received had the contract been performed. More than one type of damages (e.g., direct, incidental, and punitive) may be awarded for a single injury.

Daman and Diu \də-'män...'dē-ü\ Union territory (pop., 2001 prelim.: 158,059), western coastal India. Its capital is the town of Daman (pop., 1991: 26,900). It consists of two widely separated districts: Daman, on the GUJARAT coast north of MUMBAI (Bombay), and the island of Diu, off the southern coast of the KATHIAWAR Peninsula. Formerly Portuguese possessions, Daman and Diu were annexed by India in 1962. The population is predominantly Hindu. Agriculture and fishing are the major economic activities.

Damaraland \də-'mär-ə-,land, 'da-mə-rə-,land\ Historical region, northern central Namibia. Occupied by the HERERO and Khoisan people, who subjugated the original Bergdama people there, it extends between the NAMIB and KALAHARI deserts and from Ovamboland to Great Namaqualand, centering on WINDHOEK. The grassland region is suited both to the nomadic hunting and pastoral life of its original inhabitants and to the cattle breeding of the Europeans who, in the early 20th century, displaced the indigenous peoples and confiscated their herds.

Damascus \də-'mas-kəs\ *Arabic* **Dimashq** \di-'mäshk\ *French* **Damas** \då-'mäs\ Largest city (pop., 1994: 1,550,000) and capital of Syria. Located at an oasis near the desert at the base of the ANTI-LEBANON MTNS., it has been an important center from antiquity. Believed to be the world's oldest continuously inhabited city, it has evidence of occupation from the 4th millennium BC. The first written reference to it is in Egyptian tablets of the 15th century BC, and biblical sources refer to it as the capital of the ARAMAEANS. It changed hands repeatedly over the centuries, belonging to Assyria in the 8th century BC, then Babylon, Persia, Greece, and finally Rome in the 1st century BC. A Byzantine military outpost in the 4th century AD, it fell to the Arabs in 635; it flourished as the UMAYYAD capital, and the remains of their Great Mosque still stand. Taken by the Turks in 1516, it remained in the Ottoman empire for some 400 years. It was occupied by France in 1920 and finally regained its independence, with Syria, in 1946. Today the city is a flourishing trading center, with many educational and scientific institutions.

Damascus Document *or* **Zadokite Fragments** Document associated with the ancient Jewish community at QUMRAN. The group had fled to the desert during ANTIOCHUS IV EPIPHANES' persecutions (175–164/163 BC). The document must predate the revolt of AD 66–70, which forced the community to disband. It is known from fragments found in caves at Qumran as well as from 10th–12th-century manuscripts. The first section calls for fidelity to God's covenant and observance of the Sabbath, and also introduces the sect's leader, the Teacher of Righteousness. The second contains statutes dealing with vows, community assemblies, and admission and instruction of new members. See also DEAD SEA SCROLLS.

d'Amboise \dän-'bwäz\, **Jacques** *orig.* **Jacques Joseph Ahearn** (born 1934) U.S. dancer of the NEW YORK CITY BALLET (1949–84), noted for his athletic interpretations of classical roles. Born in Dedham, Mass., he studied at the School of American Ballet and made his debut at age 12. He joined the New York City Ballet at 15 and from the 1950s to the 1970s created leading roles in such ballets as *Western Symphony, Stars and Stripes,* and *Who Cares?* He also performed in several Broadway musicals. He later founded and directed the National Dance Institute, a nonprofit group that brings dance teaching into the public schools.

Dames, Paix des See Treaty of CAMBRAI

Damião \då-mē-'aůn\, **Frei** *orig.* **Pio Gianotti** (1898–1997) Italian-Brazilian friar. He became a Capuchin friar at 16 and later studied in Rome. In 1931 he was sent to Brazil, where he spent the rest of his life traveling in the poverty-stricken northeastern region. He soon developed a reputation as a miracle worker whose touch or prayers could relieve pain and heal disease. Doctrinally conservative, he was at odds with the region's left-wing priests, who supported LIBERATION THEOLOGY. After his death the bishop of Petrolina began the process of seeking Frei Damiao's beatification.

Damien \'dā-mē-ən\, **Father** *orig.* **Joseph de Veuster** (1840–1889) Belgian priest. After training at the College of Braine-le-Comte, he joined the Society of the Sacred Hearts of Jesus and Mary in 1858. He went as a missionary to the Sandwich (Hawaiian) Islands in 1863 and was ordained there in 1864. In 1873 he volunteered to take charge of the leper colony on Molokai Island. There he served as both physician and priest, dramatically improving living conditions and building two orphanages. He contracted leprosy himself in 1884 but refused to leave his post, and he died at Molokai five years later.

Damocles \'dam-ə-,klēz\ (fl. 4th century BC) Member of the court of DIONYSIUS I the Elder at Syracuse in Sicily. Legend holds that when Damocles spoke in extravagant terms of Dionysius' happiness, the sovereign responded by inviting Damocles to a banquet and seating him beneath a sword suspended by a thread, thereby demonstrating the precarious fortunes of men who hold power.

Damodar River \'dä-mō-,där\ River, northeastern India. It rises, with its many tributaries, in the Chota Nagpur plateau of BIHAR and flows east 368 miles (592 km) through West Bengal to join the HUGLI RIVER southwest of KOLKATA (Calcutta). Its valley includes India's most important coal- and mica-mining fields and is an area of active industrial development.

Dampier, William (1651–1715) English buccaneer and explorer. In his early years he engaged in piracy, chiefly along the western coast of South America and in the Pacific. In 1697 he published a popular book, *A New Voyage Round the World.* In 1699–1701 he explored the coasts of Australia, New Guinea, and New Britain for the British Admiralty. He was court-martialed for his cruelty, but later led a privateering expedition to the South Seas (1703–7). He was a keen observer of natural phenomena; one of his ship's logs contains the earliest known European description of a typhoon.

damping In physics, the restraint of vibratory motion, such as mechanical oscillations, NOISE, and alternating ELECTRIC CURRENTS, by dissipating ENERGY. Unless a child keeps pumping a swing, the back-and-forth motion decreases; damping by the air's friction opposes the motion and removes energy from the system. Viscous damping is caused by such energy losses as occur in liquid lubrication between moving parts or in a liquid forced through a small opening by a piston, as in automobile shock absorbers. Hysteresis damping involves energy loss within the moving structure itself. Other types of damping include electrical RESISTANCE, RADIATION, and magnetic damping.

damselfly Any of numerous insect species in the suborder Zygoptera (order Odonata) having eyes that project to each side and wings on a stalk. When at rest, the damselfly holds its narrow, membranous, net-veined wings vertically rather than horizontally, unlike DRAGONFLIES. Damselflies are delicate, weak-flying insects. Like dragonflies, they have male copulatory organs at the front part of the abdomen and commonly fly in pairs during mating.

Male jewelwing damselfly (*Calopteryx splendens*).
G.I. BERNARD—OXFORD SCIENTIFIC FILMS LTD.

Damu \'dä-ˌmü\ In MESOPOTAMIAN RELIGION, a Sumerian vegetation god and city god of Girsu on the Euphrates River. He was especially associated the flowing of sap in the spring. His name means "the child," and his cult centered on the lamentation and search for him. Damu's cult influenced and later blended with that of Dumuzi the Shepherd, a Sumerian deity of the grasslands people. Damu was also the name of a goddess of healing.

Dana, Charles A(nderson) (1819–1897) U.S. journalist. Born in Hinsdale, N.H., Dana lived at the utopian Brook Farm community for five years in the 1840s before becoming an editor for HORACE GREELEY's *New York Tribune*, where he actively promoted the antislavery cause. He became a national figure as editor and part owner of the *New York Sun* (1868–97), which under his control was much admired and imitated. With George Ripley, he edited the *New American Cyclopaedia* (1857–63). He also edited a highly successful verse anthology and wrote such books as *The Art of Newspaper Making* (1895).

Dana, James D(wight) (1813–1895) U.S. geologist, mineralogist, and naturalist. Born in Utica, N.Y., he graduated from Yale University (1833). He joined a U.S. exploring expedition to the South Seas (1838–42), acting as a geologist and zoologist. His contributions to the *American Journal of Science* stimulated U.S. geological inquiry. His research into the formation of the earth's continents and oceans led him to believe in the progressive evolution of the earth's physical features over time. By the end of his life he also came to accept the evolution of living things, as articulated by DARWIN. During his lifetime, and largely under his leadership, U.S. geology grew from a collection and classification of unrelated facts into a mature science.

Dana \'dā-nə\, **Richard Henry** (1815–1882) U.S. writer and lawyer. Born in Cambridge, Mass., he left Harvard College because of weakened eyesight and shipped out as a common sailor; after regaining his health, he returned and became a lawyer. He is remembered for his autobiographical *Two Years Before the Mast* (1840), which revealed the abuses endured by sailors. *The Seaman's Friend* (1841) became the authoritative guide to seamen's legal rights and duties. He also produced a scholarly edition of Henry Wheaton's *Elements of International Law* (1866), provided free legal aid to fugitive slaves, and served as U.S. attorney for Massachusetts.

Richard Henry Dana.
BY COURTESY OF THE LIBRARY OF CONGRESS, WASHINGTON, D.C.

Danaë \'da-nə-ˌē\ In Greek legend, the daughter of Acrisius, king of Argos. After an oracle warned her father that she would bear a son by whom he would be slain, he confined Danaë in a tower. ZEUS visited her in the form of a shower of gold, and she gave birth to PERSEUS. Mother and child were then placed in a wooden box and cast into the sea, and they drifted ashore on the island of Seriphus. Perseus grew up there, and when the island's king, Polydectes, desired Danaë, he sent the young hero off in pursuit of the MEDUSA. Perseus later rescued his mother and took her to Argos.

dance Form of expression that uses bodily movements that are rhythmic, patterned (or sometimes improvised), and usually accompanied by music. One of the oldest art forms, dance is found in every culture and is performed for purposes ranging from the ceremonial, liturgical, and magical to the theatrical, social, and simply aesthetic. Primitive dances often evolved into FOLK DANCES, which became stylized in the social dances of the 16th-century European courts. BALLET developed from the court dances and became refined by innovations in CHOREOGRAPHY and technique. In the 20th century, MODERN DANCE introduced a new mode of expressive movement. See also ALLEMANDE, BALLROOM DANCE, COUNTRY DANCE, COURANTE, GAVOTTE, GIGUE, HULA, JITTERBUG, LÄNDLER, MAZURKA, MERENGUE, MINUET, MORRIS DANCE, PAVANE, POLKA, POLONAISE, QUADRILLE, SAMBA, SARABANDE, SQUARE DANCE, SWORD DANCE, TANGO, TAP DANCE, WALTZ.

dance notation Written recording of dance movements. The earliest notation, in the late 15th century, consisted of letter-symbols. Several attempts were made in later centuries to describe dance steps, but no unified system combined both rhythm and steps until the 1920s, when RUDOLF LABAN devised his system of Labanotation. In the 1950s, the competing system of Benesh notation, or "choreology," devised by Rudolf and Joan Benesh, came into use.

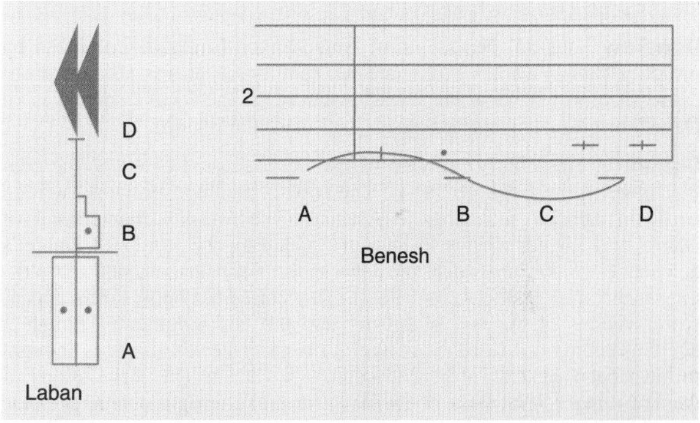

Comparison of the Laban and Benesh systems. (A) Stand with the feet together. (B) Step forward on the right foot (count 1). (C) Spring into the air. (D) Land to the left, feet together, knees bent (count 2).

dance of death *or* **danse macabre** \'däⁿs-mȧ-'kȧ-brᵊ\ *or* **skeleton dance** Medieval allegorical concept of the all-conquering and equalizing power of death, expressed in the drama, poetry, music, and visual arts of Western Europe mainly in the late Middle Ages. It is a literary or pictorial representation of a procession or dance of both living and dead figures, the living arranged in order of their rank, from pope and emperor to child, clerk, and hermit, and the dead leading them to the grave. It was given impetus by the BLACK DEATH and the HUNDRED YEARS' WAR. Though depictions declined after the 16th century, the theme was revived in literature and music of the 19th–20th century.

dandelion Any of the weedy perennial herbaceous plants that make up the genus *Taraxacum,* in the COMPOSITE FAMILY, native to Eurasia but widespread in much of temperate North America. The most familiar species, *T. officinale,* has a rosette of leaves at the base of the plant; a deep taproot; a smooth, hollow stem; and a solitary yellow flower head composed only of ray flowers (no disk flowers). The fruit is a ball-shaped cluster of many small, tufted, one-seeded fruits. The young leaves are edible; the roots can be used as a coffee substitute.

Dandie Dinmont terrier Breed of TERRIER developed in the border country of England and Scotland. First noted as a distinct breed c. 1700, it was later named after a character in Walter SCOTT's *Guy Mannering* (1815). It has a long, softly curved body, short legs, and a large, domed head crowned by a silky topknot. Its crisp-textured coat, a combination of hard and soft hairs, may be pepper- or mustard-colored. It stands 8–11 in. (20–28 cm) high and weighs 18–24 lbs (8–11 kg).

Dandolo \'dän-dō-lō\, **Enrico** (1107?–1205) Doge of the Republic of VENICE (1192–1205). After a career as a Venetian diplomat, he was elected doge at age 85. He swore the "ducal promise," spelling out the duties of his office, and instituted reforms, revising the penal code and publishing the first Venetian civil code. He also revised the coinage and sought to promote trade with the East. In 1199 he fought a victorious war against the Pisans. He was prominent in the Fourth CRUSADE, offering ships and supplies in return for payment (see Treaty of VENICE). When the crusaders were unable to pay, they agreed to help recover ZARA for Venice and helped place Alexius IV on the Byzantine throne, an action that led to the conquest of Constantinople. As a leader of the expedition, Dandolo took the title "lord of the fourth part and a half of the empire of Romania," which equaled the territory of the Byzantine Empire given to the Venetians.

dandruff Skin disorder of the scalp, a mild form of DERMATITIS. It affects most people at some time, when the scalp, which normally sheds its dead outer skin cells continuously, starts to shed them intermittently, causing a scaly buildup before shedding and noticeable flakes of skin when shedding occurs. Dandruff is not contagious and often goes away spontaneously; special shampoos can control it.

Danegeld \'dān-ˌgeld\ Tax levied in Anglo-Saxon England to buy off Danish invaders during the reign of ETHELRED II (978–1016). The term continued to be used to refer to taxes collected by the Anglo-Norman kings in the 11th and 12th century.

Danelaw \'dān-ˌlȯ\ NE region of Anglo-Saxon England. Colonized by invading Danish armies in the late 9th century AD, it was so named because the form of customary law practiced in the local courts was of Danish origin. Danish place-names still mark the region.

Daniel (c. 6th century BC) One of the OLD TESTAMENT PROPHETS, the central figure in the Book of Daniel. The book is a composite work, written partly in Hebrew and partly in Aramaic. The first six chapters tell of Daniel and his adventures in BABYLON, including the stories of Daniel's delivery from the lion's den, the Jews in the fiery furnace, and the writing on the wall at BELSHAZZAR's feast. The rest of the book offers apocalyptic visions of the end of history and the last judgment. Though it contains references to rulers of the 6th century BC, the book is thought to have been written in the 2nd century BC during the persecutions of the Jews under ANTIOCHUS IV EPIPHANES. Daniel's upright character made him a model for a persecuted community.

Daniel Romanovich \rə-'män-ə-ˌvich\ *known as* **Daniel of Galicia** (1201–1264) Ruler of GALICIA and VOLHYNIA, one of the most powerful princes in eastern central Europe. He inherited the two principalities (located in present-day Poland and Ukraine) at age 4, but pretenders to the succession kept him from ruling. He finally gained control over Volhynia in 1221 and Galicia in 1238. Daniel enriched his realm, but MONGOL invasions (1240–41) forced him to acknowledge the rule of the khan. He led a rebellion against the Mongols (1256) and succeeded briefly in driving them out of Volhynia, but another Mongol force subdued the principality in 1260.

Daniels, Josephus (1862–1948) U.S. editor, administrator, and diplomat. Born in Washington, N.C., he published a newspaper in Raleigh, N.C. (1885–1933), and became influential in the Democratic Party. In the 1912 presidential election he worked for the nomination of WOODROW WILSON, and later served as U.S. secretary of the navy (1913–21). As ambassador to Mexico (1933–44), Daniels improved relations and became FRANKLIN ROOSEVELT's most trusted adviser on Mexican issues.

Danilevsky \də-nyi-'lyef-skē\, **Nikolay (Yakovlevich)** (1822–1865) Russian naturalist and historical philosopher. He was the first to propound the philosophy of history as a series of distinct civilizations. In his *Russia and Europe* (1869), he contended that Russia and the Slavs should be indifferent to the West and concentrate on the development of political absolutism, their own special cultural heritage.

Danilova \də-'nē-lə-və\, **Alexandra (Dionisyevna)** (1903–1997) Russian-U.S. dancer and teacher, instrumental in bringing classical and modern Russian repertoires to the U.S. She attended the Imperial Ballet school in St. Petersburg and became a soloist at the MARIINSKY THEATER. In 1924 she joined the BALLETS RUSSES. From 1938 to 1952 she danced with the BALLET RUSSE DE MONTE CARLO, touring worldwide as its prima ballerina. She created leading roles in *The Triumph of Neptune, Gaîté Parisienne, Swan Lake,* and *Coppélia*. After retiring in 1957, she became a full-time faculty member at the School of American Ballet (1964–89).

Danilova in *Swan Lake.*
THE BETTMANN ARCHIVE

Danish language Official language of Denmark, belonging to the Scandinavian branch of the GERMANIC LANGUAGES. It began to separate from the other Scandinavian languages c. AD 1000. Modern Danish has lost the case system of Old Scandinavian, leaving only two noun cases; merged the masculine and feminine genders, leaving a common and a neuter gender; and acquired many Low German words. Evidence of Denmark's political influence can be seen in the stamp of the Danish language on the NORWEGIAN, SWEDISH, and ICELANDIC languages.

D'Annunzio \dän-'nünt-sē-ō\, **Gabriele** (1863–1938) Italian writer and military hero. He was a journalist before turning to poetry and fiction. His prodigious output includes *The Child of Pleasure* (1898), introducing the first of his many passionate Nietzschean-Superman heroes; *The Triumph of Death* (1894), his best-known novel; *Alcyone* (1904), considered his greatest poetic work; and the powerful play *The Daughter of Jorio* (1904). His works are marked by egocentrism, fluent and melodious style, and an overriding emphasis on sensual gratification. He urged Italy's entry into World War I, in which he distinguished himself militarily. In 1919 he set himself up as dictator of the port city Fiume in defiance of the Treaty of Versailles, and effectively secured it for Italy; he was forced to step down in 1920. He later became an ardent fascist. His eloquence, daring, political leadership, extravagant spending, and scandalous amours (especially with ELEONORA DUSE) made him one of the most striking personalities of his day.

danse macabre See DANCE OF DEATH

Dante Alighieri \'dän-tā-ˌa-lə-'gyer-ē\ (1265–1321) Italian poet. A native of Florence of noble ancestry, his life was shaped by the conflict between papal and imperial partisans (the GUELPHS AND GHIBELLINES). When the opposing political faction gained ascendancy, he was exiled (1302) from Florence, to which he never returned. His life was given direction by his spiritual love for Beatrice Portinari (died 1290), to whom he dedicated most of his poetry. His great friendship with GUIDO CAVALCANTI shaped his later career as well. *La Vita Nuova* (1293?) celebrates Beatrice in verse. In his difficult years of exile, he wrote the verse collection *The Banquet* (c. 1304–7), *De vulgari eloquentia* (1304–7; "Concerning Vernacular Eloquence"), the first theoretical discussion of the Italian literary language; and *On Monarchy* (1313?), a major Latin treatise on medieval political philosophy. He is best known for the monumental epic poem *The Divine Comedy* (written c. 1310–14; originally titled simply *Commedia*), a profoundly Christian vision of human temporal and eternal destiny. It is an allegory of universal human destiny in the form of a pilgrim's journey through hell and purgatory, guided by the Roman poet VIRGIL, then to Paradise, guided by Beatrice. By writing it in Italian rather than Latin, Dante almost singlehandedly made Italian a literary language, and he stands as one of the towering figures of European literature.

Danton \däⁿ-'tōⁿ\, **Georges (-Jacques)** (1759–1794) French revolutionary leader. A lawyer in Paris before the FRENCH REVOLUTION, he cofounded the Club of the CORDELIERS (1790) and frequently made impassioned speeches before both it and the JACOBIN CLUB. He was elected minister of justice in 1792, and he became a member of the first COMMITTEE OF PUBLIC SAFETY in April 1793. Effectively the head of government for three months, he pursued a policy of compromise and negotiation. He was not reelected to the Committee when its term expired in July, and became leader of the moderate Indulgents, which had risen from the Cordeliers. His moderation and opposition to the REIGN OF TERROR led to his own death at the guillotine.

Danube River \'dan-ˌyüb\ *German* **Donau** \'dō-ˌnau̇\ *Slovak* **Dunaj** \dü-'nī\ *Serbo-Croatian and Bulgarian* **Dunav** \'dü-näv\ *Romanian* **Dunarea** \'dü-nər-ˌyä\ *Russian* **Dunay** \dü-'nī\ River, central Europe. The second-longest European river (after the VOLGA), it rises in Germany's BLACK FOREST and flows about 1,770 mi (2,850 km) to the Black Sea, passing along or through Germany, Austria, Slovakia, Hungary, Croatia, Yugoslavia, Bulgaria, Romania, and Moldova. Its many tributaries include the DRAVA, TISZA, and SAVA rivers. It has been an important highway between central and eastern Europe from antiquity. The lower Danube is a major avenue for freight transport, and the upper Danube is an important source of hydroelectricity. A regulatory body that consists of its riparian nations was established in 1948 to oversee its use. A major hydroelectric and navigation complex was built in the 1970s at Iron Gate Gorge in Romania. A canal linking Kelheim on it and Bamberg on the MAIN RIVER, allowing traffic to flow between the North and Black seas, was completed in 1992.

The confluence of the Sava (foreground) and Danube rivers from the Kalemegdan Fortress, Belgrade, Yugos.
JEAN S. BULDAIN/BERG & ASSOC.

Danube school Tradition of German landscape painting and etching that developed in the Danube River valley between Regensburg and Vienna in the early 16th century. The most important artists associated with the movement were ALBRECHT ALTDORFER and LUCAS CRANACH the Elder; others included Wolf Huber (1485–1553) and Jörg Breu the Elder (1475/76–1537). They were among the pioneers in depicting landscape for its own sake, often in highly subjective, expressive fashion.

Danzig See GDANSK

dao See TAO

Daode jing See TAO-TE CHING

Daoism See TAOISM

Daphne \'daf-nē\ In GREEK MYTHOLOGY, the personification of the laurel tree. The beautiful daughter of a river god, Daphne lived a pastoral existence and rejected every lover. When APOLLO pursued her, she prayed to GAEA or to her father to save her, whereupon she was transformed into a laurel. Apollo took its leaves to weave garlands that were thenceforth awarded to prize-winning poets.

Daphnephoria \ˌdaf-nē-'fōr-ē-ə\ In GREEK RELIGION, a festival held every ninth year at Thebes in Boeotia in honor of Apollo Ismenius or Apollo Chalazius. It consisted of a procession and the dedication of a bronze tripod in APOLLO's temple. The festival was said to have originated in a vision of the Theban general Polematas, who was promised victory over the Aeolians and Pelasgians if the Daphnephoria was instituted.

Dapsang See K2

DAR See DAUGHTERS OF THE AMERICAN REVOLUTION

Dar es Salaam \ˌdär-ˌes-sä-'läm\ Capital, largest city (pop., 1995 est.: 1,747,000), and major port of Tanzania. Founded in 1862 by the sultan of ZANZIBAR, it came under the German East Africa Co. in 1887. It served as the capital of GERMAN EAST AFRICA (1891–1916), of Tanganyika (1961–64), and subsequently of Tanzania. It is an industrial center, and its harbor is the major outlet for Tanzania's agricultural and mineral exports. It is the site of the University of Dar es Salaam (1961).

Darby, Abraham (1678?–1717) British ironmaster. In 1709 Darby's Bristol Iron Co. became the first to successfully smelt IRON ore with COKE (see SMELTING). He demonstrated the superiority of coke in cost and efficiency by building much larger furnaces than were possible with charcoal as fuel. The quality of his iron made it possible to manufacture thin castings that outcompeted brass for pots and other hollowware; iron from his establishment was used for the cylinders of THOMAS NEWCOMEN's engines, for a cast-iron bridge, and for the first locomotive with a high-pressure boiler. See also DUD DUDLEY.

D'Arcy, William Knox (1849–1917) British businessman. After making a fortune as a gold miner in Australia, D'Arcy secured a 60-year oil-mining concession in Iran in 1901. An oil strike on these lands led to the formation of the Anglo-Persian Oil Co. in 1909. See also BRITISH PETROLEUM CO.

Dardanelles \ˌdär-dᵊn-'elz\ *ancient* **Hellespont** \'he-lə-ˌspänt\ Narrow strait between the peninsula of Gallipoli in Europe and the mainland of Turkey in Asia. Some 38 mi (61 km) long, and 0.75–4 mi (1–6 km) wide, it links the Aegean Sea with the Sea of Marmara. Strategically important from antiquity, the Dardanelles was defended by TROY from its position on the Asian side. In 480 BC XERXES crossed the strait to invade Greece, as did ALEXANDER THE GREAT in 334 BC on his expedition against Persia. Held by the Byzantine empire and later the Ottoman Turks, it is of great strategic and economic importance as the gateway from the Black Sea to Istanbul and the Mediterranean. See also GALLIPOLI.

Dardanelles Campaign *or* **Gallipoli Campaign** \gə-'li-pə-lē\ (1915–16) Unsuccessful British-led operation against Turkey in WORLD WAR I, intended to force the DARDANELLES strait and occupy Constantinople (Istanbul). In response to a Russian appeal to relieve pressure against its troops on the Caucasus front, Britain agreed to a naval action against Turkey at the Dardanelles. When bombardment alone failed, British and Australian and New Zealand (Anzac) troops landed on the GALLIPOLI peninsula in April 1915, where they met strong resistance from Turkish forces under MUSTAFA KEMAL ATATURK. After six months of standoff, the campaign was halted and allied troops were skillfully withdrawn under difficult conditions. Allied casualties numbered about 250,000. The failed campaign gave the impression that the Allies were militarily inept, prompting the resignation of WINSTON CHURCHILL, the chief promoter of the venture, as first lord of the admiralty.

Dare, Virginia (born 1587) First child born in America to English parents. Her parents were among the 120 settlers who landed at ROANOKE ISLAND, Va., in 1587. Her grandfather, JOHN WHITE, was the colony's governor; he left to collect supplies in England nine days after her birth. A relief expedition that finally reached the colony in 1590 found only the word "croatoan" carved on a post; the infant Virginia had vanished along with all the other colonists.

Darfur \där-'für\ Historical region and former province, western Sudan. It was an independent kingdom from c. 2500 BC. Its first traditional rulers, the Daju, probably traded with ancient Egypt; they were succeeded by the Tunjur. Darfur's Christian period (c. 900–1200) was ended by the advance of Islam with the empire of KANEM-BORNU. In the 1870s Darfur came under Egyptian rule, and in 1916 it became a province of Sudan.

Darién \ˌdar-ē-'en\ Traditional region, eastern Panama. Extending into northwestern Colombia, it forms the link between Central and South America. A hot, humid area of tropical rain forests, it has always been sparsely populated. The first European settlement in South America, Santa María de la Antigua del Darién, was attempted there in 1510. From this failing colony Vasco Núñez de BALBOA made his famous march to the Pacific Ocean in 1513.

Darío \dä-ˈrē-ō\, **Rubén** *orig.* **Félix Rubén García Sarmiento** (1867–1916) Nicaraguan poet, journalist, and diplomat. At 19 he began the travels in Europe and the Americas that would continue throughout his life. The diverse collection *Azul* (1888), written in an innovative simple, direct style, is his first major work. As a diplomat in Buenos Aires (from 1893), he became the center of the new MODERNISMO movement. His *Profane Hymns* (1896) was influenced by the French Symbolists. As a journalist in Europe, he became increasingly concerned with issues of imperialism and nationalism. *Songs of Life and Hope* (1905) represents the culmination of his technical experimentation and artistic resourcefulness. In addition to his poetry, he wrote about 100 short stories. Poor and run-down, he died of pneumonia at 49.

Darius I \da-ˈrī-əs\ *known as* **Darius the Great** (550–486 BC) King of Persia (522–486 BC). He was the son of Hystaspes, satrap of PARTHIA. Much of what is known of him is through his own inscriptions. He took the throne by force, killing Bardiya, a son of CYRUS THE GREAT, who had usurped power. He continued the conquests of his predecessors, subduing THRACE, MACEDONIA, some Aegean islands, and land stretching to the Indus Valley. He failed in his great expedition against the Scythians (513), but put down the IONIAN REVOLT (499), which had been supported by Eretria and ATHENS. After that he twice tried to conquer Greece, but a storm destroyed his fleet in 492 and the Athenians defeated him at the Battle of MARATHON in 490. He died before a third expedition could be launched. Among the greatest of the ACHAEMENIAN DYNASTY, he was noted for his administrative genius and his building projects, especially those at PERSEPOLIS.

Darius I seated before two incense burners, detail of a bas-relief of the north courtyard in the Treasury at Persepolis, late 6th–early 5th century BC; in the Archaeological Museum, Tehran.

BY COURTESY OF THE ORIENTAL INSTITUTE, THE UNIVERSITY OF CHICAGO

Darjeeling *or* **Darjiling** Town (metro. area pop., 1991: 73,000), northeastern India. It was purchased in 1835 from the raja of Sikkim and was developed as a sanatorium for British troops. Located at an average elevation of 7,500 ft (2,286 m), it commands views of Mount KANCHENJUNGA and Mount EVEREST. It is the summer headquarters of the Bengal government. Its economy is based primarily on tea, which is plantation-grown.

dark matter Nonluminous MATTER not directly detectable by astronomers, hypothesized to exist because the mass of the visible matter in the universe cannot account for observed gravitational effects. Long believed to exist in large quantities, it enters into many theories of the origin of the universe and its present large-scale structure and into models of GRAVITATION and other fundamental forces between particles. Numerous candidates for dark matter have been proposed over the years, but none has yet been detected.

Darlan \där-ˈlä^{n}\, **(Jean-Louis-Xavier-) François** (1881–1942) French admiral. After graduating from the French naval school (1902), he rose through the ranks to become navy commander in chief (1939). After France's defeat by Germany in World War II, he entered PHILIPPE PETAIN's government as vice premier and foreign minister (1941–42), then became commander in chief of all VICHY FRANCE military forces. In 1942 he concluded an armistice with the Allies in Algiers, then was killed by an anti-Vichy assassin.

Darling River River, southeastern Australia. It is the longest member of the Murray-Darling river system. It rises in several headstreams in the GREAT DIVIDING RANGE and flows generally southwest across NEW SOUTH WALES for 1,702 mi (2,739 km) to join the MURRAY RIVER at the VICTORIA border.

Darlington, Cyril Dean (1903–1981) British biologist. A professor at Oxford University from 1953, he believed that chromosomes were the cellular components that passed hereditary information from generation to generation. He explained the behavior of chromosomes during meiosis, formulating a theory of evolution in which the exchange of parts of chromosomes (crossing-over) was the central variable in determining the inherited characteristics of the next generation. His *Evolution of Man and Society* (1969) raised controversy by insisting that the intelligence of races was determined by inheritance.

Darnley, Lord *orig.* **Henry Stewart** (1545–1567) English nobleman, second husband of MARY, QUEEN OF SCOTS, and father of JAMES I. Son of Matthew Stewart, earl of Lennox (1516–1571), a pretender to the Scottish throne, Henry wed his cousin Mary in 1565 despite the opposition of ELIZABETH I and Scottish Protestants. It became evident, even to Mary, that superficial charm was his only positive attribute. After he played a role in the murder of Mary's secretary, DAVID RICCIO, he was himself murdered at 21 at the instigation of James Hepburn, earl of Bothwell (1535–1578), whom Mary soon married.

Darrow \ˈdar-ō\, **Clarence (Seward)** (1857–1938) U.S. lawyer and orator. Born near Kinsman, Ohio, he moved to Chicago in 1887 and immediately joined the effort to free anarchists charged with murder in the HAYMARKET RIOT. He was appointed Chicago city corporation counsel (1890), then became general attorney for the Chicago and North Western Railway. He left the railroad to defend EUGENE V. DEBS in the PULLMAN STRIKE (1894), which established his reputation as a union and criminal lawyer. He represented striking Pennsylvania coal miners, drawing attention to working conditions and the use of CHILD LABOR (1902–3); secured the acquittal of WILLIAM HAYWOOD in the assassination of Gov. Frank R. Steunenberg of Idaho (1907); and sought to defend the McNamara brothers, accused of bombing the *Los Angeles Times* building (1911). He saved Richard Loeb and Nathan Leopold from a death sentence for the murder of 14-year-old Robert Franks, and won acquittal for a black family that had fought a mob trying to expel it from its home in a white Detroit neighborhood (1925–26). Perhaps his most famous case was the SCOPES TRIAL (1925).

darshan *or* **darsan** \ˈdər-shən, ˈdär-shən\ In Hindu worship, the beholding of an auspicious deity, person, or object. The experience is often conceived to be reciprocal and results in a blessing of the viewer. In *rathayatras* (car festivals), images are carried through the streets to allow viewing by those who formerly would not have been allowed in the temple. Darshan may also be imparted by a GURU to his disciples, a ruler to his subjects, or a PILGRIMAGE shrine to its visitors. In Indian philosophy, darshan also refers to a philosophical system (e.g., VEDANTA).

Dart, Raymond A(rthur) (1893–1988) Australian-South African physical anthropologist and paleontologist whose discoveries of fossil HOMINIDS led to significant insights into the evolutionary origins of human beings. In 1924, when Asia was still believed to have been the cradle of humankind, Dart's discovery of the so-called Taung skull near the Kalahari Desert substantiated CHARLES DARWIN's prediction that such ancestral hominid forms would be found in Africa. Dart made the skull the type-specimen of a new genus and species, *AUSTRALOPITHECUS africanus*, and lived to see his findings corroborated by additional discoveries that firmly established Africa as the site of humankind's earliest origins. Dart taught at the University of Witwatersrand from 1923 to 1958.

darter Any of about 100 species of small, slender freshwater fishes (family Percidae), native to eastern North America. Darters live near the bottom of clear streams, darting quickly about when feeding on small aquatic animals such as insects and worms or when disturbed. They have two dorsal fins and often are brightly colored. Most species are 2–3 in. (5–7 cm) long, but some grow to 9 in. (23 cm). Some species lay their eggs and abandon them; the males of other species establish a nest and guard the eggs until hatched. See also SNAIL DARTER.

Dartmouth College \ˈdärt-məth\ Private institution of higher learning in Hanover, N.H., a traditional member of the IVY LEAGUE. It is consistently ranked as one of the best liberal-arts colleges in the U.S. It was founded in 1769 by Rev. Eleazar Wheelock (1711–1779) for the education of "youth of the Indian Tribes . . . English Youth and others." The original charter was approved by George III. Women were first admitted in 1972. Besides offering a broad range of undergraduate programs, it grants graduate and professional degrees in business, engineering, medicine, and the arts and sciences. Total enrollment is about 5,300. See also DARTMOUTH COLLEGE CASE.

Dartmouth College case *formally* ***Trustees of Dartmouth College vs. Woodward*** Case in which the U.S. Supreme Court held

(1819) that the charter of DARTMOUTH COLLEGE, granted in 1769 by George III, was a contract and as such could not be impaired by the New Hampshire legislature. State legislators had tried to alter the contract's terms regarding the continuance of the board of trustees, an effort rejected by the Court. The decision was far-reaching in its application to business charters, protecting businesses and CORPORATIONS from much government regulation. DANIEL WEBSTER argued Dartmouth's case.

darts Indoor target game played by throwing feathered darts at a circular board with numbered spaces. The board, usually made of cork, bristle, or elmwood, is divided into 20 sectors valued at points from 1 to 20. Six concentric rings, ranging from an inner bull's-eye to a narrow outermost ring, determine scoring. The official throwing distance in most countries is 7 ft 9¼ in. (2.37 m), though variations extend up to 9 ft (2.75 m). In Britain, darts is normally played in pubs.

Darwin *formerly* **Palmerston** Seaport (pop., 1995 est.: 82,000), capital of NORTHERN TERRITORY, Australia. Located on Port Darwin, a deep inlet of Clarence Strait in the Timor Sea, it has one of Australia's best harbors. The harbor was named in 1839 after CHARLES DARWIN. The port, settled in 1869, was known as Palmerston until 1911. Located in a largely undeveloped region, Darwin is a supply and shipping center for northern Australia. A military base in World War II, it was bombed by the Japanese in 1942, then extensively rebuilt. A cyclone in 1974 damaged or destroyed nearly all of the city; rebuilt a second time, it is now one of Australia's most modern cities.

Darwin, Charles (Robert) (1809–1882) British naturalist. The grandson of ERASMUS DARWIN and JOSIAH WEDGWOOD, he studied medicine at Edinburgh University and biology at Cambridge. He was recommended as naturalist on HMS *Beagle,* which was bound on a long scientific survey expedition to South America and the South Seas (1831–36). His zoological and geological discoveries on the voyage resulted in numerous important publications, and formed the basis of his theories of evolution. Seeing competition between individuals of a single species, he recognized that within a local population the individual with, for example, the sharper beak might have a better chance to survive and reproduce, and that if such traits were passed on to new generations they would be predominant in future populations. He saw this NATURAL SELECTION as the mechanism by which advantageous variations were passed on to later generations and less advantageous traits gradually disappeared. He worked on his theory for more than 20 years before publishing it in his famous *On the Origin of Species by Means of Natural Selection* (1859). The book was immediately in great demand and Darwin's intensely controversial theory was accepted quickly in most scientific circles; most opposition came from religious leaders. Though Darwin's ideas were modified by later developments in genetics and molecular biology, his work remains central to modern evolutionary theory. His many other important works included *Variation in Animals and Plants Under Domestication* (1868) and *The Descent of Man . . .* (1871). He was buried in Westminster Abbey. See also DARWINISM.

Darwin, Erasmus (1731–1802) British physician, grandfather of CHARLES DARWIN and FRANCIS GALTON. A freethinker and radical, Darwin often wrote his opinions and scientific treatises in verse. In *Zoonomia or the Laws of Organic Life* (1794–96), he advanced a theory of evolution similar to that of J.-B. LAMARCK, suggesting that species modified themselves by adapting to their environment in an intentional way. His conclusions, drawn from simple observation, were rejected by the more sophisticated 19th-century scientists, including his grandson Charles.

Erasmus Darwin, detail of an oil painting by Joseph Wright, 1770; in the National Portrait Gallery, London.

BY COURTESY OF THE NATIONAL PORTRAIT GALLERY, LONDON

Darwinism Theory of the evolutionary mechanism proposed by CHARLES DARWIN as an explanation of organic change. It denotes Darwin's specific view of how EVOLUTION works. Darwin developed the concept that evolution is brought about by the interplay of three principles: variation (present in all forms of life), heredity (the force that transmits similar organic form from one generation to another), and the struggle for existence (which determines the variations that will be advantageous in a given environment, thus altering the species through selective reproduction). Present knowledge of the genetic basis of inheritance has contributed to scientists' understanding of the mechanisms behind Darwin's ideas, in a theory known as neo-Darwinism.

Darwin's finch *or* **Galápagos finch** Any of 14 species (in three genera) of songbirds (family Fringillidae) whose adaptations to several ecological niches in the Galápagos Islands and Cocos Island gave CHARLES DARWIN evidence for his thesis that "species are not immutable." All the species are 4–8 in. (10–20 cm) long and brownish or black, but they differ greatly in the configuration of the bill, which is suited to each species' particular feeding habit.

Dassault \dȧ-ˈsō\, **Marcel** *orig.* **Marcel Bloch** (1892–1986) French aircraft designer and industrialist. He designed aircraft during World War I, and in 1930 started his own company to build military and civilian airplanes. Sent to Buchenwald as a Jew during World War II, he later changed his last name (to that of his brother's byname in the Resistance) and resumed his business. His company produced Europe's first supersonic plane, the Mystère, and in 1956 began production of the Mirage warplane, which would be acquired by countries worldwide.

data compression Process of reducing the amount of data needed for storage or transmission of a given piece of information (text, graphics, video, sound, etc.), typically by use of encoding techniques. Advanced techniques analyze, identify, and then replace commonly occurring text patterns with single characters and symbols (e.g., "ing to" as in "going to" could be converted to "$"). Major benefits of data compression are larger data-storage capacity, particularly on CD-ROMs; more efficient transmission by FAX machines and MODEMS; and DATA ENCRYPTION. A trade-off between time and speed characterizes most advanced methods of data compression.

data encryption Process of disguising information as "ciphertext," or data that will be unintelligible to an unauthorized person. Decryption is the process of converting ciphertext back into its original format, sometimes called plaintext (see CRYPTOGRAPHY). Computers encrypt data by applying an ALGORITHM to a block of data. A personal key known only to the message's transmitter and intended receiver is used to control the encryption. Well-designed keys are almost impregnable. A key 16 characters long selected at random from 256 ASCII characters could take far longer than the 15-billion-year age of the universe to decode, assuming the perpetrator attempted 100 million different key combinations per second. Symmetric encryption requires the same key for both encryption and decryption. Asymmetric encryption, or public-key cryptography, requires a pair of keys, one for encryption and one for decryption.

data mining Type of database analysis that attempts to discover commercially useful patterns or relationships in a group of data. The analysis uses advanced statistical methods, such as cluster analysis, and sometimes employs ARTIFICIAL INTELLIGENCE or NEURAL-NETWORK techniques. A major goal of data mining is to discover previously unknown relationships among the data, especially when the data come from different databases. Businesses can use these new relationships to develop new advertising campaigns or make predictions about how well a product will sell.

data processing Manipulation of data by a COMPUTER. It includes the conversion of raw data to machine-readable form, flow of data through the CPU and memory to output devices, and formatting or transformation of output. Any use of computers to perform defined operations on data can be included under data processing. In the commercial world, data processing refers to the processing of data required to run organizations and businesses.

data structure Way in which data are stored for efficient search and retrieval. The simplest data structure is the one-dimensional (linear) array, in which stored elements are numbered with consecutive integers and contents are accessed by these numbers. Data items stored nonconsecutively in memory may be linked by pointers (memory addresses stored with items to indicate where the "next" item or items in the structure are located). Many ALGORITHMS have been developed for sorting data efficiently; these apply to structures residing in main memory and also to structures that constitute information systems and DATABASES.

data transmission Sending and receiving data via cables (e.g., telephone lines or FIBER OPTICS) or wireless relay systems. Because ordinary telephone circuits pass signals that fall within the frequency range of voice communication (about 300–3,500 hertz), the high frequencies associated with data transmission suffer a loss of amplitude and transmission speed. Data signals must therefore be translated into a format compatible with the signals used in telephone lines. Digital computers use a MODEM to transform outgoing digital electronic data; a similar system at the receiving end translates the incoming signal back to the original electronic data. Specialized data-transmission links carry signals at frequencies higher than those used by the public telephone network. See also BROADBAND TECHNOLOGY, CABLE MODEM, DSL, ISDN, FAX, RADIO, TELETYPE, T1, WIRELESS COMMUNICATIONS

database Collection of data or information organized for rapid search and retrieval, especially by a computer. Databases are structured to facilitate storage, retrieval, modification, and deletion of data in conjunction with various DATA-PROCESSING operations. A database consists of a file or set of files that can be broken down into records, each of which consists of one or more fields. Fields are the basic units of data storage. Users retrieve database information primarily through queries. Using keywords and sorting commands, users can rapidly search, rearrange, group, and select the field in many records to retrieve or create reports on particular aggregates of data according to the rules of the DATABASE MANAGEMENT SYSTEM being used.

database, relational See RELATIONAL DATABASE

database management system (DBMS) System for quick search and retrieval of information from a DATABASE. The DBMS determines how data are stored and retrieved. It must address problems such as security, accuracy, consistency among different records, response time, and memory requirements. These issues are most significant for database systems on computer NETWORKS. Ever-higher processing speeds are required for efficient database management. Relational DBMSs, in which data are organized into a series of tables ("relations") that are easily reorganized for accessing data in different ways, are the most widely used today.

Date Line See INTERNATIONAL DATE LINE

date palm Tree *(Phoenix dactylifera)* of the PALM family, found in the Canary Islands and northern Africa, the Middle East, Pakistan, India, and California. The trunk, strongly marked with the pruned stubs of old leaf bases, ends in a crown of long, graceful, shining, pinnate leaves. The fruit, called the date, is a usually oblong brown BERRY. Dates have long been an important food in desert regions, and are the source of syrup, alcohol, vinegar, and a strong liquor. All parts of the tree yield products of economic value, being used variously for timber, furniture, basketry, fuel, rope, and packing material. The seeds are sometimes used as stock feed. The tree is grown as an ornamental along the Mediterranean shores of Europe. Its leaves are used for the celebration of Palm Sunday (among Christians) and the Feast of Tabernacles (among Jews). Date sugar, a product of India, is obtained from the sap of a closely related species, *P. sylvestris.*

dating In geology and archaeology, the process of determining an object's or event's place within a chronological scheme. Scientists may use either relative dating, in which items are sequenced on the basis of stratigraphic clues (see STRATIGRAPHY) or a presumed evolution in form or structure, or absolute dating, in which items are assigned a date independent of context. The latter type includes POTASSIUM-ARGON and CARBON-14 dating; both are based on the measurement of radioactive decay. The record of changes in polarity of the earth's magnetic field has provided a timescale for SEAFLOOR SPREADING and long-term marine SEDIMENTATION. DENDROCHRONOLOGY has proved useful in archaeology. See also FISSION-TRACK DATING, HELIUM DATING, LEAD-210 DATING, RUBIDIUM-STRONTIUM DATING, URANIUM-234–URANIUM-238 DATING, URANIUM-THORIUM-LEAD DATING.

Daubenton \dō-bäⁿ-ˈtōⁿ\, **Louis-Jean-Marie** (1716–1800) French naturalist. A prolific scientist, he completed many zoological descriptions and dissections and undertook productive studies in the comparative anatomy of recent and fossil animals, plant physiology, and mineralogy. He introduced Merino sheep to France.

Daubigny \dō-bēn-ˈyē\, **Charles-François** (1817–1878) French landscape painter of the BARBIZON SCHOOL. He was trained by his father, also a painter. He began by painting historical and religious works but soon turned to landscapes, painting rivers, beaches, and canals from a boat. His images were notable for their uncrowded composition and accurate depiction of natural light. One of the earliest proponents of painting directly from nature, he is considered the link between mid-19th-century naturalism and Impressionism.

Daudet \dō-ˈde\, **Alphonse** (1840–1897) French short-story writer and novelist. He wrote his first novel at 14. Unable to finish his schooling after his parents lost all their money, he took a post in a duke's household. He later joined the army, but fled the terrors of the PARIS COMMUNE of 1871. His health was long undermined by poverty and by the venereal disease that eventually cost him his life. He is remembered for his humorous, sentimental portrayals of the life and characters of southern France, inspired by his experiences at many social levels. His many works include the story collection *Monday Tales* (1873), the play *L'Arlésienne* (1872), the novels *The Nabob* (1877) and *Sappho* (1884), and several volumes of memoirs. His son, Léon Daudet (1867–1942), edited with CHARLES MAURRAS the reactionary review *L'Action Française* and was a virulent satirist and polemicist on the subjects of medicine and psychology as well as public affairs.

Alphonse Daudet.
H. ROGER-VIOLLET

Daughters of the American Revolution (DAR) U.S. patriotic society for direct descendants of soldiers or others who aided the cause of independence. It was organized in 1890 and chartered by Congress in 1895. Its historical division stresses the study of U.S. history and preservation of Americana. Its educational division provides scholarships and loans, helps support schools for underprivileged youth and for Americanization training, sponsors prizes, and publishes manuals. Its patriotic division publishes the *Daughters of the American Revolution Magazine* and *The National Defense News*. It was long known for its conservatism; its refusal in 1939 to let MARIAN ANDERSON perform at Washington's Constitution Hall led to her famous concert at the Lincoln Memorial.

Daumier \dōm-ˈyā\, **Honoré (-Victorin)** (1808–1879) French painter, sculptor, and caricaturist. He was born into a family of artists. From age 13 he worked for a bailiff in a law court and later as a clerk in a bookstore, where he observed and analyzed the appearance and behavior of people of different social classes. In 1829, after studying lithography, he began contributing cartoons and drawings satirizing 19th-century French politics and society to periodicals, and came to enjoy a wide reputation. He produced over 4,000 lithographs and 4,000 illustrative drawings. His paintings, drawing on literary themes and documenting contemporary life and manners, were executed in a vigorous, sketchy style; they were rarely exhibited, and he remained unknown as a painter. In sculpture he specialized in caricature heads and figures; some 15 small clay busts occupy an important place in the history of sculpture.

dauphin \ˈdȯ-fən\ Title of the eldest son of a king of France, the heir apparent to the French crown, from 1350 to 1830. The title was established through the purchase of lands known as the Dauphiné in 1349 by the future CHARLES V.

Dauphiné \ˌdō-fē-ˈnā\ Historic region and former province, southeastern France. Occupied by Burgundians and later by Franks, it formed part of the Holy Roman Empire under LOTHAIR I and was part of the kingdom of Arles. It was sold to PHILIP VI of France and ultimately became an appanage of the eldest son of the French king, who assumed the title (dauphin) attached to the land. The area had a quasi-independent status until it was annexed to France in 1457.

Davao \ˈdä-ˌvau̇\ City (pop., 1994 est.: 961,000), southeastern Mindanao Island, Philippines. Located at the mouth of the Davao River on

Davao Gulf, it is an international port and the leading commercial center in the region. It developed as a Japanese colony. Razed during World War II, the rebuilt city is a blend of Spanish, American, and Moorish influences. Largely rural outside its urban core, it is one of the world's largest cities in area, covering 854 sq mi (2,212 sq km). It is the site of the University of Mindanao (1946).

Davenant \'dav-ə-nənt\, **William** *or* **William D'Avenant** *later* **Sir William** (1606–1668) British poet, playwright, and theater manager. Early works include the comedy *The Witts* (licensed 1634) and a volume of poems, *Madagascar* (1638). He was made poet laureate in 1638. Involved in intrigues during the English Civil Wars, he was imprisoned at the Tower of London, where he worked on his verse epic *Gondibert* (1651). Later he made the first attempt to revive English drama (banned under Oliver Cromwell) and brought the first opera, painted stage sets, and female actress-singer to the English public stage. After the Restoration he continued playwriting and founded a playhouse.

Davenport, John (1597–1670) British-American Puritan clergyman. A vicar in London, he moved to Amsterdam in 1633 and served there as co-pastor of the English Church. In 1637 he left for America with Theophilus Eaton (c. 1590–1658) and their followers. They founded a colony at Quinnipiac (New Haven) in 1638; Davenport became pastor of the New Haven church and Eaton was chosen governor. After failing to prevent New Haven's union with the Connecticut colony, Davenport left in 1667 to lead the First Church in Boston.

David (died c. 962 BC) Second of the Israelite kings (r. c. 1000–c. 962 BC). David was an aide at the court of Saul until the monarch's jealousy forced him into outlawry. He became king of Israel on Saul's death. He captured Jerusalem from the Jebusites and made it his capital, defeated the Philistines, and gained control of many bordering kingdoms. He faced several revolts, including one by his third son, Absalom. He unified all Israel into one kingdom and made Jerusalem both the religious and political center. He made all other names for God mere titles or attributes for Israel's god Yahweh, who was worshiped in Jerusalem. Though the kingdom split under David's son and successor Solomon, religious unity endured, and the house of David symbolized the bond between God and Israel. The word messiah comes from *hameshiach,* the title of kings of the line of David.

David \'dä-vət\, **Gerard** (c. 1460–1523) Netherlandish painter. He worked mainly in Bruges, where he entered the painters' guild in 1484 and became dean in 1501. He became the city's leading painter after the death of Hans Memling. Most of his works are altarpieces and other panels featuring traditional religious themes, but his best-known paintings, *The Judgment of Cambyses* and *The Flaying of Sisamnes* (1498), deal with the theme of justice; they originally hung in the town hall of Bruges. His works are among the earliest Flemish paintings to feature the Italian Renaissance iconography of putti (male child angels) and garlands.

"Virgin and Child with Saints and Donor," panel painting by Gerard David, c. 1505; in the National Gallery, London.

BY COURTESY OF THE TRUSTEES OF THE NATIONAL GALLERY, LONDON; PHOTOGRAPH, J.R. FREEMAN & CO. LTD.

David \dä-'vēd\, **Jacques-Louis** (1748–1825) French painter. At 18 he entered the Royal Academy of Painting and Sculpture. In 1775 he went to Rome and became a proponent of the Neoclassical style, but also studied the work of such 17th-century painters as Nicolas Poussin and Caravaggio. He soon prospered as a painter of historical events and classical themes. He became the unchallenged painter of the French Revolution, and later was appointed official portraitist to Napoleon. He was a founding member of the new Institut de France, which replaced the Royal Academy, and produced commemorative medals and other revolutionary propaganda. Among his masterpieces is *The Death of Marat* (1793), an expression of universal tragedy as well as a portrayal of a key event of the French Revolution. He was best known as a painter of mythological and historical subjects, a great portraitist, and the principal exponent of Neoclassicism. His influence on European art was pervasive; his pupils included A.-J. Gros and J.-A.-D. Ingres.

Jacques-Louis David, self-portrait, oil painting, 1794; in the Louvre, Paris.

ALINARI—ART RESOURCE/EB INC.

David, Star of *Hebrew* **Magen David** ("Shield of David"). Jewish symbol composed of two overlaid equilateral triangles that form a six-pointed star. It appears on synagogues, tombstones, and the flag of Israel. An ancient sign not much used by Jews before the Middle Ages, it was popularized by Kabbalists for protection against evil spirits. The Jewish community of Prague adopted it as an official symbol and its use became widespread in the 17th century. Though it has neither biblical nor Talmudic authority, it became a nearly universal emblem of Judaism in the 19th century. The Nazis' use of it to identify Jews invested it with the symbolism of martyrdom and heroism.

David I (1082?–1153) King of the Scots (1124–53). The youngest of six sons of Malcolm III, he became king of Scotland on the death of his brother Alexander I. He created a rudimentary central administration, issued the first Scottish royal coinage, and admitted into Scotland an influential Norman aristocracy. David also reorganized Scottish Christianity to conform with European and English usages and founded many religious communities. He had obtained lands in central England through his marriage to the daughter of an English earl in 1113, and he won title to Northumberland from the future Henry II in 1149.

David II *known as* **David the Builder** (1073–1125) King of Georgia (1089–1125). Sometimes known as David III, he became coruler with his father, Giorgi II, in 1089. David defeated the Turks in the Battle of Didgori (1122) and captured Tbilisi. Under his leadership Georgia became the strongest state in Caucasia.

David II (1324–1371) King of the Scots from 1329. In keeping with an Anglo-Scottish peace treaty, he was married at age 4 to the sister of Edward III of England. His reign was marked by conflict with England and a decline in the prestige of the monarchy. He went into exile in France in 1334 after Edward III supported a rival for the throne, and he fought against Edward for the French king Philip VI. David returned to Scotland in 1341 and carried out raids against the English, who captured him in 1346. He was released in 1357 on the promise of ransom, and his offer to trade the Scottish throne for forgiveness of the ransom money was repudiated in Scotland.

David ap Llywelyn \'dá-vith-áp-hlə-'we-lin\ (1208?–1246) Welsh prince, ruler of the state of Gwynedd in northern Wales (1240–46). His father, Llywelyn ap Iorwerth, had made Gwynedd the center of Welsh power. David, the rightful heir, fought his half brother for power and imprisoned him in 1239. He was forced to cede part of his territory to Henry III of England (1241) and later went to war against Henry. The first Welsh ruler to declare himself prince of Wales, he fell ill and died while the war was in progress.

David of Tao \'taú\ (died 1000) Georgian prince of the Bagratid family of Tao, a region between Georgia and Armenia. A just ruler and a friend of the church, he allied with BASIL II to defeat the rebel Bardas Skleros (976–79) and was rewarded with extensive lands that made him the most important ruler in Caucasia. In 987–89 he supported Bardas Phokas against Basil but was defeated and agreed to cede his lands to Basil on his death. Despite this setback, David's heir, Bagrat III (978–1014), was able to become the first ruler of a unified Georgian kingdom.

Davidson, Bruce (born 1933) U.S. photographer and filmmaker. Born in Oak Park, Ill., he studied at the Yale University School of Design. He worked briefly at *Life* magazine and in 1958 joined the photographers' cooperative Magnum Photos. He has produced numerous outstanding photo essays, the most important being *East 100th Street* (1970), 123 photographs shot with a large-format camera in East Harlem, New York, and has also made several short films.

Davidson College Private liberal-arts college in Davidson, N.C., founded in 1837. It is affiliated with the Presbyterian church, though its approach to learning is nonsectarian. Women were first admitted in 1972. Enrollment is about 1,600.

Davies, Peter Maxwell *later* **Sir Peter** (born 1934) British composer. He studied in England, Italy, and the U.S. He cofounded the contemporary ensemble The Fires of London and was its musical director (1970–87); he wrote many of his works for the group. Since 1970 he has lived and composed primarily in the remote Orkney Islands. He has written many musical theater works and has conducted orchestras worldwide. His most famous compositions are *Eight Songs for a Mad King* (1969) and *An Orkney Wedding, with Sunrise;* his other works include *Vesalii Icones* (1969), *Miss Donnithorne's Maggot* (1974), and *Ave maris stella* (1975); the operas *Taverner* (1968), *The Martyrdom of St. Magnus* (1976), and *Le Jongleur de Notre Dame* (1978); and seven symphonies.

Davies, (William) Robertson (1913–1995) Canadian novelist and playwright. Born in Thamesville, Ontario, and educated at Oxford, he for many years edited the Peterborough (Ont.) *Examiner* and taught at the University of Toronto. He is best known for three trilogies: the *Deptford Trilogy* consists of *Fifth Business* (1970), *The Manticore* (1972), and *World of Wonders* (1975), novels examining the intersecting lives of three men from a small Canadian town; the *Salterton Trilogy*, three comedies of manners set in a provincial university town; and the so-called Cornish trilogy—*The Rebel Angels* (1981), *What's Bred in the Bone* (1985), and *The Lyre of Orpheus* (1988).

Davis, Angela (Yvonne) (born 1944) U.S. political activist. Born in Birmingham, Ala., she became a doctoral candidate at the University of California, studying under HERBERT MARCUSE. Because of her political views, her college teaching position was not renewed. A champion of the cause of black prisoners, she was arrested in 1970 for complicity in the abortive courtroom escape and kidnapping attempt led by the so-called Soledad Brothers, in which four people, including the trial judge, were killed. An all-white jury acquitted her of all charges. In 1980 she ran for vice president on the Communist Party ticket. Davis became a professor in 1991 at the University of California, Santa Cruz.

Davis, Benjamin O(liver), Jr. (1912–2002) U.S. pilot and administrator, the first black general in the U.S. Air Force. Born in Washington, D.C., he graduated from West Point and in 1941 was admitted to the Army Air Corps. He organized the 99th Fighter Squadron, the first all-black air unit, and in 1943 organized and commanded the TUSKEGEE AIRMEN. He flew 60 combat missions. In 1948 he helped plan the desegregation of the Air Force, and he later commanded a fighter wing in the Korean War. He retired as lieutenant general in 1970 and became an assistant secretary of transportation (1971–75). In 1998 he was awarded his fourth general's star, which made him a general of the highest order in the U.S. military.

Davis, Bette *orig.* **Ruth Elizabeth** (1908–1989) U.S. film actress. Born in Lowell, Mass., she played small parts on stage before going to Hollywood in 1931. After a series of minor roles, she established her reputation with *Of Human Bondage* (1934) and *Dangerous* (1935, Academy Award). Known for her intense characterizations of strong women, she gave electrifying performances in such films as *The Petrified Forest* (1936), *Jezebel* (1938, Academy Award), *Dark Victory* (1939), *The Little Foxes* (1941), *Now, Voyager* (1942), *All About Eve* (1950), and *The Virgin Queen* (1955). Later films include *What Ever Happened to Baby Jane?* (1962) and *The Whales of August* (1987).

Davis, Colin (Rex) *later* **Sir Colin** (born 1927) British conductor. Self-taught as a conductor, he first earned acclaim with a 1958 production of *The Abduction from the Seraglio*. His reputation was established when he filled in for OTTO KLEMPERER the next year. He was music director of Covent Garden 1971–86, and with the Bavarian Radio Symphony 1983–92; he remains principal conductor of the London Symphony Orchestra. He has a special affinity for the music of HECTOR BERLIOZ and JEAN SIBELIUS.

Davis, David (1815–1886) U.S. jurist. Born in Cecil Co., Md., he practiced law and was elected to the Illinois legislature in 1844. As a state circuit-court judge (1848–62) he became a close friend of ABRAHAM LINCOLN, and in 1860 he worked to secure Lincoln's election. In 1862 he was appointed to the U.S. Supreme Court, where he served until 1877. He resigned to accept election to the U.S. Senate (1877–83).

Davis, Glenn (Ashby) (born 1934) U.S. track star. Born in Wellsburg, W.V., he ran in high school and at Ohio State University. He was the world-record holder in the 400-m hurdles from 1956 to 1962 and was the first man to win the Olympic gold medal twice in that event (1956, 1960). He also won a gold medal in the 4 × 100-m relay (1960) and set a world record in the 200-m hurdles.

Davis, Jefferson (1808–1889) U.S. political leader, president of the CONFEDERATE STATES OF AMERICA (1861–65). Born in Christian Co., Ky., he graduated from West Point and served in Wisconsin Territory and later in the Black Hawk War. Elected to the U.S. House of Representatives (1845–46), he resigned to serve in the MEXICAN WAR, where he distinguished himself at the Battle of BUENA VISTA. A national hero, he served in the U.S. Senate (1847–51) and as Pres. FRANKLIN PIERCE's secretary of war (1853–57). He returned to the Senate in 1857, where he advocated states' rights but tried to discourage secession. After Mississippi seceded in 1861, he resigned and was chosen president of the Confederacy. He conducted the South's war effort in the face of a lack of manpower, supplies, and money, and hampered by discord from radicals within his administration. On Lee's surrender, he fled Richmond, hoping to continue the fight until he could secure better terms from the North. Captured and indicted for treason, he was never tried; he was released in poor health in 1867. His citizenship was restored posthumously in 1978.

Davis, Miles (Dewey) (1926–1991) U.S. trumpeter and bandleader, one of the most original and influential musicians in jazz. Born in Alton, Ill., Davis grew up in East St. Louis, Mo., and began study at the Juilliard School in New York in 1944. He worked with CHARLIE PARKER 1946–48. His early efforts as a bandleader resulted in recordings known as "Birth of the Cool" (1949), in which a relaxed aesthetic replaced the freneticism of BEBOP and launched the "cool jazz" school of the 1950s. From 1955 Davis's groups framed his spare, lyrical approach in contrast to the dense complexity of saxophonists such as JOHN COLTRANE and Wayne Shorter. His dark, brooding tone, logically paced improvisations, and frequent use of the metal Harmon mute were major influences on jazz trumpet soloists. The 1959 album *Kind of Blue* was a pioneering example of modal harmonic jazz. His music became more aggressive during the 1960s, and his use of electronic instruments by the end of the decade (*Bitches Brew,* 1969) gave rise to the jazz-rock fusion of the 1970s.

Miles Davis, 1969.

VOTAVAFOTO FROM LONDON DAILY EXPRESS—PICTORIAL PARADE

Davis, Stuart (1894–1964) U.S. abstract painter. He was born in Philadelphia, the son of a graphic artist. He studied in New York with ROBERT HENRI (1909–12), made drawings for the periodical *The Masses*, associated with the ASH CAN SCHOOL, and exhibited in the ARMORY SHOW. A visit to Paris in 1928–29 inspired his own version of Cubism; he began rearranging natural forms from everyday life into flat posterlike patterns with sharp outlines and contrasting colors (the dissonant colors and repetitive rhythms reflecting his interest in jazz), in a style that eventually led to totally abstract patterns. He is considered the outstanding U.S. artist who worked in the Cubist style.

Davis Cup Trophy awarded to the winning team of an international tennis tournament for men. The cup was donated in 1900 by Dwight F.

Davis, himself a player in the first two matches (called ties), for a competition between teams from the U.S. and Britain. Since then, the tournament has developed into a truly international event. More than 100 nations have participated, but winners have been confined to the U.S, Australia, South Africa, Britain, and a few other European nations.

Davis Strait Strait, northern Atlantic Ocean. Lying between southeastern BAFFIN ISLAND and southwestern GREENLAND, it separates BAFFIN BAY to the north from the Labrador Sea to the south, and forms part of the NORTHWEST PASSAGE. About 400 mi (650 km) north to south and 200–400 mi (325–650 km) wide, it was explored in 1585 by the English navigator John Davis. Along the coast of Greenland, the Greenland Current carries relatively warm water northward, while the cold Labrador Current transports icebergs southward along Baffin Island's eastern shore.

Davos \dä-'vōs\ Commune (pop., 1990: 11,600), eastern Switzerland. It consists of two villages, Davos-Platz and Davos-Dorf, located in a valley of the ALPS. First inhabited by Romansh-speaking people, it was settled in the 13th century by German speakers. It became the capital of the League of Ten Jurisdictions or Courts in 1436 and was ruled by Austria in 1477–1649. After the 1860s it became a fashionable health resort, and in the 20th century it developed into a center for skiing and other winter sports. In the 1990s Davos became famous for hosting the World Economic Forum, an annual gathering of international politicians and financiers who represented a transnational elite.

Davout \dȧ-'vü\, **Louis-Nicolas** *later* **prince d'Eckmühl** \dek-'mǖl\ (1770–1823) French general in the NAPOLEONIC WARS. Despite his noble origins, in 1790 he led his regiment in a pro-Revolutionary revolt and he performed with merit in the Belgian campaign of 1792–93. He accompanied NAPOLEON to Egypt (1798–99) and was promoted to division general. As a corps commander, he had a significant impact on the victories at Austerlitz (1805), Auerstedt (1806), Jena (1806), Eylau (1807), Eckmühl (1809), and Wagram (1809). Created a duke (1808) and prince (1809) by Napoleon, Davout served as minister of war during the HUNDRED DAYS.

Davy, Humphry *later* **Sir Humphry** (1778–1829) English chemist. By his early 20s his work on gases had established his reputation. His discovery of the anesthetic effect of NITROUS OXIDE in 1799 was a major contribution to surgery. He also did early research on voltaic cells and BATTERIES, TANNING, ELECTROLYSIS, and mineral analysis. In *Elements of Agricultural Chemistry* (1813) he became the first to apply chemical principles systematically to farming. He was the first to isolate POTASSIUM, SODIUM, BARIUM, STRONTIUM, MAGNESIUM, and CALCIUM; he also discovered BORON and studied CHLORINE and IODINE extensively. He analyzed many PIGMENTS, and proved that DIAMOND is a form of CARBON. He was one of the greatest exponents of the SCIENTIFIC METHOD. His research on mine explosions and flame and his invention of the safety lamp brought him great prestige, and in 1820 he was made president of the Royal Society.

daw See JACKDAW

Dawenkou culture *or* **Ta-wen-k'ou culture** \'dä-wen-ˌkō\ Chinese Neolithic culture of c. 4500–2700 BC. It was characterized by the emergence of delicate wheel-made pots of various colors; ornaments of stone, jade, and bone; walled towns; and high-status burials involving ledges for displaying grave goods, coffin chambers, and the burial of animal teeth, pig heads, and pig jawbones. See also ERLITOU CULTURE, HONGSHAN CULTURE, LONGSHAN CULTURE, NEOLITHIC PERIOD.

Dawes, Charles G(ates) (1865–1951) U.S. politician. Born in Marietta, Ohio, he practiced law in Nebraska before being appointed U.S. comptroller of the currency (1897–1902). In World War I he headed supply procurement for the American Expeditionary Force in France. In 1923 he chaired the Allied Reparations Commission and arranged the DAWES PLAN. He served as vice president (1925–29) under CALVIN COOLIDGE. He received the 1925 Nobel Peace Prize.

Dawes General Allotment *or* **Dawes Severalty Act** (1887) U.S. land-distribution law proposed by Sen. Henry L. Dawes (1816–1903) of Massachusetts as a way to "civilize" and make farmers of the American Indians. Grants of 80–160 acres were offered to each Indian head of household, though actual ownership was withheld for 25 years to guard against sales to speculators. The unintended result was a weakened tribal structure, the inability of many nomadic Indians to adjust to an agrarian existence, and a reservation life of poverty, disease, and despondency. Under the provision that made available for public sale any "surplus" reservation land, whites had acquired two-thirds of the Indian land by 1932.

Dawes Plan (1924) Arrangement for Germany's payment of REPARATIONS after WORLD WAR I, produced by a committee of experts presided over by CHARLES DAWES. The total amount of reparations was not determined, but payments were to begin at 1 billion gold marks in the first year and rise to 2.5 billion by 1928. The plan, which also provided for the reorganization of the Reichsbank and for an initial loan of 800 million marks to Germany, was later replaced by the more lenient YOUNG PLAN.

dawn redwood Coniferous, nonevergreen tree *(Metasequoia glyptostroboides),* the only living species of the genus *Metasequoia,* of the family Taxodiaceae, native to remote valleys of central China. Both branchlets and leaves grow out in pairs from points along the stem. The bright-green, feathery leaves turn reddish brown in autumn. Though *Metasequoia* fossils are abundant, the tree was thought to be extinct until living specimens were discovered in the 1940s. Only a few thousand are known to have survived, in central China. Since these stands were discovered, seeds and cuttings have been planted throughout the world.

Dawson, George Geoffrey *orig.* **George Geoffrey Robinson** (1874–1944) English journalist, influential editor of the *Times* of London. While in civil service in South Africa, he became editor of the *Johannesburg Star* as part of an effort to promote support for official policies. As editor of *The Times* in the years 1912–19 and 1923–41, he was associated with a group that sought to shape national policy through personal exchanges with leading statesmen; he saw himself as the "secretary-general of the Establishment." A firm believer in appeasement, he was instrumental in the policy that led to the MUNICH AGREEMENT of 1938.

day Time required for a celestial body to turn once on its axis; especially, the period of the earth's rotation. The SIDEREAL day is the time required for the earth to rotate once relative to the background of the stars (i.e., the time between two observed passages of a star over the same meridian of longitude). The apparent solar day is the time between two successive transits of the sun over the same meridian. Because the orbital motion of the earth makes the sun seem to move slightly eastward each day relative to the stars, the solar day is about four minutes longer than the sidereal day. The mean solar day is the average value of the solar day, which changes slightly in length during the year as the earth's speed in its orbit varies. See table on following page.

Day, Doris *orig.* **Doris von Kappelhoff** (born 1924) U.S. singer and film actress. Born in Cincinnati, she worked as a band vocalist in the 1940s and went on to great success as a solo recording artist. She made her film debut in 1948 and starred in such musicals as *Calamity Jane* (1953), *Young at Heart* (1955), and *The Pajama Game* (1957). Playing a sunny, wholesome girl-next-door, she embodied the idealized American woman of the 1950s. She played dramatic roles in *Love Me or Leave Me* (1955) and *The Man Who Knew Too Much* (1956) before starring in bedroom comedies such as *Pillow Talk* (1959) and *That Touch of Mink* (1962). She also hosted *The Doris Day Show* on television (1968–73).

Day, Dorothy (1897–1980) U.S. journalist and social reformer. Born in Brooklyn, she grew up in Chicago, then returned to New York to work for the radical journals *The Call* and *The Masses.* With the birth of her daughter (1927), she broke her ties with radicalism and converted to Roman Catholicism. After writing for the liberal Catholic journal *Commonweal,* in 1933 she and Peter Maurin (1877–1949) cofounded *The Catholic Worker,* which expressed her view of "personalism." She sought to aid the poor by establishing urban houses of hospitality as part of the Catholic Worker movement. After Maurin's death, she continued to publish the paper and manage the "hospitality houses" for the poor. Though her outspoken pacifist views were criticized by Catholic conservatives, she influenced such Catholic liberals as THOMAS MERTON and DANIEL AND PHILIP BERRIGAN.

Day-Lewis, C(ecil) (1904–1972) Irish-British poet. Son of a clergyman, he studied at Oxford University and in the 1930s became part of a circle of left-wing poets centered on W. H. AUDEN, though he later turned to an individual lyricism expressed in traditional forms. His works include translations of VIRGIL's *Georgics* (1940), *Aeneid* (1952), and *Eclogues* (1963), and the verse collections *The Room* (1965) and *The Whispering Roots* (1970). He also wrote the autobiography *The Buried Day* (1960) and several detective novels under the pseudonym

Days

Day	Derivation
Sunday	from Old English translation of Latin *solis dies* ("sun's day")
Monday	from Old English translation of Latin *lunae dies* ("moon's day")
Tuesday	from Old English *tīwesdæg* ("Tyr's day")*
Wednesday	from Old English *wōdnesdæg* ("Woden's day")*
Thursday	from Old English *thursdæg* ("Thor's day")*
Friday	from Old English *frīgedæg* ("Frigg's day")*
Saturday	from Old English translation of Latin *Saturni dies* ("Saturn's day")

*In translating the Latin names, the Germanic peoples sometimes substituted the names of their own gods. Thus, *Martis dies* ("Mars's day") became *tīwesdæg* ("Tyr's day"), *Mercurii dies* ("Mercury's day") became *wōdnesdæg* ("Woden's day"), and *Veneris dies* ("Venus's day") became *frīgedæg* ("Frigg's day").

Months

Month	Derivation
January (31 days)	from the Roman republican calendar month Januarius, named for Janus, god of beginnings
February (28, 29 in leap year)	from the Roman month Februarius, named for Februa, the festival of purification held on the 15th
March (31)	from the Roman month Martius, named for Mars
April (30)	from the Roman month Aprilis, perhaps derived from the Greek Aphrodite (the month being sacred to her Roman equivalent, Venus), or from Latin *aperire*, "to open," for the unfolding of buds and blossoms
May (31)	from the Roman month Maius, probably named for the goddess Maia
June (30)	from the Roman month Junius, probably named for Juno
July (31)	from the Roman month Julius (formerly Quintilis), named for Julius Caesar in 44 BC
August (31)	from the Roman month Augustus (formerly Sextilis), named for Augustus in 8 BC
September (30)	seventh month of the early Roman republican calendar, from Latin *septem*, "seven"
October (31)	eighth month of the republican calendar, from Latin *octo*, "eight"
November (30)	ninth month of the republican calendar, from Latin *novem*, "nine"
December (31)	tenth month of the republican calendar, from Latin *decem*, "ten"

Nicholas Blake. He became poet laureate of England in 1968. He was the father of DANIEL DAY-LEWIS.

Day-Lewis, Daniel (born 1957) British actor. The son of C. DAY-LEWIS, he made his London stage debut in 1982. He first won acclaim for his role as a gay working-class punk in *My Beautiful Laundrette* (1985). Noted for his versatility, he convincingly played characters with a range of nationalities, accents, and classes in such films as *A Room with a View* (1985), *The Unbearable Lightness of Being* (1988), *My Left Foot* (1989, Academy Award), *The Last of the Mohicans* (1992), *The Age of Innocence* (1993), *The Crucible* (1996), and *The Boxer* (1997).

day lily Any plant of the genus *Hemerocallis,* in the LILY FAMILY, consisting of about 15 species of PERENNIAL herbaceous plants distributed from central Europe to eastern Asia. Members have long-stalked clusters of funnel- or bell-shaped flowers that range in color from yellow to red and are each short-lived (hence "day" lily). Day lilies also have fleshy roots and narrow, sword-shaped leaves that are grouped at the base of the plant. The fruit is a CAPSULE. Some species are cultivated as ornamentals or for their edible flowers and buds.

Dayaks \'dī-ˌaks\ In Borneo, a non-Muslim indigenous people of the southern and western interior (modern Kalimantan). Dayak is a generic term that has no precise ethnic or tribal significance but distinguishes the indigenous people from the largely Malay population of the coastal areas. Most Dayaks are riverine people who live in small longhouse communities. Children live with their parents until marriage, and boys, who usually seek brides outside their own village, go to live in their wife's community. Their subsistence economies rest on the shifting cultivation of hill rice, supplemented by fishing and hunting. Today they number over 2 million.

Dayan \dī-'än\, **Moshe** (1915–1981) Israeli soldier and statesman. Born on Israel's first KIBBUTZ of Russian parents, he became a guerrilla fighter against Arab raiders. Later he joined the illegal Jewish defense force HAGANA. He lost an eye fighting the Vichy French in Syria during World War II. He was army chief of staff during the SUEZ CRISIS (1956) and later agriculture minister (1959–64). He was appointed defense minister just before the SIX-DAY WAR, and the Israeli victory brought him widespread adulation; he served until 1974. He joined the opposition LIKUD as foreign minister when it came into power in 1977 and helped broker the 1978 CAMP DAVID ACCORDS. See also ARAB–ISRAELI WARS.

Dayananda Sarasvati \də-'yä-nən-də-ˌsə-rəs-'və-tē\ *orig.* **Mula Sankara** (1824–1883) Hindu ascetic and social reformer. A Brahman, he rejected what he considered idol worship at 14 after seeing mice swarm over an image of SHIVA, attracted by offerings placed before it. His religious quest led him to Yoga, and to escape an arranged marriage he joined the ascetic Sarasvati order. He spent 15 years traveling in search of religious truth, and in 1863 began preaching his vision of reinstating a purified Vedic religion. He debated orthodox Hindu scholars and Christian missionaries, and in 1875 founded ARYA SAMAJ. He opposed child marriage and the ban on remarriage by widows and opened Vedic study to all castes.

daylight saving time System for uniformly advancing clocks, especially in summer, so as to extend daylight hours during conventional waking time. In the Northern Hemisphere, clocks are usually set ahead one hour in late March or in April and are set back one hour in late September or in October. In the U.S. and Canada, daylight saving time begins on the first Sunday in April and ends on the last Sunday in October.

Dayr al-Bahri See DEIR EL-BAHRI

Dayton City (pop., 2000: 166,179), southwestern Ohio. Settled on the Miami River in 1796 by a group of Revolutionary War veterans, it developed as a river port shipping agricultural produce. The 1829 opening of the Miami and Erie Canal between Dayton and CINCINNATI and the arrival in 1851 of the railroad stimulated its industrial growth. It was home to WILBUR AND ORVILLE WRIGHT and is also their place of burial. The city is a market and distribution center. It is the site of Wright-Patterson Air Force Base (established 1946) and the Air Force Institute of Technology (1947). Home to several colleges and universities, it also has an art institute and a symphony orchestra.

Daytona Beach Coastal city (pop., 2000: 64,112), northeastern Florida. Located south of JACKSONVILLE, it was founded by Mathias Day in 1870 and incorporated in 1876. In 1926 the cities of Seabreeze, Daytona, and Daytona Beach were incorporated as Daytona Beach. The Ormond-Daytona beach of hard, white sand has been used for automobile speed trials since 1903. The city is known for the Daytona International Speedway.

Dazai \dä-'zī\, **Osamu** *orig.* **Shuji Tsushima** (1909–1948) Japanese novelist. He emerged as the literary voice of his time at the end of World War II, capturing the period of postwar confusion when traditional values were discredited. The son of a wealthy landowner and politician, he often used his background as material in his fiction. *Tsugaru* (1944) is perhaps his best novel. His postwar works—*The Setting Sun* (1947), *Villon's Wife* (1947), and *No Longer Human* (1948)—were increasingly despairing in tone, reflecting the crisis that led to his suicide at 38.

DC See DIRECT CURRENT

DDT *in full* **dichlorodiphenyltrichloroethane** Synthetic INSECTICIDE belonging to the family of organic HALOGENS. In 1939 its toxicity in a wide variety of insects was discovered (by Paul Hermann Müller, who was awarded a Nobel Prize for his work) and effectively used against many disease vectors. By the 1960s, many species of insects had developed populations resistant to DDT; meanwhile, this highly stable compound was accumulating along the FOOD CHAIN and having toxic effects on various birds and fishes. During the 1960s it and similar chemicals were found to have severely reduced the populations of certain birds, including the bald eagle; its use is now tightly controlled in the U.S.

de *or* **te** \'dε\ (Chinese: "virtue") In TAOISM, the potentiality of TAO that is present in all things; in CONFUCIANISM, the virtue of internal goodness and propriety. In both systems, it is regarded as the active principle of tao, and is thus the life or moral principle. In the *TAO-TE CHING*, de is described as the unconscious functioning of the physical self, which can live harmoniously with nature. Personal de is thought to flourish when one abandons ambition and the spirit of contention for a life of naturalness, leading to an awareness of the underlying unity that permeates the universe.

De Beers Consolidated Mines World's largest producer and distributor of diamonds. Diamonds were first discovered in southern Africa in the mid-1860s on the de Beer farm. Two diamond mines dug there (no longer in operation) were at one time the world's most productive. CECIL RHODES bought a claim to the De Beers mine in 1871, and eventually bought claims to most of southern Africa's diamond mines. To keep prices high and demand steady, he formed the Diamond Syndicate (forerunner of today's Central Selling Organization) in the 1890s; it now controls nearly 80% of the world diamond trade. De Beers also has interests in explosives and chemicals, in synthetic diamonds, and in gold, coal, and copper mines.

de Colmar \di-'kōl-ˌmär\, **Charles Xavier Thomas** (1785–1870) French mathematician. In 1820, while serving in the French army, he built his first arithmometer, which could perform basic addition, subtraction, multiplication, and division. The first mechanical calculator to gain widespread use, it became a commercial success and was still being used up to World War I.

De Forest, Lee (1873–1961) U.S. inventor. Born in Council Bluffs, Iowa, he had invented many gadgets by age 13, including a working silverplating apparatus. After earning a PhD from Yale Univ., he founded the De Forest Wireless Telegraph Co. (1902) and gave public demonstrations of wireless telegraphy, including a live performance by E. CARUSO in 1910. In 1907 he patented the AUDION vacuum tube. He developed a sound-on-film optical-recording system called Phonofilm and demonstrated it in theaters (1923–27). Though he was unable to interest film producers in its possibilities, the film industry soon converted to talking pictures using a similar process. A poor businessman and a poorer judge of people, he was twice defrauded by his business partners. Eventually despairing of success in business or manufacturing, he sold his patents at low prices to such firms as American Telephone & Telegraph Co., which profited highly from their commercial development. Though embittered, he was widely honored as the father of radio and the grandfather of television.

De Gasperi \dā-gäs-'pā-rē\, **Alcide** (1881–1954) Italian prime minister (1945–53). Born in the southern Tirol under Austria-Hungary, he served in the Austrian parliament 1911–19, and sought the annexation of his region to Italy. He later served in the Italian parliament (1921–27) as a founder of the ITALIAN POPULAR PARTY. After 16 months' imprisonment as an anti-Fascist, he became a Vatican librarian in 1929. In World War II he was active in the resistance, and after the fall of the Fascist regime he returned to Italian politics as head of the newly formed CHRISTIAN DEMOCRATIC PARTY. As prime minister (1945–53), he enacted a new constitution, instituted land reform, and oversaw Italy's postwar economic reconstruction. Under his leadership Italy joined NATO, and he helped organize the Council of EUROPE and the EUROPEAN COAL AND STEEL COMMUNITY.

de Gaulle, Charles (-André-Marie-Joseph) (1890–1970) French soldier, statesman, and architect of France's FIFTH REPUBLIC. He joined the army in 1913 and fought with distinction in World War I. He was promoted to the staff of the supreme war council in 1925. In 1940 he was promoted to brigadier general and served briefly as undersecretary of state for defense under PAUL REYNAUD. After the fall of France to the Germans, he left for England and started the FREE FRENCH movement. Devoted to France and dedicated to its liberation, he moved to Algiers in 1943 and became president of the French Committee of National Liberation, at first jointly with HENRI HONORE GIRAUD. After the liberation of Paris, he returned and headed two provisional governments, then resigned in 1946. He opposed the FOURTH REPUBLIC, and in 1947 he formed the Rally of the French People (RPF), but severed his connections with it in 1953. He retired from public life and wrote his memoirs. When an insurrection in Algeria threatened to bring civil war to France, he returned to power in 1958, as prime minister with powers to reform the constitution. That same year he was elected president of the new FIFTH REPUBLIC, which ensured a strong presidency. He ended the ALGERIAN WAR and transformed France's African territories into 12 independent states. He withdrew France from NATO, and his policy of neutrality during the Vietnam War was seen by many as anti-Americanism. He began a policy of détente with Iron Curtain countries and traveled widely to form a bond with French-speaking countries. After the civil unrest of May 1968 by students and workers, he was defeated in a referendum on constitutional amendments and resigned in 1969.

de Girard \də-zhā-'rär\, **Philippe (Henri)** (1775–1845) French inventor. He devised an achromatic TELESCOPE, improved methods of preparing linen YARN for spinning, and designed a rotating STEAM ENGINE and steam cannon. He also developed a beet press, an improved WATERWHEEL, and a WIRE DRAWING machine.

De Grey River \də-'grā\ River, northwestern Western Australia. It rises as the Oakover River in the Robertson Range and flows north. Midway in its course, it turns northwest to join the Nullagine River and becomes the De Grey, continuing 118 mi (190 km) to the Indian Ocean. In 1888 the rich Pilbara goldfield attracted many settlers to the river's valley. The river supports pastureland for the grazing of sheep and cattle.

De Havilland, Geoffrey *later* **Sir Geoffrey** (1882–1965) British aircraft designer and manufacturer. In 1910 he built and flew an airplane with a 50-horsepower engine. He formed his own company in 1920 and built the commercially successful two-seater Moth. In World War II the twin-engined Mosquito was the company's most successful product. After the war he pioneered the manufacture of jet-propelled airplanes with his Comet passenger jet and Vampire and Venom jet fighters.

de Havilland \də-'ha-və-lənd\, **Olivia (Mary)** (born 1916) U.S. film actress. Born in Tokyo to British parents, she was raised in California. She made her film debut in 1935 and played the delicate heroine opposite ERROL FLYNN in such swashbucklers as *Captain Blood* (1935) and *The Adventures of Robin Hood* (1938). She revealed dramatic depth in *Gone with the Wind* (1939), *To Each His Own* (1946, Academy Award), *The Snake Pit* (1948), and *The Heiress* (1949, Academy Award). Her victory in a landmark lawsuit against WARNER BROTHERS (1945) limited actors' contracts to seven years, including suspension periods. She moved to Paris in 1955 and made only rare film appearances thereafter.

de Klerk \də-'klerk\, **F(rederik) W(illem)** (born 1936) President of South Africa (1989–94) who brought the APARTHEID system to an end and negotiated a transition to majority rule. Replacing P. W. BOTHA as leader of the NATIONAL PARTY and president, de Klerk quickly moved to release all important political prisoners, including NELSON MANDELA, and to lift the ban on the AFRICAN NATIONAL CONGRESS. He and Mandela jointly received the 1993 Nobel Peace Prize. Following the country's first all-race elections in 1994, Mandela became president and de Klerk was appointed second deputy president. He retired from politics in 1997.

de Kooning, Willem (1904–1997) Dutch-U.S. painter. He studied art in Rotterdam and entered the U.S. as a stowaway in 1926. Settling in Hoboken, N.J., he supported himself as a house painter before moving to New York City, where he came under the influence of ARSHILE GORKY. He supported himself by working for the WPA FEDERAL ART PROJECT. In the 1930s and '40s his work was both figurative and abstract; the two tendencies eventually fused in images that combined biomorphic and geometric shapes. In the 1940s he became one of the leading exponents of ABSTRACT EXPRESSIONISM, and particularly of ACTION PAINTING. Among his best-known works is a series of deliberately vulgar images of women done with roughly applied pigment and raw colors (e.g., *Woman I*, 1950–52; *Woman and Bicycle,* 1953). In 1963 he moved to East Hampton, N.Y. In his later years he produced clay sculpture that was cast into bronze.

de la Mare, Walter (John) (1873–1956) British poet and novelist. Of French Huguenot descent, he was educated in London and worked for the Standard Oil Co. (1890–1908) before turning to writing, initially under the pseudonym Walter Ramal. He wrote for both adults and children. His collection *Come Hither* (1923) was especially highly praised. *Memoirs of a Midget* (1921) was his best-known novel. His *Collected Stories for Children* appeared in 1947. He was buried in St. Paul's Cathedral.

de la Renta, Oscar (born 1932) Dominican-U.S. fashion designer. After studies in Santo Domingo and Madrid, he became staff designer for CRISTOBAL BALENCIAGA in Madrid. In 1962 he moved to New York and started his own company to produce women's ready-to-wear fashions. In 1973 he founded Oscar de la Renta Couture and expanded into household linens, menswear, and perfumes. In the 1970s he introduced the ethnic look with gypsy and Russian themes; more recently he has produced romantic evening clothes in taffeta, chiffon, velvet, brocade, and fur. Since 1993 he has been couture designer for PIERRE BALMAIN.

de la Roche \də-lä-'rōsh\, **Mazo** (1879–1961). Canadian author. Born in Newmarket, Ontario, she is best known for a series of novels centered on the Whiteoak family of Jalna, an estate in her native Ontario. These sagas of the family's history, more popular in the U.S. and Europe than in Canada, were the basis of a film, *Jalna* (1935), and a play, *Whiteoaks* (1936). She also wrote children's stories, travel books, drama, and an autobiography.

De La Warr \'de-lə-ˌwar\, **Baron** *or* **Baron Delaware** *orig.* **Thomas West** (1577–1618) English founder of Virginia. After serving under the Earl of Essex in the Netherlands and Ireland, he became a member of the Virginia Co. and was appointed governor in 1610. He and 150 settlers arrived at Jamestown as another group was abandoning the colony. He established two forts at the mouth of the James River and rebuilt Jamestown. Delaware Bay, the Delaware River, and the state of Delaware were named for him.

De Laurentiis \dā-laů-'ren-tēs, *Engl* ˌdē-lòr-'en-shəs\, **Dino** (born 1919) Italian-U.S. film producer. He produced his first film at 20 and scored his first hit with *Bitter Rice* (1948). He formed a joint production company with Carlo Ponti (born 1910) and produced such admired films as FEDERICO FELLINI'S *La strada* (1954, Academy Award) and *The Nights of Cabiria* (1956, Academy Award). In the early 1960s he built a studio, Dinocittà, where he made several epics; their lack of success forced him to sell the studio in the early 1970s. He then moved to the U.S., where he produced such films as *Serpico* (1973), *Ragtime* (1981), and *Crimes of the Heart* (1986) before a string of failures forced him into bankruptcy.

De Leon, Daniel (1852–1914) U.S. (Dutch-born) socialist. Born in Curaçao, he arrived in the U.S. in 1874. He joined the Socialist Labor Party in 1890 and soon became one of its leaders. Finding the labor union leadership insufficiently radical, he led a faction that seceded from the Knights of Labor in 1895, later forming the Socialist Trade and Labor Alliance (STLA). In 1905 he helped found the INDUSTRIAL WORKERS OF THE WORLD (IWW), which absorbed the STLA. In 1908 his leadership was rejected by extremists who favored more violent forms of political activity, and he created the unsuccessful Workers' International Industrial Union.

de Man \də-'män\, **Paul** (1919–1983) Belgian-U.S. literary critic. He emigrated to the U.S. in 1947, attended Harvard Univ., and in 1970 joined the faculty at Yale, where he remained the rest of his life. His groundbreaking *Blindness and Insight* (1971) made Yale the American center for deconstructive literary criticism (see DECONSTRUCTION). His other works include *Allegories of Reading* (1979), *The Rhetoric of Romanticism* (1984), and *Aesthetic Ideology* (1988). His reputation was undermined with the posthumous revelation of his wartime anti-Semitic writings for the pro-Nazi Belgian newspaper *Le Soir.*

de Mille \də-'mil\, **Agnes (George)** (1905–1993) U.S. dancer and choreographer who expanded the innovative use of American themes. Born in New York City, she graduated from UCLA and moved back to New York, and soon was touring the U.S. with her own mime-dance concerts (1929–40). She choreographed works for Ballet (later AMERICAN BALLET) THEATRE; in *Rodeo* (1942) she used TAP DANCING for the first time in a ballet. She choreographed many Broadway musicals, including *Oklahoma!* (1943), *Carousel* (1945), *Brigadoon* (1947), and *Paint Your Wagon* (1951). She wrote several books on dance and an autobiography.

De Niro \də-'nir-ō\, **Robert** (born 1943) U.S. film actor. Born in New York City, the son of an artist, he made his debut in 1968 and played in minor films until his critically acclaimed performance in *Bang the Drum Slowly* (1973). He starred in *Mean Streets* (1973) and other films directed by MARTIN SCORSESE, including *Taxi Driver* (1976), *Raging Bull* (1980, Academy Award), and *GoodFellas* (1990). Noted for his intensely committed performances, he also starred in *The Godfather, Part II* (1974, Academy Award), *The Deer Hunter* (1978), *True Confessions* (1981), and *Wag the Dog* (1997). He directed his first film, *A Bronx Tale,* in 1993.

De Palma \də-'päl-mə\, **Brian (Russell)** (born 1940) U.S. film director. Born in Newark, N.J., he made his first feature-length film, *The Wedding Party,* in 1964 (released 1969). The commercial success of *Carrie* (1976) established his reputation as a director of graphic horror-suspense films. After openly imitating the work of ALFRED HITCHCOCK in the 1970s, he found his own style in such films as *Dressed to Kill* (1980), *Blow Out* (1981), and *Body Double* (1984). He also directed *The Untouchables* (1987), *Casualties of War* (1989), *Carlito's Way* (1993), and *Snake Eyes* (1998).

De Quincey, Thomas (1785–1859) English essayist and critic. While a student at Oxford he first took opium to relieve the pain of facial neuralgia. He became a lifelong addict, an experience that inspired his best-known work, *Confessions of an English Opium-Eater* (1822), whose highly poetic and imaginative prose has made it an enduring masterpiece of English style. As a critic he is best known for the essay "On the Knocking at the Gate in *Macbeth*" (1823).

De Sica \də-'sē-kə\, **Vittorio** (1901–1974) Italian film director and actor. He joined an acting company in 1923 and soon became a matinee idol. He appeared on screen as a leading man in a series of light comedies, and he excelled in a dramatic role in ROBERTO ROSSELLINI'S *General della Rovere* (1959). He directed his first film in 1940 and, working with screenwriter Cesare Zavattini, made a major contribution to the Neorealism of the postwar Italian cinema with *Shoeshine* (1946, Academy Award) and *The Bicycle Thief* (1948, Academy Award). His later films include *Umberto D* (1952), *Two Women* (1961), *Yesterday, Today, and Tomorrow* (1963, Academy Award), and *The Garden of the Finzi-Continis* (1971, Academy Award).

de Soto \thā-'sō-tō, *Engl* di-'sō-tō\, **Hernando** (1496?–1542) Spanish explorer and conquistador. He joined the 1514 expedition of Pedro Arias Dávila (1440–1531) to the West Indies, and in Panama he quickly made his mark as a trader and explorer. By 1520 he had accumulated a small fortune through his slave trading in Nicaragua and on the Isthmus of Panama. He joined FRANCISCO PIZARRO on an expedition to conquer Peru in 1532, returning to Spain in 1536 with great wealth. Commissioned by the Spanish crown to conquer what is now Florida, he departed in 1538 in command of 10 ships and 700 men. On that expedition he explored the extensive region that was to become the southeastern U.S. and discovered the Mississippi River. Overcome by fever, he died in Louisiana and was buried in the Mississippi.

De Stijl See De STIJL

de Valera \ˌdev-ə-'ler-ə\, **Eamon** *orig.* **Edward** (1882–1975) Irish (U.S.-born) politician and patriot. Born in New York City to a Spanish father and an Irish mother, at age 2 he was sent to live with his mother's family in Ireland when his father died. He joined the Irish Volunteers (1913) and helped lead the rebels in the EASTER RISING. He was elected president of SINN FÉIN in 1918. Repudiating the treaty that formed the Irish Free State because it provided for the partition of Ireland, he supported the republican resistance in the ensuing civil war. In 1924 he founded FIANNA FÁIL, which won the 1932 elections. As prime minister (1932–48), he took the Irish Free State out of the British COMMONWEALTH and made his country a "sovereign" state, renamed Ireland, or Éire. He proclaimed Ireland neutral in World War II. After twice serving again as prime minister (1951–54, 1957–59), he became president of Ireland (1959–73).

De Valera, c. 1965.
BY COURTESY OF THE IRISH EMBASSY; PHOTOGRAPH, LENSMEN LTD. PRESS PHOTO AGENCY, DUBLIN

de Valois \də-vȧl-'wä\, **Ninette** *later* **Dame Ninette** *orig.* **Edris Stannus** (1898–2000) British dancer, choreographer, and founder of the precursor to the ROYAL BALLET. She appeared in revues and pantomimes from 1914, before joining the BALLETS RUSSES as a soloist in 1923. She founded the Academy of Choreographic Art in 1926 to teach movement to actors, and cofounded the Camargo Society in 1930. In 1931 she founded and directed the Vic-Wells Ballet; this became the Sadler's Wells Ballet (1946–56) and later the Royal Ballet (1956), which she directed until 1963. She choreographed many ballets in the 1930s and '40s and remained active with the company until 1971.

De Voto \di-'vō-tō\, **Bernard (Augustine)** (1897–1955) U.S. journalist, historian, and critic. Born in Ogden, Utah, he taught at Northwestern University and Harvard, briefly edited *The Saturday Review* (1936–38), and wrote a column for *Harper's* 1935–55. Known for his works on American literature and the history of the western frontier as well as his vigorous, outspoken style, he was one of the most widely read critics and historians of his day. Among his nonfiction works are *Mark Twain's America* (1932), *Across the Wide Missouri* (1948, Pulitzer Prize), and *The Course of Empire* (1952).

de Vries \də-'vrēs\, **Hugo (Marie)** (1848–1935) Dutch botanist and geneticist. He taught at Amsterdam University 1878–1918, where he introduced the experimental study of organic evolution. His rediscovery in 1900 (simultaneously with CARL ERICH CORRENS and ERICH TSCHERMAK VON SEYSENEGG) of GREGOR MENDEL's principles of HEREDITY and his own theory of biological MUTATION explained concepts about the nature of variation of species that made possible the universal acceptance and active investigation of CHARLES DARWIN's theory of organic evolution. De Vries discovered and named the phenomenon known as mutation, and also contributed to knowledge of the role of osmosis in plant physiology. See also WILLIAM BATESON.

de Wolfe, Elsie *orig.* **Ella Anderson** (1865–1950) U.S. interior designer. A New York socialite, she worked as a professional actress (1890–1904) before becoming a designer. Her design principles of simplicity, airiness, and visual unity helped change the fashion of interior design. She spent much of her life in France as a noted hostess. During World War I she nursed soldiers, for which service she received the Croix de Guerre.

DEA See DRUG ENFORCEMENT ADMINISTRATION

Dead Sea *Arabic* **Bahret Lut** \'bä-ret-'lüt\ *ancient* **Lacus Asphaltites** Landlocked salt lake between Israel and Jordan. The lowest body of water on the earth, it averages about 1,312 ft (400 m) below sea level. At 50 mi (80 km) long and up to 11 mi (18 km) wide, its northern half belongs to Jordan, while its southern half is divided between Jordan and Israel. After the 1967 ARAB-ISRAELI WAR, however, the Israeli army remained in occupation of the entire western shore. The Dead Sea lies between JUDAEA to the west and the Transjordanian plateaus to the east; the JORDAN RIVER flows in from the north. It has been associated with biblical history since the time of ABRAHAM.

Dead Sea Scrolls Caches of ancient, mostly Hebrew, manuscripts found at several sites on the northwestern shore of the Dead Sea (1947–56). The writings date from between the 3rd century BC and the 2nd century AD and total 800–900 manuscripts in 15,000 fragments. Many scholars believe that those deposited in 11 caves near the ruins of QUMRAN belonged to a sectarian community whom most scholars believe were ESSENES, though other scholars suggest SADDUCEES or Zealots. The community rejected the rest of the Jewish people and saw the world as sharply divided between good and evil. They cultivated a communal life of ritual purity, called the "Union," led by a messianic "Teacher of Righteousness." The Dead Sea Scrolls as a whole represent a wider spectrum of Jewish belief and may have been the contents of libraries from Jerusalem hidden during the war of AD 66–73. See also DAMASCUS DOCUMENT.

deafness Partial or total inability to hear. In conduction deafness, the passage of sound vibrations through the ear is interrupted. The obstacle may be earwax, a ruptured eardrum, or stapes fixation, which prevents the stapes bone from transmitting sound vibrations to the INNER EAR. In nerve deafness, a defect in the sensory cells of the inner ear (e.g., injury by excessive noise) or in the vestibulocochlear nerve prevents the transmission of sound impulses to the auditory center in the brain. Some deaf people are helped by HEARING AIDS or cochlear implants; others can learn to communicate with SIGN LANGUAGE and/or lip reading.

Deák \'de-äk\, **Ferenc** (1803–1876) Hungarian politician. He entered the Hungarian Diet in 1833, becoming a leader of the reform movement for the political emancipation of Hungary. Appointed minister of justice in 1848, he was the principal author of the reforming "April laws." In the 1860s he put forth Hungary's conditions for reconciliation with Austria in terms that led to the COMPROMISE OF 1867, establishing the dual monarchy of Austria-Hungary, and he helped to complete the legislation deriving from the Compromise.

Dean, Dizzy *orig.* **Jay Hanna** (1911–1974) U.S. baseball pitcher. Born in Lucas, Ark., he did not finish elementary school. He joined the St. Louis Cardinals in 1932, and in five seasons with them led the National League four times in complete games and four times in strikeouts. In 1937 he teamed with his brother Paul (nicknamed "Daffy") to pitch the Cardinals to a World Series victory; he won 30 games and lost seven that year, and remains the last 30-game winner in the National League. He developed arm trouble the same year and never fully regained his form. He ended his career with the Chicago Cubs after being traded for the 1938 season. He was known for his colorful personality, which, after his retirement at age 30, served him well as a broadcaster.

Dean, James (Byron) (1931–1955) U.S. film actor. Born in Marion, Ind., he played bit parts in four films before trying the Broadway stage, where his role in *The Immoralist* (1954) led to a screen test and a brilliant though brief movie career. His starring role in *East of Eden* (1955) brought him an Academy Award nomination. As a misunderstood teenager in *Rebel Without a Cause* (1955) he personified the confused and restless youth of the 1950s. He was featured as a nonconformist ranch hand in his last film, *Giant* (1956). His death at 24 in an automobile crash before the film's release caused anguish among his fans and contributed to his idolization as a cult figure.

James Dean in *Giant* (1956).

Dean, John Wesley, III (born 1938) U.S. lawyer and White House counsel. Born in Akron, Ohio, he studied law at Georgetown University and in 1970 was appointed White House counsel by Pres. RICHARD NIXON. In 1972 Nixon asked Dean to investigate whether White House personnel were involved in the Watergate Hotel break-in (see WATERGATE SCANDAL). Refusing to participate in a cover-up, Dean began telling federal investigators what he knew. He was fired by Nixon in April 1973 and two months later testified before a Senate committee about obstruction of justice by White House officials, including the president. His revelations ultimately led to Nixon's resignation.

Deane, Silas (1737–1789) U.S. diplomat. Born in Groton, Conn., he served as a delegate to the Continental Congress, which in 1776 sent him to France secretly to obtain financial and military assistance. The shiploads of arms he secured contributed to the American victory at the Battle of SARATOGA. In 1777 he, BENJAMIN FRANKLIN, and Arthur Lee (1740–1792) negotiated treaties with France for commerce and alliance. Lee later insinuated that Deane had embezzled money; though never proved, the allegations ruined him.

Dearborn City (pop., 1996 est.: 91,000), southeastern Michigan. Settled in 1795, it originated as a stagecoach stop between DETROIT and CHICAGO. It was the birthplace of HENRY FORD and the headquarters of the FORD MOTOR CO. Industrial development began with the building of the Ford assembly plant in 1917 and continued with related automotive industries. It was incorporated as a city in 1925.

Dearborn, Henry (1751–1829) U.S. army officer and secretary of war (1801–9). Born in Hampton, N.H., he fought in the American Revolution and later was appointed marshal for the District of Maine (1789–93). He represented Massachusetts in the U.S. House of Representatives (1793–97), was secretary of war under Pres. THOMAS JEFFERSON, and ordered the establishment of Fort Dearborn at "Chikago" in 1803. In the WAR OF 1812, he commanded several failed attempts to invade Canada and was recalled by Pres. JAMES MADISON.

death penalty See CAPITAL PUNISHMENT

Death Valley Valley, southeastern California. The lowest, hottest, driest portion of North America, it is about 140 mi (225 km) long and from 5 to 15 mi (8–24 km) wide. The Amargosa River flows into it from the south and contains a small pool, Badwater, that at 282 ft (86 m) below sea level is the lowest point in North America. Death Valley was formerly an obstacle to pioneer settlers (hence its name); it later was a center of borax mining. Declared a national monument in 1933, it was made a national park in 1994; the park covers 3,336,000 acres (2,351,000 hectares) and extends into Nevada.

deathwatch beetle Borer insect (BEETLE species *Xestobium refuvillosum*) that tends to be small (less than 0.5 in., or 1–9 mm) and cylindrical. When disturbed, it usually pulls in its legs and plays dead. It makes a ticking or clicking sound by bumping its head or jaws against the sides of the tunnels it creates as it bores into old furniture and wood, a sound that, according to superstition, forecasts a death.

Deathwatch beetle (*Xestobium refuvillosum*).

G. E. HYDE FROM THE NATURAL HISTORY PHOTOGRAPHIC AGENCY—EB INC.

DeBakey \də-'bā-kē\, **Michael (Ellis)** (born 1908) U.S. surgeon. Born in Lake Charles, La., he received his MD from Tulane University. In 1932 he devised the "roller pump," to be used in heart-lung machines. His work with the U.S. Surgeon General's office led to the development of mobile army surgical hospitals (MASH units). He also developed an efficient method of grafting frozen blood vessels to correct aortic aneurysms and pioneered the use of plastic tubing instead of grafts (1956). He was the first to perform a successful coronary artery bypass, and in 1963 he was the first to insert a mechanical device into the chest to assist the heart. He edited the *Yearbook of Surgery* (1958–70). His many awards include the Medal of Freedom.

déblé \'dyeb-lā, 'deb-lā\ Wooden female figure carved by the Senufo people of West Africa. It was used as a "rhythm pounder" in dance rituals to promote the fertility of the soil. The Poro (or Lo) male secret society held the figures by the upper arms and pounded them on the ground to keep the rhythm as they performed the fertility dance. The figures were also placed in the fields during digging contests.

Deborah (c. 1150–c. 1050 BC) Prophetess and political leader of ancient Israel. Her story is told in the Old Testament's Book of Judges. With her general, Barak, she is credited with defeating the Canaanite armies led by Sisera. The Israelite victory over the Canaanites, which was aided by a thunderstorm that Israel saw as the coming of God from Mount Sinai, was celebrated in the Song of Deborah (Judges 5), possibly the earliest portion of the Bible.

Debré \də-'brā\, **Michel (-Jean-Pierre)** (1912–1996) French politician. He entered the civil service and advanced steadily. In World War II he escaped from German imprisonment to join the Resistance and worked in the underground in German-occupied France. In 1945 he joined CHARLES DE GAULLE's provisional government. He served in the senate 1948–58. He was the principal author of the constitution of the FIFTH REPUBLIC and its first premier (1959–62). He served in the National Assembly 1963–68, then in various cabinet posts, including minister of defense (1969–73).

Debrecen \'de-bret-ˌsen\ City (pop., 2000 est.: 203,648), eastern Hungary. An important city in eastern Hungary, it has long been a market center and a religious, political, and cultural arena. Chartered in the 14th century, it became prominent during and after the Turkish occupation. Hungary's short-lived independence from the HABSBURGS was proclaimed there in 1849; the city later reverted to Austrian control. During World War II it was briefly the seat of the interim Hungarian government. Still a commercial and cultural center, its monuments include the Great Reformed Church; it is the site of Lajos Kossuth University (1912).

Debs, Eugene V(ictor) (1855–1926) U.S. labor organizer. Debs was born in Terre Haute, Ind., and left home at 14 to work in the railroad shops. As a locomotive fireman, he became an early advocate of industrial unionism, and he became president of the American Railway Union in 1893. His involvement in the PULLMAN STRIKE led to a six-month prison term in 1895. In 1898 he helped found the U.S. Socialist Party; he would run as its presidential candidate five times (1900–20). In 1905 he helped found the INDUSTRIAL WORKERS OF THE WORLD. Debs was charged with sedition in 1918 after denouncing the 1917 Espionage Act; he conducted his last presidential campaign from prison, winning 915,000 votes, before being released by presidential order in 1921.

Eugene V. Debs.

BY COURTESY OF THE LIBRARY OF CONGRESS, WASHINGTON, D.C.

debt Something owed. Anyone having borrowed money or goods from another owes a debt and is under obligation to return the goods or repay the money, usually with INTEREST. For governments, the need to borrow in order to finance a deficit budget has led to the development of various forms of NATIONAL DEBT. See also BANKRUPTCY, DEBTOR AND CREDITOR, USURY.

debtor and creditor Respectively, a person who owes a debt and a person to whom the debt is owed. Usually the debtor has received something from the creditor, in return for which the debtor has promised to make repayment at a later time. If the debtor fails to repay by the deadline, a formal collection process may commence. It is sometimes possible to attach the debtor's property, wages, or bank account as a means of forcing payment. Imprisonment of the debtor is a practice no longer followed. See also GARNISHMENT, LIEN.

Debussy \ˌde-byü-'sē\, **(Achille-) Claude** (1862–1918) French composer. Born into near-poverty, he showed an early gift for the piano. He entered the Paris Conservatoire in 1873, and soon thereafter was employed as pianist by Nadezhda von Meck, P. TCHAIKOVSKY's patroness. Influenced by the Symbolist poets and Impressionist painters, he was early led toward a compositional style of great originality, shunning the strictures of traditional counterpoint and harmony to achieve new effects of great subtlety through unusual voice leading and timbral colors to evoke pictorial images and moods especially of languor and hedonism. He is regarded as the founder of musical IMPRESSIONISM. His significance in weakening the hold of traditional tonal harmony equals that of F. LISZT, RICHARD WAGNER, and A. SCHOENBERG. Given his effect on such composers as M. RAVEL, I. STRAVINSKY, BELA BARTOK, A. BERG, A. WEBERN, and P. BOULEZ, he can be seen as the most influential French composer of the last three centuries. His works include the opera *Pelléas et Mélisande* (1902); the orchestral works *Prelude to The Afternoon of a Faun* (1894), *Nocturnes* (1899), *La mer* (1905), *Images* (1912), and the ballet *Jeux* (1913); a string quartet (1893); the piano sets *Estampes* (1903), *Images* (1905, 1907), *Children's Corner* (1908), 24 *Préludes* (1910, 1913), and 12 *Études* (1915); and many songs.

Debussy, painting by Marcel Baschet, 1884; in the Musée de Versailles.

GIRAUDON—ART RESOURCE

Debye \də-'bī\, **Peter** *orig.* **Petrus Josephus Wilhelmus Debije** (1884–1966) Dutch-U.S. physical chemist. His first important research, on ELECTRIC DIPOLE moments, advanced knowledge of the arrangement of ATOMS in MOLECULES and of the distances between atoms. He showed that X-ray CRYSTALLOGRAPHY worked on powders, obviating the difficult first step of preparing good crystals. In 1923 he and Erich Hückel extended SVANTE ARRHENIUS's theory of the DISSOCIATION of SALTS in solution, proving that IONIZATION is complete. He also investigated light scattering in gases. He won the Nobel Prize in 1936.

Decadents Group of poets of the end of the 19th century, including some French Symbolists (see SYMBOLIST MOVEMENT), notably STEPHANE

MALLARME and PAUL VERLAINE, and the later generation of England's Aesthetic movement (see AESTHETICISM), notably ARTHUR SYMONS and OSCAR WILDE. Many nonpoets, including the novelist J.-K. HUYSMANS and the artist AUBREY BEARDSLEY, are also often associated with the Decadents. The Decadents emphasized art for art's sake, seeing it as autonomous and opposed to nature and to the materialistic preoccupations of industrialized society, and therefore stressed the bizarre, incongruous, and artificial in both their work and their lives.

Decansky, Stefan See STEFAN DECANSKY

decapod Any of more than 8,000 species (order Decapoda) of CRUSTACEANS having five pairs of legs attached to the thorax. The shrimplike species, which can be as small as 0.5 in. (12 mm), have a slender body with a long abdomen, a well-developed fantail, and, often, long, slender legs. The crablike types, whose claw span can measure 13 ft (4 m), have a flattened body and, frequently, stout short legs and a reduced tail fan. Decapods are primarily marine and are most abundant in shallow tropical waters, but they are commercially valuable throughout the world. Some species (e.g., HERMIT and FIDDLER crabs) are adapted to terrestrial environments. See also CRAB, CRAYFISH, LOBSTER, SHRIMP.

Decapolis \di-'ka-pə-lis\ League of 10 ancient Greek cities, including DAMASCUS, in eastern PALESTINE. It was formed after the Roman conquest in 63 BC for mutual protection against their Semitic neighbors. The name also denotes the roughly contiguous territory formed by these cities, all but one of which lay east of the JORDAN RIVER. The exact number of cities varied over time. Subject to the Roman governor of Syria, the league survived until the 2nd century AD.

DeCarava, Roy (born 1919) U.S. photographer. Born in New York City, DeCarava took up photography in the late 1940s. In 1952 he was awarded a Guggenheim Fellowship in support of his project to photograph the people of his native Harlem. Many of these photos were compiled in the book *The Sweet Flypaper of Life* (1955), with text written by the poet LANGSTON HUGHES. DeCarava's interest in education led him to found A Photographer's Gallery, which sought to educate the public about photography, in 1955, and an association of black photographers in 1963. He is perhaps best known for his portraits of jazz musicians.

decathlon Composite athletic contest that consists of ten different track-and-field competitions: the 100-, 400-, and 1,500-m runs, the 110-m high hurdles, the JAVELIN and DISCUS throws, SHOT PUT, POLE VAULT, HIGH JUMP, and LONG JUMP. Introduced as a three-day event at the 1912 Olympic Games, it later became a two-day event. Competitors are scored according to a table established by the International Amateur Athletic Federation. Decathloners are often regarded as the finest all-around athletes in the world.

Decatur \di-'kā-tər\ City (pop., 2000: 81,860), central Illinois. Situated on the Sangamon River east of SPRINGFIELD, it was founded in 1829. In 1860 it was the site of ABRAHAM LINCOLN's first endorsement by a party convention for the presidential nomination. It is a commercial center for the surrounding agricultural region. Industries include the processing of corn and soybeans and the manufacture of tractors and other vehicles.

Decatur \di-'kā-tər\, **Stephen** (1779–1820) U.S. naval officer. Born in Sinepuxent, Md., he entered the navy in 1798. In the TRIPOLITAN WAR he led a daring 1804 expedition into the harbor of Tripoli to burn a captured U.S. ship. In the War of 1812 he commanded the USS *United States* and captured the British ship *Macedonian*. In 1815 he commanded a squadron in the Mediterranean that forced a peace with the Barbary states on U.S. terms. At a banquet on his return he gave a toast that included the words "Our country, right or wrong." In 1815 he was made a navy commissioner, an office he held until killed in a duel.

Deccan Peninsula of India south of the NARMADA RIVER. In a more restricted sense, it is the tableland between the Narmada and KRISHNA rivers, comprising MAHARASHTRA and parts of MADHYA PRADESH, ANDHRA PRADESH, KARNATAKA, and ORISSA. Its average elevation is about 2,000 feet (600 m). Its principal rivers, the GODAVARI, KRISHNA, and KAVERI, flow from the WEST GHATS eastward to the Bay of BENGAL. Its early inhabitants were a Dravidian population not reached by the 2d millennium BC Aryan invasion. Ruled by MAURYAN (4th–2nd century BC) and GUPTA (4th–6th century AD) dynasties, it became an independent Muslim kingdom in 1347. Later split up into five Muslim sultanates, Deccan was largely conquered by the MUGHAL DYNASTY in the 17th century. In the 18th century it was the scene of rivalry between the British and French, and subsequently of the British struggle against the MARATHA CONFEDERACY. It remained under British control until India gained independence in 1947.

Decembrist revolt (December 1825) Unsuccessful uprising by Russian revolutionaries. Following the death of ALEXANDER I, a group of liberal members of the upper classes and military officers staged a rebellion in an effort to prevent the accession of NICHOLAS I. The poorly organized revolt was easily suppressed. Afterwards 289 Decembrists were tried; five were executed, 31 imprisoned, and the rest banished to Siberia. Their martyrdom inspired later generations of Russian dissidents.

decibel (dB) Unit for measuring the relative intensities of sounds or the relative amounts of acoustic or electric power. Because it requires about a tenfold increase in power for a sound to register as twice as loud to the human ear, a logarithmic scale is useful for comparing sound intensity. Thus, the threshold of human hearing (absolute silence) is assigned the value of 0 dB and each increase of 10 dB corresponds to a tenfold increase in intensity and a doubling in loudness. The "threshold of pain" for intensity varies from 120 to 130 dB among different individuals. A related unit is the bel = 10 dB. It is named for ALEXANDER GRAHAM BELL.

Nonlinear (Decibel) and Linear (Intensity) Scales

Decibels	Intensity*	Type of sound
130	10	artillery fire at close proximity (threshold of pain)
120	1	amplified rock music; near jet engine
110	10^{-1}	loud orchestral music, in audience
100	10^{-2}	electric saw
90	10^{-3}	bus or truck interior
80	10^{-4}	automobile interior
70	10^{-5}	average street noise; loud telephone bell
60	10^{-6}	normal conversation; business office
50	10^{-7}	restaurant; private office
40	10^{-8}	quiet room in home
30	10^{-9}	quiet lecture hall; bedroom
20	10^{-10}	radio, television, or recording studio
10	10^{-11}	soundproof room
0	10^{-12}	absolute silence (threshold of hearing)

*In watts per square meter.

deciduous tree Broad-leaved tree that sheds all its leaves during one season. Deciduous forests are found in three middle-latitude regions with a temperate climate characterized by a winter season and year-round precipitation: eastern North America, western Eurasia, and northeastern Asia. They also extend into more arid regions along stream banks and around bodies of water. OAKS, BEECHES, BIRCHES, CHESTNUTS, ASPENS, ELMS, MAPLES, and BASSWOODS (or LINDENS) are the dominant trees in mid-latitude deciduous forests. Other plants that shed their leaves seasonally may also be called deciduous. See also CONIFER, EVERGREEN.

decision theory In STATISTICS and related subfields of philosophy, the theory and method of formulating and solving general decision problems. Such a problem is specified by a set of possible states of the environment or possible initial conditions; a set of available experiments and a set of possible outcomes for each experiment, giving information about the state of affairs preparatory to making a decision; a set of available acts depending on the experiments made and their consequences; and a set of possible consequences of the acts, in which each possible act assigns to each possible initial state some particular consequence. The problem is dealt with by assessing probabilities of consequences conditional on different choices of experiments and acts and by assigning a utility function to the set of consequences according to some scheme of value or preference of the decision maker. An optimal solution consists of an optimal decision function, which assigns to each possible experiment an optimal act that maximizes the utility, or value, and a choice of an optimal experiment. See also COST-BENEFIT ANALYSIS, GAME THEORY.

Decius \'dē-shəs\, **Gaius Messius Quintus Trajanus** (AD 201?–251) Roman emperor (249–251). Of uncertain origins, he served as senator, consul, and provincial military commander before taking the throne from Philip the Arabian. He resisted the Gothic invasion of MOESIA, and instituted the first organized persecution of Christians throughout the empire (250), which only served to strengthen the Christian cause. He ended the persecutions in 251, shortly before he was defeated and killed by the GOTHS.

Declaration of Independence (July 4, 1776) Document approved by the CONTINENTAL CONGRESS that announced the separation of 13 North American British colonies from Britain. The armed conflict during the AMERICAN REVOLUTION gradually convinced the colonists that separation from Britain was essential. Several colonies instructed their delegates to the Continental Congress to vote for independence. On June 7, RICHARD HENRY LEE of Virginia offered a resolution for independence. The congress appointed THOMAS JEFFERSON, JOHN ADAMS, BENJAMIN FRANKLIN, ROGER SHERMAN, and ROBERT R. LIVINGSTON to draft a declaration. Jefferson was persuaded to write the draft, which was presented with few changes on June 28. It began with a declaration of individual rights and then listed the acts of tyranny by GEORGE III that formed the justification for seeking independence. After debate and changes to accommodate regional interests, including deletion of a condemnation of slavery, it was approved on July 4 as "The Unanimous Declaration of the Thirteen United States of America." It was signed by Congress president JOHN HANCOCK, printed, and read aloud to a crowd assembled outside, then engrossed (written in script) on parchment and signed by the 56 delegates.

Declaration of the Rights of Man and of the Citizen Manifesto adopted by France's National Assembly in 1789, which contained the principles that inspired the FRENCH REVOLUTION. One of the basic charters of human liberties, it served as the preamble to the CONSTITUTION OF 1791. Its basic principle was that "all men are born free and equal in rights," specified as the rights of liberty, private property, the inviolability of the person, and resistance to oppression. It also established the principle of equality before the law and the freedoms of religion and speech. The Declaration represented a repudiation of the pre-Revolutionary monarchical regime.

Declaratory Act (1766) Declaration by the British Parliament that accompanied repeal of the STAMP ACT. It stated that Parliament's authority was the same in America as in Britain and asserted Parliament's authority to make laws binding on the American colonies.

declaratory judgment In law, a judgment merely declaring a right or establishing the legal status or interpretation of a law or instrument. It is binding but is distinguished from other judgments or court opinions in that it includes no executive element (an order that something be done); instead it simply declares or defines rights to be observed or wrongs to be eschewed by litigants, or expresses the court's view on a contested question of law.

decolonization Process by which colonies become independent of the colonizing country. Decolonization was gradual and peaceful for some British colonies largely settled by expatriates, but violent for others, where native rebellions were energized by nationalism. The postwar European nations generally lacked the wealth and political capacity necessary to suppress faraway revolts and lacked the support of the new superpowers, the U.S. and the Soviet Union, which had taken positions opposing COLONIALISM. Korea was freed in 1945 by Japan's defeat in the war. The U.S. relinquished the Philippines in 1946. Britain left India in 1947, Palestine in 1948, and Egypt in 1956; it withdrew from Africa in the 1950s and '60s, from various island protectorates in the 1970s and '80s, and from Hong Kong in 1997. The French left Vietnam in 1954 and had given up its North African colonies by 1962. Portugal gave up its African colonies in the 1970s; Macao was returned to the Chinese in 1999.

decompression chamber See HYPERBARIC CHAMBER

decompression sickness *or* **bends** *or* **caisson disease** Harmful effects of rapid change from a higher- to a lower-pressure environment. Small amounts of the gases in air are dissolved in body tissues. When pilots of unpressurized aircraft go to high altitudes, or when divers breathing compressed air return to the surface, external pressure on the body decreases and the gases come out of solution. Rising slowly allows the gases to enter the bloodstream and be taken to the lungs and exhaled; with a quicker ascent, the gases (mostly nitrogen) form bubbles in the tissues. In the nervous system, they can cause paralysis, convulsions, motor and sensory problems, and psychological changes; in the joints, severe pain and restricted mobility (the bends); in the respiratory system, coughing and difficulty breathing. Severe cases include SHOCK. Recompression in a HYPERBARIC CHAMBER followed by gradual decompression cannot always reverse tissue damage.

deconstruction Method of literary criticism that assumes that language refers only to itself rather than to an extratextual reality and that asserts multiple conflicting interpretations of a text, basing such interpretations on the metaphoric and philosophical implications of the use of language in the text rather than on the author's intention. Loosely, the "meaning" of a text is sought not in the individual author's subjectivity but rather in the play of linguistic devices (such as metaphor and metonymy) and structures in the writing itself. Deconstruction was initiated by JACQUES DERRIDA in the 1960s and has become an important part of POSTMODERNISM, especially in POSTSTRUCTURALISM and textual analysis.

Decoration Day See MEMORIAL DAY

decorative arts Arts concerned with the design and decoration of objects that are utilitarian rather than purely aesthetic, including CERAMICS, glassware, BASKETRY, JEWELRY, METALWORK, FURNITURE, and TEXTILES. The separation of the decorative arts from the fine arts is a modern distinction.

deduction In LOGIC, a type of inference distinguished by the fact that if the premises of the inference are all true, then the conclusion necessarily follows and hence is also true. This feature distinguishes deduction from INDUCTION. The above definition of deduction is hypothetical and speaks only about the formal relationship between the premises and the conclusion of a deduction; it does not imply that all the premises or the conclusion of any deduction must in fact be true. Thus, the following inference is deductive, even though the second premise and the conclusion are untrue: "No odd natural number is divisible without remainder by 2; 4 is an odd natural number; therefore, 4 is not divisible without remainder by 2."

deed See ESCROW

Deep Blue Computer chess-playing system designed by IBM. In 1996 Deep Blue made history by defeating the world champion, GARRY KASPAROV, in one of their six games—the first time a computer had won a game against a chess grandmaster under tournament conditions. In the 1997 rematch, it won the deciding sixth game in only nineteen moves; its 3.5–2.5 victory (it won two games and had three draws) marked the first time a current world champion had lost a match to a computer opponent under tournament conditions. In its final configuration, the IBM RS6000/SP computer used 256 processors working in tandem, with an ability to evaluate 200 million chess positions per second.

deep-sea trench *or* **oceanic trench** Any long, narrow, steep-sided depression in the ocean bottom in which maximum oceanic depths (24,000–36,000 ft, or 7,000–11,000 m) occur. The deepest known depression of this kind is the MARIANA TRENCH. Most trenches occur at SUBDUCTION ZONES, where one tectonic plate is thrust under another.

deep-sea vent Hydrothermal (hot-water) vent formed on the ocean floor when seawater circulates through hot volcanic rocks, often located where new oceanic crust is being formed. Vents also occur on submarine volcanoes. In either case, the hot solution emerging into cold seawater precipitates mineral deposits that are rich in iron, copper, zinc, and other metals. Outflow of these heated waters probably accounts for 20% of the earth's heat loss. Exotic biological communities are now known to exist around the vents; these ecosystems are totally independent of energy from the sun, depending not on photosynthesis but rather on chemosynthesis by sulfur-fixing bacteria.

deer Any of the RUMINANTS in the family Cervidae, which have two large and two small hooves on each foot and antlers on the males of most species and on the females of some species. Deer live mainly in forests but may be found in deserts, tundra, and swamps and on high mountainsides. They are native to Europe, Asia, North America, South America, and northern Africa and have been introduced widely elsewhere. Females are usually called does, and males bucks. Deer range in shoulder height from the 12-in. (30-cm) pudu (genus *Pudu*) to the 6.5-ft (2-m) MOOSE. They typically have a compact body, short tail, and long, slender ears. They shed their antlers each year, and new ones grow in. The general form of the antler varies among species. Deer feed on grass, twigs, bark, and shoots. They are hunted for their meat, hides, and ant-

Rival European red deer stags (*Cervus elaphus*) fighting for possession of a hind in the rutting season.
STEFAN MEYERS GDT/ARDEA LONDON

lers. See also CARIBOU, ELK, MULE DEER, MUNTJAC, RED DEER, ROE DEER, WHITE-TAILED DEER.

deer mouse *or* **white-footed mouse** Any of about 60 species (genus *Peromyscus,* family Cricetidae) of small, delicate RODENTS that are active at night and are found in habitats from Alaska to South America. They often outnumber all other mammals in an area. Deer mice are 3–6.5 in. (8–17 cm) long (excluding the long tail) and have large eyes, soft fur, and relatively large ears. Colors range from white to brown or blackish, with white underparts and feet. They eat plant and animal matter and nest in burrows or trees. Clean, easily cared for, and prolific, they are often used as laboratory animals.

Deere, John (1804–1886) U.S. inventor and manufacturer of agricultural implements. Born in Rutland, Vt., he was apprenticed to a blacksmith, and later set up his own smithy and moved to Illinois. There he found, through the frequent repairs he had to make, that wood-and-cast-iron plows, used in the eastern U.S. from the 1820s, were unsuited to the heavy, sticky prairie soils. By 1838 he had sold three newly fashioned plows of his design; by 1846 he had sold about 1,000, and by 1857 10,000. In 1868 Deere & Co. was incorporated, and it gradually began making cultivators and other farm machinery.

defamation In law, issuance of false statements about a person that injure the reputation of or deter others from associating with that person. Libel and slander are the legal subcategories of defamation. Libel is defamation in print, pictures, or any other visual symbols. A libel plaintiff must generally establish that the alleged libel refers to him or her specifically, that it was published to others (third parties), and that some injury occurred as a result. The U.S. Supreme Court has ruled that public persons (e.g., celebrities or politicians) alleging libel may recover damages only if they prove that the statement in question was made with "actual malice," that is, with knowledge that it was false or with reckless disregard for the truth (*New York Times Co. vs. Sullivan,* 1964). Slander is defamation by oral communication. An action for slander may be brought without alleging and proving special injury if the statement has a plainly harmful character, as by imputing to the plaintiff criminal guilt, serious sexual misconduct, or a characteristic affecting his or her business or profession. The defense in defamation cases often takes the form of seeking to establish the truth of the statements in question.

defecation \ˌdef-ə-ˈkā-shən\ *or* **bowel movement** Elimination of FECES from the digestive tract. PERISTALSIS moves feces through the COLON to the RECTUM, where they stimulate the urge to defecate. The rectum shortens, pushing the feces into the ANAL CANAL, where internal and external sphincters allow them to be passed or retained. Chest, abdominal, and pelvic muscles are used to pass them. Long delay of defecation causes constipation and hardened feces. See also DIARRHEA, INCONTINENCE.

Defense, U.S. Department of Federal executive division responsible for ensuring U.S. national security and supervising U.S. military forces. Based in the PENTAGON, it includes the Joint Chiefs of Staff, the departments of the U.S. ARMY, U.S. NAVY, and U.S. AIR FORCE, and numerous defense agencies and allied services. It was formed in 1947 by an act of Congress (amended 1949) combining the War and Navy Departments.

defense economics Field of national economic management concerned with peacetime and wartime military expenditures. It arose in response to the greater scale and sophistication of warfare in the 20th century. Most nations seek to avoid the vast financial and human costs of war—which include the lost earnings of those killed or injured, lifetime medical care needed for those permanently incapacitated, and losses to the economy caused by diverting resources from investments in future economic capacity—by maintaining a level of military preparedness sufficient to deter aggressors. Peacetime defense economics focuses on issues of allocation of resources between the military and civilian sectors, the relative size and character of the various armed forces, and the choice and design of their weapons.

defense mechanism In psychoanalytic theory, an often unconscious mental process (such as REPRESSION) that makes possible compromise solutions to personal problems or CONFLICTS. The compromise generally involves concealing from oneself internal drives or feelings that threaten to lower self-esteem or provoke ANXIETY. The term was first used by SIGMUND FREUD in 1894. The major defense mechanisms are repression, the process by which unacceptable desires or impulses are excluded from consciousness; reaction formation, a mental or emotional response that represents the opposite of what one really feels; projection, the attribution of one's own ideas, feelings, or attitudes (especially blame, guilt, or sense of responsibility) to others; regression, reversion to an earlier mental or behavioral level; denial, the refusal to accept the existence of a painful fact; rationalization, the substitution of rational and creditable motives for the true (but threatening) ones; and sublimation, the diversion of an instinctual desire or impulse from its primitive form to a more socially or culturally acceptable form. See also EGO, NEUROSIS, PSYCHOANALYSIS.

deficit financing In government, the practice of spending more money than is received as revenue, the difference being made up by borrowing or minting new funds. The term usually refers to a conscious attempt to stimulate the economy by lowering tax rates or increasing government expenditures. Critics of deficit financing regularly denounce it as an example of shortsighted government policy. Advocates argue that it can be used successfully in response to a RECESSION or DEPRESSION, proposing that the ideal of an annually balanced budget should give way to that of a budget balanced over the span of a BUSINESS CYCLE. See also JOHN MAYNARD KEYNES, NATIONAL DEBT.

definition In philosophy, the specification of the meaning of an expression relative to a language. Definitions may be classified as lexical, ostensive, and stipulative. Lexical definition specifies the meaning of an expression by stating it in terms of other expressions whose meaning is assumed to be known (e.g., a ewe is a female sheep). Ostensive definition specifies the meaning of an expression by pointing to examples of things to which the expression applies (e.g., green is the color of grass, limes, lily pads, and emeralds). Stipulative definition assigns a new meaning to an expression (or a meaning to a new expression); the expression defined (definiendum) may either be a new expression that is being introduced into the language for the first time, or an expression that is already current.

deflation Contraction in the volume of available money or CREDIT that results in a general decline in prices. Attempts are sometimes made to bring on deflation (through raising interest rates and tightening the MONEY SUPPLY) in order to combat INFLATION and slow the economy. Deflation is characteristic of DEPRESSIONS and RECESSIONS.

Defoe \di-ˈfō\, **Daniel** *orig.* **Daniel Foe** (1660–1731) British novelist, pamphleteer, and journalist. A well-educated London merchant, he became an acute economic theorist and began to write eloquent, witty, often audacious tracts on public affairs. A satire he published resulted in his being imprisoned in 1703, and his business collapsed. He traveled as a government secret agent while continuing to write prolifically. In 1704–13 he wrote practically single-handedly the periodical *Review,* a serious and forceful paper that influenced later essay periodicals such as *The* SPECTATOR. His *Tour Through the Whole Island of Great Britain* (3 vols., 1724–26) followed several trips to Scotland. Late in life he turned to fiction. He achieved literary immortality with the novel *Robinson Crusoe* (1719), which drew partly on memoirs of voyagers and castaways. He is also remembered for the vivid, picaresque *Moll Flanders* (1722); the nonfictional *Journal of the Plague Year* (1722), on the GREAT PLAGUE in London in 1664–65; and *Roxana* (1724), a prototype of the modern novel.

Defoe, engraving by M. Van der Gucht, after a portrait by J. Taverner, first half of the 18th century.

BY COURTESY OF THE NATIONAL PORTRAIT GALLERY, LONDON

defoliant Chemical dust or spray applied to plants to cause their leaves to drop off prematurely. Defoliants sometimes are applied to CROP plants such as COTTON to facilitate harvesting. They have also been used in warfare to eliminate enemy food crops and potential areas of concealment (as in the VIETNAM WAR). See also AGENT ORANGE.

deforestation Process of clearing forests. Rates of deforestation are particularly high in the tropics, where the poor quality of the soil has led to the practice of routine clear-cutting to make new soil available for agricultural use. Deforestation can lead to EROSION, drought, loss of biodiversity through extinction of plant and animal species, and increased atmospheric carbon dioxide. Many nations have undertaken afforestation or reforestation projects to reverse the effects of deforestation, or to increase available timber. See also GREENHOUSE EFFECT.

deformation and flow Alteration in size or shape of a body under the influence of mechanical forces. Flow is a change in deformation that continues as long as the force is applied. Gases and liquids normally flow relatively freely, while solids deform when subjected to forces. Most solids initially deform elastically (see ELASTICITY), though rigid material such as metals, concrete, or rocks can sustain large forces while undergoing little deformation. If enough force is applied, even these materials will reach their elastic limit, at which point brittle substances fracture while ductile materials (see DUCTILITY) rearrange their internal structure, the result being plastic deformation (see PLASTICITY).

Degas \də-ˈgä\, **(Hilaire-Germain-) Edgar** (1834–1917) French painter, graphic artist, and sculptor. The son of a wealthy banker, he entered the École des Beaux-Arts in 1855. He spent much time in Italy studying and copying the old masters and became a skilled draftsman, producing history paintings and portraits. In the 1860s he was introduced to IMPRESSIONISM by EDOUARD MANET and gave up his academic aspirations, turning for his subject matter to the fast-moving city life of Paris, particularly the ballet, theater, circus, racetrack, and cafés. Influenced by Japanese prints and the new medium of photography, he used displaced figure groupings and unfamiliar perspective to create figure groups seen informally and in movement, similar in effect to snapshots (e.g., *Place de la Concorde*). His fascination with the ballet and the racetrack sprang from his interest in picturing people absorbed in the practiced movements of their occupations. He worked much in pastel, his favorite medium, producing series of women, bathers, ballerinas, and horse races. From c. 1880 he modeled wax figures, which were cast in bronze after his death. He was the first of the Impressionists to achieve recognition.

degenerative joint disease See OSTEOARTHRITIS

degree, academic Title conferred by a COLLEGE or UNIVERSITY to indicate completion of a course of study or extent of academic achievement. In medieval Europe, there were only two degrees: master (a scholar of arts and grammar) and doctor (a scholar of philosophy, theology, medicine, or law). The baccalaureate, or bachelor's degree, was originally simply a stage toward mastership. Today in Anglo-American countries the Bachelor of Arts degree (BA or AB) is awarded after four years of college study, the Master of Arts (MA) after two additional years, and the Doctor of Philosophy (PhD) after several years of post-baccalaureate study and research. In the mid-20th century the Associate of Arts degree (AA) began to be awarded by U.S. COMMUNITY COLLEGES. Common professional degrees are the Doctor of Jurisprudence (JD) and the Doctor of Medicine (MD). Honorary degrees are granted without regard to academic achievement. In France the *baccalauréat* is conferred on the completion of SECONDARY EDUCATION, the *licence* on completion of three or four years of university study, the *maîtrise* on the passing of advanced examinations, and the *doctorat* on completion of several years of advanced academic studies. In Germany the doctorate is the only degree granted, though diploma examinations are offered to students who forgo the doctoral requirements.

dehydration Method of FOOD PRESERVATION in which moisture (primarily water) is removed to inhibit the growth of microorganisms; dehydration also often reduces the bulk of food. It is an ancient practice, used by prehistoric peoples in sun-drying seeds, by North American Indians in sun-drying meat slices, and by the Japanese in drying fish and rice. It was used to prepare troop rations in World War II, and in recent decades campers and relief agencies have discovered its advantages. Commercial dehydration equipment includes tunnel dryers, kilns, and vacuum dryers. A combination of dehydration and freezing is used in the process of freeze-drying, whereby solid food remains frozen while its liquid escapes as vapor. The dairy industry is one of the largest producers of dehydrated foods, including whole milk, skim milk, and eggs.

dehydration Loss of water, almost always along with SALT, from the body, caused by restricted water intake or excessive water loss. Early symptoms of water deprivation are thirst, decreased saliva, and impaired swallowing. (When more ELECTROLYTES than water are lost, osmosis pulls water into cells, and there is no thirst.) Later, tissues shrink, including the skin and eyes. Mild fever rises as PLASMA volume and cardiac output decrease, and PERSPIRATION decreases or stops, greatly reducing heat loss. URINE output falls, and the KIDNEYS cannot filter wastes from the blood. Irreversible SHOCK can occur at this point. The cause of dehydration is treated first; then water and electrolytes must be given in the correct proportions.

Deinarchus See DINARCHUS

Deinonychus \dī-ˈnä-ni-kəs\ Genus of clawed THEROPOD dinosaurs that flourished in western North America during the Early CRETACEOUS PERIOD (144–99 million years ago). *Deinonychus* walked and ran on two legs, yet its killing devices, large sickle-like talons 5 in. (13 cm) long on the second toe of each foot, required it to stand on one foot while slashing at its prey with the other. Its long, outstretched tail was enclosed in bundles of bony rods that grew out of the tail vertebrae, making it very rigid. About 8–13 ft (2.4–4 m) long and weighing 100–150 lbs (45–68 kg), it had a large brain and was evidently a fast, agile predator.

Deir el-Bahri *or* **Dayr al-Bahri** \ˈdār-el-ˈbä-rē\ Temple site, Egypt. Located on the western bank of the Nile near THEBES and opposite KARNAK, it has the remains of three temples associated with pharaohs: the funerary temple of King Mentuhotep II (built c. 1970 BC); a temple built by THUTMOSE III (c. 1435 BC); and the terraced temple of Queen HATSHEPSUT (built c. 1470 BC), much of which has been restored.

Deira \ˈdā-rə\ Anglo-Saxon kingdom, Britain. Located in the eastern part of modern YORKSHIRE, it stretched from the HUMBER ESTUARY to the TEES RIVER. Its first recorded king, Aelle, reigned from AD 560. By the last quarter of the 7th century it had been united with its neighbor BERNICIA to form the kingdom of NORTHUMBRIA.

Deirdre \ˈdir-drə, ˈdar-drā\ In medieval Irish literature, the heroine of *The Fate of the Sons of Usnech,* the great love story (written in the 8th or 9th century) of the ULSTER CYCLE. A Druid foretold at Deirdre's birth that many men would die on her account, and she was raised in seclusion. A woman of great beauty, she rejected the advances of King Conor (see CONCHOBAR), married Noísi, one of the sons of Usnech, and fled with him to Scotland. Lured back to Ireland, Noísi and his brothers were murdered, and Deirdre killed herself to avoid marrying Conor. In the 20th century the story was dramatized by WILLIAM BUTLER YEATS and JOHN MILLINGTON SYNGE.

Deism Belief in God based on reason rather than revelation or the teaching of any specific religion. A form of natural religion, Deism originated in England in the early 17th century as a rejection of orthodox Christianity. Deists asserted that reason could find evidence of God in nature and that God had created the world and then left it to operate under the natural laws he had devised. The philosopher Edward Herbert (1583–1648) developed this view in *On Truth* (1624). By the late 18th century Deism was the dominant religious attitude among Europe's educated classes; it was accepted by many upper-class Americans of the same era, including the first three U.S. presidents.

Del Monte Foods Co. Largest U.S. producer of canned fruits and vegetables. Formed in 1899 as the California Fruit Canners Assn., it began marketing a line of canned goods under the Del Monte brand (the name of a luxurious hotel in Monterey, Cal.) in 1916. It is a major grower and distributor of bananas and pineapples, and it owns numerous diverse subsidiaries.

Delacour \ˌdel-ə-ˈkür\, **Jean Theodore** (1890–1985) French-U.S. aviculturist. After his boyhood collection of more than 1,300 live birds was destroyed during World War I, he made expeditions worldwide and assembled a huge new collection at the Château de Clères in Normandy. He bred pheasants in captivity, discovered and named many new bird and mammal species, founded the magazine *L'Oiseau* (1920), and wrote the standard work *The Birds of French Indochina* (1931). When the Germans again destroyed his aviary, he emigrated to the U.S., but he later reestablished his aviary and zoo at Clères.

Delacroix \ˌde-lə-ˈkrwä\, **(Ferdinand-) Eugène (-Victor)** (1798–1863) French painter. As a young man he was strongly influenced by the English painters RICHARD PARKES BONINGTON, JOHN CONSTABLE, and J.M.W. TURNER, but painted mostly historical or contemporary events and scenes from literature. In 1822 he exhibited *Dante and Virgil in Hell*, a landmark in the development of French 19th-century Romanticism. After his success at the Paris Salon, he was commissioned to decorate government buildings; he became one of the most distinguished monumental mural painters in the history of French art. He explored the new medium of lithography and in 1827 executed 17 lithographs for an edition of *Faust.* In 1830 he painted *Liberty Leading the People* to commemorate the July Revolution that brought LOUIS-PHILIPPE to the French throne. On a trip to Morocco in 1832 he acquired a wealth of rich and exotic visual imagery on which he would draw throughout his life. His output was enormous; after his death, more than 9,000 paintings, pastels, drawings, and watercolors were found in his Paris studio (now a museum). His use of color influenced the development of IMPRESSIONISM.

"Liberty Leading the People," oil on canvas by Eugène Delacroix, 1830; in the Louvre, Paris.

GIRAUDON/ART RESOURCE, NEW YORK CITY

Delagoa Bay \ˌdel-ə-ˈgō-ə\ Bay, southeastern coast of Mozambique. Some 19 mi (31 km) long and 16 mi (26 km) wide, with Inhaca Island, a tourist resort, at its mouth, it also is the site of MAPUTO, the nation's capital. First explored by the Portuguese in 1544, it was important as an outlet for ivory and slaves, a way station for Indian Ocean trade, and a route to the South African diamond mines and goldfields. Ownership was contested by the Portuguese, Dutch, English, and Boers until it was awarded by arbitration to Portugal in 1875.

DeLancey, James (1703–1760) American administrator and jurist. Born in New York City, he studied law in London, then returned in 1729 and became a member of the governor's council. In 1731 he was appointed to New York colony's supreme court; as chief justice (1733), he presided at the libel trial of JOHN PETER ZENGER. He opposed the royal governor, GEORGE CLINTON, and obtained his recall, and later served as lieutenant governor (1753–55, 1757–60).

Delano, Jane A(rminda) (1862–1919) U.S. nurse and educator. Born in Montour Falls, N.Y., she became superintendant of nurses in Jacksonville, Fla., where she insisted on using mosquito netting to prevent the spread of yellow fever even before the mosquito was known to carry it. In Bisbee, Ariz., she established a hospital for miners with scarlet fever. She oversaw the enlistment of over 20,000 U.S. nurses for overseas duty during World War I.

Delany, Martin R(obison) (1812–1885) U.S. abolitionist and physician. Born in Charles Town, Va., he worked in Pittsburgh as a doctor's assistant. In the 1840s he founded a newspaper, *Mystery,* to publicize grievances of blacks and copublished the *North Star* (1846–49) with FREDERICK DOUGLASS. One of the first blacks admitted to Harvard Medical School (1850–51), he later practiced in Pittsburgh. He developed a strong interest in foreign colonization for blacks and went to Africa to investigate sites. He moved to Canada in 1856, but returned early in the Civil War to recruit for the 54th Massachusetts Volunteers, which he also served as surgeon. He was made a major, the first black to receive a regular army commission.

Delany, Samuel R. *in full* **Samuel Ray Delany, Jr.** (born 1942) U.S. science-fiction novelist and critic. Born in New York City into a distinguished black family, he attended CCNY and published his first novel in 1962. His highly imaginative works, which have garnered wide critical admiration, address racial and social issues, sexuality, heroic quests, and the nature of language. *Dhalgren* (1975), his most controversial novel, tells of a young bisexual man searching for identity in a large, decaying city. Other works include the novels *Babel-17* (1966, Nebula Award), *The Einstein Intersection* (1967, Nebula Award), *Triton* (1976), and *Stars in My Pocket Like Grains of Sand* (1984), and scripts for film, radio, and *Wonder Woman* comic books.

Delaunay \də-lō-ˈnā\, **Robert** (1885–1941) French painter. He spent his early career as a part-time designer of stage scenery and came under the influence of Neo-Impressionism, Fauvism, and Cubism. In 1909–11 his color experiments culminated in a series of paintings of the Eiffel Tower, which combined fragmented Cubist forms with dynamic movement and vibrant color. The introduction of bright color to Cubism, which came to be known as ORPHISM, distinguished his work from that of the more orthodox Cubist painters and influenced the artists of Der BLAUE REITER. With his wife, the Ukrainian-born painter and textile designer Sonia Terk Delaunay (1885–1979), he painted abstract mural decorations for the 1937 Paris Exposition.

"La Tour Eiffel," oil on canvas by Robert Delaunay, 1910–11; in the Kunstmuseum, Basel, Switzerland.

DEPOSITED BY EMANUEL HOFFMANN-FOUNDATION IN KUNSTMUSEUM BASEL, SWITZERLAND; PHOTOGRAPH, HANS HINZ

Delaware *or* **Lenni Lenape** \ˌle-nē-ˈle-nə-pē\ Confederation of ALGONQUIAN-speaking North American Indians who occupied the Atlantic seaboard from southern Delaware to western Long Island, especially the Delaware River Valley. They depended primarily on agriculture, but also hunted and fished. They were grouped in three clans based on maternal descent; these were in turn divided into lineages, whose members lived together in a LONGHOUSE. They were governed by a council of lineage sachems (chiefs), who directed the public affairs of the community; the eldest woman of the lineage appointed the sachem. The Delaware were the Indians most friendly to WILLIAM PENN; they were rewarded by the infamous Walking Purchase, a treaty that deprived them of their own lands and forced them to settle on lands assigned to the Iroquois. After 1690 they drifted westward. They sided with the French in the FRENCH AND INDIAN WAR (1754–63) and helped defeat the British general Edward Braddock. In 1867 most of the remaining Delaware were removed to Oklahoma. Today they number about 10,000.

Delaware State (pop., 2000: 783,600), middle Atlantic region, U.S. Covering 2,026 sq mi (5,247 sq km), its capital is DOVER. Originally inhabited by ALGONQUIAN tribes, Delaware's first permanent white settlement was by Swedes at Fort Christina, now WILMINGTON, in 1638. In 1655 New Sweden was taken by the Dutch of New Amsterdam and in 1664 by the English. Delaware was thereafter a part of New York until 1682, when it was ceded to WILLIAM PENN. It was governed by Pennsylvania until 1776, although it was granted its own assembly in 1704. The first state to ratify the U.S. Constitution in 1787, it is the nation's second smallest state but one of its most densely populated. Chemical manufacturing is the major industry, followed by food processing. Delaware's most important transportation artery is the Chesapeake and Delaware Canal, deepened for ocean shipping, which shortens the water route between PHILADELPHIA and BALTIMORE.

Delaware, University of Public university in Newark, Del., with courses also offered at sites in Wilmington, Dover, Milford, Georgetown, and Lewes. Its 11 colleges offer a curriculum in the arts, sciences, business, engineering, oceanography, education, and nursing. It traces its roots to the Academy of Newark (1765); it subsequently underwent several name changes and expansions, taking its current name in 1921. Total enrollment today exceeds 18,000.

Delaware Bay Inlet of the Atlantic Ocean. Forming part of the New Jersey–Delaware state border, it extends southeast for 52 mi (84 km) from the junction of the DELAWARE RIVER with Alloway Creek to its entrance between Cape May and Cape Henlopen. Bordered by marshy lowlands, the bay is an important link in the ATLANTIC INTRACOASTAL WATERWAY.

Delaware River River in Pennsylvania and Delaware. Formed by the junction of its eastern and western branches in southern New York, it flows some 280 mi (451 km) to empty into the Atlantic Ocean at DELAWARE BAY. Navigable to TRENTON, N.J., it is spanned by the Commodore John Barry Bridge (1,644 ft or 500 m long), completed in 1974.

Delbrück \'del-ˌbrœk\, **Max** (1906–1981) German-U.S. biologist. He received his PhD from the University of Göttingen in 1930, and in 1937 he emigrated to the U.S., where he joined the Caltech faculty. In 1939 he discovered a one-step process for growing bacteriophages that, after an hour of inactivity, would induce a phage to multiply to produce several hundred thousands of progeny. In 1946 he and A. D. HERSHEY independently discovered that the genetic material of different kinds of viruses can combine to create new types of viruses, a process previously believed to be limited to higher, sexually reproducing forms of life. In 1969 he shared a Nobel Prize with Hershey and their colleague SALVADOR LURIA.

Delcassé \del-kȧ-'sā\, **Théophile** (1852–1923) French politician. A journalist, he was elected to the Chamber of Deputies in 1885 and served in cabinet posts from 1893. As foreign minister in six successive governments (1898–1905), he reached agreement with the British that led to the ENTENTE CORDIALE. Considered the principal architect of the new system of European alliances formed before World War I, he also paved the way for the ANGLO-RUSSIAN agreement of 1907. He later served as minister of the marine (1911–13) and again as foreign minister (1914–15).

Deledda \dā-'lād-dä\, **Grazia** (1871–1936) Italian novelist. She wrote her first stories, influenced by the verismo ("realism") school, at 17. In her approximately 40 novels, including *After the Divorce* (1902), *Elias Portolu* (1903), and *Ashes* (1904), the ancient ways of her native Sardinia often conflict with modern mores. Her later novel *The Mother* (1920) and the posthumously published autobiographical novel *Cosima* (1937) were widely admired. She received the Nobel Prize in 1926.

Deleuze \də-'lœz\, **Gilles** (1925–1995) French philosopher and literary critic. He taught at the Sorbonne (1957–1960) and the Univs. of Lyon (1964–69) and Vincennes (1969–1987). He is best known for his interpretations of the history and literature of philosophy. His best-known work is *Anti-Oedipus* (1972; with Félix Guattari).

Delft City (pop., 2001 est.: 96,180), southwestern Netherlands. Founded in 1075 and chartered in 1246, it was a trade center in the 16th–17th century and was famous for its DELFTWARE pottery. It was the birthplace of jurist HUGO GROTIUS (1583) and painter JOHANNES VERMEER (1632). Landmarks include a Gothic church, a Renaissance-style town hall, and a 17th-century armory. Principal manufactures include ceramics.

delftware *or* **delft** Tin-glazed EARTHENWARE, with blue-and-white or polychrome decoration, first made in the early 17th century at Delft, Holland. Dutch potters later introduced the art of tin glazing to England along with the name, which now applies to wares manufactured in the Netherlands and England. It is distinguished from FAIENCE (made in France, Germany, Spain, and Scandinavia) and MAJOLICA (made in Italy).

Delhi \'de-lē\ Union territory (pop., 2001 prelim.: 13,782,976), northern central India. Bounded by the states of UTTAR PRADESH and HARYANA, it comprises the cities of Delhi (popularly known as Old Delhi) and NEW DELHI (India's capital) and adjacent rural areas. Delhi was the capital of a Muslim dynasty from 1206 until it was laid waste by TIMUR in 1398. It was conquered by the Mughal BABUR in 1526. Although the Mughal capital was mostly at AGRA, Delhi was beautified by SHAH JAHAN, beginning in 1638. Pillaged by NADIR SHAH in 1739, it surrendered to Marathas in 1771. Taken by the British in 1803, it was a center of the INDIAN MUTINY in 1857. Delhi replaced Calcutta (now KOLKATA) as the capital of British India in 1912, at which time construction began on the section of the city that became New Delhi. The capital was moved to New Delhi in 1931, and it became the capital of independent India in 1947. The area's economy and population center mainly in Old Delhi, while government is concentrated in New Delhi. The government is the chief employer. The territory is also the transportation hub for northern central India.

Delhi sultanate Principal Muslim sultanate in North India from the 13th to the 16th century. Its creation owed much to the campaigns of Muhammad of Ghur and his lieutenant Qutb-ud-Din Aybak between 1175 and 1206. During the reign of Sultan Iltutmish (1211–36), a permanent capital was established at Delhi and political ties with Ghur were severed. From 1290 to 1320, under the Khalji dynasty, the sultanate was an imperial power. Its power was shattered by TIMUR'S invasion (1398–99), but it somewhat recovered under the Lodi (Afghan) dynasty (1451–1526). It fell again to BABUR (1526), was reestablished briefly, then finally was subsumed into AKBAR'S Mughal empire (1556).

Delian League \'dē-lē-ən\ Confederacy of ancient Greek states led by Athens and based on the island of DELOS. Founded in 478 BC to combat Persia, its members included Aegean states and islands; Athens supplied commanders and assessed tributes of ships or money. It achieved a major victory in 467–466 when its fleet drove out Persian garrisons on the southern Anatolian coast. After 454 its leaders moved the treasury to Athens for safekeeping, used it to rebuild the city's temples, and treated the league as the Athenian empire. Most league members sided with Athens in the PELOPONNESIAN WAR, which diverted the league from its Persian campaign. After defeating Athens in battle in 405, Sparta disbanded the league in 404. Fear of Sparta helped revive the league in the early 4th century, but it weakened as Sparta declined and was crushed by PHILIP II at the Battle of CHAERONEA (338).

Delibes \də-'lēb\, **(Clément Philibert) Léo** (1836–1891) French composer. He studied at the Paris Conservatoire and worked as a church organist and as accompanist and chorus master at the Paris Opera. Though he composed almost 30 operas, operettas, and ballets, as well as many choral pieces, he is remembered today for three works: the ballets *Coppélia* (1870) and *Sylvia* (1876) and the opera *Lakmé* (1883).

DeLillo \de-'lil-ō\, **Don** (born 1936) U.S. novelist. Born in the Bronx, N.Y., to immigrant parents, he worked in advertising before beginning to write seriously. His postmodernist works portray the unrest and alienation of an America cosseted by material excess and stupefied by empty mass culture and politics. *Ratner's Star* (1976) attracted attention with its baroque comic sense and verbal facility. His vision later turned darker and his characters more willful in their destructiveness and ignorance, as in *Players* (1977), *Running Dog* (1978), *The Names* (1982), and *White Noise* (1985). *Libra* (1988) portrays LEE HARVEY OSWALD, *Mao II* (1991) tells of a writer enmeshed in political violence, and *Underworld* (1997) portrays 1950s America.

delinquency Criminal behavior carried out by a juvenile. Young males make up the bulk of the delinquent population (about 80% in the U.S.)

in all countries in which the behavior is reported. Theories regarding delinquency's causes focus on the social and economic characteristics of the offender's family, the values communicated by the parents, and the nature of youth and criminal subcultures, including gangs. In general both "push" and "pull" factors are involved. Most delinquents apparently do not continue criminal behavior into their adult life but rather adjust to societal standards. The most common method of dealing with delinquent offenders is probation, whereby the delinquent is given a suspended sentence and in return must live by a prescribed set of rules under the supervision of a probation officer. See also CRIMINOLOGY, PENOLOGY.

delirium Mental disturbance with disorientation and confused thinking. The patient is drowsy, restless, and fearful of imaginary disasters, sometimes with hallucinations. Delirium usually results from a disorder affecting the brain (e.g., fever, intoxication, head trauma). Alcoholic delirium results not from excessive alcohol consumption alone but from exhaustion, malnutrition (particularly lack of THIAMINE), and DEHYDRATION. Bewildering changes of scene may trigger delirium, which usually clears up soon after the physical causes have been dealt with.

delirium tremens (DTs) \di-ˈlir-ē-əm-ˈtrē-menz\ DELIRIUM seen in severe cases of alcohol withdrawal (see ALCOHOLISM) complicated by exhaustion, lack of food, and dehydration, usually preceded by physical deterioration due to vomiting and restlessness. The whole body trembles, sometimes with seizures, disorientation, and hallucinations. Delirium tremens lasts 3–10 days, with a reported death rate of 1–20%. Hallucinations may develop independently of delirium tremens and may last days to weeks.

Delius \ˈdē-lē-əs\, **Frederick (Theodore Albert)** (1862–1934) British-French composer. Born to German parents in England, he studied music in Leipzig and elsewhere, and in 1887 E. GRIEG convinced his parents to let him pursue a musical career. He moved to France, eventually settling in a village near Paris. After World War I he gradually succumbed to paralysis and blindness, the consequence of syphilis. His works, influenced by C. DEBUSSY, include the operas *A Village Romeo and Juliet* (1901) and *Fennimore and Gerda* (1910); the tone poems *Brigg Fair* (1907) and *On Hearing the First Cuckoo in Spring* (1912); and the choral works *Appalachia* (1903) and *A Mass of Life* (1908).

delivery See PARTURITION

Della Robbia family \ˌdāl-lä-ˈrȯb-yə\ Family of Italian artists active in Florence. The first works of Luca (di Simone di Marco) Della Robbia (1399/1400–1482) were reliefs sculptured in marble, most notably those for the Cantoria (singing-gallery) of Florence Cathedral (1432–37). He is remembered mainly for his development of glazed terra-cotta as a medium for sculpture; his major terra-cotta works include roundels of the Apostles (c. 1444) in FILIPPO BRUNELLESCHI's Pazzi Chapel in Santa Croce. In time the Della Robbia studio became a potters' workshop-industry, famous especially for its renderings of the Madonna and Child in white enamel on a blue ground. Andrea (di Marco) Della Robbia (1435–1525), Luca's nephew, assumed control of the workshop c. 1470. Trained as a marble sculptor, his best-known works are ten roundels of infants on the facade of Florence's Foundling Hospital (c. 1487). Giovanni Della Robbia (1469–1529), the most distinguished of Andrea's sons, took control of the family workshop after his father's death. His early works, notably a lavabo in Santa Maria Novella (1497) and medallions in the Loggia of San Paolo (1493–95), were collaborations with his father.

dell'Abbate, Niccolo See Niccolo dell'ABBATE

Delmarva Peninsula Peninsula, eastern U.S. Extending between CHESAPEAKE and DELAWARE bays, it is about 180 mi (290 km) long and up to 70 mi (110 km) wide. Encompassing parts of the states of Delaware, Maryland, and Virginia, a fact that gives it its name (*Del*aware, *Mary*land, *Virginia*) it includes Maryland's eastern Shore. Fishing and tourism are economically important.

Delors \də-ˈlȯr\, **Jacques (Lucien Jean)** (born 1925) French statesman. In 1962 he left his position in banking for a series of government positions, including minister of economics and finance. As president of the European Commission (EC) from 1985 to 1995, he pushed through reforms and persuaded the member states to agree to the creation of a single market in 1993, the first step toward full economic and political integration in the EUROPEAN UNION.

Delos \ˈdē-ˌläs\ *Greek* **Dhílos** \ˈt͟hē-ˌlȯs\ Island, Greece. One of the smallest of the CYCLADES, it was an ancient center of religious, political, and commercial life in the Aegean. It was the legendary birthplace of APOLLO and ARTEMIS. The DELIAN LEAGUE was established there in 478 BC, following the PERSIAN WARS. Made a free port by Rome in 166 BC, it was a flourishing commercial center and slave market. Sacked in 88 BC during the Mithradatic Wars, it gradually declined and was abandoned. Its impressive ruins have been extensively excavated.

Delphi \ˈdel-ˌfī\ Site of the ancient temple and ORACLE of APOLLO in Greece. Located on the slopes of Mount PARNASSUS, it was the center of the world in ancient Greek religion. According to legend, the oracle was originally sacred to GAEA, and Apollo acquired it by slaying her child, the serpent Python. From 582 BC Delphi was the site of the PYTHIAN GAMES. The oracle was consulted not only on private matters but also on affairs of state, such as the founding of new colonies.

delphinium See LARKSPUR

delta Low-lying plain composed of stream-borne sediments deposited by a river at its mouth. Deltas have been important to humankind since prehistoric times. Sands, silts, and clays deposited by floodwaters were extremely productive agriculturally; and major civilizations flourished in the deltaic plains of the Nile and Tigris-Euphrates rivers. In recent years geologists have discovered that much of the world's petroleum resources are found in ancient deltaic rocks. Deltas vary widely in size, structure, composition, and origin, though many are triangular (the shape of the Greek letter delta).

dema deity \ˈdā-mə\ Any of several mythical ancestral beings of the Marind-Anim people of southern New Guinea. In their mythology, the killing of a divine ancestor (a dema deity) brings about the transition from the ancestral world to the human one. In Ceramese mythology, for example, the goddess Hainuwele grows from a coconut blossom and is dismembered by dema men; when the pieces of her body are buried, they become new plant species, especially tubers, the chief food of the Ceramese. Such myths offer explanations for the origin of agriculture as well as for human sexuality and death.

deme \ˈdēm\ (Greek, *demos*) In ancient Greece, a country district or village, as distinct from a POLIS. In CLEISTHENES' democratic reforms (508–507 BC), the demes of Attica (the area around Athens) gained a voice in local and state government. The Attic demes had their own police powers, cults, and officials. Males of 18 years of age became registered members of the deme. Members decided deme matters and kept property records for taxation. Each deme sent representatives to the Athenian BOULE in proportion to its size. The term continued to be applied to local districts in Hellenistic and Roman times.

dementia \di-ˈmen-shə\ Chronic, usually progressive, deterioration of intellectual functions. Most common in the elderly, it usually begins with short-term memory loss once thought a normal result of aging but now known to result from ALZHEIMER'S DISEASE. Other common causes are Pick's disease and cerebral ARTERIOSCLEROSIS. Dementia also occurs in Huntington's CHOREA, paresis (see PARALYSIS), and some types of ENCEPHALITIS. Treatable causes include hypothyroidism (see THYROID GLAND), other metabolic diseases, and some malignant tumors. Treatment may arrest dementia's progress but usually does not reverse it. See also SENILE DEMENTIA.

Demerara River \ˌde-mə-ˈrar-ə\ River, eastern Guyana. Rising in the forests of central Guyana, it flows north for 215 mi (346 km) to the Atlantic Ocean at GEORGETOWN. Oceangoing steamers ascend 65 mi (105 km) to Linden for bauxite; smaller ships reach Malali, 25 mi (40 km) farther upstream; beyond lie numerous rapids.

Demeter \di-ˈmē-tər\ In Greek religion, a consort of ZEUS and the goddess of agricuture, especially grain. Though rarely mentioned by HOMER and not an Olympian deity, she is probably an ancient goddess. She is

Demeter of Cnidus, sculpture, mid-4th century BC; in the British Museum.
BY COURTESY OF THE TRUSTEES OF THE BRITISH MUSEUM

best remembered for her role in the story of PERSEPHONE, in which her lack of attention to the harvest causes a famine. In addition to appearing as a goddess of agriculture, Demeter was sometimes worshiped as a divinity of the Underworld and as a goddess of health, birth, and marriage.

Demetrius I Poliorcetes ("the Besieger") \də-'mē-trē-əs...,pä-lē-,ȯr-'sē-tēz\ (336–283 BC) King of Macedonia (294–288). As a young general he fought to rebuild the empire of his father, ANTIGONUS I MONOPHTHALMUS. Under his father's command, he initially failed in his assaults on Egypt and Nabataea, but later freed Athens from Macedonia (307) and defeated PTOLEMY I SOTER (306), restoring some of his father's domain. He fought alongside his father at the Battle of IPSUS (301), where Antigonus was killed, and later retook Athens (294). He became king of Macedonia after killing Alexander V (r.297–294). Driven out in 288, he surrendered to SELEUCUS I NICATOR in 285.

DeMille \də-'mil\, **Cecil B(lount)** (1881–1959) U.S. film director and producer. Born in Ashfield, Mass., the son of an Episcopal lay preacher, he made his Broadway acting debut in 1900. In 1913 he joined Jesse Lasky (1880–1958) and SAMUEL GOLDWYN to form the forerunner of PARAMOUNT COMMUNICATIONS. Their first venture, *The Squaw Man* (1914), was the first full-length feature film produced in Hollywood, and it established DeMille as a director. He made numerous comedies before creating such biblical spectacles as *The Ten Commandments* (1923, remade 1956) and *The King of Kings* (1927), becoming known for his flamboyance and his taste for huge casts and extravagant sets. Among his 70 other films are *Samson and Delilah* (1949) and *The Greatest Show on Earth* (1952, Academy Award). He also hosted the popular weekly *Lux Radio Theatre* (1936–45).

Deming, W(illiam) Edwards (1900–1993) U.S. statistician, educator, and advocate of quality-control methods in industrial production. Born in Sioux City, Iowa, he received his PhD in mathematical physics from Yale Univ., and he subsequently taught at New York University for 46 years. From the 1930s he worked with statistical analysis to achieve better industrial quality control. In 1950 he was invited to Japan to teach executives and engineers. His ideas, which centered on tallying product defects, analyzing and addressing their causes, and recording the effects of the changes on subsequent quality, were eagerly adopted there and eventually helped Japanese products dominate the market in much of the world. In 1951 Japan instituted the Deming Prize, awarded to corporations that win a rigorous quality-control competition. Deming's ideas were taken up by U.S. corporations in the 1980s, particularly under the rubric of TOTAL QUALITY MANAGEMENT.

Demiurge \'de-mē-ərj\ Subordinate god who shapes and arranges the physical world. In his dialogue *Timaeus*, PLATO identified the Demiurge as the force that fashioned the world from the preexisting materials of chaos. In GNOSTICISM of the early Christian era, the Demiurge is regarded as an inferior deity who had created the imperfect, material world and who belonged to the forces of evil opposing the supreme God of goodness.

democracy Philosophy of government in which supreme power is vested in the people and exercised by them directly or indirectly through a system of representation usually involving periodic free elections. In a direct democracy, the public participates directly in government (as in some ancient Greek city-states and some New England TOWN MEETINGS). Most democracies today are representative democracies. The concept of representative democracy arose less from ancient Greek practice than from ideas and institutions that developed in medieval Europe, during the Enlightenment, and in the American and French Revolutions. Today democracy has come to imply universal suffrage, competition for office, freedom of speech and the press, and the rule of law.

Democratic Party One of the two major political parties in the U.S., historically the party of labor, minorities, and progressive reformers. In the 1790s a group of THOMAS JEFFERSON's supporters called themselves "Democratic Republicans" or "Jeffersonian Republicans" to show their belief in the principle of popular government and their opposition to monarchical government. The party adopted its present name in the 1830s during the presidency of ANDREW JACKSON. Democrats won nearly every presidential election in the years 1836–60, but the issue of slavery split the party, the Northern Democrats, led by STEPHEN A. DOUGLAS, advocating POPULAR SOVEREIGNTY in the new territories, while the Southern Democrats called for protection of slavery in the territories. As a result, in 1860 the new antislavery Republican Party won its first national victory under ABRAHAM LINCOLN. From 1861 to 1913 the only Democratic president was GROVER CLEVELAND; in these years the party was basically conservative and agrarian-oriented, and its members were opposed to protective tariffs. It returned to power under WOODROW WILSON, instituting greater federal regulation of banking and industry, but the Republicans' frank embrace of big business drew voters amid the prosperity of the 1920s. Democrats became dominant again in 1932, electing FRANKLIN ROOSEVELT. A coalition of urban workers, small farmers, liberals, and others sustained Democrats in office until 1953, and the party regained the presidency with the 1960 election of JOSEPH P. KENNEDY. It retained majority control of Congress in the 1970s and '80s.

Democratic Party of the Left *or* **Italian Communist Party** Major Italian political party. Founded as the Partito Comunista Italiano (PCI) in 1921 by dissidents of the ITALIAN SOCIALIST PARTY's left wing, it was outlawed with other political parties by BENITO MUSSOLINI's Fascists in 1926 and went underground. It participated in the Italian Resistance in World War II. After the war it joined in coalition governments and was consistently successful at the polls. In 1956, after revelation of JOSEPH STALIN's crimes, PALMIRO TOGLIATTI tried to dissociate the PCI from the Soviet Union. ENRICO BERLINGUER, as party leader 1972–84, became a leading proponent of EUROCOMMUNISM. In 1991, to consolidate left-wing forces and broaden its base, it changed its name to Democratic Party of the Left; it became Italy's second-largest political party and Western Europe's largest communist party.

Democratic Republic of the Congo See Democratic Republic of the CONGO

Democritus \di-'mä-krə-təs\ (c. 460–370 BC) Greek philosopher. Though only a few fragments of his work survive, he was apparently the first to describe invisible "atoms" as the basis of all matter. His atoms—indestructible, indivisible, incompressible, and uniform, differing only in size, shape, and motion—anticipated with surprising accuracy those discovered by 20th-century scientists. For his amusement at human foibles, he has been called "the Laughing Philosopher." See also ATOMISM.

demography \di-'mä-grə-fē\ Statistical study of human populations, especially with reference to size and density, distribution, and vital statistics. Contemporary demographic concerns include the global "population explosion," the interplay between population and economic development, the effects of BIRTH CONTROL, urban congestion, illegal immigration, and labor force statistics. The basis for most demographic research lies in population CENSUSES and the registration of vital statistics.

demon *or* **daemon** \'dē-mən\ In religions worldwide, any of various evil spirits that mediate between the supernatural and human realms. The term comes from the Greek word *daimon,* a divine or semidivine power that determined a person's fate. ZOROASTRIANISM had a hierarchy of demons, which were in constant battle with AHURA MAZDA. In Judaism it was believed that demons inhabited desert wastes, ruins, and graves and inflicted physical and spiritual disorders on humankind. Christianity placed Satan or Beelzebub at the head of the ranks of demons, and Islam designated IBLIS or Satan as the leader of a host of evil jinn. Hinduism has many demons, called *asuras*, who oppose the DEVAS (gods). In Buddhism demons are seen as tempters who prevent the achievement of nirvana.

Demosthenes \di-'mäs-thə-,nēz\ (384–322 BC) Athenian statesman known as the greatest orator of ancient Greece. According to PLUTARCH, he was a stutterer in his youth and improved his speech by placing pebbles in his mouth and practicing before a mirror. His talents were recognized early, and powerful cli-

Demosthenes, marble statue, detail of a Roman copy of a Greek original of c. 280 BC; in the Ny Carlsberg Glyptotek, Copenhagen.

BY COURTESY OF THE NY CARLSBERG GLYPTOTEK, COPENHAGEN

ents engaged him as a speechwriter. Throughout his life he espoused democratic principles. He roused Athens against PHILIP II by his great *Philippics,* and later against Philip's son ALEXANDER THE GREAT. In so doing he incurred the enmity of AESCHINES, who argued that Philip's intentions were peaceable; Demosthenes succeeded in having Aeschines ostracized (330), but was himself later forced into exile (324). Recalled after Alexander's death (323), he fled Alexander's successor and committed suicide.

Dempsey, Jack *orig.* **William Harrison** (1895–1983) U.S. boxer. Born in Manassa, Col., he started fighting in 1914 under the name Kid Blackie, a reference to his having worked in the copper mines. After compiling an impressive number of first-round knockouts, he was matched in 1919 with the world heavyweight title-holder, Jess Willard, whom he defeated in three rounds. He held the title until his defeat by GENE TUNNEY in 1926 in a 10-round decision. In the next year's rematch, in the famous "Long Count" bout, Dempsey would not go to a neutral corner after knocking Tunney down, allowing the champion extra time to recover and win the fight. Nicknamed the "Manassa Mauler," Dempsey was known as a ferocious fighter who kept continuously on the offensive. He fought exhibition matches in the 1930s before retiring in 1940; he later became a successful restaurateur. In 84 fights he compiled a record of 62 wins, 51 by knockout.

Dempsey.
UPI

demurrer \di-ˈmər-ər\ In law, a plea in response to an allegation that admits its truth but also asserts that it is not sufficient as a cause of action. In the U.S., demurrers are no longer used in federal procedure (having been replaced by motions to dismiss or motions for more definite statement) but are still used in some states. A general demurrer challenges the sufficiency of the substance of an allegation, whereas a special demurrer challenges the structure or form of an allegation.

Demuth \də-ˈmüth\, **Charles** (1883–1935) U.S. painter. Born in Lancaster, Pa., he studied in Philadelphia and later in Europe. On his return, he became an important channel for the transmission of modern European movements into American art. He is best known as an exponent of PRECISIONISM. He excelled at watercolor and executed an outstanding series of flowers, circuses, and café scenes. Later he incorporated advertisements and billboard lettering into hard-edged, abstract cityscapes such as *Buildings, Lancaster* (1930). Among his well-known works are his so-called "poster portraits" such as *I Saw the Figure 5 in Gold* (1928), a symbolic portrait of WILLIAM CARLOS WILLIAMS.

"I Saw the Figure 5 in Gold," oil on composition board by Charles Demuth, 1928; in the Metropolitan Museum of Art, New York City.
BY COURTESY OF THE METROPOLITAN MUSEUM OF ART, NEW YORK CITY, THE ALFRED STIEGLITZ COLLECTION, 1949

Denali See Mount MCKINLEY

Denali National Park \də-ˈnä-lē\ Preserve, southern central Alaska. Established in 1980, it comprises the former Mount McKinley National Park (1917) and Denali National Monument (1978). Highlights of the park include Mount MCKINLEY, the large glaciers of the ALASKA RANGE, and abundant wildlife. The park's total area is 5,000,000 acres (2,025,000 hectares).

denaturation \dē-ˌnā-chə-ˈrā-shən\ Biochemical process modifying a PROTEIN'S CONFIGURATION. It involves breaking many weak (hydrogen and hydrophobic) bonds (see BONDING) that maintain the protein's highly ordered structure. This usually results in loss of biological activity (e.g., loss of an ENZYME's ability to catalyze reactions). Denaturation can be brought about by heating; treatment with ALKALIS, ACIDS, UREA, or DETERGENTS; or even vigorous shaking of the protein solution. It can be reversed in some cases (e.g., serum ALBUMIN, HEMOGLOBIN), if conditions favorable to the protein are restored, but not in others. The term is also used to describe the rendering of ETHANOL unfit to drink.

Dench, Judi(th Olivia) *later* **Dame Judi** (born 1934) British actress. She made her stage debut in 1957 as Ophelia in *Hamlet,* and Shakespearean works became her specialty. Also at home in musical roles, she starred in the London premiere of *Cabaret* in 1968. Among her many other notable credits were the 1981–84 TV series "A Fine Romance" and the films *84 Charing Cross Road* (1986), *Mrs. Brown* (1997)—in which she starred as Queen Victoria—and *Shakespeare in Love* (1998, Academy Award), though the stage remained her first love.

dendrochronology \ˌden-drō-krə-ˈnä-lə-jē\ Method of scientific DATING based on the analysis of tree rings. Because the width of annular rings varies with climatic conditions, laboratory analysis of timber core samples allows scientists to reconstruct the conditions that existed when a tree's rings developed. By taking thousands of samples from different sites and different strata within a particular region, researchers can build a comprehensive historical sequence that becomes a part of the scientific record. Such master chronologies are used by archaeologists, climatologists, and others.

Deneuve \də-ˈnœv\, **Catherine** *orig.* **Catherine Dorléac** (born 1943) French film actress. She appeared in films from age 13 and won fame with her role in *The Umbrellas of Cherbourg* (1964). Her cool blond beauty and skillful portrayals in ROMAN POLANSKI'S *Repulsion* (1965) and LUIS BUNUEL'S *Belle de jour* (1967) and *Tristana* (1970) made her an international star. Her numerous other films include *The Last Metro* (1980) and *Indochine* (1992).

Deng Xiaoping *or* **Teng Hsiao-p'ing** \ˈdəŋ-ˈshau̇-ˈpiŋ\ (1904–1997) Chinese Communist leader, China's most powerful figure from the late 1970s until his death. In the 1950s he became a vice-premier of the People's Republic and general secretary of the CHINESE COMMUNIST PARTY (CCP). He fell from favor during the CULTURAL REVOLUTION but was rehabilitated in 1973 under the sponsorship of ZHOU ENLAI. Though seen as a likely successor to Zhou as premier, Deng was again ousted, this time by the GANG OF FOUR, when Zhou died in 1976. When MAO ZEDONG died later that year, the ensuing power struggle resulted in the arrest of the Gang of Four and Deng's second rehabilitation. His protégés Zhao Ziyang and Hu Yaobang became premier and CCP secretary-general, respectively. Both embraced Deng's wide-reaching reform program, which abandoned many orthodox communist doctrines and introduced free-enterprise elements into the economy. After the massacre of student protesters (following Hu's death), Zhao was dismissed for supporting the students. Deng's international image was tarnished for backing the crackdown. He gradually relinquished his official posts but continued to guide China behind the scenes until his death.

dengue \ˈdeŋ-gē\ *or* **breakbone fever** *or* **dandy fever** Acute, infectious, mosquito-borne HEMORRHAGIC FEVER, temporarily disabling but rarely fatal. Other symptoms include extreme joint pain and stiffness, intense pain behind the eyes, a return of fever after brief pause, and a characteristic rash. Dengue is caused by a virus carried by mosquitoes of the genus *Aedes,* usually *A. aegypti,* which also carries YELLOW FEVER. There are four strains of virus; infection with one type does not confer immunity to the remaining three. Treatment focuses on relieving symptoms. Patients should be isolated during the first three days, when mosquitoes can pick up the disease from them. Prevention relies on mosquito control.

Dengyo Daishi See SAICHO

Denikin \dyi-ˈnyē-kyin\, **Anton (Ivanovich)** (1872–1947) Russian general. A professional in the imperial Russian army, he was a lieutenant-general in World War I. After the Russian Revolution of 1917, he and LAVR KORNILOV were arrested for conspiring to overthrow the provisional government. They fled south to the Don River region and assumed command of the anti-Bolshevik ("White") forces in the RUSSIAN

Civil War. In 1919 Denikin launched a major offensive toward Moscow, but his forces were defeated by the Red Army at Orel. Forced to retreat, he turned over his command to Pyotr Wrangel (1920), then fled Russia and later settled in France (1925–45).

denim Durable twill-woven fabric with colored (usually blue) warp (lengthwise) and white filling (crosswise) threads, also sometimes woven in colored stripes. The name originated in the French *serge de Nîmes*. Denim is usually all-cotton, though it is sometimes made of a cotton-synthetic mixture. Decades of use in the clothing industry, especially in the manufacture of overalls and trousers worn for heavy labor, have demonstrated denim's durability, a quality that, along with its comfort, made denim jeans extremely popular for leisure wear in the late 20th century.

Denis, Ruth Saint See Ruth Saint Denis

Denis \də-'nē, *Engl* 'de-nəs\, **St.** *or* **St. Denys** (died AD 258?) Patron saint of France and first bishop of Paris. Probably born in Rome, he was one of seven bishops sent to convert the people of Gaul during the reign of Decius. Little is known of his life; he is believed to have been martyred during the persecutions of the emperor Valerian. A 9th-century legend says that he was beheaded on Montmartre and that his decapitated body carried his head to the area northeast of Paris where the Benedictine abbey of St. Denis was founded.

denitrifying bacteria \ˌdē-'nī-trə-ˌfī-iŋ\ Soil microorganisms whose action results in the conversion of nitrates in soil to free atmospheric nitrogen, thus exhausting soil fertility and reducing agricultural productivity. Without denitrification, earth's nitrogen supply would eventually accumulate in the oceans, since nitrates are highly soluble and are continuously leached from the soil into nearby bodies of water. See also nitrifying bacteria.

Denmark *officially* **Kingdom of Denmark** *Danish* **Danmark** \'dän-ˌmärk\ Constitutional monarchy, northern central Europe. Area: 16,639 sq mi (43,094 sq km). Its territory includes Greenland and the Faeroe Islands, which are self-governing dependencies. Population (1997 est.): 5,284,000. Capital: Copenhagen. The majority of the population is Nordic. Language: Danish (official). Religion: Evangelical Lutheranism (official). Currency: Danish krone. Lying between the North and Baltic seas, it occupies the Jutland peninsula and an archipelago to its east. The two largest islands, Sjælland and Fyn, together make up more than one-fourth of the country's total land area. With a 4,500-mi (7,300-km) coastline, the climate is generally temperate and often wet. Denmark has a mixed economy based on services and manufacturing and boasts one of the world's oldest and largest social-welfare systems. Its standard of living is among the highest in the world. Its chief of state is the Danish monarch, while the head of government is the prime minister. Inhabited from 100,000 BC, it was settled by Danes, a Scandinavian branch of the Teutons, c. 6th century AD. During the Viking period the Danes expanded their territory, and by the 11th century the united Danish kingdom included parts of what are now Germany, Sweden, England, and Norway. Scandinavia was united under Danish rule from 1397 until 1523, when Sweden became independent; a series of debilitating wars with Sweden in the 17th century resulted in the Treaty of Copenhagen (1660), which established the modern Scandinavian frontiers. Denmark gained and lost various other territories, including Norway, in the 19th and 20th century; it went through three constitutions between 1849 and 1915 and was occupied by Nazi Germany in 1940–45. A founding member of NATO (1949), Denmark adopted its current constitution in 1953. It became a member of the European Union in 1973, and modified its membership during the 1990s. The island of Zealand, on which Copenhagen stands, was connected to the central island of Funen by a rail tunnel and bridge in 1997. This ended more than 100 years of ferry service and cut the crossing time to under 10 minutes.

Dennison, Aaron Lufkin (1812–1895) U.S. watch manufacturer. He was born in Freeport, Me. After studying the methods used at the Springfield Armory, he mastered the technical difficulties of machine production of small parts, set up a factory in Waltham, Mass., in 1850, and began to produce the first inexpensive factory-made watches with interchangeable parts. His introduction of machinery into the manufacture of paper boxes and other paper products resulted in the founding of the Dennison Manufacturing Co. He is regarded as the father of American watchmaking.

density Mass of a unit volume of a material substance. It is calculated by dividing an object's mass by its volume. In the International System of Units, and depending on the units of measurement used, density can be expressed in grams per cubic centimeter (g/cm^3) or kilograms per cubic meter (kg/m^3). The expression "particle density" refers to the number of particles per unit volume, not to the density of a single particle. See also specific gravity.

density current Any current in either a liquid or a gas that is kept in motion by the force of gravity acting on small differences in density. A density difference can exist between two fluids or between different parts of the same fluid. Density currents flow along ocean and lake bottoms, because the water entering is colder, saltier, or contains more suspended sediment and thus is denser than the surrounding water. Density currents are a factor in water pollution, as the industrial discharge of large amounts of polluted or heated water can generate density currents that affect neighboring human or animal communities.

density function In statistics, a function whose integral is calculated to find probabilities associated with a continuous random variable (see continuity, probability theory). Its graph is a curve above the horizontal axis that defines a total area, between itself and the axis, of 1. The percentage of this area included between any two values coincides with the probability that the outcome of an observation described by the density function falls between those values. Every random variable is associated with a density function (e.g., a variable with a normal distribution is described by a bell curve).

dentistry Profession concerned with the teeth and mouth. It includes repair or removal of decayed teeth, straightening and adjustment of teeth for proper occlusion, and design, manufacture, and fitting of false teeth and other prosthetic devices. X rays are used to show conditions not visible on examination. Using local anesthesia, caries in teeth are drilled to remove diseased areas and filled with various materials. Decay that reaches a tooth's root risks infection of the nerve and requires root-canal surgery. Teeth that must be extracted are replaced by crowns for single teeth and full or partial dentures for more. Dentists also educate patients on oral hygiene, examine and clean teeth and apply fluoride compounds for decay resistance.

D'Entrecasteaux Islands \ˌdōn-trə-'kas-tō\ Island group (pop., 1990: 49,000), Papua New Guinea. Located in the South Pacific Ocean, the group includes Normanby, Fergusson, and Goodenough islands and many islets, atolls, and reefs. Most are volcanic, precipitous, and forested. They have a combined land area of 1,213 sq mi (3,142 sq km). They were named by the French navigator Bruni d'Entrecasteaux in 1793. The chief settlement is Dobu, located on an islet between Normanby and Fergusson.

Denver City (pop., 1996 est.: 498,000), capital of Colorado. On the SOUTH PLATTE RIVER just east of the ROCKY MTNS., its elevation of 5,280 ft (1,609 m) gives it the nickname "Mile High City." An early stopping place for Indians and trappers, it was settled in the 1859 gold rush. The growing rival towns of Auraria and St. Charles combined in 1860 to form Denver, which became the capital in 1867. The 1870s and '80s saw a silver boom that ended in 1893, but new gold discoveries helped prevent a major decline. Modern Denver, a transportation, industrial, and commercial hub, has one of the nation's largest livestock markets. It is a major center for winter sports, with many ski areas in the vicinity. The Denver branch of the U.S. Mint (opened 1906) produces about 75% of U.S. coinage and is the nation's second-largest gold depository.

deontic logic \dē-'än-tik\ Branch of MODAL LOGIC that studies the permitted, the obligatory, and the forbidden, which are characterized as deontic modalities (Greek, *deontos:* "of that which is binding"). It seeks to systematize the abstract, purely conceptual relations between propositions in this sphere, such as the following: If an act is obligatory, then its performance must be permitted and its omission forbidden. In given circumstances, every act is such that either it or its omission is permitted. Modal logic leaves to substantive disciplines such as ETHICS and LAW the concrete questions of what specific acts or states of affairs are to be forbidden, permitted, or the like.

deontological ethics Ethical theories that maintain that the moral rightness or wrongness of an action depends on its intrinsic qualities, and not (as in CONSEQUENTIALISM) on the nature of its consequences. Deontological ethics holds that at least some acts are morally wrong in themselves (e.g., lying, breaking a promise, punishing the innocent, murder), regardless of their consequences. It often finds expression in such slogans as "Duty for duty's sake," "Virtue is its own reward," and "Let justice be done though the heavens fall." Deontological theories have been termed formalistic because their central principle lies in the conformity of an action to some rule or law. The best known exponent of deontological ethics was IMMANUEL KANT.

Depardieu \də-pär-'dyœ\, **Gérard** (born 1948) French film actor. He made his film debut in 1965 and played minor parts until his performance in *Going Places* (1974) brought him a major role in BERNARDO BERTOLUCCI's *1900* (1976). He became French cinema's top male star in the 1980s and also made films elsewhere in Europe and in the U.S. Noted for a screen image that combines sensitivity with masculine strength, he delivered compelling performances in *The Last Metro* (1980), *The Return of Martin Guerre* (1981), *Jean de Florette* (1986), *Manon of the Spring* (1986), *Cyrano de Bergerac* (1990), and *Tous les matins du monde* (1992).

department store Retail establishment that sells a wide variety of goods. These usually include ready-to-wear apparel and accessories, yard goods and household textiles, household wares, furniture, and electrical appliances and accessories. In addition to departments (supervised by managers and buyers) for the various categories of goods, there are departmental divisions of merchandising, advertising, service, accounting, and budgetary control. The BON MARCHÉ in Paris, which began as a small shop in the early 19th century, is often considered the first department store. The first U.S. department-store chains—J. J.C. PENNEY and SEARS, ROEBUCK AND CO.—date to the 1920s. See also GUM, HARRODS.

dependency In international relations, a weak state dominated by or under the jurisdiction of a more powerful state but not formally annexed by it. Examples include AMERICAN SAMOA (U.S.) and GREENLAND (Denmark). The dominant state may control certain of its affairs, such as defense, foreign relations, and internal security, and allow it autonomy in domestic affairs such as education, health, and infrastructural development. In the 1960s and '70s the term referred to an approach to understanding third-world development that emphasized the constraints imposed by the global political and economic order.

depletion allowance In tax law, the deductions from gross income allowed investors in exhaustible mineral deposits (including oil or gas) for the depletion of the deposits. The depletion allowance is intended as an incentive to stimulate investment in this high-risk industry, though critics argue that mineral deposits are valuable enough to justify high levels of investment even without tax incentives. See also DEPRECIATION.

deposit account Either of two basic bank deposit accounts. The demand deposit is payable on demand (see CHECK). Theoretically, the TIME DEPOSIT is payable only after a fixed interval of time; in practice, withdrawals from most small time-deposit accounts are paid on demand.

depreciation Accounting charge for the decline in value of an asset spread over its economic life. Depreciation includes deterioration from use, age, and exposure to the elements, as well as decline in value caused by obsolescence, loss of usefulness arising from the availability of newer and more efficient goods serving the same purpose. It does not include sudden losses caused by fire, accident, or disaster. Depreciation is often used in assessing the value of property (e.g., buildings, machinery) or other assets of limited life (e.g., a leasehold or copyright) for tax purposes. See also DEPLETION ALLOWANCE, INVESTMENT CREDIT.

depression In economics, a major downswing in the BUSINESS CYCLE characterized by sharply reduced industrial production, widespread unemployment, a serious decline or cessation of growth in construction, and great reductions in international trade and capital movements. Unlike RECESSIONS, which may be limited to a single country, severe depressions such as the GREAT DEPRESSION encompass many nations. See also DEFLATION, INFLATION.

depression Neurotic or psychotic disorder marked by sadness, inactivity, difficulty in thinking and concentration, a significant increase or decrease in appetite and time spent sleeping, feelings of dejection and hopelessness, and sometimes suicidal tendencies. Probably the most common psychiatric complaint, depression has been described by physicians from at least the time of HIPPOCRATES, who called it melancholia. Its course is extremely variable from person to person; it may be fleeting or permanent, mild or severe. Depression is more common in women than in men. The rates of incidence increase with age in men, while the peak for women is between the ages of 35 and 45. Its causes can be both psychosocial (e.g., the loss of a loved one) and biochemical (chiefly, reduced quantities of the monoamines NOREPINEPHRINE and SEROTONIN). Treatment is usually a combination of PSYCHOTHERAPY and drug therapy (see ANTIDEPRESSANT). A person who experiences alternating states of depression and extreme elation is said to suffer from BIPOLAR DISORDER.

Depression of 1929 See GREAT DEPRESSION

Depretis \dā-'pre-tēs\, **Agostino** (1813–1887) Italian politician. In 1848 he was elected to the first Piedmontese parliament, and was reelected thereafter until his death. After Italy was unified, he served in several cabinet posts (1862–67). He became premier in 1876 and was the dominant force in Italian politics until 1887. Among his notable achievements was the signing of the TRIPLE ALLIANCE and his government policy of *trasformismo,* bringing together members of different parties in the same cabinet.

depth charge *or* **depth bomb** Weapon used by ships or aircraft to attack submerged submarines. Developed by the British in World War I for use against German submarines, it consisted of a canister filled with explosives and dropped off the stern of a ship near a submerged submarine. It rarely exploded close enough to sink the submarine, but its shock waves loosened the submarine's joints and damaged its instruments, forcing it to the surface, where naval gunfire could finish it off. Modern depth charges can be fired as far as 2,000 yards (1,800 m) from a ship's deck or launched from aircraft. Atomic depth charges have a nuclear warhead and a vastly increased killing radius.

Derain \də-'raⁿ\, **André** (1880–1954) French painter, graphic artist, and designer. He studied in Paris at the Académie Carrière and Académie Julian. He developed his early style in association with his friends MAURICE DE VLAMINCK and HENRI MATISSE; the three were the principal exponents of FAUVISM. Derain's landscapes and figure studies featured brilliant colors, broken brush strokes, and impulsive lines. By the 1920s, however, he had turned to the Neoclassical style. He produced numerous book illustrations and designs for stage sets, notably for SERGEY DIAGHILEV'S BALLETS RUSSES.

Derby One of the classic English horse races (established 1780), run in June over a 1½-mi (2,400 m) course at Epsom Downs, Surrey. Many other horse races have been named for the Derby (e.g., the KENTUCKY

DERBY), and the term itself has come to signify a race or contest of any type.

Derby \'där-bē\, **Earl of** *orig.* **Edward (George Geoffrey Smith) Stanley** (1799–1869) English statesman. Having entered Parliament as a Whig in 1820, he later joined the Conservatives and became leader of the Conservative Party (1846–68) and prime minister (1852, 1858, and 1866–68). Legislation adopted during his tenure included the removal of Jewish discrimination in Parliament membership, the transfer of India's administration from the EAST INDIA CO. to the crown, and the REFORM BILL OF 1867. He is remembered as one of England's greatest parliamentary orators.

Derbyshire \'där-bē-ˌshir\ *or* **Derby** \'där-bē\ County (pop., 1995 est.: 1,059,000), central England. The landscape varies from the moorlands of the north to the Trent lowlands in the south. Industry ranges from tourism in the High Peak district to mining and engineering in the eastern and southern coalfields. Apart from gaining the rural district of Tintwistle from CHESHIRE, the traditional county was unaltered by the administrative reorganization in 1974; its county seat is MATLOCK.

derivative In mathematics, a fundamental concept of DIFFERENTIAL CALCULUS representing the instantaneous rate of change of a FUNCTION. The first derivative of a function is a function whose values can be interpreted as SLOPES of TANGENT LINES to the graph of the original function at a given point. The derivative of a derivative (known as the second derivative) describes the rate of change of the rate of change, and can be thought of physically as acceleration. The process of finding a derivative is called DIFFERENTIATION.

derivative, partial See PARTIAL DERIVATIVE

derivatives Financial contracts whose value is derived from another asset, which can include stocks, bonds, currencies, interest rates, commodities, and related indexes. Purchasers of derivatives are essentially wagering on the future performance of that asset. Derivatives include such widely accepted products as FUTURES and options. Concern over the risky nature of derivatives grew after some well-publicized corporate losses in 1994 involving PROCTER &D GAMBLE, Metallgesellschaft AG of Germany, and Orange Co., Cal., and anxiety intensified after the collapse of the London-based merchant bank Barings PLC in 1995. Securities regulators from 16 countries then agreed on measures to improve control of derivatives.

dermatitis *or* **eczema** \ig-'zē-mə, 'eg-zə-mə\ INFLAMMATION of the SKIN, usually itchy, with redness, swelling, and blistering. Causes and patterns vary. Contact dermatitis appears at the site of contact with an irritating substance or allergen. Atopic dermatitis, with patches of dry skin, occurs in infants, children, and young adults with genetic hypersensitivities (atopy). Stasis dermatitis affects the ankles and lower legs because of chronic poor blood flow in the veins. Seborrheic dermatitis appears as scaly skin, most often on the scalp (DANDRUFF) and areas rich in SEBACEOUS GLANDS. Neurodermatitis is apparently caused by repeated scratching of an itchy skin area.

dermatology Medical specialty dealing with diseases of the SKIN. Its scientific basis was established in the mid-19th century by Ferdinand von Hebra (1816–1880), whose approach was based on microscopic examination of skin lesions. Starting in the 1930s, an emphasis on biochemistry and physiology led to more sophisticated and effective treatments. Dermatology deals with fungal diseases, skin cancers, PSORIASIS, and life-threatening skin diseases such as pemphigus, SCLERODERMA, and LUPUS ERYTHEMATOSUS.

dermestid (beetle) \dər-'mes-təd\ Any member of about 700 species (family Dermestidae) of widely distributed BEETLES that are household pests. Usually brown or black, some are brightly colored or patterned, and they vary in shape from elongated to oval. Dermestids range from 0.05 to 0.5 in. (1–12 mm) long and are covered with hairs or scales that easily flake off. The wormlike larvae feed on furs, skins, feathers, horn, and hair; some feed on cheese and dried meats or on carpets, rugs, furniture, and clothing. Two are museum pests that have destroyed collections of stuffed animals; museums and collectors must either have pest-proof display shelves or continuously apply pesticides. The larvae of carrion-feeding species are sometimes used to clean the soft tissue attached to animal skeletons.

Dermot Macmurrough See DIARMAID MACMURCHADA

Déroulède \dā-rü-'led\, **Paul** (1846–1914) French politician and poet. An ardent nationalist and advocate of revenge against Germany, he helped found the revanchist *Ligue des patriotes* (League of Patriots), supported GEORGES BOULANGER, and campaigned against ALFRED DREYFUS. After trying to overthrow the government in 1899, he was exiled in 1900 but allowed to return in 1905. His patriotic poems include the collection *Chants du soldat* (1872).

Derrida \de-rē-'dä\, **Jacques** (born 1930) French (Algerian-born) philosopher. He has taught principally at the École Normale Supérieure in Paris (1965–84). His critique of Western philosophy encompasses literature, linguistics, and psychoanalysis. His thought is based on his disapproval of the search for an ultimate metaphysical certainty or source of meaning that has characterized most of Western philosophy. Instead, he offers DECONSTRUCTION, a way of reading philosophic texts intended to make explicit the underlying metaphysical suppositions and assumptions through a close analysis of the language that attempts to convey them. His works on deconstructive theory and method include *Speech and Phenomena* (1967), *Writing and Difference* (1967), and *Of Grammatology* (1967).

Derry *or* **Londonderry** District (pop., 1995 est.: 103,000), northwestern Northern Ireland. Its name was changed to Derry in 1984. It is also the name of a former traditional county for an area colonized by the English in 1609. The 1973 administrative reorganization broke the area up into several districts, including Derry. Bordered by the Irish Republic, and Lough Foyle, it is centered around the seaport city of DERRY. In 1969 the old city and the adjacent area were merged administratively, and in 1973 it became one of Northern Ireland's 26 districts.

Derry *or* **Londonderry** Seaport (pop., 1995 est.: 77,000) and district seat of DERRY, Northern Ireland. St. COLUMBA established a monastery there in the 6th century, but the settlement was repeatedly destroyed by Norse invaders. In 1600 an English force seized Derry; shortly thereafter JAMES I of England granted Derry to the citizens of London, who brought in Protestant settlers. It was officially known as Londonderry. Growth of the modern city dates from the 1850s, when linen shirt making became important, and clothing manufacture remains a major industry. Home to two cathedrals, Anglican and Roman Catholic, it has been the site of terrorist violence in the late 20th century. Its name was officially changed to Derry in 1984.

Dershowitz, Alan (Morton) (born 1938) U.S. lawyer. Born in New York City, he graduated from Yale Law School and clerked for Justice ARTHUR GOLDBERG before being appointed to the Harvard Law School faculty at age 25. Known as a civil-liberties lawyer, he appeared for the defense in many highly publicized criminal cases, including Claus von Bulow and O.J. SIMPSON. His journal articles and widely syndicated newspaper articles were collected in such volumes as *The Abuse Excuse* (1994); his other books include *Reasonable Doubts* (1966) and *The Best Defense* (1982).

dervish In Islam, a member of a Sufi fraternity. These mystics stressed emotional aspects of devotion through ecstatic trances, dancing, and whirling. Dervishes can be either resident in the community or lay members; wandering or mendicant dervishes are called fakirs and are often regarded as holy men who possess miraculous powers. Though viewed as unorthodox and extreme by most Muslims, the movement has endured to the present. See also SUFISM.

Derwent River \'dər-wənt\ River, Tasmania, Australia. Rising in Lake ST. CLAIR, it flows 113 mi (182 km) southeast to enter Storm Bay through a 3.5-mi- (5.5-km-) wide estuary. Its major upper-course tributaries are extensively developed for hydropower. The city of HOBART is situated on the estuary, 12 mi (19 km) from the river's mouth. This stretch of the river forms an excellent deepwater port and is spanned by the Tasman Bridge.

Derwent Water Lake, Cumbria, England. Located in the LAKE DISTRICT, it is about 3 mi (5 km) long and 0.5–1.25 mi (0.8–2 km) wide, with a maximum depth of 72 ft (22 m). The River Derwent enters its southern end and leaves the lake's northern end near the market town of Keswick. Several sites on its shores are National Trust property and are frequented by tourists. Lords Island, one of several in the lake, was once the residence of the earls of Derwentwater.

Des Moines \di-'mȯin\ City (pop., 1996 est.: 193,000), capital of Iowa. Located at the juncture of the Raccoon and DES MOINES rivers, Fort Des

Moines was established in 1843 to protect the Sauk and Fox Indians. The area was opened to white settlers in 1845. East Des Moines developed and by 1856 had amalgamated with Fort Des Moines to form the present city, which became the capital in 1857. The state's largest city, it is a communications hub and a major commercial manufacturing, governmental, and publishing center (especially for farm journals). It is the site of Drake University (1881) and home to the KRNT Theatre, one of the nation's largest.

Des Moines River River, southwestern Minnesota into Iowa. Rising near PIPESTONE, it flows 525 mi (845 km) southeast to join the Mississippi River near Keokuk, Iowa. Above Humboldt, Iowa, it is known as the West Fork. From the late 1830s until the end of the AMERICAN CIVIL WAR, it was the main commercial artery for central Iowa. It was early utilized for power, and, although none survive, 80 grain mills were built (1840–90) along its banks.

Des Plaines River \des-'plānz\ River, northeastern Illinois. Rising in southeastern Wisconsin, it flows south into Illinois past CHICAGO, to join the Kankakee River after a course of 150 mi (241 km). In 1900 Chicago completed a drainage canal from the southern branch of the CHICAGO RIVER to the Des Plaines. It is part of the Illinois Waterway (1933), which allows modern barge traffic to pass between the GREAT LAKES and the MISSISSIPPI RIVER.

Desai \'dā-ˌsī, de-'sī\, **Anita** *orig.* **Anita Mazumdar** (born 1937) Indian novelist and author of children's books. Considered India's premier imagist writer, she excels in evoking character and mood through visual images. Her works include *Fire on the Mountain* (1977), *Clear Light of Day* (1980), *Baumgartner's Bombay* (1988), and the popular children's book *The Village by the Sea* (1982).

Desai \de-'sī\, **Morarji (Ranchhodji)** (1896–1995) Prime minister of India (1977–79). The son of a village teacher, he joined the provincial civil service of Bombay (now Mumbai) in 1918. He joined MOHANDAS K. GANDHI's struggle in 1930 and spent almost 10 years in British jails in the 1930s and '40s. In 1969 he became chairman of the opposition to INDIRA GANDHI; he was detained in solitary confinement 1975–77 for his political activities. When elections were held in 1977, he became prime minister, but his coalition unraveled and in 1979 he resigned.

desalination *or* **desalting** Removal of dissolved salts from SEAWATER and from the salty waters of inland seas, highly mineralized GROUNDWATERS, and municipal wastewaters. Desalination makes such otherwise unusable waters fit for human consumption, irrigation, industrial applications, and other purposes. DISTILLATION is the most widely used desalination process; freezing and thawing, electrodialysis, and reverse osmosis are also used. All are energy-intensive and therefore expensive. Currently, more than 2 billion gallons (8 million cu m) of fresh water are produced each day by several thousand desalination plants throughout the world, the largest plants being in the Arabian Peninsula.

Descartes \dā-'kärt\, **René** (1596–1650) French mathematician, scientist, and philosopher, considered the father of modern philosophy. Born near Tours and educated at a Jesuit college, he joined the military in 1618 and traveled widely for the next 10 years. In 1628 he settled in Holland, where he would remain until 1649. Descartes's ambition was to introduce into philosophy the rigor and clarity of mathematics. In his *Meditations on First Philosophy* (1641), he began by methodically doubting knowledge based on authority, the senses, and reason, in the hope of arriving in the end at something indubitable. This he reached in his famous "Cogito ergo sum" ("I think, therefore I am"). His task was to build on this as a foundation, to deduce from it a series of other propositions, each following with the same self-evidence, and thus to produce a philosophical system on which people could agree as completely as they do on Euclid's geometry. He developed a dualistic system (see DUALISM) in which he distinguished radically between mind, the essence of which is thinking, and matter, the essence of which is extension in three dimensions. His metaphysics is rationalistic (see RATIONALISM), but his physics and physiology are empiricistic (see EMPIRICISM) and mechanistic (see MECHANISM). As a mathematician, he founded ANALYTIC GEOMETRY and reformed algebraic notation.

descent System of acknowledged social parentage whereby a person may claim KINSHIP ties with another. Descent systems vary widely. The practical importance of descent comes from its use as a means for individuals to assert rights, duties, privileges, or status. Descent has special influence when rights to succession, INHERITANCE, or residence follow kinship lines. One method of limiting the recognition of kinship is to emphasize the relationship through one parent only. Such unilineal kinship systems are of two main types—patrilineal systems, in which the relationships through the father are emphasized; and matrilineal systems, in which maternal relationships are stressed. These systems differ radically from cognatic systems, in which everyone has similar obligations to, and expectations from, both paternal and maternal kin. The cognatic system is somewhat vague and tends to characterize the more industrialized countries, in which individual rights and duties are increasingly defined institutionally or legally.

desensitization *or* **hyposensitization** Treatment to eliminate allergic reactions (see ALLERGY) by injecting increasing strengths of purified extracts of the substance that causes the reaction. This creates special ANTIBODIES (blocking antibodies) in the patient's serum that combine with the allergen, blocking its reaction with allergic antibodies. Desensitization can also be required when a penicillin-sensitive person needs to be treated with PENICILLIN. See also ANAPHYLAXIS, ANTIGEN.

desert Large, extremely dry area of land with fairly sparse vegetation. It is one of the earth's major types of ecosystems. Areas with a mean annual precipitation of 10 in. (250 mm) or less are generally considered deserts. They include the high-latitude circumpolar areas as well as the more familiar hot, arid regions of the low and mid-latitudes. Desert terrain may consist of rugged mountains, high plateaus, or plains; many occupy broad mountain-rimmed basins. Surface materials include bare bedrock, plains of gravel and boulders, and vast tracts of shifting sand. Wind-blown sands, commonly thought to be typical of deserts, make up only about 2% of North American deserts, 10% of the Sahara, and 30% of the Arabian desert.

desert varnish *or* **patina** Thin, dark red to black mineral coating (generally iron and manganese oxides and silica) deposited on pebbles and rocks on the surface of desert regions. As dew and soil moisture brought to the surface by capillary action evaporate, their dissolved minerals are deposited on the surface. Wind abrasion removes the softer salts and polishes the surface to a glossy finish. Both high evaporation rates and sufficient precipitation are necessary for desert varnish to form.

desertification Spread of a desert environment into arid or semiarid regions, caused by climatic changes, human influence, or both. Climatic factors include periods of temporary but severe drought and long-term climatic changes toward dryness. Human factors include artificial climatic alteration, as through the removal of vegetation (which can lead to unnaturally high EROSION), excessive cultivation, and the exhaustion of water supplies. Desertification drains an arid or semiarid land of its life-supporting capabilities. It is characterized by a declining GROUNDWATER table, salt accumulation in topsoil and water, a decrease in surface water, increasing erosion, and the disappearance of native vegetation.

Desiderio da Settignano \dā-sē-'der-yō-dä-ˌsāt-tēn-'yä-nō\ (c. 1430–64) Italian sculptor. Born into a family of stonemasons, he entered the Stone and Wood Carvers' Guild of Florence in 1453. He based his style on DONATELLO's work of the 1430s, and his skill as a marble cutter established him as a master of bas-relief. His delicate, sensitive, original technique was best expressed in portrait busts of women and children. His most important public work was the tomb of Carlo Marsuppini in the church of Santa Croce, with its rich architectural detail one of the most outstanding of all Florentine wall monuments.

designer drug Synthetic version of a controlled narcotic substance. Designer drugs are manufactured with a molecular structure slightly different from that of a related controlled substance in order to create a drug not specifically listed by law-enforcement organizations as illicit. Because they are manufactured in clandestine laboratories, often by amateurs, such drugs can be dangerous. One of the best-known is MDMA (3,4 methylenedioxymethamphetamine), a variation on methamphetamine that is known on the street especially as "ecstasy." Non-narcotic synthetic chemical compounds designed to interact with specific proteins and enzymes in order to combat disease have also been called designer drugs.

desktop publishing (DTP) Use of a personal computer to perform publishing tasks. DTP allows an individual to combine text, numerical data, and graphic elements in a document that can be output on a printer or a phototypesetter. A typical DTP system includes a personal computer, a high-resolution printer, and input devices such as an optical SCANNER. Text and graphic elements are commonly created or manipulated with several separate software programs and then combined with a page-makeup program. Powerful DTP programs offer full-featured graphics capabilities.

desmid \'dez-məd\ Any of a group of beautiful, one-celled, microscopic green ALGAE characterized by great variation in cell shape. Typically the cell is divided symmetrically into semicells connected at a central point. Desmids are found worldwide, usually in acid bogs or lakes. Since most species have a limited range, the presence of specific desmids is helpful in characterizing water samples.

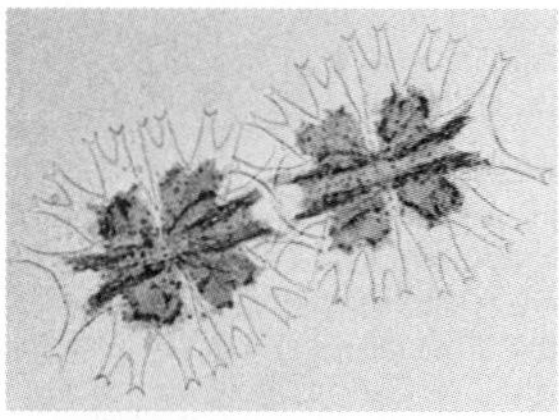

Desmid (*Micrasterias*), highly magnified.
WINTON PATNODE—PHOTO RESEARCHERS

Desmond Ancient territorial division, Ireland. From the 11th to the 17th century, the name was often used for two quite distinct areas. Gaelic Desmond extended over part of modern Counties Kerry and Cork; Anglo-Norman Desmond extended over northern Kerry, most of the modern county of Limerick, southwestern Tipperary, eastern and southern County Cork, and eastern Waterford.

Desmoulins \dā-mü-'la^{n}\, **(Lucie-Simplice-) Camille (-Benoist)** (1760–1794) French journalist influential in the French Revolution. Though a stammer had impeded him as a lawyer, he suddenly emerged as an inspiring orator when the Revolution began, inciting the storming of the Bastille. In his pamphlets and newspapers he campaigned for the deposition of the king and the establishment of a republic. Elected to the National Convention, he joined other MONTAGNARDS in a struggle against the GIRONDINS. Later he and GEORGES J. DANTON became leaders of a moderate faction, the Indulgents. After attacking the Committee of Public Safety's REIGN OF TERROR, he was guillotined along with other Dantonists.

despotism, enlightened See ENLIGHTENED DESPOTISM

Dessalines \,dā-sə-'lēn\, **Jean-Jacques** (1758?–1806) Emperor of Haiti who drove out the French in 1804. He was a slave of a black master in Saint-Domingue (Haiti) when he joined a slave rebellion in 1791. He became a lieutenant of TOUSSAINT-LOUVERTURE, but submitted to the French expedition that deposed Toussaint in 1802. NAPOLEON's decision to reintroduce slavery led Dessalines and others to rebel, and with British help they expelled the French. In 1804 Dessalines proclaimed the island independent under its Arawakan name, Haiti, and proclaimed himself emperor the following year. He made it illegal for whites to own property and killed thousands; he also discriminated against mulattoes. He was killed during a mulatto revolt.

destroyer Fast naval vessel used to protect other ships. The term was first applied to vessels built in the 1890s to protect BATTLESHIPS from TORPEDO boats. By World War I destroyers were often sent ahead of the battle fleet to scout for the enemy, beat back its destroyers with CANNON fire, and then launch torpedoes against its battleships and CRUISERS. When the SUBMARINE became the main torpedo-launching vessel, destroyers armed with DEPTH CHARGES protected convoys and battle fleets against submarine attack. In World War II, with the addition of RADAR and ANTIAIRCRAFT guns, its escort role included air defense. Modern destroyers are run by a crew of about 300 and equipped with surface-to-air missiles, antiship missiles, and one or two big guns. Many carry submarine-hunting helicopters, and some carry CRUISE MISSILES.

detached retina Separation of most layers of the RETINA of the eye from the choroid, the pigmented middle layer of the eyeball. With age, small tears can develop in the retina, and the vitreous humor inside the eyeball leaks through, separating the retina from the choroid. The disease retrolental fibroplasia or accidents can also cause retinal detachment. It usually develops slowly, without pain. Floating black spots and flashes of light appear in the affected eye, and vision becomes increasingly blurred. Without prompt treatment, it causes permanent blindness. Draining the fluid behind the retina and applying heat, a laser beam, or extreme cold causes scarring that seals the tears and prevents the retina from detaching again.

detective story Type of popular literature dealing with the step-by-step investigation and solution of a crime, usually murder. The first detective story was EDGAR ALLAN POE's "The Murders in the Rue Morgue" (1841). The genre soon expanded to novel length. Sherlock Holmes, the first fictional detective to become a household name, first appeared in ARTHUR CONAN DOYLE's *A Study in Scarlet* (1887). The 1930s was the golden age of the detective novel, exemplified by the books of DASHIELL HAMMETT. The introduction of mass-produced paperback books in the late 1930s made detective stories readily accessible to a wide public, and well-known fictional detectives were created by G.K. CHESTERTON, AGATHA CHRISTIE, DOROTHY SAYERS, RAYMOND CHANDLER, MICKEY SPILLANE, and GEORGES SIMENON.

détente \dā-'tänt\ Period of the easing of COLD WAR tensions between the U.S. and the Soviet Union from 1967 to 1979. The era was a time of increased trade and cooperation with the Soviet Union and the signing of the SALT treaties. Relations cooled again with the Soviet invasion of Afghanistan.

detergent Any of various surfactants (substances that reduce SURFACE TENSION) used to dislodge dirt from soiled surfaces and retain it in suspension, allowing it to be rinsed away. The term usually refers to synthetic substances and excludes SOAPS. The characteristic features of any detergent are a hydrophilic end and a hydrophobic end. In ionic detergents, the hydrophilic property is conferred by the ionized part of the molecule. In nonionic detergents, hydrophilicity is based on the presence of multiple hydroxyl groups or other hydrophilic residues. Besides those used in water to wash dishes and laundry, detergents that function in other SOLVENTS are used in lubricating oils, gasolines, and dry-cleaning solvents to prevent or remove unwanted deposits.

determinant In LINEAR ALGEBRA, a numerical value associated with a MATRIX having the same number of rows as columns. It is particularly useful in solving SYSTEMS OF (LINEAR) EQUATIONS and in the study of VECTORS. For a two-by-two matrix, the determinant is the product of the upper left and lower right terms minus the product of the lower left and upper right terms. Determinants of larger matrices involve more complicated arithmetic combinations of the terms and are usually solved using a calculator or computer.

determinism Theory that all events, including human decisions, are completely determined by previously existing causes. The traditional FREE WILL PROBLEM arises from the question, Is moral responsibility consistent with the truth of determinism? (See COMPATIBILISM.) PIERRE-SIMON LAPLACE framed its classical formulation in the 18th century. For Laplace, the present state of the universe is the effect of its previous state and the cause of the state that follows it. If a mind, at any given moment, could know all the laws and all the forces operating in nature and the respective positions and momenta of all its components, it could thereby know with certainty the future and the past of every entity.

deterrence Military strategy whereby one power uses the threat of reprisal to preclude an attack from an adversary. The term largely refers to the basic strategy of the nuclear powers and the major alliance systems. The premise is that each nuclear power maintains a high level of instant and overwhelming destructive capability against any aggressor. It relies on two basic conditions: the ability to retaliate after a surprise attack must be perceived as credible, and retaliation must be perceived as a possibility, if not a certainty.

Detroit City (pop., 1996 est.: 1,000,000), largest in Michigan. Located on the DETROIT RIVER, and founded by the French in 1701, it became a trading center for the GREAT LAKES region. It surrendered to the British during the FRENCH AND INDIAN WAR, then came under U.S. control in 1796. The capital of Michigan 1805–47, it grew as one of the country's shipping and flour-milling centers. In the 20th century it became the automobile capital of the world with the help of HENRY FORD. The city's industrial growth attracted migrants, at first Europeans and later Southern blacks, who by 1990 made up three-fourths of the population. The decline in the area's automotive industry brought economic hardship in the late 20th century. Wayne State University (1868) is the city's oldest college.

Detroit River River, southeastern Michigan. Forming part of the boundary between Michigan and Ontario, it connects Lake ST. CLAIR with Lake ERIE. It flows south for 32 mi (51 km) past DETROIT and WINDSOR, Ont., where a bridge and tunnel connect the two cities. The largest islands in the river are Belle Isle (a city park of Detroit) and Grosse Ile (a residential area with an airport), both in Michigan, and Fighting Island in Ontario. The river is heavily used by both pleasure craft and GREAT LAKES shipping.

deus ex machina \'dā-əs-ˌeks-'ma-ki-nə, 'dā-əs-ˌeks-mə-'shē-nə\ Stage device in Greek and Roman drama in which a god appeared in the sky by means of a crane (Greek, *mechane*) to resolve the plot of a play. Plays by SOPHOCLES and particularly EURIPIDES sometimes require the device. The term now denotes something that appears suddenly and unexpectedly and provides an artificial solution to an apparently insoluble difficulty.

deuterium \dü-'tir-ē-əm\ *or* **heavy hydrogen** ISOTOPE of HYDROGEN, chemical symbol ^2H or D, atomic number 1 (but atomic weight approximately 2). HAROLD C. UREY won a Nobel Prize for its discovery and isolation. Its nucleus contains one PROTON and one NEUTRON. A stable substance found as about 0.015% of ordinary hydrogen, deuterium can be purified by DISTILLATION of hydrogen or by ELECTROLYSIS of WATER. It enters into all the same chemical reactions as ordinary hydrogen; it forms D_2 and HD, analogous to H_2, and D_2O (HEAVY WATER), analogous to H_2O. NUCLEAR FUSION of deuterium atoms or of deuterium and TRITIUM at high temperatures releases enormous amounts of ENERGY. Such reactions have been used in NUCLEAR WEAPONS. Deuterium is useful as a tracer in research into reaction mechanisms and biochemical pathways.

deuterium oxide See HEAVY WATER

Deuteronomic Reform \ˌdü-tə-rə-'nä-mik\ Religious reformation in JUDAH during the reign of King JOSIAH (c. 640–609 BC). As Assyria's hold on Israel weakened, Josiah waged a campaign against foreign cults and had their altars and idols removed from the Temple. He called for a return to the observance of Mosaic Law, based on the book of the Law discovered in the Temple of JERUSALEM (c. 622 BC), believed to be the same book as the law code in the Book of Deuteronomy. Rural sanctuaries and fertility cults were destroyed and the worship of Yahweh (the God of Israel) was centralized at Jerusalem.

deva \'dā-və, 'dē-və\ (Sanskrit: "divine") In the VEDIC RELIGION of India, one of many divine powers, roughly divided into sky, air, and earth divinities. During the Vedic period, the gods were divided into two classes, the devas and the *asuras*. In India the devas gradually came to be more powerful, and the *asuras* came to be thought of as DEMONS. In the monotheistic systems that emerged by the late Vedic period, the devas were subordinate to one supreme being.

devaluation Reduction in the exchange value of a country's monetary unit in terms of gold, silver, or foreign CURRENCY. By decreasing the price of the home country's exports abroad and increasing the price of imports in the home country, devaluation encourages the home country's export sales and discourages expenditures on imports, thus improving its BALANCE OF PAYMENTS.

devaraja \ˌdā-və-'rä-jä\ In ancient Cambodia, the cult of the "god-king," established early in the 9th century by Jayavarman II (c. 770–850), founder of the Khmer empire. The cult taught that the king was a manifestation of the god Shiva. For centuries it provided Khmer kings with the religious basis of their royal authority.

development, biological Gradual changes in size, shape, and function during an organism's life that translate its genetic potentials (GENOTYPE) into functioning mature systems (PHENOTYPE). It includes growth but not repetitive chemical changes (METABOLISM) or changes over more than one lifetime (EVOLUTION). DNA directs the development of a fertilized egg so that cells become specialized structures that carry out specific functions. In humans, development progresses through the EMBRYO and FETUS stages before birth and continues during childhood. Other mammals follow a similar course. Amphibians and insects go through distinctive stages that are quite different. In plants, the basic pattern is determined by the arrangement of lateral buds around a central growing stem. Different rates of growth of the plant's component elements then determine its shape and that of various parts. In both animals and plants, growth is greatly influenced by HORMONES; factors within individual cells probably also play a role.

development bank National or regional financial institution designed to provide medium- and long-term capital for productive investment. Such investment is usually accompanied by technical assistance. Some development banks are government-owned and -operated, while others are private. Many have been established under the auspices of the WORLD BANK. Among the largest are the Inter-American Development Bank, the Asian Development Bank, and the African Development Bank.

developmental psychology Branch of PSYCHOLOGY concerned with changes in cognitive, motivational, psychophysiological, and social functioning that occur throughout the human life span. In the late 19th and early 20th century, developmental psychologists were concerned primarily with CHILD PSYCHOLOGY. In the 1950s they became interested in the relationship between child rearing and adult personality, as well as in examining adolescence in its own right. By the later 20th century they had become interested in all aspects of psychological development and change over the entire life span.

Devers \'dē-vərz\, **(Yolanda) Gail** (born 1966) U.S. track athlete. Born in Seattle, Wash., she had an outstanding collegiate athletic career at UCLA. Her health began to deteriorate while training for the 1988 Olympics, and she was diagnosed in 1990 as suffering from GRAVES' DISEASE. After months of painful radiation treatment, she resumed training and went on to win gold medals in the 1992 and 1996 Olympics and to win or place second in other international 100-m, 100-m hurdles, and 4 × 100-m relay races.

Devi \'dā-vē\ Term used to designate a goddess in HINDUISM. It is sometimes used as an honorific title for women, and it may also refer to local female divinities throughout India. In the 5th–6th century, Hindu texts first began to identify Devi as the Great Goddess and the embodiment of matter, energy, and illusion. She is represented in a variety of aspects, both good and evil, including the beautiful but menacing DURGA, the destructive KALI, and the sexually powerful Shakti (see SHAKTI).

devil Spirit or power of evil. Though sometimes used to refer to DEMONS, the term more often designates the prince of evil spirits. In Judaism, Christianity, and Islam, he is viewed as a fallen ANGEL who tried to usurp the position of God. In the Bible the devil is known as Satan, Beelzebub, and LUCIFER. Christian theology holds that his main task is to tempt humans to reject the way of life and redemption in favor of SIN and death. In the Quran the devil is called IBLIS; he tempts the unfaithful but not the true believer.

devil ray See MANTA RAY

devilfish See MANTA RAY

Devils Island *French* **Île du Diable** \ˌēl-dǖ-'dyäblᵊ\ Rocky islet off the Atlantic coast of FRENCH GUIANA. The smallest of the three Îles du Salut, it is a narrow strip of land 3,900 ft (1,200 m) long and 1,320 ft (400 m) wide. Part of a penal settlement since 1852, it housed the convicts' leper colony until the islands were made a maximum-security area. It shared the notoriety for cruelty of the mainland French Guiana penal colony. Spies and political prisoners, including ALFRED DREYFUS, were held there. The penal colony was phased out by the early 1950s.

Devils Tower National Monument National preserve, northeastern Wyoming. The first U.S. national monument, it was established in 1906 near the Belle Fourche River. It includes 1,347 acres (545 hectares) and features a natural rock tower, the remnant of a volcanic intrusion now exposed by erosion. The tower has a flat top and is 865 ft (263 m) high.

Devolution, War of (1667–68) Conflict between France and Spain over possession of the SPANISH NETHERLANDS. LOUIS XIV began the war on the pretext that the custom of devolution, whereby daughters of a first marriage were preferred to sons of subsequent marriages regarding property inheritance, should apply to sovereign territories also. That would mean that his wife, Marie-Thérèse (1638–1683), should succeed her father, PHILIP IV, in the Spanish Netherlands. The French army advanced into Flanders in May 1667 and easily secured its objectives. A peace was reached at Aix-la-Chapelle, whereby France gave up Franche-Comté but retained conquered towns in Flanders.

Devon \'de-vən\ County, southwestern England. It lies between CORNWALL, DORSET, and SOMERSET, and has coasts on the BRISTOL CHANNEL and ENGLISH CHANNEL. EXETER is its long-established county seat. Its area includes the moorlands of Dartmoor, inhabited from prehistoric times and now a popular tourist area. Livestock-based agriculture is the main industry; Devonshire clotted cream is still produced.

Devonian period \di-'vō-nē-ən\ Interval of geologic time from 417 to 354 million years ago; it was the fourth period of the PALEOZOIC ERA. During the Devonian, a giant continent was situated in the Southern Hemisphere (see GONDWANA), and other landmasses were located in the equatorial regions. Siberia was separated from Europe by a broad ocean, and North America and Europe were joined. Many types of primitive marine and freshwater fish appeared and proliferated, and the period is sometimes referred to as the Age of Fishes. Ferns and primitive GYMNOSPERMS diversified and created the first forests.

Devrient \dəv-rē-'aⁿ, dev-'rēnt\, **Ludwig** (1784–1832) German actor. At the Dessau court theater he developed his talent for character parts. After his Berlin debut in *The Robbers* (1814), he played Falstaff, Shylock, King Lear, and Richard III and was acclaimed the greatest German actor of the Romantic period. His eldest nephew, Karl August Devrient (1797–1872), acted in Dresden, Karlsruhe, and principally Hanover (1839–72), where he was popular in roles in plays by Shakespeare, Goethe, and Schiller. Karl's brother Eduard (1801–1877) began his career as an opera singer, then worked as an actor and stage director in Dresden (1844–52) and Karlsruhe (1852–70), where he directed German classics and made new translations of Shakespeare's plays. Karl's other brother, Emil (1803–1872), made his stage debut in 1821 and acted with the Dresden court theater (1831–68); his greatest successes were as Hamlet and as Goethe's Tasso. Eduard's son Otto (1838–1894) acted in various companies, then became a director in Karlsruhe and other German cities. In Weimar he produced his own version of Goethe's *Faust* (1876); he also wrote several tragedies. Karl's son Max (1857–1929) made his debut in Dresden in 1878 and in 1882 joined the famed Vienna Burgtheater.

Devrient, Wilhelmine Schröder- See W. SCHRODER-DEVRIENT

dew Deposit of water droplets formed at night by the condensation of water vapor from the air onto the surfaces of exposed objects. Dew forms on clear nights, when exposed surfaces lose heat by radiation and are thus usually colder than the air. The cold surface cools the air in its vicinity, and, if the air is humid enough, it may cool below its dew point, the temperature at which water vapor condenses out of the air onto the surface. See also FROST.

Dewar \'d(y)ü-ər\, **James** *later* **Sir James** (1842–1923) British chemist and physicist. In 1891 he built a machine for producing liquid oxygen in quantity. His Dewar flask for storing liquefied gases—a double-walled flask has insulating vacuum between the inner and outer walls—became essential in low-temperature scientific work; its principle is used in the Thermos bottle. Dewar was the first to liquefy and solidify hydrogen, and his 1905 discovery that cooled charcoal can help create high vacuums was useful in atomic physics.

dewberry Any BLACKBERRY (genus *Rubus*) that is so lacking woody fiber in the stems that it trails along the ground. In the eastern and southern U.S., several trailing native species of *Rubus*, especially *R. flagellaris, R. baileyanus, R. hispidus, R. enslenii,* and *R. trivialis,* produce excellent fruits. Some varieties, especially Lucretia, are cultivated.

Dewey, George (1837–1917) U.S. naval commander. Born in Montpelier, Vt., he graduated from Annapolis in 1858 and served with Union naval forces in the Civil War. In 1897 he commanded the U.S. Asiatic squadron. When the SPANISH-AMERICAN WAR began, he sailed from Hong Kong to the Philippines; he defeated the Spanish fleet at the Battle of MANILA BAY (1898), opening fire with the command "You may fire when you are ready, Gridley." His victory, with no loss of U.S. ships, led to U.S. acquisition of the Philippines. In 1899 Congress created for him the rank of admiral of the navy.

George Dewey.
BROWN BROTHERS

Dewey, John (1859–1952) U.S. philosopher and educator who was one of the founders of PRAGMATISM, a pioneer in functional psychology, and a leader of the progressive movement in U.S. education. He received his PhD (1884) from Johns Hopkins University and taught 10 years at the University of Michigan before moving to the University of Chicago. Influenced by G. STANLEY HALL and WILLIAM JAMES, he developed an instrumentalist theory of knowledge that conceived of ideas as tools for the solution of problems encountered in the environment. Believing the experimental methods of modern science provided the most promising approach to social and ethical problems, he applied this view to studies of democracy and liberalism. He believed that democracy provided citizens with the opportunity for maximum experimentation and personal growth. His writings on education, notably *The School and Society* (1899) and *The Child and the Curriculum* (1902), emphasized the interests of the child and the use of the classroom to cultivate the interplay between thought and experience. At Chicago he created laboratory schools to test his theories. His work in psychology focused on the total organism in its efforts to adjust to the environment. In 1904 Dewey joined the Columbia University faculty. In 1925 he produced his magnum opus, *Experience and Nature.*

Dewey, Melvil(le Louis Kossuth) (1851–1931) U.S. librarian. Born in Adams Center, N.Y., he graduated from Amherst College in 1874, whereupon he became acting librarian there. In 1876 he published *A Classification and Subject Index for Cataloguing and Arranging the Books and Pamphlets of a Library,* in which he outlined the DEWEY DECIMAL CLASSIFICATION system. He was one of the founders of the American Library Association and of *Library Journal* (both 1876). He set up the School of Library Economy, the first U.S. institution for training librarians. He also reorganized the N.Y. State Library (1889–1906) and established the system of traveling libraries and picture collections. A cofounder of the Spelling Reform Assn., he respelled his own name.

Dewey, Thomas E(dmund) (1902–1971) U.S. attorney and politician. Born in Owosso, Mich., he became an assistant U.S. attorney in New York in 1931 and was elected district attorney in 1937. His successful prosecution of organized crime led to three terms as governor of New York (1943–55), in which he pursued a policy of political and fiscal moderation. He received the Republican presidential nomination in 1944 but was soundly defeated by F. Roosevelt; nominated again in 1948, he was widely predicted to defeat the incumbent, HARRY TRUMAN, but Truman retained the vote of farmers and labor to prevail. Dewey retired from politics in 1955 but continued to advise Republican administrations.

Dewey Decimal Classification *or* **Dewey Decimal System** System for organizing the contents of a library based on the division of all knowledge into 10 groups, with each group assigned 100 numbers. Subdivisions eventually extend into decimal numbers; for example, the history of England is placed at 942, the history of the Stuart period at 942.06, and the history of the English Commonwealth at 942.063. The system was first formulated in 1873 by MELVIL DEWEY. Many libraries add a book number created from the Cutter, or Cutter-Sanborn, Tables, which further specify author and genre. The Library of Congress classification system has largely replaced the Dewey system in recent decades.

dextrose See GLUCOSE

Dezhnev \'dezh-nyif\, **Cape** *Russian* **Mys Deshneva** \'məs-dezh-'nyȯ-və\ Cape, extreme eastern Russia. It is the easternmost point of the Chukchi Peninsula and of the entire Eurasian landmass. It is separated from Cape Prince of Wales in Alaska by the Bering Strait (see BERING SEA).

Dga'l-dan *or* **Galdan** \'gäl-'dän\ (1644?–1697) Leader of the Dzungar tribes of MONGOLS, who conquered an empire that reached from Tibet in the southwest to the borders of Russia in the northeast. As a younger son of a powerful chief, Dga'l-dan was sent to Tibet, where he was trained as a Buddhist LAMA. His older brother's death gave Dga'l-dan the opportunity to exercise political power; he avenged the death and went on to conquer eastern Turkistan and Outer Mongolia. He led his armies toward Beijing, but was defeated by the KANGXI EMPEROR, who personally led some 80,000 troops armed with Western artillery.

Dge-lugs-pa *or* **Gelukpa** \'gā-lük-bä\ Yellow Hat sect of TIBETAN BUDDHISM, the chief religion in Tibet since the 17th century. It was founded in the 14th century by Tsong-kha-pa (1357–1419). His reforms included strict monastic discipline, celibacy, and improved education for monks. The head of the chief monastery at Lhasa first received the title of DALAI LAMA from ALTAN Khan in 1578. With his aid the Dge-lugs-pa triumphed over the Karma-pa, or Red Hat, sect. The Dge-lugs-pa ruled Tibet until the Chinese Communist takeover (1950); the sect continues to exist, but many of its members, including the Dalai Lama, remain in exile.

Dhaka *or* **Dacca** \'da-kə, 'dä-kə\ City (pop., 1991: 3,839,000; metro area population 1991: 6,501,000), capital of Bangladesh. It can be traced to the 1st millennium AD, but it did not rise to prominence until the 17th century, when it served as the MUGHAL capital of BENGAL province. It came under British control in 1765 and was the capital of Eastern Bengal and ASSAM province (1905–12). The capital of East Bengal province in 1947 and of East Pakistan in 1956, it suffered heavy damage during the war of independence in 1971. Together with its port, Dhaka is the country's leading industrial center. Its historic buildings include temples, churches, and some 700 mosques dating back to the 15th century.

Bayt ul-Mukarram Mosque and shopping mall, Dhaka, Bangladesh.
FREDERIC OHRINGER FROM THE NANCY PALMER AGENCY

Dhar \'där\ Town (pop., 1991: 59,000), western MADHYA PRADESH state, central India. On the northern slopes of the Vindhya Range, it commands one of the gaps leading to the NARMADA RIVER valley. An ancient town, it was famous in medieval India as the capital of the RAJPUTS (9th–14th century). It was conquered by the Muslims in the 14th century, was under MUGHAL dominion, and fell to the Marathas in 1730. Long a center of culture and learning, its fine historic sites include the Pillar Mosque (1405), built out of the remains of Jaina temples.

dharma In HINDUISM, the religious and moral law governing individual and group conduct. It is treated in the Dharma Sutras, the oldest collection of Hindu laws, and in the compilations of law and custom called the *Dharma Sastras*. In BUDDHISM, dharma is the universal truth common to all individuals at all times, and it is regarded as one of the primary sources of Buddhist doctrine and practice. In JAINISM, dharma signifies moral virtue as well as the eternal life force.

Dhiban See DIBON

dhow \'daù\ One- or two-masted Arab sailing vessel, usually with lateen rigging (slanting, triangular sails), common on the Red Sea and the Indian Ocean. On the larger types, called baggalas and booms, the mainsail is considerably bigger than the mizzensail. Bows are sharp, with a forward and upward thrust, and the sterns of the larger dhows may be windowed and decorated.

Di Prima \di-'prē-mə\, **Diane** (born 1934) U.S. poet. Born in New York City, she settled in Greenwich Village and became one of the few women to attain prominence in the BEAT MOVEMENT. In 1961 she cofounded *Floating Bear,* a monthly featuring notable Beat writers. Her collections include *The New Handbook of Heaven* (1963), *Poems for Freddie* (1966), *Earthsong* (1968), *The Book of Hours* (1970), *Loba* (1978), and *Pieces of a Song* (1990). She also founded two publishing houses that specialized in young poets.

diabase *or* **dolerite** Fine- to medium-grained, dark gray to black intrusive igneous rock. Diabase is one of the dark rocks known commercially as "black granite." It is extremely hard and tough and is commonly quarried for crushed stone, under the name "trap." Chemically and mineralogically, diabase closely resembles the volcanic rock basalt, but it is generally somewhat coarser grained.

diabetes insipidus \,dī-ə-'bē-tēz-in-'si-pə-dəs\ ENDOCRINE disorder causing extreme thirst and excessive production of very dilute urine, apparently due to lack of antidiuretic hormone (vasopressin, which regulates the kidney's water conservation and urine production), or failure of the kidney tubules to respond to it. Injections of animal or synthetic vasopressin-like compounds are effective if the hormone is lacking but not if the response is absent. Disorders of the hypothalamus are one cause of diabetes insipidus.

diabetes mellitus \'mel-ət-əs\ Disorder of insufficient production of or reduced sensitivity to INSULIN. Insulin, synthesized in the islets of LANGERHANS, is necessary to metabolize GLUCOSE. In diabetes, blood sugar levels increase (hyperglycemia; see GLUCOSE TOLERANCE TEST). Excess sugar is excreted in the urine (glycosuria). Symptoms include increased urine output, thirst, weight loss, and weakness. Type I, or insulin-dependent diabetes mellitus (IDDM), an AUTOIMMUNE DISEASE in which no insulin is produced, must be treated by insulin injections. Type II, or non-insulin-dependent diabetes mellitus (NIDDM), in which tissues do not respond to insulin, is linked to heredity and obesity and may be controllable by diet; it accounts for 90% of all cases, many of which go undiagnosed for years. Untreated diabetes leads to accumulation of KETONES in the blood, followed by acidosis (high blood acid content) with nausea and vomiting and then coma. Careful attention to content and timing of meals, with periodic checking of blood sugar, may manage diabetes. If not, injected or oral insulin is necessary. Complications, including heart disease, diabetic retinopathy (a leading cause of blindness), kidney disease, and nerve disorders, especially in the legs and feet, account for most deaths. Degree of blood-sugar control does not always correlate with progression of complications. Reversible diabetes may occur as a complication of pregnancy.

diagenesis Sum of all processes, chiefly chemical, that produce changes in a sediment after its deposition but before its final LITHIFICATION. Usually, not all the minerals in a sediment are in chemical equilibrium, so changes in interstitial water composition or in temperature or in both will lead to chemical alteration of one or more of the minerals present. Diagenesis is considered a relatively low-pressure, low-temperature alteration process that involves such processes as cementation, reworking, replacement, crystallization, and leaching.

Diaghilev \dē-'ä-gə-,lef\, **Sergey (Pavlovich)** (1872–1929) Russian impresario, founder-director of the BALLETS RUSSES. After studying law at the University of St. Petersburg (1890–96), he cofounded and edited (1899–1904) the avant-garde magazine *Mir Iskusstva* ("World of Art"). He then left Russia for Paris to present productions of Russian ballet and opera, to wide acclaim. In 1909 he established the Ballets Russes, in which he achieved a stunning synthesis of dance, art, and music by bringing together superb choreographers, dancers, composers, and artists and set designers. A tyrannical and mercurial personality, he led the company until his death. Diaghilev's massive influence was felt throughout the 20th-century arts.

Diaghilev, c. 1916.
DANCE COLLECTION, THE NEW YORK PUBLIC LIBRARY AT LINCOLN CENTER, ASTER, LENOX AND TILDEN FOUNDATIONS

diagnosis Identification of a disease or disorder. Diagnosis requires a medical history (including family history), a physical examination, and usually tests and diagnostic procedures (e.g., BLOOD ANALYSIS, DIAGNOSTIC IMAGING). A list of possible causes—the differential diagnosis—is developed and then narrowed down by further tests that eliminate or support specific possibilities.

diagnostic imaging *or* **medical imaging** Use of ELECTROMAGNETIC RADIATION to produce images of internal body structures for diagnosis. X RAYS have been used since 1895. Denser tissues, such as bones, absorb more X rays and show as lighter areas on X-ray film. A CONTRAST MEDIUM can be used to highlight soft tissues in still X-ray pictures, or can be followed on X-ray motion-picture films as it moves through the body or part of the body to record body processes. In COMPUTED AXIAL TOMOGRAPHY, X rays are focused on specific tissue planes, and a series of such parallel "slices" of the body are processed by computer to produce a 3-D image. The risks of X-ray exposure are reduced by more precise techniques using lower doses and by use of other imaging techniques. See also ANGIOCARDIOGRAPHY, ANGIOGRAPHY, MAGNETIC RESONANCE IMAGING, NUCLEAR MEDICINE, POSITRON EMISSION TOMOGRAPHY, ULTRASOUND.

dial gauge Any of a number of deviation-type GAUGES that indicate the amount by which an object being gauged deviates from the standard. This deviation is usually shown in units of measurement, but some gauges show only whether the deviation is within a certain range. They include dial indicators, in which movement of a gauging spindle deflects a pointer on a graduated dial; wiggler indicators, used by machinists to center or align work in MACHINE TOOLS; COMPARATORS, or visual gauges; and air gauges, used to gauge holes of various types.

dialect Variety of a language spoken by a group of people and having features of vocabulary, grammar, and/or pronunciation that distinguish it from other varieties of the same language. Dialects usually develop as a result of geographic, social, political, or economic barriers between groups of people who speak the same language. When dialects diverge to the point that they are mutually incomprehensible, they become languages in their own right. This was the case with Latin, various dialects of which evolved into the different ROMANCE LANGUAGES. See also KOINE.

dialectical materialism Philosophical approach expressed through the writings of KARL MARX and FRIEDRICH ENGELS, and later by GEORGY PLEKHANOV, VLADIMIR ILICH LENIN, and JOSEPH STALIN, the official philosophy of COMMUNISM. Its central tenet, borrowed from HEGELIANISM, is that all historical growth, change, and development results from the struggle of opposites. (In philosophical terms, a thesis is opposed by its antithesis, which results in a synthesis.) Specifically, it is the class struggle—the struggle between the capitalist and landowning classes, on the one hand, and the proletariat and peasantry, on the other—that creates the dynamic of history. The laws of historical dialectics are seen to be so powerful that individual leaders are of little historical consequence. Originally conceived as operating primarily in the social, economic, and political realm, the principle was extended in the 20th century to the scientific realm as well, with major effects on Soviet science. Marx and Engels stated their philosophical views mainly in the course of polemics and brief historical studies; there is no systematic exposition of dialectical materialism.

dialysis \dī-'a-lə-səs\ In chemistry, separation of suspended colloidal (see COLLOID) particles from dissolved IONS or small MOLECULES via their unequal rates of DIFFUSION through pores of semipermeable MEMBRANES (e.g., parchment, collodion, cellophane). A slow process, dialysis may be accelerated by heating or by applying an ELECTRIC FIELD if the particles are charged.

dialysis \dī-'a-lə-səs\ *or* **hemodialysis** \ˌhē-mō-dī-'a-lə-səs\ Process of removing blood from a patient with KIDNEY FAILURE, purifying it with a hemodialyzer (artificial kidney), and returning it to the bloodstream. Many substances (including UREA and inorganic SALTS) in the blood pass through a porous membrane in the machine into a sterile solution; particles such as blood cells and PROTEINS are too large to pass. This process controls the acid-base balance of the blood and its content of water and dissolved materials.

diamagnetism Kind of MAGNETISM characteristic of materials that line up at right angles to a nonuniform MAGNETIC FIELD and that partly expel from their interior the magnetic field in which they are placed. In most materials, the magnetic fields of the ELECTRONS balance each other and add up to zero. However, when placed in an external magnetic field, the interaction of this field with the electrons induces an internal field in the opposite direction. The substance can then be weakly repelled by magnetic poles. Examples of diamagnetic substances include BISMUTH, ANTIMONY, SODIUM CHLORIDE, GOLD, and MERCURY.

diamond Mineral composed of pure CARBON, the hardest naturally occurring substance known and a valuable gemstone. Diamonds are formed deep in the earth by tremendous pressures and temperatures over long periods of time. In the crystal structure of diamond, each carbon atom is linked to four other, equidistant, carbon atoms. This tight crystal structure results in properties that are very different from those of GRAPHITE, the other common form of pure carbon. Diamonds vary from colorless to black and may be transparent, translucent, or opaque. Most gem diamonds are transparent and colorless or nearly so. Colorless or pale blue stones are most valued, but most gem diamonds are tinged with yellow. Because of their extreme hardness, diamonds have important industrial applications. Most industrial diamonds are gray or brown and are translucent or opaque. In the symbolism of gemstones, the diamond represents steadfast love and is the birthstone for April.

diamond cutting Branch of lapidary art involving the five basic steps in fashioning a diamond: marking, cleaving, sawing, girdling, and faceting. The most popular style is the brilliant cut, a round stone with 58 facets; a round diamond with only 18 facets is known as a single cut. Any other style is known as a fancy cut. See also GEMSTONE.

Diamond Necklace, Affair of the (1785) Scandal at the court of LOUIS XVI that discredited the French monarchy on the eve of the FRENCH REVOLUTION. An adventuress, the Countess de La Motte, schemed to acquire a valuable diamond necklace by duping Cardinal de ROHAN into believing that MARIE-ANTOINETTE wanted to obtain it surreptitiously and that he could gain favor by facilitating its purchase. When the scheme came to light, Louis XVI had the cardinal arrested. Though acquitted, the arbitrary treatment of the cardinal deepened impressions of the autocratic nature of the king's government.

Diamond Sutra *in full* **Diamond-Cutter Perfection of Wisdom Sutra** Wisdom text of MAHAYANA Buddhism. It was composed c. AD 300 and translated into Chinese c. AD 400. The best known of the wisdom texts contained in the PRAJNAPARAMITA, it is written in the form of a dialogue between the BUDDHA Gautama and a questioning disciple. The work emphasizes the transitory nature of the material world and suggests that spiritual fulfillment can be attained only by transcending ephemeral phenomena and abandoning rationalism.

Dian, Lake *or* **Dian Chi** *or* **Tien Ch'ih** \'dyen-'chē\ Lake, central YUNNAN province, southern China. It is about 25 mi (40 km) long by 8 mi (13 km) wide. The area was settled by sedentary agricultural peoples as early as the 2nd century BC. It was the center of the independent state of Dian (Tien), which became tributary to the HAN DYNASTY after 109 BC.

Diana Roman goddess of nature, animals, and the hunt. As a fertility deity, she was invoked for aid in conception and childbirth. She was virtually indistinguishable from the Greek goddess ARTEMIS. In her cult in Rome she was considered the protector of the lower classes, especially slaves.

Diana, Princess of Wales *orig.* **Lady Diana Frances Spencer** (1961–1997) Consort (1981–96) of CHARLES, PRINCE OF WALES. Daughter of Viscount Althorp (later Earl Spencer), she was a kindergarten teacher at the time of her engagement to Charles, whom she married on July 29, 1981, in a globally televised ceremony. They had two sons, Princes William (1982) and Henry (1984). Her beauty and unprecedented popularity as a member of the royal family attracted intense press attention, and she became one of the most photographed women in the world. The marriage gradually broke down; Charles and Diana separated in 1992 and were divorced in 1996. She remained highly visible and continued her activities on behalf of numerous charities. In 1997 she was killed in a car crash in Paris, along with her companion, Emad Mohamed (Dodi) al-Fayed (1955–1997), and their driver. A massive public outpouring of grief for "Princess Di" surprised the royal family, which then arranged for an internationally televised funeral.

Diane de France \dyån-də-'fräⁿs\ *later* **duchesse de Montmorency et Angoulême** (1538–1619) Natural daughter (legitimated 1547) of King HENRY II of France. In 1559 she was married to François de Montmorency (1530–1579). She was known for her culture, intelligence, and beauty as well as for the influence she wielded during the reigns of HENRY III and HENRY IV.

Diane de Poitiers \dē-'ån-də-pwä-'tyā\ *later* **duchesse de Valentinois** (1499–1566) Mistress of King HENRY II of France. Diane came to the French court as a lady-in-waiting, where Henry, 20 years her junior, fell violently in love with her. After the death of her husband, Diane became Henry's mistress from c. 1536. Throughout his reign (1547–59) she held court as queen of France in all but name, while the real queen, CATHERINE DE MÉDICIS, was forced to live in comparative obscurity. Beautiful and cultivated, Diane was a patron of poets and artists.

Dianetics See Church of SCIENTOLOGY

dianthus See PINK FAMILY

diaphragm \'dī-ə-ˌfram\ Dome-shaped muscular and membranous structure between the THORACIC and ABDOMINAL cavities. The principal muscle used in RESPIRATION, it is also important in coughing, vomiting, excretion, and other expulsive functions. Spasms of the diaphragm produce HICCUPS. The AORTA passes behind the diaphragm; the inferior VENA cava and esophagus pass through it. Protrusion of part of the stomach above the diaphragm is called a hiatal hernia.

Diarmaid Macmurchada \'dir-mid-mək-'mu̇r-k̲ə-də\ *or* **Dermot Macmurrough** \'dər-mət-mək-'mər-ō\ (died 1171) Irish king of Leinster (1126–71). He faced a number of rivals in claiming the throne of his father, Enna, and he asserted his authority by killing or blinding 17 rebel chieftains (1141). He abducted another Irish king's wife in 1153, beginning a bitter feud in which he was driven from Ireland (1166). He returned with the backing of Anglo-Norman lords (including the earl of Pembroke), and in 1170 they captured Dublin. Pembroke married Dermot's daughter and became ruler of Leinster after his death. Dermot's appeal for Norman help in settling an internal dispute thus proved instrumental in the Norman conquest of Ireland.

diarrhea \ˌdī-ə-'rē-ə\ Abnormally fast passage of waste material through the large intestine, resulting in frequent defecation with loose feces and sometimes cramps. Causes range widely and can include cholera, dysentery, highly seasoned foods or high alcohol intake, poisons (including food poisoning), drug side effects, Graves' disease, and psychoneurosis. Mild cases of diarrhea are treated with bismuth subsalicylate (trade name Pepto-Bismol); extreme cases are treated with fluid and electrolyte replacement while the underlying disease passes. Traveler's diarrhea affects up to half of people who travel to developing countries. Its prevention includes taking bismuth subsalicylate tablets, drinking only bottled or canned beverages, and eating only peeled fruits, canned products, and restaurant food that is piping hot. Severe cases require antibiotics. In cases of severe malnutrition, diarrhea is potentially lethal, and it is responsible for hundreds of thousands of deaths annually in underdeveloped countries.

diary *or* **journal** Record of events, transactions, or observations kept daily or at frequent intervals; especially a daily record of personal activities, reflections, or feelings. Written primarily for the writer's use alone, the diary usually offers a frankness not found in writing done for publication. The diary form, which began to flower in the late Renaissance, is important as a record of social and political history. The most famous diary in English is that of Samuel Pepys; other notable journals include those of John Evelyn, Jonathan Swift, Fanny Burney, James Boswell, Andre Gide, and Virginia Woolf.

Dias \'dē-əsh\, **Bartolomeu** *or* **Bartholomew Diaz** \'dē-äs\ (c. 1450–1500) Portuguese navigator and explorer. Given command of an expedition to ascertain the southern limit of Africa, he set sail in 1487. He sailed farther south than previous explorers and became the first European to round the Cape of Good Hope (1488). His voyage opened the sea route to Asia via the Atlantic and Indian oceans. He later commanded a ship in an expedition under Pedro Alvares Cabral, in which he participated in the discovery of Brazil; he was lost at sea when they reached the Cape.

Diaspora \dī-'as-pə-rə, dē-'as-pə-rə\, **Jewish** All Jewish communities outside Israel. *Diaspora* (Greek: "dispersion") also carries historical and religious connotations, since Jews have a special relationship to Israel. Most Orthodox Jews hope for the return of Jews to Israel. Reform Judaism holds that dispersal of the Jews was intended by God to foster monotheism; however, support for a national Jewish state was notably greater after the Holocaust. The first Diaspora was the Babylonian Exile of 586 BC. The largest Diaspora flourished in Alexandria, where, in the 1st century BC, Jews represented 40% of the population. Diaspora Jews far outnumbered Jews in Palestine even before Jerusalem was destroyed in AD 70. Today, of the estimated 14 million Jews worldwide, some 4 million live in Israel, 4.5 million in the U.S., and 2.2 million in Russia and other republics of the former Soviet Union.

diastrophism \dī-'as-trə-ˌfi-zəm\ *or* **tectonism** Large-scale deformation of the earth's crust by natural processes, which leads to the formation of continents and ocean basins, mountain systems and rift valleys, and other features by mechanisms such as lithospheric plate movement (see plate tectonics), volcanic loading, or folding. The study of diastrophism, or tectonic processes, is the central unifying principle in modern geology and geophysics.

diathermy \'dī-ə-ˌthər-mē\ Use of high-frequency electric current for deep heating of tissues in physical therapy. Shortwave, ultrasound, and microwave diathermy heat tissues at different depths for different purposes. Low heat warms tissue to ease muscle pain. Higher degrees of diathermy destroy tissue; this is useful in surgery, particularly on the eye or nerves, to coagulate, limit bleeding, and seal off traumatized tissues.

diatom \'dī-ə-ˌtäm\ Any member of the algal division or phylum Bacillariophyta (about 16,000 species), tiny planktonic (see plankton), unicellular or colonial algae found floating in all the waters of the earth. The intricate and delicate markings of the silicified cell wall are useful in testing the resolving power of microscope lenses. The beautiful symmetry and design of diatoms justify their title "jewels of the sea." Among the most important and prolific sea organisms, diatoms serve directly or indirectly as food for many animals. Diatomaceous earth, composed of fossil diatoms, is used in filters, insulation, abrasives, paints, and varnishes, and as an insecticide.

Diatom (highly magnified).

ERIC GRAVE—PHOTO RESEARCHERS

diatomaceous earth \ˌdī-ə-tə-'mā-shəs\ *or* **kieselguhr** \'kē-zəl-ˌgu̇r\ Light-colored, porous, and friable sedimentary rock composed of the frustrules (silicate cell walls) of diatoms. It is used in industrial filtration applications; as a filler or extender in paper, paint, brick, tile, ceramics, linoleum, plastic, soap, detergent, and other products; in insulation for boilers, blast furnaces, and other high-temperature devices; as a sound insulator; and as a carrier for herbicides and fungicides. The oldest and best-known commercial use is as a very mild abrasive in metal polishes and toothpaste. Large deposits occur in California, Nevada, Washington, and Oregon; other sources are Denmark, France, Russia, and Algeria.

Díaz \'dē-ˌäs\, **Porfirio** (1830–1915) Soldier and president of Mexico (1877–80, 1884–1911). After training for the priesthood, he pursued a military career instead. When peace was restored to Mexico under Benito Juarez, Díaz resigned his command, but he soon became dissatisfied with the government. After leading two revolts, he was elected president in 1877. He succeeded in bolstering the export economy through foreign investment, while leading in the spirit of a caudillo, suppressing opposition, rigging elections, and using patronage to win the cooperation of various groups. The Mexican Revolution was launched in 1910 to end his dictatorship and reverse his policies. See also Francisco Madero, La Reforma.

Porfirio Díaz.

BY COURTESY OF THE LIBRARY OF CONGRESS, WASHINGTON, D.C.

Dibdin, Charles (1745–1814) British composer, novelist, and actor. A cathedral chorister, Dibdin began working for a music publisher at 15 and began his stage career in 1762. His first operetta was *The Shepherd's Artifice* (1764). By 1778, when he became composer to Covent Garden, he had produced eight operas, including *The Padlock* (1768), *The Waterman* (1774), and *The Quaker* (1775). He later produced his ballad opera *Liberty Hall.* He was author, singer, and accompanist for his celebrated one-man "table entertainments"; most of his popular sea songs were written for these. In all, he wrote about 100 stage works and 1,400 songs. He was the most popular British composer of the 18th century.

Dibon \'dī-ˌbän\ *modern* **Dhiban** \t͟hē-'ban\ Ancient city of Palestine. The capital of Moab, it was located north of the Arnon River in western central Jordan. Excavations have uncovered the remains of city walls and numerous buildings; pottery at the site dates from c. 3200 BC to the 7th century AD. One of the most important finds was the Moabite Stone, written in the Moabite alphabet, an important representation of the

Phoenician script. Dating from the 9th century BC, it commemorates a victory over the Israelites. See also MOABITES.

dice Set of small cubes (each called a die) marked on each face with from one to six spots and used in GAMBLING and in various social games by being shaken and thrown down to come to rest at random on a flat surface. The combined number of the spots on the topmost surface of the tossed dice decides, according to the rules of the game being played, whether the thrower (or "shooter") wins, loses, or continues to throw. In numerous board games the thrown dice determine the player's moves. Dice, which may be traced back to prehistory, were in many cultures magical devices used for the casting of lots to divine the future. In the modern era they became associated with the playing of games of chance, including CRAPS.

dickcissel \dik-'si-səl, 'dik-ˌsi-səl\ American PASSERINE (*Spiza americana,* family Fringillidae) bird that eats seeds and breeds in weedy fields of the central U.S. Most dickcissels winter in northern South America, but some stray to the Atlantic coast. The male, for whose song the species is named, is a streaky brown bird 6.5 in. (16 cm) long, with a black bib on its yellow breast, resembling a miniature MEADOWLARK.

Dickcissel (*Spiza americana*).
THASE DANIEL

Dickens, Charles (John Huffam) (1812–1870) British novelist, generally considered the greatest of the Victorian period. He was born in Portsmouth. When his father, a clerk, was thrown into debtors prison, Charles was withdrawn from school and forced to work in a factory. As a young man he worked as a reporter. His fiction career began with short pieces reprinted as *Sketches by "Boz"* (1836). The comic novel *The Pickwick Papers* (1837) made him the most popular English author of his time. *Oliver Twist* (1838), *Nicholas Nickleby* (1839), *The Old Curiosity Shop* (1841), and *Barnaby Rudge* (1841) followed. After a trip to America, he wrote *A Christmas Carol* (1843) in a few weeks, followed by *Martin Chuzzlewit* (1844). With *Dombey and Son* (1848), his novels began to express a heightened uneasiness about the evils of Victorian industrial society, which intensified in the semiautobiographical *David Copperfield* (1850), as well as *Bleak House* (1853), *Hard Times* (1854), *Little Dorrit* (1857), *Great Expectations* (1861), and *Our Mutual Friend* (1865). *A Tale of Two Cities* (1859) appeared in the period when he achieved great popularity for his public readings. *The Mystery of Edwin Drood* (1870) was left unfinished. Dickens's works are characterized by attacks on social evils and inadequate institutions, an encyclopedic knowledge of London, pathos, a vein of the macabre, a pervasive spirit of benevolence and geniality, inexhaustible powers of character creation, an acute ear for characteristic speech, and a highly individual and inventive prose style.

Dickey, James (Lafayette) (1923–1997) U.S. poet, novelist, and critic. Born in Atlanta, he earned degrees from Vanderbilt University after serving as a pilot in World War II. His poetry—published in such volumes as *Into the Stone* (1960), *Drowning with Others* (1962), *Helmets* (1964), *Buckdancer's Choice* (1965), and *The Zodiac* (1976)—combines themes of nature mysticism, religion, and history. He became widely known with his powerful novel *Deliverance* (1970; film, 1972).

Dickinson, Emily (Elizabeth) (1830–1886) U.S. poet. Granddaughter of the cofounder of Amherst College and daughter of a respected lawyer and one-term congressman, she was educated at Amherst (Mass.) Academy and Mount Holyoke Female Seminary. She subsequently spent virtually all her life, increasingly reclusive, in her family home in Amherst. She began writing in the 1850s; by 1860 she was boldly experimenting with language and prosody, striving for vivid, exact words and epigrammatic concision, while adhering to the basic quatrains and meters of the Protestant hymn. The subjects of her deceptively simple lyrics, whose depth and intensity contrast with the apparent quiet of her life, include love, death, and nature. Her numerous letters are sometimes equal in artistry to her poems. By 1870 she was dressing only in white and declining to see most visitors, and she never again left the boundaries of the house. Of her 1,775 poems, only seven were published during her lifetime. After posthumous publications (some rather inaccurate), her reputation and readership grew. Her complete works were published in 1955, and she has since become universally regarded as one of the two or three greatest American poets.

Dickinson, John (1732–1808) American statesman. Born in Talbot Co., Md., he attended the 1765 Stamp Act Congress and drafted its declaration of rights and grievances. He wrote an open letter to colonists that influenced opinion against the TOWNSHEND ACTS. A delegate to the Continental Congress, he helped draft the ARTICLES OF CONFEDERATION. He voted against the Declaration of Independence, hoping for conciliation with the British. As a Delaware delegate to the CONSTITUTIONAL CONVENTION, he signed the U.S. Constitution and urged its adoption in a series of letters signed "Fabius." He is sometimes called the "penman of the Revolution."

dicot See COTYLEDON, FLOWERING PLANT

dictator In the ROMAN REPUBLIC, a temporary magistrate with extraordinary powers. Nominated in times of crisis by a consul, recommended by the Senate, and confirmed by the Comitia Curiata, the dictator's term was six months or the duration of the crisis, and he had authority over all other magistrates. By 300 BC his powers were limited; no dictators were chosen after 202. The dictatorships of SULLA and Julius CAESAR were a new form with almost unlimited powers. Caesar became dictator for life just before his assassination; afterward the office was abolished.

dictatorship Form of government in which one person or an OLIGARCHY possesses absolute power without effective constitutional checks. With constitutional DEMOCRACY, it is one of the two chief forms of government in use today. Modern dictators usually use force or fraud to gain power and then keep it through intimidation, terror, suppression of civil liberties, and control of the mass media. In 20th-century Latin America, nationalist leaders often achieved power through the military and attempted either to maintain the privileged elite or to institute far-reaching social reform, depending on their class sympathies. In Europe's communist and fascist dictatorships, a charismatic leader of a mass party used an official ideology to maintain his regime, and terror and propaganda to suppress opposition. In postcolonial Africa and Asia, dictators have often retained power by establishing one-party rule after a military takeover.

dictionary Reference work that lists words, usually in alphabetic order, and gives their meanings and often other information such as pronunciations, etymologies, and variant spellings. The earliest dictionaries, such as those created by Greeks of the 1st century AD, emphasized explaining changes that had occurred in the meanings of words over time. The close juxtaposition of languages in Europe led to the appearance of many bilingual and multilingual dictionaries from the early Middle Ages. The movement to produce an English dictionary was partly prompted by a desire for wider literacy, so that common people could read Scripture, and partly by a frustration that no regularity in spelling existed in the language. The first purely English dictionary was Robert Cawdrey's *A Table Alphabetical* (1604), treating some 3,000 words. In 1746–47 SAMUEL JOHNSON undertook the most ambitious English dictionary to that time, a list of 43,500 words. NOAH WEBSTER's dictionary of Americanisms in the early 19th century sprang from a recognition of the changes and variations within language. The immense *OXFORD ENGLISH DICTIONARY* was begun in the late 19th century. Today there are various levels of dictionaries, general-purpose dictionaries being most common. Modern lexicographers (dictionary makers) describe current and past language but rarely prescribe its use.

Diderot \dēd-'rō\, **Denis** (1713–1784) French man of letters and philosopher. Educated by Jesuits, he later received degrees from the University of Paris. From 1745 to 1772 he served as chief editor of the 35-volume *ENCYCLOPÉDIE*, a principal work of the ENLIGHTENMENT. He composed such influential works as *Let-*

Diderot, oil painting by Louis-Michel van Loo, 1767; in the Louvre, Paris.
GIRAUDON—ART RESOURCE

ter on the Deaf and Dumb (1751), which studies the function of language, and *Thoughts on the Interpretation of Nature* (1754), acclaimed as the method of philosophical inquiry of the 18th century. The first great art critic, he was especially admired posthumously for his *Essay on Painting* (written 1765). His novels include *The Nun* (written 1760) and *Rameau's Nephew* (finished 1774); he also wrote plays and theoretical works on drama. See also JEAN LE ROND D'ALEMBERT.

Didion, Joan (born 1934) U.S. novelist and essayist. Born in Sacramento, Cal., she graduated from UC–Berkeley in 1956 and worked for *Vogue* magazine 1956–63. Her writing explores disorder and personal and social unrest. Her first novel, *Run River,* was published in 1963; later novels include *Play It as It Lays* (1970), *A Book of Common Prayer* (1977), *Democracy* (1984), and *The Last Thing He Wanted* (1996). Her essay collections include *Slouching Towards Bethlehem* (1968) and *The White Album* (1979). With her husband, John Gregory Dunne, she has written a number of screenplays, including *A Star Is Born* (1976).

Dido \'dī-dō\ In Greek legend, the founder of CARTHAGE. She fled to North Africa after the murder of her husband and bought land from a local chieftain, Iarbas. She killed herself rather than marry him. VIRGIL altered the story in his *Aeneid,* in which Dido welcomes AENEAS to Carthage during his travels, becomes his lover, and kills herself when he abandons her.

Didot family \dē-'dō\ Family of French printers, publishers, and typefounders. The family had a profound influence on the history of typography. François Didot (1689–1759) went into business as a printer and bookseller in Paris in 1713. Three successive generations kept the firm flourishing into the 19th century. Under François's elder son, François-Ambroise (1730–1804), the Didot point system of 72 points to the French inch became the standard unit of type measurement, as it remains today. François-Ambroise changed the standard of type design by increasing the contrast between thick and thin letters. His sons Pierre (1761–1853) and Firmin (1764–1836) took charge of the printing and typefounding, respectively. Pierre published acclaimed editions of French and Latin classics, and Firmin designed the Didot typeface. François's younger son, Pierre-François (1731–1793), and the latter's two sons were also active in the business, as were Firmin's three sons.

Didrikson, Babe See Babe Didrikson ZAHARIAS

Didyma \'di-də-mə\ Ancient sanctuary, south of MILETUS in modern Turkey. Its temple, the seat of an oracle of Apollo, was plundered by the Persians c. 494 BC and resanctified after ALEXANDER THE GREAT conquered Miletus in 334 BC. Around 300 BC the Milesians began to build a new temple; although it was never completed, the well-preserved remains were excavated in the early 20th century.

die Tool or device for imparting a desired shape, form, or finish to a material. Examples include a perforated block through which METAL or PLASTIC is drawn or extruded, the hardened steel forms for producing the patterns on coins and medals by pressure, and the hollow molds into which metal or plastic is forced. Modern tools and dies can be traced to the work of Honoré Blanc at the Saint-Étienne armory in France beginning in 1780. Blanc's techniques were adopted and enlarged in the U.S. by ELI WHITNEY and others, who used templates (tool-guiding patterns) and fixtures—the antecedents of today's tools and dies—to mass-produce firearms for the U.S. Army (see ARMORY PRACTICE). Today the demand for dies used in metal forming, DIE CASTING, and plastic molding is filled by tool- and die-making shops.

Die Brücke See Die BRÜCKE

die casting Forming metal objects by injecting molten metal under pressure into DIES or MOLDS. An early and important use of the technique was in the LINOTYPE machine (1884), but the mass-production automobile assembly line gave die casting its real impetus. Great precision is possible, and products range from tiny parts for sewing machines and automobile carburetors to aluminum engine-block castings.

die making See TOOL AND DIE MAKING

Diebenkorn \'dē-bən-ˌkȯrn\, **Richard** (1922–1993) U.S. painter. After studying at Stanford Univ., he taught at the California School of Fine Arts (1947–50), and there developed an abstract style under the influence of such painters as CLYFFORD STILL and MARK ROTHKO. By the mid-1950s he had achieved some commercial success, but turned to an expressionistic figurative style. He produced accomplished figure drawings, still lifes, landscapes, and interiors in the modernist tradition. Throughout his career he alternated between figuration and abstraction. His best-known works are the *Ocean Park* series, begun in the 1960s, comprising over 140 large abstract paintings that retain allusions to landscape.

Diefenbaker \'dē-fən-ˌbā-kər\, **John G(eorge)** (1895–1979) Prime minister of Canada (1957–63). Born in Grey Co., Ontario, he practiced law in Saskatchewan. Elected to the Canadian House of Commons in 1940, he became leader of the Progressive Conservative Party (1956–67) and was named prime minister in 1957. In 1963 his party lost its majority in the House of Commons. He became chancellor of the University of Saskatchewan in 1969.

dielectric \ˌdī-i-'lek-trik\ Insulating material or a very poor CONDUCTOR of ELECTRIC CURRENT. Dielectrics have no loosely bound ELECTRONS, and so no current flows through them. When they are placed in an ELECTRIC FIELD, the positive and negative charges within the dielectric are displaced minutely in opposite directions, which reduces the electric field within the dielectric. Examples of dielectrics include glass, plastics, and ceramics.

Diemen \'dē-mən\, **Anthony van** (1593–1645) Dutch colonial administrator who consolidated the Dutch empire in the Far East. He joined the Dutch EAST INDIA CO. and served in Batavia from 1618. As governor-general of the Dutch East Indian settlements (1636–45), he enabled the Dutch to gain a monopoly of the spice trade in the Moluccas, conquer cinnamon-producing areas in Ceylon (later Sri Lanka), seize the key Portuguese stronghold of Malacca, and capture all of Formosa (Taiwan). By 1645 he had established the United Provinces of the Netherlands as the paramount commercial and political power in the East Indies. Van Diemen also initiated the exploring expeditions of ABEL JANSZOON TASMAN and Frans Visscher (1642, 1644).

Dien Bien Phu \'dyen-'byen-'fü\, **Battle of** (1953–54) Decisive engagement in the first of the INDOCHINA WARS (1946–54) The French fought the VIET MINH (Lien Viet) for control of a small mountain outpost near Laos. The French occupied the outpost, but the Vietnamese cut all the roads into it, leaving the French to rely on air supplies. Gen. VO NGUYEN GIAP then attacked the base with heavy artillery and a force of 40,000 men; the base fell to him despite heavy U.S. aid to the French.

Dieppe \'dyep, dē-'ep\ Town (pop., 1995 est.: 38,000) and seaport, northern France, on the ENGLISH CHANNEL. French kings, realizing its strategic importance, granted it numerous privileges. In 1668 almost 10,000 of its people died during a plague, and in 1694 the town was almost completely destroyed by the English and Dutch fleets. In World War II it was the site of an unsuccessful Allied commando landing (1942). Its port is one of the safest on the Channel, but its shallowness hinders modern shipping.

Dies \'dīz\, **Martin, Jr.** (1901–1972) U.S. politician. Born in Colorado, Texas, he served in the U.S. House of Representatives 1931–45 and 1953–59. He originally supported the New Deal, but by 1937 had turned against it. In 1938 he was named chairman of the HOUSE UN-AMERICAN ACTIVITIES COMMITTEE; popularly known as the Dies Committee, it pursued alleged subversives in New Deal agencies and labor unions. Conservatives applauded its exposure of supposed subversives, and liberals decried Dies's tactics of smearing reputations with unproved charges.

Diesel, Rudolf Christian Karl (1858–1913) German thermal engineer. In the 1890s he invented the INTERNAL-COMBUSTION ENGINE that bears his name, producing a series of increasingly successful models of the DIESEL ENGINE that culminated in his demonstration in 1897 of a 25-horsepower, four-stroke, single vertical cylinder compression engine.

diesel engine INTERNAL-COMBUSTION ENGINE in which air is compressed to a temperature sufficiently high to ignite fuel injected into the cylinder, where combustion and expansion activate a piston (see PISTON AND CYLINDER). It converts the chemical energy stored in the fuel into mechanical energy, which can be used to power large trucks, locomotives, ships, small electric-power generators, and some automobiles. The diesel engine differs from other internal-combustion engines (such as GASOLINE ENGINES) in that it has no IGNITION SYSTEM, and so is often called a compression-ignition engine. Diesel fuel is low-grade and comparatively unrefined. Compared to other internal-combustion engines, diesel engines are expensive and heavy and produce more air pollution, noise, and vibration.

Diet Japanese national legislature. Under the MEIJI CONSTITUTION, the Diet had two houses, a House of Peers and a House of Representatives, with coequal powers. Its powers were largely negative: it could block legislation and veto budgets. Under the U.S.-sponsored constitution of 1947, the (upper) House of Councillors seats 252 members (100 at-large and 152 prefectural); the (lower) House of Representatives has 500 members. The prime minister, who leads the majority party in the lower house, must be a member.

Diet of Worms See Diet of WORMS

dietary fiber See dietary FIBER

dieting Regulating food intake to improve physical condition, especially to lose weight. Examples include diets low in FAT for weight loss, low in saturated fat and CHOLESTEROL to prevent or help treat CORONARY HEART DISEASE, or high in CARBOHYDRATES and PROTEIN to build muscle. Weight-loss diets are based on reducing CALORIE intake in different proportions of fat, carbohydrate, or protein; most result in some weight loss, but often the weight is gained back within a few years. Diets must include adequate NUTRITION and are most effective combined with exercise. Appetite suppressants may have dangerous side effects. Excessive weight loss may be a sign of ANOREXIA NERVOSA.

Dietrich \'dē-trik, *Engl* 'dē-trik\, **Marlene** *orig.* **Maria Magdalene** (1901–1992) German-U.S. film actress and singer. After joining MAX REINHARDT's theater company in 1922, she appeared in German films and became an international star as the destructive cabaret singer Lola-Lola in JOSEF VON STERNBERG's *The Blue Angel* (1930). Sternberg brought her to Hollywood, where they made many films together, including *Morocco* (1930), *Shanghai Express* (1932), *The Scarlet Empress* (1934), and *The Devil Is a Woman* (1935), which established her aura of glamorous sophistication and languid sensuality. During World War II she made over 500 appearances before Allied troops. She also starred in such films as *Destry Rides Again* (1939), *A Foreign Affair* (1948), *Witness for the Prosecution* (1957), and *Touch of Evil* (1958). She toured widely as a nightclub performer into the 1960s, singing trademark songs such as "Falling in Love Again."

Marlene Dietrich.
PICTORIAL PARADE

Dietz \'dēts\, **Howard** (1896–1983) U.S. songwriter. Born in New York City, he studied at Columbia University and later joined an advertising agency, where he designed the trademark roaring lion for Goldwyn Pictures (later MGM). He joined the studio in 1919 and became director of advertising, a post he retained until 1957. From 1923 he wrote lyrics in his spare time. In 1929 he met the composer Arthur Schwartz (1900–1984); the duo established their reputation with *The Little Show* and went on to write such Broadway shows as *Three's a Crowd* (1930), *The Band Wagon* (1931), *Flying Colors* (1932), *Revenge with Music* (1934), *At Home Abroad* (1935), *Inside U.S.A.* (1941), and *The Gay Life* (1961). Dietz wrote about 500 songs; the Dietz-Schwartz collaborations include "Something to Remember You By," "Dancing in the Dark," and "You and the Night and the Music."

Dievs \'dē-əfs\ In the pre-Christian BALTIC RELIGION, the sky god. Along with the goddess Laima, he determined the course of the world and human destiny. He was pictured as a Baltic king who lived on a farmstead in the heavens, occasionally descending to earth on horseback or in a chariot to serve as the protector of farmers and their crops. His two sons were the morning and evening stars. In modern Baltic, *dievs* refers to the Christian God.

Diez \'dēts\, **Friedrich Christian** (1794–1876) German linguist, regarded as the founder of Romance philology. He began his career as a scholar of medieval Provençal poetry, and taught literature at the University of Bonn from 1823 to the end of this life. Diez applied the methodology of comparative linguistics pioneered by JACOB GRIMM and FRANZ BOPP to the ROMANCE LANGUAGES. In his *Grammar of the Romance Languages* (1836–44) and *Etymological Dictionary of the Romance Languages* (1853), he demonstrated the relationship of "Vulgar" or Spoken LATIN to Classical Latin and the Romance languages' evolution from Spoken Latin into their modern form.

difference equation EQUATION involving differences between successive values of a FUNCTION of a discrete variable (i.e., one defined for a sequence of values that differ by the same amount, usually 1). A function of such a variable is a rule for assigning values in sequence to it. For example, $f(x + 1) = xf(x)$ is a difference equation. Methods developed for solving such equations have much in common with methods for solving linear DIFFERENTIAL EQUATIONS, which difference equations are often used to approximate.

differential In CALCULUS, an expression based on the DERIVATIVE of a FUNCTION, useful for approximating certain values of the function. The differential of an independent VARIABLE x, written Δx, is an infinitesimal change in its value. The corresponding differential of its dependent variable y is given by $\Delta y = f(x + \Delta x) - f(x)$. Because the derivative of the function $f(x)$, $f'(x)$, is equal to the RATIO $\Delta y/\Delta x$ as Δx approaches zero (see LIMIT), for small values of Δx, $\Delta y \cong f'(x)\Delta x$. This formula often enables a quick and fairly accurate approximation to be made for what otherwise would be a tedious calculation.

differential calculus Branch of mathematical ANALYSIS, devised by ISAAC NEWTON and G. W. LEIBNIZ, and concerned with the problem of finding the rate of change of a FUNCTION with respect to the variable on which it depends. Thus it involves calculating DERIVATIVES and using them to solve problems involving nonconstant rates of change. Typical applications include finding MAXIMUM and MINIMUM values of functions in order to solve practical problems in OPTIMIZATION.

differential equation Mathematical statement that contains one or more DERIVATIVES. It states a relationship involving the rates of change of continuously changing quantities modeled by functions. Differential equations are very common in physics, engineering, and all fields involving quantitative study of change. They are used whenever a rate of change is known but the process giving rise to it is not. The solution of a differential equation is generally a FUNCTION whose derivatives satisfy the equation. Differential equations are classified into several broad categories. The most important are ORDINARY DIFFERENTIAL EQUATIONS (ODEs), in which change depends on a single variable, and PARTIAL DIFFERENTIAL EQUATIONS (PDEs), in which change depends on several variables. See also DIFFERENTIATION.

differential gear In automotive mechanics, a GEAR arrangement that transmits power from the engine to a pair of driving WHEELS, dividing the force equally between them but permitting them to follow paths of different lengths, as when turning a corner or traversing an uneven road. On a straight road the wheels rotate at the same speed; when turning a corner the outside wheel has farther to go and would turn faster than the inner wheel if unrestrained. The automobile differential was invented in 1827; originally used on steam-driven vehicles, it was well known when internal-combustion engines finally appeared.

differential geometry Field of mathematics in which methods of CALCULUS are applied to the local geometry of curves and surfaces (i.e., to a small portion of a surface or curve around a point). A simple example is finding the TANGENT LINE on a two-dimensional curve at a given point. Similar operations may be extended to calculate the CURVATURE and LENGTH OF A CURVE and to analogous properties of surfaces in any number of dimensions.

differential operator In mathematics, any combination of DERIVATIVES applied to a FUNCTION. It takes the form of a POLYNOMIAL of derivatives, such as $D^2_{xx} - D^2_{xy} \cdot D^2_{yx}$, where D^2 is a second derivative and the subscripts indicate PARTIAL DERIVATIVES. Special differential operators include the GRADIENT, DIVERGENCE, CURL, and Laplace operator (see LAPLACE'S EQUATION). Differential operators provide a generalized way to look at DIFFERENTIATION as a whole, as well as a framework for discussion of the theory of DIFFERENTIAL EQUATIONS.

differentiation Mathematical process of finding the DERIVATIVE of a FUNCTION. Defined abstractly as a process involving LIMITS, in practice it may be done using algebraic manipulations that rely on three basic formulas and four rules of operation. The formulas are: (1) the derivative of x^n is nx^{n-1}, (2) the derivative of sin x is cos x, and (3) the derivative of the exponential function e^x is itself. The rules are: (1) $(af + bg)' =$

$af' + bg'$, (2) $(fg)' = fg' + gf'$, (3) $(f/g)' = (gf' - fg')/g^2$, and (4) $(f(g))' = f'(g)g'$, where a and b are constants, f and g are functions, and a prime (′) indicates the derivative. The last formula is called the chain rule. The derivation and exploration of these formulas and rules is the subject of DIFFERENTIAL CALCULUS. See also INTEGRATION.

diffraction Spreading of WAVES around obstacles. It occurs with water waves, sound, electromagnetic waves (see ELECTROMAGNETIC RADIATION), and small moving particles such as ATOMS, NEUTRONS, and ELECTRONS, which show wavelike properties. When a beam of light falls on the edge of an object, it is bent slightly by the contact and causes a blur at the edge of the shadow of the object. Waves of long WAVELENGTH are diffracted more than those of short wavelength.

diffusion Process by which there is a net flow of matter from a region of high concentration to one of low concentration. It occurs fastest in liquids and slowest in solids. Diffusion can be observed by adding a few drops of food coloring to a glass of water. The scent from an open bottle of perfume quickly permeates a room because of random motion of the vapor molecules. A spoonful of salt placed in a bowl of water will eventually spread throughout the water.

digestion Process of dissolving and chemically converting food for absorption by cells. In the mouth, food is chewed, mixed with SALIVA, which begins to break down starches, and kneaded by the tongue into a ball for swallowing. PERISTALSIS propels it through the esophagus and the rest of the alimentary canal. In the stomach, food mixes with ACID and ENZYMES, which further break it down. The mixture, called CHYME, enters the duodenum, the first part of the small intestine. BILE from the liver breaks up FAT globules. Enzymes from the pancreas and intestinal glands act on specific molecules, breaking CARBOHYDRATES down into simple SUGARS, PROTEINS into AMINO ACIDS, and fats into GLYCEROL and FATTY ACIDS. These products are absorbed by the bloodstream. Indigestible substances, such as FIBER, pass into the large intestine, where water and IONS are reabsorbed and FECES held for EXCRETION. See illustration opposite.

digestive tract See ALIMENTARY CANAL

digital camera CAMERA that captures images electronically rather than on film. The image is captured by an array of CHARGE-COUPLED DEVICES (CCDs), stored in the camera's RANDOM ACCESS MEMORY or a special diskette, and transferred to a computer for modification, long-term storage, or printing out. Since the technology produces a graphics file, the image can be readily edited using suitable software. Models designed and priced for the mass consumer market—as opposed to costly models designed for photojournalism and industrial photography—first became available in 1996. They appeal particularly to users who want to send pictures over the Internet or to crop, combine, enhance, or otherwise modify their photographs.

digital certificate Electronic credit card intended for on-line business transactions and authentications on the Internet. Digital certificates are issued by certification authorities (e.g., VeriSign). They typically contain identification information about the holder, including the person's public key (used for encrypting and decrypting messages), along with the authority's digital signature, so that the recipient can verify with the authority that the certificate is authentic. Web sites may also have digital certificates, to enable a person intending to buy its products to confirm that it is an authenticated e-commerce site.

digital computer COMPUTER capable of solving problems by processing information expressed in discrete form. By manipulating combinations of binary digits (see BINARY CODE), it can perform mathematical calculations, organize and analyze data, control industrial and other processes, and simulate dynamic systems such as global weather patterns. See also ANALOG COMPUTER.

Digital Subscriber Line See DSL

digital-to-analog conversion (DAC) Process by which digital signals (which have a binary state) are converted to analog signals (which theoretically have an infinite number of states). For example, a modem converts computer digital data to analog audio-frequency signals that can be transmitted over telephone lines.

digital video disk See DVD

digitalis \ˌdi-jə-ˈta-ləs\ Organic compound derived from leaves of the common FOXGLOVE and used as a drug that strengthens HEART muscle contraction. It was first prescribed in the 18th century. Its active principles belong to a class of STEROIDS called cardiac GLYCOSIDES. Their dosage must be carefully monitored, because the lethal dose may be only three times the effective dose. Digitoxin and digoxin are among the most commonly prescribed forms of digitalis.

diglossia \dī-ˈglȯs-ē-ə\ Coexistence of two varieties of the same language in a speech community, with each variety being more or less standardized and occupying a distinct sociolinguistic niche. Typically, one variety is more formal or prestigious while the other is more suited to informal conversation, or is taken as a mark of lower social status or less education. Classic diglossic situations can be found in ARABIC-speaking communities, where Modern Standard Arabic coexists with dozens

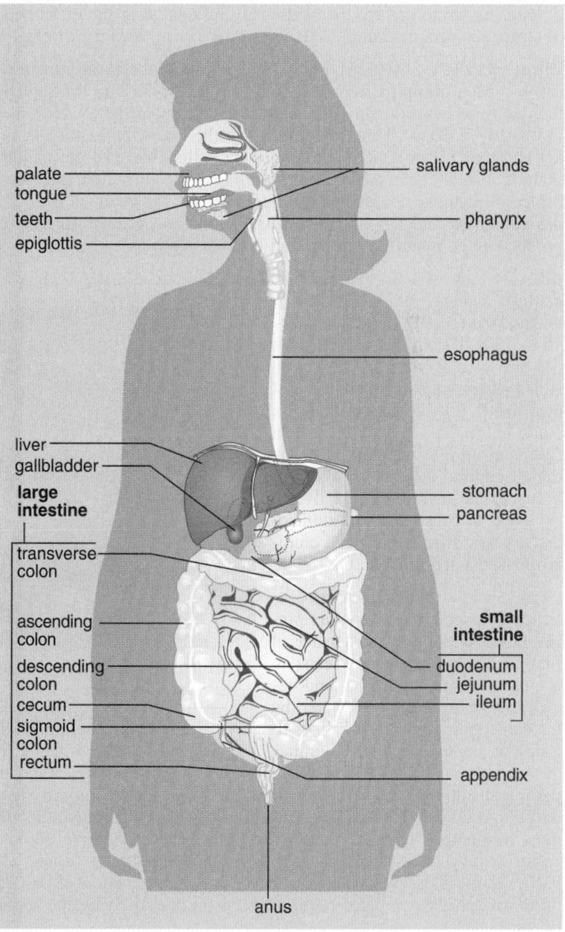

Food taken in by the mouth is moistened and lubricated with saliva secreted by the salivary glands. Enzymes in the saliva begin the breakdown of starches. Movement of the palate against the back of the pharynx helps keep food from entering the nasal cavity. The epiglottis, a flap of tissue, prevents food from entering the larynx from the pharynx during swallowing. Muscles in the esophagus wall contract in waves to move the food to the stomach. A mixture of substances secreted by the stomach (incl. enzymes, hydrochloric acid, and mucus) assist in the breakdown of food. Partly digested food passes into the small intestine, where larger molecules are broken down into sugars, amino acids, and fatty acids. The pancreas secretes digestive enzymes into the duodenum. The liver secretes bile salts that make insoluble fats entering the small intestine water-soluble and vulnerable to enzymatic action. Excess bile salts are stored in the gallbladder. Small molecules are absorbed into the bloodstream through the jejunum and ileum. The large intestine (colon) serves primarily to compact and store undigestible material, which moves into the cecum from the ileum, and muscular contractions move the feces into the rectum to be expelled from the anus.

of regional Arabic dialects, or among speakers of DRAVIDIAN LANGUAGES such as TAMIL, where different words for basic concepts such as "house" or "water" are chosen depending on the speaker's caste or religion.

Dijkstra \'dāk-strə\, **Edsger (Wybe)** (born 1930) Dutch computer scientist. He received his PhD from the University of Amsterdam while working at Amsterdam's Mathematical Center (1952–62). He taught at the Technical University of Eindhoven 1963–73; from 1984 he taught at the University of Texas. He is widely known for his 1959 solution to the shortest-path problem; his algorithm is still used to determine the fastest way between two points, as in the routing of communication networks and in flight planning. His research on the idea of mutual exclusion in communications led him to suggest in 1968 the concept of computer semaphores, which are used in virtually every modern operating system. A letter he wrote in 1968 was extremely influential in the development of structured programming. He received the Turing Award in 1972.

C
D

Dijon \dē-'zhōⁿ\ City (pop., 1999: 149,867), eastern central France. The site has been occupied from pre-Roman times. It became the capital of the duchy of BURGUNDY in 1015 and prospered under the VALOIS dynasty (1364–1477). LOUIS XI annexed the city in the late 15th century. A market and tourist center, it is surrounded by eight forts; historic buildings include a 13th-century church and 14th-century town hall (the former palace of the dukes of Burgundy). Its university was founded in 1722. It has foundries and automobile plants, but is best known for its food products (e.g., mustard, vinegar, and gingerbread).

dik-dik Any of four species of delicate African ANTELOPE (genus *Madoqua*), named for the sound it makes when alarmed. It stands 12–16 in. (30–40 cm) high at the shoulder and weighs 7–11 lbs (3–5 kg). It has an elongated snout and a soft coat that is gray or brownish above, white below. The hair on the crown forms an upright tuft and may partially conceal the short, ringed horns of the male. Dik-diks live in dry areas of dense brush in southern and eastern Africa, and feed chiefly on acacia and other shrubs.

Dik-dik (*Madoqua*).
JACK CANNON—OSTMAN AGENCY

dike Bank, usually of earth, constructed to control or confine water. Dikes were purely defensive at first, but later became a means to acquire polders, tracts of land reclaimed from a body of water by the construction of offshore dikes roughly parallel to the shoreline. After a dike is built, the polder is drained by pumping out the water. Where the land surface is above low-tide level, tide gates discharge water into the sea at low tide and automatically close to prevent reentry of seawater at high tide. To reclaim lands that are below low-tide level, the water must be pumped over the dikes. The most notable example of polder construction is the system adjacent to Holland's IJSSELMEER (Zuider Zee) barrier dam. If the Netherlands were to lose the protection of its dikes, its most densely populated portion would be inundated by the sea and rivers.

dilemma tale *or* **judgment tale** Typical African form of short story. Its ending is open to conjecture or is morally ambiguous, allowing the audience to comment or speculate on the correct solution to the problem posed, whether a conflict of loyalty, the need to choose a just response to a difficult situation, or the laying of blame when several parties seem equally guilty. Dilemma tales function both as instruction and entertainment and help establish social norms.

Dili City (pop., 1999 est.: 65,000), capital of EAST TIMOR. It lies on the northern coast of TIMOR Island on Ombai Strait. Dili has been the capital, chief port and commercial center of the eastern half of Timor since it was settled by the Portuguese about 1520. During World War II it was occupied by Japan. East Timor was under Portuguese rule until 1975, after which it was designated a province of Indonesia. Dili suffered major damage by Indonesia military "militias" after East Timor voted for independence in 1999. The city became the capital of newly sovereign East Timor in 2002.

Dilke \'dilk\, **Sir Charles Wentworth** (1843–1911) British politician. He was elected to Parliament in 1868, first as an extremist then a moderate. In 1882 he became a member of WILLIAM E. GLADSTONE's cabinet and was seen as a future prime minister. He was ruined at the height of his career when he was cited as a corespondent in a sensational divorce suit in 1886. Dilke denied the woman's story, and the accumulated evidence showed that much of it was a fabrication. He returned to the House of Commons (1892–1911), where he promoted progressive labor legislation and gained a reputation as a military expert.

dill FENNEL-like annual or biennial herb *(Anethum graveolens)* of the PARSLEY family, or its dried, ripe fruit, or seeds, and leafy tops, which are used to season foods, particularly in eastern Europe and Scandinavia. Native to Mediterranean countries and southeastern Europe, dill is now widely cultivated in Europe, India, and North America. The entire plant is aromatic, and the small stems and immature umbels are used for flavoring food. Dill has a warm, slightly sharp flavor.

Dillinger \'dil-ən-jər\, **John (Herbert)** (1903?–1934) U.S. bank robber. Born in Indianapolis, he was arrested in 1924 in the foiled holdup of a grocery and sentenced to prison, where he learned the craft of bank robbery. He was paroled in 1933. In four months he led his gang in five bank robberies in Indiana and Ohio. Again captured and incarcerated, he escaped prison and returned to bank robbery until his recapture. In 1934 he used a fake wooden pistol to effect his escape from an Indiana prison. His bank robberies continued until he was killed in an ambush involving the FBI, Indiana police, and a friend and brothel madam (the "lady in red"), who drew him to Chicago's Biograph Theater.

Dilthey \'dil-,tī\, **Wilhelm** (1833–1911) German philosopher of history. Opposed to holding the methods of the natural sciences as the ideal, he tried to establish the humanities—history, philosophy, religion, psychology, art, literature, law, politics, and economics—as interpretive sciences in their own right. He held that the essence of human beings cannot be grasped by introspection, but only from a knowledge of all of history. His major work was *Introduction to Human Science* (1883); two influential essays are "Ideas Concerning a Descriptive and Analytical Psychology" (1894) and "The Structure of the Historical World in the Human Sciences" (1910). His work influenced the study of literature.

DiMaggio \də-'mä-zhē-,ō, di-'ma-jē-,ō\, **Joe** *orig.* **Joseph Paul** (1914–1999) U.S. baseball star. Born in Martinez, Cal., he joined the New York Yankees in 1936 and stayed with them until his retirement in 1951. Regarded as one of the greatest of all center fielders, he played outfield with such languid grace that some inattentive fans thought he was lazy. Known as "Joltin' Joe" or "the Yankee Clipper," he achieved a career batting average of .325. In 1941 he accomplished one of the most remarkable of all major-league records with his feat of hitting safely in 56 consecutive games. DiMaggio helped the Yankees win 10 American League championships and nine World Series titles. His brothers Vincent and Dominic also played in the major leagues. His second wife (for nine months in 1954) was MARILYN MONROE. After his retirement he served as an executive for two major-league teams and appeared in television commercials.

dimension In mathematics, a number indicating the fewest coordinates necessary to identify a point in a geometric space; more generally, a number indicating a measurement of length (see LENGTH, AREA, AND VOLUME). One-dimensional space can be represented by a numbered line, on which a single number identifies a point. In two-dimensional space, a COORDINATE SYSTEM may be superimposed, requiring only two numbers to identify a point. Three numbers suffice in three-dimensional space, and so on.

dimensional analysis Technique used in the physical sciences and engineering to reduce physical properties such as acceleration, viscosity, energy, and others to their fundamental dimensions of length, mass, and time. This technique facilitates the study of interrelationships of systems (or models of systems) and their properties. Acceleration, for example, is expressed as length per unit of time squared; whether the units of length are in the English or metric system is immaterial. Dimensional analysis is often the basis of mathematical models of real situations.

dimethyl ketone See ACETONE

dimethyl sulfoxide \dī-'me-thəl-səl-'fäk-,sīd\ **(DMSO)** Colorless, nearly odorless liquid organic compound that mixes in all proportions with water, alcohol, and most organic SOLVENTS and dissolves a wide variety of compounds (but not aliphatic HYDROCARBONS). It readily penetrates skin and other tissues and is used to carry drugs and ANTITOXINS through the skin. It has many industrial uses, as a solvent, cleaner, pesticide, paint stripper, hydraulic fluid, preservative of cells at low temperatures, and metal complexing agent.

diminished capacity *or* **diminished responsibility** In law, any mental condition that renders a person unable to form the specific intent necessary for the commission of a crime but that does not amount to INSANITY. It is most frequently asserted as a defense to murder charges that require proof of a particular mental state (e.g., premeditation). If diminished capacity is shown, negating an element of the crime with which a defendant is charged, the defendant can be convicted only of a lesser offense that does not include the element. Though recognized as a defense in Britain, most other countries recognize only mental disease or abnormality of sufficient degree to sustain a defense of insanity.

diminishing returns, law of Economic law stating that if one input into the production of a commodity is increased while all other inputs remain fixed, a point will eventually be reached at which the input yields progressively smaller increases in output. For example, a farmer will find that a certain number of laborers on his farm will yield the maximum output per worker. If he exceeds that number, the output per worker will fall.

Dimitrov \di-ˈmē-ˌtrȯf\, **Georgi (Mikhailovich)** (1882–1949) Bulgarian communist leader. He helped found the Bulgarian Communist Party in 1919. After leading a communist uprising in 1923 that provoked fierce government reprisals, he was forced to live abroad and became head of the central European section of the COMINTERN in Berlin (1929–33). He won worldwide fame for his defense against Nazi accusations in the REICHSTAG FIRE trial (1933). He headed the Comintern in Moscow 1935–43, then returned to Bulgaria, where he served as prime minister 1945–49. He effected the communist consolidation of power that formed the Bulgarian People's Republic in 1946.

Dinarchus *or* **Deinarchus** \dī-ˈnär-kəs\ (c. 360–after 292 BC) Professional speechwriter at Athens. He rose to fame through his speeches against DEMOSTHENES and others accused of misusing the treasury. His work, however, reflects the decline of Attic oratory; his surviving speeches show little creativity, abuse instead of reason, and plagiarism.

d'Indy, Vincent See V. d'INDY

Dinesen \ˈdē-nə-sən\, **Isak** *orig.* **Karen Christence Dinesen** *later* **Baroness Blixen-Finecke** (1885–1962) Danish writer. She married her cousin, a baron, and they moved to Kenya; *Out of Africa* (1937; film, 1985), a memoir of her years on their coffee plantation (1914–31), reveals a deep love of Africa and its people. Her finely crafted stories, set in the past and pervaded with an aura of supernaturalism, incorporate themes of eros and dreams; her collections include *Seven Gothic Tales* (1934) and *Winter's Tales* (1942). Her only novel, *The Angelic Avengers* (1944), was seen as a satire of Nazi-occupied Denmark.

Ding Ling *or* **Ting Ling** \ˈdiŋ-ˈliŋ\ *orig.* **Jiang Weizhi** (1904–1986) Chinese writer. She had written three collections, many of whose stories centered on young, unconventional Chinese women, before publishing the proletarian-oriented *Flood* (1931), acclaimed as a model of SOCIALIST REALISM. She later expressed dissatisfaction with the Communist Party, for which she was censured and imprisoned for five years during the CULTURAL REVOLUTION; she was eventually reinstated in the party. Her later works include critical essays and fiction, some published in *I Myself Am a Woman* (1989).

dingo Australian wild dog *(Canis dingo)*, apparently introduced from Asia 5,000–8,000 years ago. It has short, soft fur, a bushy tail, and erect, pointed ears. It is about 4 ft (1.2 m) long, including the 12-in. (30-cm) tail, and stands about 24 in. (60 cm) high. Its color varies between yellowish and reddish brown, often with white underparts, feet, and tail tip. Dingoes hunt alone or in small groups. They formerly preyed on kangaroos but now feed mainly on rabbits and sometimes on livestock. They contributed, through competition for resources, to the extermination of the TASMANIAN WOLF and TASMANIAN DEVIL on the Australian mainland.

Dingo (*Canis dingo*).

G.R. ROBERTS

Dinka Cattle-herding people of the Nile basin in southern Sudan. They speak an eastern Sudanic language of the NILO-SAHARAN family and are closely related to the NUER. Numbering about 3 million, they are divided into independent groups of 1,000–30,000 persons. Leadership is provided by priest-chiefs. In recent years they have fought with Sudanese government troops in a struggle for greater autonomy. See also NILOTES.

dinoflagellate \ˌdī-nō-ˈfla-jə-lət\ Any of numerous one-celled, aquatic organisms that have two dissimilar flagella and characteristics of both plants (ALGAE) and animals (PROTOZOANS). Most are microscopic and marine. The group is an important component of PHYTOPLANKTON in all but the colder seas, and an important link in the food chain. Dinoflagellates also produce part of the luminescence sometimes seen in the sea. Under favorable conditions, dinoflagellate populations may reach 60 million organisms per liter of water. Such rapid growths, called blooms, result in the RED TIDES that discolor the sea and poison fish and other marine animals. See also *CERATIUM*.

dinosaur Any of the extinct REPTILES that were the dominant land animals during most of the MESOZOIC ERA (248–65 million years ago). The various species appeared at different times, and not all overlapped. Many were carnivores, but several were herbivores. Dinosaurs are classified as either ORNITHISCHIANS or SAURISCHIANS, based on PELVIC GIRDLE structure. Most had a long tail, which they held straight out, apparently to maintain balance. Most species were egg layers. Some were probably warm-blooded. Dinosaur fossils have been found on every continent. Most types of dinosaur flourished until late in the CRETACEOUS PERIOD (65 million years ago), then disappeared within the next million years. Two theories for the cause of this mass extinction, following some 140 million years of existence, are that mountain-building cycles altered habitat and changed climate or that an asteroid hit the earth, resulting in immense dust clouds that blocked sunlight for several years. The birds are thought by many to be living descendants of the dinosaurs. See also CARNOSAUR, SAUROPOD.

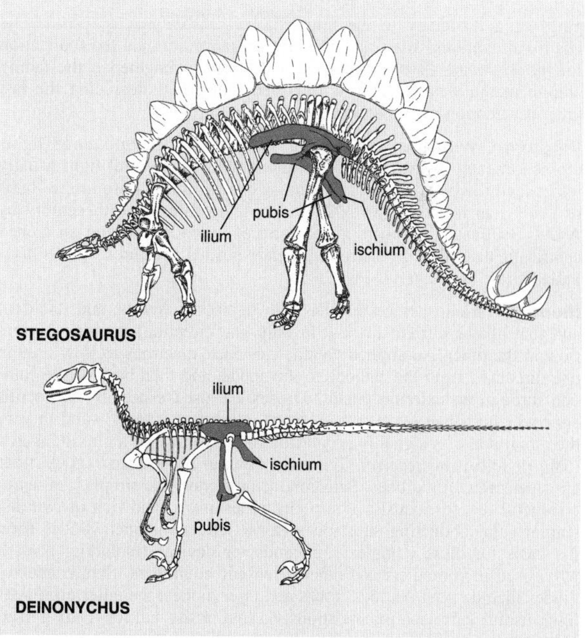

Skeletons of an ornithischian dinosaur (*Stegosaurus*) and a saurischian dinosaur (*Deinonychus*). The skeleton of *Stegosaurus* shows a pelvic arrangement resembling that of birds, with a long ilium and a pubis having a short blade that extends backward into a long thin process lying below and parallel to the ischium. The pelvic girdle of *Deinonychus* shows the triangular outline formed by the ischium, pubis, and ilium characteristic of the saurischians.

Dinosaur National Monument National preserve, northwestern Colorado and northeastern Utah. It was set aside in 1915 to preserve rich fossil beds that include dinosaur remains. It was enlarged in 1938 and again in 1978 to its present 330 sq mi (855 sq km). It protects the canyons of the Green and Yampa rivers, which contain highly colored geologic formations.

Dinwiddie \din-ˈwid-ē\, **Robert** (1693–1770) British colonial administrator. He entered government service in 1727 and was appointed surveyor general for the southern part of America (1739–51). As lieutenant governor of Virginia, he sent George Washington in 1753 to prevent the French from controlling the western frontier, an action that helped precipitate the French and Indian War. He tried to obtain intercolonial cooperation for the war effort, an issue taken up at the Albany Congress. In 1758 he returned to England.

Diocletian \ˌdī-ə-ˈklē-shən\ *Latin* **Gaius Aurelius Valerius Diocletianus** *orig.* **Diocles** (AD 245–316) Roman emperor (284–305) who restored efficient government after the near-anarchy of the 3rd century. He was serving under the emperor Carinus (r.283–85) when the co-emperor, Carinus' brother Numerian, was killed. Diocletian's army declared him emperor, but his domain was restricted to Asia Minor and possibly Syria. Carinus attacked Diocletian (285) but was assassinated before achieving victory, allowing Diocletian to become sole emperor. He sought to remove the military from politics, and established a tetrarchy (four-ruler system) to spread his influence and combat rebellions throughout the empire. Proclaiming himself and his corulers as gods, he added the trappings of a theocracy to the reign. His fiscal, administrative, and military reorganization laid the foundation for the Byzantine Empire in the east and briefly strengthened the fading empire in the west. In 303–4 he issued four edicts decreeing the last great persecution of Christians. He abdicated in 305.

Diocletian, detail of a bust in the Capitoline Museum, Rome.
ALINARI—ART RESOURCE

Diocletian window Semicircular window divided into three lights (compartments) by two vertical mullions, with the central light usually wider than the two side lights. Its name comes from its use in the Baths of Diocletian in Rome (AD 302). It was revived in the 16th century by Andrea Palladio and others in the form of a window having an arched central light flanked by narrower, square-headed apertures, known as a Palladian or Venetian window.

diode Electronic device that has two electrodes (anode and cathode) and that allows current to flow in only one direction, resisting current flow in the other. An applied voltage can cause electrons to flow only in one direction, from the cathode to the anode, and then back to the cathode through an external circuit. Diodes are used especially as rectifiers—which change alternating current into direct current—and to vary the amplitude of a signal in proportion to the voltage in a circuit, as in a radio or television receiver. The most familiar diodes are vacuum tubes and semiconductor diodes. Semiconductor diodes, the simplest of semiconductor devices, consist of two electrodes and a sandwich of two dissimilar semiconducting substances (a p-n junction). Such diodes form the basis for more complex semiconductor devices (including transistors) used in computers and other electronic equipment. Semiconductor diodes include light-emitting diodes and laser diodes; the latter emit laser light, useful for telecommunications via fiber optics and for reading compact discs.

Diogenes of Sinope \dī-ˈäj-ə-ˌnēz...sə-ˈnō-pē\ (died c. 320 BC) Greek philosopher, principal member of the Cynics. He is credited by some with originating the Cynic way of life, but he himself acknowledged his debt to Antisthenes (c. 445–365 BC). He conveyed the Cynic philosophy by personal example rather than any system of thought. He strove to destroy social conventions (including family life) as a way of returning to a "natural" life. To this end he lived as a vagabond pauper, sleeping in public buildings and begging for food. He also advocated shamelessness (performing harmless unconventional actions), outspokenness, and training in austerity.

Diomede Islands \ˈdī-ə-ˌmēd\ Two islands in the Bering Strait. Lying about 2.5 mi (4 km) apart, they are separated by the U.S.–Russian boundary, which coincides with the International Date Line. The larger island, Big Diomede (*Russian* Ratmonov), belongs to Russia and is the site of an important weather station. To the east lies Little Diomede Island, a part of Alaska.

Diomedes \ˌdī-ə-ˈmē-ˌdēz\ Greek hero in the Trojan War. He was commander of 80 ships from Argos bringing soldiers to defeat Troy. His exploits included wounding the goddess Aphrodite, killing Rhesus and his Thracian followers, and stealing the Trojan Palladium (the sacred image of Athena that protected Troy). Aphrodite punished him by making his wife unfaithful to him in his absence, and after the war he returned home to find his claim to the throne of Argos disputed. He then sailed to Italy and founded the colony of Argyripa (later Arpi) in Apulia.

Dionysia See Bacchanalia

Dionysius I *or* **Dionysius the Elder** (c. 430–367 BC) Tyrant of Syracuse (405–367). He became ruler with Spartan help and retained power until his death, basing his strength on the support of his mercenary army. He held Carthaginian expansion on Sicily in check and hoped to acquire an empire in Greek Italy. Syracuse's economy depended on war, and under Dionysius great advances were made in the technology of large-scale artillery and the manufacture of munitions. His disastrous third campaign against the Carthaginians resulted in the ceding of money and territory; he died during the next Carthaginian conflict.

Dionysius of Halicarnassus (fl. c. 20 BC) Greek historian and teacher of rhetoric. Dionysius migrated to Rome in 30 BC. His history of Rome, from its origins to the First Punic War, written from a pro-Roman standpoint but carefully researched, is, with Livy's, the most valuable source for early Roman history. Its 20 books began to appear in 7 BC; the last 10 have been lost.

Dionysius the Areopagite \ˌar-ē-ˈä-pə-ˌjīt, ˌar-ē-ˈä-pə-ˌgīt\ (fl. 1st century AD) Biblical figure, converted by St. Paul. His conversion at Athens is mentioned in Acts 17:34, and he acquired a posthumous reputation largely through confusion with later Christians similarly named. Around AD 500, a series of influential Greek treatises uniting Neoplatonism and Christian theology were forged in his name; the writer, probably a Syrian monk, is now known as Pseudo-Dionysius the Areopagite.

Dionysus \ˌdī-ə-ˈnī-səs\ Greek god of vegetation and fruitfulness, known especially as the god of wine and ecstasy. His Roman equivalent was Bacchus. His worship was introduced into Greece from Asia Minor, and he became one of the most important of all the Greek gods, while his cult remained associated with that of many Asiatic deities. A son of Zeus and (according to the standard tradition) Semele, he was brought up by the maenads, or bacchantes. The first creator of wine, he traveled widely teaching the winemaking art, with a following of satyrs, sileni (see satyr and silenus), and nymphs. He had the gift of prophecy and was received at Delphi along with Apollo, though his principal oracle was at Thrace. Festivities called Dionysia or (among the Romans) Bacchanalia were held in his honor; in their earlier years they were wild, ecstatic occasions, and they have often been the subject of artistic representation. Dionysus originally appeared as a bearded man, but later more often as a slim youth. His principal attribute was the thyrsus, a wand bound with vine leaves. The dithyramb, a choral hymn in his honor, is often seen as the basis of Western drama.

Diop \ˈjȯp\, **Birago Ismael** (1906–1989) Senegalese poet and recorder of traditional Wolof folktales. A veterinarian and diplomat, he was active in the Negritude movement in the 1930s. His output of lyric poetry is small but beautifully composed. His books containing tales told to him by his family's griot include *Tales of Amadou Koumba* (1947) and *Tales and Commentaries* (1963).

diopside \dī-ˈäp-ˌsīd\ Common silicate mineral in the pyroxene family. Diopside is a calcium and magnesium silicate ($CaMgSi_2O_6$) that occurs in metamorphosed siliceous limestones and dolomites, in skarns, and in igneous rocks. It is also found in small amounts in many chondritic meteorites. Clear specimens of good green color are sometimes cut as gems.

Dior \'dyȯr, *Engl* dē-'ȯr, 'dē-ȯr\, **Christian** (1905–1957) French fashion designer. He trained for the French diplomatic service, but in the financial crisis of the 1930s he began illustrating fashions for a weekly periodical. In 1942 he joined the house of the Parisian designer Lucien Lelong. In 1947 he introduced his revolutionary "New Look," which featured small shoulders and long, full skirts, a dramatic change from the World War II style of padded shoulders and short skirts (a consequence of wartime shortages). In the 1950s the "sack" or "H" line became the characteristic silhouette of his designs. He was instrumental in commercializing Parisian fashion on a worldwide scale.

Dior, 1957.
POPPERFOTO

diorite \'dī-ə-ˌrīt\ Medium- to coarse-grained igneous rock that commonly is composed of about two-thirds plagioclase feldspar and one-third dark-colored minerals, such as hornblende or biotite. Diorite has about the same structural properties as granite but, perhaps because of its darker color and more limited supply, is rarely used as an ornamental building material. It is one of the dark gray stones that is sold commercially as "black granite."

Dioscuri \ˌdī-əs-'kyu̇r-ī, dī-'äs-kyə-ˌrī\ *or* **Castor and Pollux** (Greek, *dioskouroi:* "sons of Zeus") Twin gods of ancient Greece. They aided shipwrecked sailors and accepted sacrifices for favorable winds. Castor was mortal and Pollux was immortal; when Castor was killed, Pollux disowned his immortality to join his brother. Zeus later changed them into the constellation GEMINI.

dioxin \dī-'äk-sən\ AROMATIC COMPOUND, any of a group of contaminants produced in making herbicides (e.g., AGENT ORANGE), disinfectants, and other agents. They have two benzene rings connected by a pair of oxygen atoms; when substituents on the rings are chlorine atoms, the molecules are particularly toxic. The best known, usually called simply dioxin, is 2,3,7,8-tetrachlorodibenzo-*p*-dioxin, or 2,3,7,8-TCDD. It is extremely stable chemically, does not dissolve in water but does in oils (and thus accumulates in body fat). Its human toxicity is disputed and the subject of continuing research.

diphtheria \dif-'thir-ē-ə\ Acute infectious BACTERIAL DISEASE caused by *Corynebacterium diphtheriae,* which usually enters through the tonsils, nose, or throat and multiplies there, forming a thick membrane that adheres to the tissues and sometimes blocks the trachea, requiring emergency treatment. The bacteria produce a TOXIN that spreads to cause other symptoms, including fever, chills, sore throat, and lesions in heart muscle and peripheral nerve tissue that may cause death from heart failure and paralysis. Diphtheria is treated with an ANTITOXIN that neutralizes the toxin and produces long-term IMMUNITY. Vaccination has greatly reduced its occurrence in Europe and North America.

Diplodocus \də-'plä-də-kəs\ genus of SAUROPOD dinosaur found as fossils in Late Jurassic rocks of North America and related to *APATOSAURUS*. *Diplodocus* and its relatives (diplodocids) were some of the longest land animals that ever lived, some approaching 100 ft (30 m). It had a long neck and extremely small brain and skull. Most diplodocids weighed about 30 tons, and some as much as 80 tons. It was formerly thought that *Diplodocus* may have spent a good deal of time in water, but fossil evidence indicates it moved freely on land, where it apparently fed on soft vegetation. It may be the most commonly displayed dinosaur.

diploidy See PLOIDY

diplomacy Art of conducting relationships for gain without conflict. It is the chief instrument of FOREIGN POLICY. Its methods include secret negotiation by accredited envoys (though political leaders also negotiate) and international agreements and laws. Its use predates recorded history. The goal of diplomacy is to further the state's interests as dictated by geography, history, and economics. Safeguarding the state's independence, security, and integrity is of prime importance; preserving the widest possible freedom of action for the state is nearly as important. Beyond that, diplomacy seeks maximum national advantage without using force and preferably without causing resentment.

diplomatic service See FOREIGN SERVICE

diplopia See DOUBLE VISION

Dipo Negoro \'dē-pō-ne-'gōr-ō\, **Pangeran (Prince)** (c. 1785–1855) Javanese leader in the 19th-century conflict known to the West as the Java War (1825–30). He was the son of the ruler of Jogjakarta, a sultanate created in 1755 by a Dutch treaty that dismembered the once-powerful Javanese kingdom of Mataram. Dutch land reforms undercut the economic position of the Javanese aristocrats, and Dipo Negoro became the aristocrats' leader against the Dutch. The Javanese saw him as a "just prince" come to save the people, and the conflict itself was seen as a Muslim holy war against the infidels. For three years Dipo Negoro's guerrilla forces had the upper hand, but the Dutch triumphed in the end, and Dipo Negoro was arrested at the peace negotiations.

dipole See ELECTRIC DIPOLE, MAGNETIC DIPOLE

dipper *or* **water ouzel** \'ü-zəl\ Any of five songbird species in the genus *Cinclus* (family Cinclidae), noted for hunting insects by walking underwater in rushing streams. The species are widely distributed in Asia, Africa, Europe, and North and South America. Dippers are plump, stub-tailed birds, about 7 in. (18 cm) long, with a thrushlike bill and legs. They are commonly blackish brown or dull gray. They nest in a dome of moss built in a crevice, often behind a waterfall. See also OUZEL.

Eurasian dipper (*Cinclus cinclus*).
H.M. BARNFATHER—BRUCE COLEMAN INC.

dipteran \'dip-tə-rən\ Any member of the more than 85,000 species in the insect order Diptera (the two-winged, or "true," flies), characterized by the use of only one pair of wings for flight and the reduction of the second pair of wings to knobs used for balance. Dipterans live in all habitats worldwide, including the subarctic and high mountains. They range in size from about 0.05 in. (1 mm) long (MIDGES) to 3 in. (8 cm) long (ROBBER FLIES). Dipteran larvae break down and redistribute organic materials, and both adults and larvae are a significant link in numerous food chains. Many species are annoying bloodsuckers, and several (e.g., HOUSEFLY, MOSQUITO, SAND FLY, TSETSE FLY) are vectors of disease. Other species cause great damage to agricultural crops. See also BLOWFLY, CRANE FLY, FRUIT FLY, GNAT, HORSEFLY, LEAF MINER.

Dirac \di-'rak\, **P(aul) A(drien) M(aurice)** (1902–1984) English mathematician and theoretical physicist. His first major contribution, in 1925–26, was a general and logically simple form of quantum mechanics. Around the same time he developed ideas of ENRICO FERMI which led to FERMI-DIRAC STATISTICS. He then applied ALBERT EINSTEIN's special theory of relativity to the quantum mechanics of the electron, and showed that the electron must have spin of ½. His theory also revealed new states later identified with the positron. He shared a 1933 Nobel Prize with ERWIN SCHRODINGER. In 1932 Dirac was appointed to the Lucasian mathematics professorship at Cambridge Univ., a chair once occupied by ISAAC NEWTON. He retired from Cambridge in 1968 and in 1971 became professor emeritus at Florida State Univ.

dire wolf Extinct WOLF *(Canis dirus)* that existed during the PLEISTOCENE EPOCH (1.6 million–10,000 years ago), probably the most common mammalian species found preserved in the LA BREA TAR PITS. It differed from the modern wolf in being larger and having a more massive skull, a smaller brain (and probably less intelligence), and relatively light limbs. The species was considerably widespread; skeletal remains have been found in Florida, the Mississippi Valley, and the Valley of Mexico.

direct current (DC) Flow of ELECTRIC CHARGE that does not change direction. Direct current is produced by BATTERIES, FUEL CELLS, rectifiers, and GENERATORS with commutators. Direct current was supplanted by ALTERNATING CURRENT (AC) for common commercial power in the late 1880s because it was then uneconomical to transform it to the high voltages

C
D

needed for long-distance transmission. Techniques developed in the 1960s overcame this obstacle, and direct current is now transmitted over very long distances, though it must ordinarily be converted to alternating current for final distribution. For some uses, such as electroplating, direct current is essential.

direct-mail marketing Method of merchandising in which the seller's offer is made through mass mailing of a circular or catalog or through a newspaper or magazine advertisement, and in which the buyer places an order by mail, telephone, or Internet. The rise of retail mail-order selling occurred in the late 19th century, when U.S. firms such as SEARS, ROEBUCK and MONTGOMERY WARD built large businesses selling goods primarily to farmers. Its use has grown steadily since the introduction of computerized mailing lists after 1960; it is now employed by tens of thousands of firms, and reaches virtually every consumer in the U.S.

directing Art of coordinating and controlling all elements in the staging of a play or making of a film. Until the late 19th century, a theatrical director was usually the play's leading actor or the company's actor-manager. Today's stage director combines such elements as the script, actors, decor, costumes, and lighting to shape an imaginative interpretation of what the playwright has written. The director must understand the art of acting and be able to choose the appropriate actor to fit a specific role. The director also composes the "stage picture" to emphasize the spoken word. The film director combines the theatrical director's responsibilities with the technical functions of CINEMATOGRAPHY, editing, and sound recording. See also ACTOR-MANAGER SYSTEM, AUTEUR THEORY.

Directoire style \dē-rek-'twär\ Style of dress, furniture, and ornament popular in France during the DIRECTORY, 1795–99. Dress for men mixed the ancient and contemporary: high boots, vests, open coats, top hats. Women's fashions featured dresses with long sleeves and V necklines, worn with ruffled caps. Directoire furniture and ornamentation were based on ancient Roman objects recently excavated at POMPEII.

Directory *French* **Directoire** \dē-rek-'twär\ (1795–99) Government set up during the FRENCH REVOLUTION by the CONSTITUTION OF 1795. Legislative power was placed in the Council of Five Hundred and the Council of Ancients, while executive power was placed in a five-member Directory. Though the Directors nominally inherited many of the powers of the COMMITTEE OF PUBLIC SAFETY, they had no funds to finance their projects or courts to enforce their will. The regime was marked by administrative chaos and corruption and by the uprisings in the VENDÉE. It was overthrown in NAPOLEON's Coup of 18–19 BRUMAIRE.

dirigible See AIRSHIP

Dirks, Rudolph (1877–1968) U.S. (German-born) cartoonist. He emigrated with his family to Chicago as a child. Largely self-taught, he moved to New York at 17 to work as a staff artist for WILLIAM RANDOLPH HEARST's *New York Journal*, where in 1897 he created the comic strip *The Katzenjammer Kids*, virtually the first strip to employ speech. In 1912, when he moved to the *New York World*, he lost the rights to the name Katzenjammer and started a new strip, *The Captain and the Kids*, featuring the same "kids," while *The Katzenjammer Kids* continued to be drawn by another artist. His strip was continued by his son after his death.

Dirksen \'dərk-sən\, **Everett McKinley** (1896–1969) U.S. politician. Born in Pekin, Ill., he served in World War I, then returned to Illinois to pursue business interests. He served in the U.S. House of Representatives 1932–48, where he voted against most New Deal measures and remained an isolationist until the U.S. entered World War II. He later served in the U.S. Senate (1950–69), becoming minority leader in 1959. He was noted for his oratorical style. Though a conservative, he helped secure passage of the Nuclear Test Ban Treaty, the Civil Rights Act, and the Voting Rights Act.

dirty sandstone See GRAYWACKE

disarmament Reduction in armaments by one or more nations. Arms reductions may be imposed by a war's victors on the defeated (as happened after Germany's defeat in World War I). Bilateral disarmament agreements may apply to a specific area (such an agreement has kept the Great Lakes weapon-free since 1817). The term is most commonly used for multilateral reduction and limitation agreements, particularly in the context of nuclear weapons. See also ARMS CONTROL.

disc jockey (DJ) Person who plays recorded music on radio or television or at a nightclub. Disc-jockey programs began in the U.S. on radio in the 1940s, when phonograph records (discs) were popular; the programs became the mainstay of many radio stations. A record's sales could depend on a popular disc jockey's preferences, and record companies sent DJs gifts and money ("payola") to win air time for their records. The practice faded after a federal investigation in 1959, but reemerged in the 1980s. With the rise of DISCO in the 1970s, nightclub DJs became adept at creating seamless musical transitions between recordings so that the dance music never stopped.

Disciples of Christ Group of U.S. Protestant churches that originated in the frontier revivals of the early 19th century. Movements founded by Thomas and Alexander Campbell (1763–1854, 1788–1866) and Barton W. Stone (1772–1844) merged in 1832 and took the name Disciples of Christ. The new denomination grew rapidly. Its goal was to unite all Protestants on the basis of NEW TESTAMENT practices. The attempt failed, and the movement itself split into two major segments: the more conservative Churches of Christ (which rejects any innovation without New Testament precedent, including musical instruments in worship) and the Christian Church (Disciples of Christ). Other conservative congregations separated from the Christian Church (Disciples of Christ) in the 1920s; they established a separate annual gathering, the North American Christian Convention, in 1927. In 1985 the Disciples of Christ entered into an ecumenical partnership with the United Church of CHRIST. The common Disciples heritage is still manifest in the meetings of the World Convention of Churches of Christ, organized in 1930.

disco Style of dance music that arose in the mid-1970s, characterized by hypnotic rhythm, repetitive lyrics, and electronically produced sounds. Disco (short for "discotheque") evolved largely from New York underground nightclubs, in which DISC JOCKEYS would play dance records for hours without interruption, taking care to synchronize the beats so as to make a seamless change between records. Artists such as Donna Summer, Chic, and the Bee Gees had many hits in the genre, which peaked with the release of the film *Saturday Night Fever* (1977). Disco faded quickly after 1980, but its powerful influence, especially its sequenced electronic beats, still continues to affect much of pop music.

discount rate *or* **bank rate** Interest rate charged by a CENTRAL BANK for loans of reserve funds to COMMERCIAL BANKS and other financial intermediaries. The discount rate is one important indicator of the condition of MONETARY POLICY in an economy. Because raising or lowering the discount rate alters the rates that commercial banks charge on loans, adjustment of the discount rate is used as a tool to combat RECESSION and INFLATION.

discovery In law, pretrial procedures providing for the exchange of information between the parties involved. Discovery may be made through interrogatories, written questions sent from one side to the other in an attempt to secure important facts. It also can be made through depositions, whereby a witness is sworn and, in the presence of attorneys for both sides, is subjected to questions. (The written record of the proceedings also is called a deposition.) Other forms of discovery include an order of production and inspection, which compels the opposing party to produce relevant documents or other evidence, and requests for medical examination in cases in which a party's mental or physical condition is at issue.

discus throw Track-and-field sport of hurling for distance a disk-shaped object known as a discus. The discus is about 220 mm (8¾ in.) in diameter and is thicker in the center than at the perimeter; it must weigh at least 2 kg (4 lbs 6½ oz) for men's events, 1 kg (2 lbs 3¼ oz) for women's. It is thrown by means of a whirling movement made by the athlete within a circle 2.5 m (8 ft 2½ in.) in diameter. The sport has been part of the PENTATHLON competition since the ancient Greek Olympics; today it is also an Olympic event in its own right.

disk, hard See HARD DISK

disk flower See COMPOSITE FAMILY

diskette See FLOPPY DISK

dislocation Displacement of the bones of a JOINT. It disrupts the LIGAMENTS, MUSCLES, and capsule (encasing membrane) holding the joint in place. The joint, painful and tender, appears misshapen and swollen, with discoloration of the overlying skin. The patient cannot use the joint and often feels a grating or grinding sensation on trying to move it. The bones must be returned to their normal position (reduction) and the joint kept immobile until healed. Recurrent and congenital dislocations usually require surgical reconstruction.

Dismal Swamp *or* **Great Dismal Swamp** Marshy region, southeastern Virginia and northeastern North Carolina. Despite much lumbering and widespread destruction by fire, the area is still heavily wooded. About 30 mi (48 km) long and 10 mi (16 km) wide, it is home to many rare birds and numerous poisonous snakes. Noted for its fishing and hunting, it is traversed by the Dismal Swamp Canal, part of the ATLANTIC INTRACOASTAL WATERWAY.

Disney, Walt(er Elias) (1901–1966) U.S. film producer and cartoonist. Born in Chicago, he grew up in Missouri. In the 1920s he joined with Ub Iwerks (1901–1971) to create animated commercials and cartoons (see ANIMATION). When a distributor cheated them, Walt moved to Hollywood, enlisted his brother Roy as his business manager, and persuaded Iwerks to join them. Together they created Mickey Mouse. The cheerful rodent—customarily drawn by Iwerks, with Disney providing the voice—starred in the first animated film with sound, *Steamboat Willie* (1928). The brothers formed Walt Disney Productions (later the DISNEY CO.) in 1929. Mickey Mouse's instant popularity led them to invent such other characters as Donald Duck, Pluto, and Goofy and to make several short cartoon films, including *The Three Little Pigs* (1933). The company grew to include a staff of cartoonists, headed by Iwerks. Their first full-length animated film, *Snow White and the Seven Dwarfs* (1937), was followed by such classics as *Pinocchio* (1940), *Fantasia* (1940), *Dumbo* (1941), *Cinderella* (1950), and *Peter Pan* (1953). Disney also produced other films, including *Mary Poppins* (1964), and television shows. He created the plans for Disneyland and initiated the construction of Disney World (see DISNEY WORLD AND DISNEYLAND).

Disney Co. U.S. entertainment corporation. It was founded by WALT DISNEY and his brother Roy as Walt Disney Productions in 1929 to incorporate their cartoon ANIMATION studio. It produced short and full-length animated cartoons in the 1930s and 1940s, then expanded in the 1950s to make nature documentaries and live-action films, as well as television programs. It expanded further with the opening of Disneyland (1955) and Walt Disney World (1971) (see DISNEYLAND AND DISNEY WORLD). It declined after Disney's death in 1966 but was revitalized under new management in the 1980s. As the Walt Disney Co. it expanded its production units and produced such films as *The Little Mermaid* (1989) and *Toy Story* (1995), the first full-length computer-animated film. The films *Beauty and the Beast* (1991) and *The Lion King* (1994) were recreated as Broadway musicals, and the company took an active role in reviving and commercializing New York's Times Square. In 1996 it acquired the ABC television network to become the world's largest media and entertainment corporation; it also operates the cable television Disney Channel. See also MICHAEL EISNER.

Disney World and Disneyland Two theme parks built by the Walt Disney Co. (see DISNEY CO.), a U.S. corporation that became the best-known 20th-cent purveyor of entertainment. Disneyland, an interactive, family-oriented fantasy environment that opened in Anaheim, Cal., in 1955, was WALT DISNEY'S response to typical amusement parks, which entertained children but not their parents. The park, whose architecture is a blend of futurism and nostalgic 19th-century reproductions, has different sections devoted to specific themes. Walt Disney World opened near Orlando, Fla., in 1971. Besides containing Epcot Center (an idealized city), Disney-MGM Studios, and the Magic Kingdom and Animal Kingdom theme parks, Disney World was the first amusement park to incorporate hotels (including two designed by MICHAEL GRAVES) and sports and other recreational facilities into its master plan.

disorderly conduct Conduct likely to lead to a disturbance of the public peace or that offends public decency. It has been held to include the use of obscene language in public, fighting in a public place, blocking public ways, and making threats. Statutes against disorderly conduct must identify the specific acts that constitute it. The offense usually carries minor penalties.

dispersion Any phenomenon associated with the propagation of individual waves at speeds that depend on their WAVELENGTHS. Wavelength determines the speeds at which waves travel through mediums. This variation in speed causes RADIATION to separate into components that have different FREQUENCIES and wavelengths. For example, when a beam of white light is sent through a glass prism, REFRACTION causes the beam to disperse into an array of its component colors of light, producing a rainbowlike effect.

displacement activity Performance by an animal of an act inappropriate for the stimulus or stimuli that evoked it. It usually occurs when an animal is torn between two conflicting drives, such as fear and aggression. Displacement activities often consist of comfort movements (e.g., grooming, scratching).

display behavior Ritualized behavior by which an animal conveys specific information. The best-known displays are visual, but others rely on sound, smell, or touch. Agonistic (aggressive) displays make it unnecessary to chase intruders from a territory or for animals to injure each other in competition for mates. One type of defensive display deceives predators or lures them away from vulnerable young. See also BIRDSONG, COURTSHIP BEHAVIOR.

disposable income Portion of an individual's income over which the recipient has complete discretion. To assess disposable income, it is necessary to determine total income, including not only wages and salaries, interest and dividend payments, and business profits, but also transfer income such as social-security benefits, pensions, and alimony. Obligatory payments, including personal income taxes and compulsory social-insurance contributions, must be subtracted. Disposable income may be used for CONSUMPTION or SAVING.

Dispur \dis-'pu̇r\ City, capital of ASSAM, India. Following an administrative reorganization in 1972, this suburb of GAUHATI became the capital of Assam.

Disraeli \diz-'rā-lē\, **Benjamin** *later* **Earl of Beaconsfield** (1804–1881) British politician and author who was twice prime minister (1868, 1874–80). Of Italian-Jewish descent, he was baptized a Christian as a child, which enabled his future career because until 1858 Jews by religion were excluded from Parliament. He first made his mark as a writer with *Vivian Grey* (1826–27); later novels included *Coningsby* (1844) and *Sybil* (1845). He was elected to Parliament as a Conservative in 1837. In 1845 he made a series of brilliant speeches against SIR ROBERT PEEL and his decision to repeal the CORN LAWS and became leader of the Parliament's Conservatives. He served three stints as chancellor of the exchequer (1852, 1858–59, 1865–68) and played a prominent role in passing the REFORM BILL OF 1867. He was prime minister briefly in 1868, then returned in his second ministry (1874–80) to promote social reform. An advocate of a strong foreign policy, he secured a triumph for imperial prestige with his acquisition of Suez Canal shares and won concessions for England at the Congress of BERLIN. A trusted friend of Queen VICTORIA, he introduced a bill conferring on her the title Empress of India. After the Conservatives were defeated in 1880, he kept the party leadership and finished his political novel *Endymion* (1880).

dissociation Breaking of a chemical COMPOUND into simpler constituents as a result of added ENERGY, as in the case of gaseous molecules dissociated by heating; also, the effect of a SOLVENT on a dissolved polar compound (ELECTROLYTE). All electrolytes dissociate into IONS to a greater or lesser extent in polar solvents (in which the molecules are ELECTRIC DIPOLES). The degree of dissociation can be used to determine the EQUILIBRIUM constant. Dissociation is used to explain electrical conductivity and many other properties of electrolytic SOLUTIONS.

dissociative identity disorder See MULTIPLE PERSONALITY DISORDER

dissonance See CONSONANCE AND DISSONANCE

dissonance, cognitive See COGNITIVE DISSONANCE

distaff Device used in hand spinning in which individual fibers are drawn out of a mass of prepared fibers held on a stick (the distaff), twisted together to form a continuous strand, and wound on a second stick (the spindle). It is most often used for making LINEN; wool does not require a distaff (see CARDING). The first stage in mechanizing spinning was to mount the spindle horizontally in bearings to rotate with a large hand-driven wheel; the distaff, carrying the mass of fiber, was held in the left hand, and the SPINNING WHEEL slowly turned with the right. The Saxon, or Saxony, wheel incorporated a BOBBIN on which the YARN was wound continuously; the distaff holding the raw fiber became a stationary vertical rod, and the wheel was activated by a foot treadle, freeing both the operator's hands.

distance formula Algebraic expression that gives the distances between pairs of points in terms of their coordinates (see COORDINATE SYSTEM). In two- and three-dimensional EUCLIDEAN SPACE, the distance formulas for points in rectangular coordinates are based on the PYTHAGOREAN THEOREM. The distance between the points (a,b) and (c,d) is given by $\sqrt{(a-c)^2+(b-d)^2}$. In three dimensional space, the distance between the points (a, b, c) and (d, e, f) is $\sqrt{(a-d)^2+(b-e)^2+(c-f)^2}$.

distemper Viral disease in two forms, canine and feline. Canine distemper is acute and highly contagious, affecting dogs, foxes, wolves, mink, raccoons, and ferrets. Most untreated cases are fatal. Infected animals are best treated with prompt injections of serum globulins; secondary infections are warded off by antibiotics. Immunity can be conferred by vaccination. Feline distemper causes a severe drop in the number of the infected cat's white blood cells. It rarely lasts more than a week, but the mortality rate is high. Vaccines offer effective immunity.

disthene See KYANITE

distillation VAPORIZATION of a LIQUID and subsequent CONDENSATION of the resultant GAS back to liquid form. It is used to separate liquids from nonvolatile solids or solutes (e.g., ALCOHOLIC BEVERAGES from the fermented materials, water from other components of seawater) or to separate two or more liquids with different BOILING POINTS (e.g., gasoline, kerosene, and lubricating oil from crude oil). Many variations have been devised for industrial applications. An important one is fractional distillation, in which liquids with similar boiling points are repeatedly vaporized and condensed as they rise through an insulated vertical column. The most volatile of the liquids emerges first, nearly pure, from the top of the column, followed in turn by less and less volatile fractions of the original mixture. This method separates the mixture's components far better than simple distillation does.

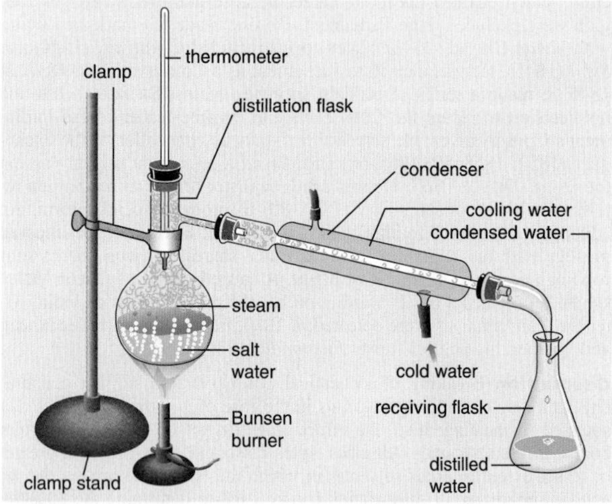

A laboratory distillation apparatus, demonstrating desalination of water. In the distillation flask, salt water is boiled to produce water vapor, while the salt remains in the liquid solution. The vapor is forced out the top of the flask and into the condenser, which consists of a glass tube within a larger tube. Cooling water flows through the outer section, the vapor in the inner section cools and condenses, and the (purified) liquid water flows down to the receiving flask.

distilled liquor ALCOHOLIC BEVERAGE (such as BRANDY, WHISKEY, RUM, or arrack) obtained by distillation from WINE or other fermented fruit juice or from various GRAINS that have first been brewed. The essential ingredient is usually a natural sugar or a starchy substance that may be easily converted into a sugar. The distillation process is based on the different boiling points of water (212°F, 100°C) and alcohol (173°F, 78.5°C). The alcohol vapors that arise while the fermented liquid boils are trapped and recondensed to create a liquid of much greater alcoholic strength. The resultant distillate is matured, often for several years, before it is packaged and sold. See also AQUAVIT, GIN, LIQUEUR, VODKA.

distribution See FREQUENCY DISTRIBUTION, NORMAL DISTRIBUTION

distributive law One of the laws relating to number operations. In symbols, it is stated: $a(b + c) = ab + ac$. The monomial factor a is distributed, or separately applied, to each term of the polynomial factor $b + c$, resulting in the product $ab + ac$. It can also be stated in words: The result of first adding several numbers and then multiplying the sum by some number is the same as first multiplying each separately by the number and then adding the products. See also ASSOCIATIVE LAW, COMMUTATIVE LAW.

District Court, U.S. See UNITED STATES DISTRICT COURT

District of Columbia Federal district of the U.S. Coextensive with the city of WASHINGTON, D.C., it is bounded by Maryland and Virginia. Originally 100 sq mi (259 sq km), the territory was authorized by Congress in 1790 and granted by Maryland and Virginia; it now occupies 68 sq mi (176 sq km). The site was chosen by Pres. GEORGE WASHINGTON and became the seat of the federal government by 1800. Part of the district (ALEXANDRIA, Va.) was retroceded to Virginia in 1847. The slave trade was forbidden in the District in 1850 and slavery was abolished in 1862. The territorial government was abolished in 1874 in favor of government by a commission appointed by the President. Residents were granted suffrage in national elections in 1961 by the 23rd Amendment to the U.S. CONSTITUTION. The mayor-council form of government was established in 1967. Originally appointees of the President, the mayor and councilors became elected officials in 1973 and received local legislative powers in 1974.

dithyramb \'dith-i-ˌram(b)\ Choric poem, chant, or hymn of ancient Greece sung by revelers at the festival in honor of DIONYSUS. The form originated about the 7th century BC in extemporaneous songs of banqueters; it was a recognized literary genre by the end of the 6th century BC. Dithyrambs were composed by ARION and PINDAR, among others. By c. 450 BC the poems had become increasingly bombastic and turgid and the form was declining.

Dittersdorf \'dit-ərs-ˌdȯrf\, **Carl Ditters von** *orig.* **Carl Ditters** (1739–1799) Austrian composer. A violin prodigy, he served as kapellmeister at the court of the Prince-Bishop of Breslau 1770–95. Though ennobled by the empress in 1773, he apparently declined the offer of the post of kapellmeister at the imperial court in Vienna. Extremely prolific, he wrote some 120 symphonies, some 40 concertos (many for violin), sacred choral works, and many chamber pieces. Most important are some 40 stage works, particularly his singspiels, including *Doctor und Apotheker* (1786) and *Die Liebe im Narrenhause* (1787).

diuretic \ˌdī-yu̇r-'e-tik\ Any drug that increases the flow of URINE. Diuretics promote removal of excess water, salts, poisons, and metabolic wastes to help relieve EDEMA, KIDNEY FAILURE, or GLAUCOMA. Most types act by decreasing the amount of fluid reabsorbed by the NEPHRONS and passed back into the blood. Diuretics that allow the body to retain POTASSIUM are used for patients with HYPERTENSION or CONGESTIVE HEART FAILURE.

Divali *or* **Diwali** \də-'wä-lē, də-'vä-lē\ In HINDUISM, a five-day religious festival in autumn. It honors LAKSHMI, goddess of wealth, or, in Bengal, the goddess KALI. During its celebration, earthenware lamps are lit and placed on the parapets of houses and temples or set adrift on rivers and streams. The fourth day of the festival marks the start of a new year, a time of gift-giving, visiting friends, decorating homes, and wearing new clothes. Divali is celebrated by Jains and Sikhs as well.

diver See LOON

divergence In mathematics, a DIFFERENTIAL OPERATOR applied to a three-dimensional vector-valued FUNCTION. The result is a function that describes a rate of change. The divergence of a vector **v** is given by

$$\text{div } \mathbf{v} = \frac{\partial \mathbf{v}_1}{\partial x} + \frac{\partial \mathbf{v}_2}{\partial y} + \frac{\partial \mathbf{v}_3}{\partial z}$$

in which $\mathbf{v}_1$, $\mathbf{v}_2$, and $\mathbf{v}_3$ are the vector components of **v**, typically a velocity field of fluid flow.

diverticulum \ˌdī-vər-'ti-kyə-ləm\ Small pouch or sac formed in the wall of a major organ, usually the ESOPHAGUS, SMALL INTESTINE, or LARGE INTESTINE (the most frequent site of problems). In the large intestine, feces pushed into a pouch can make it bulge out from the colon wall, a condition known as diverticulosis, which has no symptoms. In the more serious condition called diverticulitis, those sacs become inflamed, causing pain and cramps, chills, and sometimes fever. Mild cases need only bed rest, antibiotics, an enema, and a bland diet. In severe cases, perforation or rupture of the colon wall at the bulge can cause PERITONITIS. Rupture may require COLOSTOMY. Meckel's diverticulum, a congenital malformation of the upper intestine that causes bleeding and inflammation, may require surgical removal.

divertimento \di-,vər-ti-'men-tō\ 18th-century chamber-music genre consisting of several movements, often of a light and entertaining nature, for strings, winds, or both. Though the name was applied (c. 1750–1800) to a confusingly varied range of works, it almost always referred to pieces with a single instrument to a part, which could include string quartets and even keyboard sonatas.

dividend Individual share of earnings distributed among stockholders of a corporation or company in proportion to their holdings. Usually paid in cash, dividends may also be distributed in the form of additional shares of STOCK. Preferred stockholders receive a preferential dividend, usually at a fixed rate; common stockholders get a portion of what remains after payment of the dividends on preferred stock.

dividing engine MACHINE used to mark off equal intervals accurately, usually on precision instruments. Georg Friedrich von Reichenbach (1772–1826), a German maker of astronomical instruments, designed an early dividing engine, and Jesse Ramsden (1735–1800), a British pioneer in the design of precision tools, designed dividing engines of great accuracy for both circles and straight lines and produced highly accurate SEXTANTS, theodolites (see SURVEYING), and vertical circles for astronomical observatories.

divination Practice of discerning the hidden significance of events and foretelling the future. Divination is found in all societies, ancient and modern, though methods vary. In the West, psychics claim innate ability to predict the future, and HOROSCOPES, palm reading, and TAROT cards are popular methods of divination. Other methods involve or have involved interpreting dreams, discovering OMENS in natural events, reading the entrails of animals, casting lots, and consulting ORACLES. Divination has long been viewed as the province of specially gifted persons, such as PROPHETS, SHAMANS, and magicians. See also ASTROLOGY.

Divine, Father *orig.* **George Baker** (1877?–1965) U.S. religious leader. Born near Savannah, Ga., he began preaching c. 1900 in the South and later in Baltimore as "The Messenger." He settled in New York City in 1915 and adopted the name Major J. Devine (later altered to Father Divine). In 1919 he established his first communal settlement in Sayville, Long Island, and he founded the Peace Mission movement. His predominantly black following expanded rapidly in the 1930s and '40s, and his settlements, called "heavens," eventually numbered about 170. He taught his followers to renounce personal property and the strict moral code he preached included celibacy and a ban on alcohol and tobacco. Many of his followers, called "angels," believed him to be God.

divine kingship Religio-political concept that views a ruler as an incarnation, manifestation, mediator, or agent of the sacred. In some nonliterate societies, members view their rulers or chiefs as inheritors of the community's own magical power. The ruler may exercise this power either malevolently or benevolently, but is usually responsible for influencing the weather and the land's fertility to ensure the harvest necessary for survival. In other societies, particularly those of ancient China, the Middle East, and South America, the ruler was identified with a particular god or as a god himself; in Japan, Peru (Incas), Mesopotamia, and the Greco-Roman world, the ruler was regarded as the son of a god. In both these cases, the ruler protected the community from enemies and generally fed and cared for his flock. A third form of divine kingship, one practiced in Europe, is that of the ruler as mediator or executive agent of a god. In this form it is the institution of kingship, more than an individual ruler, that bears the mark of the sacred.

diving Sport of plunging into water, usually headfirst and often following the performance of one or more acrobatic maneuvers (such as flexing or somersaulting). It emerged as a competitive sport in the late 19th century and became part of the Olympic Games in 1904. Dives are performed from a firm platform 5 or 10 m (16.4 or 32.8 ft) above the water, or from an elastic springboard 1 or 3 m (3.3 or 9.8 ft) above the water. In Olympic contests, only the 10-m platform and 3-m springboard are used. Contestants are required to do certain dives, each rated according to its degree of difficulty, as well as dives of their own choice. Judges score each dive, and the total score is multiplied by the degree of difficulty.

diving duck Any DUCK that obtains its food by diving to the bottom in deep water rather than by dabbling in shallows (see DABBLING DUCK). Diving ducks prefer marine environments and are popularly called either bay ducks or sea ducks. Bay ducks (tribe Aythyini, family Anatidae), including CANVASBACK, redhead, SCAUP, and allied species, are found more frequently in estuaries and tidal lagoons than on the open sea. Sea ducks (20 species in tribes Mergini and Somateriini) include the bufflehead, EIDERS, GOLDENEYE, MERGANSERS, oldsquaw, and SCOTERS; some are also or mainly found on inland waters.

division of labor Specialization in the production process. Complex jobs can usually be less expensively completed by a large number of people each performing a small number of specialized tasks than by one person attempting to complete the entire job. The idea that specialization reduces costs, and thereby the price the consumer pays, is embedded in the principle of COMPARATIVE ADVANTAGE. Division of labor is the basic principle underlying the ASSEMBLY LINE in mass-production systems.

divorce Dissolution of a valid MARRIAGE, usually freeing the parties to remarry. In contexts in which religious authority is still strong and the religion holds that marriage is indissoluble (e.g., ROMAN CATHOLICISM, HINDUISM), divorce may be difficult and rare. In the U.S., nearly half of all marriages end in divorce. The most common grounds for divorce are absence from the marital home, drug or alcohol addiction, adultery, cruelty, conviction of a crime, desertion, insanity, and nonsupport. See also ANNULMENT.

Diwali See DIVALI

Dix, Dorothea (Lynde) (1802–1887) U.S. reformer for the welfare of the mentally ill. Born in Hampden, Mass. (now in Maine), she opened a school for girls in Boston in 1821. In 1841 she began teaching Sunday school in a jail, where she was distressed to see the mentally ill imprisoned with criminals. For 18 months she toured mental institutions, and in 1843 she reported their deplorable conditions to the Massachusetts legislature. After improvements were made, she expanded her campaign to other states. Through her work, special mental hospitals were built in 15 states and in Canada.

Dix, Otto (1891–1969) German painter and printmaker. He studied at the academies of Düsseldorf and Dresden and experimented with Impressionism and Dada before arriving at Expressionism with a nightmarish personal vision of contemporary social reality, depicting the horrors of war and the depravities of a decadent society with great emotional effect. He was appointed professor at the Dresden Academy in 1926 and elected to the Prussian Academy in 1931. His antimilitary works aroused the wrath of the Nazi regime and he was dismissed from his academic posts in 1933. His later work was marked by religious mysticism.

"Parents of the Artist," oil on canvas by Otto Dix, 1921; in the Öffentliche Kunstsammlung, Basel, Switzerland.

BY COURTESY OF THE OFFENTLICHE KUNSTSAMMLUNG AND THE EMANUEL HOFFMAN-STIFTUNG, BASEL, SWITZ.; PHOTOGRAPH, HANS HINZ

Dixiecrat *or* **States' Rights Democrats** Member of a right-wing Democratic splinter group in the 1948 election. Organized by Southerners who objected to the Democrats' civil-rights program, the Dixiecrats met in Birmingham, Ala., and nominated Gov. STROM THURMOND of South Carolina for president. He received over 1 million votes in the 1948 election and carried four states.

Dixieland *or* **New Orleans jazz** JAZZ played by a small ensemble featuring collective and solo improvisation. The earliest jazz ensembles grew out of the RAGTIME and brass bands of New Orleans, incorporating elements of the BLUES. In early jazz ensembles such as those led by KING OLIVER and JELLY-ROLL MORTON, the trumpet or cornet plays the melody, with clarinet and trombone providing accompaniment based on the piece's harmonic structure. The tension created by soloists contrasted with the release of ensemble refrains combine with a distinctive two-beat rhythm to give the music its character, often a joyous cacophony at fast tempos or slow, mournful dirges. Dixieland groups usually include banjo, tuba, and drums.

Dixon, Joseph (1799–1869) U.S. inventor and manufacturer. Born in Marblehead, Mass., he was largely self-taught. He began his pioneering industrial use of GRAPHITE in 1827 with the manufacture of lead pencils, stove polish, and lubricants. He discovered that graphite crucibles withstood high temperatures, and secured patents on graphite crucibles for making steel and pottery. He established a crucible steelworks in Jersey City in 1850. He also experimented with photography and photolithography and devised a technique for printing banknotes in color to prevent counterfeiting.

Dixon, Willie *orig.* **William James** (1915–1992) U.S. musician who influenced the emergence of electric BLUES and ROCK MUSIC. In 1936 Dixon moved from his native Mississippi to Chicago, won an Illinois Golden Glove boxing championship, and began selling his songs. He played double bass in several bands before joining Chess Records. His lively compositions, which he sold for as little as $30, included "Little Red Rooster," "You Shook Me," and "Back Door Man"; many were later covered by M. WATERS, E. PRESLEY, and the ROLLING STONES. Dixon toured widely throughout the U.S. and Europe.

Djakarta See JAKARTA

Djibouti \ji-'bü-tē\ *officially* **Republic of Djibouti** *formerly (1885–1967)* **French Somaliland** *(1967–77)* **French Territory of the Afars and Issas** \ä-'fär...ē-'sä, ä-'färz...ē-'säz\ Republic, eastern Africa, on the Gulf of ADEN at the entrance to the RED SEA. Area: 8,880 sq mi (22,999 sq km). Population (1997): 622,000. Capital: DJIBOUTI. Over half of the people are Issas and related Somali clans; Afars are nearly two-fifths; the balance includes Yemeni Arabs and Europeans, mostly French. Languages: French, Arabic (both official). Religion: Sunnite Islam. Currency: Djibouti franc. Djibouti is divided into three principal regions: the coastal plain; the volcanic plateaus in the country's south and center; and the mountain ranges in the north, reaching 6,654 ft (2,028 m) at Mount Mousâ. The land is primarily desert: hot, dry, and desolate; less than 1% is arable. Djibouti has a developing market economy that is almost entirely based on trade and commercial services, centering around DJIBOUTI city. The country is a republic with one legislative house; its head of state and government is the president. Settled around the 3rd century BC by the Arab ancestors of the Afars, it was later populated by Somali Issas. In AD 825, Islam was brought to the area by missionaries. Arabs controlled the trade in this region until the 16th century; it became the French protectorate of French Somaliland in 1888. In 1946 it became a French overseas territory, and in 1977 gained its independence. In the late 20th century, the country has received refugees from the Ethiopian–Somali war, and from civil conflicts in Eritrea. In the 1990s it suffered from political unrest.

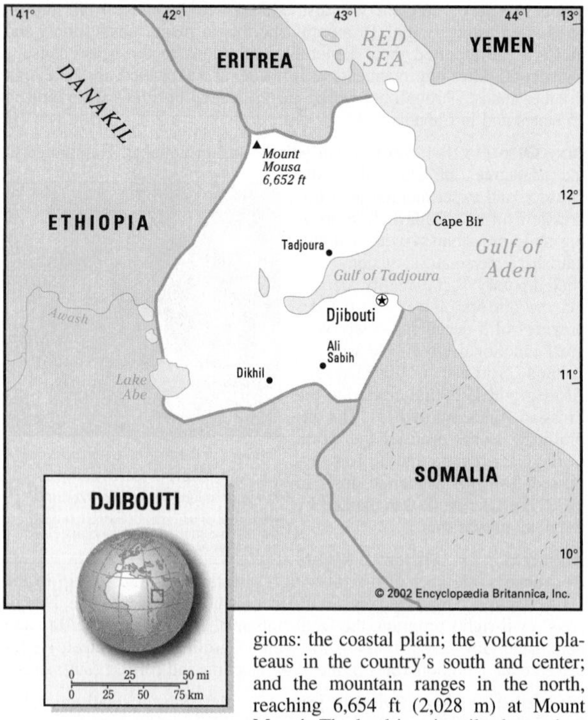

Djibouti Port city (pop., 1995 est.: 383,000) and capital of Djibouti. Located on the southern shore of the Gulf of Tadjoura in the Gulf of ADEN, it was founded by the French in 1888, and made the capital of French Somaliland in 1892. Linked by rail to ADDIS ABABA in 1917, it was made a free port in 1949. The economic life of both the city and the nation depends on the city's use as a transshipment point, especially between Ethiopia and the RED SEA trade. Built on three level areas linked by jetties, the city has a mixture of old and modern architecture. Drought and war during the 1980s and early '90s brought many refugees to Djibouti from Somalia and Ethiopia, swelling its population.

Djilas \'ji-läs\, **Milovan** (1911–1995) Yugoslav politician and political writer. His opposition to Yugoslavia's royalist dictatorship led to a prison term (1933–36). He joined the Yugoslav Communist Party's central committee in 1938 and its politburo in 1940. In World War II he played a major role in the partisan resistance to the Germans. In 1953 he became president of the Federal People's Assembly, but his criticism of the party and calls for liberalization soon led to his ouster from all political posts by TITO. He was later arrested several times after his books criticizing communism, including *The New Class* (1957), were published in the West.

Dmitry, False *or* **Pseudo-Demetrius** Any of three pretenders to the Muscovite throne who, during the Time of TROUBLES, claimed to be IVAN IV's child Dmitry Ivanovich, who had been killed while still a child, possibly at the order of BORIS GODUNOV. The first False Dmitry challenged Godunov's right to the throne and was proclaimed czar in 1605. In 1606 he was murdered by Vasily Shuysky (1552–1612), who succeeded him. Rumors spread that Dmitry had survived, and a second pretender gained a large following before being killed in 1610. A third False Dmitry appeared in 1611, gaining the allegiance of the COSSACKS and the inhabitants of Pskov, but was executed in 1612.

DNA *or* **deoxyribonucleic acid** \dē-'äk-si-ˌrī-bō-nyü-'klē-ik, dē-'äk-si-ˌrī-bō-nyü-'klā-ik\ One of two types of NUCLEIC ACID (the other is RNA); a complex organic compound found in all living CELLS and many VIRUSES. It is the chemical substance of GENES. Its structure, with two strands wound around each other in a double helix to resemble a twisted ladder, was first described (1953) by FRANCIS CRICK and JAMES D. WATSON. Each strand is a long chain (POLYMER) of repeating NUCLEOTIDES: ADENINE (A), GUANINE (G), CYTOSINE (C), and THYMINE (T). The two strands contain complementary information: A forms hydrogen bonds (see HYDROGEN BONDING) only with T; C only with G. When DNA is copied in the cell, the strands separate and each serves as a template for assembling a new complementary strand; this is the key to stable HEREDITY. DNA in cells is organized into dense protein-DNA complexes (see NUCLEOPROTEIN) called CHROMOSOMES. In EUKARYOTES these are in the NUCLEUS, and DNA also occurs in mitochondria and CHLOROPLASTS (if any). PROKARYOTES have a single circular chromosome in the CYTOPLASM. Some prokaryotes and a few eukaryotes have DNA outside the chromosomes in PLASMIDS. See also ROSALIND FRANKLIN, GENETIC ENGINEERING, MUTATION, MAURICE WILKINS. See illustration opposite on following page.

DNA computing Form of computing in which DNA molecules are used to solve basic but complex mathematical problems. The biological cell is regarded as an entity that resembles a sophisticated computer. The four bases that are constituents of DNA, traditionally represented by the letters A, T, C, and G, are used as operators, as the binary digits 0 and 1 are used in computers. DNA molecules are encoded to a researcher's specifications and than induced to recombine (see RECOMBINATION), resulting in trillions of "calculations" simultaneously. The field is in its infancy and its implications are only beginning to be explored. See also QUANTUM COMPUTING.

DNA fingerprinting Method developed by the British geneticist Alec Jeffreys (born 1950) in 1984 for isolating and making images of sequences of DNA. The procedure consists of obtaining a sample of cells containing DNA (e.g., from skin, blood, or hair), extracting the DNA, and purifying it. The DNA is then cut by ENZYMES, and the resulting fragments of varying lengths undergo procedures that permit them to be analyzed. The pattern of fragments is unique for each individual. DNA fingerprinting is used to help solve crimes and determine paternity; it is also used to locate gene segments that cause genetic diseases, to map the genetic material of humans (see HUMAN GENOME PROJECT), to engineer drought-resistant plants (see GENETIC ENGINEERING), and to produce biological drugs from genetically altered cells.

Dnieper River \'nē-pər\ *Russian* **Dnepr** \də-'nyeprᵊ\ *ancient* **Borysthenes.** River, eastern central Europe. One of the longest rivers in Europe, it rises west of MOSCOW and flows south through Belarus and Ukraine, emptying into the Black Sea after a course of 1,420 mi (2,285 km). More than 300 hydroelectric plants operate in the Dnieper basin, and it has several huge dams. Navigable for about 1,042 mi (1,677 km) during the 10 months of the year when it is not frozen, it is an important shipping artery for eastern Europe.

Dniester River \'nē-stər\ *Russian* **Dnestr** \də-'nyestrᵊ\ *ancient* **Tyras.** River, southern central Europe. Rising on the northern side of the CARPATHIAN MTNS., it flows south and east for 840 mi (1,352 km) to the Black Sea near ODESSA. It is the second-longest river in Ukraine and the main water artery of Moldova. It is navigable for 750 mi (1,200 km).

Dnipropetrovsk \də-ˌnye-prə-pē-'tròfsk\ *formerly (1783–1926)* **Ekaterinoslav** \i-ˌkà-ti-'rē-nə-ˌsläf\ City (pop., 1996 est.: 1,147,000), southern central Ukraine. Located on the DNIEPER RIVER, it was founded in 1783 and named for CATHERINE THE GREAT; it grew after the railroad arrived in the 1880s. In 1926 the Soviets gave it its current name. A railway junction and a center of the wheat trade, it has developed into one of the largest industrial cities of Ukraine, with a huge iron and steel industry. It is the site of institutes of higher education, and its cultural amenities include several theaters.

Doberman pinscher \'dō-bər-mən-'pin-chər\ Breed of working dog developed in Apolda, Germany, by Louis Dobermann, a dog-pound keeper, in the late 19th century. This sleek, agile, powerful dog stands 24–28 in. (61–71 cm) high and weighs 60–88 lbs (27–40 kg). It has a short, smooth black, blue, fawn, or red coat, with rust markings on the head, throat, chest, tail base, and feet. Dobermans have a reputation for fearlessness, alertness, loyalty, and intelligence. They have been used in police and military work, as watchdogs, and as guide dogs for the blind.

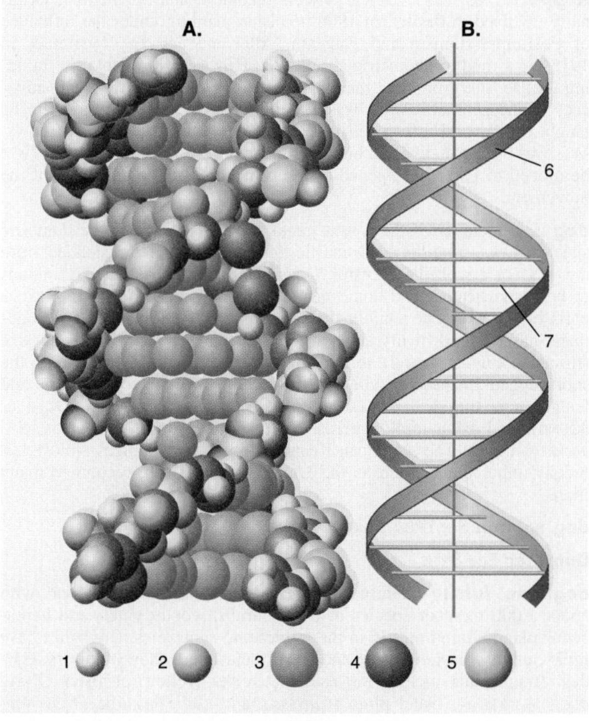

DNA double helix. A. Molecular model of DNA. The molecules include (1) hydrogen, (2) oxygen (3) carbon and nitrogen in the linked nitrogenous bases, (4) carbon in the sugar deoxyribose, and (5) phosphorus. B. Schematic representation of DNA. The twisted ladder shape consists of (6) nitrogenous base pairs joined by hydrogen bonds, on (7) a sugar-phosphate backbone.

Döblin \'dœ̄-ˌblēn\, **Alfred** (1878–1957) German novelist and essayist. He studied medicine at the Univs. of Berlin and Freiburg, specializing in psychiatry. His first novel, *The Three Leaps of Wang-lun* (1915), describes the quashing of a rebellion in China. His best-known work, *Berlin Alexanderplatz* (1929), is written in an Expressionist vein and dramatizes the miseries of working-class life in a disintegrating social order. His Jewish ancestry and socialist views compelled him to leave Germany upon the Nazi takeover, and he fled to France (1933) and then the U.S. (1940), resettling in Paris in the early 1950s.

Dobrovskyý \'dò-bròf-skē\, **Josef** (1753–1829) Czech linguist. Ordained a priest in 1786, he was able to devote himself to scholarship in Prague after 1791 due to noble patronage. His textual criticism of the Bible led him to study OLD CHURCH SLAVIC and then the SLAVIC LANGUAGES as a group. An influential scholar of the CZECH LANGUAGE and its literature, he published such works as *History of the Bohemian Language and Literature* (1792). His grammar of Czech, *Learning System of the Bohemian Language* (1809), helped standardize literary Czech, and his grammar of Old Church Slavic (1822) laid the foundation of comparative Slavic LINGUISTICS.

dobsonfly Any insect of the family Corydalidae with four net-veined wings, found in North and South America, Asia, Australia, and Africa. The species *Corydalus cornutus* has a wingspread of about 5 in. (13 cm), and the male has very large jaws (mandibles) of about 1 in. (2.5 cm) or more. Females lay eggs near streams. Larvae live in the streams and, with their strong biting mouthparts, are ferocious predators on other aquatic insects and small invertebrates. Sometimes called hellgrammites or toebiters, they can inflict painful bites on humans; they are eaten by fish, especially bass, and are used as bait by fishermen.

Dobzhansky \dəb-'zhan-skē\, **Theodosius** *orig.* **Feodosy Grigorevich Dobrzhansky** (1900–1975) Ukrainian-U.S. geneticist and evolutionist. He emigrated in 1927 to the U.S., where he taught at Caltech, Columbia Univ., and Rockefeller University. He laid the groundwork for a theory combining Darwinian evolution and Mendelian genetics by changing the then commonly held view that natural selection produced something close to the best of all possible results and that changes would be rare and slow and not apparent over one life span. He observed extensive genetic variability in wild populations of drosophila, and found that in a given population some genes would regularly change in abundance with the seasons of the year.

dock Any coarse weedy plant of the genus *Rumex*, in the BUCKWHEAT family, that has a long taproot and is sometimes used as a potherb. Most docks are native to Europe but naturalized throughout North America. Examples include curly dock *(R. crispus)* and bitter dock *(R. obtusifolius)*. The early basal leaves of patience-dock *(R. patientia)* are sometimes used in salads. The common weed *R. acetosa* is known variously as dock, common sorrel, or garden sorrel. See also SORREL.

Doctorow \'däk-tə-ˌrō\, **E(dgar) L(aurence)** (born 1931) U.S. novelist. Born in New York City, he worked as an editor and has since taught at colleges and universities. His best-selling novels have often focused on the working class and the dispossessed of earlier decades in America. *The Book of Daniel* (1971) concerned the Rosenberg spy case. *Ragtime* (1975; film, 1981) incorporates actual figures of early-20th-century America. *Loon Lake* (1980), *World's Fair* (1985), and *Billy Bathgate* (1989; film, 1991) examine the Great Depression and its aftermath. *The Waterworks* (1994) is set in 19th-century New York.

Doctors' Plot (1953) Alleged conspiracy of prominent Soviet medical specialists to murder leading government and party officials. In January 1953, the Soviet press reported that nine doctors, at least six of them Jews, had been arrested and confessed their guilt. Because of JOSEPH STALIN's death in March, no trial occurred. *Pravda* later announced that the charges against the doctors were false and their confessions obtained by torture. In his secret speech at the Communist Party's TWENTIETH CONGRESS, NIKITA KHRUSHCHEV asserted that Stalin intended to use the doctors' trial to launch a massive party purge.

Doctors Without Borders *French* **Médecins Sans Frontières** \mād-'saⁿ-säⁿ-frōⁿ-'tyer\ World's largest independent international medical relief agency, established by a group of French physicians in 1971. It aids victims of armed conflict, epidemics, and natural and man-made disasters, and others who lack health care due to geographic remoteness or ethnic marginalization, in front-line hospitals, refugee camps, disaster sites, towns, and villages. Teams provide primary health care, perform surgery, vaccinate children, rehabilitate hospitals, operate emergency nutrition and sanitation programs, and train local medical staff. Operating independently of governments, the organization depends on volunteer health professionals (over 2,000 annually) and private donations. It received the 1999 Nobel Peace Prize.

doctrine of the affections See doctrine of the AFFECTIONS

Doctrine of the Mean See ZHONG YONG

documentary Film that interprets factual material for educational or entertainment purposes. ROBERT FLAHERTY's *Nanook of the North* (1922) is considered the prototype of the genre. John Grierson's *Drifters* (1929) and Pare Lorentz's *Plow That Broke the Plains* (1936) influenced documentary filmmaking in the 1930s. LENI RIEFENSTAHL contributed aesthetically powerful documentaries to the Nazis' propaganda efforts in the 1930s. All the major belligerents in World War II produced propaganda documentaries; the U.S. made such films as FRANK CAPRA's series *Why We Fight* (1942–45), and Britain released *London Can Take It* (1940) and *Desert Victory* (1943). The popularity of documentaries on television in the 1960s and '70s led to such television miniseries as. KEN BURNS's *Civil War* (1990). See also CINÉMA VÉRITÉ.

documentary theater See theater of FACT

dodder Any of the leafless, twining, parasitic vines (see PARASITISM) that make up the genus *Cuscuta* (family Cuscutaceae), containing more than 150 species found throughout temperate and tropical regions. The stringlike stems may be yellow, orange, pink, or brown. Many species have been introduced with their host plants into new areas. Dodders contain no CHLOROPHYLL, instead absorbing water and food through rootlike organs called haustoria that penetrate the tissue of a host plant and may kill it. Dodder can do great damage to crops of CLOVER, ALFALFA, FLAX, HOPS, and BEANS. The best control is to remove the plant from fields by hand and to prevent its accidental introduction.

Dodder (*Cuscuta gronovii*).
RUSS KINNE–PHOTO RESEARCHERS

Dodge, Mary Mapes *orig.* **Mary Elizabeth Mapes** (1831–1905) U.S. author. Born in New York City, she began writing children's stories when she was suddenly widowed with two small sons. Her first collection, *Irvington Stories* (1864), was followed by *Hans Brinker; or, The Silver Skates* (1865), which became a children's classic. In 1873 she was named editor of the new children's magazine *St. Nicholas*; its success stemmed from her high standards, which attracted such writers as MARK TWAIN, LOUISA MAY ALCOTT, ROBERT LOUIS STEVENSON, and RUDYARD KIPLING.

Dodge, William E(arl) (1805–1883) U.S. mining entrepreneur. Born in Hartford, Conn., he was a dry-goods merchant before founding the metal dealership Phelps, Dodge & Co. with his father-in-law, Anson G. Phelps, in 1833. They soon established a prosperous metal-importing business. Dodge made numerous other investments in timberland, mills, and iron and copper mines. After purchasing the Copper Queen mine in Arizona in 1882, the company became a major U.S. mining concern, and today the diversified Phelps Dodge Corp. is one of the world's largest copper producers.

dodo Extinct flightless bird *(Raphus cucullatus)* of Mauritius, first seen by Portuguese sailors about 1507. Humans and the animals they introduced had exterminated the dodo by 1681. It weighed about 50 lbs (23 kg) and had blue-gray plumage, a big head, a 9-in. (23-cm) blackish bill with a reddish hooked tip, small useless wings, stout yellow legs, and a tuft of curly feathers high on its rear end. The Réunion solitaire *(R. solitarius),* also driven to extinction, may have been a white version of the dodo. Partial museum specimens and skeletons are all that remain of the dodo.

Restoration of a dodo (*Raphus cucullatus*).
BY COURTESY OF THE PEABODY MUSEUM OF NATURAL HISTORY, YALE UNIVERSITY

Dodoma \dō-'dō-mä\ City (pop., 1988: 204,000), Tanzania. Designated the national capital since 1974, it awaits complete transfer of official functions from DAR ES SALAAM, the current capital. Located in a sparsely populated agricultural region at an elevation of 3,720 ft (1,135 m), it is a market center for the surrounding area. Industries produce wood and furniture, beverages, processed food, soap, and oil.

Dodona \dō-'dō-nə\ Sanctuary of the Greek god ZEUS, located at EPIRUS. Mentioned by HOMER, it was the site of an ORACLE, where messages came through the rustling of leaves or other natural sounds. There was also a large bronze gong that vibrated in the breeze.

Doe, Samuel K(anyon) (1950/51–1990) Liberian soldier and head of state (1980–90). A member of the Krahn ethnic group, Doe led a coup in 1980 that overthrew Pres. William Tolbert (1913–1980). He suspended Liberia's constitution until 1984, and in 1985 won a presidential election widely denounced as fraudulent. His regime was considered corrupt and brutal, and his life was continually threatened by assassination attempts. In the civil war that broke out in 1989 Doe was captured and killed.

Doenitz, Karl See Karl DÖNITZ

Doesburg \'düs-ˌbœrg\, **Theo van** *orig.* **Christian Emil Maries Kupper** (1883–1931) Dutch painter, decorator, and art theorist. Originally involved in theater, in 1900 he began painting under the influence of Postimpressionism and Fauvism. After meeting PIET MONDRIAN in 1915, he turned to geometric abstraction. He was instrumental in founding the De STIJL group and the avant-garde periodical *De Stijl*. His advocacy of the geometric style was well received at the BAUHAUS, where he taught briefly and influenced LE CORBUSIER, WALTER GROPIUS, and LUDWIG MIES VAN DER ROHE. In 1926 he wrote his manifesto, *De Stijl*, and in 1930 he moved to Paris and opened a studio, which became the focus of the movement.

dog Any member of the CANINE genus *Canis,* particularly the domestic species, *Canis familiaris*. Domestic dogs seem to have decended from the WOLF or a wolflike ancestor. Dogs were apparently the first animals to be domesticated, and domestication seems to have begun in various parts of the world at roughly the same time. Selective breeding by humans has resulted in myriad domestic breeds that vary widely in size (from the tiny CHIHUAHUA to the huge MASTIFF), physical form (e.g., the short-legged DACHSHUND and the flat-faced BULLDOG), coat texture and length (e.g., the sleek DOBERMAN PINSCHER and the long-haired AFGHAN HOUND), and behavioral patterns (e.g., sporting dogs, TOY DOGS, and WORKING DOGS). The American Kennel Club now recognizes almost 150 breeds; other clubs, such as the United Kennel Club, recognize many more.

dog salmon See CHUM SALMON

Dog Star See SIRIUS

dogbane family Family Apocynaceae, of the GENTIAN order, with about 1,000 member species of trees, shrubs, woody vines, and herbaceous plants, found mostly in the tropics and subtropics. Dogbanes have milky, often poisonous juice and usually clustered, showy flowers. Garden ornamentals include PERIWINKLE, OLEANDER, yellow oleander *(Thevetia)*, FRANGIPANI, Natal plum *(Carissa),* and crepe jasmine *(Tabernaemontana coronaria)*. Some species are African SUCCULENTS. Arrow poisons are obtained from many dogbanes, and the poisonous ALKALOIDS of some species are used in medicines.

doge \'dōj\ (Venetian Italian: "duke") Highest official of the republic of VENICE in the 8th–18th century. The office originated when the city was nominally subject to the Byzantine empire and became permanent in the

8th century. The doge was chosen from among the ruling families of Venice and held office for life. He held extensive power, as evidenced by the rule of ENRICO DANDOLO (r.1192–1205), though from the 12th century the aristocracy placed limits on the doge's authority. Under Francesco Foscari (r.1423–57), Venice undertook the first conquests of the Italian mainland. The last doge was deposed when NAPOLEON conquered northern Italy in 1797.

Dogen \'dō-gen\ (1200–1253) Japanese Buddhist who introduced Soto ZEN to Japan from China. Orphaned at 7, he became a monk at 13. He studied in China under the Zen master Rujing 1223–27, and also studied with EISAI. He returned to Japan and taught Zen meditation, spending his last years at Eihei Temple, which he founded.

dogfish Any of several species of small SHARKS. The spiny dogfish (*Squalus acanthias,* family Squalidae) has a sharp spine in front of each of its two dorsal fins. It is abundant along northern Atlantic and Pacific coasts. It is gray with white spots, about 2–4 ft (60–120 cm) long, and often found in schools. It preys on fishes and invertebrates and often steals bait and damages fishing nets. It yields liver oil or is ground for fertilizer. Other well-known species are the spotted dogfishes (family Scyliorhinidae), which are sold as food, and the smooth hound or smooth dogfish (*Mustelus canis,* family Triakidae), one of the most common sharks on the U.S. Atlantic coast. See also BOWFIN.

Dogon \'dō-,gän\ People of the central plateau region of Mali, whose language is of uncertain affinity within the NIGER-CONGO family. Numbering about 350,000, the Dogon are mainly an agricultural people. They live in villages composed of elaborate mud buildings, often built on cliff faces. They are known for their fine wood sculptures, metalwork, and leatherwork.

dogsled racing Sport of racing sleds pulled by dogs over snow-covered cross-country courses. It developed from a traditional Eskimo method of transportation. Modern sleds are usually of wood (ash) construction, with leather lashings and steel- or aluminum-covered runners. Sled dogs are usually ESKIMO DOGS, SIBERIAN HUSKIES, SAMOYEDS, or ALASKAN MALAMUTES; teams typically consist of 4–10 dogs. The course is usually 12–30 mi (19–48 km) long, though some, including the IDITAROD, are considerably longer.

dogtooth violet Any of the approximately 20 species of spring-blooming plants that make up the genus *Erythronium,* in the LILY FAMILY, all native to North America except for the purple- or pink-flowered dogtooth violet of Europe *(E. dens-canis).* The nodding flowers, usually one to a plant or in small clusters, range in color from white to purple. The two leaves, borne at the base of the plant, often are covered with white or brown spots. The common dogtooth violet of North America, *E. americanum,* has yellow flowers and brown-mottled leaves. Several species are grown as rock-garden ornamentals.

dogwood Shrubs, trees, and herbaceous plants of the genus *Cornus,* in the dogwood family (Cornaceae), found in temperate and warm temperate zones and on tropical mountains. The family is noted for its woody ornamental species native to both coasts of North America and to eastern Asia and Europe. Some members, such as the flowering dogwood *(Cornus florida),* are chiefly ornamental; the European cornelian cherry *(C. mas),* also an ornamental, has edible fruit; others yield wood for furniture. In the flowering dogwoods, flowers are small and the conspicuously expanded structures are colored bracts that surround the cluster of true flowers.

Flowers of flowering dogwood (*Cornus florida*).

J.C. ALLEN AND SON

Doha \'dō-hə\ *Arabic* **Ad-Dawhah** \àd-'daù-hə\ City (pop., 1993 est.: 339,000), capital of Qatar. Located on the eastern coast of the Qatar Peninsula, it contains about three-fifths of Qatar's population. Long a center of pirate activity in the PERSIAN GULF, Doha was a small village when it became the capital of newly independent Qatar in 1971. The city has been thoroughly modernized. Its Government House (1969) was built on reclaimed waterfront land; its water supply is obtained by distilling seawater. The deepwater port, built in the 1970s, accommodates oceangoing vessels.

Doherty, Peter Charles (born 1940) Australian immunologist and pathologist. He earned a PhD at the University of Edinburgh. With ROLF ZINKERNAGEL, he found that T CELLS from mice infected with a meningitis virus destroyed virus-infected cells only from the same strain of mice, and showed that T cells must recognize two signals on an infected cell—one from the virus and one from the cell's own antigens—to destroy it. For the new understanding of general cellular immune mechanisms enabled by their research, the two men shared a 1996 Nobel Prize.

Dole, Robert J(oseph) (born 1923) U.S. politician. Born in Russell, Kan., he was seriously wounded during World War II; his recuperation from near-total paralysis left him without the use of his right hand. He returned to Kansas, earned a law degree, and held state elective office before serving in the U.S. House of Representatives (1961–69). He served in the U.S. Senate 1969–96. He was Pres. GERALD FORD's running mate in 1976. He became Senate majority leader in 1984 and minority leader in 1987. In 1996 he retired from the Senate to campaign for president; he received the Republican nomination but was defeated by WILLIAM JEFFERSON CLINTON. His wife, Elizabeth Hanford Dole (born 1936), ran unsuccessfully for the Republican nomination in 2000.

Dole, Sanford Ballard (1844–1926) Hawaiian politician. Born in Honolulu to U.S. missionaries, he served in Hawaii's legislature (1884–87) and on its supreme court (1887–93). He led the committee formed by local sugar interests that overthrew Queen LILIUOKALANI and sought annexation by the U.S., then served as the first president of the Republic of Hawaii 1894–1900. Pres. GROVER CLEVELAND blocked annexation and demanded the queen's restoration, but Dole pressed successfully for annexation and served as governor of the Territory of Hawaii 1900–3. He later became a federal district judge (1903–15).

dolerite See DIABASE

Dolin, Anton *later* **Sir Anton** *orig.* **Sydney F. P. C. Healey-Kay** (1904–1983) British dancer and choreographer. In 1921 he joined the BALLETS RUSSES, where he created leading roles as a soloist. In the 1930s and 1940s, he helped form several ballet companies; in 1949 he and his partner ALICIA MARKOVA founded the forerunner of London's Festival Ballet, of which he was artistic director and premier dancer until 1961. He created leading roles in *Le train bleu, Job,* and *Bluebeard,* choreographed such works as *Capriccioso* (1940), *The Romantic Age* (1942), and *Variations for Four* (1957), and wrote several books.

doline See SINKHOLE

doll Small-scale figure of a human being, used especially as a child's plaything. The doll is perhaps humankind's oldest toy, though some ancient dolls may have served religious or magical functions (similar to those served by the KACHINA doll). Dolls were buried in children's graves in Egypt, Greece, and Rome and in early Christian catacombs. In Europe, dolls have been commercially manufactured since about the 16th century. Doll heads were made of wood, terra-cotta, alabaster, and wax. In about 1820, glazed porcelain (Dresden) doll heads and unglazed bisque (ceramic) heads became popular. These were supplanted in the 20th century by molded plastic. In Japan, dolls are traditionally festival figures rather than playthings. In India, elaborately dressed dolls were given to child brides by both Hindus and Muslims. Today dolls are often collected as antiques.

Painted wooden Egyptian doll, 2000 BC.

BY COURTESY OF THE TRUSTEES OF THE BRITISH MUSEUM

Dollar Diplomacy U.S. foreign policy created by Pres. WILLIAM H. TAFT to ensure financial stability in a region in exchange for favorable treatment of U.S. commercial interests. It grew out of Pres. THEODORE ROOSEVELT's peaceful intervention in the Dominican Republic, where U.S. loans had been exchanged for the right to choose the head of customs (the country's major revenue source). The policy was carried out in Central America (1909) and China (1910) by Taft's secretary of state, PHILANDER KNOX. Pres. WOODROW WILSON repudiated the policy in 1913. The term has become a disparaging reference to the manipulation of foreign affairs for economic ends.

Dollfuss \'dȯl-ˌfüs\, **Engelbert** (1892–1934) Austrian politician. He rose rapidly in Austrian politics to become chancellor in 1932. Opposed to the Nazis, he welcomed BENITO MUSSOLINI as an ally, converting Austria virtually into an Italian satellite state. In 1933 he abolished the parliament and established an authoritarian regime based on conservative Roman Catholic and Italian Fascist principles. In 1934 after paramilitary groups loyal to him crushed Austria's Social Democrats, he issued a new constitution establishing a dictatorship. Germany soon incited the Austrian Nazis to civil war, and Dollfuss was assassinated in a raid on the chancellery.

Dollond \'däl-ənd\, **John and George** (1706–1761, 1774–1852) British optical scientists. John developed an achromatic (non-color-distorting) refracting TELESCOPE and a practical heliometer (a telescope that measures the sun's diameter and the angles between celestial bodies). His grandson George worked most of his life for the family firm of instrument makers, inventing various precision instruments used in astronomy, geodesy, and navigation. His MICROMETER made of rock crystal was used by astronomers; his atmospheric recorder simultaneously measured and recorded on paper tape temperature, atmospheric pressure, wind speed and direction, evaporation, and electrical phenomena.

dolmen \'dōl-mən\ Prehistoric monument usually consisting of several large stone slabs set edgewise in the earth to support a flat stone roof, all covered by a mound of earth that in most cases has weathered away. Designed as a burial chamber, the structure is typical of the NEOLITHIC PERIOD in Europe. Dolmens, though found as far east as Japan, are mainly confined to western Europe and northern Africa. See also MEGALITH, MENHIR.

Dolmen at Pentre Evan, Dyfed, Wales.

Dolmetsch \'däl-ˌmech\, **(Eugène) Arnold** (1858–1940) French-British music scholar and performer. He moved to England after studying violin with Henri Vieuxtemps (1820–1881). There he began collecting, repairing, and learning to play old instruments. He built copies of old lutes, clavichords, harpsichords, and recorders, ultimately involving his wife and children in the performance and promulgation of early music. His *Interpretation of Music of the 17th and 18th Centuries* (1915) was highly influential, and he is regarded as the father of the 20th-century early-music revival.

dolomite Type of limestone, the carbonate fraction of which is dominated by the mineral dolomite, calcium magnesium carbonate $CaMg(CO_3)_2$. The CARBONATE MINERAL dolomite occurs in marbles, talc schists, and other magnesium-rich metamorphic rocks. It occurs in hydrothermal veins, in cavities in carbonate rocks, and less often in various sedimentary rocks as a cement. It is most common as a rock-forming mineral in carbonate rocks.

Dolomites \ˌdō-lə-ˌmīts\ *Italian* **Alpi Dolomitiche** \'äl-pē-dō-lō-'mē-tē-kē\ Mountain group, northern Italian Alps. Including a number of impressive peaks, 18 of which rise to more than 10,000 ft (3,050 m), the range and its characteristic rock are named for the 18th-century French geologist Dieudonné Dolomieu, who made the first scientific study of the region. The mountains are formed of light-colored dolomitic limestone, which erosion has carved into grotesque shapes. Popular with tourists and mountain-climbers, the area has a number of resort towns.

dolphin Either of two types of animals: aquatic mammals or oceanic fishes. Mammalian dolphins are small TOOTHED WHALES, usually with a well-defined, beaklike snout. (They are often called PORPOISES, but that name is properly reserved for a blunt-snouted whale family.) The common dolphin *(Delphinus delphis)* and the BOTTLENOSE DOLPHIN, both of the family Delphinidae, are found widely in warm temperate seas. Most of the 32 delphinid species are marine, gray, blackish or brown above and pale below; and about 3–13 ft (1–4 m) long. River dolphins (family Platanistidae; four species) live mainly in freshwater in South America and Asia. The little-known dolphins of the family Stenidae (eight species), or long-snouted dolphins, inhabit tropical rivers and oceans and are sometimes grouped with the Delphinidae. One of the two fish species, *Coryphaena hippuras* (family Coryphaenidae), also called mahimahi and dorado, is a popular food and sport fish of tropical and temperate waters worldwide. The pompano dolphin *(C. equiselis)* is similar. See also KILLER WHALE.

Bottle-nosed dolphins (*Tursiops truncatus*).

Domagk \'dō-ˌmäk\, **Gerhard** (1895–1964) German bacteriologist and pathologist. While director of the Bayer Laboratory for Experimental Pathology and Bacteriology, Domagk noticed the antibacterial action of a dye, Prontosil red, against streptococcal infection in mice. Found to be an effective treatment in humans, Prontosil became the first sulfonamide drug. Awarded a Nobel Prize in 1939, Domagk was unable to accept it at the time because of Nazi policy. He also was active in research on tuberculosis and cancer.

domain name Address of a computer, organization, or other entity on a TCP/IP network such as the INTERNET. Domain names are typically in a three-level "server.organization.type" format. The top level denotes the type of organization, such as "com" (for commercial sites) or "edu" (for educational sites); the second level is the top level plus the name of the organization (e.g., "britannica.com" for Encyclopædia Britannica); and the third level identifies a specific host server at the address, such as the "www" (WORLD WIDE WEB) host server for "www.britannica.com". A domain name is ultimately mapped to an IP ADDRESS, but two or more domain names can be mapped to the same IP address. A domain name must be unique on the Internet, and must be assigned by a registrar accredited by the Internet Corporation for Assigned Names and Numbers (ICANN). See also URL.

Dombrowska, Maria See Maria DABROWSKA

dome In architecture, a hemispherical structure evolved from the ARCH, forming a ceiling or roof. Domes first appeared on round huts and tombs in the ancient Middle East, India, and the Mediterranean in forms, such as solid mounds, adaptable only to the smallest buildings. The Romans introduced the large-scale masonry hemisphere. A dome exerts thrust all around its perimeter, and the earliest monumental examples (see PANTHEON) required heavy supporting walls. Byzantine architects invented a technique for raising domes on piers, making the transition from a cubic base to the hemisphere by four PENDENTIVES. Bulbous or pointed domes were widely used in Islamic architecture. The design spread to Russia, where it gained great popularity in the form of the onion dome, a pointed, domelike roof structure. The modern geodesic dome, developed by R. BUCKMINSTER FULLER, is fabricated of lightweight triangular framing that distributes stresses within the structure itself. See illustration opposite on following page.

Dome of the Rock *or* **Mosque of Omar** Oldest existing Islamic monument. It is located on Temple Mount, previously the site of the Temple of JERUSALEM. The rock over which it is built is sacred to both Muslims and Jews. In Islam, MUHAMMAD is believed to have ascended into heaven from the site. In Judaism it is the site where ABRAHAM prepared to sacrifice his son Isaac. Built in 685–91 as a place of pilgrimage, the octagonal building has richly decorated walls and a gold-overlaid dome mounted above a circle of piers and columns.

Domenichino \ˌdō-mā-nē-'kē-nō\ *orig.* **Domenico Zampieri** (1581–1641) Italian painter. He was trained in the academy of CARRACCI FAMILY in Bologna. In 1602 he joined the Bolognese artists in Rome working under CARRACCI FAMILY in the decoration of the Farnese Palace. His easel paintings were noted for their idyllic mood and subdued color, a radical departure from the monumental classicism of his frescoes. He became Rome's leading painter and had a succession of major decorative commissions. He was an outstanding draftsman and portraitist; his paintings were regarded as second only to those of RAPHAEL throughout the 17th–18th century, and had great influence on NICOLAS POUSSIN and CLAUDE LORRAIN.

"Last Communion of Saint Jerome," oil painting by Domenichino, 1614; in the Vatican Museum.

SCALA—ART RESOURCE

Domenico Veneziano \dō-'mā-nē-kō-və-ˌnet-sē-'ä-nō\ (fl. 1438–1461) Italian painter. Born in Venice, he was active mainly in Florence. Two signed works survive: fresco fragments of the Virgin and Child from a street tabernacle (1430s) and the altarpiece for the church of Santa Lucia dei Magnoli, called the St. Lucy Altarpiece (c. 1445), one of the outstanding Florentine paintings of the mid-15th century and Domenico's most successful experiment in rendering outdoor light. He used color and texture as the basis of perspective and composition; his influence can be seen in the work of ALESSO BALDOVINETTI.

Domesday Book \'düimz-ˌdā, 'dōmz-ˌdā\ (1086) Original record or summary of WILLIAM I the Conqueror's survey of England. The most remarkable administrative feat of the Middle Ages, the survey was carried out, against popular resentment, by panels of commissioners who compiled accounts of the estates of the king and his tenants. As summarized in the Domesday Book, it now serves as the starting point for the history of most English towns and villages. Originally called "the description of England," the name Domesday Book (a reference to doomsday, when people face a final accounting of their lives) was later popularly attached to it.

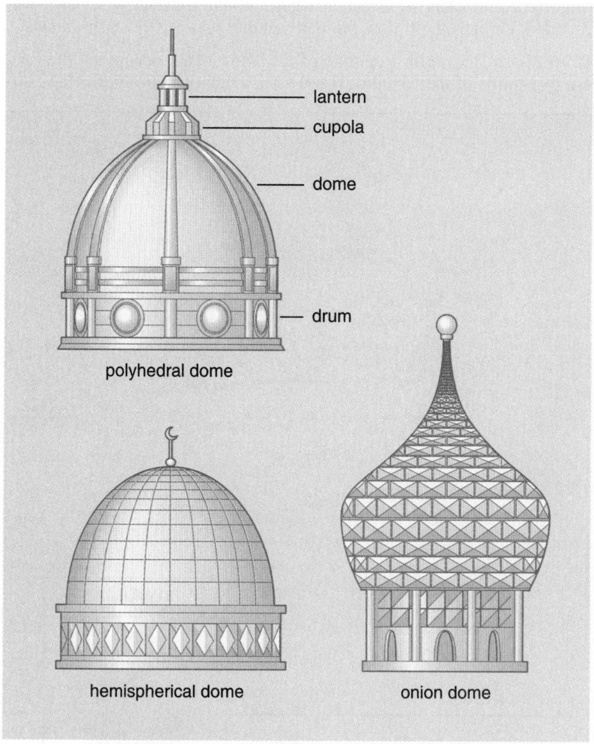

A dome is traditionally supported primarily by a cylindrical or polygonal drum; it may be surmounted by a cupola, which may have a lantern to admit light. The classic hemispherical dome has a circular base and semicircular section; the polyhedral dome has segments resting on a polyhedral base and meeting at the top; the onion dome rests on a circular base and has an ogee section.

domestic cat *or* **house cat** Domesticated CARNIVORE *(Felis catus)* that retains many of the characteristics of the larger wild CATS but differs in coat and size. Breeds are either shorthaired (e.g., SIAMESE) or longhaired (e.g., PERSIAN). Domestic cats are usually white, black, yellow, or gray, sometimes with markings of a different color. A pattern of dark stripes or swirls on a lighter background is called tabby. Males may reach lengths of 28 in. (71 cm), and females are usually about 20 in. (51 cm); weights generally vary from 6 to 10 lbs (2.5–4.5 kg). Nonpedigreed cats may weigh up to 28 lbs (13 kg). The most closely related wild species are the North African wildcats (including *Felix lybica*); as a result of their valuable mouse and rat hunting, which protected farmers' grain supplies, they were being domesticated in ancient Egypt by 1500 BC. The Cat Fanciers' Association now recognizes about 37 breeds.

domestic service Employment of hired workers by private households for tasks including housecleaning, cooking, child care, gardening, and personal service. It also includes the performance of similar tasks for hire in public institutions and businesses, including hotels and boardinghouses. In ancient Greece and Rome, domestic service was performed almost exclusively by slaves. In medieval Europe, serfs provided much of the necessary labor force. Indentured servants were widely used in colonial America, as were black slaves in the pre-Civil War South. In Victorian England, many middle- and upper-class households hired domestic servants; the royalty and gentry often employed huge staffs with an elaborate hierarchy. Domestic service has declined in the U.S. and Europe since the early 1920s, a trend attributed to the leveling of social classes, greater job opportunities for women, and the spread of labor-saving household devices.

domestic system *or* **putting-out system** Production system widespread in 17th-century. Europe in which merchant-employers "put out" materials to rural home workers, who then returned finished products to the employers for payment. The domestic system differed from the handicraft system of home production in that the workers neither bought materials nor sold products. It undermined the urban GUILDS and brought the first widespread industrial employment of women and children. The system was generally superseded by employment in FACTORIES but was retained in the 20th century in some industries, notably watchmaking in Switzerland, toy manufacturing in Germany, and many industries in India and China.

domestic tragedy Drama in which the main characters are ordinary people. This form of tragedy contrasts with classical tragedy, in which the main characters are of royal or aristocratic rank. An early domestic tragedy, *A Warning for Faire Women* (1599), dealt with the murder of a merchant by his wife. The form became popular in the mid-18th century and reached its maturity in the 19th-century bourgeois tragedies of HENRIK IBSEN. GERHART HAUPTMANN, EUGENE O'NEILL, and ARTHUR MILLER wrote important 20th-century domestic tragedies.

domestication Process of hereditary reorganization of wild animals and plants into forms more accommodating to the interests of people. In its strictest sense, it refers to the initial stage of human mastery of wild animals and plants. The fundamental distinction of domesticated animals and plants from their wild ancestors is that they are created by human labor to meet specific requirements or whims and are adapted to the conditions of continuous care people maintain for them. A variety of animals have been domesticated for food (e.g., CATTLE, CHICKENS, PIGS), clothing (e.g., SHEEP, SILKWORMS), transportation and labor (e.g., CAMELS, DONKEYS, HORSES), and pleasure (e.g., CATS, DOGS). See also BREEDING, SELECTION.

domicile Place where an individual has a fixed and permanent home for legal purposes. The term refers to the place where an organization (e.g., a corporation) is chartered or that is the organization's principal place of business. The domicile of an individual or organization determines the proper jurisdiction and venue for legal process, including taxation. For persons lacking capacity (e.g., minors), domicile is usually defined as the domicile of the guardian.

dominance In genetics, the greater influence by one of a pair of GENES (alleles) that affect the same inherited trait. If an individual pea plant that has one allele for tallness and one for shortness is the same height as an individual that has two alleles for tallness, the tallness allele is said to be completely dominant. If such an individual is shorter than an individual that has two tallness alleles but still taller than one that has two shortness alleles, the tallness allele is said to be partially or incompletely dominant and the shortness allele is said to be recessive (see RECESSIVENESS).

Domingo, Plácido (born 1941) Spanish tenor and conductor. Born in Madrid, he moved with his parents, both zarzuela singers, to Mexico in 1949. He studied voice, piano, and conducting, making his debut as a baritone. After developing his tenor range, he made his U.S. debut with J. SUTHERLAND, spent three years in Tel Aviv (singing in Hebrew), came to the New York City Opera in 1965, and debuted with the Metropolitan Opera at Lewissohn Stadium in 1966. Acclaimed for his great musicality and impressive voice, he has a repertoire of some 80 roles.

Dominic, St. *orig.* **Domingo de Guzmán** (c. 1170–1221) Founder of the Order of Friars Preachers, or DOMINICANS. Born in Spain, he joined the religious community of the cathedral of Osma c. 1196. On a visit to southern France in 1203, he encountered the Albigensian heresy (see CATHARI) and determined to fight it. He gathered a group of preachers willing to travel the roads barefoot and in poverty, and in 1206 he founded a convent of nuns converted from heresy. While designing his order devoted to preaching, Dominic may first have met St. FRANCIS OF ASSISI, who became his good friend. In 1216 he received sanction for his order from Pope HONORIUS III. He established schools of theology at his two principal houses near the Univs. of Paris and Bologna.

St. Dominic, detail of a panel by the school of Messina (?), 15th century; in the Museo Archeologico Nazionale, Palermo, Italy.
ANDERSON–ALINARI FROM ART RESOURCE

Dominica \ˌdä-mə-ˈnē-kə\ *officially* **Commonwealth of Dominica** Island republic of the LESSER ANTILLES in the Caribbean Sea, between the French islands of GUADELOUPE and MARTINIQUE. Area: 289 sq mi (749 sq km). Population (1997 est.): 74,400. Capital: ROSEAU. The majority of the people are of African or mixed African and European descent. Languages: English (official), French patois. Religion: mainly Roman Catholicism. Currency: Eastern Caribbean dollar. A mountainous island, it is broken midway by a plain drained by the Layou River. It has a warm tropical climate with heavy rainfall. Among the poorest of the Caribbean nations, its main crop is bananas. A developing tourist trade was helped by the establishment in 1975 of Morne Trois Pitons National Park, a unique tropical mountain wilderness, but the country was ravaged by hurricanes in 1979 and 1980. With financial help from Britain, it is trying to protect its coastline. It is a republic with one legislative house; its chief of state is the president, and its head of government is the prime minister. At the time of CHRISTOPHER COLUMBUS arrival in 1493, it was inhabited by the CARIBS. With its steep coastal cliffs and inaccessible mountains, it was one of the last islands to be explored by Europeans, and the Caribs remained in possession until the 18th century; it was then settled by the French and ultimately taken by Britain in 1783. Subsequent hostilities between the settlers and the native inhabitants resulted in the Caribs' near extinction. Incorporated with the LEEWARD ISLANDS in 1833 and with the WINDWARD ISLANDS in 1940, it became a member of the West Indies Federation in 1958. Dominica became independent in 1978. See also WEST INDIES.

Dominican Member of the Order of Friars Preachers, a Roman Catholic preaching and teaching order founded by St. DOMINIC. It dates officially from 1216, when Pope HONORIUS III gave it his approval, though Dominic had begun to build it at least a decade earlier. In contrast with earlier orders, the Dominicans were not organized in autonomous monastic houses, but joined the order at large and could be sent to any house or province on the order's business. The early teaching centers

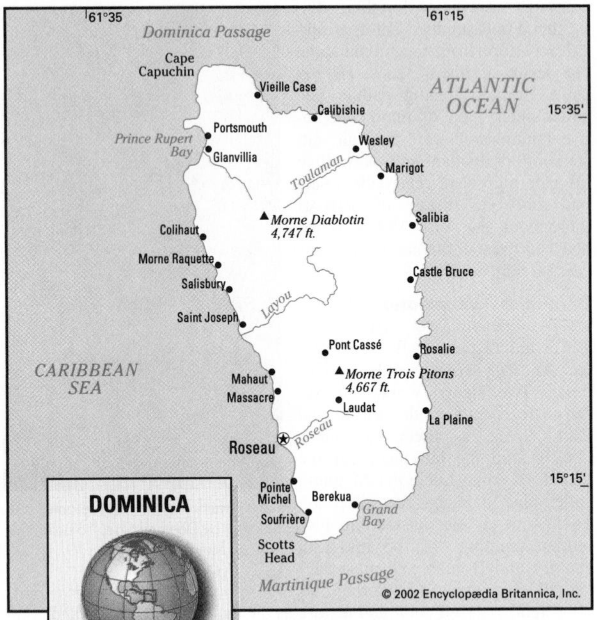

were at Bologna, Paris, Cologne, and Oxford. Dominican preachers spoke out against the CATHARI, the MOORS, and the Jews and were among the first missionaries under the Spanish and Portuguese explorers. Dominicans were put in charge of the INQUISITION when it was founded. Perhaps their most famous member was St. THOMAS AQUINAS.

Dominican Republic Republic of the WEST INDIES, occupying the eastern two-thirds of the island of HISPANIOLA, which it shares with Haiti. Area: 18,657 sq mi (48,322 sq km). Population (1997 est.): 7,802,000. Capital: SANTO DOMINGO. The majority of the people are of mixed European and African ancestry. Language: Spanish (official). Religion: mainly Roman Catholicism. Currency: Dominican peso. The country is generally mountainous, with ranges and hills running from northwest to

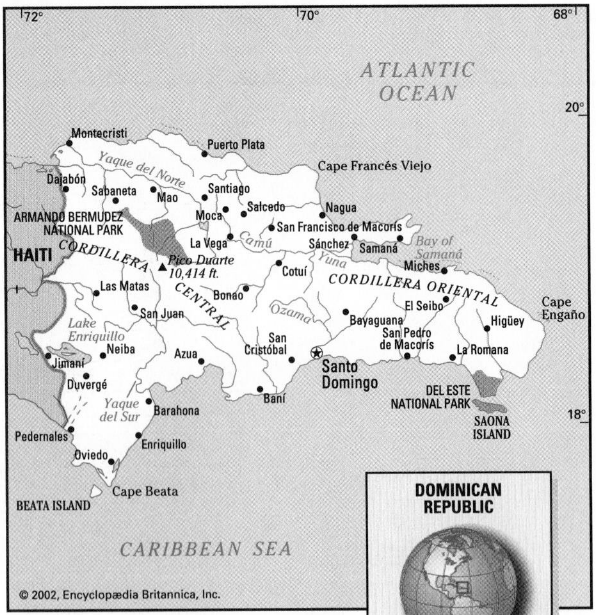

southeast. The Central Highlands reach a height of 10,417 ft (3,175 m) at Duarte Peak, the highest point in the West Indies. The Cibao Valley in the north is noted for its fertility; the western part of the country is generally dry with large stretches of desert. One of the poorest countries of the Caribbean, it has a mixed economy heavily dependent on the production and export of sugar. It is a republic with two legislative houses; its head of state and government is the president. The Dominican Republic was originally part of the Spanish colony of Hispaniola. In 1697 the western third of the island, which later became Haiti, was ceded to France; the remainder of the island passed to France in 1795. The eastern two-thirds of the island were returned to Spain in 1809, and the colony declared its independence in 1821. Within a matter of weeks it was overrun by Haitian troops and occupied until 1844. Since then the country has been under the rule of a succession of dictators, except for short interludes of democratic government, and the U.S. has frequently been involved in its affairs. The termination of the dictatorship of RAFAEL TRUJILLO in 1961 led to civil war in 1965, and U.S. military intervention. The country suffered from severe hurricanes in 1979 and 1998.

domino theory *or* **domino effect** Theory of U.S. foreign policy that if one noncommunist state "fell" to COMMUNISM, so would its neighbors. The theory was first enunciated by Pres. HARRY TRUMAN, who used it to justify sending military aid to Greece and Turkey in the late 1940s. DWIGHT D. EISENHOWER, JOHN F. KENNEDY, and LYNDON B. JOHNSON used it to justify military involvement in Asia, especially the prosecution of the VIETNAM WAR.

dominoes Game of several variations played with a set of flat rectangular blocks (dominoes) whose faces are divided into two equal parts that are blank or bear from one to six dots arranged as on DICE faces. The usual set consists of 28 pieces. Dominoes in China may date to the 12th century AD; the Eskimos have also long played a domino-like game. There is no record of dominoes in Europe before the mid-18th century. The principle in nearly all modern dominoes games is to match one end of a piece to another that is identically or reciprocally numbered. The game may be set at 50 or 100 points.

Domitian \də-'mish-ən\ *Latin* **Caesar Domitianus Augustus** *orig.* **Titus Flavius Domitianus** (AD 51–96) Roman emperor (81–96). The son of VESPASIAN, he succeeded his brother TITUS, whom he probably had killed. His administration was ostensibly egalitarian and based on precedent, but his laws were severe. Defeats in Britain and Germany undid his successes, though increased pay for the army kept it loyal. From 89 he became crueler, imposing a reign of terror over prominent senators and confiscating his victims' property to cover imperial expenses. The group that killed him included his wife and possibly his successor, NERVA.

domovoy \də-mə-'vȯi\ In Slavic mythology and folklore, a spirit-guardian of home and family. It never leaves the household to which it belongs. It favors hardworking people; when displeased with its family, it may cause trouble with farm animals or make knocking or grating noises. Its weeping, moaning, or singing are interpreted as portents of evil or good.

Dôn \'dōn\ In Welsh mythology, a mother-goddess, the counterpart of the Irish Danu. According to the MABINOGION, she was the sister of the magician-king Math and the mother of Gwydion (a master of magic and poetry) and Arianrhod, who was in turn the mother of Dylan (presumed to be a sea god) and Lleu Llaw Gyffes (probably the Welsh form of LUGUS).

Don Juan Fictional character famous as a heartless womanizer but also noted for his charm and courage. In Spanish legend, Don Juan was a licentious rogue who seduced a young girl of noble family and killed her father. Coming across a stone effigy of the father in a cemetery, he invited it home to dine with him, and the ghost of the father arrived for dinner as the harbinger of Don Juan's death. Don Juan's first literary appearance was in TIRSO DE MOLINA's tragedy *The Seducer of Seville* (1630). He was the hero-villain of W.A. MOZART's opera *Don Giovanni* (1787), of plays by MOLIÈRE and GEORGE BERNARD SHAW, and of Lord BYRON's long satiric poem *Don Juan* (1819–24).

Don Pacifico Affair (1850) Conflict between Britain and Greece that originated when the home of David Pacifico (known as Don Pacifico), a British subject living in Athens, was burned down in an anti-Semitic riot. In support of his demand for compensation, VISCOUNT PALMERSTON sent a naval squadron to blockade the Greek coast. Palmerston's policy drew protests from France and Russia as well as Britain's House of Lords, but he won the support of the Commons after arguing that Britain should protect its subjects from injustice wherever they might live.

Don River \'dȯn\ *Tatar* **Duna** \'dü-nə\ *ancient* **Tanais.** River, southwestern Russia. Rising south of MOSCOW in the central Russian uplands, it flows generally south for 1,162 mi (1,870 km) to enter the Gulf of Taganrog in the Sea of AZOV. In its middle course it flows into the Tsimlyansk Reservoir, which dominates the Don's lower course. Most of its basin is rich farmland and timberland. A major shipping artery, it is navigable (in the spring) as far as 990 mi (1,584 km) from the Sea of Azov.

Donahue, Phil (born 1935) U.S. television personality. Born in Cleveland, he began as a reporter and anchor at a Dayton radio station (1959–67), then hosted *The Phil Donahue Show* on television (1967–74). With his syndicated talk show, produced first in Chicago (1974–85) and later in New York (1985–96), he pioneered the noncelebrity talk show, in which a topical social issue was discussed by a panel of guests affected by it. His show won some 20 Emmy awards. The format he introduced gradually degenerated into confessional and confrontational spectacles that became known as "tabloid TV."

Donaldson, Walter (1893–1947) U.S. songwriter. A native of Brooklyn, he began his career as a music publisher's pianist, and would later establish his own music publishing company. After his first Broadway success with "My Mammy," introduced by A. JOLSON in *Sinbad* (1918), he continued writing for Broadway revues for more than 25 years, producing such songs as "My Buddy," "My Blue Heaven," "Carolina in the Morning," "Yes Sir! That's My Baby," and "Makin' Whoopee." He also wrote for many films, including *The Great Ziegfeld* (1936), *After the Thin Man* (1936), and *Saratoga* (1937).

donatário Recipient of a *capitanía* (captaincy), which was both a territorial division and a royal land grant in Portugal's colonies. The system was introduced to Brazil in 1533 by King John III in order to consolidate Portuguese power in the colony. Each donatário received a portion of land and was charged with gathering and protecting settlers and promoting agriculture and commerce. At one time Brazil's viability as a colony depended on the success of the donatários, but by 1754 all the captaincies had been abolished.

Donatello \ˌdō-nä-'tel-lō, *Engl* ˌdä-nə-'te-lō\ *orig.* **Donato di Niccolò** (c. 1386–1466) Italian sculptor active in Florence. He learned stone carving from the sculptors of the Florence Cathedral (c. 1400), and in 1404 joined the workshop of LORENZO GHIBERTI. He drew his inspiration from classical and medieval sources. With his marble statues of St. Mark (1411–13) and St. George (c. 1415) for the church of Or San Michele in Florence, he revolutionized the concept of sculpture; not since antiquity had the human body been rendered with such naturalism and emotional impact. He invented his own style of bas-relief with his marble panel *St. George Killing the Dragon* (c. 1417). His bronze sculpture *David,* conceived independently of any architectural setting, was the first large-scale, free-standing nude statue of the Renaissance. In Florence he worked for the MEDICI FAMILY (1433–43), producing sculptural decoration for the sacristy of San Lorenzo, the Medici family church, and in Padua (1450s) for the church of Sant'Antonio. He was the greatest European sculptor of the 15th century, influencing painters as well as sculptors, and was a founder of the Renaissance style.

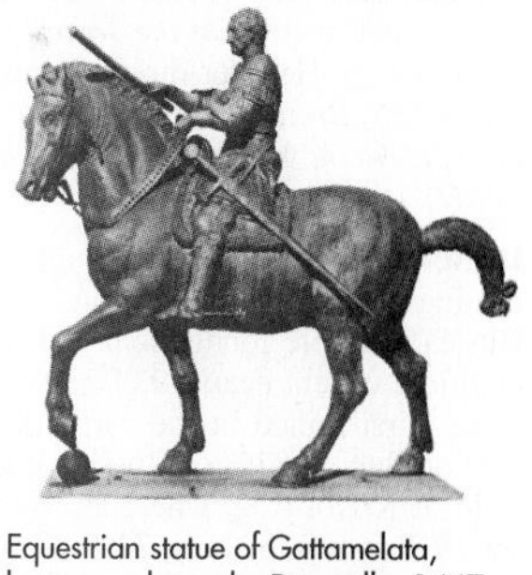

Equestrian statue of Gattamelata, bronze sculpture by Donatello, 1447–53; in the Piazza del Santo, Padua, Italy.

ANDERSON—ALINARI FROM ART RESOURCE/EB INC.

Donation of Constantine Document concerning the supposed grant by CONSTANTINE I the Great to Pope Sylvester I (314–35) and later popes of temporal power over Rome and the Western Empire. The gift was said to have been motivated by Constantine's gratitude to Sylvester for miraculously healing his leprosy and converting him to Christianity. Proved in the 15th century to be a forgery, the document was already questioned by the emperor OTTO III but was often cited in the 11th–15th century to support papal claims in the struggle between church and state.

Donation of Pepin (754) Promise made by the Frankish king PEPIN III to win for Pope STEPHEN II (III) lands in Italy conquered by the Lombards. In 756 it was written in a document that became the basis of papal rule over central Italy, which lasted until the 19th century. Pepin made the donation to repay the pope for his support when he deposed the last of the MEROVINGIANS and took the Frankish throne. Pepin won territory from the Lombard king in two military campaigns (754, 756) and gave it to the papacy. The donation was later confirmed and enlarged by CHARLEMAGNE (774).

Donatism \'dō-nə-ˌti-zəm, 'dä-nə-ˌti-zəm\ Schismatic Christian movement in North Africa in the 4th century. It arose out of the debate over the status of church leaders who had cooperated with Roman officials during persecutions of Christians. The movement's leader, Donatus (died c. AD 355), denied the validity of priestly duties performed by such leaders, insisting that lapsed Christians were not in a state of grace and thus had no authority to administer the sacraments. The struggle over the Donatist heresy came to a head in 311, when Caecilian was consecrated bishop of Carthage by a lapsed bishop. The Donatists declared the election invalid, but CONSTANTINE I decided in favor of Caecilian, prompting the Donatists to break with the Roman church in 312. Despite persecution, Donatism survived in North Africa until the advent of Islam (7th century).

Donbas See DONETS BASIN

Donders \'dȯn-dərz\, **Frans Cornelis** (1818–1889) Dutch ophthalmologist. His study of "muscae volitantes" (spots before the eyes) resulted in Donders' law, stating that the rotation of the eye around the line of sight is involuntary. His research improved diagnosis, operative treatment, and use of eyeglasses for vision problems. He found that in farsightedness the eyeball is shortened, resulting in light rays being focused behind the retina (1858). His finding that astigmatism is caused by uneven cornea and lens surfaces (1862) created the field of scientific clinical refraction. His *On the Anomalies of Accommodation and Refraction* (1864) was the first authoritative work in the field.

Donen \'dō-nən\, **Stanley** (born 1924) U.S. film director and choreographer. Born in Columbia, S.C., he began his career in the stage chorus of *Pal Joey* (1940), where he met GENE KELLY. He and Kelly choreographed *Best Foot Forward* (1941; film, 1943) and other musicals, and the two codirected *On the Town* (1949) and the acclaimed *Singin' in the Rain* (1952). He later directed and produced such films as *Seven Brides for Seven Brothers* (1954), *The Pajama Game* (1957), *Funny Face* (1957), *Damn Yankees* (1958), *Charade* (1963), and *Two for the Road* (1967).

Donets Basin \də-'nyets, *Engl* də-'nets\ *or* **Donbas** \'dän-ˌbas\ Large mining and industrial region, southeastern Ukraine and southwestern Russia. Notable for its coal and iron reserves, the exploited area of the coalfield covers nearly 9,000 sq mi (23,300 sq km) south of the DONETS RIVER. First mined in the early 19th century, by 1913 the Donets Basin was producing 87% of Russian coal. The coalfields adjoin the rich ironfield of Krivoi Rog, where an ironworks was set up in 1872 in DONETSK; by 1913 it was making 74% of all Russian pig iron. The area today is the largest single producing area of iron and steel in Ukraine and one of the world's major heavy-industrial complexes.

Donets River River, southwestern Russia and eastern Ukraine. Rising in the Central Russian Upland, it winds south and east through Russia and Ukraine for some 650 mi (1,050 km) to join the DON RIVER below Konstantinovsk. It flows along the northern DONETS BASIN industrial region, which uses it for heavy shipping and also causes severe pollution problems. A water shortage in the river and industrial area led to the construction in the 1970s of a canal connecting the DNIEPER to the Donets. Six weirs make navigation possible upstream to the city of DONETSK.

Donetsk \də-'nyetsk\ *formerly (1924–61)* **Stalino** \'stä-lyi-nō\ City (pop., 1998 est.: 1,065,400), southeastern Ukraine. In 1872 an ironworks was founded there by a Welshman, John Hughes, to produce iron rails for the growing Russian rail network. Fueled by the rich deposits of the DONETS BASIN, both coal mining and steelmaking developed rapidly. Heavy destruction in World War II led to postwar modernization, and subsequent growth has been rapid. Modern Donetsk is one of Ukraine's largest metallurgical centers.

Dong-nai River *or* **Donnai River** \'dȯŋ-'nī\ River, southern Vietnam. Rising in the central highlands, it flows southwest for about 300 mi (480 km), joining the Saigon River northeast of HO CHI MINH CITY and combining with it and other streams to form an estuary north of the MEKONG delta.

Dong Qichang *or* **Tung Ch'i-ch'ang** \'du̇ŋ-'chē-'chäŋ\ (1555–1636) Chinese painter, calligrapher, and theoretician of the late Ming period. He is noted especially for his writings on Chinese painting, which he divided into the Northern school, which taught the acquisition of truth, and the Southern school, which emphasized sudden, intuitive understanding. At the center of the scholarly ideal of the Southern school was the art of calligraphy, which expressed the true nature of the artist without the interposition of pictorial description. Dong Qichang's own paintings stress stark forms, seemingly anomalous spatial renderings, and naive handling of ink and brush. His ideas continue to influence Chinese aesthetic theory.

Dong Son culture \'dȯŋ-'sȯn\ Important prehistoric culture of Indochina that developed in the 1st millennium BC, best known for its bronzes. Excavations at the site of Dong Son in northern Vietnam revealed bronze objects, iron, pottery, and Chinese artifacts. The Dong Son were a seafaring people who traded throughout S.East Asia. They are credited with making the Red River delta area a great rice-growing region. Dong Son culture, transformed by Chinese and Indian influence, became the basis of the general civilization of Indochina. The Dong Son homeland was taken over by HAN-DYNASTY China in AD 43.

Dong Thap Muoi See Plain of REEDS

Dong Zhongshu *or* **Tung Chung-shu** \'du̇ŋ-'ju̇ŋ-'shü\ (179?–104? BC) Confucian scholar. As chief minister to WUDI of the Han dynasty, he dismissed all non-Confucian scholars from government. He established CONFUCIANISM as the empire's unifying ideology (136 BC) and set up an imperial college, instrumental in the later establishment of the Chinese civil service. As a philosopher, he made the theory of the interaction between heaven and humanity his central theme. He merged the YIN-YANG concept with Confucianism and believed that one of the emperor's duties was to preserve the balance of yin and yang. His *Chunqiu fanlu* is one of the most important philosophical works of the Han period.

Dongan \'däŋ-gən\, **Thomas** (1634–1715) British colonial governor of New York. A member of an Irish royalist family, he was exiled to France after the English Civil Wars, but recalled to England in 1677 and sent to America. As governor of New York (1682–88), he organized the colony's first representative assembly, issued a "Charter of Liberties" in 1683, and pursued a policy of cooperation with the Iroquois Confederacy against the French. He returned to England in 1691.

Dongbei See MANCHURIA

Donglin Academy *or* **Tung-lin Academy** \'du̇ŋ-'lin\ Chinese academy founded during the SONG DYNASTY and revived in 1604 by scholars and officials to protest the moral laxity and intellectual weakness undermining public life in the last years of the MING DYNASTY. Its members cultivated the antiabsolutist views of MENCIUS and rebuked the court for failing to uphold Confucian values. The court eunuch WEI ZHONGXIAN persecuted members and supporters of the Academy, practically wiping it out by 1627. It was rehabilitated after Wei's death.

Dongting, Lake *or* **Dongting Hu** *or* **Tung-t'ing Hu** \'du̇ŋ-'tiŋ-'hü\ Large, shallow lake, northeastern HUNAN province, China. Its size varies greatly from season to season. Its normal area of 1,089 sq mi (2,820 sq km) may increase up to 7,700 sq mi (20,000 sq km) in flood season. Some two-fifths of the water from the YANGTZE RIVER (Chang Jiang) flows into the lake through four channels. It also is fed by the Zi, YUAN, XIANG, and Li rivers. It discharges into the Yangtze.

Dönitz \'dœ̄-nits, *Engl* 'dər-nəts\, **Karl** *or* **Karl Doenitz** (1891–1980) German admiral. After serving as a submarine officer in World War I, he oversaw the creation of the German U-BOAT fleet in the 1930s, thus violating the Treaty of VERSAILLES. As the fleet's commander, he conducted the Battle of the ATLANTIC in World War II, then served as commander in chief of the navy 1943–45. He succeeded ADOLF HITLER as Germany's leader in the last few days of the war and executed Germany's surrender to the Allies. Convicted of war crimes at the Nuremberg Trials, he served 10 years in prison.

Donizetti \ˌdō-nēd-ˈzä-tē, *Engl* ˌdä-nə-ˈze-tē\, **Gaetano (Domenico Maria)** (1797–1848) Italian opera composer. He was tutored and guided by the opera composer Simone Mayr (1763–1845), and his opera *Zoraida di Granata* had a successful premiere in Rome in 1822, but it was *Anna Bolena* in 1830 that made his name internationally. Later successes included *L'elisir d'amore* (1832), *Lucrezia Borgia* (1833), *Lucia di Lammermoor* (1835), *Roberto Devereux* (1837), *La fille du régiment* (1840), *Linda di Chamonix* (1842), and *Don Pasquale* (1843). Enormously prolific, he could produce an entire opera in weeks. He completed almost 70 operas, as well as over 150 sacred works and hundreds of songs. Infected with syphilis, he suffered a severe four-year decline leading to his death. Donizetti, G. Rossini, and V. Bellini were the foremost Italian opera composers of the early 19th century and the principal masters of the bel canto style.

donjon \ˈdän-jən\ *or* **keep** Most heavily fortified area of a medieval castle, usually a tower, to which the occupants could retire during a siege. It contained a well, quarters, offices, and service rooms. One side often overlooked the bailey (grounds between encircling walls); the other commanded the field and approaches to the castle.

donkey *or* **burro** Descendant of the African wild ass that has been used as a beast of burden since 4000 BC. The average donkey stands about 40 in. (100 cm) high at the shoulder, but breeds range from 24 to 66 in. (61–168 cm). Coats range from white to gray or black, usually with a dark stripe from mane to tail and a crosswise stripe on the shoulders. The mane is short and upright, and the tail has long hairs only at the end. The very long ears are dark at the base and tip. Donkeys are surefooted and can carry heavy loads over rough terrain. See also mule.

Donkin, Bryan (1768–1855) British inventor. Initially apprenticed to a papermaker, Donkin perfected a version of the Fourdrinier machine. He established a factory to produce and can vegetable soups and preserved meats for the Royal Navy. With a printer he developed a forerunner of the rotary press and a composition printing roller. He became a civil engineer in London, received two gold medals from the Society of Arts, and was a founder of the British Institution of Civil Engineers (1818).

Dönme *or* **Dönmeh** \dœn-ˈme, *Engl* ˌdən-ˈmā\ Jewish-Islamic sect founded in Salonika (now Thessaloniki, Greece) in the late 17th century. Its members were followers of Shabbetai Tzevi, whom they believed to be the messiah. Arrested by Ottoman authorities in 1666, he chose conversion to Islam over death, as did his followers, who believed that his conversion was a step in the fulfillment of messianic prophecy. While accepting Islam, they secretly practiced various Jewish rites, preserved some knowledge of Hebrew, and refused to intermarry with Muslims. The community moved to Turkey in the early 20th century and gradually assimilated, resisting Jewish attempts to return them to Judaism.

Donnai River See Dong-nai River

Donne \ˈdən\, **John** (1572–1631) English poet. Born into a Roman Catholic family, he entered Oxford University at 12; he later transferred to Cambridge, and subsequently studied law. An adventurer in youth, he hoped for a high public appointment, but a clandestine marriage to his employer's daughter ruined his prospects. He converted to Anglicanism; ordained in 1615, he became a preacher of great power and eloquence and was installed as dean of St. Paul's Cathedral in 1621. The greatest of the English Metaphysical poets (see metaphysical poetry), he is noted for his love lyrics, religious verse and treatises, and sermons. His secular poetry, most written early in his career, is direct, intense, brilliantly witty, and daringly imaginative. Later his tone darkened with works such as the *Anniversaries* (1611–12), two long poems meditating on the decay of the world. His 19 famous "Holy Sonnets" (written 1607–13) were published posthumously. Among his prose works, many as dramatic and intimate as his poetry, the most enduring is *Devotions upon Emergent Occasions* (1624).

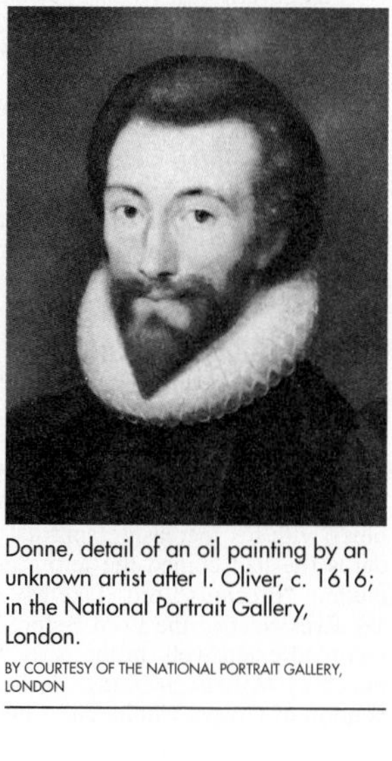

Donne, detail of an oil painting by an unknown artist after I. Oliver, c. 1616; in the National Portrait Gallery, London.

BY COURTESY OF THE NATIONAL PORTRAIT GALLERY, LONDON

Donner party Group of U.S. pioneers stranded en route to California. In late 1846, 87 immigrants led by George and Jacob Donner were trapped by heavy snow in the Sierra Nevada. Fifteen of the group set out to find help. When the others' food ran out, they resorted to cannibalism of those already dead. The 47 surviving members were rescued in February 1847. Donner Lake and Donner Pass, Cal., are named for them.

Donostia-San Sebastián See San Sebastián

Doolittle, Hilda *known as* **H.D.** (1886–1961) U.S. poet. Born in Bethlehem, Pa., she went to Europe in 1911 and remained there the rest of her life. One of the first Imagists (see Imagism), and deeply influenced by Ezra Pound, she wrote clear, impersonal, sensuous verse that combined classical themes with modernist techniques. Her later work was looser and more passionate, though it remained erudite and symbolic. Her collections include *Sea Garden* (1916), *Hymen* (1921), and *Red Roses for Bronze* (1929). She was also acclaimed for her translations, verse drama, and prose works.

Doolittle, Jimmy *orig.* **James Harold** (1896–1993) U.S. general. Born in Alameda, Cal., he enlisted in the army in World War I and became an aviator. After the war he earned a PhD in engineering, remaining in the Army Air Corps as a test pilot until 1930. He became head of aviation for Shell Oil Co. and in 1932 set a world speed record. During World War II he returned to active duty and in 1942 led a raid on Tokyo, for which he received the Congressional Medal of Honor. He commanded air operations on many fronts, including attacks on Germany in 1944–45. After the war he remained active in the aerospace industry. He received the Presidential Medal of Freedom in 1989.

door Movable barrier installed in the entry of a room or building to restrict access or provide visual privacy. Early doors were hides or textiles. With monumental architecture came pivoting doors of rigid, permanent materials; important chambers often had stone or bronze doors. Pompeiian doors looked much like modern wooden doors; they were constructed of stiles (vertical planks) and rails (horizontal planks) fastened together to support panels and occasionally equipped with locks and hinges. The typical Western medieval door was of vertical planks backed with horizontal or diagonal bracing. In the 20th century, a single, hollow-core panel door became most common. Other types include the revolving door, folding door, sliding door (inspired by the Japanese shoji), rolling door, and Dutch door (divided horizontally so that the lower or upper part can be opened separately).

Door Peninsula Peninsula, northeastern Wisconsin. Located between Green Bay and Lake Michigan, it was named for a strait at its tip known as La Porte des Mortes ("Death's Door"). About 80 mi (130 km) long and 25 mi (40 km) wide at its base, the peninsula was visited in the 17th century by French traders and missionaries. It is now a year-round vacation area, and tourism is a major business.

dopa *or* **L-dopa** *or* **levodopa** Organic chemical (L-3,4-dihydroxyphenylalanine) from which the body makes dopamine, a neurotransmitter deficient in persons with parkinsonism. Large daily doses of dopa can lessen the effects of the disease. However, it becomes less effective over time and causes abnormal involuntary movements (dyskinesia).

dopamine \ˈdō-pə-ˌmēn\ Catecholamine widely distributed in the central nervous system from which epinephrine and norepinephrine are formed. It is a central nervous system neurotransmitter essential to control of motion; it also acts as a hormone. Degeneration of certain dopamine-producing brain cells results in parkinsonism.

dopant \ˈdō-pənt\ Any impurity added to a semiconductor to modify its electrical conductivity. The most common semiconductors, silicon and germanium, form crystalline lattices in which each atom shares electrons with four neighbors (see bonding). Replacing some atoms with "donor" atoms (e.g., phosphorus, arsenic) that have five bonding electrons makes extra electrons available. The semiconductor thus doped is called n-type (for negative, because of the additional negative charge). Doping with "acceptor" atoms (e.g., gallium), with only three electrons available, creates a positively charged lattice defect; conduction can occur by migration of this "hole" through the crystal structure of such a p-type (for positive) semiconductor.

Doppler effect Apparent difference between the FREQUENCY at which WAVES—including light, sound, and radio waves—leave a source and that at which they reach an observer. The effect, first described by the Austrian physicist Christian Doppler (1803–1853), is caused by the relative motion of the observer and the wave source. It can be observed by listening to the blowing horn or siren of an approaching vehicle, whose pitch rises as the vehicle approaches the observer and falls as it recedes. It is used in RADAR and to calculate the speed of stars by observing the change in frequency of their light.

Dorchester *ancient* **Durnovaria.** Town (pop., 1995 est.: 16,000), and county seat of DORSET, England. On the River Frome, the ancient town was a sizable Roman British center, and many remains of the period have been found. By 1086 it was a royal borough, and a castle had been built by the 12th century; the Franciscan priory, founded before 1331, is thought to have been constructed from its ruins. The town is now a market center serving an extensive rural area. THOMAS HARDY was born near Dorchester, the "Casterbridge" of his Wessex novels.

Dorchester Former town, now a ward of BOSTON, Mass. It extended nearly to the Rhode Island border and included Dorchester Heights, whose fortification by GEORGE WASHINGTON's artillery led the British to evacuate Boston on March 17, 1776 at the start of the AMERICAN REVOLUTION.

Dordogne River \dȯr-'dȯnʸ\ *ancient* **Duranius.** River, southwestern France. Rising in the MASSIF CENTRAL and flowing west for 293 mi (472 km), it unites with the GARONNE RIVER north of BORDEAUX to form the Gironde Estuary. It then flows through the spa resorts of Monts Dore in the Puy-de-Dôme. The river is a source for hydroelectric power.

Doré \dȯ-'rā\, **Gustave (-Paul)** (1832–1883) French printmaker. Born in Strasbourg, in 1847 he went to Paris and began producing lithographic caricatures for a weekly journal and several albums of lithographs (1847–54). He achieved fame and wide popularity with his wood-engraved book illustrations; among the finest were editions of DANTE's *Inferno* (1861) and the Bible (1866). His vivid work is characterized by images of the grotesque and bizarre. Employing over 40 block cutters, he eventually produced more than 90 illustrated books.

Doren, Carl and Mark Van See Carl and Mark VAN DOREN

Dorgon \'dȯr-ˌgän\ *or* **Chengzong** *or* **Ch'eng-tsung** \'cheŋ-'dzu̇ŋ\ (1612–1650) Prince of the MANCHU people, instrumental in founding the QING (MANCHU) DYNASTY in China. He joined his former enemy WU SANGUI in driving the Chinese rebel LI ZICHENG from Beijing, where Li had already unseated the last MING-DYNASTY emperor. Though some wanted to put Dorgon on the throne, he saw to it that his nephew Fu-lin was proclaimed emperor (Dorgon acted as regent); this loyalty and selflessness won him the high regard of future historians.

Doria \'dȯr-yä\, **Andrea** (1466–1560) Genoese statesman, mercenary, and admiral, the foremost naval commander of his time. A member of an aristocratic family, he was orphaned at an early age and became a soldier of fortune. In 1522 he entered the service of FRANCIS I, who was fighting Emperor CHARLES V in Italy. Doria later transferred his services to Charles and in 1528 drove the French out of Genoa. He became the new ruler of Genoa and reorganized its government into an effective and stable oligarchy. He commanded several naval expeditions against the Turks, and helped Charles V extend his domination over the Italian peninsula. Though greedy and authoritarian, Doria was also a fearless commander with outstanding tactical and strategic talents.

Doria, detail of a portrait by Sebastiano del Piombo; in the Doria Palace, Rome.
ALINARI—ART RESOURCE/EB INC.

Dorians Major division of the ancient Greeks. Coming from the north and northwest, they conquered the PELOPONNESE c. 1100–1000 BC, overran the remnants of the MYCENAEAN and MINOAN civilizations, and ushered in a dark age that lasted almost three centuries, until the rise of the Greek city-states. They had their own dialect and were organized into three TRIBES. Patterns of settlement determined their alliances in later Greek conflicts. To Greek culture they gave the Doric order of architecture, the tragic choral lyric, and a militarized aristocratic government. They assimilated into Greek societies in some cases, but in Sparta and Crete they held power and resisted cultural progression.

dormer Window set vertically in a structure that projects from a sloping roof. It often illuminates a bedroom. In the late Gothic and early Renaissance periods, elaborate masonry dormers were designed. Dormers were used along with the mansard ROOF to defy a Parisian law limiting buildings to six stories; the seventh story was called a garret (or attic) and was made habitable by the dormer. See also GABLE.

dormouse Any of 20 RODENT species (family Gliridae) found throughout Eurasia and northern Africa. Dormice have large eyes, soft fur, rounded ears, and a hairy (sometimes bushy) tail. They live in trees, bushes, and rock walls and in nests of plant material. They eat fruit, nuts, birds' eggs, and some insects and small animals. Many species sleep for long periods, particularly in winter. The largest species, the edible dormouse *(Glis glis),* is gray and attains a maximum length of about 8 in. (20 cm), excluding the 6-in. (15-cm) tail.

Edible dormouse (*Glis glis*).
SCHUNEMANN—BAVARIA-VERLAG

Dornberger \'dȯrn-ˌber-gər\, **Walter Robert** (1895–1980) German-U.S. engineer. From 1932, with WERNHER VON BRAUN, he began to perfect the ROCKET engine. During World War II he directed construction of the V-2 rocket, the forerunner of all postwar spacecraft. In the U.S. after the war, he worked as an adviser on GUIDED MISSILES for the U.S. Air Force. In the 1950s he participated in the Air Force–NASA project Dyna-Soar, which eventually became the SPACE-SHUTTLE program.

Dorr, Thomas Wilson (1805–1854) U.S. politician. Born in Providence, R.I., he served in the state legislature from 1834, where he tried to introduce constitutional reform to widen white manhood suffrage. In 1841 he organized the People's Party, which held elections and installed Dorr as governor in 1842. The existing government refused to recognize his authority, labeling the action "Dorr's Rebellion." The state had two governments until 1844, when Dorr was tried for treason; though given a life sentence, he was released in 1845.

Dorset County (population 1995 est.: 379,000), southwestern England. It is located on the ENGLISH CHANNEL; its county seat is DORCHESTER. Prehistoric peoples were active in the area and left abundant monuments of Neolithic, Bronze, and Iron Age dates, including Maiden Castle, a huge earthworks just outside Dorchester. The area subsequently became part of the West Saxon kingdom. As Wessex it appears in the writings of THOMAS HARDY.

Dorsey, Thomas A(ndrew) (1899–1993) U.S. songwriter, singer, and pianist, the "Father of GOSPEL MUSIC." Born in Villa Rica, Ga., the son of a revivalist preacher, Dorsey was influenced by blues pianists in the Atlanta area and played piano in secular "hokum" music (sometimes in brothels) as "Georgia Tom." In 1926 he moved to Chicago, where he toured with Ma RAINEY and his own bands. From 1929 on, he combined blues with his increasing spiritual concerns to create many gospel standards (he had coined the term "gospel music" in the early 1920s), including "Precious Lord, Take My Hand," "Peace in the Valley," and "If We Ever Needed the Lord Before," publishing his own sheet music. He recorded extensively in the early 1930s. Many of his songs were introduced by MAHALIA JACKSON. He founded and directed the National Convention of Gospel Choirs and Choruses.

Dorsey, Tommy *orig.* **Thomas** (1905–1956) U.S. trombonist and leader of one of the most popular big bands of the SWING era. Born in Shenandoah, Pa., Dorsey led the Dorsey Brothers Orchestra from 1934 with his brother, saxophonist and clarinetist Jimmy Dorsey (1904–1957); they later separated to lead their own groups. Tommy Dorsey's band combined smooth ballad performances with up-tempo jazz arrangements featuring some of the best musicians of the period, including BUDDY RICH, F. SINATRA, and arranger Sy Oliver. Dorsey's trombone playing was technically impeccable, and his seamless phrasing and sweet tone were a major influence on singers and brass players alike.

Dortmund \'dòrt-,mùnt\ *ancient* **Throtmannia.** City (pop., 1996 est.: 599,000), North Rhine-Westphalia, western Germany. First mentioned in AD 885, it became a free imperial city in 1220 and later joined the HANSEATIC LEAGUE. A prosperous trading center in the 14th century, it declined after the THIRTY YEARS' WAR, and lost its imperial rights in 1803. The development of coal and iron-ore mining and the completion of the Dortmund-Ems Canal in 1899 stimulated its regrowth. The city was largely destroyed in World War II, but was extensively rebuilt. It is a major transportation and industrial center of the RUHR area.

Dorylaeum \,dòr-ə-'lē-əm\, **Battle of** (July 1, 1097) Battle in which a combined force of crusaders and Byzantines defeated an army of SELJUQ Turks in Anatolia. The crusaders later captured Antioch. See also CRUSADES.

Dos Passos \däs-'pa-səs\, **John (Roderigo)** (1896–1970) U.S. writer. Son of a wealthy Chicago lawyer, he attended Harvard University. His wartime service as an ambulance driver and later work as a journalist led him to see the U.S. as "two nations," one for the rich and one for the poor. His reputation as social historian, radical critic of American life, and major novelist of the postwar "lost generation" rests primarily on his powerful trilogy *U.S.A.*, comprising *The 42nd Parallel* (1930), *1919* (1932), and *The Big Money* (1936). Later works, including the trilogy *District of Columbia*, were less ambitious and more politically conservative.

Dostoyevsky \däs-tə-'yef-skē\, **Fyodor (Mikhaylovich)** (1821–1881) Russian novelist. Born in Moscow to a middle-class family, he gave up an engineering career early in order to write. In 1849 he was arrested for belonging to a radical discussion group; sentenced to be shot, he was reprieved at the last moment and spent four years at hard labor in Siberia, where he developed epilepsy and experienced a deepening of his religious faith. Later he published and wrote for several periodicals while producing his best novels. His novels are concerned especially with faith, suffering, and the meaning of life; they are famous for their psychological depth and insight and their near-prophetic treatment of issues in philosophy and politics. His first, *Poor Folk* (1846), was followed the same year by *The Double*. *The House of the Dead* (1862) is based on his imprisonment, and *The Gambler* (1866) on his own gambling addiction. Best known are the novella *Notes from the Underground* (1864) and the great novels *Crime and Punishment* (1866), *The Idiot* (1869), *The Possessed* (1872), and *The Brothers Karamazov* (1880), his masterpiece, which focuses on the problem of evil, the nature of freedom, and the characters' craving for some kind of faith. By the end of his life he was acclaimed one of his country's greatest writers, and his works had a profound influence on 20th-century literature.

Dou \'daù\, **Gerrit** *or* **Gerard Dou** (1613–1675) Dutch painter born and active in Leiden. From 1628 to 1631 he studied with REMBRANDT, adopting his subject matter, careful draftsmanship, and dramatic treatment of light and shadow. When Rembrandt left Leiden, Dou developed his own style, painting smooth, meticulously detailed small-scale domestic interiors and portraits. He used the "frame within a frame" device of surrounding his figures by a window or curtain, and excelled at scenes lit by candlelight. With JAN STEEN he was among the founders of the Guild of St. Luke at Leiden (1648).

Douala \dü-'ä-lä\ City (pop., 1992 est.: 1,200,000), chief port of Cameroon, on the Bight of BIAFRA. It was the capital of German Kamerun and later of French Cameroun, and was taken from the Germans in 1914. Cameroon's largest city, it is one of central Africa's major industrial centers, and its deepwater port handles most of the country's overseas trade. It is home to a variety of commercial, agricultural, and industrial schools; a museum and handicraft center encourage the production and preservation of Cameroonian art.

double-aspect theory *or* **dual-aspect theory** Type of mind-body MONISM that is similar to the IDENTITY THEORY, with one notable exception: According to the double-aspect theory, reality is not material; rather, the mental and material (psychological and physical) attributes are mutually complementary aspects of a unitary reality. An analogy is an undulating line that is simultaneously concave and convex; each aspect is an integral but only partial expression of the total reality. See also MIND-BODY PROBLEM.

double bass Lowest-pitched of the modern STRINGED INSTRUMENTS. It varies in size, up to 80 in (200 cm) tall. Its shape also varies; its shoulders usually slope more than those of the violin, reflecting its status as a hybrid of the VIOL and VIOLIN families (the name comes from the double-bass viol). It emerged from these families in the late Renaissance, and has always been less standardized in form than its cousins in the violin family. It normally has four strings; the orchestral instrument often has a lower fifth string (more often, an extension is added to the fourth string), and the jazz instrument has a higher fifth string. Its range is an octave below the CELLO's. It is normally bowed in orchestral music and plucked in jazz. In rock bands, the electric bass is used instead.

double jeopardy In law, the prosecution of a person for an offense for which he or she has already been prosecuted. The 5th Amendment to the U.S. CONSTITUTION states that no person shall "be subject for the same offense to be twice put in jeopardy of life and limb." The clause bars second prosecutions after acquittal or conviction and prohibits multiple convictions for the same offense. Thus a person cannot be guilty of both murder and manslaughter for the same homicide, nor can a person be retried for the same crime after the case has been resolved. A person could, however, be convicted of both murder and robbery if the murder arose from the robbery. See also rights of the ACCUSED, DUE PROCESS.

double refraction *or* **birefringence** Optical property in which a single ray of unpolarized light (see POLARIZATION) splits into two components traveling at different velocities and in different directions. One ray is refracted (see REFRACTION) at an angle as it travels through the medium, while the other passes through unchanged. The splitting occurs because the speed of the ray through the medium is determined by the orientation of the light compared with the CRYSTAL LATTICE of the medium. Since unpolarized light consists of waves that vibrate in all directions, some will pass through the lattice without being affected, while others will be refracted and change direction. Materials that exhibit double refraction include ICE, QUARTZ, and SUGAR.

double vision *or* **diplopia** Perception of two images of an object, usually caused by temporary or permanent eye-muscle paralysis. Normally, the brain fuses slightly different images from each eye by matching corresponding points on each RETINA. When an eye muscle is paralyzed, the image falls at a different point and the images do not correspond. Double vision may be an early symptom of BOTULISM or MYASTHENIA GRAVIS and occurs in other infections, head injuries, and nerve or muscle disorders.

Doubleday, Abner (1819–1893) U.S. Army officer, once thought to be the inventor of BASEBALL. Born in Ballston Spa, N.Y., he served in the Mexican War and the Seminole Wars. As a major general in the American Civil War, he gave the first order to fire at Fort Sumter, and later fought in other major battles. In 1907 a commission appointed by A.G. SPALDING concluded that Doubleday formulated the essential rules of baseball in 1839 at Cooperstown, N.Y., leading to the choice of Cooperstown as the site of the Baseball Hall of Fame. It was later proved that Doubleday was not in Cooperstown in 1839. See also ALEXANDER CARTWRIGHT.

Abner Doubleday.
CULVER PICTURES

Doubs River \'dü\ *ancient* **Dubis** River, eastern France and western Switzerland. Rising in the JURA Mtns., it flows northeast to form part of the French–Swiss border. It continues east into Switzerland, makes a hairpin turn and heads back into France, finally entering the SAÔNE

River, after a course of about 270 mi (435 km), only 56 mi (90 km) from its source.

Dougga See Thugga

Douglas, Aaron (1899–1979) U.S. painter and graphic artist. Born in Topeka, Kan., Douglas moved to New York City in 1925. There he joined the burgeoning arts scene in Harlem that later became known as the Harlem Renaissance. In his magazine illustrations and murals, he synthesized cubist forms with stylized and geometric shapes drawn from African art. Perhaps his most significant work was a series of four murals, collectively titled *Aspects of Negro Life*, for the 135th Street branch of the New York Public Library. His illustrations are widely known for their tonal gradations and Art Deco-style silhouettes. He taught at Fisk University from 1939 to 1966.

Douglas, James *later* **Sir James** (1803–1877) Canadian statesman, known as "the father of British Columbia." Born in Demerara, British Guiana, he joined the Hudson's Bay Co. in 1821 and became a senior member in charge of operations west of the Rocky Mountains. In 1849 he moved the company's headquarters from Oregon to Vancouver Island. As governor of Vancouver (1851–64) when gold was discovered on the Fraser River in 1858, he extended his authority to the mainland to preserve Britain's Pacific foothold. When Britain created the colony of British Columbia, Douglas was appointed governor (1858–64).

Douglas, Kirk *orig,* **Issur Danielovitch** *later* **Isadore Demskey** (born 1916) U.S. film actor and producer. Born in Amsterdam, N.Y., he had minor Broadway roles before making his film debut in *The Strange Love of Martha Ivers* (1946), and emerged as a major star in *Champion* (1949). Despite sensitive performances in *The Glass Menagerie* (1950) and *Paths of Glory* (1957), he became identified with the intense, forceful roles he played in such films as *The Bad and the Beautiful* (1952), *Lust for Life* (1956), *Gunfight at the O.K. Corral* (1957), and *Seven Days in May* (1964). He produced and starred in *Spartacus* (1960). He continued to appear in films into the 1990s.

Douglas, Michael (born 1944). U.S. film actor and producer. The son of Kirk Douglas, he was born in New Brunswick, N.J. He made his film acting debut in 1969 and began his career as a producer with *One Flew over the Cuckoo's Nest* (1975). He produced and acted in such films as *The China Syndrome* (1979), *Romancing the Stone* (1984), *Fatal Attraction* (1987), and *Wall Street* (1987, Academy Award), and also starred in *Basic Instinct* (1992), *Falling Down* (1993), and *The Game* (1997).

Douglas, Stephen A(rnold) (1813–1861) U.S. politician. Born in Brandon, Vt., he sat on the Illinois supreme court before serving in the U.S. House of Representatives (1843–47) and Senate (1847–61), where he strongly supported the Union and national expansion. To solve the division over slavery, he developed the policy of popular sovereignty and influenced passage of the Compromise of 1850 and the Kansas-Nebraska Act. Short and heavyset, he was dubbed "the Little Giant" for his oratorical skill. Abraham Lincoln's challenge to him for his Senate seat led to the Lincoln-Douglas Debates. The Democrats nominated Douglas for president in 1860, but a splinter group of Southerners nominated John C. Breckinridge, which divided the Democratic vote and gave the presidency to Lincoln. In 1861 he undertook a mission for Lincoln to gain support for the Union among the Southern border states and in the Northwest, where he died of typhoid.

Douglas, Tommy *orig.* **Thomas Clement** (1904–1986) Canadian (Scottish-born) politician. His family emigrated to Winnipeg in 1919. An ordained minister, he became active in the socialist Co-operative Commonwealth Federation, and he served in the Canadian Parliament 1935–44. As premier of Saskatchewan (1944–61), he led Canada's first socialist government. For establishing Medicare in the province, he is considered the father of socialized medicine in Canada. He resigned in 1961 to become leader of the New Democratic Party, a post he held until 1971.

Douglas, William O(rville) (1898–1980) U.S. jurist and public official. Born in Maine, Minn., he attended Columbia University Law School and joined a Wall Street law firm to learn the intricacies of financial and corporate law, and taught law (1927–36). He became a member of the Securities and Exchange Commission (SEC) in 1936. As SEC chairman (1937–39) he engineered the reorganization of the nation's stock exchanges, instituted measures for the protection of small investors, and began government regulation of the sale of securities. He was appointed to the U.S. Supreme Court by Pres. Franklin Roosevelt in 1939, and served until 1975. Though responsible for writing the opinions in many complicated financial cases, he became most famous for his pronouncements on civil liberties. He rejected government limitations on freedom of speech and was an outspoken defender of an unfettered press. He also strove to uphold the rights of the accused. He wrote numerous books on history, politics, foreign relations, and conservation, including *Of Men and Mountains* (1950) and *A Wilderness Bill of Rights* (1965).

Douglas fir Any of about six species of coniferous evergreen timber trees (see conifer) that make up the genus *Pseudotsuga,* in the pine family, native to western North America and eastern Asia. Long, flat, spirally arranged yellow- or blue-green needles grow directly from the branch. The North American tree commonly called Douglas fir is *P. menziesii* (sometimes *P. douglasii*). Douglas firs may grow to 250 ft (75 m) tall and 8 ft (2.4 m) in diameter. One of the best timber trees in North America, it is also a popular ornamental and Christmas tree and is used for reforestation along the Pacific Coast.

Cone of a Douglas fir (*Pseudotsuga menziesii*).
GRANT HEILMAN

Douglas-Home \'dəg-ləs-'hyüm\, **Sir Alec** *orig.* **Alexander Frederick** *later* **Baron Home (of the Hirsel of Coldstream)** (1903–1995) British statesman. A member of the House of Commons 1931–45 and 1950–51, he entered the House of Lords after inheriting the earldom of Home (1951). He served as minister of state for Scotland (1951–55), leader of the House of Lords (1957–60), and foreign secretary (1960–63) before succeeding Harold Macmillan as prime minister in 1963, relinquishing his hereditary titles. He was unable to improve the British balance-of-payments situation and antagonized Conservatives by supporting legislation against price-fixing, but gained U.S. approval for his anti-Communism. After his government fell in 1964, he became Conservative opposition spokesman on foreign affairs and later again foreign secretary 1970–1974. In 1974 he was created a life peer.

Douglass, Frederick *orig.* **Frederick Augustus Washington Bailey** (1817–1895) U.S. abolitionist. Born in Tuckahoe, Md., to a slave mother and a white father, he was sent to work as a house servant in Baltimore, where he learned to read. At 16 he was returned to the plantation, then was hired out as a ship caulker. In 1838 he fled to New York and then moved to New Bedford, Mass., changing his name to elude slave hunters. His eloquence at an 1841 antislavery convention gave him a new career as an agent for the Massachusetts Anti-Slavery Society, in which capacity he endured frequent insults and violent personal attacks. In 1845 he wrote his autobiography, now regarded as a classic. He lectured in England and Ireland (1845–47), then founded the antislavery *North Star,* which he published until 1860 in Rochester, N.Y. In 1851 he split with the radical William Lloyd Garrison and allied with the moderates led by James Birney. In the Civil War he was a consultant to Pres. Abraham Lincoln. During Reconstruction he fought for full civil rights for freedmen and supported women's rights. He served in government posts in Washington, D.C. (1877–86), and as U.S. minister to Haiti (1889–91).

Douhet \dü-'e\, **Giulio** (1869–1930) Italian general. He served as commander of Italy's first aviation unit, the Aeronautical Battalion (1912–15). In World War I his criticism of the war's conduct led to his court-martial, imprisonment, and retirement. An investigation in 1917 justified his criticisms; his conviction was reversed, and he was appointed head of the aviation service. In books such as *The Command of the Air* (1921) he advanced his ideas on strategic air power and the importance of strategic bombing. He advocated the creation of an independent air force, reduction of land and sea forces, and unification of the armed forces. Though his ideas aroused great controversy, many were adopted by the major powers.

Doukhobors *or* **Dukhobors** \'dü-kə-,bȯr\ (Russian: "Spirit Wrestler") Member of a Russian peasant religious sect. Its members, most of whom originally lived in southern Russia, objected to the liturgical reforms (1652) of Patriarch NIKON and Russia's Westernization under PETER I. They had no priests or sacraments, and their egalitarian and pacifist beliefs provoked sporadic persecution from 1773 on. LEO TOLSTOY won them the right to emigrate, and by 1899 7,500 had left for western Canada. In the early 20th century they clashed repeatedly with the Canadian government over noncompliance with land, tax, and education laws. The removal of Doukhobor children from their parents 1953–59 prompted legal action to obtain compensation in the late 1990s.

Douris \'dü-ris\ (fl. early 5th century BC) Greek vase painter. He was known for his work in RED-FIGURE POTTERY, which exhibit his fine draftsmanship and rhythmic composition. He decorated his vases with a variety of themes, including the legend of the Golden Fleece. His signature has been identified on some 40 vases; more than 200 have been attributed to him, including a cup depicting *Eos Embracing Her Dead Son Memnon*.

Douro River \'dō-,rü\ *Spanish* **Duero** \'dwā-rō\ *ancient* **Durius.** River in Spain and Portugal. The third-longest in the IBERIAN PENINSULA, it rises in the Sierra de Urbión in central Spain, and crosses the Numantian Plateau. It flows generally westward for 556 mi (895 km) across Spain and northern Portugal to the Atlantic Ocean. It has extensive barge traffic in its Portuguese section, and has been harnessed for hydroelectric power.

dove Any of certain birds of the PIGEON family (Columbidae). The names pigeon and dove are often used interchangeably. Though "dove" usually refers to the smaller, long-tailed members of the pigeon family, there are exceptions: the common street pigeon, generally typical for birds designated as pigeons, is frequently called the rock dove. The common names of these birds do not necessarily reflect their accurate biological relationships to one another.

Dove, Rita (Frances) (born 1952) U.S. writer and teacher. Born in Akron, Ohio, she studied writing at the University of Iowa and published the first of several chapbooks of her poetry in 1977. Her poems and short stories focus on the particulars of family life and personal struggle, addressing the larger dimensions of the African-American experience primarily by indirection. Her poetry collections include *Museum* (1983), *Thomas and Beulah* (1986, Pulitzer Prize), *Mother Love* (1995), and *On the Bus with Rosa Parks* (1999). She was poet laureate of the U.S. 1993–95.

Dover *ancient* **Dubris Portus** Town (pop., 1995 est.: 34,000; metro. area population 1995 est.: 104,000) and seaport on the Strait of DOVER, southeastern England. A pre-Roman settlement existed on the site, and in the 4th century AD it was guarded by a Saxon fort. During the 11th century it was chief of the CINQUE PORTS. Dover Castle, a stronghold of medieval England, was besieged by rebellious barons in 1216. The town was held by Parliamentarians in the ENGLISH CIVIL WARS. It was a naval base in World War I and was bombed by Germans in World War II. Landmarks include the castle, a Roman lighthouse, and an ancient fortress church. Famous for the white chalk cliffs rising above it, Dover is a leading passenger port.

Dover City (pop., 1996 est.: 30,000), capital of Delaware, on the St. Jones River. Laid out in 1717 as the site for a county courthouse and jail by order of WILLIAM PENN's, and named for DOVER, England, it became the capital in 1777. Its many colonial buildings include the Old State House (rebuilt 1787–92), which served as the capitol building until 1933; displayed there are King CHARLES II's original royal grant and WILLIAM PENN's deeds to Delaware (1682). The modern city is a farm trade center and shipping point for fruits, and has some light industries.

Dover, Strait of *French* **Pas de Calais** \,päd-kȧ-'lā\ *ancient* **Fretum Gallicum** Channel separating southeastern England from northwestern France. Connecting the ENGLISH CHANNEL with the NORTH SEA, it is about 20 mi (32 km) wide at its narrowest point. Lined on the British side with the famous White Cliffs, which are composed of soft chalk, it is one of the world's busiest seaways; its chief ports include DOVER and Folkestone in England and CALAIS and Boulogne in France. It was the scene of several historic naval battles, including the repulse by the English of the Spanish ARMADA in 1588. Allied troops in the DUNKIRK EVACUATION crossed to Dover in 1940.

Dover, Treaty of (1670) Pact between CHARLES II of England and LOUIS XIV in which Charles promised to support French policy in Europe in return for a French subsidy that would free him from financial dependence on Parliament. There were actually two treaties: a secret one concerning the conversion of England to the Roman Catholic faith (which never took effect), and a formal one concerning an Anglo–French military and naval alliance designed to subjugate the United Provinces of the Netherlands.

Dow, Herbert H(enry) (1866–1930) U.S. (Canadian-born) inventor and manufacturer. Born in Belleville, Ontario, he attended college in Cleveland. He developed and patented electrolytic methods (the Dow process) for extracting BROMINE from brines (concentrated water solutions of salts). In 1895 he founded the DOW CHEMICAL CO. to electrolyze brine for CHLORINE, used in insecticides. He was the first U.S. producer of IODINE (which he also extracted from brine). He eventually was granted some 65 patents as his company became one of the world's leading chemical manufacturers.

Dow Chemical Co. Leading U.S. petrochemical company that manufactures chemicals, pharmaceuticals, consumer goods, paint, and many other products for industrial and home use. It was founded in 1897 by the chemist HERBERT H. DOW, initially as a bleach plant to use wastes produced by the Midland Chemical Co. It was incorporated with Midland Chemical and the Dow Process Co. in 1900. Dow's products have included a broad range of industrial chemicals and metals, plastics and packaging materials, and bioproducts. mustard gas, NAPALM, AGENT ORANGE, and silicone breast implants, aspirin, plastic wrap, and Styrofoam.

Dow Jones average STOCK price average computed by Dow Jones & Co. Dow Jones & Co., founded in 1882 by Charles H. Dow (1851–1902) and Edward D. Jones (1856–1920), commenced publication of the *WALL STREET JOURNAL* in 1889 and began computing a daily industrials average in 1897. Today it publishes averages based on 20 transportation stocks, 15 utility stocks, and 30 selected industrial stocks, as well as a composite average of all three; the industrial-stocks average is universally followed by U.S. and international investors. The company also publishes several BOND averages. See also NASDAQ, STOCK EXCHANGE.

Dowland, John (1563–1626) English composer and lutenist. Born in London and educated at Oxford, he was refused a court position in 1594 and, believing his adoptive Catholicism had been the cause, he left for the continent. There he traveled extensively and took a position at the Danish court. In 1612, when his compositions had made him famous, he was finally appointed lutenist to the English court. He left about 80 works for solo lute and some 80 lute songs, including "Flow my tears" and "Weep you no more, sad fountains." His *Lachrimae* is a collection for viol-and-lute ensemble.

Down District (pop., 1995 est.: 61,000), Northern Ireland. Establish as a district in 1973, it fronts Strangford Lough and the IRISH SEA. Extreme southern and western Down is mountainous; the dome-shaped Mourne Mountains reach an elevation of 2,789 ft (850 m). Down is a rich agricultural district; livestock-raising is also important. The name also of a traditional county, Down was settled in prehistoric times. It was where St. PATRICK began his mission in Ireland (AD 432), and his well and bath houses are preserved near the district seat, DOWNPATRICK. In Tudor times, parts of Down were colonized by English and Scottish adventurers.

Downing, Andrew Jackson (1815–1852) U.S. horticulturist, landscape gardener, and architect. Born in Newburgh, N.Y., he educated himself in landscape gardening and architecture while working in his father's nursery. In 1850 he began collaborating with the British architect Calvert Vaux (1824–1895); the two designed a number of estates in New York's Hudson River valley and on Long Island. Recognized as the foremost U.S. landscape designer of his day, he was commissioned in 1851 to lay out the grounds for the Capitol, the White House, and the Smithsonian Institution. His death at 36 in a steamboat accident prevented him from seeing his plans to completion. His books on architecture and landscaping became standard works, and his influence on American conceptions of the middle-class home were far-reaching.

Downpatrick Town (pop., 1995 est.: 11,000), Northern Ireland. The seat of DOWN district, it is on the southwestern end of Strangford Lough, and is the Dun-da-leth-glas of Irish chroniclers. Formerly a MacDunleary stronghold, it was seized in 1177 by the Anglo-Norman adventurer

John de Courci and served as his headquarters until 1203. St. PATRICK is reputedly buried in the grounds of its cathedral.

Down's syndrome *or* **Down syndrome** *or* **trisomy 21** \'trī-ˌsō-mē\ CONGENITAL DISORDER caused by an extra CHROMOSOME (trisomy) on the chromosome 21 pair. Those with the syndrome may have broad, flat faces; up-slanted eyes, sometimes with epicanthal folds (whence its former name, mongolism); mental retardation (usually moderate); heart and/or kidney malformations; and abnormal fingerprint patterns. Many persons with Down's syndrome can live and work independently or in a sheltered environment, but they age prematurely and have a short (55-year) life expectancy. The risk of bearing a child with the disorder increases with the mother's age; it can be detected in the fetus by AMNIOCENTESIS.

C
D

dowry \'dau̇-rē\ Property that a wife or a wife's family gives to her husband upon MARRIAGE. The dowry has a long history in Europe, India, Africa, and other parts of the world. Some of its basic functions are to protect the wife against ill treatment by her husband, since a dowry can be a conditional gift; to help the husband discharge the responsibilities of marriage, since the dowry makes it possible for the young man to establish a household; to provide the wife with support in case of her husband's death; and to compensate the groom's kin for their payment of BRIDEWEALTH. In Europe, the dowry has served to build the power and wealth of great families and has even played a role in the politics of grand alliance through marriage. It began to disappear in the 19th century, as industrialization grew.

dowsing \'dau̇-ziŋ\ Occult practice used for finding water, minerals, or other hidden substances. A dowser generally uses a Y-shaped piece of hazel, rowan, or willow wood (also called a dowser or a divining rod). The dowser grasps the rod by its two prongs and appears, while walking, to be receiving transmissions from beneath the earth. If the rod quivers violently or points downward, some buried substance has been located. First practiced in Europe during the Middle Ages, dowsing is most often used to find water but may also be employed to locate precious metals, buried treasure, archaeological remains, or even dead bodies.

Doyle, Arthur Conan *later* **Sir Arthur** (1859–1930) British writer. Born in Edinburgh, he became a doctor and practiced until 1891; he was knighted for his medical work in the second SOUTH AFRICAN WAR and his public defense of the war. He is best known for his fictional detective Sherlock Holmes, who first appeared in the novel *A Study in Scarlet* (1887). Collections of his Holmes stories began with *The Adventures of Sherlock Holmes* (1892). Tiring of Holmes, he devised his death in 1893, only to be forced by public demand to restore him to life. His other Holmes novels include *The Sign of Four* (1890), *The Hound of the Baskervilles* (1902), and *The Valley of Fear* (1915). His historical romances include *The White Company* (1890).

Sir Arthur Conan Doyle, detail of a portrait by H.L. Gates, 1927; in the National Portrait Gallery, London.

BY COURTESY OF THE NATIONAL PORTRAIT GALLERY, LONDON

Drâa River \'drä\ River, southwestern Morocco. Rising from two headstreams in the Atlas Mtns., it flows south to form much of the Algerian–Moroccan frontier before emptying into the Atlantic Ocean near Cape Drâa. Although it is Morocco's longest river, of its total 700 mi (1,100 km) length, all but the headstreams and upper course are usually dry.

Drabble, Margaret (born 1939) British novelist. Sister of A. S. BYATT, she graduated from Cambridge Univ., then acted briefly before committing herself to writing. Her novels include *A Summer Bird-cage* (1962), *The Realms of Gold* (1975), and *The Gates of Ivory* (1991). She has also written literary biographies (like her husband, Michael Holroyd) and other literary studies and has edited the *Oxford Companion of English Literature* (1985).

dracaena \drə-'sē-nə\ Any of about 50–80 species of ornamental foliage plants that make up the genus *Dracaena,* in the AGAVE FAMILY, native primarily to the Old World tropics. Most have short stalks and narrow, sword-shaped leaves; some have taller stalks and resemble trees. The small flowers are red, yellow, or green. *D. sanderiana* and *D. fragrans* are often grown as houseplants. The ornamental dragon tree *(D. draco)* of the Canary Islands bears orange fruit. Its trunk contains a red gum, called dragon's blood, that was formerly used in medicines.

Draco \'drā-kō\ *or* **Dracon** (7th century BC) Athenian lawgiver. Almost nothing is known of his life. His harsh legal code (621 BC) punished most crimes, even trivial ones, with death. SOLON repealed Draco's code, retaining only the homicide statutes.

draft See BILL OF EXCHANGE

draft See CONSCRIPTION

Draft Riot of 1863 Four days of violence in New York City to protest the inequities of AMERICAN CIVIL WAR conscription. The law permitted draftees to buy their way out of army service for $300, a sum relatively few men could afford. When the drawing of names began on July 11, mobs of Irish and other foreign-born workers surged into the streets, burning draft headquarters and other buildings, and assaulting blacks, who they had feared would take their jobs. About 100 people (mostly rioters) died.

drafting Precise graphical representation of a structure, machine, or its component parts that communicates the intent of a technical design to the fabricator (or the prospective buyer) of the product. Drawings may present the various aspects of an object's form, show the object projected in space, or explain how it is built. Drafting uses orthographic projection, in which the object is viewed along parallel lines that are perpendicular to the plane of the drawing. Orthographic drawings include top views (plans), flat front and side views (elevations), and cross-sectional views showing profile. Perspective drawing, which presents a realistic illusion of space, uses a horizon line and vanishing points to show how objects and spatial relationships might appear to the eye, including diminution of size and convergence of parallel lines. Drafting was done with precision instruments (T square or parallel rule, triangle, mechanical pens and pencils) until computerization revolutionized production methods in architectural and engineering offices.

drafting See DRAWING

drag FORCE exerted by a fluid stream on any obstacle in its path or felt by an object moving through a fluid. Its magnitude and how it may be reduced are important to designers of moving vehicles, ships, suspension bridges, cooling towers, and other structures. Drag forces are conventionally described by a drag coefficient, defined irrespective of the shape of the body. DIMENSIONAL ANALYSIS reveals that the drag coefficient depends on the REYNOLDS NUMBER; the precise dependence must be elucidated experimentally, and can be used to predict the drag forces experienced by other bodies in other fluids at other velocities. Engineers use this principle of dynamic similarity when they apply results obtained with a model structure to predict the behavior of other structures. See also FRICTION, STREAMLINE.

drag racing Form of motor racing in which two contestants race side by side from a standing start over a straight quarter-mile strip of pavement. Winners go on to compete against others in their class until only one is left undefeated. There are three main classes of vehicle: (1) the Top Fuel Eliminator (called a "rail" or "slingshot"), a lightweight, long-chassied vehicle with wide rear tires that is fueled by a special mixture, such as methanol and nitromethane; (2) the "funny car," a high-performance copy of a late-model production car that uses special fuel; and (3) the standard production car, a modified version of a gasoline-powered production car. The Top Fuel class is the fastest, followed by the funny car. Drag racing is most popular in the U.S.

dragon Legendary monster usually depicted as a huge, bat-winged, fire-breathing lizard or snake with a barbed tail. The dragon symbolized evil in the ancient Middle East, and the Egyptian god Apepi was the great serpent of the world of darkness. The Greeks and Romans sometimes represented dragons as evil creatures and sometimes as beneficent powers acquainted with the secrets of the earth. In Christianity the dragon symbolized sin and paganism, and saints such as St. GEORGE were shown triumphing over it. Used as warlike emblems in many cultures, dragons were carved on the prows of Norse ships and depicted on royal ensigns in medieval England. In the Far East the dragon was a beneficent creature, wingless but regarded as a power of the air. In China it symbolized yang in the YIN-YANG of cosmology, and it served as the emblem of the royal family.

dragon worm See GUINEA WORM

dragonfly Any member of the insect suborder Anisoptera (order Odonata), characterized by four large, membranous, many-veined wings, that, when at rest, are held horizontally rather than vertically (see DAMSELFLY). Dragonflies are agile and have bulging eyes that often occupy most of the head and a wingspan of about 6 in. (16 cm). The dragonfly is one of the fastest-flying and most predaceous insects; in 30 minutes it can eat its own weight in food. Dragonflies differ from most other insects by having the male copulatory organs at the front part of the abdomen rather than at the back end. Male and female often fly in tandem during sperm transfer.

Dragonfly (*Libellula forensis*).
E.S. ROSS

dragoon In late-16th-century. Europe, a mounted soldier who fought as a light cavalryman on attack and as a dismounted infantryman on defense. The term derived from his weapon, a short MUSKET called the dragoon. Dragoons were organized in companies, and their officers bore infantry titles. By the 18th century, dragoon referred to members of certain cavalry regiments. The term and function disappeared along with cavalry in the 20th century.

Drake, Francis *later* **Sir Francis** (c. 1540–1596) English admiral, the most renowned seaman of the Elizabethan Age. Son of a tenant farmer, he went to sea at 13 to escape his family's poverty. He gained a reputation as an outstanding seaman and became wealthy through raids against Spanish colonies. In 1577 he was commissioned by ELIZABETH I to lead an expedition to South America and beyond. He set sail with five ships, but ultimately only his flagship, the *Golden Hind,* made its way through the Strait of Magellan into the Pacific and up the coast of South and North America; he then turned south to anchor off modern San Francisco, claiming the area for Elizabeth. He sailed westward to the Philippines and around the Cape of Good Hope, and returned to Plymouth in 1580 laden with treasure, the first captain ever to sail his own ship around the world and the first Englishman to sail the Pacific, the Indian Ocean, and the South Atlantic. In 1581 he was knighted and made mayor of Plymouth. Appointed vice admiral (1588), he played a crucial role in defeating the Spanish ARMADA and became England's hero, achieving a popularity unequaled until HORATIO NELSON's. On his last voyage, to the West Indies, he succumbed to fever and was buried at sea.

Sir Francis Drake, oil painting by an unknown artist; in the National Portrait Gallery, London.
BY COURTESY OF THE NATIONAL PORTRAIT GALLERY, LONDON

Drake equation *or* **Green Bank equation** Equation claimed to yield the number of technically advanced civilizations in the MILKY WAY GALAXY as a function of several factors conducive to evolution of intelligent life with technological capabilities. It was largely developed by Frank D. Drake (born 1930) in 1961 at a SETI conference in Green Bank, W.V. Of all the stars that form in the galaxy, only some will give rise to life-supporting planets, and of those planets, only some will generate life capable of high technology and yet able to avoid technological destruction. Because the numbers for each factor are poorly known, the results generated vary from zero to millions.

Drake Passage Strait, connecting the Atlantic and Pacific oceans between TIERRA DEL FUEGO and the SHETLAND ISLANDS. Located about 100 mi (660 km) north of the Antarctic Peninsula, it is 600 mi (1,000 km) wide. In this area the climate changes from cool, humid, and subpolar to the frozen conditions of Antarctica. An important trade route in the 19th and early 20th century, its stormy seas and icy conditions made the rounding of Cape HORN through the Drake Passage a difficult journey.

Drakensberg \'drä-kənz-ˌberk\ *Zulu* **Kwathlamba** \'kwät-'läm-bä\ Mountain range, southern Africa. It rises to more than 11,400 ft (3,475 m) and extends from southwest to northeast in LESOTHO and southeastern South Africa, separating the extensive high plateaus of the interior from the lower lands along the coast. It is an area of many game reserves and national parks.

Draper, Charles Stark (1901–1987) U.S. aeronautical engineer. Born in Windsor, Mo., he taught at MIT from 1935, where he developed a gunsight for naval ANTI-AIRCRAFT GUNS that was installed on most U.S. naval vessels in World War II. His inertial navigation system, called spatial inertial reference equipment (SPIRE), allowed a plane to fly thousands of miles to its destination without reference to outside navigational aids, such as radio or the positions of celestial bodies. His group at MIT also developed the guidance systems for the spacecraft of the APOLLO program.

Draper, Ruth (1884–1956) U.S. monologist. Born in New York City, she began her career by writing sketches about people she had observed and performing them at parties. She made her New York debut (1917) in a series of one-act pieces. Her London debut (1920) established her as a master monologist. She performed worldwide, playing on a bare stage with few props and creating characters and settings by subtle modulation of feature, gesture, and voice.

Drava River \'drä-və\ *German* **Drau** \'drau̇\ River, southern central Europe. It rises in the Carnic Alps and flows east through Austria, where it forms the Drautal, the longest longitudinal valley of the ALPS. Flowing southeast through Slovenia and on to northern Croatia, where it forms part of the Croatian–Hungarian border, it is 447 mi (719 km) long, and a major tributary of the DANUBE RIVER. Its valley was the chief passage through which historically invaders penetrated the alpine countries.

Dravidian languages \drə-'vi-dē-ən\ Family of more than 25 languages indigenous to and spoken principally in southern Asia by more than 210 million people. The four major Dravidian languages of southern India—TELUGU, TAMIL, KANNADA, and MALAYALAM—have independent scripts and long documented histories; they account for the overwhelming majority of all Dravidian-speakers. All have borrowed liberally from SANSKRIT. The only Dravidian language spoken entirely outside of India is Brahui, with fewer than 2 million speakers mainly in Pakistan and Afghanistan. Grammatically, Dravidian languages are agglutinative, and MORPHOLOGY is limited almost solely to suffixation. The Dravidian family, with no demonstrated relationship to other language families, is assumed to have covered a much more extensive area of South Asia prior to the spread of INDO-ARYAN and was the source of loanwords into early Indo-Aryan dialects.

drawing Art or technique of producing images on a surface, usually paper, by means of marks in graphite, ink, chalk, charcoal, or crayon. It is often a preliminary stage to work in other media. According to GIORGIO VASARI, *disegno* (drawing and design) was the foundation of the three arts of painting, sculpture, and architecture. In the Italian Renaissance, drawing became an independent technique and was associated especially with Florentine art.

drawing *or* **drafting** In YARN manufacture, process of attenuating the loose assemblage of fibers called sliver by passing it through a series of rollers, thus straightening the individual fibers and making them more parallel. Each pair of rollers spins faster than the previous one. Drawing reduces a soft mass of fiber to a firm uniform strand of usable size. In the production of man-made fibers, drawing is a stretching process applied to fibers in the plastic state, increasing orientation and reducing size. In metalworking, drawing refers to the process of shaping sheet metal into complex, three-dimensional forms with metal dies. See also CARDING, WIRE DRAWING.

drawing frame *or* **spinning frame** MACHINE for DRAWING, twisting, and winding YARN. Invented in the 1730s by LEWIS PAUL and JOHN WYATT, the spinning machine operated by drawing cotton or wool through pairs of successively faster rollers. It was eventually superseded by R. ARKWRIGHT's water frame.

Dreadnought, HMS British BATTLESHIP launched in 1906 that established the pattern of the warships that dominated the world's navies for the next 35 years. It was equipped entirely with big guns because recent improvements in naval gunnery had made preparation for short-range battle unnecessary. Powered by steam turbines instead of the steam pistons then common, it sailed at a record top speed of 21 knots. It displaced 18,000 tons (16,300 metric tons), was 526 ft (160 m) long, and carried a crew of about 800. By World War I it was nearly outclassed by faster "superdreadnoughts" carrying bigger guns. It was placed on reserve in 1919 and broken up for scrap in 1923.

dream Series of thoughts, images, or emotions occurring during SLEEP, particularly sleep accompanied by rapid eye movement (REM sleep). Dream reports range from the very ordinary and realistic to the fantastic and surreal. Humans have always attached great importance to dreams, which have been variously viewed as windows to the sacred, the past and the future, or the world of the dead. Dreams have provided creative solutions to intellectual and emotional problems and have offered ideas for artistic pursuits. A type of cognitive synthesis that facilitates conscious insight may occur subconsciously during dreaming. The most famous theory of the significance of dreams is the psychoanalytic model of SIGMUND FREUD; in Freud's view, desires that are ordinarily repressed (hidden from consciousness) because they represent forbidden impulses are given expression in dreams, though often in disguised (i.e., symbolic) form.

Dreaming, the *or* **Dream-Time** In the religion of the AUSTRALIAN ABORIGINES, the mythological time of the creation, when the environment was shaped and humanized by mythic beings who took animal or human form or changed their form at will. They took long journeys and created human life and the social order. In Aboriginal belief, they continue to exist, though they may have traveled beyond the lands of the people who sing about them or have metamorphosed into natural features such as rocky outcrops or waterholes. The places where they are thought to have performed some action or to have been transformed are sacred ritual centers. See also AUSTRALIAN RELIGION.

Dred Scott decision *formally* ***(Dred) Scott vs. Sandford*** 1857 ruling of the U.S. Supreme Court that made slavery legal in all territories. Scott was a slave whose master had taken him in 1834 from a slave state (Missouri) to a free state and free territory, then back to Missouri. Scott sued for his freedom in Missouri in 1846, saying his residence in a free state and a free territory made him free. ROGER B. TANEY declared that Scott was not entitled to rights as a U.S. citizen (and, in fact, had "no rights which any white man was bound to respect"). Taney and six justices went on to declare that the MISSOURI COMPROMISE was unconstitutional because Congress had no power to prohibit slavery in the territories (see STATES' RIGHTS). The decision, a clear victory for the South, increased Northern antislavery sentiment, strengthened the new REPUBLICAN PARTY, and fed the sectional strife that led to war in 1861.

Dreikaiserbund See THREE EMPERORS' LEAGUE

Dreiser \ˈdrī-zər\, **Theodore (Herman Albert)** (1871–1945) U.S. novelist. Born in Terre Haute, Ind., to poor German immigrant parents, he left home at 15 for Chicago. He worked as a journalist, then moved to New York in 1894 for a successful career as a magazine editor and publisher. His first novel, *Sister Carrie* (1900), about a young kept woman who goes unpunished for her transgressions, was denounced as scandalous. His subsequent novels would confirm his reputation as the outstanding American practitioner of NATURALISM. After the success of *Jennie Gerhardt* (1911), he began writing full-time, producing a trilogy consisting of *The Financier* (1912), *The Titan* (1914), and *The Stoic* (published 1947), which was followed by *The Genius* (1915) and its sequel, *The Bulwark* (published 1946). *An American Tragedy* (1925), based on a murder trial, made him a hero among social reformers. He also wrote short stories, plays, essays, and memoirs.

Theodore Dreiser.
THE GRANGER COLLECTION, NEW YORK CITY

Dresden City (pop., 1996 est.: 469,000), eastern Germany, situated on the ELBE RIVER. Originally a Slavonic settlement, it was the residence of the margraves of Meissen in the early 13th century. The Dresden china industry originated there but was moved to Meissen in 1710 (see MEISSEN PORCELAIN). NAPOLEON I made the town a center of military operations and won his last great battle there in 1813. Dresden was occupied by Prussia in 1866. In World War II, it was severely damaged by Allied bombing raids in 1945. Several of its historic buildings have been restored or reconstructed. It is known for its art galleries, museums, and other cultural institutions. Industries produce precision and optical instruments.

Dresden Codex *Latin* **Codex Dresdensis.** One of the few pre-Columbian MAYA CODICES to survive book burnings by Spanish clergy. It contains exceptionally accurate astronomical calculations, including eclipse-prediction tables and the SYNODIC PERIOD of Venus. The Mayas' reputation as astronomers is based largely on these figures.

dress Covering, or clothing and accessories, for the human body. The term encompasses such familiar garments as shirts, trousers, jackets, footwear, HATS, CORSETS, and GLOVES; hairstyles, beards, mustaches, and WIGS; and COSMETICS, JEWELRY, and other forms of body decoration. In the West up to the modern era, dress functioned as a reflection of social and economic standing; in the 20th century, improved manufacturing technologies made styles of the elite available to the general population even as the blue jeans and other informal attire once associated with the working class became ubiquitous.

dressage \drə-ˈsäzh\ (French, "training") Sport involving the execution by a trained horse of precision movements in response to barely perceptible signals from its rider. Particularly important are the animal's pace and bearing in performing walks, trots, canters, and more specialized maneuvers. Training is divided into the elementary *campagne* and the advanced *haute école.* Dressage competitions have been included in the Olympic Games since 1912. Riders compete as individuals and in teams.

Dressler, Marie *orig.* **Leila Marie Koerber** (1869–1934) Canadian-U.S. actress. Born in Cobourg, Ontario, she began her acting career as a vaudeville comedienne, and made her film debut in *Tillie's Punctured Romance* (1914), in which CHARLIE CHAPLIN also appeared. After a period of obscurity, her career revived with the coming of sound films, and in the 1930s she was known for her portrayals of self-sufficient, humorous old women (often costarring with WALLACE BEERY) in such films as *Min and Bill* (1931, Academy Award) and *Tugboat Annie* (1933).

Drew, Charles Richard (1904–1950) U.S. physician and surgeon. Born in Washington, D.C., he received his PhD from Columbia University. While researching the properties and preservation of blood plasma, he developed efficient ways to process and store plasma in blood banks. He directed the U.S. and Britain's World War II blood-plasma programs until 1942. An African-American, he resigned over the segregation of the blood of blacks and whites in blood banks. He died in an auto accident.

Drew, Daniel (1797–1879) U.S. railway financier. In 1844 he founded the Wall Street brokerage firm of Drew, Robinson, and Co., which became one of the principal traders in railroad stocks in the U.S. The "Erie War" of 1866–68, in which Drew joined JAY GOULD and JAMES FISK against CORNELIUS VANDERBILT in a struggle for control of the ERIE RAILROAD CO., eventually led to his ruin, and he filed for bankruptcy in 1876.

Drew family U.S. theatrical family. Louisa Lane (later Louisa Lane Drew; 1820–1897) began her stage career at 8 in Philadelphia, where her widowed mother had brought her from England. Her many successful parts included Lady Teazle, Mrs. Malaprop, and such "breeches" roles as Shakespeare's Romeo and Mark Antony. In 1850 she married the Irish comic actor John Drew (1827–1862), who made his U.S. debut in 1842 and comanaged the Arch Street Theatre in Philadelphia. He toured widely, and she managed the theater from 1861, directing the renamed Mrs. John Drew's Arch Street Theatre company with notable success until 1892. Their son John Drew, Jr. (1853–1927) made his debut (1873) with his mother's company, then joined the companies of

Augustin Daly (1879–92) and Charles Frohman (1892–1915). He was noted for his roles in Shakespearean comedy, society drama, and light comedies. Their daughter Georgiana Emma Drew (1856–1893) made her acting debut with her mother's company (1872). She became the wife of Maurice Barrymore and the mother of Lionel, Ethel, and John Barrymore (see BARRYMORE FAMILY).

Drexel, Anthony J(oseph) (1826–1893) U.S. banker and philanthropist. Born in Philadelphia, he and his brothers inherited his father's Philadelphia banking house and built it into a successful investment-banking concern, specializing in flotation of government bonds, railroad organization, mining development, and urban real estate. In 1891 he founded the Drexel Institute of Art, Science, and Industry, now Drexel University. He was the uncle of ST. KATHERINE DREXEL.

Drexel, St. Katherine (1858–1955) U.S. missionary. Born in Philadelphia, the niece of banker and philanthropist ANTHONY J. DREXEL, she inherited a vast fortune, which she used to fund her charitable enterprises. She built mission schools in Minnesota, South Dakota, Wyoming, and New Mexico, and in 1887 Pope LEO XIII asked her to become a missionary. In 1891 she founded the Blessed Sacrament Sisters for Indians and Colored People (now Sisters of the Blessed Sacrament), a congregation of missionary nuns dedicated to the welfare of Native Americans and African Americans. She founded several schools for minority students as well as Xavier University in New Orleans (1915). She was canonized in 2000.

Dreyer \'drī-ər\, **Carl Theodor** (1889–1968) Danish film director. He entered the film industry as a writer of subtitles and became a scriptwriter and editor. His first film as a director was *The President* (1919); after several others, he made his most famous silent film, *The Passion of Joan of Arc* (1928). He created a new directorial style based on extensive close-ups and authentic settings. His other films include *Vampire* (1932), the celebrated *Day of Wrath* (1943), *The Word* (1955), and *Gertrud* (1964). He is regarded as the most important figure in Danish cinema.

Carl Dreyer.
BY COURTESY OF THE MUSEUM OF MODERN ART FILM STILLS ARCHIVE, NEW YORK

Dreyfus \dre-'fues, *Engl* 'drī-fəs, 'drā-fəs\, **Alfred** (1859–1935) French army officer, subject of the Dreyfus Affair. Son of a Jewish textile manufacturer, he studied at the École Polytechnique, then entered the army and rose to the rank of captain (1889). He was assigned to the war ministry when, in 1894, he was accused of selling military secrets to Germany. He was convicted and sentenced to life imprisonment on Devil's Island. The legal proceedings, based on insufficient evidence, were highly irregular, but public opinion and the French press, led by its virulently anti-Semitic section, welcomed the verdict. Doubts began to grow as evidence came out suggesting that C. F. Esterhazy (1847–1923) was the true traitor. The movement for revision of Dreyfus's trial gained momentum when EMILE ZOLA wrote an open letter under the headline "J'Accuse," accusing the army of covering up its errors in making the case. After a new court-martial (1899) again found Dreyfus guilty, he was pardoned by the president of the republic in an effort to resolve the issue. In 1906 a civilian court of appeals cleared Dreyfus and reversed all previous convictions. Formally reinstated and decorated with the Legion of Honor, he later saw active service in World War I. The affair resulted in the separation of church and state in 1905.

Dreyfus, before 1894.
H. ROGER-VIOLLET

Dreyfuss \'drā-fəs\, **Henry** (1904–1972) U.S. industrial designer. Born in New York, he began designing stage sets for the Broadway theater at 17 and in 1929 opened his first industrial design office. Bell Telephone Laboratories hired him to design a series of telephones in the 1930s. Among his other notable designs was the interior of the ocean liner *Independence.* A pioneer of ergonomic design, he published several books explaining his methods, including *Designing for People* (1955, 1967).

drill Tool to make holes, usually by revolving. Drills, gimlets, and AUGERS have cutting edges that detach material to leave a hole. Drilling usually requires high speed and low TORQUE, with little material being removed during each revolution of the tool. The earliest (perhaps BRONZE AGE) drill points had sharp edges that ultimately developed into arrow shapes with two distinct cutting edges. This shape was effective and remained popular until the late 19th century, when factory-made, spiral-fluted twist drills became available at reasonable cost to displace the blacksmith-made articles. Rotating drill bits containing diamonds or other hard materials are used for drilling rock, as for tunnels or oil wells. See also DRILL PRESS.

drill In military science, the preparation of soldiers for performance of their duties through the practice of prescribed movements. It trains soldiers in battle formations, familiarizes them with their weapons, and develops a sense of teamwork and discipline. Today close-order drill is used for marching, ceremonies, and parades; combat drill is used to practice the looser routines of battle. It was introduced by the Greeks, who practiced the maneuvers of the PHALANX. Careful training of the LEGIONS was a major factor in the Roman Empire's dominance. After Rome's decline, drill largely disappeared and battles became free-for-all combats. GUSTAV II ADOLF of Sweden led in reintroducing drill techniques in early-17th-century Europe.

drill Large, short-tailed MONKEY (*Mandrillus leucophaeus,* family Cercopithecidae), formerly found from Nigeria to Cameroon, that, because of hunting and deforestation, is now restricted to remote forest regions of Cameroon. Like the related MANDRILL, the drill is stout-bodied and has vividly colored buttocks. The male is about 32 in. (82 cm) long and has a black face. Its lower lip is bright red, the hairs around the face and a tuft behind the ears are yellowish white, and the rest of the fur is olive-brown. An omnivore, it is mainly terrestrial, gregarious, and powerful; it can fight ferociously if molested.

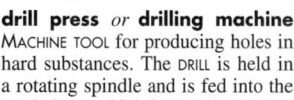

Drill (*Mandrillus leucophaeus*).
J. KOHLER—BAVARIA-VERLAG

drill press *or* **drilling machine** MACHINE TOOL for producing holes in hard substances. The DRILL is held in a rotating spindle and is fed into the workpiece, which is usually clamped in a VISE supported on a table. The drill may be gripped in a chuck with three jaws that move radially in unison, or it may have a tapered shank that fits into a tapered hole in the spindle. Means are provided for varying the spindle speed and (on some machines) for automatically feeding the drill into the workpiece. See also BORING MACHINE.

Drina River \'drē-nə\ River, central Balkans. Originating with the confluence of the Tara and Piva rivers, it follows a northerly 285 mi (459 km) course to enter the SAVA RIVER. Its upper course is through canyons, while its lower course is wider. The Drina constitutes a large part of the boundary between Bosnia and Herzegovina, and the Yugoslav republic of Serbia.

drive In psychology, an urgent need pressing for satisfaction, usually rooted in some physiological deficiency or imbalance (e.g., hunger and thirst) and impelling the organism to action. Psychologists distinguish between drives that are innate and directly related to basic physiological needs (e.g., food, air, and water) and drives that are learned (e.g., drug addiction). Among the other drives psychologists have identified are achievement, affection, affiliation, exploration, manipulation, maternity, pain avoidance, sex, and sleep.

driver Computer program that acts as an intermediary between the OPERATING SYSTEM and a device such as a disk drive, video card, printer, or keyboard. The driver must contain a detailed knowledge of the device, including its set of specialized commands. The presence of a separate driver program frees the operating system from having to understand the details of every device; instead, the operating system issues general commands to the driver, which in turn translates them into specific instructions for the device, or vice versa.

drop forging Process of shaping metal and increasing its strength. In most FORGING, an upper DIE is forced against a heated workpiece positioned on a stationary lower die. If the upper die or hammer is dropped, the process is known as drop forging. To increase the force of the blow, power is sometimes applied to augment gravity.

drop spindle See SPINDLE AND WHORL

drosophila \drō-'sä-fə-lə\ Any member of about 1,000 species in the DIPTERAN genus *Drosophila,* commonly known as vinegar flies but also called FRUIT FLIES. Some species, particularly *D. melanogaster,* are used extensively in laboratory experiments on genetics and evolution because they are easy to raise and have a short life cycle (less than two weeks at room temperature). More data have been collected concerning the genetics of drosophila than for any other animal. Its biology in its natural habitats is not well known. Its larvae may live in rotting or damaged fruits or in fungi or fleshy flowers.

Droste-Hülshoff \'drò-stə-'hᴂls-hòf\, **Annette, Freiin (baroness) von** *orig.* **Anna Elisabeth Franziska Adolphine Wilhelmine Louise Maria, Freiin von Droste zu Hülshoff** (1797–1848) German writer. One of the great women poets of Germany, she wrote religious verse (particularly *Das Geistliche Jahr,* 1851) but is most famous for detailed, evocative poems about her native Westphalia. Her stories are considered forerunners of the 19th-century realistic short story. Her only complete prose work, *The Jew's Beech* (1842), is a psychological study of a villager who murders a Jew.

Drottningholm Palace \'drüt-niŋ-ˌhòlm\ Royal palace, near Stockholm, Sweden. It was designed by Nicodemus Tessin (1615–1681) and built 1662–86. It shows French Baroque influences in its plan, gardens, and interior, but it also has Italian Classical elements and is capped by a Nordic *sateri* roof. A theater attached to it was built in the 1760s and is preserved with its original sets and stage machinery as a theatrical museum. The palace was formerly the Swedish royal family's summer residence.

drought Lack or insufficiency of rain for an extended period that severely disturbs the HYDROLOGIC CYCLE in an area. Droughts involve water shortages, crop damage, streamflow reduction, and depletion of groundwater and soil moisture. They occur when evaporation and transpiration exceed precipitation for a considerable period. Drought is the most serious hazard to agriculture in nearly every part of the world. Efforts have been made to control it by seeding clouds to induce rainfall, but these experiments have had only limited success.

drug Any chemical agent that affects the function of living things. Some, including ANTIBIOTICS, STIMULANTS, TRANQUILIZERS, ANTIDEPRESSANTS, ANALGESICS, NARCOTICS, and HORMONES, have generalized effects. Others, including LAXATIVES, heart stimulants, ANTICOAGULANTS, DIURETICS, and ANTIHISTAMINES, act on specific systems. VACCINES are sometimes considered drugs. Medicinal drugs may protect against attacking organisms (by killing them, stopping them from reproducing, or blocking their effects on the host), substitute for a missing or defective substance in the body, or interrupt an abnormal process. A drug must bind with receptors in or on cells and cannot work if the receptors are absent or its CONFIGURATION does not fit theirs. Drugs may be given by mouth, by injection, by inhalation, rectally, or through the skin. The oldest existing catalogue of drugs is a stone tablet from ancient Babylonia (c. 1700 BC); the modern drug era began when antibiotics were discovered in 1928. Synthetic versions of natural drugs led to design of drugs based on chemical structure. Drugs must be not only effective but safe; side effects can range from minor to dangerous (see MEDICINAL POISONING). Many illegal drugs also have medical uses (see COCAINE, HEROIN, DRUG ADDICTION). See also DRUG RESISTANCE, PHARMACOLOGY, PHARMACY.

drug addiction *or* **chemical dependency** Physical and/or psychological dependency on a psychoactive (mind-altering) substance (e.g., alcohol, NARCOTICS, NICOTINE), defined as continued use despite knowing that the substance causes harm. Physical dependency results when the body builds up a tolerance to a drug, needing increasing doses to achieve the desired effects and to prevent withdrawal symptoms. Psychological dependency may have more to do with one's psychological makeup; some people may have a genetic tendency to addiction. The most common addictions are to alcohol (see ALCOHOLISM), BARBITURATES, TRANQUILIZERS, and AMPHETAMINES, as well as to the stimulants nicotine and CAFFEINE. Initial treatment (detoxification) should be conducted with medical supervision. Individual and group psychotherapy are critical elements. ALCOHOLICS ANONYMOUS and similar support groups can increase the success rate of other efforts. The ability to admit addiction and the will to change are necessary first steps.

Drug Enforcement Administration (DEA) Agency of the U.S. Department of JUSTICE charged with enforcing laws that cover trafficking in controlled substances. Established in 1973, the DEA works with other agencies to control the cultivation, production, smuggling, and distribution of illicit drugs. Most of its efforts are directed against international narcotics smuggling organizations, but it also works to shut down interstate operations.

drug poisoning See MEDICINAL POISONING

drug resistance Property of a disease-causing organism that allows it to withstand drug therapy. In any population of infectious agents, some have a MUTATION that helps them resist the action of a drug. The drug then kills more of the nonresistant microbes, leaving the mutants without competition to multiply into a resistant strain. This situation is more likely if the drug is not taken properly (e.g., a course of ANTIBIOTICS not completed, anti-HIV drug doses missed) or not prescribed properly (e.g., an antibiotic given for a viral disease). Resistance factors can also be transferred between species that infect the same body. The overprescription of antibiotics in humans and the addition of antibiotics to animal feed have accelerated the evolution of resistant strains of bacteria, making it increasingly difficult to fight off certain disease-causing organisms.

Druid Member of a learned class of priests, teachers, and judges among the ancient Celtic peoples. The Druids instructed young men, oversaw sacrifices, judged quarrels, and decreed penalties; they were exempt from warfare and paid no tribute. They studied ancient verse, natural philosophy, astronomy and religious lore; their principal doctrine was belief in the immortality of the soul and the transmigration of souls. They sometimes practiced human sacrifice to cure gravely ill people or protect warriors in battle. The Druids were suppressed in Gaul by the Romans in the 1st century AD and in Britain a little later. They lost their priestly functions in Ireland after the coming of Christianity but survived as poets, historians, and judges. See also CELTIC RELIGION.

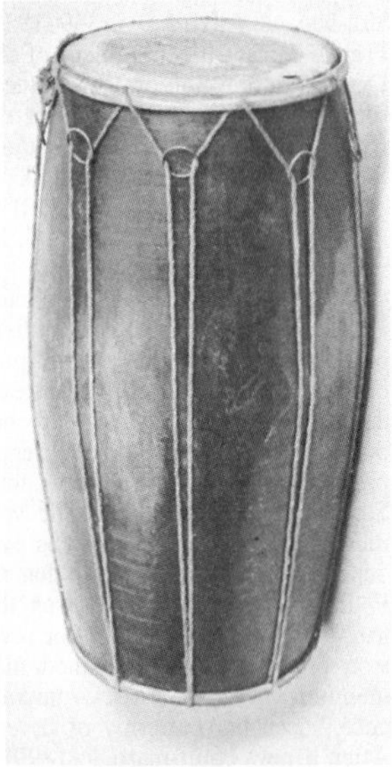

Barrel drum from India with cord-tensioned construction, in the Metropolitan Museum of Art, New York City.

BY COURTESY OF THE METROPOLITAN MUSEUM OF ART, NEW YORK CITY

drum Musical instrument whose sound is produced by the vibration of a stretched membrane. Drums are usually either cylindrical or bowl-shaped. The drum is a universal instrument and very ancient; a drum dating to 6000 BC has been found in Moravia. Drums have been important ritually in cultures worldwide. Drums may have a definite pitch or be unpitched; those of Africa, South and Southeast Asia (see TABLA), and the Middle East are mostly pitched, whereas Western drums are more often unpitched. Drumming has attained its highest degree of development in Africa and India. From the 13th century, folk dancing in Europe was accompanied by a single musician playing simultaneously the pipe or fife and the tabor, a small double-headed snare drum played with one stick.

The side drum, or snare drum, has coiled wires or gut strings strung across the lower head, which vibrate against it when the upper head is struck. The powerful bass drum is used especially in marching bands. The pitched TIMPANI are the standard orchestral drums. Until the 17th century, drum parts in Western music were entirely improvised. The drum set used in popular music is played by a single person and normally includes a snare drum, tom-toms, a pedal-operated bass drum, and suspended and hi-hat CYMBALS.

drum *or* **croaker** In biology, any of about 160 species (family Sciaenidae) of carnivorous, generally bottom-dwelling fishes. Most are marine, found along warm and tropical seashores. Most can "vocalize" by moving strong muscles attached to the air bladder, which acts as a resonating chamber, amplifying the sounds. Drums have two dorsal fins and are usually silvery. The WEAKFISHES, sea trouts, and squeteagues (genus *Cynoscion*) have a large mouth, jutting jaws, and canine teeth, but most drums have an underslung lower jaw and small teeth. The largest species, the totuava, weighs up to 225 lbs (100 kg), but other species are much smaller. Many drums are food or game fishes. See also BASS, KINGFISH.

drupe Fruit in which the outer layer is a thin skin, the middle layer is thick and usually fleshy (though sometimes tough, as in the ALMOND, or fibrous, as in the coconut), and the inner layer (the pit) is hard and stony. Within the pit is usually one seed. In aggregate fruits such as the raspberry and blackberry (which are not true BERRIES), many small drupes are clumped together. Other representative drupes are the CHERRY, PEACH, MANGO, OLIVE, and WALNUT.

Drury Lane Theatre Oldest English theater still in use. It was built in London by Thomas Killigrew for his acting company as the Theatre Royal (1663). It burned in 1672 and was rebuilt in 1674 with CHRISTOPHER WREN as architect. It prospered under such actor-managers as COLLEY CIBBER (1710–34), and later under DAVID GARRICK (1747–76) and RICHARD BRINSLEY SHERIDAN (1776–88). An expanded "fireproof" theater, opened in 1794, burned in 1809. Rebuilt in 1812 with over 2,000 seats, it declined in popularity from the 1840s, but revived in the 1880s with melodramas and spectacles and was the scene of the acting triumphs of HENRY IRVING and ELLEN TERRY. More recently it has played host to many U.S. musicals.

Drusus Germanicus \'drü-səs-jər-'ma-ni-kəs\, **Nero Claudius** (38–9 BC) Younger brother of TIBERIUS and commander of Roman forces in German territory. The reputed son of Octavian (later AUGUSTUS), he was allowed to take office five years earlier than the legal age. In 13 BC he became governor of the three GAULS, where he conducted a census and erected an altar to Augustus. In 12 he marched into Germany, reaching the Elbe three years later. During those years he was made PRAETOR in 11 and CONSUL in 9. At the Elbe he was thrown from his horse and died. His son CLAUDIUS later became emperor.

Druze *or* **Druse** \'drüz\ Highly secretive Middle Eastern religious sect. It originated in Egypt in 1017 and is named for one of its founders, Muhammad al-Darazi (died 1019/20). Strictly monotheistic and based in ISLAM, Druze beliefs include an eclectic mixture of elements from GNOSTICISM, NEOPLATONISM, JUDAISM, and IRANIAN RELIGION. The Druze believe in the divinity of al-Hakim bi-Amr Allah (985–1021?), sixth caliph of the FATIMID DYNASTY of Egypt, and expect him to return someday to inaugurate a golden age. They permit no converts, either to or from their religion, and no intermarriage. Their religious system is kept secret from the outside world, and they are permitted to deny their faith if their life is in danger. Today they number about one million, mostly in Syria and Lebanon.

dry cleaning System of cleaning textiles with chemical SOLVENTS instead of water. The chemicals, often halides or organohalogens (compounds that contain HALOGEN atoms bonded to carbon atoms), dissolve dirt and grease from fabrics. Carbon tetrachloride was once widely used as a dry-cleaning liquid, but its adverse health effects have cut back its use; other organic halogen compounds are now preferred, particularly tetrachloroethylene, which is much more stable and less toxic.

dry ice CARBON DIOXIDE in SOLID form. It is a dense, snowlike substance that passes directly from solid to vapor (see SUBLIMATION) at −109.3°F (−78.5°C). It is used chiefly to keep foods, vaccines, and other perishable products cold during shipping or storage.

dry lake See PLAYA

dry rot Symptom of fungal disease in plants (see FUNGUS), characterized by firm spongy to leathery or hard decay of the stem (branch), trunk, root, rhizome, corm, bulb, or fruit. The fungus consumes the CELLULOSE of wood, leaving a soft skeleton that is readily reduced to powder.

Dry Tortugas National Park \tȯr-'tü-gəz\ National park located on the Dry Tortugas islands, southwestern Florida. The islands are situated at the entrance to the Gulf of Mexico, west of Key West, Fla. Established in 1935 as Fort Jefferson National Park, it occupies an area of about 64,700 acres (26,200 hectares). Its current name was adopted in 1992. The park's principal features are a marine exhibit and the remains of fortifications built in 1846.

dryad \'drī-əd, 'drī-ˌad\ *or* **hamadryad** In GREEK MYTHOLOGY, tree NYMPHS. Dryads were originally the spirits of oak trees (*drys:* "oak"), but the name was later applied to all tree nymphs. They were nature spirits who took the form of beautiful young women, and it was believed that they lived only as long as the trees they inhabited.

Dryden, John (1631–1700) British poet, dramatist, and literary critic. The son of a country gentleman, he was educated at Cambridge University. His poetry celebrating the Restoration so pleased Charles II that he was named poet laureate (1668) and, two years later, royal historiographer. Even after losing the laureateship and his court patronage in 1688 with the accession of William III, he succeeded in dominating the literary scene with his numerous works, many attuned to politics and public life. Many of his nearly 30 comedies, tragedies, and dramatic operas—including *Marriage A-la-Mode* (1672), *Aureng-Zebe* (1675), and *All for Love* (1677)—were outstandingly successful. His *Of Dramatick Poesie* (1668) was the first substantial piece of modern dramatic criticism. Turning away from drama, he became England's greatest verse satirist, producing the masterpieces *Absalom and Achitophel* (1681) and *Mac Flecknoe* (1682). He also produced extensive translations of Latin poetry, including VIRGIL's *Aeneid*.

dryopithecine \ˌdrī-ō-'pi-thə-ˌsīn\ Any member of a genus *(Dryopithecus)* of extinct apelike animals that is representative of a group of generalized APES that contains the ancestors of both the modern apes and humans. Fragmentary materials found over a widespread area, including Europe, Africa, and Asia, have been attributed to other groups but were probably remains of *Dryopithecus.* Dryopithecines are found as fossils in Miocene and Pliocene deposits (23.8–1.8 million years old) and apparently originated in Africa. Several distinct forms are known, including small, medium, and large (GORILLA-sized). Dryopithecines lacked most of the specializations that distinguish modern apes from humans.

DSL *in full* **Digital Subscriber Line** Broadband digital communications connection that operates over standard copper telephone wires. It requires a DSL MODEM, which splits transmissions into two frequency bands: the lower frequencies for voice (ordinary telephone calls) and the upper band for digital data, especially for connection to the INTERNET. Data can be transferred via DSL at much higher rates than with ordinary dial-up modem service; the range of DSL signals, however, is very small. Connections can be made only within a few miles of the nearest transmitting station. DSL and "xDSL" are umbrella terms under which a variety of protocols and technologies fall. ADSL (Asymmetric DSL) is a popular type of DSL in which most of the bandwidth of the connection is devoted to downloading data from the network to the user, leaving only a small-scale connection for uploading data. In HDSL (High bit-rate DSL) and SDSL (Symmetric DSL) the data stream is symmetric; that is, the upstream and downstream rates are the same. UDSL (Unidirectional DSL), VDSL (Very high data rate DSL), and others still under development are intended to offer even greater rates of data transmission.

du Barry \dǖ-bà-'rē\, **comtesse (Countess)** *orig.* **(Marie-) Jeanne Bécu** *known as* **Madame du Barry** (1743–1793) French mistress of LOUIS XV. A Paris shop assistant, she became the mistress of Jean du Barry, who introduced her into Parisian high society. Admired for her beauty, she joined Louis XV's court in 1769 after a nominal marriage to Jean's brother, a nobleman, qualified her as Louis's official royal mistress. Though she exercised little political influence, her unpopularity contributed to the decline of the prestige of the crown in the early 1770s. After Louis's death (1774), she was banished from court. In the French Revolution she was condemned as a counterrevolutionary and guillotined.

Du Bois \dü-'bȯis\, **W(illiam) E(dward) B(urghardt)** (1868–1963) U.S. sociologist and black-rights leader. Born in Great Barrington, Mass., he received a PhD from Harvard University and began conducting empirical studies on the social situation of U.S. blacks. He concluded that change could be attained only through agitation and protest, a view that clashed with that of Booker T. Washington. His famous book *The Souls of Black Folk* appeared in 1903. In 1905 Du Bois founded the Niagara Movement, the forerunner of the NAACP. He served as the NAACP's director of research and editor of its magazine, *Crisis,* (1910–34). He taught at Atlanta University and wrote several more books. Identified with pro-Russian causes from the 1940s, he became disillusioned with the U.S., and in 1961 joined the Communist Party, moved to Ghana, and renounced his U.S. citizenship.

Du Buat \dᵫ̄-bᵫ̄-'ä\, **Pierre-Louis-Georges** (1734–1809) French hydraulic engineer. He compiled experimental data from which he determined his basic algebraic expression for discharge from pipes and open channels. Though valid only within the range of his experimental data, this equation provided the best means at the time of predicting the performance of water-supply systems and similar works. His emphasis on achieving results that would be of practical use strongly influenced the development of experimental hydraulics in the 18th–19th century.

du Cange \'kä^n^zh\, **Charles du Fresne, seigneur (Lord)** (1610–1688) French scholar. Du Cange's most important works, *A Glossary for Writers of Middle and Low Latin* (1678) and *A Glossary for Writers of Middle and Low Greek* (1688), made use of his encyclopedic knowledge not only of languages but of history, law, archaeology, and geography. His historical approach and effort to distinguish these languages' medieval vocabularies from their classical counterparts inspired later scholars to examine the development of language from a historical perspective. Frequently reedited, his dictionaries retained their usefulness through the 20th century.

Du Fu *or* **Tu Fu** \'dü-'fü\ (712–770) Chinese poet, often considered the greatest of all time. After a traditional Confucian education, he failed the important civil-service examinations and consequently spent much of his life wandering, repeatedly attempting to gain court positions, with mixed success. His early poetry, which celebrates the natural world and bemoans the passage of time, garnered him renown. He suffered periods of extreme personal hardship, and as he matured his verse began to express profound compassion for humanity. An expert in all the poetic genres of his day, he is renowned for his superb classicism and skill in prosody, though many of the subtleties of his art do not survive translation.

du Maurier \dü-'mȯr-ē-ˌā\, **Daphne** *later* **Dame Daphne** (1907–1989) British novelist and playwright. Granddaughter of George du Maurier and daughter of the actor-manager Sir Gerald Du Maurier (1873–1934), she is best known for the romantic gothic suspense novel *Rebecca* (1938), one of many successful tales set on the wild coast of Cornwall. Her other novels include *Jamaica Inn* (1936), *Frenchman's Creek* (1942), and *My Cousin Rachel* (1951). Her story "The Birds," like *Jamaica Inn* and *Rebecca,* was filmed by Alfred Hitchcock.

du Maurier, George (Louis Palmella Busson) (1834–1896) British caricaturist and novelist. Forced to abandon painting for drawing when he was blinded in one eye, his skilled draftsmanship and engaging personality quickly established his success. His drawings for *Punch*, *Once a Week,* and *The Leisure Hour* were acute commentaries on the Victorian scene. His highly successful novel *Trilby* (1894), about an artist's model who falls under the spell of the musician Svengali, has entered popular mythology. His other novels were *Peter Ibbetson* (1891) and *The Martian* (1897). His granddaughter Daphne du Maurier edited his letters (1951).

Du Mont, Allen B(alcom) (1901–1965) U.S. engineer. Born in Brooklyn, N.Y., he became interested in television in 1928, as chief engineer at the De Forest Radio Co., and concluded that television required a purely electronic system to work. In 1931 he set up what would become Allen B. Du Mont Laboratories, where he improved the cathode-ray tube and developed the modern oscilloscope. In 1937 he began manufacturing the first commercial television receivers. After World War II he marketed the first widely available TV receivers and set up one of the first TV broadcasting networks. He served with the National Television System Committee formulating broadcasting standards, and worked with the Federal Communications Commission in allocating frequencies for TV channels.

Du Pont Co. *in full* **E.I. du Pont de Nemours & Co.** \nə-'mür\ U.S. manufacturer. The company was founded near Wilmington, Del., in 1802 by a French immigrant, Éleuthère Irénée du Pont de Nemours, son of the eminent economist Pierre-Samuel du Pont de Nemours (1739–1817). The company originally manufactured gunpowder and other explosives. It was incorporated in 1899 after nearly a century as a partnership, after which it began to diversify its product line, partly through extensive acquisitions. It developed nitrocellulose plastics in 1915 and synthetic rubber in 1931, and later developed the fibers nylon, Orlon, Dacron, Kevlar, and Lycra, as well as Mylar film and Teflon resin, among many other synthetics. The company was run by the du Pont family until World War II. Today it is a highly diverse conglomerate with major electronics, automotive, and pharmaceutical branches.

Dual Alliance See Austro–German Alliance, Franco–Russian Alliance

dual-aspect theory See double-aspect theory

Dual Monarchy See Austria–Hungary

dualism Use of two irreducible, heterogeneous principles (sometimes in conflict, sometimes complementary) to analyze the knowing process (epistemological dualism) or to explain all of reality or some broad aspect of it (metaphysical dualism). Examples of epistemological dualism are being and thought and subject and object; examples of metaphysical dualism are good and evil, God and the world, and body and spirit. Dualism is distinguished from monism and pluralism. Zoroastrianism and Manichaeism are good examples of highly dualistic religions; in East Asia, the yin-yang principle demonstrates complementary dualism.

Dubayy *or* **Dubai** \dü-'bī\ Constituent emirate (pop., 2001 est.: 913,000), United Arab Emirates. It is surrounded by the emirates of Abu Dhabi, and Ash-Shariqah, and it has 45 mi (72 km) of coastline on the Persian Gulf. Occupying an area of 1,510 sq mi (3,900 sq km), it is the second most populous and second largest state of the federation. Most of its population live in or near its capital, Dubayy city (pop., 1995: 669,181). Settled in 1799 by people from Abu Dhabi, Dubayy became a locally powerful state in the early 19th century, and until the 1930s it was known for its pearl exports. It has since been enriched by oil wealth. Dubayy city is now a center for most of the banks and insurance companies of the United Arab Emirates.

Dubček \'düb-ˌchek\, **Alexander** (1921–1992) Czech politician. In World War II he took part in the underground resistance to Nazi occupation. After the war he rose in Communist Party ranks to become a member of the Presidium of the party's Central Committee (1962). In 1968 he forced Antonín Novotný (1904–1975) to resign and replaced him as head of the Communist Party. He introduced liberal reforms in the brief period known as the Prague Spring, which ended when the Soviet Union invaded Czechoslovakia in August 1968. Demoted to lesser posts, he was expelled from the party in 1970. He returned to prominence in 1989 after the Communist Party had given up its monopoly on power, and was elected speaker of the Czech parliament.

Dubinsky, David (1892–1982) Polish-U.S. labor leader. Son of a baker in Russian Poland, he was sent to Siberia in 1908 for his union activities. He escaped and emigrated to the U.S. in 1911, where he renewed his union work. In 1932 he became president of the International Ladies' Garment Workers' Union (ILGWU), a post he kept until 1966, transforming the ILGWU from a small, fractious regional organization into a model international union. He also played a significant role in the merger of the American Federation of Labor and the Congress of Industrial Organizations in 1955.

Dublin *ancient* **Eblana** City (pop., 2002 prelim.: 495,101), capital of Ireland. On the River Liffey, it was settled by Danish Vikings arriving in the area in the 9th century AD; they held it until it was taken by the Irish in the 11th century. Under English control in the 12th century, it was given a charter by Henry II, establishing it as a seat of government. It prospered in the 18th century as a center of the cloth trade, and its harbor dates from this period. In the 19th–20th century it has been the site of bloody nationalist violence, including the 1867 Fenian movement and the 1916 Easter Rising. It is the country's chief port, center of finance and commerce, and seat of culture. Its Guinness Brewery is the nation's largest private employer. Educational and cultural institutions include the University of DUBLIN, and the National Library and National Museum, housed on the grounds of Leinster House (1748), now the seat of the Irish parliament.

Dublin, University of *or* **Trinity College** Oldest university in Ireland, founded in 1591 by Elizabeth I and endowed by the city of Dublin. Trinity was originally intended to be the first of many constituent colleges of the university, but no others were established and the two names became interchangeable. The full benefits of the university (degrees, fellowships, scholarships, etc.) were for many years limited to Anglicans, but in 1873 all religious requirements were eliminated. The university has faculties of arts, humanities, business and economics, engineering, medicine and dentistry, science, and graduate studies. The library contains many illuminated manuscripts, including the *Book of Kells.* Total enrollment is about 12,000.

Dublin Bay prawn See SCAMPI

Dubnow \'düb-ˌnȯf\, **Simon Markovich** (1860–1941) Russian-Jewish historian. Largely self-educated, he gained notice as a scholar of Jewish history before the Bolshevik Revolution prompted him to leave his native Russia for Germany in 1922. He emphasized the cultural autonomy of the Jewish people throughout history, rejecting assimilation but also opposing Zionism as unrealistic. His best-known works were *History of the Jews* (10 vols., 1925–30) and *History of Hasidism* (1931). He fled Nazi Germany in 1933 for Riga, Latvia, where he was eventually killed by the Germans.

Dubos \dü-'bōz\, **René (Jules)** (1901–1982) French-U.S. microbiologist and environmentalist. He emigrated to the U.S. in 1924 and earned his PhD from Rutgers University. His pioneering research in isolating antibacterial substances from soil microorganisms led to the discovery of major antibiotics. He researched and wrote on antibiotics, acquired immunity, tuberculosis, and bacteria native to the gastrointestinal tract. In his later years, his interest shifted to the relationship of humans to the natural environment; his *So Human an Animal* (1968) won the Pulitzer Prize. See also SELMAN WAKSMAN.

Dubrovnik \'dü-ˌbrȯv-nik\ Port city (pop., 1991: 56,000), Croatia. It is situated on the southern Adriatic coast southwest of SARAJEVO. Founded in the 7th century by Roman refugees, it later came under Byzantine rule after the fall of Rome. It was under Venetian control 1205–1358, but remained largely independent and became a mercantile power. It was known as a center of Slavic literature and art in the 15th–17th century. Subjugated by NAPOLEON I in 1808, it was passed to Austria in 1815 and to Yugoslavia in 1918. It was bombed by the Serbs in 1991–92 during Croatia's struggle for independence. The old city, enclosed by medieval city walls, contains 14th-century convents and the 15th-century Rector's Palace.

Dubuffet \dǖ-bǖ-'fe\, **Jean (-Philippe-Arthur)** (1901–1985) French painter, sculptor, and printmaker. He studied painting in Paris, but in 1929 began making a living as a wine merchant. When he returned to art full-time in the early 1940s, he became a leading artist in Paris and proponent of ART BRUT. He executed crude images incised into rough impasto surfaces made of such materials as sand, plaster, tar, gravel, and ashes bound with varnish and glue, and sculptural works made of junk materials; their unfinished appearance provoked public outrage. In the 1960s he experimented with musical composition and architectural environments, and in his later years he produced large fiberglass sculptures for public spaces.

Duccio (di Buoninsegna) \'düt-chō\ (fl. c. 1278–1318/19) Italian painter. Little is known of his life, but several commission records survive, as well as two documented works, the Rucellai Madonna for the Florentine church of Santa Maria Novella (1285) and the famous *Maestà* altarpiece for Siena Cathedral (1308–11); both represent landmarks in the history of Italian painting. His style reflected the influence of CIMABUE and Byzantine art, though he introduced a warmth of human feeling that was comparable to that of GIOTTO in Florentine painting. He was the leading painter in Siena, one of Italy's most vital artistic centers in the Middle Ages.

Duchamp \dǖ-'shäⁿ\, **Marcel** (1887–1968) French artist and art innovator. In 1904 he arrived in Paris and earned his living by drawing cartoons for comic magazines. In 1913 he caused a sensation at the ARMORY SHOW with his painting *Nude Descending a Staircase, No. 2* (1912), combining the principles of Cubism and Futurism. He then abandoned conventional media and, with FRANCIS PICABIA, became the leader of the New York DADA movement. He invented the READY-MADE, notably a urinal titled *Fountain* (1917), and snubbed the traditional values of art, living by the conviction that life is meaningless and absurd. Though among the most gifted painters of his time, he lacked faith in art itself, seeking to replace aesthetic values with an aggressive intellectualism and irreverence for the common-sense world. He greatly influenced the Surrealists, and his attitude toward art and society led to POP ART and other modern and postmodern movements. A legend in his lifetime, he is considered one of the leading spirits of 20th-century art

duck Any of various relatively small, short-necked, large-billed WATERFOWL (several genera in subfamily Anatinae, family Anatidae). The legs of true ducks (Anatinae) are placed rearward (as are those of SWANS), resulting in a waddling gait. Most true ducks differ from swans and true geese (see GOOSE) in that male ducks molt twice annually, females lay large clutches of smooth-shelled eggs, and both sexes have overlapping scales on the skin of the leg and exhibit some differences between sexes in plumage and in call. All true ducks except SHELDUCKS and sea ducks (see DIVING DUCK) mature in the first year and pair only for the season. They are generally divided into three groups: perching ducks, DABBLING DUCKS, and diving ducks. The whistling duck species, also called tree ducks, are not true ducks but are more closely related to geese and swans.

duck hawk See PEREGRINE FALCON

duckbill See PLATYPUS

ductility Capacity of a material to deform permanently (e.g., stretch, bend, or spread) in response to STRESS. Most common STEELS, for example, are quite ductile and hence can accommodate local stress concentrations. Brittle materials, such as glass, cannot accommodate concentrations of stress because they lack ductility, and therefore fracture easily. When a material specimen is stressed, it deforms elastically (see ELASTICITY) at first; above a certain deformation, called the elastic limit, deformation becomes permanent.

ductus arteriosus \'dək-təs-är-ˌtir-ē-'ō-səs\ Short blood vessel between the pulmonary ARTERY and the AORTA in the fetus, which bypasses the lungs to distribute oxygen received through the placenta from the mother's blood. It normally closes once the baby is born and the lungs inflate, separating the PULMONARY and SYSTEMIC circulations. Closure before birth causes circulatory problems. If the ductus stays open after birth (patent ductus arteriosus, more common in premature births), oxygenated and deoxygenated blood mix. Alone, this may not be serious; in some heart malformations it is even necessary for life. PROSTAGLANDIN can keep the ductus open until surgery is done.

Dudley City (pop., 1991: 300,000), WEST MIDLANDS, England. It is the site of several Saxon and Norman fortifications. Coal and ironstone have been mined there since the Middle Ages. By the mid-19th century there were numerous blast furnaces, whose pollution helped to give the area to the north and east the name "Black Country." Metalworking is an important industry.

Dudley, Dud (1599–1684) English ironmaster. He is usually credited with the first SMELTING of IRON ore with COKE. CHARCOAL had been exclusively used for smelting iron until Dudley began experimenting with coke, encouraged by the English government, which was concerned about the rapid destruction of forests for fuel. Dudley patented his innovation in 1621, but the poor quality of his metal limited its sale. See also ABRAHAM DARBY.

Dudley, Robert See Earl of LEICESTER

due process Legal proceedings carried out fairly and in accord with established rules and principles (called also procedural due process). Substantive due process refers to a requirement that laws and regulations be related to a legitimate government interest (e.g., crime prevention) and not contain provisions that result in the unfair or arbitrary treatment of an individual. The 5th Amendment to the U.S. CONSTITUTION states that "no person shall . . . be deprived of life, liberty, or property, without due process of law." This right was extended to the states by the 14th Amendment (1868). The boundaries of due process are not fixed and are the subject of endless judicial interpretation and decision making. Fundamental to procedural due process are adequate notice before the government can deprive one of life, liberty, or property, and the opportunity to be heard and defend one's rights. Substantive due process limits the government's power to enact laws or regulations that affect one's life, liberty, or property rights. See also rights of the ACCUSED, DOUBLE JEOPARDY.

duel Formal combat with weapons fought between two persons in the presence of witnesses. Intended to settle a quarrel or point of honor, it represented an alternative to the usual process of justice. The judicial duel, or trial by battle, is reported in ancient sources and was prevalent in medieval Europe. A judge could order two parties to meet in a duel to settle a matter. It was believed that through such an appeal to the "judgment of God" the righteous would emerge victorious; the loser, if still alive, was dealt with according to the law. Duels of honor were private encounters over real or imagined slights or insults. Duels (later fought with pistols) continued to be fought frequently in France until the late 19th century and in Germany until World War I. The most famous U.S. duel was that between ALEXANDER HAMILTON and AARON BURR (1804). See also ORDEAL.

Duero River See DOURO RIVER

Dufay \dᵫ-'fe\, **Guillaume** (c. 1400–1474) Franco-Flemish composer, principal composer of the BURGUNDIAN SCHOOL. As a boy he sang in the choir of Cambrai Cathedral. Ordained a priest, he acquired a high reputation for learnedness. In 1428 he joined the papal singers in Rome, by which time his works had made him famous. He returned to Cambrai c. 1440, where he would supervise the cathedral's music for the rest of his life, apart from a period working for the duke of Savoy (1451–58). Many musicians came to learn under him, and he enjoyed renown as the greatest living composer. His surviving works, which employ a richly harmonic texture, include some 90 chansons, 13 isorhythmic motets, and at least six complete masses, including such early cantus-firmus masses as *Missa L'homme armé* and *Missa Se la face ay pale.*

Dufy \dᵫ-'fē\, **Raoul** (1877–1953) French painter and designer. In 1900 he studied at the École des Beaux-Arts in Paris and experimented with IMPRESSIONISM. He converted to Fauvism in 1905 under the influence of HENRI MATISSE. He developed a distinctive style characterized by rapid calligraphic drawing on backgrounds of bright, decorative color; his subjects included such recreational scenes as horse races, parades, and concerts. He also designed textiles and made numerous book illustrations. His highly accessible works did much to popularize modern art.

dugong \'dü-ˌgäŋ\ Large marine mammal (*Dugong dugon,* the sole living member of the family Dugongidae) that lives in shallow coastal waters from the Red Sea and eastern Africa to the Philippines, New Guinea, and northern Australia. It is 7–11 ft (2.2–3.4 m) long and usually weighs 500–800 lbs (230–360 kg). Its round, tapered body ends in a flipper with paired, pointed, horizontal branches. The forelimbs are rounded flippers; there are no hind limbs. The head blends into the body, and the snout is broad, square, and bristled. Dugongs live in pairs or in groups of up to six individuals. Once heavily hunted for their meat, hides, and oil, they are now protected throughout most of their range, though some populations remain in danger of extermination. See also MANATEE, SEA COW.

duiker \'dī-kər\ Any of about 14 species of small, shy ANTELOPE. They live in most of Africa but are rarely seen by humans. The gray, or bush, duiker *(Sylvicapra grimmia)* has long legs and lives in regions with bush or grass cover. It stands 22–26 in. (57–67 cm) tall at the shoulder. Only males have horns, which are straight and spiky. Forest duikers (about 13 species, genus *Cephalophus*) are short-legged, hunchbacked animals that live in dense brush and in forests. They stand 14–18 in. (36–46 cm) tall and vary from pale brown through reddish brown to nearly black. Both sexes have short, spiky horns.

Zebra duiker (*Cephalophus zebra*).

KENNETH W. FINK FROM THE NATIONAL AUDUBON SOCIETY COLLECTION/PHOTO RESEARCHERS–EB INC.

Duisburg \'dü-ēs-ˌbu̇rk, *Engl* 'düz-bərg\ City (pop., 1992 est.: 537,000), North Rhine-Westphalia state, western Germany. It lies at the junction of the RHINE and RUHR rivers and is connected with the North Sea ports by the Rhine–Herne Canal. Known to the Romans as Castrum Deutonis, it was mentioned in AD 740 as Diuspargum, a seat of the Frankish kings. It passed to Cleves in 1290 and, with Cleves, to BRANDENBURG in 1614. After suffering heavily in the THIRTY YEARS' WAR, it revived as the seat of a Protestant university from 1655 to 1818. With increasing industrialization after 1880, it is now one of the world's largest inland ports.

Dujardin \dᵫ-zhär-'da^{n}\, **Félix** (1801–1860) French biologist. His studies of microscopic animal life frequently found in decaying organic materials led him in 1834 to propose a new group of one-celled animals that he called Rhizopoda. He named the seemingly formless life substance that oozed outward through openings in certain shells sarcode; later it became known as protoplasm. This work led him in 1835 to argue against CHRISTIAN GOTTFRIED EHRENBERG's theory that microscopic organisms have the same organs as higher animals. Dujardin also studied jellyfish, corals, and sea stars; his study of flatworms laid the foundation for the later development of the study of parasites and parasitism.

Dukakis \dü-'kä-kis\, **Michael S(tanley)** (born 1933) U.S. politician. Born in Brookline, Mass., he attended law school at Harvard, served in the Massachusetts state legislature (1963–71), and was elected governor for three terms (1975–79, 1983–91), during which he coped with a budgetary crisis, restoring the state's fiscal health and strengthening its economic base. As the Democratic presidential nominee in 1988, he lost to GEORGE BUSH. He retired from politics in 1991 to teach.

Dukas \dᵫ-'käs\, **Paul (Abraham)** (1865–1935) French composer. Born into a musical family, he studied at the Paris Conservatoire. His first success was the overture *Polyeucte* (1892). Perfectionism led him to destroy much of his work. His fame rests almost entirely on the tone poem *The Sorceror's Apprentice* (1897); his other surviving works include the opera *Ariane et Barbe-bleue* (1906), the ballet *La péri* (1912), and a symphony in C (1896).

duke European title of nobility, the highest rank below a prince or king except in countries having such titles as archduke or grand duke. The wife of a duke is a duchess. The Romans gave the title *dux* to high military commanders with territorial responsibilities. It was adopted by the barbarian invaders of the Roman empire and was used in their kingdoms and also in France and Germany for rulers of very large areas. In some European countries a duke is a sovereign prince who rules an independent duchy. In Britain, where there were no ducal titles until 1337, it is a hereditary title.

Duke, James B(uchanan) (1856–1925) U.S. tobacco magnate and philanthropist. Born in Durham, N.C., he and his brother Benjamin (1855–1929) entered the family tobacco business. In 1890 James became president of the American Tobacco Co., which controlled the entire U.S. tobacco industry until it was broken up under antitrust laws in 1911 into several companies that would become the principal U.S. cigarette makers. He oversaw the family's contributions to Trinity College in Durham, which was renamed DUKE UNIV.

Duke, Vernon *orig.* **Vladimir (Aleksandrovich) Dukelsky** (1903–1969) Russian-U.S. composer. He fled Russia at 16, settling in Constantinople. From there he visited the U.S., where GEORGE GERSHWIN suggested his new name and advised him not to be afraid of "going lowbrow." He composed classical works in Europe, including *Zéphyr et Flore* (1925) for the BALLETS RUSSES, but returned to the U.S. in 1929. With lyricists including E.Y. HARBURG and HOWARD DIETZ, he wrote music for shows (including *Walk a Little Faster*, 1932) and movies (including *Cabin in the Sky*, 1943, and *Sadie Thompson*, 1944). His songs include "April in Paris," "Taking a Chance on Love," and "Banjo Eyes,"

Duke University Private university in Durham, N.C. It was created in 1924 through an endowment from JAMES B. DUKE, though the original college (Trinity) traces its roots to the mid-19th century. Duke maintained separate campuses for undergraduate men and women until the 1970s. Besides an undergraduate liberal-arts college, the university includes schools of graduate studies, engineering, law, business, divinity, medicine (including a medical center), nursing, and environmental studies. Total enrollment is about 12,000.

Dukhobor See DOUKHOBOR

Dulany \də-'lā-nē\, **Daniel** (1722–1797) American lawyer. Born in Annapolis, Md., he became a leading lawyer in the colonies and a member of the Maryland governor's council (1757–76). In 1765 he wrote an influential pamphlet criticizing the STAMP ACT, but he opposed revolt against British rule and remained a Loyalist during the American Revolution.

Dulbecco \dəl-ˈbe-kō\, **Renato** (born 1914) Italian-U.S. virologist. He received his MD from the University of Turin in 1936, and emigrated to the U.S. in 1947. With Marguerite Vogt he pioneered the culturing of animal viruses and investigated how certain viruses gain control of the cells they infect. They showed that polyoma virus inserts its DNA into the DNA of the host cell, and that the cell is then transformed into a cancer cell, reproducing the viral DNA along with its own and producing more cancer cells. Dulbecco suggested that human cancers could be caused by similar reproduction of foreign DNA fragments. He shared a 1975 Nobel Prize with two former students, Howard Temin (born 1934) and DAVID BALTIMORE. The last of his academic appointments in the U.S. and Britain was as president of the Salk Institute.

dulcimer *or* **hammered dulcimer** ZITHER whose strings are beaten with small hammers. Its soundbox is flat and usually trapezoidal; each pair of strings produces a single note, and the pairs slope upward alternately left and right to facilitate rapid playing. The Hungarian cimbalom is a large dulcimer with legs and a damper pedal, much used in Gypsy orchestras. The Appalachian dulcimer is a narrow zither with a fretted fingerboard and three to five strings, which are stopped with one hand and plucked with a plectrum held in the other.

DuLhut \dū̅-ˈlū̅t\, **Daniel Greysolon, Sieur** (1639?–1710) French soldier and explorer. He made two voyages to New France before 1674 and returned to Montreal in 1675. He negotiated fur-trade agreements with Indian tribes, rescued LOUIS HENNEPIN from the Sioux, assisted COMTE DE FRONTENAC in the campaign against Indian allies of the British, and is credited with establishing French control over the land north and west of Lake Superior. Duluth, Minn., is named for him.

Dulles \ˈdə-ləs\, **Allen W(elsh)** (1893–1969) U.S. diplomat and administrator. Born in Watertown, N.Y., he held diplomatic posts before practicing law with his brother, JOHN FOSTER DULLES. In World War II he served in the Office of Strategic Services. After the war he chaired a committee to survey the U.S. intelligence system. When the CENTRAL INTELLIGENCE AGENCY was established in 1951, he became its deputy director. As director (1953–61) he oversaw the agency's early successes, but the U-2 INCIDENT (1960) and the BAY OF PIGS INVASION (1961) led to his resignation.

Dulles, John Foster (1888–1959) U.S. secretary of state (1953–59). Born in Washington, D.C., he was counsel to the American Peace Commission at Versailles and later helped oversee the payment of World War I reparations. He helped prepare the charter of the U.N. and was a delegate to its General Assembly (1946–49). He negotiated the complex Japanese peace treaty (1949–51). As secretary of state under Pres. DWIGHT D. EISENHOWER, he advocated active opposition to Soviet actions and developed the EISENHOWER DOCTRINE. His critics considered him inflexible and harsh and a practitioner of "brinkmanship"; later assessments credit his firmness in checking Communist expansion.

Duluth \də-ˈlüth\ City (pop., 1996 est.: 84,000) and inland port, northeastern Minnesota. It is situated on Lake SUPERIOR at the mouth of the St. Louis River, opposite Superior, Wis. The combined Duluth-Superior harbor is the western terminus of the ST. LAWRENCE SEAWAY. Through it are shipped iron ore, coal, grain, and oil. The site was named after DANIEL DULHUT, one of the French voyageurs who visited the area in the 17th century. It was laid out in 1856 and incorporated as a city in 1870.

Duma *Russian* **Gosudarstvennaya Duma** ("State Assembly") Elected legislative body that, with the State Council, constituted the imperial Russian legislature (1906–17). It had only limited power to control spending and initiate legislation, and the four Dumas that convened (1906, 1907, 1907–12, 1912–17) rarely enjoyed the cooperation of the ministers or the emperor, who retained the right to rule by decree when the Duma was not in session. In the Soviet era, SOVIETS were the basic unit of government. After the fall of the Soviet Union (1991), the Russian parliament (composed of the Congress of People's Deputies and the Supreme Soviet) had legislative responsibilities until its conflicts with Pres. BORIS YELTSIN reached a crisis in 1993. Parliament's revolt was put down by military force, and a new constitution established a new parliament composed of a Federation Council (in which all 89 of Russia's republics and regions have equal representation) and a Duma, with 450 members elected through proportional representation on a party basis and through single-member constituencies. The president may override and even dissolve the legislature under certain circumstances.

Dumas \dū̅-ˈmä, *Engl* d(y)ü-ˈmä, ˈd(y)ü-ˌmä\, **Alexandre** *known as* **Dumas *père*** (1802–1870) French playwright and novelist. His first success was as a writer of melodramatic plays, including *Napoléon Bonaparte* (1831) and *Antony* (1831). His immensely popular novels, set in colorful historical backgrounds, include *The Three Musketeers* (1844), a romance about four swashbuckling heroes in the age of Cardinal RICHELIEU, and its sequel *Twenty Years After* (1845); *The Count of Monte Cristo* (1844–45); and *The Black Tulip* (1850). His illegitimate son Alexandre Dumas (1824–1895), called Dumas *fils*, is best known for his play *La Dame aux Camélias* (1848), the basis of G. VERDI's opera *La Traviata* and later of several films titled *Camille*.

Dumfries \dəm-ˈfrēs\ Town (pop., 1995 est.: 31,000), southwestern Scotland. The seat of Dumfries and Galloway region, it is the country's largest burgh. Situated near the border with England on the left bank of the River Nith, it is the main market center for an intensive livestock farming region. The poet ROBERT BURNS lived there 1791–96; he is buried there, and his house is now a museum.

Dummer, Jeremiah (1681–1739) American lawyer and colonial agent. Born in Boston, in 1708 he defended in England Massachusetts' claim to Martha's Vineyard and was appointed colonial agent for Massachusetts (1710–21) and for Connecticut (1712–30) in England. A diligent advocate for the colonies, in 1715 he wrote a pamphlet defending the charter rights of the New England colonies.

Dummett, Michael A(nthony) E(ardley) *later* **Sir Michael** (born 1925) British philosopher. In *Truth and Other Enigmas* (1978), *The Logical Basis of Metaphysics* (1991), and *The Seas of Language* (1993), he expounds his view that philosophical clarity regarding the nature of thought is best approached through the study of how thoughts are expressed in language. The proper form of a theory of meaning for a natural language would be an explicit theoretical statement of what anybody has to know in order to be proficient in using the language.

Dumont d'Urville \dū̅-mōⁿ-dū̅r-ˈvēl\, **Jules-Sébastien-César** (1790–1842) French navigator. His exploration of the South Pacific (1826–29) resulted in extensive revision of charts of South Sea waters and redesignation of island groups in Melanesia, Micronesia, Polynesia, and Malaysia. In 1830 he conveyed the exiled king CHARLES X to England. He set sail for Antarctica in 1837; though unable to penetrate the pack ice, his expedition surveyed the Straits of Magellan, discovered Joinville Island and Louis Philippe Land, and sighted the Adélie coast (named after Dumont's wife) before returning in 1840.

Dumuzi-Abzu \ˈdü-mü-zē-ˈäb-ˌzü\ In MESOPOTAMIAN RELIGION, a Sumerian fertility goddess. The city goddess of Kinirsha in the southeastern marshland region, she represented the power of new life in the marshes. Her counterpart in the central herding region was TAMMUZ.

Dumuzi-Amaushumgalana \ˈdü-mü-zē-ˌä-mä-ˈü-shu̇m-gä-ˈlä-nä\ In MESOPOTAMIAN religion, a Sumerian god who represented the power of growth and new life in the date palm. He was the young bridegroom of the fertility goddess Inanna or ISHTAR. Their marriage was celebrated annually as a harvest festival. He was also identified with the Sumerian god TAMMUZ.

Dunajec River \dü-ˈnä-yets\ River, southern Poland. Rising in the Tatra Mountains near the Slovakia border, it flows about 156 mi (251 km) northeast into the VISTULA RIVER. It was the scene of heavy fighting during World War I in the Austro-German offensive. In 1975 Czechoslovakia and Poland modified their border along the Dunajec to permit Poland to construct a dam for irrigation in the region southeast of KRAKÓW.

Dunant \dū̅-ˈnäⁿ\, **(Jean-) Henri** (1828–1910) Swiss humanitarian. An eyewitness to the Battle of SOLFERINO, he organized emergency aid services for the Austrian and French wounded. In 1862 he proposed the formation of voluntary relief services in all countries and proposed an international agreement covering the war wounded. In 1864 he founded the RED CROSS, and the GENEVA CONVENTION came into being. He continued to promote interest in the treatment of prisoners of war, the abolition of slavery, international arbitration, disarmament, and the establishment of a Jewish homeland. In 1901 he shared with Frédéric Passy (1822–1912) the first Nobel Peace Prize.

Dunaway, Faye (born 1941) U.S. film actress. Born in Bascom, Fla., she acted in several plays off-Broadway (1962–67) before making her film debut in *The Happening* (1967). She became an international star in *Bonnie and Clyde* (1967), and later starred in such films as *Chinatown* (1974), *Network* (1976, Academy Award), *Mommie Dearest* (1981), and *Barfly* (1987).

Dunbar, Paul Laurence (1872–1906) U.S. author. Born in Dayton, Ohio, the son of former slaves, he became the first black writer to try to live by his writings and one of the first to attain national prominence. He wrote for a largely white readership, using black dialect and depicting the pre-Civil War South in pastoral, idyllic tones. His verse collections include *Oak and Ivy* (1893), *Majors and Minors* (1895), and *Lyrics of Lowly Life* (1896). His poems reached a wide readership, and he gave readings in the U.S. and England. He also published four short-story collections and four novels, including *The Sport of the Gods* (1902).

Paul Laurence Dunbar, 1906.

BY COURTESY OF THE LIBRARY OF CONGRESS, WASHINGTON, D.C.

Dunbar, William (1460/65–before 1530) Scottish poet. He was attached to the court of JAMES IV. Of the more than 100 poems attributed to him, most are short occasional pieces, ranging from gross satire to hymns of religious exaltation. The longer works include the charming dream allegory *The Goldyn Targe*, the nuptial song *The Thrissill and the Rois*, and *The Flyting of Dunbar and Kennedie,* a virtuoso piece of personal abuse directed at a rival. Dunbar was the dominant makar (courtly poet) in the golden age of Scottish poetry.

Duncan, David Douglas (born 1916) U.S. photojournalist. After graduating from college he became a freelance photographer. In 1946 he joined the staff of *Life* magazine and covered the Korean War (1950); his photographs depicting the life of the ordinary soldier were published in *This Is War!* (1951). Resuming his freelance life, in 1956 he met PABLO PICASSO, with whom he became fast friends; he would publish several photographic essays on Picasso's works, including *The Private World of Pablo Picasso* (1958) and *Picasso's Picassos* (1961).

Duncan, Isadora *orig.* **Angela** (1877–1927) U.S. interpretive dancer. She was born in San Francisco. She rejected the conventions of classical ballet and based her technique on natural rhythms and movement inspired by ancient Greece, dancing barefoot in a tunic without tights. Enjoying little success in the U.S., she moved to Europe in 1898. She toured Europe giving recitals to great acclaim throughout her life, earning notoriety for her liberated unconventionality, and founded several dance schools. She was killed when her long scarf caught in the spokes of a car's wheel. Her emphasis on "free dance" made her a precursor of MODERN DANCE, and she became an inspiration to a range of avant-garde artists.

Duncan I (died 1040) King of the Scots (1034–40). The grandson of King MALCOLM II, his accession to the throne violated the system in which kingship alternated between two branches of the royal family. He was challenged by Macbeth, Mormaor (subking) of Moray, who may have had a stronger claim to the throne. Macbeth murdered Duncan in 1040, and Duncan's elder son later killed Macbeth and ruled as MALCOLM III CANMORE.

Dundee \ˌdən-ˈdē\ City (pop., 1995 est.: 168,000), headquarters of Tayside administrative region, Scotland. An important seaport, it is situated on the Firth of Tay, a NORTH SEA inlet. Earliest mention of the town dates from the late 12th century, and over the next several centuries it saw repeated sackings and much bloodshed by the English. Among surviving buildings, the City Churches, a collection of three parish churches housed under one roof, are a focal point in the modern city center. Dundee was a world center for jute manufacturing in the 19th century. Textiles are still produced, but since World War II light-engineering has become the predominant industry. The University of Dundee was founded in 1881.

dune See SAND DUNE

dung beetle Any member of one subfamily (Scarabaeinae) of SCARAB BEETLES, which shapes manure into a ball (sometimes as large as an apple) with its scooperlike head and paddle-shaped antennae. They vary from 0.2 to more than 1 in. (5–30 mm) long. In early summer it buries itself and the ball and feeds on it. Later in the season the female deposits its eggs in dung balls, on which the larvae will later feed. They are usually round with short wing covers (elytra) that expose the end of the abdomen. They can eat more than their own weight in 24 hours and are considered helpful because they hasten the conversion of manure to substances usable by other organisms.

Dungannon \dən-ˈga-nən\ District (pop., 1995 est.: 47,000), Northern Ireland. Created in 1973, it extends from Lough NEAGH to the district of FERMANAGH and from the foothills of the Sperrin Mountains to the Blackwater River and the Irish Republic. An essentially pastoral area, its early history is linked with the O'Neills, earls of TYRONE, whose chief residence was at the town of Dungannon (population 1995 est: 10,000), the district seat. The Irish Parliament's independence was first proclaimed there in 1782.

Dungeness crab \ˈdən-jə-nəs\ Edible CRAB *(Cancer magister)* found along the Pacific coast from Alaska to lower California, one of the coast's largest and most important commercial crabs. The male is 7–9 in. (18–23 cm) wide and 4–5 in. (10–13 cm) long. The reddish brown upper surface is lighter toward the back; the legs and undersurface are yellowish. It lives on sandy bottoms below the high-tide mark. Closely related North American species are the rock crab of the Atlantic coast, the Jonah crab in coastal waters from New England to Canada, and the red and Pacific rock crabs, both in Pacific coastal waters. All are edible, but their commercial importance varies.

Dunham, Katherine (born 1910) U.S. dancer, choreographer, and anthropologist noted for her interpretation of primitive and ethnic dances. In 1931 she opened a dance school in her native Chicago. In 1940 she formed the U.S.'s first all-black dance company, for which she choreographed revues based on her anthropological research in the Caribbean; her early works included *Tropics* and *Le jazz hot*. She later received a PhD in anthropology from the University of Chicago. From 1945 to 1955 she directed a dance school in New York, which trained many important black dancers. In the 1950s she toured in Europe with her company. She also choreographed Broadway stage productions, operas, and movies.

Katherine Dunham in *Tropical Revue* (1945–46).

BY COURTESY OF THE DANCE COLLECTION, NEW YORK PUBLIC LIBRARY, ASTOR, LENOX AND TILDEN FOUNDATIONS

dunite \ˈdü-ˌnīt, ˈdə-ˌnīt\ Yellowish green to green igneous rock composed almost entirely of olivine. Chromite and magnetite also occur in dunite, as do spinel, ilmenite, pyrrhotite, and platinum in some cases. Dunites may be a source of CHROMIUM. Places of occurrence include Dun Mtn., New Zealand (the source of its name), South Africa, and Sweden.

Dunkirk Evacuation (1940) In WORLD WAR II, the evacuation of the BRITISH EXPEDITIONARY FORCE and other Allied troops, cut off by the Germans, from the French seaport of Dunkirk (Dunkerque) to England. Naval vessels and hundreds of civilian boats were used in the evacuation, which began on May 26. When it ended on June 4, about 198,000 British and 140,000 French and Belgian troops had been saved. The operation's success was due to fighter cover by the RAF and (unintentionally) to ADOLF HITLER's order of May 24 halting the advance of German armored forces into Dunkirk.

Dunmore's War, Lord See LORD DUNMORE'S WAR

Dunne, Finley Peter (1867–1936) U.S. journalist and humorist. Born in Chicago of Irish immigrants, Dunne began contributing Irish-dialect sketches to Chicago newspapers in 1892. In these he created the character Martin Dooley, who commented on current events in a rich Irish brogue. Mr. Dooley soon became a force for clear thinking and tolerance in public affairs. Dunne wrote more than 700 dialect essays, some of which were republished in eight volumes, including *Mr. Dooley in Peace and War* and *Mr. Dooley's Philosophy,* from 1898 to 1919.

Dunnet Head Cape, northeastern Scotland. A rounded headland, it is the northernmost point of the Scottish mainland, jutting into the NORTH SEA. It is crowned by a lighthouse, 346 ft (105 m) high, built in 1831.

Duns Scotus \'dənz-'skō-təs\, **John** (1266?–1308) Medieval Scottish philosopher and scholastic theologian. He studied and taught at Oxford, where he joined the Franciscans, and later taught at the University of Paris, from which he was briefly exiled for supporting Pope BONIFACE VIII in his quarrel with King PHILIP IV. In 1307 he became professor of theology at Cologne, perhaps to escape charges of heresy over his defense of the doctrine of the Immaculate Conception, which the Dominicans and secular authorities opposed. His two major works are his *Ordinatio* and his *Quaestiones quodlibetales,* both left unfinished at his death.

Dunstable \'dən-stə-bəl\, **John** (c. 1390–1453) English composer. His life and career are almost completely obscure. After his death he came to be credited with the achievements of all his English contemporaries, including Leonel Power (c. 1380–1445). He left at least 50 compositions, all for three and four voices and almost all sacred. Their full triadic harmony and frequent parallel motion in the voices represented an important innovation that influenced such composers as G. DUFAY and Gilles Binchois (c. 1400–1460), softening the austerity of 14th-century polyphony.

Dunstan of Canterbury, St. (924–988) Archbishop of Canterbury. He served as a chief adviser to the kings of Wessex, beginning with Edmund I, who made him abbot of Glastonbury (c. 943). Under King Eadred he served as minister of state, working to conciliate the Danish section of the kingdom and reform the church. Dunstan was outlawed (955) under King Eadwig and went into exile in Flanders, but he was recalled by King Edgar (957) and continued his reforms, restructuring English monasticism on the continental model. He became archbishop of Canterbury in 959.

duodenum \,dü-ə-'dē-nəm, dů-'ä-dᵊn-əm\ First and shortest (9–11 in., or 23–28 cm) segment of the SMALL INTESTINE. It curves down and then up from the pylorus of the stomach, where CHYME enters it. Ducts from the pancreas and gallbladder bring in bicarbonate to neutralize stomach acid, pancreatic enzymes to further digestion, and bile salts to break up fats. Nutrient absorption begins in the lower duodenum, which has a mucous lining. Exposure to stomach acid makes the upper duodenum susceptible to PEPTIC ULCERS, the duodenum's most common problem. Compression of the lower duodenum between the liver, pancreas, and major blood vessels can require surgery.

Duparc \dᵫ-'pårk\, **(Marie Eugène) Henri** (1848–1933) French song composer. He studied music with C. FRANCK while also studying law. His composing career lasted about 16 years; he stopped composing at 36 for psychological reasons. Highly self-critical, he destroyed an incomplete opera and other works and acknowledged only 13 completed songs, including "L'invitation au voyage," "Phidylé," "Testament," and "Extase," as his lifetime oeuvre. Almost all the songs, universally admired, were originally for voice and piano; he later orchestrated eight of them.

Dupleix \dᵫ-'pleks, *Engl* dü-'pleks\, **Joseph-François** (1697–1763) French colonial administrator who attempted to establish a French empire in India. His father, a director of the French EAST INDIA CO., secured him an appointment in 1720 to the superior council of Pondicherry, capital of French India, and in 1742 he was named governor-general of French India. He fought the British in India during the War of the AUSTRIAN SUCCESSION (1744) and later attempted to undermine the British position in South India. His schemes exhausted French finances, and he was recalled to France, discredited, in 1754.

Dupuytren \dᵫ-pwʸē-traⁿ\, **Guillaume** *later* **Baron Dupuytren** (1777–1835) French surgeon and pathologist. Dupuytren was the first to excise the lower jaw and to clearly describe the pathology of congenital hip dislocation. He revised the classification of burns and devised surgery for cervical cancer and for creation of an artificial anus, among other advances. He is best known for surgical procedures to alleviate Dupuytren's contracture, in which fibrosis in the palm causes permanent retraction of one or more fingers.

Dura-Europus \'důr-ə-yů-'rō-pəs\ Ancient town on the EUPHRATES, in modern Syria. Originally a Babylonian town, it was rebuilt as a military colony c. 300 BC under the SELEUCID DYNASTY. Annexed by the Romans in AD 165, it became a frontier fortress. Shortly after 256 it was overrun and destroyed by the SASANIAN DYNASTY. Its ruins give an unusually detailed picture of everyday life there, and provide information about the fusion of Greek and Semitic culture.

Durance River \dᵫ-'räⁿs\ *ancient* **Druentia.** River, southeastern France. The principal river draining the French side of the Alps toward the Mediterranean, its origin is in the Montgenèvre region. To its confluence with the RHÔNE RIVER below AVIGNON, it is 189 mi (304 km) long. It is the site of extensive hydroelectric projects that were established after World War II.

Durand \dů-'rand\, **Asher B(rown)** (1796–1886) U.S. painter, engraver, and illustrator. Born in Jefferson Village, N.J., he had established his reputation as an engraver by 1823 with his print of JOHN TRUMBULL's *Declaration of Independence* and his portraits of prominent contemporary Americans. He later devoted himself to landscape painting, becoming a founder of the HUDSON RIVER SCHOOL and one of the earliest U.S. artists to work directly from nature. In 1826 he cofounded the National Academy of Design in New York and served as its president 1845–61.

Durango \dů-'raŋ-gō\ State (pop., 1995 est.: 1,432,000), northern central Mexico. The western portion of the state's 47,560 sq mi (123,181 sq km) territory lies within the mineral-laden Sierra Madre Occidental; semiarid plains, used for ranching, comprise the eastern portion. The Río Nazas, the largest river in the state, flows for about 375 mi (600 km); it is a main source of water for commercial agriculture. Along its lower course is the Laguna cotton district, a large state-operated cooperative that DURANGO city, the state's capital, shares with COAHUILA state. First explored by Europeans in 1562, Durango shared the colonial history of CHIHUAHUA as a major part of Nueva Vizcaya; the two became separate states in 1823.

Durango *officially* **Victoria de Durango** City (pop., 1990: 414,000) capital of DURANGO state, northern central Mexico. It lies in a fertile valley of the SIERRA MADRE, 6,197 ft (1,889 m) above sea level. North of the city is the Cerro del Mercado, a hill of nearly pure iron ore representing one of the world's largest deposits. First settled in 1556, Durango was the political and ecclesiastical capital of Nueva Vizcaya, which included Durango and CHIHUAHUA until 1823. The city, long known as a health resort, is an important commercial and mining center.

Durant \dů-'rant\, **Will(iam James) and Ariel** *orig.* **Ada Kaufman** (1885–1981, 1898–1981) U.S. writers. Will was born in North Adams, Mass., Ariel in Prosurov, Russia. After the great success of Will's *Story of Philosophy* (1926), they cowrote the 11-volume *The Story of Civilization* (1935–75), including *Rousseau and Revolution* (1967, Pulitzer Prize). Though involved in the writing of every volume, Ariel was not listed as coauthor until the seventh.

Durant, William C(rapo) (1861–1947) U.S. industrialist, founder of GENERAL MOTORS CORP. Born in Boston, he established a carriage company in 1886. He joined the Buick Motor Car Co. (founded by David Buick in 1902) in 1903–4 and quickly revived it. In 1908 he brought together several automotive manufacturers to form the General Motors Co. He lost control of the company two years later. With Louis Chevrolet (1878–1941) he founded the Chevrolet Motor Co., which acquired control of General Motors in 1915. As president of General Motors Corp. until 1920, he presided over its steady expansion.

Durante \də-'ran-tē\, **Jimmy** *orig.* **James Francis** (1893–1980) U.S. comedian. Born in New York City, by 16 he was playing piano in Bowery nightclubs. By the 1920s the team of Durante, Lou Clayton, and Eddie Jackson were stars in vaudeville and nightclubs; they appeared on Broadway in FLORENZ ZIEGFELD's *Show Girl* (1929). He made his film debut in *Roadhouse Nights* (1930) and over the next 30 years brightened many films and musicals with his gravelly voice, malapropisms, and warmhearted buffoonery. Nicknamed the "Schnozzola" for his large nose, he is remembered for ending his programs with the line "Goodnight, Mrs. Calabash, wherever you are."

C
D

Duras \dūē-'räs\, **Marguerite** *orig.* **Marguerite Donnadieu** (1914–1996) French (Indochinese-born) novelist, playwright, film director, and screenwriter. Indochina was the setting for Duras's first successful novel, *The Sea Wall* (1950). Her writing grew increasingly minimal and abstract. Among her major novels are *The Afternoon of Monsieur Andesmas* (1962), *L'Amour* (1971), *Le ravissement de Lol V. Stein* (1964), and the semiautobiographical *The Lover* (1984, Prix Goncourt; film, 1992), about a French teenage girl's love affair with an older Chinese man. Highly prolific, she was also acclaimed for her screenplays of *Hiroshima mon amour* (1959) and *India Song* (1975).

Durban City (pop., 1991: 716,000; metro. area pop.: 1,137,000) and chief seaport, South Africa. Located on Natal Bay of the Indian Ocean, it was the site of a European trading settlement from 1824 and was named Port Natal by the traders. Land was ceded to them by the Zulu king SHAKA, and the Old Fort (now a museum) was built. Durban was founded in 1835 on the site of Port Natal. In the 1840s the Boers clashed with the British over control of Durban. One of the world's major commercial ports, it is the headquarters of South Africa's sugar industry and a center of diverse manufacturing. Tourism is also important, based on the city's proximity to game and nature reserves and to beaches.

Dürer \'dūēr-ər, *Engl* 'du̇r-ər\, **Albrecht** (1471–1528) German painter and printmaker. He worked as a draftsman in his father's goldsmith workshop before being apprenticed at 15 to a painter and illustrator in his native Nuremberg. He opened his own workshop c. 1494 and began producing woodcuts and copper engravings. His extensive travel took him twice to Italy, where he was inspired by the works of ANDREA MANTEGNA, ANTONIO DEL POLLAIUOLO, and BELLINI FAMILY; Italian influence can be seen in such engravings as *The Four Witches* (c. 1497) and *Adam and Eve* (1504). He became known for his penetrating half-length portraits and self-portraits. In 1506, in Venice, he completed his great altarpiece *The Feast of the Rose Garlands* for the German chapel in the church of San Bartolommeo. Later important graphic works include his famous *Passion* series of copperplate engravings (1507–13), the *Small Passion* in woodcuts (1509–11), and his greatest engravings: *St. Jerome in His Study, Melencolia I,* and *The Knight, Death, and the Devil* (1513–14). Back in Nuremberg he worked for Emperor MAXIMILIAN I (1512–19). By 1515 he had achieved international fame. In 1518 he became a devoted follower of MARTIN LUTHER. His finest painting is the *Four Apostles* of 1526. He was the greatest Renaissance artist in northern Europe and had many pupils and imitators.

Dürer, "Self-portrait in Furred Coat," oil on wood panel, 1500; in the Alte Pinakothek, Munich.

ALTE PINAKOTHEK, MUNICH; PHOTOGRAPH, BLAUEL/GNAMM—ARTOTHEK

Durfee, William Franklin (1833–1899) U.S. engineer and inventor. Born in New Bedford, Mass., he set up his own firm after graduating from Harvard University Elected to the state legislature in 1861, he introduced the nation's first proposal for arming black recruits. In 1864, at Wyandotte, Mich., he supervised the first production of steel by the BESSEMER PROCESS in America; from this steel the first American steel rails were produced in 1865. His steelworks analytical laboratory was the first built in the U.S. He later became an innovator in copper refining.

Durga In Hinduism, one of the forms of the goddess DEVI or Shakti (see SHAKTI), and the wife of SHIVA. She was born fully grown, created out of flames that issued from the mouths of BRAHMA, VISHNU, Shiva, and other gods and embodying their collective energy (shakti). They created her to slay the buffalo-demon Mahisasura, whom they were unable to overcome. She is usually depicted riding a lion or tiger, each of her multiple arms bearing a weapon. See also DURGA-PUJA. See photograph opposite.

Durga-puja \'du̇r-gä-'pü-jä\ Hindu festival held annually in northeastern India in September–October in honor of the goddess DURGA. Images of the goddess are made, worshiped for nine days, and then immersed in water. The celebration includes colorful processions and much public and private festivity.

Durham \'dər-əm\ County (population 1995 est.: 507,000), northeastern England. It is adjacent to the North Sea coast; the county seat is DURHAM. The northern part of the county is cut by the valleys of the Rivers Wear and Tees; the Tees lowlands extend across the south. Under the Romans the region was a military outpost associated with HADRIAN'S WALL. It was later incorporated into the Saxon kingdom of NORTHUMBRIA. It was unimportant economically until the 19th century, when exploitation of its coalfields, now exhausted, made it a key area of industrial growth in Britain. The area is now a center of light industry.

Durham *Saxon* **Dunholme.** City (metro area pop., 1995 est.: 85,000), northern England. The seat of DURHAM county, it is on a peninsula in the River Wear. This natural defensive site, fortified by WILLIAM THE CONQUEROR against the Scots, became a seat of the feudal prince-bishops of Durham. Medieval Durham was a place of pilgrimage, holding the remains of St. Cuthbert in its cathedral (begun in 1093). The bishops of Durham helped establish the city as an educational center. It is the site of the Gulbenkian Museum of Oriental Art and Archaeology, part of the University of Durham.

Durham See SHORTHORN

Durham, Earl of *orig.* **John George Lambton** (1792–1840) British colonial administrator in Canada. He was a member of the British House of Commons (1813–28) and served in the cabinet of EARL GREY (1830–33). In 1838 he was appointed governor-general and lord high commissioner of Canada. He appointed a new executive council to placate the rebellious French Canadians of Lower Canada (later Quebec). Criticized in England for his action, he resigned. He later issued the Durham Report that advocated the union of Lower Canada and Upper Canada and the expansion of self-government, to preserve Canadian loyalty to Britain.

durian \'du̇r-ē-ən\ Tree *(Durio zibethinus)* of the bombax family (Bombacaceae) and its fruit, cultivated in Indonesia, the Philippines, Malaysia, and southern Thailand. The tree has oblong, tapering leaves and yellowish-green flowers and resembles the elm in shape. The spherical fruit has a hard spiny shell and contains five oval compartments, each filled with an edible cream-colored, custard-like pulp, in which are embedded one to five chestnut-sized seeds, which are edible if roasted. The ripe

Durga, Rajasthani miniature of the Mewar school, mid-17th century; in a private collection.

PRAMOD CHANDRA

fruits are eaten by many animals. Though the durian has a mild, sweet flavor, it also has a pungent foul odor. It is seldom exported.

Durkheim \dūr-'kem\, **Émile** (1858–1917) French social scientist who developed a vigorous methodology combining empirical research with sociological theory, and is widely regarded as the founder of the French school of SOCIOLOGY. His sociological reflections, never remote from the moral philosophy he was schooled in, were first expressed in *The Division of Labor in Society* (1893) and *Suicide* (1897). In his view, ethical and social structures were endangered by technology and mechanization. The DIVISION OF LABOR produced ALIENATION among workers, and the increased prosperity of the late 19th century generated greed and passions that threatened the equilibrium of society. Durkheim drew attention to ANOMIE, or social disconnectedness, and studied SUICIDE as a decision to renounce life. Following the DREYFUS affair, he came to regard education and religion as the most potent means of reforming humanity and molding new social institutions. His *Elementary Forms of the Religious Life* (1915) is an anthropological study of the origins and functions of religion, which Durkheim saw as expressing the collective conscience of a society and producing social solidarity. He also wrote influential works on sociological method. He taught at the Universities of Bordeaux (1887–1902) and Paris (1902–17). See also MARCEL MAUSS.

Durocher \dů-'rō-shər\, **Leo (Ernest)** (1905–1991) U.S. baseball player and manager. Born in West Springfield, Mass., he played for various teams from 1928 to 1938, distinguishing himself by his sharp fielding at shortstop. He gained notoriety as the cheeky, contentious manager of the Brooklyn Dodgers (1939–46, 1948); he was suspended from managing for the entire 1947 season for "conduct detrimental to baseball." He managed the New York Giants 1948–55, left to become a commentator, but returned to the game as a coach for the Los Angeles Dodgers (1961–64) and later to manage the Chicago Cubs (1966–72) and the Houston Astros (1972–73). He is credited with the observation "Nice guys finish last" (actually, "The nice guys over there are in seventh place").

Durrani, Ahmad Shah See AHMAD SHAH DURRANI

Durrell \'də-rəl\, **Lawrence (George)** (1912–1990) British (Indian-born) writer. He spent most of his life in Mediterranean countries, often in diplomatic posts. He is best known for the tetralogy *The Alexandria Quartet,* composed of the novels *Justine* (1957), *Balthazar* (1958), *Mountolive* (1958), and *Clea* (1960), which explore the erotic lives of a group of exotic characters in Alexandria, Egypt. His poetry—including *Cities, Plains and People* (1946)—and nonfiction books about locales—including *Prospero's Cell* (1945), *Reflections on a Marine Venus* (1953), and *Bitter Lemons* (1957), describing three Greek islands—are often considered his best works.

Dürrenmatt \'dœr-ən-ˌmät\, **Friedrich** (1921–1990) Swiss playwright. His plays, showing the influence of BERTOLT BRECHT as well as the theater of the ABSURD, were central to the post-1945 revival of the German theater. In his first play, *Es steht geschrieben* ("All as It Is Written"; 1947), and his next two plays, *The Marriage of Mr. Mississippi* (1952) and *An Angel Comes to Babylon* (1953), he took comic liberties with historical facts to present parables about modern life. His play *The Visit* (1956) and the modern morality play *The Physicists* (1962) earned him international acclaim. After 1970 he wrote adaptations, detective novels, radio plays, and essays. His works have been translated into more than 50 languages.

Duryea \'důr-ˌyā\, **Charles E(dgar) and J(ames) Frank** (1861–1938, 1869–1967) U.S. automotive inventors. They were born near Canton, Ill. Charles initially worked as a bicycle mechanic; after seeing a gasoline engine at a state fair, he designed a gasoline-powered automobile, and in 1893 he and his brother Frank constructed the first U.S. automobile, which they drove successfully on the streets of Springfield, Mass. In Chicago in 1895, Frank drove an improved model to win the first U.S. auto race. In 1896 their company manufactured the first commercially produced U.S. automobiles; 13 cars were sold before the company failed and the brothers separated. Both started new automobile manufacturing ventures; Frank later developed the Stevens-Duryea limousine, which was produced into the 1920s.

Dusan, Stefan See STEFAN DUSAN

Duse \'dü-zā\, **Eleonora** (1858–1924) Italian actress. Born into a family of touring actors, she appeared on stage from age 4. She acted in several French plays to great acclaim from 1878 and toured with her own company in Europe and the U.S. after 1885. She fell in love with GABRIELE D'ANNUNZIO in the 1890s and acted in several plays he wrote for her, notably *Francesca da Rimini.* Unlike her contemporary SARAH BERNHARDT, she did not try to project her own personality but instead sought to lose herself in her characters. The most fluent and expressive actress of her day, she was especially noted for her roles in HENRIK IBSEN's plays. She retired in 1909 but returned to the stage in 1921 and was touring the U.S. when she died.

Eleonora Duse.

BY COURTESY OF THE LIBRARY OF CONGRESS, WASHINGTON, D.C.

Dushanbe \'dyü-ˌshäm-bə, ˌdyü-shäm-'bā\ *formerly (until 1929)* **Dyushambe** \'dyü-ˌshäm-bə, ˌdyü-shäm-'bā\ *(1929–61)* **Stalinabad** \ˌstä-lyi-nə-'bäd\ City (pop., 1994 est.: 524,000), capital of Tajikistan. It lies on the Varzob River in southwestern Tajikistan. It was built in the Soviet period on the site of three former settlements, the largest of which, Dyushambe, was a part of the khanate of BUKHARA; it suffered severely in the fighting during the Soviet takeover in 1920. In 1924 it became the capital of the new Tajik Autonomous S.S.R., and rapid industrial and population growth followed. An important transport junction, it accounts for much of the republic's industrial output.

Dussek \'dů-sek\, **Jan Ladislav** (1760–1812) Bohemian (Czech) composer and pianist. He toured Europe with great success as a pianist and studied with C.P.E. BACH. He joined his father-in-law's music-publishing firm in London (1792–99) but fled England to escape his creditors. He served two princely patrons and spent his last years in the household of C.-M. de TALLEYRAND. A transitional figure between Classicism and Romanticism, he wrote some 60 violin sonatas, some 15 piano concertos, and some 30 admired piano sonatas, which may have influenced LUDWIG VAN BEETHOVEN

Düsseldorf \'dūe-səl-ˌdȯrf\ City (pop., 1996 est.: 572,000), capital of North Rhine-Westphalia state, western Germany. Located on the RHINE RIVER, it is the administrative and cultural center of the industrial Rhine-Ruhr area. Chartered in 1288 by the count of Berg, it passed to the Palatinate-Neuberg line in 1609. Although it suffered considerably in the THIRTY YEARS' WAR and the War of the SPANISH SUCCESSION, it later revived. It was transferred to Prussia in 1815 and grew rapidly with the establishment of iron and steel industries in the 1870s. Heavily damaged in World War II, its old buildings were repaired and new ones erected. It is the site of the first German skyscraper, the Wilhelm-Marx-Haus (1924). It was the birthplace of HEINRICH HEINE.

Dust Bowl Section of the U.S. GREAT PLAINS that extended over southeastern Colorado, southwestern Kansas, the panhandles of Texas and Oklahoma, and northeastern New Mexico. The term originated after World War I, when the area's grasslands were converted to agricultural fields. In the naturally dry climate, overcultivation added to the effect of a severe drought in the early 1930s, when heavy winds blew the loose topsoil in "black blizzards" that blocked out the sun and piled dirt in drifts. Many farmers and ranchers left the region for California and elsewhere. The planting of windbreaks and grassland enabled the area to recover by the early 1940s.

dusting See SPRAYING AND DUSTING

Dutch East India Co. See Dutch EAST INDIA CO.

Dutch East Indies See INDONESIA

Dutch elm disease Widespread disease that kills ELMS, caused by the FUNGUS *Ceratocystis ulmi.* It was first identified in the U.S. in 1930, and an eradication campaign could not stop its spread into regions wherever the very susceptible American elm *(Ulmus americana)* grew. The leaves on one or more branches of a stricken tree suddenly wilt, turn dull green to yellow or brown, curl, and may drop early. Because symptoms are easily confused with other diseases, positive diagnosis is possible only through laboratory culturing. The fungus can spread up to 50 ft (15 m) from diseased to healthy trees by natural root grafts. Overland, the fungus normally is spread by the European elm bark beetle (*Scolytus multistriatus;* see BARK BEETLE), less commonly by the American elm bark beetle *(Hylurgopinus rufipes).* Control involves exclusion of the beetles, usually by use of an insecticidal spray applied to the tree.

Dutch Guiana See SURINAME

Dutch language West GERMANIC LANGUAGE spoken by more than 20 million people in the Netherlands, northern Belgium, and a small corner of northern France; it is also an official language in Surinam and the Netherlands Antilles. Though English-speakers are accustomed to calling the main Germanic language of the Netherlands "Dutch" and that of Belgium "Flemish," the two are regarded as the same language, called Nederlands in both countries, where efforts have been made to unify spelling and literary usage. Many Dutch-speakers command both a local dialect and Standard Dutch, based approximately on the speech of the major urban centers of North and South Holland. "Flemish" (or Dutch in Belgium) has its own phonetic and lexical regionalisms.

Dutch Reformed Church See REFORMED CHURCH

Dutch Republic *officially* **Republic of the United Netherlands** Former state (1581–1795), about the size of the modern kingdom of the Netherlands. It consisted of the seven northern Netherlands provinces that formed the Union of Utrecht in 1579 and declared independence from Spain in 1581 (finally achieved in 1648). Political control shifted between the province of Holland and the princes of Orange. In the 17th century the Dutch Republic developed into a world colonial empire far out of proportion to its resources, emerging as a center of international finance and a cultural capital of Europe. In the 18th century, the republic's colonial empire was eclipsed by that of England. In 1795 the republic collapsed under the impact of a Dutch democratic revolution and invading French armies.

Dutch Wars See ANGLO–DUTCH WARS

Dutchman's-breeches Plant *(Dicentra cucullaria)* of the fumitory family (Fumariaceae) named for its sprays of tremulous, yellow-tipped white flowers that fancifully resemble the wide-legged, traditional pantaloons worn by Dutch men. The plant is native throughout eastern and midwestern North America, usually in open woodlands. The gray-green foliage grows from white underground tubers and is not as tall as the flowering stalk, which also springs directly from the ground.

Dutchman's-breeches (*Dicentra cucullaria*).
JOHN H. GERARD

Dutchman's-pipe Climbing vine *(Aristolochia durior),* also called pipe vine, of the birthwort family (Aristolochiaceae), native to central and eastern North America. It bears heart-shaped or kidney-shaped leaves and yellowish-brown or purplish-brown tubular flowers resembling a curved pipe. Exhibiting rapid growth, Dutchman's-pipe is often planted as a screen or an ornamental on porches and arbors.

Dutchman's-pipe (*Aristolochia durior*).
A.J. HUXLEY

Duvalier \dü-'val-yā\, **François** *known as* **Papa Doc** (1907–1971) President of Haiti (1957–71). He received his MD in 1934, and was appointed director general of the National Public Health Service in 1946 under Pres. Dumarsais Estimé and held other government positions until Estimé was overthrown by Paul Magloire, who became president. Duvalier led the opposition to Magloire, and became president soon after Magloire's resignation in 1956. He reduced the size of the military and organized the Tontons Macoutes ("Bogeymen"), a private force that terrorized and assassinated alleged foes of his regime. He played on the culture of VODUN to intimidate the opposition as well. Promoting a cult of his person as the semidivine embodiment of the nation, he declared himself president for life in 1964. His regime's corruption and despotism isolated Haiti, the poorest country in the hemisphere, from the rest of the world. His 19-year-old son, Jean-Claude (born 1951), succeeded him on his death. A weak ruler, dominated by his mother and later his wife, "Baby Doc" instituted slight reforms, but increasing social unrest forced him to flee into exile in France in 1986.

Dvaravati \dvə-'rä-və-tē\ Ancient kingdom of Southeast Asia (fl. 6th–13th century). The first MON KINGDOM established in what is now Thailand, it had early commercial and cultural contact with India, which influenced Mon sculpture, writing, law, and governmental forms. Conquered in turn by the Burmese, the Khmer, and the Thai, the Dvaravati Mon passed on the Indian influence to their conquerers.

DVD *in full* **digital video disk** *or* **digital versatile disk** Type of optical disk that represents the new generation of COMPACT DISC (CD) technology. Like a CD drive, a DVD drive uses a low-power LASER to read digitized (binary) data that have been encoded onto the disc in the form of tiny pits. Because it uses a digital format, a DVD can store any kind of data, including movies, music, text, and graphical images. DVDs are available in single- and double-sided versions, with one or two layers of information per side. A double-sided, dual-layer version can store about 30 times as much information as a standard CD. DVDs are made in a ROM (read-only memory) format as well as in erasable (DVD-E) and recordable (DVD-R) formats. Though DVD players can usually read CDs, CD players cannot read DVDs. It is expected that DVDs will eventually replace CDs, especially for MULTIMEDIA WORKSTATIONS.

Dvina River \dvē-'nä\, **Northern** *Russian* **Severnaya Dvina** \'syevyir-nə-yə\ River, northern Russia. Formed by the junction of the Sukhona and Yug rivers, it is one of the largest and most important waterways of the northern European part of Russia. It flows northwest for 462 mi (744 km) and enters the Dvina inlet of the WHITE SEA below the city of ARKHANGELSK. Navigable for most of its length, it was used by early fur hunters and colonists, and monasteries and towns were established at important confluences. It retains its economic importance and is linked with the VOLGA-BALTIC WATERWAY via the Sukhona River.

Dvina River, Western *Russian* **Zapadnaya Dvina** \'zä-pəd-nə-yə\ *Latvian* **Daugava** \'daù-gə-və\ River, northern central Europe. It rises in Russia's Valdai Hills and flows 632 mi (1,020 km) in a great arc south through Russia and Belarus and then northwest across Latvia. It discharges into the Gulf of RIGA on the BALTIC SEA. An important water route since early times, and connected in its upper reaches by easy portages to the DNIEPER, VOLGA, and NEVA rivers, it constituted part of the great trade route from the Baltic region to Byzantium and to the Arabic east. Many rapids and, in the 20th century, the presence of dams have restricted navigation on it.

Dvořák \'vȯr-ˌzhäk, də-'vȯr-ˌzhäk\, **Antonín (Leopold)** (1841–1904) Bohemian (Czech) composer. Son of a rural innkeeper and butcher, he was permitted to attend organ school in Prague in 1857. He played viola in a theater orchestra, often under B. SMETANA, and eventually found employment that left him ample time for composition. J. BRAHMS assisted in getting his works published, and by 1880 his fame had spread throughout Europe. He made 10 visits to England, and served as director of New York's new National Conservatory of Music 1892–95, which resulted in his "New World" Symphony (1893). His music, which frequently draws on folk tunes, is seen as an expression of Czech nationalism. Highly prolific, he is primarily known for his orchestral and chamber works; his works include nine symphonies, concertos for piano, violin, and cello, two serenades, several tone poems, 14 string quartets, two piano quartets, and two piano quintets. His many piano works include the four-hand *Slavonic Dances* (1878, 1886). His sacred music includes a *Stabat Mater* (1877), a *Requiem* (1890), and a *Te Deum* (1892). Of his 13 operas, only *Rusalka* (1900) is still performed.

dwarf star Any star of average or low luminosity, mass, and size, including WHITE DWARF STARS and red dwarf stars. Dwarf stars include most main-sequence stars (see HERTZSPRUNG-RUSSELL DIAGRAM), including the SUN. Their color can range from blue to red, corresponding to temperatures varying from over 17,500°F (10,000°C) to a few thousand degrees.

dwarfism Growth retardation resulting in abnormally short adult stature, caused by a variety of hereditary and metabolic disorders. Pituitary dwarfism is caused by insufficient GROWTH HORMONE. Hereditary dwarfisms include achondroplasia, with normal trunk size but short limbs and a large head; hypochondroplasia, similar except for normal head size; and diastrophic dwarfism, with progressive, crippling skeletal deformities. Intelligence is normal in these forms of dwarfism. Some kinds, such as CRETINISM, include mental retardation. Dwarfism may also result from inadequate nutrition in early life (see RICKETS).

dybbuk \'di-bək\ In Jewish folklore, a disembodied human spirit that must wander restlessly, burdened by former sins, until it inhabits the body of a living person. Belief in such spirits was common in Eastern Europe in the 16th–17th century. Individuals thought to be possessed by a dybbuk were taken to a BAAL SHEM, who would carry out a rite of EXORCISM. The mystic ISAAC BEN SOLOMON LURIA helped promote belief in dybbukim with his doctrine of the transmigration of souls. The folklorist S. Ansky depicted such a spirit in his classic Yiddish drama *The Dybbuk* (c. 1916).

Dyck, Anthony Van See Anthony VAN DYCK

dye Any of a class of complex organic compounds that are intensely colored, used to color textiles, leather, paper, and other materials. Major dyes known to the ancients came from plants such as INDIGO and madder (see MADDER FAMILY) or from the shells of mollusks; today most dyes are made from coal tar and PETROCHEMICALS. The chemical structure of dyes is relatively easy to modify, so many new colors and types of dyes have been synthesized. Dye molecules are deposited from solution onto materials in such a way that they cannot be removed by the original solvent. Fiber-reactive dyes form a COVALENT BOND with the fiber. Other dyes require previous application of a mordant, an inorganic material that causes the dye to precipitate as an insoluble salt, or vat dyeing, in which a soluble colorless compound is absorbed by the fibers, then oxidized (see OXIDATION-REDUCTION) to the insoluble colored compound, making it remarkably fast to washing, light, and chemicals. See also AZO DYE.

Dylan \'dil-ən\, **Bob** *orig.* **Robert Zimmerman** (born 1941) U.S. singer and songwriter. He grew up in Duluth and in the iron-range town of Hibbing, Minn., adopted the name of the poet Dylan Thomas, and traveled to New York in search of idol WOODY GUTHRIE. In the early 1960s, he performed professionally in Greenwich Village coffeehouses and released albums that made him the darling of critics and folk music devotees. "Blowin' in the Wind" and "The Times They Are a-Changin'" became anthems of the civil-rights movement. In 1965 he adopted electrically amplified instruments and the rhythms of rock and roll in a major departure. The landmark albums *Highway 61 Revisited* (1965) and *Blonde on Blonde* (1966) established him as leading figure in rock, and his lyrics, influenced partly by the BEAT MOVEMENT, brought poetic complexity to pop music. After a motorcycle accident in 1966, he underwent another musical turnabout and released several albums (notably *Nashville Skyline,* 1969) characterized by COUNTRY MUSIC elements and a muted, reflective tone. Among the most praised of his many later albums are *Blood on the Tracks* (1975), *Time Out of Mind* (1997) and *"Love and Theft"* (2001). He is perhaps the most admired and influential American songwriter of his time.

dynamics Branch of MECHANICS that deals with the MOTION of objects in relation to FORCE, MASS, MOMENTUM, and ENERGY. Dynamics can be divided into two branches, KINEMATICS and kinetics. The foundations of dynamics were laid by GALILEO, who derived the law of motion for falling bodies and was the first to recognize that all changes of velocity of a body are the result of forces. ISAAC NEWTON formulated this observation in his second law of motion (see NEWTON'S LAWS OF MOTION).

dynamite Blasting EXPLOSIVE, patented in 1867 by ALFRED P. NOBEL. Dynamite is based on NITROGLYCERIN but is much safer to handle than nitroglycerin alone. By mixing the nitroglycerin with kieselguhr, a porous silica-containing earth, in proportions that left an essentially dry and granular material, Nobel produced a solid that was resistant to shock but readily explodable by heat or sudden impact. Later, wood pulp was substituted as the absorbent, and sodium nitrate was added as an oxidizing agent to increase the strength of the explosive.

dysentery \'di-sᵊn-ˌter-ē\ Infectious intestinal disorder with INFLAMMATION, abdominal pain and straining, and DIARRHEA, often containing blood and mucus. Dysentery is spread in food or water contaminated by feces, often by infected individuals with unwashed hands. Bacillary dysentery (shigellosis), caused by *Shigella* bacteria, may be mild or may be sudden, severe, and fatal. Fluid loss causes DEHYDRATION. Advanced stages include chronic large-intestine ulceration. It is treated with antibiotics, fluid replacement, and sometimes blood transfusion. Amoebic (or amebic) dysentery, caused by the AMOEBA *Entamoeba histolytica,* has two forms, one much like bacillary dysentery and the other chronic and intermittent, sometimes with large-intestine ulcerations. It is treated with drugs that kill the amoebae.

dyslexia \dis-'lek-sē-ə\ Chronic neurological disorder causing inability or great difficulty in learning to read or spell, despite normal intelligence. It inhibits recognition and processing of graphic symbols, particularly those pertaining to language. Symptoms, including very poor reading skills, reversed word and letter sequences, and illegible handwriting, usually become evident in the early school years. With early recognition and specialized approaches to teaching reading, most dyslexics can learn to read. Anomalies have recently been found in reading-related pathways in the brains of dyslexic persons.

dysmenorrhea \ˌdis-ˌme-nə-'rē-ə\ Pain or cramps before or during MENSTRUATION. In primary dysmenorrhea, caused by endocrine imbalances, severity varies widely. Irritability, fatigue, backache, or nausea may also occur. Long assumed to be psychosomatic, it is now known to be due to excess PROSTAGLANDINS, which contract the UTERUS, causing cramps. Pain relievers that block prostaglandin formation can decrease its severity, which may also be eased after childbearing. Secondary dysmenorrhea is caused by other disorders, including genital obstructions, pelvic inflammation, infection, polyps, or tumors. Treatment is directed toward the underlying disorder.

Dyson \'dī-sən\, **Freeman (John)** (born 1923) English-U.S. physicist and educator. After studies at Cambridge Univ., he taught principally at Princeton's Institute for Advanced Study (from 1953). He has done extensive research into quantum theory, but is perhaps best known for his speculative work on human colonization of the solar system and beyond, and for his researches into modes of searching for intelligent extraterrestrial life. His books for a general audience include *Disturbing the Universe* (1979), *Weapons and Hope* (1984), and *Origins of Life* (1985).

dysphasia See APHASIA

dysphemia See STUTTERING

dysplasia \dis-'plā-zhə\ Abnormal formation of a bodily structure or tissue, usually bone, that may occur in any part of the body. Several types are well-defined diseases in humans. In the most common, epiphyseal dysplasia, the ends of children's bones (epiphyses) grow and harden very slowly; DWARFISM often results (sometimes only in the legs), and degenerative joint disease usually develops by middle age. Large dogs bred for narrow hips may have hip dysplasia, with abnormalities involving the head of the thighbone and the hip socket.

Dyushambe See DUSHANBE

Dzerzhinsky \dyir-'zhen-skē\, **Feliks (Edmundovich)** (1877–1926) Russian Bolshevik leader, head of the first Soviet secret-police organization. Son of a Polish nobleman, he was repeatedly arrested for revolutionary activities beginning in 1897. After the Russian Revolution of 1917, he headed the newly created Cheka, which became Soviet Russia's security-police agency. He organized the first concentration camps in Russia and acquired a reputation as a ruthless and fanatical communist. In 1924 he was given control of the Supreme Economic Council.

E. coli \'kō-ˌlī\ *in full* **Escherichia coli** \ˌesh-ə-'ri-kē-ə-'kō-ˌlī\ Species of bacterium that inhabits the stomach and intestines. *E. coli* can be transmitted by water, milk, food, or flies and other insects. Mutations can lead to strains that cause diarrhea by giving off toxins, invading the intestinal lining, or sticking to the intestinal wall. Therapy consists largely of fluid replacement, though specific drugs are effective in some cases. The illness is usually self-limiting, with no evidence of long-lasting effects. However, one dangerous strain causes bloody diarrhea, kidney failure, and death in extreme cases. Proper cooking of meat, washing of produce, and pasteurization of cider prevent infection from contaminated food sources.

e-commerce *in full* **electronic commerce** business-to-consumer and business-to-business commerce, as well as internal organizational transactions that support these activities, conducted by way of the INTERNET or other electronic networks. E-commerce originated in a standard for the exchange of business documents, such as orders or invoices, between suppliers and their business customers. This standard had its inception in the 1948–49 Berlin blockade and airlift. Various industries elaborated upon this system in the ensuing decades before the first general standard was published in 1975. The resulting national electronic data interchange (EDI) standard is unambiguous, independent of any particular machine, and flexible enough to handle most simple electronic transactions. As important as standard forms are for business-to-business transactions, e-commerce encompasses much wider activity. For example, secure electronic transfer of sensitive information is essential to the continued growth of e-commerce. Businesses often deploy private networks (intranets) for sharing information and collaborating within the company, usually insulated from the surrounding Internet by computer-security systems known as firewalls. Businesses also frequently rely on extranets, extensions of a company's intranet that allow portions of its internal network to be accessed by collaborating businesses. A new form of corporate cooperation known as a virtual company, which is actually a network of firms, each performing some of the processes needed to manufacture a product or deliver a service, has flourished.

e-mail *in full* **electronic mail** Messages and other data exchanged between individuals using COMPUTERS in a network. An e-mail system allows computer users to send text, graphics, and sometimes sounds and animated images to other users. It developed from large organizations using an internal messaging system as a communication link among employees. The mass provision of e-mail addresses for private individuals by INTERNET SERVICE PROVIDERS led to the development of e-mail as a system to supplement or replace communication by letter.

Ea \'ā-ä\ In MESOPOTAMIAN RELIGION, the god of water. He formed a triad of deities with ANU and BEL. Originally a local deity in the city of Eridu, he evolved into the lord of the fresh waters beneath the earth, the god of ritual purification, and a patron of sorcery and incantations. Akkadian mythology makes him the father of MARDUK. His counterpart among the Sumerians was Enki, from whose half-fish, half-goat form the astrological figure of CAPRICORN is derived.

eagle Any of many large, heavy-beaked, big-footed BIRDS OF PREY belonging to the family Accipitridae, found worldwide. Eagles are generally larger and more powerful than HAWKS and may resemble a VULTURE in build and flight characteristics, but they have a fully feathered (often crested) head and strong feet equipped with great curved talons. Most species subsist mainly on live prey, which they generally capture on the ground. Eagles have been a symbol of war and imperial power since Babylonian times. They mate for life. They nest in inaccessible places and use the same nest each year. Species vary from 24 in. to 3.3 ft (60 cm–1 m) long. The SEA EAGLES include the BALD EAGLE. See also GOLDEN EAGLE.

White-bellied sea eagle (*Haliaeetus leucogaster*) catching a fish.

© MARY PLAGE/BRUCE COLEMAN LTD.

Eakins \'ā-kənz\, **Thomas** (1844–1916) U.S. painter. After early training at the École des Beaux-Arts in Paris (1866–70), he spent most of his life in his native Philadelphia. He reinforced his study of the live model at the Pennsylvania Academy of Fine Arts by studying anatomy at a medical college. *The Gross Clinic* (1875), depicting a surgical operation, was too realistic for his contemporaries but is now seen as his masterpiece. In 1876 he began teaching at the Pennsylvania Academy, but was forced to resign in 1886 for working with nude models in mixed classes. In addition to numerous portraits, he painted boating and other outdoor scenes that reflect his fascination with the human body in motion. His interest in locomotion led him to the sequential photography of EADWEARD MUYBRIDGE, and he began producing photographs and sculpture as well as paintings. He was the outstanding U.S. painter of the 19th century.

Eales, John (born 1970) Australian rugby union player. Between 1990 and 2001 Eales, who stands 6 ft 7 in. (2.01 m), displayed exceptional all-around ability while playing second row forward (lock) for Queensland and Australia. With Australia he won two World Cups (1991, 1999) and two Tri-Nations Cups (2000, 2001), and served as captain of the Wallabies from 1996 to 2001. Many consider Eales to be among the greatest rugby players in the sport's history.

Eames \'ēmz\, **Charles and Ray** (1907–1978, 1916–1988) U.S. designers. Born in St. Louis, Charles was trained as an architect; Ray (born Ray Kaiser), a native of Sacramento, studied painting with HANS HOFMANN (1933–39). After marrying in 1941, they moved to California, where they designed movie sets and researched the uses of plywood for furniture. In 1946 an exhibit of their furniture designs at the Museum of Modern Art resulted in the mass production of their molded plywood chairs by the Herman Miller Furniture Co., and their furniture soon became known for its beauty, comfort, and elegance. After 1955 they made educational films, notably *Powers of Ten* (1969).

ear Organ of HEARING and balance. The outer ear directs sound vibrations through the auditory canal to the eardrum, which is stretched across the end of the auditory canal and which transmits sound vibrations to the middle ear. There a chain of three tiny bones conducts the vibrations to the INNER EAR. Fluid inside the cochlea of the inner ear stimulates sensory hairs; these in turn initiate the nerve impulses that travel along the auditory nerve to the brain. The inner ear is also an organ of balance: the sensation of dizziness that is felt after spinning is caused when fluid inside the inner ear's semicircular canals continues to move and stimulate sensory hairs after the body has come to rest. The eustachian tube connects the middle ear with the nasal passages; that connection allows the common cold to spread from the nasal passages to the middle ear, especially in infants and small children. The most common cause of hearing loss is otosclerosis, a surgically correctable disease in which one of the bones of the middle ear fails to vibrate. See also DEAFNESS, OTITIS. See illustration on following page.

Earhart \'er-ˌhärt\, **Amelia (Mary)** (1897–1937) U.S. aviator, the first woman to fly alone across the Atlantic Ocean. Born in Atchison, Kan., she worked as a military nurse in Canada during World War I and later as a social worker in Boston. In 1928 she became the first woman to cross the Atlantic in a plane, though as a passenger. In 1932 she accomplished the flight alone, becoming the first woman and the second person to do so. In 1935 she became the first person to fly solo from Hawaii to California. In 1937 she set out with a navigator, Fred Noonan, to fly around the world; they had completed over two-thirds of the distance when her plane disappeared without a trace in the central Pacific Ocean. Speculation about her fate has continued to the present.

earl See COUNT

Early, Jubal A(nderson) (1816–1894) U.S. and Confederate military leader. Born in Franklin Co., Va., he graduated from West Point and served in the second Seminole War and the Mexican War. He opposed secession but supported his home state of Virginia when it joined the Confederacy. He fought at the Battle of BULL RUN and in Virginia. In 1864 he led Confederate forces down the Shenandoah Valley and threatened Washington, D.C., but was defeated by Union troops under PHILIP

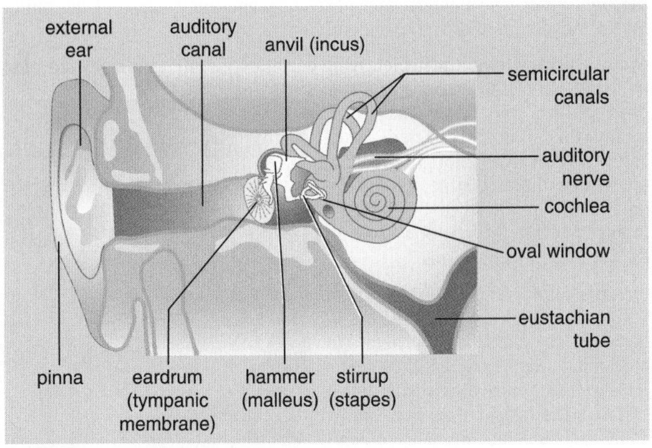

The cartilaginous pinna and auditory canal direct sound waves to the middle ear. The eardrum, stretched across the end of the canal, vibrates as sound waves reach it. Vibrations are transmitted via three small bones (hammer, anvil, stirrup) to the membranous oval window that links the middle ear to the inner ear. The cochlea is a coiled, fluid-filled tube lined with sensory hairs. Vibrations in the oval window cause movement of the cochlear fluid, stimulating the hairs to initiate impulses which travel along a branch of the auditory nerve to the brain. The eustachian tube, running from the middle ear to the nasopharynx, equalizes pressure between the middle and outer ear. The fluid-filled semicircular canals play a role in balance, as hairs in the canals respond to movement-induced changes in the fluid by initiating impulses that travel to the brain.

SHERIDAN. Relieved of command, he fled to Mexico and then Canada, returning to Virginia in 1869.

Early American furniture Furniture made in the second half of the 17th century by American colonists. The earliest pieces were massive and based on English Jacobean styles. Decoration consisted of carved flower motifs or lunettes and carved scrolls and leaves, sometimes highlighted by painting; oak and pine were the most common woods. Produced in the Connecticut River valley and Massachusetts coastal settlements, it consisted mainly of chests, cupboards, tables, stools, chairs, and beds.

Early Christian art Architecture, painting, and sculpture produced from the 3rd century AD to c. 750, particularly in Italy and the western Mediterranean. Artwork produced in the eastern part of the Roman empire is considered BYZANTINE ART. The earliest identifiable works consist of a few 2nd-century wall and ceiling paintings in the Roman catacombs. Early Christian iconography was symbolic (e.g., a fish symbolized Christ, bread and wine symbolized the Eucharist) and, like the religion, evoked mysticism and spirituality. Large-scale sculpture was not popular; the principal genres and media were relief sculpture on tombs, ivory carving, and paintings and mosaics on church walls and floors.

Early Netherlandish art Architecture, painting, sculpture, and other visual arts produced in Flanders in the late 14th and 15th century under the rule of the dukes of BURGUNDY. In 1384 PHILIP II THE BOLD acquired the countship of Flanders by marriage, and the Flemish-Burgundian political alliance remained intact until 1482. Philip embellished the churches and monasteries of his capital, Dijon, with sculpture, especially that of CLAUS SLUTER, and paintings. His grandson, PHILIP III THE GOOD, patronized the arts on a grander scale, hiring JAN VAN EYCK and ROGIER VAN DER WEYDEN. Among the masters active until the end of the alliance were ROBERT CAMPIN, PETRUS CHRISTUS, DIRCK BOUTS, HUGO VAN DER GOES, and HANS MEMLING.

Earnhardt, (Ralph) Dale (1951–2001) American STOCK-CAR RACER who was the dominant driver in the National Association for Stock Car Auto Racing (NASCAR) during the 1980s and 1990s. Ralph Earnhardt, Dale's father, raced stock cars in the American southeast during the 1960s and helped to foster his son's passion for the sport. The younger Earnhardt made his NASCAR Winston Cup debut in 1975. He continued as a part-time driver on the circuit until he landed a full time position in the Winston Cup series in 1979. That year he collected 17 top 10 finishes and earned the Rookie of the Year title. The next year he raced to five victories and 19 top five finishes in winning his first Winston Cup title. Earnhardt drove to six more Winston Cup titles (1986-87, 1990-91, 1993-94), equaling the career mark of RICHARD PETTY. Earnhardt gained a reputation as an aggressive driver and became known as "the Intimidator." He died from injuries suffered during a crash in the final lap of the 2001 Daytona 500. His son Dale, Jr., also raced in the NASCAR Winston Cup series.

Earp \'ərp\, Wyatt (Berry Stapp) (1848–1929) U.S. frontiersman. Born in Monmouth, Ill., he worked in the 1870s as a police officer in Wichita and Dodge City, where he befriended the gunmen Doc HOLLIDAY and BAT MASTERSON. He later worked as a guard for Wells Fargo. By 1881 he had moved to TOMBSTONE, Ariz., living as a gambler and a saloon guard. His brother Virgil became town marshal, and his other brothers (James, Morgan, and Warren) bought real estate and businesses. A feud with the Clanton gang ended in a shootout at the O.K. Corral in which three of the Clanton gang were killed. In 1882 Morgan was murdered, and Wyatt, Warren, and some friends killed two suspects in retaliation. Accused of murder, Wyatt fled to Colorado and later settled in California. Stuart Lake's *Wyatt Earp, Frontier Marshal* (1931), written with Earp's collaboration, portrayed him as a fearless lawman.

earth Third PLANET in distance outward from the SUN. Believed to be about 4.6 billion years old, it is about 92,960,000 mi (149,573,000 km) away from the sun. It orbits the sun at a speed of 18.5 mi (29.8 km) per second, making one complete revolution in 365.25 days. As it revolves, it spins on its axis, rotating once every 23 hours 56 minutes 4 seconds. The fifth largest planet of the SOLAR SYSTEM, it has an equatorial circumference of 24,902 mi (40,076 km). Its total surface area is roughly 197,000,000 sq mi (509,600,000 sq km), of which about 29% is land. Earth's atmosphere consists of a mixture of gases, chiefly nitrogen and oxygen. Its only natural satellite, the MOON, orbits the planet at a distance of about 238,870 mi (384,400 km). The earth's surface is subdi-

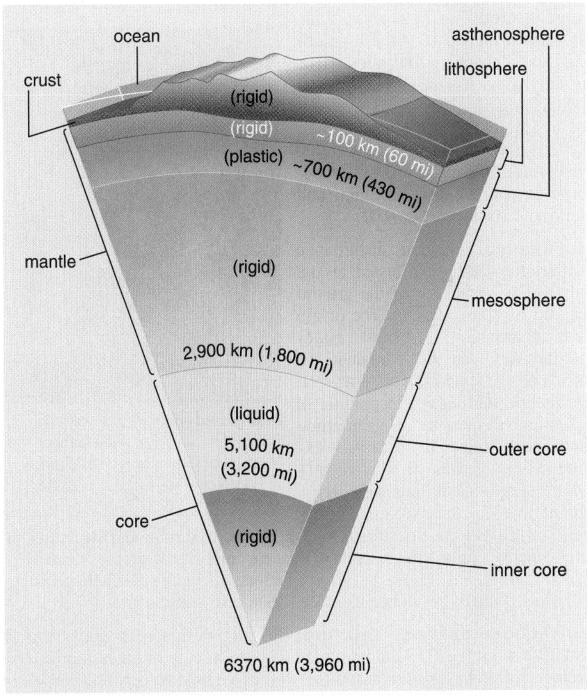

The earth's layers may be identified in two distinct ways. In chemical terms, the rock has three basic layers (left): the crust consists of granitic and basaltic rock, the mantle of silicate materials, and the core primarily of nickel and iron. Measured by physical properties, the earth has five principal layers (right): the lithosphere is a rigid outer layer, the asthenosphere is a thin layer of plastically deforming material that flows under stress, the mesosphere is a rigid layer that extends down to the core, the outer core is a viscous liquid in which the earth's magnetic field is believed to originate, and the inner core is solid. The layers are not drawn to scale.

E
F
G

vided into seven continental masses: AFRICA, ANTARCTICA, ASIA, AUSTRALIA, EUROPE, NORTH AMERICA, and SOUTH AMERICA. These continents are surrounded by the so-called World Ocean, which is broken down into three major bodies: the ATLANTIC, PACIFIC, and INDIAN oceans.

earth-crossing asteroid *or* **Apollo asteroid** ASTEROID whose path crosses earth's orbit. Some astronomers have mounted a full-scale search for such asteroids, partly to calculate whether they may collide with earth, since early detection might make it possible to deflect them. More than 400 are now cataloged, about 150 of which are larger than 0.6 mi (1 km) in diameter. Collisions between earth and asteroids of such size are believed to occur a few times every million years. Such a collision would produce an explosion with as much force as several hydrogen bombs, possibly resulting in a disturbance in the world's climate or catastrophic tidal waves. Some scientists believe the extinction of the dinosaurs at the end of the CRETACEOUS PERIOD was triggered by the impact just north of the Yucatán Peninsula of an asteroid or COMET about 6 mi (10 km) in diameter. Two other classes of asteroids with somewhat smaller and larger orbits than the Apollos—the Atens and Amors—may also make close encounters with the earth.

Earth Summit *officially* **United Nations Conference on Environment and Development** Conference held at Rio de Janeiro (June 3–14, 1992) to reconcile worldwide economic development with environmental protection. It was the largest gathering of world leaders in history, with 117 heads of state and representatives of 178 nations. Biodiversity, global warming, sustainable development, and preservation of tropical rain forests were among the topics discussed. Five international agreements were signed amid tensions between the poorer developing states, who opposed environmental restrictions without increased aid, and the industrialized nations, who would not promise the requested aid. Follow-up meetings were held in 1997 at the U.N. General Assembly in New York and in 2002 in Johannesburg.

earthenware POTTERY that has been fired at low heat and is slightly more porous and coarser than STONEWARE and PORCELAIN. For practical and decorative purposes, it is usually glazed. The earliest known pottery, a soft earthenware excavated at a Neolithic settlement in Turkey, is thought to be about 9,000 years old. Earthenware is still widely used for cooking, freezing, and serving. See also CREAMWARE.

Lead-glazed earthenware water pot, Paris, 15th century, in the National Museum of Ceramics, Sèvres, France.

BY COURTESY OF THE MUSEE NATIONAL DE LA CERAMIQUE, SEVRES

earthquake Sudden disturbance within the earth manifested at the surface by a shaking of the ground caused by SEISMIC WAVES. The origin and distribution of most major earthquakes can be explained in terms of FAULTS and the PLATE TECTONICS theory. Earthquake magnitude (a quantitative measure of amplitude and energy released) is usually expressed in terms of the RICHTER SCALE. Earthquake intensity is a qualitative measure (e.g., "barely felt" or "catastrophic destruction") of damage to terrain and structures at any given location. In general, a quake's intensity decreases with distance from its EPICENTER, but other factors, including surface geology, may significantly influence its effects. See also SEISMOLOGY.

earthquake-resistant structure Building designed to prevent total collapse, preserve life, and minimize damage in case of an earthquake or tremor. Earthquakes exert lateral as well as vertical forces, and responding to their random, often sudden motions is a complex task that is just beginning to be understood. Earthquake-resistant structures absorb and dissipate seismically induced motion by a combination of means: damping decreases the amplitude of oscillations of a vibrating structure; ductile materials (e.g., steel) fail only after considerable inelastic deformation. Skyscrapers present the problem that too much flexibility would allow tremendous swaying in its upper floors to develop during an earthquake, increasing damage to its contents. Care must be taken to provide built-in tolerance for some structural damage, resist lateral loading through stiffeners (diagonal sway bracing), and allow areas of the building to move somewhat independently.

earthshine Sunlight reflected from earth, especially that reflected onto the darkside of the MOON. For a few days before and after each new moon, this doubly reflected earthshine is powerful enough to make the whole moon visible, producing the effect, in the case of the new moon, of "the new moon holding the old moon in her arms."

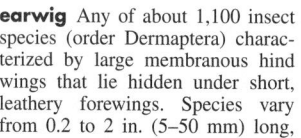

Earthshine on the moon.

BY COURTESY OF YERKES OBSERVATORY, WISCONSIN

earthworm Any of more than 1,800 species of terrestrial WORMS in the ANNELID class Oligochaeta (in particular, members of the genus *Lumbricus*). Earthworms exist in all soils of the world that have sufficient moisture and organic content. The most common U.S. species, *L. terrestris,* grows to about 10 in. (25 cm), but an Australian species can grow as long as 11 ft (3.3 m). The segmented body is tapered at both ends. Earthworms eat decaying organisms and, in the process, ingest soil, sand, and pebbles, aerating the soil, promoting drainage, and improving the soil's nutrient content for plants. They are eaten by many animals.

Earthworm (*Lumbricus terrestris*).

JOHN MARKHAM

earwig Any of about 1,100 insect species (order Dermaptera) characterized by large membranous hind wings that lie hidden under short, leathery forewings. Species vary from 0.2 to 2 in. (5–50 mm) long, and all are flat, slender, and dark, with a shiny outer covering and simple biting mouthparts. Several species can shoot a foul-smelling liquid, formed in abdominal glands, as far as 4 in. (10 cm). Earwigs have a pair of horny, forceps-like tail filaments, or pincers (cerci), at the back end of the abdomen that may function in defense, capturing prey, folding wings, or fighting courtship battles.

easement In Anglo-American property law, an interest in land owned by another that entitles its holder to a specific limited use or enjoyment, such as the right to cross the land or have a view over it continue unobstructed. It may be created expressly by a written deed of grant conveying the specific usage right, or it may be created by implication, as when an owner divides property into two parcels in such a way that an already existing, obvious, and continuous use of one parcel (e.g., for access) is necessary for the reasonable enjoyment of the other. Some U.S. states permit the creation of an easement by prescription (acquisition of an interest), as when one person makes continuous use of another's land for some specified period of time (e.g., 20 years). Utility companies often own easements in gross; these are not dependent on ownership of the surrounding estate. Numerous other kinds of easements have been important in Anglo-American law. See also REAL AND PERSONAL PROPERTY.

East, Edward Murray (1879–1938) U.S. plant geneticist, agronomist, and chemist. He finished high school at age 15 and received an MS in 1904. He was particularly interested in determining and controlling the protein and fat content of corn, both of which significantly influence its value as animal feed. His research, with that of GEORGE HARRISON SHULL, led to the development of modern-day hybrid corn. Commercial production of hybrid seed corn was made possible by the work of his student Donald F. Jones (1890–1963). East's work helped make possible studies in the field of population genetics.

East African Rift System See GREAT RIFT VALLEY

East Anglia Traditional region of England. Consisting of the counties of NORFOLK and SUFFOLK and parts of CAMBRIDGESHIRE and ESSEX, its traditional center is the city of NORWICH. The easternmost area in England, it has been settled for thousands of years; Colchester, the oldest recorded town in England, was important in pre-Roman and Roman times. East Anglia was one of the kingdoms of Anglo-Saxon England and was later ruled by Danes in the 9th century. During the medieval period it was known for its woolen products, but the region's modern economy is predominantly agricultural. Along the coast are many important fishing ports and holiday resorts.

East Asian arts Musical, visual, and performing arts of China, Korea, and Japan. China is the source of much of the Korean and Japanese arts. Painting and calligraphy are the principal fine arts in China. Korean arts feature the use of stone in architecture and sculpture and an outstanding celadon pottery glaze. Japanese arts are influenced by Chinese painting and calligraphy, indigenous themes, and Buddhist iconography. In East Asian countries, forms of music, dance, and drama evolved together and are usually linked. See also Chinese architecture, Chinese art, Japanese architecture, Japanese art, Japanese music, Korean art.

East China Sea See China Sea

East India Co. *or* **English East India Co.** English chartered company formed for trade with East and Southeast Asia and India, incorporated in 1600. It began as a monopolistic trading body, establishing early trading stations at Surat, Madras (now Chennai), Bombay (Mumbai), and Calcutta (Kolkata). Trade in spices was its original focus; this broadened to include cotton, silk, and other goods. In 1708 it merged with a rival and was renamed the United Co. of Merchants of England Trading to the East Indies. Becoming involved in politics, it acted as the chief agent of British imperialism in India in the 18th–19th century, exercising substantial power over much of the subcontinent. The company's activities in China in the 19th century served as a catalyst for the expansion of British influence there; its financing of the tea trade with illegal opium exports led to the first Opium War (1839–42). From the late 18th century it gradually lost both commercial and political control; its autonomy diminished after two acts of Parliament (1773, 1774) established a regulatory board responsible to Parliament, though the act gave the company supreme authority in its domains. It ceased to exist as a legal entity in 1873. See also Dutch East India Co., French East India Co.

East India Co., Dutch Trading company founded by the Dutch in 1602 to protect their trade in the Indian Ocean and to assist in their war of independence from Spain. The Dutch government granted it a trade monopoly in the waters between the Cape of Good Hope and the Straits of Magellan. Under the administration of forceful governors-general, it was able to defeat the British fleet and largely displace the Portuguese in the East Indies. It prospered through most of the 17th century but then began to decline as a trading and sea power; it was dissolved in 1799. See also East India Co., French East India Co.

East India Co., French Trading company founded by Jean-Baptiste Colbert in 1664, and its successors, established to oversee French commerce with India, East Africa, and other territories of the Indian Ocean and the East Indies. In competition with the established Dutch East India Co., it mounted expensive expeditions that were often harassed by the Dutch. It also suffered in the French economic crash of 1720, and by 1740 the value of its trade with India was half that of the English East India Co. Its monopoly over French trade with India was ended in 1769, and it languished until its disappearance in the French Revolution.

East Pacific Rise Submarine linear mountain range on the floor of the South Pacific Ocean, roughly paralleling the western coast of South America. The main portion of the rise lies generally about 2,000 mi (3,200 km) off the coast, and it lies about 6,000–9,000 ft (1,800–2,700 m) above the surrounding seafloor. The East Pacific Rise has a generally smooth and flattish surface, and it drops sharply away at the sides. It is composed largely of basic igneous crust, overlain or abutted by more or less flat-lying sediments.

East Prussia *German* **Ostpreussen** \'ȯst-ˌprȯis-ᵊn\ Historical region and former Prussian province, east of Pomerania. From 1815 it was known as East Prussia, part of the kingdom of Prussia, and in the 19th century it was a stronghold of Prussian Junkers, a military aristocracy. It was the scene of successful resistance against the Russians in World War I. Following the war it was separated from the rest of Germany by the Polish Corridor (1919); it was reunited with the Reich by the German conquest of Poland in 1939. Overrun by Soviet armies at the end of World War II, in 1945 it was divided between the Soviet Union and Poland.

East River Navigable tidal strait linking Upper New York Bay with Long Island Sound in New York City. It separates Manhattan and the Bronx from Brooklyn and Queens. About 16 mi (26 km) long and 600–4,000 ft (200–1200 m) wide, it connects with the Hudson River via the Harlem River and Spuyten Duyvil Creek at the northern end of Manhattan Island. Roosevelt (formerly Welfare), Wards, Randalls, and Rikers islands are in the East River, which has numerous port facilities.

East St. Louis Race Riot Outbreak of violence in East St. Louis, Ill., in July 1917, sparked by the employment of blacks in a factory holding government contracts. It was the worst of several attacks during World War I on black Americans newly employed in war industries. Some 6,000 blacks were driven from their homes; 40 blacks and 8 whites were killed.

East Sussex County (pop. 1999 est.: 496,200), southeastern England. It is located on the English Channel; the county seat is Lewes. A ridge of chalk hills, the South Downs, crosses the county along the coast; in the southeast the reclaimed marshes of Pevensey Levels have historically been an important entry point for invaders. Neolithic remains and an Iron Age hill fort have been found, as well as evidence of Roman occupation. The South Saxons came to dominate the area, and were in turn subjugated by Wessex. In 1066 William of Normandy (see William I) landed at Pevensey and fought the Battle of Hastings. Most of the county's recent growth has been along the coast, beginning with the rise of Brighton as a seaside resort.

East Timor *or* **Timor-Leste** *officially* **Democratic Republic of East Timor** Country, occupying the eastern half of the island of Timor, Southeast Asia. Bounded by the Timor Sea and by the western half of Timor, it also includes the enclave of Ambeno surrounding the town of Pante Makasar on the northwestern coast and the islands of Atauro (Kambing) and Jaco. Area: 5,743 sq mi (14,874 sq km). Population (2002 est.): 797,000. Capital: Dili. The Portuguese first settled on Timor in 1520 and were granted rule over Timor's eastern half in 1860. The Timor political

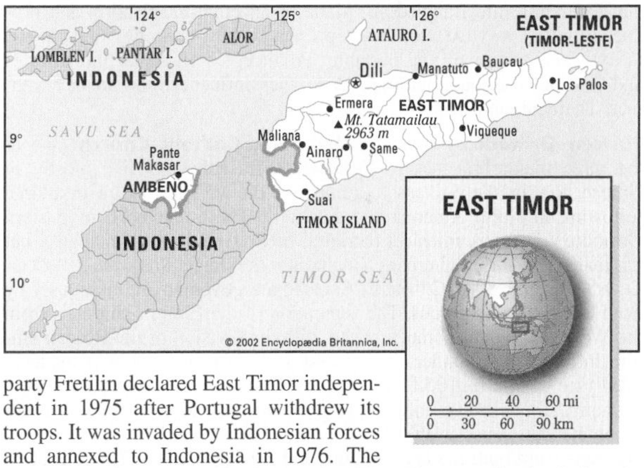

party Fretilin declared East Timor independent in 1975 after Portugal withdrew its troops. It was invaded by Indonesian forces and annexed to Indonesia in 1976. The takeover, which resulted in thousands of East Timorese deaths during the next two decades, was disputed by the United Nations. In 1999 an independence referendum won overwhelmingly; though Indonesia officially recognized the referendum, anti-independence militias killed hundreds of people and sent thousands fleeing to the western part of the island before and after the vote. A U.N.-administered interim authority imposed order and oversaw elections, the promulgation of a constitution, and the return of refugees; East Timor became a sovereign nation in 2002.

East-West Schism See Schism of 1054

East York City, southeastern Ontario. With the cities of North York, Toronto, Scarborough, York, and Etobicoke, it forms the municipality of Metropolitan Toronto. A planned industrial and residential urban complex, it was established in 1967 through the amalgamation of the former East York township (created in 1924), and the former town of Leaside (settled 1819).

Easter Major festival of the Christian church year, celebrating the resurrection of Jesus on the third day after his crucifixion. In Western churches it falls on a Sunday between March 22 and April 25, depending on the date of the first full moon after the spring equinox. The date was fixed after the Council of NICAEA (AD 325). In the Eastern Orthodox calendar, which uses a different calculation, it often falls later. A joyful festival and a time of redemption, Easter brings an end to the long period of penance that constitutes LENT. The word is probably derived from Eostre, a Germanic goddess of spring, and some of its folk customs (e.g., the decoration of eggs as symbols of new life) may have originated with ancient pagan spring festivals. From the late 2nd century, it has also been a time for BAPTISM.

Easter Island *Spanish* **Isla de Pascua** *native* **Rapa Nui** \ˈrä-pä-ˈnü-ē\ Island (pop., 2000 est.: 3,618), eastern Pacific Ocean. Located 2,200 mi (3,600 km) west of Chile, it has an area of 63 sq mi (163 sq km). Initially inhabited c. AD 400 by Polynesians from the MARQUESAS, it has long been famous for its monolithic stone statues in human form. They are 10–40 ft (3–12 m) high and some weigh more than 50 tons. They were probably erected c. 1000–1600 AD. War and disease decimated the island's population over the succeeding centuries, and the statues' origins were forgotten. Annexed by Chile in 1888, the island has been declared a WORLD HERITAGE SITE.

Easter Rising *or* **Easter Rebellion** (1916) Republican insurrection in Ireland against the British, which began on Easter Monday, April 24. Led by Patrick Pearse and Tom Clarke, some 1,560 Irish Volunteers and 200 members of the Irish Citizen Army seized the Dublin General Post Office and other strategic points in Dublin. After five days of fighting, British troops put down the rebellion, and 15 of its leaders were tried and executed. Though the uprising itself had been unpopular with most of the Irish, the executions caused revulsion against the British authorities. The uprising heralded the end of British power in Ireland.

Eastern Hemisphere Part of the earth east of the Atlantic Ocean. It includes Europe, Asia, Australia, and Africa. Longitudes 20° W and 160° E are often considered its boundaries.

Eastern Indian bronze *or* **Pala bronze** Metal sculptures produced from the 9th century in the area of modern Bihar and West Bengal in India, extending into Bangladesh. Made of an eight-metal alloy and produced by LOST-WAX CASTING, they represent various divinities (e.g., SHIVA, VISHNU) and are small and portable. Produced in Buddhist monasteries and distributed throughout South Asia, they influenced the art of Myanmar, Thailand, and Java.

Eastern Orthodoxy *officially* **Orthodox Catholic Church** One of the three major branches of CHRISTIANITY. Its adherents live mostly in Greece, Russia, the Balkans, Ukraine, and the Middle East, with a large following in North America and Australia. The titular head of Eastern Orthodoxy is the ecumenical patriarch of Constantinople (Istanbul), but its many territorial churches (including the huge RUSSIAN ORTHODOX CHURCH and the GREEK ORTHODOX CHURCH) are governed autonomously by head bishops or patriarchs. The separation of the Eastern churches from the Western, or Latin, branch began with the division of the Roman empire into two parts under CONSTANTINE I. A formal break was made in 1054 (see SCHISM OF 1054). Doctrinally, Eastern Orthodoxy differs from Roman Catholicism in not accepting the primacy of the POPE and in not accepting the clause in the Western CREED that states that the HOLY SPIRIT proceeds from both the Father (God) and the Son (Jesus). Today Eastern Orthodoxy has more than 200 million adherents worldwide.

Eastern Rite Church *or* **Eastern Catholic Church** Any of several Eastern Christian churches that trace their origins to ethnic or national Eastern churches but are united with the Roman Catholic church (see ROMAN CATHOLICISM). A few of these churches became associated with Rome in the 12th century, but most rejoined it in the 16th century or later. Eastern Rite churches acknowledge the authority of the POPE but are allowed to use their own ancient liturgies and to maintain rites and customs more typical of EASTERN ORTHODOXY, such as allowing priests to marry and admitting infants to holy communion. The Eastern Rite includes the Ukrainian Orthodox church, the MARONITE CHURCH, and some Armenians, Ruthenians, and Melchites (in Syria). Today Eastern Catholics number more than 12 million.

Eastern Woodlands Indians American Indians of the largely wooded area stretching east from the Mississippi River Valley to the Atlantic coastline and extending north into Canada and south into what are now Illinois and North Carolina. The Indians in this region spoke IROQUOIAN, ALGONQUIAN, and SIOUAN languages. Individual groups included the ABENAKI, Woodland CREE, DELAWARE, FOX, HURON, Illinois, IROQUOIS, MAHICAN, MENOMINEE, MIAMI, MICMAC, MOHAWK, MOHEGAN, MONTAGNAIS AND NASKAPI, OJIBWA, ONEIDA, Ottawa, PEQUOT, POWHATAN, SAUK, SENECA, Tuscarora, and WINNEBAGO.

Eastman, George (1854–1932) U.S. inventor and manufacturer. Born in Waterville, N.Y., Eastman in 1880 perfected a process for making dry plates for photography. In 1889 he introduced transparent film, and in 1892 he reorganized his Rochester (N.Y.) company as the EASTMAN KODAK CO. The introduction of the first Kodak (a coined word that became a trademark) camera helped promote large-scale amateur PHOTOGRAPHY. By 1927 Eastman Kodak had a virtual monopoly of the U.S. photographic industry. Eastman's bequests to the University of Rochester were acknowledged in the naming of the Eastman School of Music.

Eastman Kodak Co. Major U.S. manufacturer of film, cameras, photographic supplies, and other imaging products. The present company was incorporated in 1901 as the successor to a business founded in 1880 by GEORGE EASTMAN, whose innovations included the perfection of a process for making dry plates, roll film (1884), and the Kodak camera (1888), the first camera simple enough to appeal to large numbers of amateur photographers. The company's later innovations included the first home-movie equipment, the Kodachrome color slide film, the cartridge-loaded Instamatic cameras, and the highly automatic Disc cameras. Its headquarters are in Rochester, N.Y. See also POLAROID CORP.

Eastman School of Music CONSERVATORY in Rochester, N.Y. The DKG School of Musical Art was founded in 1914; it was soon purchased by GEORGE EASTMAN, who donated it to the University of Rochester in 1921 with an endowment fund. H. HANSON, its principal director (1924–64), built it into a world-renowned institution. Eastman's annual festival of American music (1925–71) programmed works by some 700 composers, more than a third of which were recorded. Today some 600 students are enrolled. Eastman's student orchestra has been considered of professional quality. Its faculty has included world-famous musicians, and many of its graduates have had stellar careers.

Eastwood, Clint(on) (born 1930) U.S. film actor and director. Born in San Francisco, he won attention in the television series *Rawhide* (1959–66) before his roles in three of SERGIO LEONE's "spaghetti westerns" (1964–66) made him an international star. He returned to the U.S. for the hugely successful *Dirty Harry* (1971), the first of a series of action films in which he played laconic and dangerous heroes. He combined directing with acting in such films as *Play Misty for Me* (1971), *Pale Rider* (1985), *Unforgiven* (1992, Academy Award), *A Perfect World* (1993), and *The Bridges of Madison County* (1995). His interest in jazz led him to direct and produce *Bird* (1988), about CHARLIE PARKER. His minimalist style of acting and direction gradually added critical acclaim to his long-established box-office success.

eating disorders Abnormal eating patterns, including ANOREXIA NERVOSA, BULIMIA, compulsive overeating, and pica (appetite for nonfood substances). These disorders, which usually have a psychological component, may lead to underweight, OBESITY, or MALNUTRITION. In rumination disorder, an infant repeatedly regurgitates food.

Eaton, Cyrus S(tephen) (1883–1979) Canadian-U.S. industrialist and philanthropist. Born in Pugwash, Nova Scotia, he entered business in 1907, built several electric-power plants in western Canada and soon diversified into other utilities, banking, and steel in the U.S. In 1930 he merged several steel companies to form Republic Steel, the third-largest U.S. steel company. He lost most of his fortune in the Great Depression, then made another fortune. An active advocate of nuclear disarmament and improved Soviet-U.S. relations, he helped inaugurate the PUGWASH CONFERENCES in 1957.

EB virus See EPSTEIN-BARR VIRUS

Ebb, Fred See John KANDER

Ebbinghaus \ˈe-biŋ-ˌhau̇s\, **Hermann** (1850–1909) German psychologist. He pioneered experimental methods for measuring rote learning and memory, demonstrating that memory is based on associations. His "forgetting curve" relates forgetting to the passage of time. His major works are *Memory* (1885) and *Principles of Psychology* (1902).

EBCDIC \ˈep-sə-ˌdik\ *in full* **extended binary-coded digital interchange code** Data-encoding system, developed by IBM, that uses a unique eight-BIT binary code for each number and alphabetic character as well as punctuation marks and accented letters and non-alphabetic characters. EBCDIC differs in several respects from ASCII, the most widely used system of encoding text, dividing the eight bits for each character into two four-bit zones, with one zone indicating the type of character, digit, punctuation mark, lowercase letter, capital letter, and so on, and the other zone indicating the specific character within this type.

Ebert \'ā-bert\, **Friedrich** (1871–1925) German politician. A journeyman saddler and trade unionist, he became chairman of the German SOCIAL DEMOCRATIC PARTY in 1913. Under his leadership, the Social Democratic movement gained increasing influence in German national politics. After revolution broke out in 1918, he formed a Socialist coalition government. He helped bring about the Weimar constitution and in 1919 was elected the first president of the WEIMAR REPUBLIC. Facing threats to the new government, he waged a civil war, assisted by the FREIKORPS, against Socialists and Communists and suppressed the KAPP PUTSCH. His authority was weakened in 1923 by the crisis over the RUHR OCCUPATION, his party's withdrawal from the governing coalition, and ADOLF HITLER's abortive BEER HALL PUTSCH.

Ebla *modern* **Tell Mardikh** \'tel-'mär-dik\ Ancient city, northwestern Syria. Located south of ALEPPO, it dominated northern Syria, Lebanon, and parts of northern MESOPOTAMIA during the height of its power (c. 2600–2240 BC) and enjoyed trade with states as far away as Egypt, Iran, and Sumer. The city's archives, dating to the 3rd millennium BC, were discovered virtually intact in 1975 excavations; they offer a rich source of information about the area's ancient way of life.

Ebola \ē-'bō-lə\ Virus responsible for a severe and often fatal HEMORRHAGIC FEVER. Outbreaks in primates, including humans, have been recorded. Initial symptoms are fever, severe headaches and muscle aches, and loss of appetite; blood clots and profuse uncontrollable hemorrhaging appear within days, followed by nausea, vomiting, and diarrhea. Death occurs in 8–17 days; fatality rates range from 50% to 90%. There is no known treatment. It takes its name from the Ebola River in northern Congo (Zaire), where it first emerged in 1976. The virus appears as long filaments, sometimes branched or intertwined. The virus particle contains one molecule of RNA. How it attacks cells is unknown. It can be transmitted through contact with bodily fluids; unsanitary conditions and lack of adequate medical supplies have been factors in its spread.

ebony Wood of several species of trees of the genus *Diospyros* (family Ebenaceae), found widely in the tropics. The best is very heavy, almost black, and from HEARTWOOD only. Because of its color, durability, hardness, and ability to take a high polish, ebony is used for cabinetwork and inlaying, piano keys, knife handles, and turned articles. The best Indian and Ceylon ebony is produced by *D. ebenum,* which grows in abundance west of Trincomalee in Sri Lanka. Jamaica, American, or green ebony comes from *Brya ebenus,* a leguminous tree or shrub.

Ebro River \'ā-,brō\ *ancient* **Iberus** River, northeastern Spain. It rises in the CANTABRIAN MTNS. and flows for 565 mi (910 km) in a southeasterly course to the Mediterranean Sea, between BARCELONA and VALENCIA. The second-longest Spanish river, it has the greatest discharge and largest drainage basin in the country. The Ebro is only navigable upstream for 15 mi (25 km) from its delta.

Eça de Queirós \'ē-sä-də-'kā-,rüsh\, **José Maria de** *or* **José Maria de Eça de Queiroz** (1845–1900) Portuguese novelist. The illegitimate son of a magistrate, he began a career in law but turned to writing; later he held several diplomatic posts. He was associated with the Generation of '70, a group of intellectuals committed to social and artistic reform. His novels, in which he introduced naturalism and realism to Portuguese fiction, include *The Sin of Father Amaro* (1876), *Cousin Bazilio* (1878), and his masterpiece, *The Maias* (1888), a satire exploring the consequences of decadence in Portuguese society. He is often considered his country's greatest novelist.

eccentric and rod mechanism Arrangement of mechanical parts used to obtain a reciprocating straight-line MOTION from a rotating shaft. It serves the same purpose as a slider-crank mechanism and is particularly useful when the required stroke of the reciprocating motion is small in comparison with the dimensions of the driving shaft. Because an eccentric can be attached anywhere along a shaft, it is unnecessary to form any part of the shaft into a CRANK. Eccentrics are seldom used to transmit large FORCES because FRICTION loss would be high; they are commonly used to drive the valve gears of engines.

Eccles \'ek-əlz\, **W(illiam) H(enry)** (1875–1966) English physicist. After receiving his doctorate from the Royal College of Science, he became an early advocate of OLIVER HEAVISIDE's theory that an upper layer of the atmosphere reflects radio waves, enabling their transmission over long distances. In 1912 he suggested that solar radiation accounted for wave-propagation differences between day and night.

ecclesia \ə-'klē-zē-ə\ (Greek, *ekklesia:* "gathering of those summoned") In ancient Greece, the assembly of citizens in a CITY-STATE. The Athenian ecclesia already existed in the 7th century; under SOLON it consisted of all male citizens of age 18 and over. It controlled policy, including the right to hear appeals in the public court, elect ARCHONS, and confer special privileges. After discussion, members voted by a show of hands; a simple majority determined the results. The body could not initiate new business, since motions had to originate in the BOULE. Ecclesias existed in most Greek city-states through Roman times, though their powers faded under the empire.

ecclesiastical heraldry Arms associated with the administrative and collegiate bodies of the church, particularly the Anglican/Episcopal, Roman Catholic, or Presbyterian church. Abbeys, priories, and dioceses have their own arms, and high ecclesiastical functionaries have always added their personal arms. See also coat of ARMS.

Ecevit \,e-je-'vēt\, **Bülent** (born 1925) Turkish poet, journalist, and politician. A writer for the newspaper of the Republican People's Party (RPP), he was elected as a RPP member to the Turkish parliament in 1957. As minister of labor (1961–65), he made the strike a legal weapon for labor for the first time in Turkish history. He became head of the RPP in 1972 and served as prime minister of Turkey on numerous occasions. As head of government, he declared an amnesty for all political prisoners and in 1974 authorized Turkey's military intervention in Cyprus after the Greek-led coup on that island.

Echegaray (y Eizaguirre) \,ā-chā-gä-'rī\, **José** (1832–1916) Spanish dramatist. A mathematics professor in his early life, he later held government positions, including minister of finance, and helped develop the Banco de España. His first play, *The Checkbook,* was not produced until he was 42; from then on he wrote an average of two plays a year for the rest of his life. These melodramas, now forgotten, were very popular in his day, and he was admired for his fertile imagination and his skillful stage effects. With FREDERIC MISTRAL, he won the 1904 Nobel Prize for Literature.

echidna \i-'kid-nə\ *or* **spiny anteater** Either of two species of egg-laying mammals (MONOTREME family Tachyglossidae). Echidnas are stocky and virtually tailless. They have strong-clawed feet and spines on the upper part of the brownish body. The snout is narrow, the mouth small, and the tongue long and sticky for feeding on termites and ants. New Guinea echidnas are 18–31 in. (45–78 cm) long and piglike; valued for their meat, they are declining in numbers. Echidnas of Australia and Tasmania are 14–21 in. (35–53 cm) long. Echidnas exude milk from mammary openings on the skin, and the young lap it up. See also ANTEATER, PANGOLIN.

echinacea \,e-ki-'nā-shə, ,e-ki-'nā-sē-ə\ Any member of the CONEFLOWER genus *Echinacea.* Commonly called the purple coneflower, echinacea is used as a border plant. The leaves and roots are used in herbal remedies to boost the immune system and to treat colds and flu.

echinoderm \i-'kī-nə-,dərm\ Any of various marine INVERTEBRATES (phylum Echinodermata) characterized by a hard spiny covering, a calcite skeleton, and five-rayed radial body symmetry. About 6,000 existing species are grouped in six classes: FEATHER STARS and sea lilies (Crinoidea), STARFISHES (Asteroidea), brittle stars and basket stars (Ophiuroidea), SEA URCHINS (Echinoidea), sea daisies (Concentricycloidea), and SEA CUCUMBERS (Holothurioidea). Echinoderms are found in all the oceans, from the intertidal zone to the deepest oceanic trenches. Most species have numerous tube feet that are modified for locomotion, respiration, tunneling, sensory perception, feeding, and grasping. Movement of water through a vascular system composed of five major canals and smaller branches controls extension and retraction of the tube feet. Most echinoderms feed on microscopic detritus or suspended matter, but some eat plants.

Echo In GREEK MYTHOLOGY, a mountain NYMPH transformed into a disembodied voice. According to OVID, her chatter distracted HERA from the infidelities of ZEUS, and the goddess punished her by depriving her of independent speech, rendering her able only to repeat the last words spoken by another. When NARCISSUS failed to requite her love, she faded away into a voice only.

echolocation \ˌe-kō-lō-ˈkā-shən\ Physiological process for locating distant or invisible objects (such as prey) by emitting sound waves that are reflected back to the emitter by the objects. Echolocation is used by an animal to orient itself, avoid obstacles, find food, and interact socially. Most BATS employ echolocation, as do most, if not all, TOOTHED WHALES (but apparently no BALEEN WHALES), a few SHREWS, and two kinds of birds (oilbirds and certain cave swiftlets). Echolocation pulses consist of short bursts of sound at frequencies ranging from about 1,000 Hz in birds to at least 200,000 Hz in whales. Bats use frequencies from about 30,000 to about 120,000 Hz.

Eck, Johann *orig.* **Johann Maier** (1486–1543) German Roman Catholic theologian. He was ordained in 1508, became a doctor of theology in 1510, and began a lifelong career at the University of Ingolstadt. Initially friendly with MARTIN LUTHER, Eck assailed Luther's NINETY-FIVE THESES as heretical. In 1519 he debated Luther and Andreas Karlstadt (c. 1480–1541), and LEO X commissioned Eck to publish and enforce the papal bull condemning the Theses. Eck's treatise *Enchiridion Against the Lutherans* (1525) summarized contested Catholic beliefs, Protestant objections to them, and Catholic answers to the objections; it was Eck's most popular work and the best-known Catholic polemical handbook of the 16th century.

Eckert, J(ohn) Presper, Jr. (1919–1995) U.S. engineer. Born in Philadelphia, he studied at the University of Pennsylvania. In 1946 he and JOHN W. MAUCHLY built a digital computer, the ENIAC, which contained a primitive form of the circuitry used in present-day high-speed computers. In 1949 they introduced the BINAC (Binary Automatic Computer). Their third model, UNIVAC I (Universal Automatic Computer), found many uses in commerce. Eckert received 85 patents and in 1969 was awarded the National Medal of Science.

Eckert, Wallace J(ohn) (1902–1971) U.S. astronomer. Born in Pittsburgh, he received his PhD from Yale University. He was one of the first to apply IBM punched-card equipment to the reduction of astronomical data and to describe planetary orbits numerically. As director of Columbia Univ.'s Watson Scientific Computing Laboratory from 1945, he used computers to determine precise planetary positions, and made major contributions to the study of the orbit of the moon, one of whose craters is named for him.

Eckhart, Meister *orig.* **Johannes** (c. 1260–1327/28?) German theologian and mystic. A Dominican from age 15, he studied theology at Cologne and Paris and became a popular preacher and teacher. In his mid-30s he served as vicar of Thuringia. His mystical writings examined the relationship between God and humanity; he pictured the soul achieving complete union with God and posited something (Godhead) beyond God. He took up a professorship in Cologne in his 60th year; shortly thereafter he was charged with heresy on several points in his works. He died before he could rebut a second charge.

Eckstine \ˈek-ˌstīn\, **Billy** *orig.* **William Clarence Eckstein** (1914–1993) U.S. singer and bandleader, one of the greatest interpreters of popular song and blues in jazz. Born in Pittsburgh, Eckstine sang with EARL HINES's big band 1939–43, then formed his own band in 1944. Sympathetic with the new sounds of BEBOP, Eckstine engaged many of its innovators, including DIZZY GILLESPIE, CHARLIE PARKER, and SARAH VAUGHAN. Disbanding the group in 1947, he achieved greater popular success as a solo performer, specializing in ballads featuring his deep, resonant baritone.

eclampsia See PREECLAMPSIA AND ECLAMPSIA

eclipse Complete or partial obscuring of one celestial body by another when three such objects become aligned. In one type, the eclipsing body comes between an observer and a luminous source, appearing to cover it totally or partly, as when the moon comes between earth and the sun (solar eclipse). A second type occurs when the eclipsing body comes between the luminous source and casts a shadow on the eclipsed object, which is darkened by its shadow, as when the moon enters earth's shadow (lunar eclipse). The shadow consists of the central umbra, into which no direct sunlight penetrates (total eclipse), and the penumbra, reached by light from only part of the sun's disk (partial eclipse). Eclipses are awe-inspiring and are chronicled in the oldest records of history. Some civilizations (e.g., Babylonian, Maya, Chinese) learned to predict eclipses accurately. Solar eclipses visible from different parts of earth occur two to five times a year; one total solar eclipse occurs in most years. When earth is closest to the sun and the moon farthest from earth, the moon's shadow may fall entirely within the sun's disk, with a ring of the disk visible around it (annular eclipse). Total solar eclipses have increased knowledge of the nature of the CHROMOSPHERE and CORONA, usually invisible in the glare of the PHOTOSPHERE. Lunar eclipses occur just as frequently as solar eclipses; during total lunar eclipses, the moon may appear deep red from sunlight refracted through earth's atmosphere. Eclipses of other stars and planets may provide information about them (see ECLIPSING VARIABLE STAR). See also BAILY'S BEADS. See illustration below.

eclipsing variable star *or* **eclipsing binary** BINARY STAR in an orbit whose plane passes through or very near earth. An observer on earth sees one star pass periodically over the face of the other and diminish its light through an ECLIPSE. The star Algol, in the constellation Perseus, was the first such star recognized (1782); several thousand are now known. By comparing the duration of the eclipse to the period of the orbit, astronomers can calculate the sizes of the stars. See also VARIABLE STAR.

ecliptic \i-ˈklip-tik\ Great circle that is the apparent path of the SUN among the constellations in the course of a year; from another viewpoint, the projection on the CELESTIAL SPHERE of the orbit of earth around the sun, which intersects the plane of the celestial equator at the vernal and autumnal EQUINOXES. The constellations of the ZODIAC are arranged along the ecliptic.

eclogite \ˈek-lə-ˌjīt\ Any member of metamorphic rocks whose original composition is similar to that of basalt. Eclogites consist primarily of green PYROXENE (omphacite) and red GARNET (pyrope), with small amounts of various other minerals such as KYANITE and RUTILE. These minerals in the eclogite are the result of reactions in originally igneous minerals having been subjected to extremely high pressures and moderate to relatively high temperatures.

eclogue \ˈek-ˌlȯg, ˈek-ˌläg\ Short, usually pastoral, poem in the form of a dialogue or soliloquy (see PASTORAL). The eclogue as a pastoral form first appeared in the IDYLLS of THEOCRITUS, was adopted by VIRGIL, and was revived in the Renaissance by DANTE, PETRARCH, and BOCCACCIO. EDMUND

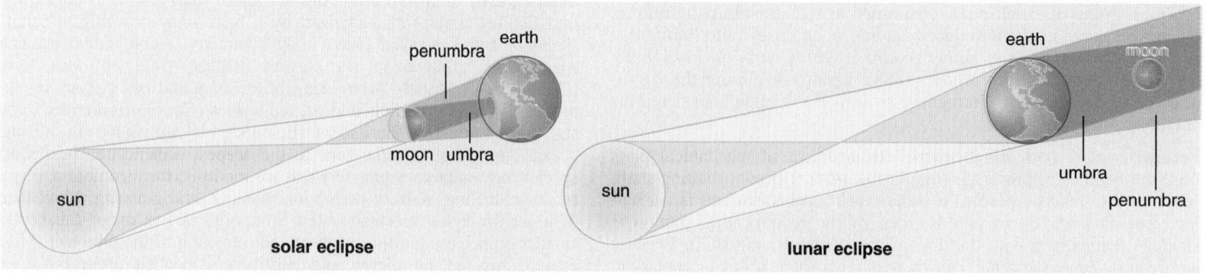

A solar eclipse occurs when the moon passes between the earth and the sun. Observers in the moon's penumbral shadow see a partial blocking of the sun; those in the umbra see the sun completely covered by the moon. A lunar eclipse occurs when the moon passes into the earth's shadow. In the penumbra, the moon may appear dimmed; when it enters the umbra, the full moon becomes quite dark and may take on a reddish tinge.

SPENSER'S *Shepheardes Calender*, a series of 12 eclogues, was the first outstanding pastoral poem in English. 18th-century English poets used the eclogue for ironic verse on nonpastoral subjects. Since then a distinction has been made between eclogue and pastoral, with eclogue referring only to the dialogue or soliloquy form.

Eco \'ā-kō, *Engl* 'e-kō\, **Umberto** (born 1932) Italian critic and novelist. He has taught since 1971 at the University of Bologna. In *The Open Work* (1962), he suggested that some literature and modern music is fundamentally ambiguous and invites the audience to participate in the interpretive and creative process. He explored other areas of communication and SEMIOTICS in *A Theory of Semiotics* (1976), *Semiotics and the Philosophy of Language* (1984), and *The Limits of Interpretation* (1991). His novels include the erudite but best-selling murder mystery *The Name of the Rose* (1980; film, 1986), *Foucault's Pendulum* (1988), and *The Island of the Day Before* (1995).

ecology Study of the relationships between organisms and their environment. Physiological ecology focuses on the relationships between individual organisms and the physical and chemical features of their environment. Behavioral ecologists study the behaviors of individual organisms as they react to their environment. Population ecology, including population GENETICS, is the study of processes that affect the distribution and abundance of animal and plant populations. Community ecology studies how communities of plant and animal populations function and are organized. Paleoecology is the study of the ecology of FOSSIL organisms. Ecologists frequently concentrate on particular taxonomic groups or on specific environments. Applied ecology applies ecological principles to the management of populations of crops and animals. Theoretical ecologists provide simulations of particular practical problems and develop models of general ecological relevance.

econometrics Statistical and mathematical analysis of economic relationships. Econometrics creates equations to describe phenomena such as the relationship between changes in price and demand. Econometricians estimate production functions and cost functions for firms, supply-and-demand functions for industries, income distribution in an economy, macroeconomic models and models of the monetary sector for policy makers, and business cycles and growth for forecasting. Information derived from these models helps both private businesses and the government make decisions and set MONETARY and FISCAL policy. See also CLIOMETRICS, RAGNAR FRISCH, MACROECONOMICS, MICROECONOMICS.

Economic Cooperation and Development, Organization for (OECD) International organization founded in 1961 to stimulate economic progress and world trade. Based in Paris, the OECD serves as a consultative assembly and a clearinghouse for economic data, and also coordinates economic aid to developing countries. Its current members are Australia, Austria, Belgium, Britain, Canada, the Czech Republic, Denmark, Finland, France, Germany, Greece, Hungary, Iceland, Ireland, Italy, Japan, Luxembourg, Mexico, The Netherlands, New Zealand, Norway, Poland, Portugal, South Korea, Spain, Sweden, Switzerland, Turkey, and the U.S.

economic development Process whereby simple, low-income national economies are transformed into modern industrial economies. Theories of economic development—the evolution of poor countries dependent on agriculture or resource extraction into prosperous countries with diversified economies—are of critical importance to Third World nations. Economic development projects have typically involved large capital investments in infrastructure (roads, irrigation networks, etc.), industry, education, and financial institutions. More recently, the realization that creating capital-intensive industrial sectors provides only limited employment and can disrupt the rest of the economy has led to smaller-scale economic development programs that aim to utilize the specific resources and natural advantages of developing countries and to avoid disruption of their social and economic structures. See also ECONOMIC GROWTH.

economic forecasting Prediction of future economic activity and developments. Economic forecasts, which range from a few weeks to many years, are widely used in business and government to help formulate policy and strategy. Macroeconomic forecasts predict the course of the aggregate economy and concentrate on variables such as interest rates, the rate of inflation, and the rate of unemployment. Forecasts of private consumption and investment, government expenditures, and net exports help government policymakers responsible for fiscal policy. For example, part of the justification for a change in taxes is a forecast of its economic effects. Microeconomic forecasts are designed to project the effects of change at the level of an industry or a firm. Most microeconomic forecasts begin with assumptions about the aggregate economy before focusing on the projected effects in the specific sector that is of interest. Manufacturers and retailers use such forecasts to formulate business plans. See also ECONOMETRICS, MACROECONOMICS, MICROECONOMICS.

economic growth Process by which a nation's wealth increases over time. The most widely used measure of economic growth is the real rate of growth in a country's total output of goods and services (gauged by the GROSS DOMESTIC PRODUCT adjusted for INFLATION, or "real GDP"). Other measures (e.g., national income per capita, consumption per capita) are also used. The rate of economic growth is influenced by natural resources, human resources, capital resources, and technological development in the economy along with institutional structure and stability. Other factors include the level of world economic activity and the terms of TRADE. See also ECONOMIC DEVELOPMENT.

economic indicator Statistic used to determine the state of general economic activity or to predict it in the future. A leading indicator is one that tends to turn up or down before the general economy does (e.g., building permits, common stock prices, and business inventories). Coincident indicators move in line with the economy; lagging indicators change direction after the economy does.

economic planning Use of government to make economic decisions with respect to the use of resources. In communist countries with a state planning apparatus, detailed and rigid planning results in a COMMAND ECONOMY; LAND, CAPITAL, and the means of production are publicly owned and centrally allocated, and the government makes both micro- and macroeconomic decisions. Microeconomic decisions include what goods and services to produce, the quantities to produce, the prices to charge, and the wages to pay. Macroeconomic decisions include the rate of investment and the extent of foreign trade. In most industrialized countries, governments influence their economies indirectly through monetary and fiscal policies. A few key economic sectors may be publicly owned, but the trend has been toward the privatization of industries that were socialized in the aftermath of the Great Depression and World War II. Japan is the most notable example of economic planning in a capitalist framework; government and industry cooperate closely in planning patterns of capital investment, research and development, and export strategies. See also CAPITALISM, COMMUNISM, SOCIALISM, ZAIBATSU.

economic system Set of principles and techniques by which a society decides and organizes the ownership and allocation of economic resources. At one extreme, usually called a free-enterprise system, all resources are privately owned. This system, following ADAM SMITH, is based on the belief that the common good is maximized when all members of society are allowed to pursue their rational self-interest. At the other extreme, usually called a pure-communist system, all resources are publicly owned. This system, following KARL MARX and VLADIMIR ILICH LENIN, is based on the belief that public ownership of the means of production and government control of every aspect of the economy are necessary to minimize inequalities of wealth and achieve other agreed-upon social objectives. No nation exemplifies either extreme. As one moves from CAPITALISM through SOCIALISM to COMMUNISM, a greater share of a nation's productive resources is publicly owned and a greater reliance is placed on ECONOMIC PLANNING. FASCISM, more a political than an economic system, is a hybrid; privately owned resources are combined into syndicates and placed at the disposal of a centrally planned state.

economic warfare Use of economic measures by governments engaged in international conflict. These may include export and import controls, shipping controls, trade agreements with neutral nations, and so on. Economic warfare among belligerents began with the BLOCKADE and interception of contraband. In World War II it was broadened to include economic pressure applied to neutral countries from which the enemy obtained its supplies. In the Cold War it often involved using measures such as an EMBARGO to deny potential enemies goods that might contribute to their war-making ability.

economics Social science that analyzes and describes the consequences of choices made concerning scarce productive resources. Economics is the study of how individuals and societies choose to employ those resources: what goods and services will be produced, how they will be produced, and how they will be distributed among the members of society. Economics is customarily divided into MICROECONOMICS and MACRO-

ECONOMICS. Of major concern to macroeconomists are the rate of economic growth, the inflation rate, and the rate of unemployment. Specialized areas of economic investigation attempt to answer questions on a variety of economic activity; they include agricultural economics, ECONOMIC DEVELOPMENT, economic history, environmental economics, industrial organization, international trade, LABOR ECONOMICS, MONEY SUPPLY and banking, public finance, urban economics, and WELFARE ECONOMICS. Specialists in mathematical economics and ECONOMETRICS provide tools used by all economists. The areas of investigation in economics overlap with many other disciplines, notably history, MATHEMATICS, POLITICAL SCIENCE, and SOCIOLOGY.

Economist, The Weekly magazine of news and opinion, founded in 1843 and published in London, generally regarded as one of the world's preeminent journals of its kind. The publication maintains the position that free markets typically provide the best method of running economies and governments.

ecosystem \'ē-kō-ˌsis-təm\ Complex of living organisms, their physical environment, and all their interrelationships in a particular unit of space. An ecosystem's abiotic (nonbiological) constituents include minerals, climate, soil, water, sunlight, and all other nonliving elements; its biotic constituents consist of all its living members. Two major forces link these constituents: the flow of energy and the cycling of nutrients. The fundamental source of energy in almost all ecosystems is radiant energy from the sun; energy and organic matter are passed along an ecosystem's FOOD CHAIN. The study of ecosystems became increasingly sophisticated in the later 20th century; it is now instrumental in assessing and controlling the environmental effects of agricultural development and industrialization. See also BIOME.

ecoterrorism *or* **ecological terrorism** *or* **environmental terrorism** destruction, or the threat of destruction, of the environment in order to intimidate or coerce governments. The term also has been applied to crimes committed against companies or government agencies in order to prevent or interfere with activities allegedly harmful to the environment. Ecoterrorism includes actions such as threats to contaminate water supplies or to destroy or disable energy utilities and practices such as the deployment of ANTHRAX. Another form of ecoterrorism, often referred to as environmental warfare, consists of the deliberate and illegal destruction, exploitation, or modification of the environment as a strategy of war or in times of armed conflict. Examples include the U.S. military's use of the defoliant AGENT ORANGE during the VIETNAM WAR and the destruction of Kuwaiti oil wells by retreating Iraqi military forces during the 1991 PERSIAN GULF WAR. The activities of some environmental activists also have been described as ecoterrorism. They include criminal trespass on the property of logging companies and other firms and obstruction of their operations through sabotage or the environmentally harmless modification of natural resources in order to make them inaccessible or unsuitable for commercial use, a practice known as "monkeywrenching."

Ecstasy Euphoria-inducing stimulant and hallucinogen. It is a derivative of the AMPHETAMINE family and a relative of the stimulant methamphetamine. Taken in pill form, it has a chemical relationship to the psychedelic drug MESCALINE. Developed in 1913 as an appetite suppressant, the drug was not originally approved for release. In the 1950s and '60s, it began to be used in psychotherapy. The drug increases the production of the neurotransmitter SEROTONIN and blocks its reabsorption in the brain; it also increases the amount of the neurotransmitter DOPAMINE. Stimulation of the central nervous system gives users feelings of increased energy and lowers social inhibitions. By the 1980s, parties and dances that featured Ecstasy use (known as "raves") became popular. Despite its ban in the U.S. and the rest of the world, the drug retained a huge following, especially among young people.

ectopic pregnancy \ek-'tä-pik\ *or* **extrauterine pregnancy** Condition in which a fertilized egg is imbedded outside the UTERUS (see FERTILIZATION). Early on, it may resemble a normal PREGNANCY, with hormonal changes, AMENORRHEA, and development of a placenta. Later, most patients have pain as the growing embryo stretches the structure it is attached to. Rupture may cause life-threatening bleeding. A tubal pregnancy may result from obstruction of the egg's passage through the fallopian tube. In an ovarian pregnancy, the egg is fertilized before it leaves the OVARY. Implantation elsewhere in the abdomen is an abdominal pregnancy.

ectotherm \'ek-tə-ˌthərm\ Any so-called cold-blooded animal; that is, any animal whose regulation of body temperature depends on external sources, such as sunlight or a heated rock surface. The ectotherms include the FISHES, AMPHIBIANS, REPTILES, and INVERTEBRATES. The body temperatures of aquatic ectotherms are usually very close to those of the water. Ectotherms do not require as much fuel as warm-blooded animals (ENDOTHERMS), but most cannot deal as well with cold surroundings.

Ecuador *officially* **Republic of Ecuador** Country, northwestern South America. Area: 105,037 sq mi (272,045 sq km), including the GALÁPAGOS ISLANDS. Population (2001): 12,879,000. Capital: QUITO. The people are about two-fifths Indian (mostly QUECHUA) and two-fifths mestizo (Indian-Spanish), with most of the rest of Spanish ancestry. Language: Spanish (official). Religion: predominantly Roman Catholicism. Currency: U.S. dollar. Its Pacific coastal lowlands rise to the peaks and highlands of the ANDES, which give way to the Ecuadorian portion of the tropical AMAZON basin in the east. The Andes rise dramatically in two north to south chains separated by high valleys. The highest peak is CHIMBORAZO; COTOPAXI, the world's highest active volcano, is nearby. The country lies in an active earthquake zone. Almost half is forested, with tropical rainforests in the east. Straddling the equator, its climate varies from tropical in the lowlands to temperate in the highlands. It has a developing economy based primarily on services, followed by manufactur-

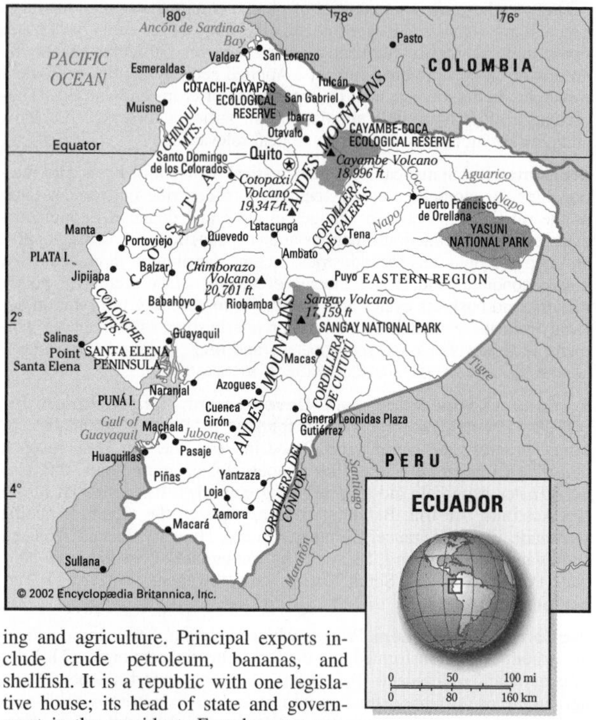

ing and agriculture. Principal exports include crude petroleum, bananas, and shellfish. It is a republic with one legislative house; its head of state and government is the president. Ecuador was conquered by the INCAS in AD 1450 and came under Spanish control in 1534. Under the Spaniards it was a part of the VICEROYALTY OF PERU until 1740, when it became a part of the viceroyalty of NEW GRANADA. It gained its independence from Spain in 1822 as part of the republic of GRAN COLOMBIA, and in 1830 became a sovereign state. A succession of authoritarian governments ruled into the mid-20th century, and economic hardship and social unrest prompted the military to take a strong role. Border disputes led to war between Peru and Ecuador in 1941; the two fought periodically until agreeing to a final demarcation in 1998. The economy, booming in the 1970s with petroleum profits, was depressed in the 1980s by reduced oil prices and earthquake damage. A new constitution was adopted in 1979. In the 1990s social unrest caused political instability and several changes of heads of state. In a controversial move to help stabilize the economy, the U.S. dollar replaced the sucre as the national currency in 2000.

ecumenism \e-'kyü-mə-ˌni-zəm, 'e-kyü-mə-ˌni-zəm\ Movement toward unity or cooperation among the Christian churches. The first major step in the direction of ecumenism was the International Missionary Conference of 1910, a gathering of Protestants. Several Protestant denominations inaugurated a Life and Work Conference in 1925 (on social and practical problems) and a Faith and Order Conference (on church doctrine and governance) in 1927. After World War II the WORLD COUNCIL OF CHURCHES was established; the International Missionary Conference joined it in 1961. The Roman Catholic church has also shown strong interest in improving interchurch relations since the Second VATICAN COUNCIL (1962–65). The more conservative or fundamentalist Protestant denominations have generally refrained from involvement. Another important factor in 20th-century ecumenism has been the creation of united churches that reconcile splintered sects, such as the United Church of Christ (1957) and the Evangelical Lutheran Church in America (1988).

eczema See DERMATITIS

Edda Body of ancient Icelandic literature. Contained in two 13th-century books, it is the fullest and most detailed source for modern knowledge of Germanic mythology. The *Prose Edda* (or *Younger Edda* or *Snorra-Edda*; c. 1222), a handbook on poetics by SNORRI STURLUSON, explains diction and meter in SKALDIC and Eddic poetry and recounts tales from Norse mythology. The *Poetic Edda* (*Elder Edda*, *Sæmundar Edda;* c. 1250–1300) is a collection of mythological and heroic poems of unknown authorship composed c. 800–1100. These austere lays are the oldest surviving antecedents of the NIBELUNGENLIED legends.

Eddington, Arthur Stanley *later* **Sir Arthur** (1882–1944) British astronomer, physicist, and mathematician. At Cambridge University he won every mathematical honor. He was chief assistant at the Royal Observatory at Greenwich 1906–13; in 1914 he became director of the Cambridge observatory. Religious and pacifistic, he declared that the world's meaning could not be discovered by science. His greatest contributions were in astrophysics, where his studies included stellar structure, subatomic sources of stellar energy, white dwarf stars, and diffuse matter in interstellar space. His philosophical ideas led him to believe that unifying quantum theory and general relativity would permit the calculation of certain universal constants.

Eddington.
BY COURTESY OF THE UNIVERSITY OF CHICAGO; PHOTOGRAPH, YERKES OBSERVATORY, WILLIAMS BAY, WIS.

Eddy, Mary Baker *orig.* **Mary Morse Baker** (1821–1910) U.S. religious leader, founder of CHRISTIAN SCIENCE. Born near Concord, N.H., she married in 1843; her husband died the following year, and she married again in 1853. She suffered from ill health for much of her life. In the early 1860s she was cured of a spinal malady by Phineas P. Quimby (1802–1866), who cured ailments without medication. She remained well until shortly after Quimby's death; in 1866 she suffered a severe fall and lost hope for recovery, only to be healed by reading the New Testament. She considered that moment her discovery of Christian Science and spent several years evolving her system. In 1875 she published *Science and Health,* which her followers regarded as divinely inspired. Having divorced in 1873, in 1877 she married one of her followers, Asa G. Eddy (died 1882). The First Church of Christ, Scientist was organized in 1879. Eddy established the Massachusetts Metaphysical College in 1881; she also founded three periodicals, notably the CHRISTIAN SCIENCE MONITOR (1908).

Mary Baker Eddy.
BY COURTESY OF THE LIBRARY OF CONGRESS, WASHINGTON, D.C.

Edelman, Gerald Maurice (born 1929) U.S. biochemist. Born in New York City, he received an MD from the University of Pennsylvania and a PhD from Rockefeller University. His work with Rodney Porter (1917–1985) on antibodies won a 1972 Nobel Prize. By modeling an entire antibody molecule, Edelman's team found it had more than 1,300 amino acids in a four-chain structure and identified the locations where antigens bind. Focusing on formation and differentiation of tissues and organs, they discovered cell-adhesion molecules, proteins that attach cells together to make tissues. Edelman's attempt at a general theory of neural development and brain function is discussed in his *Neural Darwinism* (1987).

edelweiss \'ā-dᵊl-,vīs, 'ā-dᵊl-,wīs\ Perennial plant *(Leontopodium alpinum)* of the COMPOSITE FAMILY, native to alpine areas of Europe and South America. It has 2–10 yellow flower heads in a dense cluster. Below these flower heads, 6–9 lance-shaped, woolly, white leaves are arranged in the form of a star. Most varieties are ornamentals.

Edelweiss (*Leontopodium alpinum*).
SIEGFRIED EIGSTLER—SHOSTAL

edema \i-'dē-mə\ Abnormal accumulation of watery fluid in the spaces between CONNECTIVE-TISSUE cells. Usually a symptom of diseases of the kidneys, heart, veins, or lymphatic system, which affect water balance in the cells, tissues, and blood, edema can be pitting (retaining an imprint when compressed) or nonpitting. Treatment must usually focus on the underlying cause. Edema may be local (e.g., HIVES from allergies), or generalized (also called dropsy), sometimes involving body cavities as well as tissues.

Eden, (Robert) Anthony *later* **Earl of Avon** (1897–1977) British politician. After combat service in World War I, he was elected to the House of Commons in 1923. He became foreign secretary in 1935 but resigned in 1938 to protest NEVILLE CHAMBERLAIN's policy of appeasement. He held the post again 1940–45 and 1951–55, and helped settle the Anglo–Iranian oil dispute and arranged an armistice in Indochina. Succeeding WINSTON CHURCHILL as prime minister in 1955, he attempted to ease international tension by welcoming to Britain NIKITA KHRUSHCHEV and NIKOLAY A. BULGANIN. His fall began when Egypt seized the Suez Canal and he supported an Anglo-French intervention in Egypt (see SUEZ CRISIS). He resigned in 1957, citing ill health.

Eden, photograph by Yousuf Karsh.
© KARSH FROM RAPHO/PHOTO RESEARCHERS

Eden River River, northern England. It rises in the uplands that connect the LAKE DISTRICT with the highlands of the PENNINES and flows in a meandering course 90 mi (145 km) northwest to its estuary in the Solway Firth, an IRISH SEA inlet. It is not navigable.

Ederle \'ed-ər-lē\, **Gertrude (Caroline)** (born 1906) U.S. swimmer, the first woman to swim the English Channel. Born in New York City, she set women's world freestyle records in the early 1920s, and in 1924 she shared a gold medal (400-m relay) at the Olympic Games. In 1926 she swam the 35-mi (56-km) Channel in 14 hours 31 minutes, breaking the men's record by 1 hour 59 minutes. Her record was only broken in 1950, by Florence Chadwick (13 hours 20 minutes).

Edessa \i-'de-sə\ Chief city (pop., 1991: 18,000), Macedonia, Greece. Located on a steep bluff above the valley of the Loudhiás River, it is a prominent trading and agricultural center. The assumption that it was Aigai, the first capital of ancient MACEDONIA, has been challenged by archaeological discoveries at VERGHINA. Fought over by the Bulgarians, Byzantines, and Serbs, Edessa was taken by the Turks in the 15th century. In 1912 it passed to Greece.

Edgar the Aetheling \'ath-ə-liŋ\ (died c. 1125) Anglo-Saxon prince. He was proposed as king of England after the Battle of HASTINGS (1066) but instead served the Norman kings WILLIAM I THE CONQUEROR and WILLIAM II. Rebellions in favor of the aetheling (prince) continued in England until 1069. Edgar led the Norman conquest of Apulia in southern Italy (1086) but was deprived of his Norman lands by William II in 1091. In 1097, on William's orders, he overthrew Donald Bane, a Scottish king hostile to the Normans. He later unsuccessfully opposed HENRY I in the struggle for the English throne.

Edgerton, Harold E(ugene) (1903–1990) U.S. electrical engineer and photographer. Born in Fremont, Neb., he was a graduate student at MIT in 1926 when he developed a flash tube that could produce high-intensity bursts of light in as little as 1/1,000,000 of a second; it is the flash device still used in photography today. Since it can also emit repeated bursts of light at regular brief intervals, it is an ideal STROBOSCOPE. With the new flash, Edgerton was able to photograph such things as drops of milk falling into a saucer and bullets traveling at speeds of 15,000 mph (24,000 kph); the resulting images have been appreciated for their artistic beauty and their value to industry and science.

Edgeworth, Maria (1767–1849) British-Irish writer. From age 15 she assisted her father in managing his estate, gaining a knowledge of rural economy and the Irish peasantry. Her early children's stories, published as *The Parent's Assistant* (1796), feature the first convincing child characters since Shakespeare. *Castle Rackrent* (1800), her first novel, revealed her gift for social observation and authentic dialogue. Other notable works are *Belinda* (1801); *Tales of Fashionable Life* (1809–12), a six-volume work including the novel *The Absentee*, which focused attention on abuses by absentee English landowners; *Patronage* (1814); and *Ormond* (1817).

Edgeworth-Kuiper belt See KUIPER BELT

Edinburgh \'e-dᵊn-ˌbər-ə\ City (pop., 1995: 448,900), capital of Scotland. Located in southeastern Scotland, the original burgh, now known as Old Town, arose in the 11th century AD, around Edinburgh Castle, the royal residence of Malcolm III MacDuncan. In 1329 ROBERT THE BRUCE granted Edinburgh a town charter; it became the capital of the Scottish kingdom in 1437. The city was destroyed in 1544 in the border wars with England; its characteristic use of stone architecture began with this rebuilding. The 18th century saw a cultural and intellectual renaissance in Scotland, and Edinburgh was home to such luminaries as DAVID HUME, ADAM SMITH, ROBERT BURNS, and WALTER SCOTT. It was the birthplace of the *ENCYCLOPÆDIA BRITANNICA* (1768) and the *Edinburgh Review* (1802). The city expanded in the late 18th century with the development of the Georgian-style New Town, separated from the Old Town by a valley. It is the center of Scottish culture and education and is home to the University of EDINBURGH, National Library, National Gallery, and Royal Scottish Museum. It is the site of the Scots national parliament.

Edinburgh, University of Private university in Edinburgh, Scotland. It was founded as a college under Presbyterian auspices in 1583 and achieved university status c. 1621 after a school of divinity was added. Schools of medicine and law were added in the early 18th century, and faculties of music, science, arts, social sciences, and veterinary medicine were subsequently added. The university has produced a long line of eminent cultural figures, including Sir WALTER SCOTT, JOHN STUART MILL, THOMAS CARLYLE, CHARLES DARWIN, ROBERT LOUIS STEVENSON, and ALEXANDER GRAHAM BELL. Current enrollment is about 18,000.

Edinburgh Festival International festival of the arts, with emphasis on music and drama. Founded in 1947 by RUDOLF BING, it is held for three weeks each summer. Its theatrical offerings include plays by major international theatrical companies; plays premiered at the festival include T. S. ELIOT's *The Cocktail Party* (1949) and THORNTON WILDER's *The Matchmaker* (1954). The adjunct Edinburgh Fringe attracts amateur theater groups and has launched such works as *Beyond the Fringe* (1960) and TOM STOPPARD's *Rosencrantz and Guildenstern Are Dead* (1966). Musically, it offers concerts, recitals, and operas by international companies, orchestras, and soloists.

Edirne \ā-'dir-nə\, **Treaty of** *or* **Treaty of Adrianople** \ˌā-drē-ə-'nō-pəl\ (September 14, 1829) Pact concluding the RUSSO-TURKISH WAR of 1828–29. Signed at Edirne (ancient Adrianople), Turkey, the treaty opened the Turkish straits to Russian shipping and granted Russia some territorial concessions. It strengthened Russia's position in Eastern Europe and weakened that of the Ottoman empire, and it foreshadowed the Ottoman empire's dependence on the European balance of power and the dismemberment of its Balkan possessions.

Edison, Thomas Alva (1847–1931) U.S. inventor. Born in Milan, Ohio, he had very little formal schooling. He set up a laboratory in his father's basement at age 10; at 12 he was earning money selling newspapers and candy on trains. He worked as a telegrapher (1862–68) before deciding to pursue invention and entrepreneurship. Throughout much of his career, he was strongly motivated by efforts to overcome his handicap of partial deafness. For Western Union he developed a machine capable of sending four telegraph messages down one wire, only to sell the invention to Western Union's rival, JAY GOULD, for more than $100,000. He created the world's first industrial-research laboratory, in Menlo Park, N.J. There he invented the carbon-button transmitter (1877), still used in telephone speakers and microphones today; the phonograph (1877); and the incandescent lightbulb (1879). To develop the lightbulb, he was advanced $30,000 by such financiers as J. P. MORGAN and the Vanderbilts. In 1882 he supervised the installation of the world's first permanent commercial central power system, in lower Manhattan. After the death of his first wife (1884), he built a new laboratory in West Orange, N.J. Its first major endeavor was the commercialization of the phonograph, which ALEXANDER GRAHAM BELL had improved on since Edison's initial invention. At the new laboratory Edison and his team also developed an early movie camera and an instrument for viewing moving pictures; they also developed the alkaline storage battery. Although his later projects were not as successful as his earlier ones, Edison continued to work even in his 80s. Singly or jointly, he held a world-record 1,093 patents, nearly 400 of them for electric light and power. He always invented for necessity, with the object of devising something new that he could manufacture. More than any other, he laid the basis for the technological revolution of the modern electric world.

Edmonton City (metro. area pop., 1996: 863,000), capital of Alberta. Located on the SASKATCHEWAN RIVER, in the center of the province, it began as a series of fur-trading posts built from 1795. With the arrival of the railway and an influx of settlers in the late 19th century, Edmonton began to prosper economically, and in 1905 it became the capital of the new province of Alberta. The 1947 discovery of petroleum in the area greatly stimulated the city's growth; an agricultural and oil-based economy still prevails there. It is the distribution center of northwestern Canada. Its cultural and educational institutions include the University of Alberta (1906).

Edmunds, George Franklin (1828–1919) U.S. senator and expert on constitutional law. Born in Richmond, Vt., he was a lawyer and legislator in Vermont, then served in the U.S. Senate 1866–91, where he was active in the impeachment of Pres. ANDREW JOHNSON, chaired the judiciary committee (1872–79, 1882–91), and was a principal author of the Sherman Antitrust Act (1890).

Edo period \'ed-ō\ (1603–1867) Cultural period of Japanese history corresponding to the political period of governance by the TOKUGAWA SHOGUNATE. Edo (present-day Tokyo), chosen by TOKUGAWA IEYASU as Japan's new capital, became one of the largest cities of its time and was the site of a thriving urban culture. In literature, the Edo period saw BASHO's development of the HAIKU and the virtuoso comic linked-verse compositions and humorous novels of IHARA SAIKAKU; in theater, both KABUKI (with live actors) and BUNRAKU (with puppets) entertained the townsmen (samurai, for whom theatergoing was forbidden, often attended in disguise). The development of multicolored printing techniques made it possible for ordinary people to obtain woodblock prints of popular kabuki actors or trendsetting courtesans (see UKIYO-E). Travelogues extolled the scenic beauty or historic interest of spots in distant provinces, and temple or shrine pilgrimages to distant places were popular. In scholarship, National Learning called attention to Japan's most ancient poetry and oldest written histories. Dutch Learning, the study of Europe and its sciences, became popular despite extremely limited intercourse with Europe. NEO-CONFUCIANISM was also popular. See also GENROKU PERIOD.

Edom \'ē-dəm\ Ancient country, south of the DEAD SEA. The Edomites probably occupied the area c. 13th century BC. Though closely related to the Israelites, they were in frequent conflict and were probably subject to the Israelite kingdom (11th–10th century BC). Located on the trade route between Arabia and the Mediterranean, Edom was known for its copper industry. Later conquered by the Nabataeans, the Edomites migrated to southern Judaea. Edom and neighboring Moab were known in Maccabean and Roman times as Idumaea.

education Learning that takes place in schools or schoollike environments (formal education) or in the world at large; the transmission of the values and accumulated knowledge of a society. In primitive cultures there is often little formal education; children learn from their environment and activities, and the adults around them act as teachers. In more complex societies, where there is more knowledge to be passed on, a more selective and efficient means of transmission—the school and teacher—becomes necessary. The content of formal education, its duration, and who receives it have varied widely from culture to culture and age to age, as has the philosophy of education. Some philosophers (e.g., John Locke) have seen individuals as blank slates onto which knowledge can be written; others (e.g., J.-J. Rousseau) have seen the innate human state as desirable in itself and therefore to be tampered with as little as possible, a view often taken in alternative education. See also behaviorism, John Dewey, elementary education, higher education, kindergarten, lyceum movement, progressive education, public school, special education, teaching.

education, philosophy of Application of philosophical methods to problems and issues in education (e.g., what constitutes learning and whether virtue can be taught). Some philosophers would say that philosophy of education should end with the attempt to clarify and justify educational statements and arguments, but many go beyond analysis to concern themselves with establishing value judgments and substantive goals for education.

Education, U.S. Department of Federal executive division responsible for carrying out government education programs. Established in 1980 by Jimmy Carter, it seeks to ensure access to education and to improve the quality of education nationwide. It administers programs in elementary and secondary education, higher education, vocational and adult education, special education, bilingual education, civil rights, and educational research.

educational psychology Branch of psychology concerned with the learning processes and psychological issues associated with the teaching and training of students. The educational psychologist studies the cognitive development of students and the various factors involved in learning, including aptitude and learning measurement, the creative process, and the motivational forces that influence student–teacher dynamics. Two early leaders in the field were G. Stanley Hall and Edward L. Thorndike. See also school psychology.

Edward, Lake Lake, eastern Africa. One of the great lakes of the western Great Rift Valley, it is on the border of Democratic Republic of the Congo (Zaire) and Uganda and is 48 mi (77 km) long and 26 mi (42 km) wide. On the northeast it is connected to the smaller Lake George. Lake Edward empties north through the Semliki River to Lake Albert. The lake abounds in fish; wildlife about its shores is protected within Virunga National Park and Queen Elizabeth National Park. It was named by Henry Morton Stanley, who visited the lake in 1888–89.

Edward I *known as* **Edward Longshanks** (1239–1307) King of England (1272–1307). The eldest son of Henry III, he supported his father in a civil war with the barons, contributing to Henry's defeat at the battle of Lewes (1264) but later winning out over the rebels. Edward joined the abortive Eighth Crusade in 1271–72, then returned to England to succeed his father. His reign was a time of rising national consciousness, in which he strengthened the crown against the feudal nobility. He fostered the development of Parliament and played an important role in defining English common law. He conquered Wales (1277) and crushed Welsh uprisings against English rule, but his conquest of Scotland (1296), including the defeat of William Wallace, was undone by later revolts. He expelled the Jews from England in 1290; they would not be readmitted until 1655. He died on a campaign against Robert I, who had proclaimed himself king of Scotland the previous year.

Edward II *known as* **Edward of Caernarvon** \kär-'nä-vən\ (1284–1327) King of England (1307–27). He was the son of Edward I. He angered the barons by granting the earldom of Cornwall to his favorite, Piers Gaveston; the barons drew up the Ordinances (1311), a document limiting the king's power over finances and appointments, and executed the arrogant Gaveston (1312). The English defeat by Robert I at the Battle of Bannockburn (1314) ensured Scottish independence and left Edward at the mercy of powerful barons, notably Thomas of Lancaster. He defeated and executed Lancaster in 1322, freeing himself from baronial control and revoking the Ordinances. His queen, Isabella, helped her lover Roger de Mortimer invade England with other dissatisfied nobles and depose Edward in favor of his son, Edward III. Edward II was imprisoned and probably murdered.

Edward III *known as* **Edward of Windsor** (1312–1377) King of England (1327–77). His mother, Isabella of France, deposed his father Edward II and crowned the 15-year-old Edward in his place. Isabella and her lover Roger de Mortimer governed in Edward's name for four years and persuaded him to grant the Scots their independence (1328). After having Mortimer executed in 1330, Edward became the sole ruler of England. By asserting his right to the French crown, he began the Hundred Years' War. He instituted the Order of the Garter in 1342. He defeated the French at the Battle of Crécy (1346) and captured Calais (1347), though lack of funds forced him to sign a truce. The Black Death hit England in 1348, but fighting continued. The Scots surrendered to Edward in 1356, and the same year his son Edward the Black Prince won a major victory for the English at the Battle of Poitiers. In 1360 Edward gave up his claim to the French crown in return for Aquitaine. The war later resumed when Charles V repudiated the Treaty of Calais; Edward lost Aquitaine, and he signed a new truce in 1375. In his later years he fell under the influence of his greedy mistress Alice Perrers and his son John of Gaunt.

Edward IV (1442–1483) King of England (1461–70, 1471–83). His father, a claimant to the throne, was killed in 1461, and Edward was crowned, thanks largely to his cousin the earl of Warwick. This alliance did not last, and after much intrigue and fighting Edward was deposed and fled in 1470. The next year he returned to become a leading participant in the Wars of the Roses, defeating and killing Warwick and nearly all the remaining Lancastrian leaders. After murdering Henry VI and repelling an attack on London, Edward remained secure as king for the rest of his life. He invaded France, which Henry had inherited but largely lost; though the attempt was unsuccessful, Edward made an excellent financial settlement by treaty. His administrative achievements made his reign a time of prosperity and success. Seven children survived him; his two sons were probably murdered in the Tower of London, and his eldest daughter married Henry VII.

Edward IV, portrait by an unknown artist; in the National Portrait Gallery, London.

BY COURTESY OF THE NATIONAL PORTRAIT GALLERY, LONDON

Edward VI (1537–1553) King of England and Ireland (1547–53). Son of Henry VIII and Jane Seymour, he succeeded to the throne after Henry's death. During the young king's reign, power was wielded first by his uncle the duke of Somerset (1547–49) and then by the duke of Northumberland. Facing death from tuberculosis, Edward was persuaded to exclude his two half sisters (later queens) Mary I and Elizabeth I, from the succession and to put Northumberland's daughter-in-law, Lady Lady Jane Grey, in line for the throne.

Edward VII.

THE BETTMANN ARCHIVE/BBC HULTON

Edward VII *orig.* **Albert Edward** (1841–1910) King of the United Kingdom (1901–10). Son of Queen

VICTORIA, he attended Oxford and Cambridge and in 1863 married Alexandra (1844–1925), daughter of CHRISTIAN IX. Noted for his interest in racing and yachting and his sometimes scandalous personal behavior, he was excluded by Victoria from most affairs of state until he was over 50 years old. He succeeded to the throne on her death, and his reign helped restore luster to the monarchy after her long seclusion as a widow. An immensely popular sovereign, he helped pave the way for the ENTENTE CORDIALE with his state visit to Paris in 1903.

Edward VIII (1894–1972) King of the United Kingdom (1936) who abdicated voluntarily. Son of GEORGE V, he served as a staff officer in World War I. After the war he made extensive goodwill tours of the British empire and became very popular with the English people. In 1930 he became friends with Wallis Simpson and her husband and by 1934 had fallen in love with her. In January 1936 he succeeded to the throne on his father's death. Unable to gain acceptance for their proposed marriage, he abdicated in December, becoming the only British sovereign to resign the crown voluntarily. He was created duke of Windsor and in 1937 married Simpson, who became the duchess of WINDSOR. At WINSTON CHURCHILL's invitation, he served as governor of the Bahamas during World War II, and after 1945 the couple lived in Paris. Not until 1967 were they invited to attend an official public ceremony with other members of the royal family.

The duke of Windsor (formerly Edward VIII) and duchess of Windsor on their wedding day, June 3, 1937, photograph by Cecil Beaton.
CAMERA PRESS

Edward the Black Prince (1330–1376) Prince of Wales (1343–76). Son of EDWARD III, he apparently received his sobriquet because he wore black armor. He was one of the outstanding commanders of the Hundred Years' War, winning a major victory at the Battle of Poitiers in 1356. He was prince of Aquitaine 1362–72; his rule there was a failure, for which he was largely to blame. He returned sick and broken to England and formally surrendered his principality to his father. He had no successor as prince of Aquitaine. Though the heir apparent, he never became king; his son became RICHARD II.

Edward the Confessor, St. (1003?–1066) King of England (1042–66). The son of ETHELRED II, he was exiled to Normandy for 25 years (1016–41) while the Danes held England (see CANUTE THE GREAT). For the first 11 years of his reign the real master of England was Godwine, earl of Wessex. Edward outlawed Godwine in 1051 and appointed Normans to high positions in government, thus preparing the way for the NORMAN CONQUEST. Godwine continued his opposition, and his son Harold (see HAROLD II) dominated England after 1053, subjugating Wales in 1063. Edward named Harold as his successor on his deathbed, but the duke of Normandy (the future WILLIAM I) invaded England to claim the crown earlier promised him. Though an ineffectual monarch, Edward was famous for his piety, which earned him the epithet "the Confessor."

Edwards, Blake *orig.* **William Blake McEdwards** (born 1922) U.S. film director, producer, and screenwriter. Born in Tulsa, he acted in films in the 1940s, then gained respect as a screenwriter, notably for *My Sister Eileen* (1955) and *The Notorious Landlady* (1962). He created the TV series *Peter Gunn* (1958–60). Among his successful directorial efforts are *Breakfast at Tiffany's* (1961), *The Pink Panther* (1964) and its sequels, *10* (1979), and *Victor/Victoria* (1982), which he revived in 1995 as a Broadway musical starring his wife, JULIE ANDREWS.

Edwards, Gareth (born 1947) Welsh rugby union player. Edwards, considered to be among the greatest rugby players, played scrum half on the great Welsh sides that won the Five Nations Championship 11 times in 16 seasons between 1964 and 1978. He played 53 tests plus 10 for the British Lions (1967–78). Amazingly for a scrum half, he scored 20 tries for Wales.

Edwards, Jonathan (1703–1758) U.S. theologian. Born in East Windsor, Conn., the fifth of 11 children in a strict Puritan home, he entered Yale College at 13. In 1727 he was named a pastor at his grandfather's church in Northampton, Mass. His sermons on "Justification by Faith Alone" gave rise to a revival in the Connecticut River Valley in 1734, and in the 1740s he was also influential in the GREAT AWAKENING. In 1750 he was dismissed from the Northampton church over a disagreement on who was eligible to take communion, and he became pastor in Stockbridge in 1751. He died of smallpox shortly after accepting the presidency of the College of New Jersey (now Princeton Univ.). A staunch Calvinist, he emphasized original sin, predestination, and the need for conversion. His most famous sermon, "Sinners in the Hands of an Angry God," vividly evokes the fate of unrepentant sinners in hell.

Edwards, Robert See Patrick STEPTOE and Robert Edwards

eel Any of more than 500 fish species (order Anguilliformes) that are slender, elongated, and usually scaleless, with long dorsal and anal fins that are continuous around the tail tip. Eels are found in all seas, from coastal regions to the mid-depths. Freshwater eels are active, predaceous fish with small embedded scales; they grow to maturity in freshwater and return to the sea, where they spawn and die. The transparent young drift to the coast and make their way upstream. Freshwater eels, considered valuable food fish, include species ranging from 4 in. (10 cm) to about 11.5 ft (3.5 m) long. See also MORAY.

eelworm Any of several species of NEMATODE, named for their resemblance to miniature eels. Eelworms are either free-living or parasitic, and most are about 0.005–0.05 in. (0.1–1.5 mm) long. They are found in all parts of the world. Free-living forms inhabit salt water, freshwater, and damp soil. Parasitic forms are found in the roots of many plant species; the potato-root eelworm, for example, is a serious pest of potatoes. Some species occur in both plants and animals.

efficiency *or* **mechanical efficiency** In mechanics, the measure of the effectiveness with which a system performs. It is stated as the ratio of a system's WORK output to its work input. The efficiency of a real system is always less than 1 because of FRICTION between moving parts. A machine with an efficiency of 0.8 returns 80% of the work input as work output; the remaining 20% is used to overcome friction. In a theoretically frictionless, or ideal, machine, the work input and work output are equal, and the efficiency would be 1, or 100%.

effigy mound Earthen mound in the form of a bird or animal (e.g, bear, deer, turtle, buffalo), found in the northern central U.S., especially the Ohio River valley. Little is known of the effigy mounds except that most were burial sites. The culture that produced them dates from AD 300 to the mid-17th century. See also HOPEWELL CULTURE.

Effigy Mounds National Monument National preserve, northeastern Iowa. Located on the Mississippi River, it covers 1,475 acres (597 hectares). Established in 1949, the monument has 183 known mounds, some of which are in the shape of birds and bears. The mounds were built over the course of the Woodland period (1000 BC–1200 AD), with the effigy mounds probably constructed between AD 400 and 1200. Some of the mounds have yielded copper, bone, and stone tools of Indian origin. One of the bear mounds is 137 ft (42 m) long and 3.5 ft high.

eft See NEWT

Egas Moniz \'ā-gäs-mō-'nēz\, **António Caetano de Abreu Freire** (1874–1955) Portuguese neurologist and statesman. He introduced cerebral angiography (1927–37). With Almeida Lima, he performed the first prefrontal lobotomy in 1936, and in 1949 he shared a Nobel Prize with WALTER RUDOLF HESS for the development of the lobotomy. Because of its serious side effects, he advised using lobotomy only when all other treatment failed. He also served in the Portuguese legislature and as a minister and led the Portuguese delegation at the Paris Peace Conference.

egg In biology, the female sex cell, or gamete. In zoology, the Latin term ovum is often used to refer to the single cell, whereas the word egg may be applied to the entire specialized structure or capsule that consists of the ovum, its various protective membranes, and any accompanying nutritive materials. The egg or ovum, like the male gamete (SPERM), bears only a single (haploid; see PLOIDY) set of CHROMOSOMES. When female and male gametes unite during FERTILIZATION, the double (diploid) set of chromosomes is restored in the resulting zygote. In humans, the ovum matures inside one of the OVARY's follicles (hollow group of cells) and is released when the follicle ruptures (ovulation). The ovum passes into the fallopian (uterine) tube, and will degenerate if not fertilized within about 24 hours. In animals, the amount of nutritive material (yolk) deposited in an egg is dependent on the length of time before the developing animal can feed itself or, in the case of mammals, begins to receive nourishment from the maternal circulation. Most animal eggs are enclosed by one or more membranes. Insect eggs are covered by a thick, hard outer membrane, and amphibian eggs are surrounded by a jellylike layer. The term egg also refers to the content of the hard-shelled reproductive body produced by a bird or reptile.

Eggleston, Edward (1837–1902) U.S. novelist and historian. Born in Vevay, Ind., he became an itinerant preacher at 19; he later held various pastorates and edited several periodicals. He realistically portrayed backwoods Indiana in *The Hoosier School-Master* (1871). His other novels include *The End of the World* (1872), *The Circuit Rider* (1874), *Roxy* (1878), and *The Graysons* (1888). He then turned to writing history; his *Beginners of a Nation* (1896) and *Transit of Civilization from England to America* (1900) contributed to the growth of the study of social history.

eggplant Tender perennial plant *(Solanum melongena)* of the NIGHTSHADE FAMILY. It requires a warm climate and is grown extensively in eastern and southern Asia (where it is native) and in the U.S. It is usually grown as an annual for its fleshy fruit. It has an erect, bushy stem; large ovate, slightly lobed leaves; and pendant, violet, solitary flowers. The fruit is a large, glossy, egg-shaped berry, varying in color from dark purple to red, yellowish, or white, and sometimes striped. It is a staple in cuisines of the Mediterranean region.

Eggplant (*Solanum melongena*).
INGMAR HOLMASEN

Egill Skallagrímsson *or* **Egill Skalla-Grímsson** \'ā-yil-'skä-hlä-grim-ˌsȯn\ (910?–990) Icelandic poet. One of the greatest skaldic poets (see SKALDIC POETRY), his adventurous life and verses are preserved in the *Egils saga* (1220?), attributed to his descendant SNORRI STURLUSON. In the saga Egill kills the son of King Erik Bloodax and places a curse on the king. He later falls into Erik's hands but saves his own life by composing in one night a long poem praising Erik, *Hofuthlausn* (c. 948). After the death of two sons he composes the lament *Sonatorrek* (c. 961).

Eginhard See EINHARD

eglantine See SWEETBRIER

Eglevsky \ig-'lyef-skəi\, **André** (1917–1977) U.S. (Russian-born) ballet dancer and teacher, considered the outstanding male dancer of his time. He left Russia as a child and studied in Paris, becoming a lead dancer with the BALLET RUSSE DE MONTE CARLO at age 14. He moved to the U.S. in 1937. He danced with a number of companies before joining the NEW YORK CITY BALLET (1951–58), where he created leading roles in several of GEORGE BALANCHINE's ballets, including *Scotch Symphony* and *Caracole*. He also taught at the School of American Ballet. In 1958 he opened his own ballet school and in 1961 established the Eglevsky Ballet.

Eglevsky in *Apollo*, 1944.
FRED FEHL

ego (Latin: "I") In psychoanalytic theory, the portion of the psyche experienced as the "self" or "I." It is the part that remembers, evaluates, plans, and in other ways is responsive to and acts in the surrounding physical and social world. According to SIGMUND FREUD, it coexists with the ID (the unconscious, instinctual portion of the psyche) and the SUPEREGO (the portion representing the conscience, or the internalization of societal norms). The ego is not coextensive with either the PERSONALITY or the body; rather, it serves to integrate these and other aspects of the person, such as memory, imagination, and behavior. It mediates between the id and the superego by building up various DEFENSE MECHANISMS.

egoism In ETHICS, the principle that we should each act so as to promote our own interests. The great advantage of such a position is that it avoids any possible conflict between morality and self-interest; if it is rational for us to pursue our own interest, the rationality of morality is equally clear. The prescriptive thesis of ethical egoism can be distinguished from the descriptive thesis of psychological egoism. Psychological egoism is a generalization about human motivation, namely, that everyone always acts so as to promote his or her own interests.

egret \'ē-grət\ Any of several species (mainly in the genus *Egretta*) of wading birds in the same family (Ardeidae) as HERONS and BITTERNS. Egrets live in marshes, lakes, humid forests, and other wetland environments worldwide. They catch and eat small fishes, amphibians, reptiles, mammals, and crustaceans. They nest in trees and bushes or on the ground. Most are white and develop long plumes for the breeding season. The value of plumes as ornamental objects once drove egrets to near-extinction, but changes in fashion and strict conservation measures have allowed their numbers to increase. The great white egret is about 35 in. (90 cm) long; other common species average 20–24 in. (50–60 cm) long.

Common egret (*Egretta alba*).
R.F. HEAD FROM THE NATIONAL AUDUBON SOCIETY COLLECTION/PHOTO RESEARCHERS

Egypt *officially* **Arab Republic of Egypt** *formerly* **United Arab Republic** *Arabic* **Misr** \'misr\ *ancient* **Aegyptus** Republic, North Africa. Area: 386,900 sq mi (1,002,070 sq km). Population (1997 est.): 62,110,000. Capital: CAIRO. The people are mainly a homogeneous mix of Hamitic and Semitic lineages. Language: Arabic (official). Religion: Islam (official); minority, Coptic Christianity. Currency: Egyptian pound. Egypt occupies a crossroads between Africa, Europe, and Asia. The majority of its land is in the arid Western and ARABIAN DESERTS, separated by the country's dominant feature, the NILE RIVER. The Nile forms a flat-bottomed valley, generally 5–10 mi (8–16 km) wide, that fans out into the densely populated delta lowlands north of Cairo. The Nile valley (Lower Egypt) and delta (Upper Egypt), along with scattered oases, support all of Egypt's agriculture and have more than 99% of its population. It has a developing, mainly socialist but partly free-enterprise economy, based primarily on industry, including petroleum production, and agriculture. It is a republic with one legislative house; its chief of state is the president, while the head of government is the prime minister. It is one of the world's oldest continuous civilizations. In c. 3000 BC, Upper and Lower Egypt were united, beginning a period of cultural achievement and a line of native rulers that lasted nearly 3,000 years. Egypt's ancient history is divided into the Old, Middle, and New Kingdoms, spanning 31 dynasties and lasting to 332 BC. The PYRAMIDS date from the Old Kingdom; the cult of OSIRIS and the refinement of sculpture from the Middle Kingdom; the era of empire and the EXODUS of the Jews from the New Kingdom. An Assyrian invasion occurred in the 7th century BC, and the Persian Achaemenids established a dynasty in 525 BC. The invasion by ALEXANDER THE GREAT in 332 BC inaugurated the Macedonian Ptolemaic period, and the ascendancy of ALEXANDRIA. The Romans held Egypt from 30 BC to AD 395; later it was placed under the control of Constantinople. CONSTANTINE's granting of tolerance in 313 to the Christians began the development of a formal Egyptian (COPTIC) church. Egypt came under Arab control in 642, and ultimately was transformed into an Arabic-speaking state, with ISLAM as the dominant religion. Held by the UMAYYAD and ABBASID dynasties, in 969 it became the center of the FATIMID DYNASTY. In 1250, the Mamluks established a dynasty that lasted until 1517 (see MAMLUK REGIME), when Egypt fell to the Ottoman Turks. An economic decline ensued, and with it a decline in Egyptian culture. Egypt became a

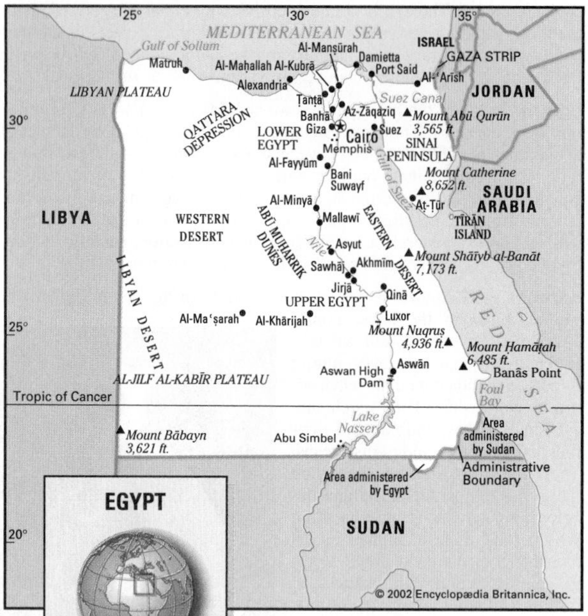

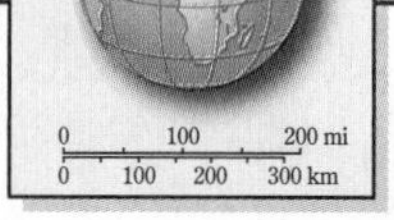

British protectorate in 1914 and received nominal independence in 1922, when a constitutional monarchy was established. A coup overthrew the monarchy in 1952, with GAMAL ABDEL NASSER taking power. Following three wars with Israel (see ARAB–ISRAELI WARS), Egypt, under Nasser's successor, ANWAR AL-SADAT, ultimately played a leading role in Middle East peace talks. Sadat was succeeded by HOSNI MUBARAK, who followed Sadat's peace initiatives, and in 1982 regained Egyptian sovereignty (lost in 1967) over the SINAI peninsula. Although Egypt took part in the coalition against Iraq during the PERSIAN GULF WAR (1991), it later began peace overtures with countries in the region, including Iraq.

Egyptian architecture Houses, palaces, temples, tombs, and other buildings of ancient Egypt. Most Egyptian towns were situated on the floodplain and have been lost, but religious structures built on higher ground have survived in many forms. Tomb architecture was often grandiose. The tomb was not simply a place to lay a corpse, but the home of the deceased, provided with goods to ensure continued existence after death. Mud brick and wood were the standard domestic building materials, but from the Old Kingdom (c. 2575–c. 2130 BC) on, stone was used for tombs and temples. Egyptian masons used stone to reproduce the forms of wood and brick buildings. MASTABAS and step pyramids were used for tomb superstructures, but the most characteristic form of the Old Kingdom was the true PYRAMID. The finest example is the monumental Great Pyramid of Khufu (Cheops) at GIZA. For nonroyal burials, simple chapel rooms with stelae (see STELE) were located at some distance from the royal burial compounds. In the New Kingdom (1539–1075 BC), royal tombs were cut into the face of cliffs to discourage looting; elaborate complexes of tombs and mortuary TEMPLES were built in the Valley of the Kings at THEBES. Two principal types of temple can be distinguished: cult TEMPLES for worship of the gods and funerary or mortuary temples. Most notable were the great stone cult temples; imposing remains can be seen at LUXOR, KARNAK, ABYDOS, and ABU SIMBEL.

Egyptian art Ancient sculptures, paintings, and decorative crafts produced in the dynastic periods of the 3rd–1st millennia BC in the Nile Valley of Egypt and NUBIA. Egyptian art served those in power as a forceful propaganda instrument that perpetuated the existing framework of society. Much of what has survived is associated with ancient tombs. The course of art in Egypt paralleled the country's political history and is divided into three periods: Old Kingdom (c. 2700–c. 2150 BC), Middle Kingdom (c. 2000–c. 1670 BC), and New Kingdom (c. 1550–c. 1070 BC). The Old Kingdom's stone tombs and temples were decorated with vigorous and brightly painted reliefs illustrating the daily life of the people. Rules for portraying the human figure were established, specifying proportions, postures, and placement of details, often linked to the subjects' social standing. An artistic decline at the end of the Old Kingdom led to a revival in the more stable political climate of the Middle Kingdom, notable for its expressive portrait sculptures of kings and its excellent relief sculptures and painting. The New Kingdom brought a magnificent flowering of the arts; great granite statues and wall reliefs glorified rulers and gods, painting became an independent art, and the decorative crafts reached new peaks, the treasure of TUTANKHAMEN's tomb typifying the variety of luxury items created. See also EGYPTIAN ARCHITECTURE.

Egyptian language Extinct AFROASIATIC LANGUAGE of the Nile valley. Its very long history comprises five periods: Old Egyptian (3000–2000 BC), best exemplified by a corpus of religious inscriptions known as the Pyramid Texts and a group of autobiographical tomb inscriptions; Middle Egyptian (2000–1300 BC), the classical literary language; Late Egyptian (1300–700 BC), known mainly from manuscripts; Demotic (700 BC–AD 500), used in the periods of Persian, Greek, and Roman dominance, and differing from Late Egyptian chiefly in its graphic system; and Coptic (AD 300–1500), the language of Christian Egypt, gradually supplanted as a vernacular by Arabic from the 9th century on but still preserved to some degree in the liturgy of the COPTIC ORTHODOX CHURCH. Egyptian was originally written in HIEROGLYPHS, out of which evolved hieratic, a cursive rendering of hieroglyphs, and demotic, a kind of shorthand reduction of hieratic. Coptic was written in a modified form of the Greek alphabet, with seven signs added from the Demotic script for sounds that did not occur in Greek.

Egyptian law Law that prevailed in Egypt from c. 3000 BC to c. 30 BC. No formal Egyptian code of law has been preserved, but legal documents (e.g., deeds and contracts) have survived. The pharaoh was the ultimate authority in the settlement of disputes. The next most powerful individual was the vizier, who directed all administrative branches of the government, sat in judgment on court cases, and appointed magistrates. Parties to a dispute were not represented by legal advocates; they spoke for themselves, presented any documentary evidence, and sometimes called witnesses. Both men and women could own and bequeath property, file lawsuits, and bear witness. Punishment for criminal offenders could be severe, but in some periods basic human rights, even those of slaves, were acknowledged. Egyptian law strongly influenced both GREEK and ROMAN law.

Egyptian religion Polytheistic belief system of ancient Egypt from the 4th millennium BC to the first centuries AD, including both folk traditions and the court religion. Local deities that sprang up along the Nile Valley had both human and animal form and were synthesized into national deities and cults after political unification c. 2925 BC. The gods were not all-powerful or all-knowing, but were immeasurably greater than humans. Their characters were not neatly defined, and there was much overlap, especially among the leading deities. One important deity was HORUS, the god-king who ruled the universe, who represented the earthly Egyptian king. Other major divinities included RE, the sun god; PTAH and ATON, creator gods; and ISIS and OSIRIS. The concept of Ma'at ("order") was fundamental: the king maintained Ma'at both on a societal and cosmic level. Belief in and preoccupation with the afterlife permeated Egyptian religion, as the surviving tombs and PYRAMIDS attest. Burial near the king helped others gain passage to the netherworld, as did spells and passwords from the BOOK OF THE DEAD.

Egyptology Study of pharaonic Egypt from the putative beginnings of Egyptian culture (c. 4500 BC) to the Arab conquest (AD 641). Egyptology began with discovery of the ROSETTA STONE (1799) and publication of *Description de l'Égypt* (1809–28) by scholars accompanying Napoleon. In the 19th century the Egyptian government opened Egypt to Europeans, many of whose collecting activities amounted to plundering. In 1880 FLINDERS PETRIE brought controlled, scientifically recorded excavation to Egypt, revolutionizing archaeology and pushing Egyptian origins back to 4500 BC. The discovery of TUTANKHAMEN's tomb in 1922 heightened public awareness. In 1975 the First International Congress of Egyptology convened in Cairo. Many little-explored sites remain.

Ehrenberg \'er-ən-ˌberk\, **Christian Gottfried** (1795–1876) German biologist, explorer, and founder of micropaleontology (the study of fossil microorganisms). He received his MD from the University of Berlin. The only survivor of a scientific expedition to the Middle East (1820–25), he identified and classified land and marine plants, animals, and microorganisms collected on that and other expeditions. He proved that fungi come from spores and demonstrated the sexual reproduction of molds and mushrooms. He was the first to study coral in detail, and he identified planktonic microorganisms as the cause of phosphorescence in the sea. He advanced the view (opposed by FELIX DUJARDIN) that all animals, including the tiniest, possess complete organ systems. Arguing that a single "ideal type" may be applied to all animals, he worked toward a comprehensive system of classification.

Ehrenburg \'er-ən-ˌbu̇rg, 'er-ən-ˌbu̇rk\, **Ilya (Grigoryevich)** (1891–1967) Russian writer and journalist. Arrested as a youth for revolutionary activity, he moved to Paris. He worked as a war correspondent, then returned to write for Soviet newspapers. His first novel and best work was *Julio Jurenito and His Disciples* (1922). He soon embraced the Soviet regime, eventually becoming one of its most effective spokesmen in the West. The vehemently anti-Western *The Fall of Paris* (1941) was followed by *The Storm* (1946–47) and *The Ninth Wave* (1951–52). After JOSEPH STALIN's death, Ehrenburg's works, including *The Thaw* (1954) and his autobiography, *People, Years, Life* (6 vols., 1960–66), turned critical of Stalin's heritage.

Ehrlich \'ər-lik\, **Paul** (1854–1915) German medical scientist. After early work on distribution of foreign substances in the body and on cell nutrition, he found uses for staining agents in diagnosis (including that of tuberculosis) and treatment. He also researched typhoid, fever medications, and eye diseases. In one paper, he showed that different tissues' oxygen consumption reflected the intensity of their cell processes. Ehrlich developed a method of stimulating production of antitoxins by injecting increasing amounts of toxin into animals; his work was crucial to the creation of a diphtheria antitoxin. He and É. METCHNIKOFF received a 1908 Nobel Prize. With Sahachiro Hata (1837–1938), he developed Salvarsan, the first effective syphilis treatment, in 1910.

Ehrlich \'ər-lik\, **Paul R(alph)** (born 1932) U.S. biologist. Born in Philadelphia, he studied at the University of Kansas and taught at Stanford University from 1959. Though much of his research was done in entomology, his overriding concern became unchecked population growth. His most influential work was *The Population Bomb* (1968). In 1990 he shared with EDWARD O. WILSON Sweden's prestigious Crafoord Prize.

Ehrlichman, John D(aniel) (1925–1999) U.S. presidential assistant central to the WATERGATE SCANDAL. Born in Tacoma, Wash., he practiced law before joining RICHARD NIXON's administration in 1969. With H.R. HALDEMAN he formed the so-called palace guard around the president. He soon established the group known as the "plumbers" to acquire political intelligence and stop information leaks. When members of the group were caught robbing Democratic headquarters, he became involved in the cover-up and was forced to resign in 1973. Convicted of conspiracy, perjury, and obstruction of justice, he served 18 months in jail.

Eichendorff \'ī-k̲ən-ˌdȯrf\, **Joseph, Freiherr (Baron) von** (1788–1857) German poet and novelist. Born to the nobility, he and his family lost their castle in the Napoleonic Wars, and he later worked in the Prussian civil service. He became associated with the national leaders of the Romantic movement while studying in Berlin. His most important prose work, *Memoirs of a Good-for-Nothing* (1826), is considered a high point of Romantic fiction. In the 1830s he wrote poetry that achieved the popularity of folk songs and inspired such composers as R. SCHUMANN, F. MENDELSSOHN, J. BRAHMS, H. WOLF, and R. STRAUSS. His epic poem *Robert und Guiscard* (1855) has the French Revolution as its subject.

Eichmann \'īk̲-ˌmän\, **(Karl) Adolf** (1906–1962) German Nazi official. In 1932 he joined the Nazi Party and became a member of HEINRICH HIMMLER's SS organization. In World War II he organized the identification, assembly, and transportation of Jews to Auschwitz and other death camps. In 1945 he was captured by U.S. troops but escaped and eventually settled in Argentina. In 1960 he was arrested near Buenos Aires and taken to Israel, where he was tried as a war criminal, with huge worldwide publicity, and hanged for his part in the HOLOCAUST.

eider \'ī-dər\ Any of several species of large DIVING DUCKS (in tribes Mergini and Somateriini) that are heavy and round-bodied, with a humped bill that produces a characteristic sloping profile. Eiders are the source of eiderdown, feathers that the hen plucks from her breast to line the nest and insulate her eggs. Eiderdown is used as a warm filling for jackets, pillows, quilts, and sleeping bags. Hens are mottled brown, but drakes (males) are boldly patterned, with a green pigment on the head. Eiders live in the cold far north.

Eider River \'ī-dər\ River, Schleswig-Holstein state, northern Germany. It rises east of Rendsburg and flows west for 117 mi (188 km) to the North Sea. It is navigable up to Rendsburg. It formed the northern limit of the Roman empire from the reign of CHARLEMAGNE (768–814), was recognized as the boundary of the HOLY ROMAN EMPIRE in 1027, and formed the traditional frontier between SCHLESWIG AND HOLSTEIN.

Eiffel Tower \'ī-fəl\ Parisian landmark built for the Centennial Exposition of 1889. Conceived by the bridge engineer Gustave Eiffel (1832–1923), the 984-ft (300-m) tower of open-lattice wrought iron was a technological masterpiece. Making use of advanced knowledge of the behavior of metal arch and TRUSS forms under loading, the structure presaged a revolution in civil engineering and architectural design. The tower was the world's tallest building until completion of the CHRYSLER BUILDING in 1930.

The Eiffel Tower, Paris, designed by Gustave Eiffel, 1887–89.
GIRAUDON—ART RESOURCE

Eigen \'ī-gən\, **Manfred** (born 1927) German physicist. He received his PhD from the University of Göttingen in 1951. He shared a 1967 Nobel Prize with Ronald Norrish (1897–1978) and George Porter (born 1920) for work on extremely rapid CHEMICAL REACTIONS. His methods, called relaxation techniques, involve applying bursts of energy to a solution and following the rates of subsequent changes (flash PHOTOLYSIS); reactions thus studied include hydrogen ion formation during water DISSOCIATION and keto–enol TAUTOMERISM.

eigenvalue \'ī-gən-ˌval-yü\ In mathematical ANALYSIS, one of a set of discrete values of a parameter, k, in an equation of the form $L\mathbf{x} = k\mathbf{x}$. Such characteristic equations are particularly useful in solving DIFFERENTIAL EQUATIONS, INTEGRAL EQUATIONS, and SYSTEMS OF EQUATIONS. In the equation, L is a LINEAR TRANSFORMATION such as a MATRIX or a DIFFERENTIAL OPERATOR, and $\mathbf{x}$ can be a vector or a function (called an eigenvector or eigenfunction). The totality of eigenvalues for a given characteristic equation is a set. In quantum mechanics, where L is an energy operator, the eigenvalues are energy values.

Eight, The Group of U.S. painters who reacted against the traditions of the National Academy of Design. The original eight—R. HENRI, Everett Shinn (1876–1953), JOHN SLOAN, Arthur B. Davies (1862–1928), Ernest Lawson (1873–1939), MAURICE PRENDERGAST, George Luks (1867–1933), and WILLIAM GLACKENS—were later joined by GEORGE WESLEY BELLOWS. In 1908 they exhibited together in New York City. Saloons, tenements, pool halls, and slums were among their favorite subjects, and their style was rough and realistic. Their careers took various directions, and a few years later they were absorbed into the ASH CAN SCHOOL.

eighteen schools Divisions of BUDDHISM that arose in India in the three centuries after the death of the BUDDHA (c. 483 BC). The number of schools, or sects, was probably closer to 30 than 18. The first division in the Buddhist community occurred as a result of the second council, held at Vaishali in the 4th century BC, where differences among disciples over the nature of the Buddha gave rise to the school known as the MAHASANGHIKAS. Other schools included the Sthaviravadins and their offshoots (3rd century BC), including the Theravadins (see THERAVADA).

Eightfold Path Buddhist doctrine, stated by the BUDDHA in his first sermon near Benares, India. The path is regarded as the way for individuals to deal with the problems named in the FOUR NOBLE TRUTHS. The path consists of right understanding (faith in the Buddhist view of existence), right thought (the resolve to practice the faith), right speech (avoidance of falsehoods, slander, and abuse), right action (abstention from taking life, stealing, and improper sexual behavior), right livelihood (rejection of occupations not in keeping with Buddhist principles), right effort (development of good mental states), right mindfulness (awareness of body, feelings, and thought), and right concentration (meditation). It is also called the Middle Path, because it steers a course between sensuality and asceticism. Following the Path leads to escape from suffering and attainment of NIRVANA.

Eijkman \'īk-,män, 'āk-,män\, **Christiaan** (1858–1930) Dutch physician and pathologist. While seeking a bacterial cause for beriberi, he noticed a resemblance between a nerve disorder in his laboratory chickens and that seen in beriberi. He eventually showed that the cause was their diet of white rather than brown rice, but believed the disorder was caused by a toxin even after it was shown to be due to thiamine deficiency. His work led to the discovery of VITAMINS and earned him a 1929 Nobel Prize, shared with F. GOWLAND HOPKINS.

Eileithyia \,ī-lī-'thī-ə\ Greek goddess of childbirth. Capable of helping or hindering labor according to her will, she was worshiped over a period of centuries from Neolithic to Roman times. The earliest evidence for her cult was found at Amnisus in Crete. In later Greek polytheism, she is sometimes described as the daughter of HERA and is sometimes identified with Hera or with ARTEMIS.

Einaudi \,ā-nä-'ü-dē\, **Luigi** (1874–1961) Italian economist and politician. He taught at the University of Turin 1900–1943, and edited the *Review of Economic History* 1936–43. An opponent of the Fascists, he fled to Switzerland in 1943. He returned in 1945 and served as governor of the Bank of Italy 1945–48. As minister of the budget (1947), he successfully curbed inflation and stabilized the currency. He was the first president (1948–55) of the Republic of Italy.

Eindhoven \'īnt-,hō-vən\ Commune (pop., 1994 est.: 196,000), southern Netherlands. Situated on the Dommel River, southeast of ROTTERDAM, it was chartered in 1232 by Henry I, duke of Brabant. After 1900 it developed from a small village into one of the largest industrial centers of the Netherlands, and in 1920 it annexed five adjoining municipalities. The city is the seat of a technical university and the headquarters of PHILIPS ELECTRONICS NV.

Einhard \'īn-,härt\ *or* **Eginhard** \'ā-gin-,härt\ (c. 770–840) Frankish historian and scholar. An adviser to CHARLEMAGNE and to LOUIS I the Pious, Einhard was made abbot of several monasteries and held extensive lands. His biography of Charlemagne (c. 830) analyzed Charlemagne's family, achievements, administration, and death and exemplified the classical renaissance at the Carolingian court.

Einstein, Albert (1879–1955) German-Swiss-U.S. scientist. Born to a Jewish family in Ulm, he grew up in Munich, and his family moved to Switzerland in 1894. He became a junior examiner at the Swiss patent office in 1902 and began producing original theoretical work that laid many of the foundations for 20th-century physics. He received his doctorate from the University of Zurich in 1905, the same year he won international fame with the publication of three articles: one on BROWNIAN MOTION, demonstrating the existence of molecules; one on the PHOTOELECTRIC EFFECT, in which he demonstrated the particle nature of light; and one on his special theory of RELATIVITY, which included his formulation of the equivalence of mass and energy ($E = mc^2$). He held several professorships before becoming director of Berlin's Kaiser Wilhelm Institute in 1914. In 1915 he published his general theory of relativity, which was confirmed experimentally during a solar eclipse in 1919 with observations of the deviation of light passing near the sun. He received a Nobel Prize in 1921 for his work on the photoelectric effect, his work on relativity still being controversial. He made important contributions to QUANTUM FIELD THEORY, and for decades he sought to discover the mathematical relationship between ELECTROMAGNETISM and GRAVITATION, which he believed would be a first step toward discovering the common laws governing the behavior of everything in the universe, but such a UNIFIED FIELD THEORY eluded him. His theories of relativity and gravitation represented a profound advance over Newtonian physics and revolutionized scientific and philosophical inquiry. He resigned his position at the Prussian Academy when ADOLF HITLER came to power and moved to Princeton, N.J., where he joined the Institute for Advanced Study. Though a longtime pacifist, he was instrumental in persuading Pres. FRANKLIN ROOSEVELT in 1939 to initiate the MANHATTAN PROJECT for the production of an atomic bomb, a technology his own theories greatly furthered, though he did not work on the project himself. The most eminent scientist in the world in the postwar years, he declined an offer to become the first prime minister of Israel and became a strong advocate for nuclear disarmament.

Einstein's mass-energy relation Relationship between MASS (m) and ENERGY (E) in ALBERT EINSTEIN's special theory of RELATIVITY, expressed $E = mc^2$, where c equals 186,000 mi/second (300,000 km/second), the speed of LIGHT. Whereas mass and energy were viewed as distinct in earlier physical theories, in special relativity a body's mass can be converted into energy in accordance with Einstein's formula. Such a release of energy decreases the body's mass (see CONSERVATION LAW).

Eisai \'ā-'sī\ (1141–1215) Japanese monk who introduced Rinzai ZEN Buddhism to Japan. Originally a Tendai (TIANTAI) monk, he visited China twice (1168, 1187) and returned to teach a strict meditational system based on the use of KOAN (riddles). He instructed DOGEN.

Eisenhower \'ī-zən-,haù-ər\, **Dwight D(avid)** (1890–1969) 34th president of the U.S. (1953–61). Born in Denison, Texas, he graduated from West Point (1915), then served in the Panama Canal Zone (1922–24) and in the Philippines under DOUGLAS MACARTHUR (1935–39). In World War II Gen. GEORGE MARSHALL appointed him to the army's war-plans division (1941), then chose him to command U.S. forces in Europe (1942). After planning the invasions of North Africa, Sicily, and Italy, he was appointed supreme commander of Allied forces (1943). He planned the NORMANDY CAMPAIGN (1944) and the conduct of the war in Europe until the German surrender (1945). He was promoted to five-star general (1944) and was named army chief of staff in 1945. He served as president of Columbia University from 1948 until being appointed supreme commander of NATO in 1951. Both Democrats and Republicans courted Eisenhower as a presidential candidate; in 1952, as the Republican candidate, he defeated ADLAI STEVENSON with the largest popular vote up to that time. He defeated Stevenson again in 1956 in an even larger landslide. His achievements included efforts to contain Communism with the EISENHOWER DOCTRINE. He sent federal troops to Little Rock, Ark., to enforce integration of a city high school (1957). When the Soviet Union launched Sputnik I (1957), he was criticized for failing to develop the U.S. space program and responded by creating NASA (1958). In his last weeks in office the U.S. broke diplomatic relations with Cuba.

Dwight D. Eisenhower, 1952.
FABIAN BACHRACH

Eisenhower Doctrine U.S. foreign-policy pronouncement by Pres. DWIGHT D. EISENHOWER (1957) that promised military and economic aid to anti-Communist governments, at a time when Communist countries were providing arms to Egypt and offering strong support to Arab states. Part of the COLD WAR policy developed by JOHN FOSTER DULLES to contain expansion of the Soviet sphere of influence, the doctrine continued pledges made under the TRUMAN DOCTRINE.

Eisenstaedt \'ī-zən-,stat\, **Alfred** (1898–1995) German-U.S. photojournalist. He became a professional photographer in Berlin in 1929 and came under the influence of ERICH SALOMON. His work appeared in many European picture magazines in the 1930s. In 1935 he emigrated to New York, where he became one of the first four photographers hired by *Life* (1936). He would contribute more than 2,500 picture stories and 90 cover photos to the magazine, including outstanding portraits of kings, dictators, film stars, and ordinary people. Collections of his work include *Witness of Our Time* (1966) and *The Eye of Eisenstaedt* (1969).

Eisenstein \'ī-zən-,stīn\, **Sergei (Mikhailovich)** (1898–1948) Russian film director and theorist. He began his career at a workers' theater in Moscow in 1920, designing costumes and scenery. After studying stage direction with VSEVOLOD MEYERHOLD, he turned to filmmaking. In *Strike* (1924) he introduced his influential concept of film montage, adding startling and often discordant images to the main action to create the maximum psychological impact. He further developed the style in *The Battleship Potemkin* (1925), a commissioned propaganda film sometimes called the greatest film of all time. Among his other films are *October* (*Ten Days that Shook the World;* 1928) and *The General Line* (1929). After a frustrating period in Hollywood and Mexico (1930–33), he returned to Russia and made two more classics, *Alexander Nevsky* (1938) and *Ivan the Terrible* (2 parts, 1945–46).

Eisner \'īz-nər\, **Kurt** (1867–1919) German journalist and politician. From 1898 he was editor of *Vorwärts,* the official SOCIAL DEMOCRATIC PARTY newspaper. He joined the Independent Social Democratic Party in 1917, later becoming its leader. In November 1918 he organized a Socialist revolution that overthrew the monarchy in Bavaria, and he became first prime minister and minister of foreign affairs of the new Bavarian republic. In February 1919 he was assassinated by a reactionary zealot.

Eisner, Michael (Dammann) (born 1942) U.S. entertainment executive. Born in Mount Kisco, N.Y., he worked at ABC-TV (1966–76) before becoming president of Paramount Pictures (1976–84), and has served as head of the DISNEY CO. since 1984. He was instrumental in reviving Disney as a major movie producer with such films as *Pretty Woman* (1990) and restored its reputation for classic animation with *Beauty and the Beast* (1991) and *The Lion King* (1995), which became hit Broadway musicals. He expanded the company into such other fields as television, publishing, home video, and cruise ships.

eisteddfod \ī-'steth-vȯd, ā-'steth-vȯd\ Formal assembly of Welsh BARDS and minstrels that originated in the traditions of medieval court bards. Early eisteddfods were competitions of musicians (especially harpists) and poets from which new musical, literary, and oratorical forms emerged. The assembly at Carmarthen in 1451 authoritatively established the arrangement of the strict meters of Welsh poetry. The modern annual National Eisteddfod, revived in the 19th century, includes awards for music, prose, drama, and art, but the investiture of the winning poet remains its high point.

ejido \ā-'hē-thō\ In Mexico, village lands held in the traditional Indian system of land tenure, blessed by Mexican law in the 1920s, that combines communal ownership with individual use. The ejido consists of cultivated land, pastureland, other uncultivated lands, and the *fundo legal,* or town site. The cultivated land is generally apportioned in family holdings, which cannot be sold but can be passed down to heirs. Though the LAND REFORM of the mid-18th century was aimed at breaking up the large church holdings, it also forced the Indians to give up their ejidos. The village lands were restored by the 1917 constitution. In 1992 the CARLOS SALINAS government revoked the ban on the sale of ejido land.

Ekaterinoslav See DNIPROPETROVSK

Ekron \'e-,krän\ Ancient Canaanite and PHILISTINE city. It was one of the five cities of the Philistine pentapolis, in what is now central Israel. Though allocated to JUDAH after the Israelite conquest, it was a Philistine stronghold in DAVID's time; it was later associated with the worship of the deity Baalzebub. Taken by Egyptians (c. 918 BC), it was tributary to ASSYRIA in the 7th century BC. The city was known as Akkaron from Hellenistic times; by the Middle Ages it had been abandoned.

El Chief deity of the West Semites. In ancient texts from Ras Shamra in Syria, El was the husband of the mother goddess Asherah and father of all the gods except BAAL. He was often depicted as an old man with a white beard and wings. The writers of the Old Testament used El as a synonym for Yahweh (the God of Israel) or as a general term for deity.

El Aaiún \ä-'yün\ *or* **Laâyoune** \lä-'yün\ Town (pop., 1998 est.: 164,000), North Africa. The capital (1940–76) of the overseas Spanish province of WESTERN SAHARA and since 1976 of the not internationally recognized Laâyoune province of Morocco, it lies in the northern part of Western Sahara, 8 mi (13 km) inland from the Atlantic Ocean. It was developed by Spain in 1938 as the administrative, military, and European population center of the former province. Nearby oases supply water.

El Alamein \,a-lə-'mān\, **Battles of** (June–July 1942; October 23–November 6, 1942) Two battles between British and Axis forces in Egypt in WORLD WAR II. Axis forces under ERWIN ROMMEL began a drive eastward along the North African coast in early 1942. Though initially checked by the British, they managed to reach El Alamein on June 30. The first engagement ended in mid-July with Rommel still there, blocked and on the defensive. In October British forces under BERNARD LAW MONTGOMERY began a devastating attack from El Alamein, routing Rommel's vastly outnumbered forces. By November 6 the British had driven the Germans back into Libya.

El Cid See The CID

El Dorado (Spanish: "The Golden") Legendary golden city sought by Spanish explorers in the New World. It was the fabulously wealthy land of a king who was said to have been covered with gold dust so many times that he was permanently gilded. Many Spanish and English expeditions in the Americas were sent in search of El Dorado. In 1540 FRANCISCO VAZQUEZ DE CORONADO ventured as far north as Kansas seeking the Seven Golden Cities of CIBOLA. WALTER RALEIGH searched for El Dorado in vain in South America, leading an expedition up the Orinoco River in 1595.

El Escorial \,es-kȯr-'yäl\ Palace-monastery northwest of Madrid, built in 1563–67 for PHILIP II. It is the burial place of Spanish sovereigns and one of the largest religious establishments in the world. It was conceived by Juan Bautista de Toledo (1530–1597) and completed by Juan de Herrera (c. 1530–1597), who is considered responsible for its architectural style. Its plan is a giant rectangle, with a domed church at the center flanked by the palace, monastery, college, library, cloisters, and courts. The massive granite walls, relieved only by a series of unadorned windows and Doric pilasters, with no concession to decorative richness, produced an austerity beyond anything the Italian Renaissance ever envisaged.

El Greco See El GRECO

El Malpais National Monument \,el-,mäl-pä-'ēs\ National monument, western New Mexico. Located at an elevation of 6,400–8,400 ft (1,950–2,560 m), it covers 114,716 acres (46,424 hectares), including a lava-flow area of 85,000 acres (34,400 hectares). Features include a 17-mi (27-km) lava tube system, a number of ice caves, volcanic cinder cones, one of New Mexico's largest natural arches, and more than 20 gas and lava spatter cones. Designated a national natural landmark with the name Grants Lava Flow in 1969, it became a national monument in 1987.

El Morro National Monument National monument, western central New Mexico. Established in 1906, it has an area of 2 sq mi (5 sq km). El Morro, or Inscription Rock, is a soft sandstone mesa rising 200 ft (60 m) above the valley floor and covering several acres. Indians, Spaniards, and Americans left their inscriptions (1605–1774) on the cliff sides of the mesa. El Morro also has a number of pre-Columbian petroglyphs, and on its top lie ruins of ZUNI Indian pueblos.

El Niño In oceanography and climatology, the appearance, every few years, of unusually warm surface waters of the Pacific Ocean along the tropical western coast of South America. It affects fishing, agriculture, and local weather from Ecuador to Chile and can cause global climatic anomalies in the equatorial Pacific, Asia, and North America. The name (Spanish for "the Christ Child") was originally used by 19th-century Peruvian fishermen to describe the annual flow of warm equatorial waters southward around Christmastime. Peruvian scientists later noted that every few years more intense changes lasting for a year or more were associated with high rainfall along the normally arid coast. The more unusual episodes gained world attention in the 20th century, and the original annual connotation of the name was replaced by that of the anomalous occurrence. See also LA NIÑA.

El Paso City (pop., 2000: 563,662), western Texas. Located on the RIO GRANDE river opposite Ciudad JUÁREZ, Mexico, it is the largest of the U.S.–Mexican border cities. The area was the site of several missions from the 16th century; the first village was built on the site of El Paso in 1827. It became U.S. territory in 1848, when an army post was erected; the town was laid out in 1859. It grew slowly until 1881, when four railways arrived; in a decade its population had increased more than tenfold. Spanish language and culture distinguish the modern city. The commercial and financial center for an extensive trade territory, it is the site of the University of Texas at El Paso (1913) and Fort Bliss (home of the U.S. Army Air Defense Center); the White Sands Missile Range is nearby.

El Salvador *officially* **Republic of El Salvador** Republic in CENTRAL AMERICA. Area: 8,124 sq mi (21,041 sq km). Population (1998 est.): 6,031,326. Capital: SAN SALVADOR. The majority of the people are mestizo (mixed European and Indian), with small numbers of Indians (mostly Pipil), and people of European descent. Language: Spanish (official).

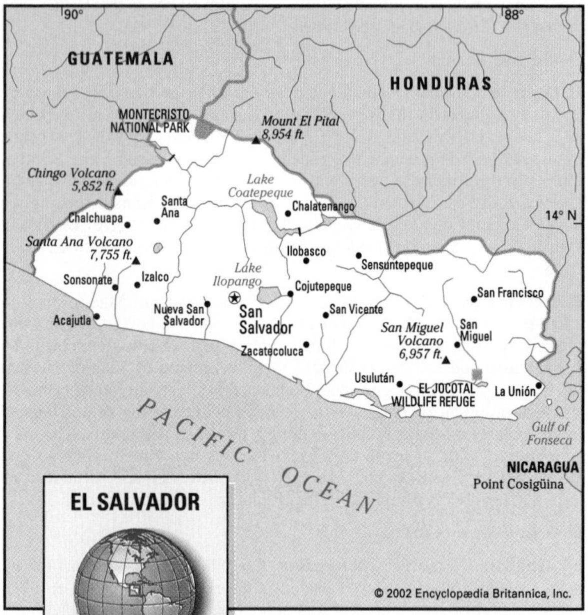

Religion: Roman Catholicism. Currency: Salvadoran colón. The smallest but most densely populated Central American country, it is crossed by two volcanic mountain ranges, with a narrow coastal region and high central plains in the southern region. The climate ranges from hot and wet in the lowlands to cooler and wetter in the highlands. Cloud forests predominate at the highest elevations. El Salvador has a developing economy based on trade, manufacturing, and agriculture, with coffee, sugarcane, and cotton the major export crops. It is a republic with one legislative house; its chief of state and head of government is the president. The Spanish arrived in the area in 1524 and subjugated the Pipil Indian kingdom of Cuzcatlán by 1539. The country was divided into two districts, San Salvador and Sonsonate, both attached to Guatemala. When independence came in 1821, San Salvador was incorporated into the Mexican empire; upon its collapse in 1823, Sonsonate and San Salvador combined to form the new state of El Salvador within the United Provinces of Central America. From its founding, it experienced a high degree of political turmoil, and was under military rule 1931–79, when the government was ousted in a coup. Elections held in 1982 set up a new government, and in 1983 a new constitution was adopted, but civil war continued through the 1980s. An accord in 1992 brought an uneasy truce.

Elagabalus \ˌe-lə-ˈga-bə-ləs\ *or* **Heliogabalus** \ˌhe-lē-ō-ˈga-bə-ləs\ *officially* **Caesar Marcus Aurelius Antoninus Augustus** *orig.* **Varius Avitus Bassianus** (AD 204–222) Roman emperor (218–22) notable for his eccentric behavior. Passed off as CARACALLA's illegitimate son, he became emperor with the support of the army. He identified himself with the Syrian god BAAL and imposed Baal worship on the empire. His execution of dissidents, promotion of favorites, and homosexual orgies outraged the Romans. After he named his cousin Alexander heir and then changed his mind, the Praetorian Guards mutinied, murdered him, and made Alexander emperor.

Elagabalus, marble bust; in the Capitoline Museum, Rome.
ALINARI—ART RESOURCE

Elam \ˈē-ləm\ Ancient country, southwestern modern-day Iran. It was located at the head of the Persian Gulf east of BABYLONIA; its capital was Susa (Elam was sometimes known as Susiana). It was closely tied culturally to MESOPOTAMIA, and was in conflict with the Sumerians (see SUMER) and Akkadians (see) from c. 3000 BC. In the 13th century BC, it became a dominant power; it included most of Mesopotamia east of the TIGRIS and reached almost to PERSEPOLIS. This domination ended when Nebuchadnezzar I of Babylon (r.1124–1103 BC) captured Susa. Later, Elam formed a satrapy of the Persian empire, and Susa became one of its capitals.

eland \ˈē-lənd\ Either of two species of easily tamed, oxlike ANTELOPE (genus *Taurotragus*) found in herds on the plains or in lightly wooded areas of central and southern Africa. The largest of the antelope, they may stand up to 6 ft (1.8 m) tall at the shoulder and weigh as much as 2,200 lbs (1,000 kg). They have a short, dark mane, a dewlap hanging from the throat, and long horns twisted in a tight spiral. The common eland is pale brown, becoming blue-gray with age, and often marked with narrow, vertical white stripes. The giant, or Derby, eland is reddish brown with a blackish neck and vertical white stripes and horns heavier than those of the common eland.

Giant eland (*Taurotragus derbianus*).
LEONARD LEE RUE III

elapid \ˈe-lə-pəd\ Any of about 200 species of venomous snakes (family Elapidae) that have short fangs fixed in the front of the upper jaw. Elapids are found in the New World, Africa, southern Asia, Pacific Islands, and Australia. Slender and agile, most are small and harmless to humans, but they include the largest and most lethal of snakes. Their venom is primarily neurotoxic but often contains substances that damage body tissues or blood cells. The relatively painless bite may cause a swift death from paralysis of the heart and lungs. See also BLACK SNAKE, BROWN SNAKE, COBRA, CORAL SNAKE, MAMBA.

elastic modulus *or* **elastic constant** In MATERIALS SCIENCE and physical METALLURGY, any of various numbers that quantify the response of a material to elastic or springy deflection. When tensile stress is applied to a material, the resulting strain is determined by Young's modulus (see THOMAS YOUNG), a constant defined as the ratio of the STRESS in a body to the corresponding STRAIN. It has dimensions of $(\text{force})/(\text{length})^2$ and is measured in units such as the PASCAL or newton per square meter (1 Pa = 1 N/m^2), dyne/cm^2, or lbs per sq in. (psi). See also ELASTICITY.

elasticity Ability of a deformed material body to return to its original shape and size when the forces causing DEFORMATION are removed. Most solids show some elastic behavior, but there is usually a limit—the material's "elastic limit"—to the force from which recovery is possible. Stresses beyond its elastic limit cause the material to yield, or flow, and the result is permanent deformation or breakage. The limit depends on the material's internal structure; for example, steel, though strong, has a low elastic limit and can be extended only about 1% of its length, whereas rubber can be elastically extended up to about 1,000%. ROBERT HOOKE, one of the first to study elasticity, developed a mathematical relation between tension and extension.

Elba Island (pop., 1991: 29,000) off the western coast of Italy, in the TYRRHENIAN SEA. Occupying an area of 86 sq mi (223 sq km), it is the largest island of the Tuscan Archipelago. France obtained Elba from Rome in 1802. When NAPOLEON abdicated in May 1814, he was exiled to Elba. The island was recognized as an independent principality with Napoleon as its ruler until February 1815, when he returned to France to begin the HUNDRED DAYS. Thereafter Elba was restored to TUSCANY.

Elbe River \ˈel-bə\ *Czech* **Labe** \ˈlä-be\ *ancient* **Albis.** River, central Europe. One of the continent's major waterways, it rises in the Krkonose (Giant) Mountains on the border of the Czech Republic and Poland and flows southwest across Bohemia. It then flows northwest across Germany and empties into the North Sea near Cuxhaven. From 1945 to 1990 it formed part of the boundary between East and West Germany. It is 724 mi (1,165 km) long, and connected by canals with the BALTIC SEA, the HAVEL RIVER and BERLIN, the RUHR industrial region and the RHINE RIVER. It is navigable for 1,000-ton barges as far upstream as PRAGUE through the VLTAVA RIVER. HAMBURG is 55 mi (88 km) upstream from its mouth.

Elbrus \el-'brüs\, **Mt.** Peak, CAUCASUS MTNS., southwestern Russia. The highest peak in the Caucasus and in Europe, it is an extinct volcano with twin cones reaching 18,510 ft (5,642 m) and 18,356 ft (5,595 m) high. There are many mineral springs along its descending streams, while 53 sq mi (138 sq km) of Elbrus is covered by 22 glaciers. It is a major center for mountaineering and tourism in the Caucasus region.

Elburz Mountains \el-'bůrz\ Mountain range, northern Iran. It is 560 mi (900 km) long and extends along the southern shore of the CASPIAN SEA, from which it is separated by a narrow coastal lowland. It includes Iran's highest peak, Mount Damavand, at 18,934 ft (5771 m) high. The forests of the Elburz cover more than 8 million acres (3 million hectares). The Hyrcanian tigers for which they were famous are now very rare, but other wild cats, including the leopard and the lynx, are still numerous.

elder Any of about 20–30 species, mainly shrubs and small trees, that make up the genus *Sambucus,* in the HONEYSUCKLE FAMILY. Most are native to forested temperate or subtropical areas. Elders are important as garden shrubs, as forest plants, and for their berries (elderberries), which provide food for wildlife and are used for wines, jellies, pies, and folk medicines. Elders have divided leaves and flat, roundish clusters of tiny, yellowish-white, saucer-shaped flowers. The American, or sweet, elder *(S. canadensis)* of North America is the most important species horticulturally.

European red elder (*Sambucus racemosa*).

A.J. HUXLEY

elder, box See BOX ELDER

Elder, John (1824–1869) Scottish marine engineer. In 1854 he developed the marine compound STEAM ENGINE (using both high- and low-pressure STEAM), which enabled seagoing vessels to save 30–40% of the coal they had been burning and helped make practical long voyages on which refueling was impossible.

Eldridge, (David) Roy (1911–1989) U.S. trumpeter, one of the most vital and creative jazz musicians of the SWING era. Born in Pittsburgh, he was influenced by saxophonists such as COLEMAN HAWKINS and developed a fast, nimble technique matched with harmonic sophistication. He played with FLETCHER HENDERSON (1935–36) and was featured with the big bands of GENE KRUPA and ARTIE SHAW in the 1940s. (A nickname reflecting his stature, Little Jazz, was also the title of a record made with Shaw). The dominant voice on his instrument in the swing style, he exerted a strong influence on BEBOP musicians.

Eleanor of Aquitaine (1122?–1204) Queen consort of LOUIS VII of France (1137–52) and HENRY II of England (1152–1204), the most powerful woman of 12th-century Europe. She inherited the duchy of Aquitaine and married the heir to the French throne. Beautiful, capricious, and strong-willed, she accompanied Louis on the Second CRUSADE (1147–49), and her conduct aroused his jealousy. The marriage was annulled (1152) despite the existence of their two daughters, and she married Henry Plantagenet, soon to be Henry II; the marriage united England, Normandy, and western France under his rule. She bore Henry five sons, including RICHARD I the Lionheart and JOHN LACKLAND, and three daughters who married into other royal houses. Her court at Poitiers became a center of culture, fostering the poetry of the TROUBADOURS. She may have spurred her sons to revolt against Henry (1173); when the rebellion failed she was captured and confined until his death (1189). She was active in government during the reign of Richard I, ruling during his crusade to the Holy Land and ransoming him from Austria. After Richard died (1199) and John became king, she saved Anjou and Aquitaine for John against French threats, then retired to a monastery.

Eleanor of Castile (1246–1290) Queen consort of EDWARD I of England. Daughter of the king of Castile, she brought Edward title to Gascony on their marriage in 1254, and she was sent to France for safety during the baronial rebellion (1264–65). She joined Edward on a crusade to the Holy Land (1270–73), and legend says she saved his life by sucking poison from a dagger wound. On her death, Edward erected Eleanor Crosses at each place where her coffin rested en route to London.

Eleatics \,el-ē-'a-tiks\ School of philosophy that flourished in the 5th century BC. One of the principal schools of PRE-SOCRATICS, it took its name from the Greek colony of Elea (Velia) in southern Italy. It is distinguished by its radical MONISM—i.e., its doctrine of the One, according to which all that exists is a static plenum of Being as such, and nothing exists that stands either in contrast or in contradiction to Being. Thus, all differentiation, motion, and change must be illusory. Its literary sources consist of fragments (most less than 10 lines long) preserved by later classical authors: 19 from PARMENIDES, four from his pupil ZENO OF ELEA, and 10 from another pupil, Melissus (fl. 5th century BC).

Eleazar ben Judah of Worms \,el-ē-'ā-zər\ *orig.* **Eleazar ben Judah ben Kalonymos** (c. 1160–1238) German-Jewish mystic and Talmudic scholar. His wife and daughters were killed by Crusaders in 1196, despite which he continued to teach a doctrine of love of humanity. After studying with JUDAH BEN SAMUEL, to whom he was related, he became a rabbi at Worms (1201). Eleazar attempted to unify the mysticism of the Kabbala with the Talmud. His greatest work was his ethical code, *Rokeah* (1505). He believed that God himself was unknowable but that the *kavod,* a ruling angel that was an emanation from God, was knowable. His writings are a major source of information on medieval HASIDISM.

election Formal process by which voters make their political choices on public issues or candidates for public office. The use of elections in the modern era dates to the emergence of representative government in Europe and North America since the 17th century. Regular elections serve to hold leaders accountable for their performance and permit an exchange of influence between the governors and the governed. The availability of alternatives is a necessary condition. Votes may be secret or public. See also ELECTORAL SYSTEM, PARTY SYSTEM, PLEBISCITE, PRIMARY ELECTION, REFERENDUM AND INITIATIVE.

elector *German* **Kurfürst** Prince of the HOLY ROMAN EMPIRE who had a right to participate in electing the German emperor. Beginning c. 1273, and with the confirmation of the GOLDEN BULL, there were seven electors: the archbishops of Trier, Mainz, and Cologne; the duke of Saxony; the count palatine of the Rhine; the margrave of Brandenburg; and the king of Bohemia. Other electorates were created much later for Bavaria (1623–1778), Hanover (1708), and Hesse-Kassel (1803), but by the 17th century the electors' office had become meaningless because the HABSBURG DYNASTY produced the de facto emperors. The office disappeared when the empire was abolished in 1806.

electoral college Constitutionally mandated process for electing the U.S. PRESIDENT and vice president. Each state appoints as many electors as it has senators and representatives in CONGRESS (U.S. senators, representatives, and government officers are ineligible); the District of Columbia has three votes. A winner-take-all rule operates in every state except Maine and Nebraska. Three presidents have been elected by means of an electoral college victory while losing the national popular vote (RUTHERFORD B. HAYES in 1877, BENJAMIN HARRISON in 1888, and GEORGE W. BUSH in 2000). Though pledged to vote for their state's winners, electors are not constitutionally obliged to do so. A candidate must win 270 of the 538 votes to win the election.

Electoral Commission (1877) Commission created to resolve the disputed 1876 presidential election between Republican RUTHERFORD B. HAYES and Democrat SAMUEL TILDEN. Tilden had won the popular vote and was only one electoral vote short of victory, but the Republicans contested the tallies in four states, charging fraud. Unable to reach a consensus, Congress appointed a 15-member commission, evenly divided between the two parties, except for one justice, Joseph P. Bradley, a Republican considered nonpartisan; Republicans pressured him, and the tally went to Hayes, who was declared the winner on March 2. See also WORMLEY CONFERENCE.

electoral system Method and rules of counting votes to determine the outcome of elections. Winners may be determined by a plurality, a majority (more than 50% of the vote), an extraordinary majority (a percentage of the vote greater than 50%), or unanimity. Candidates for public office may be elected directly or indirectly. PROPORTIONAL REPRESENTATION is used in some areas to ensure a fairer distribution of legislative seats to constituencies that may be denied representation under the plurality or majority formulas. See also PARTY SYSTEM, PLURALITY SYSTEM, PRIMARY ELECTION.

Electra In Greek legend, the daughter of AGAMEMNON and Clytemnestra. When Agamemnon was murdered by Clytemnestra and her lover Aegisthus, Electra saved her young brother ORESTES from the same fate by sending him away. Orestes later returned, and Electra helped him kill their mother and Aegisthus. She then married her brother's friend Pylades. The story is treated in plays by AESCHYLUS, SOPHOCLES, and EURIPIDES.

Electra complex See OEDIPUS COMPLEX

electric automobile Battery-powered motor vehicle. Originating in the 1880s, electric cars were used for private passenger, truck, and bus transportation in cities, where their low speeds and limited battery range were not drawbacks, and the cars became popular for their quietness and low maintenance costs. Until 1920 they were competitive with gasoline-fueled cars; they became less so after the electric self-starter made gasoline-powered cars more attractive and MASS PRODUCTION made them cheaper to produce. In Europe electric vehicles have been used as short-range delivery vans. Renewed interest in electric cars beginning in the 1970s, spurred especially by new consciousness of foreign oil dependency and environmental concern, led to improvements in speed and range. Recent laws, particularly in California, have mandated commercial production. "Hybrid" cars employing both electric and internal combustion engines and providing the best features of both technologies, have recently become commercially available. Experimental vehicles have used solar FUEL CELLS.

electric charge Quantity of ELECTRICITY that flows in ELECTRIC CURRENTS or that accumulates on the surfaces of dissimilar nonmetallic substances that are rubbed together briskly. It occurs in discrete natural units, equal to the charge of an ELECTRON or PROTON. It cannot be created or destroyed. Charge can be positive or negative; one positive charge can combine with one negative charge, and the result is a net charge of zero. Two objects that have an excess of the same type of charge repel each other, while two objects with an excess of opposite charge attract each other. The unit of charge is the coulomb, which consists of 6.24×10^{18} natural units of electric charge.

electric circuit See CIRCUIT

electric current Movement of ELECTRIC CHARGE carriers. In a wire, electric current is a flow of ELECTRONS that have been dislodged from ATOMS and is a measure of the quantity of electrical charge passing any point of the wire per unit time. Current in gases and liquids generally consists of a flow of positive IONS in one direction together with a flow of negative ions in the opposite direction. Conventionally, the direction of electric current is that of the flow of the positive ions. In ALTERNATING CURRENT (AC) the motion of the charges is periodically reversed; in DIRECT CURRENT (DC) it is not. A common unit of current is the ampere, a flow of one coulomb of charge per second, or 6.24×10^{18} electrons per second.

electric dipole \'dī-pōl\ Pair of equal and opposite ELECTRIC CHARGES, the centers of which do not coincide. An ATOM in which the center of the negative cloud of ELECTRONS has been shifted slightly away from the NUCLEUS by an external ELECTRIC FIELD is an induced electric dipole. When the external field is removed, the atom loses its dipolarity. A water molecule, in which two hydrogen atoms stick out of one side of an oxygen atom, is a permanent electric dipole. The oxygen side is always slightly negative, the hydrogen side slightly positive.

electric discharge lamp *or* **vapor lamp** Lighting device consisting of a transparent container within which a gas is energized by an applied voltage and made to glow. After practical generators were devised in the 19th century, many experimenters applied electric power to tubes of gas. From c. 1900, electric discharge lamps were in use in Europe and the U.S. Fluorescent, neon, mercury, sodium, and metal-halide lamps are of the electric discharge variety.

electric eel Eel-shaped South American fish *(Electrophorus electricus)* capable of producing an electric shock strong enough to stun a human. The electric eel (not a true EEL) is a sluggish inhabitant of slow freshwater, surfacing periodically to gulp air. Long, cylindrical, scaleless, and gray-brown, it sometimes reaches a length of 9 ft (2.75 m) and a weight of 49 lbs (22 kg). The tail region, bordered below by a long anal fin that the fish undulates to move about, contains the electric organs. The shock (up to 650 volts discharged at will) is used mainly to immobilize fish and other prey.

electric eye See PHOTOCELL

electric field Region around an ELECTRIC CHARGE in which an electric FORCE is exerted on another charge. The strength of an electric field E at any point is defined as the electric force f exerted per unit positive electric charge q at that point, or $E = F/q$. An electric field has both magnitude and direction and can be represented by lines of force, or field lines, that start on positive charges and terminate on negative charges. The electric field is stronger where the field lines are close together than where they are farther apart. The value of the electric field has dimensions of force per unit charge and is measured in units of newtons per coulomb.

electric furnace Chamber heated with electricity to very high temperatures, for melting and alloying METALS and REFRACTORIES. Modern electric furnaces generally are either ARC FURNACES or induction furnaces. Arc furnaces produce roughly two-fifths of the STEEL made in the U.S. In the induction furnace, a coil carrying alternating electric current surrounds the container or chamber of metal; circulating eddy currents induced in the metal produce extremely high temperatures.

electric potential Amount of WORK needed to move a unit ELECTRIC CHARGE from a reference point to a specific point against an ELECTRIC FIELD. The POTENTIAL ENERGY of a positive charge increases when it moves against an electric field, and decreases when it moves with the field. Electric potential can be thought of as potential energy per unit charge. The work done in moving a unit charge from one point to another, as in an electric circuit, is equal to the difference in potential energies at each point. Electric potential is expressed in units of joules per coulomb, or volts.

electric ray Any of the aquatic RAYS (families Torpedinidae, Narkidae, and Temeridae) that produce an electrical shock. They are found worldwide in warm and temperate seas, mostly in shallow water but some (genus *Benthobatis*) at depths greater than 3,000 ft (1,000 m). Slow-moving bottom-dwellers, they feed on fishes and invertebrates. They range in length from less than 1 ft (30 cm) to about 6 ft (1.8 m) and have a short, stout tail. They are soft and smooth-skinned, with a circular or nearly circular body disk formed by the head and pectoral fins. They are harmless unless touched or stepped on. The electric organs, composed of modified muscle tissue, are in the disk near the head. The shock from these organs, which may reach 220 volts and is strong enough to fell a human adult, is used for defense, sensory location, and capturing prey.

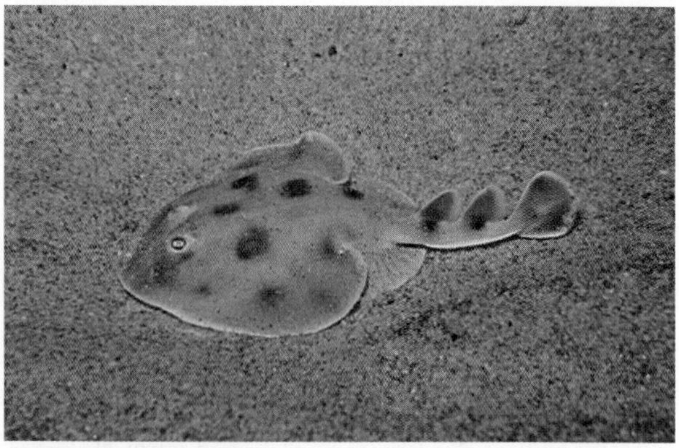

Electric ray (*Narcine brasiliensis*).
DOUGLAS FAULKNER

electric shock Physical effect of an ELECTRIC CURRENT that enters the body, ranging from a minor static-electricity discharge to a power-line accident or lightning strike but most often resulting from house current.

The effects depend on the current (not the voltage), and the worst damage occurs along its path from the entry to the exit point. Causes of immediate death are VENTRICULAR FIBRILLATION and paralysis of the brain's breathing center or of the heart. CARDIOPULMONARY RESUSCITATION is the best first aid. Though most survivors recover completely, aftereffects may include CATARACT, ANGINA, or nervous-system disorders.

electrical engineering Branch of ENGINEERING concerned with the practical applications of ELECTRICITY in all its forms, including those of ELECTRONICS. Electrical engineering deals with electric light and POWER systems and apparatuses; electronics engineering deals with wire and RADIO communication, the stored-program electronic COMPUTER, RADAR, and automatic control systems. The first practical application of electricity was the TELEGRAPH, in 1837. Electrical engineering emerged as a discipline in 1864 when JAMES CLERK MAXWELL summarized the basic laws of electricity in mathematical form and predicted that radiation of electromagnetic energy would occur in a form that later became known as radio waves. The need for electrical engineers was not felt until the invention of the TELEPHONE (1876) and the INCANDESCENT LAMP (1878).

electrical impedance \im-'pē-dᵊns\ Opposition that a circuit presents to ELECTRIC CURRENT. It includes both RESISTANCE and REACTANCE. Resistance arises from collisions of the current-carrying charged particles with the internal structure of the CONDUCTOR. Reactance is an additional opposition to the movement of electric charge that arises from the changing electric and MAGNETIC FIELDS in circuits carrying ALTERNATING CURRENT. Impedance in circuits carrying steady DIRECT CURRENTS is simply resistance. The magnitude of the impedance Z of a circuit is equal to the maximum value of the potential difference, or voltage V, across the circuit, divided by the maximum value of the current I through the circuit, or simply $Z = V/I$. The unit of impedance is the ohm.

electricity Phenomenon associated with stationary or moving ELECTRIC CHARGES. The word comes from the Greek *elektron* ("amber"); the Greeks discovered that amber rubbed with fur attracted light objects such as feathers. Such effects due to stationary charges, or static electricity, were the first electrical phenomena to be studied. Not until the early 19th century were static electricity and ELECTRIC CURRENT shown to be aspects of the same phenomenon. The discovery of the ELECTRON, which carries a charge designated as negative, showed that the various manifestations of electricity are the result of the accumulation or motion of numbers of electrons. The invention of the incandescent lightbulb (1879) and the construction of the first central power station (1881) by THOMAS ALVA EDISON led to the rapid introduction of electric power into factories and homes. See also JAMES CLERK MAXWELL.

electrification, rural See RURAL ELECTRIFICATION

electroacoustic music Music in which the sounds are produced or modified by electronic components. In the late 1940s, magnetic tape began to be used, especially in France, to modify natural sounds (playing them backward, at different speeds, etc.), creating the genre known as musique concrète. By the early 1950s, composers in Germany and the U.S. were employing assembled conglomerations of OSCILLATORS, filters, and other equipment to produce entirely new sounds. The development of voltage-controlled oscillators and filters led to the first SYNTHESIZERS in the 1950s, which effectively standardized the assemblages and made them more flexible. No longer relying on tape editing, electroacoustic music could now be created in real time. Since their advent in the late 1970s, personal computers have been used to control the synthesizers. Digital sampling—the use of actual recorded sounds corresponding to every pitch, often from acoustic (nonelectronic) instruments or even voices, activated generally by playing a keyboard—has largely replaced the use of oscillators as a sound source.

electrocardiography \i-ˌlek-trō-ˌkärd-ē-'äg-rə-fē\ Method of tracing the ELECTRIC CURRENT of a heartbeat to provide information on the HEART. Electrocardiograms (ECGs) are made by applying ELECTRODES, usually to the arms, legs, and chest wall, attached to an electrocardiograph, which records the tiny heart current. Upward and downward movements on the tracing reflect contractions of the atria and ventricles. Deviations from a patient's norm point to a possible heart disorder and its site, as well as to possible high blood pressure and other diseases.

electrochemistry Branch of CHEMISTRY concerned with the relation between ELECTRICITY and chemical change. Many spontaneous CHEMICAL REACTIONS liberate electrical ENERGY, and some of these reactions are used in BATTERIES and fuel cells to produce electric power. Conversely, electric current can bring about many reactions that do not occur spontaneously. ELECTROLYSIS is an electrochemical process. Electrochemistry is important for METALLURGY and the study of CORROSION. Passage of electricity through a GAS generally causes chemical changes, a subject that forms a separate branch of electrochemistry. See also oxidation-reduction.

electroconvulsive therapy See SHOCK THERAPY

electrocution Method of execution in which the condemned person is subjected to a heavy charge of electric current. The prisoner is shackled into a wired chair, and ELECTRODES are fastened to the head and one leg so that the current will flow through the body. One electrical shock may not be enough to kill the person; if a doctor does not confirm the death, several shocks may be applied. The electric chair was first used in 1890. Electrocution also refers to death by other causes of electrical shock (e.g., accidental contact with high-voltage wiring).

electrode Electric CONDUCTOR, usually metal, used as one of two terminals to conduct ELECTRIC CURRENT through a conducting medium. A simple voltaic cell, or BATTERY, consists of two electrodes, usually one zinc and one copper, immersed in an electrolytic solution (see ELECTROLYTE). When a chemical reaction occurs in the solution, ELECTRONS gather on the zinc electrode, or CATHODE, which becomes negatively charged. At the same time, electrons are drawn from the copper electrode, the ANODE, giving it a positive charge. The difference in charge sets up a potential difference, or voltage, between the two electrodes. When they are connected by a conducting wire, electrons flow from the cathode to the anode, producing a current.

electrodynamics, quantum See QUANTUM ELECTRODYNAMICS

electroencephalography \i-ˌlek-trō-in-ˌsef-ə-'läg-rə-fē\ Technique for recording electrical activity in the brain, whose cells emit distinct patterns of rhythmic electrical impulses. Pairs of ELECTRODES on the scalp transmit signals to an electroencephalograph, which records them as peaks and troughs on a tracing called an electroencephalogram (EEG). Different wave patterns on the EEG are associated with normal and abnormal waking and sleeping states. They help diagnose conditions such as tumors, infections, and epilepsy. The electroencephalograph was invented in the 1920s by Hans Berger (1873–1941).

electrolysis \i-ˌlek-'trä-lə-səs\ Process in which ELECTRIC CURRENT passed through a substance causes a chemical change, usually the gaining or losing of ELECTRONS (see OXIDATION-REDUCTION). It is carried out in an electrolytic cell consisting of separated positive and negative ELECTRODES immersed in an ELECTROLYTE SOLUTION containing IONS. Electric current enters through the CATHODE; positively charged CATIONS travel to it and combine with electrons. Negatively charged ANIONS give up electrons at the ANODE. Both thus become neutral molecules. Electrolysis is used extensively in METALLURGY to extract or purify METALS from ORES or compounds and to deposit them from solution (ELECTROPLATING). Electrolysis of molten SODIUM CHLORIDE yields metallic SODIUM and CHLORINE gas; that of dissolved sodium chloride yields sodium hydroxide and chlorine gas; that of WATER, HYDROGEN and OXYGEN.

electrolyte Substance that conducts ELECTRIC CURRENT as a result of DISSOCIATION of its molecules into positively and negatively charged particles called IONS. The most familiar electrolytes are ACIDS, BASES, and SALTS, which ionize when dissolved in SOLVENTS such as water or alcohol. Many salts, including SODIUM CHLORIDE, behave as electrolytes when melted in the absence of solvent, since they have IONIC BONDS. The most commonly used electrolytes are dissolved metal salts for ELECTROPLATING metals and acids in electric batteries.

electromagnet Device consisting of a core of magnetic material such as iron, surrounded by a coil through which an ELECTRIC CURRENT is passed to magnetize the core. When the current is stopped, the core is no longer magnetized. Electromagnets are particularly useful wherever controllable magnets are required, as in devices in which the MAGNETIC FIELD is to be varied, reversed, or switched on and off. Suitably designed magnets can lift many times their own weight and are used in steelworks and scrap yards to lift loads of metal. Other devices that utilize electromagnets include particle accelerators, telephone receivers, loudspeakers, and televisions.

electromagnetic field Property of space caused by the motion of an ELECTRIC CHARGE. A stationary charge produces an ELECTRIC FIELD in the surrounding space. If the charge is moving, a MAGNETIC FIELD is also produced. A changing magnetic field also produces an electric field. The interaction of electric and magnetic fields produces an electromagnetic field which has its own existence in space apart from the charges involved. An electromagnetic field can sometimes be described as a wave that transports electromagnetic ENERGY.

electromagnetic force One of the four known basic FORCES in the universe. Electromagnetism is responsible for interactions between charged particles that occur because of their charge, and for the emission and absorption of PHOTONS (ELECTROMAGNETIC RADIATION). The phenomena of ELECTRICITY and MAGNETISM are consequences of this force, and the relationships between them were first described by JAMES CLERK MAXWELL in the 1860s. The physical description of electromagnetism has since been combined with QUANTUM MECHANICS into the theory of QUANTUM ELECTRODYNAMICS. The electromagnetic force is about 10^{36} times as strong as the gravitational force (see GRAVITATION), but significantly weaker than both the WEAK FORCE and the STRONG FORCE.

electromagnetic induction Induction of an ELECTROMOTIVE FORCE in a CIRCUIT by varying the magnetic flux linked with the circuit. The phenomenon was first investigated in 1830–31 by JOSEPH HENRY and MICHAEL FARADAY, who discovered that when the MAGNETIC FIELD around an electromagnet was increased or decreased, an ELECTRIC CURRENT could be detected in a separate nearby CONDUCTOR. A current can also be induced by constantly moving a permanent magnet in and out of a coil of wire, or by constantly moving a conductor near a stationary permanent magnet. The induced electromotive force is proportional to the rate of change of the magnetic flux cutting across the circuit.

electromagnetic radiation Energy propagated through free space or through a material medium in the form of electromagnetic waves. Examples include RADIO WAVES, INFRARED RADIATION, visible LIGHT, ULTRAVIOLET RADIATION, X RAYS, and GAMMA RAYS. Electromagnetic radiation exhibits wavelike properties such as REFLECTION, REFRACTION, DIFFRACTION, and INTERFERENCE, but also exhibits particlelike properties in that its energy occurs in discrete packets, or quanta. Though all types of electromagnetic radiation travel at the same speed, they vary in FREQUENCY and WAVELENGTH, and interact with matter differently. A VACUUM is the only perfectly transparent medium; all others absorb some frequencies of electromagnetic radiation.

electromagnetic spectrum Total range of FREQUENCIES or WAVELENGTHS of ELECTROMAGNETIC RADIATION. The spectrum ranges from waves of long wavelength (low frequency) to those of short wavelength (high frequency); it comprises, in order of increasing frequency (or decreasing wavelength): long-wave RADIO WAVES, MICROWAVES, INFRARED RADIATION, visible LIGHT, ULTRAVIOLET RADIATION, X RAYS, and GAMMA RAYS. In a VACUUM, all waves of the electromagnetic spectrum travel at the same speed, 299,792,458 m/s (186,282 miles/second).

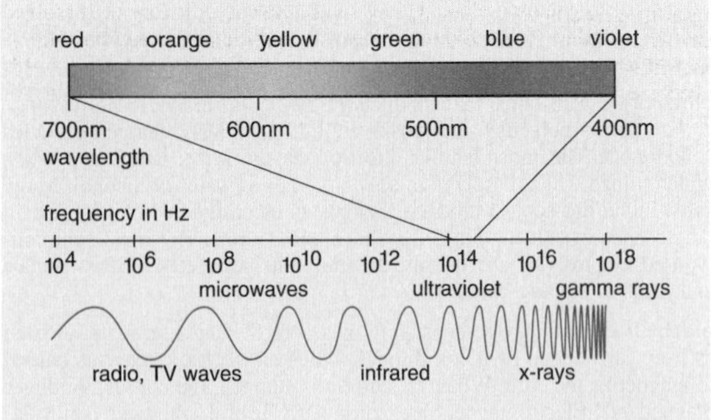

The spectrum of electromagnetic waves ranges from low-frequency radio waves to high-frequency gamma rays. Only a small portion of the spectrum, representing wavelengths of roughly 400–700 nanometers, is visible to the human eye.

electromagnetism Branch of physics that deals with the relationship between ELECTRICITY and MAGNETISM. Their merger into one concept is tied to three historical events. HANS C. ORSTED's accidental discovery in 1820 that MAGNETIC FIELDS are produced by ELECTRIC CURRENTS spurred efforts to prove that magnetic fields can induce currents. MICHAEL FARADAY showed in 1831 that a changing magnetic field can induce a current in a circuit, and JAMES CLERK MAXWELL predicted that a changing electric field has an associated magnetic field. The technological revolution attributed to the development of electric power and modern communications can be traced to these three landmarks.

electromotive force Energy per unit ELECTRIC CHARGE that is imparted by an energy source, such as an electric GENERATOR or a BATTERY. As the device does WORK on the electric charge being transferred within itself, energy is converted from one form to another. The work done on a unit of electric charge or the energy gained by the unit charge is the electromotive force *emf* (or *E*) and is characteristic of any energy source capable of driving electric charge around a circuit. A common unit of electromotive force is the volt *V*, a unit equal to the difference in electric potential between two points in a conductor carrying a current of one ampere and dissipating one watt of power between the two points.

electromyography \i-ˌlek-trō-mī-ˈäg-rə-fē\ Process of graphically recording the electrical activity of muscle, which normally generates an electric current only when contracting or when its nerve is stimulated. Electrical impulses are shown as wavelike tracings on an OSCILLOSCOPE and recorded as an electromyogram (EMG), usually along with audible signals. The EMG can show whether muscle weakness or wasting is due to nerve impairment (as in AMYOTROPHIC LATERAL SCLEROSIS and POLIOMYELITIS) or muscle impairment or disease (myopathy).

electron Lightest electrically charged SUBATOMIC PARTICLE known. It carries a negative charge (see ELECTRIC CHARGE), the basic charge of ELECTRICITY. An electron has a small mass, less than 0.1% the mass of an ATOM. Under normal circumstances, electrons move about the NUCLEUS of an atom in ORBITALS that form an electron cloud bound in varying strengths to the positively charged nucleus. Electrons closer to the nucleus are held more tightly. The first subatomic particle discovered, the electron was identified in 1897 by J. J. THOMSON.

electron microscopy \mī-ˈkräs-kə-pē\ Technique that allows examination of samples too small to be seen with a light MICROSCOPE. Electrons have much smaller wavelengths than visible light and hence higher resolving power. To be observable, samples must be made electron-dense by coating or staining with metals. Two different instruments are used. In the scanning electron microscope, a moving beam of ELECTRONS scanned across an object is focused by magnetic "lenses" to produce an image of the surface of the object similar to an image on a television screen. The photographs look three-dimensional; they may be of small organisms or their parts, of molecules such as DNA, or even of large individual atoms (e.g., uranium, thorium). In the transmission electron microscope, the electron beam passes through a very thin, carefully prepared sample and is focused onto a screen or photographic plate to visualize the interior structure of such samples as cells and tissues.

electron paramagnetic resonance See ELECTRON SPIN RESONANCE

electron spin resonance (ESR) *or* **electron paramagnetic resonance (EPR)** Technique of spectroscopic analysis (see SPECTROSCOPY) used to identify paramagnetic substances (see PARAMAGNETISM) and investigate the nature of the BONDING within molecules by identifying unpaired ELECTRONS and their interaction with their immediate surroundings. Unpaired electrons, because of their spin, behave like tiny MAGNETS and can be lined up in an applied magnetic field; energy applied by alternating MICROWAVE radiation is absorbed when its frequency coincides with that of PRECESSION of the electron magnets in the sample. The graph or spectrum of radiation absorbed as the field changes gives information valuable in chemistry, biology, and medicine.

electronic banking Use of computers and telecommunications to enable banking transactions to be done by telephone or computer rather than through human interaction. Its features include electronic funds transfer for retail purchases, automatic teller machines (ATMs), and automatic payroll deposits and bill payments. Some banks offer home banking, whereby a person with a personal computer can make transactions, either via a direct connection or by accessing a Web site. Electronic banking has vastly reduced the physical transfer of paper money and coinage from one place to another or even from one person to another.

electronic mail See E-MAIL

electronics Branch of physics that deals with the emission, behavior, and effects of ELECTRONS and with electronic devices. The beginnings of electronics can be traced to experiments with ELECTRICITY. In the 1880s THOMAS ALVA EDISON and others observed the flow of current between elements in an evacuated glass tube. A two-electrode VACUUM TUBE constructed by John A. Fleming (1849–1945) produced a useful output current. The AUDION, invented by LEE DE FOREST (1907), was followed by further improvements. The invention of the TRANSISTOR at Bell Labs (1947) initiated a progressive miniaturization of electronic components that by the mid-1980s resulted in high-density MICROPROCESSORS, which in turn led to tremendous advances in computer technology and computer-based automated systems. See also SEMICONDUCTOR, SUPERCONDUCTIVITY.

electrophile ATOM or MOLECULE that in a CHEMICAL REACTION seeks an atom or molecule containing an ELECTRON pair available for BONDING or the negative end of a polar molecule (see COVALENT BOND, ELECTRIC DIPOLE). In the Lewis electron theory (see ACID–BASE THEORY) advanced by Gilbert Lewis (1875–1946) in 1923, electrophiles are by definition Lewis acids. Examples include the hydronium ion (H_3O^+), boron trifluoride (BF_3), and the HALOGEN molecules (F_2, Cl_2, Br_2, and I_2). See also ACID, NUCLEOPHILE.

electrophoresis \i-ˌlek-trə-fə-ˈrē-səs\ Movement of electrically charged particles in a fluid under the influence of an ELECTRIC FIELD. The particles migrate toward the ELECTRODE of the opposite ELECTRIC CHARGE, often on a gel-coated slab or plate, sometimes in a fluid flowing down a paper. Originated about 1930 by Arne Tiselius (1902–1971) as a technique for ANALYSIS, electrophoresis is used to analyze and separate COLLOIDS (e.g., PROTEINS) or deposit coatings.

electroplating Process of coating with METAL by means of an ELECTRIC CURRENT. Plating metal may be transferred to conductive surfaces (e.g., metals) or to nonconductive surfaces (e.g., plastics, wood, leather) if a conductive coating has been applied. Usually the current deposits a given amount of metal on the CATHODE (workpiece) and the ANODE (source of metal) dissolves to the same extent, maintaining a fairly uniform solution. SILVER plating is used on tableware, electrical contacts, and engine bearings. The most extensive use of GOLD plating is on jewelry and watch cases. ZINC coatings prevent the corrosion of steel articles, and NICKEL and CHROMIUM plate are used on automobiles and household appliances. See also TERNEPLATE, SHEFFIELD PLATE.

electrostatic force *or* **Coulomb force** Force between two ELECTRIC CHARGES. The magnitude of the force F is proportional to the product of the two charges, q_1 and q_2, divided by the square of the distance between them, or

$$F = \frac{1}{4\pi\varepsilon_0}\frac{q_1 q_2}{r^2}$$

where ε_0 is the PERMITTIVITY of free space. The electrostatic force can be one of repulsion, such as the force between two objects having like charges, or it can be attractive, such as the force between two objects having opposite charges.

electrostatic induction Modification in the distribution of ELECTRIC CHARGE on one material under the influence of an electric charge on a nearby object. It occurs whenever any object is placed in an ELECTRIC FIELD. When a negatively charged object is brought near a neutral object, it induces a positive charge on the near side of the object and a negative charge on the far side. If the negative side of the original object is momentarily grounded, the negative charge may escape, so that the object becomes positively charged by induction.

electroweak theory Theory that describes both the ELECTROMAGNETIC FORCE and the WEAK FORCE. Though the forces appear to be different, they are actually different facets of a more fundamental force. This theory, formulated in the 1960s by Sheldon Glashow (born 1932), Steven Weinberg (born 1933), and Abdus Salam (born 1926), represents a 20th-century scientific landmark and won its authors a 1979 Nobel Prize. It was validated in the 1980s with the discovery of the W PARTICLE and Z PARTICLE, which it had predicted. See also FUNDAMENTAL INTERACTION, UNIFIED FIELD THEORY.

electrum Natural or artificial ALLOY of GOLD with at least 20% SILVER, used to make the first known coins in the Western world. Most natural electrum also contains copper, iron, palladium, bismuth, and perhaps other metals. The color varies from white-gold to brassy, depending on the percentages of the major constituents and copper. The first Western coinage, possibly begun by King Gyges of Lydia (7th century BC), consisted of irregular ingots of electrum bearing his stamp as a guarantee of negotiability at a predetermined value. See also COINAGE.

elegy \ˈe-lə-jē\ Meditative lyric poem. The classical elegy was any poem written in elegiac meter (alternating lines of dactylic hexameter and pentameter). Today the term may refer to this meter rather than to content, but in English literature since the 16th century it has meant a lament in any meter. A distinct variety with a formal pattern is the pastoral elegy, such as JOHN MILTON's "Lycidas" (1638). Poets of the 18th-century Graveyard School reflected on death and immortality in elegies, most famously THOMAS GRAY's *Elegy Written in a Country Church Yard* (1751).

element, chemical One of the 115 presently known kinds of substances that constitute all MATTER at and above the level of ATOMS, the smallest unit of any element. All atoms of an element are identical in nuclear charge (number of PROTONS) and number of ELECTRONS (see ATOMIC NUMBER), but their MASS (ATOMIC WEIGHT) may differ if they have different numbers of NEUTRONS (see ISOTOPE). Each element has a one- or two-letter CHEMICAL SYMBOL. Elements combine to form a wide variety of COMPOUNDS. All elements with atomic numbers greater than 83 (bismuth), and some isotopes of lighter elements, are unstable and radioactive (see RADIOACTIVITY). The TRANSURANIUM ELEMENTS, with atomic numbers greater than 92 (see URANIUM), artificially created by bombardment of other elements with neutrons or other heavy particles, have been discovered since 1940. The most common elements (by weight) in the earth's crust are oxygen, 49%; silicon, 26%; aluminum, 8%; and iron, 5%. Of the known elements, 11 (hydrogen, nitrogen, oxygen, fluorine, chlorine, and the six noble gases) are GASES, two (bromine and mercury) are LIQUIDS (two more, cesium and gallium, melt at about or just above room temperature), and the rest are SOLID under ordinary conditions. See also PERIODIC TABLE. See illustration and table on the following pages.

elementary education *or* **primary education** Traditionally, the first stage of formal education, beginning at age 5–7 and ending at age 11–13. Elementary education is often preceded by some form of PRESCHOOL. It usually includes middle school, or junior high school (ages 11–13), though this is sometimes regarded as part of SECONDARY EDUCATION. Nearly all nations are committed to some form of elementary education, though in many developing countries most children drop out of school before the fifth grade. The elementary curriculum usually emphasizes reading and writing, arithmetic, and basic social studies and science. A basic teaching strategy involves moving the student from the immediate and familiar to the distant and unfamiliar, an approach first formulated by JOHANN HEINRICH PESTALOZZI.

elementary particle See SUBATOMIC PARTICLE

elephant Any of three UNGULATE species in the order Proboscidea (family Elephantidae), characterized by their large size, long trunk, tusks, massive legs, large ears, and huge head. All species are grayish to brown, with sparse, coarse body hair. The trunk is used for breathing, drinking, and reaching for food. Elephants eat grasses, leaves, and fruit. The African savanna, or bush, elephant *(Loxodonta africana),* of sub-Saharan Africa, is the largest living land animal, weighing up to 16,500 lbs (7,500 kg) and standing 10–13 ft (3–4 m) tall at the shoulder. The African forest elephant (*L. cyclotis*) is smaller. The Indian elephant *(Elephas maximus),* of South and Southeast Asia, weighs about 12,000 lbs (5,500 kg) and stands about 10 ft (3 m) tall. Elephants live in habitats ranging from thick jungle to savanna, in small family groups led by old cows. Most bulls live in bachelor herds. Elephants migrate seasonally. They may eat more than 500 lbs (225 kg) of vegetation daily. All species are considered endangered.

Asian elephant (*Elephas maximus*).
E.S. ROSS

elephant bird See AEPYORNIS

PERIODIC TABLE OF THE ELEMENTS

☐ alkali metals ☐ other metals ☐ noble gases
☐ alkali earth metals ☐ other nonmetals ☐ lanthanides
☐ transition metals ☐ halogens ☐ actinides

IA	IIA	IIIB	IVB	VB	VIB	VIIB	VIII			IB	IIB	IIIA	IVA	VA	VIA	VIIA	Zero
1 H																	2 He
3 Li	4 Be											5 B	6 C	7 N	8 O	9 F	10 Ne
11 Na	12 Mg											13 Al	14 Si	15 P	16 S	17 Cl	18 Ar
19 K	20 Ca	21 Sc	22 Ti	23 V	24 Cr	25 Mn	26 Fe	27 Co	28 Ni	29 Cu	30 Zn	31 Ga	32 Ge	33 As	34 Se	35 Br	36 Kr
37 Rb	38 Sr	39 Y	40 Zr	41 Nb	42 Mo	43 Tc	44 Ru	45 Rh	46 Pd	47 Ag	48 Cd	49 In	50 Sn	51 Sb	52 Te	53 I	54 Xe
55 Cs	56 Ba	57 La	72 Hf	73 Ta	74 W	75 Re	76 Os	77 Ir	78 Pt	79 Au	80 Hg	81 Tl	82 Pb	83 Bi	84 Po	85 At	86 Rn
87 Fr	88 Ra	89 Ac	104 Rf	105 Db	106 Sg	107 Bh	108 Hs	109 Mt	110	111	112		114		116		118

Lanthanide Series	58 Ce	59 Pr	60 Nd	61 Pm	62 Sm	63 Eu	64 Gd	65 Tb	66 Dy	67 Ho	68 Er	69 Tm	70 Yb	71 Lu
Actinide Series	90 Th	91 Pa	92 U	93 Np	94 Pu	95 Am	96 Cm	97 Bk	98 Cf	99 Es	100 Fm	101 Md	102 No	103 Lr

The periodic table arranges the elements into groups (vertically) of elements sharing common physical and chemical characteristics, and into periods (horizontally) of sequentially increasing atomic number and electron-shell configuration. The elements are listed on the following page by their full names. Elements 110, 111, 112, 114, 116, and 118 have been created experimentally but have not yet been named.

Elephant Man *orig.* **Joseph (Carey) Merrick** (1862–1890) Englishman disfigured by a disease that caused overgrowths over his skin and bone surfaces. His head was 3 ft (.9 m) around, with large bags of skin hanging from it, the jaw so deformed he could not speak clearly. One arm ended in a 12-in. (.3-m) wrist and a finlike hand. His legs were similarly deformed, and a defective hip made him lame. He escaped from a workhouse at 21 to join a freak show, where a London physician, Frederick Treves, discovered him and admitted him to London Hospital. He died in his sleep at 27 of accidental suffocation. His disease was probably the very rare Proteus syndrome. A successful play and film were based on Merrick's life.

elephant seal Either of the two largest PINNIPED species: the northern elephant seal *(Mirounga angustirostris),* of coastal islands off California and Baja California, or the southern elephant seal *(M. leonina),* of sub-Antarctic regions. Both are gregarious earless SEALS. The male has an inflatable, trunklike snout. The northern species is yellowish or gray-brown, the southern species blue-gray. Males of both species reach a length of about 21 ft (6.5 m) and a weight of about 7,780 lbs (3,530 kg) and are much larger than the females. Elephant seals feed on fish and squid or other CEPHALOPODS. During the breeding season, bulls fight to establish territories along beaches and to acquire harems of up to 40 cows.

Elephant seal bull (*Mirounga*).
ANTHONY MERCIECA—ROOT RESOURCES

Eleusinian Mysteries \ˌel-yu̇-ˈsi-nē-ən\ Most famous MYSTERY RELIGION of ancient Greece. It was based on the story of DEMETER, whose daughter PERSEPHONE was kidnapped by HADES. While searching for her daughter, Demeter stopped at ELEUSIS, revealed her identity to the royal family, and taught the natives her rites. The Greater Mysteries were celebrated in autumn, beginning with a procession from Athens to the temple at Eleusis. This was followed by a ritual bath in the sea, three days of fasting, and completion of secret rites. Initiates were promised personal salvation and benefits in the afterlife.

Eleusis \i-ˈlü-səs\ *Greek* **Elevsís** \ˌe-lef-ˈsēs\ Town, with ruins of an ancient city, eastern Greece. Famous as the site of the ELEUSINIAN MYSTERIES, it is about 14 mi (23 km) west of Athens. It was independent until the 7th century BC, when Athens annexed the city and made the Eleusinian Mysteries a major Athenian religious festival. The Gothic leader ALARIC destroyed Eleusis in AD 395. Deserted until the 18th century, it was revived as the modern town of Eleusis (Greek Lepsina), now a suburb of Athens. Some of the ruins have been excavated, including the Hall of Initiation, which dates back some 3,000 years to late Mycenaean times.

elevator Car that moves in a vertical shaft to carry passengers or freight between the levels of a multistory building. The use of mechanical lifting platforms dates to Roman times. Steam and hydraulic elevators came into use in the 19th century; electric elevators had been introduced by the end of the century. Most modern elevators are electrically propelled through a system of cables and pulleys with the aid of a counterweight, though hydraulic elevators are still used in low buildings. The introduction of an automatic safety device by Elisha Otis (1811–1861) in 1853 made the passenger elevator possible. By opening the way to higher buildings, the elevator played a decisive role in creating the characteristic urban geography of modern cities.

Elgar, Edward (William) *later* **Sir Edward** (1857–1934) British composer. Son of a piano tuner, he became proficient on violin and organ. His early works succeeded in getting performed, and his reputation grew steadily. His *Enigma Variations* (1899) brought him fame, and for

Element	Symbol	Atomic no.	Atomic weight*	Element	Symbol	Atomic no.	Atomic weight*
Actinium	Ac	89	227.028	Meitnerium	Mt	109	(268)
Aluminum	Al	13	26.9815	Mercury	Hg	80	200.59
Americium	Am	95	(243)	Molybdenum	Mo	42	95.94
Antimony	Sb	51	121.75	Neodymium	Nd	60	144.24
Argon	Ar	18	39.948	Neon	Ne	10	20.180
Arsenic	As	33	74.9216	Neptunium	Np	93	237.0482
Astatine	At	85	(210)	Nickel	Ni	28	58.69
Barium	Ba	56	137.33	Niobium	Nb	41	92.9064
Berkelium	Bk	97	(247)	Nitrogen	N	7	14.0067
Beryllium	Be	4	9.01218	Nobelium	No	102	(259)
Bismuth	Bi	83	208.9804	Osmium	Os	76	190.2
Bohrium	Bh	107	(264)	Oxygen	O	8	15.9994
Boron	B	5	10.81	Palladium	Pd	46	106.42
Bromine	Br	35	79.904	Phosphorus	P	15	30.97376
Cadmium	Cd	48	112.41	Platinum	Pt	78	195.08
Calcium	Ca	20	40.08	Plutonium	Pu	94	(244)
Californium	Cf	98	(251)	Polonium	Po	84	(209)
Carbon	C	6	12.011	Potassium	K	19	39.0983
Cerium	Ce	58	140.12	Praseodymium	Pr	59	140.9077
Cesium	Cs	55	132.9054	Promethium	Pm	61	(145)
Chlorine	Cl	17	35.453	Protactinium	Pa	91	231.0359
Chromium	Cr	24	51.996	Radium	Ra	88	226.0254
Cobalt	Co	27	58.9332	Radon	Rn	86	(222)
Copper	Cu	29	63.546	Rhenium	Re	75	186.207
Curium	Cm	96	(247)	Rhodium	Rh	45	102.9055
Dubnium	Db	105	(262)	Rubidium	Rb	37	85.4678
Dysprosium	Dy	66	162.50	Ruthenium	Ru	44	101.07
Einsteinium	Es	99	(252)	Rutherfordium	Rf	104	(261)
Erbium	Er	68	167.26	Samarium	Sm	62	150.36
Europium	Eu	63	151.96	Scandium	Sc	21	44.9559
Fermium	Fm	100	(257)	Seaborgium	Sg	106	(263)
Fluorine	F	9	18.9984	Selenium	Se	34	78.96
Francium	Fr	87	(223)	Silicon	Si	14	28.0855
Gadolinium	Gd	64	157.25	Silver	Ag	47	107.868
Gallium	Ga	31	69.72	Sodium	Na	11	22.98977
Germanium	Ge	32	72.61	Strontium	Sr	38	87.62
Gold	Au	79	196.9665	Sulfur	S	16	32.07
Hafnium	Hf	72	178.49	Tantalum	Ta	73	180.9479
Hassium	Hs	108	(265)	Technetium	Tc	43	(98)
Helium	He	2	4.00260	Tellurium	Te	52	127.60
Holmium	Ho	67	164.930	Terbium	Tb	65	158.9254
Hydrogen	H	1	1.0079	Thallium	Tl	81	204.383
Indium	In	49	114.82	Thorium	Th	90	232.0381
Iodine	I	53	126.9045	Thulium	Tm	69	168.9342
Iridium	Ir	77	192.22	Tin	Sn	50	118.71
Iron	Fe	26	55.845	Titanium	Ti	22	47.867
Krypton	Kr	36	83.80	Tungsten (wolfram)	W	74	183.85
Lanthanum	La	57	138.9055	Ununnilium	Uun	110	. . .
Lawrencium	Lr	103	(262)	Uranium	U	92	238.029
Lead	Pb	82	207.2	Vanadium	V	23	50.9415
Lithium	Li	3	6.941	Xenon	Xe	54	131.29
Lutetium	Lu	71	174.967	Ytterbium	Yb	70	173.04
Magnesium	Mg	12	24.305	Yttrium	Y	39	88.9059
Manganese	Mn	25	54.9380	Zinc	Zn	30	65.39
Mendelevium	Md	101	(258)	Zirconium	Zr	40	91.224

*Parentheses indicate the mass number of the most stable isotope of a radioactive element.

the rest of his life he was a great national figure, regarded as having inaugurated the "English musical renaissance," a revival of British composition after the long lackluster era since G.F. HANDEL's death. His principal works include the five *Pomp and Circumstance Marches* (1901–7), two symphonies (1908, 1911), concertos for violin (1910) and cello (1919), the oratorio *The Dream of Gerontius* (1900), and the tone poems *Cockaigne* (1901), and *Falstaff* (1913).

Elgin \'el-gən\, **Earl of** *orig.* **James Bruce** (1811–1863) British governor-general of Canada. He was appointed governor of Jamaica in 1842, then served as governor of British North America (1847–54) and implemented the policy of responsible, or cabinet, government recommended by Lord DURHAM. Elgin supported the Rebellion Losses Act (1849), which compensated Canadians for losses during the 1837 rebellion in Lower Canada, a stand criticized by Tory opponents in England and French-Canadian rioters in Montreal. He negotiated the Reciprocity Treaty (1854) between the Canadian colonies and the U.S. In 1857 he left Canada to serve in diplomatic posts in China, Japan, and India.

Elgin Marbles \'el-gən\ Collection of ancient Greek marble sculptures and architectural fragments in the BRITISH MUSEUM. They were removed from the PARTHENON in Athens and other buildings by Thomas Bruce, Lord Elgin (1766–1841), ambassador to the Ottoman Empire, and shipped to England between 1802 and 1811. Elgin claimed he was saving the works from destruction by the Turks, who then controlled Greece. He secured permission from the Turks to remove "any pieces of stone" bearing figures or inscriptions. They remained in his private possession, amid mounting criticism, until 1816, when the crown bought them. The controversy still continues; the Greek government frequently demands their return.

Lapith fighting a Centaur; detail of a metope from the Parthenon at Athens; one of the Elgin Marbles in the British Museum.

HIRMER FOTOARCHIV, MUNCHEN

Elgon \'el-ˌgän\, **Mount** Extinct volcano on the Kenya–Uganda border. Located northeast of Lake VICTORIA, its crater, about 5 mi (8 km) in diameter, contains several peaks, of which Wagagai, at 14,178 ft (4,321 m), is the highest. The Bantu-speaking Gishu (Gisu) occupy the mountain's western slopes.

Eliade \ˌel-ē-'ä-dā\, **Mircea** (1907–1986) Romanian-U.S. historian of religion. He studied Sanskrit and Indian philosophy at the University of Calcutta, then returned to complete his PhD at the University of Bucharest, where he taught until 1939. In 1945 he moved to Paris to teach at the Sorbonne, and from 1956 he taught at the University of Chicago. Eliade considered religious experiences to be credible phenomena, manifestations of the sacred in the world, and his work traced the forms they have taken throughout the world and through time. He founded the journal *History of Religions* in 1961. His books include *The Myth of the Eternal Return* (1949) and *A History of Religious Ideas* (3 vols., 1978–85); he edited the 16-volume *Encyclopedia of Religion.*

Elijah \i-'lī-jə\ *or* **Elias** *Hebrew* **Eliyyahu** (9th century BC) Hebrew PROPHET. The Bible related that he denounced foreign cults and defeated 450 prophets of BAAL in a contest on Mount Carmel. In doing so, he earned the enmity of King AHAB and his consort, JEZEBEL, who forced him to flee into the wilderness. Later he was taken up into heaven in a whirlwind, leaving behind his successor, ELISHA. His insistence that only the God of Israel is entitled to the name of divinity expresses a fully conscious monotheism. He is also recognized as a prophet in Islam.

Elijah ben Solomon (1720–1797) Lithuanian scholar and Jewish leader. Born into a long line of scholars, he traveled in Poland and Germany before settling in Vilna, Lithuania, the cultural center of eastern European Jewry. He refused rabbinic office and lived as a recluse while devoting himself to study and prayer, but nevertheless became famous and revered in the Jewish community. His scholarly interests included biblical exegesis, Talmudic studies, folk medicine, grammar, and philosophy. A vehement opponent of HASIDISM, he denounced its claims to miracles, visions, and spiritual ecstasy, calling instead for the intellectual love of God.

Elion \'e-lē-ən\, **Gertrude (Belle)** (1918–1999) U.S. pharmacologist. Born in New York City, she graduated from Hunter College. Unable to find a research position because of her sex, she initially taught high-school chemistry. In 1944 she became GEORGE H. HITCHINGS's assistant at Burroughs Wellcome. They developed drugs for leukemia, autoimmune disorders, urinary-tract infections, gout, malaria, and viral herpes using innovative research methods. They examined the biochemistry of normal human cells and of disease-causing agents and used the results to formulate drugs that could kill or inhibit reproduction of a particular pathogen but leave normal host cells unharmed. In 1988 they shared a Nobel Prize with JAMES BLACK.

Eliot, Charles William (1834–1926) U.S. educator. Born in Boston, he studied at HARVARD UNIV. and taught mathematics and chemistry there (1858–63) and at MIT (1865–69). He was named president of Harvard in 1869 after studying European educational systems, and set about a program of fundamental reforms. He demanded a place for the sciences in liberal education, and he replaced the program of required courses for undergraduates with the elective system. Under Eliot, the graduate school of arts and sciences was created (1890), Radcliffe College was established (1894), the quality of the professional schools was raised, and the university became an institution of world renown. His reforms had widespread influence in American higher education. After resigning in 1909, he edited the 50-volume *Harvard Classics* (1909–10), wrote several books, and devoted himself to public service.

Eliot, George *orig.* **Mary Ann Evans** *later* **Marian Evans** (1819–1880) British novelist. Born in Warwickshire, she was raised with a strong evangelical piety, but broke with religious orthodoxy in her twenties. She worked as a translator, a critic, and a subeditor of the *Westminster Review* (1851–54). Later she turned to fiction. Adopting a masculine pseudonym to evade prejudice against women, she first brought out *Scenes of Clerical Life* (1858). This was followed by such classic works as *Adam Bede* (1859), *The Mill on the Floss* (1860), *Silas Marner* (1861), *Romola* (1862–63), *Felix Holt, the Radical* (1866), and *Daniel Deronda* (1876). Her masterpiece, *Middlemarch* (1871–72), provides a thorough study of every class of provincial society. The method of psychological analysis she developed would become characteristic of modern fiction. With the journalist, philosopher, and critic George Henry Lewes (1817–1878), a married man, she enjoyed a long and happy, though scandalous, liaison; their Sunday-afternoon salons were a brilliant feature of Victorian life.

George Eliot, chalk drawing by F.W. Burton, 1865; in the National Portrait Gallery, London.

BY COURTESY OF THE NATIONAL PORTRAIT GALLERY, LONDON

Eliot, John (1604–1690) English Puritan missionary to the Indians of Massachusetts Bay Colony. He emigrated to Boston in 1631 and became pastor of a church in nearby Roxbury. Supported by his congregation and fellow ministers, he began a mission to the Indians that inspired the creation in 1649 of the first genuine missionary society (financed chiefly from England). His methods set the pattern of subsequent Indian missions for almost two centuries. His translation of the Bible into the Algonquian language was the first Bible printed in North America.

Eliot, T(homas) S(tearns) (1888–1965) U.S.-British poet, playwright, and critic. Born in St. Louis, he studied at Harvard University before moving to England in 1914, where he would work as an editor from the early 1920s until his death. His first important poem, and the first modernist masterpiece in English, was the radically experimental "Love Song of J. Alfred Prufrock" (1915). *The Waste Land* (1922), which expresses with startling power the disillusionment of the postwar years, made his international reputation. His first critical volume, *The Sacred Wood* (1920), introduced concepts much discussed in later critical theory. He married in 1915; his wife was mentally unstable, and they separated in 1933. (He married again, happily, in 1957.) His conversion to Anglicanism in 1927 shaped all his subsequent works. His last great work was *Four Quartets* (1936–42), four poems on spiritual renewal and the connections of the personal and historical past and present. Influential later essays include *The Idea of a Christian Society* (1939) and *Notes Towards the Definition of Culture* (1948). His play *Murder in the Cathedral* (1935) is a verse treatment of Thomas BECKET's martyrdom; his other plays, including *The Cocktail Party* (1950), are lesser works. From the 1920s on he was the most influential English-language modernist poet. He won the Nobel Prize in 1948; from then until his death he achieved public adulation unequaled by any other 20th-century poet.

Elis \'ē-lis\ *modern* **Iliá** \ēl-'yä\ Ancient Greek region and city-state, northwestern PELOPONNESE, Greece. Bounded by Achaea, ARCADIA, Messenia, and the Ionian Sea, the region was known for its horse breeding and was the site of the OLYMPIC GAMES. As an ally of Athens in the PELOPONNESIAN WAR, Elis lost much of its territory. Later by emphasizing the sanctity of the Olympic Games, it regained some land and even some independence after the Roman occupation of Greece (146 BC), only to disintegrate with the collapse of the Roman empire. The modern-day locality contains the archaeological site of OLYMPIA, scene of the games.

Elisabethville See LUBUMBASHI

Elisha \i-'lī-shə\ (9th century BC) Hebrew prophet. As the successor of ELIJAH, he was strongly devoted to the Mosaic tradition of Israel and a potent enemy of all foreign gods and cults. He instigated a revolt against the ruling house of Israel, the dynasty of Omri, that resulted in the death of the king and his family. Elisha's story is told in the Old Testament books of I Kings and II Kings.

Elisha ben Abuyah (fl. 1st century AD) Jewish scholar and apostate. Born before the destruction of the Second Temple of Jerusalem (AD 70), he became a respected rabbi, then won notoriety for breaking Jewish laws and abandoning Judaism. He was well versed in Greek thought, and the motives for his apostasy may have been devotion to philosophy, membership in a Gnostic sect, or conversion to Christianity. He was denounced in the Talmud and was known as "Aher" ("the Other") because his apostasy made his name repugnant.

Elista \e-'lyē-stə, *Engl* ē-'lis-tə\ *formerly (1944–57)* **Stepnoy** \styip-'nȯi\ City (pop., 1999 est.: 101,700), capital of Kalmykia republic, southwestern Russia. It was founded in 1865 and became a city in 1930. In 1944, when the Kalmyks were exiled by JOSEPH STALIN for their alleged collaboration with the Germans, the republic was dissolved and the city became known as Stepnoy. The name Elista was restored in 1957. Agriculture employs the most workers.

Elizabeth (1837–1898) Empress consort of Austria (1854–98) and queen of Hungary (1867–98). Regarded as the most beautiful princess in Europe, she married her cousin, Emperor FRANCIS JOSEPH, in 1854. She was popular with her subjects but offended Viennese high society by her impatience with rigid court etiquette. The Hungarians admired her, especially for her efforts in bringing about the COMPROMISE OF 1867. During a visit to Switzerland she was assassinated by an Italian anarchist.

Elizabeth *or* **Elizabeth Stuart** (1596–1662) Titular queen of Bohemia from 1619. Daughter of the Scottish king James VI (later JAMES I of England), she came to English royal court in 1606. Noted for her beauty and charm, she became a favorite subject of the poets. In 1613 she was married to Frederick V, the Elector Palatine, who became king of Bohemia (as Frederick I) in 1619. After his defeat by the CATHOLIC LEAGUE in 1620, the couple went into exile, where she spent the next 40 years. In 1661 her nephew CHARLES II grudgingly allowed her to return to England. Her most famous son was Prince RUPERT.

Elizabeth *Russian* **Yelizaveta Petrovna** (1709–1761) Empress of Russia (1741–61). Daughter of PETER I and CATHERINE I, she was proclaimed empress after staging a coup d'état and arresting IVAN VI, his mother, and their chief advisers. She encouraged the development of education and art and left control of most state affairs to her advisers and favorites. Her reign was characterized by court intrigues, a deteriorating financial situation, and the gentry's acquisition of privileges at the expense of the peasantry. However, Russia's prestige as a major European power grew. Russia adhered to a pro-Austrian, anti-Prussian foreign policy, annexed a portion of southern Finland after fighting a war with Sweden, improved its relations with Britain, and fought Prussia in the SEVEN YEARS' WAR. Elizabeth was succeeded by her nephew PETER III.

Elizabeth City (pop., 2000: 120,568), northeastern New Jersey. Located on Newark Bay adjacent to NEWARK, it is connected by bridge to STATEN ISLAND. Settlement began in 1664 with the purchase of land from the DELAWARE Indians. The first colonial assembly met there (1668–82). It was the scene of four military engagements during the AMERICAN REVOLUTION. It grew throughout the 19th century, and is now highly industrialized, with important shipping operations. It was the original seat of PRINCETON UNIV. (1746) and home to ALEXANDER HAMILTON and AARON BURR.

Elizabeth I (1533–1603) Queen of England (1558–1603). Daughter of HENRY VIII and his second wife, ANNE BOLEYN, she displayed precocious seriousness as a child and received the rigorous education normally reserved for male heirs. Her situation was precarious during the reigns of her half brother EDWARD VI and her half sister MARY I. After Sir Thomas Wyatt's rebellion in 1554, she was imprisoned but later released. Her accession to the throne on Mary's death was greeted with public jubilation. She assembled a core of experienced advisers, including WILLIAM CECIL and FRANCIS WALSINGHAM, but she zealously retained her power to make final decisions. Important events of her reign included the restoration of England to Protestantism; the execution of MARY, QUEEN OF SCOTS; and England's defeat of the Spanish ARMADA. She lived under constant threat of conspiracies by British Catholics. Over time she became known as the Virgin Queen, wedded to her kingdom. Many important suitors came forward, and she showed signs of romantic attachment to the earl of LEICESTER, but she remained single, perhaps because she was unwilling to compromise her power. She had another suitor, the 2nd earl of ESSEX, executed in 1601 for treason. Though her later years saw an economic decline and disastrous military efforts to subdue the Irish, her reign had already seen England's emergence as a world power and her presence had helped unify the nation against foreign enemies. Highly intelligent and strong-willed, Elizabeth inspired ardent expressions of loyalty, and her reign saw a brilliant flourishing in the arts, especially literature and music. After her death, she was succeeded by JAMES I.

Elizabeth II *orig.* **Elizabeth Alexandra Mary** (born 1926) Queen of the United Kingdom from 1952. She became heir presumptive when her uncle, EDWARD VIII, abdicated and her father became king as GEORGE VI. In 1947 she married her distant cousin PHILIP, DUKE OF EDINBURGH, with whom she had four children, including CHARLES, PRINCE OF WALES. She became queen on her father's death in 1952. She made numerous visits to Commonwealth countries and paid state visits to other countries worldwide. Increasingly aware of the modern role of the monarchy, she favored simplicity in court life and took an informed interest in government business. In the 1990s the monarchy was troubled by the highly publicized marital difficulties of two of the queen's sons and criticized for what some deemed an inadequate response to the death of DIANA, PRINCESS OF WALES. In 2002 the queen's mother and sister died within two months of each other.

Elizabeth II, 1985.
KARSH—CAMERA PRESS/GLOBE PHOTOS

Elizabeth Farnese \fär-'nā-zā\ *Spanish* **Isabella Farnese** (1692–1766) Queen consort of PHILIP V of Spain. A member of the ducal FARNESE FAMILY of Parma, she became Philip's second wife in 1714 and quickly established ascendancy over her weak husband. Because his two sons by his first wife were in line to succeed him, she sought to secure Italian possessions for her own children, including CHARLES III. This quest embroiled Spain in wars and intrigues for three decades. However, she chose able and devoted ministers, who introduced beneficial internal reforms and improved Spain's economy. After Philip's death in 1746, she ceased to exert any real influence.

Elizabeth Islands Chain of small islands, southeastern Massachusetts. Extending southwest for 16 mi (26 km) from the southwestern tip of CAPE COD, the group lies between BUZZARDS BAY and Vineyard Sound. The islands were visited in 1602 by the English navigator Bartholomew Gosnold, who established a short-lived (three-week) colony on the westernmost island of Cuttyhunk 18 years before the arrival of the *Mayflower* at PLYMOUTH. Naushon, the largest island, was a British naval base during the WAR OF 1812. The islands, covering an area of about 14 sq mi (36 sq km), are mostly privately owned.

Elizabeth of Hungary, St. (1207–1231) Princess of Hungary, canonized for her devotion to the poor. She married Louis IV of Thuringia, who died of plague in 1227 en route to the Sixth CRUSADE. She then devoted her life to the poor and sick, for whom she built a hospice. According to legend, she met her husband unexpectedly on one of her charitable errands, and the loaves of bread she was carrying miraculously changed into roses.

Elizabethan literature \i-ˌli-zə-'bē-thən\ Body of works written during the reign of ELIZABETH I (1558–1603). Probably the most splendid age in the history of English literature, it saw a flowering of poetry, was a golden age of drama, and inspired a wide variety of splendid prose. It encompasses the work of SIR PHILIP SIDNEY, EDMUND SPENSER, CHRISTOPHER MARLOWE, WILLIAM SHAKESPEARE, and others. Though some patterns and themes persisted, the tone of most forms of literary expression, especially drama, darkened rather suddenly around the start of the 17th century. See also JACOBEAN LITERATURE.

elk Any of several species of large DEER in the genus *Cervus*, notably the RED DEER of Europe, the Kashmir stag, and the Himalayan shou, as well as the North American deer more correctly called WAPITI. The creature called elk in Europe is a member of the species *(Alces alces)* known in North America as MOOSE. The name is also applied to the extinct IRISH ELK.

Elkin, Stanley (Lawrence) (1930–1995) U.S. writer. Born in New York City, he grew up in Chicago; from 1960 he taught writing at Washington University. His works explore contemporary life with tragicomic wit and imaginative insight. *Criers and Kibitzers, Kibitzers and Criers* (1966) was an acclaimed collection of short stories on Jewish themes. The novel *The Franchiser* (1976) tells of Ben Flesh, who, like Elkin, suffered from multiple sclerosis, which is for Flesh both an enlightenment and a burden. *The Living End* (1979) consists of three interwoven novellas.

Ellesmere, Lake Coastal lake, eastern SOUTH ISLAND, New Zealand. Located on the southern side of BANKS PENINSULA, the tidal lake, shallow and brackish, is 14 mi (23 km) long by 8 mi (13 km) wide and is no deeper than 7 ft (2 m). The lake is host to great flocks of waterfowl.

Ellesmere Island \'elz-ˌmēr\ Island, Nunavut, Canada. The largest of the QUEEN ELIZABETH ISLANDS and lying off the northwestern coast of GREENLAND, it is believed to have been visited by Vikings in the 10th century AD. It is roughly 300 mi (500 km) wide by 500 mi (800 km) long, the most rugged in the ARCTIC ARCHIPELAGO, with towering mountains and vast ice fields. Cape Columbia is the most northerly point of Canada. Ellesmere Island National Park Reserve was established in 1986.

Ellice Islands See GILBERT AND ELLICE ISLANDS, TUVALU

Ellington, Duke *orig.* **Edward Kennedy** (1899–1974) U.S. pianist, bandleader, arranger, and composer, and a dominant figure in American music. Ellington formed his band in 1924 in his native Washington, D.C.; by 1927 it was performing regularly at the Cotton Club in Harlem. Until the end of his life Ellington's band would enjoy the highest professional and artistic reputation in jazz. First known for his distinctive "jungle" sound derived from the use of growling muted brass and sinister harmonies, Ellington's integration of blues elements became an enduring part of his music. He composed with the idiosyncratic sounds of his instrumentalists in mind. Many of his players spent most of their careers with the band, including saxophonists JOHNNY HODGES and Harry Carney, bassist JIMMY BLANTON, trombonists Tricky Sam Nanton and Lawrence Brown, and trumpeters Bubber Miley and Cootie Williams. BILLY STRAYHORN was Ellington's musical alter ego and frequent collaborator. Ellington composed a massive body of work, including music for dancing, popular songs, large-scale concert works, musical theater, and film scores. His best-known compositions include "Mood Indigo," "Satin Doll," "Don't Get Around Much Anymore," and "Sophisticated Lady."

Duke Ellington.

REPRINTED WITH PERMISSION OF DOWN BEAT MAGAZINE

ellipse Closed curve, one of the CONIC SECTIONS of ANALYTIC GEOMETRY, consisting of all points whose distances from each of two fixed points (foci) add up to the same value. The midpoint between the foci is the center. One property of an ellipse is that the reflection off its boundary of a line from one focus will pass through the other. In an elliptical room, a person whispering at one focus is easily heard by someone at the other. An oval may or may not fit the definition of an ellipse.

elliptic geometry NON-EUCLIDEAN GEOMETRY that rejects EUCLID's fifth postulate (the PARALLEL POSTULATE) and modifies his second postulate. It is also known as Riemannian geometry, after BERNHARD RIEMANN. It asserts that no line passing through a point not on a given line is parallel to that line. It also states that while any straight line of finite length can be extended indefinitely, all straight lines are the same length. Though many of elliptic geometry's theorems are identical to those of EUCLIDEAN GEOMETRY, others differ (e.g., the angles in a triangle add up to more than 180°). It can most easily be pictured as geometry done on the surface of a SPHERE where all lines are great circles.

Ellis, (Henry) Havelock (1859–1939) British sexuality researcher. A medical doctor, he gave up his practice to devote himself to scientific and literary work. His major work, the seven-volume *Studies in the Psychology of Sex* (1897–1928), was a comprehensive, groundbreaking encyclopedia of human sexual biology, behavior, and attitudes whose topics included homosexuality, masturbation, and the physiology of sexual behavior. Sale of the first volume led to a trial when the salesman was arrested on obscenity charges; the later volumes had to be published in the U.S. and were legally available only to the medical profession until 1935. Ellis viewed sexual activity as a natural expression of love and sought to dispel the widespread fear and ignorance surrounding it. He was also known as a champion of women's rights.

Havelock Ellis.

THE MANSELL COLLECTION

Ellis Island Island, Upper New York Bay, southeastern New York. It lies southwest of MANHATTAN island and has an area of about 27 acres (11 hectares). In 1808 the state of New York sold the island to the federal government. It served as the nation's major immigration station 1892–1954, when immigrant processing was moved to NEW YORK CITY proper. It became part of the STATUE OF LIBERTY NATIONAL MONUMENT in 1965; its restored main hall is the site of the Ellis Island Immigration Museum.

Ellison, Ralph (Waldo) (1914–1994) U.S. writer. Born in Oklahoma City, he studied music at Tuskegee Institute before joining the Federal Writers' Project. He won eminence for his novel *Invisible Man* (1952); narrated by a nameless young black man, it reflects bitterly on American race relations. It is regarded as among the most distinguished works of American fiction since World War II. He later published two essay collections, *Shadow and Act* (1964) and *Going to the Territory* (1986) and lectured and taught widely. An edition of his unfinished second novel was published by his literary executor, John Callahan, with the title *Juneteenth* in 1999.

Ellsworth, Oliver (1745–1807) U.S. politician, diplomat, and jurist. Born in Windsor, Conn., he served in the CONTINENTAL CONGRESS (1777–83) and coauthored the Connecticut Compromise (1787), which resolved the issue of representation in Congress. In 1789 he became one of Connecticut's first U.S. senators. He was the chief author of the Judiciary Act (1789), which established the federal court system. He was appointed chief justice of the U.S. Supreme Court in 1796; ill health forced his resignation in 1800.

elm Any of about 18 species of forest and ornamental shade trees that make up the genus *Ulmus* (family Ulmaceae), native mostly to northern temperate areas. Many are grown for their height and attractive foliage. The leaves are doubly toothed and often lopsided at the base. The flowers, which lack petals, appear before the leaves and are borne in clusters. Seeds are borne in a samara (dry, winged fruit). The American elm *(U. americana)* has dark gray, ridged bark and elliptical leaves. Many species are susceptible to DUTCH ELM DISEASE. Elm wood is important for boats and farm buildings because it is durable in water; it is also used for furniture. See also SLIPPERY ELM.

Leaves and fruit of American elm (*Ulmus americana*).

KITTY KAHOUT FROM ROOT RESOURCES

Elman, Mischa *orig.* **Mikhail Saulovitch** (1891–1967) Russian-U.S. violinist. He studied with Leopold Auer (1845–1930) in St. Petersburg from age 10 and made his professional debut in Berlin at 13. Tours of Germany and England followed, and he first played in the U.S. in 1908. With J. HEIFETZ and Efrem Zimbalist (1889–1985), he established the "Russian school" of violin playing. Admired for his full tone and passionate style, he had many pieces written for him by eminent composers.

Elsheimer \'els-ˌhī-mər\, **Adam** (1578–1610) German painter and printmaker. After study in Frankfurt, he went to Rome in 1600 and began producing images of Italian classical subjects, nocturnal scenes, and landscapes. He painted on small copper plates and executed drawings and etchings. He frequently depicted illumination by firelight, candlelight, and moonlight. His *Flight into Egypt* (1609) was the first painting to depict the constellations accurately. An important figure in the development of 17th-century landscape painting, he greatly influenced Dutch, Italian, and French artists. He died at 32.

Elssler, Fanny (1810–1884) Austrian ballerina who introduced character dance into ballet. She studied in Vienna and toured in Europe before making her Paris Opera debut in 1834. Her warm, spirited style, contrasting with the cool academic style of the then-reigning MARIE TAGLIONI, made her an immediate success. During 1840–42 Elssler toured the U.S., earning adulation and large sums of money. She returned to Europe to tour until her retirement to Vienna in 1851.

Éluard \ā-lü̅-'är\, **Paul** *orig.* **Eugène Grindel** (1895–1952) French poet. In 1919 he met ANDRE BRETON, Philippe Soupault, and LOUIS ARAGON, with whom he founded the movement they would call SURREALISM. His subsequent poetry—*Capitale de la douleur* (1926), *Les dessous d'une vie ou la pyramide humaine* (1926), *La rose publique* (1934), and *Les yeux fertiles* (1936)—is considered the best to have come out of the movement. After the Spanish Civil War he abandoned Surrealist experimentation. During World War II he wrote poems dealing with suffering and brotherhood that were circulated secretly and strengthened the morale of the Resistance. His postwar poetry, including *Le Phénix* (1951), was more lyrical.

eluviation Removal of dissolved or suspended material from a layer or layers of the soil by the movement of water when rainfall exceeds evaporation. Such loss of material in solution is often referred to as leaching. The process of eluviation influences soil composition.

Elway, John (Albert) (born 1960) U.S. football player. Born in Port Angeles, Wash., he had an outstanding athletic career at Stanford Univ., then played professional baseball briefly before joining the Denver Broncos in 1983. He is one of only three quarterbacks to have passed for more than 45,000 yards, he holds the record for victories by a starting quarterback (148), and he ranks third for pass attempts (6,392), pass completions (3,633), and total yardage (48,129). Famous for last-minute heroics, he led a total of 47 fourth-quarter game-winning or game-tying touchdown drives. He announced his retirement in 1999 after leading the Broncos to a second consecutive Super Bowl victory.

Ely \'ē-lē\, **Richard T(heodore)** (1854–1943) U.S. economist. Born in Ripley, N.Y., he studied at Columbia University and the University of Heidelberg. His work focused on labor unrest, agricultural economics, and the problems of rural poverty. He taught at Johns Hopkins University 1881–92, but resigned in the face of harsh opposition to his ideas on academic freedom and the labor movement. He was a founder of the American Economic Association (1885). At the University of Wisconsin (1892–1925), he helped create Wisconsin's progressive program of social-reform legislation.

Elysium \i-'li-zhē-əm, i-'li-zē-əm\ *or* **Elysian Fields** Ancient Greek paradise reserved for heroes to whom the gods had granted immortality. HOMER described it as a land of perfect happiness at the end of the earth, on the banks of the Oceanus River. From the time of PINDAR (c. 500 BC) on, Elysium was imagined as a dwelling place for those who had lived a righteous life.

Elytis \e-'lē-ˌtēs\, **Odysseus** *orig.* **Odysseus Alepoudhelis** (1911–1996) Greek poet. The scion of a prosperous Cretan family, he began publishing verse influenced by French Surrealism in the 1930s. His first two collections reveal his love of the Greek landscape and the Aegean Sea. During World War II he joined the antifascist resistance and became something of a bard among young Greeks. One of his best-known poems is *The Axion Esti* (1959); later works include *The Sovereign Sun* (1971) and *The Little Mariner* (1986). He won the Nobel Prize in 1979.

Elzevir family *or* **Elsevier family** \'el-zə-ˌvir\ Family of Dutch booksellers, publishers, and printers, 15 members of which were in business between 1587 and 1681. Members of the family operated at The Hague, Utrecht, and Amsterdam. They were best known for their books or editions of the Greek New Testament and the classics. Though their work enjoyed an almost legendary reputation for excellence of typography and design, it is now regarded as merely typical of the high quality that prevailed in their day in Holland.

Emain Macha \'e-vənʸ-'vä-k̲ə\ Political center of ULSTER during pre-Christian and early Christian times. Now called Navan Fort, it is located near the town of Armagh in Northen Ireland. It was the seat of the semihistorical king CONCHOBAR, a subject of the medieval Irish tales of the ULSTER CYCLE along with CU CHULAINN and other great warriors. St. PATRICK established his base near Emain Macha, and it is still the primatial see of both the Roman Catholic and Protestant churches in Ireland.

Emancipation, Edict of (1861) Manifesto issued by ALEXANDER II that freed the serfs of the Russian empire. Defeat in the CRIMEAN WAR, change in public opinion, and the increasing number and violence of peasant revolts had convinced Alexander of the need for reform. The final edict was a compromise and fully satisfied no one, particularly the peasants. It immediately granted personal liberties to the serfs, but the process by which they were to acquire land was slow, complex, and expensive. Though it failed to create an economically viable class of peasant proprietors, its psychological impact was immense.

Emancipation Proclamation (1863) Edict issued by Pres. ABRAHAM LINCOLN that freed the slaves of the Confederacy. On taking office, Lincoln was concerned with preserving the Union and wanted only to prevent slavery from expanding into the western territories; but after the South seceded, there was no political reason to tolerate slavery. In September 1862 he called on the seceded states to return to the Union or have their slaves declared free. When no state returned, he issued the proclamation on January 1, 1863. The edict had no power in the Confederacy, but it provided moral inspiration for the North and discouraged European countries from supporting the South. It also had the practical effect of permitting recruitment of blacks for the Union army; by 1865 nearly 180,000 black soldiers had enlisted. The 13th Amendment to the Constitution, ratified in 1865, officially abolished slavery.

embargo Detention of merchant vessels or other property to prevent their movement to a foreign territory. A civil embargo is the detention of national vessels in home ports; a hostile embargo is the detention of the ships or property of a foreign state. The term is also used to mean a legal prohibition on commerce. When employed as a political tool by an international organization, an embargo's effectiveness requires cooperation from nonmembers as well as members of the organization. Since 1960 the U.S. has maintained a trade embargo against Cuba, which has failed to bring down its government. Similarly, the 1974 embargo by Arab oil-producing states of petroleum shipments to the West failed to bring about desired policy changes toward Israel.

Embargo Act Legislation by the U.S. Congress in December 1807 that closed U.S. ports to all exports and restricted imports from Britain. The act was Pres. THOMAS JEFFERSON's response to British and French interference with neutral U.S. merchant ships during the NAPOLEONIC WARS. The embargo had little effect in Europe, but it imposed an unpopular restriction on New England merchants and exporters (see HARTFORD CONVENTION). Legislation passed in 1809 lifted the embargo, but continued British interference with U.S. shipping led to the WAR OF 1812.

Embden \'em-dən\, **Gustav Georg** (1874–1933) German physiological chemist. He taught at the University of Frankfurt am Main from its founding in 1914. He conducted studies on the chemistry of carbohydrate metabolism and muscle contraction and was the first to discover and link all the steps in the conversion of glycogen to lactic acid. His studies focused mainly on chemical processes in living organisms, especially intermediate metabolic processes in liver tissue. By developing a technique to prevent tissue damage, Embden discovered the liver's important role in metabolism and did preliminary studies that led to the investigation of normal sugar metabolism and of diabetes.

Embden-Meyerhof-Parnas pathway See GLYCOLYSIS

embezzlement Crime of fraudulently appropriating property entrusted to one's care and converting it to one's own use. It occurs when a person gains possession of goods lawfully and then misappropriates them. It thus stands in contrast to larceny, the taking of goods from another without the latter's consent. The most widely adopted embezzlement statutes cover custodians of public funds. Many laws subject public servants to severe penalties, even if funds are lost through improper administration rather than a clear attempt to steal. See also FRAUD, THEFT.

embolism \'em-bə-,li-zəm\ Obstruction of blood flow by an embolus—a substance (e.g., a blood clot, a fat globule from a CRUSH INJURY, or a gas bubble) not normally present in the bloodstream. Obstruction of an artery to the brain may cause STROKE. Pulmonary embolism (in the pulmonary artery or a branch) causes difficulty breathing, chest pain, and death of a section of lung tissue (LUNG INFARCTION), with fever and rapid heartbeat. Embolism in a coronary artery can cause MYOCARDIAL INFARCTION. See also THROMBOSIS.

embroidery Art of decorating textiles with needle and thread. Among the basic techniques are cross-stitch and quilting. The Persians and Greeks wore quilted garments as armor. The earliest surviving examples of embroidery are Scythian (c. 5th–3rd century BC). The most notable extant Chinese examples are the imperial silk robes of the Qing dynasty (1644–1911/12). Islamic embroideries (16th–17th century) show stylized geometric patterns based on animal and plant shapes. northern European embroidery was mostly ecclesiastical until the Renaissance. European skills and conventions prevailed in North America in the 17th–18th century. The Native Americans embroidered skins and bark with dyed porcupine quills; later the beads they acquired in trade took the place of quills. The indigenous peoples of Central America produced a kind of embroidery with feathers. The BAYEUX TAPESTRY is the most famous surviving piece of needlework.

Detail of an embroidered waistcoat, French, 1800–25; in the Metropolitan Museum of Art, New York City.

BY COURTESY OF THE METROPOLITAN MUSEUM OF ART, NEW YORK CITY, GIFT OF UNITED PIECE DYE WORKS, 1936

embryo \'em-brē-,ō\ Early stage of development of an organism in the EGG or the UTERUS, during which its essential form and its organs and tissues develop. In humans, the organism is called an embryo for the first seven or eight weeks after conception, after which it is called a FETUS. In mammals, the fertilized egg or zygote undergoes cleavage (cell division without cell growth) to form a hollow ball or blastocyst. During the second week following fertilization, gastrulation (cell differentiation and migration) results in the formation of three tissue types. These three types of tissue develop into different organ systems: the ectoderm develops into the skin and nervous system; the mesoderm develops into connective tissues, the circulatory system, muscles, and bones; and the endoderm develops into the lining of the digestive system, lungs, and urinary system. In humans, by about the fourth week, the head and trunk can be distinguished and the brain, spinal cord, and internal organs begin to develop. By the fifth week, limbs begin to appear and the embryo is about .33 in. (.8 cm) long. By the end of eight weeks, the embryo has grown to about 1 in. (2.5 cm) long and all subsequent change is limited primarily to growth and specialization of existing structures. Any CONGENITAL DISORDERS begin in this stage. See also PREGNANCY.

embryology Study of the formation and development of an embryo and fetus. Before widespread use of the microscope and the advent of cellular biology in the 19th century, embryology was based on descriptive and comparative studies. From the time of Aristotle it was debated whether the embryo was a preformed, miniature individual or an undifferentiated form that gradually became specialized. The latter theory was proved in 1827 when KARL ERNST BAER discovered the mammalian ovum (egg). The German anatomist Wilhelm Roux (1850–1924), noted for his pioneering studies on frog eggs (from 1885), became the founder of experimental embryology.

emerald Grass-green variety of BERYL that is highly valued as a gemstone. Its physical properties are those of beryl. Its refractive and dispersive powers (i.e., its capacity to deflect light and to break white light into its component colors) are not high, so cut stones display little brilliancy or fire (flashes of color). The color that gives this gem its value is due to the presence of small amounts of chromium. The most important production of fine quality gem material is from Colombia; emeralds are also mined in Russia, Australia, South Africa, and Zimbabwe. Synthetic emeralds are identical to natural crystals and may rival them in color and beauty.

emergence In the theory of EVOLUTION, the rise of a system that cannot be predicted or explained from antecedent conditions. The British philosopher of science G. H. Lewes (1817–1878) distinguished between resultants and emergents—phenomena that are predictable from their constituent parts (e.g., a physical mixture of sand and talcum powder) and those that are not (e.g., a chemical compound such as salt, which looks nothing like sodium or chlorine). The evolutionary account of life is a continuous history marked by stages at which fundamentally new forms have appeared. Each new mode of life, though grounded in the conditions of the previous stage, is intelligible only in terms of its own ordering principle. These are thus cases of emergence. In philosophy of MIND, the primary candidates for the status of emergent properties are mental states and events.

Emerson, P(eter) H(enry) (1856–1936) English photographer. Trained as a physician, he began using photography in an anthropological study of East Anglia; the images were published in several books. A proponent of photography as a medium of artistic expression, he published a handbook, *Naturalistic Photography* (1889), in which he outlined his aesthetic system, which he called naturalism, emphasizing that photographs should look like photographs rather than paintings. The book was so popular that he became known as one of the world's leading photographers, and his views influenced much of 20th-century photography.

Emerson, Ralph Waldo (1803–1882) U.S. poet, essayist, and lecturer. Born in Boston, he graduated from Harvard and was ordained a Unitarian minister in 1829. His questioning of traditional doctrine led him to resign the ministry three years later. He formulated his philosophy in *Nature* (1836); the book helped initiate New England TRANSCENDENTALISM, a movement of which he soon became the leading exponent. In 1834 he moved to Concord, Mass., the home of his friend HENRY DAVID THOREAU. His lectures on the proper role of the scholar and the waning of the Christian tradition caused considerable controversy. In 1840, with MARGARET FULLER, he helped launch *The Dial*, a journal that provided an outlet for Transcendentalist ideas. He became internationally famous with his *Essays* (1841, 1844), including "Self-Reliance." *Representative Men* (1850) consists of biographies of historical figures. *The Conduct of Life* (1860), his most mature work, reveals a developed humanism and a full awareness of human limitations. His *Poems* (1847) and *May-Day* (1867) established his reputation as a major poet.

Ralph Waldo Emerson, lithograph by Leopold Grozelier, 1859.

BY COURTESY OF THE LIBRARY OF CONGRESS, WASHINGTON, D.C.

emery Granular rock consisting of a mixture of the mineral corundum (aluminum oxide, Al_2O_3) and iron oxides such as magnetite (Fe_3O_4) or hematite (Fe_2O_3). It is a dark, dense substance that looks much like iron ore. Turkey is the world's major producer. Long used as an abrasive or polishing material, particularly in sandpapers, it has largely been replaced by synthetic materials such as alumina. Its largest application now is as a nonskid material in floors, stair treads, and pavements.

émigré nobility \,ā-mē-'grā, *Engl* 'e-mi-,grā\ Members of the French nobility who fled France during the FRENCH REVOLUTION. In exile, mainly in England, the émigrés plotted against the Revolutionary government, seeking foreign help to restore the old regime. In response, Revolutionary leaders in France decreed that those émigrés who did not return by January 1792 were liable to death as traitors, and their property was confiscated. NAPOLEON granted the great majority of émigrés amnesty in 1802. During the BOURBON RESTORATION they were an important force in French politics.

Emilia-Romagna \ā-'mēl-yä-rō-'män-yä\ Autonomous region (pop., 1996 est.: 3,924,000), northern Italy. Located on the Adriatic Sea, the area includes the PO RIVER to the north and the APENNINES to the west and south. It takes its name from the Roman Aemilian Way, built c. 187 BC; BOLOGNA is the chief city and regional capital. The region formerly comprised the duchies of Parma and Modena and the papal Romagna. It became part of the kingdom of Italy in 1861; the present political region was created in 1948. The fertile Emilian Plain in the north makes Emilia-Romagna one of the leading agricultural regions of Italy. It has a large food-processing industry, and livestock and dairy farming are extensive.

Emin Pasha \e-'mēn-pä-'shä\, **Mehmed** *orig.* **Eduard Schnitzer** (1840–1892) German physician, explorer, and administrator in Egyptian Sudan. Schnitzer adopted a Turkish name while serving as a medical officer and administrator in the Ottoman government. In 1876 he joined with British forces led by Gen. CHARLES GEORGE GORDON at Khartoum. In 1878 he was appointed governor of Equatoria province. During the MAHDIST MOVEMENT uprising, the Egyptian government abandoned the Sudan (1884), and the isolated Emin was rescued by HENRY MORTON STANLEY in 1888. On an expedition to equatorial Africa, he was killed by Arab slave-traders. Through his scholarly papers and specimen collections, he contributed vastly to the knowledge of African geography, natural history, ethnology, and languages.

eminent domain Government power to take private property for public use without the owner's consent. Constitutional provisions in most countries, including the U.S. (in the 5th Amendment to the CONSTITUTION), require the payment of just compensation to the owner. As a power peculiar to sovereign authority and coupled with a duty to pay compensation, the concept was developed by such 17th-century NATURAL-LAW jurists as HUGO GROTIUS and SAMUEL PUFENDORF. See also CONFISCATION.

emir \i-'mir\ In the Muslim Middle East, a military commander, governor of a province, or high military official. The first leader to call himself emir was the second CALIPH, UMAR IBN AL-KHATTAB. The title was used by all his successors until the abolition of the caliphate in 1924. In the 10th century the commander of the caliph's armies at Baghdad held the title. It was later adopted by the rulers of independent states in central Asia, notably Bukhara and Afghanistan. The United Arab Emirates, despite their name, are all ruled by SHEIKHS.

Emmett, Daniel Decatur (1815–1904) U.S. showman and songwriter. The son of an Ohio blacksmith, he joined the army at 17 as a fifer. In 1843 in New York he helped organize the Virginia Minstrels, one of the earliest MINSTREL-SHOW troupes. He is credited with writing "Dixie" (1859), a minstrel "walk-around" that became the Confederacy's unofficial national anthem. His other songs include "Old Dan Tucker" and "Blue-Tail Fly." He also wrote banjo tunes and music-instruction manuals.

Emmy award Annual presentation for outstanding achievement in U.S. television. Its name is taken from the nickname "immy" for the image orthicon, a television camera tube. The Emmys are presented by the National Academy of Television Arts and Sciences, founded in 1946, whose members vote on outstanding programs, actors, directors, and writers in such categories as drama, comedy, and variety.

Emory University Private university in Atlanta, Ga. It was chartered as a college in 1836 under Methodist auspices; in 1915 it merged with a school of medicine to become a university. It consists of two undergraduate colleges (one four-year and one two-year), a graduate school of arts and sciences, a division of allied health professions, and schools of law, business, theology, public health, nursing, and medicine. Research facilities include the Carter Presidential Center, the Yerkes Primate Center, and a cancer center. Total enrollment is about 11,000.

emotion Affective aspect of CONSCIOUSNESS. The emotions are generally understood as representing a synthesis of subjective experience, expressive behavior, and neurochemical activity. Most researchers hold that they are part of the human evolutionary legacy and serve adaptive ends by adding to general awareness and the facilitation of social communication. Some nonhuman animals are also considered to possess emotions, as first described by CHARLES DARWIN in 1872. An influential early theory of emotion was that proposed independently by WILLIAM JAMES and Carl Georg Lange (1834–1900), who held that emotion was a perception of internal physiological reactions to external stimuli. WALTER B. CANNON questioned this view and directed attention to the thalamus as a possible source of emotional content. Later researchers have focused on the brain-stem structure known as the reticular formation, which serves to integrate brain activity and may infuse perceptions or actions with emotional valence. Cognitive psychologists have emphasized the role of comparison, matching, appraisal, memory, and attribution in the forming of emotions. All modern theorists agree that emotions influence what people perceive, learn, and remember, and play an important part in personality development. Cross-cultural studies have shown that, whereas many emotions are universal, their specific content and manner of expression vary considerably.

emotivism In metaethics (see ETHICS), the view that moral judgments do not function as statements of fact but rather as expressions of the speaker's or writer's feelings. According to the emotivist, when we say "You acted wrongly in stealing that money," we are not expressing any fact beyond that stated by "You stole that money." It is, however, as if we had stated this fact with a special tone of abhorrence, for in saying that something is wrong, we are expressing our feelings of disapproval toward it. Emotivism was expounded by A. J. AYER in *Language, Truth and Logic* (1936) and developed by Charles Stevenson in *Ethics and Language* (1945).

empathy Ability to imagine oneself in another's place and understand the other's feelings, desires, ideas, and actions. The empathic actor or singer is one who genuinely feels the part he or she is performing. The spectator of a work of art or the reader of a piece of literature may similarly become involved in what he or she observes or contemplates. The use of empathy was an important part of the psychological counseling technique developed by CARL R. ROGERS.

Empedocles \em-'ped-ə-ˌklēz\ (c. 490–430 BC) Greek philosopher, statesman, poet, and physiologist. Nothing remains of his writings but 500 lines from two poems. He held that all matter was composed of four essential ingredients: fire, air, water, and earth. Like HERACLEITUS, he believed that two forces, love and strife, interact to bring together and separate the four substances. Believing in the transmigration of souls, he declared that salvation requires abstention from the flesh of animals, whose souls may once have inhabited human bodies.

emperor Title of the sovereigns of the ancient Roman empire and, by derivation, various later European rulers, also applied to certain non-European monarchs. Caesar AUGUSTUS was the first Roman emperor. Byzantine emperors ruled at Constantinople until 1453. CHARLEMAGNE became the first of the Western emperors (later Holy Roman emperors) in 800. After Otto I became emperor in 962, only German kings held the title. In other parts of Europe, monarchs who ruled multiple kingdoms (e.g., ALFONSO VI, who ruled Léon and Castile) sometimes took the title emperor. NAPOLEON's assumption of the title, as a putative successor of Charlemagne, was a direct threat to the HABSBURG DYNASTY. Queen VICTORIA of Britain took the title empress of India. Non-European peoples whose rulers have been called emperor include the Chinese, Japanese, Mughals, Incas, and Aztecs.

emphysema \ˌem-fə-'zē-mə, ˌem-fə-'sē-mə\ *or* **pulmonary emphysema** Abnormal distension of the lungs with air, usually associated with cigarette smoking and chronic BRONCHITIS. Elastic tissue degenerates, severely interfering with exhalation. Capillary walls disappear, leaving lung tissue dry and pale. The walls of the pulmonary alveoli (see PULMONARY ALVEOLUS) break down, so the lung fills with pools of air. Symptoms include severe breathlessness, weight loss, bluish skin, chest tightness, and wheezing. In bullous emphysema, the alveoli form large air CYSTS that may rupture, causing lung collapse (see ATELECTASIS), or require surgery. Emphysema is irreversible; it normally continues to progress even after the cessation of smoking, and may lead to death. See also PULMONARY HEART DISEASE.

Empire State Building Steel-framed 102-story building designed by Shreve, Lamb & Harmon Associates and completed in New York City in 1931. At a height of 1,250 ft (381 m), it surpassed the CHRYSLER BUILDING to become the highest structure in the world (until 1954). It is notable for its use of the SETBACK.

Empire style \'äm-ˌpir, 'em-ˌpīr\ Style of furniture and interior decoration that flourished in France during the First Empire (1804–14). It corresponds to the REGENCY STYLE in England. Responding to the desire of NAPOLEON for a style inspired by imperial Rome, the architects Charles

Percier (1764–1838) and Pierre Fontaine (1762–1853) decorated his state rooms with classical styles of furniture and ornamental motifs, supplemented by sphinxes and palm leaves to commemorate his Egyptian campaigns. The style influenced the arts (J.-L. David in painting, Antonio Canova in sculpture, the Arc de Triomphe) and fashion and spread quickly throughout Europe.

empiricism Pair of closely related philosophical doctrines, one pertaining to concepts and the other to beliefs. The doctrine concerning concepts is that concepts (e.g., "gravity") can be understood only if they are connected by their users with experiences they have had or could have (e.g., weight, unsupported objects falling). The doctrine concerning beliefs (e.g., that gravity bends space) holds that they depend ultimately and necessarily on experience for their justification (e.g., light passing near the sun appears to deviate from a straight path). Neither doctrine implies the other. Several empiricists have admitted that there are a priori propositions but denied that there are a priori concepts. On the other hand, few if any empiricists have denied the existence of a priori propositions while maintaining the existence of a priori concepts. John Locke, George Berkeley, and David Hume are classical representatives of empiricism. See also Francis Bacon.

employee training *or* **job training** *or* **occupational training** Vocational instruction for employed persons, first used commonly in the developed world during World War II. Work-related training is necessary as new techniques, new methods, new tools, new synthetic materials, new sources of power, and increased uses of automation continue to bring extensive changes. The U.N. and its agencies contribute to training programs in developing countries. See also technical education.

Empson, William *later* **Sir William** (1906–1984) British poet and critic. He studied at Cambridge, and later taught in Japan and China. His precocious *Seven Types of Ambiguity* (1930), which suggests that uncertainty or overlap of meanings in the use of a word can be an enrichment of poetry rather than a fault, had an immense influence on 20th-century criticism; its close examination of poetic texts helped lay the foundation for New Criticism. Later works include *Some Versions of Pastoral* (1935) and *The Structure of Complex Words* (1951). His verse, influenced by John Donne, is elliptical, difficult, and pessimistic.

Ems River *ancient* **Amisia.** River, northwestern Germany. It rises on the southern slope of the Teutoburg Forest in northeastern Rhine-Westphalia and flows west and northwest 230 mi (371 km) to the North Sea. Its mouth is a wide estuary bordering on the Netherlands. Canals built 1892–99 connect it with the Dortmund–Ems Canal and the Ruhr River industrial district; it carries heavy traffic.

Ems Telegram (1870) Telegram sent from Ems, Germany, to Otto von Bismarck and subsequently published by him in an edited version designed to offend the French government. The telegram reported an encounter between King William I of Prussia and the French ambassador, in which William politely refused to promise that no member of his family would seek the Spanish throne. The version published by Bismarck, which made it seem that the two men had insulted each other, precipitated the Franco–Prussian War.

emu \'ē-ˌmyü\ Ratite of Australia. After the ostrich, the emu is the second-largest living bird. They stand more than 5 ft (1.5 m) tall and often weigh more than 100 lbs (45 kg). The common emu (*Dromaius,* or *Dromiceius, novaehollandiae,* family Dromaiidae), the only survivor of several forms exterminated by settlers, has a stout body and long legs. Both sexes are brownish, with a dark-gray head and neck. Emus can run up to 30 mph (50 kph); if cornered, they kick with their large feet. They mate for life and forage in small flocks for fruits and insects but sometimes damage crops. See also cassowary.

Emu (*Dromaius novaehollandiae*).
V. SERVENTY—BRUCE COLEMAN INC./EB INC.

emulsion Mixture of two or more liquids in which one is dispersed in the other as microscopic or ultramicroscopic droplets (see colloid). Emulsions are stabilized by agents (emulsifiers) that form films at the droplets' surface (e.g., for soap or detergent molecules) or impart mechanical stability (e.g., for colloidal carbon, bentonite clay, proteins, or carbohydrate polymers). Less stable emulsions separate spontaneously into two liquid layers; more stable ones can be destroyed by inactivating the emulsifier, by freezing, or by heating. Polymerization reactions are often carried out in emulsions. Many familiar and industrial products are oil-in-water (o/w) or water-in-oil (w/o) emulsions: milk (o/w), butter (w/o), latex paints (o/w), floor and glass waxes (o/w), and many cosmetic and personal-care preparations and medications (either type).

Enabling Act Law passed by the German Reichstag in 1933 that enabled Adolf Hitler to assume dictatorial powers. Deputies from the Nazi Party, the German National People's Party, and the Center Party voted in favor of the act, which "enabled" Hitler's government to issue decrees independently of the Reichstag and the presidency. It gave Hitler a base from which to carry out the first steps of his National Socialist revolution.

enamelwork Metal objects decorated with an opaque glaze fused to the surface by intense heat. The resulting surface is hard and durable, and can be brilliantly colorful. Objects most suitable for enamelwork are delicate, small (e.g., jewelry, snuffboxes, scent bottles, watches), and made of copper, brass, bronze, or gold. The best-known processes are cloisonné and champlevé. Enamelwork was produced as early as the 13th century BC, reached its peak in the Byzantine empire, and flourished throughout medieval and Renaissance Europe. In the early 20th century, Carl Faberge produced highly prized objects made of gold, enamel, and jewels. See also Limoges painted enamel.

encephalitis \in-ˌse-fə-'lī-təs\ Inflammation of the brain, most often due to infection, usually with a virus. One class of encephalitides (including multiple sclerosis) attacks the myelin sheath that insulates nerve fibers rather than the neurons themselves. In most cases, symptoms include fever, headache, lethargy, and coma. Convulsions are most common in infants. Characteristic neurological signs include uncoordinated, involuntary movements and localized weakness. The symptoms and a lumbar puncture (to obtain cerebrospinal fluid for analysis) may establish the presence but not the cause. Treatment usually aims to relieve the symptoms and ensure quiet rest. Various symptoms may remain after recovery.

Encke's Comet \'eŋ-kəz\ Faint comet having the shortest orbital period (about 3.3 years) of any known, first observed in 1786. It was the second comet (after Halley's Comet) to have its period determined (1819), by Johann Franz Encke (1791–1865). Encke also found that the comet's period decreases by about 2½ hours in each revolution and showed that this effect could not be explained by the planets' gravitational influence. Its period continues to decrease, though more slowly, and appears to be related to the effects of outgassing.

enclosure movement Division or consolidation of communal lands in Western Europe into the carefully delineated and individually owned farm plots of modern times. Before enclosure, farmland was under the control of individual cultivators only during the growing season; after harvest and before the next growing season, the land was used by the community for the grazing of livestock and other purposes. In England the movement for enclosure began in the 12th century and proceeded rapidly from 1450 to 1640; the process was virtually complete by the end of the 19th century. In the rest of Europe, enclosure made little progress until the 19th century. Common rights over arable land have now been largely eliminated.

encomienda \en-ˌkō-mē-'en-də\ In colonial Spanish America, a system by which the Spanish crown defined the status of the Indian population in its colonies. An encomienda consisted of a grant by the crown of a specified number of Indians living in a particular area. The receiver could exact tribute from the Indians and was required to protect them and instruct them in the Christian faith. The encomienda did not include a grant of land, but in practice the *encomenderos* gained control of Indian lands. Though the original intent was to reduce the abuses of forced labor, in practice it became a form of enslavement.

encryption, data See data encryption

Encyclopædia Britannica Oldest and largest English-language general encyclopedia. Its three-volume first edition was published in 1768–71 in Edinburgh, Scotland. In subsequent editions it grew in size and reputation. The most famous editions include the ninth (1875–89), known as "the scholar's encyclopedia," and the 11th (1910–11), which, with contributions from more than 1,500 experts of world reputation, was also the first to divide the traditionally lengthy treatises into more particularized articles. With the 14th edition (1929), the encyclopedia began to be revised and reprinted annually. The current edition, the 15th (1974), embodied a new structure, dividing the major articles from the shorter ones. *Encyclopædia Britannica* now also appears in CD-ROM and online versions. A series of ownership changes led to its purchase by American publishers in 1901; since the 1940s it has been published in Chicago.

encyclopedia Reference work that contains information on all branches of knowledge or that treats a particular branch of knowledge comprehensively. It is self-contained and explains subjects in greater detail than a DICTIONARY. It differs from an ALMANAC in that its information is not dated and from pedagogical texts in its attempt to be easy to consult and to be readily understood by the layperson. Though generally written in the form of many separate articles, encyclopedias vary greatly in format and content. The prototype of modern encyclopedias is usually acknowledged to be Ephraim Chambers's *Cyclopaedia* (1728), and the first modern encyclopedia was the French *ENCYCLOPÉDIE* (1751–65). The largest general encyclopedia in English is the *ENCYCLOPÆDIA BRITANNICA*.

Encyclopédie \äⁿ-ˌsē-klō-pā-ˈdē\ French encyclopedia created in the 18th century by the PHILOSOPHES; one of the principal works of the ENLIGHTENMENT. Under the full title *Encyclopédie, ou dictionnaire raisonné des sciences, des arts et des métiers* ("Encyclopedia, or Classified Dictionary of Sciences, Arts, and Trades"), it was inspired by the success of E. Chambers's British *Cyclopaedia; or An Universal Dictionary of Arts and Sciences* (1728). Under the direction of DENIS DIDEROT and initially aided by JEAN LE ROND D'ALEMBERT, 17 volumes were published between 1751 and 1765; other volumes were added later for a total of 35. Though opposed by conservative ecclesiastics and government officials and subjected to censorship, the *Encyclopédie* attracted articles from many important thinkers of the time, including J.-J. ROUSSEAU, VOLTAIRE, and Diderot, who were called "Encyclopedists." In its skepticism, its emphasis on scientific determinism, and its criticism of the abuses perpetrated by contemporary legal, judicial, and clerical institutions, the work had widespread influence as an expression of progressive thought prior to the FRENCH REVOLUTION.

endangered species Any species of plant or animal threatened with EXTINCTION. International and national agencies work to maintain lists of endangered species, to protect and preserve natural habitats, and to promote programs for recovery and reestablishment of these species. The Species Survival Commission of the International Union for Conservation of Nature and Natural Resources (IUCN) publishes information online about endangered species worldwide as the *Red List of Threatened Species*. Separate books for animal and plant species are also published. In the United States, the Fish and Wildlife Service is responsible for the CONSERVATION and management of fish and wildlife, including endangered species, and their habitats. Its list now consists of about 1,200 domestic species of endangered or threatened animals and plants, and some 200 recovery programs are in effect.

endive \ˈen-ˌdīv, ˌän-ˈdēv\ Edible annual leafy plant *(Cichorium endivia)* of the COMPOSITE FAMILY. It is variously believed to have originated in Egypt and Indonesia, and has been cultivated in Europe since the 16th century. Its many varieties form two groups, the curly-leaved, or narrow-leaved, endive *(crispa),* and the Batavian, or broad-leaved, endive *(latifolia).* The former is used mostly for salads, the latter for cooking.

endocarditis \ˌen-dō-kär-ˈdī-təs\ INFLAMMATION of the heart lining (endocardium), in association with a noninfectious disease (e.g., systemic LUPUS ERYTHEMATOSUS) or caused by INFECTION, usually at the heart valves. Severe bacterial infection causes an acute form with fever, sweating, chills, joint pain and swelling, and EMBOLISMS. Subacute endocarditis usually comes from bacteria that do not ordinarily cause disease. Bacterial endocarditis is usually treated with long-term antibiotics. In nonbacterial thrombotic endocarditis, blood clots form along heart valve edges.

endocrine system \ˈen-də-krən\ Group of ductless GLANDS that secrete HORMONES necessary for normal growth and development, reproduction, and HOMEOSTASIS. The major endocrine glands are the HYPOTHALAMUS, PITUITARY, THYROID, islets of LANGERHANS, ADRENALS, PARATHYROIDS, OVARIES, and TESTES. Secretion is regulated either by regulators in a gland that detect high or low levels of a chemical and inhibit or stimulate secretion, or by a complex mechanism involving the hypothalamus and the pituitary. TUMORS that produce hormones can throw off this balance. Diseases of the endocrine system result from over- or underproduction of a hormone or an abnormal response to a hormone.

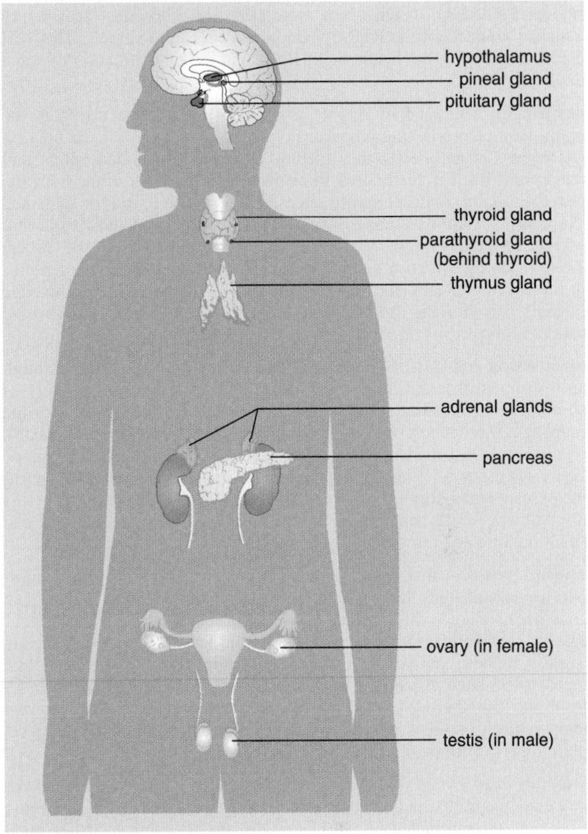

Endocrine glands of the human body.

endocrinology \ˌen-də-kri-ˈnäl-ə-jē\ Medical discipline dealing with regulation of body functions by HORMONES and other biochemicals and treatment of ENDOCRINE-SYSTEM imbalances. In 1841 FRIEDRICH GUSTAV HENLE first recognized "ductless GLANDS," which secrete products directly into the bloodstream. The field was essentially established in the early 20th century, when ERNEST H. STARLING, who introduced the term hormone, proposed that chemical and nervous regulation of physiological processes were linked. Endocrine therapy is based on replacing deficient hormones with purified extracts. Nuclear technology has led to new treatments; use of radioactive iodine for hyperthyroidism greatly reduced the need for THYROID-GLAND surgery. The detection of minute amounts of hormone with radioimmunoassays (see RADIOLOGY) permits early diagnosis and treatment of endocrine disorders.

endogamy See EXOGAMY AND ENDOGAMY

endometriosis \ˌen-dō-ˌmē-trē-ˈō-səs\ Disorder of the female reproductive system in which endometrium (uterine lining) grows in an abnormal location because some endometrial fragments traverse the fallopian tubes into the abdominal cavity and become embedded on structures there, usually the ovaries, rather than exiting the uterus via the vagina (during menstruation). Symptoms include pain on menstruation, sexual intercourse, defecation, and/or urination; heavy menstrual flow; blood in the urine; and infertility. Diagnosis is best made by LAPAROSCOPY. Treatment includes surgery and hormones to suppress ovulation for six to nine months.

endoplasmic reticulum \ˌen-də-ˈplaz-mik-rə-ˈtik-yə-ləm\ (ER) Highly intricate membrane system within the CYTOPLASM of a eukaryotic cell (see

EUKARYOTE), important in the synthesis of proteins and lipids. The ER usually makes up more than half the membrane of the cell and is continuous with the outer membrane of the nuclear envelope (see NUCLEUS). There are two distinct regions of ER: the rough ER, or RER (so called because of the protein-synthesizing RIBOSOMES attached to it), and the smooth ER (SER), which is not associated with ribosomes and mainly transfers products of the RER by budding off transport vessels. The SER is also involved in the synthesis of lipids and the detoxification of some toxic chemicals.

endorphin \en-'dȯr-fən\ Any of a group of PROTEINS occurring in the brain, with pain-relieving properties typical of OPIUM and related opiates. Discovered in the 1970s, they include enkephalin, beta-endorphin, and dynorphin. Each is distributed in characteristic patterns throughout the nervous system. Endorphins are released in response to PAIN or sustained exertion (causing the "runner's high"). They are also believed to have a role in appetite control, release of PITUITARY SEX HORMONES, and SHOCK. There is strong evidence that they are connected with "pleasure centers" in the brain, and they seem to be activated by ACUPUNCTURE. Knowledge of their behavior has implications for treating addictions and chronic pain.

endoscopy \en-'däs-kə-pē\ Examination of the body's interior through an instrument inserted into a natural opening or an incision, usually as an outpatient procedure. Endoscopes include the esophagoscope (for the esophagus), bronchoscope (for bronchi), gastroscope (for the stomach), proctosigmoidoscope (for the rectum and lower colon), and laparoscope (see LAPAROSCOPY). With FIBER OPTICS, much more maneuverable instruments can reach formerly inaccessible sites, while causing much less discomfort. Attachments can take tissue samples, excise polyps and small tumors, and remove foreign objects.

endotherm So-called warm-blooded animals; that is, those that maintain a constant body temperature independent of the environment. The endotherms include the BIRDS and MAMMALS. If heat loss exceeds heat generation, metabolism increases to make up the loss or the animal shivers to raise its body temperature. If heat generation exceeds the heat loss, mechanisms such as panting or perspiring increase heat loss. Unlike ECTOTHERMS, endotherms can be active and survive at quite low external temperatures, but because they must produce heat continuously, they require high quantities of "fuel" (i.e., food).

Energia *also called* **RKK Energia** *formerly* **OKB-1** Russian aerospace company that is a major producer of spacecraft, rockets, and missiles. Energia originated in 1946 as a department within a Soviet institute conducting work on long-range missiles. Ten years later, under SERGEY KOROLYOV, it became the independent design bureau OKB-1. In the 1950s it developed the R-7 (SS-6), the world's first inter-continental ballistic missile; a modified R-7 placed the first artificial satellite into orbit (see SPUTNIK). OKB-1 was responsible for the U.S.S.R.'s commanding early lead in the "space race," although it failed in its secret project to beat the U.S. to a manned Moon landing. In 1974 the conglomerate NPO Energia was created with OKB-1 at its center. A main focus for the company was the development and operation of space stations (see SALYUT, MIR). In the early 1990s Energia became the main contractor for the Russian portion of the INTERNATIONAL SPACE STATION (it provided the station's Zvezda habitat and control module), but its role was later reduced. In 1994 it was renamed RKK Energia and partially privatized. After the dissolution of the Soviet Union in 1991, Energia partnered with multinational satellite launching services, to which it provided its Block DM upper stage for boosting payloads to geostationary orbit.

energy Capacity for doing WORK. Energy exists in various forms—including KINETIC, POTENTIAL, THERMAL, CHEMICAL, electrical (see ELECTRICITY), and NUCLEAR—and can be converted from one form to another. For example, fuel-burning heat engines convert chemical energy to thermal energy; batteries convert chemical energy to electrical energy. Though energy may be converted from one form to another, it may not be created or destroyed; that is, total energy in a closed system remains constant. All forms of energy are associated with MOTION. A rolling ball has kinetic energy, for instance, whereas a ball lifted above the ground has potential energy, as it has the potential to move if released. HEAT and work involve the transfer of energy; heat transferred may become thermal energy. See also ACTIVATION ENERGY, BINDING ENERGY, IONIZATION ENERGY, MECHANICAL ENERGY, SOLAR ENERGY, ZERO-POINT ENERGY.

energy, conservation of Principle of physics according to which the ENERGY of interacting bodies or particles in a closed system remains constant though it may take different forms (e.g. KINETIC ENERGY, POTENTIAL ENERGY, THERMAL ENERGY, or energy in an ELECTRIC CURRENT or stored in an ELECTRIC or MAGNETIC field or in chemical bonds). With the advent of RELATIVITY physics in 1905, MASS was recognized as equivalent to energy. When dealing with a system of high-speed particles, whose mass increases as a consequence of their speed, the laws of conservation of energy and of conservation of mass become one CONSERVATION LAW. See also HERMANN VON HELMHOLTZ.

energy, equipartition of Law of STATISTICAL MECHANICS stating that, in a system in thermal EQUILIBRIUM, on average, an equal amount of energy is associated with each independent energy state. It states specifically that a system of particles in equilibrium at absolute temperature T will have an average energy of $\frac{1}{2}kT$, where k is the BOLTZMANN CONSTANT, associated with each degree of freedom. For example, an ATOM of a gas has three degrees of freedom (its three position coordinates); therefore, it will have an average total energy of $\frac{3}{2}kT$.

Energy, U.S. Department of (DOE) Federal executive division responsible for administering national energy policy. Established in 1977, it promotes energy efficiency and the use of renewable energy. Its national security programs serve to develop and oversee nuclear-energy resources. Its Office of Environmental Management oversees waste management and cleanup activities at inactive facilities. The Fossil Energy Office develops policies and regulations concerning the use of natural gas, coal, and electric energy. Its regional power administrations transmit electric power produced at federal hydroelectric projects.

Engelbart, Douglas (Carl) (born 1925) U.S. computer scientist. Born near Portland, Ore., he received his PhD from UC–Berkeley. In the 1960s he set up the Augmentation Research Center at the Stanford Research Institute in Utah. He invented HYPERTEXT, the multiwindow display, the MOUSE, and groupware. His demonstration of these capabilities in San Francisco in 1968 started the process of development that led to the Microsoft WINDOWS operating system. Engelbart's group at SRI was one of the original four members of the ARPANET, precursor of the INTERNET. Since his retirement, he has led the Bootstrap Institute, researching ways to support cooperative work by computers. In 1997 he received the Turing Award.

Engels \'eŋ-əls\, **Friedrich** (1820–1895) German Socialist philosopher. Son of a factory owner, he eventually became a successful businessman himself, never allowing his communist principles and criticism of capitalist ways to interfere with the profitable operations of his firm. As a young man he developed an interest in the philosophy of G. W. F. HEGEL as expounded by the Young Hegelians, and he became persuaded that the logical consequence of HEGELIANISM and dialectic was communism. In 1844 he published *The Condition of the Working Class in England.* With KARL MARX, whom he met in Cologne, he formed a permanent partnership to promote the socialist movement. After persuading the second Communist Congress to adopt their views, the two men were authorized to draft the *COMMUNIST MANIFESTO* (1848). After Marx's death (1883), Engels served as the foremost authority on Marx and MARXISM. Aside from his own books, he completed volumes 2 and 3 of *Das Kapital* on the basis of Marx's uncompleted manuscripts and rough notes.

engine MACHINE that can convert any of various forms of ENERGY into mechanical POWER or MOTION. The STEAM ENGINES developed during the INDUSTRIAL REVOLUTION to power stationary machinery were modified in the 19th century to propel locomotives and ships, and were joined later by steam turbines. INTERNAL-COMBUSTION ENGINES were developed by NIKOLAUS OTTO and RUDOLF DIESEL in the late 19th century. Gas turbines and rocket engines came into use in the later 20th century. See also DIESEL ENGINE, GASOLINE ENGINE, JET ENGINE, ROCKET, and ROTARY ENGINE.

engineering Professional art of applying science to the optimum conversion of the resources of nature to the uses of humankind. Engineering is based principally on physics, chemistry, and mathematics and their extensions into MATERIALS SCIENCE, solid and fluid MECHANICS, THERMODYNAMICS, transfer and rate processes, and systems analysis. A great body of special knowledge is associated with engineering; preparation for professional practice involves extensive training in the application of that knowledge. Engineers employ two types of natural resources, materials and ENERGY. Materials acquire uses that reflect their properties: their strength, ease of fabrication, lightness, or durability; their ability to insulate or conduct; and their chemical, electrical, or acoustical properties. Important sources of energy include fossil fuels (coal, petroleum, gas), wind, sunlight, falling water, and nuclear fission. See also AEROSPACE ENGINEERING, CIVIL ENGINEERING, CHEMICAL ENGINEERING. GENETIC ENGINEERING, MECHANICAL ENGINEERING, MILITARY ENGINEERING.

engineering geology *or* **geological engineering** Scientific discipline concerned with the application of geologic knowledge to engineering problems such as reservoir design and location, determination of slope stability for construction purposes, and determination of earthquake, flood, or subsidence danger in areas considered for roads, pipelines, bridges, dams, or other engineering works.

England *Latin* **Anglia** Southern part of the island of Great Britain, excluding Wales. Area: 50,351 sq mi (130,410 sq km). Population (2000 est.): 49,997,000. It is the largest constituent unit of the United Kingdom of Great Britain and Northern Ireland. England is often erroneously considered synonymous with the island of Great Britain and even with the entire kingdom. Despite the political, economic, and cultural legacy that has perpetuated its name, however, England no longer officially exists as a country and enjoys no separate political status within the United Kingdom. It is a land of low hills and plateaus, with a 2,000-mi (3,200-km) coastline. A substantial upland, the PENNINES, divides northern England; the CHEVIOT HILLS define the Scottish border. In the southwest lie the Cotswold Hills and the plateau regions of Exmoor and Dartmoor; in the southeast lie the Downs, and in the south the Salisbury Plain. English weather is diverse, with a generally mild but erratic maritime climate. England is divided into eight geographic regions, often referred to as the standard regions of England; they do not serve any administrative function. The South East, centered on LONDON, is an economically dominant area. It contains an extensive range of manufacturing and science-based industry and commercial endeavors. The WEST MIDLANDS, in western central England, is a diversified manufacturing region that centers on BIRMINGHAM. The region also includes the Shakespeare country, centered on STRATFORD-UPON-AVON. The East Midlands, in eastern central England, is also a manufacturing region and contains some of England's best farmland. EAST ANGLIA is the easternmost part of England. It is mainly an agricultural region, but high-technology industries have developed there. MANCHESTER and LIVERPOOL are the chief industrial cities of the North West; the region has long been known for textile making, but that is rapidly giving way to diversified manufacturing. The HUMBERSIDE region lies to the east and is noted for textiles and steelmaking, though its economy has become more diversified and there is extensive farmland. The North region extends north to the Scottish border. It includes the celebrated LAKE DISTRICT and is a center of engineering and pharmaceutical manufacture. The South West region, which includes CORNWALL, has a growing tourist industry, and some areas are becoming industrialized. England is especially noted for its long and rich literary tradition, as well as for its architecture, painting, theaters, museums, and universities (see University of OXFORD, University of CAMBRIDGE). It also played an integral role in the evolution of ROCK MUSIC (see BRITISH INVASION). See also GREAT BRITAIN, UNITED KINGDOM.

England, Bank of CENTRAL BANK of Britain, headquartered in London. Incorporated by act of Parliament in 1694, it soon became the largest and most prestigious financial institution in England. It did not assume the responsibilities of a central bank until the 19th century, and it was privately owned until 1946, when it was nationalized.

England, Church of English national church and the mother church of the Anglican Communion. Christianity was brought to England in the 2nd century, and though nearly destroyed by the Anglo-Saxon invasions, it was reestablished after the mission of St. AUGUSTINE OF CANTERBURY in 597. Medieval conflicts between church and state culminated in HENRY VIII's break with Roman Catholicism in the REFORMATION. When the pope refused to annul Henry's marriage to CATHERINE OF ARAGON, the king issued the Act of Supremacy (1534), which declared the English monarch to be head of the Church of England. Under Henry's successor, EDWARD VI, more Protestant reforms were instituted. After a five-year Catholic reaction under MARY I, ELIZABETH I ascended the throne (1558), and the Church of England was reestablished. The Book of COMMON PRAYER (1549) and the Thirty-nine Articles (1571) became the standards for liturgy and doctrine. The rise of PURITANISM in the 17th century led to the ENGLISH CIVIL WARS; during the Commonwealth the Church of England was suppressed, but it was reestablished in 1660. The evangelical movement in the 18th century emphasized the church's Protestant heritage, while the OXFORD MOVEMENT in the 19th century emphasized its Roman Catholic heritage. The Church of England has maintained an episcopal form of government, and its leader is the archbishop of Canterbury. In 1992 the church voted to ordain women as priests. In the U.S., the Protestant EPISCOPAL CHURCH is descended from and remains associated with the Church of England.

English Channel *or* **The Channel** *French* **La Manche** \lä-'mäüsh\ Strait between southern England and northern France. It connects the Atlantic Ocean with the North Sea through the Strait of DOVER. The French name ("The Sleeve") is a reference to its shape, which gradually narrows from about 112 mi (180 km) in the west to only 21 mi (34 km) in the east, between DOVER and CALAIS. Historically both a route for and a barrier to invaders of Britain, in the 20th century it has developed into one of the world's busiest sea routes for oil tankers and ore carriers. The CHANNEL TUNNEL, completed in 1994, now provides a land route between Paris and London.

English Civil Wars (1642–51) Armed conflict in the British Isles between Parliamentarians and supporters of the monarchy (Royalists). Tension between CHARLES I and the House of Commons had been building for some time, and after his unsuccessful attempt to arrest five members of Parliament, both sides prepared for war. The first phase of the wars (1642–46) was initially characterized by inconclusive encounters, but victories by Parliamentarian forces under OLIVER CROMWELL at the Battles of MARSTON MOOR and NASEBY turned the tide. In 1646 the Royalist forces were disbanded. In 1647 Charles I negotiated with a Scottish group for assistance, starting the second phase of the wars, a series of Royalist rebellions, and a Scottish invasion. All were defeated, and Charles I was executed in 1649. The fighting continued, and Royalist forces under CHARLES II invaded England in 1651. Parliamentary forces defeated the Royalists at Worcester in 1651 and Charles II fled abroad, effectively ending the civil wars. The wars' political consequence was the establishment of the Commonwealth and Protectorate. See also NEW MODEL ARMY, SOLEMN LEAGUE AND COVENANT.

English East India Co. See EAST INDIA CO.

English horn Large OBOE pitched a 5th below the ordinary oboe. It has a bent metal crook to hold the double reed, and a bulbous bell. It is a transposing instrument in F. It is "neither English nor a horn"; in its original name, *cor anglais, cor* ("horn") referred to its original hornlike curved shape, but the source of *anglais* ("English") is a mystery. It has remained a basically orchestral instrument since its first appearance c. 1750.

English language Language belonging to the GERMANIC LANGUAGES branch of the INDO-EUROPEAN LANGUAGE family, widely spoken on six continents. The primary language of the U.S., Britain, Canada, Australia, Ireland, New Zealand, and various Caribbean and Pacific island nations, it is also an official language of India, the Philippines, and many sub-Saharan African countries. It is the second most widely spoken native language in the world, the mother tongue of more than 350 million people, the most widely taught foreign language, and the international language of science and business. English relies mainly on word order (usually subject-verb-object) to indicate relationships between words (see SYNTAX). Written in the LATIN ALPHABET, it is most closely related to FRISIAN, GERMAN, and DUTCH. Its history began with the migration of the Jutes, Angles, and SAXONS from Germany and Denmark to Britain in the 5th–6th century. The NORMAN CONQUEST of 1066 brought many French words into English. Greek and Latin words began to enter it in the 15th century, and Modern English is usually dated from 1500. English easily borrows words from other languages and has coined many new words to reflect advances in technology.

English school Dominant school in painting in England from the 18th century to c. 1850. From 1730 to 1750 two distinctive British forms of painting were perfected by WILLIAM HOGARTH: genre scenes depicting the "modern moral subject," and the small-scale group portrait, or "conversation piece." Full-scale portraiture was popularized by JOSHUA REYNOLDS and THOMAS GAINSBOROUGH; the landscape tradition was founded by RICHARD WILSON; and historical painting was practiced by two American-born painters, BENJAMIN WEST and JOHN SINGLETON COPLEY. The flowering of English Romantic art was embodied in the landscapes of J.M.W. TURNER and JOHN CONSTABLE. The art of the period rivaled continental art in quality and had great influence on European painting.

English sparrow See HOUSE SPARROW

engraving Any of various processes of cutting a design into a plate or block of metal or wood. The cutting is done by a graver, or burin, on a copper, zinc, aluminum, or magnesium plate, and the design is printed with a roller press from ink rubbed into the incised grooves. Wood engraving derives from the WOODCUT, but the use of the hard, smooth boxwood, cut with the burin commonly used by the copper-plate engraver, produces a finer, more detailed image. By contrast with engraving from metal plates, the printing of wood engravings is done from the surface of the plate or block; the parts that are not to be printed are cut away. See also ETCHING.

ENIAC \'ē-nē-ˌak, 'en-ē-ˌak\ *in full* **Electronic Numerical Integrator and Computer.** Early electronic DIGITAL COMPUTER built in the U.S. in 1945 by J. PRESPER ECKERT and JOHN W. MAUCHLY. The massive ENIAC, which weighed 30 tons and filled an entire room, used some 18,000 VACUUM TUBES, 70,000 resistors, and 10,000 capacitors. In December 1945 it solved its first problem, calculations for the HYDROGEN BOMB. After its official unveiling in 1946, it was used to prepare artillery-shell trajectory tables and perform other military and scientific calculations.

Enigma Device used by the German military to encode strategic messages before and during World War II. The Enigma code was first broken by the Poles in the early 1930s, so that German messages were eventually intercepted and deciphered by Allied code-breakers during the war. (See also ULTRA.)

Enkidu \'en-kē-ˌdü\ Friend and companion of the Mesopotamian hero GILGAMESH. In the ancient *Epic of Gilgamesh,* Enkidu is a wild man created by the god ANU. After Gilgamesh defeats him, the two become friends (in some versions Enkidu becomes Gilgamesh's servant). He aids Gilgamesh in killing the divine bull sent by the goddess ISHTAR to destroy them. The gods then kill Enkidu in revenge, prompting Gilgamesh to search for immortality.

enlightened despotism *or* **benevolent despotism** In the 18th century, a form of government in which absolute monarchs pursued legal, social, and educational reforms inspired by the ENLIGHTENMENT. Among the most prominent enlightened despots were FREDERICK II THE GREAT, PETER I THE GREAT, CATHERINE II THE GREAT, MARIA THERESA, JOSEPH II, and LEOPOLD II. They typically instituted administrative reform, religious toleration, and economic development but did not propose reforms that would undermine their sovereignty or disrupt the social order.

Enlightenment European intellectual movement of the 17th–18th century in which ideas concerning God, reason, nature, and man were blended into a worldview that inspired revolutionary developments in art, philosophy, and politics. Central to Enlightenment thought were the use and celebration of reason. For Enlightenment thinkers, received authority, whether in science or religion, was to be subject to the investigation of unfettered minds. In the sciences and mathematics, the logics of induction and deduction made possible the creation of a sweeping new cosmology. The search for a rational religion led to DEISM; the more radical products of the application of reason to religion were SKEPTICISM, ATHEISM, and materialism. The Enlightenment produced modern secularized theories of psychology and ethics by men such as JOHN LOCKE and THOMAS HOBBES, and it also gave rise to radical political theories. Locke, JEREMY BENTHAM, J.-J. ROUSSEAU, MONTESQUIEU, VOLTAIRE, and THOMAS JEFFERSON all contributed to an evolving critique of the authoritarian state and to sketching the outline of a higher form of social organization based on natural rights. One of the Enlightenment's enduring legacies is the belief that human history is a record of general progress.

Ennin \'en-ˌnēn\ (794–864) Japanese Buddhist who founded the Sammon branch of the Tendai (TIANTAI) sect. Educated in the Enryaku-ji monastery near Kyoto, he was a disciple of SAICHO. He spent nine years studying Buddhism in China, returning home in AD 847 with 559 volumes of Chinese Buddhist texts and a system of musical notation for religious chants that is still used in Japan. He introduced to Japanese Buddhism the practice of chanting the name of Amida (AMITABHA) as a route to rebirth in Amida's paradise. He also established Tendai esotericism. He became chief priest of his order in 854, and his teachings were influential in Japanese Buddhism for centuries.

Enniskillen \ˌe-ni-'ski-lən\ *or* **Inniskilling** Town (pop., 1995 est.: 11,000), seat of FERMANAGH district, southwestern Northern Ireland. Situated on an island in the Erne River, it was a strategic crossing point of Lough ERNE. Incorporated by the English king JAMES I, it defeated a force sent by JAMES II in 1689 and gained a reputation as a Protestant stronghold. Long a garrison town, it gave its name to the Royal Inniskilling Fusiliers and the 6th (Inniskilling) Dragoons, both famous regiments of the British army. The town now functions as an agricultural market.

Ennius \'e-nē-əs\, **Quintus** (239–169 BC) Roman poet, dramatist, and satirist. The most influential of the early Latin poets, he is considered the founder of Roman literature. His epic *Annales*, a narrative poem telling the story of Rome from the wanderings of AENEAS to the poet's own day, was the national epic until it was eclipsed by VIRGIL's *Aeneid.* He excelled in tragedy, adapting 19 plays from the Greek, of which only about 420 lines survive.

ensilage See SILAGE

Ensor \'en-sȯr\, **James (Sidney)** *later* **Baron Ensor** (1860–1949) Belgian painter and printmaker. Trained in Brussels, he spent most of his life in his native Ostend. In 1883 he joined a group known as Les VINGT ("The Twenty") and began depicting skeletons, phantoms, masks, and other images of grotesque fantasy as social commentary. His *Entry of Christ into Brussels* (1888), painted in smeared, garish colors, provoked outrage. Continuing negative criticism plunged him ever deeper into cynicism until he finally became a recluse. The exhibition of *Entry of Christ* in 1929 led to his being ennobled by King Albert. He was one of the formative influences on EXPRESSIONISM.

enstatite \'enz-tə-ˌtīt\ Common silicate mineral in the PYROXENE family. It is the stable form of magnesium silicate ($MgSiO_3$, often with up to 10% iron) in magnesium- and iron-rich igneous rock types. Enstatite crystallizes in the orthorhombic system (three unequal axes at right angles to each other).

entablature Assemblage of horizontal moldings and bands supported by the columns of Classical buildings. The entablature is usually divided into three main sections: the lowest band, or architrave, which originally took the form of a beam running from support to support; the central band, or frieze, consisting of an unmolded strip with or without ornament; and the top band, or cornice, constructed from a series of moldings that project from the edge of the frieze. Most entablatures correspond to or are derived from the Doric, Ionic, or Corinthian ORDER.

entamoeba \ˌen-tə-'mē-bə\ Any PROTOZOAN of the genus *Entamoeba,* most of which are parasites in the intestines of vertebrates, including humans. *E. histolytica* causes human amebic DYSENTERY. Infection of the large intestine with *E. histolytica* often causes no symptoms; however, diarrhea, abdominal pain, and fever may result from invasion and ulceration of intestinal walls. In the worst cases, the liver, lungs, brain, and spleen may be affected. Cysts of *E. histolytica* are transmitted through food and water, often by fly and cockroach droppings. *E. gingivalis,* found especially in unhealthy mouths, has not been shown to cause disease.

entasis \'en-tə-səs\ Convex curve given to a column, spire, or similar upright member to avoid the optical illusion of hollowness or weakness that would arise from normal tapering. Exaggerated in Greek work of the Doric ORDER, it grew more and more subtle in the 5th–4th century BC. Entasis is also occasionally found in Gothic spires and in smaller Romanesque columns.

Entebbe incident \en-'te-bē\ (July 3–4, 1976) Israeli rescue of 103 hostages from a French airliner hijacked by members of the PALESTINE LIBERATION ORGANIZATION and flown to Entebbe, Uganda, where they were permitted to remain by Pres. IDI AMIN. The hijackers released 258 passengers and held the rest, demanding that Israel release 53 imprisoned PLO members. Israel airlifted in 100–200 soldiers, escorted by fighter planes; in their brilliantly executed raid, seven hijackers, one soldier, and three hostages were killed.

Entente, Little See LITTLE ENTENTE

Entente Cordiale \äⁿ-'täⁿt-kȯrd-'yäl\ (French: "Cordial Understanding") (1904) Anglo-French agreement that settled numerous colonial disputes and ended antagonisms between Britain and France. It granted freedom of action to Britain in Egypt and to France in Morocco and resolved several other imperial disputes. The agreement reduced the virtual isolation of each country and was consequently upsetting to Germany, which had benefited from Franco–British antagonism. The Entente paved the way for Anglo-French diplomatic cooperation against Germany before World War I and for later military alliances.

enthalpy \'en-thəl-pē\ Sum of the internal energy E and the product of the PRESSURE P and volume V of a thermodynamic system (see THERMODYNAMICS). So, enthalpy $H = E + PV$. Its value is determined by the temperature, pressure, and composition of the system at any given time. According to the law of conservation of energy (see CONSERVATION LAW), the change in internal energy is equal to the HEAT transferred to the system minus the WORK done by the system. If the only work done is a change of volume at constant pressure, the enthalpy change is exactly equal to the heat transferred to the system.

entitlement Generally, the granting of government assistance to individuals as mandated by law or by need. Recipients of such assistance may be entitled to it by virtue of their status, without otherwise having to qualify for it. In the U.S., historically, legally mandated entitlements include MEDICARE AND MEDICAID, and SOCIAL SECURITY. Needs-based entitlements included UNEMPLOYMENT benefits, WORKERS' COMPENSATION, and Aid to Families with Dependent Children (AFDC). With passage of the Personal Responsibility and Work Opportunity Act (PRWORA) in 1996, most needs-based assistance lost entitlement status as federal programs were replaced by state-controlled systems funded by federal block grants. See also SOCIAL INSURANCE, WELFARE.

entomology Branch of ZOOLOGY dealing with the scientific study of INSECTS, including their taxonomy, morphology, physiology, and ecology. Applied aspects of entomology, such as the harmful and beneficial impact of insects on humans, are also studied.

entropy \'en-trə-pē\ Measure of a system's ENERGY that is unavailable for WORK, or of the degree of a system's disorder. When heat is added to a system held at constant temperature, the change in entropy is related to the change in energy, the PRESSURE, the temperature, and the change in volume. Its magnitude varies from zero to the total amount of energy in a system. The concept, first proposed in 1850 by the German physicist Rudolf Clausius (1822–1888), is sometimes presented as the second law of THERMODYNAMICS, which states that entropy increases during irreversible processes such as spontaneous mixing of hot and cold gases, uncontrolled expansion of a gas into a vacuum, and combustion of fuel. In popular, nontechnical use, entropy is regarded as a measure of the chaos or randomness of a system.

enuresis \,en-yu̇-'rē-səs\ Repeated URINATION into bedding or clothing, usually at night, in a normal child old enough to have completed toilet training. Enuresis may be voluntary or involuntary. It may run in families. Stressful life events, poor toilet training, and chronic social disadvantage increase its likelihood. It usually resolves with time. Treatment includes family education, reassurance, and behavior therapy. An alarm to wake the child when urination begins has proved highly effective but takes time to achieve complete success. Drug treatment, though not the treatment of choice, is sometimes effective.

Enver Pasa \en-'ver-pä-'shä\ (1881–1922) Turkish soldier and politician. He was one of the YOUNG TURKS who deposed the Ottoman sultan ABDÜLHAMID II in 1908. He later served as governor of Benghazi, Libya (1912), army chief of staff in the Second Balkan War (1913), and minister of war during World War I. A rival of MUSTAFA KEMAL ATATURK in the postwar period, he unsuccessfully sought Soviet help to overthrow him (1920).

environmental geology Scientific field concerned with applying the findings of geologic research to the problems of land use and civil engineering. It is closely allied with urban geology and deals with the impact of human activities on the physical environment. Other important concerns of environmental geology include reclaiming mined lands; identifying geologically stable sites for constructing buildings, nuclear power plants, and other facilities; and locating sources of building materials, such as sand and gravel.

Environmental Protection Agency (EPA) U.S. government agency that sets and enforces national pollution-control standards. It was established by Pres. RICHARD NIXON (1970) to supersede a welter of confusing and ineffective state environmental laws. Its early accomplishments include the banning of use of DDT (1972), the setting of deadlines for the removal of lead from gasoline (1973), the establishing of health standards for drinking water (1974), and the monitoring of fuel efficiency in automobiles (1975). Its existence has resulted in heightened awareness and concern for the environment worldwide.

environmental sculpture 20th-century art form that involves or encompasses the spectator. The environmental sculptor can use any medium. Indoor environmental works often incorporate sculptural figures in detailed settings in gallery or museum spaces. Outdoor works in natural or urban settings include "earthworks" (large-scale alterations of the earth's surface effected by earth-moving equipment) such as Robert Smithson's *Spiral Jetty* (1970), a rock-and-dirt spiral 1,500 feet long in the Great Salt Lake. The wrapped buildings of CHRISTO are among the notable urban environmental works.

environmentalism Advocacy of the preservation or improvement of the natural environment, especially the social movement to control environmental pollution. Other specific goals of environmentalism include control of human population growth, conservation of natural resources, and restriction of the negative effects of modern technology. Environmental advocacy at the international level by NONGOVERNMENTAL ORGANIZATIONS and some states has resulted in treaties, conventions, and other instruments of environmental law addressing problems such as GLOBAL WARMING, the depletion of the OZONE LAYER, and the danger of transboundary pollution from nuclear accidents. Influential U.S. and British environmentalists have included THOMAS ROBERT MALTHUS, JOHN MUIR, RACHEL CARSON, BARRY COMMONER, PAUL R. EHRLICH, and EDWARD O. WILSON. In the social sciences, the term refers to any theory that emphasizes the importance of environmental factors in the development of culture and society.

enzyme Substance that acts as a CATALYST in living organisms, regulating the REACTION RATE at which life's CHEMICAL REACTIONS proceed without being altered in the process. Enzymes reduce the ACTIVATION ENERGY needed to start these reactions; without them, most would not take place at a useful rate. Because they are not consumed, only tiny amounts are needed. Enzymes catalyze all aspects of cell metabolism; including the digestion of food, in which large nutrient molecules (including proteins, carbohydrates, and fats) are broken down into smaller molecules, the conservation and transformation of chemical energy, and the construction of cellular materials and components. Almost all enzymes are PROTEINS; many contain a COFACTOR, either an organic compound (e.g., a VITAMIN) or an inorganic ION (e.g., iron, zinc). The enzyme-cofactor combination assumes an active CONFIGURATION, usually including an active site for the substance (substrate) involved in the reaction to fit into. Many enzymes are specific to one substrate. If a competing molecule blocks the active site or changes its shape, the enzyme's activity is inhibited. If the configuration is destroyed (see DENATURATION), its activity is lost. Enzymes are classified by the type of reaction they catalyze: (1) OXIDATION-REDUCTION; (2) transfer of a chemical group; (3) HYDROLYSIS; (4) removal or addition of a chemical group; (5) isomerization (see ISOMER, ISOMERISM); and (6) binding together of substrate units (POLYMERIZATION). Most enzyme names end in "-ase." Enzymes are chiral catalysts, producing mostly or only one of the possible stereoisomeric products (see OPTICAL ACTIVITY). FERMENTATION of wine, leavening of bread, curdling of milk into cheese, and brewing of beer all are enzymatic reactions. Uses in medicine include killing disease-causing microorganisms, promoting wound healing, and diagnosing certain diseases.

Eocene epoch \'ē-ə-,sēn\ Major division of the TERTIARY PERIOD, from 54.8 to 33.7 million years ago. It follows the Paleocene epoch and precedes the Oligocene epoch. The name, derived from the Greek *eos* ("dawn"), refers to the dawn of recent life; during the Eocene, all the major divisions, or orders, of modern mammals appeared, as well as many essentially modern bird orders. Climates were warm and humid. Temperate and subtropical forests were widespread, but grasslands were limited.

Eochaid Ollathair See DAGDA

eohippus \,ē-ō-'hi-pəs\ Former name of a genus of ancestral horses, commonly called dawn horses, that flourished in North America during the Early EOCENE EPOCH (54.8–49 million years ago). It is now classified with European species in the genus *Hyracotherium*. Eohippus stood 1–2 ft (30–60 cm) high at the shoulders and was adapted to running, with hind legs longer than the forelegs. The body was lightly constructed, with slender legs and elongated feet that were functionally three-toed (though the front feet had four toes). The skull varied from shortened (primitive) to relatively long (more horselike).

Eolie, Isole See LIPARI ISLANDS

eon Long span of geologic time. In formal usage, eons are the longest portions of geologic time (ERAS are the second-longest). Three eons are recognized: the PHANEROZOIC EON (dating from the present back to the beginning of the Cambrian period), the PROTEROZOIC EON, and the ARCHEAN EON. Less formally, eon often refers to a span of one billion years.

eon (Gnosticism) See AEON

Epaminondas \i-ˌpam-ə-ˈnän-dəs\ (c. 410–362 BC) Theban statesman, tactician, and leader. He defeated the Spartans at Leuctra in 371 using a new strategy that attacked the opponent's strongest point first with overwhelming power, and made Thebes the most powerful state in Greece. He led four more successful expeditions into the Peloponnese. In 370–369 he freed the Messenian HELOTS from Spartan enslavement. In 362, at the head of a large allied force, he defeated Sparta, Athens, and their allies at MANTINEA, but was mortally wounded.

ephemeris \i-ˈfe-mə-rəs\ Table of the positions of celestial bodies at regular intervals, often with supplementary information. Constructed as early as the 4th century BC, ephemerides are still essential to astronomers and navigators. Modern ephemerides are calculated, with heavy computing and careful checking, when a mathematical description of a heavenly body's observed motion has evolved. Various national ephemerides are published regularly; the U.S. ephemeris, first published in 1852, became the best, and is now published as *The Astronomical Almanac.*

Ephesus \ˈe-fə-səs\ Ancient Ionian Greek city; its ruins lie near the modern village of Selcuk in western Turkey. It was situated south of the Cayster River, and was the site of the Temple of ARTEMIS. Traditionally founded by the Carians, it was one of the 12 Ionian Cities and was involved in the PERSIAN and PELOPONNESIAN wars. It was taken by ALEXANDER THE GREAT c. 334 BC and prospered throughout the HELLENISTIC period. It passed to Rome in 133 BC; under AUGUSTUS it became the capital of the Roman province of Asia. It was an early seat of Christianity, visited by St. PAUL, and the recipient of the Epistle to the Ephesians. The Goths destroyed the city and temple in AD 262; neither ever recovered. There are extensively excavated ruins at the modern site.

ephor \ˈe-fər, ˈe-ˌfȯr\ (Greek, *ephoros*) Title of the five highest Spartan magistrates. With the two kings of SPARTA they formed the state's executive wing. The list of ephors dated back to 754 BC. Every male citizen was eligible for election to the ephorate, which conducted meetings of the GEROUSIA and APELLA and executed their decrees. The ephors' extensive police powers allowed them to declare war on the HELOTS annually, with legal license to attack and kill them if necessary. In an emergency they could even arrest and try a king.

epic Long narrative poem in an elevated style that celebrates heroic achievement and treats themes of historical, national, religious, or legendary significance. Primary (or traditional) epics are shaped from the legends and traditions of a heroic age and are part of oral tradition; secondary (or literary) epics are written down from the beginning, and their poets adapt aspects of traditional epics. The poems of HOMER are usually regarded as the first important epics and the main source of epic conventions in Western Europe. These conventions include the centrality of a HERO, sometimes semidivine; an extensive, perhaps cosmic, setting; heroic battle; extended journeying; and the involvement of supernatural beings.

epic theater Dramatic form developed in Germany after World War I by BERTOLT BRECHT and others, intended to provoke rational thought rather than to create illusion. It presents loosely connected scenes often interrupted by direct addresses to the audience providing analysis, argument, or documentation. Brecht's goal was to use alienating or distancing effects to block the emotional responses of the audience members and force them to think objectively about the play. Actors were instructed to keep a distance between themselves and the characters they portrayed and to emphasize external actions rather than emotions.

epicenter Point on the surface of the earth that is directly above the source (or focus) of an EARTHQUAKE. There the effects of the earthquake usually are most severe. See also SEISMOLOGY.

Epictetus \ˌep-ik-ˈtet-əs\ (c. AD 55–c. 135) Greek philosopher associated with STOICISM. His original name is not known; *epiktetos* means "acquired." He is not known to have written anything, but his teachings were transmitted by his pupil Arrian (died c. AD 180) in two works, the *Discourses* and the *Encheiridion.* True education, Epictetus believed, consists in recognizing that the only thing that belongs to an individual fully is his will. Humans are not responsible for the ideas that present themselves to their consciousness, though they are wholly responsible for how they react to them.

"Barbarian Archer in Scythian Costume," Athenian plate by Epictetus, late 6th century BC; in the British Museum.

BY COURTESY OF THE TRUSTEES OF THE BRITISH MUSEUM

Epicureanism \ˌe-pi-kyu̇-ˈrē-ə-ˌni-zəm, ˌe-pi-ˈkyu̇r-ē-ə-ˌni-zəm\ Philosophy taught by EPICURUS. In ancient polemics, as often since, the term was employed with an even more generic meaning as the equivalent of hedonism, the doctrine that pleasure or happiness is the only intrinsic good. Popularly, Epicureanism thus means devotion to pleasure, comfort, and high living, with a certain elegance of style, though these meanings are only generally related to Epicurus' actual teachings.

Epicurus \ˌe-pi-ˈkyu̇-rəs\ (341–270 BC) Greek philosopher. His school in Athens, the Garden, competed with PLATO's Academy and ARISTOTLE's Lyceum. Several fundamental concepts characterize his philosophy. In physics, these are ATOMISM, a mechanical conception of causality, limited by the idea of a spontaneous motion, or "swerve," of the atoms, which interrupts the necessary effect of a cause; the infinity of the universe and the equilibrium of all forces that circularly enclose its phenomena; and the existence of gods, conceived as beatified and immortal natures completely extraneous to happenings in the world. In ethics, his basic concepts are the identification of good with pleasure and of the supreme good and ultimate end with the absence of pain from the body and the soul. See also EPICUREANISM.

Epidaurus \ˌe-pi-ˈdȯr-əs\ Town, ancient Greece. An important commercial center in the northeastern PELOPONNESE, it was famed for its 4th-century-BC temple of ASCLEPIUS. Excavations of the sacred precinct have uncovered that temple and other buildings, including a theater, stadium, and hospital. Offerings of small clay body parts have been found, and inscriptions record divine medical cures. Originally Ionic, it became Doric under the influence of ARGOS, to which it owed religious allegiance; politically it remained independent until Roman times.

epidemiology \ˌe-pə-ˌdē-mē-ˈä-lə-jē\ Study of disease distribution in populations and the factors that determine it, chiefly through statistics. It focuses on groups rather than individuals and often takes a historical perspective. Descriptive epidemiology surveys a population to see what segments (e.g., age, sex, ethnic group, occupation) are affected by a disorder, follows changes or variations in its incidence or mortality over time and in different locations, and helps identify syndromes or suggest associations with risk factors. Analytic epidemiology conducts studies to test the conclusions of descriptive surveys or laboratory observations. Epidemiologic data on diseases is used to find those at high risk, identify causes and take preventive measures, and plan new health services.

epidote \ˈe-pə-ˌdōt\ Any of a group of colorless to green or yellow-green silicate minerals with the general chemical formula $A_2B_3(SiO_4)(Si_2O_7)O(OH)$, in which *A* is usually calcium (Ca) and *B* is generally aluminum (Al), although other elements are sometimes substituted. The epidote minerals occur as reaction products of other (earlier) minerals in low-grade (formed under relatively low-temperature, low-pressure conditions) regionally metamorphosed rocks, where their occurrence is used as an indicator of metamorphic grade.

epidote-amphibolite facies \ˈe-pə-ˌdōt-am-ˈfi-bə-ˌlīt-ˈfā-shēz\ One of the major divisions of the mineral facies classification of METAMORPHIC ROCKS, encompassing rocks that formed under moderate temperature (500–750°F, or 250–400°C) and pressure conditions. This facies grades into the GREENSCHIST FACIES under less intense metamorphic conditions and into the AMPHIBOLITE FACIES with greater temperature and pressure. Typical minerals include biotite, almandine garnet, plagioclase, epidote, and amphibole. Chlorite, muscovite, staurolite, and chloritoid may also occur.

epigram Short poem treating concisely, pointedly, and often satirically a single thought or event and often ending with a witticism or ingenious turn of thought. By extension, the term applies to a terse, sage, or witty (often paradoxical) saying, usually in the form of a generalization. Writers of Latin epigrams included CATULLUS and MARTIAL. The form was revived in the Renaissance. Later masters of the epigram have included BEN JONSON, FRANCOIS LA ROCHEFOUCAULD, VOLTAIRE, ALEXANDER POPE, SAMUEL TAYLOR COLERIDGE, OSCAR WILDE, and GEORGE BERNARD SHAW.

epilepsy *or* **cerebral seizures** *or* **convulsive disorder** Sudden, recurrent disturbances in mental function, consciousness, sensory activity, or body movements, caused by paroxysmal malfunction of neurons in the CEREBRAL CORTEX. Not a specific disease but a complex of symptoms, epilepsy includes generalized (grand mal) seizures, absence (petit mal) seizures (momentary lapses of awareness), and focal seizures (localized movements and sensations). Neurologists classify cases by clinical pattern, site of origin (often located by ELECTROENCEPHALOGRAPHY), and cause. Treatable causes include some brain tumors, infections, metabolic and endocrine-system abnormalities, and trauma. Brain surgery helps a few epileptics. In most, seizures can be controlled to varying extents by anticonvulsant drugs.

epinephrine \ˌe-pə-ˈne-frən\ *or* **adrenaline** \ə-ˈdre-nᵊl-ən\ One of two HORMONES (the other being NOREPINEPHRINE) secreted by the ADRENAL GLANDS, as well as at some nerve endings (see NEURON), where they serve as NEUROTRANSMITTERS. They are similar chemically and have similar actions on the body. They increase the rate and force of heart contractions, increasing blood output and raising BLOOD PRESSURE. Epinephrine also stimulates breakdown of GLYCOGEN to GLUCOSE in the liver, raising blood glucose levels, and both hormones increase the level of circulating free FATTY ACIDS. All these actions ready the body for action in times of stress or danger requiring increased alertness or exertion. Epinephrine is used in medical situations including cardiac arrest, ASTHMA, and acute allergic attack (see ALLERGY).

Epiphany Christian festival celebrated on January 6. One of the oldest Christian holy days (along with CHRISTMAS and EASTER), the festival originated in the Eastern church and was adopted in the Western church by the 4th century. It commemorates the first manifestation of JESUS to the Gentiles, as represented by the MAGI. The eve of Epiphany, called Twelfth Night, is thought to mark the arrival of the Wise Men in Bethlehem. Epiphany also celebrates the (much later) baptism of Jesus by JOHN THE BAPTIST and Jesus' first miracle, performed at Cana.

epiphyte Any plant that grows upon or is attached to another plant or object merely for physical support. Epiphytes are found mostly in the tropics and are also known as air plants because they have no attachment to the ground or other obvious nutrient source. They obtain water and minerals from rain and from debris on the supporting plants. ORCHIDS, FERNS, and members of the PINEAPPLE family are common tropical epiphytes. LICHENS, MOSSES, LIVERWORTS, and ALGAE are epiphytes of temperate regions.

Epirus \i-ˈpī-rəs\ Ancient country, northwestern Greece. It was bounded by ILLYRIA, MACEDONIA, THESSALY, AETOLIA, ACARNANIA, and the Ionian Sea. In the NEOLITHIC PERIOD it was populated by peoples from the southwestern Balkans, who brought with them the Greek language and who may have been among the founders of MYCENAE. It was the launching area of the DORIAN invasions (1100–1000 BC) into Greece. A princess from Epirus was married to PHILIP II of Macedon; their son was ALEXANDER THE GREAT. The area became a Roman province in the 2nd century BC and later, a part of the BYZANTINE EMPIRE. An independent state in 1204 AD, it was taken in 1430 by the Ottoman Turks. Greece gained the southern part of the region by 1919; the northern part is now in southern Albania.

episcopacy \i-ˈpis-kə-pə-sē\ System of church government by BISHOPS. It existed as early as the 2nd century AD, when bishops were chosen to oversee preaching and worship within a specific region, now called a diocese. Today local congregations are shepherded by priests and deacons, but only bishops can ordain priests, perform the rite of CONFIRMATION, and consecrate other bishops. Their special duties are closely tied to the idea of APOSTOLIC SUCCESSION. Some Protestant churches abandoned episcopacy during the REFORMATION, but it was retained by the Roman Catholic, Eastern Orthodox, Anglican, and Swedish Lutheran churches, among others.

Episcopal Church, Protestant Descendant of the Church of ENGLAND in the U.S. With the American Revolution, the Church of England was disestablished in the U.S. (1789), and American Anglicans renamed it the Protestant Episcopal Church. The church accepts both the Apostles' and NICENE CREEDS and a modified version of the Thirty-nine Articles of the Church of England. The General Convention is the highest ecclesiastical authority, and it is headed by a presiding bishop, which it elects. The Reformed Episcopal Church broke away from the main body in 1873. The church accepted the ordination of women in 1976.

episome \ˈe-pə-ˌsōm\ Any of a group of genetic elements consisting of DNA and capable of giving selective advantage to the bacteria in which they occur. Episomes may be attached to the bacterial cell membrane or become part of the CHROMOSOME. Cells with episomes act like males during conjugation, a mating process in certain bacteria. During conjugation, cells lacking the episome may receive either the episome or the episome plus the genes to which it is attached. Experiments involving gene transfers from cells in which episomes have been incorporated in the chromosomes have been used to determine the locations of genes on the chromosome.

epistatic gene \ˌe-pə-ˈsta-tik\ GENE that determines whether or not a trait determined by another gene will be expressed. For example, when the gene responsible for albinism occurs, the genes that determine skin color are present but not expressed; the gene for albinism is therefore called an epistatic gene.

epistemology Study of the origin, nature, and limits of human knowledge. Nearly every great philosopher has contributed to the epistemological literature. One major issue is whether all knowledge is derived from experience. EMPIRICISM affirms this view for all nonanalytic propositions (see analytic–synthetic distinction); RATIONALISM rejects it. Other related issues include whether beliefs that cannot be verified or falsified by experience can be considered knowledge. Philosophers have long disputed whether knowledge is a type of belief, and whether knowledge requires a special faculty in the mind or a disposition to act in certain ways. PLATO characterized knowledge as justified true belief, and most modern epistemological discussions start from that point, but do not accept that simple description.

epistolary novel \i-ˈpis-tə-ˌler-ē, ˌe-pi-ˈstōl-ə-rē\ NOVEL in the form of a series of letters written by one or more of the characters. It allows the author to present the characters' thoughts without interference, convey events with dramatic immediacy, and present events from several points of view. It was one of the first novelistic forms to be developed. It was foreshadowed by APHRA BEHN's poem cycle *Love-Letters Between a Nobleman and His Sister* (1683). The outstanding early example is SAMUEL RICHARDSON's *Pamela* (1740); distinguished later works include TOBIAS SMOLLETT's *Humphry Clinker* (1771) and PIERRE LACLOS's *Les Liaisons dangereuses* (1782). The genre remained popular up to the 19th century. Its reliance on subjective points of view makes it the forerunner of the modern psychological novel.

epitaph \ˈe-pə-ˌtaf\ Inscription in verse or prose on a tomb, or, by extension, anything written as if to be inscribed on a tomb. Probably the earliest surviving epitaphs are those written on ancient Egyptian sarcophagi and coffins. Ancient Greek examples are often of literary interest. In Elizabethan times epitaphs began to assume a more literary character. Many of the best known are literary memorials (often deliberately witty) not intended for a tomb.

epithalamium \ˌe-pə-thə-ˈlā-mē-əm\ *or* **epithalamion** \ˌe-pə-thə-ˈlā-mē-ən\ Nuptial song or poem in honor or praise of a bride and bridegroom. In ancient Greece such songs were a traditional way of invoking good fortune on a marriage and often of indulging in ribaldry. The earliest evidence for literary epithalamiums are fragments by SAPPHO; the oldest surviving Latin examples are three by CATULLUS. In the Renaissance, epithalamiums based on classical models were written in Italy, France, and England; that of EDMUND SPENSER (1595) is considered the finest in English.

epoch Unit of geologic time during which a rock series is deposited. It is a subdivision of a geologic PERIOD. Additional distinctions can be made by adding relative time terms, such as early, middle, and late. The use of the term is usually restricted to divisions of the TERTIARY and QUATERNARY PERIODS.

Epona \'e-pō-nə\ Horse goddess of the ancient CELTIC RELIGION. Associated with kingship and fertility, she was known as Epona in Gaul, Rhiannon in Wales, and Macha in Ireland. Her cult was found throughout the Western Roman empire and was spread by members of the Roman army, especially cavalry units.

epoxy \i-'päk-sē\ Any of a class of thermosetting POLYMERS, polyethers built up from MONOMERS with an ETHER group that takes the form of a three-membered epoxide ring. The familiar two-part epoxy adhesives consist of a RESIN with epoxide rings at the ends of its MOLECULES and a curing agent containing AMINES or ANHYDRIDES. When mixed, these react to yield, after curing, a complex network with ether groups linking the monomers. Stable, tough, and resistant to corrosive chemicals, epoxies are excellent adhesives and useful surface coatings.

EPROM \'ē-,präm\ *in full* **erasable programmable read-only memory** Form of computer MEMORY that does not lose its content when the power supply is cut off and that can be erased and reused. EPROMs are generally employed for programs designed for repeated use (such as the BIOS) but that can be upgraded with a later version of the program.

Epstein \'ep-,stīn\, **Jacob** *later* **Sir Jacob** (1880–1959) U.S.-British sculptor. Born in New York City, he studied in Paris and settled in England in 1905. His 18 figures known as the Strand Statues (1907–8) provoked outrage by their nudity; his nude angel on the tomb of OSCAR WILDE (1912) in Paris was attacked as indecent. In 1913 he became affiliated with VORTICISM, and developed a style characterized by simple forms and calm surfaces in pieces carved from stone, often partly retaining the shape of the original block, or modeled in plaster, such as *The Rock Drill* (1913–14). He is best known for religious and allegorical figures carved in colossal blocks of stone, and for bronze portrait busts of celebrities. Occasionally he produced monumental bronze groups, such as *St. Michael and the Devil* (1958) for Coventry Cathedral.

Epstein-Barr virus \,ep-,stīn-'bär\ *or* **EB virus (EBV)** Herpesvirus, named for two of its discoverers, that is the major cause of acute infectious MONONUCLEOSIS. The virus infects only salivary-gland cells and one type of white blood cell. Saliva is the only bodily fluid that has been proved to contain infectious EBV particles. In less-developed nations, infection with EBV occurs in almost all children before the age of 5 and is not associated with any symptoms. When EBV infection is delayed until the teen or early adult years, the body commonly responds differently, resulting in infectious mononucleosis. Other, rarer disorders have also been linked with Epstein-Barr virus, including certain cancers. There are no specific treatments for any form of EBV infection, and no vaccines have been developed.

equal-field system Chinese land-distribution system, AD 485–8th century. Borrowed by Japan in 646, it lasted about a century there. Under the system, all adults were assigned a fixed amount of land; a portion of its produce was paid as taxes. On a person's death, most of the land was returned to the government. Increases in population and a tendency for the land to come to be held permanently led to the system's collapse in China; tax-free status and additional allotments for nobles and monasteries resulted in its demise in Japan.

equal protection Guarantee under the 14th Amendment to the U.S. CONSTITUTION that a state must treat an individual or class of individuals the same as it treats other individuals or classes in like circumstances. It protects against laws that treat individuals differently without a rational basis for doing so. Until the 1960s it was applied sparingly, and primarily to cases involving discrimination against blacks. Beginning in the 1960s, the U.S. Supreme Court under EARL WARREN dramatically transformed the concept, applying it to cases involving welfare benefits, exclusionary ZONING, municipal services, and school financing. Under WARREN E. BURGER, the Court extended it to cases involving sex discrimination and the status and rights of ALIENS. Under WILLIAM REHNQUIST, the Court has applied it to cases involving homosexual rights and discrimination against persons with disabilities.

Equal Rights Amendment (ERA) Proposed but unratified amendment to the U.S. CONSTITUTION designed mainly to invalidate many state and federal laws that discriminated against women. Its central tenet was that sex should not be a determining factor in establishing the legal rights of individuals. It was first introduced in Congress in 1923, shortly after women obtained the right to vote. It was finally approved by the U.S. Senate 49 years later (1972) but was subsequently ratified by only 30 of the 50 state legislatures. Critics claimed it would cause women to lose privileges and protections, such as exemption from compulsory military service and economic support by their husbands. Supporters, led by the NATIONAL ORGANIZATION FOR WOMEN, argued that discriminatory state and federal laws left many women in a state of economic dependency.

equality Generally, an ideal of uniformity in treatment or status by those in a position to affect either. Acknowledgment of the right to equality often must be coerced from the advantaged by the disadvantaged. Equality of opportunity was the founding creed of U.S. society, but equality among all races and between the sexes has proved easier to legislate than to achieve in practice. Social or religious inequality is deeply ingrained in some cultures and thus difficult to overcome (see CASTE). Government efforts to achieve economic equality include enhancing opportunities through tax policy, subsidized training and education, redistributing wealth or resources, and preferential treatment of those historically treated unequally (see AFFIRMATIVE ACTION). See also CIVIL-RIGHTS MOVEMENT, FEMINISM, GAY-RIGHTS MOVEMENT, HUMAN RIGHTS, UNIVERSAL DECLARATION OF HUMAN RIGHTS.

equation Statement of equality between two expressions consisting of variables and/or numbers. In essence, equations are questions, and the development of mathematics has been driven by attempts to find answers to those questions in a systematic way. Equations vary in complexity from simple ALGEBRAIC EQUATIONS (involving only addition or multiplication) to DIFFERENTIAL EQUATIONS, exponential equations (involving exponential expressions), and INTEGRAL EQUATIONS. They are used to express many of the laws of PHYSICS. See also SYSTEM OF EQUATIONS.

equation, algebraic See ALGEBRAIC EQUATION

equation, difference See DIFFERENCE EQUATION

equation, quadratic See QUADRATIC EQUATION

equation of motion See equation of MOTION

equation of state See equation of STATE

equations, system of See SYSTEM OF EQUATIONS

equator Great circle around the earth that is everywhere equidistant from the geographic poles and lies in a plane perpendicular to the earth's axis. This geographic, or terrestrial, equator divides the earth into the Northern and Southern Hemispheres and forms the imaginary reference line on the earth's surface from which LATITUDE is reckoned (i.e., 0° latitude). In astronomy, the celestial equator is the great circle in which the plane of the terrestrial equator intersects the celestial sphere; it is thus equidistant from the celestial poles. When the sun lies in its plane, day and night are everywhere of equal length; this happens at the EQUINOXES.

Equatorial Africa See FRENCH EQUATORIAL AFRICA

equatorial coordinates See CELESTIAL COORDINATES

Equatorial Guinea *officially* **Republic of Equatorial Guinea** *formerly* **Spanish Guinea** Republic on the western coast of equatorial Africa, partly on the mainland, and including BIOKO Island. Area: 10,831 sq mi (28,051 sq km). Population (1997): 443,000. Capital: MALABO. The majority of the mainland population are Bantu-speaking FANG people, with a minority of other Bantu-speaking tribes (see BANTU LANGUAGES). The majority on Bioko are the Bubi, descendants of Bantu migrants from the mainland. Languages: Spanish, French (both official); pidgin English is commonly spoken. Religion: Roman Catholicism (four-fifths of the population); the Bubi retain their traditional religion. Currency: CFA franc. Bordered by Cameroon and Gabon, Equatorial Guinea's mainland region, Río Muni (Mbini), is separated by the Bight of BIAFRA from the island area of Bioko to the northwest. The mainland has a coastal plain some 12 mi (20 km) wide, with a long stretch of beach, low cliffs to the south, and hills and plateaus to the east. The Benito River divides the region. The island of Bioko consists of three extinct volcanic cones and has several crater lakes and rich lava soils. Dense tropical rain forest prevails throughout the mainland, and includes valuable hardwoods. Animal life has been decimated by overhunting. Cacao, timber, and coffee are the only exports. Equatorial Guinea is a republic with one legislative house; its chief of state is the president, and the head of government is the prime minister. The first inhabitants of the mainland region appear to have been PYGMIES. The now-prominent Fang and Bubi reached the mainland region in the 17th-century Bantu migra-

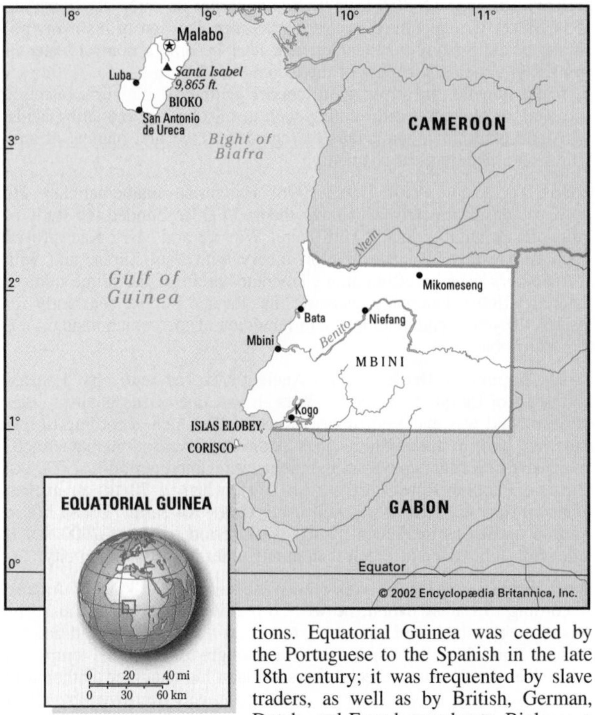

tions. Equatorial Guinea was ceded by the Portuguese to the Spanish in the late 18th century; it was frequented by slave traders, as well as by British, German, Dutch, and French merchants. Bioko was administered by British authorities (1827–58) before the official takeover by the Spanish. The mainland (Río Muni) was not effectively occupied by the Spanish until 1926. Independence was declared in 1968, followed by a reign of terror and economic chaos under the dictatorial president Macías Nguema, who was overthrown by a military coup in 1979 and later executed. A new constitution was adopted in 1982, but political unrest persisted.

eques \'e-ˌkwes, 'ē-ˌkwēz\ (Latin: "horseman") In ancient Rome, a knight. In early Rome, the equites (in full, *equites equo publico,* "horsemen with mounts provided at public expense") were of the senatorial class. They were the most influential members of the COMITIA CENTURIATA. By the early 4th century BC, non-senators could be equites, providing their own horses. AUGUSTUS reorganized them as a military class, removing them from politics; qualifications were free birth, good health and character, and wealth. In the 1st century AD, equites were permitted civil careers, and they became particularly involved in financial administration.

equilibrium Condition in which the net FORCE acting on a particle is zero. A body in equilibrium experiences no ACCELERATION and, unless disturbed by an outside force, will remain in equilibrium indefinitely. A stable equilibrium is one in which small, externally induced displacements from that state produce forces that tend to oppose the displacement and return the body to equilibrium. An unstable equilibrium is one in which the least departures produce forces tending to increase the displacement. A brick lying on the floor is in stable equilibrium, while a ball bearing balanced on a knife-edge is in unstable equilibrium.

equilibrium, chemical Condition in the course of a reversible CHEMICAL REACTION in which no net change in the amounts of reactants and products occurs: Products are reverting to reactants at the same rate as reactants are forming products. For practical purposes, the reaction under those conditions is completed. Expressed in terms of the law of MASS ACTION, the REACTION RATE to form products is equal to the reaction rate to re-form reactants. The ratio of the reaction rate constants (i.e., of the amounts of reactants and products, each raised to the proper power), defines the equilibrium constant. Changing the conditions of TEMPERATURE or PRESSURE changes the reaction's equilibrium; a high temperature or pressure may be used to "push" a reaction that at ordinary conditions makes little product. See also H.-L. LE CHÂTELIER.

equine \'ē-ˌkwīn, 'e-ˌkwīn\ Any member of the UNGULATE family Equidae, which includes the modern HORSES, ZEBRAS, and ASSES, all in the genus *Equus,* as well as more than 60 species known only from fossils. Equines descended from the dawn horse (see EOHIPPUS). Wild horses, which once inhabited much of northern Eurasia, were smaller and had shorter legs than their domesticated descendants. See also PRZEWALSKI'S HORSE.

equinox \'ē-kwə-ˌnäks, 'e-kwə-ˌnäks\ Either of two moments in the year when the sun is exactly above the EQUATOR and day and night are of equal length all over the earth. The vernal equinox, when spring begins in the Northern Hemisphere, occurs about March 21, when the sun moves north across the celestial equator. The autumnal equinox falls about September 23, as the sun crosses the celestial equator going south. The term equinox also refers to either of two points in the sky where the ECLIPTIC and the celestial equator (see CELESTIAL SPHERE) intersect. See also SOLSTICE.

equinoxes, precession of the Motion of the points where the sun crosses the celestial equator, caused by PRECESSION of earth's axis. HIPPARCHUS noticed that the stars' positions were shifted consistently from earlier measures, indicating that the earth, not the stars, was moving. This precession, a wobbling in the orientation of earth's axis with a cycle of almost 26,000 years, is caused by the gravity of the sun and the moon acting on earth's equatorial bulge. The planets also have a small influence on precession. Projecting earth's axis onto the CELESTIAL SPHERE locates the northern and southern celestial poles. Precession makes these points trace out circles on the sky and also makes the celestial equator wobble, changing its points of intersection (equinoxes) with the ECLIPTIC.

equipartition of energy See equipartition of ENERGY

equistetum See HORSETAIL

equity Finance and accounting concept. Equity represents any of three separate but related values: the money value of a property or of an interest in a property in excess of claims or liens against it; a risk interest or ownership right in property; and the common STOCK of a corporation. In CORPORATE FINANCE, a basic equation holds that a company's total assets minus total liabilities equals total owners' equity.

equity Justice according to fairness, especially as distinguished from mechanical application of rules under COMMON LAW. Courts of equity (also called chancery courts) arose in England in the 14th century in response to the increasingly strict rules of proof and other requirements of the courts of law. Equity provided remedies not available under the old WRIT system. Often these remedies involved something other than damages, such as specific performance of contractual obligations, enforcement of a TRUST, restitution of goods wrongfully acquired, imposition of an INJUNCTION, or the correction and cancellation of false or misleading documents. The equity courts eventually established their own precedents, rules, and doctrines and began to rival the law courts in power. The two systems were united in 1873. Courts of equity also developed early in U.S. history, but by the early 20th century most jurisdictions had combined them with courts of law into a single system. Modern courts apply both legal and equitable principles and offer both legal and equitable relief.

equivalence principle Fundamental principle of physics that in its weak form states that gravitational (see GRAVITATION) and inertial (see INERTIA) masses are the same. ALBERT EINSTEIN's stronger version states that gravitation and ACCELERATION are indistinguishable. It implies that the effect of gravity is removed in a suitably accelerated reference frame, such as an elevator with its cable cut, in which a person would experience FREE FALL.

equivalence relation In mathematics, a generalization of the idea of equality between elements of a SET. All equivalence relations (e.g., that symbolized by the equals sign) obey three conditions: reflexivity (every element is in the relation to itself), symmetry (element A has the same relation to element B that B has to A), and transitivity (see TRANSITIVE LAW). Congruence of triangles is an equivalence relation in geometry. Members of a set are said to be in the same equivalence class if they have an equivalence relation.

equivalent weight *or* **combining weight** Quantity of an element that exactly reacts with (equals the combining value of) 1 g of hydrogen, 8 g of oxygen, or a corresponding amount of any other element. An

E
F
G

element's equivalent weight is its ATOMIC WEIGHT divided by its VALENCE. In general, for OXIDATION-REDUCTION, including ELECTROLYSIS, the equivalent weight is the weight associated with the loss or gain of 6.02×10^{23} electrons (AVOGADRO'S NUMBER) or 96,500 coulombs; this is also the MOLECULAR WEIGHT divided by the number of electrons lost or gained. The equivalent weight of a substance with several valences differs depending on the number of electrons transferred in the given reaction. The number of equivalent weights of any substance dissolved in one liter of solution is called the solution's normality *(N)*. See also STOICHIOMETRY.

Er Hai *or* **Erh Hai** \'er-'hī\ Lake, western YUNNAN province, China. It lies in a deep basin at the foot of the Diancang range between the upper CHANG, there called the Jinsha, and MEKONG rivers; it is about 30 mi (50 km) long and 6–10 mi (10–16 km) wide. The south of the basin has connections to eastern Yunnan and to SICHUAN province and is on the main route southwest to Myanmar (Burma). The surrounding area was brought under Chinese control during the YUAN DYNASTY (late 13th century).

Er Rif \er-'rif\ *or* **Rif** Hilly coastal region, northern Morocco. Constituting the central and eastern parts of former Spanish Morocco, the hills extend from east of MELILLA to CEUTA. For the greater part of its length, the mountains hug the Mediterranean Sea, leaving only a few narrow coastal valleys suitable for agriculture or urban settlement. The higher peaks are snowcapped in winter. In the 1920s, BERBER tribes inhabiting the region rose in revolt under Abd al-Krim to resist Franco-Spanish occupation.

era Very long span of geologic time; in formal usage, a portion of geologic time of the second-greatest magnitude (eons are longer). Three eras are recognized: PALEOZOIC, MESOZOIC, and CENOZOIC. Because of the difficulties involved in establishing accurate chronologies, the PRECAMBRIAN, or earliest, eras are classified independently. An era is composed of one or more geologic PERIODS.

ERA See EQUAL RIGHTS AMENDMENT

Era of Good Feelings See Era of GOOD FEELINGS

erasable programmable read-only memory See EPROM

Erasmus \i-'raz-məs\, **Desiderius** (1469–1536) Dutch priest and humanist, considered the greatest European scholar of the 16th century. Born in Rotterdam, the illegitimate son of a priest and a physician's daughter, he entered a monastery and was ordained a priest in 1492. He studied at the University of Paris and traveled throughout Europe, coming under the influence of ST. THOMAS MORE and JOHN COLET. The book that first made him famous was the *Adagia* (1500, 1508), an annotated collection of Greek and Latin proverbs. He became noted for his editions of classical authors, Church Fathers, and the New Testament as well as for his own works, including *Handbook of a Christian Knight* (1503) and *Praise of Folly* (1509). Using the philological methods pioneered by Italian humanists, he helped lay the groundwork for the historical-critical study of the past. By criticizing ecclesiastical abuses, he encouraged the growing urge for reform, which found expression both in the Protestant REFORMATION and in the Catholic COUNTER-REFORMATION. Though he saw much to admire in MARTIN LUTHER, he came under pressure to attack him; he took an independent stance, rejecting both Luther's doctrine of predestination and the powers claimed for the papacy.

Eratosthenes of Cyrene \,er-ə-'täs-thə-,nēz\ (276?–194? BC) Greek scientific writer, astronomer, and poet. He settled in Alexandria c. 255 BC and became director of its great library. He is the first man known to have calculated the earth's circumference, though the exact length of the units (stadia) he used is uncertain. He also measured the tilt of earth's axis with great accuracy, compiled a star catalog, worked out a calendar that included leap years, and tried to fix the dates of literary and political events since the siege of Troy.

Erbakan \,er-bä-'kän\, **Necmettin** (born 1926) First Islamic-party politician to win a general election in Turkey (1995). Son of an Ottoman-era religious court judge, he studied mechanical engineering before being elected to the National Assembly in 1969. He formed an Islamic party in 1970 and again in 1972 and served twice as deputy prime minister. His third attempt to form a party created the REFAH (WELFARE) PARTY, which won the most seats in the 1995 elections. He formed a coalition government in 1996, but his party was outlawed in 1997 and he was banned from politics.

Ercker, Lazarus (1530?–1594?) German writer on early METALLURGY. In 1554 Ercker was appointed assayer at Dresden, the first of his many positions in the Saxony bureaucracy, and later became a control tester of coins. His systematic review of the techniques then in use for testing alloys and minerals of silver, gold, copper, antimony, mercury, bismuth, and lead, of obtaining and refining such metals, and of extracting acids, salts, and other compounds may be regarded as the first manual of analytical and metallurgical chemistry.

Erdös \'er-dòsh\, **Paul** (1913–1996) Hungarian mathematician. He proved a classic theorem of number theory (1933), founded the study of probabilistic number theory with Aurel Wintner and Mark Kac, proved important results in approximation theory with Paul Turan, and with Atle Selberg gave an astounding elementary proof of the prime number theorem (1949). Famously eccentric, he traveled almost constantly for his last 40 years, collaborating with hundreds of mathematicians on numerous problems.

Erech \'ē-,rek\ *or* **Uruk** \'ü-,ru̇k\ Ancient MESOPOTAMIAN city. Located northwest of UR on the EUPHRATES RIVER, it was one of the greatest cities of SUMER and was enclosed by brickwork walls which according to legend were built by the mythical hero GILGAMESH. Excavations have traced successive cities that date from the prehistoric Ubaid period (c. 5000 BC) down to Parthian times (126 BC–AD 224), when c. 70 BC an ancient school of learned scribes was still using CUNEIFORM script. Urban life in what is known as the Erech-Jamdat Nasr period (c. 3500–2900 BC) is more fully illustrated at Erech than at any other Mesopotamian city.

Erechtheus \i-'rek-,thüs, i-'rek-thē-əs\ Legendary god-king of Athens. According to HOMER's *Iliad*, he was born from the earth and raised by ATHENA, who established him in her temple at Athens. Later tradition associates him with a huge snake that was thought to live in the temple. In a lost play by EURIPIDES, Erechtheus sacrificed his daughter Chthonia to ensure a victory in war, and as punishment was destroyed by either POSEIDON or ZEUS.

eremite See HERMIT

Ereshkigal \ā-'resh-,kē-gəl\ In MESOPOTAMIAN RELIGION, the goddess of the underworld. Her chief enemy was her sister ISHTAR, a fertility goddess and guardian of life. Namtar, the death-bringing demon, was her offspring and servant. Her cult extended to Egypt, Arabia, and Asia Minor.

Eretria \e-'rē-trē-ə\ Ancient Greek town, on the island of EUBOEA. Jointly with its neighbor KHALKÍS, it founded CUMAE in Italy c. 750 BC, the first of the Greek colonies in the west. Subsequent rivalry with Khalkís culminated in war, and by the classical period Khalkís was the leading city of Euboea. In 499–498 BC Eretrian triremes sailed to support the Ionian revolt against PERSIA, for which act DARIUS destroyed the city (490 BC) and deported the population. It was rebuilt, but under Macedonian and Roman rule it became insignificant. There are extensive ruins at the site.

Erfurt \'er-,fu̇rt\ City (pop., 1996 est.: 211,000), central Germany. BONIFACE founded a bishopric there in AD 742, and by 805 it was an important center on the Frankish empire's eastern border. It was granted municipal rights c. 1250, and joined the HANSEATIC LEAGUE in the 15th century. The city passed to Prussia in 1802, forming part of Prussian SAXONY until 1945. It was the site of the first meeting of the heads of East and West Germany in 1970. It is dominated by its 12th century cathedral; other buildings include the monastery where MARTIN LUTHER was a monk (1505–8). Erfurt is an important road and railway junction and a commercial center.

ergativity Tendency of a language to pair the subject, or agent, of an intransitive verb with the object, or patient, of a transitive verb. This contrasts with the situation in nominative-accusative languages such as Latin or English, in which the subjects of both transitive and intransitive verbs are paired grammatically, and distinguished from the object of a transitive verb. Languages or language families that display ergativity to varying degrees include Sumerian, CAUCASIAN LANGUAGES, ESKIMO-ALEUT, MAYAN, AUSTRALIAN ABORIGINAL LANGUAGES, and many AMERICAN INDIAN LANGUAGES.

ergonomics See HUMAN-FACTORS ENGINEERING

ergot \'er-gət, 'er-,gät\ Disease of CEREAL GRASSES, especially RYE, caused by the FUNGUS *Claviceps purpurea.* An ear of rye infected with ergot exudes a sweet, yellowish mucus. Ergot is the source of drugs used to control postpartum hemorrhage and to treat migraine headaches. Lysergic acid, from which the powerful HALLUCINOGEN LSD is synthesized, comes from ergot. Taking an overdose of ergot-derived medications or eating flour milled from ergot-infected rye can cause ergotism (also called St. Anthony's Fire) in humans and livestock; symptoms may include convulsions, miscarriages in females, and dry gangrene, and may result in death.

Ergun River See ARGUN RIVER

Erhard \'er-ˌhärt\, **Ludwig** (1897–1977) German economist and politician. As economics minister (1949–63), he was the chief architect of West Germany's postwar economic recovery. He achieved what has been called an economic miracle through his "social market system," which was based on free-market capitalism but included special provisions for housing, farming, and social programs. In 1957 he was appointed federal vice-chancellor, and in 1963 he succeeded KONRAD ADENAUER as chancellor. His government was troubled by an economic downturn and a budget deficit, as well as Erhard's relative weakness as a leader, and he was forced to resign in 1966.

Eric the Red See ERIK THE RED

erica \'er-i-kə\ Any of the approximately 500 species of low evergreen shrubs that make up the genus *Erica,* in the HEATH FAMILY, most native to South Africa. Some also occur in the Mediterranean and in northern Europe, and species have been introduced to North America. They have small, narrow leaves arranged in whorls set closely together on the shoots. Some African species are large bushes or trees. The white, or tree, heath *(E. arborea)* is also known as BRIER. Some southern African species are cultivated in cool greenhouses and outdoors in southwestern North America.

Erickson, Arthur (Charles) (born 1924) Canadian architect. Born in Vancouver, he first earned wide recognition with his plan for Simon Fraser University (1963–65), designed with Geoffrey Massey, which included an enormous skylit indoor plaza, a sensitive response to a cool, rainy climate. Robson Square, Vancouver (1978–79), a large civic center, incorporates waterfalls, a roof garden, plazas, and stairs with integrated ramps. Other works include UBC's Museum of Anthropology (1976), with its succession of concrete piers and broad expanses of glass, and the Canadian Embassy in Washington, D.C. (1989), a blend of contemporary and neoclassical elements that echo its surroundings.

Ericsson, John (1803–1889) Swedish-U.S. naval engineer and inventor. He moved to England in 1826, where he constructed a steam locomotive (1829) and later devised a caloric engine and patented a screw propeller. He emigrated to the U.S in 1839. During the Civil War he proposed, designed, and built a novel warship, the *MONITOR*. Its battle with the *Merrimack* led the government to place an order for many more such vessels. Wholly steam-powered and with a screw propeller and an armored revolving turret, it set a new pattern for U.S. warships that continued until the 20th century. He later developed a TORPEDO and investigated solar-powered motors.

Eridu \'er-i-ˌdü, e-'rē-dü\ Ancient city, on the Persian Gulf. While it was the chief seaport of SUMER and BABYLONIA, and was located near UR and the EUPHRATES, its coastline has filled in, and the site is now 120 mi (193 km) inland, in modern Iraq. It was revered as the oldest city in Sumer, and its patron god was Enki (EA). Founded on sand dunes c. 5th millennium BC, its ruins show the sequence of the preliterate Ubaid civilization, with a long succession of superimposed temples portraying the development of an elaborate mud-brick architecture. It was occupied until c. 600 BC.

Eridu Genesis \e-'rē-dü\ Sumerian creation epic. It recounted the origins of the world and humanity, the founding of cities, and the great flood sent by the gods to destroy humanity. Forewarned by the god EA, a man named Ziusudra, known for his humility and obedience, built a huge boat in which to ride out the flood. As a reward for his good life, the gods later granted him immortality.

Erie City (pop., 1996 est.: 105,000), northwestern Pennsylvania. Named for the Erie Indians, it was the site of a French fort (1753) on Lake ERIE. The site was acquired by the U.S. in 1795, when the town was laid out. Nearby naval shipyards built most of the fleet that defeated the British at the Battle of Lake Erie (1813) in the WAR OF 1812. Economic development began with the opening (1844) of the Erie and Pittsburgh Canal and with railway construction in the 1850s. Pennsylvania's only port on the ST. LAWRENCE SEAWAY, it is a shipping point for many products, including lumber, coal, and petroleum. While early industries were largely agricultural, manufactures, including electrical equipment and construction machinery, are now well diversified.

Erie, Lake Lake, in U.S. and Canada. The fourth largest of the five GREAT LAKES, it lies between lakes HURON and ONTARIO and forms the boundary between Canada (Ontario) and the U.S. (Michigan, Ohio, Pennsylvania, and New York). It is 240 mi (388 km) long and has a maximum width of 57 mi (92 km), with a surface area of 9,910 sq mi (22,666 sq km). The DETROIT RIVER carries inflow from Lake Huron to the west, and the lake discharges at its eastern end through the NIAGARA RIVER. It is an important link in the ST. LAWRENCE SEAWAY; its ports handle steel, iron ore, coal, and grain. The area was once inhabited by Erie Indians; when the French arrived in the 17th century they found the Iroquois living there. The British were in the region in the 18th century, and the U.S. shores were settled after 1796. It was the site of the Battle of Lake Erie, an important engagement of the WAR OF 1812.

Erie Canal Historic waterway, northern U.S. It stretches from BUFFALO, N.Y., on Lake ERIE to ALBANY, N.Y., on the HUDSON RIVER. Commissioned by Gov. DEWITT CLINTON of New York, it opened in 1825. It connected the GREAT LAKES with NEW YORK CITY and contributed greatly to the settlement of the Midwest, allowing for the transport of people and supplies. Enlarged several times, the canal is 340 mi (547 km) long, 150 ft (46 m) wide, and 12 ft (4 m) deep. Now used mainly for pleasure boating, it is part of the New York State Canal System.

Erie Railroad Co. Former railroad running between New York City, Buffalo, and Chicago. Incorporated in 1832 and completed in 1851, the Erie became known as "the scarlet woman of Wall Street" in the mid-19th century, when it was the object of financial struggles between DANIEL DREW, JAY GOULD, JAMES FISK, and CORNELIUS VANDERBILT. Manipulations of its stock by Gould and Fisk became notorious. It went bankrupt four times, and in 1976 it was taken over by CONRAIL.

Erigena \ə-'rē-ge-nə\, **John Scotus** *Latin* **Johannes Scotus Eriugena** (c. AD 810–877?) Irish-born theologian, translator, and commentator. In his philosophical system, which came to be known as Scotism, he attempted to integrate Greek and Neoplatonist philosophy with Christian belief in such works as *On Predestination* (851), which was condemned by church authorities. *On the Division of Nature* (862–66) tries to reconcile NEOPLATONISM with the Christian doctrine of creation; for its pantheistic implications, it too was condemned. His Latin translations of major works of Greek PATRISTIC LITERATURE made them accessible to Western thinkers. Remembered for the nonconformity of his thought, he is said to have been stabbed to death by his students with their pens for attempting to make them think.

Erik the Red *orig.* **Erik Thorvaldson** (late 10th century) Founder of the first European settlement on Greenland (c. 986) and father of LEIF ERIKSSON. A native of Norway, Erik grew up in Iceland; exiled for manslaughter c. 980, he set sail and landed on Greenland. With 350 colonists he founded a colony that numbered about 1,000 settlers by 1000 AD. In 1002 the colony was ravaged by sickness, and it gradually died out, though other Norse settlements in Greenland continued. Erik's story is told in the Icelandic *Eiríks saga.*

Erikson, Erik H(omburger) (1902–1994) German-U.S. psychoanalyst. Trained in Vienna by ANNA FREUD, he emigrated to the U.S. in 1933, where he practiced child psychoanalysis in Boston and joined the Harvard Medical School faculty. In 1936 he moved to Yale Univ., and in 1938 he began his first studies of cultural influences on psychological development, working with Sioux Indian children and later with the Yurok Indians. He later taught at UC–Berkeley; he left in 1950 after refusing to sign a loyalty oath. Personality development, in Erikson's view, takes place through a series of identity crises that must be overcome and internalized in preparation for the next developmental stage; he posited eight such stages. His other concerns included social psychology and the interactions of psychology with history, politics, and culture. His works include *Childhood and Society* (1950), *Young Man Luther* (1958), *Gandhi's Truth* (1969), and *Life History and the Historical Moment* (1975).

Eriksson, Leif See LEIF ERIKSSON THE LUCKY

Eris \'er-is\ Ancient Greek personification of strife. Her Roman counterpart was Discordia. The daughter of Nyx and the sister of ARES, she was best known for her role in starting the TROJAN WAR. When she alone was not invited to the wedding of Peleus and Thetis, she threw down among the guests a golden apple inscribed "for the most beautiful." HERA, ATHENA, and APHRODITE each claimed it, and ZEUS assigned the task of judging to the Trojan PARIS. He awarded the apple to Aphrodite, who in turn helped him carry off the beautiful HELEN, an act that triggered war.

Eritrea \ˌer-ə-'trē-ə, ˌer-ə-'trā-ə\ *officially* **State of Eritrea** *Tigrinya* **Ertra** Country, eastern Africa. It extends for about 600 mi (1,000 km) along the Red Sea coast, and includes the Dahlak Archipelago. Area: 46,770 sq mi (121,100 sq km). Population (2001 est.): 4,298,000 (including about 350,000 refugees from The Sudan). Capital: ASMARA. There is no official religion or language. The varied population is about half Tigrinya-speaking (see TIGRAY) Christians, with a large minority of Muslims and diverse other peoples. Arabic, English, and Italian are also spoken. Currency: Nafka. Eritrea's land varies from temperate central highlands to coastal desert plain, with savanna and open woodlands in the western lowlands. Its economy is based on livestock herding and subsistence agriculture. Industry, based in Asmara, includes food products, textiles, and leather goods; exports include salt, hides, cement, and gum arabic. Eritrea's form of government is a transitional regime with one interim legislative body; the head of state and government is the president. As the site of the main ports of the Aksumite empire, it was linked to the beginnings of the Ethiopian kingdom, but it retained much of its independence until it came under Ottoman rule in the 16th century. In the 17th–19th century, control of the territory was disputed among Ethiopia, the Ottomans, the kingdom of Tigray, Egypt, and Italy; it became an Italian colony in 1890. Eritrea was used as the main base for the Italian invasions of Ethiopia (1896 and 1935–36), and in 1936 became part of Italian East Africa. It was captured by the British in 1941, federated to Ethiopia in 1952, and made a province of Ethiopia in 1962. Thirty years of guerrilla warfare by Eritrean secessionist groups ensued. A provisional Eritrean government was established in 1991 after the overthrow of the Ethiopian government, and independence came in 1993. A new constitution was ratified in 1997. A border war with Ethiopia that began in 1998 ended in an Ethiopian victory in 2000.

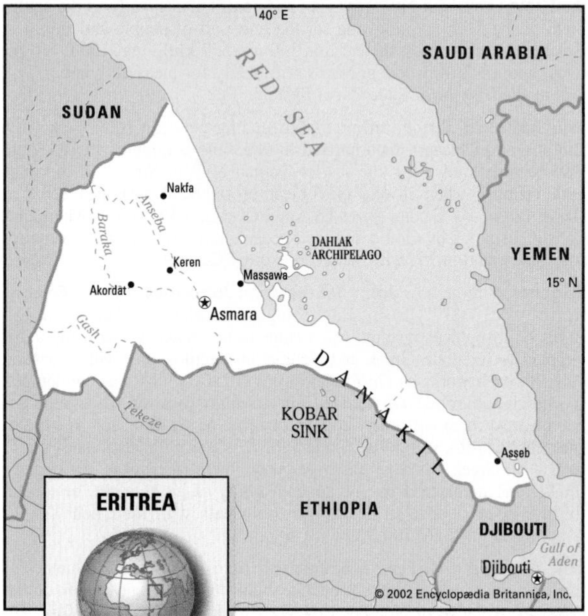

Erivan See YEREVAN

Erlitou culture \'er-lē-'tō\ Neolithic culture (1900–1350 BC) of the central plains of northern China. It was the first state-level society in China, and its remains are taken to be correlates of the XIA DYNASTY. Remains of palatial buildings, royal tombs, and paved roads have been uncovered, leading to hypotheses that the site represents a Xia capital. The society employed advanced bronze technology. The relationship between Erlitou bronzes and those produced earlier at Qijia in Gansu remains unclear. See HONGSHAN CULTURE, NEOLITHIC PERIOD.

ermine \'ər-mən\ Any of several WEASEL species (genus *Mustela,* family Mustelidae) whose white winter coat is the ermine of the fur trade. Ermines are found in northern North America, Eurasia, and North Africa. They are most abundant in thickets, woodland, and semitimbered areas. In summer they are brown, with whitish throat, chest, and belly. Species are 5–12 in. (13–29 cm) long (excluding the 2–5-in., or 5–12-cm, tail) and weigh less than 11 oz (0.3 kg). Voracious carnivores, ermines feed on small mammals, birds, eggs, frogs, and occasional invertebrates. The ermine used in the Middle Ages for royal robes was from a species called stoat *(M. erminea).*

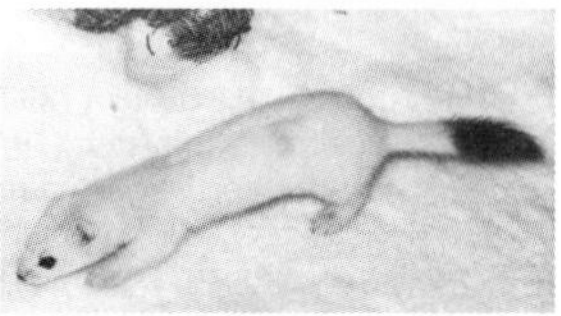

Ermine (*Mustela erminea*).

Ernst, Max \'ernst, 'ərnst\ (1891–1976) German-French painter and sculptor. He gave up studying philosophy and psychology at Bonn University for painting. After serving in World War I, he became the leader of the DADA movement in Cologne (1919), working in collage and photomontage. In 1922 he settled in Paris and was among the founders of SURREALISM. His work was imaginative and experimental; he pioneered the technique of FROTTAGE. After 1934 the irrational and whimsical imagery seen in his paintings appeared also in his sculpture. In 1941 he moved to New York, where he married PEGGY GUGGENHEIM and began collaborating with MARCEL DUCHAMP. He returned to France in 1953 and continued to produce lyrical and abstract works.

Max Ernst, photograph by Yousuf Karsh, 1965.

Eros \'er-ˌäs, 'ir-ˌäs\ Greek god of love. Though HESIOD declared him one of the primeval gods born of CHAOS, he was later said to be the son of APHRODITE. His Roman counterpart was CUPID. Eros was depicted as a beautiful winged youth carrying a bow and a quiver of arrows. In later literature and art he became increasingly younger, ending as an infant. His cult center was at Thespiae, but he also shared a sanctuary with Aphrodite at Athens.

Eros First ASTEROID found to travel mainly inside the orbit of Mars and the first to be landed on by a spacecraft. Discovered in 1898 and named for the Greek god of love, Eros is an elongated body about 20.5 mi (33 km) in its greatest dimension. It can approach to within 14 million mi (22 million km) of the earth. In 2000 the Near Earth Asteroid Rendezvous (NEAR Shoemaker) spacecraft orbited Eros, collecting a full year of data, and in 2001 it set down gently on Eros's surface.

erosion Removal of surface material from the earth's crust and transportation of the eroded materials by natural agencies from the point of removal. Erosion is caused by wind action, river and stream processes, marine processes (sea waves), and glacial processes. The complementary actions of erosion and deposition or sedimentation operate through wind, moving water, and ice to alter existing landforms and create new landforms. Erosion will often occur after rock has been disintegrated or altered through WEATHERING. Moving water is the most important natural agent of erosion. Sea wave erosion results primarily from the impact of waves striking the shore and the abrasive action of sand and pebbles agitated by wave action. Erosion by rivers is caused by the scouring action of the sediment-containing flowing water. Glacial erosion occurs by surface abrasion as the ice, embedded with debris, moves slowly over the ground accompanied by the plucking of rock from the surface. Wind plays a key role in arid regions as blowing sand breaks down rock and dislodges surface sand from unprotected sand dunes. Human intervention, as by the removal of natural vegetation for farming or grazing purposes, can lead to or accelerate erosion by wind and water. See also SHEET EROSION.

error In applied mathematics, the difference between a value and an estimate of that value. In statistics, a common example is the difference between the mean age of a given group of people (see MEAN, MEDIAN, AND MODE) and that of a sample drawn from the group. In NUMERICAL ANALYSIS, an example of round-off error is the difference between the true value of PI and commonly substituted expressions like 22/7 and shorter versions like 3.14159. Truncation error results from using only the first few terms of an infinite series. Relative error is the ratio of the size of an error to the size of the quantity measured, and percentage error is relative error expressed as a percent.

Erskine \'ər-skən\, **Thomas** *later* **Baron Erskine (of Restormel)** (1750–1823) Scottish lawyer. Son of an earl, he left military service to become a lawyer in 1778. His practice flourished after he won a seminal libel case, and he went on to make important contributions to the protection of personal liberties. His defense of politicians and reformers on charges of treason and related offenses, including an unsuccessful defense of THOMAS PAINE (1792), checked repressive measures taken by the British government in the aftermath of the French Revolution. He contributed to the law of criminal responsibility by defending, on the novel ground of insanity, a would-be assassin of GEORGE III. He served in Parliament (1783–84, 1790–1806) until elevated to the peerage (1806), and was lord chancellor (1806–7) in William Grenville's "ministry of all talents." In 1820 he defended Queen Caroline, whom GEORGE IV had brought to trial before the House of Lords for adultery in order to deprive her of her rights and title. His brothers David Steuart Erskine (1742–1829) and Henry Erskine (1746–1817) were notable for defending Scottish sovereignty in the selection of peers and defending constitutionality in the face of sedition and treason laws.

Erté \'er-'tā\ *orig.* **Roman Tertov** *later* **Romain de Tertoff** (1892–1990) Russian-French fashion illustrator and designer. In 1912 he left his native St. Petersburg for Paris, where he worked briefly with the couturier PAUL POIRET. From 1916 to 1937 he published elegant, highly stylized illustrations depicting models in mannered poses against Art Deco interiors in *Harper's Bazaar*. He also designed theatrical scenery and costumes for the Folies-Bergère in Paris (1919–30), and in the 1920s he costumed performers in U.S. musicals, most notably the *Ziegfeld Follies*. His designs continue to be widely reproduced.

Afternoon dress of black and white satin designed by Erté for *Harper's Bazaar*, 1924.

© SEVENARTS LIMITED

Ervin, Sam *orig.* **Samuel James Ervin, Jr.** (1896–1985) U.S. senator (1954–74). Born in Morganton, N.C., he served on the state supreme court (1948–54) before being appointed to a vacant U.S. Senate seat. An eloquent expert on the Constitution, he sat on the Senate committee that censured Sen. JOSEPH MCCARTHY and helped investigate labor racketeering. In the 1960s he led Southern filibusters against civil-rights laws while acting as a leading champion of civil liberties. As chairman of the special committee investigating the WATERGATE SCANDAL, he became a folk hero for his unceasing pursuit of evidence against White House claims of executive privilege, dispensing wisdom and earthy humor in a distinctive accent.

Erving, Julius (Winfield) (born 1950) U.S. basketball star. Born in Roosevelt, N.Y., he played two years at the University of Massachusetts before joining the pros. At 6 ft 7 in. (2 m), "Doctor J" played forward for the Virginia Squires (1971–73) of the ABA, the New York Nets (1973–76), and the Philadelphia 76ers (1977–87), and was known for his fast breaks, balletic leaps, and climactic slam dunks. He is one of only three professional players (with KAREEM ABDUL-JABBAR and WILT CHAMBERLAIN) whose career point totals exceeded 30,000 (with 30,026).

erythema \ˌer-ə-'thē-mə\ Abnormal skin redness from increased blood flow, caused by dilation and irritation of surface CAPILLARIES. It has a variety of manifestations. In erythema multiforme, a symptom complex seen in several diseases, spots appear suddenly, often with a bull's-eye pattern. It may become life-threatening in severe cases; in mild cases symptoms may recur. Hormone treatment may be effective. In erythema nodosum, a hypersensitivity reaction usually associated with strep infection (see STREPTOCOCCUS), drugs, or the disease sarcoidosis, painful red nodules appear in the deeper skin layer of the lower legs. They usually disappear over several weeks and do not recur. Another form of erythema is PELLAGRA.

Erythrae \'er-ə-ˌthrē\ Ancient city of LYDIA. Located on the Aegean coast opposite the island of CHIOS, it was one of the 12 Ionian Cities. The original site of the settlement is uncertain, but from the 4th century BC it was located at modern Ildir, where traces of the wall circuit, theater, and citadel are visible. It was involved in 5th century BC Greek politics on various sides, came under Persian control, and was freed by ALEXANDER THE GREAT in 334 BC. A free city in the Roman province of Asia, it was noted for its wine and goats, as well as its prophetic SIBYLS, Herophile and Athenais.

erythroblastosis fetalis \i-ˌrith-rə-ˌblas-'tō-səs-fi-'ta-ləs\ *or* **hemolytic disease of the newborn** ANEMIA in an infant, caused when a pregnant woman produces ANTIBODIES to an ANTIGEN in her fetus's red blood cells. An Rh-negative woman (see RH BLOOD-GROUP SYSTEM) with an Rh-positive fetus whose ABO blood group (see ABO BLOOD-GROUP SYSTEM) matches hers is likely to have an immune reaction after the first such pregnancy, which sensitizes her when fetal red blood cells enter her bloodstream, usually during labor. If BLOOD TYPING shows incompatibility, an anti-Rh antibody injection given to the mother after the birth can destroy the fetal red cells, thus preventing trouble in a future pregnancy. If AMNIOCENTESIS detects products of blood destruction, Rh-negative blood transfusions to the fetus before birth or exchange transfusion after it may save the baby's life. ABO incompatibilities are more common but usually less severe.

erythrocyte \i-'rith-rə-ˌsīt\ *or* **red blood cell** *or* **red corpuscle** Blood cell that carries oxygen, carbon dioxide, nutrients, and waste for exchange with other tissues. HEMOGLOBIN gives the cell—and whole blood—its color. Red cells are small, round, flexible, and concave on both sides, and lack a NUCLEUS. They develop continuously in BONE MARROW in several stages and are stored in the SPLEEN. The mature form lives 100–120 days. Adult human blood has about 5.2 million red cells per cu mm. Some conditions change their shape (e.g., PERNICIOUS ANEMIA, SICKLE-CELL ANEMIA) or number (e.g., ANEMIA, polycythemia).

Erzberger \'erts-ˌber-gər\, **Matthias** (1875–1921) German politician. Elected to the Reichstag in 1903, he became the leader of the left wing of the CENTER PARTY. During World War I, he was involved in the Reichstag resolution proposing a negotiated peace with no territorial gains. He headed the German delegation that signed the Armistice, and he advocated acceptance of the Treaty of Versailles. In 1919–20 he served as vice-chancellor and finance minister. As a supporter of the republican-democratic system, he became the victim of a slander campaign from the extreme right. He resigned his ministry and was later assassinated by nationalist partisans.

Esagila \ˈā-sä-'gē-lä\ Temple complex in ancient BABYLON dedicated to MARDUK. The huge edifice was 660 ft (202 m) long, with three vast courtyards surrounded by many chambers. It took centuries to construct; most of the work being done in the 6th century BC during the reign of NEBUCHADNEZZAR II. Its wealth was famous in antiquity, but by the time Babylon was excavated in 1899–1917 it had been thoroughly plundered.

Esaki, Leo *orig.* **Esaki Reiona** (born 1925) Japanese physicist. In 1956 he became chief physicist of the Sony Corp., and in 1960 he was awarded an IBM fellowship for further research in the U.S., subsequently joining IBM's research laboratories in Yorktown, N.Y. He worked intensively on TUNNELING in semiconductors, and constructed the tunnel diode, which found broad applications in computers and other devices. He shared a 1973 Nobel Prize with Ivar Giaever (born 1929) and BRIAN JOSEPHSON.

escalator Moving staircase used as transportation between floors or levels in stores, airports, subways, and other mass pedestrian areas. The name was first applied to a moving stairway shown at the Paris Exposition of 1900. Modern escalators are electrically powered, driven by chain and sprocket, and held in place by two tracks. As the treads approach a landing, they pass through a comb device; a switch cuts off power if an object becomes jammed between comb and treads.

escape velocity Speed sufficient for a body to escape from a gravitational center of attraction without accelerating further. It decreases with altitude and equals the square root of 2 (about 1.414) times the speed needed to maintain a circular orbit at the same altitude. At the surface of earth, disregarding atmospheric resistance, escape velocity is about 6.96 mi/second (11.20 km/second). Escape velocity from the surface of the moon is about one-third of this.

eschatology \ˌes-kə-ˈtä-lə-jē\ Theological doctrine of the "last things," or the end of the world. Mythological eschatologies depict an eternal struggle between order and chaos, and celebrate the eternity of order and the repeatability of the origin of the world. Historical eschatologies are grounded in datable events that are perceived as fundamental to the progress of history. Judaism, Christianity, and Islam have historical eschatologies. Old Testament eschatology sees the catastrophes that beset the people of Israel as due to their disobedience to the laws and will of God, and holds that conformity to God's will result in renewal and the fulfillment of God's purpose. In Christianity, the end times are thought to have begun with the life and ministry of Jesus, the MESSIAH who will return to establish the KINGDOM OF GOD. MILLENNIALISM focuses especially on Christ's second coming and the reign of the righteous on earth. In SHIITE Islam, the MAHDI, or restorer of the faith, will come to inaugurate the last judgment, in which the good will enter HEAVEN and the evil will fall into HELL.

Escher \ˈe-shər\, **M(aurits) C(ornelis)** (1898–1972) Dutch graphic artist. He became well known for prints in which he used realistic detail to achieve bizarre optical illusions, such as staircases that appear to lead both up and down from the same level. His work assumed a Surrealist flavor as he began depicting unexpected metamorphoses of mundane objects. His works were of interest to mathematicians, cognitive psychologists, and the general public, and were widely reproduced throughout the 20th century.

Encounter, lithograph printed in black by M.C. Escher, 1944; in the Museum of Modern Art, New York City.

COLLECTION, THE MUSEUM OF MODERN ART, NEW YORK CITY; GIFT OF THE INTERNATIONAL GRAPHIC ARTS SOCIETY

Escoffier \es-kȯf-ˈyā\, **(Georges-) Auguste** (1846–1935) French chef known for his innovations in haute cuisine. He earned a worldwide reputation as director of the kitchens at the Grand Hotel at Monte Carlo and at César Ritz's Savoy (1890–99) and Carlton (1899–1922) hotels in London. He helped reform *grande cuisine* by simplifying and refining it and making its preparation more efficient. He wrote *Guide culinaire* (1903), *Ma cuisine* (1934), and other classic works. He is often called the greatest chef of all time.

Escorial, El See EL ESCORIAL

escrow \ˈes-ˌkrō\ Instrument, such as a deed, money, or PROPERTY, that constitutes evidence of obligations between two or more parties and is held by a third party. It is delivered by the third party only upon fulfillment of some condition. In commercial usage, this condition is most often the performance of an act (e.g., payment) by the party who is to receive the instrument. Escrow is also used in family transactions (e.g., when a death in the family results in an instrument being delivered to another family member).

Esdraelon \ˌez-drə-ˈē-lən\, **Plain of** *Hebrew* **Emeq Yizreel** \ˈe-mek-ˌyēz-rā-ˈel\ Plain, northern Israel. About 25 mi (40 km) long, it divides the hilly areas of GALILEE in the north and SAMARIA in the south. Part of the ancient passage between Egypt and the FERTILE CRESCENT, it was an avenue of commerce and a scene of conflict from remotest antiquity. At the northwest is the site of ancient MEGIDDO. Owing to poor natural drainage, it was sparsely inhabited for many centuries, but since 1920 the land has been reclaimed, and dozens of settlements, combining intensive agriculture with light industry, have been set up. Afula is the principal urban center.

Esenin, Sergey See Sergey YESENIN

Esfahan \ˌes-fä-ˈhän\ *or* **Isfahan** \ˌis-fä-ˈhän\ City (pop., 1996: 1,266,072), western central Iran. An ancient Median town, it was known as Aspadana. A major city of the SELJUQ DYNASTY (11th–13th century AD) and of the SAFAVID DYNASTY of Iran (16th–18th century), its golden age began in 1598 when Shah ABBAS I made it his capital and rebuilt it into one of the 17th century's largest cities. At its center he created the immense Meydan-i-Shah, or Royal Square, a great rectangular garden enclosing the noted MASJID-I-SHAH (Royal Mosque). In 1722 Afghanis took the city, and it went into decline. Recovery began in the 20th century, and it is now a major textile center, whose industries include steelmaking and petroleum refining.

Eshnunna \esh-ˈnən-ə\ *or* **Tell Asmar** \ˌtel-ˈas-mər\ Ancient city ruins, eastern Iraq. Occupied before 3000 BC, it was, during the 3rd dynasty of UR, the seat of an ensi (governor). After the collapse of Ur, it became independent but was later conquered by HAMMURABI. Stone tablets found near Babylon, called the "Laws of Eshnunna," predate the Code of HAMMURABI by about two generations, and help show the development of ancient law. After Hammurabi's time it fell into decline. Sumerian artifacts from the site include stone statuettes dating from the 3rd millennium BC.

Statuettes found at Tell Asmar, Early Dynastic II (c. 2775–c. 2650 BC); in the Oriental Institute, the University of Chicago.

BY COURTESY OF THE ORIENTAL INSTITUTE, THE UNIVERSITY OF CHICAGO

Eskimo *or* **Inuit** \ˈi-nü-wət\ Group of peoples who, with the closely related ALEUT, constitute the native population of the Arctic and subarctic regions of Greenland, Alaska, Canada, and far eastern Siberia. Self-designations include such names as Inuit, Inupiat, Yupik, and Alutiit, each being a variant of "the people." The name Eskimo, first applied by Europeans, may derive from a Montagnais word for snowshoes; it is favored by Arctic peoples in Alaska, while those in Canada and Greenland prefer Inuit. The Eskimo are of Asian origin, like the American Indians, but are distinguishable from the latter by their climatic adaptations, the presence of the B blood type, and their languages (Eskimo-Aleut), all of which suggest that they are of distinctive origin. Traditional Eskimo culture was totally adapted to an extremely cold, snow- and ice-bound environment in which vegetable foods were almost nonexistent and caribou, fish, and marine mammals were the major food source. Harpoons and one-person kayaks or larger umiaks were used for hunting on the sea. Clothing was fashioned of caribou furs and sealskins. Snow-block igloos or semisubterranean sod and stone houses were used in winter, while in summer animal-skin tents were erected. Dogsleds were the basic means of land transport. Religion centered on the unseen world of spirits. Today snowmobiles have replaced dogsleds, and rifles harpoons. Many Eskimo have abandoned their nomadic hunting pursuits and moved into northern towns and cities. Some have formed cooperatives to market their handicrafts and other wares. There are about 43,000 Eskimo in Alaska, 21,000 in Canada, 51,000 in Greenland and Denmark, and 1,600 in Siberia.

Eskimo-Aleut languages \ˌal-ē-ˈüt\ Family of languages spoken in Greenland, Canada, Alaska, and eastern Siberia by the Eskimo and Aleut peoples. Aleut, distantly related to the Eskimo languages, consists of eastern and western dialects; today both are spoken by fewer than 400 people. The Eskimo languages have two subgroups: Yupik (five languages), spoken on the Chukchi Peninsula in Siberia and in southwestern Alaska; and Inupiaq-Inuktitut, a continuum of dialects spoken across arctic Alaska and Canada to the coasts of Labrador and Greenland. Yupik languages are spoken today by around 13,000 people, while Inupiaq-Inuktitut has over 100,000 speakers, nearly half speakers of Greenlandic Inuktitut.

Eskimo dog Breed of hunting and sled dog found near the Arctic Circle. It is believed by some to be representative of a pure breed 25,000–50,000 years old and by others to be descended from wolves (wolf). It is powerfully built and big-boned, standing about 20–25 in. (51–64 cm) high and weighing 65–85 lbs (30–39 kg). Its long, waterproof outer coat, variable in color, covers a thick, woolly undercoat. See also spitz.

Eskimo dog team.
HARRY GROOM FROM RAPHO/PHOTO RESEARCHERS

esophagus \i-ˈsä-fə-gəs\ Muscular tube that conveys food by peristalsis from the pharynx to the stomach. Both ends are closed off by sphincters (muscular constrictions), which relax to let food through and close to keep it from backing up. Disorders include ulceration and bleeding, heartburn from stomach acid, achalasia (failure of one or both sphincters to open), and muscle spasms. Scleroderma may involve the esophagus.

ESP See extrasensory perception

espalier \is-ˈpal-yər\ Tree or other plant trained to grow flat against a support (such as a trellis or wall). The term is also used for the support itself, as well as for the method or technique. The technique was developed in Europe to encourage fruit-tree production in an incompatible climate; it originally used a wall to provide heat as well as support. Decorative or space-saving espaliers use metal, wire, or wooden frames to create ornamental shapes for shrubbery or to train trees on trellises, walls, or fences. Evergreens such as loquat, fire thorn, sweet bay magnolia, and upright yew, as well as dwarf apple and pear trees, make excellent espaliers.

Español, Pedro See Pedro Berruguete

Espartero \ˌä-spär-ˈtā-rō\, **Baldomero** *later* **Príncipe (Prince) de Vergara** (1793–1879) Spanish general and politician. After the accession of Isabella II he joined the government forces opposed to Don Carlos (see Carlism) and helped win the First Carlist War. He became head of the government in 1840 and was appointed regent in 1841. In 1843 a generals' revolt forced him to flee to England, where he lived until 1849. He returned to Spain, then shared control of the government (1854–56) with Gen. Leopoldo O'Donnell (1809–1867), before returning to retirement.

esparto \is-ˈpär-tō\ Either of two species of gray-green needlegrasses *(Stipa tenacissima* and *Lygeum spartum),* native to southern Spain and northern Africa, or the fiber produced by esparto. *L. spartum* grows in rocky soil on the high plains. *S. tenacissima* flourishes in sandy, iron-rich soils in dry, sunny locations on the seacoast. Esparto fiber has great strength and flexibility; it is used for making ropes, sandals, baskets, mats, and other durable articles. Esparto leaves are used in the manufacture of paper.

Esperanto \ˌes-pə-ˈrän-tō\ Artificial language created in 1887 by Lazarus Ludwig Zamenhof (1859–1917), a Polish oculist, for use as an international second language. Zamenhof's *Fundamento de Esperanto* (1905) outlines its basic principles. All words, derived from roots commonly found in the European languages, are spelled as pronounced, and grammar is simple and regular. Nouns have no gender and end in *-o*, and there is only one definite article, *la* (e.g., *la amiko,* "the friend"). Adjectives are marked by the ending *-a*. Verbs are regular and have only one form for each tense or mood. The Universal Esperanto Association (founded 1908) has members in 83 countries. Estimates of the number of Esperanto-speakers range from 100,000 to several million.

espionage \ˈes-pē-ə-ˌnäzh\ Process of obtaining military, political, commercial, or other secret information by means of spies, secret agents, or illegal monitoring devices. It is sometimes distinguished from the broader category of intelligence gathering by its aggressive nature and its illegality. Counterespionage efforts are directed at detecting and thwarting espionage by others.

Espíritu Santo *formerly* **Marina** Island, northwestern Vanuatu, South Pacific Ocean. The country's largest island, it is 76 mi (122 km) long and 45 mi (72 km) wide, and covers 1,420 sq mi (3,677 sq km). Volcanic in origin, it has a mountain range running along its western coast; Mount Tabwémasana rises to 6,165 ft (1,879 m). It is heavily wooded and has broad, fertile, well-watered valleys. Agriculturally developed, its principal settlement is Luganville (Santo) on the southeastern coast.

Esquire U.S. monthly magazine, founded in 1933 by Arnold Gingrich. It began as an oversized magazine for men that featured a sophisticated style and drawings of scantily clad young women. It later abandoned its titillating role but continued to cultivate the image of affluence and refined taste. It pioneered the treatment of unconventional topics and feature stories and attracted a general-interest audience with pieces by well-known writers. In the 1940s, because of its early notoriety, it was the object of an ultimately unsuccessful court case challenging its worthiness for mailing privileges at desirable rates. *Esquire* has in recent years largely ceased to publish the kind of fiction and nonfiction that once made it distinctive.

essay Analytic, interpretative, or critical literary composition, usually dealing with its subject from a limited and often personal point of view. Flexible and versatile, the essay was perfected by Michel de Montaigne, who chose the name *essai* to emphasize that his compositions were "attempts" to express his thoughts and experiences. The essay has been the vehicle of literary and social criticism in some countries, while in others it became semipolitical, earnestly nationalistic, and often polemical, playful, or bitter.

Essen City (pop., 1996 est.: 615,000), North Rhine-Westphalia state, western Germany. Located on the Ruhr River; it is the site of the most extensive iron- and steelworks in Europe. It was originally the seat of a convent (founded 852), whose 15th century cathedral still stands. It became a city in the 10th century and was locally sovereign until 1802, when Essen passed to Prussia. The development of ironworks, steelworks, and coal mines stimulated growth in the 19th century. The city was largely destroyed in World War II, targeted as a center of the German war industry. It has since been rebuilt with large, modern buildings, including concert halls, an economic research institute, and an art institute.

Essene \i-ˈsēn, ˈe-sēn\ Member of a Jewish sect active in Palestine from the 2nd century BC to the 1st century AD. The Essenes formed small monastic communities whose members strictly observed the laws of Moses and the Sabbath and held their property in common. They withdrew from society, avoiding temple worship in Jerusalem and supporting themselves by manual labor. They usually excluded women. It is likely that the DEAD SEA SCROLLS were composed, copied, or collected by the Essenes.

essential oil Any of a class of highly volatile (readily evaporating) organic compounds found in plants and usually named for them (e.g., rose oil, peppermint oil). They have been known and traded since ancient times. Many contain ISOPRENOIDS. Some, such as oil of wintergreen (methyl salicylate) and orange oil (*d*-limonene), have one predominant component, but most have dozens or hundreds. Trace components impart the characteristic odor, which synthetic or blended oils can rarely duplicate. Essential oils have three primary commercial uses: as odorants in perfumes, soaps, detergents, and other products; as flavors in baked goods, candies, soft drinks, and many other foods; and as pharmaceuticals, in dental products and many medicines (see AROMATHERAPY).

essentialism In ONTOLOGY, the assertion that there are two classes into which we can divide an object's properties: properties the object could have lacked (accidental properties), and properties it could not possibly have lacked (essential properties). The essence of a thing is conceived as the totality of its essential properties.

Essequibo River \ˌe-se-ˈkwē-bō\ River, eastern central Guyana. The largest river between the AMAZON and the ORINOCO rivers, and the longest in Guyana, it rises in the Acarai Mountains on the Brazilian border. It flows north for 630 mi (1,010 km) to empty into the Atlantic Ocean 13 mi (21 km) from GEORGETOWN. Its estuary, 20 mi (32 km) wide, is obstructed by islands and silt but is navigable by small ocean vessels to Bartica, 50 mi (80 km) inland.

Essex County (population 1995 est.: 1,578,000), eastern England. It extends along the North Sea coastline between the THAMES RIVER and STOUR RIVER estuaries; the county seat is CHELMSFORD. The ancient county stretched west as far as MIDDLESEX, but GREATER LONDON now incorporates its southwestern corner. It was a Roman center until the 5th-century Saxon invasions, and an Anglo-Saxon kingdom of the Heptarchy with its center at London. It came under Danish control in the 9th century and was later reconquered by WESSEX. The modern county now takes much of London's overflow. Though much of the country is still farmed, it is the site of petroleum installations on the Thames River and of a nuclear power plant.

Essex, 1st Earl of *orig.* **Walter Devereux** (1541–1576) English soldier. Born to an English titled family, he helped suppress a rebellion in northern England in 1569 and was made earl of Essex in 1572. In 1573 he offered to subdue and colonize, at his own expense, a portion of Ulster that had not accepted English overlordship. There he treacherously captured and executed the Irish rebel leaders and massacred hundreds of the populace, contributing to Irish bitterness toward the English. ELIZABETH I commanded him to break off the enterprise in 1575. He died of dysentery shortly after returning to Ireland from England.

Essex, 2nd Earl of *orig.* **Robert Devereux** (1567–1601) English soldier and courtier. Son of the 1st Earl of ESSEX, as a young man he became the aging ELIZABETH I's favorite, though their relationship was stormy. In 1591–92 he commanded the English force in France that helped HENRY IV fight the French Roman Catholics, and in 1596 he commanded forces in the sack of Cádiz. In 1599 Elizabeth sent him to Ireland as lord lieutenant, where he fought an unsuccessful campaign against Irish rebels and concluded an unfavorable truce, leading Elizabeth to deprive him of his offices in 1600. In 1601 he made an unsuccessful attempt to raise the populace of London in revolt against Elizabeth; he was captured, tried by his former mentor FRANCIS BACON, and beheaded.

Robert Devereux, 2nd earl of Essex, detail of a painting after Marcus Gheeraerts the Younger, late 16th century; in the National Portrait Gallery, London.

BY COURTESY OF THE NATIONAL PORTRAIT GALLERY, LONDON

Essex, 3rd Earl of *orig.* **Robert Devereux** (1591–1646) English military commander. Son of the 2nd Earl of ESSEX, he began his military career in 1620 and commanded forces for CHARLES I until the LONG PARLIAMENT deposed Charles's ministers (1640). As the ENGLISH CIVIL WARS began, he was appointed to command the Parliamentary army. He fought against the Royalists at the indecisive Battle of Edgehill (1642) and advanced on London in 1643. His army was besieged at Lostwithiel, Cornwall, in 1644, and all surrendered except Essex, who escaped by sea. He resigned his command in 1645.

Essex Junto \ˈjən-ˌtō\ Informal group of FEDERALIST political leaders in Massachusetts, mainly from Essex Co. Its members supported ALEXANDER HAMILTON and friendship with Britain and opposed THOMAS JEFFERSON, the EMBARGO ACT, and the WAR OF 1812. Its leaders, including TIMOTHY PICKERING, tried to form a separate confederation in New England and participated in the HARTFORD CONVENTION. They declined in importance after 1814.

establishment clause *or* **establishment-of-religion clause** Clause in the 1st Amendment to the U.S. CONSTITUTION forbidding Congress from establishing a state religion. It prevents the passage of any law that gives preference to or forces belief in any one religion. It is paired with a clause that prohibits limiting the free expression of religion.

estate law Laws governing the nature and extent of an owner's rights with respect to REAL AND PERSONAL PROPERTY. When used in connection with PROBATE proceedings, it refers to the laws governing the disposition of the total property of whatever kind owned by a person at the time of death. See also ESTATE TAX, PROPERTY, PROPERTY TAX.

estate tax Levy on the value of property changing hands at the death of the owner, fixed mainly by reference to its total value. Estate tax is generally applied only to estates evaluated above a set amount and is applied at graduated rates. An estate tax was first instituted in the U.S. in 1898 to help finance the Spanish-American War; it was repealed in 1902 but permanently reimposed in 1916, initially to help finance mobilization for World War I. Methods of avoiding estate tax (e.g., gifts and trust funds) were largely foiled by the U.S. Tax Reform Act of 1976.

Estates General *or* **States General** *French* **États-Généraux.** In pre-Revolutionary France, the representative assembly of the three "estates" or orders of the realm: the clergy and the nobility (both privileged minorities) as well as the THIRD ESTATE, which represented the majority of the people. Usually summoned by monarchs in times of crisis, the Estates General met at irregular intervals from the 14th century on; it was of limited effectiveness because the monarchy usually dealt with local Estates instead. The last meeting of the Estates General was at the start of the FRENCH REVOLUTION in 1789, when the deputies of the Third Estate led in founding the NATIONAL ASSEMBLY.

Este family \ˈes-tā\ Princely family of Lombard origin prominent in the history of medieval and Renaissance Italy. The Estensi, a branch of the 10th-century dynasty of the Obertenghi, took their name from the township and castle of Este, near Padua. The founder of the family was the margrave Alberto Azzo II (died 1097), through whose son Folco I (died 1136?) descended the House of Este. The family first gained prominence as leaders of the Guelphs in the wars between the GUELPHS AND GHIBELLINES. Members of the family ruled in Ferrara in the 13th–16th century. After Alfonso II (1533–1597), the fifth and last duke of Ferrara, died childless, direct papal rule was established in Ferrara in 1598, and the main branch of the Este family came to an end. The family also ruled in Modena and Reggio from the late Middle Ages to the late 18th century. In addition to their political prominence, members of the family also played an important role as promoters of art and culture.

Estenssoro, Víctor Paz See Victor PAZ ESTENSSORO

ester Any of a class of organic compounds that can react with water (see HYDROLYSIS) to produce an ALCOHOL and an organic or inorganic ACID. They are formed by the reverse process, esterification: Acid reacts with alcohol to form an ester and water. Esters of CARBOXYLIC ACIDS, the most common, contain the acid's carbonyl group (—C=O; see FUNCTIONAL GROUP); the carbon's fourth bond is with the alcohol's oxygen atom. Hydrolysis of esters in the presence of an ALKALI (saponification) is used to make SOAPS from FATS and OILS. Carboxylic acid esters of low molecular weight are colorless, volatile liquids with pleasant odors; they give flavor and fragrance to fruits and flowers and are used as synthetic flavors and fragrances. Others, such as ethyl acetate and butyl acetate, are used as SOLVENTS for lacquers, paints, and varnishes. Certain POLYMERS are esters, including LUCITE (polymethyl methacrylate), and Dacron (polyethylene terephthalate). Esters of alcohols and inorganic acids include nitrate esters (e.g., NITROGLYCERIN), which are explosive; phosphate esters, including such biologically important compounds as NUCLEIC ACIDS; and others used as flame retardants, solvents, plasticizers, gasoline and oil additives, and insecticides.

Esterházy family \'es-tər-,hä-zē\ Aristocratic MAGYAR family, dating from at least the 15th century, that produced numerous Hungarian diplomats, army officers, and patrons of the arts. By the 18th century the Esterházys were the largest landowners in Hungary and possessed a private fortune even larger than that of the Habsburg emperors, whom they supported. The great Esterházy palace was built at Eisenstadt, on NEUSIEDLER LAKE. F.J. HAYDN spent most of his career as music director at the palace. The family's various members held important governmental, ecclesiastical, diplomatic, and military posts in Hungary well into the 20th century.

Estes \'es-tēz\, **William K(aye)** (born 1919) U.S. psychologist. Born in Minneapolis, he worked with B. F. SKINNER on instrumental learning in the 1940s, and in 1950 he introduced stimulus sampling theory (SST), a model for describing learning mathematically. His later work has focused on "cognitive architectures." His works include *Learning Theory and Mental Development* (1970), *Statistical Models in Behavioral Research* (1991), and *Classification and Cognition* (1994). He has taught at Stanford, Rockefeller, and Harvard universities. In 1997 he received the National Medal of Science.

Esther OLD TESTAMENT heroine, central figure in the Book of Esther. She was a beautiful Jewish woman, the wife of the Persian king Ahasuerus (XERXES I). She and her cousin MORDECAI persuaded the king to cancel an order for the extermination of Jews in his realm, plotted by the king's chief minister, Haman. Instead, Haman was hanged on the gallows he had built for Mordecai, and the Jews were given permission to destroy their enemies. The Jewish festival of PURIM celebrates this event. The Book of Esther was probably written in the 2nd century BC.

Estienne \ā-'tyen\, **Henri II** (1528–1598) French scholar-printer. As a young man he traveled Europe studying ancient manuscripts and visiting scholars before returning to his father's Geneva printing firm to publish the first printed editions of several Greek texts. In 1566 he published a Latin edition of HERODOTUS with a controversial apologia in which he bitterly satirized his own age. His voluminous output of classical scholarship also included a 13-volume Greek and Latin text of PLUTARCH and a five-volume Greek dictionary, *Thesaurus graecae linguae* (both 1572). New editions of the dictionary, his greatest work, were printed into the 19th century.

estimation In mathematics, use of a FUNCTION or formula to derive a solution or make a prediction. Unlike approximation, it has precise connotations. In statistics, for example, it connotes the careful selection and testing of a function called an estimator. In calculus, it usually refers to an initial guess for a solution to an equation, which is gradually refined by a process that generates closer estimates. The difference between the estimate and the exact value is the ERROR.

Estonia *officially* **Republic of Estonia** *Estonian* **Eesti** \'ā-stē\ Country, northeastern Europe. It consists of a mainland area and some 1,500 islands and islets in the Baltic Sea. Area: 17,413 sq mi (45,100 sq km). Population (1997 est.): 1,463,000. Capital: TALLINN. Estonians are nearly two-thirds of the population. Russians account for almost one-third, and there are Ukrainian, Finnish, and Belarusian minorities. Language: Estonian (official). Religions: Estonian Orthodoxy, Lutheranism, Methodism. Currency: kroon. The land is low and hilly, with numerous lakes and forests and many rivers. It has a cool-temperate and humid climate. The economy is mainly industrial, producing shale oil, machinery, fabricated metal products, and building materials. It is noted for its textiles, and woodworking is a traditional and important industry. It is a republic with one legislative body; the chief of state is the president, while the head of government is the prime minister. It was invaded by Vikings in the 9th century AD and later by Danes, Swedes, and Russians, but the Estonians were able to withstand the assaults until the Danes took control in 1219. In 1346 the Danes sold their sovereignty to the TEUTONIC ORDER, which was then in possession of LIVONIA (S Estonia and Latvia). In the mid-16th century, Estonia was once again divided, with northern

Estonia capitulating to Sweden, and Poland gaining Livonia, which it surrendered to Sweden in 1629. Russia acquired Livonia and Estonia in 1721. Nearly a century later, serfdom was abolished, and from 1881 Estonia underwent intensive Russification. In 1918 Estonia obtained independence from Russia, which lasted until the Soviet Union occupied the country in 1940 and forcibly incorporated it into the U.S.S.R. Germany held the region (1941–44) during World War II, but the Soviet regime was restored in 1944, after which Estonia's economy was collectivized and integrated into that of the Soviet Union. In 1991, along with other parts of the former U.S.S.R., it proclaimed its independence, and subsequently held elections. Estonia continued negotiations with Russia to settle their common border.

Estremadura See EXTREMADURA

estrogen \'es-trə-jən\ Organic compound, any of a class of SEX HORMONES that primarily influence the female REPRODUCTIVE SYSTEM's development, maturation, and function. The three major estrogens—estradiol, estrone, and estriol—are produced mainly by the OVARIES and PLACENTA; the ADRENAL GLANDS and the TESTES secrete smaller amounts. Estrogens affect the OVARIES, VAGINA, fallopian tubes, UTERUS, and MAMMARY GLANDS and play crucial roles in PUBERTY, MENSTRUATION, PREGNANCY, and PARTURITION. They also influence the structural differences between female and male bodies. In experimental animals, loss of estrogens diminishes mating desires and other behavioral patterns.

estrus Period in the sexual cycle of female MAMMALS, except the higher PRIMATES, during which they are in heat (ready to accept a male for mating). Some animals (e.g., DOGS) have only one heat during a breeding season; others (e.g., GROUND SQUIRRELS) will come into heat repeatedly during the breeding season until impregnated. During estrus the female secretes PHEROMONES that signal her receptivity to the males; her genital area may become swollen, and she may also give behavioral signals.

estuary \'es-chə-,wer-ē\ Partly enclosed coastal body of water in which river water is mixed with seawater. An estuary is thus defined by salinity rather than geography. Many coastal features designated by other names are in fact estuaries (e.g., Chesapeake Bay). Some of the oldest continuous civilizations have flourished in estuarine environments (e.g., the Tigris and Euphrates rivers, the Nile delta, the Ganges delta, and the lower Huang River valley). Cities such as London (Thames River), New York (Hudson River), and Montreal (St. Lawrence River) developed on estuaries and became important commercial centers.

E F G

Etana Epic \ā-'tä-nä\ Ancient Mesopotamian myth concerning dynastic succession. The gods chose Etana as the first king, but his wife, though pregnant, could not give birth, and thus Etana had no heir. The god SHAMASH answered Etana's prayers by directing him to rescue a maimed eagle, which rewarded Etana by carrying him high up in the sky, near heaven, where Etana could obtain the birth plant to help his wife. Surviving texts are incomplete and divergent: in one version Etana makes it to heaven (but the text then breaks off); in another he falls to earth. A king named Etana ruled Kish in southern Mesopotamia sometime in the 3rd millennium BC.

etching Method of engraving in which lines or textures are bitten, or etched, into a metal plate, usually copper, with acid. The image produced has a spontaneity of line that comes from drawing on the plate in the same direct way as with pen or pencil on paper. The first etchings date from the early 16th century, but the basic principle had been used earlier for the decoration of armor. Among the pioneers of the medium were ALBRECHT ALTDORFER, ALBRECHT DURER, and PARMIGIANINO; the greatest of all etchers was REMBRANDT. In the 20th century, etching has been especially popular for book illustration. See also AQUATINT, ENGRAVING.

ethanol \'e-thə-ˌnȯl\ *or* **ethyl alcohol** *or* **grain alcohol** Organic compound, most important of the ALCOHOLS, chemical formula CH_3CH_2OH. Produced by FERMENTATION, it is the intoxicating ingredient in ALCOHOLIC BEVERAGES. In the U.S., ethanol for industrial purposes is made by chemical synthesis, purified by DISTILLATION, and, to avoid the tax on ethyl alcohol for drinking, made unfit to drink (see DENATURATION) by mixing it with METHANOL, CAMPHOR, BENZENE, or KEROSENE. Ethanol has many uses as a solvent, raw material, extraction medium, antifreeze, antiseptic, and gasoline additive and substitute. It is toxic, depressing the central NERVOUS SYSTEM, and addictive to some persons (see ALCOHOLISM). Moderate amounts depress the inhibitory activities of the brain, and so appear to stimulate the mind, but larger amounts seriously impair coordination and judgment, and excessive consumption can cause COMA and death. Taking ethanol in combination with BARBITURATES or related drugs is especially dangerous.

Ethelbert I *or* **Aethelberht I** (died 616) King of Kent (560–616). He married the Christian Bertha, daughter of the king of Paris, and when AUGUSTINE OF CANTERBURY and other missionaries arrived in Kent in 597, he welcomed them and gave them a dwelling at Canterbury. Though baptized by Augustine along with thousands of his subjects, he did not try to establish Christianity by decree. He produced the first written laws in Anglo-Saxon (see ANGLO-SAXON LAW).

Ethelred II *or* **Aethelred Unraed** *known as* **Ethelred the Unready** (968?–1016) King of the English (978–1013, 1014–16). He became king after his half brother's assassination, and was suspected of involvement in the murder. An ineffectual ruler, he failed to mount an organized defense against the Danish invasions (from 980); his massacre of Danish settlers (1002) provoked further attacks. When SWEYN I was accepted as king in England in 1013, Ethelred fled to Normandy. He returned to the throne on the death of Sweyn in 1014, but on his death he was succeeded by the Dane CANUTE THE GREAT. His epithet "Unraed" means "evil counsel," and has been translated incorrectly as "the Unready."

ether \'ē-thər\ Any of a class of organic compounds whose molecular structure has an oxygen atom interposed between two carbon atoms, with the general chemical formula R_1OR_2. Ethers resemble ALCOHOLS but generally are less dense, less soluble in water, more volatile, and more inert. They are used in chemical processing, for extraction and separation of chemicals, and as solvents. Some are used as insecticides and soil fumigants. They are also used in medicine and pharmacology. CODEINE is the methyl ether of MORPHINE. "Ether" often refers to ethyl ether ($C_2H_5OC_2H_5$), best known as an anesthetic but also used as a solvent, an extractant, and a reaction medium.

Etherege \'eth-rij\, **George** *later* **Sir George** (c. 1635–1692?) British playwright. He is remembered as the creator of the Restoration comedy of manners. His first comedy, *Love in a Tub* (1664), was an immediate success and introduced realistic scenes of lively comedy and life of the day. He also wrote *She Wou'd if She Cou'd* (1668) and the popular *The Man of Mode* (1676). Though his own plays ceased to be performed after the 18th century, his style of comedy was adopted by later playwrights and persisted into modern times.

Ethernet Telecommunications networking PROTOCOL introduced by Xerox Corp. in 1979. It was developed as an inexpensive way of sending information quickly between office machines connected together in a single room or building, but it rapidly became a standard computer interconnection method. The original data rate of 10 megabits per second has been increased to 100 megabits per second for a new standard known as fast ethernet. The original specification required COAXIAL CABLE as the communications medium, but costs have been reduced through the employment of simple paired wires. See also computer NETWORK.

ethical relativism Philosophical view that what is right or wrong and good or bad is not absolute but variable and relative, depending on the person, circumstances, or social situation. Rather than claiming that an action's rightness or wrongness can depend on the circumstances, or that people's beliefs about right and wrong are relative to their social conditioning, it claims (in one common form) that what is truly right depends solely on what the individual or the society thinks is right. Because what people think will vary with time and place, what is right will also vary. If, however, changing and even conflicting moral principles are equally valid, there is apparently no objective way of justifying any principle as valid for all people and all societies. This conclusion is rejected by consequentialists (see CONSEQUENTIALISM) and deontologists (see DEONTOLOGICAL ETHICS) alike.

ethics Branch of philosophy that inquires into the nature of ultimate value and the standards by which human actions can be judged right or wrong. Ethics may be subdivided into normative ethics, metaethics, and applied ethics. Normative ethics seeks to set norms or standards for conduct; a crucial question of normative ethics is whether actions are to be judged right or wrong solely on the basis of their consequences. Those theories that judge actions by their consequences have traditionally been known as TELEOLOGICAL ETHICS, or CONSEQUENTIALISM, while those that judge actions according to their intrinsic moral quality have been referred to as DEONTOLOGICAL ETHICS. Metaethics is concerned with the analysis of the logical and semantic aspects of moral language; major metaethical theories include naturalism (see NATURALISTIC FALLACY), nonnaturalism (or INTUITIONISM), EMOTIVISM, and PRESCRIPTIVISM. Applied ethics is the application of normative ethical theories to practical moral problems (e.g., abortion). Among the major fields of applied ethics are bioethics, business ethics, legal ethics, and medical ethics.

Ethiopia \ˌē-thē-'ō-pē-ə\ *officially* **Federal Democratic Republic of Ethiopia** *formerly* **Abyssinia** Country, eastern Africa. It is situated on the Horn of Africa, the continent's easternmost projection. Area: 437,794 sq mi (1,133,882 sq km). Population (2001): 65,892,000. Capital: ADDIS ABABA. The people are about one-third AMHARA and one-third OROMO, with the balance mostly Tigray, Afar, Somali, Saho, and Agew. Languages: Amharic, Oromo. Religions: Ethiopian Orthodoxy (three-fifths of the population), Islam (one-fourth of the population), animism (one-tenth of the population). Currency: birr. The landlocked country is mountainous in the north, with lowlands to the east and west. The central Ethiopian Plateau is split by the GREAT RIFT VALLEY, which divides the eastern and western highlands. The climate is temperate in the highlands, which are mainly savanna, and hot in the arid lowlands. Excessive lumbering has led to severe erosion; this, along with periodic droughts, has led to food shortages. The country's once abundant wildlife has been decimated; many species are endangered. Ethiopia is one of the world's poorest countries. Agriculture is mainly for subsistence, with cereals the main crop. Livestock is also important. Coffee is the main export, followed by hides and skins. A new republic was established in 1995: it has two legislative houses; the chief of state is the president, and the head of government is the prime minister. Ethiopia, the Biblical land of CUSH, was inhabited from earliest antiquity, and was once under ancient Egyptian rule. Geez-speaking agriculturalists established the kingdom of Daamat in the 2nd millennium BC. After 300 BC they were superseded by the kingdom of AKSUM, whose king Menilek I, according to legend, was the son of King SOLOMON and the Queen of Sheba. Christianity was introduced in the 4th century AD and became widespread (see ETHIOPIAN ORTHODOX CHURCH). Ethiopia's prosperous Mediterranean trade was cut off by the Muslim Arabs in the 7th–8th century and the area's interests were directed eastward. Contact with Europe resumed in the late 15th century with the arrival of the Portuguese. Modern Ethiopia began with the reign of TEWODROS II, who began the consolidation of the country. In the wake of European encroachment, the coastal region was made an Italian colony in 1890, but under Emper-

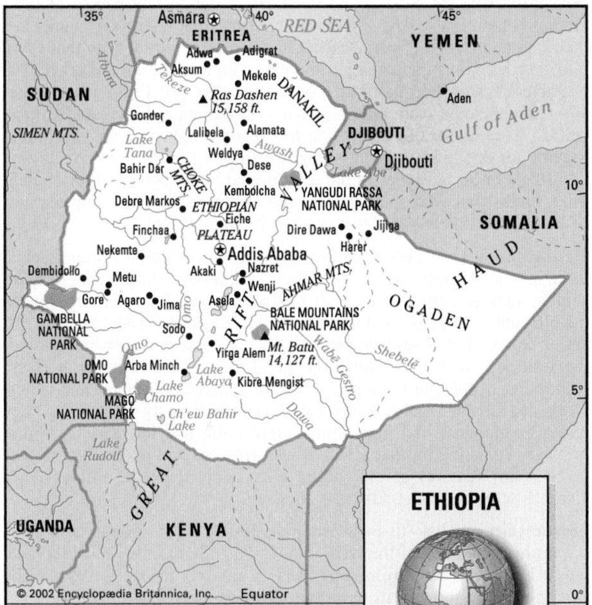

or MENILEK II, the Italians were defeated and ousted in 1896. Ethiopia prospered under his rule, and his modernization programs were continued by emperor HAILE SELASSIE in the 1930s. In 1936 Italy again gained control of the country, and held it as part of Italian Africa until 1941, when it was liberated by the British. Ethiopia incorporated ERITREA in 1952. In 1974 Haile Selassie was deposed and a Marxist government, plagued by civil wars and famine, controlled the country until 1991. In 1993 Eritrea gained its independence, but border conflicts with it and neighboring Somalia continued in the 1990s.

Ethiopian Orthodox Church Independent Christian patriarchate in Ethiopia. Founded in the 4th century by St. Frumentius and his brother Aedesius and based in Addis Ababa, the church adheres to Monophysite doctrine (see MONOPHYSITE HERESY). It accepts the honorary primacy of the Coptic PATRIARCH of Alexandria, who appointed its ARCHBISHOPS from the 12th century until 1959, when an autonomous Ethiopian patriarchate was established. Its customs include circumcision, rigorous fasting, and the participation of laypeople known as *debtera,* who perform liturgical music and dances and act as astrologers, scribes, and fortune-tellers. Its principal adherents are the Amhara and Tigray peoples of the northern and central highlands. See also COPTIC ORTHODOX CHURCH.

Ethiopic languages \ˌē-thē-ˈō-pik\ Group of about 22 languages, spoken by more than 25 million people in Eritrea and Ethiopia, that constitutes part of the South Semitic branch of the SEMITIC LANGUAGE family. Ethiopic has been divided by linguists into North Ethiopic, comprising Ge'ez, Tigré, and Tigrinya (or Tigrai), and South Ethiopic, comprising the rest of the languages. Ge'ez (or Ethiopic) is the oldest Ethiopian Semitic language, first attested in inscriptions from the Kingdom of AKSUM. It became the language of Christianity in the Aksumite period, and—though probably extinct as a vernacular sometime before the 10th century AD—it remained the classical language of highland Ethiopian civilization and the liturgical language of the ETHIOPIAN ORTHODOX CHURCH into the 20th century. Tigré has about 800,000 speakers in northern Eritrea, while Tigrinya has about 4 million speakers. The estimated 1.3 million Tigrinya-speakers in Eritrea constitute about 50% of the country's population. The most important South Ethiopic language is AMHARIC.

ethnic cleansing The creation of an ethnically homogeneous geographic area through the elimination of unwanted ethnic groups by deportation, forcible displacement, or GENOCIDE. Ethnic cleansing also has involved attempts to remove any physical vestiges of the targeted group in the territory, often through the destruction and desecration of their monuments, cemeteries, and houses of worship. Although some critics of the term have claimed that ethnic cleansing is simply a form of genocide, defenders of the usage have noted that, whereas the murder of an ethnic, racial, or religious group is the primary intention of a genocidal policy, the chief goal of ethnic cleansing is the establishment of ethnically homogeneous lands, which may be achieved by any of a number of methods including genocide. The term ethnic cleansing was widely employed in the early 1990s to describe the brutal treatment of Bosniacs (Bosnian Muslims), ethnic Serbs in the Krajina region of Croatia, and ethnic Albanians in the Serbian province of Kosovo during the conflicts that erupted in the wake of the disintegration of Yugoslavia.

ethnic group Social group or category of the population that, in a larger society, is set apart and bound together by common ties of RACE, LANGUAGE, nationality, or CULTURE. Ethnic diversity is one aspect of the social complexity found in most contemporary societies, the legacy of political conquests and migrations. The nation-state has traditionally been uneasy with ethnic diversity, and nation-states have often attempted to eliminate or expel ethnic groups. Most nations today practice some form of PLURALISM, which usually rests on a combination of toleration, interdependence, and separatism. The concept of ethnicity is more important today than ever, as a result of the spread of doctrines of freedom, self-determination, and democracy. See also CULTURE CONTACT, ETHNIC CLEANSING, ETHNOCENTRISM, RACISM.

ethnocentrism Tendency to interpret or evaluate other cultures in terms of one's own. Generally considered a human universal, it is evident in the widespread practice in the West, especially in previous centuries, of labeling non-Western peoples as "savages" or "barbarians" simply because their societies differed from those of the West. Even anthropologists, who are supposed to be sensitive to cultural differences, might characterize all nonliterate peoples as being without religion (as did Sir John Lubbock) or as having a "prelogical mentality" (as did Lucien Lévy-Bruhl) merely because their ways of thinking did not correspond with those of western Europe. The opposite of ethnocentrism is cultural relativism, the understanding of cultural phenomena within the context in which they occur.

ethnography \eth-ˈnä-grə-fē\ Descriptive study of a particular human society, or the process of making such a study. Contemporary ethnography is based almost entirely on fieldwork. The ethnographer lives among the people who are the subject of study for a year or more, learning the local language and participating in everyday life while striving to maintain a degree of objective detachment. He or she usually cultivates close relationships with "informants" who can provide specific information on aspects of cultural life. Contemporary ethnographies have both influenced and been influenced by literary theory. See also BRONISLAW MALINOWSKI, CULTURAL ANTHROPOLOGY.

ethnomusicology Scholarly study of music as an aspect of culture. Taking an anthropological approach (it was originally called "comparative musicology"), it has tended to focus on non-Western music, particularly music of oral traditions. The field's origins lie in the late 19th century with the work of such scholars as F.-J. Fétis (1784–1871) and Carl Stumpf (1848–1936), and much work was motivated by the search for musical universals, under the assumption that prehistory could be studied through research into "primitive" cultures of the present. Recognizing that traditional societies were quickly disappearing with the modern world's encroachment, it soon put its highest priority on collection (by field recording, using the new recording technology) and transcription (using newly devised pitch calibrations). A number of classification schemes for comparative analysis of different musics have been proposed, but the natural focus remains on diversity.

ethology \ē-ˈthä-lə-jē\ Study of animal behavior, a combination of laboratory and field science, with strong ties to other disciplines (e.g., neuroanatomy, ECOLOGY, EVOLUTION). Though many naturalists have studied aspects of animal behavior through the centuries, the modern science of ethology is considered to have arisen as a discrete discipline with the work in the 1920s of NIKOLAAS TINBERGEN and KONRAD LORENZ. Interested in the behavioral process rather than in a particular animal group, ethologists often study one type of behavior (e.g., aggression) in various unrelated animals.

ethyl alcohol See ETHANOL

ethylene Simplest OLEFIN (CH_2CH_2), a colorless, flammable gas with a sweetish taste and odor. The highest-volume PETROCHEMICAL, it occurs in PETROLEUM and NATURAL GAS but is usually produced by heating higher HY-

DROCARBONS (usually ethane and ethane–propane mixtures). Ethylene is polymerized to POLYETHYLENE either at high pressures and temperatures or by CATALYSIS. It reacts with numerous other chemicals to produce ETHANOL, solvents, gasoline additives, ANTIFREEZE, detergents, and various plastics. In plants, ethylene is a hormone that inhibits growth and promotes leaf fall and fruit ripening.

ethylene glycol \'e-thə-,lēn-'glī-,kòl\ Simplest member of the GLYCOL family, also called 1,2-ethanediol ($HOCH_2CH_2OH$). It is a colorless, oily liquid with a mild odor and sweet taste. Widely used as an ANTIFREEZE in automobile cooling systems, it is also used in many other chemical processes. It and some of its derivatives are fairly toxic.

ethyne See ACETYLENE

Etna, Mt. Active volcano, eastern coast of Sicily. The highest active volcano in Europe, its topmost elevation is more than 10,000 ft (3,200 m); its circumference is about 93 mi (150 km). It has erupted repeatedly over the centuries, most violently in 1669, when the lava flow destroyed villages on the lower slope and submerged part of the town of CATANIA. Activity was almost continuous in the decade following 1971, and in 1983 an eruption that lasted four months prompted authorities to explode dynamite there in an attempt to divert lava flows.

Etobicoke \i-'tō-bə-,kōk\ City, southeastern Ontario. Along with the cities of NORTH YORK, SCARBOROUGH, YORK, and Toronto and the borough of EAST YORK, it forms the Municipality of Metropolitan TORONTO. The city occupies an area of 49 sq mi (127 sq km). It was established in 1967 through the amalgamation of the township of Etobicoke, the towns of New Toronto and Mimico, and the village of Long Branch. Its name is an Indian word meaning "place where the alders grow."

Eton College \'ē-tən\ Largest public school (independent secondary school) in England and one of the most prestigious. It is located in Eton, Berkshire. It was founded by Henry VI in 1440–41, the same year he founded King's College, Cambridge. By tradition, 24 scholarships are reserved at Cambridge for Etonians. Boys enter Eton about age 13. Most come from England's wealthiest families, though 70 scholarships are awarded on the basis of competitive examination. Total enrollment is about 1,000. See also COLLEGE.

Etosha National Park \ē-'tō-shə\ National reserve, northern Namibia. Covering some 8,598 sq mi (22,269 sq km), it centers on the Etosha Pan, a vast expanse of salt with lone salt springs, used by animals as salt licks. It has one of the largest accumulations of big-game species in the world, including lions, elephants, rhinoceros, elands, zebras, and springbok.

Etruria \i-'trùr-ē-ə\ Ancient country, central Italy. It covered the region that now constitutes TUSCANY and part of UMBRIA. It was inhabited by the ETRUSCANS, who established a civilization by the 7th century BC. Their chief confederation, traditionally including 12 cities, developed a culture that reached its height in the 6th century BC. Etruscan power extended into northern and southern Italy at its peak, but the cities of Etruria were gradually absorbed by Rome during the 3rd century BC.

Etruscan art Art of the people of ETRURIA (c. 8th–4th century BC). The art of the ETRUSCANS falls into three categories: funerary, urban, and sacred. Because of Etruscan attitudes toward the afterlife, most of the art that remains is funerary. Characteristic achievements are the wall frescoes—painted in two-dimensional style—and realistic terra-cotta portraits found in tombs. Bronze reliefs and sculptures are also common. Tombs found at Caere, carved underground out of soft volcanic rock, resemble houses. Urban architecture was another specialty; Etruscans were among the first in the Mediterranean to lay out cities with a grid plan, a practice copied by the Romans. In the sacred area, Etruscan temples had a deep front porch with columns and abundant terra-cotta roof sculptures, such as those from the temple at Veii (late 6th century). Etruscan art was influenced by Greek art, and in turn influenced the development of realistic portraiture in Italy.

Etruscan language Language spoken by the ancient people of ETRURIA in Italy. Its proposed relations with the INDO-EUROPEAN family have not been generally accepted, and Etruscan remains a linguistic isolate. Known mainly from inscriptions dating from the 7th century BC to the 1st century AD, Etruscan was written in an alphabet derived from one of the GREEK ALPHABETS.

Etruscan religion Beliefs and practices of the ancient people of ETRURIA in western Italy. The ETRUSCANS believed that the gods manifested their nature and will in every aspect of the natural world, such that every bird and berry was a potential source of knowledge of the gods. The characteristics of their more than 40 deities were often vague or changeable, though some were later equated with the major Greek and Roman deities. Famous for DIVINATION, the Etruscans sought to learn the future, looking for divine signs in lightning, the livers of sacrificed animals, and the flights of birds. Belief in the afterlife led to the construction of elaborate tombs that were furnished as houses for the dead. Many features of Etruscan religion were later adopted by the Romans.

Etruscans Ancient people of ETRURIA, whose urban civilization reached its height in the 6th century BC. Their origins are obscure. By the 7th century they had incorporated all of TUSCANY into their territory, and in the 6th century they pushed north to the Po River valley and became rulers of Rome. The Etruscans gave the city its first public works, including walls and a sewer system. By the end of the 6th century, pressure from other peoples in the region, including Greeks, Romans, and Gauls, weakened Etruria. The Romans expelled their dynasty in 509 BC. They had a commercial and agricultural civilization and left a rich cultural heritage, including art that featured wall frescoes and realistic tomb portraits. Many features of the culture were adopted by the Romans. See also ETRUSCAN LANGUAGE, ETRUSCAN RELIGION.

eubacteria \,yü-bak-'tir-ē-ə\ Group consisting of the true BACTERIA, one of two major groups of the PROKARYOTES. The other is the ARCHAEBACTERIA, which are as different from eubacteria as either is from EUKARYOTES. The two groups are thought to have evolved separately from a common ancestor early in earth's history, and they differ in fundamental ways. Virtually all the familiar bacteria that cause diseases (e.g., *E. COLI*, STAPHYLOCOCCUS and SALMONELLA strains, mycobacteria) or are important in food, agriculture, biotechnology, and other industrial activity (e.g., *LACTOBACILLUS*, NITRIFYING and DENITRIFYING bacteria, and LACTOBACILLUS and STREPTOMYCES strains) are eubacteria.

Euboea \yù-'bē-ə\ *Greek* **Évvoia** \'e-vē-ä\ Island, Aegean Sea. One of the largest in Greece, it is about 110 mi (180 km) long and 4–30 mi (6–48 km) wide. The island, mainly mountainous, includes the fertile plain of the Lílas River, which was in antiquity a famous horse-breeding region. It is connected with BOEOTIA by a bridge built by the Chalcidians. It was dominated by Athens for much of the 5th century BC, while its main cities of KHALKÍS and ERETRIA were involved in the PERSIAN and PELOPONNESIAN wars. From 146 BC it was part of the Roman province of Macedon. It was controlled by Venice from 1366, conquered by the Turks in 1470, and passed to Greece in 1830.

eucalyptus \,yü-kə-'lip-təs\ Any of the more than 500 species of mostly very large trees in the genus *Eucalyptus,* in the MYRTLE family, native to Australia, New Zealand, Tasmania, and nearby islands. Many species are grown widely throughout the temperate regions of the world as shade trees or in forestry plantations. Because they grow rapidly, many species attain great height. The leaf glands of many species, especially *E. salicifolia* and *E. globulus,* contain a volatile, aromatic oil known as eucalyptus oil, used mostly in medicines. Eucalyptus wood is used extensively in Australia as fuel, and the timber is commonly used in buildings and fencing. The bark of many species is used in papermaking and tanning.

Eucharist \'yü-kə-rəst\ *or* **Holy Communion** *or* **Lord's Supper** Christian rite commemorating the Last Supper of JESUS with his disciples. On the night before his death, Jesus consecrated bread and wine and gave them to his disciples, saying "this is my body" and "this is my blood." A central rite of Christian worship, the Eucharist involves consecration of bread and wine by the clergy and their consumption by worshipers. Intended as a means of fostering unity in the church, it has also been a source of division because of differing interpretations of its nature. In Roman Catholicism the Eucharist is a SACRAMENT, and the bread and wine are thought to become the actual body and blood of Jesus through TRANSUBSTANTIATION. Anglicans and Lutherans also emphasize the divine presence in the offering and recognize it as a sacrament, while others regard it as a memorial with largely symbolic meaning.

Eucken \'òi-kən\, **Rudolf Christoph** (1846–1926) German philosopher. He taught primarily at the University of Jena (1874–1920). Eucken maintained that it is a human duty and privilege to overcome nature by incessant active striving after the spiritual life. A strident critic of naturalism, he held that the human soul differentiated humans from the rest of the natural world and that the soul could not be explained by natural processes. He was known as an interpreter of ARISTOTLE, and he wrote works in ethics and religion, including *Socialism* (1920) and *Individual and Society* (1923). He won the Nobel Prize for Literature in 1908.

Euclid \'yü-kləd\ (fl. c. 300 BC) Greek mathematician of antiquity, known primarily for his highly influential treatise on geometry, the *Elements.* He founded a school in Alexandria during the reign of PTOLEMY I. Little is known of his life, but there are many anecdotes. In the most famous, asked by Ptolemy if there is a shorter way to geometry than through his *Elements,* Euclid replies, "There is no royal road to geometry." The *Elements,* based on the works of earlier mathematicians, is a brilliant synthesis of old and new. It has been a major influence on rational thought and a model for many philosophical treatises, and has set a standard for logical thinking and methods of proof in the sciences. The starting point not just of EUCLIDEAN GEOMETRY but of an approach to reasoning, it is sometimes said to be the most translated, published, and studied work after the Bible.

Euclidean geometry Study of points, lines, angles, surfaces, and solids based on EUCLID's AXIOMS. Its importance lies less in its results than in the systematic method Euclid used to develop and present them. This axiomatic method has been the model for many systems of rational thought, even outside mathematics, for over 2,000 years. From 10 axioms and postulates, Euclid deduced 465 theorems, or propositions, concerning aspects of plane and solid geometric figures. This work was long held to constitute an accurate description of the physical world and to provide a sufficient basis for understanding it. During the 19th century, rejection of some of Euclid's postulates resulted in two NON-EUCLIDEAN GEOMETRIES that proved just as valid and consistent.

Euclidean space In geometry, a two- or three-dimensional space in which the axioms and postulates of EUCLIDEAN GEOMETRY apply; also, a space in any finite number of dimensions, in which points are designated by coordinates (one for each dimension) and the distance between two points is given by a DISTANCE FORMULA. The only conception of physical space for over 2,000 years, it remains the most compelling and useful way of modeling the world as it is experienced. Though non-Euclidean spaces, such as those that emerge from ELLIPTIC GEOMETRY and HYPERBOLIC GEOMETRY, have led scientists to a better understanding of the universe and of mathematics itself, Euclidean space remains the point of departure for their study.

eudaemonism \yu̇-'dē-mə-ˌni-zəm\ In ETHICS, the view that the end of human existence consists in some function or activity appropriate to human beings as such. Whatever that function or activity turns out to be, virtue is excellence in its performance. The ultimate rationale for morality in TELEOLOGICAL ETHICS lies in its contribution to making possible the achievement of one's potential as a human being, one's natural telos. Eudaemonists may conceive virtue either as an instrumental means to happiness (e.g., honesty produces a good reputation, which is a means to wealth and political power) or as a constitutive means to happiness (e.g., honesty is an essential part of leading a happy life).

Eudocia Macrembolitissa \yu̇-'dō-shə-ˌmak-rəm-ˌbä-lə-'ti-sə\ (1021–1096) Byzantine empress and regent, called the wisest woman of her time. As the wife of Constantine X Ducas, she became regent for her three sons after his death (1067). To fend off the Seljuq Turks, she married a Cappadocian general, Romanus Diogenes (later ROMANUS IV DIOGENES). After his capture at the Battle of MANZIKERT (1071), Eudocia and her son Michael ruled jointly and deposed Romanus. After Michael succeeded to the throne, Eudocia entered a convent.

Eugene City (pop., 1996 est.: 124,000), western Oregon. Located on the Willamette River, it was settled by Eugene Skinner in 1846. Named Eugene City in 1853, it grew as an agricultural and lumber center with the arrival of the railroad in 1870. It is the site of the University of OREGON (founded 1872) and Northwest Christian College (1895). It is a tourist center for the MacKenzie River recreational area and Willamette National Forest.

Eugene of Savoy *orig.* **François-Eugène, prince de Savoie-Carignan** (1663–1736) French-Austrian general. Born in Paris, he was the son of the comte de Soissons, of the House of Savoy-Carignan, and of Olympe Mancini (see MANCINI FAMILY), niece of JULES MAZARIN. LOUIS XIV severely restrained Eugene's ambitions, prompting him to leave France and enter the service of Emperor LEOPOLD I. He later served Joseph I and CHARLES VI. He quickly distinguished himself in battle and advanced in rank to imperial field marshal at 29. He fought notably against the Turks in central Europe and the Balkans and against France in the War of the GRAND ALLIANCE and the War of the SPANISH SUCCESSION. With his friend the duke of MARLBOROUGH, he won the important victory at the Battle of BLENHEIM (1704) and ousted the French from Italy. In 1718 he won a great triumph over the Turks, taking the city of Belgrade. He later served as governor in the AUSTRIAN NETHERLANDS (1714–24). An outstanding strategist and an inspired leader, he was regarded as one of the greatest soldiers of his generation.

eugenics \yu̇-'je-niks\ Study of human improvement by genetic means. The first thorough exposition of eugenics was made by FRANCIS GALTON, who in *Hereditary Genius* (1869) proposed that a system of arranged marriages between men of distinction and women of wealth would eventually produce a gifted race. The American Eugenics Society, founded in 1926, supported Galton's theories. U.S. eugenicists also supported restriction on immigration from nations with "inferior" stock, such as Italy, Greece, and countries of eastern Europe, and argued for the sterilization of insane, retarded, and epileptic citizens. Sterilization laws were passed in more than half the states, and isolated instances of involuntary sterilization continued into the 1970s. The assumptions of eugenicists came under sharp criticism beginning in the 1930s and were discredited after the German Nazis used eugenics to support the extermination of Jews, blacks, and homosexuals. See also GENETICS, RACE, SOCIAL DARWINISM.

Eugénie \œ̄-zhā-'nē\ *orig.* **Eugénia María de Montijo de Guzmán** (1826–1920) Wife of NAPOLEON III and empress of France (1853–70). Daughter of a Spanish noble, she married Napoleon III in 1853, and came to have an important influence on her husband's foreign policy. As a devoted Roman Catholic, she favored a strong papacy and supported Ultramontane causes. She also encouraged French opposition to a Prussian candidate for the Spanish throne in the controversy that precipitated the Franco–Prussian War. After the French defeat at Sedan, she joined her family in exile in England.

Eugenius III \yu̇-'jē-nē-əs\ *orig.* **Bernard of Pisa** (died 1153) Pope (1145–53). A Cistercian abbot, he was elected pope when Rome was on the verge of anarchy, and in 1146 he was forced into exile. While in France he supported LOUIS VII's intention to launch the Second CRUSADE to free Edessa, an effort that ended in failure. He returned to Italy (1148), but the hostility of the Senate often kept him away from Rome. In the Treaty of Constance (1153) Eugenius fixed conditions for the coronation of FREDERICK I BARBAROSSA, but died before it could take place.

euhemerism \yü-'hē-mə-ˌri-zəm\ Attempt to find a historical basis for mythical beings and events. It takes its name from Euhemerus (fl. 300 BC), a Greek scholar who examined popular mythology in his *Sacred History* and asserted that the gods originated as heroes or conquerors who were admired and later deified. Though modern scholars do not accept euhemerism as the sole explanation for the origin of gods, it is thought to be valid in some cases.

eukaryote \yü-'kar-ē-ˌōt\ Any organism composed of one or more cells, each of which contains a clearly defined nucleus enclosed by a membrane, along with organelles (small, self-contained, cellular parts that perform specific functions). The organelles include mitochondria, CHLOROPLASTS, a Golgi apparatus (which packages large molecules for transport), an ENDOPLASMIC RETICULUM, and LYSOSOMES. All organisms except BACTERIA are eukaryotes; bacteria are PROKARYOTES.

Eulenspiegel \'ȯi̇l-ən-ˌshpē-gəl, *Engl* 'ȯil-ən-ˌspē-gəl\, **Till** German peasant trickster of folk and literary tales. The historical Till is said to have died in 1350; anecdotes associated with his name were printed c. 1500 in Low German and from 1515 in High German. In the tales the stupid yet cunning peasant demonstrates his superiority to the narrow, dishonest, condescending townsman, as well as to the clergy and nobility. The tales were translated into Dutch and English (c. 1520), French (1532), and Latin (1558).

Euler \'ȯi-lər\, **Leonhard** (1707–1783) German mathematician. In 1733 he succeeded Daniel Bernoulli (see BERNOULLI FAMILY) at the St. Petersburg Academy of Sciences. There he developed the theory of trigonometric and logarithmic functions and advanced mathematics generally. Under the patronage of Frederick the Great, he worked at Berlin

Academy for many years (1744–66), where he developed the concept of function in mathematical analysis and discovered the imaginary logarithms of negative numbers. Throughout his life he was interested in NUMBER THEORY. In addition to inspiring the use of arithmetic terms in writing mathematics and physics, Euler introduced many symbols that became standard, including Σ for summation; $\int n$ for the sum of divisors of *n*; *e* for the base of the natural LOGARITHM; and *a*, *b*, and *c* for the sides of a triangle and A, B, and C for the opposite angles; $f(x)$ for a function; π for the ratio of the circumference to the diameter of a circle; and *i* for $\sqrt{-1}$. Much of his work was done after he was blinded in 1766. He is considered one of the greatest mathematical minds of all time.

Euler's formula Either of two important mathematical theorems of LEONHARD EULER. The first is a topological invariance (see TOPOLOGY) relating the number of faces, vertices, and edges of any POLYHEDRON. It is written $f + V = E + 2$, where f is the number of faces, V the number of vertices, and E the number of edges. A cube, for example, has 6 faces, 8 vertices, and 12 edges, and satisfies this formula. The second formula, used in TRIGONOMETRY, says $e^{ix} = \cos x + i\sin x$ where e is the base of the natural LOGARITHM and i is the square root of -1 (see IRRATIONAL NUMBER). When x is equal to π or 2π, the formula yields two elegant expressions relating π, e, and i: $e^{i\pi} = -1$ and $e^{2i\pi} = 1$.

Eumenes II \'yü-mə-ˌnēz\ (died 160/159 BC) King of PERGAMUM (197–c. 160 BC). He continued the policy of his father, ATTALUS I SOTER, of cooperation with Rome. He helped defeat ANTIOCHUS III, thus enlarging his realm. He brought his kingdom to its height and made it a great center of Greek culture, and is credited in particular with constructing nearly all the public buildings and sculpture on the Pergamum acropolis. He was suspected of disloyalty in the Roman struggle against PERSEUS; Rome subsequently withdrew its support, and Eumenes' power and the glory of Pergamum declined. His brother Attalus II became coruler c. 160 BC.

Eumolpus \yü-'mäl-pəs\ Mythological ancestor of the priestly class, the Eumolpids, at ELEUSIS in ancient Greece. His name means "sweet singer." Three divergent identities for him exist in legend: he is the father, son, or pupil of Musaeus, a mythical singer connected with ORPHEUS, in one; an originator of the ELEUSINIAN MYSTERIES in another; and a king of Thrace and son of POSEIDON in a third.

eunuch \'yü-nək\ Castrated human male. From remote antiquity on, eunuchs were employed in the Middle East and China as guards and servants in harems or other women's quarters, and as chamberlains to kings. The eunuchs' confidential position frequently enabled them to exercise an important influence over their royal masters. Many of the patriarchs of Constantinople during Byzantine times were eunuchs. Eunuch advisers as a class only disappeared with the end of the Ottoman empire. See also CASTRATO.

euonymus \yu̇-'ä-nə-məs\ Any of about 170 species of shrubs, woody climbers, and small trees that make up the genus *Euonymus* (family Celastraceae), native to temperate Asia, North America, and Europe, including many popular landscape ornamental shrubs and ground covers. The winged spindle tree *(E. alata),* also called burning bush, is a handsome shrub with corky winged stems. Wood of the common spindle tree *(E. europaea)* is used for pegs and spindles; several varieties are grown as ornamentals.

euphonium \yu̇-'fō-nē-əm\ *or* **tenor tuba** Large valved BRASS INSTRUMENT, the leading lower-pitched instrument in military bands. It developed from the valved BUGLE and CORNET in Germany c. 1840. It has four valves and a wide conical bore resembling the tuba's. Its range is an octave below the trumpet and cornet. It is played either vertically or with the bell facing forward. The very similar baritone has the same range and transposition, and is distinguished only by its narrower bore. Both are essential members of bands of all kinds, and are often given significant solo roles.

euphorbia See SPURGE

Euphranor \yu̇-'frā-nȯr\ (c. 390–c. 325 BC) Greek sculptor and painter active in Athens. The only surviving work identified as his are fragments of a colossal marble statue of Apollo (c. 330 BC) found in the agora at Athens. Other recorded (but lost) works suggest that he was one of the foremost Athenian artists of the mid-4th century BC. He also wrote treatises on proportion and color.

Euphrates River \yu̇-'frā-tēz\ *Turkish* **Firat Nehri** \fə-'rät-ne-'rē\ *Arabic* **Al-Furat** \ˌäl-fu̇-'rät\ River, western Asia. The largest river in western Asia, it rises in Turkey and flows southeast across Syria and southern Iraq. Formed by the confluence of the Kara and the Murat in the high Armenian plateau, the Euphrates descends between major ranges of the TAURUS MTNS. and drops nearly 1,000 ft (300 m) to the Syrian plateau. It then flows through western and central Iraq to unite with the TIGRIS, and continues, as Shatt al Arab, to the PERSIAN GULF. In all, it is 2,235 mi (3,596 km) long. Its valley was heavily irrigated in ancient times, and many great cities, some of whose ruins remain, lined its banks. With the Tigris, it defined the area known as MESOPOTAMIA.

Euphronius *or* **Euphronios** \yu̇-'frō-nē-əs\ (fl. c. 520–500 BC) Greek vase painter and potter active in Athens. His signature has been identified on 20 vessels, eight that he signed as painter and 12 as potter. He was an outstanding early proponent of RED-FIGURE POTTERY. His best-known work as a painter is a krater in the Louvre depicting Herakles wrestling Antaeus. As a potter he worked with the finest vase painters of his time. His greatest rival was EUTHYMIDES.

Eure River \'œr\ River, northern France. From its source in the Perche Hills it flows chiefly through agricultural and wooded regions on its 140-mi (225-km) course, passing through CHARTRES below the cathedral, which is located on high ground on its left bank. It joins the SEINE above ROUEN.

Euripides \yu̇-'ri-pə-ˌdēz\ (484?–406 BC) Greek playwright. With AESCHYLUS and SOPHOCLES, he is recognized as one of Athens' three great tragic dramatists. An associate of ANAXAGORAS, he expressed his questions about Greek religion in his plays. Repeatedly chosen to compete in the dramatic festival of Dionysus, beginning in 455 BC, he won his first victory in 441. He competed 22 times, writing four plays for each occasion. Of his 92 plays, about 19 survive, including *Medea* (431 BC), *Hippolytus* (428), *Electra* (418), *The Trojan Women* (415), *Ion* (413), *Iphigenia at Aulis* (406), and *The Bacchae* (406). Many of his plays include prologues and rely on a DEUS EX MACHINA. Unlike Aeschylus and Sophocles, Euripides made his characters' tragic fates stem almost entirely from their own flawed natures and uncontrolled passions. Chance, disorder, and human irrationality and immorality frequently result in apparently meaningless suffering that is looked on with indifference by the gods.

Euripus See KHALKIS

Euripus Strait See EVRIPOS STRAIT

euro Unit of exchange adopted in January 1999 that represents the combined currencies of 12 countries of the EUROPEAN UNION (EU), including the German deutsche mark, the French franc, and the Italian lira. The new currency was intended to strengthen Europe as an economic power, increase international trade, simplify monetary transactions, and lead to pricing equality throughout Europe. The euro replaced the national currencies of participating countries on March 1, 2002. A few members of the EU, notably Britain, announced that they would wait until the currency went into effect before deciding whether to join.

Eurocommunism Trend among European communist parties toward independence from Soviet COMMUNIST PARTY doctrine in the 1970s and '80s. The term, coined in the mid-1970s, received wide publicity after the publication of Santiago Carrillo's *Eurocommunism and the State* (1977). The Eurocommunist movement rejected the Soviet doctrine of one monolithic world communist movement and advocated instead that each country's communist party base its policies on the traditions and needs of its own country. With MIKHAIL GORBACHEV's encouragement, all communist parties took independent courses in the late 1980s. Most of the European communist parties declined after the breakup of the Soviet Union.

Eurodollar U.S. dollar that has been deposited outside the U.S., especially in Europe. Foreign banks holding Eurodollars are obligated to pay in U.S. dollars when the deposits are withdrawn. Most Eurodollars are used to finance trade, but many central banks also operate in the Eurodollar market. See also CURRENCY, FOREIGN EXCHANGE.

Europa \yu̇-'rō-pə\ In GREEK MYTHOLOGY, the daughter either of Phoenix or of Agenor, king of Phoenicia. Her beauty inspired the love of ZEUS, who approached her in the form of a white bull and carried her off across the sea to Crete. After bearing Zeus three sons, she married the king of Crete, who adopted her sons. They grew up to become King MINOS of Crete, King Rhadamanthus of the Cyclades, and Prince Sarpedon of Lycia. On Crete she was worshiped under the name Hellotis. The continent of EUROPE is named for her.

Europe Second smallest continent on earth. It is bordered by the Arctic Ocean, the Atlantic Ocean, and the Mediterranean, Black, and Caspian seas. The continent's eastern boundary runs along the URAL MTNS. and the URAL RIVER. Its area includes numerous islands, archipelagoes, and peninsulas. Indented by bays, fjords, and seas, continental Europe's irregular coastline is about 24,000 mi (38,000 km) long. Area: 4,000,000 sq mi (10,400,000 sq km). Population (1997 est.): 542,578,000. The greater part of Europe combines low elevations with low relief; about three-fifths of the land is at an elevation of less than 600 ft (180 m) above sea level, and another one-third is between 600 and 3,000 ft (180 and 900 m) above sea level. The highest points are in the mountain systems crossing the southern part of the continent, including the PYRENEES, ALPS, APENNINES, CARPATHIANS, and BALKAN MTNS. A well-watered continent with many rivers, it has few sizable lakes. Glaciers cover an area of about 44,800 sq mi (116,000 sq km), mostly in the north. Roughly one-third of Europe is arable, and about half of that land is devoted to cereals, principally wheat and barley. One-third is forested. It was the first of the world's regions to develop a modern economy based on commercial agriculture and industry, and remains one of the world's major industrial regions, with average per capita income among the world's highest. The people of Europe constitute about one-seventh of the world's population, and the vast majority belong to the European (or Caucasoid) geographic race, although there are many divisions of language and nationality. Most of its approximately 60 native languages belong to either the ROMANCE, GERMANIC, or SLAVIC languages. Europe's population is overwhelmingly Christian. Modern humans supplanted the scanty NEANDERTHAL population in Europe about 40,000 years ago, and by the beginning of the 2nd millennium BC the general population groups that would become the historical peoples and nations of Europe were in place. The Greek civilizations were the earliest in Europe, and in the Classical period the Greeks were a conduit for the advanced civilizations of the Middle East, which, along with the unique Greek contribution, laid the foundation for European civilization. By the mid-2nd century BC the Greeks had come under Roman control, and the vast Roman empire brought to the conquered parts of Europe the civilization the Greeks had begun. It was through the Romans that Christianity penetrated into Europe. The Roman empire in the west finally collapsed in the 5th century AD, leading to an extensive breakdown of classical civilization, not to be revived until the RENAISSANCE in the 15th–16th century, which began the modern European traditions of science, exploration, and discovery. The Protestant REFORMATION of the 16th century ended the dominance of the Roman church over western and northern Europe, and the ENLIGHTENMENT of the 17th–18th century stressed the primacy of reason. In the late 18th century, Enlightenment ideals helped spur the FRENCH REVOLUTION, which toppled Europe's most powerful monarchy and spearheaded the movement toward democracy and equality. The late 18th century also marked the beginning of the INDUSTRIAL REVOLUTION, which led to Europe's military and political dominance over much of the world for the next century. In the early 20th century the European powers were divided in World War I, which led to the effective end of monarchy in Europe and created a host of new nations in central and eastern Europe. World War II marked the passing of world power from the states of western Europe and saw the rise of communism in eastern Europe with the Soviet Union and its satellites sharply dividing the continent. In the late 20th century, with the collapse of communism in the U.S.S.R., many of its member states became independent and East and West Germany were reunified. See also EUROPEAN UNION, NATO. See map on following page.

Europe, Council of Organization of more than 40 European states formed to promote European unity, protect human rights, and facilitate social and economic progress. Established in 1949 by 10 Western European states, it has devised international agreements on human rights and established a number of special bodies and expert committees on social, legal, and cultural issues. It is headquartered in Strasbourg, France.

European Aeronautic Defence and Space Co. (EADS)European aerospace company that is one of the world's largest. It was formed (2000) from the merger of Aerospatiale Matra of France, Daimler-Chrysler Aerospace (Dasa) of Germany, and Construcciones Aeronáuticas S.A. (CASA) of Spain. It holds an 80-percent share in the AIRBUS INDUSTRIE consortium and is responsible for the final assembly of Airbus aircraft. It has a controlling interest in the trinational venture Astrium (created 2000), whose facilities in France, Germany, and Great Britain cover a broad range of the space business from ground systems and launch vehicles to satellites and orbital infrastructure. Its Eurocopter subsidiary produces military and civil helicopters. It also has stakes in Arianespace, which markets the commercial services of Ariane launch vehicles; the Eurofighter consortium to develop a multirole combat aircraft; and the French aerospace firm Dassault.

European Atomic Energy Community (EURATOM) International organization established in 1958 to form a common market for developing peaceful uses of atomic energy. It originally had six members; it now includes all members of the EUROPEAN UNION. Among its aims were to facilitate the establishment of a nuclear-energy industry on a European rather than a national scale, coordinate research, encourage construction of power plants, establish safety regulations, and establish a common market for trade in nuclear equipment and materials. In 1967 its governing bodies were merged into the EUROPEAN COMMUNITY.

European Coal and Steel Community (ECSC) Administrative agency established by a treaty ratified in 1952, designed to integrate the coal and steel industries of France, West Germany, Italy, Belgium, the Netherlands, and Luxembourg. It originated in ROBERT SCHUMAN's plan (1950) to establish a common market for coal and steel by those countries willing to submit to an independent authority; the ECSC now includes all members of the EUROPEAN UNION. It initially removed barriers to trade in coal, coke, steel, pig iron, and scrap iron; it later supervised the reduction of its members' excess production. In 1967 its governing bodies were merged into the EUROPEAN COMMUNITY.

European Community (EC) Organization formed in 1967 with the merger of the EUROPEAN ECONOMIC COMMUNITY, EUROPEAN COAL AND STEEL COMMUNITY, and EUROPEAN ATOMIC ENERGY COMMUNITY. The merger created a single Commission of the European Community and a single Council of Ministers. Other executive, legislative, and judicial bodies were also collected under the umbrella of the EC. In 1993 the EC became the basis for the EUROPEAN UNION, and the European Economic Community was renamed the European Community.

European Court of Justice Judicial branch of the EUROPEAN UNION (EU), established in 1958 to ensure the observance of international agreements negotiated by predecessor organizations of the EU. It reviews the legality of the acts of EU executive bodies and rules on cases of civil law between member states or private parties. It can invalidate the laws of EU members when they conflict with EU law. Its bench, which is appointed by member governments, consists of 15 judges and eight advocates-general. See also INTERNATIONAL COURT OF JUSTICE.

European Defense Community (EDC) Attempt by Western European powers, with U.S. support, to counterbalance the overwhelming conventional military ascendancy of the Soviet Union in Europe by creating a supranational European army, including West German forces. A treaty was concluded in 1952, but the French parliament's refusal to ratify the treaty in 1954 brought an end to the project. One consequence of the French action was the decision in 1955 to rearm West Germany and allow its entry into NATO. In 1955 the EDC was replaced by the WESTERN EUROPEAN UNION.

European Economic Community (EEC) *later* **European Community (EC)** *known as* **the Common Market** Economic association of European countries to promote European economic unity. It was established by the Treaty of Rome in 1957 to develop the economies of the member states into one large common market and build a political union of the states of Western Europe. The EEC also sought to establish a single commercial policy toward nonmember countries, to coordinate transportation systems, agricultural policies, and general economic policies, and to remove measures restricting free competition. It also assured the mobility of labor, capital, and entrepreneurship among member states. The liberalized trade policies it sponsored from the 1950s were highly successful in increasing trade and economic prosperity in Western Europe. In 1967 its governing bodies were merged into the EUROPEAN COMMUNITY. In 1993 the EEC was renamed the European Community (EC); it is now the principal organization within the EUROPEAN UNION.

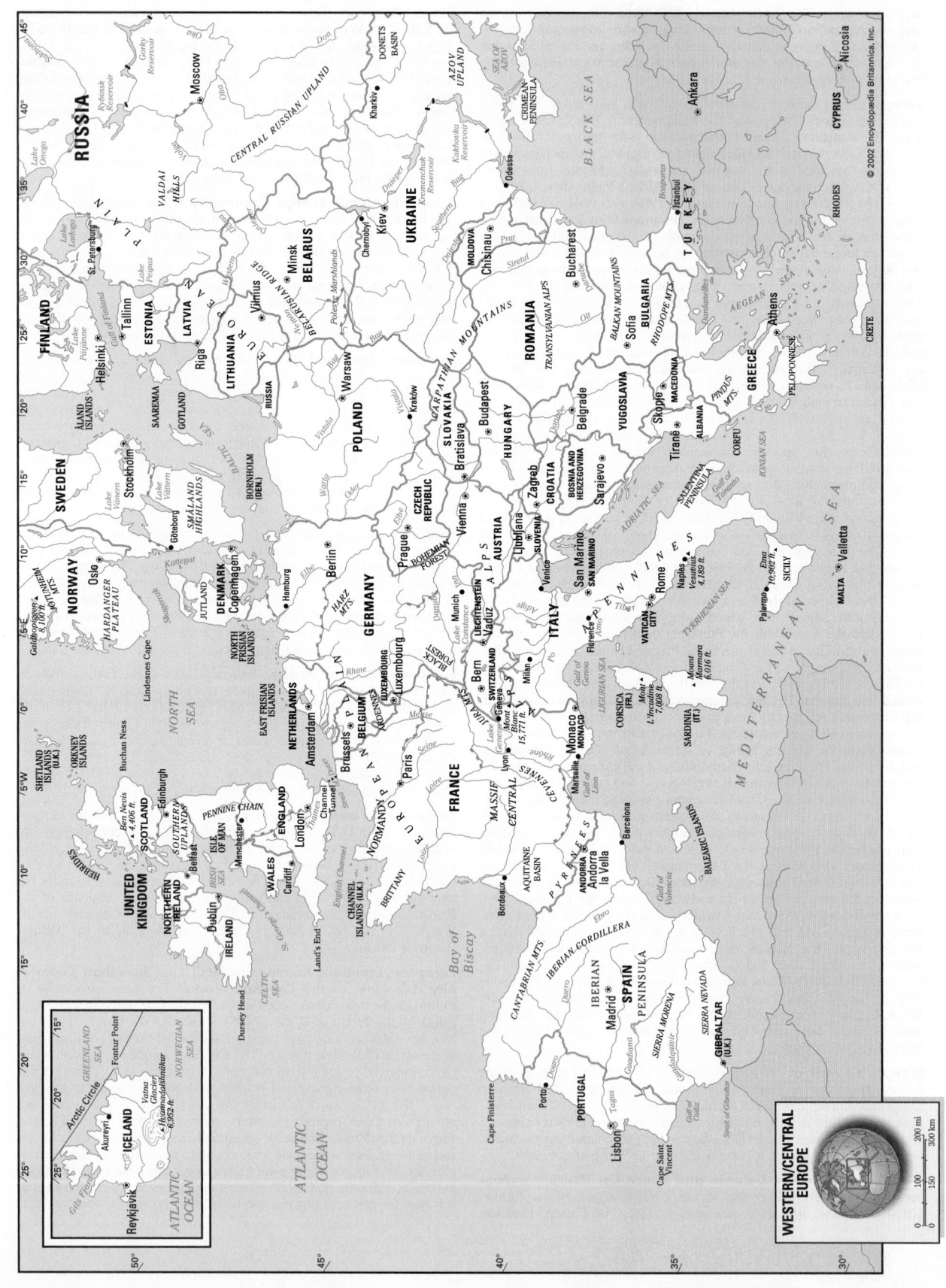

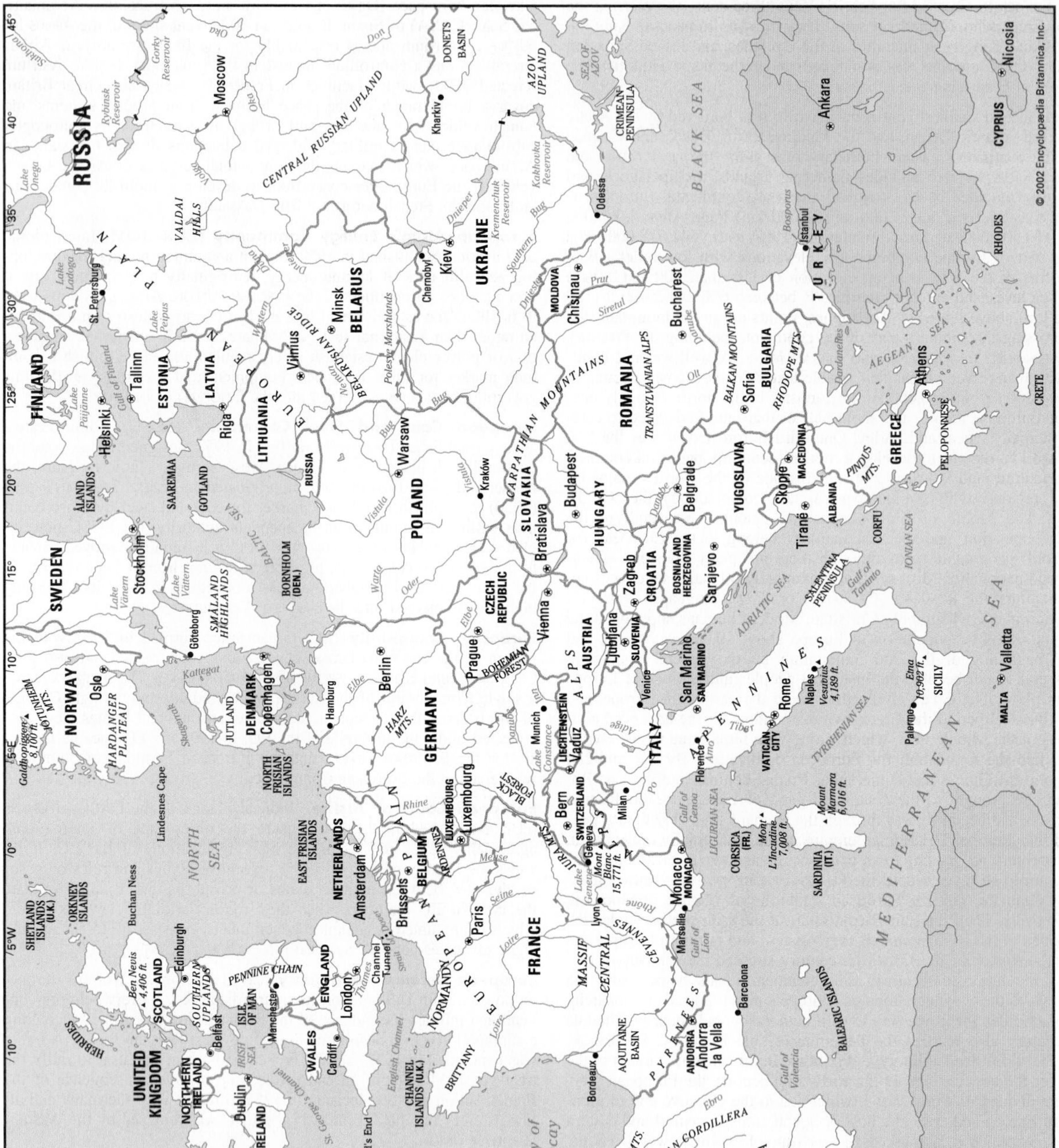
WESTERN/CENTRAL EUROPE
0 100 200 mi
0 150 300 km
© 2002 Encyclopædia Britannica, Inc.
RUSSIA
Moscow
Lake Onega
Rybinsk Reservoir
Gorky Reservoir
Oka
Volga
VALDAI HILLS
CENTRAL RUSSIAN UPLAND
Don
DONETS BASIN
AZOV UPLAND
SEA OF AZOV
CRIMEAN PENINSULA
Kharkiv
Kakhovka Reservoir
Kremenchuk Reservoir
Dnieper
Odessa
BLACK SEA
Lake Ladoga
St. Petersburg
Lake Peipus
EUROPEAN PLAIN
FINLAND
Helsinki
Lake Päijänne
Gulf of Finland
Tallinn
ESTONIA
LATVIA
Riga
LITHUANIA
Vilnius
Minsk
BELARUS
BELARUSIAN RIDGE
Polesye Marshlands
Chernobyl
Kiev
UKRAINE
MOLDOVA
Chisinau
Prut
Siretul
Bucharest
ROMANIA
TRANSYLVANIAN ALPS
CARPATHIAN MOUNTAINS
BALKAN MOUNTAINS
BULGARIA
Sofia
RHODOPE MTS.
Istanbul
Bosporus
TURKEY
Ankara
CYPRUS
Nicosia
RHODES
AEGEAN SEA
Dardanelles
Athens
CRETE
PELOPONNESE
GREECE
PINDUS MTS.
ALBANIA
Tiranë
MACEDONIA
Skopje
YUGOSLAVIA
Belgrade
BOSNIA AND HERZEGOVINA
Sarajevo
CROATIA
Zagreb
HUNGARY
Budapest
SLOVAKIA
Bratislava
Kraków
POLAND
Warsaw
Vistula
Bug
RUSSIA
ÅLAND ISLANDS
SAAREMAA
GOTLAND
BALTIC SEA
BORNHOLM (DEN.)
SWEDEN
Stockholm
Lake Vänern
Lake Vättern
SMÅLAND HIGHLANDS
Göteborg
NORWAY
Oslo
JOTUNHEIM MTS.
Galdhøpiggen 8,100 ft.
HARDANGER PLATEAU
Skagerrak
Kattegat
DENMARK
Copenhagen
JUTLAND
Lindesnes Cape
NORTH SEA
NORTH FRISIAN ISLANDS
EAST FRISIAN ISLANDS
Hamburg
Elbe
Berlin
HARZ MTS.
GERMANY
Oder
Warta
CZECH REPUBLIC
Prague
BOHEMIAN FOREST
Vienna
AUSTRIA
ALPS
Munich
Danube
Lake Constance
LIECHTENSTEIN
Vaduz
BLACK FOREST
SWITZERLAND
Bern
Geneva
Lake Geneva
Mont Blanc 15,771 ft.
JURA MTS.
Milan
Po
Ljubljana
SLOVENIA
Venice
Adige
ITALY
San Marino
SAN MARINO
Florence
Arno
Tiber
APENNINES
VATICAN CITY
Rome
Naples
Vesuvius 4,189 ft.
TYRRHENIAN SEA
ADRIATIC SEA
SALENTINA PENINSULA
Gulf of Taranto
IONIAN SEA
CORFU
Palermo
Etna 10,902 ft.
SICILY
MALTA
Valletta
LIGURIAN SEA
Gulf of Genoa
CORSICA (FR.)
Mont L'incudine 7,008 ft.
SARDINIA (IT.)
Mount Marmara 6,016 ft.
MEDITERRANEAN SEA
Monaco
MONACO
Marseille
Gulf of Lion
Rhône
CÉVENNES
MASSIF CENTRAL
Lyon
FRANCE
Paris
Seine
Loire
Meuse
NORMANDY
EUROPEAN PLAIN
BRITTANY
AQUITAINE BASIN
Bordeaux
PYRENEES
ANDORRA
Andorra la Vella
Barcelona
BALEARIC ISLANDS
Gulf of Valencia
Ebro
IBERIAN CORDILLERA
CANTABRIAN MTS.
IBERIAN PENINSULA
SPAIN
Madrid
Duero
Tagus
Guadiana
SIERRA MORENA
SIERRA NEVADA
Guadalquivir
GIBRALTAR (U.K.)
Strait of Gibraltar
Gulf of Cadiz
PORTUGAL
Porto
Douro
Lisbon
Cape Saint Vincent
Cape Finisterre
Bay of Biscay
ATLANTIC OCEAN
CHANNEL ISLANDS (U.K.)
English Channel
Channel Tunnel
Strait of Dover
Thames
NETHERLANDS
Amsterdam
BELGIUM
Brussels
ARDENNES
LUXEMBOURG
Luxembourg
Rhine
UNITED KINGDOM
ENGLAND
London
WALES
Cardiff
Manchester
ISLE OF MAN
PENNINE CHAIN
SOUTHERN UPLANDS
SCOTLAND
Edinburgh
Ben Nevis 4,406 ft.
HEBRIDES
SHETLAND ISLANDS (U.K.)
ORKNEY ISLANDS
Buchan Ness
NORTHERN IRELAND
Belfast
IRISH SEA
St. George's Channel
IRELAND
Dublin
Dursey Head
CELTIC SEA
Land's End
ICELAND
Reykjavík
Akureyri
Vatna Glacier
Hvannadalshnúkur 6,952 ft.
Arctic Circle
Fontur Point
GREENLAND SEA
NORWEGIAN SEA
ATLANTIC OCEAN
Gils Fjord

European Free Trade Association (EFTA) Group of four countries—Iceland, Liechtenstein, Norway, and Switzerland—organized to remove barriers to trade in industrial goods among themselves, but with each nation maintaining its own commercial policy toward countries outside the group. The organization was formed in 1960 by Austria, Denmark, Norway, Portugal, Sweden, Switzerland, and Britain as an alternative to the EUROPEAN ECONOMIC COMMUNITY (EEC). Some of those countries later left the EFTA and joined the EEC.

European Parliament Legislative assembly of the EUROPEAN UNION (EU), established in 1958. Its members were originally selected by the member nations' legislatures; since 1979, they have been elected by direct universal suffrage. They are apportioned according to the member nations' populations, and currently number over 500. The parliament's leadership is shared by a president and 14 vice presidents, elected for 30-month terms. The EU Council of Ministers, which represents the member states, consults the parliament, which is empowered to discuss whatever matters it wishes. The parliament, whose powers were expanded with passage of the MAASTRICHT TREATY (1993), remains subordinate to the Council of Ministers and does not function with the authority of the U.S. CONGRESS or other national legislatures.

European Space Agency (ESA) *French* **Agence Spatiale Européenne** Western European space and space-technology research organization headquartered in Paris. It was founded in 1975 from the merger of the European Launcher Development Organisation (ELDO) and the European Space Research Organisation (ESRO), both established in 1964. Members are Austria, Belgium, Britain, Denmark, Finland, France, Germany, Ireland, Italy, the Netherlands, Norway, Portugal, Spain, Sweden, and Switzerland. Canada, through a special cooperative agreement, participates in some projects. The ESA developed the Ariane series of space launch vehicles, and it supports a launch facility in French Guiana. It has launched a system of meteorological satellites (Meteosat) as well as the Giotto space probe, which examined the nucleus of HALLEY'S COMET, and Hipparcos, a satellite that measured the parallaxes, positions, and proper motions of more than 100,000 stars.

European Union (EU) Organization of most of the states of Western Europe, formed in 1993, to oversee the economic and political integration of these states. It was created by the MAASTRICHT TREATY and ratified by all members of the EUROPEAN COMMUNITY (EC), out of which the EU developed. The successful EC had made its members more receptive to greater integration and provided a framework for unified action by member countries in security and foreign policy and for cooperation in police and justice matters. In its major goal to create a common monetary system, the EU established the EURO, which replaced national currencies. The 15-member European Union's principal institutions are the European Community, the Council of Ministers (its forum for individual ministries), the European Commission (its administrative bureaucracy), the EUROPEAN PARLIAMENT, and the EUROPEAN COURT OF JUSTICE.

Eurotunnel See CHANNEL TUNNEL

eurypterid \yu̇-ˈrip-tə-rəd\ Member of an extinct order (Eurypterida) of ARTHROPODS, similar in body plan to the HORSESHOE CRAB, that lived c. 505–245 million years ago. Frequently referred to as giant scorpions, most eurypterids were small, although *Pterygotus buffaloensis,* a species from the SILURIAN PERIOD, was the largest arthropod ever known, reaching a length of about 10 ft (3 m). The eurypterids lived in brackish waters. Some were predators; others were probably bottom-dwelling scavengers.

eurythmics \yu̇-ˈrith-miks\ Method of musical training for young children developed by E. JAQUES-DALCROZE in the early years of the 20th century. It called for movements of the arms and legs in specific ways in response to changing rhythms and pitches. The initial aim was to encourage a physical response to music in the young, in the hope that they would ultimately find learning and playing it easier and that it would generally enhance their mental and physical functions. Very popular in the early 20th century, it has declined in recent decades.

Eusebius of Caesarea \yu̇-ˈsē-bē-əs…ˌsē-zə-ˈrē-ə\ (fl. 4th century AD) Bishop and historian of early Christianity. Baptized and ordained at Caesarea in Palestine, he may have been imprisoned during the Roman persecutions. His fame rests on his *Ecclesiastical History* (AD 312–24), which preserves portions of works no longer extant. He became bishop of Caesarea c. 313. Accused of Arianism, he was excommunicated in 325 but was soon exonerated by the Council of Nicaea. He was a staunch supporter of CONSTANTINE I's attempts to unify and standardize Christian doctrine, and his writings include the *Life of Constantine*.

euthanasia \ˌyü-thə-ˈnā-zhə\ *or* **mercy killing** Painless killing of a person with a painful, incurable disease or incapacitating disorder. Most legal systems consider it murder, though in many jurisdictions a physician may lawfully decide not to prolong life or may give drugs to relieve pain even when they may shorten life. Associations promoting legal euthanasia exist in many countries. The legalization movement has gained ground with advancing medical technology, which has been used to prolong the lives of patients enduring extreme suffering or patients who are comatose or unable to communicate their wishes. Euthanasia was legalized in The Netherlands in 2001 and in Belgium in 2002. In 1997 Oregon became the first state in the United States to decriminalize physician-assisted suicide. See also LIVING WILL.

Euthymides \yu̇-ˈthi-mə-ˌdēz\ (fl. c. 515–500 BC) Greek red-figure vase painter. He was a contemporary of EUPHRONIUS. His signature has been found on eight extant vases, six that he signed as a painter and two as a potter. He was noted for his mastery of foreshortening and studies in movement. The amphora now in Munich's Antiquities Museum showing foreshortened figures in three-quarter view is an outstanding example of his draftsmanship.

eutrophication \yu̇-ˌtrō-fə-ˈkā-shən\ Gradual increase in the concentration of PHOSPHORUS, NITROGEN, and other plant nutrients in an aging aquatic ecosystem such as a lake. The productivity or fertility of such an ecosystem increases as the amount of organic material that can be broken down into nutrients increases. This material enters the ecosystem mainly through runoff that carries debris. WATER BLOOMS often develop on the surface, preventing the light penetration and oxygen absorption necessary for underwater life. See also WATER POLLUTION.

Evagoras \i-ˈva-gə-rəs\ (died 374 BC) King of SALAMIS, Cyprus (c. 410–374). He pursued a policy of friendship with Athens and the promotion of Hellenism. He secured Persian aid for Athens against Sparta. With help from Athens and Egypt, he extended his rule over most of Cyprus and part of Anatolia. Relations with Persia later became hostile, and he was defeated by Persia in 381. Though he remained king of Salamis in name, he was in fact a vassal of Persia.

evangelicalism \ˌe-ˌvan-ˈje-li-kə-ˌli-zəm\ Protestant movement that stresses conversion experiences, the Bible as the only basis for faith, and evangelism at home and abroad. The religious revival that occurred in Europe and America during the 18th century was generally referred to as the evangelical revival. It included PIETISM in Europe, METHODISM in Britain, and the GREAT AWAKENING in America. In London in 1846, the Evangelical Alliance was organized by evangelical Christians from several denominations and countries. In the U.S., the National Association of Evangelicals was formed in 1942. Evangelicals tend to be more ecumenical than fundamentalists. See Christian FUNDAMENTALISM, PENTECOSTALISM.

Evans, Arthur (John) *later* **Sir Arthur** (1851–1941) British archaeologist. Son of the archaeologist Sir John Evans (1823–1908), he served as a curator at Oxford's Ashmolean Museum (1884–1908). Beginning in 1899 he devoted several decades to excavating the ruins of the ancient city of KNOSSOS in Crete, uncovering evidence of a sophisticated BRONZE AGE civilization that he named MINOAN. His work, one of archaeology's major achievements, greatly advanced the study of European and eastern Mediterranean prehistory. He published his definitive account in *The Palace of Minos* (4 vols., 1921–36).

Evans, Bill *orig.* **William John** (1929–1980) U.S. pianist and composer, one of the most influential musicians in modern jazz. Born in Plainfield, N.J., Evans was classically trained and influenced by pianists BUD POWELL, HORACE SILVER, and LENNIE TRISTANO. His subtle harmonies and lyrical melodic sensitivity were particularly well suited to modal improvisation, demonstrated on the landmark MILES DAVIS recording *Kind of Blue* (1959). As leader of his own trio, Evans established near-telepathic communication with his fellow musicians, creating music of rare depth and introspection. His best-known composition is "Waltz for Debby."

Evans, Edith (Mary) *later* **Dame Edith** (1888–1976) British actress. She made her stage debut as Cressida in WILLIAM SHAKESPEARE's *Troilus and Cressida* (1912) and joined the OLD VIC company in 1925. One of the finest actresses of the 20th century, she appeared in London and on Broadway in plays by Shakespeare, GEORGE BERNARD SHAW, and NOEL COWARD. She played Lady Bracknell in OSCAR WILDE's *The Importance* *of Being Earnest* on stage and screen (1952). Her other films include *Look Back in Anger* (1959), *Tom Jones* (1963), *The Chalk Garden* (1964), and *The Whisperers* (1967).

Dame Edith Evans as Mrs. Ross in *The Whisperers*, 1967.

BY COURTESY OF SEVEN PINES PRODUCTIONS LTD.; PHOTOGRAPH, PICTORIAL PARADE

Evans, Frederick H(enry) (1853–1943) British photographer. He first attracted attention as a popular London bookseller and champion of the work of GEORGE BERNARD SHAW and AUBREY BEARDSLEY. Around 1890 he began to photograph English and French cathedrals, and from 1898 he devoted himself exclusively to photography. His belief that only static views of idealized beauty were worth photographing clashed with the early-20th-century tendency to photograph fleeting images, but his architectural photographs are considered among the world's finest.

Evans, George Henry (1805–1856) U.S. (British-born) newspaper editor and social reformer. He emigrated to the U.S. in 1820 and in 1829 founded the *Working Man's Advocate,* the first major U.S. labor newspaper, and cofounded the WORKINGMEN'S PARTY. He organized the National Reform Association to lobby Congress for free homesteads in the West as a means to draw surplus workers from the East and improve workers' lives; this later led to passage of the Homestead Act. He also fought for the abolition of slavery and advocated equal rights for women.

Evans, Janet (born 1971) U.S. swimmer. Born in Placentia, Cal., she first swam competitively at age 4. In 1987, at 15, she set three world records and won four gold medals at the U.S. national championships. She won three gold medals at the 1988 Olympics and one in 1992.

Evans, Lee (Edward) (born 1947) U.S. sprinter. Born in Madera, Cal., he ran in college for San Jose State University. His winning time in the 400-m event at the 1968 Olympic Games (43.86 seconds) set a world record (broken by Butch Reynolds in 1988), and he anchored the U.S. team that won the 4 × 400-m relay in world-record time.

Evans, Maurice (Herbert) (1901–1989) British-U.S. actor. He made his professional stage debut in 1926 and achieved his first success in *Journey's End* (1929). He moved to the U.S. in 1935 and triumphed in Shakespearean roles on Broadway. During World War II he entertained U.S. troops with a short version of *Hamlet.* He later starred in Broadway revivals of four GEORGE BERNARD SHAW comedies, notably *Man and Superman* (1947). His greatest Broadway hit was *Dial M for Murder* (1952). He starred in a television production of *Macbeth* (1961, Emmy award) and appeared in 17 films, including *Rosemary's Baby* (1968).

Evans, Oliver (1755–1819) U.S. inventor. Born in Newport, Del., Evans began early to apply himself to industrial problems. He invented an improved CARDING device for use in the newly mechanized production of textiles. In 1784 he built a flour mill, for which he created the first continuous production line in any industry: all movement was automatic, power being supplied by waterwheels, and grain was passed by conveyors and chutes through the stages of milling and refining to emerge as finished flour. His high-pressure STEAM ENGINE (patented 1790) deserves to share the credit for the invention often given solely to RICHARD TREVITHICK. His Amphibious Digger (1805), a steam-engine scow that could run on both land and water, was the first powered road vehicle to operate in the U.S. His Mars Iron Works (founded 1806) made more than 100 steam engines for use with screw presses for processing cotton, tobacco, and paper.

Evans, Walker (1903–1975) U.S. photographer. Born in St. Louis, he was influenced early by the photographs of EUGENE ATGET. In 1934 his images of New England architecture were exhibited in the first one-man photographic show at the Museum of Modern Art. From 1935 he photographed rural victims of the Great Depression for the Farm Security Administration; these images were published in *American Photographs* (1938). He collaborated with JAMES AGEE to document the life of Alabama sharecroppers in *Let Us Now Praise Famous Men* (1941). He was later an editor of *Fortune* magazine (1945–65) and a professor at Yale University (1965–74).

Evans-Pritchard, E(dward) E(van) *later* **Sir Edward** (1902–1973) British social anthropologist whose studies of African systems of belief, witchcraft, religion, politics, and oral tradition remain foundational to the study of African societies and non-Western systems of thought. The most influential British social anthropologist since BRONISLAW MALINOWSKI and A. R. RADCLIFFE-BROWN, he succeeded the latter at Oxford University (1946), where he served as mentor to a generation of students. Among his major works are *Witchcraft, Oracles and Magic among the Azande* (1937), *The Nuer* (1940), and (with M. Fortes) *African Political Systems* (1940).

Evansville City (pop., 1996 est.: 124,000), southwestern Indiana. A port on the OHIO RIVER, it was founded in 1812, and grew as the southern terminus of the Wabash and Erie Canal (1853), which connected Lake ERIE with the Ohio River. Coal deposits and oilfields as well as fertile farmlands surround the city, and its location as a transportation hub has made it the metropolis of southwestern Indiana and adjacent states. Diversified manufactures include pharmaceuticals, and refrigeration and air conditioning equipment. It is the seat of the University of Evansville (1854). Angel Mounds State Memorial, a large prehistoric archaeological site, is nearby.

evaporation Change of a liquid into the gaseous state; in particular, the process by which liquid water enters the atmosphere as water vapor. Evaporation, mostly from the sea and from vegetation, replenishes the humidity of the air. It is an important part of the exchange of energy in the earth-atmosphere system that produces atmospheric motion, and therefore weather and climate. The rate of evaporation depends on the temperature difference between the evaporating surface and the air, the relative humidity, and wind.

evaporator Industrial apparatus for converting LIQUID into GAS or vapor. The single-effect evaporator consists of a container or surface and a heating unit; the multiple-effect evaporator uses the vapor produced in one unit to heat a succeeding unit. Double-, triple-, or quadruple-effect evaporators may be used in industrial and steam heating plants. Some evaporators are used to concentrate a solution by vaporizing and eliminating water (e.g., in a concentration plant for sugar and syrup). In purification processes such as DESALINATION, evaporators convert the water to vapor, leaving mineral residues behind; the vapor is then condensed into (desalinated) water. In a REFRIGERATION system, the cooling is produced as the rapid evaporation of the liquid refrigerant absorbs heat.

evaporite \i-ˈva-pə-ˌrīt\ Any of a variety of minerals found in sedimentary deposits of soluble salts that result from the evaporation of water. Typically, evaporite deposits occur in closed marine basins where evaporation exceeds inflow. The most important such minerals include anhydrite, halite, calcite, gypsum, polyhalite, and potassium and magnesium salts such as sylvite, carnallite, kainite, and kieserite.

evapotranspiration Loss of water from the soil both by evaporation from the soil surface and by TRANSPIRATION from the leaves of the plants growing on it. Factors that affect the rate of evapotranspiration include the amount of solar radiation, atmospheric vapor pressure, temperature, wind, and soil moisture. Evapotranspiration accounts for most of the water lost from the soil during the growth of a crop. Estimation of evapotranspiration rates is thus important in planning IRRIGATION schemes.

Evarts \ˈe-vərts\, **William Maxwell** (1818–1901) U.S. lawyer. Born in Boston, he served as counsel for Pres. ANDREW JOHNSON in his impeachment trial (1868). After Johnson's acquittal, he served as U.S. attorney general (1868–69), then represented the U.S. in the *ALABAMA* CLAIMS arbitration at Geneva (1872). He was Republican chief counsel in the RUTHERFORD B. HAYES–S. TILDEN election dispute (1876). As Hayes's secretary of state (1877–81), he asserted U.S. interests over a canal in Panama. He later served in the U.S. Senate (1885–91).

Eve, Joseph (1760–1835) U.S. scientist and inventor. Born in Philadelphia, he moved with his family to the Bahamas in his teens. There he invented a COTTON GIN, which was being used on the islands by 1787. He returned to the mainland c. 1800 and continued to manufacture gins. His other patents included a cottonseed huller (1803) and two steam engines (1818, 1826).

Evelyn \'ēv-lən, 'ev-lən\, **John** (1620–1706) British writer. A country gentleman from a wealthy landowning family, he wrote some 30 books on the fine arts, forestry, and religious topics. His *Diary* (published 1818), which he kept from 1631 to 1706, is an invaluable source of information on 17th-century social, cultural, religious, and political life. His *Life of Mrs. Godolphin* (published 1847) is one of the most moving of 17th-century biographies.

evening grosbeak North American GROSBEAK *(Hesperiphona vespertina)* that is brown, yellow, black, and white. Like all other grosbeaks, it has a large conical bill. It eats seeds and tends to form loose flocks in flight.

evening primrose Any of various species of herbaceous plants of the genus *Oenothera* (family Onagraceae). They are noted for their showy flowers, especially the yellow-flowered biennial *O. biennis*, which is found widely throughout North America and and has been introduced to Europe. It has been grown by geneticists to determine certain principles of heredity. The true PRIMROSE belongs to the family Primulaceae.

Evenki See SIBERIAN PEOPLES

event horizon Boundary marking the limits of a BLACK HOLE. At the event horizon, the escape velocity is equal to the speed of LIGHT. Since general RELATIVITY states that nothing can travel faster than the speed of light, nothing inside the event horizon can ever cross the boundary and escape beyond it, including light. Thus, nothing that enters a black hole can get out, or can be observed from outside the event horizon. Likewise, any radiation generated inside the horizon can never escape beyond it. For a nonrotating black hole, the SCHWARZSCHILD RADIUS delimits a spherical event horizon. Rotating black holes have distorted, nonspherical event horizons. Since the event horizon is not a material surface but rather merely a mathematically defined demarcation boundary, nothing prevents matter or radiation from entering a black hole, only from exiting one. Though black holes themselves may not radiate energy, particles may be radiated from just outside the event horizon via HAWKING RADIATION.

ever-normal granaries Price-stabilizing granaries first established in the 1st century BC. Under the QING DYNASTY they were set up by all Chinese provinces in each county to keep grain on hand to offset regional food shortages in years of crop failure. By keeping the supply of grain stable ("ever normal"), the granaries stabilized prices, and even undeveloped regions of the country were protected from famine.

Everest, Mt. *Tibetan* **Chomolungma,** *or Nepali* **Sagarmatha** \ˌchō-mō-'lu̇ŋ-mə\ Peak on the crest of the HIMALAYAS, in Asia. The highest point on earth, with a summit at 29,035 ft (8,850 m), it lies on the border between Nepal and Tibet. Numerous attempts to climb Everest were made from 1921; the summit was finally reached by EDMUND HILLARY of New Zealand and TENZING NORGAY of Nepal in 1953. In dispute is whether the English explorer George Mallory, whose body was discovered below Everest's peak in 1999, had actually reached the peak earlier, in 1924, and was descending it when he died. The formerly accepted elevation of 29,028 ft (8,848 m), established in the early 1950s, was recalculated in the late 1990s.

Everglades Subtropical saw-grass marsh region, southern Florida. Covering about 4,000 sq mi (10,000 sq km) of southern Florida, the area has water moving slowly through it from the lip of Lake OKEECHOBEE to mangrove swamps bordering the Gulf of MEXICO and Florida Bay. Everglades National Park, established in 1934, encompasses the southwestern portion of the marsh, covering 2,354 sq mi (6,097 sq km). The largest subtropical wilderness left in the continental U.S., it has a mild climate, which provides an environment for myriad birds, alligators, snakes, and turtles. A large portion of the glades has been reclaimed by drainage canals, altering the habitats of many species.

evergreen Any plant that retains its leaves through the winter and into the following summer or through several years. Many tropical species of broad-leaved FLOWERING PLANTS are evergreen, but in cold-temperate and Arctic areas the evergreens commonly are cone-bearing shrubs or trees (CONIFERS), such as PINES and FIRS. The leaves of evergreens usually are thicker and more leathery than those of DECIDUOUS TREES and often are needlelike or scalelike in cone-bearing trees. A leaf (or needle) may remain on an evergreen tree for two years or longer and may fall during any season.

everlasting Any of several plants that retain their form and color when dried and are used in dry bouquets and flower arrangements. Popular everlastings include several species of the COMPOSITE FAMILY, especially the true everlastings, or immortelles, species of the genus *Helichrysum*, native to North Africa, Crete, and the parts of Asia bordering on the Mediterranean and cultivated in many parts of Europe. One of the best-known everlastings is the strawflower *(H. bracteatum)* of Australia. Many GRASSES with showy plumes or spikes are classified as everlastings.

Evers \'e-vərz\, **Medgar (Wiley)** (1925–1963) U.S. black civil-rights activist. Born in Decatur, Miss., he served in World War II and entered business in Mississippi. He organized local affiliates of the NAACP and in 1954 became its first field secretary in Mississippi. He traveled throughout the state recruiting members and organizing economic boycotts. In June 1963, hours after a speech on civil rights by Pres. JOHN F. KENNEDY, Evers was shot and killed in an ambush outside his home. A white segregationist was charged but set free after two trials in 1964 resulted in hung juries; he was finally convicted after a third trial in 1994. Evers's widow, Myrlie Evers-Williams, later headed the NAACP (1995–98).

Evert, Chris(tine Marie) *formerly* **Chris Evert Lloyd** (born 1954) U.S. tennis player. Born in Fort Lauderdale, Fla., she became in 1971 the youngest player to reach the semifinals of the U.S. championship. She won the U.S. Open women's singles six times (1975–78, 1980, 1982), and repeatedly won the Wimbledon singles (1974, 1976, 1981), the French Open singles (1974, 1975, 1979, 1980, 1983, 1985, 1986), and the Australian Open singles (1982, 1984), for a total of 18 Grand Slam titles. She retired in 1989.

evidence In law, something (e.g., testimony, documents, or physical objects) presented at a judicial or administrative proceeding for the purpose of establishing the truth or falsity of an allegation of fact. To preserve legal DUE PROCESS and to prevent the jury from being misled, an extensive body of rules has sprung up regarding the handling of evidence. In the U.S., all federal and many state courts adhere to the *Federal Rules of Evidence,* which covers such elements as types of evidence, admissibility, relevance, competency of witnesses, confessions and admissions, expert testimony, and authentication. Most evidence received at trial is in the form of verbal statements of witnesses, who are subject to questioning by attorneys from both sides. Two important categories of evidence are direct evidence, which is offered by a witness whose knowledge of a factual matter is firsthand (as through sight or hearing), and CIRCUMSTANTIAL EVIDENCE. See also EXCLUSIONARY RULE.

evil eye Superstition holding that a glance can cause injury or death to those on whom it falls. The belief was found in ancient Greece and Rome as well as in folk cultures around the world, and it has persisted into modern times. Children and animals are believed to be particularly vulnerable. The evil eye is often thought to stem from envy and malice toward prosperity and beauty, and thus in many cultures unguarded praise of one's possessions or children is thought to invite misfortune. Safeguards include amulets, charms, and sacred texts; in Asia children may have their faces blackened for protection.

Evita See Eva PERÓN

evolution Biological theory that animals and plants have their origin in other types and that the distinguishable differences are due to modifications in successive generations. It is one of the keystones of modern biological theory. In 1858 CHARLES DARWIN and ALFRED RUSSEL WALLACE published a paper on evolution that revolutionized all later biological study. The heart of Darwinian evolution is the mechanism of NATURAL SELECTION. Surviving individuals, who vary (see VARIATION) in some way that enables them to live longer and reproduce, pass on their advantage to succeeding generations. In 1937 THEODOSIUS DOBZHANSKY applied Mendelian genetics (see GREGOR MENDEL) to Darwinian theory, contributing to the new understanding of evolution as the cumulative action of natural selection on small genetic variations in whole populations. Part of the proof of evolution is in the fossil record, which shows a succession of gradually changing forms leading up to those known today. Structural similarities and similarities in embryonic development among living forms also point to common ancestry. Molecular biology (especially the study of genes and proteins) provides the most detailed evidence of evolutionary change. Though the theory of evolution is accepted by nearly the entire scientific community, it has sparked much controversy from

Darwin's time to the present; most objections have come from religious leaders and thinkers (see CREATION SCIENCE). See also HUGO DE VRIES, ERNST HAECKEL, HUMAN EVOLUTION, ERNST MAYR, PARALLEL EVOLUTION, PHYLOGENY, SOCIOCULTURAL EVOLUTION, SPECIATION.

Evripos Strait \'e-vrē-ˌpȯs\ *or* **Euripus Strait** \yu̇-'rī-pəs\ Narrow strait in the Aegean Sea. Located between the Greek island of EUBOEA and the mainland of central Greece, it is 5 mi (8 km) long, and varies from 130 ft (40 m) to 1 mi (1.6 km) in width. It has strong tidal currents that reverse directions seven or more times a day, a phenomenon still not fully understood. The main port on the strait is KHALKÍS, an important trading center since the times of ancient Greece. A 130-ft (40-m) movable bridge spans the strait at Khalkís, replacing earlier structures that dated back to 411 BC.

Ewald \'ā-vəlt\, **Johannes** (1743–1781) Danish poet and dramatist. By age 19 he was becoming known as a writer. At 30, addicted to alcohol, he adopted a more solitary life and began producing his mature works, including *The Death of Balder* (1774), in which he became the first Danish poet to use themes from Scandinavian myth and saga. Of his dramatic works, only the operetta *Fiskerne* (1779; "The Fishermen") is still performed. He is especially known for his great personal odes and for songs such as "King Christian Stood by the Lofty Mast," used as a national anthem, and "Lille Gunver," the first Danish romance. He is considered one of Denmark's greatest lyric poets. His memoirs (published 1804) are his greatest prose work.

Ewe \'ā-wā\ Peoples of southeastern Ghana, southern Benin, and southern Togo who speak dialects of Gbe, a KWA LANGUAGE of the NIGER-CONGO family. The Ewe never formed a single centralized state, remaining a collection of independent communities that made temporary alliances in time of war. Most Ewe are farmers; some coastal Ewe fish. Spinning, weaving, pottery making, and blacksmithing are important crafts. Many have been converted to Christianity. Today they number about 3.5 million.

Ewing \'yü-iŋ\, **(William) Maurice** (1906–1974) U.S. geophysicist. Born in Lockney, Texas, he taught many years at Columbia University (1944–74) and also directed the Lamont-Doherty Geological Observatory (1949–74). Studying the structure of the earth's crust and mantle, he made seismic refraction measurements in the Atlantic basins, along the Mid-Atlantic Ridge, and in the Mediterranean and Norwegian seas. In 1935 he took the first seismic measurements in open seas. He was among those who proposed that earthquakes are associated with the central oceanic rifts that encircle the globe, suggesting that sea-floor spreading may be worldwide and episodic in nature. In 1939 he took the first deep-sea photographs.

Ewing \'yü-iŋ\, **Patrick (Aloysius)** (born 1962) U.S. basketball player. Born in Kingston, Jamaica, the 7-ft (2-m 13-cm) Ewing had an outstanding collegiate career at Georgetown University and was ranked no. 1 overall in the 1985 college draft. A center for the New York Knicks from 1985, he holds numerous team records and was selected as an NBA All-Star 11 times in 13 seasons. In 1999 he became the twelfth player in NBA history to score over 20,000 points and collect over 10,000 rebounds.

excavation In archaeology, the exposure, recording, and recovery of buried material remains. The techniques employed vary by the type of site, but all forms of archaeological excavation require great skill and careful preparation. The process begins with site location, through aerial photography, remote sensing, or, commonly, accidental discovery by construction crews. This is followed by careful surveying and mapping, site sampling, and development of an excavation plan. The actual digging consists of the removal of surplus dirt and the painstaking examination, through observation, sifting, and other means, of remaining soil, artifacts, and context. Common tools include the trowel, penknife, and brush. The excavation phase is followed by artifact classification, analysis, DATING, and publication of results. The excavation of a site may last decades or be a short-term emergency salvage operation (as when a site is threatened by development).

exchange, bill of See BILL OF EXCHANGE

exchange control Governmental restrictions on private transactions in foreign money or claims on foreign money. Residents are required to sell foreign money coming into their possession to a central bank or specialized government agency at EXCHANGE RATES set by the government. The chief function of most systems of exchange control is to maintain a favorable BALANCE OF PAYMENTS. See also FOREIGN EXCHANGE.

exchange rate Price of one country's money in relation to another's. Exchange rates may be fixed or flexible. An exchange rate is fixed when two countries agree to maintain a fixed rate through the use of MONETARY POLICY. Historically, the most famous fixed exchange-rate system was the GOLD STANDARD; in the late 1850s, one ounce of gold was defined as being worth 20 U.S dollars and 4 pounds sterling, resulting in an exchange rate of 5 dollars per pound. An exchange rate is flexible, or "floating," when two countries agree to let international market forces determine the rate through SUPPLY AND DEMAND. The rate will fluctuate with a country's exports and imports. Most world trade currently takes place with flexible exchange rates that fluctuate within relatively fixed limits. See also EXCHANGE CONTROL, FOREIGN EXCHANGE.

Exchequer \iks-'che-kər, 'eks-ˌche-kər\ English government department responsible for receiving and dispersing public revenue. It was established by HENRY I in the 12th century, and its name refers to the checkered cloth on which the reckoning of revenues took place. Originally, the lower Exchequer was an office for the receipt and payment of money, while the upper Exchequer was a court sitting twice a year to regulate accounts. The English judicial system grew out of the upper Exchequer, and the lower Exchequer became the Treasury. "Exchequer" is still the unofficial name of the Treasury in Britain.

excitation Addition of a discrete amount of energy to a system that changes it usually from a state of lowest energy (ground state) to one of higher energy (excited state). For example, in a hydrogen atom, an excitation energy of 10.2 electron volts is required to move the lone electron from its ground state to its first excited state. The excitation energy stored in excited atoms and nuclei is usually emitted as ULTRAVIOLET RADIATION from atoms and as gamma radiation (see GAMMA RAY) from nuclei as they return to their ground states.

exclusionary rule In U.S. law, the principle that evidence seized by police in violation of constitutional protection from unreasonable SEARCH AND SEIZURE may not be used against a criminal defendant at trial. The U.S. Supreme Court established the validity of the rule in *Weeks vs. U.S.* (1914), expanded its federal coverage in *Wolf vs. Colorado* (1949), and extended it to state criminal courts in *Mapp vs. Ohio* (1961). In *U.S. vs. Leon* (1984), the Court allowed an exception to the rule, holding that evidence obtained "in good faith" with a search warrant later ruled invalid is admissible.

excommunication Form of censure by which a member of a religious body is excluded from the congregation of believers and from the rites of the church. Excommunication has been used in various religions, notably Christianity, as a punishment for grave offenses such as HERESY. In Roman Catholicism, an excommunicated person is barred from receiving the SACRAMENTS and from burial in consecrated ground. The offender may be absolved by a priest (in some cases, only by a bishop or the pope) and received back into the church after confessing his or her SIN and doing penance for it. In Protestant denominations, other terms, such as "church discipline," may be attached to essentially the same censure.

excretion Bodily process for disposing of undigested food waste products and nitrogenous by-products of METABOLISM, regulating water content, maintaining acid-base balance, and controlling osmotic pressure to promote HOMEOSTASIS. It refers to both URINATION and DEFECATION and to the processes that take place in the digestive and URINARY systems, as the KIDNEY and LIVER filter wastes, toxins, and drugs from the blood and food reaches the last stage of digestion. Ammonia from PROTEIN digestion, the primary excretory product, is converted to UREA to be excreted in URINE.

executive In politics, a person or persons constituting the branch of government charged with executing or carrying out the laws and appointing officials, formulating and instituting foreign policy, and providing diplomatic representation. In the U.S., a system of CHECKS AND BALANCES keeps the power of the executive more or less equal to that of the JUDICIARY and the LEGISLATURE. See also MAYOR, PRESIDENT, PRIME MINISTER.

exegesis \ˌek-sə-'jē-səs, 'ek-sə-ˌjē-səs\ Scholarly interpretation of religious texts, using linguistic, historical, and other methods. In Judaism and Christianity, it has been used extensively in the study of the BIBLE. Textual criticism tries to establish the accuracy of biblical texts. Philological criticism deals with grammar, vocabulary, and style in pursuit of faithful translation. Literary criticism classifies texts according to style and attempts to establish authorship, date, and audience. Tradition criticism seeks the sources of biblical materials and traces their development. Redaction criticism examines the way pieces of the tradition have been assembled into a literary composition by editors. Form criticism studies the way narratives are shaped by the cultures that produce them. Historical criticism looks at a text's historical context.

Exekias \ek-'sek-yəs\ (fl. c. 540–520 BC) Greek potter and the most famous of the black-figure vase painters. His name is found on 13 surviving vases. He is known for his elegant drawing; his greatest gift was for conveying pathos and insight rather than overt action. Some 40 unsigned vases are attributed to him on stylistic grounds. He also made clay plaques designed to decorate tombs.

exercise Training of the body to improve health and fitness. Different types have different purposes, including AEROBICS for heart and respiratory function and weight loss, weight-bearing exercise for bone strength, weight training for muscle strength, and stretching for flexibility. Specific exercises are used in PHYSICAL MEDICINE AND REHABILITATION. Benefits include lower BLOOD PRESSURE, higher HDL CHOLESTEROL, improved disease resistance, and better general well-being.

Exeter \'ek-sə-tər\ *ancient* **Isca Dumnoniorum** City (pop., 1991: 101,000), seat of DEVON, England. Located on the River Exe about 10 mi (16 km) above the English Channel, it commands an important river crossing. An early British tribe, the Dumnonii, made Exeter their center; when it was taken by the Romans, they named it Isca Dumnoniorum. The main town in southwestern England during the Middle Ages, it was subjected to a number of sieges. ALFRED the Great twice held it against the Danes (877 and c. 894); they finally took the city in 1003 but lost it in 1068 to WILLIAM THE CONQUEROR. Exeter's Norman cathedral, consecrated in 1133, houses the Exeter Book, the largest collection extant of OLD ENGLISH poetry. The city has light manufacturing and is a service center for an extensive region.

existential import In SYLLOGISTIC, a universal proposition (i.e., a proposition of the form "All S is P" or "No S is P") said to have existential import if it is interpreted so as to logically imply the corresponding particular statement (i.e., "Some S is P" or "Some S is not P," respectively). The validity of some syllogistic figures (see SYLLOGISM) depends on whether universal statements are interpreted as having existential import.

existentialism Philosophical movement oriented toward two major themes, the analysis of human existence and the centrality of human choice. Existentialism's chief theoretical energies are thus devoted to questions about ONTOLOGY and decision. It traces its roots to the writings of SOREN KIERKEGAARD and FRIEDRICH NIETZSCHE. As a philosophy of human existence, existentialism found its best 20th-century exponent in KARL JASPERS; as a philosophy of human decision, its foremost representative was J.-P. SARTRE. Sartre finds the essence of human existence in freedom—in the duty of self-determination and the freedom of choice—and therefore spends much time describing the human tendency toward "bad faith," reflected in humanity's perverse attempts to deny its own responsibility and flee from the truth of its inescapable freedom.

Exmouth Gulf Inlet of the Indian Ocean, Western Australia, between North West Cape and the mainland. It is 55 mi (90 km) long and 30 mi (48 km) across the mouth. Fishing, pearling, prawning, and tourism are the main local industries. Nearby Cape Range National Park is important for the conservation of the rare yellow-footed rock WALLABY.

Exodus Second book of the OLD TESTAMENT. The title refers to the departure of the Israelites from Egypt under MOSES in the 13th century BC. The book begins with the story of the Israelites' enslavement in Egypt and God's call to Moses to become a prophet. It tells of the plagues sent to persuade the pharaoh to free the Israelites, and it recalls their crossing of the Sea of Reeds (or the Red Sea) and their 40 years of wandering in the Sinai desert. It also recounts how God made a COVENANT with Israel at Mount SINAI, handing down the TEN COMMANDMENTS. In Exodus God establishes his reliability as Israel's protector and savior, and lays claim to its loyalty and obedience.

exogamy and endogamy \ek-'sä-gə-mē...en-'dä-gə-mē\ Practices controlling the relation of the sexes and the selection of marital partners. Exogamous groups require their members to marry outside the group, sometimes even specifying the group into which members must marry. Such groups are usually defined in terms of KINSHIP rather than in terms of politics or territory. Exogamy is usually characteristic of unilineal DESCENT groups, in which descent is reckoned either patrilineally or matrilineally. In endogamous groups, marriage outside one's group may be forbidden, or there may merely be a tendency to marry within the group. Endogamy is characteristic of aristocracies and religious and ethnic minorities in industrialized societies, but also of the CASTE system in India and of class-conscious nonliterate societies such as the MASAI of eastern Africa.

exophthalmic goiter See GRAVES' DISEASE

exorcism In Christianity, a ceremony used to drive DEMONS out of a person they have possessed. Jesus healed people tormented by evil spirits, casting them out with a word, and his followers later drove out demons "in his name." By the 3rd century this task was assigned to a specially trained class of lower clergy. Rituals for exorcism of people and places also exist in many other traditions.

expanding universe Current understanding of the state of the universe. It is based on the finding that all GALAXIES are moving away from each other. Application of general RELATIVITY to cosmology, along with detection of RED SHIFT outside the galaxy, led to the realization in the 1920s that all galaxies are receding (see EDWIN HUBBLE). It is unknown whether the universe will expand indefinitely (open) or eventually collapse (closed) into an extremely dense, congested state, as it began, according to the BIG-BANG model. See also FRIEDMANN UNIVERSE.

experimental psychology Branch or type of psychology concerned with employing empirical principles and procedures in the study of psychological phenomena. The experimental psychologist seeks to carry out tests under controlled conditions in order to discover an unknown effect or law, to examine or establish a hypothesis, or to illustrate a known law. The areas of study that rely most heavily on the experimental method include those of SENSATION and PERCEPTION, LEARNING and MEMORY, MOTIVATION, and PHYSIOLOGICAL PSYCHOLOGY. Experimental approaches are also used in CHILD PSYCHOLOGY, CLINICAL PSYCHOLOGY, EDUCATIONAL PSYCHOLOGY, and SOCIAL PSYCHOLOGY.

experimentalism See INSTRUMENTALISM

expert system Computer-based system designed to respond like a human expert in a given field. Expert systems are built on knowledge gathered from human experts, analogous to a DATABASE but containing rules that may be applied to solving a specific problem. An interface allows the user to specify symptoms and to clarify a problem by responding to questions posed by the system. Software tools exist to help designers build a special-purpose expert system with minimal effort. An outgrowth of work in ARTIFICIAL INTELLIGENCE, expert systems show promise for an ever-widening range of applications. There are now widely used expert systems in the fields of medicine, personnel screening, and education.

explanation In philosophy, the answer to a question of why something is, occurs, or acts as it is or does. The class of things that may be objects of explanation is highly diverse and includes facts, events, objects, properties, human actions, and assertions. Among the most common forms of explanation are causal explanation (see CAUSATION), which involves explaining an event by reference to its cause(s), and deductive-nomological explanation (see COVERING-LAW MODEL), which involves subsuming a fact, statement, or event under a scientific law of which it is an instance.

Explorer Any of the largest (55-member) series of unmanned U.S. spacecraft, launched between 1958 and 1975. Explorer 1, the first satellite sent into orbit by the U.S., discovered the innermost VAN ALLEN RADIATION BELT. Other notable craft in this series include Explorer 38 (1968), which measured galactic radio sources and studied low frequencies in space, and Explorer 53 (1975), which explored X-ray sources within and beyond the Milky Way.

explosive Any substance or device that can produce a volume of rapidly expanding GAS in an extremely brief period. Mechanical explosives, depending on a physical reaction (e.g., overloading a container with compressed air) are little used except in mining. Nuclear explosives (see NUCLEAR WEAPON) use either NUCLEAR FISSION or NUCLEAR FUSION. Chemical explosives are of two types: detonating (high) explosives (e.g., TNT, DYNAMITE) have extremely rapid decomposition and development of high pressure; deflagrating (low) explosives (e.g., black powder, smokeless powder) merely burn fast and produce relatively low pressure. Primary detonating explosives are ignited by a flame, spark, or impact; secondary ones require a detonator and sometimes a booster. Modern high explosives use mixtures of ammonium nitrate and fuel oil or water gels (along with TNT and other fuels).

exponential function In mathematics, a FUNCTION in which a constant base is raised to a VARIABLE power. Exponential functions are used to model changes in population size, in the spread of diseases, and in the growth of investments. They can also accurately predict types of decline typified by radioactive decay (see HALF-LIFE). The essence of exponential growth, and a characteristic of all exponential growth functions, is that they double in size over regular intervals. The most important exponential function is e^x, the INVERSE of the natural logarithmic function (see LOGARITHM).

Export-Import Bank of the United States (Ex-Im Bank) One of the principal U.S. government agencies in international finance. Originally incorporated as the Export-Import Bank of Washington in 1934, its goal is to help finance U.S. exports, principally by lending money to foreign buyers of U.S. goods and services. Such assistance often consists of credits to foreign banks and governments in connection with development projects. See also DEVELOPMENT BANK.

Expressionism Artistic style in which the artist depicts not objective reality but the subjective emotions that objects or events arouse. This aim is accomplished through distortion and exaggeration of shape and the vivid or violent application of color. Its roots are found in the works of VINCENT VAN GOGH, EDVARD MUNCH, and JAMES ENSOR. In 1905 the movement took hold with a group of German artists known as Die BRÜCKE; their works influenced such artists as GEORGES ROUAULT, CHAIM SOUTINE, MAX BECKMANN, KATHE KOLLWITZ, and ERNST BARLACH. The group of artists known as Der BLAUE REITER were also considered Expressionists. Expressionism was the dominant style in Germany after World War I; postwar Expressionists included GEORGE GROSZ and OTTO DIX. See also ABSTRACT EXPRESSIONISM.

extensor muscle Muscle that increases the angle between members of a limb, as by straightening the elbow or knee or bending the wrist or spine backward. The movement allowed by this muscle is usually directed backward, with the notable exception of the knee joint. See also FLEXOR MUSCLE.

extenuating circumstance *or* **mitigating circumstance** In law, a factor in the commission of an act that lessens the degree of criminal culpability. Under many Anglo-American legal systems, provocation of the accused by the victim can reduce first-degree murder to manslaughter or second-degree murder. In England, a charge of murder may be reduced to manslaughter if the accused is found to be suffering DIMINISHED CAPACITY. The Italian penal code allows consideration of motives of honor. Extenuating circumstances also are a factor in many civil actions.

extinction (of species) Dying out or termination of a species. It occurs when a species can no longer reproduce at replacement levels. Most past extinctions are thought to have resulted from environmental changes that the doomed species was either unable to adapt to or that caused it to adapt so thoroughly that it became a distinctly new species. The effect of humans on the environment, especially through habitat destruction, has become the principal factor in plant and animal extinctions.

extortion Unlawful exaction of money or property through intimidation or undue exercise of authority. It may include threats of physical harm, criminal prosecution, or public exposure. Some forms of threat, especially those made in writing, are occasionally singled out for separate statutory treatment as blackmail. See also BRIBERY.

extradition Process by which one state, at the request of another, returns a person for trial for a crime punishable by the laws of the requesting state and committed outside the state of refuge. Extradition is regulated within countries by extradition acts and between countries by treaties. Some principles of extradition are common to many countries. Most decline to surrender their own nationals. Countries also generally recognize the right of political ASYLUM. In view of the solidarity of nations in the repression of crime, however, countries are usually willing to cooperate in bringing criminals to justice.

extrasensory perception (ESP) Perception that involves awareness of information about something (such as a person or event) not gained through the SENSES and not deducible from previous experience. Classic forms of ESP include telepathy, clairvoyance, and precognition. No conclusive demonstrations of the existence of ESP in any individual have been given, but popular belief in the phenomenon remains widespread. See also PARAPSYCHOLOGY.

extrauterine pregnancy See ECTOPIC PREGNANCY

Extremadura *or* **Estremadura** \es-ˌtrā-mə-ˈthü-rä, *Portuguese* ˌish-tri-mə-ˈdür-ə\ Historical region, and autonomous community (pop., 1996 est.: 1,070,000), western central Spain. It encompasses the southwestern provinces of Cáceres and Badajoz and covers an area of 16,063 sq mi (41,603 sq km); its capital is MÉRIDA. During the Christian reconquest of the IBERIAN PENINSULA, the name Extremadura was used to refer to the zones outside of Moorish territory. From the later Middle Ages the term was applied to an area approximating the modern region. The countryside remains partitioned into latifundios (large estates); wheat, grapes, and olives are important crops.

extreme sports Sports characterized by high speed or high risk. Such sports include aggressive inline skating, wakeboarding, street luge, skateboarding, freestyle parachuting (a mixture of free-form acrobatic and gymnastic maneuvers by the diver combined with relative work involving a videographer), and freestyle bicycle events (wherein tricks such as back flips are performed on a bicycle). Many of the events—snowboarding, skateboarding, and freestyle biking are examples—are performed on ramps and inclines or in a halfpipe, some with walls as high as 50 ft (15 m), which allows the athletes to get air, or achieve the height necessary to rotate 960° on a bicycle. Many of these sports were made popular by the X Games (championship competitions sponsored by the cable network ESPN). The 1998 and 2002 Olympic Games featured extreme snowboarding events in a halfpipe, in which boarders performed jumps, rotations, and mid-air maneuvers.

extrovert See INTROVERT AND EXTROVERT

extrusion Process in which metal or other material is forced through a series of DIES to create desired shapes. Many CERAMICS are manufactured by extrusion, because the process allows efficient, continuous production. In a commercial screw-type extruder, a screw AUGER continuously forces the plastic feed material through an orifice or die, resulting in simple shapes such as cylindrical rods and pipes, rectangular solid and hollow bars, and long plates. In metalworking, extrusion converts a billet of metal into a length of uniform cross-section by forcing the billet through the orifice of a die; aluminum is easily extruded. Formed sheet aluminum is used for opaque curtain-wall panels and window frames.

extrusive rock Any IGNEOUS ROCK derived from MAGMA that is poured out or ejected at the earth's surface. Extrusive rocks are usually distinguished from INTRUSIVE ROCKS on the basis of their texture and mineral composition. Lava flows and pyroclastic debris (fragmented volcanic material) are extrusive; they are commonly glassy (e.g., obsidian) or finely crystalline (e.g., basalts and felsites).

Exupéry, Antoine de Saint- See Antoine de SAINT-EXUPERY

Exxon Mobil Corporation U.S.-based oil and gas company formed in 1999 through the merger of Exxon Corp. and MOBIL CORP. It has investments and operations in petroleum and natural gas, coal, nuclear fuels, chemicals, and ores. It also operates pipelines and one of the world's largest fleets of tankers. Exxon Mobil engages in every phase of the petroleum industry from oil fields to service stations. Both Exxon and Mobil had their origins in Standard Oil (see STANDARD OIL CO. AND TRUST) and were founded in the late 1800s. In 1926 the New Jersey subsidiary of Standard Oil, Exxon's predecessor, introduced the Esso brand name. The name was changed to Exxon in 1972. As of 2002 Exxon Mobil was the world's largest integrated oil company.

Eyasi \ā-ˈyä-sē\, **Lake** Lake, northern Tanzania. At an elevation of about 3,400 ft (1,040 m), the lake covers an area of about 400 sq mi (1,050 sq km) and occupies the bottom of a bowl-like depression. Its walls are purple lava, enclosing a broad expanse of white alkaline shallows. Flamingos inhabit the lakeshore in vast flocks. Hominid fossils were found nearby.

Eybeschütz \ˈī-bə-ˌshēts\, **Jonathan** (c. 1690–1764) Polish rabbi and Talmudic scholar. Born in Kraków, he served as rabbi in a number of European towns, and his scholarship gained him a loyal following. He was reputed to have mystic powers, and when the women of his congregation asked him to give them protection from death in childbirth, he offered them amulets that contained a prayer to the false messiah SHABBETAI TZEVI. A prominent German rabbi, Jacob Emden (1697–1776), denounced the amulets. The dispute that ensued between Emden and Eybeschütz divided the European Jewish community.

Eyck \'īk\, **Jan van** (1395–1441) Flemish painter. He is recorded in 1422 as a master painter working for John of Bavaria, count of Holland, and later was employed by PHILIP III THE GOOD, duke of Burgundy. Securely attributed paintings survive only from the last decade of his career; 10 are signed and dated, an unusually large number for the period. He produced portraits and religious subjects that are unmatched for their technical brilliance, their intellectual complexity, and the richness of their symbolism. His masterpiece is the *Adoration of the Lamb* (1432), known as the Ghent Altarpiece, which he painted with his brother Hubert (c. 1370–1426). He is commonly regarded as the greatest northern European artist of the 15th century. His works were widely copied and avidly collected.

eye Organ that receives light and visual images. Non-image forming, or direction, eyes are found among worms, mollusks, cnidarians, echinoderms, and other invertebrates; image-forming eyes are found in certain mollusks, most arthropods, and nearly all vertebrates. Arthropods are unique in possessing a compound eye, which results in their seeing a multiple image that is partially integrated in the brain. Lower vertebrates such as fish have eyes on either side of the head, allowing a maximum view of the surroundings but producing two separate fields of vision. In predatory birds and mammals, binocular vision became more important. Evolutionary changes in the placement of the eyes permitted a larger overlap of the two visual fields, resulting in the higher mammals in a parallel line of direct sight. The human eye is roughly spherical. Light passes through its transparent front and stimulates receptor cells on the retina (cones for color vision, rods for black-and-white vision in faint light), which in turn send impulses through the optic nerve to the brain. Vision disorders include near- and farsightedness and ASTIGMATISM (correctable with EYEGLASSES or CONTACT LENSES), COLOR BLINDNESS, and night blindness. Other eye disorders (including DETACHED RETINA and GLAUCOMA) can cause VISUAL-FIELD DEFECTS or BLINDNESS. See also OPHTHALMOLOGY, PHOTORECEPTION.

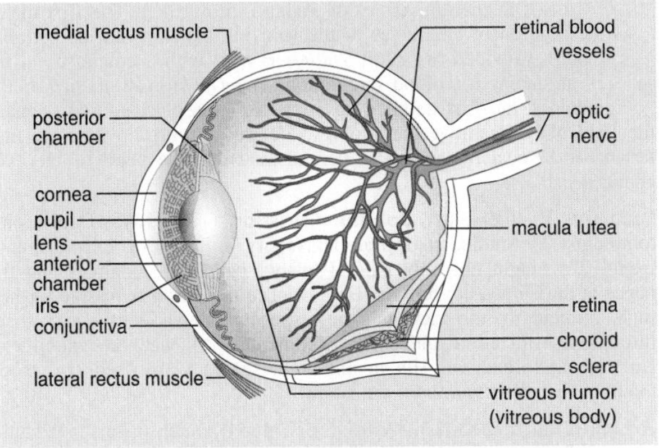

Structure of the human eye. The outer portion consists of the white protective sclera and transparent cornea, through which light enters. The middle layer includes the blood-supplying choroid and pigmented iris. Light passing into the interior through the pupil is regulated by muscles that control the pupil's size. The retina comprises the third layer and contains receptor cells (rods and cones) that transform light waves into nervous impulses. The lens, lying directly behind the iris, focuses light onto the retina. The macula lutea, in the center of the retina, is a region of high visual acuity and color discrimination. Nerve fibers pass out through the optic nerve to the brain's visual center. The eye's anterior and posterior chambers contain a watery fluid that nourishes the cornea and lens. The vitreous humor helps maintain the eye's shape. A thin layer of mucous membrane (conjunctiva) protects the eye's exposed surface. External muscles, incl. the medial rectus and lateral rectus muscles, connect and move the eye in its socket.

eyeglasses LENSES set in frames to wear in front of the eyes to aid vision or correct vision defects (see OPHTHALMOLOGY, OPTOMETRY). Their use for farsightedness and nearsightedness has been known since the late Middle Ages. In 1784 BENJAMIN FRANKLIN invented bifocals, with divided lenses for distant and near vision. Eyeglasses can also correct ASTIGMATISM. Most lenses are made of glass or plastic (lighter and more shatterproof than glass but easily scratched). Sunglass lenses are tinted to reduce glare and often treated to reduce ultraviolet light exposure. See also CONTACT LENS.

Eyre \'ar\, **Lake** Salt lake, northeastern South Australia. With a total area of 3,700 sq mi (9,300 sq km) and a maximum depth of 4 ft (1 m), it contains the lowest point in Australia, 50 ft (15 m) below sea level. It consists of two sections: Lake Eyre North, 90 mi (144 km) long and 40 mi (65 km) wide, is joined by the narrow Goyder Channel to Lake Eyre South, which is 40 mi (65 km) long and about 15 mi (24 km) wide. Lake Eyre is normally dry, and it fills completely only an average of twice in a century. When filled, the lake takes about two years to dry up again.

Eyre Peninsula Large promontory, South Australia. Projecting into the Indian Ocean, it is about 200 mi (320 km) long, and lies between the GREAT AUSTRALIAN BIGHT and Spencer Gulf. It supports wheat, sheep, and barley; iron is extracted in the Middleback Ranges to the northeast. There are numerous resort and fishing towns along the coasts.

Ezekiel \i-'zēk-yəl\ (fl. 6th century BC) Priest and PROPHET of ancient Israel. He was the subject and partial author of the Old Testament Book of Ezekiel. He began to prophesy to the Jews in Palestine c. 592 BC, pronouncing God's judgment on a sinful nation. He witnessed the conquest of Jerusalem by BABYLON and saw his fellow Israelites taken away into captivity. He offered a promise of Israel's restoration in his famous vision of a valley of dry bones that revive and assemble themselves. He envisaged a theocratic community revolving around a restored Temple in Jerusalem.

Ezhov, Nikolay See Nikolay YEZHOV

Ezra (fl. 5th–4th century BC) Jewish religious leader and reformer. He restored the Jewish community after its exile in BABYLON, persuading the people of JUDAH to return to a strict observance of Mosaic law. He served as a commissioner of the Persian government, which was tolerant of other religions but required order and authority. His efforts led to a restoration of traditional worship in the rebuilt Temple of JERUSALEM and the dissolution of all mixed marriages. For creating a Jewish community based on Law, which could exist without political statehood, he is often considered the founder of modern JUDAISM. His story is told in the books of Ezra and NEHEMIAH.

F-15 *or* **Eagle** Twin-engine jet fighter built by the MCDONNELL DOUGLAS CORP. F-15s were delivered to the U.S. Air Force (1974–94) and have been sold to U.S. allies in the Middle East. The F-15 is powered by two turbofan engines that can accelerate it to more than twice the speed of sound. The single-seat F-15 is armed with a 20-mm rotary CANNON and an array of short-range and medium-range air-to-air missiles. The fighter-bomber version, known as the Strike Eagle, includes a second seat for the weapons officer, who controls the delivery of missiles and bombs. It carried out much of the nighttime precision bombing of Iraqi installations in the PERSIAN GULF WAR.

F-16 *or* **Fighting Falcon** Single-seat, single-engine jet FIGHTER built by GENERAL DYNAMICS CORP. The first model was delivered to the U.S. Air Force in 1978; it has since been sold to more than a dozen other countries. Produced to fill the need for a lightweight, cost-effective fighter, it is 49 ft (15 m) long and has a wingspan of 31 ft (9.5 m). It can accelerate to more than twice the speed of sound, and its weaponry includes a 20-mm rotary cannon and attachments under the wings and fuselage for a variety of bombs and missiles.

F-86 See SABRE

Fa-hsien See FAXIAN

Faber \'fä-bər\, **Lothar von** (1817–1896) German manufacturer of writing products and art supplies. He took over the family pencil business in Bavaria and transformed it into a worldwide firm, establishing branches throughout Europe and the U.S. and contracting in 1856 for exclusive control of all graphite being mined in Siberia. His brother John Eberhard Faber (1822–1879) settled in the U.S. in 1849 and built a large Faber manufacturing plant; the Eberhard Faber Pencil Co. was incorporated in 1898.

Fabergé \fȧ-ber-'zhā\, **(Peter) Carl** *orig.* **Karl Gustavovich** (1846–1920) Russian goldsmith, jeweler, and designer. Educated in Europe and England, he took over his father's jewelry business in St. Petersburg in 1870. The objects he designed quickly won him the patronage of European and Russian royalty. Specializing in gold, silver, malachite, jade, lapis lazuli, and gemstones, he manufactured not only conventional jewelry but objects of fantasy, much of it inspired by the decorative arts of the LOUIS XVI STYLE. He opened workshops in Moscow, Kiev, and London and became most famous for his jeweled Easter eggs for ALEXANDER III and NICHOLAS II. His workshops were shut down after the 1917 revolution, and he died in exile.

Fabian Society \'fā-bē-ən\ Socialist society founded in 1883–84 in London, to establish a democratic socialist state in Britain. The name derived from FABIUS MAXIMUS CUNCTATOR, whose elusive tactics in avoiding pitched battles led to victory over stronger forces. Fabians believed in evolutionary socialism rather than revolution, and used public meetings and lectures, research, and publishing to educate the public. Important early members included GEORGE BERNARD SHAW and SIDNEY AND BEATRICE WEBB. They helped organize a separate party that became the LABOUR PARTY in 1906, and many Labour members of Parliament have been Fabians.

Fabius Maximus Cunctator \'fā-bē-əs-'mak-si-məs-ˌkəŋk-'tā-tər\, **Quintus** (died 203 BC) Roman commander and statesman. He served as CONSUL in 233 BC (an office he would hold five times) and censor in 230. Elected DICTATOR in 217, he used a strategy of harassment and attrition in the Second PUNIC WAR against HANNIBAL (218–201). These cautious delaying tactics (Cunctator means "delayer") allowed Rome to recover and take the offensive, but Roman impatience led to defeat at the Battle of CANNAE. He unsuccessfully opposed SCIPIO AFRICANUS' invasion of Africa in 205.

fable Narration intended to enforce a useful truth, especially one in which animals or inanimate objects speak and act like human beings. Unlike a folktale, it has a moral that is woven into the story and often explicitly formulated at the end. The Western fable tradition began with tales ascribed to AESOP. It flourished in the Middle Ages, reached a high point in 17th-century France in the works of JEAN DE LA FONTAINE, and found a new audience in the 19th century with the rise of children's literature. Fables also have ancient roots in the literary and religious traditions of India, China, and Japan.

Fables of Bidpai See PAÑCA-TANTRA

fabliau \'fa-blē-ˌō\ *or* **fableau** \fa-'blō\ Short metrical tale made popular in medieval France by JONGLEURS. Fabliaux were characterized by vivid detail and realistic observation and were usually comic, coarse, and cynical, especially in their treatment of women. Though understandable to the bourgeois and common people, they frequently contain an element of BURLESQUE that depends for its appreciation on considerable knowledge of courtly society, love, and manners. About 150 fabliaux survive, by both amateur and professional writers.

Fabre \'fȧbrᵊ\, **Jean Henri** (1823–1915) French entomologist. Largely self-taught, Fabre did important research on three insect orders: bees and wasps (Hymenoptera), beetles (Coleoptera), and grasshoppers and crickets (Orthoptera). On the basis of his observations of the paralyzing actions of wasps in response to stimulating zones in their prey, he described the importance of inherited instinct as a behavior pattern in insects. Fabre wrote many books to popularize science. Though he never accepted the theory of EVOLUTION, his work was respected by CHARLES DARWIN.

Fabriano, Gentile da See GENTILE DA FABRIANO

Fabricius (ab Aquapendente) \fə-'brish-əs\, **Hieronymus** *Italian* **Girolamo Fabrici** (1537–1619) Italian surgeon and anatomist. He studied under and later succeeded GABRIEL FALLOPIUS at the University of Padua (1562–1613). The first clear description of the valves of the veins, in his *De venarum ostiolis* (1603), provided his pupil WILLIAM HARVEY with a crucial point in his argument for blood circulation. His *De formato foetu* (1600) contained the first detailed description of the placenta and opened the field of comparative embryology. He was the first to perceive the larynx as a vocal organ and to demonstrate that the pupil of the eye changes size.

Fabricius \fȧ-'brē-sē-ůs\, **Johann Christian** (1745–1808) Danish entomologist. He studied at Uppsala University with CAROLUS LINNAEUS, and from 1775 taught not only natural history but also economics and finance at the University of Kiel. He advanced theories progressive for his time, particularly the view that new species and varieties could arise through hybridization and by environmental influence on anatomical structure and function. His taxonomic research was based on insect mouthparts rather than their wings.

Fabritius \fȧ-'brēt-sē-ɯ̅s\, **Carel** (1622–1654) Dutch painter. He studied with REMBRANDT in the early 1640s, then settled in Delft, entering its painters' guild in 1652. The earliest work attributed to him, *The Raising of Lazarus* (c. 1645), was strongly influenced by Rembrandt, but he soon developed a personal style marked by cool color harmonies, subtle lighting effects, and illusionistic perspective. His portraits and his genre and narrative paintings influenced PIETER DE HOOCH and JOHANNES VERMEER. All but about a dozen of his paintings were destroyed by an explosion of the Delft powder magazine, which killed him as well.

fabula \'fab-yə-lə, 'fäb-yů-lä\ Drama of ancient Rome. Particular types included the *fabula Atellana,* the earliest form of native farce in ancient Italy; the *fabula crepidata,* a form of Roman tragedy based on Greek models; the *fabula palliata,* an ancient Roman comedy based on Greek NEW COMEDY and treating a Greek subject; the *fabula praetexta,* an ancient Roman drama with a theme from Roman history or legend; and the *fabula togata,* a Roman comedy based on Greek models but featuring Roman life and dress.

face Front part of the head, extending from the forehead to the chin and housing the eyes, nose, mouth, and jaws. The receding of the jaw and the increasing size of the brain in human evolution has made the face essentially vertical, with two distinctively human features: a prominent, projecting nose and a clearly defined chin. The face and braincase follow different patterns of growth. While the face grows more slowly, it ends up much larger compared to the braincase in adults than at birth. The facial muscles move the features to express emotion.

fact, theater of *or* **documentary theater** Movement to bring social issues to the stage by emphasis on factual information over aesthetic considerations. An outgrowth of the Living Newspaper technique employed by the WPA Federal Theater Project in the 1930s, the form became popular in the 1960s. In Germany Rolf Hochhuth's *The Representative* (1963), PETER WEISS's *The Investigation* (1965), and Heinar Kipphardt's *In the Matter of J. Robert Oppenheimer* (1964) examined recent historical events through authentic documentary sources, such as trial transcripts and statistics. The movement influenced later political drama in Europe and the U.S.

fact–value distinction In philosophy, the ontological distinction between what is (facts) and what ought to be (values). DAVID HUME gave the distinction its classical formulation in his dictum that it is impossible to derive an "ought" from an "is." See also NATURALISTIC FALLACY.

factor In multiplication, one of two or more numerical or algebraic components of a product. A whole number's factors are the whole numbers that divide evenly into it (e.g., 1, 2, 3, 4, 6, and 12 are factors of 12). To factor a counting number means to break it down into its PRIME NUMBER factors. To factor a POLYNOMIAL is to find its prime polynomial factors, a basic procedure for solving ALGEBRAIC EQUATIONS. According to the fundamental theorem of ARITHMETIC, the prime factorization of any number or polynomial is unique.

factorial For any whole number, the product of all the counting numbers up to and including itself. It is indicated with an exclamation point: 4! (read "four factorial") is $1 \times 2 \times 3 \times 4 = 24$. In order for certain formulas involving PERMUTATIONS AND COMBINATIONS to work, 0! is defined to be 1. Factorials are particularly useful in calculating the number of ways an event can occur, for example, the number of possible orders of finish in a race.

factoring In finance, the selling of ACCOUNTS RECEIVABLE on a contract basis to an agency known as a factor in order to obtain cash payment before the accounts come due. The factor assumes full responsibility for credit analysis of new accounts, payments collection, and credit losses. Factoring is most often used in seasonal industries such as textiles and shoes to shift the functions of CREDIT and collection to a specialized agency.

factory Structure in which work is organized to meet the need for production on a large scale usually with power-driven machinery. In the 17th–18th century, the DOMESTIC SYSTEM of work in Europe began giving way to larger units of production, and capital became available for investment in industrial enterprises. The movement of population from country to city also contributed to change in work methods. MASS PRODUCTION, which transformed the organization of work, came about by the development of the MACHINE-TOOL industry. With precision equipment, large numbers of identical parts could be produced at low cost and with a small workforce. The ASSEMBLY LINE was first widely used in the U.S. meat-packing industry; HENRY FORD designed an automobile assembly line in 1913. By mid-1914, chassis assembly time had fallen from 12½ man-hours to 93 man-minutes. Some countries, particularly in Asia and South America, began industrializing in the 1970s and later. See also AMERICAN SYSTEM OF MANUFACTURE.

factory farming System of modern animal farming designed to yield the most meat, milk, and eggs in the least amount of time and space possible. The term, descriptive of standard farming practice in the U.S., is frequently used by animal-rights activists, who maintain that animal-protection measures routinely ignore farm animals. Animals are often fed growth hormones, sprayed with pesticides, and fed antibiotics to mitigate the problems of infestation and disease that are exacerbated by crowded living conditions. Chickens spend their lives crowded into small cages, often so tightly that they cannot turn around; the cages are stacked in high batteries, and the length of "day" and "night" are artificially controlled to maximize egg laying. Veal calves are virtually immobilized in narrow stalls for their entire lives. These and numerous other practices have long been decried by critics.

Fadhlallah \fäd-'ləl-lə\, **Ayatollah Sayyid Muhammad Hussayn** (born 1935) Shiite cleric and spiritual leader of HIZBULLAH, the "party of God," in Lebanon. Born in Iraq of Lebanese parents, he moved to Lebanon in 1966 and quickly established a reputation as a leading religious authority. Hizbullah, founded after the 1982 Israeli invasion of Lebanon, became public in 1985. Fadhlallah's eloquence led many to believe that he was Hizbullah's leader, but both he and the Party of God deny this, while acknowledging his strong spiritual influence. While agreeing with many Hizbullah positions, he has opposed others. In 1985 it was widely reported that he was the target of an aborted U.S.-Saudi car-bomb assassination, a charge denied by U.S. and Saudi authorities.

Faenza majolica \fä-'en-zä-mə-'jä-li-kə\ Tin-glazed EARTHENWARE produced in the Italian city of Faenza from the late 14th century. Early Faenza jugs were decorated in green and purple with Gothic lettering and heraldic lions; the first major MAJOLICA piece is a wall plaque dated 1475. In the 15th century, Renaissance motifs appeared in dark blue, rich orange, and copper-green; vases with a peacock-feather design and a globular two-handled jar are characteristic of Faenza. The factory's most outstanding wares date from the late 15th to the mid-16th century. See also FAIENCE.

Faeroe Islands *or* **Faroe Islands** \'far-ō\ Group of islands (pop., 1994 est.: 45,000), in the Atlantic Ocean. Lying north of the British Isles, the islands are a self-governing region within the kingdom of Denmark. There are 17 inhabited islands and many islets and reefs, with a total area of 540 sq mi (1,399 sq km). The largest, Strømø, holds the capital of TÓRSHAVN. The islands are high and rugged, with coasts that are deeply indented with fjords. The economy is based on fishing and sheep-raising. First settled by Irish monks (c. 700), the islands were colonized by the Vikings (c. 800) and were ruled by Norway from the 11th century until 1380, when they passed to Denmark. They unsuccessfully sought independence in 1946, but received self-government in 1948.

Fahrenheit, Daniel (Gabriel) (1686–1736) German physicist and instrument maker. Born in Danzig, he spent most of his life in the Netherlands, where he devoted himself to the study of physics and the manufacture of precision meteorological instruments. He is best known for inventing a successful alcohol thermometer (1709) and mercury thermometer (1714) and for developing the Fahrenheit temperature scale, setting zero at the freezing point of an equal mixture of ice and salt. He discovered that water can remain liquid below its freezing point and that the boiling point of liquids varies with atmospheric pressure.

Faidherbe \fe-'derb\, **Louis (-Léon-César)** (1818–1889) Governor of French Senegal (1854–61, 1863–65) and a founder of France's colonial empire in Africa. Faidherbe was trained as a military engineer and served in Algeria and Senegal before becoming the colonial governor of Senegal. Alarmed by the growing power of the Islamic leader Umar Tal, he took the offensive, driving off Umar Tal, subjugating the Moorish tribes in the north, and transforming his colony into the region's dominant power. In 1857 he founded the capital city of DAKAR.

faience \fā-'äns, fī-'ä^{n}s\ Tin-glazed EARTHENWARE made in France, Germany, Spain, and Scandinavia, similar to FAENZA MAJOLICA, for which it was named. The term is also applied to glazed earthenware made in ancient Egypt, where it was used for beads, amulets, jewelry, and small animal and human figures, most notably the blue-glazed hippopotamus figures of the Middle Kingdom (c. 2000–c. 1670 BC). Faience tiles, first made in the early dynasties, were used to decorate the walls of the subterranean chambers of the pyramids. In the New Kingdom (c. 1550–c. 1070 BC), polychrome tiles with floral designs were used in houses and palaces.

German faience lobed dish painted with chinoiserie in blue and manganese, Frankfurt am Main, c. 1690; in the Victoria and Albert Museum, London.

BY COURTESY OF THE VICTORIA AND ALBERT MUSEUM, LONDON

fair Temporary market where buyers and sellers gather to transact business. Fairs are held at regular intervals, generally at the same location and time of year. An important form of commerce before the INDUSTRIAL REVOLUTION, fairs solved the problem of distribution and made possible the demonstration of arts and crafts and the sale and BARTER of goods. They were a fixture of the Roman Empire and medieval Europe, where they were held at major caravan-route intersections and near religious festivals. The rules of the fair eventually became the basis of European business law. Fairs began to die out as cities grew larger and transportation networks became more extensive, though some continued to exist as religious festivals or recreational events. County, agricultural, and livestock fairs are still held in the U.S. and Europe. The TRADE FAIR, in which exhibitors from one industry display their goods, gained popularity in the 20th century.

fair-trade law In the U.S., any law allowing manufacturers of brand-name or trademarked goods to fix the actual or minimum resale prices of these goods. (Elsewhere the practice is called price maintenance.) Fair-trade laws were passed by many states during the GREAT DEPRESSION in an effort to protect independent retailers from price-cutting by large chain stores and consequent loss of employment in distributive trades, but most were later repealed at the state level. Critics argued that such laws restricted competition; the complexity of post–World War II marketing channels also made enforcement impracticable. In 1975 the few that remained in existence were repealed by an act of Congress.

Fairbairn \'fer-,bern\, **William** *later* **Sir William** (1789–1874) Scottish civil engineer and inventor. In 1835 he established a shipbuilding yard in London, where he constructed several hundred vessels. He was the first to use WROUGHT iron for ship hulls, bridges, mill shafting, and structural beams. He experimented with the strength of IRON and the relative merits of hot and cold blast in iron manufacture (see BLAST FURNACE). In 1845 he and ROBERT STEPHENSON designed two tubular railway bridges in Wales; Fairbairn designed the hydraulic riveters used in constructing one of them.

Fairbanks City (pop., 2000: 30,224), eastern central Alaska, situated at the junction of the Tanana and Chena rivers. Founded in 1902 after a gold strike, it was named for Charles W. Fairbanks. As the northern terminus of the ALASKA HIGHWAY and the railroad, it is the main supply center for the northern Alaskan oil business (see TRANS-ALASKA PIPELINE). Located nearby are Fort Wainwright, Eielson Air Force Base, and the University of Alaska, Fairbanks (1917). It is the site of the annual 800-mi (1,290-km) Yukon Marathon boat race and the North American Championship Sled Dog Races.

Fairbanks, Douglas *orig.* **Douglas Elton Ulman** (1883–1939) U.S. film actor. Born in Denver, he was a Broadway star by 1910, noted for his exuberance and physical agility. He made his film debut in *The Lamb* (1915). As cofounder of UNITED ARTISTS (1919), he produced and starred in such films as *The Mark of Zorro* (1920), *Robin Hood* (1922), and *The Thief of Baghdad* (1924). His films were so popular that he was called the "King of Hollywood" in the 1920s. His 15-year marriage to MARY PICKFORD ended in 1935. His son (by his first wife), Douglas Fairbanks, Jr. (1909–2000), was a debonair leading man in U.S. and British films, including *Catherine the Great* (1934), *The Prisoner of Zenda* (1937), and *State Secret* (1950). In the 1960s he hosted and sometimes acted in the British TV drama series *Douglas Fairbanks Presents*.

Fairchild, David (Grandison) (1869–1954) U.S. botanist and agricultural explorer. Born in Lansing, Mich., he studied at Kansas State University of Agriculture. From 1904 to 1928, as head of the section of plant pathology of the U.S. Department of Agriculture, he supervised the introduction of many useful plants into the U.S., including alfalfa, dates, mangos, horseradish, and bamboos.

Fairfax (of Cameron), Thomas, Baron Fairfax (1612–1671) Commander in chief of the Parliamentary army during the ENGLISH CIVIL WARS. His tactical skill and courage helped bring about many Parliamentary victories, including the Battle of MARSTON MOOR. As commander in chief of the NEW MODEL ARMY, he defeated CHARLES I at the Battle of NASEBY. Fairfax disapproved of the purge of Parliament by his soldiers in 1648 and refused to serve on the commission that condemned Charles to death. In 1650 he resigned as commander in chief to protest the proposed invasion of Scotland. In 1658 he helped GEORGE MONCK restore Parliamentary rule in the face of opposition from the army. He was a member of the Parliament that invited Charles's son to return to England as CHARLES II.

Fairweather, Mt. Mountain, British Columbia. It is located on the Alaska border in the Fairweather Range of the ST. ELIAS MTNS., at the southwestern end of the GLACIER BAY NATIONAL PARK. The highest peak in the province, it reaches 15,299 ft (4,663 m). It was named by Capt. JAMES COOK, who saw the peak in 1778 while navigating the bay in "fair weather."

fairy In folklore, any of a race of supernatural beings who have magic powers and sometimes meddle in human affairs. Some have been described as of human size, while others are "little people" only a few inches high. The term was first used in medieval Europe. Fairy lore is especially common in Ireland, Cornwall, Wales, and Scotland. Though usually beneficent in modern children's stories, the fairies of the past were powerful and sometimes dangerous beings who could be friendly, mischievous, or cruel, depending on their whim. Fairies were thought to be beautiful, to live much longer than human beings, and to lack souls. They sometimes carried off human infants and left changelings as substitutes. They occasionally took human lovers, but to enter fairyland was perilous for humans, who were obliged to remain forever if they ate or drank there. See also LEPRECHAUN.

fairy shrimp Any of the CRUSTACEANS in the order Anostraca, named for their graceful movements and pastel colors. Some grow to about 1 in. (2.5 cm) or more in length. They live in freshwater ponds in Europe, Central Asia, western North America, the drier regions of Africa, and Australia. See also SHRIMP.

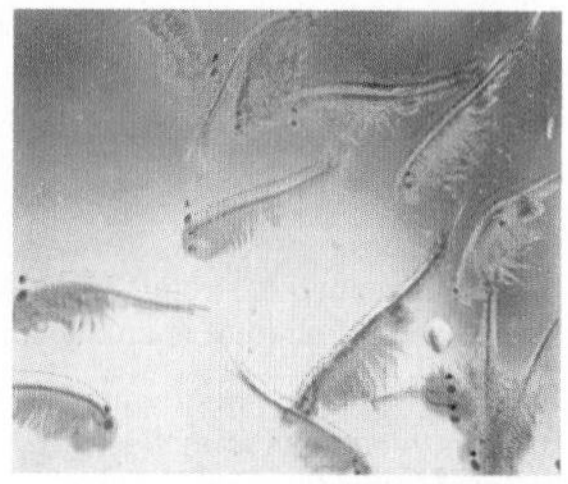

Fairy shrimp (*Eubranchipus vernalis*).

WILLIAM JAHODA–NATIONAL AUDUBON SOCIETY FROM PHOTO RESEARCHERS/EB INC.

fairy tale Simple narrative dealing with supernatural beings (such as fairies, magicians, ogres, or dragons) that is typically of folk origin and written or told for the amusement of children, or a more sophisticated narrative containing supernatural or obviously improbable events, scenes, and personages and often having a whimsical, satirical, or moralistic character. The term embraces popular folktales such as "Cinderella" and "Puss in Boots," as well as art fairy tales of later invention, such as those by HANS CHRISTIAN ANDERSEN. It is often difficult to distinguish between tales of literary and oral origin, because folktales have received literary treatment from early times and literary tales can often be traced back to oral tradition.

Faisal I \'fī-səl\ (1885–1933) Arab statesman and king of Iraq (1921–33). Son of HUSAYN IBN ALI, he helped his father plot Arab nationalist rebellion against the OTTOMAN EMPIRE during World War I. When the Arab revolt was declared in 1916, he played an important part in anti-Ottoman military campaigns. In 1918 an Arab military force occupied Damascus, and Faisal was declared king of Syria. Two years later France invaded Syria and Faisal went into exile in London. The British sponsored him as king of Iraq, in anticipation of a treaty providing for Iraqi independence; he was crowned in 1921, and Iraq became independent in 1932.

Faisalabad \'fī-sə-lə-,bad\ *formerly (until 1979)* **Lyallpur** \'līl-,pu̇r\ City (pop., 1998: 1,977,246) and district, PUNJAB province, Pakistan. Founded in 1890, it became headquarters of the Lower Chenab colony and in 1898 was incorporated as a municipality. A distributing center located in the central Punjab plain, its industries produce chemicals and synthetics, textiles, and food products. It is the site of West Pakistan Agricultural University (1961), and a number of colleges affiliated with the University of the Punjab.

faith healing Curing of an illness or disability by recourse to divine power, without the use of traditional medicine. A healer such as a clergy member or an inspired layperson may act as intermediary. Certain places, such as the grotto at LOURDES, France, are believed to effect cures among believers. In ancient Greece, temples honoring the god of medicine, ASCLEPIUS, were built near springs with healing waters. In Christianity, support for faith healing is based on the miraculous cures wrought by Jesus during his ministry. CHRISTIAN SCIENCE is noted for faith healing, and it is also practiced in a more dramatic way in PENTECOSTALISM through such customs as the laying on of hands.

Fakhr al-Din al-Razi \'fä-k̲ər-äl-'dēn-är-'rä-zē\ (1149–1209) Islamic scholar and theologian. Born in Persia, he traveled widely before settling in Herat (in modern Afghanistan). The author of more than 100 books (on subjects as diverse as medicine, mineralogy, and grammar), he gained fame and wealth through his scholarship and skill in debate, in which he often presented unorthodox views fully and favorably before refuting them. Though this led to accusations of heresy, it has preserved information about little-known sects. His works include one of the major commentaries on the Quran, *The Keys to the Unknown* (or *The Great Commentary*), and *Collection of the Opinions of Ancients and*

Moderns, a classic of KALAM. His bad temper earned him many enemies, and he may have been poisoned.

Falange \fä-'län-hä, *Engl* 'fā-lanj\ (Spanish: "Phalanx") Extreme nationalist political group in Spain. Founded in 1933 by JOSE ANTONIO PRIMO DE RIVERA and influenced by Italian FASCISM, the Falange gained popularity in opposition to the POPULAR FRONT government of 1936. Gen. FRANCISCO FRANCO merged the group with other right-wing factions by decree in 1937 and became the Falange's absolute chief. 150,000 Falangists served in Franco's armed forces in the SPANISH CIVIL WAR. After their victory, the Falange's fascism was subordinated to the Franco regime's conservative values. On Franco's death in 1975 a law was passed permitting other "political associations," and the Falange was abolished in 1977.

Falasha \fə-'lä-shə\ Jewish Ethiopians. The Falasha call themselves House of Israel and claim descent from Menilek I, son of King SOLOMON and the Queen of SHEBA. Probably descended from local Agew peoples converted by Jews in southern Arabia, they remained faithful to Judaism after the Ethiopian kingdom was converted to Christianity in the 4th century AD. Persecuted by Christians, they settled in the area around Lake Tana in northern Ethiopia. Though ignorant of the TALMUD, members adhered strictly to the Mosaic law and observed some festivals of Judaism. In 1975 the Israeli rabbinate affirmed that Falashas were Jews, and from 1980 to 1992 some 45,000 Falasha emigrated to Israel, leaving probably only a few thousand in Ethiopia.

falcon Any of nearly 60 species of diurnal BIRDS OF PREY in the family Falconidae, characterized by long, pointed wings and swift, powerful flight. The name is sometimes restricted to the more than 35 species of true falcons, genus *Falco*. Species range from 6 to 24 in. (15–60 cm) long. Females of the genus *Falco* are larger and bolder than males and are preferred for FALCONRY. Falcons, found worldwide, commonly nest in treeholes or on cliff ledges. Some species capture birds in midair; others live on hares, mice, lizards, and insects. See also GYRFALCON, HAWK, KESTREL, MERLIN, PEREGRINE FALCON.

Falconet \fål-kò-'ne\, **Étienne-Maurice** (1716–1791) French sculptor. After being apprenticed to a carpenter, he studied sculpture in Paris. He developed an intimate style with a taste for erotic figures. Through Madame de POMPADOUR's influence, he became director of the Sèvres porcelain factory (1757–66); many of his figures were reproduced in Sèvres biscuit ware. From 1766 to 1778 he worked in Russia; his masterpiece, the colossal equestrian statue of PETER I THE GREAT in St. Petersburg (made famous as *The Bronze Horseman* by ALEKSANDR PUSHKIN), was unveiled in 1782. After suffering a stroke (1783), he gave up sculpture and devoted his time to writing. He is best known for adapting the classical style of the French baroque period to the Rococo ideal.

falconry Sport of employing FALCONS or other HAWKS in hunting game. Falconry has been practiced in the Middle East at least since the 8th century BC. It flourished among the privileged classes in Europe in the Middle Ages. It began to die out after the advent of the shotgun and the enclosure of open lands in the 17th century. Today its popularity is limited to various hawking clubs and associations. The bird most commonly used is the PEREGRINE FALCON, though the goshawk and sparrow hawk have also been used. Birds are caught wild or raised from birth. Training involves selective use of a leather hood (called a rufter) and leg thongs (jesses) to keep the animal under control while familiarizing it with its new environment. During the hunt the trained bird is released to bring down its prey; it then returns to the hawker or is collected at the kill site.

Faldo, Nick (born 1957) British golfer. He turned professional in 1976 and played the first of 11 successive Ryder Cup matches in 1977. He subsequently won three Masters (1989, 1990, 1996), three British Opens (1987, 1990, 1992), and many other international tournaments. In 1990 he became the first non-American to be named PGA Player of the Year.

Falk, Peter (born 1927) U.S. actor. Born in New York City, he acted in off-Broadway plays from 1955 before appearing on Broadway in NEIL SIMON's *Prisoner of Second Avenue* (1971, Tony award) and in such films as *Murder Inc.* (1960), *Pocketful of Miracles* (1961), and *A Woman Under the Influence* (1974). He is best known as the eccentric detective in the television series *Columbo* (1971–78, three Emmy awards) and in TV movies based on the series.

Falkland Islands *Spanish* **Islas Malvinas** \'ēs-,läs-mäl-'ḇē-näs\ British self-governing colony (pop., 1993 est.: 2,000), in the southern Atlantic Ocean. Located about 300 mi (480 km) northeast of the southern tip of South America, it is made up of two main islands, East Falkland and West Falkland, and about 200 smaller islands; they cover some 4,700 sq mi (12,200 sq km). The capital is Stanley, on East Falkland. The population is English-speaking and of British descent. The economy is based on sheep-raising. The French founded the islands' first settlement on East Falkland in 1764, and the British settled West Falkland in 1765. In 1770 the Spanish purchased the French settlement and expelled the British, but the latter's settlement was restored in 1771. In 1820 Argentina proclaimed its sovereignty over the Falklands, but the British took them back in 1833. Argentina invaded in 1982, and the British reclaimed the islands after a brief conflict (see FALKLAND ISLANDS WAR).

Falkland Islands War *or* **Malvinas War** (1982) Brief undeclared war fought between Argentina and Britain over control of the FALKLAND ISLANDS and associated island dependencies. Both countries had long claimed sovereignty over the Falklands. In 1982, giving up on protracted negotiations with Britain, Argentina invaded the islands with some 10,000 troops. MARGARET THATCHER responded by sending out a naval task force, and in three months Britain had reoccupied the islands. Britain lost about 250 men, Argentina about 700. Argentina's defeat discredited its military government and helped lead to the restoration of civilian rule in 1983.

Fall, Albert Bacon (1861–1944) U.S. secretary of the interior (1921–23). Born in Frankfort, Ky., he practiced law in New Mexico Territory before being elected to the U.S. Senate, where he served 1913–21. An investigation after he left the Interior Department revealed that he had accepted a bribe while in office in return for government oil-reserve leases in the TEAPOT DOME SCANDAL. Convicted of bribery in 1929, he was imprisoned for nine months.

Falla \'fä-yə\, **Manuel de** (1876–1946) Spanish composer. He studied with F. PEDRELL, and conceived a powerful musical nationalism. His first major work was the opera *La vida breve* (1905). He lived in Paris 1907–14, where he imbibed the music of C. DEBUSSY, M. RAVEL, and others. The intensely Spanish ballet *El amor brujo* (1915) gained him further acclaim. The Spanish Civil War caused him to leave Spain for Argentina c. 1938, and he never returned. His other works include *Nights in the Gardens of Spain* (1915), *The Three-Cornered Hat* (1919), the puppet opera *El retablo de maese Pedro* (1923; with FEDERICO GARCIA LORCA), a harpsichord concerto (1926), and the huge unfinished oratorio *L'Atlántida*. He is regarded as the greatest Spanish composer of recent centuries.

fallacy, formal and informal In philosophy, reasoning that fails to establish its conclusion because of deficiencies in wording or form. Fallacies have traditionally been divided into formal and informal classes. Formal fallacies are deductively invalid arguments that typically commit an easily recognizable logical error. The class of informal fallacies can in turn be divided into material and verbal fallacies. The material fallacies are also known as fallacies of presumption, because the premises "presume" too much, either covertly assuming the conclusion or avoiding the issue in view; an example is the fallacy of *petitio principii* ("begging the question"), which occurs when the premises presume the very conclusion that is to be proved. Verbal fallacies, or fallacies of ambiguity, arise when the conclusion is achieved through an improper use of words, as where a term has one meaning in a premise and another in the conclusion.

Fallen Timbers, Battle of (August 20, 1794) Decisive victory of Gen. ANTHONY WAYNE over the northwestern Indian Confederation, securing white settlement of former Indian territory, mainly in Ohio. Wayne led over 1,000 soldiers to confront the 2,000 Indians, who had been promised British support and who had gathered behind a protective tangle of fallen trees along the Maumee River (near modern Toledo). The Indians, abandoned by the British, fled in disarray. A treaty in 1795 ceded Indian lands to the U.S. and ended British influence in the area.

Fallopius \fə-'lō-pē-əs\, **Gabriel** *Italian* **Gabriello Fallopio** (1523–1562) Italian anatomist. He contributed greatly to knowledge of the ear and reproductive system. His observations of the dissection of cadavers are outlined in *Observationes anatomicae* (1561). He discovered the fallopian tubes, which connect the ovaries to the uterus, and several major nerves of the head and face. He described the semicircular canals in the ear and named the vagina, placenta, clitoris, palate, and cochlea. He and

ANDREAS VESALIUS overturned many of GALEN's principles, a development essential to Renaissance medicine.

fallout Descent of radioactive materials from the atmosphere to the earth. Radioactivity in the atmosphere may arise from natural causes such as COSMIC RAYS as well as from nuclear explosions and atomic reactor operations. The explosion of NUCLEAR WEAPONS leads to three types of fallout: local, tropospheric, and stratospheric. The first, intense but relatively short-lived, occurs as larger radioactive particles are deposited near the site of the explosion. Tropospheric fallout occurs when the finer particles enter the TROPOSPHERE, and it spreads over a larger area in the month after the explosion. Stratospheric fallout, made of fine particles in the STRATOSPHERE, may continue years after the explosion, and the distribution is nearly worldwide. Many different radioisotopes are formed during a nuclear explosion, but only long-lived isotopes (e.g., CESIUM-137, STRONTIUM-90) are deposited as stratospheric fallout.

Falloux Law \fȧ-ˈlü\ (1850) Act granting legal status to independent secondary schools in France. It was sponsored by Count Frédéric-Alfred-Pierre de Falloux (1811–1886), minister of education in the SECOND REPUBLIC, and one of its main architects was a Catholic bishop, Félix-Antoine-Philibert Dupanloup (1802–1878). Under the guise of freedom of education, it restored much of the church's traditional influence.

False Decretals \di-ˈkrē-təlz, ˈde-krə-təlz\ Collection of church law from the 9th century, containing some forged documents. They are also called the Decretals of Pseudo-Isidore because they were issued under the name of St. ISIDORE OF SEVILLE. They were intended to establish the independence of the church and end its subjection to the Carolingian empire. They consist of laws, papal letters, and decrees of councils, some genuine but many (including the famous DONATION OF CONSTANTINE) forgeries. Widely accepted by the end of the 10th century, the collection was not proved a hoax until the 17th century.

falsework *or* **centering** Temporary framework used during construction to support arches and similar structures while the mortar or concrete is setting or the steel is being joined. As soon as the work is set and the structure is self-supporting, the centering is struck (carefully removed).

Falun Gong \ˈfä-ˌlůn-ˈgȯŋ\ *or* **Falun Dafa** \ˈdä-fä\ Controversial spiritual movement combining healthful exercises with meditation for the purpose of "moving to higher levels." Its teachings draw from Buddhism, Confucianism, Taoism, and the Western New Age Movement. It was founded in China in 1992 by Li Hongzhi, a former grain-bureau clerk from Jilin province. He originally registered it as a form of the natural-healing discipline *qigong*, but later withdrew it from China's Qigong Research Association to stress its spiritual (rather than health-related) emphasis. Its members nevertheless claim great health benefits from its practice. It claims a worldwide following of 100 million, with 70 million in China; Chinese authorities claim it has as few as 2 or 3 million members. The movement has been regarded as a threat by the Chinese government, which started arresting its followers in mid-1999. Many Falun Gong members were later tried and given long prison sentences. Li emigrated to the U.S. in 1998.

Falwell \ˈfȯl-ˌwel\, **Jerry L.** (born 1933) Protestant evangelist. Born in Lynchburg, Va., he originally studied engineering before turning to religion. He founded Thomas Road Baptist Church in 1956 and later founded Liberty Baptist College. His "Old-Time Gospel Hour" television show serves as outreach for his church. In 1979 he organized the Moral Majority to encourage his followers to become involved in politics; he withdrew from its leadership in 1990 to return to preaching. A fundamentalist interpreter of the Bible, he is known for his sometimes extreme conservatism.

Familist \ˈfa-mə-list\ Member of the Family of Love religious sect. It was founded by a 16th-century Dutch merchant, Hendrik Niclaes, whose goal was to end religious wrangling and unite all "lovers of truth" in one great Christian fellowship of peace. His largest following was in England, where his works were privately published. ELIZABETH I issued a proclamation against the Family of Love in 1580. The sect died out after the restoration of the English monarchy in 1660; some of its members may have joined the Society of FRIENDS.

family Basic social unit consisting of persons united by ties of marriage (affinity), "blood," (consanguinity), or adoption and usually representing a single household. The essence of the family group is the parent-child relationship, whose outlines nevertheless vary widely among cultures. One prominent familial form is the nuclear family, consisting of the marital pair and their offspring living in a separate dwelling. While some scholars believe this to be the oldest form, others point to the inconclusive prehistorical record and the widespread existence of other forms such as the polygynous family (a husband, two or more co-wives, and their offspring) and the extended family (parents, married children, and their offspring). The family as an institution provides for the rearing and socialization of children, the care of the aged, sick, or disabled, the legitimation of procreation, and the regulation of sexual conduct in addition to supplying basic physical, economic, and emotional security for its members. See also MARRIAGE.

family In PEDOLOGY, a group of soils that have similar profiles and include one or more subdivisions called series. The primary characteristics that define each of the nearly 6,600 identified soil families are the physical and chemical properties—especially texture, mineral composition, temperature, and depth—that are important for the growth of plants.

family planning Use of measures designed to regulate the number and spacing of children within a family, largely to curb population growth and ensure each family's access to limited resources. The first attempts to offer family planning services began with private groups and often aroused strong opposition. Activists such as MARGARET SANGER in the U.S., Marie Stopes in England, and Dhanvanthis Rama Rau in India eventually succeeded in establishing clinics for family planning and health care. Today many countries have established national policies and encourage the use of public family services. The UNITED NATIONS and the WORLD HEALTH ORGANIZATION offer technical assistance. See also BIRTH CONTROL.

family practice *or* **family medicine** *or* **general practice** Field of medicine that stresses comprehensive primary health care, emphasizing the family unit. Practitioners must be familiar to some degree with medical specialties and, especially in health maintenance organizations, are now often gatekeepers who refer patients to specialists when necessary. Once virtually the only kind of medicine, family practice has been defined as a separate field only since increasing specialization in medicine led to a shortage of practitioners. A 1963 World Health Organization report stressing the need for medical education to focus on the patient as a whole throughout life led to specific programs in family practice.

family sagas See ICELANDERS' SAGAS

famine Extreme and protracted shortage of food, resulting in widespread hunger and a substantial increase in the death rate. General famines affect all classes or groups in the region of food shortage; class famines affect some classes or groups much more severely than others; regional famines affect only a particular region of a country. Causes may be natural or human. Natural causes include drought, flooding, unfavorable weather conditions, plant disease, and insect infestation. The chief human cause is war; others include overpopulation, bad distribution systems, and high food prices. In the 20th century severe famines have occurred in China (1928–29, 5–10 million dead; 1959–60, several million), Russia (1921–22, 1.25–5 million; 1932–34, 5 million), India (1943–44, 1.5 million), Cambodia (1975–79, 1 million), and sub-Saharan Africa.

fan Rigid or folding hand-held device used for cooling, air circulation, or ceremony or as a sartorial accessory throughout the world from ancient times. As evidenced by Egyptian reliefs, early fans were of the rigid type, with a handle or stick attached to a rigid leaf or to feathers. In China, the folding fan came into fashion during the Ming dynasty (1368–1644); much significance came to be attached to the fan in the Far East, and many great Chinese painters devoted their talents to fan decoration. Portuguese traders in the 15th century brought fans to Europe from China and Japan. Through the 19th century in the West, fan decoration and size varied with European fashion.

Fan Zhongyen *or* **Fan Chung-yen** \ˈfän-ˈjůŋ-ˈyən\ (989–1052) Chinese scholar-reformer whose reforms anticipated those of WANG ANSHI. He attempted to abolish nepotism and corruption, reclaim unused land, equalize landholdings, create a strong local militia system, reduce corvée labor, and reform the civil-service examination system. He proposed the establishment of a national school system to train men to deal with the problems of history and politics; the proposal was adopted in 1044. See also NEO-CONFUCIANISM, SONG DYNASTY.

Fanfani \fän-'fä-nē\, **Amintore** (1908–1999) Italian premier who formed and led the center-left coalition that dominated Italian politics in the late 1950s and 1960s. Elected to Italy's constituent assembly (1946), he became secretary-general of the Christian Democratic Party (1954) after serving briefly as premier. With his party's victory in 1958, he became premier (1958–59) and stressed social reforms. He returned as premier (1960–63) after widespread public reaction against neofascist activity and again promoted a reformist program. He gained Italy's election to the U.N. Security Council (1958) and served as president of the U.N. General Assembly in 1965. He again served as premier in 1982–83 and 1987.

Fang \'faŋ\ Bantu-speaking peoples of southern Cameroon, mainland Equatorial Guinea, and northern Gabon. The Fang number about 3.6 million. Under colonial rule they engaged in ivory trading, and after World War I in cocoa farming. By 1939 much of the population was Christian, but since 1945 there has been a rapid growth of syncretistic sects. They are politically influential, especially in Gabon.

Fang Lizhi \'fäŋ-'lē-'jē\ (born 1936) Chinese astrophysicist and dissident held partially responsible for the 1989 student rebellion in TIANANMEN SQUARE. In 1957 he was expelled from the CHINESE COMMUNIST PARTY for a paper decrying the Marxist position on physics. He later taught at Beijing's University of Science and Technology (Keda); in 1966 he was sent to a communal farm to be reeducated. After Mao's death, Fang's party membership was restored. Appointed a vice president of one branch of Keda in 1985, he began work on restructuring it and reforming educational policy. During the demonstrations in Tiananmen Square he took refuge in the U.S. embassy, and in 1990 he and his wife were allowed to leave China.

Fanon \fȧ-'nō^{n}\, **Frantz (Omar)** (1925–1961) French (West Indian) psychoanalyst and social philosopher. Born in Martinique, he served in the French army in World War II, earned a medical degree, and became head of the psychiatric department in an Algerian hospital, where he edited the newspaper of the NATIONAL LIBERATION FRONT (from 1956). In 1960 he was appointed ambassador to Ghana by the rebel provisional government. His widely read book *The Wretched of the Earth* (1961) urged colonized peoples to purge themselves of their degradation in a "collective catharsis" by violence. He died of leukemia at 36.

fantasia \fan-'tā-zhə, ˌfan-tə-'zē-ə\ Musical composition free in form and inspiration, often for an instrumental soloist. Most fantasias try to convey the impression of improvisation. The first were Italian works for lute (c. 1530). Keyboard fantasias became common in the late 16th century; both organ and harpsichord fantasias flourished in the 17th–18th century in Britain, Germany, and France. Fugal, imitative texture, sometimes highly learned in character, was common from the beginning, often alternating with running passagework and highly chromatic chordal passages in free rhythms. Ensemble fantasias were widely composed as well. Important composers include J.P. SWEELINCK, G. FRESCOBALDI, J. J. Froberger, H. PURCELL, and J.S. BACH.

fantasy Mental images or imaginary narratives that distort or entirely depart from reality. Primary fantasies arise spontaneously from the UNCONSCIOUS, while secondary fantasies are consciously summoned and pursued. SIGMUND FREUD saw fantasy as a vehicle for the expression of repressed desires (see REPRESSION). Fantasy is important in the lives of children and is a vital element in PLAY. In adult life it is crucial to creative thinking and the making of art. Fantasy can become destructive if it serves as a constant refuge from the world of reality and a source of delusions.

Fante *or* **Fanti** \'fan-tē\ AKAN people of the southern coast of Ghana who speak a language of the KWA group. As intermediaries in colonial-era trade between the ASHANTI to the north and the Europeans to the south, the Fante established several independent kingdoms that formed a confederacy in the late 17th century. It aided the British in wars against the Ashanti in the 19th century but was disbanded in 1873 under British pressure. Today the Fante number about 250,000. A military organization called the *asafo* also serves political, social, and religious functions.

Fante \'fan-tē\, **John** (1909–1983) U.S. writer. Born in Colorado to Italian immigrant parents, he moved to Los Angeles in the early 1930s. His first novel, *Wait Until Spring, Bandini* (1938), was followed by his best-known book, *Ask the Dust* (1939), the first of his novels set in Depression-era California. Other books included the story collection *Dago Red* (1940) and the novels *Full of Life* (1952) and *Brotherhood of the Grape* (1977). He also wrote numerous screenplays, including *Creature from the Black Lagoon* (1954), *Full of Life* (1956), and *A Walk on the Wild Side* (1962). Long eclipsed, he began to be rediscovered in the 1990s.

Fantin-Latour \fä^{n}-ta^{n}-lȧ-'tür\, **(Ignace-) Henri (-Jean-Théodore)** (1836–1904) French painter and printmaker. He was trained by his father, a portrait painter, and at the École des Beaux-Arts. Though he associated with progressive artists (GUSTAVE COURBET, EUGENE DELACROIX, EDOUARD MANET), he was a traditionalist best known for his portraits and still lifes with flowers. His portrait groups, reminiscent of 17th-century Dutch guild portraits, depict literary and artistic persons of the time; his flower paintings were especially popular in England, thanks to JAMES M. WHISTLER and JOHN EVERETT MILLAIS, who found patrons to support him. His later years were devoted to lithography.

"Still Life," oil on canvas by Henri Fantin-Latour, 1866; in the National Gallery of Art, Washington, D.C.

BY COURTESY OF THE NATIONAL GALLERY OF ART, WASHINGTON, D.C., CHESTER DALE COLLECTION

Farabi \fȧ-'rä-bē\, **al-** *in full* **Muhammad ibn Muhammad ibn Tarkhan ibn Uzalagh al-Farabi** ***Latin*** **Alpharabius** ***or*** **Avennasar** (878?–c. 950) One of the great philosophers of medieval Islam. Born in Turkistan, he was probably the son of one of the caliph's Turkish bodyguards, and he grew up in Baghdad. From 942 he resided at the court of Prince Sayf al-Dawlah. Greatly influenced by Baghdad's Greek heritage in philosophy, especially the writings of ARISTOTLE, he regarded reason as superior to revelation and saw religion as a symbolic rendering of truth. Like PLATO, he believed it was the philosopher's task to provide guidance to the state. He wrote more than 100 works, notably *The Ideas of the Citizens of the Virtuous City*.

Faraday, Michael (1791–1867) English physicist and chemist. Son of a blacksmith, he received only a basic education in a church Sunday school, but went to work as an assistant to HUMPHRY DAVY, from whom he learned chemistry. He discovered a number of new organic compounds, including benzene, and was the first to liquefy a "permanent" gas. His major contributions were in the fields of electricity and magnetism. He was the first to report induction of an electric current from a magnetic field. He invented the first electric motor and dynamo, demonstrated the relation between electricity and chemical bonding, discovered the effect of magnetism on light, and discovered and named DIAMAGNETISM. He also provided the experimental, and much of the theoretical, foundation on which JAMES CLERK MAXWELL built his electromagnetic field theory. In 1833 he was appointed professor at the Royal Institution. After 1855 he retired to a house provided by Queen Victoria, but he declined a knighthood.

Farah, Nuruddin (born 1945) Somali writer, Somalia's first novelist and first English-language author. His first published novel, *From a Crooked Rib* (1970), describes a woman's determination to maintain her dignity in a sexist society. His other works include a trilogy—*Sweet and Sour Milk* (1979), *Sardines* (1981), and *Close Sesame* (1983)—about life under an African dictatorship. *Maps* (1986) examines identity and boundaries. The political nature of his fiction forced him into exile, and he has taught in Europe, North America, and elsewhere in Africa.

farce Light dramatic composition that uses highly improbable situations, stereotyped characters, violent horseplay, and broad humor. Farce is generally regarded as intellectually and aesthetically inferior to COMEDY in its crude characterizations and implausible plots, but it has remained popular throughout the West from ancient times to the present.

Fargo City (pop., 1996 est.: 84,000), eastern North Dakota. The state's largest city, it is located on the Red River of the North. It was founded in 1871 by the NORTHERN PACIFIC RAILWAY, and named for William G. Fargo of WELLS, FARGO & CO. The development of wheat-growing in the area consolidated the city's role as a transportation, marketing, and distribution center. North Dakota State University (1890) is a noted center of agricultural research. Local industries include the manufacture of farm implements and fertilizer. The meat-packing plants and stockyards in suburban West Fargo rank among the nation's largest.

Farinelli *orig.* **Carlo Broschi** (1705–1782) Italian castrato soprano. After being castrated, he became a student of the composer Nicola Porpora (1686–1768), making his debut in 1720. Renowned for his vocal power and amazing agility, he was persuaded by Porpora to go to London in 1734, where he became the greatest opera star of his time. In 1747 he abandoned the public stage for the court of PHILIP V in Madrid, where his singing revived the ailing monarch. Farinelli took over the court's musical establishment and engaged in highly extravagant projects. In 1759 he retired to Bologna, where he received illustrious guests, including JOSEPH II and W.A. MOZART, in great style at his villa.

Farley, James A(loysius) (1888–1976) U.S. politician. Born in Grassy Point, N.Y., he entered New York Democratic politics in 1912. As secretary of the state Democratic committee in 1928, he organized FRANKLIN ROOSEVELT's successful gubernatorial campaigns in 1928 and 1930. As national Democratic Party chairman (1932–40), he directed Roosevelt's 1932 and 1936 presidential campaigns. He served as postmaster general (1933–40) but resigned that post and the party chairmanship in opposition to Roosevelt's bid for a third term.

farm machinery Mechanical devices, including tractors and implements, used in farming to save labor. The great variety of farming devices covers a wide range of complexity, from simple hand-held implements used since prehistoric times to the complex harvesters of modern mechanized agriculture. From the early 19th century to the present, the chief source of power in farming has changed from animals to steam power, then to gasoline and finally to diesel. In developed countries, the number of farm workers has steadily declined in the 20th century, while farm production has increased because of the use of machinery.

Farmer, Fannie (Merritt) (1857–1915) U.S. cookery expert. Born in Boston, she became director of the Boston Cooking School in 1894, and in 1896 published *The Boston Cooking-School Cook Book*. The first cookbook to standardize the methods and measurements of recipes, it became one of the best-selling cookbooks of all time. In 1902 she established Miss Farmer's School of Cookery, with courses designed to train housewives rather than teachers of cookery.

Farmer-Labor Party (1918–44) Minor political party in Minnesota. An outgrowth of the NONPARTISAN LEAGUE, it was composed mainly of small farmers and urban laborers. It supported ROBERT LA FOLLETTE in the 1924 presidential election, and its candidate, Floyd B. Olson, was elected governor in 1930. It supported FRANKLIN ROOSEVELT in 1932 and 1936 before merging with the DEMOCRATIC PARTY in 1944 to form the Democrat-Farmer-Labor Party.

Farmer's Almanac U.S. annual journal, now called *Old Farmer's Almanac*, containing long-term weather predictions, planting schedules, astronomical tables, astrological lore, recipes, anecdotes, and sundry pleasantries of rural interest. First published by Robert B. Thomas in 1792 (for the year 1793), it went on to outlast dozens of competitors. It issued long-range weather forecasts, based on obscure interpretations of natural phenomena, long before any weather service existed, and generations of farmers planted and harvested according to its advice. Now published in Dublin, N.H., it sells some 4 million copies annually.

Farmington River River, western Liberia. The country's only river of commercial importance, it rises in the Bong Range and flows southwest for 75 mi (120 km) to the Atlantic coast. It is navigable for 10 mi (16 km) below Harbel, the port from which rubber is shipped to MONROVIA for export.

Farnese, Alessandro *later* **duca (Duke) di Parma e Piacenza** (1545–1592) Regent of the Netherlands (1578–92) for PHILIP II of Spain. He was educated at the court of Madrid, where he had been sent to prove his father's loyalty to the Habsburgs. In 1578 Philip II appointed him governor-general of the Netherlands, where his mother, MARGARET OF PARMA, had been regent earlier. His great achievement was the restoration of Spanish rule in the southern provinces and perpetuation of Roman Catholicism there. He succeeded by astute statesmanship and military operations against the alliance of rebellious Protestant provinces led by WILLIAM THE SILENT. In 1586 he succeeded his father as duke of Parma and Piacenza, but he never returned to Italy to rule.

Farnese, Elizabeth See ELIZABETH FARNESE

Farnese family \fär-'nā-sā\ Italian family that ruled the duchy of Parma and Piacenza from 1545 to 1731. The family became noted for its statesmen and soldiers, especially in the 14th–15th century, as well as by contracting politically useful marriages. In 1545 Pope PAUL III, a Farnese, detached Parma and Piacenza from the papal dominions and made them into duchies. The first duke was his illegitimate son, Pier Luigi Farnese (1503–1547), whose son Ottavio (1542–1586), the 2nd duke, made Parma the capital and consolidated the family's power. The 3rd duke, ALESSANDRO FARNESE, was Spain's regent of the Netherlands and duke in name only. His son, Ranuccio I (1569–1622), and grandson, Odoardo I (1612–1646), left heavy financial and diplomatic debts by inconclusive military campaigns in the THIRTY YEARS' WAR. In 1649 Pope Innocent X accused the Farnese of the murder of an ecclesiastic and seized the fief. Ranuccio II (1630–1694) declared war and was defeated, and the duchy survived precariously. Francesco Farnese (1678–1727) tried to save the state, but his only important success was the marriage of his niece ELIZABETH FARNESE to PHILIP V of Spain (1714). In 1731 the duchy passed from the last Farnese of the male line, Antonio (1679–1731), to Elizabeth's son, the future CHARLES III.

Farnsworth, Philo T(aylor) (1906–1971) U.S. engineer and inventor of electronic television. Born in Beaver, Utah, he attended Brigham Young University. While still in high school he began developing the early technology required for TELEVISION, and in 1927 he successfully transmitted the first image using electronic means. He formed Farnsworth Television (later Farnsworth Radio and Television Corp.) in 1929 and invented numerous devices related to television, including equipment for converting an optical image into an electrical signal; amplifier, cathode-ray, and vacuum tubes; and electrical scanners and photoelectric materials. He held some 165 patents.

faro One of the oldest gambling games played with cards. Its name probably derives from the picture of a pharaoh on an early set. It was popular in Europe in the 18th–19th century and in the U.S. in the 19th century. The game involves betting on the rank, or number, of a card drawn from a dealing box. It is still played in a few casinos.

Faroe Islands See FAEROE ISLANDS

Farouk I \fə-'rük\ *Arabic* **Faruq Al-Awwal** (1920–1965) King of Egypt (1936–52). Son of King Fuad I (1868–1936), he was educated in Egypt and England and ascended the throne in 1936. Farouk's administration was hampered by internal rivalries. His alienation of the military, especially after its loss to Israel (1948), led to his own downfall. In 1952 a coup led by GAMAL ABDEL NASSER forced him to abdicate. He was succeeded by his infant son, Fuad II, but in 1953 Egypt became a republic.

Farquhar \'fär-kər, 'fär-kwər\, **George** (1678–1707) Irish playwright. His early experience as an actor in Dublin was the source of the originality of dialogue and stage sense that gave his work its great comic power. His plays, written for the London stage and enthusiastically received, included *Love and a Bottle* (1699), *The Constant Couple* (1699), and *Sir Harry Wildair* (1701). His real contribution to English drama came with *The Recruiting Officer* (1706) and particularly *The Beaux' Stratagem* (1707), in which he introduced a verbal vigor and love of character reminiscent of Elizabethan dramatists.

Farragut \'far-ə-gət\, **David G(lasgow)** (1801–1870) U.S. naval officer. Born near Knoxville, Tenn., he served in the War of 1812 and received his first command in 1824. During the Civil War, he commanded the Union blockade of the western Gulf of Mexico; in the Battle of NEW ORLEANS he captured the port through which the Confederacy received much of its war supplies. In 1863 he helped secure victory at the Battle of VICKSBURG, bringing the Mississippi River under Union control. In 1864 he successfully attacked in the Battle of MOBILE BAY, leading his ships across a blockade of mines, or torpedoes,

Farragut, daguerreotype.
BY COURTESY OF THE LIBRARY OF CONGRESS, WASHINGTON, D.C.

with the order "Damn the torpedoes, full speed ahead!" He became a full admiral in 1866.

Farrakhan \'fär-ə-ˌkän, 'far-ə-ˌkan\, **Louis** *orig.* **Louis Eugene Walcott** (born 1933) U.S. religious leader. Born in New York City, he joined the Black Muslims in 1955, and for a time he assisted MALCOLM X in Boston. After the latter converted to SUNNI Islam, the two became enemies, and Farrakhan replaced Malcolm as minister of Mosque No. 7 in Harlem. He has repeatedly denied involvement in Malcolm's assassination, suspicions of which were based in part on an article he had published in a Muslim newspaper some months earlier. When W. Deen Muhammad, ELIJAH MUHAMMAD's successor as leader of the Nation of ISLAM, gradually began integrating the organization into the orthodox Muslim community, Farrakhan broke away and formed his own organization, also called Nation of Islam (1978). A strong proponent of black self-help and unity, he is known for his forceful speeches marked by calls for racial separatism as well as by anti-Semitism and conspiracy theories. He was the main organizer of the Million Man March on Washington in 1995.

Farrar \fə-'rär\, **Geraldine** (1882–1967) U.S. soprano. Born in Melrose, Mass., she received vocal training in New York and Paris and made her debut in C. GOUNOD's *Faust* in 1901. Coached by Lilli Lehmann (1848–1929), she made her Metropolitan Opera debut in 1906, performed in the American premiere of *Madama Butterfly* opposite E. CARUSO (1907), and was later a celebrated Carmen. She retired in 1922.

Farrar, Straus & Giroux \'far-ər-'strau̇s...zhir-'ü\ Publishing company in New York City noted for its literary excellence. It was founded in 1945 by John Farrar and Roger Straus as Farrar, Straus & Co. After various changes in personnel and name, it took its present name in 1964, with the addition of Robert Giroux as editor in chief. The company became established as a leading independent trade publisher of writers of the first rank, including many Nobel and Pulitzer Prize winners. In 1994 a controlling interest was sold to the German publisher Georg von Holtzbrinck.

Farrell \'far-əl\, **James T(homas)** (1904–1979) U.S. novelist and short-story writer. A native of Chicago and a graduate of the University of Chicago, he is known for his realistic portraits of the city's lower-middle-class Irish population, drawn from his own experiences. His well-known *Studs Lonigan* trilogy—*Young Lonigan* (1932), *The Young Manhood of Studs Lonigan* (1934), and *Judgment Day* (1935)—traces the self-destruction of a spiritually crippled young man. He later planned a cycle of 25 novels, of which he completed 10. Of the 25 novels he published, *The Face of Time* (1953) is among the best. He also produced 17 short-story collections.

Farrell, Suzanne *orig.* **Roberta Sue Ficker** (born 1945) U.S. ballet dancer. She was born in Cincinnati. She trained at the School of American Ballet and joined the NEW YORK CITY BALLET at 16, becoming a soloist at 18. She danced many roles created for her by GEORGE BALANCHINE in ballets such as *Meditation, Don Quixote,* and *Slaughter on Tenth Avenue*. After several years as principal dancer with MAURICE BEJART's Ballet of the 20th Century (1970–75), she returned to the City Ballet in 1975 as principal dancer, continuing to create leading roles until she retired in 1989 and joined the faculty of the School of American Ballet.

Farsi language See PERSIAN LANGUAGE

fascia \'fā-shə\ In architecture, a continuous flat band or molding parallel to the surface that it ornaments and either projecting from or slightly receding into it, as in the face of a Classical Greek or Roman ENTABLATURE. Today the term refers to any flat, continuous band, such as that adjacent and perpendicular to a ceiling soffit, the portion of a wall above built-in cabinets, or the outer face of a parapet wall or projecting roof.

fascism \'fa-ˌshi-zəm\ Philosophy of government that stresses the primacy and glory of the state, unquestioning obedience to its leader, subordination of the individual will to the state's authority, and harsh suppression of dissent. Martial virtues are celebrated, while liberal democratic values are denigrated. 20th-century fascism arose partly out of fear of the rising power of the lower classes and differed from contemporary communism (as practiced under JOSEPH STALIN) by its protection of the corporate and landowning powers and preservation of a class system. The fascist governments that ruled Italy (1922–43), Germany (1933–45), and Spain (1939–75) were led by charismatic politicians (BENITO MUSSOLINI, ADOLF HITLER, FRANCISCO FRANCO), who represented to their publics the strength that could rescue their nation from chaotic political and economic conditions. Japanese fascists (1936–45) fostered belief in the uniqueness of the Japanese spirit and reinforced the virtues of subordination to the state and personal sacrifice. See also TOTALITARIANISM.

fashion Any mode of dressing or adornment that is popular during a particular time or in a particular place (i.e., the current style). It can change from one period to the next, from generation to generation. It serves as a reflection of social and economic status, a function that explains the popularity of many styles throughout costume history; in the west, courts have been a major source of fashion. See also DRESS.

Fashoda Incident \fə-'shō-də\ (September 18, 1898) Climax, at Fashoda (now Kodok), Egyptian Sudan, of a series of territorial disputes between Britain and France. Britain had sought to extend its empire from Cairo to the Cape of Good Hope, while France had sought to extend its own from Dakar to the Sudan. A French force under Jean-Baptiste Marchand was the first to arrive at a strategically located fort at Fashoda, soon followed by a British force under Lord KITCHENER. After a tense standoff the French withdrew, but they continued to press claims to other posts in the region. In March 1899 the French and British agreed that the watershed of the Nile and the Congo rivers should mark the frontier between their spheres of influence.

Fassbinder \'fäs-ˌbin-dər\, **Rainer Werner** (1946–1982) German film director. He was involved in the avant-garde theater movement in Munich and helped form the Antitheater (1967). His first full-length film (1969) was followed by 40 others, produced in an astonishingly short period, including *The Bitter Tears of Petra von Kant* (1972), *Effi Briest* (1974), *The Marriage of Maria Braun* (1979), the 15-hour *Berlin Alexanderplatz* (1980), *Lola* (1981), and *Veronika Voss* (1982). Regarded as a leader of the German New Wave, he helped revitalize German cinema in the 1970s and 1980s. Defiantly homosexual and provocative, he led an outrageous life and died from a drug overdose at 36.

fasteners In construction, connectors between structural members. Bolted connections are used when it is necessary to fasten two elements tightly together, especially to resist shear and bending, as in column and beam connections. Threaded metal BOLTS are always used in conjunction with nuts. Another threaded fastener is the SCREW, which has countless applications, especially for wood construction. The wood screw carves a mating thread in the wood, ensuring a tight fit. Pins are used to keep two or more elements in alignment; since the pin is not threaded, it allows for rotational movement, as in machinery parts. Riveted connections, which resist shearing forces, were in wide use for steel construction before being replaced by welding. The rivet, visibly prominent on older steel bridges, is a metal pin fastener with one end flattened into a head by hammering it through a metal gusset plate. The common NAIL, less resistant to shear or pull-out forces, is useful for cabinet and finishing work, where stresses are minimal.

fasting Abstaining from food, usually for religious or ethical reasons. In ancient religions it was used to prepare worshipers or priests to approach deities, to pursue a vision, to demonstrate penance for sins, or to assuage an angered deity. All the major world religions include fasting among their practices. Judaism has several fast days, notably YOM KIPPUR. For Christians LENT is set aside as a 40-day period of penitence before Easter, including the traditional fast days of Ash Wednesday and Good Friday. In Islam the month of RAMADAN is observed as a period of total abstention from food from dawn to dusk. Fasting to make a political protest is often referred to as a hunger strike; hunger strikes have been employed by, among others, 19th-century female suffragists, MOHANDAS K. GANDHI, and late-20th-century Irish nationalists. Moderate fasting is also sometimes practiced for its claimed health benefits.

Fastnachtsspiel \'fäst-ˌnäḵt-ˌshpēl\ Carnival or Shrovetide play that emerged in the 15th century as the first truly secular drama of pre-Reformation Germany. Usually performed on open-air platform stages by amateur actors, students, and artisans, the plays mixed popular comic and religious elements, reflecting the tastes of their predominantly bourgeois audiences. They often contained satirical attacks on greedy clergymen and other traditional dislikes of German burghers, and are believed to have been influenced by pre-Christian folk traditions.

fat Any organic compound of plant or animal origin that is not volatile, does not dissolve in water, and is oily or greasy. Chemically, fats from animals and from vegetables (OILS) are identical, consisting mainly of TRIGLYCERIDES (ESTERS of GLYCEROL with FATTY ACIDS); the differences are in the melting temperature and physical state (solid or liquid) of each, which depends on the SATURATION of the fatty acids and the length of the carbon chain. The glycerides may have only a few component fatty acids or as many as 100 (in butterfat). Almost all natural fats and oils are constructed from two-carbon units and thus contain only fatty acids with an even number of carbon atoms. Natural fats such as corn oil have small amounts of compounds besides triglycerides, including PHOSPHOLIPIDS, plant STEROIDS, tocopherols (VITAMIN E), VITAMIN A, WAXES, carotenoids, and many others, including decomposition products of these. Fats in foods come from ripe seeds and fruits (corn, peanuts, olives, avocados) and from animal sources (meat, eggs, milk). They contain more than twice as much energy (CALORIES) per unit of weight as PROTEINS and CARBOHYDRATES. DIGESTION of fats in foods, often partial, is done by ENZYMES called lipases. The breakdown products are absorbed from the intestines into the blood, which carries microscopic fat droplets reconstituted from digested fats or synthesized in cells to sites of storage or use. Fats are readily broken down, primarily into glycerol and fatty acids, by HYDROLYSIS, a first step for many of their numerous industrial uses. See also LIPID.

Fatah \'fät-ᵊh, *Engl* 'fä-tä\ Inverted acronym of Harakat al-Tahrir al-Watani al-Filastini (Palestine National Liberation Movement), which also means "conquest" in Arabic. Founded by YASIR ARAFAT and Khalil al-Wazir in the late 1950s, the movement relied on guerrilla warfare and occasional acts of terrorism in an attempt to free Palestine from Israeli control. It eventually became the largest faction within the PALESTINE LIBERATION ORGANIZATION and attacked Israeli interests worldwide. Originally based in Damascus, it was forced to relocate several times before a political agreement was reached with Israel in 1993. A number of factions within Fatah were against peace with Israel and split from the main organization. Fatah faced further difficulty in its attempt to transform itself from a liberation movement to a more conventional political organization.

Fates In Greek and Roman mythology, the three goddesses who determined human destiny. The Fates were usually depicted as old women: Clotho, the Spinner; Lachesis, the Allotter; and Atropos, the Inflexible. Clotho spun the thread of human life, Lachesis dispensed it, and Atropos cut the thread. They determined the length of each person's life as well as its share of suffering. Their Roman names were Nona, Decuma, and Morta.

Father's Day See MOTHER'S DAY AND FATHER'S DAY

fatigue In engineering, manifestation of progressive FRACTURE in a solid under cyclic loading, as in the case of a metal strip that ruptures after repeated bending back and forth (see METAL FATIGUE). Fatigue fracture begins with one or several cracks that spread in the course of repeated application of forces until complete rupture suddenly occurs when the small unaffected portion is too weak to sustain the load. See also DUCTILITY, TESTING MACHINE.

Fatima *or* **Fatimah** \'fa-tə-mə\ (c. 605–633) Daughter of MUHAMMAD and the object of veneration in SHIITE Islam. In 622 she emigrated with her father from Mecca to Medina, where she married her cousin ALI. Their sons HASAN and al-HUSAYN IBN ALI are considered by Shiites the rightful inheritors of the tradition of Muhammad. Fatima's marriage was unhappy, but she and her husband were reconciled by the Prophet, and she cared for her father in his last illness (632). She clashed with his successor, ABU BAKR, over property and died a year later. Later tradition added to the majesty of her life, and the FATIMID DYNASTY derived its name from hers.

Fátima \'fa-tə-mə\ Village in central Portugal, site of a shrine dedicated to the Virgin MARY. From May to October 1917, three peasant children reported a vision of a woman who identified herself as the Lady of the Rosary. On October 13, a crowd of about 70,000 witnessed an amazing solar phenomenon just after the children had seen their vision. The first national pilgrimage to the site occurred in 1927. Construction of a basilica started in 1928; now flanked by retreat houses and hospitals, it faces a square where many miraculous cures have been reported.

Fatimid dynasty \'fa-tə-məd\ (909–1171) Political and religious Ismaili Shiite dynasty of North Africa and the Middle East. Its members traced their descent from FATIMA. As Shii Muslims, they opposed the Sunni ABBASID caliphate, which they were determined to supplant. From Yemen they expanded into North Africa and Sicily, and in 909 their imam emerged to proclaim the new dynasty. The first four Fatimid caliphs ruled from Tunisia, but the conquest of Egypt in 969 occasioned the building of a new capital, Cairo. At its height, the dynasty controlled Mecca and Medina, Syria, Palestine, and Africa's Red Sea coast. Seeking to overthrow the Abbasids, the Fatimids maintained a network of missionaries and agents in Abbasid territories. In 1057–59 the Fatimid caliph was briefly proclaimed in Baghdad, the Abbasid capital, but Fatimid fortunes declined thereafter, Ismaili Shiism ultimately proving unacceptable to Sunni Muslims. Attacks by crusaders, Turks, and Byzantines and factionalism in the armed forces weakened the caliphate, and the rise of the ASSASSINS sealed its fate. The last caliph died in 1171. See also SALADIN.

fatty acid Organic compound that is an important component of LIPIDS in plants, animals, and microorganisms. Fatty acids are CARBOXYLIC ACIDS with a long HYDROCARBON chain, usually straight, as the fourth substituent group on the carboxyl (—COOH) group (see FUNCTIONAL GROUP) that makes the molecule an acid. If the carbon-to-carbon bonds (see BONDING) in that chain are all single, the fatty acid is saturated; artificial SATURATION is called HYDROGENATION. A fatty acid with one double bond is monounsaturated; one with more is polyunsaturated. These are more reactive chemically. Most unsaturated fats are liquid at room temperature, so food manufacturers hydrogenate them to make them solid (see MARGARINE). A high level of saturated fatty acids in the diet raises blood CHOLESTEROL levels. A few fatty acids have branched chains. Others (e.g., PROSTAGLANDINS) contain ring structures. Fatty acids in nature are always combined, usually with GLYCEROL as TRIGLYCERIDES in FATS. Oleic acid (unsaturated, with 18 carbon atoms) is almost half of human fat and is abundant in such oils as olive, palm, and peanut. Most animals, including mammals, cannot synthesize some unsaturated "essential" fatty acids; humans need linoleic, linolenic, and arachidonic acids in their diet.

fatty tissue See ADIPOSE TISSUE

Faulhaber \'fau̇l-ˌhä-bər\, **Michael von** (1869–1952) German religious leader and prominent opponent of the Nazis. Ordained in 1892, he was bishop of Speyer before becoming cardinal and Munich's archbishop. In 1923 he contributed to the failure of ADOLF HITLER'S BEER HALL PUTSCH. During the Nazi regime he delivered the famous sermons later published as *Judaism, Christianity, and Germany* (1934), which emphasized the Jewish background of Christianity and asserted that Christian values were fundamental to German culture. Despite attempts on his life, he vigorously criticized Nazism in his sermons until the collapse of the Third Reich. After the war, he received West Germany's highest award.

Faulkner \'fȯk-nər\, **William (Cuthbert)** *orig.* **William Cuthbert Falkner** (1897–1962) U.S. writer. Born in New Albany, Miss., he dropped out of high school and only briefly attended college. He spent most of his life in Oxford, Miss. He is best known for his cycle of works set in fictional Yoknapatawpha Co., which becomes an emblem of the American South and its tragic history. His first major novel, *The Sound and the Fury* (1929), was marked by radical technical experimentation, including stream of consciousness. His American reputation, which lagged behind his European reputation, was boosted by *As I Lay Dying* (1930), *Light in August* (1932), *Absalom, Absalom!* (1936), and *Go Down, Moses* (1942), which contains the story "The Bear." *The Portable Faulkner* (1946) finally brought his work into wide circulation, and he won the Nobel Prize in 1949. His *Collected Stories* (1950) won the National Book Award. He also wrote movie scripts, a play, and two volumes of poems. Both in the U.S. and abroad, especially in Latin America, he was among the most influential writers of the 20th century.

fault In geology, a fracture in the rocks of the earth's crust, where compressional or tensional forces cause the rocks on the opposite sides of the fracture to be displaced relative to each other. Faults range in length from a few inches to hundreds of miles, and displacement may also range from less than an inch to hundreds of miles along the fracture surface (the fault plane). Most, if not all, EARTHQUAKES are caused by rapid movement along faults. Faults are common throughout the world. A well-known example is the San Andreas Fault near the western coast of the U.S. The total movement along this fault during the last few million years appears to have been several miles.

fauna All the species of animals found in a particular region, period, or special environment. Five faunal realms, based on terrestrial animal species, are generally recognized: Holarctic, including Nearactic (North

America) and Paleartic (Eurasia and northern Africa); Paleotropical (tropical Africa and S.East Asia); Neotropical (Central and South America); Australian; and Antarctic.

faunal succession, law of Observation that taxonomic groups of animals follow each other in time in a predictable manner. Sequences of successive strata and their corresponding fauna have been matched to form a composite picture detailing the history of the earth, especially from the beginning of the CAMBRIAN PERIOD. Faunal succession is the fundamental tool of STRATIGRAPHY and is the basis for the geologic time scale. Floral (plant) succession is also an important tool. Climate and conditions throughout the earth's history can be studied using the successive groups because living organisms reflect their environment.

Faunus \'fȯ-nəs\ Ancient Italian rural deity, the Roman counterpart of the Greek god PAN. The grandson of SATURN, he was depicted as half-man, half-goat, like a satyr. He was first worshiped as a god who bestowed fertility on fields and flocks, but he ended as a woodland deity. His companions were known as fauns.

Faure \'fōr\, **(François-) Félix** (1841–1899) President of the French THIRD REPUBLIC (1895–99). A successful industrialist in Le Havre, he was elected to the Chamber of Deputies (1881). After serving in several cabinet posts, he was elected president of France in an unexpected victory that was a rebuff to the political left. He opposed reopening the case of ALFRED DREYFUS, the dominating issue of his presidency, and his position encouraged agitation from both left and right political factions. He died suddenly, and his funeral was the scene of a confrontation between pro- and anti-Dreyfus groups.

Fauré \fō-'rā\, **Gabriel (Urbain)** (1845–1924) French composer. Born into the minor aristocracy, he enrolled at age 9 in a Paris music school, where he studied with C. SAINT-SAENS and remained 11 years. He held the prestigious organist positions at the churches of St. Sulpice (1871–74) and the Madeleine (1896–1905). In 1896 he also became professor of composition at the Paris Conservatoire, where he taught such students as M. RAVEL and NADIA BOULANGER. He served as its director 1905–20. In 1909 he accepted the presidency of the Société Musicale Indépendante, a group of dissident young composers. His works include the operas *Prométhée* (1900), *Pénélope* (1913), and *Masques et bergamasques* (1919), the orchestral suite *Pelléas et Mélisande* (1898), two piano quartets (1879, 1886), numerous piano *Nocturnes* and *Barcarolles,* a famous *Requiem* (1900), and many beautiful songs.

Gabriel Fauré, portrait by J.S. Sargent; in a private collection.

GIRAUDON–ART RESOURCE/EB INC.

Fauset \'fō-sət\, **Jessie Redmon** (1882–1961) U.S. novelist, critic, poet, and editor. Born in Snow Hill, N.J., she studied at Cornell and the University of Pennsylvania. As literary editor of *The Crisis* (1919–26), she discovered and encouraged writers of the HARLEM RENAISSANCE, including LANGSTON HUGHES, COUNTEE CULLEN, CLAUDE MCKAY, and Jean Toomer. In her own works, including her best-known novel, *Comedy: American Style* (1933), she portrayed mostly middle-class black characters forced to deal with self-hate as well as racial prejudice.

Faust \'faůst\ Legendary German necromancer or astrologer who sold his soul to the devil for knowledge and power. There was a historical Faust (perhaps two; both died c. 1540), who traveled widely performing magic, referred to the devil as his crony, and had a wide reputation for evil. The *Faustbuch* (1587), a collection of tales purportedly by Faust, told of such reputed wizards as MERLIN and ALBERTUS MAGNUS. It was widely translated; an English version inspired CHRISTOPHER MARLOWE's *Tragicall History of D. Faustus* (1604), which emphasized Faust's eternal damnation. Magic manuals bearing Faust's name did a brisk business; the classic *Magia naturalis et innaturalis* was known to JOHANN W. VON GOETHE, who, like GOTTHOLD LESSING, saw Faust's pursuit of knowledge as noble; in Goethe's great *Faust* the hero is redeemed. Inspired by Goethe, many artists took up the story, including H. BERLIOZ (in the dramatic cantata *The Damnation of Faust*) and C. GOUNOD (in the opera *Faust*).

Faust, detail from the title page of the 1616 edition of *The Tragicall History of D. Faustus,* by Christopher Marlowe.

BY COURTESY OF THE TRUSTEES OF THE BRITISH LIBRARY; PHOTOGRAPH, R.B. FLEMING

Fauvism \'fō-ˌvi-zəm\ Style of painting that flourished in France c. 1898–1908, characterized by the use of intensely vivid color and turbulent emotionalism. The dominant figure of the group was HENRI MATISSE; others were ANDRE DERAIN, MAURICE DE VLAMINCK, RAOUL DUFY, GEORGES BRAQUE, and GEORGES ROUAULT. The name derives from the judgment of a critic who visited their first exhibit in Paris (1905) and referred to them disparagingly as "les fauves" ("wild beasts"). They were influenced by the masters of POSTIMPRESSIONISM, VINCENT VAN GOGH and PAUL GAUGUIN. Fauvism was a transitional phase for most of the artists, who by 1908, having renewed their interest in PAUL CEZANNE's vision of order and structure, abandoned Fauvism for CUBISM. Matisse alone continued on the course he had pioneered.

favela \fə-'ve-lə\ In Brazil, a slum or shantytown. A favela gets its start when squatters occupy vacant land at the edge of a city and construct shanties of salvaged or stolen materials. Communities form over time, often developing an array of social and religious organizations and forming associations to obtain such services as running water and electricity. Sometimes the *favelados* manage to gain title to the land and then are able to improve their homes. Because of crowding, unsanitary conditions, poor nutrition, and pollution, disease is rampant in the poorer favelas and infant mortality rates are high.

Fawkes, Guy (1570–1606) British conspirator. A convert to Roman Catholicism and a religious zealot, Fawkes joined the Spanish army in the Netherlands in 1593 and became noted for his military skill. In 1604 he was enlisted by the Catholic leaders of a plot to blow up the Parliament building. When details of the GUNPOWDER PLOT were discovered, Fawkes was arrested. After being tortured to reveal the names of his accomplices, he was tried and executed in 1606, opposite the building. The proposed date of the explosion, November 5, is celebrated as Guy Fawkes Day with fireworks, masked children begging "a penny for the guy," and the burning of Fawkes's effigy.

fax *in full* **facsimile** Device for the transmission and reproduction of documents by digitized signals sent over telephone lines. Fax machines scan printed text and graphics and convert the image into a digital code: 1 for dark areas, 0 for white areas. The code is transmitted through the telephone network to similar devices, where the documents are reproduced in close to their original form. Though the concepts for fax technology were developed in the 19th century, widespread use did not occur until the 1970s, when inexpensive means of adapting digitized information to telephone circuits became common.

Faxa Bay \'fäk-sä\ Inlet of the northern Atlantic Ocean, southwestern coast of Iceland. At 30 mi (50 km) deep and 50 mi (80 km) long, it is the largest in Iceland. The main ports along the bay are Akranes and REYKJAVÍK, Iceland's capital. A U.S. air base is at Keflavík on the southern shore.

Faxian *or* **Fa-hsien** \'fä-'shyen\ *orig.* **Sehi** (5th century AD) Chinese Buddhist monk who initiated relations with India. Eager to learn of his religion at its source, he traveled to India in 402 and spent a decade visiting the major Buddhist shrines and seats of learning, especially sites in eastern India, including Kapilavastu, Bodh Gaya, and Pataliputra. He deepened his knowledge by conversing with monks and gathered sacred texts that had not yet been translated into Chinese. He returned to China by sea in 412, after spending two years in Ceylon. His *Record of Buddhist Kingdoms* contains valuable information about Indian Buddhism in this era.

fayd \'fīd\ In Islamic philosophy, the emanation of created things from God. The term is not used in the Quran, but Muslim philosophers such as al-FARABI and AVICENNA borrowed the notion from NEOPLATONISM. They conceived of creation as a gradual process arising from God's superabundance. Creation begins at the most perfect level, God, and descends

E F G

through the world of the spirit to the least perfect level, the world of matter. The *fayd* theory was refuted by al-GHAZALI in the 11th century.

FDA See FOOD AND DRUG ADMINISTRATION

feather Component structure of the outer covering and flight surfaces of all modern birds. Unique to birds, feathers apparently evolved from the scales of birds' reptilian ancestors. Feathers are variously specialized for insulation, flight, formation of body contours, display, and sensory reception. Unlike the hair of most mammals, feathers do not cover the entire skin surface of birds but are arranged in symmetrical tracts alternating with areas of bare skin, which may contain the small, soft feathers called down. A typical feather consists of a central shaft (rachis), with serial paired branches (barbs) forming a flattened, usually curved surface—the vane. The barbs possess further branches, the barbules, and the barbules of adjacent barbs are attached to one another by hooks, stiffening the vane.

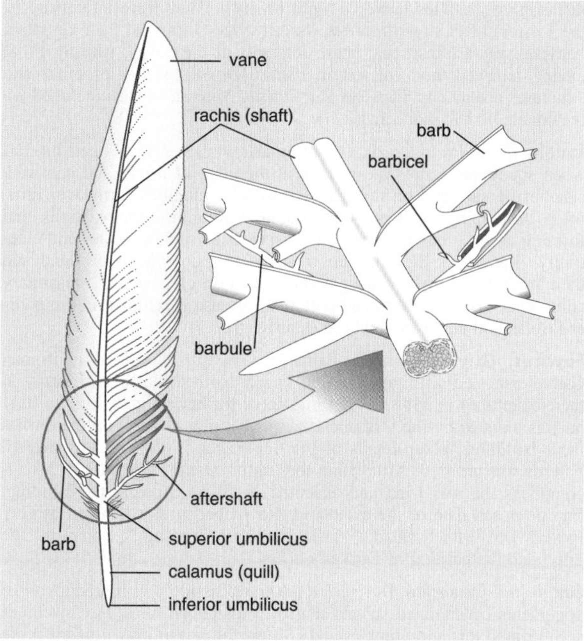

General features of a contour feather, with an enlarged view.

feather star Any of the 550 living species of crinoid ECHINODERMS (class Crinoidea) that lack the stalk that their relatives the sea lilies use to attach themselves to the ocean bottom. Most species have five feathery-fringed arms. Feather stars usually attach themselves to a surface or a floating object and feed on drifting microorganisms, trapping them in their sticky arm grooves. They live mainly on rocky bottoms in shallow water. Most abundant from the Indian Ocean to Japan, they are also found in the Atlantic.

Feather star (*Comantheria grandicalyx*).

featherbedding LABOR-UNION practices that require the employer to pay for the performance of unnecessary work or to employ workers who are not needed. Featherbedding provisions in labor contracts may result from the continuation of work rules that were once efficient but that have become obsolete because of changed technology. A union may insist on the continuation of such work rules to protect the job security of its members. See also COLLECTIVE BARGAINING.

February Revolution (1848) Rioting in France that led to the overthrow of the JULY MONARCHY and precipitated the REVOLUTIONS OF 1848. The years 1840–49 brought a flowering of socialist thought by CHARLES FOURIER, P.-J. PROUDHON, and others that fueled urban workers' discontent. A major recession in 1846–47 added to popular unrest, as did the increasing arbitrariness of the rule of King LOUIS-PHILIPPE. An opposition campaign brought police action, and crowds of students and workers gathered in the streets and clashed with police. The king tried to appease the demonstrators, but when an army unit killed 40 of them he abdicated rather than face civil war.

feces \ˈfē-ˌsēz\ *or* **excrement** *or* **stools** Solid bodily waste discharged from the COLON through the anus during DEFECATION. Normal feces are 75% water. The rest is about 30% dead BACTERIA, 30% indigestible food matter, 10–20% CHOLESTEROL and other FATS, 10–20% inorganic substances, and 2–3% PROTEIN. The color and odor are produced by bacterial action on chemical constituents. Many disorders produce abnormalities in the feces, usually constipation or DIARRHEA. Bleeding in the stomach or intestines may show up as dark red to black stools. Tests are needed to detect small amounts (occult blood). High fat content usually indicates disease of the pancreas or small intestine. Many diseases are spread by contamination of food with feces of infected persons.

Fechner \ˈfek̲-nər, *Engl* ˈfek-nər\, **Gustav Theodor** (1801–1887) German physicist and philosopher who founded the science of PSYCHOPHYSICS. He taught at the University of Leipzig (1834–40) but left because of ill health. He developed experimental procedures, still useful in experimental psychology, for measuring sensations in relation to the physical magnitude of stimuli, establishing that, as physical stimulation increases logarithmically, sensation increases arithmetically. Most important, he devised an equation to express WEBER'S LAW. His principal scientific work was *Elements of Psychophysics* (1860).

Federal Bureau of Investigation (FBI) Largest investigative agency of the U.S. government. It was founded in 1908 as the Bureau of Investigation within the U.S. Justice Department. J. EDGAR HOOVER was named its director in 1924 and served for 48 years. Since 1968 its director, who reports to the attorney general, has been appointed by the president for a 10-year term, subject to Senate approval. It now has 6,000–7,000 special agents. Its responsibilities include investigating violations of federal criminal law (including civil-rights and organized-crime cases), collecting evidence in civil cases to which the U.S. is a party, and providing internal security.

Federal Communications Commission (FCC) Independent U.S. agency. Established in 1934, it regulates interstate and foreign communications by radio, television, wire, satellite, and cable. Its standards and regulations apply only to the technical aspects, including frequency and equipment, of communication systems, not broadcast content (apart from certain rules covering obscenity and slander).

Federal Deposit Insurance Corp. (FDIC) Independent U.S. government corporation created to insure bank deposits against loss in the event of a bank failure and to regulate certain banking practices. Established after the bank holiday in early 1933, the FDIC was intended to restore public confidence in the system. It insures bank deposits in eligible banks up to $100,000 for each deposit. All members of the FEDERAL RESERVE SYSTEM are required to insure their deposits with the FDIC, and almost all COMMERCIAL BANKS in the U.S. choose to do so.

Federal Reserve System U.S. CENTRAL BANK system consisting of 12 Federal Reserve districts with a Reserve bank in the principal commercial city of each district. The system is supervised by a board of governors in Washington, D.C., as well as various advisory councils and committees. As a result of the Federal Reserve Act of 1913, all NATIONAL BANKS are required to join the system; state banks may join if they meet membership qualifications. The Federal Reserve is responsible for MONETARY POLICY. The original act set fixed reserve requirements for the U.S. FRACTIONAL RESERVE BANKING SYSTEM. It allowed each district bank to determine its DISCOUNT RATE, the rate it charged on loans to member banks. The modern Federal Reserve resulted from the Federal Reserve Act of 1935, which allowed the board to determine reserve requirements within defined limits. It became responsible for approving the discount rates of the district banks. Most importantly, the act created the Federal Reserve

Open Market Committee, which is responsible for conducting operations in financial markets that increase or decrease the amount of reserves in the system. If the Federal Reserve wants to ease monetary policy, it will use OPEN-MARKET OPERATIONS and increase the amount of reserves through the purchase of financial assets. Conversely, it can tighten monetary policy through the sale of financial assets.

Federal style Neoclassical style of American architecture and interior design that flourished 1785–1820 (later in governmental buildings) and was influenced by the GEORGIAN STYLE and the work of James and ROBERT ADAM. Inspired by the Roman republic, which the new nation believed it resembled, it was especially associated with THOMAS JEFFERSON and BENJAMIN H. LATROBE. Characteristics include shallow arches, slender proportions, delicate decoration, and symmetry; entrances are often framed by columns and pediments, with a fanlight over the door. The University of Virginia (1817–26) was Jefferson's greatest Federal-style project.

Federal Trade Commission (FTC) Independent U.S. agency charged with preventing unfair or deceptive trade practices. It regulates advertising, marketing, and consumer credit practices, and also prevents antitrust agreements and other unfair practices. Though it has no authority to punish violators, it can monitor compliance with trade laws, conduct legal investigations, issue cease-and-desist orders, convene public hearings, file civil suits in U.S. district courts, and ensure that court orders are followed.

federalism Political system that binds a group of states into a larger, noncentralized, superior state while allowing its constituent members to maintain their own political identities. Certain characteristics and principles are common to all successful federal systems: a written constitution or basic law stipulating the distribution of powers; diffusion of power among the constituent elements, which are substantially self-sustaining; and territorial divisions to ensure neutrality and equality in the representation of various groups and interests. Changes require the consent of those affected. Successful federal systems also have a sense of common nationality and direct lines of communication between the citizens and all the governments that serve them. See also *The* FEDERALIST, FEDERALIST PARTY.

Federalist, The Eighty-five essays on the proposed U.S. CONSTITUTION and the nature of republican government, published in 1787–88 by ALEXANDER HAMILTON, JAMES MADISON, and JOHN JAY in an effort to persuade New York State voters to support ratification. Most first appeared serially in New York newspapers, were reprinted in other states, and then published as a book in 1788; a few were issued separately later. All were signed "Publius." They presented a masterly exposition of the federal system and the means of attaining the ideals of justice, general welfare, and rights of individuals.

Federalist Party Early U.S. political party that advocated a strong central government. "Federalist" was first used in 1787 to describe supporters of the U.S. CONSTITUTION, with its emphasis on a federal union; the *Federalist Papers* was a series of 85 papers (1787–88) published by ALEXANDER HAMILTON, JAMES MADISON, and JOHN JAY to persuade New York voters to ratify the Constitution. By the 1790s other policies defined the party, including Hamilton's fiscal program, creation of a central bank, a tariff system, favorable treatment for U.S. shipping, friendship with Britain, and neutrality in foreign affairs. It elected JOHN ADAMS as president in 1796 but was unable to organize effectively after 1801. It lost favor for its opposition to the EMBARGO ACT and the WAR OF 1812; an internal split by the New England faction (see HARTFORD CONVENTION) further weakened the party. By the 1820s most of its original principles had been adopted by the opposition Democratic Party, and the Federalist Party disappeared. Notable Federalists included JOHN MARSHALL, RUFUS KING, TIMOTHY PICKERING, and CHARLES PINCKNEY.

fee In law, an inheritable FREEHOLD estate in real property (see REAL AND PERSONAL PROPERTY). The word derives from FIEF, as used in feudal law. Modern property law includes several varieties of fee, including fee simple (alienable and of indefinite duration), fee tail (granted to an individual and his or her descendants but subject to reversion if a tenant dies with no descendants), and life fee or life estate (held only during the lifetime of the grantee).

feed Foodstuff grown or developed for LIVESTOCK and POULTRY to maintain the health of the animals and increase the quality of such end products as meat, milk, or eggs. Modern feeds are derived from crops grown specifically for research or from by-products of surplus crops or foods produced for human consumption. Feeds are categorized as either concentrates (high in digestibility of nutrients but low in fiber content) or roughages (high in fiber and comparatively low in digestive nutrients). Most diets consist of a combination of feeds.

feedback inhibition Suppression of the activity of an ENZYME by a product of the sequence of reactions in which the enzyme is participating. When the product accumulates in a cell beyond an optimal amount, it decreases its own production by inhibiting an enzyme involved in its synthesis. After the product has been used or broken down, inhibition is relaxed and formation of the product resumes. Enzymes whose ability to catalyze a reaction depends on molecules other than the substances on which they act directly are said to be under ALLOSTERIC CONTROL.

feeding behavior Any action of an animal directed toward obtaining nutrients. Each species evolves methods of searching for, obtaining, and ingesting food for which it can successfully compete. Some species eat only one type of food; others eat a variety. Among invertebrates food choices are instinctual; among vertebrates they are learned.

Feiffer, Jules (born 1929) U.S. cartoonist and dramatist. Born in New York City, Feiffer learned his trade while assisting comic-strip artists. He became famous for "Feiffer," a satirical strip whose verbal elements are usually monologues in which the speaker (sometimes pathetic, sometimes pompous) exposes his or her own insecurities. His drawings, syndicated from 1959, are collected in books beginning with *Sick, Sick, Sick* (1958). In 1986 he received a Pulitzer Prize. His plays, including *Little Murders* (1967; film, 1971), also blend farce and social criticism. His other works include novels, screenplays (including *Carnal Knowledge,* 1971), and, in the 1990s, children's books.

Feininger \'fī-niŋ-ər\, **Andreas (Bernhard Lyonel)** (1906–1999) French-U.S. photographer and writer. Son of LYONEL FEININGER, he graduated from the BAUHAUS in 1925. After studying architecture, he moved to Sweden in 1933 and established a firm specializing in architectural and industrial photography. In 1939 he settled in New York, and from 1943 to 1962 he worked for *Life* magazine. Among his many books are *The Complete Photographer* (1966) and the collection *The World Through My Eyes* (1964).

Feininger \'fī-niŋ-ər\, **Lyonel (Charles Adrian)** (1871–1956) U.S.-German painter. Born in New York City, he went to Germany in 1887 to study music, but ended up studying painting instead. Around 1910, under the influence of Cubism, he developed a unique style, using prismatic interpenetrating planes of color to depict architectural and marine subjects. He exhibited with Der BLAUE REITER in Berlin in 1913 and was later an influential teacher at the BAUHAUS (1919–33). His work was a synthesis of art, science, and technology; he is noted for introducing compositional discipline and lyrical color to German Expressionism. After the Nazis came to power, he returned to the U.S. He was the father of ANDREAS FEININGER.

feldspar Any of a group of aluminosilicate (containing aluminum and silicon) minerals that also contains calcium, sodium, or potassium. Feldspars are the most common minerals in the earth's CRUST and are the major component in nearly all IGNEOUS ROCKS found on the earth, on the moon, and in some meteorites. They also are common in metamorphic and some sedimentary rocks. Their complex chemical and structural properties make them useful for interpreting the origins of rocks. Natural feldspars can be divided into ALKALI and PLAGIOCLASE feldspars.

feldspar, alkali See ALKALI FELDSPAR

feldspathoid \feld-'spath-ˌȯid\ Any of a group of alkali aluminosilicate minerals similar to the FELDSPARS in composition but having a lower silica-alkali ratio or containing chloride, sulfide, sulfate, or carbonate. Their physical and chemical properties lie between those of the feldspars and ZEOLITES. The most abundant feldspathoids are nepheline and leucite. Other significant varieties include kalsilite, sodalite, nosean, and haüynite. Feldspathoids are found chiefly in igneous and metamorphic rocks; they are used as raw materials in the production of alum, glass, and ceramics.

Feller, Bob *orig.* **Robert William Andrew** (born 1918) U.S. baseball pitcher. Born in Van Meter, Iowa, he played for the Cleveland Indians from 1936 to 1956, frequently leading the American League in strikeouts and games won, earning the nickname "Rapid Robert" for his fastball. He was the first 20th-century pitcher to pitch three no-hit games (1940, 1946, 1951), and his record of 348 season strikeouts (1946) stood for 19 years. He ended his career with the outstanding won-loss record of 266–162.

Fellini, Federico (1920–1993) Italian film director. After collaborating with ROBERTO ROSSELLINI on the screenplays for *Open City* (1945) and *Paisan* (1946), he undertook his first solo venture in 1952. It failed, but his next film, *I vitelloni* (1953), was a critical success. He won international acclaim with *La strada* (1954, Academy Award), *The Nights of Cabiria* (1957, Academy Award), and *La dolce vita* (1960). He continued his distinctive autobiographical style of filmmaking—a kind of poetic surrealism that displayed a sympathetic fascination with the bizarre—in *8½* (1963, Academy Award), but turned to gaudy spectacle in *Juliet of the Spirits* (1965) and *Fellini Satyricon* (1969). The best of his later films were *Amarcord* (1973, Academy Award) and the nostalgic *Ginger and Fred* (1985). His wife, Giulietta Masina (1920–1994), starred in several of his films. He was awarded a special Academy Award for lifetime achievement in 1992.

Federico Fellini, 1965.
PARIS MATCH—PICTORIAL PARADE

felony and misdemeanor In Anglo-American law, two categories of criminal offense. A crime is classed as one or the other according to its seriousness. In U.S. law, a felony is typically defined as a crime punishable by a term of imprisonment of not less than one year. Misdemeanors are often defined as offenses punishable only by fines or by short terms of imprisonment in local jails. Crimes in England are classified into indictable offenses (which may be tried by a jury) and summary offenses (which may be tried by a judge without juries). Codes in Europe distinguish offenses of greater dangerousness from lesser crimes.

felsic rock IGNEOUS ROCK dominated by the light-colored, silicon- and aluminum-rich minerals FELDSPAR and QUARTZ. The presence of these minerals gives felsic rock its characteristic light gray color. The presence of small amounts of dark minerals rich in magnesium and iron produces slight color variations. Typical felsic rocks include granite and rhyolite.

felting See FULLING

female circumcision See CLITORIDECTOMY

feminism Social movement that seeks equal rights for women. Widespread concern for women's rights dates from the ENLIGHTENMENT; its first important expression was MARY WOLLSTONECRAFT's *A Vindication of the Rights of Woman* (1792). The 1848 SENECA FALLS CONVENTION, convened by ELIZABETH CADY STANTON, LUCRETIA MOTT, and others, called for full legal equality with men, including full educational opportunity and equal compensation, and the WOMEN'S SUFFRAGE MOVEMENT began to gather momentum. From America the movement spread to Europe. American women gained the right to vote by constitutional amendment in 1920, but their participation in the workplace remained limited, and prevailing notions tended to confine women to the home. Milestones in the rise of modern feminism included SIMONE DE BEAUVOIR's *The Second Sex* (1949) and BETTY FRIEDAN's *The Feminine Mystique* (1963) and the founding in 1966 of the NATIONAL ORGANIZATION FOR WOMEN. See also EQUAL RIGHTS AMENDMENT, WOMEN'S LIBERATION MOVEMENT.

feminist philosophy Philosophical movement that criticizes, and seeks to redress, the exclusion of women and women's concerns from the academic discipline, the historical canon, and the traditional problematic of philosophy and other endeavors. Feminist philosophy has drawn attention to the very important question of the relevance of gender to philosophy. Feminist philosophers argue that traditional philosophical notions such as rationality and objectivity incorporate an inherent gender bias because they represent a specifically male point of view that does not do justice to female perspectives on the same issues. An important issue is that of defining such key concepts as female, feminine, and woman.

Fen River River, SHANXI province, northern China. After rising in the Guancen Mountains in northwestern Shanxi, it flows southeast to Taiyuan and then southwest through the central valley of Shanxi to join the HUANG near Hejin. Its total length is about 340 mi (550 km). With a torrential course and steep gradients, it is a useful waterway only in its lower reaches. Its valley was an early center of civilization and has remained an important route, linking the BEIJING area with the strategically vital Shanxi province and the major land routes to Central Asia.

fencing Sport involving attack and defense with a light sword, specifically a foil, épée, or saber that has a covered point. There is evidence of swordplay in ancient times, but it died out during the Middle Ages. In the 14th century swordplay became important both in war and the European gentleman's daily life, and by the 15th century guilds of fencing masters had formed. Strokes that were originally jealously guarded secrets of the individual guilds eventually became orthodox fencing moves. By the later 17th century, various rules and conventions had been imposed. In modern competition, hits are made with the point only, except in saber matches, and, in matches using épées, are restricted to certain areas of the body. Defense is effected by the blade. Each valid hit scores one or more points, depending on which part of the opponent's body is struck. Men's fencing was included in the first modern Olympic Games in 1896, women's in the 1924 games. Electrical scoring was introduced in 1936 to eliminate the frequent inaccuracy of human judgment.

Fénelon \fān-ˈlō^{n}\, **François de Salignac de La Mothe-** (1651–1715) French archbishop, theologian, and man of letters. Though generally conservative, his *The Education of Young Gentlewomen* (1687), based on his experience directing a women's college, supported liberal education and argued against coercing Protestants to convert. As tutor to a grandson of Louis XIV, he composed his best-known work, the novel *Les aventures de Télémaque* (1699), but the political ideas it seemed to express offended Louis, who banished him from the court. He was similarly condemned by the church for his leanings toward Quietism, which emphasized spiritual passivity. Fénelon's beliefs. His liberal views on politics and education exerted a lasting influence on French culture.

Feng shui \ˈfəŋ-ˈshwā\ Traditional Chinese method of arranging the human and social world in auspicious alignment with the forces of the cosmos, including QI and YIN-YANG. It was devised during the HAN DYNASTY (206 BC–AD 220). Specialists, called diviners, use compasslike instruments to determine the exact cosmic forces affecting a site, appropriate sites being chosen particularly in relation to bodies of water and mountains. Feng shui, especially as it affects interior design, has recently become popular in Britain and the U.S.

fenghuang *or* **feng-huang** \ˈfəŋ-ˈhwäŋ\ (Chinese: "phoenix") In Chinese mythology, a creature whose rare appearances portend a great event or indicate the greatness of a ruler. The female counterpart of the male dragon, the fenghuang has the breast of a goose, the hindquarters of a stag, the neck of a snake, the tail of a fish, the forehead of a fowl, the back of a tortoise, the face of a swallow, and the beak of a cock. It was reportedly about 9 ft (2.5 m) high. Legend tells of its appearance before the death of the Yellow Emperor in the 3rd millennium BC.

Fenian cycle \ˈfē-nē-ən\ *or* **Fionn cycle** \ˈfin\ *or* **Ossianic cycle** Irish tales and ballads centering on the deeds of the legendary Finn MacCumhaill (MacCool) and his war band, the Fianna Éireann. An elite volunteer corps of warriors and huntsmen skilled in poetry, the Fianna flourished in the 3rd century. Fenian lore attained its greatest popularity c. 1200, when its outstanding story, *The Colloquy of the Old Men,* was written down. The cycle remains a vital part of Irish folklore and contains many of the country's best-loved folktales.

Fenian movement Irish nationalist society active chiefly in Ireland, the U.S., and Britain, especially in the 1860s. The name derived from the Fianna Éireann, a legendary band of Irish warriors led by FINN MACCUMHAILL. Plans for a rising against British rule in Ireland miscarried, but in the U.S., Fenians staged abortive raids into British Canada and caused friction between the U.S. and British governments. The Irish wing was sometimes called the Irish Republican Brotherhood, and as such continued after Fenianism died out in the early 1870s. See also SINN FÉIN.

fennec \ˈfe-nik\ Desert-dwelling FOX *(Fennecus zerda)* found in northern Africa and the Sinai and Arabian peninsulas. It is small (head and body length of 14–16 in., or 36–41 cm), weighs about 3.5 lbs (1.5 kg), and has large ears (6 in., or 15 cm, or more in length). It has long, thick, whitish to sand-colored fur and a black-tipped tail 7–12 in. (18–31 cm) long. Mainly nocturnal, it spends most of the day underground in its burrow. It feeds on insects, small animals, and fruit.

Fennec (*Fennecus zerda*).

ANTHONY MERCIECA—THE NATIONAL AUDUBON SOCIETY COLLECTION/PHOTO RESEARCHERS

fennel Perennial or biennial aromatic herb *(Foeniculum vulgare)* of the PARSLEY family, native to southern Europe and Asia Minor and widely cultivated. The greenish-brown to yellowish-brown oblong oval seeds smell and taste similar to ANISE. The seeds and extracted oil are used for scenting soaps and perfumes and for flavoring candies, liqueurs, medicines, and foods, particularly pastries, sweet pickles, and fish. The thickened base of Florence fennel (*F. vulgare dulce*) is eaten as a vegetable.

Fenrir \ˈfen-rər\ In Norse mythology, a monstrous wolf. He was the son of the god LOKI and a giantess. The gods bound Fenrir to a rock with a magical chain, where he is destined to remain until doomsday, or RAGNAROK, when he will break his chains and fall upon the gods. In one version of the myth, he will devour the sun and swallow the chief god, ODIN, only to be slain by Vidar, Odin's son. Fenrir figures prominently in Norwegian and Icelandic poetry of the 10th–11th century.

Fenton, Roger (1819–1869) British photographer. In 1853 he helped found the Royal Photographic Society of London. In 1854 he was appointed the government's official photographer and sent to document the Crimean War. He shot some 360 photographs of the war; they largely represent a glorified overview, showing very little of the real action or agony of war. On his return he exhibited successfully in London and Paris. His reputation was built on his still lifes and landscapes, which were extremely popular in the Victorian era.

fenugreek \ˈfen-yə-ˌgrēk\ Slender, annual, herbaceous legume *(Trigonella foenum-graecum)* or its dried seeds, used as a food, a flavoring, and a medicine. Native to southern Europe and the Mediterranean, the plant is cultivated in central and southeastern Europe, western Asia, India, and northern Africa. The seeds smell and taste strong, sweetish, and somewhat bitter, like burnt sugar. Mealy in texture, they may be mixed with flour for bread or eaten raw or cooked. The herb is a characteristic ingredient in some curries and chutneys and is used to make imitation maple syrup.

fer-de-lance \ˈfer-dᵊl-ˈants\ (French: "spearhead") Extremely venomous PIT VIPER (genus *Bothrops*), found in diverse tropical American habitats, from cultivated lands to forests. It has a broad, triangular head and is gray or brown, marked by a series of black-edged diamonds often bordered in a lighter color. It is usually about 4–7 ft (1.2–2 m) long. Its bite can be fatal to humans. The name is sometimes applied to all members of the Central and South American genus *Bothrops* and to an Asian genus, *Trimeresurus*.

Fer Díad \ˈfär-ˌdē-əd\ Foster brother of the legendary Irish hero CÚ CHULAINN. *TÁIN BÓ CÚAILGNE,* the longest tale in the ULSTER CYCLE, deals with a conflict between Ulster and Connaught over the famous brown bull of Cooley. Joining the forces of Connaught in an expedition to seize the bull, Fer Díad engages in a three-day battle with Cú Chulainn and is defeated.

Ferber, Edna (1885–1968) U.S. novelist and short-story writer. Born in Kalamazoo, Mich., she began her career at 17 as a reporter in Wisconsin. Her early stories were collected in *Emma McChesney & Co.* (1915) and other volumes. She won critical acclaim for such novels as *So Big* (1924, Pulitzer Prize) and *Show Boat* (1926), which, with music by JEROME KERN, became a seminal work of the American musical theater. Among her later works is the novel *Giant* (1952; film, 1956). Her works offer a compassionate, lively portrait of middle-class Midwestern America.

Ferdinand (1793–1875) Emperor of Austria (1835–48). He was the eldest son of Emperor FRANCIS II, who sought to protect the principle of succession and insisted that Ferdinand be the heir, despite Ferdinand's feeblemindedness and epilepsy. He was crowned king of Hungary in 1830 and became emperor of Austria in 1835. Government affairs were controlled by a body of counselors, led by the chancellor, KLEMENS, FURST VON METTERNICH. Ferdinand was the last HABSBURG king of Bohemia (1836), and in 1838 he was crowned king of Lombardy and Venetia. In the REVOLUTION OF 1848 hostility was directed against his counselors, and Ferdinand abdicated in favor of his nephew, FRANCIS JOSEPH.

Ferdinand (Karl Leopold Maria) (1861–1948) King of Bulgaria (1908–18). Elected prince of Bulgaria in 1887, he proclaimed Bulgaria's independence from the Ottoman empire in 1908 and assumed the title of king or czar. He spearheaded the formation of the BALKAN LEAGUE (1912), which led to the first BALKAN WAR. Bulgaria was defeated in the second Balkan War (1913), and Ferdinand's resentments against his former allies determined Bulgaria's participation in WORLD WAR I on the side of the CENTRAL POWERS. Following military defeat in 1918, he was forced to abdicate in favor of his son, Boris III.

Ferdinand I (1503–1564) Holy Roman emperor (1558–64). The brother of Emperor CHARLES V, he was Charles's deputy in the Habsburg German lands (1522–58). In 1526 he took possession of Bohemia without difficulty, but he faced rival claimants in Hungary and fought periodically against the Ottoman empire, finally agreeing in 1562 to pay tribute to the Ottoman sultan for Austria's share of Hungary. He helped Charles defeat the Protestant SCHMALKALDIC LEAGUE, and later compromised on the Protestant issue and signed the Peace of AUGSBURG (1555), ending the era of religious strife in Germany. Elected emperor after Charles's abdication, which separated the Habsburg domains into Spanish and Austrian parts, Ferdinand centralized the imperial administration.

Ferdinand I, engraving by Barthel Beham, 1531.

ARCHIV FUR KUNST UND GESCHICHTE, BERLIN

Ferdinand I (1751–1825) King of the Two SICILIES (1816–25). He became king of Naples in 1759, as Ferdinand IV, when his father ascended the Spanish throne as CHARLES III. A weak ruler, he was greatly influenced by his wife, Maria Carolina of Austria (1752–1814). He engaged Naples in the Austro-English coalition against the French Revolution in 1793. The French then invaded Naples, and he fled to Sicily (1798–99, 1806–16). He returned to Naples in 1816 after the fall of NAPOLEON, as king of the united kingdom of the Two Sicilies. His despotic rule led to an uprising in 1820, after which he was forced to grant a constitution. With Austria's aid, he overthrew the constitutional government in 1821.

Ferdinand II (1578–1637) Holy Roman emperor (1619–37), archduke of Austria, king of Bohemia (1617–19, 1620–27) and king of Hungary (1618–25). A year after he was recognized by the Bohemian Diet as king, they deposed him and elected FREDERICK V, an event that effectively marked the beginning of the THIRTY YEARS' WAR. After annihilating the rebel army in 1620, he greatly reduced the Diet's power. A rigidly Catholic ruler, he forcibly catholicized Bohemia and suppressed Protestantism throughout his lands. He maintained much of his power through the victories of ALBRECHT W. E. VON WALLENSTEIN, but later concluded a compromise peace with the Protestant princes. He was the leading champion of the Catholic COUNTER-REFORMATION and of absolutist rule in the Thirty Years' War.

Ferdinand II (1810–1859) King of the Two SICILIES (1830–59). He followed his father, Francis I, as king, and initially instituted reforms, but his rule gradually became authoritarian, and he severely repressed a number of liberal and national revolts. His heavy bombardment of Sicilian cities in 1848 earned him the name "King Bomba." His government's increasingly absolute character denied the Kingdom of the Two Sicilies a role in the RISORGIMENTO and caused its collapse and incorporation into Italy in 1860.

Ferdinand III (1608–1657) Holy Roman emperor (1637–57), archduke of Austria (1621–57), king of Hungary (1625–57) and king of Bohemia (1627–57). Denied command of the Habsburg armies in the THIRTY YEARS' WAR, Ferdinand conspired to overthrow Gen. ALBRECHT W. E. VON WAL-

LENSTEIN, whom he replaced as commander (1634–35). His leadership of the so-called peace party at the imperial court led to the Peace of Prague in 1635. As emperor from 1637, he refused to allow religious freedom in his own domains, but he compromised with Europe's Protestant powers and agreed to the Peace of WESTPHALIA, ending 30 years of religious strife in central Europe.

Ferdinand V *known as* **Ferdinand the Catholic *Spanish* Fernando el Católico** (1452–1516) King of Castile from 1474 (joint sovereign with Queen ISABELLA I until 1504), king of Aragon (as Ferdinand II) from 1479, king of Sicily (as Ferdinand II, 1468–1516), and king of Naples (as Ferdinand III, 1503–16). The son of John II of Aragon (1398–1479), Ferdinand married Isabella of Castile in 1469, and fought to impose his authority over the nobles in the two kingdoms. As part of an effort to modernize Castile, they banned all religions other than Roman Catholicism, leading to the SPANISH INQUISITION (1478) and the expulsion of the Jews (1492). Conquest of Granada in 1492 made it possible to support CHRISTOPHER COLUMBUS's voyages to the New World. Ferdinand furthered his expansionary policies in the Mediterranean and in Africa. After the conquest of Naples in 1503, during the ITALIAN WARS, Spain rivaled France as the most powerful state in Europe. By uniting the Spanish kingdoms into the nation of Spain, Ferdinand began Spain's entry into the modern period of imperial expansion.

Ferdinand VI *Spanish* **Fernando** (1713–1759) King of Spain (1746–59). He was the second son of PHILIP V and his first wife. The influence of his father's second wife, ELIZABETH FARNESE, kept Ferdinand out of politics during his father's reign. During his own reign, he tried to avoid conflicts while relying on his father's minister to bring about reforms. Ferdinand, the second BOURBON Spanish king, and his beloved wife, Maria Bárbara, were patrons of the arts and learning. On his death, the crown passed to his half brother, CHARLES III.

Ferdinand VII *Spanish* **Fernando** (1784–1833) King of Spain (1808, 1813–33). He became king briefly in 1808 after the French invasion of Spain forced the abdication of his father, CHARLES IV. NAPOLEON soon replaced him as king with JOSEPH BONAPARTE, and held Ferdinand in France 1808–13. The Spanish populace rose against the French invaders in the name of Ferdinand, who became known as "the Desired." In 1812 independent Spaniards adopted a liberal constitution, which Ferdinand overthrew on his return as king in 1813 to rule in an absolutist style. His reign saw the loss of most of Spain's possessions in the Americas. He abolished the Salic Law to allow his daughter, the future ISABELLA II, to succeed him, instead of his brother, Don Carlos (1788–1855), which caused the rise of CARLISM.

Ferdowsi \fər-'dau̇-sē\ *or* **Firdusi** *or* **Firdousi** \fər-'dü-sē\ *orig.* **Abu ol-Qasem Mansur** (935?–1020/26?) Persian poet. Though many legends surround his name, few facts are known about his life. He gave the final and enduring form to the Persian national epic, the *Shah-nameh*, or *Book of Kings* (completed c. 1010), a poem based mainly on an earlier prose history. His language is still readily intelligible to modern Iranians, who regard the poem's nearly 60,000 couplets as a sonorous, majestic evocation of a glorious past. He reportedly worked on the poem for 35 years to earn a dowry for his only daughter.

Ferenczi \'fer-ənt-sē\, **Sándor** (1873–1933) Hungarian psychoanalyst. After receiving his M.D. from the University of Vienna and serving as an army doctor, he met SIGMUND FREUD in 1908 and became a member of Freud's inner circle, the Vienna Psychoanalytic Society. He founded the Hungarian Psychoanalytic Society in 1913 and began teaching psychoanalysis at the University of Budapest in 1919. He experimented with techniques of therapy and diverged from classic psychoanalytic practice in some respects (e.g., arguing that recovery of traumatic memories was not essential for modifying neurotic behavior, and emphasizing the need for therapists to create a loving, permissive atmosphere). His works include *The Development of Psychoanalysis* (with OTTO RANK; 1924).

Fergana Valley *or* **Fergana Basin** \,fir-gə-'nä\ Enormous valley, western central Asia, between the TIAN SHAN and Gissar and Alay mountain systems. It is mainly in eastern Uzbekistan and partly in Tajikistan and Kyrgyzstan, and has an area of 8,500 sq mi (22,000 sq km). One of the most densely populated areas of Central Asia, it is a major producer of cotton, fruit, and raw silk. Among the mineral deposits exploited are coal, oil, and mercury. It was conquered by the Arabs (8th century AD), GENGHIS KHAN (13th century), and TIMUR (14th. century). The khans of Kokand (see QUQON) ruled it from the late 18th century until it was taken by Russia in 1876.

Fergus Warrior king in the ULSTER CYCLE of Gaelic literature. In *TÁIN BÓ CÚAILGNE,* Fergus, an exile from Ulster, recalls the deeds of CÚ CHULAINN's youth. Another story tells of the revelation of the *Táin* in the 7th century by the ghost of Fergus. Fergus is also the subject of poems by WILLIAM BUTLER YEATS. He is said to have been shipwrecked off the coast of Northern Ireland c. AD 320, at the place known as Carrickfergus ("rock of Fergus").

Ferguson, Maynard (born 1928) Canadian trumpeter and bandleader, known for his mastery of the trumpet's highest register. Ferguson led a big band with his brother in his native Montreal while still a teenager. Moving to the U.S. in 1948, he performed with Jimmy Dorsey (1904–1957), CHARLES BARNET, and STAN KENTON before forming his own big band in 1956. His recording of "Gonna Fly Now" from the film *Rocky* brought commercial success in 1978. A versatile, energetic performer (he also plays many of the woodwind and lower brass instruments), he has inspired brass players for decades with his strong tone and sure technique.

Ferlinghetti \,fer-liŋ-'ge-tē\, **Lawrence (Monsanto)** *orig.* **Lawrence Ferling** (born 1919) U.S. poet. Born in Yonkers, N.Y., he attended Columbia University and the Sorbonne. A founder of the BEAT MOVEMENT in San Francisco in the mid-1950s, he established the City Lights bookstore, an early gathering place of the Beats. The publishing arm of City Lights was the first to print the Beats' poetry. His own poetry—lucid, witty, and composed to be read aloud—became popular in coffeehouses and on college campuses. His collections include *Pictures of the Gone World* (1955), the widely popular *A Coney Island of the Mind* (1958), and *Endless Love* (1981).

Fermanagh \fər-'ma-nə\ District (pop., 1995 est.: 55,000), and former county, extreme southwestern Northern Ireland. Located chiefly in the Erne River basin, it was established as a district within the boundaries of the traditional county in 1973; the district seat is ENNISKILLEN. Settled from prehistory, it is scattered with megaliths and cairns, and early Celtic Christian antiquities. Devenish Island, in Lower Lough ERNE, is the site of an ancient monastery. During the reign of JAMES I (1603–25) many English Anglicans were settled here. It is one of the most important tourist areas in Northern Ireland.

Fermat \fer-'mä\, **Pierre de** (1601–1665) French mathematician. Of Basque origin, Fermat studied law at Toulouse and developed interests in foreign languages, classical literature, ancient science, and mathematics. A jurist by profession, he produced major mathematical breakthroughs independently and collaboratively. A contemporary of RENE DESCARTES, he discovered independently the basic principles of ANALYTIC GEOMETRY, but because his work was published after his death, the field became known as Cartesian geometry. He found equations for TANGENT LINES to curves through processes equivalent to DIFFERENTIATION and INTEGRATION and was coauthor (with BLAISE PASCAL) of PROBABILITY THEORY. His work in NUMBER THEORY, especially divisibility, led to some of its most important theorems. He seldom demonstrated his results, which led to a centuries-long quest to prove a famous conjecture Fermat claimed was easily shown (see FERMAT'S LAST THEOREM).

Fermat, portrait by Roland Lefèvre; in the Narbonne City Museums, France.

BY COURTESY OF THE MUSEES DE LA VILLE DE NARBONNE, FRANCE

Fermat's last theorem Statement that there are no natural numbers x, y, and z such that $x^n + y^n = z^n$, in which n is a natural number greater than 2. About this, PIERRE DE FERMAT wrote in 1637 in his copy of Diophantus' *Arithmetica*, "I have discovered a truly remarkable proof but this margin is too small to contain it." Mathematicians were long unable either to prove or disprove the statement, though it has been proved for many specific values of n. In 1994 the British mathematician

Andrew Wiles (born 1953) and his former student Richard Taylor (born 1962) announced a proof, thereby solving one of the most famous of all mathematical problems.

fermentation Process that allows respiration to occur in the absence of oxygen. Biologically, it allows cells to obtain energy from fuel molecules (e.g., glucose) anaerobically. Glycolysis, the breakdown of glucose, is a form of fermentation. Alcoholic fermentation occurs when yeast cells convert carbohydrate sources to ethanol and carbon dioxide. Fermentation reactions are common in muscle cells, yeasts, some bacteria, and plants. See also BEER, WINE.

Fermi, Enrico (1901–1954) Italian-U.S. physicist. As a professor at the University of rome, he began the work, later fully developed by P. A. M. DIRAC, that led to FERMI-DIRAC STATISTICS. He developed a theory of BETA DECAY that applies to other reactions through the WEAK FORCE, which was not improved until 1957, when the weak force was found not to conserve PARITY. He discovered neutron-induced radioactivity, for which he was awarded a 1938 Nobel Prize. After receiving the award in Sweden, he never returned to fascist Italy but instead moved directly to the U.S., where he joined the faculty of Columbia University and soon became one of the chief architects of practical nuclear physics. A member of the MANHATTAN PROJECT, he was an important figure in the development of the atomic bomb; in 1942 he directed the first controlled nuclear chain reaction. He received the Congressional Medal of Merit in 1946. In 1954 he became the first recipient of the U.S. Dept. of Energy's Enrico Fermi Award. Element number 100, fermium, was named in his honor.

Fermi-Dirac statistics In QUANTUM MECHANICS, one of two possible ways (the other being BOSE-EINSTEIN STATISTICS) in which a system of indistinguishable particles can be distributed among a set of energy states. Each available discrete state can be occupied by only one particle. This exclusiveness accounts for the structure of ATOMS, in which ELECTRONS remain in separate states rather than collapsing into a common state. It also accounts for some aspects of electrical conductivity. This theory of statistical behavior was developed first by ENRICO FERMI and then by P. A. M. DIRAC (1926–27). The statistics apply only to particles such as electrons that have half-integer values of SPIN; the particles are called fermions.

fermion Any of a group of SUBATOMIC PARTICLES having odd half-integral SPIN (½, 3⁄2). Fermions are named for the FERMI-DIRAC STATISTICS that describe their behavior. They include particles in the class of LEPTONS, BARYONS, and nuclei of odd mass number (e.g., tritium, helium-3, uranium-233). They obey the PAULI EXCLUSION PRINCIPLE. Fermions are produced and undergo ANNIHILATION in particle-antiparticle pairs. See also BOSON.

fern Any of about 10,000–12,000 species (division Filicophyta) of nonflowering VASCULAR PLANTS that have true roots, stems, and complex leaves and reproduce by SPORES. Though ferns were once classified with the primitive HORSETAILS and CLUB MOSSES, botanists have since made a clear distinction between the scalelike, one-veined leaves of those plants and the more complexly veined fronds of the ferns, which are more closely related to the leaves of SEED PLANTS. Ferns come in a wide variety of sizes and shapes. Many are small, fragile plants; others are treelike (see TREE FERN). The life cycle is characterized by an ALTERNATION OF GENERATIONS between the mature, fronded form (the SPOROPHYTE) familiar in greenhouses and gardens and the form that strongly resembles a MOSS or LIVERWORT (the GAMETOPHYTE). Ferns are popular houseplants. See illustration opposite.

Fernando Póo See BIOKO

Ferrara \fer-'rä-rä\ City (pop., 1995 est.: 135,000), northern Italy. Situated near the PO RIVER, it is probably the site of the ancient Forum Alieni. It first appears in historical record in AD 753, when it was captured from RAVENNA by the Lombards. It became a cultural center and the seat of a principality, but it declined after its incorporation into the PAPAL STATES in 1598. The site of an Austrian garrison from 1832, it became part of the kingdom of Italy in 1861. It was severely damaged in World War II. Sites of interest include a 12th-century cathedral, a 14th-century moated castle, and the University of Ferrara (founded 1391).

Ferrara-Florence, Council of (1438–54) Ecumenical council held in an attempt to reunify the Eastern Orthodox and Roman Catholic churches. It was called by Pope Eugenius IV; the Eastern church was represented by Emperor JOHN VIII PALAEOLOGUS and others. Fear of facing the Turks without Western support led the Eastern participants to sign the Decree of Union (1439), but on their return to Constantinople most renounced it. Union was officially declared in HAGIA SOPHIA in 1452, but the following year the OTTOMAN EMPIRE captured Constantinople and the few partisans of the union fled. In 1448 a council of Eastern bishops condemned it officially.

Ferraro, Geraldine (Anne) (born 1935) U.S. politician. Born in Newburgh, N.Y., she practiced law in New York (1961–74), served as assistant U.S. district attorney (1974–78), and served in the U.S. House of Representatives (1978–84). In 1984 she became the first woman nominated for vice president by a major political party when she was chosen for the Democratic ticket by WALTER MONDALE. Investigations of

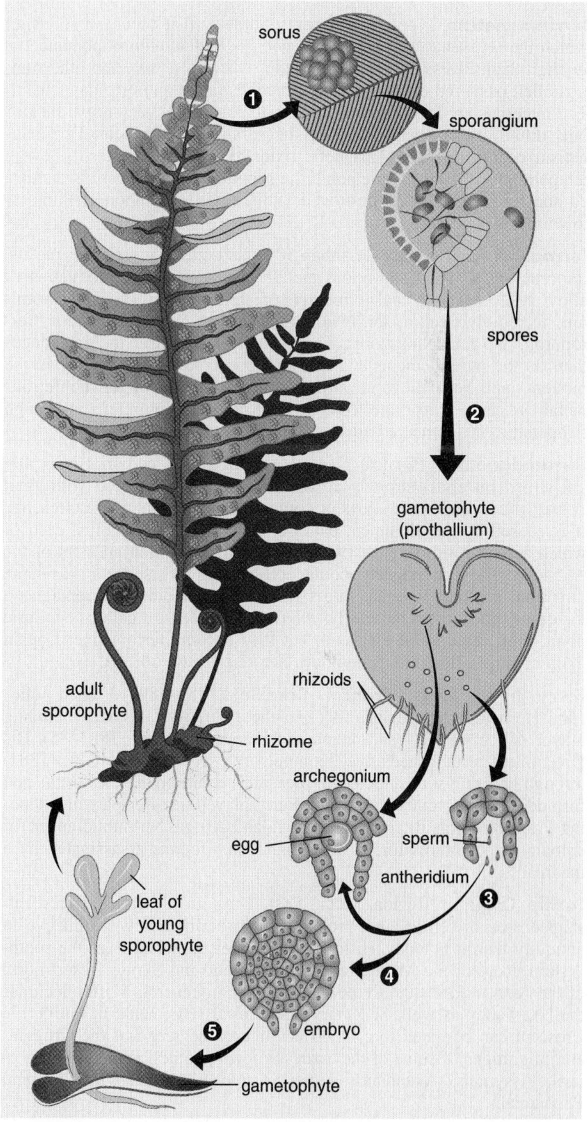

The life cycle of the fern. (1) Clusters (sori) of sporangia (spore cases) grow on the undersurface of mature fern leaves. (2) Released from its spore case, the haploid spore is carried to the ground, where it germinates into a tiny, usually heart-shaped, gametophyte (gamete-producing structure), anchored to the ground by rhizoids (rootlike projections). (3) Under moist conditions, mature sperm are released from the antheridia and swim to the egg-producing archegonia that have formed on the gametophyte's lower surface. (4) When fertilization occurs, a zygote forms and develops into an embryo within the archegonium. (5) The embryo eventually grows larger than the gametophyte and becomes a sporophyte.

her husband's finances undermined the campaign. In 1992 and 1998 she ran unsuccessfully for the U.S. Senate.

ferret Either of two species in the CARNIVORE family Mustelidae. The common ferret *(Mustela putorius furo)* is a domesticated form of the European POLECAT. It has a long, lithe body and is brown, black, or white (albino). Its average length is 20 in. (51 cm), including the 5-in. (13-cm) tail, and it weighs about 2 lbs (1 kg). It was originally domesticated for hunting mice, rats, and rabbits; today ferrets are commonly kept as pets. The black-footed ferret *(M. nigripes),* of the North American plains, has a black mask across the eyes and brownish black markings on the feet and tail tip. It is an endangered species, owing to the loss of its main source of food, the PRAIRIE DOG.

ferrimagnetism Type of permanent MAGNETISM that occurs in solids, in which the MAGNETIC FIELDS associated with individual atoms spontaneously align themselves, some parallel (as in FERROMAGNETISM), and others antiparallel, or paired off in opposite directions (as in antiferromagnetism). The materials are less magnetic than ferromagnets, as the antiparallel atoms dilute the magnetic effect of the parallel arrangement. Ferrimagnetism occurs mainly in magnetic oxides known as ferrites. Above a temperature called the Curie point, the spontaneous alignment is disrupted and ferrimagnetism is destroyed, but it is restored upon cooling below the Curie point.

ferroalloy ALLOY of IRON (less than 50%) and one or more other metals, important as a source of various metallic elements in the production of alloy STEELS. The principal ferroalloys are ferromanganese, ferrochromium, ferromolybdenum, ferrotitanium, ferrovanadium, ferrosilicon, ferroboron, and ferrophosphorus. They usually have lower melting ranges than do the pure elements and can be incorporated more readily in the molten steel. Ferroalloys are prepared from charges of the nonferrous metal ORE, iron or iron ore, COKE or COAL, and FLUX by treatment at high temperature in submerged-arc ELECTRIC FURNACES.

ferromagnetism Physical phenomenon in which certain electrically uncharged materials strongly attract others. It is associated with IRON, COBALT, NICKEL, and some alloys or compounds containing these elements. It is caused by the alignment patterns of the material's atoms, each of which acts as a simple ELECTROMAGNET, due to the motion and SPIN of the ELECTRONS. The tiny magnets spontaneously align themselves in the same direction, so their MAGNETIC FIELDS reinforce each other. Ferromagnetic materials are magnetized easily. Above a temperature called the Curie point, they cease to be magnetic, but they become ferromagnetic again upon cooling below the Curie point. See also FERRIMAGNETISM.

Ferry \fe-ˈrē\, **Jules (-François-Camille)** (1832–1893) French politician. He held a number of offices in the early THIRD REPUBLIC, including mayor of Paris (1870) and premier of France (1880–81, 1883–85). His government established free, compulsory, secular education (1882) through enacting such anticlerical measures as dissolving the Jesuits and forbidding their members to teach. Ferry played a major part in extending France's colonial territories in Asia and Africa, but public anger for colonial expenditures forced his resignation. He was assassinated by a madman.

Fertile Crescent Region, MIDDLE EAST. The term describes a crescent-shaped area of fertile land, probably more agriculturally productive in antiquity than it is today. Historically the area stretched from the southeastern coast of the Mediterranean Sea around the Syrian Desert north of the ARABIAN PENINSULA to the PERSIAN GULF; in general, it often includes the NILE valley as well. Sedentary agricultural settlements in the Fertile Crescent can be dated to c. 8000 BC. It was the scene of the struggles and migrations of some of the earliest known peoples, including Sumerians, Assyrians, Akkadians, some Semitic tribes, Babylonians, and Phoenicians.

fertility Ability of an individual or couple to reproduce through normal sexual activity. About 80% of healthy, fertile women are able to conceive within one year if they have intercourse regularly without CONTRACEPTION. Normal fertility requires the production of enough healthy SPERM by the male and viable EGGS by the female, successful passage of the sperm through open ducts from the male TESTES to the female fallopian tubes, penetration of a healthy egg, and implantation of the fertilized egg in the lining of the UTERUS (see REPRODUCTIVE SYSTEM). A problem with any of these steps can cause INFERTILITY.

fertilization Reproductive process in which a male sex cell (SPERM) unites with a female sex cell (EGG). During the process, the chromosomes of the egg and sperm will merge to form a zygote, which will divide to form an EMBRYO. In humans, sperm travel from the VAGINA through the uterus to a fallopian tube, where they surround an egg released from an OVARY usually two or three days earlier. Once one sperm has fused with the egg cell membrane, the outer layer becomes impenetrable to other sperm. See also CROSS-FERTILIZATION, SELF-FERTILIZATION.

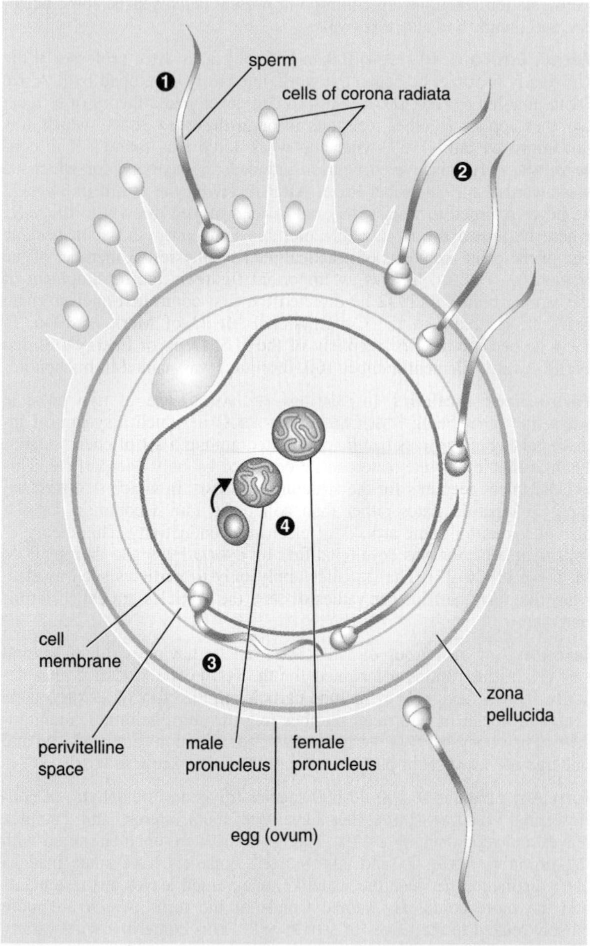

Fertilization of a human egg. (1) The sperm release enzymes that help disperse the corona radiata and bind to the zona pellucida. (2) The outer sperm head layer is sloughed off, exposing enzymes that digest a path through the zona pellucida. (3) The sperm fuses with the egg cell membrane, causing the zona pellucida to become impenetrable to other sperm. (4) The tail separates from the sperm head, and the male pronucleus enlarges and travels to the female pronucleus in the center of the cell. Chromosomes merge to form a fertilized egg.

fertilizer Natural or artificial substance containing the chemical elements that improve growth and productiveness of plants. Fertilizers enhance the natural fertility of the soil or replace the chemical elements taken from the soil by previous CROPS. The use of MANURE and COMPOSTS as fertilizers is probably almost as old as agriculture. Modern chemical fertilizers include one or more of the three elements most important in plant nutrition: NITROGEN, PHOSPHORUS, and POTASSIUM. Of secondary importance are the elements SULFUR, MAGNESIUM, and CALCIUM.

Fès \ˈfes\ *or* **Fez** \ˈfez\ *Arabic* **Fas** \ˈfas\ City (pop., 1994: 510,000), northern Morocco. The oldest of Morocco's four imperial cities, it was founded on opposite banks of the Wadi Fès by IDRIS I c. 789 and Idris II c. 809. The two parts were united by the ALMORAVIDS in the 11th century to become a major Islamic city. Fès reached its zenith under the MARINIDS as a center of learning and commerce in the mid-14th century and has kept its religious primacy through the ages. The site of the oldest mosque in northern Africa, it is also the seat of an Islamic university founded in 859. A center for trade and traditional crafts, it was until the late 19th century the only place where the fez hat was made.

fescue Any of about 100 species of GRASSES that make up the genus *Festuca* (family Poaceae, or Gramineae), native to temperate and cold regions of the Northern Hemisphere. Several species are important pasture and fodder grasses, and a few are used in lawn mixtures. One variety, blue fescue *(F. ovina* 'glauca'), has smooth, silvery leaves and is planted in ornamental borders.

Fessenden, William Pitt (1806–1869) U.S. politician. Born in Boscawen, N.H., he practiced law in Maine before serving in the U.S. House of Representatives (1841–43) and Senate (1854–64, 1865–69). Originally a Whig, he opposed the extension of slavery to the new territories and helped found the REPUBLICAN PARTY (1854) to further his views. Despite a dislike for Pres. ANDREW JOHNSON, he cast the deciding vote against Johnson's impeachment in the Senate trial.

fetal alcohol syndrome (FAS) Various CONGENITAL DISORDERS in a newborn caused by heavy drinking of alcohol by the mother around conception or during pregnancy. The main symptoms are retarded growth, central-NERVOUS-SYSTEM abnormalities, and certain face and head abnormalities. The child may be mentally retarded. Behavioral problems (e.g., poor concentration, impulsiveness) are sometimes the only obvious symptoms. The syndrome is common in babies born to chronic alcoholics, but even moderate alcohol consumption during pregnancy may cause mild symptoms. Other disorders have been linked to alcohol in breast milk.

fetial \'fē-shəl\ Any of a group of 20 Roman priestly officials who dealt with foreign relations. Selected from noble families and appointed for life, they acted as emissaries to foreign lands in times of conflict. When Rome was offended by another city-state, the fetials would visit the city-state and demand satisfaction. They also delivered treaties and made formal declarations of war, based on the decisions of the SENATE. This priesthood had faded by the late republic, but was later revived by AUGUSTUS.

fetish Object believed to have magical power to protect or aid its owner, and by extension, an object regarded with superstitious or extravagant trust or reverence. In the 18th century it was applied to West African amulets; it has also been used for various items in American Indian religion. In psychology, a fetish is an object that substitutes for a person as the focus of sexual desire. See also FETISHISM.

fetishism In psychology, erotic attachment to an inanimate object or an ordinarily asexual part of the human body or the necessity to use a nongenital object in order to achieve sexual gratification. The object is most commonly some other body part or an article of clothing. The condition occurs almost exclusively among men. See also FETISH.

fetus \'fēt-əs\ Unborn young of any vertebrate, particularly mammals, after it has acquired its basic form. In humans, this stage begins about eight weeks after conception (see EMBRYO). The fetal stage, marked by increased growth and full development of the organ systems, climaxes in birth (see PREGNANCY, PARTURITION). By the end of the third month, the arms and legs of the human fetus begin to move and reflexive movements (such as sucking) begin. Four months after conception, the fetus is about 5.3 in. (135 mm) long and weighs about 6 oz (170 g). During the fifth month, downy hairs (lanugo) cover the body and the skin becomes less transparent. At seven months, a protective greasy substance (vernix caseosa) covers the reddish, wrinkled skin. Fat is deposited under the skin during the eighth month, when the fetus typically weighs about 5 lbs (2.2 kg). A full-term fetus is about 266 days old.

feudal land tenure System by which land was held by tenants from lords. In England and France, the king was lord paramount and master of the realm. He granted land to his lords, who granted land to their vassals and so on down to the occupying tenant. Tenures were divided into free and unfree. Free tenure included tenure in CHIVALRY, as in the case of KNIGHT service, and socage (tenure by agricultural service fixed in amount and kind). The main type of unfree tenancy was villenage, a limited form of servitude. See also FEUDALISM, FIEF, LANDLORD AND TENANT, MANORIALISM.

feudalism Term that emerged in the 17th century that has been used to describe economic, legal, political, social, and economic relationships in the European MIDDLE AGES. Derived from the Latin word *feudum* (FIEF) but unknown to people of the Middle Ages, the term "feudalism" has been used most broadly to refer to medieval society as a whole, and in this way may be understood as a socio-economic system that is often called MANORIALISM. It has been used most narrowly to describe relations between lords and vassals that involve the exchange of land for military service. Feudalism in this sense is thought to have emerged in a time of political disorder in the 11th century as a means to restore order, and it was later a key element in the establishment of strong monarchies. "Feudalism" also has been applied, often inappropriately, to non-Western societies where institutions similar to those of medieval Europe are thought to have existed. The many ways "feudalism" has been used have drained it of specific meaning, however, and caused some scholars to reject it as a useful concept for understanding medieval society.

Feuerbach \'fȯi-ər-ˌbäk\, **Ludwig (Andreas)** (1804–1872) German philosopher. Son of an eminent jurist, he studied under G. W. F. HEGEL in Berlin, but abandoned Hegelian idealism for a naturalistic materialism. In *Thoughts on Death and Immortality* (1830), he attacked the concept of personal immortality. His *Abälard und Heloise* (1834) and *Pierre Bayle* (1838) were followed by *On Philosophy and Christianity* (1839), in which he claimed that "Christianity has in fact long vanished not only from the reason but from the life of mankind." In *The Essence of Christianity* (1841), he proposed that God is merely the outward projection of mankind's inward nature. Some of his views were later endorsed by KARL MARX, FRIEDRICH ENGELS, and other leaders of the revolt of labor against capitalism.

Feuillants \fœ-'yäⁿ\, **Club of the** Conservative French political club in the FRENCH REVOLUTION, which met in the former monastery of the Feuillants (Reformed Cistercians) in Paris. It was founded in 1791 by deputies who left the JACOBIN CLUB in opposition to a petition calling for the replacement of the king. The Feuillants feared that the continuation of the Revolution would lead to destruction of the monarchy and private property. The club represented a substantial group in the Legislative Assembly, but it disappeared when the insurrection of 1792 overthrew the monarchy.

fever *or* **pyrexia** \pī-'rek-sē-ə\ Abnormally high body temperature or a disease characterized by it. It most often occurs with INFECTION. Normal core body temperature, measured orally, does not exceed 99°F (37.2°C). Up to 105°F (40.6°C), fever causes weakness and is best treated with ASPIRIN, ACETAMINOPHEN, or other antipyretic drugs. At 108°F (42.2°C) or more, it can lead to convulsions and death. In treatment, it is important to know the underlying cause. Fever appears to be a defense against infectious disease, stimulating LEUKOCYTES and increasing ANTIBODY production and perhaps killing or inhibiting BACTERIA and VIRUSES that live within a narrow temperature range.

Feydeau \fā-'dō\, **Georges (-Léon-Jules-Marie)** (1862–1921) French playwright. An actor and director, he wrote 39 plays between 1881 and 1916, taking the farce to new heights on the French stage. His plots often depended on farfetched cases of mistaken identity, and he used complicated mechanical props and elaborate stage settings. His plays included *The Girl from Maxim's* (1899), *A Flea in Her Ear* (1907), and *Keep an Eye on Amélie!* (1908). His farces have remained in the repertoire of the COMÉDIE-FRANÇAISE.

Feynman \'fīn-mən\, **Richard P(hillips)** (1918–1988) U.S. theoretical physicist. Born in New York City, he received his PhD from Princeton University. During World War II he worked on the Manhattan Project. From 1950 he taught at Caltech. The FEYNMAN DIAGRAM was one of the many problem-solving tools he invented. With Julian Schwinger (born 1918) and Shinichiro Tomonaga (1906–1979), he shared a 1965 Nobel Prize for his brilliant work on QUANTUM ELECTRODYNAMICS. He was principally responsible for identifying the cause of the 1986 *CHALLENGER* disaster. Famed for his wit, he also wrote best-selling books on science. His work, which tied together all the varied phenomena at work in light, radio, electricity, and magnetism, altered the way scientists understand the nature of waves and particles.

Feynman diagram Graphical method of representing the interactions of elementary particles. It was invented by RICHARD P. FEYNMAN, who introduced the diagrams as an aid to calculating the processes that occur between ELECTRONS and PHOTONS. A Feynman diagram consists of two ax-

E
F
G

es, one representing space, the other representing time. Electrons are represented as straight lines, while photons are shown as wavy lines. The interaction between particles appears as a junction of three lines, or a vertex. Feynman diagrams are now used to show all types of particle interactions.

Fez See FÈS

Fezzan \fe-ˈzan\ *Arabic* **Fazzan** \fà-ˈzän\ *ancient* **Phazania** Historic region, southwestern Libya. A part of the SAHARA desert, most of its nearly 200,000 inhabitants dwell in oases in the center. southern Fezzan is noted for its date palms, which cover several hundred thousand acres scattered in numerous oases. It was conquered by the Romans in the 1st century BC and by the Arabs in the 7th century AD. The Turks made it part of the Ottoman empire in 1842. Fezzan was made part of Tripoli by the Italians in 1912, and it became a province of the United Kingdom of Libya (1951–63).

Fianna Fáil \ˈfē-ə-nə-ˈfȯil\ (Irish: "Warriors of Ireland") Political party in Ireland; also called, loosely, the Republican Party. It was formally constituted in 1926 by those opposed to the treaty with Britain that in 1921 brought about the Irish Free State, and was organized and led by EAMON DE VALERA. Fianna Fáil remained the principal governing party from 1932 until 1973, but from 1961 it did so with the aid of other parties. It returned to power in coalition governments in the 1980s and '90s. Its main opposition has been from FINE GAEL.

Fiat SpA International holding company and major Italian manufacturer of automobiles, trucks, and industrial vehicles and components. It is the world's sixth-largest automaker. In 1899 Giovanni Agnelli (1866–1945) founded the firm that was incorporated as Fiat in 1906; he led the firm until his death. His grandson Giovanni Agnelli (born 1921) became chairman in 1966. In 1979 the corporation converted to a holding company; in 1986 it acquired the sports-car manufacturer Alfa Romeo SpA. Among its automotive names are Ferrari and Lancia.

Fibber McGee and Molly See Jim and Marian JORDAN

fiber, dietary Food material not digestible by the human small intestine and only partially digestible by the large intestine. Fiber is beneficial in the diet because it relieves and prevents constipation, appears to reduce the risk of colon cancer, and reduces plasma CHOLESTEROL levels and therefore the risk of heart disease. Fiber also slows gastric emptying and contributes to satiety. The typical American diet is deficient in fiber; doctors have been urging its increased consumption in recent years. Whole grains, vegetables, nuts, and fruits are all good sources. See also NUTRITION.

fiber optics Thin transparent fibers of glass or plastic that transmit light through their length by internal reflections, used for transmitting data, voice, and images. Fiber-optic technology has virtually replaced copper wire in long-distance TELEPHONE lines and is used to link computers in LOCAL AREA NETWORKS, with digitized light pulses replacing the electric current formerly used for the signal. TELECOMMUNICATION using fiber optics is usually conducted with infrared light. Fiber optics uses light in the visible wavelengths to transmit images directly, in various technical devices such as those developed for ENDOSCOPY.

fiberglass *or* **glass fiber** Fibrous form of GLASS, developed in the 1930s. Liquid glass issues in fine streams through hundreds of fine nozzles, and the solidifying streams are gathered into a single strand and wound onto a spool. Strands can be twisted into yarns, woven into fabrics, or chopped into short pieces and then bonded into mats. Glass filaments and yarns add strength and electrical resistivity to molded plastic products. Glass fabrics are used as electrical insulators and as reinforcing belts in automobile tires. Discontinuous fibers are formed into wools, mats, or boards, commonly used in buildings, appliances, and plumbing.

Fibiger \ˈfē-bē-gər\, **Johannes Andreas Grib** (1867–1928) Danish pathologist. He found that rats that had suffered stomach-tissue inflammation caused by the larvae of a worm infecting cockroaches the rats had eaten subsequently developed stomach tumors, and induced tumors in mice and rats by feeding them infected cockroaches. His work, for which he received a 1926 Nobel Prize, supported the prevailing concept that cancer is caused by tissue irritation, and led to production of chemical carcinogens for use in cancer research.

Fibonacci sequence \ˌfi-bə-ˈnä-chē\ In mathematics, a sequence of numbers with surprisingly useful applications in botany and other natural sciences. Beginning with two 1's, each new term is generated as the sum of the previous two: 1, 1, 2, 3, 5, 8, 13, ... The 13th-century mathematician Leonardo of Pisa (c. 1170–after 1240), also known as Fibonacci, discovered the sequence but did not explore its uses, which have turned out to be wide and various. For example, the number of petals in most types of flowers and numbers involved in branching and seed-formation patterns come from the Fibonacci sequence. The ratio of any two successive terms approaches the value of the GOLDEN RATIO as the terms become large.

fibrillation See ATRIAL FIBRILLATION, VENTRICULAR FIBRILLATION

fibrolite See SILLIMANITE

fibromyalgia Chronic syndrome that is characterized by musculoskeletal pain, often at multiple sites. The cause is unknown. A significant number of persons with fibromyalgia also have mental disorders, especially depression. Many also have overlapping symptoms of other so-called functional somatic syndromes—especially chronic fatigue syndrome—such as fatigue, stiffness, irritable bowel syndrome, and sleep disturbances. It is common in young and middle-aged women. No treatment has been proved fully effective, although medications, physical therapy, or counseling may reduce disability and help the patient cope.

Fichte \ˈfik-tə\, **Johann Gottlieb** (1762–1814) German philosopher and patriot. Fichte's *Science of Knowledge* (1794), incited by IMMANUEL KANT's critical philosophy and especially by Kant's *Critique of Practical Reason* (1788), was his most original and characteristic work. To demonstrate that PRACTICAL REASON is really the root of reason in its entirety, the absolute ground of all knowledge as well as of humanity altogether, he started from a supreme principle, the ego, which was supposed to be independent and sovereign, so that all other knowledge was deduced from this principle. He attempted to rally German nationalists against Napoleon in his famous patriotic lectures *Reden an die deutsche Nation* (1807–8). He is regarded as one of the great transcendental idealists. His son Immanuel Hermann von Fichte (1796–1879) was also a philosopher.

Fichte, lithograph by F.A. Zimmermann after a painting by H.A. Daehling.
DEUTSCHE FOTOTHEK, DRESDEN, GER.

Ficino \fē-ˈchē-nō\, **Marsilio** (1433–1499) Italian philosopher, theologian, and linguist. His translations and commentaries on the writings of Plato and other classical Greek authors generated the Florentine Platonist Renaissance. In conceiving the universe as a hierarchy of substances that descends from God to matter, he was strongly influenced by NEOPLATONISM and medieval views. The CAMBRIDGE PLATONISTS and related movements in France and Italy reflect Ficino's original Platonist revival. Of his original writings, the *Platonic Theology* (1482) and the *Book on the Christian Religion* (1474) are most significant.

fiddler crab Any of about 65 species of DECAPODS (genus *Uca*) whose males holds one claw, always much larger than the other, somewhat like a violin. Both claws of the female are relatively small. Fiddler crabs often live in large numbers on beaches in temperate to tropical regions of the world. They inhabit water-covered burrows up to about 1 ft (30 cm) deep and feed on algae and other organic matter. Common North American species (e.g., marsh fiddler, china-back fiddler) live all along the U.S. Atlantic coast. Brightly colored, they range in body size from about 1 to 1.2 in. (2.5–3 cm).

Fides \ˈfī-dēz\ Roman goddess of good faith and honesty, who oversaw the integrity of the Romans. She was closely associated with JUPITER, and her temple was built near his on the Capitoline Hill in 254 BC. In the later Roman period she was called Fides Publica ("Public Faith") and was considered the guardian of treaties and other state documents, which were placed in her temple for safekeeping.

fiduciary \fə-'dü-shē-,er-ē\ In law, one in a position of authority whom the law obligates to act solely on behalf of the person he or she represents (as when managing money or property) and in good faith. Examples are agents, executors, trustees, GUARDIANS, and officers of CORPORATIONS. Unlike people in an ordinary business relationship, fiduciaries may not seek personal benefit from their transactions with those they represent.

Fiedler \'fēd-lər\, **Arthur** (1894–1979) U.S. conductor. Born in Boston, son of a distinguished violinist, he was trained in Berlin and joined the Boston Symphony Orchestra in 1915. In the 1920s he began conducting and recording with his own Boston Sinfonietta and various choral groups. In 1929 he organized a series of open-air concerts, which was successful enough to eventually become an institution, the Boston Pops. Thereafter his name was inextricably linked with the Pops, which achieved enormous success under him.

fief \'fēf\ In European FEUDALISM, a vassal's source of income, granted to him by his lord in exchange for his services. The fief usually consisted of land and the labor of peasants who were bound to cultivate it. The income it provided supported the vassal, who fought for his lord as a knight. Dignities, offices, and money rents were also given in fief.

field In physics, a region in which each point is affected by a force. Objects fall to the ground because they are affected by the force of earth's gravitational field (see GRAVITATION). A paper clip, placed in the MAGNETIC FIELD surrounding a magnet, is pulled toward the magnet, and two like magnetic poles repel each other when one is placed in the other's magnetic field. An ELECTRIC FIELD surrounds an ELECTRIC CHARGE; when another charged particle is placed in that region, it experiences an electric force that either attracts or repels it. The strength of a field, or the forces in a particular region, can be represented by field lines; the closer the lines, the stronger the forces in that part of the field. See also ELECTROMAGNETIC FIELD.

Field, Joshua (1787?–1863) British civil engineer. He joined HENRY MAUDSLAY's noted engineering firm, which soon became Maudslay, Sons, and Field. In 1838 they completed a pair of powerful combined steam engines that applied power to a paddle-wheel shaft by a crank (rather than cogwheels) and installed them on I. K. BRUNEL's *Great Western;* on its maiden voyage it crossed the Atlantic in only 13½ days, and it became the first regular transatlantic steamer. He was a cofounder of the Institution of Civil Engineers (1817).

Field, Marshall (1834–1906) U.S. department-store owner. Born near Conway, Mass., he became an errand boy for a dry-goods store at age 16. He moved to Chicago and was hired in 1856 by a mercantile house, in which he later attained full partnership. In 1867 he and a partner attained full ownership of a merchandising firm they had joined two years earlier; in 1888 he bought out his partner, and the firm became Marshall Field and Co. Field emphasized customer service, stressing liberal credit, the one-price system, and the privilege of returning merchandise. His DEPARTMENT STORE was the first to have a restaurant for shoppers.

Field, Sally (born 1946) U.S. film actress. Born in Pasadena, Cal., she played undemanding television roles in *Gidget* (1965–66) and *The Flying Nun* (1967–70) before developing her talent at the ACTORS STUDIO (1973–75), from which she emerged as a dramatic actress in the television movie *Sybil* (1977, Emmy award). Hollywood finally rewarded her with strong roles in *Norma Rae* (1979, Academy Award), *Absence of Malice* (1981), *Places in the Heart* (1984, Academy Award), and *Steel Magnolias* (1989). Her other films include *Punchline* (1987), *Mrs. Doubtfire* (1993), and *Eye for an Eye* (1996).

Field, Stephen J(ohnson) (1816–1899) U.S. jurist. Born in Haddam, Conn., he practiced law in New York with his brother, the legal reformer David Dudley Field (1805–1894). In 1849 he moved to California, where he later joined the state supreme court. He was appointed to the U.S. Supreme Court in 1863, and served until 1897. He became chief architect of the constitutional approach that largely exempted U.S. industry from government regulation after the American Civil War, basing his interpretation principally on the 14th Amendment (1868), which had been passed as a civil-rights measure. Field's stance toward industry would be maintained by the Court until the 1930s.

field hockey Game played between two teams of 11 players each on a turfed field 100 yards (91.4 m) by 60 yards (55 m) in size. The object is to direct a ball into the opponent's goal with a curve-ended hockey stick. Field hockey began to be played in English schools in the late 19th century, and the British Army introduced it into India and the Far East. By 1928 it had become India's national game. Men's hockey has been included in the Olympic Games since 1908, women's since 1980. The game was introduced into the U.S. in 1901 and became particularly popular at women's schools, colleges, and clubs. Several international championship tournaments are held during the year, including the World Cup.

field mouse *or* **wood mouse** In general, any MOUSE that normally lives in fields; more strictly, any of about seven species of small, long-tailed mice in the genus *Apodemus* (family Muridae). Field mice in this genus are found in fields, woodlands, and mountain meadows in the warm and temperate parts of Eurasia. They are grayish or light or reddish brown and are 2–5 in. (6–12 cm) long excluding the tail. They generally live in burrows and build nests of grass and other plants. They eat seeds, roots, and other plant material, occasionally damaging crops or young trees.

Field of Cloth of Gold Setting for meetings between HENRY VIII of England and FRANCIS I of France in June 1520, near Calais, France. Splendid temporary palaces were erected for each king, and jousts and other entertainments were held. The splendor of the meetings vastly impressed contemporaries, but the political results were negligible. In July Henry met Emperor CHARLES V, Francis's rival, near Calais, and they agreed to make no new alliances with France for two years.

field theory In mathematics, a branch of higher algebra dealing with a special type of system that consists of a set of objects (e.g., numbers) and two combining operations (e.g., addition and multiplication). Together, these satisfy AXIOMS stipulating that the set of objects forms a commutative group under addition (see GROUP THEORY), that when zero is excluded the set is also a commutative group under multiplication, and that the two operations satisfy the distributive law $a(b + c) = ab + ac$. The most commonly encountered fields are the RATIONAL NUMBERS, the REAL NUMBERS, and the COMPLEX NUMBERS, along with ordinary addition and multiplication. The investigation of polynomial equations and their solutions led to the discovery of field theory.

field trial Competitive trial of sporting dogs under conditions that approximate or simulate those found in the hunting field. Dogs representing individual breeds, or classes of breeds (e.g., bird dogs, spaniels, hounds), are judged on such factors as pace, range, keenness of nose, handling response, hunting ability, and game and gun manners.

Fielding, Henry (1707–1754) British novelist and playwright. He attended Eton College but left early and lost his family's support. In his 25 plays, all written early, he was essentially a satirist of political corruption; because of his sharp commentary he was eventually effectively banished from the theater, whereupon he took up the study of law. In 1748 he was appointed a magistrate, in which role he established a new tradition of justice and suppression of crime in London. He probably wrote *Shamela* (1741), a burlesque of SAMUEL RICHARDSON's *Pamela* that he never claimed. In the entertaining and original *Joseph Andrews* (1742) he also parodies Richardson's novel. *Tom Jones* (1749), his most popular work, is noted for its great comic gusto, vast gallery of characters, and contrasted scenes of high- and lowlife. The more sober *Amelia* (1751) anticipates the Victorian domestic novel. In these works he helped develop the English novel as a planned, realistic narrative genre surveying contemporary society.

fieldlark See PIPIT

Fields, Dorothy (1904–1974) U.S. lyricist and librettist. Born in New Jersey to a family active in theater (her father Lew was a comedian and impresario, and her brothers Herbert and Joseph were librettists), Fields taught drama and wrote poetry, and later wrote songs for Broadway and COTTON CLUB revues with J. MCHUGH, including "I Can't Give You Anything But Love" and "On the Sunny Side of the Street." With J. KERN, she later wrote songs for Hollywood, including "The Way You Look Tonight." Returning to Broadway, she wrote the book or lyrics for many musicals, including *Annie Get Your Gun* (1946) and *Sweet Charity* (1966).

Fields, Gracie *orig.* **Grace Stansfield** *later* **Dame Gracie** (1898–1979) English music-hall comedienne. She performed in music halls from age 13 and gained notice in the touring revue *Mr. Tower of London* (1918–25). She became tremendously popular with an act composed of

E
F
G

low-comedy songs such as "The Biggest Aspidistra in the World" and sentimental ballads such as "My Blue Heaven," performing on radio and television and in films such as *Sally in Our Alley* (1931) and *Sing As We Go* (1934), and selling many recordings.

Fields, W. C. *orig.* **William Claude Dukenfield** (1880–1946) U.S. actor and screenwriter. Born in Philadelphia, he was a vaudeville headliner as a juggler and appeared for seven seasons (1915–21) in the *Ziegfeld Follies.* His starring role in the stage hit *Poppy* (1923) brought him to Hollywood for its film adaptation, *Sally of the Sawdust* (1925). He emerged as a top film comedian only after the advent of sound pictures, when audiences could hear his distinctive raspy voice. His screen personality—an unlovable but hilarious con man, braggart, misanthrope, and hater of children and dogs—was largely his own. Fields wrote and improvised the action for most of his films, which included such comedies as *You Can't Cheat an Honest Man* (1939), *My Little Chickadee* (1940), *The Bank Dick* (1940), and *Never Give a Sucker an Even Break* (1941). His only serious role was Mr. Micawber in *David Copperfield* (1935).

Fiennes \'finz\, **Ralph (Nathaniel)** (born 1962) British actor. Trained at the Royal Academy of Dramatic Art, he joined London's National Theatre in 1987 and the Royal Shakespeare Co. in 1989. His television performance in *A Dangerous Man: Lawrence after Arabia* (1991) led to the role of a Nazi commandant in *Schindler's List* (1993), which launched his film career. His later films include *Quiz Show* (1994), *Strange Days* (1995), *The English Patient* (1996), and *Oscar and Lucinda* (1997). He also appeared on Broadway in *Hamlet* (1995, Tony award).

Fiesole, Mino da See MINO DA FIESOLE

Fife Historical area and administrative region (pop., 1995 est.: 352,000), eastern Scotland. An ancient Pictish kingdom, Fife became one of Scotland's leading provinces, and one of the kingdom's seven earldoms. Modern Fife consists largely of an agricultural northeast and an industrial southwest. Coal mining has long dominated its industry, which is supplemented now by manufacturing and light industries. The administrative region's headquarters is GLENROTHES.

Fifth Republic System of government in France from 1959 to the present. Under the constitution crafted by CHARLES DE GAULLE with the help of MICHEL DEBRE, executive power was increased at the expense of the National Assembly. It came into being in 1959 after de Gaulle was elected president, with Debré as his prime minister. In 1962 de Gaulle pushed through a constitutional amendment that provided for direct popular election of the president, and in 1965 he became the first French president elected by popular vote since 1848. He was succeeded by GEORGES POMPIDOU (1969–74), VALERY GISCARD D'ESTAING (1974–81), FRANCOIS MITTERRAND (1981–95), and JACQUES CHIRAC (from 1995).

fig Any plant of the genus *Ficus,* in the MULBERRY FAMILY, especially *Ficus carica,* the common fig. Yielding the well-known figs of commerce, *F. carica* is native to an area from Asiatic Turkey to northern India, but natural seedlings grow in most Mediterranean countries, where figs are used extensively, both fresh and dried. It is a bush or small tree with broad, rough, deciduous leaves (see DECIDUOUS TREE). Hundreds of different varieties are grown in various parts of the world. The fig was one of the first fruit trees to come under cultivation. Its fruit contains significant amounts of calcium, potassium, phosphorus, and iron.

Figaro, Le Morning daily newspaper published in Paris, once one of the great newspapers of France and of the world. Founded in 1826 as a witty gossip sheet on the arts, by 1866 it was a well-written daily filled with political discourse. Though the paper's reputation faltered at times and it suspended publication during World War II, in the postwar years it became the voice of the French upper middle class, providing broad subject coverage while maintaining an independent editorial stance. In the 1960s and '70s the staff was rent by conflicts over its leadership. In 1975 the paper was bought by the conservative Robert Hersant, who ran it until his death in 1996.

fighter aircraft Aircraft designed primarily to secure control of essential airspace by destroying enemy aircraft in combat. Designed for high speed and maneuverability, they are armed with weapons capable of striking other aircraft in flight. Developed early in World War I, they engaged in aerial combat with other fighters, shot down enemy bombers, and conducted various tactical missions. Most were biplanes with wooden frames and cloth skins, equipped with light machine guns synchronized to fire through the propeller. World War II saw the development of all-metal monoplanes that exceeded speeds of 450 mph (725 kph). Famous fighters of the period included the FOCKE-WULF 190, the P-47 and P-51, and the ZERO. Jet aircraft were produced at the end of the war, and jet fighters such as the U.S. SABRE and the Soviet MIG saw extensive service in the Korean War and later conflicts. See also AIR WARFARE, F-15, F-16, NIGHT FIGHTER.

Fighting Falcon See F-16

fighting fish See SIAMESE FIGHTING FISH

Figueres (Ferrer) \fē-'ger-ās\, **José** (1906–1990) Costa Rican statesman and president (1948–49, 1953–58, 1970–74). Educated in Costa Rica, Mexico, and the U.S., he became an opponent of the right-wing regime of Rafael Ángel Calderón, and in 1948 led an uprising to force Calderón to yield the presidency to the democratically elected Otilio Ulate. A junta dominated by Figueres wrote a new constitution that abolished the army and gave women the right to vote, and the presidency was turned over to Ulate in 1949. Figueres himself was elected president by a landslide in 1953; governing as a moderate socialist, he adopted a pro-U.S. policy and quickly outlawed the Communist Party. Returned to power in 1970, he became a symbol of the democratic left, and is given much credit for Costa Rica's enduring stability and democracy.

figure of speech Form of expression used to convey meaning or heighten effect, often by comparing or identifying one thing with another that has a meaning or connotation familiar to the reader or listener. An integral part of language, figures of speech are found in oral literatures as well as in polished poetry and prose and in everyday speech. Common figures of speech include SIMILE, METAPHOR, personification, hyperbole, IRONY, ALLITERATION, onomatopoeia, and puns.

figure skating Sport in which ice skaters, singly or in pairs, perform various jumps, spins, and dance movements. The figure skate blade has a special serrated toe pick, or toe rake, at the front. Until 1991, competition included a compulsory section in which prescribed figures were traced. Figure-skating events, held in the 1908 and 1920 Olympic Games, have constituted part of the Winter Olympics since they were inaugurated in 1924. Competition for individuals includes two free-skating programs: a shorter, technical program that must incorporate a number of prescribed elements or maneuvers; and a long program designed to show the skater's skill and grace that has no mandatory requirements. Jumps fall into two main groups: the edge jumps (such as the Axel, the Salchow, and the loop), which take off from one foot; and the toe jumps (such as the toe loop, the flip, and the Lutz), which are edge jumps assisted by a vault off the toe pick of the other foot. Jumps are further classified as single, double, and so on. Additional pair moves, involving a man and a woman skating together, include lifts, pair spins, and throw jumps. Figure-skating programs are judged on both technical merit and artistic impression. See also ICE DANCING.

Lift in pair figure skating performed by Yekaterina Gordeyeva and Sergey Grinkov (U.S.S.R.) at the world championships, Budapest, 1988.
ALL-SPORT USA/VANDYSTADT

figured bass Style of music notation used for the CONTINUO part in baroque music. It consists of a bass line notated in the standard way, but with numerals below the staff (e.g., 6, 6/4, 7) representing INTERVALS to be played above the bass tone. The figures were read principally by the continuo's keyboard player. They began to appear c. 1600, and by mid-century had been adopted universally. Figured bass permitted very rapid notation by the composer, and performers quickly mastered the technique of reading it. It was highly important as the conceptual underpinning of composition in the 17th–18th century. Vestiges of the figures can still be found in the chord symbols of jazz and popular music.

figurehead Ornamental symbol or figure placed on a prominent part of a ship, usually at the bow. It could be a religious symbol, a national emblem, or a figure symbolizing the ship's name. The custom of decorating a ship probably began in ancient Egypt or India and was followed by the Chinese, Phoenicians, Greeks, and Romans. As early as 1000 BC, the stem- and sternposts were carved and painted to distinguish one ship from another. The Vikings built ships with high bows and a projecting stem bearing a menacing figurehead, similar to the ships of William I the Conqueror as seen in the BAYEUX TAPESTRY. Figureheads have historically varied in size from 18 in. (45 cm) to 8–9 ft (2.5 m). They remained popular until after World War I.

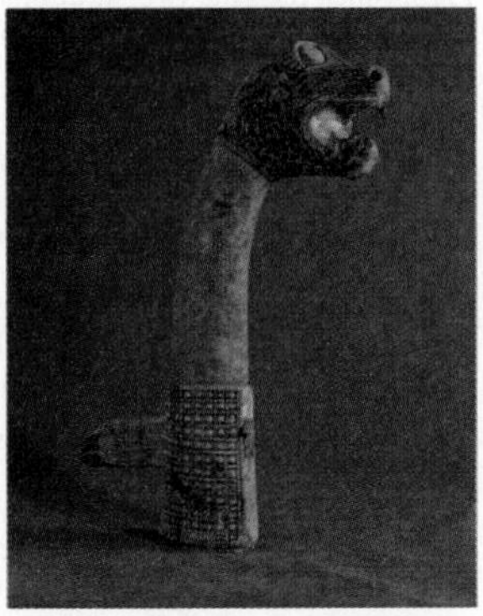

Figurehead from the Oseberg ship, Viking, about AD 800; in the Museum of National Antiquities, Oslo.

figwort Any of about 200 species of coarse plants that make up the genus *Scrophularia* (family Scrophulariaceae), native to open woodlands in the Northern Hemisphere. Figworts are tall, frequently foul-smelling plants with purple, greenish, or yellow flowers in large branched spikes.

Fiji *officially* **Republic of Fiji** *Fijian* **Viti** Nation and archipelago, South Pacific Ocean. It lies east of Vanuatu and southwest of Samoa. Area: 7,055 sq mi (18,272 sq km). Population (1997 est.): 778,000. Capital: SUVA. The majority of Fijians are of mixed Melanesian-Polynesian stock. Languages: English (official), Fijian. Religions: Methodism, Hinduism (among the large Asian Indian minority). Currency: Fiji dollar. It lies 1,300 mi (2,100 km) north of New Zealand, and comprises some 540 islets and 300 islands, of which about 100 are inhabited. The main islands are Viti Levu and Vanua Levu. It also includes, since 1881, Rotuma, an island located about 400 mi (640 km) to the northwest. The two large Fiji islands are mountainous and volcanic in origin, rising abruptly from densely populated coasts to forested central mountains. The smaller islands are formed mostly of coral reefs. The coastal deltas of the principal rivers contain most of Fiji's fertile arable land. It has a tropical oceanic climate. It has a market economy based largely on agriculture (particularly sugar production), tourism, and light industries; significant quantities of gold, silver, and limestone are mined. It is a republic with two legislative houses; its chief of state is the president, while the head of government is the prime minister. Archaeological evidence shows that the islands were occupied in the late 2nd millennium BC and had developed pottery by c. 1300 BC. The first European sighting was by the Dutch in the 16th century; in 1774 the islands were visited by Capt. JAMES COOK, who found a mixed Melanesian-Polynesian population with a complex society. Traders and the first missionaries arrived in 1835. In 1857 a British consul was appointed, and in 1874 Fiji was proclaimed a crown colony. It became independent as a member of the COMMONWEALTH in 1970, and was declared a republic in 1987 following a military coup. Elections in 1992 restored civilian rule. A new constitution was approved in 1997.

Filarete \ˌfē-lä-ˈre-tā\ *orig.* **Antonio di Pietro Averlino** (c. 1400–1469) Italian architect and sculptor. In 1451 he entered the service of the duke of Milan. He designed the Ospedale Maggiore in Milan (1457–65), among the first Renaissance buildings in Lombardy. He is chiefly important for his *Trattato d'architettura*, which describes an ideal Renaissance city called Sforzinda. Among the projects he envisioned was a tower of vice and virtue, with a brothel on the first floor and an astronomical observatory on the 10th.

filarial worm Any of a group of parasitic NEMATODES that usually require two hosts to complete the life cycle: an ARTHROPOD and another animal, which is bitten by the arthropod. The female worm produces large numbers of microscopic, active embryos, called microfilariae, that pass into the bloodstream of the primary host. These enter the body of an insect when it bites the infected animal; within the insect the microfilariae grow into larvae, which are passed to an animal the insect bites, where they complete their growth. See also HEARTWORM.

filbert *or* **hazel(nut)** Any of about 15 species of deciduous trees and shrubs that make up the genus *Corylus,* in the BIRCH family, native to the northern temperate zone; also, the edible NUTS they produce. Choice nuts are produced by two Eurasian trees, the European filbert *(C. avellana)* and the giant filbert *(C. maxima),* and by hybrids of these species. Some varieties are valuable HEDGEROW and ornamental trees. An oil from *C. avellana* is used in food products, perfumes, and soaps; the tree yields a soft, reddish-white timber that is useful for small articles such as tool handles and walking sticks.

file In hardware and metalworking, bar- or rod-shaped tool of hardened steel with many small cutting edges raised on its surfaces. Files are used for smoothing or forming objects, especially of metal. A file's cutting or abrading action results from rubbing it, usually by hand, against the workpiece. The single-cut file has rows of parallel teeth cut diagonally across the working surfaces. The double-cut file has rows of teeth crossing each other. Rasp teeth are disconnected and round on top; rasp files are usually very coarse and are used primarily on wood and soft materials.

file transfer protocol See FTP

filibuster Tactic of delaying action on a bill by talking long enough to wear down the majority in order to win concessions or force withdrawal of the bill. The tactic is normally employed by a group that cannot muster enough votes to defeat a bill by vote. Filibustering is possible in the U.S. Senate because Senate rules allow unlimited debate on a bill. A filibuster may be carried out by a group or a single member, and the speech need not be related to the bill under discussion. Calling for a vote to limit debate (cloture)—which requires 60 votes, the votes of three-fifths of the entire membership, in the U.S. Senate—or holding around-the-clock sessions to tire the speakers are measures used to defeat filibusters.

Fillmore, Millard (1800–1874) 13th president of the U.S. (1850–53). Born into poverty in Locke, N.Y., he became an indentured apprentice at 15. He studied law with a local judge and began to practice in Buffalo in 1823. Initially identified with the Anti-Masonic Party (1828–34), he followed his political mentor, THURLOW WEED, to the Whigs and was soon a leader of the party's northern wing. He served in the U.S. House of Representatives (1833–35, 1837–43), where he became a follower of HENRY CLAY. In 1848 the Whigs nominated Fillmore as vice president, and he was elected with ZACHARY TAYLOR. He became president on Taylor's death in 1850. Though he abhorred slavery, he supported the Compromise of 1850 and insisted on federal enforcement of the FUGITIVE SLAVE ACT. His stand, which alienated the North, led to his defeat by WINFIELD SCOTT at the Whigs' nominating convention in 1852 and effectively led to the death of the party. Throughout his career he advocated U.S. internal development and was an early champion of expansion in the Pacific. In 1853 he sent MATTHEW PERRY with a U.S. fleet to Japan, forcing its isolationist government to enter into trade and diplomatic relations. He returned to Buffalo and was nominated for president by the KNOW-NOTHING PARTY in 1856.

Millard Fillmore.

film See MOTION PICTURE

film noir \ˈnwär\ (French: "black film") Film genre that offers dark or fatalistic interpretations of reality. The term is applied to U.S. films of the late 1940s and early '50s that portrayed a seamy or criminal underworld and cynical characters, often shot at night or in shadowy interiors. The genre includes such films as JOHN HUSTON's *The Maltese Falcon* (1941), MICHAEL CURTIZ's *Casablanca* (1942), ALFRED HITCHCOCK's *Spellbound* (1945), and BILLY WILDER's *Double Indemnity* (1944) and *Sunset Boulevard* (1950). The trend had all but disappeared by the mid-1950s, but a few outstanding examples continued to be made, including ROMAN POLANSKI's *Chinatown* (1974) and STEPHEN FREARS's *The Grifters* (1990).

film theory Theory developed to explain the nature of films and how they produce emotional and mental effects on the audience. It recognizes the cinema as a distinct art form. See also AUTEUR THEORY, DOCUMENTARY film, SERGEI EISENSTEIN, FILM NOIR, NEW WAVE.

filter-pressing Process that occurs during crystallization of certain IGNEOUS ROCKS, in which liquid is separated from the crystals by pressure. As the crystals grow and accumulate in MAGMA, a crystal mesh may be formed. Pressure applied by the weight of crystals above or by outside forces may force the more mobile liquid out of the mesh and also may fracture or crush the remaining crystals. Filter-pressing has been used to explain the formation of rocks consisting of only one kind of mineral.

fin whale *or* **finback whale** *or* **razorback whale** *or* **common rorqual** \'rȯr-kwəl\ Swift, slender-bodied BALEEN WHALE *(Balaenoptera physalus)* named for the ridge on its back. It is 59–89 ft (18–27 m) long, with a triangular dorsal fin, short baleen, and several dozen grooves along its throat and chest. It is gray, with white on the underparts and on the right side of the lower jaw. It is found in oceans worldwide, in groups of a few to several hundred. It lives in polar waters in summer, feeding on crustaceans and small fishes, and moves to warmer waters in winter to breed. Once commercially valuable, it has been substantially reduced in numbers by overhunting and is now listed as an endangered species.

finance Process of raising funds or capital for any kind of expenditure. Consumers, business firms, and governments often do not have the funds they need to make purchases or conduct their operations, while savers and investors have funds that could earn interest or dividends if put to productive use. Finance is the process of channeling funds from savers to users in the form of credit, loans, or invested capital through agencies including COMMERCIAL BANKS, SAVINGS AND LOAN ASSOCIATIONS, and such nonbank organizations as CREDIT UNIONS and investment companies. Finance can be divided into three broad areas: BUSINESS FINANCE, personal finance, and public finance. All three involve generating budgets and managing funds for the optimum results. See also CORPORATE FINANCE.

finance company Specialized financial institution that supplies credit for the purchase of consumer goods and services. Finance companies purchase unpaid customer accounts at a discount from merchants and collect payments due from customers. They also grant small loans directly to consumers at a relatively high rate of interest.

Financial Times Morning daily newspaper published in London. Founded in 1888, it competed for many years with four other finance-oriented papers, finally in 1945 absorbing the last of them. Known as one of England's best papers, it specializes in reporting international business and financial news while maintaining an independent editorial outlook. It has had a strong influence on the British government's financial policies, and its circulation is one of the world's highest among financial newspapers.

finback whale See FIN WHALE

finch Any of several hundred species of small, conical-billed, seed-eating songbirds (in several families), including the BUNTING, CANARY, CARDINAL, CHAFFINCH, crossbill, DARWIN'S (GALÁPAGOS) FINCH, GOLDFINCH, grass finch, GROSBEAK, SPARROW, and weaver. Finches are small, compact birds 3–10 in. (10–27 cm) long. Most use their heavy bill to crack seeds; many also eat insects. Many finches are brightly colored, often with shades of red and yellow. Found throughout the temperate areas of the Northern Hemisphere and South America and in parts of Africa, finches are among the dominant birds in many areas, both in numbers of individuals and species. They are often kept as singing cage birds.

Finch, Peter (1916–1977) Australian-British actor. From 1935 he acted in Australia on the stage, in films, and on radio. He moved to London in 1949 and became a leading actor in such British and U.S. films as *A Town Like Alice* (1956), *Kidnapped* (1960), *The Pumpkin Eater* (1964), *Far from the Madding Crowd* (1967), *Sunday Bloody Sunday* (1971), and *Network* (1976, Academy Award).

Fine Gael \'fē-nə-'gāl\ (Irish: "Gaelic Nation") Major political party in Ireland, also known as United Ireland Party. It was founded in 1933 in the amalgamation of several parties, including the Cumann na nGaedheal ("Society of Gaels"), which had been formed by members of the Dáil (assembly) who accepted the Anglo-Irish treaty of 1921. It held power briefly in 1948, but FIANNA FÁIL dominated Irish politics until 1973. Since then the two parties have vied for power, with Fine Gael coalition governments in power in 1973–77, 1981–82, 1982–87, and 1994–97.

finery process Early method of converting CAST IRON to WROUGHT IRON, superseding the BLOOMERY PROCESS after BLAST FURNACES became widespread. Pieces of cast iron (see PIG IRON) were placed on a finery hearth, on which CHARCOAL was being burned with a plentiful supply of air, so that CARBON in the iron was removed by oxidation, leaving semisolid malleable iron behind. From the 15th century on, this two-stage process gradually replaced direct making of malleable iron. It was in turn replaced by the PUDDLING PROCESS.

Finger Lakes Group of narrow, glacial lakes, western New York state. They lie in north-to-south valleys between SYRACUSE and Geneseo. The region, which embraces more than 20 state parks, is noted for its scenery, has many resorts, and produces fruits (especially grapes) and vegetables. Seneca Lake, the largest in the group, is 67 sq mi (174 sq km).

fingerprinting Act of taking an impression of a person's fingerprint. Because every person's fingerprints are unique, fingerprinting is used as a method of identification, especially in police investigations. The standard method of fingerprint classification was developed by Sir FRANCIS GALTON and Sir Edward Henry; their system was officially introduced at SCOTLAND YARD in 1901. The FEDERAL BUREAU OF INVESTIGATION maintains a fingerprint file on more than 90 million people; fingerprints retrieved from a crime scene may be compared with those on file to identify suspects. DNA analysis, which examines regions of DNA unique to each person, is sometimes called DNA FINGERPRINTING.

Fink, Mike (1770?–1823) U.S. keelboatman. Probably born near Fort Pitt (now Pittsburgh), Pa., he won fame in his youth as a local marksman and Indian scout, and soon became known as "king of the keelboatmen" on the Ohio and Mississippi rivers. Renowned as a marksman, roisterer, and champion rough-and-tumble fighter, his reputation made him a legendary hero of the American tall tale; even in his own time, his name was synonymous with the braggadocio of Western frontiersmen. He later became a trapper, and was shot and killed on an expedition to the Rockies.

Finke River \'fiŋk\ River, central Australia. Rising south of Mount Ziel in the MACDONNELL RANGES, it flows southeast for some 400 mi (640 km) through the southern Northern Territories and northern South Australia. It reaches Lake EYRE in South Australia only during times of flood, when it may spread for hundreds of square miles beyond its banks. It contains Finke Gorge National Park.

Finland *officially* **Republic of Finland** *Finnish* **Suomi** \'swȯ-mē\ Country, northern Europe. Area: 130,559 sq mi (338,145 sq km). Population (2000 est.): 5,178,000. Capital: HELSINKI. The majority of the people are Finns; there is a small SAMI (Lapp) population in LAPLAND. Languages: Finnish, Swedish (both official); the Sami speak a Finno-Ugric language. Religions: Lutheranism, Finnish (Greek) Orthodoxy. Monetary unit: euro. Finland is about 725 mi (1,165 km) long and 340 mi (550 km) at its widest; a third of the country is north of the Arctic Circle. Heavily forested, it contains thousands of lakes, numerous rivers, and extensive areas of marshland. Except for a small highland region in the extreme northwest, the country is a lowland less than 600 ft (180 m) above sea level. The south has relatively mild weather; the north has severe and prolonged winters and short summers. Finland has a developed free-market economy combined with state ownership of a few key industries. It is among the wealthiest countries in Europe and in the world. Lumbering is a major industry, and manufacturing is highly developed; service industries are also notable. It is a republic with one legislative house; its chief of state is the president, and the head of government is the prime minister. Recent archaeological discoveries have led some to suggest that human habitation in Finland dates back at least 100,000 years. Ancestors of the Sami apparently were present in Finland by about 7000 BC. The ancestors of the present-day Finns came from the southern shore of the Gulf of Finland in the 1st millennium BC. The area was gradually Christianized from the 11th century. From the 12th century Sweden and Russia contested for supremacy in Finland, until in 1323 Sweden ruled most of the country. Russia was ceded part of Finnish territory in 1721; in 1808 ALEXANDER I of Russia invaded Finland, which in 1809 was formally ceded to Russia. The subsequent period saw the growth of Finnish nationalism. Russia's losses in World War I and the

Russian Revolution of 1917 set the stage for Finland's independence in 1917. It was defeated by the Soviet Union in the Russo–Finnish War (1939–40) but then sided with Nazi Germany against the Soviets during World War II and regained the territory it had lost. Facing defeat again by the advancing Soviets in 1944, it reached a peace agreement with the U.S.S.R., ceding territory and paying reparations. Finland's economy recovered after World War II. It joined the European Union in 1995.

Finlay \fin-'lī\, **Carlos J(uan)** (1833–1915) Cuban epidemiologist. He is known for his discovery that yellow fever is transmitted by a mosquito. Though he published experimental evidence in 1886, his ideas were ignored for nearly 20 years. In 1900 Walter Reed confirmed Finlay's theory, leading to the eradication of yellow fever in Cuba and Panama by William Gorgas.

Finnbogadóttir, Vigdís (born 1930) Teacher, cultural figure, and politician who served as president of Iceland from 1980 to 1996. She was the first woman in the world to be elected head of state in a national election. After graduating from Reykjavík College in 1949, Finnbogadóttir attended the University of Grenoble and the Sorbonne in France and the University of Uppsala in Sweden. She also studied in Denmark and at the University of Iceland, where she later taught. From 1972 to 1980, while serving as director of the Reykjavík Theatre Company, Finnbogadóttir presented French lessons and cultural programming on Iceland State Television. In 1980, despite being a divorced single mother, Finnbogadóttir was drafted as a candidate for the presidency of Iceland and was narrowly elected. She was reelected three times (1984, 1988, and 1992) before retiring in 1996. In the same year she became founding chair of the Council of Women World Leaders at the John F. Kennedy School of Government at Harvard University; two years later she was appointed president of the United Nations Educational, Scientific and Cultural Organization World Commission on the Ethics of Scientific Knowledge and Technology.

Finney, Albert (born 1936) British actor. The son of a bookie, he established himself as a Shakespearean actor in the late 1950s. In 1960 he won praise as a working-class rebel in the play *Billy Liar* and the film *Saturday Night and Sunday Morning.* He played the lead in *Luther* on Broadway and became an international star in the film *Tom Jones* (1963). He later starred in such films as *Two for the Road* (1967), *The Dresser* (1983), *Under the Volcano* (1984), and *A Man of No Importance* (1994).

Finnish language Finno-Ugric language of Finland, spoken by close to 6 million people worldwide, including perhaps 200,000 speakers in North America. Finnish was an unwritten language until the 16th century, when Mikael Agricola (1509–1557) produced an alphabet book (1543) and a translation of the New Testament (1548); he is regarded as the founder of the Finnish literary language. Finnish was accorded official status in 1809, when Finland entered the Russian Empire after six centuries of Swedish domination. The publication in 1835 of the national folk epic, the *Kalevala,* created from folk songs collected by Elias Lonnrot, gave increased impetus to the movement to forge a common national language encompassing all dialect areas. Finnish shares with other Baltic Finnic languages a stock of ancient loanwords from Germanic, Baltic, Slavic, and Sami (see Finno-Ugric languages).

Finno-Ugric languages \'yü-grik\ Branch of the Uralic language family spoken by about 25 million people in northeastern Europe, northern Asia, and (through immigration) North America. More than 20 million are accounted for by two languages, Finnish and Hungarian. The Ugric subbranch comprises Hungarian and Ob-Ugrian. The latter consists of two language complexes of western Siberia, Khanty (Ostyak) and Mansi (Vogul), spoken by fewer than 15,000 people. The Finnic branch comprises the Sami (Saami, Lappish) languages, the Baltic Finnic (Fennic) languages, Mordvin, Mari, and the Permic languages. Sami is spoken by some 20,000 people in northern Scandinavia and adjacent Russia. Baltic Finnic comprises Finnish, Estonian (with 1.1 million speakers worldwide), and a string of declining languages in Latvia and Russia. Mordvin (Mordva) is spoken by 1.1 million people in scattered enclaves of central European Russia. Mari (Cheremis) is also spoken in central Russia and in scattered areas east toward the Urals; its two major varieties have about 600,000 speakers. The Permic (Permian) languages, spread over a broad swath of northeastern European Russia, comprise Udmurt (spoken by some 500,000 people) and Komi (spoken by fewer than 400,000 people but with two literary forms). Finno-Ugric languages written in Russia use variants of the Cyrillic alphabet, while those outside Russia use the Latin alphabet.

Finno-Ugric religion \ˌfi-nō-'yü-grik\ Pre-Christian belief systems of the Finno-Ugric peoples, who lived in northern Scandinavia, Siberia, the Baltic region, and central Europe. Surviving Finno-Ugric groups include the Sami (Lapps), Finns, Estonians, and Magyars. The geographic and cultural diversity of these peoples led to the evolution of varying religious beliefs. The most common Finno-Ugric creation myth is the earth-diver myth, in which the devil is forced to dive into the sea and gather sand, from which God forms the earth. Another myth tells of the creation of the world from a cosmic egg. The chief deities usually included a sky god and an earth mother. While the major gods were remote, there were guardian spirits at hand to regulate daily life; they resided in households, natural sites such as lakes and forests, and natural phenomena such as wind or fire. Ancestor worship was practiced. Religious functionaries included shamans, sacrificing priests, guardians of the sanctuary, professional weeping women, and performers of wedding ceremonies. Cult centers ranged from home sanctuaries to sacred groves and sacrificial stones.

Fionn cycle See Fenian cycle

fiord See fjord

Fiordland National Park \'fyȯrd-ˌland\ Park, southern South Island, New Zealand. Established in 1952, it is one of the largest national parks in the world, with an area of 4,834 sq mi (12,519 sq km), and renowned for the grandeur of its fjords, mountains, forests, waterfalls, and lakes. It is bordered by mountains on the east and by the Tasman Sea on all other sides. It is the site of Sutherland Falls, one of the highest waterfalls in the world, which drops 1,904 ft (580 m) in three cascades.

fir Properly, any of about 40 species of trees that make up the genus *Abies,* in the pine family. Many other evergreen conifers (e.g., Douglas fir, hemlock fir) are also commonly called firs. True firs are native to North and Central America, Europe, Asia, and northern Africa. They are distinguished from other genera in the pine family by their needlelike leaves, which grow directly from the branch and have bases, shaped like suction cups, that leave conspicuous circular scars when the leaves fall. North America boasts 10 native species of fir, found chiefly from the Rocky Mountains westward. The wood of most western North American firs is inferior to that of pine or spruce but is used for lumber and pulpwood. Of the two fir species that occur in the eastern U.S. and Canada, the better known is the balsam fir *(A. balsamea),* a popular ornamental and Christmas tree.

Firdusi See FERDOWSI

fire Rapid burning of combustible material, producing heat and usually accompanied by flame. For eons, LIGHTNING was the only source of fire. The earliest controlled use of fire seems to date to c. 1,420,000 years ago, but not until c. 7000 BC did Neolithic humans acquire reliable fire-making techniques, including friction from hardwood drills and sparks struck from flint against PYRITES. Fire was used initially for warmth, light, and cooking; later it was used in fire drives in hunting and warfare, and for clearing forests of underbrush to facilitate hunting. The first agriculturalists used fire to clear fields and produce ash for fertilizer; such "slash-and-burn" cultivation is still used widely today. Fire also came to be used for firing pottery and for smelting bronze (c. 3000 BC) and later iron (c. 1000 BC). Much of the modern history of technology and science can be characterized as a continual increase in the amount of energy available through fire and brought under human control.

fire ant Any of a genus *(Solenopsis)* of insects in the ANT family, several species of which are common in North America. They are red or yellowish and can inflict a severe sting. The semipermanent nest consists of a loose mound with open craters for ventilation. The workers (see CASTE) are notorious for damaging planted grain and attacking poultry.

fire escape Means of rapid egress from a building, primarily intended for use in case of fire. Building codes define an exit as an enclosed and protected path of escape in the event of a fire, leading from an exit access through a combination of corridors, stairways, and doors to an exit discharge at an exterior court or public way. The term fire escape usually refers to open iron or steel balconies with steep stairways on the outside of buildings; often a retrofit of older buildings, these are rare in new construction. Other means of escape are by balconies leading to adjacent buildings, or through chutes, often used in hospitals.

Fire Island Elongated sandspit, off the southern shore of LONG ISLAND, New York state. Measuring 32 mi (51 km) long and 0.5 mi (1 km) at its widest, its name refers to fires that were built there as signals to ships during the WAR OF 1812; a lighthouse was built at its western tip in 1858. Now a popular summer resort, it is connected to Long Island by two bridges and by ferry. Fire Island (now Robert Moses) State Park was opened in 1908, and a 19,000-acre (7,700-hectare) section of the island was dedicated as a national seashore in 1964.

fire walking Religious ceremony that involves walking across hot coals, red-hot stones, or burning wood. It has been practiced in many parts of the world, including ancient Greece, India, Japan, China, Tahiti, New Zealand, Bulgaria, and Spain. The most common form of fire walking involves striding across a layer of embers spread thinly over the bottom of a shallow trench. More rarely, devotees may walk through a blazing log fire. The reasons for fire walking include purification and as an ordeal to prove innocence. Devotees believe that only those who lack faith will be burned, and many fire walkers do escape without injury.

firefly *or* **lightning bug** Any of the nocturnal luminous BEETLES of the family Lampyridae, consisting of about 1,900 species that inhabit tropical and temperate regions (including the common GLOWWORM). Adult fireflies are 0.2–1 in. (5–25 mm) long and have light-producing organs on the underside of the abdomen. The soft, flattened, dark-brown or black body is often marked with orange or yellow. Some adult fireflies do not eat; others feed on pollen and nectar. Most fireflies produce short, rhythmic flashes in a pattern that is characteristic of the species and an important mating signal.

fireplace Opening made in the base of a chimney to hold an open fire. The opening is framed, usually ornamentally, by a mantel (or mantelpiece). A medieval development that replaced the open central hearth for heating and cooking, the fireplace was sometimes large enough to accommodate a sitting space called an inglenook. Early fireplaces were made of stone; later, brick came into use. In 1624 Louis Savot developed a fireplace in which air was drawn through passages under the hearth and discharged into the room through a grill, a design adapted in the 20th century.

fireproofing Use of fire-resistant materials in a building to prevent structural collapse and allow safe egress of occupants in case of fire. The fire-resistive ratings of various materials and constructions are established by laboratory tests and usually specified in terms of hours a material or assembly can be expected to withstand exposure to fire. Building codes require application of cementitious material or insulation to structural steel frames, fire-resistant construction (e.g., using concrete block) of enclosures around exits, flame-spread ratings of finish materials such as carpeting and wall coverings, and use of such inherently fire-resistant materials as reinforced concrete and heavy timber.

Firestone, Harvey S(amuel) (1868–1938) U.S. industrialist. Born in Columbiana, Ohio, he established a retail tire business in 1896. In 1904 he began manufacturing automobile tires. Sales to FORD MOTOR CO. helped put Firestone Tire and Rubber Co. at the top of the U.S. tire industry. Firestone promoted the use of trucks for hauling freight and lobbied for the construction of vast highway systems. He ran his company until 1932, when his son replaced him.

firewall Computer security system that controls the flow of data from one computer or NETWORK to another. Firewalls are mainly intended to protect the resources of a private network from being directly accessed by a user from an external network, especially via the Internet. Users inside the private network may also be prevented from directly accessing external computers. To accomplish this, all communications are routed through a "proxy server" that determines whether a message or file will be allowed to enter or exit the private network.

fireweed Perennial wildflower *(Epilobium angustifolium)* of the EVENING-PRIMROSE family. Its spikes of whitish to magenta flowers, which grow up to 5 ft (1.5 m) high, can be a spectacular sight on prairies of the temperate zone. Its seeds can lie dormant for many years, awaiting the warmth necessary for germination. Fireweed is one of the first plants to appear after a forest or brush fire; it also rapidly covers scrub or woodland areas that have been cleared by machine. It has limited use in wild gardens, where it must be carefully checked and confined.

fireworks EXPLOSIVES or combustibles used for display. Of ancient Chinese origin, fireworks evidently developed out of military rockets and explosive missiles, and accompanied the spread of military explosives westward during the European Middle Ages. In force-and-spark compositions, potassium nitrate, sulfur, and ground charcoal are used; additional ingredients produce various types of sparks. In flame compositions, such as the stars that shoot out of rockets, potassium nitrate, salts of antimony, and sulfur may be used; for colored fire, potassium chlorate or perchlorate is combined with a metal salt that determines the color. Rockets are lifted by recoil from the jet of fire thrown out by the burning composition.

first cause In philosophy, the uncreated or self-created cause to which every series of causes must ultimately be traced. Used by ancient Greek thinkers, the concept was adopted by the Christian tradition and became the basis of one version of the COSMOLOGICAL ARGUMENT for the existence of God, according to which every observed event is the result of a series of causes that must end in a first cause, which is God. The argument was given its classic formulation by ST. THOMAS AQUINAS. It was rejected by many later thinkers, including DAVID HUME and IMMANUEL KANT.

First International *officially* **International Working Men's Association.** Federation of workers' groups, founded in 1864 by British and French trade-union leaders. Its structure was highly centralized, based on local groups that were integrated into national federations. It was split by conflicting schools of socialist thought, including those of KARL MARX, P.-J. PROUDHON, LOUIS AUGUSTE BLANQUI, and MIKHAIL BAKUNIN. A clash between Marx's centralized SOCIALISM and Bakunin's ANARCHISM in 1872 caused the International to split, and it was dissolved in 1876. Though it was feared at the time as a formidable power with millions of members, and several countries tried to have it outlawed, its membership was never more than 20,000 and it served mainly as a unifying force for labor in Europe.

first lady Wife of the president of the United States. Although the first lady's role has never been codified or officially defined, she figures prominently in the country's political and social life. Representative of her husband on official and ceremonial occasions both at home and abroad, the first lady is closely watched for some hint of her husband's thinking and for a clue to his future actions. The wife of the president of the U.S. played a public role from the founding of the republic, but the title *first lady* did not come into general use until much later, near the end of the 19th century. By the end of the 20th century, the title had been absorbed into other languages and was often used, without translation, for the wife of the country's leader—even in countries where the leader's consort received far less attention and exerted much less influence than did her counterpart in the U.S. Although unpaid and unelected, her prominence provides her a platform from which to influence behavior and opinion, and some first ladies have used their influence to affect legislation on important matters such as temperance reform, housing improvement, and women's rights.

FIS See ISLAMIC SALVATION FRONT

fiscal policy Measures employed by governments to stabilize the economy, specifically by adjusting the levels and allocations of taxes and government expenditures. When the economy is sluggish, the government may cut taxes, leaving taxpayers with extra cash to spend and thereby increasing levels of CONSUMPTION. An increase in public-works spending may likewise pump cash into the economy, having an expansionary effect. Conversely, a decrease in government spending or an increase in taxes tends to cause the economy to contract. Fiscal policy is often used in tandem with MONETARY POLICY. Until the 1930s, fiscal policy aimed at maintaining a balanced budget; since then it has been used "countercyclically," as recommended by JOHN MAYNARD KEYNES, to offset the cycle of expansion and contraction in the economy. Fiscal policy is more effective at stimulating a flagging economy than at cooling an inflationary one, partly because spending cuts and tax increases are unpopular and partly because of the work of ECONOMIC STABILIZERS. See also BUSINESS CYCLE.

Fischer, Bobby *orig.* **Robert James** (born 1943) U.S. chess master, the youngest grand master in history. Born in Chicago, he became a grand master at the age of 15. In 1972 Fischer defeated BORIS SPASSKY to become the first U.S. player to hold the title of Chess Champion of the World. An intense and eccentric personality, he was a devout Christian fundamentalist who frequently condemned the Soviet Union for godlessness; he was deprived of his title in 1975 after refusing to meet his Soviet challenger, ANATOLY KARPOV. He remained out of the game thereafter except for a victorious private rematch with Spassky in Yugoslavia in 1992; the game violated U.S. sanctions against Yugoslavia, and Fischer has remained abroad since.

Bobby Fischer, 1971.

AP/WIDE WORLD PHOTOS

Fischer, Emil (Hermann) (1852–1919) German organic chemist. He received his PhD in 1874. He determined the structures of URIC ACID, CAFFEINE, and related compounds, showing that all are derivatives of a single compound he named PURINE. This led him to study PROTEIN structure and the ways in which AMINO ACIDS are combined in proteins. He determined the molecular structures of GLUCOSE, FRUCTOSE, and many other SUGARS, verifying his results by synthesizing each, and distinguished the 15 stereoisomers of glucose (see ISOMER, CONFIGURATION, OPTICAL ACTIVITY). His researches into the sugars were of unparalleled importance to organic chemistry and earned him in 1902 the second Nobel Prize for Chemistry. His investigations of FERMENTATION laid the foundations of ENZYME chemistry.

Fischer-Dieskau \'fi-shər-'dēs-ˌkau̇\, **Dietrich** (born 1925) German baritone and conductor. Born in Berlin, he had his first extensive performance experience as a prisoner of war in Italy, and he made his professional debut in 1947. One of the most remarkable singers of his time, he was equally successful in the often mutually exclusive realms of opera and lied. He recorded most of the standard art-song repertoire, as well as numerous unusual and contemporary works; his many premieres included BENJAMIN BRITTEN's *War Requiem* (1962). His voice lost beauty in later years, but his musicianship and intelligence more than compensated.

Fischer projection Method of representing the three-dimensional structures of MOLECULES on the page devised by EMIL FISCHER. By convention, horizontal lines represent bonds on the side toward the viewer, and vertical lines represent bonds on the side away from the viewer. Fischer projections are a convenient way to depict chiral molecules (see OPTICAL ACTIVITY) and distinguish between pairs of enantiomers (see RACEMATE). They are most often used to depict ISOMERS of the SUGARS. See also CHEMICAL FORMULA.

fiscus (Latin: "basket") Treasury of the Roman emperor, so-called because the money was stored in baskets. Funds were also stored in the public treasury, the AERARIUM. The fiscus took in taxes from imperial provinces, forfeited property, and unclaimed lands. After VESPASIAN, it became independent of the aerarium and controlled most of the empire's income, supplying funds for the army and fleet, official salaries, and postal subsidies.

fish Any of various cold-blooded VERTEBRATES found worldwide in freshwater and salt water. Living species range from the primitive LAMPREYS and HAGFISHES through the cartilaginous SHARKS, SKATES, and RAYS to the

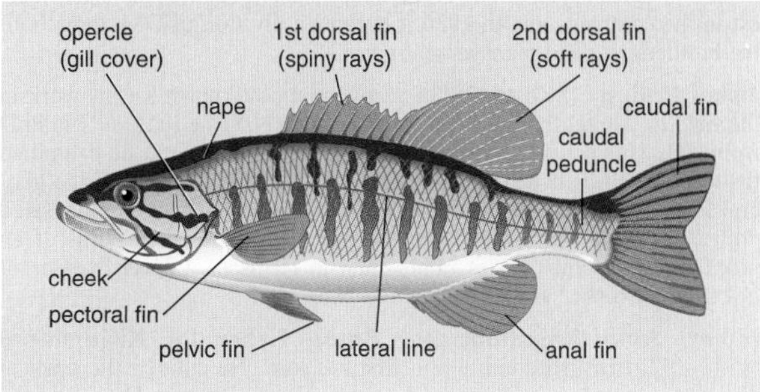

External features of a bony fish.

© 2002 MERRIAM-WEBSTER INC.

abundant and diverse BONY FISHES. Species range in length from 0.4 in. to more than 60 ft (10 mm–20 m). The body is generally tapered at both ends. Most species that inhabit surface or midwater regions are streamlined or are flattened side to side; most bottom-dwellers are flattened top to bottom. Tropical species are often brightly colored. Most species have paired fins and skin covered with either bony or toothlike scales. Fish generally respire through gills. Most bony fishes have a swim bladder, a gas-filled organ used to adjust swimming depth. Most species lay eggs, which may be fertilized externally or internally. Fishes first appeared more than 450 million years ago.

Fish, Hamilton (1808–1893) U.S. secretary of state (1869–77). Born in New York City, he served as lieutenant governor (1847–48), governor (1849–50), and U.S. senator (1851–57). As secretary of state in ULYSSES S. GRANT's administration, he skillfully promoted peaceful arbitration of explosive international situations, producing agreements with Britain in several disputes, including the *ALABAMA* CLAIMS, and with Spain over seizure of the *Virginius*. He helped draft the Treaty of Washington (1871), which provided for international arbitration. As a respected member of Grant's cabinet, he worked to counter graft, improper appointments, and violations of blacks' civil liberties.

Fish.

BY COURTESY OF THE LIBRARY OF CONGRESS, WASHINGTON, D.C.

fish duck See MERGANSER

fish farming See AQUACULTURE

fish hawk See OSPREY

fish poisoning Illness from eating varieties of poisonous fishes. Most cases are caused by one of three TOXINS: ciguatera poisoning, from fishes in whose flesh DINOFLAGELLATES have produced toxins; tetraodon poisoning, from a nerve toxin in certain pufferlike fish (fugu); and scombroid poisoning from spoilage bacteria in fish of the mackerel family. Shellfish poisoning from eating certain mussels, clams, and oysters has in some instances been traced to the plankton they sometimes feed on.

fisher (marten) Rare North American CARNIVORE (*Martes pennanti*, family Mustelidae) of northern forests. Related to the WEASEL and similarly shaped, it has a bushy tail, tapered muzzle, and low, rounded ears.

Adults are usually 20–25 in. (50–63 cm) long, excluding the 13–17-in. (33–43-cm) tail, and weigh 3–15 lbs (1.4–6.8 kg). Fishers hunt on the ground and in trees, attacking various rodents and other animals; they also eat fruits and sometimes nuts. It has been trapped for its valuable brownish black fur. See also MARTEN.

Fisher, Frederic (John) (1878–1941) U.S. automobile-body manufacturer. Born in Sandusky, Ohio, he worked for his father, a carriage maker, before moving to Detroit in 1902. From 1908 to 1916 he and his five brothers formed several companies building bodies for cars. When merged in 1916 as Fisher Body Corp., they were producing almost 400,000 bodies a year. In 1919 General Motors bought a majority interest in the company, and in 1926 it became a division of GM, though all the brothers retained management posts.

Fisher, Irving (1867–1947) U.S. economist best known for his work in the field of capital theory. Born in Saugerties, N.Y., he received his PhD from Yale University. As a professor at Yale (1892–1935), he examined the relationship between changes in the quantity of money and the general level of prices. He also promoted the concept of the "compensated dollar"—a dollar of constant purchasing power, defined in terms of an index of commodity prices rather than in terms of a given weight of gold. See also PRICE INDEX.

Fisher, John Arbuthnot *later* **Baron Fisher (of Kilverstone)** (1841–1920) British admiral and first sea lord. He entered the navy at 13 and saw combat in Crimea, China, and Egypt. Promoted to the admiralty board in 1892, he became first sea lord in 1904. He reorganized and strengthened the British navy to counter the rapid expansion of the German navy, and his reforms and innovations—including the conception of the battleship *DREADNOUGHT*, which revolutionized naval construction—ensured the Royal Navy's dominance in World War I. He retired in 1910; recalled in 1914 by WINSTON CHURCHILL, he resigned the next year in protest against the DARDANELLES CAMPAIGN.

Fisher, R(onald) A(ylmer) *later* **Sir Ronald** (1890–1962) British statistician and geneticist. As statistician for an agricultural research institute, he investigated the linkage of genes for different traits. To avoid unintentional bias in selection of materials used in experiments, he introduced the principle of randomization. It states that before an experimental effect can be attributed to a given cause or treatment, the experiment must be repeated on control units of the material and that all material used in experiments must be selected at random from the whole population it intends to represent. He also developed the concept of the analysis of variance, a statistical procedure used to design experiments that answer several questions at once.

fishing *or* **sport fishing** Sport of catching fish, freshwater or saltwater, typically with rod, line, and hook. Fishing is as old as the human ability to use tools to capture prey. The first significant modern innovations, including use of a reel, a rod with line guides, and a hook with an offset point, came in the late 17th and early 18th century. Horsehair was used as line until the mid-19th cent, when it was replaced by textile materials, in turn replaced in the 1930s by nylon. Wood and bamboo rods yielded to rods of fiberglass and other synthetic materials. Forms of sport fishing practiced today include fly fishing (freshwater), in which a fly-like hook is repeatedly cast upon the water surface to attract biting fish; bait fishing (fresh- and saltwater), in which live or artificial bait is set or drawn below the surface; and big-game fishing (saltwater), in which heavy-duty tackle is used to land large marine species (including tuna, marlin, and swordfish) from a motorized boat.

fishing industry Taking, processing, and marketing of fish and other seafood from oceans, rivers, and lakes. Fishing is one of the primary forms of food production; it ranks with farming and probably predates it. The fishing industry employs more than 5 million people worldwide. The major countries engaged in marine fishing are Japan, China, the U.S., Chile, Peru, India, South Korea, Thailand, and the countries of northern Europe. The aquatic life harvested includes both marine and freshwater species of fish, shellfish, mammals, and seaweed. They are processed into food for human consumption, animal feeds, fertilizers, and ingredients for use in other commercial commodities.

Fisk, James (1834–1872) U.S. financier. Born in Bennington, Vt., he worked his way up from circus hand to stockbroker and corporate official. He joined DANIEL DREW and JAY GOULD against CORNELIUS VANDERBILT in the "Erie War," in which the three tried to maintain control of the ERIE RAILROAD CO. by issuing fraudulent stock. They also attempted to corner the gold market by inflating the price, a venture that led to the panic of 1869. Known as "the Barnum of Wall Street," Fisk produced theatrical shows and dallied with showgirls; he was fatally shot by an associate at age 37 after quarreling over business matters and a mistress.

Fisk University Private, historically black university in Nashville, Tenn. Founded in 1865, it is affiliated with the United Church of Christ. It offers bachelor's degree programs in the arts and sciences as well as master's programs in several fields. Enrollment is about 1,000.

fission-track dating Method of determining the age of a mineral that utilizes the damage done by the spontaneous fission of uranium-238, the most abundant isotope of URANIUM. The fission results in radiation damage, or fission tracks, that can be made visible by preferential leaching (removal of material by solution) of the host substance with a suitable chemical reagent; the leaching process allows the etched fission-track pits to be viewed and counted under a microscope. The amount of uranium present can be determined by irradiation that produces thermal fission of uranium-235, which produces another population of tracks, related to the uranium concentration of the mineral. Thus, the ratio of naturally produced, spontaneous fission tracks to induced fission tracks is a measure of the age of the sample.

fitnah \'fit-nə\ (Arabic: "trial" or "test") In Islam, trials or temptations that test the unity of the Muslim community. There were four in the early history of Islam. The first (656–661), the murder of the caliph Uthman, resulted in the schism between the Sunni and the Shia (see SUNNI, SHIITE). The second coincided with the caliphates of YAZID I and his three successors (680–715); it was a continuation of the struggle between claimants to the caliphate. The third (744–50) resulted in the ascendancy of the ABBASIDS. The fourth (833–48) was a conflict over the nature of the QURAN. See also ALI, HUSAYN IBN ALI, AL-MUAWIYAH I.

FitzGerald, Edward (1809–1883) British writer. After graduating from Cambridge Univ., he lived chiefly in seclusion. He is best known for *The Rubáiyát of Omar Khayyám* (1859), a free adaptation from OMAR KHAYYAM's verses that is itself a classic of English literature. Many of its images, such as "A jug of wine, a loaf of bread, and thou" and "The moving finger writes, and, having writ, moves on" have passed into common currency. He also freely translated *Six Dramas of Calderón* (1853).

Fitzgerald, Ella (1917–1996) U.S. singer, the dominant female vocalist of American popular standards and jazz. Born in Newport News, Va., Fitzgerald won an amateur contest at Harlem's Apollo Theater in 1934 and became the star of drummer Chick Webb's big band the following year. Her association with manager and impresario Norman Granz in the late 1940s led to performances with Jazz at the Philharmonic and a famous series of "Songbook" recordings, each featuring the work of a single popular-song composer. One of the greatest scat singers in jazz, her clear, girlish voice and virtuosity made her one of the best-selling vocal recording artists in history.

Fitzgerald, F(rancis) Scott (Key) (1896–1940) U.S. novelist and short-story writer. Born in St. Paul, Minn., he attended Princeton Univ., but dropped out with bad grades. In 1920 he married Zelda Sayre (1900–1948), daughter of a respected Alabama judge. His works, including the early novels *This Side of Paradise* (1920) and *The Beautiful and Damned* (1922) and the story collections *Tales of the Jazz Age* (1922) and *All the Sad Young Men* (1926), capture the Jazz Age's vulgarity and dazzling promise. His brilliant *The Great Gatsby* (1925), a story of American wealth and corruption, was eventually acclaimed one of the century's greatest novels. In 1924 Scott and Zelda became part of the expatriate community on the French Riviera, the setting of *Tender Is the Night* (1934). His fame and prosperity proved disorienting to them both, and he became seriously alcoholic. Zelda never fully recovered from a mental breakdown in 1932, and spent most of her remaining years in a sanitarium. In 1937 Scott moved to Hollywood to write film scripts; the experience inspired the unfinished *The Last Tycoon* (1941). He died of a heart attack at 44.

Fitzroy River River, eastern QUEENSLAND, Australia. Formed by the confluence of the Dawson and Mackenzie rivers, on the slopes of the Eastern Highlands, it flows northeast across the Broadsound Range and then southeast to enter the CORAL SEA after a course of 180 mi (290 km). It is navigable 35 mi (56 km) from its mouth.

Fitzroy River River, northern WESTERN AUSTRALIA. It rises in the Durack Range and flows southwest through the King Leopold Ranges and the Geikie Gorge (where freshwater crocodiles are found). Turning northwest, it completes its flow of 350 mi (560 km), emptying into the Indian Ocean at King Sound. Sandbars and snags prevent navigation. Fitzroy Crossing, a town on the upper river, is in an area of large waterholes that sustain wildlife; just above it is the Geikie Gorge National Park.

Fiume question \'fyü-mā\ Post–World War I controversy over control of the Adriatic port of Fiume (modern Rijeka, Croatia). The secret Treaty of LONDON (1915) had assigned Fiume to Yugoslavia, but the Italians claimed it at the PARIS PEACE CONFERENCE. In 1919 GABRIELE D'ANNUNZIO mustered a small force and occupied Fiume. After Italy concluded the Treaty of Rapallo (1920) with Yugoslavia, which provided for a free state, it sent a battleship to scare him off. When BENITO MUSSOLINI came to power, he pressed for a new treaty (1924) that recognized Fiume as Italian and the suburb of Susak as Yugoslav. After World War II, Fiume became part of Yugoslavia.

Five, The See MIGHTY FIVE

Five Articles Oath See CHARTER OATH

Five Classics *Chinese* **Wujing.** Five ancient Chinese books associated with CONFUCIUS. For more than 2,000 years they were invoked as authorities on Chinese society, government, literature, and religion. Chinese students usually studied the shorter FOUR BOOKS before attempting the Five Classics, which consist of the *YI JING* ("Classic of Changes"), the *SHU JING* ("Classic of History"), the *Classic of Poetry,* the *Collection of Rituals,* and the *CHUNQIU* ("Spring and Autumn Annals"). The Five Classics were taught from 136 BC (when CONFUCIANISM became the state ideology of China) until the early 20th century. Proficiency in the texts was required for any scholar applying for a post in the vast government bureaucracy. After 1950 only selected texts were taught in public schools. See CHINESE EXAMINATION SYSTEM.

Five Dynasties Period in Chinese history betweeen the fall of the TANG DYNASTY (907) and the founding of the SONG DYNASTY (960), when five would-be dynasties (the Hou Liang, the Hou Tang, the Hou Jin, the Hou Han, and the Hou Zhou) followed one another in quick succession in northern China. The period is also called the Ten Kingdoms because of the 10 regimes that dominated separate regions of southern China in the same period. Though unstable politically, culturally it was a period of great accomplishment. Printing with wooden blocks was fully developed; the first complete printing of the Confucian Classics was completed in 953. The form of lyric poetry called *ci (tz'u)* flourished, and flower painting, previously distinctively Buddhist, became a branch of nonreligious painting.

Five Pecks of Rice Taoist-inspired popular movement that occurred near the end of China's HAN DYNASTY (206 BC–AD 220) and greatly weakened the government. It became a prototype of the religiously inspired popular rebellions that were to erupt periodically in China throughout its history. Its founder, ZHANG DAOLING, is considered the first patriarch of the Taoist church in China. He was originally a faith healer, and the movement's name came from the five pecks of rice a year that clients paid him for their cure or as dues to the cult. During a time of poverty and misery, Zhang's grandson Zhang Lu set up an independent theocratic state that grew to encompass all of present-day Sichuan province. In AD 215 Zhang Lu surrendered to CAO CAO. See also TAOISM, WHITE LOTUS, YELLOW TURBANS.

Five-Year Plans Method of planning economic growth over limited periods, through the use of quotas, used first in the Soviet Union and later in other socialist states. In the Soviet Union, the first Five-Year Plan (1928–32), implemented by JOSEPH STALIN, concentrated on developing heavy industry and collectivizing agriculture, at the cost of a drastic fall in consumer goods. The second plan (1933–37) continued the objectives of the first. Collectivization led to terrible famines, especially in the Ukraine, that caused the deaths of millions. The third (1938–42) emphasized the production of armaments. The fourth (1946–53) again stressed heavy industry and military buildup, angering the Western powers. In China, the first Five-Year Plan (1953–57) stressed rapid industrial development, with Soviet assistance; it proved highly successful. Shortly after the second plan began in 1958, the GREAT LEAP FORWARD was announced; its goals conflicted with the five-year plan, leading to failure and the withdrawal of Soviet aid in 1960.

fjord *or* **fiord** \fē-'ord\ Long, narrow arm of the sea, often extending well inland, that results from marine inundation of a glaciated valley. Many fjords are remarkably deep; it is assumed that the huge glaciers that formed in these valleys were so heavy that they eroded the bottoms of the valleys far below sea level. After the glaciers melted, the waters of the sea invaded the valleys.

Bradshaw Sound, Fiordland, west coast of South Island, New Zealand.

BY COURTESY OF THE NEW ZEALAND GEOLOGICAL SURVEY; PHOTOGRAPH, T. ULYATT

flag Combination of symbols represented on a piece of cloth, which serves as a medium of social, typically political, communication. It is usually rectangular and attached by one edge to a staff or is hoisted on a pole with halyards. Flags appear to be as old as civilized human society, though their origin is not well understood. The Chinese may have been the first to develop cloth flags, and it is believed that they were introduced to Europe by returning Crusaders. Most national flags in use today were designed in the 19th and 20th centuries.

flagellants \'fla-jə-lənts\ Medieval religious sects that included public beatings with whips as part of their discipline and devotional practice. Flagellant sects arose in northern Italy, and had become large and widespread by c. 1260. Groups marched through European towns, whipping each other to atone for their sins and calling on the populace to repent. They gained many new members in the mid-14th century while the BLACK DEATH was ravaging Europe. Though periodically suppressed by the authorities, flagellant sects enjoyed sporadic resurgences into the 16th century.

flagellum \flə-'jel-əm\ Hairlike structure that acts mainly as an organelle of movement in the cells of many living organisms. Characteristic of the PROTOZOAN group Mastigophora, flagella also occur on the sex cells of ALGAE, fungi (see FUNGUS), MOSSES, and SLIME MOLDS. Flagellar motion causes water currents necessary for respiration and circulation in SPONGES and CNIDARIANS. Most motile BACTERIA move by means of flagella. The structures and patterns of movement of flagella in PROKARYOTES differ from those in EUKARYOTES. See also CILIUM.

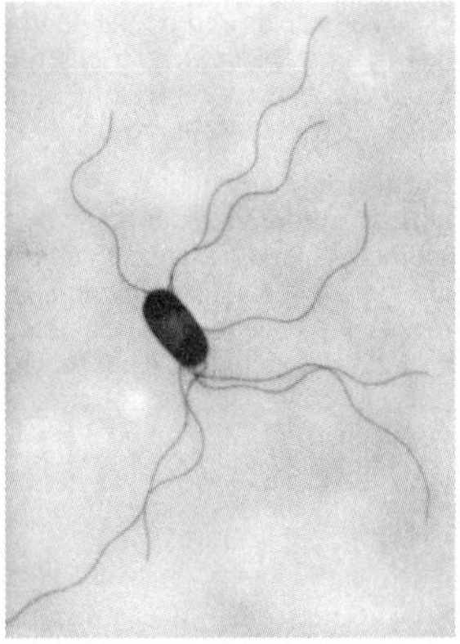
The bacterium *Proteus vulgaris* (greatly magnified) showing flagella.

© LEE D. SIMON—PHOTO RESEARCHERS

Flagler, Henry M(orrison) (1830–1913) U.S. financier. Born in Hopewell, N.Y., he initially worked as a grain merchant. His friendship with JOHN D. ROCKEFELLER, led to their establishing a firm that in 1870 became the STANDARD OIL CO. He served as a director of Standard Oil of New Jersey until 1911. He was hugely influential in the development of Florida as a vacation center, organizing and extending the Florida East Coast Railway, dredging Miami's harbor, and building a chain of luxury hotels.

Flagstad \'fläg-stä, *Engl* 'flag-ˌstad\, **Kirsten (Marie)** (1895–1962) Norwegian soprano. Born to musician parents, she made her operatic debut in 1913. In 1934 she was invited to sing Sieglinde in *Die Walküre* and Gutrune in *Götterdämmerung* at Bayreuth. Recognized as the greatest Wagnerian soprano of her generation, she made her Metropolitan Opera debut in 1935. With New York as base, she toured widely until 1941, returning to Norway to be with her husband, a member of VIDKUN QUISLING's government. Though cleared of charges of collaboration with the Germans, her later U.S. appearances were controversial.

Flaherty \'flä-ər-tē, 'fla-ər-tē\, **Robert (Joseph)** (1884–1951) U.S. filmmaker, considered the father of the DOCUMENTARY. Born in Iron Mountain, Mich., he grew up in remote northern Canada and later led explorations of the area (1910–16). He returned in 1920 to film the Eskimos' way of life, living with them for 16 months. His resulting film, *Nanook of the North* (1922), was an international success and established the model for the documentary film. His later documentaries include *Moana* (1926), *Tabu* (1931), *Man of Aran* (1934), *The Land* (1942), and *Louisiana Story* (1948).

flake tool Stone Age devices, usually flint (see chert and flint), shaped by flaking off small particles or by breaking off a large flake to use as a tool. Prehistoric humans preferred flint and similar siliceous stones because of the ease with which they could be chipped and for their sharp cutting edges. They also used sandstones, quartzites, quartz, obsidian, and volcanic rocks. Stone tools were chipped by striking a block of flint with a hammer of stone, wood, or bone or by striking the block itself on the edge of a fixed stone. Pressure flaking consists of applying pressure by means of a pointed stick or bone near the edge of a flake or blade, to detach small flakes, and was used mostly to put the finishing touches on tools. See also stone-tool industry.

Flamboyant style Phase of late Gothic architecture in 15th-century France and Spain. It evolved out of the Rayonnant style's increasing emphasis on decoration. Its most conspicuous feature is the dominance in stone window tracery of a flamelike S-shaped curve. Wall surface was reduced to the minimum to allow an almost continuous window expanse. Structural logic was obscured by covering buildings with elaborate tracery. Attractive French examples include Notre-Dame d'Épine near Châlons-sur-Marne, Saint-Maclou in Rouen (c. 1500–14), and the northern spire of Chartres Cathedral. Spanish Flamboyant architects developed their own intricate forms of vaulting with curvilinear patterns; the Capilla del Condestable in Burgos Cathedral (1482–94) and Segovia Cathedral (begun 1525) provide examples. Flamboyant Gothic, which became increasingly ornate, gave way in France to Renaissance forms in the 16th century.

flamen \'flā-mən\ One of 15 priests in ancient Rome, each of whom was devoted to the service of a specific god. The most important were those who served Jupiter, Mars, and Quirinus. Chosen from the patrician class and supervised by the pontifex maximus (chief priest), they offered daily sacrifices and led strictly regulated lives. Their wives assisted them and were also bound by ritual regulations. In imperial times a group of *flamines* were devoted to the worship of deified emperors.

flamenco \flə-'meŋ-kō\ Form of song, dance, and instrumental (mostly guitar) music commonly associated with the Andalusian Gypsies of southern Spain. (There, the Gypsy, or Roma, people and their language are known as Caló, or Gitano.) The roots of flamenco, though somewhat mysterious, seem to lie in the Gypsy migration from Rajasthan (in northwest India) to Spain between the 9th and 14th centuries. Its essence is *cante*, or song, often accompanied by guitar music and improvised dance. The *cante jondo* ("profound song" or "deep song"), thought to be the oldest form, is characterized by profound emotion and deals with themes of death, anguish, despair, or religious doubt. After the mid-19th century, flamenco song was usually accompanied by guitar music and a *palo seco* (Spanish: "dry stick," a stick that was beat on the floor to keep time) and a dancer performing a series of choreographed dance steps and improvised styles. *Baile*, or dance, has been the dominant element of flamenco since that time, though it is never performed without accompaniment. Essential to traditional flamenco is the *duende*, an intensely focused, trancelike state of transcendent emotion. It is usually enhanced by rhythmic hand clapping and encouraging interjections (*jaleo*) from fellow performers.

flamethrower Military assault weapon that projects a stream of blazing oil or gasoline against enemy positions. It consists of one or more fuel tanks, a cylinder of compressed gas to supply the propelling force, and a flexible hose with a trigger-nozzle that ignites and sprays the fuel. Portable flamethrowers are carried on the backs of ground troops; larger units may be installed on tank turrets. Modern flamethrowers, first used in combat in World War I, were used by all major powers in World War II and later wars. They are often used in areas of dense underbrush and against fortified positions at close range.

flamingo Any of four species of tall wading birds constituting the family Phoenicopteridae. The plumage is mainly pink, and the face is bare. Flamingos have webbed feet, a slender body, a long thin neck, large wings, and a short tail. They are about 3–5 ft (90–150 cm) tall. Flamingos flock by the hundreds (sometimes by the millions) in flight formations and wading groups. They tramp the shallows, stirring up organic matter, especially tiny mollusks and crustaceans, which they strain from the muddy water with their sievelike bills. The various species are found along Atlantic and Gulf coasts of tropical and subtropical North America and in South America, Africa, southern Europe, Asia, Madagascar, and India.

Flamininus \ˌflam-ə-'nī-ē-nəs\, **Titus Quinctius** (227?–174 BC) Roman general and consul (198 BC). As consul he tried to formulate a peace treaty with Philip V of Macedonia, but negotiations broke down and fighting broke out. He defeated Philip at Cynoscephalae (197) and granted freedom to the Greeks (196), for which he was hailed as a savior. He kept Roman troops in Greece until 194. After the defeat of Antiochus III and Aetolia at Thermopylae (191), he helped reestablish peace in Greece.

Flaminius \flə-'min-ē-əs\, **Gaius** (died 217 BC) Roman political leader. As tribune (232) he supported Roman expansion in northern Italy; his land bill (232) gave land to Roman plebeians and gained him great popularity, but he was held responsible for the Gallic invasion of 225 (repelled in 223), claimed to have been caused by the bill's passage. He was elected consul in 223 and 217. As censor (220) he built the Circus Flaminius in Rome and the Via Flaminia to Ariminum (Rimini). He died fighting Hannibal in the Second Punic War.

Flanders *Flemish* **Vlaanderen** \'vlän-də-rən\ Medieval principality extending along the coast of the Low Countries. Its lands are now divided among France, Belgium, and the Netherlands. Ruled by Baldwin I in 862, its strategic location between the Mediterranean Sea and the Scandinavian and Baltic countries fostered its growth as a commercial center. It passed to Burgundy in 1384 and then to the Austrian Habsburgs in 1477. It remained part of the Netherlands under Spanish rule in the 17th century. It was the scene of fighting during both World Wars. Limited autonomy was granted to Belgian Flanders in the 1980s, and it became one of the three regions in the new federation of Belgium in 1993.

Flandin \flä^n-'da^n\, **Pierre-Étienne** (1889–1958) French politician. He served in the Chamber of Deputies 1914–40, and held various ministerial posts in the Third Republic, serving briefly as premier (1934–35). As foreign minister when the Germans marched into the Rhineland in 1936, he failed to convince the French and British governments to act. As foreign minister (1940–41) in the Vichy regime, he resisted German demands. Later charged with treason, he was acquitted in 1946.

flare star Star that varies in brightness repeatedly but sporadically, sometimes by more than one magnitude, within a few minutes. The cause is thought to be the eruption of flares like those observed on the sun but much larger. Proxima Centauri, in Alpha Centauri, the closest star to the sun, is a flare star.

flat See playa

flatfish Any of about 600 species (order Pleuronectiformes) of oval-shaped, flattened bony fishes (e.g., flounder, turbot), found from tropical to cold waters. Most are marine and live at moderate depths along the continental shelf, but some enter or live permanently in freshwater. Flatfishes are carnivorous bottom-dwellers that habitually rest on one side, often partly buried in the sand or mud. Some can also change color to blend with their surroundings. Both eyes are on one side of the head. The eyed side of the fish (uppermost as it lies on the bottom) is pigmented, but the lower, blind side is normally white. Species vary from 4 in. (10 cm) to 7 ft (2 m) long, and some (e.g., the Atlantic halibut) may weigh as much as 720 lbs (325 kg). Many species are highly valued as food. See also plaice, sole.

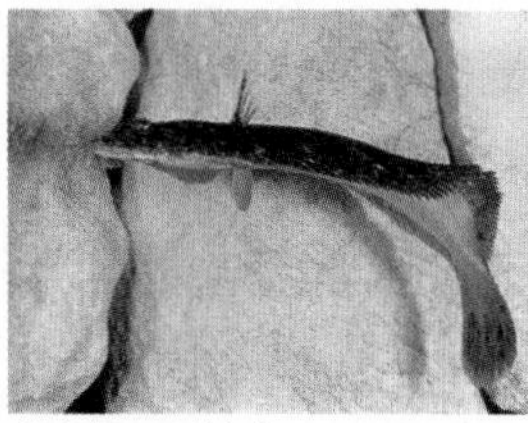

Flatfish (*Scophthalmus*).
JACQUES SIX

flatfoot Congenital or acquired flatness of the arch of the foot, in which the foot and heel usually also roll outward, resulting in a splay-footed position. Initially, it may result from ligament stretching and muscle weakness. Later, altered shape of the bones may make the deformity rigid. In a few cases it seems to result from excessive weight or an injury. Symptoms may include pain, spasm, and awkward gait, but many patients have no disability or pain. Treatment to correct arch and heel position employs proper shoes and muscle strengthening; arch supports are indicated only for severe pain or excessive fatigue.

Flathead North American Indian people of SALISHAN LANGUAGE stock who inhabited what is now western Montana. Salish was the native name of the tribe, but Flathead is now customary; they themselves did not practice head-flattening, but some of their slaves came from tribes that did. The Flatheads were the easternmost group of the PLATEAU INDIANS but exhibited many cultural traits of the PLAINS INDIANS just east over the Rockies. They acquired horses and went on bison hunts on the Plains, often warring with Plains tribes. The Plains TEPEE was the usual dwelling. Western Flatheads used bark canoes, and for all groups fishing was important. Religious belief centered on guardian spirits, with whom one communicated in visions. Since 1872 the Flatheads have resided primarily on a reservation north of Missoula, Mont. Today they number about 4,000.

Flathead River River, southeastern British Columbia and western Montana. Rising in the MacDonald Range, it flows south for 240 mi (385 km) across the Canada–U.S. boundary into Montana. After passing between the Whitefish Range and GLACIER NATIONAL PARK, it enters Flathead Lake and emerges to join the CLARK FORK. The Flathead Valley is a resort region with diversified farming and fruit growing, lumbering, and mining.

Flatt, Lester (1914–1979) U.S. BLUEGRASS and country-music guitarist and singer. He was born in Overton Co., Tenn., and worked in textile mills until the late 1930s, when he and his wife Gladys began performing as a duo. In 1945 he joined BILL MONROE's Blue Grass Boys. There he met Earl Scruggs (born 1924), a native of Flint Hill, N.C., who had played banjo since age 5 and had begun playing on radio by 15. Scruggs eventually perfected a picking technique involving the thumb and first two fingers of the right hand that came to be called the "Scruggs style." In 1948 the two men left Monroe's band to form Flatt and Scruggs and the Foggy Mountain Boys. They made dozens of records in the 1950s and '60s, and hosted their own syndicated radio and TV shows. Scruggs's original instrumental compositions, including "Foggy Mountain Breakdown," were especially popular. They parted ways in 1969 when Scruggs joined his sons Gary and Randy (and later Steve) in the Earl Scruggs Revue.

flatworm *or* **platyhelminth** Any of a phylum (Platyhelminthes) of soft-bodied, usually much-flattened WORMS, including both free-living and parasitic species. Flatworms live in a variety of marine, freshwater, and terrestrial habitats worldwide. They range in length from much less than an inch (a fraction of a millimeter) to 50 ft (15 m) and are of three main types: turbellarians (including the PLANARIAN), trematodes (see FLUKE), and cestodes (see TAPEWORM). Flatworms are bilaterally symmetrical and lack respiratory, skeletal, and circulatory systems and a body cavity. Turbellarians are mostly free-swimming, but trematodes and cestodes are parasites.

Flaubert \flō-'ber\, **Gustave** (1821–1880) French novelist. Born in Rouen, he abandoned law studies at 22 for a life of writing. His masterpiece, *Madame Bovary* (1857), a sharply realistic portrayal of provincial bourgeois boredom and adultery, led to his trial (and narrow acquittal) on charges of immorality. His other novels include the exotic *Salammbô* (1862), set in ancient Carthage; *A Sentimental Education* (1869), a classic bildungsroman of disillusionment in a time of social and political change; and *The Temptation of Saint Anthony* (1874), notable for its depiction of spiritual torment. *Trois Contes* (1877), contains three novellas set in the ancient, medieval, and contemporary periods. His collected letters are considered perhaps the finest such collection of all time. Renowned for his lapidary style, he is regarded as the foremost exponent of French REALISM.

Flaubert, detail of a drawing by E.F. von Liphart, 1880; in the Bibliothèque Municipale, Rouen, Fr.

BY COURTESY OF THE BIBLIOTHEQUE MUNICIPALE, ROUEN; PHOTOGRAPH, ELLEBE

Flavian dynasty \'flā-vē-ən\ (AD 69–96) Ancient Roman imperial dynasty of VESPASIAN and his sons TITUS and DOMITIAN, members of the Flavia gens, or clan. Vespasian sought to give the office of emperor permanent form, by means of a formal system of titles to replace personal names, an insistence on the rights of office, and a move to make Caesarism (dictatorship) hereditary by natural descent or adoption. Worship of the deified caesars (subemperors) became the symbol of imperial continuity and legitimacy.

flavin \'flā-vən\ Any of a class of organic compounds, pale yellow biological pigments that fluoresce green. They occur in compounds essential to life as COENZYMES in METABOLISM. Plants and microbes can synthesize them, but animals must consume them in the diet. RIBOFLAVIN is the best-known flavin.

flavonoid \'flā-və-ˌnȯid\ *or* **flavone** Organic compound, any member of a class of biological PIGMENTS containing no nitrogen, found in many plants. They include anthoxanthins, which give yellow colors, often to flower petals, and anthocyanins, largely responsible for the red coloring of buds and young shoots and the purple and purple-red colors of autumn leaves. Their biological function is unknown; they may attract pollinators and seed dispersers.

flax family Family Linaceae (order Linales), composed of about 14 genera of herbaceous plants and shrubs found throughout the world. The genus *Linum* includes flax, perhaps the most important member of the family, grown for LINEN fiber and linseed oil and as a garden ornamental. *Reinwardtia* species are primarily low shrubs, grown in greenhouses and outdoors in warm climates; *R. indica,* yellow flax, is notable for its large yellow flowers, borne in profusion in late fall and early winter.

Flaxman, John (1755–1826) British sculptor, illustrator, and designer. In 1770 he entered the Royal Academy schools. After 1775 he worked for JOSIAH WEDGWOOD, producing designs based on classical antiquity. He directed the Wedgwood studio in Rome (1787–94), but his book illustrations were of far greater importance; his *Iliad* (1793), *Odyssey* (1795), and *Divine Comedy* (1807) became very well known. The leading Neoclassical artist in England, he became the Royal Academy's first professor of sculpture (1810). His reputation as a sculptor, notably of monuments with large groups of free-standing figures, was exceeded only by that of ANTONIO CANOVA and BERTEL THORVALDSEN.

flea Any member of 1,600 species and subspecies of small, wingless, bloodsucking (parasitic) INSECTS (order Siphonaptera), found from the Arctic Circle to the Arabian deserts. Specialized anatomical structures allow the flea to attach itself to the skin of mammals or birds and consume their blood. Though domestic cats and dogs are well-known hosts, rodents are the mammals most commonly afflicted by fleas. The adult flea is 0.04–0.4 in. (1–10 mm) long and lives from a few weeks to more than a year. Powerful leg muscles allow it to jump distances up to 200 times its body length. Flea infestations have had enormous consequences; fleas were the principal transmission agents of the bubonic PLAGUE in the medieval epidemics.

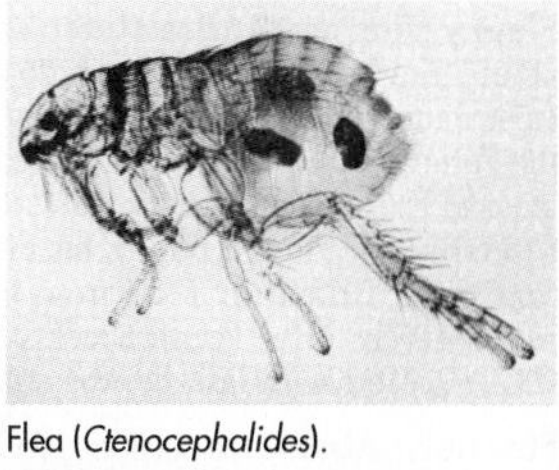

Flea (*Ctenocephalides*).

WILLIAM E. FERGUSON

flea beetle Any member of the BEETLE subfamily Alticinae (family Chrysomelidae), found worldwide. It is tiny (less than 0.25 in., or 6 mm, long) and dark or metallic in color. The enlarged hindlegs are adapted for jumping. Flea beetles are important PESTS of cultivated plants (e.g., grapes, cucumbers, melons, tobacco, potatoes, and tomatoes). The adults feed on the leaves and the larvae on the roots. Some flea beetles carry plant diseases (e.g., early potato BLIGHT).

Fleischer, Dave and Max (1894–1979, 1883?–1972) U.S. animators. Max was born in Vienna, Dave in New York City. The brothers worked as newspaper cartoonists before founding their own studio in 1921 to make animated cartoons. In the mid-1920s they produced the first sound-on-film animations. They later created and produced the popular cartoon series *Betty Boop* (1931–39), *Popeye the Sailor* (1929–42), and

Superman (1941–42) and the feature-length cartoon *Gulliver's Travels* (1939).

Fleming, Alexander *later* **Sir Alexander** (1881–1955) Scottish bacteriologist. While serving in the Royal Army Medical Corps in World War I, he conducted research on antibacterial substances that would be nontoxic to humans. In 1928 he inadvertently discovered penicillin when he noticed that a mold contaminating a bacteria culture was inhibiting the bacteria's growth. He shared a 1945 Nobel Prize with ERNST BORIS CHAIN and HOWARD WALTER FLOREY, who both carried Fleming's basic discovery further in isolating, purifying, testing, and producing penicillin in quantity.

Fleming, Ian (Lancaster) (1908–1964) British suspense novelist. He worked as a Moscow journalist, banker and stockbroker, naval intelligence officer, and newspaper manager before publishing *Casino Royale* (1953), the first of 12 novels featuring James Bond, the stylish, high-living secret-service agent 007, one of the most successful heroes of 20th-century fiction. Packed with violent action, espionage, and sex, all 12 books—including *From Russia, with Love* (1957), *Dr. No* (1958), *Goldfinger* (1959), and *Thunderball* (1961)—became popular movies.

Fleming, Peggy (Gale) (born 1948) U.S. figure skater. Born in San Jose, Cal., she won the first of five consecutive Senior Ladies' championships when she was 15. She finished second (1965) and then first (1967) in the North American title competition, won the world championship three consecutive years (1966–68), and won a gold medal in the 1968 Olympics. She turned professional that year.

Flemish art Art of the 15th to early 17th century in Flanders. The precursors of the Flemish school were located in Dijon, the first capital of the dukes of BURGUNDY, who established a powerful Flemish-Burgundian political alliance that lasted from 1363 to 1482. PHILIP III the Good moved the Burgundian capital to Bruges and in 1425 hired JAN VAN EYCK as his painter. The next generation of artists built on van Eyck's heritage and, toward the end of the 15th century, began looking to Italy for pictorial inspiration. ROGIER VAN DER WEYDEN, PETRUS CHRISTUS, DIRCK BOUTS, HUGO VAN DER GOES, HANS MEMLING, and GERARD DAVID brought innovation, but little of their work compared with van Eyck's artistic vision. In the 16th century, PIETER, THE ELDER BRUEGEL, under the influence of HIERONYMUS BOSCH, depicted peasant life with an eye for the grotesque. The great master of the 17th century, PETER PAUL RUBENS, demonstrated unrivaled skill in oil painting; his style epitomized the Flemish baroque period. See also EARLY NETHERLANDISH ART.

Fletcher, John See Francis BEAUMONT

Fleury \flœ-'rē\, **André-Hercule de** (1653–1743) French cardinal and chief minister of LOUIS XV (1726–43). A priest, he was made almoner (distributor of alms) for LOUIS XIV. In 1715 he was appointed tutor for the future LOUIS XV, who later created Fleury a cardinal and minister of state (1726). Domestically, he restored economic and financial stability to France; in foreign policy, his efforts prevented the hostilities between Spain and Britain in 1727 from becoming a European conflict. Drawn into the War of the POLISH SUCCESSION (1733–38) on the side of STANISLAW I, Louis's father-in-law, he was able to limit the conflict's scope.

Flexner, Abraham (1866–1959) U.S. educator. Born in Louisville, Ky., he taught high school for almost 20 years. When the Carnegie Foundation asked him to evaluate the 155 U.S. and Canadian medical colleges, his report (1910) had a sensational impact; many of the colleges he severely criticized closed, and others revised their policies and curricula. Flexner thereafter channeled over half a billion dollars from the Rockefeller Foundation into improving U.S. medical education. In 1930 he founded the Institute for Advanced Study in Princeton, N.J., to which he brought some of the world's outstanding scientists.

flexor muscle Muscle that decreases the angle of a JOINT (e.g., bends the elbow). Bending the wrist or spine forward is also considered flexion. The movement is usually directed forward, except at the knee. See also EXTENSOR MUSCLE.

Flick, Friedrich (1883–1972) German industrialist. Before World War II he built an industrial empire that included iron-ore and coal mines, steel mills, trucks, airplanes, and munitions. He became ADOLF HITLER's biggest industrial supplier, and at the NUREMBERG TRIALS he was convicted of using slave labor in his mines and plants. Though much of his empire was confiscated, he later amassed another fortune in coal and steel, and at the time of his death was probably Germany's wealthiest man.

flicker Any of six species of New World WOODPECKERS (genus *Colaptes*) noted for spending much time on the ground eating ants. The sticky saliva of the flicker is alkaline, perhaps to counteract the formic acid that ants secrete. Its bill is more slender than that of most woodpeckers and is slightly downcurved. Most flickers have a white rump, black breast band, and varied head markings, and most are about 13 in. (33 cm) long.

Yellow-shafted flicker (*Colaptes auratus*).
B.M. SHAUB

flight recorder Instrument that records the performance and condition of an aircraft in flight. REGULATORY AGENCIES require these devices on commercial aircraft to make possible the analysis of crashes or other unusual occurrences. They are housed in heavy steel within layers of insulation, protecting them against impacts and fires. The recording tape is also protected against inadvertent erasure and contact with seawater. It records airspeed, altitude, heading, vertical acceleration, and aircraft pitch. It also includes a separate device that records voice communication within the aircraft and by radio. Both recorders are carried in the tail of the aircraft.

Flinders, Matthew (1774–1814) British mariner and hydrographer. In two expeditions (1795–99, 1801–3) he circumnavigated Australia and Tasmania, charting their coasts and waters. His *Voyage to Terra Australis* (1814) recounted his adventures. His name was given to several geographical entities in Australia. FLINDERS PETRIE was his grandson.

Flinders Ranges Mountain region, SOUTH AUSTRALIA. It extends some 500 mi (800 km) north from Gulf SAINT VINCENT. Beyond Peterborough to the northeast, the highland region continues as the Mount Lofty Ranges. The Flinders exceed 3,000 ft (900 m) at several points, reaching 3,825 ft (1,166 m) at St. Mary Peak, the state's second-highest peak. The ranges feature scenic landscapes and include Flinders Ranges National Park and Gammon Ranges National Park.

Flinders River River, QUEENSLAND, Australia. It rises on the southwestern slopes of the Gregory Range and flows west and then north to the Gulf of CARPENTARIA through two mouths, the second known as the Bynoe River, after a course of 520 mi (837 km). The river's valley was first settled in 1864; its lands are used in part for raising cattle and sheep. Only its lowest 70 mi (113 km) are usually perennial.

Flint City (pop., 1996 est.: 135,000), eastern Michigan. Originally the site of a trading post, the city was laid out in 1836 and became a fur-trading and agricultural center. Abundant supplies of timber led to the development in 1886 of the Durant-Dort Carriage Co., and by 1900 it was producing over 100,000 horse-drawn vehicles a year. Some of the companies became suppliers for what would become the GENERAL MOTORS CORP. By the 1950s, the city was second only to DETROIT in U.S. automobile manufacturing. The closing of various G.M. plants in the 1980s and '90s left Flint with a shrinking economy. The GMI Engineering and Management Institute (1919) and the University of Michigan–Flint (1956) are located there.

flint See CHERT AND FLINT

flintlock Ignition system for firearms developed in the early 16th century. It superseded the MATCHLOCK and the WHEEL LOCK and remained in use until the mid-19th century. The most successful version, the true flintlock, was invented in France in the 17th century. When the trigger was pulled, a spring action caused the frizzen (striker) to strike the flint, showering sparks onto the gunpowder in the priming pan; the ignited powder, in turn, fired the main charge in the bore, propelling the ball.

Flodden, Battle of (September 9, 1513) English victory over the Scots, fought in Flodden Field, near Branxton, Northumberland. To honor his alliance with France and divert troops from the main English army, then in France under HENRY VIII, JAMES IV of Scotland crossed the border on August 22 with an army of about 30,000 men supported by artillery. Henry's lieutenant, the future 3rd duke of NORFOLK, gathered an army of 20,000 and issued a challenge to James, who agreed to fight on September 9. By nightfall the Scottish army had been annihilated and James was dead, together with over 10,000 of his subjects.

flood High-water stage in which water overflows its natural or artificial banks onto normally dry land, such as a river inundating its floodplain. Uncontrollable floods likely to cause considerable damage commonly result from excessive rainfall in a brief period, but they may also result from ice jams during the spring rise in rivers, and from TSUNAMIS. Common measures of flood control include improving channels, constructing protective levees and storage reservoirs, and implementing programs of soil and forest conservation to retard and absorb runoff from storms.

floor Rigid building assembly that divides space horizontally into stories. It forms the bottom of a room. It may consist of joist-supported wood planks or panels, decking or panels supported by wood or steel beams, a slab of stone or concrete on the ground, or a reinforced-concrete slab carried by concrete beams and columns. The floor assembly must support its own dead load plus the live load of occupants, activities, and furnishings. The horizontal supports beneath its top surface—and the vertical supports into which they frame—must be sufficiently large and spaced closely enough to prevent sagging of the assembly.

floor covering Finish material on floors, including wood strips, parquet, linoleum, vinyl, asphalt tile, rubber, cork, epoxy resins, ceramic tile, and carpeting. Wood-strip flooring, attached to a subfloor of plywood, is most popular, especially for residences. Vinyl tiles and sheets have displaced LINOLEUM in most residential and commercial work. Nonslip rubber and cork are used for commercial and industrial applications. TERRAZZO provides a hard, durable surface for public spaces. The Greeks used pebble mosaics as early as the 8th century BC. Tessellated pavement (mosaics of regularly shaped cubes) appeared in the Hellenistic Age and by the 1st century AD had come into popular use in and around buildings throughout the Roman empire. Inlaid stone, popular in Byzantine, Renaissance, and Gothic architecture, is now only occasionally applied in lobbies and entranceways of grand spaces.

floor exercise Event in GYMNASTICS competition consisting of various ballet and tumbling movements (including jumps, somersaults, and handstands) performed without apparatus. Women's routines are performed with musical accompaniment, men's routines without it. The whole routine must be performed with rhythm and harmony, and must be designed to use a major portion of an area 12 m (39 ft 4 in.) square. It was included as an Olympic medal event for men in 1936 and for women in 1952.

floppy disk *or* **diskette** Magnetic storage medium used with COMPUTERS. Floppy disks are made of flexible plastic coated with a magnetic material, and are enclosed in a hard plastic case. They are typically 3.5 in. (9 cm) in diameter. Data are arranged on their surfaces in concentric tracks. A disk is inserted in the computer's floppy disk drive, an assembly of magnetic heads and a mechanical device for rotating the disk for reading or writing purposes. A small electromagnet, called a magnetic head, writes a binary digit (1 or 0) onto the disk by magnetizing a tiny spot on the disk in different directions, and reads digits by detecting the magnetization direction of the spots. With the increasing use of E-mail attachments and other means to transfer files from computer to computer, the use of floppy disks has waned, though they are still widely used to keep second (backup) copies of valuable files.

Flora Roman goddess of flowering plants. Her cult was supposedly introduced into Rome during its earliest years by the Sabine king Titus Tatius. Her temple stood near Rome's Circus Maximus, and her festival, the Floralia, was instituted in 238 BC.

flora All species of plants that are found in a particular region, period, or special environment. Six floral kingdoms are commonly distinguished: Boreal (Holarctic), Paleotropical, Neotropical, South African (Capensic), Australian, and Antarctic. These kingdoms are further broken down into subkingdoms and regions, over which there is some dispute.

floral decoration Art of arranging living or dried plant material for adornment of the body or home, for public and religious ceremonies, or for festivals. Line, form, color, texture, balance, porportion, and scale are important aspects of floral arrangement, as is the container. The earliest pictorial example is a 2nd-century Roman mosaic from the villa of HADRIAN at Tivoli depicting a basket of cut flowers. Dutch and French still-life paintings of the 17th–18th century show the popularity of floral arrangements. Their long history in China and Japan is often associated with religious and philosophical beliefs; Japanese forms have become influential in the West. See also IKEBANA.

Florence *Italian* **Firenze** \fē-'rent-sä\ City (pop., 2000 est.: 376,682), capital of TUSCANY region, central Italy. Built on both sides of the ARNO RIVER, the city has been during its long history a republic, a seat of the duchy of Tuscany, and a capital (1865–71) of Italy. Founded as a Roman military colony in the 1st century BC, it was controlled in turn by the Goths, Byzantines, and Lombards. A leading city of Tuscany by the late 12th century, it was ruled after 1434 by the powerful MEDICI FAMILY. It became a republic under religious reformer SAVONAROLA, after whose downfall the Medici were restored as dukes of Florence (1531). Florence's vernacular became the Italian language, and from the 14th to the 16th century, Florence was among the greatest cities of Europe, preeminent in commerce, finance, learning, and the arts. Over time, many notables flourished there, including LEONARDO DA VINCI, MICHELANGELO, BRUNELLESCHI, DANTE, MACHIAVELLI, and GALILEO. Its buildings, including the Baptistery of St. John, the Gothic Duomo, and the UFFIZI GALLERY, are works of art themselves abounding in yet more works of art. Among its palaces and parks are the Pitti Palace and its Boboli gardens. Its university was founded in 1321. Florence's economy is based primarily on tourism, though it also has developed newer sectors such as information technology and high-fashion clothing. The region around the city has a modern and dynamic economy based on small industrial production and quality exports.

Florentine canvas work See BARGELLO

Florey, Howard Walter *later* **Baron Florey** (1898–1968) Australian pathologist. Educated in Britain and the U.S., Florey taught at Oxford University from 1935. Investigating tissue inflammation and secretion of mucous membranes, he succeeded in purifying lysozyme, a bacteria-destroying enzyme found in tears and saliva, and characterized the substances it acted on. He surveyed other naturally occurring antibacterial substances, concentrating on PENICILLIN, which, with ERNST BORIS CHAIN, he isolated and purified for general clinical use. The two demonstrated penicillin's curative properties in human studies and developed methods for producing it in quantity. In 1945 he shared a Nobel Prize with Chain and ALEXANDER FLEMING, and in 1965 he was created a life peer.

floriculture Branch of ornamental HORTICULTURE concerned with growing and marketing flowers and ornamental plants, as well as with flower arrangement. Because flowers and potted plants are largely produced in plant-growing structures in temperate climates, floriculture is largely thought of as a GREENHOUSE industry; however, many flowers are cultivated outdoors. Both the production of BEDDING PLANTS and the production of CUTTINGS to be grown in greenhouses or for indoor use (foliage plants) are usually considered part of floriculture. See also NURSERY.

Florida State (pop., 1997 est.: 14,654,000), southeastern U.S. It comprises a peninsula and adjoining mainland areas, and covers 58,664 sq mi (151,940 sq km); its capital is TALLAHASSEE. Indian groups entered Florida from the north as early as 10,000 years ago. It was explored by JUAN PONCE DE LEON c. 1513, and in 1565 Spaniards founded ST. AUGUSTINE. Florida became a British possession in 1763 after the FRENCH AND INDIAN WARS. The area reverted to Spanish control after the AMERICAN REVOLUTION (1783) but was used by the British as a base of operations during the WAR OF 1812. ANDREW JACKSON's capture of Pensacola during that war led to the cession of Florida to the U.S. in 1819. A war with the SEMINOLE Indians followed (see SEMINOLE WARS). Florida became a state in 1845. It seceded from the Union in 1861, then was readmitted in 1868. In the late 20th century, it became one of the fastest growing states in the U.S. It produces about 75% of the nation's citrus fruits, and is second only to California in vegetable production. Tourism is a leading industry, with DISNEY WORLD a major attraction. Electronics manufacture is important, and the aerospace industry, centered on the Kennedy Space Center (see Cape CANAVERAL), employs many thousands of people.

The state, and especially the city of MIAMI, with its large Cuban population, plays a major economic role in the Caribbean region. Among its many recreational areas is EVERGLADES National Park.

Florida, Straits of Passage connecting the Gulf of Mexico with the Atlantic Ocean. Extending for about 110 mi (180 km) between the Florida Keys on the north and Cuba and the Bahamas on the south, the straits mark the area where the Florida Current, the initial part of the GULF STREAM, flows east out of the Gulf of MEXICO. The Spanish explorer JUAN PONCE DE LEON de León first recorded sailing through the straits in 1513.

Florida, University of Public university in Gainesville, Fla. It was formed in 1906 through the merger of a land-grant college and a seminary. It is a comprehensive research university, consisting of numerous schools and colleges, among them colleges of law, medicine, and various health professions; schools of accounting, building construction, and forestry; a center for Latin American studies; and a division of military science. Important research facilities include a brain science center, a marine laboratory, a center for exercise science, and a wildlife sanctuary. Total enrollment is about 40,000.

Florida Controversy, West See WEST FLORIDA CONTROVERSY

flotation *or* **froth flotation** Most widely used process for extracting many MINERALS from their ORES. The method separates and concentrates ores by altering their surfaces so that they are either repelled or attracted by water. Unwetted particles, which adhere to air that is bubbled through the water, will float in the froth, while wetted particles will sink. The process was developed on a commercial scale early in the 20th century to remove very fine mineral particles that formerly had gone to waste in gravity concentration plants. With its use to concentrate copper, lead, and zinc minerals, which commonly accompany one another in their ores, many complex ore mixtures formerly of little value have become major sources of certain metals.

flounder Any of about 300 species of FLATFISHES (order Pleuronectiformes). When born the flounder is bilaterally symmetrical, with an eye on each side, and it swims near the sea's surface. After a few days, it begins to lean to one side, and the eye on that side migrates to what eventually becomes the top side. With this development come changes in bones, nerves, and muscles, and the underside loses its color. As an adult, the flounder lives on the bottom, with the eyed side on top.

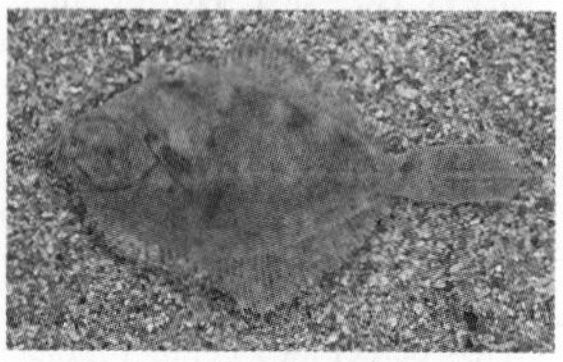

Flounder (*Platichthys*).

F. GREENAWAY FROM NATURAL HISTORY PHOTOGRAPHIC AGENCY

flour Finely ground meal of CEREAL grain, usually WHEAT, used as a basic ingredient of baked goods (see BAKING). In the production of refined flour, milling is used to separate the starchy endosperm from the other parts of the kernel. In the production of whole-wheat flour, all parts of the kernel are used. Following milling, the particles of endosperm (called semolina) are ground to flour and often bleached to imitate natural aging. Flour grades are based on the residual amount of branny particles. When flour is mixed with water to make dough, its protein content is converted to gluten, an elastic substance that forms a continuous network throughout the dough and is capable of retaining gas, thus causing the baked product to expand, or rise.

flow See DEFORMATION AND FLOW, LAMINAR flow, TURBULENT FLOW

flow meter Device that measures the velocity of a GAS or LIQUID. It has applications in medicine as well as in chemical engineering, aeronautics, and meteorology. Examples include PITOT TUBES, VENTURI TUBES, and rotameters (tapered graduated tubes with a float inside that is supported by the flowing fluid at a level that depends on the flow rate). Ultrasonic flow meters, in which reflecting ultrasound off a flowing liquid leads to a Doppler shift (see DOPPLER EFFECT) that is calibrated to provide the flow rate of the liquid, have important industrial applications and have also been used to measure arterial blood flow.

flowchart Graphical representation of a process, such as a manufacturing operation or a computer operation, indicating the various steps taken as the product moves along the production line or the problem moves through the computer. Individual operations can be represented by closed boxes, with arrows between boxes indicating the order in which the steps are taken and divergent paths determined by variable results.

flower Reproductive portion of any FLOWERING PLANT (angiosperm). Popularly, the term applies especially when part or all of the reproductive structure is distinctive in color and form. Flowers present a multitude of combinations of color, size, form, and anatomical arrangement. In some plants, individual flowers are very small and are borne in a distinctive cluster (INFLORESCENCE). Each flower consists of a floral axis that bears the essential organs of reproduction (STAMENS and PISTILS) and usually accessory organs (sepals and petals); the latter may serve both to attract pollinating insects (see POLLINATION) and to protect the essential organs. Flower parts are arrayed usually in whorls, but sometimes spirally. Four distinct whorls are common: the outer calyx (sepals), the corolla (petals), the androecium (stamens), and, in the center, the gynoecium (pistils). The sepals are usually greenish and often resemble reduced leaves; the petals are usually colorful and showy. POLLEN is produced in the stamens. A pollen-receptive stigma rests atop each pistil. The pistil, made up of one or more CARPELS, encloses an ovary that contains the ovules, or potential SEEDS. After fertilization, the ovary enlarges to form the FRUIT. Flowers have been symbols of beauty in most civilizations of the world, and flower giving is still among the most popular of social amenities.

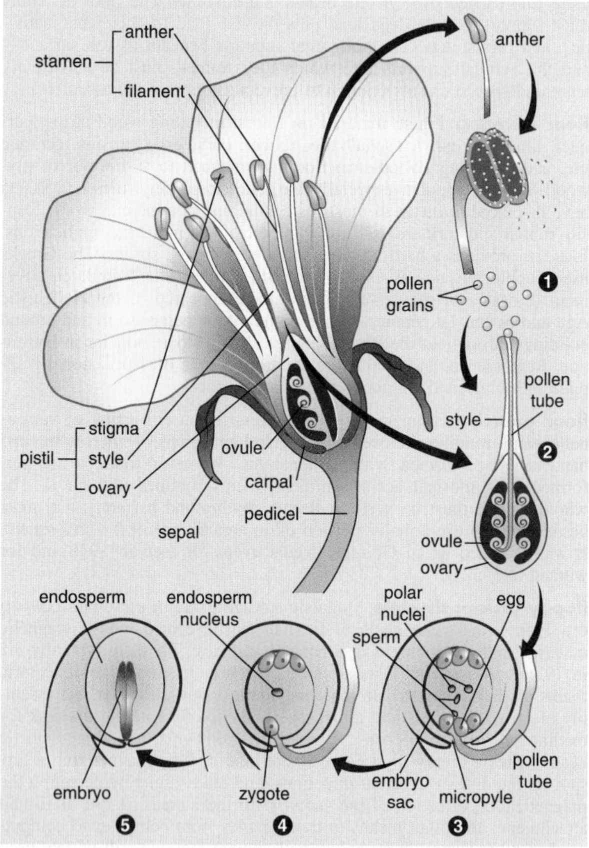

The life cycle of a flowering plant. (1) A pollen grain is released from the anther and settles on the stigma. (2) A pollen tube forms and grows through the style toward the ovule opening (micropyle). (3)Two of the nuclei (polar nuclei) in the ovule's embryo sac migrate to the center to form a single cell. Three cells migrate to the micropyle, and one enlarges to become the egg. Two sperm that have formed from mitotic division of the pollen grain's generative cell enter the embryo sac through the micropyle. (4) One sperm fuses with the egg, resulting in a fertilized egg (zygote), which develops into an embryo. The second sperm fuses with the two polar nuclei to form a triploid nucleus (containing three sets of chromosomes). (5) This nucleus divides to form a tissue (endosperm) that provides nutrients for the developing embryo.

flowering plant Any of the more than 250,000 species of angiosperms (division Magnoliophyta) having roots, stems, leaves, and well-developed conductive tissues (XYLEM and PHLOEM). They are often differentiated from GYMNOSPERMS by their production of seeds within a closed chamber (the ovary) within the flower, but this distinction is not always clear-cut. The division is composed of two classes: monocots and dicots (see COTYLEDON). Monocots have flower parts in threes, scattered conducting strands in the stem, and usually prominent parallel veins in the leaves, and they lack a CAMBIUM. Dicots have flower parts in fours or fives, conducting strands arranged in a cylinder, a net-veined pattern in the leaves, and a cambium. Flowering plants reflect an immense diversity in habit, size, and form; they account for more than 300 families growing on every continent, including Antarctica. Flowering plants have also adapted to an almost infinite variety of habitats. Most reproduce sexually by seeds via the specialized reproductive organs that are present in all flowers.

flu See INFLUENZA

flugelhorn Valved BUGLE. It has three valves and a wider bore than the CORNET and is usually pitched in B-flat. It was invented in Austria in the 1830s. It has maintained its identity—particularly its bore and its squat shape—better than has the formerly very similar cornet. It has long been part of European military bands; today it is also used in jazz and popular music.

fluid Any liquid or gas that cannot sustain a shearing force when at rest and that undergoes a continuous change in shape (see flow) when subjected to such a STRESS. Compressed fluids exert an outward PRESSURE that is perpendicular to the walls of their containers. A perfect fluid lacks VISCOSITY, but real fluids do not.

fluid mechanics Study of the effects of forces and energy on liquids and gases. One branch of the field, HYDROSTATICS, deals with fluids at rest; the other, fluid dynamics, deals with fluids in motion and with the motion of bodies through fluids. Liquids and gases are both treated as fluids because they often have the same equations of motion and exhibit the same flow phenomena. The subject has numerous applications in fields varying from aeronautics and marine engineering to the study of blood flow and the dynamics of swimming.

fluke *or* **trematode** Any member of almost 6,000 species of parasitic FLATWORMS. Flukes are found worldwide and range in size from about 0.2 to 4 in. (5–100 mm) long. They most commonly parasitize fish, frogs, and turtles, but also humans, domestic animals, and invertebrates such as mollusks and crustaceans. They include external parasites (ectoparasites), internal parasites (endoparasites), and semi-external parasites (those that attach to the lining of the mouth, to gills, or to the cloaca). Most flukes are flattened and leaflike or ribbonlike and have muscular suckers on the bottom surface, as well as hooks and spines, for attachment to the host. Fluke infestations may cause illness (e.g., SCHISTOSOMIASIS) or death in humans.

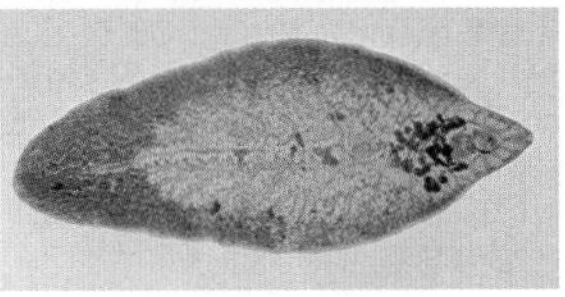

Liver fluke (*Fasciola hepatica*).
GRANT HEILMAN

fluorescence Emission of ELECTROMAGNETIC RADIATION, usually visible light, caused by EXCITATION of ATOMS in a material, which then reemit almost immediately (within about 10^{-8} seconds). The initial excitation is usually caused by absorption of energy from incident radiation or particles, such as X rays or electrons. Because re-emission occurs so quickly, the fluorescence ceases as soon as the exciting source is removed, unlike PHOSPHORESCENCE, which persists as an afterglow. A fluorescent lightbulb is coated on the inside with a powder and contains a gas; electricity causes the gas to emit ultraviolet radiation, which then stimulates the tube coating to emit light. The pixels of a television or computer screen fluoresce when electrons from an electron gun strike them. Fluorescence is often used to analyze molecules, and the addition of a fluorescing agent with emissions in the blue region of the spectrum to detergents causes fabrics to appear whiter in sunlight. X-ray fluorescence is used to analyze minerals.

fluorescent lamp Type of ELECTRIC DISCHARGE LAMP consisting of a glass tube filled with a mixture of argon and mercury vapor. A current of electricity causes the vapor to produce ultraviolet radiation that, in turn, excites a phosphor coating on the inside of the tube, causing it to fluoresce, or reradiate the energy as visible light. Fluorescent lamps are cooler and more efficient than INCANDESCENT LAMPS. They are commonly installed with diffusers as part of a suspended ceiling system. See also FLUORESCENCE.

fluoridation of water Addition of FLUORINE or fluoride compounds to water (at one part per million) to reduce dental CARIES. This practice is based on the lower rates of caries seen in areas with moderate natural fluoridation of water and on studies showing that sound teeth contain more fluoride than cavity-prone teeth and that fluorides help prevent or reduce dental caries. Fluoridation decreases the number of decayed, missing, and filled teeth in children (which increases if fluoridation is stopped), but it has provoked controversy in some cases. Excess fluorine may cause tooth mottling (a problem of appearance only) and, in higher doses, bone abnormalities. Fluoridation also helps prevent RICKETS in infants and children and helps the THYROID maintain a normal basal metabolic rate.

fluorine \'flu̇r-ˌēn, 'flȯr-ˌēn\ Nonmetallic chemical ELEMENT, chemical symbol F, atomic number 9. The lightest HALOGEN, it is the most reactive element, forming compounds with all others except helium, neon, and argon (the lighter NOBLE GASES). Its only VALENCE is 1, in F_2 (the diatomic molecule) and fluorides. A toxic pale yellow gas with a pungent odor, it can be produced only by ELECTROLYSIS under special conditions. Its chief source is FLUORITE; it also occurs in cryolite, fluorapatite, seawater, bones, and teeth. Hydrogen fluoride (HF) is a raw material for many other fluorides. Its water solution, hydrofluoric acid, is used to clean metals and polish, etch, or frost glass. Other fluorides are useful CATALYSTS and raw materials. Sodium fluoride (NaF) is added to water and tin fluoride (SnF_2) dental-care products to reduce dental CARIES (see FLUORIDATION OF WATER). Fluorocarbons are HYDROCARBONS in which some hydrogens have been replaced by fluorines; examples include FREONS and TEFLON.

fluorite *or* **fluorspar** Common HALIDE MINERAL, calcium fluoride (CaF_2); the principal fluorine mineral. Fluorite occurs most commonly as a vein mineral and is often associated with lead and silver ores; it also occurs in cavities, sedimentary rocks, pegmatites, and hot-springs areas. It is widespread in China, South Africa, Mongolia, France, Mexico, Russia, and the central U.S. Fluorite is used in the manufacture of steel, aluminum fluoride, artificial cryolite, and aluminum. It is used in glassmaking, in iron and steel enamelware, in the production of hydrofluoric acid, in the refining of lead and antimony, and (as a catalyst) in the manufacture of high-octane fuels.

Flushing Northern section, QUEENS, New York City. Located at the head of Flushing Bay in the EAST RIVER, it was settled in 1645 by English nonconformists, and became a center for Quakers (see Society of FRIENDS). In the late 18th and early 19th century, it flourished as a township and then a village until it was absorbed by Queens in 1898. Flushing Meadow-Corona Park was the site of the 1939–40 and 1964–65 New York world's fairs (the Hall of Science remains as an exhibition center), and in 1946–49 it was the temporary headquarters for the U.N. Flushing is the scene of the U.S. Open tennis championships and home to Shea Stadium.

flute WOODWIND INSTRUMENT whose sound is produced by blowing against a sharp edge. In its broad sense, a flute may be end-blown, like the RECORDER, or may have a globular shape, like the ocarina. In its narrow sense, discussed below, flute refers to the transverse flute of Western music. The transverse flute, a tubular instrument held sideways to the right, appeared in Greece and Etruria by the 2nd century BC. By the 16th century a family of boxwood flutes, with fingerholes but no keys, was in use in Europe. Keys began to be added in the late 17th century. T. BOEHM's 19th-century innovations resulted in the modern flute, which permits thorough expressive control and great agility. The cylindrical tube may be made of wood or, more often, a precious metal or alloy. Its range is from about middle C to the C three octaves higher. The flute family includes the piccolo (pitched an octave higher), the alto flute, and the rare bass flute. See also SHAKUHACHI.

flux In METALLURGY, any substance introduced in the SMELTING of ores to promote fluidity and to remove objectionable impurities in the form of SLAG. LIMESTONE is commonly used for this purpose in smelting IRON ores. Other materials used as fluxes are silica, dolomite, lime, borax, and fluorite. In SOLDERING, the flux removes oxide films, promotes wetting, and prevents reoxidation of the surfaces during heating. Rosin is widely used as a noncorrosive flux when electronic equipment is soldered; in other applications, a water solution of zinc chloride and ammonium chloride may be used.

Fluxus \'flək-səs\ International avant-garde group of artists founded in Germany by the American artist George Maciunas (1931–1978) in 1962. Its members included JOSEPH BEUYS, J. CAGE, and YVES KLEIN. Opposed to tradition and professionalism in the arts, the Fluxus group shifted the emphasis from what an artist makes to the artist's personality, actions, and opinions. Throughout the 1960s and '70s they staged "action" events, engaged in politics and public speaking, and produced sculptural works featuring unconventional materials. Though it was an influential movement in Europe, the group's work frequently conflicted with authority and aroused much controversy.

fly In general, almost any small flying insect. In entomology, the term refers specifically to the approximately 85,000 species of two-winged, or "true," flies (DIPTERANS). Other insects called flies have wing structures that differ from that of dipterans.

Fly River River, New Guinea Island. One of the island's largest rivers, it flows almost wholly through Papua New Guinea. For a short stretch of its middle course, it forms the border between Papua New Guinea and Indonesia. Rising in the Victor Emanuel Range in the central highlands, it flows south for about 700 mi (1,100 km) to the CORAL SEA; much of it is navigable.

flycatcher Any of various PASSERINE species that capture insects on the wing, particularly several Old World species (songbird family Muscicapidae) and about 367 species called New World tyrant flycatchers. The most common Old World species, the spotted flycatcher *(Muscicapa striata),* is 5.5 in. (14-cm) long and streaked grayish brown. It inhabits open woodlands and gardens eastward from Europe, where it breeds, through Asia. Most tyrant flycatchers have a large head, short legs, and a broad bill (e.g., PHOEBE).

flying buttress Masonry structure typically consisting of an inclined bar carried on a half arch that extends ("flies") from the upper part of a wall to a pier some distance away and carries the thrust of a roof or vault. A pinnacle (vertical ornament of pyramidal or conical shape) often crowns the pier, adding weight and enhancing stability. The flying buttress evolved in the Gothic era from earlier simpler, hidden supports. The design increased the supporting power of the BUTTRESS and allowed for the creation of the high-ceilinged churches typical of GOTHIC ARCHITECTURE.

flying fish Any of about 40 species of oceanic fishes (family Exocoetidae) found worldwide in warm waters and noted for their ability to "fly." All species are less than 18 in. (45 cm) long and have winglike, rigid fins and an unevenly forked tail. Two-winged species have only the pectoral fins enlarged; four-winged species have both the pectoral and the pelvic fins enlarged. Rather than flying, they actually glide. They can make several consecutive glides; the strongest fliers can travel as much as 600 ft (180 m) in a single glide, and compound glides may cover 1,300 ft (400 m). Flight is primarily a means for escaping predators.

Flying Fortress See B-17

flying shuttle MACHINE that represented an important step toward automatic WEAVING. It was invented by JOHN KAY in 1733. In previous LOOMS, the SHUTTLE was thrown, or passed, through the threads by hand, and wide fabrics required two weavers seated side by side passing the shuttle between them. Kay mounted his shuttle on wheels in a track and used paddles to shoot the shuttle from side to side when the weaver jerked a cord. Using the flying shuttle, one weaver could weave fabrics of any width more quickly than two could before.

flying squirrel Any member of two distinct groups of RODENTS that are able to make gliding leaps by means of parachute-like membranes connecting their forelegs and hind legs on each side. North American and Eurasian flying squirrels, in the SQUIRREL family (Sciuridae), are slender, long-limbed forest dwellers with soft fur and large eyes. They are 3–24 in. (8–60 cm) long, excluding the often-flattened tail, and feed on nuts, fruit, other plant material, and insects. They seldom descend to the ground. They can glide 200 ft (about 60 m) or more from one tree to another. The scaly-tailed flying squirrels of Africa (family Anomaluridae) have rows of scales on the underside of their tufted tail that help them climb and cling to trees. They are similar in appearance and feeding preferences to the sciurids and are about 4–16 in. (10–40 cm) long without the tail.

Flying Tigers *or* **American Volunteer Group** Group of U.S. civilian volunteer pilots recruited by Col. CLAIRE CHENNAULT to fight the Japanese in Burma and China in 1941–42. Surprise, mobility, precision flying, and unorthodox tactics enabled the Tigers to outwit the Japanese and inflict considerable damage on their air and ground forces.

Flynn, Errol (Leslie Thomson) (1909–1959) Australian-U.S. film actor. He sought adventure in New Guinea before turning to acting in Australia and England. In 1935 Warner Brothers brought him to Hollywood, and he became an instant success as the swashbuckling hero of *Captain Blood.* He continued to play dashing heroes through the 1940s in such films as *The Charge of the Light Brigade* (1936), *The Adventures of Robin Hood* (1938), *The Sea Hawk* (1940), *They Died with Their Boots On* (1941), and *Gentleman Jim* (1942). After a period marred by scandal and bad roles, he returned to critical and popular praise in *The Sun Also Rises* (1957).

flysch \'flish\ Sequence of shales interbedded with thin, hard, GRAYWACKE-like sandstones. Such sequences are usually thousands of yards thick, but the individual beds are only a few inches to a few yards thick. The occasional presence of fossils indicates marine deposition. The term originally was applied to a formation of the TERTIARY PERIOD in the northern Alpine region, but it now denotes similar deposits of other ages and places.

flytrap See VENUS'S-FLYTRAP

flywheel Heavy wheel attached to a rotating shaft to smooth out delivery of power from a motor to a machine. The inertia of the flywheel opposes and moderates fluctuations in the speed of the engine and stores the excess energy for intermittent use. In automobile engines, the flywheel smooths out the pulses of energy provided by the combustion in the cylinders and provides energy for the compression stroke of the pistons. In power presses the actual punching, shearing, and forming are done in only a fraction of the operating cycle. During the longer, nonactive period, the speed of the flywheel is built up slowly by a comparatively low-powered motor. When the press is operating, most of the required energy is provided by the flywheel.

FM *in full* **frequency modulation** Variation of the frequency of a carrier wave (commonly a RADIO WAVE) in accordance with variations in the audio signal being sent. Developed by American electrical engineer EDWIN H. ARMSTRONG in the early 1930s, FM is less susceptible to outside interference and noise (e.g., thunderstorms, nearby machinery) than is AM. Such noise generally affects the amplitude of a radio wave but not its frequency, so an FM signal remains virtually unchanged. FM is also better able to transmit sounds in stereo than AM. Commercial FM broadcasting stations transmit their signals in the frequency range of 88 megahertz (MHz) to 108 MHz.

Fo, Dario (born 1926) Italian playwright. He and his wife, Franca Rame, founded a theater company that developed a leftist theater of politics and later established an acting troupe with funding from the Italian Communist Party. In 1970 they set up a touring collective to perform in factories and other public sites. Fo's popular one-man show *Mistero Buffo* (1973) was censured by the Vatican. He has written over 70 plays, including the satire *Accidental Death of an Anarchist* (1974) and *The Pope and the Witch* (1989). He was awarded the Nobel Prize in 1997.

Foch \'fôsh, *Engl* 'fäsh\, **Ferdinand** (1851–1929) French commander of Allied forces in WORLD WAR I. He entered the artillery corps in 1873 and from 1885 periodically taught military strategy at the war college, becoming its commandant in 1908. After World War I broke out, he commanded an army detachment and planned the strategy that enabled JOSEPH-JACQUES-CESAIRE JOFFRE to win the First Battle of the MARNE. After commanding at the Battles of YPRES and the SOMME, he was appointed chief of the general staff (1917), adviser to the Allied armies, and then commander in chief of all Allied armies (May 1918), in which capacity he prevailed in the battle of wills with ERICH LUDENDORFF. When Germany was forced to ask for an armistice, the conditions were dictated by now-Marshal Foch. Considered the leader most responsible for the Allied victory, he was showered with honors after the war, and was buried near Napoleon in the Invalides.

Focke-Wulf 190 (Fw 190) \'fò-kə-'vůlf\ FIGHTER AIRCRAFT of Nazi Germany, second in importance only to the MESSERSCHMITT 109 in the German air force in World War II. It began service in 1941, was superior to all its opponents until 1942–43, and remained a successful fighter and fighter-bomber until the war ended. A single-seater, it was armed with four 7.9-mm machine guns; later versions also carried cannons. The model produced near the end of the war had a top speed of about 430 mph (690 kph).

fog Cloud of small water droplets near ground level that is dense enough to reduce horizontal visibility to less than about 3,000 ft (1,000 m). Fog may also refer to clouds of smoke particles (SMOG), ice particles, or mixtures of these components. When visibility is more than 3,000 ft, the phenomenon is termed mist or haze, depending on whether it is caused by water drops or by solid particles. Fog is formed by the condensation of water vapor on condensation nuclei that are always present in natural air. The most stable fogs occur when the surface is colder than the air above. Fogs can also occur when cold air moves over a warm, wet surface and becomes saturated by the evaporation of moisture from the surface. Convection currents carry the fog upward as it forms, and it appears to rise as steam or smoke from the wet surface.

Foix \'fwä\ Historical region, southern France. Corresponding approximately to the modern department of Ariège, it was a quasi-independent power in the 11th–15th century. Bounded by LANGUEDOC, and by the territories of the counts of Roussillon and the kings of ARAGON, it became part of the crown lands at the ascension of HENRY IV as king of France (1589).

Fokine \fō-'kēn\, **Michel** *orig.* **Mikhail Mikhaylovich** (1880–1942) Russian-U.S. dancer and choreographer. He trained at the Imperial Ballet school in St. Petersburg and debuted with the MARIINSKY THEATER at age 18. Following his creation of *The Dying Swan* for ANNA PAVLOVA in 1905, he was in demand as a choreographer. When his ambitious synesthetic scenario for a ballet on the story of Daphnis and Chloe was rejected, SERGEY DIAGHILEV engaged him at the BALLETS RUSSES in 1909, where he produced such unified creations as *The Firebird* (1910), *Le spectre de la rose* (1911), *Petrushka* (1911), and *Daphnis and Chloe* (1912). He returned to Russia in 1914, toured from 1918, and moved to New York in 1923, choreographing over 60 works for companies in the U.S. and Europe.

Fokine as Perseus in *Medusa.*

BY COURTESY OF THE DANCE COLLECTION, THE NEW YORK PUBLIC LIBRARY AT LINCOLN CENTER, ASTOR, LENOX AND TILDEN FOUNDATIONS

Fokker, Anthony *orig.* **Anton Herman Gerard** (1890–1939) Dutch-U.S. aircraft designer and manufacturer. He built his first plane in 1910 and taught himself to fly. In 1912 he established a small aircraft factory near Berlin. In World War I he produced over 40 types of airplanes for Germany, having originally offered his designs to both sides. He also developed a gear system that allowed a machine gun to fire through a spinning propeller's field. In 1922 he moved to the U.S. and opened an aircraft factory, where he produced numerous commercial aircraft that were used in the newly developing U.S. airlines business.

Anthony Fokker.

ULLSTEIN BILDERDIENST

fold In geology, an undulation or wave in the stratified rocks of the earth's CRUST. Stratified rocks were originally formed from sediments that were deposited in flat, horizontal sheets, although in some places the strata are no longer horizontal but have warped. The warping may be so gentle that the inclination of the strata is barely perceptible, or it may be so pronounced that the strata of the two flanks are essentially parallel or nearly flat. Folds vary widely in size; the tops of large folds are commonly eroded away on the earth's surface.

foliation Planar arrangement of structural or textural features in any rock type, but particularly that resulting from the alignment of constituent mineral grains of a METAMORPHIC ROCK along straight or wavy planes. Foliation commonly occurs parallel to original bedding, but it may not be obviously related to any other structural direction. Foliation is exhibited most prominently by sheety minerals, such as mica or chlorite.

folic acid \'fō-lik\ *or* **folate** Organic compound essential to growth and health and needed by bacteria as a growth factor. Part of the VITAMIN B COMPLEX, folic acid is necessary for synthesis of NUCLEIC ACIDS and formation of the heme component of HEMOGLOBIN in red blood cells. To prevent NEURAL TUBE DEFECTS in babies, it should ideally be taken by the mother starting at least a month before conception. Dietary folate sources include leafy and dark green vegetables, citrus fruits, cereals, beans, poultry, and egg yolks, but free folic acid occurs only in supplements. Low intake leads to FOLIC-ACID-DEFICIENCY ANEMIA.

folic-acid-deficiency anemia ANEMIA resulting from too little FOLIC ACID, needed for red-blood-cell maturation (see ERYTHROCYTE). White-cell and platelet levels are also often low. Progressive gastrointestinal problems develop. It may result from poor diet or from malabsorption, CIRRHOSIS of the liver, or anticonvulsant drugs; it may also occur in the last three months of pregnancy and in severe hemolytic anemia (in which red cells break down). The blood profile resembles that of PERNICIOUS ANEMIA. Taking folic acid causes rapid improvement; an adequate diet cures cases caused by malnutrition.

Folies Bergère \fō-'lē-ber-'zher\ MUSIC HALL AND VARIETY THEATER in Paris. It opened in 1869 and soon became a major music hall, presenting operettas and pantomimes. By the 1890s its repertory also included vaudeville sketches, acrobats, ballets, and magicians. After the vogue of nudity appeared in music halls (1894), its sensational displays of women in scanty but opulent costumes overshadowed its other performances. Under the management of Paul Derval (1918–1966), the Folies achieved an international reputation and became one of Paris's major tourist attractions. Each show requires about 10 months of preparation, 40 sets, and 1,000 costumes.

folk art Art produced in a traditional fashion by peasants, seamen, country artisans, or tradespeople with no formal training, or by members of a social or ethnic group that has preserved its traditional culture. It is predominantly functional, typically produced by hand for use by the maker or by a small group or community. Paintings are usually incorporated as decorative features on clock faces, chests, chairs, and interior and exterior walls. Sculptural objects in wood, stone, and metal include toys, spoons, candlesticks, and religious items. Folk architecture may include public and residential buildings, such as eastern European wooden churches and U.S. frontier log cabins. Other examples of visual folk arts are woodcuts, scrimshaw, pottery, textiles, and traditional clothing.

folk dance Dance that has developed without a choreographer and reflects the traditional life of the common people of a country or region. The term was coined in the 18th century and is sometimes used to distinguish between dances of the people and those of the aristocracy. Courtly and formal dances of the 16th–20th century often developed from folk dances; these include the GAVOTTE, GIGUE, MAZURKA, MINUET, POLKA, SAMBA, TANGO, and WALTZ. See also COUNTRY DANCE, HULA, MORRIS DANCE, SQUARE DANCE, SWORD DANCE, TAP DANCE.

folk music Music held to be typical of a nation or ethnic group, known to all segments of its society, and preserved usually by oral tradition. Knowledge of the history and development of folk music is largely conjectural. Musical notation of folk songs and descriptions of folk music culture are occasionally encountered in historical records, but tend to reflect primarily the literate classes' indifference or even hostility. As Christianity expanded in medieval Europe, attempts were made to suppress folk music because of its association with heathen rites and customs, and uncultivated singing styles were denigrated. During the Renaissance, new humanistic attitudes encouraged acceptance of folk music as a genre of rustic antique song, and composers made extensive use of the music; folk tunes were often used as raw material for motets and masses, and Protestant hymns borrowed from folk music. In the 17th century folk music gradually receded from the consciousness of the literate classes, but in the late 18th century it again became important to art music. In the 19th century, folk songs came to be considered a "national treasure," on a par with cultivated poetry and song. National and regional collections were published, and the music became a means of promoting nationalistic ideologies. Since the 1890s, folk music has been collected and preserved by mechanical recordings. Publications and recordings have promoted wide interest, making possible the revival of folk music where traditional folk life and folklore are moribund. After World War II, archives of field recordings were developed throughout the world. While research has usually dealt with "authentic" (i.e., older) material not heavily influenced by urban popular music and the mass media, the influence of such singer-songwriters as W. Guthrie, P. Seeger, and B. Dylan expanded the genre to include original music that largely retains the form and simplicity of traditional compositions.

folk psychology Ways of conceptualizing mind and the mental that are implicit in our ordinary, everyday attributions of mental states to ourselves and others. Philosophers have adopted different positions about the extent to which folk psychology and its generalizations (e.g., those portraying human actions as governed by intention) are supported by the findings of scientific psychology. Some consider it indispensible to understanding human conduct. Others ("eliminative materialists") think that it can and perhaps will be replaced by scientific psychology.

folklore Oral literature and popular tradition preserved among a people. Its subject matter includes fairy tales, ballads, epics, folk plays, proverbs, and riddles as well as music, dance, and traditional arts and crafts. Studies of folklore began in the early 19th century and first focused on rural peasants and others believed to be untouched by modern ways. The aim was to trace archaic customs and beliefs. In Germany Jacob and Wilhelm Grimm published their classic collection of fairy tales in 1812. James George Frazer's *The Golden Bough* (1890) reflects the use of folklore as a tool to reconstruct ancient beliefs and rituals. Nationalism was another motive for the study of folklore, which reinforced ethnic identity and figured in struggles for political independence. The catalog of motifs of folktales and myths developed by Antti Aarne and Stith Thompson encouraged comparisons of variants of the same tale or other item from different regions and times. After World War II folklorists studied urban as well as rural people and looked at folk arts in their present-day context.

folly In architecture, an eccentric, generally nonfunctional (and often deliberately unfinished) structure erected to enhance a romantic landscape. Follies were particularly in vogue in England in the 18th and early 19th century. They might resemble medieval towers, ruined castles overgrown with vines, or crumbling Classical temples complete with fallen, eroded columns. In the U.S., the term has been applied to ornate gazebos. It may also be applied to any unusual building that is extravagant or whimsical in style.

Folsom complex Prehistoric culture of North America on the eastern side of the Rocky Mountains that is characterized by flint projectile points having a concave base with side projections and a longitudinal groove on each face. The complex was first identified at Folsom, N.M., and includes a variety of scrapers, knives, and blades. It is generally dated to 8000–9000 BC and, like the earlier Clovis complex, is considered to be part of a Paleo-Indian big-game hunting tradition.

Iron statue of the god of arms and war, made by the Fon of Benin, in the Musée de l'Homme, Paris.

MARC AND EVELYNE BERNHEIM—WOODFIN CAMP AND ASSOCIATES

Fon \'fän\ People of southern Benin and adjacent parts of Togo who speak a dialect of the Kwa language Gbe. Numbering about 2 million, the Fon are mainly farmers. Craft specialists include male ironworkers, sculptors, and weavers and female potters. The primary Fon social unit is the polygynous family, each woman and her children occupying a house within a compound. The village under a hereditary chief is the traditional political unit. The kingdom of Dahomey was peopled principally by Fon.

Fonda, Henry (Jaynes) (1905–1982) U.S. actor. Born in Grand Island, Neb., he achieved success on Broadway in *The Farmer Takes a Wife* (1934), which led him to Hollywood for the film version (1935). He portrayed a thoughtful man of integrity in such films as *Young Mr. Lincoln* (1939), *The Grapes of Wrath* (1940), and *The Ox-Bow Incident* (1943). He also made such comedies as *The Lady Eve* (1941) and *The Male Animal* (1942) and dramas such as *Twelve Angry Men* (1957) and *Advise and Consent* (1961). He returned to the stage in *Mister Roberts* (1948, Tony award; film, 1955). His last film, *On Golden Pond* (1981, Academy Award), also starred his daughter Jane Fonda. His son Peter (born 1939) achieved fame in *The Wild Angels* (1966), *The Trip* (1967), and especially *Easy Rider* (1969), which he also cowrote and produced; his later career was revived in *Ulee's Gold* (1997).

Fonda, Jane (Seymour) (born 1937). U.S. film actress, political activist, and fitness enthusiast. Born in New York City, the daughter of Henry Fonda, she made her film debut in *Tall Story* (1960), which began a career that took dizzying turns. After playing comic roles in such films as *Cat Ballou* (1965) and *Barefoot in the Park* (1967), she appeared as a sex kitten in Roger Vadim's futuristic *Barbarella* (1968). She then plunged into leftist political activity, marrying the activist Tom Hayden and condemning the Vietnam War, and made socially conscious films including *They Shoot Horses, Don't They?* (1969), *Klute* (1971, Academy Award), and *Coming Home* (1978, Academy Award). She later marketed a series of hugely popular exercise books and videotapes. After marrying Ted Turner in 1991 (divorced 2001), she retired from the screen.

Fonseca \fȯn-'sä-kə\, **Gulf of** Inlet of the Pacific Ocean, Central America. Bounded by El Salvador, Honduras, and Nicaragua, it reaches inland about 40 mi (65 km) and widens to about 50 mi (80 km). Its entrance, marked by Cape Amapala in El Salvador and Cape Cosigüina in Nicaragua, is about 20 mi (32 km) across. The Conchagua Volcano rises sharply from its shore in the west.

font *or* **typeface** *or* **type family** Assortment or set of type (alphanumeric characters used for printing), all of one coherent style. Before the advent of computers, fonts were expressed in cast metal that was used as a template for printing. Fonts are now stored as digitized images that can be scaled and otherwise modified for printing on electronic printers or digital phototypesetters. Fonts typically include the normal typeface (roman) as well as italic, bold, bold italic, and sometimes extra-bold versions. See also typesetting, typography. See illustration opposite on following page.

Fontaine, Jean de La See Jean de La Fontaine

Fontainebleau \fō^{n}-ten-'blō\ Château in northern France, southeast of the town of Fontainebleau. One of the largest structures built by the kings of France, it was originally a medieval hunting lodge, but was rebuilt (from 1528) under Francis I. Its numerous renovations show the transition from early Renaissance to Mannerist (Late Renaissance) styles. The château is a succession of five courts of different shapes. Of particular interest is the Gallery of Francis I (c. 1533–45), a long, narrow room decorated with stucco relief sculpture and painting by Rosso Fiorentino.

"Diana the Huntress," oil painting by an anonymous artist of the school of Fontainebleau, c. 1550; in the Louvre, Paris.

GIRAUDON—ART RESOURCE/EB INC.

Fontainebleau, school of French and foreign artists associated with the court at Fontainebleau in the 16th century. In 1528 Francis I began to rebuild the palace and hired Rosso Fiorentino and FRANCESCO PRIMATICCIO to produce the mural decoration, stuccowork, and sculptural reliefs; also among the Italian artists was BENVENUTO CELLINI. Many engravings were made of the work being done, and much of the most decorative painting and sculpture can still be seen there. The Italian masters successfully adapted their own styles to the French taste and were assisted by French and Flemish artists; together they produced a distinctive style of Mannerism. The innovation of stucco ornament in combination with mural painting had great influence on French art of the time.

Fontane \fōn-'tä-nə\, **Theodor** (1819–1898) German writer. He began his career as a journalist and wrote books based on his travels before turning to the novel late in life. *Before the Storm* (1878) is considered a masterpiece of historical fiction. *Effi Briest* (1895), known for its superb characterizations and skillful portrayal of his native Brandenburg, is one of his several sympathetic treatments of women in circumscribed domestic lives. He is considered the first master of modern German REALISM.

fontanel *or* **fontanelle** \'făn-tə-,nel\ One of six soft spots at the junctions (sutures) of the cranial bones in an infant's skull, covered with tough, fibrous membrane. They allow molding of the head during birth. Some close by three months, others after a year, and still others by two years.

Fontanne, Lynn See Alfred LUNT and Lynn Fontanne

Fonteyn \făn-'tān\, **Margot** *later* **Dame Margot** *orig.* **Margaret Hookham** (1919–1991) British ballerina. She debuted with the Vic-Wells (later ROYAL) BALLET in 1934 and soon became its leading dancer, creating many roles in works by FREDERICK ASHTON, including *Horoscope, Symphonic Variations,* and *Ondine.* In the 1960s she won worldwide acclaim for her appearances with RUDOLF NUREYEV in such ballets as *Swan Lake, Raymonda,* and *Le corsaire.* She continued to dance as a guest artist into the mid-1970s. She is considered one of the greatest dancers of the 20th century.

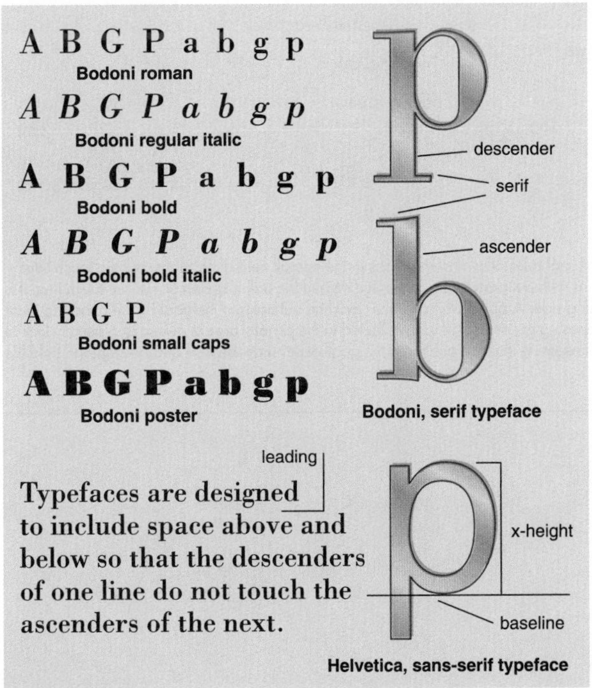

The term *font* commonly refers to a type family such as Bodoni or Helvetica, which includes the entire alphabet in various weights (regular, bold, extra bold, etc.) and styles (roman, italics, or display type such as Bodoni Poster). Type can be set in capitals ("caps"), lowercase, or small caps. The x-height of a font (the height of a lowercase letter that has no ascender or descender) will vary from typeface to typeface. The space between lines of type is referred to as "leading"—a term that dates back to a time when spacing was added with strips of lead. The specification of the example above is indicated as 10/11, or 10-point type with 11 points from baseline to baseline.

Foochow See FUZHOU

Food and Agriculture Organization (FAO) U.N. agency based in Rome, whose purpose is to improve nutrition and eliminate hunger by coordinating government efforts in agriculture, forestry, and fisheries. It also assists countries through research, training, development, and field missions, and has helped with disaster and emergency relief. From the 1960s, it has concentrated on developing high-yield grain, eliminating protein deficiencies, supporting rural development, and encouraging agricultural exports. It is governed by a biennial conference composed of member states, which elects a council drawn from members' representatives. See also WORLD FOOD PROGRAMME.

Food and Drug Administration (FDA) Agency of the U.S. Department of HEALTH AND HUMAN SERVICES. Established in 1927, it inspects, tests, approves, and sets safety standards for foods and food additives, drugs, chemicals, cosmetics, and household and medical devices. It can prevent untested products from being sold, and take legal action to halt the sale of undoubtedly harmful products or of products that involve a health or safety risk. Its authority is limited to interstate commerce.

food chain Sequence of transfer of matter and energy from organism to organism in the form of food. These interconnected feeding relationships intertwine locally into a food web because most organisms consume or are consumed by more than one other type of organism. PLANTS and other photosynthetic organisms (such as PHYTOPLANKTON), which convert solar energy to food, are the primary food source. In a predator chain, a plant-eating animal is eaten by a larger animal. In a parasite chain (see PARASITISM), a smaller organism consumes part of a larger host and may itself be parasitized by even smaller organisms. In a saprophytic chain, microorganisms live on dead organic matter. Because energy, in the form of heat, is lost at each step, or trophic level, chains do not normally encompass more than four or five trophic levels.

food poisoning Acute gastrointestinal illness from eating foods containing TOXINS, whether natural POISONS in plants and animals, chemical contaminants, or toxic products of microorganisms. Most cases are due to bacteria (including SALMONELLA and STAPHYLOCOCCUS) and their toxins (including BOTULISM). Normally harmless bacteria, such as *E. COLI*, may develop harmful strains. Chemical poisons include heavy metals (see MERCURY POISONING), either from food or leached out from cookware by acidic foods. Food additives may have a long-term cumulative toxic effect. The term ptomaine poisoning, coined to describe food poisoning (because of the foul smell associated with both putrefying food and a decomposing corpse, or *ptoma*), is an unscientific one. See also FISH POISONING, MUSHROOM POISONING.

food preservation Any method by which food is protected against spoilage by oxidation, bacteria, molds, and microorganisms. Traditional methods include DEHYDRATION, smoking, salting, controlled FERMENTATION (including pickling), and candying; certain spices have also long been used as antiseptics and preservatives. Among the modern processes for food preservation are REFRIGERATION (including FREEZING), CANNING, PASTEURIZATION, irradiation, and the addition of chemical preservatives.

fool *or* **jester** Comic entertainer whose madness or imbecility, real or pretended, made him a source of amusement and gave him license to abuse and poke fun at even his most exalted patrons. Professional fools flourished in diverse societies from ancient Egyptian times until the 18th century. Often deformed, dwarfed, or crippled, fools were kept for luck as well as amusement, in the belief that deformity can avert the evil eye and that abusive raillery can transfer ill luck from the abused to the abuser. In some societies, they were regarded as inspired with poetic and prophetic powers. The greatest literary characterization of the fool is found in WILLIAM SHAKESPEARE's *King Lear.*

fool's gold See PYRITE

foot In MEASUREMENT, any of numerous lineal measures (commonly 9.8–13.4 in., or 25–34 cm) based on the length of the human foot and used exclusively in English-speaking countries. In most countries and in all scientific applications, the foot (with its multiples and subdivisions) has been superseded by the METER. In a few countries the foot was retained, but it eventually (by 1893 in the U.S.) became defined in terms of the meter. In the U.S. the definition of the foot as exactly 30.48 cm took effect in 1959. See also INCH, INTERNATIONAL SYSTEM OF UNITS, YARD.

foot End part of the LEG, consisting of the heel, arch, and toes, on which a person stands. Its major function is locomotion. The human foot cannot grasp and is adapted for running and striding (a step unique to humans that can cover great distances with minimal energy expenditure). Its arched structure helps it support the body's weight. See also PODIATRY.

foot, metrical Basic unit of verse meter, consisting of any of various fixed combinations or groups of stressed and unstressed (or long and short) syllables. The prevailing kind and number of feet determines the meter of a poem. The most common feet in English verse are the iamb, an unstressed followed by a stressed syllable; the trochee, a stressed followed by an unstressed syllable; the anapest, two unstressed syllables followed by a stressed syllable; and the dactyl, a stressed syllable followed by two unstressed syllables. See also PROSODY.

Foot, Michael (born 1913) Leader of Britain's LABOUR PARTY (1980–83). He worked as a newspaper editor and columnist (1937–74) and served in Parliament 1945–55 and 1960–92. He served in HAROLD WILSON's cabinet as secretary of state for employment (1974–76) and leader of the House of Commons (1976–79). A left-wing socialist, Foot became the party's chief in 1980 by defeating its right-wing candidate. This and other left-wing trends caused some Labourites to resign and found the Social Democratic Party. His books include *Aneurin Bevan* (2 vols., 1962, 1973).

foot-and-mouth disease (FMD) *or* **hoof-and-mouth disease** Highly contagious viral disease of cloven-footed mammals (including cattle), spread by ingestion and inhalation. The afflicted animal develops fever and painful blisters on the tongue, lips, other tissues of the mouth, muzzle or snout, teats, and feet. FMD is endemic in many places, and because of its rapid spread and impact on animal productivity, it is considered the most economically devastating livestock disease in the world. It is not a human health hazard. No effective treatment exists; vaccines control epidemics but have not eliminated them. Since the virus can persist, quarantine, slaughter, cremation or burial of carcasses, and decontamination must be rigorous. Strict surveillance has kept North America largely FMD-free since 1929. In early 2001 a major outbreak occurred in the United Kingdom, followed shortly by outbreaks in The Netherlands and France.

football *or* **association football** *or* **soccer** Game in which two 11-member teams try to propel a ball into the opposing team's goal, using any part of the body except the hands and arms. Only the goalkeeper, when positioned within the penalty area in front of the goal, may use hands and arms. The first uniform set of soccer rules was put in place in 1863, when England's Football Association was created. Professional leagues began appearing in the late 1880s, first in England and then in other countries. The Fédération Internationale de Football Association (FIFA) was founded in 1904, and has hosted the WORLD CUP every four years since 1930. Soccer has been included in the OLYMPIC GAMES since 1908. Now played on all continents in over 150 nations, with over 40 million registered players, it is the world's most popular ball game. See also AUSTRALIAN RULES FOOTBALL, GAELIC FOOTBALL, FOOTBALL, GRIDIRON, and RUGBY.

football, gridiron Game played predominantly in the United States and Canada. In the United States, it is played between two teams of 11 players each on a rectangular field having two goalposts at each end, whose object is to get an oblong ball, in possession of one side at a time, over a goal line or between goalposts by running, passing, or kicking. A team must advance the ball 10 yards in four attempts (called downs), in order to continue to have the ball for another four downs. A run or completed pass over the goal line (touchdown) counts as six points. A kick through the goalposts (field goal) counts as three points. A post-touchdown goal kick, or extra point, counts as one point; two points are awarded if the ball is run or passed over the goal line. Gridiron football (so-called because of the markings on the field) evolved in the 19th century as a combination of RUGBY and SOCCER. The first intercollegiate match was played in 1869 between Princeton University and Rutgers College. In 1873 the first collegiate rules were standardized and the IVY LEAGUE was formed. Collegiate football grew into one of the most popular U.S. sports. In 1998 the NATIONAL COLLEGIATE ATHLETIC ASSOCIATION implemented a point plan for picking the country's top two teams, which would meet in a post-season national championship game. Professional football began in the 1890s but did not become a major sport until after World War II. The NATIONAL FOOTBALL LEAGUE was formed

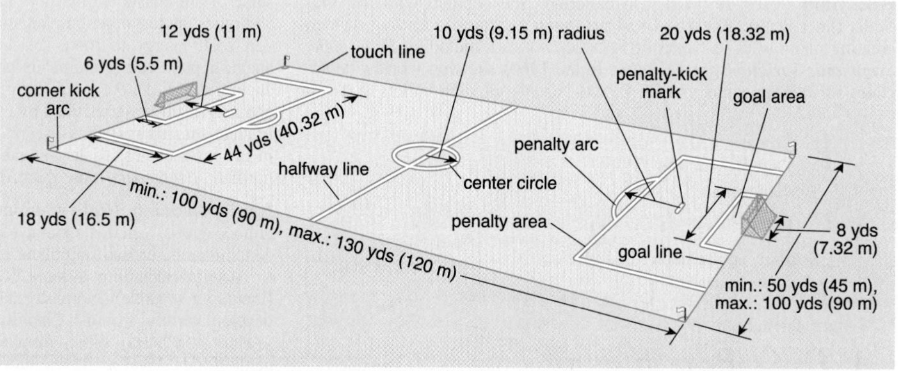

A professional football (soccer) field. International rules allow for variations in the overall field dimensions, but the touch lines must be longer than the goal lines. Play begins with a kickoff at the center line. When the ball is driven across the touch line, it is put back in play by a throw-in by the opposing side. A ball driven over the goal line but not into the goal by the attacking team is returned to play with a goal kick by the opposing goalkeeper. A player fouled in the penalty area is awarded a penalty kick at the goal, which is defended only by the goalkeeper. Within the goal area the goalkeeper may use his hands to stop and hold the ball.

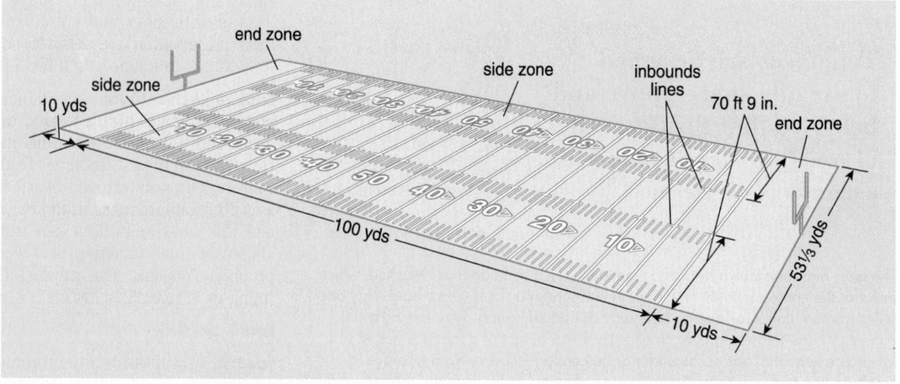

An American professional football field. The standard college field is nearly identical but has a wider inbounds zone. Whenever the ball is downed in a side zone, it is put in play on the next down at the nearest inbounds line. The line marking the end zone (within which the ball may be caught) is the goal line.

(from an earlier association) in 1922; in 1966 it subsumed the rival American Football League (created in 1959). The NFL is now divided into an American and a National conference; the conference winners compete for the SUPER BOWL championship. A Football Hall of Fame is located in Canton, Ohio. Canadian football differs from U.S. football principally by having 12 players on a team rather than 11, employing a larger field, and allowing only three downs to make a first down. These variations cause a more wide-open style of game, with emphasis on passing. See also CANADIAN FOOTBALL LEAGUE.

Foote, (Albert) Horton (born 1916) U.S. dramatist. Born in Wharton, Texas, he studied acting at the Pasadena Playhouse in California and in New York. He is best known for a series of plays about rural Texas, the Orphans' Home Cycle; these include *The Widow Claire, Valentine's Day*, and *1918.* His screenplays include *To Kill a Mockingbird* (1962, Academy Award) and *Tender Mercies* (1983, Academy Award). His low-key but insightful play *The Young Man from Atlanta* (1994) won the Pulitzer Prize.

footlights Row of lights set across the front of a stage floor to light the scene. The oil lamps and candles in use in the 17th century eventually gave way to gas and electricity. As more advanced overhead lighting techniques were developed, footlights became less necessary, except to create special shadows on actors' faces.

forage \'fȯr-ij\ Vegetable food of wild or domestic animals, including CORN and HAY. Harvested, processed, and stored forage is called SILAGE. Forage should be harvested in early maturity to avoid a decrease in protein and fiber content as crops mature.

Forbes, Edward (1815–1854) British naturalist. After studying medicine, he left the field to devote himself to natural history. He conducted extensive research on mollusks and sea stars, participating in dredgings and expeditions. While studying ocean life, he developed an interest in the geographical distribution of animals. Later he divided the plants of Britain into five well-defined groups, maintaining that most of them, like land animals, had migrated to the islands over continuous land during three separate periods: before, during, and after the glacial passage. He held numerous institutional and academic posts, and was a major figure in establishing the fields of oceanography, biogeography, and paleoecology.

Forbes family US. publishing family. Bertie Charles Forbes (1880–1954) was born in Scotland and emigrated to the U.S. in 1904. He founded *Forbes* magazine, a business and finance magazine, in 1916. He became a U.S. citizen in 1917. His son, Malcolm S. Forbes (1919–1990), was born in New York. He was decorated for his service in World War II, and later took over the publishing business, then foundering, and turned it into a success. He ran unsuccessfully in New Jersey's 1957 gubernatorial election. On his death, his son Malcolm S. ("Steve") Forbes, Jr. (born 1947), took over the magazine, assisted by his three brothers. He ran unsuccessfully for president in 1996 and 2000.

Forbidden City Imperial Palace complex in Beijing, containing hundreds of buildings and some 9,000 rooms. It served the emperors of China from 1421 to 1911. No commoner or foreigner was allowed to enter it without special permission. The moated palaces, with their golden tiled roofs and red pillars, are surrounded by high walls with a tower on each corner. The palaces consist of the outer throne halls and an inner courtyard, each palace forming an architectural whole. North of the front gate, a great courtyard lies beyond five marble bridges. Farther north, raised on a marble terrace, is the massive, double-tiered Hall of Supreme Harmony, once the throne hall, one of the largest wooden structures in China. The palaces and buildings are now public museums.

Forcados River \fȯr-'kä-dōs\ River, southern Nigeria. A navigable channel of the NIGER RIVER, it leaves the main course of the Niger about 20 mi (32 km) downstream from Aboh and flows 123 mi (198 km) westerly to the Bight of BENIN. Since c. 1900 it has been the chief link for small-ship traffic between the Niger and the Gulf of GUINEA.

force Action that tends to maintain or alter the position of a body or to distort it. It is a VECTOR quantity, having both magnitude and direction. Force is commonly explained in terms of NEWTON'S LAWS OF MOTION. All known natural forces can be traced to the FUNDAMENTAL INTERACTIONS. Force is measured in newtons (N); a force of 1 N will accelerate a mass of one kilogram at a rate of one meter per second per second. See also CENTRIFUGAL FORCE, CORIOLIS FORCE, ELECTROMAGNETIC FORCE, ELECTROSTATIC FORCE, MAGNETIC FORCE, STRONG FORCE, WEAK FORCE.

Force Acts Series of four acts passed by the U.S. Congress (1870–75) to protect the rights guaranteed to blacks by the 14th and 15th Amendments to the CONSTITUTION. The acts authorized federal authorities to penalize any interference with the registration, voting, officeholding, or jury service of blacks. Violations produced over 5,000 indictments and 1,250 convictions throughout the South. The Supreme Court later ruled sections of the acts unconstitutional.

Ford, Ford Madox *or* **Ford Madox Hueffer** \'hwəf-ər*orig.* **Ford Hermann Hueffer** (1873–1939) English novelist, editor, and critic. He collaborated with J. Conrad on *The Inheritors* (1901) and *Romance* (1903). As the founder of the *English Review* (1908), he generously encouraged younger writers. He was gassed and shell-shocked in World War I; after the war he changed his name to Ford. Of more than 70 published works, the best known are *The Good Soldier* (1915), a novel about the demise of aristocratic England; and the tetralogy *Parade's End—Some Do Not* (1924), *No More Parades* (1925), *A Man Could Stand Up* (1926), and *Last Post* (1928)—which explores the breakdown of Edwardian culture and the emergence of new values.

Ford, Gerald R. *in full* **Gerald Rudolph Ford, Jr.** ***orig.*** **Leslie Lynch King, Jr.** (born 1913) 38th president of the U.S. (1974–77). Born in Omaha, Neb., he was an infant when his parents divorced, and his mother later married Gerald R. Ford. He attended the University of Michigan and Yale law school, and practiced law in Michigan after World War II. He served in the U.S. House of Representative 1948–73, becoming minority leader in 1965. After SPIRO AGNEW resigned as vice president in 1973, RICHARD NIXON nominated Ford to fill the vacant post. When the WATERGATE SCANDAL forced Nixon's departure, Ford became the first president who had not been elected to either the vice presidency or the presidency. A month later he pardoned Nixon; to counter widespread outrage, he voluntarily appeared before a House subcommittee to explain his action. His administration gradually lowered the high inflation rate it inherited. Ford's relations with the Democratic-controlled Congress were typified by his more than 50 vetoes, of which more than 40 were sustained. In the final days of the Vietnam War in 1975, he ordered an airlift of 237,000 anti-Communist Vietnamese refugees, most of whom came to the U.S. Reaction against Watergate contributed to his defeat by JIMMY CARTER in 1976.

Ford, Harrison (born 1942) U.S. film actor. Born in Chicago, he played minor roles on screen and television before achieving stardom in GEORGE LUCAS's hit *Star Wars* (1977) and its sequels, *The Empire Strikes Back* (1980) and *Return of the Jedi* (1983). He also starred in the adventure film *Raiders of the Lost Ark* (1981) and its sequels (1984, 1989). He graduated to dramatic roles in *Witness* (1985), *Patriot Games* (1992), *Clear and Present Danger* (1994), and *Air Force One* (1997). His rugged good looks and wry charm made him, by some measures, the most popular actor of his time.

Ford, Henry (1863–1947) U.S. industrialist and pioneer automobile manufacturer. Born in Wayne Co., Mich., he worked his way up from a machinist's apprentice (at age 15) to the post of chief engineer at the Edison Co. in Detroit. He built his first experimental car in 1896. In 1903, with several partners, he formed the FORD MOTOR CO. In 1908 he designed the MODEL T; demand became so great that Ford developed new MASS-PRODUCTION methods, including the first moving ASSEMBLY LINE in 1913. He developed the Model A in 1928 to replace the Model T, and in 1932 he introduced the V-8 engine. He observed an eight-hour workday and paid his workers far above the average, holding that well-paid laborers become the consumers that industrialists require, but strenuously opposed labor unions. As the first to make car ownership affordable to large numbers of Americans, he exerted a vast and permanent influence on American life. See also FORD FOUNDATION.

Ford, John (1586–1639?) British dramatist. Early in his career he studied law and wrote collaboratively with several other playwrights, but little more is known of his life, and the dating of many of his works is uncertain. His revenge tragedies are characterized by scenes of austere beauty, insight into human passions, and poetic diction of a high order. His reputation rests on the first four plays he wrote alone: *The Broken Heart*; *The Lover's Melancholy* (1628); *Perkin Warbeck;* and *'Tis Pity She's a Whore*, an eloquently sympathetic story of incestuous lovers that is his best-known work.

Ford, John *orig.* **Sean Aloysius O'Feeney** *or* **Sean Aloysius O'Fearna** (1895–1973) U.S. film director. Born in Cape Elizabeth, Me., he joined his actor brother in Hollywood in 1914 and became a director of westerns, achieving success with *The Iron Horse* (1924). His distinctive style united action and colorful characterization and reflected his sense of history and his skill in the creation of mood. He is best remembered for such westerns as *Stagecoach* (1939), *My Darling Clementine* (1946), *She Wore a Yellow Ribbon* (1949), and *The Man Who Shot Liberty Valance* (1962). He also directed such historical dramas as *Mary of Scotland* (1936) and *Young Mr. Lincoln* (1939). He received Academy Awards for *The Informer* (1935), *The Grapes of Wrath* (1940), *How Green Was My Valley* (1941), and *The Quiet Man* (1952). and also for his wartime documentaries *The Battle of Midway* (1942) and *December 7th* (1943).

Ford, Richard (born 1944) U.S. novelist and short-story writer. Born in Jackson, Miss., he studied at Michigan State Univ., Washington University Law School, and UC–Irving, and has taught at several colleges and universities. His first novel, *A Piece of My Heart* (1976), showed the influence of WILLIAM FAULKNER. *The Sportswriter* (1986) and its sequel, *Independence Day* (1995, Pulitzer Prize), drew on his experience as a writer for a sports magazine in the 1980s. His story collection *Rock Springs* (1987) examines the lives of the lonely and alienated.

Ford, Tennessee Ernie *orig.* **Ernest Jennings** (1919–1991) U.S. COUNTRY-MUSIC singer. Born in Bristol, Tenn., he studied music in Cincinnati. After World War II he worked in radio in the Los Angeles area and soon signed a recording contract with Capitol. His "Mule Train" and "Shot Gun Boogie" had made him famous by 1951. He became a staple on the GRAND OLE OPRY and had many crossover hits, including "Sixteen Tons" and "Ballad of Davy Crockett." He later concentrated on GOSPEL MUSIC; his 1957 album *Hymns* enjoyed great success. He continued recording into the 1970s.

Ford Foundation U.S. philanthropic foundation. It was established in 1936 with gifts and bequests from HENRY FORD and his son Edsel (1893–1943). Its assets in 2000 surpassed $10 billion. Its chief concerns have been international affairs (particularly population control and alleviation of food shortages), humanities and the arts, communications (especially public television), and, in later years, resources and the environment.

Ford Motor Co. U.S. automotive corporation. Founded in Detroit in 1903 by HENRY FORD and a group of investors, the company introduced the hugely successful MODEL T in 1908 and by 1923 was producing more than half of all U.S. automotive vehicles. Through the Lincoln Motor Co. (acquired in 1922), Ford produced luxury Lincolns and Continentals. After years of declining sales, the Model T was succeeded by the Model A in 1927; other companies such as General Motors took the opportunity to make serious inroads into Ford's dominance. The company was reincorporated in 1919, with Ford and his family acquiring full ownership. Henry's son Edsel served as president 1919–43, and Henry's grandson Henry Ford II led the company 1945–79, reviving its fortunes considerably. Its stock was first publicly traded in 1956. Ford acquired the British Jaguar firm in 1989–90. The company continues to manufacture passenger cars, trucks, and tractors as well as parts and accessories.

foreclosure Legal proceeding by which a borrower's rights to a mortgaged property may be extinguished if the borrower fails to live up to the obligations agreed to in the loan contract. The lender may then declare the entire debt due and owing and may seek to satisfy it by foreclosing. Foreclosure is commonly by a court-decreed sale of the property to the highest bidder, who is often the lender. See also MORTGAGE.

foreign aid Transfer of capital, goods, or services from a donor country to a recipient country. Foreign aid may be given in the form of either cash or technical assistance, for either civilian or military purposes. Its use in the modern era began in the 18th century when Prussia subsidized some of its allies. After World War II, foreign aid developed from a subsidy into a more sophisticated instrument of foreign policy, and the U.N. Relief and Rehabilitation Administration showed that rich nations were beginning to view official international aid as an essential element of postwar reconstruction. International organizations were created to provide aid to war-ravaged countries and newly freed colonies. Donor countries often attach conditions to their aid, including the requirement to buy goods from the donor country. See also INTERNATIONAL MONETARY FUND, MARSHALL PLAN, WORLD BANK.

foreign exchange Purchase or sale of one national CURRENCY in exchange for another nation's currency, usually conducted in a market setting. Foreign exchange makes possible international transactions such as imports and exports and the movement of capital between countries. The value of one foreign currency in relation to another is defined by the EXCHANGE RATE.

Foreign Legion *French* **Légion Étrangère** French military corps consisting originally of foreigners but now including many Frenchmen. It was founded in 1831 as a highly disciplined professional army to help control French colonies in Africa. Since its founding, it has been in almost continuous combat; its forces have fought or been stationed in such places as Europe, the Crimea, Mexico, Syria, and Indochina. The new volunteer swears to serve not France but the legion; after serving one enlistment (five years) with good conduct, foreign-born soldiers are eligible for French citizenship. Since it keeps a volunteer's past secret, it has been romanticized as a haven for those seeking new identities, including criminals, but most legionnaires are professional soldiers who enjoy combat. Originally headquartered in Algeria, the legion moved its headquarters to France after Algerian independence.

Foreign Ministers, Council of Organization of the foreign ministers of the U.S., Britain, France, and the Soviet Union—the World War II ALLIED POWERS. In meetings between 1945 and 1972, they attempted to reach postwar political agreements. They produced treaties of peace with Italy, Hungary, Romania, Finland, and Bulgaria and resolved the TRIESTE problem in 1946. They convened the Geneva Conference on the KOREAN WAR in 1954, and in 1955 agreed on an Austrian treaty. They recessed after failing to agree on German unification in 1959; in 1972 they paved the way for both East and West Germany to enter the U.N.

foreign policy Underlying direction of the activities and relationships of one state in its interactions with other states. Development of foreign policy is influenced by domestic considerations, the policies or behavior of other states, or a plan to advance a specific geopolitical design. LEOPOLD RANKE emphasized the primacy of geography and external threats in shaping foreign policy, but later writers emphasized domestic needs. DIPLOMACY is the tool of foreign policy, and war, alliances, and international trade may all be manifestations of it.

foreign service *or* **diplomatic service** Staff of a state's international-affairs department that represents the state's interests in foreign countries. It fulfills two functions, diplomatic and consular. The standards for foreign-service jobs are similar in most countries. Before the 20th century, wealth, aristocratic standing, and political connections were the chief requirements for high-ranking diplomatic positions. Political appointees still hold the top positions in many foreign missions, but their subordinates generally must demonstrate their education and intellectual ability through a competitive examination. Foreign-service personnel have special legal rights (e.g., they do not have to pay taxes to their host country). See also AMBASSADOR.

foreign workers Those who work in a foreign country without initially intending to settle there and without the benefits of CITIZENSHIP in the host country. Some are recruited to supplement the workforce of a host country for a limited term or to provide skills on a contractual basis that the host country seeks. Others are recruited directly by a private employer, which may need to certify that it cannot find workers among the country's own citizens. Host countries may also import foreign workers for jobs their citizens refuse to do. Large influxes of foreign workers can awaken xenophobia, particularly when the host country's population is ethnically and culturally homogeneous and the foreign workers' culture and appearance are significantly different or when economic downturns heighten the tendency to assign blame to others.

Foreman, George (born 1949) U.S. boxer. Born in Marshall, Texas, he won the Olympic gold medal in 1968. His first world heavyweight title victory was his second-round knockout of Joe Frazier in 1973. He had won all 40 of his professional bouts, many by knockout, before he fell in eight rounds to MUHAMMAD ALI in 1974 in the so-called "Rumble in the Jungle" in Kinshasa, Zaire, one of the most famous matches in boxing history. He retired in 1978, but began a remarkable comeback in 1987 at age 38; he regained the title in ten rounds against Michael Moorer in 1994 to become, at 45, the oldest titleholder ever. He announced his retirement again the next year, but fought a few more times in 1996–97. He has been an ordained minister since 1977.

forensic medicine Science of applying medical knowledge to legal questions, recognized as a specialty since the early 19th century. Its primary tool has always been the AUTOPSY, to identify the dead (e.g., plane-crash victims) or determine cause of death, which can significantly affect trials dealing with insurance and inheritance. Forensic psychiatry determines the mental health of an individual about to stand trial. Forensic genetics allows paternity to be determined and can identify blood or other tissue samples as coming from a particular person (see DNA FINGERPRINTING). Forensic TOXICOLOGY, concerned with such topics as intentional poisonings and drug use, is increasingly important in cases of industrial and environmental poisoning.

forensic psychology Application of psychology to legal issues, often for the purpose of offering expert testimony in a courtroom. In civil and criminal cases, forensic psychologists may evaluate individuals to determine such questions as competency to stand trial, relationship of a mental disorder to an accident or crime, and potential for future dangerous behavior. In addition to conducting interviews and administering psychological tests, they usually gather a forensic history that includes such information as hospital records, police reports, and statements of witnesses. They are also expected to have a grasp of relevant legal questions. In a child-custody case, a psychologist may be asked to evaluate home environments, parents, and the character of the child in order to recommend a custody decision in the child's best interests.

forest Complex ECOSYSTEM in which trees are the dominant life form. Tree-dominated forests can occur wherever the temperatures rise above 50°F (10°C) in the warmest months and the annual precipitation is more than 8 in. (200 mm). They can develop under various conditions within these limits, and the kind of soil, plant, and animal life differs according to the extremes of environmental influences. In cool, high-latitude subpolar regions, TAIGA (boreal) forests are dominated by hardy CONIFERS. In more temperate high-latitude climates, mixed forests of both conifers and broad-leaved DECIDUOUS TREES predominate. Broad-leaved deciduous forests develop in midlatitude climates. In humid equatorial climates, tropical RAIN FORESTS develop. There heavy rainfall supports EVERGREENS that have broad leaves instead of the needle leaves of cooler evergreen forests. Forests are among the most complex ecosystems in the world, with extensive vertical layering. Conifer forests have the simplest structure: a tree layer, a shrub layer that is spotty or even absent, and a ground layer covered with LICHENS, MOSSES, and LIVERWORTS. Deciduous forests are more complex (the tree canopy is divided into an upper and lower story), and rain-forest canopies are divided into at least three layers. Forest animals have highly developed hearing, and many are adapted for vertical movement through the environment. Because food other than ground plants is scarce, many ground-dwelling animals use forests only for shelter. The forest is nature's most efficient ecosystem, with a high rate of PHOTOSYNTHESIS affecting both plant and animal systems in complex organic relationships.

Forest, Lee De See Lee DE FOREST

Forester, C(ecil) S(cott) (1899–1966) British novelist and journalist. He abandoned medicine for writing and achieved success with his first novel, *Payment Deferred* (1926). He is best known as the creator of the naval officer Horatio Hornblower, whose rise from midshipman to admiral and peer during the Napoleonic Wars is told in 12 novels published 1937–67. Many of his novels were adapted to movies, including *The African Queen* (1935; film, 1951).

forestry Management of forested land (see FOREST), together with associated waters and wasteland, primarily for harvesting timber but also for CONSERVATION and recreation purposes. The science of forestry is built around the principle of multiple-use land management, though the harvesting and replanting of timber are the primary activities. The main objective is to maintain a continuous supply of timber through carefully planned harvest and replacement. The forest manager is also responsible for the application of other land controls, including the protection of wildlife and the implementation of programs to protect the forest from weeds, insects, fungal diseases (see FUNGUS), EROSION, and fire. The planned management of forests originated in early medieval Europe, where laws regulated the felling of timber and the use of forests for hunting. In the 19th century private forestry schools were established in Europe; and in 1891 the U.S. government authorized its first reserves of forested land. During the 20th century many nations have undertaken reforestation or afforestation programs.

forge Open furnace for heating METAL ORE and metal for working and forming, or a workshop containing forge hearths and related equipment. From earliest times, smiths (see SMITHING) heated IRON in forges and formed it by hammering on an ANVIL. A BELLOWS operated by an assistant or by a foot treadle provided the forced draft for raising the temperature of the fire. Later, a waterwheel or animal power was often used to operate the bellows; modern forges have mechanically powered bellows or rotary blowers.

forgery In law, the making of a false writing with the intent to defraud. "Writing" need not be handwriting: the law of forgery also covers printing, engraving, and keyboarding. COUNTERFEITING is usually regarded as a specific type of forgery. Checks, negotiable instruments, contracts, wills, and deeds are examples of documents that may be forged. Evidence may also be forged. Forgery requires fraudulent intent; it is not forgery to sign another's name, fill in blanks, or alter a genuine writing in the honest, though mistaken, belief that such conduct is authorized.

forget-me-not Any of about 50 species of plants that make up the genus *Myosotis,* in the BORAGE family, native to temperate Eurasia and North America and to mountains of the Old World tropics. Some are favored as garden plants for their clusters of blue flowers. The woods forget-me-not *(M. sylvatica),* like most other species, changes color from pink to blue as the tubular, flaring, five-lobed flower matures.

Woods forget-me-not (*Myosotis sylvatica*).

INGMAR HOLMASEN

forging In METALLURGY, the process of shaping METAL and increasing its strength by hammering or pressing. In most forging an upper DIE is forced against a heated workpiece positioned on a stationary lower die. To increase the force of the blow, power is sometimes applied to augment gravity. The number of blows struck is carefully gauged by the operator to give maximum effect with minimum wear on the die. Forging presses employ hydraulic or mechanical pressure instead of blows; most can exert only a few hundred tons of pressure, but giant presses, used for forging parts of jet aircraft, are capable of up to 50,000 tons of pressure. See also DROP FORGING.

form In the philosophy of PLATO and SOCRATES, an intelligible essence that exists separately from the material world yet is central in its intelligible structure. The relationship between the material world and the forms was described by Plato as one of participation. There was, as Plato put it, a "place accessible to the intelligence," the realm of forms, which has a hierarchical order, the highest level being that of the form of the good. Whereas the physical world, perceived with the senses, is in constant flux and knowledge derived from it restricted and variable, the realm of forms, apprehensible only by the mind, is eternal and changeless. Each form is the pattern of a particular category of things in this world; thus, there are forms of human, stone, shape, color, beauty, and justice. Yet the things of this world are only imperfect copies of these perfect forms.

formal system In LOGIC, a formal language together with a deductive apparatus by which some well-formed formulas can be derived from others. Each formal system has a formal language composed of primitive symbols that figure in certain rules of formation (statements concerning the expressions allowable in the system) and a set of THEOREMS developed by inference from a set of AXIOMS. In an AXIOMATIC system, the primitive symbols are undefined and all other symbols are defined in terms of them. In EUCLIDEAN GEOMETRY, for example, such concepts as "point," "line," and "lies on" are usually posited as primitive terms. From the primitive symbols, certain formulas are defined as well formed, some of which are listed as axioms; and rules are stated for inferring one formula as a conclusion from one or more other formulas taken as premises. A theorem within such a system is a formula capable of proof through a finite sequence of well-formed formulas, each of which either is an axiom or is validly inferred from earlier formulas.

formaldehyde \fȯr-ˈmal-də-ˌhīd\ *or* **methanal** \ˈme-thə-ˌnal\ Simplest ALDEHYDE, chemical formula HCHO. Formaldehyde (37%) in water solution (formalin) is used as a preservative, embalming agent, and disinfectant. Large amounts of formaldehyde are used in the manufacture of various familiar PLASTICS: Bakelite (the first plastic) is the trademark name for formaldehyde and PHENOL POLYMER; Formica is the trademark name for formaldehyde and UREA polymer. The reaction of formaldehyde with PROTEINS (called amino formylation) leads to its use in the tanning industry and for treating various vegetable proteins to render them fibrous.

formalism See NEW CRITICISM

Formalism *or* **Russian Formalism** Russian school of literary criticism that flourished 1914–28. Making use of the linguistic theories of FERDINAND DE SAUSSURE, Formalists were concerned with what technical devices make a literary text literary, apart from its psychological, sociological, biographical, and historical elements. Though influenced by the SYMBOLIST MOVEMENT, they sought to make their analyses more objective and scientific than those of the Symbolists. The movement was condemned by the Soviet authorities in 1929 for its lack of political perspective. Later it became influential in the West, notably in NEW CRITICISM and STRUCTURALISM.

Forman, Milos (born 1932) Czech-U.S. film director. He began his career as a scriptwriter, then directed his first feature film in 1964. Success followed with the ironic comedies *Loves of a Blonde* (1965) and *The Fireman's Ball* (1967). He moved to the U.S. in 1969 and successfully applied his light touch to the generation gap in *Taking Off* (1971), then triumphed with *One Flew Over the Cuckoo's Nest* (1975, Academy Award). He directed successful screen adaptations of the musicals *Hair* (1979) and *Ragtime* (1981); his later films include *Amadeus* (1984, Academy Award), *Valmont* (1989), and *The People vs. Larry Flynt* (1996).

formes fixes \'fȯrm-'fēks\ Principal forms of music and poetry in 14th- and 15th-century France. Three forms predominated. The rondeau followed the pattern *ABaAabAB*. (*A (a)* and *B (b)* represent repeated musical phrases; capital letters indicate repetition of text in a refrain, while lowercase letters indicate new text.) The ballade employed the pattern *aabC*. The virelai used the pattern *AbbaA*. The TROUVÈRE Adam de la Halle (born c. 1250) wrote the first polyphonic settings of the formes fixes. G. DE MACHAUT wrote both text and music for many monophonic and polyphonic CHANSONS in the formes fixes. Later composers, including G. DUFAY, favored the rondeau.

formic acid Simplest CARBOXYLIC ACID, chemical formula HCOOH. It is secreted by some insects, especially red ANTS (its name comes from the Latin word for ant), in their bite or sting. It has many industrial uses, in textile and leather manufacture, as an industrial solvent, and as an intermediate.

Formosa See TAIWAN

Formosa Strait See TAIWAN STRAIT

formula weight Sum of the ATOMIC WEIGHTS of all ATOMS in a chemical formula. The term is generally applied to a substance that consists of ions (see IONIC BOND) rather than individual molecules (and thus does not have a MOLECULAR WEIGHT). An example is sodium chloride, or table salt. Such a substance's chemical formula describes the simplest ratio of the number of atoms of the constituent ELEMENTS. See also STOICHIOMETRY.

formwork Mold used to form concrete into structural shapes (beams, columns, slabs, shells) for building. Formwork can be of timber, steel, plastic, or fiberglass. The inside surface is coated with a bond breaker (plastic or oil) to keep the concrete from sticking to the mold. Important for high-rise construction is slipforming, whereby a vertical concrete element is continuously cast using a short section of formwork that is repeatedly disassembled and moved upward as each section is finished or that moves slowly and continuously as concrete is being placed. This is sometimes called a climbing form.

Fornes \'fōr-nās\, **Maria Irene** (born 1930) Cuban-U.S. dramatist. Her family moved to the U.S. in 1945, and she became a painter before beginning to write plays in the early 1960s. She has written some 35 stage works, and has directed her own works as well as classic drama. Her innovative dramas have made her one of the most successful and frequently produced of off-Broadway playwrights. Her best-known play, *Fefu and Her Friends* (1977), explores women's relationships with one another.

Forrest, Edwin (1806–1872) U.S. actor. Born in Philadelphia, he made his stage debut there in 1820. He played Othello in New York (1826) to great acclaim and became known for his Shakespearean roles. His feud with WILLIAM MACREADY sparked the so-called Astor Place riot (1849) when Forrest's supporters mobbed the theater where Macready was appearing. The militia was called out, the rioters attacked, and the militia fired, killing 22 and wounding 36. Forrest's reputation never fully recovered; it was further damaged by his filing a divorce suit on grounds of adultery.

Forrestal, James V(incent) (1892–1949) U.S. secretary of defense (1947–49). Born in Beacon, N.Y., he served in naval aviation in World War I, then returned to work in a New York investment firm. Appointed undersecretary of the navy in 1940, he directed the huge naval expansion and procurement programs of World War II. He became secretary of the navy in 1944. As the first secretary of defense, he began to reorganize and coordinate the armed services. He resigned in 1949, suffering depression similar to battle fatigue, and entered Bethesda Naval Medical Center; soon after, he plunged to his death from a window.

Forrester, Jay W(right) (born 1918) U.S. electrical engineer and management expert. Born in Anselmo, Neb., he taught and conducted research at MIT, where in 1945 he founded the Digital Computer Laboratory. There he invented the magnetic core random-access memory (RAM) used in digital computers for information storage. At MIT's Sloan School of Management (from 1956), he applied computer simulation to real-world relationships, such as the flow of materials in a factory, by feeding a series of interconnected equations to a computer.

Forssmann \'fȯrs-ˌmän\, **Werner** (1904–1979) German surgeon. He shared with ANDRE COURNAND and Dickinson W. Richards (1895–1973) a 1956 Nobel Prize for contributions to the development of cardiac catheterization. He used himself as the first human subject, watching the progress of the catheter in a mirror in front of a fluoroscope screen. Severely criticized for this, he abandoned cardiology for urology. His procedure, put into practice by Richards and Cournand, has become an invaluable diagnostic and research tool.

Forster, E(dward) M(organ) (1879–1970) British writer. From an upper-middle-class family, he attended Cambridge University and from c. 1907 was a member of the informal BLOOMSBURY GROUP. His early works include *Where Angels Fear to Tread* (1905), *The Longest Journey* (1907), *A Room with a View* (1908), and his first major success, *Howard's End* (1910), novels that show acute observation of middle-class life and its values. After periods in India and Alexandria, he wrote his finest novel, *A Passage to India* (1924), examining the failure of human understanding between ethnic and social groups under British rule. *Maurice*, a novel with a homosexual theme written in 1913, appeared posthumously. *Aspects of the Novel* (1927) is a classic discussion of aesthetics and the creative process. Awarded an honorary fellowship in 1946 at Cambridge, he lived there until his death.

E.M. Forster.
BBC HULTON PICTURE LIBRARY

forsterite-fayalite series \'fȯr-stər-ˌīt-fī-'ä-ˌlīt\ Most important minerals in the OLIVINE family, and possibly the most important constituents of the earth's MANTLE. These minerals occur as green to yellow, glassy crystals in many basic and ultrabasic rocks (see ACID AND BASIC ROCKS) and are also abundant in chondritic meteorites. They also occur in dolomitic limestones, marbles, and metamorphosed iron-rich sediments. They are sometimes used in the manufacture of brick.

forsythia \fər-'si-thē-ə\ Any of the seven species of ornamental shrubs that make up the genus *Forsythia,* in the OLIVE family, native to eastern Europe and East Asia. In some species the yellow flowers borne along the stems appear before the leaves in early spring. The narrow leaves occasionally have three parts; the star-shaped flowers have four. Common forsythia *(F. intermedia)* has arching stems to about 20 ft (6 m) and bright yellow flowers.

Fort-de-France \ˌfȯr-də-ˈfräⁿs\ City (pop., 1995: 104,000), capital of MARTINIQUE, West Indies. Located on the island's western coast, it was formerly called Fort-Royal, and has been Martinique's capital since 1680. Until 1918, when its commercial growth began, it had an inadequate water supply, was partly surrounded by swamps, and was notorious for yellow fever; the swamps have since been drained. It is the French West Indies' largest town, chief port, and busiest commercial center and has long sheltered the French fleet in the West Indies. Sugarcane, cacao, and rum are exported.

Fort Knox U.S. military reservation, northern Kentucky, southwest of Louisville. Occupying an area of 110,000 acres (44,510 hectares), it was established in 1918 as Camp Knox and became a permanent military post in 1932. The U.S. Gold Bullion Depository, a bombproof structure protected by elaborate security devices, was built there in 1936 to hold the bulk of the nation's gold. Since 1940 it has been the U.S. Army Armor Headquarters and the site of associated training schools.

Fort-Lamy See N'DJAMENA

Fort Lauderdale City (pop., 1996 est.: 152,000), southeastern Florida. It is located on the Atlantic Ocean, 25 mi (45 km) north of MIAMI. A fort built there in 1838 gave its name to the town, which was established in 1895 and later developed as a shipping and commercial center and residential resort. The ATLANTIC INTRACOASTAL WATERWAY is connected to the city's deepwater port, Port Everglades. The city is interlaced with recreational waterways and has extensive boating facilities, which have given rise to a marine industry.

Fort Matanzas National Monument National reserve, northeastern Florida. Established in 1924 and covering 228 acres (92 hectares), it centers around a Spanish fort on Rattlesnake Island, 14 mi (23 km) south of ST. AUGUSTINE. Originating in 1569 as a wooden tower and completed in 1742, the fort is near the site of the slaughter of 300 French HUGUENOT colonists by Spaniards in 1565.

Fort McHenry Military fort and national monument, BALTIMORE. During the WAR OF 1812, the British bombarded it in 1814 but failed to capture the city it defended. FRANCIS SCOTT KEY witnessed the battle while being held aboard a British ship, and the sight of the U.S. flag flying above the fort inspired him to write "The Star-Spangled Banner." The fort was used as a federal prison during the AMERICAN CIVIL WAR and then served as a military post until 1900, when it was abandoned. Occupying an area of 43 acres (17 hectares), it was named a national park in 1925 and a national monument in 1939.

Fort Stanwix, Treaties of (1768, 1784) Agreements by which the IROQUOIS CONFEDERACY ceded land in what is now western Pennsylvania, Kentucky, West Virginia, and New York, opening vast tracts to white exploration and settlement. In 1768 about 3,400 Iroquois gathered at Fort Stanwix (now Rome), N.Y., to sign a new treaty with the British that replaced the PROCLAMATION OF 1763. Pressure from white settlers and fur traders for additional land forced the new U.S. government to renegotiate the treaty. Weakened by the frontier campaign against them during the American Revolution, the Iroquois were persuaded to cede more land and in 1784 to sign the second treaty, also called the Treaty with the Six Nations.

Fort Sumter National Monument National preserve, on Sullivan's Island at the entrance to the harbor of CHARLESTON, S.C. Construction of the fort began in 1829 and was still in progress in 1861, when it became the site of the first engagement of the AMERICAN CIVIL WAR, April 12, 1861. The national monument, established in 1948, also includes Fort Moultrie, site of an American victory against the British (June 28, 1776) in the AMERICAN REVOLUTION, when the fort was called Fort Sullivan. The Seminole Indian leader OSCEOLA is buried there.

Fort Wayne City (pop., 1995 est.: 185,000), northeastern Indiana. Once the chief town of the MIAMI Indians, it was the site of a French trading post in the late 17th century. It was taken by the English (1760) and then by Indians under PONTIAC (1763). A log stockade built in 1794 by Gen. ANTHONY WAYNE gave the town its name. The city's industrial growth began with the building of the Wabash and Erie Canal in the 1830s. It now manufactures a range of machinery, including automotive and electrical equipment. It is the site of educational institutions, including Concordia Theological Seminary (1846) and St. Francis College (1890). Johnny APPLESEED, the pioneer orchard planter, is buried there.

Fort Worth City (pop., 1996 est.: 480,000), northern Texas. It lies on the Trinity River and constitutes the western part of the Dallas–Fort Worth urban complex. Founded in 1849 as a military outpost against COMANCHE raids, it was a stopover point for cattle drives on the CHISHOLM TRAIL. It became a cattle-shipping boomtown after the railroad arrived in 1876. Oil finds brought the petroleum-refining industry in 1920, and in 1949 aircraft manufacturing began there, expanded now to include aerospace and electronic equipment. It is the seat of Texas Christian University (1873) and Texas Wesleyan University (1890), and its attractions include the Amon Carter Museum of Western Art.

Fortaleza \ˌfōr-tə-ˈlā-zə\ Port city (pop., 1991: 743,000; metro. area pop., 1995: 2,660,000), northeastern Brazil. It lies at the mouth of the Pajeú River. Originating as a small village adjoining a Portuguese fort, it took the name of Villa do Forte da Assumpção in 1654. In 1810 it became the capital of Ceará captaincy, and in 1823 it was given city status. It became the capital of a province under the name of Fortaleza Nova de Bragança. It is a textile manufacturing center; its port handles exports.

Fortas, Abe (1910–1982) U.S. jurist. Born in Memphis, he graduated from Yale University Law School (1933), where he studied under WILLIAM O. DOUGLAS before following him to the SECURITIES AND EXCHANGE COMMISSION. He cofounded a major Washington, D.C. law firm in 1946, and represented some of the largest U.S. corporations. In 1963 he successfully argued the case of *Gideon vs. Wainwright,* which established the right of the ACCUSED to counsel in criminal trials, regardless of ability to pay. Pres. LYNDON B. JOHNSON, a close friend, nominated Fortas to the U.S. Supreme Court in 1965. When Johnson attempted to elevate him to chief justice in 1968, the nomination failed to win Senate approval, and Fortas resigned in 1969 following a threat of impeachment over securities dealings.

Fortescue \ˈfȯrt-ə-ˌskyü\, **John** *later* **Sir John** (c. 1385–1479?) English jurist. He served as chief justice of the King's Bench from 1442. He was the first to state the basic principle that it is better that the guilty escape than that the innocent be punished. He fled to Scotland after HENRY VI's defeat in 1461. Hoping for a restoration of the House of LANCASTER, he educated Prince Edward in France, and he wrote for Edward's instruction *De laudibus legum Angliae*, the first book about law written for the layperson. Returning to England in 1471, he was captured by Yorkists but was allowed to retire to his home.

Forth River, southern central Scotland. It flows east for 116 mi (187 km) from its headwaters on the slopes of Ben Lomond to enter the Firth of Forth, an estuary extending inland from the North Sea for 48 mi (77 km); the estuary varies in width from 1.5 to 17.5 mi (2.4–28 km). The river has a short highland section and a longer lowland section; the latter, called the Links of Forth, was the site of the Battle of BANNOCKBURN (1314).

fortification Structure erected to strengthen a military position against attack. The defense of cities and trade centers, usually by high walls, has been important for centuries. The citadel was the fortress of the ancient world, appearing in cities of Egypt, Greece, and the Roman empire. By Classical Greek times, fortress architecture began incorporating ramparts (walled embankments) and towers. Roman fortresses of the 2nd century tended to be square or rectangular, and were usually of dressed (cut) stone. The medieval castle remained almost impregnable until gunpowder came into use.

FORTRAN Procedural computer PROGRAMMING LANGUAGE developed for numerical analysis by JOHN W. BACKUS and others at IBM in 1957. The name derives from FORmula TRANslation. For many years it was the most widely used high-level language for scientific and engineering computations. Though other languages, such as various versions of C, are now popular for such uses, FORTRAN is still the language of choice for numerical analysis. It has been revised several times and now includes capabilities for handling structured data, dynamic ("on-the-fly") data allocation, recursions (procedures that call themselves), and other features.

Fortune Brands, Inc. U.S. industrial conglomerate. Its corporate history begins with the American Tobacco Co. (founded in 1890), which grew out of the tobacco business established in North Carolina by the Duke family (see JAMES B. DUKE) and which controlled the U.S. tobacco industry until broken up under antitrust laws in 1911. American Tobacco continued to esell such brands as Lucky Strike and Pall Mall. Its parent company, American Brands, Inc., began diversifying in the 1960s, and in 1994 American Tobacco was sold to a British conglomerate. In 1996 American Brands changed its name to Fortune Brands, Inc., to signal its departure from the tobacco industry. Its subsidiaries now include Jim Beam whiskey and Master Lock padlocks.

forum In ancient Roman cities, a centrally located open area surrounded by public buildings and colonnades and serving as a multipurpose public gathering place. The forum was an adaptation of the Greek AGORA and ACROPOLIS. In Rome the *forum Romanum* referred to the flat and formerly marshy space between the Palatine and Capitoline hills. In the Roman republic, this was the site of public meetings, law courts, and gladiatorial games and was lined with shops and open-air markets. Under the Roman empire, when the forum evolved into a center for religious and secular ceremonies and spectacles, it held many of Rome's most imposing temples, basilicas, and monuments. New forums were built, some devoted to judicial or administrative affairs and some to trade. The aesthetic harmony of Trajan's Forum (2nd century AD), with its complex of buildings and courtyards and its tiers of shops, influenced many subsequent town planners.

Trajan's Forum, Rome, designed by Apollodorus of Damascus, early 2nd century AD; one of the semicircular colonnaded exedrae.

FOTOTECA UNIONE, ROME

Foscolo \ˈfȯs-kō-lō\, **Ugo** *orig.* **Niccolò Foscolo** (1778–1827) Italian poet and novelist. His works articulated the feelings of many Italians during the turbulent epoch of the French Revolution, the Napoleonic Wars, and the restoration of Austrian rule. After Austria regained Italy in 1814, he fled first to Switzerland and then to Britain. His popular novel *The Last Letters of Jacopo Ortis* (1802) bitterly denounced Napoleon's cession of Venetia to Austria. Among his poems are the patriotic "Dei sepolcri" (1807) and the acclaimed but unfinished *Le grazie* (1803, 1818, 1822).

Fosse \ˈfȯs-ē\, **Bob** *orig.* **Robert Louis** (1927–1987) U.S. theater and film choreographer and director. Born into a vaudeville family in Chicago, Fosse began dancing professionally at age 13. He won his first Tony award for choreographing the Broadway musical *The Pajama Game* (1954) and went on to win six more for his choreography. His later hit shows included *Damn Yankees* (1955) and *Sweet Charity* (1966)—both starring his wife, Gwen Verdon (1925–2000)—as well as *Pippin* (1973) and *Dancin'* (1978). He directed the film musical *Cabaret* (1972, Academy Award); his film *All That Jazz* (1979) was a thinly disguised autobiography.

Fossey, Dian (1932–1985) U.S. zoologist. Born in San Francisco, she was working as an occupational therapist when, on a trip to Africa in 1963, she met LEAKEY FAMILY, who persuaded her to return to study the mountain gorilla in its natural habitat. By accustoming the gorillas in Rwanda's Virunga Mountains to her presence, she gathered detailed knowledge of their habits, communication, and social structure. She obtained a PhD in 1974 and taught at Cornell University while remaining involved with the Karisoke Research Center in Africa, which she had established in 1967. She recounted her observations in *Gorillas in the Mist* (1983; film, 1988). The drastic measures she took to protect the Virunga gorillas from poachers and farmers apparently led to her being murdered at her campsite.

fossil Remnant, impression, or trace of an animal or plant of a past geologic age that has been preserved in the earth's CRUST. The data recorded in fossils, known as the fossil record, constitute the primary source of information about the history of life on the earth. Only a small fraction of ancient organisms are preserved as fossils, and usually only organisms that have a solid skeleton or shell. A shell or bone that is buried quickly after deposition may retain organic tissue, though it becomes petrified (converted to a stony substance) over time. Unaltered hard parts, such as the shells of clams, are relatively common in sedimentary rocks. The soft parts of animals or plants are rarely preserved. The embedding of insects in amber and the preservation of mammoths in ice are rare but striking examples of the fossil preservation of soft tissues. Traces of organisms may also occur as tracks, trails, or even borings.

fossil fuel Any of a class of materials of biologic origin occurring within the earth's crust that can be used as a source of energy. Fossil fuels include COAL, PETROLEUM, and SHALE OIL. They all contain carbon and were formed as a result of geologic processes acting on the remains of (mostly) plants and animals that lived and died hundreds of millions of years ago. All fossil fuels can be burned to provide heat, which may be used directly, as in home heating, or to produce steam to drive a generator for the production of electricity. Fossil fuels supply nearly 90% of all the energy used by industrially developed nations.

Foster, Abigail Kelley *orig.* **Abigail Kelley** (1810–1887) U.S. abolitionist. Born in Pelham, Mass., she became active in a branch of the Female Anti-Slavery Society in the 1830s. In 1838 she helped WILLIAM LLOYD GARRISON organize the New England Non-Resistance Society. Her long career as a political lecturer brought national fame and notoriety because she addressed audiences of both men and women. In 1845 she married Stephen S. Foster (1809–1881), a prominent abolitionist who joined her lecture tour. In the 1850s she added temperance and women's rights to her lecture topics.

Foster, Jodie *orig.* **Alicia Christian** (born 1962) U.S. film actress and director. Born in Los Angeles, she was a professional actress by age 3, and continued to play child roles in family films, while earning praise as a teenage prostitute in *Taxi Driver* (1976) and a seductive speakeasy queen in an all-child cast in *Bugsy Malone* (1976). As an adult she won acclaim in such films as *The Accused* (1988, Academy Award), *The Silence of the Lambs* (1991, Academy Award), *Nell* (1994), and *Contact* (1997). She turned to directing with *Little Man Tate* (1991) and *Home for the Holidays* (1995).

Foster, Stephen (Collins) (1826–1864) U.S. songwriter. Born in Lawrenceville, Penn., Foster began writing songs as a child, despite his lack of formal tutoring. His musical influences came in part from black church services he attended with the family's servant and from songs sung by black laborers. In 1842 he published "Open Thy Lattice, Love," and in 1848 he sold "Oh! Susanna" for $100; it quickly became an international hit. He later entered into a contract with the publisher Firth, Pond & Co. He was commissioned to write songs for Edwin P. Christy's minstrel show; his "Old Folks at Home" became one of the most popular songs of the century. In 1857, drinking heavily and in financial difficulties, he sold all rights to his future songs to his publishers for about $1,900. In 1860 he moved to New York; he died penniless at 37 from a fall in a Bowery hotel. He left about 200 songs, including "Camptown Races," "My Old Kentucky Home," "Jeanie with the Light Brown Hair," and "Beautiful Dreamer," and is universally regarded as the greatest American songwriter of the 19th century.

Foster, William Z(ebulon) (1881–1961) U.S. labor organizer. Born in Taunton, Mass., he joined the Industrial Workers of the World in 1909 and came to national prominence as an AFL leader in the steel strike of 1919. In 1921 the Soviet Communists chose him as a leader of the U.S. Communist Party, and he ran as its presidential candidate in 1924, 1928, and 1932 on a platform that envisioned the ultimate demise of capitalism and the establishment of a workers' republic. Ill health forced his resignation in 1932. Soviet dissatisfaction with his successor, EARL BROWDER, brought him back as chairman (1945–56), but he fell from favor and was made chairman emeritus in 1957.

Foucault \fü-ˈkō\, **Jean (-Bernard-Léon)** (1819–1868) French physicist. Though educated in medicine, his interests lay in physics. In 1850 he measured the speed of light with extreme accuracy. He invented the FOUCAULT PENDULUM and used it to provide experimental proof that earth rotates on its axis. He also discovered the existence of eddy currents (Foucault currents) in a copper disk moving in a strong magnetic field, and invented (1859) a simple but extremely accurate method of testing telescope mirrors for surface defects.

Foucault \fü-ˈkō\, **Michel (Paul)** (1926–1984) French structuralist philosopher and historian. A professor at the Collège de France from 1970, he examined the codes and concepts by which societies operate, especially the "principles of exclusion" (such as the distinctions between the sane and the insane) by which a society defines itself. He theorized that, by surveying social attitudes in relation to institutions such as asylums, hospitals, and prisons, one can examine the development and omnipresence of power. His books, including *Madness and Civilization* (1961), *The Order of Things* (1966), *The Archaeology of Knowledge* (1969), *Discipline and Punish* (1975), and *History of Sexuality* (3 vols., 1976–84), made him one of the most influential intellectuals of his time. An outspoken homosexual, he died of AIDS. See also STRUCTURALISM.

Foucault pendulum \fü-'kō\ Large PENDULUM that is free to swing in any direction. As it swings back and forth, the earth rotates beneath it, so its perpendicular plane of swing rotates in relation to the earth's surface. Devised by J.-B.-L. FOUCAULT in 1851, it provided the first laboratory demonstration that the earth spins on its axis. A Foucault pendulum always rotates clockwise in the Northern Hemisphere and counterclockwise in the Southern Hemisphere (a consequence of the CORIOLIS FORCE). The rate of rotation depends on the latitude, becoming slower as the pendulum is placed closer to the equator; at the equator, a Foucault pendulum does not rotate.

Fouché \fü-'shā\, **Joseph** *later* **duc (Duke) d'Otrante** (1758?–1820) French police organizer. In the French Revolution, he was elected to the National Convention and voted for LOUIS XVI's death. He was sent on missions to the provinces to ensure their loyalty, and in Lyon he ordered the massacre of rebels. He became minister of police in 1799; he supported NAPOLEON's Coup of 18–19 BRUMAIRE, and subsequently organized the secret police. Though Napoleon made him duc d'Otrante in 1809, he had intrigued against Napoleon from 1807. He was dismissed after ordering a levy of the national guard (1809), but was brought back several times to undertake missions for Napoleon. He was minister of police during the HUNDRED DAYS, but was ultimately exiled as a regicide in 1816.

foundation Part of a structural system that supports and anchors the superstructure of a building and transmits its loads directly to the earth. To prevent damage from repeated freeze-thaw cycles, the bottom of the foundation must be below the frost line. The foundations of low-rise residential buildings are nearly all supported on spread footings, wide bases (usually of concrete) that support walls or PIERS and distribute the load over a greater area. A concrete grade beam supported by isolated footings, piers, or PILES may be placed at ground level, especially in a building without a basement, to support the exterior wall. Spread footings are also used—in greatly enlarged form—for high-rise buildings. Other systems for supporting heavy loads include piles, concrete CAISSON columns, and building directly on exposed rock. In yielding soil, a floating foundation—consisting of rigid, boxlike structures set at such a depth that the weight of the soil removed to place it equals the weight of the construction supported—may be used.

foundation Nongovernmental, nonprofit organization, with assets provided by donors and managed by its own officials and with income expended for socially useful purposes. Foundations can be traced back to ancient Greece. The late 19th century first saw the establishment of large foundations with broad purposes and great freedom of action have been established, usually originating in the fortunes of wealthy industrialists. Today foundations are classified as community (having support from many donors and located in a specific community), corporation-sponsored, and independent. Notable examples include the SMITHSONIAN INSTITUTION (1846), the Carnegie Corp. of New York (1911), the ROCKEFELLER FOUNDATION (1913), and the FORD FOUNDATION (1936), the largest in the world.

foundationalism In EPISTEMOLOGY, the view that some beliefs can justifiably be held directly (e.g., on the basis of sense perception or rational intuition) and not by inference from other justified beliefs. Other types of beliefs (e.g., beliefs about material objects or about theoretical entities of science) are not regarded as basic or foundational in this way but are held to require inferential support. Foundationalists have typically recognized self-evident truths and reports of SENSE-DATA as basic, in the sense that they do not need support from other beliefs. Such beliefs thus provide the foundations on which the edifice of knowledge can properly be built. See also COHERENTISM.

founder principle In genetics, the principle whereby a daughter or migrant population may differ in genetic composition from its parent population because the founders of the daughter population were not a representative sample of the parent population. For example, if only blue-eyed inhabitants of a town whose residents included brown-eyed people decided to found a new town, their descendants would all be blue-eyed. The principle may explain why American Indians—unlike the Mongoloid geographical race, from which they presumably originated—have no blood type B (see BLOOD TYPING). See also GENETIC DRIFT.

founding Process of pouring molten metal into a MOLD. When the metal solidifies, the result is a CASTING, a metal object conforming to that shape. Multitudinous metal objects are molded at some point during their manufacture. Modern foundries capable of large-scale production are characterized by a high degree of mechanization, automation, and robotics; microprocessors accurately control the automated systems. Advances in chemical binders have resulted in stronger molds and cores and in more accurate castings. Accuracy and purity are increased in vacuum conditions, and further advances are expected from zero-gravity casting in space.

fountain Artificially produced jet of water, and the structure from which it rises. Fountains have been an important feature of landscape design from ancient times. Displaced for a time by the medieval well, the fountain reemerged in the late Middle Ages. It reached its peak in the Renaissance and baroque era, with designs in which sculpture became prominent (e.g., Rome's Trevi Fountain). Supplying water through conduits to multiple fountains, as at the Palace of VERSAILLES, was an important feat. In Muslim countries, fountains for drinking and for ablutions are of great importance. A common type is the simple spout and basin enclosed in a graceful niche; more ambitious designs take the form of a richly decorated pavilion.

Fouquet \fü-'ke\, **Jean** (c. 1420–1481) French painter. Little is known about his early life or training, but a trip to Rome in the 1440s exposed him to Italian Renaissance art, which influenced his own native northern European style. His most famous works were produced for Charles VII's secretary, Étienne Chevalier: a large *Book of Hours* with some 60 full-page miniatures, and a diptych from Notre-Dame at Melun (c. 1450), with Chevalier's portrait on one panel and a Madonna and Child on the other. The altarpiece of the Pietà in the church at Nouans is his only monumental painting. In 1475 he became royal painter to LOUIS XI. He broadened the range of miniature painting to include vast panoramas of architecture and landscape and made brilliant use of aerial perspective and color tonality. He was the preeminent French painter of the 15th century.

Fouquet \fü-'ke\, **Nicolas** (1615–1680) French finance minister (1653–61) in the early years of the reign of LOUIS XIV. He was a wealthy supporter of the powerful Cardinal MAZARIN and of the royal government during the turmoil of the FRONDE (1648–53), when he lent large sums to the treasury. In 1653 he was appointed superintendent of finance. After Mazarin's death (1661), J.-B. COLBERT sought to succeed Fouquet by destroying his reputation with the king. Fouquet was arrested for embezzlement, while Colbert suppressed papers that would have absolved him. Though public opinion was in his favor, he was sentenced in 1664 to imprisonment in the fortress of Pignerol, where he died.

Four Books *Chinese* **Sishu** Ancient Confucian texts used as the basis of study for civil-service examinations (see CHINESE EXAMINATION SYSTEM) in China 1313–1905. They served as an introduction to CONFUCIANISM and were traditionally studied before the more difficult FIVE CLASSICS. The publication of the four texts as a unit in 1190 with commentaries by ZHU XI helped revitalize Confucianism in China. The texts are *DA XUE*; *ZHONG YONG;* the *Analects,* which reputedly contains direct quotations from CONFUCIUS and is deemed the most reliable source of his teachings; and *MENCIUS*.

four-color map problem In TOPOLOGY, a long-standing conjecture asserting that no more than four colors are required to shade in any map such that each adjacent region is colored differently. First posed in 1852 by Francis Guthrie, a British math student, it was solved by Kenneth Appel and Wolfgang Haken using a computer-assisted proof in 1976.

Four Freedoms Essential social and political objectives described by Pres. FRANKLIN ROOSEVELT in his State of the Union message in January 1941: freedom of speech, freedom of religion, freedom from want, and freedom from fear of physical aggression. He called for the last freedom to be achieved through a "worldwide reduction in armaments." In August 1941 he and WINSTON CHURCHILL included the four freedoms in the ATLANTIC CHARTER.

Four Horseman Name given by the sportswriter Grantland Rice to the backfield of the University of NOTRE DAME's undefeated football team of 1924: quarterback Harry Stuhldreher, halfbacks Don Miller and Jim Crowley, and fullback Elmer Layden. They and their teammates, coached by KNUTE ROCKNE, lost only two of 30 games in the years 1922–24.

Four Hundred, Council of the (411 BC) Oligarchical council that briefly took power in ATHENS during the PELOPONNESIAN WAR in a coup inspired by ANTIPHON and ALCIBIADES. An extremely antidemocratic council, it was soon replaced, at the insistence of the Athenian fleet, by a more moderate oligarchy, the Five Thousand. The new council lasted only 10 months, but full democracy was restored in 410 and a commission set up to prevent a recurrence. See also THERAMENES.

Four Noble Truths Statement of the basic doctrines of BUDDHISM. They were formulated by the BUDDHA GAUTAMA in his first sermon. The truths are (1) existence is suffering; (2) desire, or thirst, is its cause; (3) the cessation of suffering is possible; and (4) the way to accomplish this is to follow the EIGHTFOLD PATH. Though differently interpreted, these four truths are recognized by virtually all Buddhist schools.

four-o'clock Ornamental perennial plant (*Mirabilis jalapa;* family Nyctaginaceae), also called marvel-of-Peru or beauty-of-the-night, native to the tropical New World. It is a quick-growing species up to 3 ft (1 m) tall, with oval leaves on short leafstalks. The stems are swollen at the joints. The plant is called four-o'clock because its flowers, which vary from white and yellow to shades of pink and red, sometimes streaked and mottled, open in late afternoon (and close by morning).

Fourdrinier machine \ˌfȯr-drə-ˈnir\ Machine for producing PAPER, paperboard, and other fiberboards, consisting of a moving endless belt of wire or plastic screen that receives a mixture of pulp and water and allows excess water to drain off, forming a continuous sheet for further drying by suction, pressure, and heat. CALENDERING smooths the paper or board and imparts gloss or other desired finish to the surface. The first machine to produce a continuous web (roll), the Fourdrinier machine was patented in France in 1799 by Louis Robert and later improved in England by Henry (1766–1854) and Sealy (died 1847) Fourdrinier. With further improvements over the years, it is still in use today.

Fourier \für-ˈyā, *Engl* ˈfu̇r-ē-ˌā\, **(François-Marie-) Charles** (1772–1837) French social theorist. He advocated a reconstruction of society based on communal associations of producers known as phalanges (phalanxes). His system became known as Fourierism. He felt that phalanges would distribute wealth more equitably than under capitalism and that they would contribute both to a cooperative lifestyle and to individual self-fulfillment. After inheriting his mother's estate in 1812, he devoted himself to writing and refining his theories. Cooperative settlements based on Fourierism were started in France and the U.S., including BROOK FARM.

Charles Fourier, engraving by Samuel Sartain after a painting by Jean-François Gigoux.
CULVER PICTURES

Joseph Fourier, lithograph by Jules Boilly, 1823; in the Académie des Sciences, Paris.
GIRAUDON—ART RESOURCE/EB INC.

Fourier \ˈfu̇r-ē-ˌā\, **(Jean-Baptiste-) Joseph** *later* **Baron Fourier** (1768–1830) French mathematician and Egyptologist. While an engineer on Napoleon's Egyptian expedition, he conducted (1798–1801) anthropological investigations and wrote the preface to the monumental *Description de l'Égypte,* whose publication he oversaw (1809–28). In 1808 he was created a baron by Napoleon. In mathematics, he is primarily known for his work in heat conduction (1807–22), for his use of the FOURIER SERIES to solve DIFFERENTIAL EQUATIONS, and for the related concept of the FOURIER TRANSFORM. As a scientist and a humanist, he epitomized the spirit of French intellectualism of the revolutionary era.

Fourier series In mathematics, an INFINITE SERIES used to solve special types of DIFFERENTIAL EQUATIONS. It consists of an infinite sum of sines and cosines, and because it is periodic (i.e., its values repeat over fixed intervals), it is a useful tool in analyzing periodic FUNCTIONS. Though investigated by LEONHARD EULER, among others, the idea was named for JOSEPH FOURIER, who fully explored its consequences, including important applications in engineering, particularly in heat conduction.

Fourier transform In mathematical ANALYSIS, an INTEGRAL TRANSFORM useful in solving certain types of PARTIAL DIFFERENTIAL EQUATIONS. A function's Fourier transform is derived by integrating the product of the function and a kernel function (an exponential function raised to a negative complex power) over the interval from $-\infty$ to $+\infty$. The Fourier transform of a function g is given by

$$\frac{1}{\sqrt{2\pi}}\int_{-\infty}^{+\infty} g(t)e^{itx}dt.$$

Such transforms, discovered by JOSEPH FOURIER, are particularly useful in studying problems concerning electrical potential.

Fourneyron \für-ne-ˈrōⁿ\, **Benoît** (1802–1867) French inventor of the water TURBINE. He first built a small, six-horsepower unit in which water was directed outward from a central source onto blades or vanes set at angles in a rotor, and eventually produced a turbine capable of 2,300 revolutions per minute, 80% EFFICIENCY, and 60 horsepower, with a wheel 1 ft (30 cm) in diameter weighing 40 lbs (18 kg). Besides its more obvious advantages over the WATERWHEEL, Fourneyron's turbine could be installed horizontally with a vertical shaft. Immediately successful, it powered industry in continental Europe and the U.S., notably the New England textile industry. In 1895 Fourneyron turbines were installed on the U.S. side of Niagara Falls to generate electric power.

Fourteen Points Outline of proposals by Pres. WOODROW WILSON for a post–World War I peace settlement, given in an address in January 1918. The emphasis on "open covenants of peace, openly arrived at" was proposed to change the usual method of secret diplomacy practiced in Europe. Other points outlined territorial adjustments following the war. The last point called for "a general association of nations," which presaged the LEAGUE OF NATIONS.

fourth-generation language (4GL) Fourth-generation computer PROGRAMMING LANGUAGE. 4GLs are closer to human language than other high-level languages and are accessible to people without formal training as programmers. They allow multiple common operations to be performed with a single programmer-entered command. They are intended to be easier for users than machine languages (first-generation), ASSEMBLY LANGUAGES (second-generation), and older high-level languages (third-generation).

Fourth of July See INDEPENDENCE DAY

Fourth Republic Government of the French Republic from 1947 to 1958. The postwar provisional president CHARLES DE GAULLE resigned in 1946, expecting that public support would bring him back to power with a mandate to impose his constitutional ideas. Instead, the constituent assembly chose the Socialist Félix Gouin to replace him. The assembly submitted two draft constitutions to a popular vote in 1946, and the revision was narrowly approved. The structure of the Fourth Republic was remarkably like that of the THIRD REPUBLIC. The lower house of parliament, renamed the National Assembly, was the locus of power. Shaky coalition cabinets succeeded one another, and the lack of a clear-cut majority hampered coherent action. Political leaders included GEORGES BIDAULT, LEON BLUM, FELIX FAURE, PIERRE MENDES-FRANCE, RENE PLEVEN, and ROBERT SCHUMAN.

Fowler, H(enry) W(atson) (1858–1933) English lexicographer and philologist. With his brother, Francis George Fowler, he wrote *The King's English* (1906) and *The Concise Oxford Dictionary of Current English* (1911). Francis George died in 1918. H. W. Fowler's major work, planned with his brother, was *A Dictionary of Modern English*

Usage (1926), an alphabetical listing of points of grammar, syntax, style, pronunciation, and punctuation, whose depth, style, and humor have made it a classic.

Fowler, William A(lfred) (1911–1995) U.S. nuclear astrophysicist. Born in Pittsburgh, he received his PhD from Caltech and became a professor there in 1939. His theory of element generation suggests that, as stars evolve, chemical elements are synthesized progressively (light to heavy) by means of nuclear fusion that also produces light and heat, and that the heaviest elements are synthesized in supernovas. For his theory he shared a 1983 Nobel Prize with SUBRAHMANYAN CHANDRASEKHAR. He is also known for his work in radio astronomy with FRED HOYLE.

Fowles, John (Robert) (born 1926) British novelist. His richly allusive and descriptive works combine psychological probings—chiefly of sex and love—with an interest in the social and philosophical context of human behavior. His first novel, *The Collector* (1963; film, 1965), about a shy man who kidnaps a girl in a hapless search for love, was followed by *The Magus* (1966; film, 1968) and *The French Lieutenant's Woman* (1969; film, 1981), his most famous work, set in Victorian England. Later works include *The Ebony Tower* (1974) and *Daniel Martin* (1977).

Fox ALGONQUIAN-speaking Native American people who traditionally lived in what is now northeastern Wisconsin. Their permanent villages—near fields in which women cultivated corn, beans, and squash—were occupied in summer; in winter they hunted bison on the prairies. A chief and council administered tribal affairs. Families were grouped into CLANS. Religious life centered on the Grand Medicine Society, whose members enlisted supernatural aid to heal the sick and ensure success in warfare. In the 18th century the Fox joined with the SAUK (Sac) to war against the French and English. Though unconquered, they retreated south to Illinois and later west to Iowa. In 1832 BLACK HAWK led a group of Fox and Sauk in an unsuccessful attempt to return to their Illinois lands. Today most Fox (numbering about 1,500) live on tribally owned land in Iowa.

fox Any of various CANINES resembling small to medium-sized, bushy-tailed dogs. Foxes have long fur, pointed ears, relatively short legs, and a narrow snout. They have often been hunted for sport or fur. In a more restricted sense, the name refers to about 10 species of true foxes (genus *Vulpes*), especially both the Old and New World RED FOXES. See also ARCTIC FOX, BAT-EARED FOX, FENNEC, GRAY FOX.

Fox, Charles James (1749–1806) British politician. He entered Parliament in 1768 and became leader of the Whigs in the House of Commons, where he used his brilliant oratorical skills to strongly oppose Britain's policy toward the American colonies. Almost always in the political opposition; he conducted a vendetta against GEORGE III and was later an enemy of WILLIAM PITT. He served as Britain's first foreign secretary (1782, 1783, 1806). He achieved two important reforms by steering through Parliament a resolution pledging it to end the slave trade, and enacting the 1792 Libel Act, which restored to juries their right to decide what constituted libel and whether or not a defendant was guilty of it. He is remembered as a great champion of liberty.

Fox, George (1624–1691) English preacher and founder of the Society of FRIENDS, or Quakers. The son of a weaver, he left home at 18 in search of religious experience. Probably beginning as a Puritan, he reacted even more strongly than the Puritans against the tradition of the Church of ENGLAND, and came to regard personal experience as the true source of authority, placing God-given "inward light," or inspiration, above creeds and Scripture. He traveled the countryside on foot, preaching to small groups, and he and other preachers established congregations. The Society of Friends arose in the 1650s. The Quakers' denunciation of ministers and public officials and their refusal to pay tithes or take oaths led to persecution, and Fox was imprisoned eight times between 1649 and 1673. He made missionary trips to Ireland, the Caribbean islands, North America, and northern Europe. His *Journal* gives an account of his life and of the rise of Quakerism.

Fox, Michael J. *orig.* **Michael Andrew** (born 1961) Canadian film and television actor. Born in Edmonton, Alberta, he grew up on Canadian military bases and moved to Los Angeles at 18. He won three Emmy awards for his role on the popular television series *Family Ties* (1983–89), where he worked with Tracy Pollan, his future wife, and later starred in the series *Spin City* (from 1996). He appeared in the hit film comedy *Back to the Future* (1985) and its sequels (1989, 1990) as well as in such films as *Casualties of War* (1989) and *Mars Attacks!* (1996).

Fox, Vicente Quesada (born 1942) President of Mexico (2000–) whose election ended 71 years of uninterrupted rule by the INSTITUTIONAL REVOLUTIONARY PARTY (PRI). After earning a degree in business administration from the Ibero-American University in Mexico City, Fox took classes at Harvard Business School. He later worked for the Coca-Cola Company, serving as its chief executive in Mexico (1975–79). In 1987 he joined the National Action Party (PAN) and the following year was elected to the national Chamber of Deputies. Elected governor of Guanajuato in 1995, he left the post in 1998 to focus on his national campaign. As president he sought to improve relations with the United States and calm civil unrest in such areas as Chiapas and Tabasco.

Fox Broadcasting Co. U.S. television broadcasting company. Founded in 1986 by RUPERT MURDOCH, it began with 79 affiliated stations that reached 80% of U.S. homes. The network gradually expanded its broadcast hours to seven nights a week and gained more affiliates to make it available across the U.S. Concentrating on shows that appealed to affluent young viewers, it added programming divisions for children, sports, and news in the 1990s.

fox hunting Chase of a fox by horsemen with a pack of hounds. In England, home of the sport, it dates from at least the 15th century, when it probably developed out of stag and hare hunting. Modern fox hunting became popular among the upper classes in the 19th century. A hunt is led by a master; the dogs (usually 15–20 matched pairs) are controlled by the huntsman and two or three assistants. The hunt may take place on any grounds (woodlands, heath, or fields) where a fox is suspected to be. The riders, outfitted in distinctive red uniforms, meet at a host's house, and the hounds are sent off to search out the fox; when it is found, the hunt begins. The fox is chased until it either escapes or is cornered and killed. Fox hunting reached its peak in popularity before World War I; it continued into the late 20th century despite the decreasing number of large estates and popular opposition on grounds of cruelty and elitism.

fox terrier Well-known breed of dog developed in England to drive foxes from their dens. The wirehaired variety was developed from a rough-coated black-and-tan TERRIER; the smooth-haired variety was developed from the BEAGLE, GREYHOUND, BULL TERRIER, and a smooth-coated black-and-tan terrier. Both are sturdy, lively looking dogs with a tapered muzzle and folded, V-shaped ears. They stand about 15 in. (37–39 cm) high and weigh 15–19 lbs (7–8.5 kg). Predominantly white with black or black-and-tan markings, fox terriers are noted for their bold, energetic nature.

Wirehaired fox terrier.
SALLY ANNE THOMPSON

foxglove Any of 20–30 species of herbaceous plants of the genus *Digitalis,* in the SNAPDRAGON FAMILY, especially *D. purpurea,* the common, or purple, foxglove. Native to Europe, the Mediterranean region, and the Canary Islands, foxgloves typically produce ovate to oblong leaves toward the lower part of the stem, which is capped by a tall, one-sided cluster of pendulous, bell-shaped, purple, yellow, or white flowers, often marked with spots within. *D. purpurea* is cultivated as the source of the heart-stimulating drug DIGITALIS.

Foxglove (*Digitalis*).
DEREK FELL

foxhound Either of two breeds of dogs traditionally kept in packs for fox hunting. The English foxhound stands 21–25 in. (53–64 cm) high and weighs 60–70 lbs (27–32 kg). It has a short coat, which is usually a combination of black, tan, and white. The American foxhound resembles the English breed in appearance and size but is more lightly built. It is the oldest breed of sporting dog in the U.S., developed from English foxhounds imported beginning in 1650. Both breeds have been bred for strength, speed, and versatility; they are rarely kept as house pets.

Foxx, Jimmie *orig.* **James Emory** (1907–1967) U.S. baseball player. Born in Sudlersville, Md., he batted right-handed and played mostly at first base, principally with the Philadelphia Athletics (1925–35) and the Boston Red Sox (1936–42). In two of his 20 seasons he hit over 50 home runs. His career home runs totaled 534 when he retired in 1945, making him the second man in major-league history (after BABE RUTH) to hit 500 home runs.

Foxx, 1940.
UPI—EB INC.

Foyt, A(nthony) J(oseph), Jr. (born 1935) U.S. automobile racing driver. Born in Houston, he began racing at age 17. He became the first four-time winner of the Indianapolis 500 (1961, 1964, 1967, 1977), and is the only driver to have won the Indy 500, the Daytona 500, and the Le Mans Grand Prix. He was national champion stock-car driver in 1968, 1978, and 1979, and he also amassed numerous wins in sports- and midget-car racing.

Fracastoro \,frä-kä-'stȯ-rō\, **Girolamo** *Latin* **Hieronymus Fracastorius** (1478?–1553) Italian physician, poet, astronomer, and geologist. He is best known for *Syphilis sive morbus Gallicus* (1530; "Syphilis, or the French Disease"), an account in rhyme of the disease he named. His intense study of epidemic diseases led to his *De contagione et contagiosis morbis* (1546; "On Contagion and Contagious Diseases"). The first scientific statement of the true nature of contagion, infection, disease germs, and modes of disease transmission, it stated that each disease is caused by a different type of rapidly multiplying minute body, transmitted by direct contact, by carriers such as soiled clothing, or through the air. Widely praised in his time, Fracastoro's theory, soon obscured by the mystical doctrines of PARACELSUS, fell into general disrepute until LOUIS PASTEUR and ROBERT KOCH proved it 300 years later. As an astronomer, he prefigured the Copernican model of the solar system in his *Homocentrica sive de stellis liber* (1538).

fractal geometry In mathematics, the study of complex shapes with the property of self-similarity. A self-similar object's component parts resemble the whole, so that each part, and each of *its* parts, when magnified, looks roughly like the whole object. This phenomenon can be seen in objects like snowflakes and tree bark. The term fractal was coined by BENOIT B. MANDELBROT in 1975. This new system of geometry has had a significant impact on such diverse fields as physical chemistry, physiology, and fluid mechanics; fractals can describe irregularly shaped objects or spatially nonuniform phenomena that cannot be described by EUCLIDEAN GEOMETRY. Fractal simulations have been used to plot the distributions of galactic clusters and to generate lifelike images of complicated, irregular natural objects, including rugged terrains and branching patterns. See also CHAOS THEORY.

fraction In arithmetic, a number expressed as a quotient, in which a numerator is divided by a denominator. In a simple fraction, both are integers. A complex fraction has a fraction in the numerator or denominator. In a proper fraction, the numerator is less than the denominator. If the numerator is greater, it is called an improper fraction and can also be written as a mixed number—a whole-number quotient with a proper-fraction remainder. Any fraction can be written in decimal form by carrying out the division of the numerator by the denominator. The result may end at some point, or one or more digits may repeat without end.

fractional reserve system Banking system followed by all modern banks, in which less than 100% of bank deposits are held in the bank. The vast majority of the deposits are invested in loans and securities to earn income for the bank, and interest paid on deposits comes from this income. The minimum percentage the bank must hold (its reserve) is set by custom or, as in the U.S., by law. The need for a reserve is based on the fact that, on a given day, the amount of money a bank takes in may be less than what it must pay out. Reserve requirements are established both by the FEDERAL RESERVE SYSTEM and by state banking authorities. When the banking system as a whole is in need of reserves, the Federal Reserve is likely to increase them through OPEN-MARKET OPERATIONS. When an individual bank needs more reserves, it can call in loans, sell financial assets, or borrow them either from the Federal Reserve at the DISCOUNT RATE or from other banks at what is known as the Federal funds rate.

fracture In mineralogy, the appearance of a surface broken in directions other than along CLEAVAGE planes. There are several kinds of fractures: conchoidal (curved concavities resembling shells, as in glass); even (rough, approximately plane surfaces); uneven (rough and completely irregular surfaces, the commonest type); hackly (sharp edges and jagged points and depressions); and splintery (partially separated splinters or fibers).

fracture In engineering, rupture of a material too weak to sustain the forces on it. A fracture of the workpiece during forming can result from flaws in the metal; these often consist of nonmetallic inclusions such as oxides or sulfides trapped in the metal during refining. Laps are another type of flaw, in which part of a metal piece is inadvertently folded over on itself but the two sides of the fold are not completely welded together. Structural and machine parts subject to vibrations and other cyclic loading must be designed to avoid FATIGUE fracture. See also DUCTILITY, METALLURGY, STRENGTH OF MATERIALS, TESTING MACHINE.

fracture Break in a BONE, caused by stress. It causes pain, tenderness, and inability to use the part with the fracture. The site appears deformed, swollen, and discolored, and the bone moves in abnormal ways. It must be protected from weight bearing and movement between the broken ends while it heals, producing puttylike new tissue that hardens to join the broken pieces together. Complications include failure to heal, healing in the wrong position, and loss of function despite good healing. Fractures in joints present a particularly serious problem, often requiring surgery. See also OSTEOPOROSIS.

fracture zone, submarine See SUBMARINE FRACTURE ZONE

Fraenkel-Conrat \,freŋ-kəl-'kȯn-rät\, **Heinz L(udwig)** (1910– 1999) German-U.S. biochemist. He received his PhD from the University of Edinburgh and moved to the U.S. in 1936, eventually joining the faculty at UC–Berkeley. Studying the tobacco mosaic virus, he broke it down into its noninfectious protein and nearly noninfectious nucleic-acid components, and, by recombining them, successfully reconstituted the fully infective virus, which led to the discovery that the nucleic-acid portion is responsible for its infectivity and, in the absence of the viral protein, is broken down by RNA-splitting enzymes (nucleases).

Fragonard \frà-gȯ-'när\, **Jean-Honoré** (1732–1806) French painter. He studied with FRANCOIS BOUCHER in Paris c. 1749. He subsequently won a Prix de Rome, and while in Italy (1756–61) he traveled extensively and executed many sketches of the countryside, especially the gardens at the Villa d'Este at Tivoli, and developed a great admiration for the work of GIOVANNI BATTISTA TIEPOLO. In 1765 his large historical painting *Coresus Sacrifices Himself to Save Callirhoë* was purchased for LOUIS XV and won him election to the French Royal Academy. He soon abandoned this style to concentrate on landscapes in the manner of JACOB VAN RUISDAEL, portraits, and the decorative, erotic outdoor party scenes for which he became famous (e.g., *The Swing,* c. 1766). After 1767 he gave up exhibiting in the official Salon and worked primarily for private patrons. He tried to adapt to the fashionable Neoclassical style, but his close associations with royalty made his work unacceptable during the French Revolution, and he lost patrons and his livelihood. His works, with those of Boucher, epitomize the Rococo period.

"The Swing," detail, oil on canvas by Jean-Honoré Fragonard, c. 1766; in the Wallace Collection, London.
BY COURTESY OF THE TRUSTEES OF THE WALLACE COLLECTION, LONDON

frambesia See YAWS

Frame, Janet *in full* **Janet Paterson Frame Clutha** (born 1924) New Zealand novelist, short-story writer, and poet. After an impoverished childhood, she trained as a teacher. Her first book was the story collection *The Lagoon* (1951). Several times committed to mental institutions, she narrowly escaped undergoing a frontal lobotomy. Her novel *Owls Do Cry* (1957) incorporated poetry and prose in its investigation of the border between sanity and madness. Her many other novels, several of which draw on Maori legends, include *Scented Gardens for the Blind* (1963) and *The Carpathians* (1988). One of her three volumes of memoirs, *An Angel at My Table* (1984), was filmed by JANE CAMPION.

frame of reference See REFERENCE FRAME

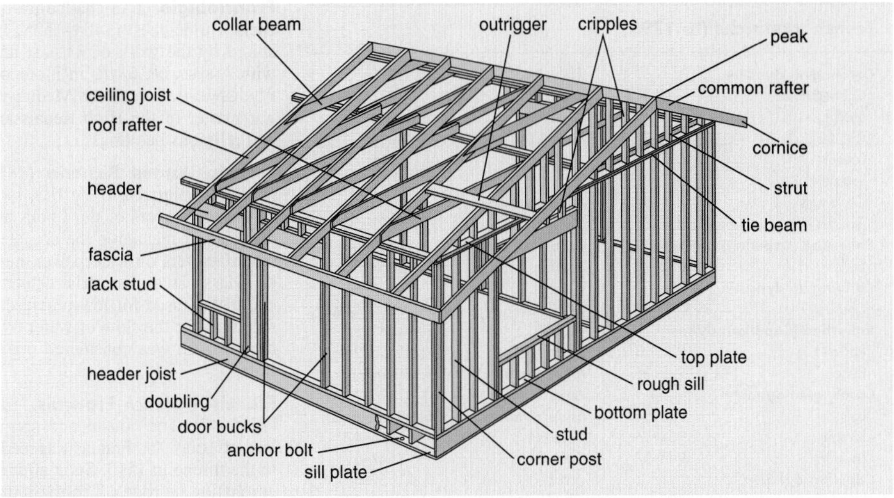

Frame of a simple wooden frame house. The frame's most important elements are the studs (uprights to which sheathing, paneling, or laths are fastened), joists (small horizontal timbers that support a floor or ceiling), and rafters (parallel beams that support a roof). The frame is usually built from 2″ × 4″ pieces of lumber ("two-by-fours"); heavier lumber is used for joists and other supporting timbers. Framed structures traditionally were constructed individually at each house site; today framing is usually mass-produced in sections and assembled on site. The lightweight wood-frame structure remains popular today in residential construction.

framed structure *or* **frame structure** Structure supported mainly by a skeleton, or frame, of wood, steel, or reinforced concrete rather than by load-bearing walls. Rigid frames have fixed joints that enable the frames to resist lateral forces; other frames require diagonal bracing or SHEAR WALLS and diaphragms for lateral stability. Heavy TIMBER FRAMING was the most common type of construction in eastern Asia and northern Europe from prehistoric times to the mid-19th century. It was supplanted by the balloon frame and the platform frame (see LIGHT-FRAME CONSTRUCTION). Steel's strength, when used in steel framing, made possible buildings with longer spans. Concrete frames impart greater rigidity and continuity; various advancements, such as the introduction of the shear wall and slipforming (see FORMWORK) have made concrete a serious competitor with steel in high-rise structures.

framing, timber See TIMBER FRAMING

France *officially* **French Republic** *French* **République Française** \rā-pü̅-'blēk-frä^{n}-'sez\ Republic, western Europe. It includes the principality of MONACO and the island of CORSICA. Area: 210,026 sq mi (543,965 sq km). Population (2001 est.): 59,090,000. Capital: PARIS. The people are mainly French. Language: French (official). Religions: Roman Catholicism (three-fourths), Protestantism, Islam. Monetary unit: euro. It has extensive plains, rivers, and a number of mountain ranges, including the PYRENEES and the ALPS. France's climate is generally moderate. About three-fifths of the land is suitable for agriculture, and forests, largely unexploited, cover about one-fourth of the area. France has a developed, mixed economy with a preponderance of small firms. Its chief of state is the president, and the head of government is the prime minister; the legislature consists of two houses. It is one of the major economic powers of the world and was a founding member of the European Community (see EUROPEAN UNION). Culturally, France has enjoyed a significant role in the world from the early Middle Ages. Archaeological excavations in France indicate continuous settlement from Paleolithic times. In c. 1200 BC the Gauls migrated into the area and in 600 BC Ionian Greeks established several settlements, including one at MARSEILLE. JULIUS CAESAR completed the Roman conquest of Gaul in 50 BC. During the 6th century AD, the Salian FRANKS ruled; by the 8th century power had passed to the CAROLINGIANS, the greatest of whom was CHARLEMAGNE. The HUNDRED YEARS' WAR (1337–1453) resulted in the return to France of land that had been held by the British; by the end of the 15th century, France approximated its modern boundaries. The 16th century was marked by the WARS OF RELIGION between Protestants (HUGUENOTS) and Roman Catholics. HENRY IV's EDICT OF NANTES (1598) granted substantial religious toleration, but this was revoked in 1685 by LOUIS XIV, who helped to raise monarchical absolutism to new heights. In 1789 the FRENCH REVOLUTION proclaimed the rights of the individual and destroyed the ancien régime. NAPOLEON ruled from 1799 to 1814, after which a limited monarchy was restored until 1871, when the THIRD REPUBLIC was created. World War I (1914–18) ravaged the northern part of France. After Nazi Germany's invasion during World War II, the collaborationist

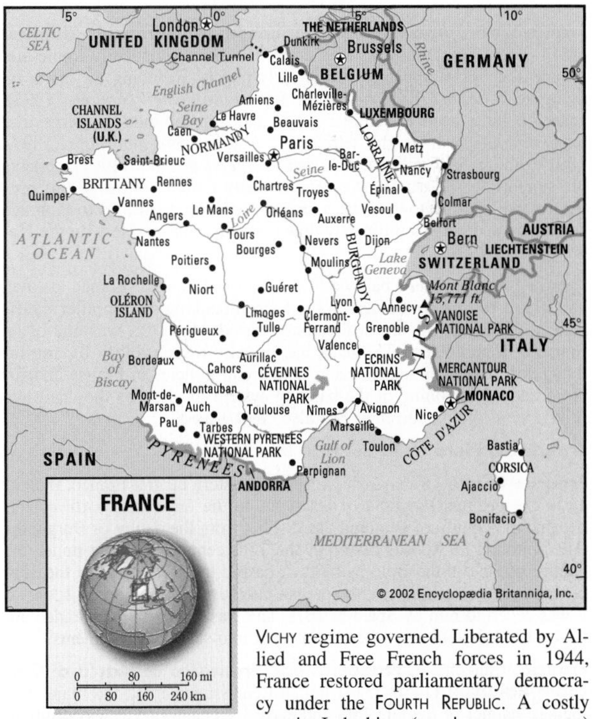

VICHY regime governed. Liberated by Allied and Free French forces in 1944, France restored parliamentary democracy under the FOURTH REPUBLIC. A costly war in Indochina (see INDOCHINA WARS) and rising nationalism in French colonies during the 1950s overwhelmed the Fourth Republic. The FIFTH REPUBLIC was established in 1958 under CHARLES DE GAULLE, who presided over the dissolution of most of France's overseas colonies (see ALGERIAN WAR, FRENCH EQUATORIAL AFRICA,

French monarchs (to 1795)

Carolingian dynasty		Philip III	1270–85
Charlemagne	768–814	Philip IV	1285–1314
Louis I	814–40	Louis X	1314–16
Charles II	843–77	John I	1316
Louis II	877–79	Philip V	1316–22
Louis III	879–82	Charles IV	1322–28
Carloman	879–84	**Valois dynasty**	
Charles (III)	884–87	Philip VI	1328–50
Robertian (Capetian) dynasty		John II	1350–64
Eudes	888–98	Charles V	1364–80
Carolingian dynasty		Charles VII	1422–61
Charles III	893/98–922	Charles VI	1380–1422
Robertian (Capetian) dynasty		Louis XI	1461–83
Robert I	922–23	Charles VIII	1483–98
Rudolf	923–36	**Valois dynasty (Orléans branch)**	
Carolingian dynasty		Louis XII	1498–1515
Louis IV	936–54	**Valois dynasty (Angoulême branch)**	
Lothair	954–86	Francis I	1515–47
Louis V	986–87	Henry II	1547–59
Capetian dynasty		Francis II	1559–60
Hugh Capet	987–96	Charles IX	1560–74
Robert II	996–1031	Henry III	1574–89
Henry I	1031–60	**House of Bourbon**	
Philip I	1059/60–1108	Henry IV	1589–1610
Louis VI	1108–37	Louis XIII	1610–43
Louis VII	1137–80	Louis XIV	1643–1715
Philip II	1179–1223	Louis XV	1715–74
Louis VIII	1223–26	Louis XVI	1774–92
Louis IX (St. Louis)	1226–70	Louis (XVII)	1793–95

FRENCH WEST AFRICA). In 1981 France elected its first Socialist president, FRANCOIS MITTERRAND. During the 1990s, the French government, balancing right- and left-wing forces, moved toward solidifying European unity.

France \'frä^{n}s\, **Anatole** *orig.* **Jacques-Anatole-François Thibault** (1844–1924) French novelist and critic. His characteristically ironic and urbane skepticism appeared in his early novels, including *Le crime de Sylvestre Bonnard* (1881) and *At the Sign of the Reine Pédauque* (1893). Later he introduced both bitter satire and humanitarian concerns into many works, such as the tetralogy *L'histoire contemporaine* (1897–1901), whose final volume, *Monsieur Bergeret in Paris* (1901), reflects his support for ALFRED DREYFUS. The comedy *Crainquebille* (1903) proclaims the hostility toward the bourgeois order that led him to embrace socialism, and he was ultimately drawn to communism. He won the Nobel Prize in 1921.

France, Banque de \'bä^{n}k-də-'frä^{n}s\ National bank of France, created in 1800 to restore confidence in the French banking system after the financial upheavals of the revolutionary period. NAPOLEON was one of its founding shareholders. The bank has primary responsibility for formulating and implementing monetary and credit policies in France and for the orderly functioning of the banking system. It also has the exclusive privilege of issuing currency. See also CENTRAL BANK.

Francesca, Piero della See PIERO DELLA FRANCESCA

Franche-Comté \,frä^{n}sh-kō^n-'tā\ Region, eastern central France. Included in the original kingdom of BURGUNDY in the 5th century AD, it later became the county of Burgundy as distinct from the duchy of Burgundy. Part of the HOLY ROMAN EMPIRE in the 11th century, it came under the control of PHILIP II the Bold in 1384. It passed to MAXIMILIAN I in the 15th century, and from him, to the Spanish HABSBURGS. Occupied by LOUIS IX, it was ceded to him by Spain in 1678, and was a province of France until the 1789 Revolution, when it was split into several departments.

Francia \frän-'chē-ä\, **Francesco** *orig.* **Francesco di Marco di Giacomo Raibolini** (1450–1517) Italian Renaissance artist, the major Bolognese painter of the late 15th and early 16th century. He was originally a goldsmith. His early works were influenced by the Ferrarese painter Lorenzo Costa (c. 1460–1535), though the strongest influences on his style were the works of PERUGINO and RAPHAEL. His workshop produced numerous sweet, excessively refined Madonnas; he also specialized in portraiture.

Franciabigio \,frän-chä-'bē-jō\ *or* **Francesco di Cristofano de Giudicis** \'jü-dē-chēs\ (1484–1525) Italian Renaissance painter. He was inspired by the work of RAPHAEL and for some years maintained a studio with ANDREA DEL SARTO in Florence. He and Andrea's student JACOPO DA PONTORMO decorated the Medici villa at Poggio a Caiano. He was a minor master of the High Renaissance style, best known for his portraits and religious paintings.

Francis, James Bicheno (1815–1892) British-U.S. hydraulic engineer. He emigrated to the U.S. in 1833, and at 22 became chief engineer of the Proprietors of the Locks and Canals on the Merrimack River. In 40 years of managing the company's waterpower interests and advising manufacturers on waterpower, he contributed greatly to the rise of LOWELL, Mass., as an industrial center. He invented the mixed-flow, or Francis, TURBINE used for low-pressure installations. He is also known for his formulas for the flow of water over weirs and many other studies in HYDRAULICS. He was considered one of the foremost civil engineers of his time.

Francis I *French* **François** \frä^n-'swä\ (1494–1547) King of France (1515–47). The cousin and son-in-law of LOUIS XII, Francis succeeded to the throne in 1515. Soon after his coronation he rode off to the ITALIAN WARS (1515–16) and recovered the Duchy of Milan. He was a Renaissance patron of the arts, a humanist, and a popular king who traveled throughout France, curtailing abuses by nobles and providing games and processions for the people. All this ended with the election in 1519 of CHARLES V as emperor. Charles was already king of Spain, and his lands now encircled France. Francis vainly sought an alliance with HENRY VIII on the FIELD OF CLOTH OF GOLD, then waged a series of wars with Charles from 1521. Francis was taken captive in 1525 and languished in prison, refusing to accede to Charles's exorbitant demands, until in 1526 the French ambassadors concluded a treaty. The war with Charles resumed in 1536, and one of Francis's last diplomatic achievements was an alliance with the Turks against the emperor.

Francis I, portrait by Pierre Dumonstier, after a drawing by Jean Clouet; in the Bibliothèque Nationale, Paris.

BY COURTESY OF THE BIBLIOTHEQUE NATIONALE, PARIS

Francis I *German* **Franz** (1708–1765) Holy Roman emperor (1745–65). The son of the duke of Lorraine, he succeeded to the duchy in 1729 (as Francis Stephen). In 1736 he married MARIA THERESA, heiress to Emperor CHARLES VI, who agreed to the marriage on the condition that Francis cede Lorraine to STANISLAW I, in compensation for which Francis was granted Tuscany (1737). He served with Maria Theresa as coregent (1740–45), and was elected emperor during the War of the AUSTRIAN SUCCESSION. He was overshadowed by his wife during his rule, but was remembered for his cultural interests.

Francis II *French* **François** (1544–1560) King of France (1559–60). He was the son of HENRY II and CATHERINE DE MÉDICIS and was married in 1558 to Mary Stuart (later MARY, QUEEN OF SCOTS), a relation of the powerful GUISE family. Sickly and weak-willed, Francis was dominated throughout his brief reign by the Guises, who tried to use him to break the strength of the HUGUENOTS. His premature death temporarily ended the Guises' dominion. He was succeeded by his brother, CHARLES IX.

Francis II *German* **Franz** (1768–1835) Last Holy Roman emperor (1792–1806) and emperor of Austria as Francis I (1804–35); king of Hungary (1792–1835), and king of Bohemia (1792–1835). He succeeded his father, LEOPOLD II, in 1792. An absolutist who hated constitutionalism, he supported the first coalition war against France (1792–97). Twice defeated by France, he elevated Austria to an empire (1804) soon after NAPOLEON made himself emperor of France. Napoleon dictated the dissolution of the Holy Roman Empire, and Francis abdicated in 1806. Though he despised Napoleon, he was forced by reasons of state to marry his daughter MARIE-LOUISE to Napoleon in 1810. Francis helped destroy Napoleon's power in battles in 1813–14. After the Congress of VIENNA (1815), he supported his chief minister, KLEMENS, FURST VON

METTERNICH, in instituting a conservative and restrictive political system in Germany and Europe.

Francis II *Italian* **Francesco** \frän-'chā-skō\ (1836–1894) King of the Two SICILIES (1859–60), the last of the BOURBON kings of Naples. He succeeded his father, FERDINAND II, in 1859 and on his accession rejected proposals made by Count CAVOUR that he join Piedmont-Sardinia in the war against Austria and grant liberal reforms on its conclusion. Alarmed by the invasion of Sicily by GIUSEPPE DE GARIBALDI in 1860, Francis capitulated to the liberals in his kingdom and restored the constitution of 1848, granted freedom of the press, and promised new elections. It was too late to save the monarchy, however; the Bourbon forces were defeated by Garibaldi and less than a month later Francis was deposed by a plebiscite. He then lived in exile in Rome and Paris.

Francis de Sales, St. (1567–1622) Roman Catholic bishop of Geneva and Doctor of the Church. Born in Savoy, he studied in Paris and at Padua and was ordained in 1593. He was consecrated bishop of Geneva in 1602. In 1610, with St. Jane Frances de Chantal, he founded the Visitation of Holy Mary (the Visitation Nuns), a teaching order. His *Introduction to a Devout Life* (1609) argued that spiritual perfection is possible for ordinary individuals busy with worldly affairs. He was an active opponent of CALVINISM. Pius XI named him patron saint of writers.

Francis Ferdinand *German* **Franz Ferdinand** (1863–1914) Archduke of Austria, whose assassination was the immediate cause of WORLD WAR I. Nephew of Emperor FRANCIS JOSEPH, he became heir apparent in 1896. His desire to marry Sophie, Countess von Chotek, a lady-in-waiting, brought him into sharp conflict with the emperor, and the marriage was only allowed after he agreed to renounce his future children's rights to the throne. From 1906 he exerted influence in military matters and became inspector general of the army (1913). While on an official visit in Sarajevo in June 1914, he and his wife were assassinated by the Serb nationalist GAVRILO PRINCIP. In July, Austria declared war against Serbia, precipitating World War I.

Francis Joseph *German* **Franz Josef** (1830–1916) Emperor of Austria (1848–1916) and king of Hungary (1867–1916). He became emperor during the REVOLUTIONS OF 1848 after the abdication of his uncle, FERDINAND I. With his prime minister, FELIX, FURST ZU SCHWARZENBERG, he achieved a powerful position for Austria, in particular with the OLMÜTZ convention in 1850. His harsh, absolutist rule within Austria produced a strong central government but also led to rioting and an assassination attempt. Following Austria's defeat by Prussia in the SEVEN WEEKS' WAR (1866), he responded to Hungarian national unrest by accepting the COMPROMISE OF 1867. He adhered to the THREE EMPERORS' LEAGUE and formed an alliance with Prussian-led Germany that led to the TRIPLE ALLIANCE (1882). In 1898 his wife was assassinated, and in 1889 his son and heir apparent RUDOLF died in a suicide love pact. In 1914 his ultimatum to Serbia following the murder of the next heir presumptive, FRANCIS FERDINAND, led Austria and Germany into WORLD WAR I.

Francis Joseph, 1908.

BY COURTESY OF THE TRUSTEES OF THE BRITISH MUSEUM; PHOTOGRAPH, J.R. FREEMAN & CO. LTD.

Francis of Assisi, St. *orig.* **Francesco di Pietro di Bernardone** (1181/82–1226) Italian saint and founder of the FRANCISCAN religious order. Born into a wealthy family, he was a soldier and prisoner of war before experiencing a conversion in his early twenties. He sold his property, gave the proceeds to the church, and began a life of poverty and devoutness. He soon attracted followers, whom he sent to preach throughout Europe, and in 1209 INNOCENT III gave approval for the Franciscan order. The Rule of St. Francis stressed the need to imitate the life of Jesus. In many ways a mystic, Francis viewed all nature as a mirror of God, calling all creatures his brothers and sisters. In 1212 he allowed formation of an order for women, called the Poor Clares. In 1219 he went to Egypt, preached to the sultan, and visited the holy places of Jerusalem. In 1224, after a vision, he became the first person to receive the STIGMATA. His influence helped restore popular faith in a church much corrupted by wealth and political aspirations.

Saint Francis of Assisi, detail of a fresco by Cimabue, late 13th century; in the lower church of S. Francesco, Assisi, Italy.

ALINARI—ANDERSON FROM ART RESOURCE

Franciscan Member of a Christian religious order founded in 1209 by St. FRANCIS OF ASSISI. The Franciscans actually consist of three orders. The First Order comprises priests and lay brothers who have sworn to a life of prayer, preaching, and penance. The Second Order (founded 1212) consists of cloistered nuns known as the Poor Clares. The Third Order consists of religious members and laypersons who observe Franciscan principles in teaching, charity, and social service. The Rule of St. Francis stipulated that Franciscan friars could own no property of any kind, either individually or communally. The friars wandered and preached among the people, helping the poor and sick. Their impact was immense; within 10 years they numbered 5,000. A milder version of the rule was approved in 1223, and after the death of St. Francis in 1226 the order was divided by conflicts over the vow of poverty. A moderate interpretation of the rule was established while St. BONAVENTURE was minister general of the order (1257–74), and the friars spread throughout Europe, their missionaries penetrating as far as Syria and Africa. Though continuing dissent led to divisions of the order into the 19th century, the Franciscans flourished, and they remain the largest Roman Catholic religious order.

Franck \'fräŋk\, **César (Auguste)** (1822–1890) Belgian-French composer. A piano prodigy, he arrived in Paris at 14 to study at the Paris Conservatoire. In 1858 he became organist at the large church of Ste. Clotilde, where he would remain the rest of his life. In 1872 he also became professor of organ at the Conservatoire. His compositions, which tend to be serious, German-influenced, and often religious, include the famous Symphony in D (1888); the tone poems *Les Éolides* (1876), *Le chasseur maudit* (1882), and *Psyché* (1888); the oratorio *Les béatitudes* (1879); chamber works including a piano quintet (1879), a violin sonata (1886), and a string quartet (1889); and many works for organ and piano.

Franco \'fräŋ-kō, *Engl* 'fraŋ-kō\, **Francisco** *in full* **Francisco Paulino Hermenegildo Teódulo Franco Bahamonde** (1892–1975) Spanish general and head of the government of Spain (1939–75). A career army officer, he was noted as a skillful leader and became army chief of staff in 1935. He joined the insurgents in the SPANISH CIVIL WAR and was named caudillo (head) of the Nationalist forces (1936). In 1937 he reorganized the fascist FALANGE party into a more pluralistic group and made it the regime's official political movement. Though in sympathy with the AXIS POWERS in WORLD WAR II, Spain remained formally neutral, but after the war Franco was ostracized as the "last surviving Fascist dictator." Relations with other nations regularized with the onset of the COLD WAR, as Franco became a leading anticommunist statesman. In the 1950s and '60s, his domestic policies moderated and Spain made great economic progress. He provided for his succession by an official referendum in 1947 that made the Spanish state a monarchy, ratifying his powers as regent for life. In 1969 he designated Prince JUAN CARLOS as his successor.

Franco-Cantabrian school \kan-'tā-brē-ən\ Oldest and most complete of several artistic traditions of the PALEOLITHIC PERIOD that flourished in southwestern France and the Cantabrian Mountains of northern Spain c. 40,000–10,000 BC. It developed in huge limestone caves, such as those at ALTAMIRA and LASCAUX, which served as ceremonial centers for ancient hunters. Inspired by magical-religious beliefs, the art consists of large numbers of cave paintings of single, lively, unrelated animals, which may have been used in rituals invoking success in the hunt and animal fertility. Small carved figurines incised with linear details have also been found.

E F G

Franco–Prussian War *or* **Franco–German War** (1870–71) War in which a coalition of German states led by Prussia defeated France, ending French hegemony in continental Europe and creating a unified Germany. The immediate cause was the candidacy of Prince LEOPOLD OF HOHENZOLLERN-SIGMARINGEN for the Spanish throne, which raised the possibility of a combination of Prussia and Spain against France. Following diplomatic maneuvers to block Leopold's candidacy, the Prussian chancellor OTTO VON BISMARCK published the EMS TELEGRAM to provoke the French government into declaring war, which it did. The other German states sided with Prussia, and German troops under Gen. HELMUTH VON MOLTKE, superior in numbers and organization, scored repeated victories. After NAPOLEON III surrendered at the Battle of SEDAN, French resistance was carried on by a new government, which deposed the emperor and established the THIRD REPUBLIC. Paris surrendered, but while treaty negotiations were going on, an insurrection by radicals in Paris created a short-lived government, the PARIS COMMUNE. After its suppression, a harsh peace treaty was implemented: Germany annexed Alsace and half of Lorraine, and France was occupied until a large indemnity was paid. The German empire was established when WILLIAM I of Prussia was proclaimed German emperor in 1871. The peace was an unstable one, marked by France's determination to recover Alsace-Lorraine and Germany's mounting imperialism, led by Prussian militarism. Their mutual animosity was a driving force that led to WORLD WAR I.

Franco-Russian Alliance *or* **Dual Alliance** (1894) Political and military pact between France and Russia that was one of the basic European alignments of the pre–World War I era. In the event of war, France wanted support against Germany, and Russia against Austria-Hungary. The alliance was formalized through an exchange of letters in order to preserve secrecy, and it was to be in force as long as the opposing TRIPLE ALLIANCE. The alliance was renewed and strengthened in 1899 and 1912.

Franconia *German* **Franken** Former duchy, southern central Germany. A medieval duchy, after AD 843 it was the German part of the former CAROLINGIAN empire. After the Carolingian line died out, its duke became the first elected German king as CONRAD I. It was divided into Rhenish (west) and East Franconia, the latter alone retaining the name of Franconia after the 12th century. The name was abolished in 1806 but revived in 1837 by the kingdom of BAVARIA in its subdivisions. It is part of present-day Bavaria state.

frangipani \ˌfran-jə-ˈpa-nē\ Any of the shrubs or small trees that make up the genus *Plumeria,* in the DOGBANE FAMILY, native to the New World tropics and widely cultivated as ornamentals; also, a perfume derived from or imitating the odor of the flower of one species, *P. rubra.* The white-edged, yellow flowers of the Mexican frangipani *(P. rubra acutifolia)* are a popular component of the Hawaiian lei.

Frank \ˈfräŋk, *Engl* ˈfraŋk\, **Anne(lies Marie)** (1929–1945) German diarist. She was a young Jewish girl who kept a record of the two years her family spent in hiding in Amsterdam to escape Nazi persecution. After their discovery by the Gestapo in 1944, the family was transported to concentration camps; Anne died of typhus at Bergen-Belsen. Friends searching the hiding place found the diary, which her father published as *The Diary of a Young Girl* (1947). Precocious in style and insight, it traces her emotional growth amid adversity and is a classic of war literature.

Frank \ˈfräŋk\, **Jacob** *orig.* **Jacob Leibowicz** (1726–1791) Jewish false MESSIAH. Born in Galicia, he was an uneducated visionary who claimed to be the reincarnation of SHABBETAI TZEVI. He proclaimed himself messiah in 1751 and founded the Frankist, or Zoharist, sect, based on the SEFER HA-ZOHAR, which he sought to put in the place of the TORAH. The sect rejected traditional Judaism, and their practices, including orgiastic rites, led the Jewish community to excommunicate them in 1756. Protected by Roman Catholic authorities, who hoped Frank would help in the conversion of the Jews, Frank and his followers were baptized in Poland. In 1760 he was imprisoned by the Inquisition, who had realized that Frank's followers regarded Frank, not Jesus, as the messiah. Freed in 1773 by invading Russians, he settled in Germany and lived as a baron until his death.

Frank, Robert (born 1924) Swiss-U.S. photographer. In the 1940s he worked as a fashion photographer for *Harper's Bazaar* in Paris. He abandoned fashion work in 1947 to travel in the U.S. and South America and explore the use of the 35-mm camera. His collection *The Americans* (1959), with its gritty, discordant images of 1950s America, had enormous influence and established Frank as a major figure. After 1959 he turned to filmmaking; his short film *Pull My Daisy* (1959), a collaboration with JACK KEROUAC, became an underground classic. A major later collection is *Robert Frank: Moving Out* (1994).

Frankel, Zacharias (1801–1875) Hungarian-German rabbi and theologian. He graduated from the University of Budapest and served as rabbi in several German communities. As chief rabbi in Dresden (1836–54), he developed a theology called positive-historical Judaism, which diverged from Orthodox Judaism in its willingness to accept scientific and historical research as well as changes in the liturgy but adhered to traditional customs more firmly than Reform Judaism. In 1854 he became president of Breslau's Jewish Theological Seminary, and his theology spread through central Europe and to the U.S., where it took root as CONSERVATIVE JUDAISM. His books include *Introduction to the Mishna* (1859) and *Introduction to the Palestinian Talmud* (1870).

Frankenheimer \ˈfraŋ-kən-ˌhī-mər\, **John** (1930–2002) U.S. film director. Born in Malba, N.Y., he worked for CBS television from 1953 and directed numerous plays, special programs, and series, including *Playhouse 90* (1954–59). His first film, *The Young Stranger* (1957), was followed by the well-received *The Young Savages* (1961) and three further successes: *All Fall Down, Birdman of Alcatraz,* and *The Manchurian Candidate* (all 1962). After the thriller *Seven Days in May* (1964), he spent nearly a decade in Europe. His thriller *Ronin* (1998) was made in France. *Reindeer Games* appeared in 2000.

Frankenthaler, Helen (born 1928) U.S. painter. She studied with RUFINO TAMAYO in high school and at Bennington College, then returned to her native New York City and joined the "second generation" of Abstract Expressionists. Influenced by JACKSON POLLOCK and ARSHILE GORKY, she developed a style featuring abstract color combinations within large expanses of bare canvas. She perfected the color stain technique, producing diaphanous color by thinning the oils and letting them soak into the unprimed canvas. In the 1960s she began to use acrylic paints. Though abstract, many of her paintings (e.g., *Ocean Desert,* 1975) evoke landscapes and are noted for their lyricism. Her work influenced the color-field painters MORRIS LOUIS and Kenneth Noland. She was married to ROBERT MOTHERWELL (1958–71).

Frankfort \ˈfraŋk-fərt\ City (pop., 2000: 27,741), capital of Kentucky. Located on the Kentucky River, it was founded in 1786 and has been the capital since statehood (1792). Twice during its early history the capitol was burned, and both times the larger cities of LOUISVILLE and LEXINGTON tried to become the state capital. Frankfort was retained, however, because of its central location. It is a trading center for the BLUEGRASS REGION, producing tobacco, corn, and Thoroughbred horses, and the site of Kentucky State University (1886).

Frankfurt (am Main) City (population 1998 est.: 643,469), western Germany. Located on the MAIN RIVER, it was the site of a Roman military settlement in the 1st century AD. It served as a royal residence of the CAROLINGIANS from the 9th century through the Middle Ages. A free imperial city 1372–1806, it lost its status under NAPOLEON but regained it in 1815. It was the capital of Germany (1816–66). It was annexed by Prussia in 1866. Its Old Town, once the largest surviving medieval city in Germany, was mostly destroyed in World War II; some landmarks survive, including its red sandstone cathedral, dedicated in 1239. International trade fairs have been held in Frankfurt since 1240; the modern-era annual book, automobile, and computer fairs are popular events. Among the city's manufactures, including machinery and printing materials, are the high-quality sausages known as frankfurters. It was the birthplace of JOHANN W. VON GOETHE.

Frankfurt National Assembly *officially* **German National Assembly** (1848–49) German national parliament that tried and failed to create a united German state during the liberal REVOLUTIONS OF 1848. Meeting in FRANKFURT AM MAIN, it proposed a constitution that provided for universal suffrage and a parliamentary government, with a hereditary emperor. The assembly offered the crown to FREDERICK WILLIAM IV of Prussia, but he was too conservative to receive a German imperial crown from any hands but those of the other German princes, and he refused. Lacking support from either Prussia or Austria, the assembly was forced to disband.

Frankfurt school Group of thinkers associated with the Institut für Sozialforschung (Institute for Social Research), founded in Frankfurt in

1923 by Felix J. Weil, Carl Grünberg, Max Horkheimer, and Friedrich Pollock. Closed by the Nazis, it reopened in 1949. Though it was originally conceived as a center for neo-Marxian social research, there is no doctrine common to all those associated with it. Intellectually, the school owes most to the writings of G. W. F. Hegel and the Young Hegelians (see Hegelianism), Immanuel Kant, Karl Marx, Wilhelm Dilthey, Friedrich Nietzsche, and Sigmund Freud. Important Frankfurt-school thinkers include Theodor Adorno, Walter Benjamin, Herbert Marcuse, and Jurgen Habermas. See also critical theory.

Frankfurter, Felix (1882–1965) U.S. (Austrian-born) jurist and public official. He emigrated to the U.S. at the age of 12 and graduated from Harvard Law School, where he later taught (1914–39). He served as secretary of war (1911–13) under Pres. William H. Taft. He advised Woodrow Wilson at the Paris Peace Conference (1919) and counseled Franklin Roosevelt on New Deal legislation (1933–39). He promoted Zionism in the U.S. and helped found the American Civil Liberties Union; his friend Louis Brandeis secretly encouraged his attacks on the Sacco-Vanzetti conviction. On the U.S. Supreme Court (1939–62) he became a leading exponent of judicial restraint, holding that judges should adhere closely to precedent and largely disregard their personal opinions; his opinions evince a hands-off attitude toward legislative action and a concern with the integrity of government, sometimes at the expense of individual liberties.

Frankfurter.
BY COURTESY OF THE LIBRARY OF CONGRESS, WASHINGTON, D.C.

Frankfurter Allgemeine Zeitung \ˈfräŋk-fu̇r-tər-ˈäl-ge-ˌmī-nə-ˈtsī-tu̇ŋ\ (German: "Frankfurt General Newspaper") Daily newspaper published in Frankfurt am Main, one of the most prestigious and influential in Germany. It was created after World War II by journalists who had worked on the highly respected *Frankfurter Zeitung* before the war. When control of the press was turned over to the new West German government in 1949, FAZ began publication. It was the first daily of truly national scope and quickly won a high reputation. Its editorial policy is regarded as conservative because it champions private enterprise.

frankincense Fragrant gum resin obtained from trees of the genus *Boswellia* (family Burseraceae), particularly several varieties found in Somalia, Yemen, and Oman. This important incense resin was used in ancient times in religious rites and in embalming. It constituted part of the Jewish incense of the sanctuary and is frequently mentioned in the Pentateuch; it was one of the gifts of the magi to the infant Jesus. It is used today in incense and fumigants and as a fixative in perfumes.

Franklin, Aretha (born 1942) U.S. popular singer. Her family moved from Memphis to Detroit when she was 2. Her father, C. L. Franklin, was a well-known revivalist preacher; his church and home were visited by such luminaries as Aretha's aunt Clara Ward, Mahalia Jackson, B.B. King, and Dinah Washington. She made her first recording at 12. At first she performed only on the gospel and "chitlin" circuits, but in 1967 her powerful and fervent voice took the country by storm in a string of songs including "I Never Loved a Man," "Respect," "Chain of Fools," "Think," and "Natural Woman." Her later albums include *Amazing Grace* (1972), *Sparkle* (1976), *Who's Zoomin' Who* (1985), and *One Lord, One Faith, One Baptism* (1989). She was the first woman inducted into the Rock and Roll Hall of Fame.

Franklin, Benjamin (1706–1790) American statesman, scientist, philosopher, and publisher. Born in Boston, he was apprenticed at 12 to his brother, a local printer. He taught himself to write effectively, and in 1723 he moved to Philadelphia, where he founded the *Pennsylvania Gazette* (1730–48) and wrote *Poor Richard's Almanack* (1732–57), whose proverbs and aphorisms emphasized prudence, industry, and honesty. He became prosperous and promoted public services in Philadelphia, including a library, fire department, hospital, and insurance company, and an academy that became the University of Pennsylvania. His inventions included the Franklin stove and bifocal spectacles, and his experiments in electricity led to the invention of the lightning rod. He served as a member of the colonial legislature (1736–51). He was a delegate to the Albany Congress (1754). He represented the colony in England in a dispute over land and taxes (1757–62); he returned there in 1764 as agent for several colonies. His initial belief in a unified colonial government under British rule gradually changed over the issue of taxation. He helped secure repeal of the Stamp Act. He served as a delegate to the second Continental Congress and a member of the committee to draft the Declaration of Independence. In 1776 he went to France to seek aid for the American Revolution. Lionized by the French, he negotiated a treaty that provided loans and military support for the Revolution (1778). In 1781 he helped negotiate a preliminary peace treaty with Britain. As a member of the 1787 Constitutional Convention, he was instrumental in achieving adoption of the U.S. Constitution. He is regarded as one of the most extraordinary and brilliant public servants in U.S. history.

Franklin, John Hope (born 1915) U.S. historian. Born in Rentiesville, Okla., he attended Fisk University and received graduate degrees from Harvard, and has taught at many colleges and universities, including Howard, Chicago, and Duke. He first gained international attention with *From Slavery to Freedom* (1947). He helped fashion the legal brief that led to the landmark *Brown vs. Board of Education* decision. He was the first black president of the American Historical Association (1978–79) and was awarded the Presidential Medal of Freedom in 1995.

John Hope Franklin, 1990.
AMPIX PHOTOGRAPHY

Franklin, Rosalind (Elsie) (1920–1958) British biologist. After graduating from Cambridge Univ., she did important experimental work for the coal and coke industries. She later produced the excellent X-ray diffraction pictures that allowed James D. Watson and Francis Crick to deduce that the three-dimensional form of DNA was a double helix. In studies of the tobacco mosaic virus, she helped show that its RNA is located in its protein rather than in its central cavity, and that this RNA is a single-stranded helix rather than the double helix found in the DNA of bacterial viruses and higher organisms. Her death from cancer at age 37 probably cost her a share of the 1962 Nobel Prize awarded to Watson, Crick, and Maurice Wilkins.

Franklin and Marshall College Private liberal-arts college in Lancaster, Pa. Franklin College (founded 1787), named for Benjamin Franklin, and Marshall College (1835), named for John Marshall, merged to create Franklin and Marshall College in 1853. Enrollment is about 1,800.

Franks Germanic-speaking people who invaded the western Roman Empire in the 5th century AD. The Franks lived east of the Rhine in the 3rd century and came under Roman influence. They gained control of northern Gaul by 494 and southern Gaul by 507, and the conversion of their leader, Clovis I, to Christianity helped unite them as a people. They established one of the most powerful kingdoms of the early Middle Ages, ruling lands in present-day France (to which they gave their name), Belgium, and western Germany. The Merovingian dynasty to which Clovis belonged was succeeded by the Carolingian dynasty, whose most notable ruler was Charlemagne. The Frankish kingdom disintegrated in the 10th century.

Franz \ˈfränts\, **Robert** *orig.* **Robert Franz Knauth** (1815–1892) German song composer. In 1842 he became director of the Singakademie of his native Halle, and the choral festivals he organized helped restore Halle to its former status as a musical city. He sent R. Schumann a set of songs, which Schumann had published in 1843 without consulting Franz. F. Liszt became another influential supporter, and would publish his own book about Franz in 1872. By 1867 Franz had become almost completely deaf and was obliged to relinquish his posts, including his professorship at the University of Halle. He experienced mental instability in his later years, when honors were increasingly heaped upon him. His 300 songs, though conservative in style, make him one of the significant figures in the history of the LIED.

Franz Josef See FRANCIS JOSEPH

Franz Josef Land *Russian* **Zemlya Frantsalosifa** \zim-ˈlyä-ˈfränts-sə-ˈyȯ-sə-fə\ Archipelago, northeastern BARENTS SEA. Consisting of about 190 islands, it is the northernmost territory of Russia, and the most northerly land of the Eastern Hemisphere. With a land area of about 8,000 sq mi (20, 720 sq km), the islands comprise a series of lowland plateaus, 85% of whose surface is ice-covered. The arctic climate supports polar bears and the Arctic fox, with numerous bird species. The Soviet Union annexed the islands in 1926 and maintained permanent weather stations there.

Fraser, Dawn (born 1937) Australian swimmer. She broke the women's world record for the 100-m freestyle race nine successive times between 1956 and 1964, and became the first woman swimmer to win gold medals in three consecutive Olympic Games. Her 1964 100-m freestyle record of 58.9 seconds stood for eight years. She set world marks (all later broken) in freestyle swimming at six different distances.

Fraser, George MacDonald (born 1925) British novelist. He trained as a journalist and served as deputy editor of the *Glasgow Herald* 1968–69. The success of his first novel, *Flashman* (1969), led him to become a full-time writer. In it and subsequent novels filled with historical color and detail, the bully of THOMAS HUGHES's *Tom Brown's Schooldays* is his hero. Recent novels include *Black Ajax* (1998) and *Flashman and the Tiger* (2000). He has also written screenplays.

Fraser, Simon (1776–1862) Canadian explorer and fur trader. Born in Bennington, N.Y., he moved to Canada in 1784. He was a clerk in the North West Co. (1791) and became a partner in 1801. In 1805 he set out to search for more suitable trade routes for the fur company. He discovered a river (later FRASER RIVER) that he mistook for the Columbia River, only realizing his error after having followed its course for over a year. In 1817, as head of the company's Red River Valley department, he was arrested for his alleged participation in the SEVEN OAKS MASSACRE. After his acquittal, he retired to farm in Ontario. SIMON FRASER UNIV. is named for him.

Fraser River \ˈfrā-zər, ˈfrā-zhər\ River, southern central British Columbia. Rising in the ROCKY MTNS. near Yellowhead Pass, it flows northwest and south nearly to the U.S. border. It then turns west through the Coast Mountains in a spectacular canyon to empty into the Strait of GEORGIA south of VANCOUVER; it is 850 mi (1368 km) long. The Cariboo gold rush, which began in 1858, took place in the Fraser River basin; lumbering is now the main industry.

Fratellini family \ˌfra-tə-ˈlē-nē\ European circus family best known for the Fratellini Brothers clown trio—Paul (1877–1940), François (1879–1951), and Albert (1886–1961). They grew up in the circus, where their father was a trapeze artist and acrobat. They worked as clowns in pairs until their eldest brother died in 1909, then formed their unique triple act. The makeup Albert designed for himself—high black brows, exaggerated mouth, and bulbous red nose—influenced that of many later clowns. The brothers toured in Europe and Russia before joining the Cirque Medrano in Paris, where they were widely admired for their wit and charm. Many of their children became successful clowns, notably Paul's son Victor (1901–1979) and granddaughter Annie (born 1932).

fraternity and sorority In the U.S., student organizations for social or scholastic activities, fraternities being for men and sororities for women. Most such organizations, which are usually residential, use combinations of letters of the Greek alphabet as names and require new members ("pledges") to partake in initiation rites. Certain honorary societies, such as Phi Beta Kappa, are also called fraternities; membership is based on general undergraduate scholarship. See also SECRET SOCIETY.

fraud In law, the deliberate misrepresentation of fact for the purpose of depriving someone of a valuable possession or legal right. Any omission or concealment that is injurious to another or that allows a person to take unconscionable advantage of another may constitute criminal fraud. The most common type is the obtaining of property by giving a check for which there are insufficient funds in the signer's account. Another is the assumption of someone else's or a fictitious identity with the intent to deceive. Also important are mail and wire fraud (fraud committed by use of the postal service or electronic devices, such as the telephone). A TORT action based on fraud is sometimes referred to as an action of deceit.

Fraunhofer lines In astronomical SPECTROSCOPY, dark lines in a star's SPECTRUM caused by selective absorption of its radiation at specific wavelengths by the various chemical ELEMENTS in its atmosphere. First observed in 1802, they are named for the German physicist Joseph von Fraunhofer (1787–1826), who from c. 1814 plotted over 500 of them and designated the brightest A through G, a system of stellar classification still in use. About 25,000 Fraunhofer lines are now known to exist in the sun's spectrum, between the wavelengths of 2,950 and 10,000 angstroms.

Fray Jorge National Park \ˌfrī-ˈhȯr-hā\ National park, northern central Chile. Established in 1941, and covering 39 sq mi (100 sq km), it preserves a pocket of subtropical forest in a semiarid region. Botanists conjecture that this unusual area probably exists because the relatively warm discharge of a nearby river into the cold Pacific Ocean creates an almost continuous fog, giving the park's plants their moisture.

Frazer, James George *later* **Sir James** (1854–1941) British anthropologist, folklorist, and classical scholar, best known as the author of *The Golden Bough.* Frazer attended Glasgow University and Cambridge Univ., where he became a professor and remained the rest of his life. In *The Golden Bough* (1890; enlarged to 12 vols., 1911–15), Frazer examines the evolution of modes of thought from the magical to the religious and, finally, to the scientific. Although the evolutionary sequence is no longer accepted, Frazer's synthesis of the new science of CULTURAL ANTHROPOLOGY with traditional humanistic concerns and his lively descriptions of exotic cultural beliefs and practices had a wide influence among men of letters. His other works include *Totemism and Exogamy* (1910) and *Folk-Lore in the Old Testament* (1918).

Frazier \ˈfrā-zhər\, **E(dward) Franklin** (1894–1962) U.S. sociologist. Born in Baltimore, he studied at Howard and Clark universities. At Morehouse College he organized the Atlanta University School of Social Work (for blacks). His controversial article "The Pathology of Race Prejudice" (1927) forced him to leave Morehouse; he obtained a PhD at the University of Chicago in 1931, then taught at Fisk University (1929–1934) and Howard University (1934–59). His *The Negro Family in the United States* (1939) is among the first sociological works on blacks researched and written by a black.

Frears, Stephen (born 1941) British film and television director. He worked as an assistant director in theater and film while directing numerous television plays. He made his film debut with *Gumshoe* (1972). After more television work, he won acclaim for the unconventional *My Beautiful Laundrette* (1985). He continued to garner praise with three films made in the U.S.—*Dangerous Liaisons* (1988), *The Grifters* (1990), and *The Hero* (1992)—before returning to Britain for *The Snapper* (1993), *Mary Reilly* (1996), and *The Van* (1997).

Fredegund \ˈfre-də-gənd\ (died 597) Queen consort of the Frankish king CHILPERIC I. Originally a servant, she became Chilperic's mistress after he killed his wife (c. 568). The murder set off a 40-year feud with the family of his half brother SIGEBERT I, whose assassination Fredegund ordered in 575. Known for her ruthlessness and appetite for intrigue, she also made attempts on the lives of his widow and son. After Chilperic was murdered (584) she took his riches and fled to Paris.

Frederick I *German* **Friedrich** *known as* **Frederick Barbarossa ("Redbeard")** (1123?–1190) Duke of SWABIA (1147–90) and German king and Holy Roman Emperor (1152–90). He signed the Treaty of Constance (1153), which promised him the imperial crown in return for his allegiance to the papacy. In 1154 he launched the first of six military campaigns against northern Italy, and on his second campaign in 1158 he conquered Milan. His support for a rival pope against ALEXANDER III led to his excommunication in 1160. Renewed expeditions against Italy met with opposition from the LOMBARD LEAGUE. In the Peace of VENICE (1177) he acknowledged Alexander III as the true pope, and a treaty with the Lombards was confirmed in 1183. Frederick conquered Lübeck in 1180 and broke the power of his chief rival, Duke Henry the Lion. He strengthened the feudal system and curbed the power of the princes by creating a stronger imperial administration. He launched the Third CRUSADE in 1189 but drowned while crossing a river in Turkey.

Frederick I *German* **Friedrich** \'frē-ˌdrik\ (1657–1713) King of Prussia (1701–13). In 1688 he succeeded his father, Frederick William, as elector of Brandenburg (as Frederick III). In European politics, Frederick allied himself with Austria, England, and Holland against France. Prussia's contingents in the imperial army distinguished themselves in the wars of the Grand Alliance and in the War of the Spanish Succession. Austria and Prussia signed a secret treaty that permitted Frederick to crown himself king of Prussia, which was obliged to support Austria militarily and in imperial affairs. As a monarchy, Prussia's diverse Hohenzollern lands were turned into provinces, and Frederick freed the new kingdom from imperial control and increased its revenues.

Frederick II *German* **Friedrich** (1194–1250) King of Sicily (1197–1250), duke of Swabia (1228–35), German king (1212–50), and Holy Roman Emperor (1220–50). The grandson of Frederick I Barbarossa, he became king of Sicily at age 3 but did not gain control over the strife-ridden country until 1212. He defeated his rival Otto IV in 1214, and though the planned union of Sicily and Germany alarmed the pope (1220), he negotiated a compromise and was crowned emperor. A delay in departing for the Sixth Crusade brought excommunication (1227), later revoked. By 1229 Frederick was king of Jerusalem. On his return he quelled a rebellion in Germany led by his son Henry, who had allied with the Lombard League. Seeing Frederick as a growing threat to papal authority, Gregory IX excommunicated him again in 1239; the emperor responded by invading the Papal States. He tried and failed (1245) to negotiate peace with Innocent IV, and his struggle with the papacy continued. By the time of his death Frederick had lost much of central Italy, and his support in Germany was uncertain.

Frederick II *German* **Friedrich** *known as* **Frederick the Great** (1712–1786) King of Prussia (1740–86). The son of Frederick William I, he suffered an unhappy early life, subject to his father's capricious bullying. After trying to escape in 1730, he submitted to his father but continued to pursue intellectual and artistic interests. On his father's death (1740), Frederick became king and asserted his leadership. He seized parts of Silesia during the War of the Austrian Succession, strengthening Prussia considerably. He invaded Saxony in 1756 and marched on into Bohemia. Frederick was almost defeated in the Seven Years' War (1756–63), until his admirer Peter III signed a Russo-Prussian peace treaty that lasted until 1780. The First Partition of Poland in 1772 led to enormous territorial gains for Prussia. Austro-Prussian rivalry led to the War of the Bavarian Succession (1778–79), a diplomatic victory for Frederick, but continued fear of Habsburg ambitions led him to form a league of German states against Joseph II. Under Frederick's leadership Prussia became one of the great states of Europe, with vastly expanded territories and impressive military strength. In addition to modernizing the army, Frederick also espoused the ideas of enlightened despotism and instituted numerous economic, civil, and social reforms.

Frederick III *German* **Friedrich** (1415–1493) Holy Roman emperor (1452–93) and king of Germany (as Frederick IV) from 1440. By 1439 he was the senior member of the Habsburg dynasty, and he united the Austrian holdings of two rival branches of the dynasty (partitioned in 1379), helping lay the foundations for the greatness of the House of Habsburg in European affairs. His greatest achievement was marrying his son Maximilian (later Maximilian I) to Mary, daughter of Charles the Bold, which gave the House of Habsburg a large part of Burgundy and made the Austrians a European power. He was the last emperor to be crowned in Rome by a pope.

Frederick V *German* **Friedrich** *known as* **Frederick the Winter King** (1596–1632) Elector Palatine of the Rhine (1610–23) and king of Bohemia (as Frederick I) for one winter (1619–20). The Protestant Bohemian estates revolted against the Catholic emperor Ferdinand II and offered the crown to Frederick (1619), making him head of the Protestant union against Catholic Austria at the beginning of the Thirty Years' War. He was soon abandoned by his allies and was routed in the Battle of White Mountain. In 1622 he went into exile in Holland. In 1623 he was deprived of his rights as an elector, and in 1628 the Upper Palatinate was annexed by Bavaria.

Frederick VII *Danish* **Frederik** \'frith-rik\ (1808–1863) King of Denmark (1848–63). After the popular demonstrations of 1848, he appointed a liberal ministry, renounced absolute rule, and adopted a representative government. His policy in Schleswig resulted in the duchy's incorporation into Denmark and war with Austria and Prussia soon after his death (see Schleswig-Holstein Question). The childless Frederick was succeeded by Christian IX.

Frederick Henry *Dutch* **Frederik Hendrik** \'frā-də-rək-'hen-drək\ (1584–1647) Third hereditary stadtholder (1625–47) of the Dutch Republic. He succeeded his half brother, Maurice of Nassau, as prince of Orange and count of Nassau. Like his father, William I the Silent, he continued the war of independence against Spain. By establishing hereditary succession to the stadtholdership for the House of Orange, he exercised semimonarchical powers. A successful strategist, he was responsible for the United Provinces' foreign policy, beginning negotiations that led to a favorable treaty with Spain in 1648.

Frederick William *German* **Friedrich Wilhelm** *known as* **the Great Elector** (1620–1688) Elector of Brandenburg (1640–88) who restored the Hohenzollern dominions after the Thirty Years' War. At his accession to the electorship, Brandenburg was ravaged by war and occupied by foreign troops. He cautiously maintained neutrality between the warring Swedes and Habsburgs, started to build a standing army, and added to his territories with the Peace of Westphalia (1648). In the First Northern War (1655–60) he gained sovereignty over the duchy of Prussia. In the complex power struggles in Europe starting in 1661, he shifted allegiance by always joining with the weaker party, hoping to maintain the balance of power. He issued the Edict of Potsdam in 1685, granting asylum to Huguenots expelled from France. When he died, he left a centralized political administration, sound finances, and an efficient army, laying the foundation for the future Prussian monarchy.

Frederick William I *German* **Friedrich Wilhelm** (1688–1740) King of Prussia (1713–40). The son of Frederick I, he received valuable military experience in the War of the Spanish Succession. Realizing that Prussia's military and financial weakness made it dependent on the relations between the great powers, he built up an army that became a strong military presence on the Continent, instituted economic and financial reforms, centralized his administration, encouraged industry and manufacture, mandated compulsory primary education (1717), and freed the serfs on his own domains (1719). He was succeeded by his son, Frederick II the Great.

Frederick William II *German* **Friedrich Wilhelm** (1744–1797) King of Prussia from 1786. He succeeded his uncle Frederick II the Great. Prussia expanded under his rule, adding territories it gained in the second (1793) and third (1795) Partitions of Poland and acquiring additional German lands. He entered into an Austro-Prussian alliance, chiefly in opposition to the French Revolution, but signed a separate treaty with France and withdrew from the alliance in 1795 after defeat in the French Revolutionary Wars. Cultural activities, especially music, flourished in his reign; both W.A. Mozart and Ludwig van Beethoven visited the king and dedicated music to him.

Frederick William III *German* **Friedrich Wilhelm** (1770–1840) King of Prussia (1797–1840). The son of Frederick William II, he pursued a policy of neutrality in the early years of the Napoleonic Wars, which accelerated the decline of Prussia's prestige. Prussia joined the third coalition against France in 1806 and suffered crushing defeat at the Battles of Jena and Auerstedt. Defeat convinced the king of the need to make decisive changes. He allowed Prussian statesmen such as Karl August, Furst von Hardenberg and Karl, Freiherr vom und zum Stein to make domestic reforms, though the state remained absolutist. The Congress of Vienna confirmed Prussia's acquisition of Westphalia and much of Saxony, but the last 25 years of the king's reign brought a downward trend in Prussia's fortunes.

Frederick William IV *German* **Friedrich Wilhelm** (1795–1861) King of Prussia (1840–61). The son of Frederick William III, he was a disciple of the German Romantic movement and an artistic dilettante, but his conservative policies helped spark the Revolution of 1848. In 1849 he refused the imperial crown offered by the Frankfurt National Assembly. His subsequent efforts to create a German union under Prussian leadership were thwarted by Austria (see Humiliation of Olmütz). A stroke left him paralyzed in 1857, and his brother, the future William I, became regent in 1858.

Fredericksburg, Battle of (December 13, 1862) Engagement of the American Civil War fought at Fredericksburg, Va., that resulted in a decisive victory for the Confederate forces. Over 120,000 Union troops under Ambrose E. Burnside were met at Fredericksburg by an entrenched

E
F
G

Confederate force of 78,000 under ROBERT E. LEE. The Union attack failed with over 12,500 casualties, compared with 5,000 for the Confederates. Burnside was relieved of his command, and the victory restored Confederate morale lost after the defeat in the Battle of ANTIETAM.

Fredericton City (pop., 1995 est.: 49,000), capital of New Brunswick. Located on the ST. JOHN RIVER, and originally the site of a French fort (1692), Fredericton was laid out as the provincial capital in 1785. Across the river, the village of St. Anne's Point had been settled by the French c. 1740. After 1825 Fredericton became a British garrison town, and its reconstructed military compound is a federal historic site. Now primarily an administrative and educational center, it is the seat of the University of NEW BRUNSWICK and St. Thomas University. It is the shopping and distribution center for central New Brunswick.

free association See ASSOCIATION

Free Democratic Party (FDP) German centrist political party that advocates individualism and free economic competition. It was formed in 1948 by liberal delegates in the U.S., British, and French zones of occupation. Though relatively small, the party has made and broken governments by forming coalitions with larger parties, including the CHRISTIAN DEMOCRATIC UNION and the SOCIAL DEMOCRATIC PARTY.

free energy Measure of the total combined energies derived from heats of transformation, disorder, and other forms of internal energy (e.g., electrostatic charges). A system will change spontaneously to achieve a lower total free energy. Thus, free energy is the driving force toward equilibrium conditions. The change in free energy between an initial and a final state is useful in evaluating certain thermodynamic processes and can be used to judge whether transformations will occur spontaneously. There are two forms of free energy, with different definitions and applications: the Helmholtz (see HERMANN VON HELMHOLTZ) free energy, sometimes called the work function, and the Gibbs (see J. WILLARD GIBBS) free energy.

free-enterprise system See CAPITALISM

free fall In mechanics, the state of a body that moves freely in any manner in the presence of gravity. The planets are in free fall in the gravitational field of the sun. A body in free fall follows an orbit such that the sum of gravitational and inertial forces equals zero See also GRAVITATION, NEWTON'S LAWS OF MOTION.

Free French French movement to continue warfare against Germany after France's 1940 defeat in WORLD WAR II. Led by CHARLES DE GAULLE in exile in London, the Free French Forces gained power in 1942 with the growing underground RESISTANCE movement in France and the defection of many VICHY FRANCE troops stationed in North Africa. After a power struggle with HENRI HONORE GIRAUD, commander in chief of French forces in North Africa, de Gaulle succeeded by 1944 in controlling the entire French war effort. The 300,000 Free French forces took part in the Allied invasions of southern France and Normandy (see NORMANDY CAMPAIGN) and were the first Allied troops to liberate Paris.

free-market economy See CAPITALISM

free radical *or* **radical** MOLECULE containing at least one unpaired ELECTRON. Most molecules contain even numbers of electrons, and their COVALENT BONDS normally consist of shared electron pairs. Cleavage of such bonds produces two separate free radicals, each with an unpaired electron (in addition to any paired electrons). They may be electrically charged or neutral and are highly reactive and usually short-lived. They combine with one another or with atoms that have unpaired electrons. In reactions with intact molecules, they abstract a part to complete their own electronic structure, generating new radicals, which go on to react with other molecules. Such chain reactions are particularly important in decomposition of substances at high temperatures and in POLYMERIZATION. In the body, oxidized (see OXIDATION-REDUCTION) free radicals can damage tissues. ANTIOXIDANT nutrients (e.g., VITAMIN C and VITAMIN E, SELENIUM) may reduce these effects. Heat, ULTRAVIOLET RADIATION, and ionizing radiation (see RADIATION INJURY) all generate free radicals. They are magnetic, so their properties can be studied with such techniques as magnetic susceptibility and electron paramagnetic resonance measurements.

Free Silver Movement Late-19th-century U.S. political movement that advocated unlimited coinage of silver. Proponents included owners of western silver mines, farmers who wanted higher crop prices, and debtors who believed an expanded currency would allow them easier payment. A depression in the mid-1870s led to an 1878 law requiring the U.S. Treasury to purchase millions of dollars in silver and coin it. After farm prices rose briefly, farm and land prices collapsed in 1887, reviving the demand of farmers for free silver. In 1890 Congress again increased silver purchases, and free silver was an objective of the POPULIST MOVEMENT in the 1892 election. In 1893 the amount of gold in the treasury dropped sharply, precipitating a panic. Congress repealed the act of 1890, angering farmers. In 1896 the Democrats nominated WILLIAM JENNINGS BRYAN for president and backed free silver. The Republican WILLIAM MCKINLEY narrowly won. In 1900 a Republican Congress enacted the Gold Standard Act.

Free Soil Party Minor but influential political party that opposed extension of slavery into the western territories. In 1846 proponents of the WILMOT PROVISO and other antislavery factions formed a party; in 1848 it nominated former Pres. MARTIN VAN BUREN for president. Though Van Buren lost, many party supporters were elected to the U.S. House of Representatives. By 1854 the party was absorbed into the REPUBLICAN PARTY.

Free State See ORANGE FREE STATE

free-tailed bat Any of about 90 species of BATS (family Molossidae), found worldwide in warm regions, that are named for the way part of the tail extends beyond the membrane attached between the hind legs. Also known as mastiff or bulldog bats because of their facial resemblance to those dogs, free-tailed bats are swift fliers with a stout body and long, slender wings. They are about 1.6–5 in. (4–13 cm) long, excluding the 0.6–3-in. (1.5–8-cm) tail, and typically have small eyes, a heavy snout, large ears, and dark fur. They eat insects and roost in tree hollows, caves, and buildings. Most species live in groups; some, including the Mexican free-tailed bat, form colonies of several million. In the past, GUANO from such colonies was mined for fertilizer and for sodium nitrate (used to make gunpowder).

free trade Policy in which a government does not discriminate against imports or interfere with exports. A free-trade policy does not necessarily imply that the government abandons all control and taxation of imports and exports, but rather that it refrains from actions specifically designed to hinder international trade, such as TARIFF barriers, currency restrictions, and import QUOTAS. The theoretical case for free trade is based on ADAM SMITH's argument that the division of labor among countries leads to specialization, greater efficiency, and higher aggregate production. The way to foster such a division of labor, Smith believed, is to allow nations to make and sell whatever products can compete successfully in an international market.

free-trade zone Area within which goods may be landed, handled, and re-exported freely. The purpose is to remove obstacles to trade and to permit quick turnaround of ships and planes. Only when the goods are moved to consumers within the country in which the zone is located do they become subject to tariffs and customs regulation. Free-trade zones are found around major seaports, international airports, and national frontiers; there are more than 200 such zones in the U.S. alone.

free verse Poetry organized according to the cadences of speech and image patterns rather than according to a regular metrical scheme. Its rhythms are based on patterned elements such as sounds, words, phrases, sentences, and paragraphs, rather than on the traditional units of metrical feet (see metrical FOOT). Free verse thus eliminates much of the artificiality and some of the aesthetic distance of poetic expression. It became current in English poetics in the early 20th century. See also PROSODY.

free will problem Problem arising from the apparent inconsistency between causal DETERMINISM in nature and the human power or capacity to choose among alternatives or act freely in certain situations, thus independently of natural, social, or divine compulsions. Itssignificance derives from the fact that free will is generally considered a necessary presupposition of moral responsibility, while determinism has (at least until the advent of QUANTUM MECHANICS) been regarded a necessary presupposition of natural science. Arguments for free will are based on the subjective experience of freedom, on sentiments of guilt, on revealed religion, and on the supposition of responsibility for personal actions that underlies the concepts of law, reward, punishment, and incentive. In theology, the existence of free will must be reconciled with God's foreknowledge, with divine omniscience and goodness (in allowing humans to choose badly), and with divine grace, which allegedly is necessary for any meritorious act.

Freed, Arthur *orig.* **Arthur Grossman** (1894–1973) U.S. film producer and lyricist. Born in Charleston, S.C., he performed in vaudeville and wrote songs in the 1920s. MGM hired him in 1929 to write lyrics for musicals, and over the next decade he produced such hits as "Singin' in the Rain," "Temptation," and "You Are My Lucky Star." After serving as associate producer of *The Wizard of Oz* (1939), he was promoted to producer. He was largely responsible for the high quality of MGM's musicals of the 1940s and '50s, including *Meet Me in St. Louis* (1944), *Easter Parade* (1948), *An American in Paris* (1951, Academy Award), *Singin' in the Rain* (1952), *Gigi* (1958, Academy Award), and *Bells Are Ringing* (1960).

Freedmen's Bureau (1865–72) U.S. agency established during RECONSTRUCTION to help freed black Americans in their transition to freedom. Officially named the U.S. Bureau of Refugees, Freedmen, and Abandoned Lands, it was directed by OLIVER O. HOWARD. It built hospitals and provided medical assistance to over 1 million freed blacks and 21 million rations for blacks and whites. It also built over 1,000 black schools and helped found black colleges and teacher-training institutes but had little success in safeguarding civil rights and promoting land redistribution. Congress responded to pressure from white Southerners by terminating the bureau.

freedom of speech Right, as stated in the 1st and 14th Amendments to the U.S. CONSTITUTION, to express information, ideas, and opinions free of government restrictions based on content. It may be restricted if it poses a "clear and present danger," a risk or threat to safety or other public interests that is serious and imminent (hence the prohibitions against falsely setting off a fire alarm or inciting others to violence). Restraints on speaking and publishing (freedom of the press), and upon action generally (including artistic expression), are fewer today than at any time in U.S. history. Many cases involving freedom of speech and of the press have also concerned DEFAMATION, OBSCENITY, and prior restraint (see PENTAGON PAPERS). See also CENSORSHIP.

freehold In Anglo-American law, ownership of a substantial interest in real property (see REAL AND PERSONAL PROPERTY) held for an indefinite period. The term originally designated the owner of an estate held in free tenure, who possessed, under the MAGNA CARTA, the rights of a free man. Today a freehold is distinguished from a leasehold, a contract to hold real property for a specified period. See also COPYHOLD, FEE, LANDLORD AND TENANT.

Freemasonry Teachings and practices of the fraternal order of Free and Accepted Masons, the largest worldwide SECRET SOCIETY. Originating with the GUILDS of medieval stonemasons, the organization became an honorary society in the 17th and 18th century, adopting the rites and trappings of ancient religious orders and chivalric brotherhoods. The first association of lodges, the Grand Lodge, was founded in England in 1717, and Freemasonry soon spread to other countries in the British Empire. Freemasons took an active role in the American Revolution and later in U.S. politics, and in the 19th century popular fears of their influence led to the ANTI-MASONIC MOVEMENT. Membership is extended only to adult males willing to express belief in a Supreme Being and the immortality of the soul. In Latin countries, the lodges have often attracted freethinkers and anticlerical types; in Anglo-Saxon nations, membership has mostly been drawn from white Protestants. Freemasonry has also given rise to social organizations such as the Ancient Arabic Order of the Noble Mystic Shrine, or Shriners.

freesia \'frē-zhə\ Any of the approximately 20 species of South African plants that make up the genus *Freesia,* in the IRIS FAMILY, with CORMS, grassy foliage, and wiry spikes of bell-like, lemon-scented flowers in white, yellow, orange, and blue. The flower spikes usually turn at right angles from the stem, displaying the flowers in a horizontal line. Two species much used in hybridization are *F. refracta,* greenish-yellow to yellow or white, and *F. armstrongii,* tinged rose-purple. The plants are grown indoors in pots or in gardens in mild climates.

Freetown Capital (pop., 1985: 470,000; metro. area pop., 1990 est.: 669,000) and largest city of Sierra Leone. Located at the mouth of the Sierra Leone River, it has the best harbor in western Africa. It was founded in 1787 by an English abolitionist, Granville Sharp, as a haven for freed African slaves from England. Later, more freed slaves from Nova Scotia and runaway slaves from Jamaica settled there. Their descendants, known as Creoles, are now outnumbered by Mende and Temne immigrants from the interior. In 1821 it became the seat of government for Britain's West African possessions. Incorporated as a municipality in 1893, Freetown became the nation's capital in 1961. It is the nation's commercial, educational, and transportation center.

freezing Method of FOOD PRESERVATION in which low temperatures (0°F, −18°C, or lower) are used to inhibit the growth of microorganisms. Used for centuries in cold regions, it was not until the advent of mechanical REFRIGERATION in the mid-19th century that the process became widely applicable commercially. In the 20th century, quick (or flash) freezing was developed by CLARENCE BIRDSEYE. Except for beef and venison, which benefit from an aging process, meat is frozen as promptly as possible after slaughter. Fruits and vegetables are often frozen in a syrup or vacuum-sealed to exclude air and prevent oxidation and desiccation.

freezing point Temperature at which a liquid becomes a solid. When the PRESSURE surrounding the liquid is increased, the freezing point is raised. The addition of some solids can lower the freezing point of a liquid, a principle used when salt is applied to melt ice on frozen surfaces. For pure substances, the freezing point is the same as the MELTING POINT. In mixtures and certain organic compounds, the early solid formation changes the composition of the remaining liquid, usually steadily lowering its freezing point, a principle that is applied in mixture separation. The freezing point of pure water at standard atmospheric pressure is 32°F (0°C). To change a liquid at its freezing point to a solid at the same temperature, the heat of fusion (see LATENT HEAT) must be removed.

Frege \'frā-gə\, **(Friedrich Ludwig) Gottlob** (1848–1925) German mathematician and logician, founder of modern mathematical LOGIC. He taught at the University of Jena 1871–1917. In his *Begriffsschrift* (1879), he first presented a system of mathematical logic in the modern sense. In discovering the fundamental ideas that have made possible the modern development of logic, and devising the notation of quantifiers and variables (see PREDICATE CALCULUS), Frege invented an entire discipline. He also made significant contributions to the philosophy of language, including a highly influential theory of the distinction between sense and reference.

Frei (Montalva) \'frā\, **Eduardo** (1911–1982) Chilean politician and president (1964–70). He earned a degree in law (1933). Though a conservative as a young man, he ran successfully for president as a center-left candidate. He offered a moderate program of agrarian reform, economic stabilization, "Chileanization" of U.S.-owned copper interests, and a more equitable distribution of wealth. Though he raised expectations of major change and made marked progress in expanding educational opportunities for the poor, most of his reform efforts failed to achieve their objectives, and his administration was plagued by inflation and labor unrest. His son Eduardo Frei Ruiz-Tagle (born 1942) has served as president since 1994. See also SALVADOR ALLENDE.

Freiburg (im Breisgau) \'frī-ˌbu̇rk\ City (pop., 1996 est.: 199,000), southwestern Germany. It is situated on the western slopes of the BLACK FOREST. Chartered in 1120, in 1218 it passed to the counts of Urach (later Freiburg). It was ruled by the HABSBURGS from 1368 to 1806, when it passed to BADEN. It was heavily bombed by the Allies during World War II. Since rebuilt, it is now the cultural and economic center of the Black Forest region. It is the seat of the Albert Ludwig University of Freiburg (founded 1457).

Freikorps \'frī-ˌkȯr\ (German: "Free Corps") Private German paramilitary groups that first appeared in late 1918 after Germany's defeat in World War I. Composed of ex-soldiers and unemployed youth and led by ex-officers, they eventually included over 65 corps of varying sizes. Most were nationalistic and radically conservative, and they were employed unofficially to put down left-wing revolts throughout Germany. Initially sanctioned by the government, they came to be viewed as a nuisance and a threat and were supplanted by regular army and police or absorbed by new units of the Nazis and other political parties.

Freire \'frā-rē\, **Paulo** (1921–1997) Brazilian educator. His ideas developed from his experience teaching literacy to Brazil's peasants. His interactive methods, which encouraged students to question the teacher, often led to literacy in as little as 30 hours of instruction. In 1963 he was appointed director of the Brazilian National Literacy Program, but he was jailed following a military coup in 1964. He went into exile, returning in 1979 to help found the Workers Party. His seminal work was *Pedagogy of the Oppressed* (1970).

Frelinghuysen \'frē-liŋ-,hī-zᵊn\, **Frederick Theodore** (1817–1885) U.S. politician. Born in Millstone, N.J., into a prominent political family, he helped found the New Jersey Republican Party and served as state attorney general 1861–66. He was appointed, then elected, to the U.S. Senate (1866–69, 1871–77). As secretary of state (1881–85) he obtained Pearl Harbor in Hawaii as a U.S. naval base and opened treaty relations with Korea (1882).

Fremont City (pop., 1996 est.: 188,000), California. It is located on the southeastern shore of San Francisco Bay (there spanned by the Dumbarton Bridge). The site of Mission San José de Guadalupe (founded 1797), the city was formed in 1956 through the amalgamation of five communities: Centerville, Irvington, Niles, Mission San José, and Warm Springs. Freeway connections stimulated residential and industrial growth as part of the San Francisco Bay development.

Frémont \'frē-,mänt\, **John C(harles)** (1813–1890) U.S. explorer. Born in Savannah, Ga., in 1838 he helped Jean-Nicolas Nicollet (1786–1843) survey and map the upper Mississippi and Missouri rivers. Aided by the influence of THOMAS HART BENTON, who became his sponsor and, in 1841, father-in-law, he led government survey expeditions to map much of the area between the Mississippi River valley and the Pacific Ocean. In 1845, on an expedition to California (on which he may have carried secret instructions for action in case of war), he supported the BEAR FLAG REVOLT. In the Mexican War he was appointed a major and with ROBERT F. STOCKTON helped conquer California, of which he was appointed military governor. In a dispute with Gen. STEPHEN KEARNY, he was arrested and court-martialed; he later resigned. He became wealthy in the gold rush and was elected one of California's first U.S. senators (1850–51). As the new Republican Party's presidential candidate in 1856, he was defeated by JAMES BUCHANAN. In the 1870s he embarked on railroad ventures and lost his fortune. He served as governor of Arizona Territory 1878–83.

French, Daniel Chester (1850–1931) U.S. sculptor. Born in Exeter, N.H., he produced his first important commission for the town of Concord, Mass.—the famous statue of *The Minute Man* (1874). He was the leading American turn-of-the-century sculptor, with studios in Boston, Concord, Washington, and New York. His best-known work, the seated marble figure of ABRAHAM LINCOLN in the Lincoln Memorial, was dedicated in 1922. His other notable public monuments include the equestrian statues of ULYSSES S. GRANT in Philadelphia (1898) and GEORGE WASHINGTON in Paris (1900), and groups representing *Europe, Asia, Africa,* and *America* in front of the New York Custom House (1907).

French, John (Denton Pinkstone) *later* **Earl of Ypres** \'ēprᵊ\ (1852–1925) British military leader. A soldier from 1874, he successfully led the British cavalry in the SOUTH AFRICAN WAR. He was appointed inspector general in 1907 and chief of the army general staff in 1913. As commander of the British Expeditionary Force from the beginning of World War I, he was criticized for his indecisive leadership at Ypres and elsewhere that caused large numbers of British casualties. Forced to resign in 1915, he served as commander in chief in Britain and later as lord lieutenant of Ireland (1918–21).

French 75 Field GUN with a 75-mm bore, devised in 1894 by the French army. It was distinguished from other CANNON of its time by its recoil system: the barrel and breech recoiled on rollers, while the gun carriage remained in place instead of jumping or rolling backward. Introduced in 1897, it was used by French and Allied armies until the fall of France in World War II.

French and Indian War North American phase of a war between France and Britain to control colonial territory (1754–63). The war's more complex European phase was the SEVEN YEARS' WAR. Earlier phases of the quest for overseas mastery were KING WILLIAM'S WAR (1689–97), QUEEN ANNE'S WAR (1702–13), and KING GEORGE'S WAR (1744–48). The North American dispute was whether the upper Ohio River valley was a part of the British empire or part of the French empire; the bigger question was which national culture would dominate the heart of North America. British settlers were the majority in the coveted area, but French exploration, trade, and Indian alliances predominated. In 1754 the French ousted a British force, including a colonial militia under Col. GEORGE WASHINGTON, at Fort Necessity, Pa. Until 1757 the French continued to dominate, but in 1758 Britain increased aid to its troops and won victories at Louisbourg, Fort Frontenac, and Fort Duquesne (Pittsburgh). The final British victory at the Battle of QUEBEC (1759) led to the fall of NEW FRANCE (1760). In the Treaty of PARIS (1763) France ceded its North American territory to Britain.

French Broad River River, western North Carolina. Rising in the BLUE RIDGE MTNS. and flowing 210 mi (340 km) north through the GREAT SMOKY MTNS. into Tennessee, it then turns west to join the Holston River near KNOXVILLE, forming the TENNESSEE RIVER. Douglas Dam, part of the TENNESSEE VALLEY AUTHORITY (TVA), is on the river near the junction.

French Communist Party French branch of the international communist movement. It was founded in 1920 by the left wing of the FRENCH SOCIALIST PARTY but did not gain significant influence until it affiliated with LEON BLUM's Popular Front coalition government in 1936. From 1945 to 1968 it won almost 25% of the vote in each election and had a large representation in the National Assembly. It lost ground when CHARLES DE GAULLE was elected in 1958, but in 1965 it formed an alliance with other left-wing parties. In the early 1980s it allied with the Socialist Party. It has since lost many of its traditional working-class supporters.

French Community (French, *la Communauté*) Association of overseas territories created in 1958 by the constitution of the FIFTH REPUBLIC to replace the FRENCH UNION in dealing with matters of foreign policy, defense, currency and economic policy, and higher education. As the former colonies gained full independence in the 1960s and '70s, the Community became obsolete; it was defunct by the late 1970s.

French East India Co. See French EAST INDIA CO.

French Equatorial Africa *formerly* **French Congo** Former federation of French possessions, western central Africa. It was in existence from 1910 to 1959; its capital was BRAZZAVILLE. With independence in 1960, the former territory of Ubangi-Shari, to which Chad had been attached in 1920, became the Central African Republic and the Republic of Chad; the Middle Congo became the Republic of the Congo; and Gabon became the Republic of Gabon.

French Guiana \gē-'a-nə, gē-'ä-nə\ *French* **Guyane Française** \gwē-'yàn-fräⁿ-'sez\ Overseas department (pop., 1993 est.: 128,000) of France, northeastern coast of South America. It has an area of 33,399 sq mi (86,504 sq km) and is bounded by Brazil, Suriname, and the Atlantic Ocean. The capital is CAYENNE. Most of French Guiana is low-lying, with mountains in the south and a swampy coastal plain. The MARONI RIVER forms the border with Suriname. French Guiana's population is mostly Creole. The principal languages are French (official) and Creole; 90% of the people are Roman Catholic. Originally settled by the Spanish, French, and Dutch, the territory of French Guiana was awarded to France in 1667, and the inhabitants were made French citizens after 1877. By 1852 the French began using the territory as a penal colony with one, on DEVIL'S ISLAND, especially notorious. It became a department of France in 1946; the penal colonies were closed by 1947.

French Guinea See GUINEA

French horn Valved circular horn with a wide bell. It is normally a transposing instrument in F. It has a wide bore and three (sometimes four) rotary valves; its conical mouthpiece produces a mellower tone than the cup-shaped mouthpieces of other BRASS INSTRUMENTS. Horns long relied on separable crooks—circular lengths of tubing that could be attached and removed rapidly—for music modulating to new keys. Since c. 1900 the standard horn has been a "double" instrument, with built-in crooks in F and B-flat that can be selected rapidly by means of a thumb valve. The modern symphony orchestra usually includes four horns. Though difficult to play and prone to producing conspicuous errors, its tone is widely admired.

French Indochina Former name (until 1950) for eastern part of INDOCHINA peninsula, South Asia. After establishing its rule by 1893, France governed it through the Indochinese Union. During World War II it was occupied by Japan, and in 1945 it was made the autonomous state of Vietnam. After the Japanese surrender, the VIET MINH under HO CHI MINH proclaimed the Democratic Republic of Vietnam. Laos and Cambodia were reoccupied by the French, who founded the Indochinese Federation. The First INDOCHINA WAR soon erupted, and the French ratified treaties (1949–50) that recognized Vietnam, Laos, and Cambodia as independent states within the FRENCH UNION. The area achieved true independence after the Geneva Conference of 1954.

French language ROMANCE LANGUAGE spoken as a first language by about 72 million people in France, Belgium, Switzerland, Canada (mainly Quebec), and many other countries and regions formerly governed by France. French is an official language of more than 25 countries. Its earliest written materials date from the 9th century. Numerous regional DIALECTS were eventually pushed aside by Francien, the dialect of Paris, adopted as the standard language in the mid-16th century. This largely replaced the dialects of northern and central France, known as the *langue d'oïl* (from *oïl,* the northern word for "yes"), and greatly reduced the use of the OCCITAN LANGUAGE of southern France, known as *langue d'oc* (from *oc,* Occitan for "yes"). Regional dialects survive mostly in uneducated rural speech. French grammar has been greatly simplified from Latin. Nouns do not have cases, and masculine and feminine gender are marked not in the noun but in its article or adjective. The verb is conjugated for three persons and for singular and plural; though spelled differently, several of these forms are pronounced identically.

French Polynesia *French* **Polynésie Française** \pȯ-lē-nā-'zē-fräⁿ-'sez\ *formerly* **French Oceania** \ˌō-shē-'a-nē-ə\ French overseas territory (pop., 1993 est.: 212,000), in the southern Pacific. It comprises 130 islands in five archipelagoes: the SOCIETY ISLANDS, the TUAMOTU ARCHIPELAGO, the GAMBIER ISLANDS, the MARQUESAS ISLANDS, and the AUSTRAL ISLANDS. TAHITI, in the Society group, is the largest island and the site of the capital, PAPEETE. While the islands cover an area of some 1,550 sq mi (4,000 sq km), more than two-thirds of the population lives on Tahiti. The islands became French protectorates in the 1840s, and in the 1880s the French colony of Oceania was established. It became an overseas territory of France after World War II, and was granted partial autonomy in 1977.

French republican calendar Dating system adopted in 1793 during the FRENCH REVOLUTION. It sought to replace the Gregorian calendar with a scientific and rational system that avoided Christian associations. The 12 months each contained three *décades* (instead of weeks) of 10 days each; the year ended with five (six for leap year) supplementary days. The year began with the autumnal equinox (September 22, 1792) as 1 Vendémiaire, year I. The other autumn months were named Brumaire and Frimaire; they were followed by the winter months Nivôse, Pluviôse, and Ventôse, the spring months Germinal, Floréal, and Prairial, and the summer months Messidor, Thermidor, and Fructidor. (All the names were derived from words for natural phenomena.) On January 1, 1806, the Gregorian calendar was reestablished by the Napoleonic regime.

French Revolution Movement that shook France between 1787 and 1799 and ended the ANCIEN RÉGIME. Causes included a large underfed population, loss of peasant support for the feudal system, an expanding bourgeoisie that was excluded from political power, and a fiscal crisis worsened by participation in the AMERICAN REVOLUTION. The efforts of the regime in 1787 to increase taxes levied on the privileged classes initiated a crisis. In response, LOUIS XVI convened the ESTATES-GENERAL, made up of clergy, nobility and the THIRD ESTATE (commoners) in 1789. Trying to pass reforms, it swore the TENNIS COURT OATH not to disperse until France had a new constitution. The king grudgingly concurred in the formation of the NATIONAL ASSEMBLY, but rumors of an "aristocratic conspiracy" led to the GREAT FEAR of July 1789, and Parisians seized the BASTILLE on July 14. The assembly drafted a new constitution that introduced the DECLARATION OF THE RIGHTS OF MAN AND OF THE CITIZEN, proclaiming liberty, equality, and fraternity. The CONSTITUTION OF 1791 also established a short-lived constitutional monarchy. The Assembly nationalized church lands to pay off the public debt and reorganized the church (see CIVIL CONSTITUTION OF THE CLERGY). The king tried to flee the country, but was apprehended at Varennes. France, newly nationalistic, declared war on Austria and Prussia in 1792, beginning the FRENCH REVOLUTIONARY WARS. Revolutionaries imprisoned the royal family and massacred nobles and clergy at the Tuileries in 1792. A new assembly, the NATIONAL CONVENTION—divided between GIRONDINS and the extremist MONTAGNARDS—abolished the monarchy and established the First Republic in September 1792. Louis XVI was judged by the Convention and executed for treason on January 21, 1793. The Montagnards seized power and adopted radical economic and social policies that provoked violent reactions, including the Wars of the VENDÉE and citizen revolts. Opposition was broken by the REIGN OF TERROR. Military victories in 1794 brought a change in the public mood, and MAXIMILIEN ROBESPIERRE was overthrown in the Convention on 9 Thermidor, year II, and executed the next day (see THERMIDORIAN REACTION). Royalists tried to seize power in Paris but were crushed by NAPOLEON on 13 Vendémaire, year IV (1795). A new constitution placed executive power in a DIRECTORY of five members. The war and schisms in the Directory led to disputes that were settled by coups d'état, chiefly those of 18 FRUCTIDOR and 18–19 BRUMAIRE, in which Napoleon abolished the Directory and declared himself leader of France. See also COMMITTEE OF PUBLIC SAFETY, CONSTITUTION OF 1795, CONSTITUTION OF THE YEAR VIII, CHARLOTTE CORDAY, Club of the CORDELIERS, GEORGES J. DANTON, Club of the FEUILLANTS, JACOBIN CLUB, J.-P. MARAT, MARIE-ANTOINETTE, LOUIS DE SAINT-JUST, E.-J. SIEYÈS.

French Revolutionary Wars (1792–99) Series of wars undertaken to defend and then to spread the ideas of the FRENCH REVOLUTION. After the National Assembly established its ascendancy over LOUIS XVI, in 1791 Austria and Prussia called on European rulers to assist Louis in reestablishing power. France declared war in 1792 and soon had occupied all of Belgium. The First Coalition (Prussia, Spain, the United Provinces, and Britain) was formed against France in 1793, and in response the French declared a levy on all Frenchmen, creating a massive army. By 1795 France had defeated the allies on every front; Prussia signed a peace treaty, and the Netherlands became the French-influenced Batavian Republic. NAPOLEON took over as commander of the Italian campaign in 1796 and by the Treaty of CAMPO FORMIO (1797) forced Austria to cede the AUSTRIAN NETHERLANDS and recognize the French-organized Cisalpine and Ligurian republics in northern Italy. He then sailed an army to Egypt to conquer the Ottoman empire, but was defeated by Britain in the Battle of the NILE (1798). Meanwhile, other French forces had occupied new territories and established republican regimes in Rome, Switzerland (the Helvetic Republic), and Italy (the Parthenopean Republic). The Second Coalition, comprising Britain, Russia, the Ottoman empire, Naples, Portugal, and Austria, was short-lived. By the time Napoleon became first consul of France in 1799, the danger of foreign intervention was over. Conflict between France and other European powers continued in the NAPOLEONIC WARS.

French Shore Area, coast of Newfoundland. French fishermen were allowed by the English to fish and to dry their catch in the region after France gave up all other claims to Newfoundland in 1713. As defined by the Treaty of Paris (1783), the French Shore extended west around the island from Cape St. John in the north to Cape Ray in the southwest. In the 1880s Newfoundland began to develop a lobster fishery and the treaty came under dispute. France sold its claims to the territory in 1904.

French Socialist Party *originally (1905–69)* **French Section of the Workers' International** Political party founded in 1905 that supported far-reaching nationalization of the economy. Socialism in France evolved from such 19th-century theorists as HENRI DE SAINT-SIMON, CHARLES FOURIER, LOUIS AUGUSTE BLANQUI, and LOUIS BLANC and the activities of French Marxists. Led by JEAN JAURES, the party grew quickly, though it suffered a setback with the separation of the left wing into the FRENCH COMMUNIST PARTY (1920). In the 1930s it was central to LEON BLUM's Popular Front government. In World War II it participated in the RESISTANCE and cooperated with CHARLES DE GAULLE, emerging after the war as France's second-largest party. It soon lost strength; in 1969 it won only 5% of the vote. Renamed the Socialist Party in 1969, it was revived by FRANCOIS MITTERRAND, but lost its dominant position in the 1990s.

French Somaliland See DJIBOUTI

French Union Political entity created by the constitution of 1946 of the FOURTH REPUBLIC. It replaced the French colonial empire with a semifederal entity that absorbed the colonies (overseas departments and territories) and gave former protectorates limited local autonomy, with some voice in decision making in Paris. By the constitution of 1958, the French Union was replaced by the FRENCH COMMUNITY.

French West Africa Former federation of French dependencies, western Africa. It consisted of what are now the independent republics of BENIN, BURKINA FASO, GUINEA, IVORY COAST, MALI, MAURITANIA, NIGER, and SENEGAL. The capital was at DAKAR. The federation was established in 1895 and dissolved 1958–59. By 1960 the former colonial territories had become independent republics.

Freneau \fre-ˈnō\, **Philip (Morin)** (1752–1832) U.S. poet, essayist, and editor, known as the "poet of the American Revolution." After the outbreak of the revolution he began to write anti-British satire. Not until his return from two years in the Caribbean, during which he wrote such poems as "The Beauties of Santa Cruz" and "The House of Night," did he become an active participant in the war. He was captured and imprisoned by the British, an experience he bitterly recounted in the poem *The British Prison-Ship* (1781).

Freon Trademark name for any of several organic compounds containing FLUORINE (fluorocarbons) and sometimes CHLORINE (CHLOROFLUOROCARBONS, or CFCs). Nonflammable, nontoxic, and noncorrosive, they have conveniently low boiling points, which makes them useful as refrigerants. By the mid-1970s, they were in wide use in refrigeration and air conditioning systems, as blowing agents for plastic foams, as fire-extinguishing agents, and in aerosol sprays. Evidence has accumulated that their decomposition in the stratosphere destroys OZONE there (see OZONE LAYER), so most of their uses have been banned. International agreements signed by most of the industrialized countries now call for the phasing out of chlorofluorocarbon use.

frequency Number of waves that pass a fixed point per unit time; also, the number of cycles or VIBRATIONS undergone in unit time by a body in PERIODIC MOTION. Frequency f is the reciprocal of the time T taken to complete one cycle (the period), or $1/T$. The frequency with which earth rotates is once per 24 hours. Frequency is usually expressed in units called hertz (Hz). One hertz is equal to one cycle per second; one kilohertz (kHz) is 1,000 Hz, and one megahertz (MHz) is 1,000,000 Hz. The musical pitch A above middle C (the A string of a violin) has been widely standardized as 440 Hz.

frequency distribution In statistics, a graph or data set organized to show the frequency of occurrence of each possible outcome of a repeatable event observed many times. Simple examples are election returns and test scores listed by percentile. A frequency distribution can be graphed as a HISTOGRAM or pie chart. For large data sets, the stepped graph of a histogram is often approximated by the smooth curve of a distribution function (called a DENSITY FUNCTION when normalized so that the area under the curve is 1). The famed bell curve or NORMAL DISTRIBUTION is the graph of one such function. Frequency distributions are particularly useful in summarizing large data sets and assigning probabilities.

frequency modulation See FM

fresco painting Method of wall painting in which water-based pigments are applied to wet, freshly laid lime plaster. The dry-powder colors, when mixed with water, penetrate the surface and become a permanent part of the wall. This technique is also known as *buon fresco*, or "true" fresco, to distinguish it from *fresco secco*, or "dry" fresco (painting on dry plaster). Early Minoan, Greek, and Roman wall paintings were frescoes. The Italian Renaissance was the greatest period of fresco painting, as seen in the works of CIMABUE, GIOTTO, MASACCIO, Fra ANGELICO, CORREGGIO, and others. MICHELANGELO's frescoes in the Sistine Chapel and RAPHAEL's in the Vatican are the most famous of all. By the 18th century, fresco had been largely replaced by oil painting. In the early 20th century it was revived by DIEGO RIVERA and others, often as a medium for political art. Fresco painting is also found in China and India.

Frescobaldi \ˌfres-kə-ˈbäl-dē\, **Girolamo** (1583–1643) Italian composer and organist. In 1608 he became organist at St. Peter's, where, except for a six-year sojourn at the Florentine court, he would remain the rest of his life. He was highly celebrated for both his playing and his diverse and ingenious compositions. He wrote numerous toccatas, ricercars, and canzonas for organ and harpsichord, along with many sacred vocal works and secular songs. His most famous work is *Fiori musicali* (1635), a large collection of organ music for the mass.

Fresnel lens \frə-ˈnel\ Series of concentric rings, each consisting of a thin part of a simple LENS, assembled on a flat surface. G.-L.-L. BUFFON (1748) first had the idea of dividing a lens surface into concentric rings to reduce the weight. In 1820 his idea was adopted by Augustin-Jean Fresnel (1788–1827) for the construction of lighthouse lenses. Fresnel lenses have the optical properties of much thicker and heavier lenses. They are used in spotlights, floodlights, railroad and traffic signals, and decorative lights. Some thin Fresnel lenses are molded in plastic, the width of the rings being only a few thousandths of an inch; such lenses are used in cameras and small projectors.

Fresno \ˈfrez-nō\ City (pop., 1996 est.: 396,000), central California. Located in the SAN JOAQUIN RIVER valley, it was settled in 1872 as a station on the Central Pacific Railroad, and became an agricultural community in the 1880s. A marketing and shipping center, it processes cotton, grain, fruits, wines, and dairy products. It is headquarters of the Sierra National Forest and a gateway to resort areas of the SIERRA NEVADAS. It is the home of California State Univ., Fresno (1911).

Freud \ˈfrȯid\, **Anna** (1895–1982) Austrian-British psychiatrist, founder of the field of child psychiatry. Daughter of SIGMUND FREUD, she pioneered in developing psychoanalytic theory and practice. In *The Ego and Defense Mechanisms* (1936), Freud called repression the principal human defense mechanism. This gave a strong, new impetus to the role of ego in psychology. She and her terminally ill father escaped Nazi-dominated Austria for London in 1938. She coauthored three books on the effects of war on children. Her thought is summarized in *Normality and Pathology in Childhood* (1968).

Anna Freud, c. 1970.
ARCHIV FUR KUNST UND GESCHICHTE, WEST BERLIN

Freud, Lucian (born 1922) British (German-born) painter. Grandson of SIGMUND FREUD, he moved with his family to London when he was 10. He is known for somber, realistic figure paintings that represent his subjects' raw physical characteristics and inner tensions; his highly individualistic, coarse style makes no attempt to idealize its usually nude subjects. His work has been internationally influential in reviving a representational style. In 1993 he was awarded the Order of Merit.

Freud, Sigmund (1856–1939) Austrian neuropsychologist, founder of PSYCHOANALYSIS, and one of the major intellectual figures of the 20th century. Trained in Vienna as a neurologist, Freud went to Paris in 1885 to study with J.-M. CHARCOT, whose work on hysteria led Freud to conclude that mental disorders might be caused purely by psychological rather than organic factors. Returning to Vienna (1886), Freud collaborated with the physician Josef Breuer (1842–1925) in further studies on hysteria, resulting in the development of some key psychoanalytic concepts and techniques, including free association, the unconscious, resistance (later defense mechanisms), and neurosis. In 1899 he published *The Interpretation of Dreams,* in which he analyzed the complex symbolic processes underlying dream formation: he proposed that dreams are the disguised expression of unconscious wishes. In his controversial *Three Essays on the Theory of Sexuality* (1905), he delineated the complicated stages of psychosexual development (oral, anal, and phallic) and the formation of the Oedipus complex. During World War I, he wrote papers that clarified his understanding of the relations between the unconscious and conscious portions of the mind and the workings of the id, ego, and superego. Freud eventually applied his psychoanalytic insights to such diverse phenomena as jokes and slips of the tongue, ethnographic data, religion and mythology, and modern civilization. Works of note include *Totem and Taboo* (1913), *Beyond the Pleasure Principle* (1920), *The Future of an Illusion* (1927), and *Civilization and Its Discontents* (1930). Freud fled to England when the Nazis annexed Austria in 1938; he died shortly thereafter. Despite the relentless and often compelling challenges mounted against virtually all of his ideas, both in his lifetime and after, Freud has remained one of the most influential figures in contemporary thought.

Freyberg \ˈfrī-ˌbərg\, **Bernard Cyril** *later* **Baron Freyberg (of Wellington and of Munstead)** (1889–1963) New Zealand (British-born) military leader. He emigrated to New Zealand with his parents in 1891. He fought in many of the fiercest battles of World War I, and at 27 he became the youngest brigadier general in the British army. He served as commander in chief of New Zealand forces in World War II.

After the war he served as governor-general of New Zealand (1946–52). In 1951 he was created a baron.

Freyja \'frā-yə\ Most important Norse goddess, one of a group of fertility deities called Vanir. Her father was the sea god Njörd, and her brother and male counterpart was Freyr. She was the goddess of battle and death as well as love and fertility. Half the heroes slain in battle went to her domain, Folkvangr, the other half to Odin's Valhalla. She taught a powerful magic to the Aesir, probably involving sexuality.

Freyr \'frār\ *or* **Frey** \'frā\ Norse god of peace, fertility, rain, and sun, one of a group of fertility deities called Vanir. The son of Njörd and brother of Freyja, he was especially venerated in pre-Christian Sweden, where he was considered the progenitor of the royal line. The best-known story about him told of his love and lust for the giantess Gerd, who was wooed and won for him by his servant. His worship was believed to bring good weather and great wealth.

Frick, Henry Clay (1849–1919) U.S. industrialist. Born in West Overton, Pa., he began building and operating coke ovens in 1870 and organized his own company in 1871. From 1889 he served as chairman of Carnegie Steel Co., the world's largest manufacturer of steel and coke. His role in the violent steel strike of 1892 in Homestead, Pa., provoked an anarchist to shoot and stab him, but he survived. He was instrumental in the formation of the U.S. Steel Corp. in 1901. A noted art collector and philanthropist, he bequeathed the Frick Collection to New York City. See also Andrew Carnegie.

friction Force that resists sliding or rolling of one solid object over another. Some friction is beneficial, such as the traction used to walk without slipping. Most friction, though, is undesirable opposition to motion, such as between moving parts of machines. For example, about 20% of the work done by an automobile engine is needed to overcome friction between moving parts. Friction is a result of attractive forces between the contact regions of two bodies, and the amount of friction is almost independent of the area of contact. Kinetic friction arises between surfaces in relative motion, static friction acts between surfaces at rest with respect to each other, and rolling friction occurs when an object rolls over a surface.

Friedan, Betty \fri-'dan\ *orig.* **Betty Naomi Goldstein** (born 1921) U.S. feminist. Born in Peoria, Ill., she attended Smith College and worked in New York before marrying and having children. Her dissatisfaction with her role as housewife prompted her to write *The Feminine Mystique* (1963), the work that sparked the modern American feminist movement. In 1966 she cofounded the National Organization for Women. Her later books include *The Second Stage* (1981).

Friedland \'frēt-ˌlänt\, **Battle of** (June 14, 1807) Victory against Russia for Napoleon in the Napoleonic Wars that led to the Peace of Tilsit. Near Friedland in eastern Prussia (modern Pravdinsk, Russia), an isolated French corps, greatly outnumbered, held off Russian attacks for nine hours while Napoleon concentrated his forces. He then attacked with 65,000 men, pushing half the Russian army into the village of Friedland, where they were killed or captured. A Prussian ally withdrew his forces from Königsberg, which the French then occupied.

Friedman \'frēd-mən\, **Milton** (born 1912) U.S. conservative economist. Born in Brooklyn, N.Y., he studied at Rutgers and Columbia before joining the faculty of the University of Chicago in 1946. There he became the leading U.S. advocate of monetarism. He oversaw the economic transition in Chile after the overthrow of Salvador Allende. In the 1980s his ideas were taken up by Pres. Ronald Reagan and Britain's Margaret Thatcher. His many books include *A Theory of the Consumption Function* (1957) and *Capitalism and Freedom* (1962), both with Rose Friedman, and *A Monetary History of the United States, 1867–1960* (1963) and *Monetary Trends of the United States and the United Kingdom* (1981), with Anna Schwartz. He received the Nobel Prize in 1976.

Friedmann universe \'frēt-man\ Model universe developed in 1922 by the Russian meteorologist and mathematician Aleksandr Friedmann (1888–1925). He believed that Albert Einstein's general theory of relativity required a theory of the universe in motion, as opposed to the static universe that scientists until then had proposed. He hypothesized a big bang followed by expansion, then contraction and an eventual big crunch. His model supposes a closed universe, but similar solutions involve an open universe (which expands infinitely), and a flat universe, in which expansion continues infinitely but gradually approaches a rate of expansion of zero. See also Edwin Hubble.

Friedrich \'frē-drik\, **Caspar David** (1774–1840) German painter. He studied at the Copenhagen Academy. After 1798 he settled in Dresden and began his career as a topographical draftsman in pencil and sepia wash. His first important oil painting, *The Cross in the Mountains* (1807–8), achieves an overwhelming sense of isolation. In 1824 he was appointed professor at the Dresden Academy. His vast, mysterious landscapes and seascapes, proclaiming human helplessness against the forces of nature, did much to establish the sublime as a primary focus of the Romantic movement. Interest in his work revived with the rise of Symbolism around the beginning of the 20th century.

Friel \'frēl\, **Brian** (born 1929) Irish dramatist and short-story writer. Born in Northern Ireland, he taught school in Londonderry before settling in Co. Donegal, Ireland. After the *New Yorker* began publishing his stories, he turned to writing full time. His first dramatic success was *Philadelphia, Here I Come!* (1963). Later he wrote about the dilemmas of Irish life and the troubles in Northern Ireland in such plays as *The Freedom of the City* (1973) and *Making History* (1988). Many of his plays—notably *Translations* (1980) and the *Dancing at Lughnasa* (1990, Tony Award; film, 1998)—deal with family relationships and their connection to language, customs, and the land. His short-story collections include *The Diviner* (1983).

Friendly, Fred W. *orig.* **Ferdinand Friendly Wachenheimer** (1915–1998) U.S. broadcast producer and journalist. Born in New York City, he began his career in radio in 1938 and later joined CBS. In the 1950s he collaborated with Edward R. Murrow to produce the radio news series *Hear It Now* and the television series *See It Now.* Friendly also produced *CBS Reports* (1961–71) and many special programs. He served as president of CBS News (1964–66), then taught at Columbia Univ.'s school of journalism. An outspoken critic of the quality of most TV programming, he became a communications adviser for the Ford Foundation (1966–80) and was instrumental in establishing the PBS network.

friendly society Mutual-aid organization formed voluntarily by individuals to protect members against debts incurred through illness, death, or old age. Friendly societies arose in 17th- and 18th-century Europe and England and became most numerous in the 19th century. They trace their roots to the burial societies of Greek and Roman artisans and the guilds of medieval Europe. In attempting to define the magnitude of the risk against which they guarded and to determine how much members should contribute to meet that risk, friendly societies used what is now the basic principle of insurance.

Friends, Society of *known as* **Quakers** Protestant denomination that arose in England in the mid-17th century. The movement began with radical English Puritans called Seekers, who rejected the Anglican church and other existing Protestant sects. They took their faith from itinerant preachers such as George Fox, who emphasized "inward light," or inward apprehension of God, as the source of religious authority. Quaker meetings are characterized by patient silence in which members wait for inspiration to speak. The movement grew rapidly after 1650 (when a judge gave them their name because "we bid them tremble at the word of God"), but its members were often persecuted or imprisoned for rejecting the state church and refusing to pay tithes or swear oaths. Some emigrated to America, where they were persecuted in Massachusetts Bay Colony but found toleration in Rhode Island and in the Quaker colony of Pennsylvania, which was chartered by Charles II under the sponsorship of William Penn in 1681. Other marks that became characteristic of Quakerism were plain speech and dress, pacifism, and opposition to slavery. The group also emphasizes philanthropy, especially aid to refugees and famine victims; the American Friends Service Committee and (British) Friends Service Council shared the 1947 Nobel Peace Prize.

Fries's Rebellion \'frēz\ (1799) Uprising, in opposition to a federal property tax, by farmers in eastern Pennsylvania. To raise money for an anticipated war with France, in 1798 the U.S. Congress voted a direct tax on real property. The tax was widely resented, and an armed group of German farmers, led by John Fries (c. 1750–1818), forced the release of tax resisters held by federal marshals. Pres. John Adams sent federal troops to arrest the rebels, who were tried for treason. Fries was convicted and sentenced to be hanged, but Adams pardoned him in 1800.

frieze \'frēz\ Any long, narrow, horizontal panel or ornamental band used for decorative purposes around the walls of a room or exterior walls of a building. In Greco-Roman architecture it is a horizontal band, often decorated with relief sculpture, between the architrave and cornice of a building. The most famous decorative frieze is on the outer wall of the PARTHENON in Athens, a 525-ft (160-m) representation of the ritual procession of the Panathenaic festival.

frigate \'fri-gət\ Either of two different types of warships, of the 17th–19th century and of World War II and after. The sailing ship known as a frigate was a three-masted, fully rigged vessel, often carrying 30–40 guns in all. Smaller and faster than SHIPS of the line, frigates served as scouts or as escorts protecting merchant convoys; they also cruised the seas as merchant raiders themselves. With the transition to steam, the term gradually gave way to CRUISER. In World War II, Britain revived the term frigate to describe escort ships equipped with SONAR and DEPTH CHARGES and used to guard convoys from submarines. In the postwar decades, it also adopted an antiaircraft role, adding RADAR and surface-to-air missiles. Modern frigates may displace more than 3,000 tons (2,700 metric tons), sail at a speed of 30 knots, and carry a crew of 200.

Battle between the frigates HMS *Shannon* and USS *Chesapeake* off Boston during the War of 1812; detail of a lithograph by J.C. Schetky.
THE NATIONAL MARITIME MUSEUM, LONDON

frigate bird *or* **man-o'-war bird** Any member of five species of large seabirds constituting the family Fregatidae, found worldwide along tropical and semitropical coasts and islands. About the size of a hen, frigate birds have extremely long, slender wings, which span up to about 8 ft (2.3 m), and long, deeply forked tails. Most adult males are all black; most females are marked with white below. Both sexes have a bare-skinned throat pouch, tiny feet, and a long hooked bill that is used to attack and rob other seabirds of their fish. The courting male's throat pouch becomes bright red and is inflated to the size of a person's head. Perhaps the most aerial of all birds except the SWIFTS, frigate birds land only to sleep or tend the nest.

Great frigate bird (*Fregata minor*).
JEN AND DES BARTLETT—BRUCE COLEMAN INC./EB INC.

Frigg \'frig\ *or* **Friia** \'frē-ə\ Norse goddess, the wife of ODIN and mother of BALDER. She was considered the patron of marriage and fertility. Some Icelandic stories depict her as a devoted mother, while others stress her loose morals. Frigg was also known to other Germanic peoples, and her name survives in the word Friday ("Friia's day").

Friml \'fri-məl\, **(Charles) Rudolf** (1879–1972) Czech-U.S. composer. Born in Prague, he studied under A. DVORAK, and he emigrated to the U.S. in 1906. In 1912, replacing V. HERBERT, he composed the highly successful operetta *The Firefly* (with Otto Harbach). The next major success of his approximately 30 operettas, *Rose Marie* (1924; with "Indian Love Call"), was followed by *The Vagabond King* (1925; with "Song of the Vagabonds" and "Some Day") and *The Three Musketeers* (1928), among the last operettas to enjoy popular success.

fringe benefit Any nonwage payment or benefit granted to employees by employers. Examples include PENSION plans, PROFIT-SHARING programs, vacation pay, and company-paid LIFE, HEALTH, and UNEMPLOYMENT INSURANCE. Employers' payments for fringe benefits are included in employee-compensation costs and therefore are not usually taxed. If the cost of fringe benefits were paid directly as wages, the worker would pay taxes on this amount and therefore have less to spend when purchasing equivalent benefits independently.

Frisch \'frish\, **Karl von** (1886–1982) Austrian-born zoologist, a pioneer of behavioral physiology. He received his PhD from the University of Munich, where he subsequently taught. Best known for his studies of bees, he found that bees communicate the distance and direction of a food supply to other members of the colony by two types of rhythmic movement, or dance. Circling indicates that food is within about 250 ft (75 m) of the hive; wagging indicates a greater distance. In 1949 he established that bees, through their perception of polarized light, use the sun as a compass even when it is not visible. He also established that fish can hear and distinguish colors. He shared a 1973 Nobel Prize with KONRAD LORENZ and NIKOLAAS TINBERGEN.

Frisch, Max (Rudolf) (1911–1991) Swiss dramatist and novelist. Originally a journalist, he later worked as an architect, a career he abandoned for writing in 1955. He is noted for his Expressionist depictions of the moral dilemmas of 20th-century life. His early drama *Santa Cruz* (1947) established the central theme of his subsequent works: the predicament of the complicated, skeptical individual in modern society. Other plays include *The Chinese Wall* (1947), *The Fire Raisers* (1958), and *Andorra* (1961). Among his novels are *I'm Not Stiller* (1954), *Homo Faber* (1957), *A Wilderness of Mirrors* (1964), and *Man in the Holocene* (1979).

Frisch \'frish\, **Ragnar (Anton Kittil)** (1895–1973) Norwegian economist. He received his PhD from the University of Oslo, and taught there from 1931 to 1965. He was a pioneer of ECONOMETRICS and one of the founders of the Econometric Society. He is famous for the development of large-scale econometric modeling linked to economic planning and national income accounting. In 1969 he shared the first Nobel Prize in Economics with JAN TINBERGEN.

Frisian Islands \'fri-zhən\ Chain of islands, North Sea. They extend 3–20 mi (5–32 km) off the northern European mainland, along the Dutch and German coasts and the southern part of Denmark's JUTLAND peninsula. Although they form a single physical feature, it is customary to subdivide them into the West Frisian Islands (owned by the Netherlands), East Frisian Islands (owned by Germany), and North Frisian Islands (owned by Germany and Denmark). The islands are separated from the mainland by shallow waters and tidal mud flats. The Dutch and German governments have spent large sums to protect the islands' seaward coasts and reclaim the land for farming. The beaches and resorts attract many tourists.

Frisian language \'fri-zhən\ West GERMANIC LANGUAGE most closely related to English. Formerly spoken from the province of North Holland in the Netherlands to the province of Schleswig in northern Germany, Frisian is now spoken only in three small areas, each with its own DIALECT. West Frisian is spoken in the province of Friesland in the Netherlands, East Frisian in the Saterland west of Oldenburg, Germany, and North Frisian along the western coast of Schleswig on the FRISIAN ISLANDS. Written records in Old Frisian date from the end of the 13th century. From the late 16th century to the late 19th century, written Frisian was seldom used. In modern times, there has been a revival of West Frisian, considered an official language by the Dutch government.

fritillary \'fri-tᵊl-ˌer-ē\ Any of the approximately 80 species of bulbous, mostly perennial, ornamental herbaceous plants that make up the genus *Fritillaria*, in the LILY FAMILY, native primarily to the northern temperate zone. Members have bell-shaped, nodding, usually solitary flowers. In many species the flower has a checkered appearance. The fruit, a CAPSULE, contains many seeds. Snake's head, or toad lily *(F. meleagris),* a species with poisonous bulbs, and crown imperial *(F. imperialis),* a strong-smelling plant, are commonly cultivated as garden flowers.

Snake's head (*Fritillaria meleagris*).
INGMAR HOLMASEN

fritillary \'fri-tᵊl-ˌer-ē\ Name applied to BUTTERFLIES in several genera (family Nymphalidae). Large fritillaries, or silverspots, belong to the genus *Speyeria* and usually have silver markings on the undersides of their wings. Many of the smaller fritillaries are members of the genus *Boloria.* Many fritillary larvae are nocturnal and feed on violet leaves.

Fritz, John *orig.* **Johann** (1822–1913) U.S. (German-born) authority on IRON and STEEL manufacture. He was associated with the Bethlehem Iron Co. from 1860 and was among the first to introduce the BESSEMER PROCESS in the U.S. He also introduced open-hearth furnaces (see OPEN-HEARTH PROCESS) and other improvements.

Friuli-Venezia Giulia \frē-'ü-lē-vā-'net-sē-ä-'jül-yä\ Autonomous region (pop., 1996 est.: 1,189,000), northeastern Italy. It borders on Austria, Slovenia, and the Adriatic Sea; its capital is TRIESTE. Known in Roman times as the Julian region, it was divided after the barbarian invasions into a coastal part, dominated by the Byzantines, and an inland zone, ruled by the dukes of Friuli and the counts of Gorizia. From the 15th century it was controlled by Austria and Venice, and after 1815 it came under HABSBURG rule. Divided after World War II between Yugoslavia and the free territory of Trieste, the region was restored to Italy in 1954. One of Italy's most seismic areas, it suffered a severe earthquake in 1976. It is known for its ham and dairy products. Its larger cities, including Trieste, have become industrialized.

Frizzell \fri-'zel\, **Lefty** *orig.* **William Orville** (1928–1975) U.S. singer and songwriter. Born in Corsicana, Texas, he was a fan of JIMMIE RODGERS from childhood. Also a semiprofessional boxer (the source of his nickname), Frizzell sang in honky-tonks and on radio in the Southwest, and had his first hit with "If You've Got the Money, I've Got the Time" (1950). He had several hits over the next two years, including "Always Late (with Your Kisses)," but his last and biggest hit was "Saginaw, Michigan" (1963). He died of a stroke at 47.

Froben \'frō-bən\, **Johann** *or* **Johannes Frobenius** (c. 1460–1527) German-Swiss scholar and printer active in Basel. His first publication was a Latin Bible (1491). By 1515 he and three partners owned four presses, and later seven. His contributions to printing in Basel included popularizing roman type, introducing italic and Greek fonts, experimenting with cheaper and smaller books, and employing talented artists, such as HANS, THE ELDER HOLBEIN the Younger, as illustrators. About 250 of his publications are known.

Frobisher, Martin *later* **Sir Martin** (1535?–1594) English navigator and early explorer of Canada's northeastern coast. Searching for a Northwest Passage to the Pacific Ocean, he crossed the Atlantic in 1576 and reached Labrador and Baffin Island, discovering FROBISHER BAY. Returning to England with reports of possible gold mines, he obtained royal backing for further expeditions in 1577 and 1578; when he brought back nothing of value, his backing collapsed. In 1585 he sailed as vice admiral of FRANCIS DRAKE's expedition to the West Indies, and in 1588 he played a prominent part in the campaign against the Spanish ARMADA.

Frobisher Bay \'frō-bi-shər\ Inlet of the North Atlantic Ocean. Extending northwest from the southeastern tip of BAFFIN ISLAND, Canada, it is about 150 mi (240 km) long and 20–40 mi (32–64 km) wide, and has a maximum depth of 400 ft (120 m). It was discovered in 1576 by MARTIN FROBISHER. The town of IQALUIT at the head of the bay is the capital of NUNAVUT.

Frobisher Bay See IQALUIT

Froebel \'frœ-bəl\, **Friedrich (Wilhelm August)** (1782–1852) German educator and founder of the KINDERGARTEN. Influenced by the theories of JOHANN HEINRICH PESTALOZZI, he founded an infant school in 1837 that he later called the Kindergarten, or "garden of children." He believed in "self-activity" and play as essential factors in child education, the teacher's role being not to drill or indoctrinate but rather to encourage self-expression through play. He greatly influenced modern techniques in PRESCHOOL EDUCATION, including the ideas of JOHN DEWEY.

frog Any of various tailless AMPHIBIANS in the order Anura. The name may be limited to any member of the family Ranidae (true frogs); more broadly, it often distinguishes smooth-skinned, leaping anurans from squat, warty, hopping ones (TOADS). Frogs generally have protruding eyes, strong, webbed hind feet adapted for leaping and swimming, and smooth, moist skin. Most are predominantly aquatic, but some live on land. They range in length (snout to anus) from 0.4 to 12 in. (9.8 mm–30 cm). Though frogs have poisonous skin glands, they rely on camouflage for protection from predators. Most eat insects and other small arthropods or worms, but several also eat other frogs, rodents, and reptiles. They usually breed in freshwater, where they lay eggs that hatch into TADPOLES. Since 1989 researchers have become increasingly alarmed by striking declines in frog populations worldwide, suspected to be linked to climatic factors or a fungal disease.

Costa Rican flying tree frog (*Agalychnis spurrelli*).
HEATHER ANGEL

froghopper See SPITTLEBUG

Froissart \frwä-'sär\, **Jean** (1333?–1400/01) French court historian and poet. As a scholar Froissart traveled widely and lived among the nobility of several European courts. His *Chronicles,* a firsthand narrative covering the HUNDRED YEARS' WAR from 1325 to 1400, including events in Flanders, Spain, Portugal, France, and England, is the most important and detailed document of feudal times and the best contemporary exposition of chivalric and courtly ideals. He also wrote ballades, rondeaux, and allegorical poetry celebrating courtly love.

Froissart (seated) writing his *Chroniques,* miniature from a mid-15th-century manuscript; in the Bibliothèque de l'Arsenal, Paris (Ms. 5190).
BY COURTESY OF THE BIBLIOTHEQUE DE L'ARSENAL, PARIS; PHOTOGRAPH, STUDIO STA PHOTO

Fromm, Erich (1900–1980) German-U.S. psychoanalyst and social philosopher. A disciple of SIGMUND FREUD, Fromm joined the FRANKFURT SCHOOL in the 1920s and left Nazi Germany for the U.S in 1933. Taking issue with Freud, he came to believe in the interaction of psychology and society and argued that psychoanalytic principles could be applied

E
F
G

to cure cultural ills. He taught at various institutions, including the National University of Mexico (1951–67) and NYU (from 1962). His many books, which had popular as well as academic success, included *Escape from Freedom* (1941), *The Sane Society* (1955), and *The Crisis of Psychoanalysis* (1970); *The Art of Loving* (1956) became a durable best-seller.

Fronde \'frō^{n}d\, **the** (1648–53) Series of civil wars in France during the minority of LOUIS XIV. The Fronde (named for the "sling" of a game played in the streets of Paris in defiance of authorities) was in part an attempt to check the growing power of royal government, but its failure paved the way for the absolutism of LOUIS XIV's reign. The first phase, the Fronde of the Parlement (1648–49), was an attempt to place constitutional limits on the queen regent, ANNE OF AUSTRIA, and her chief minister, JULES MAZARIN. Uprisings forced the government to concede to the Parlement's demands. The more serious second phase, the Fronde of the Princes (1650–53), sprang from aristocratic opposition to Mazarin. The military leader the Great CONDÉ was arrested, causing his friends to rebel (in the so-called first war of the princes). His supporters joined the Parisian party (the Old Fronde) in successfully calling for Condé's release and Mazarin's resignation. Condé lost his position when Anne joined with the Old Fronde against him, precipitating the second war of the princes (1651–53). After losses in battle, he fled. The king entered Paris in triumph in 1652, followed by Mazarin in 1653. The Fronde was the last serious challenge to the monarchy until the FRENCH REVOLUTION.

front In meteorology, the interface or transition zone between two air masses of different density and temperature. Frontal zones are frequently accompanied by low barometric pressure, marked changes in wind direction and relative humidity, and considerable cloudiness and precipitation.

Frontenac \frō^{n}-tə-'nåk\, **comte (Count) (de Palluau et) de** *orig.* **Louis de Buade** (1622–1698) French courtier and governor of New France (1672–82, 1689–98). Despite a record of misgovernment, he encouraged exploration that led to the expansion of the French empire in Canada. He established fur-trading posts that brought him into conflict with the Montreal fur traders, later expanding the posts west. He engaged in disputes with the officials and clergy of New France. The IROQUOIS CONFEDERACY, which had remained on good terms with the French until 1675, turned against the French, and the colony was left defenseless. LOUIS XIV recalled Frontenac in 1682; reappointed when the FRENCH AND INDIAN WAR started (1689), he distinguished himself by repulsing British attacks on Quebec.

Frontinus \frän-'tī-nəs\, **Sextus Julius** (c. AD 35–103?) Roman governor of Britain and author of *De aquis urbis Romae* ("The Waters of the City of Rome"). He was PRAETOR in Rome in 70; later made governor of Britain, he subdued the Silures in southeastern Wales (75) and held other tribes in check. In 97 he took charge of the aqueducts at Rome and compiled a history full of technical details and regulations governing their use and other matters of importance in the history of civil engineering.

frost Atmospheric moisture that crystallizes directly on the ground and on exposed objects. The term also refers to the occurrence of subfreezing temperatures that affect plants and crops. Frost crystals, sometimes called hoarfrost in the aggregate, form when water vapor in the atmosphere passes into the ice-crystal phase without going through the intermediate liquid phase. Frost forms under conditions that would form DEW if the temperature were above freezing. In agriculture, frost refers to the freezing of the water in plant cells, which causes the cells to burst and thereby destroys the plant.

Frost, David (Paradine) *later* **Sir David** (born 1939) British television producer. He worked in television from 1961 and hosted several programs in the U.S. and Britain, including *That Was the Week That Was* (1962–63) and *The Frost Reports* (1966–67). He conducted interviews with world leaders on *The David Frost Show* (1969–72), winning two Emmy awards. He was a cofounder of London Weekend Television and in 1983 of Britain's TV-AM.

Frost, Robert (Lee) (1874–1963) U.S. poet. He was born in San Francisco, but his family soon moved to New England. After stints at Dartmouth and Harvard colleges and a difficult period as a teacher and farmer, he moved to England and published his first collections, *A Boy's Will* (1913) and *North of Boston* (1914). At the outbreak of war he returned to New England to farm and to pursue a distinguished teaching career at Amherst and Dartmouth colleges and elsewhere. He acutely observed the details of rural life and in his poetry endowed them with universal, even metaphysical, meaning, using colloquial language, familiar rhythms, and symbols taken from common life to express both the pastoral ideals and the dark complexities of New England life. His collections include *Mountain Interval* (1916), *New Hampshire* (1923; Pulitzer Prize), *West-Running Brook* (1928), *Collected Poems* (1930; Pulitzer Prize), *A Further Range* (1936; Pulitzer Prize), *A Witness Tree* (1942; Pulitzer Prize), *Steeple Bush* (1947), and *In the Clearing* (1962). He was unique among American poets of the 20th century in simultaneously achieving wide popularity and deep critical admiration.

Robert Frost, 1954.
RUOHOMAA–BLACK STAR

frostbite Freezing of living tissue, when it loses enough heat in below-freezing weather for ice to form. High winds, wet skin, tight clothes, and alcohol use increase the risk of frostbite. Cell damage, tissue dehydration, and oxygen depletion caused by freezing and thawing can lead to blood-cell disruption, clotting in capillaries, and GANGRENE. The toes, fingers, ears, and nose are usually affected first, becoming cold, hard, white, or bloodless. The lack of pain is dangerous. Core temperature should be brought to near normal before rapid thawing in warm (under 115°F, or 46°C) water. Toxoid booster injections are recommended. The outlook is best when freezing is short-term, thawing is by rapid rewarming, and large blisters extending to the end of the part develop early. Tissue that is refrozen after thawing must almost always be amputated. Affected parts become more susceptible to recurrence. Frostbite is best prevented by wearing dry, layered, loose clothing and remaining alert. See also HYPOTHERMIA, TEMPERATURE STRESS.

froth flotation See FLOTATION

frottage \frò-'täzh\ (French: "rubbing") Technique of obtaining an impression of a raised, incised, or textured surface by placing a piece of paper over it and rubbing it with a soft pencil or crayon. Brass rubbings taken from gravestones and funerary monuments are obtained in this way. MAX ERNST pioneered the technique in the 20th century. It was much favored by the Surrealists, since it provided a point of departure for a painting or collage expressing the imagery of the subconscious.

Froude \'früd\, **James Anthony** (1818–1894) English historian and biographer. He was influenced by the Oxford Movement, which sought a renewal of Roman Catholic practices within the Church of England, but later broke with it. Among his historical works, which display both carelessness and his anti-Catholic bias, the best known is *History of England from the Fall of Wolsey to the Defeat of the Spanish Armada* (1856–70), which fundamentally altered the direction of Tudor studies. Immensely prolific, he was attacked by reviewers but was popular with the reading public. He later produced a biography (1882–84) of his friend THOMAS CARLYLE.

Froude, William (1810–1879) British engineer and naval architect. The brother of JAMES ANTHONY FROUDE, in 1837 he became an assistant to I. K. BRUNEL, for whom he oversaw railway construction. For the British Admiralty he conducted experiments using scale models of ships to determine the physical laws governing full-sized ships, using a testing tank he built at his home. The information he gained greatly influenced ship design for many decades, and a similar technique was later used by pioneers in aerodynamics. Late in life he built a successful dynamometer for use on large marine engines.

Fructidor \früẹk-tē-'dòr, *Engl* 'frək-ti-ˌdòr\, **Coup of 18** (September 4, 1799) Purge of ultraconservatives during the French DIRECTORY period. Fearing it was losing popularity, the government called for a general to command troops guarding the legislative assembly at the Tuileries. On 18 Fructidor, year V, Gen. Pierre F. C. Augereau (1757–1816) purged more than 130 royalists and counterrevolutionaries from the legislative body; many others, including journalists and a director, were deported to French Guiana. The republican constitution was also overthrown, which confirmed the new power of the army and led to the Coup of 18–19 BRUMAIRE and NAPOLEON's military despotism.

fructose \'frək-ˌtōs, 'frük-ˌtōs\ *or* **levulose** \'lev-yə-ˌlōs\ *or* **fruit sugar** Organic compound, one of the simple SUGARS (MONOSACCHARIDES), chemical formula $C_6H_{12}O_6$. It occurs in fruits, honey, syrups (especially corn syrup), and certain vegetables, usually along with its ISOMER, GLUCOSE. Fructose and glucose are the components of the disaccharide SUCROSE (table sugar); HYDROLYSIS of sucrose yields "invert sugar," a 50:50 mixture of fructose and glucose. The sweetest of the common sugars, fructose is used in foods and medicines.

fruit In its strict botanical sense, the fleshy or dry ripened ovary (enlarged portion of the PISTIL) of a FLOWERING PLANT, enclosing the seed or seeds. APRICOTS, BANANAS, and GRAPES, as well as BEAN pods, CORN grains, TOMATOES, CUCUMBERS, and (in their shells) ACORNS and ALMONDS, are all technically fruits. Popularly, the term is restricted to the ripened ovaries that are sweet and either succulent or pulpy. The principal botanical purpose of the fruit is to protect and spread the seed. There are two broad categories of fruit: fleshy and dry. Fleshy fruits include BERRIES, such as tomatoes, oranges, and cherries, which consist entirely of succulent tissue; aggregate fruits, including BLACKBERRIES and STRAWBERRIES, which form from a single flower with many PISTILS, each of which develops into fruitlets; and multiple fruits, such as PINEAPPLES and mulberries, which develop from the mature ovaries of an entire INFLORESCENCE. Dry fruits include the LEGUMES, CEREAL grains, CAPSULES, and NUTS. Fruits are important sources of dietary fiber and vitamins (especially vitamin C). They can be eaten fresh; processed into juices, jams, and jellies; or preserved by dehydration, canning, fermentation, and pickling.

fruit bat Any of numerous tropical Old World BATS in the family Pteropodidae, distributed widely from Africa to South Asia and Australasia. Most species rely on vision rather than on ECHOLOCATION to avoid obstacles. Some species are solitary, some gregarious; most roost in the open in trees, though some inhabit caves, rocks, or buildings. Some are red or yellow, and some are striped or spotted. They eat fruit or flowers (including pollen and nectar). The smallest species in the family, the long-tongued fruit bats, reach a head and body length of about 2.5 in. (6–7 cm) and a wingspan of about 10 in. (25 cm). The same family contains the largest of all bats, the flying foxes, which attain lengths up to 16 in. (40 cm) and a wingspan of 5 ft (1.5 m).

fruit fly Any DIPTERAN species of two families: large fruit flies (Trypetidae) and small fruit flies, or vinegar flies (family Drosophilidae; see DROSOPHILA). The larvae feed on fruit or other vegetation. The adults' wings are banded or spotted with brown. Many species attack cultivated fruits, sometimes causing enough damage to create significant economic loss. Some species are LEAF MINERS; others burrow in plant stems. Well-known fruit-fly pests include the MEDITERRANEAN FRUIT FLY and the apple maggot of the U.S., the Mexican and Oriental fruit flies, and the olive fruit fly of the Mediterranean region.

Fruit fly (Trypetidae).
E.S. ROSS

Frunze See BISHKEK

Frunze \'frün-zyə\, **Mikhail (Vasilyevich)** (1885–1925) Soviet army officer and military theorist. An active revolutionary from 1905, he became an outstanding commander in the RUSSIAN CIVIL WAR. With the support of JOSEPH STALIN, Frunze replaced LEON TROTSKY as commissar for war in 1925. His "unitary military doctrine" asserted that the army should be trained to offensive action, united by its determination to carry out the Communist Party's task of promoting world revolution. He introduced peacetime compulsory military service and standardized military formations, drills, and uniforms. Frunze is regarded as one of the fathers of the RED ARMY.

Fry, Christopher *orig.* **Christopher Harris** (born 1907) British playwright. He worked as an actor, director, and playwright before achieving success with *The Lady's Not for Burning* (1948), an ironic medieval comedy in verse. Noted for his wit and his religious preoccupations, he wrote other verse plays including *Venus Observed* (1950), *A Sleep of Prisoners* (1951), *The Dark Is Light Enough* (1954), and *A Yard of Sun* (1970). He also wrote several television plays and collaborated on the screenplays of *Ben Hur* (1959) and *Barabbas* (1962).

Fry, Roger (Eliot) (1866–1934) British art critic and artist. He gave up a career in science to study art in Italy. As a curator at the Metropolitan Museum of Art (1906–10), he discovered the work of the Postimpressionists, and in 1910 he introduced the Postimpressionists to Britain by organizing the first of two highly significant exhibitions. With CLIVE BELL, he preached the importance of "significant form" over content in the artwork. Associated with the BLOOMSBURY GROUP, he and several group members cofounded the Omega Workshops for arts and crafts in 1913. He was known as a brilliant lecturer and the author of numerous books.

Frye, (Herman) Northrop (1912–1991) Canadian literary critic. Born in Sherbrooke, Quebec, he was educated in Canada and Britain and from 1939 taught at Victoria College. In *Anatomy of Criticism* (1957), his most influential work, he analyzed various modes of literary criticism and stressed the recurring importance of archetypal symbols in literature. His other critical works include the influential *Fearful Symmetry: A Study of William Blake* (1947), *The Well-Tempered Critic* (1963), *The Secular Scripture* (1976), *The Great Code: The Bible and Literature* (1982), and *Northrop Frye on Shakespeare* (1986).

FTP *in full* **file transfer protocol** INTERNET PROTOCOL that allows a computer to send files to or receive files from another computer. Like many Internet resources, FTP works by means of a CLIENT-SERVER ARCHITECTURE; the user runs client software to connect to a SERVER on the Internet. On the FTP server, a program called a daemon allows the user to download and upload files. Before the WORLD WIDE WEB was introduced, FTP was one of the most popular methods of exchanging information over the Internet and many Web sites still use it to disseminate their larger files.

Fuchau See FUZHOU

Fuchs \'fu̇ks\, **(Emil) Klaus (Julius)** (1911–1988) German physicist and spy. He joined the German Communist Party in 1930 but fled Germany after the Nazi takeover in 1933. He settled in Britain, earned a doctorate at the University of Edinburgh, and became a British citizen in 1942. He worked on the ATOMIC BOMB in Britain and the U.S. In 1943 he began passing scientific secrets to the Soviet Union, which accelerated Soviet development of the atomic bomb by at least a year. His activities were detected in 1950 and he was imprisoned until 1959. After his release, he moved to East Germany, where he was appointed deputy director of the Central Institute for Nuclear Research.

fuchsia \'fyü-shə\ Any of about 100 species of flowering shrubs and trees in the genus *Fuchsia* (family Onagraceae), native to tropical and subtropical regions of Central and South America and to New Zealand and Tahiti. Several species are grown in gardens as bedding plants, small shrubs, or miniature treelike specimens; others are grown as pot plants or in hanging baskets for indoor or greenhouse cultivation. Fuchsias are valued for their showy pendulous flowers, tubular to bell-shaped, in shades of red and purple to white.

fuel cell Device that converts CHEMICAL ENERGY of a fuel directly into ELECTRICITY (see ELECTROCHEMISTRY). Fuel cells are intrinsically more efficient than most other energy-conversion devices. Electrolytic chemical reactions cause ELECTRONS to be released on one ELECTRODE and flow through an external circuit to a second electrode. Whereas in BATTERIES the electrodes are the source of the active ingredients, which are altered and depleted during the reaction, in fuel cells the gas or liquid fuel (often hydrogen, methyl alcohol, hydrazine, or a simple hydrocarbon) is supplied continuously to one electrode and oxygen or air to the other from an external source. So, as long as fuel and oxidant are supplied, the fuel cell will not run down or require recharging. Fuel cells can be used in place of virtually any other source of electricity. They are especially being developed for use in ELECTRIC AUTOMOBILES, in the hope of achieving enormous reductions in pollution.

fuel injection In an INTERNAL-COMBUSTION ENGINE, introduction of fuel into the cylinders by a pump rather than by the suction created by the movement of the pistons (see PISTON AND CYLINDER). On DIESEL ENGINES, which lack SPARK PLUGS, the heat created by compressing air in the cylinders ignites the fuel, which has been pumped in as a spray. In engines with spark ignition, fuel-injection pumps are often used instead of conventional CARBURETORS. Fuel injection distributes the fuel more evenly to the cylinders than does a carburetor; more power can be developed and undesirable emissions are reduced. In engines with continuous combustion, such as gas TURBINES and liquid-fueled ROCKETS, which have no pistons to create suction, fuel-injection systems are necessary.

Fuentes \fü-'en-tās\, **Carlos** (born 1928) Mexican writer and diplomat. The son of a career diplomat, he traveled widely before studying law and entering the diplomatic service. He is best known for his experimental novels. His first, *Where the Air Is Clear* (1958), a bitter indictment of Mexican society, won him national prestige. *The Death of Artemio Cruz* (1962), about the final hours of an unscrupulous former revolutionary, made his international reputation. Among his later novels are *Terra Nostra* (1975), *The Hydra Head* (1978), *Distant Relations* (1980), and *The Old Gringo* (1985). *The Buried Mirror* (1992) is a long essay on Hispanic cultures.

Fugard \fü-'gärd\, **Athol (Harold Lannigan)** (born 1932) South African playwright, director, and actor. He wrote two plays before *The Blood Knot* (1961), a penetrating analysis of apartheid, established his international reputation. He resumed the theme in *Hello and Goodbye* (1965) and *Boesman and Lena* (1969; film, 1973, with Fugard as Boesman). He experimented with an imagist approach to drama in *Orestes* (1971) and three other works, then returned to more traditionally structured plays. His *"Master Harold" . . . and the Boys* (1982), *The Road to Mecca* (1984), and *My Children! My Africa!* (1989) were acclaimed in London and New York. Fugard acted in *Marigolds in August* (1980), *Gandhi* (1982), and *The Killing Fields* (1984).

Fugger family \'fü-gər\ German mercantile and banking dynasty that dominated European business in the 15th–16th century. The family traced its origins to Hans (Johannes) Fugger (1348–1409), a weaver in Augsburg. Under his grandsons Ulrich (1441–1510), Georg (1453–1506), and especially Jakob (1459–1525), the company became established in international trade, including the lucrative spice and slave trades, and built a fortune in copper and silver mining. Their loans to various kings and emperors and involvement with the sale of papal INDULGENCES made the family highly influential in European politics and earned them the criticism of MARTIN LUTHER. It declined after the 16th century, but three titled lines survived into the 20th century.

Fugitive Slave Acts U.S. laws of 1793 and 1850 (repealed in 1864) that provided for the seizure and return of runaway slaves. The 1793 law authorized a judge alone to decide the status of an alleged fugitive slave. Northern opposition led to enactment of state personal-liberty laws that entitled slaves to a jury trial and as early as 1810 prompted individuals to aid the UNDERGROUND RAILROAD. Increased pressure from the South brought passage of the second statute in 1850, as part of the COMPROMISE OF 1850. It imposed penalties on federal marshals who refused to enforce the law and on individuals who helped slaves to escape; fugitives could not testify on their own behalf, nor were they permitted a jury trial. Its severity led to increased interest in the abolition movement. Additional personal-liberty laws enacted by northern states to thwart the act were cited by South Carolina as justification for its SECESSION in 1860.

fugue \'fyüg\ Musical composition characterized by systematic imitation of one or more themes in COUNTERPOINT. Fugues vary greatly in their actual form. The principal theme (subject) is imitated—i.e., repeated successively in similar form at different pitch levels by different parts or voices—in the so-called exposition. The countersubject is the continuation of the subject that accompanies the subject theme's subsequent entries in the other voices. Episodes using modified themes often separate the subject's entries. The fugue emerged gradually from the imitative polyphony of the 13th century. J.S. BACH's keyboard fugues are the most famous of all. The works of Bach and G.F. HANDEL inspired the later fugues of W.A. MOZART, LUDWIG VAN BEETHOVEN, and others, many of whom commonly included fugues in the final movements of symphonies, string quartets, and sonatas.

Fuji, Mt. *Japanese* **Fujisan** Mountain, central Japan. The highest mountain in Japan, it rises to 12,388 ft (3,776 m) near the Pacific coast in central HONSHU. Mount Fuji, with its graceful volcanic cone (dormant since 1707), has become famous internationally. It is considered a sacred symbol of Japan, and thousands of Japanese climb to the shrine on its peak every summer. The mountain is the major feature of Fuji-Hakone-Izu National Park, created in 1936.

Fujian \'fü-'jyen\ *or* **Fukien** \'fü-'kyen\ Province (pop., 1996 est.: 32,370,000), southeastern China. Located on the southeastern coast, it is bounded by ZHEJIANG, the CHINA SEA, Taiwan Strait, GUANGDONG, and JIANGXI; its capital is FUZHOU. The province's boundaries were established during the SONG DYNASTY (1127–1279), when it became an important shipbuilding and commercial center for overseas and coastal trade. It declined when the MING DYNASTY (1368–1644) banned maritime commerce. Its coastal cities were occupied by the Japanese in World War II, and it was taken by the Communist regime in 1949. In addition to being an important agricultural region, it is an area of special economic zones established in 1979 to attract foreign investment to China.

Fujimori \ˌfü-jē-'mó-rē\, **Alberto (Kenyo)** (born 1938) President of Peru (1990–2000). The son of Japanese immigrants, he graduated from Agrarian National University in 1961. He served as its rector 1984–89, and only entered politics in 1989 at the head of the new political party Cambio 90 ("Change 90"). He won a surprise victory in the 1990 presidential election and implemented fiscal-austerity measures that controlled Peru's severe inflation and indebtedness. In 1992 he dissolved the National Congress and took other steps to concentrate power in the presidency. He claimed credit for the capture of the leader of the SHINING PATH rebel movement later that year and, in 1997, the successful storming of the Japanese ambassador's residence in Lima, where TUPAC AMARÚ guerrillas had held dozens of hostages. He was reelected in 1995 and asserted victory, despite charges of fraud, in the 2000 election, but scandal involving his secret-police chief caused him to flee to Japan. The Japanese government declared in 2001 that he had dual Peruvian-Japanese citizenship.

Fujiwara family \'fü-jē-'wä-rä\ Dynastic family that dominated Japanese court government in the 9th–12th century. The family maintained a close relationship to the imperial family by marrying its daughters to emperors so that their grandsons and nephews became emperors. The Fujiwara acted as regents for child emperors and later created the post of *kampaku,* or chancellor, essentially a regent for an adult emperor. Fujiwara Michinaga (966–1028), who married three daughters to emperors and a fourth to an heir apparent, epitomized Fujiwara power and glory; his ascendancy marked the height of the HEIAN PERIOD and saw the creation of MURASAKI SHIKIBU's *Tale of Genji.* The family's power at court waned after Michinaga and was eliminated in the 12th century. See also SUGAWARA MICHIZANE.

Fujiwara style Japanese sculptural style of the late HEIAN PERIOD (897–1185). The style of the principal icons accorded with the emotional appeal of PURE LAND BUDDHISM, introduced to counter the older esoteric sects. The sculpted figures, though still full and fleshy, were more elegant and heavily polychromed, with elaborate cut-gold *(kirikane)* patterns in the drapery. The facial type was aristocratic. Delicacy of expression was achieved by a joined-wood technique invented by JOCHO. Interest in decorative effects can be seen in the applied jewelry, which in earlier periods had been painted or modeled on the sculpture's surface.

Fukuoka \ˌfü-kü-'ō-kä\ City (pop., 1995: 1,285,000) and port, Japan. It incorporates the former city of Hakata and is located on the southern coast of Hakata Bay. An ancient port, it was the scene of attempted invasions by KUBLAI KHAN in the 13th century. It is now a regional commercial, industrial, administrative, and cultural center. It contains an active fishing port and is the site of Kyushu University (1911). Hakata

Kichijo-ten (Sanskrit Mahasri; the goddess of good luck), Fujiwara style polychromed wood sculpture, late 12th century, Late Heian period; at Joruri-ji, near Nara, Japan.
ASUKA-EN, JAPAN

ningyo, elaborately costumed ceramic figurines found in most Japanese homes, are made there.

Fulani \'fü-ˌlä-nē\ Primarily Muslim people, numbering about 18 million, found in many parts of western Africa, from Lake Chad west to the Atlantic coast. Their language is Fula (of the ATLANTIC LANGUAGES of the NIGER-CONGO family). Originally they were herders, but interaction with other groups produced marked cultural changes. In the 1790s the Fulani priest USMAN DAN FODIO led a holy war (JIHAD) that created a large empire. Its decay in the 19th century aided the establishment of British rule over northern Nigeria. Many Fulani of northern Nigeria have adopted the HAUSA LANGUAGE and culture and established themselves as an urban aristocracy.

Fulani chieftain riding up to salute the emir of Katsina at the end of the Muslim festival of Ramadan in northern Nigeria.
KEN HEYMAN—RAPHO/PHOTO RESEARCHERS

Fulbright, J(ames) William (1905–1995) U.S. politician. Born in Sumner, Mo., he earned degrees from the University of Arkansas and Oxford Univ.; he returned to the University of Arkansas to teach law, and served as its president 1939–41. In 1942 he was elected to the U.S. House of Representatives, where in 1943 he introduced a resolution favoring U.S. participation in what would become the U.N. In the U.S. Senate (1945–75), he initiated the international exchange program known as the FULBRIGHT SCHOLARSHIP. As chairman of the foreign-relations committee (1959–74), he presided over influential televised hearings in 1966 on U.S. policy in the VIETNAM WAR and became a leading advocate for ending the bombing of North Vietnam and opening peace talks. In 1974 he lost his bid for reelection.

Fulbright scholarship Educational grant under an international exchange program created to increase understanding between the U.S and other countries. The program was conceived by Sen. J. WILLIAM FULBRIGHT and instituted by the Fulbright Act of 1946 and the Fulbright-Hays Act of 1961. Most participants are graduate students, but teachers, advanced researchers, trainees, and observers may also qualify. The program is administered by the U.S. Dept. of State.

Fulda River River, central Germany. Rising in the Rhön Mtns., it flows north to unite with the Werra at Münden and form the WESER RIVER; it is 135 mi (218 km) long. The river valley served as a trade route between northern and southern Germany during the Middle Ages. Today the Fulda basin has many recreational areas.

Fuller, J(ohn) F(rederick) C(harles) (1878–1966) British military theoretician and historian. He served as chief of staff of the British tank corps in World War I. He planned the surprise attack of 381 tanks at the Battle of Cambrai (November 20, 1917), the first massed tank assault in history. After the war he launched a crusade for the mechanization and modernization of the British army. His emphasis on the armored offensive met with resistance among English military tacticians, but his teachings were largely vindicated by World War II. His works include *Tanks in the Great War* (1920), *Machine Warfare* (1942), and *A Military History of the Western World* (1954–56).

Loie Fuller.
BY COURTESY OF THE DANCE COLLECTION, THE NEW YORK PUBLIC LIBRARY AT LINCOLN CENTER

Fuller, Loie *orig.* **Marie Louise Fuller** (1862–1928) U.S. improvisational dance performer and pioneer of modern dance. Born in Fullersburg, Ill., she began acting at age 4, appearing with stock companies and vaudeville shows. From 1892 in Paris she gained attention with her "serpentine dance," in which she used yards of flowing silk illuminated by theatrical lighting. She added a "fire dance" (dancing on an illuminated pane of glass) and other acts, attracting critical and public adulation, especially in Europe.

Fuller, (Sarah) Margaret (1810–1850) U.S. critic, teacher, and woman of letters. Born in Cambridgeport, Mass., she became part of the Transcendentalist circle (see TRANSCENDENTALISM), a close friend of RALPH WALDO EMERSON, and eventually the founding editor of the Trancendentalist magazine *The Dial* (1840–42). Her *Summer on the Lakes, in 1843* (1844), a study of frontier life, was followed by *Woman in the Nineteenth Century* (1845), a demand for women's political equality and a plea for women's intellectual and spiritual fulfillment. She traveled to Europe in 1846 as a correspondent for the *New York Tribune*. In Italy she married a revolutionary marquis; forced into exile, they perished in a shipwreck off Fire Island, N.Y., while returning to the U.S.

Fuller, Melville (Weston) (1833–1910) U.S. jurist. Born in Augusta, Me., he graduated from Bowdoin College and Harvard Law School. He built up a major legal practice in Chicago (from 1856), becoming prominent in Democratic politics. Though unknown nationally, he was appointed chief justice of the U.S. Supreme Court in 1888 by Pres. GROVER CLEVELAND; he would remain on the Court until his death. His colleagues included OLIVER WENDELL, JR. HOLMES, and JOHN MARSHALL HARLAN. He wrote an opinion on the *POLLOCK VS. FARMERS' LOAN AND TRUST CO.* case. He served on the Hague Court of International Arbitration 1900–10.

Fuller, R(ichard) Buckminster (1895–1983) U.S. inventor, futurist, architect, and author. The grandnephew of MELVILLE FULLER, he was born in Milton, Mass. Expelled twice from Harvard Univ., he never completed his college education. Failure in a prefab construction business led him to search for design patterns that would most efficiently use the earth's resources for humanity's greatest good. His innovations included the inexpensive, lightweight, factory-assembled Dymaxion House and the energy-efficient, omnidirectional Dymaxion Car. He developed a vectorial system of geometry that he called "Energetic-Synergetic geometry"; its basic unit is the tetrahedron, which, when combined with octahedrons, forms the most economic space-filling structures, which led Fuller to the geodesic dome.

fullerene Any of a class of closed, hollow compounds discovered in 1985, ALLOTROPES of CARBON whose MOLECULES have 12 pentagonal and differing numbers of hexagonal faces. The best known, C_{60} (buckminsterfullerene, or "buckyballs"), has the shape of a standard soccer ball. It is named for R. BUCKMINSTER FULLER, whose geodesic dome design is similar to its molecular structure. The molecules are exceptionally stable, withstanding high temperatures and pressures. Certain other molecules can become trapped in the hollow interior, a unique and exciting feature.

Fullerton City (pop., 1996 est.: 120,000), southern California. Laid out in 1887, it developed as a citrus center after the arrival of the Santa Fe Railroad in 1888. Residential and industrial growth has been rapid since World War II. The city produces transportation equipment, aircraft parts, and oil.

fulling *or* **felting** *or* **milling** Process that increases the thickness and compactness of WOOL by subjecting it to moisture, heat, friction, and pressure until shrinkage of 10–25% is achieved. Shrinkage occurs in both the warp and weft (see WEAVING), producing a smooth, tightly finished fabric that may be so compact that it resembles felt.

fulmar \'fu̇l-mər, 'fu̇l-ˌmär\ Any of several species of gull-like oceanic birds in the family Procellariidae. The northern fulmar *(Fulmaris glacialis)* ranges from temperate to Arctic waters, and the southern fulmar *(F. glacialoides)* from temperate to Antarctic waters. The much larger giant fulmar, or giant petrel *(Macronectes giganteus),* is 3 ft (90 cm) long and has a wingspan of more than 6.5 ft (200 cm). It nests around the Antarctic Circle. Fulmars eat almost anything; their natural foods are small fish, squid, and crustaceans, but they often take ships' garbage and will come ashore for carrion. They fly low over the waves of the open ocean, thus resembling their narrower-winged relatives, the SHEARWATERS, in flight.

Fulton, Robert (1765–1815) U.S. inventor and engineer. Born in Pennsylvania to Irish immigrant parents, he studied painting with BENJAMIN

WEST in London but soon turned to engineering. After designing a system of inland waterways, he tried unsuccessfully to interest the French and British governments in his prototypes of submarines (see *NAUTILUS*) and torpedoes. In 1801 he was commissioned by ROBERT R. LIVINGSTON to build a steamboat, and in 1807 Fulton's *Clermont* made the 150-mi (240-km) journey up the Hudson from New York to Albany in 32 hours, cutting 64 hours off the usual sailing time. It became the first commercially successful steamboat in the U.S. He later designed several other steamboats, including the world's first steam warship (1812). He was a member of the commission that recommended building the ERIE CANAL.

fumarole \'fyü-mə-ˌrōl\ Vent from which volcanic vapors issue. Fumaroles, like geysers, are caused by HOT SPRINGS, which disperse groundwater from the upper parts of the earth's CRUST after it has been heated by MAGMA. As magma begins to solidify, the gases in it, mostly water vapor, become concentrated by the pressure of the remaining liquid. When the pressure becomes high enough, the liquid is forced into cracks in the surrounding rock. A fumarole forms if a crack extends to the surface.

Funafuti \ˌfü-nä-'fü-tē\ Coral atoll (pop., 1995 est.: 4,000), location of capital of TUVALU, western central Pacific Ocean. It comprises some 30 islets, including Fongafale, Tuvalu's administrative center, and has a total land area of 0.9 sq mi (2.4 sq km). It encircles a lagoon that affords good anchorage. A U.S. military base was established there in 1943; the U.S. dropped its claim to the atoll in 1983. Fongafale village has a hotel, a hospital, and an airstrip.

Funchal \fün-'shäl\ City (pop., 1991: 126,000) and capital of the autonomous region of MADEIRA, Portugal. Lying on the southern coast of Madeira island in the North Atlantic, it is the center of industry, commerce, and communications for Madeira. It was founded in 1421 by the Portuguese navigator João Gonçalves Zarco and later came under Spanish (1580–1640) and British (1807–14) control. The city's scenery and mild year-round climate attract many tourists.

function In mathematics, an expression, rule, or law that defines a relationship between one VARIABLE (the independent variable) and another (the dependent variable), which changes along with it. Most functions are numerical; that is, a numerical input value is associated with a single numerical output value. The formula $A = \pi r^2$, for example, assigns to each positive real number r the area A of a circle with a radius of that length. The symbols $f(x)$ and $g(x)$ are typically used for functions of the independent variable x. A multivariable function such as $w = f(x,y)$ is a rule for deriving a single numerical value from more than one input value. A periodic function repeats values over fixed intervals. If $f(x + k) = f(x)$ for any value of x, f is a periodic function with a period of length k (a constant). The TRIGONOMETRIC FUNCTIONS are periodic. See also DENSITY FUNCTION, EXPONENTIAL FUNCTION, HYPERBOLIC FUNCTION, INVERSE FUNCTION, TRANSCENDENTAL FUNCTION.

functional analysis Branch of mathematical ANALYSIS dealing with functionals, or FUNCTIONS of functions. It emerged as a distinct field in the 20th century, when it was realized that diverse mathematical processes, from arithmetic to CALCULUS procedures, exhibit very similar properties. A functional, like a function, is a relationship between objects, but the objects may be numbers, vectors, or functions. Groupings of such objects are called spaces. DIFFERENTIATION is an example of a functional because it defines a relationship between a function and another function (its derivative). INTEGRATION is also a functional. Functional analysis focuses on classes of functions, such as those that can be differentiated or integrated.

functional group In MOLECULES, any of numerous combinations of ATOMS that undergo characteristic CHEMICAL REACTIONS themselves and in many cases influence the reactivity of the rest of the molecule. Organic compounds are often classified according to the functional groups they contain. Common functional groups include hydroxyl (—OH), in ALCOHOLS and PHENOLS; carboxyl (—COOH), in CARBOXYLIC ACIDS; carbonyl (—C=O), in ALDEHYDES, KETONES, AMIDES, CARBOXYLIC ACIDS, ESTERS, and QUINONES; and NITRO ($—NO_2$) and amino ($—NH_2$), in certain organic nitrogen compounds.

Functionalism In architecture, the doctrine that a building's form should be determined by practical considerations of use, material, and structure, and not by a preconceived picture in the designer's mind. Though not an exclusively modern conception, it is closely associated with the modernist architecture of the second quarter of the 20th century. The fight for an "honest" form of expression on the part of LOUIS SULLIVAN, LE CORBUSIER, and others came about as a result of changes in building techniques, new types of buildings required, and discontent with historical revivalism, which had been paramount in the 19th and early 20th century.

functionalism In the social sciences, a theory that stresses the interdependence of the patterns and institutions of a society and their interaction in maintaining cultural and social unity. In sociology, functionalism emerged from the work of É. DURKHEIM, who viewed society as a kind of "organism" that carried with it certain "needs" that must be fulfilled. Similar views were adopted in anthropology by A. R. RADCLIFFE-BROWN, who attempted to explain social structures as enduring systems of adaptation, fusion, and integration; and by BRONISLAW MALINOWSKI, who looked at culture as the expression of the totality of individual and collective achievement, where "every custom, material object, idea and belief fulfills some vital function." The U.S. sociologist TALCOTT PARSONS analyzed large-scale societies in terms of their social, psychological, and cultural components and focused on problems of social order, integration, and equilibrium. Later writers argued that functionalism was too rigid to account for the breadth, depth, and contingencies of human social life and that it ignored the role of history in shaping society.

functionalism In psychology, a broad school of thought that originated in the U.S. in the late 19th century and emphasized the total organism in its endeavors to adjust to the environment. Reacting against the school of structuralism led by EDWARD BRADFORD TITCHENER, functionalists such as WILLIAM JAMES, GEORGE HERBERT MEAD, and JOHN DEWEY stressed the importance of empirical, rational thought over an experimental trial-and-error philosophy. The movement concerned itself primarily with the practical applications of research (see APPLIED PSYCHOLOGY) and was critical of early forms of BEHAVIORISM.

fundamental interaction In physics, the effect of any of the four fundamental forces—gravitational, electromagnetic, strong, and weak. All known natural forces can be traced to these fundamental interactions. GRAVITATION is the attractive force between any two objects that have MASS; it causes objects to fall to the ground and maintains the orbits of planets around the sun. ELECTROMAGNETIC FORCE is responsible for the attraction and repulsion between ELECTRIC CHARGES and explains the chemical behavior of ATOMS and the properties of LIGHT. The STRONG FORCE binds QUARKS together in PROTONS, NEUTRONS, and other HADRONS, and also holds the protons and neutrons of an atomic NUCLEUS together, overcoming the repulsion of the positively charged protons for each other. The WEAK FORCE is observed in certain forms of radioactive decay (see RADIOACTIVITY) and in reactions that fuel the sun and other stars.

fundamentalism, Christian Conservative Protestant movement that arose out of 19th-century MILLENNIALISM in the U.S. It emphasized as fundamental the literal truth of the Bible, the imminent physical Second Coming of Jesus, the virgin birth, resurrection, and atonement. It spread in the 1880s and '90s among Protestants dismayed by labor unrest, Catholic immigration, and biblical criticism. Scholars at Princeton Theological Seminary provided intellectual arguments, published as 12 pamphlets (1910–15). Displeasure over the teaching of EVOLUTION, which many believed could not be reconciled with the Bible, and over biblical criticism gave fundamentalism momentum in the 1920s. In the 1930s and '40s, many fundamentalist Bible institutes and colleges were established, and fundamentalist groups within some Baptist and Presbyterian denominations broke away to form new churches. In the later 20th century, fundamentalists made use of television as a medium for evangelizing and became vocal in politics as the "Christian right." See also EVANGELICALISM, PENTECOSTALISM.

fundamentalism, Islamic Conservative religious movement that seeks a return to Islamic values and Islamic law (see SHARIA) in the face of Western modernism, which is seen as corrupt and atheistic. Though popularly associated in the West with Middle Eastern terrorists, only a few Islamic fundamentalists are terrorists, and not all Arab terrorists are fundamentalists. The Iranian revolution of 1979 established an Islamic fundamentalist state, and the TALIBAN has established its version of the same in much of Afghanistan. Islamic fundamentalist movements have varying degrees of support in North Africa, Pakistan, Bangladesh, and Muslim S.East Asia, but Islamic fundamentalism represents a minority viewpoint in the context of world Islam.

Fundy, Bay of Inlet of the Atlantic Ocean, southeastern Canada. Located between the provinces of New Brunswick and Nova Scotia, it extends 94 mi (151 km) inland, and is 32 mi (52 km) wide at its entrance. It is noted for its fast-running tides, which may produce rises as great as 70 ft (21 m), the highest in the world. Noted also for the spectacular rock formations and forests of its shorelines, it has several deepwater harbors, including one at ST. JOHN, New Brunswick. In 1948, a 51,000-acre (20,700-hectare) section of the bay's New Brunswick coast was set aside as Fundy National Park.

fungal diseases *or* **mycoses** Diseases caused by any FUNGUS that invades the tissues. Superficial fungal infections (e.g., athlete's foot) are confined to the skin. Subcutaneous infections, which extend into tissues and sometimes adjacent structures such as bone and organs, are rare and often chronic. In systemic infections, fungi spread through the body of a normal (or, more often, an immunosuppressed) host. Some fungal diseases (e.g., YEAST infections) may be either superficial or systemic, affecting certain target organs.

fungicide \'fən-jə-ˌsīd, 'fəŋ-gə-ˌsīd\ Any TOXIN used to kill or inhibit growth of fungi (see FUNGUS) that cause economic damage to crop or ornamental plants (including rusts in cereals, blight in potatoes, mildew in fruits) or endanger the health of domestic animals or humans. Most are applied as sprays or dusts; seed fungicides are applied as a protective coating to seeds before germination. COPPER compounds, especially copper sulfate, and SULFUR (Bordeaux mixture) have long been used for this purpose, but now synthetic organic compounds are commonly used. Many antifungal substances occur naturally in plant tissues.

fungus Any of about 50,000 species of organisms of the kingdom Fungi, or Mycota, including YEASTS, rusts, SMUTS, MOLDS, MUSHROOMS, and MILDEWS. Though formerly classified as plants and still considered plants in some systems, they lack CHLOROPHYLL and the organized plant structures of stems, roots, and leaves. Fungi contribute to the disintegration of organic matter that results in the release of carbon, oxygen, nitrogen, and phosphorus from dead plants and animals into the soil or the atmosphere. They can be found in the water, soil, air, plants, and animals of all regions of the world that have sufficient moisture to enable them to grow. Essential to many household and industrial processes, fungi are also used in the production of ENZYMES, organic acids, VITAMINS, and ANTIBIOTICS. They also can destroy crops, cause such diseases as ATHLETE'S FOOT and RINGWORM, and ruin clothing and food with mildew and rot. The THALLUS, or body, of a typical fungus consists of a MYCELIUM through which CYTOPLASM flows. The mycelium generally reproduces by forming SPORES, either directly or in special fruiting bodies that are generally the visible part of the fungus. The soil provides an ideal habitat for many species. Lacking chlorophyll, fungi are unable to carry out PHOTOSYNTHESIS and must obtain their carbohydrates by secreting enzymes onto the surface on which they are growing to digest the food, which they absorb through the mycelium. Saprophytic fungi live off dead organisms and are partly responsible for the decomposition of organic matter. Parasitic fungi invade living organisms, often causing disease and death (see PARASITISM). Fungi establish symbiotic relationships with ALGAE (forming LICHENS), plants (forming mycorrhizae; see MYCORRHIZA), and certain insects.

Funk, I(saac) K(auffman) (1839–1912) U.S. publisher. Born in Clifton, Ohio, he was ordained a Lutheran minister in 1861, but resigned the pulpit in 1872 to travel in Europe and the Middle East. In 1877, with Adam Willis Wagnalls (1843–1924), he founded I. K. Funk & Co., later Funk & Wagnalls Co. (1891). The firm became best known for its *Standard Dictionary of the English Language* (1893), whose successors remained in print through the next century.

fur seal Any of nine species of eared SEALS valued for their fur, especially the chestnut-colored underfur. Fur seals live in groups and feed on fish and other animals. Driven nearly to extinction by fur hunters, most species are now protected by law. The northern fur seal *(Callorhinus ursinus)* is a migratory inhabitant of northern seas. The male is deep brown, has a grayish mane, grows to about 10 ft (3 m) long, and weighs about 650 lb (300 kg). The dark-gray female is much smaller. The eight species of southern fur seals (genus *Arctocephalus*) occur in the Southern Hemisphere and on Guadalupe Island. They are brown or black and average 4–6 ft (1.2–1.8 m) long.

Furchgott, Robert F(rancis) (born 1916) U.S. pharmacologist. He received his PhD from Northwestern University. With L.J. IGNARRO and FERID MURAD, he found that NITRIC OXIDE acts as a signaling molecule in the cardiovascular system. Furchgott demonstrated that cells in the endothelium of blood vessels produce a molecule called endothelium-derived relaxing factor (EDRF), which signals smooth muscle cells in blood vessel walls to relax, dilating the vessels. Ignarro later concluded that EDRF was nitric oxide. The research done by Furchgott, Murad, and Ignarro was key to the development of the drug VIAGRA, which treats impotence. The three men shared a 1998 Nobel Prize.

Furies Group of Greco-Roman goddesses of vengeance. The Furies lived in the underworld and ascended to earth to pursue the wicked. They were known to the Greeks as the Erinyes, but those who feared to speak their name often called them by euphemisms such as Eumenides ("Kind Ones"). According to HESIOD, they were daughters of GAEA, the earth goddess. AESCHYLUS made them the terrifying chorus of his tragedy *Eumenides,* and EURIPIDES was the first to speak of them as three in number.

furniture Household equipment made of wood, metal, plastics, marble, glass, fabrics, and related materials, designed for a variety of purposes. It ranges from the simple pine chest or country chair to the most elaborate marquetry-work cabinet or gilded console table. It is usually movable, though it can be built in, such as kitchen cabinets and bookcases. Stylistically it is related to architecture and interior design. Throughout history the functional and decorative aspects of furniture have been influenced by economics and FASHION. In the 14th–18th century, furniture making flourished with ever-increasing affluence. In the 1920s and '30s architects designed chairs made of such modern materials as tubular steel and plastic. See also BENTWOOD FURNITURE, EARLY AMERICAN FURNITURE, SHAKER FURNITURE.

Furtwängler \'fu̇rt-ˌveŋ-lər\, **(Gustav Heinrich Ernst Martin) Wilhelm** (1886–1954) German conductor and composer. After private composition studies with Joseph Rheinberger (1839–1901), he debuted in 1906. His revised *Te Deum* (1910) established him as a composer, and in 1917 a guest-conducting job in Berlin earned the phrase "Furtwängler miracle." He succeeded R. STRAUSS at the Berlin State Opera, and Arthur Nikisch (1855–1922) at the Leipzig Gewandhaus and Berlin Philharmonic, becoming especially associated with the music of LUDWIG VAN BEETHOVEN and RICHARD WAGNER. Though criticized for staying in Germany during the Nazi era, he was no friend of the regime, continuing to program modern music, helping Jewish musicians escape, and being peripherally involved in a 1944 plot to assassinate ADOLF HITLER.

furuncle See BOIL

fuse In ELECTRICAL ENGINEERING, a safety device that protects electric CIRCUITS from the effects of excessive ELECTRIC CURRENTS. A fuse commonly consists of a current-conducting strip or wire of easily fusible metal; whenever the circuit is made to carry a current larger than that for which it is intended, the strip melts to interrupt it.

Fuseli \fyü-'zel-ē\, **Henry** *orig.* **Johann Heinrich Füssli** (1741–1825) Swiss-British painter and writer on art. The son of a portrait painter, he trained in theology as well as in art and art history. He left his native Zurich for London in 1764. Encouraged by Sir JOSHUA REYNOLDS, he went to Italy in 1770 and stayed for eight years; on his return to England, his works exhibited at the Royal Academy, such as *The Nightmare* (1781), his most famous work, secured his reputation. His subject matter was chiefly literary and his images portrayed macabre fantasies and the grotesque. He was elected a full academician in 1790 and taught painting at the Academy 1799–1805.

Fustel de Coulanges \fᵫ̄-stel-də-kü-'läⁿzh\, **Numa Denis** (1830–1889) French historian. He had a brilliant teaching career at the University of Strasbourg (1860–70) and later received other academic appointments. He championed the importance of objectivity and the unreliability of secondary sources, which became important tenets of modern historiography, and his insistence on the use of contemporary documents led to the very full use of the French national archives in the 19th century. Most of his work, including *La cité antique* (1864) and *La Gaule romaine* (1891), dealt with Roman Gaul and the Germanic invasions of the Roman empire.

fusulinid \ˌfyü-zə-'lī-nəd\ Any of a large group of extinct foraminiferans, single-celled organisms related to amoebas but having complex shells that are easily preserved as fossils. The fusulinids first appeared

E F G

during the CARBONIFEROUS PERIOD, perhaps c. 320 million years ago, and persisted until the end of the PERMIAN PERIOD, 248 million years ago. They have been extremely useful for correlating different rock units in widely separated regions and for dividing geologic time into smaller units. Petroleum geologists also use them to help locate economically valuable deposits of oil and natural gas.

Futabatei Shimei \fü-ˈtä-bä-tā-ˈshē-mā\ *orig.* **Hasegawa Tatsunosuke** (1864–1909) Japanese novelist and translator. He is best known for *Ukigumo* (1887–89; "The Drifting Clouds"), his first novel, and for his translations of stories by IVAN TURGENEV. In these he used a style called *gembun itchi* ("unification of spoken and written language"), one of the first attempts at a modern colloquial idiom. His later works include the novels *An Adopted Husband* (1906) and *Mediocrity* (1907). He is credited with bringing modern realism to the Japanese novel.

futhark See RUNIC WRITING

Futuna Islands \fü-ˈtü-nä\ *or* **Hoorn Islands** \ˈhōrn\ Island group (pop., 1996: 4,638), South Pacific Ocean. The islands, Futuna and Alofi, form the southwestern part of the French overseas territory of WALLIS AND FUTUNA, and lie northeast of FIJI. Their combined land area is 36 sq mi (93 sq km). Futuna is the site of Mount Singavi, 2,493 ft (760 m) high. The islands became a French protectorate in 1888. Both are well watered, and Alofi is heavily wooded. The main villages are on the southern coast of Futuna. Alofi is uninhabited.

futures Commercial contracts calling for the purchase or sale of specified quantities of a good at specified future dates. The good in question may be grain, livestock, precious metals, or financial instruments such as TREASURY BILLS. Up until the time the contract calls for the delivery of the good, the contract is subject to speculation. Futures contracts originated in the trade in agricultural commodities; for example, American grain farmers were able to sell their harvest in advance on the Chicago BOARD OF TRADE, a COMMODITY EXCHANGE.

Futurism Early-20th-century art movement, centered in Italy, that celebrated the dynamism, speed, and power of the machine and the vitality and restlessness of modern life. The term was coined by FILIPPO MARINETTI, who in 1909 published a manifesto glorifying the new technology of the automobile and the beauty of its speed and power. In 1910, UMBERTO BOCCIONI and others published a manifesto on painting. They adopted the Cubist technique of depicting several views of an object simultaneously with fragmented planes and outlines, and used rhythmic spatial repetitions of the object's outlines in transit to render movement. Their preferred subjects were speeding cars and trains, racing cyclists, and urban crowds; their palette was more vibrant than the Cubists'. With Boccioni, the most prominent Futurist artists were his teacher, Giacomo Balla (1871–1958), and Gino Severini (1883–1966). Boccioni's death in 1916 and World War I brought an end to the movement, which had a strong influence in postrevolutionary Russia and on DADA.

Futurism Literary, artistic, and political movement begun in Italy about 1909 and marked especially by violent rejection of tradition and an effort to give formal expression to the dynamic energy and movement of mechanical processes. Its most significant results were in the visual arts and poetry. Futurism was first announced in a manifesto by FILIPPO MARINETTI. The principal Italian Futurist artists were Giacomo Balla (1871–1958), UMBERTO BOCCIONI, Carlo Carrà (1881–1966), and Gino Severini (1883–1966). Russian Futurism, founded soon afterward by VLADIMIR MAYAKOVSKY and Velimir Khlebnikov (1885–1922), went beyond the Italian model in its revolutionary political and social outlook. The movement's influence had ceased to be felt by 1930.

futurology Study of current trends in order to forecast future developments. The field originated in the "technological forecasting" developed near the end of World War II and in studies examining the consequences of nuclear conflict. Studies in the 1960s sought to anticipate future social patterns and needs. *The Limits of Growth* by Dennis Meadows et al. (1972) focused on global socioeconomic trends, projecting a Malthusian vision in which the collapse of the world order would result if population growth, industrial expansion, pollution, food production, and natural-resource use continued at current rates. Later reports reiterated many of these concerns, with critics contending that futurologists' models were flawed and futurologists responding that their analytic techniques were becoming increasingly sophisticated. Other notable works include Alvin Toffler's *Future Shock* (1970), Daniel Bell's *The Coming of Post-Industrial Society* (1973), Jonathan Schell's *The Fate of the Earth* (1982), and Nigel Calder's *The Green Machines* (1986).

Fuzhou \ˈfü-ˈjō\ *or* **Fu-chou** *or* **Foochow** \ˈfü-ˈchau̇\ *formerly* **Minchow** City (pop., 1999 est.: 1,057,372), capital of FUJIAN province, China. Located on the bank of the MIN RIVER, it was the capital of the kingdom of Yue in the 2nd century BC. Fuzhou, important militarily in the 1st century AD, came later under the TANG DYNASTY. During the SONG DYNASTY (960–1279), it was a center for overseas trade and also an important cultural center. It reached its height of prosperity when it was opened as a treaty port after the OPIUM WAR of 1839–42. It is now a center for industrial chemicals. In the city and nearby hills are notable examples of Chinese architecture, including pagodas and temples.

Fuzulî \fü-zü-ˈlē\, **Mehmed bin Süleyman** (c. 1480–1556) Turkish poet. Considered the greatest figure in classical Turkish literature, he composed poems with equal facility and elegance in Turkish, Persian, and Arabic. His works transcended the highly formalized Islamic literary aesthetic and influenced many poets up to the 19th century. His most famous poems include his rendition of the Muslim classic *Leyla ve Mecnun*, a celebrated allegory depicting the attraction of the human spirit for divine beauty. His two poetry anthologies, one in Azerbaijani Turkish and one in Persian, contain his most lyrical verses.

fuzzy logic LOGIC based on the concept of fuzzy sets, in which membership is expressed in varying probabilities or degrees of truth—that is, as a continuum of values ranging from 0 (does not occur) to 1 (definitely occurs). As additional data are gathered, many fuzzy-logic systems are able to adjust the probability values assigned to different parameters. Because some such systems appear able to learn from their mistakes, they are often considered a crude form of ARTIFICIAL INTELLIGENCE. The term and concept date from a 1965 paper by Lotfi A. Zadeh (born 1921). Fuzzy-logic systems achieved commercial application in the early 1990s. Advanced clothes-washing machines, for example, use fuzzy-logic systems to detect and adapt to patterns of water movement during a wash cycle, increasing efficiency and reducing water consumption. Other products using fuzzy logic include camcorders, microwave ovens, and dishwashers. Other applications include EXPERT SYSTEMS, self-regulating industrial controls, and computerized speech- and handwriting-recognition programs.

Fw 190 See FOCKE-WULF 190

Fyn \ˈfūēn\ Island of Denmark. It is located between Sjælland and the JUTLAND Peninsula; its administrative center and largest city is ODENSE. Fyn, which has an area of 1,346 sq mi (3,486 sq km), is a fertile agricultural and fruit-growing region. Road and rail bridges and ferries connect the island with the rest of Denmark.

Fyodor I \ˈfyō-dər\ *Russian* **Fyodor Ivanovich** (1557–1598) Czar of Russia (1584–98) whose death ended the rule of the RURIK dynasty. The son of IVAN IV, Fyodor was feebleminded and took no part in the government, which was dominated by his wife's brother, BORIS GODUNOV. Godunov was responsible for the major achievements of Fyodor's reign, including elevation of the metropolitan see of Russia to a patriarchate (1589), recovery of lands near the Gulf of Finland (1595), and strengthening of Russia's control over western Siberia and territory in the Caucasus. The childless Fyodor was succeeded by Godunov.

Fyodor II *Russian* **Fyodor Borisovich Godunov** (1589–1605) Czar of Russia for three months in 1605, during the Time of TROUBLES. The son and successor of BORIS GODUNOV, Fyodor was immediately challenged by the first False DMITRY. After his military commander shifted his support to the pretender, Fyodor's mother tried to take power. Her action angered the BOYARS, who provoked a Moscow mob to riot and murder Fyodor and his mother. The pretender then assumed the throne.

Fyodor III *Russian* **Fyodor Alekseyevich** (1661–1682) Czar of Russia (1676–82). He ascended the throne on the death of his father, ALEXIS, but youth and poor health prevented him from actively participating in government. Various advisers dominated his administration, notably VASILY GOLITSYN, who instituted military reforms, limited the power of the aristocracy, and fostered the development of Western culture. The childless Fyodor was succeeded by his brother IVAN V and half brother PETER I THE GREAT, for whose widespread reforms Fyodor's reign had laid the groundwork.

G. intestinalis See GIARDIA LAMBLIA

Gabar \'ga-bər\ Derogatory name applied to Iranian Zoroastrians. The word may derive from the Arabic *kafir* ("infidel"). After the Muslim conquest of Persia in the 7th century BC, the Zoroastrians became an outcast minority, saddled with many social and economic disabilities. Since the 19th century they have received support from the PARSIS of India. Persecuted after the Islamic fundamentalist revolution of 1978–79, they currently number a few thousand. See also ZOROASTRIANISM AND PARSIISM

gabbro Any of several medium- or coarse-grained rocks that consist primarily of PLAGIOCLASE feldspar and PYROXENE. Gabbros are found widely on the earth and on the moon. They are sometimes quarried for dimension stone ("black granite"), but the direct economic value of gabbro is minor. Far more important are the nickel, chromium, and platinum minerals that occur almost exclusively in association with gabbroic or related rocks. Magnetite (iron) and ilmenite (titanium) are also found in gabbroic complexes.

Gabin \gà-'ba^{n}\, **Jean** *orig.* **Jean-Alexis Moncorgé** (1904–1976) French film actor. The son of a music-hall comedian, he began as a performer at the Folies Bergère (1923). After his film debut in 1931, he earned critical and popular acclaim in *Maria Chapdelaine* (1934), *Pépé le moko* (1937), *Grand Illusion* (1937), *The Human Beast* (1938), and *Daybreak* (1939), often portraying the silent, tough antihero surviving in a world of social outcasts. He appeared in several films as Inspector Maigret and also in *Speaking of Murder* (1959), *Money, Money, Money* (1962), and *The Upper Hand* (1967).

gable Triangular section formed by a roof with two slopes, extending from the eaves to the ridge where the two slopes meet. It may be miniaturized over a DORMER window or entranceway. If the gable end projects above the roof level to form a parapet, the edge is often trimmed to form an ornamental silhouette (e.g., curved or stepped), as in Dutch town houses of the 16th–17th century. In Asia, gables often feature projecting roof tiles and grotesque sculptures of animals at the ridge and eaves.

Gable, (William) Clark (1901–1960) U.S. film actor. Born in Cadiz, Ohio, he debuted on Broadway in 1928 and went to Hollywood in 1930. After an initial rejection MGM signed him, and within a year he was playing romantic leads. He triumphed in *It Happened One Night* (1934, Academy Award). With his sardonic virility and lighthearted charm, appealing to men as well as women, he became known as "the King." Among his 70-odd films are *Mutiny on the Bounty* (1935), *San Francisco* (1936), *Saratoga* (1937), and, most memorably, *Gone with the Wind* (1939). After the death of his third wife, CAROLE LOMBARD, he joined the Army Air Corps and received the Distinguished Flying Cross and Air Medal for his wartime bombing missions. He later starred in such films as *The Hucksters* (1947), *Mogambo* (1953), and *The Misfits* (1961).

Gable, Dan(iel Mack) (born 1948) U.S. freestyle wrestler and coach. Born in Waterloo, Iowa, he never lost a match in his high-school years. After an outstanding career at Iowa State Univ., he won the 1971 world and Pan-American championships. At the 1972 Olympics he won a gold medal, not losing a single point. From 1972 he coached at the University of Iowa, winning nine consecutive national titles and 12 Big Ten championships, and he coached the 1980 and 1984 U.S. Olympic wrestling teams.

Gabo \'gä-bō\, **Naum** *orig.* **Naum Pevsner** (1890–1977) Russian-U.S. sculptor. He studied at the University of Munich, and in 1913 he was introduced to avant-garde art in Paris by his brother, ANTOINE PEVSNER. In 1920 the brothers returned to Russia and issued the *Realist Manifesto*, setting forth the principles of European CONSTRUCTIVISM. Gabo produced abstract works of such unorthodox materials as glass, plastic, and wire to achieve a sense of movement. After some years in Europe, he settled in the U.S. in 1946 and taught at Harvard's architecture school. He received many awards and public commissions. A pioneer of the Constructivist movement, he was one of the earliest artists to experiment with KINETIC SCULPTURE.

Gabon \gà-'bō^{n}\ *officially* **Gabonese Republic** Country, central Africa. Area: 103,347 sq mi (267,667 sq km). Population (1997 est.): 1,190,000. Capital: LIBREVILLE. Gabon has more than 40 ethnic groups: the FANG make up a majority and live north of the OGOOUÉ RIVER; the largest groups south of the river are the Punu, Sira, and Nzebi. Languages: French (official); indigenous languages. Religion: Christianity, primarily Roman Catholicism. Currency: CFA franc. Gabon straddles the equator on the western coast of Africa. It has a narrow coastal plain and becomes hilly in the south and north. The basin of its chief river, the Ogooué, covers most of the country; about three-fourths is equatorial rain forest, which supports numerous plant and animal species. Gabon has reserves of manganese that are among the largest in the world; it also has huge deposits of high-grade iron ore. Gabon has a mixed, developing economy based largely on the exploitation of these mineral and timber resources. Its head of state is the president, and the head of government is the prime minister; the parliament consists of two houses. Artifacts dating from late Paleolithic and early Neolithic times have been found in Gabon, but it is not known when the BANTU speakers who established Gabon's ethnic composition arrived. PYGMIES were probably the original inhabitants. The Fang arrived in the late 18th century and were followed by the Portuguese and by French, Dutch, and English traders. The SLAVE TRADE dominated commerce in the 18th and much of the 19th century. The French then took control, and Gabon was administered (1843–86) with FRENCH WEST AFRICA. In 1886 the colony of French Congo was established to include both Gabon and the Congo; in 1910 Gabon became a separate colony within FRENCH EQUATORIAL AFRICA. An overseas territory of France from 1946, it became an autonomous republic within the FRENCH COMMUNITY in 1958 and declared its independence in 1960. Rule by a sole political party was established in the 1960s, but discontent with it led to riots in Libreville in 1989. Legalization of opposition parties led to new elections in 1990. Peace negotiations with neighboring Chad rebels and with the Republic of the Congo were ongoing in the 1990s.

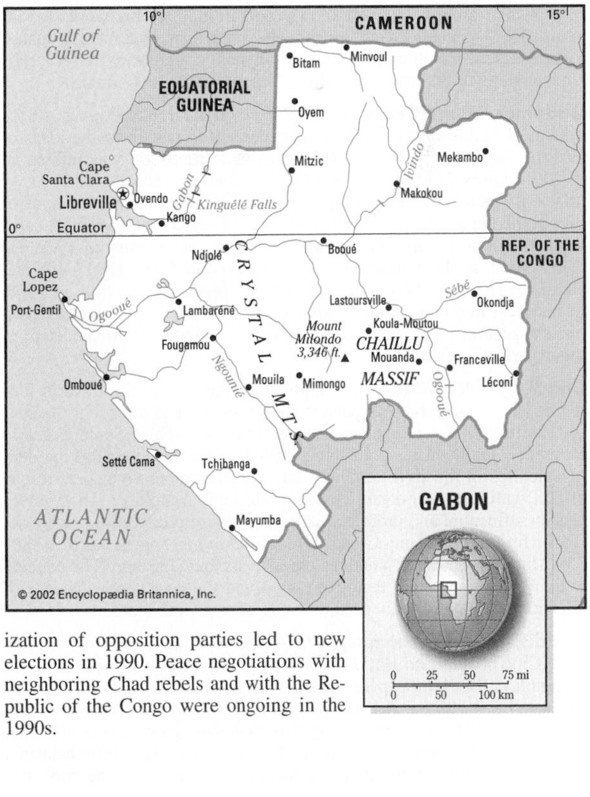

Gaborone \ˌgä-bō-ˈrō-nā\ *formerly (until 1969)* **Gaberones** \ˌgä-bə-ˈrō-nəs\ City (pop., 1997: 183,487), capital of Botswana. It is located in southeastern Botswana, near the border with South Africa. The seat of government was transferred there from Mafikeng, South Africa, in 1965, one year before Botswana became independent of Britain. Gaborone is on the Cape–Zimbabwe railway and is the site of government offices, parliament buildings, health facilities, a thermal power station, and an airport. It is the seat of the University of Botswana (1976) and also has a national museum and art gallery (1968).

Gabriel In the Bible, one of the archangels. In the Old Testament he was the heavenly messenger sent to explain DANIEL's visions, and in the New Testament he revealed to Zechariah the coming birth of JOHN THE BAPTIST and appeared to MARY in the Annunciation to tell her she was to be the mother of JESUS. In Christian tradition it is believed that he will blow the trumpet on Judgment Day. In the Quran, he is known as JIBRIL.

Gabriel *or* **Gabriel Prosser** (1775?–1800) American slave who planned the first slave rebellion in U.S. history. Born near Richmond, Va., to an African-born mother, he grew up as the slave of Thomas H. Prosser. In 1800 the deeply religious Gabriel planned a slave insurrection to create an independent slave state in Virginia with himself as king. Intending to attack Richmond and kill all whites except Frenchmen, Methodists, and Quakers, he assembled 1,000 slaves outside the city on August 30, but a violent rainstorm washed out bridges and scattered the rebels. Before they could reassemble, Gov. JAMES MONROE learned of the plot and ordered out the state militia. Gabriel and 34 others were arrested, tried, and hanged.

Gabrieli \ˌgä-brē-ˈe-lē\, **Andrea and Giovanni** (died 1586, c. 1555–1612) Italian composers. Andrea was born in Venice, worked at the Bavarian court, and in 1566 became an organist at ST. MARK'S BASILICA in Venice, where he remained the rest of his life. He wrote over 200 madrigals and much other secular vocal music. His sacred vocal works, which number over 150, include many splendid settings for church festivals employing separated choirs *(cori spezzati);* many were published posthumously in a collection called *Concerti* (1587). His nephew and student Giovanni joined him as organist at St. Mark's in 1584. Like Andrea, he wrote numerous festive works for separated choirs and instrumental groups. His best-known works today are his works for instruments, especially wind instruments (canzonas, ricercars, sonatas, toccatas, etc.), which employ dramatic dynamic and spatial effects. His student HEINRICH SCHUTZ conveyed the Venetian style to Germany.

Gadamer, Hans-Georg (1900–2002) German philosopher whose system of philosophical hermeneutics, derived in part from the ideas of WILHELM DILTHEY, EDMUND HUSSERL, and MARTIN HEIDEGGER, was influential in 20th-century CONTINENTAL PHILOSOPHY, AESTHETICS, THEOLOGY, and LITERARY CRITICISM. The son of a chemistry professor, Gadamer studied the humanities at the universities of Breslau, Marburg, Freiburg, and Munich, earning a doctorate in philosophy under Heidegger at Freiburg in 1922. He later taught at the universities of Frankfurt am Main (1947–49) and Heidelberg (from 1949), where he became professor emeritus in 1968. In his most important work, *Truth and Method* (1960), Gadamer developed a general theory of understanding and interpretation modeled on the experience of art.

Gaddi \ˈgäd-dē\, **Taddeo** (c. 1300–1366) Italian painter active in Florence. He was the son of a painter and mosaicist and a student of GIOTTO. His best-known works are frescoes in the church of Santa Croce in Florence. He directed a flourishing workshop for three decades, producing pictures in the style of Giotto but featuring more vivid picturesque effects with narrative detail. His son and pupil Agnolo (c. 1350–1396) was an influential and prolific artist who likewise produced a notable series of frescoes for Santa Croce, *The Legend of the True Cross* (c. 1388–93). Many extant panel paintings are also attributed to him. His concentration on design rather than expression and the decorative elegance of his cool, pale colors influenced the style of late Gothic art.

Gaddis, William (Thomas) (1922–1998) U.S. novelist. Born in New York City, he attended Harvard University and later wrote speeches and screenplays. His long experimental novels are characterized by complex and allusive plotting and language and a dark (if often humorous) view of contemporary American society. His first, *The Recognitions* (1955), a multileveled examination of spiritual bankruptcy, was only belatedly recognized as a masterpiece. Discouraged by its reception, he published nothing more until *JR* (1975, National Book Award), which depicts greed, hypocrisy, and banality in business. His later novels are *Carpenter's Gothic* (1985) and *A Frolic of His Own* (1994, National Book Award).

Gadsden, James (1788–1858) U.S. soldier and diplomat. Born in Charleston, S.C., he was appointed an officer in the U.S. Army in 1812. In 1820 he established military posts in Florida and supervised the removal of Seminole Indians to reservations in Florida and later in the West (1823–32). He served as president of a South Carolina railroad 1840–50. In 1853 he was appointed U.S. minister to Mexico and instructed to buy land from Mexico for a southern railroad route (see GADSDEN PURCHASE).

Gadsden Purchase (December 30, 1853) U.S. purchase of land in Mexico. Following the conquest of much of northern Mexico in the MEXICAN WAR (1848), advocates of a southern transcontinental railroad endorsed the purchase of 30,000 sq mi (78,000 sq km) of northern Mexican territory, now southern Arizona and southern New Mexico. The purchase was negotiated by JAMES GADSDEN, U.S. minister to Mexico, for $10 million. The acquisition fixed the borders of the later 48 contiguous states.

gadwall Small DABBLING DUCK *(Anas strepera)* that is a popular game bird, found throughout the upper Northern Hemisphere. Its largest breeding populations in North America are in the Dakotas and in Canada's prairie provinces. The gadwall is brownish gray with white patches, visible only during flight, on the rear of the wings. Its preferred diet is stems and leaves of aquatic plants, supplemented by seeds and algae. Gadwalls often live in shallow freshwater ponds and marshes, often in mixed flocks with WIGEONS. Unlike wigeons, they rarely feed on land.

Gaea \ˈjē-ə\ Greek goddess of the earth. She was both mother and wife to URANUS, or Heaven, from whom she was separated by her son CRONUS, a TITAN. According to HESIOD, she was the mother of all 12 Titans, as well as of the FURIES and the Cyclopes (see CYCLOPS). She may have originated as a mother goddess worshiped in pre-Hellenic Greece before the introduction of the cult of ZEUS.

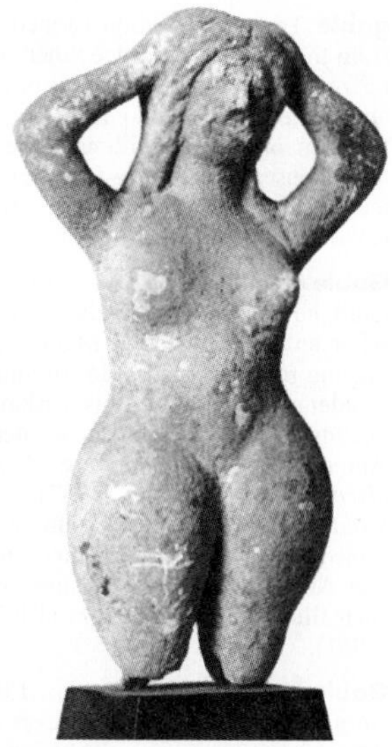

Gaea, terra-cotta statuette from Tanagra, Greece; in the Musée Borély, Marseille.

GIRAUDON—ART RESOURCE/EB INC.

Gaelic See IRISH LANGUAGE, SCOTTISH GAELIC LANGUAGE

Gaelic football \ˈgā-lik\ Irish sport, an offshoot of the extremely violent medieval game mêlée. In the modern game, sides are limited to 15. Players may not throw the ball but may dribble it with hand or foot, and may punch or punt it toward their opponents' goal. Goals count as either one or three points, depending on whether the ball passes above (one) or below (three) a crossbar attached to the goalposts. It is played mostly in Ireland and the U.S.

Gaelic revival Resurgence of interest in Irish language, literature, history, and folklore inspired by the growing Irish nationalism of the early 19th century. With the 17th-century English conquest and settlement of Ireland, Irish almost disappeared as a literary language. By the mid-19th century, translations of heroic tales from ancient Irish manuscripts led to the popularity, among the educated classes, of poets who wrote in patterns echoing ancient bardic verse. The revival laid the scholarly and nationalistic groundwork for the IRISH LITERARY RENAISSANCE. See also BARD.

gag rule Parliamentary device to limit debate; specifically, one of a series of resolutions passed by the U.S. Congress that tabled without discussion petitions regarding slavery (1836–40). It was introduced by proslavery members to postpone consideration of antislavery petitions encouraged by the AMERICAN ANTI-SLAVERY SOCIETY. It was repealed in 1844 due to efforts of JOHN QUINCY ADAMS and others.

gagaku \gä-ˈgä-kü\ Traditional court and religious music of Japan. It first appeared as an import from Korea in the 5th century AD and became established at court by the 8th century. Though little notation from before the 12th century survives, a mostly later body of music continues to be performed at Shinto ceremonies. Gagaku employs transverse flute *(ryuteki),* double-reed pipe *(hichiriki),* mouth organ *(sho),* gong *(shoko),* drums, and stringed instruments including the *biwa* (see PIPA) and KOTO. It may accompany dance (BUGAKU) or be played independently *(kangen)*; it is further classified either as Chinese (or Left) music *(togaku)* or as Korean (or Right) music *(komagaku).*

Gagarin \gə-ˈgär-ən\, **Yury (Alekseyevich)** (1934–1968) Soviet cosmonaut. Son of a carpenter on a collective farm, he graduated from the Soviet Air Force cadet school in 1957. In April 1961, aboard VOSTOK 1, he became the first human to travel into space. The spacecraft orbited earth once in 1 hour and 29 minutes. Gagarin's flight brought him worldwide fame, and he was much honored in the Soviet Union. He never went into space again, but trained other cosmonauts. He was killed at 34 when his jet crashed during a training flight.

Gahadavala dynasty \gə-hə-də-ˈvä-lə\ (c. 1050–c. 1250) One of the many ruling families of North India on the eve of the 12th–13th century Muslim conquests. Its history illustrates all the features of the early medieval North Indian polity—dynastic hostilities and alliances, feudal-state structure, absolute dependence on Brahmanical social ideology, and vulnerability in the face of external aggression. Muslim expansion eclipsed the Gahadavala dynasty in the early 13th century.

Gahanbar \gä-ˌhän-ˈbär\ In ZOROASTRIANISM, any of six festivals occurring at irregular intervals during the year and marking the change of seasons in Iran. Globally they are aligned with the six stages in the creation of the world: the heavens, water, the earth, vegetation, animals, and humanity. Each festival lasts five days. The PARSIS celebrate the Gahanbar festivals in two stages, beginning with liturgical rites and sacrificial offerings and concluding with a solemn feast.

Gaia hypothesis \ˈgī-ə\ Model of the earth in which its living and nonliving parts are viewed as a complex interacting system that can be thought of as a single organism. Developed c. 1972 largely by British chemist James E. Lovelock and U.S. biologist Lynn Margulis, the Gaia hypothesis is named for the Greek earth goddess. It postulates that all living things have a regulatory effect on earth's environment that promotes life overall; the earth is homeostatic in support of life-sustaining conditions. The theory is highly controversial.

Gainsborough, Thomas (1727–1788) British painter. At 13 he left his native Suffolk to study in London. By c. 1750, back in Suffolk, he had established a reputation in portraiture and landscape painting. He painted landscapes for pleasure; portraiture was his profession. In 1759 he moved to the fashionable spa of Bath, where his works would be seen by a wider and wealthier public. In 1768 he became a founding member of the Royal Academy of Art. He developed an elegant, formal portrait style inspired by ANTHONY VAN DYCK, whose influence can be seen in such portraits as his famous *Blue Boy* (1770). In 1774 he moved to London and became a favorite of the royal family, preferred above the official court painter, JOSHUA REYNOLDS. His love of landscape came from studying 17th-century Dutch artists and later PETER PAUL RUBENS, whose influence is evident in *The Watering Place* (1777). His output was prodigious; he produced many landscape drawings in various media, and in his later years seascapes, pastoral subjects, and children. Among the great portrait painters of the era, he alone devoted serious attention to landscapes.

"The Morning Walk," oil on canvas by Thomas Gainsborough, 1785; in the National Gallery, London.

BY COURTESY OF THE TRUSTEES OF THE NATIONAL GALLERY, LONDON

Gaitskell, Hugh (Todd Naylor) (1906–1963) British politician. He taught political economy at the University of London and in World War II served in the ministry of economic warfare. He entered the House of Commons in 1945 and became minister of fuel and power (1947–50) and chancellor of the exchequer (1950–51). Chosen to succeed CLEMENT R. ATTLEE as Labour Party leader in 1955, he reunited the party and moderated its policies before his sudden death.

Gajah Mada \ˈgä-jä-ˈmä-dä\ (died 1364) Prime minister of the MAJAPAHIT EMPIRE and a national hero in Indonesia. Born a commoner, Gajah Mada rose to power on his intelligence, courage, and loyalty to King Jayanagara (1309–1328), whom he restored to power after an insurrection. His feelings for the king changed when the latter took possession of his wife, and he subsequently had the king killed. During the reigns of Jayanagara's daughter Tribhuvana and grandson Hayam Wuruk (r.1350–89), Gajah Mada was the most powerful figure in Majapahit, conquering territories that may have included the entire Indonesian archipelago and part of Malaysia. A law book that had great significance in Javanese history was compiled under his instructions, and the principal poet of the era, Prapancha (fl. 14th century), eulogized Gajah Mada (his patron) in *Nagarakrtagama,* the epic of Majapahit.

Terra-cotta head identified as Gajah Mada; in the Trawulan Site Museum, Indonesia.

BY COURTESY OF THE TRAWULAN MUSEUM, INDONESIA

Gajdusek \ˈgī-də-ˌshek\, **D(aniel) Carleton** (born 1923) U.S. physician and researcher. Born in Yonkers, N.Y., he received his MD from Harvard University. He provided the first medical description of the central-nervous-system disorder kuru, unique to the Fore people of New Guinea, and concluded that it was spread by their funeral custom of ritually eating the deceased's brains. With Clarence Gibbs, Jr., he proposed that it was caused by an extremely slow-acting virus. Though kuru is now known to be caused by prions, his study had significant implications for research into multiple sclerosis, parkinsonism, and other degenerative neurological conditions. He shared a 1976 Nobel Prize with BARUCH BLUMBERG.

galactic cluster See OPEN CLUSTER

galactic coordinate In astronomy, a galactic latitude or longitude, useful for describing the relative positions and motions of components of the Milky Way galaxy. Galactic latitude is measured in degrees north or south of the plane of the Milky Way. Galactic longitude is measured in degrees east of the galactic center in the constellation Sagittarius.

galactic halo In astronomy, a nearly spherical volume of thinly scattered stars, GLOBULAR CLUSTERS, and tenuous gas observed surrounding spiral GALAXIES. It may extend far beyond the disk and contain most of the galaxy's mass. The halo of the MILKY WAY GALAXY is thought to have a radius of some 50,000 light-years and may be dominantly composed of DARK MATTER.

galactic nucleus See ACTIVE GALACTIC NUCLEUS

galactose \gə-ˈlak-ˌtōs\ Organic compound, a MONOSACCHARIDE, chemical formula $C_6H_{12}O_6$. It is usually found in nature combined with other sugars, for example, in LACTOSE, in POLYSACCHARIDES, and in glycolipids, CARBOHYDRATE-containing LIPIDS that occur in the brain and other nervous tissues of most animals. It has uses in organic synthesis and in medicine.

galago \gə-ˈlā-gō, gə-ˈlä-gō\ Any of six species of small, tree-dwelling PRIMATES (genus *Galago*) found in forests of sub-Saharan Africa. Galagos are gray, brown, or red-

Bush babies (*Galago senegalensis*).

GEORGE HOLTON—PHOTO RESEARCHERS

dish or yellowish brown animals with large eyes and ears, long hind legs, soft woolly fur, and a long tail. They are active at night, feeding on fruits, insects, and small birds. Smaller forms, such as the bush baby, are particularly active and agile in the trees. On the ground, galagos sit upright and move by jumping with their hind legs. They range in length from 4.5–6 in. (11–16 cm), excluding the 7–8-in. (18–20-cm) tail, to 12–15 in. (30–37 cm), excluding the 16.5–18.5-in. (42–47-cm) tail.

Galahad \'gal-ə-,had\ In Arthurian legend, the pure knight who achieved a vision of God through the Holy Grail. The illegitimate son of Lancelot and the princess Elaine, he alone was worthy to sit in the Siege Perilous at the Round Table, reserved for the one destined to succeed in the quest for the Grail. Unlike his father, who was given to earthly and adulterous love, Galahad was chaste and filled with spiritual fervor. By finding the grail he healed the Fisher King and brought fertility back to the land. He appears in many Arthurian romances, notably in Sir Thomas Malory's *Morte Darthur.* See also Perceval.

Galápagos finch See Darwin's finch

Galápagos Islands \gə-'lä-pə-gəs\ *Spanish* **Archipiélago de Colón** \,är-chē-'pyā-lä-gō-thā-kō-'lōn\ Island group, eastern Pacific Ocean. A province (pop., 1997 est.: 15,000) of Ecuador, the Galápagos are a group of 19 islands lying on the equator 600 mi (1,000 km) west of the mainland. Their total land area of 3,086 sq mi (7,994 sq km) is scattered over 23,000 sq mi (59,500 sq km) of ocean. Visited by the Spanish in 1535, they had been unclaimed when Ecuador took official possession of them in 1832. They became internationally famous when visited in 1835 by Charles Darwin; their unusual fauna, including the giant tortoise (Spanish, *galápago*), contributed to his ideas on natural selection. Ecuador made the Galápagos a wildlife sanctuary in 1935, and a national park in 1968.

Galati \gȧ-'läts, gȧ-'lät-sē\ *German* **Galatz** \'gä-,läts\ City (pop., 1994: 327,000), southeastern Romania. Located at the confluence of the Danube and Siret rivers, it was occupied by the Turks from the early 16th century until 1829; its growth was encouraged by its status as a free port (1837–83). During World War II, retreating German troops devastated the town and reduced the population, substantially Jewish, to less than half. Extensively rebuilt, it is one of Romania's chief ports and the site of the country's largest shipyard.

Galatia \gə-'lā-shə\ Ancient district, central Asia Minor. It was occupied early in the 3rd century BC by Celtic tribes who were then overpowered by the Seleucid king Antiochus I Soter in 275 BC. At that point the Celts, called Galatae (Galatians) by 3rd-century-BC writers, settled in the territory to which they gave their name. Passing successively under the rule of Pergamum and Pontus, Galatia became a Roman protectorate in 85 BC. By the 2nd century AD, the region had become absorbed into the Hellenistic civilization.

galaxy Any of the billions of systems of stars and interstellar matter that make up the universe. Galaxies vary considerably in size, composition, and structure, but nearly all are arranged in groups, or clusters, of from a few to as many as 10,000. Each is composed of millions to trillions of stars; in many, as in the Milky Way galaxy, nebulae (see nebula) can be detected. Roughly 70% of the bright galaxies in the sky are spiral galaxies, with a main disk in which spiral arms wind out from the center. The arms contain the greatest concentration of a spiral galaxy's interstellar gas and dust, where stars can form. Surrounding the center (nucleus) is a large, usually nearly spherical nuclear bulge. Outside this and the disk is a sparse, more or less spherical galactic halo. In elliptical galaxies, which vary greatly in size, stars are distributed symmetrically in a spherical or spheroidal shape. Dwarf ellipticals (with only a few million stars) are by far the most common kind of galaxy, though none is conspicuous in the sky. Irregular galaxies, such as the Magellanic Clouds, are relatively rare. Radio galaxies are very strong sources of radio waves. Seyfert galaxies, with extremely bright nuclei, often emit radio waves and may be related to quasars.

Galba \'gal-bə, 'gȯl-bə\ *in full* **Servius Galba Caesar Augustus** ***orig.*** **Servius Sulpicius Galba** (3 BC–AD 69) Roman emperor (68–69). A member of the Senate, he became consul in 33, received command of the Upper German Army in 39, and was made governor of Nearer Spain in 60. Fearing his own assassination, he led a rebellion in 68 against Nero, who committed suicide. After being accepted as emperor by the Senate, Galba executed many important Romans, including some responsible for his accession. His seven-month administration was priggish and cruel, his advisers allegedly corrupt. He reneged on promises to the army; when he chose a successor unacceptable to the Praetorian Guard, they killed him and his chosen heir.

Galba, marble bust; in the Uffizi, Florence.
ALINARI—ART RESOURCE/EB INC.

Galbraith \'gal-,brāth\, **John Kenneth** (born 1908) Canadian-U.S. economist and public servant. Born in Iona Station, Ontario, he studied at the Univs. of Toronto and California (PhD, 1934). He held important government posts during the New Deal and World War II. As a professor at Harvard University (1949–75) he was active in public affairs, serving as an adviser to Pres. John F. Kennedy and as ambassador to India (1961–63). His influentially liberal writings, often praised for their literary merit, examine the strengths and weaknesses of U.S. capitalism and consumerism. *The Affluent Society* (1958) called for less emphasis on production and more attention to public services, and *The New Industrial State* (1967) traced similarities between "managerial" capitalism and socialism.

Galdan See Dga'l-dan

Galdós, Benito Pérez See Benito Perez Galdos

Galen \'gā-lən\ *Latin* **Galenus** (AD 129–c. 200) Greek physician, writer, and philosopher. Born in Pergamum, Asia Minor, he became chief physician to the gladiators in AD 157. Later, in Rome, he became a friend of Marcus Aurelius and physician to Commodus. Galen saw anatomy as fundamental and, based on animal experiments, described cranial nerves and heart valves and showed that arteries carry blood, not air. However, in extending his findings to human anatomy he was often in error. Following Hippocratic concepts (see Hippocrates), he believed in three connected body systems—brain and nerves for sensation and thought, heart and arteries for life energy, and liver and veins for nutrition and growth—and four humors (body fluids)—blood, yellow bile, black bile, and phlegm—that needed to be in balance. Few had the skills to challenge his seductive physiological theory. He wrote about 300 works, of which about 150 survive. As they were translated, his influence spread to the Byzantine empire, Arabia, and then Western Europe. A revival of interest in the 16th century led to new anatomical investigations, which caused the overthrow of his ideas when Andreas Vesalius found anatomical errors and William Harvey correctly explained blood circulation.

galena \gə-'lē-nə\ *or* **lead glance** Gray lead sulfide (PbS), the chief ore mineral of lead. One of the most widely distributed sulfide minerals, it occurs in many types of deposits and in many localities. In the U.S., galena is mined principally in the Mississippi River Valley. Galena often contains silver and so is often mined for that metal as well as for lead. Other commercially important minerals that frequently occur in close association with galena are antimony, copper, and zinc.

Galerius \gə-'lir-ē-əs\ *in full* **Gaius Galerius Valerius Maximianus** (died AD 311) Roman emperor (305–11) notorious for his persecution of Christians. As caesar and a victorious commander, he apparently induced Diocletian to begin the persecutions. In 305 Galerius became augustus (senior emperor) of the East and briefly made himself supreme ruler. He imposed a harsh poll tax on the urban population and kept up the ruthless persecution of Christians. He fell ill in 311; fearing the Christian God was taking vengeance, he issued an edict of tolerance.

Galicia \gə-'li-shə\ *Polish* **Halicz** \'häl-ich\ *Russian* **Galitsiya** \gə-'lēt-sē-yə\ Historic region, eastern Europe. Covering 30,645 sq mi (79,371 sq km), it included the northern slopes of the Carpathian Mtns. and the valleys of the upper Vistula, Dniester, Bug, and Seret rivers. In 1199, eastern Galicia, situated near the principalities of Kiev and Volhynia was taken by Prince Roman of Volhynia who united Volhynia and Galicia. In 1349 the Polish king Casimir III annexed Galicia. When Poland was partitioned, beginning in 1772, the territory passed to Austria. Restored to Poland after World War I, eastern Galicia was taken by the Soviet Union in World War II and united to the Ukrainian S.S.R. After the war, eastern Galicia remained a part of the U.S.S.R. (after 1991, part of Ukraine), while western Galicia was attached to Poland.

Galicia \gə-ˈlē-shə\ *ancient* **Gallaecia** Autonomous community (pop., 2000 est.: 2,731,900) and ancient kingdom, northwestern Spain. Bounded by the Atlantic Ocean and covering 11,365 sq mi (29,435 sq km), Galicia's name is derived from the Celtic Gallaeci, who lived there when the region was conquered by the Romans c. 137 BC. Taken by the VISIGOTHS in AD 585, it next passed to the Moors, and became part of the kingdom of Asturias in the 8th–9th century. It lost much of its political autonomy after the unification of CASTILE and Aragon in 1479. The region was made an autonomous community in 1981; its capital is SANTIAGO DE COMPOSTELA. Agriculture, forestry, and fishing dominate the economy.

Galilean satellite \ˌga-lə-ˈlē-ən, ˌga-lə-ˈlā-ən\ Any of the four large satellites of JUPITER discovered by GALILEO in 1610. In order of distance from Jupiter: Io (the most volcanically active body in the solar system), Europa (suspected to contain a liquid ocean under its frozen surface), Ganymede (the largest satellite in the solar system), and Callisto. Both Ganymede and Callisto are larger than Pluto and Mercury.

Galilee *Hebrew* **Ha-Galil** Northernmost region of biblical and modern Israel. It contains two of the four holy cities of Judaism, TIBERIAS and Zefat. It was the boyhood home of JESUS Christ and the setting for much of his ministry. It became the center of Jewish scholarship after the destruction of Jerusalem (AD 70). In the modern era, the first wave of Jewish immigrants settled there (1882). The first KIBBUTZ, Deganya, was established in 1909 on the shore of the Sea of GALILEE, through which flows the JORDAN RIVER.

Galilee, Sea of *or* **Lake Tiberias** Freshwater lake, northern Israel. It is 13 mi (21 km) long and 7 mi (11 km) wide; it lies about 700 ft (212 m) below sea level, and receives most of its inflow from the JORDAN RIVER. The region has been inhabited for millennia: archaeological finds dating to some 500,000 years ago are among the oldest in the Middle East. In the 1st century AD, the region was rich and populated; it was the scene of many episodes in the life of JESUS. Today the lake's waters irrigate the surrounding agricultural region. Modern health resorts have grown up and the baths at TIBERIAS are among Israel's winter resort attractions.

Galileo \ˌga-lə-ˈlē-ō, ˌga-lə-ˈlā-ō\ *in full* **Galileo Galilei** (1564–1642) Italian mathematician, astronomer, and physicist. Son of a musician, he studied medicine before turning his attention to mathematics. His invention of the hydrostatic balance (c. 1586) made him famous. In 1589 he published a treatise on the center of gravity in solids, which won him the post of mathematics lecturer at the University of Pisa. There he disproved the Aristotelian contention that bodies of different weights fall at different speeds; he also proposed the law of uniform acceleration for falling bodies and showed that the path of a thrown object is a parabola. The first to use a TELESCOPE to study the skies, he discovered (1609–10) that the surface of the moon was irregular, that the Milky Way was composed of stars, and that Jupiter had moons (see GALILEAN SATELLITE). His findings led to his appointment as philosopher and mathematician to the grand duke of Tuscany. During a visit to Rome (1611), he spoke persuasively for the COPERNICAN SYSTEM, which put him at odds with Aristotelian professors and led to Copernicanism's being declared false and erroneous (1616) by the Church. Obtaining permission to write about the Copernican system so long as he discussed it noncommittally, he wrote his *Dialogue Concerning the Two Chief World Systems* (1632). Though considered a masterpiece, it enraged the Jesuits, and Galileo was tried before the INQUISITION, found guilty of heresy, and forced to recant. He spent the rest of his life under house arrest, continuing to write and conduct research even after going blind in 1637.

Galileo NASA mission to study JUPITER and its GALILEAN SATELLITES with an orbiting spacecraft and an atmospheric probe, launched in 1989. Though the failure of its high-gain antenna resulted in its data being transmitted back to earth very slowly, the mission returned a wealth of valuable data. En route to Jupiter, the craft took the first detailed images of two asteroids. On arrival in 1995, it released the atmospheric probe into Jupiter's clouds, discovering large thunderstorms. In a series of flybys of the Galilean moons, it discovered evidence of volcanoes on Io hotter than any on earth, evidence of a liquid ocean below Europa's icy surface, a magnetic field around Ganymede, and evidence of a possible subsurface ocean on Callisto.

Galissonnière, Marquis de La See Marquis de LA GALISSONNIÈRE

gall Abnormal, localized outgrowth or swelling of plant tissue caused by infection from bacteria, fungi, viruses, or nematodes, or by irritation by insects and mites. The common plant disease CROWN GALL, characterized by the proliferation of galls on the roots and lower stems, is caused by the bacterium *Agrobacterium tumefaciens.*

gall See BILE

Gall, Franz Joseph (1758–1828) German anatomist and physiologist, founder of phrenology. Convinced that mental functions reside in specific brain areas and determine behavior, he assumed that the skull surface reflected development of these areas. The first concept was proved correct when PAUL BROCA located the brain's speech center in 1861. The second was invalidated when it was found that the skull's thickness varies, so its shape does not reflect the brain's. Gall was the first to identify gray matter with active tissue (nerves) and white matter with conducting tissue.

Galla See OROMO

Galland \gä-ˈlänt\, **Adolf (Joseph Ferdinand)** (1912–1996) German fighter ace. A skillful glider pilot by 20, he flew hundreds of missions in the SPANISH CIVIL WAR. In World War II he led a fighter squadron in the Battle of BRITAIN, destroying 100 British planes, and became commander of the Luftwaffe's fighter arm. Blamed by ADOLF HITLER and HERMANN GORING for the collapse of Germany's air defense against Anglo-American bombing raids, he was relieved of his command in 1945. Briefly imprisoned at the war's end, he later became an adviser to the Argentine air force and an aviation consultant in West Germany.

Gallant \ga-ˈlant\, **Mavis** *orig.* **Mavis de Trafford Young** (born 1922) Canadian-French writer. Born in Montreal, she moved to Europe in 1950 and settled in Paris. Her essays, novels, plays, and especially short stories delineate in unsentimental prose and with trenchant wit the isolation, detachment, and fear that afflict rootless North American and European expatriates. The *New Yorker* has published more than 100 of her stories (more than of any other writer) and much of her nonfiction.

Gallatin \ˈga-lə-tᵊn\, **(Abraham Alfonse) Albert** (1761–1849) Swiss-U.S. secretary of the treasury (1801–14). At 19 he emigrated to Pennsylvania, where he became successful in business and finance. In the U.S. House of Representatives (1795–1801), he set up its finance committee, the forerunner of the ways and means committee. As secretary of the treasury he reduced the national debt by $23 million. He opposed the War of 1812 and was instrumental in negotiating the Treaty of Ghent in 1814. He served as minister to France (1816–23) and to Britain (1826–27) and became president of the National (later Gallatin) Bank in New York City (1831–39).

Gallatin, portrait by Rembrandt Peale, 1805; in Independence National Historical Park, Philadelphia.

BY COURTESY OF THE INDEPENDENCE NATIONAL HISTORICAL PARK COLLECTION, PHILADELPHIA

Gallaudet \ˌgal-ə-ˈdet\, **Thomas Hopkins** (1787–1851) U.S. philanthropist. Born in Philadelphia, he graduated from Yale College and later studied in England and France, where he learned the sign method of communication. In 1816 he established the first free American school for the deaf at Hartford, Conn.; for over 50 years it would remain the main American training center for instructors of the deaf. GALLAUDET UNIV. is named in his honor.

Gallaudet University \ˌgal-ə-ˈdet\ Private university for deaf and hard-of-hearing students in Washington, D.C. It has its roots in a school for deaf and blind children founded in 1856 by Amos Kendall and headed 1857–1910 by Edward M. Gallaudet, son of THOMAS GALLAUDET, founder of the first school for the deaf in the U.S. It consists of a college of arts and sciences, a graduate school, and schools of communications, management, education and human services, and continuing education. Total enrollment is about 2,000.

gallbladder Muscular membranous sac under the liver that stores and concentrates BILE. Pear-shaped and expandable, it holds about 1.7 fluid oz (50 ml). Its inner surface absorbs water and inorganic salts from bile, which becomes 5–18 times more concentrated than when it leaves the liver. The gallbladder contracts to discharge bile through the bile duct into the DUODENUM. Disorders include GALLSTONES and inflammation (cholecystitis). Surgical removal of the gallbladder (cholecystectomy) has no serious side effects.

Gallé \gà-'lā\, **Emile** (1846–1904) French glass and furniture designer. From 1867 he worked in his father's faience and furniture factory in Nancy. His deeply colored opaque pieces, layered and carved or etched with plant motifs, were a great success at the Paris Exhibitions of 1878 and 1889 and were widely imitated. He used wheel cutting, acid etching, casing, and such special effects as metallic foil and air bubbles to produce what he called "marquetry of glass." His furniture designs featured floral inlay and carving; some incorporated inlaid quotations from well-known authors. A proponent of the Art Nouveau style, he collaborated with many colleagues, notably LOUIS MAJORELLE.

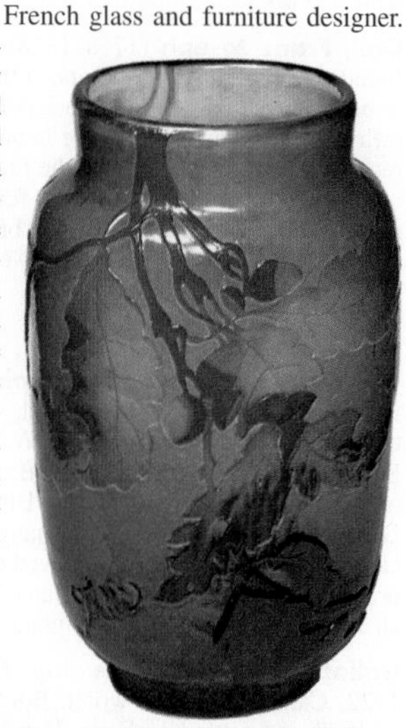

Vase with relief decoration by Émile Gallé, c. 1895; in the Victoria and Albert Museum, London.

BY COURTESY OF THE VICTORIA AND ALBERT MUSEUM, LONDON

gallery In architecture, a long, covered space open on one side, such as a PORTICO or a COLONNADE. It may be recessed into a wall or elevated on columns or CORBELS, and often serves as a passageway. Within an interior, a gallery may be a platform or upper floor projecting from a wall (e.g., in a legislative house) with seating for spectators. In a church NAVE, the long, narrow platforms supported by colonnades are called tribune galleries. In a theater, the gallery is the highest balcony and generally has the cheapest seats. Galleries appeared in Renaissance houses as long, narrow rooms used as promenades and to exhibit art. The modern art gallery is their descendant.

galley Large seagoing vessel propelled primarily by oars. The Egyptians, Cretans, and other ancient peoples used sail-equipped galleys for war and commerce. The Phoenicians apparently introduced the bireme (c. 700 BC), which had two banks of oars staggered on either side. The Greeks first built the TRIREME c. 500 BC. War galleys would cruise in columns, usually several abreast, and would engage the enemy as a PHALANX, again abreast. A galley could also confront the enemy with its bow, which was equipped with a RAM, grappling irons, and missile-hurling devices. Invention of the lateen (fore-and-aft) sail and the stern rudder rendered the galley obsolete for commerce, but its greater maneuverability maintained its military importance into the 16th century. See also LONGSHIP.

Galli Bibiena family \'gäl-lē-bēb-'yen-ä\ 18th-century Italian architects and theatrical designers. The family took its final name from the birthplace of its progenitor, the artist Giovanni Maria Galli (1625–1665). His descendants are noted for dazzling theatrical designs of spacious proportions achieved by intricate perspective. Giovanni's son Ferdinando Galli Bibiena (1657–1743) studied painting and architecture and worked for the duke of Parma. He designed scenery for court festivities and operas in Barcelona and Vienna, and was architect of the royal theater at Mantua. His brother Francesco (1659–1739) was the ducal architect at Mantua and built theaters in Vienna, Nancy (France), Verona, and Rome. Ferdinando's son Giuseppe (1696–1757), the most distinguished of the family, remained in Vienna to become chief organizer of splendid court functions. Engravings of his stage sets were published in three series (1716, 1723, 1740–44). He designed the interior of the theater at Bayreuth in 1748. His brothers Alessandro and Antonio were also architects and designers of note. His son Carlo (1728–1787), the last of the illustrious family, worked in theaters throughout Europe.

Gallia Narbonensis See NARBONENSIS

Gallic Wars (58–50 BC) Campaigns in which Julius CAESAR conquered GAUL. Clad in his bloodred cloak as a "distinguishing mark of battle," he led his troops to victories throughout the province, relying on superior strategy, tactics, discipline, and military engineering. In 58 he drove back the Helvetii from Rome's northwestern frontier, then subdued the Belgic group of Gallic peoples in the north (57), reconquered the Veneti (56), crossed the Rhine River to raid Germany (55), and crossed the Channel to raid Britain (55, 54). His major triumph was the defeat of VERCINGETORIX in 52. He described the campaigns in *De bello Gallico* ("On the Gallic War").

Gallicanism \'ga-lə-kə-ˌni-zəm\ French eccelesiastical and government policies designed to restrict the papacy's power. It affirmed the independence of the French king in the temporal realm, the superiority of an ecumenical council over the pope, and the union of king and clergy to limit the intervention of the pope within France. Gallicanism was opposed to Ultramontanism, which championed papal authority. The doctrine was important in the medieval struggle between church and state. In 1438, after several conflicts between kings and popes, Charles VII issued the PRAGMATIC SANCTION OF BOURGES, affirming that a pope was subject to a general council and that his jurisdiction was conditioned by the royal will.

Gallieni \gàl-yā-'nē\, **Joseph Simon** (1849–1916) French army officer. As governor of the French Sudan (1886–88), he successfully combated rebel Sudanese forces. After service in Indochina (1892–96), he returned to Africa as governor-general of Madagascar (1896–1905) and won a reputation as a judicious and flexible colonial master. He successfully integrated both African territories into the French colonial empire. Named military commander of Paris just before World War I, he fought in the First Battle of the MARNE and became minister of war in 1915. He was posthumously created marshal of France (1921).

Gallienus \ˌgal-ē-'ē-nəs\, **Publius Licinius Egnatius** (AD 218?–268) Roman emperor who ruled jointly with his father, VALERIAN (253–60), then alone (260–68). With the empire disintegrating under foreign invasions, the Senate made him co-emperor. He took charge of the western frontiers, winning a series of battles against the Goths and others. When the Persians devastated the East and his father died in captivity, he was left with only Italy and the Balkans. Later the Goths attacked anew; he was killed during his defense while trying to put down an insurgency. His reforms as emperor included the transfer of army command to professional equestrian officers, expansion of the cavalry, and an intellectual renaissance at Rome, discernible in its art and literature.

gallinule \'ga-lə-ˌnül\ Any of several species of marsh birds (family Rallidae) found in temperate, tropical, and subtropical regions worldwide. Gallinules are about 12–18 in. (30–45 cm) long, with a compressed body like those of the related RAILS and COOTS. They have a fleshy plate on the forehead and long, thin toes that enable them to run over floating vegetation. Many species have brightly colored areas of plumage or skin. They are noisy, inquisitive, and less secretive than most rails. Many are migratory. They build a bulky nest of rushes on or near the water. See also MOORHEN.

Purple gallinule (*Porphyrula martinica*).

RUTH CORDNER FROM ROOT RESOURCES—EB INC.

Gallipoli \gə-'li-pə-lē\ *Turkish* **Gelibolu** \ˌge-lē-bȯ-'lü\ *ancient* **Callipolis.** Seaport and town (pop., 1990: 18,000), European Turkey. It lies on a narrow peninsula at the entrance to the Sea of MARMARA, southwest of ISTANBUL. First colonized by the Greeks, it was the site of an important Byzantine fortress. It became the first Ottoman conquest in Europe (c. 1356) and was used as a naval base because of its strategic importance for the defense of Istanbul. Much of the town was destroyed in World War I during the DARDANELLES CAMPAIGN. Historic sites include a 14th-century Ottoman castle and the tombs of Thracian kings.

Gallipoli Campaign See DARDANELLES CAMPAIGN

Galloway, Joseph (1731?–1803) American colonial lawyer and legislator. Born in West River, Md., he became a lawyer in Philadelphia. He was elected to the colonial legislature in 1756 and served as speaker 1766–75. A Loyalist, he opposed the independence of the colonies; his efforts to peacefully settle the differences with Britain narrowly missed adoption by the Continental Congress. During the American Revolution he joined the British army under WILLIAM HOWE, then became a civil administrator during the British occupation of Philadelphia. When the Continental Army reentered the city in 1778, he fled to England.

gallstone Mass of crystallized substances that forms in the GALLBLADDER. The most common type occurs when the liver secretes BILE with too much CHOLESTEROL to stay in solution. Liver damage, chronic gallbladder disease, or biliary-tract cancer may predispose to stone formation. In the gallbladder, stones may cause INFLAMMATION or produce no symptoms. A stone obstructing the bile duct causes severe pain (biliary colic). Gallstones usually must be removed with the gallbladder or broken up with ULTRASOUND. In some cases a stone can be treated by giving the patient bile salts, which help redissolve cholesterol. If the gallbladder must be removed, LAPAROSCOPY is now the method of choice.

Gallup, George (Horace) (1901–1984) U.S. public-opinion statistician. Born in Jefferson, Iowa, he taught journalism at Drake University and Northwestern University until 1932, when a New York advertising firm hired him to conduct public-opinion surveys for its clients. He became a pioneer in the scientific sampling of public opinion, and his Gallup Poll, as well as other public-opinion polls, gained credibility after correctly forecasting FRANKLIN ROOSEVELT's 1936 presidential victory. Gallup founded the American Institute of Public Opinion (1935), the British Institute of Public Opinion (1936), and the Audience Research Institute (1939).

Galsworthy \'gȯlz-ˌwər-t͟hē\, **John** (1867–1933) English novelist and playwright. He gave up a law career to become a writer, and many of his works have legal themes. He published several works before *The Man of Property* (1906), the first novel of *The Forsyte Saga* (completed 1922). The family chronicle by which he is chiefly remembered, it consists of three novels linked by two interludes. He continued the story of the Forsytes in three further novels collected in *A Modern Comedy* (1929). His plays, written in a naturalistic style, usually examine a controversial ethical or social problem; they include *The Silver Box* (1906), *Strife* (1909), *Justice* (1910), and *Loyalties* (1922). He won the Nobel Prize in 1932.

Galt, Alexander Tilloch *later* **Sir Alexander** (1817–1893) British-Canadian statesman. He emigrated to Lower Canada (later Quebec) in 1835 and worked for the British-American Land Co., serving as high commissioner 1844–55. He served in the Canadian legislature (1849–50, 1853–72), becoming leader of the English-speaking minority. As finance minister (1858–62, 1864–67), he advocated federation, then served as the first finance minister of the Dominion government (1867–68). After retiring from Parliament in 1872, he advocated Canadian independence and served as the first Canadian high commissioner in London (1880–83).

Galton, Francis *later* **Sir Francis** (1822–1911) British explorer, anthropologist, and eugenicist, known for his pioneering studies in a variety of fields. Galton, a cousin of CHARLES DARWIN, studied medicine at Cambridge University but never took a degree. As a young man he traveled widely in Europe and Africa, making useful contributions in zoology and geography. He was among the first to recognize the implications of Darwin's theory of evolution, eventually coining the word EUGENICS to denote the science of planned human betterment through selective mating. His aim was the creation not of an aristocratic elite but of a population consisting entirely of superior men and women. He also wrote important works on human intelligence, fingerprinting, applied statistics, twins, blood transfusions, criminality, meteorology, and measurement.

Galton, detail of an oil painting by G. Graef, 1882; in the National Portrait Gallery, London.

BY COURTESY OF THE NATIONAL PORTRAIT GALLERY, LONDON

Galvani \gäl-'vä-nē\, **Luigi** (1737–1798) Italian physician and physicist. His early research focused on comparative anatomy, including the structure of kidney tubules and the middle ear. His developing interest in electricity was inspired by the fact that dead frogs underwent convulsions when attached to an iron fence to dry. He experimented with muscular stimulation by electrical means, using an electrostatic machine and a Leyden jar, and from the early 1780s animal electricity remained his major field of investigation. His discoveries led to the invention of the voltaic pile, a kind of battery that makes possible a constant source of current electricity.

galvanizing Protection of IRON or STEEL against exposure to the atmosphere and consequent rusting by application of a ZINC coating. Properly applied, galvanizing may protect from atmospheric CORROSION for 15–30 years or more. If the coating is damaged, the iron or steel continues to be protected by sacrificial corrosion, a phenomenon in which atmospheric oxidation spares the iron and affects the zinc (as long as it lasts). See also TERNEPLATE.

galvanometer \ˌgal-və-'nä-mə-tər\ Instrument for measuring small ELECTRIC CURRENTS by deflection of a moving coil. A common galvanometer consists of a light coil of wire suspended from a metallic ribbon between the poles of a permanent magnet. As current passes through the coil, the MAGNETIC FIELD it produces reacts with the magnetic field of the permanent magnet, producing a TORQUE. The torque causes the coil to rotate, moving an attached needle or mirror. The angle of rotation, which provides a measure of the current flowing in the coil, is measured by the movement of the needle or by the deflection of a beam of light reflected from the mirror.

Galveston City (pop., 1994 est.: 59,000) and port of entry, southeastern Texas. Located at the northeastern end of Galveston Island in the Gulf of Mexico, it was the pirate JEAN LAFFITE's headquarters (1817–21). Settlement of the island then began, and the town of Galveston was laid out in 1834; during the Texas revolt against Mexico (1835–36), it briefly served as the capital. During the AMERICAN CIVIL WAR it was an important Confederate supply port. Although the city has suffered from several hurricanes in the 20th century, it remains a major deepwater port, with shipping and oil refining facilities.

Gálvez \'gäl-ˌves\, **José** *later* **marqués (Marquess) de la Sonora** (1720–1787) Spanish colonial administrator. He was noted for his work as inspector general in New Spain (Mexico), 1765–71, where he reorganized the tax system, formed a government tobacco monopoly, and occupied Upper California. As minister of the Indies (from 1775), he worked to expand commerce. He devised the intendancy system that was introduced in 1786. Gálvez is considered Spain's greatest colonial administrator.

Galway \'gȯl-ˌwā\ County (pop., 1995 est.: 179,000), western Ireland. With an area of 2,293 sq mi (5,939 sq km), it is bounded on the west by the Atlantic Ocean. Its seat, the town of Galway (pop., 1995 est.: 51,000), is at the head of Galway Bay. The descendants of the followers of the Norman Richard de Burgh, who assumed rule in the area in the 1230s, became known as the tribes of Galway. After 1652 the land settlement of OLIVER CROMWELL established a new class of landed proprietors. Galway is still largely an agricultural region. It has the largest Gaelic-speaking population of any Irish county.

Galway, James (born 1939) Irish flutist. Born in Belfast, he went to London as a teenager to study flute, completing his studies with J.-P. RAMPAL and Marcel Moyse (1889–1984) in Paris. He was principal flutist of the Royal Philharmonic (1966–69) and later of the Berlin Philharmonic (1969–75). He subsequently enjoyed great success as a soloist in light classical and popular music.

Gama, Vasco da *later* **conde (Count) da Vidigueira** (c. 1460–1524) Portuguese navigator. On his first voyage to India (1497–99), he traveled around the Cape of Good Hope with four ships, visiting trading cities in Mozambique and Kenya en route. Portugal's King MANUEL I acted quickly to open trade routes with India, but a massacre of Portuguese in India caused him to dispatch a fleet of 20 ships in 1502, led by da Gama, to establish Portuguese supremacy in the region. Da Gama, now an admiral, forced allegiance along the way from local rulers and attacked Arab shipping. After various battles, he secured obedience to Portuguese rule and returned home. In 1524 he was appointed Portuguese viceroy in India but died shortly after arriving in Goa. His voyages to India opened the sea route from Western Europe to the East.

Gamaliel I \gə-ˈmā-lē-əl\ *or* **Rabban Gamaliel** \rä-ˈbän\ (fl. 1st century AD) Early rabbinic figure and patriarch of the Jewish community of Israel. Grandson of the renowned HILLEL, he became a respected scholar of the Torah and a member of the Sanhedrin. Known for his mastery of Jewish oral law, he was the first to be granted the title of rabban. He is mentioned in the New Testament as a teacher of St. PAUL and a friend of the early Christians.

Gamaliel II *or* **Gamaliel of Jabneh** \ˈjab-nə\ (fl. late 1st/early 2nd century AD) Rabbi and president of the SANHEDRIN. Grandson of GAMALIEL I, he rallied the Jews who had taken refuge in the city of Jabneh after the fall of Jerusalem to the Romans in AD 70. He became patriarch of the Jewish community of Israel c. AD 80. One of the greatest legal scholars of his era, Gamaliel is frequently cited in the MISHNA. He helped unify the Jews by regulating prayer ritual and the Jewish calendar.

Gambetta \ˌgäⁿ-bə-ˈtä, *Engl* gam-ˈbe-tə\, **Léon** (1838–1882) French republican statesman who helped found the THIRD REPUBLIC. He became famous as a lawyer defending republican critics of the SECOND EMPIRE and was elected to the legislative assembly in 1869. He helped direct the defense of France during the FRANCO-PRUSSIAN WAR and played a principal role in the provisional government formed after NAPOLEON III's capture in 1870. He used his persuasive skill to push for ratification of the CONSTITUTIONAL LAWS OF 1875, which became the basis of the new parliamentary republic. As president of the Chamber of Deputies (1879–81) and premier (1881–82), he continued his advocacy of democratic ideals and national unity.

Gambetta, photograph by Étienne Carjat; in the Bibliothéque Nationale, Paris.

BY COURTESY OF THE BIBLIOTHEQUE NATIONALE, PARIS

Gambia *officially* **Republic of the Gambia** Republic, western Africa. Constituting an enclave in Senegal, it lies along the GAMBIA RIVER stretching inland 295 mi (475 km) from the Atlantic Ocean. Area: 4,127 sq mi (10,689 sq km). Population (1997 est.): 1,248,000. Capital: BANJUL. About two-fifths of the population is MALINKE, followed by FULANI (about one-fifth), WOLOF (about one-seventh), and other groups. Language: English (official). Religion: Islam. Monetary unit: dalasi. Gambia is generally hilly and the climate subtropical, with savanna in the uplands and swamps in low-lying areas. It has a developing market economy based largely on the production and export of peanuts, though only about one-sixth of the country is arable. The river serves as a major transportation artery. Tourism is an important source of revenue. It is a republic with one legislative body; its head of state and government is the president. Beginning around the 13th century AD, the Wolof, Malinke, and Fulani peoples settled in different parts of what is now Gambia and established villages and then kingdoms in the region. European exploration began when the Portuguese sighted the Gambia River in 1455. In the 17th century, when Britain and France both settled in the area, the British Fort James, on an island about 20 mi (32 km) from the river's mouth, was an important collection point for the SLAVE TRADE. In 1783 the Treaty of Versailles reserved the Gambia River for Britain. After the British abolished slavery in 1807, they built a fort at the mouth of the river to block the continuing slave trade. In 1889 Gambia's boundaries were agreed upon by Britain and France; the British declared a protectorate over the area in 1894. Independence was proclaimed in 1965, and Gambia became a republic within the Commonwealth in 1970. It formed a limited confederation with Senegal in 1982, which was dissolved in 1989. During the 1990s, the government was in turmoil. See map above.

Gambia River River, western Africa. Rising in Guinea and flowing northwest through Senegal and west through Gambia to the Atlantic Ocean, it is 700 mi (1,120 km) long. It is the only western African river

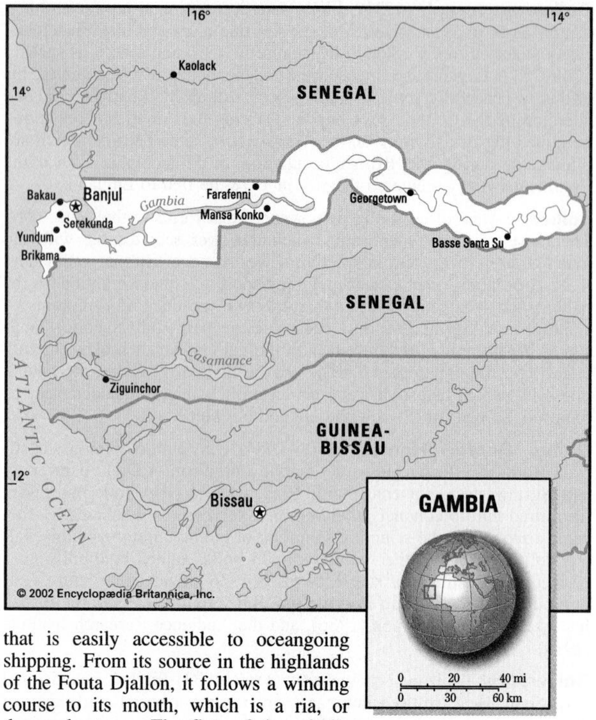

that is easily accessible to oceangoing shipping. From its source in the highlands of the Fouta Djallon, it follows a winding course to its mouth, which is a ria, or drowned estuary. The flats of the middle and upper river support rice and peanuts and are more heavily settled than the area around the river's lower course.

Gambier Islands \ˈgam-ˌbir\ Island group, FRENCH POLYNESIA. It is the southeasternmost extension of the TUAMOTU ARCHIPELAGO. The largest island, Mangareva, is 5 mi (8 km) long and encircled by a barrier reef 40 mi (64 km) in circumference. It rises to about 1,444 ft (440 m) in the peaks Duff and Mokoto; the chief village of Rikitea is on its eastern side. It was annexed by the French in 1881. The economy is based on subsistence agriculture.

gambling Betting or staking of something of value on the outcome of a game or event. Commonly associated with gambling are HORSE RACING, BOXING, numerous playing-card and DICE games, COCKFIGHTING, JAI ALAI, and recreational BILLIARDS and DARTS. BINGO and LOTTERY also represent forms of gambling. In most gambling games it is customary to express the idea of probability in terms of "odds against winning." Casino gambling, once highly restricted, is now legal in many states, and lotteries are employed by many states to raise revenues. See also BOOKMAKING, CASINO.

game show *or* **quiz show** Radio or television show designed to test the knowledge or luck of contestants or experts. Among the shows popular on U.S. radio were *Dr. I.Q.* (1939–49), *Information, Please* (1938–48), and *The Quiz Kids* (1940–53). The genre was adopted by television and cash awards were increased, so that radio's *$64 Question* became television's *$64,000 Question*. In the mid-1950s, to increase their shows' popularity, some producers began feeding answers to contestants chosen to win. An accusation of unfair practices on *Twenty-one* (1958) led to a government investigation and the quick demise of the big-money shows. The game show later regained popularity when it was revived in formats with lower stakes and easier questions, as on *The Price is Right*, *Jeopardy!*, and *Wheel of Fortune*.

game theory Branch of applied mathematics devised to analyze certain situations in which there is an interplay between parties that may have similar, opposed, or mixed interests. Game theory was originally developed by JOHN VON NEUMANN and Oscar Morgenstern in their book *The Theory of Games and Economic Behavior* (1944). In a typical game, decision-making "players," who each have their own goals, try to outsmart one another by anticipating the others' decisions; the game is finally resolved as a consequence of these decisions. A solution to a game prescribes the decisions the players should make and describes the game's appropriate outcome. See also DECISION THEORY, PRISONER'S DILEMMA.

gamelan \'ga-mə-,lan\ Indigenous orchestra of Java and Bali, and more generally of Indonesia and Malaysia, usually consisting largely of gongs, xylophones, and metallophones (rows of tuned metal bars struck with a mallet). Gamelan polyphony is complex and many-voiced. The melody is taken by the voice, flute, or rebab (a bowed stringed instrument); under it, most of the other instruments provide rhythmic paraphrases of the melody, producing a shimmering, variegated texture. The gamelan has influenced such Western composers as C. DEBUSSY, O. MESSIAEN, J. CAGE, S. REICH, and P. GLASS.

Gamelin \,gàm-'laⁿ, *Engl* ,ga-mə-'lan\, **Maurice (-Gustave)** (1872–1958) French army commander. He entered the army in 1893 and rose to division command in World War I and army chief of staff in 1931. He supported the defensive strategy based on the MAGINOT LINE and, as commander of Allied forces when World War II broke out, took no offensive action during the PHONY WAR. Surprised by the German assault in the Ardennes (May 1940), he was dismissed and replaced by MAXIME WEYGAND, but France collapsed the next month. He was tried by the Vichy government and interned in Germany 1943–45.

gametophyte \gə-'mē-tə-,fīt\ In certain plants, the sexual phase (or an individual representing the phase) in the ALTERNATION OF GENERATIONS. The alternate, nonsexual phase is the SPOROPHYTE. In the gametophyte phase, male and female organs (gametangia) develop and produce eggs and sperm (gametes), which unite in fertilization (syngamy). The fertilized egg (zygote) develops into the sporophyte, which produces numerous single-celled SPORES, which in turn develop directly into new gametes.

gamma decay Type of RADIOACTIVITY in the most common form of which an unstable atomic nucleus dissipates energy by gamma emission, producing GAMMA RAYS. Gamma decay also includes two other processes, internal conversion and internal PAIR PRODUCTION. In internal conversion, excess energy in a NUCLEUS is transferred to one of its own orbiting ELECTRONS and the electron is ejected from the ATOM. In internal pair production, excess energy is converted into an electron and a POSITRON, which are emitted together. Typical half-lives (see HALF-LIFE) for gamma emission range from about 10^{-9} to 10^{-14} second.

gamma globulin \'gläb-yə-lən\ Subgroup of the GLOBULINS. In humans and many other mammals, most ANTIBODIES are in the gamma globulin fraction of blood. A human gamma globulin preparation may be administered (by injection) to persons lacking IMMUNITY, either generally or to a particular disease, after exposure or before expected exposure.

gamma ray Penetrating very short-wavelength ELECTROMAGNETIC RADIATION, similar to an X ray but of higher energy, that is emitted spontaneously by some radioactive substances (see GAMMA DECAY, RADIOACTIVITY). Gamma radiation also originates in the decay of certain SUBATOMIC PARTICLES, and in particle-antiparticle ANNIHILATION (see also ANTIMATTER). Gamma rays can initiate nuclear fission, can be absorbed by ejection of an electron (see PHOTOELECTRIC EFFECT), and can be scattered by free electrons (see COMPTON EFFECT).

gamma-ray astronomy Study of astronomical objects that emit GAMMA RAYS. Gamma-ray telescopes are designed to study high-energy astrophysical systems, including stellar CORONAS, WHITE DWARF STARS, NEUTRON STARS, BLACK HOLES, SUPERNOVA remnants, CLUSTERS OF GALAXIES, and diffuse gamma-ray COSMIC BACKGROUND RADIATION. Puzzling gamma-ray bursts were first detected in the early 1960s. They were widely hypothesized to be produced by neutron stars in the Milky Way, but their even distribution (unlike the distribution of stars in this galaxy) makes their origin likely to be extragalactic. In the early 1970s the first gamma-ray observatory satellite, launched to collect data from above the atmosphere (which absorbs gamma rays), detected a bright gamma-ray source with no obvious optical counterpart. Its nature remained a mystery until 1992, when detection of periodic X-ray and gamma-ray emission suggested that it is a PULSAR, the nearest yet detected.

Gamow \'ga-,mȯf\, **George** *orig.* **Georgy Antonovich Gamov** (1904–1968) Russian-U.S. nuclear physicist and cosmologist. After studying at Leningrad University with Aleksandr Friedmann (1888–1925), he subsequently developed his quantum theory of radioactivity, the first successful explanation of the behavior of radioactive elements. His "liquid drop" model of atomic nuclei served as the basis for modern theories of nuclear fission and fusion. After emigrating to the U.S. in 1934, he collaborated with EDWARD TELLER in researching beta decay (1936) and developing a theory of the internal structures of red giant stars (1942). In the 1950s he became interested in biochemistry, proposing theories of genetic-code structure that were later found to be true. Throughout his career he also wrote popular works on such difficult subjects as relativity and cosmology.

Gan River *or* **Kan River** \'gän\ River, southeastern China. Located in JIANGXI province, it flows north through Poyang Lake to enter the CHANG (YANGTZE) RIVER after a course of 537 mi (864 km). A major southern tributary of the Chang, its valley provided an important route in historical times from GUANGZHOU to the Chang valley and the north.

Gäncä \gän-'jä\ *formerly (1804–1918)* **Yelizavetpol** \yi-li-zə-'vyet-,pȯl\ *(1935–89)* **Kirovabad** \,kē-rə-və-'bät\ City (pop., 1995 est.: 292,000), western Azerbaijan. It lies along the Gäncä River. A town was founded nearby in the 5th century AD, destroyed by earthquake in 1139, and rebuilt on the present site. Taken by the Mongols in 1231, it was captured in 1606 by the Persians, who made it the center of the Gäncä khanate. The Russians annexed it in 1804 and renamed it Yelizavetpol. In 1935 it was renamed Kirovabad and developed industrially to become one of the largest cities of Azerbaijan. It manufactures aluminum, machinery, and instruments and is an agricultural processing center. Notable buildings include Dzhuma-Mechet Mosque (1620) and the mausoleum of the Persian poet NEZAMI.

Gance \'gäⁿs\, **Abel** *orig.* **Eugène Alexandre Péréthon** (1889–1981) French film director and screenwriter. He worked in the cinema from 1909, finally winning acclaim with *Mater dolorosa* (1917) and *Tenth Symphony* (1918). His *J'accuse* (1918) and *The Wheel* (1923) were hailed as masterpieces. He devoted four years to his masterpiece, *Napoléon* (1927), in which he used experimental techniques to emphasize cinematic movement. Battle sequences were shot with three synchronized cameras and the images were projected on a triple screen to produce a three-dimensional effect, and the film pioneered in the use of stereophonic sound. A triumph in Europe, it fared badly in a harshly cut version in the U.S. but was finally released in its original glory in 1981. Gance's later films, largely controlled by the studios, gave inadequate scope for his creative genius.

Gance, 1954.
H. ROGER-VIOLLET

Ganda *or* **Baganda** People of southern Uganda who speak Luganda, a BANTU LANGUAGE of the BENUE-CONGO group. Numbering 3.7 million, the Ganda are Uganda's largest ethnic group. Traditionally hoe cultivators, they also grow cotton and coffee for export and keep livestock. In the 19th century the Ganda developed the centralized state known as BUGANDA.

Gandhara art Style of Buddhist art that developed in what is now northwestern Pakistan and eastern Afghanistan from the 1st to the 7th century AD. It was contemporaneous with MATHURA ART. The Gandhara region had earlier been a site of much Buddhist missionary activity, and the Kushan rulers maintained contact with Rome; the Gandhara school incorporated motifs and techniques from classical Roman art

The Buddha preaching, relief from Gandhara, schist, c. 2nd century AD; in the Prince of Wales Museum of Western India, Bombay.
P. CHANDRA

(e.g., vine scrolls, cherubs with garlands, tritons, centaurs), but the iconography was based on the interpretation of Buddhist legends. Sculptural materials included green phyllite, gray-blue mica, and stucco; sculptures were originally painted and gilded. See also KUSHAN ART.

Gandhi \'gän-dē\, **Indira (Priyadarshini)** *orig.* **Indira Priyadarshini Nehru** (1917–1984) Prime minister of India (1966–77, 1980–84). The only child of JAWAHARLAL NEHRU, she studied in India and at Oxford University. In 1942 she married Feroze Gandhi (died 1960), a fellow member of the INDIAN NATIONAL CONGRESS. In 1959 she was given the largely honorary position of party president, and in 1966 she achieved actual power when she was made leader of the Congress Party and, consequently, prime minister. She instituted major reforms, including a strict population-control program. In 1971 she mobilized Indian forces against Pakistan in the cause of East Bengal's secession. She oversaw the incorporation of Sikkim in 1974. Convicted in 1975 of violating election laws, she declared a state of emergency, jailing opponents and passing many laws limiting personal freedoms. She was defeated in the following election, but she returned to power in 1980. In 1984, in response to Sikh separatist violence, she ordered an army attack on the Golden Temple, the holiest Sikh shrine, which resulted in over 450 Sikh deaths. She was later shot and killed by her own Sikh bodyguards in revenge.

Indira Gandhi.
AP/WIDE WORLD PHOTOS

Gandhi, Mohandas K(aramchand) *known as* **Mahatma Gandhi** (1869–1948) Preeminent leader of Indian nationalism and prophet of nonviolence in the 20th century. Gandhi grew up in a home steeped in religion, and he took for granted ahimsa (noninjury to all living beings) and religious tolerance. He studied law in England, but, too diffident to make a successful lawyer, he ended up taking a job with an Indian firm in South Africa. There he became an effective advocate for Indian rights. In 1906 he first put into action SATYAGRAHA, his technique of nonviolent resistance. His success in South Africa had given him an international reputation by the time he returned to India in 1914, where within a few years he had become the leader of a nationwide struggle for Indian home rule. By 1920 Gandhi commanded influence hitherto unattained by any political leader in India. He refashioned the INDIAN NATIONAL CONGRESS into an effective political instrument of Indian nationalism and undertook major campaigns of nonviolent resistance in 1920–22, 1930–34 (including his momentous march to the sea to collect salt to protest a government monopoly), and 1940–42. In the 1930s he also campaigned to end discrimination against India's untouchable class and concentrated on educating rural India and promoting cottage industry. India achieved dominion status in 1947, but the fact that the country was partitioned into India and Pakistan was a great disappointment to Gandhi, who had long worked for Hindu-Muslim unity. In September 1947 he ended rioting in Calcutta (now Kolkata) by fasting. In January 1948 he was shot down by a young Hindu fanatic. Gandhi won the affection and loyalty of millions and became known as the Mahatma, or great soul.

Gandhi, Rajiv (Ratna) (1944–1991) Indian politician, prime minister of India (1984–89). Son of INDIRA GANDHI, he studied engineering at Cambridge University and became a commercial airline pilot in 1968. He entered politics after the death of his brother Sanjay in 1980. Sworn in as prime minister the day his mother was assassinated (October 31, 1984), he led the Congress (I) Party to a landslide victory in elections that year. His administration took vigorous measures to reform the government bureaucracy and liberalize the country's economy, but his attempts to discourage separatist movements failed, and his government became embroiled in financial scandals. He resigned in 1989 but remained leader of the Congress (I) Party. He was assassinated in 1991 while running for reelection.

Gandhinagar \ˌgən-də-'nə-gər\ City (pop., 1991: 122,000), capital of GUJARAT state, western central India. It lies on the banks of the Sabarmati River, north of the former capital of AHMADABAD. Built to supplant the former capital, after the state of BOMBAY was divided, the city was begun in 1966 and named for MOHANDAS K. GANDHI. The first state government offices were transferred there in 1970, and the city continued to grow through the 1990s.

Gando See GWANDU

Ganesha *or* **Ganesa** \gə-'nā-shə\ Elephant-headed Hindu god, the son of SHIVA and PARVATI. He is also revered in Jainism, and he is important in the art and mythology of Buddhist Asia. As the remover of obstacles, Ganesha is invoked when beginning worship or starting any new venture. He was popular with Indian nationalists, who saw British colonialism as one obstacle to be removed. The patron of letters and learning, he is the legendary scribe who wrote down the *MAHABHARATA*. His popularity continued to grow through the 20th century. His festival is especially popular in the Indian state of MAHARASHTRA.

Ganesa dancing, relief from Farrukhabad, Uttar Pradesh, India, 10th century AD; in the State Museum, Lucknow, India.
PRAMOD CHANDRA

Gang of Four Most powerful members of a radical political elite convicted for implementing the harsh policies of MAO ZEDONG during the CULTURAL REVOLUTION. The four were Wang Hongwen, Zhang Chunqiao, Yao Wenyuan, and Mao's third wife, JIANG QING. Manipulating the youthful RED GUARDS, the Gang of Four controlled four areas: intellectual education, basic theories in science and technology, teacher-student relations and school discipline, and party policies regarding intellectuals. The turmoil of the Cultural Revolution subsided after 1969, but the Gang of Four maintained their power until Mao's death in 1976, when they were imprisoned; they stood trial in 1980–81.

Ganga dynasty \'gäŋ-gə\ Either of two distinct but remotely related Indian dynasties. The Western Gangas ruled in MYSORE state c. AD 250–1004. They encouraged scholarly work, built some remarkable temples, and encouraged cross-peninsular trade. The Eastern Gangas ruled KALINGA from 1028 to 1434–35. They were great patrons of religion and the arts; the temples of the Ganga period rank among the masterpieces of Hindu architecture. Both dynasties interacted with the CALUKYA and COLA dynasties.

Ganges Delta *or* **Ganges-Brahmaputra Delta** Region in WEST BENGAL, India, and Bangladesh. An area of about 220 mi (354 km) wide along the Bay of BENGAL, it is covered by the streams forming the mouths of the GANGES and BRAHMAPUTRA rivers. In Bangladesh, the Brahmaputra is joined by the Tista River, and from there to its junction with the Ganges is known as the Jamuna River. The main streams, the Ganges and the Jamuna, unite to form the Padma River. The river farthest west that enters the Bay of Bengal is the HUGLI RIVER. Many smaller streams of the Delta form a swamp region (about 6,526 sq mi or 16,902 sq km in area) known as the Sunderbans. The Delta was struck in 1970 by one of history's most devastating cyclones.

Ganges River \'gan-ˌjēz\ *Hindi* **Ganga** \'gəŋ-gə\ River, northern India. Held sacred by followers of HINDUISM, it is formed from five headstreams rising in northern UTTAR PRADESH state. On its 1,560-mi (2,510-km) course, it flows southeast through the Indian states of BIHAR and WEST BENGAL. In central Bangladesh it is joined by the BRAHMAPUTRA and MEGHNA rivers. Their combined waters empty into the Bay of BENGAL and form a delta 200 mi (320 km) wide, which is shared by India and Bangladesh. Its plain is one of the most fertile and densely populated regions in the world.

Gangetic Plain \gan-'je-tik\ *or* **Indo-Gangetic Plain** Fertile region in north-central India stretching westward from the BRAHMAPUTRA River valley and the GANGES DELTA to the INDUS RIVER valley. It contains the subcontinent's richest and most densely populated areas. The greater part of the plain is made up of alluvial soil, deposited by the Ganges,

Brahmaputra, and Indus rivers. The eastern part of the plain has summer rainfall so heavy that vast areas become swamps or shallow lakes. It becomes progressively drier toward the west, where it incorporates the THAR DESERT.

ganglion \'gaŋ-glē-ən\ Aggregate of nerve-cell bodies outside the central NERVOUS SYSTEM (CNS). The spinal ganglion contains the nerve-cell bodies of the nerve fibers that carry impulses toward the CNS (afferent neurons in dorsal root ganglia) or away from it (efferent neurons in ventral root ganglia).

gangrene Localized soft-tissue death (necrosis) from prolonged blood-supply blockage. It can occur in ARTERIOSCLEROSIS, DIABETES MELLITUS, or decubitus ULCER, and after severe BURNS or FROSTBITE. In dry gangrene, gradual blood-supply decrease turns the part discolored and cold, then dark and dry. Treatment requires improving blood flow. Moist gangrene comes from a sudden blood-supply cutoff. Bacterial infection causes swelling, discoloration, and then a foul smell. Along with antibiotics, tissue removal may be needed to prevent spread, which can be fatal. A more virulent form, gas gangrene, is named for gas bubbles under the skin produced by a highly lethal toxin from CLOSTRIDIUM bacteria. The wound oozes brownish, smelly pus. Infection spreads rapidly, causing death. All dead and diseased tissue must be removed and antibiotics given; an antitoxin can also be used.

Gangtok \'gəŋ-ˌtȯk\ Town (pop., 2001 est.: 29,162), capital of SIKKIM state, northeastern India. At an elevation of 5,600 ft (1,700 m), it overlooks the Ranipool River. It was the governmental seat of the kingdom of Sikkim until the monarchy was abolished (1975) and India annexed Sikkim (1976). It was an important point on the India–Tibet trade route until the border with Tibet was closed in 1962. The former royal palace and chapel are located there; the noted Buddhist monastery of Rumtek is nearby.

Ganioda'yo See HANDSOME LAKE

gannet Any of three oceanic bird species (family Sulidae) closely related to the BOOBIES. Gannets are found in the North Atlantic, where they are the largest seabirds, and in temperate waters around Africa, Australia, and New Zealand. Adults are mainly white with black-tipped wing feathers and a large, yellowish or buff-colored head marked with black around the eyes. They have a tapered beak and pointed tail. They dive with half-closed wings to catch fish and squid. They waddle on land but are expert fliers, spending most of their lives over water. They nest in dense colonies on cliffs. The largest species is the 40-in. (100-cm) northern gannet.

Northern gannets (*Morus bassanus*).
WILLIAM AND LAURA RILEY

Gannett Co., Inc. One of the largest newspaper groups in the U.S. It was founded by Frank Ernest Gannett (1876–1957), who in 1906 began buying small newspapers in upstate New York. It was incorporated in 1923. Its stock was first publicly traded in 1967. In 1982 it began publishing *USA TODAY*, the first national general-interest newspaper in the U.S. By 2002 it owned about 94 daily papers, with a total circulation of 7.7 million. It also owns about 20 television stations.

Gansu *or* **Kansu** \'gän-'sü\ Province (pop., 1999 est.: 25,430,000), northern central China. For centuries a passage between the Upper HUANG HE (Yellow River) region and western China, it became part of Chinese territory in the 3rd century BC. It was renowned as the entranceway into China used by MARCO POLO. Eastern Gansu is the main site of earthquakes in China; in 1920 an earthquake there caused 200,000 deaths. Gansu's capital is LANZHOU. Wheat is the province's chief crop, and wheat flour rather than rice is the basis of the local diet.

Ganymede In Greek legend, the son of King Tros (or Laomedon) of Troy. Because of his unusual beauty, he was carried off by ZEUS disguised as an eagle, and he became cupbearer to the gods. Other versions of the legend trace his abduction to other gods or to King MINOS of Crete. The story has long been held to have homosexual implications, and the word catamite is derived from his Latin name, Catamitus.

Ganymede and Zeus in the form of an eagle, antique marble statue; in the Vatican Museum.
ANDERSON–ALINARI FROM ART RESOURCE/EB INC.

GAO See GENERAL ACCOUNTING OFFICE

Gao Xingjian (born 1940) Chinese émigré novelist and playwright. His novel *Lingshan* (1989; *Soul Mountain*) resulted from a pilgrimage in the form of a 10-month walking tour along the YANGTZE RIVER. Gao's works were banned in China after the publication of *Taowang* (1989; *Fugitives*), which reflected the 1989 events in TIANANMEN SQUARE. In 1987 he settled in France and later became a French citizen. He was awarded the Nobel Prize for Literature in 2000.

gar Any of several large North or Central American fishes (genus *Lepisosteus*) related to the BOWFIN and dating back to the EOCENE EPOCH. Gars are confined chiefly to freshwater, though some species enter brackish or salt water. They frequently bask at the surface in sluggish waters and commonly breathe atmospheric air. Their jaws and face form a sharp-toothed beak, and their body is encased in an armor of diamond-shaped, thick scales. Their eggs are toxic to predators. They are highly voracious predators, with long rows of needlelike teeth. The alligator gar of the southern U.S. reaches a length of about 10 ft (3 m) and is one of the largest freshwater fishes.

Garand \gə-'rand, 'gar-ənd\, **John C(antius)** (1888–1974) U.S. (Canadian-born) firearms engineer. Born in St. Rémi, Quebec, he moved with his family to Connecticut in 1898. From 1919 he worked at the SPRINGFIELD ARMORY; after 17 years, he devised a gas-operated weapon of .30-in. caliber that was 43 in. (109 cm) long yet weighed only 9.5 lbs (4.3 kg). Adopted in 1936, the M1 became the world's first standard-issue autoloading infantry rifle; it gave U.S. troops in World War II and the Korean War a great advantage. Garand signed over all patents of his invention to the U.S. government.

garbanzo See CHICKPEA

Garbo, Greta *orig.* **Greta Louisa Gustafsson** (1905–1990) Swedish-U.S. film star. She was working as a salesgirl when she was chosen to appear in publicity films. Her modest success encouraged her to study at the Royal Dramatic Theatre's training school, where the film director Mauritz Stiller discovered her. He cast her in *The Story of Gösta Berling* (1924) and became her mentor and coach. They were hired by MGM in 1925, and Garbo's beauty and enigmatic personality made her a star in her first U.S. film, *The Torrent* (1926). Aloof, mysterious, yet passionate, she mesmerized audiences in such films as *Anna Christie* (1930), *Grand Hotel* (1932), *Anna Karenina* (1935), *Camille* (1936), and *Ninotchka* (1939). Her reclusive life after her early retirement added to her mystique.

Greta Garbo in *Camille* (1936).
CULVER PICTURES

García Lorca \gär-'thē-ä-'lȯr-kä\, **Federico** (1898–1936) Spanish poet and dramatist. He studied literature, painting, and music, and later was a founder, director, and musician for La Barraca, a theatrical company that brought classical drama to rural audiences. He was an established experimental poet when he became famous for *The Gypsy Ballads* (1928), a verse collection lyrically combining his musical, poetical, and spiritual impulses; as in many of his later works, its themes and images were drawn from folk traditions. Of his many poems of death, "Lament for the Death of a Bullfighter" (1935), written for a friend, is his most famous poem and the finest elegy in modern Spanish literature. His dramatic trilogy consisting of *Blood Wedding* (produced 1933), *Yerma* (produced 1934), and *The House of Bernarda Alba* (produced 1936) is the best known of his masterpieces. As if fulfilling the premonition of violent death that haunts his works, he was shot without trial by fascists during the Spanish Civil War.

García Márquez \gär-'sē-ä-'mär-kās\, **Gabriel (José)** (born 1928) Latin-American writer. He worked many years as a journalist in Latin-American and European cities, and later also as a screenwriter and publicist, before settling in Mexico. His best-known work, the novel *One Hundred Years of Solitude* (1967), recounts the history of the fictional village of Macondo, the setting of much of his work; enormously admired and influential, it became the principal vehicle for the style known as magic realism. Later novels include *The Autumn of the Patriarch* (1975), *Chronicle of a Death Foretold* (1981), *Love in the Time of Cholera* (1985), and *The General in His Labyrinth* (1989). His collections of short stories and novellas include *No One Writes to the Colonel* (1968) and *Leaf Storm* (1955). He received the Nobel Prize in 1982.

García Márquez, 1982.
© LUTFI OZKOK

Gard, Roger Martin du See Roger Martin du Gard

Garda, Lake *ancient* **Lacus Benacus.** Lake, northern Italy. Largest of the Italian lakes, it is 34 mi (54 km) long and 2–11 mi (3–18 km) wide, with a shoreline of 77.5 mi (125 km). It borders Lombardy, Veneto, and Trentino-Alto Adige. Separated from the Adige River valley by the narrow ridge of Mount Baldo, it is fed by the Sarca River at its northern end, while the Mincio flows out toward the Po River to the south. The lake is encircled by the Gardesana scenic route, opened in 1931, and is sheltered by the Alps to the north, which promotes a temperate Mediterranean climate. It is a popular resort area.

garden Plot of ground where herbs, fruits, flowers, vegetables, or trees are cultivated. The earliest surviving detailed garden plan is Egyptian and dates from about 1400 BC; it shows tree-lined avenues and rectangular ponds. Mesopotamian gardens were places where shade and cool water could be enjoyed; Hellenistic gardens were conspicuously luxurious in their display of precious materials, a tradition carried over by Byzantine gardens. Islamic gardens made use of water, often in pools and fed by narrow canals resembling irrigation channels. In Renaissance Europe, gardens reflected confidence in human ability to impose order on the external world; Italian gardens emphasized the unity of house and garden. French 17th-century gardens were rigidly symmetrical, and French cultural dominance in Europe popularized this style into the next century. In 18th-century England, increasing awareness of the natural world led to the development of "natural" gardens that made use of irregular, nonsymmetrical layouts. Chinese gardens have generally harmonized with the natural landscape, and have employed rocks gathered from great distances as a universal decorative feature. Early Japanese gardens imitated Chinese principles; later developments were the abstract garden, which might feature only sand and rocks, and miniature gardens made in trays (see bonsai).

garden city Ideal planned community as envisioned by the British town planner Ebenezer Howard (1850–1928). It was to be a small city that combined the amenities of urban and rural life; it would be compact, with contained growth. At the center would be a garden ringed with a civic and cultural complex, a park, housing, and industry, the whole surrounded by an agricultural green belt. Traffic would move along radial avenues and ring roads. The first garden city was built at Letchworth, England, in 1903. Though Howard's ideas have been widely influential, imitators have often ignored his stipulation that the town be a self-contained, true mixed-use community.

Garden Grove City (pop., 1996 est.: 149,000), southwestern California. Located south of Anaheim, it is a growing suburban residential area. It is the site of the Crystal Cathedral, a church sheathed in 10,000 panes of glass, designed by Philip Johnson.

gardenia Any of the approximately 200 species of ornamental shrubs and trees in the genus *Gardenia,* in the madder family, native to tropical and subtropical Africa and Asia. Gardenias have white or yellow tubular flowers, evergreen leaves, and large, berrylike fruits containing a sticky, orange pulp. Cape jasmine *(G. jasminoides),* native to China, is the fragrant species sold by florists.

gardening Laying out and tending of a garden. Though palatial gardens existed in ancient times, small home gardens became prevalent only in the 19th century. Gardening as a pastime grew with the increase in home ownership and leisure time. A well-designed flower garden displays blends and contrasts of colors and forms, and takes into account the effect of seasonal changes. Essential tasks include soil maintenance, control of weeds, and protection of plants from pests and diseases. Chemical means are widely used, though environmentally sensitive methods such as organic supplements and hand-weeding have become increasingly popular.

Gardiner, Samuel Rawson (1829–1902) English historian whose career was dedicated to the study of the English Civil Wars. He taught at King's College, London, and was a fellow at Oxford. His researches among manuscript collections gave unrivaled authority to his monumental undertaking. Its principal volumes were *History of England from the Accession of James I to the Outbreak of the Civil War, 1603–1642* (1883–84); *History of the Great Civil War, 1642–1649* (1886, 1893); and *History of the Commonwealth and Protectorate, 1649–1660* (1903).

Gardner, Alexander (1821–1882) Scottish-U.S. photographer. In 1856, the year he emigrated from Scotland, he was hired by Mathew B. Brady as a portrait photographer, and within two years he opened a studio for Brady in Washington, D.C. In 1861 he began to assist Brady in making a photographic record of the Civil War. Brady refused to give him public credit, so in 1863 he opened his own portrait studio and continued photographing the war on his own. He published a collection of 100 original prints in 1866. From 1867, as photographer for the Union Pacific Railroad in Kansas, he chronicled the building of the railroad and the new settlements built around it.

Gardner, Ava (Lavinia) (1922–1990) U.S. film actress. Born to a tenant farmer in Smithfield, N.C., she appeared in minor film parts until her role in *The Killers* (1946) made her a star. She played temptresses and seductive heroines in such films as *One Touch of Venus* (1948), *Show Boat* (1951), *The Snows of Kilimanjaro* (1952), and *The Barefoot Contessa* (1954). A sensuous, dark-haired beauty, she was praised for her powerful and touching performances in such films as *Mogambo* (1953), *On the Beach* (1959), and *The Night of the Iguana* (1964).

Gardner, Erle Stanley (1889–1970) U.S. detective novelist. Born in Malden, Mass., he dropped out of college, and was admitted to the California bar after three years as a law-firm typist. While practicing trial law, he wrote pulp fiction, basing the courtroom scenes and brilliant legal maneuvers on his own tactics. He gave up the law following the success in 1933 of his first novels featuring the lawyer-detective Perry Mason, *The Case of the Velvet Claws* and *The Case of the Sulky Girl*, and 80 Perry Mason novels followed. He also wrote two other series of detective stories, one under the pseudonym A. A. Fair.

James A. Garfield, 1880.
BY COURTESY OF THE LIBRARY OF CONGRESS, WASHINGTON, D.C.

Garfield, James A(bram) (1831–1881) 20th president of the U.S. (1881). Born in Orange, Ohio, he graduated from Williams College, then returned to Ohio to teach and head an academy that became Hiram College. In the Civil War he led the 42nd Ohio Volunteers and fought at Shiloh and Chickamauga. He resigned as a major general to serve in the U.S. House of Representatives (1863–80). A RADICAL REPUBLICAN during Reconstruction, he served on the ELECTORAL COMMISSION in the 1876 election, and was the House Republican leader from 1876 to 1880, when he was elected to the Senate. At the 1880 Republican nominating convention, the delegates supporting ULYSSES S. GRANT and JAMES BLAINE became deadlocked. On the 36th ballot Garfield was nominated as a compromise presidential candidate, with CHESTER ARTHUR as vice president, and won by a narrow margin. His brief term, less than 150 days, was marked by a dispute with Sen. ROSCOE CONKLING over patronage. On July 2 he was shot at Washington's railroad station by Charles J. Guiteau, an Arthur supporter. He died on September 19 after 11 weeks of public debate over the ambiguous constitutional conditions for presidential succession (later clarified by the 20th and 25th Amendments).

Garfunkel, Art See Paul SIMON

Gargano Promontory \gär-ˈgä-nō\ *ancient* **Garganum.** Mountainous promontory jutting into the Adriatic Sea from eastern coast of Italy. Called the spur of the Italian boot, it is 40 mi (65 km) long and 25 mi (40 km) at its widest, rising to 3,494 ft (1,065 m) at Mount Calvo. The northern coast has citrus and olive groves and vineyards along the shore; the southern slopes, facing the Foggia plain, are known for producing red wines.

Gargas Cave in southern France, discovered in 1887, containing murals from the AURIGNACIAN Period. On its clay walls and ceiling are finger tracings and engraved pictures of wild horses, bison, and mammoths cut into the rock with a sharp tool. They may have functioned as magical images related to hunting and animal fertility. The most distinctive feature is the numerous human hand silhouettes painted in red and black, both as "negative" prints (made by paint blown around and between the fingers while the hand is pressed against the wall) and as "positive" prints (made by hands dipped in paint). The oldest form of painting known (dating to c. 30,000 BC), hand silhouettes are widespread in the art of hunter-and-gatherer societies worldwide.

gargoyle Carved spout that drains water from a rooftop gutter. The Gothic gargoyle was usually a grotesque bird or animal sitting on the back of a cornice and projecting forward for several feet in order to throw the water far from the building. The term is often loosely applied to any grotesque or fantastic beast, such as the *chimères* (chimeras) that decorate the parapets of NOTRE-DAME DE PARIS.

Garibaldi \ˌgar-ə-ˈbȯl-dē\, **Giuseppe** (1807–1882) Italian patriot and soldier of the RISORGIMENTO. He came under the influence of GIUSEPPE MAZZINI in 1834, took part in a failed mutiny intended to provoke a republican revolution in Piedmont, and escaped to France. He lived in exile in South America (1836–48) and learned guerrilla warfare tactics during liberation attempts in Brazil and Uruguay. He returned to Italy in 1848 with his small band of "Red Shirts" and fought in Milan in the war of independence against Austria. After Pope Pius IX fled Rome (1848), Garibaldi for a while defended the city from the French when they attempted to reinstate papal rule. His bold retreat through central Italy made him a well-known figure. He lived in exile again until 1854, and in 1859 he led an army in another war against Austria. In 1860, with no government backing, he raised an army of about 1,000 men and attacked Sicily; by the end of his campaign, he commanded 30,000 men, with whom he seized Naples. He handed all of southern Italy over to VICTOR EMMANUEL II and hailed him as the first king of a united Italy. With secret support from Victor Emmanuel, he led unsuccessful campaigns into the Papal States in 1862 and 1867.

Giuseppe Garibaldi, 1866.
DEUTSCHE FOTOTHEK, DRESDEN

Garland City (pop., 1996 est.: 190,000), northern Texas. Bordering DALLAS, it was founded when two rival railroad communities, Duck Creek and Embree, were consolidated in 1887. Its economy is industrialized and supplemented by the farm crops grown on the nearby Blacklands Belt. Manufactures include electronic equipment, chemicals, and scientific instruments.

Garland, Judy *orig.* **Frances Gumm** (1922–1969) U.S. singer and film actress. Born in Grand Rapids, Minn., into a family of vaudeville performers, she made her stage debut at 3. She toured with her sisters until her debut in a short film, *Every Sunday* (1936). She was a hit in *Broadway Melody of 1938* and starred as a wholesome girlfriend in nine films with MICKEY ROONEY, including *Love Finds Andy Hardy* (1938). She became an international star as Dorothy in *The Wizard of Oz* (1939). Among her other musical hits are *Meet Me in St. Louis* (1944), *Easter Parade* (1948), and *Summer Stock* (1950). Her sweet but powerful voice and emotional range made her legendary as a concert performer. After record-breaking engagements at the London Palladium and New York's Palace Theatre, she returned to the screen in triumph in *A Star Is Born* (1954), and she was acclaimed for her role in *Judgment at Nuremberg* (1961). Her life was troubled by broken marriages and reliance on drugs, which led to her early death. Her daughters, Liza Minnelli (by VINCENTE MINNELLI) and Lorna Luft, followed her to the musical stage.

Judy Garland, 1945.
BROWN BROTHERS

Garland Sutra See AVATAMSAKA-SUTRA

garlic Bulbous perennial plant *(Allium sativum)* of the LILY FAMILY, native to central Asia and growing wild in Italy and southern France. The bulbs are used as a flavoring. A classic ingredient in many national cuisines, garlic has a powerful, onionlike aroma and pungent taste; its wide use in the U.S. originated among European immigrant groups. Since ancient and medieval times it has been prized for its medicinal properties; it was formerly carried as a charm against vampires and other evils. Garlic bulbs are used sliced or ground to flavor sauces, stews, and salad dressings. The membranous skin of the garlic bulb encloses up to 20 edible bulblets called cloves. See also ALLIUM.

Garmo Peak See COMMUNISM PEAK

Garner, Erroll (Louis) (1921–1977) U.S. pianist and composer, one of the most virtuosic and popular pianists in jazz. Born in Pittsburgh, Garner was influenced by FATS WALLER and was entirely self-taught. He spelled ART TATUM in the latter's trio in 1945 and subsequently formed his own three-piece group, achieving commercial success with *Concert by the Sea* (1958), one of the best-selling albums in jazz. Like Waller and Tatum, Garner was adept at performing both with a rhythm section and unaccompanied, often establishing great momentum with his sure sense of swing. His best-known composition is "Misty."

Garner, John Nance (1868–1967) U.S. politician. Born in Red River Co., Texas, he practiced law before serving in the U.S. House of Representatives (1903–33), where he rose to become speaker in 1931. Adept at backstage maneuvering, he supported the graduated income tax and the Federal Reserve System and by 1917 was regarded as highly influential. Elected vice president under FRANKLIN ROOSEVELT in 1932 and 1936, he was a conservative within the New Deal administration, and he broke with Roosevelt in his second term over the effort to pack (enlarge) the U.S. Supreme Court. He retired to his Texas ranch in 1941.

garnet Any of a group of common SILICATE MINERALS with identical crystal structure but highly variable chemical composition. Garnets are most often found in metamorphic rocks but also occur in certain types of igneous rocks, and, usually in minor amounts, in some sedimentary rocks. They may be colorless, black, or many shades of red and green. Garnets are hard, and they fracture with sharp edges. They are used as abrasives for fine sanding and polishing of wood, leather, glass, metals, and plastics, as sandblasting agents, and in nonskid surface coatings. Garnet is the birthstone for January. Garnets have been mined in New York, Maine, and Idaho in the U.S., the world's leading producer; notable quantities have also been found in Australia, China, India, and elsewhere.

Garnet, Henry Highland (1815–1882) U.S. clergyman and abolitionist. Born a slave in New Market, Md., he escaped in 1824 to New York, where he became a Presbyterian minister. He joined the AMERICAN ANTI-SLAVERY SOCIETY and agitated for emancipation; in a 1843 speech he called on slaves to revolt and murder their masters, but he later renounced his radical views and served as pastor in several pulpits. He favored emigration of U.S. blacks to Africa and in 1881 was appointed U.S. minister to Liberia.

Garnier \gärn-'yā\, **Francis** *French* **Marie-Joseph-François Garnier** (1839–1873) French naval officer, colonial administrator, and explorer. Son of an army officer, he joined the navy and participated in the French advance into southern Vietnam in 1861. An enthusiastic believer in France's imperial destiny, he promoted the exploration of the Mekong River and took part in the first European expedition to enter Yunnan from the south (1866–68). His account, *Voyage d'exploration en Indo-Chine, 1866–68* (1873), is a valuable record of the political and economic situation of the countries through which he passed. Summoned to Saigon in 1873 to rein in unauthorized trading with China, he instead tried to seize territory for France in northern Vietnam and was killed in the attempt.

Garnier \gärn-'yā\, **Tony** (1869–1948) French architect. The son of Charles Garnier (see PARIS OPERA), he held the position of architect of Lyon 1905–19. He is known chiefly for his Cité Industrielle, a farsighted plan for an industrial city. Most striking is his depiction of simplified REINFORCED-CONCRETE forms inspired by the pioneering work of Auguste Perret. The most important work in Lyon to emerge from his Cité Industrielle was the large stockyard complex of 1908–24.

garnishment In law, attachment of a debtor's wages to satisfy a judgment. Under a garnishment order, the court requires the employer to deduct and pay to the creditor a percentage of the debtor's salary until the debt is satisfied. As legal redress, the practice can be traced to ROMAN LAW. See also DEBTOR AND CREDITOR.

Garonne River \gä-'rōn\ *ancient* **Garumna.** River, southwestern France. The most important river of southwestern France, it is 357 mi (575 km) long. Formed by two glacial headstreams in the central Spanish PYRENEES, it flows north through mountain passes and descends to flow east across France. It continues to TOULOUSE and then to BORDEAUX, where it is 1,800 ft (550 m) across. Flowing by the wine-growing Entre-deux-Mers peninsula, it unites with the DORDOGNE RIVER 16 mi (26 km) north of Bordeaux to form the vast GIRONDE ESTUARY.

Garrett, Pat(rick Floyd) (1850–1908) U.S. lawman. Born in Chambers Co., Ala., he worked as a cowboy and buffalo hunter until 1879, when he settled in Lincoln Co., N.M., and became sheriff. In 1881 he tracked down and shot the escaped BILLY THE KID. He later became a rancher, sheriff of Dona Ana Co., N.M., and customs collector in El Paso. He was fatally shot in a dispute over a ranch lease, but suspicion lingered that he was executed by an enemy from his days as sheriff.

Garrick, David (1717–1779) British actor, producer, and playwright. Tutored in his boyhood by SAMUEL JOHNSON, he settled in London as a wine merchant before winning fame with his debut as Richard III in 1741. In diverse roles in such plays as *King Lear, Hamlet,* and BEN JONSON's *The Alchemist,* he was acclaimed for his naturalistic style and came to be regarded as one of England's greatest actors. As part owner and manager of the DRURY LANE THEATRE (1747–76) he reformed theatrical stage practices, replaced many Restoration adaptations of Shakespeare with his own versions, and made it London's most prosperous theater. He wrote over 20 plays.

Garrison, William Lloyd (1805–1879) U.S. journalist and abolitionist. Born in Newburyport, Mass., he joined the abolitionist movement at 25 and edited several local newspapers dedicated to moral reform. In 1829 he and BENJAMIN LUNDY edited the *Genius of Universal Emancipation.* In 1831 he founded *The Liberator,* which became the most radical of the antislavery journals. In 1833 he helped found the AMERICAN ANTI-SLAVERY SOCIETY. Following a split within the society, partly over women's participation (which he favored), he became president of the smaller society (1840–65). A pacifist, he demanded in 1844 that the North secede peacefully from the South. As his influence waned, his radicalism increased; through *The Liberator* he denounced the Compromise of 1850, the Kansas-Nebraska Act, and the Dred Scott decision, and hailed JOHN BROWN's raid. In the Civil War he forswore pacifism to support Pres. ABRAHAM LINCOLN and welcomed the Emancipation Proclamation. In 1865 he retired but continued to press for women's suffrage, temperance, and free trade.

Garrison.
BY COURTESY OF THE LIBRARY OF CONGRESS, WASHINGTON, D.C.

Garson, Greer (1903?–1996) British-U.S. film actress. A stage actress in England from 1932, she was acclaimed in her first U.S. film, *Goodbye, Mr. Chips* (1939), and later in *Mrs. Miniver* (1942, Academy Award). Known for portrayals of women of moral courage and virtue, she starred in such films as *Pride and Prejudice* (1940), *Madame Curie* (1943), and *Mrs. Parkington* (1944). She retired around 1955 but returned to the screen as ELEANOR ROOSEVELT in *Sunrise at Campobello* (1960).

Garter, (The Most Noble) Order of the English order of knighthood founded by EDWARD III in 1348 and considered the highest British honor. Legend holds that it was created after an incident in which Edward was dancing with the Countess of Salisbury, when one of her garters dropped to the floor. As bystanders snickered, Edward gallantly picked up the garter and put it on his own leg, admonishing the courtiers in French with what is now the order's motto, "Honi soit qui mal y pense" ("Shame to him who thinks evil of it"). Membership consists of the British sovereign and the prince of Wales, each with 25 "knight companions."

garter snake Any of more than a dozen species of snakes (genus *Thamnophis,* family Colubridae) with a striped pattern that resembles a garter: usually one or three longitudinal yellow or red stripes, with checkered blotches between. Forms in which the stripes are obscure or lacking are called grass snakes. Found in gardens and vacant lots, garters are among the most common snakes from Canada to Central America. They are small (usually less than 24 in., or 60 cm, long) and harmless, though some will strike if provoked. They eat insects, earthworms, and amphibians.

Garuda \'gə-rü-də\ In Hindu mythology, the bird (similar to a kite or eagle) on whom the god VISHNU rides. Garuda was a younger brother of Aruna, charioteer of the sun god SURYA. His mother was enslaved by NAGAS (hence the emnity between kites and serpents) and was released only after Garuda brought the serpents an elixir of immortality. He is associated with royalty in several S.East Asian countries.

Garvey, Marcus (Moziah) (1887–1940) Jamaican-U.S. black-nationalist leader. In 1914 he founded the UNIVERSAL NEGRO IMPROVEMENT ASSN.; after moving to the U.S. in 1916, he established branches in New York's Harlem and other ghettos in the North. By 1919 the rising "Black Moses" claimed a following of about 2 million, to whom he spoke of a "new Negro," proud of being black. His newspaper, *Negro World* (1919–33), advocated an independent black economy within the framework of white capitalism, and he established black-run businesses, including the Black Star shipping line. In 1920 he convened an international convention to unify blacks and encourage trade between Africa and the U.S. His influence

Garvey, 1922.
UPI

declined rapidly when he was indicted in 1922 for mail fraud. After he had served two years in prison, his sentence was commuted and he was deported (1927). His movement, the first important black-nationalist movement in the U.S., soon died out.

Gary City (pop., 1996 est.: 111,000), northwestern Indiana. Located at the southern end of Lake MICHIGAN, it was laid out by the U.S. STEEL CORP. in 1906. Gary prospered until a decline in the steel industry in the 1980s led to plant closings. City revitalization efforts were introduced in the 1990s. It was the scene, in the early 20th century, of a development in public education when William A. Wirt (1874–1938) established the work-study-play school, popularly known as the platoon school.

Gary, Elbert H(enry). (1846–1927) U.S. businessman, chief organizer of the U.S. STEEL CORP. Born near Wheaton, Ill., he entered law practice in 1871, becoming an authority on corporate law, and served as judge of DuPage Co. 1882–90. In 1898 he became president of Federal Steel Co.; when Federal merged with other companies to become U.S. Steel Corp in 1901, Gary was elected chairman of the board of directors. As chief executive officer for 26 years, he presided over its growth and development. He promoted profit sharing, higher wages, and better working conditions, but was a firm opponent of unions. GARY, Ind., named in his honor, was laid out in 1906 by U.S. Steel.

gas One of the three fundamental states of MATTER, in which matter has no definite shape, is very fluid, and has a density about 0.1% that of LIQUIDS. Gas is very compressible but tends to expand indefinitely, and fills any container. A small change in temperature or pressure produces a substantial change in its volume; these relationships are expressed as equations in the GAS LAWS. The KINETIC THEORY OF GASES, developed in the 19th century, described gases as assemblages of tiny particles (ATOMS or MOLECULES) in constant motion and contributed much to our understanding of their behavior. The term gas can also mean GASOLINE, NATURAL GAS, or the anesthetic NITROUS OXIDE. See also SOLID.

gas, intestinal See INTESTINAL GAS

gas chromatography (GC) Type of CHROMATOGRAPHY with a GAS mixture as the mobile phase. In a packed column, the packing or solid support (held in a tube) serves as the stationary phase (vapor-phase chromatography, or VPC) or is coated with a liquid stationary phase (gas-liquid chromatography, or GLC). In capillary columns, the stationary phase coats the walls of small-diameter tubes. The sample of gas or volatile liquid to be analyzed is injected into the inlet; its components move through with a carrier gas (usually hydrogen, helium, or argon) at rates influenced by their degree of interaction with the stationary phase. The temperature, nature of the stationary phase, and column length can be varied to improve separation. The gas stream issuing from the column's end may pass through a thermal conductivity detector or a flame ionization detector, where its properties are compared with those of known reference substances. GC is used to measure air pollutants, ESSENTIAL OILS, gases or alcohol in blood, and composition of industrial process streams.

gas laws Laws that relate the PRESSURE, volume, and TEMPERATURE of a GAS. Boyle's law—named for ROBERT BOYLE—states that, at constant temperature, the pressure P of a gas varies inversely with its volume V, or $PV = k$, where k is a constant. Charles's law—named for J.-A.-C. Charles (1746–1823)—states that, at constant pressure, the volume V of a gas is directly proportional to its absolute (Kelvin) temperature T, or $V/T = k$. These two laws can be combined to form a single generalization of the behavior of gases known as an equation of state, $PV = nRT$, where n is the number of gram-moles of a gas and R is called the universal gas constant. Though this law describes the behavior of an ideal gas, it closely approximates the behavior of real gases. See also JOSEPH GAY-LUSSAC.

gas reservoir In geology, a naturally occurring storage area, characteristically a folded rock formation, that traps and holds natural gas. The reservoir rock must be permeable and porous to contain the gas, and it has to be capped by impervious rock in order to form an effective seal and prevent the gas from escaping. Typical reservoir rocks are sedimentary and include SANDS, SANDSTONES, ARKOSES, and fissured LIMESTONES and DOLOMITES. In the U.S. and certain other countries, artificial gas reservoirs are being created from depleted oil and gas fields, particularly near salt domes and in sedimentary basins, to store gas during periods of low consumption for later use.

Gascony \'gas-kə-nē\ *French* **Gascogne** \gà-'skȯnʸ\ *ancient* **Vasconia.** Historical region, southwestern France. It consisted of the northern foothills of the PYRENEES, and extended east from the BASQUE COUNTRY along the France–Spain border to TOULOUSE on the upper GARONNE RIVER. Under Roman rule it was the province of Novempopulana. Taken by the Visigoths in the 5th century AD and by the Franks in 507, it was overrun from 561 by the Basques, or Vascones; in 602 the Frankish kings recognized Vasconia, or Gascony, as a duchy. In 1052 it was conquered by AQUITAINE, and in the 12th century it passed to the PLANTAGENET kings of England. In the HUNDRED YEARS' WAR, it retained English allegiance until the French reconquest in the mid-15th century.

Gascony, Gulf of See Bay of BISCAY

Gascoyne River \'gas-ˌkȯin\ River, western Western Australia. It rises west of the GIBSON DESERT and flows west for 475 mi (760 km) through gold-mining and sheep-raising country and empties into the Indian Ocean at Carnarvon on Shark Bay.

Gaskell \'gas-kəl\, **Elizabeth (Cleghorn)** *orig.* **Elizabeth Cleghorn Stevenson** *known as* **Mrs. Gaskell** (1810–1865) British writer. The daughter and wife of Unitarian ministers, she began writing in middle age. *Cranford* (1853), her most popular novel, and the unfinished *Wives and Daughters* (1864–66), perhaps her best, are about the lives of country villagers. *Mary Barton* (1848), *Ruth* (1853), and *North and South* (1855) examine social problems of the urban working class. She wrote the first biography of her friend CHARLOTTE BRONTE (1857).

Elizabeth Gaskell, chalk drawing by George Richmond, 1851; in the National Portrait Gallery, London.

BY COURTESY OF THE NATIONAL PORTRAIT GALLERY, LONDON

gasoline *British* **petrol** Mixture of volatile, flammable HYDROCARBONS derived from PETROLEUM, used as fuel for INTERNAL-COMBUSTION ENGINES (also as a solvent for OILS and FATS). Gasoline became the preferred automobile fuel because it releases so much ENERGY when burned, it mixes readily with air in a CARBURETOR, and initially was cheap due to a large supply. Costs have now increased greatly except where subsidized. Gasoline was first produced by DISTILLATION. Later processes increased the yield from crude oil by splitting large molecules into smaller ones. Still other methods, such as conversion of straight-chain hydrocarbons into their branched-chain ISOMERS, followed. The result is a complex mixture of hundreds of hydrocarbons. A gasoline's octane number indicates its ability to resist knocking (which means combustion is too rapid) and can be altered by changing the proportions of certain components. LEAD, once used to reduce knocking, has been banned as toxic. Other additives include DETERGENTS, ANTIFREEZES, and ANTIOXIDANTS. Since the mid-20th century gasoline fumes have been a major component of urban AIR POLLUTION. Efforts to reduce dependence on gasoline, which is a nonrenewable resource, include use of "gasohol," a 90:10 mix of gasoline and ETHANOL, and the development of ELECTRIC AUTOMOBILES.

gasoline engine Most widely used form of INTERNAL-COMBUSTION ENGINE, found in most AUTOMOBILES and many other vehicles. Gasoline engines vary significantly in size, weight per unit of power generated, and arrangement of components. The principal type is the reciprocating-piston engine. In four-stroke engines, each cycle requires four strokes of the piston—intake, compression, power (expansion), and exhaust—and two revolutions of the crankshaft. In a two-stroke cycle, the compression and power strokes of the four-stroke cycle are carried out without the inlet and exhaust strokes, in one upstroke and one downstroke of the piston and one revolution of the crankshaft. The size, weight, and cost of the engine per horsepower are therefore less, and two-stroke-cycle engines are used in motorcycles and smaller machines (e.g., lawnmowers and power rakes). See also COMPRESSION RATIO, PISTON AND CYLINDER, ROTARY ENGINE.

Gasparini, Angelo See Gasparo ANGIOLINI

Gaspé Peninsula \gä-ˈspā\ Peninsula, southeastern Quebec. It extends east to northeast for 150 mi (240 km) from the Matapédia River into the Gulf of ST. LAWRENCE, lying south of the ST. LAWRENCE RIVER and north of CHALEUR BAY and New Brunswick. Much of the region is within conservation areas, including Gaspesian Provincial Park and Forillon National Park. Famous for its scenery, it is also noted for hunting and fishing. The chief settlements are along the coast.

Gasperi, Alcide De See Alcide DE GASPERI

Gasprinski \gəs-ˈprin-skē\, **Ismail** (1851–1914) Russian journalist. Born in the Crimea and educated in Moscow, his travels brought him to Paris, where he met Ottoman refugees who inspired him to take up the Turkish cause at home. He wrote about the cultural problems of Turkic Muslims for a Russian newspaper and later for his own bilingual paper (founded 1883), which became Russia's most influential Turkish newspaper, advocating Pan-Islamic and Pan-Turkic causes.

Gastein \gä-ˈshtīn\, **Convention of** (1865) Agreement between Austria and Prussia following their seizure of the duchies of Schleswig and Holstein from Denmark in 1864. The pact provided that Prussia was to administer Schleswig, Austria was to administer Holstein, and the emperor of Austria and king of Prussia were to be sovereign over the duchies. Both duchies were admitted to the ZOLLVEREIN. Joint administration led to disputes that ended with Austria's defeat and expulsion from Germany in 1866. See also SCHLESWIG-HOLSTEIN QUESTION.

gastrectomy \ga-ˈstrek-tə-mē\ Surgical removal of all or part of the STOMACH to treat PEPTIC ULCERS. It eliminates the cells that secrete acid and halts the production of gastrin, the hormone that stimulates them. Once a common operation, it is now a last resort. The usual procedure, antrectomy, removes the lower half of the stomach (antrum), the chief site of gastrin secretion. The remaining stomach is joined to the DUODENUM. Subtotal gastrectomy removes up to three-quarters of the stomach. The greatest drawback is malnutrition caused by decreased appetite and ability to digest food.

gastritis \ga-ˈstrī-təs\ INFLAMMATION in the STOMACH. Acute gastritis, usually caused by ingesting something irritating or by infection, starts suddenly, with severe pain, vomiting, thirst, and diarrhea, and subsides rapidly. Treatment involves a short fast and then a bland diet, sedatives, and antispasmodics. Chemical gastritis, from ingestion of corrosive chemicals, requires emptying and washing out the stomach. Chronic gastritis has vague symptoms, including abdominal discomfort or pain, poor appetite, gas, and irregular bowel movements. Causes include prolonged use of aspirin or other irritating drugs, infection with *Helicobacter pylori*, or pernicious anemia.

gastroenteritis \ˌga-strō-ˌen-tə-ˈrī-təs\ Acute infectious syndrome of the stomach lining and intestines. Symptoms include diarrhea, vomiting, and abdominal cramps. Severity varies from transient diarrhea to life-threatening DEHYDRATION, children and the very old being more at risk for the latter. Many microorganisms produce it, either by secreting TOXINS or by invading the gut walls. Forms of gastroenteritis include FOOD POISONING, CHOLERA, and traveler's diarrhea. Depending on cause and severity, treatment includes antibiotics or simply supportive care.

gastroesophageal reflux disease (GERD) Disorder characterized by frequent passage of gastric contents from the stomach back into the esophagus. Symptoms of GERD may include heartburn, coughing, frequent clearing of the throat, and difficulty in swallowing. It can be caused by relaxation of the muscle that connects the esophagus and the stomach, delayed emptying of the esophagus or stomach, hiatal hernia, obesity, or pregnancy. Treatment is with antacids or acid-inhibiting medications and lifestyle changes such as not eating before bedtime, avoiding acidic or fatty foods or beverages, cessation of smoking, and weight loss. Surgery may be necessary in severe cases.

gastronomy Art of selecting, preparing, serving, and enjoying fine food. Two early centers of gastronomy were China (from the 5th century BC) and Rome, the latter noted for the vulgarity and ostentation of its banquets. The foundations of Western gastronomy were laid during the Renaissance, particularly in Italy and France. The influential *grande cuisine* of France reached its apex in the works of M.-A. CARÊME and G.-A. ESCOFFIER. Regardless of regional differences in cuisine, a primary consideration in food preparation is freshness. Others include complementarity or opposition of taste, juxtaposition of textures, and overall appearance, including color harmony and accent. See also NOUVELLE CUISINE.

gastropod Any member of the class Gastropoda, the largest group of MOLLUSKS, including about 65,000 species. Gastropods, which include the SNAILS, CONCHS, WHELKS, LIMPETS, PERIWINKLES, ABALONES, SLUGS, and sea slugs (see NUDIBRANCH), are found worldwide, in marine, freshwater, and terrestrial environments. Gastropods typically have a large foot with a flat sole for crawling, a single coiled shell that covers the soft body, and a head that bears a pair of eyes and tentacles. However, they are so diverse that some forms lack shells, while animals in one genus have shells with two halves, like BIVALVES. Most feed by using a radula, a ribbon of small horny teeth that tear food into pieces. They may be herbivores, carnivores, predators, parasites, or filter feeders of plankton and detritus.

Gates, Bill *orig.* **William Henry Gates III** (born 1955) U.S. computer programmer and businessman. Gates was born in Seattle, Wash. As a teenager, he helped form a group of computer programmers who computerized their high school's payroll system and founded a company that sold traffic-counting systems to local governments. At 19 he dropped out of Harvard University and cofounded MICROSOFT CORP. with Paul G. Allen (born 1954). Microsoft began its domination of the fledgling microcomputer industry when Gates licensed the operating system MS-DOS to IBM in 1980 for use in IBM's first personal computer. As the company's largest shareholder, Gates became a billionaire in 1986, and within a decade he was the world's richest private individual. Beginning in 1995, Gates refocused Microsoft on the development of software solutions for the INTERNET, and he also moved the company into the computer hardware and gaming markets with the Xbox video machine. In 1999 he and his wife created the largest charitable foundation in the United States.

Gates, Henry Louis, Jr. (born 1950) U.S. critic and scholar. Born in Keyser, W.V., he attended Yale and Cambridge universities. He has chaired Harvard Univ.'s esteemed department of Afro-American Studies for many years. In such works as *Figures in Black* (1987) and *The Signifying Monkey* (1988) he has used the term "signifyin'" to represent a practice that can link African and African-American literary histories; his other books include *Thirteen Ways of Looking at a Black Man* (1998). He has edited many anthologies, including *Reading Black, Reading Feminist* (1990) and the *Norton Anthology of African American Writers* (1997), and has restored and edited many lost works by black writers. He writes frequently to a general public, notably in *The New Yorker*, and he wrote the television series *Wonders of the African World* (1999).

Gates, Horatio (1728?–1806) British-American general. He served in the British army during the French and Indian War. In 1772 he emigrated to Virginia, where he sided with colonial interests. He was made adjutant general of the Continental Army (1775) and succeeded Gen. PHILIP SCHUYLER in New York (1777). Assisted by BENEDICT ARNOLD, he forced the surrender of the British forces under JOHN BURGOYNE at the Battle of Saratoga (1777). Congress chose Gates as president of the Board of War. Supporters, including THOMAS CONWAY, sought to have Gates replace GEORGE WASHINGTON, but the plan failed, and Gates returned to his New York command. In 1780 he was transferred to the South, where he attempted to oust the British forces under CHARLES CORNWALLIS but was defeated at the battle of Camden, S.C. An official inquiry was ordered, but charges never were pressed. He retired to Virginia, then freed his slaves in 1790 and moved to New York.

Gates of the Arctic National Park National preserve, northern Alaska. Its area of 11,756 sq mi (30,448 sq km) is entirely north of the ARCTIC CIRCLE. Proclaimed a national monument in 1978, the area underwent boundary changes and was renamed in 1980. It includes a portion of the Central BROOKS RANGE. The southern slopes are forested, contrasting with the barren northern reaches at the edge of Alaska's North Slope.

Gatling gun Hand-cranked MACHINE GUN. The first reliable version of the machine gun, it was invented by Richard J. Gatling (1818–1903) during the American Civil War. Making use of the newly invented brass cartridge, he assembled a cluster of 10 barrels rotated by a crank, each of which was loaded and fired once during a complete rotation. The barrels were loaded by gravity and the action of the cartridge container, and the spent cartridge cases were ejected. Without equal in the era of hand-operated machine guns, it could fire as many as 3,000 rounds per minute. It became obsolete in the 1880s when the invention of smokeless powder led to development of a truly automatic machine gun.

GATT See GENERAL AGREEMENT ON TARIFFS AND TRADE

Gatun Lake \gä-'tün\ *Spanish* **Lago Gatún** \'lä-gō-gä-'tün\ Lake, Panama. Constituting part of the PANAMA CANAL system, its area is 166 sq mi (430 sq km). It was formed by damming the CHAGRES RIVER. Its dam (completed 1912) and spillway serve to hold sufficient water in the Gaillard Cut for canal passage and for use in the canal's locks during dry spells. Guacha Island, a wildlife sanctuary, lies in the center of the lake.

Gauches, Cartel des See CARTEL DES GAUCHES

gaucho Any of the nomadic and colorful horsemen of the Argentine and Uruguayan PAMPAS, who remain folk heros famed for hardiness and lawlessness. Gauchos flourished from the mid-18th to the mid-19th century. At first they rounded up the herds of horses and cattle that roamed freely on the vast grasslands east of the Andes. In the early 19th century they fought in the armies that defeated the Spanish colonial regime and then for the CAUDILLOS who jockeyed for power after independence. Argentine writers celebrated the gauchos, and *la literatura gauchesca* (gaucho literature) is an important part of the Argentine cultural tradition.

gaucho literature Latin-American poetic genre that imitates the *payadas* ("ballads") traditionally sung to guitar accompaniment by wandering GAUCHO minstrels of Argentina and Uruguay. The term also includes the body of Latin-American literature about the gaucho way of life and philosophy. Long a part of folk literature, gaucho lore became a subject of 19th-century Romantic verse, as well as prose that often explores themes of conflict between the old and new.

Gaudí (i Cornet) \'gaù-thē\, **Antoni** *Spanish* **Antonio Gaudí y Cornet** (1852–1926) Spanish (Catalan) architect. Though his early works were Mudéjar (Spanish Muslim-Christian) in effect, his work after 1902 eluded all convention. He began to produce "equilibrated" structures able to stand on their own without bracing; his system employed piers and columns that tilt to transmit diagonal forces and thin-shell, laminated-tile vaults. Works such as the Park Güell (1900–14), Casa Milá (1905–10), and Casa Batlló (1904–6) feature undulating surfaces and polychrome decoration (e.g., pieces of broken ceramic). Much of his later career was occupied with the extraordinary Church of the Holy Family (Sagrada Familia), still unfinished at his death, whose original Gothic style was transformed into a complex forest of flowing forms and exuberant detail, with spiral-shaped piers, vaults, towers, and a hyperbolic paraboloid roof.

Gaugamela \,gò-gə-'mē-lə\, **Battle of** (331 BC) Clash between the forces of ALEXANDER THE GREAT and Darius III of Persia that brought the fall of the Persian empire. Attempting to stop Alexander's incursions, Darius prepared a battleground on the Plain of Gaugamela in northern Iraq and, with his much larger army, waited for Alexander. His plans were undone by Alexander's brilliant tactics; when he saw defeat was imminent, he fled and his army was cut down. Alexander's victory gave him control of South Asia.

gauge \'gāj\ In MANUFACTURING and ENGINEERING, a device used to determine whether a dimension is larger or smaller than a reference standard. A snap gauge, for example, is formed like the letter C, with outer "go" and inner "not go" jaws, and is used to check diameters, lengths, and thicknesses. Screw-thread pitch gauges have triangular serrations spaced to correspond with various pitches, or numbers of threads per inch or per centimeter. Deviation-type or DIAL GAUGES indicate the amount by which an object deviates from the standard.

Gauguin \gō-'gaⁿ\, **(Eugène-Henri-) Paul** (1848–1903) French painter, sculptor, and printmaker. Born in Paris, he spent his childhood in Lima (his mother was a Peruvian Creole). From c. 1872 he was a successful stockbroker in Paris. In the 1870s, inspired by IMPRESSIONISM, he started painting. He met CAMILLE PISSARRO in 1874, and throughout the 1880s he exhibited with the Impressionists. In 1883 he lost his job and became a full-time painter. Disillusioned with bourgeois materialism, in 1886 he moved to Pont-Aven, Brittany, where he became the focus of a group of artists who emulated his style (see PONT-AVEN SCHOOL). A meeting with VINCENT VAN GOGH (1886) and a trip to Martinique (1887) changed his life; he broke with Impressionism and in 1891 moved to Tahiti. His works became open protests against materialism, most notably his immense canvas *Where Do We Come From? What Are We? Where Are We Going?* (1897), a dreamlike allegory of life unspoiled by civilization. He was an influential innovator; FAUVISM owed much to his use of color, he inspired PABLO PICASSO, and his primitivism and stylistic simplifications led to an appreciation of African art and the development of CUBISM. See also POSTIMPRESSIONISM.

Gauhati \gaù-'hä-tē\ *or* **Guwahati** \,gü-wə-'hä-tē\ Town (pop., 1991: 584,000), western ASSAM state, northeastern India. Located on the BRAHMAPUTRA River, it was the capital of the Hindu kingdom of Kamarupa (under the name of Pragjyotisa) c. AD 400. Taken by the Ahoms, it became the seat of the Ahom governor of Lower ASSAM in 1681. It was ceded to the British in 1826 and was the administrative seat for Assam until 1874. Gauhati is now an important river port and Assam's main commercial center. The nearby temples of Kamakhya and Umananda are places of Hindu pilgrimage.

Gaul *Latin* **Gallia** Ancient country, Europe, located generally south and west of the RHINE, west of the ALPS, and north of the PYRENEES. The Gauls north of the PO RIVER harried Rome from c. 400 BC; by 181 BC Rome had subjugated and colonized that area of northern Italy they called Cisalpine Gaul. Rome conquered the region known as Transalpine Gaul over the next century. It included most of modern France and Belgium and parts of Switzerland, Germany, and the Netherlands. Julius CAESAR completed the conquest of Gaul (see GALLIC WARS) in 58–50 BC; Lugdunum (LYON) became the capital. The entire area was reorganized in the 1st century AD into several provinces, including NARBONENSIS, AQUITANIA, LUGDUNENSIS, and BELGICA. By AD 260 it had become a center of unrest; by the 6th century, Rome had given up all its Gallic territories.

Gaulle, Charles de See Charles DE GAULLE

Gaullists See RALLY FOR THE REPUBLIC

Gauss \'gaùs\, **Carl Friedrich** *orig.* **Johann Friedrich Carl Gauss** (1777–1855) German mathematician, astronomer, and physicist. Born to poor parents, he was a prodigy of astounding depth. By his early teens he had already performed astonishing proofs who also distinguished himself in ancient languages. He published over 150 works and made such important contributions as the fundamental theorem of ALGEBRA (in his doctoral dissertation), the LEAST SQUARES METHOD, Gauss-Jordan elimination (for solving MATRIX equations), and the bell curve (or Gaussian error curve) (see NORMAL DISTRIBUTION). After he died, many important papers were found that he had not published because they did not meet his high standards. His development of NON-EUCLIDEAN GEOMETRY went unnoticed for decades. Gauss also made important contributions to physics and astronomy and pioneered the application of mathematics to gravitation, electricity, and magnetism. He also developed the fields of potential theory and real analysis. With ARCHIMEDES and NEWTON, he is one of the greatest mathematicians of all time.

Gaussian distribution See NORMAL DISTRIBUTION

Gautier \gō-'tyā\, **Théophile** (1811–1872) French poet, novelist, critic, and journalist. He lived most of his life in Paris, where he initially studied painting. He insisted on the sovereignty of the beautiful in such works as the novel *Mademoiselle de Maupin* (1835). He developed a poetic technique for recording his exact impressions of works of art, as in the formally perfect poems of *Émaux et camées* (1852). Travel inspired some of his best poetry, in *España* (1845), and finest prose, in *Voyage en Espagne* (1845). He also wrote copious art and drama criticism. His works inspired such poets as CHARLES BAUDELAIRE, whose *Fleurs du Mal* was dedicated to him, and his prodigious and varied output influenced literary sensibilities for decades.

gavotte \gə-'vät\ Folk dance of French peasant origin, supposedly danced by the people of Gap (Gavots). The dance became popular as a court dance in the 17th–18th century, developing more complicated steps under the direction of ballet masters. Its slow, walking steps were danced to music in 4/4 time. Musically it included three parts and was an optional movement of the SUITE.

Gawain \gə-'wān, 'gä-,wān\ Knight of King Arthur's Round Table. A nephew of Arthur, he appears in early ARTHURIAN LEGEND as a model of perfection. In later romances, his character is marred by arrogance and by an inability to perceive the significance of the GRAIL. In the 14th-century Middle English poem *Sir Gawain and the Green Knight*, he accepted a challenge from a mysterious Green Knight, who offered to let Gawain chop off his head if he could return the blow one year later. When the blow was struck, the Knight picked up his head and left the court, and Gawain set out in search of him. After passing through a series of temptations, Gawain met the Green Knight's blows and suffered only a small wound, his neck protected by a magical green sash.

Gay, John (1685–1732) British poet and dramatist. From an ancient but impoverished Devonshire family, Gay was apprenticed to a silk mercer in London but was released early. He soon cofounded the journal *The British Apollo*. His poetry collections included *Rural Sports* (1713) and *Trivia* (1716). He is best known for the BALLAD OPERA *The Beggar's Opera* (1728), which ran for 62 performances (the longest run to that date). The play, with music by J. C. Pepusch (1667–1752), was a cynical tale of thieves and highwaymen intended to mirror the moral degradation of society; its success made it a landmark in music-theater history. It was adapted by BERTOLT BRECHT and K. WEILL as *The Threepenny Opera* (1928). Gay was buried in Westminster Abbey.

Gay, oil painting by William Aikman; in the Scottish National Portrait Gallery, Edinburgh.

BY COURTESY OF THE SCOTTISH NATIONAL PORTRAIT GALLERY, EDINBURGH

Gay-Lussac \gel-ǖ-'säk\, **Joseph (-Louis)** (1778–1850) French chemist and physicist. He showed that all gases expand by the same fraction of their volume for a given temperature increase; this led to the devising of a new temperature scale whose profound thermodynamic significance was later established by Lord KELVIN. Taking measurements from a balloon at over 20,000 ft (6,000 m), he concluded that earth's magnetic intensity and atmospheric composition were constant to that altitude. With ALEXANDER VON HUMBOLDT, he determined the proportions of hydrogen and oxygen in water. He is remembered as a pioneer investigator of the behavior of gases and techniques of chemical analysis and a founder of meteorology

gay rights movement *or* **homosexual rights movement** Civil rights movement that advocates equal rights for gay men, lesbians, bisexuals, and transsexuals; seeks to eliminate sodomy laws barring homosexual acts between consenting adults; and calls for an end to discrimination against gay men and lesbians in employment, credit, lending, housing, public accommodations, and other areas of life. The first group to campaign publicly was founded in Berlin in 1897 by Magnus Hirschfeld (1868–1935) and had 25 local chapters in Europe by 1922; suppressed by the Nazis, it did not survive World War II. The first U.S. support group, the Mattachine Society, was founded in Los Angeles c. 1950; the Daughters of Bilitis, for lesbians, was founded in San Francisco in 1955. The COC (founded 1966), a prominent European group, is headquartered in Amsterdam. The U.S. movement gained a militant momentum in 1969 with the STONEWALL REBELLION. "Stonewall" came to be commemorated annually by Gay and Lesbian Pride Week in cities around the world. The International Lesbian and Gay Association (founded 1978), headquartered in Brussels, lobbies for human rights and fights discrimination against lesbian, gay, bisexual, and transgendered persons.

Gaye, Marvin (Pentz) *orig.* **Marvin Pentz Gay** (1939–1984) U.S. singer and songwriter. Born in Washington, D.C., son of a Pentecostal minister, he learned music in church. He signed a contract with Harvey Fuqua (born 1924) in 1959, and followed him to Motown, where he played drums on early S. ROBINSON hits. His own hits (from 1962) climaxed in "I Heard It Through the Grapevine" (1967). He paired with female singers, including Tammi Terrell (1946–1970), in songs by Nick Ashford (born 1943) and Valerie Simpson (born 1948). With *What's Goin' On?* (1971) his songs became more socially conscious. Troubled in his personal relationships and finances, he reemerged in 1982 with "Sexual Healing." He was shot to death by his father in a quarrel.

Gayomart \ˌga-yō-'märt\ In later ZOROASTRIANISM, the first man and the progenitor of humankind. Created by AHURA MAZDA, he was made incarnate after 3,000 years of life as a spirit. His existence at first immobilized Ahriman, the evil spirit who wanted to invade creation, but after 30 years of attacks Ahriman destroyed Gayomart. His body became the earth's minerals; gold was his seed, and from it sprang the human race.

Gaza Strip *Arabic* **Qita Ghazzah** \kē-'tä-'gà-zə\ *Hebrew* **Rezuat azza** \re-zü-'ät-'äz-ə\ Territory, southeastern Mediterranean Sea coast. Occupying 140 sq mi (363 sq km) northeast of the SINAI Peninsula, it is also the location of the city of Gaza, which was a prosperous trading center for much of its history and was first mentioned in the 15th century BC. Often besieged by invaders, including Israelites, Assyrians, Babylonians, and Persians, it declined in importance after the Crusades. It was ruled by the OTTOMAN EMPIRE from the 16th century. After World War I, the city and the strip became part of the British mandate of PALESTINE. Following the first ARAB-ISRAELI WAR (1948–49), the territory was occupied by Egypt, and the city became that country's headquarters in Palestine. The occupied area was later reduced to an area 25 mi (40 km) long, which became known as the Gaza Strip, still under Egyptian control. In the SIX-DAY WAR (1967) the area was captured by Israel. The area's chief economic problem was the large number of Palestinian Arab refugees who lived there in extreme poverty. In 1987, rioting among Gaza's Palestinians marked the birth of the INTIFADA. Continued unrest led, in 1993, to an agreement between Israel and the PALESTINE LIBERATION ORGANIZATION granting limited self-rule to the Palestinian population of the Gaza Strip and West Bank. A breakdown in further negotiations in 2000 led to another outbreak of violence.

gazebo \gə-'zē-bō\ Lookout in the form of a turret, cupola (small, lanternlike dome), or garden house set on a height to give an extensive view. Few late-18th- and 19th-century rustic gazebos survive, but 17th-century turrets built up in an angle of the garden wall are not uncommon. The term now often refers specifically to a freestanding roofed structure, typically octagonal, with open or latticework sides.

gazel See GHAZEL

gazelle Any of numerous species of graceful ANTELOPE (genus *Gazella*) found on open plains and semideserts from Mongolia to the Atlantic coast of North Africa and throughout eastern and central tropical Africa. Gazelles are 2–3 ft (60–90 cm) high at the shoulder. They range in herds that usually contain five to 10 individuals but may include several hundred. They are generally brown with white underparts and rump, and many have a horizontal dark band along each side. A light stripe runs down each side of the face. The horns are short to medium in length, with numerous raised rings, and are variously shaped, but all are slightly upturned at the ends. Some species are considered endangered.

Thomson's gazelle (*Gazella thomsoni*).

E.R. DEGGINGER

Gazelle Peninsula Peninsula, extending northeast from the island of NEW BRITAIN, South Pacific Ocean. It is about 50 mi (80 km) wide but tapers to 20 mi (32 km) where it joins the mainland. From coastal plains its surface rises to 7,999 ft (2,438 m) at Mount Sinewit in the central Baining Mountains. It is volcanically active and highly fertile, with cocoa and copra plantations along the coast. It is the most populous portion of the island, and was the base of German settlement late in the 19th century.

Gaziantep \ˌgä-zē-än-'tep\ *formerly* **Aintab** \īn-'täb\ City (pop., 1997: 712,800), southern central Turkey. Located north of ALEPPO, it was strategically situated near ancient trade routes, and has been occupied since the early 4th millennium BC. Known as Hamtap in the Middle Ages, it was an important stronghold guarding Syrian routes. Captured by Turks in 1183, it later changed hands among various invaders until its absorption into the OTTOMAN EMPIRE in the early 16th century. Called Aintab under the Ottomans, it was occupied by the British and French after World War I. By then it was a center of Turkish nationalist resistance to European occupation, and upon its return to Turkey in 1922, it was renamed in honor of its heroic stand (Turkish *gazi*: "champion of Islam").

Gdańsk \gə-'dänsk\ *German* **Danzig** \'dänt-sik\ City (pop., 1996 est.: 463,000), capital of Gdańsk province, northern Poland. Located at the mouth of the Vistula River on the Baltic Sea, it was first mentioned in the late 10th century as a Polish town. The capital of the dukes of Pomerania in the 13th century, it was taken by the Teutonic Knights in 1308. In 1466 Casimir IV regained the territory for Poland, and Gdańsk expanded greatly. From 1793 it was controlled mainly by Prussia; following World War I, it was a free city governed by Poland. In 1938 Adolf Hitler demanded that Gdańsk be given back to Germany; Poland's refusal was the excuse for his attack on Poland in 1939, which precipitated World War II. The city, greatly damaged during the war, was returned to Poland in 1945. It is now fully restored, with renewed port facilities. The independent labor union Solidarity was founded there in 1980.

Gdańsk, Gulf of Inlet of the Baltic Sea. Bordered by Poland on the west and south and Russia on the east, it extends 40 mi (64 km) from north to south and 60 mi (97 km) east to west, reaching a maximum depth of more than 371 ft (113 m). Coastal activities include shipbuilding, fishing, and the resort trade.

GDP See GROSS DOMESTIC PRODUCT

GE See General Electric Co.

Ge Hong *or* **Ko Hung** \'gə-'hůŋ\ (AD 283?–343) Chinese alchemist and Taoist philosopher. He received a Confucian education but later became interested in the Taoist cult of physical immortality. His writings blended the occult doctrines of Taoism with the ethics of Confucius. His major work, *Baopuzi* ("He Who Holds to Simplicity"), discusses alchemy, diet, sexual hygiene, and meditation as well as the importance of ethical principles.

gear Machine component consisting of a toothed wheel attached to a rotating shaft. Gears operate in pairs, the teeth of one engaging the teeth of a second, to transmit and modify rotary MOTION and TORQUE. To transmit motion smoothly, the contacting surfaces of gear teeth must be carefully shaped to a specific profile. The smaller of a gear pair is often known as the pinion. If the pinion is on the driving shaft, the pair acts to reduce speed and to amplify torque; if the pinion is on the driven shaft, the pair acts to increase speed and reduce torque.

Geb \'geb\ *or* **Keb** In ancient Egyptian religion, the god of the earth and the physical support of the world. Geb and his sister Nut belonged to the second generation of deities at Heliopolis. In Egyptian art he was often depicted as lying at the feet of the air god, Shu, with Nut, the sky goddess, arched above them. He was the third divine ruler among the gods, and the pharaohs claimed descent from him.

gecko Any of about 750 species of harmless but noisy LIZARDS in the family Gekkonidae: small, usually nocturnal reptiles that have soft skin, a short, stout body, a large head, and weak limbs often equipped with suction-padded digits. The pads contain tiny hairlike projections with microscopic hooks that cling to small surface irregularities, allowing geckos to climb absolutely smooth and vertical surfaces and even to run across ceilings. Most are 1–6 in. (3–15 cm) long, including the tail, and they are usually drably colored, with gray, brown, or white predominating. They live in habitats ranging from deserts to jungles in warm areas worldwide. When kept as pets in houses or apartments, they are allowed to run free and eat undesirable insects.

Gedrosia \yə-'drō-zhə\ Historic region, South Asia. It was west of the Indus River, in what is now the Baluchistan region of Pakistan. In 325 BC Alexander the Great's forces suffered disastrous losses there on his return from India. They captured the area, but after Alexander's death his general Seleucus I Nicator was forced to make peace by trading Gedrosia and all his territories east of the Hindu Kush for 500 elephants. His departure ended Greek intervention on the subcontinent of India.

Geertgen tot Sint Jans \'gart-gən-tòt-sint-'yäns\ (fl. c. 1475–1495) Dutch painter. Little is known of his career. His name means "Little Gerard of the Brethren of St. John," after the religious order in Haarlem of which he was a lay brother. His only documented work, a large triptych of *The Crucifixion,* was painted for the Brethren's monastery. Paintings attributed to him include a luminous nocturnal *Nativity* (National Gallery, London) and *St. John the Baptist in the Wilderness* (Staatliche Museum, Berlin).

Geertz \'gərts\, **Clifford (James)** (born 1926) U.S. cultural anthropologist, a leading proponent of a form of anthropology that stresses the importance of SYMBOLS and interpretation in human social life. Culture, according to Geertz, is "a system of inherited conceptions expressed in symbolic forms"—forms that serve to impose meaning on the world and make it understandable. Geertz's writings have been influential both within and outside of anthropology; they include *The Religion of Java* (1960), *The Interpretation of Cultures* (1973), *Local Knowledge* (1983), and *Works and Lives* (1988). He has taught at the University of Chicago (1960–70) and has been a fellow at the Institute for Advanced Study in Princeton, N.J. See also CULTURAL ANTHROPOLOGY.

Gegenbaur \'gā-gən-ˌbau̇r\, **Karl** (1826–1903) German anatomist. A strong supporter of Charles Darwin's theory of evolution, he showed that comparative anatomy supplies evidence of it. His *Elements of Comparative Anatomy* (1859) stressed that structural similarities in different animals, especially parts with a common origin (e.g., human arm, horse's foreleg, and bird's wing), give clues to their evolutionary history.

gegenschein \'gā-gən-ˌshīn\ *or* **counterglow** Oval patch of faint light exactly opposite the sun in the night sky, so faint it can be seen only in the absence of moonlight, away from city lights, with the eyes adapted to darkness. It is lost in the light of the Milky Way except in February, March, April, August, September, and October. The gegenschein and the ZODIACAL LIGHT form the most notable parts of a band of very faint light along the ECLIPTIC.

Gehrig \'ger-ig\, **(Henry) Lou(is)** (1903–1941) U.S. baseball player, one of the game's great hitters. Born in New York City, he attended Columbia University before joining the New York Yankees. From 1925 to 1939, Gehrig (nicknamed "the Iron Horse") played in 2,130 consecutive games as a left-handed-hitting first baseman for the Yankees, a record not broken until 1995 (see Cal Ripken). In 1932 he became the first player to hit four home runs in a single game. He batted in 150 or more runs in a season seven times. In two seasons (1934, 1936) he hit 49 home runs. He left baseball with a career batting average of .340 and 493 home runs. His 1,990 runs batted in place him third in history, behind Hank Aaron and Babe Ruth. In 1939 it was learned that he was dying of AMYOTROPHIC LATERAL SCLEROSIS, which came to be known as Lou Gehrig's disease.

Lou Gehrig, 1939.
AP/WIDE WORLD PHOTOS

Gehry \'ger-ē\, **Frank (Owen)** (born 1929) Canadian-U.S architect. Born in Toronto, he studied at USC and Harvard University. His use of inexpensive materials (chain-link fencing, plywood, corrugated steel) gave many of his early buildings an unfinished, whimsical air. His structures often use unconventional or distorted shapes and have a sculptural or fragmented, collage-like quality. In designing public buildings, he tended to cluster small units within a larger space rather than creating monolithic structures, thus emphasizing human scale. Of particular note is his Guggenheim Museum in Bilbao, Spain (1997), a shimmering pile of sharply twisting, curving shapes surfaced in titanium. Gehry won the Pritzker Architecture Prize in 1989.

Geiger \'gī-gər\, **Abraham** (1810–1874) German-Jewish theologian. He served as rabbi in Wiesbaden from 1832 and in Breslau 1838–63. He helped found a theological journal in 1835 and served as its editor. Geiger urged the need for simplified ritual, liturgy in one's native language, and emphasis on the prophetic writings as the core of Judaism, and stressed the process of change and growth in Jewish religious consciousness, a basic idea in Reform Judaism.

Geiger \'gī-gər\, **Theodor Julius** (1891–1952) German sociologist. An early critic of the Nazis, Geiger fled to Copenhagen, where in 1938 at the University of Århus he became Denmark's first professor of sociology. He studied social stratification and mobility, examining Danish intellectuals and the people of Århus. His posthumous *Democracy Without Dogma* (1964) expressed his vision of a society depersonalized by ideology but redeemed by human relationships.

Geiger counter *or* **Geiger-Müller counter** Device used for detecting and counting individual particles of RADIATION. Invented by the German physicist Hans Geiger (1882–1945) and later refined with help from Walther Müller, the device is a gas-filled metal tube with a wire through its axis and a high voltage applied to the wire. As particles enter the tube, they create a large avalanche of IONIZATION in the gas, which then discharges, creating a brief electric pulse. The tube produces the same large output pulse for virtually every charged particle that passes through the gas and so is useful for detecting individual particles. It can therefore indicate lower levels of radiation than is possible with other types of detectors.

Geisel \'gī-zəl\, **Theodor Seuss** *known as* **Dr. Seuss** (1904–1991) U.S. writer and illustrator. Born in Springfield, Mass., he studied at Dartmouth College and did doctoral work at Oxford. He began working in 1927 as a freelance cartoonist, illustrator, and writer. Under his pseudonym, Geisel began creating immensely popular children's books peopled with outlandish invented creatures and brimming with nonsense words. *And to Think That I Saw It on Mulberry Street* (1937), his first Dr. Seuss book, was followed by such huge successes as *Horton Hatches the Egg* (1940), *The Cat in the Hat* (1957), *How the Grinch Stole Christmas* (1957), *Yertle the Turtle* (1958), and *Green Eggs and Ham* (1960). Such perennial best-sellers, and his posthumous *Oh, the Places You'll Go!* (1993), have made him the best-selling children's author in the world.

geisha \'gā-shə\ Member of a professional class of women in Japan whose traditional occupation is to entertain men. A geisha must be adept at singing, dancing, and playing the samisen in addition to being skilled at making conversation. The geisha system is thought to have emerged in the 17th century to provide a class of well-trained entertainers set apart from courtesans and prostitutes: though geisha sometimes had sexual relationships with their clients, they were supposed to entertain primarily through their accomplishments. The numbers of geisha have declined from some 80,000 in the 1920s to a few thousand at present, almost all confined to Tokyo and Kyoto, where they are patronized by only the wealthiest businessmen and most influential politicians. Ordinary businessmen seek out bar hostesses, who, though not trained in traditional singing or dance, like geisha excel at supportive conversation.

Gelasius I \jə-'lā-shē-əs\, **St.** (died 496) Pope (492–96). He combatted the Acacian Schism in the East, which advocated the MONOPHYSITE HERESY. He maintained papal authority and established Roman primacy in ecclesiastical affairs. In 494 he changed the pagan LUPERCALIA festival into the feast of the Purification.

gelatin \'je-lə-tᵊn\ Animal PROTEIN substance having gel-forming properties, used primarily in food products. Derived from COLLAGEN, it is extracted by boiling animal skin and bones. It is commonly produced as granules or as a ground mix with added sugars, flavors, and colors. Immersed in a liquid, it takes up moisture and swells. It is used to make such foods as molded desserts, jellied meats, soups, candies, and aspics and to stabilize such emulsion and foam food products as ice cream and marshmallows. It is nutritionally an incomplete protein. It is also used in various pharmaceutical products.

Gell-Mann \'gel-ˌmän\, **Murray** (born 1929) U.S. physicist. Born in New York City, he entered Yale University at 15 and earned his PhD from MIT in 1951. From 1955 he taught at Caltech, becoming Millikan professor of theoretical physics in 1967. In 1953 he introduced the concept of "strangeness," a quantum property that accounted for decay patterns of certain MESONS. In 1961 he and Yuval Ne'eman (born 1925) proposed a scheme (the "Eightfold Way") that grouped mesons and BARYONS into multiplets of 1, 8, 10, or 27 members on the basis of various properties. He speculated that it was possible to explain certain properties of known particles in terms of even more fundamental particles, or building blocks, which he later called QUARKS. He was awarded a 1969 Nobel Prize.

Geltzer \'gyelt-syir\, **Yekaterina (Vasilyevna)** (1876–1962) Russian prima ballerina of the BOLSHOI BALLET. She graduated from the Bolshoi Theater's ballet school in 1894 and joined the company, becoming prima ballerina in 1901. She was known for dramatic roles, including that of the heroine of *The Red Poppy* (1927), in a career that lasted more than 40 years. After the 1917 Revolution, she and her husband, VASILY TIKHOMIROV, helped preserve the classical technique and repertoire of the Imperial Russian ballet.

Gelukpa See DGE-LUGS-PA

Gemara \gə-'mär-ə, gə-mä-'rä\ Commentary on the collection of Jewish law known as the MISHNA. Written by Jewish scholars in Palestine and Babylonia c. AD 200–500, it is printed around the relevant passage of the Mishna. See also TALMUD.

Gemini \'jem-ə-ˌnī\ (Latin: "Twins") In astronomy, the constellation lying between Cancer and Taurus; in ASTROLOGY, the third sign of the ZODIAC, governing approximately the period May 21–June 21. It is represented by a set of twins. The twins are most often identified as the mythological Castor and Pollux (DIOSCURI), but have also been equated with other famous pairs such as ROMULUS AND REMUS.

Gemini \'je-mə-ˌnī, 'je-mə-ˌnē\ Series of 12 two-person spacecraft launched into earth orbit by the U.S. between 1964 and 1967, after the one-person MERCURY program and before the three-person APOLLO program. Designed to test astronauts' ability to maneuver spacecraft manually, the Gemini series helped develop techniques for orbital rendezvous and docking with a target vehicle used later in the Apollo moon-landing program. It also gave NASA engineers a chance to improve spacecraft environmental control and electrical power systems.

Gemistus Plethon \jə-'mis-təs-'plē-ˌthän\, **George** (c. 1355–1450/52) Byzantine philosopher and humanist scholar. He served as lay theologian with the Byzantine delegation to the 1438–45 general council of FERRARA-FLORENCE. His treatise *On the Difference Between Aristotle and Plato* revived interest in PLATO and led to Cosimo de' MEDICI's founding of the Platonic Academy of Florence. Its clarification of the distinction between Platonic and Aristotelian thought proved seminal in determining the philosophic orientation of the Italian Renaissance.

Gemma Augustea \ˌjem-ə-ˌȯ-gəs-'tē-ə\ ("Gem of Augustus") Sardonyx CAMEO depicting the glorification of Caesar AUGUSTUS. He is sitting next to the goddess Roma, and both are trampling the armor of defeated enemies. Now in the Art History Museum in Vienna, it was probably carved during the reign of CALIGULA (AD 37–41). It is one of the most impressive carved cameos of a series of Roman gems representing imperial personages.

Gempei War \'gem-ˌpā\ (1180–85) Final struggle between two Japanese warrior clans, the Minamoto (Genji) and the Taira (Heike), for supremacy in Japan, resulting in the Minamoto's victory and the establishment of the KAMAKURA SHOGUNATE. Stories of the rise and fall of the two families, with their Buddhist overtones of evanescence and their sense of heroic tragedy, have a popularity in Japan akin to that of ARTHURIAN LEGENDS in English-speaking countries.

Gemsbok National Park \'gemz-ˌbȯk\ National preserve, southwestern Botswana. It borders on the Republic of South Africa's KALAHARI GEMSBOK NATIONAL PARK. It was established as a game reserve in 1932 to protect migratory animal populations that cross the border between the two countries; it became a national park in 1971. Its wildlife includes large herds of gemsbok, gnu (wildebeest), and springbok.

gemstone Any of various minerals prized for beauty, durability, and rarity. A few noncrystalline materials of organic origin (e.g., pearl, red coral, and amber) also are classified as gemstones. Of the more than 3,500 identified natural minerals, fewer than 100 are used as gemstones and only 16 have achieved importance: beryl, chrysoberyl, corundum, diamond, feldspar, garnet, jade, lazurite, olivine, opal, quartz, spinel, topaz, tourmaline, turquoise, and zircon. Some of these (e.g., BERYL and CORUNDUM) provide more than one type of gem. In virtually all cases, the minerals have to be cut and polished for use in jewelry. See illustration opposite on following page.

gender In language, a grammatical category contrasting distinctions of sex or animateness. Gender marking may be natural, with linguistic markers of gender corresponding to real-world gender, or purely grammatical, with markers of gender in part semantically based and in part semantically arbitrary. In languages with grammatical gender, nouns are partitioned into sets. Membership of a noun in a set may be expressed by its form and/or by the forms of other parts of speech controlled by the noun. Closely related to gender systems in language are class systems, as in BANTU LANGUAGES, in which the number of sets into which nouns are partitioned is much larger, with distinct categories for things such as plants, animals, and tools, though, as with nouns in European languages, assignment of most nouns to classes is semantically arbitrary.

gender gap Difference in viewpoints and attitudes between men and women, especially as reflected in differing responses to public and private issues and sometimes to political candidates, parties, or programs. Such political differences were little noted in the U.S. until the 1980s, men and women until then having shown very similar voting habits. Since then, women have been seen to support the Democratic Party and liberal policies in significantly greater numbers than men particularly on matters of equal employment opportunity, child care, and gun control.

gene Unit of HEREDITY that occupies a fixed position on a CHROMOSOME. Genes achieve their effects by directing PROTEIN synthesis. They are composed of DNA, except in some viruses that contain RNA instead. The sequence of nitrogenous bases along a strand of DNA determines the GENETIC CODE. When the product of a particular gene is needed, the portion of the DNA molecule that contains that gene splits, and a complementary strand of RNA, called messenger RNA (mRNA), forms and then passes to RIBOSOMES, where proteins are synthesized. A second type of RNA, transfer RNA (tRNA), matches up the mRNA with specific AMINO ACIDS, which combine in series to form polypeptide chains, the building blocks of proteins. Experiments have shown that many of the genes within a cell are inactive much or even all of the time, but they can be switched on and off. MUTATIONS occur when the number or order of bases in a gene is disrupted. See also GENETIC ENGINEERING, GENETICS, HARDY-WEINBERG LAW, HUMAN GENOME PROJECT, LINKAGE GROUP.

gene flow Introduction of genetic material (by interbreeding) from one population of a species to another, thereby changing the composition of the gene pool of the receiving population. The introduction of new characteristics through gene flow increases variability within the population and makes possible new combinations of traits. In humans, gene flow usually comes about through human MIGRATION.

gene therapy *or* **gene transfer therapy** Introduction of a normal GENE into an individual in whom that gene is not functioning, either into those tissue cells that normally express the gene (curing that individual only) or into an early embryonic cell (curing the individual and all future offspring). Prerequisites for each procedure include finding the best delivery system (often a virus) for the gene, demonstrating that the transferred gene can express itself in the host cell, and establishing that the procedure is safe. Diseases for which gene-therapy research is advanced include cystic fibrosis, Huntington's disease, and familial hypercholesterolemia; research continues on its application for Alzheimer's disease, breast and other cancers, and diabetes. Some aspects of gene therapy, including genetic manipulation and selection, research on embryonic tissue, and experimentation on human subjects, have aroused ethical controversy.

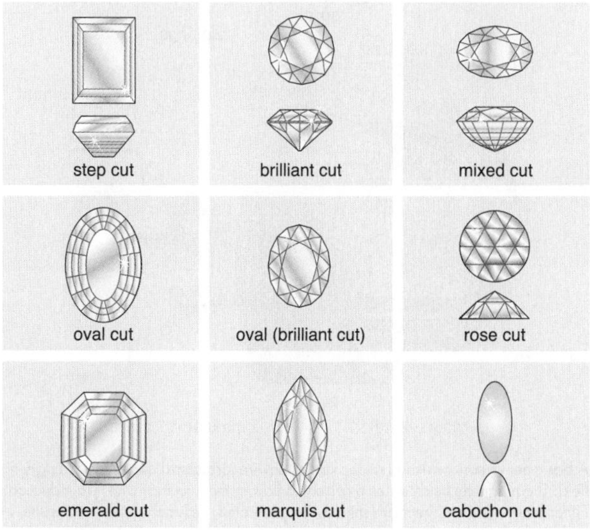

Several traditional gemstone cuts.

genealogy Study of family origins and history. It is found in most parts of the world and is international in scope. Originally concerned with tracing royal, aristocratic, or clerical lines, genealogy has broadened its scope over the centuries, and many ordinary people now pursue it as a hobby. In preliterate cultures genealogical information was transmitted orally, usually as a list of names; later generations recorded this information. Divine origins were often ascribed to kings and heroes. Modern genealogists use artifacts, including ancient records, coins, deeds, tapestries, paintings, and monuments, to help them in their work.

Genée, Dame Adeline *orig.* **Anina Margarete Kirstina Petra Jensen** (1878–1970) Danish-born British dancer, choreographer, and teacher. She made her debut in Norway at age 10. In 1897 she was engaged at the Empire Theatre in London, where she became one of the leading figures of the Edwardian theater. After 1909 she occasionally performed in ballets she herself produced, including *La Danse* (1912), which addressed the history of ballet. In 1920 she established an organization that in 1936 became the Royal Academy of Dancing. In 1950 she was made a Dame of the British Empire.

General Accounting Office (GAO) U.S. legislative agency. Established in 1921, it audits and evaluates government programs and activities to ensure effective receipt and disbursement of public funds. As the investigative arm of Congress, it performs reviews requested by committee chairs and ranking minority members, as well as those required by law or initiated by the GAO itself.

General Agreement on Tariffs and Trade (GATT) Set of multilateral trade agreements aimed at the abolition of QUOTAS and the reduction of TARIFF duties among the signing nations. Originally signed by 23 countries at Geneva in 1947, GATT became the most effective instrument in the massive expansion of world trade in the later 20th century. By 1995, when GATT was replaced by the WORLD TRADE ORGANIZATION (WTO), 125 nations had signed its agreements, which governed 90% of world trade. GATT's most important principle was trade without discrimination, in which member nations opened their markets equally to one another. Once a country and its largest trading partners agreed to reduce a tariff, that tariff cut was automatically extended to all GATT members. GATT also established uniform customs regulations and sought to eliminate import quotas. It sponsored many treaties that reduced tariffs, the last of which, signed in Uruguay in 1994, established the WTO.

General Dynamics Corp. Major U.S. defense contractor. Its forerunner, the Electric Boat Co., was founded in 1899 and built the *Holland*, the first submarine purchased by the U.S. Navy. After World War II it diversified into military aircraft, armored vehicles (including the M-1 battle tank), and natural-gas tankers. The company was incorporated under its present name in 1952, and in 1954 it launched the *Nautilus*, the first nuclear-powered submarine; it later produced the Trident submarines. Its Gulfstream Aerospace subsidiary manufactures business jet aircraft.

General Electric Co. (GE) Major U.S. corporation and one of the largest companies in the world. Its products include electrical and electronic equipment, plastics, aircraft engines, medical imaging equipment, and financial services. The company was incorporated in 1892, acquiring all the assets of the Edison General Electric Co. (founded as Edison Electric Light Co. by THOMAS ALVA EDISON in 1878) and two other electrical companies. The company established a research laboratory in 1900, and many of its later products, including various home appliances, were developed by in-house scientists. In 1986 GE purchased the RCA CORP., including its television network, NBC. GE's headquarters are in Fairfield, Conn.

General Mills, Inc. Leading U.S. producer of packaged foods, especially flour, breakfast cereals, snacks, and prepared mixes. General Mills was incorporated in 1928 to acquire Washburn Crosby Co. and four other milling companies. Specializing in cereals and flour products, the company introduced Wheaties and Cheerios breakfast cereals, Gold Medal flour, and Bisquick baking mix, as well as the Betty Crocker line of products. It diversified into such industries as toys and fashion in the 1960s, but by the 1990s was again dealing exclusively with consumer foods. Its headquarters are in Minneapolis.

General Motors Corp. (GM) U.S. corporation, the world's largest automotive manufacturer for most of the 20th century. It was founded in 1908 by WILLIAM C. DURANT to consolidate several motorcar companies, and it soon included the makers of Buick, Oldsmobile, Cadillac, and Oakland (later Pontiac) autos. GM acquired the Chevrolet auto company in 1918. By 1929 GM had passed FORD MOTOR CO. to become the leading U.S. auto manufacturer, and had added such overseas operations as Vauxhall of England. GM bought Electronic Data Systems Corp. in 1984, and Hughes Aircraft Co. in 1986. The company faced severe competition from Japanese automakers in the 1970s and '80s, and in 1984 it founded a new automotive division, Saturn, to compete with Japanese imports.

general practice See FAMILY PRACTICE

General Services Administration (GSA) Executive agency of the U.S. government that manages federal equipment and property. Established in 1949, the GSA is responsible for purchasing and distributing supplies to government agencies and maintaining supplies of critical materials. It also oversees the construction of government buildings and maintains the computer and communications systems used by the federal government. It was rocked by scandal in 1978 when an investigation uncovered bribery, theft, and wasteful management; new rules and procedures were later put into place to prevent such abuses.

general staff Group of military officers that assists the commander of a division or larger unit by helping to formulate and disseminate policy and by transmitting orders and overseeing their execution. It is distinguished from staffs that consist of technical specialists (e.g., medical, police, communications, and supply officers). It appeared in its modern form in the Prussian army in the early 19th century and in other European countries after 1870. The U.S. Army created a general staff in 1903.

general strike Stoppage of work by a substantial proportion of workers in each of a number of industries in an organized effort to achieve economic or political objectives. The idea of a general STRIKE spanning a variety of industries apparently began in Britain in the early 19th century; it was envisioned as a tactic of COLLECTIVE BARGAINING or, by more radical thinkers, as an instrument of social revolution. Notable general strikes occurred in Russia during the Revolution of 1905, in Britain in 1926 (carried on by various LABOR UNIONS in support of striking coal miners), and in France in 1967 (touched off by student demands for educational reform).

General Telephone and Electronics Corp. See GTE CORP.

generative grammar \'je-nə-rə-təv\ Finite set of formal rules that will produce all the grammatical sentences of a language. The idea of a generative grammar was first definitively articulated by NOAM CHOMSKY in *Syntactic Structures* (1957). The generative grammarian's task is ideally not just to define the interrelation of elements in a particular language, but also to characterize universal grammar—that is, the set of rules and principles intrinsic to all natural languages, which are thought to be an innate endowment of the human intellect. See also GRAMMAR, SYNTAX.

generator Machine that converts mechanical ENERGY to ELECTRICITY for transmission and distribution over power lines to domestic, commercial, and industrial customers. Generators also produce the electric power required for automobiles, aircraft, ships, and trains. The mechanical power for an electric generator is usually obtained from a rotating shaft and is equal to the shaft TORQUE multiplied by the rotational, or angular, velocity (speed). The mechanical power may come from various sources: TURBINES powered by water, wind, steam, or gas; GASOLINE ENGINES; or DIESEL ENGINES. See illustration opposite.

Genesee River \ˌje-nə-'sē, 'je-nə-ˌsē\ River, Pennsylvania and New York. It flows north from its headwaters in Pennsylvania, bisecting ROCHESTER, N.Y., to enter Lake ONTARIO after a course of 158 mi (254 km). Midway along its course, it flows into a 25-mi (40-km) gorge with sides rising at times 800 ft (245 m) above its banks. Called the "Grand Canyon of the East," it is the focal point of Letchworth State Park.

Genesis \'je-nə-səs\ First book of the BIBLE. Its name, taken from its first verse, means "beginning." Genesis provides the creation story for Judaism and Christianity and begins the history of the Israelite people. In addition to God's creation of the universe, it includes the story of ADAM AND EVE, CAIN AND ABEL, NOAH and the Flood, the Tower of BABEL, and God's COVENANT with the three patriarchs, ABRAHAM, Isaac, and JACOB, concluding with the story of Jacob's son JOSEPH. It is traditionally ascribed to MOSES, but modern scholarship has identified at least three literary strains in it, dating from 950 BC to the 5th century BC, though incorporating material from much earlier. It is one of the five books of the OLD TESTAMENT that make up the Pentateuch (see TORAH).

Genêt, Citizen Edmond See CITIZEN GENÊT AFFAIR

Genet \zhə-'nā\, **Jean** (1910–1986) French novelist and dramatist. An illegitimate child abandoned by his mother, he began to write while imprisoned for burglary. His first novel, *Our Lady of the Flowers* (1944), portrays an underworld of thugs, pimps, and hustlers. *Miracle of the Rose* (1945–46) is based on his adolescence at a notorious reform school, and *The Thief's Journal* (1949) recounts his life as a tramp, pickpocket, and prostitute. He became a leading figure in avant-garde theater with such plays as *The Maids* (1947), *The Balcony* (1956), and *The Blacks* (1958), stylized Expressionist dramas designed to shock and implicate an audience by revealing its hypocrisy and complicity in an exploitative social order. Admired by the Existentialists, he was the subject of J.-P. SARTRE's huge and adulatory biography *Saint Genet* (1952).

genetic code Sequence of NUCLEOTIDES in DNA and RNA that determines the AMINO-ACID sequence of PROTEINS. A messenger RNA molecule synthesized from the DNA directs the synthesis of the protein. Three adjacent nucleotides constitute a unit known as a codon; each codon codes for a single amino acid. There are 64 possible codons, 61 of which specify the 20 amino acids that make up proteins. Because most of the 20 amino acids are coded for by more than one codon, the code is called degenerate. Once thought to be identical in all forms of life, the genetic

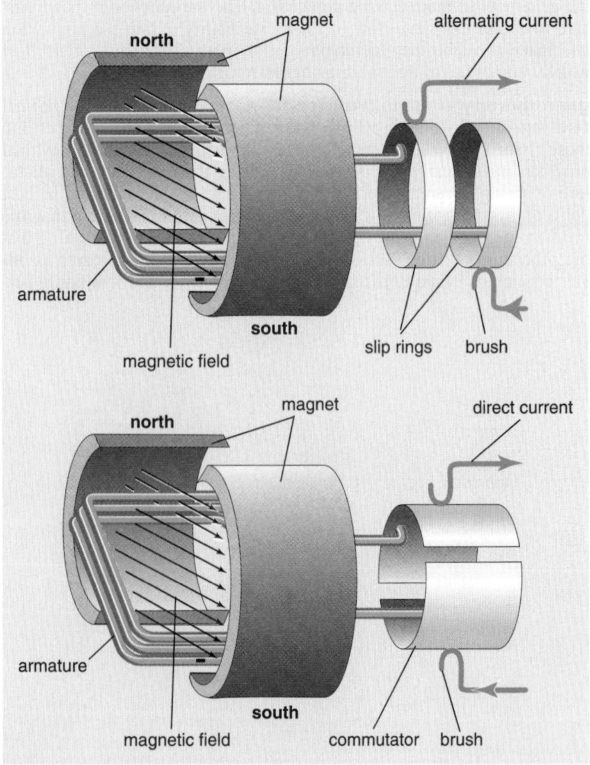

A basic generator consists of a loop or coil of wire (armature) rotating in a magnetic field. The magnetic field causes a current to flow in the (moving) wire, via induction. Either alternating or direct current may be generated, depending on whether the ends of the looped wire are attached to a set of slip rings (top: AC) or to a commutator (bottom: DC).

E
F
G

code has been found to vary slightly in certain organisms and in the mitochondria of some eukaryotes.

genetic drift Change in the pool of GENES of a small population that takes place strictly by chance. Genetic drift can result in genetic traits being lost from a population or becoming widespread in a population without respect to the survival or reproductive value of the gene pairs (alleles) involved. A random statistical effect, genetic drift can occur only in small, isolated populations in which the gene pool is small enough that chance events can change its makeup substantially. In larger populations, any specific allele is carried by so many individuals that it is almost certain to be transmitted by some of them unless it is biologically unfavorable. See also FOUNDER PRINCIPLE.

genetic engineering Artificial manipulation, modification, and RECOMBINATION of DNA or other NUCLEIC-ACID molecules in order to modify an organism or population of organisms. The term initially meant any of a wide range of techniques for modifying or manipulating organisms through heredity and reproduction. Now the term denotes the narrower field of recombinant-DNA technology, or gene cloning, in which DNA molecules from two or more sources are combined, either within cells or in test tubes, and then inserted into host organisms in which they are able to reproduce. This technique is used to produce new genetic combinations that are of value to science, medicine, agriculture, or industry. Through recombinant-DNA techniques, bacteria have been created that are capable of synthesizing human insulin, human interferon, human growth hormone, a hepatitis-B vaccine, and other medically useful substances. Recombinant-DNA techniques, combined with the development of a technique for producing antibodies in great quantity, have made an impact on medical diagnosis and cancer research. Plants have been genetically adjusted to perform nitrogen fixation and to produce their own pesticides. Bacteria capable of biodegrading oil have been produced for use in oil-spill cleanups. Genetic engineering also introduces the fear of adverse genetic manipulations and their consequences (e.g., antibiotic-resistant bacteria or new strains of disease). See also BIOTECHNOLOGY, MOLECULAR BIOLOGY.

genetics Study of HEREDITY in general and of GENES in particular. Modern genetics began with the work of GREGOR MENDEL, who formulated the basic laws of heredity. WALTER S. SUTTON proposed that CHROMOSOMES were the site of Mendel's hereditary factors. The HARDY-WEINBERG LAW established the mathematical basis for studying heredity in populations. THOMAS HUNT MORGAN provided evidence that genes occur on CHROMOSOMES and that adjacent genes on the same chromosome form LINKAGE GROUPS. OSWALD AVERY showed that DNA is the chromosome component that carries genetic information. DNA's molecular structure was deduced by JAMES D. WATSON and FRANCIS CRICK. These and other developments led to the deciphering of the GENETIC CODE of the DNA molecule, which in turn made possible the RECOMBINATION techniques of GENETIC ENGINEERING. An understanding of genetics is useful for the diagnosis, prevention, and treatment of hereditary diseases, the breeding of plants and animals, and the development of industrial processes that use microorganisms. See also BEHAVIOR GENETICS.

Geneva \jə-ˈnē-və\ *French* **Genève** \zhə-ˈnev\ *German* **Genf** \ˈgenf\ *Italian* **Ginevra** \jē-ˈnā-vrä\ City (pop., 1996 est.: 174,000), capital of Geneva canton, southwestern Switzerland. At the tip of Lake GENEVA on the RHONE RIVER, it was, by the 6th century BC, a center of the Celtic Allobroges, and was later conquered by the Romans. In the 16th century JOHN CALVIN transformed Geneva into a theocratic state and the intellectual center of Protestant Europe. In the 18th century, as the birthplace of JEAN-JACQUES ROUSSEAU and the sanctuary of VOLTAIRE, it attracted the elite of the ENLIGHTENMENT. It joined the Swiss Confederation in 1814. It was the site of the GENEVA CONVENTION in 1864, and the LEAGUE OF NATIONS was founded there in 1919. An international center of commerce and finance, it is the headquarters of the International RED CROSS (1864) and the European branch of the UNITED NATIONS.

Geneva, Lake *French* **Lac Léman** \ˈläk-lā-ˈmän\ *German* **Genfersee** \ˈgen-fər-ˌzā\ Lake, lying between southwestern Switzerland and southeastern France. About 134 sq mi (347 sq km) of the lake's area are Swiss, and 90 sq mi (234 sq km) are French. It is formed by the RHONE RIVER, which enters at the eastern end and leaves at the western end through the city of GENEVA. Lying at an elevation of 1,220 ft (372 m), it is 45 mi (72 km) long, with an average width of 5 mi (8 km). The water is subject to fluctuations of level known as seiches, in which the lake's mass rhythmically swings from shore to shore.

Geneva, University of Institution of higher learning in Geneva. It was founded by JOHN CALVIN and Théodor de Bèze (1519–1605) in 1559 as Schola Genevensis (later called the Academy), a theological seminary. The natural sciences, law, and philosophy were later added to the curriculum, and in the 19th century a medical faculty was established. In the 1930s the Institut Jean-Jacques Rousseau, a private school of education founded in 1912, became part of the university. Today many foreign students are attracted by its reputation in international studies, botany, and education. Total enrollment is about 14,000.

Geneva Conventions Series of four international agreements (1864, 1906, 1929, 1949) signed in Geneva that established the humanitarian principles by which the signatory nations are to treat an enemy's military and civilian nationals in wartime. The first convention was initiated by J.-H. DUNANT; it established that medical facilities were not to be war targets, that hospitals should treat all wounded impartially, that civilians aiding the wounded should be protected, and that the RED CROSS symbol should serve to identify those covered by the agreement. The second convention amended and extended the first. The third stated that prisoners of war should be treated humanely and that prison camps should be open to inspection by neutral countries. The 1949 conventions made further provisions for civilians falling into a belligerent's hands. Two 1977 amendments extended protection to guerrilla combatants; the U.S. did not sign them. Public opinion and disapprobation are the only sanctions that can be applied to violators. See also HAGUE CONVENTIONS, WAR CRIME.

Geneva Protocol *officially* **Protocol for the Pacific Settlement of International Disputes** (1924) LEAGUE OF NATIONS draft treaty to ensure collective security in Europe. Submitted by EDVARD BENES, the protocol proposed sanctions against an aggressor nation and provided a mechanism for the peaceful settlement of disputes. States would agree to submit all disputes to the Permanent Court of International Justice, and any state refusing arbitration was to be deemed the aggressor. The French enthusiastically supported the protocol, but it was rejected by the British.

Geneva Summit (1955) Meeting in Geneva of the leaders of the U.S., France, Britain, and the Soviet Union that sought to end the COLD WAR. Such issues as disarmament, unification of Germany, and increased economic ties were discussed. Though no agreements were reached, the conference was considered an important first step toward easing Cold War tension.

Genghis Khan \ˈgeŋ-gəs-ˈkän, ˈjeŋ-gəs-ˈkän\ *or* **Chinggis Khan** \ˈchiŋ-gəz-ˈkän\ *orig.* **Temüjin** (c. 1160–1227) Mongolian warrior-ruler who consolidated nomadic tribes into a unified Mongolia and whose troops fought from China's Pacific coast to Europe's Adriatic Sea, creating the basis for one of the greatest continental empires of all time. The leader of a destitute clan, Temüjin fought various rival clans and formed a Mongol confederacy, which in 1206 acknowledged him as Genghis Khan ("Universal Ruler"). By that year the united Mongols were ready to move out beyond the steppe. He adapted his method of warfare, moving from dependence on pure cavalry to the use of sieges, catapults, ladders, and other equipment and techniques suitable for the capture and destruction of cities. In less than 10 years he took over most of Juchen-controlled China; he then destroyed the Muslim KHWAREZM-SHAH DYNASTY while his generals raided Iran and Russia. He is infamous for his slaughter of whole cities and destruction of fields and irrigation systems, but admired for his military brilliance and ability to learn. He died on a military campaign, and the empire was divided among his sons and grandsons.

genie See JINNI

genius Person of extraordinary intellectual power. The genius displays originality, CREATIVITY, and the ability to think and work in areas not previously explored. Though geniuses have usually left their unique mark in a particular field, studies have shown that the general INTELLIGENCE of geniuses is also exceptionally high. Genius appears to be a function of both hereditary and environmental factors. See also GIFTED CHILD.

genius In ancient ROMAN RELIGION, the attendant spirit of a person or place. It originally represented the housefather, who gave continuity to a family or clan over generations; its female counterpart was the housemother, called the *juno*. In later times, the *genius* was seen as an individual's guardian spirit or higher self, and it was worshiped by that individual, especially on his birthday. There were also *genii* of places and of groups such as legions, states, and guilds.

Genoa \'je-nō-ə\ *Italian* **Genova** \'je-nō-və\ *ancient* **Genua.** City (pop., 2000 est.: 636,104) and seaport, northwestern Italy. Capital of LIGURIA region, it is the center of the Italian RIVIERA. Flourishing under the Romans, it went on to become a chief Mediterranean commercial city (12th–13th century), rivaled only by VENICE. Its fortunes declined in the 14th–15th century, after it lost a century-long struggle with Venice for control of the LEVANT. Taken by NAPOLEON in the early 19th century, it later regained its independence and prospered, especially after Italian unification. Although the city was badly damaged in World War II, a number of historic buildings survive. The birthplace of CHRISTOPHER COLUMBUS, Genoa is still noted for its maritime tradition, with shipbuilding its major industry; its university (founded 1471) is known for its economic and maritime studies.

Genoa, Conference of (1922) Post–World War I meeting at Genoa, Italy, to discuss the economic reconstruction of Central and Eastern Europe and to improve relations between Soviet Russia and Western Europe. Representatives of 30 European countries sought ways to enlist foreign capital for the "restoration of Russia." Negotiations broke down when France and Belgium, Russia's main creditors, insisted on repayment of prewar loans and restitution of confiscated foreign-owned property in Russia. Announcement of the German-Soviet Treaty of RAPALLO further strained relations.

genocide \'je-nə-ˌsīd\ Deliberate and systematic destruction of a racial, religious, political, or ethnic group. The term was coined after the Nazi era (1933–45) to define a legal concept describing a premeditated effort to destroy a population (see HOLOCAUST). In 1946 the U.N. General Assembly declared genocide a punishable crime, whether committed by an individual, group, or government, even against one's own people, in either peacetime or wartime (this last point distinguishing it from "crimes against humanity," whose legal definition specifies wartime). Suspects may be tried by a court in the country where the act was committed or by an international court (see INTERNATIONAL CRIMINAL COURT). An example of genocide in addition to the Holocaust is the slaughter of Tutsis by Hutus in Rwanda in the 1990s.

genotype \'jē-nə-ˌtīp\ Genetic makeup of an organism. The genotype determines the hereditary potentials and limitations of an individual. Among organisms that reproduce sexually, an individual's genotype comprises the entire complex of GENES inherited from both parents. Sexual reproduction guarantees that each individual has a unique genotype, except for identical twins, who come from the same fertilized egg. See also PHENOTYPE, VARIATION.

Genovese \ˌje-nə-'vē-zē\, **Eugene D(ominick)** (born 1930) U.S. historian. Born in New York City, he earned a doctorate at Columbia University and has taught at Rutgers, Columbia, Cambridge, and elsewhere. He is known for his writings on the American Civil War and slavery, especially *Roll, Jordan, Roll* (1974) and *The Slaveholders' Dilemma* (1992).

genre painting \'zhän-rə\ Painting of scenes from everyday life, of ordinary people at work or play, depicted in a realistic manner. In the 18th century, the term was used derogatorily to describe painters specializing in one type of picture, such as flowers, animals, or middle-class life. By the mid-19th century it was being used more approvingly, and it is still popularly used to describe works by 17th-century Dutch and Flemish painters such as JAN STEEN, GERARD TERBORCH, ADRIAEN VAN OSTADE, and JOHANNES VERMEER, and later masters such as J.-B.-S. CHARDIN in France, PIETRO LONGHI in Italy, and GEORGE CALEB BINGHAM in the U.S.

genro \'gen-'rō\ (Japanese: "principal elders") Extraconstitutional oligarchy that dominated the Japanese government from the promulgation of the MEIJI CONSTITUTION (1889) to the early 1930s. The genro were men who had played a leading role in the 1868 MEIJI RESTORATION. Their caretaking role outside the official government structure continued the Japanese tradition of having actual authority wielded by forces other than the titular authority. See also FUJIWARA FAMILY, HOJO FAMILY, ITO HIROBUMI, YAMAGATA ARITOMO.

Genroku period \ˌgen-'rō-ˌkü\ (1688–1704) Period in Japanese history characterized by a flourishing of the culture of the non-samurai city dweller. The term is often used to cover the period c. 1675–1725. Ostentatious displays of wealth were prohibited, but the affluent townsmen of Kyoto, Osaka, and Edo (Tokyo) found means to display their wealth. Much time and money was spent in the pleasure quarters, districts where theaters, brothels, and teahouses were located, and this "floating (i.e., fleeting) world," or *ukiyo,* was commemorated in brightly colored woodblock prints (see UKIYO-E). The Genroku period set the standards for an urban culture that continued throughout the Edo period.

gens \'jenz\ Ancient Roman clan whose members were all descended from a common male ancestor. The descendants revered the original male ancestor and identified their relationship by using his name as their second name (e.g., Gaius *Valerius* Catullus). Marriage between members of a gens was commonly discouraged.

gentian family \'jen-shən\ Family Gentianaceae (order Gentianales), composed of some 1,100 species of annual and perennial herbaceous plants and, rarely, shrubs, native mostly to northern temperate regions. The four or five united petals that make up the flower may be deeply divided; they overlap and are twisted in the bud. Some species are used in herbal remedies and in the making of dyes. Several species of gentians (genus *Gentiana*) bear attractive flowers and are cultivated as garden ornamentals. Gentians occur widely in moist meadows and woods.

Gentile \jen-'tē-lā\, **Giovanni** (1875–1944) Italian philosopher sometimes called the "philosopher of Fascism." A university professor, he and BENEDETTO CROCE edited the journal *La Critica* (1903–22). He served in education posts in BENITO MUSSOLINI's government. His philosophy of "actual idealism," strongly influenced by G. W. F. HEGEL, denied the existence of individual minds and of any distinction between theory and practice, subject and object, past and present. He planned and edited the *Enciclopedia Italiana* (1936) and wrote prolifically on education and philosophy. Among his works are *The Reform of Education* (1920), *The Philosophy of Art* (1931), and *My Religion* (1943). He was killed by anti-Fascist communists.

Gentile da Fabriano \jen-'tē-lā-dä-ˌfäb-rē-'ä-nō\ *orig.* **Gentile di Niccolò di Massio** (c. 1385–1427) Italian painter. He was probably trained in the Lombardy region. In 1409 he was commissioned to decorate the Doges' Palace in Venice with historical frescoes, now lost. His most important fresco cycle, also destroyed, was in the church of St. John Lateran in Rome. His major surviving painting is the celebrated Strozzi Altarpiece (1423), featuring *The Adoration of the Magi*. Its combination of naturalism and rich ornamentation influenced Italian artists throughout the century, notably Fra ANGELICO and BENOZZO GOZZOLI, and established Gentile as one of Italy's greatest proponents of the International Gothic style. He was the most important Italian painter of the first quarter of the 15th century.

Gentileschi \ˌjän-tē-'les-kē\, **Artemisia** (1593–1652/53) Italian painter. The daughter of ORAZIO GENTILESCHI, she studied with him and with the landscape painter Agostino Tassi. Her earliest known work is *Susanna and the Elders* (1610), formerly attributed to Orazio. In 1616 she joined the Academy of Design in Florence and began to develop a powerful style of her own. She was one of the greatest of CARAVAGGIO's followers and the most violent, arguably as a result of her rape by Tassi and the trial at which she was forced under torture to give evidence against him. She favored such subjects as Judith beheading Holofernes and other images of heroic women. She worked in Rome and Naples, and spent three years with her father in London (1638–41). The first woman artist to attain an international reputation, she is admired today as the earliest to show a feminist consciousness in her work.

"The Annunciation," painting by Orazio Gentileschi, 1623; in the Galleria Sabauda, Turin, Italy.

SCALA—ART RESOURCE

Gentileschi, Orazio *orig.* **Orazio Lomi** (1562–1639) Italian painter. Born in Pisa, he went to Rome c. 1576–78 and painted frescoes in various churches (c. 1590–1600). His paintings of the early 17th century reveal the influence of CARAVAGGIO's strong chiaroscuro and contemporary figure types; though more refined than Caravaggio's works, they lack the master's power and uncompromising realism. Invited to England by CHARLES I in 1626, he remained there as court painter the rest of his life. ARTEMISIA GENTILESCHI was his daughter.

Gentz \'gents\, **Friedrich** (1764–1832) German political journalist. Strongly influenced by EDMUND BURKE, he published journals and pamphlets analyzing events from the viewpoint of a conservative liberal and compared the French Revolution unfavorably to the American Revolution. After serving in the Prussian civil service (1785–1803), he moved to Vienna, where he became KLEMENS, FURST VON METTERNICH's propagandist and confidential adviser from 1812. He served as secretary-general to the various congresses that convened after Napoleon's defeat.

genus Biological classification that ranks below family and above SPECIES, consisting of structurally or phylogenetically (see PHYLOGENETIC TREE) related species or a single species exhibiting unusual differences. For example, the species of roses collectively form the genus *Rosa,* and those of horses, donkeys, and zebras form the genus *Equus.* The genus name, capitalized and usually italicized, is the first word of a scientific name in the system of BINOMIAL NOMENCLATURE.

geochemical cycle Developmental path followed by individual elements or groups of elements in the crustal and subcrustal zones of the earth and on its surface. The concept encompasses geochemical differentiation (natural separation and concentration of elements) and heat-assisted recombination processes. Changes may not be apparent over a short term, but over a long term changes of great magnitude occur, including the evolution of continents and oceans.

geochemistry Scientific discipline dealing with the relative abundance, distribution, and migration of the earth's chemical elements and their isotopes. Historically, geochemistry was concerned primarily with defining elemental abundances in minerals and rocks. Modern geochemical research also includes study of the continual recycling of the earth's constituent materials through geologic processes, the cyclic flow of individual elements (and their compounds) between living and nonliving systems, and certain areas of COSMOLOGY.

geochronology Dating and interpretation of geologic events in the history of the earth. The classical technique of geochronology was STRATIGRAPHY, including faunal succession. Since the mid-20th century, radiometric dating has provided absolute age data to supplement the relative dates obtained from the fossil record. Radiometric dating is based on the principle that radioactive isotopes in geologic material decay at constant, known rates to daughter isotopes. See also CARBON-14 DATING.

geode Hollow mineral body found in limestones and some shales, commonly a slightly flattened globe 1–12 in. (2.5–30 cm) in diameter and containing a CHALCEDONY layer surrounding an inner lining of crystals. The hollow interior often is nearly filled with inward-projecting crystals, new layers growing on top of old. The crystals are often of quartz but sometimes of other minerals.

geodesy \jē-'ä-də-sē\ Scientific discipline concerned with the size and shape of the earth, its gravitational field, and the location of fixed points. Originally, all geodesic work was based on land surveys. Now satellites are used in conjunction with the land-based system.

geoduck \'gü-ē-ˌdək\ Marine BIVALVE *(Panopea generosa)* that inhabits the intertidal zone of the Pacific coast from southern Alaska to Baja California. It is the largest known burrowing bivalve, with a shell about 7–9 in. (18–23 cm) long and siphons that extend up to about 4 ft (1.3 m). It may weigh as much as 8 lbs (3.6 kg). Though highly prized for food, it lives in deep burrows and is difficult to dig out (the name probably derives from an Indian phrase meaning "dig deep"). Similar species are found in other parts of the world.

Geoffrey of Monmouth \'jef-rē...'män-məth\ (died 1155) Medieval British chronicler. He was probably an Oxford cleric for most of his life. His mostly fictional *History of the Kings of Britain* (c. 1135–39) traced the descent of British princes from the Trojans; it brought the figure of Arthur (see ARTHURIAN LEGEND) into European literature and introduced the enchanter MERLIN, whose story he related in the *Vita Merlini* (c. 1148–51?). Though denounced from the first by other historians, the *History* was one of the most popular books of the Middle Ages and had an enormous influence on later chroniclers.

geographic information system (GIS) Computerized system that relates and displays data collected from a geographic entity in the form of a map. The ability of GIS to overlay existing data with new information and display it in color on a computer screen is used primarily to conduct analyses and make decisions related to geology, ecology, land use, demographics, transportation, and other domains, most of which relate to the human use of the physical environment. Through the process of geocoding, geographic data from a database is converted into images in the form of maps.

geography Science of the earth's surface, which describes and analyzes the spatial variations in physical, biological, and human phenomena that occur on the surface of the globe and treats their interrelationships and their significant regional patterns. Once associated entirely with mapping and the exploration of the earth, the field today is wide-ranging, and geographers use a variety of methods and techniques drawn from numerous disciplines. Subfields of geography include physical, human, and regional geography, which may range in scale from worldwide to a continent, a country, or a city.

geologic oceanography See MARINE GEOLOGY

geologic time Interval of time occupied by the earth's geologic history, extending from c. 3.9 billion years ago (corresponding to the age of the oldest known rocks) to the present day. It is, in effect, the part of the earth's history that is recorded in rock strata. The geologic time scale is classified in nested intervals distinguished by characteristic geologic and biologic features. From longest to shortest duration, the intervals are EON, ERA, PERIOD, and EPOCH. See table on following page.

geological engineering See ENGINEERING GEOLOGY

geology Scientific study of the earth, including its composition, structure, physical properties, and history. Geology is commonly divided into subdisciplines concerned with the chemical makeup of the earth, including the study of minerals (MINERALOGY) and rocks (PETROLOGY); the structure of the earth (STRUCTURAL GEOLOGY) and volcanic phenomena (VOLCANOLOGY); landforms and the processes that produce them (GEOMORPHOLOGY and GLACIOLOGY); geologic history, including the study of fossils (PALEONTOLOGY), the development of sedimentary strata (STRATIGRAPHY), and the evolution of planetary bodies and their satellites (astrogeology); and ECONOMIC GEOLOGY and its various branches, such as mining geology and petroleum geology. Some major fields closely allied to geology are GEODESY, GEOPHYSICS, and GEOCHEMISTRY. See also ENVIRONMENTAL GEOLOGY.

geomagnetic field Magnetic field associated with the earth. It is essentially dipolar (i.e., it has two poles, the northern and southern magnetic poles) on the earth's surface. Away from the surface, the field becomes distorted. Most geomagnetists explain the field by means of dynamo theories, whereby a source of energy in the earth's CORE causes a self-sustaining magnetic field. In the dynamo theories, fluid motion in the earth's core involves the movement of conducting material within an existing magnetic field, thus creating a current and a self-enforcing field.

geomagnetic reversal Alternation of the earth's magnetic polarity. The earth's internal magnetic field reverses, on average, about every 300,000 to 1 million years. This reversal is very sudden on a geologic time scale, apparently taking about 5,000 years. The time between reversals is highly variable, sometimes less than 40,000 years and at other times as long as 35 million years. No regularities or periodicities have yet been discovered. A long interval of one polarity may be followed by a short interval of opposite polarity. See also POLAR WANDERING.

geomagnetics Branch of geophysics concerned with all aspects of the earth's magnetic field, including its origin, variation through time, and manifestations in the form of magnetic poles, the magnetization of rocks, and local or regional magnetic anomalies.

Geometric style Style of vase painting that flourished in Athens c. 1000–700 BC. Vases decorated in this style feature horizontal bands filled with geometric patterns such as zigzags, triangles, and swastikas in dark paint on a light ground. The rhythmic effect is similar to that of basketry. The abstract motifs developed into stylized animal and human forms in such narrative scenes as funerals, dances, and boxing matches.

Geologic Time

Eon	Era	Periods and systems	Epochs and series	Beginning of interval*	Biological forms
Phanerozoic	Cenozoic	Quaternary	Holocene	0.01	
			Pleistocene	1.8	Earliest humans
		Tertiary	Pliocene	5	
			Miocene	24	Earliest hominids
			Oligocene	34	
			Eocene	55	Earliest grasses
			Paleocene	65	Earliest large mammals
	Cretaceous-Tertiary boundary (65 million years ago): extinction of dinosaurs				
	Mesozoic	Cretaceous	Late	99	
			Early	144	Earliest flowering plants; dinosaurs in ascendance
		Jurassic		206	Earliest birds and mammals
		Triassic		248	Age of Dinosaurs begins
	Paleozoic	Permian		290	
		Carboniferous			
		Pennsylvanian		323	Earliest reptiles
		Mississippian		354	Earliest winged insects
		Devonian		417	Earliest vascular plants (incl. ferns and mosses) and amphibians
		Silurian		443	Earliest land plants and insects
		Ordovician		490	Earliest corals
		Cambrian		543	Earliest fishes
Proterozoic	Precambrian			2,500	Earliest colonial algae and soft-bodied invertebrates
Archean				4,000	Life appears; earliest algae and primitive bacteria

*In millions of years before the present.

Small bronze and clay figurines, elaborately decorated fibulas, and limestone seals were also produced. The patterns remained popular and influenced much later Greek art.

geometry See ALGEBRAIC GEOMETRY, ANALYTIC GEOMETRY, DIFFERENTIAL GEOMETRY, ELLIPTIC GEOMETRY, EUCLIDEAN GEOMETRY, FRACTAL GEOMETRY, HYPERBOLIC GEOMETRY, NON-EUCLIDEAN GEOMETRY, PROJECTIVE GEOMETRY

geomorphology Scientific discipline that describes and classifies the earth's topographic features. Many systems of classifying landforms have been devised. Some systems describe and group topographic features primarily according to the processes that shaped or modified them. Others take additional factors into consideration (e.g., character of the surface rocks and climatic variations) and include the developmental stage of landforms as an aspect of their evolution over geologic time.

geophysics Major branch of earth science that applies the principles and methods of physics to the study of the earth. Geophysics deals with such geologic phenomena as the temperature distribution of the earth's interior; the source, configuration, and variations of the GEOMAGNETIC FIELD; and the large-scale features of the terrestrial CRUST, such as rifts, continental sutures, and oceanic ridges. Modern geophysical research also examines phenomena of the outer parts of the earth's atmosphere and even the physical properties of other planets and their satellites. See also MARINE GEOPHYSICS.

geopolitics Analysis of geographic influences on power relationships in international politics. The term was employed in 1916 by the Swedish political scientist Rudolph Kjellén (1864–1922) in his discussion of the importance of geography in the development of national policies—in particular, the acquisition of natural boundaries, access to important sea routes, and control of strategically important land areas. Improvements in communications and transportation have lessened the importance of such factors, and the term is now used with broader meanings.

George, David Lloyd See David LLOYD GEORGE

George, Henry (1839–1897) U.S. land reformer and economist. Born in Philadelphia, he left school before age 14 to work as a clerk and then at sea. In 1858 he went to California, where he worked for newspapers (briefly founding his own) and took part in Democratic party politics. In 1879 he published *Progress and Poverty,* in which he proposed that the state tax away all economic rent—the income from the use of the bare land, but not from improvements—and abolish all other taxes. George envisaged that the government's annual income from this "single tax" would be so large that there would be a surplus for expansion of public works.

George, Lake Lake, northeastern New York. It is 32 mi (51 km) long and 1–4 mi (1.6–6.4 km) wide, and is connected to Lake CHAMPLAIN through a series of waterfalls. In the foothills of the ADIRONDACKS, it is noted for its scenic beauty, and is a popular resort area. Memorialized in JAMES FENIMORE COOPER's novels as Lake Horicon, the real lake was the scene of numerous battles during the FRENCH AND INDIAN WAR and the AMERICAN REVOLUTION. Fort Ticonderoga is located on the falls at the lake's outlet.

George, St. (fl. c. 3rd century) Early Christian martyr and patron saint of England. His historical existence is uncertain, but from the 6th century he was the subject of legends as a warrior-saint. He was said to have rescued a Libyan king's daughter from a dragon, which he killed in return for a promise that the king's subjects would be baptized. In art, the young saint often wears knight's armor ornamented with a scarlet cross. He probably became England's patron saint in the 14th century, when EDWARD III made him patron of the Order of the GARTER.

George \gā-'ȯr-gə\, **Stefan** (1868–1933) German poet. George traveled widely, becoming associated with STEPHANE MALLARME and the SYMBOLIST MOVEMENT in Paris and the Pre-Raphaelites in London. Returning to Germany, he edited the journal *Blätter fur die Kunst* 1892–1919 and became the center of the "George Circle," gathering young poets around him in a close-knit aesthetic band. His collections include *Hymnen* (1890), *Das Jahr der Seele* (1897), *Der siebente Ring* (1907), and *Der Stern des Bundes* (1914). A supporter of "pure poetry," he opposed not only the debasement of the language but also materialism and naturalism. Though politically conservative, he turned down Nazi offers of money and honors, preferring exile. His collected works include translations of DANTE and WILLIAM SHAKESPEARE's sonnets as well as prose sketches.

George I *orig.* **George Louis** ***German*** **Georg Ludwig** (1660–1727) First king of England (1714–27) from the House of HANOVER. He succeeded his father as the elector of Hanover (1698) and fought with distinction in the War of the SPANISH SUCCESSION. As a great-grandson of JAMES I of England and under the Act of SETTLEMENT, George succeeded to the English throne in 1714. He formed a Whig ministry and left internal politics to his ministers, including 1ST EARL STANHOPE, VISCOUNT TOWNSHEND, and ROBERT WALPOLE. He was unpopular because of his German manner and German mistresses and their involvement in the SOUTH SEA

BUBBLE crisis, but he strengthened Britain's position by forming the QUADRUPLE ALLIANCE (1718). He was succeeded by his son, GEORGE II.

George I *Greek* **Georgios** *orig.* **Prins Vilhelm af Danmark (Prince William of Denmark)** (1845–1913) King of Greece. Son of CHRISTIAN IX of Denmark, he served in the Danish navy and in 1862 was nominated to the Greek throne by Britain, France, and Russia after the Greek king, Otto, was deposed. Accepted by the Greek National Assembly, he ascended the throne as George I in 1863. He oversaw the incorporation of territory in Thessaly and Epirus into Greece as well as the annexation of Crete. In the unrest caused by the BALKAN WARS, he was assassinated at Salonika; he was succeeded by his son, Constantine I. His long reign was the formative period for the development of Greece as a modern European state.

George II *orig.* **George Augustus** *German* **Georg August** (1683–1760) King of Great Britain and elector of Hanover (1727–60). His father, the elector of Hanover, became GEORGE I of England; he succeeded him in both roles in 1727. He retained ROBERT WALPOLE as his key minister until 1742. His new minister, John Carteret (1690–1763), brought England into the War of the AUSTRIAN SUCCESSION, where George fought courageously at the Battle of Dettingen (1743), the last time a British king appeared on the battlefield. The parliament and ministers forced Carteret's resignation and the appointment of WILLIAM PITT. George lost interest in politics, and Pitt's strategy brought about a British victory in the SEVEN YEARS' WAR.

George II *Greek* **Georgios** (1890–1947) King of Greece (1922–24, 1935–47). He became king when his father, CONSTANTINE I, was deposed in 1922, but the royal family was unpopular and George fled Greece in 1923. The National Assembly proclaimed Greece a republic in 1924. George remained in exile until the conservative Populist Party, with army support, gained control of the legislature and restored the monarchy in 1935. IOANNES METAXAS seized power in 1936 with the king's support. George was forced into exile in 1941 in World War II; republican sentiment threatened his throne, but he was restored by a plebiscite and returned to Greece in 1946.

George III *orig.* **George William Frederick** (1738–1820) King of Great Britain and Ireland (1760–1820); also elector (1760–1814) and king (1814–20) of Hanover. The grandson of GEORGE II, he ascended the throne during the SEVEN YEARS' WAR. His chief minister, Lord BUTE, forced WILLIAM PITT's resignation and caused intrigue rather than stability within the government. Bute resigned in 1763, but George's political overtures to others were snubbed, until Lord NORTH became prime minister in 1770. England was in financial distress caused by the war, and George supported attempts to raise funds through taxation of the American colonies, which led to the AMERICAN REVOLUTION. With North, he was blamed for prolonging the war and losing the colonies. He reasserted his power when North and CHARLES JAMES FOX planned to take control of the EAST INDIA CO.; he forced them to resign and reaffirmed his control through a new "patriotic" prime minister, WILLIAM PITT. George supported him until the war with Revolutionary France (1793) and fears of related uprisings in Ireland caused Pitt to propose political emancipation of the Roman Catholics. George's vehement opposition led to Pitt's resignation in 1801. In 1811 George's ill health and a return of the madness that had afflicted him for short periods earlier in his life caused Parliament to enact the regency of his son, the future GEORGE IV.

George IV *orig.* **George Augustus Frederick** (1762–1830) King of the United Kingdom (1820–30) and king of Hanover (1820–30). The son of GEORGE III, he earned his father's ill will by his extravagances and dissolute habits, contracting a secret marriage that was annulled by his father. In 1811 George became regent for his father, who had been declared insane. Retaining his father's ministers rather than appointing his Whig friends, he saw Britain and her allies triumph over Napoleon in 1815. A patron of the architect JOHN NASH, he sponsored the restoration of WINDSOR CASTLE.

George V *orig.* **George Frederick Ernest Albert** (1865–1936) King of the United Kingdom (1910–36). The second son of the future EDWARD VII, he succeeded his father in 1910. Early in his reign, he faced problems resulting from the constitutional struggle to restrict the power of the House of LORDS. Respect for the new king increased during World War I, and he visited the front in France several times. After the war he faced both serious industrial unrest and the resignation as prime minister of ANDREW BONAR LAW (1923), who was replaced by STANLEY BALDWIN. After the collapse of the pound and the subsequent financial crisis in 1931, he persuaded JAMES RAMSAY MACDONALD to remain in office and form a national coalition government. He was succeeded successively by his sons EDWARD VIII and GEORGE VI.

George V.
CAMERA PRESS

George VI *orig.* **Albert Frederick Arthur George** (1895–1952) King of the United Kingdom (1936–52). The second son of GEORGE V, he was proclaimed king following the abdication of his brother, EDWARD VIII. He was an important symbolic leader of the British people during World War II, supporting the wartime leadership of WINSTON CHURCHILL and visiting his armies on several battlefronts. In 1949 he was formally recognized as head of the COMMONWEALTH by its member states. He earned the respect of his people by scrupulously observing the responsibilities of a constitutional monarch and by overcoming the handicap of a severe stammer. He was succeeded by his daughter, ELIZABETH II.

George VI.
KEYSTONE

George Washington Birthplace National Monument National monument, eastern Virginia. Established in 1930, it consists of 538 acres (218 hectares), located along the POTOMAC RIVER. "Wakefield," the house where GEORGE WASHINGTON (born February 22, 1732) spent the first three years of his life, burned in 1779. The present Memorial House was reconstructed in 1931–32 and represents a typical 18th-century Virginia plantation dwelling with a period garden.

George Washington University, The Private university in Washington, D.C. It was chartered in 1821, the original impetus for a university in the capital having come from GEORGE WASHINGTON. It consists of an undergraduate and graduate college and schools of international affairs, law, medicine and health sciences, business and public management, engineering, and education. It is home to the Institute for European, Russian, and Eurasian Studies and the Space Policy Institute. Total enrollment is about 19,000.

Georges Bank Submerged sandbank in the Atlantic Ocean, east of Massachusetts. It has long been an important fishing ground, with scallops harvested in its northeastern portion. Navigation is made dangerous by crosscurrents and fog. In 1994 it was closed to commercial fishing in order to replenish depleted stock.

George's War, King See KING GEORGE'S WAR

Georgetown *formerly (1784–1812)* **Stabroek** \'stä-ˌbrůk\ City (pop., 1995 est.: 254,000), capital of Guyana. The nation's chief port, it lies on the Atlantic Ocean at the mouth of the DEMERARA RIVER. It was founded by the British in 1781 and named after GEORGE III; it was largely rebuilt by the French by 1784. Known during the Dutch occupation as Stabroek, it was established as the seat of government of the combined colonies of Essequibo and Demerara in 1784. When the British regained control in 1812, the name was changed back to Georgetown. The modern city is the chief commercial and manufacturing center of Guyana.

Georgetown University Private university in Washington, D.C. Founded in 1789, it was the first Roman Catholic (Jesuit) college in the U.S. It has always been open to people of all faiths. It includes a college of arts and sciences, a graduate school, and schools of foreign service, law, medicine, nursing, business, and languages and linguistics. Important facilities include a seismological observatory, the Woodstock Theological Center, and various medical research centers. Total enrollment is about 13,000.

Georgia State (pop., 1997 est.: 7,486,000), southeastern U.S. One of the original, and the last, of the 13 English colonies, it covers 58,910 sq mi (152,577 sq km) and is the largest state east of the Mississippi River; its capital is ATLANTA. The area was inhabited by the CREEK and CHEROKEE Indians when Spanish missions arrived in the 16th century. English settlement began in 1733 at SAVANNAH when JAMES OGLETHORPE established a refuge for debtors. European settlement accelerated after the AMERICAN REVOLUTION, and the last of the Indians were forcibly removed in the 1830s. Georgia seceded from the Union in 1861, and the AMERICAN CIVIL WAR was particularly hard on the state. It was the last former Confederate state to be readmitted to the Union in 1870. Its landscape sweeps from the BLUE RIDGE Mountains in the north to the OKEFENOKEE SWAMP (which it shares with Florida) on the south. For most of the 19th century it was the capital of the cotton empire of the South; in the 20th century industry predominated. The state's population has grown throughout the 20th century, with Atlanta especially attracting national corporations.

Georgia *officially* **Republic of Georgia** *Georgian* **Sakartvelo** \sä-'kärt-ve-ˌlō\ Republic, South Asia. In the Caucasus Mtns., on the southeastern shores of the Black Sea, it includes the autonomous republics of Abkhazia and Adzharia. Area: 26,831 sq mi (69,492 sq km). Population (1997 est.): 5,377,000. Capital: TBILISI. Two-thirds of the people are Georgian (Karttvelebi); minorities include Armenians, Russians, and Azerbaijanis. Language: GEORGIAN (official). Religion: Georgian Orthodoxy. Currency: lari. Most of Georgia is mountainous; many peaks rise higher than 15,000 ft (4,600 m). The Caucasus protect it against cold air from the north, and the climate is mainly subtropical. Fertile lowlands lie near the shores of the Black Sea. It has a well-developed industrial

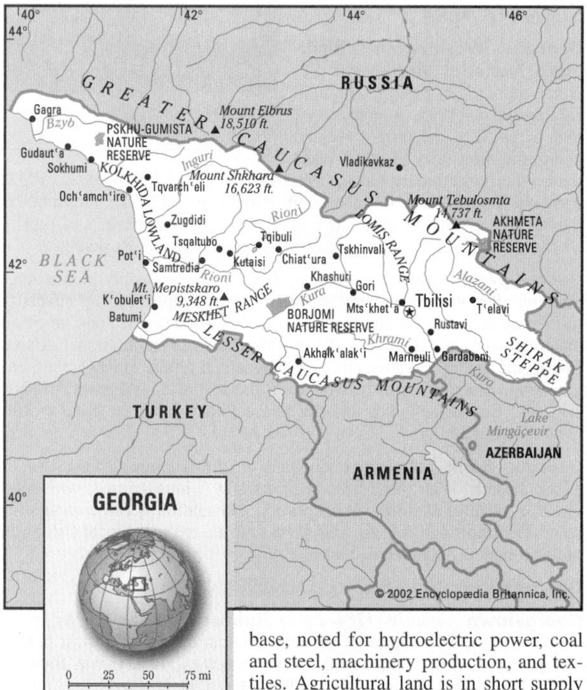

base, noted for hydroelectric power, coal and steel, machinery production, and textiles. Agricultural land is in short supply and difficult to farm; crops include tea, citrus fruits, wine grapes, sugar beets, and tobacco. It is a republic with one legislative body; its head of state and government is the president. Ancient Georgia was the site of the kingdoms of Iberia and COLCHIS, whose fabled wealth was known to the ancient Greeks. The area was part of the Roman empire by 65 BC, and became Christian in AD 337. For the next three centuries it was involved in the conflicts between the Byzantine and Persian empires; after 654 it was controlled by Arab caliphs, who established an emirate in Tbilisi. It was controlled by the Armenian Bagratids from the 8th to the 12th century, and the zenith of Georgia's power was reached in the reign of Queen Tamara, whose realm stretched from Azerbaijan to Circassia, forming a pan-Caucasian empire. Invasions by Mongols and Turks in the 13th–14th century disintegrated the kingdom, and the fall of Constantinople (now ISTANBUL) to the Ottoman Turks in 1453 isolated it from western Christendom. The next three centuries saw repeated invasions by the Armenians, Turks, and Persians. Georgia sought Russian protection in 1783, and in 1801 was annexed to Russia. After the RUSSIAN REVOLUTION OF 1917, the area was briefly independent; in 1921 a Soviet regime was installed, and in 1936 Georgia became the Georgian S.S.R., a full member of the Soviet Union. In 1990 a noncommunist coalition came to power in the first free elections ever held in Soviet Georgia, and in 1991, Georgia declared independence. In the 1990s, while Pres. EDUARD SHEVARDNADZE tried to steer a middle course, internal dissention resulted in conflicts with the Abkhaz Republic, and external distrust of Russian motives in the area grew.

Georgia, Strait of Channel in the Pacific Ocean, southwestern Canada and northwestern U.S. Located between VANCOUVER ISLAND, the southwestern mainland of British Columbia, and northwestern Washington state, it is 150 mi (241 km) long and 30 mi (28 km) at its widest. To the north the strait ends in a jumble of islands separating it from Johnstone and Queen Charlotte straits. The southern end is marked by the San Juan Islands of Washington and joins Haro Strait, forming a link in the INSIDE PASSAGE sea route between SEATTLE, Wash., and Skagway, Alaska.

Georgia, University of Public university in Athens, Ga. Founded in 1785, it was the first state college in the U.S. It is part of the University System of Georgia and is a land- and sea-grant institution. It includes colleges of arts and sciences, agricultural and environmental sciences, business, education, environmental design, family and consumer sciences, journalism and mass communications, pharmacy, and veterinary medicine, and schools of forest resources, law, and social work. Campus facilities include a botanical garden, an institute for African-American studies, and a center for East–West trade policy. Total enrollment is about 30,000.

Georgia Institute of Technology Public institution of higher learning in Atlanta, founded in 1885. It consists of colleges of architecture, computing, engineering, sciences, and public policy and administration. Undergraduate and graduate degrees are offered. Georgia Tech is home to a nuclear research center and several other research-and-development centers. Total enrollment is about 13,000.

Georgian Bay Inlet, Lake HURON, southeastern Ontario. Sheltered from the lake by Manitoulin Island and the Bruce Peninsula, it is 120 mi (190 km) long and 50 mi (80 km) wide; its maximum depth is 540 ft (165 m). The Georgian Bay Islands National Park, established in 1929, comprises some 40 islands in the southeastern and western parts of the bay. The Thirty Thousand Islands along the bay's eastern shore constitute a popular summer resort area.

Georgian language CAUCASIAN LANGUAGE of the Republic of Georgia, spoken by about 4.1 million people worldwide. Georgian is unique among Caucasian languages in having an ancient literary tradition. The earliest attestation of the language is an inscription of AD 430 in a church in Palestine, in a script ancestral to that used for Old Georgian (5th–11th century). The civil script used to write Modern Georgian, with 33 characters and no distinction between upper- and lowercase, was an offshoot of a script that first appeared in the 10th century. The origins of Georgian writing are uncertain, though it was presumably a free adaptation of the GREEK ALPHABET, with new characters invented for the sounds peculiar to Georgian. Georgian has features typical of other Caucasian languages, including a large consonant inventory (with clusters of up to six consonants in word-initial position), complex agglutinative MORPHOLOGY, and ergative features in some tense systems (see ERGATIVITY).

Georgian poetry Body of lyrical poetry produced in Britain in the early 20th century. Desiring to make new poetry more accessible to the public, RUPERT BROOKE and Sir Edward Marsh produced five anthology volumes—containing works by ROBERT GRAVES, WALTER DE LA MARE, Siegfried Sassoon (1886–1967), and others—called *Georgian Poetry* (1912–22). "Georgian" was meant to suggest the opening of a new poetic age with the accession in 1910 of GEORGE V; however, much of the Georgians' work was conventional, and the name came to refer to literature rooted in its time and backward-looking.

Georgian style Architecture, interior design, and decorative arts of Britain during the reigns (1714–1830) of the first four Georges. It encompassed Palladianism (see ANDREA PALLADIO), turned to an austere Neoclassicism, moved on to GOTHIC REVIVAL, and ended with the REGENCY

STYLE. The era is said to mark the summit of house design in Britain. Its legacy can be seen in the city squares of uniform, symmetrical brick London townhouses, their facades employing Classical pilasters, pedimented doors and windows, and graceful moldings. Their interiors, often furnished with Chippendale and Sheraton pieces, were characterized by harmonious proportions, quiet colors, and Roman-derived stucco ornamentation.

geosyncline Linear trough of subsidence of the earth's crust, in which vast amounts of sediment accumulate. The filling of a geosyncline with thousands or tens of thousands of feet of sediment is accompanied by folding, crumpling, and faulting of the deposits. Intrusion of crystalline igneous rock and regional uplift complete the transformation into a belt of folded mountains. The concept was introduced by JAMES HALL in 1859 and is basic to the theory of mountain building. See also ANDEAN GEOSYNCLINE, APPALACHIAN GEOSYNCLINE, CORDILLERAN GEOSYNCLINE.

geothermal energy Power obtained by using heat from the earth's interior. Most geothermal resources are in regions of active VOLCANISM. Hot springs, geysers, pools of boiling mud, and fumaroles are the most easily exploited sources. The ancient Romans used hot springs to heat baths and homes, and similar uses are still found in Iceland, Turkey, and Japan. Geothermal energy's greatest potential lies in the generation of electricity. It was first used to produce electric power in Italy in 1904. Today geothermal power plants are in operation in New Zealand, Japan, Iceland, Mexico, the U.S., and elsewhere.

Gerald of Wales See GIRALDUS CAMBRENSIS

geranium Any of the approximately 300 species of perennial herbaceous plants or shrubs that make up the genus *Geranium* (family Geraniaceae), native mostly to subtropical southern Africa. They are among the most popular bedding and greenhouse plants. The closely related genus *Pelargonium* contains some 280 species of annual, biennial, and perennial herbaceous plants also commonly called geraniums. The showy, or Martha Washington, geraniums *(P.* x *domesticum)* have large pansylike flowers, few to the cluster. Some geraniums are grown as basket plants indoors and out; they are also used as ground covers in warm areas. Some species have fragrant leaves. Geranium oil smells like roses and is used chiefly in perfumes, soaps, and ointments.

Hybrid geranium (*Pelargonium* × *hortorum*).
JOHN H. GERARD

gerbil \'jər-bəl\ Any of almost 100 species of burrowing mouselike RODENTS (in the family Cricetidae) found in Africa and Asia, usually in dry, sandy areas but also in grasslands, cultivated fields, or forests. Gerbils have large eyes and ears and soft, brown or grayish fur. Most are 4–6 in. (10–15 cm) long, excluding the long, hairy tail. Many species have long hind legs used for leaping. Gerbils feed primarily on seeds, roots, and other plant material. One species *(Meriones unguiculatus)* is a popular pet. The great gerbil *(Rhombomys opimus)* sometimes damages crops and embankments in Russia, and members of one African genus *(Tatera)* are possible carriers of bubonic PLAGUE.

Gere, Richard (born 1949) U.S. film actor. Born in Philadelphia, he starred in the stage musical *Grease* in London (1973) before attracting attention in the film *Looking for Mr. Goodbar* (1977), and went on to star in such other hits as *Days of Heaven* (1978), *American Gigolo* (1979), and *An Officer and a Gentleman* (1982). In the 1980s he became an advocate for Tibetan Buddhism and for Latin American political refugees. His later films include *Pretty Woman* (1990) and *Runaway Bride* (1999).

geriatrics See GERONTOLOGY AND GERIATRICS

Géricault \,zhā-ri-'kō\, **(Jean-Louis-André-) Théodore** (1791–1824) French painter. Under Pierre Guérin (1774–1833) he developed great skill in figure construction and composition, and under JOSEPH VERNET he became adept at capturing animal movement. He was inspired by the coloration of PETER PAUL RUBENS and the contemporary subject matter of A.-J. GROS. On a trip to Italy (1816–17), he became an admirer of MICHELANGELO and art of the baroque period. On his return to Paris, the macabre subject matter and political overtones of his huge *Raft of the Medusa* (1818–19) aroused great controversy. In 1820–21 he went to England and produced a large body of lithographs, watercolors, and oils of jockeys and horses. An avid horseman, he died after a riding accident. His work had enormous influence, most notably on EUGENE DELACROIX, and on the development of Romantic art in France.

germ-plasm theory Concept of the physical basis of HEREDITY expressed by the biologist August Weismann (1834–1914). It claimed that germ plasm, which Weismann believed to be independent from all other cells of the body, was the essential element of germ cells (eggs and sperm) and was the hereditary material passed from generation to generation. First proposed in 1883, his view contradicted J.-B. LAMARCK's then-prevalent theory of acquired characteristics. Though its details have been altered, its idea of the stability of hereditary material is the basis of the modern understanding of physical inheritance.

germ theory Theory that certain diseases are caused by invasion of the body by microorganisms. LOUIS PASTEUR, JOSEPH LISTER, and ROBERT KOCH are given much of the credit for its development and acceptance in the later 19th century. Pasteur showed that organisms in the air cause FERMENTATION and spoil food; Lister was first to use an ANTISEPTIC to exclude germs in the air to prevent infection; and Koch first linked a specific organism with a disease (ANTHRAX). The full implications of germ theory for medical practice were not immediately apparent after it was proven; surgeons operated without masks or head coverings as late as the 1890s.

germ warfare See BIOLOGICAL WARFARE

Germain \zher-'ma^{n}\, **Thomas** (1674–1748) French silver- and goldsmith. He studied painting as a boy and in 1691 was apprenticed to a silversmith in Rome. From 1706 to the 1720s, back in France, he worked on church commissions, such as a silver-gilt monstrance for Notre-Dame de Paris (1716). He became a master in the guild in 1720, and in 1723 LOUIS XV appointed him a royal goldsmith. Among his patrons were the queen of Spain, the king and queen of Naples, and the Portuguese court; his workshop produced some 3,000 silver objects for the palace at Lisbon over a 40-year period. He is best known for elaborate objects in Rococo style, though some of his pieces are simple and elegant.

German Civil Code *German* **Bürgerliches Gesetzbuch.** Body of codified private law that went into effect in the German empire in 1900. The code, since modified, grew out of a desire for a truly national law that would override the often conflicting customs and law codes of the various German territories. Divided into five parts, it covers personal rights and legal personality, the law of contracts and sales, property, domestic relations, and inheritance or succession. It contains elements of Germanic tribal, feudal, and common law, as well as ROMAN LAW. See also GERMANIC LAW.

German Confederation (1815–66) Organization of the states of central Europe, established by the Congress of VIENNA to replace the destroyed HOLY ROMAN EMPIRE. It was a loose political association of 39 German states, formed for mutual defense, with no central executive or judiciary. Delegates met in a federal diet, dominated by Austria. Amid a growing call for reform and economic integration, conservative leaders, including KLEMENS, FURST VON METTERNICH, persuaded the confederation's princes to pass the repressive CARLSBAD DECREES (1819), and in the 1830s he led the federal Diet in passing additional measures to crush liberalism and nationalism. The formation of the ZOLLVEREIN and the REVOLUTIONS OF 1848 undermined the confederation; it was dissolved with the Austro-Prussian War (1866) and the establishment of the NORTH GERMAN CONFEDERATION.

German East Africa Former dependency of imperial Germany, corresponding to present-day Rwanda and Burundi, the continental portion of Tanzania, and a small section of Mozambique. German commercial agents arrived in 1884, and in 1891 the German imperial government took over administration of the area. During World War I, it was occupied by the British, who received a mandate to administer the greater part of it (Tanganyika Territory) by the Treaty of VERSAILLES (1919). A smaller portion (RUANDA-URUNDI) was entrusted to Belgium.

German historical school of economics Branch of economic thought, developed chiefly in Germany in the later 19th century, in which the economic situation of a nation is understood as the result of its total historical experience. Objecting to the deductively reasoned "laws" of CLASSICAL ECONOMICS, exponents of the historical approach examined the development of the entire social order, of which economic motives and decisions were only one component. They viewed government intervention in the economy as a positive and necessary force. Early founders, including Wilhelm Roscher and Bruno Hildebrand, developed the idea of the historical method and sought to identify general stages of economic development through which all countries must pass. Members of the later school, notably Gustav von Schmoller (1813–1917), carried out more detailed historical research and attempted to discover cultural trends through historical inquiry.

German language Official language of Germany and Austria and one of the official languages of Switzerland, used by over 100 million speakers. It belongs to the West Germanic group of the GERMANIC LANGUAGES. German has four noun cases and masculine, feminine, and neuter genders. Its many DIALECTS belong to either the High German *(Hochdeutsch)* or Low German *(Plattdeutsch)* groups. Modern High German, spoken in the central and southern highlands of Germany, Austria, and Switzerland, is now standard written German, used in administration, higher education, literature, and the mass media in both High and Low German speech areas.

German measles See RUBELLA

German National People's Party (DNVP) (1919–33) Radical right-wing political party active in the Reichstag of the WEIMAR REPUBLIC. Hostile to the republic, it supported the restoration of the monarchy and a united Germany. During a controversy (1929–30) over paying war reparations to the Allies, the party, led by ALFRED HUGENBERG, allied with the NAZI PARTY in favor of stopping payments. In 1933 it joined a coalition that supported ADOLF HITLER as chancellor and passed the ENABLING ACT; along with all German political parties except the Nazis, the party was dissolved three months later.

German People's Party (DVP) Right-liberal political party founded by GUSTAV STRESEMANN in 1918, made up largely of the educated and propertied. Since Stresemann was essentially a monarchist, when he decided to cooperate with the WEIMAR REPUBLIC the DVP was at first excluded as being among the "national opposition." When Stresemann became chancellor in 1923, the DVP was part of the "Great Coalition," composed of representatives of the Social Democrats, the Center, and the German Democrats. It dwindled c. 1927, and large sections of it went over to the extreme right.

German shepherd *or* **Alsatian** Breed of WORKING DOG developed in Germany from traditional herding and farm dogs. A strongly built, long-bodied dog, it stands 23–25 in. (58–64 cm) high and weighs 75–95 lbs (34–43 kg). Its coat is of coarse, medium-long outer hair and shorter, dense inner hair and ranges from white or pale gray to black; often it is gray and black or black and tan. Noted for intelligence, alertness, and loyalty, it is used as a guide for the blind, as a watchdog, and in police and military work.

German shepherd.
SALLY ANNE THOMPSON—EB INC.

German-Soviet Nonaggression Pact (1939) Agreement stipulating mutual nonaggression between the Soviet Union and Germany. The Soviet Union approached Germany after proposing a collective-security agreement to Britain and France and being rebuffed. In the pact, the two states pledged publicly not to attack each other; its secret provisions divided Poland between them and gave the Soviet Union control of Latvia, Lithuania, Estonia, and Finland. The Soviets hoped to buy time to build up their forces in the face of German expansionism; Germany wished to proceed with its invasion of Poland and the countries to its west without worrying about the Red Army. News of the pact shocked and horrified the world. Nine days after its signing, Germany began WORLD WAR II. The agreement was voided when Germany attacked the Soviet Union in 1941.

Germanic languages \jər-ˈma-nik\ Branch of the INDO-EUROPEAN LANGUAGE family, comprising languages descended from Proto-Germanic. These are divided into West Germanic, including ENGLISH, GERMAN, FRISIAN, DUTCH, AFRIKAANS, and YIDDISH; North Germanic, including DANISH, SWEDISH, ICELANDIC, NORWEGIAN, and Faeroese (the language of the Faeroe Islands); and East Germanic, now extinct, comprising GOTHIC and the languages of the Vandals, Burgundians, and a few other tribes. The Gothic Bible of AD 350 is the earliest extensive Germanic text. The West Germanic languages developed around the North Sea and in overseas areas colonized by their speakers. The North Germanic, or Scandinavian, languages, were carried as far west as Greenland and as far east as Russia in the Viking expansion of the early Middle Ages. The continental Scandinavian languages were strongly influenced by Low German in the late Middle Ages, but Icelandic and Faeroese have preserved many characteristics of Old Scandinavian grammar.

Germanic law Law of the various Germanic peoples from ancient times to the Middle Ages. It was essentially unwritten tribal custom, which evolved from popular practice and moved with the tribe. With the spread of Christianity, ecclesiastical law, derived from ROMAN LAW, gained importance, especially in matters of marriage and succession. A mercantile law, developed by the 12th century to meet the needs of traders, further eroded the power of local law.

Germanic religion Beliefs, rituals, and mythology of the pre-Christian Germanic peoples, in a geographic area extending from the Black Sea across central Europe and Scandinavia to Iceland and Greenland. The religion died out in central Europe with the conversion to Christianity (4th century) but continued in Scandinavia until the 10th century. The Old Norse literature of medieval Iceland, notably the *Poetic* EDDA (c. 1200) and the *Prose Edda* (c. 1222), recounts the lore of the Germanic gods. The earth was held to have been created out of a cosmic void called Ginnungagap; in another account the first gods formed it from the body of a primeval giant, AURGELMIR. There were two sets of gods in the Germanic pantheon, the warlike AESIR and the agricultural VANIR. Germanic religion also encompassed belief in female guardian spirits, elves, and dwarfs. Rites were conducted in the open or in groves and forests; animal and human sacrifice was practiced. RAGNAROK is the Germanic doomsday.

Germanicus Caesar \jər-ˈma-ni-kəs\ (15 BC–AD 19) Nephew and adopted son of TIBERIUS, brother of CLAUDIUS, and father of CALIGULA and AGRIPPINA THE YOUNGER. A successful and popular general, he stifled a rebellion in the West on the death of AUGUSTUS (AD 14). Though urged to take imperial power, he deferred to Tiberius, under whom he had served. In the East he came into conflict with Gnaeus Calpurnius Piso, governor of Syria. Germanicus' death may have been due to poisoning ordered by Piso, though Tiberius was also suspected; Piso's suicide left the matter unsolved. Only his premature death prevented Germanicus from becoming emperor.

germanium Chemical ELEMENT with physical properties similar to SILICON, used especially in SEMICONDUCTOR devices. Discovered in 1886, germanium became economically significant after 1945, when its semiconductor properties were put to use in electronics. It remains of primary importance in the manufacture of TRANSISTORS and of components for other devices such as rectifiers and photocells. It is also used as a component of alloys, in phosphors for fluorescent lamps, and in the glasses of certain optical components, such as camera and microscope lenses.

Germantown, Battle of (October 4, 1777) Abortive attack in the AMERICAN REVOLUTION by 11,000 American troops on 9,000 British regulars stationed at Germantown (now part of Philadelphia). GEORGE WASHINGTON's daring dawn raid, a four-pronged attack, failed partly because of dense fog that confused the American troops into firing on one of their own columns. Despite its failure, this and the colonial victory at the Battle of SARATOGA impressed the French with Washington's strategic ability and influenced them to offer military aid.

Germany *officially* **Federal Republic of Germany** *German* **Deutschland** \ˈdȯich-ˌlänt\ Republic, northern central Europe. Area: 137,846 sq mi (357,021 sq km). Population (2000 est.): 82,225,000. Capital: BERLIN. The majority of the people are German. Language: German (official). Religions: Lutheranism, Roman Catholicism. Monetary unit: euro. The land is generally flat in the north and hilly in the northeast and central region, rising to the Bavarian Alps in the south. The RHINE RIVER basin dominates the central and western part of the country, while other

important rivers are the ELBE, DANUBE, and ODER. It has a developed free-market economy largely based on services and manufacturing; it is one of the richest countries in the world. Exports include motor vehicles and iron and steel products. The chief of state is the president, and the head of government is the chancellor. Federal power is centered in the bicameral Parliament. Germanic tribes entered Germany c. 2nd century BC, displacing the Celts. The Romans failed to conquer the region, which only became a political entity with the division of the CAROLINGIAN empire in the 9th century AD. The monarchy's control was weak, and power increasingly devolved upon the nobility, organized in feudal states. The monarchy was restored under Saxon rule in the 10th century, and the HOLY ROMAN EMPIRE, centering on Germany and northern Italy, was revived. Continuing conflict between the Holy Roman emperors and the Roman Catholic popes undermined the empire, and its dissolution was accelerated by MARTIN LUTHER's revolt in 1517, which divided Germany, and ultimately Europe, into Protestant and Catholic camps, culminating in the THIRTY YEARS' WAR (1618–48). Germany's population and borders were greatly reduced, and its numerous feudal princes gained virtually full sovereignty. In 1862 OTTO VON BISMARCK came to power in PRUSSIA and over the next decade reunited Germany in the German empire. It was dissolved in 1918 after the German defeat in World War I. Germany was stripped of much of its territory and all of its colonies. In 1933 ADOLF HITLER's became chancellor and established a totalitarian state, the THIRD REICH, dominated by the NAZI PARTY. Hitler's invasion of Poland in 1939 plunged the world into World War II. Following its defeat in 1945, Germany was divided by the Allied Powers into four zones of occupation. Disagreement with the Soviet Union over their reunification led to the creation in 1949 of the Federal Republic of Germany (WEST GERMANY) and the German Democratic Republic (EAST GERMANY). Berlin, the former capital, remained divided. West Germany became a prosperous parliamentary democracy, East Germany a one-party state under Soviet control. The East German communist government was overthrown peacefully in 1989, and Germany was reunited in 1990. After the initial euphoria over unity, the former West Germany sought to incorporate the former East Germany both politically and economically, resulting in heavy financial burdens for the wealthier western Germans. However, the country continued to move toward deeper political and economic integration with Western Europe through its membership in the EUROPEAN UNION.

Germany, East *officially* **German Democratic Republic** Former republic (1945–90), northern central Europe. It is now the eastern portion of the Federal Republic of Germany. In 1945, occupied Germany was divided into U.S., British, French, and Soviet zones. In 1949 the U.S., British, and French zones were combined as WEST GERMANY, while the Soviet zone formed East Germany as a Communist state. Declared a sovereign nation in 1955, it became a founding member of the WARSAW PACT. The regimes of WALTER ULBRICHT and later ERICH HONECKER were harshly repressive. The BERLIN WALL was constructed at its border with BERLIN in 1961 to stem the flight of its citizens to the West. The Communist government was dismantled in 1989–90, and the country adopted the constitution and official name of Germany when the states were united in October 1990.

Germany, West *officially* **Federal Republic of Germany** Former republic (1949–90), western central Europe. It consisted of the western two-thirds of what is now the Federal Republic of Germany. It was formed in 1949 when the U.S., British, and French zones of occupation in Germany were united, while the Soviet zone became EAST GERMANY. It became a sovereign nation and a member of NATO in 1955, though its occupiers retained military bases. It united with SAARLAND in 1957, and joined the U.N. in 1973. It was reunited with East Germany in October 1990.

germinal mutation See MUTATION

germination Sprouting of a SEED, SPORE, or other reproductive body, usually after a period of dormancy. Absorption of water, passage of time, chilling, warming, oxygen availability, and light exposure may all operate in initiating the germination process. The carefully controlled mass germination of cereal seeds supplies enzymes for the making of alcoholic beverages and for other industries; spores of the commercially cultivated mushroom *Agaricus brunescens* are also mass germinated.

Gérôme \zhā-'rōm\, **Jean-Léon** (1824–1904) French painter, sculptor, and teacher. Son of a goldsmith, he studied in Paris and painted melodramatic and often erotic historical and mythological compositions, excelling as a draftsman in the linear style of J.-A.-D. INGRES. His best-known works are Oriental scenes, inspired by several visits to Egypt. In his later years he produced mostly sculpture. He exerted much influence as a teacher at the École des Beaux-Arts; his pupils included ODILON REDON and THOMAS EAKINS. A staunch defender of the academic tradition, he tried in 1893 to block the government's acceptance of the Impressionist works bequeathed by GUSTAVE CAILLEBOTTE.

Geronimo \jə-'rä-nə-,mō\ (1829–1909) Chiricahua APACHE leader. In the 1870s Geronimo led a revolt of 4,000 Apaches who had been forcibly removed by U.S. authorities to a barren reservation in eastern central Arizona. Years of turmoil and bloodshed followed; Geronimo finally surrendered in 1884, only to escape with a band of followers. On a false promise of safe return to Arizona, Geronimo was arrested (1886) and put to hard labor, then placed on a reservation at Fort Sill, Okla.; there he dictated his autobiography, *Geronimo: His Own Story.*

gerontology and geriatrics \jer-ən-'täl-ə-jē...,jer-ē-'a-triks\ Scientific and medical disciplines, respectively, concerned with all aspects of health and disease in the elderly and with the normal aging process. Gerontology is concerned primarily with the changes that occur between maturity and death and with the factors that influence these changes. It addresses the social and economic effects of an aging population and the physiological and psychological aspects of aging to learn about the aging process and possibly minimize disabilities. Geriatrics deals with prevention and treatment of diseases once assumed to be inevitable in old people. See also AGING, OLD AGE.

gerousia \jə-'rü-zhē-ə\ In ancient SPARTA, the council of elders, one of two chief organs of the Spartan state, the other being the APELLA. The gerousia prepared business submitted to the apella and had extensive judicial powers: it alone pronounced sentences of death or exile. Its 30 members, the *gerontes* ("elders"), including the two kings, were chosen for life by acclamation of the citizens from among candidates of age 60 or older.

Gerry \'ger-ē\, **Elbridge** (1744–1814) U.S. statesman. Born in Marblehead, Mass., he was an early advocate for independence; as a delegate to the Continental Congress, he signed the Declaration of Independence. He served in the U.S. House of Representatives 1789–93, and in 1797 was sent to France with JOHN MARSHALL and CHARLES C. PINCKNEY to resolve disputes that resulted in the XYZ AFFAIR. He served as governor of Massachusetts 1810–11; during his term the state legislature redrew the district lines to favor Democratic-Republican candidates against the Federalists, a practice that became known as GERRYMANDERING. In 1812 he advocated war with Britain and was elected vice president on the ticket with JAMES MADISON.

gerrymandering \'jer-ē-,man-driŋ\ Drawing of electoral district lines to give one political party unfair advantage. The practice is named after Massachusetts Gov. ELBRIDGE GERRY, who submitted a state-senate redistricting plan that would have concentrated the voting strength of the FEDERALIST PARTY in just a few districts, thereby giving disproportionate representation to the Democratic-Republican Party. Some of Gerry's new districts were necessarily odd-shaped; one district's outline, seen to resemble a salamander, gave rise to the scornful term gerrymander. The practice has persisted to the present day, and redistricting battles in the state legislatures have often had to be decided by the courts.

Gershwin, George *orig.* **Jacob Gershvin** (1898–1937) U.S. composer. Born in East New York to Russian-Jewish immigrants, he heard jazz performed live from about age 6. He worked as a song plugger in his teens, and in 1914 he published his first song. In 1918 his "Swanee," performed by A. JOLSON, achieved extraordinary success. His first complete score was *La, La Lucille* (1919). PAUL WHITEMAN commissioned from him the hugely successful orchestral work *Rhapsody in Blue* (1924). Gershwin's first major Broadway success, *Lady, Be Good!* (1924), was a collaboration with his brother IRA GERSHWIN. They soon established themselves as one of the great teams in Broadway history; their shows included *Tip-Toes* (1925), *Oh, Kay!* (1926), *Strike Up the Band* (1927), *Funny Face* (1927), *Girl Crazy* (1930), and the satire *Of Thee I Sing* (1931), the first musical to win a Pulitzer Prize. He also scored several successful films. His most ambitious work was the "folk opera" *Porgy and Bess* (1935), a collaboration with Ira and DuBose Heyward. His classical compositions include a piano concerto (1925) and the tone poem *An American in Paris* (1928). Gershwin died at 38 of a brain tumor.

George Gershwin, working on the score *Porgy and Bess* (1935).
PICTORIAL PARADE—EB INC.

Gershwin, Ira *orig.* **Israel Gershvin** (1896–1983) U.S. lyricist, brother of GEORGE GERSHWIN. He briefly attended CCNY, then did odd jobs until his brother asked him to write lyrics for his melodies; their first collaboration was "The Real American Folk Song," in *Ladies First* (1918). The fabled Gershwin partnership resulted in such idiomatic and ingenious lyrics as "'S Wonderful," "I Got Rhythm," "Embraceable You," "Summertime," and "It Ain't Necessarily So." After his brother's death Ira collaborated on *Lady in the Dark* with K. WEILL (1940), *Cover Girl* with J. KERN (1944), and *A Star Is Born* with H. ARLEN (1954), among other shows.

Gesell \gə-'zel\, **Gerhard A(lden)** (1910–1993) U.S. judge. Born in Los Angeles, he earned a law degree from Yale University. In 1967 Pres. LYNDON B. JOHNSON appointed him to the Federal District Court in Washington, D.C. There he struck down a local ban on abortion (1969) and allowed the resumption of publication of the PENTAGON PAPERS (1971). He ruled that national security was not a valid reason for the 1971 WATERGATE break-in (1974), and made other significant rulings regarding the scandal. He presided over the criminal trial of OLIVER NORTH in 1989. He remained on the bench until his death.

gesneriad \ges-'nir-ē-,ad\ Any of more than 1,800 species of mostly tropical and subtropical herbaceous or slightly woody plants in the family Gesneriaceae. None are of economic importance except as horticultural ornamentals; among the latter are the AFRICAN VIOLETS and GLOXINIAS.

Gesta Romanorum \,jes-tə-,rō-mə-'nō-rəm\ (Latin: "Deeds of the Romans") Latin collection of anecdotes and tales, probably compiled in early-14th-century England. Very popular in its time, it became a source for much later literature, including works by GEOFFREY CHAUCER and WILLIAM SHAKESPEARE. It contains stories from classical history and legend and from various Oriental and European sources, many about magicians and monsters, ladies in distress, and escapes from perilous situations, all unified by their moral purpose and realistic detail. Though its author is unknown, it may have been intended as a manual for preachers.

Gestalt psychology \gə-'stält, ge-'shtält\ 20th-century school of psychology that provided the foundation for the modern study of PERCEPTION. The German term Gestalt, referring to how a thing has been "put together" *(gestellt),* is often translated as "pattern" or "configuration" in psychology. Its precepts, formulated as a reaction against the atomistic orientation of previous theories, emphasized that the whole of anything is different from the sum of its parts: organisms tend to perceive entire patterns or configurations rather than bits and pieces. The school emerged in Austria and Germany at the end of the 19th century and gained impetus through the works of MAX WERTHEIMER, WOLFGANG KOHLER, and Kurt Koffka (1886–1941); its principles were later expanded by KURT LEWIN. A form of PSYCHOTHERAPY only loosely related to Gestalt principles and influenced by EXISTENTIALISM and PHENOMENOLOGY was developed by Frederick S. (Fritz) Perls (1893–1970) in the 1940s. Gestalt therapy directs the client toward appreciating the form, meaning, and value of his or her perceptions and actions.

Gestapo \gə-'stä-pō\ *in full* **Geheime Staatspolizei** (German: "Secret State Police") Political police of Nazi Germany. It was created by HERMANN GORING in 1933 from the political and espionage units of the Prussian police and by HEINRICH HIMMLER from the police of the remaining German states. Himmler was given command in 1934. The Gestapo operated without civil restraints, and its actions were not subject to judicial appeal. Thousands of Jews, leftists, intellectuals, trade unionists, political clergy, and homosexuals disappeared into concentration camps after being arrested by the Gestapo. In World War II the Gestapo suppressed partisan activities in the occupied territories, and a section of the Gestapo under ADOLF EICHMANN organized the deportation of Jews to the extermination camps in Poland.

Gesualdo \jā-'swäl-dō\, **Carlo, principe (Prince) of Venosa** (1561?–1613) Italian composer. Nobly born, he was a passionate musical dilettante. In 1590 he had his wife and her lover (a duke) murdered, which earned him great notoriety but no punishment. His later marriage to the duke of Ferrara's niece made the cosmopolitan Ferrara court his second home. His steadily deepening melancholia was reflected in his music, which included some 125 madrigals and about 75 sacred vocal works. His extreme chromaticism and abrupt changes in tempo and dynamics, exaggerating such traits in the madrigals of his time, would have no rival until the 20th century, when his works were rediscovered.

get Jewish divorce document written in Aramaic and obtained from a rabbinic court. In ORTHODOX and CONSERVATIVE JUDAISM it is the only valid way to end a marriage, though outside Israel a civil divorce is required first. In REFORM JUDAISM a civil divorce suffices. To obtain a get, mutual consent of husband and wife is usually required, except in special cases such as apostasy, impotence, insanity, or refusal to cohabit.

Gethsemane \geth-'se-mə-nē\ Garden outside JERUSALEM on the Mount of OLIVES. It is where JESUS is said to have prayed after the Last Supper and where he was arrested by Roman soldiers. The name *Gethsemane* originates from the Hebrew term for "oil press," suggesting that the garden was a grove of olive trees. Though its exact location cannot be determined, Armenian, Greek, Latin, and Russian churches have accepted an olive grove on the western slope of the Mount of Olives as the site.

Getty, J(ean) Paul (1892–1976) U.S. oil billionaire, reputed to be the richest man in the world at his death. Born in Minneapolis, the son of an oil millionaire, he began buying and selling oil leases in Oklahoma in 1913. He acquired Pacific Western Oil Corp. in 1932 and soon gained control of several independent oil companies. He renamed his oil concern Getty Oil Co. in 1956. His most lucrative venture was a 60-year oil concession in Saudi Arabia. His financial empire eventually encompassed some 200 enterprises. A zealous art collector, he founded the J. PAUL GETTY MUSEUM near Malibu, Cal., in 1953.

Getty Museum, J. Paul Museum established by JEAN PAUL GETTY to house his large collection of artworks, to which he continued to add. The original museum occupied a wing added to his ranch house in Malibu, Cal. His collections soon outgrew that location, and in 1974 they were moved to a new building in Malibu, a lavish re-creation of a Roman villa uncovered at Herculaneum. On Getty's death the museum became the most richly endowed in the world. It now is housed in the Getty Center, a striking six-building complex in Los Angeles designed by

RICHARD MEIER, which opened with great publicity in 1997. Its collections include European paintings, sculpture, drawings, and decorative arts to 1900, illuminated manuscripts, and photographs. Greek and Roman antiquities remain in the Malibu villa. The collections reflect Getty's preference for paintings of the Renaissance and the baroque period and for French furniture.

Getty Trust, J. Paul Private operating foundation founded in 1953 by JEAN PAUL GETTY to establish the J. PAUL GETTY MUSEUM. Originally located in Malibu, Cal., it now occupies five buildings in the Getty Center in Los Angeles, each building housing one of the institutes it established when it diversified its activities in 1983. One institute develops computerized databases on art-historical information; the others support art restoration and conservation, interdisciplinary research in art history and the related humanities, art education, and training in museum management. The Getty Grants Program supports projects around the world involving the history and understanding of art and its conservation.

Gettysburg Town (pop., 1996 est.: 9,000), southern Pennsylvania. The site of the momentous AMERICAN CIVIL WAR battle (see Battle of GETTYSBURG), the town and the surrounding area are now in Gettysburg National Military Park, which preserves 3,865 acres (1,564 hectares), including the battlefield. The Soldiers' Monument in Gettysburg National Cemetery marks the spot where Pres. ABRAHAM LINCOLN delivered his GETTYSBURG ADDRESS. The site includes more than 1,200 Civil War monuments, markers, and tablets.

Gettysburg, Battle of (July 1–3, 1863) Major engagement in the AMERICAN CIVIL WAR at Gettysburg, Pa., regarded as the war's turning point. After defeating Union forces at the Battle of CHANCELLORSVILLE, ROBERT E. LEE decided to invade the North with 75,000 troops. When he learned that the Union's Army of the Potomac had a new commander, GEORGE MEADE, he led his own troops to Gettysburg, a strategic crossroads. On the first day of battle, Meade's advance force under John Buford held the site until reinforcements arrived. On the second day, the Confederates attacked Union lines at Little Round Top, Cemetery Hill, Devil's Den, the Wheatfield, and the Peach Orchard. On the third day, Lee sent 15,000 troops to assault Cemetery Ridge, held by 10,000 Union troops under WINFIELD S HANCOCK. A Confederate spearhead broke through the Union artillery defense but was stopped by a fierce Union counterattack on three sides. At night under cover of a heavy rain on July 4, Lee led his troops back to Virginia; Meade was later criticized for not pursuing him. Losses totaled about 23,000 casualties among 88,000 Union troops and over 20,000 casualties among 75,000 Confederates.

Gettysburg Address (November 19, 1863) Speech by Pres. ABRAHAM LINCOLN at the dedication of a cemetery at Gettysburg, Pa., for those killed at the Battle of GETTYSBURG during the American Civil War. The main address was delivered by the renowned orator Edward Everett (1794–1865) and lasted two hours. Lincoln's brief speech, honoring the Union dead and the principles of democracy and equality they died for, lasted two minutes. Soon recognized as an extraordinary piece of prose poetry, it remains the most famous speech ever delivered in the U.S.

Getz, Stan(ley) (1927–1991) U.S. jazz saxophonist. Born in Philadelphia, Getz was influenced by LESTER YOUNG and became known for his light tone and ethereal approach while one of the "Four Brothers" of WOODY HERMAN's Second Herd (1947–49). He dominated popularity polls on his instrument with the advent of the cool jazz of the 1950s, and his incorporation of Brazilian bossa-nova music in the early 1960s brought him to a wider public and commercial success.

Geulincx \'gœ̄-liŋks\, **Arnold** *known as* **Philaretus** \ˌfi-lə-'rē-təs\ (1624–1669) Flemish metaphysician and logician. He taught at the University of Louvain from 1646, but was dismissed in 1658, probably because of his sympathy with JANSENISM. Taking refuge at Leiden, Holland, he became a Calvinist. He lived in poverty until 1662, when he obtained a position at the University of Leiden. He was a major exponent of the doctrine known as OCCASIONALISM. His major works include *De Virtute* (1665), *Gnothi Seauton* (1675; "Know Thyself"), and *Metaphysica Vera* (1691; "True Metaphysics").

geyser \'gī-zər\ (Icelandic *geysir,* "to rush forth") Any hot spring that discharges jets of steam and water intermittently, generally associated with recent volcanic activity and produced by the heating of underground waters that have come into contact with, or are very close to, MAGMA. Geyser discharges as high as 1,600 ft (500 m) have been recorded, but 160 ft (50 m) is much more common (e.g., Old Faithful in Yellowstone National Park). Occasionally, a geyser will adopt an extremely regular and predictable pattern of intermittent activity and discharge for a few minutes every hour or so.

Gezira \jə-'zē-rə\ *or* **Al-Jazirah** \ˌal-jə-'zē-rə\ Region, eastern central Sudan. Southeast of the confluence of the Blue NILE and the White Nile rivers, it is the site of one of the largest irrigation projects in the world. Begun by the British in 1925, the project distributes the waters of the Blue Nile through a 2,700-mi (4,300-km) network of canals and ditches. It has made the region the most productive agricultural area of the Sudan.

Ghadamis *or* **Ghudamis** \gə-'dä-mis\ Oasis and town (pop., 1981 est.: 30,000), northwestern Libya. Located near the Libyan–Algerian border, it is at the junction of ancient Saharan caravan routes. It was the Roman stronghold Cydamus (whose ruins remain), and an episcopal see under the Byzantines; columns of the Christian church still remain in the Sidi Badri Mosque. A center for the Arab slave trade through the 19th century, it is now a caravan depot linked to the Mediterranean coast.

Ghaghara River \'gä-gə-rə\ *formerly* **Gogra** \'gō-grə\ *Nepali* **Karnali** \kär-'nä-lē\ River, northern India, Nepal, and China. A major tributary of the GANGES, it rises as the Karnali in the Tibetan Himalayas and flows southeast into Nepal. Cutting south across the Siwalik Hills, it splits into two branches, to rejoin in India and form the Ghaghara proper. It flows southeast to enter the Ganges after a 600 mi (970 km) course. Together with the Ganges and its tributaries, it formed the vast alluvial plain of northern BIHAR. Along its lower course it is also called the Sarju River and the Deoha.

E
F
G

Ghana \'gä-nə\ *officially* **Republic of Ghana** *formerly* **Gold Coast** Republic, western Africa. Area: 92,098 sq mi (238,533 sq km). Population (1997 est.): 18,101,000. Capital: ACCRA. Ghana is home to some 75 different tribes; the most numerous are the AKAN, followed by the Mole-Dagbani (MOSSI). Language: English (official). Religions: Christianity (both Protestantism and Roman Catholicism) and indigenous religions. Currency: cedi. The land is generally flat, dominated by the VOLTA RIVER basin. The north is characterized by grassland plains; the south is heavily forested. The southern coastal plain, called the Gold Coast, extends inland for 30–50 mi (50–80 km). Its varied wildlife includes lion, leopard, and elephant. It has a developing mixed economy

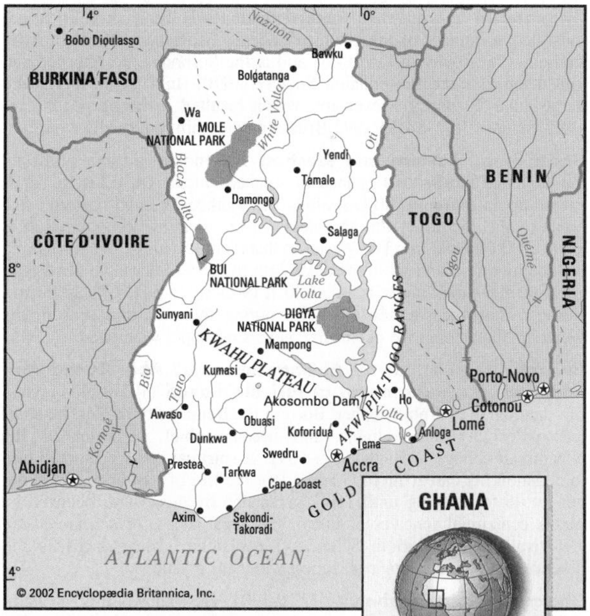

based largely on agriculture and mining. Cacao is the mainstay of the economy; mineral exports include gold and diamonds. It is a republic with one legislative house; its head of state and government is the president. The modern state of Ghana is named after the ancient GHANA EMPIRE that flourished until the 13th century AD in the western Sudan, about 500 mi (800 km) northwest of the modern state. The Akan peoples then founded their first states in modern Ghana. Gold-seeking Mande traders arrived by the 14th century and HAUSA merchants by the 16th century. During the 15th century the Mande founded the states of Dagomba and Mamprussi in the northern half of the region. The ASHANTI, an Akan people, originated in the central forest region and formed a strongly centralized empire that was at its height in the 18th–19th century. European exploration of the region began early in the 15th century, when the Portuguese landed on the Gold Coast; they later established a settlement at Elmina as headquarters for the SLAVE TRADE. By the mid-18th century the Gold Coast was dominated by numerous forts controlled by Dutch, British, and Danish merchants. Britain made the Gold Coast a crown colony in 1874, and British protectorates over the Ashanti and the northern territories were established in 1901. In 1957 the Gold Coast became the independent state of Ghana. Since independence, numerous political coups have occurred, but that of 1981 produced a government that lasted into the 1990s.

Ghana empire First of the great medieval trading empires of western Africa (7th–13th century), located in what is now southeastern Mauritania and part of Mali. Its inhabitants acted as intermediaries between Arab and BERBER salt traders to the north and gold and ivory producers to the south. Gold was secured through barter from those living at the empire's southern limit and exchanged in the capital for commodities, especially salt. As the empire grew richer it extended its reach, incorporating gold-producing southern lands and cities to the north. The king exacted tribute from the princes of subject tribes. Ghana began to decline with the rise of the Muslim ALMORAVIDS; the Almoravid leader ABU BAKR seized the Ghanaian capital of Kumbi in 1076, the empire's subject peoples began to break away, and in 1240 the empire's remains were incorporated into the SUNDIATA empire of Mali.

Ghannouchi \gän-'nü-shē\, **Rachid** (born 1941) Tunisian political activist and cofounder of the Islamic Tendency Movement (NAHDA). After studying philosophy in Damascus and at the Sorbonne, he returned and joined the Quranic Preservation Society (1970). In 1981 he organized the Islamic Tendency Movement, which resulted in his imprisonment 1981–84 and 1987–88. In 1993 Britain granted him political asylum.

Ghats \'gȯts\, **Eastern and Western** Two mountain ranges forming the edges of the DECCAN plateau in southern India. The Eastern Ghats extend about 500 mi (800 km) along the southeastern and eastern coast north to the mouth of the Mahanadi River; their average elevation is about 2,000 ft (600 m). The Western Ghats run 800 mi (1,290 km) along the southwestern and western coast north to the mouth of the Tapti River; their elevations range from 3,000 ft (900 m) to 5,000 ft (1,500 m). Because they receive heavy rainfall during the monsoon season, the Western Ghats comprise peninsular India's principal watershed.

Ghazali \gä-'za-lē\, **al-** *or* **Al-Ghazzali** *in full* **Abu Hamid Muhammad ibn Muhammad al-Tusi al-Ghazali** (1058–1111) Muslim theologian and philosopher. Born in the Iranian city of Tus, he studied philosophy and religion and became chief professor of the Nizamiyah college in Baghdad in 1091. A spiritual crisis prompted him to abandon his career in 1095 and adopt the life of a poor Sufi. He did not return to teaching until 1106, persuaded by those who believed he was a centennial renewer of Islam. His great work, *Ihya ulum al-din* ("Revival of the Religious Sciences"), explained Islamic doctrines and practices and traced their connection with Sufi mysticism.

Ghazan \gä-'zän\, **Mahmud** (1271–1304) Best-known Il-Khan (subordinate KHAN) to rule the Mongol dynasty in Persia. In 1284 his father, the Persian ruler Arghun, made him viceroy of northeastern Persia, where he defended the frontier against the Chagatai Mongols. In 1295 he converted from Buddhism to Islam before taking the throne. He successfully fought his family's hereditary enemy, the Mamluks (see MAMLUK REGIME), in Syria, defeating their army at Homs. The Mamluks reoccupied Syria on his departure, and despite three more attempts to defeat them he died leaving Damascus in their hands. He spoke many languages and was adept at handicrafts; he commissioned a history of the Mongols, later expanded to include all those with whom the Mongols had come in contact.

ghazel *or* **ghazal** *or* **gazel** \'gaz-el, *Arabic* 'gȧ-zȧl\ In Islamic literature, a lyric poem, generally short and graceful in form and typically dealing with love. The genre developed in late-7th-century Arabia. The poems begin with a rhymed couplet whose rhyme is repeated in all subsequent even lines, while the odd lines are unrhymed. The two main types of ghazel are native to the Hejaz and Iraq. It reached its greatest refinement in the works of HAFEZ. American poets such as ADRIENNE RICH have used variations of the form.

Ghaznavid dynasty \'gœz-nə-vəd\ (977–1186) Turkish dynasty that ruled in Khorasan (NE Iran), Afghanistan, and northern India. It was founded by Sebüktigin (r.977–97), a former slave. His son MAHMUD (998–1030) enlarged the empire to its greatest extent; during his reign, FERDOWSI wrote the epic *Shahnameh* ("Book of Kings"). Mahmud's grandson Masud I (1031–41) lost the western half of the empire to the SELJUQ DYNASTY. The Ghaznavids continued to rule their eastern provinces until suffering defeat at Ghurid hands in 1186. They are noted for their architecture and their theories of governance, and epic poetry and poetic romances flourished under their rule.

Ghent \'gent\ *Flemish* **Gent** \'kent\ *French* **Gand** \'gä^n\ City (pop., 1996 est.: 226,000), capital of East Flanders province, northwestern Belgium. One of the chief towns of the medieval county of FLANDERS, it was by the 13th century one of the largest towns in northern Europe. Its prosperity was based on its manufacture of luxury cloths, which were famous throughout Europe. It began to decline in the late 16th century, when its cloth was unable to compete with England's. Its economy revived with the introduction of cotton-spinning machinery (in particular, a power loom smuggled out of England), and it subsequently became the center of the Belgian textiles industry. Belgium's second-largest port, it is also a horticultural center.

Ghent, Pacification of (1576) Declaration by which the northern and southern provinces of the LOW COUNTRIES put aside their religious differences and united in revolt against the Spanish Habsburgs. As the first major expression of the Netherlands' national consciousness, it called for the expulsion of Spanish troops from the Low Countries, the restoration of provincial and local prerogatives, and an end to the persecution of Calvinists. The Spanish governor soon resumed hostilities, however, and religious differences within the region caused a split in 1579 between the Calvinist north (the Union of Utrecht) and the Catholic south (the Union of Arras). The general union ended in 1584.

Gheorghiu-Dej \'gyȯr-gyü-'dā\, **Gheorghe** (1901–1965) Romanian politician. He became head of the Communist Party in 1944 and held government economic posts 1946–52. After purging the party of rivals closely identified with Soviet policies, he became prime minister (1952–55) and gradually adopted economic and foreign policies that served Romania's national interests. As president of the State Council (1961–65), he pursued a program of industrialization, despite the objections of other Soviet-bloc countries that wanted Romania to remain agricultural. He further demonstrated Romania's independence by forming cordial relations with non-communist nations and with China.

Gherardo delle Notte See Gerrit van HONTHORST

ghetto Street or quarter of a city set apart as a legally enforced residence area for Jews. The name comes from an island (the site of a foundry, or *ghetto*) where Venetian Jews were forced to live. Forced segregation of Jews spread throughout Europe in the 14th–15th century. Ghettos were customarily enclosed with walls and gates and kept locked at night and during Christian festivals. Since lateral expansion was usually impossible, most ghettos grew upward; congestion, fire hazards, and unsanitary conditions often resulted. Ghettos were abolished in Western Europe in the 19th century; those revived by the NAZI PARTY (see WARSAW GHETTO UPRISING) were overcrowded holding places preliminary to extermination. More recently, the term ghetto has been applied to impoverished urban areas exclusively settled by a minority group and perpetuated by economic and social pressures rather than legal measures.

Ghibellines See GUELPHS AND GHIBELLINES

Ghiberti \gē-'ber-tē\, **Lorenzo** (c. 1378–1455) Italian sculptor, goldsmith, and designer active in Florence. He was trained as a goldsmith and painter. In 1402 he won a competition for the commission to make a pair of bronze doors for the Baptistery of Florence Cathedral, defeating FILIPPO BRUNELLESCHI. The honor brought him immediate fame and prominence. Work on the doors lasted from 1403 to 1424. In 1425 he was asked to make a second pair, known as the Gates of Paradise, which he completed in 1452. The reliefs on the first door are the major sculptural works of the International Gothic style in Italy; those on the second, in a more advanced style, are among the finest examples of Italian Renaissance art. Among his other commissions were three bronze statues for Or San Michele (1413–29) and two reliefs for the Baptistery of Siena Cathedral (1417–27). He directed a large workshop with many assistants, including DONATELLO and PAOLO UCCELLO. His treatise on art history and theory includes the earliest surviving autobiography of an artist.

Ghirlandaio \ˌgir-lən-ˈdä-yō\, **Domenico** *orig.* **Domenico di Tommaso Bigordi** (1449–1494) Italian painter of the Early Renaissance, active in Florence. He trained with ALESSO BALDOVINETTI. In 1481–82 he painted several frescoes, including the *Calling of Sts. Peter and Andrew,* in the Vatican's Sistine Chapel. His greatest fresco cycle, commissioned by an agent of the MEDICI, was painted in the choir of Santa Maria Novella in Florence (1485–90); depicting scenes from the lives of the Virgin and St. John the Baptist in contemporary dress against detailed patrician interiors, it has become a major source of current knowledge on the furnishings of a late-15th-century Florentine palace. With his two brothers he directed one of the most prosperous workshops in Florence; they also produced numerous altarpieces. His finest portrait is *The Old Man and His Grandson* (c. 1480–90).

ghost Soul or specter of a deceased person. Belief in ghosts has been common since ancient times and is reflected in folklore around the world. It is based on the notion that the spirit is separable from the body and can continue its existence after the death of the body. Ghosts are believed to inhabit the netherworld and to be capable of returning to the world of the living, appearing as living beings or in a nebulous likeness of the deceased. They are thought to be especially likely to haunt places or people connected with some strong emotion of their past life, such as fear, remorse, or the terror of a violent death. The traditional visual manifestations of haunting include ghostly apparitions, the movement of objects, or the appearance of strange lights; auditory signs include disembodied laughter and screams, knocking, or footsteps.

Ghost Dance 19th-century cult that represented an attempt by Indian peoples in the western U.S. to rehabilitate their traditional cultures. It arose in 1889, when the PAIUTE prophet-dreamer WOVOKA announced the imminent return of the dead (hence "ghost"), the ousting of the whites, and the restoration of Indian lands, food supplies, and way of life, all of which would be hastened by dances and songs revealed in Wovoka's spiritual visions. The Ghost Dance spread rapidly; it coincided with the SIOUX outbreak of 1890, which culminated in the massacre at WOUNDED KNEE, where the "ghost shirts" failed to protect the wearers as promised by Wovoka. The cult soon became obsolete.

Ghulam Ahmad \ˈgü-lam-ˈak̲-mad\, **Mirza** (c. 1839–1908) Indian Muslim leader, founder of the AHMADIYA sect. Born into a prosperous family, he led a life of contemplation and religious study. Claiming in 1889 to have had a special revelation from God, he gathered a small band of disciples. He declared himself to be the MAHDI and the reincarnation of MUHAMMAD, JESUS, and KRISHNA. He was opposed by the orthodox Muslim community, but a number of his teachings became the basis of the beliefs of the Ahmadiya. He attempted to establish missionary organizations and schools on the Christian model, but did not try to reconcile Christian and Muslim doctrine.

GI Bill (of Rights) *or* **Servicemen's Readjustment Act** (1944) U.S. legislation that provided benefits to World War II veterans. Through the Veterans Administration (VA), the bill provided grants for school and college tuition, low-interest mortgage and small-business loans, job training, hiring privileges, and unemployment payments. Amendments to the act provided for full disability coverage and the construction of additional VA hospitals. Later legislation extended the benefits to all who had served in the armed forces.

GIA See GROUPE ISLAMIQUE ARMÉE

Giacometti \ˌjä-kə-ˈme-tē\, **Alberto** (1901–1966) Swiss sculptor and painter. His father was a Postimpressionist painter and his brother Diego was a well-known furniture designer. He studied art in Geneva (1919–20) and Paris (1922–25). He developed a style related to the Cubist sculpture of ALEXANDER ARCHIPENKO and JACQUES LIPCHITZ, partly inspired by African and Oceanic art. By the 1940s he had developed his signature style, producing thin, attenuated sculptures of solitary, skeletal figures and heads. He became well known, especially in the U.S., through two exhibitions in New York (1948, 1950) and an essay on his art by J.-P. SARTRE. His work evokes a sense of existential tragedy comparable to that produced by the existentialist writers. In 1963 he designed the stage set for SAMUEL BECKETT

Giacometti, photograph by Yousuf Karsh, 1965.

Giambologna \ˌjäm-bō-ˈlōn-yä\ *or* **Giovanni da Bologna** *or* **Jean Boulogne** \bü-ˈlȯn^y\ (1529–1608) Flemish-Italian sculptor. After studies under Jacques Dubroeucq, he went to Rome in 1550, where his style was influenced by Hellenistic sculpture and the works of MICHELANGELO, and settled in Florence in 1552. He produced many of his most important works for the MEDICI FAMILY, but it was the *Fountain of Neptune* (1563–66) in Bologna that made him famous. His bronze equestrian statue of Cosimo I de' MEDICI (1587–93), the first of its kind made in Florence, became a pattern for similar statues all over Europe. His garden sculptures—notably for Florence's Boboli Gardens and for three Medici villas, including the colossal *Apennine* (1570–80) at Pratolino—enjoyed great popularity. He was also a prolific manufacturer of bronze statuettes; many of his working models still survive. He was the outstanding sculptor of Italian MANNERISM.

Giannini \ˌjē-ə-ˈnē-nē\, **A(madeo) P(eter)** (1870–1949) U.S. banker. Born in San Jose, Cal., the son of Italian immigrants, he left school at 13 to work in the family wholesale produce business, becoming a partner in 1889. In 1904 he and five partners founded the Bank of Italy in San Francisco. Their bank followed an unorthodox program of making loans to small farmers and businessmen and actively soliciting customers. In 1909 he began buying banks elsewhere in California, eventually creating the first statewide branch-banking system in the U.S. After acquiring a second network of branch banks, he merged the two in 1930 under the name Bank of America National Trust and Savings Association. By the time of his death, Bank of America had more than 500 branch banks, with more than $6 billion in deposits.

giant See GIGANTISM

giant order See COLOSSAL ORDER

giant sequoia See BIG TREE

giant silkworm moth See SATURNIID MOTH

giant star Star with a relatively large radius for its mass and temperature; this yields a large radiating area, so such stars are bright. Subclasses include SUPERGIANT STARS, red giants (with low temperatures, but very bright), and subgiants (with slightly reduced radii and brightness). Some giants are hundreds of thousands of times brighter than the sun. Giants and supergiants sometimes have masses 10–30 times that of the sun and volumes millions of times greater, and are thus low-density stars.

Giap, Vo Nguyen See VO NGUYEN GIAP

Giardia lamblia \jē-ˈär-dē-ə-ˈlam-blē-ə\ *or* **G. intestinalis** Single-celled PROTOZOAN parasite. Pear- or beet-shaped, the cells have two nuclei and eight flagella, and attach to human intestinal mucous membrane with a sucking organ. They cause the disease giardiasis. Generally spread by ingesting traces of human feces containing the parasite, giardiasis is most common among children in close contact with other children, but also occurs among adults. Diarrhea, pain, and distension of the stomach may occur. It is common wherever there is contamination of surface or domestic water in lakes, rivers, and reservoirs, and is a major cause of diarrhea worldwide. Beaver feces are often responsible for giardiasis among campers who take water from lakes and rivers.

gibbon \'gi-bən\ Any of about six species (genus *Hylobates*) of lesser APES (family Hylobatidae), found in Indo-Malayan forests. Gibbons use their long arms to swing from branch to branch. They walk erect on the ground, live in small groups, and feed on shoots and fruits, as well as on some insects, birds' eggs, and young birds. They have long hair and are about 16–26 in. (40–65 cm) long. Their coats vary from tan or silvery to brown or black. They have large canine teeth, and their voices are noted for their volume, musical quality, and carrying power.

Gibbons (genus *Hylobates*).
EDMUND APPEL—PHOTO RESEARCHERS

Gibbon \'gi-bən\, **Edward** (1737–1794) British historian. Educated at Oxford and in Switzerland, he wrote his early works in French. In London he became a member of SAMUEL JOHNSON's brilliant intellectual circle. On a trip to Rome he was inspired to write the history of the city. His *Decline and Fall of the Roman Empire* (6 vols., 1776–88) is a continuous narrative from the 2nd century AD to the fall of Constantinople in 1453. Though Gibbon's conclusions have been modified by later scholars, his acumen, historical perspective, and superb literary style have given his work its lasting reputation as the greatest historical work ever written in English.

Gibbons, Orlando (1583–1625) English composer and organist. Son of a musician, he became organist of the Chapel Royal c. 1605 and remained there the rest of his life, serving also as organist at Westminster Abbey for his last two years. A versatile composer, he wrote several Anglican services, some 40 anthems, about 50 secular keyboard pieces, about 35 fantasias for chamber ensembles, and some 15 madrigals.

Gibbons v. Ogden U.S. Supreme Court decision (1824) that established that states could not, by legislative enactment, interfere with the power of Congress to regulate INTERSTATE COMMERCE. The state of New York had authorized a monopoly on steamboat operation in its waters, an action upheld by a state chancery court, but the Supreme Court ruled that competing steamboat operators were protected by the terms of a federal license to engage in trade along a coast. The decision, an important development in the interpretation of the COMMERCE CLAUSE of the U.S. CONSTITUTION, freed all navigation from monopoly control.

Gibbs, J(osiah) Willard (1839–1903) U.S. theoretical physicist and chemist. Born in New Haven, Conn., he became the first person to earn an engineering doctorate from Yale Univ., where he taught from 1871 until his death. He began his career in engineering but turned to theory, analyzing the EQUILIBRIUM of JAMES WATT's steam-engine governor. His major works were on fluid thermodynamics and the equilibrium of heterogeneous substances, and he developed STATISTICAL MECHANICS. Gibbs was the first to expound with mathematical rigor the "relation between chemical, electrical, and thermal energy and capacity for WORK." Though little of his work was appreciated during his lifetime, his application of THERMODYNAMIC theory to chemical reactions converted much of physical chemistry from an empirical to a deductive science, and he is regarded as one of the greatest U.S. scientists of the 19th century.

Gibbs, William Francis (1886–1967) U.S. naval architect. Born in Philadelphia, he initially studied law but turned to naval architecture, studying for a year in seclusion, and with his brother Frederick H. Gibbs designed a transatlantic liner. During World War I they designed ships for the U.S. government, and after the war they were commissioned to recondition the *Leviathan*. Gibbs's design for the *Malolo* (1927), with its numerous watertight compartments and other safety features, became an industry standard. In 1940 he designed a cargo ship suitable for mass production; using prefabrication techniques, he reduced production time from as long as four years to as little as four days, an innovation of enormous value in World War II. His passenger liner *United States* (1952) set speed records in transatlantic service.

Gibeon \'gi-bē-ən\ Ancient city of CANAAN. It is located northwest of JERUSALEM at modern Al-Jib. According to the Bible, its inhabitants made an alliance with the Israelite military leader Joshua at the time of the conquest of Canaan but were instead made slaves. Excavations in 1956 by a U.S. expedition revealed that the site had been occupied during the Early and Middle BRONZE AGES, and in the latter part of the Late Bronze Age, just before Joshua's conquest of Canaan; the town then was a dependency of Jerusalem and probably not fortified.

Gibraltar \jə-'bròl-tər\ British colony (pop., 1995 est.: 31,000), Mediterranean coast in southern Spain. The site of a British air and naval base that guards the Strait of GIBRALTAR, it occupies a narrow peninsula 3 mi (5 km) long and 3/4 mi (1.2 km) wide, known as the Rock. It appears from the east as a series of sheer, inaccessible cliffs, which makes it strategically important. The Moors held Gibraltar from 711 to 1501, when it was annexed by Spain. Captured by the British in 1704, it became a British crown colony in 1830. It was an important port in World Wars I and II. It remained the center of a sovereignty dispute between Spain and England, even though its residents voted in 1967 to remain part of Britain.

The Rock of Gibraltar.
HANS HUBER

Gibraltar, Strait of *ancient* **Fretum Herculeum.** Channel, connecting the Mediterranean Sea with the Atlantic Ocean. Lying between southernmost Spain and northwesternmost Africa, it is 36 mi (58 km) long and narrows to 8 mi (13 km) between Point Marroquí (Spain) and Point Cires (Morocco). At the strait's eastern extreme, 14 mi (23 km) apart, stand the PILLARS OF HERCULES, which have been identified as the Rock of Gibraltar and Jebel Musa in CEUTA. It has long been of great strategic and economic importance.

Gibran \ji-'brän\, **Khalil** *orig.* **Jubran Khalil Jubran** (1883–1931) U.S. (Lebanese-born) philosophical essayist, novelist, poet, and artist. He emigrated with his parents to Boston in 1895 and later settled in New York City. His works, written in both Arabic and English, are full of lyrical outpourings and express his deeply religious and mystical nature. *The Prophet* (1923), a book of poetic essays, achieved cult status among American youth for several generations. His other English works include *The Madman* (1918), *Sand and Foam* (1926), and *Jesus, the Son of Man* (1928).

Gibson, Althea (born 1927) U.S. tennis player. Born in Silver, S.C., she moved to New York City when she was 3, later returning south to attend Florida A&M University. She was the first black to win the French (1956) and Wimbledon and U.S. singles championships (1957–58). She also won the U.S. mixed doubles, Australian women's doubles (both 1957), and U.S. professional women's title (1960), for a total of 11 Grand Slam events. Ranked no. 1 in the U.S. in 1957 and 1958, she was voted Female Athlete of the Year by the Associated Press both years, the first black to receive that honor.

Gibson, Bob *orig.* **Robert** (born 1935) U.S. baseball pitcher. Born in Omaha, he was an outstanding high-school baseball and basketball player. As a right-handed pitcher for the St. Louis Cardinals (1961–75), he won seven of nine World Series games and in 1968 had an earned run average of 1.12 (fourth all-time) and 13 shutouts (tied for second all-time). His career total of 3,117 strikeouts made him the first pitcher to accumulate more than 3,000 since WALTER JOHNSON in the 1920s.

Gibson, Charles Dana (1867–1944) U.S. illustrator. Born in Roxbury, Mass., he studied at New York's Art Students League and began to contribute drawings to *Life, Scribner's, Harper's,* and *Century*. His "Gibson girl" drawings, relying on his wife as a model, defined the U.S. ideal of spirited feminine beauty at the turn of the century, and his refined pen-and-ink style was widely imitated. *Collier's* reportedly paid him the unprecendented sum of $50,000 to produce a double-page illustration every week for a year. He also published several collections of satirical drawings of high society.

Gibson, Eleanor J(ack) *orig.* **Eleanor Jack** (born 1910) U.S. psychologist. Born in Peoria, Ill., she taught at Smith College (1931–49) and Cornell University (from 1949). In her major work, *Principles of Perceptual Learning and Development* (1969), she proposed that perceptual learning is a process of discovering how to transform previously overlooked potentials of sensory stimulation into effective information. In books such as *The Psychology of Reading* (1975), she also contributed to studies of the reading process. She received the National Medal of Science in 1992. JAMES J. GIBSON was her husband.

Gibson, James J(erome) (1904–1979) U.S. psychologist and philosopher. Born in McConnelsville, Ohio, he taught at Smith College (1928–49) and Cornell University (1949–72). He is best known for his adherence to realism and his extensive experimental studies of visual perception explicating that view. In his first major work, *The Perception of the Visual World* (1950), he proposed that perception is unmediated by associations or information processing, but rather is direct. He argued for an examination of the organism's dynamic world in search of the information that specified the state of that world. He developed his position in *The Senses Considered as Perceptual Systems* (1966) and *The Ecological Approach to Visual Perception* (1979). His followers organized the International Society for Ecological Psychology. ELEANOR J. GIBSON was his wife.

Gibson, Josh(ua) (1911–1947) U.S. baseball player. Born in Buena Vista, Ga., he played as a catcher in the Pittsburgh Crawfords (1927–29, 1932–36) and the Homestead (Pa.) Grays (1930–31, 1937–46). Though precise records do not exist, he is believed to have led the NEGRO LEAGUES in home runs for 10 consecutive seasons and to have had a career batting average of .347. His catching ability was praised by major-league stars against whom he played in exhibition games. Often called "the black Babe Ruth," he was one of the greatest players kept from the major leagues by the unwritten rule against black ballplayers. He was elected to the Baseball Hall of Fame in 1972.

Gibson, Mel (Columcille) (born 1956) Australian (U.S.-born) film actor. He moved with his family to Australia at age 12. After his screen debut in 1977, he won a following in the futuristic action film *Mad Max* (1979), which was followed by the sequels *Road Warrior* (1981) and *Beyond Thunderdome* (1985). He won international acclaim for his roles in *Gallipoli* (1981), *The Year of Living Dangerously* (1983), and *The Bounty* (1984), played a tough cop in the violent *Lethal Weapon* (1987) and its sequels (1989, 1992, 1998), and directed and starred in *The Man Without a Face* (1993) and *Braveheart* (1995, Academy Awards for best picture and director).

Gibson, William (Ford) (born 1948) U.S.-Canadian science-fiction writer. Born in Conway, S.C., he attended the University of British Columbia. With his first novel, *Neuromancer* (1984), he emerged as a leading exponent of cyberpunk, a school of science fiction whose works are characterized by countercultural antiheroes trapped in a dehumanized, high-tech future. His concept of "cyberspace" (a term he coined), a computer-simulated reality, is a major contribution to the genre. His later books include *Count Zero* (1986), *Burning Chrome* (1986), *Mona Lisa Overdrive* (1988), *The Difference Engine* (1990; with BRUCE STERLING), and *Virtual Light* (1993).

Gibson Desert Arid zone, WESTERN AUSTRALIA. Located south of the GREAT SANDY DESERT, it now constitutes Gibson Desert Nature Reserve, and is home to many desert animals. Measuring about 250 mi (400 km) from north to south, and 520 mi (840 km) from east to west, it was named for Alfred Gibson, an explorer who was lost there in the 1870s.

Giddens, Anthony (born 1938) British political adviser and educator. Trained as a sociologist and social theorist, he lectured at universities in Europe, North America, and Australia before cofounding an academic publishing house (Polity Press, 1985). In 1997 he became director of the London School of Economics and Political Science. An influential adviser to TONY BLAIR, his concept of a "third way"—a political program not limited by the traditional left–right political dichotomy—is seen as underpinning Blair's Labour government.

Gide \'zhēd\, **André (-Paul-Guillaume)** (1869–1951) French writer. Son of a law professor, he began writing at an early age. His early prose poem *Fruits of the Earth* (1897) reflects his increasing awareness of his homosexuality. The novellas *The Immoralist* (1902) and *Strait Is the Gate* (1909) showed his mastery of classical construction, and *Lafcadio's Adventures* displayed his gift for mordant satire. In 1908 he cofounded *La nouvelle revue française,* the literary review that would unite progressive French writers for 30 years. The autobiographical *If It Die . . .* (1924) is among the great works of confessional literature. *Corydon* (1924), a defense of homosexuality, was violently attacked. *The Counterfeiters* (1926) is his most complex novel. He become a champion of society's victims and outcasts, and was for a time attracted to communism; with the outbreak of World War II he gained a greater appreciation for tradition. He received the Nobel Prize in 1947.

Gide, oil painting by P.A. Laurens, 1924; in the National Museum of Modern Art, Paris.

© A.D.A.G.P. 1970; PHOTOGRAPH, GIRAUDON—ART RESOURCE

Gideon Judge and hero of ancient Israel, whose deeds are described in the Old Testament Book of Judges. The book contains two versions of Gideon's story. In one account, he led his tribe of Manasseh in a victorious campaign against the Midianites, then fashioned an idolatrous image from the booty and led Israel into immorality. In another version, he replaced worship of the local deity, BAAL, with that of Yahweh (the God of Israel), and the power of Yahweh enabled his tribe to destroy the Midianites.

Gielgud \'gil-ˌgu̇d, 'gēl-ˌgu̇d\, **(Arthur) John** *later* **Sir John** (1904–2000) British actor and director. He made his London debut in 1921 and joined the OLD VIC company in 1929, becoming widely acclaimed for a series of Shakespearean performances, notably Hamlet and Richard II, and also excelling in such plays as *The School for Scandal, The Importance of Being Earnest, The Seagull,* and *Tiny Alice.* He directed several repertory seasons in the 1940s and toured the world with the solo recital *Ages of Man* (1958–59). He appeared in many films in Britain and the U.S. from 1924, including *Arthur* (1981, Academy Award), *Gandhi* (1982), *Prospero's Books* (1991), and *Shine* (1996). For almost 70 years he was regarded as one of the finest actors in the English language.

Giers \'gyērs\, **Nikolay (Karlovich)** (1820–1895) Russian foreign minister in the reign of ALEXANDER III. Succeeding ALEKSANDR, PRINCE GORCHAKOV as foreign minister in 1882, he tried to maintain the THREE EMPERORS' LEAGUE with Germany and Austria-Hungary, but when it lapsed (1887) he negotiated the REINSURANCE TREATY with Germany only. When that alliance was not renewed (1890), he concluded a formal Russo-French agreement (1894) that became the basis for the Russo-Franco-British alliance against the CENTRAL POWERS in World War I.

GIF \'gif\ *in full* **Graphics Interchange Format** Standard computer file format for graphic images. GIF files use data compression to reduce the file size. The original version of the format was developed by CompuServe in 1987. The current version supports animated GIFs (a graphics image that moves). GIF and JPEG are the most commonly used graphics formats on the INTERNET.

gift exchange Transfer of goods or services that, although regarded as voluntary by those involved, is part of expected social behavior. First studied by MARCEL MAUSS, the gift-exchange cycle entails obligations to give, receive, and return, each phase being surrounded with sanctions and calculations involving prestige and the maintenance of social relations. Some SACRIFICES may be viewed as gifts to supernatural powers from which a return in the form of aid or approval is expected; and the transfer of women in MARRIAGE between kin groups usually involves social obligations similar to those found in gift exchange. See also POTLATCH.

gifted child Child having great natural ability or talent. The best indications of giftedness are often those provided by teachers and parents, supplemented by data from IQ tests and cumulative school records. Some school districts specify an IQ level (variously, 120–135) above which a child is deemed gifted and may qualify for advanced educational programs. See also GENIUS.

gigantism Excessive growth, resulting from heredity, diet, or growth regulation disorder. ANDROGEN deficiency causes long bones to continue growing after they would normally stop. Overproduction of GROWTH HORMONE—usually due to a tumor—causes pituitary gigantism (see PITUITARY GLAND). With gradual but continuous growth, height may reach 8 ft (240 cm), with normal proportions. Greater susceptibility to infection, injury, and metabolic disorders shortens the life span. Surgery or radiation can be employed to curtail further growth. Gigantism often occurs with ACROMEGALY.

gigue \'zhēg\ Dance derived from the English jig that was popular as a lively court dance in 17th-century Europe. Though originally a solo dance, in its courtly form it was danced by couples in formal ballet style to music in 6/8 or 12/8 time. As a musical form, it became the last movement in the standard SUITE.

Gijón \k̲ē-'k̲ōn\ Seaport city (pop., 1998 est.: 265,491), on the Bay of BISCAY, northwestern Spain. Founded before Roman times, it was captured by the Moors early in the 8th century. It was retaken c. 737 and served as the capital of the kingdom of ASTURIAS until 791. It was burned during civil wars in 1395. In the 16th–17th century it suffered many pirate attacks. The remnants of the Spanish ARMADA took refuge there in 1588. It is the site of Roman baths and medieval palaces.

Gil Robles (y Quinoñes) \k̲ēl-'rō-blās\, **José María** (1898–1980) Spanish politician. A lawyer, in 1931 he formed the Catholic party Acción Popular, which became the main component of the right-wing coalition CEDA, a powerful bloc in the Spanish Second Republic after 1933. In 1935 he served as minister of war. In 1936 he led an alliance of CEDA and other conservative parties in the Cortes, but the majority of seats were held by the leftist Popular Front. When the SPANISH CIVIL WAR broke out, he purchased arms for the rebels, then lived in exile in Portugal (1936–53, 1962–64). He worked to establish a Christian Democratic party in Spain and after Franco's death (1975) reemerged briefly as a political leader.

Gila Cliff Dwellings National Monument \'hē-lə\ National preserve, southwestern New Mexico. Located in the Gila National Forest near the headwaters of the GILA RIVER, it contains groups of small but well-preserved PUEBLO INDIAN dwellings in natural cavities of an overhanging cliff 150 ft (45 m) high. The dwellings were inhabited c. AD 100–1300. Established in 1907, the monument occupies 533 acres (216 hectares).

Gila monster One of the only two species (both in the family Helodermatidae) of venomous LIZARDS, named for the Gila River basin and found in the southwestern U.S. and northern Mexico. The Gila monster *(Heloderma suspectum)* grows to about 20 in. (50 cm) long, is stout-bodied with black and pink blotches or bands, and has beadlike scales. During warm weather, it feeds at night on small mammals, birds, and eggs and stores fat in the tail and abdomen for the winter. It is sluggish but has a strong bite. The venom (a neurotoxin) is conducted along grooves in the teeth from glands in the lower jaw. Bites are rarely fatal to humans. The other venomous species is the Mexican beaded lizard *(H. horridum)*.

Gila River River, New Mexico and Arizona. Rising in southwestern New Mexico in the Elk Mtns., near the GILA CLIFF DWELLINGS NATIONAL MONUMENT, it flows 630 mi (1,015 km) west over desert land to the COLORADO RIVER at Yuma, Ariz. Coolidge Dam (1928) on the Gila near Globe, Ariz., is used for irrigation; the dam, together with Roosevelt Dam on the SALT RIVER, stores all available surface water, so the Gila River bed is dry down to the Colorado. Its valley is the chief habitat of the GILA MONSTER.

Gilbert, Cass (1859–1934) U.S. architect. Born in Zanesville, Ohio, he briefly attended MIT, then worked briefly for the firm of McKim, Mead & White. For some years his 60-story Woolworth Building (1910–13) in New York, with its Gothic detail in terra-cotta over a steel frame, was regarded as a model of tall commercial building design (it was for years the tallest building in the world). Other works include the U.S. Supreme Court Building, Washington, D.C. (completed 1935) and the campuses of the Univs. of Minnesota and Texas. Though not highly original, Gilbert was an acknowledged leader of his profession in the U.S. during a period in which monumental architecture predominated.

Gilbert, Humphrey *later* **Sir Humphrey** (1539?–1583) English soldier and navigator. The half brother of WALTER RALEIGH, he proposed in his *Discourse* (1566) a voyage in search of the NORTHWEST PASSAGE. Queen ELIZABETH I rejected the idea and sent him to Ireland (1567–70), where he ruthlessly suppressed an uprising, for which he was knighted. In 1578 he set out with seven ships, intending to colonize North America, but through his poor leadership some ships returned to England and others turned to piracy. He sailed again in 1583, this time arriving in Newfoundland, which he claimed in the name of the queen.

Gilbert, W(illiam) S(chwenck) *later* **Sir William** (1836–1911) British librettist. His early ambition was for a legal career, but in 1861 he began to publish comic ballads, illustrated by himself and signed "Bab." In 1870 he met A. SULLIVAN, and they soon produced the light opera *Thespis* (1871), which was followed by *Trial by Jury* (1875) and four productions staged by Richard D'Oyly Carte (1844–1901): *The Sorcerer* (1877), *H.M.S. Pinafore* (1878), *The Pirates of Penzance* (1879), and *Patience* (1881). Carte built the Savoy Theatre in 1881 for productions of the partners' work, which became known as the "Savoy Operas"; these later operettas included *Iolanthe* (1882), *Princess Ida* (1884), *The Mikado* (1885), *Ruddigore* (1887), *The Yeomen of the Guard* (1888), and *The Gondoliers* (1889). Mounting tensions between Gilbert and Sullivan led to a break, but they reunited in 1893 to produce *Utopia Limited* and later *The Grand Duke* (1896). Gilbert died of a heart attack brought on while rescuing a woman from drowning. His lyrics include some of the finest comic verse ever written in English.

Gilbert and Ellice Islands Former British colony, western central Pacific Ocean. The colony consisted of the GILBERT ISLANDS, TUVALU (formerly Ellice islands), the northern LINE ISLANDS, and the PHOENIX ISLANDS. First visited by Europeans by the early 19th century, the group was proclaimed a British protectorate in 1892 and made a crown colony in 1916. In 1979 the colony was divided and formed parts of independent Kiribati and Tuvalu.

Gilbert Islands Group of 16 coral atolls (pop., 1995: 65,939), part of the island nation of KIRIBATI, western Pacific Ocean. The islands, including TARAWA, the largest, occupy a total land area of 105 sq mi (272 sq km). The British visited them in the 18th–19th century, and in 1892 they became a British protectorate. In 1916 they became part of the Gilbert and Ellice Islands Crown Colony. They were occupied by Japanese forces 1941–43, and saw heavy fighting. Made a separate territory in 1976, they became part of Kiribati in 1979.

Gilchrist \'gil-krist\, **Percy Carlyle** (1851–1935) British metallurgist. In 1876–77, with his cousin Sidney Gilchrist Thomas (1850–1885), he devised the BASIC BESSEMER PROCESS of making steel in Bessemer converters from phosphorus-containing pig iron. In the Thomas-Gilchrist process, the lining used in the converter is basic rather than acidic, and it captures the acidic phosphorus oxides formed on blowing air through molten iron made from the high-phosphorus iron ore prevalent in Europe. The process subsequently became widely used.

Gilead \'gi-lē-əd\ Area of ancient Palestine, east of the JORDAN RIVER. Now northwestern Jordan, it was bounded in the north by the Yarmuk River and in the southwest by what were known then as the plains of Moab. Sometimes "Gilead" is used in a more general sense for all the region east of the Jordan River. The name first appears in the biblical account of the last meeting of Jacob and Laban (Gen. 31:21–22). The scene of the battle between Gideon and the Midianites, it was also the home of the prophet ELIJAH.

Gilgamesh \'gil-gə-ˌmesh, gil-'gä-məsh\ Hero of the ancient AKKADIAN-LANGUAGE *Epic of Gilgamesh.* The great literary work of ancient MESOPOTAMIA, the epic is known from 12 incomplete tablets discovered at NINEVEH in the library of ASHURBANIPAL. Gaps in the narrative have been filled in with fragments found elsewhere. The character Gilgamesh is probably based on the Gilgamesh who ruled Uruk in the 3rd millennium BC. The epic presents Gilgamesh as a great warrior and builder, who rejects the marriage proposal of the goddess ISHTAR. With the aid of his friend and companion ENKIDU, he kills the divine bull that Ishtar sends to destroy him. Enkidu's death prompts Gilgamesh to seek Utnapishtim, survivor of the legendary flood, to learn how to escape death. He obtains a youth-renewing plant only to have it stolen. The epic ends with the return of the spirit of Enkidu, who gives a dismal report on the underworld.

Gill, Brendan (1914–1997) U.S. writer. Born in Hartford, Conn., he is chiefly known for his pieces in the *New Yorker*, where he spent some 60 years, many of them as staff film critic (1960–67), theater critic (1968–87), and architecture critic (1992–97). His many books include the memoir *Here at The New Yorker* (1975). On the death of JOSEPH CAMPBELL he denounced his one-time friend as a bigot and reactionary. A leading preservationist, he led the successful fight to save GRAND CENTRAL STATION.

Gilles de Rais See BLUEBEARD

Gillespie, Dizzy *orig.* **John Birks** (1917–1993) U.S. jazz trumpeter, composer, arranger, and bandleader, one of the primary innovators of BEBOP. Born in Cheraw, S.C., Gillespie was influenced by ROY ELDRIDGE and played with the big bands of CAB CALLOWAY, EARL HINES, and BILLY ECKSTINE before leading small groups in the mid-1940s. He pioneered bebop with saxophonist CHARLIE PARKER and pianist THELONIOUS MONK. Bringing this approach to his big band in the late 1940s, Gillespie popularized the use of Afro-Cuban rhythms in jazz. Alternating between large and small ensembles for the rest of his career, his virtuosity and comic wit (in addition to his puffed cheeks and trademark 45° upturned trumpet bell) made him one of the most charismatic and influential musicians in jazz.

Dizzy Gillespie, 1955.
UPI

Gilman, Charlotte (Anna) Perkins (Stetson) (1860–1935) U.S. feminist theorist, writer, and lecturer. Born in Hartford, Conn., she gained worldwide fame as a lecturer on women, ethics, labor, and society. In her best-known work, *Women and Economics* (1898), she proposed that women's sexual and maternal roles had been overemphasized to the detriment of their social and economic potential and that only economic independence could bring true freedom. Her other works include the celebrated short story "The Yellow Wallpaper" (1899) and her autobiography, *The Living of Charlotte Perkins Gilman* (1935).

Gilmore, Patrick (Sarsfield) (1829–1892) Irish-U.S. bandmaster. He emigrated to the U.S. at 19. In 1859 he took over the Boston Brigade Band (later known as Gilmore's Band). During the Civil War the entire band enlisted in the Union Army. A flamboyant showman, Gilmore organized extravaganza performances in 1869 and 1872 with more than 10,000 performers; the first featured cannon fire and 100 firemen beating anvils, and the second employed a chorus of 20,000. From 1872 until his death he led the New York 22nd Regiment Band, giving 150 concerts in Europe in 1878. His innovations reduced the heavy reliance on brass instruments in favor of the higher proportion of reeds characteristic of modern concert bands.

gin Colorless DISTILLED LIQUOR made from neutral grain spirits flavored with JUNIPER berries and aromatics (such as ANISE and CARAWAY seeds). Its origin is attributed to a 17th-century Dutch medical researcher, Franciscus Sylvius. Two principal types are marketed: a malty-flavored and full-bodied Netherlands type (alcohol content about 35% by volume) and a dry, purified type favored in Britain and the U.S. (40–47% alcohol by volume). Dry gin, which has more flavoring ingredients, is served either unmixed or in cocktails. Dutch gins are usually served unmixed or with water.

gin rummy RUMMY game for two players in which each is dealt 10 cards and a player may win a hand by matching or sequencing by suit all the cards in it by drawing from a deck. Play may also end when the unmatched cards count up to 10 points or less. If a player matches all the cards he is "gin." The first player to reach 100 points wins. The game was introduced in New York in 1909.

ginger Herbaceous perennial plant (*Zingiber officinale;* family Zingiberaceae), probably native to South Asia, or its aromatic, pungent RHIZOME, which is used as a spice, flavoring, food, and medicine. The spice has a slightly biting taste and is used, usually dried and ground, to flavor breads, sauces, curry dishes, confections, pickles, and ginger ale. The fresh rhizome, green ginger, is used in cooking. The leafy stems of the plant bear flowers in dense, conelike spikes. Oil distilled from the rhizome is used in foods and perfumes.

gingerbread In architecture and design, elaborately detailed embellishment, either lavish or superfluous. Though the term is occasionally applied to such highly detailed and decorative styles as the ROCOCO, it usually refers to the hand-carved and -sawn wood ornamentation of the CARPENTER GOTHIC style.

ginkgo Tree (*Ginkgo biloba,* family Ginkgoaceae) that is the only living representative of the gymnosperm order Ginkgoales. Native to China, it is often termed a living fossil because it is unclear whether uncultivated groups can be found in the wild. It has been planted since ancient times in Chinese and Japanese temple gardens and is now valued in many parts of the world as an attractive, fungus- and insect-resistant ornamental tree. It tolerates cold weather and, unlike most gymnosperms, can survive the adverse atmospheric conditions of urban areas. Pyramidal in shape, it has a columnar, sparingly branched trunk. The light-colored wood, soft and weak, has little economic value. The fan-shaped, leathery leaves, most divided into two lobes by a central notch, resemble the leaflets of the maidenhair fern. The silvery nut, when roasted, is considered a delicacy. Studies have suggested that *Ginkgo biloba* supplements can enhance memory function in the elderly and delay the onset of Alzheimer's disease.

Ginkgo (*Ginkgo biloba*).
GRANT HEILMAN

Ginsberg, Allen (Irwin) (1926–1997) U.S. poet. Born in Newark, N.J., the son of a poet, he attended Columbia Univ., where he met JACK KEROUAC. His epic poem *Howl* (1956), a denunciation of the failings of American society, became the most famous poem of the BEAT MOVEMENT; in it and later works, largely inspired by WALT WHITMAN, he celebrated the pleasures of psychotropic drugs, footloose wandering, and homosexuality. *Kaddish* (1961) is a long confessional poem about his mother's insanity and suicide. His collections include *Reality Sandwiches* (1963), *Planet News* (1968), *The Fall of America* (1972), and *Mind Breaths* (1978). His life was one of ceaseless travel, poetry readings, and left-wing political activity, and he was an influential guru of the American youth counterculture in the 1960s and '70s.

Ginsburg, Ruth Bader *orig.* **Ruth Joan Bader** (born 1933) U.S. jurist. Born in New York City, she graduated at the top of her class at Columbia Law School in 1959, but was turned down for numerous jobs because of her sex. From 1972 to 1980 she taught at Columbia, where she became the first tenured female professor. As director of the Women's Rights Project of the AMERICAN CIVIL LIBERTIES UNION, she argued six landmark cases on gender equality before the U.S. Supreme Court. In 1980 she was appointed to the U.S. Court of Appeals, and in 1993 she was appointed by Pres. WILLIAM JEFFERSON CLINTON to the Supreme Court as its second female justice in history. On the Court she has generally favored moderation and restraint.

ginseng \'jin-ˈseŋ\ Either of two herbs of the family Araliaceae or their roots, which have long been used as a drug in China and as the ingredient for a stimulating tea. *Panax quinquefolium,* the North American ginseng, is native from Quebec and Manitoba southward to the coasts of the Gulf of Mexico. Asian ginseng *(P. schinseng)* is native to Manchuria and Korea and is cultivated in Korea and Japan. Ginseng has a sweetly aromatic flavor. Its root has long been regarded by the Chinese as a panacea for illness; its purported effects include improved mental performance, ability to learn, and memory and sensory awareness.

Gioberti \jō-ˈber-tē\, **Vincenzo** (1801–1852) Italian philosopher and politician whose writings helped bring about the unification of the Italian states. Ordained a priest (1825), he became court chaplain of Sardinia (1831), but was briefly imprisoned (1833) for involvement in a republican plot. He exiled himself to Paris and Brussels, where he published works advocating a united Italy headed by the pope. He returned to Italy in 1847 and became premier of Sardinia-Piedmont (1848–49). His philosophy centered on his concept of being and is termed "ontologism."

Giolitti \jō-ˈlēt-tē\, **Giovanni** (1842–1928) Italian politician and prime minister five times between 1892 and 1921. He served in parliament 1882–1928. As a political leader, he used the technique later called *giolittisma*, which emphasized personal deals rather than party loyalty, as well as electoral corruption. As prime minister (1892–93), he instituted reforms but became enveloped in a bank scandal; he cleared himself but greatly damaged his successor, FRANCESCO CRISPI. As minister of the interior (1901–3) and prime minister (1903–5, 1906–9), he was both praised and criticized for his calm attitude toward widespread strikes. In his fourth ministry (1911–14) he oversaw the ITALO-TURKISH WAR, then opposed Italy's entrance into World War I. In his final term as premier (1920–21), he undertook Italy's reconstruction. He tolerated the early Fascists but in 1924 withdrew his support.

Giordano \jōr-ˈdä-nō\, **Luca** (1634–1705) Italian painter active in Naples. He was inspired by the work of JOSE DE RIBERA and (after extensive travel in Florence, Rome, and Venice) that of PAOLO VERONESE and PIETRO DA CORTONA, whose influence is most evident in his huge ceiling fresco in the gallery of the Medici-Riccardi Palace (1682–85/86), Florence. In 1692 he went to Spain as court painter to CHARLES II; his frescoes in EL ESCORIAL are considered his best works of the period. In 1702 he returned to Naples, where he completed his last great work, the ceiling of the Treasury Chapel of the Certosa di San Martino (1704). His oil and fresco output was enormous, and his subject matter ranged from religious to mythological themes. Many of his frescoes in Naples were destroyed or damaged in World War II.

Giorgione \jȯr-ˈjō-nē\ *or* **Giorgio da Castelfranco** *orig.* **Giorgio Barbarelli** (c. 1477–1510) Italian painter active in Venice. Nothing is known of his early life. The technique, color, and mood of his pictures suggest that he studied with Giovanni Bellini in Venice in the 1490s. His major public commission was the execution of frescoes on the exterior of the German Exchange, now known only through engravings and ruined fragments. Of the few paintings attributed to Giorgione, two were completed by other artists after his death, one by TITIAN. Though almost every aspect of his work is controversial, including the attribution, dating, and interpretation of paintings associated with him, it is clear that he was a pioneer in the technique of oil painting on canvas and a master of creating mood and mystery, as epitomized in *The Tempest* (c. 1505), a milestone in Renaissance landscape painting. He had far-reaching influence on portraiture; many early 16th-century artists imitated his style. See also VENETIAN SCHOOL.

Giotto (di Bondone) \ˈjȯt-tō\ (c. 1267–1337) First of the great Italian painters, active in Florence. He decorated chapels and churches in Assisi, Rome, Padua, Florence, and Naples with frescoes and panel paintings. His works in Rome include the heavily restored mosaic of *Christ Walking on the Water* over the entrance to St. Peter's Basilica and an altarpiece from St. Peter's, now in the Vatican Museum. In Padua, his fresco of the Last Judgment decorates the western wall of the Arena Chapel, and the rest of the chapel is covered with his narrative frescoes featuring scenes from the lives of the Virgin Mary and Christ. Later in his career he executed frescoes in four chapels in the church of Santa Croce in Florence, two of which survive. In 1334 he was appointed surveyor of Florence Cathedral; his design for the campanile was altered after his death. The most important extant panel painting attributed to him is *The Madonna in Glory* (c. 1305–10). He achieved great fame in his lifetime. For breaking with the impersonal stylizations of Byzantine art and introducing new ideals of naturalism and humanity, three-dimensional space and three-dimensional form, he is considered the father of European painting. The course of Italian painting was dominated by his students and followers, notably TADDEO GADDI, ANDREA ORCAGNA, and PIETRO AND AMBROGIO LORENZETTI.

"Lamentation," fresco by Giotto, c. 1305–06; in the Arena Chapel, Padua, Italy.
SCALA/ART RESOURCE, N.Y.

Giovanni da Bologna See GIAMBOLOGNA

Giovanni di Paolo (di Grazia) \jȯ-ˈvän-nē-dē-ˈpau̇-lō\ (c. 1399–1482) Italian painter active in Siena. A prolific artist, he produced his most characteristic works from the 1440s, notably the monumental altarpiece *The Presentation of Christ in the Temple* (1447–49), 12 scenes from the life of St. John the Baptist, and a Madonna (1463) altarpiece in Pienza Cathedral. He also painted countless other religious panels. His tormented spirituality and expressionistic style were little appreciated until his reputation was revived in the 20th century.

Gippsland \ˈgips-ˌland\ Region, southeastern VICTORIA, Australia. It extends northwest from Western Port (near MELBOURNE) to the NEW SOUTH WALES border and south from the Eastern Highlands to the coast; it has an area of 13,600 sq mi (35,200 sq km). Fertile and well watered, Gippsland is the focus of the state's dairy industry, while its petroleum and natural gas are tapped from offshore wells in BASS STRAIT. Tourism is also important in the southeastern area, which has coastal resorts and the Lakes National Park. The first settlers were attracted by gold finds in the 1850s; farmers arrived after the completion of a rail line from Melbourne in 1887.

giraffe RUMINANT (Giraffa camelopardalis, family Giraffidae) that is the tallest of all mammals, reaching an overall height of 18 ft (5.5 m) or more. It has extremely long legs and neck, a short body, a tufted tail, a short mane, and two to four short, skin-covered horns. The back slopes downward to the hindquarters. The coat is pale buff, with reddish brown spots. It feeds primarily on ACACIA leaves. It lives in herds on savannas and in open bush country and is native to most of sub-Saharan Africa. Giraffes are still numerous in eastern Africa, where they are protected, but hunting by humans has reduced their populations elsewhere. The only other member of the family is the OKAPI.

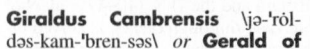

Giraffe (*Giraffa camelopardalis*).
© ANIMALS ANIMALS, 1971

Giraldus Cambrensis \jə-ˈrȯl-dəs-kam-ˈbren-səs\ *or* **Gerald of Wales** (1146?–1223?) Historian and archdeacon of Brecknock, Wales (1175–1204). Educated in Paris, he returned to Wales and struggled unsuccessfully to become bishop of St. David's, hoping to make it independent of Canterbury. He advised HENRY II of England and Henry's son JOHN, especially on Welsh and Irish issues. His accounts of life in the late 12th century have proved valuable to historians.

Girard \zhē-'rȧr, *Engl* jə-'rärd\, **Stephen** (1750–1831) French-U.S. financier and philanthropist. He became a sailor at 14 and by 1774 commanded a French ship involved in American trade with the West Indies. He settled in Philadelphia during the American Revolution, then resumed trading in 1783. He developed a worldwide trading fleet and amassed a fortune. In 1812 he bought out the BANK OF THE U.S., renaming it the Bank of Stephen Girard. During the War of 1812 he purchased government bonds, which by 1814 constituted 95% of the U.S.'s war loan. He bequeathed his fortune to social-welfare institutions.

Girardon \zhē-rȧr-'dōⁿ\, **François** (1628–1715) French sculptor. Born in Troyes, he studied there and in Rome, and in 1657 became a member of the French Royal Academy. In 1666 he received his most famous commission, the *Apollo Tended by the Nymphs,* for the Grotto of Thetis at VERSAILLES. Of his other works at Versailles, the most notable are *The Bath of the Nymphs* (1668–70) and *The Rape of Persephone* (1677–79). Works in Paris include an equestrian statue of LOUIS XIV (1683–92), destroyed in the French Revolution, and the tomb of Cardinal RICHELIEU in the church of the Sorbonne (1675–94). Though influenced by the work of G.-L. BERNINI, his own style was more restrained.

Giraud \zhē-'rō\, **Henri (-Honoré)** (1879–1949) French army officer. In World War II he commanded forces in northern France but was captured by the Germans in 1940. He escaped in 1942 and soon became commander in chief of the French forces in North Africa. In 1943 he was copresident with CHARLES DE GAULLE of the French Committee of National Liberation, but retired in 1944 over differences with de Gaulle.

Giraudoux \zhē-rō-'dü\, **(Hyppolyte-) Jean** (1882–1944) French novelist, essayist, and playwright. He made the diplomatic service his career, while becoming known as an avant-garde writer with early poetic novels such as *Suzanne et le Pacifique* (1921). He created an impressionistic form of drama by emphasizing dialogue and style rather than realism. In such works as *Électre* (1937) and *Cantique des cantiques* (1938), he sought inspiration in classical or biblical tradition. His most famous works are *Tiger at the Gates* (1935), about the Trojan War, and *The Madwoman of Chaillot* (1946).

girder In building construction, a large main supporting BEAM, commonly of steel or REINFORCED CONCRETE, that carries a heavy transverse (crosswise) load. In a floor system, beams and joists transfer their loads to the girders, which in turn frame into the columns.

Gironde Estuary \zhē-'rōⁿd\ Estuary on the Bay of BISCAY, southwestern France. Formed by the confluence of the GARONNE and DORDOGNE rivers, it extends for about 45 mi (72 km) inland. It is navigable for oceangoing vessels, although it has sandbanks and strong tides.

Girondin \jə-'rän-din\ *or* **Girondist** Moderate republican member in the Legislative Assembly during the FRENCH REVOLUTION. Many members were originally from the department of Gironde; as followers of J.-P. BRISSOT, they were initially called Brissotins. Dominant in the assembly in 1791–92, they supported foreign war as a means to unite the people behind the Revolution. In 1792 the NATIONAL CONVENTION was divided between them and the more radical MONTAGNARDS; in 1793 they were driven from the National Convention and the Montagnards seized power. Many Girondins were guillotined in the REIGN OF TERROR.

GIS See GEOGRAPHIC INFORMATION SYSTEM

Giscard d'Estaing \zhis-kär-des-'taⁿ\, **Valéry** (born 1926) French political leader, third president of the Fifth Republic (1974–81). He was elected to the National Assembly in 1956. He served as finance minister under CHARLES DE GAULLE (1962–66) and GEORGES POMPIDOU (1969–74); in his first term of office France attained its first balanced budget in 30 years, but his conservative policies helped cause a recession and he was dismissed. In 1974 he became president after defeating FRANCOIS MITTERRAND, who, in turn, defeated him in 1981.

Giscard d'Estaing, 1985.
©1985 THIERRY BOCCON-GIBOD/BLACK STAR

Gish, Lillian (Diana) (1893–1993) U.S. film and theater actress. Born in Springfield, Ohio, she acted on Broadway and with touring companies from age 5, often with her sister, Dorothy (1898–1968). Their screen careers began when D. W. GRIFFITH featured them in *An Unseen Enemy* (1912). Lillian won international fame in *The Birth of a Nation* (1915) and starred as the heroine of such other Griffith films as *Broken Blossoms* (1919) and *Orphans of the Storm* (1921). Dorothy was a star through the 1920s, but her career was overshadowed by her sister's fame. After the hits *La Bohème* and *The Scarlet Letter* (both 1926), Lillian's film career waned and she returned to the stage in such plays as *Uncle Vanya* (1930), *Life with Father* (1940), and *The Trip to Bountiful* (1953). Returning to the screen, she was acclaimed in *The Night of the Hunter* (1955), *A Wedding* (1978), and *The Whales of August* (1987).

Gislebertus \,gēz-lə-'ber-tůs\ (fl. c. 1120–1140) French sculptor. His most notable works are the tympanum sculpture of the western doorway of the cathedral at Autun, depicting the Last Judgment; a large-scale nude Eve for the northern doorway; and some 60 carved capitals in the interior and doorways illustrating biblical scenes. His work had a lasting effect on the development of French GOTHIC ART.

Gissing, George (Robert) (1857–1903) British novelist. He had a brilliant academic career but an unhappy personal life; twice involved in miserable marriages, he experienced the life of near poverty and constant drudgery that he described in *New Grub Street* (3 vols., 1891), his best-known work, and *The Private Papers of Henry Ryecroft* (1903). Inspired by HONORE DE BALZAC, he wrote a cycle of 22 novels, which included *Born in Exile* (1892) and *The Odd Women* (1893). His realistic novels of lower-middle-class life are noted for their acute perception of women's social position and psychology.

Giuliani, Rudolph W(illiam) *known as* **Rudy Giuliani** (born 1944) New York City mayor (1994–2002). Born and educated in New York, he was the city's first Republican mayor in two decades. Credited with cutting crime, improving the quality of life, and benefiting business, he won a second and final term in 1997, though critics charged that he defended police misconduct and gutted essential programs. After the SEPTEMBER 11 ATTACKS in 2001, Giuliani drew high praise for his strong leadership of the city through the crisis.

Giulini \jü-'lē-nē\, **Carlo Maria** (born 1914) Italian conductor. He studied viola and composition at Santa Cecilia in Rome, and after several years as a violist, became a conductor in 1944. After several years at La Scala, he left opera at the peak of his international career in 1967, fed up with lack of rehearsal time. His recordings of operas and choral works by W.A. MOZART and G. VERDI became widely acclaimed, and he subsequently held important orchestral posts in Chicago (1968–78), Vienna (1973–76), and, his last, in Los Angeles (1978–86).

Giulio Romano \'jü-lē-ō-rō-'mä-nō\ *orig.* **Giulio Pippi** (1499?–1546) Italian painter and architect. Apprenticed to RAPHAEL in Rome, he became his master's principal heir and artistic executor, completing several of Raphael's Vatican frescoes. From 1524 he lived in Mantua, where he came to dominate artistic activity and developed a personal, anticlassical style. His most important commission, the Palazzo del Te (begun 1526), was one of the first Mannerist buildings to deliberately flout the tenets of Classical architecture. He achieved great fame in his lifetime, and his work presaged the illusionistic ceiling painting of the baroque period.

Givenchy \zhē-väⁿ-'shē\, **Hubert de** (born 1927) French fashion designer. After studying art at the École des Beaux-Arts, he designed for the Paris fashion houses of Robert Piguet, Lucien Lelong, and ELSA SCHIAPARELLI. In 1952 he opened his own house and introduced his first collection. In 1957 he and CRISTOBAL BALENCIAGA introduced the "sack" silhouette (clothes without waistlines). His designs for AUDREY HEPBURN in *Breakfast at Tiffany's* (1961) popularized the high-bosomed dress without sleeves or belt. In the 1960s, his ready-to-wear boutiques brought high fashion at low prices to women throughout the world.

Giza \'gē-zə\ *or* **Al-Jizah** \ál-'jē-zə\ City (pop., 1996: 2,221,868), Upper Egypt. Located on the western bank of the Nile, it is a suburb of CAIRO. A noted entertainment district, it is also the center of Egypt's motion-picture industry. Five mi (8 km) west of the city lie the Great

Sphinx and the three great PYRAMIDS of the PHARAOHS, built during Egypt's 4th dynasty (c. 2613–c. 2494 BC).

Gjellerup \'gyel-ə-rüp\, **Karl Adolph** (1857–1919). Danish poet and novelist. The son of a parson, he studied theology, but after coming under the influence of Darwinism and the ideas of GEORG BRANDES, he considered himself an atheist, which he proclaimed in *An Idealist* (1878) and *The Teutons' Apprentice* (1882). In his later years he would embrace Buddhism and other East Asian religions. His other works include *Minna* (1889) and *The Pilgrim Kamanita* (1906). He shared the 1917 Nobel Prize with HENRIK PONTOPPIDAN.

glacial age See ICE AGE

glacier Large mass of perennial ice that forms on land through the recrystallization of snow and that moves forward under its own weight. The term ice sheet is commonly applied to a glacier that occupies an extensive tract of relatively level land and that flows from the center outward. Glaciers occur where snowfall in winter exceeds melting in summer, conditions that prevail only in high mountain areas and polar regions. Glaciers occupy about 11% of the earth's land surface but hold roughly three-fourths of its fresh water; 99% of glacier ice lies in Antarctica and Greenland.

Glacier Bay Narrow inlet of the Pacific Ocean, southeastern Alaska coast. About 60 mi (97 km) long, it contains 16 active glaciers that descend from ST. ELIAS MTNS. to the east and Fairweather Range to the west. The bay has fjordlike inlets and many largely treeless islands, used as rookeries by thousands of seabirds. It is the focus of GLACIER BAY NATIONAL PARK.

Glacier Bay National Park National park, southeastern Alaska. Located on the Gulf of ALASKA, it was proclaimed a national monument in 1925 and renamed in 1980. It covers 3,225,284 acres (1,305,226 hectares). It includes GLACIER BAY, the northwestern slope of Mount FAIRWEATHER, and the U.S. portion of the Alsek River. Among the notable features of the park are great tidewater glaciers, one of which, Muir Glacier, rises 265 ft (81 m) above the water and is nearly 2 mi (3 km) wide. The park also includes numerous plant species and such wildlife as brown and black bears, mountain goats, whales, seals, and eagles.

Glacier National Park National preserve, British Columbia. Lying in the heart of the SELKIRK MTNS., within the northern bend of the COLUMBIA RIVER, it was established in 1886; it occupies an area of 521 sq mi (1,349 sq km). Snowcapped peaks flanked by ice fields and glaciers form an alpine panorama. Outstanding features are the Illecillewaet Glacier and the Nakimu Caves in the Cougar Valley.

Glacier National Park National preserve, northwestern Montana. Set in the state's ROCKY MTNS. wilderness, it adjoins the Canadian border and Canada's WATERTON LAKES NATIONAL PARK. The two parks together compose the Waterton-Glacier International Peace Park, dedicated in 1932. Glacier National Park was established in 1910 and encompasses 1,013,572 acres (410,178 hectares). The park, with its active glaciers, straddles the CONTINENTAL DIVIDE.

glaciology \glā-shē-'ä-lə-jē\ Scientific discipline concerned with all aspects of ice on landmasses. It deals with the structure and properties of GLACIER ice, its formation and distribution, the dynamics of ice flow, and the interactions of ice accumulations with climate. Glaciological research is conducted in a variety of ways, including radar sounding, boreholes, lateral tunnels, and remote sensing with satellite-borne infrared and multispectral scanners.

Glackens, William (James) (1870–1938) U.S. painter. Born in Philadelphia, he worked as a newspaper illustrator there and later in New York. In 1891 he met ROBERT HENRI, and he subsequently became a member of The EIGHT and the ASH CAN SCHOOL. He favored colorful street scenes of urban middle-class life (e.g., *Hammerstein's Roof Garden*, 1902), heavily influenced by Impressionism. He was a prolific draftsman, and his drawings (e.g., *Seated Woman*, 1902) reveal an elegant style not seen in his paintings. In 1912 he traveled to Europe to buy paintings for the collection of ALBERT BARNES. In 1913 he helped organize and exhibited in the ARMORY SHOW.

gladiator (Latin: "swordsman") Professional combatant in ancient Rome who engaged in fights to the death as sport. Gladiators originally performed at ETRUSCAN funerals, the intent being to give the dead man armed attendants in the next world. At Rome gladiator matches were wildly popular from 264 BC. By the time of Julius CAESAR, 300 pairs would fight at a single show; by the time of TRAJAN, 5,000 combatants of various classes would fight. In the late ROMAN REPUBLIC, the audience called for death with thumbs downward (or thumbs toward their breasts) and for mercy with handkerchiefs (or thumbs downward, according to some sources). The victor earned palm branches or money, and after a few victories a gladiator could be freed. Most were slaves or criminals, but a talented or handsome one could become a favorite of society; since they often served as bodyguards, they occasionally became politically important. DOMITIAN delighted in using dwarfs and women as gladiators. With the coming of Christianity the games began to fall into disfavor, but they may have continued into the 6th century. See also SPARTACUS.

gladiolus \,gla-dē-'ō-ləs\ Any of about 300 species of flowering plants of the genus *Gladiolus,* in the IRIS FAMILY, native to Europe, Africa, and the Mediterranean and widely cultivated for cut flowers. The flowering spike, which springs from a CORM, reaches 2–3 ft (60–90 cm) in height and has many funnel-shaped flowers, all clustered on one side of the stem. There are six petallike floral parts and sparse, swordlike leaves. Cultivated gladioli, which come in all colors, have been developed mostly from southern and eastern African species.

Gladstone, William E(wart) (1809–1898) British politician and prime minister (1868–74, 1880–85, 1886, 1892–94). He entered Parliament in 1833 as a Tory, but after holding various government posts, including chancellor of the exchequer (1852–55, 1859–66), he slowly converted to liberalism and became Liberal party leader in 1866. In his first term as prime minister (1868–74), he oversaw national education reform, voting reform (see BALLOT ACT), and the disestablishment of the Irish Protestant church (1869). In 1875–76 he denounced the indifference of BENJAMIN DISRAELI's government to the BULGARIAN HORRORS. In his second term, he secured passage of the REFORM BILL OF 1884. His cabinet authorized the occupation of Egypt (1882), but his failure to rescue Gen. CHARLES GEORGE GORDON in Khartoum (1885) cost Gladstone much popularity and his government's defeat. In 1886 he was able to use Irish HOME RULE to regain control of Parliament, but when his Home Rule Bill was rejected he resigned. He devoted the next six years to trying to convince the electorate to grant Home Rule to Ireland. Liberals won a majority again in 1892, and in his fourth cabinet he piloted through another Home Rule Bill, but it was soundly rejected by the House of Lords. He is buried in Westminster Abbey.

Gladstone.
CULVER PICTURES

Glåma River \'glò-mə\ River, eastern Norway. The longest river in SCANDINAVIA, it rises in a series of small streams near the Swedish–Norwegian border. It flows south, then west into Øyeren (lake). From there it continues south to Sarpsborg and enters Oslofjorden at Fredrikstad, after a course of 380 mi (610 km). It is a major source of hydroelectric power. It is navigable up to the Sarpsfoss (Sarps Falls) at Sarpsborg.

gland Collection of cells or tissue that removes specific substances from the blood, alters or concentrates them, and then either releases them for further use by the body or eliminates them. Typically, the functional cells of a gland rest on a MEMBRANE and are surrounded by a meshwork of blood vessels. Endocrine, or ductless, glands (e.g., PITUITARY, THYROID, ADRENAL) discharge HORMONES into the bloodstream directly rather than through ducts (see ENDOCRINE SYSTEM). Exocrine glands (e.g., digestive, MAMMARY, SALIVARY, SWEAT) discharge their products through ducts.

glandular fever See infectious MONONUCLEOSIS

Glaser \'glā-zər\, **Donald (Arthur)** (born 1926) U.S. physicist. Born in Cleveland, he received his PhD from Caltech, then joined the faculty at the University of Michigan. There he developed the BUBBLE CHAMBER, an instrument that became widely used in the study of subatomic particles because it allows precise measurement of the particles' paths. He was awarded a 1960 Nobel Prize.

Glasgow \'glas-gō\ City (pop., 1999 est.: 611,440), western Scotland, located on the River CLYDE, 20 mi (32 km) from its mouth on the Atlantic coast. The largest city in Scotland, Glasgow began to develop with the arrival, c. 550 AD, of St. Kentigern (St. Mungo), who established a religious community there. The present cathedral (13th century) was built on the site of the chapel. Made a royal burgh in 1450, it prospered in the 18th century, when the Americas' tropical produce (tobacco, sugar, and rum) made fortunes for Glasgow merchants. Its economy wavered as the tobacco trade was cut off by the AMERICAN REVOLUTION and the cotton industry, by the AMERICAN CIVIL WAR. With the INDUSTRIAL REVOLUTION came coal mining, iron founding, and, especially, shipbuilding. Its manufactures now include textiles, food and beverages, and chemicals. A notable education center, Glasgow has many cultural amenities.

Glasgow, Ellen (Anderson Gholson) (1873–1945) U.S. novelist. Born in Richmond, Va., she was irregularly schooled and lived the life of a Southern belle. With *Virginia* (1913), she completed a five-novel series (begun 1900) depicting the state's social history. She was past 50 when she gained critical notice for *Barren Ground* (1925). *The Sheltered Life* (1932) is part of a trilogy of ironic novels of manners. Later works include the novel *In This Our Life* (1941, Pulitzer Prize) and the posthumous memoir *The Woman Within* (1954). Her realistic depiction of Virginia life helped direct Southern literature away from sentimentality and nostalgia.

Ellen Glasgow, miniature by an unknown artist; in the collection of the Virginia Historical Society.
BY COURTESY OF THE VIRGINIA HISTORICAL SOCIETY

Glasgow, University of Public university in Glasgow, Scotland. It was founded in 1451 and reorganized in 1577. In the 18th century its faculty included such eminent figures as ADAM SMITH and JAMES BLACK; JAMES WATT was an assistant there. In the 19th century the faculty included JOSEPH LISTER and Lord KELVIN. There are currently six faculties: arts, divinity, law, medicine, science, and engineering. The rector is elected triennially by the students. Total enrollment is about 17,000.

Glashow \'gla-shō\, **Sheldon Lee** (born 1932) U.S. theoretical physicist. Born in New York City, he joined the faculty at Harvard University in 1967. With Steven Weinberg (born 1933) and Abdus Salam (1926–1996), he received a 1979 Nobel Prize for formulation of the ELECTROWEAK THEORY, unifying electromagnetism and the WEAK FORCE. In extending the early, limited theory of Weinberg and Salam to include more classes of elementary particles, he had to invent an important new property (CHARM) for QUARKS.

glasnost \'gläs-ˌnōst, 'glas-ˌnōst\ (Russian: "openness") Soviet policy of open discussion of political and social issues. It was instituted by MIKHAIL GORBACHEV in the late 1980s and began the democratization of the Soviet Union. Glasnost also permitted criticism of government officials and allowed the media freer dissemination of news and information. See also PERESTROIKA.

glass Solid material, typically a mix of inorganic compounds, usually transparent or translucent, hard, brittle, and impervious to the natural elements ("vitreous properties"). It is made by cooling molten ingredients fast enough so no visible crystals form. A poor conductor of heat and electricity, glass takes on colors when certain metal OXIDES are included in the mix. Most glass breaks easily. OBSIDIAN is a naturally occurring glass. Everyday glass ("soda-lime" or "soda-lime-silica") is made of silica (silicon dioxide), soda (sodium carbonate), and LIMESTONE (calcium carbonate), with magnesia (magnesium oxide) for sheet glass or alumina (aluminum oxide) for bottle glass. Fused silica is an excellent glass but expensive because of pure silica's very high melting point. Borosilicate glass (Pyrex) is used for cookware and laboratory glassware because it expands very little when heated. LEAD crystal is used for fine tableware. It has a heavy feel and a sparkle due to its high REFRACTION index. Even more specialized glasses include optical, photosensitive, metallic, and fiber-optic. Since glass has no sharp melting point, most types can be shaped while hot by many techniques, mostly blowing or molding. See also VOLCANIC GLASS.

glass, architectural Glass used in structures. Glass was first used for windows in Roman imperial times. Lack of transparency and the difficulty encountered in making any but small panes eventually led to the introduction of STAINED-GLASS windows in the 12th century. Clear, colorless glass proved difficult to achieve until the Venetian manufacture of cristallo (see VENETIAN GLASS). Large sheets of glass first became practicable when the French introduced plate glass in the 17th century. Mechanization of glass forming did not occur until the late 19th century. The float-glass method currently in use, which eliminated the need for grinding and polishing, was introduced in the 1950s. Special glass products today include insulated (multipane) assemblies, laminated security glass (wired glass), and glass blocks and bricks (see MASONRY).

Glass, Carter (1858–1946) U.S. politician. Born in Lynchburg, Va., he became a journalist and from 1888 owned two newspapers in Lynchburg. In the U.S. House of Representatives (1902–18), he sponsored legislation that established the Federal Reserve System. As secretary of the treasury (1918–20) he supported WOODROW WILSON's fight for the League of Nations. Appointed, then elected, to the U.S. Senate (1920–46), he became a leader of the conservative Southern Democratic bloc. An expert on monetary policy, he cowrote the bill that established the Federal Deposit Insurance Corp. (1933). He initially supported FRANKLIN ROOSEVELT's NEW DEAL but became a severe critic.

glass, decorative See AMELUNG GLASS, BACCARAT GLASS, BOHEMIAN GLASS, CAMEO GLASS, CUT GLASS, LUSTERED GLASS, STAINED GLASS, VENETIAN GLASS, WATERFORD GLASS

Glass, Philip (born 1937) U.S. composer. Born in Chicago, he studied at the Juilliard School and with N. BOULANGER in Paris, but his later studies with RAVI SHANKAR in 1966 and the tabla player Alla Rakha produced a radical shift in his compositional style. He became the leading exponent of musical "minimalism," employing insistently repeated notes and chords, subtly shifting timbres, and blocklike harmonic progressions without contrapuntal voice leading. He achieved fame suddenly with the opera *Einstein on the Beach* (1975), and has since written about 20 more operas, including *Satyagraha* (1980), *Akhnaten* (1984), and *The Voyage* (1992); some 50 film scores, including *Koyaanisqatsi* (1983) and *The Thin Blue Line* (1988); and such other works as *Glassworks* (1981) and *Songs from Liquid Days* (1986). His collaborators have included Robert Wilson, ALLEN GINSBERG, DORIS LESSING, D. BOWIE, and P. SIMON. His work has appealed to fans of rock and popular music, and he is today perhaps the world's most famous living composer.

glass fiber See FIBERGLASS

glaucoma \glau̇-'kō-mə, glȯ-'kō-mə\ Disease caused by increased pressure in the EYE as a result of blockage of the flow of fluid (aqueous humor) at the outer edge of the iris. This pressure is transmitted to the optic nerve head and the RETINA. Chronic glaucoma can be treated with drugs that contract the pupil. Acute glaucoma may be intermittent. Permanent relief requires surgery to provide an outlet for the fluid. Either type causes vision impairment or blindness if untreated.

glaucophane schist facies \'glȯ-kə-ˌfān-'shist-'fā-shēz\ One of the major divisions of the mineral facies classification of metamorphic rocks, encompassing rocks whose peculiar mineralogy suggests that they formed under conditions of high pressure and relatively low temperature (generally less than about 662°F, or 350°C); such conditions are not typical of the normal geothermal gradient in the earth. The minerals that chiefly occur include soda amphibole (glaucophane), soda pyroxene (jadeite), garnet, lawsonite, and pumpellyite. Quartz, muscovite, chlorite, epidote, and plagioclase may also be present. Classic deposits occur in western California.

Glaucus \'glȯ-kəs\ Name of several figures in GREEK MYTHOLOGY. One Glaucus was the young son of King MINOS; he fell into a jar of honey and died, and the court seer restored him to life with a magic herb. Glaucus Pontius was a sea god; originally a fisherman and diver, he ate a magic plant and became divine. Glaucus, son of SISYPHUS and father of BELLEROPHON, fed his horses human flesh and was torn to pieces by them. Another Glaucus was a grandson of Bellerophon, who assisted King Priam in the TROJAN WAR.

Glazunov \'gla-zə-ˌnȯf\, **Alexander (Konstantinovich)** (1865–1936) Russian composer. A compositional prodigy, he achieved success with his Symphony No. 1 at 16. He became a protégé of the art patron Mitrofan Belaev, who took him to Western Europe, where he began to build his international reputation. He became director of the St. Petersburg Conservatory in 1905. Though honored by the government after the revolution, from 1928 he lived largely abroad. His music is generally conservative and Romantic. His works include the ballets *Raymonda* (1897) and *The Seasons* (1899); eight symphonies; concertos for piano (two), violin, and saxophone; and many orchestral tone poems and suites.

Gleason, Jackie *orig.* **Herbert John** (1916–1987) U.S. comedian and actor. Born in Brooklyn, N.Y., he performed in carnivals and nightclubs and later played minor roles in films and on stage. He achieved success in the television comedy series *Cavalcade of Stars* (1950–52), *The Jackie Gleason Show* (1952–59, 1961–70), and *The Honeymooners* (1955–56). He starred on Broadway in *Take Me Along* (1959, Tony award), and appeared on screen as Minnesota Fats in *The Hustler* (1961), and later in *Smokey and the Bandit* (1977) and its sequels (1980, 1983). He is remembered as one of television's most beloved stars.

Glendale City (pop., 1996 est.: 182,000), southern central Arizona. Located in the SALT RIVER valley, west of PHOENIX, it was founded in 1892, and is an agricultural trading center for fruits, vegetables, and cotton. It is one of the fastest growing cities in the U.S. Nearby is the American Graduate School of International Management, which trains employees of U.S. firms for work abroad

Glendale City (pop., 1996 est.: 184,000), southwestern California. Located north of Los Angeles, at the southeastern end of the San Fernando Valley, it was laid out in 1886. It was part of Rancho San Rafael (1784), the first Spanish land grant in California. Aircraft, optical instruments, and pharmaceuticals are among its manufactures. The city's Forest Lawn Memorial Park is known for its elaborate statuary.

Glendower \glen-'dau̇-ər\, **Owen** *Welsh* **Owain Glyndwr** (1354?–1416?) Self-proclaimed prince of Wales who led an unsuccessful rebellion against England. Educated in England, he returned to Wales and touched off an uprising against HENRY IV (under whom he had previously fought) in northern Wales in 1400. He was soon in control of most of Wales and had set up a Welsh Parliament. In 1403 his alliance with English nobles was crushed at Shrewsbury, and a later French alliance also failed; his strongholds at Aberystwyth and Harlech fell to the future HENRY V in 1408–9. Glendower nonetheless remained active as a guerrilla warrior as late as 1412. His rebellions were the last major Welsh attempts to throw off English rule.

Glenn, John H(erschel), Jr. (born 1921) U.S. astronaut and senator. Born in Cambridge, Ohio, he flew 59 missions as a Marine Corps pilot in World War II and 90 during the Korean War. The oldest of the seven astronauts selected in 1959 for the Mercury project's spaceflight training, he was a backup pilot for ALAN B. SHEPARD and Virgil I. Grissom (1926–1967), who made the first two U.S. suborbital flights into space. Glenn was selected for the orbital flight, and in February 1962 his space capsule, Friendship 7, was launched and made three orbits. He retired from the space program in 1964 and pursued his interest in politics, serving as U.S. Senator from Ohio 1975–99. In 1998, at 77, he made his second spaceflight (as part of the crew of the space shuttle *Discovery*), becoming the oldest person to go into space.

Glenrothes \glen-'rä-this\ Town (pop., 1995 est.: 36,000), eastern Scotland. The administrative seat of the FIFE region, it was established in 1948 as the country's second new town, to provide housing for coal miners near the experimental Rothes Colliery. When the coal-mining industry declined, new industries were developed, including the manufacture of electronic components, computers, and plastics.

gley \'glā\ Sticky clay soil or soil layer formed under the surface of some waterlogged soils. Characteristic of poorly drained areas, gley soils contain reduced amounts of iron and other elements and are gray and mottled in color.

glider Nonpowered heavier-than-air craft capable of sustained flight. Early experimenters in glider flight included GEORGE CAYLEY, who built the first man-carrying glider in 1853, and Otto Lilienthal (1848–1896), who introduced tail stabilizers on his first practical man-carrying craft in 1891. Improvements by Octave Chanute (1832–1910) in 1896 and by WILBUR AND ORVILLE WRIGHT in 1902 perfected the control needed for developing the Wrights' powered airplane in 1903. The slender-winged glider was launched by being towed behind an airplane or a car. Gliders were used in World War II to carry troops. Today they are mainly used for recreation; the sailplane type is built for soaring on the lift from thermals. See also HANG GLIDING.

gliding See SOARING

Glinka, Mikhail (Ivanovich) (1804–1857) Russian composer. He studied in Italy and Berlin, and in 1836 his first opera, *A Life for the Czar*, immediately earned him the reputation of Russia's leading composer. Elements of Russian folk music were heard even more clearly in the opera *Ruslan and Ludmila* (1842) and the orchestral work *Kamarinskaya* (1848). The influence of these works on later Russian composers, including PYOTR ILYICH TCHAIKOVSKY and NIKOLAI RIMSKY-KORSAKOV, was significant, and Glinka is regarded as the father of the Russian national school.

Global Positioning System (GPS) Precise, satellite-based navigation and location system developed for U.S. military use but available to the general public with the use of proper equipment. GPS is a fleet of 24 communications satellites that transmit signals globally around the clock. With a GPS receiver one can quickly and accurately determine the latitude, longitude, and in most cases the altitude of a point on or above the earth's surface. A single GPS receiver can find its own position in seconds from GPS satellite signals, to an accuracy of 10 meters; accuracy within one meter can be achieved with sophisticated military-specification receivers. This capability has reduced the cost of acquiring spatial data for making maps while increasing cartographic accuracy. Other applications include measuring the movement of polar ice sheets, or even finding the best auto route between given points.

global warming Potential increase in average global atmospheric temperatures resulting from enhancement of the GREENHOUSE EFFECT by AIR POLLUTION. Many scientists predict that this increase will significantly alter climate patterns, increasing global average temperatures by as much as 9°F (5°C) by the middle of the 21st century. Such global warming would cause the polar ice caps and mountain glaciers to melt rapidly, significantly raising the levels of coastal waters, and would produce new patterns and extremes of drought and rainfall, seriously disrupting food production in certain regions. Other scientists maintain that such predictions are overstated. The 1992 EARTH SUMMIT and the 1997 conference of the UN Framework Convention on Climate Change attempted to address the issue of global warming, but in both cases the cause was hindered by conflicting national economic agendas and disputes between rich and poor nations over the cost and consequences of reducing emissions of greenhouse gases.

globalization Process by which the experience of everyday life, marked by the diffusion of commodities and ideas, is becoming standardized around the world. Factors that have contributed to globalization include increasingly sophisticated communications and transportation technologies and services, mass migration and the movement of peoples, a level of economic activity that has outgrown national markets through industrial combinations and commercial groupings that cross national frontiers, and international agreements that reduce the cost of doing business in foreign countries. Globalization offers huge potential profits to companies and nations but has been complicated by widely differing expectations, standards of living, cultures and values, and legal systems as well as unexpected global cause-and-effect linkages. See also FREE TRADE.

Globe and Mail, The Daily newspaper published in Toronto, the most prestigious and influential journal in Canada. It was formed in 1936 when George McCullagh bought and merged two competing papers, the liberal *Globe* (founded 1844) and the conservative *Mail and Empire* (founded 1872 as *The Mail*). The paper sees its role as "independent but not neutral." Its publication of the texts of speeches, parliamentary debates, and other documents has made it Canada's newspaper of record. It is especially strong in international news coverage.

Globe Theatre London theater in which the plays of WILLIAM SHAKESPEARE were performed after 1599. It was built by two brothers, Cuthbert and RICHARD BURBAGE; half the shares were kept by the Burbages, and the rest were assigned equally to Shakespeare and other members of the CHAMBERLAIN'S MEN. The wooden theater, built in the shape of an O with no roof over the central area, was destroyed by fire in 1613, rebuilt in 1614, and finally pulled down in 1644. Reconstructed near its original site, it inaugurated its first regular season in 1996.

globular cluster Any large group of Population II (see POPULATIONS I AND II) stars closely packed in a symmetrical, somewhat spherical form. About 100 have been identified in the MILKY WAY GALAXY. Globular clusters contain many more stars (10,000–1 million) than OPEN CLUSTERS do and can be several hundred light-years in diameter. Because they are so distant from the solar system, most are not visible to the unaided eye. OMEGA CENTAURI and a few others can be seen without a telescope as hazy patches of light.

globulin \'gläb-yə-lən\ Any of a major class of PROTEINS insoluble in pure water and soluble in dilute saline (salt) SOLUTIONS. In their natural state, the protein chain is folded into a globular form. Globulins are found in many plants, especially cereals. Globulins in animal fluids include ENZYMES, ANTIBODIES (the GAMMA GLOBULINS), LIPOPROTEINS, COMPLEMENT components, TRANSPORT proteins, and various types of fibrous and contractile proteins.

glockenspiel \'glä-kən-ˌspēl, 'glä-kən-ˌshpēl\ Percussion instrument consisting of a set of tuned steel bars, arranged like a piano keyboard, which are struck with hammers. An alternative form of the instrument is played by means of an actual keyboard. Its normal range is 2½ octaves. The bell lyre, held vertically, is the portable form of glockenspiel used in marching bands.

Glorious Revolution *or* **Bloodless Revolution** *or* **Revolution of 1688** In English history, the events of 1688–89 that resulted in the deposition of JAMES II and the accession of his daughter MARY II and her husband WILLIAM III. James's overt Roman Catholicism, his suspension of the legal rights of dissenters, and the prospect of a Catholic heir to the throne brought discontent to a head, and seven eminent Englishmen invited the Protestant William of Orange to bring an army to redress the nation's grievances. James's supporters turned against him and he fled to France. The Convention Parliament asked William and Mary to rule jointly and set out the BILL OF RIGHTS.

glossolalia See gift of TONGUES

Gloucester \'gläs-tər\ *ancient* **Glevum.** City (pop., 1995 est.: 107,000), southwestern England. The seat of GLOUCESTERSHIRE, it lies on the River SEVERN, and is linked by ship canal to docks in the Severn estuary. It was founded as the Roman colony of Glevum in AD 96–98. An abbey was founded there in 681; the town later became the capital of the Anglo-Saxon kingdom of MERCIA. Important economically even before the NORMAN CONQUEST (1066), it was incorporated in 1483 and continued to flourish as a trading center. It has varied industries, including the manufacture of railway rolling stock and aircraft, and light and heavy engineering works.

Gloucestershire \'gläs-tər-ˌshir\ County (pop., 1995 est.: 553,000), western England. It is located at the head of the SEVERN RIVER estuary on the Welsh border; GLOUCESTER is the county seat. The Severn bisects the county from north to south. Prehistoric peoples were active in the area; later, the Romans had military camps within the county, and Gloucester was a Roman town of note. After the departure of the Romans, the Saxons occupied the area. Throughout the Middle Ages Gloucestershire was a battlefield, reflected in the imposing Norman defensive castles built on the Welsh frontier. While the county's Cotswold area is important economically, most of its eastern half is scenic, and a large area is set aside as the Dean National Forest Park.

glove Covering for the hand with separate sections for the fingers and the thumb, usually extending over the wrist or part of the arm. Linen gloves were found in the tomb of TUTANKHAMEN in Egypt. Medieval European nobles wore both fabric and leather gloves, often jeweled and embroidered. In the 16th century, Catherine de Médicis, queen consort of HENRY II of France, made gloves for women fashionable. Glovemaking became an industry in 1834 when the glove-cutting die was invented in France. Fabric gloves of antiquity were made of woven material, but modern fabric gloves are knitted of cotton, wool, or synthetic fibers. See photograph opposite.

glowworm Any crawling, luminous insect that emits light either continuously or in prolonged glows rather than in the brief flashes characteristic of most FIREFLIES. Glowworms include larvae and adult (often wingless) females of fireflies and certain other BEETLE species and larvae of certain GNAT species. They are widely distributed. The great diversity in the size, number, location, and structure of the bioluminescent organs suggests that the light-producing ability of the various species evolved independently.

gloxinia \gläk-'si-nē-ə\ Any of the 20 plant species that make up the genus *Sinningia,* in the GESNERIAD family, native to Brazil, especially *S. speciosa,* an ornamental pot plant. Gloxinias produce large, erect bell-shaped flowers in rich, velvety colors, usually violet or purple. The genus *Gloxinia* of the same family contains six species that are not cultivated.

Gluck \'glu̇k\, **Christoph Willibald** *later* **Ritter (Knight) von Gluck** (1714–1787) German opera composer. Son of a forester, he ran away to study music in Prague. He traveled widely, writing operas for various cities, before settling in Vienna in 1750, where he would remain—except for an interlude in Paris (1773–79)—the rest of his life. In 1762, with the librettist Ranieri di Calzabigi (1714–1795), he wrote his famous opera *Orfeo ed Euridice,* in which he borrowed aspects of French opera to achieve a simplified dramatic style that decisively broke with the static and calcified Italian style. His preface to *Alceste* (1767) laid out the musico-dramatic principles of his "reform opera." He became court composer to the emperor. In 1773 he moved to Paris, where his former pupil MARIE-ANTOINETTE was on the verge of becoming queen. There he won acclaim for *Iphigénie en Aulide* (1774), *Armide* (1777), and *Iphigénie en Tauride* (1779). His other operas (of more than 40 in all) include *Paride ed Elena* (1770) and *Echo et Narcisse* (1779). He wrote five ballets, of which *Don Juan* (1761) was one of the first successful *ballets d'action.*

glucose *or* **dextrose** *or* **grape sugar** *or* **corn sugar** Organic compound, a simple SUGAR (MONOSACCHARIDE), chemical formula $C_6H_{12}O_6$. The product of PHOTOSYNTHESIS in plants, it is found in fruits and honey. As the major circulating free sugar in blood, it is the source of energy in cell function and a major participant in METABOLISM. Control of its level and metabolism is of great importance (see INSULIN). Glucose and FRUCTOSE make up SUCROSE. Glucose units in long chains make up POLYSACCHARIDES (e.g., CELLULOSE, GLYCOGEN, STARCH). Glucose is used in foods, medicine, brewing, and wine making and as the source of various other organic chemicals.

English kid glove, embroidered in silk and metal thread, c. 1600; in the Metropolitan Museum of Art, New York City.

BY COURTESY OF THE METROPOLITAN MUSEUM OF ART, NEW YORK CITY, PURCHASE, ROGERS FUND, 1953

glucose tolerance test Test of ability to metabolize GLUCOSE, the main blood sugar. It helps diagnose DIABETES MELLITUS, HYPOGLYCEMIA, and other impairments of glucose metabolism. After an initial blood sample, the subject drinks a solution high in glucose. Blood and urine samples are taken a half hour, one hour, two hours, and three hours later. Normally, blood glucose peaks within an hour and returns to its normal range within two and a half hours.

glue Adhesive substance resembling GELATIN, extracted from animal tissue, particularly hides and bones, or from fish, casein (milk PROTEIN), or vegetables. Glue was used as early as 3000 BC in wooden-furniture construction in Egypt. Synthetic RESIN adhesives such as the EPOXIES are replacing glue for many uses, but glue is still widely used as an adhesive in woodworking and in certain manufacturing and other industrial processes.

glue-laminated timber *or* **glulam** Structural lumber product made by bonding together thin layers of wood with the grain of all boards parallel, used for beams, columns, arches, and decking. Glulam has several advantages over solid-wood components: Large members of various sizes and shapes impossible to make from solid wood can be fabricated, the individual boards may be properly dried, and defects such as knots may be removed. Glulam arches, which undergo bending and gluing during manufacture, are often used in long-span structures such as sports arenas.

Glueck \'glůk\, **Sheldon and Eleanor** *orig.* **Eleanor Touroff** (1896–1980, 1898–1972) U.S. criminologists. Sheldon came to the U.S. from Poland as a child. He and Eleanor (born in Cambridge, Mass.) were married in 1922. As researchers at Harvard Law School, they studied the careers of criminals and juvenile delinquents and are especially known for the Gluecks' Social Prediction Tables, which attempted to identify potential delinquents at the age of 6 or even younger.

glutamic acid \glü-'ta-mik\ One of the nonessential amino acids, closely related to glutamine. The two constitute a substantial fraction of the amino acids in many proteins (10–20% in many cases and up to 45% in some plant proteins). An important metabolic intermediate as well as a neurotransmitter molecule in the central nervous system, glutamic acid finds uses in medicine and biochemical research. Its sodium salt is monosodium glutamate (MSG).

glutamine \'glü-tə-ˌmēn\ One of the nonessential amino acids, closely related to glutamic acid. It is especially important in the cellular metabolism of animals as the only amino acid capable of readily crossing the blood-brain barrier. It is used in medicine and biochemical research and as a feed additive.

gluten Mixture of proteins not readily soluble in water that occurs in wheat and most other cereal grains. Its presence in flour makes production of leavened baked goods (see baking) possible because the chainlike gluten molecules form an elastic network that traps carbon dioxide gas and expands with it. The properties of gluten vary with its composition, which differs according to the source. Thus, doughs range from soft and extensible to tough and elastic, depending on the gluten in the flours. Persons with an allergy to gluten can often eat rice or spelt products.

glycerol \'gli-sə-ˌrȯl\ *or* **glycerin** Clear, colorless, viscous, sweet-tasting liquid organic compound of the alcohol family, chemical formula $HOCH_2CHOHCH_2OH$. With three hydroxyl (—OH) groups, it can form three types of esters (monoglycerides, diglycerides, and triglycerides). Mono- and diglycerides are common food additives. Fats and oils are triglycerides; their processing into soap was the chief source of glycerol until the mid-20th century, when industrial synthesis took over. Glycerol has thousands of uses, including as an emulsifier, softening agent, plasticizer, and stabilizer in baked goods, ice cream, and tobacco; in skin lotions, mouthwashes, and cough medicines; as a protective medium for freezing red blood cells, sperm, corneas, and other tissues; in printing inks and in the gums and resins in paints and coatings; in antifreeze mixtures; as a nutrient in fermentation, and as a raw material for nitroglycerin.

glyceryl trinitrate See nitroglycerin

glycine \'glī-ˌsēn\ One of the nonessential amino acids. The simplest amino acid (NH_2CH_2COOH), it occurs in many proteins, especially silk fibroin and gelatin. It has a sweet taste and is used to reduce the bitter flavor of saccharin. Other uses are in organic synthesis and biochemical research, as a nutrient and feed additive, and to retard rancidity in animal and vegetable fats.

glycogen \'glī-kə-jən\ Principal storage carbohydrate of animals, occurring primarily in the liver and resting muscles. It is also found in various bacteria, fungi, and yeasts. Glycogen is a branched polysaccharide, a long chain of glucose units, into which it is broken down when energy is needed.

glycogen storage disease *or* **glycogenosis** \ˌglī-kə-jə-'nō-səs\ Any of numerous types of hereditary enzyme deficiency resulting in altered metabolism of glycogen. The problems are classified in two groups, those affecting the liver and those involving striated muscle, both primary glycogen storage sites. Symptoms in the liver group range from symptomatic hypoglycemia with ketosis to asymptomatic liver enlargement (hepatomegaly). In the muscle group, they range from weakness and cramps to fatal heart enlargement.

glycol \'glī-ˌkȯl\ Any of a class of organic compounds of the alcohol family in which two hydroxyl groups (—OH; see functional group) are attached to different carbon atoms. The term is often used for the simplest of the class, ethylene glycol (1,2-ethanediol). Propylene glycol (1,2-propanediol), much like ethylene glycol but not toxic, is used extensively in foods, cosmetics, and oral hygiene products as a solvent, preservative, and moisture-retaining agent. Other important glycols include 1,3-butanediol and 1,4-butanediol, used as raw materials for plastics and other chemicals; 2-ethyl-1,3-hexanediol, an insect repellent; and 2-methyl-2-propyl-1,3-propanediol, the raw material of the tranquilizer meprobamate.

glycolysis \glī-'kä-lə-səs\ *or* **glycolytic pathway** *or* **Embden-Meyerhof-Parnas pathway** \'em-dən-'mī-ər-ˌhōf-'pär-nəs\ Sequence of 10 chemical reactions taking place in most cells that breaks down glucose, releasing energy that is then captured and stored in ATP. One molecule of glucose (plus coenzymes and inorganic phosphate) makes two molecules of pyruvate (or pyruvic acid) and two molecules of ATP. The pyruvate enters into the tricarboxylic acid cycle if enough oxygen is present or is fermented into lactic acid or ethanol if not. Thus, glycolysis produces both ATP for cellular energy requirements and building blocks for synthesis of other cellular products. See also Gustav Georg Embden, Otto Meyerhof.

glycoside \'glī-kə-ˌsīd\ Any of a wide variety of naturally occurring organic compounds in which a carbohydrate portion consisting of one or more sugars or sugar derivatives is combined with a hydroxy compound (a compound containing an —OH group). Since sugars themselves are hydroxy compounds, polysaccharides are glycosides by definition. Other glycosides include various flower and fruit pigments, several antibiotics (e.g., streptomycin), and the cardiac glycosides (see digitalis).

GM See General Motors Corp.

Gnadenhütten Massacre \jə-'nā-dən-ˌhə-tən\ (March 8, 1782) Murder of 96 Indians, mostly Delawares, by American troops at an Ohio village during the American Revolution. The Indians, converted peaceful Christians, were under suspicion because of their neutrality in the war. An American officer, David Williamson, and his militia, seeking revenge for Indian raids on frontier settlements, pretended friendship with the Indians, then disarmed them and returned to kill them in cold blood; two scalped boys escaped to relate the slayings.

Gnam-ri strong-btsan \'näm-'rē-'strȯŋ-bət-'sän\ (c. 570–619?) Descendant of a line of rulers of Yarlong, united tribes in central and southern Tibet that became known to China's Sui dynasty (581–618). After his assassination, he was succeeded by his son, who continued his father's military expansion, establishing his capital at Lhasa. The son became so powerful that the Tang dynasty (618–907) entered into a marriage alliance with him in 641.

gnat Any member of several species of small dipterans, most of which bite or annoy humans. Midges are also sometimes called gnats. In North America the name is also applied to the blackfly, fruit fly, and other small flies that hover about the eyes of humans and other animals.

Blue-gray gnatcatcher (*Polioptila caerulea*).
KARL H. MASLOWSKI

gnatcatcher Any of about 11 species of small songbirds (genus *Polioptila*) often treated as a subfamily of the Old World warbler family Sylviidae. The blue-gray gnatcatcher, 4.5 in. (11 cm) long, with its long white-edged tail, looks like a tiny mockingbird. It breeds locally from eastern Canada and California to the Bahamas and Guatemala and winters from the southern U.S. southward. The black-tailed gnatcatcher lives in the deserts of the southwestern U.S.; the other species are found in Central and South America and Cuba.

Gneisenau \'gnī-zə-ˌnau̇\, **August (Wilhelm Anton), Graf (Count) Neidhardt von** (1760–

1831) Prussian field marshal and military reformer. Along with GERHARD J. D. VON SCHARNHORST, he remolded the Prussian army shattered by NAPOLEON (1806) from a mercenary force into an instrument of modern warfare, introducing universal military service. In 1811–12 he traveled on secret missions to negotiate a new war against Napoleon. The war of liberation renewed in 1813, and as chief of staff to GEBHARD VON BLUCHER he planned Prussian, and sometimes Russian, strategy. Gneisenau's insistence on the decisive battle and relentless pursuit proved successful at the Battle of WATERLOO.

gneiss \'nīs\ Medium- to coarse-grained metamorphic rock with parallel, somewhat irregular banding that has little tendency to split along planes. Gneiss is the principal rock over extensive metamorphic terrains. Orthogneiss is formed by the metamorphism of igneous rocks; paragneiss results from the metamorphism of original sedimentary rocks. Pencil gneiss contains rod-shaped individual minerals or segregations of minerals, and augen gneiss contains large lenticular mineral grains or mineral aggregates having the appearance of eyes scattered through the rock.

Gnosticism \'näs-tə-ˌsi-zəm\ Religious and philosophical movement popular in the Roman world in the 2nd–3rd century AD. The term, based on the Greek *gnosis* ("knowledge"), was not coined until the 17th century, when it was applied liberally to ancient Christian heretical sects, especially those described by their orthodox contemporaries as radically dualistic and world-denying, and who sought salvation through esoteric revelation and mystical spirituality. Late-19th- and early-20th-century research replaced that view of Gnosticism with several groupings. Lesser-known varieties of ancient Christianity are represented in the *Gospel of Thomas* and the *Gospel of Mary* (which portrays MARY MAGDALENE as a leading apostle). They emphasized the teachings of JESUS, rather than his death and resurrection, as the key to salvation. The Valentian Gnostics were another group. Other texts previously considered Gnostic are now assigned to distinct religious traditions, especially Hermeticism (see HERMETIC WRITINGS), MANDAEANISM, and MANICHAEISM. The texts of the Sethians have the best claim to the designation "Gnostic"; they describe one supreme, good God and the creation, by a junior heavenly being (Sophia), of an arrogant creature who then claims to be God. That creature withholds from humanity moral knowledge and eternal life, but Sophia plants the divine spirit within people to save them. Male and female saviors (including Jesus) were sent from the world above to instruct humanity in the knowledge of the true God and humanity's own divine nature.

gnu \'nü\ *or* **wildebeest** Either of two species of African ANTELOPE (genus *Connochaetes*). The gnu stands higher at the shoulder than at the rump, reaching a shoulder height of 3–4 ft (1–1.3 m). The southern African form, the white-tailed gnu, or black wildebeest, is dark brown with long black tufts on the snout, chin, throat, and chest, and a black mane and flowing white tail. Today it exists only in national parks and preserves. The brindled gnu, or blue wildebeest, is reasonably abundant over much of central and South Africa. It is silvery gray with dark vertical bands on the sides and has a black mane, tail, and face, whitish cheeks, and a tuft of dark hair on chin and throat. Both sexes of both species have horns. Gnu live in often large, constantly moving herds and graze on the grasses and scrub of open plains.

White-bearded gnu (*Connochaetes taurinus albojubatus*).
LEONARD LEE RUE III

Go Japanese game played between two players who alternately place black and white stones on a board checkered by 19 vertical lines and 19 horizontal lines. The players attempt to conquer territory by surrounding vacant areas or capture stones by surrounding them. Points are awarded by conquering and capturing, and reduced by losing one's stones. Go originated in either India or China as early as 2356 BC and was brought to Japan c. AD 500.

Go-Daigo \'gō-dī-'gō\ (1288–1339) Emperor of Japan whose efforts to overthrow the KAMAKURA SHOGUNATE resulted in a split in the imperial family. When Go-Daigo came to the throne in 1318, political authority was divided between the de jure government of the emperor and the de facto government of the SHOGUN in Kamakura, though neither emperor nor shogun had real power, their positions being controlled by powerful families. Go-Daigo sought to hold the reins of government himself; but he alienated Ashikaga Takauji (see ASHIKAGA FAMILY), whose support had been crucial to his victory, by neglecting to appoint him to the position of shogun. Takauji rebelled and, victorious, elevated another member of the imperial family to the throne. Go-Daigo fled south to the Yoshino Mountains and established court there. The period of Northern and Southern Courts *(nanboku cho)* that followed lasted until 1392. See also HOJO FAMILY, INSEI.

Goa \'gō-ə\ State (pop., 1991: 1,169,700), India. Located on the western coast, it is bordered by MAHARASHTRA and KARNATAKA states and has a 62-mi (100-km) coastline on the Arabian Sea. It has an area of 1,429 sq mi (3,702 sq km), which includes the offshore island of Goa. The capital is PANAJI. Ruled by Hindu dynasties until 1472, it came under the Portuguese in 1510. Their settlement of Old Goa became the capital of Portuguese India. After attaining independence in 1947, India demanded that Portugal cede Goa. Indian troops finally occupied Goa in 1961; it was incorporated into India in 1962, as part of the territory of Goa, Daman, and Diu. It became a state in 1987. It is predominantly agricultural; its distinctive architecture and fine beaches make it a popular tourist resort.

goat Any hollow-horned RUMINANT in the BOVID genus *Capra.* Goats have a lighter build and straighter hair than SHEEP; their horns arch backward; and the tail is short. Males usually have a beard. Wild goats include the IBEX and markhor. Domesticated goats are descended from the pasang, which is probably native to Asia. In China, Great Britain, Europe, and North America, the domestic goat is primarily a MILK producer; much of the milk is used to make cheese. Some breeds, notably the ANGORA and cashmere, are raised for their WOOL; young goats are the source of kid leather.

goatsucker See NIGHTJAR

Gobelin family \gȯ-'bla^{n}\ French dyers and clothmakers. In the late 15th century, the brothers Jean (died 1476) and Philibert Gobelin discovered a scarlet dye and opened a dyeing factory near Paris, which flourished until the late 16th century. In 1601 HENRY IV brought in Flemish weavers and they began to produce tapestries. In 1662 LOUIS XIV reorganized the factory and appointed CHARLES LE BRUN director; it produced tapestry and upholstery furnishings for the royal palaces until 1694. By the 18th century only tapestries were manufactured, under the inspection of J.-B. OUDRY and FRANCOIS BOUCHER. The factory was closed during the French Revolution but reopened by Napoleon. Since 1826 it has manufactured carpets and tapestries.

Gobi Desert \'gō-bē\ Desert, central Asia. One of the great desert and semidesert regions of the world, the Gobi stretches across Central Asia over large areas of Mongolia and China. It occupies an arc of land 1,000 mi (1,609 km) long and 300–600 mi (500–1,000 km) wide, with an estimated area of 500,000 sq mi (1,300,000 sq km). Contrary to the image often associated with a desert, much of the Gobi is not sand but bare rock.

Gobind Singh \gō-'bin-də-'siŋ-gə, 'gō-ˌbind-'siŋ\ *orig.* **Gobind Rai** (1666–1708) Sikh GURU. Son of the Guru Tegh Bahadur (1664–1675), he was trained in the martial arts in the Punjab. When he was 9 his father was executed, and he became the 10th and last Guru of SIKHISM, presiding over the Sikh court at Anandpur. A scholar and poet, he is credited with putting the ADI GRANTH into its final form. His other great achievement was the founding (1699) of the Khalsa, the egalitarian community that gave Sikhism its political and religious definition and galvanized its martial energies. He was continually at war with local Hindu chiefs and the Mughal authorities, who together forced the Sikhs out of Anandpur in 1704 and killed his four sons. After the death of AURANGZEB, he supported the claim of the future emperor, Bahadur Shah (1643–1712), to the throne. He was assassinated before he could persuade Bahadur Shah to allow the Sikhs' return to Anandpur.

Gobineau \gȯ-bē-'nō\, **Joseph-Arthur, comte (Count) de** (1816–1882) French diplomat and writer. While serving in the diplomatic service (1849–77), he wrote the *Essay on the Inequality of Human Races* (1853–55), which asserted the superiority of the white race over others and labeled the "Aryans," or Germanic peoples, as the summit of civilization. He claimed that white societies flourished as long as they remained free of black and yellow strains and that dilution would lead to corruption. The *Essay* influenced such figures as ROBERT F WAGNER, HOUSTON STEWART CHAMBERLAIN, and ADOLF HITLER.

goby Any of more than 800 species of carnivorous fishes (suborder Gobioidei, order Perciformes), found worldwide but especially abundant in the tropics. Most species are small bottom-dwellers with a weak suction cup formed by the fusion of their pelvic fins. About 700 species are typically elongated, sometimes scaleless, fishes found along shores and among reefs in tropical and temperate seas. They have two dorsal fins and a rounded tail, lack a lateral line (sensory organ along the side of the body), and are often brightly colored. Most adults are no longer than 4 in. (10 cm).

God Deity or Supreme Being. Each of the major monotheistic world religions worships a Supreme Being, who is the sole god of the universe, the maker of all things, omniscient and all-powerful. God is also good. In ancient Israel God was named Yahweh. The God of the Hebrew Bible also became the God of Christianity, but generic words, such as *theos* in Greek or *Deus* in Latin, were often used to refer to him. In Islam the term is ALLAH. See also MONOTHEISM.

god and goddess Generic terms for the many deities of ancient and modern polytheistic religions. There may be deities of earthly and celestial phenomena as well as deities related to human values, pastimes, and institutions, including love, marriage, hunting, war, and the arts. They may be capable of being killed but are often immortal and always more powerful than humans, though they are often described in human terms, with all the flaws, thoughts, and emotions of humans. See also POLYTHEISM.

Godard \gȯ-ˈdär\, **Jean-Luc** (born 1930) French film director. He wrote film criticism for the influential journal *Cahiers du cinéma* before astonishing audiences with his first feature film, the improvisatory and original *Breathless* (1960), which established him as the apostle of the NEW WAVE. He continued to explore new techniques in such films as *My Life to Live* (1962), *Pierrot le fou* (1965), *Alphaville* (1965), and *Weekend* (1968), using the camera creatively to express political commentary. He returned to themes of more universal concern with *Every Man for Himself* (1979) and *Passion* (1982), but shocked audiences and the Vatican with his updated Nativity story in *Hail Mary!* (1985).

Godavari River \gō-ˈdä-və-rē\ River, central India. It rises in the Western GHATS and flows east across the DECCAN Plateau, along the Maharashtra–Andhra Pradesh border. It crosses ANDHRA PRADESH state, and turns southeast for its last 200 mi (320 km) before reaching the Bay of BENGAL. Its total length is about 910 mi (1,465 km). The development of an irrigation-canal system, linking its delta with that of the KRISHNA RIVER to the southwest, has made the land one of the richest rice-growing areas of India. The Godavari, throughout its entire length, is sacred to the Hindus.

Goddard, Robert Hutchings (1882–1945) U.S. inventor, regarded as the father of modern rocketry. Born in Worcester, Mass., he received his doctorate from Clark Univ., where he later taught for most of his career. His experiments with ROCKETS began in 1908, when he proved that thrust and consequent propulsion can take place in a vacuum. He was the first to develop a rocket motor using liquid fuels (tested in 1926) and the first to explore mathematically ratios of energy and thrust per weight of liquid oxygen and liquid hydrogen. In 1935 he first shot a liquid-fueled rocket faster than the speed of sound. He patented the first practical automatic steering apparatus for rockets, developed step rockets designed to gain great altitudes, and developed the first rocket-fuel pumps, self-cooling rocket motors, and other components of an engine designed for space exploration. Much of his work anticipated that of WERNHER VON BRAUN in Germany, but was ignored by the U.S. government until after his death at the end of World War II.

Goddard family New England cabinetmakers. Of English ancestry, the Goddards intermarried with the TOWNSEND FAMILY, equally famous cabinetmakers. John Goddard (1723–1785), the son of a carpenter, moved in the 1720s from Massachusetts to Newport, R.I., where he and his brother worked for Job Townsend. By the 1760s Goddard had established his own workshop and become Newport's leading cabinetmaker, producing simple adaptations in the QUEEN ANNE STYLE. He originated the blockfront, a distinctive front for desks, secretaries, and cabinets, decorated with his characteristic carved shell ornaments; pieces were made of mahogany from the West Indies and South America. Some 20 Goddard and Townsend craftsmen of four generations are known. Goddard-Townsend furniture was among the finest made in North America in the 18th century.

Godden, Rumer *orig.* **Margaret Rumer Godden Haynes-Dixon** (1907–1998) British writer. She grew up in India, and after attending school in Britain she returned to spend many years there. *Black Narcissus* (1939; film, 1947) tells of a group of English nuns in the Himalayas and deals with her recurring themes of cultural conflicts and obsessive love. She often wrote about children, as in *The River* (1946; filmed by JEAN RENOIR in 1951) and *The Greengage Summer* (1958; film, 1961), and wrote almost two dozen books for children.

Gödel \ˈgœ-dəl, *Engl* ˈgə(r)-dəl\, **Kurt** (1906–1978) Austrian-U.S. mathematician and logician. He began his career on the faculty of the University of Vienna, where he produced his groundbreaking proof (see GÖDEL'S THEOREM) in the early 1930s. He emigrated to the U.S. in 1940 and taught at the Institute for Advanced Study at Princeton. There, his close friendship with ALBERT EINSTEIN led him into the field of general relativity theory, and to solutions of some of Einstein's equations. A quiet and unassuming man, Gödel did not at first recognize the importance of his famous theorem, and later in life declined many of the honors that it brought him.

Gödel's theorem Principle of the foundations of MATHEMATICS. One of the most important discoveries of 20th-century mathematics, it states the impossibility of defining a complete system of AXIOMS that is also consistent (does not give rise to contradictions). Any formal system (e.g., a computer program or a set of mathematical rules and axioms) powerful enough to generate meaningful statements can generate statements that are true but that cannot be proven or derived within the system. As a consequence, mathematics cannot be placed on an entirely rigorous basis. Named for KURT GODEL, who published his proof in 1931, it immediately had consequences for philosophy (particularly logic) and other areas. Its ramifications continue to be debated.

Godey's Lady's Book \ˈgō-dēz\ Monthly magazine for women, one of the most successful and influential periodicals in 19th-century America. Founded in 1830 in Philadelphia by Louis Antoine Godey, it became an important arbiter of fashion and etiquette. It also published works by such writers as RALPH WALDO EMERSON, HENRY W. LONGFELLOW, and NATHANIEL HAWTHORNE. Edited by Godey until 1836, the magazine was then edited by SARA JOSEPHA HALE until 1877. It ceased publication in 1898.

Godfrey, Arthur (Morton) (1903–1983) U.S. radio and television entertainer. Born in New York City, his relaxed manner and affable banter as a radio host won him such a wide following that he had two daily shows and a weekly show on CBS in the 1940s. His variety show, transferred to television as *Arthur Godfrey's Talent Scouts,* and later *The Arthur Godfrey Show* (1948–60), launched the careers of numerous popular entertainers.

Godfrey of Bouillon \bü-ˈyōⁿ\ (c. 1060–1100) Duke of Lower Lorraine (1089–1100) and a leader of the First CRUSADE, who became the first Latin ruler in Palestine (1099). He joined the crusade in 1096 and captured Jerusalem from the Muslims in 1099; refusing the title of king, he was instead called Defender of the Holy Sepulchre. He made truces with nearby Muslim cities and fought off an Egyptian attack, but he alienated other crusaders and left the kingdom weakened.

Godfrey of Saint-Victor (1125?–1194) French monk, philosopher, theologian, and poet. Around 1160 Godfrey entered the monastery of Saint-Victor in Paris. He left after 20 years for a rural priory, where he wrote his principal work, *Microcosmus*, an attempt to systematize history and knowledge into a rational structure. Recalling classical philosophy and that of the early Church Fathers, it asserts that mankind is a microcosm containing the material and spiritual elements of reality. In his other notable work, *Fons philosophiae* (c. 1176; "The Fount of Philosophy"), he proposed a classification of learning. His writings are considered prime examples of 12th-century humanism.

godi \ˈgō-dē\ In pre-Christian Scandinavia, a priest-chieftain. Worship of the Norse gods was organized around them, and in Iceland, where there was no king, they became the ruling class. They dominated the Icelandic assembly, made laws, and appointed judges. When Iceland was converted to Christianity c. 1000, they controlled the organization of the new religion. Many of them built churches, and some were ordained priests.

Godiva \gə-'dī-və\, **Lady** (fl. c. 1040–1080) Anglo-Saxon gentlewoman famous for her legendary ride while nude through Coventry, England. She was the wife of Leofric, earl of Mercia (died 1057), with whom she founded a monastery at Coventry. There is no evidence connecting the rider with the historical Godiva. According to the legend, Leofric, exasperated over Godiva's ceaseless imploring that he reduce Coventry's heavy taxes, declared he would do so if she rode naked through the crowded marketplace. She did so, her long hair covering all of her body except her legs; as a result Leofric removed all tolls except those on horses. A later chronicle asserts that Godiva required the townsmen to remain indoors at the time fixed for her ride. Peeping Tom, a citizen who looked out his window, became part of the legend in the 17th century, and in most accounts he was struck blind or dead.

Godoy \gō-'dȯi\, **Manuel de** (1767–1851) Spanish politician. He entered the royal bodyguard in 1784 and soon became the lover of Maria Luisa, wife of the future CHARLES IV. On Charles's accession (1788) Godoy continued as a royal favorite and was made duke de Alcudia and prime minister (1792–98, 1801–8). In 1795 Godoy negotiated a favorable peace after Spain's defeat by France and was awarded the title Prince of the Peace. He allied Spain with France against England, which brought a Spanish naval defeat at Cape St. Vincent (1797) and the disastrous defeat at the Battle of TRAFALGAR. In 1808, when it was learned that NAPOLEON planned to seize parts of Spain in the PENINSULAR WARS, the Spanish court tried to flee. Charles was forced to abdicate, and Godoy accompanied him into exile.

Godthåb See NUUK

Godunov \'gō-dᵊn-,ȯf\, **Boris (Fyodorovich)** (1551?–1605) Czar of Russia (1598–1605). After serving in the court of IVAN IV, he was named guardian to Ivan's dim-witted son FYODOR I and became the virtual ruler of Russia as Fyodor's chief adviser from 1584. When Fyodor's little brother Dmitry died mysteriously in 1591, Godunov was suspected of having had him put to death. When Fyodor died without heirs in 1598, an assembly of clergy and gentry elected Godunov czar. A capable ruler, he instituted many reforms, but continuing BOYAR opposition and a general famine (1601–3) eroded his popularity. The False DMITRY led an army into Russia, and on Boris's sudden death resistance broke down and the country lapsed into the Time of TROUBLES.

Godwin, William (1756–1836) British writer. He became a Presbyterian minister, but soon lost his faith. His *Enquiry Concerning Political Justice* (1793) captivated SAMUEL TAYLOR COLERIDGE, WILLIAM WORDSWORTH, ROBERT SOUTHEY, and PERCY B. SHELLEY (who was to become his son-in-law), condemning the institution of marriage, among other things. *The Adventures of Caleb Williams* (1794) was his masterpiece. He married MARY WOLLSTONECRAFT in 1797, but she died soon after the birth of their daughter, MARY SHELLEY, conceived before their marriage.

Goebbels \'gœ-bəls, *Engl* 'gə(r)-bəlz\, **(Paul) Joseph** (1897–1945) German Nazi leader. After earning a doctorate from Heidelberg Univ., he joined the NAZI PARTY and was appointed district leader in Berlin by ADOLF HITLER in 1926. A gifted speaker, Goebbels also edited the party's journal and began to create the Führer myth around Hitler, instituting the party demonstrations that helped convert the masses to Nazism. After Hitler seized power in 1933, Goebbels took control of the national propaganda machinery. During World War II he carried on a personal propaganda blitz to raise hopes on the home front. Named chancellor in Hitler's will, he remained with Hitler to the end. One day after Hitler's death, Goebbels and his wife killed themselves and their six children.

Goebbels, c. 1935.
INTERFOTO-FRIEDRICH RAUCH, MUNICH

Goerdeler \'gœr-də-lər\, **Karl Friedrich** (1884–1945) German politician. He served as second mayor of Königsberg 1920–30, and mayor of Leipzig 1930–37. A member of the rightist GERMAN NATIONAL PEOPLE'S PARTY, he had to resign as mayor of Leipzig when his relations with the NAZI PARTY deteriorated. He collaborated with conservative generals led by LUDWIG BECK against Hitler, after whose overthrow Goerdeler was to become chancellor. When the JULY PLOT failed in 1944, he went into hiding, but was soon arrested by the Gestapo in Poland and hanged.

Goering, Hermann See Hermann GÖRING

Goes \'güs\, **Hugo van der** (c. 1440–1482) Flemish painter. Nothing is known of his life before 1467, when he became a master in the painters' guild in Ghent. He received numerous commissions from the town of Ghent (processional banners, heraldic shields, etc.) through 1475. He was elected dean of the guild in 1474. The next year, at the height of his career, he entered a monastery near Brussels as a lay brother, though he continued to paint and travel. A mental breakdown in 1481 led to a suicide attempt, and he died the following year. His masterpiece and only documented work is a large triptych known as the Portinari Altarpiece (c. 1473–78); an outstanding early example of northern realism, it shows psychological insight and an emotional intensity unprecedented in Flemish art. A poignant and disturbing *Death of the Virgin* is attributed to him.

Goethals \'gō-thəlz\, **George Washington** (1858–1928) U.S. Army officer and engineer. Born in Brooklyn, N.Y., he graduated from West Point, then served in the Army Corps of Engineers and taught engineering at West Point. Appointed by Pres. THEODORE ROOSEVELT to build the PANAMA CANAL, he was forced to solve complex engineering problems while supervising the living conditions and production of 30,000 workers from many nations; the esprit de corps he engendered became legendary. He was appointed the Canal Zone's first governor (1914–17). In World War I, he directed procurement for and the movement of U.S. troops at home and abroad. After retiring in 1919 he served as a consultant to many organizations, including the Port of New York Authority.

Goethe \'gœ̄-tə, *Engl* 'gə(r)-tə\, **Johann Wolfgang von** (1749–1832) German poet, novelist, playwright, and natural philosopher. Born in Frankfurt, he studied law in Leipzig and Strasbourg. In 1773 he provided the STURM UND DRANG movement with its first major drama, *Götz von Berlichingen*, and in 1774 with its first novel, *The Sorrows of Young Werther*, an extraordinarily popular work in its time, in which he created the prototype of the Romantic hero. In 1775 he accepted an appointment at the ducal court at Weimar, where he would remain the rest of his life; his presence would establish Weimar as a literary and intellectual center. His poetry includes lyrics in praise of natural beauty and ballads such as "The Erl-King" (1782) that echo folk themes. Many early works were inspired by a series of passionate loves. Contact with classical Greek and Romantic culture during an Italian sojourn helped shape his plays, including *Iphigenie auf Tauris* (1787), *Egmont* (1788), and *Torquato Tasso* (1790), and the poems in *Roman Elegies* (1795). From 1794, his friendship with FRIEDRICH SCHILLER became the most important of his life. *Wilhelm Meister's Apprenticeship* (1795–96) is often called the first BILDUNGSROMAN; it was followed many years later by *Wilhelm Meister's Travels* (1821–29). His masterpiece, the philosophical drama *Faust* (Part I, 1808; Part II, 1832), concerns the struggle of the soul for knowledge, power, happiness, and salvation. He also wrote extensively, if idiosyncratically, on botany, optics, and other scientific topics. In his late years he was celebrated as a sage and visited by world luminaries. The greatest figure of German Romanticism, he is regarded as a giant of world literature.

goethite \'gər-,tīt, 'gō-,thīt\ Widespread iron hydroxide mineral, α-FeO(OH), the most common ingredient of iron rust. In terms of relative abundance, it is second only to hematite (α-Fe_2O_3) among iron oxides. Goethite varies in color from yellow-brown to red and is the source for the pigment known as yellow ocher; it is also the primary mineral in some important iron ores, such as those in the Alsace-Lorraine basin in France. Other important deposits are found in the southern Appalachian Mountains of the U.S. and in Brazil, South Africa, Russia, and Australia.

Goffman, Erving (1922–1982) Canadian-U.S. sociologist. Born in Manville, Alberta, he taught principally at the Univs. of California and Pennsylvania. He studied primarily face-to-face communication and re-

E
F
G

lated rituals of social interaction; his *The Presentation of Self in Everyday Life* (1959) laid out the dramaturgical perspective he used in subsequent studies, such as *Asylums* (1961) and *Stigma* (1964). In *Frame Analysis* (1979) and *Forms of Talk* (1981), he focused on the ways people "frame" or define social reality in the communicative process. See also INTERACTIONISM.

Gogh, Vincent van See Vincent VAN GOGH

Gogol \'gō-ˌgȯl\, **Nikolay (Vasilyevich)** (1809–1852) Russian writer. Born in Ukraine, he tried acting and worked at minor government jobs in St. Petersburg before achieving literary success with *Evenings on a Farm near Dikanka* (1831–32). His pessimism emerged in such stories as "Taras Bulba" (1835) and "Diary of a Madman" (1835). His farcical drama *The Government Inspector* (1836) lampooned a corrupt government bureaucracy. From 1836 to 1846 he lived in Italy. He laid the foundations of 19th-century Russian realism with his masterpiece, the novel *Dead Souls* (1842), a satire about serfdom and bureaucratic inequities in which he hoped to castigate abuses and guide his countrymen through laughter, and his story "The Overcoat" (1842). His collected stories (1842) received great acclaim. He soon lost his creative abilities and came under the influence of a fanatical priest who prompted him to burn the manuscript of the second volume of *Dead Souls*. He died a few days later at 42, perhaps of intentional starvation, on the verge of madness.

Gogra River See GHAGHARA RIVER

Goibniu \'gȯv^{y}-n^{y}ü\ Ancient Celtic blacksmith god. In Irish tradition he was one of a trio of divine craftsmen. He had the gift of brewing an ale that bestowed immortality and was the provider of the sacred otherworld feast, the Fled Goibnenn. In Christian times, as Gobbán Saer, he was a legendary builder of churches. His Welsh counterpart, Gofannon, appeared in the *MABINOGION*.

goiter Enlargement of the THYROID GLAND, causing a prominent swelling at the throat. The thyroid can grow to 50 times normal weight, interfere with breathing and swallowing, and cause a choking feeling. Simple (endemic) goiter, the most common, is due to low IODINE intake. It and related conditions result from various defects in thyroid hormone synthesis (hypothyroidism). Advanced cases are treated with thyroid hormone, or surgical removal of the thyroid if it obstructs breathing. The cause of sporadic goiter, which occurs in areas where iodine intake is more than adequate, remains a mystery. An enlarged thyroid may have normally functioning tissue or may produce too much hormone (hyperthyroidism). See also GRAVES' DISEASE.

Golan Heights \'gō-ˌlän\ *Arabic* **Al-Jawlan** \äl-ˌjau̇-'län\ Hilly area (pop., 1988 est.: 24,000), southwestern Syria. It overlooks the upper JORDAN RIVER valley; its maximum elevation is 7,297 ft (2,224 m). It was held by Syria (1941–67), then came under Israeli military occupation (see SIX-DAY WAR). After the ARAB-ISRAELI WAR of 1973, a U.N. buffer zone was established between Syrians and Israelis in the heights. In 1981 Israel unilaterally annexed the part of the Golan that it held. In early 2000, the two countries began talks to resolve the situation.

Golconda \gäl-'kän-də\ Fortress and ruined city, ANDHRA PRADESH state, southern India. Located 5 mi (8 km) west of modern HYDERABAD, it was the capital (1512–1687) of one of the five Muslim sultanates of the DECCAN. It was conquered in 1687 by the emperor AURANGZEB and was annexed to the MUGHAL empire. The fortress, with palaces and mosques, remains intact. Historically, Golconda was famous for its diamonds, mined in the nearby hills.

gold Metallic chemical ELEMENT, one of the TRANSITION ELEMENTS, chemical symbol Au, atomic number 79. It is a dense, lustrous, yellow, malleable precious METAL, so durable that it is virtually indestructible, often found uncombined in nature. Jewelry and other decorative objects have been crafted from gold for thousands of years. It has been used for coins, to back paper currencies, and as a reserve asset. Gold is widely distributed in all IGNEOUS ROCKS, usually pure but in low concentrations; its recovery from ores and deposits has been a major preoccupation since ancient times (see CYANIDE PROCESS). The world's gold supply has seen three great leaps, with CHRISTOPHER COLUMBUS's arrival in the Americas in 1492, with discoveries in California (see GOLD RUSH) and Australia (1850–75), and discoveries in Alaska, Yukon (see KLONDIKE), and South Africa (1890–1915). Pure gold is too soft for prolonged handling; it is usually used in ALLOYS with SILVER, COPPER, and other metals. In addition to being used in jewelry and as currency, gold is used in electrical contacts and circuits, as a reflective layer in space applications and on building windows, and in filling and replacing teeth. Dental alloys are about 75% gold, 10% silver. In jewelry, its purity is expressed in 24ths, or karats: 24-karat is pure, 12-karat is 50% gold, etc. Its compounds, in which it has VALENCE 1 or 3, are used mainly in plating and other decorative processes; a soluble chloride compound has been used to treat RHEUMATOID ARTHRITIS.

Gold Coast Section of the coast of the Gulf of GUINEA, western Africa. Extending approximately from Axim, Ghana, in the west to the VOLTA RIVER in the east, it was so called because it was an important source of gold. It was an area of intense colonial rivalry from the 17th century. Acquired by the British in the 19th century and named the Gold Coast colony, the area achieved independence as the Republic of Ghana in 1960.

Gold Coast See GHANA

gold reserve Fund of gold bullion or coin held by a government or bank. In the past, banks accumulated gold reserves to fulfill their promise to pay their depositors in gold. COMMERCIAL BANKS received deposits subject to repayment in gold on demand and issued notes redeemable in gold on demand. Most gold reserves eventually shifted to CENTRAL BANKS, which took over the function of issuing paper money. Gold reserves were moved again in the 1930s, when many governments required their central banks to turn over to the national treasuries all or most of their gold holdings. In the U.S., the Gold Reserve Act of 1934 required Federal Reserve banks to turn over all gold bullion or coin to the U.S. Treasury, which placed most of the reserves at FORT KNOX.

gold rush Rapid influx of fortune seekers to the site of newly discovered gold deposits. The first major gold strike occurred in California in 1848, when John Marshall, a carpenter building a sawmill for JOHN SUTTER, found gold. Within a year about 80,000 "forty-niners" had flocked to the California gold fields, and 250,000 had arrived by 1853. Some mining camps grew into permanent settlements, and the demand for food, housing, and supplies propelled the new state's economy. As gold became more difficult to extract, companies and mechanical mining methods replaced individuals. Smaller gold rushes occurred in Colorado (1859, 1892), Nevada (1859), Idaho (1861), Montana (1863), South Dakota (1876), Arizona (1877), and Alaska (1898) and resulted in settlement of many areas; where gold veins proved small, the settlements became ghost towns. Major gold rushes also occurred in Australia (1851), South Africa (1886), and Canada (1896). See also KLONDIKE GOLD RUSH.

gold standard Monetary system in which the standard unit of CURRENCY is a fixed quantity of GOLD or is freely convertible into gold at a fixed price. The gold standard was first adopted in Britain in 1821. Germany, France, and the U.S. instituted it in the 1870s, prompted by North American gold strikes that increased the supply of gold. The gold standard ended with the outbreak of World War I in 1914; it was reestablished in 1928, but because of the relative scarcity of gold, most nations adopted a gold-exchange standard, supplementing their gold reserves with currencies (U.S. dollars and British pounds) convertible into gold at a stable rate of exchange. Though the gold-exchange standard collapsed again during the Great Depression, the U.S. set a minimum dollar price for gold, an action that allowed for the restoration of an international gold standard after World War II. In 1971 dwindling gold reserves and an unfavorable BALANCE OF PAYMENTS led the U.S. to suspend the free convertibility of dollars into gold, and the gold standard was abandoned. See also BIMETALLISM, EXCHANGE RATE, SILVER STANDARD.

Goldberg, Arthur J(oseph) (1908–1990) U.S. jurist. Born in Chicago, he first gained national attention as counsel for the Chicago Newspaper Guild in its 1938 strike, and he was instrumental in the merger of the AFL–CIO in 1955. After serving as U.S. secretary of labor (1961–62), he was appointed to the U.S. Supreme Court (1962–65). He gave up his seat at the request of Pres. LYNDON B. JOHNSON to become U.S. ambassador to the U.N. (1965–68), but resigned in protest over the continued escalation of the Vietnam War. He twice served as ambassador-at-large for Pres. JIMMY CARTER.

Goldberg, Rube *orig.* **Reuben Lucius** (1883–1970) U.S. cartoonist. After receiving a degree in engineering and briefly designing sewer pipes for San Francisco, he worked as a sportswriter and cartoonist for San Francisco newspapers (1904–7), then moved east and joined the

New York Evening Mail (1907–21), where he created three long-running comic strips and the cartoon character Professor Lucifer Gorgonzola Butts, an inventor of contraptions that did simple tasks in hilariously roundabout ways. From 1938 until he retired in 1964, he did editorial cartooning for the *New York Sun*, among other publications, winning a 1948 Pulitzer Prize.

Goldberg, Whoopi *orig.* **Caryn Johnson** (born 1949) U.S. actress and comedian. A New York native, she moved in the mid-1970s to California, where she cofounded the San Diego Repertory Theater. She took her stage name from a family surname. Her one-woman *Spook Show* (1984–85) ran on Broadway and led to her film debut in the lead role in *The Color Purple* (1985). Her other films include *The Long Walk Home* (1989), *Ghost* (1990, Academy Award), *Sister Act* (1992), and *Ghosts of Mississippi* (1996). Her work in television includes *Star Trek: The Next Generation* (1992–93) and *The Whoopi Goldberg Show* (1994, 1996).

Golden Bull of 1356 Constitution for the Holy Roman Empire promulgated by Charles IV. Stamped with a golden seal, the document gave seven electors the power to choose the ruler of Germany by a simple majority. It also specified the electors and established succession by primogeniture. Intended to eliminate papal influence in German political affairs, it did away with the pope's previous right to examine rivals and approve results, and also increased the power of the princes.

golden eagle Dark-brown eagle *(Aquila chrysaetos)* with golden, leaf-shaped nape feathers, dark eyes, gray beak, fully feathered legs, large yellow feet, and large talons. Its wingspread reaches almost 8 ft (2.3 m). It ranges from central Mexico (where it is the national bird) along the Pacific coast and through the Rocky Mountains to Alaska, and small numbers are found from Newfoundland to North Carolina. Also found in North Africa, it is more common across Russia, to southern China and Japan. It nests in cliff caves or in lone trees. The species is protected in the U.S.

Golden eagle (*Aquila chrysaetos*).
© ALAN AND SANDY CAREY

Golden Gate Bridge Suspension bridge spanning the Golden Gate, San Francisco. From its completion in 1937 until the completion of New York's Verrazano-Narrows Bridge in 1964, it had the longest main span in the world, 4,200 ft (1,280 m). It remains incomparable in its magnificence. Its construction, supervised by Joseph B. Strauss (1870–1938), involved many difficulties: rapidly running tides, frequent storms and fogs, and the problem of blasting rock under deep water to plant earthquake-resistant foundations.

Golden Gate Bridge, San Francisco.
GEORGE HALL—WOODFIN CAMP

Golden Horde Russian designation for the western part of the Mongol empire. The Golden Horde flourished from the mid-13th century to the end of the 14th century. The name is traditionally said to derive from the golden tent of Batu, a grandson of Genghis Khan, who expanded the domain of the Golden Horde in a series of brilliant campaigns that included the sacking and burning of Kiev in 1240. At its peak, its territory included most of European Russia. The outbreak of the Black Death in 1346 marked the beginning of its disintegration; in the 15th century it broke into several smaller khanates.

golden lion tamarin *or* **golden lion marmoset** Species of tamarin *(Leontideus rosalia),* having a thick, lionlike mane, black face, and long, silky, golden fur. A striking-looking animal, it is found in South America, where it is listed as critically endangered.

golden ratio/rectangle/section Numerical proportion considered to be an aesthetic ideal in classical design. It refers to the ratio of the base to the height of a rectangle or to the division of a line segment into two in such a way that the ratio of the shorter part to the longer is equal to that of the longer to the whole. It works out to about 1.61803:1. A rectangle constructed from golden sections (segments in this ratio) is called a golden rectangle.

Golden Temple *Punjabi* **Darbar Sahib** *or* **Harimandir.** Chief house of worship for the Sikhs of India (see Sikhism) and their most important pilgrimage site, located in the city of Amritsar in Punjab state. Founded by Guru Ramdas (1574–1581) and completed by Guru Arjan in 1604, the temple has entrances on four sides, signifying a welcome to all creeds and castes. Though destroyed in the 1760s by Afghan invaders, it was rebuilt and in the early 19th century it acquired its marble walls and gold-plated copper domes. The surrounding buildings include a meeting hall, reference library, and museum, as well as the shrine known as the Akal Takhat. In a 1984 confrontation with Sikh separatists, government troops attacked and seriously damaged the complex, but it has since been restored.

goldeneye *or* **whistler** Either of two species of small, yellow-eyed diving ducks that produce a whistling sound with their rapidly beating wings. The common goldeneye *(Bucephala clangula)* breeds throughout the Northern Hemisphere; Barrow's goldeneye *(B. islandica)* breeds primarily in northwestern North America and Iceland. Both winter mainly in northern coastal waters. Both are about 18 in. (46 cm) long and have a black back marked with white, white sides and breast, and conspicuous white patches in front of the eyes. The head of the common is dark green; that of the Barrow's is purplish black. Both nest in tree cavities and prefer a diet of aquatic invertebrates. They are prized as game birds.

goldenrod Any of the approximately 100 species of weedy, usually perennial herbaceous plants that make up the genus *Solidago,* in the composite family. Most are native to North America; a few grow in Europe and Asia. They have toothed leaves and clustered yellow flower heads composed of both disk and ray flowers. Characteristic plants in eastern North America, they are found almost everywhere—in woodlands, swamps, on mountains, in fields, and along roadsides—and are a prominent feature of autumn from the Great Plains east to the Atlantic. Unlike ragweed, which blooms at the same time, they are not a cause of hay fever.

goldenseal Perennial herb (Hydrastis canadensis) native to woods of the eastern U.S. Its rootstocks have medicinal properties. The plant has a single greenish-white flower, the sepals of which fall as they open, followed by a cluster of small red berries. Goldenseal is sometimes planted in the shady wild garden but is also grown commercially for the yellow rootstocks, which yield hydrastine, an alkaloid. Used medicinally by American Indians, it is now a popular herbal supplement taken for minor pain and infections.

Goldenseal (*Hydrastis canadensis*).
KITTY KOHOUT FROM ROOT RESOURCES

goldfinch Any of several species (genus *Carduelis,* family Carduelidae) of songbirds that have a short, notched tail and much yellow in the plumage. All have a bill that is more delicate and sharply pointed than that of most finches. They live in flocks, feeding on weeds in fields and gardens. They have high, lisping calls. Various species live in western Eurasia and North and South America and have been introduced into New Zealand and Australia. They are typically 4–5.5 in. (10–14 cm) long. The male of the American goldfinch (or wild canary), found across North America, is bright yellow, with black cap, wings, and tail.

goldfish Ornamental aquarium and pond fish *(Carassius auratus)* of the CARP family, native to East Asia but introduced into many other areas. The goldfish was domesticated by the Chinese at least as early as the Song dynasty (960–1279). It is naturally greenish brown or gray, but its color varies. Selective breeding has produced more than 125 breeds, including the common, petshop comet and the veiltail, with a three-lobed, flowing tail. They feed on plants and small animals, and, in captivity, on small crustaceans and other foods. They have become naturalized in many parts of the eastern U.S.

Goldfish (*Carassius auratus*).
W.S. PITT–ERIC HOSKING

Golding, William (Gerald) *later* **Sir William** (1911–1993) British novelist. Educated at Oxford, he worked as a schoolmaster until 1960. His first and best-known novel was *Lord of the Flies* (1954), about a group of boys isolated on an island who revert to savagery. Later works, several of which are likewise parables of the human condition that show the thinness of the veneer of civilization, include *The Inheritors* (1955), *Pincher Martin* (1956), *Free Fall* (1959), *The Spire* (1964), *Darkness Visible* (1979), *Rites of Passage* (1980, Booker Prize), and *Close Quarters* (1987). He won the Nobel Prize in 1983.

Goldman, Emma (1869–1940) U.S. (Lithuanian-born) anarchist. She emigrated to the U.S. in 1885, and in 1889 she met and formed a long-time relationship with the Russian anarchist Alexander Berkman (1870–1936). For an assassination attempt on HENRY CLAY FRICK, Berkman was imprisoned 1892–1906, during which they corresponded regularly. Goldman lectured on anarchism and was jailed in 1893 for inciting a riot in New York. She founded and edited (1906–17) the anarchist magazine *Mother Earth* and wrote on anarchism, feminism, birth control, and other social problems. After Berkman's release she continued anarchist activities with him until 1917, when they were arrested for obstructing the military draft. On her release from prison in 1919, she and other anarchists were deported to Russia. She moved to England in 1921, and later to Canada and Spain, continuing to lecture throughout Europe.

Goldmark, Peter Carl (1906–1977) Hungarian-U.S. engineer. He earned a doctorate from the University of Vienna before emigrating to the U.S. in 1933. From 1936 to 1972 he worked at Columbia Broadcasting System Laboratories. In 1940 he demonstrated the first commercial color-television system; based on a rotating three-color disk, his system found wide application in closed-circuit television for industry, medical institutions, and schools because his camera was much smaller, lighter, and easier to maintain than those that eventually came to be used in commercial television. In 1948 he introduced the long-playing (LP) phonograph record, which revolutionized the recording industry. In 1950 he developed the scanning system that would allow the U.S. Lunar Orbiter spacecraft (launched in 1966) to relay photographs 238,000 mi (380,000 km) from the moon to earth.

Goldoni, Carlo (1707–1793) Italian playwright. He practiced law but preferred to write plays, beginning with *Belisario* (1734). He renovated the COMMEDIA DELL'ARTE form by replacing its masked stock figures with realistic characters, its repetitive action with tightly constructed plots, and its predictable farce with spontaneity in such plays as *Pamela* (1750), based on SAMUEL RICHARDSON's novel. His comedy of manners *La locandiera* (1753) is still performed (as *Mine Hostess*). When rivals ridiculed his innovations, he took his realistic comedy to Paris, where he directed the Comédie-Italienne and wrote many plays in French. He later rewrote them for Italian audiences, and *Il vantaglio* (1763, *The Fan*) became one of his greatest successes.

Goldschmidt, Victor Moritz (1888–1947) Swiss-Norwegian mineralogist and petrologist. He became director of the Mineralogical Institute of the University of Kristiania (now Oslo) in 1914. The dearth of raw materials during World War I led Goldschmidt to research in GEOCHEMISTRY. His work in that area, and more general studies after the war, marks the beginnings of modern geochemistry. His *Geochemical Laws of the Distribution of the Elements* (8 vols., 1923–38) laid the foundations of inorganic crystal chemistry. During the 1930s he studied the relative cosmic abundance of the elements. In 1942 he escaped a Nazi concentration camp and fled to England; after the war he returned to Oslo.

Goldsmith, Oliver (1730–1774) Irish-British essayist, poet, novelist, and dramatist. He attended Trinity College before studying medicine in Edinburgh. Settling in London, he began writing essays, some of which were collected in *The Citizen of the World* (1762). In 1764 he became an original member of SAMUEL JOHNSON's famous Club. He won a reputation as a poet with *The Traveller* (1764), confirmed by his famous pastoral elegy *The Deserted Village* (1770). *The Vicar of Wakefield* (1766) revealed his skill as a novelist. The charming farce *She Stoops to Conquer* (1773) was his most effective play. He is noted for his exceptionally graceful, lively style, and was a friend of many literary lights of his day, who agreed that he was one of the oddest personalities of his time.

Oliver Goldsmith, oil painting from the studio of Sir Joshua Reynolds, 1770; in the National Portrait Gallery, London.
BY COURTESY OF THE NATIONAL PORTRAIT GALLERY, LONDON

Goldwater, Barry M(orris) (1909–1998) U.S. senator. Born in Phoenix, Ariz., he headed the family department-store business from 1937, and did wartime service as an Air Force pilot (1941–45). In his initial term as senator (1953–64), he established himself as a strong conservative, calling for a harsh diplomatic stance toward the Soviet Union, opposing arms-control negotiations with that country, and charging the Democrats with creating a quasi-socialist state at home. His 1964 presidential bid against Pres. LYNDON B. JOHNSON was doomed by the charge that his extremist views might prompt war with the Soviets, and Johnson won a landslide victory. Returning to the Senate (1969–87), he helped persuade RICHARD NIXON to resign; his views moderated, and he became a symbol of high-minded conservatism.

Goldwyn, Samuel *orig.* **Schmuel Gelbfisz** ***later*** **Samuel Goldfish** (1879–1974) U.S. film producer. He emigrated alone at 13 from Poland to New York, where he worked in a glove factory and became a salesman. He formed a film company with his brother-in-law, Jesse L. Lasky (1880–1958), and CECIL B. DEMILLE in 1913. In 1917 he left the company and with Edgar Selwyn established Goldwyn Pictures Corp. By the time that company merged into MGM (1924), he had become an independent producer. Now in total control, he emerged as a great showman, employing top screenwriters, directors, and actors to produce films of high quality, including *Wuthering Heights* (1939), *The Little Foxes* (1941), *The Best Years of Our Lives* (1946), *Guys and Dolls* (1955), and *Porgy and Bess* (1959).

golem \'gō-ləm\ In Jewish folklore, an image that comes to life. From the Middle Ages stories were told of wise men who could bring clay effigies to life by means of magic charms or sacred words. Golems began as perfect servants, whose only fault lay in fulfilling their master's commands too literally or mechanically. Later golems were imagined as protectors of the Jews in times of persecution, but also had a frightening aspect.

Golem (right) in the German film *Der Golem* (1920).
BY COURTESY OF FRIEDRICH-WILHELM MURNAU-STIFTUNG, WIESBADEN; PHOTOGRAPH, MUSEUM OF MODERN ART FILM STILLS ARCHIVE, NEW YORK

golf Game in which a player using special clubs (limited in number to 14) attempts to sink a small, dimpled ball with as few strokes as possible into each of the nine or 18 successive holes on an outdoor course. A hole includes (1) a teeing area, a clearing from which the ball is initially driven toward the actual hole, or cup; (2) a fairway, a long, closely mowed, and often angled lane; (3) a putting green, a smooth grassy area containing the hole; and (4) often one or more natural or artificial hazards (such as bunkers).

Each hole has associated with it a par, or score standard, usually from par 3 to par 5. Golf developed in Scotland, where it was played as early as the 15th century; the courses were originally fields of grass that herds of sheep had clipped short in their characteristic grazing style. Golf balls were originally made of wood; wood was replaced in the 17th century by boiled feathers in leather, in the 19th century by gutta-percha, and in the 20th century by hard rubber. Clubs are known by the traditional names of "irons" (primarily for mid-range to short shots) and "woods" (primarily for longer shots); today irons are more likely made of stainless steel, and the heads of woods are usually made of metal such as steel or titanium. The principal men's tournaments include the U.S. Open, the MASTERS, the British Open, and the PGA championship. The RYDER CUP is an important international team tournament.

Golgi \'gȯl-jē\, **Camillo** (1843/44–1926) Italian physician and cytologist. He devised a way to stain nerve tissue and with it discovered a NEURON, now called the Golgi cell, that has many short, branching extensions (dendrites) and connects other neurons. This led to identification of the neuron as the basic structural unit of the nervous system. He also discovered the Golgi tendon organ (the point at which sensory nerve fibers branch out within a tendon), and the Golgi apparatus (a cell organelle that packages large molecules for transport). He shared a 1906 Nobel Prize with Santiago Ramón y Cajal (1852–1934).

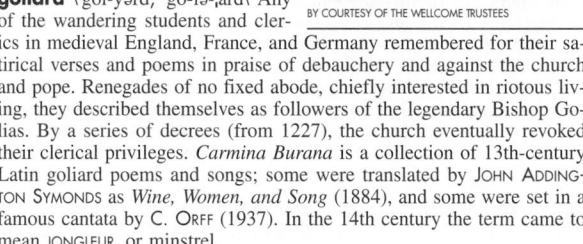

Golgi, 1906.
BY COURTESY OF THE WELLCOME TRUSTEES

Golgotha See CALVARY

goliard \'gōl-yərd, 'gō-lə-ˌärd\ Any of the wandering students and clerics in medieval England, France, and Germany remembered for their satirical verses and poems in praise of debauchery and against the church and pope. Renegades of no fixed abode, chiefly interested in riotous living, they described themselves as followers of the legendary Bishop Golias. By a series of decrees (from 1227), the church eventually revoked their clerical privileges. *Carmina Burana* is a collection of 13th-century Latin goliard poems and songs; some were translated by JOHN ADDINGTON SYMONDS as *Wine, Women, and Song* (1884), and some were set in a famous cantata by C. ORFF (1937). In the 14th century the term came to mean JONGLEUR, or minstrel.

Golitsyn, Vasily (Vasilyevich), Prince (1643–1714) Russian statesman and chief adviser to SOPHIA Alekseyevna. After commanding in the Ukraine, he served in the court of FYODOR III and reorganized the Russian army. When Sophia became regent in 1682, she appointed her lover Golitsyn head of the foreign office. He negotiated an alliance with Poland (1686) against the Ottoman Turks, but failed in his two campaigns against the Turks (1687, 1689). He also concluded the Treaty of NERCHINSK with China. In 1689 he was exiled to Siberia after a coup displaced Sophia and placed PETER I on the throne.

Golitsyn family \gə-'lyēt-sən\ Russian noble family descended from the 14th-century Lithuanian grand duke Gediminas. Three members played prominent roles as statesmen around the time of PETER I THE GREAT (r.1682–1725). VASILY GOLITSYN was chief adviser to Peter's regent, SOPHIA Alekseyevna. Boris Golitsyn (1654–1714) was court chamberlain (1676) and Peter's tutor; he participated in the coup that placed Peter on the throne and was associated with the major achievements of Peter's early reign. Peter dismissed him after his despotic rule of a province in the lower Volga resulted in a major revolt. Dmitry Golitsyn (1665–1737) held several posts under Peter from 1697 but opposed Peter's reforms and in 1724 was deprived of all public duties. In 1727 he became a member of the Supreme Privy Council, which governed for PETER II until his death (1730). He urged the council to offer the throne to ANNA Ivanovna if she would sign a set of conditions transferring crucial prerogatives to the council. She initially agreed, then dissolved the council. He was condemned to death (1736) for his antiautocratic beliefs, but Anna commuted his sentence to life imprisonment.

Gollancz \gə-'lants\, **Victor** *later* **Sir Victor** (1893–1967) British publisher, writer, and humanitarian. Born to a family of orthodox Jews, Gollancz evolved a religious outlook strongly influenced by Christian ethics. In 1928 he founded the publishing firm of Victor Gollancz, Ltd., issuing best-sellers and works supporting his favored causes, including social welfare, pacifism, and abolition of capital punishment. Through the Left Book Club, which he founded in 1936, he worked against fascism, and after World War II he led relief efforts.

Goltzius \'gȯlt-sē-œs\, **Hendrick** (1558–1617) Dutch printmaker and painter. He set up his own copperplate engraving business in Haarlem and became the leading master of Dutch Mannerist engraving. His early works included reproductions of prints by ALBRECHT DURER and LUCAS VAN LEYDEN. Among his best-known original prints are an engraving of the *Farnese Hercules* (c. 1592), the chiaroscuro woodcut *Hercules Killing Cacus* (1588), and the series *Roman Heroes* (1586). His miniature portrait drawings are outstanding, and his landscape drawings anticipate the great 17th-century landscapes. His paintings, done late in his career, are less impressive, but his technique as an engraver was unsurpassed.

Gomal Pass See GUMAL PASS

Gombrowicz \gȯm-'brȯ-vēch\, **Witold** (1904–1969) Polish novelist, story writer, and dramatist. He is best known for his novel *Ferdydurke* (1937). He spent 24 years (1939–63) in voluntary exile in Buenos Aires, and later settled in France. His often bizarre and satirical works explore themes of sadomasochistic dependency and innate human immaturity, in sometimes eccentric prose. His writings were long banned in Poland, and he published his postwar works abroad, including the absurdist satires *Trans-Atlantyk* (1953), *Pornografia* (1960), and *Kosmos* (1965) and his journals (3 vols., 1957–66).

Gomel See HOMYEL

Gómez \'gō-mās\, **Juan Vicente** (1857?–1935) Dictator of Venezuela (1908–35). Though he had almost no formal education, he rose to power by joining a private army that captured Caracas and the government. In 1908 he seized control from his former commander; thereafter he ruled either as president or through puppet governments until his death. Under Gómez, Venezuela achieved a measure of independence and economic progress, but he controlled the nation through force and terror. He was reputedly the wealthiest man in South America at the time of his death.

Gomorrah See SODOM AND GOMORRAH

Gompers, Samuel (1850–1924) U.S. (British-born) labor leader, first president of the American Federation of Labor. He emigrated to New York with his family in 1863, where he became a cigar maker and a union organizer. Known for his opposition to radicalism, Gompers argued that unions should avoid political involvement and focus on economic goals, bringing about change through strikes and boycotts. He stressed the primacy of the national organization over local and international affiliations, as well as the need for written contracts. In 1886 he led the national organization of cigar makers out of the KNIGHTS OF LABOR to form the American Federation of Labor (AFL), of which he served as president from 1886 to 1924 (except 1895). See also AFL-CIO.

Samuel Gompers, 1911.
BY COURTESY OF THE LIBRARY OF CONGRESS, WASHINGTON, D.C.

Gomulka \gō-'mu̇l-kə\, **Wladyslaw** (1905–1982) Leader of the Polish Communist Party (1956–70). In 1926 he joined the underground Communist Party and became a union organizer. In World War II he was active in the communist underground in Warsaw. After the Soviet liberation of Poland, he ascended through the party ranks quickly. Though ruthless in eliminating opposition to communist rule, he publicly opposed some Soviet policies and was accused of "nationalist deviation" by JOSEPH STALIN in 1948 and arrested in 1951. He was rehabilitated in 1956 and elected party first secretary. At first universally supported, he adopted halfhearted reforms that were ultimately disappointing. In

1970 he was ousted along with other top leaders following workers' riots over food prices.

Gonçalves \gō^{n}n-'säl-vish\, **Nuno** (fl. 1450–1471) Portuguese painter. He is recorded as court painter to Alfonso V in 1450, but his works for the Portuguese court have not survived. His altarpiece for Lisbon Cathedral was destroyed in the great earthquake of 1755. His six-paneled St. Vincent altarpiece (c. 1460–70), discovered only in 1882, is the outstanding Portuguese painting of the 15th century, a remarkable portrait gallery of scrupulously realistic, stiffly posed figures, with affinities to Italian and Flemish art.

Gonçalves Dias \gō^{n}n-'säl-vish-'dē-ȧsh\, **Antônio** (1823–1864) Brazilian poet. A respected ethnologist and scholar, he lived much of the time abroad. He drowned at 41. His songs, collected in *First Poems* (1847), *More Poems* (1848), and *Last Poems* (1851), continually celebrated the New World, with exuberance and longing, as a tropical paradise. His "Song of Exile" (1843) is known to every Brazilian schoolchild, and he is regarded as the national poet of Brazil.

Goncourt \gō^{n}-'kür\, **Edmond (-Louis-Antoine Huot de) and Jules (-Alfred Huot de)** (1822–1896, 1830–1870) French writers. The Goncourt brothers were enabled by a legacy to devote their lives largely to writing. They produced a series of social histories (from 1854) as well as a body of art criticism. The most lasting of their meticulously detailed naturalistic novels is *Germinie Lacerteux* (1864), which explores working-class life. Their published journals (kept 1851–96) represent both a revealing autobiography and a monumental history of social and literary life in 19th-century Paris. By his will Edmond established the Académie Goncourt, which annually awards the Prix Goncourt, France's preeminent literary prize, to the author of an outstanding work of French literature.

Gondwana *or* **Gondwanaland** Hypothetical former supercontinent in the Southern Hemisphere, which included modern South America, Africa, southern Europe, India, Australia, and much of the Middle East and Antarctica. The concept that the continents were at one time joined was first set forth in detail by Alfred Wegener in 1912. He envisioned a single great landmass, Pangaea, which supposedly began to separate late in the Triassic period. Subsequent workers distinguished between a southern landmass, Gondwana, and Laurasia to the north. See also continental drift.

Góngora (y Argote) \'gȯn-gō-rä\, **Luis de** (1561–1627) Spanish poet. Very influential in his era, he developed the difficult, complex poetic style that became known as *gongorismo;* it provoked scorn and enmity from many of his contemporaries and was so exaggerated by less gifted imitators that his reputation suffered until the 20th century, when his poems began to be appreciated for their cold beauty. *Soledades* (1613; "Solitudes") is perhaps his most outstanding work in the style. His lighter poetry— *romances* (folk ballads), *letrillas* (short lyric poems), and sonnets—achieved greater popular success.

gonorrhea \ˌgä-nə-'rē-ə\ Sexually transmitted disease with genitourinary inflammation, caused by the bacterium *Neisseria gonorrhoeae* (gonococcus). Symptoms in men include burning on urination, discharge of pus, and, with deeper infection, frequent urination, sometimes with blood. Women may have mild vaginal discharge and burning, but there is usually no sign until a sex partner is infected or complications—sometimes serious—arise from its spread beyond the cervix. If spontaneous recovery does not occur, it may cause sterility in both sexes but is rarely fatal. Gonorrhea is common worldwide. Penicillin, generally a successful treatment, reduced its incidence, but resistant strains are increasingly found. Many cases are not reported. Penicillin may also mask coexisting syphilis (since the dose to cure gonorrhea does not cure syphilis).

Gonzaga dynasty \gōn-'dzä-gä\ Italian dynasty that ruled Mantua 1328–1707 and Montferrat and Casale 1536–1707. Its history began with Luigi I (or Lodovico; 1267–1360), who gained control of Mantua in 1328. Its rulers, many noted as military and political leaders and patrons of the arts, included Giovan Francesco II (died 1444), a general and founder of the first school based on humanistic principles (1423); and Federigo II (died 1540), captain general of the papal forces who was made duke of Mantua in 1530. Mantua was annexed by Austria in 1708.

Good Feelings, Era of (1815–25) Period of U.S. national unity and complacency. A Boston newspaper coined the term in 1817 to describe a nation free from the influence of European political and military events. The good feelings were stimulated by two events of 1816, during James Madison's presidency: enactment of the first U.S. protective tariff, and establishment of the second national bank. The presidency of James Monroe (1817–25) was marked by the dominance of the Democratic-Republican Party and the decline of the Federalist Party.

Good Friday Friday before Easter, commemorating the crucifixion of Jesus. As early as the 2nd century it was kept by Christians as a day of penance and fasting. The Eastern Orthodox and Roman Catholic churches have special liturgies for the day, which include readings and prayers commemorating Christ's sufferings on the cross. Protestant churches also hold special services on Good Friday.

Good Hope, Cape of (province) See Cape Province

Good Hope, Cape of Rocky promontory, southwestern coast, Western Cape province, South Africa. It was sighted by the Portuguese navigator Bartolemeu Dias in 1488 on his return voyage to Portugal after finding the southern limits of the African continent. Known for the stormy weather and rough seas encountered there, the cape lies at the convergence of warm currents from the Indian Ocean and cool currents from Antarctic waters. A part of the Cape of Good Hope Nature Reserve established in 1939, the cape was the site of the first Dutch settlement at Table Bay in 1652.

Good Neighbor Policy Popular name for the policy toward Latin America pursued by Pres. Franklin Roosevelt in the 1930s. In a marked departure from the traditional U.S. interventionism abhorrent to Latin Americans, the U.S. repudiated its assumed right to intervene unilaterally in Latin American affairs, abrogated the Platt Amendment of 1901, and withdrew its Marines from Haiti. U.S. anticommunist policies after World War II led to renewed distrust between North and Latin America and an end to the non-interventionism of the Good Neighbor Policy.

Goodall, Jane (born 1934) British ethologist. Soon after finishing high school, she fulfilled her childhood ambition of traveling to Africa, where she assisted Louis Leakey, who suggested she study chimpanzees. She received a PhD from Cambridge University for her work, and remained at the research center she founded in Gombe, Tanzania, until 1975. Her observations established, among other things, that chimpanzees are omnivorous rather than vegetarian, can make and use tools, and have complex and highly developed social behaviors. Noteworthy among her writings are *In the Shadow of Man* (1971) and *The Chimpanzees of Gombe* (1986).

Goodman, Benny *orig.* **Benjamin David** (1909–1986) U.S. jazz clarinetist and leader of the most popular band of the swing era. Born in Chicago, Goodman formed a big band in 1934, using arrangements by Fletcher Henderson. The band's sensational broadcast from Los Angeles's Palomar Ballroom in 1935 is seen as the beginning of the swing era. Goodman's band featured trumpeters Bunny Berigan, Ziggy Elman, and Harry James and drummer Gene Krupa, all of whom would establish big bands of their own. Goodman's small group was among the first racially integrated ensembles known to a wide public. His virtuosity and immense popularity earned him the sobriquet "King of Swing."

Goodpasture, E(rnest) W(illiam) (1886–1960) U.S. pathologist. Born in Tennessee, he spent most of his career (1924–55) at Vanderbilt University. His method for cultivating viruses and rickettsias in fertile chicken eggs, developed in 1931, made possible the production of vaccines for such diseases as smallpox, influenza, yellow fever, typhus, Rocky Mountain spotted fever, and other illnesses caused by agents that can be propagated only in living tissue.

Goodson, Mark (1915–1992) U.S. radio and television producer. Born in Sacramento, Cal., he worked as a radio announcer from 1939. In the late 1940s he and Bill Todman developed such hit radio shows as *Stop the Music* (1947) and *Hit the Jackpot* (1948), and later such long-running television game shows as *What's My Line?* (1950–67), *I've Got a Secret* (1952–67), *To Tell the Truth* (1956–67), and *The Price Is Right* (1957–64). He received an Emmy award for lifetime achievement in 1990.

Goodyear, Charles (1800–1860) U.S. inventor of the vulcanization process that permitted the commercial use of rubber. He was born in New Haven, Conn. Interested in treating rubber so that it would lose its adhesive quality and not melt, he discovered vulcanization in 1839 when he accidentally dropped a rubber-sulfur mixture onto a hot stove. The process would prove profoundly important for the future uses of rubber. He patented it in 1844, but had to fight numerous patent infringements in the U.S. and Europe. He never profited from his discovery and died in debt. The Goodyear Tire and Rubber Co. (founded 1898) honors his name.

gooney See ALBATROSS

goose Any large, heavy-bodied WATERFOWL (family Anatidae) of the genera *Anser* (so-called gray geese) and *Branta* (so-called black geese), all found in the Northern Hemisphere. Intermediate in size and build between large DUCKS and SWANS, geese are less fully aquatic than either, and their legs are farther forward, allowing them to walk readily. Geese have a specially modified bill for grasping sedges and grasses, their main diet. The sexes are alike in coloration; males (called ganders) are usually larger than females. Both sexes utter loud honking or gabbling cries while on the wing or when danger appears. Geese pair for life. Flocks traveling in V-formation migrate between their breeding grounds and wintering grounds far south. See also BARNACLE GOOSE, CANADA GOOSE, GREYLAG, NENE.

gooseberry Hardy fruit bush of the Northern Hemisphere, often placed in the genus *Ribes* with the CURRANT (or alternatively assigned to the genus *Grossularia* as its sole member), in the family Saxifragaceae. The spiny bushes bear clusters of greenish to greenish-pink flowers. The tart, oval berries may be prickly, hairy, or smooth. They are eaten ripe and often made into jellies, preserves, pies and other desserts, or wine. Because gooseberry is an alternate host for white-pine BLISTER RUST, growing it is illegal in some states where white pine is an important resource.

Gooseberry (*Ribes*).
DEREK FELL

GOP See REPUBLICAN PARTY

gopher *or* **pocket gopher** Any of about 40 species (family Geomyidae) of stocky RODENTS found in North and Central America. Gophers range in length from 5 to 18 in. (13–45 cm), including a short, sparsely haired tail. They have chisel-like front teeth and long, strong claws on their forefeet; large fur-lined pouches open externally on each side of the mouth. Coat color varies from almost white to brown or black. Gophers live alone in extensive, shallow underground burrows marked by a series of rounded earth mounds on the surface. They feed on the underground parts of plants, which they obtain as they tunnel along.

Eastern pocket gopher (*Geomys*).
WOODROW GOODPASTER—THE NATIONAL AUDUBON SOCIETY COLLECTION/PHOTO RESEARCHERS

Gorbachev \\,gȯr-bə-'chȯf, 'gȯr-bə-,chef\\, **Mikhail (Sergeyevich)** (born 1931) Soviet official and last president of the Soviet Union (1990–91). After earning a law degree from Moscow State University (1955), he rose through the ranks to become a full Politburo member (1980) and general secretary of the COMMUNIST PARTY OF THE SOVIET UNION (1985–91). His extraordinary reform policies of GLASNOST and PERESTROIKA were resisted by party bureaucrats; to reduce their power, Gorbachev changed the Soviet constitution in 1988 to allow multi-candidate elections and removed the monopoly power of the party in 1990. He cultivated warmer relations with the U.S., and in 1989–90 he supported the democratically elected governments that replaced the communist regimes of Eastern Europe. In 1990 he was awarded the Nobel Peace Prize. Russia's economic and political problems led to a 1991 coup attempt by hard-liners. In alliance with president BORIS YELTSIN, Gorbachev quit the Communist Party, disbanded its Central Committee, and shifted political powers to the Soviet Union's constituent republics. Events outpaced him, and the various republics formed the COMMONWEALTH OF INDEPENDENT STATES under Yeltsin's leadership. On December 25, 1991, Gorbachev resigned the presidency of the Soviet Union, which ceased to exist that same day.

Gorbachev, 1985.
COLTON/PICTURE SEARCH—BLACK STAR

Gorchakov \\,gȯr-chə-'kȯf\\, **Aleksandr (Mikhailovich), Prince** (1798–1883) Russian politician and diplomat. A career diplomat, he became foreign minister in 1856, succeeding KARL, COUNT NESSELRODE, and immediately began to establish cordial relations with France and Prussia. He was named imperial chancellor in 1866. He renounced the ban on Russian warships on the Black Sea (1870) and allied Russia with Germany and Austria-Hungary in the THREE EMPERORS' LEAGUE (1873). His influence waned when he was unable to maintain the League and failed, after the RUSSO-TURKISH WAR, to prevent the harsh Treaty of SAN STEFANO from being imposed on the defeated Turks or to stop the European powers from replacing it with a treaty far less favorable to Russia.

gordian worm See HORSEHAIR WORM

Gordimer, Nadine (born 1923) South African writer. The daughter of Jewish immigrants, she published her first book, the story collection *The Soft Voice of the Serpent*, in 1952. Her later works include *The Conservationist* (1974, Booker Prize), *Burger's Daughter* (1979), *July's People* (1981), *A Sport of Nature* (1987), *My Son's Story* (1990), *None to Accompany Me* (1994), and *The House Gun* (1998). Her works, written in a clear, controlled, unsentimental style, often concern exile and alienation. She was a strong opponent of her country's apartheid policy, and concerns about black–white relations are frequently expressed in her fiction. She received the Nobel Prize in 1991.

Gordium Ancient city, capital of PHRYGIA. Located in what is now northwestern Turkey, its ruins have yielded important information about ancient Phrygian culture. Excavations revealed Early BRONZE AGE and HITTITE settlements, but the city achieved its greatest prominence as the flourishing capital of Phrygia in the 9th–8th century BC. According to legend, it was founded by the peasant Gordius, who contrived the knot later cut by ALEXANDER THE GREAT. Gordium remained the political center of Phrygia until the Cimmerians overran it in the early 7th century BC. Though rebuilt under the Persians, it never regained its former splendor.

Gordon, Charles George (1833–1885) British general who became a national hero for his exploits in China and his ill-fated defense of KHARTOUM. He distinguished himself as a young officer in the CRIMEAN WAR (1853–56), and subsequently volunteered for the second OPIUM WAR (1856–60). In 1862 he helped defend Shanghai during the TAIPING REBELLION. These exploits earned him the epithet "Chinese" Gordon. In 1873 the Egyptian ruler Isma'il Pasha, who regularly employed Europeans, appointed Gordon governor of the province of Equatoria in southern Sudan (1874–76) and as governor-general of the Sudan (1874–80). In that post he acted to crush rebellions and suppress the slave trade. He was again sent to the Sudan by Britain in 1884 to evacuate Anglo-Egyptian forces from Khartoum, which was threatened by MAHDIST MOVEMENT insurgents. After his arrival, the city was besieged and remained isolated for several months until it finally succumbed (January 26, 1885). Gordon was killed in the action.

Charles George Gordon, portrait by Lady Julia Abercromby; in the National Portrait Gallery, London.
BY COURTESY OF THE NATIONAL PORTRAIT GALLERY, LONDON

E F G

Gordon, Dexter (Keith) (1923–1990) U.S. tenor saxophonist, one of the most influential saxophonists in modern jazz. Born in Los Angeles, Gordon played in the big bands of LIONEL HAMPTON and BILLY ECKSTINE in the early 1940s, later working in small groups with CHARLIE PARKER, Tadd Dameron, and fellow tenorist Wardell Gray. He was incarcerated on narcotics charges in the early 1950s, and moved to Denmark in 1962. A starring role in the film *Round Midnight* (1986) revived his career.

Gordon, George, Lord (1751–1793) English instigator of the anti-Catholic Gordon riots. The third son of the duke of Gordon, he entered Parliament in 1774. In 1779 he organized the Protestant associations formed to secure the repeal of the Catholic Relief Act (1778). In 1780 he led a mob to Parliament to present a petition against the act. The ensuing riot lasted a week, causing great property damage and nearly 500 casualties. Gordon was charged with, but not convicted of, high treason. Convicted of libeling the queen of France in 1787, he was imprisoned in Newgate, where he died.

Gordon River River, southwestern TASMANIA, Australia. It rises in the central highlands and then flows south and west to enter the Indian Ocean at MACQUARIE HARBOUR after a course of 115 mi (185 km). The river is navigable only in its lowest 20 mi (32 km). Gordon Dam, built in 1978, created Lake Gordon, one of the largest freshwater storage reservoirs in Australia.

Gordy, Berry, Jr. See MOTOWN

Gore, Al *in full* **Albert Arnold Gore, Jr.** (born 1948) U.S. politician. Born in Washington, D.C., he was the son of Albert Gore, future senator from Tennessee. After graduating from Harvard Univ., he briefly attended divinity school before serving in the Vietnam War as a military reporter (1969–71). He worked as a reporter for *The Tennessean* in Nashville (1971–76) while attending first divinity school and then law school at Vanderbilt University. He served in the U.S. House of Representatives (1977–85) and later the Senate (1985–93). A moderate Democrat, he was nominated as vice president in 1992 with WILLIAM JEFFERSON CLINTON; they were reelected in 1996. As the Democratic presidential nominee in 2000, he surpassed GEORGE W. BUSH in the popular vote but lost the electoral vote when the U.S. Supreme Court ended a recount in the decisive state of Florida.

Gorée \gō-'rā\, **Île de** *or* **Gorée Island** Island, Senegal. Inhabited by the Lebu people when it was occupied by the Portuguese in the mid-15th century, it was later occupied by the Dutch, and then taken by the French in 1677. It was a major Atlantic slave trading center until 1848. Millions of Africans are said to have been shipped through the island; many died there. Under French control until Senegal's independence in 1960, it later lost importance with the rise of St.-Louis and DAKAR on the mainland. It is now a WORLD HERITAGE SITE; a museum there displays slavery artifacts.

Goremykin \ˌgȯr-ə-'mē-kən\, **Ivan (Longinovich)** (1839–1917) Russian politician. He served as minister of the interior (1895–99) and briefly as premier (1906). A conservative who supported russification of the minorities, he became closely associated with GRIGORY RASPUTIN. He served again as premier 1914–16; in 1915 he opposed government reforms that were supported by many ministers, regarding them as an attempt to undermine the autocracy. After the revolution, he was arrested, imprisoned, and murdered by the BOLSHEVIKS in the Caucasus.

Goren, Charles H(enry) (1901–1991) U.S. contract BRIDGE authority. Born in Philadelphia, he learned bridge while a law student at McGill University. His innovative system of point-count bidding and repeated successes in tournaments made him one of the world's most famous and influential players. His several popular books include the widely translated *Goren's Bridge Complete* (1963).

Gorey, Edward (St. John) (1925–2000) U.S. writer, illustrator, and designer. Born in Chicago, he studied at Harvard University and worked as an illustrator before publishing his first children's book, *The Doubtful Guest,* in 1957. In this and such later books as *The Hapless Child* (1961) and *The Gashlycrumb Tinies* (1962), his arch nonsense verse and mock-Victorian prose accompany pen-and-ink drawings of beady-eyed, blank-faced individuals in Edwardian costume whose dignified demeanor is undercut by silly, often macabre events. They have been anthologized in *Amphigorey* (1972), *Amphigorey Too* (1975), and *Amphigorey Also* (1983).

Gorgas, Josiah (1818–1883) U.S. army officer. Born in Dauphin Co., Pa., he served in the U.S. Army from 1841. Following the sympathies of his Alabama-born wife, he resigned his commission when the South seceded. As chief of ordnance for the Confederate army, he sought arms from abroad while establishing factories in the South to produce rifles, small arms, bullets, powder, and cannons. He was promoted to brigadier general in 1864.

Gorgas \'gȯr-gəs\, **William (Crawford)** (1854–1920) U.S. Army surgeon. Born in Mobile, Ala., son of the Confederate general Josiah Gorgas (1818–1883), he served in the U.S. Army for many years. In charge of sanitation measures in Havana with the army's medical corps in 1898, he conducted experiments on mosquito transmission of YELLOW FEVER and effectively eliminated it from the area. Sent to Panama in 1904, he eradicated yellow fever from the Canal Zone and brought MALARIA under control, removing the chief obstacles to building the Panama Canal. He was surgeon general of the U.S. Army 1914–18.

Gorges \'gȯr-jəz\, **Ferdinando** *later* **Sir Ferdinando** (1566?–1647) British colonist. After a military career, he sought royal grants to establish settlements in North America. Believing that colonizing should be a royal endeavor, he obtained a charter in 1620 to develop the Council for New England, planning to distribute land as manors and fiefs to fellow aristocrats on the Council. Since the self-governing English colonies at Plymouth and Massachusetts Bay had received their charters directly from the crown, Gorges's Council was bypassed. He received the charter for Maine in 1639, but could not effect his plan.

Gorgon One of three monsters in GREEK MYTHOLOGY, the most famous of which was MEDUSA. According to HESIOD, the three Gorgons were daughters of the sea god Phorcys. Another tradition held that they were created by the earth goddess, GAEA, to aid her sons, the TITANS, in their struggle with the gods. Classical art depicts them as winged females with snakes for hair.

Gorgon, carved marble mask of the early 6th century BC; in the Acropolis Museum, Athens.
ALINARI—ART RESOURCE

gorilla Largest of the great APES. A stocky, powerful forest dweller native to equatorial Africa, the gorilla *(Gorilla gorilla)* has black skin and hair, large nostrils, and prominent brow ridges. Adults have long, powerful arms; short, stocky legs; an extremely thick, strong chest; and a protruding abdomen. Adult males have a prominent crest on top of the skull and a "saddle" of gray or silver hairs on the lower part of the back. Males, about twice as heavy as females, may reach a height of about 5.5 ft (1.7 m) and a weight of 300–600 lbs (135–275 kg). Gorillas are mainly terrestrial, walking about on all four limbs. They live in stable family groups of six to 20 animals that are led by one or two silverbacked males. They eat leaves, stalks, and shoots. They are unaggressive and even shy unless provoked. They are calmer and more persistent than chimpanzees; though not as adaptable, gorillas are highly intelligent and capable of problem solving. Hunted for its meat, and with its habitat disappearing, the gorilla is an endangered species throughout its range; the mountain gorilla subspecies is critically endangered.

Male gorilla (*Gorilla gorilla*).
KENNETH W. FINK—ROOT RESOURCES

Göring \'gœ̄-riŋ\, **Hermann** *or* **Hermann Goering** (1893–1946) German Nazi leader. He fought in World War I with the German air force. In 1922 he joined the NAZI PARTY and was given command of the SA. After the abortive BEER HALL PUTSCH, he escaped to Austria, then returned to Germany (1927) and was elected to the Reichstag. Chosen president of the Reichstag (1932), his power mounted after ADOLF HITLER was named chancellor in 1933. As Hitler's most loyal supporter, Göring held numerous posts, including minister of the interior in Prussia, where he established the GESTAPO. He also became head of the German air force (Luftwaffe) and minister of economic affairs. After the Luftwaffe failed to win the Battle of BRITAIN, Göring lost face and semiretired to his country estate, where he displayed the vast art collection he had confiscated from Jews in occupied countries. In 1946 he was condemned to death at the NUREMBERG TRIALS, but committed suicide by taking a poison capsule.

Göring, as commander of the Sturmabteilung, 1933.
HEINRICH HOFFMANN, MUNICH

Gorki See NIZHNIY NOVGOROD

Gorky, Arshile *orig.* **Vosdanik Adoian** (1904–1948) Armenian-U.S. painter. In 1920 he emigrated from Turkish Armenia to the U.S. In 1925, after study at RISD, he settled in New York City, where he studied and then taught at the Grand Central School of Art (1926–31). He sought to assimilate the aesthetic visions of PAUL CEZANNE, JOAN MIRO, and PABLO PICASSO by painting in their styles until he encountered the émigré European Surrealists, when he developed his own style of abstraction with biomorphic forms suggesting plants or human viscera floating over a background of melting colors. After a series of personal calamities, including a studio fire that destroyed many of his paintings, a crippling car accident, cancer, and abandonment by his wife, he hanged himself. He is the most important direct link between SURREALISM and ABSTRACT EXPRESSIONISM.

Gorky, Maxim *orig.* **Aleksey Maksimovich Peshkov** (1868–1936) Russian writer. After a childhood of poverty and misery (his assumed name, Gorky, means "bitter"), he became a wandering tramp. His early works offered sympathetic portrayals of the social dregs of Russia; they include the stories "Chelkash" (1895) and "Twenty-six Men and a Girl" (1899) and the successful play *The Lower Depths* (1902). For his revolutionary activity, he spent the years 1906–13 abroad as a political exile. His works include the autobiographical trilogy *My Childhood* (1913–14), *In the World* (1915–16), and *My Universities* (1923). Though initially an open critic of VLADIMIR ILICH LENIN and the Bolsheviks, after 1919 he cooperated with Lenin's government. He soon became the undisputed leader of Soviet writers; as the first president of the Union of Soviet Writers, he helped establish SOCIALIST REALISM. He lived in Italy 1921–28. He died suddenly while under medical treatment, possibly killed on JOSEPH STALIN's orders

gorse Any of several related plants of the genera *Ulex* and *Genista*. Common gorse *(U. europaeus)* is a spiny, yellow-flowered leguminous shrub native to Europe and naturalized in the Middle Atlantic states and on Vancouver Island. The large green spines and green twigs of Spanish gorse *(G. hispanica),* native to Spain and northern Italy, make it appear evergreen in winter. Both species bear yellow, pea-like flowers and grow well in dry soil.

Gorsky, Alexander (Alexeievich) (1871–1924) Russian dancer and choreographer, and influential director of the BOLSHOI BALLET. He trained in St. Petersburg and joined the MARIINSKY THEATER, where he became a soloist in 1895 and introduced Vladimir Stepanov's new dance-notation system at the ballet school. He directed several ballets before moving to Moscow in 1900 as lead dancer and stage manager of the Bolshoi. He reshaped the repertoire and introduced realism in scenery and costume that revived interest in the company and led to its increased importance in the 20th century.

Gortyn \'gȯr-ˌtīn\ Ancient city, southern central CRETE, Greece. Although unimportant in Minoan times, it later displaced Phaestus as the dominant city. It shared or disputed control of Crete with KNOSSOS until the Roman annexation in the 1st century BC, when it became the administrative capital of the Roman province of Crete and Cyrenaica. Among the city's ruins, the great civic law code of Gortyn, discovered in the 19th century, is the most extensive account of Greek law before the Hellenistic Age.

goryo \gō-'ryō\ In Japanese mythology, vengeful spirits of the dead. They were originally thought to be spirits of nobles who had been killed unjustly and who avenged themselves by bringing about natural disasters, disease, and wars. Identified by divination, they were appeased by being granted status as gods. Later the belief arose that anyone could become a goryo by willing it at the moment of death or by meeting an untimely death. Various forms of exorcism and magical practices have been used to ward them off.

Gosden, Freeman F(isher) and Charles J. Correll (1899–1982, 1890–1972) U.S. comedians. Gosden was born in Richmond, Va., Correll in Peoria, Ill. They performed comedy routines in traveling variety shows before creating two black characters, Sam and Henry, for a Chicago radio show (1926–28). In 1929 they broadened their appeal by devising a larger cast of characters for a new nightly radio program, *Amos 'n' Andy,* thus creating the first SITUATION COMEDY. As Amos the cab driver and his sidekick Andy, they became the mainstays of radio's most popular program in the 1930s, and their popularity ensured the success of radio broadcasting as a form of mass entertainment. Their show, which became a weekly, ended in 1954, partly in response to criticism that its humor was offensive to blacks.

goshawk \'gäs-ˌhȯk\ Any of the more powerful accipiters (HAWKS in the genus *Accipiter*), primarily short-winged, forest-dwelling bird catchers. Best known is the northern goshawk, which reaches about 2 ft (60 cm) in length with a 4.3-ft (1.3-m) wingspread and has finely barred gray plumage. Long used for FALCONRY, the goshawk takes game as large as foxes and grouse. In the wild it lives in temperate to northern forests throughout the Northern Hemisphere, though it has become rare in the British Isles and is declining in North America. Several other species are found in the Southern Hemisphere.

Northern goshawk (*Accipiter gentilis*).
KARL H. MASLOWSKI

Gospel Any of the four NEW TESTAMENT books narrating the life and death of JESUS. The Gospels of MATTHEW, MARK, LUKE, and JOHN are placed at the beginning of the New Testament and make up about half its total text. The first three are often called the Synoptic Gospels, because they give similar accounts of the ministry of Jesus, often in identical language.

gospel music Form of black American music derived from 19th-century Pentecostal church services and from spiritual and BLUES singing. Recordings of Pentecostal preachers' sermons were immensely popular among American blacks in the 1920s. Taking the scriptural direction "Let everything that breathes praise the Lord" (Psalms, 150), Pentecostal churches welcomed timbrels, pianos, banjos, guitars, other stringed instruments, and even brass into their services. Choirs often featured the extremes of female vocal range in antiphonal counterpoint with the preacher's sermon. Other forms of gospel music have included the singing and acoustic-guitar playing of itinerant street preachers, and harmonizing male quartets, whose acts included dance routines and stylized costumes. Its principal composers and practitioners included THOMAS DORSEY, who coined the term; the Rev. C. A. Tindley (1851–1933); the blind wandering preacher Rev. Gary Davis (1896–1972); Sister Rosetta Tharpe (1915–1973), whose performances took gospel into nightclubs and theaters in the 1930s; and MAHALIA JACKSON. Gospel music was a significant influence on RHYTHM AND BLUES and SOUL MUSIC, which have in turn strongly influenced contemporary gospel music.

Gosplan \gȯs-'plän\ Central board that supervised various aspects of the planned economy of the former Soviet Union. The name is an abbreviation of the Russian for "State Planning Committee." Established in 1921, Gosplan originally advised the government but assumed a more comprehensive planning role in 1928, when the First FIVE-YEAR PLAN was adopted in an effort to bring about rapid INDUSTRIALIZATION and collectivization. Throughout the existence of the Soviet Union it was responsible for translating general economic objectives outlined by the Communist Party into specific national plans. See also COMMAND ECONOMY, UNION OF SOVIET SOCIALIST REPUBLICS.

Gossart \'gós-ärt\, **Jan** *or* **Jan Gossaert** *known as* **Mabuse** \mä-'bu̅e̅-zə\ (c. 1478–1532) Flemish painter. After a stay in Italy in 1508–9, Gossart turned from the ornate style of the Antwerp school to the High Renaissance style. *Neptune and Amphitrite* (1516) reflects his attempt to assimilate the art of classical antiquity and the Italian Renaissance. Despite his efforts to develop a fully Italianate style, his nudes seldom avoid the stiffness of his earlier figures, and ultimately he retained the jewellike technique and careful observation of traditional Early Netherlandish art. He was among the first to introduce the Italian Renaissance style into the Low Countries.

Gosse \'gós\, **Edmund** *later* **Sir Edmund** (1849–1928) British literary historian and critic. He worked principally as a librarian and translator (of HENRIK IBSEN's plays, among many other works). He wrote the literary histories *18th Century Literature* (1889) and *Modern English Literature* (1897), as well as biographies of THOMAS GRAY, JOHN DONNE, Ibsen, and others, and introduced many works by continental European writers to English readers. Many of his critical essays were collected in *French Profiles* (1905), and his autobiography, *Father and Son* (1907), has been much admired.

E
F
G

Göteborg \'yœ-tä-,bór^y\ *or* **Gothenburg** \'gäth-^{ə}n-,bərg\ City (pop., 1997 est.: 454,800), southwestern Sweden. The country's chief seaport and second-largest city, it lies along the Göta River estuary, about 5 mi (8 km) above the KATTEGAT. The city, founded in 1603, was destroyed in the Kalmar War with Denmark (1611–13), but was refounded in 1619. Many of the early inhabitants were Dutch, who built urban canals and laid out the city center. A prosperous period began with the completion of the Göta Canal (1832) and the start of a transoceanic shipping service. It retains some historic architecture, and a moat still encircles the old part of the city. The port's principal exports are automobiles (Volvo), ball bearings, and paper.

Gothic, Carpenter See CARPENTER GOTHIC

Gothic architecture Architectural style in Europe that lasted from the mid-12th century to the 16th century, particularly a style of masonry building characterized by cavernous spaces with the expanse of walls broken up by overlaid TRACERY. In the 12th–13th century, feats of engineering permitted increasingly gigantic buildings. Solutions to the problem of building a very tall structure while preserving as much natural light as possible were the rib VAULT, FLYING BUTTRESS, and pointed (Gothic) arch. Stained-glass window panels rendered startling sun-dappled interior effects. One of the earliest buildings to combine these elements into a coherent style was the abbey of Saint-Denis, Paris (c. 1135–44). The High Gothic years (c. 1250–1300), heralded by CHARTRES CATHEDRAL, were dominated by France, especially with the development of the RAYONNANT STYLE. Britain, Germany, and Spain produced variations of this style, while Italian Gothic stood apart in its use of brick and marble rather than stone. Late Gothic (15th-century) architecture reached its heights in Germany's vaulted HALL CHURCHES. Other late Gothic styles include the British PERPENDICULAR STYLE and the French and Spanish FLAMBOYANT STYLE.

Gothic art Architecture, sculpture, and painting that flourished in Western and central Europe in the Middle Ages. It evolved from ROMANESQUE ART and lasted from the mid-12th century to the end of the 15th century. Its loftiest form of expression is architecture, as in the great cathedrals of northern Europe. Sculpture was closely tied to architecture and often used to decorate the exteriors of cathedrals and other religious buildings. Painting evolved from stiff, two-dimensional forms to more natural ones. Religious and secular subjects were depicted in illuminated manuscripts. Panel and wall painting evolved into the Renaissance style in Italy in the 15th century, but retained its Gothic features until the early 16th century elsewhere in Europe. See also GOTHIC ARCHITECTURE.

Gothic language Extinct GERMANIC LANGUAGES spoken by the GOTHS. Its records antedate those of other Germanic languages by about four centuries. Best known from a translation of the Bible into Gothic in AD 350, it died out among the OSTROGOTHS after the fall of their kingdom in Italy in the 6th century and among the VISIGOTHS around the time of the Arab conquest in 711. It persisted longer in the Crimea, where a form of Gothic was spoken as late as the 16th century.

gothic novel European Romantic, pseudo-medieval fiction with a prevailing atmosphere of mystery and terror. Such novels were often set in castles or monasteries equipped with subterranean passages, dark battlements, and hidden panels, and had plots involving ghosts, madness, outrage, superstition, and revenge. HORACE WALPOLE's *Castle of Otranto* (1765) initiated the vogue, which peaked in the 1790s. ANN RADCLIFFE's *The Mysteries of Udolpho* (1794) and *The Italian* (1797) are among the finest examples. MATTHEW GREGORY LEWIS's *The Monk* (1796) introduced more horrific elements into the English gothic. Gothic traits appear in MARY SHELLEY's *Frankenstein* (1818) and BRAM STOKER's *Dracula* (1897) and in the works of many major writers, and persist today in thousands of paperback romances.

Gothic Revival Architectural movement (c. 1730–c. 1930) most commonly associated with Romanticism. The first nostalgic imitation of GOTHIC ARCHITECTURE appeared in the 18th century, when scores of houses with castle-style battlements were built in England, but only toward the mid-19th century did a true Gothic Revival develop. The mere imitation of Gothic forms and details then became its least important aspect, as architects focused on creating original works based on underlying Gothic principles. French architects, particularly E.-E. VIOLLET-LE-DUC, were the first to think about applying the Gothic skeleton structure to a modern age. Though the movement began losing force toward the end of the century, Gothic-style churches and collegiate buildings continued to be constructed in Britain and the U.S. well into the 20th century.

Gothic script See BLACK LETTER SCRIPT

Goths Germanic people whose two branches, the OSTROGOTHS and the VISIGOTHS, harassed the Roman Empire for centuries. Legend holds that they originated in southern Scandinavia, crossed to the southern shore of the Baltic Sea, then migrated to the Black Sea in the 2nd century AD. They raided the Roman provinces in Asia Minor and the Balkan peninsula in the 3rd century and drove the Romans out of the province of Dacia during the reign of AURELIAN. The adjective "Gothic" was applied disparagingly and inappropriately to medieval architecture by much later writers.

Gotland Island (pop., 1997: 58,000), southeastern Sweden. Located in the Baltic Sea, it covers 1,159 sq mi (3,001 sq km). A trading center since the BRONZE AGE, Gotland became part of Sweden in the 9th century. By the 12th century. Gotland's traders dominated the routes between Russia and western Europe. German merchants, who settled in the major town, Visby, brought it into the HANSEATIC LEAGUE. It was at the height of its prosperity when it was taken by the Danish in 1361. It was finally returned to Sweden in 1645, and was fortified in the late 19th century. The island's modern economy centers on agriculture, fishing, and tourism.

Goto Islands \'gō-,tō\ Island chain, CHINA SEA, part of Nagasake prefecture, Japan. Lying off the western coast of Japan, the chain comprises more than 100 islands, of which 34 are inhabited. The five main ones are Fukue, Hisaka, Naru, Uku, and Nakadori; the capital is Fukue, on Fukue island. They have a total area of 266 sq mi (689 sq km), stretching about 60 mi (100 km) from northeast to southwest. The islands were a gateway to Japan for the introduction of Chinese culture. Fishing is the major activity in the northern islands; agriculture predominates in the southern islands.

gotra \'gō-trə\ Lineage segment within an Indian CASTE, indicating common descent from a mythical ancestor. Marriage by members of the same gotra was traditionally prohibited. The custom was intended to prevent inbreeding as well as to broaden the influence of each gotra through marriage alliances. The term originally denoted segments of the BRAHMAN caste descended from seven ancient seers. The number of Brahman gotras later increased, and some non-Brahman Hindu groups also established gotras.

Gottfried von Strassburg \'gót-,frēt-fón-'shträs-,búrk\ (fl. c. 1210) German poet, one of the greatest of the Middle Ages. Little is known of his life. His courtly epic *Tristan und Isolde* (c. 1210) is the classic version of the famous love story. The unfinished poem is based on an Anglo-Norman version of the story, which came from Celtic legend. One of the most perfect creations of the medieval courtly spirit, it is distinguished by its refined and elevated tone and its skillful technique.

Gottfried von Strassburg (right of centre), miniature from the Heidelberger Liederhandschrift; in the Universitätsbibliothek, Heidelberg, Ger.

BY COURTESY OF THE UNIVERSITATSBIBLIOTHEK, HEIDELBERG, GER

Göttingen \'gœ-tiŋ-ən\, **University of** *German* **Georg-August-Universität zu Göttingen.** Eminent European university, founded in 1737 in Göttingen, Germany. It was one of the first and most influential secular universities. In the late 18th century it was the center of the Göttinger Hain, a circle of poets who were forerunners of German Romanticism. In the late 19th century its Mathematical Institute, headed at various times by CARL FRIEDRICH GAUSS, BERNHARD RIEMANN, and DAVID HILBERT, attracted students from all over the world. In the 20th century its physics faculty included MAX BORN, WERNER HEISENBERG, and MAX VON LAUE. Current enrollment is about 27,000.

Gottschalk \'gät-ˌshȯk\, **Louis Moreau** (1829–1869) U.S. composer and pianist. Born in New Orleans to an English father and a French mother, he was exposed early to the colorful life of the city's Caribbean and Latin American population. Sent to France at 13 to study music, he quickly became known throughout Europe as a piano virtuoso and a composer of exotic piano works. He returned in 1853 and toured widely throughout the New World, though in 1865 he left the U.S. permanently because of a sex scandal. Though he wrote operas and symphonies, he is known for his more than 200 piano pieces, including *Bamboula, Le bananier, Le banjo, L'Union,* and *The Dying Poet.* Gottschalk was the first American pianist to achieve international recognition.

Gottwald \'gȯt-ˌvält\, **Klement** (1896–1953) Czechoslovak communist politician and journalist. A charter member of Czechoslovakia's Communist Party (1921), he became its leader in 1927 and a member of the Czechoslovak parliament in 1929. Opposed to the MUNICH AGREEMENT, he lived in Moscow through World War II, making several broadcasts to the Czechoslovak underground. After the war, he was appointed deputy premier (1945–46), then premier (1946–48). Inaugurated as president in 1948 after EDVARD BENES's resignation, he quickly consolidated his position, purging rivals and adopting a Stalinist model of government, and served until his death.

gouache \'gwäsh\ Opaque watercolor. Also known as poster paint, designer's color, and body color, it differs from transparent WATERCOLOR in that the pigments are bound by liquid glue, which is used as a thinner. The addition of white pigment lightens the tone and lends opacity. Gouache paints dry to a matte finish and, if desired, without visible brush marks. They can be applied thinly or thickly. A wide range of colors are available, including fluorescent and metallic pigments. The suede finish and crisp lines characteristic of many Indian and Islamic miniature paintings is produced by this medium; it is used in Western screen and fan decoration and was used by modern artists such as GEORGES ROUAULT and PAUL KLEE.

Goulart \gü-'lärt\, **João (Belchior Marques)** (1918–1976) Reformist president of Brazil (1961–64). Son of a wealthy rancher, he earned a law degree and became a protégé of Pres. GETULIO VARGAS, in whose administration he served as minister of labor, industry, and commerce. Elected vice president (1956–61), he became president when Pres. Jânio Quadros resigned. He undertook a program of radical reforms, winning passage of a law limiting the amount of profits that foreign companies could export. He attempted LAND REFORM but was unable to secure majority support for his legislative program. Inflation reached alarming proportions, the cost of living tripling. He was ousted by the military in 1964 and died in exile.

Goulburn River \'gōl-bərn\ River, central VICTORIA, Australia. Rising on Mount Singleton in Fraser National Park, it flows north for 280 mi (450 km) through the Eildon, Goulburn, and Waranga reservoirs and Lake Nagambie to join the MURRAY RIVER. Goulburn River National Park lies along its banks.

Gould \'güld\, **Chester** (1900–1985) U.S. cartoonist. Born in Pawnee, Okla., he studied cartooning through a correspondence school. His "Dick Tracy" action comic strip, first distributed in 1931 by the Chicago Tribune–New York News Syndicate, became the first popular cops-and-robbers series. Drawn with hard outlines and accurate in the details of crime and criminal investigation, the widely syndicated strip featured a clean-cut detective with a jutting jaw, whose methods made him the nemesis of a gallery of grotesquely caricatured criminals. Gould retired from the strip in 1977.

Gould \'güld\, **Glenn (Herbert)** (1932–1982) Canadian pianist. He planned to concentrate on composing, but the acclaim that greeted his first recording of J.S. BACH's *Goldberg Variations* (1955) led to an international career as a pianist. His interpretations of Bach (and occasionally of other composers) set a new standard with their technical brilliance and subtle intelligence. Famously eccentric, he often wore gloves while playing and was intensely hypochondriac. Never happy performing, in 1964 he left the concert stage forever for the recording studio. He later composed radio "documentaries" (including "The Idea of North") that fall somewhere between typical examples of the genre and musique concrète.

Gould \'güld\, **Jay** *orig.* **Jason** (1836–1892) U.S. railroad executive, speculator, and unscrupulous robber baron. Born in Roxbury, N.Y., he first worked as a surveyor, then bought a tannery, and by 1859 was speculating in the stocks of small railways. In 1867 he became a director of the Erie Railroad and joined with DANIEL DREW and JAMES FISK to keep CORNELIUS VANDERBILT from buying control of the railroad. He bribed New York legislators to legalize the sale of watered stock. He and Fisk joined with WILLIAM MARCY TWEED to profit from further stock manipulations. In 1869 they attempted to corner the gold market, causing the BLACK FRIDAY panic. In 1872 public outcry forced Gould to cede control of the Erie. With a fortune of $25 million he controlled the Union Pacific by 1874, and by 1881 he owned 15% of all U.S. rail mileage. He sold his Union Pacific stock to amass a rail system southwest of St. Louis that by 1890 included half the region's rail mileage. He gained control of Western Union (1881), owned the New York *World* (1879–83) and the Manhattan Elevated Railroad (1886), and remained ruthless to the end.

Gould, Shane (born 1956) Australian (Fiji-born) swimmer. At the 1972 Olympic Games, at age 15, she dominated women's swimming, winning five medals (three gold, one silver, one bronze). She set world records in all five freestyle distances (100, 200, 400, 800, and 1,500 m). In 1973 she became the first woman to break the 17-minute barrier in the 1500-m freestyle (16 minutes 59.6 seconds).

Gould, Stephen Jay (1941–2002) U.S. paleontologist and evolutionary biologist. Born in New York City, he received a PhD in paleontology from Columbia University and joined the faculty of Harvard University in 1967. With Niles Eldredge (born 1943), he developed the controversial theory of punctuated equilibrium (1972), a revision of DARWINISM that proposed that the evolutionary creation of new species occurs in rapid bursts over periods as short as thousands of years, which are followed by long periods of stability. He was widely known as a popularizing writer on biological and evolutionary topics, especially in *Natural History* magazine; his numerous books include *The Panda's Thumb* (1980), *The Mismeasure of Man* (1981), and *The Structure of Evolutionary Theory* (2002).

Gounod \gü-'nō\, **Charles (François)** (1818–1893) French composer. He studied music at the Paris Conservatoire and in Rome. He also studied for the priesthood and worked as an organist, and he remained torn between the theater and the church. His reputation largely rests on his hugely popular opera *Faust* (1859). His 15 other operas include *Roméo et Juliette* (1867), *Le médecin malgré lui* (1858), *Philémon et Baucis* (1860), and *Mireille* (1864); other works include 17 masses, more than 150 songs, and two symphonies.

Dwarf gourami (*Colisa lalia*).

JANE BURTON—BRUCE COLEMAN LTD.

gourami \gü-'rä-mē\ Any of several of the freshwater, tropical labyrinth fishes (order Perciformes), especially *Osphronemus goramy,* an East Indian fish caught or raised for food. A compact, oval fish with a long, filamentous ray extending from each pelvic fin, it weighs up to 20 lbs (9 kg). Adults are brown or gray with a paler belly. Other gouramis, several of them popular in home aquariums, are Asian members of different genera and families. Generally deep-bodied and small-mouthed, they include the giant gourami *(Colisa fasciata),* a blue-green and reddish brown fish 5 in. (12 cm) long; the dwarf gourami *(C. lalia),* 2.5 in. (6 cm) long, brightly striped in red and blue; and the kissing gourami *(Helostoma temmincki),* a greenish or pinkish white fish noted for its "kissing" activities.

gourd Any of the approximately 700 species of food and ornamental plants that make up the family Cucurbitaceae (order Violales), including MELONS, SQUASHES, and PUMPKINS. Most species are prostrate or climb by tendrils. They are annual herbaceous plants native to temperate and tropical areas. Economically important food gourds include pumpkin, CUCUMBER, WATERMELON, CHAYOTE, and squash. Gourds are generally low in nutrients; one exception is winter squash (certain cultivars of *Cucurbita maxima, C. moschata, C. pepo,* etc.). The hard shells of many gourds have made them useful as containers and utensils. Colorful and oddly shaped gourds are picked for ornamental use.

Gourmont \gür-'mō^{n}\, **Rémy de** (1858–1915) French novelist, poet, playwright, and philosopher. He worked 10 years at the national library; his dismissal resulted from an allegedly unpatriotic article in the *Mercure de France,* a journal he had cofounded. A painful skin disease later kept him a semirecluse. One of the most intelligent critics from the SYMBOLIST MOVEMENT, he had a major role in disseminating its aesthetic doctrines. His 50 published volumes are mainly collections of essays. His novels include *Very Woman* (1890), *The Dream of a Woman* (1899), and *A Virgin Heart* (1907).

gout Hereditary metabolic disorder in which excess URIC-ACID salts, normally excreted in urine, are deposited as needle-sharp crystals in joints, causing attacks of severe INFLAMMATION. The most common site is the base of the big toe. One of the oldest diseases in medical literature, gout is far more common in men. Attacks usually do not begin until middle age. They cause heat, redness, and extreme tenderness and pain, and often subside in a week or two. Colchicine is used to treat acute attacks. Drugs such as allopurinol inhibit uric-acid synthesis.

government Political system by which a body of people is administered and regulated. Different levels of government typically have different responsibilities. The level closest to those governed is local government. Regional governments comprise a grouping of individual communities. National governments nominally control all the territory within internationally recognized borders and have responsibilities not shared by their subnational counterparts. Most governments exercise EXECUTIVE, legislative (see LEGISLATURE), and judicial (see JUDICIARY) powers and split or combine them in various ways. Some also control the religious affairs of their people; others avoid any involvement with religion. Political forms at the national level determine the powers exercised at the subnational levels; these have included autocracy, DEMOCRACY, FASCISM, MONARCHY, OLIGARCHY, plutocracy (government by the wealthy), THEOCRACY, and TOTALITARIANISM.

government budget Forecast of governmental expenditures and revenues for the ensuing fiscal year. In modern industrial economies, the budget is the key instrument for the execution of government economic policies. Because government budgets may promote or retard economic growth in certain areas of the economy and because views about priorities in government spending differ widely, government budgets are the focus of competing political interests. In the U.S. the federal budget is prepared by the president's Office of Management and Budget. The U.S. Congress has considerable input, influencing the budget's preparation through negotiations with the president and considering it in detail on its official submission to Congress.

governor In technology, a device that automatically maintains the rotary speed of an engine within reasonably close limits regardless of the load. A typical governor regulates an engine's speed by varying the rate at which fuel or working fluid is furnished to it. Nearly all governors work by CENTRIFUGAL FORCE and consist of a pair of masses rotating about a spindle driven by the engine and kept from flying outward, usually by springs. With an increase in speed, the controlling force of the springs is overcome and the masses move outward, opening valves supplying the engine with its working fluid or fuel. JAMES WATT invented a governor for controlling steam engines. Modern governors are used to regulate the flow of gasoline to INTERNAL-COMBUSTION ENGINES and the flow of steam, water, or gas to various types of TURBINES. See also FLYWHEEL.

Gower \'gaů-ər, 'gȯr\, **John** (1330?–1408) English poet. His works, in the tradition of COURTLY LOVE and moral allegory, strongly influenced other poets of his day. His friend GEOFFREY CHAUCER called him "moral Gower." His *Speculum meditantis* (c. 1374–78), written in French, is an allegorical work on vices and virtues. *Vox clamantis* (1385?), his major Latin poem, owes much to OVID. His greatest work in English is the *Confessio Amantis* (begun c. 1386), a long collection of exemplary tales of love.

Goya (y Lucientes), Francisco (José) de (1746–1828) Spanish painter and printmaker. He came to maturity in 1775 with the first of some 60 cartoons for the royal tapestry factory of Santa Bárbara, painted through 1792. In 1780 he was elected to the Royal Academy in Madrid and in 1786 was appointed painter to CHARLES III. By 1799, under the patronage of CHARLES IV, he had become the most successful and fashionable artist in Spain; his famous *The Family of Charles IV* was painted at this time (1800). Though he welcomed his honors and success, the record he left of his patrons and their society is ruthlessly penetrating. The eroticism of his famous *Naked Maja* and *Clothed Maja* (c. 1800–5) caused him to be summoned before the Inquisition in 1815. After an illness left him permanently deaf in the 1790s, his work took on an exaggerated realism that borders on caricature. His 80 *Caprices* (publ. 1799), satirical prints attacking political, social, and religious abuses, was an outstanding achievement in the history of printmaking. When Napoleon's invaded Spain (1808–15), Goya produced the 82-etching series *The Disasters of War* (1810–20). He settled in Bordeaux, France, in 1824, resigned as court painter in 1826, and began working in lithography. Exceptionally prolific and versatile, he completed some 500 oil paintings and murals, 300 etchings and lithographs, hundreds of drawings, and more than 200 portraits. He is said to have acknowledged three masters: DIEGO VELAZQUEZ, REMBRANDT, and nature. He had no immediate followers, but his work profoundly influenced 19th-century European art.

Goyen \'k̲üi-ə, *Engl* 'gȯi-ən\, **Jan Josephs(zoon) van** (1596–1656) Dutch painter and etcher. He studied in Leiden and Haarlem before settling at The Hague in 1632. Confining himself primarily to the scenery of Holland, he painted on wood panels; intricate detail, low horizons, and subtle atmospheric effects characterize his work. He excelled at capturing the moods of sky and water, Dutch cities (e.g., *View of Leiden,* 1643), and lowland winter scenes. A prolific draftsman, he also executed many landscape etchings. He had numerous imitators. With SALOMON VAN RUYSDAEL, he was the outstanding master of tonal landscape painting in 17th-century Holland.

Gozzoli \gȯt-'tsȯ-lē\, **Benozzo** *orig.* **Benozzo di Lese** \'lā-sā\ (c. 1420–1497) Italian Renaissance painter. Early in his career he assisted

Detail with Lorenzo de' Medici from "Procession of the Magi," fresco by Gozzoli, 1459; in the Medici-Riccardi Palace, Florence.

SCALA—ART RESOURCE

LORENZO GHIBERTI on the east doors of the Baptistery in Florence and Fra ANGELICO on frescoes in Florence, Rome, and Orvieto. His reputation today rests on the breathtaking fresco cycle *The Journey of the Magi* (1459–61) in the chapel of Florence's Medici-Riccardi Palace. His work as a whole was undistinguished. He painted several altarpieces and a series of 25 frescoes of Old Testament scenes, now badly damaged, for the Camposanto in Pisa (1468–84).

GPS See GLOBAL POSITIONING SYSTEM

Grable, Betty (1916–1973) U.S. film actress. Born in St. Louis, Mo., she performed as a chorus-line dancer in 1930s musicals, then was featured in such musicals as *Down Argentine Way* (1940) and *Moon over Miami* (1941). Noted for her shapely legs, she became a top star and the favorite pinup girl of U.S. troops in World War II. After the war, she starred in such films as *Mother Wore Tights* (1947) and *How to Marry a Millionaire* (1953), but her film career declined with the decline of the film musical.

Gracchus \'gra-kəs\, **Gaius Sempronius** (154?–121 BC) Roman TRIBUNE (123–122 BC). He joined the outcry over the murder of his brother, Tiberius GRACCHUS, and helped implement the latter's agrarian law. He combined the votes of plebeians and equites to pass reforms aimed at curbing the corruption of the nobility. His attempts to extend citizenship to Rome's Italian allies and more freedom to plebeians were unpopular. Though he came from an aristocratic family, his policies were seen by extreme conservatives as an attempt to destroy the aristocracy. He committed suicide while under siege on the Aventine Hill.

Gracchus, Tiberius Sempronius (163?–133 BC) Roman aristocrat and TRIBUNE (133). He sponsored agrarian reforms to restore the class of small independent farmers on which the Roman economy and military depended. Though a traditional system only 30 years before, it was seen as radical by his Senate enemies. He was assassinated in a riot sparked by senatorial opponents angered by his unorthodox political tactics.

Grace One of a group of Greek goddesses who personified charm and beauty. Originally fertility goddesses, they were frequently associated with APHRODITE. Their number varied in different legends, but often there were three. They were sometimes said to be the daughters of ZEUS and HERA and sometimes of HELIOS and Aegle, daughter of Zeus.

grace In Christian theology, the unmerited gift of divine favor, which brings about the SALVATION of a sinner. The concept of grace has given rise to theological debate over the nature of human depravity and the extent to which individuals may contribute to their own salvation through free will. Though in principle the ideas of merit and grace are mutually exclusive, the question of whether grace may be given as a reward for good works or for faith alone was important in the Protestant REFORMATION. There has also been controversy over the means of grace: Roman Catholics, Eastern Orthodox, and some Protestants believe that it is conferred through the SACRAMENTS, while some other Protestants (e.g., Baptists) hold that participation in grace results from personal faith alone. See also JUSTIFICATION, ORIGINAL SIN.

Grace, W.G. *in full* **William Gilbert Grace** (1848–1915) Greatest cricketer in Victorian England. Although he practiced medicine, cricket was his first love, and Grace evolved the modern principles of batting and achieved many notable performances on rough and unpredictable wickets such as are unknown to modern players. In his career in first-class cricket (1865–1908), Grace scored 54,896 runs, registered 126 centuries (100 runs in a single innings), and, as a bowler, took 2,876 wickets. In 84 matches for Gentlemen versus Players he amassed 6,000 runs and took 271 wickets. In 1880 he was on the English team that played the first Test match against Australia in England.

grackle Any of several songbird species (in the family Icteridae) having iridescent black plumage and a long tail; also called crow-blackbird. Grackles use their stout, pointed bill to snap up insects, dig grubs from the soil, and kill small vertebrates, including fishes and baby birds; they can also crack hard seeds. The common grackle *(Quiscalus quiscula)* of North America is about 12 in. (30 cm) long. The males of two *Cassidus* species (boat-tailed and great-tailed grackles) have a long, deeply keeled tail; these species are found in arid lands of the southwestern U.S. to Peru and in salt marshes from New Jersey to Texas, where they are locally called JACKDAWS. See also BLACKBIRD, MYNAH. See photograph opposite.

gradient In mathematics, a DIFFERENTIAL OPERATOR applied to a three-dimensional vector-valued FUNCTION to yield a VECTOR whose three components are the PARTIAL DERIVATIVES of the function with respect to its three variables. The symbol for gradient is ∇. Thus, the gradient of a function f, written grad f, or ∇f, is $\nabla f = \mathbf{i}f_x + \mathbf{j}f_y + \mathbf{k}f_z$ where f_x, f_y, and f_z are the first partial derivatives of f and the vectors **i**, **j**, and **k** are the unit vectors of the VECTOR SPACE. If in physics, for example, f is a temperature field (giving the temperature at every point in a space), ∇f is the direction of the heat-flow vector in the field.

Graf, Steffi *orig.* **Stephanie Maria** (born 1969) German tennis player. At the age of 13 she became the second-youngest player ever to earn an international ranking. In 1987 she won her first Grand Slam event (the French Open), and in 1988 she won all four Grand Slam events (French, Australian, U.S., and Wimbledon) and an Olympic gold medal. Sidetracked by knee surgery in 1997, she played her way back to the top, winning the French Open in 1999, for her 22nd Grand Slam title (including seven Wimbledon championships). She announced her retirement later that year.

Gräfe \'grä-fə\, **Albrecht Friedrich Wilhelm Ernst von** (1828–1870) German ophthalmologist. Using HERMANN VON HELMHOLTZ's ophthalmoscope, he developed several operations for eye disorders, including iridectomy (removal of part of the iris) for glaucoma and lens extraction for cataract. He traced blindness and visual defects in some cerebral disorders to optic-nerve inflammation. Gräfe's sign (diagnostic for Graves' disease) is failure of the upper eyelid to follow the eyeball when looking downward. His writings include a *Manual of Comprehensive Ophthalmology* (7 vols., 1874–80). He is considered the founder of modern ophthalmology.

graffiti (Italian: "scratched") Any casual writing or design marked on a wall. Graffiti have been made throughout history; they are found in abundance on the monuments of ancient Egypt. Technically the term applies to a design scratched through a layer of paint or plaster, but its meaning is extended to other markings. Graffiti produced with spray paint became notorious in New York City in the 1970s and have appeared in cities all over the U.S. and Europe. The 20th-century preoccupation with accidental and other manifestations of the subconscious stimulated this form of expression and produced a brief vogue for "graffiti art." Graffiti are sometimes considered a form of folk art.

graft In horticulture, the act of placing a portion of one plant (called a bud or scion) into or on a stem, root, or branch of another (called the stock) in such a way that a union forms and the partners continue to grow. Grafting is used for various purposes: to repair injured trees, produce dwarf trees and shrubs, strengthen plants' resistance to certain diseases, retain varietal characteristics, adapt varieties to adverse soil or climatic conditions, ensure pollination, produce multifruited or multiflowered plants, and propagate certain species (such as hybrid roses) that can be propagated in no other way. In theory, any two plants that are closely related botanically and that have a continuous CAMBIUM can be grafted. Grafts between species of the same genus are often successful and between genera occasionally so, but grafts between families are nearly always failures. See illustration on following page.

Common grackle (*Quiscalus quiscula*).
THASE DANIEL

Graham, Billy *in full* **William Franklin Graham, Jr.** (born 1918) U.S. Christian evangelist. Born in Charlotte, N.C., son of a dairy farmer, he underwent a conversion experience at 16 during a revival. After attending Bob Jones College and the Florida Bible Institute, he was ordained a Southern Baptist clergyman in 1939. He later earned a degree in anthropology from Wheaton College. He won numerous converts with his tent revivals and radio broadcasts, and by 1950 he had become fundamentalism's leading spokesman. He led a series of widely televised interna-

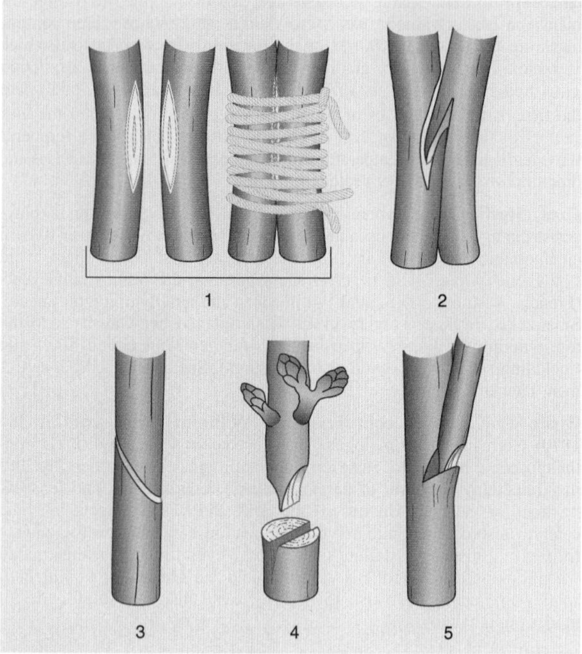

Some methods of grafting: (1) simple splice graft, showing cut surfaces of stock and scion and the cut surfaces joined and bound, (2) tongued graft, (3) whip graft, (4) cleft graft, (5) side cleft graft.

tional revival crusades through the Billy Graham Evangelistic Association in Minneapolis, and he became spiritual adviser to a series of U.S. presidents.

Graham \'grā-əm, 'gram\, **Jorie** (born 1951) U.S. poet. Born in New York City, she studied at NYU and the University of Iowa, where she has since taught. Her abstract, intellectual verse is known for its visual imagery, complex metaphors, and philosophical content. Her first volume of verse, *Hybrids of Plants and of Ghosts* (1980), contains compact, intricate poems that explore death, beauty, and change. Later volumes include *The Dream of the Unified Field* (1995, Pulitzer Prize).

Graham, Katharine *orig.* **Katharine Meyer** (1917–2001) U.S. owner and publisher of news publications. Born in New York City, the daughter of Agnes and Eugene Meyer (1875–1959), owner and publisher of *The Washington Post* (1933–46), she studied at Vassar College and the University of Chicago. In 1940 she married Philip Graham, who later became the *Post*'s publisher. The Grahams acquired the paper from Meyer in 1948. After her husband's suicide in 1963, she stepped in as head of the Washington Post Co. Under her leadership the *Post* became one of the nation's most powerful newspapers, particularly with its coverage of the Watergate scandal. Her best-selling autobiography, *Personal History*, earned the PULITZER PRIZE in 1997.

Graham, Martha (1894–1991) U.S. dancer, teacher, choreographer, and foremost exponent of MODERN DANCE. Born in Pittsburgh, she studied from 1916 with TED SHAWN at the Denishawn school. She left in 1923 for New York, where she founded her own school in 1927 and a performing company in 1929. She choreographed over 160 works, creating unique "dance plays" and using a variety of themes to express emotion and conflict. Many are based on American themes, including *Appalachian Spring* (1944). She collaborated for many years with Louis Horst, her musical director, and with ISAMU NOGUCHI, who designed many of her sets. She retired from dancing in 1970 but continued to teach and choreograph. Her technique became the first significant alternative to classical BALLET, and her influence extended worldwide through her choreography and her students.

Graham, Otto (Everett, Jr.) (born 1921) U.S. football player and coach. Born in Waukegan, Ill., he was a star tailback at Northwestern University. He is best remembered as quarterback (switching from his college position) of the Cleveland Browns during a 10-year period (1946–55) in which they won 105 games, lost 17, and tied five in regular season play and won seven of 10 championship games. Graham's career average yardage per pass (8.63) was not surpassed until the 1980s. His coaching career was mainly with the U.S. Coast Guard Academy (1959–66) and the Washington Redskins (1966–68).

Grahame, Kenneth \'grā-əm, 'gram\ (1859–1932) British writer of children's books. Born in Edinburgh, he worked as a banker in London while contributing articles and stories to journals, which he collected in such books as *The Golden Age* (1895) and *Dream Days* (1898). He is best known for his classic *The Wind in the Willows* (1908; dramatized by A.A. MILNE as *Toad of Toad Hall*, 1930), whose animal characters—principally Mole, Rat, Badger, and Toad—captivatingly combine human traits with authentic animal habits.

Grahn, Lucile *orig.* **Lucina Alexia** (1819–1907) Danish ballerina, ballet mistress, and choreographer. She was trained in Copenhagen by AUGUST BOURNONVILLE. In 1839 she was engaged at the Paris Opéra; this marked the beginning of her international career as one of the greatest Romantic ballerinas. After 1846 she toured Europe, frequently producing the ballets in which she appeared, including her own original works. In 1856 Grahn retired from the stage. From 1858 to 1875 she worked as a ballet mistress and director in Germany. At the Court Opera in Munich she produced a number of ballets and also worked with the composer RICHARD WAGNER on the production of several of his operas.

grail *or* **Holy Grail** In ARTHURIAN LEGEND, a sacred cup that was the object of a mystical quest by knights of the Round Table, notably Sir GALAHAD. The grail legend may have been inspired by classical and Celtic stories of magic cauldrons and horns of plenty. It was first given Christian significance as a mysterious, holy object by CHRÉTIEN DE TROYES in the 12th-century romance *Perceval, or the Count of the Holy Grail.* The grail was sometimes said to be the same cup used by JESUS at the Last Supper and later by Joseph of Arimathea to catch the blood flowing from the wounds of Jesus on the cross.

grain See CEREAL

grain alcohol See ETHANOL

grain elevator Storage building for grain, usually a tall frame, metal, or concrete structure with a compartmented interior; also, the device for loading grain into a building. One common mechanism consists of a hopper, a long rectangular open trough, and an endless vertical belt or chain with flights (crosspieces) for conveying the grain to the top of the stack. The force of gravity enables elevated grain to be unloaded quickly and easily from chutes.

grain mill Structure for grinding CEREAL. WATERWHEELS were first exploited for such tasks. Geared mills turning grindstones (see GEAR) were used in the Roman Empire, but their fullest development occurred in medieval Europe, in, for example, the great grain mill near Arles, France, which may have met the needs of 80,000 people. WINDMILLS were also among the prime movers that replaced animal muscle as a source of power. They were used for centuries in various parts of the world, and remain of major industrial importance in developing nations.

Grainger, (George) Percy (Aldridge) (1882–1961) Australian-U.S. composer and pianist. After studying music in Frankfurt, he established himself as a piano virtuoso in England, while also pursuing ethnomusicological interest, collecting folk tunes in England and Denmark. He moved to the U.S. permanently in 1914, teaching in Chicago and New York, and established an ethnomusicological center at the University of Melbourne. Though an inveterate experimenter in the realms of timbre, rhythm, harmony, and texture, he is known for his tuneful short works for orchestra, piano, and concert band, including *Country Gardens, Molly on the Shore, Mock Morris,* and *Lincolnshire Posy.*

gram Unit of MASS or WEIGHT used especially in the centimeter-gram-second (CGS) system of MEASUREMENT. One gram is equal to 0.001 kg, about 0.035 oz, or 15.43 grains. The gram is very nearly equal to the mass of 1 cc of pure water at its maximum density. The gram of FORCE is equal to the weight of a gram of mass under standard gravity. For greater precision, the mass may be weighed at a point at which the acceleration due to gravity is 980.655 cm/sec^2. See also GRAVITATION, METRIC SYSTEM.

gram stain Universally used staining technique for the initial identification of BACTERIA, devised in 1884 by the Danish physician Hans Christian Gram (1853–1938). The stain reveals basic differences in the biochemical and structural properties of a living cell. A slide containing a smear of bacteria is treated with a purple dye; the slide is then dipped in an iodine solution, followed by an organic solvent (such as alcohol) that can dissolve the dye. Gram-positive bacteria remain purple because they have a thick cell wall that the solvent cannot easily penetrate; gram-negative bacteria lose their color because they have thin cell walls that allow the solvent to penetrate and remove the dye.

gramadevata \'grä-mə-'dā-və-ˌtä\ Folk deities widely worshiped in rural India. Often female figures, they may have originated as agricultural deities, and they are offered animal sacrifices to ward off disease, crop failures, and other natural disasters. Many are purely local, spirits of a place (e.g., a crossroads) or of a person who has died an untimely death. They are worshiped in the form of stones or earthenware icons fixed in simple shrines or set up under a village tree.

grammar Rules of a language governing its PHONOLOGY, MORPHOLOGY, SYNTAX, and SEMANTICS; also, a written summary of such rules. The first Europeans to write grammar texts were the Greeks, notably the Alexandrians of the lst century BC. The Romans applied the Greek grammatical system to Latin. The works of the Latin grammarians Donatus (4th century AD) and PRISCIAN (6th century) were widely used to teach grammar in medieval Europe. By 1700, grammars of 61 vernacular languages had been printed. These were mainly used for teaching and were intended to reform or standardize language. In the 19th–20th century, linguists began studying languages to trace their evolution rather than to prescribe correct usage. Descriptive linguists (see FERDINAND DE SAUSSURE) studied spoken language by collecting and analyzing sample sentences. Transformational grammarians (see NOAM CHOMSKY) examined the underlying structure of language (see GENERATIVE GRAMMAR). The older approach to grammar as a body of rules needed to speak and write correctly is still the basis of primary and secondary teaching.

Grammy Awards Annual awards given by the Recording Academy (officially the National Academy of Recording Arts and Sciences). The first Grammies (the name is a dimunitive of "gramophone") were given in 1958. The awards, which reflect the votes of the Academy's large membership of musicians, producers, and other music professionals, have expanded considerably to reflect the variety of musical taste and production; today awards are given in dozens of categories.

Grampian *or* **Grampian Hills** Mountain system, Scotland. Extending across central Scotland, it forms a natural boundary between the Scottish Highlands and Scottish Lowlands. Its highest peak, BEN NEVIS, is the highest mountain in Britain.

Grampians, the Mountain range, western VICTORIA, Australia. Composed mainly of hard sandstone, the range is noted for deep gorges, weathered rock formations, and wildflowers. The highest peak, Mount William, rises to 3,827 ft (1,166 m). The range was named after the GRAMPIAN of Scotland.

Gramsci \'gräm-shē\, **Antonio** (1891–1937) Italian intellectual and politician. After entering the University of Turin, he joined the ITALIAN SOCIALIST PARTY in 1914. In 1921 he left the Socialists to found the Italian Communist Party (see DEMOCRATIC PARTY OF THE LEFT), and spent two years in the Soviet Union. In 1924 he became head of the party and was elected to the national legislature. The party was outlawed by the fascist government in 1926, and Gramsci was arrested and imprisoned for 11 years; in poor health, he was released to die at 46. His influential *Letters from Prison* (1947) and other writings outline a version of communism less dogmatic than Soviet communism. His work has influenced sociology, political theory, and international relations.

Gran Chaco \grän-'chä-kō\ *Spanish* **Chaco** *or* **El Chaco** Plain, southern central South America. An arid lowland, it is bounded by the ANDES, the PARAGUAY and PARANÁ rivers, a marshy area in Bolivia, and by the Río SALADO in Argentina. Its area is about 280,000 sq mi (725,000 sq km). The region's main part, in the fork of the Paraguay and PILCOMAYO rivers, was fought over by Bolivia and Paraguay, in the 1932–35 CHACO WAR. By a 1938 treaty, a larger eastern part went to Paraguay and a smaller western part to Bolivia. Chaco's wildlife is abundant, and there are at least 60 known species of snake. Cattle grazing is a major economic activity.

Gran Colombia \'grän-kō-'lōm-bē-ä\ Former South American republic 1822–30. Formerly the viceroyalty of NEW GRANADA, it included roughly the modern nations of Colombia, Panama, Venezuela, and Ecuador. Gran Colombia was formed in 1819 during the war for independence from Spain, with its capital at BOGOTÁ. SIMON BOLIVAR was its creator and first president. Gran Colombia had a vigorous existence during the war, becoming independent in 1822, and was dissolved with the secession of Venezuela and Ecuador in 1830.

Gran Paradiso National Park \'grän-ˌpä-rä-'dē-zō\ Park, northwestern Italy. Established in 1836 as a hunting zone, in 1856 it became the Royal Hunting Reserve of the Gran Paradiso, and in 1947 received national park status. It covers an area of 153,240 acres (62,000 hectares) and extends along the upper Valle d'Aosta region; it contains the highest peak in the Graian Alps, Gran Paradiso, at 13,323 ft (4,061 m). The terrain is typically alpine, with numerous glaciers and coniferous tree-lined slopes.

Granada \grä-'nä-t͟hä\ City (pop., 1992 est.: 256,200; metro area population 1995: 273,000), capital of Granada province, ANDALUSIA, southern Spain. Located at the northwestern slope of the Sierra Nevada, it was the site of the Iberian settlement Elibyrge in the 5th century BC and of the Roman Illiberis. As the seat of the Moorish kingdom of Granada, it was the final stronghold of the MOORS in Spain, until 1492. Nearby is the ALHAMBRA, as well as the Alcazaba fortress that guarded it. The city has fine Renaissance, baroque, and neoclassical architecture and is a major tourist center. It has been the see of an archbishop since 1493; the University of Granada was founded in 1526.

Granados (y Campiña) \grä-'nä-t͟hōs\, **Enrique** (1867–1916) Spanish composer. He studied composition with F. PEDRELL and concertized as a pianist. From 1901 he taught at the Academia Granados, the music school he founded in Barcelona. He wrote four zarzuelas, including *María del Carmen* (1898), and two "poemas" (also stage works), as well as songs and chamber works. His fame rests on the piano suite *Goyescas* (1911). His opera of the same name was performed successfully at New York's Metropolitan Opera in 1916; returning to Europe, Granados's ship was torpedoed by a German submarine.

Grand Alliance, War of the (1689–97) Third major war of LOUIS XIV of France, in which his expansionist plans were blocked by an alliance led by Britain, the United Provinces of the Netherlands, and the Austrian Habsburgs. The deeper issue underlying the war was the rivalry between the BOURBON and HABSBURG dynasties. Louis launched a campaign in the 1680s to position the Bourbons for future succession to the Spanish throne. To oppose him, the Habsburg emperor LEOPOLD I joined other European nations in the League of AUGSBURG. The league proved ineffective, but in 1690 Britain, Brandenburg, Saxony, Bavaria, and Spain, alarmed at Louis's successes, joined with Leopold to form the Grand Alliance. As war broke out in Europe and in overseas colonies, including America (see KING WILLIAM'S WAR), Louis found his military inadequately prepared, and France suffered heavy naval losses. In 1695 Louis started secret peace negotiations, which culminated in the Treaty of Rijswijk (1697). The underlying conflict between the Habsburg and Bourbon rulers and English–French conflicts remained unresolved and resurfaced four years later in the War of the SPANISH SUCCESSION.

Grand Banks Portion of North American continental shelf, in the Atlantic Ocean. Lying southeast and south of NEWFOUNDLAND, it is a noted international fishing ground and extends 350 mi (560 km) north–south and 420 mi (675 km) east–west. The cold Labrador Current and the warm GULF STREAM meet in its vicinity, causing heavy fogs. The banks were first reported in 1498 by JOHN CABOT. In 1977 Canada extended its fishing claim to encompass most of the Grand Banks; it has since given limited fishing rights to other countries.

Grand Canal Series of waterways in northern China that link Hangzhou with Beijing. 1,085 mi (1,747 km) in length, it is the world's longest man-made waterway. It was build to enable successive Chinese regimes to transport surplus grain from the agriculturally rich Chang (Yangtze) and Huai river valleys to feed the capital cities and large standing armies in the north. The oldest portion, in the south, may date from the 4th century BC. Expanded over the centuries, it continues to be used today for shipping and irrigation.

Grand Canyon Gorge cut by the COLORADO RIVER, northwestern Arizona. Noted for its rock formations and coloration, it is about 0.1–18 mi

(0.2–29 km) wide, and extends from northern Arizona to Grand Wash Cliffs, near the Nevada border, a distance of about 277 mi (446 km). The deepest section, 56 mi (90 km) long, is within Grand Canyon National Park, which covers the river's length from Lake Powell to Lake MEAD. The surrounding plateau is 5,000–9,000 ft (1,500–2,750 m) above sea level, and the canyon is in places more than a mile deep. The national park, now containing 1,904 sq mi (4,931 sq km), was created in 1919. The former Grand Canyon National Monument, established in 1932, was added, with other lands, in 1975.

Grand Canyon series Major division of rocks in northern Arizona dating from PRECAMBRIAN TIME. The rocks of the series consist of about 10,600 ft (3,400 m) of quartz sandstones, shales, and thick sequences of carbonate rocks. Spectacular exposures of these rocks occur in the Grand Canyon.

Grand Central Station Railroad terminal in New York City designed and built (1903–13) by Reed & Stem in collaboration with the firm of Warren & Wetmore, who receive credit for the aesthetics of the huge structure. The concourse, with its 125-ft (43-m) ceiling vault painted with constellations, was one of the largest enclosed spaces of its time. A gem of BEAUX-ARTS STYLE, the terminal looks as though it could have been transported from 1870s France. Atop the symmetrical main facade is a large clock and sculptures of an American eagle and Roman deities.

Grand Falls See CHURCHILL FALLS

Grand Guignol \grän-gēn-'yȯl\ Short plays of violence, horror, and sadism popular in 20th-century Parisian CABARETS. The name probably derives from the violent plots that featured the puppet Guignol. The plays were performed mainly at the Théâtre du Grand Guignol, from 1897 to 1962. The genre was introduced into England in 1908, but it remained mainly a Parisian theatrical form.

grand jury Jury that examines accusations against persons charged with crime and, if the evidence warrants it, makes formal charges on which the accused are later tried. It does not decide guilt or innocence, only whether there is "probable cause" to believe that a person has committed a crime, and issues or elects not to issue an indictment. Public officials (prosecutors and police) provide information and summon witnesses for the jury. The proceedings are usually secret. Some U.S. states have abolished the grand jury and authorize indictments by prosecutors.

Grand National British STEEPLECHASE horse-racing event held annually in Liverpool. Established in 1839, it attracts more attention throughout the world than any other such event because of its extreme difficulties and dangers. The course is covered twice for a distance of 4 miles 855 yards (7,219 m), including 31 jumps, some of them spectacularly hazardous.

Grand Ole Opry COUNTRY-MUSIC radio show in Nashville, Tenn. Founded in 1925 by George Dewey Hay, who had helped organize Chicago's "WLS National Barn Dance," the show was originally known as the "WSM Barn Dance"; it acquired its lasting name in 1926. Its music developed from D. MACON's ballads, the string bands, cowboy music, and western swing of the 1930s, and later the traditional music characterized by the career of ROY ACUFF. After World War II, the honky-tonk style of ERNEST TUBB and later H. WILLIAMS, the bluegrass of BILL MONROE, and the voices of EDDY ARNOLD and KITTY WELLS all became Opry staples, as did comedy routines, notably by Minnie Pearl (1912–1996). In 1941 the Opry became a live stage show. In 1974 it moved to the Opryland amusement park and entertainment center. The Opry initiated and promoted the creation of Nashville as the center of country music.

Grand Portage National Monument Historic site, northeastern corner of Minnesota. Located on Lake SUPERIOR near the Canadian border, it was designated a national historic site in 1951 and a national monument in 1958. It covers a 9-mi (14-km) overland trail from Lake Superior's northern shore that bypassed the obstacles to early canoe travel. Used by early explorers, the portage marked the end of travel on the GREAT LAKES and the beginning of the interior river route. The portage trail now bisects the reservation of the Grand Portage tribe of the Minnesota Chippewa Indians.

Grand Prix racing \'grän-'prē\ Automobile racing in which formula cars (open-wheel, open-cockpit, rear-engine vehicles) are run on closed highways or other courses somewhat simulating road conditions. The cars used (known as Formula One cars) are generally smaller than those used in speedway races such as the INDIANAPOLIS 500. Grand Prix racing began in 1906 and today comprises more than 15 major international events. Its popularity grew particularly from the 1950s, when world championships were established.

Grand Rapids City (pop., 1996 est.: 188,000), western Michigan. Located on the Grand River, it was founded in 1826 as a trading post. Ample lumber from nearby forests soon fueled a woodworking industry. After Grand Rapids furniture was shown at the Philadelphia Centennial in 1876, the city became known as the furniture capital of America. Its industry diversified with the advent of World War I, and metal-based manufacturing thereafter exceeded furniture. Its public library contains important collections of books on furniture design; its educational institutions include Kendall College of Art and Design (1928). It was the boyhood home of Pres. GERALD FORD.

Grand River See NEOSHO RIVER

Grand Staircase–Escalante National Monument National preserve, southern Utah. Created a national monument in 1996, it covers 1.7 million acres (.7 million hectares). Its western section has cliffs and plateaus, and its eastern section has canyons along the Escalante River. Dinosaur tracks have been found there. The area was once inhabited by the ANASAZI people.

Grand Teton National Park \'tē-ˌtän\ National preserve, northwestern Wyoming. In 1950 most of Jackson Hole National Monument (a fertile valley) was incorporated into the park, which was established in 1929 and now covers 484 sq mi (1,254 sq km). The snow-covered peaks of its TETON RANGE are 7,000 ft (2,100 m) above the nearby SNAKE RIVER valley.

Grand Traverse Bay \'tra-vərs\ NE arm of Lake MICHIGAN, indenting northwestern Michigan. Located off the coast of the Lower Peninsula, the head of the bay is 32 mi (52 km) long and 12 mi (19 km) wide. It is divided into the East and West arms by Old Mission Peninsula, with Traverse City at its base. The Leelanau Peninsula lies west of the bay, which is noted for its year-round fishing. The area is an important summer-resort region.

Grand Trunk Railway Early Canadian railway line, incorporated in 1852–53 to connect the key cities of eastern Canada with Portland, Me. By completing its final link in July 1853 between Montreal and Portland, it became North America's first international railroad. The main Canadian line between Montreal and Toronto opened in 1856, and the Grand Trunk eventually became the main rail system of Quebec and Ontario. It merged with the Great Western Railway (1882) and became part of the CANADIAN NATIONAL RAILWAYS (1919–23).

grand unified theory *or* **grand unification theory** (GUT) Theory that attempts to unify the electroweak force (see ELECTROWEAK THEORY) with the STRONG FORCE. The unification of all four FUNDAMENTAL INTERACTIONS is sometimes called UNIFIED FIELD THEORY. Such theories generally predict that a PROTON decays into lighter particles. So far, no successful GUTs have been devised.

Grande, Río See RIO GRANDE

grande école \grän-dā-'kȯl\ (French: "great school") Any of several preeminent specialized institutions of higher learning in France. The École Polytechnique (Polytechnic School) was founded in 1794 to recruit and train technicians for the army. The École Normale Supérieure (Normal Superior School) serves mainly to prepare future university and *lycée* (senior secondary-school) teachers. The École Normale d'Administration trains the highest ranks of civil servants. The internationally renowned Collège de France (founded 1530) is a research institution that offers lectures by eminent scholars; it does not grant degrees or certificates. Other grandes écoles include institutes for advanced study in social science, architecture, and the arts.

grandfather clause Constitutional provision enacted by seven Southern U.S. states (1895–1910) to deny suffrage to black men. It exempted descendants of men who voted before 1867 from meeting new literacy and property requirements. Since black men were not granted voting rights until passage of the 15th Amendment in 1870, this clause effectively excluded them, and many impoverished and illiterate whites, from voting. The U.S. Supreme Court declared the clause unconstitutional in 1915.

Grandi \'grän-dē\, **Dino, conte (Count) di Mordano** (1895–1988) Italian politician. He made an unsuccessful bid for leadership of Italy's Fascists in 1921, losing to BENITO MUSSOLINI, but then held a succession of high government posts (1924–43), including foreign minister (1929–33). In July 1943, as chair of the Grand Council of Fascism, he attacked Mussolini and proposed a motion of no confidence; passage of the resolution deposed Mussolini. Grandi fled to Lisbon, then moved to Brazil, but eventually returned to Italy.

Grandma Moses See Grandma MOSES

Grange, Red *orig.* **Harold** (1903–1991) U.S. football player. Born in Forksville, Pa., he had an outstanding collegiate career at the University of Illinois, where in 1924 he ran for five touchdowns in a single game against the University of Michigan. In 1925 he joined the Chicago Bears, where his exploits earned him the nickname "the Galloping Ghost" and stimulated public interest in professional football. After suffering a knee injury in 1927, he was never again a dangerous runner. He retired in 1934 and subsequently worked as a sportscaster.

Red Grange, 1920s.
THE BETTMANN ARCHIVE

Granger movement \'grān-jər\ Coalition of U.S. farmers, mainly in the Midwest, that fought monopolistic grain-transport practices in the 1870s. Oliver H. Kelley (1826–1913), a U.S. Department of Agriculture employee, organized the Patrons of Husbandry in 1867 to bring farmers together to learn new farming methods. By the mid-1870s almost every state had at least one branch, or Grange, and national membership passed 800,000. The Grangers influenced some states to pass regulatory legislation to counter the price-fixing by railroads and grain-storage facilities. Outgrowths of the Granger movement included the GREENBACK and POPULIST movements. The Grangers dropped to about 100,000 members by 1880; they rebounded in the early 20th century, but declined again subsequently.

Granicus \grə-'nī-kəs\, **Battle of the** (334 BC) First victory won by ALEXANDER THE GREAT in his invasion of the Persian empire. Against heavy odds at the Granicus River, Alexander's army defeated the Persians under Darius III, who fled. Alexander himself charged the Persian generals, killing two of Darius' relatives and almost losing his own life. The Macedonians reportedly lost only 115 men. The victory gave western Asia Minor to Alexander, and most cities hastened to open their gates.

Granit \grä-'nēt\, **Ragnar Arthur** (1900–1991) Finnish-Swedish physiologist. His "dominator-modulator" theory states that in addition to the retina's three kinds of cone cells, which respond to different colors, certain optic-nerve fibers (dominators) respond either to the whole spectrum or to specific colors (modulators). He also proved that light inhibits as well as stimulates optic-nerve impulses; other research helped determine the nerve pathways and processes by which receptors in muscle coordinate muscle action. He shared a 1967 Nobel Prize with GEORGE WALD and HALDAN KEFFER HARTLINE.

granite Coarse- or medium-grained INTRUSIVE ROCK that is rich in quartz and ALKALI FELDSPAR. One of the most common rocks of the earth's crust, it is formed by the cooling of MAGMA. Granite was once used extensively as paving blocks and building stone, but today its principal uses are as roadway curbing, veneer for building faces, and tombstones. Granite characteristically forms irregular masses of extremely variable size, ranging from less than 5 mi (8 km) in maximum dimension to larger masses (BATHOLITHS) that are often hundreds of square miles in area.

granodiorite \ˌgra-nō-'dī-ə-ˌrīt\ Medium- to coarse-grained rock that is one of the most abundant INTRUSIVE ROCKS. It contains quartz and is distinguished from granite by having more PLAGIOCLASE feldspar than ORTHOCLASE feldspar; its other mineral constituents include hornblende, biotite, and augite. Granodiorite is similar to granite in appearance but darker.

Grant, Cary *orig.* **Archibald Alexander Leach** (1904–1986) British-U.S. film actor. He performed with an acrobatic comedy troupe in England before he found parts in stage musicals. He made his film debut in *This Is the Night* (1932) and earned stardom with MAE WEST in *She Done Him Wrong* (1933). His debonair charm and stunning good looks, combined with a distinctive voice, made him a longtime popular star in such sophisticated comedies as *Topper* (1937), *Bringing Up Baby* (1938), *His Girl Friday* (1940), and *The Philadelphia Story* (1941). He also starred in ALFRED HITCHCOCK's thrillers *Suspicion* (1941), *Notorious* (1946), *To Catch a Thief* (1955), and *North by Northwest* (1959). He received an honorary Academy Award in 1970.

Cary Grant, 1957.
THE MUSEUM OF MODERN ART/FILM STILLS ARCHIVE, NEW YORK CITY

Grant, Ulysses S. *orig.* **Hiram Ulysses** (1822–1885) U.S. general and 18th president of the U.S. (1869–77). Born in Point Pleasant, Ohio, he served in the Mexican War under ZACHARY TAYLOR; he resigned his commission in 1854 when he could not afford to bring his family west. Allegations that he became a drunkard in the lonely years in the West and in later life, though never proved, would affect his reputation. He worked unsuccessfully at farming in Missouri and at his family's leather business in Illinois. When the AMERICAN CIVIL WAR began (1861), he was appointed brigadier general; his 1862 attack on Fort Donelson, Tenn., produced the first major Union victory. He drove off a Confederate attack at Shiloh but was criticized for heavy Union losses. He devised the campaign to take the stronghold of VICKSBURG, Miss., in 1863, cutting the Confederacy in half from east to west. Following his victory at the Battle of CHATTANOOGA in 1864, he was appointed commander of the Union army. While WILLIAM T. SHERMAN made his famous march across Georgia, Grant attacked ROBERT E. LEE's forces in Virginia, bringing the war to an end in 1865. Grant's administrative ability and innovative strategies were largely responsible for the Union victory. His successful Republican presidential campaign made him, at 46, the youngest man yet elected president. His two terms were marred by administrative inaction and political scandal involving members of his cabinet, including the CRÉDIT MOBILIER SCANDAL and the WHISKEY RING operation. He was more successful in foreign affairs, in which he was aided by his secretary of state, HAMILTON FISH. He supported amnesty for Confederate leaders and protection for black civil rights. His veto of a bill to increase the amount of legal tender (1874) diminished the currency crisis in the next 25 years. In 1881 he moved to New York; when a partner defrauded an investment firm co-owned by his son, the family was impoverished. His memoirs were published by his friend MARK TWAIN.

Ulysses S. Grant.
BY COURTESY OF THE LIBRARY OF CONGRESS, WASHINGTON, D.C.

granulite facies \'gran-yə-ˌlīt-'fā-shēz\ One of the major divisions of the mineral facies classification of metamorphic rocks, encompassing rocks that formed under intense temperature-pressure conditions (higher than 950°F, or 500°C). The minerals found in the rocks of granulite facies include hornblende, pyroxene, biotite, garnet, calcium plagioclase, and quartz or olivine. See also AMPHIBOLITE FACIES.

Granville-Barker, Harley (1877–1946) British producer, playwright, and critic. An actor from age 15, he directed his own first play, *The Marrying of Ann Leete,* in 1901. As comanager of the Court Theatre (1904–7) he produced many of Shaw's early plays as well as plays by HENRIK IBSEN, MAURICE MAETERLINCK, and JOHN GALSWORTHY, and also produced his own *The Voysey Inheritance* (1905) and *Waste* (1907). He influenced 20th-century theater with his naturalistic stagings of Shakespeare's plays, which emphasized continuous action on an open stage and rapid, lightly stressed speech. He moved to Paris after World War I and there wrote his classic *Prefaces to Shakespeare* (1927–46).

grape Any of the 60 plant species that make up the genus *Vitis* (family Vitaceae), native to the northern temperate zone, including varieties that may be eaten as table fruit, dried to produce raisins, or crushed to make grape juice or WINE. *V. vinifera* is the species most commonly used in wine making. The grape is usually a woody vine, climbing by means of tendrils. In arid regions it may form an almost erect shrub. Botanically, the fruit is a BERRY. Grapes contain such minerals as calcium and phosphorus and are a source of vitamin A. All grapes contain sugar (glucose and fructose) in varying quantities.

Grape (*Vitis*).
GRANT HEILMAN

grape hyacinth Any of the approximately 50 species of small bulbous perennial plants that make up the genus *Muscari,* in the LILY FAMILY, native to the Mediterranean region. Most species have dense clusters of blue, white, or pink urn-shaped flowers borne at the tip of a leafless flower stalk. Some species have a musky odor. Grape hyacinths often are planted as spring-flowering garden ornamentals.

grape phylloxera \ˌfī-ˌläk-ˈsir-ə, fə-ˈläk-sə-rə\ Small, greenish yellow insect (*Phylloxera vitifoliae,* order Homoptera) that is highly destructive to grape plants in Europe and the western U.S. It sucks fluid from grapevines, causing GALLS to form on leaves and nodules on roots; eventually the plants rot. It was introduced into Europe from the eastern U.S. in the mid-19th century and within 25 years had almost destroyed the grape and wine industries in France, Italy, and Germany. Vines were saved by grafting European plants to rootstocks of resistant vines native to the U.S. Hybrids and fumigants are used to combat the pest.

grape sugar See GLUCOSE

grapefruit Tree *(Citrus paradisi)* of the RUE FAMILY and its edible fruit. It probably originated in Jamaica and spread from there to the West Indies and then the New World mainland. The dark, shiny green foliage is very dense. The large, white flowers are borne singly or in clusters. Lemon-yellow when ripe, the fruit is 4–6 in. (100–150 mm) in diameter, about twice as large as a medium-sized orange. The mildly acidic pulp—light yellowish, pink, or red and juicy—is an excellent source of vitamin C. It is popular as breakfast fruit in various parts of the world.

Grapefruit (*Citrus paradisi*).
GRANT HEILMAN

graph Visual representation of a data set or a mathematical EQUATION, INEQUALITY, or FUNCTION to show relationships or tendencies that these formulas can only suggest symbolically and abstractly. Though HISTOGRAMS and pie charts are also graphs, the term usually applies to point plots on a COORDINATE SYSTEM. For example, a graph of the relationship between real numbers and their squares matches each real number on a horizontal axis with its square on a vertical axis. The resulting set of points in this case is a PARABOLA. A graph of an inequality is usually a shaded region on one side of a curve, whose shape depends not only on the equation or inequality but on the coordinate system chosen.

graph theory Mathematical theory of networks. A graph consists of nodes (also called points or vertices) and edges (lines) connecting certain pairs of nodes. An edge that connects a node to itself is called a loop. In 1735 LEONHARD EULER published an analysis of an old puzzle concerning the possibility of crossing every one of seven bridges (no bridge twice) that span a forked river flowing past an island. Euler's proof that no such path exists and his generalization of the problem to all possible networks are now recognized as the origin of both graph theory and TOPOLOGY.

graphic art Traditional category of fine arts, including any form of visual artistic expression (e.g., PAINTING, DRAWING, PHOTOGRAPHY, PRINTMAKING), usually produced on flat surfaces. Design in the graphic arts often includes TYPOGRAPHY, but also encompasses original drawings, plans, and patterns for the decorative arts (e.g., furniture, ceramics), interiors, engineering, and architecture.

graphic design The art and profession of selecting and arranging visual elements—such as typography, images, symbols, and colors—to convey a message to an audience. Sometimes graphic design is called "visual communications." It is a collaborative discipline: writers produce words and photographers and illustrators create images that the designer incorporates into a complete visual message. Although graphic design has been practiced in various forms throughout history, it emerged as a specific profession during the job-specialization process that occurred in the late 19th century. Its evolution has been closely bound to developments in image-making, typography, and reproduction processes. Prominent graphic designers include Jules Chéret, Piet Zwart, Paul Rand, Alexey Brodovitch, Milton Glaser, and David Carson.

graphical user interface (GUI) Computer display format that allows the user to select commands, call up files, start programs, and do other routine tasks by using a MOUSE to point to pictorial symbols (icons) or lists of menu choices on the screen as opposed to having to type in text commands. The first GUI to be used in a PERSONAL COMPUTER appeared in Apple Computer's Lisa, introduced in 1983; its GUI became the basis of Apple's extremely successful Macintosh (1984). The Macintosh's GUI style was widely adapted by other manufacturers of personal computers and PC software. In 1985 Microsoft Corp. introduced WINDOWS, a GUI (which later grew into an operating system) that gave MS-DOS–based computers many of the same capabilities as the Macintosh. In addition to being used for operating-system interfaces, GUIs are used in other types of software, including BROWSERS and application programs.

graphite *or* **plumbago** \ˌpləm-ˈbā-gō\ *or* **black lead** Mineral ALLOTROPE of CARBON. It is dark gray to black, opaque, and very soft. Its layered structure, with rings of six ATOMS arranged in widely spaced horizontal sheets, gives it its slippery quality. It occurs in nature and is used (mixed with clay) as the "lead" in pencils as well as in lubricants, crucibles, polishes, arc lamps, batteries, brushes for electric motors, and nuclear-reactor cores.

graptolite \ˈgrap-tə-ˌlīt\ Any member of an extinct group of small, aquatic colonial invertebrates that first became apparent during the CAMBRIAN PERIOD and persisted into the Early Carboniferous period (354–323 million years ago). Graptolites were floating animals that had tentacles and a hard outer covering. They have most often been preserved as impressions on black shales. Graptolite fossils show a gradual development through time, and evolutionary relationships between different graptolite groups have been discovered and analyzed.

grass Any of many low, green, nonwoody plants that make up the families Poaceae (or Gramineae), Cyperaceae (SEDGES), and Juncaceae (RUSHES). Only the approximately 8,000–10,000 species in the family Poaceae are true grasses. They are economically the most important of all flowering plants because of their nutritious grains and soil-forming function, and they have the most widespread distribution and the largest number of individuals. The CEREAL grasses include wheat, corn (maize), rice, rye, oats, barley, and millet. Grasses provide forage for grazing animals, shelter for wildlife, and construction materials, furniture, utensils, and food for humans. Some species are grown as garden ornamentals, cultivated as TURF for lawns and recreational areas, or used as cover plants for erosion control. Most have round stems that are hollow between the joints, bladelike leaves, and extensively branching fibrous root systems.

Grass \ˈgräs\, **Günter (Wilhelm)** (born 1927) German novelist, poet, and playwright. Born in Danzig (now Gdánsk, Poland), Grass passed through the Hitler Youth movement, was drafted at 16 and wounded in battle, and became a prisoner of war. His extraordinary first novel, *The Tin Drum* (1959), brought him worldwide fame, and he became the literary spokesman for the German generation that grew up in the Nazi era. It was followed by *Cat and Mouse* (1961) and *Dog Years* (1963); the three novels form a trilogy set in Danzig. His other works, all politically topical, include *The Flounder* (1977); *Meeting at Telgte* (1979), *Headbirths* (1980); *The Call of the Toad* (1992), about the uneasy relationship between Poland and reunified Germany; *A Broad Field* (1995), controversial for expressing his view that reunification was a mistake; and *My Century* (1999). He is also a sculptor and printmaker. He received the Nobel Prize in 1999.

Grass.
AUTHENTICATED NEWS INTERNATIONAL

grasshopper Any of the leaping insects of the family Acrididae (short-horned grasshoppers) or Tettigoniidae (long-horned grasshoppers), both in the order Orthoptera. Grasshoppers are most common in tropical forests, semiarid regions, and grasslands. Colors range from green to olive or brown, sometimes with yellow or red markings. Grasshoppers eat plant material and may damage crops. Some species are more than 4 in. (11 cm) long. The male can produce a buzzing sound either by rubbing its front wings together or by rubbing toothlike ridges on the hind legs against a raised vein on each front wing. Grasshoppers are a favorite food of many birds, frogs, and snakes. See also KATYDID, LOCUST.

Short-horned grasshopper (Acrididae).
EARL L. KUBIS—ROOT RESOURCES

Grateful Dead U.S. rock group, formed in San Francisco in the mid-1960s by Jerry Garcia (1942–1995) on guitar, Phil Lesh (born 1940) on bass, Ron "Pigpen" McKernan (1945–1973) on keyboards, Bob Weir (born 1947) on guitar, and Bill Kreutzmann (born 1946) on drums. The Grateful Dead emerged from the Haight-Ashbury psychedelic-drug-and-music scene, later gaining fame for performing at the Monterey Pop Festival (1967) and WOODSTOCK. Though they regularly released albums, their focus was on live music. They became one of the country's most successful touring bands, known for Garcia's marathon four-hour musical meanderings and for their entourage of "Deadheads," a devoted legion of nomadic fans who followed the band in spirited makeshift communities. In the late 1980s, a new generation of fans made the Grateful Dead the most successful touring band in the world. They stopped touring after Garcia died of a heart attack at a drug rehabilitation center.

Gratian \'grā-shən\ *Latin in full* **Flavius Gratianus Augustus** (359–383) Roman emperor (367–83). He originally shared the office with his father, VALENTINIAN I (364–75), and his uncle, VALENS (364–78). He later shared authority with his 4-year-old half brother, who was supported by the army. On his uncle's death he became ruler of the Eastern Empire, and summoned THEODOSIUS I to share power with him. Influenced by St. AMBROSE, Gratian omitted the words *pontifex maximus* ("supreme priest") from his title. He was murdered opposing the usurper Magnus Maximus.

Grattan \'gra-tᵊn\, **Henry** (1746–1820) Irish politician. He entered the Irish Parliament in 1775 and, as a brilliant orator, soon became the leading spokesperson of the Irish nationalist agitation. His movement gained momentum; he forced the British in 1779 to remove restraints on Irish trade, and in 1782 to relinquish its right to legislate for Ireland. In 1800 he headed the unsuccessful opposition to the union of England and Ireland. In 1805 he was elected to the English House of Commons, where he fought for Catholic emancipation for his last 15 years.

gravel Aggregate of more or less rounded rock fragments coarser than sand (i.e., more than 0.08 in., or 2 mm, in diameter). Gravel beds in some places contain heavy metallic ore minerals, such as cassiterite (a major source of tin), or native metals, such as gold, in nuggets or flakes. Deposits accumulate in parts of stream channels or on beaches where the water moves too rapidly to permit sand to remain. Because of changing conditions, gravel formations generally are more limited and more variable in coarseness, thickness, and configuration than sand or clay deposits. In many regions gravel terraces (or raised beaches) extend great distances inland, indicating that the sea at one time stood higher than it does today. Gravels are widely used building materials.

Graves, Michael (born 1934) U.S. architect and designer. Born in Indianapolis, he studied at Harvard University and in 1962 began a long teaching career at Princeton Univ., while designing private houses in the abstract and austere style of orthodox modernism. In the late 1970s he rejected modernist expression and began seeking a richer, postmodernist vocabulary. The hulking masses of the Portland Building in Portland, Ore. (1980), and the Humana Building in Louisville, Ky. (1982), display his highly personal, Cubistic rendering of such classical elements as colonnades and loggias. Though considered somewhat awkward, these and his later buildings (e.g., Indianapolis Art Center, 1996) have been acclaimed for their ironic interpretation of traditional forms.

Graves, Robert (von Ranke) (1895–1985) British-Spanish man of letters. His first three volumes of poetry were published during World War I, in which he was severely wounded; they include some of the finest English love poems of the century. In 1926 he began a 13-year relationship with the American poet Laura Riding (1901–1991), with whom he founded a press, briefly published a journal, and collaborated as a writer. After 1929 he lived principally in Mallorca, Spain. The most famous of his more than 120 books are *Good-bye to All That* (1929), a grim memoir of the war; the historical novel *I, Claudius* (1934; televised in 1976); and erudite, controversial studies in mythology, notably *The White Goddess* (1948).

Graves, Robert James (1796–1853) Irish physician. In 1821 he set up the Park Street School of Medicine, where he gave his advanced students responsibility for patients (under supervision) and lectured in English, not Latin. He was a founder and editor of the *Dublin Journal of Medical Science.* His *Clinical Lectures on the Practice of Medicine* (1848) established his reputation. He introduced timing of the pulse by watch and giving patients with fevers nourishment instead of withholding it. He was a leader of the Irish (Dublin) school of diagnosis, which stressed observation of patients, and was one of the first to fully describe exophthalmic goiter (GRAVES' DISEASE).

Graves' disease *or* **toxic diffuse goiter** *or* **exophthalmic goiter** \ˌek-säf-'thal-mik\ Most common type of hyperthyroidism (oversecretion of thyroid hormone), usually with GOITER and exophthalmos (eyeball protrusion). Increased thyroid hormone levels result in increased cardiac output, rapid heartbeat, and possibly heart failure. Stress may trigger a severe worsening (thyroid storm), which can lead to circulatory collapse and death. Graves' disease is considered an autoimmune disease. It can sometimes be controlled by drugs; severe cases require partial or total removal of the THYROID GLAND.

gravitation Universal force of attraction that acts between all bodies that have MASS. Though it is the weakest of the four known forces, it shapes the structure and evolution of stars, galaxies, and the entire universe. The laws of gravity determine the trajectories of bodies in the solar system and the MOTION of objects on earth, where all bodies experience a downward gravitational force exerted by earth's mass, the force experienced as weight. ISAAC NEWTON was the first to develop a quantitative theory of gravitation, holding that the force of attraction between two bodies is proportional to the product of their masses and inversely proportional to the square of the distance between them. ALBERT EINSTEIN proposed a whole new concept of gravitation involving the four-dimensional continuum of SPACE-TIME which is curved by the presence of matter. In his general theory of RELATIVITY, he showed that a body undergoing uniform acceleration is indistinguishable from one that is stationary in a gravitational field.

gravitational radius See SCHWARZSCHILD RADIUS

gravity, center of Imaginary point where the total weight of a material body may be thought to be concentrated. Since weight and MASS are proportional, the same point may also be called the center of mass, but the center of mass does not require a gravitational field. A body's center of gravity may coincide with its geometric center, especially if the body is symmetric and composed of homogeneous material. In asymmetric, unhomogeneous, or hollow objects, the center of gravity may be at some distance from the geometric center, or even at a point in space external to the object, such as between the legs of a chair.

gravure printing \grə-ˈvyu̇r\ PRINTING processes used for catalogs, magazines, newspaper supplements, cartons, floor and wall coverings, textiles, and plastics. The Bohemian Karel Klíč (1841–1926) made photogravure a practical commercial process in 1878. An image is etched in the copper surface of the printing cylinder, as pits or wells of different depths. In rotogravure printing, the cylinder rotates through a trough filled with fast-drying ink. A thin steel doctor blade removes the ink from the surface, but not from the wells. The cylinder comes in contact with the paper, which draws the ink out of the wells. Because of the various depths of the wells, a full range of tonal values can be printed; in reproducing illustrations, gravure comes closest to simulating continuous-tone copy. In COLOR PRINTING, a separate cylinder is prepared for each color. See also LETTERPRESS PRINTING, OFFSET PRINTING.

Gray, Asa (1810–1888) U.S. botanist. Born in Sauquoit, N.Y., he received a medical degree from Fairfield Medical School, where he spent his spare time studying plant specimens. He collaborated with John Torrey (1796–1873) on *Flora of North America* (1838–43) and in 1842 joined the faculty at Harvard Univ., where he would teach until 1873. His donation of his thousands of books and plant specimens established Harvard's botany department. He was largely responsible for the unification of the taxonomic knowledge of the North American flora; his most widely used book, commonly called *Gray's Manual* (1848), remains a standard work. He was the chief early American supporter of the theories of CHARLES DARWIN.

Gray, Thomas (1716–1771) British poet. He studied and later settled at Cambridge, where he wrote poems of wistful melancholy filled with truisms phrased in striking, quotable lines. Though his output was small, he became the dominant poetic figure in his day. He is remembered especially for *An Elegy Written in a Country Church Yard* (1751), one of the best known of English lyric poems and the greatest work of the English "graveyard school." After its overwhelming success, his next two poems met a disappointing response, and he virtually ceased writing.

Thomas Gray, detail of an oil painting by John Giles Eccardt; in the National Portrait Gallery, London.

BY COURTESY OF THE NATIONAL PORTRAIT GALLERY, LONDON

gray fox Grizzled, gray-furred New World FOX *(Urocyon cinereoargenteus)* found in forested, rocky, and brush-covered country from Canada to northern South America. Distinguished by the reddish color on its neck, ears, and legs, it grows to a length of about 20–30 in. (50–75 cm), excluding its 12–16-in. (30–40-cm) tail, and a weight of about 7–13 lbs (3–6 kg). Unlike other foxes, it commonly climbs trees. Primarily nocturnal, it takes a variety of foods, including small birds and mammals, insects, and fruits.

grayhound See GREYHOUND

grayling Any of several game fishes (genus *Thymallus*) similar to TROUT that are found in cold, clear streams of Eurasia and northern North America. Graylings are silvery-purple and reach a length of about 16 in. (40 cm). They have relatively large scales, a small mouth with weak teeth, and a sail-like, brightly colored dorsal fin. They feed primarily on insects and spawn in shallow water in the spring. Pollution of streams has reduced the numbers of this excellent food fish.

graywacke \ˈgrā-ˌwak\ *or* **dirty sandstone** Sedimentary rock composed of sand-sized grains in a fine-grained clay matrix. The sand-sized grains frequently include rock fragments of wide-ranging mineralogies (e.g., pyroxenes, amphiboles, feldspars, and quartz). The clay matrix may constitute up to 50% of the volume. Of the clay minerals, chlorite and biotite are most abundant. The matrix tends to bind the grains strongly and form a relatively hard rock.

Graz \ˈgräts\ City (pop., 2001: 226,424), capital of Styria state, southeastern Austria. The country's second-largest city, it lies on the Mur River at the foot of the Styrian Alps. It grew from a fortress settlement and received town rights c. 1240 AD. It became the center of Steiermark (Styria) during the Middle Ages, and was the residence of the Leopoldine HABSBURGS after 1379. Its fortifications, built in the 15th–16th century, successfully withstood numerous sieges by Hungarians and Turks; the fortifications were converted into parks in the 19th century. Astronomer JOHANNES KEPLER taught at its university, founded in 1585. A rail and industrial center, Graz has an active trade in agricultural products; tourism is also important.

Graziani \ˌgrät-sē-ˈä-nē\, **Roldolfo, marchese (Marquess) di Neghelli** (1882–1955) Italian field marshal and adherent of BENITO MUSSOLINI. He was commander in chief of Italian forces in Libya (1930–34), governor of Italian Somaliland (1935–36), and viceroy of Ethiopia (1936–37). At the outbreak of World War II, he advanced against Egypt from Libya, was defeated by the British under ARCHIBALD PERCIVAL WAVELL, and resigned his post in 1941. After the Italian armistice of 1943, he became defense minister of the German-backed Italian republic. Sentenced to 19 years' imprisonment in 1950, he was released that year. He later became a leader of the Italian neofascist movement.

Great Atlantic & Pacific Tea Co. (A&P) U.S. corporation operating one of the largest supermarket chains in the U.S., mostly under the A&P name. The company had its start in 1859, when the Great American Tea Co. was founded in New York as a direct-mail operation to trade in tea from the cargoes of clipper ships. The first retail stores were incorporated in 1869 under the name Great Atlantic & Pacific Tea Co. By 1925 it was the largest U.S. grocery chain, and in 1936 A&P opened its first supermarket. By 1969 it was the largest supermarket chain in the U.S., but it declined thereafter, and in 1979 a controlling portion of its stock was bought by a German supermarket giant. A&P purchased Shopwell, Inc., in 1986.

Great Attractor Proposed concentration of mass (equivalent to tens of thousands of galaxies) that influences the movement of many galaxies, including the MILKY WAY. In 1986 a group of astronomers noted that the Milky Way and neighboring galaxies exhibit systematic deflections from the motion predicted by EDWIN HUBBLE's theory of the expanding universe. One possible explanation is a "Great Attractor" exerting a gravitational pull on the surrounding galaxies; its center would lie in the direction of the constellations Hydra or Centaurus in the southern sky, about 200 million light-years from earth.

great auk Flightless seabird *(Pinguinus impennis)* extinct since 1844. Great auks bred in colonies on rocky islands off North Atlantic coasts; fossil remains have been found as far south as Florida, Spain, and Italy. Their bodies were about 30 in. (75 cm) long; the wings, used for swimming underwater, were less than 6 in. (15 cm) long. They stood erect on land and had a black back and head, a white front, and a large white spot between the eye and the black bill. Great auks were hunted to extinction for food and bait. About 80 specimens are preserved in museums. See also AUK.

Great Australian Bight Bay of the Indian Ocean, southern Australian coast. Its generally accepted boundaries are from Cape Pasley, Western Australia, to Cape Carnot, South Australia—a distance of 720 mi (1,160 km). The head of the bight abuts on the arid NULLARBOR PLAIN and is bounded by cliffs 200–400 ft (60–120 m) high. Near Eucla on the bight's shores is the Nuytsland Reserve. Lying in the track of the winter western winds, the bight has a reputation for storms and rough seas.

Great Awakening Religious revival in British North America from 1720 into the 1740s. It was part of a movement, known as PIETISM or Quietism on the European continent and evangelicalism in England, that swept Western Europe in the late 17th and early 18th century under the leadership of preachers such as JOHN WESLEY. In North America the Great Awakening was a Protestant evangelical reaction against formalism and rationalism in religion, and it had a strong Calvinist element. Revivalist preachers emphasized the need for sinners to fear punishment and to hope for the unearned gift of GRACE from God. George Whitefield (1714–1770) was one of the most popular, preaching to huge crowds throughout the colonies in 1739–40. JONATHAN EDWARDS also helped inspire the Great Awakening and was its most important theologian. Among its results were missions to the Indians and the founding of colleges (including Princeton Univ.). Another revival known as the Second Great Awakening occurred in New England and Kentucky in the 1790s.

E
F
G

Great Barrier Reef Long stretch of CORAL REEF, off the northeastern coast of QUEENSLAND, Australia. The largest deposit of CORAL in the world, it extends for more than 1,250 mi (2,000 km) along the Australian coast and has an area of 80,000 sq mi (207,000 sq km). The reef has been formed over millions of years from the skeletons of a mass of living marine organisms. In addition to 350 species of coral, marine life includes anemones, worms, gastropods, lobsters, crayfish, prawns, crabs, and a variety of fishes. Encrusting red ALGAE form the purplish red algal rim that is one of the reef's characteristic features.

Great Basin National Park National preserve, eastern Nevada. Made a national park in 1986, the area was previously part of the Humboldt National Forest. It has an area of 121 sq mi (313 sq km) and consists of the southern part of the Snake Mtns., a chain that rises abruptly from the desert floor to reach a height of 13,063 ft (3,982 m) at Wheeler Peak. A park attraction is the Lehman Caves, a group of limestone caverns.

Great Bear Lake Lake, Northwest Territories. Lying astride the Arctic Circle, it was visited before 1800 by NORTH WEST CO. traders and later named for the bears that inhabited its shores. Containing many small islands, Great Bear Lake is roughly 200 mi (320 km) long and 25–110 mi (40–175 km) wide and has a maximum depth of 1,356 ft (413 m). It is the largest lake entirely within Canada and the fourth largest in North America. The lake's waters abound with fish, including the speckled trout.

Great Britain *or* **Britain** Kingdom, western Europe. Comprising ENGLAND, SCOTLAND, and WALES, the kingdom, which entirely occupies the largest island in Europe, covers 88,150 sq mi (228,300 sq km). With Northern IRELAND, it constitutes the UNITED KINGDOM of Great Britain and Northern Ireland. Less formally, the names Great Britain and Britain are used to refer to the entire United Kingdom.

Great Dane Breed of WORKING DOG developed at least 400 years ago in Germany, where it was used for BOAR hunting. Tallest of the working breeds, it stands 28–32 in. (71–81 cm) tall and weighs 120–150 lbs (54–68 kg). It has a massive, square-jawed head and elegant body lines. Its short coat is black, golden brown, brindle, blue-gray, or white with black patches. It is typically swift and alert and is noted for courage, friendliness, and dependability. There is no known reason to associate Denmark with the breed.

Great Depression *or* **Depression of 1929** Longest and most severe economic depression ever experienced by the Western world. It began in the U.S. with the New York STOCK MARKET CRASH OF 1929 and lasted until about 1939. By late 1932 stock values had dropped to about 20% of their previous value, and by 1933 11,000 of the U.S.'s 25,000 banks had failed. This led to much-reduced levels of demand and hence of production, resulting in high unemployment (by 1932, 25–30%). Since the U.S. was the major creditor and financier of postwar Europe, the U.S. financial collapse led to collapses of other economies, especially those of Germany and Britain. Nations sought to protect domestic production by imposing tariffs and quotas, reducing the value of international trade by more than half by 1932. The Great Depression contributed to political upheaval. It led to the election of FRANKLIN ROOSEVELT in the U.S. and major changes in the structure of the U.S. economy brought about by his NEW DEAL. It directly contributed to ADOLF HITLER's rise to power in Germany in 1933 and to political extremism in other countries. Before the Great Depression, governments relied on impersonal market forces to achieve economic correction; afterward, government action came to assume a principal role in ensuring economic stability.

Great Dismal Swamp See DISMAL SWAMP

Great Dividing Range Entire extent of mountain ranges roughly paralleling the coasts of QUEENSLAND, NEW SOUTH WALES, and VICTORIA, Australia. Beginning in the north on Cape York Peninsula, Queensland, they range south to become the AUSTRALIAN ALPS, near the New South Wales–Victoria border. Bending west in Victoria, they end in the GRAMPIANS, while a southern spur emerges from the BASS STRAIT to form the central uplands of TASMANIA. The range stretches for 2,300 mi (3,700 km). First traversed by Europeans (1813) moving into the Australian outback, the region is now important for agriculture, lumbering, and mining, while national parks attract tourists.

Great Fear (1789) In the FRENCH REVOLUTION, a period of panic and riot by peasants and others amid rumors of an "aristocratic conspiracy" by the king and the privileged to overthrow the THIRD ESTATE. The gathering of troops around Paris provoked insurrection, and on July 14 the Parisian rabble seized the BASTILLE. In the provinces the peasants rose against their lords, attacking châteaux and destroying feudal documents. To check the peasants, the National Constituent Assembly decreed the abolition of the feudal regime and introduced the DECLARATION OF THE RIGHTS OF MAN AND OF THE CITIZEN.

Great Fire of London (September 2–5, 1666) Worst fire in London's history. It destroyed a large part of the city, including most of the civic buildings, ST. PAUL'S CATHEDRAL, 87 parish churches, and about 13,000 houses. It began accidentally at the house of the king's baker in Pudding Lane near London Bridge, and a violent east wind encouraged the flames. On the fourth day houses were blown up by gunpowder to master the fire. The Thames River swarmed with vessels filled with people trying to save their goods, and some fled to the hills of Hampstead and Highgate, but most of the houseless Londoners settled in Moorfields.

Great Fish River River, southeastern Eastern Cape province, South Africa. Flowing southeast for much of its 400 mi (644 km) run, it joins the Koonap River before entering the Indian Ocean southeast of Grahamstown. In the early 19th century, the lower Great Fish valley formed a battle zone between mostly British settlers moving east from the Cape and tribal settlements to the northeast.

Great Game Rivalry between Britain and Russia in Central Asia in the late 19th century. The term was used by RUDYARD KIPLING in his novel *Kim* (1901). British attitudes were influenced by the reports of official, semiofficial, and private adventurers enjoying the thrill of clandestine operations beyond the frontiers of India, reports that frequently embellished (or even invented) accounts of Russian machinations and the vacillating loyalties of local chieftains.

great hall Main space in a medieval manor house, monastery, or college, in which meals were eaten. In large manor houses it also served other purposes: Justice was administered there, entertainment enjoyed, and often at night its stone floor was strewn with rushes so that servants could sleep there.

great horned owl HORNED OWL species (Bubo virginianus) that ranges from Arctic tree limits south to the Strait of Magellan. A powerful, mottled-brown predator, it is often more than 2 ft (60 cm) long, with a wingspan often approaching 80 in. (200 cm). It usually eats small rodents and birds, but has been known to carry off larger prey. Adapted to desert and forest, the species migrates only when food is scarce.

Great Indian Desert See THAR DESERT

Great Lakes Group of large lakes located chiefly in the GREAT RIFT VALLEY, eastern central Africa. It includes the lakes TURKANA, ALBERT, VICTORIA, TANGANYIKA, and MALAWI.

Great Lakes Chain of lakes, central North America. Comprising Lakes SUPERIOR, MICHIGAN, HURON, ERIE, and ONTARIO, they form a natural boundary between the U.S. and Canada. They cover an area of about 94,850 sq mi (245,660 sq km), and constitute the largest freshwater surface in the world. They are connected to form a single waterway that discharges down the ST. LAWRENCE RIVER into the Atlantic Ocean. With the ST. LAWRENCE SEAWAY they form a 2,000-mi (3,200-km) shipping lane that carries oceangoing traffic as far west as DULUTH, Minn. Large quantities of iron ore, coal, grain, and manufactured goods are moved between lake ports and shipped overseas. While commercial fishing was once a major industry on the lakes, pollution and other factors led to its collapse; recovery has been slow and partial. The lakes are used for many recreational activities, including boating and sailing.

Great Lakes trout See LAKE TROUT

Great Leap Forward Failed industrialization campaign undertaken by the Chinese Communists between 1958 and early 1960. MAO ZEDONG hoped to develop labor-intensive methods of industrialization that would emphasize manpower rather than the gradual purchase of heavy machinery, thereby putting to use China's dense population and obviating the need to accumulate capital. Rather than large new factories, he proposed developing backyard steel furnaces in every village. Rural people were organized into communes where agricultural and political decisions emphasized ideological purity rather than expertise. The program was implemented so hastily and zealously that many errors occurred; these were exacerbated by a series of natural disasters and the withdrawal of

Soviet technical personnel. China's agriculture was so disrupted that about 20 million people died of starvation from 1958 to 1962. By early 1960 the government began to repeal the Great Leap Forward; private plots were returned to peasants and expertise began to be emphasized again.

Great Mosque See MASJID-I-JAMI

Great Mother of the Gods *or* **Cybele** \'si-bə-lē\ Deity of the ancient Mediterranean world. Her cult originated in Phrygia in Asia Minor and spread to the Greek world, where she was identified with RHEA. It reached Rome by the 3rd century BC and became a major cult during the empire. Known by a variety of local names, Cybele was venerated as the universal mother of gods, humans, and animals. Her lover was the fertility god ATTIS. Her priests, the Galli, castrated themselves when they entered her service, and on her festival day they spattered their blood on her altar and her sacred pine tree.

Cybele, terra-cotta statuette, from Camirus, Rhodes, early 5th century BC; in the British Museum, London.

BY COURTESY OF THE TRUSTEES OF THE BRITISH MUSEUM

Great Northern Railway Co. U.S. railroad founded by JAMES J. HILL in 1890. Hill bought a Minnesota railroad, the St. Paul and Pacific Railroad, in 1878, and extended it north to the Canadian border and west to the Pacific coast, encouraging thousands of homesteaders to settle along its tracks. Together with J. P. MORGAN of the NORTHERN PACIFIC RAILWAY CO., Hill bought control of the Chicago, Burlington & Quincy Railroad in 1901 and set up a HOLDING COMPANY to control the three railroads. In 1904 the U.S. Supreme Court declared the company in violation of antitrust laws and ordered it dissolved, but the Burlington continued under control of the Great Northern and the Northern Pacific. In 1970 the three were merged under the name Burlington Northern, Inc.

Great Northern War See Second NORTHERN WAR

Great Ouse River See OUSE RIVER

Great Plague of London (1664–66) Epidemic of plague that ravaged London, killing over 75,000 of a total population estimated at 460,000. As early as 1625, 40,000 Londoners had died of the plague, but this was the worst and the last of the epidemics. The greatest devastation was in the city's outskirts in areas where the poor were densely crowded. The disease spread throughout the country, but from 1667 only sporadic cases appeared until 1679. The plague's decline was attributed to various causes, including the GREAT FIRE OF LONDON. DANIEL DEFOE's *Journal of the Plague Year* (1722) provided a valuable picture of the time.

Great Plains Continental slope of central North America. It stretches from the RIO GRANDE at the U.S.–Mexico border in the south to the MACKENZIE RIVER delta along the Arctic Ocean in the north and from the Interior Lowlands and the Canadian Shield in the east to the ROCKY MTNS. in the west. The plains embrace parts of ten U.S. states and four Canadian provinces, covering an area of about 1,125,000 sq mi (2,900,000 sq km). A high plateau of semiarid grassland, these prairie regions in both the U.S. and Canada produce the major proportion of wheat grown in each country and are also important cattle- and sheep-herding areas. Parts of the plains have reserves of coal and lignite, petroleum, and natural gas.

Great Proletarian Cultural Revolution See CULTURAL REVOLUTION

Great Red Spot Storm on the planet JUPITER that moves in longitude but remains centered at about latitude 22° south. A high-pressure center, it is oval, measuring about 8,700 mi (14,000 km) north to south, roughly the diameter of earth, and averaging twice as wide east to west. Its discovery in the 1660s is attributed to GIAN DOMENICO CASSINI or ROBERT HOOKE. Its color, whose cause is unknown, varies from brick-red to brownish; it tends to change color over a period of years.

Great Rift Valley *or* **Rift Valley** *or* **East African Rift System** Rift system (see RIFT VALLEY), extending from Jordan in the Middle East south to Mozambique in South Africa. It is some 4,000 mi (6,400 km) long and averages 30–40 mi (48–64 km) wide. The rift has been forming for some 30 million years, as Africa and the Arabian Peninsula separate, and has produced such massifs as KILIMANJARO and Mount KENYA. The system's main branch, the Eastern Rift Valley, is occupied in the north by the JORDAN RIVER, the DEAD SEA, and the Gulf of AQABA. It continues south along the RED SEA to several lakes in Kenya. Less obvious in Tanzania, with its eastern rim eroded, it continues south to the Indian Ocean near BEIRA, Mozambique. The western branch of the system, the Western Rift Valley, extends north from the northern end of Lake MALAWI in an arc that includes lakes RUKWA, TANGANYIKA, KIVU, EDWARD, and ALBERT.

Great St. Bernard Pass *ancient* **Mons Jovis.** Pass in the ALPS. One of the highest of the alpine frontier passes, at 8,100 ft (2,469 m), it lies on the Italian–Swiss border east of the MONT BLANC group and connects Valais, Switzerland, with AOSTA, Italy. Historically the most important transalpine route, it was often used by pilgrims to Rome and later by medieval armies. In 1800 it was crossed by NAPOLEON and his 40,000 troops on their way to northern Italy. A famous hospice on the pass, founded by St. Bernard of Menthon in the 11th century, is still kept by Augustinian monks who, with their ST. BERNARD dogs, provide services to travelers. The old road, open only five months a year, has been partly superseded by a tunnel beneath the pass, which allows year-round travel.

Great Salt Lake Lake, northern Utah. It is the largest inland body of salt water in the western Hemisphere and one of the most saline in the world. It fluctuates greatly in size, depending on rates of evaporation and the flow of the rivers into it. Its surface area has varied from about 2,400 sq mi (6,200 sq km) at its highest levels in 1873 and the mid-1980s to about 950 sq mi (2,460 sq km) at its low level in 1963. At times of median water level, it is generally less than 15 ft (4.5 m) deep. Surrounded by stretches of sand, salt land, and marsh, the lake remains isolated, though in recent years it has become important as a source of minerals and as a beach and water-sports attraction and a wildlife preserve.

Great Sand Dunes National Monument National monument, southern central Colorado. At the eastern edge of the San Luis Valley, it parallels for about 10 mi (16 km) the western base of the SANGRE DE CRISTO RANGE. Established in 1932, the 60-sq-mi (155-sq-km) region contains some of the highest inland sand dunes in the U.S., with changing crests that rise to 700 ft (215 m).

Great Sandy Desert Wasteland, northern WESTERN AUSTRALIA. It extends from Eighty Mile Beach on the Indian Ocean eastward into NORTHERN TERRITORY and from Kimberley Downs south to the TROPIC OF CAPRICORN and the GIBSON DESERT. An arid expanse of salt marshes and sand hills, it roughly coincides with the sedimentary Canning basin. Canning Stock Route (1,000 mi, or 1,600 km, long) spans the region from Wiluna via Lake Disappointment to Halls Creek.

Great Schism See Western SCHISM

great sea otter See SEA OTTER

Great Slave Lake Lake, southern central Northwest Territories. Named for the Slave Indians, it is fed by several rivers, including the SLAVE, and drained by the MACKENZIE RIVER into the Arctic Ocean. The lake, with an area of 11,031 sq mi (28,570 sq km), is the fifth largest in North America. It is 300 mi (500 km) long and 30–140 mi (50–225 km) wide, with a maximum depth of more than 2,000 ft (600 m). While supporting a fishing industry, the lake is an integral part of the Mackenzie River waterway.

Great Smoky Mountains West range of the APPALACHIAN MTNS. It extends along the North Carolina–Tennessee boundary and blends into the BLUE RIDGE Mountains to the east. The highest part lies within the GREAT SMOKY MOUNTAINS NATIONAL PARK and includes Clingmans Dome, which at 6,643 ft (2,025 m) is the highest peak. Covered by forests, it was originally the domain of the CHEROKEE, and the area includes the Cherokee Indian Reservation and parts of the Pisgah and Cherokee national forests. The mountains form a popular resort area that includes part of the APPALACHIAN NATIONAL SCENIC TRAIL, and the Blue Ridge Parkway.

Great Smoky Mountains National Park National preserve, eastern Tennessee and western North Carolina. It is 20 mi (32 km) wide and extends southwest for 54 mi (87 km) from the Pigeon River to the Little Tennessee River. Established in 1934 to preserve the U.S.'s last remaining sizable area of southern primeval hardwood forest, it covers 520,269 acres (210,553 hectares) and contains some of the highest peaks in the APPALACHIAN MTNS. Summits are crowned with dense forest, while lower elevations have mountain laurel, rhododendron, and azaleas. The region's first settlers established themselves in the area's valleys, and some of their homes are preserved in the park. It was designated a WORLD HERITAGE SITE in 1983.

Great Society Slogan used in 1965 by Pres. LYNDON B. JOHNSON to identify his legislative program of national reform. In his first State of the Union address, Johnson described his vision of a "Great Society" that would include a "war on poverty" and federal support for education, medical care for the elderly, and legal protection for blacks deprived of voting rights by state regulations. He also proposed a new department of housing and urban development to coordinate federal housing projects. Congress enacted almost all his programs, the largest number of legislative programs since the NEW DEAL. See also CIVIL RIGHTS ACT OF 1964, MEDICARE AND MEDICAID.

Great Trek Emigration of some 12,000–14,000 AFRIKANERS from Cape Colony, South Africa, between 1835 and the early 1840s, in rebellion against British policies and in search of fresh pasturelands. The trek, regarded by Afrikaners as the origin of the South African nation, enabled the settlers to establish temporary military supremacy over rival African kingdoms, to penetrate into Natal and the Highveld, and to carry white settlement north to the Limpopo River. See also A PRETORIUS.

Great Victoria Desert Arid region, WESTERN and SOUTH AUSTRALIA. Lying between GIBSON DESERT on the north and NULLARBOR PLAIN on the south, it extends east from Kalgoorlie almost to the Stuart Range. Much of its eastern end is occupied by the Central and North West Aboriginal reserves. A vast expanse of sand hills, it is crossed by the Laverton-Warburton Mission Track, which links the mission station in the Warburton Range with Laverton, 350 mi (560 km) southwest. There are several national parks and reserves in the area, including the Great Victoria Desert Nature Reserve and the Nullarbor National Park.

Great Wall (of China) *Chinese* **Wanli Changcheng** \'wän-'lē-'chäŋ-'cheŋ\ Defensive wall, northern China. One of the largest building-construction projects ever carried out, it runs (with all its branches) about 4,000 mi (6,400 km) east to west from BO HAI to a point deep in central Asia. Parts of the fortification date from the 4th century BC. In 214 BC SHI HUANGDI connected existing defensive walls into a single system fortified by watchtowers. These served both to guard the rampart and to communicate with the capital, Xianyang, near XI'AN, by signal—smoke by day and fire by night. Originally constructed partly of masonry and earth, it was faced with brick in its eastern portion. It was rebuilt in later times, especially in the 15th–16th century. The basic wall is about 30 ft (9 m) high, and the towers rise to about 40 ft (12 m). It was designated a WORLD HERITAGE SITE in 1987.

great white shark *or* **white shark** Large, aggressive SHARK (*Carcharodon carcharias,* family Isuridae), considered the species most dangerous to humans. It is found in tropical and temperate regions of all oceans and is noted for its voracious appetite. Its diet may include fishes, sea turtles, birds, sea lions, and ships' garbage. It is heavy-bodied and has a crescent-shaped tail and large, saw-edged, triangular teeth. It may reach a length of about 35 ft (11 m) and is generally gray, bluish, or brownish, with the color shading suddenly into a whitish belly. Though it is widely feared, only a few hundred humans are known to have ever been killed by the great white shark.

Great Zimbabwe See ZIMBABWE

Greater London Metropolitan county (pop., 1995 est.: 7,007,000), England. It lost its administrative functions in 1986, and now exists in name only. Covering an area of 632 sq mi (1,637 sq km), it comprises the City of LONDON and 32 other boroughs; 13 constitute Inner London and the others, Outer London. Lying on both sides of the River THAMES, the Greater London conurbation extends as far as 45 mi (72 km) from the center. It is a major political, industrial, cultural, and financial center.

Greater Manchester Metropolitan county (pop., 1995 est.: 2,578,000), northwestern England. It lost its administrative functions in 1986, and now exists in name only. It is one of the major conurbations of the country, including the city of MANCHESTER and several boroughs. Its area is 497 sq mi (1,287 sq km); it is a major British commercial and transportation center.

grebe Any of about 18 species of diving birds (family Podicipedidae) found in most tropical and temperate areas and often in subarctic regions. Most species can fly, and some are migratory. Grebes have a pointed bill, short narrow wings, and a vestigial tail. The position of their legs, set at the rear of the body, makes walking awkward. They feed chiefly on fish or invertebrates. Courting or rival males perform elaborate aquatic dances in pairs. Species range from about 8 to 29 in. (21–73 cm) long.

Slavonian, or horned, grebe (*Podiceps auritus*).

INGMAR HOLMASEN

Greco, El (Spanish: "The Greek") *orig.* Domenikos Theotokopoulos (c. 1541–1614) Cretan-Spanish painter, the first great master of Spanish painting. Documentation on his early life is limited, but it is known that he was in Venice c. 1566–70 and may have studied in TITIAN's workshop. In 1572 he was a member of the guild of St. Luke in Rome. His first commission in Spain (1577) was for altarpieces for the church of Santo Domingo el Antiguo in Toledo (1577–79); the paintings for the high altar, *The Assumption of the Virgin* and *The Trinity*, show the influence of Titian and MICHELANGELO. Their elongated human figures became his signature style. His masterpiece, *The Burial of the Count of Orgaz* (1586–88), portrays a supernatural, semiabstract vision of heaven above, filled with tall, phantomlike figures, and a normal view of earth below. From 1590 until his death his output was prodigious. His major commissions included the complete altar composition for the Hospital de la Caridad at Illescas (1603–5), for which he also worked as architect and sculptor. He excelled as a portraitist. Two landscapes survive, notably his *View of Toledo* (c. 1610). His workshop produced many replicas of his works, but his style was so individual that his only followers were his son and a few forgotten imitators.

Greco–Persian Wars See PERSIAN WARS

Greco-Roman wrestling Style of WRESTLING in which the legs are prohibited from being used to obtain a fall and in which no holds may be taken below the waist. It originated in France in the early 19th century, in imitation of classical Greek and Roman representations of the sport. It eventually came to be favored by most other countries and was, until the acceptance of freestyle wrestling in the late 20th century, the style practiced exclusively in Olympic and international amateur competition.

Greco–Turkish Wars (1897, 1921–22) Two military conflicts between the Greeks and the Turks. The first, or Thirty Days' War, took place after an 1896 rebellion on Turkish-ruled Crete between Christian residents and their Muslim rulers. Greek troops occupied the island in 1897. The European powers imposed a blockade to prevent assistance to the island. Unable to reach Crete, the Greeks sent a force to attack the Turks in Thessaly, but it was overwhelmed by the superior Turkish army. Though a peace treaty forced the Greeks to withdraw, Turkish troops also left Crete, which had been made an international protectorate and was later (1913) ceded to Greece. The second war occurred after World War I, when the Greeks attempted to claim territories assigned to them by the Treaty of SÈVRES (1920). In 1921 the Greek army launched an offensive in Anatolia against nationalist Turks who would not recognize the treaty. The Greek forces were driven out by MUSTAFA KEMAL ATATURK, and the Treaty of LAUSANNE (1923) returned the disputed territories to Turkey.

Greece *officially* **Hellenic Republic** *Greek* **Ellás** \e-'läs\ *ancient* **Hellas.** Country, BALKAN PENINSULA, southern Europe. Area: 50,949 sq mi (131,957 sq km). Population (2000 est.): 10,562,000. Capital: ATHENS. The people are mainly ethnic Greek. Language: Greek (official). Reli-

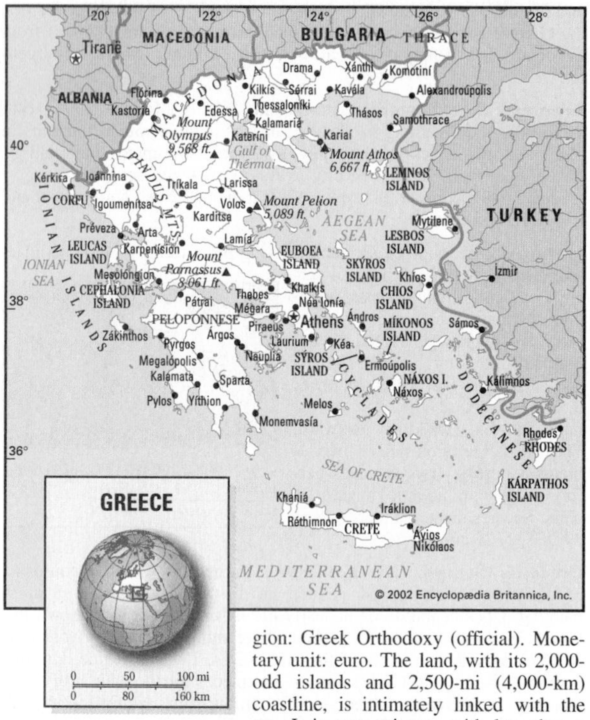

gion: Greek Orthodoxy (official). Monetary unit: euro. The land, with its 2,000-odd islands and 2,500-mi (4,000-km) coastline, is intimately linked with the sea. It is mountainous, with less than a fourth in lowland, much of this as coastal plains along the Aegean or mountain valleys and small plains near river mouths. The country's interior is dominated by the Pindus Mountains, which extend from Albania on Greece's northwestern border into the PELOPONNESE. Mount Olympus is the country's highest peak. Among its islands are the AEGEAN and IONIAN groups and CRETE. Greece has a Mediterranean climate. It has an advanced developing, mainly private-enterprise, economy based on agriculture, manufacturing, and tourism. It is a multiparty republic with one legislative house; the chief of state is the president, and the head of government is the prime minister. The earliest urban society in Greece was the palace-centered MINOAN civilization, which reached its height on Crete c. 2000 BC. It was succeeded by the mainland MYCENAEAN civilization, which arose c. 1600 BC following a wave of Indo-European invasions. In c. 1200 BC a second wave of invasions destroyed the BRONZE AGE cultures, and a dark age followed, known mostly through the epics of HOMER. At the end of this time, classical Greece began to emerge (c. 750 BC) as a collection of independent city-states, including SPARTA in the Peloponnese and ATHENS in Attica. The civilization reached its zenith after repelling the Persians at the beginning of the 5th century BC (see PERSIAN WARS) and began to decline after the civil strife of the PELOPONNESIAN WAR at the century's end. In 338 BC the Greek city-states were taken over by PHILIP II of Macedon, and Greek culture was spread by Philip's son ALEXANDER THE GREAT throughout his empire. The Romans, themselves heavily influenced by Greek culture, conquered the Greek states in the 2nd century BC. After the fall of Rome, Greece remained part of the BYZANTINE EMPIRE until the mid-15th century, when it became part of the expanding OTTOMAN EMPIRE; it gained its independence in 1832. It was occupied by Nazi Germany during World War II. Civil war followed and lasted until 1949, when communist forces were defeated. In 1952 Greece joined NATO. A military junta ruled the country from 1967 to 1974, when democracy was restored and a referendum declared an end to the Greek monarchy. In 1981 Greece joined the European Community (see EUROPEAN UNION), the first eastern European country to do so. Upheavals in the Balkans in the 1990s strained Greece's relations with some neighboring states, including the former Yugoslav entity that became the Republic of Macedonia.

Greek alphabet Writing system developed in Greece c. 1000 BC, the direct or indirect ancestor of all modern European ALPHABETS. Derived from the North Semitic alphabet via that of the PHOENICIANS, it modified an all-consonant alphabet to represent vowels. Letters for sounds not found in Greek became the Greek letters *alpha, epsilon, iota, omicron,* and *upsilon,* representing the vowels *a, e, i, o,* and *u.* This greatly increased the accuracy and legibility of the new system. While the Chalcidian version of the Greek alphabet probably gave rise to the Etruscan alphabet and thus indirectly to the LATIN ALPHABET, in 403 BC Athens officially adopted the Ionic version. This became the classical Greek alphabet, which had 24 letters, all capitals—ideal for monuments; various scripts better suited to handwriting were later derived from it.

Letters	English Sound	Names	Letters	English Sound	Names
Α α	*a*	alpha	Ν ν	*n*	nu
Β ϐ, β	*b*	beta	Ξ ξ	*x*	xi
Γ γ	*g*	gamma	Ο ο	*o*	omicron
Δ δ	*d*	delta	Π π	*p*	pi
Ε ε	*e*	epsilon	Ρ ρ	*rh, r*	rho
Ζ ζ	*z*	zeta	Σ σ, ς	*s*	sigma
Η η	*ē*	eta	Τ τ	*t*	tau
Θ θ	*th*	theta	Υ υ	*y, u*	upsilon
Ι ι	*i*	iota	Φ φ	*ph*	phi
Κ κ	*k*	kappa	Χ χ	*kh*	chi
Λ λ	*l*	lambda	Ψ ψ	*ps*	psi
Μ μ	*m*	mu	Ω ω	*ō*	omega

The modern Greek alphabet, with English sound equivalents.

Greek Civil War (1944–45, 1946–49). Two-stage conflict during which Greek communists unsuccessfully tried to gain control of Greece. The two principal Greek guerrilla forces that had resisted Nazi Germany's occupation—the communist-controlled National Liberation Front–National Popular Liberation Army (EAM–ELAS) and the Greek Democratic National Army (EDES)—came into conflict after EAM–ELAS set up a provisional government that rejected the Greek king and his government-in-exile. When Germany withdrew from Greece in 1944, the communists and royalist guerrillas were brought together by the British in an uneasy coalition. Because the communist guerrillas refused to disband their forces, a bitter civil war broke out in late 1944 that was put down by British forces. After elections that the communists did not participate in, the Greek king was restored to his throne. In 1946 a full-scale guerrilla war was reopened by the communists. The U.S. government took over the defense of Greece, creating the TRUMAN DOCTRINE as justification. After fierce skirmishes in the mountains, in 1949 the communists announced the end of open hostilities. An estimated 50,000 Greeks died in the conflict, which left a legacy of bitterness.

Greek fire Any of several flammable mixtures used in ancient and medieval warfare, particularly a petroleum-based mixture invented by the Byzantine Greeks in the 7th century. Flammable materials such as pitch and sulfur had been used in war since ancient times, but true Greek fire was especially deadly. Thrown in pots or discharged from tubes, it apparently caught fire spontaneously, and water could not put it out. Greek fire launched from tubes mounted on ship prows wrought havoc on the Arab fleet attacking Constantinople in 673. Its effectiveness was a prime reason for the long survival of the Byzantine Empire. The recipe was so secret that its precise composition remains unknown.

Greek Independence, War of (1821–32) Rebellion of Greeks within the Ottoman Empire. The revolt began under the leadership of Alexandros Ypsilanti (1792–1828). He was soon defeated, but in the meantime other rebels in Greece and on several islands gained control of the Peloponnese and declared Greek independence (1822). Three times the Turks attempted invasions. Internal rivalries prevented the Greeks from extending their control and consolidating their position. With Egyptian reinforcements, the Turks successfully invaded the Peloponnese and captured several cities, but the intervention of the European powers saved the Greek cause. A settlement was finally reached at an 1830 London conference, declaring Greece an independent monarchical state.

Greek language Indo-European language spoken mostly in Greece. Its history can be divided into four phases: Ancient Greek, Koine, Byzantine Greek, and Modern Greek. Ancient Greek is subdivided into Mycenaean Greek and Archaic and Classical Greek. The language of the latter periods had numerous dialects (e.g., Ionic, Attic). The second phase, Koine (Hellenistic Greek), arose during Alexander the Great's reign in the 4th century BC. A common language with simplified grammar, it spread throughout the Hellenized world. Purists who rejected Koine as a corruption of Attic Greek successfully advocated adoption of the Classical language for all writing. Thus, the written form, Byzantine Greek (5th–15th century AD), stayed rooted in the Attic tradition while the spoken language continued to develop. Modern Greek, dating from the 15th century, has many local dialects. Standard Modern Greek, Greece's official written and spoken language, is largely based on a form called Demotic (used in popular speech) but includes elements of Katharevusa, the written language formerly used in government and public life.

Greek law Legal systems of the ancient Greeks. Each city-state administered its own laws, many of which were laid down in written statutes. The harsh law code of Draco and the more humane one of Solon are two of the most famous. Unlike Roman law, Greek law produced little analytical jurisprudence, though the philosophers examined abstract concepts of justice. Those who sat in judgment based their verdicts less on notions of equity than on the statutes' literal meaning. Both private and criminal procedures began with the summoning of the defendant to the magistrate and the filing of a written complaint. A type of arbitration was available in civil suits. Enforcement of a judgment was generally left to the plaintiff.

Greek mythology Oral and literary traditions of the ancient Greeks concerning their gods and heroes and the nature and history of the cosmos. The Greek myths and legends are known today primarily from Greek literature, including such classic works as Homer's *Iliad* and *Odyssey*, Hesiod's *Works and Days* and *Theogony*, Ovid's *Metamorphoses*, and the dramas of Aeschylus, Sophocles, and Euripides. The myths deal with the creation of the gods and the world, the struggle among the gods for supremacy and the triumph of Zeus, the love affairs and quarrels of the gods, and the effects of their adventures and powers on the mortal world, including their link with natural phenomena such as thunderstorms or the seasons and their connection with cultic sites or rituals. Among the great stories of Greek mythology and legend are those of the Trojan War, the voyage of Odysseus, Jason's search for the Golden Fleece, the exploits of Heracles, the adventures of Theseus, and the tragedy of Oedipus. See also Greek religion.

Greek Orthodox Church Independent Eastern Orthodox church of Greece. The term is sometimes used erroneously for Eastern Orthodoxy in general. It remained under the patriarch of Constantinople until 1833, when it became independent. It is governed by 67 metropolitan bishops, presided over by an archbishop.

Greek pottery Pottery made in ancient Greece. Its painted decoration has become the primary source of information about the development of Greek pictorial art. It was made in a variety of sizes and shapes, according to its intended use; large vessels were used for storage and transportation of liquids (wine, olive oil, water), smaller pots for perfumes and unguents. The earliest style, known as the Geometric style (c. 1000–700 BC), features geometric patterns and, eventually, narrative scenes with stylized figures. From the late 8th to the early 7th century BC, a growing Eastern influence resulted in the "Orientalizing" of motifs (e.g., sphinx, griffin), notably in pieces made in Corinth (c. 700 BC), where the painters developed black-figure pottery. Athenians adopted the black-figure style and from 600 BC on became the dominant manufacturers of Greek pottery. They invented red-figure pottery c. 530 BC. By the 4th century BC the figured decoration of pottery had declined, and by the end of the century it had died out in Athens.

Greek religion Beliefs, rituals, and mythology of the ancient Greeks. Though the worship of the sky god Zeus began as early as the 2nd millennium BC, Greek religion in the established sense began c. 750 BC and lasted for over a thousand years, extending its influence throughout the Mediterranean world and beyond. The Greeks had numerous gods who controlled various natural or social forces (e.g., Poseidon the sea, Demeter the harvest, Hera marriage). Different deities were worshiped in different localities, but Homer's epics helped create a unified religion, in which the major gods were believed to live on Mount Olympus under the rule of Zeus. The Greeks also worshiped various gods of the countryside: Pan, nymphs, naiads, dryads, Nereids, and satyrs (see satyr and Silenus), along with the Furies and the Fates. Heroes from the past, such as Heracles and Asclepius, were also venerated. Animal sacrifices were of great importance, usually made at a temple on the altar of the god. Other cultic activities included prayers, libations, processions, athletic contests, and divination, particularly through oracles and birds. Great religious festivals included the City Dionysia at Athens and the festival of Zeus in the western Peloponnese that included the Olympic Games. Death was seen as a hateful state; the dead lived in the realm of Hades, and only heroes enjoyed Elysium. Great wrongdoers suffered in Tartarus. Mystery religions emerged to satisfy the desire for personal guidance, salvation, and immortality. Greek religion faded with the rise of Christianity and lost its last great advocate with the death of Julian in AD 363. See also Greek mythology.

Greek Gods and Goddesses

Aeolus	god of the winds	Helios	god of the sun
Aphrodite	goddess of love, beauty, and procreation	Hephaestus	god of fire and metalworking
Apollo	god of sunlight, prophecy, music, and poetry	Hera	queen of heaven, goddess of marriage and women
Ares	god of war	Hermes	messenger god and god of commerce, fertility, and dreams
Artemis	goddess of the animals, hunting, and fertility		
Athena	goddess of wisdom	Hestia	goddess of the hearth
Boreas	god of the north wind	Iris	goddess of the rainbow, messenger of the gods
Cybele	mother of the gods, humans, and animals	Morpheus	god of dreams
Demeter	goddess of fruit, crops, and vegetation	Nemesis	goddess of vengeance
		Nike	goddess of victory
Dionysus	god of wine	Pan	god of pastures, forests, and herds
Eos	goddess of the dawn		
Eros	god of love	Persephone	goddess of the underworld
Gaea	goddess of the earth		
Hades or Pluto	god of the underworld	Poseidon	god of the sea
		Rhea	mother of the gods
Hebe	goddess of youth	Selene	goddess of the moon
Hecate	goddess of magic, ghosts, and witchcraft	Uranus	god of the sky
		Zeus	lord of heaven

Greek Revival Architectural style, based on 5th-century-BC Greek temples, which spread throughout Europe and the U.S. in the early 19th century. The revival was symptomatic of the public's preoccupation with Greek culture at the time. Architects often tacked majestic facades with Grecian columns onto existing buildings; banks and institutions became imitation Doric temples, and Greek Revival houses often sport large porticoes made up of heavy pilasters and reinterpreted pediments. In the U.S., where the style was adopted on a large scale, many strange distortions found acceptance. The British Museum (1847), utilizing the Greek Ionic order on a massive scale, is the most powerful English example of the style. See also Neoclassical architecture.

Greeley, Horace (1811–1872) U.S. newspaper editor and political leader. Born in Amherst, N.H., Greeley was a printer's apprentice in Vermont before moving to New York City, where he edited a literary magazine and weeklies for the Whig Party. In 1841 he founded the highly influential *New York Tribune*, a daily paper dedicated to reforms, economic progress, and the elevation of the masses. He edited it for the rest of his life, becoming known especially for his articulation of the

North's antislavery sentiments in the 1850s. After the onset of the American Civil War (1861), he pursued a politically erratic course. His unrealized lifelong ambitions for public office culminated in 1872 in an unsuccessful run for president on the Liberal Republican Party ticket.

Greeley.

© ARCHIVE PHOTOS

Green, Adolph See Betty COMDEN

Green, Hetty *orig.* **Henrietta Howland Robinson.** (1835–1916) U.S. financier, reputedly the wealthiest U.S. woman of her time. She was born in New Bedford, Mass. In 1865 her father and aunt both died, leaving her an estate valued at $10 million. By shrewd management she increased it to more than $100 million at her death. See photograph below.

Hetty Green, 1897.

BY COURTESY OF THE LIBRARY OF CONGRESS, WASHINGTON, D.C.

Green, Julian *or* **Julien Green** (1900–1998) French-American writer. Born in France of American parents, Green grew up in the south of France. He lived mostly in France, though he taught for a few years in the United States. Green's novels are written in French and are usually set in French provincial towns or in the American South. In the intense, claustrophobic atmosphere of these novels, neurotic characters engage in obsessive relationships marked by secrecy, guilt, betrayal, sexual passion, and violence. In 1970 the Académie Française awarded him its grand prize for literature in appreciation of his masterful French prose style, which is marked by clarity, precision, and simplicity. Green's works were collected in *Complete Works,* 10 vol. (1954–65).

Green, William (1873–1952) U.S. labor leader, president of the American Federation of Labor (AFL). Born in Coshocton, Ohio, he was a coal miner from age 16. He worked his way up through the union hierarchy and was finally elected president of the AFL in 1924, a post he kept until his death. The formation in 1935 of the Committee for Industrial Organization (CIO), headed by JOHN L. LEWIS, led to bitter public disputes between the two men, ending in the expulsion of the CIO from the AFL in 1936. See also AFL-CIO, LABOR UNION.

Green Bank equation See DRAKE EQUATION

Green Bay City (pop., 1996 est.: 102,000), northeastern Wisconsin. Located on the Fox River at Green Bay, an inlet of Lake MICHIGAN, it was the site of French trading posts from 1634 until the WAR OF 1812. The U.S. took possession when the army built Fort Howard there in 1816. With the decline of the fur trade and the opening of the ERIE CANAL, it developed as a lumbering and agricultural center. A GREAT LAKES port of entry with heavy shipping, it has a large wholesale and distributing business. The city is famous for its professional football team, the Green Bay Packers, which it has supported since 1919. It is the site of a University of Wisconsin branch and a technical college.

Green Berets \bə-ˈrāz\ *or* **Special Forces** Elite unit of the U.S. Army specializing in counterinsurgency. The Green Berets (whose berets can be colors other than green) came into being in 1952. They were active in the Vietnam War, and they have been sent to areas of conflict around the world to assist governments supported by the U.S. to employ guerrilla warfare tactics against insurgents.

green manure Crop grown and plowed under for its beneficial effects to the soil and subsequent crops, though during its growth it may be grazed. These crops are usually ANNUALS, either GRASSES or LEGUMES. They add nitrogen to the soil, increase the general fertility level, reduce EROSION, improve the physical condition of the soil, and reduce nutrient loss from leaching. They are usually planted in the fall and turned under in the spring before the summer crop is sown. See also COVER CROP.

Green Mountains Part of the APPALACHIAN MTNS. system. It extends for 250 mi (402 km) through the center of Vermont, and has a maximum width of 30 mi (50 km). Many peaks rise to more than 3,000 ft (900 m); the highest is Mount Mansfield, at 4,393 ft (1,339 m). Known for their skiing facilities, the mountains are traversed by the Long Trail (part of the APPALACHIAN NATIONAL SCENIC TRAIL). The Green Mountains National Forest which covers 214,000 acres (86,600 hectares), was established in 1932.

green revolution Great increase in production of food grains (especially WHEAT and RICE) that resulted in large part from the introduction into developing countries of new, high-yielding varieties, beginning in the mid-20th century. Its early dramatic successes were in Mexico and the Indian subcontinent. The new varieties require large amounts of chemical fertilizers and pesticides to produce their high yields, raising concerns about cost and potentially harmful environmental effects. Poor farmers, unable to afford the fertilizers and pesticides, have often reaped even lower yields with these grains than with the older strains, which were better adapted to local conditions and had some resistance to pests and diseases. See also NORMAN BORLAUG.

Green River River, western U.S. It flows from western Wyoming, south into Utah, where it turns east to make a loop through the northwestern corner of Colorado. Turning south in Utah, it enters the COLORADO RIVER in CANYONLANDS NATIONAL PARK, after a course of 730 mi (1,175 km). Originally known as the Spanish River, it was renamed in 1824, probably for its color, derived in places from green soapstone banks along its course.

Greenaway, Kate *orig.* **Catherine** (1846–1901) British artist and children's-book illustrator. The daughter of a draftsman and wood engraver, she studied art in London. In 1868 she began to exhibit drawings, contribute illustrations to magazines, and design Christmas and Valentine cards. Her first book, *Under the Window* (1878), was followed by *The Birthday Book* (1880), *Mother Goose* (1881), and many others that were enormously successful and strongly affected contemporary fashions. Her yearly almanacs (1888–97) also became very popular.

Illustration for "When We Went Out with Grandmamma" by Kate Greenaway for *Marigold Garden,* 1885.

MARY EVANS PICTURE LIBRARY, LONDON

Greenback movement (1868–88) Campaign mainly by U.S. farmers to maintain or increase the amount of paper money in circulation. To finance the AMERICAN CIVIL WAR the U.S. government issued paper money not backed by gold and printed in green ink, called greenbacks. After the war fiscal conservatives called for an end to greenbacks, but farmers and others who wanted to maintain high prices opposed the move. In 1868 the Democrats endorsed a plan to redeem some war bonds with new greenbacks. The depression after the panic of 1873 intensified the demand for more greenbacks or unlimited silver coinage. After passage of the Resumption Act (1875), which provided for redemption of greenbacks in gold, the newly formed Greenback-Labor Party sought its repeal. In 1878 it elected 14 members of Congress, but support waned after 1884. See also FREE SILVER MOVEMENT, POPULIST MOVEMENT.

Greenberg, Clement (1909–1994) U.S. art critic. After graduating from Syracuse Univ., he returned to his native New York City and began writing for such publications as *Partisan Review* and *The Nation,* promoting an approach to looking at art that became known as "Greenberg formalism." The chief arbiter of art in the U.S. from the late 1940s through the 1950s, he exerted extraordinary influence as a champion of

ABSTRACT EXPRESSIONISM and its leading exponent, JACKSON POLLOCK. He routinely visited galleries and artists' studios and promoted the work of many, including HELEN FRANKENTHALER, MARK ROTHKO, and DAVID SMITH. He disavowed such later movements as POP ART and CONCEPTUAL ART and wrote little after the 1960s.

Greenberg, Hank *orig.* **Henry Benjamin** (1911–1986) U.S. baseball player. Born in the Bronx, N.Y., he began his professional career at first base with the Detroit Tigers in 1933. He twice helped the Tigers win the World Series (1935, 1940) and was named the American League's Most Valuable Player both years. In 1938 he hit 58 home runs. He often encountered prejudice on the field, but his refusal to play on Jewish holidays won him praise. He served four years in the military in World War II, then returned to the Tigers; traded to the Pittsburgh Pirates in 1947, he retired in 1948. He was part owner and general manager of the Cleveland Indians until 1957, and general manager of the Chicago White Sox 1959–63. The first Jewish star player in the major leagues, he was elected to the Baseball Hall of Fame in 1956.

Greenberg, Joseph H(arold) (1915–2001) U.S. anthropologist and linguist. Born in Brooklyn, N.Y., he received his PhD from Northwestern University. He eschewed more orthodox methods of historical LINGUISTICS for the approach he termed "mass" or "multilateral" comparison, which involved looking for phonetic resemblances among words in many languages simultaneously. His 1963 classification of AFRICAN LANGUAGES into four families (AFROASIATIC, NIGER-CONGO, NILO-SAHARAN, and KHOISAN) was widely accepted. However, his 1987 classification of all AMERICAN INDIAN LANGUAGES into just two families, Amerind and Na-Dene (see ATHABASKAN LANGUAGES) provoked a rancorous denunciation by specialists, who faulted both his data and his method.

Greene, Charles Sumner and Henry Mather (1868–1957, 1870–1954) U.S. architects. Born in Brighton, Ohio, the Greene brothers established a partnership in Pasadena, Cal., in 1894. Using a modernist approach, they pushed the older STICK STYLE further than it had ever gone. In the years 1904–11, they pioneered the influential California bungalow, a single-storied house with a low-pitched roof. Their bungalows feature wide, low volumes, the use of balconies and verandas to achieve a melding of indoor and outdoor space, and frank utilization of wood members (sticks), exquisitely worked and extending gracefully beyond the edges of the spreading GABLES.

Greene, (Henry) Graham (1904–1991) British author. After studying at Oxford Univ., he converted to Roman Catholicism in 1926. Beginning c. 1930, he worked principally as a freelance journalist for several decades, during which he traveled widely. *Stamboul Train* (1932; also titled *Orient Express*; film, 1934) was the first of his "entertainments," thrillers with considerable moral complexity and depth; others included *A Gun for Sale* (1936; also titled *This Gun For Hire*; film, 1942), *The Confidential Agent* (1939; film, 1945), and *The Third Man* (1949; film, 1949). His finest novels—*Brighton Rock* (1938; film, 1948), *The Power and the Glory* (1940; film, 1962), *The Heart of the Matter* (1948; film, 1954), and *The End of the Affair* (1951; film, 1999)—all have distinctly religious themes. Third-world nations on the brink of political upheaval were the settings of *The Quiet American* (1955; film, 1957), *Our Man in Havana* (1958; film, 1959), *A Burnt-Out Case* (1961), and *The Comedians* (1966; film, 1967). Later works included *The Honorary Consul* (1973; film, 1983) and *The Human Factor* (1978; film, 1979).

Greene, Nathanael (1742–1786) American general. Born in Potowomut, R.I., he served in the colonial legislature and as commander of the colonial militia (1775). He led troops in the Continental Army at Boston and New York, then fought in the battles at Trenton, Brandywine, and Germantown. He succeeded Gen. HORATIO GATES as commander in chief of the southern army (1778), and his strategy so weakened the British troops that Gen. CHARLES CORNWALLIS abandoned plans to conquer North Carolina (1781). Greene began the reconquest of inner South Carolina, and by late June he had forced the British back to Charleston. He presided at the court-martial of JOHN ANDRE in the BENEDICT ARNOLD affair (1780).

Greengard, Paul (born 1925) U.S. molecular and cellular biologist. He received his PhD from Johns Hopkins University. Greengard discovered how DOPAMINE and other neurotransmitters work in the nervous system. He showed that slow synaptic transmission involves protein phosphorylation, a chemical reaction in which a phosphate molecule is linked to a protein, thus changing the protein's function. Along with ERIC KANDEL and ARVID CARLSSON, he was awarded a Nobel Prize in 2000. The findings of these three men resulted in the development of new drugs for PARKINSONISM and other disorders.

greenhouse Building designed for the protection of tender or out-of-season plants against excessive cold or heat. Usually a glass- or plastic-enclosed structure with a framing of aluminum, galvanized steel, or such woods as redwood, cedar, or cypress, it is used for the production of fruits, vegetables, flowers, and any other plants requiring special temperature conditions. It is heated partly by the sun and partly by artificial means. This controlled environment can be adapted to the needs of particular plants.

greenhouse effect Warming of the earth's surface and lower atmosphere that tends to intensify with an increase in atmospheric carbon dioxide and certain other gases. Visible light from the sun heats the earth's surface. Part of this energy is reradiated in the form of long-wave INFRARED RADIATION, much of which is absorbed by molecules of carbon dioxide and water vapor in the atmosphere and reradiated back toward the surface as more heat. This process is analogous to the glass panes of a greenhouse that transmit sunlight but hold in heat. The trapping of infrared radiation causes the earth's surface and lower atmosphere to warm more than they otherwise would, making the surface habitable. The increase in atmospheric carbon dioxide caused by widespread combustion of FOSSIL FUELS may intensify the greenhouse effect and cause long-term climatic changes. An increase in atmospheric concentrations of other trace gases such as CHLOROFLUOROCARBONS, NITROUS OXIDE, and METHANE may also aggravate greenhouse conditions. It is estimated that since the beginning of the industrial revolution the amount of atmospheric carbon dioxide has increased 30%, while the amount of methane has doubled. Today the U.S. is responsible for about one-fifth of all human-produced greenhouse-gas emissions. See also GLOBAL WARMING.

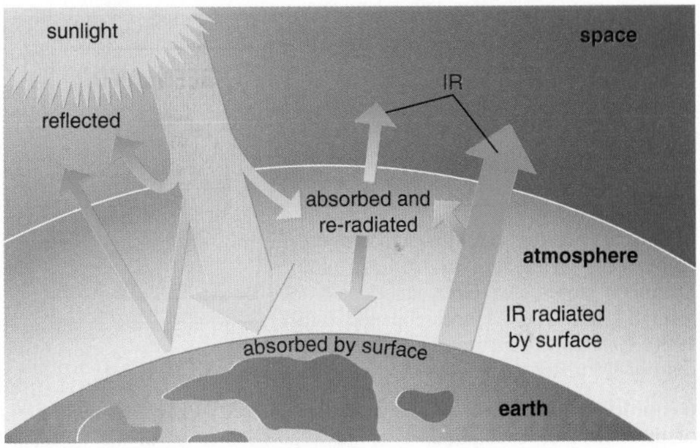

Some incoming sunlight is reflected by the earth's atmosphere and surface, but most is absorbed by the surface, which is warmed. Infrared (IR) radiation is then emitted from the surface. Some IR radiation escapes to space, but some is absorbed by the atmosphere's greenhouse gases (especially carbon dioxide, water, and methane) and re-radiated in all directions, some to space and some back toward the surface, where it further warms the surface and lower atmosphere.

Greenland *Danish* **Grønland** \'grœ̄n-,län\ *Greenlandic* **Kalaallit Nunaat** \kä-'lät-lēt-nu̇-'nät\ Island (pop., 1991 est.: 57,000), northeastern North America. The world's largest island (excluding Australia), it covers 840,000 sq mi (2,175,600 sq km), is located in the North Atlantic Ocean and is a dependency of Denmark. Its capital is NUUK. Two-thirds of the island lies within the Arctic Circle; it is dominated by the massive GREENLAND ICE SHEET. While fishing is central to the economy, there are commercial mineral deposits, including a large gold deposit discovered in 1989. More than four-fifths of the population are native Greenlanders, principally of Inuit (see ESKIMO) descent. The Inuit probably crossed to northwestern Greenland from North America, along the islands of the Canadian Arctic, from 4000 BC to AD 1000. The Norwegian ERIK THE RED visited Greenland in 982; his son, LEIF ERIKSSON, introduced Christianity in the 11th century. Greenland came under joint Danish-Norwegian rule in the late 14th century. The original Norse settlements became extinct

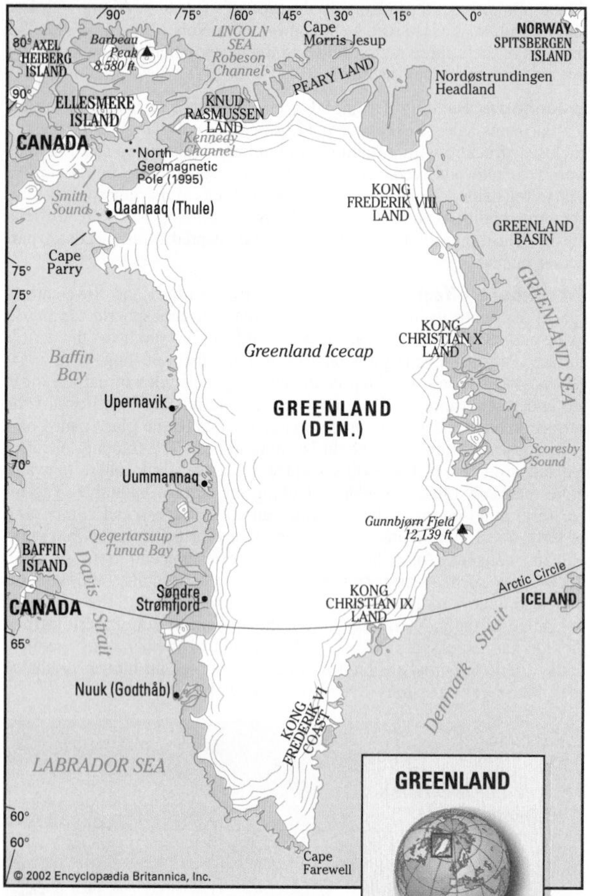

in the 15th century, but Greenland was recolonized by Denmark in 1721. In 1776 Denmark closed the Greenland coast to foreign trade; it was not reopened until 1950. Greenland became part of the kingdom of Denmark in 1953, and home rule was established in 1979.

Greenland Ice Sheet Single ice cap, GREENLAND. Covering about 80% of the island of Greenland, it is the largest ice mass in the Northern Hemisphere, second only to the Antarctic. It extends 1,570 mi (2,530 km) north to south, has a maximum width of 680 mi (1,094 km) near its northern margin, and an average thickness of about 5,000 ft (1,500 m). The ice sheet rises to two domes; the northern dome, reaching more than 10,000 ft (3,000 m), is its thickest and coldest point. In volume it contains 12% of the world's glacial ice. If it melted, the sea level would rise 20 ft (6 m).

Greenpeace International environmental organization. Founded in Canada in 1971 to oppose U.S. nuclear testing in Alaska, it later expanded its goals to include saving endangered species, stopping environmental abuses, and increasing public environmental awareness. It has specialized in "direct, nonviolent action" in protests often designed to garner wide publicity. Its members have frequently steered small inflatable craft between the harpoon guns of whalers and their prey. In 1985 the *Rainbow Warrior,* a Greenpeace ship being used to obstruct French nuclear testing in the South Pacific, was sunk by French agents, resulting in the death of a photographer. Greenpeace has offices in some 30 countries.

Greens, the *German* **die Grünen.** Environmentalist political party founded in West Germany in 1979. A merger of about 250 ecological and environmentalist groups, it sought to organize public support for the control of nuclear energy and of air and water pollution. A national party from 1980, it called for the dismantling of the WARSAW PACT and NATO and the demilitarization of Europe. It first won representation in the Bundestag in 1983. It experienced almost constant ideological tensions between its left wing and a more pragmatic faction. The German Greens were the first such party, but by the end of the 1980s almost every country in Europe had Green parties.

Greensboro City (pop., 1996 est.: 195,000), northern central North Carolina. Established in 1808 as the county seat, it was named for Gen. NATHANAEL GREENE. Toward the end of the AMERICAN CIVIL WAR, Greensboro was the temporary capital of both the Confederacy and North Carolina. It is a large wholesale distribution point and an important insurance center. Textiles dominate its diversified industries. It is the site of several colleges and universities.

greenschist facies \'grēn-,shist-'fā-shēz\ One of the major divisions of the mineral facies classification of metamorphic rocks, encompassing the rocks that formed under farily low temperatures (from about 480°F to 660°F, or 250°C to 350°C) and pressure conditions and usually produced by regional METAMORPHISM. The minerals commonly found in such rocks include quartz, orthoclase, muscovite, chlorite, serpentine, talc, and epidote; carbonate minerals and amphibole (actinolite) may also be present.

Greenspan, Alan (born 1926) U.S. economist and chairman of the board of the FEDERAL RESERVE SYSTEM. Born in New York, he grew up an only child and initially wanted to be a professional musician. He received his doctorate from New York University in 1977. Having become a private economic consultant, Greenspan served as chairman of the president's Council of Economic Advisers under Pres. GERALD FORD. From 1981 to 1983 he chaired the bipartisan National Commission on Social Security Reform. In 1987 Pres. RONALD REAGAN appointed him chairman of the Federal Reserve Board, a position he continued to hold under Pres. G. Bush and Pres. W. Clinton. As Federal Reserve chairman, he has fought inflation through controlling the DISCOUNT RATE.

Greenwich \'gre-nich, 'gri-nij\ Borough (pop., 1991: 201,000), GREATER LONDON, on the southern bank of the THAMES RIVER. The meridian that passes through the borough serves as the basis for standard time as well as for reckonings of longitude throughout the world. Greenwich Park was enclosed by the duke of Gloucester in 1423; it was the site of the Royal Observatory 1675–c. 1958. Other historic buildings include the Queen's House, now part of the National Maritime Museum, and the Royal Naval College, established in 1873. The Millennial Dome, constructed in the 1990s, was used to usher in celebrations for the year 2000.

Greenwich Mean Time (GMT) Former name for mean solar time of the longitude (0°) of the former Royal Observatory at Greenwich, England, or Greenwich meridian. GMT was used to avoid potentially confusing references to local time systems (zones). In accord with tradition, 0000 GMT (denoting the start of a solar day) occurred at noon. In 1925 the numbering system for GMT was changed so that the day (like the civil day) began at midnight. Some confusion resulted, and in 1928 the International Astronomical Union changed the designation of the standard time of the zero meridian to UNIVERSAL TIME, which remains in general use. The term GMT is still used for some purposes (including navigation) in English-speaking countries.

Greenwich Village Residential section, Lower MANHATTAN, NEW YORK CITY. A village settlement during colonial times, it became in successive stages an exclusive residential area, a tenement district, and, after 1910, a rendezvous for writers, artists, students, bohemians, and intellectuals. The quaintness of its old townhouses led to rising rents in the 1980s and 1990s. Washington Square, in its center, is dominated by Washington Arch and NEW YORK UNIV.

Grégoire \grā-'gwär\, **Henri** (1750–1831) French prelate who defended of the Constitutional Church in the FRENCH REVOLUTION. Elected to the National Assembly (1789), he worked to unite the clergy with the THIRD ESTATE. Initially opposed to the CIVIL CONSTITUTION OF THE CLERGY, he later became the Constitutional bishop of Loir-et-Cher (1790). In the de-Christianizing campaign of 1793–94, he continued to wear clerical dress and profess his faith openly. After the collapse of the JACOBIN regime, he was a leader in restoring freedom of worship and reorganizing the church. He opposed NAPOLEON's regime and the CONCORDAT OF 1801 that ended the Constitutional Church.

Gregorian calendar Solar dating system now in general use. It was proclaimed in 1582 by Pope GREGORY XIII as a reform of the Julian calendar. By the Julian reckoning, the solar year comprised 365½ days. The addition of a "leap day" every four years was intended to maintain correspondence between the calendar and the seasons; however, a slight inaccuracy in the measurement of the solar year caused the calendar dates of the seasons to regress almost one day per century. By Pope Gregory's time, the Julian calendar was 10 days out of sync with the seasons; in 1582, to bring the vernal equinox (and thus Easter) back to its proper date, 10 days were dropped (October 5 became October 15). The Gregorian calendar differs from the Julian only in that no century year is a leap year unless it is exactly divisible by 400 (e.g., 1600, 2000). A further refinement, the designation of years evenly divisible by 4,000 as common (not leap) years, will keep the calendar accurate to within one day in 20,000 years.

Gregorian chant Liturgical music of the Roman Catholic church consisting of unaccompanied melody sung in unison to Latin words. It is named for Pope GREGORY I the Great, who may have contributed to its collection and codification, and who was traditionally represented as having received all the melodies directly from the Holy Spirit. Of the five bodies of medieval Latin liturgical music, it is the dominant repertoire, and the name is often used broadly to include them all. It apparently derived principally from Jewish cantillation, with other elements entering from the Eastern Church (see BYZANTINE CHANT) and elsewhere. Chant has traditionally been performed at the MASS and the canonical hours (the eight prayer services traditionally held daily in monasteries). Its texts come primarily from the biblical psalms, metrical hymns, and texts specific to the mass and the hours. The melodies are classified as belonging to one or another of the eight CHURCH MODES. Chant rhythm is not strictly metrical, and its notation does not indicate rhythm. Since the Second VATICAN COUNCIL, the performance of chant has diminished greatly. See also CANTUS FIRMUS.

Gregory, Augusta *orig.* **Isabella Augusta Persse** *known as* **Lady Gregory** (1852–1932) Irish playwright and theater manager, an important figure in the IRISH LITERARY RENAISSANCE. With WILLIAM BUTLER YEATS, she helped found the Irish Literary Theatre (1898) and the ABBEY THEATRE (1904). She wrote many dialect comedies based on Irish peasant life, including those collected in *Seven Short Plays* (1909). She also translated plays by Molière and others into an Anglo-Irish dialect called Kiltartan, and translated and arranged Irish sagas into continuous narratives, published as *Cuchulain of Muirthemne* (1902) and *Gods and Fighting Men* (1904).

Gregory I, St. *known as* **Gregory the Great** (c. 540–604) Pope (590–604) and doctor of the church. A Roman patrician, by age 30 he had attained the office of prefect, Rome's highest civil office. He then felt called to the religious life; he built several monasteries and served as a papal representative before being elected pope in 590, to which he only reluctantly assented. He became the architect of the medieval papacy. He strove to curb corruption by centralizing the papal administration. In 598 he won temporary peace with the Lombards, and he allowed the Byzantine usurper Phocas to make permanent peace with them in 602. Eager to convert pagan peoples, Gregory sent AUGUSTINE OF CANTERBURY on a mission to England (596). Under Gregory, Gothic Arian Spain (see ARIANISM) became reconciled with Rome. He laid the basis for the PAPAL STATES. He was a strong opponent of slavery, and he extended tolerance to Jews and heathens. He wrote the *Pastoral Rule,* a guide for church government, and other works. His extensive recodification of the liturgy and chant led to his name being given to GREGORIAN CHANT. He is remembered as perhaps the greatest of all the medieval popes.

Gregory VII, St. *orig.* **Hildebrand** (c. 1020–1085) Pope (1073–85). Educated in a monastery in Rome where his uncle was abbot, he rose to become a cardinal and archdeacon of Rome and was finally chosen pope in 1073. One of the great medieval reformers, Gregory attacked simony and clerical marriage and insisted that his papal legates had authority over local bishops. He is remembered chiefly for his conflict with Emperor HENRY IV in the INVESTITURE CONTROVERSY. Gregory's excommunication of the emperor gave rise a bitter quarrel that ended when Henry begged for forgiveness in a memorable scene at Canossa, Italy, in 1077. A renewed quarrel led Gregory to excommunicate the emperor again in 1080, and Henry's forces took Rome in 1084. Gregory was rescued by ROBERT GUISCARD, but the devastation of Rome forced the pope to withdraw to Salerno, where he died.

Gregory IX *orig.* **Ugo di Segni** (c. 1170–1241) Pope (1227–41) who founded the papal INQUISITION. In 1227 he excommunicated FREDERICK II when the emperor delayed in keeping his pledge to lead a crusade. Gregory ordered an attack on the kingdom of Sicily in the emperor's absence, but his forces were defeated. In 1234 he published the Decretals, a code of canon law that remained fundamental to Catholicism until World War I. Attacking heresy in southern France and northern Italy, he strengthened the Inquisition. Frederick's invasion of Sardinia, a papal fief, led Gregory to renew his excommunication (1239); he sought support in northern Italy but died before the struggle was resolved.

Gregory X *orig.* **Tebaldo Visconti** (c. 1210–1276) Pope (1271–76). He kept the Holy Roman Empire from disintegrating by securing the election of RUDOLF I as emperor. Rudolf in return promised to lead a new crusade and renounced claims in Rome and the papal territories. In 1274 Gregory issued a new constitution reforming the assembly of cardinals that elects a new pope. He also initiated a crusade and worked to unify the Greek and Roman churches.

Gregory XIII *orig.* **Ugo Buoncompagni** (1502–1585) Pope (1572–85) who promulgated the GREGORIAN CALENDAR. After teaching at the University of Bologna, he served as a delegate to the Council of Trent, became a cardinal in 1565, and was elected pope in 1572. A promoter of the COUNTER-REFORMATION, he sought to execute the reform decrees of the council. He compiled the *INDEX LIBRORUM PROHIBITORUM* and founded several colleges and seminaries, delegating their direction to the Jesuits. Aided by an astronomer and a mathematician, he corrected the errors in the Julian calendar and issued the Gregorian calendar (1582), which was later adopted worldwide.

Gregory of Nazianzus \ˌnā-zē-ˈan-zəs\, **St.** (c. 330–389?) One of the church fathers of EASTERN ORTHODOXY. Born in Asia Minor, he was ordained a priest in Nazianzus in 362. He helped his friend BASIL THE GREAT combat Arianism. Though consecrated bishop of Sasima in 372, he did not take possession of the bishopric, instead retiring to a life of contemplation and study. He was noted for his defense of the doctrine of the Holy Trinity and of the Nicene Creed. In 380 he took over the Great Church of Constantinople, but after being denied acknowledgment as bishop he once again retired.

Gregory of Nyssa \ˈnis-ə\, **St.** (c. 335–394?) Eastern Orthodox theologian and mystic. Initially a teacher of rhetoric, he turned to religion under the influence of his brother, BASIL THE GREAT, and was consecrated bishop of Nyssa in 372. Deposed by Arian opposition in 376, he was restored to office in 378 after the death of the Arian emperor, Valens. An associate of GREGORY OF NAZIANZUS, he became a leading defender of the doctrine of the Holy Trinity. His writings include *The Great Catechesis,* a classic outline of orthodox theology that examines the place of the sacraments in the church. A Christian Platonist, he shared ORIGEN's hope for ultimate universal salvation.

Gregory of Tours \ˈtu̇r\, **St.** *orig.* **Georgius Florentius** (538/539–594/595) Frankish bishop and writer. Born into an aristocratic family that had supplied several bishops of what is today central France, Gregory succeeded his cousin as bishop of Tours in 573. The complicated political situation of the period involved him in numerous political events and in open dispute with the king, CHILPERIC I. His fame rests on his *History of the Franks,* a chief source for knowledge of the 6th-century Franco-Roman kingdom. His other writings, including *Lives of the Fathers,* on the lives of saints, and seven books of miracles, afford unique evidence of life in Merovingian France.

Grenada \grə-ˈnā-də\ Self-governing state, WINDWARD ISLANDS, West Indies. Area: 133 sq mi (344 sq km). Population (2001 est.): 102,000. Capital: SAINT GEORGE'S. Blacks, mulattoes, and East Indians make up most of the population. Language: English (official). Religion: Roman Catholicism. Currency: Eastern Caribbean dollar. Grenada is the most southerly of the Windward Islands, lying about 100 mi (160 km) north of Venezuela; its territory includes the southern GRENADINES. Volcanic in origin, it is dominated by a thickly forested mountain ridge rising to 2,757 ft (840 m) at Mount St. Catherine. The southern coast is indented with beaches and natural harbors. Its tropical maritime climate supports rich vegetation. Often called the Isle of Spice, it is known for its nutmeg, cinnamon, and vanilla, as well as cocoa. It has a developing market economy dependent on agricultural exports and tourism. The chief of state is the British sovereign, represented by the governor-general; the head of government is the prime minister. The warlike CARIB Indians

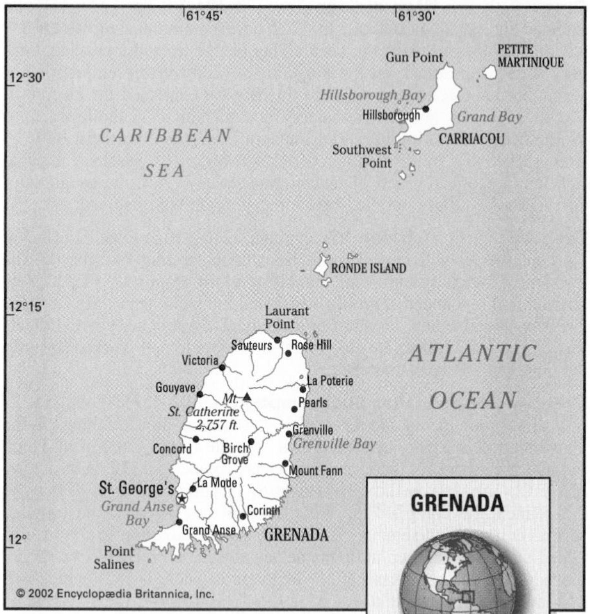

dominated Grenada when Christopher Columbus sighted the island in 1498 and named it Concepción; they ruled it for the next 150 years. In 1672 it became subject to the French crown and remained so until 1762, when British forces captured it. In 1833 the island's black slaves were freed. Grenada was the headquarters of the government of the British Windward Islands 1885–1958 and a member of the West Indies Federation 1958–62. It became a self-governing state in association with Britain in 1967 and gained its independence in 1974. In 1979 a left-wing government took control in a bloodless coup. Relations with its U.S.-oriented Latin-American neighbors became strained as Grenada leaned toward Cuba and the Soviet bloc. In order to counteract this trend, the U.S. invaded the island in 1983; democratic self-government was reestablished in 1984. Its relations with Cuba, once suspended, were restored in 1997.

grenade Small explosive, chemical, or gas bomb used at short range. Invented in the 15th century, it became so important that 17th-century European armies had specially trained grenade throwers, or grenadiers. After c. 1750 grenades were largely abandoned because the increasing range and accuracy of firearms had lessened opportunities for close combat. They returned to widespread use in the 20th century, when their effectiveness in World War I trench warfare made them a standard part of the combat infantryman's equipment, which they have remained. Most common is the explosive grenade, with a core of TNT or another high explosive encased in an iron jacket and a fuse that detonates it either on impact or after a brief (usually four-second) delay. Chemical and gas grenades generally burn rather than explode.

Grenadines \ˌgre-nə-'dēnz\, **The** Chain of about 600 islands and islets, southeastern Lesser Antilles, West Indies. The islands span over 60 mi (100 km) at the eastern end of the Caribbean Sea. The northern Grenadines are administratively part of St. Vincent and the Grenadines, while the southern islands are a dependency of Grenada. The St. Vincent group consists of Bequia, Canouan, Mayreau, Mustique, Union Island, and associated islets. Carriacou Island, the largest of the Grenada group, has an area of 13 sq mi (34 sq km). Rainfall is low, and few of the islands are inhabited.

Grenfell, Wilfred (Thomason) *later* **Sir Wilfred** (1865–1940) English medical missionary. Having joined the Royal National Mission to Deep Sea Fishermen, he initiated missionary service to the fishermen of Labrador and became absorbed in improving conditions there. He raised funds through speaking tours and books. When the Mission withdrew its support, he founded the International Grenfell Assn., which helped found six hospitals, four hospital ships, seven nursing stations, two orphanages, two large schools, 14 industrial centers, and a cooperative lumber mill in Labrador.

Grenoble \grə-'nȯblᵊ, *Engl* grə-'nō-bəl\ City (pop., 1995 est.: 155,000), southeastern France. It lies along the Isère River, which divides the city into two parts. The old town occupies the cramped right bank, while the newer part of the town spreads out into the plain on the left bank. It is the former capital of the Dauphiné. It was a center of the French Resistance during World War II. Sites of interest include a 13th-century cathedral, the 15th-century Palais de Justice, and the University of Grenoble (founded 1339).

Grenville, George (1712–1770) English politician. He entered Parliament in 1741, held a number of ministerial appointments, then served as prime minister 1763–65. His policy of taxing the American colonies, initiated by his Revenue Act of 1764 and the Stamp Act of 1765, started the train of events leading to the American Revolution. He was unpopular for the prosecution of John Wilkes for seditious libel and his clumsy handling of the Regency Act of 1765, alienating George III and leading to the fall of his ministry. In opposition thereafter, Grenville helped bring about the passage of the Townshend Acts (1767).

Gresham's law Observation that "bad money drives out good." It is named for Sir Thomas Gresham (1519–1579), financial agent of Queen Elizabeth I, who was one of the first to elucidate it (he had been preceded by Copernicus). The meaning expressed is that, if two coins have the same face value but are made from metals of unequal value, the cheaper will tend to drive the other out of circulation; the more valuable coin will be hoarded or used for foreign exchange instead of for domestic transactions.

Grettis saga Latest of the Icelanders' sagas, written c. 1320. It tells of the brave and wellborn Grettir, who at 14 kills a man and is outlawed. He spends his years of exile performing brave deeds. Returning to Iceland, he saves the people from a ghost that is ravaging the countryside, which in dying curses him with a growing fear of the dark. Outlawed again, his increasing fear keeps him from hiding himself, and he is finally overwhelmed with the aid of witchcraft. The saga's distinction rests on its hero's complex character and its skillful incorporation of folklore motifs.

Gretzky, Wayne (Douglas) (born 1961) Canadian ice-hockey player, considered the greatest in the history of the game. Born in Brantford, Ontario, he was the youngest player and leading scorer in Junior League Cup competition in 1977. As center and captain for the Edmonton Oilers (1979–88), he led his team to four Stanley Cup victories, becoming the first player to average more than two points a game. He was traded successively to the Los Angeles Kings (1988), the St. Louis Blues (1996), and the New York Rangers (1996), with whom he ended his career in 1999, by which time he held 61 National Hockey League records. He holds the all-time NHL records for goals (894), assists (1,963), and points (2,857), as well as corresponding seasonal records (92 goals, 163 assists, 215 points). He is the only player to have led the league in scoring for seven consecutive years (1980–87) and the only one named most valuable player eight consecutive seasons (1979–87). His modesty and courtesy in an often brutal sport brought him respect as a model of sportsmanship.

Greuze \'grœ̄z, *Engl* 'grə(r)z\, **Jean-Baptiste** (1725–1805) French painter. He studied at the Royal Academy in Paris. His first exhibited painting, *The Father Reading the Bible to His Children*, won him immediate success at the Salon of 1755. Throughout the 1760s he won acclaim with such sentimental works as *The Village Betrothal* (1761) and *Prodigal Son* (c. 1765). Hoping to gain admission to the Academy as a history painter, he submitted a large historical work; when it was rejected, he refused to exhibit anywhere but his own studio for 30 years. He earned a living with morality pictures and images of young women in innocent disarray, but in time his popularity waned. The reaction against his sentimental genre paintings resulted in critical neglect of his drawings and portraits, which display great technical gifts.

Grévy \grā-'vē\, **(François-Paul-) Jules** (1807–1891) French politician who served as president (1879–87) in the Third Republic. A lawyer, he was a leader of the liberal opposition in the legislature, then became president of the National Assembly (1871–73) and of the Chamber of Deputies (1876). In 1879 he was elected to the presidency and sought to minimize presidential powers, preferring a strong legislature. He resisted nationalist demands for revenge against Germany after the FRANCO-PRUSSIAN WAR and opposed colonial expansion. He was forced to resign in 1887 by scandals affecting his son-in-law, though he himself was not implicated.

Grew, Nehemiah (1641–1712) British botanist. A physician and professor, Grew's training in animal anatomy led to his interest in that of plants. His writings noted the existence of cells and coined such terms as radicle (for the embryonic root), plume (for the primary bud of a plant embryo; now called plumule), and parenchyma (for unspecialized cells). His highly significant *Anatomy of Plants* (1682) contained the first thorough account of plant anatomy; its many excellent wood engravings represented the three-dimensional, microscopic structure of plant tissue. Among other fundamental discoveries, he suggested that the stamen (with its pollen) is the male sex organ and the pistil corresponds to the female sex organ. With MARCELLO MALPIGHI, he is considered a founder of the science of plant anatomy.

Grey, Earl *orig.* **Charles Grey** (1764-1845) British politician, leader of the Whig Party, and prime minister (1830–34). Grey entered Parliament in 1786 and soon became prominent among the aristocratic Whigs, led by CHARLES JAMES FOX, in opposition to WILLIAM PITT's conservative government. In 1806 Grey became first lord of the admiralty in Lord Grenville's government, and when Fox died the same year Grey became foreign secretary and leader of the Foxite Whigs. In 1807 the dismissal of the ministry and the loss of his seat for Northumberland because of his Catholic sympathies left Grey with a distaste for office. From 1815 to 1830 he was more patron than leader of the divided Whig opposition. In 1830 he became prime minister with popular backing for parliamentary reform. After considerable debate and conflict, he won adoption of the REFORM BILL OF 1832.

Grey, Sir Edward *later* **Viscount Grey of Fallodon** (1862–1933) British statesman. A relative of Earl GREY, he entered Parliament as a Liberal (1885) and became foreign secretary in 1905. During the MOROCCAN CRISES (1905, 1911), he supported France against Germany, but with equivocations that caused diplomatic confusion. After the assassination of FRANCIS FERDINAND (1914), Grey proposed that Austria-Hungary obtain satisfaction from Serbia by occupying Belgrade. When all peace moves failed, he maneuvered a divided British cabinet into World War I, about which he commented, "The lamps are going out all over Europe; we shall not see them lit again in our lifetime." He was responsible for the secret Treaty of LONDON (1915).

Grey, Lady Jane (1537–1554) Titular queen of England for nine days in 1553. The great-granddaughter of HENRY VII, she was married in May 1553 to the son of the duke of NORTHUMBERLAND. Northumberland persuaded the dying EDWARD VI to set aside his half sisters as successors in favor of the Protestant Lady Jane. She was proclaimed queen on July 10, despite popular support for Edward's half sister Mary Tudor (see MARY I). Mary was proclaimed queen on July 19 after Lady Jane gladly relinquished the crown. Committed to the Tower of London, Lady Jane and her husband were sentenced to death in 1554. The sentence was initially suspended, but her father's participation in Wyatt's rebellion sealed her fate, and she was beheaded.

Lady Jane Grey, detail of a panel attributed to Master John, c. 1545; in the National Portrait Gallery, London.

BY COURTESY OF THE NATIONAL PORTRAIT GALLERY, LONDON

Grey, Zane *orig.* **Pearl Grey** (1872–1939) U.S. novelist. Born in Zanesville, Ohio, he began his career as a dentist. He first visited the American West in 1906. His first novel set there, *The Heritage of the Desert* (1910), achieved success, and his second, *Riders of the Purple Sage* (1912), became the most popular of all his novels. With these books he helped created a new literary genre, the WESTERN. His later westerns, numbering more than 80, include *The Lone Star Ranger* (1915) and *Code of the West* (1934). He moved to California in 1918 and formed his own film production company. He was also a world-champion fisherman. He remains one of the best-selling authors of all time.

greyhound *or* **grayhound** Fastest dog, one of the oldest breeds (dating from about 3000 BC in Egypt), and long symbolic of the aristocracy. It has a narrow head; long neck; deep chest; long, muscular hindquarters; a long, slim tail; and a short, smooth coat, of various colors. It stands 25–27 in. (64–69 cm) high and weighs 60–70 lbs (27–32 kg). Streamlined and slender, it can reach a speed of about 45 mph (72 kph). Greyhounds hunt by sight and may be used to hunt hares, deer, foxes, and small game. They are frequently raced for sport.

Greyhound.

SALLY ANNE THOMPSON

Greyhound Lines, Inc. U.S. corporation that has provided the major intercity bus transportation in the U.S. and Canada. It was founded in 1926 as Motor Transit Management. Backed by the railroads, the company soon had a network of lines spreading across the country. It adopted its current name in 1930. By 1933 Greyhound's routes covered 40,000 mi (65,000 km). In the early 1980s deregulation of the bus-transit industry led Greyhound to drop many local bus lines. In 1987 Greyhound Corp. sold its bus operations, and Greyhound Lines, Inc., became an independent corporation devoted to intercity bus transportation. It was purchased in 1999 by Canada's Laidlaw Inc., a waste-management company.

greylag Most common Eurasian representative *(Anser anser)* of the so-called gray GOOSE, and ancestor of all Occidental domestic geese. It nests in temperate regions and winters from Britain to North Africa, India, and China. It is pale gray with pink legs; the bill is pink in the eastern race and orange in the western race.

Grieg \'grig\, **Edvard (Hagerup)** (1843–1907) Norwegian composer. His parents were persuaded by OLE BULL to send him to Leipzig for music study, and he later studied with Niels Gade and others in Copenhagen, where he became inspired with the ideal of a Norwegian national music. He frequently performed as a pianist, and often accompanied his wife in recitals of his songs. His incidental music to HENRIK IBSEN's *Peer Gynt* (1875), which the playwright invited him to write, became, with his piano concerto (1868), perhaps his most popular work. By the end of his life he was a national institution, and he is still regarded as Norway's greatest composer. His other works include *Symphonic Dances* (1897), *Lyric Suite* (1904), over 150 songs, and many works for piano, including 66 *Lyric Pieces* (1867–1901) and *From Holberg's Time* (1884).

Grien, Hans Baldung See Hans BALDUNG

Grierson \'grir-sən\, **George Abraham** *later* **Sir George** (1851–1941) Anglo-Irish civil servant and linguist. While holding a succession of British government posts in Bengal (1873–98), Grierson carried out pioneering research on South Asian, particularly INDO-ARYAN, languages. In 1898 he began work on the 19-volume *Linguistic Survey of India,* and spent the next 30 years publishing data on hundreds of languages and dialects. While his work was of enormous value, his hypothetical linguistic constructs such as "Rajasthani," "Bihari," and "Lahnda" tended to be regarded as real languages by nonspecialists, and obscured both South Asians' own notions of what they spoke and other possible interpretations of the data.

Griffes \'grif-əs\, **Charles T(omlinson)** (1884–1920) U.S. composer. Born in Elmira, N.Y., he studied music in Berlin with E. HUMPERDINCK and others, then returned and taught at a boys' school in Tarrytown, N.Y., for the rest of his short life. His early works reflect German Romanticism, but his mature style combined Impressionism and orientalism. His principal works are for piano, though some were later orchestrated: *The Pleasure-Dome of Kubla Khan* (1912), a piano sonata (c. 1912), and *Roman Sketches* (including "The White Peacock") (1915).

Griffey, Ken *orig.* **George Kenneth Griffey, Jr.** (born 1969) U.S. baseball player. Born in Donora, Pa., he began his professional career in 1987. As a left-handed hitting center fielder for the Seattle Mariners from 1989, he averaged .300 or better in hitting in seven of his first nine seasons and hit 40 or more home runs in four of those seasons, reaching 56 in 1997 and 1998. His father, Ken Griffey, Sr. (born 1950), was also an outstanding professional baseball player.

Griffin, Merv (Edward) (born 1925) U.S. television producer and entrepreneur. Born in San Mateo, Cal., he hosted a radio show (1945–48) and sang with Freddy Martin's Orchestra (1948–52) before creating and hosting the popular *Merv Griffin Show* on television (1962–63, 1965–72, syndicated 1972–86). He also created the successful game shows *Jeopardy!* and *Wheel of Fortune.* He later owned hotels, resorts, and casinos.

Griffith, Andy *orig.* **Andrew Samuel** (born 1926) U.S. actor. Born in Mount Airy, N.C., he made his Broadway debut in *No Time for Sergeants* (1955) and starred in its screen version (1958) after making a strong film debut in *A Face in the Crowd* (1957). He starred in many television shows, using his native Blue Ridge drawl to portray homespun characters such as the sheriff in the popular comedy series *The Andy Griffith Show* (1960–68). He later starred in the dramatic series *Matlock* (1986–91).

Griffith, Arthur (1872–1922) Irish journalist and nationalist, principal founder of Sinn Féin. As a young man he edited political newspapers and urged passive resistance to British rule. He lost influence with the extreme nationalists when he did not participate in the Easter Rising (1916), but regained it when the British jailed him with other Sinn Féin members. In 1918 the Irish members of the House of Commons declared a republic and chose Eamon de Valera as president and Griffith as vice president. In 1921 Griffith led the Irish delegation to the self-government treaty conference and was the first Irish delegate to accept partition, embodied in the Anglo-Irish Treaty (1921). When the Dáil narrowly approved it in 1922, de Valera resigned and Griffith was elected president. Exhausted from overwork, he died soon after.

Griffith, D(avid) W(ark) (1875–1948) U.S. film director. He was born in Floydsfork, Ky. After acting in touring companies, he sold film scenarios to the Biograph Co., which hired him as a director (1908–13). In over 400 films for Biograph he developed filmmaking as an art form with such techniques as the close-up, the scenic long shot, and crosscutting, and he collaborated with cinematographer Billy Bitzer to create fade-out, fade-in, and soft-focus shots. He nurtured the careers of such future stars as Mary Pickford, Lillian Gish, Mack Sennett, and Lionel Barrymore. His epic dramas *The Birth of a Nation* (1915) and *Intolerance* (1916) greatly influenced later filmmakers. After cofounding United Artists Corp. in 1919, he directed *Broken Blossoms* (1919), *Way Down East* (1920), and *Orphans of the Storm* (1921). His last films were *Abraham Lincoln* (1930) and *The Struggle* (1931). He is regarded as one of the seminal figures in the history of motion pictures.

Griffith, Emile (Alphonse) (born 1938) U.S. boxer. Born in the U.S. Virgin Islands, Griffith began his professional career in 1958. He won three world championships as a welterweight (1961, 1962, 1963) and two as a middleweight (1966, 1967), an achievement surpassed only by Sugar Ray Robinson's total of six. He retired in 1977 with a record of 85–24–2.

Griffith Joyner, (Delorez) Florence *orig.* **Delorez Florence Griffith** (1959–1998) U.S. sprinter. Born in Los Angeles, she started running at 7 and attended UCLA. At the 1984 Olympics she won a silver medal in the 200-m race and became a celebrity with her long, decorated fingernails and eye-catching racing suits. In 1987, she married Al Joyner, an Olympic gold medalist and brother of Jackie Joyner-Kersee. At the 1988 Olympic trials, she set a world record in the 100-m sprint (10.49 sec); at the games themselves, "FloJo" captured gold medals (in the 100-m, 200-m, and 4 x 100-m relay) and a silver (4 x 400-m relay). Her world-record time in the 200 m (21.34 sec) and her earlier 100-m record still stood at the time of her death, which was attributed to a brain seizure.

Grijalva River \grē-ˈhäl-və\ River, southeastern Mexico. Its headstreams rise in the Sierra Madre of Guatemala and the Sierra de Soconusco of Mexico. It flows northwest through Chiapas state (where it is known locally as the Río Chiapa), then roughly parallels the Chiapas–Tabasco state border, veers north at Villahermosa, and empties into the Bay of Campeche after some 400 mi (640 km). A portion is navigable by shallow-draft vessels.

Grillparzer \ˈgril-ˌpärt-sər\, **Franz** (1791–1872) Austrian dramatist. He spent much of his life in government service. His early tragedies include *The Ancestress* (1817), *Sappho* (1818), and the pessimistic *The Golden Fleece* (1821). He was discouraged by the reception given *King Ottocar, His Rise and Fall* (1825), a story based on Napoleon's life which met censorship difficulties. *The Waves of Sea and Love* (1831) is often considered his greatest tragedy; another masterpiece is *A Dream Is Life* (1834), an Austrian *Faust.* Three other tragedies were found among his papers after his death. His tragedies were belatedly recognized as the greatest works of the Austrian stage.

Grimké \ˈgrim-kē\, **Sarah (Moore) and Angelina (Emily)** (1792–1873, 1805–1879) U.S. antislavery crusaders and women's-rights advocates. The sisters were born in Charleston, S.C., to a wealthy slaveholding family but developed an early dislike of slavery. In the mid-1820s they became Quakers and moved to the North. From 1835 they wrote letters and pamphlets urging Southern women to use moral force against slavery, and they freed the slaves they had persuaded their mother to apportion to them as their inheritance. They lectured on antislavery throughout New England as the first female agents of the American Anti-Slavery Society, enlisting women in the abolitionist cause and becoming pioneers in the women's-rights movement. In 1838 Angelina married Theodore Weld, and the sisters collaborated with him.

Grimm, Jacob (Ludwig Carl) and Wilhelm (Carl) *known as* **the Brothers Grimm** (1785–1863, 1786–1859) German folklorists and philologists. They spent most of their lives in literary research as librarians and professors at the Univs. of Göttingen and Berlin. They are most famous for *Kinder- und Hausmärchen* (1812–15), known in English as *Grimm's Fairy Tales*, a collection of 200 tales taken mostly from oral sources, which helped establish the science of folklore. Together and separately, they also produced many other scholarly studies and editions. Wilhelm's chief solo work was *The German Heroic Tale* (1829); Jacob's *German Mythology* (1835) was a highly influential study of pre-Christian German faith and superstition. Jacob's extensive *Deutsche Grammatik* (1819–37), on the grammars of all Germanic languages, elaborating the important principle now known as Grimm's law, became strongly influential. In the 1840s the brothers began work on the *Deutsches Wörterbuch*, a vast historical dictionary of the German language that required several generations to complete and remains the standard work of its kind.

Jacob (right) and Wilhelm Grimm, oil portrait by Elisabeth Jerichau-Baumann, 1855; in the National-Galerie, Berlin.

BY COURTESY OF THE STAATLICHE MUSEEN ZU BERLIN

grinding machine Machine tool that uses a rotating abrasive grinding wheel to change the shape or dimensions of a hard, usually metallic, workpiece. Grinding is the most accurate of all the basic machining processes. All grinding machines use a wheel made from one of the manufactured abrasives, silicon carbide or aluminum oxide. To grind a cylindrical form, the workpiece rotates as it is fed against the grinding wheel. To grind an internal surface, a small wheel moves inside the hollow of the workpiece, which is gripped in a rotating chuck. On a surface grinder, the workpiece is held in place on a table that moves under the rotating abrasive wheel.

Grinnell College \gri-ˈnel\ Private liberal-arts college in Grinnell, Iowa. It was the first college to be established west of the Mississippi River (1846) and the first U.S. college to establish a political-science department (1883). It awards the bachelor's degree in a variety of fields. Total enrollment is about 1,300.

griot \ˈgrē-ˌō\ African tribal storyteller. The griot's role was to preserve the genealogies and oral traditions of the tribe. Griots were usually among the oldest men. In places where written language is the prerogative of the few, the place of the griot as cultural guardian is still maintained. In Senegal, for example, the griot—without resorting to fantasy—recites poems or tells stories of warriors, drawing on his own sources of inspiration.

grippe See INFLUENZA

Griqua, 19th-century people, of mixed Khoikhoin and European ancestry, who occupied the region of central South Africa just north of the Orange River. In 1861, having been forced to sell their land rights to Orange Free State, one group of Griqua moved to the southern hills of the Drakensberg. This new home became Griqualand East. Other Griqua living around Kimberley met no serious challenge to their land rights until diamonds were discovered there. Though with the aid of the British this group resisted absorption into the Orange Free State, Griqualand West in 1871 was annexed to the British crown and the Griqua were recognized as British subjects.

Gris \'grēs\, **Juan** *orig.* **José Victoriano González Pérez** (1887–1927) Spanish painter active in Paris. He studied engineering at the Madrid School of Arts and Manufactures (1902–4). In 1906 he moved to Paris and began producing drawings in the Art Nouveau style for newspapers. He became involved with the Cubist artists, notably PABLO PICASSO, and soon developed his own version of Synthetic CUBISM, a style more severe and calculated than that of other Cubists. His works, typically still lifes, are characterized by rigorously geometric compositions. His technique included the use of paper collage. He also produced sculpture, book illustrations, and sets and costumes for SERGEY DIAGHILEV's Ballets Russes.

grisaille \grē-'zī, grə-'zāl\ Painting technique by which an image is executed entirely in shades of gray and usually modeled to produce the illusion of sculpture or relief. It was used especially by 15th-century Flemish painters (e.g., JAN VAN EYCK's Ghent Altarpiece, 1432) and in the late 18th century to imitate classical sculpture in wall and ceiling decoration. It is sometimes used to produce monotone underpainting for translucent oil colors. In the 16th century, grisaille enamels were developed in Limoges, France; the technique achieves a dramatic effect of light and shade and a pronounced sense of three-dimensionality.

Grisaille stained glass, detail of the Five Sisters Window, 13th century, Cathedral of St. Peter, York, North Yorkshire, Eng.

Grisham, John (born 1955) U.S. novelist. Born in Jonesboro, Ark., he earned a law degree and served in the Mississippi legislature before turning to writing. His best-selling novels of legal suspense include *A Time to Kill* (1989), *The Firm* (1991; film, 1993), *The Pelican Brief* (1992; film, 1993), *The Client* (1993; film, 1994), *The Rainmaker* (1995; film, 1997), and *The Testament* (1999). Fast-paced and adrenalin-charged, they typically feature innocent people who become heroes by fighting corruption.

Grisi, Carlotta *orig.* **Caronna Adela Giuseppina Maria Grisi** (1819–1899) Italian ballerina of the Romantic era. She trained at the ballet school of La Scala in Milan. In 1834 she became the protégé of the dancer and ballet master JULES PERROT. She was engaged at the Paris Opéra, where her first creation was *Giselle* (1841). Grisi remained the undisputed principal ballerina of the Opéra until 1849 and was praised for her seemingly spontaneous and effortless style. She retired in 1853.

grizzly bear Large North American BROWN BEAR whose forms, including the Alaskan brown BEARS, are usually considered races or subspecies of a single species *(Ursus arctos)*. The more than 80 forms once ranged over open regions of western North America from Mexico to Alaska, but their numbers have dwindled. Grizzlies have humped shoulders, an elevated forehead, and brownish to buff fur. They may grow to about 8 ft (2.5 m) long and weigh 900 lbs (410 kg). One variety, the Kodiak bear, is the largest living land carnivore, reaching lengths of more than 10 ft (3 m) and a weight of 1,700 lbs (750 kg). Grizzlies feed on game, fish, berries, and occasionally grass. They have been known to attack humans and are prized as big game.

Grizzly bear (*Ursus arctos*).

Gromyko \grə-'mē-kō\, **Andrey (Andreyevich)** (1909–1989) Soviet foreign minister (1957–85) and president (1985–88) of the Presidium of the Supreme Soviet. Though never strongly identified with any political faction, he served dependably as a skilled emissary and spokesman. He was ambassador to the U.S. 1943–46, Soviet representative to the U.N. Security Council 1946–48, and ambassador to Britain 1952–53. In 1957 he began his long tenure as foreign minister and became renowned for his negotiating skills. In 1985 he was promoted to the presidency, with great prestige but little power, after MIKHAIL GORBACHEV came to power.

Gropius \'grō-pē-əs\, **Walter (Adolph)** (1883–1969) German-U.S. architect. The son of an architect, he studied in Munich and Berlin and joined the office of PETER BEHRENS in 1907. In 1919 he became director of the Staatliches Bauhaus Weimar. He designed a new school building and housing for the BAUHAUS when it moved to Dessau (1925). With its dynamic INTERNATIONAL STYLE composition, asymmetrical plan, smooth white walls set with horizontal windows, and flat roof, it became a monument of the modernist movement. In 1934 Gropius fled Germany for Britain, and in 1937 he arrived in the U.S, taking a position at Harvard University. At the Bauhaus and as chair (1938–52) of Harvard's architecture department, he established a new prototype of design education, which ended the 200-year supremacy of the French École des BEAUX-ARTS. Chief among his ideas was the belief that all design requires systematic study of the particular needs and problems involved, taking into account modern construction materials and techniques without reference to previous forms or styles.

Gros \'grō\, **Antoine-Jean** (1771–1835) French painter. He was trained by his father, a painter of miniatures, and later by J.-L. DAVID in Paris. In the 1790s he accompanied NAPOLEON on his campaigns as his official battle painter. The dramatic power of such paintings as *Napoleon Visiting the Pesthouse at Jaffa* (1804) influenced THEODORE GERICAULT and EUGENE DELACROIX. When David went into exile after Napoleon's defeat, Gros took over his studio and tried to work in the Neoclassical style. His best works after 1815 were portraits. Haunted by a sense of failure, he drowned himself in the Seine. He was a leading figure in the development of Romanticism.

Gros Morne National Park \grō-'mȯrn\ National park, Newfoundland. Covering 458,000 acres (185,500 hectares) and established as a national park in 1973, it includes mountains of the Long Range and takes its name from Gros Morne Peak, which rises to 2,644 ft (806 m). The park also includes beaches, forests, shifting dunes, and a tidal inlet.

Gros Ventres \'grō-ˌvänt\ (French: "Big Bellies") Name applied to two distinct North American Indian groups: the HIDATSA, or Gros Ventres of the Missouri, and the Atsina, or Gros Ventres of the Prairie (or Plains).

grosbeak \'grōs-ˌbēk\ Any of several songbird species in the family Fringillidae that have an exceptionally large, conical bill. Most eat seeds. Species are found in North America (e.g., rose-breasted, black-headed, blue, and EVENING GROSBEAKS) and northern Eurasia (pine grosbeak). See also CARDINAL.

Evening grosbeak (*Hesperiphona vespertina*).

Gross, Michael (born 1964) German swimmer. Born in Frankfurt, the 6-ft 7-in. (2-m) Gross acquired the nickname "the Albatross." He won six Olympic medals (two gold and two silver in 1984, one gold and one bronze in 1988), and set world records in the 200-m freestyle and 100-m butterfly.

Gross, Samuel David (1805–1884) U.S. surgeon, teacher of medicine, and author. Born in Easton, Pa., he was apprenticed to a local country doctor before receiving formal medical training. His most celebrated work, *Elements of Pathological Anatomy* (1839), was a pioneering effort that organized knowledge on the subject in English. His *System of Surgery* (2 vols., 1859) had a profound effect on surgical thought worldwide. His *Manual of Military Surgery* (1861) was written at the government's request. He also invented many surgical tools. He was memorably portrayed in THOMAS EAKINS's masterpiece *The Gross Clinic*.

gross domestic product (GDP) Total market value of the goods and services produced by a nation's economy during a specific period of time. GDP is customarily reported on an annual basis. It is defined to include all final goods and services—that is, those that are produced by the economic resources located in that nation regardless of their ownership, and are not resold in any form. GDP differs from gross national product (GNP), which is defined to include all final goods and services produced by resources owned by that nation's residents, whether located in the nation or elsewhere.

Grosseteste \'grōs-ˌtest\, **Robert** (c. 1175–1253) English bishop and scholar. He introduced Latin translations of Greek and Arabic writings in philosophy and science to Europe. After serving as chancellor of the University of Oxford (c. 1215–21), he served as first lecturer in theology to the Franciscans, whom he greatly influenced. As bishop of Lincoln from 1235, he promoted a belief in the importance of the cure of souls, a centralized, hierarchical view of the church, and a belief in the superiority of the church over the state.

Grossglockner \'grōs-ˌglȯk-nər\ Highest peak in Austria, in the HOHE TAUERN range. It reaches an elevation of 12,457 ft (3,797 m) and was first climbed in 1800. A noted glacier on the mountain is the Pasterze Glacier, 5 mi (8 km) long and 3 mi (5 km) wide. Winter sports, mountain climbing, and beautiful scenery have made Grossglockner a tourist attraction.

Grosvenor \'grōv-nər\, **Gilbert H(ovey)** (1875–1966) U.S. geographer, writer, and editor. Born in Constantinople, Grosvenor attended Amherst College and was hired by ALEXANDER GRAHAM BELL, president of the NATIONAL GEOGRAPHIC SOCIETY, as an editorial assistant for its magazine. As editor in chief of *National Geographic Magazine* (1903–54), he transformed it from a small scholarly journal into an interesting and superbly illustrated magazine with a large circulation. In 1920 he was elected president of the society. He contributed many articles and photographs to the magazine, wrote a history of the society and other books, and was long a leader in conservation and wildlife protection.

Grosz \'grōs\, **George** *orig.* **Georg** (1893–1959) German-U.S. painter, draftsman, and illustrator. After studying art in Dresden and Berlin, he began selling caricatures to magazines. During World War I he served in the German army; discharged as unfit in 1917, he moved into a garret studio in Berlin, and by the end of the war he had developed a graphic style that combined a highly expressive use of line with ferocious social satire. His depictions of war and depravity provided some of the most vitriolic social criticism of his time. From 1918 to 1920 he was a prominent member of the DADA group in Berlin. His *Face of the Ruling Class* (1921) and *Ecce Homo* (1922), collections of drawings featuring greedy capitalists, war profiteering, and social decadence, earned him an international reputation. In 1932 he emigrated to the U.S., where he taught at New York's Art Students League while continuing to produce magazine cartoons, nudes, and landscapes.

grotesque In architecture and decorative art, a mural or sculptural decoration combining animal, human, and plant forms. The word derives from the Italian *grottesco*, in reference to the grottolike underground rooms *(grotte)* where such ornaments were found during the excavation of Roman buildings c. 1500. The grotesque was revived in the Renaissance, and a fashion for it in 16th-century Italy quickly spread to the rest of Europe; it was used most frequently in fresco decoration (painted, carved, or molded) until the 19th century.

Grotius \'grō-shē-əs\, **Hugo** *orig.* **Huigh de Groot** (1583–1645) Dutch jurist, humanist, and poet. Born in Delft, he enrolled at Leiden University at 11 and as a teenager accompanied Johan Van OLDENBARNEVELT on a mission to France, where he remained to study law and publish a book on politics (1598). Appointed the official historiographer of Holland, he wrote the history of the Dutch revolt against Spain. Increasingly involved in politics, he wrote a defense of Dutch trading rights for the Dutch EAST INDIA CO., and called for free access to the ocean for all nations. He became attorney general of Holland in 1607. Imprisoned in 1618 when his patron Oldenbarnevelt was executed by Prince Maurice, he escaped to Paris in 1621 (by hiding in a trunk of books) and returned 10 years later, having achieved great international prestige. His legal works advance the idea that nations are bound by NATURAL LAW; his masterpiece, *De Jure Belli ac Pacis* (1625; "On the Law of War and Peace"), one of the first great contributions to modern INTERNATIONAL LAW, prescribes rules for the conduct of war. He also published many translations and works of classical scholarship.

Grotius, detail of a portrait by M.J. van Mierevelt; in the Rijksmuseum, Amsterdam.

BY COURTESY OF THE RIJKSMUSEUM, AMSTERDAM

Grotowski \grȯ-'tȯv-skē\, **Jerzy** (1933–1999) Polish-U.S. stage director. He joined the Polish Laboratory Theatre of Wroclaw in 1959 and founded a permanent company in 1965. The Laboratory Theatre made its U.S. debut with *Akropolis* (1969); it was followed by *Undertaking Mountain* (1977) and *Undertaking Earth* (1977–78), by which time Grotowski was living largely in the U.S. Known as an avant-garde theorist, he sought to create dramatic tension by setting up emotional confrontations between audience and actors. His book *Towards a Poor Theater* (1968) emphasized the centrality of the actor and advocated minimal stage sets. He strongly influenced U.S. experimental theater movements, notably the LIVING THEATER.

ground squirrel Any of numerous relatively short-legged, terrestrial RODENTS of the SQUIRREL family (Sciuridae), found in North America, Mexico, Africa, Europe, and Asia. The name is often applied to CHIPMUNKS. Ground squirrels belong to the genera *Ammospermophilus, Xerus, Atlantoxerus,* and *Spermophilus.* They live in burrows, sometimes in colonies. Though primarily herbivores, some feed on insects and other small animals and on carrion. Many species collect food, carrying it in their cheek pouches, and store it in their burrows. Those in cold areas may hibernate in winter; those in dry areas may become dormant in summer. Species range from about 7 to 20 in. (17–52 cm) in length, including the tail.

California ground squirrel (*Spermophilus beecheyi*).

KENNETH W. FINK FROM ROOT RESOURCES—EB INC.

groundhog See WOODCHUCK

Groundhog Day (February 2) In the U.S., the day that the groundhog predicts whether spring will be coming soon. If, on emerging from his hole, he sees his shadow, there will be six more weeks of winter; if not, spring is imminent. The tradition stems from English beliefs about seeing shadows on CANDLEMAS (also February 2).

groundnut Any of several plants that bear edible fruit or other nutlike parts. Three are LEGUMES: *Arachis hypogaea,* the PEANUT, the fruit of which is a legume or pod rather than a true NUT; *Apois americana,* also called wild bean and potato bean, the TUBERS of which are edible; and *Lathyrus tuberosa,* also called earth-nut pea. *Cyperus esculentus,* nut sedge or yellow nut grass, is a PAPYRUS relative (SEDGE FAMILY) that also bears edible tubers, especially in the variety called chufa or earth almond.

groundwater *or* **subsurface water** Water that occurs below the surface of the earth, where it occupies spaces in soils or geologic strata. Most groundwater comes from precipitation, which gradually percolates into the earth. Typically, 10–20% of precipitation eventually enters AQUIFERS. Most groundwater is free of pathogenic organisms, and purification for domestic or industrial use is not necessary. Furthermore, groundwater supplies are not seriously affected by short droughts and are available in many areas that do not have dependable surface water supplies.

groundwater table See WATER TABLE

Group of Seven See Group of SEVEN

Group Theatre New York theater company (1931–41), founded by HAROLD CLURMAN, CHERYL CRAWFORD, and LEE STRASBERG to present U.S. plays of social significance. Embracing the acting principles of the STANISLAVSKY METHOD, the company—which also included such actors and directors as ELIA KAZAN, Lee J. Cobb, and Stella Adler—staged *Success Story* (1931), *Men in White* (1933), CLIFFORD ODETS's *Waiting for Lefty* (1935) and *Golden Boy* (1937), Irwin Shaw's *Bury the Dead* (1936), and WILLIAM SAROYAN's *My Heart's in the Highlands* (1939), among many other plays.

group theory In modern algebra, a system consisting of a set of elements and an operation for combining the elements, which together satisfy certain AXIOMS. These require that the group be closed under the operation (the combination of any two elements produces another element of the group), that it obey the ASSOCIATIVE LAW, that it contain an identity element (which, combined with any other element, leaves the latter unchanged), and that each element have an inverse (which combines with an element to produce the identity element). If the group also satisfies the COMMUTATIVE LAW, it is called a commutative, or abelian, group. The set of integers under addition, where the identity element is 0 and the inverse is the negative of a positive number or vice versa, is an abelian group. See also FIELD THEORY.

group therapy Form of PSYCHOTHERAPY in which several patients or clients discuss their personal problems, usually in the presence of a therapist or counselor. In one approach to group therapy, the chief aim is to raise members' awareness and morale and combat feelings of isolation by cultivating a sense of belonging to the group; an outstanding example is ALCOHOLICS ANONYMOUS. The other principal approach strives to foster free discussion and uninhibited self-revelation; members are helped to self-understanding and more successful behavior through mutual examination of their reactions to people in their lives, including one another.

Groupe Islamique Armée (GIA) \ˈgrüp-is-lȧ-ˈmēk-är-ˈmā\ (French: "Armed Islamic Group") Algerian militant group formed in 1992 after the government aborted the likely victory of the ISLAMIC SALVATION FRONT (FIS) in 1991 legislative elections. The group began a series of violent, armed attacks against the government and foreigners and is accused of civilian massacres—although it has been alleged that many such atrocities were committed by security-service infiltrators and special military units. Estimates of GIA strength have varied from hundreds to several thousand guerrillas, with some support from abroad.

grouper Any of numerous species of fishes (family Serranidae) widely distributed in warm seas, especially members of the genera *Epinephelus* and *Mycteroperca*. Groupers are characteristically large-mouthed, heavy-bodied fishes. Some species grow larger than 6 ft (about 2 m) long and 500 lbs (225 kg). Groupers are usually dull green or brown; some species can change their color pattern, and deepwater individuals may be much redder than nearshore ones. They are prime food fishes and provide sport for anglers and spearfishermen. A few species carry a toxic substance in their flesh and can cause poisoning when consumed. See also JEWFISH, SEA BASS.

grouse Any of various game birds in the family Tetraonidae (order Galliformes), including the PRAIRIE CHICKEN and PTARMIGAN, or the sandgrouse (order Columbiformes). The best-known Old World species is the black grouse *(Lyrurus tetrix)* of Wales, Scotland, Scandinavia, and northern central Europe. The male (blackcock), iridescent blue-black with white wing bars, may be 22 in. (55 cm) long and weigh about 4 lbs (almost 2 kg); the smaller female is mottled brown and barred with black. Grouse are noted for the male's communal courtship dances. The best-known North American species is the RUFFED GROUSE.

Blackcock (*Lyrurus tetrix*).
INGMAR HOLMASEN

Grove, Andrew S. (born 1936) U.S. (Hungarian-born) businessman. He studied at CCNY before earning his PhD from UC–Berkeley in 1963. After working for Fairchild Semiconductor 1963–67, he helped found INTEL CORP. in 1968. At Intel he has served as president (1979–97), CEO (1987–97), and chairman of the board (from 1997), and is widely credited with the company's enormous success. He has lectured at Stanford University from 1991. He holds several patents on semiconductor devices and technology, and is the author of several books. In 1997 he was named *Time* magazine's "Man of the Year."

Grove, George *later* **Sir George** (1820–1900) British musicologist. He was trained as a civil engineer, and he erected lighthouses in Jamaica and Bermuda. He became secretary of the Crystal Palace in 1852, and he would write program notes for its concerts for 40 years. His extensive contributions to William Smith's *Dictionary of the Bible* led to his establishing the Palestine Exploration Fund in 1865. He served as editor of *Macmillan's Magazine* 1868–83. In 1873 he began work on his four-volume *Dictionary of Music and Musicians*; expanded to 20 volumes in subsequent editions, it is today the world's foremost music encyclopedia. He served as first director of the Royal College of Music (1883–92), an institution he was largely responsible for placing on a firm professional and physical foundation.

growing season Period of the year, also called frost-free season, during which growing conditions for native vegetation and cultivated crops are the most favorable. It usually becomes shorter as distance from the equator increases. In equatorial and tropical regions the growing season ordinarily lasts all year; at higher latitudes (e.g., the tundra), it may last as little as two months or less. It also varies according to elevation above sea level: higher elevations tend to have shorter growing seasons.

growth hormone (GH) *or* **human growth hormone (HGH)** *or* **somatotropin** \sō-ˌmə-tə-ˈtrō-pən\ PEPTIDE HORMONE secreted by the anterior lobe of the PITUITARY GLAND. It promotes growth of bone and other body tissues by stimulating PROTEIN synthesis and FAT breakdown (for energy). Excessive production causes GIGANTISM, ACROMEGALY, or other malformations; deficient production results in DWARFISM, dramatically relieved if GH is given before puberty. GENETIC ENGINEERING techniques now permit large-scale production of adequate amounts of GH for that purpose.

growth ring In a cross section of the stem of a woody plant, the amount of wood added during a single growth period. In temperate regions this period is usually one year, in which case the growth ring may be called an annual ring. In tropical regions growth rings may not be discernible or are not annual. Even in temperate regions growth rings are occasionally missing; and sometimes a second, or "false," ring may be deposited during a single year (e.g., following defoliation by insects). Nevertheless, annual rings have been used in dating ancient wooden structures, especially those of American Indians in the dry U.S. Southwest. Changes in ring width are a source of information about ancient climates.

Gruen, Victor (1903–1980) Austrian-U.S. architect and city planner. Trained in Vienna, he moved in 1938 to the U.S., where he established Victor Gruen Associates, comprising professionals from engineering, architecture, and planning, to solve problems of urban areas. The firm produced the master plan for Tehran, and Gruen served as planning consultant for cities worldwide. He is best known as a pioneer of regional shopping centers and of the renewal and revitalization of city core areas.

Grünewald \ˈgrᴇ̄-nə-ˌvält, *Engl* ˈgrü-nə-ˌwȯld\, **Matthias** *orig.* **Mathis Gothardt Neithardt** *or* **Mathis Gothart Nithart** (c. 1475/80–1528) German painter. Details of his early life are vague. By c. 1509 he was court painter to the archbishop of Mainz and had established a successful career, concentrating on religious themes. Around 1511 he was commissioned to add two wings to the *Assumption of the Virgin* altarpiece recently completed by ALBRECHT DURER. In 1515 he completed his most important commission, the wings of the Isenheim Altarpiece in the Antonite monastery in southern Alsace (now in the museum in Colmar, France). Considered his masterpiece, it features distorted figures, extreme emotional intensity, brooding color, and draperies that expand and contract in accordion pleats, a hallmark of his style. About 10 paintings and 35 drawings survive. He had no known pupils and, unlike his contemporaries, did not produce woodcuts or engravings, but his painterly achievement remains one of the most striking in the history of northern European art.

grunion \ˈgrən-yən\ Edible Pacific fish *(Leuresthes tenuis)* found along the western coast of the U.S. In the warm months, it lays its eggs in beach sand during a full or new moon when the tide cycle is at its peak.

The young hatch and enter the ocean on the next spring tide, two weeks later. Grunion reach a length of about 8 in. (20 cm).

GTE Corp. *formerly (1959–82)* **General Telephone and Electronics Corp.** U.S. HOLDING COMPANY for several U.S. and international telephone companies. It provides telephone service mainly to rural areas and manufactures electronic equipment. The company, founded in 1926 as Associated Telephone Utilities to unite various independent phone companies, went bankrupt in the Great Depression and was reorganized as General Telephone. In the 1950s it became a manufacturer of electronic phone equipment, merging with Sylvania Electronics in 1958. GTE and Bell Atlantic (one of the "Baby Bells") merged to become Verizon Communications in 2000.

Gtsang dynasty \'tsäŋ\ (1565?–1642) Last secular native ruling house in Tibet. The Gtsang kings allied themselves with the Karma-pa order of Buddhists against the new reformed DGE-LUGS-PA order. The Dge-lugs-pa gained the support of the Mongol ALTAN Khan, and although the Gtsang attacked their headquarters in Lhasa, the dynasty was finally dethroned in 1642, when temporal authority was given to the Mongol-backed DALAI LAMA.

Guacanayabo \ˌgwä-kä-nä-'yä-bō\, **Gulf of** Inlet of the Caribbean Sea, southeastern Cuba. It stretches in a broad horseshoe from the southern coast of Camagüey province about 70 mi (110 km) to the southwestern shore of Granma province. It is shallow and dotted with coral reefs; its chief port is Manzanillo (pop., 1990 est.: 107,700).

Guadalajara \ˌgwä-dᵊl-ə-'hä-rə\ City (pop., 1990: 1,629,000), capital of JALISCO state, western central Mexico. Mexico's second-largest city, it lies near the Río Grande de Santiago, at an altitude of 5,141 ft (1,567 m). Founded by the Spanish in 1531, it was relocated several times under pressure from Indians. In 1810 it was occupied briefly by MIGUEL HIDALGO. Since 1940 it has become a major industrial producer, while retaining a rich agricultural trade. The governor's palace, begun in 1743, is a noted example of Spanish Mexican architecture. Guadalajara is the site of two universities.

Guadalcanal \ˌgwä-dᵊl-kə-'nal\ Island, SOLOMON ISLANDS, South Pacific Ocean. The largest in the island group, it has an area of 2,047 sq mi (5,302 sq km). The economy is based mainly on fishing and agriculture; gold-mining began in the 1990s. It was visited by the Spanish in the 16th century and by the English in the late 18th century; it was annexed in 1893 by the British as part of the Solomon Islands protectorate. During World War II it was the scene of prolonged fighting between U.S. and Japanese forces (1942–43), which resulted in the Allied capture of a Japanese airbase there. Several naval battles were also fought in the area. The national capital, HONIARA, lies on the northern coast.

Guadalquivir River \ˌgwä-dᵊl-ki-'vir\ *Arabic* **Wadi al-Kabir** \'wä-dē-ˌäl-kə-'bir\ *ancient* **Baetis.** River, southern Spain. Rising in the mountains of Jaén province, it flows west 408 mi (657 km) to empty into the Gulf of Cádiz. Spain's second-longest river, its natural environment is one of the most varied in Europe, containing representatives of half of the continent's plant species and nearly all those of the North African region. Its fauna also includes a great variety of European and North African species.

Guadalupe \ˌgwä-t͟hä-'lü-pā, *Engl* 'gwä-də-ˌlüp\ City (pop., 1990: 535,000), central NUEVO LEÓN state, northeastern Mexico. It lies 672 ft (205 m) above sea level on the Santa Catarina River, just east of MONTERREY. It serves as the commercial center of an agricultural area.

Guadalupe Hidalgo \ˌgwä-dᵊl-'ü-pä-ē-'t͟häl-gō\, **Treaty of** (February 2, 1848) Treaty between the U.S. and Mexico that ended the MEXICAN WAR, named for the Mexico City neighborhood where it was signed. It drew the U.S.–Mexico boundary at the Rio Grande and the Gila River. For $15 million the U.S. received more than 525,000 sq mi (1.36 million sq km) of land and agreed to settle the more than $3 million in claims made by U.S. citizens against Mexico. By leaving Mexicans unsure of their country's future and reopening the question of the expansion of slavery in the vast territory ceded to the U.S., the treaty was a factor in the civil wars that followed in both countries.

Guadalupe Mountains National Park \ˌgwä-də-'lü-pä\ National park, western Texas, east of EL PASO. Established in 1972, it occupies an area of 86,416 acres (34,998 hectares). It is centered around two peaks: Guadalupe Peak, which reaches 8,751 ft (2,667 m), and El Capitan, which rises to 8,078 ft (2,462 m). The park is an area of great geological interest, with a major PERMIAN limestone fossil reef.

Guadeloupe \'gwä-də-ˌlüp, ˌgwä-də-'lüp\ Overseas department of France (pop., 1996: 427,000), eastern WEST INDIES. Consisting of the islands of Basse-Terre and Grande-Terre and several smaller islands, its land area is 687 sq mi (1,780 sq km); the capital is BASSE-TERRE. St.-Barthélemy and the northern two-thirds of ST. MARTIN are dependencies, lying 150 mi (240 km) northwest of it. Forests and tree crops such as coffee, abound on the mountains of Basse-Terre, while sugarcane is cultivated on Grande-Terre. The Carib Indians held off the Spanish and French for a number of years before the islands became part of France in 1674. The British occupied Guadeloupe for short periods in the 18th–19th century; the islands became officially French in 1815. In 1946 it was made a department of France. Tourism has benefited the economy in recent decades.

Guadiana River \ˌgwä-dē-'ä-nə\ River, in Spain and Portugal. One of the longest in the IBERIAN PENINSULA, it flows 483 mi (778 km) through southern central Spain and southeastern Portugal, forming parts of the countries' borders, to the Gulf of Cádiz. Its headwaters rise in the mountains of Spain's Cuenca province; west of Daimiel they form marshy lakes, known as Ojos del Guadiana ("Eyes of the Guadiana"), a noted wildfowl sanctuary. As it continues west, it cuts a series of gorges through the Toledo Mtns., now the sites of several dams that provide hydroelectric power.

Guainía, Rio See Rio NEGRO

Guajira Peninsula \gwä-'hē-rä\ Peninsula, northwestern coast of South America. It is bounded by the Caribbean Sea and the Gulf of Venezuela. Much of the peninsula lies in Colombia, the rest in Venezuela. Ríohacha (pop., 1992 est.: 126,000), is its principal town; natural gas fields nearby are connected by pipeline with BARRANQUILLA, to the southwest.

Guam \'gwäm\ Island (pop., 1993 est.: 143,000), largest and southernmost of the MARIANA ISLANDS, Micronesia. Guam is an unincorporated U.S. territory; its capital is AGANA. With an area of 209 sq mi (541 sq km), it is divided into a northern plateau and a southern chain of volcanic hills. The native people are the Chamorro, of Malayo-Indonesian stock with a considerable admixture of Spanish, Filipino, and Mexican. They speak Chamorro in addition to English, the official language. Possibly visited by FERDINAND MAGELLAN in 1521, it was formally claimed by Spain in 1565 and remained Spanish for two centuries. It was ceded to the U.S. after the SPANISH–AMERICAN WAR in 1898. In World War II the Japanese occupied the island 1941–44. It subsequently became a major U.S. air and naval base. In 1950 it was made a U.S. territory and placed under the Department of the Interior. The naval and air bases are the island's economic mainstay, followed by tourism.

Guan Hanqing *or* **Kuan Han-ch'ing** \'gwän-'hän-'chiŋ\ (1241?–1320?) Chinese dramatist, often considered the greatest playwright of the Chinese classical theater. He belonged to a writers' guild that provided plays for performing groups, and his plays often dealt with everyday events and portrayed women of low social standing with sympathy. He wrote over 60 plays, 14 of which survive, including *Injustice Suffered by Doue, Butterfly Dream,* and *Saving a Prostitute.*

Guan Yu *or* **Kuan Yü** \'gwän-'yü\ *or* **Guan Di** (died 219) Military hero of the THREE KINGDOMS era (3rd century AD) who started his career as the bodyguard of Liu Bei, the founder of one of the three kingdoms. He was captured and executed but his fame and popularity continued to grow. China's rulers conferred ever greater titles upon him until in 1594 he was canonized as god of war and protector of China. Thousands of temples were constructed in his honor. His cult spread to Korea in the 17th century, where it was believed that he saved the country from Japanese invasion.

guanaco \gwə-'nä-kō\ Slender-bodied South American lamoid (see ALPACA). The guanaco *(Lama guanacoe)* has long legs and neck, a short tail, and large, pointed ears. It lives in small bands of females, usually led by a male, and grazes on grass and other plants, ranging from the snowline to sea level throughout the Andes from Peru and Bolivia to Tierra del Fuego. The adult stands 43 in. (110 cm) high at the shoulder and is pale brown above and white below, with a grayish head. The downy fiber covering the young is valued for textiles, and guanaco pelts are used by the fur industry.

Guanajuato \ˌgwä-nä-ˈhwä-tō\ State (pop., 2000: 4,656,761), central Mexico. It lies on the interior plateau at an average elevation of about 6,000 ft (1,800 m) and has an area totaling 11,773 sq mi (30,491 sq km); the capital is Guanajuato city. The north is mountainous, while the south, consisting of fertile plains, is largely devoted to agriculture. The state is drained by several rivers, including the Lerma. The first Spanish settlement was at San Miguel de Allende (1542). During colonial times it was an important silver-mining area. The region became a state in 1824. The principal industry is mining (silver, gold, tin, lead, and opals).

Guanajuato City (pop., 2000: 74,874), capital of Guanajuato state, Mexico. It lies 6,725 ft (2,050 m) above sea level. Founded in 1554, it is an outstanding example of the Spanish colonial city. One of the greatest silver-mining centers of the 16th century, the city's wealth was manifest in its richly endowed churches, including La Valenciana, San Francisco (1671), and San Diego (1663). In 1810 it was the first major city to fall to the independence leader Miguel Hidalgo. It later declined until increased tourist trade and federal support of mining and agriculture in the 1930s brought recovery. It is the site of the University of Guanajuato (1945).

Guangdong *or* **Kwangtung** \ˈgwäŋ-ˈdùŋ\ Southernmost mainland province (pop., 2000 est.: 86,420,000), China. It is bounded by the China Sea to the south, and along its coast are Hong Kong and Macao. It has an area totaling 76,100 sq mi (197,100 sq km). The capital is Guangzhou (Canton). It was first incorporated into the Chinese empire in 222 BC. Overseas trade through Guangzhou swelled the population of the province in the 16th–17th century. It was the site of illicit opium importation by the British, which led to the First Opium War in 1841. Kowloon was ceded to Britain in 1860 and Macao to Portugal in 1887; they both reverted to China in the late 1990s. Guangdong was a base for the Nationalists under Sun Yat-sen from 1912. Japanese forces occupied the province in 1938–45. Its centuries of foreign contact have given it a degree of self-sufficiency that sets it apart from the rest of China.

Guangwudi *or* **Kuang-wu ti** \ˈgwäŋ-ˈwü-ˈdē\ *orig.* **Liu Xiu** (5? BC–AD 57) Chinese emperor who restored the Han dynasty after the interlude of the Xin dynasty (AD 9–25) created by the usurper Wang Mang. The restored Han dynasty is often called the Later Han or Eastern Han. His reign was spent consolidating his rule and subduing numerous domestic rebellions, including the Red Eyebrows revolt.

Guangxi (Zhuangzu) *or* **Kwangsi (Chuang)** \ˈgwäŋ-ˈshē\ Autonomous region (pop., 2000 est.: 44,890,000), southeastern China. Bounded by northern Vietnam, it is largely hilly, with river valleys where rice is grown. It has an area totaling 85,100 sq mi (220,400 sq km). Its capital is Nanning. Its recorded history dates from 45 BC, and it was given its present name during the Yüan dynasty in AD 1279. With Guangdong, it became the base of the Nationalists under Sun Yat-sen in the early 20th century. Local leaders later formed the Guangxi Clique in opposition to Chiang Kai-shek, who crushed their revolt in 1929. Guangxi was declared a province of the People's Republic of China in 1949, and in 1958 it became the Zhuang Autonomous Region of Guangxi. Noted for its agricultural production, it is also an important source for forest products.

Guangzhou *or* **Kuang-chou** \ˈgwäŋ-ˈjō\ *English* **Canton** City (pop., 1999 est.: 3,306,277), capital of Guangdong province, China. Located on the Zhu River about 80 mi (130 km) from the sea, it is southern China's chief port. Incorporated in the Chinese empire in the 3rd century BC, it later became an important city under the Ming dynasty. The first Chinese seaport opened to foreigners, it was regularly visited by Arab and Hindu traders and, in the 16th century, by the Portuguese. The English arrived in the late 17th century followed by the French and Dutch. Its resistance to the English opium trade led to war (1839–42), and it was occupied by the British and French in 1856–61. In the 19th century it was the seat of Nationalist ideas promoted by the Guomindang. Occupied by the Japanese 1938–45, it was taken by the Chinese communists in 1949. Its industrial growth expanded, and with Communist China's renewed ties to the West, it was designated as one of several economic investment areas for foreigners in 1984. One of China's largest cities, its expanding economy added to its continued growth.

guanine \ˈgwä-ˌnēn\ Organic compound of the purine family, often called a base, consisting of two rings, each containing both nitrogen and carbon atoms, and an amino group. It occurs in combined form in many important biological molecules, particularly nucleic acids, and free or combined in various natural sources, including guano, sugar beets, yeast, and fish scales. In DNA its complementary base is cytosine. It or its corresponding nucleoside or nucleotide may be prepared from nucleic acids by selective techniques of hydrolysis.

guano \ˈgwä-nō\ Accumulated excrement and remains of birds, bats, and seals, valued as fertilizer. Bird guano comes mainly from islands off the coasts of Peru, Baja California, and Africa that are heavily populated by cormorants, pelicans, and gannets. Bat guano is found in caves throughout the world, and seal guano has accumulated to great depths on islands off northwestern Peru; both are lower in fertilizer value than bird guano.

Guantánamo \gwän-ˈtä-nə-ˌmō\ City (pop., 1994 est.: 207,796), capital of Guantánamo province, eastern Cuba. Lying in the mountains 21 mi (34 km) north of strategic Guantánamo Bay, it was founded in 1819. French refugees from Haiti aided in colonizing the area, and many cultural characteristics, including the architecture, show their influence. Catalans were also among the early settlers. It is the center of an agricultural region producing sugarcane and coffee.

Guantánamo Bay Inlet of the Caribbean Sea, southeastern Cuba. It is one of the largest bays in the world: its harbor is about 6 mi (9 km) wide and 12 mi (19 km) long. Its strategic importance was recognized during the Spanish–American War, when U.S. marines landed there in 1898. A U.S. naval base, established in 1903, remained there even after hostilities erupted between the two countries in 1959, and it served as an internment facility for Islamic militants beginning in 2002.

Guanyin See Avalokitesvara

Guaporé River \ˌgwä-pō-ˈrā\ *in Brazil* **Iténez** \ē-ˈtā-nes\ River, western central South America. Rising in southwestern Brazil, it flows northwest past Mato Grosso city. It continues northwest, forming the border between Bolivia and Brazil, and empties into the Mamoré River above the town of Guajará-Mirim. It is navigable along its entire 1,087-mi (1,749-km) course. In contrast with the brown, silt-laden Mamoré, the Guaporé has unusually clear water; for several miles below their juncture, the two colors remain distinct.

Guarani \ˌgwär-ə-ˈnē\ South American Indian group that inhabited eastern Paraguay and adjacent areas of Brazil and Argentina. Aboriginal Guarani were warlike and took captives to be sacrificed (and allegedly eaten). Their slash-and-burn agriculture required them to move their settlements every few years. The descendants of Guarani women and Spanish ranchers are modern Paraguay's rural population. Only a few scattered communities of true Guarani remain, but Paraguay still claims a strong Guarani heritage, and most of the million peasants living along the Paraguay River near Asunción speak a version of the aboriginal Guarani language.

guaranteed minimum income Income-maintenance program administered through the taxation system for which eligibility is determined by income and family size. Such programs are predicated on the assumption that the government's responsibility to provide for the welfare of its citizens includes ensuring its citizens a minimum standard of living. A system of income guarantees has existed in Britain since 1966; similar programs have been proposed in the U.S. but never enacted. Unlike unemployment-based welfare programs, income maintenance programs base eligibility solely on income, and therefore the working poor are not excluded. See also welfare, welfare state.

Guardi \ˈgwär-dē\, **Francesco** (1712–1793) Italian landscape painter. He and his two brothers collaborated in a flourishing studio-workshop in Venice; their sister was married to Giovanni Battista Tiepolo. By the 1750s Francesco was producing *vedute* (view paintings) of Venice. His many romantic impressions of the city never achieved the popularity of Canaletto's near-photographic records of its architecture, and his work came to be appreciated only after the rise of Impressionism.

guardian In law, one who has, or is legally appointed to, the care and management of another, usually a minor. A natural guardian is a guardian by natural relationship (usually the father or mother). A guardian may be appointed by the court when it decides that a child needs one (usually when the parents have died or disappeared).

Guardian, The Influential newspaper published in London and Manchester, considered one of Britain's best papers. Founded in 1821 as the weekly *Manchester Guardian,* it became a daily in 1855; 100 years later "Manchester" was dropped from the name, as it had become a national daily with an international reputation. Owned by a trust and financially secure, the paper has always taken an independent liberal stance in its editorials and maintained great breadth and depth of news coverage.

Guare \'gwar\, **John** (born 1938) U.S. dramatist. Born in New York, he studied at the Yale School of Drama. In 1971 he earned critical acclaim for *The House of Blue Leaves. Two Gentlemen of Verona* (1972, with Mel Shapiro), a rock-musical version of WILLIAM SHAKESPEARE's comedy, won him Tony and New York Drama Critics Circle awards. His later works include *Six Degrees of Separation* (1990; film, 1993) and *Four Baboons Adoring the Sun* (1992). His screenplays include *Atlantic City* (1981).

Guarini \gwä-'rē-nē\, **(Giovanni) Battista** (1538–1612) Italian poet. In 1567 he entered the service of Alfonso II, Duke of Ferrara, as courtier and diplomat. In 1579 he replaced his friend TORQUATO TASSO as court poet. With Tasso, he is credited with developing the genre of PASTORAL drama. Guarini retired in 1582 and wrote his best-known work, *Il pastor fido* (1590; "The Faithful Shepherd"), a pastoral tragicomedy that became one of the most famous and widely translated works of the age.

Guarneri \gwär-'ner-ē\, **Andrea** (1626–1698) Italian musical-instrument maker. He apprenticed with NICOLA AMATI 1641–54. Setting up his own shop in Cremona, he made violas and cellos as well as violins. His sons Pietro (1655–1720) and Giuseppe (1666–1740?) worked with their father; by 1683 Pietro had moved to Mantua and set up his own business, though he made few instruments. Giuseppe inherited the Cremona business from his father in 1698. During his lifetime his name was obscured by A. STRADIVARI's fame, but his violins and cellos are today highly prized. His sons Pietro (1695–1762) and Bartolomeo (1698–1744) were also instrument makers; Bartolomeo, called Guarneri del Gèsu, was one of the finest in history; his violins show the influence of both his father and Stradivari and are known for their full sound.

Guatemala \,gwä-tə-'mä-lə\ *officially* **Republic of Guatemala** Country, CENTRAL AMERICA. Area: 42,042 sq mi (108,889 sq km). Population (1997 est.): 11,242,000. Capital: GUATEMALA. Mayan Indians are

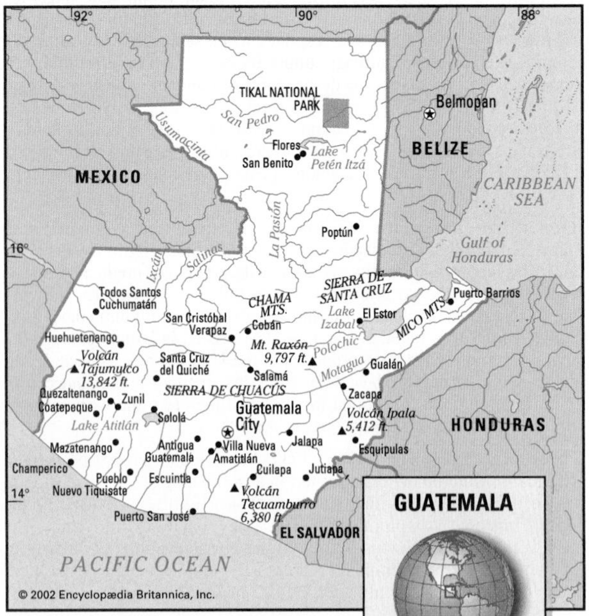

about 55% of the population; Ladinos, mostly of mixed Hispanic-Indian origin, are about 42%. Language: Spanish (official). Religion: Roman Catholicism. Currency: quetzal. Guatemala has extensive lowlands in the Petén portion of the YUCATÁN PENINSULA and the Caribbean littoral in the north. Mountains comprise about half the total area and cut across the country's midsection. The northern tropical rain forests of the Petén are rich in fine woods and rubber. It has a developing market economy based largely on agriculture, and is Central America's leading coffee producer. It is a republic with one legislative body; its head of state and government is the president. From simple farming villages dating to 2500 BC, the MAYA of Guatemala and the Yucatán developed an impressive civilization. Its heart was the northern Petén, where the oldest Mayan stelae and the ceremonial center of TIKAL are found. Mayan civilization declined after AD 900, and the Spanish began the subjugation of their descendants in 1523. Independence from Spain was declared by the Central American colonies in Guatemala City in 1821, and Guatemala was incorporated into the Mexican empire until its collapse in 1823. In 1839 Guatemala became an independent republic under the first of a series of dictators who held power almost continuously for the next century. In 1945 a liberal-democratic coalition came to power and instituted sweeping reforms. Attempts to expropriate land belonging to U.S. business interests prompted the U.S. government in 1954 to sponsor an invasion. In the following years Guatemala's social revolution came to an end and most of the reforms were reversed. Chronic political instability and violence henceforth marked Guatemalan politics; most of the 200,000 deaths that resulted were blamed on government forces. In 1991 it abandoned its long-standing claims of sovereignty over Belize and the two countries established diplomatic relations. It continued to experience violence as guerrillas sought to seize power. A peace treaty was signed in 1996, and the country started slowly to recover from its civil war.

Guatemala *or* **Guatemala City** City (metro area pop., 1993 est.: 1,130,000), capital of Guatemala. The largest city in CENTRAL AMERICA, it lies in the central highlands at an elevation of 4,897 ft (1,493 m). Founded in 1776, it replaced earthquake-damaged Antigua Guatemala as the capital of the captaincy general of Guatemala. After independence, it served as capital of the province of Central America under the Mexican empire of AGUSTIN DE ITURBIDE, and later of the Republic of Guatemala. It is the country's political, social, cultural, and economic center and the site of the San Carlos University of Guatemala (1676); its museums include the National Archaeological Museum, with its rare collection of Mayan artifacts. The modern city was largely rebuilt after the earthquakes of 1917–18; it was severely damaged again in 1976.

Guatimozin See CUAUHTÉMOC

guava Any of many trees and shrubs of the genus *Psidium* (MYRTLE family), native to the New World tropics. The two important species are common guava *(P. guajava)* and cattley, or strawberry, guava *(P. littorale* or *P. cattleianum)*. The sweet pulp of the common guava fruit has a musky, sometimes pungent odor. The pulp of the strawberry guava fruit has a strawberry-like flavor. Guavas are processed into jams, jellies, and preserves. Fresh guavas are rich in vitamins A, B, and C; they are eaten raw or sliced and are served as desserts.

Guaviare River \gwäv-'yä-rā\ River, central and eastern Colombia. It rises in the ANDES in southwestern central Colombia, and is known as the Guayabero in its upper course. It meanders northeast before joining the ORINOCO RIVER on the Colombia–Venezuela border, after a course of about 650 mi (1,050 km). Frequent rapids obstruct navigation.

Guayaquil \,gwī-ä-'kēl\ *in full* **Santiago de Guayaquil** Largest city (pop., 1997 est.: 1,974,000) and chief port, Ecuador. It is situated on the GUAYAS RIVER, 45 mi (72 km) from the Pacific Ocean. Founded by the Spanish at its present site in 1537, it was frequently attacked by buccaneers. In 1822 it was the scene of a historic conference between SIMON BOLIVAR and JOSE DE SAN MARTIN, after which Bolívar emerged as sole leader of the South American liberation movement. As the focus of Ecuador's international trade and domestic commerce, it has become a major Pacific port. It is the site of three universities.

Guayas River \'gwī-äs\ River, western Ecuador. Its two principal tributaries, the Daule and Babahoyo rivers, rise on the western slopes of the ANDES and unite just above the city of GUAYAQUIL. Below the city it flows through a low-lying delta and enters the Gulf of Guayaquil. Its length to the end of the longest tributary is about 200 mi (320 km). Its floodplain is Ecuador's most fertile region and the source of almost all of its banana crop.

Guchkov \güch-'kȯf\, **Aleksandr (Ivanovich)** (1862–1936) Russian politician. After NICHOLAS II issued the OCTOBER MANIFESTO (1905), Guchkov helped found the Octobrist Party. As a member of the Duma, he attempted to enact more reforms but became increasingly critical of the government for its disdain for the constitution and for the influence of GRIGORY RASPUTIN. When the RUSSIAN REVOLUTION OF 1917 broke out, he was sent to receive Nicholas's abdication, and later served briefly as minister of war and the navy. After the Bolsheviks seized power in October, he emigrated to Paris.

Gudbrandsdalen \'gůd-ˌbräns-ˌdä-lən\ Valley, southern central Norway. It extends about 140 mi (225 km) above Lake MJØSA and Lillehammer. It was the scene of severe fighting in World War II, in which the Norwegians and British attempted to hold off a German invasion. It is the setting for HENRIK IBSEN's play *Peer Gynt.*

Guderian \gü-'dā-rē-än\, **Heinz (Wilhelm)** (1888–1954) German general and tank expert. His book *Attention! Tanks!* (1937) incorporated theories by the British general J. F. C. FULLER and by CHARLES DE GAULLE. As a principal architect of armored warfare and the BLITZKRIEG, he contributed decisively to Germany's victories early in World War II in Poland, France, and the Soviet Union. In 1943, as inspector general of armored troops, he simplified and accelerated tank production. After the JULY PLOT against ADOLF HITLER, he became acting chief of staff (1944–45).

Guderian.
ULLSTEIN BILDERDIENST

Gudrun See KRIEMHILD

Guelph \'gwelf\, **University of** Public university in Guelph, Ontario. It is an important center for research in scientific agriculture, having been established (1964) through the merger of Ontario Agricultural College (1874), Ontario Veterinary College (1862), and a newly created liberal-arts college. Facilities include the headquarters of the Canadian Network of Toxicology Centres, a center for the study of livestock genetics, and a gerontology research center. Total enrollment is about 13,000.

Guelphs and Ghibellines \'gwelfs...'gi-bə-ˌlēnz\ Opposing factions in German and Italian politics during the Middle Ages. The terms Guelph (see WELF DYNASTY) and Ghibelline (from Waiblingen, the castle of the Welfs' HOHENSTAUFEN opponents) first acquired significance in Italy during the reign of the Hohenstaufen emperor FREDERICK I BARBAROSSA, who tried to assert imperial authority over northern Italy and was opposed by Pope ALEXANDER III. The split between the Guelphs, who sided with the papacy, and the Ghibellines, who were sympathetic to the Holy Roman emperors, contributed to chronic strife in the cities of northern Italy in the 13th–14th century, reflected in DANTE's *Divine Comedy.*

Guercino \gwār-'chē-nō\, **Il (Italian: "The Squinter")** *orig.* **Giovanni Francesco Barbieri** (1591–1666) Italian painter. Strongly influenced by the BOLOGNESE SCHOOL, he was called to Rome in 1621 by the Bolognese pope Gregory XV and, among other commissions, decorated the Villa Ludovisi; the ceiling fresco *Aurora* is painted to appear as if there were no ceiling, so that Aurora's chariot is seen to float directly over the building. He returned to his native town of Cento in 1623. In 1642, on the death of GUIDO RENI, he moved to Bologna and was its leading painter until his death. One of the outstanding draftsmen of his age, he had a profound impact on the development of 17th-century baroque decoration.

Guernsey \'gərn-zē\ Second largest of the CHANNEL ISLANDS (pop., 1995 est.: 59,000). Situated in the ENGLISH CHANNEL just west of NORMANDY, France, it has an area of 24 sq mi (62 sq km). With Alderney and Sark, Herm, Jethou, and other islets, it forms the bailiwick of Guernsey; its capital is St. Peter Port (pop., 1991: 17,000). The island was known as Sarnia to the Romans. It was home to VICTOR HUGO 1855–70. The GUERNSEY breed of cattle originated there.

Guernsey \'gərn-zē\ Breed of dairy CATTLE that originated on the Channel Island of Guernsey. Like the JERSEY, it is thought to have descended from French cattle. Larger than Jerseys, Guernseys are fawn-colored and marked with white. Their milk has a pronounced yellow color. First exported to the U.S. in 1830, they are found also in Australia and Canada.

Guerrero \gār-'rā-rō\ State (pop., 1995 est.: 2,917,000), southwestern Mexico. Bounded by the Pacific Ocean, its 24,819-sq-mi (64,281-sq-km) territory, except for its narrow coastal plain, lies entirely within the Sierra Madre del Sur, the valleys of which are fertile but difficult to access. Its principal river is the Balsas. Named after the independence leader Vicente Guerrero (1783–1831), the region became a state in 1849. Its capital is CHILPANCINGO, but its best-known cities are ACAPULCO and Taxco, a preserved colonial town. It derives its income from agriculture, mining, and tourism.

guerrilla \gə-'ri-lə\ Member of an irregular military force fighting small-scale, limited actions, in concert with an overall political-military strategy, against conventional military forces. Guerrilla tactics involve constantly shifting attacks, sabotage, and TERRORISM. The word (the diminutive of the Spanish *guerra,* "war") was first used to describe the Spanish-Portuguese irregulars who helped drive the French from the Iberian Peninsula in the early 19th century. The underlying strategy is to harass the enemy until the guerrillas have sufficient military strength to win or can pressure the enemy to seek peace. The Chinese general SUNZI (4th century BC) laid down the rules of guerrilla tactics.

Guesde \'ged\, **Jules** *orig.* **Mathieu Basile** (1845–1922) French labor organizer. He consulted with KARL MARX in 1880 on a socialist program, adopted by a French labor congress, that called on workers to elect representatives who would "conduct the class struggle in the halls of parliament." He was opposed by "possibilists," who advocated collective bargaining and support for progressive candidates regardless of party affiliation. He founded the socialist weekly *L'Égalité,* served in the Chamber of Deputies from 1893, and was minister without portfolio (1914–15).

Guesde, 1906.
BBC HULTON PICTURE LIBRARY

Guest, Edgar (Albert) (1881–1959) U.S. (British-born) writer. His family emigrated to the U.S. when he was 10. He became an office boy for the *Detroit Free Press,* and later a reporter and writer of daily sentimental rhymes. These became so popular that they were syndicated throughout the country. His first book, *A Heap o' Livin'* (1916), became a best-seller and was followed by similar collections of optimistic verse on such subjects as home, mother, and the virtue of hard work.

Guevara \ge-'vär-ə\, **Che** *orig.* **Ernesto Guevara de la Serna** (1928–1967) Theoretician and tactician of guerrilla warfare and prominent figure in FIDEL CASTRO's revolution in Cuba (1956–59). Born to a middle-class family in Argentina, he completed medical studies in 1953 and subsequently traveled widely in Latin America, eventually settling in Guatemala. The overthrow of Guatemala's Pres. JACOBO ARBENZ persuaded him that the U.S. would always oppose leftist governments and that only violent revolution would end the poverty of the Latin American masses. He left Guatemala for Mexico, where he met Castro and joined his cause. After the Cuban revolution he held several key posts as one of Castro's most trusted aides; handsome and charismatic, he served as one of the revolution's most effective voices. He left Cuba in 1965 to organize guerrilla fighters in Congo and later Bolivia. Captured and shot by the Bolivian army, he immediately achieved international fame and the status of a martyred hero among leftists worldwide.

Che Guevara.
LEE LOCKWOOD—BLACK STAR

Guggenheim \'gü-gən- ˌhīm\, **Meyer and Daniel** (1828–1905, 1856–1930) U.S. industrialists, father and son, who developed worldwide mining interests that yielded a vast fortune. Born in Switzerland, Meyer emigrated to the U.S. in 1847 and built an import firm specializing in Swiss embroideries. His investments in two Colorado copper mines in the 1880s were the foundation of extensive mining interests. His seven sons, especially Daniel, built a large organization of smelting and refining operations. In 1901 the Guggenheims merged their holdings with the American Smelting and Refining Co., a trust composed of the country's largest metal-processing plants. Daniel directed the trust until 1919 and acquired mines throughout the world. Philanthropies include the John Simon Guggenheim Memorial Foundation (1925) to award fellowships to artists and scholars studying abroad, and the Solomon R. Guggenheim Foundation (1937), which oversees New York's GUGGENHEIM MUSEUM and the Guggenheim Collection in Venice. See also SOLOMON GUGGENHEIM.

Guggenheim, Peggy *orig.* **Marguerite** (1898–1979) Art collector and patron of the NEW YORK SCHOOL of artists. Granddaughter of MEYER & DANIEL GUGGENHEIM, she inherited a large fortune in 1921. In 1930 she moved to Paris, where she took up a bohemian life, and in 1932 to London. She returned to New York in 1941, married MAX ERNST, and in 1942 opened a gallery where she exhibited many of the artists she supported, among them JACKSON POLLOCK, ROBERT MOTHERWELL, MARK ROTHKO, and HANS HOFMANN. After World War II she settled in Venice and exhibited her outstanding collection of Cubist, abstract, and Surrealist art; the Peggy Guggenheim Collection is still open to the public.

Guggenheim, Solomon (Robert) (1861–1949) Businessman and art collector. Born in Philadelphia, he became a partner in his father's Swiss embroidery import business. He also worked in the family mining industry and was a director of many family companies. After retiring from business in 1919, he devoted his time to collecting modernist paintings. He established the Solomon R. Guggenheim Foundation (1937), which provided the funds for the Solomon GUGGENHEIM MUSEUM (1959). See also MEYER & DANIEL GUGGENHEIM.

Guggenheim Museum \'gü-gən-ˌhīm\ Museum in New York City housing the Solomon R. Guggenheim collection of modern art. An example of the "organic architecture" of FRANK LLOYD WRIGHT, the building (constructed 1956–59) represents a radical departure from traditional museum design, spiraling upward and outward in a smooth coil of massive, unadorned white concrete. The exhibition space, which has been criticized for upstaging the artwork displayed, consists of a six-story-high spiral ramp encircling an open center volume lighted by a dome of glass supported by stainless steel.

Guggenheim Museum Bilbao \bil-'baü\ Art museum, Bilbao, northern Spain. It opened in 1997 as a cooperative venture between the Guggenheim Foundation and the Basque regional administration of northwestern Spain. The museum complex, designed by FRANK GEHRY, consists of interconnected buildings whose extraordinary free-form titanium-sheathed mass suggests a gigantic work of abstract sculpture. The interior space, organized around a large atrium, is mainly devoted to modern and contemporary art.

GUI See GRAPHICAL USER INTERFACE

Guianas \gē-'ä-nəz, gī-'a-nəz\, **the** Region, northern South America. Located on the Atlantic and Caribbean coasts, it lies between the ORINOCO, NEGRO, and AMAZON rivers, and covers an area of about 181,000 sq mi (468,800 sq km). It consists of Guyana (formerly British Guiana), Suriname (formerly Dutch Guiana), and FRENCH GUIANA; most of it is covered by dense forests containing valuable wood. Settlements are largely confined to the coast and river valleys. The earliest known inhabitants were the Surinam Indians. Its coast was sighted by CHRISTOPHER COLUMBUS in 1498, and the area was explored by the Spanish in the early 16th century. The Dutch founded settlements c. 1580, and the French and English, in the early 17th century.

guide dog *or* **Seeing Eye dog** Dog professionally trained to guide and protect its blind master. They have also been used to assist persons with hearing impairments and restricted mobility. Systematic training of guide dogs originated in Germany during World War I to aid blinded veterans. At the age of approximately one year, the dog is trained for three or four months. RETRIEVERS and GERMAN SHEPHERDS are the most widely used breeds.

guided missile Projectile provided with means for altering its direction after it leaves its launching device. Almost all modern MISSILES are propelled by ROCKET OF JET ENGINES and have guidance mechanisms, usually including sensors, to help the missile find its target. Heat-seeking missiles, for example, carry infrared sensors that allow them to home in on the exhaust of jet engines.

Guido d'Arezzo \'gwē-dō-dä-'rāt-sō\ (991?–after 1033) Italian music theorist. A Benedictine monk charged with training the choristers in the cathedral of Arezzo, he is credited with two important advances: the invention of the staff for notating exact pitches, and the use of different syllables to sing each pitch, or SOLMIZATION. In his famous *Micrologus* (1026–33), he describes the use of at least a two-line staff and the use of syllables as a mnemonic device for singing musical pitches. The famous "Guidonian hand," an aid to modulation from one HEXACHORD to another by using the joints of the hand to represent different pitches, is not mentioned in his extant writings.

Guienne *or* **Guyenne** \gē-'en\ *ancient* **Aquitania** Historical region, southwestern France. An old duchy whose capital was at BORDEAUX, it was near the GARONNE and DORDOGNE rivers. From Roman times until the Middle Ages it was part of the region of AQUITAINE. Under English control during much of the later Middle Ages, Guienne was retaken by the French at the beginning of the HUNDRED YEARS' WAR, but in 1360 it was restored, with Aquitaine, to the English. France later reconquered the area, and from the 17th century until 1789, Guienne was part of the French *gouvernement* of Guienne and Gascony.

guild Association of craftsmen or merchants formed for mutual aid and for the advancement of their professional interests. Guilds flourished in Europe between the 11th and 16th century and were of two types: merchant guilds, including all the merchants of a particular town or city; and craft guilds, including all the craftsmen in a particular branch of industry (e.g., weavers, painters, goldsmiths). Their functions included establishing trade monopolies, setting standards for quality of goods, maintaining stable prices, and gaining leverage in local governments in order to further the interests of the guild. Craft guilds also established hierarchies of craftsmen based on level of training (e.g., masters, journeymen, and apprentices).

Guild Socialism Movement that called for workers' control of industry through a system of national guilds, organized internally on democratic lines, and state ownership of industry. It began in England in 1906 with publication of Arthur J. Penty's *The Restoration of the Gild System* and was organized into the National Guilds League in 1915. It reached its apex with the left-wing shop stewards' movement during World War I and, after the war, with building guilds that built houses for the state. Both movements collapsed after the economic slump of 1921, and the League was dissolved in 1925.

Guillemin \gē-ə-'maⁿ\, **Roger C(harles) L(ouis)** (born 1924) French-U.S. physiologist. He and his colleagues discovered, isolated, analyzed, and synthesized hypothalamic hormones that regulate thyroid activity, cause the pituitary to release growth hormone, and regulate the activities of the pituitary and the pancreas. He shared a 1977 Nobel Prize with ANDREW V. SCHALLY and ROSALYN YALOW. Guillemin is also known for his discovery of ENDORPHINS.

guillemot \'gi-lə-ˌmät\ Any of three species of black-and-white seabirds (genus *Cepphus,* family Alcidae). Guillemots have a pointed, black bill and red legs. Guillemots are deep divers that feed at the bottom. The best-known species, the black guillemot, breeds around the Arctic Circle and winters south to the British Isles, Maine, and the Bering Strait; it is about 14 in. (35 cm) long. The similar pigeon guillemot breeds along both coasts of the North Pacific, south to Japan and southern California; the spectacled guillemot breeds from Japan to the Kuril Islands. In British usage, the name also refers to birds called MURRES in the U.S.

guillotine \ˌgē-ə-'tēn, 'gi-lə-ˌtēn\ Instrument for inflicting capital punishment by decapitation. A minimal wooden structure, it supported a heavy blade that, when released, slid down in vertical guides to sever the victim's head. It was introduced in France in 1792 in the FRENCH REVOLUTION, though similar devices had been used in Scotland, England, and other European countries, often for executing criminals of noble birth. The name derived from a French physician and member of the National Assembly, Joseph-Ignace Guillotin (1738–1814), who was instrumental in passing a law requiring all sentences of death to be carried out "by means of a machine," so that execution by decapitation would no longer be confined to nobles and executions would be as painless as possible. The last execution by guillotine in France took place in 1977.

Guin, Ursula Le See Ursula LE GUIN

Guinea \'gi-nē\ *officially* **Republic of Guinea** *formerly* **French Guinea** Country, western Africa. Area: 94,926 sq mi (245,857 sq km). Population (1997 est.): 7,405,000 (including 700,000 refuges from Liberia and Sierra Leone). Capital: CONAKRY. The FULANI people are in the majority, followed by the MALINKE and many other groups. Language: French (official). Religion: Islam. Currency: Guinean franc. Facing the Atlantic Ocean to the west, Guinea has four topographical regions. Lower Guinea comprises the coast and coastal plain, which are sandy and interspersed with lagoons and mangrove swamps. To the east the Fouta Djallon highlands rise sharply from the coastal plain to elevations above 3,000 ft (900 m); western Africa's three major rivers—the NIGER, SÉNÉGAL, and GAMBIA—originate there. Upper Guinea comprises the Niger Plains. The Forest Region, an isolated forested highland in the southeast, rises to 5,748 ft (1,752 m) at Mount Nimba, the country's highest peak. Most of the country has a humid tropical climate, while more than two-fifths is covered by tropical rain forest. Export crops include rice, bananas, and coffee. Guinea is the world's second-largest producer of bauxite. Its developing, mixed economy is based on agriculture, mining, and trade. It is a multiparty republic with one legislative house; the head of state and government is the president, assisted by the prime minister. In c. AD 900, successive migrations of the Susu swept down from the desert and pushed the original inhabitants, the Baga, to the Atlantic coast. Small kingdoms of the Susu rose in importance in the 13th century and later extended their rule to the coast. In the mid-15th century the Portuguese visited the coast and developed a slave trade. In the 16th century the Fulani established domination over the Fouta Djallon region; they ruled into the 19th century. In the early 19th century the French arrived, and in 1849 proclaimed the coastal region a French protectorate. In 1895 French Guinea became part of the federation of FRENCH WEST AFRICA. In 1946 it was made an overseas territory of France, and in 1958 achieved independence. Following a military coup in 1984, Guinea began implementing Westernized government systems. A new constitution was adopted in 1991, and the first multiparty elections were held in 1993. During the 1990s, Guinea accommodated several hundred thousand war refugees from neighboring Liberia and Sierra Leone.

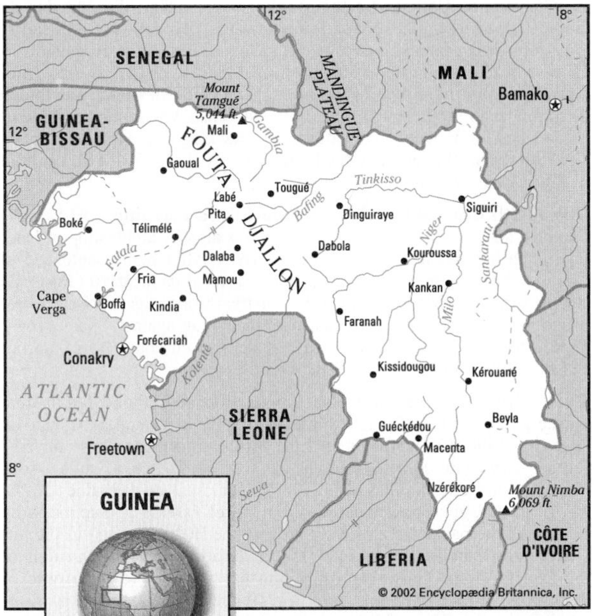

Guinea, Gulf of Great inlet of the Atlantic Ocean, western central African coast. It includes the Bights of BENIN and BIAFRA, and its major tributaries are the CASAMANCE, VOLTA, and NIGER rivers. Its natural resources include offshore oil deposits and metal ore deposits. Its coastline forms part of the western edge of the African tectonic plate and corresponds remarkably to the continental margin of South America from Brazil to the Guianas, providing one of the clearest confirmations of the theory of CONTINENTAL DRIFT.

Guinea-Bissau \'gi-nē-bi-'saù\ *officially* **Republic of Guinea-Bissau** *formerly (until 1974)* **Portuguese Guinea** Country, western Africa. Its territory includes the Bijagós Archipelago, off the Atlantic coast to the southwest. Area: 13,948 sq mi (36,125 sq km). Population (1997 est.): 1,179,000. Capital: BISSAU. The four major ethnic groups are the Balanta Brassa, FULANI, MALINKE, and Mandyako. Language: Portuguese (official); each tribe speaks its own vernacular. Religion: Islam; traditional beliefs. Currency: CFA franc. Most of the country consists of low, marshy terrain and flat plateau. The climate is generally hot and tropical. Much of the country's wildlife is aquatic; crocodiles, snakes, and such birds as pelicans and flamingos abound. It has a developing, primarily agricultural economy; cashews and peanuts are the main cash crops. It is a multiparty republic with one legislative house, its chief of state is the president, and the head of government is the prime minister. More than 1,000 years ago the coast of Guinea-Bissau was occupied by iron-using agriculturists. They grew irrigated and dry rice and were also the major suppliers of marine salt to the western Sudan. At about the same time, it came under the influence of the MALI EMPIRE and became a tributary kingdom known as Gabú. After 1546 Gabú was virtually autonomous; vestiges of the kingdom lasted until 1867. The earliest overseas contacts came in the 15th century with the Portuguese, who imported slaves from the Guinea area to the offshore CAPE VERDE Islands. Portuguese control of Guinea-Bissau was marginal despite their claims to sovereignty there.

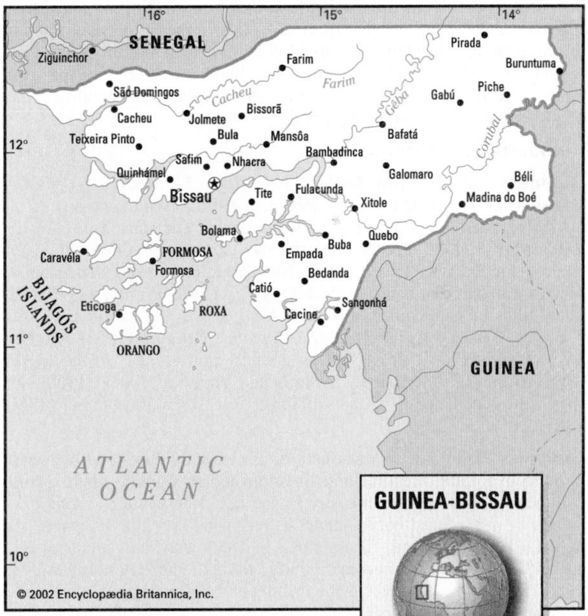

The end of the slave trade forced the Portuguese inland in search of new profits. Their subjugation of the interior was slow and sometimes violent; it was not effectively achieved until 1915, though sporadic resistance continued until 1936. Guerrilla warfare in the 1960s led to the country's independence in 1974, but political turmoil continued and the government was overthrown by a military coup in 1980. A new constitution was adopted in 1984, and the first multiparty elections were held in 1994. A destructive civil war in 1998 was followed by a military coup in 1999.

guinea fowl Any of a family (Numididae) of African birds, sometimes placed in the family Phasianidae. One species *(Numida meleagris)* is widely domesticated for its flesh and, because it gabbles loudly at the least alarm, as a "watchdog" on farms. Wild forms of this species are known as helmet guinea fowl because of their large bony crest. Many varieties are widespread in the savannas and scrublands of Africa, and the guinea fowl has been introduced into the West Indies and elsewhere. About 20 in. (50 cm) long, in its typical form it has a bare face, brown eyes, red and blue wattles at the bill, white-spotted black plumage, and a hunched posture. It lives in flocks and feeds on seed tubers and some insects.

Vulturine guinea fowl (*Acryllium vulturinum*).

S.C. BISSEROT—BRUCE COLEMAN INC.

guinea pig Domesticated species *(Cavia porcellus)* of South American CAVY (family Caviidae). It resembles most other cavies in being stout, short-legged, and about 10 in. (25 cm) long. It has small ears, no external tail, and a coat that is black, tan, cream-colored, brown, white, or a combination of these colors. Hair length and texture vary among varieties. It feeds largely on grass and other green plants. Domesticated in pre-Incan times, it was introduced into Europe in the early 16th century. It is a popular pet and a valuable research animal.

guinea worm *or* **medina worm** *or* **dragon worm** NEMATODE *(Dracunculus medinensis)* that is a common parasite of humans and other mammals in tropical Asia and Africa and has been introduced into the West Indies and tropical South America. The female grows to 20–48 in. (50–120 cm) long; the male, which dies upon mating, is only about 0.5–1.1 in. (12–29 mm) long. Both sexes live in the connective tissue of the host animal. Humans become infected when they drink water containing tiny crustaceans (e.g., COPEPODS) that have eaten guinea-worm larvae. The disease the guinea worm carries, called dracunculiasis, can be extremely debilitating and painful.

Guinevere See ARTHURIAN LEGEND

Guinness \'gi-nəs\, **(de Cuffe), Alec** *later* **Sir Alec** (1914–2000) British actor. He made his stage debut in 1934. His reputation soared after 1936, when he joined the OLD VIC company and starred in plays by WILLIAM SHAKESPEARE, GEORGE BERNARD SHAW, and ANTON CHEKHOV. A versatile actor, he won the praise of New York critics and audiences in Shakespearean roles and in T. S. ELIOT's *The Cocktail Party* (1946). His many films include comedies such as *Kind Hearts and Coronets* (1949), *The Lavender Hill Mob* (1951), *The Captain's Paradise* (1953), and *Our Man in Havana* (1959) as well as dramas such as *The Bridge on the River Kwai* (1957, Academy Award) and *Tunes of Glory* (1960). He won a new generation of fans in three *Star Wars* films (1977, 1980, 1983).

Guinness PLC \'gi-nəs\ Manufacturer of distilled liquors and brewer of a distinctive, dark, creamy stout. It originated in Dublin, where Arthur Guinness bought a small brewery in the late 18th century. From 1799 the brewery produced only Guinness stout, which became known as the national beer of Ireland. Incorporated in 1886 as Arthur Guinness Son and Co. Ltd., it did not become a public limited company until 1982. In 1955, to help settle trivia disputes in pubs, it began publishing *The Guinness Book of Records*, which has become perhaps the best-selling book (annually) in the world. In 1997 it merged with Grand Metropolitan PLC, the parent company of Burger King, to form the London-based Diageo PLC.

Guiscard, Robert See ROBERT GUISCARD

Guise, 2nd duc (Duke) de *orig.* **François de Lorraine** (1519–1563) French soldier and loyal servant to the French crown, the greatest figure produced by the House of GUISE. He fought in FRANCIS I's army and was badly wounded at the siege of Boulogne (1545), earning him the nickname "the Scarred." He led French armies in other victories against the English and the Spanish. On the accession of FRANCIS II (1559), Guise became grand master of the royal household. The BOURBONS launched a conspiracy to overthrow the Guises, who learned of the plot and ruthlessly suppressed it (1560). When CATHERINE DE MÉDICIS became regent (1560), she supported the Bourbons (who were leaders of the HUGUENOT movement) and religious toleration, as against the Guises and Catholic dominance. The first of the resultant Wars of RELIGION again showed Guise to be an outstanding soldier. He was assassinated by a Huguenot in 1563.

Guise, 3rd duc (Duke) de *orig.* **Henri I de Lorraine** (1550–1588) French leader of the Catholic party and the HOLY LEAGUE during the French Wars of RELIGION. When CATHERINE DE MÉDICIS turned to the Guises in 1572 for help in removing the Huguenot GASPARD II DE COLIGNY, Henri, who blamed Coligny for the murder of his father, the 2nd duc de GUISE, helped plan the SAINT BARTHOLOMEW'S DAY MASSACRE. Fearing Guise's growing popularity, HENRY III made peace with the Huguenots in 1576, and Guise angrily countered by forming the HOLY LEAGUE. After Guise's victory in the War of the THREE HENRYS (1588), Henry was forced to surrender to the League's demands, and Guise was appointed lieutenant general of France. Soon afterward, the king's bodyguard stabbed Guise to death; the next day his brother, Louis II (1555–1588), cardinal de Guise, was also murdered.

Guise, 5th duc (Duke) de *orig.* **Henri II de Lorraine** (1614–1664) French leader of the House of GUISE. He was already archbishop of Rheims when he became duc de Guise in 1640. After being sentenced to death for his part in a conspiracy against Cardinal de RICHELIEU (1641), he fled to Brussels and commanded the Austrian troops against France. He unsuccessfully led the Neapolitans in their war against Spain (1647, 1654), then spent the rest of his life at the French court, trying unsuccessfully to revive the power of the Guise dynasty.

Guise \'gēz\, **House of** Noble French Roman Catholic family that played a major role in French politics during the REFORMATION. Claude de Lorraine (1496–1550) was created the 1st duc (duke) de Guise in 1527 for his service to FRANCIS I in the defense of France. Claude's sons François, 2nd duc de GUISE, and Charles, cardinal de Lorraine (1524–1574), gained great power during the reign of FRANCIS II. Supported by Spain and the papacy, their persecution of the HUGUENOTS led to the unsuccessful Amboise Conspiracy (1560), an attempted assassination of the leaders of the Guise party and transfer of power to the House of BOURBON. The Guise-led massacre of a Huguenot congregation at Vassy precipitated the Wars of RELIGION, in which Henri I, 3rd duc de GUISE, was a prominent leader. Charles de Lorraine, 4th duc de Guise (1571–1640), lived through the rapid decline of the family's power. Henri II, 5th duc de GUISE, tried unsuccessfully to revive the family's power; the direct line expired with the death of his grand-nephew in 1675.

guitar Plucked STRINGED INSTRUMENT. It normally has six strings, a fretted fingerboard, and a soundbox with a pronounced waist. It probably originated in Spain in the early 16th century. By 1800 it was being strung with six single strings; 19th-century innovations gave it its modern form. Modern classical-guitar technique owes much to Francisco Tárrega (1852–1909), and A. SEGOVIA gave the instrument prominence in the concert hall. However, it has always been primarily an amateur's instrument, and it remains an important folk instrument in many countries. The 12-string guitar is strung in six double courses. The Hawaiian or steel guitar is held horizontally and the strings are stopped by the pressure of a metal bar, producing a sweet glissando tone. The electric guitar represented a major development. Electric pickups were attached to the acoustic guitar in the 1920s, and electroacoustic guitars were soon being

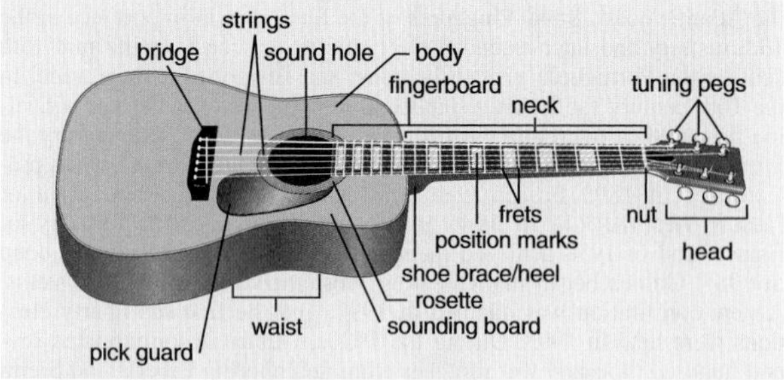

Features of a modern acoustic guitar.

© 2002 MERRIAM-WEBSTER INC.

produced. In the 1940s LES PAUL invented the solid-body guitar; lacking a soundbox, it transmits only the string vibrations. With its long-sustained notes, affinity for strong amplification, and capacity for producing wailing melodic lines as well as harshly percussive rhythms, it soon became the principal instrument of Western popular music.

Guitry \gē-'trē\, **Sacha** (1885–1957) Russian-French actor and dramatist. Born in St. Petersburg, son of the actor Lucien Guitry (1860–1925), he appeared on the Russian stage with his father's company. At 21 he achieved success with his first play, *Nono.* He had over 90 plays produced, including *Pasteur* (1919) and *Béranger* (1920), written for his father to act in. He wrote, directed, and acted in many films, of which the best known was *Roman d'un tricheur* (1936).

Guiyang \'gwē-'yäŋ\ *or* **Kuei-yang** \'gwā-'yäŋ\ City (pop., 1991 est.: 1,530,000), capital of GUIZHOU province, southern China. It is situated south of CHONGQING. The SUI (581–618) and TANG (618–907) dynasties established military outposts there, but the city developed only after the MONGOL invasion of southwestern China in 1279. Chinese settlement followed, and under the MING (1368–1644) and QING (1644–1911) dynasties, Guiyang became the seat of a prefecture. The SINO-JAPANESE WAR spurred its growth into a major provincial city and industrial center.

Guizhou \'gwē-'jō\ *or* **Kuei-chou** \'gwā-'jō\ *or* **Kweichow** \'gwā-'chau̇\ Province (pop., 1996 est.: 35,080,000), southwestern China. It has rough topography, poor communications, and consequent isolation. The capital is GUIYANG. About three-fourths of the people are Han Chinese; there are also aboriginal peoples, including the Miao. Guizhou came under Chinese influence during the MING DYNASTY (1368–1644), when it was made a province. During the QING DYNASTY (1644–1911), struggles between the minorities, involving especially the Miao, were common. Serious revolts occurred in the 19th century and in 1941–44, as a result of exploitation by local warlords. The Communists took the area in 1949. Its mineral resources are rich and support some mining.

Guizot \gē-'zō\, **François (-Pierre-Guillaume)** (1787–1874) French political figure and historian. He studied law but became a professor of history at the University of Paris in 1812. He emerged as a leader of the conservative constitutional monarchists and during the JULY MONARCHY (1830–48) was the dominant minister in France, holding such offices as minister of education, foreign minister, and premier. Forced to resign by the REVOLUTION OF 1848, he spent most of his remaining days in relative political isolation. His works include *General History of Civilization in Europe* (1828) and *The History of France from the Earliest Times to the Year 1789* (1872–76).

Guizot, 1855.
ARCHIVES PHOTOGRAPHIQUES, PARIS

Gujarat \ˌgü-jə-'rät\ State (pop., 1994 est.: 44,235,000) and historic region, western India. Bounded by the Arabian Sea, with a coastline of 992 mi (1,596 km) long, and Pakistan, it has an area of 75,685 sq mi (196,024 sq km); the capital is GANDHINAGAR. During the 4th–5th century AD, it was ruled by the GUPTA DYNASTY; it derived its name from the Gurjaras, who ruled the area in the 8th–9th century. After a period of economic and cultural achievement, it fell successively under Arabic Muslim, Mughal, and Maratha rule. In 1818 it came under British control, and after 1857 was a province of British India. Following Indian independence in 1947, most of Gujarat was included in the state of Bombay, which was divided into Gujarat and Maharashtra in 1960. Gujarat is a leading industrialized state of India, and a major petroleum producer. It is also famous for its art and craft products.

Gulag \'gü-ˌläg\ System of Soviet labor camps and prisons that from the 1920s to the mid-1950s housed millions of political prisoners and criminals. The term (an abbreviation of the Russian words for Chief Administration of Corrective Labor Camps) was largely unknown in the West until the 1973 publication of ALEKSANDR SOLZHENITSYN's *Gulag Archipelago.* The Gulag consisted of hundreds of camps, under the control of the secret police, where prisoners felled timber, worked in the mines, or labored on construction projects. At least 10% died each year from harsh working conditions, inadequate food, and summary executions. The Gulag reached its height in the years of collectivization of Soviet agriculture (1929–32), during JOSEPH STALIN's purges (1936–38), and immediately after World War II, shrinking only after Stalin's death in 1953. An estimated 15–30 million Russians died in the camps.

Gulbenkian, Calouste (Sarkis) (1869–1955) Turkish-British financier, industrialist, and philanthropist. In 1911 he helped found the Turkish Petroleum Co. (later Iraq Petroleum Co.) and became the first to exploit Iraqi oil; his 5% share made him one of the world's richest men. From 1948 he negotiated Saudi Arabian oil concessions to U.S. firms. He amassed an outstanding art collection of some 6,000 works, now in Lisbon's Calouste Gulbenkian Museum. The Lisbon-based Calouste Gulbenkian Foundation supports activities worldwide in science, art, social welfare, cultural relations, health, and education.

gulf Any large coastal indentation, similar to a BAY but larger. Most existing gulfs were formed or greatly extended as a result of the rise in sea level that accompanied the ending of the last ice age. Some, such as the Gulf of California and the Gulf of Oman, resulted from warping, folding, or downfaulting of the earth's crust, which caused parts of the shoreline to drop below sea level. Most gulfs are connected with the sea by one or more straits. A gulf may have a group of islands at its mouth or may open into another gulf. Gulfs may differ from the adjoining sea in water properties and sedimentation.

Gulf & Western Inc. Former U.S. corporation, founded in 1958 by Charles Bluhdorn. One of the most highly diversified conglomerates in the U.S., Gulf & Western took control of the Paramount Pictures Corp. in 1966 and changed its name to PARAMOUNT COMMUNICATIONS in 1989. It was acquired by the media conglomerate Viacom Inc. in 1994.

Gulf Cooperation Council Persian Gulf–based international organization founded in Abu Dhabi in 1981. Its members include Kuwait, Saudi Arabia, Bahrain, Qatar, the United Arab Emirates, and Oman. Its purpose is to facilitate cooperation among members in the fields of international commerce, education, shipping, and travel. Its headquarters are in Saudi Arabia and it meets twice a year. Its administrative structure includes a supreme council, a council of foreign ministers, an arbitration commission, and a general secretariat.

Gulf Intracoastal Waterway System of inland waterways, including rivers and canals, along the U.S. coast of the Gulf of MEXICO. It extends from Apalachee Bay, Fla., west to the Mexican border at Brownsville, Texas, a distance of more than 1,100 mi (1,770 km). It includes MOBILE BAY and Mississippi Sound, passes through NEW ORLEANS, and takes in the Sabine-Neches Waterway and the ship canal at HOUSTON. Together with its counterpart, the ATLANTIC INTRACOASTAL WATERWAY, it forms the Intracoastal Waterway, a shipping route that extends for 3,000 mi (4,800 km) in the southern and eastern U.S.

Gulf of Tonkin Resolution (August 5, 1964) Resolution by the U.S. Congress authorizing Pres. LYNDON B. JOHNSON to use "all necessary measures" to repel armed attacks against U.S. forces in Vietnam. It was drafted in response to the alleged shelling of two U.S. navy ships by North Vietnam in the Gulf of Tonkin. Later information disputed the severity of the attack. The resolution was cited as authorization for the subsequent expansion of the VIETNAM WAR; many in Congress came to see it as a blank check, and it was repealed in 1970.

Gulf Oil Corp. Major U.S. petroleum company. Gulf Oil began with an oil gusher near Beaumont, Texas, in 1901 and was incorporated in 1907. The oil well was developed by the Pittsburgh Mellon family (see ANDREW W. MELLON). Gulf became the first oil company to enter the consumer gasoline market when it opened a drive-in filling station in Pittsburgh in 1913. By 1923 the Gulf refinery in Port Arthur, Texas, was the largest in the world. Gulf Oil continued to develop oil fields in Texas, Oklahoma, and Louisiana, as well as in Mexico and Venezuela. In 1984 it was bought by Chevron, another oil company.

Gulf Stream Warm ocean current, part of a general clockwise-rotating system of currents in the North Atlantic. A major contribution of the Gulf Stream is its warming effect on the climates of adjacent land areas. In winter, the air over the ocean west of Norway is more than 40°F (22°C) warmer than the average for that latitude, one of the greatest temperature anomalies in the world. Winters in southwestern England are extraordinarily mild for this northern latitude because of the Gulf

E
F
G

Stream. Regions of the Gulf Stream, such as the Grand Banks, have been among the most productive commercial fishing grounds in the world.

Gulf War syndrome Cluster of illnesses in veterans of the Persian Gulf War (1990–91) characterized by variable and nonspecific symptoms such as fatigue, muscle and joint pains, headaches, memory loss, and post-traumatic stress reactions. The cause is unknown. The disorder does not appear to be fatal but can be associated with considerable distress and disability.

gull Any of more than 40 species of heavily built, web-footed seabirds (family Laridae) that are most abundant as breeders in temperate to arctic regions of the Northern Hemisphere. Adults are mainly gray or white, with variable head markings. The bill is strong and slightly hooked, sometimes with a spot of color. Species differ in bill and leg colors and in wing patterns. Wingspreads range from 24 to 63 in. (0.6–1.6 m). Gulls feed on insects, mollusks, and crustaceans on beaches; worms and grubs in plowed fields; and fish and garbage from ships and along shores. Some large gulls prey on the eggs and young of other birds, including their own kind. See also HERRING GULL, KITTIWAKE.

Herring gull (*Larus argentatus*).
JOHN MARKHAM

Gull, William Withey *later* **Sir William** (1816–1890) British physician. A famous and popular teacher, Gull was one of the first clinicians to describe pathological lesions in TABES DORSALIS (1856), intermittent hemoglobin in the urine, arteriosclerotic atrophy of the kidney, and MYXEDEMA, known as Gull's disease. He believed in minimal use of drugs and defended vivisection and clinical investigation. He was the leading British physician of his time; his patients included Queen Victoria.

Gullstrand, Allvar (1862–1930) Swedish ophthalmologist. He contributed to knowledge of the cornea and of astigmatism, improved post-cataract-surgery corrective lenses, and devised the Gullstrand slit lamp, a valuable diagnostic tool for detailed study of the eye. He won a 1911 Nobel Prize for research on the eye as a light-refracting apparatus.

gum *or* **gingiva** \'jin-jə-və, jin-'jī-və\ Mucous MEMBRANE attached to and surrounding the necks of the teeth and the alveolar bone of the jaw. The edges of the gums around the teeth are free and extend into the spaces between the teeth. Fibers of the ligament that holds the teeth in their sockets enter the gum and hold it tightly against the teeth. Pink, speckled, and tough, healthy gums have limited sensitivity to pain, temperature, and pressure. Changes in color, loss of speckling, or abnormal sensitivity are early signs of gingivitis, in which pockets form between the gum and teeth and become infected, with inflammation, bleeding, and, in severe cases, loss of teeth.

gum In botany, an adhesive substance of vegetable origin, mostly obtained as exudate from the bark of trees or shrubs belonging to the PEA family. Gum arabic (from a species of ACACIA) is used in lithography. Gum tragacanth (from several shrub species in the genus *Astragalus*) is used as a coating and binding agent in pill manufacture, as an emulsifier in processed foods, and as a thickener in sauces. Some plant gums are used in the manufacture of cosmetics.

GUM \'güm\ Largest DEPARTMENT STORE in Russia. Situated in Moscow's Red Square, it occupies a huge, ornate building (constructed 1889–93) that once housed more than 1,000 shops. The name is an acronym for the Russian meaning "State Department Store." GUM now includes about 150 shops selling food, clothing, home appliances, watches and cameras, and many other goods. It functions more like a Western-style shopping mall than a department store and is a popular tourist attraction.

gum, chewing See CHEWING GUM

gum tree See TUPELO

Gumal Pass \gə-'məl\ *or* **Gomal Pass** \gō-'məl\ Mountain pass, southern North-West Frontier Province, Pakistan. Lying along the Gumal River valley in the SULAIMAN RANGE, it is the most important pass between the KHYBER and Bolan passes, and connects Ghazni in eastern Afghanistan with Dera Ismail Khan in Pakistan. Actually a 4-mi (6-km) gorge, it is the oldest trade route in the area, traditionally used by nomadic Afghan traders called Powindahs, whose entry into Pakistan is now restricted.

gumbo In soil science, any of various fine-grained, rich, black, alluvial soils, especially of the central U.S., that when wet become impenetrable and soapy or waxy and very sticky. When dried, gumbo "bakes" and becomes extremely hard.

gun Weapon consisting essentially of a metal tube from which a missile or projectile is shot by the force of exploding GUNPOWDER or some other propellant. The term is often limited today to the so-called big guns, CANNON larger than a howitzer or MORTAR. It may also be used to refer to military small arms such as the RIFLE, MACHINE GUN, and PISTOL, as well as to nonmilitary firearms such as the SHOTGUN. Though the Chinese used gunpowder in warfare from the 9th century, guns were not developed until the Europeans acquired gunpowder in the 13th century. The earliest guns (c. 1327) resembled old-fashioned soda bottles; they apparently were fired by applying a red-hot wire to a touchhole drilled through the top. Separating the barrel and the powder chamber resulted in breechloaders, which continued to be used in naval swivel guns and fortress wallpieces well into the 17th century. Small arms, as distinguished from hand cannon, did not exist until the development of the MATCHLOCK in the 15th century. See also FLINTLOCK, WHEEL LOCK.

gunasthana \'gü-nəs-'tä-nə\ In JAINISM, any of the 14 stages of spiritual development through which a soul passes on its way to liberation. The goal is to gradually purify the soul and to gain release from the cycle of birth and death. The thirteenth stage was that of an ARHAT. In the final stage the soul achieves the release known as MOKSHA. See also EIGHTFOLD PATH, NIRVANA.

gunite See SHOTCRETE

Gunn, Thom(son William) (born 1929) British-U.S. poet. Educated at Cambridge and Stanford universities, he has lived in San Francisco since the 1950s and began teaching at UC–Berkeley in 1958. His early verse appeared in *Fighting Terms* (1954) and *The Sense of Movement* (1957); in the late 1950s his poems became more experimental. *My Sad Captains* (1961), *Moly* (1971), *Jack Straw's Castle* (1976), and *The Passages of Joy* (1982) discuss his homosexuality; *The Man with Night Sweats* (1992) has AIDS as a subject.

gunpowder Any of several mixtures used as propelling charges in guns and as blasting agents in mining. The first such EXPLOSIVE was black powder, a mixture of SALTPETER (potassium nitrate), sulfur, and charcoal. It originated in the 9th century in China and made its way west in the 13th century. The recipe was refined and finally fixed in the 14th century; black powder is still widely used for ignition charges, primers, fuses, blank charges in military ammunition, and fireworks. In 1838 it was discovered that cotton could be made explosive by dipping it in concentrated nitric acid, and the form of nitrocellulose known as guncotton came into use as an ingredient of gunpowder in the 1860s. In the 1880s Paul Vieille (1854–1934) used nitrocellulose to create the first smokeless gunpowder; modern gunpowder consists of either nitrocellulose alone or a combination of nitrocellulose and NITROGLYCERIN.

Gunpowder Plot (1605) Conspiracy by English Roman Catholic zealots to blow up Parliament and kill JAMES I. Angered by James's refusal to grant more religious toleration to Catholics, a group of conspirators led by Robert Catesby (1573–1605) recruited GUY FAWKES to their plot. One member warned his brother-in-law Lord Monteagle not to attend Parliament on the appointed day (November 5, 1605), and Monteagle alerted the government. Fawkes was arrested in a rented cellar under the palace at Westminster, where he had concealed 20 barrels of gunpowder. Under torture, he revealed the names of the conspirators, and they were all either killed while resisting arrest or executed in 1606. The plot bitterly intensified Protestant suspicions of Catholics.

Gunther, John (1901–1970) U.S. journalist and author. Born in Chicago, he worked for the *Chicago Daily News* London bureau (1924–36) before publishing *Inside Europe* (1936), the first of his highly successful sociopolitical books describing and interpreting various regions of the world, including *Inside Asia* (1939), *Inside Latin America* (1941), *Inside Africa* (1955), *Inside Russia Today* (1958), *Inside Europe Today* (1961), and *Inside South America* (1967). He was also a war correspondent and radio commentator.

Guo Moruo \'gwò-'mò-'rwò\ *or* **Kuo Mo-jo** \'gwò-'mò-'jò\ *orig.* **Guo Kaizhen** (1892–1978) Chinese scholar and writer. In youth he abandoned medical studies to devote himself to foreign literature, producing a popular translation of JOHANN W. VON GOETHE's *Sorrows of Young Werther* (1922). He wrote prolifically in every genre, including poetry, fiction, plays, nine autobiographical volumes, translations of Western works, and historical and philosophical treatises, including a monumental study of ancient inscriptions. Initially a liberal democrat, he became a Marxist in the 1920s, and his work was banned by the Guomindang. Following the 1949 revolution, he was named to the highest official literary positions, and later to the presidency of the Chinese Academy of Sciences.

Guo Xiang *or* **Kuo Hsiang** \'gwò-'shyäŋ\ (died AD 312) Chinese Neo-Taoist philosopher. He was a high government official who adapted and completed an unfinished commentary on the *Zhuangzi* (writings of ZHUANGZI). Interpreting TAO ("the way") as nothingness, he argued that it cannot produce being and cannot be a first cause. He concluded that there is no agent of causality in the universe: all things spontaneously produce themselves, and everything has its own nature. Happiness comes from following that distinctive nature, and dissatisfaction and regret come from failing to follow it. He also interpreted Taoist "nonaction" to mean spontaneous action rather than sitting still, a deviation from original Taoism that agreed with Zhuangzi's thought.

Guomindang \'gwō-'min-'däŋ\ See NATIONALIST PARTY

guppy Colorful, freshwater, live-bearing topminnows (*Lebistes reticulatus* and *Poecilia reticulata;* see KILLIFISH) popular as pets in home aquariums. Guppies are hardy, energetic, easily kept, and prolific. The male, smaller and much more brightly colored than the female, grows to about 1.5 in. (4 cm). Guppies have been bred in various ornate strains characterized by color or pattern and by shape and size of the tail and dorsal fins.

(Top) Male and (bottom) female guppies (*Lebistes reticulatus*).
JANE BURTON—BRUCE COLEMAN LTD.

Gupta dynasty \'gu̇p-tə\ (4th–6th century) Rulers of an empire in northern and parts of central and western India. The dynasty was founded by Candra Gupta I (r.320–c. 330). The Gupta era was once regarded as India's Classical period, but new archaeological evidence gives the MAURYAN EMPIRE that designation. Nevertheless, the Gupta period is noted for the flourishing of Sanskrit literature (see KALIDASA), its sophisticated metal coins, its advanced mathematics (at that time more advanced than anywhere else), which made use of decimal notation and zero, and its astronomical advances.

Gur languages \'gu̇r\ *or* **Voltaic languages** \väl-'tā-ik\ Branch of the huge NIGER-CONGO family of languages. Gur comprises more than 70 languages and language complexes spoken mainly in Burkina Faso, northern Ivory Coast, northern Ghana, and northern Togo. Mooré (Moré) in Burkina Faso has the largest number of speakers, more than 4 million (see MOSSI). Formerly considered a Gur language, Dogon, spoken by about 350,000 people in Mali (see DOGON), is of uncertain affiliation within Niger-Congo.

Gurdjieff \gər-'jēf\, **George (Ivanovitch)** *orig.* **George S. Georgiades** (1872?–1949) Armenian mystic and philosopher. He apparently traveled in the Middle East, Africa, and Central Asia as a young man. He taught in Moscow and St. Petersburg, and in 1919 he founded the Institute for the Harmonious Development of Man at Tiflis (now Tbilisi), Georgia. In 1922 he reestablished the institute at Fontainebleau, France, gathering a group of followers who lived communally, engaging in philosophical dialogue, ritual exercises, and dance. His basic assertion was that ordinary living was akin to sleep and that through spiritual discipline it was possible to achieve heightened levels of vitality and awareness. The Fontainebleau center closed in 1933, but Gurdjieff continued to teach in Paris until his death.

gurdwara \gu̇r-'dwä-rä\ Sikh place of worship. Each gurdwara houses a copy of the ADI GRANTH and serves as a meeting place for worship, including recitation, singing, and explication of scripture. A community kitchen and often a school are attached to the building. In private homes a room set aside for devotion is also called a gurdwara. Pilgrimages are often made to the gurdwaras associated with the Sikh GURUS' lives, notably the GOLDEN TEMPLE.

Gurjara-Pratihara dynasty \gu̇r-'jä-rə-prə-tē-'hä-rə\ Either of two dynasties of medieval Hindu India. The Pratiharas were the most important dynasty of medieval northern India. The line of Haricandra ruled in Mandor, Marwar (present-day Jodhpur, Rajasthan), in the 6th–9th century, generally with feudatory status. The line of Nagabhata ruled first at Ujjain and later at Kannauj in the 8th–11th century. This line is generally considered the more important one; at its peak of prosperity and power (c. 836–910), it rivaled the GUPTA DYNASTY in the extent of its territory. The last important Pratihara king was driven from Kannauj by MAHMUD OF GHAZNA (1018). Other Gurjara lines existed, but they did not take the surname Pratihara.

Guru Title of the first 10 leaders of SIKHISM. The first was NANAK, who before his death (1539) began the tradition that allowed the Guru to name his successor. He was followed by Angad (1539–1552), AMAR DAS, Ramdas (1574–1581), ARJAN, HARGOBIND, HARI RAI, Hari Krishen (1661–1664), Tegh Bahadur (1664–1675), and GOBIND SINGH. In time the Guru became as much a military as a spiritual leader. Gobind Singh discontinued the office in 1708 and vested its authority in the Sikh sacred scripture, the ADI GRANTH. See also GURU.

guru In HINDUISM, a personal spiritual teacher. In ancient India, knowledge of the VEDAS was transmitted through oral teaching from guru to pupil. The rise of the BHAKTI movement further increased the importance of gurus, who were often looked on as living embodiments of spiritual truth and were identified with the deity. They prescribed spiritual disciplines to their devotees, who followed their dictates in a tradition of willing service and obedience. Men or women may be gurus, though generally only men have established lineages. See also GURU.

Gustafson \,gəs-'taf-sən\, **Ralph (Barker)** (1909–1995) Canadian poet. A native of Quebec, Gustafson attended Oxford Univ.; he settled in New York after World War II, but later returned to Canada. His work shows a development from traditional form and manner to an elliptical style reflecting the influence of Anglo-Saxon verse and the metrical experiments of GERARD MANLEY HOPKINS. His later works, usually considered his better writings, include *Rivers Among Rocks* (1960), *Conflicts of Spring* (1981), and *Shadows in the Grass* (1991). He also published collections of short stories.

Gustav I Vasa *orig.* **Gustav Eriksson Vasa** (1496?–1560) King of Sweden (1523–60) and founder of the VASA DYNASTY. The son of a Swedish senator, Gustav joined the rebellion against CHRISTIAN II of Denmark, who controlled most of Sweden. He became leader of the rebels (1520) and secured crucial aid from the rich free city of Lübeck. This aid enabled Gustav to establish Sweden's independence, and in 1523 he was elected king. Gustav imposed heavy taxes to pay his debts to Lübeck and to strengthen royal authority and lands. He hoped to seize the Roman Catholic church's wealth, and he pushed Sweden toward becoming a Protestant (Lutheran) country. An autocratic ruler, he built a strong monarchy and an efficient administration.

Gustav II Adolf *Latin* **Gustavus Adolphus** (1594–1632) King of Sweden (1611–32) who made Sweden a major European power. The son of CHARLES IX, Gustav inherited his father's dynastic quarrels with SIGISMUND III VASA and until 1629 faced a legitimist invasion from Poland. He ended the war with Denmark in 1613, but Sweden was forced to pay a crushing war indemnity. He ended the war with Russia (1617) and annexed Ingria and Kexholm. Internal tensions were largely resolved by his trusted chancellor, AXEL GUSTAFSSON OXENSTIERNA. Gustav's sweeping domestic reforms included establishing an efficient central administration and improving education. Resuming the war with Sigismund in 1621, Gustav obtained much of Polish Livonia (Latvia and Estonia). He saw his Polish campaigns as part of the struggle of PROTESTANTISM against the COUNTER-REFORMATION. He entered the THIRTY YEARS' WAR in 1630 as a defensive maneuver, to secure the Swedish state and

E
F
G

church from danger. An outstanding military tactician, he led an army of unusual quality, and his position was strengthened by alliances with France, Brandenburg, and Saxony. Success in the Battle of Breitenfeld let him sweep through central Germany and claim large territorial cessions, particularly Pomerania (1631). At Lützen in 1632, the Swedes defeated ALBRECHT W. E. VON WALLENSTEIN's army, but Gustav was killed in battle.

Gustav III (1746–1792) King of Sweden (1771–92). The son of King Adolf Frederick (1710–1771), he succeeded to a weakened Swedish throne. Unable to mediate between the contending factions of the Riksdag (legislature), in 1772 he established a new constitution that increased the crown's power. He introduced numerous enlightened reforms, which antagonized the nobility. He waged an unpopular war on Russia (1788–90), and when a group of Swedish officers mutinied, he again augmented royal authority in a new constitution (1789). Gustav planned to form a league of European monarchs to oppose the French Revolution, but the Swedish nobility remained opposed to him and had him assassinated. A patron of the arts and a playwright, Gustav's reign was known as the Swedish enlightenment.

Gustav IV Adolf (1778–1837) King of Sweden (1800–1809). Son of the assassinated GUSTAV III, he came to the throne in 1792 under the regency of his uncle Charles, duke of Södermanland (later CHARLES XIII). In 1805 Gustav brought Sweden into the European coalition against NAPOLEON. When Russia joined with France in 1807, Gustav remained in the field, though he knew it would mean a Russian attack on Finland. Denmark-Norway also declared war on Sweden, causing the loss of additional territory. In 1809 Gustav was overthrown in a coup and his heirs were declared ineligible to succeed him. He and his family left Sweden for exile, settling in Switzerland.

Gustav V *orig.* **Oscar Gustaf Adolf** (1858–1950) King of Sweden (1907–50). The son of Oscar II (1829–1907), he entered the army and traveled widely before succeeding his father in 1907. In a period of expanding democracy within his country, Gustav proved a capable constitutional monarch. Though he favored the Allies in World Wars I and II, he was a firm proponent of Swedish neutrality.

Gut of Canso See Strait of CANSO

Gutenberg \'gü-tᵊn-ˌbərg\, **Johannes (Gensfleisch zur Laden zum)** (c. 1395–1468) German inventor of a method of PRINTING from movable type. Born to a patrician family in Mainz, he apparently worked at such crafts as goldsmithing and gem cutting in Mainz and Strasbourg, and was experimenting with printing by 1438. He obtained backing in 1450 from the financier Johann Fust (c. 1400–1466); Fust's impatience and other factors led to Gutenberg's loss of his establishment to Fust in 1455. Gutenberg's masterpiece, and the first book ever printed from movable type, is the "Forty-Two-Line" Bible, completed no later than 1455. A magnificent Psalter was published in 1457, after the loss of his press. The only other works still attributed to him are minor. His invention's unique elements included a mold, with which type could be cast precisely and in large quantities; a type-metal alloy; a new press, derived from those used in winemaking, papermaking, and bookbinding; and an oil-based printing ink. None of these features existed in Chinese or Korean printing, in the existing European technique of stamping letters on various surfaces, or in woodblock printing. Gutenberg's invention, seminal to the course of Western civilization, remained the source of the basic elements of typesetting for 500 years.

Guthrie, (William) Tyrone *later* **Sir Tyrone** (1900–1971) British theater director and producer. After his first London production in 1931, he became director of the Shakespeare Repertory Company (1933–45), which performed at the OLD VIC and Sadler's Wells theaters. Noted for his original approach to Shakespeare, he also directed such operas as *Peter Grimes* (1946) and *Carmen* (1949) and his own play, *Top of the Ladder* (1950). He helped found and direct the STRATFORD FESTIVAL in Canada (1953–57), strongly influencing the development of Canadian theater. He directed the Minneapolis (later Tyrone Guthrie) Theatre (1961–63).

Guthrie, Woody *orig.* **Woodrow Wilson** (1912–1967) U.S. singer and songwriter, one of the legendary figures of American FOLK MUSIC. Born in Okemah, Okla., Guthrie left home at 15 to travel the country by freight train. With his guitar and harmonica he sang in the hobo and migrant camps of the Great Depression, later becoming a musical spokesman for labor and populist sentiment. He wrote over 1,000 songs, including "So Long (It's Been Good to Know Yuh)," "Hard Traveling," and "Union Maid." In New York he joined P. SEEGER and others in the Almanac Singers, with whom he continued to perform for farmer and worker groups after serving in World War II. His "This Land Is Your Land" became an unofficial national anthem. His autobiography, *Bound for Glory* (1943), was filmed in 1976. His son Arlo (born 1947) also achieved success as a songwriter and singer.

Guwahati See GAUHATI

Guy-Blaché, Alice (1873–1968) Pioneer of French and American film industries. The first woman director, she is also generally acknowledged to be the first director to film a narrative story. She directed her first film, *La Fée aux choux* ("The Cabbage Fairy"), in 1896 to demonstrate the entertainment possibilities of the motion-picture camera manufactured by her employer, Léon Gaumont. She became the Gaumont film company's head of production, directing nearly all early Gaumont films. About 1901 Guy began to work on longer, more elaborate projects, notably *Esmeralda* (1905), based on VICTOR HUGO's *The Hunchback of Notre Dame*, and *La Vie du Christ* (1906; "The Life of Christ"). From 1906 to 1907 she directed about 100 films, using experimental sound technology. She married cameraman Herbert Blaché in 1907 and followed him to the United States, where in 1910 she founded the successful Solax Company. As president of Solax, she directed about 45 films and supervised nearly 300 other productions. Only a handful of the hundreds of films she made survive.

Guyana \gī-'ä-nə\ *officially* **Co-operative Republic of Guyana** *formerly (until 1966)* **British Guiana** Republic, northeastern South America. Area: 83,044 sq mi (215,083 sq km). Population (1997 est.): 773,000. Capital: GEORGETOWN. The people are about half East Indian, with a large black (Afro-Guyanese) minority. Language: English (official). Religion: Christianity, Hinduism. Currency: Guyana dollar. It has a narrow Atlantic coastal plain that extends up to 10 mi (16 km) inland and includes reclaimed land protected by sea walls and canals. The tropical forest zone begins some 40 mi (64 km) inland and covers more than 80% of the country. The Pacaraima Mountains in the west provide headwaters for the ESSEQUIBO RIVER. It has a developing market economy with both public and private ownership. Major exports are sugar, rice, bauxite and aluminum. It is a multiparty republic with one legislative house; its head of state and government is the president. It was colonized by the Dutch in the 17th century; during the NAPOLEONIC WARS the British occupied the territory and afterward purchased the

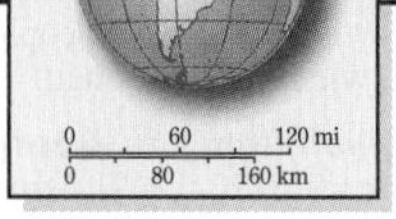

colonies of Demerara, Berbice, and Essequibo, united in 1831 as British Guiana. The slave trade was abolished in 1807, but emancipation of the 100,000 slaves in the colonies was not complete until 1838. From the 1840s, East Indian and Chinese indentured servants were brought to work the plantations; by 1917 almost 240,000 East Indians had migrated to British Guiana. It was made a crown colony in 1928 and granted home rule in 1953. Political parties began to emerge, developing on racial lines as the People's Progressive Party (largely East Indian) and the People's National Congress (largely black). The PNC formed a coalition government and led the country into independence as Guyana in 1966. In 1970 Guyana became a republic within the COMMONWEALTH; in 1980 it adopted a new constitution. Venezuela has long claimed land west of the Essequibo River, and the U.N. has continued to arbitrate the issue.

Guyenne See GUIENNE

Guzmán (Fernández) \güs-ˈmän\, **(Silvestre) Antonio** (1911–1982) President of the Dominican Republic (1978–82). Son of a textile merchant, he managed textile stores before being elected president as a left-of-center candidate, despite attempts by followers of the incumbent, JOAQUIN BALAGUER, to halt the vote count. Responding to the collapse of world sugar prices, he launched an aggressive agricultural policy that quickly enabled the country to achieve self-sufficiency in rice and beans. Though he inherited a turbulent political and economic situation, he left behind a stable economy and democratic institutions guaranteeing civil liberties. His death was an apparent suicide.

Gwalior \ˈgwä-lē-ˌȯr\ City (pop., 1991: 691,000), MADHYA PRADESH state, northern central India. The city, now an important commercial and industrial center, is built around a walled fortress situated on a cliff 300 ft (90 m) above the plain. First known from c. AD 525, it was under Hindu rule until 1232 and then changed hands several times between Muslims and Hindus until 1751; thereafter it remained a Maratha stronghold, though it was taken by the British several times. The fortress contains outstanding examples of Hindu architecture, including reservoirs, palaces, temples, and a mosque. Just below the fort's walls are 15th-century rock-cut Jain statues that are nearly 60 ft (18 m) high.

Gwandu \ˈgwän-dü\ *formerly* **Gando** \ˈgän-dō\ Traditional emirate, northwestern Nigeria. Originally settled by the Kebbawa, the area was part of the the Kebbi kingdom in the 16th century. The emirate's town of Gwandu became important during the FULANI jihad (1804–12), and from 1815 it was one of the two capitals of the Fulani empire until it came under British control in 1903. The Gando emirate was reduced in size by British cessions to FRENCH WEST AFRICA in 1907. Its emir, however, remains an important Muslim traditional leader in Nigeria. The town of Gwandu is a local agricultural market.

Gwent Historical region, southeastern Wales. Its heart is the plain of Gwent, and it includes a coastal plain along the SEVERN RIVER estuary. Gwent was and still is the gateway between England and southern Wales. The Romans built a military headquarters and major fortress there, and the Normans erected castles. Now a Welsh administrative county, with its seat at CWMBRÂN, Gwent's economy relies on both agriculture and industry.

Gwyn, Nell *orig.* **Eleanor** (1650–1687) British actress. She was selling oranges at the DRURY LANE THEATRE when she became the mistress of its leading actor, Charles Hart, who trained her for the stage. She became the leading comedienne of the King's Company (1666–69) and as "pretty, witty Nell" was in demand as a speaker of impudent prologues and epilogues. She became the mistress of CHARLES II (1669–85) and was popular with the public, who found her high spirits and frank recklessness welcome antidotes to Puritanism.

Gwynedd *or* **Gwyneth** \ˈgwi-ˌneth\ Historical region, northwestern Wales. The ancient region of Gwynedd comprised most of northern Wales. The Normans built castles at Caernarvon and Conwy but did not penetrate inland. It thus remained a stronghold of Welsh culture, with a high proportion of Welsh-speaking people. Made a Welsh county in 1974 with its seat at CAERNARVON, it includes SNOWDONIA NATIONAL PARK (1951), which covers about half its total area. Tourism is economically important.

gymnasium In Germany, a state-maintained secondary school that prepares pupils for higher academic education. This type of nine-year school originated in Strasbourg in 1537. Though the usual graduation age is 19 or 20, pupils may terminate their studies at the age of 16 and enter a vocational school. Secondary or postprimary education is also provided by middle schools *(Mittelschulen)*, teachers colleges, and commercial schools.

gymnastics Competitive sport in which individuals perform optional and prescribed acrobatic exercises, mostly on special apparatus, in order to demonstrate strength, balance, and body control. Part of the ancient Olympic Games, gymnastics in its modern form was virtually reinvented in the modern era by the German Friedrich Jahn (1778–1852). The sport became part of the revived Olympics in 1896; women's gymnastics was instituted in 1936. Men's events include the HORIZONTAL BAR, PARALLEL BARS, SIDE HORSE (pommel horse), VAULTING, RINGS, and FLOOR EXERCISES. Women's events include the balance beam, UNEVEN PARALLEL BARS, vaulting, floor exercises, and RHYTHMIC SPORTIVE GYMNASTICS.

gymnosperm \ˈjim-nə-ˌspərm\ Any woody plant that reproduces by means of a seed (or ovule) in direct contact with the environment, as opposed to an angiosperm, or FLOWERING PLANT, whose seeds are enclosed by mature ovaries, or fruits. The four surviving gymnosperm divisions are Coniferophyta (CONIFERS, the most widespread), Cycadophyta (CYCADS), Ginkgophyta (GINKGOS), and Gnetophyta. More than half are trees; most of the rest are shrubs. Gymnosperms occur on all continents except Antarctica, and especially in the temperate latitudes. Those widely found in the Northern Hemisphere are JUNIPERS, FIRS, LARCHES, SPRUCES, and PINES; in the Southern Hemisphere, podocarps *(Podocarpus)*. The wood of gymnosperms is often called SOFTWOOD to differentiate it from the HARDWOOD of angiosperms. Many timber and pulp trees are also planted as ornamentals. Gymnosperms also are a minor source of food; of essential oils used in soaps, air fresheners, disinfectants, pharmaceuticals, cosmetics, and perfumes; of tannin, used for curing leather; and of TURPENTINES. Gymnosperms were a major component in the vegetation that was compressed over millions of years into COAL. Most are EVERGREEN. They produce male and female reproductive cells in separate male and female strobili (see CONE).

gynecology See OBSTETRICS AND GYNECOLOGY

gynecomastia \ˌgī-nə-kō-ˈmas-tē-ə\ Breast enlargement in a male. It usually involves only the nipple and nearby tissue of one breast. More rarely, the whole breast grows to a size normal in a female. True gynecomastia is related to an increase in ESTROGENS. Testicular or pituitary-gland TUMORS commonly cause gynecomastia. Similar conditions (pseudogynecomastia) are caused by excessive body fat, inflammatory disorders, granular lesions, or growth of tumors. Treatment involves hormone therapy, correction of the estrogen disorder, or tumor removal.

Gypsies *or* **Roma** People originating in northern India but now living worldwide, principally in Europe. Most speak ROMANY in addition to the local language. It is thought that Gypsy groups left India in successive migrations, reaching Western Europe by the 15th century. In the 20th century they spread to North and South America and Australia. Because of their often nomadic and marginalized lives, population figures are largely guesswork; estimates in the early 21st century range from 2 to 3 million. How many Gypsies remain nomadic is unclear, but those that migrate do so at least seasonally along patterned routes that ignore national boundaries. They have often been persecuted and harassed; the Nazis killed about 400,000 Gypsies in extermination camps. They pursue occupations compatible with a nomadic life. In the past they were often livestock traders, tinkers, fortune-tellers, and entertainers; today they are often car mechanics, auto-body repairmen, and workers in traveling circuses and amusement parks. Confederations of 10–100 families elect chieftains for life, but their title is not heritable. Women are organized as a group within the confederation and represented by a senior woman. Modern Gypsy culture faces erosion from urban influences; integrated housing, economic independence, and intermarriage with non-Gypsies have weakened Gypsy law.

gypsum \ˈjip-səm\ Common SULFATE mineral, hydrated calcium sulfate ($CaSO_4{\cdot}2H_2O$), of great commercial importance. Deposits occur in many countries, but the U.S., Canada, France, Italy, and Britain are among the leading producers. Crude gypsum is used as a fluxing agent, soil conditioner, filler in paper and textiles, and retarder in portland cement. About three-fourths of the total production is calcined for use as plaster of paris and as building materials in plaster, board products, and tiles and blocks.

E F G

gypsy moth Species *(Lymantria dispar)* of TUSSOCK MOTH, a serious pest of trees. The European strain was introduced into eastern North America c. 1869. The heavy-bodied, weak-flying female is white with black zigzag markings and a wingspan of 1.5–2 in. (38–50 mm). The smaller, darker male is a stronger flier. The voracious larvae can completely defoliate deciduous trees within weeks. The larger Asian gypsy moth (wingspan of about 3.5 in., or 90 mm) is even more threatening because the female is a stronger flier, enabling it to spread quickly, and the larvae eat the leaves of both conifers and deciduous trees. It was introduced into northwestern North America in 1991. Sprayed insecticides remain the most effective means of control.

Gypsy Rose Lee See Gypsy Rose LEE

gyrfalcon \ˈjər-ˌfal-kən\ Arctic BIRD OF PREY *(Falco rusticolus),* the largest FALCON. It may reach 2 ft (60 cm) in length. It breeds only in the North Pole region (and in some Central Asian highlands) but is sometimes seen at lower latitudes when food is scarce. It varies from pure white with black speckling to dark gray with barring. Its legs are fully feathered. It hunts near the ground for hares, rodents, and birds of the tundra and seacoast. In traditional FALCONRY, the gyrfalcon was the bird of kings.

Gyrfalcon (*Falco rusticolus*) with prey.
SHELLY GROSSMAN–WOODFIN CAMP

gyroscope \ˈjī-rə-ˌskōp\ Device consisting of a rapidly spinning wheel set in a framework that permits it to tilt freely in any direction, or to rotate about any axis. The MOMENTUM of such a wheel causes it to retain its attitude when the framework is tilted. Because of this ability, gyroscopes are used in compasses, in automatic pilots on ships and aircraft, in the steering mechanisms of torpedoes, in antiroll equipment on large ships, and in inertial guidance systems.

E
F
G

H-R diagram See Hertzsprung-Russell diagram

Ha-erh-pin See Harbin

Ha Jin (born 1956) Chinese-U.S. writer. Born in China, Ha Jin joined the army at age 14. He received a doctorate at Brandeis University in the U.S., where he remained. His book of stories *Under the Red Flag* (1997) concerns the Cultural Revolution. His novel *Waiting* (1999), about Chinese society, won the National Book Award, as well as the 2000 PEN/Faulkner Award for fiction.

Haakon IV Haakonsson \'hä-kȯn...'hä-kȯns-ˌsȯn\ *known as* **Haakon the Old** (1204–1263) King of Norway (1217–63). After he became king his mother answered doubts about his paternity by passing through an ordeal of hot irons. He established Norwegian sovereignty over Iceland and Greenland (1261–62) and died defending the Hebrides and the Isle of Man from the Scots. He was a noted patron of the arts, and his reign began the "golden age" in medieval Norwegian history.

Haakon VII \'hȯ-kən\ *orig.* **Christian Frederik Carl Georg Valdemar Axel** (1872–1957) King of Norway (1905–57). Born Prince Carl of Denmark, he was offered the Norwegian crown after the restoration of the country's independence in 1905. He accepted only after receiving approval by a plebiscite, and he took the Old Norse name of Haakon. In World War II he fled to England after the German invasion of Norway (1940), and his refusal to abdicate inspired the Norwegians to resist the German occupation.

Haarlem City (pop., 2001 est.: 148,377), western Netherlands. It lies along the Spaarne River, west of Amsterdam. By the 12th century it had become a fortified town and the residence of the counts of Holland. It was chartered in 1245, and incorporated in the United Netherlands in 1577. Its prosperity peaked in the 17th century, when it was a refuge for Huguenots and also an artistic center. An industrial city now, it is also the center for a tulip-growing region.

Haas \'häs\, **Mary Rosamond** (1910–1996) U.S. linguist. Born in Richmond, Ind., she studied with Edward Sapir at Yale University. Her dissertation was on Tunica, a moribund American Indian language, and she continued her fieldwork on and studies of American Indian languages, especially of the southeastern U.S., including Natchez and Muskogean languages, for the rest of her life. She directed the Survey of California Indian Languages while on the UC Berkeley faculty (1945–77).

Habakkuk \hə-'bak-ək, 'hab-ə-ˌku̇k\ (6th or 7th cent. BC) One of the 12 Minor Prophets of the Old Testament, traditional author of the Book of Habakkuk. (His prophecy is part of a larger book, The Twelve, in the Jewish canon.) He was perhaps a Temple musician as well as a prophet. He denounced the sins of Judah but also predicted the final triumph of righteousness.

habeas corpus \'hā-bē-əs-'kȯr-pəs\ (Latin: "you should have the body") In common law, any of several writs issued to bring a party before a court. The most important such writ *(habeas corpus ad subjiciendum)* is used to correct violations of personal liberty by directing judicial inquiry into the legality of a detention. Common grounds for relief include a conviction based on illegally obtained evidence, a denial of effective assistance of counsel, or a conviction by a jury that was improperly selected or impaneled. The writ may be used in civil matters to challenge a person's custody of a child or the institutionalization of a person declared incompetent.

Haber \'hä-bər\, **Fritz** (1868–1934) German physical chemist. After early research in electrochemistry and thermodynamics, he developed, with his brother-in-law Carl Bosch (1874–1940), the Haber–Bosch process for making ammonia. Intensely patriotic, he directed Germany's World War I chemical-warfare efforts, under which poison gas was introduced. Haber was awarded the 1918 Nobel Prize for Chemistry. In 1933 the Nazi Party's anti-Semitic policies led him to resign as head (since 1911) of the Kaiser Wilhelm Institute.

Haber-Bosch process \'hä-bər-'bȯsh\ *or* **Haber ammonia process** *or* **synthetic ammonia process** First economically feasible method of directly synthesizing ammonia from hydrogen gas and atmospheric nitrogen. It was developed c. 1909 by Fritz Haber and Carl Bosch (1874–1940), prompted by rapidly increasing demand for nitrogen fertilizer. It was the first industrial process to use high pressure (200–400 atmospheres) for a chemical reaction. A catalyst (usually iron) lets it take place at a moderate temperature (750–1,200°F, or 400–650°C), and immediate removal of ammonia as it is formed favors formation of more of it. Still the cheapest means of industrial nitrogen fixation, it is a basic process of the chemical industry.

Habermas \'hä-bər-ˌmäs\, **Jürgen** (born 1929) German philosopher associated with the Frankfurt school. He has taught primarily at the University of Frankfurt, and also formerly directed the Max Planck Institute in Starnberg (1971–80). In *Theory of Communicative Action* (1981), he argues that while instrumental reason (which starts from the assumption of a subject confronting an independent object that the subject seeks to understand in order to control) has dominated modern social thought, only communicative reason (which postulates a community of subjects engaged in communication for the purpose of universal emancipation) holds out the possibility of forging a truly democratic society.

Habima *or* **Habimah** \hə-'bē-mə\ (Hebrew: "Stage") Hebrew theater company. Organized in Poland in 1912, it was reestablished in 1917 in Moscow, where it was encouraged by Konstantin Stanislavsky. Habima's production of *The Dybbuk* (1922) established it as a company of high artistic merit, and it became affiliated with the Moscow Art Theatre. After producing *The Golem* (1925), the group toured Europe and the U.S. In 1931 most of the group moved to Tel Aviv. In 1958 it became the National Theatre of Israel.

habit In psychology, any regularly repeated behavior that requires little or no thought and is learned rather than innate. Some habits (e.g., tying a shoelace) may conserve higher mental processes for more demanding tasks, but others promote behavioral inflexibility or are unhealthy. Five methods are commonly used to break unwanted habits: replacing the old response with a new one, repeating the behavior until it becomes unpleasant, separating the individual from the stimulus that prompts the response, habituation, and punishment.

habitat Place where an organism or a community of organisms lives, including all living and nonliving factors or conditions of the surrounding environment. A host organism inhabited by parasites is as much a habitat as a place on land such as a grove of trees or an aquatic locality such as a small pond. "Microhabitat" refers to the conditions and organisms in the immediate vicinity of a plant or animal.

habituation Reduction of an animal's behavioral response to a stimulus, as a result of a lack of reinforcement during continual exposure to the stimulus. Habituation is usually considered a form of learning in which behaviors not needed are eliminated. It may be separated from most other forms of decreased response on the basis of permanence; the habituated animal either does not resume its earlier reaction to the stimulus after a period of no stimulus, or, if the normal action is resumed on reexposure to the stimulus, it wanes more quickly than before. Vital responses (e.g., flight from a predator) cannot be truly habituated.

Habsburg dynasty \'haps-ˌbərg\ *or* **Hapsburg dynasty** Royal German family, one of the chief dynasties of Europe from the 15th to the 20th century. As dukes, archdukes, and emperors, the Habsburgs ruled Austria from 1282 until 1918. They also controlled Hungary and Bohemia (1526–1918) and ruled Spain and the Spanish Empire for almost two centuries (1504–6, 1516–1700). One of the earliest Habsburgs to rise to great power was Rudolf I, who became German king in 1273. Frederick IV, the Habsburg king of Germany, was crowned Holy Roman emperor as Frederick III in 1452, and Habsburgs continued to hold that title until 1806. Frederick's son Maximilian I acquired the Netherlands, Luxembourg, and Burgundy through marriage. The zenith of Habsburg power came in the 16th century under the emperor Charles V. See also Holy Roman Empire.

Hachiman \'hä-chē-ˌmän\ One of the most popular of Japan's Shinto deities. Referred to as the god of war, he is believed to be the deification of Ojin, the fifteenth emperor. He is the patron of the Minamoto clan and of warriors in general. His first shrine was built in 725, and today half the Shinto shrines are dedicated to him. In the 8th century Hachiman was accepted as a Buddhist divinity.

hacienda \ˌ(h)ä-sē-ˈen-də\ In Latin America, a large landed estate. The hacienda originated in the colonial period and survived into the 20th century. Laborers, ordinarily Indians, were theoretically free wage earners on haciendas, but in practice their employers, who controlled the local governments, were able to bind them to the land, primarily by keeping them in a state of perpetual indebtedness. By the 19th century, as much as half of Mexico's rural population was entangled in the peonage system. Many haciendas were broken up by the MEXICAN REVOLUTION. Haciendas are known as *estancias* in Argentina and *fazendas* in Brazil.

Hackman, Gene *orig.* **Eugene Alden** (born 1930) U.S. film actor. Born in San Bernardino, Cal., he won a leading role on Broadway in *Any Wednesday* (1964), which led to his film debut in *Lilith* (1964). Praised for his performances in *Bonnie and Clyde* (1967) and *I Never Sang for My Father* (1970), he attained star status in *The French Connection* (1971, Academy Award). Noted for his portrayals of ordinary men, he won further acclaim for *The Conversation* (1974), *Mississippi Burning* (1988), and *Unforgiven* (1992, Academy Award). Among his other films are *Superman* (1978) and its sequels (1980, 1987).

Hadar remains \ˈhä-där\ HOMINID fossils found since 1973 near the Awash River, about 185 mi (300 km) from Addis Ababa in Ethiopia. The remains, representing at least 30 hominid individuals, including LUCY and the so-called "First Family" of 13 AUSTRALOPITHECUS *afarensis* individuals who probably perished together, date from 3.4–2.9 million years ago. In the Middle Awash region just to the south, researchers have found some of the oldest known (c. 4 million years old) hominid fossils, and in the adjacent Gona area some of the oldest known (c. 2.6 million years old) stone tools have been identified.

haddock Valuable North American food fish (*Melanogrammus aeglefinus,* family Gadidae). A bottom-dweller that feeds on invertebrates and fishes, it resembles the COD, with its chin barbel (fleshy feeler) and two anal and three dorsal fins, but is distinguished by a dark (rather than light) lateral line and a distinctive dark spot on each shoulder. It is gray or brownish above, paler below. It grows to about 3 ft (90 cm) long and 25 lbs (11 kg).

Haddock (*Melanogrammus aeglefinus*).
PAINTING BY JEAN HELMER

Hades \ˈhā-ˌdēz\ Greek god of the underworld. He was also known as Pluto; his Roman equivalent was Dis. Hades was the son of the TITANS RHEA and CRONUS and the brother of ZEUS and POSEIDON. His queen was PERSEPHONE, the daughter of DEMETER, whom he kidnapped from earth and carried off to the underworld. Stern and pitiless, unmoved by prayer or sacrifice, he presided over the trial and punishment of the wicked after death. His name was also sometimes used to designate the dwelling place of the dead, and it later became a synonym for Hell.

Hadith \hȧ-ˈdēth\ In ISLAM, the oral traditions attributed to the Prophet MUHAMMAD, his family, and the COMPANIONS OF THE PROPHET. Hadith is revered by Muslims as a major source of religious law and moral guidance. It consists of two parts: the oral law itself and the ISNAD, or chain of authorities who passed it down to posterity. The various collections of Hadith provide the major source for studying the development of Islam in its first few centuries.

Hadrian \ˈhā-drē-ən\ *Latin* **Caesar Traianus Hadrianus Augustus** ***orig.*** **Publius Aelius Hadrianus** (AD 76–138) Roman emperor (117–38), TRAJAN's nephew and successor. After years of intrigue, he was adopted and named successor just before Trajan's death. He executed his senatorial opponents, abandoned Trajan's conquests in Armenia and Mesopotamia, and coped with unrest in Mauretania and Parthia. He traveled widely, and many of his accomplishments were related to his visits abroad. He began construction of HADRIAN'S WALL, and he visited and disciplined troops in Algeria and elsewhere. An admirer of Greek civilization, he completed the temple of Zeus in Athens and created a federation of Greek cities. He launched a building program at Delphi and was initiated into the ELEUSINIAN MYSTERIES. After his young companion Antinoüs drowned in the Nile (130), he grieved openly; he erected statues of the boy throughout the realm, and cults sprang up widely. He named ANTONINUS PIUS his successor, to be followed by MARCUS AURELIUS.

Hadrian, bust in the National Archaeological Museum, Naples.
ANDERSON—ALINARI FROM ART RESOURCE/EB INC.

Hadrianopolis, Battle of See Battle of ADRIANOPLE

Hadrian's Villa HADRIAN's country residence, built (c. AD 125–34) at Tivoli near Rome. A sumptuous imperial complex with parks and gardens on a grand scale, it included baths, libraries, sculpture gardens, theaters, alfresco dining areas, pavilions, and private suites. The buildings, which covered about 7 sq mi (18 sq km), were reproductions of celebrated structures the emperor had seen in his travels. The uneven terrain made necessary large flights of steps and terraces. Significant portions have survived to modern times.

Hadrian's Wall Continuous Roman defensive barrier, begun by HADRIAN in AD 122, that guarded the northwestern frontier of the province of Britain from barbarian (particularly Celtic) invaders. It extended 73 mi (118 km) from coast to coast, from Wallsend (Segedunum) to Bowness. It had towers, gates, and forts at regular intervals; a ditch fronted it and an earthwork (the *vallum*) ran behind it. Though briefly abandoned in favor of the ANTONINE WALL, it returned to use until c. 410. Portions remain visible today.

hadron \ˈha-ˌdrän\ Any of the SUBATOMIC PARTICLES that are built from QUARKS and thus interact via the STRONG FORCE. The hadrons fall into two groups: MESONS and BARYONS. Except for protons and neutrons, which are bound in nuclei, all hadrons have short lives and are produced in high-energy collision of subatomic particles. All hadrons are subject to GRAVITATION; charged hadrons are subject to ELECTROMAGNETIC FORCES. Some hadrons break up by way of the WEAK FORCE (as in radioactive decay); others decay via the strong and electromagnetic forces.

Haeckel \ˈhe-kəl\, **Ernst (Heinrich Philipp August)** (1834–1919) German zoologist and evolutionist. After taking a degree in medicine in 1857, he obtained a doctorate in zoology from the University of Jena, and from 1862 to 1909 he taught zoology at Jena. His work concentrated on diverse marine invertebrates. Influenced by CHARLES DARWIN, Haeckel saw evolution as the basis for an explanation of all nature and the rationale of a philosophical approach. He attempt-

Haeckel, c. 1870.
THE BETTMANN ARCHIVE

ed to create the first genealogical tree of the entire animal kingdom. He proposed that each species illustrates its evolutionary history in its embryological development ("Ontogeny recapitulates phylogeny"). Through his theories of the evolution of humans (some of them wrong), he brought attention to important biological questions. Through his numerous books, he was an influential popularizer of evolutionary theory.

haematite See HEMATITE

Haemophilus \hē-ˈmä-fə-ləs\ Genus of tiny rod-shaped BACTERIA. All are strict parasites occurring in the respiratory tracts of warm-blooded animals, including humans, and in certain cold-blooded animals. They are gram-negative (see GRAM STAIN), do not move, and require a growth factor found in blood. Some require oxygen, others do not. One species causes a sexually transmitted disease in humans known as chancroid, or soft CHANCRE. Another causes secondary infection in persons suffering from influenza.

Hafez \ˈk̲ō-fez\ *or* **Hafiz** \ˈk̲ō-fiz\ *orig.* **Mohammad Shams od-Din Hafez** (1325/26–1389/90) Persian poet. The recipient of a traditional religious education (Hafez designates someone who has learned the Quran by heart), he served as court poet to several rulers of Shiraz. He perfected the GHAZEL as a verse form of 6–15 couplets linked by unity of subject and symbolism rather than by a logical sequence of ideas. His poems are notable for their simple, often colloquial, musical language and his unaffected use of homely images and proverbial expressions. His most famous work is the *Divan.* He is regarded as one of the greatest Persian lyric poets.

Hafsid dynasty \ˈhaf-səd\ BERBER dynasty of the 13th–16th century founded by the ALMOHAD governor Abu Zakariyya Yahya in northern central Africa c. 1229. His son Mustansir (r.1249–77) enlarged the empire to its peak of power and prestige. It had trade relations with Italian, Spanish, and Provençal communities despite running pirate operations in the Mediterranean. It resisted periodic Marinid invasions (see MARINID DYNASTY). Dynastic struggles after 1452 weakened the Hafsids, allowing Arabs to take over. Spanish and Turkish forces later competed for the Hafsid territory, and the Turks incorporated its land into a province in 1574.

Hagana \hä-gä-ˈnä\ Zionist military organization (1920–48). It was organized to combat the attacks of Palestinian Arabs on Jewish settlements, and effectively defended them despite being outlawed by the British authorities and poorly armed. Through World War II its activities were moderate by contrast with more extreme Zionist militias, but it turned to terrorism after the war when the British refused to permit unlimited Jewish immigration to Palestine. In 1947 it clashed openly with British forces and with the forces of the Palestinian Arabs and their allies. With the creation of Israel in 1948, the Hagana became its national army.

Hagen, Walter (Charles) (1892–1969) U.S. golfer. Born in Rochester, N.Y., he won numerous important championships from the mid-1910s to the late 1920s and captained the U.S. Ryder Cup team 1927–37. A colorful, self-confident man, he insisted that professional golfers be treated as gentlemen (not always previously the case). Among his well-known remarks is the observation that, in life, one should take the time to "stop and smell the roses."

Walter Hagen, 1936.
UPI—EB INC.

hagfish Any of about 30 species of primitive jawless fishes in two families of the class Agnatha. The Myxinidae are found in every ocean; the Eptatretidae are found everywhere but the North Atlantic. Hagfishes are eel-like, scaleless, and soft-skinned and have paired thick barbels on the end of the snout. Species grow to 16–32 in. (40–80 cm) long. They have a cartilaginous skeleton. The mouth is a slitlike, sucking opening with horny teeth. Found in cold seawater, to depths of over 4,000 ft (1,200 m), they habitually lie buried in burrows on soft bottoms. They eat invertebrates and dead or crippled fishes, and may bore their way into the bodies of fish caught on lines or in nets and eat the fish from the inside. They secrete extraordinary amounts of slime when handled. See also LAMPREY.

Haggadah *or* **Haggada** \ˌhä-gä-ˈdä, hə-ˈgä-də\ In Judaism, the text that guides the performance of ritual acts and prayers at the SEDER dinner celebrating PASSOVER. The Haggadah retells the story of EXODUS, offering commentaries that provide a religious philosophy of Jewish history and supplying answers to the traditional questions asked by children at the beginning of the Seder. More broadly, the term Haggadah can refer to the part of rabbinical literature not concerned with the law (e.g., stories, parables, legends, history, and astronomy).

Haggai \ˈhag-ē-ˌī, ˈhag-ˌī\ (fl. 6th century BC) One of the 12 Minor Prophets of the OLD TESTAMENT, traditional author of the Book of Haggai. (His prophecy is part of a larger book, The Twelve, in the Jewish canon.) Born during the Babylonian Exile, he returned to Israel when it ended and helped mobilize the Jewish community to rebuild the Temple of JERUSALEM. His book consists of four prophecies delivered in 521 BC. He attributes the economic distress of the returned exiles to their delay in reconstructing the Temple and promises that the new house of God will be greater than the first.

Haggard, H(enry) Rider *later* **Sir Rider** (1856–1925) British novelist. After holding a series of official posts in South Africa (1875–81), he began writing stories set in Africa. Of his 34 colorful adventure novels, the best-known is *King Solomon's Mines* (1885); others include *She* (1887), *Allan Quatermain* (1887), *Cleopatra* (1889), and *Ayesha* (1905). Also a farmer, he wrote *A Farmer's Year* (1899) and *Rural England* (2 vols., 1902), and he was knighted in 1912 for his work on agricultural commissions.

Haggard, Merle (Ronald) (born 1937) U.S. COUNTRY-MUSIC singer and songwriter. Poverty marked Haggard's childhood, and in his teens he began a career of theft and burglary. After his release from San Quentin prison in 1960, he became a professional musician in his native Bakersfield, Cal. He was soon producing hit recordings regularly, including "Mama Tried," "The Bottle Let Me Down," "The Fightin' Side of Me," "Okie from Muskogee" (controversial for its apparent attack on hippies), and later hit duets with GEORGE JONES and W. NELSON.

Hagia Sophia \ˈhä-gē-ə-sō-ˈfē-ə, ˈhä-jē-ə-sō-ˈfē-ə\ (Greek: "Holy Wisdom") Church in Istanbul, later a mosque and now a museum. It is the masterpiece of BYZANTINE ARCHITECTURE. Designed under JUSTINIAN I by Anthemius of Tralles and Isidorus of Miletus, the original building was completed in less than six years (AD 532–37). It combined a longitudinal BASILICA and a centralized building in a wholly original manner, with a huge main dome (rebuilt 563) supported on PENDENTIVES and semidomes on either side. In plan it is almost square. There are three aisles separated by columns with galleries above and great marble piers rising up to support the dome. The walls above the galleries, as well as the base of the dome, are pierced by windows, whose light obscures the supports, giving the impression that the canopy floats on air.

hagiography \ˌha-gē-ˈä-grə-fē, ˌhā-jē-ˈä-grə-fē\ Literature describing the lives of the saints. Christian hagiography includes stories of saintly monks, bishops, princes, and virgins, with accounts of their martyrdom and of the miracles connected with their relics, tombs, icons, or statues. Written as early as the 2nd century and popular during the Middle Ages, hagiographies focus on lives of individual saints or on stories of a class of saints (e.g., martyrs).

Hagler, Marvin (born 1954) U.S. middleweight boxing champion. Born in Newark, N.J., "Marvelous Marvin" won the world title in 1980 and defended it 12 times between 1981 and 1986. He finally lost it in a controversial 12-round split decision to SUGAR RAY LEONARD in 1987. Of his 62 career wins, 52 were by knockout.

Hague \ˈhāg\, **The** *Dutch* **'s-Gravenhage** \ˌsk̲räv-ᵊn-ˈhä-k̲ə\ *or* **Den Haag** \den-ˈhäk̲\ City (pop., 1996 est.: 443,000), seat of government of the Netherlands. Located 4 mi (6 km) from the North Sea, it is the administrative capital of the nation and the home of the court and government, though AMSTERDAM, located 33 mi (53 km) NW, is the official capital. The counts of Holland built a castle there in 1248 that became their principal residence. The complex now forms the Binnenhof in the old quarter of the city, which became the seat of the Dutch government in

1585. The city grew rapidly in the 19th and 20th century. A center of government, international law, and corporate administration, most of its businesses are engaged in trade, banking, and insurance. The U.N. International Court of Justice is housed in the Peace Palace (1913). The city is filled with notable architecture, despite heavy damage during the German occupation in World War II.

Hague Conventions Series of international agreements signed at The Hague (1899, 1907). The first conference was requested by Russia to discuss rules to limit warfare and attempt arms limitations. Twenty-six countries attended and approved several proposed conventions, including prohibition of the use of asphyxiating gases (not renewed in 1907) and creation of a Permanent Court of Arbitration. The 1907 meeting, called by Theodore Roosevelt, was attended by 44 countries and also had arms limitation as a goal, which again went unmet. An agreement to reconvene in eight years confirmed the principle that international conferences were the best way to handle international problems. Though World War I prevented the next meeting from taking place, the conferences influenced creation of the League of Nations and the United Nations. See also Geneva Conventions.

Hahn, Otto (1879–1968) German physical chemist. He worked at the Kaiser Wilhelm Institute for Chemistry 1912–44, serving as director from 1928. With Lise Meitner he discovered several radioelements. In 1938, with Meitner and Fritz Strassmann (1902–1980), he found the first chemical evidence of nuclear-fission products, created when they bombarded uranium with neutrons. For his discovery of nuclear fission, Hahn was awarded a 1944 Nobel Prize. He became president of the Max Planck Society; a respected public figure, he spoke out strongly against further development of nuclear weapons. In 1966 he shared the Enrico Fermi Award with Meitner and Strassmann.

Hahnemann \'hä-nə-mən\, **(Christian Friedrich) Samuel** (1755–1843) German physician, founder of homeopathy. Struck by the similarity of the symptoms quinine produced in the healthy body to those of the disorders it cured, he theorized that "likes are cured by likes" and proposed his doctrine that substances used this way are most effective in small doses. His chief work, *Organon of Rational Medicine* (1810), expounds his system. His *Pure Pharmacology* (6 vols., 1811) detailed the symptoms produced by testing a large number of drugs on healthy subjects.

Hai River \'hī\ River, Hebei province, China. A short part of the Bai River, the name Hai properly belongs only to the stream from Tianjin that flows into the Bo Hai some 43 mi (70 km) away. It is, however, also used as the general name for the system of tributary streams that discharge into the sea through this channel. Because of the streams' heavy inflow, the Hai River often floods; in 1939 Tianjin was submerged for a month. The river is now the site of a comprehensive water-control project.

Haida \'hī-də\ Northwest Coast Indian people of the Queen Charlotte Islands, British Columbia, and southern Prince of Wales Island, Alaska. There were two major tribal divisions, or moieties, to one of which a child was assigned at birth based on maternal descent. Each moiety consisted of lineages that owned rights to land, had their own chiefs, waged war, held ceremonies such as potlatches, and functioned as economically independent units. Haida economy was based on fishing and hunting. The Haida continue to be known for their craftsmanship and their art, which includes totem poles. Today they number about 3,500.

Haidarabad See Hyderabad

Haifa \'hī-fə\ *ancient* **Sycaminum.** City (pop., 1997 est.: 255,000) and chief port, northwestern Israel. Located on the Bay of Haifa overlooking the Mediterranean Sea, it is first mentioned in the Talmud (c. 1st–4th century AD). Conquered in 1100 by the Crusaders, it was taken by Napoleon in 1799, and by Egyptian general Ibrahim Pasha in 1839. Occupied by British forces in 1918, it became part of mandated Palestine. It came under Israeli control in 1948, during the Arab–Israeli War. Situated on the northern slopes of Mount Carmel, with the exception of its port section on the bay, it is a tourist resort and a commercial center. Haifa is the world headquarters of the Baha'i movement.

Haig, Douglas *later* **Earl Haig** (1861–1928) British general in World War I. A career army officer, he was promoted to general in 1914 and led British forces in northern France. In 1915 he succeeded John French as commander in chief of the British Expeditionary Force. Advocating a strategy of attrition, he was criticized for the enormous British losses at the Battles of the Somme (1916) and Ypres (1917). He was promoted to field marshal in 1916. In 1918 he secured the appointment of Ferdinand Foch as commander of Allied forces; the two worked well together, and after helping stop the last German offensive Haig led the victorious Allied assault in August 1918.

haiku \'hī-,kü\ Unrhymed Japanese poetic form consisting of 17 syllables arranged in three lines containing five, seven, and five syllables, respectively. Haiku expresses much and suggests more in the fewest possible words. The form gained distinction in the 17th century, when Basho elevated it to a highly refined art. It remains Japan's most popular poetic form. The Imagist poets (1912–30) and others have imitated the form in English and other languages.

hail Precipitation of balls or pieces of ice with a diameter of 0.2–4 in. (5 mm–10 cm). Small hail (also called sleet, or ice pellets) has a diameter of less than 0.2 in. Hail can be extremely destructive to buildings and crops; if it is large enough, it may be dangerous to animals. Hailstones 6 in. (15 cm) in diameter have fallen during storms in the U.S. Midwest. Hailstorms are most common in the middle latitudes and usually last around 15 minutes. They ordinarily occur in middle to late afternoon and may accompany thunderstorms.

Hail Mary *Latin* **Ave Maria** Principal Roman Catholic prayer addressed to the Virgin Mary. It begins with the greetings spoken to Mary by the Archangel Gabriel and by her cousin Elizabeth in the Gospel of Luke: "Hail Mary, full of grace, the Lord is with thee. Blessed art thou among women and blessed is the fruit of thy womb, Jesus." A closing petition, "Holy Mary, Mother of God, pray for us sinners, now and at the hour of our death," came into general use by the end of the 14th century. Churchgoers who attend confession are often asked to repeat the prayer as penance for sins.

Haile Mariam, Mengistu See Mengistu Haile Mariam

Haile Selassie \'hī-lē-sə-'las-ē\ *orig.* **Tafari Makonnen** (1892–1975) Emperor of Ethiopia (1930–74) and messiah of the Rastafarians. Tafari was a son of Ras Makonnen, a chief adviser to Emperor Menilek II. After Menilek's daughter, Zauditu, became empress (1917), Ras (Prince) Tafari, who had married Menilek's great-granddaughter, was named regent and heir apparent to the throne. When Zauditu died (1930), Tafari took the name of Haile Selassie ("Might of the Trinity") to mark his imperial status. As emperor he sought to modernize his country and steer it into the mainstream of African politics. He brought Ethiopia into the League of Nations and the U.N. and made Addis Ababa the center for the Organization of African Unity (OAU). Through most of his reign he remained popular among the majority Christian population. He was deposed in 1974 in a military coup by Mengistu Haile Mariam and kept under house arrest. He was apparently killed by his captors.

Haile Selassie, 1967.
AP/WIDE WORLD PHOTOS

Hainan *or* **Hai-nan** \'hī-'nän\ Province (pop., 1996 est.: 7,240,000) and island of China. The province also includes the Paracel and Spratly islands. It is located in the China Sea, separated from Guangdong by a narrow strait. The southernmost province of China and the smallest, it was for centuries part of Guangdong province; it became a separate province in 1988. Its capital is Haikou. Under Chinese rule since the 2nd century BC, it was not closely controlled until the Tang dynasty (AD 618–907). Chinese began settling the island in 12–13th century, gradually forcing the indigenous peoples into the interior. Occupied by the Japanese 1939–45, it came under Communist control in 1950. Although the government has tried to stimulate economic development there, it is one of China's less prosperous regions.

Hainaut \ā-'nō\ *Flemish* **Henegouwen** \'hā-nə-ˌka̱u̇-ə\ Medieval county, now a province in southwestern Belgium. The area was once part of the county of Hainaut, which was larger than the modern province, and was bounded by FLANDERS on the north. United with Flanders several times in the 11th–13th century, it was later ruled by many, including the duke of BURGUNDY. Gradually annexed to France in the 17th–18th century, part of the county stayed with France (now the Nord department), and the rest passed to the Netherlands in 1814 and to Belgium in 1831. Most of the province is a well-farmed region; animals, including Belgian draft horses, are also raised.

Haiphong \'hī-'fȯŋ\ Seaport city (pop., 1992 est.: 783,000), northern Vietnam. Lying on the RED RIVER delta, off the Gulf of TONKIN, it is the nation's third largest city and serves as the port of the capital, HANOI, 60 mi (97 km) to the west. Established in 1874, it developed commercially as a port and as the terminus of a railway. It became a leading industrial center, and after 1954 many new plants were built there with aid given by Soviet-bloc countries and by China. It sustained heavy damage from U.S. bombing during the VIETNAM WAR.

hair Threadlike outgrowths of the SKIN. Babies shed a layer of downy, slender hairs (lanugo) before or just after birth. The fine, short, unpigmented hairs (vellus) then grow. Starting at puberty, terminal hair, longer, coarser, and more pigmented, develops in the armpits, crotch, sometimes on parts of the trunk and limbs, and, in males, on the face. Scalp hair, eyebrows, and eyelashes are different types. The number of scalp hairs, which grow about 0.5 in. (13 mm) per month, averages 100,000–150,000. The hair shaft (above the skin) is dead tissue, composed of KERATIN. Only a few growing cells at the base of the root are alive. Hair is formed by cell division at the base of the follicle (a tiny pocket in the skin), part of a cycle of growing, resting, and falling out. Vellus lasts about four months, scalp hairs three to five years.

hairstreak Any BUTTERFLY in the subfamily Theclinae (family Lycaenidae), sometimes known as gossamer-winged butterflies. Adults are delicate and have a 0.75–1.5-in. (18–38-mm) wingspan. Rapid fliers, hairstreaks usually have iridescent wings and are typically brown or gray with delicate stripes on the bottoms of the wings. Larvae are short, broad, and sluglike. Some species eat plants, many are cannibals, and still others secrete honeydew, a sweet by-product of digestion that attracts ANTS. Found in open areas on every continent, hairstreaks are most abundant in the New World tropics.

hairworm See HORSEHAIR WORM

Haiti \'hā-tē\ *officially* **Republic of Haiti** Country, WEST INDIES. It occupies the western third of the island of HISPANIOLA, with the Dominican Republic to the east. Area: 10,695 sq mi (27,700 sq km). Population (2000 est.): 6,868,000. Capital: PORT-AU-PRINCE. Almost the entire population is black or mulatto. Language: Haitian Creole and French (both official). Religion: Roman Catholicism; voodoo (voudou). Currency: gourde. Most of its land is mountainous, with about two-fifths above 1,600 ft (490 m). The mountain ranges alternate with fertile but overpopulated lowlands. Its climate is tropical, modified by the mountains, and subject to periodic droughts and hurricanes. Its longest river is the ARTIBONITE. The poorest country in the Americas, it has a developing market economy based in large part on agriculture and light industries; coffee is the main cash crop. It is a multiparty republic with two legislative houses; the chief of state is the president, and the head of government is the prime minister. For its early history, see HISPANIOLA. Haiti gained its independence when the former slaves of the island, initially led by TOUSSAINT-LOUVERTURE, and later by JEAN-JACQUES DESSALINES, rebelled against French rule in 1791–1804. The new republic encompassed the entire island of Hispaniola, but the eastern portion was restored to Spain in 1809. It was reunited under Haitian Pres. Jean-Pierre Boyer (1818–43); after his overthrow the eastern portion revolted and formed the Dominican Republic. Haiti's government was marked by instability, with frequent coups and assassinations. It was occupied by the U.S. in 1915–34. In 1957 the dictator FRANCOIS ("PAPA DOC") DUVALIER came to power. Despite an economic decline and civil unrest, Duvalier ruled until his death in 1971. He was succeeded by his son, Jean-Claude ("Baby Doc") Duvalier, who was forced into exile in 1986. Haiti's first free presidential elections, held in 1990, were won by JEAN-BERTRAND ARISTIDE. He was deposed by a military coup in 1991, after which tens of thousands of Haitians attempted to flee to the U.S. in small boats. The military government stepped down in 1994, and Aristide returned from

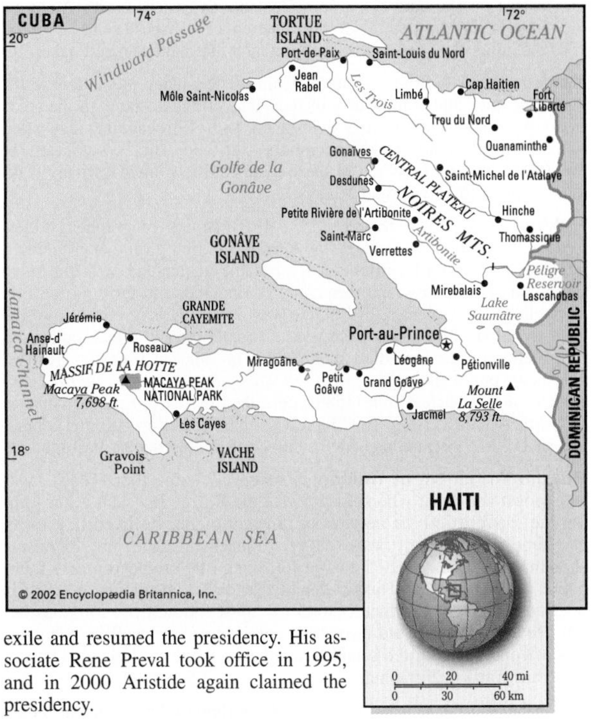

exile and resumed the presidency. His associate Rene Preval took office in 1995, and in 2000 Aristide again claimed the presidency.

Haitink \'hī-tiŋk\, **Bernard (Johann Hermann)** (born 1929) Dutch conductor. Originally a violinist, he first performed with the Concertgebouw Orchestra in 1956. From 1961 to 1988 he was its permanent conductor, and he left a wide-ranging recorded legacy. He has also had a noteworthy opera career as head of the Glyndebourne (1978–88) and Covent Garden (from 1988) operas.

hajj \'hȧj\ In ISLAM, the pilgrimage to MECCA required of all Muslims at least once in their lifetime, provided they are physically and financially able. It is one of the Five Pillars of ISLAM. By tradition the pilgrimage is undertaken between the seventh and twelfth days of the last month of the Islamic year. At Mecca, the pilgrims are obliged to perform several rituals, including walking seven times around the KAABA shrine. They must also visit holy places outside Mecca and sacrifice an animal in honor of ABRAHAM's near-sacrifice of Isaac. In conclusion, they return to Mecca and perform a farewell circling of the shrine.

Hajjaj (ibn Yusuf al-Thaqafi) \k̲ä-'jäj\, **al-** (661–714) Provincial governor under the UMAYYAD DYNASTY (661–750), first in Mecca and then in Iraq. He ruthlessly suppressed a rebellion in Mecca in 692 but was known for promoting prosperity and security in Iraq, striking new coins, keeping the irrigation system working, and improving agricultural production.

hake Any of several large marine fishes (genus *Merluccius*) usually considered part of the COD family. Hakes are elongated, large-headed fishes with large, sharp teeth, two dorsal fins (one notched), and a notched anal fin. They are swift carnivores and, though somewhat soft-fleshed, are used as food. Hakes are found throughout the Atlantic, in

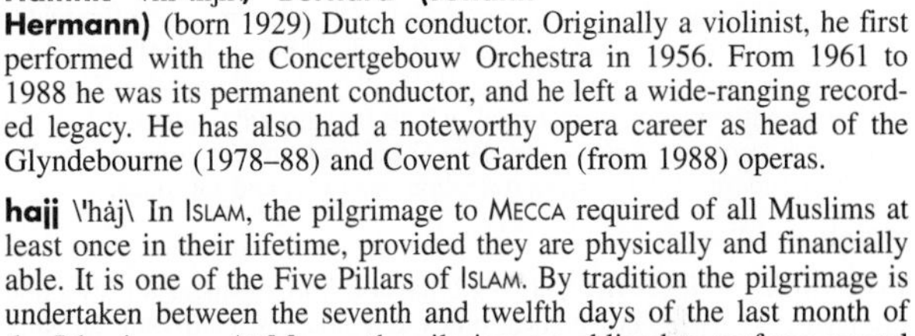

Silver hake (*Merluccius bilinearis*).
PAINTING BY JEAN HELMER

the eastern Pacific, and along New Zealand. In eastern North America, the name is also applied to several related marine fishes (genus *Urophycis*), including the economically important white hake and red hake.

Hakka \'häk-'kä\ Ethnic group of China. Their name is Cantonese for "guest people" and is indicative of their unassimilated status in the areas of southern China where they live. In the 18th–19th century, they often feuded with their non-Hakka neighbors over land. The TAIPING REBELLION (1850–64) initially grew out of these local conflicts; after it, many Hakka emigrated to Taiwan and Malaysia.

Hakluyt \'hak-ˌlüt\, **Richard** (1552?–1616) British geographer. A clergyman, he gave public lectures and became the first professor of modern geography at Oxford University. He became acquainted with the most important sea captains and merchants of England, and took on the role of publicist for explorers. In 1583 he was sent to Paris as chaplain to the English ambassador and also served as an intelligence officer, collecting information on the Canadian fur trade and on other overseas enterprises. His major publication, *The principall Navigations, Voiages and Discoveries of the English nation* (1589), described the early English voyages to North America. After 1600 he advised ELIZABETH I on colonial affairs, and in 1612 he became a charter member of the Northwest Passage Co.

Hakuin \'hä-kù-ˌēŋ\ *or* **Hakuin Ekaku** \'e-kä-kù\ (1686–1769) Japanese priest and artist who helped revive the Rinzai ZEN sect. After joining the sect c. 1700, he became an itinerant monk. He lived in poverty at a time when many priests sought advancement under the Tokugawa shogunate, and he attracted a large following that provided a new foundation for Rinzai Zen. Hakuin taught that direct knowledge of truth is open to all people and that a moral life must follow from religious belief. He used KOANS to aid meditation and invented the well-known paradox of contemplating the sound of one hand clapping. He is also known as an artist and calligrapher.

hal In SUFISM, a state of mind reached from time to time by mystics during their journey towards God. The ahwal (plural of hal) are God-given graces that appear when a soul is purified of its attachments to the material world. Unlike MAQAMS, which are based on merit, ahwal cannot be acquired or retained through an individual's own efforts; the Sufi can only wait patiently for their arrival, which fill him with spiritual joy and renew his desire to seek God. The ahwal most often referred to are watching, nearness, ecstasy, intoxication, sobriety, and intimacy.

Halab See ALEPPO

Halakhah *or* **Halakha** \ˌhä-lä-'kä, hä-'lä-kə\ In Judaism, all laws and ordinances evolved since biblical times to regulate worship and the daily lives of the Jewish people. In contrast to the laws written in the TORAH, the Halakhah represents an oral tradition. These laws were passed from generation to generation before being written down in the 1st–3rd century AD in the compilation called the MISHNA, which became the foundation of the TALMUD.

Halas \'ha-ləs\, **George Stanley** (1895–1983) U.S. coach and team owner. Born in Chicago, he graduated from the Univ.of Illinois and briefly played baseball for the New York Yankees. In 1920 he founded the Chicago Bears football team, and he served as its coach for most of the next 50 years (1920–30, 1933–43, 1946–55, 1958–67). He is noted for having revived the T-formation with a man-in-motion, variations of which are still in wide use. Under his coaching the Bears won seven league championships and four divisional titles. He retained ownership of the Bears until his death. He helped found the NATIONAL FOOTBALL LEAGUE.

halberd Weapon consisting of an ax blade and a sharp spike mounted on the end of a long staff. Usually about 5–6 ft (1.5–2 m) long, it was an important weapon in middle Europe in the 15th and early 16th century. It enabled a foot soldier to contend with an armored man on horseback; the spiked head kept the rider at a distance, and the ax blade could strike a heavy cleaving blow. Firearms and the declining use of ARMOR made the halberd obsolete.

Haldane \'hòl-ˌdān\, **J(ohn) B(urdon) S(anderson)** (1892–1964) British geneticist. Son of JOHN SCOTT HALDANE, he began studying science as his father's assistant at age 8 and later received his MA from Oxford. Haldane, R. A. FISHER, and SEWALL WRIGHT, in separate mathematical arguments based on analyses of MUTATION rates, size, reproduction, and other factors, related CHARLES DARWIN's evolutionary theory and GREGOR MENDEL's laws of heredity. Haldane also contributed to the theory of enzyme action and to studies in human physiology.

J.B.S. Haldane.
BASSANO AND VANDYK STUDIOS

Haldane, John Scott (1860–1936) British physiologist and philosopher. He developed procedures for studying the physiology of breathing and of the blood, and devices for measuring hemoglobin and for analyzing blood gas and mixtures of gases. He discovered that breathing is regulated in large part by the effect of the amount of carbon dioxide in the blood on the brain's respiratory center. He studied the effects of low air pressure, investigated the action of gases in mine suffocations and explosions (an important contribution to mine safety), and developed a staged decompression method for ascent from deep-sea dives. He also tried to clarify the philosophical basis of biology. He was the brother of RICHARD BURDON HALDANE and the father of J.B.S. HALDANE.

Haldane, Richard Burdon *later* **Viscount Haldane (of Cloan)** (1856–1928) Scottish lawyer and statesman. As British secretary of state for war (1905–12), he instituted important military reforms; the speedy mobilization of British forces in 1914 was largely due to his planning. He was lord chancellor (1912–15) in H. H. ASQUITH's government and again (1924) in JAMES RAMSAY MACDONALD's Labour Party government.

Haldeman \'hòl-də-mən\, **H(arry) R(obbins)** (1926–1993) U.S. White House aide. Born in Los Angeles, he worked as an advertising executive there 1949–68. He managed several of RICHARD NIXON's political campaigns, including his 1968 presidential campaign. Named White House chief of staff, he became Nixon's close adviser along with JOHN D. EHRLICHMAN. He participated in the White House cover-up surrounding the Watergate break-in (see WATERGATE SCANDAL) as well as other "dirty tricks" used in the 1972 campaign. Forced to resign in 1973, he was tried and convicted for conspiracy, perjury, and obstruction of justice in 1975; he served 18 months in jail.

Hale, George E(llery) (1868–1938) U.S. astronomer. Born in Chicago, he studied at Harvard and in Berlin. In 1888 he organized the Kenwood Observatory in Chicago. In 1892 he joined the faculty of the University of Chicago and began organizing the Yerkes Observatory, of which he was director until 1904; there he built the 40-in. (1-m) refracting telescope that remains the largest of its type in the world. He established the *Astrophysical Journal* in 1895. In 1904 he organized the MOUNT WILSON OBSERVATORY, and was its director until 1923. There he built solar apparatus of great power as well as the huge 60-in. (1.5-m) and 100-in. (2.5-m) reflecting telescopes. In 1928 he began work on a 200-in. (5-m) reflecting telescope at Caltech's PALOMAR OBSERVATORY; completed in 1948, it was named in his honor. As a researcher, he is known particularly for his discovery of magnetic fields in sunspots.

Hale, John Parker (1806–1873) U.S. politician and reformer. Born in Rochester, N.H., he was elected to the U.S. House of Representatives (1843–45), where he achieved prominence opposing slavery. In the U.S. Senate (1847–53, 1855–65), he sponsored a bill abolishing flogging in the navy. His antislavery position won him the nomination as the FREE SOIL PARTY's presidential candidate in 1852. He returned to the Senate as a Republican and became a leader of the new party. He later served as U.S. minister to Spain (1865–69).

Hale, Matthew *later* **Sir Matthew** (1609–1676) British legal scholar. Orphaned at age 5, he planned to become a minister but ultimately chose the law. He defended Archbishop LAUD and other Royalists during the ENGLISH CIVIL WARS (1642–51). As a COMMON PLEAS justice (1654–58) and member of Parliament (1654–60), he played a major role in reforming the legal system and promoting CHARLES II's restoration. He later became chief baron of the exchequer (1660) and chief justice of the King's Bench (1671–76). One of the greatest scholars of the history of English

COMMON LAW, he is best known for his *History of the Pleas of the Crown* (1680; first published 1736).

Hale, Nathan (1755–1776) American Revolutionary officer. Born in Coventry, Conn., he attended Yale University and became a schoolteacher. He joined a Connecticut regiment in 1775 and took part in the siege of Boston. Made a captain in 1776, he helped capture a British provision sloop on Long Island. Volunteering for spy duty, he penetrated British lines but was captured while returning and hanged without trial the next day at 21. His last words reportedly were "I only regret that I have but one life to lose for my country."

Hale, Sarah Josepha *orig.* **Sarah Josepha Buell** (1788–1879) U.S. writer and editor. Born in Newport, N.H., Hale turned to writing in 1822 as a widow trying to support her family. She edited the *Ladies' Magazine* (1828–37) and then GODEY'S LADY'S BOOK (1837–77); as the first female magazine editor, she shaped many of the attitudes and ideas of women of the period. Her books include *The Ladies' Wreath* (1837), a collection of poetry by women that sold widely; and *Woman's Record* (1853). She is also remembered for her verse "Mary Had a Little Lamb" (1830).

Hale-Bopp, Comet COMET discovered in 1994 by the amateur astronomers Alan Hale and Thomas Bopp at a distance of about seven ASTRONOMICAL UNITS, beyond JUPITER's orbit and farther than any comet detected before by amateurs. Astronomers estimated its nucleus to be about 25 mi (40 km) in diameter, far larger than most comets. At its closest approach to the sun in April 1997, it was one of the intrinsically brightest comets in several centuries, though not the brightest as seen from earth. The comet triggered the mass suicide near San Diego, Cal., in 1997 of 39 members of a religious cult known as Heaven's Gate, whose leader maintained that they would be reincarnated in a spacecraft following in the comet's wake.

Haleakala National Park \ˌhä-lā-ä-kä-ˈlä\ National park, eastern Maui Island, Hawaii. Established in 1960, it occupies an area of 28,655 acres (11,597 hectares). Its central feature is Haleakala Crater, the world's largest dormant volcanic crater, more than 2,500 ft (762 m) deep and about 20 mi (32 km) in circumference. The crater floor, covering more than 19 sq mi (49 sq km), has areas of forest, desert, and meadow. It is the site of Science City, a research-observatory complex operated by the U.S. Department of Defense and the universities of HAWAII and MICHIGAN.

Haley, Alex (Palmer) (1921–1992) U.S. writer. Born in Ithaca, N.Y., and raised in North Carolina, he served in the Coast Guard (1939–59) and later became a journalist. An interview with MALCOLM X led to the best-selling *Autobiography of Malcolm X* (1965; film, 1992). His greatest success was *Roots* (1976, special Pulitzer Prize), a history of seven generations of his ancestors beginning with their enslavement. Adapted for television, it became one of the most popular American television shows ever and spurred great interest in genealogy, though Haley later admitted that it was partly fictional.

Haley, Bill *orig.* **William John Clifton** (1925–1981) U.S. singer and guitarist, one of the pioneers of rock and roll (see ROCK MUSIC). Born in Michigan, Haley worked as a disc jockey and sang and played guitar for several COUNTRY-MUSIC bands in the late 1940s, later forming his own band, the Saddlemen. Marrying elements of country to RHYTHM AND BLUES, he renamed his band Bill Haley and His Comets, and recorded some of rock's earliest hits, including "Shake Rattle and Roll" (1954) and "Rock Around the Clock" (1955). He continued to tour as a nostalgia act into the 1970s.

Haley, William (John) *later* **Sir William** (1901–1987) English journalist and editor. Haley began to study journalism in 1918 and joined the staff of the *Manchester Evening News* in 1922. He held the post of director of the *Manchester Guardian and Evening News* before becoming director general of the BBC (1944–52) and then editor of *The Times* of London (1952–66), the most important and influential position in British journalism.

half-life Interval of time required for one-half of the atomic nuclei of a radioactive sample to decay (change spontaneously into other nuclear species by emitting particles and energy), or the time required for the number of disintegrations per second of a radioactive material to decrease by one-half. Half-lives are characteristic properties of the various unstable atomic nuclei and the particular way in which they decay. ALPHA DECAY and BETA DECAY are generally slower processes than GAMMA DECAY.

halftone process In PRINTING, a technique of breaking up an image into a series of dots to permit reproduction of the full tone range of a photograph or artwork. It is traditionally done by placing a glass screen printed with a tight grid of lines over the plate being exposed. The grid breaks up the image into hundreds of tiny dots, each of which is read by the camera as either black or white—or, in the case of color art, as either a single printing color or white. The resulting image, called a halftone, is then rephotographed for printing. Screens are made with a varying number of lines per inch, depending on the application; for newspapers the range is about 80–120, whereas glossy magazines usually require 133–175 lines per inch.

Haliburton, Thomas Chandler (1796–1865) Canadian writer. He served in the legislature of his native Nova Scotia and later served as a judge of the Supreme Court (1841–54), where he maintained the strong conservatism that informs his writings. He moved to England in 1856 and was a member of Parliament from 1859 until his death. He is best known for creating the character Sam Slick, a Yankee clock peddler and cracker-barrel philosopher whose escapades first appeared in the newspaper *Nova Scotian* and were later published in *The Clockmaker* (1836, 1838, 1840) and other volumes.

halibut Any of various FLATFISHES, especially the Atlantic and Pacific halibuts (genus *Hippoglossus,* family Pleuronectidae), both of which have eyes and color on the right side. The Atlantic halibut, found on both sides of the North Atlantic, is the largest flatfish; it may reach a length of about 7 ft (2 m) and a weight of 720 lbs (325 kg). It is brown, blackish, or deep green on the eyed side. The smaller and slimmer Pacific halibut is found on both sides of the North Pacific. Other edible halibut include the Greenland halibut, of Arctic and near-Arctic parts of the Atlantic, and the California halibut (family Bothidae), found along the California coast.

Halicarnassus \ˌha-lə-kär-ˈna-səs\ *modern* **Bodrum** \bō-ˈdrüm\ Ancient Greek city, southwestern CARIA. Now a location in modern Turkey, on a peninsula in the Aegean Sea, it became the capital of Caria (c. 370 BC) under MAUSOLUS, who built a great wall, public buildings, and a secret dockyard and canal. His widow erected (c. 350 BC) the Mausoleum in his memory. It was one of the SEVEN WONDERS of the Ancient World; its remains are now in the BRITISH MUSEUM. Halicarnassus was the birthplace of the Greek HERODOTUS. It came under Roman rule in 129 BC, and in early Christian times was a bishopric. The ruins of the castle of the Knights of St. John, founded c. AD 1400, dominate the ancient site.

halide mineral \ˈha-ˌlīd, ˈhā-ˌlīd\ Any of a group of naturally occurring inorganic compounds that contain a halogen such as fluorine, chlorine, iodine, or bromine as the anion. Such compounds, with the notable exceptions of FLUORITE, HALITE, and sylvite, are rare and of very local occurrence.

Halifax City (pop., 1995 est.: 121,000), capital of Nova Scotia. Located on Halifax Harbor, an inlet of the Atlantic Ocean, it was settled by the British in 1749 as a counterbalance to French holdings at CAPE BRETON. It served as a British army and navy base until its defenses were taken over by the Canadian government in 1906. The city suffered from a munitions-ship explosion in 1917 that killed nearly 2,000 people. During World Wars I and II, Halifax was Canada's most important naval base. The city is Nova Scotia's leading commercial and industrial center, and its port is one of the busiest in Canada. Its educational institutions include DALHOUSIE UNIV. (1818); historic buildings include St. Paul's Church (1750), Canada's oldest Protestant church.

The Old Town Clock on Citadel Hill, Halifax, Nova Scotia.
JOHN DE VISSER

Halifax, Earl of *orig.* **Edward Frederick Lindley Wood** (1881–

1959) British statesman. He was elected to Parliament in 1910. As viceroy of India (1925–31), he worked on terms of understanding with MOHANDAS K. GANDHI and accelerated constitutional advances. His tenure as foreign secretary (1938–40) in NEVILLE CHAMBERLAIN's government was controversial because of Chamberlain's policy of appeasement toward ADOLF HITLER, but Halifax kept the post into WINSTON CHURCHILL's ministry. As ambassador to the U.S. (1941–46), he greatly served the Allied cause in World War II, for which he was created earl of Halifax in 1944.

halite \'ha-ˌlīt, 'hā-ˌlīt\ Naturally occurring SODIUM CHLORIDE (NaCl), common or rock salt. Halite occurs on all continents, in beds that range from a few feet to more than 1,000 ft (300 m) in thickness. Termed EVAPORITE deposits because they formed by the evaporation of saline water in partially enclosed basins, they characteristically are associated with beds of limestone, dolomite, and shale. Halite is found in large deposits in New York and in Russia, France, India, and Canada.

Hall, Charles Martin (1863–1914) U.S. chemist. Born in Thompson, Ohio, he attended Oberlin College, where, soon after graduating in 1885, he discovered the method of producing ALUMINUM by ELECTROLYSIS (simultaneously with Paul Héroult), an innovation that brought the metal into wide commercial use. Supported by the Mellon family, he formed the Pittsburgh Reduction Co. (later ALCOA). The need for cheap and plentiful power led the company to Niagara Falls, where in 1895 it became the first customer for Niagara's new power plant.

Hall, G(ranville) Stanley (1844–1924) U.S. psychologist. Born in Ashfield, Mass., he studied in Germany under WILHELM WUNDT and HERMANN VON HELMHOLTZ, returning to the U.S. to earn the first psychology PhD granted in America (Harvard, 1878). After teaching at Johns Hopkins Univ., he helped establish Clark University (1888) in Worcester, Mass., and worked there to shape experimental psychology into a science. He is frequently regarded as the founder of child psychology and educational psychology; he also did much to direct into the psychological currents of his time the ideas of CHARLES DARWIN and SIGMUND FREUD. He founded several journals, including the *American Journal of Psychology,* and helped found the American Psychological Assn., of which he was the first president. Hall's work gave early impetus and direction to the development of psychology in the U.S.

hall, hypostyle See HYPOSTYLE HALL

Hall, James *later* **Sir James** (1761–1832) Scottish geologist and physicist. He founded experimental geology by artificially producing various rock types in the laboratory. He saw that he could obtain different kinds of rocks by melting minerals and cooling them at a controlled rate. Later, he produced a rock that closely resembled natural marble by heating calcium carbonate under pressure. He experimented extensively with igneous rocks from Scotland and showed that they had been produced by intense heat.

Hall, James (1811–1898) U.S. geologist and paleontologist. Born in Hingham, Mass., he made extensive explorations in the St. Lawrence Valley while teaching at Rensselaer Polytechnic Institute (1832–36). In 1836 he was appointed state geologist for the Geological Survey of New York; his studies culminated in the massive *Geology of New York* (part 4, 1843), a classic in American geology that introduced the geosynclinal theory of mountain building. He was state geologist of Iowa 1855–58 and of Wisconsin 1857–60. He served as director of New York State's Museum of Natural History 1871–98. His major later work was the huge *Paleontology of New York* (13 vols., 1847–94).

Hall, John H(owe) (1881–1953) U.S. metallurgist. Born in South Portsmouth, R.I., he attended Harvard University. He worked at various foundries and obtained numerous patents on steel processes. During World War II he produced the first successful heavy steel castings used as armor. He wrote the standard texts *The Steel Foundry* (1914) and *Steel Foundry Practice* (1955).

Hall, Peter (Reginald Frederick) *later* **Sir Peter** (born 1930) British theater, opera, and film director. After producing and acting in over 20 plays at Cambridge Univ., he entered the professional theater. At London's Arts Theatre (1955–56) he staged London premieres of important continental plays. Especially renowned for his Shakespearean productions, he served as managing director of the Royal Shakespeare Co. 1962–68, and continued to direct plays for it long afterward. He succeeded LAURENCE OLIVIER as managing director of London's National Theatre (1973–88). He formed his own theatrical production company in 1988. He has also directed the Covent Garden Opera and many operas at Glyndebourne, as well as several films.

Hall, Radclyffe *orig.* **Marguerite Radclyffe-Hall** (1880–1943) English writer. Born to a wealthy family and educated at King's College, London, Hall began her literary career by writing verses, which eventually were collected into five volumes. She won prizes for her novel *Adam's Breed* (1926), a plea for animal rights. She was condemned for writing openly and sympathetically about lesbianism in *The Well of Loneliness* (1928), one of the first lesbian novels in English. It was judged obscene and banned in Britain; the ban was overturned on appeal after Hall's death. Most of her five other novels express her strong Christian beliefs.

hall church Type of church with side aisles approximately equal in height to the NAVE, unlike the typical BASILICA. The interior is lit by large aisle windows instead of a CLERESTORY, with chapels sometimes arranged alongside the nave. Hall churches originated in Germany and were characteristic of the Late Gothic period there. Special features of German hall churches include lofty nave arcades and immense roofs. St. Elizabeth in Marburg (c. 1257–83) is an archetypal example.

Hall effect Development of a transverse ELECTRIC FIELD in a solid material carrying an ELECTRIC CURRENT and placed in a MAGNETIC FIELD perpendicular to the current. Discovered in 1879 by Edwin H. Hall (1855–1938), the Hall field results from the force exerted by the magnetic field on the moving particles of the current. The Hall effect can be used to measure certain properties of current carriers as well as to detect the presence of a current on a magnetic field.

Hallaj \k̲a-'laj\, **al-** (858?–922) Muslim teacher of SUFISM. Brought up in the Iraqi city of Wasit, he was drawn to asceticism at an early age and studied with a series of Sufi teachers. From c. 895 he traveled extensively as a teacher and preacher, making three pilgrimages to Mecca and gathering a large following. These travels and his popularity alienated his Sufi masters, and his demands for reform earned him the enmity of non-Sufi Muslims. Accused of fomenting rebellion and claiming to be divine, he was arrested, imprisoned (c. 911–22), and eventually crucified and tortured to death.

Halle (an der Saale) \'hä-lə\ City (pop., 1996 est.: 283,000), eastern central Germany. Lying on the SAALE RIVER, Halle's location was the site of settlements that centered around the local salt deposits and flourished c. 1000–400 BC. Halle and its valuable saltworks were granted to the archbishopric of Magdeburg in AD 968. It was a member of the HANSEATIC LEAGUE 1281–1478. The capital of Halle district in East Germany (1952–90), it is an important rail junction and a principal commercial and industrial center. It was the birthplace of G.F. HANDEL.

Halleck \'hal-ək\, **Henry W(ager)** (1815–1872) U.S. general. Born in Westernville, N.Y., he graduated from West Point. After touring military facilities in Europe (1844), he wrote a textbook on war (1846) that became widely used. In 1861 he commanded in the western department of Missouri, organizing and training large volunteer armies. In 1862 he was appointed general in chief of Union forces, but failed to achieve an overall battle strategy, and his victories were attributed to his subordinates ULYSSES S. GRANT and JOHN POPE. Held responsible for Union reverses in Virginia, he was replaced by Grant in 1864.

Halley \'ha-lē, 'hā-lē\, **Edmond** (1656–1742) English astronomer and mathematician. He studied at Oxford University. In 1676 he set sail for the South Atlantic with the intention of compiling an accurate catalog of the stars of the Southern Hemisphere. His star catalogue (1678) recorded the position of 341 stars. In 1684 he met ISAAC NEWTON at Cambridge, which led to his prominent role (with ROBERT HOOKE and CHRISTOPHER WREN) in the devel-

Halley, detail of an oil painting by R. Phillips, c. 1720; in the National Portrait Gallery, London.

BY COURTESY OF THE NATIONAL PORTRAIT GALLERY, LONDON

opment of Newton's law of gravitation. Halley edited Newton's *Philosophiae naturalis principia mathematica,* bringing it to print in 1687. He produced the first meteorological chart (1686, showing the distribution of prevailing winds in the world's oceans) and magnetic charts of the Atlantic and Pacific (1701). In astronomy, he described the parabolic orbits of 24 comets observed in the years 1337–1698. He showed that three of these were so similar they must have been the same comet and accurately predicted its return in 1758 (see Halley's Comet).

Halley's Comet First comet whose return was predicted, proving that at least some comets are members of the solar system. Edmond Halley showed in 1705 that comets seen in 1531, 1607, and 1682 were really one comet, and he predicted its return in 1758. Later calculations identified it with the large, bright comet seen during the Norman Conquest (and depicted in the Bayeux Tapestry) and with other comet sightings at intervals of about 76 years, the first in 240 BC. The only easily seen comet that returns in a single lifetime, it approached earth twice in the 20th century (1910, 1985–86). It is roughly 9 mi (15 km) across.

hallmark Symbol stamped on an item of silver or gold to indicate that it conforms to legal standards of purity. Hallmarking in Britain dates from 1300; no gold or silver could be sold until tested for purity and struck with the king's mark. A maker's mark was introduced in 1363; at first a symbol, such as a fish or key, it came to include or be replaced by initials. A "hallmark" was a mark made at Goldsmith's Hall, London. In the U.S., no hallmarks were initially required. In the late 18th and early 19th century, local regulations were established in New York, Boston, Baltimore, and elsewhere; makers' marks appeared and the words "coin" and "sterling" were stamped on silver objects. In 1906 the use of the words came under federal regulation. Hallmarks on gold, similar to those on silver, are also subject to federal regulation.

Halloween Holiday observed on October 31, the eve of All Saints' Day. Its pagan origins can be traced to the Celtic festival of Samhain, celebrated in ancient England and Ireland to mark the beginning of the Celtic new year. The souls of the dead were supposed to revisit their homes on Samhain eve, and witches, goblins, black cats, and ghosts were said to roam abroad. The night was also thought to be the most favorable time for divinations concerning marriage, luck, health, and death. The pagan observances influenced the Christian festival of All Hallows' Eve, celebrated on the same date. The holiday was gradually secularized and was introduced into the U.S. by the late 19th century. Still associated with evil spirits and the supernatural, it is celebrated by children in costume who gather candy by ringing doorbells and calling out "trick or treat," "trick" referring to the pranks and vandalism that are also part of the Halloween tradition.

Hallstatt \'häl-ˌshtät, *Engl* 'hȯl-ˌstat\ Site in upper Austria where objects characteristic of the Early Iron Age (from c. 1100 BC) were first identified. More than 2,000 graves were near a salt mine that preserved implements, parts of clothing, and bodies of miners. The remains are divided into four phases (A, B, C, D), differing according to burial practices, presence of low grave mound or tumulus, relative quantity of bronze and iron, and style of pottery, weapons, jewelry, and clothing. Decoration in general is geometric and symmetrical, with a tendency toward the extravagant.

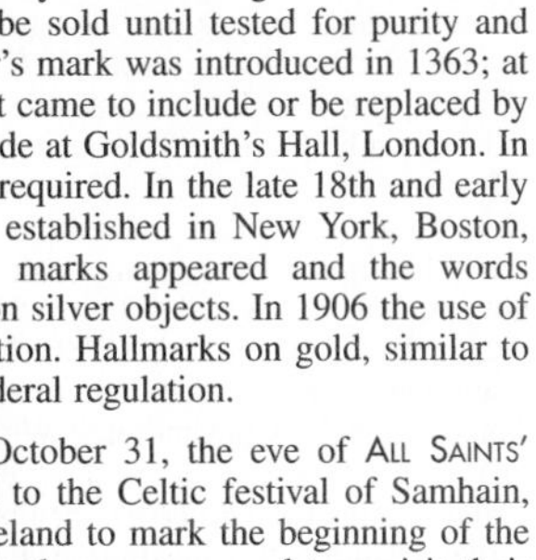

Bronze bucket found at Early Iron Age cemetery at Hallstatt, Austria, about 6th century BC.

BY COURTESY OF THE TRUSTEES OF THE BRITISH MUSEUM

hallucination Perception of objects, sounds, or sensations having no demonstrable reality, usually arising from a disorder of the nervous system or in response to certain drugs (see hallucinogen). Hallucinations are in many ways similar to dreams: they derive their content from perceptions known to memory, though these can be greatly transformed. Hallucinations can result when attention collapses from intense arousal due to extreme anxiety, fatigue, excitement, or other causes. They figure prominently in the diagnosis of schizophrenia.

hallucinogen \hə-'lü-sᵊn-ə-jən\ Substance that produces psychological effects normally associated only with dreams, schizophrenia, or religious visions. It produces changes in perception (ranging from distortions in what is sensed to perceptions of objects where there are none), thought, and feeling. Those that have aroused the most controversy include LSD, mescaline, psilocybin (from certain mushrooms), and bufotenine (from the skin of toads); some would add marijuana. The mode of action is still not clear to science; serotonin, epinephrine, or other neurotransmitters may be affected.

Halmahera \ˌhal-mə-'her-ə\ *Dutch* **Djailolo** \jī-'lō-lō\ Largest island of the Moluccas, Indonesia. It is made up of four peninsulas enclosing three great bays; politically it includes the small islands of Ternate and Tidore. Its area is 6,865 sq mi (17,780 sq km). It is dominated by heavily wooded mountain chains, with three active volcanoes on the northern peninsula. The indigenous population, whose descendants inhabit the interior, were probably Papuan; the coastal people include many elements from surrounding islands. In 1683 the Dutch obtained a foothold in Halmahera with the aid of the sultan of Ternate. With the Moluccas, it was incorporated into the Republic of Indonesia in 1949.

halogen \'ha-lə-jən\ Any of the five nonmetallic elements with similar chemical properties: fluorine, chlorine, bromine, iodine (I), and astatine (At). They occur next to the rightmost column of the periodic table as usually arranged. All are highly reactive oxidizing agents (see oxidation-reduction) with valence 1 (for fluorine, the only valence). They combine readily with most metals and nonmetals to form a variety of compounds and never occur uncombined in nature. Astatine occurs naturally in minute amounts as an intermediate decay product; it has no stable nonradioactive isotope. Halogen salts with metals (halides) are very stable; sodium chloride is the most familiar. Halogen compunds coating fluorescent lamps phosphoresce to produce light in response to electric discharges inside the lamp (see electric discharge lamp).

halogen lamp *or* **tungsten-halogen lamp** Incandescent lamp with a quartz bulb and a gas filling that includes a halogen. It gives brilliant light from a compact unit. The halogen combines with the tungsten evaporated from the hot filament to form a compound that is attracted back to the filament, thus extending the filament's life. The evaporated tungsten is also prevented from condensing on the bulb and darkening it, an effect that reduces the light output of ordinary incandescent lamps. First used in the late 1960s in motion-picture production, halogen lamps are now also used in automobile headlights, underwater photography, and residential lighting.

Hals \'hälz, 'häls\, **Frans** (1581/85–1666) Dutch portrait painter. Born in Antwerp, he spent his life in Haarlem, where he was registered as a master by the Guild of St. Luke in 1610. His group portraits of members of local guilds and military societies, notably the monumental *Banquet of Officers of the Civic Guard of St. George* (1616), were painted with a technique close to Impressionism in its looseness, unique in Dutch art at the time. He introduced a jovial spirit that revolutionized portraiture and set him apart from his contemporaries. His subjects exude joie de vivre, with an occasional hint of sadness. After 1650 he portrayed elderly people who nervously display the spark of life even as it flickers; these portraits, such as *The Women Regents of the Almshouse at Haarlem* (1664), are his masterpieces. His work greatly influenced Edouard Manet, Vincent van Gogh, and Robert Henri.

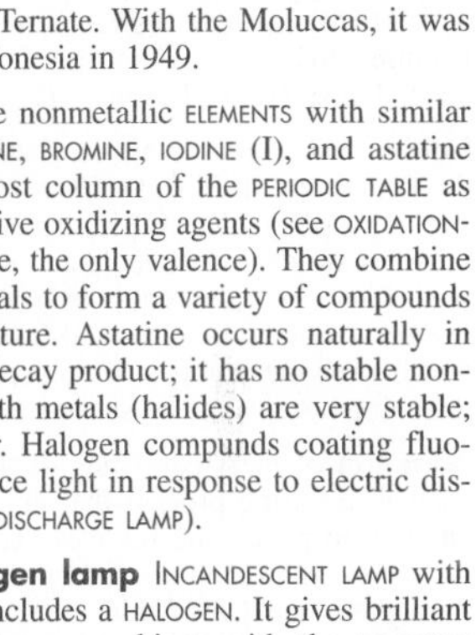

"The Merry Toper," oil on canvas by Frans Hals, c. 1628–30; in the Rijksmuseum, Amsterdam.

BY COURTESY OF THE RIJKSMUSEUM, AMSTERDAM

Halsey \'hȯl-sē, 'hȯl-zē\, **William F(rederick), Jr.** *known as* **Bull Halsey** (1882–1959) U.S. admiral. Born in Elizabeth, N.J., he graduated from Annapolis, commanded a destroyer in World War I, became a naval aviator, and was promoted to vice admiral in 1940. When the Japanese attacked Pearl Harbor, his fleet was at sea; the only U.S. naval presence in the Pacific for months, it carried out surprise attacks against the Japanese in the Marshall and Gilbert islands. A leading exponent of carrier-based aircraft, he became famous for his daring and imaginative tactics. As commander of the South Pacific naval forces, he was instrumental in the Japanese defeat at GUADALCANAL. In 1944 he became commander of the 3rd Fleet, leading his carrier task force in brilliant air strikes. He was responsible for finding and destroying the Japanese fleet at the Battle of LEYTE GULF. He was promoted to fleet admiral in 1945 and retired in 1947.

Halsted, William Stewart (1852–1922) U.S. pioneer of scientific surgery. Born in New York City, he graduated from the College of Physicians and Surgeons. In 1881 he discovered that blood could be aerated and reinfused. He developed conduction anesthesia (1885) by experimenting with injecting cocaine into his own nerve trunks, subsequently becoming addicted (later cured). At Johns Hopkins University he established the first surgical school in the U.S. An early champion of antiseptic procedures, Halsted introduced the use of thin rubber gloves in surgery (1890). He emphasized homeostasis during surgery, gentleness in handling living tissue, and precise realignment of severed tissues. He created hospital surgical residencies.

haltia \'häl-tē-ä\ Among the Balto-Finnic peoples, a guardian spirit of the household. In Finland it was the spirit of the first person to claim a site as property. Identical in appearance to this original owner, the haltia presided over the household and served as a moral force to discourage misbehavior. A haltia could only be transported to a new home by carrying fire or ashes from the old one. On farms there were barn-spirits to watch over the animals, a mill-spirit to keep the miller awake, and a threshing-house spirit to supervise the drying of the grain.

ham Cut of meat consisting of the thigh of a HOG, usually preserved through a curing process that involves salting, smoking, or drying. In addition to preserving the meat, curing gives it additional flavor. Sugar or honey is sometimes added to further enhance flavor. Produced throughout the Old World except where forbidden by religious edict (principally by observant Muslims and Jews), ham became a favored food on the farms of North America. The distinctive qualities of hams of various regions of the world result from unique combinations of hog-raising and meat-processing technologies. Virginia hams, for example, are cut from razorback hogs fed on peanuts and peaches, and smoked over apple- and hickory-wood fires. Ham is a compact source of high-grade animal protein, thiamine, and iron.

hamadryad See DRYAD

Hamas \hä-'mäs\ *officially* **Harakat-al-Muqawima al-Islamiyya (Islamic Resistance Movement)** Militant Palestinian Islamic movement dedicated to the destruction of Israel and the creation of a Palestinian Islamic state. It was founded in 1988 by Sheikh Ahmad Yasin, and its leadership comes from the MUSLIM BROTHERHOOD. Hamas's aims are more militant: it takes the position that Palestine cannot be surrendered to non-Muslims. It opposes the 1993 peace agreement between the PALESTINE LIBERATION ORGANIZATION and Israel.

Hamburg \'häm-,bu̇rk, *Engl* 'ham-,bərg\ City (pop., 1997 est.: 1,708,000), constituting a state, northern Germany. Located on the ELBE RIVER, it is Germany's largest port. It grew around the 9th-century castle of Hammaburg. Treaties with LÜBECK in the mid-13th century led to the formation of the HANSEATIC LEAGUE, of which it was a leader. Incorporated into the French empire in 1810–14, it became a member of the GERMAN CONFEDERATION as a free city in 1815. In World War II Allied firebombing killed some 55,000 people and devastated the city. It was rapidly rebuilt after the war. The birthplace of F. MENDELSSOHN and J. BRAHMS and home to the Hamburg Opera, it has enjoyed a distinguished musical history. It is Germany's foremost industrial city and northern Germany's chief economic center.

Hamhung \'häm-,hu̇ŋ\ City (pop., 1987 est.: 701,000), eastern central North Korea. It was the commercial and administrative center of North Korea during the CHOSON dynasty (1392–1910) and developed as a modern industrial city in the 1920s. During the KOREAN WAR, most industrial plants in the area were destroyed by U.S. bombing raids, but they were rebuilt. In addition to its manufacturing importance, it is the site of several institutions of learning.

Hamilton City (pop., 1995 est.: 1,100), capital of BERMUDA. It lies on Great Bermuda island in the western Atlantic, along the shore of a deep-water harbor. Founded in 1790, it succeeded St. George as capital in 1815. To encourage business and employment, it was made a free port in 1956. Tourism is the economic mainstay; cruise ships dock along the main street.

Hamilton City (pop., 1995 est: 335,000; metro. area pop., 1996: 624,000), southeastern Ontario. Located on Hamilton Harbor at the western end of Lake ONTARIO, it was settled by British loyalists fleeing the AMERICAN REVOLUTION. The opening of the Burlington Canal (1830), linking the harbor to Lake Ontario, led to the city's development as an important port and rail center. It is now one of Canada's leading industrial centers and a financial hub, and the site of MCMASTER UNIV. The center of an extensive fruit-growing district, it is the site of one of Canada's largest open-air markets.

Hamilton, Alexander (1755?–1804) U.S. statesman. Born on Nevis in the Leeward Islands, he arrived in New Jersey in 1772. In the American Revolution he joined the Continental Army and showed conspicuous bravery at the Battle of Trenton. He served as aide-de-camp to Gen. GEORGE WASHINGTON (1777–81) and, fluent in French, became a liaison with French commanders. After the war he practiced law in New York. At the Continental Congress, he argued for a strong central government. As a delegate to the Annapolis Convention in 1786, he drafted the address that led to the Constitutional Convention. With JAMES MADISON and JOHN JAY, he wrote articles for *The FEDERALIST* that explained the new Constitution and helped win its ratification. Appointed the first secretary of the treasury (1789), he established national fiscal policies that strengthened the national government and helped institute the BANK OF THE U.S. Opposition to his policies by THOMAS JEFFERSON led to the rise of political parties; Hamilton became leader of the FEDERALIST PARTY, and Madison and Jefferson created the Democratic-Republican Party. Hamilton favored friendship with Britain and influenced Washington to take a neutral stand toward the French Revolution. He caused a rift in the Federalist Party by opposing its nomination of JOHN ADAMS for president in 1796. In 1800 he tried to prevent Adams's reelection, circulating a private attack which AARON BURR, long at odds with Hamilton, obtained and published. When Jefferson and Burr both defeated Adams but received equal electoral votes, Hamilton helped persuade the Federalists in the House of Representatives to choose Jefferson. In 1804 he opposed Burr's candidacy for governor of New York. This affront, coupled with alleged remarks questioning Burr's character, led Burr to challenge Hamilton to a duel, in which Hamilton was mortally wounded.

Alexander Hamilton, detail of an oil painting by John Trumbull; in the National Gallery of Art, Washington, D.C.

BY COURTESY OF THE NATIONAL GALLERY OF ART, WASHINGTON, D.C., ANDREW MELLON COLLECTION

Hamilton, Edith (1867–1963) U.S. (German-born) scholar and educator. Brought up in Fort Wayne, Ind., she decided on a teaching career. After graduating from Bryn Mawr, she was invited to head its preparatory school when she was 29. Preferring classical studies to school administration, she retired to write such historical works as *The Greek Way* (1930) and *The Roman Way* (1932). Her *Mythology* (1943) was studied by millions as a textbook. She became an honorary citizen of Athens at the age of 90.

Hamilton, Emma, Lady *orig.* **Amy Lyon** (1761?–1815) English social figure, mistress of HORATIO NELSON. In 1786 she became the mistress, and in 1791 the wife, of Sir William Hamilton (1730–1803), British envoy to Naples. A beautiful woman whose portrait was frequently painted by GEORGE ROMNEY, she was a favorite in Neapolitan society. She became Nelson's mistress in 1798 and gave birth to their daughter, Horatia, in 1801, then lived with Nelson after her husband's death (1803). She later squandered the money both men left her, was imprisoned for debt (1813–14), and died in poverty.

Hamilton College Private liberal-arts college in Clinton, N.Y. It was founded in 1793 as an academy for the children of ONEIDA Indians and white settlers, but was reorganized as a college in 1812. In 1968 it opened a sister school for women; the two schools were merged in 1978. Enrollment is about 1,700.

Hamito-Semitic languages See AFROASIATIC LANGUAGES

Hamm, Mia *in full* **Mariel Margaret Hamm** (b. 1972) U.S. soccer player. At the age of 15 Hamm became the youngest person ever to play on the U.S. national soccer team. In 1989 she entered the University of North Carolina at Chapel Hill, and by the time she graduated in 1994 she had won numerous awards and helped her team win four National Collegiate Athletic Association (NCAA) championships. The university honored her by retiring her uniform number (19). She had also helped the U.S. team win the World Cup in 1991and 1999. Hamm became one of the most popular players on the U.S. women's Olympic team, which won the gold medal in 1996 and the silver in 2000. She broke the all-time international scoring record for either men or women on May 16, 1999, against Brazil with her 108th career goal. In 2001 Hamm began her professional career with the Washington (D.C.) Freedom of the nascent Women's United Soccer Association (WUSA).

Hammar \ˌhȧm-ˈmär\, **Hawr al** Large swampy lake, southeastern Iraq. Lying south of the junction of the TIGRIS and EUPHRATES rivers, and fed by distributaries of the Euphrates, the lake is 750 sq mi (1,950 sq km) in area; it drains through a short channel into the SHATT AL-ARAB near BASRA. It was once a reed-filled marshland but was later used for irrigating the delta region. Home to the Madan or Marsh Arabs, a tribe of seminomadic marsh dwellers, it was drained in 1992 by the government in an attempt to drive out SHIITE guerrillas who had taken refuge there. By 1993 one-third of the lake was dry; thousands of the residents had fled deeper into the marshes or to Iran.

Hammarskjöld \ˈha-mər-ˌshəld\, **Dag (Hjalmar Agne Carl)** (1905–1961) Second secretary-general of the UNITED NATIONS (1953–61). His father was prime minister of Sweden and chairman of the Nobel Prize Foundation. Hammarskjöld studied law and economics in Uppsala and Stockholm, then taught at Stockholm (1933–36). He joined the civil service, serving in the finance ministry, as president of the board of the Bank of Sweden, and in the foreign ministry, where he became chair of the Swedish delegation to the U.N. (1952). He was appointed secretary-general in 1953, and reappointed in 1957. His first three years were quiet, but he subsequently dealt with the SUEZ CRISIS, conflict in Lebanon and Jordan, and civil strife following the creation of the Republic of the Congo (1960). He died in a plane crash on a mission to Africa. He was posthumously awarded the Nobel Peace Prize (1961). His journals, published as *Markings* (1963), reveal a man of deep religious convictions.

hammer Tool for pounding or delivering repeated blows. Hand hammers have a handle and striking head. Surfaces of hammerheads vary in size, angle of orientation to the handle (parallel or inclined), and type of face (flat or convex). Carpenters' hammers often have a claw on the head for extracting NAILS. Weights range from a few ounces or grams up to 15 lbs (7 kg) for hammers used in breaking stones. Steam hammers often use, in addition to gravity, a downward thrust from a steam-activated piston. Pneumatic (air-driven) hammers include the hammer drill, for rock and concrete, and the riveting hammer, for construction operations involving steel girders and plate.

Hammer, Armand (1898–1990) U.S. industrialist and philanthropist. Born in New York City, Hammer made his first million dollars in pharmaceuticals before earning his medical degree from Columbia University. He went to Soviet Russia in 1921 to provide medical aid to famine victims, and was persuaded by VLADIMIR ILICH LENIN to remain. His ventures, including a pencil-manufacturing firm, were bought out by the Soviets in the late 1920s, and he returned to the U.S. laden with artworks formerly owned by the ROMANOV family. He increased his fortune in the U.S. with whiskey making and cattle raising and retired in 1956, but an investment in wildcat oil wells led to another career as head of the Occidental Petroleum Corp. (1957–90). He was a longtime advocate of broadening U.S.-Soviet trade ties. The Armand Hammer Museum in Los Angeles houses his art collection.

hammer-beam roof English medieval timber roof system used when a long span was needed. Not a true TRUSS, the construction is similar to corbeled masonry (see CORBEL) in that each set of beams steps upward (and inward) by resting on the ones below by means of curved braces and struts. The roof of RICHARD II's Westminster Hall in London (1402), with a 70-ft (21-m) span, is an excellent example.

hammer throw Athletic event in which a 16-lb (7.26-kg) metal ball attached to a spring steel handle (not more than 3 ft 11¾ in. long) is thrown for distance. The thrower makes three full, quick turns of the body before flinging the weight. The sport developed centuries ago in the British Isles; it has been a regular part of TRACK-AND-FIELD competitions there since 1866, and an Olympic sport since 1900.

hammered dulcimer See DULCIMER

Hammerfest \ˈhä-mər-ˌfest\ Northernmost town in Europe (pop., 1990 est.: 7,000), on the island of Kvaløya, northwestern Norway. Chartered in 1789, most of it was destroyed by fire in 1891. Norway's first municipal hydroelectric station was built with its reconstruction. Germans occupied the town 1940–44; on their withdrawal, they blew up the installations and evacuated the population. The town has since been rebuilt. Despite its latitude, its harbor is ice-free year-round because of the warming North Atlantic Current. The sun shines continuously May 17–July 29; there is no sunlight from November 21 to January 21. Tourism and fish-oil processing are important economically.

hammerhead shark Any of the swift, powerful SHARKS in the family Sphyrnidae, having a broad, flattened, hammer- or spade-shaped head, with the eyes and nostrils at the ends of the sidewise projections. Widely distributed in all oceans, in warm and temperate waters, they feed on fish, stingrays, skates, and other sharks. Some species are fished for leather and oil. Three species seem to be particularly dangerous to humans: the great hammerhead (the largest hammerhead, growing to 15 ft, or 4.5 m, or more), the scalloped hammerhead, and the smooth hammerhead. All three are grayish and found throughout the tropics.

Hammerstein \ˈha-mər-ˌstīn, ˈha-mər-ˌstēn\, **Oscar, II** (1895–1960) U.S. lyricist, musical-comedy author, and producer. Grandson of the opera impresario Oscar Hammerstein (1846–1919), he was born in New York City and studied law at Columbia University before beginning his theater career. Among his early musicals are *Rose Marie* (1924; music by R. FRIML), *The Desert Song* (1925; music by S. ROMBERG), and the J. KERN musicals *Sunny* (1925) and *Show Boat* (1927), the latter a musical-theater landmark. In the early 1940s he began a famous collaboration with R. RODGERS; the two soon became the preeminent figures in the American musical theater, creating *Oklahoma!* (1943; Pulitzer Prize), *Carousel* (1945), *State Fair* (1945), *Allegro* (1948), *South Pacific* (1949; Pulitzer Prize), *The King and I* (1951), *Me and Juliet* (1953), *Flower Drum Song* (1958), and *The Sound of Music* (1959). They formed the publishing firm Williamson Music, and from 1949 were theatrical producers as well.

Hammett, (Samuel) Dashiell (1894–1961) U.S. detective novelist. Born in St. Mary's Co., Md., he left school at 13. He spent eight years as a private detective before beginning to publish fiction in pulp magazines. His first novels were *Red Harvest* (1929) and *The Dain Curse* (1929). *The Maltese Falcon* (1930; film, 1941), considered his finest work, introduced Sam Spade, the prototype of the hard-boiled detective. It was followed by the story collection *The Continental Op* (1930) and the novel *The Glass Key* (1931). *The Thin Man* (1934), featuring the witty detective couple Nick and Nora Charles, spawned a popular series of movies. Nora was based on LILLIAN HELLMAN, with whom Hammett had a romantic alliance from 1930 until his death. He later worked as a screenwriter. For refusing to answer questions about his Communist Party affiliations and betray his associates, he served a prison sentence in the 1950s.

Hammett.
CULVER PICTURES, INC.

Hamming, Richard W(esley) (1915–1998) U.S. mathematician. Born in Chicago, he received his PhD from the University of Nebraska.

In 1945 he went to work for the MANHATTAN PROJECT and managed the computers used in the first atomic bombs. He also made important contributions to communication theory and computing, especially in the areas of probability, orthogonal arrays, and error detection and correction in data storage and transmission. He invented the Hamming code to deal with error correction. Much of his work was done at Bell Labs. In 1968 he received the Turing Award.

Hammurabi \ˌha-mə-ˈrä-bē\ (died c. 1750 BC) Sixth and best-known Babylonian ruler of the Amorite dynasty. His kingdom was one of several prominent realms in BABYLONIA. His desire to control the Euphrates led him to conquer the cities of Uruk (ERECH) and Isin in 1787 BC, but he gave up on further military campaigns in that area, turning instead to the northwest and the east in 1784. Twenty years of peace followed, and then 14 years of almost continuous warfare that resulted in a unified MESOPOTAMIA. He used control of waterways (damming them to deny his enemies water or to create a flood by releasing them) to defeat his enemies. He also engaged in building and restoring temples, city walls, public buildings, and canals. His laws, collected in the Code of HAMMURABI, demonstrate his desire to be a just ruler.

Hammurabi, limestone relief; in the British Museum.

BY COURTESY OF THE TRUSTEES OF THE BRITISH MUSEUM; PHOTOGRAPH, J.R. FREEMAN & CO. LTD.

Hammurabi, Code of Most complete and perfect extant collection of Babylonian laws, developed during the reign of HAMMURABI. It consists of 282 of his legal decisions, collected toward the end of his reign and inscribed on a diorite stela set up in the temple of MARDUK. The text is in the AKKADIAN LANGUAGE. Despite a few references to family solidarity, trial by ordeal, and the *lex talionis* (an eye for an eye, a tooth for a tooth), it represents an advance over tribal custom in that it recognizes no blood feud, private retribution, or marriage by capture. The principal portion of the code is preserved in the Louvre Museum in Paris.

Hampden, John (1594–1643) English Parliamentary leader. In 1635 he refused to pay 20 shillings in SHIP MONEY, a levy by CHARLES I for outfitting his navy, on the ground that only Parliament was empowered to levy taxes. Though the court ruled in favor of Charles, resistance to the tax became widespread. In the LONG PARLIAMENT (1640), Hampden attacked royal policies and was one of the five members who evaded arrest by the king in 1642. The ship-money episode was one of the controversies that led to the ENGLISH CIVIL WARS, in which Hampden was mortally wounded.

Hampshire \ˈhamp-ˌshir\ County (pop., 2000 est.: 1,252,600), southern central England. It lies on the English Channel; WINCHESTER is the county seat. The Test and Avon are major rivers. Evidence of prehistoric settlement ranging from the Bronze Age to the Iron Age exists in the area. Towns developed at Silchester and Winchester during the Roman occupation. The region suffered from attacks of Norsemen, but during the Middle Ages it was comparatively peaceful and came to be known for its woolens. PORTSMOUTH and Gosport form one of Britain's principal naval centers, while SOUTHAMPTON is a major passenger port.

Hampton City (pop., 2000: 146,437), southeastern Virginia. Located on CHESAPEAKE BAY and the northern shore of HAMPTON ROADS, it forms part of a metropolitan complex that includes NEWPORT NEWS, NORFOLK, VIRGINIA BEACH, CHESAPEAKE, and PORTSMOUTH. It originated around a fort built by the British in 1609 on the site of an Indian village. Permanent settlement dates from 1610–11, making it the nation's oldest continuously settled community of English origin. It was burned by its Confederate residents in 1861 to prevent the Union occupancy; it was rebuilt after the AMERICAN CIVIL WAR. Military installations and tourism are important to the economy. Hampton University (1868) was established there by the FREEDMEN'S BUREAU to educate former slaves.

Hampton, Lionel (1908–2002) U.S. jazz vibraphonist and drummer, leader of one of the most popular and enduring big bands. Born in Louisville, Ky., Hampton's first vibraphone recording, accompanying LOUIS ARMSTRONG, was made in 1930. He became well known as a member of BENNY GOODMAN's small groups (1936–40) before forming his own big band. The rhythmic drive and excitement of Hampton's band highlighted his virtuosic playing and extroverted showmanship and became one of the direct progenitors of RHYTHM AND BLUES.

Hampton, Wade (1818–1902) U.S. military leader. Born in Charleston, S.C., he managed his family's plantations and served in the state legislature (1852–61). In the AMERICAN CIVIL WAR he organized and led "Hampton's Legion" of South Carolina troops, fighting at Bull Run and Gettysburg and serving as second in command under JEB STUART. After Stuart died, he was promoted to major general and led the cavalry (1864). After the war he sought reconciliation but opposed the policies of Reconstruction, and as governor of South Carolina (1876–79) he led the fight to restore white supremacy. He served in the U.S. Senate 1879–91.

Wade Hampton.

BY COURTESY OF THE LIBRARY OF CONGRESS, WASHINGTON, D.C.

Hampton Roads Channel through which the JAMES, Elizabeth, and Nansemond rivers flow into CHESAPEAKE BAY. About 4 mi (6 km) wide and 40 ft (12 m) deep, it has been an important military base since colonial days. In 1862 it was the scene of the Battle of the MONITOR AND MERRIMACK. The port cities of NEWPORT NEWS, NORFOLK, and PORTSMOUTH comprise the Port of Hampton Roads, one of the busiest U.S. seaports.

Hampton Roads Conference (February 3, 1865) Informal and unsuccessful peace talks at Hampton Roads, Va., during the AMERICAN CIVIL WAR. Pres. ABRAHAM LINCOLN agreed to meet with the Confederate vice president, ALEXANDER H. STEPHENS, to reach a peace settlement. Lincoln's terms called for a reunion of the nation, emancipation of the slaves, and disbanding of Confederate troops. Since Stephens had been authorized to accept independence only, no settlement was reached.

hamster Any of various stout Old World RODENTS (in the family Muridae) with a short tail, soft fur, and long cheek pouches for carrying food. Hamsters are nocturnal and generally live in burrows; they feed on fruits, grain, and vegetables, though some species also eat insects and other small animals. The common hamster of Europe and western Asia is 8–12 in. (20–30 cm) long, without the 1–2.5-in. (3–6-cm) tail; its coat is brown above and black below, with white patches along each side. The golden hamster of Syria is a popular pet and is widely used as a laboratory animal; it is golden brown with white underparts and 6–8 in. (15–20 cm) long, including the tail.

Golden hamster (*Mesocricetus auratus*).

JOHN MARKHAM

Hamsun \ˈhäm-ˌsün\, **Knut** *orig.* **Knut Pedersen** (1859–1952) Norwegian novelist, dramatist, and poet. Of peasant origin, he had almost no formal education. His semiautobiographical first novel, *Hunger* (1890), about a starving young writer, revealed his impulsive, lyrical style. It was followed by such works as *Mysteries* (1892), *Pan* (1894), and *Victoria* (1898), with which he established himself as a leader of the Neoromantic revolt against social realism. *Growth of the Soil* (1917) and his many other novels express a message of fierce individualism and back-to-nature philosophy. He won the Nobel Prize in 1920. His antipathy to modern Western culture led to his support of Nazi Germany during its wartime occupation of Norway; he was imprisoned and tried after the war, and his reputation was seriously damaged.

han Fief controlled by a DAIMYO, or territorial lord, during the EDO PERIOD (1603–1868) in Japan. Collectively, the han resembled a confederation of principalities united under the TOKUGAWA SHOGUNATE. In 1869 the daimyo were requested to surrender their domains to the MEIJI EMPEROR; in 1871 they were abolished and replaced by the present-day prefectures.

Han dynasty \'hän\ (206 BC–AD 220) Second great Chinese imperial dynasty. In contrast to the preceding QIN DYNASTY, the Han was a period of cultural flowering. One of the greatest of the early histories, the *Shiji* by Sima Qian, was composed, and the *fu,* a poetic form that became the norm for creative writing, began to flourish. The Yuefu, or Music Bureau, collected and recorded not only ceremonial chants but also the songs and ballads of ordinary people. Lacquerware, first developed during the SHANG DYNASTY, reached a level of great mastery, and silk was woven for export trade, which reached as far as Europe. Buddhism entered China during the Han. Paper was invented, time was measured with water clocks and sundials, and calendars were published frequently. So thoroughly did the Han dynasty establish what was thereafter considered Chinese culture that the Chinese word for Chinese people is Han.

Han Gaozu See LIU BANG

Han Kao-tsu See LIU BANG

Han River \'hän\ River, east-central China. A principal tributary of the YANGTZE RIVER (Chang Jiang), it has a total length of about 750 mi (1,200 km). It rises in the mountains in southwestern SHAANXI province; known by various names in its upper course, it becomes the Han at Hanzhong and flows through a fertile basin some 60 mi (100 km) long and 12 mi (19 km) wide, then cuts through a series of deep gorges and emerges into the central Yangtze basin in HUBEI province. Its lower course forms a dense network of water transport covering the southern part of the North China Plain.

Han Yongun \'hän-'yòŋ-'ùn\ *or* **Manhae** (1879–1944) Korean poet and religious and political leader. After participating in the failed TONGHAK UPRISING, he fled to Mount Solok and studied Buddhism. He became a priest in 1905 and set out to restore and nationalize Buddhism in Korea. In 1910, when Korea came under Japanese rule, he joined the independence movement. He helped draft a Korean Declaration of Independence in 1919 and was arrested and jailed for three years. In 1927 he led in the establishment of the Singanhoe society, a united national independence front. His best-known work is a volume of poetry, *The Silence of the Lover.*

Han Yu *or* **Han Yü** \'hän-'yǖ\ (768–824) Chinese poet and prose writer, the first proponent of NEO-CONFUCIANISM. An orphan, he joined the Chinese bureaucracy and served in several high government posts. He attacked Taoism and Buddhism, which were then at the height of their influence, and sought to restore Confucianism to its former status. He revived interest in the writings of MENCIUS and other neglected Confucian classics. His own works were written in a simple prose style unlike the elaborate manner popular at the time, and he became known as the Prince of Letters.

Han Yü, portrait by an unknown artist; in the National Palace Museum, Taipei.

BY COURTESY OF THE COLLECTION OF THE NATIONAL PALACE MUSEUM, TAIPEI, TAIWAN, REPUBLIC OF CHINA

Hanafi, Alam al-din al- See AL-HANAFI

Hancock, Herbie *orig.* **Herbert Jeffrey** (born 1940) U.S. pianist, composer, and bandleader. Born in Chicago, he was educated at Grinnell College in Iowa. Part of the superb rhythm section of MILES DAVIS's mid-1960s group, he led the group after Davis left. In the 1970s he became involved in funk music, and later disco, while continuing to tour with jazz groups, including WYNTON MARSALIS. In 1986 he acted in and scored *Round Midnight* (1986, Academy Award). His later career has been notably diverse.

Hancock, John (1737–1793) American Revolutionary leader. Born in Braintree, Mass., he entered his wealthy uncle's mercantile business in Boston in 1754. His identification with the patriot cause dated from the STAMP ACT, which, as a leading merchant, he protested. He was elected to the Massachusetts legislature in 1769, soon after the British seized one of his ships, and he chaired the Boston town committee formed after the BOSTON MASSACRE. He became president of the provincial congress (1774–75), and he and SAMUEL ADAMS led the Massachusetts Patriots. In 1775 both were forced to flee from British troops sent to arrest them for treason. Hancock was a member of the Continental Congress 1775–80, serving as its president 1775–77; the bold flourish with which he signed the DECLARATION OF INDEPENDENCE has made his name synonymous with "signature." As governor of Massachusetts (1780–85, 1787–93), he presided over the state's ratification of the Constitution in 1788.

Hancock, Winfield Scott (1824–1886) U.S. general and politician. Born in Montgomery Co., Pa., he graduated from West Point and served in the Mexican War. Appointed a brigadier general of volunteers at the start of the AMERICAN CIVIL WAR, he became a corps commander in the Army of the Potomac (1863–65), and held a key Union defense in the Battle of GETTYSBURG. After the war he commanded the military division of Louisiana and Texas, where he maintained the civil authorities, winning the support of Democrats and, as a result, their presidential nomination in 1880; he lost the election to JAMES GARFIELD.

hand End part of the ARM, consisting of the wrist joint, palm, thumb, and fingers. The hand has great mobility and flexibility to carry out precise movements. Bipedal locomotion in humans frees the hands for grasping and manipulation. The opposable thumb allows them to pick up small items and grip objects from both sides. Dexterity in the hands and increased brain size are believed to have evolved together in humans.

Hand, (Billings) Learned (1872–1961) U.S. jurist. Born in Albany, N.Y., he studied philosophy (under WILLIAM JAMES, JOSIAH ROYCE, and GEORGE SANTAYANA) and law at Harvard. In 1909 he was appointed a federal district judge, and in 1924 he was elevated to the U.S. Circuit Court of Appeals, on which he served as chief judge from 1939 to 1951. His 52-year tenure on the federal bench represents a record. Several of his decisions, including in the Alcoa antitrust case (1945) and a 1950 case involving communist-conspiracy charges, are considered landmarks. Though he never reached the U.S. Supreme Court, his reputation surpasses that of all but a few who have sat there.

handball Game played in a three- or four-walled court or against a single wall by two or four players (in singles or doubles games, respectively) who use their hands to strike a small rubber ball, attempting to place it beyond the reach of their opponents. The game runs to 21 points. Handball games were played in ancient Rome and later (as PELOTA) in Spain and France. Modern handball developed in Ireland, where it is still popular. It was widely played particularly among late-19th-century Irish immigrants in New York, whence it eventually spread around the continent. It is a forerunner of modern JAI ALAI.

Handel, George Frideric *orig.* **Georg Friederich Händel** (1685–1759) German-British composer. Born to a barber-surgeon in Halle, he had to struggle to study organ, violin, and composition. Moving to Hamburg in 1703, he played in the opera orchestra under Reinhard Keiser (1674–1739), and his first opera was produced there in 1705. A Medici prince invited him to Florence; there and in Rome, patronized by cardinals and nobility, he wrote oratorios, cantatas, and more operas. Hired as kapellmeister by the elector at Hanover (1710), he asked permission to visit London before assuming his responsibilities. There his opera *Rinaldo* (1711) immediately made his name; forsaking Hanover, he remained in England the rest of his life. In 1714 the German elector became GEORGE I of England; any annoyance at Handel's defection dissipated, and the king

George Frideric Handel, detail of an oil painting after Thomas Hudson, 1756; in the National Portrait Gallery, London.

BY COURTESY OF THE NATIONAL PORTRAIT GALLERY, LONDON

became one of his patrons. Handel became musical director of the new Royal Academy of Music, an opera house, which thrived until the public taste shifted away from Italian opera. In 1732 he revised his oratorio *Esther* for a public performance, the first public oratorio performance in England. Its success was followed by many more English-language oratorios, including his great *Messiah* (1741). Handel was renowned as virtually the greatest organist and harpsichordist in the world. His posthumous reputation grew to mammoth proportions and dominated English music for more than a century. He wrote about 45 Italian operas, including *Giulio Cesare* (1723), *Orlando* (1733), and *Alcina* (1735). His oratorios include *Israel in Egypt* (1739), *Saul* (1739), and *Jephtha* (1752). His church music includes the *Chandos Anthems* (1718) and *Coronation Anthems* (1727). His orchestral works include the famous *Water Music* (1717) and *Royal Fireworks Music* (1749), the 18 concerti grossi of Op. 3 and Op. 6, and 17 organ concertos.

handicap In sports and games, a method of offsetting the varying abilities or characteristics of competitors in order to equalize their chances of winning. In horse racing, for example, a track official may assign weights to horses according to their speed in previous performances. In golf a poorer player may reduce his score by a few strokes. See also BOOKMAKING; GAMBLING.

Handke \'hänt-kə\, **Peter** (born 1942) Austrian writer. He studied law before beginning to write seriously. He earned an early reputation as a member of the avant-garde. His plays, which generally lack conventional plot, dialogue, and characters, include *Offending the Audience* (1966), in which actors analyze the nature of theater and alternately insult the audience and praise its "performance," and *Kaspar* (1968). His novels, mostly ultraobjective, deadpan accounts of characters in extreme states of mind, include *The Goalie's Anxiety at the Penalty Kick* (1970) and *The Left-Handed Woman* (1976). A dominant theme is the deadening effects and underlying irrationality of ordinary language, everyday reality, and rational order.

Handsome Lake *or* **Ganioda'yo** \ˌgän-yō-'dī-yō\ (1735?–1815) Seneca Indian chief. Born in Ganawaugus, N.Y., he led a somewhat dissolute life before becoming seriously ill in 1799; on recovering, he reported a vision revealing the will of the Great Spirit. He developed a religion he called Gai'wiio (Good Message) that combined elements of Christianity and Indian beliefs; as an itinerant preacher, he urged his people to refrain from adultery, drunkenness, laziness, and witchcraft. The religion revitalized the demoralized Iroquois.

Handy, W(illiam) C(hristopher) (1873–1958) U.S. composer, cornetist, and bandleader known for integrating BLUES elements into RAGTIME, changing the course of popular music. Born in Florence, Ala., Handy worked as a soloist and conductor with several bands around the turn of the century and became active as a music publisher in Memphis (1908) and later New York (1918). Handy's compositions, including "St. Louis Blues," "Beale Street Blues," and "Memphis Blues," became favorites of singers and instrumentalists in the 1920s, helping to codify the blues as a framework within which to improvise.

Hanfeizi \'han-'fā-'tsə\ *or* **Han-fei-tzu** \'han-'fā-'dzü\ (died 233 BC) Greatest of China's legalist philosophers. Much about his life is unknown; it ended when he was sent on a diplomatic mission to the court of the first Qin emperor, who had admired his writings, and found himself imprisoned and was made to drink poison. His works are collected in the *Hanfeizi,* presumably compiled after his death. In 55 sections of varying lengths, it presents a synthesis of legal theories up to his time. To Hanfeizi it was axiomatic that political institutions must change with changing historical circumstances and must be adapted to the prevailing pattern of human behavior, which is determined not by moral sentiments but by economic conditions. The ruler should not try to make people good but only to restrain them from doing evil.

hang gliding Use of a kitelike GLIDER by a harnessed rider in gliding down usually from a cliff or hill. The hang glider was developed as a flexible-wing parachute by NASA officials in the 1960s, but soon was redesigned as a glider for recreational and competitive sport. World championships have been held and records kept since 1976.

Hangzhou *or* **Hang-chou** \'häŋ-jō\ *or* **Hangchow** \'haŋ-'chau̇\ City (pop., 1999 est.: 1,346,148), capital of ZHEJIANG province, China. It lies at the head of Zhejiang Bay and is the southern terminus of the GRAND CANAL. Its buildings and gardens are renowned, and some of China's most famous monasteries are located nearby. As Lin'an, it was the capital of the SONG DYNASTY c. AD 1126–1279. A prosperous center of commerce with an estimated population then of 1–1.5 million, it was visited in the late 13th century by MARCO POLO, who called it Kinsai. Its importance as a port decreased as the bay silted up, but it remained a commercial center, and was opened to foreign trade in 1896. In addition to its cultural importance, it is also the center for an industrial area.

haniwa \'hä-nē-ˌwä\ Terra-cotta cylinders and sculptures arranged on and around Japanese tombs during the Tumulus period (c. AD 250–552). The earliest haniwa were barrel-shaped hollow cylinders used to mark the borders of a burial ground. By the 4th century the cylinders were topped with sculptures of warriors, attendants, dancers, animals, boats, birds, and military equipment. After the introduction of Buddhism and the practice of cremation, the making of haniwa declined.

Hanks, Tom *orig.* **Thomas J.** (born 1956) U.S. film actor. Born in Concord, Cal., he displayed a flair for light comedy in the television series *Bosom Buddies* (1980–82), then became a film star in the comedies *Splash* (1984) and *Big* (1988). After winning praise for *A League of Their Own* (1992) and the romantic hit *Sleepless in Seattle* (1993), he proved himself an accomplished dramatic actor in *Philadelphia* (1993, Academy Award), *Forrest Gump* (1994, Academy Award), *Apollo 13* (1995), *Saving Private Ryan* (1998), and *Cast Away* (2000). He made his debut as director and screenwriter with *That Thing You Do* (1996).

Hanlin Academy \'hän-ˌlin\ Elite scholarly institution founded in the 8th century in China to perform secretarial, archival, and literary tasks for the court and establish the official interpretations of the Confucian Classics (see FIVE CLASSICS). By the time of the MING DYNASTY, admittance was granted only to those who did exceptionally well in the CHINESE EXAMINATION SYSTEM. Hanlin scholars functioned as the emperor's close advisers and confidential secretaries. The academy was closed when the QING DYNASTY was overthrown in 1911.

Hanna, Mark *orig.* **Marcus Alonzo** (1837–1904) U.S. industrialist and political kingmaker. Born in New Lisbon, Ohio, he became a businessman in Cleveland, with interests in banking, coal and iron, transportation, and publishing. Convinced that business success depended on the success of the Republican Party, in 1880 he began to gain industrialists' support for its candidates. In 1892 he helped WILLIAM MCKINLEY secure the Ohio governorship, and his corporate fund-raising for McKinley's 1896 presidential campaign allowed Republicans to spend an unprecedented $3.5 million, overwhelm the opposition of WILLIAM JENNINGS BRYAN, and cement the growing alliance between big business and the party. He served in the U.S. Senate 1897–1904.

Hanna, William (Denby) (1910–2001) U.S. animator known for his collaborative productions with Joseph (Roland) Barbera (born 1911). Hanna was born in Melrose, N.M., Barbera in New York City. Both worked as story editors in film studios before Hanna joined MGM in 1937 and collaborated with Barbera to create the Tom and Jerry cartoon characters. From 1940 to 1957 they produced over 200 *Tom and Jerry* cartoons, seven of which won Academy Awards. They founded Hanna-Barbera Productions in 1957 and collaborated on such popular television cartoon series as *The Flintstones, Yogi Bear,* and *Huckleberry Hound.*

Hannibal (247–183? BC) Carthaginian general, one of the great military leaders of antiquity. Taken to Spain by his father, the Carthaginian general Hamilcar Barca (died 229/228 BC), he was sworn to eternal enmity with Rome. After the death of his father and brother-in-law, he took charge of Carthage's army in Spain (221). He secured Spain, then crossed the Ebro River into Roman territory, and entered Gaul. He marched over the Alps into Italy; encumbered by elephants and horses, he was beset by Gallic tribes, harsh winter weather, and defection of his Spanish troops. He defeated FLAMINIUS but was severely harassed by FABIUS MAXIMUS CUNCTATOR. In 216 he won the Battle of CANNAE. In 203 he left for northern Africa to help Carthage fend off SCIPIO's forces. He lost decisively to Scipio's ally MASINISSA at the Battle of ZAMA, but escaped. He headed the Carthaginian government (c. 202–195); forced to flee, he sought refuge with ANTIOCHUS III, whose fleet he commanded against Rome, with disastrous results. After the Battle of Magnesia (190) the Romans demanded he be handed over; he eluded them until, seeing no escape, he took poison.

Hanoi \ha-'nȯi\ City (pop., 1993 est: 2,155,000), capital of Vietnam. Located in northern Vietnam on the western bank of the RED RIVER, it became the capital of Vietnam's Ly dynasty in 1010. It was the main capital of Vietnam until 1802, when the NGUYEN DYNASTY transferred the capital south to HUE. Under French rule, Hanoi again became an important administrative center, and in 1902 it was made the capital of French INDOCHINA. It became the capital of North Vietnam after the French defeat in 1954. During the VIETNAM WAR, many of its monuments and palaces were destroyed by U.S. bombing. As the capital of a united Vietnam since 1975, it has steadily been rebuilt and its industrial base has grown.

Hanotaux \à-nò-'tō\, **(Albert-Auguste-) Gabriel** (1853–1944) French politician and historian. An archivist in the foreign ministry from 1880, he advanced rapidly and was appointed foreign minister in 1894. He oversaw French colonial expansion in French West Africa, Madagascar, and Tunisia. In 1898 he advocated a strong stand at Fashoda (see FASHODA INCIDENT). He also championed a Franco-Russian alliance. His large body of historical writings centered on early modern institutional history and contemporary diplomatic affairs.

Hanover \'ha-ˌnō-vər\ *German* **Hannover** \hä-'nō-fər\ City (pop., 1996 est.: 523,000), capital of Lower Saxony state, northwestern Germany. Located on the Leine River, it is first mentioned in documents in AD 1100. It joined the HANSEATIC LEAGUE in 1386. From 1495 it belonged to the WELF DYNASTY (later the House of HANOVER). It was capital of the kingdom of Hanover (1815–66), then was annexed by Prussia. It became the capital of Lower Saxony in 1946. It suffered destruction in World War II but was rebuilt. It is now an educational, financial, and commercial center with highly diversified industries.

Hanover, House of British royal house of German origin. It was descended from George Louis, elector of Hanover, who succeeded to the British crown as GEORGE I in 1714. The dynasty also provided the monarchs GEORGE II, GEORGE III, GEORGE IV, WILLIAM IV, and VICTORIA. By the Act of SETTLEMENT (1701) the crown was to go to ANNE (of the House of STUART) and then, if she lacked issue, to Sophia (1665–1714), electress of Hanover (granddaughter of JAMES I) and her descendants. The House of Hanover was succeeded in 1901 by the House of Saxe-Coburg-Gotha, renamed in 1917 the House of WINDSOR.

Hansberry, Lorraine (1930–1965) U.S. playwright. She was born in Chicago, and her childhood experiences in a black family in a hostile white neighborhood lent power to her first play, *A Raisin in the Sun* (1959). The first play by a black woman produced on Broadway, it won high critical praise and was filmed in 1961. Her next play, *The Sign in Sidney Brustein's Window* (1964), had a modest Broadway run. Her promising career was cut short by her early death from cancer.

Hanseatic League \ˌhan-sē-'a-tik\ *or* **Hansa** (from German *Hanse*, "association") Organization founded in the late medieval period by northern German towns and merchant communities to protect their trading interests. The league dominated commercial activity in northern Europe from the 13th to the 15th century. It protected transport of goods by quelling pirates and brigands and fostered safe navigation by building lighthouses. Most important, it sought to organize and control trade by winning commercial privileges and monopolies and by establishing trading bases overseas. In extreme cases its members resorted to warfare, as when they raised an armed force that defeated the Danes in 1368 and confirmed the league's supremacy in the Baltic Sea. Over 150 towns were at some point associated with the league, including BREMEN, HAMBURG, and LÜBECK.

Hansen's disease See LEPROSY

Hanson, Howard (Harold) (1896–1981) U.S. composer, conductor, and educator. Born in Wahoo, Neb., he was awarded the Rome Prize in 1921 and studied in Italy with O. RESPIGHI. Returning to the U.S., he became director of the EASTMAN SCHOOL OF MUSIC (1924), and remained there 40 years, building the school into a world-renowned institution. Despite his keen scholarly interest in modern developments, his own music is neo-Romantic; he is best known for his seven symphonies—including the second ("Romantic") and fourth ("Requiem"; Pulitzer Prize)—and his opera *Merry Mount* (1934).

hantavirus Genus of VIRUSES of the family Bunyaviridae that cause PNEUMONIA and HEMORRHAGIC FEVERS. Carried by rodents, they spread to humans directly or by inhalation but apparently are not transmitted from one person to another. An outbreak in the 1990s in the southwestern U.S. caused a mysterious, often fatal, flulike illness with rapid respiratory failure in previously healthy adults. The culprit was a hantavirus type carried by mice and not previously associated with human illness in the U.S.

Hanukkah \'hä-nə-kə, 'k̲ä-nə-kə\ In Judaism, a holiday celebrating the rededication of the Second Temple of JERUSALEM in 164 BC, after its desecration three years earlier by order of ANTIOCHUS IV EPIPHANES. The MACCABEES recaptured Jerusalem and reconsecrated the Temple after leading a successful revolt against Syrian rule. The lighting of the MENORAH recalls the story that a one-day supply of oil burned miraculously in the Temple for eight days until new oil could be obtained. Sometimes called the Feast of Dedication or Feast of Lights, it is celebrated for eight days in December, during which the ceremonial candles are lit and children play games and receive gifts. Originally a minor holiday, it has become more lavishly celebrated as a result of its proximity to CHRISTMAS.

Hanuman \'hə-nu̇-ˌmän, ˌhə-nu̇-'män\ Monkey god of Hindu mythology, a central figure in the *RAMAYANA*. He was a guardian spirit, the offspring of a nymph and the wind god. His great heroic exploit was recovering RAMA's wife, SITA, from captivity by the demon RAVANA. Hanuman also flew to the Himalayas and carried back a mountain of medicinal herbs to cure Rama's grievously wounded brother Laksmana. Worshiped in the form of a monkey, he is an important deity because of his strength and his faithfulness to Rama.

haplite See APLITE

haploidy See PLOIDY

Hapsburg dynasty See HABSBURG DYNASTY

Hara Kei \'hä-rä-'kā\ *or* **Hara Takashi** \'tä-kä-shē\ (1856–1921) Prime minister of Japan (1918–21) and cofounder of one of Japan's first political parties, the RIKKEN SEIYUKAI. Hara lowered the property qualifications for voting, thus enlarging the electorate to include small landholders, who supported the Seiyukai. He attempted to reduce the power of the military, which led to his assassination by a right-wing fanatic.

hara-kiri See SEPPUKU

harai \hä-'rī\ Purification ceremonies in the SHINTO religion, used to cleanse an individual before he may approach a deity. Salt, water, and fire are the chief agents of purification, and the rites range from bathing in the cold sea to washing the hands before entering a temple. Priests undergo more rigorous harai rites intended to regulate the body, heart, environment, and soul. Great purification ceremonies are held twice a year in Japan, on June 30 and December 31.

Harald III Sigurdsson *known as* **Harald Hardraade** \'hȯr-ˌrȯ-də*or* **Harald the Ruthless** (1015–1066) King of Norway (1045–66). The son of a Norwegian chieftain, he fought against the Danes in 1030, then fled the country, taking service in the Russian and Byzantine armies. He returned in 1045 to take the throne. He struggled unsuccessfully to wrest the Danish throne from Sweyn II (1045–62). He expanded Norway's possessions in the Orkney, Shetland, and Hebrides islands, and he attempted to conquer England in 1066 but was defeated and killed at Stamford Bridge.

Harare \hä-'rä-rā\ *formerly* **Salisbury** \'sȯlz-bə-rē\ City (pop., 1992: 1,184,000), capital of Zimbabwe. Located in northeastern Zimbabwe, it was founded as Salisbury by the British in 1890. It was the capital, successively, of the colony of Southern Rhodesia, the Federation of Rhodesia and Nyasaland (1953–63), and RHODESIA (1965–79). Under the new government of independent Zimbabwe (1980), it was renamed Harare. It is a cultural and educational center and the site of the University of Zimbabwe (1957). The center of Zimbabwe's industry and commerce, it is the distribution point for the area's agricultural produce. There are important gold mines nearby.

Harbin \'här-bən, här-'bin\ *or* **Ha'erbin** *or* **Ha-erh-pin** \'hä-'ər-'bin\ City (pop., 1999 est.: 2,586,978), capital and largest city of HEILONGJIANG province, northeastern China. Located on the SONGHUA RIVER in the center of MANCHURIA, it grew with the arrival of the Chinese Eastern Railway, built by the Russians in the late 19th century. A Russian military base during the RUSSO-JAPANESE WAR, it was a haven for Russian refugees after the RUSSIAN REVOLUTION OF 1917 and had the largest Russian population of any city outside the Soviet Union. Chinese communist forces took the city in 1946 and from it directed their conquest of Manchuria. Since 1949 it has become the chief industrial base of northeastern China, and is a shipping center for agricultural products.

harbor seal Nonmigratory, earless SEAL *(Phoca vitulina)* found throughout the Northern Hemisphere. Harbor seals are whitish or grayish at birth, generally gray with black spots as adults. The adult male may reach a length of about 6 ft (1.8 m) and a weight of almost 300 lbs (130 kg); the female is somewhat smaller. Found along coastlines and in a few freshwater lakes in Canada and Alaska, the harbor seal is a gregarious animal that feeds on fish, squid, and crustaceans. It is of little economic value and in some areas is considered a nuisance by fishermen.

Harburg, E(dgar) Y(ipsel) *orig.* **Isidore Hochberg** (1898–1981) U.S. lyricist, producer, and director. Born in New York City, Harburg attended CCNY with his friend IRA GERSHWIN. When his electrical-appliance business went bankrupt in 1929, he devoted himself to songwriting for Broadway, writing such songs as the Depression anthem "Brother, Can You Spare a Dime?" (with Jay Gorney). From 1935 Harburg and H. ARLEN wrote songs for many films, including *The Wizard of Oz* (1939) and *Cabin in the Sky* (1943). Blacklisted for his political views, Harburg returned to Broadway to write musicals, notably *Finian's Rainbow* (1947; with BURTON LANE).

hard coal See ANTHRACITE

hard disk Magnetic storage medium for a MICROCOMPUTER. Hard disks are flat, circular plates made of aluminum or glass and coated with a magnetic material. Hard disks for PERSONAL COMPUTERS can store up to several gigabytes (billions of bytes) of information. Data are stored on their surfaces in concentric tracks. A small electromagnet, called a magnetic head, writes a binary digit (1 or 0) by magnetizing tiny spots on the spinning disk in different directions and reads digits by detecting the magnetization direction of the spots. A computer's hard drive is a device consisting of several hard disks, read/write heads, a drive motor to spin the disks, and a small amount of circuitry, all sealed in a metal case to protect the disks from dust. In addition to referring to the disks themselves, the term hard disk is also used to refer to the whole hard drive.

hard water Water that contains mineral salts of calcium and magnesium, principally as bicarbonates, chlorides, and sulfates, and sometimes iron. Hardness caused by calcium bicarbonate is known as temporary, because boiling converts the bicarbonate to the insoluble carbonate; hardness from the other salts is called permanent. Water is softened on a large scale by adding just enough lime to precipitate the calcium as carbonate and the magnesium as hydroxide, and then sodium carbonate is added to remove the remaining calcium salts. Home water softeners make use of the ion exchange properties of natural or synthetic ZEOLITE minerals.

Hardanger Fjord \här-ˈdäŋ-ər-ˌfyȯrd\ Fjord, southwestern Norway. The country's second-largest fjord, it extends inland 70 mi (113 km) from the North Sea to the Hardanger Plateau. It has a maximum depth of 2,922 ft (891 m). Waterfalls pour from the surrounding mountains, which rise to about 5,000 ft (1,500 m). Frequented by tourists, the area has many branch fjords. A 17th-century baronial mansion stands at Rosendal, near the fjord's mouth.

Hardee, William J(oseph) (1815–1873) U.S. military leader. Born near Savannah, Ga., he graduated from West Point in 1838. In 1855 he wrote *Rifle and Light Infantry Tactics,* a popular manual that was later used by both sides in the Civil War. When Georgia seceded in 1861, he resigned his commission and assumed command of Confederate forces in northeastern Arkansas, later demonstrating his military skills at the battles of Shiloh and Chattanooga. He later took command of the military department of South Carolina, Georgia, and Florida, and attempted to halt WILLIAM T. SHERMAN's march across Georgia. After the war he retired to his plantation.

Harden, Arthur *later* **Sir Arthur** (1865–1940) British biochemist. His more than 20 years of study of sugar fermentation advanced knowledge of metabolic processes in all living forms. In 1929 he shared the Nobel Prize for Chemistry with Hans von Euler-Chelpin. He also produced pioneering studies of bacterial enzymes and metabolism. He was knighted in 1936.

Hardenberg \ˈhär-dən-ˌberk\, **Karl August, Fürst (Prince) von** (1750–1822) Prussian statesman who preserved the integrity of the Prussian state during the NAPOLEONIC WARS. He won the abiding trust of FREDERICK WILLIAM III in 1798, and served as foreign minister 1804–6. He was forced to withdraw from political life, at NAPOLEON's behest, after Prussia's collapse in the war of 1806–7 against France. When Prussia was faced with insolvency and could not pay war indemnities in 1810, Napoleon agreed to Hardenberg's reinstatement and he became prime minister with full powers. He continued the domestic reforms introduced by KARL, FREIHERR VOM UND ZUM STEIN and liberalized financial, economic, and agricultural policies. In foreign affairs he exchanged Prussia's alliance with France for an alliance with Russia in 1813, and in 1814–15 he represented Prussia at the peace negotiations in Paris and Vienna.

hardening In METALLURGY, an increase in HARDNESS of a METAL induced, deliberately or accidentally, by hammering, ROLLING, drawing (see WIRE DRAWING), or other physical processes. The first few deformations imposed by such treatment weaken the metal, but because of the crystalline structure of metal its strength increases with continued deformations. Crystals slip against each other; but, because of the complexity of the crystal structure, the more such slips are multiplied, the more they tend to place obstacles in the way of further slippage, as the various dislocation lines crisscross each other. See also CARBURIZING, HEAT TREATING, TEMPERING.

hardening of the arteries See ARTERIOSCLEROSIS

Hardie, J(ames) Keir (1856–1915) British labor leader. A coal miner, he led strikes and helped form unions, then worked as a journalist and founded two newspapers. Elected to Parliament in 1892, he helped organize the Independent Labour Party. In 1906 he became the first leader of the LABOUR PARTY in the House of Commons. A pacifist, he sought unsuccessfully to bind the SECOND INTERNATIONAL to declaring a general strike in all countries in the event of war. From 1903 he also acted as chief adviser to the militant suffragists headed by EMMELINE PANKHURST.

Harding, Warren G(amaliel) (1865–1923) 29th president of the U.S. (1921–23). Born in Corsica, Ohio, he became a newspaper publisher in Marion, where he was allied with the Republican Party's political machine. He served successively as state senator (1899–1902), lieutenant governor (1903–4), and U.S. senator (1915–21), supporting conservative policies. At the deadlocked 1920 Republican presidential convention, he was chosen as the compromise candidate. Pledging a "return to normalcy" after World War I, he defeated JAMES COX with over 60% of the popular vote, the largest margin to that time. On his recommendation, Congress established a budget system for the federal government, passed a high protective tariff, revised wartime taxes, and restricted immigration. His administration convened the WASHINGTON CONFERENCE (1921–22). His ill-advised cabinet and patronage appointments, including ALBERT FALL, led to the TEAPOT DOME SCANDAL and characterized his administration as corrupt. While in Alaska, he received word of the corruption about to be exposed and headed back. He arrived in San Francisco exhausted, reportedly suffering from food poisoning and other ills, and died there on August 2 under unclear circumstances. He was succeeded by his vice president, CALVIN COOLIDGE.

Warren G. Harding.

BY COURTESY OF THE LIBRARY OF CONGRESS, WASHINGTON, D.C.

hardness Resistance of a MINERAL to scratching, described relative to a standard scale of 10 minerals known as the MOHS HARDNESS scale. Hardness is an important diagnostic property in mineral identification. There is a general link between hardness and chemical composition (via CRYSTAL structure); thus, most hydrous minerals, halides, carbonates, sulfates, and phosphates are relatively soft; most sulfides are relatively soft (two exceptions being marcasite and pyrite); and most anhydrous oxides and silicates are hard. See also HARDENING.

hardness scale See MOHS HARDNESS

hardpan Cemented or compacted and often clayey layer in soil that cannot be penetrated by roots. Lime, gypsum, iron, and other minerals may be carried up to the surface of soil by capillary action and deposited to form a natural concrete. In agricultural situations, special equipment may be used to chisel away hardpan so that crop plants can grow.

hardware Computer machinery and equipment, including memory, cabling, power supply, peripheral devices, and circuit boards. Computer operation requires both hardware and SOFTWARE. Hardware design specifies a computer's capability; software instructs the computer on what to do. The advent of MICROPROCESSORS in the late 1970s led to much smaller hardware assemblies and accelerated the proliferation of computers. Today's PERSONAL COMPUTERS are as powerful as the early MAINFRAMES, while mainframes are now smaller and have vastly more computing power than the early models.

hardwood Timber obtained from broad-leaved, flower-bearing trees. Hardwood trees are DECIDUOUS TREES, except in the warmest regions. The term, a classification of material, applied originally to such hard European woods as beech and oak but also includes some of the softest of woods. Included in the category are EBONY, various mahoganies (see MAHOGANY FAMILY), MAPLE, TEAK, and American black WALNUT.

Hardy, Oliver See LAUREL AND HARDY

Hardy, Thomas (1840–1928) British novelist and poet. Son of a country stonemason and builder, he practiced architecture before beginning to write poetry, then prose. Many of his novels, beginning with his second, *Under the Greenwood Tree* (1872), are set in the imaginary county of Wessex. *Far from the Madding Crowd* (1874), his first success, was followed by *The Return of the Native* (1878), *The Mayor of Casterbridge* (1886), *The Woodlanders* (1887), *Tess of the D'Urbervilles* (1891), and *Jude the Obscure* (1895), all expressing his stoical pessimism and his sense of the inevitable tragedy of life. Their continuing popularity (many have been filmed) owes much to their richly varied yet accessible style and their combination of romantic plots with convincingly presented characters. Hardy's works became increasingly at odds with Victorian morality, and public indignation at *Jude* so disgusted him that he wrote no more novels. He returned to poetry with *Wessex Poems* (1898), *Poems of the Past and the Present* (1901), and *The Dynasts* (1910), a huge poetic drama of the Napoleonic Wars.

Hardy-Weinberg law Equation that describes genetic balance within a population. It may be stated as follows: In a large, random-mating population, the proportion of dominant and recessive genes (see DOMINANCE and RECESSIVENESS) tends to remain constant from generation to generation unless outside forces act to change it. Forces that can disturb this natural balance are SELECTION, MUTATION, GENE FLOW, and NATURAL SELECTION. Certain gene-controlled traits are selected for or against by the partners involved. The law is used to calculate the probability of human matings that may result in defective offspring, and to determine whether the number of harmful mutations in a population is increasing as a result of radiation from industrial processes, medical techniques, and fallout.

hare Bounding mammal (in the family Leporidae) whose young, unlike those of RABBITS, are born fully haired, with open eyes, and sufficiently advanced to hop about a few minutes after birth. The common hare *(Lepus europaeus)* is native to central and southern Europe, the Middle East, and Africa; introduced into Australia, it has become a pest there. In North America the JACKRABBIT and SNOWSHOE HARE are widespread. Many other species occur naturally on all principal landmasses except Australia. Hares have well-developed hind legs, and the ears are usually longer than the head. Species vary in length from 16 to 28 in. (40–70 cm), without the short tail. Hares in northern latitudes are white in winter and grayish brown in summer; elsewhere, they are usually grayish brown year-round. Hares are primarily herbivorous.

Black-tailed jackrabbit (*Lepus californicus*).

Hare Krishna movement \'här-ē-'krish-nə\ *officially* **International Society for Krishna Consciousness (ISKCON)** 20th-century Hindu religious movement. It was founded in the U.S. by A.C. Bhaktivedanta Swami (1896–1977) in 1965. The organization claims a lineage of spiritual masters dating back to CAITANYA (1485–1534?), whom it regards as an incarnation of KRISHNA. Hare Krishna became popular in the U.S. and Europe among young people of the 1960s and '70s counterculture, who often appeared in public places dressed in saffron robes, chanting, dancing, and asking for contributions. Members of the group are vegetarians. They renounce alcohol and drugs and chant several hours every day. Peace and joy are to be gained by surrendering to Krishna. Since the founder's death in 1977, the communes in which many members live have been governed by an international commission. The movement has endured several schisms since its founding and was among the first groups to be attacked by anticult organizations.

harebell Widespread, slender-stemmed perennial plant *(Campanula rotundifolia),* also called Scottish bluebell, of the BELLFLOWER family, native to woods, meadows, and cliffsides of northern Eurasia and North America and of mountains farther south. It bears nodding, blue, bell-like flowers. There are more than 30 named wild varieties. Each of its delicate stems, growing in clumps, bears one to several drooping blue-violet bells.

harem In Muslim countries, that part of a house set apart for the women of the family or from which nonfamily males are excluded. Harems existed in the pre-Islamic civilizations of the Middle East; in the courts of pre-Islamic Assyria, Persia, and Egypt, they were often the sites of political intrigues involving rival court factions. Large harems for wives and concubines were common in wealthy Arab households into the 20th century; the great harem of the Turkish sultans (15th–20th century) contained several hundred women, guarded by eunuchs. By the later 20th century, the full harem system existed only among conservative elements of Arab society. The harem also existed in the courts of China and Japan as well as in India and S.East Asia.

Hargobind \ˌhər-'gō-bin-də, ˌhər-'gō-bind\ (1595–1644) Sixth Sikh GURU (1606–44). He became Guru after the execution of his father, Guru ARJAN, by the Mughal rulers of India. Until his time, Sikhism had been a passive and peace-loving religion, but Hargobind gave it a strong military character in response to the enmity of the Mughals. He created an army, fortified cities, and built a defensive encampment near the holy city of Amritsar. For this he was jailed 12 years by the emperor. After his release he defeated the armies of SHAH JAHAN, ending the notion of Mughal invincibility. He was succeeded by his grandson, HARI RAI.

Hargreaves, James *or* **James Hargraves** (c. 1725–1778) British inventor of the SPINNING JENNY. A poor, uneducated spinner and weaver, he is said to have conceived the idea when he observed a SPINNING WHEEL accidentally overturned; as the SPINDLE continued to revolve while upright, he reasoned that many spindles could be so turned, and went on to construct the first machine (patented 1770) with which one person could spin several threads at once.

Hari Rai \'hə-rē-'rä-ē\ (1630–1661) Seventh Sikh GURU (1644–61). He was nominated as Guru by his grandfather, Guru HARGOBIND, and his leadership marked a decline in the fortunes of his followers. Contemplative by temperament, he shunned military obligations and weakened the Sikhs in their struggle against India's Mughal emperors. He made a political blunder by helping the brother of the emperor AURANGZEB foment a rebellion. His son, Ram Rai, won him a pardon, but did it by altering a line of the ADI GRANTH; Hari Rai punished him for this blasphemy by passing him over in selecting the next Guru.

Haring, Keith (1958–1990) U.S. painter and draftsman. Born in Reading, Pa., he studied at New York's School of Visual Arts and developed a unique style inspired by graffiti, cartoons, and comic strips, which he displayed in works drawn clandestinely at night on subway-station walls around the city. In graffiti style he filled the page from edge to edge, using signs, abstract symbols, and human and animal figures writhing and wriggling in a spaceless, airless design. In the 1980s he executed murals in New York and exhibited internationally, achieving great commercial success. His early death resulted from AIDS.

Haringvliet \'har-iŋ-ˌvlēt\ Freshwater channel, southwestern Netherlands. A distributary of the Hollandsch Canal, the Haring flows about 20 mi (32 km) to discharge into the North Sea. Its low shores were devastated by tidal surge floods in 1953. As part of a plan for land reclamation and flood protection, a dam was completed at its mouth in 1971; it incorporates a lock that allows the channel to remain open to shipping.

Harlan, John Marshall (1833–1911) U.S. jurist. Born in Boyle Co., Ky., he practiced law there in the 1850s, commanded a Union regiment in the American Civil War, and served as state attorney general (1863–67) before being appointed to the U.S. Supreme Court by Pres. Rutherford B. Hayes. On the Court (1877–1911) he became one of the most forceful dissenters in its history. His best-known dissents, such as those in *Plessy vs. Ferguson* (1896) and the Civil-Rights Cases (1883), favored the rights of blacks. He also issued famous dissents in favor of the federal income tax (1895) and opposing monopolies in cases arising under the Sherman Antitrust Act of 1890 (he favored trust-busting). His grandson John Marshall Harlan (1899–1971) also served on the Supreme Court (1955–71).

Harlem District occupying part of northern Manhattan Island, New York City. It lies north of Central Park, with its business district centered on 125th Street. Founded by Peter Stuyvesant in 1658 as Nieuw Haarlem, it was named after Haarlem in the Netherlands. During the American Revolution it was the site of the Battle of Harlem Heights (September 16, 1776). It was a farming area in the 18th century and a fashionable residential district in the 19th century. A black residential and commercial area by World War I, in the 1920s it was the center of the cultural movement known as the Harlem Renaissance.

Harlem Globetrotters All-black professional U.S. basketball team. The Globetrotters play exhibition games all over the world, displaying spectacular ball handling and humorous antics. Their usual opposition is another traveling team, the Washington Generals, which is never allowed to win. The team was organized in 1927 by the promoter Abe Saperstein, who owned it until his death in 1966.

Harlem Renaissance *or* **New Negro Movement** Period of outstanding literary vigor and creativity centered in New York's black ghetto of Harlem in the 1920s. Its leading figures included Alain Locke (1886–1954), James Weldon Johnson, Claude McKay, Countee Cullen, Langston Hughes, Zora Neale Hurston, Jessie Redmon Fauset, Jean Toomer (1894–1967), Wallace Thurman (1902–1934), and Arna Bontemps. The movement, which coincided with the great creative and commercial growth of jazz, altered the character of much black American literature away from dialect works and conventional imitations of white writers and toward sophisticated explorations of black life and culture that revealed and stimulated new confidence and racial pride.

harlequin \'här-li-k(w)ən\ Principal stock character of the Italian commedia dell'arte. He began in the 16th century as a wily, unscrupulous comic servant, and by the 17th century he was a faithful valet involved in amorous exploits. His costume of peasant clothes covered with colored patches developed into a tight-fitting costume decorated with bright triangles and diamond shapes. He carried a *batte* or slapstick and wore a black half-mask. In mid-18th-century England the harlequin was portrayed by John Rich in dance pantomimes (see mime and pantomime). It was also the principal character of the slapstick form called the harlequinade.

Harley, Robert *later* **Earl of Oxford** (1661–1724) English politician. Elected to Parliament in 1688, he led a coalition of Whigs and moderate Tories. He was speaker of the House of Commons 1701–5, and secretary of state 1704–8. A favorite of Queen Anne, he changed his politics to ally with the Tories. He became chancellor of the exchequer and head of the Tory ministry in 1710. Created Earl of Oxford (1711) and lord treasurer, he secured a reasonable peace at the Peace of Utrecht (1713). He was exiled from power by the Hanoverian succession and imprisoned (1715–17), after which he retired from politics.

Harlow, Jean *orig.* **Harlean Carpenter** (1911–1937) U.S. film actress. Born in Kansas City, Mo., she worked as an extra and played bit parts before her first success, in *Hell's Angels* (1930). With her platinum-blonde hair and flashy vulgarity, she became Warner Brothers' resident sex symbol in *The Public Enemy* and *Platinum Blonde* (1931). MGM revealed her as an able actress with a flair for comedy in such films as *Dinner at Eight* (1933), *China Seas* (1935), *Libeled Lady* (1936), and *Saratoga* (1937). After surviving two divorces, the suicide of her second husband, and public scandal, she died of uremic poisoning at 26.

Jean Harlow.
BROWN BROTHERS

harmonic See overtone

harmonic motion See simple harmonic motion

harmonica *or* **mouth organ** Small rectangular wind instrument consisting of free metal reeds set in slots in a small wooden frame and blown through two parallel rows of wind channels. Successive notes of the scale are obtained by alternately blowing and sucking; the tongue covers channels not required. In chromatic models, a finger-operated stop selects either of two sets of reeds tuned a semitone apart. The harmonica was invented by Friedrich Buschmann of Berlin in 1821 (also inventor of the accordion), who borrowed the basic principle from the Chinese *sheng*. It is widely used in blues as well as folk and country music.

harmonium *or* **reed organ** Free-reed keyboard instrument in which wind from a foot-operated bellows causes metal reeds to vibrate. Pitch is determined by the size of the reed; there are no pipes. Separate sets of reed produce different tone colors, the sound quality being determined by the size and shape of the tone chamber surrounding each reed. The harmonium developed in the early to mid-19th century in Europe and America, and was a very popular church and household instrument into the 1930s.

Harmonium by Jacob Alexandre, Paris, 19th century.
BEHR PHOTOGRAPHY

harmony Combination and relation of simultaneous musical notes, and the science of the structure, relation, and progression of individual harmonies in a piece of music. Harmony has always existed as the "vertical" aspect of older music that is primarily contrapuntal; the rules of counterpoint are intended to control consonance and dissonance, which are fundamental aspects of harmony. However, the sense of harmony as dominating the individual contrapuntal lines followed on the invention of figured bass and the continuo c. 1600. The most influential theory of harmony, that of J.-P. Rameau, followed in the 18th century and employed the symbols of figured bass. Tonality is principally a harmonic concept, and is based not only on a seven-note scale of a given key but on a set of harmonic relations and progressions based on triads (three-note chords) drawn from the scale.

Harmsworth, Alfred See Viscount Northcliffe

harness racing Sport of racing standardbred horses harnessed to lightweight, two-wheeled, bodiless (seat-only) vehicles known as sulkies. Its origins date to ancient chariot races. Today two types of horse are used, trotters and pacers. The former employ a gait in which the legs move in diagonal pairs, the latter a gait in which the legs move in lateral pairs. Since the establishment of pari-mutuel racing under lights in the 1940s, the sport has grown tremendously in popularity.

Harnett, William (Michael) (1848–1892) U.S. (Irish-born) still-life painter. Brought to Philadelphia as a child, he was trained as an engraver and soon developed outstanding skill in trompe l'oeil painting. While traveling in Europe he painted his best-known work, *After the Hunt* (1885). In 1886 he settled in New York. Among his other notable paintings are *The Old Violin* (1886) and *The Faithful Colt* (1890). His work, popular with the public, was generally dismissed by critics.

Harold I *known as* **Harold Harefoot** (died 1040) King of England (1035–40). The illegitimate son of CANUTE THE GREAT, he served as regent of England for his half brother Hardecanute, king of Denmark. In 1036 he murdered the royal claimant, Alfred the Aetheling, and proclaimed himself king. He fended off Welsh and Scottish invaders and was succeeded by Hardecanute.

Harold II *known as* **Harold Godwineson** (c. 1020–1066) King of England (1066). The son of the politically powerful Godwine, earl of Wessex, he inherited his father's earldom and power in 1053. When EDWARD THE CONFESSOR died in January 1066, Harold's supporters dominated the WITAN (king's council) and chose him as king. He was opposed by King HARALD III of Norway, whom he defeated on September 25, 1066, at Stamford Bridge near York. He then marched south to meet William, duke of Normandy, and was killed at the Battle of HASTINGS.

Harold III (Norway) See HARALD III SIGURDSSON

harp Plucked STRINGED INSTRUMENT in which the resonator is perpendicular to the plane of the strings. Harps are roughly triangular. In early harps and many folk harps, the strings are strung between the resonating "body" and the "neck." Early harps and many folk harps lack the forepillar or column—forming the third side of the triangle—that characterizes frame harps; the column permits high string tension and higher-pitched tuning. Small, primitive harps date back to at least 3000 BC in the ancient Mediterranean and Middle East. In Europe they became particularly important in Celtic societies. The large modern orchestral harp emerged in the 18th century. It has 47 strings and a range of almost seven octaves. It plays the entire chromatic scale by means of seven pedals, each of which can alter the pitch of a note (in all octaves) by two semitones through tightening or relaxing the strings by turning a forklike projection against it; it is thus known as the double-action harp. Its massive resonator permits considerable volume of tone. See also AEOLIAN HARP.

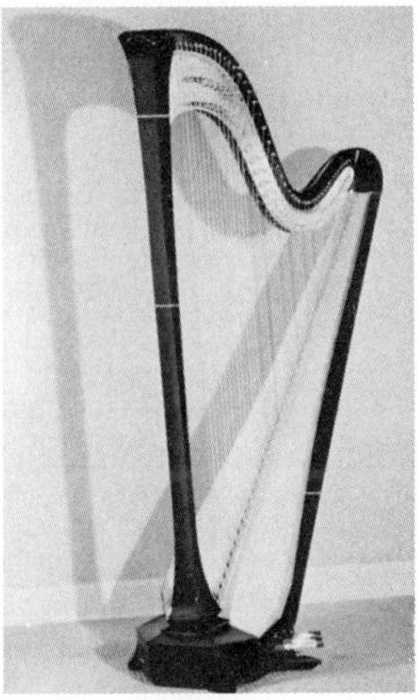

Double-action pedal harp.

BY COURTESY OF LYON-HEALY

harp seal Migratory earless SEAL *(Pagophilus groenlandicus,* sometimes *Phoca groenlandica)* of the North Atlantic and Arctic oceans. The adult male is light grayish or yellowish, with brown or black on the head and a similarly colored U-shaped marking on the back and sides. The female is less clearly marked. Adults are about 6 ft (1.8 m) long and 400 lbs (180 kg). Strong swimmers, they feed on fish and crustaceans and spend much of the year at sea. They breed near Newfoundland and in the Greenland and White seas. Until two weeks old, the pups bear a fluffy white coat highly valued by the fur trade; public indignation over hunting methods (including clubbing) has led to increased regulation and supervision of sealing activities in the Newfoundland area.

Harper brothers U.S. printers and publishers. The two oldest brothers, James (1795–1869) and John (1797–1875), established J. & J. Harper in 1817; their siblings Joseph (1801–1870) and Fletcher (1806–1877) joined in 1823 and 1825. The firm took the name Harper & Brothers in 1833. The company began publishing periodicals in 1850 with *Harper's New Monthly Magazine* (see HARPER'S MAGAZINE), which was followed by *Harper's Weekly* (1857) and *Harper's Bazaar* (1867). In 1900 the business passed out of family hands. Two of the Harper magazines are still being published; the name Harper also survives in the international book-publishing firm HarperCollins.

Harpers Ferry National Historical Park National preserve, West Virginia, in the BLUE RIDGE MTNS. at the point where West Virginia, Virginia, and Maryland converge. Authorized as a national monument in 1944 and a historical park in 1963, it covers 1,909 acres (772 hectares). It is located at the confluence of the Shenandoah and POTOMAC rivers, and consists primarily of the town of Harpers Ferry, W.V. (population 1990: 300). It is the site of the 1859 raid by abolitionist JOHN BROWN, an incident that precipitated the AMERICAN CIVIL WAR, and of several battles during the war.

Harper's Magazine Monthly magazine published in New York City, one of the oldest and most prestigious literary and opinion journals in the U.S. Founded in 1850 as *Harper's New Monthly* by the printing and publishing firm of the HARPER BROTHERS, it was a leader in publishing works by illustrious British and U.S. authors. By 1865 it had become the most successful periodical in the U.S. In the 1920s its format changed to that of a forum on public affairs, balanced with short stories. It was threatened with economic problems from the 1960s on, and in 1980 its demise was averted by grants from a philanthropic organization, the MacArthur Foundation. Since 1976 it has been edited almost continuously by Lewis Lapham (born 1935).

harpsichord Keyboard instrument whose strings are set in vibration by a plucking mechanism. The latter consists of plectra made of quill (or sometimes leather) mounted on vertical wooden jacks that are activated by the keys. A cloth damper touches the string when the player releases the key. It often has two parallel keyboards (or manuals) and generally has two or more sets of strings; these permit the simultaneous sounding of pitches an octave higher or lower than the note struck as well as alternative tone colors (produced by plectra of different material plucking the strings at different points), and can be activated or deactivated by knobs called stops. The notes' loudness is not affected by the power with which the keys are struck, and there is no way to sustain a note after the key is released. Primitive harpsichords existed by the mid-15th century. In the 17th–18th century the harpsichord became a very important solo, accompanimental, and ensemble instrument. From c. 1750 the pianoforte, with its greater dynamic capacity, began to displace it, and by 1820 the harpsichord had largely vanished. It was revived in the 20th century by scholars, performers, and builders.

Harpsichord with soundboard by Hans Ruckers, Amsterdam, 1612.

FROM THE NATIONAL TRUST PROPERTY, FENTON HOUSE, HAMPSTEAD, LONDON; BY GRACIOUS PERMISSION OF HER MAJESTY QUEEN ELIZABETH, THE QUEEN MOTHER

Harpy In Greek and Roman mythology, a bird of prey with a woman's face. Often depicted on tombs, Harpies may originally have been conceived of as ghosts. In early Greek literature, including the writings of HOMER and HESIOD, they were wind spirits and were not represented as ugly or repellent. In the legend of JASON and the Argonauts, however, the Harpies were hideous, foul-smelling birds with the faces of women, sent to punish King Phineus of Thrace by defiling his food; they were frightened away by the sons of Boreas.

harrier Any of about 11 species of HAWKS (subfamily Circinae; family Accipitridae) that are plain-looking, long-legged, long-tailed, and slender. Harriers cruise low over meadows and marshes looking for mice, snakes, frogs, small birds, and insects. They are about 20 in. (50 cm) long and have a small beak and face feathers that form a facial disk. They nest in marshes or tall grass. The best-known harrier is the marsh hawk *(Circus cyaneus),* commonly called hen harrier in Britain, which breeds in temperate and northern regions throughout the Northern Hemisphere. Other common species are found in Africa, South America, Europe, and Asia.

Harriman, Edward H(enry) (1848–1909) U.S. financier and railroad magnate. Born in Hempstead, N.Y., he worked as an office boy and then a stockbroker on Wall Street. He began his career in railroad management as an executive with the Illinois Central. In 1898 he organized a syndicate to acquire the UNION PACIFIC RAILROAD CO., which he soon brought out of bankruptcy into prosperity. Using unpopular business methods, he acquired several other lines, notably the Southern Pacific. His abortive 1901 contest with JAMES J. HILL for control of the NORTHERN PACIFIC led to one of Wall Street's most serious financial crises. The railway trust he formed with J. P. MORGAN was dissolved by the U.S. Supreme Court in 1904.

Harriman, W(illiam) Averell (1891–1986) U.S. diplomat. Born in New York City, the son of EDWARD H. HARRIMAN, he worked for the

Union Pacific Railroad Co. from 1915, serving as board chairman 1932–46. Pres. FRANKLIN ROOSEVELT appointed him in 1934 to the National Recovery Administration. He went to Britain in 1941 to expedite lend-lease aid, and he later served as ambassador to the Soviet Union (1943–46) and Britain (1946), secretary of commerce (1947–48), and special U.S. representative to supervise the MARSHALL PLAN (1948–50). He served as governor of New York 1954–58. In 1961 he was appointed assistant secretary of state for Far Eastern affairs by Pres. JOHN F. KENNEDY, for whom he helped negotiate the Nuclear Test Ban Treaty. As ambassador-at-large for Pres. LYNDON B. JOHNSON, Harriman led the U.S. delegation to the Paris peace talks with North Vietnam (1968–69).

Harris, Arthur Travers *later* **Sir Arthur** (1892–1984) British air officer. He served in World War I and after the war in various posts in the Royal Air Force (RAF). Nicknamed Bomber Harris, as air marshal and commander of the RAF bomber command (1942) he developed the saturation technique of mass bombing (concentrating clouds of bombers in a giant raid on a single city) that was applied with destructive effect on Germany in World War II.

Harris, Joel Chandler (1848–1908) U.S. writer. Born in Eatonton, Ga., he became known as a humorist in his pieces for various newspapers, including the *Atlanta Constitution* (1876–1900). He created a vogue for a distinct type of dialect literature with "Tar-Baby" (1879) and later stories that drew on folklore and featured the character Uncle Remus, a wise, genial old black man who weaves his philosophy of life into tales about Brer Rabbit, Brer Fox, and other animals.

Harris, Julie (Ann) (born 1925) U.S. actress. Born in Grosse Pointe Park, Mich., she made her stage debut in 1945 and won acclaim for her role in *The Member of the Wedding* (1950), recreated in her film debut (1952). On Broadway she received Tony awards for *I Am a Camera* (1952), *The Lark* (1956), *Forty Carats* (1969), *The Last of Mrs. Lincoln* (1973), and *The Belle of Amherst* (1977). She played memorable roles in such films as *East of Eden* (1955), *Requiem for a Heavyweight* (1962), and *Harper* (1966), and in many television plays, winning Emmy awards for *Little Moon of Alban* (1959) and *Victoria Regina* (1962). She also appeared in the TV series *Knots Landing* (1979–87).

Harris, Roy *orig.* **LeRoy Ellsworth** (1898–1979) U.S. composer. Born near Chandler, Okla., he farmed and did odd jobs to support his music studies. After World War I, he attended UC–Berkeley. In the 1920s he studied with Arthur Farwell (1872–1952) and N. BOULANGER, building a reputation for craft and seriousness of purpose. Of his 12 completed symphonies, the third (1937) is the best known. His music, while unmistakably modern, has roots in folk song and is often somber and plainspoken.

Harris, Townsend (1804–1878) U.S. diplomat. Born in Sandy Hill, N.Y., he became president of New York City's board of education and helped found the Free Academy (later CCNY). In 1847 he left New York to embark on trading voyages in the Pacific and Indian oceans. In 1853 he met MATTHEW PERRY in Shanghai and tried to accompany him to Japan, but was rejected. In 1856 he secured an appointment as consul general to Japan; he was unwelcome at first, but changing attitudes in Japan and Harris's perseverance produced a commercial treaty in 1858 that opened Japanese ports to U.S. trade.

Harrisburg City (pop., 1994 est.: 54,000), capital of Pennsylvania. Located in southeastern Pennsylvania on the SUSQUEHANNA RIVER, the site was first established c. 1718 as a trading post and ferry service by John Harris, who named it Harris' Ferry. Laid out in 1785, it became known as Harrisburg and was made the state capital in 1812. In 1839 it was the scene of the first national WHIG PARTY convention, which nominated WILLIAM H. HARRISON. After completion of the PENNSYLVANIA RAILROAD's main line from Harrisburg to PITTSBURGH in 1847, it developed as a transportation center. The state capitol, with a dome patterned after St. Peter's in Rome, was completed in 1906.

Harrison, Benjamin (1833–1901) 23rd president of the U.S. (1889–93). Born in North Bend, Ohio, the grandson of WILLIAM H. HARRISON, he practiced law in Indianapolis from the mid-1850s. He served in the Union army in the Civil War, rising to brigadier general. He served in the U.S. Senate 1881–87. Though defeated when he ran for reelection, he was nominated for president by the Republicans. He defeated the incumbent, GROVER CLEVELAND, even though Cleveland won more of the popular vote than Harrison. As president, his domestic policy was marked by passage of the SHERMAN ANTITRUST ACT. His foreign policy expanded U.S. influence abroad. His secretary of state, JAMES BLAINE, presided at the conference that led to the establishment of the PAN-AMERICAN UNION, resisted pressure to abandon U.S. interests in the Samoan Islands (1889), and negotiated a treaty with Britain in the BERING SEA DISPUTE (1891). Defeated for reelection by Cleveland in 1892, he returned to Indianapolis to practice law. In 1898–99 he was the leading counsel for Venezuela in its boundary dispute with Britain.

Benjamin Harrison, photograph by George Prince, 1888.

BY COURTESY OF THE LIBRARY OF CONGRESS, WASHINGTON, D.C.

Harrison, John (1693–1776) British horologist. The son of a carpenter, in 1735 he invented the first practical marine CHRONOMETER. He followed it with three later instruments, each smaller and more accurate than its predecessor, and in 1762 his No. 4 chronometer was found to be in error by only five seconds (1 1/4′ longitude) after a voyage from England to Jamaica. Chronometers gave mariners their first practical method of fixing position at sea from celestial observations. See also FERDINAND BERTHOUD.

Harrison, Rex *orig.* **Reginald Carey** *later* **Sir Rex** (1908–1990) British actor. He made his debut in films and on the London stage in 1930, later appearing in such successful plays as *French Without Tears* (1936). After World War II he returned to the screen as a suave leading man in such films as *Blithe Spirit* (1945) and *Notorious Gentleman* (1945). He made his U.S. film debut in *Anna and the King of Siam* (1946). His most famous role, as Prof. Henry Higgins in *My Fair Lady* (1956, Tony award), won him equal acclaim in its film version (1964, Academy Award). He was an impressive Julius Caesar in *Cleopatra* (1963).

Harrison, William Henry (1773–1841) Ninth president of the U.S. (1841). Born in Charles City Co., Va., to a political family, he enlisted in the army at 18 and served under ANTHONY WAYNE at the Battle of FALLEN TIMBERS. In 1798 he became secretary of the Northwest Territories, and in 1800 governor of the new Indiana Territory. In response to pressure from white settlers, he negotiated treaties with the Indians that ceded millions of acres of additional land to the U.S. When TECUMSEH organized an uprising in 1811, Harrison led a U.S. force to defeat the Indians at the Battle of TIPPECANOE, a victory that largely established his reputation in the public mind. In the WAR OF 1812 he was made a brigadier general and defeated the British and their Indian allies at the Battle of the THAMES in Ontario. After the war he moved to Ohio, where he became prominent in the WHIG PARTY. He served in the U.S. House of Representatives (1816–19) and Senate (1825–28). As the Whig candidate in the 1836 presidential election, he lost narrowly. In 1840 he and his running mate, JOHN TYLER, won election with a slogan emphasizing Harrison's frontier triumph: "Tippecanoe and Tyler too." The 68-year-old Harrison delivered his inaugural speech without a hat or overcoat in a cold drizzle, contracted pneumonia, and died one month later, the first president to die in office.

William Henry Harrison, detail of an oil painting by Abel Nichols; in Essex Institute, Salem, Massachusetts, U.S.

BY COURTESY OF ESSEX INSTITUTE, SALEM, MASSACHUSETTS

Harrods \'har-ədz\ Renowned London DEPARTMENT STORE. It was founded by a miller, Henry Charles Harrod, as a grocery store in 1849. The store expanded in the late 1800s, and many new departments were added.

Though Harrods still sells gourmet food, it now emphasizes fashionable clothing. Known for its zealous customer service, it is considered the best department store in Britain. In 1985 it was bought by Mohammed al-Fayed (born 1933).

Harrow School Educational institution in Harrow, Greater London. Its founder, John Lyon (died 1592), was a yeoman of neighboring Preston who yearly set aside 20 marks for the education of poor children of Harrow. ELIZABETH I granted the school's charter in 1571, and the first building was opened in 1611. It has long been renowned as one of the two or three greatest English public (i.e., independent) schools; its graduates include RICHARD BRINSLEY SHERIDAN, Lord BYRON, SIR ROBERT PEEL, and WINSTON CHURCHILL.

Harsa \'hər-shə\ *or* **Harsavardhana** \'hər-shə-'vər-də-nə\ (c. 590–647?) Ruler of a large empire in northern India 606–47. He was a Buddhist convert in a Hindu era. He brought what is now Uttar Pradesh and parts of Punjab and Rajasthan under his hegemony, but he contented himself with tribute and homage and never built a centralized empire. His chroniclers, including the Chinese pilgrim XUANZANG, describe him as benevolent and energetic. He set up institutions to benefit the poor and the sick and established the first diplomatic relations between India and China (641). A patron of men of learning, he was himself a poet.

Hart, Albert Bushnell (1854–1943) U.S. historian. Hart taught at Harvard University 1883–1926. His books include *Formation of the Union* (1892), *Guide to the Study of American History* (1896, with Edward Channing), *Foundations of American Foreign Policy* (1901), and *Essentials of American History* (1905). He also edited several series of histories, including *Epochs of American History* (1891–1926) and *The American Nation* (1903–18).

Hart, Basil Liddell See Basil LIDDELL HART

Hart, Lorenz (Milton) (1895–1943) U.S. lyricist. A descendant of HEINRICH HEINE, Hart was born in New York City and initially worked as a translator of German. In 1918 he met R. RODGERS, then 16, at Columbia University. Their many Broadway hits would include *The Garrick Gaieties* (1925), *A Connecticut Yankee* (1927), *The Boys from Syracuse* (1938), and *Pal Joey* (1940). Their 25-year collaboration (often difficult because of Hart's alcoholism and aversion to deadlines) yielded nearly 1,000 songs, including "Blue Moon" (their only song not introduced on stage or film), "My Funny Valentine," "The Lady Is a Tramp," and "Bewitched, Bothered, and Bewildered." He died of liver failure at 48.

Hart, Moss (1904–1961) U.S. playwright and director. Born in New York City, he wrote his first play at 17, and hit his stride when he collaborated with GEORGE S. KAUFMAN on *Once in a Lifetime* (1930). That success led to their popular comedies *You Can't Take It with You* (1936, Pulitzer Prize; film, 1938) and *The Man Who Came to Dinner* (1939; film, 1942). Hart wrote the book for IRVING BERLIN's *Face the Music* (1932) and C. PORTER's *Jubilee* (1934), wrote and directed such plays as *Lady in the Dark* (1941; film, 1944) and *Winged Victory* (1943; film, 1944), and directed the long-running musicals *My Fair Lady* (1956, Tony award) and *Camelot* (1960). Among his screenplays are *Gentleman's Agreement* (1947) and *A Star Is Born* (1954). He wrote a best-selling autobiography, *Act One* (1959).

William S. Hart in *The Gunfighter*, 1916–17.

MUSEUM OF MODERN ART—FILM STILLS ARCHIVE

Hart, William S. (1870–1946) U.S. stage and film actor. Born in Newburgh, N.Y., he made his stage debut in 1889 and portrayed a series of western heroes in the plays *The Squaw Man* (1905), *The Virginian* (1907), and *The Trail of the Lonesome Pine* (1912). In 1914 he went to Hollywood, where his stern, taciturn performances made him a star and the first cowboy hero. Among his numerous films, many of which he wrote and directed, were *The Passing of Two-Gun Hicks* (1914–15), *The Square-Deal Man* (1917), *Wild Bill Hickok* (1923), and *A Lighter of Flames* (1923).

Hartack, Bill *orig.* **William John** (born 1932) U.S. jockey. Born in Ebensburg, Pa., he became the second jockey (after EDDIE ARCARO) ever to win five Kentucky Derbies (1957, 1960, 1962, 1964, 1969). In 1956 he became the first jockey to win $2 million in a single year; he surpassed $3 million the following year. In 1972 he became the fifth jockey ever to win over 4,000 races.

Harte, Bret *orig.* **Francis Brett Harte** (1836–1902) U.S. writer. Born in Albany, N.Y., he left for California in 1854. He briefly experienced camp life in California mining country before becoming a newspaper and periodical editor and writer. His works, which helped create the local-color school in American fiction, include the short stories "The Luck of Roaring Camp" (1868) and "The Outcasts of Poker Flat" (1869), the poem "The Heathen Chinee" (1870), and the play *Ah Sin* (1877; with MARK TWAIN). In an era when the West was a popular subject, they made him internationally famous. His writing slumped in the 1870s, and he accepted consulships in Europe, never returning to the U.S.

Harte.

BY COURTESY OF THE LIBRARY OF CONGRESS, WASHINGTON, D.C.

hartebeest \'här-tə-,bēst\ Either of two species of swift, slender ANTELOPE (genus *Alcelaphus*) found in herds on open plains and scrublands of sub-Saharan Africa. They often mingle with herds of other antelope or ZEBRAS. Hartebeests stand about 4 ft (1.2 m) tall at the shoulder, and the back slopes downward from heavy forequarters to narrow hindquarters. The long face is accentuated, in both sexes, by ringed, lyre-shaped horns united at the base. The red hartebeest is pale reddish brown with a lighter rump. Two subspecies (Swayne's hartebeest and the tora) are listed as endangered.

Coke's hartebeest (*Alcelaphus buselaphus cokii*).

LEONARD LEE RUE III

Hartford City (pop., 1996 est.: 133,000), capital of Connecticut. Lying on the CONNECTICUT RIVER, it was settled by Dutch traders in the 1630s. The Fundamental Orders of Connecticut, which later served as a model for the U.S. CONSTITUTION, were adopted (1639) in Hartford. The city's insurance industry, its major business, dates from 1794, when the first Hartford fire insurance policy was issued. Its statehouse (1796) was designed by CHARLES BULFINCH. Its institutions of higher learning include TRINITY COLLEGE. The birthplace of J. P. MORGAN, it was the home of HARRIET BEECHER STOWE and MARK TWAIN, whose houses are preserved.

Hartford Convention (December 5, 1814–January 5, 1815) Secret meeting of FEDERALIST PARTY delegates from New England states who opposed the WAR OF 1812. It adopted a strong states'-rights position in opposition to the mercantile policies of Pres. JAMES MADISON and the Embargo Act of 1807 and other measures that prohibited trade with Britain and France. News of the signing of the Treaty of Ghent on December 24, 1814, which ended the war, discredited the nascent separatist movement at the convention and weakened Federalist influence.

Hartley, Marsden (1877–1943) U.S. painter. After attending the Cleveland School of Art, he settled in New York, but also lived sporadically in France and Germany. From 1900 he spent most summers in his native Maine, painting landscapes. He first exhibited them at ALFRED STIEGLITZ's New York gallery in 1909. In 1913 he exhibited with Der

Blaue Reiter in Berlin and at the ARMORY SHOW. His early style of painting abstracts with strongly outlined forms and brilliant colors evolved into a personal interpretation of Expressionism, most evident in his bold and brooding Maine landscapes. He produced a dramatic series of pastels and oil paintings of New Mexico (1918–20), and in 1932 a notable series of the volcano Popocatépetl in Mexico.

Hartline, Haldan Keffer (1903–1983) U.S. physiologist. Born in Bloomsburg, Pa., he received his MD from Johns Hopkins University Experimenting on horseshoe crabs, he was the first to record the electrical impulses sent by a single optic-nerve fiber. He found that when one of the eye's receptor cells is stimulated, others nearby are depressed, enhancing contrast and sharpening perception of shapes. He showed how simple retinal mechanisms constitute vital steps in the integration of visual information. In 1967 he shared a Nobel Prize with GEORGE WALD and RAGNAR ARTHUR GRANIT.

Hartmann von Aue \'härt-mən-fòn-'au̇-ə\ (fl. 1190–1210) Middle High German poet. Apparently a member of the Swabian court, he took part in the crusade of 1197. He is noted for his courtly epics, the Arthurian romances *Erec* (c. 1180–85) and *Iwein* (c. 1200), both based on works by CHRÉTIEN DE TROYES. Through *Erec*, ARTHURIAN LEGEND first entered German literature. *Der arme Heinrich* ("Poor Heinrich"), his finest poem, is a didactic religious epic. He also wrote lyrics and allegorical love poems.

Hartree, Douglas R(ayner) (1897–1958) English physicist, mathematician, and computer pioneer. At Manchester University in the mid-1930s, he built a differential analyzer for solution of differential equations, based on the machine of VANNEVAR BUSH. During World War II he was involved with the ENIAC project in the U.S. At Cambridge Univ., he publicized American computer activities and supported British efforts to build stored-program computers. He introduced the self-consistent field approximation scheme that is the basis for most atomic calculations and for the prevailing physical understanding of the wave mechanics of atoms. The Hartree method—sometimes called the Hartree-Fock method to acknowledge Vladimir Fock (1898–1974), who generalized Hartree's scheme—is widely used to describe electrons in atoms, molecules, and solids.

Harun al-Rashid \hȧ-'rün-ȧl-rȧ-'shēd\ (c. 765–809) Fifth Abbasid caliph (see ABBASID DYNASTY), who ruled the Arabian empire from Baghdad at its peak of size and wealth (786–809). His father was the third caliph. His mother and his tutor, Yahya (see BARMAKIDS), helped him rise to power, and he succeeded to the caliphate after the mysterious death of his brother, the fourth caliph. Despite localized rebellions, Harun's reign oversaw great industrial development and trade expansion, which created vast wealth for the caliphate, as described in the *THOUSAND AND ONE NIGHTS*. He divided the empire for inheritance by two of his sons, thereby acknowledging a split between Persian and Arab interests.

Harvard University Oldest institution of higher learning in the U.S. (founded 1636) and perhaps the most prestigious. Harvard College was named for a Puritan minister, John Harvard (1607–1638), who left the school, in Cambridge, Mass., his books and half of his estate. Its schools of divinity, law, and medicine were established in the early 19th century. CHARLES ELIOT, during his long tenure as president (1869–1909), made Harvard an institution with national influence. Harvard has educated seven U.S. presidents, many Supreme Court justices, cabinet officers, and congressional leaders, and dozens of major literary and intellectual figures. Its undergraduate school, Harvard College, contain about one-third of the total student body. Radcliffe College (1879) was a coordinate undergraduate women's college. From 1960 women graduated from both Harvard and Radcliffe, and in 1999 Radcliffe was absorbed by Harvard, the name surviving in the Radcliffe Institute for Advanced Study. Harvard University also has graduate or professional schools of medicine, law, business, divinity, education, government, dentistry, architecture and landscape design, and public health. Among its affiliated research institutes are the Museum of Comparative Zoology, the Peabody Museum of Archaeology and Ethnology, and the Fogg Art Museum. Its Widener Library is one of the largest and most important libraries in the world. Total enrollment is about 18,000.

harvestman See DADDY LONGLEGS

Harvey, Paul (born 1915) U.S. radio commentator and news columnist. Born in Tulsa, Okla., he worked as an announcer and radio station director in the Midwest in the 1940s. He became a news commentator and analyst for ABC in 1944 and a syndicated columnist from 1954. Noted for his firm, staccato delivery and his conservative but individualistic opinions on current events, he has enjoyed an almost unparalleled longevity as a national broadcaster.

Harvey, William (1578–1657) English physician. He studied at Cambridge University and later at the University of Padua, then considered the best medical school in Europe. After receiving a medical diploma, he was appointed to St. Bartholemew's Hospital (1609). He became one of JAMES I's physicians c. 1618, and continued as a king's physician for CHARLES I, whose personal friend he became. Harvey's elucidation of blood circulation overturned the work of GALEN and advanced that of ANDREAS VESALIUS and HIERONYMUS FABRICIUS. To reach his conclusions, Harvey depended on his own observations and reasoning, numerous animal dissections, autopsies, and clinical observations. His *Anatomical Exercise Concerning the Motion of the Heart and Blood in Animals* (1628) recorded his findings. It clarified the function of heart valves, proved that blood did not pass through the septum in the heart, explained the purpose of valves in the veins and of the pulmonary circulation, showed that blood is pumped from the atria into the ventricles and then into the rest of the circulatory system, and proved that the pulse reflected heart contractions.

Haryana \ˌhär-ē-'ä-nə\ State (pop., 2001 est.: 21,082,989), northern India. It occupies an area of 17,070 sq mi (44,212 sq km). The city of CHANDIGARH is the joint administrative capital of Haryana and PUNJAB. The region is the legendary birthplace of HINDUISM, and its festivals attract many pilgrims. Most of Haryana lies on the flat GANGETIC PLAIN, an area that has seen waves of migration from the time of ALEXANDER THE GREAT. It came under the control of the British EAST INDIA CO. in 1803, became a part of Punjab in 1858, and became a separate state in 1966. Its economy is mainly agricultural.

Harz Mountains \'härts\ Mountain range, central Germany. Lying between the WESER and ELBE rivers, it is 60 mi (100 km) long and about 20 mi (32 km) wide. The northwestern and highest portion is known as the Oberharz, and the more extensive southeastern part is the Unterharz; the Brocken group, dividing the two, is considered part of the Oberharz. The highest peak is Mount BROCKEN. It was intensively developed in the 10th–16th century for mining. Its most important modern industry is tourism.

Hasan \'hȧ-sȧn\ *in full* **Hasan ibn Ali ibn Abi Talib** (624–680) Grandson of MUHAMMAD, the elder son of Muhammad's daughter FATIMA. He is one of the five most revered persons in the SHIITE branch of Islam. After the murder of his father ALI in 661, he was seen by many as the Prophet's rightful heir. When MUAWIYAH I opposed Hasan's succession and began to prepare for war, Hasan raised an army to meet him. Plagued by defections, however, he opened peace negotiations within the year and abandoned the caliphate to his opponent. For the rest of his life he lived quietly in Medina.

Hasan al-Basri \'hȧ-sȧn-ȧl-bäs-'rē\, **al-** *in full* **Abu Said ibn Abi al-Hasan Yasar al-Basri** (642–728) Muslim ascetic and major figure in early Islam. Born in Medina, he took part in the conquest of eastern Iran as a young soldier. He then settled at Basra, and from 684 he was a popular preacher. He emphasized the practice of religious self-examination and asserted that true Muslims must live in a state of anxiety about their destiny after death. Rejecting determinism, he held that people are entirely responsible for their actions. Political opposition forced him into hiding 705–14, but he afterwards lived openly in Basra. He is considered a founder of the two major schools of early SUNNI Islam, the MUTAZILA and the ASHARIYA.

Unglazed pot from Hasanlu, 9th century BC; in the Metropolitan Museum of Art, New York City.

BY COURTESY OF THE METROPOLITAN MUSEUM OF ART, NEW YORK CITY, PURCHASE, 1960, ROGERS FUND

Hasanlu \'hä-sən-ˌlü\ Archaelogical site, northwestern Iran. Excavations have revealed the area's prehistory, especially the late 2nd and early 1st millennia BC. It was inhabited c. 2100–c. 825 BC, but the richest period, often called Mannaean, dates to the 10th–9th century BC. It was crowned by a high citadel surrounded by a fortification wall. The outer town, which was unfortified, consisted primarily of ordinary dwellings and a cemetery. Many metal artifacts, including a solid gold bowl and two bronze vessels in the shape of horse heads, have been found.

Hasdeu \häsh-'dyü\, **Bogdan Petriceicu** (1836–1907) Romanian linguist. He collected and published ancient Slavic and Romanian documents in *The Historical Archive of Romania* (1865–67) and in his subsequent writings initiated the critical investigation of Romanian history. He became director of the state archives in 1876 and was appointed professor of philology at the University of Bucharest in 1878. His *Words of the Ancestors* (1878–81) was the first history of apocryphal literature in Romania.

Hašek \'hä-shek\, **Jaroslav** (1883–1923) Czech writer. He published 16 volumes of short stories before World War I, when he became a prisoner of war. After his release he devoted himself to writing a six-volume war novel, *The Good Soldier* Schweik, but died after completing only four volumes (published 1921–23). Even in its incomplete state, it is considered one of the world's masterpieces of satire.

hashish \ha-'shēsh\ Hallucinogenic drug preparation derived from RESIN from the flowers of HEMP plants. MARIJUANA, a product of the same plant, is far less potent. Hashish is smoked or eaten. The active ingredient, tetrahydrocannabinol (THC), makes up 10–15% of hashish.

Hasidism \'hä-sə-ˌdi-zəm\ Pietistic and mystical movement in JUDAISM that originated in 18th-century Poland. It was a reaction against rigid legalism and Talmudic learning in favor of a joyful form of worship that served as a spiritual outlet for the common people. Hasidism began with the preaching of the man later known as the BAAL SHEM TOV. Teaching that God was immanent in all things and that piety was more important than scholarship, he won followers known as Hasidim ("loyalists"). Dov Baer founded the first Hasidic community c. 1710, and countless small communities soon sprang up in Poland, Russia, Lithuania, and Palestine, each led by a ZADDIK. Communal services were marked by dancing, shouting, and singing, through which participants reached a state of spiritual ecstasy. Though excommunicated from ORTHODOX JUDAISM in 1772, the Hasidim continued to flourish. By the 19th century Hasidism had become an ultraconservative movement. Huge numbers of Hasidim fell victim to the HOLOCAUST, but their survivors established vital movements in Israel and the U.S. The Lubavitcher sect, based in Brooklyn, N.Y., numbers about 200,000.

Haskala *or* **Haskalah** \ˌhäs-kä-'lä\ Intellectual movement in European JUDAISM in the 18th–19th century, which sought to supplement traditional Talmudic studies with education in secular subjects, European languages, and Hebrew. Partly inspired by the ENLIGHTENMENT, the Haskala was sometimes called the Jewish Enlightenment. It originated with prosperous and socially mobile Jews, who hoped to use reforms to enable the Jews to escape ghetto life and enter the mainstream of European society and culture. This meant adding secular subjects to the school curriculum, adopting the language of the larger society in place of Yiddish, abandoning traditional garb, and reforming synagogue services. One of its leaders was MOSES MENDELSSOHN, who began a revival of Hebrew writing. Haskala's emphasis on the study of Jewish history and ancient Hebrew as a means of reviving Jewish national consciousness influenced ZIONISM, and its call to modernize religious practices led to the emergence of REFORM JUDAISM.

Hasmonean dynasty \ˌhaz-mə-'nē-ən\ Dynasty of ancient JUDAEA, descendants of the MACCABEE family. The name derives from their ancestor Hasmoneus, but the first of the ruling dynasty was Simon Maccabeus, who became leader of the Maccabean revolt against the SELEUCID king c. 143 BC and, in victory, was made high priest, ruler, and ethnarch of Judaea. The last Hasmonean was deposed and executed in 37 by the Romans under Mark ANTONY.

Hassam \'has-əm\, **(Frederick) Childe** (1859–1935) U.S. painter and printmaker. Born in Boston, he studied there and in Paris before settling in New York. City life was his favorite subject, but his landscapes of New England and rural New York State also became popular. Paintings such as *Washington Arch, Spring* (1890) are characterized by clear, luminous atmosphere and brilliant color. He also produced some 400 etchings and lithographs. From 1898 to 1918 he exhibited together with a group of New York and Boston painters known as The Ten, who became the foremost proponents of U.S. IMPRESSIONISM.

Hassan II \'hȧ-sȧn, *Engl* ha-'sän\ *orig.* **Mawlay Hassan Muhammad ibn Yusuf** (1929–1999) King of Morocco (1961–99). On his succession to the throne, he introduced a new constitution providing for a popularly elected legislature, but exercised authoritarian rule from 1965 to 1970, instituting a new constitution in 1970. He claimed the former Spanish Sahara, which Algeria also claimed; Morocco's annexation of it led to ongoing hostilities. In 1986 he became the second Arab leader to meet publicly with an Israeli leader. He condemned the 1990 invasion of Kuwait by Iraq. Under his leadership Morocco achieved political stability and some economic and social development, though human rights remained an issue. See also MUHAMMAD V, SAHARAN ARAB DEMOCRATIC REPUBLIC.

Hassler \'häs-lər\, **Hans Leo** (1564–1612) German composer and organist. Born into a family of organists, he studied with A. & G. GABRIELI in Venice. He served as chamber organist to the FUGGER FAMILY of Augsburg 1586–c. 1600. His compositions became widely known and were granted copyright protection by the emperor in 1591. A Protestant, he eventually left Catholic Augsburg to take posts in Nuremberg, Ulm, and Dresden. He is best known for his sacred Latin choral music, including masses, psalms, and motets, but also composed Italian madrigals, German part-songs (several became Protestant hymns), and instrumental music.

Hassuna \ha-'sü-nə\ Archaeological site, northern Iraq. An ancient Mesopotamian town located south of MOSUL, it was excavated in 1943–44, and was found to represent an advanced village culture that apparently spread throughout northern Mesopotamia. At Hassuna itself, six layers of houses were uncovered, each progressively more substantial. Vessels and pottery dating to c. 5600–5350 BC were discovered. Similar wares found elsewhere in the Middle East show that even as early as the 6th millennium BC an extensive trade network existed in the region.

Hastings, Battle of (October 14, 1066) Battle that ended in the defeat of HAROLD II of England by William, duke of Normandy, and established the NORMANS as rulers of England. On his deathbed EDWARD THE CONFESSOR had granted the English throne to Harold, earl of Wessex, despite an earlier promise to make William his heir. William crossed to England from Normandy with a skilled army of 4,000–7,000 men, landing at Pevensey in Sussex and moving eastward along the coast to Hastings. Harold met the Norman invaders with an army of 7,000 men, many of whom were untrained peasants. The English were defeated after a daylong battle in which Harold was killed, and the Norman duke was crowned WILLIAM I. See also NORMAN CONQUEST.

Hastings, Warren (1732–1818) British colonial administrator in India. He worked for the English EAST INDIA CO. from 1750, rising to membership in its council in Bengal (1761–64) and Madras (now Chennai; 1769). As governor of Bengal (1772–74), he moved the central government to Calcutta (now Kolkata) under direct British control and remodeled the justice system. In 1774 he acquired the new title of governor-general, with responsibilities for supervising other British settlements in India. His powers were shared with a council of four, several of whom tried to blame Hastings for the continuing abuses of power by Englishmen. From 1777 to 1783 he sought to counter the instability created by the fall of the Mughal empire and tried to maintain peaceful relations with neighboring states but was drawn into the MARATHA WARS. This disrupted the company's trade and antagonized opinion in England, as did several dubious ventures Hastings entered into to raise extra funds. In 1785, leaving an India at peace, he retired to England. In 1786 EDMUND BURKE introduced an impeachment process against him on charges of corruption; after a trial that lasted from 1788 to 1795, Hastings was acquitted.

Warren Hastings, oil painting by Tilly Kettle; in the National Portrait Gallery, London.

BY COURTESY OF THE NATIONAL PORTRAIT GALLERY, LONDON

hat Head covering of any of various styles, used for warmth, fashion, or religious or ceremonial purposes. Through the Middle Ages men wore hats in the form of caps or hoods and women wore veils, hoods, or head draperies. The silk top hat originated in Florence c. 1760. The derby (bowler) was introduced in 1850. The cloth cap with visor was for decades the international standard for workingmen and boys. Women's hats went through periods of ostentation. In the East, colorful turbans are the traditional headgear; in eastern and southern Mediterranean countries, men wear the fez; in Asia, the Chinese devised the simple coolie hat and the Japanese the elaborate cap-shaped *kammuri*; in India, the Gandhi cap, fez, and turban are in general use. In Latin America and the southwestern U.S., the broadbrimmed sombrero is still popular. Since c. 1960 the wearing of hats by both men and women has greatly declined in Western industrialized countries.

Hatch Act (1939, amended 1940) Legislation enacted by the U.S. Congress to eliminate corrupt practices in national elections. The bill was sponsored by Sen. Carl Hatch of New Mexico (1889–1963) in response to allegations that officials of the WORKS PROGRESS ADMINISTRATION were using their positions to win votes for the Democratic Party in the 1936 election. It forbade intimidation or bribery of voters and restricted political campaign activities by federal employees. It also limited campaign contributions by individuals and spending by campaign committees.

hate crime In law, crime directed at a person or persons on the basis of characteristics such as race, religion, ethnicity, or sexual orientation. The concept emerged in the U.S. in the late 1970s, and since then laws have been passed in many U.S. states mandating additional penalties for violent crimes motivated by bias or bigotry against particular groups. Several other Western countries, including Australia, Britain, and Canada, have adopted laws designed to curb violent crime against racial and religious minorities. German law forbids public incitement and instigation of racial hatred, including the distribution of Nazi propaganda. Critics of hate-crime legislation have argued that the groups it is designed to protect are arbitrarily selected (e.g., no such legislation protects the elderly) and that the offender's attitude toward the group to which the victim belongs is irrelevant to the criminal nature of the offense.

Hatfields and McCoys Two families of the U.S. Appalachian Mountains who engaged in a backwoods feud in the late 19th century. The families, each with at least 13 children and numerous other relatives, lived on opposite sides of a border stream, the Hatfields in West Virginia and the McCoys in Kentucky. The feud may have originated in opposing allegiances in the Civil War. In 1882 the first murder of a Hatfield was followed by the murder of three McCoys. Retaliatory raids and murders continued with little interference from local police. In 1888 a posse of McCoys led by a deputy sheriff captured nine Hatfields and took them to Kentucky to stand trial for murder. The trials resulted in one sentence of death and eight of imprisonment. Flare-ups gradually abated by the 1920s.

Hathor \'hä-tȯr\ *or* **Athyr** \'ä-'thir\ In ancient EGYPTIAN RELIGION, the goddess of the sky, of women, and of fertility and love. Her principal animal form was a cow, and she was strongly associated with motherhood. Her worship was linked at Heliopolis with that of RE, whose wife or daughter she was said to be. In Upper Egypt she was worshiped with HORUS, and in the NECROPOLIS at Thebes she was held to be the patroness of the dead.

Hatshepsut, limestone sculpture, c. 1485 BC; in the Metropolitan Museum of Art, New York City.
BY COURTESY OF THE METROPOLITAN MUSEUM OF ART, NEW YORK, ROGERS FUND AND CONTRIBUTIONS FROM EDWARD S. HARKNESS, 1929

Hatshepsut \hat-'shep-süt\ Queen of Egypt (c. 1472–1458 BC). Daughter of Thutmose I and wife of Thutmose II, she first acted as regent for her stepson, THUTMOSE III, but soon ordered herself crowned as pharaoh. She attained unprecedented power, adopting the titles and regalia of a pharaoh, complete with a false beard. She devoted much of the profit from expanded trade and tribute to an extensive building program, most notably to a splendid temple at Dayr al-Bahri. Thutmose III, who had become head of the army, succeeded her; whether she died naturally or was deposed and killed is uncertain.

Hatta \'hä-tä\, **Mohammad** (1902–1980) Indonesian independence leader and prime minister (1948–50). While studying in the Netherlands (1922–32), he became president of a group of Indonesian nationalist students studying overseas. He was imprisoned in a concentration camp in West New Guinea for his activities and then exiled to the island of Bandanaira. He collaborated with the Japanese during World War II. He became prime minister in 1948 and gained support from Western countries that year by suppressing a communist revolt. Hatta helped guide Indonesia to complete independence in 1949. He became vice president under SUKARNO in 1950, but resigned in 1956. After Sukarno's downfall, he served as an adviser to SUHARTO.

Hatteras \'ha-tə-rəs\, **Cape** Long, narrow, curved sandbar forming a promontory on Hatteras Island, North Carolina. It extends 70 mi (113 km) along the OUTER BANKS between the Atlantic Ocean and PAMLICO SOUND. Much of it is included in Cape Hatteras National Seashore, established in 1937. It is the site of the tallest lighthouse in the U.S., 208 ft (63 m) high.

Hauhau \'hau̇-,hau̇\ Member of the Pai Marire, a religious-military cult of the MAORI people of New Zealand. The cult was founded in 1864 by Te Ua Haumene, who claimed to have been visited by the angel GABRIEL and to have sacrificed his child in repentance for the straying of the Maori people. A mixture of Jewish, Christian, and Maori beliefs, the movement held that the Maori were a new chosen people and charged them with driving out the Europeans and recovering the ancestral lands. The effort failed, though fighting lasted until 1872. Some cult beliefs have persisted among the Maoris.

Hauptmann \'hau̇pt-,män\, **Gerhart (Johann Robert)** (1862–1946) German playwright and poet. He studied sculpture before turning to literature in his early twenties. His first play, the starkly realistic social drama *Before Dawn* (1889), made him famous and signaled the end of the highly stylized German drama. His naturalistic plays on themes of social reality and proletarian tragedy, including *The Weavers* (1892), *The Beaver Coat* (1893), and *Drayman Henschel* (1898), made him the most prominent German playwright of his era. He was awarded the Nobel Prize in 1912. In his novels, stories, epic poems, and later plays, he abandoned naturalism for mystical religiosity and mythical symbolism.

Gerhart Hauptmann, etching by Hermann Struck, 1904; in the Schiller-Nationalmuseum, Marbach, Ger.
BY COURTESY OF THE SCHILLER-NATIONALMUSEUM, MARBACH, GER

Hauptmann \'hau̇pt-,män\, **Moritz** (1792–1868) German musicologist. He studied composition and violin with L. SPOHR. From 1842 he was cantor of the music school at J.S. BACH's former church in Leipzig. In 1850 he cofounded the Bach Gesellschaft, devoted to publishing Bach's complete works; he served as its president the rest of his life and edited its first three volumes. As a theorist, he is known for his emphasis on the harmonic dualism of major and minor.

Hausa \'hau̇-sə\ People of northwestern Nigeria and southern Niger who speak the HAUSA LANGUAGE. The Hausa, numbering 30 million, are the largest ethnic group in the area. In the mid-14th century a confederation of Hausa states was formed, influenced by the spread of Islam from the kingdom of MALI EMPIRE. Hausa society has traditionally been organized on a feudal basis. The head of an emirate is surrounded by titled officeholders who hold villages as fiefs, from which their agents collect taxes. The economy has traditionally rested on agriculture, though craftwork and trade are also important. Hausa society is markedly hierarchical; the ranking, both of offices and social classes, is expressed in an elaborate etiquette. See also FULANI.

Hausa language \'haů-sə, 'haů-zə\ Chadic language of West Africa (see AFROASIATIC LANGUAGES), with some 30 million first-language speakers in northern Nigeria and southern Niger. Outside of Hausaland, communities of HAUSA merchants have stimulated the use of Hausa as a LINGUA FRANCA across a broad area of the African Sahel and savanna region. In common with most or all other Chadic languages, Hausa is tonal (see TONE), has a system of glottalized consonants (marked in Roman script by hooks on *b, d* and *k*), distinguishes two grammatical GENDERS, and has the customary word order subject-verb-object. Hausa is now customarily written in the LATIN ALPHABET, introduced in the early 20th century, though writing in an adaptation of the ARABIC ALPHABET, attested about a century earlier, continues in Koranic schools and some other contexts.

hausen See BELUGA

Haushofer \'haůs-,hō-fər\, **Karl (Ernst)** (1869–1946) German officer and leading proponent of GEOPOLITICS. As an army officer in Japan (1908–10), he studied its expansionist policies in Asia and later wrote several books on Japan's role in 20th-century politics. Retiring from the army (1919), he founded the *Journal for Geopolitics* (1924) and taught at the University of Munich (1921–39). Haushofer's influence in military circles was considerable, and in World War II he attempted to justify Germany and Japan in their drives for world power. Investigated for war crimes after the war, he and his wife committed suicide.

Haussmann \ōs-'mån\, **Georges-Eugène** *later* **Baron Haussmann** (1809–1891) French administrator and city planner. He entered the French civil service in 1831 and rose to become prefect of the Seine department (1853–70). He inaugurated a wide-reaching program of municipal improvements in Paris, including a new water supply and sewage system, the creation of wide avenues through Paris's mass of small streets, the landscape gardening of the BOIS DE BOULOGNE, and the construction of the PARIS OPERA and Les Halles market. Many of his planning concepts were used in the designs of other cities.

Haüy \à-'wʸē\, **René-Just** (1743–1822) French mineralogist, one of the founders of the science of CRYSTALLOGRAPHY. He studied theology and was a professor at the Collège de Navarre for 21 years. He became a professor of mineralogy at the Museum of Natural History (1802) and at the Sorbonne (1809). By experimentation he derived a theory of crystal structure, and he subsequently applied his theory to the classification of minerals. He was also known for his studies of pyroelectricity and PIEZOELECTRICITY in crystals.

Havana *Spanish* **La Habana** \,lä-ä-'b̲ä-nä\ City (pop., 1995 est.: 2,241,000), capital of Cuba. The city, which is also a province, lies on the island's northern coast. The largest city in the Caribbean, it is Cuba's chief port, and has one of the best harbors in the Western Hemisphere. It was founded by the Spanish in 1515 and moved to its present location in 1519. Made the capital of Cuba in 1592, it was Spain's chief naval station in the New World. Its harbor was the scene of the destruction of the U.S. battleship *MAINE* in 1898, the immediate cause of the SPANISH-AMERICAN WAR. Before 1959, when FIDEL CASTRO came to power, Havana was a haven for U.S. tourists, offering gambling and showy nightlife. In addition to being Cuba's commercial and industrial center, it contains many buildings reflecting Spanish colonial style, including the cathedral (1704) that formerly contained CHRISTOPHER COLUMBUS's tomb, the Palace of the Captains General, and Morro Castle. Central Havana is now a WORLD HERITAGE SITE.

Havel \'hä-vəl\, **Václav** (born 1936) Czech playwright and dissident, first president of the Czech Republic (from 1993). He worked in a Prague theater from 1959 and became resident playwright by 1968. His plays, including *The Memorandum* (1965), are absurdist, satirical examinations of bureaucratic routines that explore the moral compromises made by those living under totalitarianism. They were banned by the communist authorities, and Havel was repeatedly arrested and imprisoned in the 1970s and '80s. During antigovernment demonstrations in 1989, he became the leading figure in the Civic Forum, a coalition of groups pressing for democratic reforms. The Communist Party capitulated (in the bloodless "Velvet Revolution") and formed a coalition government with the Civic Forum, and Havel was elected president in 1989. In 1993 he was elected president of the new Czech Republic.

Havel River \'hä-fᵊl\ River, northeastern Germany. It flows south out of Mecklenburg to Spandau (in BERLIN), where it is joined by the SPREE RIVER. Curving past POTSDAM and BRANDENBURG, the Havel heads northwest to join the ELBE RIVER after a course of 213 mi (343 km). Over much of its course it forms part of a canal system that links the Elbe with the ODER RIVER.

Havelok (the Dane) \'ha-və-,läk\ Middle English metrical ROMANCE of some 3,000 lines, written c. 1300. Of the literature produced after the Norman Conquest, it offers the first view of ordinary life. Composed in a Lincolnshire dialect and containing many local traditions, it tells the story of the English princess Goldeboru and the orphaned Danish prince Havelok, who defeats a usurper to become king of Denmark and part of England.

Haverford College Private liberal-arts college in Haverford, Pa., near Philadelphia. Founded by QUAKERS in 1833 as a men's college, it became coeducational in 1980. It is consistently ranked as one of the top U.S. colleges. It maintains cooperative programs with BRYN MAWR and SWARTHMORE colleges and the University of PENNSYLVANIA. Enrollment is about 1,200.

Havre, Le See LE HAVRE

Hawaii *formerly* **Sandwich Islands** State (pop., 1997 est.: 1,187,000), U.S., comprising a group of islands in the central Pacific Ocean that covers 6,471 sq mi (16,760 sq km). Its capital is HONOLULU. Located 2,397 mi (3,857 km) west of San Francisco, the state's major islands are, from west to east, Niihau, Kauai, OAHU, Molokai, Lanai, Kahoolawe, Maui, and HAWAII; there are over 120 islets. The state's active volcanoes include MAUNA LOA and KILAUEA. People of at least part-Hawaiian descent constitute about one-eighth of Hawaii's total population, followed by those of Japanese ancestry, who constitute one-fourth. The majority of the state's residents live on Oahu. The original Hawaiians were of Polynesian origin and came from the MARQUESAS ISLANDS c. AD 400. Capt. JAMES COOK visited the islands in 1778, and called them the Sandwich Islands. In 1796 KAMEHAMEHA I united the group under his rule. American whalers began to stop there; they were followed in 1820 by New England missionaries, and Western influences changed the islands. While Kamehameha III in 1851 placed Hawaii under U.S. protection, a coup later fomented by U.S. sugar interests resulted in the monarchy's overthrow and the establishment of a Republic of Hawaii (1893). In 1898 the new republic and the U.S. agreed on annexation, and in 1900 Hawaii became a U.S. territory. The bombing of PEARL HARBOR by the Japanese in 1941 led to U.S. involvement in WORLD WAR II, and Hawaii became a major naval station. Hawaii became the 50th state in 1959. Its largest industry is tourism. It is also a world astronomy center, with telescopes atop MAUNA KEA.

Hawaii Volcanic island, part of the state of Hawaii. It lies south of Maui and constitutes Hawaii county, with Hilo (pop., 1990: 38,000) the island's main town. Known as the Big Island, it is the largest in area at 4,028 sq mi (10,433 sq km), and southeasternmost of the Hawaiian Island group. It is the youngest geologically and was formed by five volcanoes connected by lava ridges. KILAUEA, the world's most active volcano, is located there in HAWAII VOLCANOES NATIONAL PARK. The island has other volcanic peaks, including MAUNA KEA. Sugar, tourism, cattle, orchids, and coffee are the basis of the economy.

Hawaii, University of State university system consisting of a main campus in Honolulu (Manoa) and several other campuses, some of them two-year community colleges. The main campus, founded in 1907, offers a comprehensive range of undergraduate and graduate degree programs, and includes schools of law and medicine. Important university facilities include a volcano research center, a marine center, and a biomedical center. Total enrollment is about 20,000.

Hawaii Volcanoes National Park National preserve, southeastern shore of HAWAII island. Established in 1916, it occupies an area of 358 sq mi (927 sq km) and includes the active volcanoes MAUNA LOA and KILAUEA, 25 mi (40 km) apart. Other highlights are Kau Desert, an area of lava formations near Kilauea, and a tree-fern forest that receives nearly 100 in. (2,500 mm) of annual rainfall.

Hawaiian goose See NENE

Hawaiians Aboriginal people of Hawaii, descendants of Polynesians who migrated to Hawaii in two waves: the first from the Marquesas Islands probably c. AD 400; the second from Tahiti in the 9th or 10th century. Without metals, pottery, or beasts of burden, Hawaiians made implements of stone, wood, shell, teeth, and bone. They had a highly developed oral culture and possessed percussion, string, and wind instruments. Their basic unit of land, the *ahupuaa*, usually extended from the shore to the mountaintop, providing the occupants with the means to grow and gather all they needed. Hawaiians had four principal gods and many lesser deities. Their laws, which included intricate taboos, bore heavily upon the masses, especially women. After the arrival of Christian missionaries in 1820, some of the more repressive laws and taboos were abolished, but the native population was devastated by Western diseases. Numbering about 300,000 in 1778, full-blooded Hawaiians today number fewer than 10,000.

hawk Any of many small to medium-sized, diurnal BIRDS OF PREY, particularly those in the genus *Accipiter*. The term is often applied to other birds in the Accipitridae family (including BUZZARDS, HARRIERS, and KITES) and sometimes to certain FALCONS. Hawks usually eat small mammals, reptiles, and insects but occasionally kill birds. There is often no difference in plumage between sexes. Hawks are found on the six major continents. Most nest in trees, but some nest on the ground or on cliffs. True hawks (accipiters) can usually be distinguished in flight by their long tails and short, rounded wings. They are exemplified by the 12-in (30-cm) sharp-shinned hawk *(A. striatus),* gray above with fine rusty barring below, found throughout much of the New World. See also GOSHAWK, SPARROW HAWK.

Red-tailed hawk (*Buteo jamaicensis*).
ALAN CAREY

hawk moth *or* **sphinx moth** Any MOTH of the LEPIDOPTERAN family Sphingidae. Found worldwide, these stout-bodied moths have long, narrow forewings and shorter hind wings, with wingspans ranging from 2 to 8 in. (5–20 cm). Many species pollinate flowers while sucking nectar; the proboscis of some species is up to 13 in. (32.5 cm) long. Some hawk moths migrate. The larvae, which are smooth and have a dorsal "horn," are called hornworms; larvae of two North American species—the tobacco, or southern, hornworm, and the tomato, or northern, hornworm—attack tomato, tobacco, and potato crops.

Hawkesbury River River, New South Wales, Australia. Rising in the GREAT DIVIDING RANGE, it flows 293 mi (472 km) northeast to the TASMAN SEA north of SYDNEY. Known as the Wollondilly in its upper course and as the Warragamba after receiving the Nattai River, it becomes the Hawkesbury after its junction with the Grose. It continues for 100 mi (160 km), becoming a salt tidal stream.

Hawking, Stephen W(illiam) (born 1942) English theoretical physicist. He studied at Oxford University and later received his PhD from Cambridge. He has worked primarily in the field of general RELATIVITY and particularly on the physics of BLACK HOLES. In 1971 he suggested that after the big bang, numerous objects formed having as much as 1 billion tons of mass but only the size of a proton. These "mini–black holes" are unique in being subject to both the laws of relativity, due to their immense mass and gravity, and the laws of QUANTUM MECHANICS, due to their minute size. In 1974 he proposed that black holes "evaporate" by what is now known as HAWKING RADIATION. His work greatly spurred efforts to theoretically delineate the properties of black holes. His work also showed the relationship of these properties to the laws of classical thermodynamics and quantum mechanics. Hawking's achievements, despite near-total paralysis from amyotrophic lateral sclerosis, have earned him extraordinary honors. His books include the best-selling *A Brief History of Time* (1988).

Hawking radiation Radiation theoretically emitted from just outside the EVENT HORIZON of a BLACK HOLE. STEPHEN W. HAWKING proposed in 1974 that subatomic particle pairs arising naturally near the event horizon may result in one particle's escaping the vicinity of the black hole while the other particle, of negative energy, disappears into it. The flow of particles of negative energy into the black hole reduces its mass until it disappears completely in a final burst of radiation.

Hawkins, Coleman (Randolph) (1904–1969) U.S. musician, the first important tenor-saxophone soloist in jazz. Born in St. Joseph, Mo., Hawkins came to prominence as a member of FLETCHER HENDERSON's big band (1924–34), with which he absorbed the style of LOUIS ARMSTRONG and developed the smooth legato phrasing and robust tone that set the technical standard for all tenor players. He worked in Europe 1934–39, and soon after his return recorded "Body and Soul," which became a commercial success and one of the masterpieces of improvised jazz. Hawkins was receptive to the harmonic advances made by younger players, who widely acknowledged his influence.

Coleman Hawkins, c. 1943.
REPRINTED WITH PERMISSION OF DOWN BEAT MAGAZINE

Hawkins, Erick (1909–1994) U.S. modern dancer. Born in Trinidad, Col., he worked with GEORGE BALANCHINE (1935–37) before joining the MARTHA GRAHAM company in 1938, with which he became a leading dancer. He and Graham were married 1946–54. He stayed with her company until 1951, when he organized his own troupe. He was interested in kinesiology and would only perform to live music.

Hawkins, John *later* **Sir John** (1532–1595) English naval administrator and commander. A relative of FRANCIS DRAKE, he became a merchant in the African trade and the first English slave trader. After a successful slave-trading voyage in 1562–63, a group that included ELIZABETH I provided money for a second expedition. A Spanish fleet attacked him on his third voyage (1567–69), with Drake, beginning the quarrel between England and Spain that led to war in 1585. As treasurer (1577) and controller (1589) of the navy, he rebuilt older ships and helped design the faster ships that withstood the Spanish ARMADA in 1588. He later devised the naval blockade to intercept Spanish treasure ships. One of the foremost seamen of 16th-century England, he was the chief architect of the Elizabethan navy.

Hawks, Howard (Winchester) (1896–1977) U.S. film director, screenwriter, and producer. Born in Goshen, Ind., he served as a pilot in World War I, then wrote screenplays in Hollywood (from 1922) and directed several projects before making his first major film, *A Girl in Every Port* (1928). A master technician and storyteller, he created a sense of intimacy by filming from the eye level of a spectator. He directed over 40 films (many of which he also produced and wrote) in a variety of genres: adventure (*The Dawn Patrol*, 1930), crime (*Scarface*, 1932), comedy (*Bringing Up Baby*, 1938), war (*Sergeant York*, 1941), musicals (*Gentlemen Prefer Blondes*, 1953), film-noir thrillers (*The Big Sleep*, 1946), science fiction (*The Thing*, 1951), and westerns (*Red River*, 1948; *Rio Bravo*, 1959).

hawkweed Any of the approximately 200 species of weedy plants that make up the genus *Hieracium,* in the COMPOSITE FAMILY, native to temperate regions. Mouse-ear hawkweed *(H. pilosella),* orange hawkweed *(H. aurantiacum),* and common hawkweed *(H. vulgatum)* are widely distributed weeds. Some species are cultivated as garden ornamentals for their attractive flower clusters.

Hawr al Hammar See Hawr al HAMMAR

hawthorn Any of various thorny shrubs or small trees of the genus *Crataegus,* in the ROSE family, native to the northern temperate zone. Many species are native to North America. The simple leaves are usually toothed or lobed. Hawthorns bear white or pink flowers, usually in clusters, and small applelike, red (rarely blue or black) fruits. Many cultivated varieties are grown as or-

Hawthorn (*Crataegus*).
WALTER CHANDOHA

namentals for their attractive flowers and fruits. The hawthorn is well suited for HEDGEROWS; its combination of sturdy twigs, hard wood, and many thorns makes it a formidable barrier to cattle and hogs.

Hawthorne, Nathaniel (1804–1864) U.S. novelist and short-story writer. Descended from Puritans of Salem, Mass., he was imbued with a deep moral earnestness. After producing several unexceptional works, he wrote some of his greatest tales, including "My Kinsman, Major Molineux" (1832), "Roger Malvin's Burial" (1832), and "Young Goodman Brown" (1835). His story collections include *Twice-Told Tales* (1837), *Mosses from an Old Manse* (1846), and *The Snow-Image* (1851). He is best known for the novels *The Scarlet Letter* (1850), a story of adultery set in colonial New England that ranks as one of the greatest American novels, and *The House of the Seven Gables* (1851), the story of a family that lives under a curse for generations. His later works include *The Blithedale Romance* (1852) and *The Marble Faun* (1860). A skilled literary craftsman and a master of allegory and symbolism, he ranks among the greatest American fiction writers.

Nathaniel Hawthorne, photograph by Mathew Brady.

THE GRANGER COLLECTION, NEW YORK CITY

hay In agriculture, dried GRASSES and other foliage used as animal FEED. Typical hay crops are TIMOTHY, ALFALFA, and CLOVER. Usually the material is cut in the field while still green and then either dried in the field or mechanically dried by forced hot air. Balers compress hay into tightly packed rectangular or cylindrical bales tied with wire or twine. Loose hay may also be "vacuumed" off the field and then blown into stacks in a barn or other storage facility. Properly cured hay with 20% or less moisture may be stored for months without danger of spoilage.

Hay, John (Milton) (1838–1905) U.S. diplomat and writer. Born in Salem, Ind., he studied law in Springfield, Ill., where he met ABRAHAM LINCOLN. He served as Pres. Lincoln's private secretary (1861–65), then held diplomatic posts in Europe (1865–70). After writing editorials for the *New York Tribune* (1870–75), he served as assistant secretary of state (1879–81). He coauthored a 10-volume biography of Lincoln (1890). He was appointed by Pres. WILLIAM MCKINLEY as ambassador to Britain (1897–98). As secretary of state (1898–1905), he helped negotiate the end of the Spanish-American War, supported the decision to retain the Philippines for the U.S., promulgated the OPEN DOOR POLICY, and negotiated treaties to give the U.S. exclusive rights to build the Panama Canal.

hay fever Seasonal sneezing, nasal congestion, and tearing and itching of the eyes caused by ALLERGY to the POLLEN of certain plants, chiefly those pollinated by the wind (e.g., RAGWEED in North America, TIMOTHY grass in Britain). ANTIHISTAMINES may provide temporary relief, but the most effective long-range treatment is DESENSITIZATION. Unless properly treated, about one-third of patients with hay fever develop ASTHMA.

Haya de la Torre \ä-yä-thā-lä-'tōr-rā\, **Víctor Raúl** (1895–1979) Peruvian political theorist and activist. The son of wealthy parents, in 1914 he founded APRA, a left-of-center reformist party. He ran for president repeatedly, but was always thwarted by the military and other conservative forces. He spent much of his life in prison, exile, or hiding, influencing Peruvian politics through his underground activities and writings. See also INDIGENISMO.

Hayashi Razan \hä-'yä-shē-rä-'zän\ (1583–1657) Japanese Neo-Confucian scholar. Originally a student of Buddhism, he became a loyal adherent of NEO-CONFUCIANISM, and from 1607 he served the Tokugawa shogunate. He established the Neo-Confucian teachings of ZHU XI as the ideology of the shogunate, emphasizing loyalty and a hierarchical social order. Hayashi also reinterpreted Shinto from the point of view of Zhu Xi's philosophy, laying the foundation for the Confucianized Shinto of later centuries. In 1630 the third Tokugawa shogun gave him an estate in Edo, where he founded an academy.

Haydarabad See HYDERABAD

Haydn \'hī-dᵊn\, **Franz Joseph** (1732–1809) Austrian composer. Intended for the priesthood, he was recruited at 8 to the choir at St. Stephen's Church, Vienna, where he learned violin and keyboard. On leaving the choir, he began supporting himself by teaching and playing violin, while undertaking rigorous study of counterpoint and harmony. He came to the attention of PIETRO METASTASIO, and through him became factotum to the composer Nicola Porpora (1686–1768) in exchange for lessons. Gaining entrée to high society, in 1761 he became head of the musical establishment at the great palace of the ESTERHÁZY FAMILY, which would support him for most of his career. In this position of artistic isolation but with excellent resources, Haydn felt free to experiment and was forced to become original. By his late years he was recognized internationally as the greatest living composer. He composed important works in almost every genre, and his elegant and ingratiating works balance wit and seriousness, custom and innovation. The first great symphonist, he composed 108 symphonies, including the popular last 12 "London symphonies" (1791–95); he virtually invented the string quartet, and his 68 quartets remain the foundation of the quartet literature. His choral works include 15 masses and the oratorios *The Creation* (1798) and *The Seasons* (1801). He also wrote 48 piano sonatas and more than 100 beautiful works for the cello-like baryton. The principal shaper of the Classical style, he exerted major influence on his friend WOLFGANG AMADEUS MOZART and his student LUDWIG VAN BEETHOVEN.

Hayek \'hī-ak\, **Friedrich (August) von** (1899–1992) Austrian-British economist. He moved to London in 1931 and held positions at the University of London and the London School of Economics, becoming a British citizen in 1938. Later posts included a professorship at the University of Chicago (1950–62). In his works he opposed the theories of JOHN MAYNARD KEYNES and criticized government intervention in the free market, arguing that it is destructive of individual values and ultimately ineffective against such economic ailments as inflation, unemployment, and recession. His books include *The Road to Serfdom* (1944), *The Constitution of Liberty* (1960), and *The Political Order of a Free People* (1979). His views have been highly influential among conservatives, including MARGARET THATCHER. In 1974 he shared the Nobel Prize with GUNNAR MYRDAL.

Hayes, Bob *orig.* **Robert Lee** (1942–2002) U.S. sprinter and football player. Born in Jacksonville, Fla., he was a star sprinter running back for Florida A&M University. Along with nine other runners, he held the world record in the 100-m dash (10 seconds) from 1960 to 1968. After winning two gold medals at the 1964 Olympic Games (100-m dash and 4×100-m relay), he joined the Dallas Cowboys football team as a wide receiver (1965–76) and eventually set team records for pass receptions and kick returns.

Hayes (Brown), Helen (1900–1993) U.S. actress. Born in Washington, D.C., she began her stage career at 5 and made her Broadway debut at 9. She went on to an illustrious career, starring in such Broadway productions as *Caesar and Cleopatra* (1925), *What Every Woman Knows* (1926), and *The Animal Kingdom* (1932) and becoming known as "First Lady of the American Theater." Her small size belied a majestic stage presence that made her memorable in *Mary of Scotland* (1933–34) and *Victoria Regina* (1935–39). She starred in revivals of *The Skin of Our Teeth* (1955), *The Glass Menagerie* (1956), and *Long Day's Journey into Night* (1971), acted in numerous radio and television plays, and won Academy Awards for her films *The Sin of Madelon Claudet* (1931) and *Airport* (1970), as well as three Tony awards and the Presidential Medal of Freedom. She was married to CHARLES MACARTHUR.

Hayes, Rutherford B(irchard) (1822–1893) 19th president of the U.S. (1877–81). Born in Delaware, Ohio, he practiced law in Cincinnati, representing defendants in several fugitive-slave cases and becoming associated with the new Republican Party. After fighting in

Rutherford B. Hayes, 1877.

BY COURTESY OF THE LIBRARY OF CONGRESS, WASHINGTON, D.C.

H I J K

the Union army, he served in the U.S. House of Representatives (1865–67). As governor of Ohio (1868–72, 1875–76), he advocated a sound currency backed by gold. In 1876 he won the Republican nomination for president. His opponent, SAMUEL TILDEN, won a larger popular vote, but Hayes's managers contested the electoral-vote returns in four states, and a special ELECTORAL COMMISSION awarded the election to Hayes. As part of a secret compromise reached with Southerners (see WORMLEY CONFERENCE), he withdrew the remaining federal troops from the South, ending RECONSTRUCTION, and promised not to interfere with elections there, ensuring the return of white Democratic supremacy. He introduced civil-service reform based on merit, incurring a dispute with ROSCOE CONKLING and the conservative "stalwart" Republicans. At the request of state governors, he used federal troops against strikers in the railroad strikes of 1877. Declining to run for a second term, he retired to work for humanitarian causes.

Haymarket Riot (May 4, 1886) Violent confrontation between police and labor protesters in Chicago that dramatized the labor movement's struggle for recognition. Radical unionists had called a mass meeting in Haymarket Square to protest police brutality in a strike action. A bomb was thrown into the crowd, killing seven policemen and injuring 60 others. Police and workers fired on each other. Public demand for action led to the arrest of eight anarchists (see ANARCHISM). Convicted of conspiracy to murder, they were sentenced to death; four were executed and one committed suicide. In 1893 the three survivors were pardoned by Gov. JOHN PETER ALTGELD.

Hayne, Robert Young (1791–1839) U.S. politician. Born in Colleton District, S.C., he practiced law from 1812. In the U.S. Senate 1823–32, he became a spokesman for the South and the doctrine of states' rights. In his famous 1830 debate with DANIEL WEBSTER on the Constitution, he set forth the doctrine of NULLIFICATION. In 1832 he developed an ordinance at the South Carolina nullification convention that declared federal tariff laws null and void in the state. Resigning from the Senate, he served as governor (1832–34) and as mayor of Charleston (1834–37).

Hays Office *formally* **Motion Picture Producers and Distributors of America** U.S. organization that promulgated a moral code for films. In 1922, after a number of scandals involving Hollywood personalities, film-industry leaders formed the organization to counteract the threat of government censorship and to create favorable publicity for the industry. Under Will H. Hays (1879–1954), a politically active lawyer, it initiated a blacklist, inserted morals clauses into actors' contracts, and in 1930 developed a Production Code that detailed what was morally acceptable on the screen. The code was supplanted in 1966 by a voluntary rating system.

Haywood, William D(udley) (1869–1928) U.S. labor leader. Born in Salt Lake City, he became a miner at 15. In 1905 he chaired the founding convention of the INDUSTRIAL WORKERS OF THE WORLD and led its organizing efforts. After his acquittal in 1907 on a charge of involvement in the murder of Idaho's antilabor former governor, Frank Steunenberg (1861–1905), "Big Bill" Haywood made a speaking tour for the Socialist party and supported numerous strikes. He was later forced out of the party for advocating violence. In 1917 he was convicted of sedition for his opposition to World War I and sentenced to 20 years in prison; in 1921, while free on bail, he fled to Russia.

Hayworth, Rita *orig.* **Margarita Carmen Cansino** (1918–1987) U.S. film actress. Born in Brooklyn, N.Y., she danced with her father in nightclubs from age 12 and played bit parts in films from 1935. She cultivated a sophisticated glamour in *Only Angels Have Wings* (1939), *Strawberry Blonde* (1941), and *Blood and Sand* (1941). The musicals *You'll Never Get Rich* (1941), *You Were Never Lovelier* (1942), and *Cover Girl* (1944) made her a star and a favorite pinup of U.S. GIs. Her worldly, erotic role in *Gilda* (1946) confirmed her status as Hollywood's love goddess. Her later films included *The Lady from Shanghai* (1948), *Pal Joey* (1957), and *Separate Tables* (1958). She suffered from Alzheimer's disease for the last 15 years of her life.

hazel See FILBERT

Hazeltine \ˈhā-zəl-ˌtin\, **(Louis) Alan** (1886–1964) U.S. electrical engineer and physicist. Born in Morristown, N.J., in the early 1920s he invented the neutrodyne circuit, which made commercial radio possible by neutralizing the noise that plagued all radio receivers of the time; by 1927 some 10 million radio receivers were using the device. Hazeltine later advised the U.S. government on regulation of radio broadcasting, and during World War II he served on the National Defense Research Committee.

Hazlitt, William (1778–1830) British essayist. He studied for the ministry, but to remedy his poverty he became instead a prolific critic, essayist, and lecturer. He began contributing to journals, notably LEIGH HUNT's *Examiner,* and to essay collections, notably *The Round Table* (1817). His lecture courses were published as *On the English Poets* (1818) and *On the English Comic Writers* (1819). Many of his most brilliant essays appeared in his two most famous books, *Table Talk* (1821) and *The Plain Speaker* (1826). *The Spirit of the Age* (1825) contains some of his most effective writing.

H.D. See Hilda DOOLITTLE

Head, Bessie *orig.* **Bessie Amelia Emery** (1937–1986) South African-Botswanan writer. Born in South Africa of an illegal union between a white mother and a black father, she suffered rejection and alienation from an early age. She described the contradictions and shortcomings of pre- and postcolonial African society in morally didactic novels and stories, including *When Rain Clouds Gather* (1969), *Maru* (1971), *A Question of Power* (1973), *The Collector of Treasures* (1977), *Serowe, Village of the Rainwind* (1981), *A Bewitched Crossroad* (1984), and *The Cardinals* (1993).

Head, Edith (1898–1981) U.S. costume designer. Born in San Bernardino, Cal., she became chief designer at Paramount Studios in 1933, and later worked at Universal. Hollywood's best-known designer, she was noted for the wide range of her costumes, from the elegantly simple to the elaborately flamboyant. She won a record eight Academy Awards for her work in such films as *All About Eve* (1950), *Roman Holiday* (1953), and *The Sting* (1973).

head louse See human LOUSE

head rhyme See ALLITERATION

headache Pain in the upper portion of the head. Episodic tension headaches are the most common, usually causing mild to moderate pain on both sides. They result from sustained contraction of face and neck muscles, often due to fatigue, stress, or frustration. Headaches are treated with ASPIRIN, ACETAMINOPHEN, or other NSAIDs. Chronic daily headaches are similar but more frequent. They usually have a psychological cause and respond to certain antidepressants. They may also come from overuse of pain relievers. MIGRAINE and CLUSTER headaches are vascular headaches. Headaches may also be caused by distension of arteries at the base of the brain, from fever, hangover, or an attack of high blood pressure. Headache can be a symptom of MENINGITIS, hemorrhagic STROKE, or TUMOR.

Heade \ˈhēd\, **Martin Johnson** (1819–1904) U.S. painter. Born in Lumberville, Pa., he studied in Europe and Britain, then returned to take up portrait and landscape painting. An avid naturalist, he made extensive trips in South and Central America and the Caribbean (1863–70), where he produced luminous, meticulously detailed images of the tropical forests and landscapes (e.g., *Orchids and Hummingbird*, c. 1865). The New England coast and the rocky shore of Lake George (N.Y.) also inspired notable paintings (e.g., *Salt Marshes, Newport, R.I.*, c. 1863). He was a leading exponent of LUMINISM.

headhunting Practice of removing, displaying, and in some cases preserving human heads. Headhunting arises in some cultures from a belief in the existence of a more or less material soul matter that resides in the head. The headhunter seeks, through decapitation of his enemies, to transfer this soul matter to himself and his community. Headhunting is thus sometimes found with certain forms of CANNIBALISM as well as with HUMAN SACRIFICE. It has been practiced worldwide and may go back to Paleolithic times. Among the MAORI of New Zealand, the heads of enemies were dried and preserved so that tattoo marks and the facial features were recognizable. In South America, the skulls were removed and the skin packed with hot sand to create a shrunken head.

health Extent of continuing physical, emotional, mental, and social ability to cope with one's environment. Good health is harder to define than bad health (which can be equated with presence of disease) because it must convey a more positive concept than mere absence of disease, and there is a variable area between health and disease. A person may be in good physical condition but have a cold or be mentally ill.

Someone may appear healthy but have a serious condition (e.g., cancer) that is detectable only by physical examination or diagnostic tests, or not even by these.

Health and Human Services, U.S. Department of Federal executive division responsible for carrying out government programs and policies relating to human health, welfare, and income security. Established in 1980 when responsibility for education was removed from the Department of Health, Education and Welfare, it consists of five major components: the Administration for Children and Families, the Administration on Aging, the Health Care Financing Administration, the Public Health Service, and the Substance Abuse and Mental Health Services Administration.

health insurance System for the advance financing of medical expenses through contributions or taxes paid into a common fund to pay for all or part of health services specified in an insurance policy or law. The key elements are advance payment of premiums or taxes, pooling of funds, and eligibility for benefits on the basis of contributions or employment without an income or assets test. Health insurance may apply to a limited or comprehensive range of medical services and may provide for full or partial payment of the costs of specific services. Benefits may consist of the right to certain medical services or reimbursement of the insured for specified medical costs. Private health insurance is organized and administered by an insurance company or other private agency; public health insurance is run by the government (see SOCIAL INSURANCE). Both forms of health insurance are to be distinguished from socialized medicine and government medical-care programs, in which doctors are employed directly or indirectly by the goverment, which also owns the health-care facilities (e.g., Britain's NATIONAL HEALTH SERVICE). See also INSURANCE.

health maintenance organization (HMO) Public or private organization providing comprehensive medical care to subscribers on the basis of a prepaid contract. HMOs deliver a broad range of health services for a fixed fee. In the prepaid group-practice model, physicians are organized into a group practice with one insuring agency. A medical care foundation, or individual practice association, usually involves multiple insurance companies and reimburses members of a loose network of individual physicians from subscribers' prepaid fees. Originally viewed as a way to control health-care costs and meet increased demand for health services, HMOs have become controversial because some limit care by refusing to pay for tests or treatment against their own doctors' advice.

Healy, T(imothy) M(ichael) (1855–1931) Irish political leader. Soon after he entered Parliament in 1880, the "Healy Clause" of the Land Act of 1881, protecting tenant farmers' agrarian improvements from rent increases, made him popular in Ireland. Associated with CHARLES STEWART PARNELL, he broke with him in 1886. Later, dissatisfied with both the Liberals and the Irish Nationalists after the 1916 EASTER RISING, he supported SINN FÉIN after 1917. He was supported by both the British and Irish ministries as governor-general (1922–28) of the new Irish Free State.

Heaney \'hē-nē\, **Seamus (Justin)** (born 1939) Irish poet. After studying at Queen's University in Belfast, he became a teacher and lecturer. Appalled by the violence in his native Northern Ireland, he moved to the Republic of Ireland in 1972. In recent years he has taught at Harvard, Oxford, and Cambridge. His works, rooted in Northern Irish rural life, evoke historical events and draw on Irish myth, but also reflect the land's recent troubled decades. His collections include *Death of a Naturalist* (1966), *Door into the Dark* (1969), *North* (1975), *Station Island* (1984), *The Haw Lantern* (1987), *Seeing Things* (1991), and *The Spirit Level* (1996). *Preoccupations* (1980) consists of essays on poetry and poets. He received the Nobel Prize in 1995.

hearing In law, a trial, or more specifically the formal examination of a cause before a judge according to the laws of the land. In popular usage the term often refers to a formal proceeding before a magistrate prior to the inception of a case, and in particular to a preliminary hearing, where a magistrate or judge determines whether the evidence justifies proceeding with the case.

hearing *or* **audition** *or* **sound reception** Physiological process of perceiving SOUND. Hearing entails the transformation of sound vibrations into nerve impulses, which travel to the brain and are interpreted as sounds. Members of two animal groups, ARTHROPODS and VERTEBRATES, are capable of sound reception. Hearing enables an animal to sense danger, locate food, find mates, and, in more complex creatures, engage in communication (see ANIMAL COMMUNICATION). All vertebrates have two ears, often with an inner chamber housing auditory hair cells (papillae) and an outer eardrum that receives and transmits sound vibrations. Localization of sound depends on the recognition of minute differences in intensity and in the time of arrival of the sound at the two ears. Sound reception in mammals is generally well developed and often highly specialized, as in bats and dolphins, which use ECHOLOCATION, and whales and elephants, which can hear mating calls from tens or even hundreds of miles away. Dogs and other canines can similarly detect faraway sounds. The human ear can detect frequencies of 20–20,000 hertz (Hz); it is most sensitive to those between 1,000 and 3,000 Hz. Impulses travel along the central auditory pathway from the cochlear nerve to the medulla to the CEREBRAL CORTEX. Hearing may be impaired by disease, injury, or old age; some disorders, including DEAFNESS, may be congenital. See also HEARING AID.

hearing aid Device that increases the loudness of sounds in the user's EAR. Its principal components are a microphone, an amplifier, and an earphone. Hearing aids are increasingly smaller and less conspicuous, fitting behind the earlobe or within the ear canal. They have widely differing characteristics, amplifying different components of speech sounds for maximum comprehension by each wearer. Hearing aids with automatic volume control vary the amplification automatically with the input.

Hearn, (Patricio) Lafcadio (Tessima Carlos) *Japanese* **Koizumi Yakumo** (1850–1904) Irish-U.S.-Japanese writer, translator, and teacher. He emigrated to the U.S. at 19 and worked as a reporter and translator, writing on a wide range of subjects. In 1890 he traveled as a magazine writer to Japan, where he soon became a teacher, took a Japanese wife and name, and became a Japanese subject. Articles and books about Japan's customs, religion, and literature followed, including *Glimpses of Unfamiliar Japan* (1894), *Exotics and Retrospective* (1898), *In Ghostly Japan* (1899), *Shadowings* (1900), and *A Japanese Miscellany* (1901); *Kwaidan* (1904) was a collection of supernatural stories and haiku translations. It was Hearn who, perhaps more than any other single person, introduced the broad culture of Japan to the West.

Hearst \'hərst\, **William Randolph** (1863–1951) U.S. newspaper publisher. Born in San Francisco, Hearst in 1887 took over the struggling *San Francisco Examiner,* which he remade into a successful blend of investigative reporting and lurid sensationalism. After buying the *New York Morning Journal* (later *New York Journal-American*) in 1895, he fought fierce circulation wars with other papers and helped bring about the era of YELLOW JOURNALISM, employing circulation-boosting strategems that profoundly influenced U.S. journalism. Distorted reportage in Hearst papers fanned public sentiment against Spain that led to the SPANISH-AMERICAN WAR. He served in Congress (1903–7) but ran unsuccessfully for other offices. In the 1920s he built a grandiose castle in SAN SIMEON, Cal. At the peak of his fortune in 1935 he owned 28 major newspapers, 18 magazines, radio stations, movie companies, and news services. Extravagance and the Depression weakened him financially, and by 1940 he had lost control of his empire. He spent his last years in virtual seclusion.

William Randolph Hearst, 1906.
BY COURTESY OF THE LIBRARY OF CONGRESS, WASHINGTON, D.C.

heart Organ that pumps blood, circulating it to all parts of the body (see CIRCULATION). The human heart is a four-chambered double pump with its right and left sides fully separated by a septum and subdivided on both sides into an atrium above and a ventricle below. The right heart receives venous blood from the superior and inferior venae cavae (see VENA CAVA) and propels it into the PULMONARY CIRCULATION. The left heart takes in blood from the pulmonary veins and sends it into the SYSTEMIC CIRCULATION. Electrical signals from a natural PACEMAKER cause the heart muscle to contract. Valves in the heart keep blood flowing in one direc-

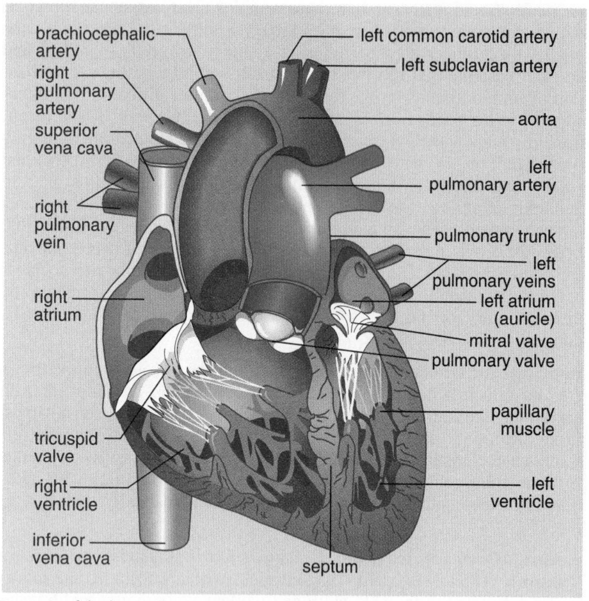

Structure of the human heart. Oxygen-rich blood from the lungs enters the heart through the pulmonary veins, passing into the left atrium and on to the left ventricle. Contraction of the muscles of the left ventricle forces blood into the aorta. The mitral valve prevents blood from moving back into the left atrium during contraction. Various arteries branch off from the aorta to supply blood to all parts of the body. Oxygen-poor blood draining from the body into the superior vena cava and inferior vena cava flows to the right atrium, through the tricuspid valve, and into the right ventricle. As the right ventricle contracts, oxygen-poor blood passes through the pulmonary valve into the pulmonary arteries and on to the lungs to receive oxygen.

tion. Their snapping shut after each contraction causes the sounds heard as the heartbeat. See also CARDIOVASCULAR SYSTEM.

heart attack See MYOCARDIAL INFARCTION

heart clam See COCKLE

heart disease Any disorder of the heart, including CORONARY HEART DISEASE, HEART MALFORMATION, and PULMONARY HEART DISEASE, as well as rheumatic heart disease (see RHEUMATIC FEVER), hypertensive heart disease (see HYPERTENSION), inflammation of the heart muscle (myocarditis) or of its inner or outer membrane (ENDOCARDITIS, pericarditis), and heart valve disease. Abnormalities of the heart's natural PACEMAKER or of the nerves that conduct its impulses cause CARDIAC ARRHYTHMIAS. Some CONNECTIVE-TISSUE diseases (notably systemic LUPUS ERYTHEMATOSUS, RHEUMATOID ARTHRITIS, and SCLERODERMA) can affect the heart. HEART FAILURE may result from many of these disorders.

heart failure Inability of one or both sides of the HEART to pump enough blood for the body. Causes include PULMONARY HEART DISEASE, HYPERTENSION, and coronary atherosclerosis (see ARTERIOSCLEROSIS). A person with left-sided heart failure experiences shortness of breath after exertion, difficulty in breathing while lying down and night breathlessness, and abnormally high pressure in the pulmonary veins. A person with right-sided failure experiences abnormally high pressure in the systemic veins, liver enlargement, and accumulation of fluid in the legs. A person with failure of both ventricles has an enlarged heart and a three-beat heartbeat. Treatment includes bed rest, DIGITALIS, restricted SODIUM intake and increased sodium excretion, and elimination of the underlying cause. See also CONGESTIVE HEART FAILURE.

heart malformation *or* **congenital heart disease** Deformity of the HEART. It includes septal defect (opening in the septum between the sides of the heart; severity depends on size and site); ATRESIA or stenosis of one or more valves; tetralogy of Fallot (with four components: ventricular septal defect, pulmonary valve stenosis, right ventricular enlargement, and positioning of the AORTA so that it receives blood from both ventricles); and transposition of the great vessels (so the PULMONARY and SYSTEMIC circulations each receive blood from the wrong side of the heart). Such defects can prevent enough oxygen from reaching the tissues, so the skin has a bluish cast. Many are fatal if not corrected surgically soon after birth—or, rarely, before it, if detected prenatally. Abnormalities of the large vessels are usually less serious (see coarctation of the AORTA, DUCTUS ARTERIOSUS).

heart transplant Procedure to remove a diseased HEART and replace it with a healthy one from a legally dead donor. The first was performed in 1967 by CHRISTIAAN BARNARD. The diseased heart is removed (except for some atrial tissue to preserve nerve connections to the natural PACEMAKER). The new heart is put in place and connected to the recipient's blood vessels. Patients and donors are matched for tissue type, but the patient's IMMUNE SYSTEM must still be suppressed to prevent rejection (see IMMUNOSUPPRESSION). A successful TRANSPLANT can enable the recipient to have an active life for many years.

heartwood Dead, central wood of trees. Its cells usually contain tannins or other substances that make it dark and sometimes fragrant. Heartwood is mechanically strong, resistant to decay, and less easily penetrated by wood-preservative chemicals than other types of wood. One or more layers of living and functional sapwood cells are periodically converted to heartwood.

heartworm Species *(Dirofilaria immitis)* of FILARIAL WORM that parasitizes mammals, especially dogs. Up to 500 adult heartworms, which can grow to 6–12 in. (15–30 cm) long, live in the dog's heart, and the microfilariae (embryonic larvae) pass into the blood. Mosquitoes transfer infested blood from dog to dog. Both adult and larval heartworms tax the heart and restrict blood flow to the lungs, kidneys, and liver. By the time visible symptoms (chronic cough, labored breathing, listlessness, heart failure) develop, it may be too late for treatment. Preventive medicines and treatments, including surgery, exist.

heat Energy transferred from one body to another as the result of a difference in temperature. Heat flows from a hotter body to a colder body when the two bodies are brought together. This transfer of energy usually results in an increase in the temperature of the colder body and a decrease in that of the hotter body. A substance may absorb heat without an increase in temperature as it changes from one PHASE to another—that is, when it melts or boils. The distinction between heat (a form of energy) and temperature (a measure of the amount of energy) was clarified in the 19th century by such scientists as J.-B. FOURIER, GUSTAV KIRCHHOFF, and LUDWIG BOLTZMANN.

heat capacity Ratio of heat absorbed by a material to the change in temperature. It is usually expressed as calories per degree in terms of the amount of the material being considered. Heat capacity and its temperature variation depend on differences in energy levels for ATOMS. Heat capacities are measured with a CALORIMETER and are important as a means of determining the ENTROPIES of materials. See also SPECIFIC HEAT.

heat exchanger Any of several devices that transfer HEAT from a hot to a cold FLUID. In many engineering applications, one fluid needs to be heated and another cooled, a requirement economically accomplished by a heat exchanger. In double-pipe exchangers, one fluid flows inside the inner pipe, and the other in the annular space between the two pipes. In shell-and-tube exchangers, many tubes are mounted inside a shell; one fluid flows in the tubes and the other flows in the shell, outside the tubes. Special-purpose devices such as boilers, evaporators, superheaters, condensers, and coolers are all heat exchangers. Heat exchangers are used extensively in fossil-fuel and NUCLEAR POWER plants, gas TURBINES, heating and AIR CONDITIONING, REFRIGERATION, and the chemical industry. See also COOLING SYSTEM.

heat exhaustion *or* **heat prostration** Response of the body to excessive heat. The body temperature rises moderately and heavy PERSPIRATION persists. Heat exhaustion results from inadequate water and salt intake and can lead to DEHYDRATION and collapse. It may progress to HEATSTROKE if not treated by lying down in a cool place and drinking fluids, preferably water with salt added. See also TEMPERATURE STRESS.

heat pump Device for transferring heat from a substance or space at one temperature to another at a higher temperature. It consists of a compressor, a condenser, a throttle or expansion valve, an evaporator, and a working fluid (refrigerant). The compressor delivers vaporized refrigerant to the condenser in the space to be heated. There, cooler air condenses the refrigerant and becomes heated during the process. The liquid refrigerant then enters the throttle valve and expands, coming out as a liquid-vapor mixture at a lower temperature and pressure. It then enters the evaporator, where the liquid is evaporated by contact with the warmer space. The vapor then passes to the compressor and the cycle is repeated. A heat pump is a reversible system and is commonly used both to heat and to cool buildings. It operates on the same thermodynamic principles as REFRIGERATION.

heat treating Changing the properties of METALS (including IRON, STEEL, ALUMINUM, COPPER, and TITANIUM) by processes involving heating. It is used to harden metals that have different crystal structures at low and high temperatures. The metal is heated and then quenched (cooled rapidly) to retain the high-temperature constituent. Mild heating (tempering) may then be used to attain the desired hardness. Heating followed by slow cooling (annealing) is used to soften metals.

Heath, Edward (Richard George) *later* **Sir Edward** (born 1916) British politician, prime minister of Britain (1970–74). He held various government positions after being elected to Parliament in 1950, and after the Conservative defeat in 1964 he became a major opposition figure. As prime minister, he faced the crisis of violent conflict in Northern Ireland, over which he imposed direct British rule in 1972, and won French acceptance of British entry into the EUROPEAN ECONOMIC COMMUNITY. Unable to cope with Britain's mounting economic problems, chiefly rising inflation and unemployment and crippling labor strikes, he was succeeded by HAROLD WILSON in 1974 and replaced as party leader by MARGARET THATCHER in 1975.

heath family Family Ericaceae, made up mostly of shrubs and small trees, including AZALEAS, RHODODENDRONS, MOUNTAIN LAUREL, BLUEBERRIES, and the low EVERGREEN shrubs of the genus *Erica* (see ERICA). A large percentage of the family's approximately 110 genera and 4,000 species are cultivated. Members are widely distributed, extending into the subarctic and along mountain chains through the tropics. They are often evergreen species that thrive on open, barren land with usually acid and poorly drained soils. See also HEATHER.

Heathcoat, John (1783–1861) British inventor. The LACEMAKING machine he patented in 1809, the most complex textile machine then in existence, produced an exact imitation of handmade pillow lace. His lace factory was destroyed by LUDDITES in 1816. He later developed means for ornamenting net in the course of manufacture, for making ribbons as well as plaited and twisted net, and for winding raw silk from cocoons.

heather *or* **Scotch heather** Low evergreen shrub *(Calluna vulgaris)* of the HEATH FAMILY, widespread in western Europe and Asia, North America, and Greenland. It is the chief vegetation on many wastelands of northern and western Europe. *C. vulgaris* is distinguished from true heaths, which are sometimes loosely called heather, by the lobes of its calyx (see FLOWER), which conceal the petals; in true heaths the petals cover the calyx. Scotch heather has purple stems, close-leaved green shoots, and feathery spikes of bell-shaped flowers. It has various economic uses: large stems are made into brooms, shorter ones are tied into bundles that serve as brushes, and long trailing shoots are woven into baskets.

heating Process of raising the temperature of an enclosed space. Heat can be delivered by CONVECTION, RADIATION, and THERMAL CONDUCTION. With the exception of the ancient Romans, who developed a form of central heating, most cultures relied on direct heating methods such as FIREPLACES and stoves. Central heating, adopted for use again in the 19th century, is a method of indirect heating: heat is produced away from the occupants and then conveyed to them. In warm-air heating, air heated by a furnace rises through ducts to rooms above, where it is emitted through grills. In hot-water systems, a pump circulates water from a boiler through a system of pipes to radiators or convectors in rooms. In steam systems, steam is generated in the boiler and led to radiators through pipes. The high temperature of the steam makes it hard to control, and steam heating has been largely superseded. A common type of electric heating system converts electric current to heat by means of resistors that emit radiant energy. See also RADIANT HEATING, SOLAR HEATING.

heatstroke Debility caused by exposure to heat and humidity, usually for many hours, called sunstroke when caused by direct sunlight. Body temperature is 106–110°F (41–43°C) or higher. Perspiration almost stops, leading to the rapid temperature rise, collapse, and coma. Cooling with ice-water baths or packs, with massage to promote circulation, is urgent to save the victim's life. Even after body temperature drops, circulatory disorder and brain damage may cause death. See also HEAT EXHAUSTION.

heaven Dwelling place of God or the gods and the abode of the blessed dead. The term also refers to the celestial sphere, the place of the sun, moon, planets, and stars and the source of light, which symbolizes good. For later Judaism and Christianity, heaven is the destination of the faithful after a general resurrection of the dead, in contrast to HELL, the place of punishment for the wicked. Islam has a similar belief. In Chinese religion, heaven is equated with the divine will, which guides the operation of all physical and moral laws. In some Mahayana Buddhist sects, heaven is a paradise for those who have received the saving grace of AMITABHA.

"The Angel Shows John the Heavenly Jerusalem," from the *Apocalypse of St. John*, c. 1020; in the Staatsbibliothek Bamberg, Germany (MS. 140).

BY COURTESY OF THE STAATSBIBLIOTHEK BAMBERG, GERMANY

Heaven's Gate U.S. religious group that committed mass suicide in 1997 and that had been founded on a belief in UNIDENTIFIED FLYING OBJECTS. Established by Marshall H. Applewhite (1932–1997) and Bonnie Nettles (1927–1985) in 1972, the group assumed a variety of names over the years, including Human Individual Metamorphosis. As preparation for the "transition" to a new life on a spaceship, it advocated self-renunciation to the point of castration. Settling finally in the San Diego area in 1996, the group support itself by creating sites on the WORLD WIDE WEB and quietly preparing for the end time. They believed that the comet HALE-BOPP was followed by a spaceship that would take them to a better place. On March 26, 1997, as the comet approached, the remaining 39 members of the group took poison and committed suicide in a carefully orchestrated manner.

Heaviside \'he-vē-ˌsīd\, **Oliver** (1850–1925) English physicist. In 1902 he predicted the presence of the IONOSPHERE. Since Arthur Kennelly (1861–1939) had made a similar prediction, the ionosphere was long known as the Kennelly-Heaviside layer. Heaviside's work on telephone theory made long-distance service practical. In his *Electromagnetic Theory* (1893–1912), he postulated that an electric charge would increase in mass as its velocity increased, anticipating one aspect of ALBERT EINSTEIN's special theory of relativity. He also developed the system of mathematical transforms known as Heaviside calculus.

heavy hydrogen See DEUTERIUM

heavy metal Type of ROCK MUSIC marked by highly amplified "power chords" on electric guitar, a hard beat, thumping bass, and often dark lyrics. It evolved in Britain and the U.S. in the late 1960s from the heavy, blues-oriented music of Steppenwolf, J. HENDRIX, and others, later defining itself as a genre through the music of such bands as Led Zeppelin, Black Sabbath, Grand Funk Railroad, and Aerosmith. After a period of decline, a new generation of bands, including Iron Maiden and Mötley Crüe, revived the genre in the 1980s, along with the careers of many of its pioneers, including Ozzy Osbourne.

heavy spar See BARITE

heavy water *or* **deuterium oxide** \dü-'tir-ē-əm\ Water composed of two DEUTERIUM atoms and one OXYGEN atom, chemical formula D_2O. Ordinary water from most natural sources contains about 0.015% deuterium oxide; this can be enriched or purified by DISTILLATION, ELECTROLYSIS, or chemical processing. Heavy water is used as a moderator in NUCLEAR POWER plants, slowing down the fast neutrons so that they can react with the fuel in the reactor. Heavy water is also used in research as an isotopic tracer for chemical reactions and biochemical pathways. Water with TRITIUM (T_2O) rather than deuterium may also be called heavy water.

Heb-Sed festival One of the oldest festivals of ancient Egypt, celebrated by the king after 30 years of rule and repeated every three years thereafter. The event was probably a ritual reenactment of the unification of Egypt by Menes c. 3000 BC. After beginning the celebration by offering a sacrifice to the gods, the king was crowned with the white crown of Upper Egypt, followed by the red crown of Lower Egypt. He then ran a ritual course four times, before being carried in procession to the chapels of HORUS and SETH.

Hebbel, (Christian) Friedrich (1813–1863) German poet and dramatist. After an early life marked by poverty, he became famous with the prose play *Judith* (1840), based on the biblical story. Among his later tragedies, *Maria Magdalene* (1843), portraying the lower middle class, and *Gyges and His Ring* (1856), probably his most mature and subtle work, are realistic psychological tragedies that make use of G. W. F. HEGEL's concepts of history and moral values. The mythological trilogy *Die Nibelungen* (1862) grandiosely depicts the clash between heathen and Christian.

Hebe \'hē-bē\ Greek goddess of youth, daughter of ZEUS and HERA. She served as cupbearer to the gods, and when HERACLES ascended into heaven after his painful death, she became his bride. She was generally worshiped along with her mother.

Hebe carrying nectar and ambrosia, detail of a vase painting; in the Jatta Museum, Ruvo di Puglia, Italy.

ALINARI—GIRAUDON FROM ART RESOURCE

Hebei \'hə-'bā\ *or* **Hopeh** \'hō-'bā\ *formerly* **Chihli** \'jə-'lē\ Province (pop., 2000 est.: 67,440,000), northern China. BEIJING city forms an enclave in its center. Historically a chief barrier to northern invasion, it contains part of the GREAT WALL of China. From 1644 to 1912 it was ruled by the QING DYNASTY. Occupied by the Japanese in 1937, it was taken by the Chinese Communists in 1949. The provincial capital was at Baoding until 1958, when it was transferred to TIANJIN, then to SHIJIAZHUANG in 1967. Culturally and economically, Hebei is the most advanced province in northern China. The North China Plain covering southern Hebei has been inhabited by humans for several millennia. The fossil remains of *Homo erectus pekinensis* were discovered there.

Hébert, Anne (1916–2000) Canadian novelist and poet. Daughter of a poet and critic, Hébert began her career by writing poetry. After the mid-1950s, however, she moved to Paris, where she produced a number of novels that are psychological examinations of violence, rebellion, and the quest for personal freedom. She was three times the recipient of Canada's highest literary award, the Governor General's Award, once for her poetry in *Poems* (1960) and twice for her fiction (*Kamourska*, 1970, and *Burden of Dreams*, 1992).

Hébert \ā-'ber\, **Jacques (-René)** *known as* **Père Duchesne** \per-dü-'shen\ (1757–1794) French Revolutionary political journalist and chief spokesman for the extremist SANSCULOTTES. He wrote political satires under his pen name, and his newspaper, *Le père Duchesne,* was widely read. He became influential in the Club of the CORDELIERS and with his followers, called Hébertists, helped overthrow the monarchy in 1792. He had the Cathedral of Notre-Dame and 2,000 other churches converted to the worship of Reason. As spokesman for the sansculottes, he pressured the Jacobin regime to institute the REIGN OF TERROR. By 1794 he was regarded as a dangerous extremist, and the Committee of Public Safety had him arrested and guillotined.

Hebraic law Law codes of ancient Israel found in the Jewish Scripture (OLD TESTAMENT). Three separate codes are usually distinguished: the Book of the Covenant, the Deuteronomic Code, and the Priestly Code. The Book of the Covenant is found in Exodus 20–23 and is similar to the much earlier Code of HAMMURABI in Babylon. The Deuteronomic Code in Deuteronomy 12–26 is a revision of earlier Israelite laws and was used in the effort to purify the worship of Yahweh (God) from Canaanite and other influences (see DEUTERONOMIC REFORM). The Priestly Code, found in parts of Exodus, all of Leviticus, and much of Numbers, covers mostly ceremonial practices.

Hebrew alphabet Script used to write the HEBREW LANGUAGE and a number of other languages used as vernaculars by Jews, including LADINO and YIDDISH. The modern 22-letter ALPHABET in use today differs only slightly from the script adapted by Jewish scribes in the early centuries BC from the square script used to write Imperial ARAMAIC. Prior to this adaptation, Hebrew was written in a linear script borrowed ultimately from the Phoenicians, and first attested in the 9th century BC; though the linear script passed out of favor among Jews, Samaritans, adherents of an ancient offshoot of Judaism, continued to use it into modern times. Hebrew is written from right to left, and the letter shapes—at least originally—represented only consonants. Later certain of the consonants were utilized to denote vowels in certain positions, and by c. AD 600 a system of diacritics, or "points," were used to show all vowels in the text of the Bible.

Hebrew calendar See Jewish CALENDAR

Hebrew language NW SEMITIC LANGUAGE that is both a sacred language of Judaism and a modern vernacular in the state of Israel. Like ARAMAIC, to which it is closely related, Hebrew has a documented history of nearly 3,000 years. The earliest fully attested stage of the language is Biblical Hebrew: the earlier parts ("Standard Biblical Hebrew") date before 500 BC and include even older poetic passages; the later parts ("Late Biblical Hebrew") were composed c. 500–200 BC. Post-Biblical Hebrew, variously termed Rabbinic or Mishnaic Hebrew (see MISHNA), is characterized by an early period when Hebrew was still probably to some degree a vernacular, and a later period, after c. AD 200, when Aramaic became the everyday speech of Jews in South Asia. The 6th and 7th century marked a transition to Medieval Hebrew. The resurrection of Hebrew as a vernacular is closely linked with the 18th-century HASKALA movement and 20th-century ZIONISM. Contemporary Israeli Hebrew is spoken by about 5 million people in Israel and abroad. Pronunciation represents on the whole a leveling of differences between the Ashkenazic and Sephardic traditions (see ASHKENAZI, SEPHARDI). See also HEBREW ALPHABET.

Hebrew University of Jerusalem Independent university in Jerusalem, founded in 1925. The foremost university in Israel, it attracts many Jewish students from abroad; Arab students also attend. It has faculties of humanities, science, social science, law, agriculture, dentistry, and medicine; schools of education, social work, pharmacy, home economics, and applied science and technology; and a graduate library school. Total enrollment is about 23,000.

Hebrides \'he-brə-,dēz\ *or* **Western Isles** *ancient* **Ebudae** Group of islands, west of Scotland. They are separated into two groups, the Outer Hebrides (comprising the Western Isles administrative region) and the Inner Hebrides, divided by the Little Minch Strait. Composed of more than 40 islands, only a few of which are inhabited, the islands' original inhabitants were Celts. Norse raids, which led to Norse rule, began after the 8th century and lasted until 1266, when the islands were ceded to Scotland. Their economy centers on farming, fishing, and weaving, the latter noted especially for Harris tweed.

Hebron \'he-brän\ *Arabic* **Al-Khalil** \,al-kä-'lēl\ City (pop., 1997: 119,401), southwest of JERUSALEM. It is a sacred city of JUDAISM and ISLAM as the home of ABRAHAM and the site of his burial place, at the Cave of Machpelah. King DAVID made Hebron his capital briefly in the 10th century BC. Muslims ruled the city from AD 635 until after World War I, except in 1100–1260, when the Crusaders controlled it. It was part of Palestine from 1923 until its annexation by Jordan in 1948. Captured by Israel during the SIX-DAY WAR (1967), it became part of the WEST BANK territory under Israeli administration. In 1997 Israel and the PLO agreed on a partial Israeli pullout from Hebron.

Hecate \'he-kə-tē\ Greek goddess of magic and spells. She probably originated in Asia Minor. HESIOD held her to be the daughter of the Titan Perses and represented her as the bestower of wealth and the blessings of daily life. She witnessed the abduction of PERSEPHONE by HADES and assisted in the search for her. Pillars called Hecataea were erected at doorways and crossroads to ward off evil spirits. She was sometimes depicted as three bodies back to back, so that she could look in all directions at a crossroads.

Hecatompylos \ˌhe-kə-ˈtäm-pə-ˌläs\ Ancient city, western KHORASAN, Iran. For a time the capital of the kingdom of PARTHIA, it was located at the southern foot of the eastern ELBURZ MTNS. It was a SELEUCID military outpost c. 300 BC. By c. 200 BC it was the Iranian ARSACID capital. Known to have been on the SILK ROAD between the Near East and China, it may have been located between the Iranian cities of Damghan and Shahrud, but its precise site has not been established.

Hecht \ˈhekt\, **Ben** (1894–1964) U.S. journalist, novelist, playwright, and film writer. Born in New York City, he worked for Chicago newspapers 1910–22; at the *Daily News* he perfected a type of human-interest sketch that was widely emulated. Later he divided his time between New York and Hollywood. With CHARLES MACARTHUR he wrote the plays *The Front Page* (1928), which influenced both the public's and the newspaper industry's ideas about the newspaper world; *Twentieth Century* (produced 1932); and *Ladies and Gentlemen* (produced 1939). His film scripts, often written with MacArthur, include *Gunga Din* (1938), *Wuthering Heights* (1939), *Spellbound* (1945), and *Notorious* (1946).

Heckman, James J. (b. 1944) U.S. economist and winner of the 2000 NOBEL PRIZE in Economic Sciences, along with DANIEL MCFADDEN, for development of methods for analyzing individual or household behaviour. Born in Chicago, Heckman studied mathematics at Colorado College (B.A. 1965) and economics at Princeton University (M.A. 1968, Ph.D. 1971). He has taught at Columbia University (1970–74) and the University of Chicago (1973–). The "Heckman correction," a two-step statistical approach, offers a means of addressing errors in statistical sampling. He received the John Bates Clark medal from the American Economics Association in 1983.

Heckscher \ˈhek-shər\, **Eli Filip** (1879–1952) Swedish economist and economic historian. He taught at the Stockholm School of Economics from 1909 and was a founder and director of the Stockholm Institute for Economic History. He wrote mainly on economic history, producing such works as *The Continental System* (1922) and *Mercantilism* (1935). He originated the concept of commodity points, which limit the fluctuation of paper currencies, and argued in favor of FREE TRADE, asserting that differing productive factors were responsible for differing commodities trading advantages among nations. This hypothesis, expanded on by his student Bertil Ohlin (1899–1979), is now known as the Heckscher-Ohlin theory.

Hector In Greek legend, the eldest son of PRIAM and HECUBA, the husband of Andromache, and the chief warrior of the Trojan army. In HOMER's *Iliad* he is notable not only for his military prowess but also for his nobility of character. He was a favorite of APOLLO, who helped him slay Achilles' friend Patroclus in combat; in reprisal, Achilles killed Hector in battle and dragged his naked body around the walls of Troy.

Hecuba \ˈhe-kyə-bə\ In Greek legend, the wife of the Trojan king PRIAM and mother of HECTOR. At the end of the TROJAN WAR she was taken prisoner. According to EURIPIDES, her youngest son, Polydorus, had been placed in the care of Polymestor, king of Thrace. When she arrived in Thrace, she learned that Polydorus had been murdered. In revenge, she blinded Polymestor and killed his two sons. In other versions of the legend, she was later turned into a dog, and her grave beside the Hellespont became a landmark for ships.

hedgehog Any of 14 species of insectivores in the family Erinaceidae. All prefer animal food but will eat plant material. The nine species of spiny hedgehogs have short, barbless spines on the back, a round body, small head, pointed face, and little or no tail. Species range from 4 to 17 in. (10–44 cm) long. Spiny hedgehogs are native to Britain, northern Africa, and Asia; one species was introduced into New Zealand. The five species of gymnure, or hairy hedgehog, are Asian. They have coarse guard hairs but no spines and are extremely malodorous. The common gymnure may be 18 in. (46 cm) long and have a 12-in. (30-cm) tail. See also PORCUPINE.

hedgerow Fence or boundary formed by a dense row of shrubs or low trees. Hedgerows enclose or separate fields, protect the soil from wind erosion, and serve to keep cattle and other livestock enclosed. To lay a hedge, the trunks of closely planted saplings of species suitable for hedgerows (e.g., HAWTHORN) are cut a good portion of the way through and the sapling laid down on the ground. New growth rises vertically, forming an impenetrable mesh of branches. In Britain, hedgerows have been a feature of the countryside since the ENCLOSURE MOVEMENT and provide a habitat for numerous songbirds and small animals. As large-scale mechanized farming has become dominant, hedgerows are being removed to combine small fields into larger ones.

hedging Method of reducing the RISK of loss caused by price fluctuation. It consists of the purchase or sale of equal quantities of the same or very similar commodities in two different markets at approximately the same time, with the expectation that a future change in price in one market will be offset by an opposite change in the other market. For example, a grain-elevator operator may agree to buy a ton of wheat and at the same time sell a FUTURES contract for the same quantity of wheat; when the wheat is sold, he buys back the futures contract. If the grain price has dropped, he can buy back the futures contract for less than he sold it for; his profit from doing so will be offset by his loss on the grain. Hedging is also common in the securities and foreign-exchange markets. See also STOCK OPTION.

Heeger, Alan J. (b. 1936) U.S. chemist. Born in Sioux City, Iowa, he received a Ph.D. from the University of California at Berkeley in 1961. With ALAN G. MACDIARMID and HIDEKI SHIRAKAWA, Heeger determined that certain plastics can be chemically modified to conduct electricity almost as readily as metals. The finding led to the discovery of other conductive polymers and contributed to the emerging field of molecular electronics. Heeger, who taught at several institutions, founded the UNIAX Company in 1990. In 2000 he shared the Nobel Prize for Chemistry with MacDiarmid and Shirakawa.

Hefei \ˈhə-ˈfā\ *or* **Ho-fei** \ˈhō-ˈfā\ *formerly* **Luchow** City (pop., 1990: 730,000), central China. The capital of ANHUI province since 1949, the present city dates from the SONG DYNASTY (960–1126). It is a natural center of communications, with easy water transport to the CHANG (YANGTZE) RIVER and important land routes running through it. A railway built in the 1930s transports much of its produce. It is the main location of China's University of Science and Technology.

Hefner, Hugh (Marston) (born 1926) U.S. magazine founder and entrepreneur. Born in Chicago, he studied at the University of Illinois. In 1953 he founded *Playboy* magazine for men. With its intellectually respectable articles and its forthright philosophy of hedonism, *Playboy* was a seminal influence on the "sexual revolution" of the 1960s. Hefner later expanded his enterprise into nightclubs and then into other entertainment media and product marketing.

Hegel \ˈhā-gəl\, **Georg Wilhelm Friedrich** (1770–1831) German philosopher. After working as a tutor, he was headmaster of the gymnasium at Nuremberg (1808–16) and then taught principally at the University of Berlin (1818–31). His work, following on that of IMMANUEL KANT, JOHANN GOTTLIEB FICHTE, and F. W. SCHELLING, marks the pinnacle of post-Kantian German IDEALISM. As an absolute idealist inspired by Christian insights and grounded in his mastery of a vast fund of knowledge, Hegel found a place for everything—logical, natural, human, and divine—in a dialectical scheme that repeatedly swung from thesis to antithesis and back again to a higher and richer synthesis. His panoramic system engaged philosophy in the consideration of all the problems of history and culture, none of which could any longer be deemed foreign to its competence. At the same time, it deprived all the implicated elements and problems of their autonomy, reducing them to symbolic manifestations of the one process, that of the Absolute Spirit's quest for and conquest of its own self. His principal works are *Phenomenology of Mind* (1807), *Encyclopedia of the Philosophical Sciences* (1817), and *Philosophy of Right* (1821). HEGELIANISM has been as fertile in the reactions it precipitated—in SOREN KIERKEGAARD, KARL MARX, G. E. MOORE, and the VIENNA CIRCLE—as in its positive impact. Hegel is regarded as the last of the great philosophical system builders.

Hegelianism \hi-ˈgā-lē-ə-ˌni-zəm\ Diversified philosophical movement that developed out of G. W. F. HEGEL's system of thought. Four stages can be distinguished. The first consists of the Hegelian school in Germany in the period 1827–50. The school divided into three currents. The right, or "Old Hegelians," sought to uphold Hegelianism's compatibility with evangelical orthodoxy and conservative political policies. The left, or "Young Hegelians," interpreted Hegel's identification of the rational with the real in a revolutionary sense. The center preferred to fall back on interpretations of the Hegelian system in its genesis and significance. In the second phase (1850–1904), usually called Neo-Hegelian, the works of the center played a preponderant role. After WILHELM DILTHEY discovered unpublished papers from Hegel's youth in the early 20th cen-

H I J K

tury, there arose in Germany yet another movement; this third phase, the Hegel renaissance, stressed the reconstruction of the genesis of Hegel's thought. In the fourth stage, after World War II, the revival of Marxist studies in Europe finally thrust into the foreground the value of the Hegelian heritage for MARXISM.

Hegira *or* **Hejira** \hi-ˈjī-rə, ˈhe-jə-rə\ (Arabic *Hijra,* "flight") Flight of MUHAMMAD from MECCA to MEDINA in AD 622 in order to escape persecution and found a community of believers. The date represents the beginning of ISLAM. The second caliph, UMAR IBN AL-KHATTAB, began the practice of using the event as the starting point for the Muslim calendar; years are now denoted by the initials AH (Latin, *Anno Hegirae:* "in the year of the Hegira"). The disciples who fled with Muhammad to Medina were called the COMPANIONS OF THE PROPHET.

Heh See HU, SIA, AND HEH

Heian period \ˈhā-ˈän\ (794–1185) Period of Japanese history named for the capital city of Heian-kyo (Kyoto). It is known mainly for the flourishing culture of the court aristocracy, which devoted itself to the pursuit of aesthetic refinement as displayed in poetry and calligraphy. MURASAKI SHIKIBU's contemporaneous novel *The Tale of Genji* depicts that life. A less refined view of Heian Japan is offered in one portion of *Konjaku monogatari,* a collection of stories and folktales. Aesthetics were also emphasized by the SHINGON Buddhist sect, which, along with the broadly syncretic Tendai (Chinese: Tiantai) sect, replaced the earlier Nara Buddhist sects in influence. Pietism gained popularity in the late Heian, leading to the founding of the PURE LAND sect by HONEN. Politically, civilians dominated until 1156, when warriors were called in to settle a political dispute and never left. A brief period of rule by the Taira military clan ensued. See also FUJIWARA FAMILY GEMPEI WAR, SUGAWARA MICHIZANE, TAIRA KIYOMORI.

Heidegger \ˈhī-di-gər\, **Martin** (1889–1976) German philosopher. He taught at the Univs. of Marburg (1923–27) and Freiburg (1927–44). In 1927 he published his magnum opus, *Sein und Zeit (Being and Time).* It strongly influenced Jean-Paul SARTRE and other existentialists, and, despite Heidegger's protestations, he was classed as the leading atheistic existentialist. His declared purpose was to raise anew the question of the meaning of being. His preliminary analysis of human existence (*Dasein,* or "being-there") employed the method of PHENOMENOLOGY. In the early 1930s his thought underwent a *Kehre* ("turning around"), which some have seen as an abandonment of the problem of *Being and Time.* Heidegger joined the NAZI PARTY in 1933 and supported Hitler's policies as rector of Freiburg (1933–34) and less actively to the end of the war. His complicity with the Nazis, which he never publicly disavowed, has prompted debates about whether his philosophy is inherently "totalitarian." Heidegger's work strongly influenced HERMENEUTICS and POSTSTRUCTURALISM.

Martin Heidegger.
CAMERA PRESS

Heidelberg \ˈhīd-ᵊl-ˌbərk\ City (pop., 1996 est.: 139,000), southwestern Germany, situated on the NECKAR RIVER. First mentioned in historical record in 1196, it was the capital of the Rhenish PALATINATE and the residence of the electoral counts Palatine until 1720. It was a center of German CALVINISM in the 16th century. It was devastated during the THIRTY YEARS' WAR (1622) and by the French in 1689 and 1693. It is the site of the 13th-century Heidelberg Castle, a major tourist attraction, and of the University of HEIDELBERG (1386), the oldest in Germany.

Heidelberg, University of *German* **Ruprecht-Karl-Universität Heidelberg.** Autonomous university at Heidelberg, Germany. It was founded in 1386 and modeled on the University of PARIS. The first college was founded by the Cistercian order. The university suffered a decline in the 17th–18th century but regained its prestige after a reorganization in the early 19th century, becoming a center of sciences, law, and philosophy, and its lively student life became the subject of many Romantic stories. Current enrollment is about 28,000.

Heiden, Eric (Arthur) (born 1958) U.S. speed skater. Born in Madison, Wisc., he became the first American to win the world speed-skating championship, retaining the title for three years (1977–79). In the 1980 Winter Olympics he became the first to win gold medals in all five speed-skating events. He later turned to competitive cycling. His younger sister, Beth, was also a world-class skater.

Heidenstam \ˈhā-dən-ˌstám\, **(Carl Gustaf) Verner von** (1859–1940) Swedish poet and novelist. His first book of poems, *Pilgrimage and Wander Years* (1888), drew on his years living in southern Europe and the Middle East and was an immediate success. With his essay "Renaissance" (1889), he became a leader of the opposition in Sweden to NATURALISM, calling for a rebirth of the literature of fantasy, beauty, and nationalism. Many of the poems he wrote in this vein are translated in *Sweden's Laureate* (1919). He also wrote historical fiction, including *The Charles Men* (1897–98) and *The Tree of the Folkungs* (1905–7). He was awarded the Nobel Prize in 1916.

Heifetz \ˈhī-fəts\, **Jascha** (1901–1987) Russian-U.S. violinist. He studied with his father from age 5, performing F. MENDELSSOHN's concerto at 8. From 1909 to 1914, despite its being illegal for a Jew to live in St. Petersburg, he studied there with Leopold Auer (1845–1930). He emigrated to the U.S. in 1917, where for many years he performed in a trio with ARTHUR RUBINSTEIN and Gregor Piatigorsky (1903–1976). Despite an aloof stage manner, Heifetz had impeccable technique and musical flair, and he became perhaps the world's most famous violinist. He retired in 1972, having taught at USC from 1959.

Heilong River See AMUR RIVER

Heilongjiang \ˈhā-ˈlȯŋ-ˈjyäŋ\ *or* **Heilungkiang** \ˈhā-ˈlu̇ŋ-ˈjyäŋ\ Province (population 1996 est.: 37,010,000), northeastern China. It borders on the AMUR RIVER and is China's northernmost province; its capital is HARBIN. It was part of an area formerly known as MANCHURIA. Little developed before the late 19th century, it was under Russian dominance until 1917, when it came under Chinese control. It was taken by Japan in 1931, but retaken by Soviet forces in 1945, who returned it to Chinese (Communist) control. After the 1960 Sino-Soviet rift, its border was the scene of frequent clashes. The area is now one of expanding industrialization.

Heimdall \ˈhām-ˌdäl\ In Norse mythology, the watchman of the gods. Called the shining god, he was noted for his white skin, and he dwelt at the entrance to ASGARD and guarded the rainbow bridge that connected it with earth. Endowed with extraordinary vision and hearing, Heimdall carried a horn that could be heard throughout heaven and earth; with it he would one day announce RAGNAROK, the end of the world, and on that day he and his enemy LOKI would kill each other.

Heimlich maneuver \ˈhīm-lik\ Emergency procedure for dislodging a foreign body from a choking victim's throat, devised by the U.S. surgeon Henry J. Heimlich. It is used only when the airway is totally obstructed, as shown by inability to speak or breathe. The rescuer reaches around the victim from behind, grasps one fist in the other just below the victim's rib cage, and makes several upward thrusts into the victim's belly. This expels the foreign object with air from the victim's own lungs. An unconscious victim is laid faceup and the thrusts are given by a kneeling or squatting rescuer.

Heine \ˈhī-nə\, **(Christian Johann) Heinrich** *orig.* **Harry Heine** (1797–1856) German-French poet. Born of Jewish parents, he converted to Protestantism to enter careers that he never actually pursued. He established his international literary reputation with *The Book of Songs* (1827), a collection of bittersweet love poems. His prose *Pictures of Travel* (4 vols., 1826–31) was widely imitated. After 1831 he lived in Paris. His articles and studies on social and political matters, many critical of German conservatism, were censored there, and German spies watched him in Paris. His second verse collection, *New Poems* (1844), reflected his social engagement. His third, *Romanzero* (1851), written while suffering failing health and financial reverses, is notably bleak but has been greatly admired. He is regarded as one of Germany's greatest lyric poets, and many of his poems were set as songs by such composers as F. SCHUBERT, R. SCHUMANN, and J. BRAHMS.

Heinlein \'hīn-līn\, **Robert A(nson)** (1907–1988) U.S. science-fiction writer. Born in Butler, Mo., he pursued graduate study in physics and mathematics, and began his writing career in the pulp magazine *Astounding Science Fiction* in the 1930s. The first of his many novels and story collections was *Rocket Ship Galileo* (1947). *Stranger in a Strange Land* (1961), his best-known work, attracted a large cult following. His other books include *Double Star* (1956), *Methuselah's Children* (1958), *Starship Troopers* (1959), *The Moon Is a Harsh Mistress* (1966), and *I Will Fear No Evil* (1970). He won an unprecedented four Hugo Awards, and his sophisticated works did much to develop the genre.

Heinz, H(enry) J(ohn) (1844–1919) U.S. entrepreneur, founder of a major manufacturer of processed foods. He was born in Pittsburgh, where he entered his father's brick-manufacturing business. He simultaneously built up a produce business, delivering produce grown on his own land to local grocers. In 1876, with a brother and a cousin, he formed the F. & J. Heinz Co., a maker of pickles, ketchup, baked beans, and other prepared foods. It was reorganized in 1888 as the H. J. Heinz Co. and incorporated in 1905. Heinz served as its president until his death.

heir One who inherits or is entitled to succeed to the possession of property after the death of its owner. In most jurisdictions, statutes of descent determine transfer of title to property if no WILL names the recipient. One may be either heir apparent or heir presumptive during the lifetime of the property holder. An heir apparent's right to an inheritance cannot be voided or undone except by exclusion under a valid will. An heir presumptive's right to inherit may be defeated by the birth of a nearer relative. In Britain, the heir apparent of the monarch is the eldest son. If there are no sons, the eldest daughter is heiress presumptive. See also PRIMOGENITURE.

Heisei emperor See AKIHITO

Heisei period \'hā-'sā\ Japanese reign period that began in 1989 when AKIHITO became emperor on the death of his father, HIROHITO. The Heisei period has been a sober one for the Japanese, marked by turbulent politics (with nine prime ministers in its first nine years), an economic slowdown, and crises in the financial world. A devastating earthquake in KOBE and AUM SHINRIKYO's nerve-gas attack on a Tokyo subway line (both in 1995) have contributed to the dark picture of the period to date. Positive events include the wedding of the crown prince and the hosting of the 1998 Winter Olympics in Nagano. See also KEIZO OBUCHI, SHOWA PERIOD.

Heisenberg \'hī-zᵊn-bərg\, **Werner (Karl)** (1901–1976) German physicist. Educated at Munich and Göttingen, he taught at the University of Leipzig 1927–41 and directed the Max Planck Institute for Physics 1942–76. In 1925 he solved the problem of how to account for the stationary discrete energy states of an anharmonic oscillator, a solution that launched the development of QUANTUM MECHANICS. In 1927 he published his famous UNCERTAINTY PRINCIPLE. He also made important contributions to the theories of the hydrodynamics of turbulence, the atomic nucleus, ferromagnetism, cosmic rays, and subatomic particles. He was awarded a Nobel Prize in 1932 for his work on quantum mechanics.

Heisenberg uncertainty principle See UNCERTAINTY PRINCIPLE

Heisman, John (William) (1869–1936) U.S. collegiate football coach and one of the game's greatest innovators. Born in Cleveland, he played for both Brown University and the University of Pennsylvania. He was responsible for legalizing the forward pass in 1906, and he originated the center snap and the "hike" count signals of the quarterback in starting play. He coached at several colleges between 1892 and 1927, compiling a record of 185 wins, 68 losses, and 18 ties. The HEISMAN TROPHY was named for him.

Heisman Trophy Cup awarded annually to the outstanding college football player in the U.S., as determined by a poll of sportswriters. The trophy was instituted in 1935 by New York's Downtown Athletic Club, and officially named the following year for its first athletic director, the player-coach JOHN HEISMAN.

Hejaz \he-'jaz\ *Arabic* **Al-Hijaz** \,al-hē-'jaz\ Region of western Saudi Arabia. It occupies an area of 134,600 sq mi (348,600 sq km) along the Red Sea coast of the ARABIAN PENINSULA, from Jordan to Asir province. Its northern portion was inhabited by the 6th century BC. In the 7th century AD its cities of MECCA and MEDINA saw the birth of ISLAM, and they remain (with JERUSALEM) Islam's holiest cities. In 1258 it fell to the Egyptians and in 1517 to the Turks. In 1916 Sharif HUSAYN IBN ALI revolted and proclaimed himself king of Hejaz. IBN SAUD, the sultan of NEJD, assumed the title in 1926, and in 1932 united Hejaz, Nejd, and other districts to form the Kingdom of Saudi Arabia.

Hejira See HEGIRA

Hel In Norse mythology, the realm of the dead and, later, the goddess of the dead. She was the daughter of LOKI. Her kingdom, Niflheim, or the World of Darkness, was divided into several sections. Murderers, perjurers, and adulterers suffered torment in a castle filled with serpents' venom, while the dragon Nidhogg sucked their blood. Those who fell in battle went to VALHALLA and thus avoided Hel.

Helen In GREEK MYTHOLOGY, the most beautiful woman in Greece, who was the indirect cause of the TROJAN WAR. She was a daughter of ZEUS, either by LEDA or by NEMESIS. Her brothers were the DIOSCURI, and her sister was Clytemnestra, wife of AGAMEMNON. Helen was the wife of MENELAUS. When PARIS, son of PRIAM, was asked to decide which goddess was the most beautiful, he chose APHRODITE, who rewarded him with the most beautiful woman in the world. Seducing Helen with the goddess's help, Paris carried her off to Troy, and the Greeks sent a military force to pursue them. At the war's end, with Paris dead, Helen returned to Sparta with Menelaus.

Helena \'he-lə-nə\ City (pop., 1995 est.: 28,000), capital of Montana. Located near the Missouri River in western central Montana, in an area visited by the LEWIS AND CLARK EXPEDITION (1805), it was settled after gold was discovered there in 1864 (in Last Chance Gulch, now the city's main street). It became capital of the territory in 1875 and of the state in 1889. In addition to state government activities, Helena is an agricultural and livestock trade center and has light manufactures. The capitol building has a copper-covered dome surmounted by a reproduction of the Statue of Liberty.

Helena, St. (AD 248?–328?) Mother of CONSTANTINE I. She was the wife of CONSTANTIUS I CHLORUS before he became caesar (subemperor), and she bore Constantine before being renounced for political reasons. She became a Christian under her son's influence. Implicated in the execution of her daughter-in-law (326), she made a pilgrimage to the Holy Land and had churches built in Jerusalem and Bethlehem on the sites of the Ascension and the Nativity. By the late 4th century she was reputed to have found Christ's cross.

Helga, St. See St. OLGA

helicon See SOUSAPHONE

Helicon, Mt. Mountain, eastern central Greece, part of the Helicon range, a continuation of the higher Parnassus range. Located near the Gulf of Corinth, it is 5,738 ft (1,749 m) high. It was celebrated by the ancient Greeks as the home of the MUSES; on it were the fountains of Aganippe and Hippocrene, the supposed sources of poetic inspiration.

helicopter Aircraft with one or more power-driven horizontal PROPELLERS or rotors that enable it to take off and land vertically, move in any direction, or remain stationary in the air. It is often described as a rotary-wing aircraft, in contrast to a conventional fixed-wing AIRPLANE. One of the earliest ideas for flying, it appeared in China and Renaissance Europe as a toy and in LEONARDO DA VINCI's designs. The Frenchman Paul Cornu made the first manned flight in 1907. IGOR SIKORSKY produced the first successful prototype in 1939, which was followed by rapid development in the U.S. and Europe. It was widely used by the military in the Korean and Vietnam wars to move and rescue troops. It is also used for civilian rescue work and various commercial purposes.

helioflagellate \,hē-lē-ō-'fla-jə-lət\ Any of a class of freshwater PROTOZOANS. They are sometimes considered relatives of heliozoans (organisms that for movement have extensions of CYTOPLASM called pseudopodia, but no flagella) because of their slender, radiating pseudopodia. The cores of the pseudopodia of some helioflagellates radiate from a central granule, as they do in some heliozoans. Helioflagellate life cycles alternate between flagellate and heliozoan phases. Some members are spherical, others oval.

Heliogabalus See ELAGABALUS

heliopause Boundary between the heliosphere, the teardrop-shaped region around the SUN filled with solar-magnetic fields and outward-moving solar gas, and the zone of transition to the INTERSTELLAR MEDIUM. Its tail is estimated to reach 50–100 ASTRONOMICAL UNITS from the sun, encompassing the orbits of all the major planets. Its shape changes, influenced by a wind of interstellar gas produced by the sun's motion through it.

Heliopolis \ˌhē-lē-ˈä-pə-ləs\ *biblical* **On.** Ancient holy city, Egypt. The city, mainly now ruins lying northeast of CAIRO, was the seat of worship of the Egyptian sun god Ra. Its great temple of Ra was second in size only to that of Amon at THEBES, and its priesthood wielded great influence. In the New Kingdom, the temple became the repository of royal records. The city's surviving monument is the obelisk of Sesostris I, the oldest in existence. Two obelisks erected there by THUTMOSE III and known as Cleopatra's Needles now stand on the THAMES RIVER embankment in London and in CENTRAL PARK, New York City.

Helios \ˈhē-lē-ˌōs\ Sun god of ancient Greece. He drove his chariot from east to west across the sky each day and sailed across the ocean each night in a huge cup. He was especially worshiped on Rhodes, where he was considered the chief god as early as the 5th century BC. In Greece he was later displaced by APOLLO. The Romans worshiped him as SOL.

heliotrope \ˈhē-lē-ə-ˌtrōp\ Any of about 250 species of tropical or temperate, mostly herbaceous, plants that make up the genus *Heliotropium,* in the BORAGE family, found throughout the world. Included are many weedy species. The best known is garden heliotrope *(H. arborescens),* a shrubby perennial that bears fragrant, purple to white, flat-clustered, five-lobed flowers in coiled sprays, similar to FORGET-ME-NOTS.

Garden heliotrope (*Heliotropium arborescens*).
WALTER DAWN

helium Chemical ELEMENT, chemical symbol He, atomic number 2. A NOBLE GAS, it is colorless, odorless, tasteless, completely unreactive, and nontoxic. First found by SPECTROSCOPY of the sun's atmosphere in 1868, it is the second most abundant and second-lightest element in the universe (after hydrogen). Helium makes up a tiny proportion of the atmosphere but as much as 7% of NATURAL GAS. It is the product of radioactive decay (see RADIOACTIVITY) and is used in HELIUM DATING. It is used as an inert gas in welding, rocket propulsion, BALLOON flight, HYPERBARIC CHAMBERS, deep-sea DIVING (see NITROGEN NARCOSIS), GAS CHROMATOGRAPHY, luminous signs, and CRYOGENICS. Liquid helium, which exists only below −452°F (−268.9°C, about 4°C above ABSOLUTE ZERO), is a "quantum fluid" (see FLUID MECHANICS), with unique properties, including SUPERFLUIDITY, SUPERCONDUCTIVITY, and near-zero VISCOSITY.

helium dating Method of age determination that depends on the production of helium during the decay of radioactive isotopes of uranium and thorium. Because of this decay, the helium content of any mineral or rock capable of retaining helium will increase during the lifetime of that mineral or rock, and the ratio of helium to its radioactive progenitors then becomes a measure of geologic time. Fossils may also be dated by helium dating. The relatively large amount of helium produced in rocks may make it possible to extend helium dating to rocks and minerals as young as a few tens of thousands of years old.

hell Abode of evildoers after death, or the state of existence of souls damned to punishment after death. Most ancient religions included the concept of a place that divided the good from the evil or the living from the dead (e.g., the gloomy subterranean realm of HADES in Greek religion, or the cold and dark underworld of Nilfheim or HEL in Norse mythology). The view that hell is the final dwelling place of the damned after a last judgment is held by Zoroastrianism, Judaism, Christianity, and Islam. The Jewish concept of Gehenna as an infernal region of punishment for the wicked was the basis for the Christian vision of hell as the fiery domain of Satan and his evil angels and a place of punishment for those who die without repenting of their sins. In Hinduism hell is only one stage in the career of the soul as it passes through the phases of reincarnation. The schools of Buddhism have varying conceptions of hell, usually entailing some kind of punishment or purgatory. In Jainism, hell is a purgatory in which sinners are tormented by demons until the evil of their lives has been exhausted.

hellbender SALAMANDER (*Cryptobranchus alleganiensis,* family Cryptobranchidae) found in swift-flowing rivers in the eastern and central U.S. It grows to about 25 in. (63 cm) long, has a stout body, flat head, broad tail fin, and wrinkled sides, and is typically brownish gray with black spots. Adults have lungs, but a gill slit persists from the larval stage on each side behind the head. Wrinkled fleshy folds on the body and legs increase surface area for respiration through the skin, the principal mode of oxygen intake. Hellbenders lie under stones during the day, emerging at night to feed on crayfish, small fishes, and worms.

hellebore \ˈhe-lə-ˌbōr\ Member of either of two genera of poisonous herbaceous plants, *Helleborus* (BUTTERCUP family) and *Veratrum* (LILY FAMILY). Some are grown as garden ornamentals. *Helleborus* consists of about 20 species of PERENNIAL plants native to Eurasia; most are nearly stemless, with thick roots and long-stalked, divided leaves and showy flowers. *Veratrum* contains about 45 species, better called false hellebores, native widely to damp areas of the Northern Hemisphere. They have simple leaves and clusters of small flowers.

Green hellebore (*Helleborus viridis*).
G.E. HYDE FROM THE NATURAL HISTORY PHOTOGRAPHIC AGENCY

Hellenistic Age In the eastern Mediterranean and the Middle East, the period between the death of ALEXANDER THE GREAT (323 BC) and the conquest of Egypt by Rome (30 BC). Alexander and his successors established Greek monarchies that controlled the area from Greece to Afghanistan. The Macedonian ANTIGONID kingdom, the Middle Eastern SELEUCID kingdom, and the Egyptian Ptolemaic kingdom spread Greek culture, mixed Greek and non-Greek populations, and fused Greek and Oriental elements. They produced effective bureaucracies and a common, creative culture based at ALEXANDRIA. A great flowering of the arts, literature, and science occurred particularly in the period 280–160. The decline of the Hellenic states occurred as Rome gained strength and won wars against Macedonia and against MITHRADATES VI EUPATOR, turning the kingdoms and their allies into Roman provinces. Egypt was the last to fall, after having been drawn into the civil war between Mark ANTONY and Octavian (AUGUSTUS).

Heller, Joseph (1923–1999) U.S. writer. Born in Brooklyn, N.Y., Heller flew 60 combat missions as a bombardier in World War II before finishing his studies at Columbia and Oxford and working as an advertising copywriter. His satirical novel *Catch-22* (1961), based on his wartime experiences, was one of the most significant works of postwar protest literature and a huge critical and popular success. His later novels include *Something Happened* (1974), *Good as Gold* (1979), *God Knows* (1984), and *Closing Time* (1994).

Heller, Yom Tov (Lipmann ben Nathan Ha-Levi) (1579–1654) Bohemian Jewish religious scholar. After serving as rabbi in Moravia and Vienna, he became chief rabbi in Prague in 1627. He was forced to collect a heavy tax imposed on Jews by FERDINAND II during the Thirty Years' War, damaging his reputation in the Jewish community. Later, as rabbi in Volhynia, he earned the enmity of wealthy Jews for denouncing simony. From 1643 he was chief rabbi in Kraków. He is best known for his commentary on the Mishna, *The Additions of Yom Tov* (1614–17).

Hellespont See DARDANELLES

Hellman, Lillian (Florence) (1905–1984) U.S. playwright. Born in New Orleans, she worked as a book reviewer, press agent, and play reader while writing plays. Her first major success, *The Children's Hour* (1934), concerned two schoolteachers falsely accused of lesbianism. She examined family infighting in her hit *The Little Foxes* (1939) and political injustice in *Watch on the Rhine* (1941). All were made into successful films. Called before the House Un-American Activities Committee in 1952, she refused to testify. She adapted VOLTAIRE's *Candide* for a musical version by LEONARD BERNSTEIN (1956). Her *Toys in the Attic* (1960) was also made into a film. She wrote several memoirs and edited the works of her longtime companion, DASHIELL HAMMETT.

Hells Canyon Gorge of the SNAKE RIVER. Forming part of the Idaho–Oregon boundary, it is 125 mi (200 km) long and for 40 mi (64 km) is more than a mile deep. A maximum depth of 7,900 ft (2,400 m) makes it the deepest gorge in North America. With its surrounding area of 662,000 acres (268,000 hectares), Hells Canyon was designated a national recreation area in 1975.

Helmand River *or* **Helmund River** \'hel-mənd\ *ancient* **Etymander** River, southwestern Afghanistan and eastern Iran. Rising in eastern central Afghanistan, it flows southwest across more than half the country before flowing north for a short distance through Iran and emptying into the Helmand (SISTAN) swamps on the Afghan– Iranian border. At 870 mi (1,400 km) long, it is one of Afghanistan's most important rivers and has been extensively developed for irrigation. A long-standing dispute between Afghanistan and Iran has centered on Iran's claim to a portion of the Helmand's waters.

Helmholtz \'helm-ˌhōlts\, **Hermann (Ludwig Ferdinand) von** (1821–1894) German scientist, one of the greatest of the 19th century. After training in medicine, he taught physiology and later physics at several German universities. His interests continually shifted to new disciplines, in which he applied his earlier insights to every problem he examined. He made fundamental contributions to physiology, optics, electrodynamics, mathematics, acoustics, and meteorology, but is best known for his statement (1847) of the law of conservation of ENERGY. His approach was strongly empirical at a time when many scientists embraced deductions from mental concepts. He invented several measurement instruments, including the myograph, ophthalmoscope, and ophthalmometer. He described body heat and energy, nerve conduction, and the physiology of the eye. His mathematical analysis of vortices in fluids (1858) was a tour de force. His work in electrodynamics built on that of MICHAEL FARADAY and JAMES CLERK MAXWELL but was eventually superseded by that of ALBERT EINSTEIN.

Helmont, Jan Baptista van (1580–1644) Belgian chemist, physiologist, and physician. Though he tended to mysticism, he was a careful observer and exact experimenter. The first to recognize gases other than air, he coined the word "gas" and discovered that the "wild spirits" (carbon dioxide) produced by burning charcoal and by fermenting grape juice were the same. For applying chemical principles to digestion and nutrition, he has been called the "father of biochemistry." His collected works were published in 1648.

helots \'he-ləts\ Native peoples of Laconia and Messenia conquered and controlled by SPARTA. They were state-owned serfs or slaves who worked the land to feed and clothe the Spartan population, whom they vastly outnumbered. Their masters could not free them or sell them. The Spartans lived in constant fear of a helot revolt, and annually declared war on them to legally keep them in place by force. During wartime helots attended their masters on campaigns, serving as troops and as rowers in the fleet. The Messenian helots were liberated c. 370 BC, those in Laconia not until the 2nd century BC.

Helper, Hinton Rowan (1829–1909) U.S. antislavery writer. Born in Davie Co., N.C., in 1857 he wrote *The Impending Crisis of the South,* attacking slavery as the cause of the South's economic weakness and using statistics to show that the use of free black labor victimized nonslaveholding whites and inhibited economic progress. His book became influential in the antislavery movement in the North; in the South it caused a furor and was banned by several states. For his safety Helper moved to New York. After the Civil War, he wrote three bitter racist tracts advocating deportation of blacks to Africa or Latin America.

Helpmann, Robert (Murray) *later* **Sir Robert** (1909–1986) Australian ballet dancer, choreographer, actor, and director. After dancing and acting in Australia, in 1933 he went to London to study, joining the Vic-Wells (later ROYAL) BALLET, where he became a regular partner of M. FONTEYN. His own ballets included *Hamlet* (1942), *Miracle in the Gorbals* (1944), and *Adam Zero* (1946). He danced in the films *The Red Shoes* and *Tales of Hoffmann,* acted in many Shakespeare plays, and also directed several plays. He was artistic codirector of the Australian Ballet (1965–76).

Helsinki *Swedish* **Helsingfors** City (pop., 1997 est.: 532,000), capital of Finland. Located in southern Finland on a peninsula with natural harbors, it is the country's leading seaport. Often called the "white city of the north" because many of its buildings are made of a local light-colored granite, it was founded by Sweden in 1550 and moved to its present site in 1640. With Finland it came under Russian rule in 1808. Under the Russian czar ALEXANDER I it became the capital of the grand duchy of Finland in 1812, and remained as the capital of the country. In 1917 Finland declared independence from Russia, and a brief but bloody civil war ensued in the capital. In subsequent decades it developed into an important trade center. It was damaged by Russian bombing during World War II (see RUSSO-FINNISH WAR), but was rebuilt. It was the site of a 1975 international conference (see HELSINKI ACCORDS).

Helsinki Accords International agreement signed in 1975 to reduce tension between the Soviet and Western blocs by securing their common acceptance of the post–World War II status quo in Europe, including Germany's division. The accords, signed by all the countries of Europe (except Albania) as well as the U.S. and Canada, were nonbinding and lacked treaty status. They were sought by the Soviet Union to gain implicit recognition of its postwar hegemony in Eastern Europe. In return, the U.S. and its Western European allies pressed for respect for human rights and cooperation in economic, scientific, and other humanitarian areas. Follow-up meetings in Belgrade (1977–78), Madrid (1980–83), and Ottawa (1985) saw strong criticism of Soviet human-rights abuses, with Soviet counteraccusations. A 1990 conference in Paris formally ended the COLD WAR and recognized German reunification.

Helvetic Republic Republic founded in March 1798, constituting the greater part of Switzerland, after it had been conquered by France in the FRENCH REVOLUTIONARY WARS. The government was patterned after that of the DIRECTORY in France. Delegates called on NAPOLEON to mediate in factional disputes, and in 1803 he substituted a new Swiss Confederation for the republic, forcing it into close association with France.

Helvétius \el-vās-'yu̅s\, **Claude-Adrien** (1715–1771) French philosopher, controversialist, and patron of the PHILOSOPHES. He is remembered for his hedonism (see AXIOLOGY), his attack on the religious foundations of ethics, and his educational theory. His *On the Mind* (1758) immediately became notorious for its attack on all forms of morality based on religion. He held that all men are equally capable of learning, a belief that led him to argue against J.-J. ROUSSEAU'S *Émile* and claim that education's possibilities for solving human problems were unlimited.

Hemacandra \ˌhā-mə-'chən-drə\ *orig.* **Candradeva** (1088–1172) Sage of Jainism. His birth was attended by auspicious omens, and he was educated by Jain priests. Ordained in 1110, he became an adviser to King Kumarapala in 1125, and by converting the king he firmly entrenched Jainism in Gujarat. His many writings include works on almost every branch of Indian philosophy and the sciences as well as literary writings such as his Sanskrit epic, *Lives of the 63 Great Personages.* In accordance with Jain tradition, he fasted to death.

hemangioma \ˌhē-ˌman-jē-'ō-mə\ Congenital benign TUMOR made of blood vessels in the skin. Capillary hemangioma (nevus flammeus, port-wine stain), an abnormal mass of CAPILLARIES on the head, neck, or face, is pink to dark bluish-red and even with the skin. Size and shape vary. It becomes less noticeable or disappears with age. Immature hemangioma (hemangioma simplex, strawberry mark), a reddish nub of dilated small blood vessels, enlarges in the first six months and may become ulcerated but usually recedes after the first year. Cavernous hemangioma, a rare, red-blue, raised mass of larger blood vessels, can occur in skin or in mucous membranes, the brain, or the viscera. Fully developed at birth, it is rarely malignant. Hemangiomas can often be removed by cosmetic surgery.

hematite *or* **haematite** \'hē-mə-ˌtīt\ Heavy and relatively hard OXIDE MINERAL, ferric oxide (Fe_2O_3), that constitutes the most important iron ore because of its high iron content and its abundance. Much hematite (from the Greek word meaning "blood," for its red color) occurs in a soft, fine-grained, earthy form called red ocher or ruddle. Red ocher is used as a paint pigment; a purified form, rouge, is used to polish plate glass. The world's largest production comes from the Hamersley Range in western Australia.

hematology \ˌhē-mə-'tä-lə-jē\ Branch of medicine concerned with the nature, function, and diseases of the BLOOD. It covers the cellular and serum composition of blood, the COAGULATION process, BLOOD-CELL FORMATION, HEMOGLOBIN synthesis, and disorders of all these. MARCELLO MALPIGHI, in the 17th century, was the first to examine red blood cells (ERYTHROCYTES). In the 18th century, the British physiologist William Hewson

(1739–1774) examined the lymphatic system and blood clotting. In the 19th century, the bone marrow was recognized as the site of blood-cell formation and diseases of the blood such as ANEMIA and LEUKEMIA were identified. In the early 20th century, the ABO BLOOD-GROUP SYSTEM was discovered and the role of nutrition in blood formation was studied. Post–World War II studies have delved further into the nature of blood diseases and improved treatments, and have examined hemoglobin synthesis and the role of PLATELETS in blood coagulation.

hematopoiesis See BLOOD-CELL FORMATION

hematuria \\,hē-mə-'tu̇r-ē-ə\\ Blood in the urine. It usually indicates injury or disease of the kidney or another structure of the urinary system or possibly, in males, the reproductive system. It may result from infection, inflammation, tumors, kidney stones, or other disorders. How the blood looks and when it appears in the urine stream reflect whether it originates in the urethra, the bladder, or the kidney.

Hemingway, Ernest (Miller) (1899–1961) U.S. writer. Born in Oak Park, Ill., he began work as a journalist after high school. He was wounded while serving as an ambulance driver in World War I. He later became part of a famous group of expatriate writers in Paris, and soon embarked on a life of travel, skiing, fishing, and hunting that would be reflected in his work. His story collection *In Our Time* (1925) was followed by the novel *The Sun Also Rises* (1926). Later novels included *A Farewell to Arms* (1929) and *To Have and Have Not* (1937). His lifelong love for Spain (including a fascination with bullfighting) led to his working as a correspondent during the Spanish Civil War, which resulted in the novel *For Whom the Bell Tolls* (1940). Other short-story collections include *Men Without Women* (1927), *Winner Take Nothing* (1933), and *The Fifth Column* (1938). He lived primarily in Cuba from c. 1940, the locale of his novella *The Old Man and the Sea* (1952, Pulitzer Prize). He was awarded the Nobel Prize in 1954. He left Cuba shortly after its 1959 revolution; a year later, depressed and ill, he shot himself. *A Moveable Feast* (1964) is a posthumously published Paris memoir. The succinct and concentrated prose style of his early works strongly influenced many British and American writers for decades.

Hemingway, photograph by Yousuf Karsh, 1959.

BY COURTESY OF MARY HEMINGWAY; PHOTOGRAPH, © KARSH FROM RAPHO/PHOTO RESEARCHERS

hemispheric asymmetry See LATERALITY

hemlock Any of 10 species of coniferous evergreen trees that make up the genus *Tsuga,* in the PINE family, native to North America and central and eastern Asia. Some are important timber trees, and many are popular ornamentals. Other plants commonly called hemlock include ground hemlock (see YEW) and POISON HEMLOCK and water hemlock (PARSLEY family). A true hemlock is a tall, pyramidal tree with purplish or reddish-brown bark, slender horizontal or drooping branches, and short, blunt leaves that grow from woody cushionlike structures on the twigs.

hemodialysis See DIALYSIS

hemoglobin \\'hē-mə-,glō-bən\\ PROTEIN in the blood of many animals (in vertebrates it is in red blood cells) that transports OXYGEN from the lungs to the tissues and CARBON DIOXIDE back. It is bright red when combined with oxygen and purple-blue in the deoxygenated state. Each molecule is made up of a globin (a type of protein) molecule and four heme groups. Heme, a complex HETEROCYCLIC COMPOUND, is an organic molecule derived from PORPHYRIN with an IRON atom at the center (see LIGAND, TRANSITION ELEMENT). Abnormal hemoglobins (see SICKLE-CELL ANEMIA, HEMOGLOBINOPATHY) can be used to trace past human migrations and to study genetic relationships among populations.

hemoglobinopathy \\,hē-mə-,glō-bə-'nä-pə-thē\\ Any of a group of disorders caused by genetic abnormality of the HEMOGLOBIN molecule. The most prominent types are SICKLE-CELL ANEMIA and thalassemia, a set of disorders whose symptoms range from none to fatal ANEMIA.

hemolytic disease of the newborn See ERYTHROBLASTOSIS FETALIS

hemophilia \\,hē-mə-'fi-lē-ə\\ Hereditary bleeding disorder caused by deficiency of a COAGULATION factor. Lack of factor VIII causes classic hemophilia; other types are caused by deficiency of factor IX or XI. The first two are transmitted by sex-linked heredity; the third has dominant inheritance and occurs in females as well as males. Spontaneous bleeding may occur. Even trivial injury can cause life-threatening blood loss. Drugs can be given to stop bleeding. Heavy blood loss requires blood transfusions.

hemorrhage \\'he-mə-rij\\ Escape of blood from blood vessels into surrounding tissue. When a vessel is injured, hemorrhage continues as long as the vessel remains open and the pressure in it exceeds the pressure outside of it. Normally, COAGULATION closes the vessel and stops the bleeding. Uncontrolled hemorrhage can result from ANTICOAGULANT therapy, HEMOPHILIA, or severe blood-vessel damage, leading to excessive blood loss and SHOCK.

hemorrhagic fever \\,he-mə-'ra-jik\\ Disease with high fever, HEMORRHAGE of internal organs and in small spots in the skin, HYPOTENSION and SHOCK, and sometimes neurologic effects. It is caused by several kinds of virus (of which EBOLA is the best known), some carried by ticks or mosquitoes and some apparently by animals. A subtype, epidemic hemorrhagic fever, also causes head, muscle, joint, and abdominal pain; nausea and vomiting; sweating and thirst; and coldlike symptoms. It comes on suddenly and can cause severe kidney damage.

hemorrhoid \\'he-mə-,rȯid\\ *or* **pile** Mass formed by distension of the network of veins supplying the anal canal. It may develop from infection or increased abdominal pressure (as in pregnancy or heavy lifting). Mild hemorrhoids may require only ointments, laxatives, and baths. If clotting, bleeding, or pain occurs, surgical removal may be needed. Internal hemorrhoids, with little nerve supply, can be destroyed in several ways without anesthesia. External hemorrhoids, under the skin, are cut out under local anesthesia.

hemp Stout, aromatic, erect annual herbaceous plant (*Cannabis sativa,* family Cannabaceae), the sole species of CANNABIS; also, its fiber. Hemp originated in Central Asia and is now cultivated widely in the northern temperate zone. A tall, canelike variety is raised for the fiber; a short, more branched variety is prized as the more abundant source of MARIJUANA. Hemp fiber is strong and durable and is used for cordage and for artificial sponges and such coarse fabrics as sacking (burlap) and canvas. Hemp is grown primarily for fiber in most countries.

Hemp (*Cannabis sativa*).

JOHN KOHOUT FROM ROOT RESOURCES

Henan *or* **Honan** \\'hə-'nän\\ Province (pop., 1996 est.: 91,000,000), eastern central China. Its capital is ZHENGZHOU. Early evidence of Chinese civilization were found there that gave rise to the SHANG DYNASTY (18th–12th century BC), the first of several that ruled until c. AD 936. KAIFENG became the capital under the Northern SONG DYNASTY which was overthrown by the MONGOLS in 1127; Zhengzhou then was made the capital. Henan's principal crop is wheat. It has large deposits of coal, petroleum, and natural gas which fuel the economies of its major cities. It is also a railroad transportation hub.

henbane Plant *(Hyoscyamus niger)* of the NIGHTSHADE FAMILY, native to Britain and found growing wild in waste places and on rubbish heaps. It also occurs in central and southern Europe and in western Asia extending to India and Siberia, and has long been naturalized in the U.S. The whole plant has a powerful, nauseating odor. Commercial henbane, which consists of the dried leaves of *H. niger* and sometimes of *H. muticus,* of Egypt, yields three dangerous drugs: ATROPINE, hyoscyamine,

H I J K

and scopolamine. Isolated and purified, these drugs are valuable remedies for spasmodic muscular contractions, nervous irritation, and hysteria.

Henderson, Fletcher (Hamilton) (1897–1952) U.S. pianist, arranger, and leader of one of the most influential big bands in jazz. Born in Cuthbert, Ga., Henderson formed a dance band in New York in 1923. The band soon distinguished itself in two ways: the engagement of LOUIS ARMSTRONG as principal soloist placed greater emphasis on swinging improvisation, and the arrangements by Henderson and Don Redman (1900–1964) codified the roles of the sections within the ensemble to replace the collective improvisation of early jazz groups. Nearly all big bands subsequently followed their example. A poor businessman, he was forced to dissolve his band several times, but his arrangements played a key role in the success of BENNY GOODMAN in the late 1930s, and provided a template for much of the music of the SWING era.

Hendricks, Thomas A(ndrews) (1819–1885) U.S. politician. Born near Zanesville, Ohio, he practiced law in Indiana before serving in the U.S. House of Representatives (1851–55) and Senate (1863–69) and later as governor (1873–77). He was the Democratic nominee for vice president in 1876 (with SAMUEL TILDEN) and again in 1884, when he was elected with GROVER CLEVELAND. He died shortly after taking office.

Hendrix, Jimi *orig.* **James Marshall** (1942–1970) U.S. BLUES and rock guitarist (see ROCK MUSIC). Born in Seattle of mixed black-Cherokee ancestry, the left-handed Hendrix taught himself to play the guitar, which he held upside down. He served as an army paratrooper, and later toured as guitarist for LITTLE RICHARD and others. In 1966 he moved to London and formed a trio, The Jimi Hendrix Experience, which rapidly became popular in Europe. His sensational appearance at the Monterey Pop Festival in 1967 and the success that year of the album *Are You Experienced?* lifted him to instant stardom, and his subsequent albums were among the most influential of the 1960s. He died at 27 of an apparently accidental overdose of barbiturates.

Henie \'he-nē\, **Sonja** (1912–1969) Norwegian-U.S. figure skater. Born in Kristiania, she was trained in ballet. She won the world amateur championship for women 10 consecutive years (1927–36) and won three gold medals in the Winter Olympics (1928, 1932, 1936). With her dancer's training, she was largely responsible for converting a predictable series of colorless exercises into a spectacular and popular exhibition. She achieved further renown as a professional ice skater and movie actress. In 1941 she became an American citizen.

Sonja Henie performing in her *Hollywood Ice Revue* of 1950.
PICTORIAL PARADE

Henle \'hen-lə\, **Friedrich Gustav Jacob** (1809–1885) German pathologist and anatomist. He published the first descriptions of the composition and distribution of the surface tissue of anatomical structures (epithelium) and of fine eye and brain structures. Henle embraced GIROLAMO FRACASTORO's unpopular microorganism theory. His *Comprehensive Anatomy* (1841) was the first systematic histology treatise. His *Handbook of Rational Pathology* (2 vols., 1846–53) described diseased organs in relation to their normal functions, opening the era of modern pathology.

Henlein \'hen-līn\, **Konrad** (1898–1945) Sudeten-German politician. In 1933 he became leader of the Sudeten-German Home Front, the second-strongest party in the Czech parliament. After a revolt broke out in the SUDETENLAND in 1938, the government suspended his party for treasonable activities and Henlein fled to Germany. After the MUNICH AGREEMENT ceded the Sudetenland to Germany, he was appointed commissioner for the territory. While in Allied custody at the end of World War II, he committed suicide.

Henley, William Ernest (1849–1903) British poet, critic, and editor. After a tubercular disease forced the amputation of one foot and radical surgery on the other leg, Henley began writing free-verse impressionistic poems about hospital life which would eventually make his reputation. They appeared in *A Book of Verses* (1888). His most popular poem, "Invictus" (1875), dates from the same period. He later edited several journals, the most brilliant of which, the *Scots Observer* (later the *National Observer*), published the early work of THOMAS HARDY, GEORGE BERNARD SHAW, H.G. WELLS, JAMES M. BARRIE, and RUDYARD KIPLING.

henna Tropical shrub or small tree *(Lawsonia inermis)* of the LOOSESTRIFE family, native to northern Africa, Asia, and Australia, and the reddish-brown dye obtained from its leaves. The plant bears small opposite leaves and small, fragrant, white to red flowers. In addition to being grown for its dye, it is used as an ornamental.

Hennepin \ˌe-nə-'paⁿ, *Engl* 'he-nə-pən\, **Louis** (1626–1701?) French missionary and explorer. A Franciscan, he traveled to Canada in 1675 with RENE-ROBERT LA SALLE. They explored the Great Lakes region, founding Fort Crèvecoeur (near Peoria, Ill.) in 1680. When La Salle returned for supplies, Hennepin and others explored the upper Mississippi River. They were captured by Sioux Indians and taken to a site he named the Falls of St. Anthony (later Minneapolis); after four months they were rescued by DANIEL DULHUT. Hennepin returned to France in 1682 and wrote an account of his journeys.

Henri \'hen-rē\, **Robert** *orig.* **Robert Henry Cozad** (1865–1929) U.S. painter. Born in Cincinnati, he studied in Philadelphia and Paris, taught art in Philadelphia, and, after settling in New York in 1900, became the leader of the young artists known as The EIGHT. He exhibited with The Eight in 1908 and later at the ARMORY SHOW (1913). As a portrait painter he demonstrated facile brushwork, lively colors, and an ability to catch fleeting gestures and expressions. He is best remembered as a teacher, principally at New York's Art Students League (1915–28), where he became one of the most influential art teachers in the U.S. and a powerful force in turning young artists away from academicism and toward the rich subject matter of modern city life. His belief in the artist as a social force led to the formation of the ASH CAN SCHOOL.

Henri I de Lorraine See 3rd duc de GUISE

Henri II de Lorraine See 5th duc de GUISE

Henrietta Maria *French* **Henriette-Marie** (1609–1669) French-born English queen, wife of CHARLES I and mother of CHARLES II and JAMES II. The daughter of HENRY IV of France and MARIE DE MÉDICIS, she was no stranger to political intrigue. By openly practicing Roman Catholicism at court, she alienated many of Charles's subjects. As the ENGLISH CIVIL WARS approached, she sought without success to instigate a military coup to overthrow the Parliamentarians. Her further efforts to enlist support for Charles from the Pope, the French, and the Dutch infuriated many Englishmen. Deterioration of the Royalist position caused her to flee to France in 1644, and she never again saw her husband, who was executed in 1649.

Henry, Cape Promontory, at the southern entrance to CHESAPEAKE BAY, southeastern Virginia. Located in VIRGINIA BEACH city, it is opposite Cape Charles, to which it is connected by the Chesapeake Bay Bridge Tunnel. It is the site of Cape Henry Memorial, which marks the 1607 landing of the first permanent English settlers in America. The memorial, part of Colonial National Historical Park, includes the Old Lighthouse, the first in the U.S. (1792). The nearby New Lighthouse (1881) has one of the world's most powerful lights, visible offshore for 20 mi (32 km).

Henry, Joseph (1797–1878) U.S. physicist. Born in Albany, N.Y., he aided SAMUEL F. B. MORSE in developing the telegraph. He discovered several important principles of electricity, including self-induction. He observed electromagnetic induction a year before MICHAEL FARADAY announced its discovery. He made improvements to electromagnets, discovered the laws on which the transformer is based, investigated electric discharge, and demonstrated that sunspots radiate less heat than the general solar surface. In 1846 he became the first secretary and director of the Smithsonian Institution, where he organized a corps of volunteer weather observers that led to creation of the U.S. Weather Bureau. He was a chief technical adviser to ABRAHAM LINCOLN during the Civil War and a primary organizer of the National Academy of Science. In 1893 the standard unit of electrical inductance, the henry, was named in his honor.

Henry, O. *orig.* **William Sydney Porter** (1862–1910) U.S. short-story writer. Born in Greensboro, N.C., he wrote for newspapers and later worked as a bank teller in Texas, where he was convicted of embezzlement; he began writing stories in prison as O. Henry. He moved to New York, where his tales romanticizing the commonplace, particularly the life of ordinary New Yorkers, and often using coincidence and surprise endings, became highly popular. His collections include *Cabbages and Kings* (1904); *The Four Million* (1906), including "The Gift of the Magi"; *The Trimmed Lamp* (1907), including "The Last Leaf"; and *Whirligigs* (1910), including "The Ransom of Red Chief."

Henry, Patrick (1736–1799) American Revolutionary leader. Born in Studley, Va., he became a lawyer; his oratorical skill was revealed in the Parson's Cause trial (1763). A member of the Virginia House of Burgesses, he opposed the Stamp Act and was a leader in the radical opposition to the British. He was a founding member of the Committees of Correspondence and a delegate to the Continental Congress. In 1775 at a Virginia assembly he made his famous defense of liberty, "Give me liberty or give me death," and presented resolutions to arm the Virginia militia in the expected war. He helped draft the state's first constitution and served as governor 1776–79 and 1784–86. He supported Gen. George Washington and authorized the expedition of George Rogers Clark. In 1788 he opposed ratification of the U.S. Constitution, which he felt did not secure individual liberties, and he was instrumental in the adoption of the Bill of Rights.

Henry I *known as* **Henry Beauclerc** \'bō-kler\ **("Good Scholar")** (1069–1135) King of England (1100–35) and ruler of Normandy (1106–35). The youngest son of William I, he became king on the death of William II. His eldest brother, Robert Curthose (Robert II), returned from the First Crusade to claim the English throne in 1101; Henry placated him by giving him Normandy, but Robert ruled it badly, and in 1106 Henry seized Normandy and imprisoned his brother. Henry quarreled with Anselm of Canterbury over the issue of investiture (see Investiture Controversy), but they were reconciled in 1107. He maintained control of Normandy despite attacks by Robert's son, and named his daughter Matilda his heir.

Henry II *known as* **Henry of Anjou** \'an-jü\ *or* **Henry Plantagenet** \plan-'ta-jə-nət\ (1133–1189) Duke of Normandy (from 1150), count of Anjou (from 1151), duke of Aquitaine (from 1152), and king of England (from 1154). The son of Matilda and grandson of Henry I, he gained vast territories in France by marrying Eleanor of Aquitaine (1152). He invaded England and in settlement of the war King Stephen named Henry as heir (1153). As king, Henry extended his holdings in northern England and western France, strengthened royal administration, and reformed the court system. His attempt to assert royal authority at the expense of the church (see Constitutions of Clarendon) led to a quarrel with the archbishop of Canterbury, his former close friend St. Thomas Becket, which ended with Becket's murder and Henry's subsequent penance at Canterbury (1174). His reign was plagued by disputes among family members, especially struggles for precedence among his sons, including Richard I the Lionheart and John (Lackland). Richard allied with Philip II of France to drive Henry from the throne in 1189.

Henry II *French* **Henri** \än-'rē\ *orig.* **duc (Duke) d'Orléans** (1519–1559) King of France (1547–59). The second son of Francis I, he had strong differences with his father, accentuated by the rivalry between their mistresses and by Henry's support of the constable Anne, duc de Montmorency (1493–1567). Though he continued many of his father's policies, Henry raised the Catholic House of Guise to favor, and he vigorously suppressed Protestantism within his kingdom. He made a number of administrative reforms. In foreign affairs Henry continued his father's warfare against Emperor Charles V until 1559, when he signed the Treaty of Cateau-Cambrésis. The treaty was to be cemented by the marriage of Henry's daughter to Philip II of Spain; during the festivities he was hit in the head by a lance, and he died from the wound.

Henry II *or* **St. Henry** *German* **Heinrich** (973–1024) Duke of Bavaria (as Henry IV, 995–1005), German king (1002–24), and Holy Roman emperor (1014–24), the last of the Saxon dynasty. He led a series of military campaigns against Poland before making peace in 1018. To protect the papacy he fought Greeks and Lombards in Italy (1021). He fostered cooperation between church and state and established the German bishops as secular rulers as well as ecclesiastical princes.

Henry III (1207–1272) King of England (1216–72). He inherited the throne at age 9 but did not begin to rule until French-backed rebels were expelled (1234). He alienated the barons by his indifference to tradition and his agreement to supply Innocent IV with funds in exchange for the Sicilian crown. The barons forced him to accept the Provisions of Oxford, but Henry renounced the agreement in 1261. His former favorite Simon de Montfort led a rebellion in 1264, defeating and capturing the king. Henry's son Edward (later Edward I) turned the tables a year later, and Henry, weak and senile, allowed Edward to take charge of the government.

Henry III *French* **Henri** *orig.* **duc** (Duke) d'Anjou (1551–1589) King of France (1574–89). The third son of Henry II and Catherine de Médicis, he commanded the royal army against the Huguenots in the Wars of Religion. He was crowned king after the death of his brother Charles IX. During the continuing civil wars he made concessions to the Huguenots, causing the Roman Catholics to form the Holy League. The Catholics were further alarmed in 1584 when the Protestant Henry of Navarre (later Henry IV) became heir to the throne. Henry III tried to placate the Holy League, but he was forced by a mob to flee Paris. In 1588 he had the Catholic leaders Henry, 3rd duc de Guise, and Cardinal Louis II de Lorraine assassinated. In 1589 Henry was himself assassinated by a fanatical Jacobin friar.

Henry III *German* **Heinrich** (1017–1056) Duke of Bavaria (as Henry VI, 1027–41), duke of Swabia (as Henry I, 1038–45), German king (1039–56), and Holy Roman emperor (1046–56). He gained sovereignty over Bohemia and Moravia and arranged the election of Pope Clement II, who crowned him emperor. The last emperor to dominate the papacy, Henry appointed three more popes in succeeding years. He championed the church reform advocated by the monasteries of Cluny and Gorze. He was nearly deposed in a revolt (1054–55), and in his later years his influence faltered in northeastern Germany, Hungary, southern Italy, and Lorraine.

Henry IV *orig.* **Henry Bolingbroke** (1366–1413) King of England (1399–1413), first of three 15th-century monarchs of the House of Lancaster. Son of John of Gaunt, he initially supported Richard II against the duke of Gloucester, but turned against him after being banished in 1398. He invaded England in 1399, forcing Richard's surrender and abdication. Having gained the crown by usurpation, he successfully consolidated his power in the face of repeated uprisings of powerful nobles. However, he failed to subdue the Welsh under Owen Glendower, was defeated by the Scots, and was unable to overcome the fiscal and administrative weaknesses that contributed to the eventual downfall of the Lancastrian dynasty. He was succeeded by his son, Henry V.

Henry IV *or* **Henry of Navarre** *French* **Henri de Navarre** (1553–1610) First Bourbon king of France (1589–1610) and king of Navarre (as Henry III, 1572–89), one of the most popular figures in French history. Henry was brought up as a Protestant and received his military training from the Huguenot leader Gaspard II de Coligny in the Wars of Religion. He married Margaret of Valois in 1572; the marriage provided the opportunity for the St. Bartholomew's Day Massacre six days later. Henry was held at the French court from 1572 to 1576, when he escaped to join the forces against Henry III. He fought the War of the Three Henrys and prevailed as unrivaled leader. He became king after Henry III was assassinated in 1589, but was forced to fight the Holy League for nine years to secure his kingdom. In 1593 he converted to Roman Catholicism to remove all pretext for resistance to his rule. He entered Paris amid cheers in 1594, but he had to wage war (1595–98) against Spain, which supported the remaining resistance to him in France. Henry signed the Edict of Nantes in 1598, ending 40 years of civil war. With the aid of his ministers, including the duc de Sully, Henry brought order and new prosperity to France. His earlier marriage was annulled and in 1600 he married Marie de Médicis. In 1610 he was assassinated by a fanatical Roman Catholic.

Henry IV *German* **Heinrich** (1050–1106) Duke of Bavaria (1055–61), German king (1054–1106), and Holy Roman emperor (1084–1105/6). He inherited the imperial throne at age 6; his unworldly mother was regent until 1062, and Henry gained control of the government in 1065. His reassertion of royal rights provoked rebellion in Saxony (1073–75). He engaged in a long struggle with Pope Gregory VII on the issue of lay investiture (see Investiture Controversy). Gregory excommunicated him and absolved his subjects of their oaths of loyalty. Seeking absolution, Henry was forced to cross the Alps in winter and, according to tradition, stand barefoot in the snow three days before the castle at Canossa where the pope was staying before the latter would rescind his order. The German princes deserted Henry (1077) and elected RUDOLF I as king. In 1080 Gregory excommunicated Henry again and recognized Rudolf, and Henry responded by conquering Rome (1084) and installing a new pope. In his last years his sons Conrad and Henry led rebellions against his rule.

Henry V (1387–1422) King of England (1413–22) of the House of LANCASTER. The eldest son of HENRY IV, he fought Welsh rebels (1403–8). As king he harshly suppressed a Lollard uprising (1414) and a Yorkist conspiracy (1415). He claimed extensive lands in France and launched an invasion (1415), and his stunning victory at the Battle of AGINCOURT made England one of the greatest powers in Europe. His continuing victories forced the French to sign the Treaty of Troyes (1420), in which Henry was named heir to the French throne and regent of France. He married Catherine, daughter of the French king, but died of camp fever before he could return home.

Henry VI (1421–1471) King of England (1422–61, 1470–71). Son of HENRY V, he became king as an infant, and grew up a pious and studious recluse, who suffered episodes of mental instability. England's political affairs were dominated by the rivalries of a series of overpowerful ministers of the Houses of Lancaster and York, and Henry's incapacity for government became one of the causes of the Wars of the ROSES. In 1461 a Yorkist was proclaimed EDWARD IV. Henry fled, but returned in 1464 in an unsuccessful Lancastrian rising and was eventually captured and imprisoned. After a quarrel in the York faction, he was restored to the throne in 1470. Edward fled, but soon returned to defeat and kill the earl of WARWICK and regain the throne. The death in battle of Prince Edward, Henry's heir, sealed Henry's fate, and he was murdered in the Tower of London soon afterward.

Henry VI *German* **Heinrich** (1165–1197) German king (1169–97) and Holy Roman Emperor (1191–97) of the HOHENSTAUFEN DYNASTY who acquired the kingdom of Sicily by marriage. He took over government of the Holy Roman Empire when his father, FREDERICK I BARBAROSSA, embarked on a crusade to the Holy Land in 1189. Soon after his coronation he faced revolts by Henry the Lion in Germany and TANCRED in Sicily, but he succeeded in making peace in 1194. His effort to make the imperial crown hereditary was unsuccessful, but his son FREDERICK II became emperor after him.

Henry VII *orig.* **Henry Tudor, Earl of Richmond** (1457–1509) King of England (1485–1509) and founder of the TUDOR dynasty. As earl of Richmond and a kinsman in the House of LANCASTER, he fled to Brittany after the triumph of the Yorkist forces in 1471. He later returned to England, rallied the opponents of RICHARD III, and defeated him at the Battle of BOSWORTH FIELD (1485). He married Elizabeth of York and ended the Wars of the ROSES, though Yorkist plots continued. He made peace with France (1492), the Netherlands (1496), and Scotland (1499) and used his children's marriages to build European alliances. His commercial treaties and promotion of trade made England wealthy and powerful. He was succeeded by his son HENRY VIII.

Henry VII *German* **Heinrich** (c. 1270–1313) Count of Luxembourg (as Henry IV), German king (1308–13), and Holy Roman Emperor (1312–13). The first German king of the House of Luxembourg, he strengthened the position of his family by obtaining the throne of Bohemia for his son. He became ruler of Lombardy (1311) but faced conflicts between GUELPHS AND GHIBELLINES. Though crowned emperor at Rome, he was unable to subdue Florence or Naples, and he failed in his attempt to bind Italy firmly to the empire.

Henry VIII (1491–1547) King of England (1509–47). Son of HENRY VII, Henry married his brother's widow, CATHERINE OF ARAGON (the mother of MARY I), soon after his accession in 1509. His first chief minister, THOMAS, CARDINAL WOLSEY, exercised nearly complete control over policy 1515–27. In 1527 Henry pursued a divorce from Catherine to marry ANNE BOLEYN, but Pope CLEMENT VII denied him an annulment. Wolsey, unable to help Henry, was ousted. The new minister, THOMAS CROMWELL, in 1532 initiated a revolution when he decided that the English Church should separate from Rome, allowing Henry to marry Anne in 1533. A new archbishop, THOMAS CRANMER, declared the first marriage annulled. A daughter, ELIZABETH I, was born soon after. Becoming head of the Church of ENGLAND represented Henry's major achievement, but had wide-ranging consequences. Henry, once profoundly devoted to the papacy and rewarded with the title Defender of the Faith, was excommunicated, and he was obliged to settle the nature of the newly independent church. In the 1530s his power was greatly enlarged, especially by transferring to the crown the wealth of the monasteries and by new clerical taxes, but his earlier reputation as a man of learning became buried under his enduring fame as a man of blood. Many, including ST. THOMAS MORE, were killed because they refused to accept the new order. The king grew tired of Anne, and in 1536 she was executed for adultery. He immediately married JANE SEYMOUR, who bore him a son, EDWARD VI, but died in childbirth. Three years later, at Cromwell's instigation, he married ANNE OF CLEVES, but he hated her and demanded a quick divorce, and he had Cromwell beheaded in 1540. By now Henry was becoming paranoid, as well as enormously fat and unhealthy. In 1540 he married CATHERINE HOWARD, but had her beheaded for adultery in 1542. In 1542 he waged a financially ruinous war against Scotland. In 1543 he married CATHERINE PARR, who survived him. He was succeeded on his death by his son Edward.

Henry Beauclerc See HENRY I (ENGLAND)

Henry of Anjou See HENRY II (ENGLAND)

Henry Plantagenet See HENRY II (ENGLAND)

Henry the Navigator *Portuguese* **Henrique o Navegador** *orig.* **Henrique, infante (Prince) de Portugal, duque (Duke) de Viseu, senhor (Lord) da Covilha** (1394–1460) Portuguese prince and patron of explorers. He helped his father JOHN I capture the Moroccan city of Ceuta in 1415 and served as governor of Ceuta and later of the Portuguese province of Algarve. He established his own court at Sagres and sponsored voyages of discovery in the Madeira Islands and along the western coast of Africa. As grand master of the Order of Christ, he gained funds for backing voyages aimed at the conversion of pagans. His patronage led to the development of the Portuguese caravel and improved navigational instruments and the advancement of cartography.

Henslowe, Philip (c. 1550–1616) English theater owner and manager. He settled in London before 1577, marrying a wealthy widow, and became the owner of several theaters, among them the Rose Theatre, which he built (with a partner) in 1587. The most lavish was the Fortune, built in 1600 for the Admiral's Men, the chief rivals of WILLIAM SHAKESPEARE's company. Henslowe's theaters gave the first productions of many Elizabethan dramas. His diary (edited 1904–08 by Sir Walter Gregg) is an important source for theatrical history.

Henson, Jim *orig.* **James Maury** (1936–1990) U.S. puppeteer and producer. Born in Greenville, Miss., he created a puppet show for a television station while in college and developed the first Muppets (melding "marionettes" and "puppets"). In the 1960s he made TV commercials. When PBS featured the Muppets on *Sesame Street* (from 1969), Henson achieved nationwide popularity. His *Muppet Show* premiered on television in 1976 and gained audiences in over 100 countries. He also produced and directed *The Muppet Movie* (1979) and its sequels.

Henze \'hent-sə\, **Hans Werner** (born 1926) German-Italian composer. He studied with Wolfgang Fortner (1907–1987) and later with René Leibowitz (1913–1972). After an early association with the avant-garde at Darmstadt under Leibowitz's influence, the more traditional grounding received from Fortner reasserted itself. He moved permanently to Italy in 1953. He is best known for his operas, which include *Der König Hirsch* (1955), *Elegy for Young Lovers* (1961), *Der junge Lord* (1964), and *The Bassarids* (1965). He has also written numerous major symphonies and concertos. His longtime commitment to Marxism has expressed itself in many of his works. Though never known widely in the U.S., in Europe Henze is considered one of the major composers of the later 20th century.

heparin \'he-pə-rən\ Organic compound, short-term ANTICOAGULANT used to prevent THROMBOSIS during and after surgery and for initial treatment of various heart, lung, or circulatory disorders in which there is an increased risk of BLOOD clotting. A mixture of complex CARBOHYDRATE molecules called mucopolysaccharides, it occurs naturally in liver and lung tissues. It was discovered in 1922 and originally used to prevent clotting in blood taken for laboratory tests.

hepatitis INFLAMMATION of the LIVER. There are seven known types of viral hepatitis (A–G). Types A, spread mainly through food contaminated with feces, and B, transmitted sexually or by injection, cause JAUNDICE and flulike symptoms. The hepatitis C virus spreads mostly by shared needles in intravenous drug use and can cause liver CIRRHOSIS and cancer after a long latent period. Until recently there was no test to detect it in blood, and many people were exposed through blood transfusions. Hepatitis D becomes active only in the presence of type B; it causes severe chronic liver disease. Type E, like Type A, is transmitted by contaminated food or water; its symptoms are more severe than Type A's and can result in death. The hepatitis F virus (HFV), which was first reported in 1994, is spread like Type A and E. The hepatitis G virus (HGV), isolated in 1996, is believed to be responsible for many sexually transmitted and bloodborne cases of hepatitis. HGV causes both acute and chronic forms of the disease and often infects persons already infected with Type C. Vaccines exist for types A and B (the second also prevents type D). Drug treatment for B and C is not always effective. The other types may not need drug treatment. Chronic active hepatitis causes spidery and striated skin markings, acne, and abnormal hair growth. It results in liver tissue death (necrosis) progressing to cirrhosis. Alcoholic hepatitis, from long-term overconsumption of alcohol, can be reversed and cirrhosis prevented by early treatment including quitting or sharply reducing drinking. Other drugs can also cause noninfectious hepatitis. An autoimmune hepatitis affects mainly young women and is treated with corticosteroids to relieve symptoms.

hepatolenticular degeneration See WILSON'S DISEASE

Hepburn, Audrey *orig.* **Edda van Heemstra Hepburn-Ruston** (1929–1993) Belgian-U.S. film actress. After spending World War II in Nazi-occupied Holland, she studied ballet and acting in London. She was discovered by COLETTE, who insisted she play the lead in *Gigi* on Broadway (1951). She made her U.S. film debut in *Roman Holiday* (1953, Academy Award), then returned to Broadway in *Ondine* (1954, Tony award). She projected a radiant elfin innocence combined with elegance in such films as *Sabrina* (1954), *War and Peace* (1956), *Funny Face* (1957), *Breakfast at Tiffany's* (1961), *My Fair Lady* (1964), and *Wait Until Dark* (1967). She later devoted herself to charity work and was a goodwill ambassador for UNICEF.

Hepburn, Katharine (Houghton) (born 1907) U.S. actress. Born in Hartford, Conn., she made her Broadway debut in 1928 and became a star with her first film, *A Bill of Divorcement* (1932). Her following grew with *Morning Glory* (1933, Academy Award), *Little Women* (1933), and *Bringing Up Baby* (1938), to which she brought a spirited individuality and strength of character. She starred in the Broadway hit *The Philadelphia Story* (1939; film, 1940). Among her other notable films were *The African Queen* (1951), *Summertime* (1955), and *Suddenly Last Summer* (1959). She made eight films with her longtime lover SPENCER TRACY, including *Woman of the Year* (1942), *Pat and Mike* (1952), and *Guess Who's Coming to Dinner* (1967, Academy Award), and won two more Oscars for *The Lion in Winter* (1968) and *On Golden Pond* (1981).

Katharine Hepburn.
BROWN BROTHERS

Hephaestus *or* **Hephaistos** \hi-ˈfes-təs\ Greek god of fire. He was originally a deity of Asia Minor and nearby islands (especially Lemnos); his Roman counterpart was Vulcan. Born lame, or crippled at an early age, he was cast out of heaven by his parents, ZEUS and HERA. His wife was APHRODITE, goddess of love. He was the patron of smiths and craftsman and was often depicted working at his forge. Volcanoes were believed to be the fires of his workshops.

Hepplewhite, George (died 1786) British cabinetmaker. He was apprenticed to a furniture maker in Lancaster and later opened a shop in London. His reputation is based on his *Cabinet-Maker and Upholsterer's Guide* (1788), containing some 300 designs. Pieces based on his designs are rare and none can be definitely attributed to his firm, nor can his personal responsibility for the designs be established; the plates in the book are unsigned. The designs have the simplicity, elegance, and utility associated with the graceful Neoclassical style (e.g., chairs with straight, tapered legs and oval backs). His designs were borrowed by THOMAS SHERATON and DUNCAN PHYFE.

heptathlon Women's athletics competition in which contestants take part in seven different TRACK-AND-FIELD events: 100-m hurdles, SHOT PUT, HIGH JUMP, LONG JUMP, JAVELIN THROW, and 200- and 800-m runs. The two-day event replaced the women's PENTATHLON in the Olympic Games after 1981.

Hepworth, (Jocelyn) Barbara *later* **Dame Barbara** (1903–1975) British sculptor. Her work, naturalistic at first, had become abstract by the 1930s, and she produced severe geometrical pieces with straight edges. As her work matured, her sculptures became increasingly perforated, emphasizing interior space. By the 1950s she was internationally famous, and she received many prestigious commissions, including *Single Form* (1963), a memorial to DAG HAMMARSKJOLD at the United Nations Building, New York. She became, with HENRY MOORE, a leader of the modern movement in England and one of the most influential sculptors of the mid-20th century.

Hera Greek queen of the gods and sister-wife of ZEUS. Her Roman counterpart was JUNO. She was worshiped as queen of heaven and patron of marriage and women. She also held the title Eileithyia, the goddess of birth. She was the patron deity of Samos and Argos, which held celebrations and processions in her honor. Her sacred animal was the cow. In literature she was depicted as a jealous wife who vindictively pursued the women Zeus seduced.

Heracleitus *or* **Heraclitus** \ˌher-ə-ˈklī-təs\ (c. 540–480 BC) Greek philosopher. Little is known of his life; the one book he apparently wrote is lost, and his views survive only in short fragments attributed to him. In his cosmology, fire forms the basic material principle of an orderly universe; he called the world order an "ever-living fire kindling in measures and being extinguished in measures," and extended fire's manifestations to include the ether in the upper atmosphere. The persistence of unity despite change is illustrated by his famous analogy of life to a river: "Upon those who step into the same rivers, different and ever different waters flow down."

Heracles \ˈher-ə-ˌklēz\ *Latin* **Hercules** Legendary hero of ancient Greece and Rome. Known for his great strength, he was the son of ZEUS and Alcmeme, the granddaughter of PERSEUS. Zeus's jealous wife HERA sent two serpents to kill Heracles in his cradle, but the infant strangled them. He grew up to marry a princess, then killed her in a fit of rage sent by Hera and was forced to become the servant of Eurystheus, ruler of Greece. Eurystheus obliged Heracles to perform the famous 12 labors, including cleansing the Augean stables, fetching the golden apples of the Hesperides, and descending into Hades to bring back the three-headed dog Cerberus. He married Deianeira, who later sent him a shirt smeared with poison, which she mistakenly believed was a love potion.

Heracles breaking the horns of the hind of Arcadia, flanked by Athena and Artemis, detail of a Greek vase painting, c. 540 BC; in the British Museum.
BY COURTESY OF THE TRUSTEES OF THE BRITISH MUSEUM; PHOTOGRAPH, THE HAMLYN GROUP PICTURE LIBRARY

In agony, Heracles burned himself to death on a pyre, and his spirit ascended to heaven. He became an immortal and married HEBE.

heraldry Art and science of devising, displaying, and granting armorial insignia and of tracing and recording genealogies. The use of heraldic symbols as a means of identification spread throughout the European nobility in the 13th century. The principal vehicle for displaying the heraldic devices is the shield; the crest, a subsidiary device that emerged in the 14th century, was modeled onto the helm (helmet). Pictorial representations show the shield with the helm and crest above. Arms are hereditary; all male descendants of the first person to whom they were granted bear the arms. As insignia of honor, they are protected by law in the European monarchies, Ireland, Switzerland, South Africa, and Zimbabwe. See also coat of ARMS, ECCLESIASTICAL HERALDRY.

herb See SPICE AND HERB

herbal Ancient manual of plants used for medicinal purposes. Hundreds or thousands of medicinal plants were known in ancient India, China, and Greece and medieval Europe. In the later 16th century, European herbals began to include plants from the Western Hemisphere. Their accuracy varies widely, but many of the plants in herbals later became sources for drugs (e.g., DIGITALIS).

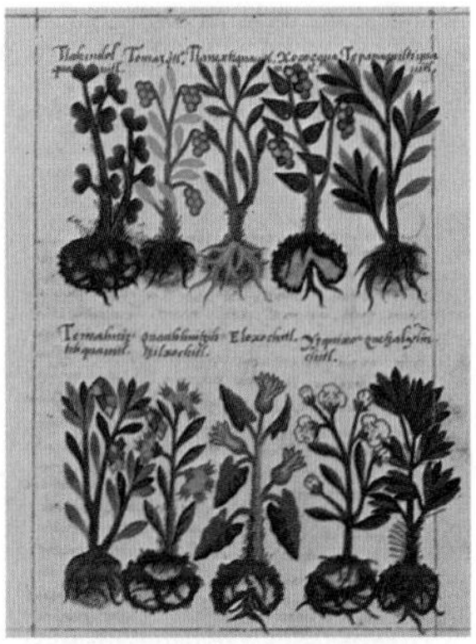

Watercolor illustration from the *Badianus Manuscript,* an Aztec herbal in Latin by Juan Badianus and Martinus de la Cruz, 1552; in the Vatican Library.

BY COURTESY OF THE VATICAN LIBRARY, VATICAN CITY

herbarium Collection of dried plant specimens mounted on sheets of paper, identified by experts and labeled by their proper scientific names, together with other information (where they were collected, how they grew, etc.). These specimens are filed in cases according to families and genera, available for ready reference. Like BOTANICAL GARDENS and ARBORETUMS, herbaria are the "dictionaries" of the plant kingdom, the reference specimens essential to the proper naming of unknown plants.

Herbert, George (1593–1633) British Metaphysical poet. He was elected orator of Cambridge University in 1620, a position that involved him with the royal court. He was later ordained and became a rector at a rural parish, to which he devoted himself unstintingly until his death. His poems, only published after his death in *The Temple* (1633), concern personal, doctrinal, and ritual matters, and are noted for their mastery of metrical form, use of allegory and analogy, and religious devotion. Some are pattern poems, the lines forming the shape of the subject.

Herbert, Victor (August) (1859–1924) Irish-U.S. composer and cellist. After his widowed mother married a German doctor, he was raised in Stuttgart, and he studied at its conservatory. He married the soprano Therese Forrester in 1886 and they moved to the U.S., she to sing and he to play in the orchestra at the new Metropolitan Opera. He was soon active as a conductor, cellist, composer, and teacher. His solid training, orchestrating skill, and melodic gift found natural expression in more than 40 operettas, including *Babes in Toyland* (1903), *Mlle Modiste* (1905), *The Red Mill* (1906), and *Naughty Marietta* (1910).

Herbert, Zbigniew (1924–1998) Polish poet and essayist. Herbert started writing at age 17, but published little before 1956. His poetry expresses an ironic moralism in free verse laden with classical and other historical allusions. His most distinguished collection of poetry, *Elegy for an Exit*, was published in 1990.

herbicide Agent, usually chemical, for killing or inhibiting the growth of unwanted plants (weeds). Modern weed killers are put in two categories, selective (affecting specific plant species) and nonselective (affecting plants generally). These in turn are classified as foliage-applied and soil herbicides. Contact herbicides (e.g., SULFURIC ACID, diquat, paraquat) kill only the plant organs with which they are in contact. Translocated herbicides (e.g., amitrole, picloram, 2,4-D) are effective against roots or other organs, to which they are transported from aboveground treated surfaces (soil). See also DEFOLIANT.

herbivore \'ər-bə-ˌvȯr\ Animal adapted to subsist solely on plant tissues. Herbivores range from insects (e.g., aphids) to large mammals (e.g., elephants), but the term is most often applied to UNGULATES. Adaptations for a herbivorous diet include the four-chambered stomach of RUMINANTS, the ever-growing incisor teeth of RODENTS, and the specialized grinding molars of cattle, sheep, and goats. Certain herbivores eat only one type of food (e.g., the KOALA), but most have at least moderate variety in their diet.

Herblock *orig.* **Herbert Lawrence Block** (1909–2001) U.S. editorial cartoonist. Born in Chicago, he first published his cartoons in the *Chicago Daily News* (1929). Later he worked for the Newspaper Enterprise Association (1933–43) and the *Washington Post* (from 1946). A leading spokesman for liberalism, he attacked injustices in politics, big business, industry, labor, and economics throughout his 70-year career. He is best known for his 1950s cartoons attacking Senator JOSEPH MCCARTHY. The winner of three Pulitzer Prizes (1942, 1954, 1979), he received the Presidential Medal of Freedom in 1994.

Herculaneum \ˌhər-kyü-'lā-nē-əm\ Ancient city, Campania, Italy. Located at the northwestern foot of VESUVIUS, it was destroyed, together with POMPEII and Stabiae, by the eruption of AD 79. It was buried under a mass of tufa about 50–60 ft (15–18 m) deep, which made excavation difficult but preserved many fragile items. Excavation began in the 18th century and uncovered numerous artifacts, including paintings and furniture. Later work uncovered the palaestra (sports ground), and a vast central swimming pool.

Hercules See HERACLES

Herder, Johann Gottfried von (1744–1803) German critic and philosopher. Trained in theology and literature, he initially worked as a teacher and preacher at Riga. As court preacher at Bückeburg, he produced works, including *Plastik* (1778) and *Essay on the Origin of Language* (1772), that made him the leading figure of the STURM UND DRANG literary movement. In 1770 he met JOHANN W. VON GOETHE, who would be his associate for many years, and with whom he would help lay the groundwork for German ROMANTICISM. He moved to Goethe's Weimar in 1776; his *Zerstreute Blätter* (1785–97; "Sporadic Papers") and the unfinished *Outlines of a Philosophy of the History of Man* (1784–91), attempting to show that nature and history obey one system of laws, mark him as an innovator in the philosophy of history and an early proponent of the idea that a common culture, rather than political boundaries, defines a people. His later estrangement from Goethe resulted in a bitter enmity toward the whole classical movement in German poetry and philosophy.

heredity Transmission of physical and mental traits from parents to offspring through GENES. From his studies in the late 19th century, GREGOR MENDEL derived certain basic laws of heredity, which eventually became the foundation for the modern science of GENETICS. Each member of the parental generation transmits only half its genes to the offspring; and different offspring of the same parents receive different combinations of genes. Many characteristics are polygenic (i.e., influenced by more than one gene). Many genes exist in numerous variations (alleles) throughout a population. The polygenic and multiple allelic nature of many traits gives a vast potential for variability among hereditary characteristics. While the GENOTYPE (an individual's total hereditary makeup) determines the broad limits of features an individual may develop, the actual features that do develop (the PHENOTYPE) are dependent on complex interactions between genes and their environment. See also VARIATION. See illustration on following page.

Hereford \'hər-fərd\ Popular breed of beef CATTLE, the product of generations of breeding in the English county of Herefordshire. The characteristic color, red with white face and white markings, has been fixed for only a comparatively short time. Its outstanding characteristics are uniformity of color, early maturity, and ability to thrive under adverse conditions. Introduced into the U.S. in 1817, it has become the predominant breed in the range areas of North America from Canada to Mexico.

Hereford and Worcester \'her-i-fərd...'wu̇s-tər\ County (population 1995 est.: 694,000), western England. It extends from the Welsh borderland to the industrial Midlands; WORCESTER is the county seat. Formed in 1974 by the amalgamation of the former counties of Herefordshire and

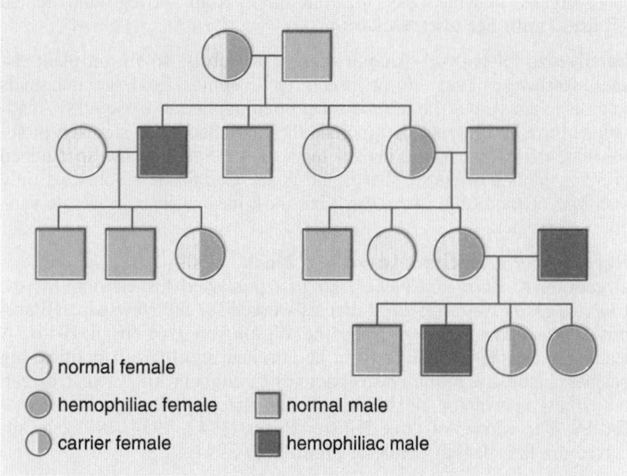

A pedigree chart tracing the inheritance of hemophilia, a sex-linked trait, through three familial generations. The recessive gene for hemophilia is carried on the X chromosome. Males inheriting one affected X chromosome from the mother and, less commonly, females inheriting an affected X chromosome from both mother and father experience the disease. Females who inherit an affected X chromosome from either mother or father are carriers for the disease. In the first generation here, a normal male and a female carrier produce a normal son and daughter, a son with hemophilia, and a carrier daughter.

Worcestershire, it includes lowland plains, the Forest of Dean plateau, the Black Mtns., the rich valleys of the Rivers SEVERN and AVON, and the Cotswolds. There are remains of Norman strongholds, Benedictine abbeys, and a perfectly preserved priory church. Agriculture is a major activity; there is some heavy industry.

Herero \hə-ˈrer-ō\ Group of closely related Bantu-speaking peoples of South Africa (central Namibia, eastern Botswana, southern Angola). The Herero formerly subsisted mainly on the milk and meat of their cattle, but following European contact in the mid-19th century many came to depend on horticulture as well. A series of uprisings against German colonial encroachment (1904–7) led to the extermination of three-fourths of their population and the resettlement of survivors in the mostly inhospitable sand veld of the western Kalahari. Today the Herero number over 200,000.

heresy \ˈher-ə-sē\ Doctrine rejected as false by religious authorities. In Christianity, the orthodox theology of the church is thought to be based on divine revelation, and heretics are viewed as perversely rejecting the guidance of the church. Numerous Christian heresies appeared from the 2nd century onwards. Early heresies included ARIANISM, the MONOPHYSITE HERESY, PELAGIANISM, and DONATISM. Some heresies, such as MONTANISM, expressed faith in a new prophet who added to the body of Christian revelation. Some types of GNOSTICISM were heretical branches of Christianity. The major means of combating heretics in the early church was EXCOMMUNICATION. In the 12th–13th century, the INQUISITION was established to combat heresy, and heretics who refused to recant were often executed. In the 16th century the Protestant REFORMATION brought an end to the doctrinal unity of Western Christendom, and the concept of heresy became less important in the various Christian churches, though it continues to exist. The concept of heresy also exists in Judaism, Buddhism, Hinduism, and Islam.

Heritage Foundation U.S. conservative THINK TANK "committed to rolling back the liberal welfare state and building an America where freedom, opportunity, and civil society flourish." Founded in 1973 by two Congressional aides, Edwin Feulner and Paul Weyrich, it provides research on pending political issues to Congress, policymakers, news media, and academic communities. It flourished during the presidency of RONALD REAGAN, and its Mandate for Leadership provided the basis for his administrative system.

herm In GREEK RELIGION, a sacred stone object connected with the worship of HERMES. Herms were used as cult objects, for milestones, and for boundary markers. In time, these stones were replaced by pillars topped with a likeness of the head of Hermes or by statues of the god. In Roman sculpture the heads of JUPITER or the forest god Silvanus were often substituted.

Herman, Jerry *orig.* **Gerald** (born 1933) U.S. songwriter. Born in New York City, Herman studied drama in Miami and wrote for TV, but soon switched to theater. After some off-Broadway successes, his *Milk and Honey* opened on Broadway (1961, Tony Award). The hugely successful *Hello, Dolly!* (1964; film, 1969) won ten Tony Awards. Later Herman musicals include *Mame* (1966) and *La Cage Aux Folles* (1983).

Herman, Woody *orig.* **Woodrow Charles** (1913–1987) U.S. clarinetist, saxophonist, singer, and leader of one of the most popular big bands in jazz. Born in Milwaukee, Herman formed his first band in 1936. Known as "The Band That Plays the Blues," the group had a hit in 1939 with the riff tune "Woodchopper's Ball." His 1940s bands, the "Thundering Herds," evolved into powerful and colorful ensembles that combined a light rhythm-section sound with explosive, forward-looking arrangements. He led his band almost continuously for over 50 years, and many notable jazz musicians gained early professional exposure there.

hermaphroditism \hər-ˈma-frə-ˌdī-ˌti-zəm\ Condition of having both male and female reproductive organs (see REPRODUCTIVE SYSTEM). It is normal in most flowering plants and in some invertebrate animals. True human hermaphrodites are extremely rare. Tissue of the OVARY and TESTES may occur separately or be combined, external genitals may show traits of both sexes, and XY and XX sex CHROMOSOME pairs are present. If the condition is detected at birth, the child's sex can be chosen, usually on the basis of which sex organs dominate; those of the other sex are removed surgically. Individuals raised as members of one sex who develop characteristics of the other at puberty may be treated with surgery, and SEX HORMONES may help them continue to live according to the sexual identity they are accustomed to.

hermeneutics \ˌhər-mə-ˈnü-tiks\ Study of the general principles of biblical interpretation. Its primary purpose is to discover the truths and values of the Bible, which is seen as a receptacle of divine revelation. Four major types of hermeneutics have emerged: literal (asserting that the text is to be interpreted according to the "plain meaning"), moral (seeking to establish the principles from which ethical lessons may be drawn), allegorical (interpreting narratives as having a level of reference beyond the explicit), and anagogical or mystical (seeking to explain biblical events as they relate to the life to come). More recently the word has come to refer to all "deep" reading of literary and philosophical texts.

Hermes \ˈhər-ˌmēz\ Greek god, son of ZEUS and Maia. The earliest center of his cult was probably Arcadia, where he was worshiped as a god of fertility. He was also associated with the protection of cattle and sheep. In HOMER's *Odyssey* he appears as the messenger of the gods and the conductor of the dead to HADES. As a messenger he also became the god of roads and doorways and the protector of travelers. He was also the god of dreams. His Roman counterpart was MERCURY.

Hermes leading a satyr chorus, vase by Douris, 5th century BC; in the British Museum.

Hermetic writings Occult texts on philosophical or theological subjects ascribed to Hermes Trismegistos ("Hermes the Thrice-Greatest"), identical to the Egyptian god THOTH, who was credited with inventing writing. The collection, written in Greek and Latin, was probably put together in the 1st–3rd century AD. Written in the form of dialogues, it synthesizes Near Eastern religion, PLATONISM, STOICISM, and other philosophies. It also reflects ideas and beliefs widely held in the early Roman empire on ASTROLOGY, ALCHEMY, and MAGIC. The goal of the writings was the deification of humanity through knowledge of the transcendent God.

Hermeticism \hər-'me-ti-ˌsi-zəm\ *or* **Hermetism** *Italian* **Ermetismo** Modernist poetic movement originating in Italy in the early 20th century. Works produced within the movement are characterized by unorthodox structure, illogical sequences, and highly subjective language. Its formalistic devices were partly derived from FUTURISM, but the cryptic brevity, obscurity, and involution of the Hermetics was forced on them by fascist censors. GIUSEPPE UNGARETTI, SALVATORE QUASIMODO, and EUGENIO MONTALE were the principal exponents of the movement, which was named for Hermes Trismegistos, a reputed author of occult symbolic works (see HERMETIC WRITINGS).

hermit *or* **eremite** Individual who shuns society to live in solitude, often for religious reasons. The first Christian hermits appeared in Egypt in the 3rd century AD, escaping persecution by withdrawing to the desert and leading a life of prayer and penance. The first hermit was probably Paul of Thebes c. AD 250. Other famous hermits included St. ANTHONY OF EGYPT, who established an early form of Christian MONASTICISM in the 4th century, and the pillar hermit SIMEON STYLITES. The communal life of monasteries eventually tempered the austerities of the hermit's life. In Western Christianity the eremitic life died out, but it has persisted in Eastern Christianity.

hermit crab Any CRAB (families Paguridae and Coenobitidae) that uses empty shells or other hollow objects as a shelter for partial containment and protection of the body. They are found worldwide in sandy- or muddy-bottomed waters and occasionally on land and in trees. They have two pairs of antennae and four pairs of legs; the first pair of legs is modified to form pincers, shaped to cover the shell entrance when the animal is inside. As the crab grows, it periodically leaves its shell and finds a larger one to occupy. The reddish brown large hermit crab (*Pagurus pollicaris;* 4–5 in., or 10–12 cm, long) and the small hermit crab *(P. longicarpus)* are found in North American Atlantic coastal waters.

Hermit crab (*Pagurus samuelis*).
RUSS KINNE—PHOTO RESEARCHERS

Hermitage (museum) \er-mi-'täzh, *Engl* 'hər-mə-tij\ Largest museum in Russia and one of the most important in the world. Located in St. Petersburg, it derives its name from the "Hermitage" pavilion adjoining the Winter Palace, built in 1764–67 for CATHERINE II the Great as a private gallery for her treasured collections. On her death in 1796, the imperial collections were estimated to total 4,000 pictures. After the Winter Palace was destroyed by fire in 1837, the Hermitage was reconstructed and opened to the public by NICHOLAS I in 1852. After the Bolshevik Revolution, the collections were transferred to public ownership. The museum is now housed in five interconnected buildings, including the Winter Palace and the Small, Old, and New Hermitages. Along with thousands of art objects from Central Asia, India, China, Egypt, the pre-Columbian Americas, Greece, and Rome, the Hermitage houses outstanding collections of Western painting. Russian history is represented by archaeological material from prehistoric times on.

Hermon, Mt. *Arabic* **Jabal ash-Shaykh** \'jà-bál-àsh-'shīk\ Snow-capped mountain on the Lebanon–Syria border. Located west of DAMASCUS, and rising to 9,232 ft (2,814 m), it is the highest point on the eastern coast of the Mediterranean Sea and is sometimes considered the southernmost extension of the ANTI-LEBANON MTNS. A sacred landmark in Hittite, Palestinian, and Roman times, it represented the northwestern limit of Israelite conquest under MOSES and JOSHUA. Since the SIX-DAY WAR (1967), about 40 sq mi (100 sq km) of its southern and western slopes have been part of the Israeli-administered GOLAN HEIGHTS.

Hermonthis \hər-'män-thəs\ Ancient town, Upper Egypt. Located near THEBES on the western bank of the NILE, and now an archaeological site, it was the seat of a sun cult and was a crowning place of kings. It was the original home of the rulers of THEBES, who reunited Egypt after c. 2130–1939 BC. Excavations (1929–38) uncovered the Bucheum (the necropolis of the mummified Buchis bulls), cemeteries of various periods, and part of the town area, including the temple of the war god Mentu.

Hermosillo \ˌer-mō-'sē-yō\ City (pop., 1990: 449,000), capital of SONORA state, northwestern Mexico. On the coastal plain near the confluence of the Sonora and San Miguel rivers, it is south of Nogales on the Mexico–U.S. border. In addition to its administrative functions, it is a commercial and manufacturing center for the surrounding irrigated farmlands. The city houses the University of Sonora (1938) and is a popular winter resort.

Herne, James A. *orig.* **James Ahearn** (1839–1901) U.S. playwright. Born in Cohoes, N.Y., he worked as a traveling actor before achieving success with his first play, *Hearts of Oak* (1879; written with DAVID BELASCO). *Margaret Fleming* (1890) is considered his major achievement, though *Shore Acres* (1892) was his most popular play. He helped bridge the gap between 19th-century melodrama and the 20th-century drama of ideas.

hernia Protrusion of any organ or tissue from its normal cavity. The term usually refers to an abdominal hernia, which may be a CONGENITAL DISORDER or acquired after birth. Tissue may protrude through the abdominal muscle at the groin (inguinal), upper thigh (femoral), or navel (umbilical); its circulation can become cut off, leading to INFLAMMATION, INFECTION, and GANGRENE. If the tissue cannot be pushed back into place and kept there by a truss, surgery may be necessary. Other common hernias are hiatal hernia (protrusion of part or all of the stomach above the diaphragm) and herniated disk (protrusion of tissue from a disk in the vertebral column through its outer layer).

hero Mythological or legendary figure, often of divine descent, who is endowed with great strength or ability, like the heroes celebrated in early EPICS such as *GILGAMESH*, HOMER's *Iliad*, *BEOWULF*, or the *CHANSON DE ROLAND*. Usually illustrious warriors or adventurers, heroes are often represented as fulfilling a quest (e.g., AENEAS, in VIRGIL's *Aeneid*, founding the Roman state, or Beowulf ridding his people of their enemies). Heroes often possess special qualities such as unusual beauty, precocity, and skills in many crafts. Inclined to boasting and foolhardiness, they defy pain and death to live fully, creating a moment's glory that survives in the memory of their descendants.

Hero and Leander \lē-'an-dər\ Lovers celebrated in Greek legend. Hero, a virgin priestess of APHRODITE, was seen by Leander of Abydos during a festival, and the two fell in love. He swam the Hellespont nightly to be with her, guided by a light from her tower. One stormy night the lamp was extinguished, and Leander drowned. When Hero saw his body on the shore, she threw herself from the tower into the sea. The story was told by OVID and was treated by CHRISTOPHER MARLOWE in his play *Hero and Leander* and by Lord BYRON in *The Bride of Abydos*.

Hero of Alexandria *or* **Heron of Alexandria** (fl. c. AD 60) Greek mathematician and inventor. He is remembered for his formula for the area of a triangle and for inventing the aeolipile, the first STEAM ENGINE, which, in his design, was a forerunner of the jet engine. Of his many treatises, one contains a method for approximating the square root of a number. His writings on mechanics include discussions of the five simple MACHINES, mechanical problems of daily life, and the construction of many kinds of engines.

Herod *or* **Herod the Great** (73–4 BC) Roman-appointed King of JUDAEA (37–4 BC). A practicing Jew, he was of Arab origin. He was critical to imperial control of Judaea, despite his earlier support of Mark ANTONY, and the Roman emperor increased his territory. Judaea prospered under his early reign, during which he increased trade and built fortresses, aqueducts, and theaters, but he could not give full rein to his desire to build and thrive because he feared the PHARISEES, Judaism's controlling faction. He lost favor through increasing cruelty, manifest in the murder of his wife, her sons, and other relatives. His grip on his kingdom weakened as he became increasingly mentally unstable and physically debilitated. He killed his eldest son, and he slew the infants of Bethlehem (see JESUS) shortly before his own death after a bungled suicide attempt.

Herod Agrippa I \ə-'grip-ə\ *orig.* **Marcus Julius Agrippa** (c. 10 BC–AD 44) King of JUDAEA (AD 41–44). Grandson of HEROD THE GREAT and nephew of HEROD ANTIPAS, he became friends in Rome with the emperor TIBERIUS and CALIGULA. Caligula made him king of his uncle's realm in northeastern Palestine and of Galilee, and after Caligula's death Herod's support of CLAUDIUS earned him the kingdom of Judaea, where he won the support of the Jews and repressed Jewish Christians. He built public buildings in Beirut and hosted games at Caesarea to honor Claudius. He died suddenly during the games.

Herod Antipas \'an-ti-pəs\ (21 BC–AD 39) Son of HEROD THE GREAT and TETRARCH of GALILEE (4 BC–AD 39) throughout JESUS's ministry. He was responsible for the death of JOHN THE BAPTIST (demanded by his wife, Herodias, and stepdaughter, SALOME) but later refused to cooperate when Pontius PILATE pressed him to conduct the trial of Jesus. He was caught up in the intrigue between the Syrians and Nabataeans. After denouncing HEROD AGRIPPA I, he was banished by CALIGULA to Gaul. A notable accomplishment was the building of TIBERIAS.

Herodotus \hə-'rä-də-təs\ (484?–430/420 BC) Greek historian. He was probably born at Halicarnassus, in Asia Minor, and resided in Athens and then in Thurii in southern Italy. His travels covered a large part of the Persian empire. He is the author of the first great narrative history produced in the ancient world, the *History* of the PERSIAN WARS. It is a unified artistic masterpiece, with many illuminating digressions and anecdotes skillfully worked into the narrative. Despite many inaccuracies, it remains the leading source of original information about the history of Greece between 550 and 479 BC, as well as that of much of western Asia and Egypt.

heroin HETEROCYCLIC COMPOUND, a highly addictive ALKALOID derivative of MORPHINE (chemically, it is diacetylmorphine) that makes up a large portion of illicit NARCOTICS traffic. Easily made from morphine, it was developed and first used as an ANALGESIC, but its undesirable effects outweighed its value, and it is illegal in most countries. Injection brings an ecstatic, warm, glowing sensation, followed by relaxation and contentment. Within half a day withdrawal symptoms set in, with a craving for more. Development of tolerance, requiring ever greater amounts for the same effects, leads to DRUG ADDICTION. Illegal street heroin is usually only 2–5% pure; unwitting injection of relatively pure heroin is a major cause of overdose, resulting in depressed respiration, coma, and death.

heron Any of about 60 species of long-legged wading birds in the same family (Ardeidae) as EGRETS and BITTERNS. They are found worldwide but are most common in the tropics. They wade in the shallow waters of pools, marshes, and swamps, catching frogs, fishes, and other aquatic animals. They nest on rough stick platforms in bushes or trees near water. Herons commonly stand with their neck bent in an southern shape and fly with their legs trailing and their head held back. They have broad wings and a long, straight, sharp-pointed bill. They are subdivided into typical herons (including the 50-in., or 130-cm, great blue heron of North America), night herons, and tiger herons.

Heron's formula \'hir-ˌänz\ Formula for finding the area of a triangle in terms of the lengths of its sides. In symbols, if a, b, and c are the lengths of the sides:

$$\text{Area} = \sqrt{s(s-a)(s-b)(s-c)}$$

where s is half the perimeter, or $\frac{1}{2}(a + b + c)$.

Herophilus \hə-'räf-ə-ləs\ (335?–c. 280 BC) Alexandrian physician, often called the father of anatomy. He performed public dissections on human corpses; studied the cavities of the brain, which he regarded as the center of the nervous system; traced the sinuses of the dura mater to their junction (the torcular Herophili); and classified nerve trunks as motor and sensory, distinguishing them from tendons and blood vessels. He described the eye, liver, salivary glands, pancreas, genitals, duodenum, and prostate gland (naming the last two) and was the first to measure the pulse. A student of HIPPOCRATES' doctrine, he emphasized the curative powers of drugs, diet, and gymnastics. He wrote at least nine works, including a commentary on Hippocrates and a book for midwives, all lost in the destruction of the library of Alexandria.

herpes simplex \'hər-ˌpēz\ Infection caused by herpes simplex virus. Type I typically produces a cluster of small blisters (cold sores, or fever blisters), usually on the lips or face; it can also infect the eyes. Type II, transmitted mostly through sexual contact, causes genital blisters, which rupture, becoming very painful. Oral sex can give either type the chance to infect the usual site of the other. The virus can also infect nerves. In both types, the virus remains after symptoms end and can reactivate, causing blisters to reappear. Babies born to mothers with active herpes can become infected during birth; this can be prevented by cesarean section. There is no cure, but drugs can reduce severity and risk of transmission.

herpes zoster See SHINGLES

Herrera \(h)ə-'rer-ə\, **Francisco** Name of two Spanish painters. Francisco Herrera the Elder (c. 1590–1654) was a painter and engraver. His early works are in the Mannerist style. Under the influence of FRANCISCO ZURBARAN, he developed the naturalistic style seen in his four scenes from the life of St. Bonaventure (1627). Around 1650 he moved to Madrid. His last documented work, a painting of St. Joseph (1648) influenced by ANTHONY VAN DYCK, features elongated forms and elaborate draperies. He achieved considerable fame in Seville, where DIEGO VELAZQUEZ was briefly his pupil. His son Francisco Herrera the Younger (1627–1685) worked as a painter and architect. His religious works are in the theatrical style of Roman baroque art, which he introduced in Seville. In 1660 he was appointed co-president (with BARTOLOME ESTEBAN MURILLO) of Seville's new Academy of Painting, but he soon left for Madrid and was active there as a painter of frescoes and altarpieces. In 1672 he was appointed painter to CHARLES II, and in 1677 master of the Royal Works. His greatest architectural achievement was the church of El Pilar at Saragossa (begun 1681).

Herrick, James Bryan (1861–1954) U.S. physician and clinical cardiologist. Born in Oak Park, Ill., he received his MD from Rush Medical College. His case report on a black patient with anemia included the first description of the crescent-shaped ERYTHROCYTES characteristic of sickle-cell anemia, later shown to be the precipitating factor of the disease. Herrick was also the first observer to identify and describe coronary thrombosis.

Herrick, Robert (1591–1674) English poet. Educated at Cambridge and later ordained, he became known as a poet in the 1620s and by the end of that decade had become a country vicar in Devonshire. A disciple of BEN JONSON, he wrote classically influenced lyrics whose appeal is in their freshness and their perfection of form and style. The only book he published was *Hesperides* (1648), containing 1,400 poems, mostly short, many of them EPIGRAMS. He is best remembered for the line "Gather ye rosebuds while ye may."

Robert Herrick, detail of an engraving by W. Marshall, from the frontispiece to *Hesperides*, 1648.

Herriman, George (Joseph) (1881–1944) U.S. cartoonist. Born in New Orleans, he started cartooning after a fall from a scaffold prevented him from working as a house painter. His first comic strip, *Lariat Pete*, appeared in 1903 in the *San Francisco Chronicle;* it was followed by several others. His best-known strip, *Krazy Kat*, appeared in 1910 and settled in for a run of more than 30 years in the WILLIAM RANDOLPH HEARST newspapers. *Krazy Kat*'s fantasy, drawing, and dialogue were of such high quality that some people consider it the finest comic strip ever published.

herring Either the Atlantic or the Pacific subspecies of *Clupea harengus* (once considered two separate species), slab-sided, northern fishes that are small-headed and streamlined, with silvery iridescent sides and a deep-blue, metallic-hued back. The name also refers to some other members of the family Clupeidae. Adults range in length from 8 to 15 in. (20–38 cm). One of the most abundant species of fish, herring travel in enormous schools. They eat planktonic crustaceans and fish larvae. In Europe they are processed and sold as kippered herring; in eastern Canada and the northeastern U.S., most of the herring used are young fishes canned as sardines. Herring taken in the Pacific are used mainly to make fish oil and meal.

herring gull Most common of the Atlantic GULLS in the Northern Hemisphere. The herring gull *(Larus argentatus)* has a gray mantle, flesh-colored legs and feet, and black-and-white-spotted wing tips. Herring gulls are primarily scavengers; their populations are generally increasing because of expanding food supplies, chiefly garbage and sewage in or near coastal waters.

Herriot \ˌer-ē-ˈō\, **Édouard** (1872–1957) French politician and writer. He became mayor of Lyon in 1905 and kept the post for most of his life. Elected as a member of the Radical Party to the Chamber of Deputies (1919), he led the opposition to the BLOC NATIONAL as head of the CARTEL DES GAUCHES (1924). As prime minister (1924–25) he forced the resignation of the president, ALEXANDRE MILLERAND, and led France to accept the DAWES PLAN and recognize the Soviet Union. In 1926 he was prime minister for three days, and he held the position again in 1932. He abstained from voting when the National Assembly gave full powers to PHILIPPE PETAIN at Vichy in 1940, then was arrested and deported to Germany (1942–45). He returned to France and served as president of the National Assembly 1947–54. In his long career he served in nine different cabinets.

Herriot \ˈher-ē-ət\, **James** *orig.* **James Alfred Wight** (1916–1995) British veterinarian and writer. Wight joined the practice of two veterinarian brothers working in the Yorkshire Dales and at age 50 was persuaded by his wife to write down his collection of anecdotes. His humorous, fictionalized reminiscences were published under the name James Herriot in *If Only They Could Talk* (1970) and *It Shouldn't Happen to a Vet* (1972), which were issued in the U.S. as *All Creatures Great and Small* (1972). The instant best-seller inaugurated a series of highly popular books, which was adapted for two films and a long-running television series.

Herrmann, Bernard (1911–1975) U.S. composer. Born in New York City, he studied at NYU and Juilliard and was one of a group of young composers around C. IVES in the 1930s. Active in radio from 1930, his work with ORSON WELLES led to a career in movies. He wrote scores for Welles's *Citizen Kane* (1941) and *The Magnificent Ambersons* (1942); other films included *All That Money Can Buy* (1941, Academy Award). He scored eight of ALFRED HITCHCOCK's films, including *Vertigo* (1958), *North by Northwest* (1959), and *Psycho* (1960).

Herschel family \ˈhər-shəl\ British family of astronomers. The German-born William Herschel (1738–1822) emigrated to England in 1757 and initially supported himself through music. In order to study distant celestial objects, he ground his own mirrors, producing the best telescopes of the day. His discovery of Uranus catapulted him to fame at 43. He hypothesized that nebulae are composed of stars and developed a theory of stellar evolution. He also discovered infrared radiation. He was knighted in 1816. His sister, Caroline Lucretia Herschel (1750–1848), contributed to her brother's researches, carrying out many of the necessary calculations. She also detected by telescope three nebulae and eight comets. In 1787 the king gave her an annual pension in recognition of her work. She continued to work for decades after William's death. William's son John (1792–1871) studied mathematics at Cambridge University and from 1816 assisted his father. He later undertook a journey to the Southern Hemisphere to survey its skies there; he returned in 1838 having recorded the locations of 68,948 stars. Also an accomplished chemist, he invented (independently of WILLIAM HENRY FOX TALBOT) the process of photography on sensitized paper. He was knighted in 1831. His sons Alexander Stewart (1836–1907) and John (1837–1921) also became astronomers.

Hersey, John (Richard) (1914–1993) U.S. (Chinese-born) novelist and journalist. Born to missionaries, he worked as a correspondent in the Far East, Italy, and Russia in the years 1937–46. His novel *A Bell for Adano* (1944, Pulitzer Prize) depicts the Allied occupation of a Sicilian town. *Hiroshima* (1946), about the experiences of atomic-blast survivors, and *The Wall* (1950), about the Warsaw Ghetto uprisings, combine fact and fiction. His later novels include *A Single Pebble* (1956), *The Child Buyer* (1960), and *The Conspiracy* (1972).

Hersh, Seymour (Myron) (born 1937) U.S. journalist. Born in Chicago, he graduated from the University of Chicago in 1954. He began his journalistic career in 1959 as a police reporter, and later worked for UPI and the *New York Times* and as a national correspondent for the *Atlantic Monthly.* His report on the MY LAI INCIDENT won him a 1970 Pulitzer Prize; he also wrote about domestic spying by the CIA and produced many other investigative reports. His *The Dark Side of Camelot* (1997) was a controversial negative look at JOHN F. KENNEDY; *Against All Enemies* (1998) discussed the ailments suffered by Persian Gulf War veterans.

Hershey, A(lfred) D(ay) (1908–1997) U.S. biologist. Born in Owosso, Mich., he worked principally at the Carnegie Institution in Washington, D.C. He and SALVADOR LURIA independently demonstrated the occurrence of spontaneous MUTATION in both bacteriophages and hosts. Later, Hershey and MAX DELBRUCK independently discovered the occurrence of genetic RECOMBINATION in phages. Delbrück incorrectly interpreted his results, but Hershey proved that the results he had obtained were recombinations by showing that the genetic processes in question correspond with the crossing-over of parts of similar chromosomes observed in cells of higher organisms. He showed that phage DNA is the main component entering the host cell during infection, and that DNA, rather than protein, is the phage's genetic material. In 1969 he shared a Nobel Prize with Luria and Delbrück.

Hertford \ˈhär-fərd\ Town (pop., 1995 est.: 23,000), seat of HERTFORDSHIRE, southeastern England. Located on the northern periphery of London, Hertford was first recorded as the scene of a general synod led by Theodore of Tarsus in AD 672. The oldest buildings extant are 15th-century timber-framed houses. The town has light engineering industries and many agricultural connections, in addition to its government functions.

Hertfordshire \ˈhär-fərd-ˌshir\ County (population 1999 est.: 1,043,000), southern England. It adjoins London on its northern side; its county seat is HERTFORD. It includes the two early "garden cities"—Letchworth (1903) and Welwyn Garden City (1920)—and four of the eight new towns planned around London since World War II. With an array of direct road and rail links to London, it houses light industries, offices, film studios, and thousands of exurbanites.

Hertz \ˈherts, *Engl* ˈhərts\, **Heinrich (Rudolf)** (1857–1894) German physicist. While a professor at Karlsruhe Polytechnic (1885–89), he produced electromagnetic waves in the laboratory and measured their length and velocity. He showed that the nature of their vibration and their susceptibility to reflection and refraction were the same as those of light and heat waves, and proved that light and heat are electromagnetic radiations. He was the first to broadcast and receive radio waves. In 1889 he was appointed professor at the University of Bonn, where he continued his research on the discharge of electricity in rarefied gases. The hertz (Hz), a unit of frequency in cycles per second, is named for him.

Hertzog \ˈhert-ˌsȯk\, **J(ames) B(arry) M(unnik)** (1866–1942) Prime minister of the Union of South Africa (1924–39). His political principles were "South Africa First" (i.e., ahead of the British Empire) and the "Two Streams Policy," under which British and AFRIKANER would be free from domination by each other. He served in the cabinet of LOUIS BOTHA (1910–12), but broke with Botha over his accommodationist policies and formed the NATIONAL PARTY. As prime minister, Hertzog gave the Union its flag, made AFRIKAANS an official language, promoted APARTHEID, and affirmed the equality of British and Afrikaner rights under the Union. In 1933 he was forced to accept a coalition with JAN SMUTS, and in 1939 he resigned over the issue of neutrality in World War II.

Hertzsprung-Russell diagram \ˈhert-sprůŋ-ˈrə-səl\ *or* **H-R diagram** Graph in which the absolute MAGNITUDES of STARS are plotted against their color. Of great importance to theories of stellar evolution, it evolved from charts begun independently in 1911 by the Danish astronomer Ejnar Hertzsprung (1873–1967) and the U.S. astronomer Henry Norris Russell (1877–1957). On the diagram, stars are ranked from bottom to top in order of increasing brightness and from right to left by increasing temperature. Stars tend to cluster in certain parts of the diagram, especially along a diagonal line, the "main sequence," which is the locus of hydrogen-burning stars of different masses.

Hervey Bay Inlet and city, southeastern QUEENSLAND, Australia. Named in 1770 by Capt. JAMES COOK and surveyed in 1804, the bay measures 55 by 40 mi (89 by 64 km). Hervey Bay city (pop., 1993 est.: 33,000) comprises a complex of bayside resorts, which also serve a district of sugarcane and pineapple plantations.

Herzegovina See BOSNIA AND HERZEGOVINA

Herzen \ˈhert-sən\, **Aleksandr (Ivanovich)** (1812–1870) Russian writer and political activist. As a student at the University of Moscow, he joined a socialist group, for which he was exiled to work in the provincial bureaucracy (1834–42). Returning to Moscow, he joined the Westernizers but then turned to anarchist socialism. After inheriting a considerable fortune, he left Russia. In Paris he proclaimed Western institutions "dead" and developed the theory of a unique Russian path to socialism known as peasant populism. He moved to London in 1852 and founded the Free Russian Press, as well as the influential newspaper *Kolokol* ("The Bell") in 1857; smuggled into Russia, the paper was read by both reformers and revolutionaries. When the Emancipation Act was enacted in 1861, he denounced it as a betrayal of the peasants. He then turned his energies to writing *My Past and Thoughts* (1861–67), considered one of the greatest works of Russian prose.

Herzl \'hert-sᵊl\, **Theodor** (1860–1904) Hungarian Zionist leader. Growing up Jewish in Hungary, he believed that assimilation was the best strategy to deal with the anti-Semitism he encountered. He became a Zionist while covering the Alfred Dreyfus affair as a journalist in Paris. In 1897 he organized a world congress of Zionism, which was attended by about 200 delegates, and he became the first president of the World Zionist Organization, established by the congress. Herzl's indefatigable organizing, propagandizing, and diplomacy had much to do with making Zionism a political movement of worldwide significance. Though he died more than 40 years before the establishment of the state of Israel, his remains were moved to Jerusalem in 1949 and entombed on a hill now known as Mount Herzl.

Herzog \'hert-sȯk\, **Werner** *orig.* **Werner H. Stipetic** (born 1942) German filmmaker. He won two awards for his first feature film, *Signs of Life* (1967), which introduced the theme of descent into madness that was to reappear repeatedly in his later films, most powerfully in *Aguirre, the Wrath of God* (1972), *Nosferatu* (1979), and *Fitzcarraldo* (1982). His own grand obsession with the filming of *Fitzcarraldo*, which was shot in the Amazon rainforest and called for a ship to be dragged over the mountains, became legendary. His surreal and exotic films were among the best of the highly praised postwar West German cinema. After *Scream of Stone* (1991) he worked mainly on documentaries.

Heschel \'he-shəl\, **Abraham Joshua** (1907–1972) Polish-U.S. Jewish philosopher and theologian. He studied at the University of Berlin and taught Jewish studies in Germany until he was deported by the Nazis in 1938. After coming to the U.S., he taught at Hebrew Union College and later at Jewish Theological Seminary. His goal was to devise a modern philosophy of religion based on ancient and medieval Judaic traditions, and he emphasized Judaism's prophetic and mystical aspects. Emphasizing social action as an expression of pious ethical concerns, he worked for black civil rights and against the Vietnam War. His writings include *Man Is Not Alone* (1951) and *God in Search of Man* (1956).

Heshen *or* **Ho-shen** (1750–1799) Infamous Chinese courtier who abused his influence with the Qianlong emperor to assume high ministerial positions and control the disbursement of revenue and the recruitment of personnel. His embezzlement of funds intended for suppressing the White Lotus rebellion resulted in prolonging the fighting and drove the imperial troops to looting, consequently undermining the authority of the Qing dynasty. He was arrested by the Qianlong emperor's successor and forced to commit suicide.

Hesiod \'hē-sē-əd, 'he-sē-əd\ (fl. c. 700 BC) Greek poet. One of the earliest Greek poets, he is often called the father of Greek didactic poetry. A native of Boeotia, in central Greece, he may have been a professional reciter of poetry. Two complete epics have survived: the *Theogony*, relating stories of the gods, and the *Works and Days*, describing peasant life and expressing his views on the proper conduct of men. His works reveal his essentially serious outlook on life and portray a less glamorous world than Homer's. His poems won renown during his lifetime, and the power of his name was such that epics by others were later attributed to him.

Hess, (Walter Richard) Rudolf (1894–1987) German Nazi leader. He joined the fledgling Nazi Party in 1920 and soon became Adolf Hitler's friend. After participating in the Beer Hall Putsch (1923), he escaped but returned voluntarily to prison, where he took down dictation for Hitler's *Mein Kampf.* He became Hitler's private secretary and, in 1933, deputy party leader. In the early days of World War II his power waned. In 1941 he created an international sensation when he secretly landed by parachute in Scotland on an abortive mission to negotiate peace between Britain and Germany. The British government held him as a prisoner of war, and his initiative was rejected by Hitler. He was given a life sentence at the Nuremberg Trials, and from 1966 he was the sole inmate at Spandau prison.

Hess, Victor Francis (1883–1964) Austrian-U.S. physicist. He received his doctorate from the University of Vienna in 1906. His research dealt chiefly with radioactivity and atmospheric electricity. His experiments proved what had long been suspected: an extremely penetrating radiation of extraterrestrial origin permeates the atmosphere (see cosmic ray). Further investigation of this radiation, named cosmic rays in 1925, led Carl D. Anderson (1905–1991) to discover the positron and opened up new fields of research in modern physics. For his work Hess shared with Anderson a Nobel Prize in 1936.

Hess, Walter Rudolf (1881–1973) Swiss physiologist. He worked at the University of Zurich 1917–51. His interests centered on the nerves that control automatic functions such as digestion and excretion, and that also trigger the activities of a group of organs that respond to complex stimuli, such as stress. Using fine electrodes to stimulate or destroy specific areas of the brain in cats and dogs, Hess mapped the control centers for each function to such a degree that he could bring about the physical behavior pattern of a cat confronted by a dog simply by stimulating the proper points on the cat's hypothalamus He shared a 1949 Nobel Prize with Antonio Egas Moniz.

Hesse \'hes\ *German* **Hessen** State (pop., 2000 est.: 6,052,000), western central Germany. Occupying an area of 8,152 sq mi (21,114 sq km), it was formed in 1945 through the amalgamation of former Prussian provincial units. Its capital is Wiesbaden. The Hessians are thought to be descended from the Frankish tribe of the Chatti, who were Christianized by St. Boniface in the early 8th century AD. Hesse was twice partitioned in the 15th century, but Philip reunited the territory. The area today has small farms, while the state's industries are centered in the Rhine-Main area. On the banks of the Weser River are many ruined castles and old churches and palaces.

Hesse \'hes-ə\, **Eva** (1936–1970) U.S. (German-born) sculptor. She arrived in New York with her family in 1939, fleeing the Nazi regime. She attended Pratt Institute, Cooper Union, and Yale University. In 1964 she married and moved briefly to Germany and began making sculpture, developing a style featuring sensuous shapes and unconventional materials (including rubber tubing, synthetic resins, cord, cloth, and wire). In the 1960s she exhibited throughout the U.S. and achieved some critical acclaim. In 1969 she underwent the first of three unsuccessful operations for a brain tumor. Her influence since her death has been widespread.

Hesse \'hes-ə\, **Hermann** (1877–1962) German novelist and poet. He left a seminary because of his inability to adapt to the life there. His first novel was *Peter Camenzind* (1904); it was followed by *Beneath the Wheel* (1906), *Gertrud* (1910), and *Rosshalde* (1914). An opponent of militarism, he settled permanently in Switzerland at the outbreak of World War I. His later works deal with the individual's search for spiritual fulfillment, often through mysticism. *Demian* (1919), influenced by his experience with psychoanalysis, made him famous. *Siddhartha* (1922), about the early life of Buddha, reflects a visit to India. *Steppenwolf* (1927), *Narcissus and Goldmund* (1930), and *The Glass Bead Game* (or *Magister Ludi;* 1943) concern duality and the conflict between the contemplative and the active life. He won the Nobel Prize in 1946. His mysticism and his appeal for self-realization made him posthumously a cult figure among young people.

Hermann Hesse, 1957.
WIDE WORLD PHOTOS

Hestia Greek goddess of the hearth and one of the 12 chief deities of Mount Olympus. She was the daughter of Rhea and Cronus. When Apollo and Poseidon became suitors for her hand, she swore to remain a maiden forever, whereupon Zeus gave her the honor of presiding over all sacrifices. Though mainly a goddess of the family hearth and domestic life, she was sometimes also worshiped at the civic hearth in public buildings.

Heston, Charlton *orig.* **John Charlton Carter** (born 1924) U.S. actor. Born in Evanston, Ill., he made his Broadway debut in *Antony and Cleopatra* (1947) and his film debut in *Dark City* (1950). He became a star in *The Greatest Show on Earth* (1952) and was a muscular and dignified stalwart in *The Ten Commandments* (1956), *Ben-Hur* (1959, Academy Award), and *The Greatest Story Ever Told* (1965). He later starred in *Airport 1975* (1974) and *Earthquake* (1974) and directed and acted in *Antony and Cleopatra* (1972) and *Mother Lode* (1982). He was president of the Screen Actors Guild (1966–71) and was elected president of the NATIONAL RIFLE ASSOCIATION in 1998.

Hesychius of Alexandria \hə-'si-kē-əs\ (fl. 5th century AD) Greek scholar and linguist. He compiled the *Alphabetical Collection of All Words*, the most complete Greek lexicon known from antiquity. Though preserved only in a 15th-century abridgment by a Venetian editor, it is valued as a basic authority for the dialects and vocabularies of ancient inscriptions and poetry as well as the sacred writings of the Greek Church Fathers (see PATRISTIC LITERATURE).

heterocyclic compound \,he-tə-rō-'sī-klik\ Any of a class of organic compounds whose molecules contain one or more rings of atoms with at least one atom (the "hetero-atom") being an element other than carbon, most frequently oxygen, nitrogen, or sulfur. As in HYDROCARBONS, the BONDING may be saturated (see SATURATION), unsaturated, or aromatic (see AROMATIC COMPOUND), and the compound may consist of a single ring or have fused rings (in which adjoining rings share two carbon atoms). Five-membered heterocyclics include CHLOROPHYLL, HEMOGLOBIN, INDIGO, TRYPTOPHAN, and certain polymers. Six-membered heterocyclics include PYRIDINE, pyridoxine (vitamin B_6; see VITAMIN B COMPLEX), VITAMIN E, NICOTINE, QUININE, and MORPHINE, and the pyran nucleus, which is found in sugars and the anthocyanin pigments. Other important heterocyclic compounds are PYRIMIDINES, which occur in BARBITURATES, and PURINES, which occur in CAFFEINE and related compounds; pyrimidine and purine are the parent compounds of the NUCLEIC ACIDS.

heterosis \,he-tə-'rō-səs\ *or* **hybrid vigor** Increase in such characteristics as size, growth rate, fertility, and yield of a hybrid organism over those of its parents. Plant and animal breeders exploit heterosis by mating two different purebred lines that have desirable traits. The first-generation offspring generally show, in greater measure, the desired characteristics of both parents. Since this vigor may decrease if the hybrids are actually mated together, the parental lines must be maintained and crossed for each new crop or group desired.

heterozygote See HOMOZYGOTE AND HETEROZYGOTE

Heuss \'hȯis\, **Theodor** (1884–1963) German politician and author. A member of the German Democratic Party during the WEIMAR REPUBLIC, he served in the Reichstag (1924–28, 1930–33). After ADOLF HITLER came to power, Heuss's books, on political science, were burned as "un-German." After World War II, he helped found the FREE DEMOCRATIC PARTY and served (1948–49) on the parliamentary council that wrote the West German constitution. He served as president of the new state from 1949 until his retirement in 1959.

Hewish, Antony (born 1924) British astrophysicist. In 1967 Hewish determined that the regularly patterned radio signals (pulses) that JOCELYN BELL BURNELL had detected were not caused by earthly interference or, as some speculated, by intelligent life-forms trying to communicate with distant planets but were energy emissions from certain stars. For this work in identifying PULSARS as a new class of stars, he shared a 1974 Nobel Prize with MARTIN RYLE.

Hewitt, Abram S(tevens) (1822–1903) U.S. industrialist and politician. Born in Haverstraw, N.Y., he formed an iron-making business with Edward and PETER COOPER in New York City in 1845; he later helped establish the COOPER UNION school (1859). He produced gun-barrel iron for the government during the Civil War and in 1870 produced the first commercial-grade steel in the U.S. In 1871 he helped SAMUEL TILDEN oust WILLIAM MARCY TWEED's ring, which controlled the TAMMANY HALL Democratic organization and the municipal government of New York City. He served in the U.S. House of Representatives (1875–79, 1881–86). As mayor of New York (1887–88), he initiated major reforms that broke Tammany Hall's influence.

Hewitt, Don S. (born 1922) U.S. television producer. Born in New York City, he served as a war correspondent in World War II, joined CBS in 1948, and directed its first televised evening news broadcast, with Douglas Edwards (1948–62). He was executive producer of *CBS News with Walter Cronkite* (1962–81), and he created the popular *60 Minutes* in 1968.

Hewlett-Packard Co. U.S. manufacturer of computers, computer printers, and measuring instruments. Founded in 1938 in Palo Alto, Cal., by William Hewlett (1913–2001) and David Packard (1912–1996), the company grew along with the electronics sector of the U.S. defense industry after World War II. In 1966 it developed its first computer, and in 1968 one of the earliest desktop electronic calculators. Hewlett-Packard entered the personal-computer market in 1980 with the HP-85, and its HP LaserJet printer dominated the market for computer printers in the 1980s. By the 1990s the company was a leading maker of minicomputers used by businesses and institutions and a leader in the field of laser and inkjet printers. In 2002 the company bought rival Compaq Computer for $25 billion.

hexachord (Greek: "six strings") In music, a group of six tones in a specified pattern, specifically the INTERVAL pattern *tone-tone-semitone-tone-tone* (as in G-A-B-C-D-E). The hexachord was apparently conceived when GUIDO D'AREZZO noticed that the scales of the CHURCH MODES could be seen to overlap in their interval patterns. His system of SOLMIZATION gave each hexachord the same syllables (ut-re-mi-fa-sol-la), and by means of overlapping hexachords the theorist could represent the complete "gamut" of pitches. Though counterintuitive to modern musicians, who think in terms of octaves, the concept of hexachords was fundamental to music theory throughout the Middle Ages and Renaissance.

Heydrich \'hī-drik\, **Reinhard (Tristan Eugen)** (1904–1942) German Nazi official. He resigned from the navy in 1931 to join the SS, becoming SS chief for Berlin (1934), head of the Reich Security Central Office (1939), and HEINRICH HIMMLER's chief deputy. Noted for his ruthlessness against "enemies of the state," in the early years of World War II he organized mass executions in the German-occupied territories and became known as "the Hangman." In 1942 he chaired the WANNSEE CONFERENCE. Appointed deputy adminstrator of Bohemia and Moravia, he was assassinated by Czech patriots; in retaliation the Gestapo demolished Lidice and executed its male population of about 200.

Heyerdahl \'hā-ər-,däl\, **Thor** (1914–2002) Norwegian ethnologist and adventurer. After a trip to Polynesia convinced him that Polynesian culture bore traces of South American cultures, he built a raft, the *Kon-Tiki*, and sailed it from South America to Polynesia in 1947 to demonstrate the possibility of such contact, a trip recounted in his best-selling *Kon-Tiki* (1950). In 1969 he sailed a reconstruction of an ancient Egyptian reed boat (the *Ra*) from Morocco to the Caribbean to show that the Egyptians could have preceded CHRISTOPHER COLUMBUS to the New World. In 1977 he took the reed craft *Tigris* from the Tigris River in Iraq across the Arabian Sea to Pakistan and back to the Red Sea to demonstrate the possibility of two-way trading journeys that could have spread ancient Sumerian culture eastward. His theories have not been generally accepted by academic anthropologists.

Heyerdahl.
PIERRE VAUTHEY—GAMMA/LIAISON

Heyse \'hī-zə\, **Paul (Johann Ludwig von)** (1830–1914) German writer. An independent scholar, he led a circle of writers in Munich who sought to preserve traditional artistic values from the encroachment of political radicalism, materialism, and realism. His admired short stories and novellas were collected in numerous volumes; he also published novels, including *Children of the World* (1873) and *Merlin* (1892), and many unsuccessful plays. Among his best works are his translations of GIACOMO LEOPARDI and other Italian and Spanish poets; many were set to music by HUGO WOLF. His popularity was already declining when he was awarded the Nobel Prize in 1910.

Heywood, John (1497?–after 1575) British playwright. His witty, satirical verse interludes (dialogues on a set subject) helped put English drama on the road to the fully developed comedy of the Elizabethans. His interludes, which replace biblical allegory with representations of everyday life and manners, include *The Play of the Wether, A Play of Love,* and *Wytty and Wytless* (all printed 1533), and *The Playe Called the Foure P.P.: A Palmer, a Pardoner, a Potycary, a Pedler* (printed c. 1544). He also wrote epigrams, ballads, and a verse allegory, *The Spider and the Flie* (1556).

Hezbollah See HIZBULLAH

Hezekiah \ˌhe-zə-ˈkī-ə\ (fl. late 8th and early 7th century BC) King of JUDAH at Jerusalem. The dates of his reign are uncertain but are often given as 715–686 BC. He was a reformer who tried to discourage foreign cults and assert the religious traditions of Israel during a time of Assyrian supremacy. The rebellion that broke out in Palestine c. 703 BC was probably led by Hezekiah. Though he fortified Jerusalem, other cities of Judah fell, and the revolt was put down in 701 BC. The Assyrians demanded a heavy tribute of gold, but tradition holds that a plague devastated the Assyrian army and Jerusalem was spared.

Hialeah \ˌhī-ə-ˈlē-ə\ City (pop., 1996 est.: 205,000), southeastern Florida. Settled in 1910 by the aviation pioneers James Bright and GLENN H. CURTISS, the town took its name from a Seminole Indian word meaning "pretty prairie." The city serves mainly as a residential suburb of MIAMI. It is the site of the horse-racing track Hialeah Park (1925).

Hiawatha \ˌhī-ə-ˈwȯ-thə\ Legendary chief (c. 1450) of the Onondaga tribe of North American Indians, regarded by native tradition as the founder of the IROQUOIS CONFEDERACY. His story is told in HENRY W. LONGFELLOW's popular poem *Song of Hiawatha* (1855), though Longfellow perpetuated an error of HENRY ROWE SCHOOLCRAFT's that placed Hiawatha in a Midwestern tribe.

hibernation State of greatly slowed METABOLISM and low body temperature in winter in certain animals. True hibernators include many cold-blooded animals and a few mammals (e.g., bats, hedgehogs) that go into a near-dead state with a near-freezing body temperature and very slow breathing and heart rate. Mammals such as bears that sleep in dens with only slightly lowered body temperature wake easily and are not considered true hibernators. Most hibernators build up a reserve of body fat or store food ahead of time. They may wake and eat several times during the winter. Cold-blooded animals must hibernate where the weather drops below freezing. Hibernation's warm-weather equivalent is estivation.

Hiberno-Saxon style Decorative style that resulted when Irish (Hibernian) monks went to England in 635. It mingled the Celtic decorative tradition—curvilinear and "trumpet" forms, scrolls, spirals, and a double-curve motif—with the interlaced zoomorphic patterns and bright color of the pagan Anglo-Saxons. Mediterranean art entered as an element when St. AUGUSTINE OF CANTERBURY's mission arrived from Rome, introducing the human figure in art objects, but the style's basic characteristics remained geometric, with interlaced designs and areas of bright color, as seen in the LINDISFARNE GOSPELS and the Book of KELLS. It was taken to Europe by Irish and Saxon Christian missionaries and there exerted strong influence on CAROLINGIAN ART. See also ANGLO-SAXON ART.

hibiscus \hī-ˈbis-kəs\ Any of about 250 species of shrubs, trees, and herbaceous plants that make up the genus *Hibiscus,* in the MALLOW FAMILY, native to warm temperate and tropical regions. Several are cultivated as ornamentals for their showy flowers. The tropical Chinese hibiscus, or China rose *(H. rosa-sinensis),* has large, somewhat bell-shaped reddish blossoms. The East African hibiscus *(H. schizopetalus),* a drooping shrub, is often grown in hanging baskets indoors. Other members of the genus include OKRA, ROSE OF SHARON, and many flowering plants known by the common name mallow.

China rose (*Hibiscus rosa-sinensis*).
SVEN SAMELIUS

hiccup Spasmodic contraction of the DIAPHRAGM that causes a sudden breath in, cut off when the vocal cords snap together, creating the characteristic sound. Causes include overdistended stomach, gastric irritation, and nerve spasms. The many folk remedies for hiccups interrupt the rhythm of the spasms. The most common and effective treatment is to hold the breath as long as possible. Hiccups usually stop within minutes, though they may last days, weeks, or longer. Prolonged severe hiccups are treated with nerve blocks or by surgically cutting the nerve that supplies the diaphragm.

Hickok, Wild Bill *orig.* **James Butler** (1837–1876) U.S. frontiersman. Born in Troy Grove, Ill., he moved to Kansas to farm and later served as a constable in Monticello, Kan. While working as a stage driver in 1861, he shot and killed the outlaw Dave McCanles, which launched legends of his marksmanship. He was a Union scout and spy in the Civil War, then was appointed deputy U.S. marshal (1866–67). His ironhanded rule as sheriff of Hays City (1869–71) and marshal of Abilene (1871) helped tame these Kansas towns. He toured with Buffalo Bill's WILD WEST SHOW 1872–74. While visiting the goldfields in the Dakota Territory, he was at a poker table in a Deadwood saloon when he was shot dead by a drunken stranger, Jack McCall.

Hickok.
CULVER PICTURES

hickory Any of about 18 species of deciduous timber and nut-producing trees that make up the genus *Carya,* in the WALNUT family. About 15 species are native to eastern North America, and three to eastern Asia. The fruit is an egg-shaped nut enclosed in a fleshy husk. The nuts of some species—principally shagbark hickory *(C. ovata),* shellbark hickory *(C. laciniosa),* mockernut hickory *(C. tomentosa),* and PECAN—contain large, sweet-tasting, edible seeds. The pecan, the most valuable species economically, is cultivated for its flavorful nuts and its light-colored wood. The wood of other hickories is used as fuel and for tool handles, sports equipment, furniture, and flooring.

Hicks, Edward (1780–1849) U.S. naive painter. Born in Attleboro, Pa., he was a coach and sign painter from an early age. In middle age he began to produce paintings of farm scenes and landscapes. Fearing that art was contrary to his Quaker religion but believing that it might bring meaning to life, he often framed his pictures with edifying verse. He painted his best-known subject, *The Peaceable Kingdom,* about 100

"The Cornell Farm," oil on canvas by Edward Hicks, 1848; in the National Gallery of Art, Washington, D.C.
BY COURTESY OF THE NATIONAL GALLERY OF ART, WASHINGTON, D.C., GIFT OF EDGAR WILLIAM AND BERNICE CHRYSLER GARBISCH

times; some 25 versions survive. In this charming Quaker pageant, WILLIAM PENN appears on the left making his treaty with the Indians, while beasts are gathered on the right with little children playing among them.

Hicks, John R(ichard) *later* **Sir John** (1904–1989) British economist. He taught at several institutions, notably Oxford Univ., and was knighted in 1964. His classic work *Value and Capital* (1939) helped resolve basic conflicts between business-cycle theory and the equilibrium theory, which holds that economic forces tend to balance one another rather than simply reflect cyclical trends. He shared the 1972 Nobel Prize with KENNETH ARROW.

Hidalgo \hi-'dal-gō\ State (pop., 1995 est.: 2,112,000), eastern central Mexico. With an area of 8,036 sq mi (20,813 sq km), it was part of the state of MEXICO until 1869, when it was established as a separate state in honor of the revolutionary patriot MIGUEL HIDALGO. Containing some of the most mountainous areas in Mexico, it has extensive mineral deposits, including silver and gold. In pre-Columbian times it was the center of the TOLTEC civilization; Tula, west of PACHUCA, the state capital, was once capital of the Toltecs and is an archaeological site. The state has major metalworking factories, as well as agricultural production.

Hidalgo (y Costilla) \ē-'t͟häl-gō\, **Miguel** (1753–1811) Mexican priest, called the father of Mexican independence. Ordained in 1789, he had an uneventful early career, during which he endeavored to improve his parishioners' economic well-being. In the town of Dolores (now Dolores Hidalgo), he joined a group plotting independence from Spain in the light of Napoleon's invasion of that country. On September 16, 1810, when his group was betrayed, he rang the church bell and addressed his parishioners with his *Grito de Dolores* (Cry of Dolores), calling them to revolution. Thousands of Indians and mestizos joined him, and he succeeded in capturing Guanajuato and other cities in the region before reaching Mexico City, where his hesitation led to their defeat and his execution. The martyred Hidalgo became a potent symbol of the independence movement that eventually succeeded, and each September 16—now celebrated as Mexico's Independence Day—the president shouts a version of the *Grito de Dolores* from the National Palace balcony.

Hidatsa \hi-'dät-sə\ *or* **Gros Ventres (of the Missouri)** \'grō-,vänt\ PLAINS INDIAN people of Siouan stock who lived on the upper Missouri River in semipermanent villages. They raised corn, beans, and squash, and hunted bison. Hidatsa social organization included age-graded military societies; there were also various clans based on maternal descent. The SUN DANCE was the major religious ceremony. Together with the MANDAN, with whom they had peaceful relations for more than 200 years, they exchanged native goods with European traders for guns, knives, and other items. In the mid-1800s disease and war with the Dakota (SIOUX) sharply reduced their number. Today 1,200 Hidatsa live on a reservation in North Dakota.

Hideyoshi See TOYOTOMI HIDEYOSHI

Hierakonpolis \,hī-ə-rə-'kän-pə-ləs\ Ancient city, Upper Egypt. Located south of THEBES, it was the prehistoric residence of the kings of Upper Egypt. Now an archaeological site, it reveals the beginning of Egypt's historical period. It was at its height from 3400 BC to the Old Kingdom (c. 2575 BC). THUTMOSE III later completely rebuilt the archaic temple. During the New Kingdom, el-Kab, across the river, became economically more important, but Hierakonpolis retained its place as a religious and historic center.

Hierapolis \,hī-ə-'ra-pə-ləs\ Ancient city, now in Syria. Its remains lie northeast of ALEPPO. As a center of the worship of the Syrian goddess ATARGATIS, it became known to the Greeks as the Holy City (Hierapolis). One of the great cities of Syria in the 3rd century AD, it thereafter declined. HARUN AL-RASHID restored it at the end of the 8th century. Captured by Crusaders in the 12th century but reclaimed by SALADIN in 1175, it later became the headquarters of the MONGOLS, who completed its ruin.

hieroglyph \'hī-rə-,glif\ Character in any of several systems of WRITING that is pictorial in nature, though not necessarily in the way it is read. The term was originally used for the oldest system of writing Ancient Egyptian (see EGYPTIAN LANGUAGE). Egyptian hieroglyphs could be read iconically (the representation of a house enclosure stood for the word *pr,* "house"), phonetically (the "house" sign could have the phonetic value *pr*), or associatively (a sign representing one thing could stand for a homophone meaning something else). Unlike contemporary CUNEIFORM WRITING, phonetic hieroglyphs denoted consonants, not syllables, so there was no regular way to write vowels; by convention, Egyptologists insert the vowel *e* between consonants in order to pronounce Egyptian words. The standardized orthography of the Middle Kingdom (2050–1750 BC) employed about 750 hieroglyphs. In the early centuries AD, use of hieroglyphs declined—the last dated text is from AD 394—and the meaning of the signs was lost until their decipherment in the early 19th century (see J.-F. CHAMPOLLION, ROSETTA STONE). The term "hieroglyph" has been applied to similar systems of writing, notably a script used to write the ancient ANATOLIAN LANGUAGE Luvian and a script used by the Mayas (see MAYAN HIEROGLYPHIC WRITING).

hierophant \'hī-ə-rə-,fant, hī-'er-ə-fənt\ Chief priest of the ELEUSINIAN MYSTERIES in ancient Greece. His main task was to display the sacred objects during the celebration of the mysteries and explain their secret meaning to initiates. The priest was usually an old, celibate man with a forceful voice, chosen from the Eumolpids, one of the original clans of Eleusis. Upon election, he cast aside his former name and was called only *hierophantes.*

hieros gamos \'hē-ə-,rȯs-'gä-,mȯs\ (Greek: "sacred marriage") Sexual relations of fertility deities enacted in myths and rituals, characteristic of societies based on cereal agriculture (e.g., Mesopotamia, Phoenicia, and Canaan). At least once a year, people dressed as gods engaged in sexual intercourse to guarantee the fertility of the land. The festival began with a procession to the marriage celebration, which was followed by an exchange of gifts, a purification rite, the wedding feast, preparation of the wedding chamber, and a secret nocturnal act of intercourse.

Higgs particle *or* **Higgs boson** Carrier of an all-pervading fundamental field (Higgs field) that is hypothesized as a means of endowing MASS on some elementary particles through its interactions with them. It was named for Peter W. Higgs (born 1929) of the University of Edinburgh, one of those who first postulated the idea. The Higgs mechanism explains why the carriers of the WEAK FORCE are heavy, while the carrier of the ELECTROMAGNETIC FORCE has a mass of zero. There is no direct experimental evidence for the existence of either the Higgs particle or the Higgs field.

high blood pressure See HYPERTENSION

High Commission, Court of English ecclesiastical court instituted by HENRY VIII to enforce the Act of SUPREMACY (1534). It became a controversial instrument of repression, used against those who refused to acknowledge the authority of the Church of ENGLAND. Its main function, and the most controversial, was administration of the oath ex officio, committing one to answer even self-incriminating questions; those who refused to take the oath were turned over to the feared Court of STAR CHAMBER. Opposition, mainly from the Puritans and the common lawyers, resulted in the court's abolishment by Parliament in 1641. See also PREROGATIVE COURT.

High Court of Admiralty In England, formerly the court presided over by the deputy of the admiral of the fleet. It was established c. 1360 to deal with matters of discipline and cases of PIRACY and prizes (ships and goods captured at sea), but it eventually had jurisdiction over mercantile and shipping matters. In 1875 it was merged with the other great courts of England into the High Court of Justice.

high-definition television (HDTV) Any system producing significantly greater picture resolution than that of the ordinary 525-line (625-line in Europe) TELEVISION screen. Conventional television transmits signals in analog form. Digital HDTV systems, by contrast, transmit pictures and sounds in the form of digital data. These numerical data are broadcast using the same high radio frequencies that carry analog waves, and computer processors in the digital television set then decode the data. Digital HDTV can provide sharper, clearer pictures and sound with very little interference or other imperfections. Of perhaps greater importance, digital television sets will potentially be able to send, store, and manipulate images as well as receive them, thereby merging the functions of the television set and the computer.

high-energy physics See PARTICLE PHYSICS

high jump Jump for height over a horizontal bar in a TRACK-AND-FIELD contest. The sport's equipment includes a semicircular runway allowing an approach run of at least 15 m (49 ft), the raised bar and its vertical supports, and a cushioned landing area. Jumpers must leave the ground from one foot. Early jumping styles, including the near-erect scissors jump and the facedown Western roll-and-straddle, were largely superseded from 1968 by the "Fosbury flop," a backward-twisting dive named for its originator, the U.S. jumper Dick Fosbury (born 1947).

high place *Hebrew* **bama** In ancient Israel or CANAAN, a shrine built on an elevated site. For Canaanites the shrines were devoted to fertility deities, to the BAALS, or to the Semitic goddesses called the Asherot. The shrines often included an altar and a sacred object such as a stone pillar or wooden pole. One of the oldest known high places, dating from c. 2500 BC, is at MEGIDDO. The Israelites also associated elevated places with the divine presence, and after conquering Canaan they used Canaanite high places to worship Yahweh (God). Later the Temple of JERUSALEM on Mount Zion became the only accepted high place.

high-rise building Multistory building taller than the maximum height people are willing to walk up, thus requiring vertical mechanical transportation. The introduction of safe passenger ELEVATORS made practical the erection of buildings more than four or five stories tall. The first high-rise buildings were constructed in the U.S. in the 1880s. Further developments were made possible by the use of steel structural frames and glass CURTAIN-WALL systems. High-rises are used for residential apartments, hotels, offices, and sometimes retail, light manufacturing, and educational facilities. See also SKYSCRAPER.

high school In the U.S., any three- to six-year SECONDARY school serving students about 14–18 years of age. Four-year schools are by far the most common; their grade levels are designated freshman (9th grade), sophomore (10th), junior (11th), and senior (12th). Comprehensive high schools offer both general academic courses and specialized commercial, trade, and technical subjects. Most U.S. high schools are tuition-free, supported by state funds. Private high schools are usually classed as either PAROCHIAL or PREPARATORY schools.

high seas In maritime law, the waters lying outside the TERRITORIAL WATERS of any and all states. In the Middle Ages, a number of maritime states asserted sovereignty over large portions of the high seas. The doctrine that the high seas in time of peace are open to all nations was first proposed by HUGO GROTIUS (1609), but it did not become an accepted principle of INTERNATIONAL LAW until the 19th century. Activities permitted on the high seas include navigation, fishing, the laying of submarine cables and pipelines, and overflight of aircraft.

high-speed steel ALLOY of STEEL introduced in 1900. It doubled or trebled the capacities of machine shops by permitting the operation of machine tools at twice or three times the speeds possible with CARBON STEEL (which loses its cutting edge when the temperature produced by the friction of the cutting action is above about 400°F, or 210°C). A common type of high-speed steel contains 18% tungsten, 4% chromium, 1% vanadium, and only 0.5–0.8% carbon. See also HEAT TREATING, STAINLESS STEEL.

higher education Education beyond the secondary level. Institutions of higher education include not only COLLEGES and UNIVERSITIES but also professional schools in such fields as law, theology, medicine, business, music, and art. They also include teacher-training schools, COMMUNITY COLLEGES, and institutes of technology. At the end of a prescribed course of study, a DEGREE, diploma, or certificate is awarded. See also CONTINUING EDUCATION.

Highland Games Athletic games originating in the Scottish Highlands and now held there and in various parts of the world, usually under the auspices of a local Caledonian society. Events include flat and hurdle races, long and high jumps, hammer and weight throws, and the caber toss, the hurling end-over-end of a tapered fir pole about 17 ft (5 m) long and 90 lbs (40 kg) in weight. Competitions in bagpipe playing and Highland dancing also form an important part of the meetings.

Tossing the caber at a Braemar gathering.
ABERDEEN JOURNALS LTD.

hijacking Crime of seizing possession or control of a vehicle from another by force or threat of force. Although by the late 20th century hijacking most frequently involved the seizure of an airplane and its forcible diversion to destinations chosen by the air pirates, when the term was coined in the 1920s in the U.S. hijacking generally referred to in-transit thefts of truckloads of illegally manufactured liquor or to the similar seizure of rumrunners at sea. Airplane hijacking is also known as skyjacking. The first reported case of such hijacking occurred in Peru in 1931. Between 1968 and 1970 alone there were nearly 200 hijackings. The participants often were politically motivated Palestinians or other Arabs who commandeered airplanes while in flight and threatened harm to the passengers and crew unless certain of their comrades were released from jail in Israel or some other location. Air hijackings continued in the 1980s and '90s, though new airport security measures and international agreements on terrorism probably deterred many more. The deadliest act of air piracy ever occurred in September 2001, when suicide terrorists simultaneously hijacked four airliners in the United States and flew two of them into the World Trade Center complex in New York City and one into the Pentagon in Washington, D.C.; the fourth crashed outside Pittsburgh, Pennsylvania. The crashes killed 266 people aboard the airplanes and thousands more in the buildings and on the ground. See also PIRACY.

Hijaz, Al- See HEJAZ

Hijra See HEGIRA

hiking Walking, often among hills or mountains, as recreational sport. It represents an activity in its own right and also figures in BACKPACKING, CAMPING, HUNTING, MOUNTAINEERING, and ORIENTEERING. Hiking programs are offered by youth groups and other organizations, such as the U.S. Wilderness Society. Trails are preserved in most U.S. federal and state parklands. Most European cities have hiking trails outside them. One of the longest U.S. hiking trails is the APPALACHIAN NATIONAL SCENIC TRAIL.

Hilbert, David (1862–1943) German mathematician whose work aimed at establishing the formalistic foundations of mathematics. He finished his PhD at the University of Königsberg (1884) and moved to the University of Göttingen in 1895. In 1900 at the International Mathematical Congress in Paris, he laid out 23 research problems as a challenge to the 20th century. Many have since been solved, in each case to great fanfare. Hilbert's name is prominently attached to an infinite-dimensional space called a Hilbert space (see INNER PRODUCT SPACE), a concept useful in mathematical ANALYSIS and QUANTUM MECHANICS.

Hildebrand, Joel Henry (1881–1983) U.S. educator and chemist. Born in Camden, N.J., he taught principally at the University of Pennsylvania and UC–Berkeley. His 1924 monograph on the solubility of nonelectrolytes, *Solubility*, was the classic reference for almost half a century. His many scientific papers and chemistry texts include *An Introduction to Molecular Kinetic Theory* (1963) and *Viscosity and Diffusivity* (1977). He received the Distinguished Service Medal in 1918 and the King's Medal (British) in 1948.

Hildegard von Bingen \'hil-də-ˌgärt-fȯn-'biŋ-ən\ (1098–1179) German abbess and visionary mystic. She became prioress at the Benedictine cloister of Disibodenberg in 1136. Having experienced visions since childhood, she was eventually permitted to write *Scivias* (1141–52), in which she recorded 26 prophetic, symbolic, and apocalyptic visions; it was followed by two more such collections. She founded a convent at Rupertsberg c. 1147, where she continued to prophesy; she became known as the "Sibyl of the Rhine," and her advice was sought by the most powerful and eminent figures of Europe. Her other works include a morality play, a book of saints' lives, treatises on medicine and natural history, and extensive correspondence. Her *Symphonia armonie celestium revelationum* consists of 77 lyrical poems, all with monophonic melodies; she is apparently the first woman composer in the Western tradition whose music is known. Though long regarded as a saint, she has never been formally canonized.

Hill, David Octavius, and Robert Adamson (1802–1870, 1821–1848) Scottish photographers. Hill, originally a painter, was a founding member of the Royal Scottish Academy and its secretary for 40 years. In 1843 he enlisted the help of Adamson, a chemist experienced in photography, in photographing the delegates to the founding convention of the Free Church of Scotland. They used the calotype process, by which an image was developed from a paper negative. Their portraits demonstrate a masterly sense of form and composition and a dramatic use of light and shade. Their five-year partnership resulted in some 3,000 photographs, including many views of Edinburgh and small fishing villages.

Hill, James J(erome) (1838–1916) Canadian-U.S. financier and railroad builder. Born near Guelph, Ontario, he began his career in St. Paul overseeing steamboat transportation. In 1873 he reorganized a bankrupt railroad as the St. Paul, Minneapolis, and Manitoba Railway Co.; he served as its president from 1882. The GREAT NORTHERN RAILWAY CO. absorbed the St. Paul line in 1890, and Hill became its president (1893–1907) and chairman of the board (1907–12). The NORTHERN PACIFIC and the Chicago, Burlington and Quincy railroads also came under Hill's control; E. Harriman's attempt to seize control of Northern Pacific from him (1901) triggered a Wall Street panic. Hill's banking activity as president of Northern Securities Co. was declared in violation of the Sherman Anti-Trust Act in 1904. See also EDWARD H. HARRIMAN.

Hill, Joe *orig.* **Joel Emmanuel Hägglund** (1879–1915) Swedish-U.S. songwriter and organizer for the INDUSTRIAL WORKERS OF THE WORLD (IWW). Hill emigrated to the U.S. c. 1902 and joined the IWW in 1910. His songs of protest and solidarity—including "The Preacher and the Slave," in which he coined the phrase "pie in the sky" as a mocking description of the reward awaiting the meek in the next world—became widely popular. In 1914 he was arrested in Salt Lake City and charged with the murder of a grocer and his son during a robbery. Convicted on circumstantial evidence despite mass demonstrations on his behalf, Hill was executed by a firing squad. His death made him a martyr in the eyes of the radical U.S. labor movement.

Hill painting See PAHARI PAINTING

Hillary, Edmund (Percival) *later* **Sir Edmund** (born 1919) New Zealand mountain climber and explorer. Born in Auckland, he became a professional beekeeper but enjoyed climbing in the New Zealand Alps. With TENZING NORGAY, he became the first person to reach the summit of Mount EVEREST (1953), an achievement that brought him worldwide fame. In 1958 he participated in the first crossing of Antarctica by vehicle. From the 1960s he has helped build schools and hospitals for the Sherpa people.

Hillary, 1956.
UPI

Hillel (fl. 1st century BC–1st century AD) Jewish sage and architect of RABBINIC JUDAISM. Born in Babylonia, he went to Palestine to complete his studies under the PHARISEES. He became the revered head of the school known by his name, the House of Hillel, and his carefully applied method of exegesis came to be called the Seven Rules of Hillel. He liberated texts from a slavish literal interpretation and sought to make obedience to Law feasible for all Jews. His legal writings were very influential in the compilation of the TALMUD, which also contains many stories and legends about his life. He is remembered as a model scholar and communal leader, whose brilliance, patience, and goodness are to be emulated by all RABBIS.

Hilliard \ˈhil-yərd\, **Nicholas** (1547–1619) British painter. Son of a goldsmith, he trained as a jeweler and began painting miniatures in his youth. In 1570 was appointed miniature painter to ELIZABETH I. He produced many portraits of her and of such members of her court as FRANCIS DRAKE and WALTER RALEIGH. He retained his appointment on the accession of JAMES I (1603), while also practicing as a goldsmith and jeweler. The first great native-born English painter of the Renaissance, he raised the art of MINIATURE PAINTING to its highest point of development and influenced English portraiture through the early 17th century.

Hillman, Sidney *orig.* **Simcha** (1887–1946) Lithuanian-U.S. labor leader. He emigrated to the U.S. in 1907, became a garment worker, and was elected president of the Amalgamated Clothing Workers of America in 1914. Under his leadership the union greatly increased its membership, secured unemployment insurance, and organized two banks. He served in various NEW DEAL labor organizations, including the NATIONAL RECOVERY ADMINISTRATION. He helped found the Congress of Industrial Organizations and was active in it until his death. See also AFL-CIO, JOHN L. LEWIS.

Hillquit, Morris *orig.* **Morris Hillkowitz** (1869–1933) Latvian-U.S. Socialist leader. He emigrated to the U.S. in 1886, joined the Socialist Labor Party, and helped found the United Hebrew Trades in 1888. When the party split, he led a moderate faction to help form the Social Democratic Party, which in 1901 became the Socialist Party. As the party's chief theoretician, he defined its position of pacifism during World War I and defended many Socialists in court. He was twice the party's unsuccessful candidate for mayor of New York (1917, 1932).

Hilton, Conrad (Nicholson) (1887–1979) U.S. businessman, founder of one of the world's largest hotel organizations. Born in San Antonio, N.M., as a boy he helped his father turn the family's adobe house into an inn for traveling salesmen. After his father's death in 1918 he bought several hotels in Texas, and by 1939 he was building, leasing, and buying hotels in California, New York, Illinois, and elsewhere. In 1946 the Hilton Hotels Corp. was organized; in 1948, as the business expanded overseas, it became Hilton International Co. Later diversification included a credit-card company and a car-rental firm. His son Barron succeeded him as president in 1966.

Hilton, James (Glen Trevor) (1900–1954) British novelist. Educated at Cambridge Univ., he later wrote numerous novels, but is principally remembered for three best-selling works that led to popular films: *Lost Horizon* (1933; film, 1937), *Good-Bye Mr. Chips* (1934; film, 1939), and *Random Harvest* (1941; film, 1942). He eventually moved to California to work as a screenwriter.

Himachal Pradesh \hə-ˈmä-chəl-prə-ˈdesh\ State (pop., 1994 est.: 5,530,000), northern India. Located in the western HIMALAYAS, it covers an area of 21,490 sq mi (55,659 sq km); its capital is SIMLA. The area's history dates back to the VEDIC period; later the ARYANS assimilated the indigenous peoples. It was exposed to successive invasions through the centuries, ending with British domination in the 19th century. Between 1948 and the achievement of statehood in 1971, the state underwent various changes in size and administrative status. It is one of the least urbanized states in India, and most of the people are subsistence-level farmers.

Himalayas \ˌhi-mə-ˈlā-əz, hi-ˈmä-lə-yəz\ *or* **the Himalaya** Mountain system, southern Asia. It forms a barrier between the Tibetan Plateau to the north and the plains of the Indian subcontinent to the south. It constitutes the greatest mountain system on earth and includes 30 mountains rising to heights above 24,000 ft (7,300 m), including Mount EVEREST. The system extends some 1,500 mi (2,400 km) from east to west and covers about 230,000 sq mi (595,000 sq km). It is traditionally divided into four parallel ranges: from north to south, the Trans-Himalayas, the Great Himalayas (including the major peaks), the Lesser Himalayas (including peaks of 7,000–15,000 ft, or 2,000–4,500 m), and the Outer Himalayas (including the lowest peaks). Between the eastern and western extremities of the broad Himalayan arc lie several Indian states and the kingdoms of Nepal and Bhutan. It acts as a great climatic divide, causing heavy rain and snow on the Indian side but aridity in TIBET, and represents at many points a virtually impassable barrier, even by air. The mountains' glaciers and snows are the source of 19 major rivers, including the INDUS, GANGES, and BRAHMAPUTRA.

Himera \ˈhi-mə-rə\ Ancient Greek city, northern coast of SICILY. It was founded c. 649 BC by Syracusan exiles and Chalcidian inhabitants of Zancle (see MESSINA). An unsuccessful Carthaginian invasion of Sicily ended in the death of Hamilcar at the Battle of Himera in 480 BC. It was finally destroyed in 409 BC by Hamilcar's grandson HANNIBAL. Its only visible relic is a Doric temple (480 BC); many of its lion-head spouts are exhibited in the Palermo Museum.

Himmler, Heinrich (1900–1945) German Nazi police administrator who became the second most powerful man in the Third Reich. He joined the NAZI PARTY in 1925 and rose to become head of ADOLF HITLER's SS. He was put in command of most German police units after 1933, taking charge of the GESTAPO in 1934, and established the Third Reich's first concentration camp, at Dachau. He soon built the SS into a powerful network of state terror and by 1936 he commanded all the Reich's police forces. In World War II he expanded the Waffen-SS (Armed SS) until it rivaled the army; after 1941 he organized the death camps in Eastern Europe. In the war's final months he intrigued to surrender Germany to the Allies; Hitler ordered his arrest, but when he attempted to escape he was captured by the British and committed suicide by taking poison.

Himmler.
CAMERA PRESS

Hims See HOMS

Hinayana \ˌhē-nə-ˈyä-nə\ Name given to the more conservative schools of BUDDHISM. A Sanskrit word meaning "Lesser Vehicle" (because it is concerned with the individual's salvation), it was first applied pejoratively to the established Buddhist schools by followers of the more liberal MAHAYANA ("Greater Vehicle," because it is concerned with universal salvation) tradition. The ancient Hinayana schools continued to prosper after the rise of the Mahayana in the 1st century AD, but THERAVADA Buddhism was the only Hinayana school that maintained a strong position after the collapse of Indian Buddhism in the 13th century.

Hincmar of Reims \ˈhiŋk-ˌmär...ˈrēmz\ (806?–882) French archbishop and theologian. The most influential churchman of the Carolingian era, he advised the French kings LOUIS I and CHARLES II and was chosen archbishop of Reims in 845. He maintained his influence despite the hostility of LOTHAIR I, and secured the succession of Charles as Holy Roman Emperor. His theological writings included treatises on predestination, in which he argued that God does not damn a sinner in advance, and a defense of the Christian opposition to divorce.

Hindemith \ˈhin-də-ˌmit\, **Paul** (1895–1963) German composer. His talent was noticed early, and he received thorough training on viola, violin, clarinet, and piano. He became concertmaster of the Frankfurt Opera at 20, and began drawing attention as a composer at new-music festivals. Because his wife was Jewish and his music was considered "degenerate" by the Nazis, he left Germany in 1938, coming to the U.S. in 1940. Advocating *Gebrauchsmusik* ("useful music"), he wrote solo sonatas and concertos for many of the standard orchestral instruments. *Mathis der Maler* (1935) is the best known of his six operas; the symphony based on it, and the *Symphonic Metamorphosis on Themes of Weber* (1943), are widely performed. His extensively worked-out tonal theories resulted in his rewriting (but not necessarily improving) many of his earlier compositions.

Hindenburg, Paul von *in full* **Paul Ludwig Hans Anton von Beneckendorff und von Hindenburg** (1847–1934) German field marshal and second president (1925–34) of the WEIMAR REPUBLIC. Born to an aristocratic Prussian family, he retired from the Prussian army as a general in 1911. Recalled to duty in World War I, he commanded German forces in East Prussia and became a national hero after the Battle of TANNENBERG (1914). With ERICH LUDENDORFF as his chief aide, he nominally commanded all German forces until the end of the war, then retired again in 1919. Supported by conservative groups, he was elected president of Germany in 1925. When the GREAT DEPRESSION led to a political crisis, he was pressured to make the government more independent of parliamentary controls. In 1930 he allowed Chancellor HEINRICH BRUNING to dissolve the Reichstag, and in the new elections the Nazis emerged as the second-largest party. In 1932 he was reelected president by opponents of the Nazis; however, his advisers considered the Nazis useful, and in 1933 he was persuaded to appoint ADOLF HITLER chancellor.

Hindenburg.
CULVER PICTURES

Hindenburg disaster Explosion of the dirigible *Hindenburg,* the largest rigid AIRSHIP ever constructed. Launched in 1936 in Germany, it started the first commercial air service across the North Atlantic and made 10 successful round trips. On May 6, 1937, as it was landing in Lakehurst, N.J., its hydrogen gas burst into flames, destroying the airship and killing 36 of the 97 persons aboard. The disaster, recorded on film and tape, effectively ended the use of rigid airships in commercial transportation.

Hindi language INDO-ARYAN LANGUAGE of India, spoken or understood by more than 30% of the country's population. Modern Standard Hindi is a LINGUA FRANCA (as well as native language) of millions of people in North India and the official language of the Indian Union. It is effectively a continuation of Hindustani, which developed from Khari Boli, the speech of certain classes and districts in Delhi affiliated with the Mughal court in the 16th–18th century. A heavily Persianized variant of Khari Boli used by Muslim authors formed the basis for URDU. Hindustani was codified by the British at Fort William College in Calcutta (now Kolkata). There Hindu intellectuals promoted a Sanskritized form of Hindustani (see SANSKRIT LANGUAGE) written in the Devanagari script (see INDIC WRITING SYSTEMS) in the late 18th and early 19th century; it became the progenitor of modern literary Hindi as used by Hindu authors. During the Indian independence movement, Hindustani was regarded as a national unifying factor, but after the partition in 1947 this attitude changed, and the name has practically dropped from use in favor of either Hindi or Urdu. Linguists, particularly GEORGE ABRAHAM GRIERSON, have also used the term Hindi to refer collectively to all the dialects and regional literary languages of the northern Indian plain (see INDO-ARYAN LANGUAGES). Hindi has drastically simplified the complex grammar of Old Indo-Aryan while preserving certain phonetic features.

Hindu-Arabic numerals Set of 10 symbols—1, 2, 3, 4, 5, 6, 7, 8, 9, 0—that represent numbers in the decimal NUMBER SYSTEM. They originated in India in the 6th or 7th century and were introduced to Europe through Arab mathematicians around the 12th century (see AL-KHWARIZMI). They represented a profound break with previous methods of counting, such as the ABACUS, and paved the way for the development of ALGEBRA.

Hindu Kush \ˈhin-dü-ˈku̇sh\ *Latin* **Caucasus Indicus.** Mountain system, Central Asia. Some 600 mi (950 km) long, it forms a water divide between the AMU DARYA River valley to the northwest and the INDUS RIVER valley to the southeast, and runs from the PAMIRS in the east near the Pakistan–China border through Pakistan to western Afghanistan. Its passes have historically been of great military significance, providing access to the northern plains of India. It includes about two dozen summits of more than 23,000 ft (7,000 m), including the highest, Tirich Mir, at 25,260 ft (7,699 m).

Hinduism Oldest of the world's major religions. It evolved from the VEDIC RELIGION of ancient India. Though the various Hindu sects each rely on their own set of scriptures, they all revere the ancient VEDAS, which were brought to India by Aryan invaders after 1200 BC. The philosophical Vedic texts called the UPANISHADS explored the search for knowledge that would allow mankind to escape the cycle of REINCARNATION. Fundamental to Hinduism is the belief in a cosmic principle of ultimate reality called BRAHMAN, and its identity with the individual soul, or ATMAN. All creatures go through a cycle of rebirth, or SAMSARA, which can only be broken by spiritual self-realization, after which liberation, or MOKSHA, is attained. The principle of KARMA determines a being's status within the cycle of rebirth. The greatest Hindu deities are BRAHMA, VISHNU, and SHIVA. The numerous other Hindu gods are mostly viewed as incarnations or epiphanies of the main deities, though some are survivors of the pre-Aryan era. The major sources of classical mythology are the *MAHABHARATA* (which includes the BHAGAVADGITA, the most important religious text of Hinduism), the *RAMAYANA*, and the PURANAS. The hierarchical social structure of the CASTE system is important in Hinduism; it is supported by the principle of DHARMA. The major branches of Hinduism are VAISHNAVISM and SHAIVISM, each of which includes many different sects.

Major Hindu Holidays

Date	Name	Significance
Caitra (Mar.–Apr.) Shukla ("waxing fortnight") 9	Ramanavami ("ninth of Rama")	celebrates the birth of Rama
Vaishakha (Apr.–May)		
Jyaistha (May–June)		
Asadha (June–July) Sh. 2	Rathayatra ("pilgrimage of the chariot")	famous Jagannatha festival of the temple complex at Puri, Orissa
Shravana (July–Aug.) Krsna ("waning fortnight") 8	Janmastami ("eighth day of the birth")	birthday of the god Krishna
Bhadrapada (Aug.–Sept.) Sh. 4	Ganeshacaturthi ("fourth of Ganesha")	honors Ganesha, a particular favorite in Maharashtra
Ashvina (Sept.–Oct.) Sh. 7–10	Durga-puja ("homage to Durga")	special to Bengal, in honor of the goddess Durga
Ashvina Sh. 7–10	Dashahra ("ten days"), or Dussera	celebrating Rama's victory over Ravana; traditional beginning of the warring season
Ashvina Sh. 15	Lakshmipuja ("homage to Lakshmi")	date on which commercial books are closed, and new annual records begun
Karttika (Oct.–Nov.) K. 15 and Sh. 1	Dipavali, Divali ("strings of lights")	festival of lights, when light is carried from the waning to the waxing fortnight
Margashirsa (Nov.–Dec.) K. 13	Maha-shivaratri ("great night of Shiva")	honors Shiva on the blackest night of the month
Pausa (Dec.–Jan.) Sh. 15	Guru Nanak Jayanti	birthday of Nanak, founder of Sikhism
Magha (Jan.–Feb.)		
Phalguna (Feb.–Mar.) Sh. 14	Holi (name of a demoness)	fertility and role-changing festival, scene of great teasing of superiors
Phalguna Sh. 15	Dolayatra ("swing festival")	scene of the famous hook-swinging rites of Orissa

In the 20th century Hinduism blended with Indian nationalism to become a potent political force.

Hindustan Name for India. It was historically applied to northern India, in contrast to the DECCAN, or southern India. It included the region bounded on the north by the HIMALAYAS and on the south by the Vindhya Mountains and Narmada River, comprising the GANGES RIVER valley from the PUNJAB to ASSAM. The name was also applied to a small area comprising the upper basin of the Ganges.

Hine, Lewis (Wickes) (1874–1940) U.S. photographer. Born in Oshkosh, Wis., he was trained as a sociologist. In 1904 he began to photograph immigrants at ELLIS ISLAND and the tenements and sweatshops where they lived and worked. In 1911 he was hired by the National Child Labor Committee to record child labor conditions. Traveling throughout the East, he produced appalling pictures of exploited children. In World War I he worked as a photographer with the Red Cross. On returning to New York, he photographed the construction of the EMPIRE STATE BUILDING. For the rest of his life he photographed government projects.

Hines, Earl (Kenneth) (1903–1983) U.S. pianist and bandleader who had a profound influence on the development of jazz piano. Hines was born in Duquesne, Pa. Known as "Fatha" Hines, he was a pianist of amazing technical command and tireless energy. Breaking with the stride tradition, he emulated the single-note instruments (e.g., trumpet) in creating melodic variations of the melody with the right hand. Hines led a successful Chicago-based big band from 1928 to 1948. He was influenced by LOUIS ARMSTRONG, and the two performed together frequently throughout their careers; their recorded encounters from the late 1920s, particularly "Weather Bird," are jazz classics.

hip-hop See RAP

Hipparchus *or* **Hipparchos** \hi-'pär-kəs\ (died after 127 BC) Greek astronomer and mathematician. He discovered the PRECESSION of the equinoxes, calculated the length of the year to within 6.5 minutes, compiled the first known star catalog, and made an early formulation of trigonometry. His observations were painstaking and extremely accurate. He rejected all astrology but also sun-centered views of the universe; his views had a profound influence on PTOLEMY. His star catalog logged the positions of the stars in terms of CELESTIAL COORDINATES, listed about 850 stars, and specified their brightnesses by a system of six magnitudes similar to today's. He determined that the moon has an elliptical, somewhat irregular orbit. His main contribution to geography was to apply rigorous mathematical principles to the determination of places on the earth's surface, and he was the first to do so by specifying latitude and longitude.

Hippias (died 490 BC) Tyrant of Athens (528/527–510). He succeeded his father PEISISTRATUS as TYRANT. He was a patron of poets and craftsmen, and Athens prospered under his rule, but he became repressive after the assassination of his brother Hipparchus (514). He was overthrown by the Spartans (510) and exiled himself to Asia Minor. A Spartan attempt to restore him failed, and he sought Persian help. He went with the Persians to attack the Athenians, and it was he who advised DARIUS I in 490 to land at MARATHON, which resulted in a major Persian defeat.

Hippocrates \hi-'pä-krə-,tēz\ (460?–377? BC) Greek physician regarded as the father of medicine. Meno, a pupil of ARISTOTLE, stated that Hippocrates believed that disease was caused by the excreted vapors of undigested food. His philosophy was to see the body as a whole. He apparently traveled widely in Greece and Asia Minor, practicing and teaching. The "Hippocratic Collection" supposedly belonged to the library of a medical school (probably at Cos, Hippocrates' birthplace) and then to the library at Alexandria. An unknown proportion of the 60 or so surviving manuscripts—the earliest dating from the 10th century AD—are actually by Hippocrates. The collection deals with anatomy, clinical subjects, diseases of women and children, prognosis, treatment, surgery, and medical ethics. The Hippocratic Oath (not actually written by Hippocrates), also part of the Hippocratic Collection, is divided into two major sections, the first setting out the physician's obligations to his students and his pupils' duties to him, the second pledging him to prescribe only beneficial treatments, refrain from causing harm or hurt, and live an exemplary life.

Hippocrates, Roman bust copied from a Greek original, c. 3rd century BC; in the collection of the Antichità Di Ostia, Italy.

BY COURTESY OF THE SOPRINTENDENZA ALLE ANTICHITA DI OSTIA, ITALY

hippopotamus Amphibious African mammal *(Hippopotamus amphibius)*, the largest nonruminating, even-toed UNGULATE. Once found throughout sub-Saharan Africa, it is now restricted to parts of eastern and southeastern Africa. It has a barrel-shaped body, an enormous mouth, short legs, and four toes on each foot. It may reach a length of 15 ft (4.6 m), a height of 5 ft (1.5 m) at the shoulder, and a weight of 6,500–10,000 lbs (3,000–4,500 kg). The skin is very thick, nearly hairless, and grayish brown above, lighter and pinkish below. The ears and nostrils protrude above water when the rest of the body is submerged. Hippopotamuses live near rivers, lakes, swamps, or other permanent bodies of water, usually in groups of seven to 15. During the day, they sleep and rest in or near the water. At night they go on land to feed on grasses, which they crop with their horny lips. In water they can swim fast, walk along the bottom, and remain submerged (with ears and nostrils closed) for as long as 10 minutes.

Hira \'hir-ə\ *Arabic* **al-Hirah** \ȧl-'hir-ə\ Ancient kingdom, South Asia. Occupying the area of the lower EUPHRATES RIVER valley and the upper part of the PERSIAN GULF, it was ruled by the Lakhmid dynasty (3rd century AD–602), who themselves were subordinate to the SASANIANS of Persia. Its chief town, also named Hira, was a diplomatic, political, and military center, and an important station on the Persia–Arabia caravan route. Tradition holds that the Arabic script was developed there. Also the seat of a bishopric for NESTORIAN Christians, it promoted Christian monotheism in the ARABIAN PENINSULA. Hira began to decline early in the 7th century, and in 633 the town was taken by the Muslims.

Hirata Atsutane \ˌhē-ˈrä-tä-ˌä-tsu̇-ˈtä-nā\ (1776–1843) Leader of the Japanese Restoration SHINTO school. Born in Akita, he settled in Edo (modern Tokyo) at 20 and became a disciple of MOTOORI NORINAGA. Hirata sought to develop a Shinto theological system offering principles for social and political action. He proclaimed the natural superiority of Japan and championed the imperial line. For criticizing the TOKUGAWA SHOGUNATE, which had reduced the emperor to a powerless symbol, he was punished by being confined to his birthplace for the rest of his life. His theories helped bring about the shogunate's overthrow, and he influenced 20th-century Shinto and Japanese nationalism.

Hirohito \ˌhir-ō-ˈhē-tō\ *or* **Showa emperor** \ˈshō-ə\ (1901–1989) Longest-reigning of Japan's monarchs (1926–89). His rule coincided with Japan's 20th-century militarism and its aggression against China and S.East Asia and in the Pacific Ocean during World War II. Though the MEIJI CONSTITUTION invested the emperor with supreme authority, in practice he merely ratified the policies formulated by his ministers and advisers. Historians debate whether Hirohito could have diverted Japan from its militaristic path and what responsibility he should bear for the actions of the government and military during the war. In August 1945 he broke the precedent of imperial silence when he made a national radio broadcast to announce Japan's surrender, and in 1946 he made a second broadcast to repudiate the traditional quasi-divine status of Japan's emperors.

Hiroshige Ando \ˌhir-ə-ˈshē-gā-ˈän-dō\ *known as* **Utagawa Hiroshige** *or* **Ichiyusai Hiroshige** *orig.* **Ando Tokutaro** (1797–1858) Japanese artist and master of the color woodblock print. He became a pupil of the UKIYO-E master Utagawa Toyohiro in Edo (now Tokyo) c. 1811. In 1833–34 a series of 55 landscape prints, *Fifty-three Stages on the Tokaido,* established him as one of the most popular *ukiyo-e* artists of all time. Demand for his figure-with-landscape designs became so great that overproduction diminished their quality. He produced more than 5,000 prints, and 10,000 copies were made from some of his woodcuts. His genius was first recognized in the West by the Impressionists and Postimpressionists, on whom he exerted much influence. See also EDO PERIOD.

Hiroshima \hə-ˈrō-shə-mə, ˌhir-ə-ˈshē-mə\ City (pop., 1996 est.: 1,109,000), southwestern HONSHU, Japan. Founded as a castle town in the 16th century, it was from 1868 a military center. In 1945 it became the first city ever to be struck by an ATOMIC BOMB, dropped by the U.S. in an effort to end World War II. Rebuilding began in 1950, and Hiroshima is now the largest industrial city in the region. It has become a spiritual center of the peace movement to ban atomic weapons; Peace Memorial Park is dedicated to those killed by the bomb, and Atomic Bomb Memorial Dome is the remains of the only building to survive the blast.

Cenotaph in Peace Memorial Park, Hiroshima, Japan; Atomic Bomb Dome is visible through the arch.
BOB GLAZE—ARTSTREET

Hirsch \ˈhirsh\, **Samson Raphael** (1808–1888) German Jewish scholar. He served as rabbi in Oldenburg, Emden, Nikolsburg, and Frankfurt am Main. In his *Nineteen Letters of Ben Uziel* (1836), he expounded his system of Neo-Orthodoxy, which helped make ORTHODOX JUDAISM viable in 19th-century Germany. He advocated blending strict schooling in the Torah with modern secular education, and he argued that Orthodox Jews should separate from the larger Jewish community in defense of their traditions. His many works include commentaries on the Pentateuch and an Orthodox textbook on Judaism.

Hirschfeld, Al(bert) (born 1903) U.S. caricaturist. Born in St. Louis, he has lived mostly in New York. He studied art in Europe and traveled in the Far East, where Japanese and Javanese art influenced his graphic style. He is especially known for his stylish drawings in the *New York Times* over many decades (since 1929) portraying show-business personalities, in which readers have long enjoyed hunting for the name of his daughter, Nina. Hirschfeld has also illustrated many books and produced watercolors, lithographs, etchings, and sculptures.

His \ˈhis\, **Wilhelm** (1863–1934) Swiss cardiologist. His father, Wilhelm His (1831–1904), first realized that each nerve fiber stems from a single neuron, and invented the microtome, a device used to slice thin tissue sections for microscopic examination. The younger His discovered (1893) the specialized muscle fibers (bundle of His) running along the septum between the heart's left and right chambers. He found that they help communicate a single rhythm of contraction to all parts of the heart, and he was one of the first to recognize that the heartbeat originates in individual cells of heart muscle.

Hispaniola \ˌhis-pən-ˈyō-lə\ *Spanish* **Española** \ˌes-pä-ˈnyō-lä\ Island, central West Indies. The second-largest West Indian island, it lies east of Cuba. It is divided into Haiti to the west and the Dominican Republic to the east. The island is some 400 mi (650 km) long and 150 mi (241 km) wide at its widest point. CHRISTOPHER COLUMBUS landed there in 1492. The Spanish wiped out the natives and settled the island with African slaves. The slaves rebelled in the late 18th century; led by TOUSSAINT-LOUVERTURE and J.-J. DESSALINES, it became independent in 1804, forming the Republic of Haiti. In 1843 the eastern part rebelled and the Dominican Republic was formed.

Hiss, Alger (1904–1996) U.S. government official. Born in Baltimore, he attended Harvard Law School and clerked for OLIVER WENDELL, JR. HOLMES. He worked at the U.S. State Department in the 1930s, attended the Yalta Conference as an adviser to F. Roosevelt, was briefly temporary secretary general of the fledgling U.N., and served as head of the Carnegie Endowment for International Peace 1946–49. In 1948 WHITTAKER CHAMBERS testified before the House Committee on Un-American Activities that Hiss had been a fellow member of a Communist spy ring in the 1930s. Hiss sued Chambers for slander when the charge was made public, unprotected by congressional immunity. When Chambers produced State Department documents that Hiss had allegedly given him to pass to the Soviets, Hiss was indicted for perjury. His first trial ended with a hung jury in 1949; at his second trial (1950) he was found guilty. He was released from jail in 1954, still protesting his innocence. In 1992 newly opened Russian archives found no evidence that Hiss was a Soviet spy, but in 1996 U.S. security documents suggested that he could have been the Soviet agent "Ales." The Hiss case ushered in the JOSEPH MCCARTHY era and brought RICHARD NIXON fame as a congressional investigator.

histamine \ˈhis-tə-ˌmēn\ Organic compound found in nearly all animal tissues, in microorganisms, and in some plants. Its release makes blood vessels dilate and become more permeable, causing the runny nose, watery eyes, and tissue swelling of HAY FEVER and some other ALLERGIES; histamine also affects gastric juice secretion and smooth muscle contraction and is implicated in anaphylactic shock (see ANAPHYLAXIS). Stinging nettles and certain insect VENOMS contain histamine. In humans, histamine is formed by removal of a carboxyl group from HISTIDINE. Its effects are counteracted by ANTIHISTAMINES.

histidine \ˈhis-tə-ˌdēn\ One of the essential AMINO ACIDS, first isolated in 1896. It occurs abundantly in HEMOGLOBIN and can be isolated from blood corpuscles. It is used in medicine and biochemical research and as a dietary supplement and feed additive.

histogram *or* **bar graph** GRAPH using vertical or horizontal bars whose lengths indicate quantities. Along with the pie chart, the histogram is the most common format for representing statistical data. Its advantage is that it not only clearly shows the largest and smallest categories but gives an immediate impression of the distribution of the data. In fact, a histogram is a representation of a FREQUENCY DISTRIBUTION.

histology \his-ˈtä-lə-jē\ Branch of biology concerned with the composition and structure of plant and animal tissues in relation to their specialized functions. Its aim is to determine how tissues are organized at all structural levels, from cells and intercellular substances to organs. Histologists examine extremely thin slices of human tissue under microscopes, using dye to increase the contrast between cellular components.

histone Any of a class of rather simple PROTEINS occurring in cell nuclei and in combination with DNA to form NUCLEOPROTEINS. They can be obtained from both plants and animals. Unlike most proteins, they dissolve readily in water. They were discovered c. 1884.

historical school of economics See GERMAN HISTORICAL SCHOOL OF ECONOMICS

historiography \hi-ˌstōr-ē-ˈä-grə-fē\ Writing of history, especially that based on the critical examination of sources and the synthesis of chosen particulars from those sources into a narrative that will stand the test of critical methods. Two major tendencies in history writing are evident from the beginnings of the Western tradition: the concept of historiography as the accumulation of records and the concept of history as storytelling, filled with explanations of cause and effect. In the 5th century BC the Greek historians HERODOTUS and, later, THUCYDIDES emphasized firsthand inquiry in their efforts to impose a narrative on contemporary events. The dominance of Christian historiography by the 4th century introduced the idea of world history as a result of divine intervention in human affairs, an idea that prevailed throughout the Middle Ages in the work of such historians as BEDE. HUMANISM and the gradual secularization of critical thought influenced early modern European historiography. The 19th and 20th century saw the development of modern methods of historical investigation of scientific history based on the use of primary source materials. Modern historians, aiming for a fuller picture of the past, have tried to reconstruct a record of ordinary human activities and practices; the French *Annales* school has been influential in this respect.

history, philosophy of Branch of philosophy concerned with questions about the meaningfulness of history and the nature of historical explanation. Philosophy of history in the traditional sense is conceived to be a first-order inquiry, its subject matter being the historical process as a whole and its broad aim being to provide an overall elucidation of its course. As a second-order inquiry, philosophy of history focuses on the methods by which practicing historians treat the human past. The former, often referred to as speculative philosophy of history, has had a long and varied career; the latter, known as critical or analytical philosophy of history, rose to prominence only in the 20th century.

history play See CHRONICLE PLAY

Hitchcock, Alfred *later* **Sir Alfred** (1899–1980) British-U.S. film director. He worked in the London office of a U.S. film company from 1920 and was promoted to director in 1925. His film *The Lodger* (1926) concerned an ordinary person caught in extraordinary events, a theme that was to recur in many of his films. Fascinated with voyeurism and crime, he proved himself the master of the thriller with *The Man Who Knew Too Much* (1934), *The 39 Steps* (1935), and *The Lady Vanishes* (1938). For his first U.S. film, *Rebecca* (1940), he created a suspenseful psychological drama out of a romantic novel, and his virtuosity was evident in such celebrated later films as *Lifeboat* (1944), *Spellbound* (1945), *Notorious* (1946), *Rear Window* (1954), *Vertigo* (1958), *North by Northwest* (1959), *Psycho* (1960), *The Birds* (1963), and *Frenzy* (1972).

Hitchings, George Herbert (1905–1998) U.S. pharmacologist. Born in Hoquiam, Wash., he earned a PhD from Harvard University. Over nearly 40 years, he and GERTRUDE ELION designed a variety of new drugs that work by interfering with replication or other vital functions of specific disease-causing agents, including drugs to treat leukemia, severe rheumatoid arthritis and other autoimmune diseases (also useful for suppressing rejection after organ transplants), gout, malaria, urinary and respiratory-tract infections, and herpes simplex. In 1988 he shared a Nobel Prize with Elion and JAMES BLACK.

Hitler, Adolf (1889–1945) Dictator of Nazi Germany (1933–45). Born in Austria, he had little success as an artist in Vienna before moving to Munich in 1913. As a soldier in the German army in World War I, he was wounded and gassed. After the war, resentful about defeat and the peace terms, he joined the German Workers' Party in Munich (1919). In 1920 he became head of propaganda for the renamed National Socialists, or NAZI PARTY, and in 1921 party leader. He set out to create a mass movement, using unrelenting propaganda. The party's rapid growth climaxed in the BEER HALL PUTSCH (1923), for which he served nine months in prison; there he started to write his virulent autobiography, *Mein Kampf*. Regarding inequality between races as part of the natural order, he exalted the "Aryan race" while propounding anti-Semitism, anticommunism, and extreme German nationalism. The economic slump of 1929 renewed his power. In the Reichstag elections of 1930 the Nazis became the country's second-largest party, and in 1932 the largest. Hitler ran for president in 1932 and lost, but he entered into intrigues to gain legitimate power, and in 1933 PAUL VON HINDENBURG invited him to be chancellor. Adopting the title of *Führer* ("Leader"), he gained dictatorial powers by the ENABLING ACT and suppressed opposition with assistance from HEINRICH HIMMLER and JOSEPH GOEBBELS. Hitler also began to enact anti-Jewish measures, leading to the HOLOCAUST. His aggressive foreign policy led to the signing of the MUNICH AGREEMENT. He became allied with BENITO MUSSOLINI in the ROME–BERLIN AXIS. The GERMAN–SOVIET NONAGGRESSION PACT (1939) enabled him to invade Poland, precipitating WORLD WAR II. After early successes in the war, he often ignored his generals and met dissent with ruthlessness. As defeat grew imminent in 1945, he married EVA BRAUN in an underground bunker in Berlin, and the next day they committed suicide.

Hitler–Stalin Pact See GERMAN–SOVIET NONAGGRESSION PACT

Hitler Youth *German* **Hitler-Jugend** \ˌyü-gent\ Organization set up by ADOLF HITLER in 1933 for educating and training male youths aged 13–18 in Nazi principles. Under the leadership of Baldur von Schirach (1907–1974), by 1935 it included almost 60% of all German boys, and by 1936 it became a state agency that all young "Aryan" Germans were expected to join. The youths lived a Spartan life of dedication, fellowship, and Nazi conformity, with little parental guidance. A parallel organization, the League of German Girls, trained girls for domestic duties and motherhood.

Hito-no-michi \hē-ˈtō-ˌnō-ˈmē-chē\ Japanese religious sect founded by Miki Tokuharu (1871–1938). It was based on an earlier religious movement founded by Kanada Tokumitsu (1863–1919), who taught that the sufferings of his followers could be transferred to him by divine mediation so that he could endure their troubles vicariously. Though compelled by the government to ally itself with SHINTO, Hito-no-michi continued its unorthodox teachings and gathered a following of more than 600,000 by 1934. It was ordered disbanded in 1937; Tokuharu and his son Miki Tokuchika were jailed, and Tokuharu died the next year. In 1945 Miki Tokuchika was released, and he revived the sect under the name PL KYODAN.

Hitomaro See KAKINOMOTO NO HITOMARO

Hittite \ˈhi-ˌtīt\ Indo-European people whose empire (Old Kingdom c. 1700–1500 BC, New Empire c. 1500–1380 BC) was centered in Anatolia and northern Syria. Old Kingdom records detail Hittite territorial expansion; New Empire documents contain accounts of the battle of KADESH fought against Egypt, one of the greatest battles of the ancient world. Hittite kings had absolute power and were deputies of the gods, at death becoming gods themselves. Hittite society was feudal and agrarian; iron-working technology was developed. The empire fell abruptly, possibly because of large-scale migrations of SEA PEOPLES and Phrygians to the area.

HIV *in full* **human immunodeficiency virus** RETROVIRUS associated with AIDS. HIV attacks and gradually destroys the IMMUNE SYSTEM, leaving the host unprotected against infection. It cannot be spread through casual contact, but instead is contracted mainly through exposure to blood and blood products (e.g., by sharing hypodermic needles or by accidental needle sticks), semen and female genital secretions, or breast milk. A pregnant woman can pass the virus to her fetus across the placenta. The virus first multiplies in lymph nodes near the site of infection. Once it spreads through the body, usually about 10 years later, symptoms appear, marking the onset of AIDS. Multi-drug "cocktails" can delay onset, but missing doses can lead to DRUG RESISTANCE. Like other viruses, HIV needs a host cell to multiply. It attacks helper T CELLS and can infect other cells. A rapid MUTATION rate helps it foil both the immune system and treatment attempts. No vaccine or cure exists. Abstinence from sex, use of condoms or other means to prevent sexual transmittal of the disease, and avoidance of needle sharing have reduced infection rates in some areas.

hives *or* **urticaria** \ˌər-tə-ˈkar-ē-ə\ Allergic skin reaction in which slightly raised, flat-topped, very itchy swellings appear suddenly. The acute form, probably most often caused by food ALLERGIES, subsides in 6–24 hours, but the chronic form, believed to be due to emotional and mental stress, lasts much longer. Acute hives may also be triggered by drugs, especially PENICILLIN, inhaled allergens or TOXINS, or diseases. Treatment involves identifying and avoiding the allergen; EPINEPHRINE and ANTIHISTAMINES may help the acute skin symptoms.

Hiwassee River \hī-ˈwä-sē\ River, southeastern U.S. Rising in the BLUE RIDGE MTNS. in northern Georgia, it flows 132 mi (213 km) into North

Carolina and southeastern Tennessee to join the Tennessee River at the Chickamauga Reservoir. It has three major Tennessee Valley Authority dams. The endangered snail darter was transplanted to the Hiwassee in the 1970s.

Hizbullah *or* **Hezbollah** \ˌhiz-bu̇l-ˈlä\ (Arabic: "Party of God") Militant Islamist organization founded in 1982 in southern Lebanon in response to the Israeli invasion and the Iranian Revolution (1979). Its goals are to push Israel out of Lebanon and to form an Iranian-style Shiite Islamic republic in Lebanon. Its political stance is anti-West, and it is suspected of involvement in many of the terrorist activities of the 1980s in Lebanon, including kidnappings, bombings, and hijackings. In the 1990s Hizbullah candidates won seats in Lebanon's parliamentary elections. See also Ayatollah Sayyid Muhammad Hussayn Fadhlallah.

HMO See health maintenance organization

Hmong \ˈhmȯŋ\ *or* **Miao** \mē-ˈau̇\ Mountain-dwelling peoples of China, Vietnam, Laos, and Thailand who speak Sino-Tibetan dialects. Agriculture is the chief means of subsistence for the Hmong throughout their territories; they grow corn and rice and raise opium as a cash crop. Most venerate spirits, demons, and ancestral ghosts, and animal sacrifice is widespread. Households are multigenerational. In China many Hmong follow the Chinese practice of arranged marriage.

Hmong-Mien languages \ˈməŋ-ˈmyen\ *or* **Miao-Yao languages** \mē-ˈau̇-ˈyau̇\ Language family of southern China, northern Vietnam, Laos, and northern Thailand, with more than 9 million speakers. Hmong (Miao, Meo) has been divided into three dialect groups, Western, Central, and Northern. Beginning in the 18th century, groups of Western dialect speakers emigrated into northern Indochina. In the aftermath of the Indochina wars that ended in 1975, many Hmong fled from Laos to Thailand. Some were eventually resettled in the U.S., which now has perhaps 150,000 Western dialect speakers. Mien (Yao) has three major dialects; the largest, Mien (Mian), accounts for about 85% of Mien-speakers. Though structurally similar to other languages of the area, most notably Chinese, no genetic relationship between Hmong-Mien and any other language family has been demonstrated.

Ho Chi Minh *orig.* **Nguyen Sinh Cung** (1890–1969) President (1945–69) of the Democratic Republic of Vietnam (North Vietnam). Son of a poor scholar, he was brought up in a rural village. In 1911 he found work on a French steamer and traveled the world, then spent six years in France, where he became a socialist. In 1923 he went to the Soviet Union; the next year he went to China, where he started organizing exiled Vietnamese. He founded the Indochina Communist Party in 1930 and its successor, the Viet Minh, in 1941. In 1945 Japan overran Indochina, overthrowing its French colonial rulers; when they surrendered to the Allies, Ho and his Viet Minh forces took Hanoi and proclaimed Vietnamese independence. France refused to relinquish its former colony, and the First Indochina War broke out in 1946. Ho's forces defeated the French in 1954 at Dien Bien Phu, after which the country was partitioned into North and South Vietnam. Ho, who ruled in the north, was soon embroiled with the U.S.-backed regime of Ngo Dinh Diem in the south in what became known as the Vietnam War; North Vietnamese forces prevailed six years after Ho's death.

Ho Chi Minh City *formerly* **Saigon** \ˈsī-ˌgän\ City (pop., 1993 est.: 4,322,000), southern Vietnam. It lies along the Saigon River north of the Mekong River delta. The Vietnamese first entered the region, then part of the kingdom of Cambodia, in the 17th century. In 1862 the area, including the town, was ceded to France. After World War II Vietnam declared its independence, but French troops seized control and the First Indochina War began. The Geneva conference in 1954 divided the country, and Saigon became the capital of South Vietnam. In the Vietnam War, it was the headquarters for U.S. military operations; it was captured by North Vietnamese troops in 1975 and renamed for Ho Chi Minh. Rebuilding since the war has promoted its commercial importance.

Ho Chi Minh Trail Former trail system, extending from northern Vietnam to southern Vietnam. It was opened in 1959 and used by North Vietnamese troops in the Vietnam War as the major military supply route. Starting south of Hanoi, the main trail traversed Laos and Cambodia on its way to South Vietnam and required more than a month's march to travel. With underground support facilities, including hospitals and weapons caches, it was the main route for the invasion of South Vietnam in 1975.

Ho-fei See Hefei

Ho-shen See Heshen

Hoar, Ebenezer R(ockwood) (1816–1895) U.S. politician. Born in Concord, Mass., he became a lawyer known for his outspoken antislavery views. He was elected to the state senate as a member of the antislavery Whigs, or "Conscience Whigs." Later he helped form the Free Soil and Republican parties in Massachusetts. He served on the state supreme court (1859–69), was briefly U.S. attorney general (1869–70), and was elected to the U.S. House of Representatives (1873–75).

Hoar, George Frisbie (1826–1904) U.S. politician. Born in Concord, Mass., he became a lawyer and helped form the Free Soil Party in Massachusetts. With his brother, Ebenezer Hoar, and father, Samuel Hoar (1778–1856), he helped organize the Republican Party. He served in the U.S. House of Representatives (1869–77) and Senate (1877–1904). He championed civil-service reform and was an outspoken foe of the American Protective Assn.

Hoare, Sir Samuel (John Gurney) *later* **Viscount Templewood (of Chelsea)** (1880–1959) British statesman. As secretary of state for India (1931–35), he had the immense task of developing and defending in debate the new Indian constitution and was a chief architect of the Government of India Act (1935). For his role in developing the unpopular Hoare–Laval Pact while foreign secretary (1935), he was forced to resign. As home secretary (1937–39) he helped develop the Munich Agreement, which marked him as an appeaser and damaged his reputation. In World War II he was ambassador to Spain (1940–44).

Hoare-Laval Pact (1935) Secret plan to offer Benito Mussolini most of Ethiopia (then called Abyssinia) in return for a truce in the Italo–Ethiopian War. It was put together by British foreign secretary Sir Samuel Hoare and French premier Pierre Laval, who tried and failed to achieve a rapprochement between France and Italy. When news of the plan leaked out, it drew immediate and widespread denunciation.

Hobart City (pop., 1995: 195,000), chief port, and capital, Tasmania, Australia. Located on the Derwent River estuary at the base of Mount Wellington, it is Tasmania's largest and Australia's most southerly city. Established in 1803, it became a major port for ships whaling in the southern oceans. Its lack of natural resources limited its development. It now has a deepwater port, rail lines, and an airport, making it a focus of communications and trade. The city is the site of Anglican and Roman Catholic cathedrals and the first Jewish synagogue in Australia (built 1843–45).

Hobbema \ˈhä-bə-mə\, **Meindert** *orig.* **Meyndert Lubbertsz(oon)** (1638–1709) Dutch landscape painter. He worked principally in Amsterdam, painting quiet rural scenes studded with trees, rustic buildings, peaceful streams, and water mills. In 1689 he produced his masterpiece, *The Avenue, Middelharnis*. Though he apparently had little success in his lifetime, his work became popular and influential in England in the 19th century.

Hobbes \ˈhäbz\, **Thomas** (1588–1679) British philosopher and political theorist. The son of a vicar who abandoned his family, Hobbes was raised by his uncle. He graduated from Oxford Univ., then became a tutor and traveled with his pupil in Europe, where he engaged Galileo in philosophical discussions on the nature of motion. He later turned to political theory and wrote out his support for absolutism, which put him at odds with the rising antiroyalist sentiment of the time. He fled to Paris in 1640, where he tutored the future Charles II of England and wrote his best-known work, *Leviathan* (1651), in which he reasserted his absolutist position and argued against separation of church and state. He returned to Britain in 1651 after the death of Charles I. In 1666 Parliament threatened to investigate

Hobbes, detail of an oil painting by John Michael Wright, in the National Portrait Gallery, London.

BY COURTESY OF THE NATIONAL PORTRAIT GALLERY, LONDON

him as an atheist. He is regarded as a pioneer of UTILITARIANISM (he justified obedience to moral rules as the means to peaceable, comfortable living), modern POLITICAL SCIENCE, and RATIONALISM.

Hobby, Oveta Culp *orig.* **Oveta Culp** (1905–1995) U.S. publisher and government official. Born in Killeen, Texas, she became parliamentarian of the Texas legislature (1925–31). She married William P. Hobby, publisher of the *Houston Post-Dispatch*, and became its executive vice president (1938). She headed the Women's Auxiliary Army Corps (later WOMEN'S ARMY CORPS) 1942–45. In 1953 she was appointed director of the Federal Security Agency, which was reorganized as the Department of Health, Education, and Welfare; as secretary of the department (1953–55), she was the second woman to hold a U.S. cabinet position. She became chairman of the *Post*'s board in 1965.

Hobhouse, L(eonard) T(relawny) (1864–1929) British sociologist known for his comparative studies of social development. He sought to correlate social change with its contribution to the general advance of the community, focusing especially on the intellectual, moral, and religious elements of change. He taught at the Universities of Oxford and London. Among his works are *Morals in Evolution* (1906), *The Rational Good* (1921), and *Elements of Social Justice* (1922).

Hobsbawm \'häbz-ˌbȯm\, **Eric J(ohn Ernest)** (born 1917) English historian. He received his PhD from Cambridge Univ., where he was a fellow 1949–55. Since 1982 he has been professor emeritus in economics at the University of London. His books include *Industry and Empire* (1968) and *The Invention of Tradition* (1983), but he is best known for his four-volume history of the West from 1789 to 1991, comprising *The Age of Revolution* (1962), *The Age of Capital* (1975), *The Age of Empire* (1987), and *The Age of Extremes* (1994).

Hockney, David (born 1937) British painter, draftsman, printmaker, photographer, and stage designer. He studied at the Bradford College of Art and the Royal College of Art in London. In the mid-1960s he taught at the Univs. of Iowa, Colorado, and California, and in 1978 he settled permanently in Los Angeles. His portraits, self-portraits, still lifes, and quiet scenes of friends are characterized by a frank, mundane realism and brilliant colors derived from Pop art. The California swimming pool became one of his favorite themes, as in *A Bigger Splash* (1967). A brilliant draftsman and printmaker, he published series of etchings, including illustrations for *Six Fairy Tales of the Brothers Grimm* (1969). In the 1970s he achieved prominence as a set designer for the opera and ballet. He later experimented with photography and photocollage, and still later with computer technology and printers.

Hodges, Johnny *orig.* **John Cornelius** (1907–1970) U.S. saxophonist, one of the greatest alto-saxophone stylists in jazz. Born in Cambridge, Mass., Hodges was encouraged and influenced by SIDNEY BECHET in the mid-1920s. He joined DUKE ELLINGTON's band in 1928 and quickly became its most prominent soloist. Except for a period when he led his own small group (1951–55), Hodges would remain with Ellington for the rest of his career. His peerless, soulful tone and rhythmic poise made him a master interpreter of both ballads and BLUES, and Ellington and BILLY STRAYHORN composed many pieces expressly for him.

Hodgkin, Dorothy M(ary) *orig.* **Dorothy Mary Crowfoot** (1910–1994) English chemist. After studying at Oxford and Cambridge, she went to work at Oxford. From 1942 to 1949 she worked on a structural analysis of penicillin. In 1948 she and her colleagues made the first X-ray photograph of vitamin B_{12}, one of the most complex nonprotein compounds, and they eventually completely determined its atomic arrangement. In 1969 she completed a similar three-dimensional analysis of insulin. Her work won her a 1964 Nobel Prize. She was chancellor of Bristol University 1970–88, and was known for her work for peace and international scientific cooperation. In 1965 she became the second woman ever awarded the Order of Merit.

Hodgkin's disease *or* **lymphoreticuloma** \ˌlim-fō-ri-ˌtik-yə-'lō-mə\ Most common malignant LYMPHOMA. It starts with local, painless swelling of lymph nodes and sometimes of the spleen, liver, or other organs, followed by weight loss, weakness, and lassitude. Diagnosis can be confirmed only by biopsy, usually from a lymph node. The cause remains unknown. Treatment with chemotherapy, radiation, or both depends on the stage of the disease. More than 90% of patients diagnosed early can be cured, as can many with advanced disease.

Hodgkinson, Eaton (1789–1861) British mathematician and civil engineer. From 1847 he taught at University College in London. Researching the STRENGTH OF MATERIALS, including CAST IRON, he developed a concept for determining the neutral line (where stress changes from tension to compression) in a beam subject to bending. His work led to experiments in materials strength to determine the strongest construction beam, and to the eventual design of the I-beam, also known as the "Hodgkinson's beam."

Hodna, Chott el *Arabic* **Shatt al-Hodna** \'shat-al-'hȯd-nə\ Shallow saline lake, northern central Algeria. At the bottom of an arid depression in the Hodna Plain, it acts as an interior drainage basin. It is subject to extreme evaporation and varies in size; it is often dry. Roman and premedieval settlement is evident in the vicinity, but there is little modern development.

Hoe, Robert and Richard (March) (1784–1833, 1812–1886) British-U.S. inventors. Father and son, they were born respectively in Hoes, Leicestershire (England), and New York City. They emigrated to the U.S. in 1803. In New York Robert cofounded a printing-equipment company, and in 1827 he introduced the cast-iron frame, which would soon replace the standard wooden frames used for printing presses. His improved version of the Napier cylinder PRINTING press was so superior that it supplanted all English-made presses in the U.S. Richard joined the company in 1827 and became its head on his father's death. He replaced the flatbed press with the first successful ROTARY PRESS (patented 1847). He followed this with the web press (1865) and the web perfecting press (1871), revolutionary improvements that made possible the large-circulation daily newspaper.

Hoff, Jacobus van't See Jacobus H. VAN'T HOFF

Hoffa, Jimmy *orig.* **James Riddle** (1913–1975?) U.S. labor leader. Born in Brazil, Ind., he moved with his family to Detroit in 1924, left school at 14, and began work as a stockboy and warehouseman. He became a labor organizer in the 1930s, rising in the TEAMSTERS UNION during the next two decades until he reached the office of president, which he held from 1957 to 1971. Known throughout the trucking industry as a tough bargainer, he played a key role in forging the first national freight-hauling agreement and helped make the Teamsters the largest labor union in the U.S. Long associated with underworld figures, he was sent to prison in 1967 for jury tampering, fraud, and conspiracy; his sentence was commuted by Pres. RICHARD NIXON in 1971. In 1975 he disappeared from a restaurant near Detroit; he is believed to have been murdered to prevent his retaking control of the union. His son, James Riddle Hoffa, Jr. (born 1941), was elected president of the Teamsters in 1999.

Hoffman, Abbie *orig.* **Abbott** (1936–1989) U.S. political radical. Born in Worcester, Mass., he attended Brandeis University and UC–Berkeley and became active in the civil rights movement. In 1968 he organized the Youth International Party (Yippies), which protested the Vietnam War and the U.S. political system. Arrested for disrupting the Democratic Party convention in Chicago in 1968, he gained widespread media attention for his antics at the trial of the so-called Chicago Seven. After he was arrested for selling drugs (1973), he went underground, underwent plastic surgery, and used the alias "Barry Freed" to work as an environmentalist in New York. He resurfaced in 1980, served a year in jail, and resumed his environmental work. Subject to depression, he committed suicide.

Hoffman, Dustin (born 1937) U.S. actor. Born in Los Angeles, he acted in off-Broadway plays from 1965 and made his screen debut in *The Graduate* (1967), a phenomenal hit. He played a remarkable range of characters in such films as *Midnight Cowboy* (1969), *Little Big Man* (1970), *All the President's Men* (1976), *Kramer vs. Kramer* (1979, Academy Award), *Tootsie* (1982), *Rain Man* (1988, Academy Award), and *Wag the Dog* (1997). He returned to the Broadway stage in a revival of *Death of a Salesman* (1984), repeating the role for television (1985, Emmy award), and played Shylock in *The Merchant of Venice* in London (1989) and New York (1990).

Hoffman, Samuel (Kurtz) (1902–1995) U.S. propulsion engineer. Born in Williamsport, Pa., he spent most of his career in the aviation industry. At North American Aviation (from 1949), he vastly increased the power of rocket engines, and he completed the prototype of the Jupiter C that launched the first U.S. SATELLITE and placed the first U.S. astronauts in space. His work was essential to the early development of intercontinental and intermediate-range ballistic missiles (see ICBM). From 1958 he oversaw development of the engines for SATURN launch vehicles, which eventually carried U.S. astronauts to the moon.

Hoffmann \'hóf-män\, **E(rnst) T(heodor) A(madeus)** *orig.* **Ernst Theodor Wilhelm** (1776–1822) German writer and composer, a major figure of German ROMANTICISM. He initially supported himself as a legal official (the conflict between the ideal world of art and daily bureaucratic life is evident in many of his stories), and later turned to writing and music, which he often pursued simultaneously. His story collection *Fantasy Pieces in the Style of Callot* (1814–15) established his reputation as a writer. His later popular collections *Hoffmann's Strange Stories* (1817) and *The Serapion Brethren* (1819–21) combine wild flights of imagination with vivid examinations of human character. He also worked as a conductor, music critic, and theatrical musical director. The most successful of his many original musical works were the ballet *Arlequin* (1811) and the opera *Undine* (performed 1816). He died at 46 of progressive paralysis. His stories inspired notable operas and ballets by J. OFFENBACH *(Tales of Hoffmann),* L. DELIBES *(Coppélia),* P. TCHAIKOVSKY *(The Nutcracker),* and P. HINDEMITH *(Cardillac).*

Hoffmann \'hóf-män\, **Josef** (1870–1956) Austrian architect and designer. Born in Moravia, he studied under OTTO WAGNER in Vienna, but in 1899 he helped found the Vienna SEZESSION, which broke free of Wagner's classicism. He cofounded, and for 30 years (1903–33) directed, the Wiener Werkstätte (Vienna Workshop), an important center for arts and crafts. His Stoclet House (1905) in Brussels is considered his masterpiece; the exterior of this opulent structure achieved an elegance not often associated with design based on straight lines and white squares and rectangles. He designed the Austrian pavilions for the 1914 Deutscher Werkbund Exhibition in Cologne and for the 1934 Venice Biennale. In 1920 he was appointed city architect of Vienna.

Hofmann, Hans (1880–1966) German-U.S. painter and art teacher. From 1898 he studied art in Munich, and in 1904 he moved to Paris, where he was inspired by the work of HENRI MATISSE and ROBERT DELAUNAY. In 1915 he opened his first school of painting in Munich. He moved to the U.S. in 1930 and taught at New York's Art Students League. In 1933 he opened the Hans Hofmann School of Fine Art, where he would exert strong influence on young abstract painters of the 1930s and '40s, including WILLEM DE KOONING and JACKSON POLLOCK. His style evolved into total abstraction, and he pioneered the paint-dripping technique later associated with Pollock. He closed the school in 1958 to devote the rest of his life to his painting. He was one of the most influential art teachers of the 20th century and a significant figure in the development of ABSTRACT EXPRESSIONISM.

Hans Hofmann, photograph by Arnold Newman, 1960.

Hofmannsthal \'hóf-mäns-,täl\, **Hugo von** (1874–1929) Austrian poet, dramatist, and essayist. Born into an aristocratic banking family, he made his reputation with lyric poems (the first published when he was 16) and verse plays, including *The Death of Titian* (1892) and *Death and the Fool* (1893). He renounced lyrical poetry in a 1902 essay and thereafter turned to theater; his later plays include *Christina's Journey Home* (1910), *Everyman* (1911), *The Difficult Man* (1921), and *The Tower* (1925). In 1906 he began a celebrated collaboration with the composer R. STRAUSS; their remarkable first opera, *Elektra* (1908), was followed by *Der Rosenkavalier* (1910), *Ariadne auf Naxos* (1912, revised 1916), *Die Frau ohne Schatten* (1919), *Die ägyptische Helena* (1928), *Arabella* (1933), and *Die Liebe der Danae* (1940). In 1920 he cofounded the Salzburg Festival with MAX REINHARDT.

Hofstadter \'hōf-,sta-tər\, **Richard** (1916–1970) U.S. historian. He attended the University of Buffalo and Columbia Univ., where he later taught from 1946 until his death. His books of U.S. history, which contain much sociological thought, were often best-sellers; they include *The American Political Tradition* (1948), *The Age of Reform* (1955, Pulitzer Prize), *Anti-Intellectualism in American Life* (1963, Pulitzer Prize), and *American Violence* (1970).

hog Heavy, fat-producing domesticated PIG developed in the U.S. in the late 19th and early 20th century. As the growing use of cheaper vegetable oils decreased the importance of lard as a source of fat, meatpackers sought hogs yielding more lean meat and less fat, and breeders (mostly European) began crossbreeding programs to obtain lean meat and vigorous animals. Today the term hog is often used for any pig weighing more than 120 lbs (54 kg).

hog cholera *or* **swine fever** Often fatal viral disease of swine in Europe, North America, and Africa, transmitted by vehicles used to carry pigs, people dealing with them, and uncooked garbage in feed. Fever progresses to symptoms that include appetite loss; affected eyes and digestive tract; respiratory difficulty; rash; and inflamed mouth and throat. The pig moves reluctantly and staggers; later it cannot rise; coma follows. Antiserum is rarely effective. Survivors become chronically ill and can spread the virus. Illness must be reported, infected animals slaughtered, and quarantine instituted. A vaccine can control it. The African strain causes death sooner and has no effective prevention or treatment.

hogan Dwelling of the NAVAJO Indians of Arizona and New Mexico. The hogan is roughly circular and constructed usually of logs, which are stepped in gradually to create a domed roof. The whole structure is then covered with mud and sod except for a circular opening in the roof that allows smoke to escape. The entrance generally faces the rising sun.

Hogan, Ben *orig.* **William Benjamin** (1912–1997) U.S. golfer. Born in Dublin, Texas, he turned professional in 1929. He won the U.S. PGA championship (1946, 1948), the U.S. Open (1948, 1950, 1951, 1953), the Masters Tournament (1951, 1953), and the British Open (1953), several of which victories followed severe injuries suffered in a 1949 car accident. Known for his demanding practice regimen, his singleminded determination, and the extraordinary accuracy of his shotmaking, he won 63 championships in his career.

Hogarth, William (1697–1764) British painter and engraver. Apprenticed at 15 to a silversmith, he opened his own engraving and printing shop at 22. He took private drawing lessons while earning a living as an engraver of book illustrations. His first major work, *Masquerades and Operas*, attacking contemporary taste and questioning the art establishment, won him many enemies. In 1728 he embarked on a painting career with *A Scene from "The Beggar's Opera,"* revealing his interest in theater and comic subject matter; he also painted "conversation pieces" (informal group portraits) for wealthy clients. His engravings of modern morality subjects, often in sequential sets, were aimed at a wide public, and their outstanding success established his financial independence. To safeguard his livelihood against pirated editions, he fought for legislation protecting artists' copyright. Britain's first copyright act was passed in 1735, the year he published his satirical eight-part series *The Rake's Progress.* His other satirical series include *A Harlot's Progress* (1730–31) and *Marriage à la Mode* (1743–45). The teaching academy he established led to the founding of the Royal Academy (1768).

"The Painter and His Pug," self-portrait by William Hogarth, oil on canvas, 1745; in the Tate Gallery, London.

Hogg, James (1770–1835) Scottish poet. A shepherd, he was almost entirely self-educated. The talents of "the Ettrick Shepherd" were discovered by WALTER SCOTT when Hogg supplied material for Scott's *Minstrelsy of the Scottish Border*, and his popularity accompanied the ballad revival of the early Romantic movement. Hogg's other writings include the poetry collection *The Queen's Wake* (1813) and *The Private Memoirs and Confessions of a Justified Sinner* (1824), a novel about religious mania with a psychopathic hero that anticipates the modern psychological thriller.

Hoggar Mountains See Ahaggar Mtns.

hognose snake Any of three or four species (genus *Heterodon,* family Colubridae) of harmless North American snakes named for their upturned snout, which is used for digging. When threatened, they flatten the head and neck, then strike with a loud hiss, but rarely bite. If their bluff fails, they roll over, writhing, and then act dead, with mouth open and tongue lolling. They eat chiefly toads and frogs. Heavy-bodied and blotchy, they are usually about 24 in. (60 cm) long. Though not adders, they are sometimes called puff adders or blow snakes.

Hohe Tauern \'hō-ə-'tau̇-ərn\ Segment of the eastern Alps, in southern Austria. It extends 70 mi (113 km) east from the Italian border in Tirol. Its many lofty peaks include the Grossglockner, Austria's highest. The region is popular for mountain climbing and skiing.

Hohenlohe-Schillingsfürst \,hō-ən-'lō-ə-'shi-liŋs-,fu̇rst\, **Chlodwig (Karl Viktor), Fürst (Prince) zu** (1819–1901) Imperial German chancellor and Prussian prime minister (1894–1900). Active in Bavarian politics from 1846, he served as minister president (1866–70) after Prussia's defeat of Bavaria in the Seven Weeks' War. He favored a unified Germany, and in 1871 he entered the service of the German empire. He was appointed German chancellor in 1894. His wide experience and fatherly relationship with Emperor William II failed to prevent his sovereign's demagogic excesses, and his influence largely ended in 1897 when Bernhard von, Prince Bulow became foreign secretary.

Hohenstaufen dynasty \,hō-ən-'shtau̇-fən\ German dynasty that ruled the Holy Roman Empire (1138–1208, 1212–54). It was founded by Count Frederick (died 1105), who built Staufen Castle and was appointed duke of Swabia as Frederick I (1079). Hohenstaufen emperors included Frederick I Barbarossa (r.1155–90), Henry VI (r.1191–97), and Frederick II (r.1220–50). The dynasty continued the struggle with the papacy begun under their predecessors. See also Guelphs and Ghibellines.

Hohenzollern dynasty \,hō-ənt-'sȯ-lərn\ Dynasty prominent in European history, chiefly as the ruling house of Brandenburg-Prussia (1415–1918) and of imperial Germany (1871–1918). The first recorded ancestor, Burchard I, was count of Zollern in the 11th century. Two main branches were formed: the Franconian line (including burgraves of Nuremberg, electors of Brandenburg, kings of Prussia, and German emperors) and the Swabian line (including counts of Zollern, princes of Hohenzollern-Sigmaringen, and princes and then kings of Romania). The Franconian branch became Lutheran at the Reformation but turned to Calvinism in 1613 and acquired considerable territory in the 15th–17th century. Both Prussian and German sovereignties were lost at the end of World War I. The Swabian line remained Catholic at the Reformation and ruled in Romania until 1947. The Hohenzollern monarchs included Frederick William I, Frederick II the Great, Frederick William II, and Frederick William III of Prussia; William I and William II of Germany; and Carol I and Carol II of Romania.

Hohhot \'hə-'hȯt\ *or* **Hu-ho-hao-t'e** \'hü-'hə-'hau̇-'tā\ *or* **Huhehot** \'hü-,hə-'hȯt\ *Mongol* **Kukukhoto** \,kü-kü-'k̲ō-tō\ City (pop., 1999 est.: 754,749), capital of Nei Monggol, northern China. The original Mongol city was an important religious center for Tibetan Buddhism (Lamaism) and later a Muslim trading community. After World War II it developed into an industrial center with sugar refining, woolens, and an iron and steel industry. Its university (1957) was the first in Nei Monggol. The city is a regional cultural center.

Hohokam culture \'hō-hō-,käm\ Culture of a group of North American Indian peoples who lived c. 300 BC–AD 1400 in the Sonoran Desert (Arizona), especially along the Gila and Salt rivers. The Hohokam Indians developed complex networks of canals for irrigation, an agricultural-engineering feat unsurpassed in pre-Columbian North America. Some 14th-century canals have been restored for use. Corn was the major crop; beans and squash were added after contact with the Anasazi. For unknown reasons, Hohokam culture disintegrated in the early 15th century. The Pima and Papago peoples are probably direct descendants.

Hojo family Family of hereditary regents to the shogunate of Japan who exercised actual power from 1199 to 1333. Hojo Tokimasa (1138–1215) joined the cause of Minamoto Yoritomo against Taira Kiyomori, then ruler of Japan. Together they prevailed, and Yoritomo became Japan's new ruler, taking the title of shogun. Tokimasa's daughter married Yoritomo, and when Yoritomo died in 1199 Tokimasa became regent to Yoritomo's heir, his own grandson. The position of shogunal regent became hereditary; this office oversaw the constables and tax collectors that the shogunate placed in each province. The system worked well through the first half of the 13th century; its decline was due to depletion of resources stemming from the defense of Japan against two Mongol invasions and to the personal failings of the last Hojo regent. Hojo rule ended when Ashikaga Takauji captured Kyoto in the name of Go-Daigo and the Ashikaga family assumed the title of shogun. See also Kamakura shogunate.

Hokan languages \'hō-kən\ Hypothetical superfamily of North American Indian languages uniting a number of languages and language families of the western U.S. and Mexico. The Hokan hypothesis was first proposed by Roland B. Dixon and Alfred L. Kroeber in 1913 and refined by Edward Sapir; like Penutian, it was an attempt to reduce the number of unrelated language families in one of the most linguistically heterogeneous areas of the world. Its core consisted of languages of aboriginal California and the Southwest, with outlying members from Sonora and Oaxaca in Mexico. Except for some Yuman languages (spoken in southern California, Arizona, and Baja California), all were either extinct or spoken almost exclusively by older adults by the end of the 20th century.

Hokkaido \hō-'kī-dō\ *formerly* **Yezo** \'ye-zō\ Island (pop., 2000 est.: 5,683,000) and province, northern Japan. Northernmost of the four main islands of Japan, it is bordered by the Sea of Japan, the Sea of Okhotsk, and the Pacific Ocean, and has an area of 30,107 sq mi (77,978 sq km). Its administrative headquarters is Sapporo. Its several high mountains include Asahi (7,513 ft, or 2,290 m). It includes Japan's longest river, the Ishikari. Long the domain of the aboriginal Ainu, it attracted serious Japanese settlement beginning in 1869. It has a varied economy, supported by iron and steel, and the largest coal deposits in Japan. The Seikan Tunnel (1988) under the Tsugaru Strait links it with Honshu.

Hokusai \'hō-kü-,sī\ *orig.* **Katsushika Hokusai** (1760–1849) Japanese painter, draftsman, printmaker, and book illustrator. Apprenticed to a woodcut engraver at 15, he became a student of the leading ukiyo-e master, Katsukawa Shunsho, in 1778. His first published works, prints of kabuki actors, appeared the following year. He soon turned to historical and landscape subjects and prints of children. He developed an eclectic style and achieved success with book illustrations and *surimono* prints ("printed things" for special occasions, such as cards and announcements), picture books and novelettes, erotic books and album prints, paintings, and ink sketches. He experimented with Western-style perspective and coloring and later concentrated on samurai themes and Chinese subjects. His *Thirty-six Views of Mount Fuji* (1826–33) were unsurpassed in concept and execution. He had numerous followers, though none had his power or versatility.

Holbein \'hōl-,bīn\, **Hans, the Younger** (c. 1497/98–1543) German painter, draftsman, and designer renowned for the precise rendering of his drawings and the compelling realism of his portraits, particularly those recording the court of King Henry VIII of England. Holbein was a member of a family of important artists. His father, Hans Holbein the Elder, and his uncle Sigmund were renowned for their somewhat conservative examples of late Gothic painting in Germany. Holbein the Younger no doubt first studied with his father in Augsburg. He moved to Basel c. 1515, entered the painters' corporation in 1519, and was executing important murals by 1521. He also designed book illustrations and woodcuts for publishers, notably a series of over 40 scenes illustrating the medieval allegory of the Dance of Death (1523–26). His portraits, including that of Desiderius Erasmus (1523), featured rich color, psychological depth, detailed accessories, and dramatic silhouette. In 1526 he went to England, where he painted portraits of German merchants and court personalities, and by 1536 he had entered the service of Henry VIII. In his last 10 years he produced some 150 life-size and miniature portraits of the royalty and nobility. He also designed fashions for the court and state robes for the king. He was one of the greatest portraitists of all time.

Holberg \'hōl-berg\, **Ludvig** *later* **Friherre** (Baron) Holberg (1684–1754) Norwegian-Danish man of letters. Educated in Denmark and England, he traveled in various European countries before becoming a professor at the University of Copenhagen, where he began to create a new class of humorous literature. His seriocomic epic *Peder Paars* (1719), a parody of VIRGIL's *Aeneid,* is the earliest classic of the Danish language. He was soon producing a steady flow of stage comedies, including *The Political Tinker* (1723), *The Weathercock* (1723), *Jean de France* (1723), *Jeppe of the Hill* (1723), *The Fussy Man* (1731), and *Erasmus Montanus* (1731), many of which are still produced. His other works include the satirical novel *The Journey of Niels Klim to the World Underground* (1741). The outstanding Scandinavian literary figure of the ENLIGHTENMENT, he is claimed by both Norway and Denmark as a founder of their literatures.

Hölderlin \'hœl-dər-ˌlēn\, **(Johann Christian) Friedrich** (1770–1843) German poet. He qualified for ordination, but found himself more drawn to Greek mythology than to Christian dogma. In 1793 he was befriended by FRIEDRICH SCHILLER, who helped him publish his early poetry. He produced works of passionate, expressive intensity, including his only novel, *Hyperion* (1797–99), the unfinished tragedy *The Death of Empedocles,* and a number of odes, elegies, and verse translations. In these works he naturalized the forms of classical Greek verse in German and lamented the loss of an idealized classical Greek world. His behavior became erratic and in 1805 he succumbed irretrievably to schizophrenia; he spent his last 36 years in a carpenter's house under the shadow of insanity. Little recognized in his lifetime, he was forgotten until the 20th century, when he came to be ranked among the finest of German lyric poets.

Hölderlin, pastel by Franz Karl Hiemer, 1792; in the Schiller-Nationalmuseum, Marbach, Ger.

BY COURTESY OF THE SCHILLER-NATIONALMUSEUM, MARBACH, GER

holding company Corporation that owns enough voting STOCK in one or more other companies to exercise control over them. A holding company provides a means of concentrating control of several companies with a minimum of investment; other means of gaining control, such as MERGERS or consolidations, are more complicated legally and more expensive. A holding company can reap the benefits of a subsidiary's goodwill and reputation while limiting its liability to the proportion of the subsidiary's stock that it owns. The parent company in a conglomerate corporation is usually a holding company.

Holi \'hō-lē\ Hindu spring festival. It is held on the full-moon day of Phalguna (Feb.–Mar.) and celebrated with reckless abandon. All distinctions of CASTE, age, sex, and status are disregarded. Participants throw colored powders on each other, and street celebrations are noisy and riotous. The festival is especially associated with the worship of KRISHNA, and it is considered an imitation of his play with the wives and daughters of the cowherds.

Holiday, Billie *orig.* **Eleanora Fagan** (1915–1959) U.S. singer, one of the greatest interpreters of song in jazz. Born in Baltimore, Holiday was discovered singing in a Harlem nightclub in 1933. Recordings with BENNY GOODMAN and DUKE ELLINGTON led to a series of outstanding small-group records (1935–42) featuring such musicians as LESTER YOUNG (who gave her the sobriquet Lady Day) and TEDDY WILSON. Exposure with the big bands of COUNT BASIE (1937) and ARTIE SHAW (1938) brought greater public attention; for the rest of her life she would remain one of the best known of jazz singers. Personal crises and drug and alcohol addiction plagued her career, and she was incarcerated in 1947 on narcotics charges. Her voice could reveal a sweet, often sensual expressiveness or disturbing bitterness in the service of a lyric: her clear projection of emotion represents a landmark of personal expression.

Billie Holiday, 1958.

REPRINTED WITH PERMISSION OF \<E>DOWN BEAT\</E> MAGAZINE

Holiness movement Fundamentalist religious movement that arose in the 19th century among Protestant churches in the U.S. It was characterized by the doctrine of sanctification, according to which believers were enabled to live a perfect life after a conversion experience. It originated in the teachings of JOHN WESLEY, founder of METHODISM, who issued a call for Christian "perfection" (the transformation of a sinner into a saint through God's intercession). In 1843 a group of Holiness ministers founded the Wesleyan Methodist Church of America, which became popular in the rural Midwest and South; another Holiness church of this era was the Free Methodist Church of North America, founded in 1860. Between 1880 and World War I a new set of Holiness groups appeared, including the Church of the Nazarene, established to minister to the urban poor, and the Church of God.

Holinshed \'hä-lən-ˌshed\, **Raphael** (died c. 1580) English chronicler. From c. 1560 Holinshed lived in London, where he was employed as a translator by Reginald Wolfe, who was preparing a universal history. He is remembered for the abridged history he published after Wolfe's death, *Chronicles of England, Scotlande, and Irelande* (1577), compiled largely uncritically from many sources of varying degrees of trustworthiness. It enjoyed great popularity and was quarried by Elizabethan dramatists, especially WILLIAM SHAKESPEARE, who drew on its second edition (1587) for *Macbeth, King Lear, Cymbeline,* and many of his historical plays.

holism \'hō-ˌli-zəm\ In the philosophy of the social sciences, the view that denies that all large-scale social events and conditions are ultimately explicable in terms of the individuals who participated in, enjoyed, or suffered them. Methodological holism maintains that at least some social phenomena must be studied at their own autonomous, macroscopic level of analysis, that at least some social "wholes" are not reducible to or completely explicable in terms of individuals' behavior (see EMERGENCE). Semantic holism denies the claim that all meaningful statements about large-scale social phenomena (e.g., "The industrial revolution resulted in urbanization") can be translated without residue into statements about the actions, attitudes, relations, and circumstances of individual men and women.

holistic medicine \hō-'lis-tik\ Doctrine of prevention and treatment that emphasizes looking at the whole person—body, mind, emotions, and environment—rather than a single function or organ. It promotes use of a wide range of health practices and therapies, including ACUPUNCTURE, HOMEOPATHY, and nutrition, stressing "self-care" with traditional commonsense essentials. In the extreme, it may accord equal validity to a wide range of health-care approaches, some incompatible and not all scientific. It does not ignore mainstream Western medical practices, but does not see them as the only effective therapies. See also ALTERNATIVE MEDICINE.

Holland Historic region, the Netherlands, occupying the northwestern portion of the modern country. It originated in the early 12th century as a fief of the HOLY ROMAN EMPIRE. In 1299 it was united with HAINAUT. Members of the house of WITTELSBACH served as counts of Holland, Zeeland, and Hainaut until 1433, when they ceded the titles to PHILIP III THE GOOD, duke of Burgundy. It passed to the HABSBURGS in 1482, and became a center of the revolt against Spain in 1572. Holland and six other northern Netherlands provinces declared their independence from Spain in 1579, proclaiming the United Provinces of the Netherlands. Its capital, AMSTERDAM, became Europe's foremost commercial center in the 18th century. The Napoleonic kingdom of Holland occupied the territory 1806–10. In 1840 it was divided into the provinces of North Holland and South Holland.

Holland (of Foxley and of Holland), Baron *orig.* **Henry Richard Vassall Fox** (1773–1840) British Whig politician. He was the nephew and disciple of CHARLES JAMES FOX, whose ideas he expounded in the House of Lords. As lord privy seal in GEORGE GRENVILLE's "Ministry of All the Talents" coalition (1806–7), he helped secure the abolition of the slave trade in the British colonies. He later served as chancellor of the duchy of Lancaster (1830–34, 1835–40).

Holland, Brian and Eddie *orig.* **Edward** U.S. songwriters and producers. In 1962 the Detroit-born brothers Brian (born 1941) and Eddie (born 1939) formed a team with Lamont Dozier (born 1941) which subsequently created a series of hits for almost every artist on the MOTOWN label, and helped define its characteristic sound through blending elements of GOSPEL music and RHYTHM AND BLUES with elaborate arrangements. Their songs include "Baby Love," "Stop! In the Name of Love" (two of the seven no. 1 hits they wrote for the SUPREMES), "Heat Wave," "Baby I Need Your Loving," and dozens of other hits for such artists as MARVIN GAYE and the Temptations.

Hollerith, Herman (1860–1929) U.S. inventor. Born in Buffalo, N.Y., he attended Columbia Univ.'s School of Mines and later assisted in the 1880 U.S. census. By the time of the 1890 census, he had invented machines to record statistics by electrically reading and sorting punched cards, and the census results were consequently obtained in one-third the time required in 1880. In 1896 he founded the Tabulating Machine Co., which later became IBM. Hollerith's electromechanical sensing and punching devices were forerunners of the input/output units of later computers.

Holley, Alexander Lyman (1832–1882) U.S. metallurgist and mechanical engineer. Born in Lakeville, Conn., he brought the rights to the BESSEMER PROCESS to the U.S. in 1863 and became the first in the U.S. to begin steel production by the Bessemer process at his plant in Troy, N.Y. He made significant improvements in the converter, and designed numerous large steelworks.

Holley, Robert William (1922–1993) U.S. biochemist. Born in Urbana, Ill., he received his PhD from Cornell University Holley and others showed that transfer RNA was involved in the assembly of amino acids into proteins. He was the first to determine the sequence of nucleotides in a NUCLEIC acid, a process that required digesting the molecule with enzymes, identifying the pieces, and then figuring out how they fit together. It has since been shown that all transfer RNA has a similar structure. He shared a 1968 Nobel Prize with MARSHALL WARREN NIRENBERG and HAR GOBIND KHORANA.

Holliday, Doc *orig.* **John Henry** (1852–1887) U.S. gambler and gunman. Born in Griffin, Ga., he graduated from dental school in 1872, then moved west for a drier climate to treat his tuberculosis. He soon abandoned dentistry for gambling and began drifting, settling in Tombstone, Ariz., in 1880. There he joined WYATT EARP and his brothers in the famous gunfight at the O.K. Corral (1881). Having earned a reputation as a gunman, he continued to drift through the West until his death from tuberculosis at 35.

Hollweg, Theobald von Bethmann See Theobald von BETHMANN HOLLWEG

holly Any of approximately 400 species of red- or black-berried ornamental shrubs and trees that make up the genus *Ilex* (family Aquifoliaceae), including the popular Christmas hollies. English holly *(I. aquifolium)* bears shiny, spiny, dark, evergreen leaves; American holly *(I. opaca)* has oblong, prickly leaves; both have usually red fruits. There are spineless and yellow-fruited forms of both species.

American holly (*Ilex opaca*).

© NOBLE PROCTOR FROM THE NATIONAL AUDUBON SOCIETY COLLECTION/PHOTO RESEARCHERS

Holly, Buddy *orig.* **Charles Hardin Holley** (1936–1959) U.S. singer and songwriter. Born in Lubbock, Texas, he played in country-music bands while in high school. Later switching to rock and roll, in 1957 Holly and his band, the Crickets, had hits with such songs as "That'll Be the Day," "Peggy Sue," and "Oh, Boy!" Holly died at 22 in a plane crash, along with the singers Richie Valens (born 1941) and The Big Bopper (Jape Richardson, born 1930). He left behind many recordings which were released posthumously, and he soon attained legendary stature; he was part of the first group inducted into the Rock and Roll Hall of Fame.

hollyhock Herbaceous plant *(Althaea rosea)* of the MALLOW family, native to China but widely cultivated for its handsome flowers. The several varieties include annual, biennial, and perennial forms. The stalk, growing about 5–9 ft (1.5–2.7 m) tall, bears leaves with five to seven lobes and, along the upper portion, commonly white, pink, red, or yellow flowers. See photograph above.

Hollyhock (*Althaea rosea*).

LEFEVER/GRUSHOW FROM GRANT HEILMAN PHOTOGRAPHY, INC.

Hollywood District of the city of LOS ANGELES. Its name is synonymous with the U.S. movie industry. In 1887 it was laid out as a subdivision by Horace Wilcox, a prohibitionist who envisioned a community based on his religious principles. It was consolidated with Los Angeles in 1910 and became the center of the movie industry by 1915. By the 1960s it also was the source of much U.S. network television programming.

Hollywood City (pop., 2000: 139,357), southeastern Florida. Lying along the Atlantic coast, the site was a palmetto jungle when the developer Joseph W. Young laid out the town in 1921. It is now primarily a resort-residential city with some diversified industry. Nearby are Port Everglades (a docking and warehousing facility) and a SEMINOLE reservation.

Hollywood Ten Group of U.S. movie producers, directors, and screenwriters who refused to answer questions about communist affiliations before the HOUSE UN-AMERICAN ACTIVITIES COMMITTEE in 1947. The Ten—Alvah Bessie, Herbert Biberman, Lester Cole, Edward Dmytryk, Ring Lardner, Jr., John Howard Lawson, Albert Maltz, Samuel Ornitz, Adrian Scott, and Dalton Trumbo—were charged with contempt of Congress and given prison sentences of six months to a year. After their release, they were blacklisted and unable to find work in Hollywood, though some wrote scripts under pseudonyms. The blacklist gradually disappeared in the early 1960s.

Holm, Hanya *orig.* **Johanna Eckert** (1898?–1992) German-U.S. choreographer of modern dance and Broadway musicals. After training in Germany, she worked at Mary Wigman's Central Institute as a dancer and teacher and later codirector. In 1931 she opened a Wigman school in New York, which became the Hanya Holm Studio in 1936. In addition to works for her own company, she choreographed such musicals as *My Fair Lady* (1956) and *Camelot* (1960). She promoted the use of DANCE NOTATION, and her choreography for *Kiss Me, Kate* (1948) was the first to be copyrighted.

Hanya Holm, 1929.

BY COURTESY OF THE DANCE COLLECTION, THE NEW YORK PUBLIC LIBRARY AT LINCOLN CENTER, HANYA HOLM COLLECTION

Holmes, Larry (born 1949) U.S. heavyweight boxing champion. Born in Cuthbert, Ga., he won 19 of 23 amateur bouts before turning professional. From 1973 to 1978 Holmes won 28 consecutive bouts, culminating in a victory over the reigning champion, Ken Norton. He defended the title 17 times between 1978 and 1983, once (1980) against MUHAMMAD ALI. He lost the title to Michael Spinks in 1985. Only JOE LOUIS held the heavyweight crown longer than Holmes.

Holmes, Oliver Wendell (1809–1894) U.S. physician, poet, and humorist. He joined the Harvard faculty in 1847, and later became dean of its medical school. He won national acclaim with his poem "Old Ironsides" (1830). From 1857 he published his "Breakfast-Table" essays in the *Atlantic Monthly,* later republished in such collections as *The Autocrat of the Breakfast-Table* (1858) and *The Professor of the Breakfast-Table* (1860). Other works include the poem "The Chambered Nautilus" and the novel *Elsie Venner* (1861). OLIVER WENDELL, JR. HOLMES, was his son.

Holmes, Oliver Wendell, Jr. (1841–1935) U.S. jurist, legal historian, and philosopher. He was born in Boston to OLIVER WENDELL HOLMES and

Amelia Lee Jackson, daughter of a Massachusetts supreme court justice. As an officer in the American Civil War, he was seriously wounded three times. He practiced law in Boston from 1867, eventually serving as an associate justice (1882–99) and then chief justice (1899–1902) of the state supreme court. In *The Common Law* (1881), he advanced the notion of law as accumulated experience rather than science. Appointed to the U.S. Supreme Court by Pres. THEODORE ROOSEVELT in 1902, Holmes advocated judicial restraint, maintaining that lawmaking was the business of legislative bodies rather than courts. In *Schenk vs. U.S.* (1919), he stated the "clear and present danger" test for FREEDOM OF SPEECH. Many of his vigorous and lucid opinions, including dissenting opinions (he was known as The Great Dissenter), became classic interpretations of the law, and he is regarded as one of the foremost jurists of the modern age. He served until 1932.

Holocaust *Hebrew* **Sho'ah** Era of Nazi persecution of Jews and other minorities (1933–45), marked by increasing barbarization of methods in the expanding territories under German rule. It climaxed in the "final solution," the attempted extermination of European Jewry. ADOLF HITLER'S persecution of Jews in Germany began soon after he became chancellor. Under the NUREMBERG LAWS (1935), Jews lost their citizenship. Almost every synagogue in Germany was destroyed in the KRISTALLNACHT pogrom in 1938, and thereafter Jews were imprisoned in CONCENTRATION CAMPS. German victories in the early years of WORLD WAR II brought most of European Jewry under the Nazis and their satellites. As German armies moved eastward into Poland, the Balkans, and the Soviet Union, special mobile killing units, the *Einsatzgruppen*, rounded up and killed Jews, Roma (Gypsies), and many non-Jewish Slavs; other groups targeted by the Nazis included homosexuals, the mentally retarded, physically disabled, and emotionally disturbed. After the WANNSEE CONFERENCE (1942), Jews from all over occupied Europe were systematically evacuated to concentration and extermination camps. Underground resistance movements were active in several nations, and Jewish risings took place against overwhelming odds in the ghettos of Poland (see WARSAW GHETTO UPRISING). Individuals such as RAOUL WALLENBERG saved thousands by their efforts, but the Allied governments failed to provide effective aid to the Jews. By the end of the war, an estimated six million Jews and millions of others had been killed by Nazi Germany and its collaborators.

Holocaust Remembrance days International commemoration of the millions of victims of Nazi Germany's exterminationist policies. The commemoration, observed on different days in different countries, often marks the victims' efforts at resistance and concentrates on contemporary efforts to battle hatred and anti-Semitism. From 1951 Jews have observed Holocaust Remembrance Day on the 27th of Nisan, shortly after Passover, in the Jewish calendar. The Israeli parliament declared that day Yom Hashoah ve Hagevurah (Holocaust Remembrance and Heroism Day), marking not only destruction but resistance.

Holocene epoch \'hō-lə-ˌsēn\ *formerly* **Recent epoch** Latest interval of the earth's geologic history, dating from 10,000 years ago to the present. The younger of the two epochs that constitute the QUATERNARY PERIOD, the Holocene follows the last glacial stage of the PLEISTOCENE EPOCH. It is characterized by relatively warm climatic conditions. During this epoch humans have refined the skills that led to the present level of civilization.

holography \hō-'lä-grə-fē\ Method of recording or reproducing a three-dimensional image, or hologram, by means of a pattern of interference produced using a LASER beam. To create a hologram, a beam of coherent light (a laser) is split; half the beam falls on a recording medium (such as a photographic plate) unaltered, and the other half is first reflected off the object to be imaged. The two beams together produce an INTERFERENCE pattern of stripes and whorls on the plate. The developed plate is the hologram. When light is shone on the hologram, a three-dimensional image of the original object is produced by the recorded interference pattern. Some holograms require laser light to reproduce the image; others may be viewed in ordinary white light. Holography was invented in 1947 by the Hungarian-British physicist Dennis Gabor (1900–1979), who won a 1971 Nobel Prize for his invention.

Holst, Gustav(us Theodore von) (1874–1934) British composer. Son of an organist, he played organ and conducted as a child. At the Royal College of Music he met R. VAUGHAN WILLIAMS, who became a friend for life. He made his living first by playing trombone, then as a teacher. Always frail, he gave up teaching after a collapse in 1923 to devote the rest of his life to composition. His most popular piece is the vividly orchestrated suite *The Planets* (1916); other works include the charming *St. Paul's Suite* for strings (1913), the *Hymn of Jesus* (1917), and the *Choral Fantasia* (1930).

Holstein See SCHLESWIG-HOLSTEIN

Holstein \'hōl-stēn\ *or* **Holstein-Friesian** \'frē-zhən\ Breed of large dairy CATTLE that originated in northern Holland and Friesland. Its chief characteristics are its large size and black-and-white-spotted markings, sharply defined rather than blended. Probably selected for their dairy qualities c. 2,000 years ago, they have long been distributed over the fertile lowlands of continental Europe. In the U.S., Holsteins outnumber all other dairy breeds and produce 90% of the milk supply. Their milk has a relatively low butterfat content.

Holstein \'hōl-ˌshtīn\, **Friedrich (August) von** (1837–1909) German diplomat. A member of the German foreign office from 1876, he never became foreign minister but exercised power behind the scenes, earning the nickname "the gray eminence." He broke with OTTO VON BISMARCK over his alignment with Russia, as Holstein advocated a firm alliance with Austria and Britain. After Bismarck's dismissal in 1890, Holstein advised against the renewal of the REINSURANCE TREATY. He held important posts under Chancellors LEO VON CAPRIVI, CHLODWIG, FURST ZU HOHENLOHE-SCHILLINGFURST, and BERNHARD VON, PRINCE BULOW, but he proved powerless to oppose the policies of Emperor WILLIAM II and was dismissed in 1906.

Holy Alliance Loose organization of most of the European sovereigns, formed in 1815 by ALEXANDER I of Russia, Francis I of Austria, and FREDERICK WILLIAM III of Prussia, after the final defeat of NAPOLEON. Its avowed purpose was to promote the influence of Christian principles in the affairs of nations, but it accomplished little and became a symbol of conservatism and repression in Central and Eastern Europe. See also Congress of LAIBACH.

Holy Communion See EUCHARIST

Holy Cross, College of the Private institution of higher learning in Worcester, Mass. Affiliated with the JESUIT order, it was founded as a men's college in 1843; women were first admitted in 1972. It offers a traditional liberal-arts curriculum as well as cooperative degree programs with other universities in engineering and business. Total enrollment is about 2,600.

Holy Grail See GRAIL

Holy Island See LINDISFARNE

Holy League (1576–98) Association of Roman Catholics during the French Wars of RELIGION. It was first organized under the leadership of the 3rd duc de GUISE, to oppose concessions granted to the Protestant HUGUENOTS by HENRY III. In 1584, when the Huguenot leader Henry of Navarre (later HENRY IV) became heir to the throne, the League set up an alternative candidate, with Spain's assistance. To put an end to the League, which challenged his authority, Henry III had the duc de Guise assassinated (1588), an act which, rather than destroying the League, led to Henry's own assassination in 1589. The League opposed the accession of Henry IV, but when he became a Roman Catholic in 1593 the League's power waned.

Holy of Holies Innermost and most sacred area of the ancient Temple of Jerusalem, accessible only to the Israelite high priest and only once a year, on YOM KIPPUR. The Holy of Holies was located at the western end of the temple. At its entrance stood a small cedar altar overlaid with gold. In the First Temple (see Temple of JERUSALEM) the Holy of Holies held the ARK OF THE COVENANT.

Holy Roman Empire *German* **Heiliges Römisches Reich** Realm of varying extent in medieval and modern western and central Europe. Ruled initially by Frankish kings and later by Germans, it existed from CHARLEMAGNE'S coronation by Pope Leo III in AD 800 until the renunciation of the imperial title by FRANCIS II in 1806. The reign of the German OTTO I the Great, who greatly enlarged the empire and succeeded in dominating his allies, is sometimes regarded as the beginning of the empire, whose name (not adopted until the reign of FREDERICK I BARBAROSSA) reflected Charlemagne's claim that his empire was the successor of the Roman empire, and that this temporal power was augmented by his status as God's principal vicar in the temporal realm (parallel to the pope's in the spiritual realm). The empire's core consisted of Germany, Austria,

Bohemia, and Moravia. Switzerland, the Netherlands, and northern Italy sometimes formed part of it; France, Poland, Hungary, and Denmark were initially included, and Britain and Spain were nominal components. From the mid-11th century the emperors engaged in a great struggle with the papacy for dominance, and particularly under the powerful HOHENSTAUFEN DYNASTY (1138–1254) they fought with the popes over control of Italy. RUDOLF I became the first Habsburg emperor in 1273, and from 1438 the HABSBURG DYNASTY held the throne permanently. Until 1356 the emperor was chosen by the German princes; thereafter he was formally elected by the ELECTORS. Outside of their personal hereditary domains, emperors shared power with the imperial diet. During the REFORMATION, the German princes largely defected to the Protestant camp, opposing the Catholic emperor, and after 1562 emperors were no longer crowned by the pope. At the end of the THIRTY YEARS' WAR, the Peace of WESTPHALIA recognized the individual sovereignty of the empire's states; the empire thereafter became a loose federation of states and the title of emperor principally honorific. In the 18th century, issues of imperial succession resulted in the War of the AUSTRIAN SUCCESSION and the SEVEN YEARS' WAR. The greatly weakened empire was brought to an end by the victories of NAPOLEON. See also GUELPHS AND GHIBELLINES, INVESTITURE CONTROVERSY, Concordat of WORMS.

Holy Roman Emperors

Carolingian dynasty	
Charlemagne (Charles I)	800–14
Louis I	814–40
Civil War	840–43
Lothair I	843–55
Louis II	855–75
Charles II	875–77
Interregnum	877–81
Charles III	881–87
Interregnum	887–91
House of Spoleto	
Guy	891–94
Lambert	894–98
Carolingian dynasty	
Arnulf	896–99
Louis III	901–5
House of Franconia	
Conrad I	911–18
Carolingian dynasty	
Berengar	915–24
House of Saxony (Liudolfings)	
Henry I	919–36
Otto I	936–73
Otto II	973–83
Otto III	983–1002
Henry II	1002–24
Salian dynasty	
Conrad II	1024–39
Henry III	1039–56
Henry IV	1056–1105/6
Rival claimants	
Rudolf	1077–80
Hermann	1081–93
Conrad	1093–1101
Henry V	1105/6–25
House of Supplinburg	
Lothair II	1125–37
House of Hohenstaufen	
Conrad III	1138–52
Frederick I (Barbarossa)	1152–90
Henry VI	1190–97
Philip	1198–1208
Welf dynasty	
Otto IV	1198–1215
House of Hohenstaufen	
Frederick II	1215–50
Rival claimants	
Henry (VII)	1220–35
Henry Raspe	1246–47
William of Holland	1247–56
Conrad IV	1250–54
Great Interregnum	
Richard	1257–72
Alfonso (Alfonso X of Castile)	1257–75
House of Habsburg	
Rudolf I	1273–91
House of Nassau	
Adolf	1292–98
House of Habsburg	
Albert I	1298–1308
House of Luxembourg	
Henry VII	1308–13
House of Habsburg	
Frederick (III)	1314–26
House of Wittelsbach	
Louis IV	1314–46
House of Luxembourg	
Charles IV	1346–78
Wenceslas	1378–1400
House of Wittelsbach	
Rupert	1400–10
House of Luxembourg	
Jobst	1410–11
Sigismund	1410–37
House of Habsburg	
Albert II	1438–39
Frederick III	1440–93
Maximilian I	1493–1519
Charles V	1519–56
Ferdinand I	1556–64
Maximilian II	1564–76
Rudolf II	1576–1612
Matthias	1612–19
Ferdinand II	1619–37
Ferdinand III	1637–57
Leopold I	1658–1705
Joseph I	1705–11
Charles VI	1711–40
House of Wittelsbach	
Charles VII	1742–45
House of Habsburg	
Francis I	1745–65
Joseph II	1765–90
Leopold II	1790–92
Francis II	1792–1806

Holy Spirit *or* **Holy Ghost** *or* **Paraclete** In Christianity, the third person of the Holy TRINITY. Though references to the spirit of Yahweh (God) abound in the Old Testament, Christian teaching about the Holy Spirit is derived mainly from the GOSPELS. The Holy Spirit descended on JESUS at his baptism, and outpourings of the Spirit are mentioned in the Acts of the Apostles, in which healing, prophecy, exorcism, and speaking in tongues are associated with its activity. The Holy Spirit also came to the disciples during PENTECOST. The definition of the Holy Spirit as a divine person equal in substance to the Father and the Son was made at the Council of CONSTANTINOPLE (AD 381).

Holy Synod \'si-nəd\ Ecclesiastical governing body created by Czar PETER I in 1721 to head the RUSSIAN ORTHODOX CHURCH, replacing the patriarchate of Moscow. Peter created the Synod, made up of representatives of the hierarchy obedient to his will, to subject the church to the state, and appointed a secular official, the chief procurator, to supervise its activities. The Synod persecuted all dissenters and censored publications, and Peter disposed of church property and revenues for state purposes at his own discretion. In 1917 a church council reestablished the patriarchate, but the new Soviet government soon nationalized all church-held lands.

holy war Any war fought by divine command or for a primarily religious purpose. The concept is found in the Bible (e.g., the Book of Joshua) and has played a role in many religions. The CRUSADES are Europe's best-known example. In Islam, the concept is called JIHAD. Wars in which religion plays a secondary or exacerbating role are not generally called holy wars.

Holyfield, Evander (born 1962) U.S. boxer. Born in Atmore, Ala., he became the only boxer aside from MUHAMMAD ALI to win the heavyweight championship three separate times. His first title win was against J. "Buster" Douglas in 1990. He lost the title to Riddick Bowe in 1992, recaptured it in 1993, lost it to Michael Moorer in 1994, and regained it from MIKE TYSON in 1996. In his title defense against Tyson in 1997, Tyson was disqualified for biting Holyfield's ear.

Holzer \'hȯlt-sər\, **Jenny** (born 1950) U.S. conceptual artist. She studied at Duke Univ., the University of Chicago, and RISD. In the late 1970s she became involved with CONCEPTUAL ART and the Art and Language group of artists, known for their "word art" involving the display of words and text instead of visual images. Her "truisms," slogans and brief confrontational statements, were initially written on walls but came to be displayed in other modes resembling advertising technology (e.g., *Electronic Signboard*, 1990).

Home, Alec Douglas- See Sir Alec DOUGLAS-HOME

home page See WEB SITE

Home Rule, Irish Movement to secure internal autonomy for Ireland within the British empire. The slogan "Home Rule" was popularized in 1870 when the Home Government Association (later the Home Rule League) called for an Irish parliament. It was led from 1878 by CHARLES STEWART PARNELL, whose obstructionist tactics in the British Parliament publicized his country's grievances. The Home Rule bills introduced by Prime Minister WILLIAM E. GLADSTONE in 1885 and 1893 were defeated. A third bill became law in 1914 but was militantly opposed by Ulster Unionists and republicans in Ireland. A system akin to home rule was established in the six counties of Ulster (Northern Ireland) in 1920. In 1921 the remaining 26 counties in the south achieved dominion status, but the link with the British Commonwealth was severed in 1949.

Homel See HOMYEL

homeopathy \ˌhō-mē-'ä-pə-thē\ System of THERAPEUTICS founded in 1796 by SAMUEL HAHNEMANN on the principle that "like cures like." That is, substances that in healthy persons would produce the symptoms from which the patient suffers are used to treat the patient. Hahnemann further stated that the potency of a curative agent increases as the substance is diluted. When it was introduced, homeopathy was a mild, welcome alternative to heavy-handed therapies such as bleeding, but it has since been criticized for focusing on symptoms rather than causes. With the rise of ALTERNATIVE MEDICINE, it has seen a resurgence.

homeostasis \ˌhō-mē-ō-'stā-səs\ Any self-regulating process by which a biological or mechanical system maintains stability while adjusting to changing conditions. Systems in dynamic EQUILIBRIUM reach a balance in which internal change continuously compensates for external change in a feedback control process to keep conditions relatively uniform. An example is temperature regulation—mechanically in a room by a THERMOSTAT or biologically in the body by a complex system controlled by the HYPOTHALAMUS, which adjusts breathing and metabolic rates, blood-vessel dilation, and blood-sugar level in response to changes caused by factors including ambient temperature, hormones, and disease.

Homer (fl. 9th or 8th century BC) Greek poet, one of the greatest and most influential writers of all time. Though almost nothing is known of his life, he was probably an Ionian, and tradition holds that he was blind. The ancient Greeks attributed to him the great epic poems the *Iliad* and the *Odyssey*. Modern scholars generally agree that he composed (but probably did not literally write) the *Iliad*, most likely relying on oral traditions, and at least inspired the composition of the *Odyssey*. The *Iliad*, set during the TROJAN WAR, tells the story of the wrath of ACHILLES; the *Odyssey* tells the story of ODYSSEUS as he travels home from the war. The two epics provided the basis of Greek education and culture in the classical age and formed the backbone of humanistic education down to the Roman empire and the spread of Christianity.

Homer, Winslow (1836–1910) U.S. painter. Born in Boston, he served an apprenticeship with a Boston lithographer, then became a freelance illustrator in New York. He exhibited at the National Academy of Design in 1860 and was elected a member in 1865. During a stay in France in 1866, he was attracted to French naturalism and Japanese prints, but they had little effect on his generally bright and happy work, including *Snap the Whip* (1872). He became a master of watercolor and his oil paintings matured, focusing increasingly on solitary, withdrawn figures. He spent 1881–82 in the English village of Tynemouth, on the North Sea, where the coastal atmosphere, the sea, and the stoic people are the subjects of some of his most powerful images. In 1883 he moved permanently to Prout's Neck, Me., and his dominant theme became the sea and the endless struggle against an uncaring nature. In his later years he continued to paint vigorously and in near-total isolation. Though he was recognized in his lifetime as a leading U.S. painter, appreciation of his enormous achievement came only after his death.

Homestead Movement Mid-19th-century drive for free land in the U.S. Midwest, Great Plains, and West. It began in the 1830s as laborers and reformers joined farmers in calling for public land to be given free to settlers. In 1848 the FREE SOIL PARTY advocated the homestead proposal. Opposition from industrial employers and Southern slaveholders blocked legislation until the 1860 election, when the winning Republican Party supported a homestead measure. In 1862 the Homestead Act was passed, providing 160 acres of public land free to any adult citizen or head of family who had lived on the land for five years. By 1900, 600,000 homesteaders had claimed 80 million acres.

Homestead National Monument Memorial, southeastern Nebraska. Established in 1936 as a memorial to the hardships of pioneer life, it is the site of the first claim under the Homestead Act of 1862 and has exhibits tracing the development of the HOMESTEAD MOVEMENT. It occupies 163 acres (66 hectares) and includes a homestead log cabin.

Homestead Strike U.S. labor strike at ANDREW CARNEGIE's steelworks in Homestead, Pa., in July 1892. When the Amalgamated Association of Iron and Steel Workers went on strike following a wage cut, the company's manager, HENRY CLAY FRICK, hired strikebreakers, with Pinkerton Agency detectives to protect them. A gun battle resulted, in which several people were killed and many injured; the governor sent state militiamen to support the company. The broken strike represented a major setback to the union movement that was felt for decades.

homicide Killing of one human being by another. Homicide is a general term; it includes murder, manslaughter, and other criminal homicides as well as noncriminal killings. Murder is the crime of intentionally and unjustifiably killing another. First-degree murder is a homicide committed with premeditation or in the course of a serious FELONY (e.g., KIDNAPPING). Second- and third-degree murder involve lesser degrees of intent. Manslaughter is commonly divided into voluntary (or first-degree) and involuntary (or second- and third-degree) manslaughter. The first type encompasses any homicide resulting from an intentional act done without malice or premeditation and while in the heat of passion or on sudden provocation; the second type is variously defined in different jurisdictions but often includes an element of unlawful recklessness or negligence. Noncriminal homicides include killings committed in defense of oneself or another and deaths resulting from accidents caused by persons engaged in lawful acts. See also SELF-DEFENSE.

hominid \'hä-mə-ˌnid\ Any creature of the family Hominidae (order Primates), of which only one species exists today—*HOMO SAPIENS*, or human beings. Extinct species of the family are indicated in fossil remains, some of which are now quite well known: *Ardipithecus ramidus*, various species of *AUSTRALOPITHECUS*, *HOMO HABILIS*,, and *HOMO ERECTUS*. The family most closely related to the Hominidae today is the Pongidae, or anthropoid apes, including the GORILLA, the CHIMPANZEE, and the ORANGUTAN. These are believed to have diverged from a common ancestral line 5–8 million years ago. The physical characteristics that distinguish hominids from the pongids are erect posture, bipedal locomotion, rounded skulls with larger brains, small teeth (including unspecialized canines), and such behavioral characteristics as communication through language.

Homo Genus of the family Hominidae of PRIMATES characterized by a relatively large cranium (braincase), limb structure adapted to an erect posture and a two-footed gait, well-developed and fully opposable thumb, hand capable of power and precision grips, and the ability to make precision tools. The genus includes modern humans (*HOMO SAPIENS*), the extinct species *H. HABILIS* and *H. ERECTUS*, and the extinct forms of *H. sapiens* called NEANDERTHAL and CRO-MAGNON.

Homo erectus ("erect man") Extinct species of early HOMINID that is generally thought to be a direct ancestor of modern *HOMO SAPIENS*. H. erectus flourished from c. 1.6 million years ago to 250,000 years ago, ranging widely from Africa (where the species originated) to Asia to parts of Europe. Most of the anatomical differences between *H. erectus* and *H. sapiens* concern the skull and teeth, *H. erectus* showing a low, thick braincase (800–1,100 cc) with jutting brow ridges and a wide nose, palate, and jaw together with large teeth that are nevertheless hominid and not apelike. The limb bones are similar to those of *H. sapiens*, indicating that *H. erectus* was of medium stature and walked upright. The species is associated with the ACHEULIAN tool tradition and was the first hominid to master fire and inhabit caves. See also HUMAN EVOLUTION, JAVA MAN, ZHOUKOUDIAN.

Homo habilis \ˌhō-mō-'ha-bə-ləs\ ("dexterous man") Extinct species of early HOMINID that inhabited parts of sub-Saharan Africa 2.5–1.5 million years ago and is generally regarded as the earliest member of the genus *Homo*. *H. habilis* remains were first discovered in 1959 and 1960 at OLDUVAI GORGE in northern Tanzania; additional remains have since been found in the LAKE TURKANA region of northern Kenya and, arguably, at STERKFONTEIN in South Africa. The cranial capacity of *H. habilis* ranged from 600 to 800 cc. Limb bones suggest that the species walked efficiently bipedally, and the fossil of a hand suggests that *H. habilis* was capable of precise manipulation of objects. Crude tools found along with *H. habilis* remains provide further evidence that this species could shape stone. See also HUMAN EVOLUTION, OLDOWAN INDUSTRY.

Homo sapiens ("man the wise") Genus and species to which all modern human beings (*Homo sapiens sapiens*) belong and whose oldest known fossil remains date to c. 120,000 years ago, or much earlier (c. 400,000 years ago) if evidence of certain "archaic" varieties is included. *H. sapiens* is distinguished from earlier HOMINID species by characteristics and habits such as bipedal stance and gait, brain capacity averaging about 1,350 cc, high forehead, small teeth and jaw, defined chin, construction and use of tools, and ability to use SYMBOLS. Many scholars believe that modern humans developed in Africa c. 150,000 years ago and spread to the Near East c. 100,000 years ago and to other parts of Eurasia c. 40,000–50,000 years ago (this is known as the "single-origin" model). Some consider this dispersion to have occurred even more recently (50,000–65,000 years ago). Others contend that modern humans developed from various regional populations of archaic *H. sapiens* in Eurasia beginning c. 250,000 years ago (the "regional-continuity" model). In the first model the genetic differences that exist between the peoples of the world would not be very old; in the second model they would be significantly older. In any case, by c. 11,000 BC *H. sapiens sapiens* had peopled virtually the entire globe. See also CRO-MAGNON, CULTURE, HUMAN EVOLUTION, NEANDERTHAL.

homology Similarity of the structure, physiology, or development of different species of organisms based on their descent from a common evolutionary ancestor. Analogy, by contrast, is a functional similarity of structure that is based not on common evolutionary origins but on mere similarity of use. The forelimbs of such widely differing mammals as humans, bats, and deer are homologous; the form of construction and the number of bones in each are practically identical and represent adaptive modifications of the forelimb structure of their shared ancestor. The wings of birds and insects, on the other hand, are merely analogous; they are used for flight in both types of organisms but do not share a common ancestral origin.

homosexual-rights movement See GAY-RIGHTS MOVEMENT

homosexuality Quality or state in some human beings characterized by a tendency to direct sexual desire toward another of the same sex. Female homosexuality is frequently referred to as LESBIANISM (from Lesbos, the Aegean island where SAPPHO taught). The word "gay" is often used as an alternative for both "homosexual" and "lesbian," though it may refer specifically to male homosexuality. At different times and in different cultures, homosexual behavior has variously been approved of, tolerated, punished, and banned. Homosexuality was not uncommon in ancient Greece and Rome, particularly between adult and adolescent males. Judeo-Christian and Muslim cultures have generally viewed it as sinful, although many religious leaders have said it is the act, and not the inclination, that their faiths proscribe. Until the early 1970s the American Psychiatric Association had classified homosexuality as a mental illness, but that designation was dropped in 1973. Traditional beliefs about homosexuals (such as that there is a single identifiable homosexual "type" and that gay men are effeminate and gay women aggressive and masculine) have faded as a result of the increased candor with which sexual preference and practices can be discussed and the growing acceptance, particularly in areas with large homosexual populations, of homosexuality as a common variant of human sexuality. Homosexual orientation apparently results from a combination of hereditary or constitutional factors and environmental or social influences, and it tends to coexist with heterosexual feelings in varying degrees in different individuals. Although conditions for homosexuals had generally improved in most of Europe and North America by the turn of the 21st century, elsewhere in the world, violence against gays and lesbians continued.

homozygote and heterozygote Two genetic possibilities for a fertilized egg. If the two sex cells (gametes) that fuse during FERTILIZATION carry the same form of a GENE for a specific trait, the organism is said to be a homozygote for that trait. If the gametes carry differing forms of the gene, the result is a heterozygote. Because genes may be either dominant or recessive (see DOMINANCE and RECESSIVENESS), the genetic composition (GENOTYPE) of an organism cannot always be determined by the organism's physical appearance (PHENOTYPE).

Homs \'hȯms, *Engl* 'hȯmz\ *or* **Hims** \'hims\ *ancient* **Emesa** City (pop., 1994 est.: 644,000), central Syria. Located near the ORONTES RIVER, as Emesa it contained a great temple to the sun god El Gebal and was the birthplace of the priest-king ELAGABALUS, who became Roman emperor in AD 218. The emperor AURELIAN defeated Queen ZENOBIA of PALMYRA here in 272. It was taken in 636 by the Muslims, who renamed it Hims. In 1516 it passed into Ottoman hands, where it remained until the creation of SYRIA after World War I. Homs is a thriving agricultural market center, and has oil and sugar refineries. It is the central link between the interior cities and the Mediterranean coast.

Homyel \kȯ-'myel\ *or* **Gomel** \gȯ-'mel\ *or* **Homel** \hȯ-'mel\ City (pop., 1996 est.: 512,000), capital of Gomel province, southeastern Belarus. First mentioned in AD 1142 as Gomy, it passed to Lithuania in the 14th century and later to Poland; it was acquired by Russia in 1772. In the late 19th century it developed as a major railway junction, and industries began to flourish. The city, on the Sozh River, now is an important port, with river connections to towns on the DNIEPER RIVER. It is also an industrial center.

Honan See HENAN

Honda Motor Co. Japanese manufacturer of motorcycles and automobiles. Founded as a maker of small, efficient engines by the engineer Honda Soichiro in 1946, the company was incorporated as Honda Motor Co. in 1948. The Honda C-100, a small-engine motorcycle, was introduced in 1953 and by 1959 was the largest-selling motorcycle in the world. In 1959 the company established a U.S. subsidiary. The company's sales now come largely from automobiles, which it began manufacturing in 1963. Especially known for lightweight, fuel-efficient passenger cars such as the Civic and Accord, it is today one of the largest automobile companies in the world. Its headquarters are in Tokyo.

Honduras *officially* **Republic of Honduras** Republic. Area: 43,277 sq mi (112,088 sq km). Population (1997 est.): 5,823,000. Capital: TEGUCIGALPA. The population is predominantly mestizo (mixed European and Indian). Language: Spanish (official). Religion: Roman Catholicism (majority). Currency: Honduran lempira. The second-largest country of CENTRAL AMERICA, Honduras has a 400-mi (645-km) coastline on the Caribbean to the north and a 45-mi (72-km) one on the Pacific to the south. More than three-fourths of Honduras is mountainous and wooded. The eastern lowlands include part of the MOSQUITO COAST. Most of the people live in isolated communities in the mountainous interior, where the climate is hot and rainy. The economy is primarily agricultural, with bananas, coffee, and sugar for export and corn as the chief domestic staple. Honduras is a multiparty republic with one legislative house, and the head of state and government is the president. It was part of the

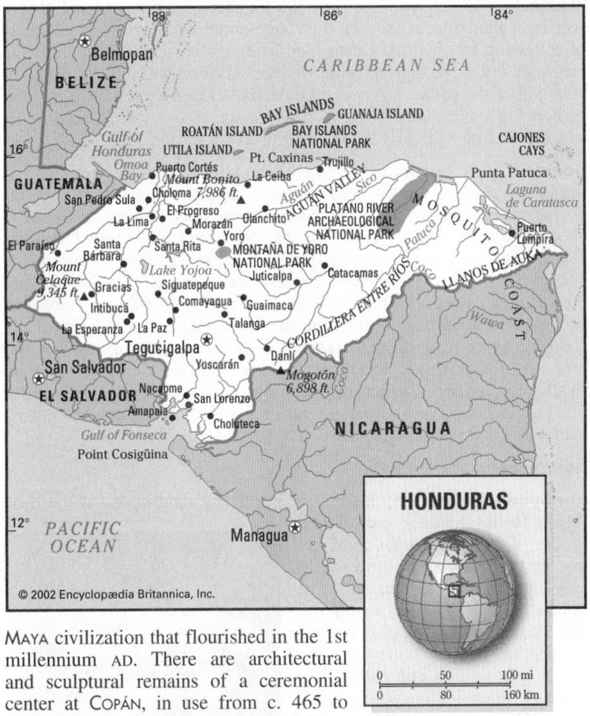

MAYA civilization that flourished in the 1st millennium AD. There are architectural and sculptural remains of a ceremonial center at COPÁN, in use from c. 465 to 800. CHRISTOPHER COLUMBUS reached Honduras in 1502, and permanent settlement followed. A major war between the Spaniards and the Indians broke out in 1537, culminating in the decimation of the Indian population through disease and enslavement. After 1570 it was part of the captaincy general of Guatemala until Central American independence in 1821. Part of the United Provinces of Central America, it withdrew in 1838 and declared its independence. In the 20th century, under military rule, there was constant civil war and some intervention by the U.S. A civilian government was elected to office in 1982. The military remained in the background, however, as the activity of leftist guerrillas increased. Flooding caused by a hurricane in 1998 devastated the country, killing several thousand people and leaving hundreds of thousands homeless. In 2001 Honduras was hit by a severe drought.

Honecker \'hō-nə-kər\, **Erich** (1912–1994) German communist head of East Germany's Socialist Unity Party (1971–89) and chairman of the Council of State (1976–89). A member of the German Communist Party, he was imprisoned by the Nazis 1935–45. In 1946 he cofounded and led the Free German Youth movement in East Germany. In 1961 he oversaw the building of the BERLIN WALL. He succeeded WALTER ULBRICHT as head of East Germany, which under his rule was one of the most repressive but also one of the most prosperous of the Soviet-bloc countries. He allowed the growth of some trade and travel ties with West Germany in return for West German financial aid. He was forced to resign with the collapse of communism in 1989.

H
I
J
K

Honegger \ȯ-nā-'ger, *Engl* 'hä-ni-gər\, **Arthur** (1892–1955) French composer. Born to Swiss-French parents, he studied in Zurich, then at the Paris Conservatory. One of the group known as Les Six, though not truly in sympathy with its aims, he first gained international renown for his oratorio *Le roi David* (1921). His exciting orchestral piece *Pacific 231* (1923), portraying a locomotive, caused a sensation. Prolific throughout his life, he composed five symphonies (including no. 3, "Liturgique," for the end of World War II), the oratorio *Jeanne d'Arc au bûcher* (1938), and numerous scores for ballet, theater, and films (including Abel Gance's *Napoleon*).

Honen \'hō-nen\ *orig.* **Seishimaru** (1133–1212) Japanese Buddhist leader. As a monk at the Mount Hiei monastery of the Tendai (Tiantai) sect, he learned the Pure Land doctrines of Chinese Buddhism (see Pure Land Buddhism), which taught salvation by the mercy of Amitabha Buddha, and he subsequently became the founder of the Pure Land (Jodo) sect in Japan. Honen believed that few people were spiritually capable of following the Buddha's own path to enlightenment, and in 1175 he proclaimed that the only thing needed for salvation was the *nembutsu,* or chanting of the name of Amida (Amitabha). Honen settled at Kyoto and gathered disciples, including Shinran. Persecuted by other Buddhists, he was driven into exile in 1207 but returned to Kyoto in 1211.

honey Sweet, viscous liquid food, dark golden in color, produced in the honey sacs of various bees from the nectar of flowers. Honey has played an enormous role in human nutrition since ancient times; until about 250 years ago, it was almost the sole sweetening agent. Commercial honeys are often produced from clover by the domestic honeybee. The nectar is ripened into honey by inversion of most of its sucrose into the sugars levulose (fructose) and dextrose (glucose) and the removal of excess moisture. Honey is stored in the beehive or nest in a honeycomb, a double layer of uniform hexagonal cells constructed of beeswax and propolis (a plant resin). The honey and comb are used in winter as food for the bee larvae and other members of the colony. Honey extracted for human consumption is usually heated to destroy fermentation-causing yeasts and then strained. See also beekeeping.

honey bear See sun bear

honeybee Broadly, any bee that makes honey (any insect of the tribe Apini, family Apidae); more strictly, one of the four species constituting the genus *Apis.* The term is usually applied to one species, the domestic honeybee *(A. mellifera),* also known as the European domestic bee or western honeybee. The other *Apis* species are confined to Asia. *A. mellifera* is usually about 0.5 in. (1.2 cm) long. All honeybees are social insects that live in nests or hives. They have three castes: workers (undeveloped females), queens, and drones (stingless males). See also beekeeping.

Honeybee (*Apis mellifera*).

INGMAR HOLMASEN

honeysuckle family Family Caprifoliaceae, containing approximately 500 species. It is well known for its many ornamental woody shrubs and vines, composed mostly of northern temperate species but including some tropical mountain plants. The genus *Lonicera* contains shrubs with opposite leaves and often showy flowers rich in nectar. One member, Japanese honeysuckle *(L. japonica),* is a highly fragrant flowering vine that kills other plants by climbing over them and shutting out the light. Also included in this family is the elder.

Hong Kong *or* **Xianggang** \'shyäŋ-'gäŋ\ Special administrative region of China (pop., 1997 est.: 6,491,000). Located off China's southern coast in the South China Sea, it comprises the island of Hong Kong and adjacent islets, ceded by China to the British in 1842, and the Kowloon Peninsula and the New Territories, both of which were leased by the British from China for 99 years (1898–1997). The entire territory was returned to China in 1997. It covers 398 sq mi (1,031 sq km); the New Territories, lying north of the Kowloon Peninsula, and constituting an enclave in China's Guangdong province, are more than nine-tenths of the total area. The administrative center of Victoria on Hong Kong island's northwestern coast is also the center of economic activities. Hong

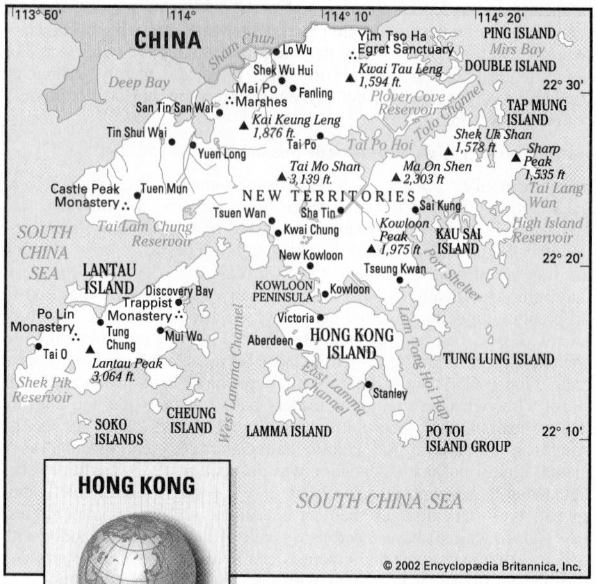

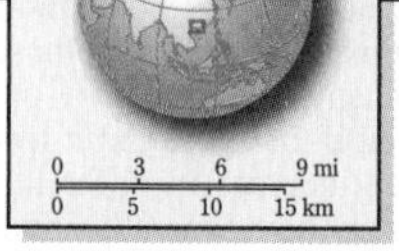

Kong has an excellent natural harbor and is one of the world's major trade and financial centers. It has many educational institutions, including the University of Hong Kong (1911).

Hong Kyong-nae Rebellion \'hȯŋ-'kyȯŋ-nä\ Peasant uprising in northern Korea in 1812 organized by Hong Kyong-nae, a fallen yangban, in response to oppressive taxation and forced labor during a time of famine caused by crop failure. The rebels prevailed for several months and were only put down after a concerted military campaign. A similar rebellion occurred in the 1860s.

Hong Xiuquan *or* **Hung Hsiu-ch'üan** \'hu̇ŋ-shē-'ü-chæ-'än\ (1814–1864) Chinese religious prophet, leader of the Taiping Rebellion. Born into a poor Hakka family, Hong showed signs of great intelligence but failed three times to obtain even the lowest degree on the civil-service exams. Suffering an emotional collapse, he had a vision in which he was instructed to rid the world of evil demons. He became the leader of his own brand of Christianity, demanded the abolition of opium smoking and prostitution, and promised an ultimate reward to his followers. In 1850 he began plotting a rebellion; the next year he declared himself Heavenly King of the Heavenly Kingdom of Great Peace (Taiping Tianguo). His army of more than a million men and women soldiers captured Nanjing, which became Hong's new capital. Power struggles culminated in his leaving affairs of state to his incompetent older brothers; he withdrew and committed suicide in 1864 after a lingering illness.

Hongli See Qianlong emperor

Hongshan culture *or* **Hung-shan culture** \'hu̇ŋ-'shän\ (4000–3000 BC) Prehistoric culture of the far north of China. It appears to have had a three-tiered elite whose members were honored with complex burials. Painted pottery found there may link it to Yangshao culture, while its beautiful jade artifacts link it to other jade-working cultures on the eastern coast, such as Liangzhu (3300–2200 BC). See also Erlitou culture, Longshan culture.

Hongshui River *or* **Hung-shui River** \'hu̇ŋ-'shwē\ River, southern China. Rising in eastern Yunnan, it flows south and east forming part of the boundary between Guizhou and Guangxi provinces. Flowing for 700 mi (1,125 km), it unites with the Xiang River in Guiping to form the Xi River.

Hongtaiji \'hu̇ŋ-'tī-'jē\ *or* **Abahai** *or* **Tiancong** \'tyän-'kȯŋ\ (1592–1643) Creator of the Qing empire in Manchuria. Under him, Inner Mongolia and Korea became vassal states of the Manchus. On the advice of his Chinese advisers, Hongtaiji began the conquest of China. He did not live to see its completion a year later, but his reign greatly strengthened the foundations of Manchu rule and he became the first emperor of the QING DYNASTY. See also DORGON, NURHACHI.

Hongwu emperor *or* **Hung-wu emperor** \'hu̇ŋ-wü\ *orig.* **Zhu Yuanzhang** (1328–1398) Founder of China's MING dynasty. A poor peasant orphaned at 16, he entered a monastery to avoid starvation. Later, as a rebel leader, he came in contact with educated gentry from whom he received an education and political guidance. He was advised to present himself not as a popular rebel but as a national leader against the foreign MONGOLS whose YUAN DYNASTY was on the point of collapse. Defeating rival national leaders, Zhu proclaimed himself emperor in 1368, establishing his capital at Nanjing and adopting Hongwu as his reign title. He drove the last Yuan emperor from China that year and reunified the country by 1382. His rule was despotic: he eliminated the posts of prime minister and central chancellor and had the next level of administration report directly to him. He prohibited EUNUCHS from participating in government and appointed civilian officials to control military affairs.

Hongze Hu *or* **Hung-tse Hu** \'hu̇ŋ-'dzə-'hü\ Lake, eastern China. Located in the HUAI RIVER valley between JIANGSU and ANHUI provinces, it was smaller in the 7th–10th century AD than its present surface area of 502 sq mi (1,300 sq km). In the 11th century, canals were constructed to make it part of a canal system between KAIFENG and Zhuzhou, joining the lake to the Huai. In 1194 the HUANG changed course, forcing the waters of the Huai into the lake, which then grew to its present size. In the 19th century flooding in the area was severe, and in the 1930s a new channel (improved in the 1950s) was dug from the lake's eastern shore direct to the sea.

Honiara \ˌhō-nē-'är-ə\ Town (pop., 1996 est.: 44,000), capital of the SOLOMON ISLANDS, South Pacific Ocean. Situated at the mouth of the Mataniko River on the north coast of GUADALCANAL, it is a port and communications center which trades chiefly in coconuts, timber, fish, and some gold. It developed during World War II around the site of the U.S. military headquarters and became the capital in 1952.

Honnecourt, Villard de See VILLARD DE HONNECOURT

Honolulu City (pop., 1996 est.: 423,000), capital, and principal port of Hawaii, on OAHU island. It is the crossroads of trans-Pacific shipping and air routes, the focus of inter-island services, and the commercial and industrial center of the state. Its area of 597 sq mi (1,545 sq km) includes some outlying islets, which constitute the Hawaiian and Pacific Islands National Wildlife Refuge. Honolulu has about 80% of the state's population. The area was settled from c. 1100, according to Hawaiian legends. During the 19th century, Honolulu flourished as a trade center especially for whalers. In 1898 it passed with the rest of Hawaii to U.S. control. In December 1941 the city and adjacent PEARL HARBOR were bombed by the Japanese. It became a prime staging area for the rest of WORLD WAR II, and later for the KOREAN and VIETNAM wars. The military remains an important source of income. The port serves numerous manufacturing plants. Nearby Waikiki Beach is a prime tourist site.

Honor, Legion of See LEGION OF HONOR

Honorius III \hō-'nōr-ē-əs\ *orig.* **Cencio Savelli** (died 1227) Pope (1216–27). He extended INNOCENT III's policies on church reform and the recovery of the Holy Land, proclaiming a crusade to regain Jerusalem in 1215 (see CRUSADES). He crowned FREDERICK II as Holy Roman Emperor (1220) but threatened to excommunicate him if he failed to join the crusade. Honorius also undertook a crusade against the Moors in Spain (1218) and settled the Barons' War in England (1223). He continued the ALBIGENSIAN CRUSADE against the heretics of southern France. He approved the Dominican, Franciscan, and Carmelite orders and authorized the first official book of canon law.

Honshu \'hȯn-ˌshü\ Island (pop., 1990: 100,254,000), Japan. The largest of the four main islands of Japan, its coastline extends 6,266 mi (10,084 km); it has an area of 87,992 sq mi (227,898 sq km). It is regarded as the Japanese mainland, and much of the country's early history took place in its southern region. The Pacific coast is the country's main economic center, lined with the metropolitan areas of TOKYO-Yokohama and OSAKA-Kobe. Honshu contains Japan's largest mountain, Mount FUJI, and its largest lake, Lake BIWA.

Hontan, Baron de La See Baron de LA HONTAN

Honthorst \'hȯnt-ˌhȯrst\, **Gerrit van** *known as* **Gherardo delle Notti (Italian: "Gerard of the Night Scenes")** (1592–1656) Dutch painter. During 10 years in Italy (c. 1610–20) he enjoyed the patronage of the nobility and assimilated the style of CARAVAGGIO. The dramatic effects of artificial light in his early paintings, as in such nocturnal scenes as *Supper Party* (1620), earned him his nickname. He was court painter at The Hague 1637–52. Some of REMBRANDT's early works were inspired by his use of CHIAROSCURO. With HENDRIK TERBRUGGHEN, he was a leader of the UTRECHT SCHOOL.

Hooch \'hōk\, **Pieter de** *or* **Pieter de Hoogh** \'hōk\ (1629–1684) Dutch genre painter. He trained in Haarlem and was a member of the painters' guild of Delft 1655–57. In style and subject matter, his work is similar to that of JOHANNES VERMEER; he was noted for his small interiors and sunny outdoor scenes, with figures engaged in humble, domestic activities in settings of serene simplicity. In his best works, such as *A Woman and Her Maid in a Court* (1658) and *The Pantry* (c. 1658), he was concerned with the effect of enclosures on light intensity, tonal variations, and linear perspective. After he moved to Amsterdam (c. 1661), his paintings increased in quantity but declined in quality. He died in a madhouse.

Hood, Mt. Peak, northwestern Oregon. Located in the CASCADE RANGE, at 11,235 ft (3,424 m) high, it is an extinct volcano that last erupted c. 1865. The snowcapped peak, the highest mountain in the state, is the focal point of Mount Hood National Forest, a popular tourist and recreation area.

Hood, Raymond M(athewson) (1881–1934) U.S. architect. Born in Pawtucket, R.I., he studied at MIT and the École des Beaux-Arts in Paris. He and John Mead Howells (1868–1959) won first prize in the 1922 Chicago Tribune Building competition; their design would be one of their many Neo-Gothic skyscrapers influenced by CASS GILBERT's Woolworth Building. Later he turned away from the revival of past styles; his Daily News (1930; with Howells) and McGraw-Hill (1930–31; with J. A. Fouilhoux) buildings, both in New York, have cleaner lines, foreshadowing the ROCKEFELLER CENTER complex.

hoof-and-mouth disease See FOOT-AND-MOUTH DISEASE

Hooghly River See HUGLI RIVER

Hooke, Robert (1635–1703) English physicist. From 1665 he taught at Oxford University. His achievements and theories were bewilderingly diverse. His important law of elasticity, known as Hooke's law (1660), states that the stretching of a solid is proportional to the force applied to it. He was one of the first to build and use a reflecting telescope. He suggested that Jupiter rotates on its axis, and his detailed sketches of Mars were later used to determine its rate of rotation. He suggested that a pendulum could be used to measure gravitation, and attempted to show that the earth and moon follow an elliptical orbit around the sun. He discovered diffraction, and proposed the wave theory of light to explain it. He was one of the first proponents of the theory of evolution. He was the first to state in general that all matter expands when heated and that air is made up of particles separated from each other by relatively large distances. He invented a marine barometer, contributed improvements to clocks, the quadrant, and the universal joint, and anticipated the steam engine.

Hooker, Joseph (1814–1879) U.S. Army officer. Born in Hadley, Mass., he attended West Point and served in the Mexican War. Appointed brigadier general of volunteers at the outbreak of the Civil War, he participated in major campaigns and became known as "Fighting Joe." He succeeded AMBROSE E. BURNSIDE as commander of the Army of the Potomac after the disastrous Battle of FREDERICKSBURG. He reorganized the army but failed to defeat ROBERT E. LEE at the Battle of Chancellorsville, incurring heavy Union casualties. He resigned just

Joseph Hooker.
BY COURTESY OF THE LIBRARY OF CONGRESS, WASHINGTON, D.C.

H I J K

before the Battle of GETTYSBURG, but later helped secure the Union victory at the Battle of CHATTANOOGA.

Hooker, Richard (1554?–1600) English clergyman and theologian. He attended Oxford Univ., became a fellow of Corpus Christi College in 1577, and was ordained in 1581. He served as master of the Temple Church (1585–91) and later was vicar of churches at Drayton Beauchamp, Boscombe, and Bishopsbourne. He created a distinctive Anglican theology during a time when the Church of ENGLAND was threatened by both ROMAN CATHOLICISM and PURITANISM. His great work was *Of the Laws of Ecclesiastical Polity* (1594–97), in which he defended the threefold authority of the Bible, church tradition, and human reason.

Hooker, Thomas (1586–1647) British-American colonial clergyman. He held pastorates in England (1620–30), where he was attacked for Puritan leanings. He fled to Holland, and emigrated to the Massachusetts Bay Colony in 1633. As pastor of a company of Puritans, he moved them to Connecticut to settle Hartford in 1636. He helped frame the Fundamental Orders (1639), which later formed the basis of the Connecticut constitution.

Hooper, Franklin Henry (1862–1940) U.S. editor. Born in Worcester, Mass., he was the brother of HORACE EVERETT HOOPER, publisher of *ENCYCLOPÆDIA BRITANNICA*. He joined the *Britannica* staff in 1899, and over the next 30 years he was connected with five editions of the *Britannica,* serving as editor in chief 1932–38.

Hooper, Horace Everett (1859–1922) U.S. publisher. Born in Worcester, Mass., Hooper left school at 16 and became involved in bookselling. With the collaboration of *The TIMES* of London, he produced a highly successful reprint of the *ENCYCLOPÆDIA BRITANNICA*'s ninth edition (1875–89). In 1901 he and Walter Jackson purchased *Britannica* outright; it was sold in 1920. He planned and published the 10th edition (1902–3), of which his brother FRANKLIN HENRY HOOPER was an editor; the 11th edition (1910–11), famed for being wholly new and the pinnacle of literary style in the *Britannica;* and the 12th edition (1922).

Hoorn Islands See FUTUNA ISLANDS

Hoover, Herbert (Clark) (1874–1964) 31st president of the U.S. (1929–33). Born in West Branch, Iowa, he became a mining engineer, and administered engineering projects on four continents (1895–1913), then headed Allied relief operations in England and Belgium. During World War I he was appointed U.S. national food administrator (1917–19) and instituted programs that furnished food to the Allies and famine-stricken areas of Europe. Appointed U.S. secretary of commerce (1921–27), he reorganized the department, creating divisions to regulate broadcasting and aviation. He oversaw commissions to build Boulder (later Hoover) Dam and the St. Lawrence Seaway. In 1928, as the Republican presidential candidate, he soundly defeated ALFRED E. SMITH. His hopes for a "New Day" program were quickly overwhelmed by the GREAT DEPRESSION. As a believer in individual freedom, he vetoed bills to create a federal unemployment agency and to fund public-works projects, instead favoring private charity. In 1932 he finally allowed relief to farmers through the RECONSTRUCTION FINANCE CORP. He was overwhelmingly defeated in 1932 by FRANKLIN ROOSEVELT. He continued to speak out against relief measures and criticized New Deal programs. After World War II he participated in famine-relief work in Europe and was appointed head of the HOOVER COMMISSION.

Hoover, J(ohn) Edgar (1895–1972) U.S. director of the FEDERAL BUREAU OF INVESTIGATION. Born in Washington, D.C., he became a lawyer in the U.S. justice department, and assisted Attorney General A. MITCHELL PALMER in the deportation cases of suspected Bolsheviks. In 1924 he was named director of the Bureau of Investigation, which he remade into a professional, merit-based organization. In the 1930s he successfully publicized its achievements in capturing gangsters and expanded the size of the renamed FBI. He received authorization to investigate the activities of communists and fascists, which he expanded to include surveillance of all radicals and activists, including the KU KLUX KLAN and MARTIN LUTHER KING. He gave little attention to organized crime but kept secret files on many politicians, which he used to discourage presidents and others from criticizing his work and conduct. Despite criticism from other sources, he retained his post for 48 years until his death.

J. Edgar Hoover.
AP/WIDE WORLD PHOTOS

Hoover Commission (1947–49, 1953–55) Advisory body headed by former Pres. HERBERT HOOVER to examine the organization of the U.S. executive branch. The first commission, officially titled the Commission on Organization of the U.S. Executive Branch, was appointed by Pres. HARRY TRUMAN to reduce the number of federal government departments. Recommendations from this and a second commission appointed by Pres. DWIGHT D. EISENHOWER were largely adopted. Some agencies were consolidated and new bodies were created, including the Department of Health, Education, and Welfare and the General Services Administration.

Hoover Dam *formerly* **Boulder Dam** Highest concrete arch DAM in the U.S., built on the Colorado River at the Arizona–Nevada border. It impounds Lake MEAD. The dam, completed in 1936, is used for flood and silt control, electric power, irrigation, and domestic and industrial water supplies. It is 726 ft (221 m) high and 1,244 ft (379 m) long (along the crest), has a power capacity of 1,345 megawatts, and a volume of 4.4 million cu yd (3.36 million cu m).

Hoover Institution on War, Revolution and Peace THINK TANK founded in 1919 (as the Hoover War Library) by HERBERT HOOVER. It is located at, but has no institutional connection with, Stanford Univ., in Palo Alto, Cal. It houses source materials on social and political developments connected to the two World Wars. Resident and visiting scholars in such fields as economics, political science, history, international relations, and law study, write, and publish the results of their work. Known for its conservative bent, the institution holds that free enterprise and limited government are foundation blocks of the American way of life, which it undertakes to safeguard through its studies of war and humanity's efforts to secure peace.

hop In botany, either of two species of the genus *Humulus,* nonwoody annual or perennial vines in the HEMP family, native to temperate North America, Eurasia, and South America. The hops used in the brewery industry (see BEER) are the dried female flower clusters (CONES) of the common hop *(H. lupulus),* a long-lived perennial with rough twining stems. Hops impart a mellow bitterness and delicate aroma to brewed beverages and aid in their preservation. The Japanese hop *(H. japonicus)* is a quick-growing annual species used as a screening vine.

Hop (*Humulus lupulus*).
GRANT HEILMAN

hop, step, and jump See TRIPLE JUMP

Hope, Bob *orig.* **Leslie Townes** (born 1903) U.S. (British-born) actor. His family emigrated to Ohio when he was 4. He created a song-and-comedy vaudeville act and in 1933 won his first substantial role in a musical, *Roberta.* Success in radio led to his first film, *The Big Broadcast of 1938,* in which he sang his theme song, "Thanks for the Memory." He hosted the highly rated *Bob Hope Show* (1938–50) on radio, and later hosted and appeared in numerous popular television specials. He costarred with BING CROSBY and Dorothy Lamour in seven popular "Road" pictures, beginning with *The Road to Singapore* (1940), and won fans in *The Paleface* (1948), *My Favorite Spy* (1951), and *The Seven Little Foys* (1955). For over 40 years he performed with his variety show for U.S. troops overseas.

Hope diamond Blue diamond from India, one of the largest blue diamonds known. Named for the London banker Thomas Hope, who purchased it in 1830, the 45.5-carat diamond is on display in the Smithsonian Institution. See photograph on following page.

The Hope diamond; in the Smithsonian Institution, Washington, D.C.
LEE BOLTIN

Hopeh See HEBEI

Hopewell culture *formerly* **Mound Builders** Most notable ancient Indian culture of eastern central North America. It flourished c. 200 BC–AD 500, chiefly in the Illinois and Ohio river valleys. (The name derives from a farm where the first site was explored.) The Hopewell Indians built earthen mounds for enclosure, burial, religious rites, and defense. Hopewell villages lay along rivers and streams. The inhabitants raised corn and possibly beans and squash but still relied upon hunting and gathering. They produced pottery and metalwork. Trade routes were evidently well developed. After AD 400 Hopewell culture gradually disappeared. See also WOODLAND CULTURES.

Hopi \'hō-pē\ Westernmost group of PUEBLO INDIANS, living on reservation lands in northeastern Arizona surrounded by the NAVAJO Reservation. They speak a language of the UTO-AZTECAN stock. Most of their traditional settlements were on high mesas and consisted of terraced PUEBLO structures of stone and adobe. Their precise origin is unknown, though they are usually considered descendants of the ANASAZI peoples. Matrilineal descent was the rule. They supported themselves by growing corn, beans, squash, and melons and by sheepherding. Hopi life was steeped in religious ceremony and involved secret rites held in semi-underground KIVAS (pit-houses) and the use of masks and costumes to impersonate KACHINAS (ancestral spirits). The Hopi number about 6,000 today.

Hopkins, Anthony *later* **Sir Anthony** (born 1937) British actor. He joined London's National Theatre in 1965, where he starred in Shakespearean roles. A subtle actor able to convey volcanic emotion with a small gesture, he made an acclaimed Broadway debut in *Equus* (1974) and stayed on in the U.S. for such films as *The Elephant Man* (1980) and such television productions as *The Bunker* (1981, Emmy award). At the National Theatre he triumphed in *King Lear* and *Antony and Cleopatra*. His later films include *The Silence of the Lambs* (1991, Academy Award), *Howards End* (1992), *The Remains of the Day* (1993), and *Amistad* (1997).

Hopkins, Esek (1718–1802) American naval officer. Born in Providence, R.I., he took command of a merchant fleet by 1754. In the French and Indian War he was a privateer. In 1775 he was appointed the first commander of the Continental Navy. Instructed to attack the British fleet in Chesapeake Bay, he sailed instead for the Bahamas, where he captured the British post at New Providence. He returned to Rhode Island, where the fleet became largely inactive. In 1776 an investigation by Congress led to his censure for disobedience. The fleet's continuing inactivity led to his suspension from command (1777) and dismissal (1778).

Hopkins, Frederick Gowland *later* **Sir Frederick** (1861–1947) British biochemist. He discovered the AMINO ACID TRYPTOPHAN (1901) and showed that it and certain others are essential in the diet and cannot be made in the body from other substances. For his discovery of VITAMINS, he shared a 1929 Nobel Prize with CHRISTIAAN EIJKMAN. He demonstrated that working muscles accumulate LACTIC ACID and isolated the tripeptide (see PEPTIDE) glutathione (1922) and showed that it is vital to utilization of oxygen by cells. He was knighted in 1925.

Hopkins, Gerard Manley (1844–1889) British poet. After studies at Oxford, he converted to Roman Catholicism and eventually became a Jesuit priest. He burned his youthful verses as inappropriate to his profession; he began writing again in 1875, but was increasingly troubled by the tension between his religious vocation and his delight in the sensuous world. One of the most individual of Victorian writers, he is noted for intense language, compressed syntax, and innovations in prosody, including SPRUNG RHYTHM. His best-known poems include "The Wreck of the Deutschland," "Pied Beauty," "God's Grandeur," and "The Windhover." He died of typhoid at 44. His work, though not published in collected form until 1918 (by his friend ROBERT BRIDGES), influenced many 20th-century poets.

Hopkins, Harry L(loyd) (1890–1946) U.S. NEW DEAL official. Born in Sioux City, Iowa, he worked as a social worker in New York in the 1920s. He directed the state's emergency relief agency from 1931. After FRANKLIN ROOSEVELT became president, Hopkins became head of the Federal Emergency Relief Administration. In 1934 he created the WORKS PROGRESS ADMINISTRATION. He served as U.S. commerce secretary (1938–40). He resigned to make several trips for the president to London and Moscow to discuss assistance and military strategy, and he later directed the LEND-LEASE program. He was regarded as Roosevelt's closest personal adviser during World War II.

Hopkins, Johns (1795–1873) U.S. merchant and financier. Born in Anne Arundel Co., Md., he worked with an uncle as a wholesale grocer before establishing Hopkins Brothers wholesalers with his brothers in 1819. The firm soon prospered in several states, accepting payment for goods in whiskey, which it then sold as Hopkins' Best. Hopkins retired in 1847 a wealthy man, and continued investing in Baltimore real estate and the Baltimore and Ohio Railroad. In his will he left $7 million to fund the establishment of JOHNS HOPKINS UNIV. and Johns Hopkins Hospital, and also endowed an orphanage for black children.

Hopkins, Mark (1814–1878) U.S. entrepreneur. Born in Richmond Co., Va., he was brought up in North Carolina. After an unprofitable attempt to mine gold in California in 1851, he began selling groceries and established one of the most prosperous mercantile houses in the state. With three other merchants he planned a transcontinental railroad, and in 1861 they organized the CENTRAL PACIFIC RAILROAD. In 1869 the main line was completed, meeting the UNION PACIFIC at Promontory, Utah.

Hopkins, Pauline (Elizabeth) (1859–1930) U.S. novelist and playwright. Born in Portland, Me., she performed with her family's singing group before writing her first novel, *Contending Forces* (1900). Later novels include *Hagar's Daughter* (1902), *Winona* (1902), *Of One Blood* (1903), and *Topsy Templeton* (1916). The novels reflect the influence of W. E. B. DU BOIS and uses the form of the traditional romance novel to explore racial and social themes. She also worked as an editor of the *Colored American Magazine*.

Hopkins, Sarah Winnemucca *or* **Sarah Hopkins Winnemucca** *or* **Thocmectony** (1844?–1891) U.S. educator, lecturer, tribal leader, and writer. Born to a Northern Paiute family in Humboldt Sink, Mexico (now Nevada), she lived as a child with a white family and attended a convent school, and later served as an army interpreter and scout. Her lecture tours in the East in the 1880s publicized the plight of her tribe and protested government policies. Her writings, of which *Life Among the Piutes* (1883) is the best known, are valuable for their description of Indian life and their insights into the impact of white settlement, and are among the few contemporary Native American works.

Hopkinson, Francis (1737–1791) U.S. political leader and writer. Born in Philadelphia, he practiced law in New Jersey. Appointed to the governor's council in 1774, he wrote anti-British political satires. A delegate to the Continental Congress in 1776, he signed the Declaration of Independence. He later wrote articles that helped win ratification of the U.S. Constitution. He served as judge of the admiralty court for Pennsylvania 1779–89, and as U.S. district judge 1789–91. He was also known for his musical compositions and his design of numerous governmental and organizational seals.

hoplite \'häp-,līt\ Heavily armed foot soldier of ancient Greece whose function was to fight in close formation. They probably first appeared in the late 8th century BC. They were equipped with new and heavier armor, including a metal helmet, breastplate, and shield; each had a sword and a 6-ft (2-m) spear for thrusting rather than throwing. From then on, battles were won not by individual champions but through the weight of massed hoplite PHALANXES breaking through enemy ranks. Though the phalanx was unwieldy and the equipment cumbersome, Greek hoplites were the best fighters in the Mediterranean world.

Hoppe \'hä-pē\, **Willie** *orig.* **William Frederick** (1887–1959) U.S. billiards player. Born in Cornwall-on-the-Hudson, N.Y., he was taught billiards by his hotelkeeper father. A master of carom technique, he became one of the most durable of all sports champions, winning 51 world titles between 1906 and 1952. In the 1940 tournament in Chicago he was undefeated in 20 matches. He retired in 1952.

Hopper, Edward (1882–1967) U.S. painter. Born in Nyack, N.Y., he was initially trained as an illustrator and later studied painting with ROBERT HENRI. In 1913 he exhibited in the ARMORY SHOW but spent much of his time on advertising art and illustrative etchings. In the mid-1920s he turned to watercolors and oil paintings of urban life. His *House by the Railroad* (1925) and *Room in Brooklyn* (1932) depict still, anonymous figures and within geometric building forms, producing the haunting sense of isolation that was to be his hallmark. He used light to isolate figures and objects, as in *Early Sunday Morning* (1930) and *Nighthawks* (1942). His mature style was already formed in the 1920s; his later development showed constant refinement and an even greater mastery of light. He strongly influenced the Pop art and New Realist painters of the 1960s and '70s.

Hopper, Grace Murray *orig.* **Grace Brewster Murray** (1906–1992) U.S. mathematician and rear admiral. Born in New York City, she received her PhD from Yale University in 1934 and taught at Vassar College 1931–44. As a U.S. Navy officer (1943–86), she worked on Harvard's Mark I (1944) and Mark II (1945) computers, and in 1949 helped design an improved compiler for translating a programmer's instructions into computer codes. She helped devise UNIVAC I, the first commercial electronic computer (1951), and wrote naval applications for COBOL. She received the National Medal of Technology in 1991.

Horace *Latin* **Quintus Horatius Flaccus** (65–8 BC) Latin lyric poet and satirist. The son of a former slave, he was educated in Rome. He fought in BRUTUS' army in the upheaval after Julius CAESAR'S murder, but later gained the favor of Brutus' conqueror, Octavian (later AUGUSTUS), and achieved virtually the status of poet laureate. His early works include books of *Satires* and *Epodes*, but his fame rests chiefly on his books of lyrical *Odes* and verse *Epistles*, including the treatise *Ars poetica*, which sets down rules for the composition of poetry. The *Odes* and *Epistles,* frequently on themes of love, friendship, and philosophy, significantly influenced Western poetry from the Renaissance through the 19th century.

Horbat Qesari See CAESAREA

Horeb, Mt. See Mount SINAI

horizon In PEDOLOGY, a distinct layer of soil forming part of the vertical sequence in a soil profile. Each horizon differs from the one above or below it in color, chemical composition, texture, and structure. The horizons become differentiated during soil development because conditions vary with depth. There are generally three major layers within any given soil profile, and they are designated, from surface downward, as A, B, and C horizons. The A horizon generally contains more organic matter than the others; it is also the most weathered and leached. The B horizon tends to be a zone of accumulation, since all or part of the mineral matter removed from the A horizon in solution may be deposited in it. The C horizon consists chiefly of the materials from which the A and B layers were derived; called parent materials, these are only slightly altered, because they are in general not subjected to soil-forming processes.

horizontal bar Event in men's gymnastics competition in which a steel bar fixed about 8 ft (2.4 m) above the floor is used for swinging exercises. Competitors generally wear hand protectors and perform routines that last 15–30 seconds. Exercises include the giant swing and various vaults (such as the straddle vault). It has been an Olympic event since the first modern Olympic Games in 1896.

horizontal integration See VERTICAL INTEGRATION

Horkheimer, Max (1895–1973) German philosopher and social theorist. Together with THEODOR ADORNO and HERBERT MARCUSE, he became a leading figure of the FRANKFURT SCHOOL and also director of the Institute for Social Research, a Marxist-oriented research center. He moved with the institute to New York when the Nazis came to power (1933), returning to Frankfurt in 1949. His books include *Dialectic of Enlightenment* (with Adorno, 1947), *Eclipse of Reason* (1947), and *Critical Theory* (1968), which expounded the Frankfurt school's basic principles.

hormone Organic compound (often a STEROID or PEPTIDE) that is produced in one part of a multicellular organism and travels to another part to exert its action. Hormones regulate physiological activities including growth, REPRODUCTION, and HOMEOSTASIS in vertebrates; MOLTING and maintenance of the larval state (see LARVA) in insects; and growth, bud dormancy, and leaf shedding in plants. Most vertebrate hormones originate in specialized tissues (see ENDOCRINE SYSTEM, GLAND) and are carried to their targets through the CIRCULATION. Among the many mammalian hormones are ACTH, SEX HORMONES, THYROXINE, INSULIN, and EPINEPHRINE. Insect hormones include ecdysone, thoracotropic hormone, and juvenile hormone. Plant hormones include abscisin, AUXINS, gibberellins, and cytokinins.

Hormuz \hȯr-'müz\ *formerly* **Ormuz** \ȯr-'müz\ Island and town, southern Iran. In the Strait of HORMUZ, the island is 5 mi (8 km) off the coast. Hormuz village on the island is the only permanent settlement. After the Arab conquest, Hormuz town was an important market and by AD 1200 it monopolized India's and China's trade. MARCO POLO twice visited there. Taken by the Portuguese in 1514, it was retaken by Persia in 1622. The town declined after the removal of its trade to Bandar Abbas on the mainland.

Hormuz, Strait of *formerly* **Strait of Ormuz** Channel linking the PERSIAN GULF with the Gulf of OMAN and the Arabian Sea. It is 35–60 mi (55–95 km) wide and separates Iran from the Arabian Peninsula. It contains the islands of Qeshm, HORMUZ, and Hengam, and is strategically and economically importance as a route for oil tankers collecting from various ports on the Persian Gulf.

Horn, Cape Cape, at southern extremity of South America. Located on Horn Island, in southern TIERRA DEL FUEGO archipelago, it projects south into DRAKE PASSAGE. It was named Hoorn for the birthplace of Dutch navigator W. C. Schouten, who rounded it in 1616. Navigation of the rough waters around the cape is hazardous, and the climate is windy and cold year-round.

Horn of Africa Region of eastern Africa. The easternmost African extension of land between the INDIAN OCEAN and the Gulf of ADEN, it is occupied by Ethiopia, Eritrea, Somalia, and Djibouti, whose cultures have been linked throughout their long history.

hornbill Any of about 45 species of Old World tropical birds (family Bucerotidae) noted for the bony helmet on the bill of some species. Hornbills range from 16 to 63 in. (40–160 cm) long, and typically have a large head, prominent bill, thin neck, broad wings, long tail, and brown or black plumage, usually with bold white markings. They nest in cavities, usually in large trees. The male of most species walls up the female in the nest, closing the hole with mud, except for a small opening through which he passes food. The female breaks out after the eggs hatch, but the young may be walled up again.

Red-billed hornbill (*Tockus erythrorhynchus*).
MARK BOULTON—THE NATIONAL AUDUBON SOCIETY COLLECTION/PHOTO RESEARCHERS

hornblende Any of a subgroup of AMPHIBOLE minerals that are calcium-iron-magnesium-rich and monoclinic in crystal structure. Hornblende, whose generalized chemical formula is $(Ca,Na)_2(Mg,Fe,Al)_5(Al,Si)_8O_{22}(OH)_2$, occurs widely in metamorphic and igneous rocks. Common hornblende is dark green to black in color and usually found in middle-grade metamorphic rocks (formed under medium conditions of temperature and pressure). Such metamorphic rocks with abundant hornblende are called AMPHIBOLITES.

Hornblower, Jonathan Carter (1753–1815) British inventor. He and his father, Jonathan (1717–1780), worked for JAMES WATT. Seeking to improve on Watt's STEAM-ENGINE design, he devised the first reciprocating compound steam engine (patented 1781); his engine had two cylinders (see PISTON AND CYLINDER), a significant contribution to EFFICIENCY. In 1799 it was judged an infringement on Watt's patent.

Hornbostel \'hȯrn-,bȯs-tᵊl\, **Erich (Moritz) von** (1877–1934) Austrian ethnomusicologist. Born into a musical family in Vienna, he was by his teens a skilled pianist and composer. After taking a doctorate in chemistry, he became involved in psychological research, and his studies of tonal perception led to his becoming one of the founders of ETHNOMUSICOLOGY. He helped establish the research program for the field and the methods used to carry it out, including field recordings. In 1912 he devised, with C. SACHS, the cross-cultural system of classification of musical instruments still in use.

Horne, Lena (Calhoun) (born 1917) U.S. singer and actress. Born in Brooklyn, Horne danced in her youth at Harlem's Cotton Club, and by 18 she was singing with popular bands. She starred in many films, including *Cabin in the Sky* (1943), *Stormy Weather* (1943), *Death of a Gunfighter* (1969), and *The Wiz* (1978). Her album *Lena Horne at the Waldorf-Astoria* (1957) was a great success, as was her appearance in the musical *Jamaica* (1957). Her one-woman show, *Lena Horne: The Lady and Her Music* (1981), was hailed as her masterpiece. She continued to perform and record into the 1990s.

Horne, Marilyn (born 1934) U.S. mezzo-soprano. Born in Bradford, Pa., she studied with Lotte Lehmann (1888–1976) and dubbed the leading role in the film *Carmen Jones* (1954). In 1960 she sang in A. BERG's *Wozzeck* in San Francisco and Chicago. Her long and influential association with the bel canto repertoire began in 1962, and she played an important role in the revival of operas by G.F. HANDEL and G. ROSSINI. Her distinctive voice was even throughout its remarkably wide range, and she had virtuoso control of breath and pitch. She retired in 2000 after a long career.

horned owl Any OWL of the genus *Bubo* (family Strigidae), with hornlike tufts of feathers, especially the GREAT HORNED OWL. Other horned owls, all BIRDS OF PREY, are found in Europe, Asia, and northern Africa (the eagle owl, or Eurasian eagle owl) and in Africa, India, Myanmar (Burma), and the Indonesian archipelago. They typically prey on rodents.

Great horned owl (*Bubo virginianus*).
E.R. DEGGINGER–VAN CLEVE PHOTOGRAPHY

horned toad *or* **horned lizard** Any of about 14 species of LIZARDS (genus *Phrynosoma,* family Iguanidae) that usually have daggerlike head spines (horns) and a flattened oval body with pointed fringe scales along the sides. Species range from about 3 to 5 in. (8–13 cm) long. They are found from British Columbia south to Guatemala and from Arkansas and Kansas westward, usually in desert or semidesert sandy country. They eat mainly ants. They hide by changing their color pattern and wriggling sideways into the sand until all but the head is covered. They may defend themselves by inflating the body quickly and (rarely) spurting blood from the eyes.

Horney \'hȯr-ˌnī\, **Karen** *orig.* **Karen Danielsen** (1885–1952) German-U.S. psychoanalyst. After receiving her M.D., she underwent psychoanalytic training with KARL ABRAHAM, and from 1920 to 1932 she conducted a private practice in Berlin and taught at the Berlin Psychoanalytic Institute. Settling in New York City in 1934, she began teaching at the New School for Social Research. She departed from some of SIGMUND FREUD's basic principles, rejecting his concept of penis envy and emphasizing the need to help patients identify and cope with the specific causes of current anxieties rather than focus on childhood traumas and fantasies. Expelled from the New York Psychoanalytic Institute in 1941, she organized a new group, the Association for the Advancement of Psychoanalysis. Her works include *The Neurotic Personality of Our Time* (1937) and *New Ways in Psychoanalysis* (1939).

Hornsby, Rogers (1896–1963) U.S. baseball player. Born in Winters, Texas, he played second base most of his career. He played for the St. Louis Cardinals (1915–26). His career batting average of .358 is second only to TY COBB's .367. For five years (1921–25) he averaged .401; his 1924 average of .424 was the highest attained in the 20th century. He and TED WILLIAMS are the only players to have twice led their league in home runs, runs batted in, and batting average. After retiring he became a baseball manager.

Hornsby, 1926.
UPI COMPIX

hornwort Any member of four to six genera of creeping annual or perennial plants of the class Anthocerotopsida. Hornworts usually grow on damp soils or on rocks in tropical and warm temperate regions. The GAMETOPHYTE typically is a flattened structure covered with small irregular lobes; the SPOROPHYTE forms a tapered cylinder (see ALTERNATION OF GENERATIONS). Rhizoids (rootlike structures) on the undersurface anchor the plant. Cavities in the gametophyte sometimes contain colonies of the cyanobacterium *Nostoc* (see CYANOBACTERIA, NOSTOC). Hornworts have a region of continuous growth at the base of the sporophyte, and a large, irregular foot. The stalk that attaches the foot to the spore-bearing capsule in LIVERWORTS is absent in hornworts.

horoscope Astrological chart showing the positions of the sun, moon, and planets in relation to the signs of the ZODIAC at a specific time. It is used to analyze the character of individuals born at that time, providing information about the current state of their life and predicting their future. Basic to a horoscope is the belief that each heavenly body has its own character, which is modified according to its relation to other celestial bodies at a given moment. To cast a horoscope, the heavens are divided into 12 zones called houses; these influence such aspects of human life as health, wealth, marriage, friendships, or death. See also ASTROLOGY.

Horowitz, Vladimir (1903–1989) Russian pianist. He attended the Kiev Conservatory and made his debut in 1921. His stunning technique gained him a large international reputation, and he became an inveterate touring performer, giving 100 concerts a year in the U.S. alone. In 1933 he married A. TOSCANINI's daughter, Wanda. Always susceptible to nervous strain, in 1953 he decided to quit public performance; his return to the concert stage in 1965 was attended by great publicity. He favored the works of Romantics such as R. SCHUMANN, F. CHOPIN, F. LISZT, and his friend S. RACHMANINOFF. He was sometimes criticized for employing his dazzling capacities to insufficiently profound interpretations.

horror story Story that focuses on creating a feeling of fear. Such tales are of ancient origin and form a substantial part of folk literature. They may feature supernatural elements such as ghosts, witches, or vampires, or address more realistic psychological fears. In Western literature, the literary cultivation of fear and curiosity for its own sake emerged in the 18th century with the GOTHIC NOVEL. Classic practitioners of the horror and gothic genres include Horace WALPOLE, MARY SHELLEY, E.T.A. HOFFMANN, EDGAR ALLAN POE, Sheridan Le Fanu (1814–1873), WILKIE COLLINS, BRAM STOKER, AMBROSE BIERCE, H. P. Lovecraft (1890–1937), and STEPHEN KING.

horse EQUINE species (Equus caballus) long used by humans as a means of transport and as a draft animal. Its earliest ancestor was the dawn horse (see EOHIPPUS). The only living horse not descended from the domestic horse is PRZEWALSKI'S HORSE. The horse was apparently first domesticated by nomadic peoples of central Asia in the 3rd millennium BC. Horses were primarily used in warfare for many centuries. The SADDLE was introduced in China in the first centuries AD. Horses were reintroduced to the New World, after wild horses had become extinct there some 10,000 years earlier, by the Spanish in the 16th century. A mature male is called a stallion or, if used for breeding, a stud; mature females are called mares. A castrated stallion is called a gelding. Young horses (foals) are also known as colts (males) and fillies (females). A horse's height is measured in 4-in. (10.2-cm) units, or hands, from the highest point of the back (withers) to the ground. Breeds are classified by size and build: draft (heavy) horses (e.g., Belgian, PERCHERON) are heavy-limbed and up to 20 hands high; PONIES (e.g., SHETLAND, Iceland) are less

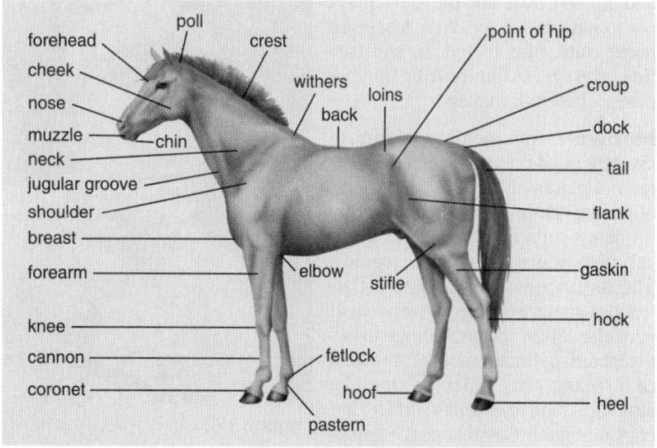

External features of a horse.

than 14.2 hands high; and light horses (e.g., Arabian, Thoroughbred) are intermediate, rarely taller than 17 hands.

horse-chestnut family Family Hippocastanaceae, composed of the buckeyes and the horse chestnuts (genus *Aesculus*), native to the northern temperate zone. The best-known species of horse chestnut is the common, or European, horse chestnut *(A. hippocastanum),* native to southeastern Europe but widely cultivated as a large shade and street tree. The Champs-Élysées in Paris is lined with rows of horse-chestnut trees.

horse racing Sport of running horses at speed, mainly Thoroughbreds with a rider astride or Standardbreds with the horse pulling a conveyance with a driver. Though racing has an ancient lineage, the first regularly organized national races were established in England under Charles II (r.1660–85), and the first in North America were held on Long Island in 1665. These early races were match events between two or three horses and were run in heats; a horse had to complete at least two heats to be judged the winner. By the mid-18th century, larger fields of runners and single-race "dash" events were the norm. Handicap racing emerged in the mid-18th century as well, as gambling came to be a standard part of horse racing. Pari-mutuel betting was instituted in the 20th century. Thoroughbred racing, conducted on a flat, elliptical, mile-long track, attracts the largest purses, followed by harness racing and quarter-horse racing. The most important U.S. Thoroughbred races are the Kentucky Derby, Preakness Stakes, and Belmont Stakes. See also steeplechase.

horsefly Any member of the dipteran genus *Tabanus* or, more generally, of the family Tabanidae. These stout flies range from as small as a housefly to as large as a bumblebee. Sometimes called greenheaded monsters, horseflies have metallic or iridescent eyes. Adults are fast, strong fliers usually found around streams, marshes, and wooded areas. They may carry animal diseases, including anthrax, tularemia, and trypanosomiasis. The bites of the bloodsucking females can be painful, and a swarm may suck more than 3 oz (about 90 ml) of blood a day from an animal. Males feed on nectar, honeydew, and plant sap. Horseflies of the genus *Chrysops,* usually called deerflies, are smaller and have dark markings on the wings.

horsehair worm *or* **hairworm** *or* **gordian worm** Any of about 250–300 species (class Nematomorpha, or Gordiacea; phylum Aschelminthes) of long, thin worms. The young are parasites in arthropods; the adults are free-living in the sea or in freshwater. The hairlike body sometimes grows to a length of about 39 in. (1 m).

horsemanship Art of training, riding, and handling horses. Good horsemanship requires that a rider control the animal's direction, gait, and speed with maximum effectiveness and minimum effort. Natural aids are a rider's balance, hands, voice, and legs; artificial aids include bits, reins, saddles, and spurs. Horsemanship was important to cavalrymen and cowboys, and is the fundamental element of dressage.

horsepower Common unit of power, the rate at which work is done. In the English system, one horsepower equals 33,000 foot-pounds of work per minute—that is, the power necessary to lift a total of 33,000 lbs mass one foot in one minute. This value was adopted by James Watt in the late 18th century after experiments with strong dray horses, and is actually about 50% more than the rate an average horse can sustain for a working day. The electrical equivalent of one horsepower is 746 watts in the International System of Units; the heat equivalent is 2,545 BTU per hour. The metric horsepower (see metric system) equals 4,500 kg-m per minute (32,549 foot-pounds per minute), or 0.9863 horsepower.

horseradish Hardy perennial plant *(Armoracia lapathifolia)* of the mustard family, native to Mediterranean lands and grown throughout the temperate zones. Its hotly pungent, fleshy root is used as a condiment and is traditionally considered medicinal. In many cool, moist areas it has become a troublesome weed. The plant bears small white flowers, small oblong pods, and large, coarse, glossy-green basal leaves arising on long stems from the crown atop the large white root.

horseshoe crab Any of four extant species of marine arthropods (order Xiphosura, subphylum Chelicerata), found on the eastern coasts of Asia (three species) and North America (one species). Despite the name, horseshoe crabs are not crabs; they are more closely related to scorpions. Fossil relatives date back 505 million years. They are most abundant in estuarine waters. The North American species, *Limulus polyphemus,* can grow to more than 2 ft (60 cm) long. The body consists of three parts hinged together: a broad, horseshoe-shaped cephalothorax; a much smaller, segmented abdomen; and a long, sharp tail-spine, or telson. They spawn on sandy beaches in spring and summer. Adults feed on marine worms; larvae feed on small organisms.

Horseshoe crab (*Limulus polyphemus*).

horseshoe pitching Game for two or four players in which a horseshoe is thrown so as to encircle or land as close as possible to a stake. A horseshoe encircling the stake is called a ringer and counts for the highest score. The game may have derived from quoits, and it became especially popular in the U.S. and Canada. Regulation games are played to a winning score of 50, informal games to 21.

horsetail Any of the 30 species of rushlike (see rush), conspicuously jointed, perennial herbaceous plants, also called scouring rushes, that make up the genus *Equisetum.* They grow in moist, rich soils everywhere except Australasia. Some are evergreens; others send up new shoots every year. The stems contain abundant silicate and other minerals. The leaves are merely sheaths that encircle the shoots. An ancient plant, the horsetail's relatives date to the Carboniferous period. The common horsetail *(E. arvense)* is widespread along stream banks and in meadows in North America and Eurasia. Though poisonous to livestock, horsetails are used by humans in folk medicines. Because of their abrasive stems, some species are used in polishing tools.

Horta, Victor, Baron (1861–1947) Belgian architect. From 1892 he designed numerous buildings in Brussels, becoming a leading exponent of the Art Nouveau style. His Hôtel Tassel (1892–93) was a pioneering example of the new style. His chief work was the Maison du Peuple (1896–99), the first structure in Belgium to have a largely iron-and-glass facade. From 1912 he directed the Académie des Beaux-Arts, and he designed the Palais des Beaux-Arts (1922–28).

Horthy \'hȯr-tē\, **Miklós (Nagybányai)** (1868–1957) Hungarian naval officer and regent (1920–44). He served with distinction as a naval commander in World War I and was promoted to admiral in 1918. In 1919 he led an army against the communist regime of Bela Kun. In 1920 the Hungarian parliament voted to restore the monarchy and elected Horthy regent of Hungary, but he thwarted the efforts of Charles IV to recover his throne. He supported Germany in World War II, though his efforts to extricate Hungary from the war led to his forced abdication and abduction by the Germans in 1944. Released in 1945, he retired to Portugal.

horticulture Branch of agriculture concerned with the cultivation of garden plants—generally fruits, vegetables, flowers, and ornamentals such as plants used for landscaping (see landscape gardening). Propagation, the controlled perpetuation of plants, is the most basic horticultural practice. Its objectives are to increase the numbers of a plant and to preserve its essential characteristics. Propagation may be achieved sexually by use of SEEDS or asexually by use of techniques such as CUTTING, grafting (see GRAFT), and TISSUE CULTURE. Successful horticulture depends on extensive control of the environment, including light, water, temperature, soil structure and fertility, and pests. Two important horticultural techniques are training (changing a plant's orientation in space) and pruning (judicious removal of plant parts), used to improve the appearance or usefulness of plants. See also FLORICULTURE.

Horus Ancient Egyptian god with the head of a falcon, whose eyes were the sun and moon. The kings of Egypt were called living incarnations of Horus. During the 1st dynasty Horus was known principally as an opponent of SETH, but after 2350 BC he became associated with the OSIRIS cult and was identified as the son of Osiris. He destroyed Seth, the killer of Osiris, and became ruler of all Egypt. His left eye (the moon) was damaged by Seth but was healed by THOTH. In the Ptolemaic period, the victory of Horus over Seth became a symbol of Egypt triumphing over its occupiers.

Horus offering a libation, bronze statue, 22nd dynasty (c. 800 BC); in the Louvre, Paris.
GIRAUDON–ART RESOURCE

Horyu-ji \'hōr-yü-jē\ *or* **Horyu Temple** Buddhist complex near Nara, Japan, comprising the oldest known wood buildings in the world. The temple was founded by Prince SHOTOKU in 607, during the Asuka period, destroyed by fire in 670, and reconstructed c. 680–708. It retains the *chu-mon* (middle gate) of the roofed cloister enclosing the rectangular temple precinct, a five-storied PAGODA, and a *kondo* (main hall).

Hosea \hō-'zā-ə, hō-'zē-ə\ (fl. 8th century BC) First of the 12 Minor Prophets in the OLD TESTAMENT, traditional author of the Book of Hosea. (His prophecy is part of a larger book, The Twelve, in the Jewish canon.) He began to prophesy during the reign of Jeroboam II and continued until near the fall of the northern kingdom of Israel in 721 BC. The book is an allegory in which the prophet is presented as a man married to a harlot or an adulterous wife. This troubled relationship stands for the betrayal of God by Israel, which has "played the harlot" by dallying with Canaanite religion.

hosiery Knit or woven coverings for the feet and legs, worn inside shoes. In the 8th century BC, HESIOD referred to linings for shoes; the Romans wrapped their feet, ankles, and legs in long strips of leather or woven cloth. Knitted socks were discovered in Egyptian tombs of the 3rd–6th century AD. The first KNITTING MACHINE was invented in England in the 16th century. Full-fashioned stockings were knitted flat, then shaped and seamed up the back by hand. In the 19th century, seamless stockings, mostly of cotton, were knitted on circular machines, but they did not fit well; seamless hose did not become popular until the 1940s, when nylon replaced silk for dress hose. Pantyhose were introduced in the 1960s.

hospice Home or hospital for relieving physical and emotional suffering of dying persons. In patients expected to live only months or weeks, hospice care offers an alternative to aggressive life-prolonging measures, which often only increase discomfort and isolation. Hospices provide a sympathetic environment in which prevention (not just control) of physical pain has top priority, along with patients' emotional and spiritual needs. Care may be provided in a health facility, on an outpatient basis, or at home.

hospital Institution for diagnosing and treating the sick or injured, housing them during treatment, examining patients, and managing childbirth. Outpatients, who can leave after treatment, come in for emergency care or are referred for services not available in a private doctor's office. Hospitals may be public (government-owned) or private (profit-making or not-for-profit); in most nations except the U.S., most are public. They may also be general, accepting all types of medical or surgical cases, or special (e.g., children's hospitals, mental hospitals), limiting service to a single type of patient or illness. However, general hospitals usually also have specialized departments, and special hospitals tend to become affiliated with general hospitals.

Hospitallers See KNIGHTS OF MALTA, TEUTONIC ORDER

hosta \'hä-stə, 'hō-stə\ Any of about 40 species of hardy herbaceous perennials, also called plantain lily, of the genus *Hosta,* in the LILY FAMILY, native to eastern Asia. They prefer light shade but will grow under a variety of conditions. They are frequently grown for their conspicuous foliage, which may be light to dark green, yellow, blue, or variegated. The ribbed leaves grow in a cluster at the base, and stalks bearing clusters of tubular white or bluish-purple flowers emerge from the leaves.

hot rod Automobile rebuilt or modified for high speed, fast acceleration, or sporty appearance. A wide range of automobiles may be called hot rods, including some of those used in DRAG RACING as well as those used in recreational cruising. They may be composed of used or new parts. Some are intended primarily for exhibition.

hot spot Region of earth's upper mantle that upwells to melt through the crust to form a volcanic feature. Most VOLCANOES that cannot be ascribed either to a subduction zone or to seafloor spreading at mid-ocean ridges are attributed to hot spots. The 5% of known world volcanoes not closely related to such plate margins (see PLATE TECTONICS) are regarded as hot-spot volcanoes. Hawaiian volcanoes are the best examples of this type, occurring near the center of the northern portion of the Pacific Plate. A chain of extinct volcanoes or volcanic islands (and seamounts), such as the Hawaiian chain, can form over millions of years where a lithospheric plate moves over a hot spot. The active volcanoes all lie at one end of the chain or ridge, and the ages of the islands or the ridge increase with their distance from those sites of volcanic activity.

hot spring *or* **thermal spring** Spring that issues water at temperatures substantially higher than the air temperature of the surrounding region. Most hot springs result from the interaction of groundwater with MAGMA or with solid but still-hot igneous rocks. Some, however, are not related to volcanic activity. In such cases, deep circulation of water is thought to carry the water to the lower parts of the earth's CRUST, where the temperature of the rocks is high.

Hot Springs National Park National park, central Arkansas. Established in 1921, it occupies an area of 5,839 acres (2,365 hectares). It is centered on 47 thermal springs, from which over 1 million gallons of water, with an average temperature of 143°F (62°C), flow daily. The springs, long used by the Indians and probably visited by HERNANDO DE SOTO in 1541, drew Spanish and French visitors in search of health benefits in the 1700s. The town of Hot Springs (pop., 1995 est: 36,000), now a health and tourist resort, was settled in 1807 and incorporated in 1876.

hotel Building that provides lodging, meals, and other services to the traveling public on a commercial basis. Inns have existed since ancient times (e.g., along the Roman road system during the Roman Empire) to serve merchants and other travelers. Medieval European monasteries operated inns to guarantee haven for travelers in dangerous regions. The spread of travel by stagecoach in the 18th century stimulated the development of inns, as did the Industrial Revolution. The modern hotel was largely the result of the railroads; when traveling for pleasure became widely popular, large hotels were often built near railroad stations. In 1889 the Savoy Hotel in London set a new standard, with its own electricity and a host of special services; the Statler Hotel in Buffalo, N.Y. (1908), another landmark, catered to the growing class of business travelers. After World War II, new hotels tended to be larger and were often built near airports. Hotel chains became common, making purchasing, sales, and reservations more efficient. Hotels fall into three categories: transient hotels; resort hotels, intended primarily for vacationers; and residential hotels, essentially apartment buildings offering room and meal service. See also MOTEL.

Hottentots See KHOIKHOI

Houdini \hü-'dē-nē\, **Harry** *orig.* **Erik Weisz** (1874–1926) U.S. magician. Born probably in Hungary, from age 1 he lived with his family in Wisconsin. He began as a trapeze performer and from 1882 played in vaudeville in New York. From c. 1900 he earned an international reputation for his daring feats of escape from locked boxes, often submerged, while shackled in chains and handcuffed. His success depended on his great strength and agility and his unusual skill in manipulating locks. He exhibited his skills in several films (1916–23). He later wrote books debunking magicians and mind readers who claimed supernatural powers, including those of JEAN-EUGENE ROBERT-HOUDIN, from whom he had taken his name.

Houdini.

PICTORIAL PARADE—EB INC.

Houdon \ü-'dō^{n}\, **Jean-Antoine** (1741–1828) French sculptor. He studied with J.-B. PIGALLE in Paris and in 1761 won the Prix de Rome. In Rome (1764–68) he achieved immediate fame with an anatomical study of a standing man (c. 1767), casts of which were widely used in art academies. He became a member of the Royal Academy in Paris (1777) with his reclining *Morpheus.* He produced numerous religious and mythological works, but his greatest strength was in the individuality of his portrait busts of such luminaries as DENIS DIDEROT, CATHERINE II THE GREAT, BENJAMIN FRANKLIN, the Marquis de LAFAYETTE, and VOLTAIRE. In the U.S. he made a marble statue of GEORGE WASHINGTON (1788). The vividness of physiognomy and character in his busts places him among the greatest portrait sculptors in history.

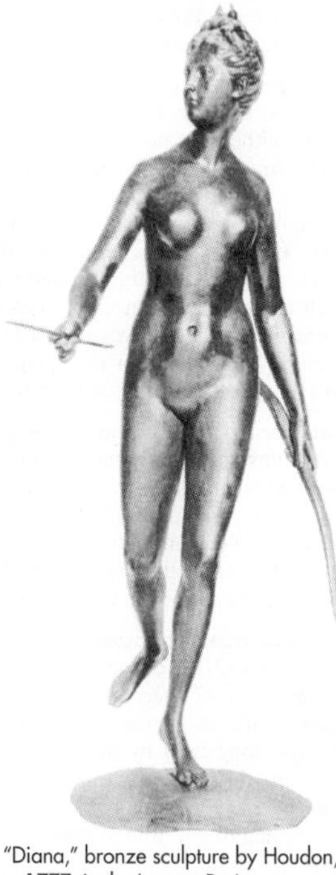

"Diana," bronze sculpture by Houdon, c. 1777; in the Louvre, Paris.

GIRAUDON—ART RESOURCE/EB INC.

hound Classification of hunting dogs that is more general than setter, retriever, pointer, or other sporting dog categories. Most hounds were bred and trained to track by scent or sight. Scent hounds (e.g., BLOODHOUND, DACHSHUND) are trained to scent in the air or on the ground. Sight hounds (e.g., SALUKI, AFGHAN HOUND) were developed to chase game by sight over long distances. Hounds such as BEAGLES, BASSET HOUNDS, and FOXHOUNDS run in packs; Afghan hounds, BORZOIS, salukis, and others run alone.

Houphouët-Boigny \üf-'we-bwän-'yē\, **Félix** (c. 1905–1993) President of Ivory Coast from independence until his death (1960–93). He worked as a rural doctor and planter before entering politics in the 1940s. In the late 1950s he was a member of France's National Assembly and cabinet, and simultaneously president of the territorial assembly and mayor of Abidjan. As president he pursued liberal free-enterprise politics and developed a strong cash-crop economy, cooperating closely with the French. Under his rule Ivory Coast became one of the most prosperous nations in sub-Saharan Africa. His later years were marred by an economic downturn, civil unrest, and criticism of the enormous Roman Catholic basilica that he had built at YAMOUSSOUKRO, his birthplace.

House, Edward M(andell) *known as* **Col. House** (1858–1938) U.S. diplomat. Born in Houston, he was an independently wealthy businessman, but turned to politics and served as an adviser to Texas governors (1892–1904), one of whom gave him the honorary title of colonel. He was active in WOODROW WILSON's presidential campaign and became his adviser (1912–19). He was the president's chief liaison with the Allies during World War I, helped draft the FOURTEEN POINTS program and the LEAGUE OF NATIONS covenant, and was a delegate to the PARIS PEACE CONFERENCE.

House, 1920.

BY COURTESY OF THE LIBRARY OF CONGRESS, WASHINGTON, D.C.

house cat See DOMESTIC CAT

house mouse Common MOUSE species (*Mus musculus,* family Muridae), the mouse most often encountered in buildings. The house mouse has been distributed by humans from Eurasia to all inhabited areas of the world and usually seeks shelter and food in human dwellings. Brown or gray, it grows up to 8 in. (20 cm) long, including a 4-in. (10-cm) tail. It consumes almost anything edible, even sampling soap, paste, and glue. It matures quickly and is ready to mate two to three months after birth. In warm areas or heated buildings, it breeds throughout the year.

house sparrow *or* **English sparrow** One of the world's best-known and most abundant small birds (*Passer domesticus,* family Passeridae or Ploceidae). It lives in towns and on farms worldwide, having accompanied Europeans from its original home in Eurasia and northern Africa. Introduced into North America in 1852, it spread across the continent within a century. It is about 6 in. (15 cm) long and buffy-brown; the male has a black bib. House sparrows breed nearly year-round in warm regions. See also SPARROW.

House sparrow (*Passer domesticus*).

ERIC HOSKING

House Un-American Activities Committee (HUAC) Committee of the U.S. House of Representatives, established in 1938 under MARTIN DIES as chairman, that conducted investigations through the 1940s and '50s into alleged communist activities. Those investigated included many artists and entertainers, including the HOLLYWOOD TEN, ELIA KAZAN, P. SEEGER, BERTOLT BRECHT, and ARTHUR MILLER. RICHARD NIXON was an active member in the late 1940s, and the committee's most celebrated case was perhaps that of ALGER HISS. Its actions resulted in several contempt-of-Congress convictions and the blacklisting of many who refused to answer its questions. Highly controversial for its tactics, it was criticized for violating First Amendment rights by "engaging in exposure for exposure's sake." Its influence had waned by the 1960s; in 1969 it was renamed the Internal Security Committee, and in 1975 it was dissolved.

housefly Common DIPTERAN *(Musca domestica),* accounting for about 90% of all flies in human dwellings. The adult is dull gray with dirty-yellowish areas on the abdomen. Body size ranges from 0.2 to 0.3 in. (5–7 mm), and the conspicuous compound eyes have some 4,000 facets. Because it has spong-

Housefly (*Musca domestica*) on a doughnut.

AVRIL RAMAGE—© OXFORD SCIENTIFIC FILMS LTD.

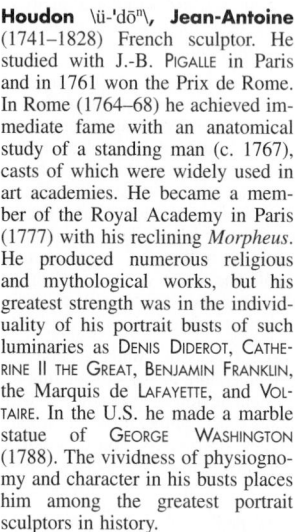

ing or lapping mouthparts, it cannot bite. It is a problem wherever decomposing organic waste and garbage are allowed to accumulate. Its feet may carry millions of microorganisms, some of which cause diseases, including CHOLERA, DYSENTERY, and TYPHOID.

Houseman, John *orig.* **Jacques Haussmann** (1902–1988) U.S. producer and actor. Born in Romania and educated in England, he emigrated to the U.S. in 1924. In 1934 he directed the opera *Four Saints in Three Acts*. In 1937 he collaborated with ORSON WELLES to found the Mercury Theatre. In World War II he directed radio operations for the Office of War Information. He later produced 19 films, including *Letter from an Unknown Woman* (1948), *They Live by Night* (1949), and *Lust for Life* (1956), produced and directed Broadway plays and TV specials (winning three Emmy awards), and directed the American Shakespeare Festival. His most notable acting role was in the film *The Paper Chase* (1973, Academy Award) and the later television series.

houseplant Plant adapted for growing indoors, commonly a member of a species that flourishes naturally only in warm climates. Two factors contribute to the success of the huge number of species grown as houseplants: they must be easy to care for, and they must be able to tolerate the fairly low levels of light and humidity found in most homes. Houseplants are selected for their foliage or flowers or both.

Housing and Urban Development, U.S. Department of (HUD) Federal executive division responsible for carrying out government housing and community development programs. Established in 1965 under Pres. LYNDON B. JOHNSON, it ensures equal access to housing and community-based employment opportunities; finances new housing, public housing, and housing rehabilitation projects; insures mortgages; and carries out programs that serve the housing needs of low-income and minority families, the elderly, disabled, and mentally ill. It also protects consumers against fraudulent practices by land developers, ensures the safety of manufactured homes, and defends homebuyers against abusive mortgage-loan practices.

Housman, A(lfred) E(dward) (1859–1936) English scholar and poet. While working as a Patent Office clerk, he studied Latin texts and wrote journal articles that led to his appointment as a professor at University College, London, and later at Cambridge. His major scholarly effort was an edition of Marcus Manilius (1903–30). His first poetry volume, *A Shropshire Lad* (1896), was based on classical and traditional models, and the lyrics express a Romantic pessimism in a spare, simple style. It gradually grew popular, and his second volume, *Last Poems* (1922), was extremely successful. Other works include the lecture *The Name and Nature of Poetry* (1933) and the posthumous collection *More Poems* (1936). His brother, the novelist and playwright Laurence Housman (1865–1959), is known for his plays *Angels and Ministers* (1921), *Little Plays of St. Francis* (1922), and *Victoria Regina* (1934).

A.E. Housman, detail of a drawing by William Rothenstein, 1906; in the National Portrait Gallery, London.

BY COURTESY OF THE NATIONAL PORTRAIT GALLERY, LONDON

Houston City (pop., 2000: 1,953,631), southern Texas. An inland port, it is linked by the Houston Ship Channel to the Gulf of MEXICO and the GULF INTRACOASTAL WATERWAY at GALVESTON. Founded in 1836, it was named for SAM HOUSTON; it was the capital of the Republic of Texas 1837–39. The state's largest city and leading port, it is a center for oil, petrochemical, and aerospace research and development (see also NASA). The area is also important for rice, cotton, and cattle. It has several institutions of higher learning, including RICE UNIVERSITY and Baylor College of Medicine.

Houston, Charles H(amilton) (1895–1950) U.S. lawyer and educator. Born in Washington, D.C., he graduated from Amherst College and taught two years at Howard University before serving as an officer in World War I. At Harvard Law School he became the first black editor of the *Harvard Law Review*. He practiced law with his father (1924–50), also serving as special counsel to the NAACP (1935–40). Before the U.S. Supreme Court in *State ex rel. Gaines vs. Canada* (1939), he successfully questioned racial segregation in public schools in areas where no "separate but equal" facilities existed; the decision was a forerunner of *BROWN VS. BOARD OF EDUCATION* (1954). He served as teacher and mentor to THURGOOD MARSHALL.

Houston, Sam(uel) (1793–1863) U.S. politician. Born in Rockbridge Co., Va., he lived as a youth with the Cherokee in Tennessee. He fought in the War of 1812 under ANDREW JACKSON, then became a lawyer in Nashville and served in the U.S. House of Representatives (1823–27), and as governor (1827–29). After his marriage failed, he resigned and again lived among the Cherokee. He exposed fraud perpetrated by government agents against the Indians, and in 1832 was sent by Pres. Jackson to negotiate Indian treaties in Texas, then a Mexican province. When armed rebellion began in 1835, the provisional government chose him to command its army, and he defeated the Mexicans at San Jacinto, securing Texas independence. He served as president of the Republic of Texas (1836–38, 1841–44) and helped win it statehood (1845), then served in the U.S. Senate (1846–59). He was elected governor in 1859 but his pro-Union views were opposed by Democratic state leaders, who voted to secede in 1861. After he refused to swear allegiance to the Confederacy, he was deposed. The city of Houston was named in his honor.

Sam Houston, photograph by Mathew Brady.

BY COURTESY OF THE LIBRARY OF CONGRESS, WASHINGTON, D.C.

Hovenweep National Monument \'hō-vən-ˌwēp\ National monument, southwestern Colorado and southeastern Utah. Established in 1923, and covering 785 acres (318 hectares), it consists of six groups of pre-Columbian Indian ruins, whose towers are excellent examples of PUEBLO INDIAN architecture of the period AD 1100–1300. Hovenweep is a UTE Indian word meaning "deserted valley."

hovercraft See AIR-CUSHION VEHICLE

Hovhaness \hō-'vä-nəs\, **Alan** *orig.* **Alan Hovhaness Chakmakjian** (1911–2000) U.S. composer. Born in Somerville, Mass., he started to compose as a child. Studies at the New England Conservatory led him to pursue an interest in non-Western music. Affected by the music of his Armenian heritage and his own lifelong mysticism, he composed over 400 works, including more than 60 symphonies and many other orchestral works, often on sacred themes, sometimes incorporating aleatory or natural sounds, as in *And God Created Great Whales* (1970).

Howard, Catherine (c. 1520–1542) Fifth wife of HENRY VIII of England. The granddaughter of the 2nd duke of NORFOLK, she became a maid of honor to ANNE OF CLEVES, Henry's fourth wife. After Henry had his marriage to Anne annulled, he married Catherine (1540). In 1541 he learned that Catherine had had several affairs before their marriage and that she had probably committed adultery as well. Incensed, he had Parliament pass a bill in 1542 declaring it treason for an unchaste woman to marry the king. Catherine was beheaded two days later in the Tower of London.

Howard, Henry See Earl of SURREY

Howard, John (Winston) (born 1939) prime minister of Australia from March 1996 and leader of the Liberal Party. Born in Sydney, N.S.W., Howard became a solicitor to New South Wales's Supreme Court. In 1974 he was elected to Parliament as a member of the Liberal Party and served under Prime Minister Malcolm Fraser as minister for business and consumer affairs (1975–77) and as federal treasurer (1977–83). Howard became leader of the Liberal Party in 1985, but, after failing to unseat the Labor Party in 1987, he was defeated in his bid to retain leadership in 1989. He regained power in 1995 and engineered the defeat of Labor in the elections of March 1996. He was reelected in 1998 and again in 2001.

Howard, Leslie *orig.* **Leslie Howard Steiner** (1893–1943) British actor. He became a popular stage actor in London and later on Broadway, where he won acclaim for *Her Cardboard Lover* (1927), *The Petrified Forest* (1935), and *Hamlet* (1936). Noted for his quiet, persuasive English charm, he made his U.S. film debut in *Outward Bound* (1930) and later starred in *Of Human Bondage* (1934), *Pygmalion* (1938), *Intermezzo* (1939), and *Gone with the Wind* (1939). He died during World War II when his plane was shot down en route from Lisbon to London.

Howard, Oliver O(tis) (1830–1909) U.S. Army officer. Born in Leeds, Me., he graduated from West Point and served in the Civil War as a major general of Maine volunteers, fighting at Bull Run, Antietam, Chancellorsville, and Gettysburg. He commanded the Army of the Tennessee (1864) and marched with WILLIAM T. SHERMAN through Georgia. During Reconstruction he was named commissioner of the FREEDMEN'S BUREAU. He helped found HOWARD UNIV. (1867), which was named in his honor, and served as its president 1869–74. He resigned to return to military service, fighting against the Indians (1877) and later serving as superintendent at West Point (1880–82).

Oliver O. Howard.

BY COURTESY OF THE LIBRARY OF CONGRESS, WASHINGTON, D.C.

Howard, Ron (born 1954) U.S. actor and director. Born in Duncan, Okla., he became a child star of television and films, appearing in *The Music Man* (1962) and on television's *Andy Griffith Show* (1960–68) and *Happy Days* (1974–80). He returned to movies in *American Graffiti* (1973), made his directorial debut with *Grand Theft Auto* (1977), and went on to direct such successful films as *Splash* (1984), *Cocoon* (1985), *Apollo 13* (1995), and *A Beautiful Mind* (2001, Academy Award). He heads his own production company.

Howard family Famous English family, founded in 1295, whose head, the duke of Norfolk, is the premier duke and hereditary earl marshal of England. The earls of Suffolk, Carlisle, and Effingham and Lord Howard of Glossop and Lord Stafford represent the family in its younger lines. Thomas Howard, 3rd duke of NORFOLK, held high offices under HENRY VIII, who married two of Howard's nieces, ANNE BOLEYN and CATHERINE HOWARD. The 4th duke of NORFOLK was executed for intrigues against ELIZABETH I, but Charles, 2nd Lord Howard of Effingham (1536–1624), was lord high admiral under Elizabeth and commanded the fleet that defeated the Spanish ARMADA. The family's Roman Catholicism kept it from prominence during certain periods.

Howard University Predominantly black university in Washington, D.C., the most prominent black educational institution in the U.S. It is financially supported by the U.S. government but is privately controlled. Though open to students of any race or ethnicity, it was founded (1867) with a special obligation to educate African-American students. It has a college of liberal arts, a graduate school of arts and sciences, and schools or colleges of business and public administration, engineering, human ecology, medicine, dentistry, and law, among others. Its library is the leading research library on black American history.

Howe, Earl *orig.* **Richard Howe** (1726–1799) British admiral who commanded the English fleet to victory in the Battle of the First of June (1794) in the FRENCH REVOLUTIONARY WARS. As vice admiral (from 1775), he commanded in North America 1776–78, defeating French attempts to take Newport, R.I. After returning to England, he commanded the Channel fleet against the French and Spaniards and served as first lord of the admiralty 1783–88. In 1793 he again commanded the Channel fleet. His victory against the French on June 1, 1794, provided an example of tactical excellence for his successors, including HORATIO NELSON.

Howe, Elias (1819–1867) U.S. inventor. Born in Spencer, Mass., the nephew of WILLIAM HOWE, he began work as a mechanic. In 1846 he was granted a patent for the first practical SEWING MACHINE. It attracted little attention, and he moved to England and worked to perfect his machine for use with leather and similar materials. When he returned the next year, he found that sewing machines were being widely made and sold; he finally established his patent rights in 1854. His invention soon revolutionized the garment industry. See also ISAAC MERRITT SINGER.

Howe, Frederick W(ebster) (1822–1891) U.S. inventor and manufacturer. Born in Danvers, Mass., he produced classic designs of several machine tools while still in his twenties: a profiling machine, a barrel-drilling and -rifling machine, and the first commercially viable universal milling machine. His rifles built with INTERCHANGEABLE PARTS led to his establishing his own armory in Newark, N.J., in 1856. He perfected the manufacture of the SPRINGFIELD RIFLE during the Civil War, and as president of the Brown & Sharpe Co. created new sewing machines and other tools.

Howe, Gordie *orig.* **Gordon** (born 1928) Canadian-U.S. hockey player, regarded as one of the greatest of all time. Born in Floral, Saskatchewan, he began playing hockey at the age of 5. In 26 seasons (1945–71) in the NHL, 25 of them playing right wing with the Detroit Red Wings, he set all-time career records for goals (801), assists (1,049), and points (1,850). (His records were later broken by WAYNE GRETZKY and also, in the case of assists, by Paul Coffey.) Howe went on to play for or manage non-NHL teams before retiring in 1980.

Gordie Howe, 1969.

BY COURTESY OF THE NATIONAL HOCKEY LEAGUE

Howe \ˈhau̇\, **Irving** (1920–1993) U.S. critic and educator. Raised in New York tenements, Howe graduated from CCNY and taught at Brandeis and Stanford universities and the City University of New York. He helped found the left-wing magazine *Dissent,* which he edited from 1953. He wrote critical works on SHERWOOD ANDERSON (1951), WILLIAM FAULKNER (1952), and THOMAS HARDY (1967) and synthesized his political and literary interests in such works as *Politics and the Novel* (1957). *World of Our Fathers* (1976) is a major study of Jewish immigrants in New York.

Howe, James Wong *orig.* **Wong Tung Jim** (1899–1976) U.S. cinematographer. At age 5 he emigrated with his family from China to the U.S. He worked in Hollywood from 1917 and became a cameraman for CECIL B. DEMILLE. He developed innovations in lighting in the 1920s and pioneered the use of the wide-angle lens, deep focus, and the handheld camera. His low-key cinematography is seen in such films as *Kings Row* (1942), *Body and Soul* (1947), *Picnic* (1956), *The Rose Tattoo* (1955, Academy Award), and *Hud* (1963, Academy Award).

Howe, Julia Ward *orig.* **Julia Ward** (1819–1910) U.S. abolitionist and social reformer. Born in New York City, she worked in the abolitionist movement from her early years. She is best known for her stirring patriotic poem "Battle Hymn of the Republic" (1862). Moved by the plight of Civil War widows, she became involved in the fight for equal opportunities for women, partly as a founder and first president (1868–77, 1893–1910) of the New England Woman Suffrage Association. She also wrote travel books, biography, drama, verse, and children's songs, and edited *Woman's Journal* (1870–90). In 1908 she became the first woman elected to the American Academy of Arts and Letters. In 1843 she married Samuel Gridley Howe (1801–1876), the first director of the Perkins School for the Blind (1832–76), who lobbied strenuously for legisla-

Julia Ward Howe, 1902.

BY COURTESY OF THE LIBRARY OF CONGRESS, WASHINGTON, D.C.

tion on behalf of the blind, the deaf, the mentally ill, and mentally handicapped children.

Howe, William *later* **Viscount Howe** (1729–1814) British military commander. The brother of Adm. Richard Howe, he entered the army in 1746 and was noted as a brilliant general in the French and Indian War. In the American Revolution, he succeeded Thomas Gage as supreme commander of British forces in North America in 1776. He soon captured New York City and the surrounding area, and in 1777 he led British troops to victories at the Battles of the Brandywine and Germantown. Moving his forces to Philadelphia, he left troops under John Burgoyne vulnerable in New York state, which contributed to the British defeat at the Battle of Saratoga. He resigned in 1778 and was succeeded by Henry Clinton.

Howe Caverns Cavern system, eastern central New York. Located west of Albany, and named for Lester Howe, who discovered them in 1842, the limestone caves have grotesque rock formations and underground channels. Elevators and boat rides are available. A second group, Secret Caverns, with underground waterfalls and fossilized marine life, is nearby.

Howel Dda See Hywel Dda

Howells, William Dean (1837–1920) U.S. novelist and critic. Born in Martins Ferry, Ohio, he wrote a campaign biography of Abraham Lincoln (1860) and served as consul in Venice during Lincoln's administration. As editor of the *Atlantic Monthly* (1871–81), he became a preeminent figure in late-19th-century American letters. A champion of literary realism, he was one of the first to recognize the genius of Mark Twain and Henry James. His own novels (from 1872) depict America as it changed from a simple, egalitarian society where luck and pluck were rewarded to one in which social and economic gulfs were becoming unbridgeable. His best-known work, *The Rise of Silas Lapham* (1885), is about a self-made man's efforts to fit into Boston society. He risked his livelihood with his plea for clemency for the anarchists involved in the Haymarket Riot, and his deepening disillusionment with American society is reflected in the late novels *Annie Kilburn* (1888) and *A Hazard of New Fortunes* (1890).

howler monkey Any of several species of slow-moving tropical American monkeys (genus *Alouatta*) noted for their roaring cries, which carry over a distance of 2–3 mi (3–5 km). Five widely distributed species are the largest New World monkeys, generally reaching lengths of 16–28 in. (40–70 cm), excluding the 20–30-in. (50–75-cm) tail. Howlers are stoutly built and bearded, with a hunched appearance and a thickly furred, prehensile tail. Their hair is long and thick, and, depending on the species, black, brown, or red. Howlers live in groups in territories mapped out by howling matches with neighboring clans. They feed primarily on leaves.

Hoxha \'hȯ-jä\, **Enver** (1908–1985) Albanian leader, first Albanian communist chief of state (1944–85). A schoolteacher, he opposed the Albanian fascists in World War II and in 1941 helped found the Albanian Communist Party, which he controlled until his death. He became prime minister (1944–54) and in 1946 he forced King Zog to abdicate. Albania's economy was revolutionized under Hoxha's rule, and he transformed the country from a semifeudal relic of the Ottoman empire into an industrialized economy. To enforce his radical programs he resorted to brutal Stalinist tactics, making Albania the most tightly controlled society in Europe. An ardent nationalist, he broke with the Soviet Union in 1961 and with China in 1978, declaring that Albania would become a model socialist republic on its own.

Hoyle, Edmond (1671/72–1769) British writer on card games. Little is known of his early life. He wrote *A Short Treatise on the Game of Whist* in 1742, and in 1760 established a set of rules for whist that remained in effect until 1864. His codification of the laws of backgammon (1743) is still largely in force. He is memorialized in the phrase "according to Hoyle" and in various game-rule books that contain his name in the title as an indication of authority.

Hoyle, Fred *later* **Sir Fred** (1915–2001) British mathematician and astronomer. He was educated at Cambridge University, where he became a lecturer in 1945. Within the framework of Albert Einstein's theory of relativity, Hoyle formulated a mathematical basis for the steady-state theory of the universe, making the expansion of the universe and the creation of matter interdependent. Controversy about the theory grew in the late 1950s and early '60s. New observations of distant galaxies and other phenomena supported the big-bang model and weakened the steady-state theory, which has since generally fallen out of favor. Though forced to alter some of his conclusions, Hoyle persistently tried to make his theory consistent with new evidence. He is known also for his popular science works and fiction.

Hrabanus Maurus See Rabanus Maurus

Hrosvitha *or* **Roswitha** \rȯs-'vē-tä\ (c. 935–c. 1000) German writer, regarded as the first German woman poet. Of noble birth, she lived as a nun in a Benedictine convent most of her life. There she wrote six prose comedies in Latin (c. 960), based in form on Terence but embodying Christian themes, to edify her fellow nuns. She also wrote narrative poems based on Christian legends and two verse chronicles.

Hrozný \'hrȯz-nē\, **Bedřich** (1879–1952) Czech archaeologist and linguist. He was the first to decipher Hittite cuneiform writing, a major advance in the study of the ancient Near East. In *Language of the Hittites* (1915), he argued that Hittite (see Anatolian languages) was one of the Indo-European languages. He later substantiated his claim by translating a number of Hittite documents. In 1925 he led an expedition to Turkey that excavated the ancient city of Kanesh.

Hrozný.
CTK

Hsi-an See Xi'an

Hsi Hsia See Xi Xia

Hsi-ning See Xining

Hsi River See Xi River

Hsi Wang Mu See Xi Wang Mu

Hsi-tsang See Tibet

Hsia dynasty See Xia dynasty

Hsiang River See Xiang River

Hsiang Yü See Xiang Yu

hsiao See xiao

Hsing-K'ai Hu See Lake Khanka

Hsiung-nu See Xiongnu

Hsüan-hsueh See Xuanxue

Hsüan-tsang See Xuanzang

Hsüan Tsung See Xuanzong

Hsün-tzu See Xunzi

HTML *in full* **HyperText Markup Language** Markup language derived from SGML that is used to prepare hypertext documents. Relatively easy for nonprogrammers to master, HTML is the language used for documents on the World Wide Web. The text coding consists of commands contained in angle brackets <> that affect the display of elements such as titles, headings, text, font style, color, and references to other documents, which can be interpreted by an Internet browser according to style rules.

HTTP *in full* **HyperText Transfer Protocol** Standard application-level protocol used for exchanging files on the World Wide Web. HTTP runs on top of the TCP/IP protocol. Web browsers are HTTP clients that send file requests to Web servers, which in turn handle the requests via an HTTP service. HTTP was originally proposed in 1989 by Tim Berners-Lee, who was a coauthor of the 1.0 specification. HTTP in its 1.0 version was "stateless": each new request from a client established a new connection instead of handling all similar requests through the same connection between a specific client and server. Version 1.1 includes persistent connections, decompression of HTML files by client browsers, and multiple domain names sharing the same IP address.

Hu-ho-hao-t'e See Hohhot

Hu Shi *or* **Hu Shih** \'hü-'shir\ (1891–1962) Chinese Nationalist scholar and diplomat who helped establish the vernacular as the official written language. Hu studied under JOHN DEWEY at Columbia University and was profoundly influenced by Dewey's philosophy and pragmatic methodology. Back in China, he began writing in vernacular Chinese, the use of which spread rapidly. Because he eschewed dogmas such as Marxism and anarchism as solutions for China's problems, he found himself opposed by the Communists but also distrusted by the Nationalists. In 1937, when war broke out with Japan, he and the Nationalists were reconciled, and Hu became ambassador to the U.S. He finished his life as president of Taiwan's Academia Sinica.

Hu, Sia, and Heh \'hü...'sē-ə...'heh\ In ancient EGYPTIAN RELIGION, the forces of nature responsible for the creation and continuance of the universe. They were personified abstractions whose meanings can be translated as "creative command," "intelligence," and "eternity." Hu and Sia served as crew members in the solar ship of the sun god RE, and they were also regarded as two of the divine attributes of every king. Heh was the personification of infinite space, portrayed as a squatting man with a sun disk on his head.

Huai River \'hwī\ River, eastern China. It flows east for 660 mi (1,100 km) to discharge into HONGZE HU (lake) in JIANGSU province. With its many tributaries, it is subject to extensive flooding; work to control the flooding is ongoing. River traffic from the Huai joins the GRAND CANAL, providing water transport routes north to the HUANG (YELLOW) RIVER and south to the CHANG (YANGTZE) RIVER.

Huainanzi *or* **Huai-nan-tzu** \'hwī-'nän-'dzə̇\ Chinese Taoist classic written c. 139 BC under the patronage of the nobleman Huainanzi. The work deals with cosmology, astronomy, and statecraft. It asserts that the TAO originated from vacuity, which produced the universe, which in turn produced material forces. These material forces combined to form YIN-YANG, which give rise to the multiplicity of things. Many of the teachings of the *Huainanzi* are still accepted as orthodox by Taoist philosophers as well as by Confucianists. See also TAOISM.

Huallaga River \wä-'yä-gä\ River, western and northern Peru. It rises in the ANDES and descends north, carving a valley between the Cordillera Central and the Cordillera Azul and emerging into the AMAZON RIVER basin to join the MARAÑÓN RIVER. The Huallaga is estimated to be 700 mi (1,100 km) long, and is mostly unnavigable.

Huang Chao *or* **Huang Ch'ao** \'hwäŋ-'chau̇\ (died 884) Chinese rebel leader whose revolt against the TANG DYNASTY, though ultimately defeated, so weakened the dynasty that it collapsed shortly thereafter. A salt smuggler turned rebel, Huang captured Guangzhou (Canton) in 879 and the Tang capital of CHANGAN in 881. There he proclaimed himself emperor, but was driven out by an alliance of government troops and Turkish nomads. One of his generals overthrew the Tang (907) and founded the first of the short-lived FIVE DYNASTIES.

Huang Hai See YELLOW SEA

Huang He , *or* **Huang Ho** *English* **Yellow River** River, northern central and eastern China. The second-longest river in China, it flows 3,395 mi (5,464 km) from the Plateau of Tibet east to the YELLOW SEA (Huang Hai). In its lower reaches it has often overflowed its banks, flooding millions of acres of rich farmland, China's rice granary. Its outlet has shifted over the years to enter the Yellow Sea at points as far apart as 500 mi (800 km). Irrigation and flood-control works have been maintained for centuries, and dams, begun in 1955, exploit the river's hydroelectric potential.

Huang-Lao \'hwäŋ-'lau̇\ Political ideology based on the tenets attributed to the Yellow Emperor HUANGDI and on the Taoist teachings of LAOZI. This method of governance, which stressed the principles of reconciliation and noninterference, became the dominant ideology of the imperial court in the early Western Han (206 BC–AD 25). The Huang-Lao masters believed that Laozi's *TAO-TE CHING* perfectly described the art of rulership, and they venerated the legendary Yellow Emperor as the founder of a golden age. Their teachings constitute the earliest Taoist movement for which there is clear historical evidence. See also TAOISM.

Huangdi *or* **Huang-ti** \'hwäŋ-'dē\ *or* **Yellow Emperor** Third of ancient China's mythological emperors and a patron saint of TAOISM. According to legend, he was born in 2704 BC and became emperor in 2697. He is remembered as a paragon of wisdom who established a golden age, seeking to create an ideal kingdom in which his people would live in keeping with natural law. Tradition holds that his reign saw the introduction of wooden houses, carts, boats, the bow and arrow, writing, and governmental institutions. His wife was reputed to have taught women how to breed silkworms and weave silk.

Hubbard, Elbert (Green) (1856–1915) U.S. editor, publisher, and author. Born in Bloomington, Ill., Hubbard became a freelance newspaperman and businessman. He retired in 1892 and the next year founded the Roycroft Press, modeled on WILLIAM MORRIS's communal Kelmscott Press. In 1895 he began issuing his monthly "Little Journey" booklets, biographical essays on famous people in which fact was interwoven with commentary. He started the magazine *The Philistine*, in which his well-known moralistic essay "A Message to Garcia" (1899) appeared. He died in the sinking of the *LUSITANIA*. Collections of his writings include *Little Journeys* (1915) and *Selected Writings* (1923).

Elbert Hubbard.
BY COURTESY OF THE LIBRARY OF CONGRESS, WASHINGTON, D.C.

Hubbard, L(afayette) Ron(ald) (1911–1986) U.S. novelist and founder of the Church of SCIENTOLOGY. Born in Tilden, Neb., he grew up in Helena, Mont., and studied engineering at George Washington University. In the 1930s and '40s he became a successful science-fiction novelist. After serving in the Navy in World War II, he published *Dianetics* (1950), which detailed his theories of the human mind. The spiritual component of Dianetics grew to have increasing importance for Hubbard, and in 1954 he founded the Church of SCIENTOLOGY to explore that spiritual dimension more fully. A controversial figure, often at odds with tax authorities as the church's wealth accumulated, he lived many years on a yacht and remained in seclusion for his last six years.

Hubble, Edwin P(owell) (1889–1953) U.S. astronomer. Born in Marshfield, Mo., he earned a degree in mathematics and astronomy at the University of Chicago, then made a brief foray into law before returning to astronomy. After earning his PhD he began working at Mount Wilson Observatory. In 1922–24 he discovered that certain nebulae contained CEPHEID VARIABLES; he determined that these were several hundred thousand light-years away (outside the Milky Way galaxy) and that the nebulae they were in were actually other galaxies. In studying those galaxies he made his second remarkable discovery (1927): that the galaxies were receding from the Milky Way at rates that increased with distance. This implied that the universe, long considered unchanging, was expanding; even more remarkable, the ratio of the galaxies' speed to their distance was a constant (see HUBBLE'S CONSTANT). Hubble's calculation of the constant was incorrect; it made the Milky Way larger than all other galaxies and the entire universe younger than the surmised age of earth. Later astronomers determined that galaxies were systematically more distant, resolving the discrepancy.

Hubble Space Telescope (HST) Most sophisticated optical observatory ever placed into orbit around earth. Because it is above the earth's obscuring ATMOSPHERE, it can obtain images much brighter, clearer, and more detailed than ground-based telescopes can. Named for EDWIN HUBBLE, it was built under NASA supervision and deployed on a 1990 SPACE-SHUTTLE mission. The large reflecting telescope's mirror optics gather light from celestial objects and direct it into two cameras and two spectrographs (see SPECTROSCOPY). A defect in the primary mirror initially caused it to produce fuzzy images; in 1993 another mission corrected this and other problems, and the telescope has since returned spectacular photographs of various cosmic phenomena.

Hubble's constant Constant used to relate the velocities of remote galaxies to their distances from earth. Denoted H and named in honor of EDWIN HUBBLE, it expresses the rate of expansion of the universe. Its value is estimated at between about 9 and 19 mi/second (15–30 km/second) per million light-years. Hubble used the RED SHIFTS of distant galaxies measured by Vesto Slipher (1875–1969) and his own distance estimates of those galaxies to establish the cosmological velocity-distance law (Hubble law): velocity = $H \times$ distance, according to which the greater a galaxy's distance, the faster it is receding. Derived from theoretical considerations and confirmed by observations, the Hubble law has made secure the concept of an EXPANDING UNIVERSE.

Hubei *or* **Hupeh** *or* **Hu-pei** \'hü-'bā\ Province (pop., 1999 est.: 59,380,000), eastern central China. It lies north of the YANGTZE RIVER; its capital is WUHAN. It was part of the 1st millennium B.C. kingdom ruled by the Zhou dynasty, and came under the Chinese empire during the HAN DYNASTY rule. Until the reign of KANGXI, Hubei and HUNAN formed one province; they were divided in the mid-17th century. The area was the scene of battles after the 1850 TAIPING REBELLION. The Revolution of 1911 (see NATIONALIST PARTY) began in Hubei. It was heavily bombed during the SINO-JAPANESE WAR. Restoration began after the communist Chinese takeover. In addition to agricultural production, Hubei has important heavy industrial production.

Hubel \'hyü-bəl\, **David (Hunter)** (born 1926) Canadian-U.S. neurobiologist. Born in Windsor, Ontario, he studied medicine at McGill University and in 1959 joined the faculty of Harvard Medical School. In 1981 he shared a Nobel Prize with TORSTEN WIESEL and ROGER SPERRY for investigations of visual perception, one of their achievements being analysis of the flow of nerve impulses from the retina to the brain's sensory and motor centers.

Hubertusburg \hü-'ber-təs-ˌbu̇rk\, **Peace of** (1763) Treaty between Prussia and Austria ending the SEVEN YEARS' WAR in Germany. Signed five days after the Treaty of PARIS, it guaranteed that FREDERICK II THE GREAT maintained his possession of SILESIA and confirmed Prussia's stature as a major European power.

huckleberry Small, fruit-bearing, branching shrub of the genus *Gaylussacia,* in the HEATH FAMILY, resembling in habit the English BILBERRY, to which it is closely related. It bears fleshy fruit with 10 nutlike seeds, differing in this respect from the BLUEBERRY. The common huckleberry of the northern U.S. is *G. baccata,* also called black, or highbush, huckleberry. The florists', or evergreen, huckleberry is actually a blueberry. The red huckleberry of the southern U.S. is commonly called the southern cranberry.

HUD See U.S. Department of HOUSING AND URBAN DEVELOPMENT

Hudson, Henry (1565?–1611) English navigator and explorer. Sailing for the Muscovy Co. of London in search of the NORTHEAST PASSAGE to the Far East, he was blocked by ice fields. In 1609 he set out in the *Half Moon* to find a similar passage for the Dutch EAST INDIA CO., but when stopped by storms he instead sought the NORTHWEST PASSAGE, which he had recently heard about from other explorers, and cruised along the Atlantic coast and up the HUDSON RIVER. In 1610 he set out again for America, this time on behalf of the Muscovy Co. and the English EAST INDIA CO., and discovered HUDSON BAY. Finding no outlet to the Pacific and in the close confinement of an Arctic winter, Hudson's crew fell to quarreling, and on the homeward voyage they mutinied and set Hudson adrift in a small boat, never to be found. His discoveries formed the basis for Dutch colonization of the Hudson River and for English claims to much of Canada.

Hudson, Rock *orig.* **Roy Harold Scherer** (1925–1985) U.S. film actor. Born in Winnetka, Ill., he worked at odd jobs before making his film debut in *Fighter Squadron* (1948). His manly, wholesome good looks made him a popular star in such dramas as *Magnificent Obsession* (1954) and *Giant* (1956), and he displayed a flair for comedy in a series of films with DORIS DAY, including *Pillow Talk* (1959), *Come September* (1961), and *Send Me No Flowers* (1964). He later starred in the television series *McMillan and Wife* (1971–77). His death from AIDS greatly increased awareness of the disease.

Hudson, W(illiam) H(enry) (1841–1922) Argentinian-British author and naturalist. The son of Americans living in Argentina, he spent his youth studying the local flora and fauna and observing both natural and human dramas on what was then a lawless frontier. He settled in England in 1869. He produced a series of ornithological studies, and later achieved fame with his books on the English countryside, including *Hampshire Days* (1903) and *Afoot in England* (1909), which helped foster the back-to-nature movement of the 1920s and '30s. He is best known for the exotic romance *Green Mansions* (1904).

Hudson Bay Inland sea, indenting eastern central Canada. With an area of 480,000 sq mi (1,243,000 sq km), it is bounded by Nunavut, Manitoba, Ontario, and Quebec. It is connected with the Atlantic Ocean via the HUDSON STRAIT and with the Arctic Ocean via the Foxe Channel. Named for HENRY HUDSON, who navigated its eastern coast in 1610, the bay and the surrounding area, known as RUPERT'S LAND, were controlled by the HUDSON'S BAY CO. 1821–69. Hudson Bay is shallow, with an average depth of 330 ft (100 m); the coast is mainly a marsh-ridden lowland. The islands it contains are administratively part of Nunavut Territory. For conservation purposes, the Canadian government has designated the whole Hudson Bay basin a "mare clausum" (closed sea).

Hudson River River, New York. Originating in the ADIRONDACK MTNS. and flowing for about 315 mi (507 km) to NEW YORK CITY, it was named for HENRY HUDSON, who explored it in 1609. Dutch settlement of the Hudson Valley began in 1629. The river became a strategic waterway during the AMERICAN REVOLUTION, and was the scene of many battles. Linked by canals with the GREAT LAKES and with the DELAWARE RIVER and lower ST. LAWRENCE RIVER valleys, the Hudson is now a major commercial route; its southern end forms the New York–New Jersey boundary.

Hudson River school U.S. landscape painters of several generations, active c. 1825–70. The first of them were inspired by the natural beauty of New York's Hudson Valley and Catskill Mountains. The leading figures were THOMAS COLE, ASHER B. DURAND, and Thomas Doughty (1793–1856). Others, such as FREDERIC EDWIN CHURCH and GEORGE INNESS, had studied in Europe and found inspiration in the grandiose landscapes of J.M.W. TURNER. By mid-century they were widely admired for their depictions of a common theme, the splendor of the untamed U.S. landscape. The name, applied retrospectively, is extended to artists of the same vision who painted imposing scenes of the Rocky Mtns., Grand Canyon, and Yosemite Valley. The first native school of painting in the U.S., it remained the dominant school of landscape painting throughout the 19th century.

Hudson Strait Arm of the Atlantic Ocean between BAFFIN ISLAND and northern Quebec, northeastern Canada. Linking HUDSON BAY and Foxe Basin with the Labrador Sea, it is about 500 mi (800 km) long and 40–150 mi (65–240 km) wide. It is navigable only during late summer and early autumn, but icebreakers make the passage most of the year. Partly explored in 1578 by English navigator MARTIN FROBISHER, it was fully navigated by HENRY HUDSON in 1610, and became a main route for the HUDSON'S BAY CO.'s ships.

Hudson's Bay Co. Corporation prominent in Canadian economic and political history. It was incorporated in England (May 2, 1670) to seek the NORTHWEST PASSAGE to the Pacific, to occupy lands adjacent to HUDSON BAY, and to carry on commerce. The lands granted to the company, known as RUPERT'S LAND, extended from Labrador west to the Rocky Mountains and from the headwaters of the Red River on the southern Canadian border north to Chesterfield Inlet on Hudson Bay. The company first engaged in the fur trade and established trading posts around Hudson Bay. By 1783 competitors had formed the NORTH WEST CO., and armed clashes continued until the two companies merged in 1821. The company was given exclusive fur-trade rights until 1858, when the monopoly was not renewed and independent companies entered the fur trade. In 1870 the company sold its territories to the government in exchange for £300,000 and mineral rights to lands around the posts and a fertile portion of western Canada. It remained a large fur-collecting and marketing agency until 1991, with extensive real-estate interests and many department stores.

Hue \hü-'ā, 'wā\ City (pop., 1992 est.: 219,000), central Vietnam. The seat of the Chinese military authority in the kingdom of Nam Viet c. 200 BC, it passed to the Chams c. AD 200. In 1306 it was ceded to Dai Viet (Vietnam). It is the site of the imperial citadel, from which the NGUYEN family reigned from the mid-16th to the mid-20th century. It was occupied by the Japanese 1940–45. It became the seat of a committee of noncommunist Vietnamese in April 1947, but lost this role in 1949, when the newly declared state of Vietnam chose Saigon (see HO CHI MINH CITY) as its capital. Hue was largely destroyed during the 1968 Tet offensive of the VIETNAM WAR; it has since been rebuilt.

Hueffer, Ford Madox See Ford Madox FORD

Huerta \'wer-tä\, **Victoriano** (1854–1916) Mexican president (1913–14). Born of Indian parents, he rose through the ranks of the army to become a general during the rule of Porfirio Diaz. He overthrew Díaz's successor, the liberal Francisco Madero, and established a repressive military dictatorship. Constitutionalist forces united against him and gained the support of U.S. Pres. Woodrow Wilson, who sent troops to assist the rebels. Huerta was defeated in 1914 and fled to Spain; from there he moved to the U.S., where he was arrested for fomenting rebellion in Mexico and died in custody.

Hugenberg \'hü-gən-ˌberk\, **Alfred** (1865–1951) German industrialist and political leader. As chairman of the Krupp family's industrial concern (1909–18), he built a huge newspaper and film empire and greatly influenced German public opinion during the Weimar Republic. As head of the conservative German National Peoples' Party (from 1928) he contributed to Adolf Hitler's rise to power. In 1931 he formed an alliance of nationalist and conservative elements to topple the Weimar government; though his effort failed, large contributions from German industrialists aided the Nazi Party's growth. In 1933 he briefly served in Hitler's cabinet, but his party was dissolved that same year.

Huggins, Charles B(renton) (1901–1997) Canadian-U.S. surgeon and urologist. Born in Halifax, Nova Scotia, he studied at the University of Chicago and subsequently taught there for several decades. He found that using estrogen to block male hormones could slow the growth of prostate cancer. He also showed that removing the ovaries and adrenal glands, which produce estrogen, could reverse tumor growth in some breast cancers. Drugs are now used to block estrogen production in such cases. He shared a 1966 Nobel Prize with Peyton Rous (1879–1970).

Hugh Capet \'kā-pət\ (938?–996) King of France (987–96), the founder of the Capetian dynasty. The son of a Frankish duke, he inherited vast estates in the regions of Paris and Orléans, which made him one of the most powerful vassals in France and a serious threat to the Carolingian king, Lothair. By 985 Hugh was the ruler of France in all but name, and two years later he was elected king. He immediately crowned his own son to ensure the line of succession, a practice continued until the time of Louis VII. He mediated disputes among French nobles and survived a conspiracy to betray him to Otto III.

Hugh of St.-Victor (1096–1141) Scholastic theologian who began the tradition of mysticism of the school of St.-Victor, Paris. He was influenced by St. Augustine of Hippo and by Dionysius the Areopagite and contributed to the development of natural theology. His theology anticipated some of the works of St. Thomas Aquinas.

Hughes, Charles Evans (1862–1948) U.S. jurist and statesman. Born in Glens Falls, N.Y., he became prominent in 1905 as counsel to New York legislative committees investigating abuses in the life-insurance and utilities industries. He won two terms as governor (1906–10), which were marked by extensive reform. He was appointed to the U.S. Supreme Court in 1910, but resigned in 1916 to run as the Republican presidential candidate. He lost to Woodrow Wilson in a close race, and returned to his law practice. As secretary of state (1921–25), he planned and chaired the Washington Conference (1921–22). He was a member of the Hague Tribunal (1926–30) and the Permanent Court of International Justice (1928–30) before being appointed chief justice of the U.S. Supreme Court in 1930 by Pres. Herbert Hoover. He led the Court through the great controversies arising out of Pres. Franklin Roosevelt's New Deal legislation. He generally favored the exercise of government power, though he spoke for the Court in invalidating (in *Schechter Poultry Corp. vs. U.S.*) a principal New Deal statute. He attacked Roosevelt's court-packing plan (1937), and he wrote the opinion sustaining collective bargaining under the Wagner Act. He served until 1941.

Hughes, Howard (Robard) (1905–1976) U.S. manufacturer, aviator, and movie producer. Born in Houston, he left college at 17 to take control of his late father's Hughes Tool Co., which owned the patent to an oil-drilling tool; the company would form the future basis for Hughes's vast fortune. In the early 1930s he founded Hughes Aircraft Co. In 1935 he set a speed record of 352 mph (567 kph) in a plane he designed. In 1938 he flew around the world in a record 91 hours. In 1947 he built and piloted the only flight of a wooden eight-engine flying boat unflatteringly nicknamed "the Spruce Goose." In the 1930s he produced several movies in Hollywood, and he owned RKO Pictures in the early 1950s. He held controlling stock in Trans World Airlines but was forced to sell it in 1966 following legal action. After about 1950 he became a famously eccentric recluse, and after his death his forged memoirs and his several wills became a source of scandal.

Hughes, (James Mercer) Langston (1902–1967) U.S. poet and writer. Born in Joplin, Mo., he published the poem "The Negro Speaks of Rivers" when he was 19, briefly attended Columbia Univ., and worked on an Africa-bound freighter. His career was dramatically launched when Hughes, working as a busboy, presented his poems to Vachel Lindsay as he dined. His poetry collections include *The Weary Blues* (1926) and *Montage of a Dream Deferred* (1951). His later *The Panther and the Lash* (1967) reflects black anger and militancy. Among his other works are short stories (including *The Ways of White Folks*, 1934), autobiographies, many works for the stage (including lyrics for K. Weill's *Street Scene*), anthologies, and translations of poetry by Federico García Lorca and Gabriela Mistral. His well-known comic character Jesse B. Semple, called Simple, appeared in his newspaper columns.

Langston Hughes, photograph by Jack Delano, 1942.

BY COURTESY OF THE LIBRARY OF CONGRESS, WASHINGTON, D.C.

Hughes, Samuel *later* **Sir Samuel** (1853–1921) Canadian soldier and politician. Born in Darlington, Canada West (later Ontario), he acquired and edited an Ontario newspaper (1885–97) and served in the Canadian House of Commons (1892–99, 1902–21). He was a commander in the South African War, and in 1911 he became Canadian minister of militia and defense. At the start of World War I, he organized, trained, and equipped the Canadian Expeditionary Force for service in Europe.

Hughes, Ted *orig.* **Edward James** (1930–1998) British poet. The son of shopkeepers, he studied at Cambridge University. He married the American poet Sylvia Plath in 1956. His first volumes of verse were *The Hawk in the Rain* (1957) and *Lupercal* (1960). After Plath's 1963 suicide he wrote little for three years, then began publishing prolifically, often in collaboration with illustrators or photographers. His collections include *Wodwo* (1967), *Crow* (1970), *Cave Birds* (1975), *Gaudete* (1977), and *Wolf Watching* (1989). His most characteristic work emphasizes the cunning and savagery of animal life in harsh, sometimes disjunctive lines. He wrote many volumes for children (including *The Iron Man,* 1968) and edited the journal *Modern Poetry in Translation.* In 1984 he became Britain's poet laureate. *Birthday Letters* (1998), published shortly before his death, consists of revealing poems about his relationship with Plath.

Hughes, Thomas (1822–1896) British reformer and novelist. An adherent of Christian Socialism, he served as a judge and member of Parliament (1865–74). He was a cofounder and principal of the Working Men's College. He is best known for *Tom Brown's School Days* (1857), on life at an English boys' boarding school, which created the image of the typical public-school boy and popularized Thomas Arnold's doctrine of "muscular Christianity." *Tom Brown at Oxford* (1861) was its sequel.

Hugli River *or* **Hooghly River** \'hü-glē\ River, northeastern India. The most westerly and commercially the most important arm of the Ganges River, it provides access to Kolkata (Calcutta) from the Bay of Bengal. Formed by the junction of the Bhagirathi and Jalangi rivers, it flows south about 160 miles (260 km) through a heavily industrialized area home to more than half of West Bengal's population. Above Kolkata the river is silted up, but it is navigable to the city by ocean liners. It enters the Bay of Bengal through an estuary 3–20 miles (5–32 km) wide, which is spanned by two bridges.

Hugo, Victor (-Marie) (1802–1885) French poet, dramatist, and novelist. The son of a general, he was an accomplished poet before he was 20. With his verse drama *Cromwell* (1827) he emerged as an important figure in Romanticism. The production of his poetic tragedy *Hernani* (1830) was a famous victory for Romantics over traditional classicists. His later plays included *Le roi s'amuse* (1832) and *Ruy Blas* (1838). His best-known novels are *The Hunchback of Notre Dame* (1831), an evocation of medieval life, and *Les misérables* (1862), the story of the convict

Jean Valjean; their huge popularity made him the most successful writer in the world. In later life he was a politician and political writer. He spent the years 1851–70 in exile for his republican views, producing his most extensive and original works, including *Les châtiments* (1853), poems of political satire, *Les contemplations* (1856), *Les chansons des rues et des bois* (1865), and *The Legend of the Centuries* (1859, 1877, 1883). He was made a senator in 1876, and he was buried in the Pantheon as a national hero.

Hugo, photograph by Nadar (Gaspard-Félix Tournachon).
ARCHIVES PHOTOGRAPHIQUES

Hugo Award Byname of the Science Fiction Achievement Award, referring to any of several trophies awarded annually by a professional organization for notable achievement in SCIENCE FICTION or science fantasy. The award was established in 1953 in honor of Hugo Gernsback, who founded *Amazing Stories*, the first magazine exclusively for science fiction. It is given in five writing categories—novel, novella, novelette, short story, and nonfiction. Awards for best new writer and special awards are also occasionally presented.

Huguenots \'hyü-gə-ˌnäts\ French Protestants of the 16th–17th century, many of whom suffered severe persecution for their faith. The first French Huguenot community was founded in 1546, and the confession of faith drawn up by the first synod in 1559 was influenced by the ideas of JOHN CALVIN. Their numbers increased rapidly and they became a political force, led by GASPARD II DE COLIGNY. Conflicts with the Roman Catholic government and others, including the House of GUISE, led to the Wars of RELIGION (1562–98). A Huguenot political party was formed in 1573 to fight for religious and civil liberties. The powerful anti-Huguenot HOLY LEAGUE was formed in 1576. HENRY IV ended the civil wars by abjuring Protestantism in 1593 and converting to Catholicism, but in 1598 he promulgated the Edict of NANTES, granting rights to Protestants. Civil wars occurred again in the 1620s, the Huguenots lost their political power, and they continued to be harassed and forcibly converted. In 1685 LOUIS XIV revoked the Edict of Nantes; over the next several years, more than 400,000 French Protestants left France.

Huhehot See HOHHOT

Hui \'hü-ē\ Chinese Muslims. Their ancestors were merchants, soldiers, craftsmen, and scholars who came to China from Islamic Persia and Central Asia from the 7th to the 13th century and intermarried with the Han Chinese and other local nationalities. Now thoroughly Chinese, they live in all parts of China but are concentrated in the west.

Huineng \'hwā-'nəŋ\ (638–713) Chinese religious leader, sixth patriarch of ZEN Buddhism. As a young and illiterate peddler of firewood, he heard the Diamond Sutra and traveled 500 miles to northern China to study with the fifth patriarch, Hongren. He returned home to Canton in 676 and was ordained a priest. He asserted that all people are basically pure and possess the Buddha-nature, and he held that if one seeks one's own nature and cultivates tranquillity, enlightenment will come suddenly, without external help. He founded the Southern school, which became the dominant school of Zen in both China and Japan.

Huitzilopochtli \ˌwēt-sē-lō-'pōcht-lē\ AZTEC sun and war god. He was usually portrayed as a hummingbird or as a warrior with a helmet of feathers and a turquoise snake staff. His animal disguise was the eagle. His mother was an earth goddess, his brothers stars in the sky, and his sister a moon goddess. Some myths presented him as the divine leader of the tribe during the long migration that brought the Aztecs to the Valley of Mexico. The fifteenth month of the ceremonial year was dedicated to him, and human sacrifices were made in his honor, in keeping with the belief that he needed human blood and hearts as daily nourishment.

Huizinga \'hœi-ziŋ-ä\, **Johan** (1872–1945) Dutch historian. He was professor of history at Groningen (1905–15) and then at Leiden until 1942, when he was held as a hostage by the Nazis; he remained under open arrest until his death. His first studies dealt with Indian literature and cultures, but he became internationally recognized for *The Waning of the Middle Ages* (1919), a lively examination of life in France and Holland in the 14th–15th century. His other works include *Erasmus* (1924), *In the Shadow of Tomorrow* (1935), and *Homo Ludens* (1938).

Huizong *or* **Hui-tsung** \'hwē-'dzùŋ\ *or* **Song Huizong** *orig.* **Zhao Ji** (1082–1135) Penultimate emperor of the Northern SONG DYNASTY in China. A painter and calligrapher, Huizong preferred the arts to government. He urged the painters in his academy to be extremely literal in their representations; his own paintings of birds and flowers are detailed, accurately colored, and perfectly composed. While he constructed an extravagant new palace garden, political disputes went unresolved and his favorite EUNUCHS gained unprecedented power in the government. His alliance with the JUCHEN tribes of Manchuria against the LIAO led to the Juchen invasion that overthrew the Northern Song.

Hukbalahap Rebellion \'hùk-bä-lä-'häp\ (1946–54) Peasant uprising in Luzon, Philippines. The rich Luzon plain was farmed by a large tenant-farmer population working on vast estates, a situation that led to periodic peasant revolts. The area became a focal point for communist organizers in the 1930s. One communist organization, the Hukbalahap, was a successful anti-Japanese guerrilla group during World War II. By the war's end it had also seized most of the Luzon large estates, established a government, and was collecting taxes. When the Philippines became independent in 1946, the Huks, prevented from taking government seats to which they had been elected, began a rebellion. For four years they were successful, and in 1950 they nearly seized Manila. Defeated by U.S. weaponry and by the rise of the popular RAMON MAGSAYSAY, their leader, Luis Taruc (born 1913), surrendered in 1954, though the Huk movement continued into the 1970s.

hula Sinuous Polynesian dance that combines undulating movement of the hips and mimetic hand gestures, often performed to chants and instruments such as the ukulele. Originally a religious dance performed to praise the chiefs, contemporary hulas tell a story or describe a place and are danced exclusively by women. The costume is typically a raffia skirt with a lei around the neck.

Hull *in full* **Kingston upon Hull** City (pop., 1995 est.: 269,000), seat of HUMBERSIDE, England. It lies on the northern bank of the HUMBER ESTUARY at its junction with the River Hull, 22 mi (35 km) from the North Sea. Hull had a medieval wool port, which passed to EDWARD I in 1293. For more than 400 years it was the chief shipping port for the inland waterways converging on the Humber Estuary. Granted city status in 1897, it is a major national seaport, accommodating large oceangoing vessels. The medieval part of the city retains a number of historic buildings; its grammar school was founded in 1486.

Hull, Bobby *orig.* **Robert Martin** (born 1939) Canadian hockey player. Born in Pointe Anne, Ontario, he played center and forward for the Chicago Black Hawks (1957–72), where his swinging slap shot and fast skating made him a dominant figure, and he scored 50 or more goals in each of five seasons. By the time he retired from the NHL, he had scored 609 goals, 555 assists, and 1,164 points. He went on to play in the now-defunct World Hockey Association (1972–81) before leaving the sport.

Bobby Hull, 1969.
CANADA WIDE—PICTORIAL PARADE

Hull, Clark L(eonard) (1884–1952) U.S. psychologist. Born in Akron, N.Y., he taught at the University of Wisconsin 1918–29, and was a member of Yale Univ.'s Institute of Human Relations 1929–52. He engaged in three distinct research endeavors. His study of psychometrics culminated in *Aptitude Testing* (1929). His study of hypnosis resulted in *Hypnosis and Suggestibility* (1933). His major effort was reserved for an intensive study of learning that produced the dominant learning theory of the 1940s and '50s. His important *Mathematico-Deductive Theory of Rote Learning* (1940) was followed by his highly influential *Principles of Behavior* (1943). Relying on the work of EDWARD L. THORNDIKE and JOHN B. WATSON, he attempted to develop a rigorous theory of learning that would account for all behaviors, human and animal. He and his followers were enormously productive of experiments and theoretical concepts, and their work dominated the experimental literature for more than two decades, but eventually was replaced by a more cognitive psychology that provided a role for mental events.

Hull, Cordell (1871–1955) U.S. politician and diplomat. Born in Overton Co., Tenn., he practiced law and served in the U.S. House of Representatives (1907–21, 1923–31), where he wrote the first income-tax bill (1913) and the inheritance-tax law (1916). He served briefly in the U.S. Senate 1931–33. As secretary of state under FRANKLIN ROOSEVELT (1933–44), he initiated a reciprocal trade program that lowered tariffs and expanded world trade. He improved Latin American relations by fostering the GOOD NEIGHBOR POLICY, and in negotiations in 1941 he supported China, urging Japan to abandon its mainland military conquests. He began early in World War II to plan an international postwar peacekeeping body, causing Roosevelt to describe him as the "father of the UNITED NATIONS"; his work earned him the 1945 Nobel Peace Prize.

Hull, Isaac (1773–1843) U.S. naval officer. Born in Huntington, Conn., a nephew of WILLIAM HULL, he was master of a ship by 19. Commissioned a lieutenant on the USS *CONSTITUTION* in 1798, he served in the Tripolitan War and in 1810 became its commander. Early in the War of 1812 he engaged the British frigate *Guerrière* and after a fierce battle rendered it a wreck. His victory united the U.S. behind the war effort, and his ship became known as "Old Ironsides." He commanded the U.S. squadrons in the Pacific (1824–27) and in the Mediterranean (1839–41).

Hull, William (1753–1825) U.S. army officer. Born in Derby, Conn., he fought in American Revolutionary campaigns in Connecticut, New York, and New Jersey. In 1805 he was appointed governor of Michigan Territory. At the outbreak of the WAR OF 1812, he was appointed brigadier general to defend Michigan and attack Canada. His poorly planned invasion of Canada forced him to retreat to Detroit, where he surrendered without a fight. He was court-martialed and convicted of cowardice and neglect of duty; his death sentence was remitted by Pres. JAMES MADISON because of his earlier service.

Hulse, Russell Alan (born 1950) U.S. physicist. Born in New York City, he earned a PhD from the University of Massachusetts. With his professor, JOSEPH H., JR. TAYLOR, he discovered dozens of PULSARS. One pulsar, PSR 1913 + 16, proved to be a binary star; the two stars' enormous interacting gravitational fields provided the first means of detecting gravity waves, predicted by ALBERT EINSTEIN in his general theory of RELATIVITY. For their discovery of PSR 1913 + 16, Hulse and Taylor shared a 1993 Nobel Prize.

human being See *HOMO SAPIENS*

human evolution Evolution of modern human beings from nonhuman and extinct HOMINID forms. Genetic evidence points to an evolutionary divergence between the lineages of humans and the great apes (Pongidae) on the African continent 5–8 million years ago. The oldest known hominid remains, dating to at least 4 million years ago, are classified as belonging to the genus *AUSTRALOPITHECUS* and are found only in Africa. One of the australopithecines, either *A. afarensis* or *A. africanus,* probably gave rise to the species representing the next major evolutionary stage, *HOMO HABILIS,* which inhabited sub-Saharan Africa until c. 1.5 million years ago. *H. habilis,* in turn, appears to have been supplanted by a taller and more human species, *HOMO ERECTUS*. This species lived from c. 2 million to 250,000 years ago and gradually migrated into Asia and parts of Europe. Archaic forms of *HOMO SAPIENS* with features resembling those of both *H. erectus* and modern humans appeared c. 400,000 years ago in Africa and perhaps parts of Asia, but fully modern humans emerged only 250,000–150,000 years ago, probably descended from *H. erectus.*

human-factors engineering *or* **human engineering** *or* **ergonomics** Profession of designing machines, tools, and work environments to best accommodate human performance and behavior. It aims to improve the practicality, efficiency, and safety of a person working with a single machine or device (e.g., using a telephone, driving a car, or operating a computer terminal). Taking the user into consideration has probably always been a part of tool design; for example, the scythe, one of the oldest and most efficient human implements, shows a remarkable degree of ergonomic engineering. Examples of common devices that are poorly designed ergonomically include the snow shovel and the computer or typewriter keyboard.

Human Genome Project U.S. research effort initiated in 1990 by the U.S. Department of Energy and the National Institutes of Health to analyze the DNA of human beings. The project, intended to be completed in 15 years, proposed to identify the chromosomal location of every human GENE, to determine each gene's precise chemical structure in order to show its function in health and disease, and to determine the precise sequence of nucleotides of the entire set of genes (the genome). Another project was to address the ethical, legal, and social implications of the information obtained. The information gathered will be the basic reference for research in human biology and will provide fundamental insights into the genetic basis of human disease. The new technologies developed in the course of the project will be applicable in numerous biomedical fields. In 2000 the government and the private corporation Celera Genomics jointly announced that the project had been virtually completed, five years ahead of schedule.

human growth hormone See GROWTH HORMONE

human immunodeficiency virus See HIV

human nature Fundamental dispositions and traits of humans. Theories about the nature of humankind form a part of every culture. In the West, debate has traditionally centered on whether humans are selfish and competitive (see, e.g., THOMAS HOBBES and JOHN LOCKE) or social and altruistic (KARL MARX, EMILE DURKHEIM). Recent research in genetics, evolutionary biology, and cultural anthropology suggests that humans may be both, and that there is a complex interaction between genetically inherited factors ("nature") and developmental and social factors ("nurture"). Basic drives shared with other PRIMATES include food, sex, security, play, and SOCIAL STATUS. GENDER differences include greater investment in reproduction and child-rearing among females, hence less risk-taking; and concomitantly less investment and greater risk-taking among males. See also BEHAVIOR GENETICS, *HOMO SAPIENS*, PERSONALITY, PHILOSOPHICAL ANTHROPOLOGY, SOCIOBIOLOGY.

human rights Rights that belong to an individual as a consequence of being human. The term came into wide use after World War II, replacing the earlier phrase "natural rights," which is thought to have originated in NATURAL LAW and STOICISM. As understood today, human rights occupy a wide continuum that reflects the diversity of human circumstances, history, and values. They are seen as universal and general and as fundamental. Some theorists limit human rights to the right to life, or to life and freedom of opportunity. In Europe and the U.S. in the 17th–18th century, thinkers such as JOHN LOCKE stressed civil and political rights (including freedom of speech, freedom of religion, and freedom from slavery, torture, and arbitrary arrest). In the 19th century, the focus moved to economic and social rights (including the right to work and the right to a minimum standard of living). The adoption of the UNIVERSAL DECLARATION OF HUMAN RIGHTS in 1948 was a landmark. In the late 20th century, the concept was sometimes extended to include such rights as self-determination, peace, and a healthy environment.

human sacrifice Offering of the life of a human being to a god. In some ancient cultures, the killing of a human being, or the substitution of an animal for a person, was an attempt to commune with the god and to participate in the divine life. It also sometimes served as an attempt to placate the god and expiate the sins of the people. It was especially common among agricultural people (e.g., in the ancient Near East), who sought to guarantee the fertility of the soil. The AZTECS sacrificed thousands of victims (often slaves or prisoners of war) annually to the sun, and the INCAS made human sacrifices on the accession of a ruler. In ancient Egypt and elsewhere in Africa, human sacrifice was connected with ANCESTOR WORSHIP, and slaves and servants were killed or buried alive along with dead kings in order to provide service in the afterlife. A similar tradition existed in China. The Celts and Germanic peoples are among the European peoples who practiced human sacrifice.

humanism In Renaissance Europe, a cultural impulse characterized by a revival of classical letters, an individualistic and critical spirit, and a shift of emphasis from religious to secular concerns. It dates to the 14th century and the poet PETRARCH, though earlier figures are sometimes described as humanists. Its diffusion was facilitated by the universal use of Latin and the invention of movable type. The term became identified more narrowly with classroom studies of the classics. Today it is often used loosely to mean an emphasis on a human-centered rather than a God-centered universe.

humanistic psychology 20th-century movement in psychology, developed largely in reaction against BEHAVIORISM and PSYCHOANALYSIS, that emphasizes the importance of values, intentions, and meaning in the compass of the individual. The concept of the "self" is a central focus for most humanistic psychologists. Architects of the humanistic approach included ABRAHAM MASLOW, CARL R. ROGERS, and Rollo May (1909–1994). Types of humanistic therapies have included sensory awareness, encounter groups, existential analysis, Gestalt therapy, logotherapy, and various transpersonal, human-potential, holistic-health, and addiction-recovery schools.

humanities Branches of knowledge that investigate human beings, their culture, and their self-expression. Distinguished from the physical and biological sciences and, less decisively, from the social sciences, the humanities include the study of languages and literatures, the arts, history, and philosophy. The modern conception of the humanities has roots in the classical Greek *paideia,* a course in general education dating from the 5th century BC that prepared young men for citizenship. It also draws on CICERO's *humanitas,* a program of training for orators set forth in 55 BC. The Renaissance humanists contrasted studies of humanity with studies of the divine; by the 19th century the distinction was instead drawn between the humanities and the sciences.

Humanities, National Endowment for the See NATIONAL ENDOWMENT FOR THE HUMANITIES

Humber Estuary *or* **Humber River** *ancient* **Abus** Estuary, NORTH SEA inlet, on the eastern coast of England. Originating with the confluence of the OUSE and TRENT rivers, it is 40 mi (64 km) long and more than 7 mi (11 km) wide at its mouth. The Humber Bridge, one of the longest suspension bridges in the world (main span 4,626 ft, or 1,410 m), was constructed (1981) chiefly to aid the economic development of the estuary's banks, which are lined by several major ports, including HULL.

Humberside Former county, eastern England. It extended along the NORTH SEA coast from Flamborough Head south across the mouth of the River HUMBER; its administrative center was HULL. The Yorkshire Wolds, high rolling plains, rise from white chalk cliffs at Flamborough Head. Prehistoric peoples were followed by Roman settlements, Anglo-Saxons, and Scandinavians.

Humboldt, (Friedrich Wilhelm Heinrich) Alexander, (Baron) von (1769–1859) German naturalist and explorer. In 1792 he joined the mining department of the Prussian government, where he invented a safety lamp and established a technical school for miners. From 1799 he explored Central and South America, traveling in the Amazon jungles and the Andean Highlands. During these journeys he discovered the connection between the Amazon and Orinoco river systems and surmised that altitude sickness was caused by lack of oxygen. He studied the oceanic current off the western coast of South America; it became known as the Humboldt current (now the Peru current). He returned to Europe in 1804. His research helped lay the foundation for comparative climatology, drew a connection between a region's geography and its flora and fauna, and added to an understanding of the development of the earth's crust. In Paris he used his financial resources to help LOUIS AGASSIZ and others launch careers. In 1829 he traveled to Russia and Siberia and made geographical, geological, and meteorological observations of Central Asia. During the 1830s he investigated magnetic storms. The last 25 years of his life were spent writing *Kosmos,* an account of the structure of the universe as then known.

Alexander von Humboldt, oil painting by Friedrich Georg Weitsch, 1806; in the Staatliche Museen zu Berlin.

BY COURTESY OF THE STAATLICHE MUSEEN ZU BERLIN

Humboldt, (Karl) Wilhelm *later* **Freiherr (Baron) von Humboldt** (1767–1835) German linguist and educational reformer. The elder brother of ALEXANDER VON HUMBOLDT, he held Prussian government posts, including minister of education (1809) and ambassador to Vienna (1812). He raised elementary education standards and was instrumental in founding Friedrich Wilhelm University (now Humboldt Univ., or University of BERLIN) in Berlin. Humboldt also contributed greatly to the philosophy of language, contending that its character and structure express the speaker's culture and individuality and that humans perceive the world through the medium of language. He also carried out research on the BASQUE LANGUAGE and Kawi (old Javanese).

Humboldt River River, northern Nevada. Rising in Elko county, it flows west and southwest for 290 mi (467 km) to Humboldt Lake (also called Humboldt Sink). Named by JOHN C. FREMONT for ALEXANDER VON HUMBOLDT, it was an important route for emigrants going from Salt Lake City to the gold fields in central California.

Humboldt University of Berlin See University of BERLIN

Hume, David (1711–1776) Scottish philosopher, historian, and economist. His first book, the important *Treatise of Human Nature* (1739–40), was his attempt to formulate a full-fledged philosophical system; its initial reception was disappointing. His *Essays Moral and Political* (1741–42), was well received, and strongly influenced the economic thinking of his friend ADAM SMITH. His *Political Discourses* (1752) was followed by his huge *History of England* (5 vols., 1754–62). He conceived of philosophy as the inductive, experimental science of human nature. Taking ISAAC NEWTON's scientific method as his model and building on JOHN LOCKE's EMPIRICISM, he tried to describe how the mind works in acquiring knowledge. He concluded that no METAPHYSICS is possible, that there can be no knowledge of anything beyond experience. He concluded that humans are more creatures of sentiment than of reason. He was led to question the objective validity of the concepts of substance and causal necessity and of the method of INDUCTION. His influence was widely felt. IMMANUEL KANT conceived his critical philosophy in direct reaction to Hume, and Hume was important in leading AUGUSTE COMTE to POSITIVISM. In Britain, Hume's positive influence is seen in JEREMY BENTHAM, who was moved to UTILITARIANISM by Hume's *Treatise*, and more extensively in JOHN STUART MILL.

Hume, John (born 1937) Leader of the Social Democratic and Labour Party (SDLP) in Northern Ireland from 1979 to 2001 and corecipient with DAVID TRIMBLE of the Nobel Prize for Peace in 1998. A schoolteacher, he became a Roman Catholic leader in the Northern Ireland civil rights movement in the 1960s. He was elected to the Northern Ireland parliament in 1969 and became the leader of the SDLP in 1979. A moderate, he condemned the use of violence by the IRISH REPUBLICAN ARMY (IRA). In the late 1980s he attempted to persuade the IRA to abandon the armed struggle against Britain and enter democratic politics. He risked his personal safety to engage in sometimes secret dialogues with leaders of SINN FÉIN, the IRA's political wing, and he played a leading role in negotiating the Good Friday Agreement, the multiparty peace accord between unionists and nationalists reached in April 1998. Elected to the new Northern Ireland Assembly in June, he resigned his seat two years later because of ill health.

humidity Amount of water vapor in the air. One of the most variable characteristics of the atmosphere, humidity is an important factor in climate and weather: it regulates air temperature by absorbing thermal radiation both from the sun and the earth; it is directly proportional to the latent energy available for the generation of storms; and it is the ultimate source of all forms of condensation and precipitation. Humidity varies because the water-holding capacity of air is determined by temperature. When a volume of air at a given temperature holds the maximum amount of water vapor possible, the air is said to be saturated. Relative humidity is the water-vapor content of the air relative to its content at saturation. Saturated air has a relative humidity of 100%; near the earth the relative humidity rarely falls below 30%.

Humiliation of Olmütz See Humiliation of OLMÜTZ

Hummel \'hùm-əl\, **Johann Nepomuk** (1778–1837) Austrian composer, pianist, and conductor. Born in Pressburg (Bratislava, in present-day Slovakia), he was a piano prodigy. Moving at 8 to Vienna, where his father was a conductor, he studied two years with W.A. MOZART. After five years of touring, he returned for further study and gave up public performance. He replaced F.J. HAYDN as music director at the Esterházy palace, but made his living teaching and composing for the theater. In 1814 he recommenced performing with huge success, and he died wealthy. He composed a number of concertos and much chamber music.

Hummert, Anne and Frank (1905–1996, 1890?–1966) U.S. radio producers. From 1927 Anne (originally Anne Schumacher) worked as a copywriter for the Chicago advertising agency co-owned by Frank. As radio entered its golden age, they began to write soap operas. Their *Just Plain Bill* (1932–55), *The Romance of Helen Trent* (1933–60), *Ma Perkins* (1933–60), and *Backstage Wife* (1935–59) became such hits that they formed Hummert Radio Productions. Creating the basic plots and assigning an assembly line of writers to complete the scripts, they produced more than 40 radio shows, including the soap operas *Stella Dallas* (1938–55) and *Young Widder Brown* (1938–56); the mystery shows *Mr. Keen, Tracer of Lost Persons* (1937–54) and *Mr. Chameleon* (1948–51); and the musical programs *The American Album of Familiar Music* (1931–51) and *Manhattan Merry-Go-Round* (1933–49).

hummingbird Any of about 320 species of New World birds (family Trochilidae), many of which have glittering colors and elaborately specialized feathers. They are most abundant in South America; about 12 species are found in the U.S. and Canada. Hummingbirds range in length from slightly more than 2 in. (5 cm) to 8 in. (20 cm), weigh 0.07–0.7 oz (2–20 g), and have a long, slender bill. The bee hummingbird of Cuba is the smallest living bird. Hummingbirds can fly forward, straight up and down, sideways, and backward and can hover in front of flowers to obtain nectar and insects. Smaller species can beat their wings as fast as 80 beats per second.

Allen's hummingbird (*Selasphorus sasin*).
ARVIL L. PARKER

humor *or* **humour** (Latin: "fluid") One of the four body fluids thought to determine a person's temperament and features, according to a physiological theory widely accepted in ancient times and the Middle Ages. As hypothesized by GALEN, the four cardinal humors were blood, phlegm, choler (yellow bile), and melancholy (black bile). The variant mixture of these humors in each person determined his "complexion" or temperament and his mental and physical qualities. The ideal person had the perfectly proportioned mixture of the four fluids; a disproportionate amount of one humor created a personality dominated by one set of related emotions (e.g., a choleric man was easily angered, proud, ambitious, and vengeful).

humpback whale Thickset BALEEN WHALE *(Megaptera novaeangliae,* or *M. nodosa)* that lives along all major ocean coasts, sometimes swimming close inshore or even into harbors and up rivers. Humpbacks grow to 40–52 ft (12–16 m) long. They are black above, with some white below, and have very long, narrow pectoral fins and large knobs on the head and jaws. The humpback migrates between polar waters in summer and tropical or subtropical breeding grounds in winter. It feeds on shrimplike crustaceans, small fish, and plankton. It is probably the most vocal of all whales (with "songs" of 5–35 minutes) and one of the most acrobatic (capable of turning a somersault). Much reduced in number by overhunting, humpbacks have been protected worldwide since the 1960s and are no longer listed as endangered.

Humperdinck, Engelbert (1854–1921) German composer. He studied piano, organ, cello, and composition with Ferdinand Hiller (1811–1885). His compositions won prizes, and in 1879 he met RICHARD WAGNER in Naples and became a member of his circle. Invited to help prepare *Parsifal* for its premiere, including copying the score and rehearsing the chorus, he came to be considered Wagner's chosen successor by some. He is known today for the highly popular opera *Hänsel und Gretel* (1892); his later works include the opera *Königskinder* (1897).

Humphrey, Doris (1895–1958) U.S. dancer and modern-dance choreographer. Born in Oak Park, Ill., she joined the Denishawn troupe in 1917. She left in 1928 to cofound, with CHARLES WEIDMAN, a school and performing dance group, which was active until 1944. Her choreography expressed an innovative use of conflict between balance and imbalance, fall and recovery; her works included *Water Study* (1928), *The Shakers* (1931), and *New Dance* (1935). She retired as a performer in 1945 but continued as artistic director for JOSE LIMON's company, creating such works as *Day on Earth* (1947) and *Ruins and Visions* (1953).

Doris Humphrey.
CULVER PICTURES

Humphrey, Hubert H(oratio) (1911–1978) U.S. politican. Born in Wallace, S.D., he worked as a pharmacist before becoming Minnesota campaign manager for Pres. FRANKLIN ROOSEVELT in 1944. He helped merge the state's Democratic and FARMER-LABOR parties. His public career began when he was elected mayor of Minneapolis (1945–48). In the U.S. Senate (1949–64), he proved to be a skilled parliamentary leader who helped forge bipartisan support for the Nuclear Test-Ban Treaty and the 1964 Civil Rights Act. As vice president under LYNDON B. JOHNSON (1965–69), he defended U.S. participation in the VIETNAM WAR, compromising his earlier reputation as a liberal "do-gooder." He won the Democratic presidential nomination in 1968, but narrowly lost the election to RICHARD NIXON. He served again in the Senate 1971–78.

humus \'hyü-məs\ Nonliving, finely divided organic matter in soil, derived from microbial decomposition of plant and animal substances. Ranging in color from brown to black, it consists primarily of carbon but also contains nitrogen and smaller amounts of phosphorus and sulfur. As it decomposes, its components are changed into forms usable by plants. Humus is classified according to how well it is incorporated into the mineral soil, the types of organisms involved in its decomposition, and the vegetation from which it is derived. It is valued by farmers and gardeners because it provides nutrients essential for plant growth, increases the soil's water absorption, and improves soil workability.

Hunan \'hü-'nän\ Province (pop., 1999 est.: 65,320,000), central China. It lies south of the YANGTZE RIVER; its capital is CHANGSHA. Part of the 3rd century BC kingdom of CHU, it passed to the QIN DYNASTY, and became part of the Chinese empire during the HAN DYNASTY (206 BC– AD 220). With part of modern HUBEI, it was a province until the mid-17th century. It was invaded in 1852 by Taiping rebels, and in 1934 Mao led the LONG MARCH from Hunan. The scene of bitter fighting during the SINO-JAPANESE WAR, it became part of communist China in 1949. Much of the terrain is mountainous, and it is the site of Mt. Heng, one of China's sacred mountains. The province's economy is basically agricultural; it is one of China's great rice-producing regions.

Hundred Days *French* **Cent Jours** (1815) In French history, the period between NAPOLEON's arrival in Paris after escaping from exile on Elba and the return of LOUIS XVIII to Paris. Napoleon landed on French soil on March 1 and reached Paris on March 20. Austria, Britain, Prussia, and Russia swiftly concluded an alliance against Napoleon and forced a series of military engagements that led up to the Battle of WATERLOO. On June 22 Napoleon abdicated a second time and was removed to St. Helena; Louis returned to Paris on July 8.

Hundred Years' War (1337–1453) Intermittent armed conflict between England and France over territorial rights and the issue of succession to the French throne. It began when EDWARD III invaded Flanders in 1337 in order to assert his claim to the French crown. Edward won a major victory at the Battle of CRÉCY (1346); after his son EDWARD THE BLACK PRINCE managed to capture JOHN II at the Battle of POITIERS (1356), the French were obliged to surrender extensive lands under the treaties of BRÉTIGNY and Calais (1360). When John II died in captivity, his son CHARLES V refused to respect the treaties and reopened the conflict, putting the English on the defensive. After Charles V's death in 1380 both countries were preoccupied with internal power struggles, and the war lapsed into uncertain peace. In 1415, however, HENRY V decided to take advantage of civil war in France to press English claims to the French throne (see Battle of AGINCOURT). By 1422, the English and their Burgundian allies controlled Aquitaine and all France north of the Loire, including Paris. A turning point came in 1429, when Joan of Arc raised the English siege of Orléans. The French king Charles VII conquered Normandy and then retook Aquitaine in 1453, leaving the English in possession only of Calais. The war laid waste to much of France and caused enormous suffering; it virtually destroyed the feudal nobility and thereby brought about a new social order. By ending England's status as a power on the continent, it led the English to expand their reach and power at sea.

Hung Hsiu-ch'üan See Hong Xiuquan

Hung-shan culture See Hongshan culture

Hung-shui River See Hongshui River

Hung T'ai-chi See Hongtaiji

Hung-tse Hu See Hongze Hu

Hung-wu emperor See Hongwu emperor

Hungarian language Finno-Ugric language of Hungary, with substantial minority populations in Slovakia, Transylvania in Romania, and northern Serbia. Hungarian has about 14.5 million speakers worldwide—more than any other Uralic language—including 400,000–500,000 in North America. The earliest known text in Hungarian dates from the late 12th century; a continuous literary tradition begins in the 15th century. Though more heavily influenced by European languages than any other Uralic language, Hungarian retains some typical Uralic features, such as vowel harmony (agreement of vowel features across syllables), a complex nominal case system, expression of possession by suffixes, and a distinction in transitive verbal conjugation between verbs having definite and indefinite objects. Contact with Turkic, Iranian, and Slavic languages, and, more recently, High German dialects and Latin, has given Hungarian many loanwords.

Hungarian Revolution (1956) Popular uprising in Hungary following a speech by Nikita Khrushchev in which he attacked the period of Joseph Stalin's rule. Encouraged by the new freedom of debate and criticism, a rising tide of unrest and discontent in Hungary broke out into active fighting in October 1956. Rebels won the first phase of the revolution, and Imre Nagy became premier, agreeing to establish a multiparty system. On November 1 he declared Hungarian neutrality and appealed to the U.N. Western powers failed to respond, and on November 4 the Soviet Union invaded Hungary to stop the revolution. Nevertheless, Stalinist-type domination and exploitation did not return, and Hungary thereafter experienced a slow evolution toward some internal autonomy.

Hungary *officially* **Republic of Hungary** *Hungarian* **Magyar Köztársaság** \'mó-ˌjór-kœs-'tär-shó-ˌshäg\ Republic, central Europe. Area: 35,919 sq mi (93,030 sq km). Population (2002 est.): 10,162,000. Capital: Budapest. The people are an amalgam of Magyars and various Slavic, Turkish, and Germanic peoples. Language: Hungarian (Magyar) (official). Religions: Roman Catholicism, Protestantism. Currency: forint. The Great Alföld (Great Hungarian Plain), with fertile agriculture land, occupies nearly half the country. Hungary's two most important rivers are the Danube and Tisza. Lake Balaton, in the Transdanubian highlands, is the largest lake in central Europe. Forests cover nearly one-fifth of its land. It is one of the more prosperous nations of eastern Europe, and a major world producer of bauxite. A conversion from a socialist to a free-market economy was begun in the late 1980s. It is a multiparty republic with one legislative house; the chief of state is the president, and the head of government is the prime minister. The western part of Hungary was incorporated into the Roman empire in 14 BC. The Magyars, a nomadic people, settled in the Great Alföld in the late 9th century. Stephen I, crowned in 1000, Christianized the country and organized it into a strong and independent state. Invasions by the Mongols in the 13th century and by the Ottoman Turks in the 14th century devastated the country, and by 1568 the territory of modern Hungary had been divided into three parts: Royal Hungary fell to the Habsburgs; Transylvania gained autonomy in 1566 under the Turks; and the central plain remained under Turkish control until the late 17th century, when the Austrian Habsburgs took over. Hungary declared its independence from Austria in 1849, and in 1867 the dual monarchy of Austria-Hungary was established. Its defeat in World War I resulted in the dismemberment of Hungary, leaving it only those areas in which Magyars predominated. In an attempt to regain some of this lost territory, Hungary cooperated with the Germans against the Soviet Union during World War II. After the war, a pro-Soviet provisional government was established, and in 1949 the Hungarian People's Republic was formed. Opposition to this Stalinist regime broke out in 1956 but was suppressed (see Hungarian Revolution). Nevertheless, in 1956–88 communist Hungary grew to become the most tolerant of the Soviet-bloc nations of eastern Europe. It gained its independence in 1989 and soon attracted the largest amount of direct foreign investment in eastern central Europe. In 1999 it joined NATO.

Hunkar Iskelesi, Treaty of See Treaty of Unkiar Skelessi

Hunkers and Barnburners Two factions of the New York state Democratic Party in the 19th century. The party split over slavery in the 1840s. The conservative Hunkers (so called by their opponents as those who "hunkered" or "hankered" after political office), led by William Marcy, favored the annexation of Texas and denounced antislavery agitation. The radical and reformist Barnburners (so called by their opponents as those who burned the barn to get rid of the rats), led by Martin Van Buren, opposed slavery's extension into new territories. At the 1848 Democratic national convention, the Barnburners joined the Free Soil Party, nominating Van Buren for president. In the 1850s some Barnburners returned to the Democratic Party while others joined the new Republican Party.

Huns Nomadic pastoralist people who invaded southeastern Europe c. AD 370. Appearing from central Asia after the mid-4th century, they first overran the Alani, who occupied the plains between the Volga and Don rivers, and then overthrew the Ostrogoths living between the Don and Dniester rivers. About 376 they defeated the Visigoths living in what is now approximately Romania and reached the Danubian frontier of the Roman empire. As warriors they inspired almost unparalleled fear throughout Europe; they were accurate mounted archers, and their rapid, ferocious charges brought them overwhelming victories. They extended their power over many of the Germanic peoples of central Europe and allied themselves with the Romans. By 432 the leadership of the various groups of Huns had been centralized under a single king, Rua (Rugila). After his death (434), he was succeeded by his two nephews, Bleda and Attila. By a peace treaty with the eastern Roman empire, the Romans agreed to double the subsidies they had been paying the Huns; when they apparently failed to pay the stipulated sums, Attila launched a heavy assault on the Roman Danubian frontier (441), and other attacks spread the Huns' control into Greece and Italy. After Attila's death (453), his many sons divided up his empire and began a series of costly struggles with their subjects. The Huns were finally routed in 455 by an alliance of Gepidae, Ostrogoths, Heruli, and others in a great battle in PANNONIA. The eastern Roman government then closed the frontier to the Huns, who gradually disintegrated as a social and political unit.

Hunt, H(aroldson) L(afayette) (1889–1974) U.S. oilman. Born in Ramsey, Ill., Hunt purchased a tract of land in eastern Texas in 1930 that proved one of the richest oilfields in the U.S. He continued his shrewd investments through his Hunt Oil Co. (founded 1936), which became the largest independent oil and gas producer in the country. In the 1960s he exploited vast oil deposits in Libya. He also invested in publishing, cosmetics, pecan farming, and health food. He promoted his ultraconservative views on his own radio programs and newspaper column in the 1950s. Two of his sons, N. Bunker and W. Herbert, tried unsuccessfully to corner the world silver market in 1980, causing its near collapse.

Hunt, (James Henry) Leigh (1784–1859) British essayist, critic, journalist, and poet. He was an editor of influential journals, particularly the reformist weekly *The Examiner* (1808–21), in an age when the periodical was at the height of its power. He was the first publisher of his friends PERCY B. SHELLEY and JOHN KEATS. He was imprisoned (1813–15) for attacks in *The Examiner* on the prince regent. "Abou Ben Adhem" and "Jenny Kissed Me" are his best-known poems. His autobiography (1850) provides a vivid picture of the era.

Hunt, Richard Morris (1827–1895) U.S. architect. Born in Brattleboro, Vt., he studied in Europe 1843–54, becoming the first U.S. architecture student at the École des Beaux-Arts in Paris. He returned to the U.S. to establish the BEAUX-ARTS STYLE. His work was eclectic, ranging from ornate early French Renaissance to monumental classicism to a picturesque villa style. He worked on the extension of the U.S. CAPITOL and designed the Tribune building in New York City (1873; since destroyed) and the facade of the METROPOLITAN MUSEUM OF ART (1900–2). Among his mansions for the new commercial aristocracy is The Breakers in Newport, R.I. (1892–95), in an opulent Renaissance style for the Vanderbilts. Hunt was a founder of the American Institute of Architects.

Hunt, William Holman (1827–1910) British painter and cofounder of the Pre-Raphaelite Brotherhood (see PRE-RAPHAELITES). He attended the Royal Academy schools and achieved his first public success with *The Light of the World* (1854). His paintings are characterized by hard color, minute detail, and an emphasis on moral or social symbolism; their moral earnestness made them extemely popular in Victorian England. He spent two years in Syria and Palestine painting biblical scenes, such as *The Scapegoat* (1855), depicting the outcast animal on the shores of the Dead Sea. His autobiographical *Pre-Raphaelitism and the Pre-Raphaelite Brotherhood* (1905) is the basic sourcebook of the movement.

Hunter, John (1728–1793) British surgeon. He never attempted to become a medical doctor, but assisted in the preparation of dissections for a course of anatomy taught by his brother WILLIAM HUNTER. In the early 1770s he began giving his own lectures on surgery and in 1776 he was named physician extraordinary to George III. He carried out many highly diverse and important studies in comparative biology, anatomy, physiology, and pathology, and is considered the founder of pathological anatomy in Britain. He was an important influence on EDWARD JENNER.

Hunter, William (1718–1783) British obstetrician, educator, and medical writer. The brother of JOHN HUNTER, he studied medicine at the University of Glasgow and became a licensed physician in London in 1756. He introduced the French practice of providing individual medical students with cadavers for dissection to Britain. After 1756 his medical practice was devoted principally to obstetrics; he became the most successful specialist of his day, and was made physician extraordinary to Queen Charlotte in 1762. His work did much to remove obstetrics from the purview of midwives and establish it as an accepted branch of medicine.

Hunter River River, eastern NEW SOUTH WALES, Australia. Rising in the Mount Royal Range of the Eastern Highlands, it flows southwest through Glenbawn Reservoir and past Denman. There, joined by its major tributary, the GOULBURN RIVER, the Hunter turns southeast, entering the TASMAN SEA at Newcastle, after a course of 287 mi (462 km). Its estuary forms one of the state's largest harbors.

Hunters' Lodges Secret organization of Canadian rebels and U.S. adventurers dedicated to freeing Canada from British colonial rule. It was formed after the failure of the 1837 rebellion and was concentrated in the northern U.S. border states. In 1838 two attempts to invade Upper Canada (now Ontario) were stopped by local British Canadian militia. Minor border raids continued until Pres. MARTIN VAN BUREN ordered the lodges disbanded in accordance with U.S. neutrality laws.

hunting Pursuit of game, principally as sport. To early humans, hunting was a necessity, and it remained so in many societies until recently. In the modern era, hunters have learned to limit their means, and codes have been established that give the quarry a fair chance to escape and avoid unnecessary suffering of wounded game. Game laws now protect game and limit hunting. Weapons include the rifle and the bow and arrow, and methods include stalking, still-hunting (lying in wait), tracking, driving, and calling. Dogs are sometimes employed to track, flush, or capture prey.

hunting and gathering society Any human society that depends on hunting, fishing, or the gathering of wild plants for subsistence. Until c. 8,000 years ago, all peoples were foragers of wild food. Many foraging peoples continued to practice their traditional way of life into the 20th century, but today all such peoples have developed extensive contacts with settled groups. In the traditional hunting-and-gathering society, social groups were small, usually made up of either individual family units or a number of related families collected together in a BAND. The diet was well balanced and ample, and food was shared. The men usually did the hunting while the women gathered plants and did most domestic chores. The remainder of the time was spent on social and religious activities.

Huntington, Collis P(otter) (1821–1900) U.S. railroad magnate. Born in Harwinton, Conn., he worked as a peddler before becoming a prosperous merchant in Oneonta, N.Y. In 1849 he moved to Sacramento and joined MARK HOPKINS in selling miners' supplies during the gold rush. He became interested in a plan to link California with the eastern U.S. by rail. In 1861 he joined Hopkins, LELAND STANFORD, and Charles Crocker (1822–1888)—called "the Big Four"—to form the CENTRAL PACIFIC RAILROAD. During its construction (1863–69), Huntington lobbied for the company, securing funding and favorable federal legislation. In 1865 the Big Four formed the Southern Pacific Railroad. In 1869 Huntington bought the CHESAPEAKE AND OHIO RAILWAY to link with the Southern Pacific, forming the first transcontinental railroad, of which he became president in 1890.

Huntington, Samuel P(hillips) (born 1927) U.S. political scientist. After receiving a doctorate from Harvard Univ., he spent most of his career teaching at Harvard, specializing in defense and international affairs. He has been a consultant to many government agencies. Among his many books, his *Clash of Civilizations and the Remaking of the World Order* (1996) predicted conflicts between the world's major cultures in the post–Cold War era.

Huntington Beach City (pop., 1996 est.: 191,000), southwestern California. Located on the Pacific coast, it was first called Shell Beach and after its subdivision (1901) was known as Pacific City. To encourage its promotion as a seaside resort, it was renamed Huntington Beach for the railroad magnate Henry E. Huntington. Its major economic assets are oil wells and refineries.

Huntington's chorea relatively rare, hereditary neurological disease that is characterized by irregular and involuntary movements of the muscles. Huntington's CHOREA is caused by a genetic mutation that causes degeneration of neurons in a part of the brain that controls movement. Symptoms usually appear between ages 35 and 50. They begin with occasional jerking or writhing movements, which are absent during sleep, and progress to random, uncontrollable, and often violent twitchings and jerks. Symptoms of mental deterioration begin later and include memory loss, dementia, bipolar disorder, or schizophrenia. There is no effective therapy or cure, and the disease invariably proves fatal. A child of a person with Huntington's chorea has a 50% chance of developing the disease.

Huntsman, Benjamin (1704–1776) British inventor of the CRUCIBLE PROCESS. A clockmaker and instrument maker, Huntsman opened a plant in SHEFFIELD c. 1740, where he produced STEEL for clock and watch springs. His new process yielded cast steel more uniform in composition and free from impurities than any previously produced. Sheffield steelmakers used the crucible process to achieve worldwide dominance in the production of tool and other high-quality steels.

Huntsville City (pop., 1996 est.: 170,000), northern Alabama. Originally called Twickenham, it was the first community in Alabama to be granted a city charter, in 1811. It was the site of Alabama's first constitutional convention (1819), and served briefly as the state capital. Settled around Big Spring (still used as a water supply), it is a commercial center for hay, cotton, corn, and tobacco. The George C. Marshall Space Flight Center and the University of Alabama in Huntsville (1950) are located there.

Hunyadi \'hu̇-nyȯd-ē\, **János** (1407?–1456) Hungarian general. Son of a knight, he saw military service under King SIGISMUND. While in Italy he learned new military techniques from FRANCESCO SFORZA; returning to southern Hungary, he repelled Turkish attacks (1437–38) and was made governor of Transylvania. With aid from Venice and the pope, he mounted a campaign against the Turks (1441–43) that broke the Ottoman empire's hold on the Balkan states, though he was defeated in a Turkish counterattack at the Battle of VARNA (1444). In 1446 he was elected regent for the young king, Laszlo V, and he served as governor of the kingdom of Hungary 1446–52. In 1456 he raised the Turkish siege of Belgrade before dying of disease. For stopping the supposedly invincible Turkish armies, he is considered a Hungarian national hero.

Huon River \'hyü-ən\ River, southern TASMANIA, Australia. Rising on the slopes of Mts. Wedge, Bowen, and Anne, it flows south and then east to be joined by its tributaries, the Weld and Picton rivers, below Huon Gorge. It passes Huonville at the limit of navigation and enters a wide estuary after a course of 105 mi (170 km), and flows into the D'Entrecasteaux Channel. The river's lower valley is intensively cultivated, containing the island's leading apple-growing area, and is also a popular tourist region.

Hupeh See HUBEI

Hupei See HUBEI

hurdling TRACK-AND-FIELD sport of running races over a series of obstacles called hurdles. Runners must remain in assigned lanes throughout a race, and, though they may knock hurdles down while running over them, they may do so only with a leg or foot, not a hand. Modern hurdlers use a sprinting style between hurdles, a double-arm forward thrust and exaggerated forward lean while clearing the hurdle, and then bring a trailing leg through at nearly a right angle to the body, enabling them to continue forward without breaking stride after clearing the hurdle. Hurdling distances are 110 m and 400 m for men and 100 m and 400 m for women.

hurdy-gurdy Pear-shaped fiddle whose strings are sounded by the rim of a rosined wooden wheel turned by a handle. A row of keys is used to produce the melody by stopping one or two strings; the remaining strings sound a constant drone. A hurdy-gurdy-like instrument existed in Europe by the 12th century; it took its present shape from the 13th century on. It has long been associated with street musicians and beggars, and is still played as a folk instrument in Europe. The name is also often used for the barrel organ, in which a hand crank rotates a barrel inside the case, on which several tunes are encoded, causing a small pipe organ to play.

Hurdy-gurdy played by a French lady of fashion, 18th century.

H. ROGER-VIOLLET

Hurley, Patrick J(ay) (1883–1963) U.S. diplomat. Born in Indian Territory (now Oklahoma), he served as U.S. secretary of war 1929–33. In World War II, he was promoted to brigadier general and sent to the Philippines to attempt the relief of U.S. troops on Bataan and sent on diplomatic missions to the eastern front, the Middle East, China, and Afghanistan. As ambassador to China (1944–45), he tried unsuccessfully to reconcile the Nationalists and Communists.

hurling Irish game resembling both FIELD HOCKEY and LACROSSE, played between 15-player teams. The game is mentioned in Irish manuscripts dating back to the 13th century BC. The stick used—a tapered, slightly curved device with a cupped blade at the end—is called a hurley. A point is scored by hitting the ball over the crossbar of the opposing team's goalposts, three points by driving it under the crossbar. It is considered the national pastime of Ireland.

Hurok \'hyu̇r-ˌäk\, **Sol(omon Israelovich)** (1888–1974) Russian-U.S. impresario. He came to the U.S. in 1905 and in 1913 inaugurated the concert series Music for the Masses, which led to his representing many famous Eastern European artists when they toured abroad, including F. CHALIAPIN, M. ELMAN, ANNA PAVLOVA, and Arthur RUBINSTEIN. The most famous impresario of his time, he made a significant contribution to the cause of peace by arranging visits of Russian opera and ballet companies to the U.S. at the height of the Cold War.

Huron \'hyu̇r-ˌän\ IROQUOIAN-speaking North American Indian people who lived in Huronia, between Georgian Bay and Lake Ontario. The Huron lived in villages, sometimes palisaded, consisting of large, bark-covered dwellings that housed several families related through maternal descent. Crops included corn, beans, squash, sunflowers, and tobacco. Hunting and fishing were of lesser importance. Villages were divided into CLANS, the chiefs of which formed councils. Women were influential in Huron affairs, clan matrons having the responsibility of selecting political leaders. The Huron were bitter enemies of tribes of the IROQUOIS CONFEDERACY, with whom they competed in the fur trade. Iroquois invasions in 1648–50 devastated the tribe, forcing a remnant westward. Today the Huron (or Wyandot, as they came to call themselves in the U.S.) number about 2,000.

Huron, Lake Lake, U.S. and Canada. The second-largest of the GREAT LAKES of North America, it is bounded by Michigan and Ontario, and is about 206 mi (330 km) long with an area of 23,000 sq mi (59,570 sq km). Inflow comes from Lake SUPERIOR, Lake MICHIGAN, and numerous streams; the lake discharges at its southern end into Lake ERIE. It contains many islands, including MACKINAC, and Saginaw Bay indents the Michigan coast. As part of the ST. LAWRENCE SEAWAY, it supports heavy commercial traffic from April to December. The first of the Great Lakes seen by Europeans, it was explored by the French (1615–79), who named it after the HURON Indians.

hurricane See TROPICAL CYCLONE

Hurston, Zora Neale (1903–1960) U.S. folklorist and writer. Born in Eatonville, Fla., she joined a traveling theatrical company, ending up in New York, where she studied anthropology with FRANZ BOAS at Columbia University and became associated with the HARLEM RENAISSANCE. She collaborated with LANGSTON HUGHES on the play *Mule Bone* (1931). Her first novel, *Jonah's Gourd Vine* (1934), was followed by the controversial but widely acclaimed *Their Eyes Were Watching God* (1937). She also wrote an autobiography, *Dust Tracks on a Road* (1942).

Hurt, John (born 1940) British actor. He made his film and stage debuts in 1962. Known as an insightful character actor, his films include *A Man for All Seasons* (1966), *The Elephant Man* (1980), and *Rob Roy* (1995). His stage performances include *The Dwarfs* (1963) and *Travesties* (1974). On television he portrayed Quentin Crisp in *The Naked Civil Servant* (1975) and Caligula in the series *I, Claudius* (1977).

Hurt, William (born 1950) U.S. film actor. Born in Washington, D.C., he acted in repertory companies before making his screen debut in *Altered States* (1980). He became a leading actor with *Body Heat* (1981), which was followed by *The Big Chill* (1983), *Kiss of the Spider Woman* (1985, Academy Award), *Children of a Lesser God* (1986), *Broadcast News* (1987), *The Accidental Tourist* (1988), and *Smoke* (1995).

Hus \'həs, 'hu̇s\, **Jan** *or* **Jan Huss** (c. 1370–1415) Bohemian religious reformer. He studied and taught at the University of Prague, where he was influenced by JOHN WYCLIFFE. As rector of the university from 1402, he became leader of a reform movement that criticized the corruption of the Roman Catholic clergy. The movement was threatened when Wycliffe's teachings were condemned by the church, and Hus's position was further undermined by his stand in the power struggles among rival popes. He was excommunicated in 1411, but continued to preach. Renewed sale of indulgences by the antipope John XXIII earned Hus's criticism, which in turn led to a revival of the case of heresy against him. He was invited to the Council of CONSTANCE to explain his views; though promised safe conduct, he was arrested, tried for heresy, and burned at the stake. His writings were important in the development of the Czech language as well as in the theology of church reform, and his followers were called HUSSITES.

Husain, Maqbul Fida (born 1915) Indian artist. His narrative paintings, executed in a modified Cubist style, can be caustic and funny as well as serious and somber. His themes—usually treated in series—include topics as diverse as Gandhi, Mother Teresa, the *Ramayana*, the *Mahabharata*, the British raj, and motifs of Indian urban and rural life. One of the most celebrated and internationally recognized Indian artists of the 20th century, he has also received recognition as a printmaker, photographer, and filmmaker.

Husak \'h(y)ü-ˌsäk\, **Gustav** (1913–1991) Leader of Czechoslovakia (1969–89). He helped direct the antifascist Slovak national uprising of 1944, and after the war he began a career as a government official and Communist Party functionary. He became a deputy premier of Czechoslovakia under Alexander Dubcek. When Dubček was deposed by Soviet forces, Husak was installed as first secretary of the Communist Party (1969). He reversed Dubček's reforms and purged the party of its liberal members. He became president in 1975. When Communist rule collapsed in 1989, he resigned as president.

Husayn ibn Ali \hu̇-'sān-ˌib-ən-ä-'lē\, **al-** (626–680) Grandson of Muhammad and son of the fourth caliph, Ali. After his father's assassination, he accepted the rule of the first caliph of the Umayyad dynasty, Muawiyah I, but refused to accept Muawiyah's son, Yazid I. He was invited to join a revolt against the Umayyads, but was intercepted by an Iraqi force, which killed him. His martyrdom in the battle of Karbala is commemorated during the first 10 days of Muharram. See also fitnah, Shiite.

Husayn ibn Ali, Sharif (c. 1854–1931) Ottoman-appointed sharif and emir of Mecca (1908–16) and self-proclaimed king of the Arabs (1916–24). His claim to be the new caliph (1924) led to war with Ibn Saud and Ibn Saud's victory. Husayn was exiled to Cyprus. One of his sons, Abdullah, became king of Transjordan (present-day Jordan); another became king of Syria and later Iraq as Faisal I.

Husayni \hu̇-'sā-nē\, **Amin al-** (1897–1974) Grand mufti of Jerusalem (1921–37). In 1921 the British appointed him mufti and president of the Supreme Muslim Council. In 1936 Arab groups formed the Arab High Committee, with Husayni as chairman, demanding an end to Jewish immigration. The British forced him out in 1937 and he went to Lebanon; he spent World War II in Germany and fled to Egypt after the war.

Husaynid dynasty \hu̇-'sā-nəd\ Ruling dynasty of Tunisia 1705–1957, established by an Ottoman-appointed officer, al-Husayn ibn Ali. He was allowed to rule autonomously and made treaties with European powers. European pressure led later Husaynid rulers to suppress piracy (1819), abolish slavery, and ease restrictions on Jews (1837–55). Husaynid rulers became mere figureheads by 1883. The monarchy was abolished when Tunisia gained its independence in 1957.

hussar \hə-'zär\ Member of a European light-cavalry unit used for scouting, modeled on the 15th-century Hungarian light-horse corps. The brilliantly colored Hungarian hussar's uniform was imitated in other European armies; it consisted of a busby (high cylindrical cloth cap), a jacket with heavy braiding, and a dolman (loose coat worn hanging from the left shoulder). Several hussar regiments of the British army were converted from light dragoons in the 19th century.

Hussein, Saddam (born 1937) President of Iraq (from 1979). He joined the Baath Party in 1957. Following a failed attempt to assassinate Iraqi president Abd al-Karim Qasim in 1959, he fled to Cairo, where he briefly attended law school. He returned to Iraq when the Baath gained power in 1963. Jailed when the Baath was overthrown, he escaped and helped reinstall the party to power in 1968. He led the nationalization of the oil industry in 1972. He took over the presidency with the aims of replacing Egypt as leader of the Arab world and gaining hegemony over the Persian Gulf, and he launched wars against Iran (1980–90) and Kuwait (1990–91), both of which he lost. He instituted a brutal dictatorship, and directed intensive campaigns against minorities within Iraq, particularly the Kurds. U.S. fears regarding his development of weapons of mass destruction led to Western sanctions against Iraq. See also Pan-Arabism, Iran-Iraq War, and Persian Gulf War.

Hussein I \hu̇-'sān\ *in full* **Hussein ibn Talal** (1935–1999) King of Jordan (1952–99). Educated in Britain, he succeeded his father, King Talal, while still in his teens. His nation's precarious geographic and economic position and the many Palestinians living there (to whom, unlike other Arab rulers, he offered citizenship and a passport) forced him to chart a cautious course in international relations. Though he carried on secret talks with all Israeli leaders except Menachem Begin, he fought with other Arab nations in the Six-Day War. When the Jordan-based Palestine Liberation Organization (PLO) threatened his reign, Hussein expelled it (1971). Thereafter he sought to repair relations with the PLO without antagonizing Israel or the U.S. He surrendered Jordan's claim to the West Bank in 1988 to the PLO. He considered his 1994 peace treaty with Israel his crowning achievement.

King Hussein of Jordan.
GAMMA

Husserl \'hu̇-sə-rəl\, **Edmund** (1859–1938) German philosopher, founder of phenomenology. He lectured at the University of Halle 1886–1901. In 1900–1 he published *Logical Investigations*; it employed a method of analysis he described as "phenomenological," which was an effort to resolve the opposition between empiricism and rationalism by tracing all philosophical and scientific systems and developments of theory to their sources in pure experience. He spent 1901–16 at the University of Göttingen. In the *Ideas* (1913) Husserl presented phenomenology as a universal philosophical science. In 1916 he moved to the University of Freiburg. In *First Philosophy* (1923–24) he proposed that phenomenology, with its method of reduction, is the way to the realization of mankind's ethical autonomy. His work was strongly influential, especially on his successor at Freiburg, Martin Heidegger.

Husserl, c. 1930.
ARCHIV FUR KUNST UND GESCHICHTE, BERLIN

Hussite \'hə-ˌsīt, 'hu̇-ˌsīt\ Member of a group of 15th-century Bohemian religious reformers, followers of Jan Hus. After Hus's death in 1415, the Hussites broke with Rome. In addition to giving communion in both bread and wine, they supported freedom of preaching, poverty of the clergy, civil punishment of notorious sinners, and expropriation of church property. Many were nobles and knights, and a papal crusade against them failed in 1431. During peace negotiations in 1433 the Hussites split into two factions, the moderate Utraquists and the radical Taborites. The Utraquists joined the Catholics and defeated the Taborites at the battle of Lipany in 1434; they survived schisms until 1620, when they were absorbed by the Catholics. Another segment of Hussites, Unitas Fratrum, set up an independent organization in 1467 and lasted until the Counter-Reformation. In 1722 a group of Hussites fled Moravia and settled on the estate of Count Nikolaus Ludwig von Zinzendorf (1700–1760) in Saxony, establishing the community of Herrnhut and founding the Moravian church.

Huston \'hyü-stən\, **John** (1906–1987) U.S. film director and screenwriter. Born in Nevada, Mo., the son of Walter Huston, he was briefly a boxer, Mexican cavalry officer, reporter, and actor before becoming a scriptwriter. His first work as a director, *The Maltese Falcon* (1941), began an illustrious career studded with film classics: *The Treasure of the Sierra Madre* (1948, Academy Awards for best director and screenplay), *Key Largo* (1948), *The Asphalt Jungle* (1950), *The African Queen* (1951), *The Night of the Iguana* (1964), *Prizzi's Honor* (1985), and *The Dead* (1987). He wrote screenplays for many of his own films and such others as *Jezebel* (1938), *Juarez* (1939), and *High Sierra* (1941). He continued to act throughout his career, notably in *Chinatown* (1974). His daughter Anjelica (born 1951) proved herself an accomplished actress in *Prizzi's Honor* (1985, Academy Award) and other films.

Huston, Walter *orig.* **Walter Houghston** (1884–1950) Canadian-U.S. actor. He made his stage debut in his native Toronto in 1902 and his New York debut in 1905. He and his second wife were a popular vaudeville song-and-dance team (1909–24). On Broadway he won praise in *Desire Under the Elms* (1924), *Dodsworth* (1934; film, 1936), and *Knickerbocker Holiday* (1938), in which he sang "September Song." He appeared in over 50 films, including *Abraham Lincoln* (1930), *Rain* (1932), and *The Treasure of the Sierra Madre* (1948, Academy Award), directed by his son JOHN HUSTON.

Hutchins, Robert Maynard (1899–1977) U.S. educator and foundation president. Born in Brooklyn, N.Y., he became dean of Yale Law School. At the University of CHICAGO as president (1929–45) and chancellor (1945–51), he encouraged liberal education based on the study of the great books of the Western tradition, deplored any tendency toward vocationalism, and dismantled the intercollegiate athletic program. Hutchins later headed various foundations, including the FORD FOUNDATION. He served as chairman of the board of editors of ENCYCLOPÆDIA BRITANNICA (1943–74) and edited the 54-volume *Great Books of the Western World* (1952). He expounded his views on education in *Higher Learning in America* (1936).

Hutchinson, Anne *orig.* **Anne Marbury** (1591–1643) British-American religious leader. In 1612 she married William Hutchinson, and they followed JOHN COTTON to the MASSACHUSETTS BAY COLONY in 1634. She organized weekly religious meetings of Boston women, criticizing the narrow Puritan orthodoxy and espousing a "covenant of grace." Her opponents accused her of believing that God's grace had freed Christians from the need to observe established moral precepts. Tried for "traducing the ministers," she was sentenced to banishment; refusing to recant, she was excommunicated. In 1638 she and her husband established a colony at Aquidneck Island, which became part of Rhode Island.

Hutchinson, Thomas (1711–1780) American colonial administrator. Son of a wealthy Boston merchant, he pursued business ventures before serving in local and provincial legislatures (1737–49) and as a delegate to the Albany Congress. He served as lieutenant governor (1758–71) and simultaneously as chief justice of the state superior court (1760–69). As governor (1771–74), he strictly enforced British rule. After he was accused of initiating the STAMP ACT, a mob sacked his home. His insistence that a shipment of tea be landed in Boston led to the BOSTON TEA PARTY. He was replaced by Gen. Thomas Gage.

Hutchinson family U.S. singing group, significant figures in the development of a native popular music tradition. Born and raised in Milford, N.H., the Hutchinson brothers Judson (1817–1859), John (1821–1908), and Asa (1823–1884) and sister Abby (1829–1892) formed a quartet and began giving concerts around New England in 1841. In contrast to the prevailing sentimental and minstrel songs of the period, their songs embraced political causes, including women's suffrage, prohibition of alcohol, and opposition to the Mexican War. They sang at many antislavery rallies, including a Boston rally that drew 20,000 people. With some members replaced by other family members, the family continued to tour into the 1880s.

Hutterite \'hə-tə-ˌrīt\ Member of the Hutterite Brethren, an ANABAPTIST sect that takes its name from its Austrian founder, Jakob Hutter, who was burned as a heretic in 1536. His followers modeled themselves on the early church in Jerusalem by holding their goods in common. Persecuted in Moravia and the Tirol, they moved eastward to Hungary and the Ukraine. In the 1870s many emigrated to the U.S. and settled in South Dakota. The society still exists in the western U.S. and Canada, where it has colonies of 60–150 members, who operate collective farms. Hutterites are pacifists who take no part in politics and remain separate from outside society.

Hutton, James (1726–1797) Scottish geologist, chemist, and naturalist. After short careers in law and medicine, he followed his interest in chemistry and developed an inexpensive manufacturing process for sal ammoniac. He settled in Edinburgh (1768) to pursue a life of science. In two papers presented in Edinburgh in 1785 (published 1788), he elaborated his theory of UNIFORMITARIANISM. Its ability to explain earth's geologic processes without reference to the Bible and its emphasis on an immensely long, cyclical process of erosion, deposition, sedimentation, and volcanic upthrust were revolutionary.

Hutu Bantu-speaking people of RWANDA and BURUNDI, with a large refugee population in the Congo (Zaire). Numbering about 9.5 million, the Hutu comprise the vast majority in both countries but were traditionally subject to the TUTSI, who under German and Belgian colonial regimes succeeded in cultivating a lord-vassal relationship. The two cultures are deeply intertwined; both speak Rwanda and Rundi and adhere to similar religious beliefs (traditional and Christian). The Tutsi remained dominant in Rwanda until 1961, when the Hutu expelled most of them and took over the government. After an unsuccessful Hutu coup attempt in Burundi in 1965, that country's Hutu remained subordinate under a Tutsi-dominated military government. Violent clashes occurred in Burundi in 1972, 1988, and 1993, and in Rwanda in 1990 and 1994–96, the later including a Hutu-initiated genocidal campaign in which over a million people were killed and 1–2 million forced into refugee camps in Zaire (now Congo) and Tanzania.

Huxley, Aldous (Leonard) (1894–1963) British novelist and critic. Grandson of T.H. HUXLEY and brother of JULIAN HUXLEY, he was partially blind from childhood. He is known for works of elegant, witty, pessimistic satire, including *Crome Yellow* (1921) and *Antic Hay* (1923), which established him as a major novelist, and *Point Counter Point* (1928). The celebrated *Brave New World* (1932) is a nightmarish vision of a future society that expresses his distrust of trends in politics and technology. Beginning with *Eyeless in Gaza* (1936), his works reveal a growing interest in Hindu philosophy and mysticism. Later works include the nonfiction *The Devils of Loudun* (1952) and *The Doors of Perception* (1954), about his experiences with hallucinogens.

Aldous Huxley, 1959.
ROBERT M. QUITTNER—BLACK STAR

Huxley, Julian (Sorell) *later* **Sir Julian** (1887–1975) British biologist, philosopher, and author. He was a grandson of T.H. HUXLEY and brother of ALDOUS HUXLEY. His research on hormones, developmental processes, ornithology, and ecology influenced the modern development of embryology, classification, and studies of behavior and evolution. He applied his scientific knowledge to social and political problems, formulating an ethical theory of "evolutionary humanism." His many books written for the general public, including *The Science of Life* (1931; with H.G. WELLS), were widely read. He served as the first director-general of UNESCO (1946–48).

Huxley, T(homas) H(enry) (1825–1895) British biologist. The son of a schoolmaster, he earned a medical degree. After working as a surgeon on a surveying expedition in the South Pacific (1846–50), during which he carried out extensive studies of marine organisms, he taught for many years at the Royal School of Mines in London (1854–85). In the 1850s he established his reputation with his important papers on animal individuality, certain mollusks, the methods of paleontology, the methods and principles of science and science education, the structure and functions of nerves, and the vertebrate skull. He was one of the earliest and strongest supporters of Darwinism; his 1860 debate with Bishop Samuel Wilberforce gained widespread attention. In the 1860s Huxley did valuable work in paleontology and classification, especially classification of birds. Later in life he turned to theology; he is said to have coined the word *agnostic* to describe his views. Few scientists have been as influential over such a wide field of scientific development and as effective in the total movement of thought and action within his own generation,

Christiaan Huygens, portrait by C. Netscher, 1671; in the Collection Haags Gemeentemuseum, The Hague.
BY COURTESY OF THE COLLECTION HAAGS GEMEENTEMUSEUM, THE HAGUE

Huygens \'hī-gənz, 'hȯi-gənz\, **Christiaan** *or* **Christian Huyghens** (1629–1695) Dutch mathematician, astronomer, and physicist. He was the first to use a pendulum to regulate a clock (1656). He invented a method of grinding and polishing telescope lenses, and used his telescopes to discover the true shape of Saturn's rings (1659). He developed explanations of reflection and refraction based on the principle of secondary wave fronts, now called Huygens' principle. He developed the wave theory of light (1678), and also contributed to the science of dynamics. His work on rotating bodies led to solutions of problems involving oscillation of a pendulum and uniform circular motion. He was also the first to determine acceleration due to gravity.

Huysmans \wēs-'mä^{n}s\, **Joris-Karl** *orig.* **Charles-Marie-Georges** (1848–1907) French DECADENT writer. His early works, influenced by contemporary naturalism, were followed by far more individual and violent works. The first was *À vau-l'eau* (1882; *Down Stream*). His best-known novel, *À rebours* (1884; *Against the Grain*), relates experiments in decadence by the bored survivor of a noble line. The controversial and clearly autobiographical *Là-bas* (1891; *Down There*) is a tale of 19th-century satanists. His final novels concern his return to Roman Catholicism. He also wrote perceptive art criticism.

Joris-Karl Huysmans, detail of an oil painting by Jean-Louis Forain.
J.E. BULLOZ

Hwang River See HUANG RIVER

Hwange National Park \'hwäŋ-gā\ *formerly* **Wankie National Park** \'wäŋ-kē\ National preserve, northwestern Zimbabwe. Located on the Botswana frontier, it was established in 1928 as a game reserve and in 1930 as a national park. The land, with an area of 5,657 sq mi (14,651 sq km) is largely flat, with hardwood forests of mukwa and teak. It is one of Africa's largest elephant sanctuaries; its abundant wildlife can be observed from platforms overlooking the water holes.

Hwarangdo \'hwä-'räŋ-'dō\ Military and philosophical code developed in the Korean state of Silla during the 6th century. It formed the basis for training an elite society of young warriors known as the *hwarang,* who were instrumental in unifying Korea under the SILLA dynasty (668–935). Their moral code, derived from BUDDHISM and CONFUCIANISM, emphasized loyalty to the king, filial piety, faithfulness to friends, courage in battle, and the evil of indiscriminate killing. The *hwarang* were disbanded during the CHOSON dynasty (1392–1910), but interest in the code revived in the late 20th century with a style of Korean martial arts known as hwarangdo.

hyacinth Any of the approximately 30 species of bulbous ornamental herbaceous plants that make up the genus *Hyacinthus* (LILY FAMILY), native primarily to the Mediterranean region and tropical Africa. The common garden hyacinths are derived from *H. orientalis.* Most species have narrow, untoothed leaves at the base of the plant and fragrant flowers (usually blue, but sometimes pink, white, or other colors in cultivated varieties) borne in a cluster at the top of the leafless stems. See also GRAPE HYACINTH.

Hyacinthus \ˌhī-ə-'sin-thəs\ In GREEK MYTHOLOGY, a young man of great beauty who attracted the love of APOLLO. The god killed him accidentally in discus throwing, and from his blood grew the flower *hyacinthos* (not the modern hyacinth), whose petals were marked with the words AI, AI ("Alas"). His death was celebrated at Amyclae, his native town in Sparta, with an early summer festival known as the Hyacinthia. The festival marked the transition from spring to summer.

Hyades \'hī-ə-ˌdēz\ OPEN CLUSTER of several hundred stars in the constellation Taurus. The bright star Aldebaran appears to be a member of the cluster but is much closer to earth than the Hyades, which are about 130 light-years away. Five genuine members of the group are visible to the unaided eye.

hyaline membrane disease See RESPIRATORY DISTRESS SYNDROME

hybrid Offspring of parents that differ in genetically determined traits (see GENETICS). The parents may be of two different species, genera, or (rarely) families. The terms "mongrel" and "crossbreed" refer usually to animals or plants resulting from a cross between two races, breeds, strains, or varieties of the same species. Because of basic biological incompatibilities, sterile hybrids (those that cannot produce living young) such as the mule (a hybrid between a jackass and a mare) commonly result from crosses between species. Some species hybrids, however, are fertile and can be sources for the formation of new species. Many economically or aesthetically important cultivated plants (e.g., bananas, coffee, peanuts, dahlias, roses, bread wheats, alfalfa, etc.) originated through natural or artificially induced hybridization. Hybridization is important biologically because it increases necessary genetic VARIATION within a species.

hybrid vigor See HETEROSIS

Hyde, Edward See Earl of CLARENDON

Hyder Ali \'hī-dər-ä-'lē\ (1722–1782) Muslim ruler of Mysore, in southern India. He organized the first Indian-controlled corps of Indian soldiers armed with Western weapons, obtained a command in the Mysore army, and eventually overthrew Mysore's raja. He conquered neighboring areas and joined a confederacy with the Nizam Ali Khan and the Marathas against the British. He fought the British for over a decade, but at the end of his life, recognizing that he could not defeat them, he urged his son to make peace.

Hyderabad \'hī-də-rə-ˌbäd\ *formerly* **Haidarabad** *or* **Nizam's Dominions** \ni-'zämz\ Former princely state, southern central India. Originally part of the ancient kingdom of GOLCONDA, it became part of the Mughal empire in 1687. The independent kingdom of Hyderabad was founded by NIZAM-AL-MULK in 1724. In 1798 it was placed under British protection, although the Nizams continued to rule over their princely state. At Indian partition in 1947, the Nizam chose to resume its independent status, but India invaded the state (1948) and took control. The area is now divided among the states of ANDHRA PRADESH, KARNATAKA, and MAHARASHTRA.

Hyderabad City (pop., 1991: 3,146,000), capital of ANDHRA PRADESH state, southern India. Founded by the sultans of GOLCONDA in the 16th century, the town was plundered and destroyed following the Mughal occupation in 1685. In 1724 it became the capital of the independent kingdom of HYDERABAD. A walled city, it has many buildings in a blend of Hindu and Muslim styles. Adjacent Secunderabad grew as a British cantonment, connected to Hyderabad by a mile-long embankment. It is the site of Osmania University (1918) and the University of Hyderabad (1974).

Hyderabad *or* **Haydarabad** City (pop., 1981: 795,000), SIND province, Pakistan. Located east of the INDUS RIVER, it was founded in 1768 by Ghulam Shah Kalhora. It remained the capital of Sind until 1843 when it surrendered to the British and the capital was transferred to KARACHI. It is now a communications, commercial, and industrial center. Notable antiquities include the tombs and palaces of former rulers; characteristic of the city are *badgirs* ("wind-catchers") fixed to housetops to catch sea breezes during the hot season.

hydra Any of 20–30 species of freshwater CNIDARIANS (genus *Hydra*). The POLYP-type body is a thin, usually translucent tube that measures up to slightly more than 1 in. (25 mm) long. Food is ingested and wastes are ejected from the open, tentacled end. Individuals are usually hermaphroditic (see HERMAPHRODITISM). Reproduction by budding is also common. Species differ in color, tentacle length and number, and gonad position and size. All hydras feed on other small invertebrates (e.g., crustaceans).

hydrangea \hī-'drān-jə\ Any of approximately 23 species of erect or climbing woody shrubs that make up the genus *Hydrangea* (family Hydrangeaceae), native to the Western Hemisphere and eastern Asia. Several species are grown in greenhouses and gardens for their showy, usually ball-like flower clusters. Cultivated varieties of the French hydrangea, or hortensia *(H. macrophylla),* bearing large globular flower clusters in various colors, are the florist's hydrangeas.

hydraulic jump Sudden change in water level, analogous to a shock wave, commonly seen below weirs and sluice gates where a smooth stream of water suddenly rises at a foaming front. The fact that the speed of water waves varies with wavelength and with amplitude leads to a wide variety of effects. Tidal bores, which may be observed on some estuaries, are large-scale examples. See also BERNOULLI'S PRINCIPLE.

hydraulic press Machine consisting of a cylinder fitted with a piston (see PISTON AND CYLINDER) that uses liquid under pressure to exert a compressive force upon a stationary ANVIL or baseplate. The liquid is forced into the cylinder by a pump. The hydraulic press is widely used in industry for forming metals and for other tasks where a large force is required. It is manufactured in a wide variety of styles and sizes and in capacities ranging from 1 ton (0.9 metric ton) or less to 10,000 tons (9,000 metric tons) or more. See also PUNCH PRESS.

hydraulics Branch of science concerned with the practical applications of FLUIDS, primarily LIQUIDS, in MOTION. It is related to FLUID MECHANICS, which in large part provides its theoretical foundation. Hydraulics deals with such matters as the flow of liquids in pipes, rivers, and channels and their confinement by dams and tanks. Some of its principles apply also to GASES, usually when variations in density are relatively small. The scope of hydraulics extends to such mechanical devices as actuators and control systems. See also BERNOULLI'S PRINCIPLE, PASCAL'S LAW, PUMP.

hydride \'hī-ˌdrīd\ Inorganic compound of HYDROGEN with another ELEMENT. Three common types are differentiated by their BONDING. In saline (ionic) hydrides (see IONIC BOND), the hydrogen is an ANION, H^-, and behaves like a HALOGEN. Saline hydrides such as sodium hydride (NaH) and calcium hydride (CaH_2) react vigorously with water, giving off hydrogen gas (H_2), and are used as portable sources of it. Metallic hydrides, such as titanium hydride (TiH_2), are alloylike materials (see ALLOY) with some properties of METALS, such as luster and electrical conductivity. Covalent hydrides (see COVALENT BOND) are mostly compounds of hydrogen and nonmetallic elements; they include WATER, AMMONIA, hydrogen sulfide (H_2S), and METHANE. In polymeric hydrides, the hydrogen forms bridges between other atoms (e.g., hydrides of boron and aluminum). Those hydrides give off large amounts of energy when burned and may be useful as rocket fuels.

hydrocarbon Any of a class of organic compounds composed only of CARBON and HYDROGEN. The carbon atoms form the framework, and the hydrogen atoms attach to them. Hydrocarbons, the principal constituents of PETROLEUM and NATURAL GAS, serve as fuels, lubricants, and raw materials for production of plastics, fibers, rubbers, solvents, explosives, and industrial chemicals. All burn to CARBON DIOXIDE and WATER with enough OXYGEN or to CARBON MONOXIDE without it. The two major categories are aliphatic, with the carbon atoms in straight or branched chains or in nonaromatic rings, and aromatic (see AROMATIC COMPOUND). Aliphatic compounds may be saturated (PARAFFINS) or, if any carbon atoms are joined by double or triple bonds, unsaturated (e.g., OLEFINS, alkenes, alkynes). All but the simplest hydrocarbons have ISOMERS (see ISOMERISM). ETHYLENE, METHANE, ACETYLENE, BENZENE, TOLUENE, and NAPHTHALENE are hydrocarbons.

hydrocephalus \ˌhī-drō-'se-fə-ləs\ Accumulation of CEREBROSPINAL FLUID (CSF) in the ventricles (cavities) of the brain, caused by overproduction, congenital blockage that prevents drainage (see NEURAL TUBE DEFECT), or complications of head injuries or infections. Normally, CSF circulates through the brain and spinal cord and drains into the circulation. In infants and young children, hydrocephalus causes the brain and skull to enlarge, because the FONTANELS have not yet closed. Without surgery to divert the excess fluid into the blood or abdomen, accumulating fluid eventually compresses the brain, causing convulsions, mental retardation, and death.

hydrochemistry See CHEMICAL HYDROLOGY

hydrochloric acid *or* **muriatic acid** Solution in water of hydrogen chloride (HCl), a gaseous inorganic compound. It is a strong ACID, virtually completely dissociated (see DISSOCIATION) into hydronium CATIONS (H_3O^+) and chloride ANIONS (Cl^-), and is corrosive and irritating. The acid reacts with most METALS to produce HYDROGEN and the metal's chloride, and with OXIDES, HYDROXIDES, and many SALTS. It is used extensively in industrial processing of metals and concentrating of some ores; in boiler scale removal, food processing, metal cleaning and pickling; and as a chemical intermediate, laboratory reagent, and alcohol denaturant (see ETHANOL). Hydrochloric acid is present in the stomach's gastric juice and can cause PEPTIC ULCERS.

hydroelectric power ELECTRICITY produced from GENERATORS driven by water TURBINES that convert the energy in falling or fast-flowing water to mechanical ENERGY. Water at a higher elevation flows downward through large pipes or tunnels (penstocks). The falling water rotates turbines, which drive the generators, which convert the turbines' mechanical energy into electricity. The advantages of hydroelectric POWER over such other sources as fossil fuels and nuclear fission are that it is continually renewable and produces no pollution. Norway, Sweden, Canada, and Switzerland rely heavily on hydroelectricity because they have industrialized areas close to mountainous regions with heavy rainfall. The U.S., Russia, China, India, and Brazil get a much smaller proportion of their electric power from hydroelectric generation. See also TIDAL POWER.

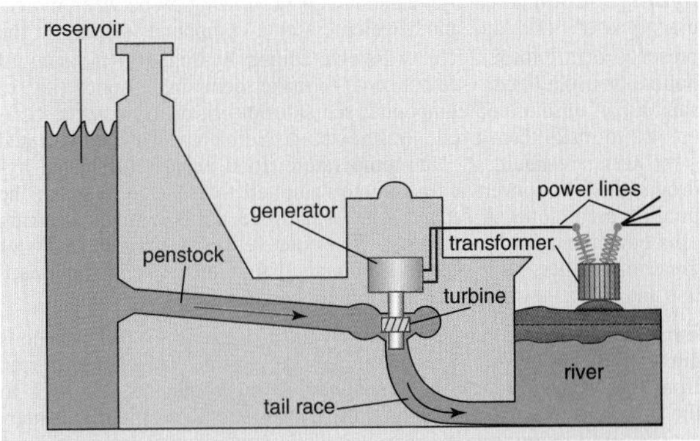

A hydro station generates power by the controlled release of water from the reservoir of a dammed river. The flowing water turns a turbine, which powers a generator, creating electricity. The voltage is stepped up by a transformer to allow long-distance power transmission.

hydrogen Lightest chemical ELEMENT, chemical symbol H, atomic number 1. A colorless, odorless, tasteless, flammable GAS, it occurs as the diatomic molecule H_2. Its ATOM consists of one PROTON (the nucleus) and one ELECTRON; the ISOTOPES DEUTERIUM and TRITIUM have an additional one and two NEUTRONS, respectively. Though only the ninth most abundant element on earth, it represents about 75% of all MATTER in the universe. Hydrogen was formerly used to fill AIRSHIPS; nonflammable helium has replaced it. It is used to synthesize AMMONIA, ETHANOL, ANILINE, and METHANOL; to treat PETROLEUM fuels; as a reducing agent (see REDUCTION) and to supply a reducing atmosphere; to make hydrogen chloride (see HYDROCHLORIC ACID) and hydrogen bromide; and in HYDROGENATION. Liquid hydrogen (boiling point −487°F, or −252.8°C) is used in the laboratory to produce extremely low temperatures, in BUBBLE CHAMBERS, and as a rocket fuel. Combustion of hydrogen with oxygen produces WATER. The properties of most ACIDS, especially in water solutions, arise from the hydrogen ION (H^+, also referred to as the hydronium ion, H_3O^+, the form in which H^+ is found in a water environment) See also HYDRIDE, HYDROCARBON.

hydrogen bomb *or* **H-bomb** *or* **thermonuclear bomb** Weapon whose enormous explosive power is generated by the fusion of HYDROGEN ISOTOPES at high temperatures to form HELIUM. The high temperatures required for the reaction are produced by detonating an ATOMIC BOMB (which draws its energy from NUCLEAR FISSION rather than NUCLEAR FUSION). The bomb's explosion produces a blast that can destroy any building within a radius of several miles, an intense white light that can cause blindness, and heat fierce enough to set off firestorms. It also creates radioactive FALLOUT that contaminates air, water, and soil. Hydrogen bombs, which may be thousands of times more powerful than atomic bombs, can be made small enough to fit in the warheads of ICBMs, which can travel halfway across the globe in 20–25 minutes. EDWARD TELLER and other U.S. scientists developed the first H-bomb and tested it at Enewetak atoll (November 1, 1952). The Soviet Union first tested an H-bomb in 1953, followed by Britain (1957), China (1967), and France (1968). By the late 1980s about 40,000 H-bombs were stored in the world's arsenals; this number declined after the fall of the Soviet Union.

hydrogen bonding Interactions between pairs of ATOMS in adjoining MOLECULES, weaker than IONIC or COVALENT bonds but stronger than VAN

DER WAALS FORCES, aligning them and keeping them together. One member of the pair (the donor) has HYDROGEN atoms covalently bonded to NITROGEN or OXYGEN atoms (—NH or —OH); the other member of the pair (acceptor) has northern or O atoms or negatively charged particles. The donor molecule effectively shares its hydrogen with the acceptor by sharing its electrons with the acceptor nitrogen or oxygen atom. Water is a good SOLVENT for ionic compounds and many others because it forms hydrogen bonds between the solute and the solvent readily. Hydrogen bonds between AMINO ACIDS in PROTEINS determine their tertiary structures. Hydrogen bonds between nitrogenous bases in NUCLEOTIDES on the two chains of DNA (GUANINE with CYTOSINE, ADENINE with THYMINE) hold the key to the transmission of genetic information.

hydrogenation \hī-ˌdrä-jə-ˈnā-shən\ CHEMICAL REACTION between molecular HYDROGEN (H_2) and another element or a compound, usually in the presence of a CATALYST. It may involve adding hydrogen at the sites of double or triple bonds (see BONDING) to make them single bonds (i.e., to saturate an unsaturated compound; see SATURATION), or to AROMATIC COMPOUNDS to make them cyclic HYDROCARBONS. Edible OILS with unsaturated FATTY ACIDS are liquid at room temperature; food manufacturers use hydrogenation to convert a fraction to saturated FATTY ACIDS to make the product more solid. A second type of hydrogenation involves breaking up a compound (hydrogenolysis, or destructive hydrogenation) and is of great importance in the PETROLEUM industry. Numerous processes in GASOLINE and PETROCHEMICAL manufacturing are based on it.

hydrologic cycle \ˌhī-drə-ˈlä-jik\ Cycle that involves the continuous circulation of water in the earth-atmosphere system. Water is transferred from the oceans through the atmosphere to the continents and back to the oceans by means of evaporation, transpiration, precipitation, interception, infiltration, subterranean percolation, overland flow, runoff, and other complex processes. Although the total amount of water within the cycle remains essentially constant, its distribution among the various processes is continually changing.

hydrology Scientific discipline concerned with the waters of the earth, including their occurrence, distribution, circulation via the HYDROLOGIC CYCLE, and interactions with living things. It also deals with the chemical and physical properties of water in all its phases.

hydrolysis \hī-ˈdrä-lə-səs\ CHEMICAL REACTION in which WATER (H_2O or HOH) and another reactant exchange FUNCTIONAL GROUPS to form two products, one containing the H and the other the OH. In most hydrolyses involving organic compounds, the other reactants and products are neutral; for example, an ESTER can be hydrolyzed to form a CARBOXYLIC ACID and an ALCOHOL. Such reactions are often accelerated by ENZYMES (as in much of DIGESTION and METABOLISM in general) or other CATALYSTS. In hydrolyses of compounds with IONIC BONDS, the nonwater reactants are SALTS, ACIDS, or BASES, participating in DISSOCIATION reactions.

hydrometallurgy Extraction of METAL from ORE by dissolving the metal (as one of its SALTS) and then recovering it from the solution. The operations usually involved are leaching (dissolving in water), commonly with additional agents; separating the waste and purifying the leach solution; and precipitating the metal or one of its pure compounds from the leach solution by chemical or electrolytic means. Though hydrometallurgy originated in the 16th century, its principal development took place in the 20th century. The development of ion exchange, solvent extraction, and other processes now permits more than 70 metallic elements to be produced by hydrometallurgy, including most GOLD, much SILVER, and large tonnages of COPPER and ZINC.

hydroponics Cultivation of plants in nutrient-enriched water, with or without the mechanical support of an inert medium such as sand or gravel. Fertilizer solution is pumped through the system periodically. As the plants grow, concentration of the solution and frequency of pumping are increased. A wide variety of vegetables and florist crops can be grown satisfactorily in gravel. Automatic watering and fertilizing saves on labor, but installation costs are high and fertilizer solution must be tested frequently. Yields are about the same as for soil-grown crops.

hydrosphere Discontinuous layer of water at or near the earth's surface. It includes all liquid and frozen surface waters, groundwater held in soil and rock, and atmospheric water vapor. Virtually all of these waters are in constant circulation through the HYDROLOGIC CYCLE. Although the components of the hydrosphere are undergoing continuous change of state and location, the total water budget remains in balance. The components of the hydrosphere have been seriously affected by the water-polluting activities of modern society.

hydrostatics Branch of PHYSICS that deals with the characteristics of FLUIDS at rest, particularly with the pressure in a fluid or exerted by a fluid (gas or liquid) on an immersed body. In applications, the principles of hydrostatics are used for problems relating to pressure in deep water (pressure increases with depth) and high in the atmosphere (pressure lessens with altitude).

hydrotherapy External use of water for medical treatment. Wet heat helps relieve pain, improves circulation, and promotes relaxation. Wet cold causes blood vessels to close, reducing swelling and pain after injury. Underwater exercise helps strengthen weak muscles, restore joint motion after injury, clean and heal burned flesh, aid muscle function after stroke, and treat arthritic deformity and pain. Whirlpool baths and showers are also used. Hydrotherapy is usually employed by specialists in PHYSICAL MEDICINE AND REHABILITATION.

hydrothermal ore deposit Any concentration of metallic minerals formed by the release of solids from hot mineral-laden water (hydrothermal solution). The solutions are thought to arise in most cases from the action of deeply circulating water heated by MAGMA. Another source of heating that may be involved includes energy released by radioactive decay.

hydroxide Any compound with one or more FUNCTIONAL GROUPS made up of one ATOM each of HYDROGEN and OXYGEN, bonded together and acting as the hydroxyl group or hydroxide ANION (OH^-). Hydroxides include the familiar ALKALIES of laboratory and industrial processes. Those of the ALKALI METALS (LITHIUM, SODIUM, POTASSIUM, rubidium, and CESIUM), the strongest BASES, are the most stable and soluble; those of the ALKALINE EARTH METALS (CALCIUM, BARIUM, and STRONTIUM), also soluble strong bases, are less stable. The hydroxides of most other metals are only slightly soluble but neutralize ACIDS; some are "amphoteric," reacting with both acids and bases.

hyena Any of three species of coarse-furred, doglike CARNIVORES (family Hyaenidae) found in Asia and Africa. Actually more closely related to cats than to dogs, they have four toes on each foot, long forelegs, nonretractile claws, and enormously strong jaws and teeth. They live alone or in packs and may be active by night or day. Hyenas are noted for scavenging but will also attack live prey. The spotted, or laughing, hyena, whose calls alternately resemble wailing and maniacal laughter, ranges through much of sub-Saharan Africa. Yellowish or grayish with dark spots, it is about 6.5 ft (1.8 m) long, including the 12-in. (30-cm) tail, and weighs up to 175 lbs (80 kg). It has been known to attack people and even carry off young children.

Hyksos \ˈhik-ˌsōs\ Group of mixed Semitic-Asiatics who settled in northern Egypt in the 18th century BC. They seized power c. 1630 BC and ruled Egypt for 108 years thereafter. They were superficially Egyptianized and did not interfere with Egyptian culture. Their chief deity was SETH, whom they identified with an Asiatic storm god. The Hyksos introduced the horse and chariot, the compound bow, improved battle-axes, and advanced fortification techniques. Hyksos pharaohs tried to halt the spread of a Theban revolt, but their dynasty fell to Ahmose in 1521.

hylomorphism \ˌhī-lə-ˈmȯr-ˌfiz-əm\ Metaphysical view according to which every natural body consists of two intrinsic principles, one potential (namely, primary matter) and one actual (namely, substantial form). It was the central doctrine of ARISTOTLE's philosophy of nature. He based his argument for hylomorphism chiefly on the analysis of change. If a being changes (e.g., from being cold to being hot), something permanent must exist that remains throughout the change; in addition, there must be an actual principle that differentiates the earlier from the later state. The permanent principle is matter, the actual principle form.

hylozoism \ˌhī-lə-ˈzō-ˌiz-əm\ View that all matter is alive, either in itself or by participation in the operation of a world soul or some similar principle. Hylozoism is logically distinct both from early forms of ANIMISM, which personify nature, and from panpsychism, which attributes some form of consciousness or sensation to all matter. The word was coined in the 17th century by RALPH CUDWORTH, who with Henry More (1614–1687) spoke of "plastic nature," an unconscious, incorporeal substance that controls and organizes matter and thus produces natural events as a divine instrument of change.

Hymen Greek god of marriage. He was usually thought to be a son of APOLLO by one of the MUSES, perhaps CALLIOPE. Other accounts called him the son of DIONYSUS and APHRODITE. In Attic legend he was a beautiful youth who rescued a group of young women, including his beloved, from a gang of pirates. He obtained the girl in marriage, and their happy life was invoked in many wedding songs.

hymn Song used in Christian worship, usually sung by the congregation and written in stanzas with rhyme and meter. The term comes from the Greek *hymnos* ("song of praise"), but songs in honor of God or the gods exist in all civilizations. Christian hymnody grew out of the singing of PSALMS in the Temple of JERUSALEM. The earliest known Christian hymn dates from c. AD 200. Hymns were prominent in the Byzantine liturgy from early times, and in the Western church they were sung by congregations until the Middle Ages, when choirs took over hymn singing. Congregational singing was reestablished during the REFORMATION. MARTIN LUTHER and his followers were great hymn writers, while the Calvinists preferred setting psalms to music. The compositions of I. WATTS and JOHN WESLEY were notable in English hymnody. The COUNTER-REFORMATION led to the composition of many Roman Catholic hymns, and the Roman Catholic church restored congregational singing of hymns after the Second VATICAN COUNCIL in the 1960s.

Hyndman \'hīnd-mən\, **Henry M(ayers)** (1842–1921) British Marxist political leader. Educated at Cambridge Univ., he worked as a journalist before founding the socialist Democratic Federation, and in *England for All* (1881), the first English socialist book in almost 50 years, he expounded the ideas of KARL MARX. He steered many British socialists toward Marxism, but FRIEDRICH ENGELS, who disliked Hyndman, encouraged many to break away and form the Socialist League. During World War I Hyndman took a patriotic and pro-French line, causing his ouster from the Socialist Party, whereupon he formed the National Socialist Party (1916), later renamed the Social Democratic Federation.

hyperactivity See ATTENTION DEFICIT DISORDER

hyperbaric chamber \,hī-pər-'bar-ik\ *or* **decompression chamber** *or* **recompression chamber** Sealed chamber supplying a high-pressure atmosphere. Breathing air at high pressure increases the oxygen level in tissues. This is used to inhibit growth of anaerobic bacteria (as in TETANUS or gas GANGRENE); to increase the chance that babies with certain heart malformations will survive heart surgery; or to cause air bubbles (as in air EMBOLISM or DECOMPRESSION SICKNESS) to be redissolved, carried to the lungs, and exhaled as pressure is gradually returned to normal.

hyperbola \hī-'pər-bə-lə\ Curve with two separate branches, one of the CONIC SECTIONS. It can be defined in terms of EUCLIDEAN GEOMETRY as the intersection of a plane and a right circular cone when the plane is parallel to the axis of the cone. If the cone's lines continue beyond its vertex to form a second, inverted cone, the cross section is the two arcs of a hyperbola. In ANALYTIC GEOMETRY, a hyperbola is the set of all points whose distances from each of two fixed points (foci) differ by a constant. Hyperbolas have many important physical attributes that make them useful in the design of LENSES and ANTENNAS.

hyperbolic function \,hī-pər-'bä-lik\ In mathematics, one of a set of functions related to the HYPERBOLA in the same way the TRIGONOMETRIC FUNCTIONS relate to the circle. They are the hyperbolic sine, cosine, tangent, secant, cotangent, and cosecant (written "sinh," "cosh," etc.). The hyperbolic equivalent of the fundamental trigonometric identity is $\cosh^2 z - \sinh^2 z = 1$. The hyperbolic sine and cosine, particularly useful for finding special types of INTEGRALS, can be defined in terms of EXPONENTIAL FUNCTIONS:

$$\sinh x = (e^x - e^{-x}) \div 2 \text{ and } \cosh x = (e^x + e^{-x}) \div 2.$$

hyperbolic geometry NON-EUCLIDEAN GEOMETRY, useful in modeling interstellar space, that rejects the PARALLEL POSTULATE, proposing instead that at least two lines through any point not on a given line are parallel to that line. Though many of its theorems are identical to those of EUCLIDEAN GEOMETRY, others differ. For example, two parallel lines converge in one direction and diverge in the other, and the angles of a triangle add up to less than 180°.

hypernephroma See RENAL CARCINOMA

hypertension *or* **high blood pressure** Condition in which BLOOD PRESSURE is abnormally high. Over time, it damages the kidneys, brain, eyes, and heart. Hypertension accelerates ARTERIOSCLEROSIS, increasing the risk of MYOCARDIAL INFARCTION, STROKE, and KIDNEY FAILURE. More common in the elderly and blacks, it usually has no symptoms but can be detected by a routine blood-pressure test. Secondary hypertension, caused by another disorder (most often kidney disease or hormone imbalance), accounts for 10% of cases. The other 90% have no specific cause (essential hypertension). A low-salt diet, weight loss, quitting smoking, limiting alcohol intake, and exercise can prevent or treat hypertension or reduce medication if drug therapy proves necessary. Malignant hypertension, a severe, rapidly progressing form, requires emergency treatment with drugs to dilate the blood vessels.

hypertext *or* **hyperlink** Linking of related information by electronic connections in order to allow a user easy access between them. Conceptualized by VANNEVAR BUSH (1945) and invented by DOUGLAS ENGELBART in the 1960s, hypertext is a feature of some computer programs that allows the user to select a word and receive additional information, such as a definition or related material. In Internet BROWSERS, hypertext links (hotlinks) are usually denoted by highlighting a word or phrase with a different font or color. Hypertext links create a branching or network structure that permits direct, unmediated jumps to related information. Hypertext has been used most successfully as an essential feature of the WORLD WIDE WEB (see HTML, HTTP). Hyperlinks may also involve objects other than text (e.g., selecting a small picture may provide a link to a larger version of the same picture).

HyperText Markup Language See HTML

HyperText Transfer Protocol See HTTP

hypnosis State that resembles SLEEP but is induced by a person (the hypnotist) whose suggestions are readily accepted by the subject. The hypnotized individual seems to respond in an uncritical, automatic fashion, ignoring aspects of the environment (e.g., sights, sounds) not pointed out to him or her by the hypnotist. Even the subject's memory and awareness of self may be altered by suggestion, and the effects of the suggestions may be extended (posthypnotically) into the subject's subsequent waking activity. Hypnotism is as old as the arts of sorcery and magic. It was popularized in the 18th century by FRANZ ANTON MESMER (as "mesmerism"), and was studied in the 19th century by the Scottish surgeon James Braid (1795–1860). SIGMUND FREUD relied on it in exploring the UNCONSCIOUS, and it eventually came to be recognized in medicine and psychology as useful in helping to calm or anesthetize patients, modify unwanted behaviors, and uncover repressed memories. There remains no generally acceptable explanation for hypnosis, though one prominent theory focuses on the possibility of discrete dissociative states affecting portions of CONSCIOUSNESS.

hypochondriasis \,hī-pə-kən-'drī-ə-səs\ Mental disorder in which an individual is excessively preoccupied with his own health and inclined to treat insignificant physical signs or symptoms as evidence of a serious disease. The hypochondriac may become convinced that he is ill even though he has no symptoms at all, or may exaggerate the importance of minor aches and pains, becoming obsessed with the fear of a life-threatening illness. A doctor's reassurances often have only a slight or temporary effect on the hypochondriac's anxieties. Hypochondriasis usually first manifests itself in early adulthood and is equally common among males and females. In some cases it may represent a psychological coping mechanism that the individual resorts to in order to deal with stressful life situations.

hypoglycemia \,hī-pō-glī-'sē-mē-ə\ Below-normal levels of blood GLUCOSE, quickly reversed by administration of oral or intravenous glucose. Even brief episodes can produce severe brain dysfunction. Fasting hypoglycemia can be life-threatening; it occurs most often in patients with DIABETES MELLITUS who mistime INSULIN therapy or miss meals. It also results from insulin-producing tumors, starvation, or metabolic disorders. Reactive hypoglycemia occurs when the body produces too much insulin in response to sugar intake. Symptoms range from irritability to confusion and seizures, leading to coma and death in severe cases.

hypophosphatemia \,hī-pō-,fäs-fä-'tē-mē-ə\ Low PHOSPHATE levels in blood. It usually occurs in conjunction with other metabolic disturbances, disrupting energy metabolism and impairing delivery of oxygen to tissues. Acute hypophosphatemia causes neurological symptoms (weakness, tremors, and confusion). Chronic hypophosphatemia, from long-term deficiency, causes general weakness and appetite loss. Treatment involves correcting the metabolic problem and giving phosphate supplements. Familial hypophosphatemia, an inherited disorder, is a major cause of RICKETS in developed nations. See also ATP.

hyposensitization See DESENSITIZATION

hypostyle hall \'hī-pə-,stīl\ Imposing interior space whose flat roof rests on many rows of columns. The design allows for the construction of large spaces without arches. It was used extensively in ancient Egypt (e.g., Temple of Amon at KARNAK) and Persia. The elaborately carved pillars consumed much of the floor space, and therefore assumed great importance. Hypostyles are rarely seen in more recent architecture because of more effective means of roof support.

hypotension *or* **low blood pressure** Condition in which BLOOD PRESSURE is abnormally low. It may result from reduced blood volume (e.g., from heavy bleeding or PLASMA loss after severe burns) or increased blood-vessel capacity (e.g., in SYNCOPE). Orthostatic hypotension—drop in blood pressure on standing—results from failure of the reflexes that contract muscles and constrict blood vessels in the legs to offset gravity as one rises. Hypotension is also a factor in POLIOMYELITIS, SHOCK, and BARBITURATE poisoning.

hypothalamus \,hī-pō-'tha-lə-məs\ Region of the brain containing a control center for many AUTONOMIC-NERVOUS-SYSTEM functions, whose complex interaction with the PITUITARY GLAND makes it an important part of the ENDOCRINE SYSTEM. As a critical link between the body's two control systems, the hypothalamus regulates HOMEOSTASIS. Nervous and hormonal pathways connect it with the pituitary, which it stimulates to release various HORMONES. The hypothalamus influences food intake, weight regulation, fluid intake and balance, thirst, body heat, and the SLEEP cycle. Disorders can produce pituitary dysfunction, DIABETES INSIPIDUS, INSOMNIA, and temperature fluctuations.

H | I | J | K

hypothermia Abnormally low body temperature, with slowing of physiologic activity. It is artificially induced (usually with ice baths) for certain surgical procedures and cancer treatments. Accidental hypothermia can result from falling into cold water or overexposure in cold weather. Underlying conditions such as cerebrovascular disease or intoxication increase the risk from exposure. Hypothermia is serious when body temperature is below 95°F (35°C) and an emergency below 90°F (32.2°C), at which point shivering stops. PULSE, respiration, and BLOOD PRESSURE are depressed. Even when the victim appears dead, revival may be possible with very gradual passive rewarming (e.g., with blankets). See also FROSTBITE, TEMPERATURE STRESS.

hypothesis testing In statistics, a method for testing how accurately a mathematical model based on one set of data predicts the nature of other data sets generated by the same process. Hypothesis testing grew out of quality control, in which whole batches of manufactured items are accepted or rejected based on testing relatively small samples. An initial hypothesis (null hypothesis) might predict, for example, that the widths of a precision part manufactured in batches will conform to a NORMAL DISTRIBUTION with a given mean (see MEAN, MEDIAN, AND MODE). Samples from new batches either confirm or disprove this hypothesis, which is refined based on these results.

hypoxia \,hip-'äk-sē-ə, hī-'päk-sē-ə\ Condition in which tissues are starved of oxygen. The extreme is anoxia (absence of oxygen). There are four types: hypoxemic, from low blood oxygen content (e.g., in ALTITUDE SICKNESS); anemic, from low blood oxygen-carrying capacity (e.g., in carbon monoxide poisoning); stagnant, from low blood flow (e.g., generally in SHOCK or locally in ARTERIOSCLEROSIS); and histotoxic, from poisoning (e.g., with CYANIDE) that keeps cells from using oxygen. If not reversed quickly, hypoxia can lead to necrosis (tissue death), as in MYOCARDIAL INFARCTION.

hyrax \'hī-,raks\ Any member of three genera of small, hoofed, quadruped, rodentlike mammals (order Hyracoidea) native to Africa and extreme South Asia. Hyraxes have a squat body, a short neck and tail, and short, slender legs. Adults are 12–20 in. (30–50 cm) long and weigh 8–11 lbs (4–5 kg). They are primarily herbivores. They are agile and climb well with the aid of special pads on their feet. Their relationship to UNGULATES is unclear. See also CONY.

Rock hyrax (*Heterohyrax*).
LEONARD LEE RUE III

hyssop \'hi-səp\ Small perennial garden herb *(Hyssopus officinalis)* of the MINT family, native to the area from southern Europe east to Central Asia and naturalized in North America. Its flowers and evergreen leaves have long been used as a flavoring for foods and beverages and as a folk medicine for nose, throat, and lung afflictions. The plant has a sweet scent and a warm, bitter taste. It is used to flavor both sweet and savory foods, and such liqueurs as absinthe. Hyssop honey is considered especially fine.

Hyssop (*Hyssopus officinalis*).
WALTER DAWN

hysterectomy \,his-tə-'rek-tə-mē\ Surgical removal of the UTERUS, either completely (total hysterectomy) or leaving the cervix (subtotal hysterectomy). It is performed in the presence of cancer or a benign fibroid tumor if the fibroid is large or rapidly growing, causes excessive bleeding or discomfort, or seems to be breaking down. Hysterectomy may also be performed after CESAREAN SECTION in cases of complications such as uncontrolled bleeding, gross infection, or cancer of the cervix. Once misused in the belief that removing the uterus (and often the OVARIES) would control what were considered inappropriate sexual urges and ambitions, it is still the most common unnecessary surgery.

hysteresis \,his-tə-'rē-səs\ Lagging of the magnetization of ferromagnetic material (see FERROMAGNETISM), such as IRON, behind variations of the magnetizing field. When such a material is placed in a coil of wire carrying an ELECTRIC CURRENT, the MAGNETIC FIELD so created forces atoms in the material to align with the field. This increases the total magnetic field to a maximum when all the atoms are aligned, though the total field lags behind the magnetizing field. When the intensity of the magnetizing field is decreased to zero, some field remains in the material, and if the magnetizing field is reversed the total magnetization also reverses but again lags behind. The complete cycle, known as a hysteresis loop, dissipates energy in the form of heat as the magnetization is reversed.

hysteria Term formerly used in psychology to designate a NEUROSIS marked by emotional excitability and disturbances of psychic, sensory, vasomotor, and visceral functions. The concept was used frequently in the first half of the 20th century to explain a wide variety of symptoms and behaviors observed particularly in women. (The term derives from the Greek word for "womb," reflecting the Greeks' belief that the condition resulted from disturbances of the uterus.) It was eventually dropped from the *Diagnostic and Statistical Manual of Mental Disorders* as overly broad. Disorders with symptoms similar to those of traditional hysteria include conversion disorder, factitious disorder, dissociative disorder, and PERSONALITY DISORDER (histrionic type).

Hywel Dda *or* **Howel Dda** \'hə-wel-'thä\ *or* **Hywel the Good** (died 950) Welsh chieftain called "king of all Wales." He inherited Seisyllwg and secured Dyfed by marriage, thereby creating the kingdom of Deheubarth. Eventually Gwynedd and POWYS also came under his rule. By 942 his realm was larger than that of any earlier Welsh ruler. He codified Welsh law during his peaceful reign and accepted the status of subking to the Anglo-Saxon king of Wessex.

Afghanistan

Albania

Algeria

Andorra*

Angola

Antigua and Barbuda

Argentina

Armenia

Australia

Austria*

Azerbaijan

The Bahamas

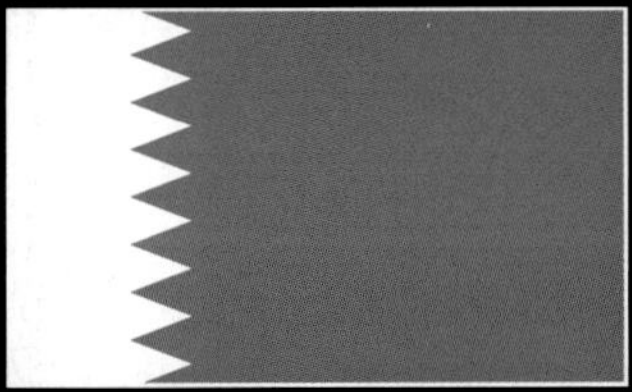
Bahrain

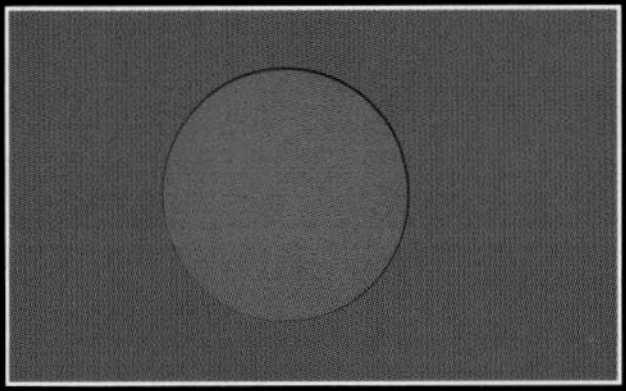
Bangladesh

Barbados

Belarus

Belgium

Belize

Benin

Bhutan

Bolivia*

Civil flags are shown except where marked thus(*); in these cases, government flags are shown in order to illustrate emblems. Both styles are official national flags.

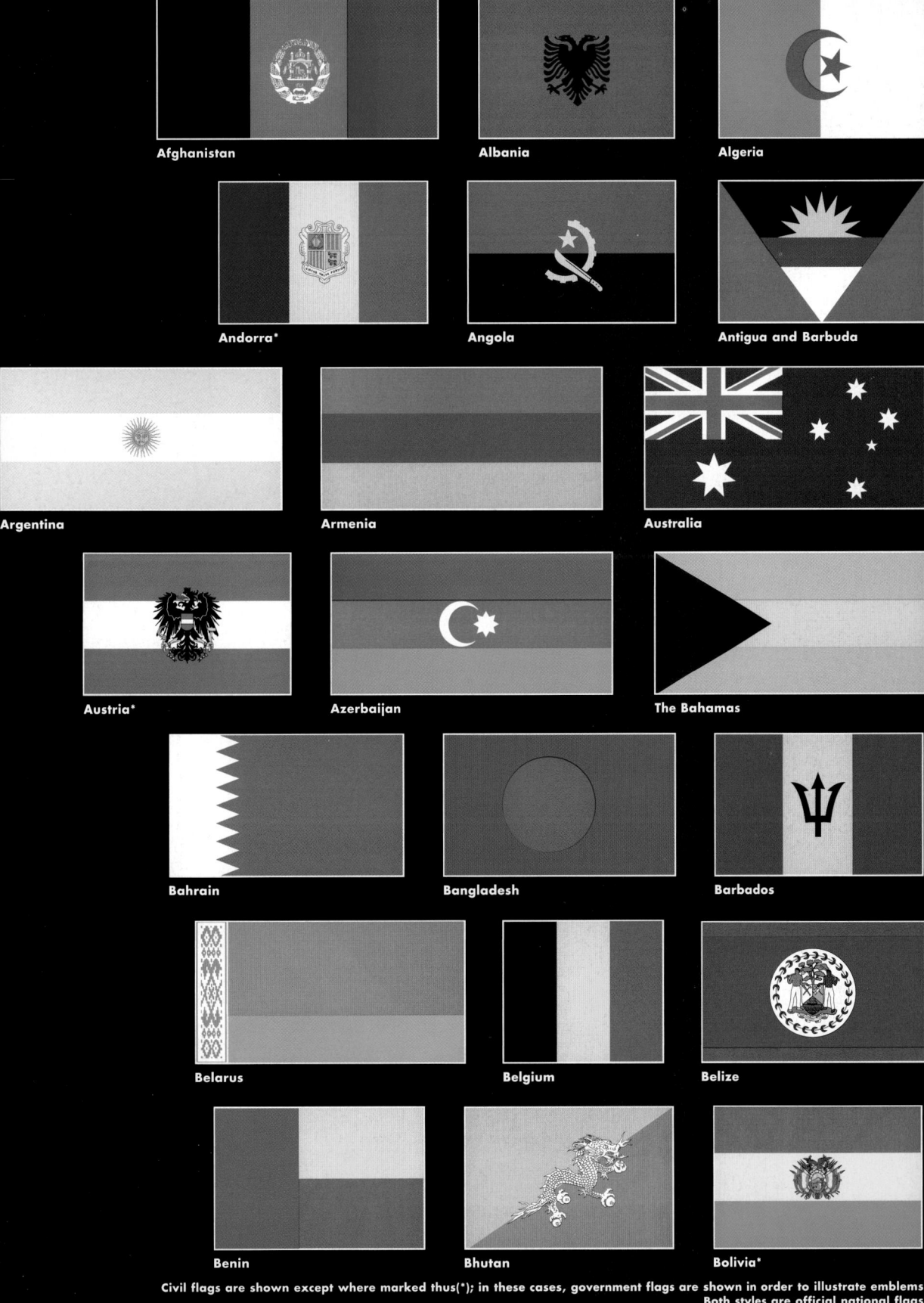

Bosnia and Herzegovina

Botswana

Brazil

Brunei

Bulgaria

Burkina Faso

Burundi

Cambodia

Cameroon

Canada

Cape Verde

Central African Republic

Chad

Chile

China

Colombia

Comoros

Democratic Republic of the Congo

Republic of the Congo

Costa Rica*

Côte d'Ivoire

Croatia

Cuba

Civil flags are shown except where marked thus(*); in these cases, government flags are shown in order to illustrate emblems. Both styles are official national flags.

Cyprus

Czech Republic

Denmark

ti

Dominica

Dominican Republic*

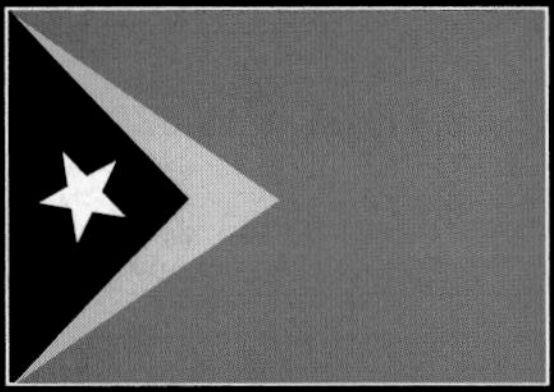

East Timor

Ecuador*

Egypt

Salvador

Equatorial Guinea

Eritrea

Ethiopia

Fiji

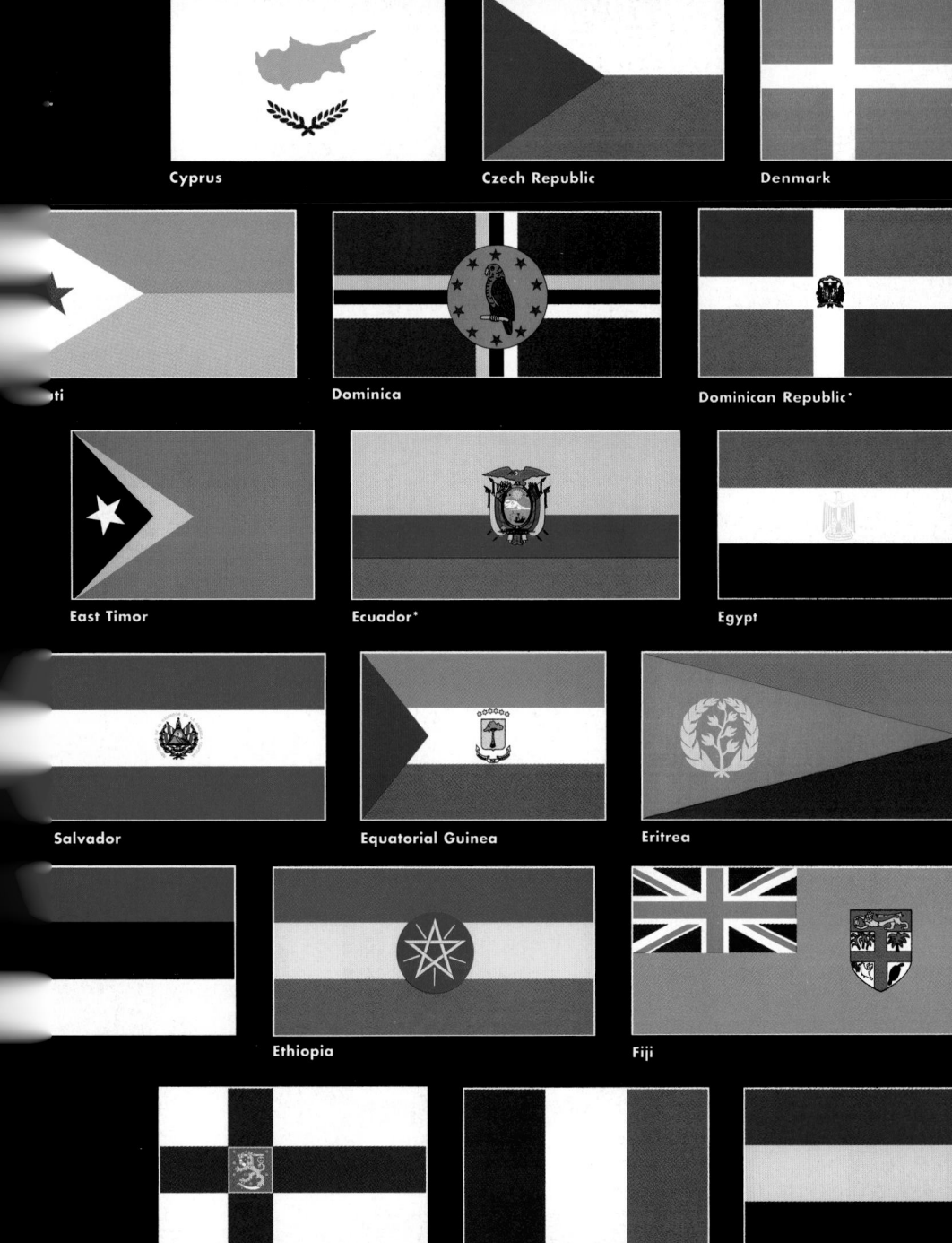

Ghana

Greece

Grenada

Guatemala*

Guinea

Guinea-Bissau

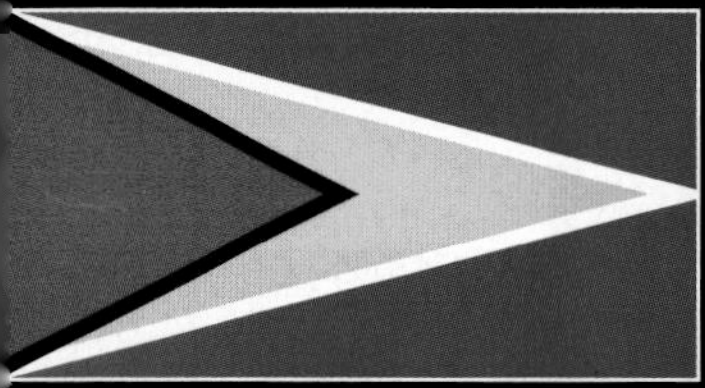
Guyana

Haiti*

Honduras

Hungary

Iceland

India

Indonesia

Iran

Iraq

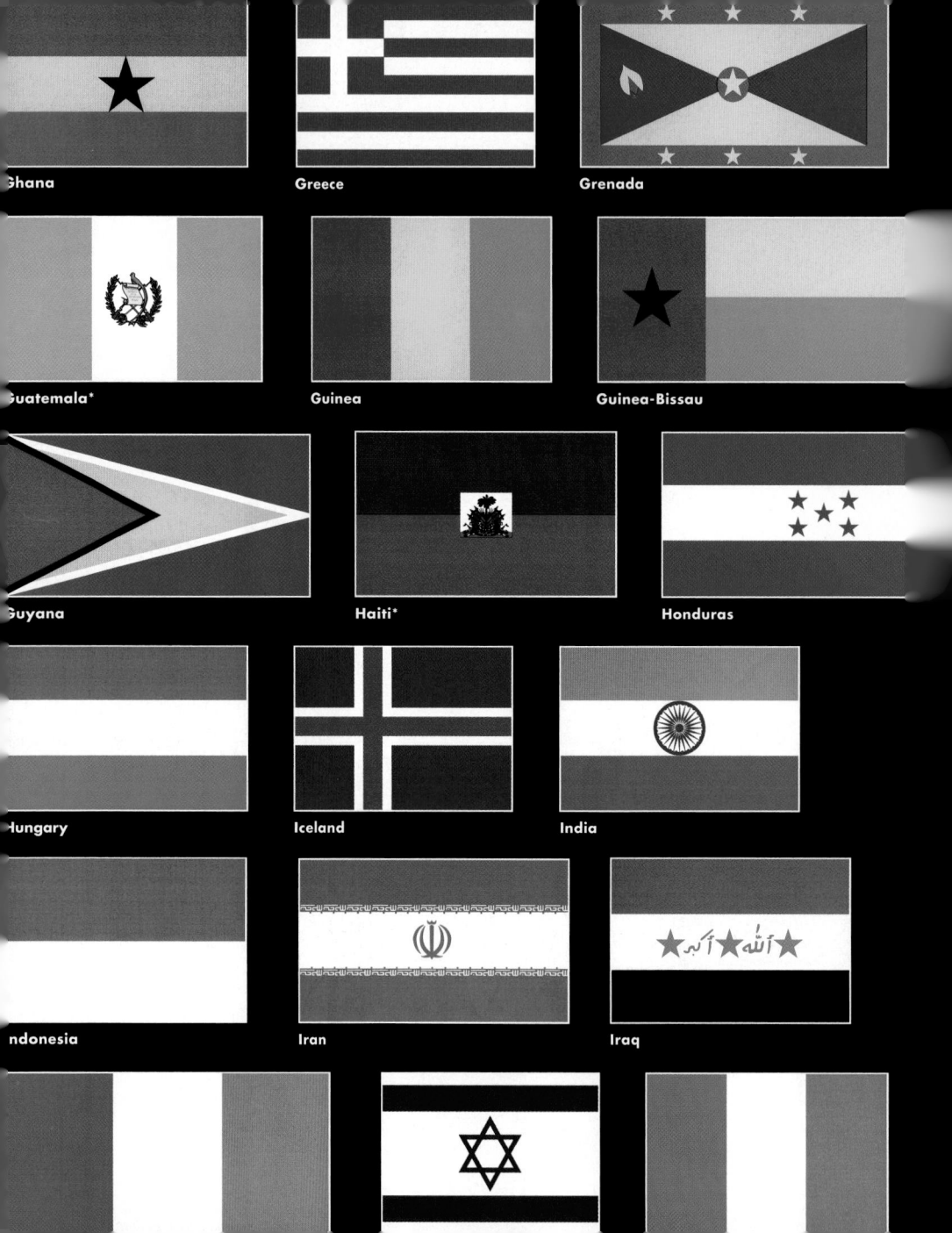

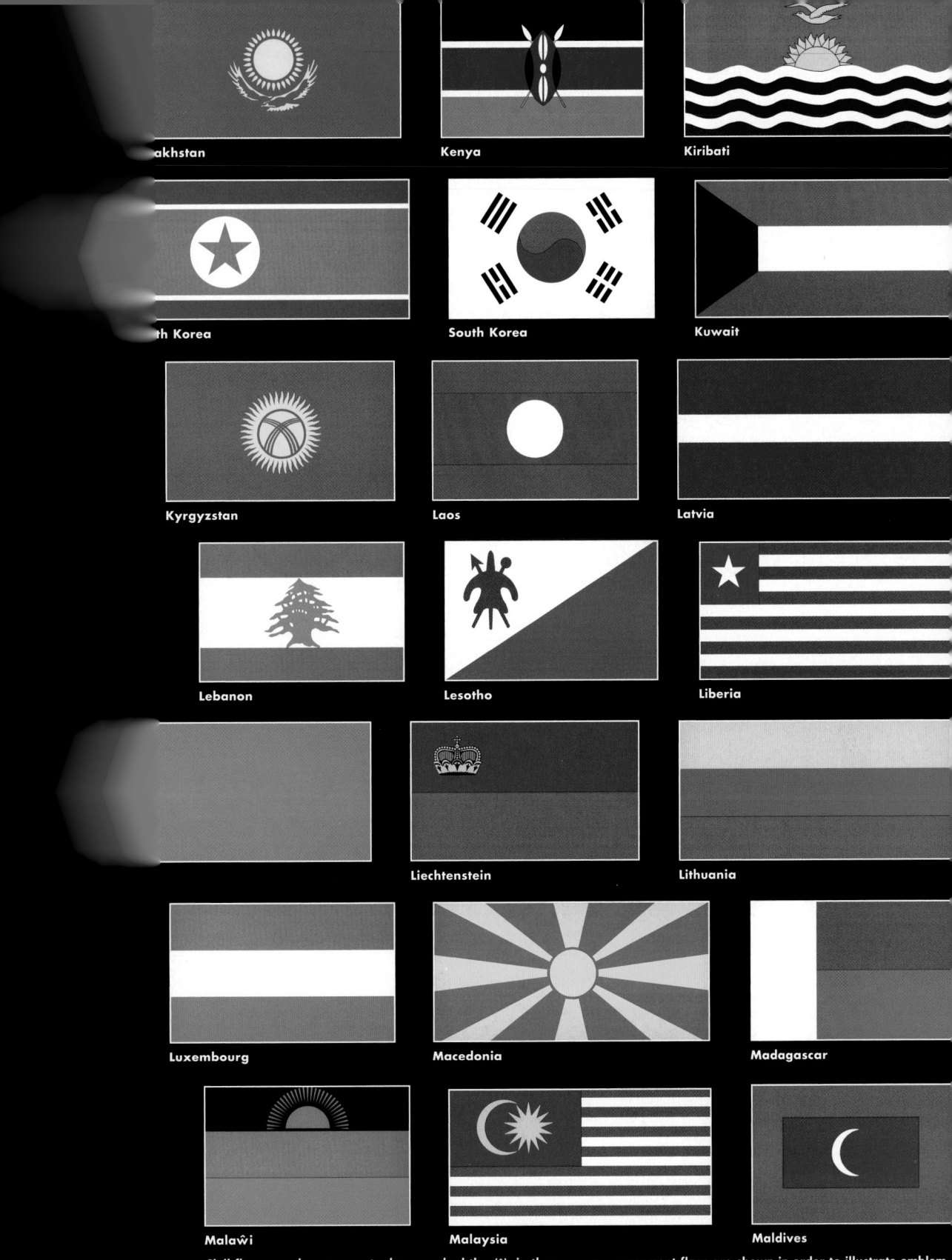

akhstan

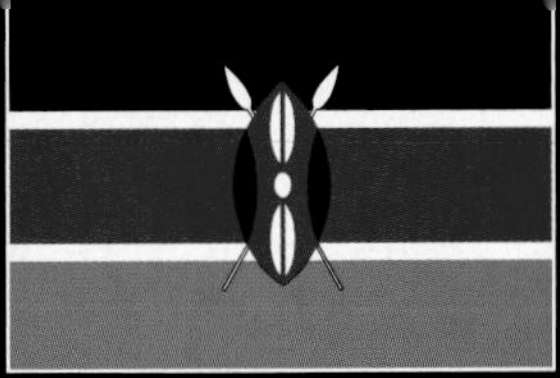
Kenya

Kiribati

th Korea

South Korea

Kuwait

Kyrgyzstan

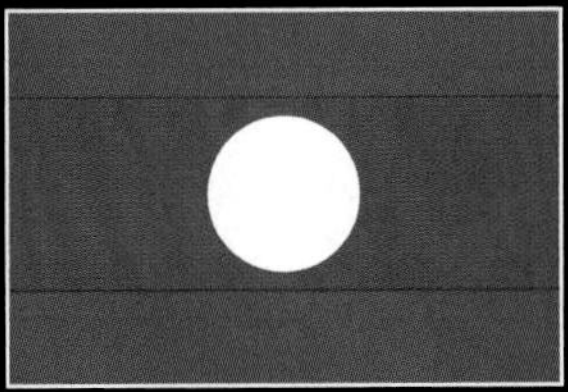
Laos

Latvia

Lebanon

Lesotho

Liberia

Liechtenstein

Lithuania

Luxembourg

Macedonia

Madagascar

Malaŵi

Malaysia

Maldives

Mali

Malta

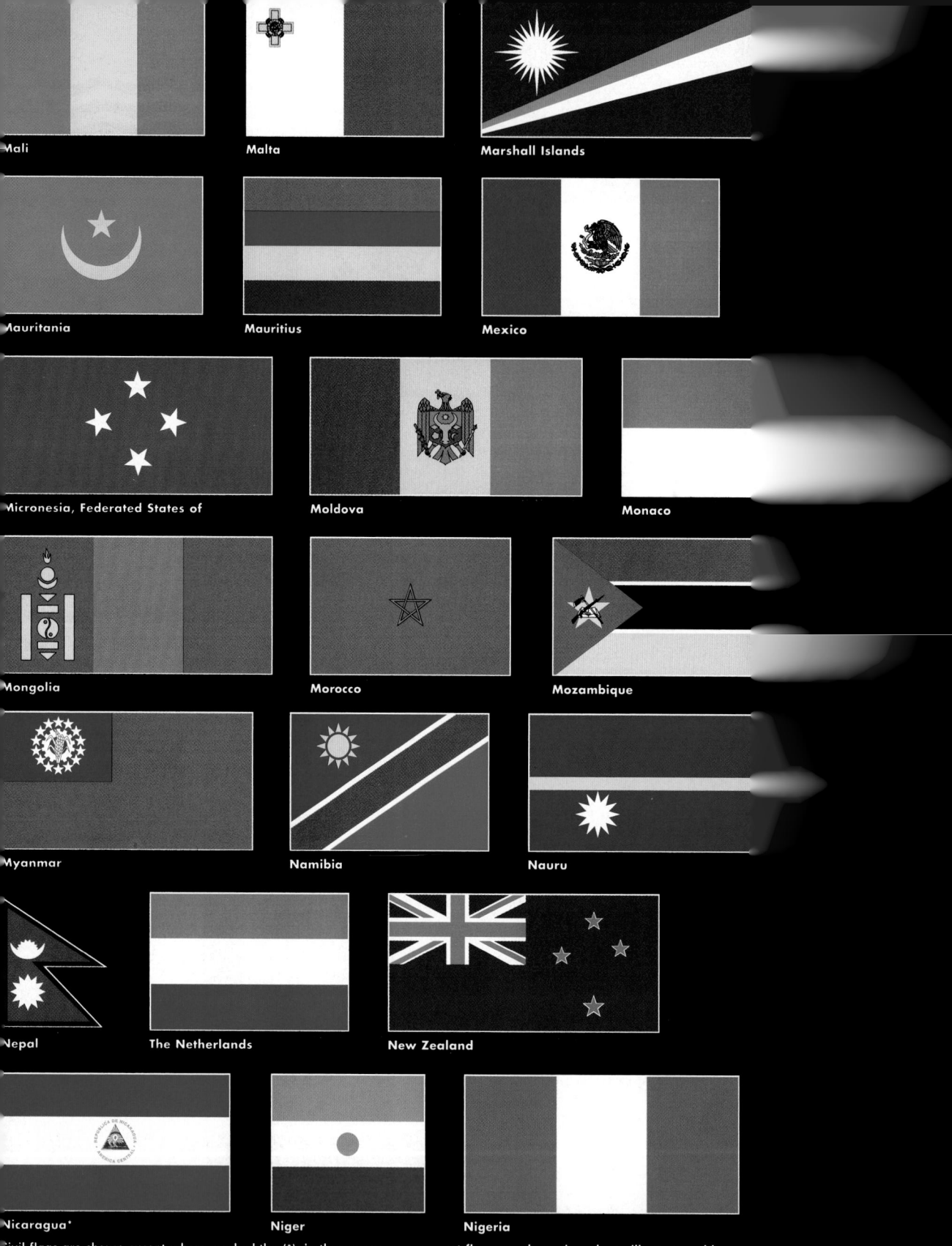

Marshall Islands

Mauritania

Mauritius

Mexico

Micronesia, Federated States of

Moldova

Monaco

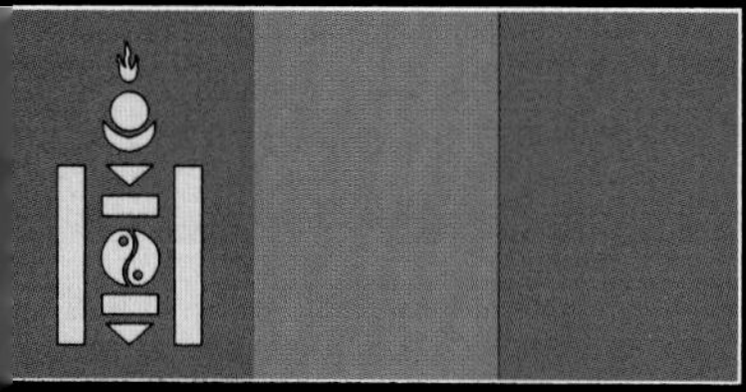
Mongolia

Morocco

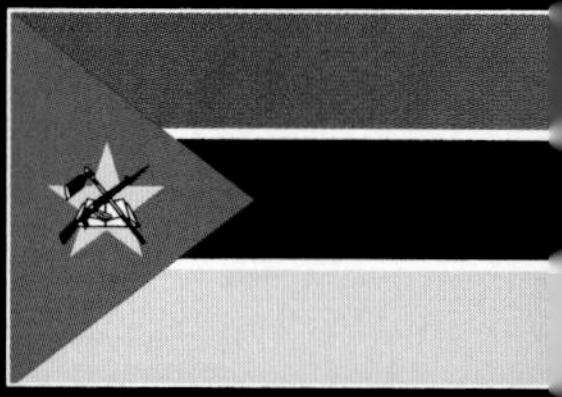
Mozambique

Myanmar

Namibia

Nauru

Nepal

The Netherlands

New Zealand

Nicaragua*

Niger

Nigeria

Civil flags are shown except where marked thus(*); in these cases ...

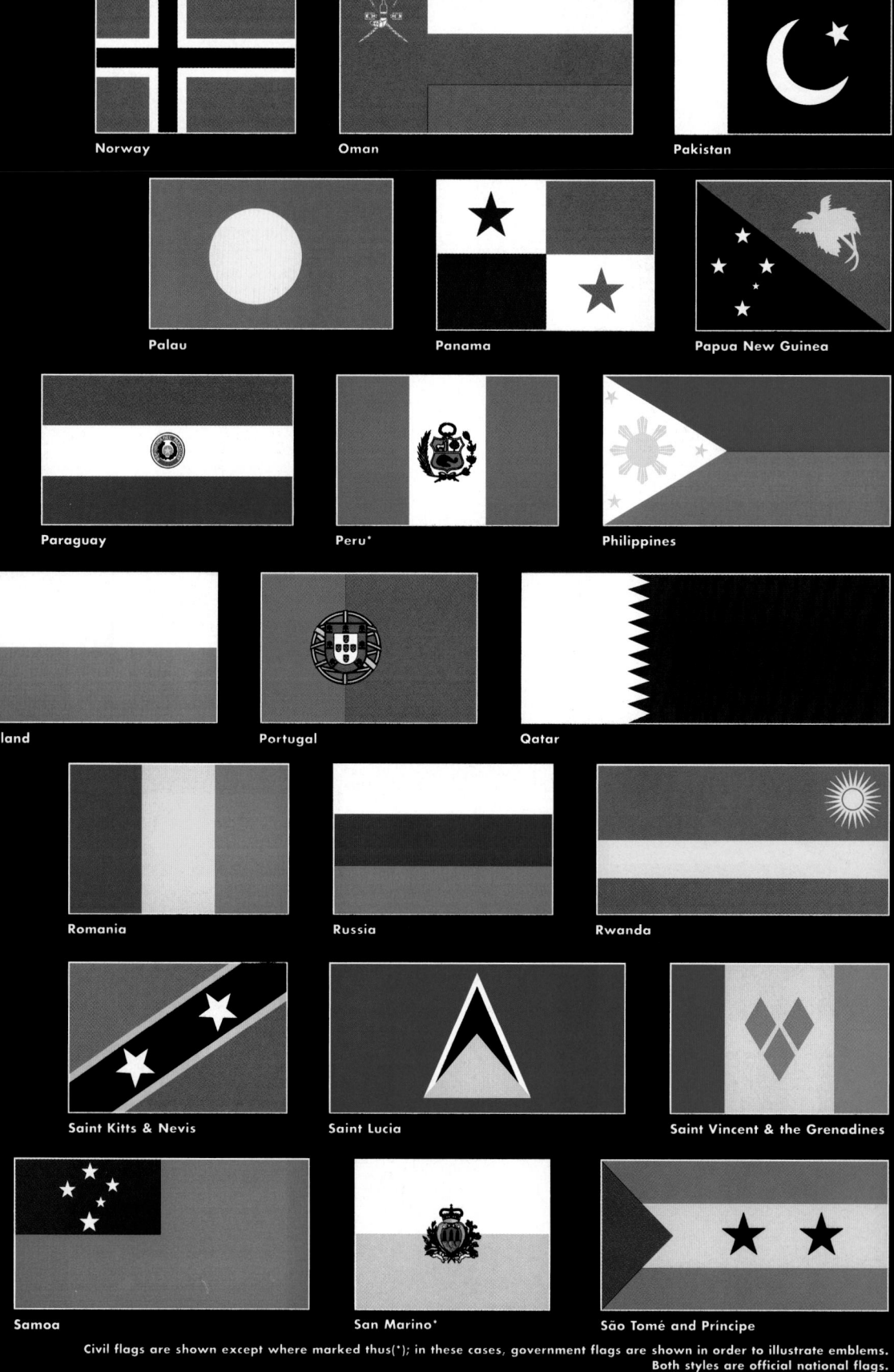

Norway

Oman

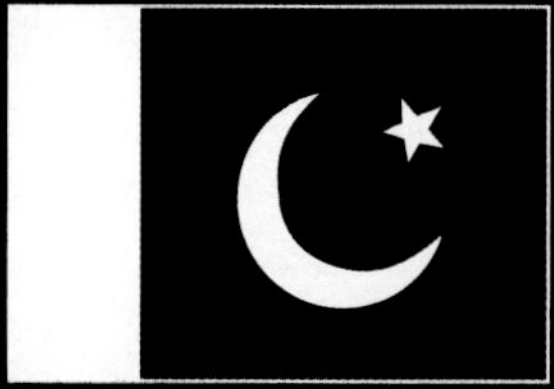

Pakistan

Palau

Panama

Papua New Guinea

Paraguay

Peru*

Philippines

Poland

Portugal

Qatar

Romania

Russia

Rwanda

Saint Kitts & Nevis

Saint Lucia

Saint Vincent & the Grenadines

Samoa

San Marino*

São Tomé and Príncipe

Civil flags are shown except where marked thus(*); in these cases, government flags are shown in order to illustrate emblems. Both styles are official national flags.

Saudi Arabia

Senegal

Seychelles

Sierra Leone

Singapore

Slovakia

Slovenia

Solomon Islands

Somalia

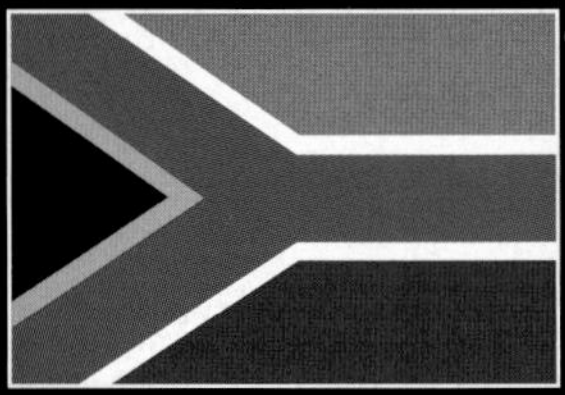
South Africa

Spain

Sri Lanka

Sudan

Suriname

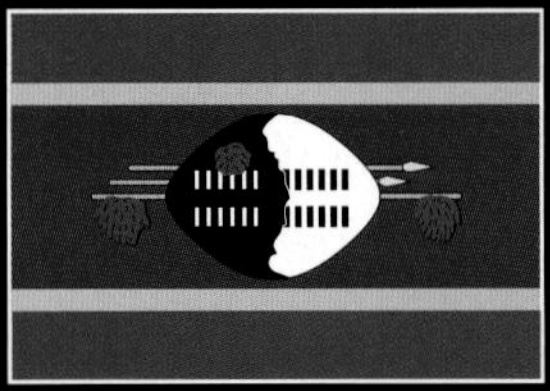
Swaziland

Sweden

Switzerland

Syria

Taiwan

Tajikistan

Tanzania

Thailand

Civil flags are shown except where marked thus(*); in these cases, government flags are shown in order to illustrate emblems. Both styles are official national flags.

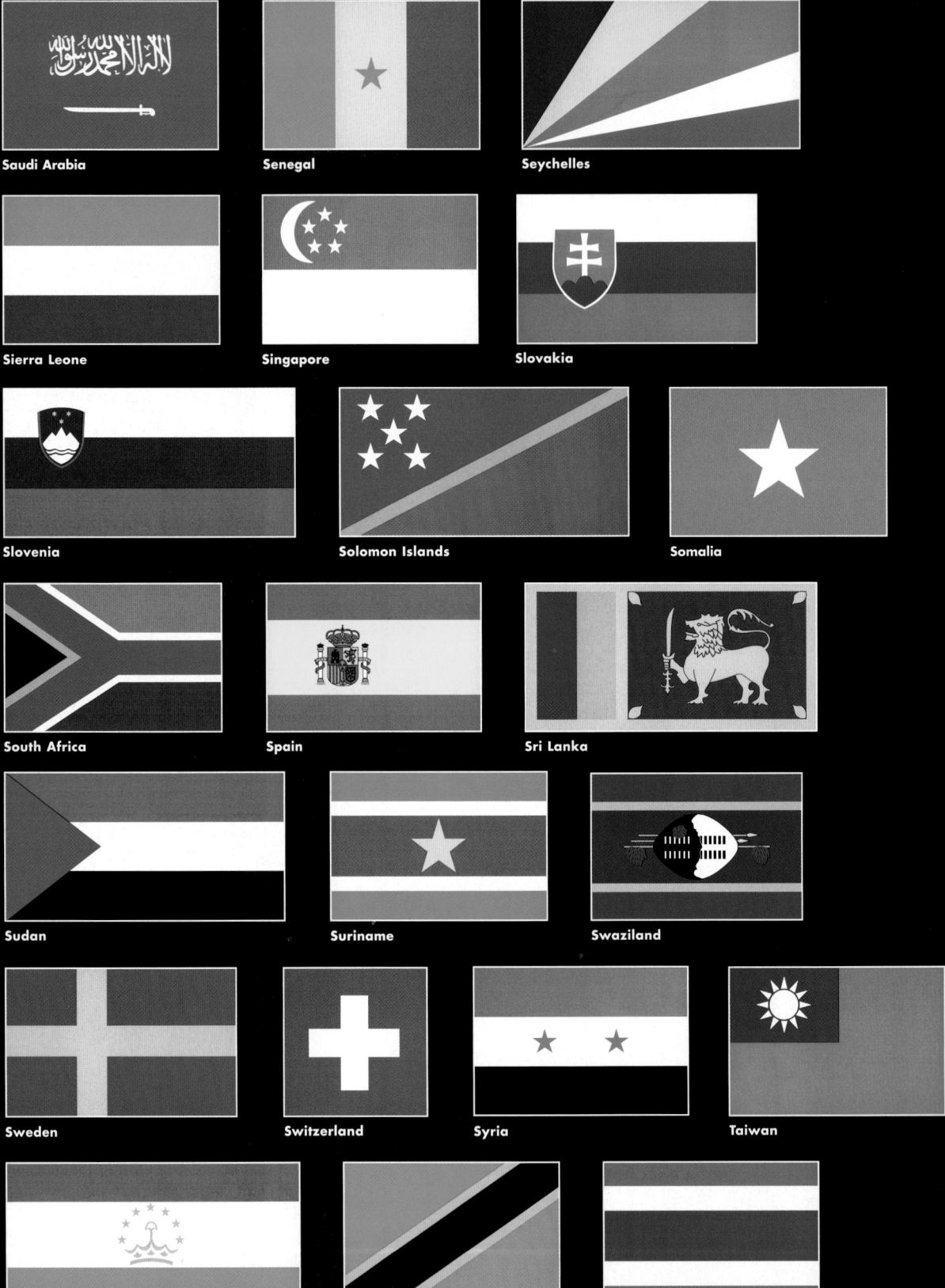

Togo

Tonga

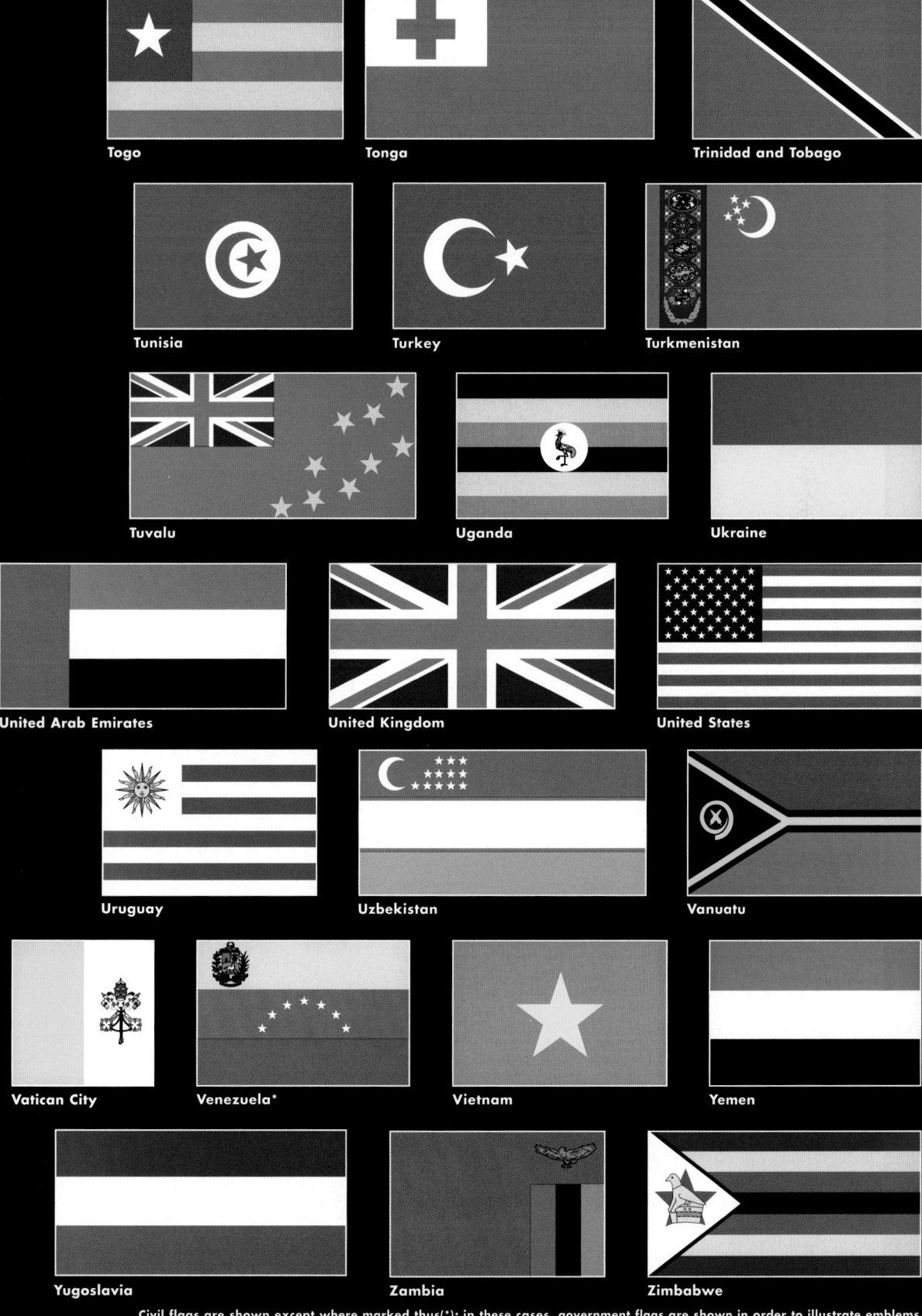

Trinidad and Tobago

Tunisia

Turkey

Turkmenistan

Tuvalu

Uganda

Ukraine

United Arab Emirates

United Kingdom

United States

Uruguay

Uzbekistan

Vanuatu

Vatican City

Venezuela*

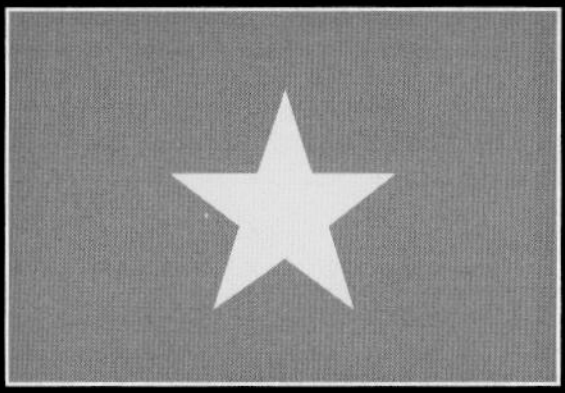
Vietnam

Yemen

Yugoslavia

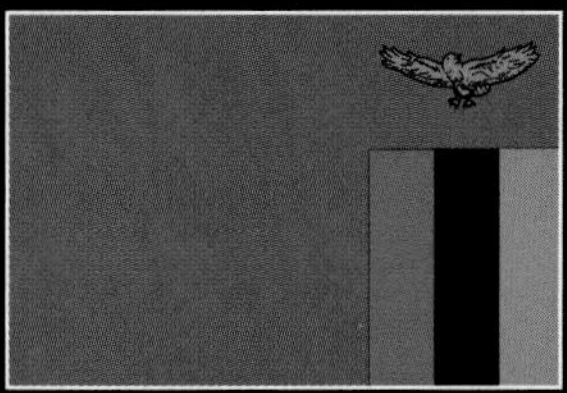
Zambia

Zimbabwe

Civil flags are shown except where marked thus(*); in these cases, government flags are shown in order to illustrate emblems. Both styles are official national flags.

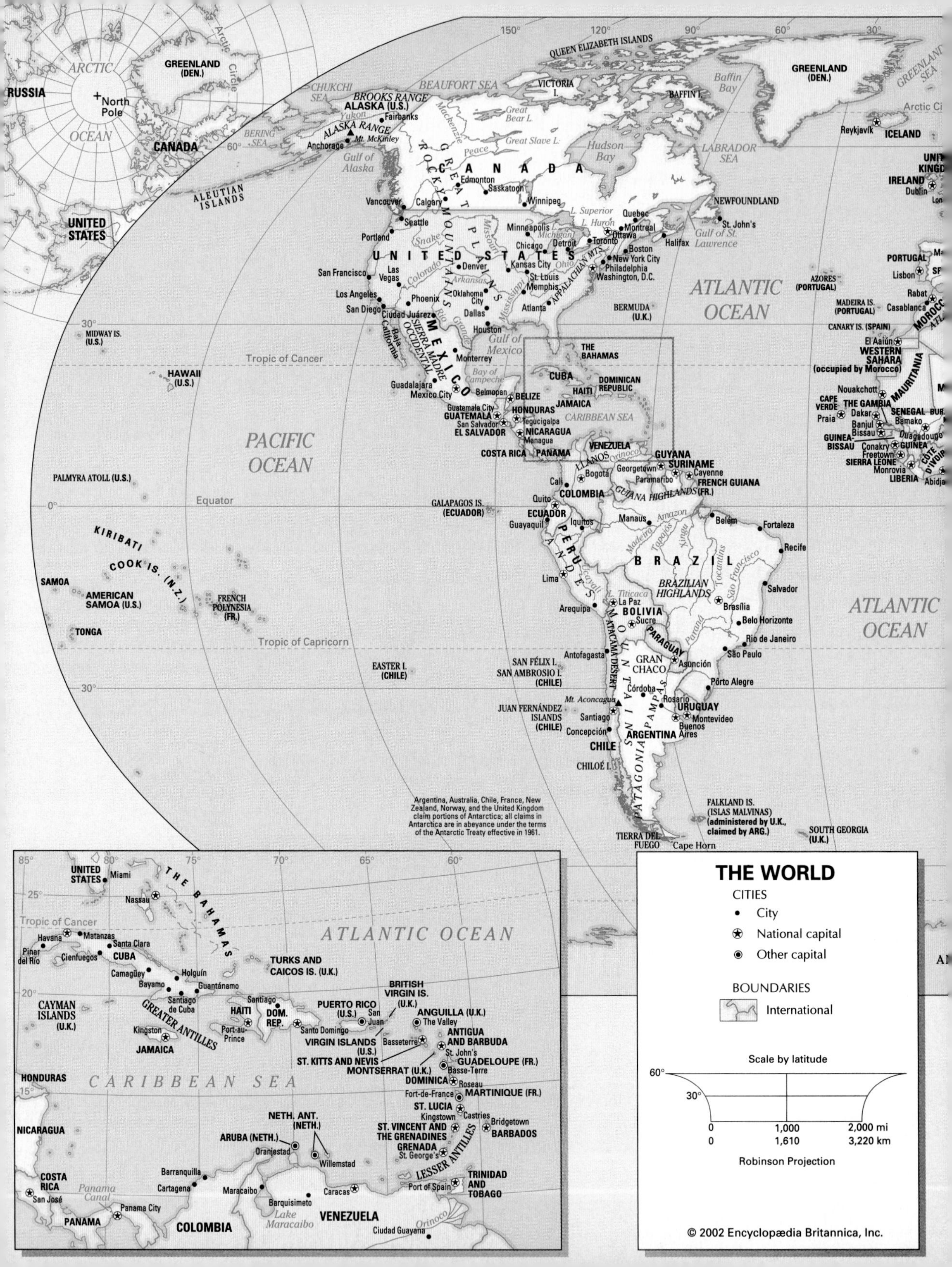
THE WORLD
CITIES
City
National capital
Other capital
BOUNDARIES
International
Scale by latitude
60°
30°
0 1,000 2,000 mi
0 1,610 3,220 km
Robinson Projection
© 2002 Encyclopædia Britannica, Inc.
ARCTIC OCEAN
North Pole
RUSSIA
GREENLAND (DEN.)
CANADA
UNITED STATES
ALEUTIAN ISLANDS
BERING SEA
CHUKCHI SEA
BEAUFORT SEA
QUEEN ELIZABETH ISLANDS
VICTORIA I.
BAFFIN I.
Baffin Bay
LABRADOR SEA
Hudson Bay
ALASKA (U.S.)
BROOKS RANGE
ALASKA RANGE
Mt. McKinley
Fairbanks
Anchorage
Gulf of Alaska
Great Bear L.
Great Slave L.
Edmonton
Saskatoon
Calgary
Vancouver
Winnipeg
Seattle
Portland
ROCKY MOUNTAINS
GREAT PLAINS
NEWFOUNDLAND
St. John's
Quebec
Montreal
Ottawa
Toronto
Halifax
Gulf of St. Lawrence
L. Superior
L. Huron
Minneapolis
Chicago
Detroit
Boston
New York City
Philadelphia
Washington, D.C.
APPALACHIAN MTS.
San Francisco
Las Vegas
Denver
Kansas City
St. Louis
Memphis
Los Angeles
San Diego
Phoenix
Oklahoma City
Dallas
Atlanta
Houston
Ciudad Juárez
Baja California
SIERRA MADRE OCCIDENTAL
MEXICO
Monterrey
Guadalajara
Mexico City
Gulf of Mexico
Bay of Campeche
BERMUDA (U.K.)
ATLANTIC OCEAN
AZORES (PORTUGAL)
MADEIRA IS. (PORTUGAL)
CANARY IS. (SPAIN)
Reykjavík
ICELAND
IRELAND
Dublin
PORTUGAL
Lisbon
Rabat
Casablanca
MOROCCO
El Aaiún
WESTERN SAHARA (occupied by Morocco)
MAURITANIA
Nouakchott
CAPE VERDE
Praia
THE GAMBIA
Dakar
Banjul
Bissau
SENEGAL
Bamako
GUINEA BISSAU
Conakry
GUINEA
Freetown
SIERRA LEONE
Monrovia
LIBERIA
MIDWAY IS. (U.S.)
Tropic of Cancer
HAWAII (U.S.)
THE BAHAMAS
CUBA
DOMINICAN REPUBLIC
HAITI
JAMAICA
Belmopan
BELIZE
Guatemala City
GUATEMALA
HONDURAS
Tegucigalpa
San Salvador
EL SALVADOR
NICARAGUA
Managua
COSTA RICA
PANAMA
CARIBBEAN SEA
VENEZUELA
GUYANA
SURINAME
Georgetown
Paramaribo
Cayenne
FRENCH GUIANA (FR.)
GUIANA HIGHLANDS
LLANOS
Orinoco
PACIFIC OCEAN
PALMYRA ATOLL (U.S.)
Equator
Bogotá
Cali
COLOMBIA
Quito
ECUADOR
Guayaquil
GALAPAGOS IS. (ECUADOR)
Iquitos
Manaus
Amazon
Belém
Fortaleza
Recife
BRAZIL
PERU
ANDES
Lima
BRAZILIAN HIGHLANDS
Salvador
Brasília
KIRIBATI
COOK IS. (N.Z.)
SAMOA
AMERICAN SAMOA (U.S.)
FRENCH POLYNESIA (FR.)
TONGA
Tropic of Capricorn
L. Titicaca
La Paz
Arequipa
BOLIVIA
Sucre
Belo Horizonte
Rio de Janeiro
São Paulo
PARAGUAY
Asunción
GRAN CHACO
Antofagasta
ATACAMA DESERT
EASTER I. (CHILE)
SAN FÉLIX I. SAN AMBROSIO I. (CHILE)
Pôrto Alegre
Córdoba
Rosario
Mt. Aconcagua
URUGUAY
Montevideo
Buenos Aires
JUAN FERNÁNDEZ ISLANDS (CHILE)
Santiago
Concepción
ARGENTINA
PAMPAS
CHILE
PATAGONIA
CHILOÉ I.
Argentina, Australia, Chile, France, New Zealand, Norway, and the United Kingdom claim portions of Antarctica; all claims in Antarctica are in abeyance under the terms of the Antarctic Treaty effective in 1961.
FALKLAND IS. (ISLAS MALVINAS) (administered by U.K., claimed by ARG.)
SOUTH GEORGIA (U.K.)
TIERRA DEL FUEGO
Cape Horn
UNITED STATES
Miami
Nassau
Tropic of Cancer
ATLANTIC OCEAN
Havana
Matanzas
Santa Clara
Pinar del Río
Cienfuegos
CUBA
Camagüey
Holguín
Bayamo
Guantánamo
Santiago de Cuba
GREATER ANTILLES
TURKS AND CAICOS IS. (U.K.)
CAYMAN ISLANDS (U.K.)
HAITI
Port-au-Prince
Santiago
DOM. REP.
Santo Domingo
Kingston
JAMAICA
PUERTO RICO (U.S.)
San Juan
BRITISH VIRGIN IS. (U.K.)
ANGUILLA (U.K.)
The Valley
VIRGIN ISLANDS (U.S.)
Basseterre
ST. KITTS AND NEVIS
ANTIGUA AND BARBUDA
St. John's
MONTSERRAT (U.K.)
GUADELOUPE (FR.)
Basse-Terre
DOMINICA
Roseau
Fort-de-France
MARTINIQUE (FR.)
ST. LUCIA
Castries
Kingstown
ST. VINCENT AND THE GRENADINES
Bridgetown
BARBADOS
GRENADA
St. George's
LESSER ANTILLES
HONDURAS
CARIBBEAN SEA
NICARAGUA
NETH. ANT. (NETH.)
ARUBA (NETH.)
Oranjestad
Willemstad
TRINIDAD AND TOBAGO
Port of Spain
Barranquilla
Cartagena
Maracaibo
Lake Maracaibo
Barquisimeto
Caracas
VENEZUELA
COSTA RICA
San José
Panama Canal
Panama City
PANAMA
COLOMBIA
Ciudad Guayana
Orinoco

30°
60°
90°
120°
150°
ARCTIC OCEAN
SVALBARD (NORWAY)
FRANZ JOSEF LAND
NOVAYA ZEMLYA
KARA SEA
NORWEGIAN SEA
NEW SIBERIAN IS.
EAST SIBERIAN SEA
VERKHOYANSK MTS.
KOLYMA MTS.
Kolyma
Lena
Yenisey
Ob
URAL MOUNTAINS
WEST SIBERIAN PLAIN
RUSSIA
Arkhangelsk
NORWAY
SWEDEN
FINLAND
ESTONIA
LATVIA
LITHUANIA
DEN.
BELARUS
GERMANY
POLAND
CZECH REP.
SLOVAKIA
UKRAINE
MOLDOVA
AUS.
HUNG.
ROMANIA
ALPS
ITALY
YUGOS.
BULG.
GREECE
TURKEY
CYPRUS
BLACK SEA
Nizhny Novgorod
Moscow
Perm
Kazan
Ufa
Samara
Volgograd
Volga
Yekaterinburg
Chelyabinsk
Omsk
Novosibirsk
Novokuznetsk
Barnaul
Krasnoyarsk
Astana
KAZAKHSTAN
Lake Balqash
ARAL SEA
CASPIAN SEA
Yakutsk
Lake Baikal
STANOVOY MTS.
Irkutsk
Chita
SEA OF OKHOTSK
KAMCHATKA PEN.
BERING SEA
SAKHALIN I.
Amur
Khabarovsk
Ulaanbaatar
MONGOLIA
GOBI DESERT
TIEN SHAN
Bishkek
KYRGYZSTAN
Tashkent
TAJIKISTAN
UZBEKISTAN
TURKMENISTAN
GEORGIA
ARMENIA
AZERBAIJAN
Harbin
Shenyang
Beijing
Tianjin
Vladivostok
NORTH KOREA
P'yŏngyang
Seoul
SOUTH KOREA
Pusan
HOKKAIDO
JAPAN
HONSHU
Tokyo
Ōsaka
SHIKOKU
KYUSHU
Huang He
KUNLUN MTS.
CHINA
Lanzhou
Xi'an
YELLOW SEA
PLATEAU OF TIBET
Chang Jiang
HIMALAYAS
Nanjing
Shanghai
Wuhan
Chongqing
Lhasa
Kabul
AFGHANISTAN
Islāmābād
Lahore
Delhi
New Delhi
NEPAL
Kāthmāndu
Mt. Everest
BHUTAN
Thimphu
BANGLADESH
Dhākā
PAKISTAN
Indus
Ganges
Karāchi
Ahmadābād
INDIA
Calcutta (Kolkata)
Bombay (Mumbai)
Nāgpur
Hyderābād
Bangalore
Madras (Chennai)
ARABIAN SEA
Bay of Bengal
Colombo
SRI LANKA
MALDIVES
Male
TAIWAN
Taipei
Kao-hsiung
Xi
MYANMAR
LAOS
Hanoi
Vientiane
SOUTH CHINA SEA
Yangôn
Bangkok
THAILAND
VIETNAM
CAMBODIA
Phnom Penh
Ho Chi Minh City
LUZON
Manila
PHILIPPINES
PHILIPPINE SEA
MINDANAO
Koror
PALAU
ANDAMAN IS. (INDIA)
NICOBAR IS. (INDIA)
Kuala Lumpur
MALAYSIA
BRUNEI
Bandar Seri Begawan
Medan
SINGAPORE
SUMATRA
BORNEO
CELEBES
Palembang
INDONESIA
Jakarta
Bandung
Semarang
Surabaya
JAVA
NEW GUINEA
PAPUA NEW GUINEA
Port Moresby
EAST TIMOR
ARAFURA SEA
PACIFIC OCEAN
NORTHERN MARIANA IS. (U.S.)
GUAM (U.S.)
MARSHALL IS.
FEDERATED STATES OF MICRONESIA
Palikir
Majuro
Bairiki
KIRIBATI
SOLOMON ISLANDS
Honiara
TUVALU
Vaiaku
VANUATU
Vila
ÉFATÉ
FIJI
Suva
CORAL SEA
NEW CALEDONIA (FR.)
ARNHEM LAND
GREAT SANDY DESERT
GREAT ARTESIAN BASIN
GREAT DIVIDING RANGE
Great Barrier Reef
AUSTRALIA
GREAT VICTORIA DESERT
Brisbane
Perth
Darling
Adelaide
Sydney
Canberra
Great Australian Bight
Melbourne
TASMANIA
Hobart
TASMAN SEA
Auckland
NEW ZEALAND
Wellington
AUCKLAND IS. (N.Z.)
INDIAN OCEAN
BRITISH INDIAN OCEAN TERRITORY (U.K.)
COCOS IS. (AUSTL.)
SOCOTRA I. (YEMEN)
SEYCHELLES
Victoria
MAURITIUS
Port Louis
RÉUNION (FR.)
AMSTERDAM I. (FR.)
SAINT PAUL I. (FR.)
CROZET IS. (FR.)
PRINCE EDWARD IS. (SOUTH AFRICA)
KERGUELEN IS. (FR.)
TUNISIA
Tripoli
LIBYA
EGYPT
SAHARA
L. Nasser
Nile
TIBESTI MTS.
SAHEL
NIGER
CHAD
L. Chad
THE SUDAN
NIGERIA
Abuja
Porto-Novo
Niamey
CAMEROON
CENTRAL AFRICAN REPUBLIC
Bangui
Yaoundé
EQ. GUIN.
GABON
Libreville
REP. OF THE CONGO
Brazzaville
Congo
DEM. REP. OF THE CONGO
Kinshasa
CABINDA (ANGOLA)
Luanda
ANGOLA
UGANDA
Kampala
RWANDA
BURUNDI
Lake Victoria
KENYA
Nairobi
Kilimanjaro
TANZANIA
Dar es Salaam
Lake Tanganyika
MALAWI
Lake Nyasa
ZAMBIA
Lusaka
Lilongwe
Harare
ZIMBABWE
MOZAMBIQUE
Mozambique Channel
COMOROS
Moroni
MADAGASCAR
Antananarivo
NAMIBIA
Windhoek
NAMIB DESERT
BOTSWANA
Gaborone
Pretoria
Maputo
Mbabane
Johannesburg
Maseru
SWAZILAND
LESOTHO
Orange
SOUTH AFRICA
Cape Town
Cape of Good Hope
ERITREA
DJIBOUTI
Gulf of Aden
Addis Ababa
ETHIOPIA
ETHIOPIAN PLATEAU
SOMALIA
Mogadishu
White Nile
SYRIA
LEBANON
ISRAEL
JORDAN
IRAQ
IRAN
ZAGROS MOUNTAINS
KUWAIT
Persian Gulf
BAHRAIN
SAUDI ARABIA
QATAR
U.A.E.
RED SEA
RUB' AL-KHALI DESERT
OMAN
YEMEN
MEDITERRANEAN SEA
ANTARCTIC PEN.
WEDDELL SEA
QUEEN MAUD LAND
Antarctic Circle
Ronne Ice Shelf
ANTARCTICA
MARIE BYRD LAND
South Pole
Ross Ice Shelf
ROSS SEA
WILKES LAND
0°
10°
20°
30°
40°
60°
50°
55°
NORWAY
Oslo
SWEDEN
Stockholm
FINLAND
Helsinki
Tallinn
St. Petersburg
Lake Ladoga
ESTONIA
NORTH SEA
DENMARK
Copenhagen
LATVIA
Riga
BALTIC SEA
RUSSIA
LITHUANIA
Vilnius
Moscow
Hamburg
THE NETHERLANDS
Amsterdam
Berlin
POLAND
Warsaw
Łódź
BELARUS
Minsk
Homyel
GERMANY
Brussels
BELGIUM
Luxembourg
LUXEMBOURG
Prague
CZECH REPUBLIC
Kraków
UKRAINE
Kiev
Kharkiv
Dnipropetrovsk
Donetsk
LIECHTENSTEIN
Vienna
SLOVAKIA
Bratislava
Bern
Zürich
Vaduz
Munich
AUSTRIA
SWITZ.
Budapest
MOLDOVA
Chişinău
Odessa
CRIMEAN PEN.
Lyon
ALPS
HUNGARY
Ljubljana
Zagreb
ROMANIA
Turin
Milan
SLOVENIA
CROATIA
BOSNIA AND HERZEGOVINA
Bucharest
SAN MARINO
Sarajevo
Belgrade
YUGOSLAVIA
MONACO
ITALY
Danube
BLACK SEA
CORSICA (FRANCE)
Adriatic Sea
Sofia
BULGARIA
Rome
Tiranë
Skopje
Istanbul
SARDINIA (ITALY)
ALBANIA
MACEDONIA
Ankara
TURKEY
GREECE
İzmir
SICILY (ITALY)
Athens
MALTA
MEDITERRANEAN SEA
CYPRUS
CROATIA
ROMANIA
CRIMEAN PEN.
RUSSIA
KAZAKHSTAN
ARAL SEA
Sarajevo
BOS.-HER.
Belgrade
Bucharest
YUGOSLAVIA
BULGARIA
Sofia
BLACK SEA
ITALY
Tiranë
Skopje
Istanbul
Samsun
GEORGIA
Tbilisi
UZBEKISTAN
ALBANIA
MACEDONIA
Bursa
Ankara
Yerevan
AZERBAIJAN
Baku
ARMENIA
CASPIAN SEA
TURKMENISTAN
Eskişehir
TURKEY
Kayseri
GREECE
İzmir
Antalya
Gaziantep
Diyarbakır
Tabrīz
Ashgabat
Athens
Mersin
Aleppo
Mosul
SICILY (ITALY)
CYPRUS
Nicosia
SYRIA
Dayr az-Zawr
Tehrān
Mashhad
Beirut
Euphrates
Baghdad
LEBANON
Damascus
IRAN
AFGHANISTAN
MEDITERRANEAN SEA
ISRAEL
Amman
Tigris
Banghāzī
Alexandria
Jerusalem
West Bank*
IRAQ
Ahvāz
Eşfahān
Cairo
JORDAN
Basra
Suez Canal
Gaza Strip*
Kuwait
Shīrāz
LIBYA
KUWAIT
Tabūk
BAHRAIN
Manama
Persian Gulf
OMAN
Sabhā
EGYPT
Buraydah
Riyadh
Doha
Abu Dhabi
Nile
Medina
SAUDI ARABIA
QATAR
Al-Fujayrah
Muscat
TIBESTI MTS.
Lake Nasser
Aswān
Jiddah
Mecca
UNITED ARAB EMIRATES
RED SEA
SAHARA
Port Sudan
OMAN
Largeau
ERITREA
Asmera
YEMEN
ARABIAN SEA
Khartoum
Şan'ā'
Al-Mukallā
Lake Chad
CHAD
THE SUDAN
Ta'izz
N'Djamena
DJIBOUTI
Djibouti
Gulf of Aden
ETHIOPIA
* Final status to be determined by Israel and the Palestinian Authority.

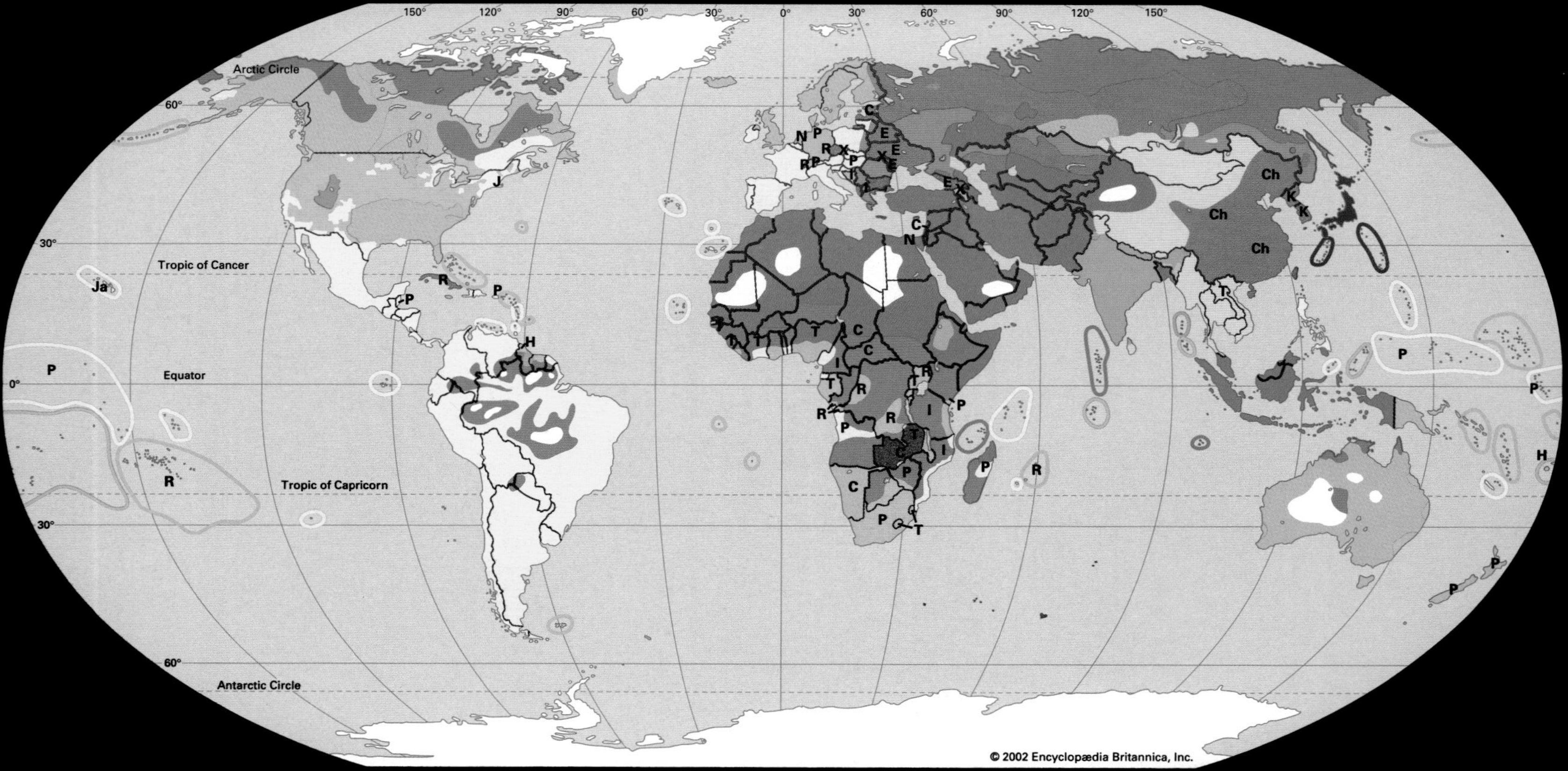

- Buddhism
- **Ch** Chinese religions[1]
- **C** Christianity, undifferentiated by branch[2]
- **E** Eastern Orthodoxy[3]
- **H** Hinduism
- **N** Independent churches of Eastern Christianity[4]
- **T** Indigenous (tribal) religions
- Islam, predominantly Sunni
- Islam, predominantly Shiʿite
- **Ja** Japanese religions[1]
- **J** Judaism
- **K** Korean religions[1]
- Mormonism
- Sikhism
- **P** Protestantism
- **R** Roman Catholicism
- **X** Nonreligious
- No dominant religion
- Uninhabited

Footnotes:

1 In certain eastern Asian areas, many of the people have plural religious affiliations. Chinese and Korean religions include Buddhism, Taoism, Confucianism, and folk cults. The Japanese religions include Shintō and Buddhism.

2 Chiefly mingled Protestantism and Roman Catholicism, neither predominant.

3 Including Greek and Russian Orthodox Christianity.

4 Including Armenian, Coptic, Ethiopian, East and West Syrian.

Note:

The majority of the inhabitants in each of the areas colored on the map share the religious tradition indicated. Letter symbols show religious traditions shared by at least 25 percent of the inhabitants within areas no smaller than 1,000 square miles. Therefore minority religions of city dwellers have generally not been represented.

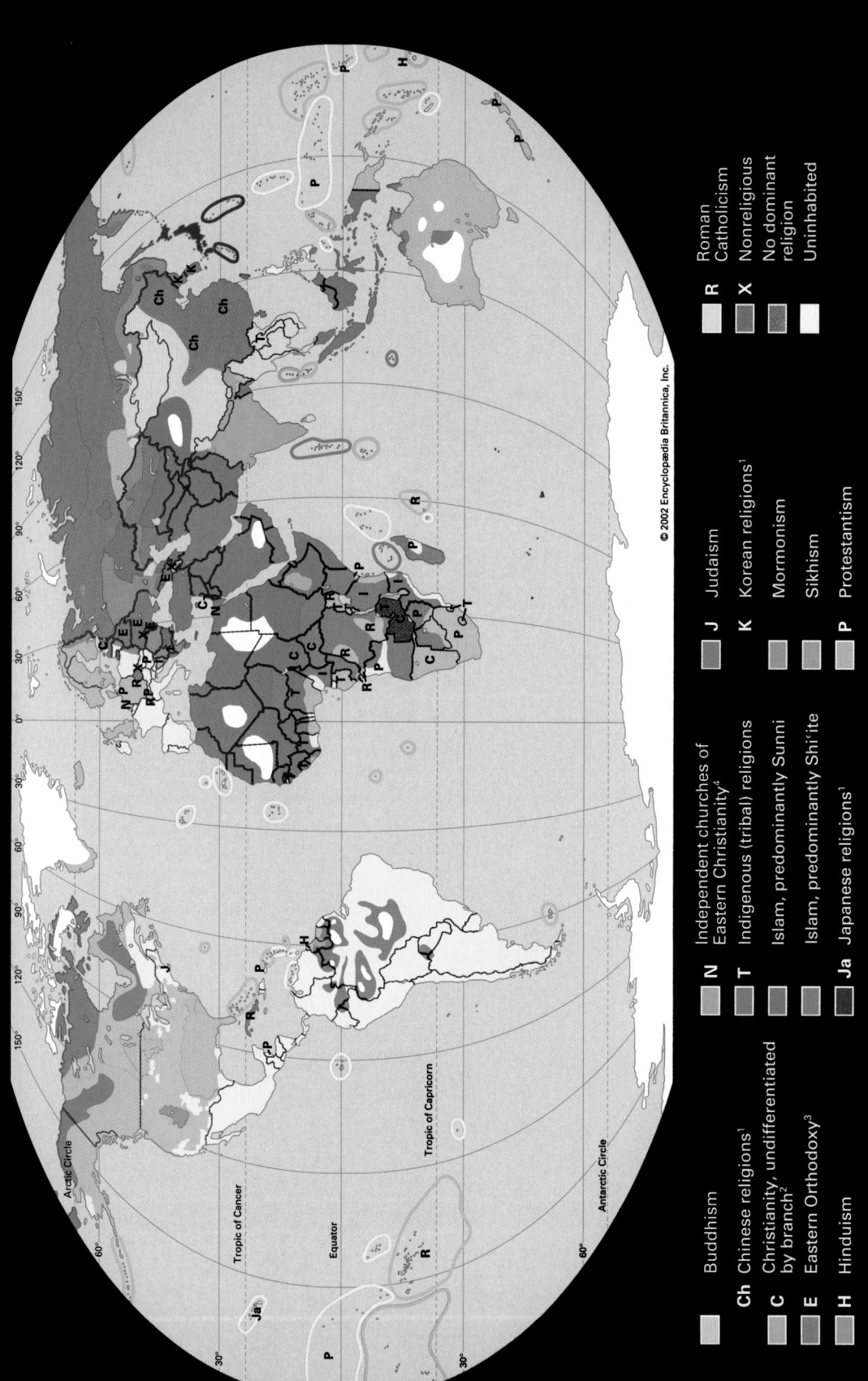

World Population Density

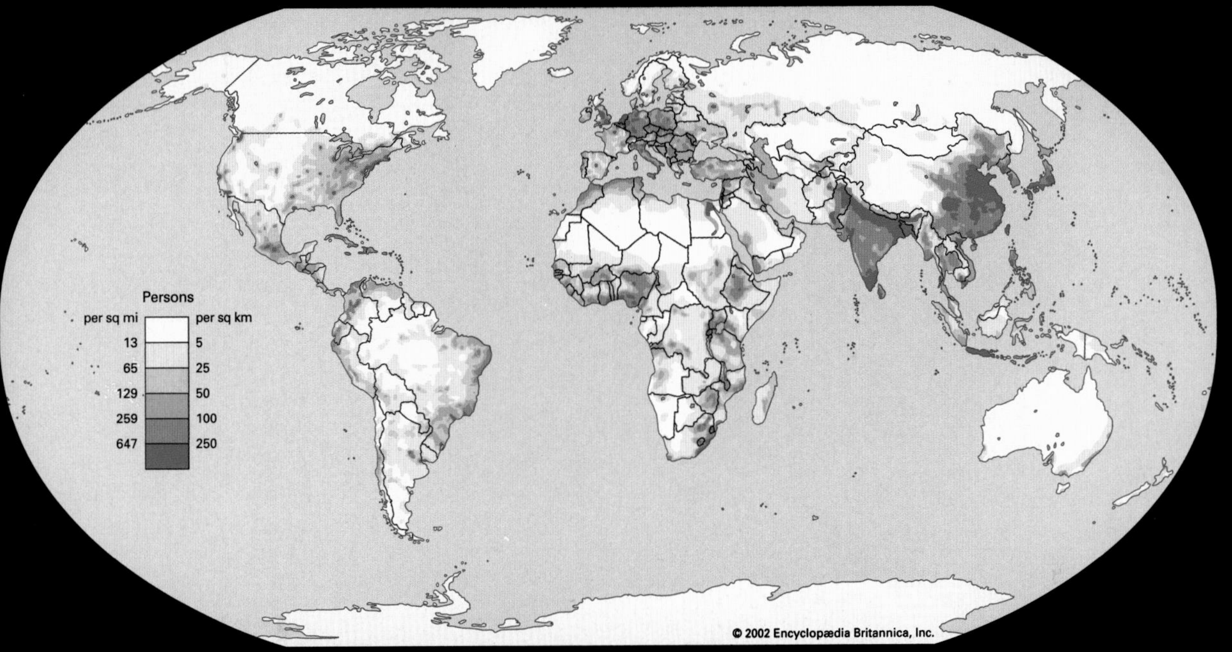

Indigenous Skin Color

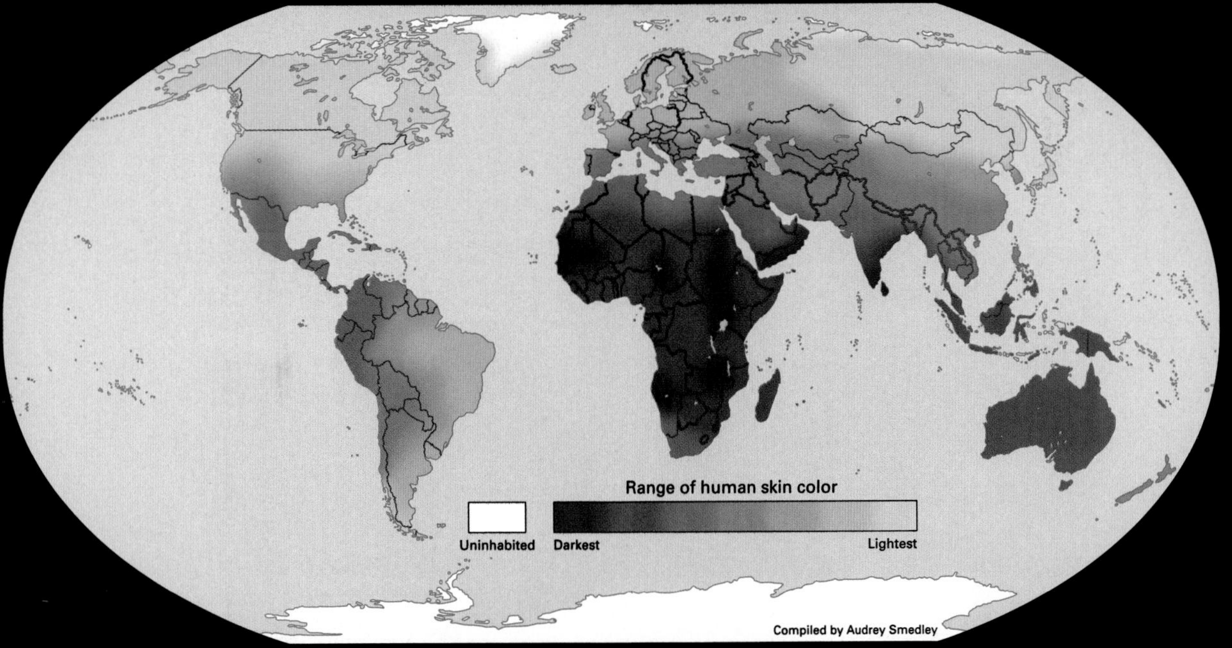

The distribution of skin color variations of indigenous populations before colonization by Europeans.
This map represents a reconstruction of populations based on a number of sources. In some cases, areal characteristics have been estimated from descriptions (or drawings) of first contact by the earliest Europeans. In other cases, where there was little European contact or where there is scant information about native populations (as, for example, the populations of Inner Asia), skin color was estimated from surrounding populations and geographic and climatological information. On a map of this scale, it is difficult to give more than a representation of current understanding. It must also be noted that many populations, even before the modern era, were quite heterogeneous in skin color, and this heterogeneity is difficult to depict accurately on any scale. In areas of the world where the indigenous population was sparse and widely scattered (such as Australia), the map's color density can be misleading. Further, some populations, such as the Tasmanians (who are virtually extinct) and Maoris (who have been widely mixed with Europeans), present only a few examples of "unmixed" individuals in historical records.

On this plate and the adjoining one is a sampling of official World Heritage sites, as designated by the United Nations Educational, Scientific and Cultural Organization (UNESCO).

This page (clockwise from top): Kilauea erupting, in Hawaii Volcanoes National Park, Hawaii, U.S. The limestone pillars of Ha Long Bay, on the Gulf of Tonkin, northern Vietnam. One of several figures among the Nazca Lines, which date from *c.* 200 BC to AD 600, in southern Peru. The ancient Acropolis of Athens, Greece. The Great Wall of China, sections of which were begun during the 7th century BC. Most of the sections still standing date from *c.* AD 1500.

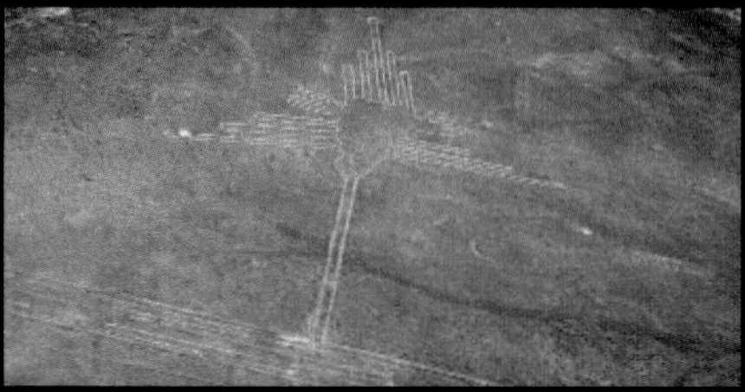

This page (clockwise from top): San Bartolomé Island, one of the Galapagos Islands, located about 600 miles (1,000 km) west of the mainland of Ecuador. The Pyramid of the Sun, in the ancient ruined city of Teotihuacán, Mexico. The Taj Mahal, considered the world's finest example of Mughal architecture, in Agra, northern India. African elephants traveling across the Serengeti Plain after a thunderstorm, in Serengeti National Park, northern Tanzania. The Segovia aqueduct, built during the reign of the Roman emperor Trajan (AD 98–117), in Segovia, Spain. The historic capital of Yemen.

Plate 15: Photographs (clockwise from top) Andrea Toback; all other photographs, Corbis: Werner Forman; Robert Holmes; W. Perry Conway; Vanni Archive; Charles and Josette Lenars.

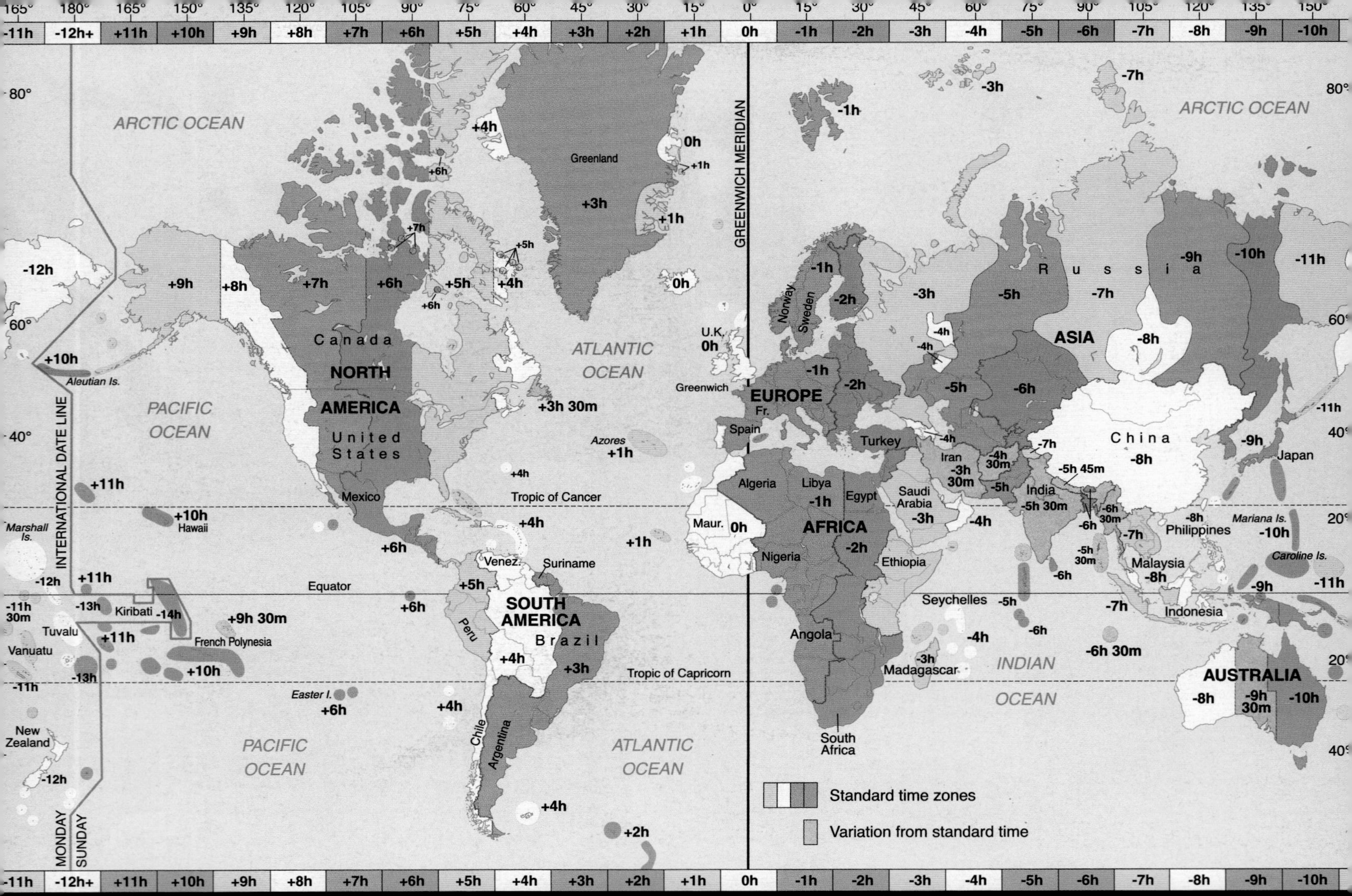

Time is calculated from the meridian of Greenwich, England. The middle of the zero time zone passes through Greenwich with its east and west limits 7°30' on each side. Each 15° zone east and west of the initial zone

I Am movement U.S. religious movement founded in the 1930s by Guy Ballard (1878–1939) and his wife, Edna (1886–1971). They taught that the Mighty I Am is the source of power in everything, a power available to individuals through a number of Ascended Masters, including Jesus. Another important Ascended Master, St. Germain, spoke to Guy Ballard at Mount Shasta in northern California and revealed Ballard's many previous lives. The movement suffered a setback when Guy died in 1939 and another when Edna and her son were indicted for fraud in 1940; though the indictment was set aside in 1946, the movement had by then lost its vitality.

I-ch'ang See Yichang

I ching See Yi jing

I-pin See Yibin

Iacocca \ˌī-ə-ˈkō-kə\, **Lee** *orig.* **Lido Anthony** (born 1924) U.S. automobile executive. Born in Allentown, Pa., he was hired as an engineer by Ford Motor Co. but soon moved to its sales department. He rose rapidly, becoming president of Ford in 1970. His brash manner led to his dismissal by Henry Ford II in 1978. A year later he was hired by the nearly bankrupt Chrysler Corp. He persuaded Congress to lend Chrysler $1.5 billion in 1980 and carried out layoffs, wage cuts, and plant closings to make the company more efficient, shifted the company's emphasis to more fuel-efficient cars, and embarked on an aggressive advertising campaign. Within a few years Chrysler was showing record profits, and Iacocca was a national celebrity with a best-selling autobiography, *Iacocca* (1984). He retired in 1992.

Iao Valley \ˈē-ˈau̇\ *or* **Wailuku Valley** \wī-ˈlü-kü\ Canyon, eastern slope of Mount Puu Kukui, on northwestern Maui Island, Hawaii. Formed by erosion, it is 5 mi (8 km) long and 4,000 ft (1,200 m) deep. Iao Needle, a volcanic monolith 2,250 ft (686 m) high, soars nearly straight up from the valley floor.

Iasi \ˈyäsh\ *German* **Jassy** \ˈyä-sē\ City (pop., 1994 est.: 340,000), northeastern Romania. Located west of the border with Moldova and northeast of Bucharest, it is on the Bahlui River. It was settled as early as the 7th century, and in the 15th century it became a customs post on the trade routes along the Prut River valley. From 1565 to 1862 it was the capital of Moldavia. It was burned by Tatars in 1513, by Turks in 1538, and by Russians in 1686. It is the site of a university, the 16th-century Church of St. Nicholas, and a national theater.

Ibadan \i-ˈbä-dᵊn, ˌē-bä-ˈdän\ City (pop., 1996 est.: 1,432,000), southwestern Nigeria. Situated northeast of Lagos, it is the nation's second largest city. The modern city grew from a camp set up by the armies of the Ife, Ijebu, and Oyo peoples in 1829; it was taken by the British in 1893. An important commercial center, it contains six parks, including Agodi Garden. It is the seat of the University of Ibadan.

Ibagué \ˌē-bä-ˈgā\ City (pop., 1997 est.: 420,000), central Colombia. It is located on the eastern slopes of the Andean Cordillera Central. Founded in 1550 on the site of an Indian village, it was moved to its present location because of Indian attacks. It was the republic's capital briefly in 1854. Its location on a road linking the cities of Armenia and Bogotá has made it a busy commercial center. It is the seat of Tolima Univ.

Ibáñez (del Campo) \ē-ˈbän-yās\, **Carlos** (1877–1960) Chilean soldier and president (1927–31, 1952–58). After a 30-year military career, he helped overthrow Pres. Arturo Alessandri Palma in 1924 and effectively controlled Chile until 1931. Backed by the army, he exiled or jailed all opponents, but failed in his attempt to rescue the ailing nitrate industry despite the help of U.S. capital. As the economy crumbled, discontent with Ibáñez's authoritarianism became overt and he fled the country. After twice attempting to regain power with the help of Chilean fascists, he won the 1952 presidential election by appealing to depressed workers, and proved to be a more democratic leader than expected. See also Juan Peron.

Ibara Saikaku See Ihara Saikaku

Ibarra, José Velasco See Jose Velasco Ibarra

Ibárruri (Gómez) \ē-ˈbä-rü-rē\, **(Isidora) Dolores** *known as* **La Pasionaria** (1895–1989) Spanish Communist leader. The daughter of a poor miner, she became radicalized in her youth. In 1918 she published an article using her pseudonym ("The Passionflower"), and in 1920 she joined Spain's new Communist Party. After a turbulent career, she emerged as a deputy in the Republican parliament. By the outbreak of the Spanish Civil War in 1936 she had won fame as a fiery and even violent street orator, and she coined the Republican battle cry, "No pasarán!" ("They shall not pass!"). With Francisco Franco's victory in 1939 she fled to the Soviet Union; she returned in 1977 after his death and the party's relegalization. Reelected to parliament, she resigned because of ill health, but remained honorary president of the party until her death.

Iberian Peninsula *or* **Iberia** Peninsula, southwestern Europe, occupied by Spain and Portugal. Its name derives from its ancient inhabitants whom the Greeks called Iberians, probably after the Ebro (Iberus) River, the peninsula's second longest river. The Pyrenees form a land barrier in the northeast from the rest of Europe, and in the south at Gibraltar the peninsula is separated from North Africa by a narrow strait. Its western and northern coasts are bordered by the Atlantic Ocean, and its eastern coast by the Mediterranean Sea. It includes Cape da Roca, in Portugal, the most westerly point of continental Europe.

Iberians Prehistoric people of southern and eastern Spain. They were largely untouched by the migrations of Celtic peoples to northern and central Spain from the 8th century BC on. Culturally they were influenced by Greek and Phoenician trading colonies. On the eastern coast, tribes seem to have formed independent city-states; in the south, they formed monarchies. Their economy was based on agriculture, mining, and metallurgy. Their non-Indo-European language continued into Roman times.

Iberville \ē-ber-ˈvēl\, **Pierre Le Moyne d'** (1661–1706) French-Canadian colonist and explorer. Son of a Montreal fur trader, he led raids on English fur-trading posts on Hudson Bay. He commanded expeditions against British settlements that by 1697 had expanded the area controlled by New France. He was sent south to fortify the Mississippi River delta and secure claims by Rene-Robert La Salle. The settlement he founded on Biloxi Bay (1699) and forts he built below present-day New Orleans (1700) and on the Mobile River (1702) led to the later colonization of Louisiana.

ibex \ˈī-ˌbeks\ Any of several species of surefooted, sturdy wild goats found in the mountains of Europe, Asia, and North Africa. Ibex are typically about 3 ft (90 cm) tall at the shoulder and have brownish gray fur that is darker on the underparts. The male has a beard and large, semicircular horns.

Ibibio \ˌib-ə-ˈbē-ō\ People of southeastern Nigeria who speak Ibibio, a Benue-Congo language of the Niger-Congo family. The Ibibio, numbering 3 million, are mainly rainforest cultivators. Lineage heads serve as guardians of ancestral shrines. Secret societies are prominent. The Ibibio are noted for their wood sculptures of ancestor figures (*ekpu*).

ibis \ˈī-bəs\ Any of about 20 species of medium-sized wading birds (subfamily Threskiornithinae) of the same family as the spoonbills. Ibises are found in all warm regions except on South Pacific islands. They wade in shallow lagoons, lakes, bays, and marshes, using their slender, down-curved bill to feed on small fishes and soft mollusks. Species range from 22 to 30 in. (55–75 cm) long. Ibises fly with neck and

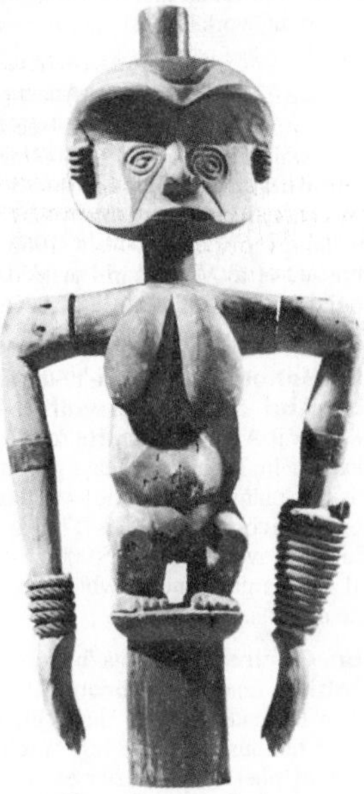

Carved figure from a male dancer's headdress, Ibibio people, Nigeria, in the Metropolitan Museum of Art, New York City.

BY COURTESY OF THE METROPOLITAN MUSEUM OF ART, NEW YORK CITY, THE MICHAEL C. ROCKEFELLER MEMORIAL COLLECTION, GIFT OF THE MATTHEW J. MELLON

legs extended, alternately flapping and sailing. They usually breed in vast colonies.

Ibiza \ē-ˈbē-zä\ Third largest island (pop., 1995 est.: 70,000) of the BALEARIC ISLANDS, Spain. Situated in the western Mediterranean, southwest of MAJORCA, it has an area of 221 sq mi (572 sq km); its capital is the town of Ibiza (pop., 1991: 28,000). A flourishing settlement in ancient times, it was inhabited by the Phoenicians and Carthaginians and has notable archaeological sites. Its landscape is hilly, and its rugged northern coast has cliffs exceeding 800 ft (245 m) in height. Its beaches and mild winter climate make it a popular tourist center.

Iblis \i-ˈblēs\ In ISLAM, the personal name of the DEVIL. Iblis was one of God's ANGELS who refused to venerate ADAM at creation. He and his followers were thrown down from heaven and await punishment at the Last Judgment. Until then he is allowed to tempt everyone but true believers to do evil. It was he who tempted ADAM AND EVE in the Garden of Eden and caused the Fall.

IBM Corp. *in full* **International Business Machines Corp.** Leading U.S. computer manufacturer, headquartered in Armonk, N.Y. It was incorporated in 1911 as the Computing-Tabulating-Recording Co., a consolidation of three office-products companies. It adopted its present name in 1924 under the leadership of THOMAS J. WATSON SR., who built it into the major U.S. manufacturer of punch-card tabulators. IBM bought an electric-typewriter company in 1933 and soon secured a large share of that market. In the early 1950s it entered the computer industry, investing heavily in development, and in the 1960s it produced 70% of the world's computers. Its initial specialty was mainframe computers, but in 1981 it produced its first PERSONAL COMPUTER, the IBM PC. IBM quickly became a leader in this field, but fierce competition undermined its market share and forced the company to retrench in the 1990s. In 1995 IBM bought the software manufacturer Lotus Development Corp.

Ibn al-Arabi \ˌib-nu̇l-ȧr-ȧ-ˈbē\ (1165–1240) Islamic mystic and theologian. Born in Spain, he traveled widely in Spain and North Africa in search of masters of Sufism. In 1198 he began a pilgrimage to the Near East, visiting Mecca, Egypt, and Anatolia before settling in Damascus in 1223. Famous and honored as a spiritual master, he spent the rest of his life in contemplation, teaching, and writing. His great work was *The Meccan Revelations*, a personal encyclopedia covering all the esoteric sciences in Islam and his own inner life. He also wrote one of the most important works in Islamic mystical philosophy, *The Bezels of Wisdom* (1229).

Ibn Aqil \ˌi-bən-a-ˈkēl\ (1040–1119) Islamic theologian. Trained in the tenets of the Hanbali school (see AHMAD IBN HANBAL), the most traditional school of Islamic law, he outraged his teachers by striving to incorporate liberal theological ideas into the tradition. He sought to use reason and logical inquiry to interpret religion, and he was influenced by the teachings of al-HALLAJ. In 1066 he was appointed professor at the mosque of al-Mansur in Baghdad, but persecution by conservative theologians soon led to his retirement, and in 1072 he was forced to retract his beliefs publicly.

Ibn Battutah \ˌib-ən-ba-ˈtü-tä\ *in full* **Abu Abd Allah Muhammad ibn Abd Allah al-Lawati al-Tanji ibn Battutah** (1304–1368/69) Medieval Arab traveler. He received a traditional juristic and literary education in Tangier. After a pilgrimage to Mecca (1325), he decided to visit as many parts of the world as possible, vowing "never to travel any road a second time." His 27-year wanderings through Africa, Asia, and Europe covered some 75,000 mi (120,000 km). On his return, he dictated his reminiscences, which became one of the world's most famous travel books, the *Rihlah*.

Ibn Gabirol \ˌi-bən-gä-ˈbē-ro̊l\ *in full* **Solomon ben Yehuda ibn Gabirol** *Latin* **Avicebron** (1022?–1058/70?) Jewish poet and philosopher. Educated in both the Hebrew and Arabic literary heritages, he became famous at age 16 for his religious hymns in Hebrew, and was later a court poet of the vizier of Granada. The more than 200 secular and 200 religious poems that survive make him an outstanding figure of the Hebrew school of poetry that flourished in Moorish Spain. Other works include influential writings of Neoplatonic philosophy and a collection of proverbs in Arabic.

Ibn Hazm \ˌi-bən-ˈk̲ä-zəm\ *in full* **Abu Muhammad Ali ibn Ahmad ibn Said ibn Hazm** (994–1064) Islamic scholar and theologian. Born in Spain, he lived through the civil war that ended the Spanish Umayyad caliphate and was afterwards imprisoned for having supported it. As a leader of the Zahiri school of jurisprudence, he taught that legal theory must rely on a literal interpretation of the Quran and tradition. His beliefs were often attacked, and his books were burned in public. His scholarship included not only jurisprudence and theology but also logic, literature, and history. Famed for his mastery of Arabic, he wrote about 400 books, fewer than 40 of which survive.

Ibn Ishaq \ˌi-bən-ēs-ˈhȧk\ *in full* **Muhammad ibn Ishaq ibn Yasar ibn Khiyar** (704?–767) Arab biographer of Muhammad. His father and two uncles collected and transmitted information about Muhammad in Medina, and Ibn Ishaq soon became an authority on the Prophet's campaigns. He studied in Alexandria and moved to Iraq, during which time he met many people who provided him with information for his biography, which became the most popular biography of Muhammad in the Muslim world.

Ibn Janah \ˌib-ən-ja-ˈnak̲\ *or* **Rabbi Jonah** (c. 990–c. 1050) Spanish scholar famed as a Hebrew grammarian and lexicographer. A practicing physician and a devout Jew, he founded the study of Hebrew syntax, establishing the rules of biblical exegesis and clarifying many difficult passages. His principal work was the two-volume *Book of Exact Investigation*, a Hebrew grammar and lexicon. All his writings were in Arabic, and he made extensive comparisons of Hebrew and Arabic words.

Ibn Khaldun \ˌib-ən-k̲al-ˈdün\ *in full* **Abu Zayd Abd al-Rahman ibn Khaldun** (1332–1406) Arab historian. Born in Tunis, he was employed in court posts by various rulers in Tunis, Fez, and Granada. After retiring from politics in 1375, he wrote his masterpiece, the *Muqaddimah* ("Introduction to History"), in which he examined the nature of society and social change and developed one of the earliest nonreligious philosophies of history. He also wrote a definitive history of Muslim North Africa, *Kitab al-ibar*. In 1382 he went to Cairo, where he was appointed professor and religious judge. Caught in TIMUR's siege of Damascus in 1400, he negotiated the freedom of civilians before the sack of the city. He is regarded as the greatest of medieval Arab historians.

Ibn Rushd See AVERROËS

Ibn Saud \ˌib-ən-sȧ-ˈüd\, **Abdulaziz** (c. 1880–1953) Founder of modern-day Saudi Arabia. Though the Sauds had ruled much of Arabia from 1780 to 1880 (see SAUD DYNASTY), in Ibn Saud's infancy the family was forced out by its rivals, the Rashids. At 21 Ibn Saud led a daring raid against the Rashids and recaptured the Saudi capital, Riyadh. He was driven out two years later, but reconstituted his forces and fought on, using religion to rally nomadic tribesmen to his cause, and in 1920–22 he defeated the Rashids and doubled his own territory. In 1924 he conquered the HEJAZ (see Sharif HUSAYN IBN ALI). In 1932 he formally created the kingdom of Saudi Arabia, which he ruled as an absolute monarch. He signed his first oil deal in 1933 but remained virtually penniless until the 1950s, when oil revenues began pouring in. His sons succeeded him.

Ibn Saud.
CAMERA PRESS

Ibn Sina See AVICENNA

Ibn Taymiya \ˌi-bən-tī-ˈmē-ä\ (1263–1328) Islamic theologian. Born in Mesopotamia, he was educated in Damascus, where he joined the Pietist school. He sought to return Islam to a strict interpretation of its sources in the Quran and the sunna, and to rid it of customs he considered contrary to the law, including the worship of saints. He was imprisoned repeatedly in Cairo after his outspoken criticisms offended religious authorities. He spent his last 15 years as a schoolmaster in Damascus, where he gathered many disciples. He died in prison. His writings are the source of the Wahhabi movement, founded by Muhammad ibn Abd al-WAHHAB.

Ibn Tibbon \ˌi-bən-ˈti-bən\, **Judah ben Saul** (1120–c. 1190) Jewish physician and translator. He was born in Granada, but persecutions of the Jews forced him to flee Spain, and he settled in southern France in 1150 to practice medicine. His translations of philosophical works by Arabic-speaking Jews helped disseminate Arabic and Greek culture in medieval Europe. His son and grandson were also noted scholars and translators.

Ibn Tulun Mosque \ˌi-bən-tü-ˈlün\ Huge, majestic red-brick complex built 876–79 at present-day Cairo by Ahmad ibn Tulun (835–884), the Turkish governor of Egypt and Syria. The mosque's crenellated walls have merlons (see BATTLEMENT) that are shaped and perforated in a decorative pattern, and its three courts are lined with arcades of broad arches and heavy pillars. The arches are decorated with elaborately carved stucco. The main space is divided by pillars into five long aisles originally ornamented with panels of carved wood. Classed as a historic monument in 1890, the mosque has since been completely restored.

Ibo See IGBO

Ibrahim Pasha \ib-rä-ˈhēm-ˈpash-ä\ (1789–1848) Egyptian general. After helping train the new Egyptian army, he won military fame in Syria, defeating an Ottoman force, and Syria and Adana were ceded to Egypt, with Ibrahim as governor-general (1833). His administration was relatively enlightened; he created a consultative council and suppressed the feudal regime. Sultan Mahmud II (r.1808–39) then sent an Ottoman army to invade Syria, and Ibrahim won his greatest victory in 1839 when the Ottoman fleet deserted to Egypt. However, the European powers, fearing the disintegration of the OTTOMAN EMPIRE, forced the Egyptians to evacuate the occupied territories. Ibrahim became viceroy of Egypt in 1848 shortly before his death.

Ibsen \ˈip-sən, *Engl* ˈib-sən\, **Henrik (Johan)** (1828–1906) Norwegian playwright. At 23 he became theater director and resident playwright of the new National Theater at Bergen, charged with creating a "national drama." He directed the Norwegian Theater from 1857 to 1863, when the theater went bankrupt. He then set off on extended travels in Europe, beginning a self-imposed exile that would last until 1891. In Italy he wrote the troubling moral tragedy *Brand* (1866) and the buoyant *Peer Gynt* (1867). After the satire *Pillars of Society* (1877) he found his voice and an international audience with powerful studies of middle-class morality in *A Doll's House* (1879), *Ghosts* (1881), *An Enemy of the People* (1882), *The Wild Duck* (1884), and *Rosmersholm* (1886). His more symbolic plays, most of them written after his return in 1891, include *Hedda Gabler* (1890), *The Master Builder* (1892), *Little Eyolf* (1894), and *When We Dead Awaken* (1899). Emphasizing character over plot, Ibsen addressed social problems such as political corruption and the changing role of women as well as psychological conflicts stemming from frustrated love and destructive family relationships. He greatly influenced European theater and is regarded as the founder of modern prose drama.

Ibsen, 1870.

UNIVERSITETSBIBLIOTEKET, OSLO

ibuprofen \ˌī-byu̇-ˈprō-fən\ ANALGESIC, one of the NSAIDs, especially effective against DYSMENORRHEA, dental pain, and RHEUMATOID-ARTHRITIS pain. It reduces pain, fever, and inflammation by inhibiting PROSTAGLANDIN synthesis. It may irritate the gastrointestinal tract and should not be taken by anyone who has an ALLERGY to ASPIRIN or takes ANTICOAGULANTS. Brand names include Advil, Motrin, and Nuprin. See also ACETAMINOPHEN.

IC See INTEGRATED CIRCUIT

Icarus See DAEDALUS

ICBM *in full* **intercontinental ballistic missile** GUIDED MISSILE with a range of more than 3,300 mi (5,300 km). The MX Peacekeeper has a range of more than 6,000 mi (9,600 km). ICBMs include the silo-launched MINUTEMAN MISSILE and the submarine-launched TRIDENT MISSILE. The first ICBMs were developed by the Soviet Union in 1958, but within four years the U.S. had achieved significant superiority.

ice SOLID form of WATER and water vapor. Below 32°F (0°C), liquid water forms a solid and water vapor forms frost on surfaces and snowflakes in clouds. Unlike most liquids, water expands on freezing, so ice is less dense than liquid water and therefore floats. It consists of compact aggregates of many CRYSTALS (with hexagonal symmetry), but ice formed from liquid does not normally have crystal faces. Molecules in the crystal are held together by hydrogen bonds (see HYDROGEN BONDING). With a very high DIELECTRIC constant, ice conducts electricity much better than most nonmetallic crystals. At very high pressures, at least five other crystal forms of ice occur.

ice age *or* **glacial age** Any geologic period during which thick ice sheets cover vast areas of land. Such periods of large-scale glaciation may last several million years and drastically reshape surface features of entire continents. A number of major ice ages have occurred throughout the earth's history; the most recent periods were during the PLEISTOCENE EPOCH (1.6 million–10,000 years ago).

ice cream Frozen dairy food made from CREAM or butterfat, MILK, sugar, and flavorings. Fruit ices (fruit-flavored nondairy frozen desserts) were introduced into Europe from the East sometime after being first described by MARCO POLO in his journals. Creation of the first true creamed ice is credited to a Parisian café owner named Tortoni in the late 18th century. The ice-cream cone originated at the 1904 World's Fair in St. Louis, Mo. Commercial ice cream is made by heating and blending its ingredients to form a mix, which is then pasteurized and homogenized. The mix is ripened for several hours and then agitated while being frozen to incorporate air; the highest-quality ice creams incorporate the least air. Ice cream is now available in hundreds, if not thousands, of flavors.

ice dancing Sport in which ice-skating pairs perform to music routines similar to BALLROOM DANCES. Ice dancers are judged on the difficulty and originality of their dance steps, their interpretation of the music, and their timing and unison. Unlike FIGURE SKATING, ice dancing does not allow movements of strength or technical skill (particularly overhead lifts, jumps, and spins of more than one-and-a-half rotations). It has been an Olympic event since 1976.

French ice dancers Isabelle and Paul Duchesnay competing at the World Ice-Dance Championships.

© DUOMO PHOTOGRAPHY

ice formation Any mass of ice that occurs on the earth's continents or surface waters. Such masses form wherever substantial amounts of liquid water freeze and remain in the solid state for some period of time. Examples include glaciers, icebergs, pack ice, and ground ice associated with PERMAFROST.

ice hockey Game played on an ice rink by two teams of six players on skates whose object is to drive a puck (a small, hard rubber disk) into the opponents' goal with a hockey stick, thus scoring one point. The first true hockey game was played in 1875 between two student teams at Montreal's McGill University. The NATIONAL HOCKEY LEAGUE, consisting of U.S. and Canadian professional teams, was organized in 1917. Hockey was introduced at the Olympic Games in 1920. It is a very aggressive game; the puck is often stripped from a player by means of a hit (check) to the body, though some hits are illegal and draw penalties. A game consists of three 20-minute periods. See also STANLEY CUP.

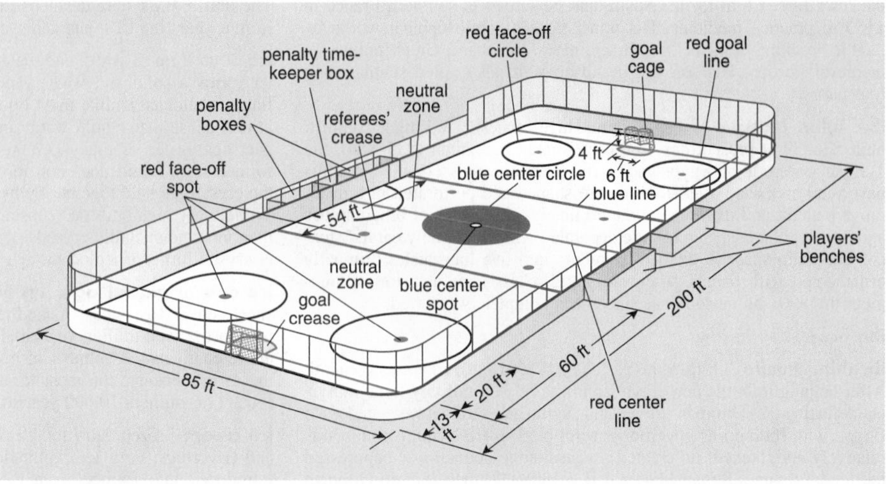

A typical professional North American ice-hockey rink. U.S. college rinks are usually wider (100 ft), and international rinks vary in both length and width. Blue lines mark the respective off-sides areas; the space between them is called the neutral zone. The puck is put into play by being dropped between two players at the face-off spots; all players except those facing off must stand outside the face-off circle. A major penalty requires that a player go to the penalty box for five minutes while his team plays shorthanded.

iceberg Floating mass of ice that has broken from the seaward end of a glacier or a polar ice sheet. Icebergs are typically found in open seas, especially around Greenland and Antarctica. They form mostly during the spring and summer, when warmer weather increases the rate of calving (separation) of icebergs at the boundaries of the Greenland and Antarctic ice sheets and smaller outlying glaciers. In the Northern Hemisphere, about 10,000 icebergs are produced each year from the Greenland glaciers, and an average of 375 flow into the North Atlantic shipping lanes, where they are a hazard to navigation, especially because only about 10% of an iceberg is exposed above the surface of the sea.

Iceland *officially* **Republic of Iceland** *Icelandic* **Ísland** \'ē-ˌslänt\ Island country, located in the northern Atlantic Ocean, lying between Norway and Greenland. Area: 40,000 sq mi (100,000 sq km). Population (1997) est.: 271,000. Capital: REYKJAVIK. The people are overwhelmingly

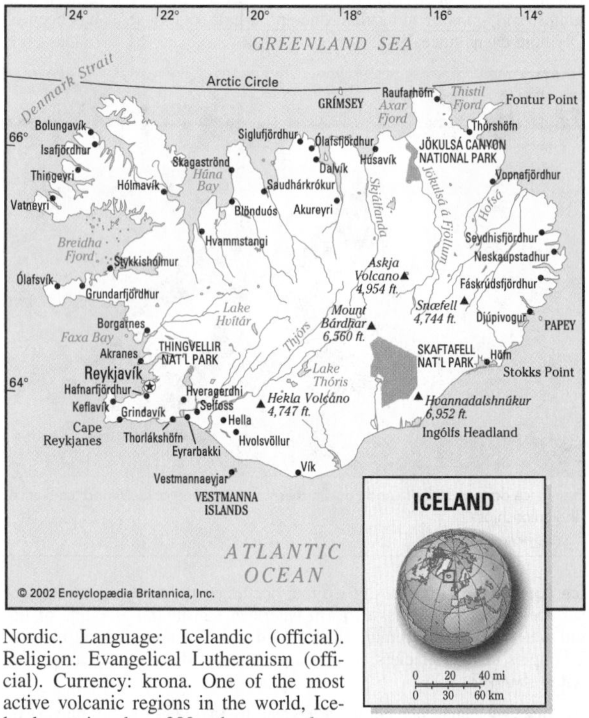

Nordic. Language: Icelandic (official). Religion: Evangelical Lutheranism (official). Currency: krona. One of the most active volcanic regions in the world, Iceland contains about 200 volcanoes and accounts for one-third of the earth's total lava flow. One-tenth of its area is covered by cooled lava beds and glaciers, including VATNAJÖKULL. Its rugged coastline is 3,700 mi (6,000 km) long. The economy is based heavily on fishing and fish products but also includes hydropower production, livestock, and aluminum processing. It is a republic with one legislative house; its chief of state is the president, and the head of government is the prime minister. Iceland was settled by Norwegian seafarers in the 9th century and was Christianized by 1000. Its legislature, the Althing, was founded in 930, making it one of the oldest legislative assemblies in the world. Iceland united with NORWAY in 1262 and with DENMARK in 1380. It became an independent state of Denmark in 1918, but severed those ties to become an independent republic in 1944. Vigdís Finnbogadóttir became the world's first female elected president in 1980. Much of Iceland's 1990s economic growth was in the expansion of its aluminum production capacity.

Icelanders' sagas *or* **family sagas** Class of heroic prose narratives written in the 13th century about the great families who lived in Iceland 930–1030. They represent the zenith of classical Icelandic saga writing and are far in advance of any contemporary medieval literature in their realism, controlled style, character delineation, and overwhelming tragic dignity. Their artistic unity, length, and complexity suggest that they were written by individual authors rather than composed orally. Justice, not courage, is often the primary virtue, as in the greatest of the family sagas, *NJÁLS SAGA*.

Icelandic language National language of Iceland, one of the GERMANIC LANGUAGES. It developed from the Norse speech brought to Iceland by settlers from western Norway in the 9th–10th century. Old Icelandic (see OLD NORSE) is the language of the SAGAS and other medieval poems. In grammar, vocabulary, and spelling, modern Icelandic is the most conservative of the Scandinavian languages; Icelanders can still read Old Norse sagas. Icelandic once borrowed words from Danish, Latin, and the Celtic and Romance languages, but a purist movement that began in the early 19th century has replaced most of these loanwords with words formed only from Icelandic elements.

Iceman, The Body of a man found sealed in a glacier in the Tirolean Ötztal Alps in 1991 and dated to 3300 BC. It has revealed significant details of everyday life during the NEOLITHIC PERIOD. The Iceman (also called Similaun Man or Ötzi, after the glacier and valley) is tattooed on parts of his body and has trimmed hair; it had previously been thought that tattooing and hair cutting began much later in Europe. He wore neatly stitched deerskin clothing, a woven grass cape, and leather shoes stuffed with grass for insulation. He carried two fungi on leather thongs, probably for medicinal purposes, and a birchbark box containing food supplies. His other equipment included a copper ax, a flint dagger, a yew bow, and a deerskin quiver holding expertly finished arrows. Although it was initially believed that he had died of freezing, X-ray examination in 2001 showed that an arrowhead was lodged in his left shoulder, suggesting that he had likely bled to death after being shot.

Ichikawa, Kon (born 1915) Japanese motion-picture director. Ichikawa graduated from the Ichioka Commercial School in Osaka. He worked in the animation department at the J.O. motion-picture studio and entered the Toho Motion Picture Company in 1942, when J.O. was merged with Toho. He directed his first motion picture, *Musume Dojo-ji* (*A Girl at Dojo Temple*), in 1946. *Sambyaku rokujugo ya* (1948; "Three Hundred and Sixty-five Nights") was his first big box-office success. He collaborated with his wife, Natto Wada, a screenwriter, on the screenplays for many of his early films. Ichikawa introduced sophisticated Western-style comedy to Japan in the 1950s and later became concerned with more serious subjects such as antiwar sentiment and modern man's search for identity.

ICI See IMPERIAL CHEMICAL INDUSTRIES PLC

Ickes \'i-kəs\, **Harold L(eClair)** (1874–1952) U.S. social activist and public official. Born in Frankstown Township, Pa., he practiced law in Chicago, doing frequent pro bono work and fighting for municipal reform. As a liberal Republican, he helped swing progressive votes to the Democrats in 1932. Appointed secretary of the interior by FRANKLIN ROOSEVELT (1933–46), he fought for the preservation of natural resources against private exploitation. He also headed the PUBLIC WORKS ADMINISTRATION (1933–39), spending over $5 billion on highways, public buildings, and dams. His scrutiny of each project ensured that it was graft-free but delayed the intended economic stimulus.

icon In EASTERN ORTHODOXY, the representation of sacred persons or events in murals, mosaics, or paintings on wood. After the Iconoclastic Controversy of the 8th–9th century, which disputed the religious function and meaning of icons (see ICONOCLASM), the Eastern churches formulated an official doctrine that approved their use, stating that since God had assumed material form in the person of Jesus, he and other sacred personages could be represented in works of art. Usually depicting Jesus or Mary but also sometimes saints, icons are relied on as objects of veneration and as tools for instruction.

"Annunciation," reverse of a double-sided painted panel icon from Constantinople, early 14th century; in the Skopolije Museum, Skopje, Macedonia.
HIRMER FOTOARCHIV, MUNCHEN

iconoclasm Destruction of religious images. In Christianity and Islam, iconoclasm was based on the Old Testament prohibition against making graven images, which were associated with idolatry. The making of portraits of Christ and the saints was opposed in the early Christian church, but ICONS had become popular in Christian worship by the end of the 6th century, and defenders of icon worship emphasized the symbolic nature of the images. Opposition to icons by LEO III in 726 led to the Iconoclastic Controversy, which continued in the Eastern church for more than a century before icons were again accepted. Statues and portraits of saints and religious figures were also common in the Western church, though some Protestant sects eventually rejected them. Islam still bans all icons, and iconoclasm has played a role in the conflicts between Muslims and Hindus in India.

iconostasis \ˌī-kə-'näs-tə-səs\ In Eastern Christian churches of Byzantine tradition, a solid screen of stone, wood, or metal separating the sanctuary from the NAVE. It has a royal door in the center and two smaller doors on either side. Covered with panel icons, it always includes the icon of the Incarnation (mother with child) on the left and the second coming of Christ on the right; icons of the four Evangelists, the Annunciation, and the Last Supper cover the royal doors themselves.

id In Freudian psychoanalytic theory, one of the three aspects of the human personality, along with the EGO and SUPEREGO. The id is the source of instinctual impulses such as sex and aggression as well as primitive needs that exist at birth. It is entirely nonrational and functions according to the pleasure-pain principle, seeking immediate fulfillment of its impulses whenever possible. Its working processes are completely unconscious in the adult, but it supplies the energy for conscious mental life, and it plays an especially important role in modes of expression that have a nonrational element, such as the making of art. The primary methods for unmasking its content, according to SIGMUND FREUD, are dream analysis and free association.

Ida, Mt. Name of both a mountain in Turkey and the highest mountain in CRETE, Greece. The Turkish mountain, near the site of ancient TROY, was a classical shrine, where PARIS passed judgment on the rival goddesses. From its highest point, about 5,800 ft (1,800 m), the gods are said to have witnessed the TROJAN WAR. The Greek mountain, in western central Crete, reaches 8,058 ft (2,456 m). It too was a classical shrine, containing the legendary cave where ZEUS was reared.

Idaho State (pop., 1997 est.: 1,210,000), northwestern U.S. It covers 83,557 sq mi (216,413 sq km); its capital is BOISE. It is dominated by the ROCKY MTNS., which extend from the Canadian border to southern central Idaho and along the Wyoming border. Its most extensive valley surrounds the SNAKE RIVER, which flows through HELLS CANYON, the deepest gorge in North America. First occupied by American Indians, the region was explored by the LEWIS AND CLARK EXPEDITION in 1805. It was part of the disputed Oregon Country that passed to the U.S. when Britain relinquished its claims by treaty in 1846. Discovery of gold in 1860 brought an influx of settlers. It became Idaho Territory in 1863 and was admitted to the Union as the 43rd state in 1890. Labor protests during 1890–1910 involving the INDUSTRIAL WORKERS OF THE WORLD erupted frequently. During the late 20th cent, Idaho developed its agriculture and industry, and promoted its natural wilderness.

Idaho, University of Public university with a main campus in Moscow and branch campuses in Coeur d'Alene, Boise, and Idaho Falls. It offers a wide range of bachelor's degree programs and is the state's primary center of graduate education. A land-grant university, it was established in 1889. It is noted for degree programs relating to the environment, natural resources, and their management. Total enrollment is about 11,000.

ideal gas See PERFECT GAS

idealism In METAPHYSICS, the view that stresses the central role of the ideal or the spiritual in the constitution of the world and in mankind's interpretation of experience. Idealism may hold that the world or reality exists essentially as spirit or consciousness, that abstractions and laws are more fundamental in reality than sensory things, or, at least, that whatever exists is known to mankind in dimensions that are chiefly mental—that is, through and as ideas. Metaphysical idealism asserts the ideality of reality; epistemological idealism holds that in the knowledge process the mind can grasp only its own contents. Metaphysical idealism is thus directly opposed to MATERIALISM, and epistemological idealism is opposed to REALISM. Absolute idealism (see G. W. F. HEGEL) includes the following principles: (1) the everyday world of things and persons is not the world as it really is but merely as it appears in terms of uncriticized categories; (2) the best reflection of the world is in terms of a self-conscious mind; (3) thought is the relation of each particular experience with the infinite whole of which it is an expression; and (4) truth consists in relationships of coherence between thoughts, rather than in a correspondence between thoughts and external realities (see COHERENTISM). See also GEORGE BERKELEY.

Idelsohn \'ē-dᵊl-ˌzōn\, **Abraham (Zevi)** (1882–1938) Latvian musicologist. After studies in Germany, he served as a synagogue cantor (from 1903) before moving to Johannesburg, Israel, the U.S., and after a stroke in 1934, back to Johannesburg. His monumental comparative studies of Jewish music in many parts of the world established that the tradition had remained relatively unchanged over time and also suggested connections between Jewish chant and the origins of Gregorian chant. He composed the first Hebrew opera, *Yiftah* (1922), and the song "Hava nagila."

Identity Christianity North American Christian movement that identifies Anglo-Saxon and other European peoples with the lost tribes of ISRAEL. Anti-Semitic and racist, Identity Christianity posits that God's COVENANT was actually with the European peoples and that the Jews are the offspring of Eve and Satan, and it characterizes blacks as subhuman.

H
I
J
K

Though it has been largely unsuccessful in persuading "white Israelites" of their purported identity, small churches are active (mainly in the northwestern U.S.) and the movement proselytizes through publications, recordings, and the Internet.

identity of indiscernibles Principle enunciated by G. W. LEIBNIZ that denies the possibility of two objects being numerically distinct while sharing all their qualitative properties in common. More formally, it states that if *x* is not identical to *y*, then there is some property *P* such that *P* holds of *x* and does not hold of *y*, or that *P* holds of *y* and does not hold of *x*. Equivalently, if *x* and *y* share all their properties, then *x* is identical to *y*. Its converse, the principle of the indiscernibility of identicals (also known as Leibniz's Law), asserts that if *x* is identical to *y*, then every property of *x* is a property of *y*, and vice versa. In extensional logic, the principle of the indiscernibility of identicals is indisputable and has the status of a law of logic.

identity theory Response to the MIND–BODY PROBLEM that asserts that mental and physical properties, however capable of being logically distinguished, are in actuality but different expressions of a single reality that is material. Strong emphasis is placed on the empirical status of such statements as "Thought is reducible to motion in the brain."

ideology System of ideas that seeks both to explain the world and to change it. The word was coined in 1796 by the French writer A. L. C. Destutt de Tracy (1754–1836) as a label for his "science of ideas." Certain characteristics of his thought proved generally true of ideologies, including a more or less comprehensive theory of society, a political program, anticipation of a struggle to implement that program (thus requiring committed followers), and intellectual leadership. Destutt de Tracy's ideas were adopted by the French DIRECTORY in building its version of a democratic, rational, and scientific society. Napoleon first gave the word a negative connotation with his scorn for what he called *idéologues.* Ideology is often contrasted unfavorably with PRAGMATISM. The significance of ideology follows from the fact that power is rarely exercised without some ideas or beliefs that justify support.

idiopathic respiratory distress syndrome See RESPIRATORY DISTRESS SYNDROME

idiot savant People of subnormal intelligence or severely limited emotional range who have prodigious intellectual gifts in a specific area. Mathematical, musical, artistic, and mechanical abilities have been among the talents demonstrated by idiot savants. Examples include performing rapid mental calculations of huge sums, playing lengthy compositions from memory after a single hearing, and repairing complex mechanisms without training. About 10% of autistic people are idiot savants; mentally retarded people may also be savants, though the incidence is much lower. See also AUTISM.

Iditarod (Trail Sled-Dog Race) \ˌī-ˈdit-ə-ˌräd\ Annual dogsled race held in March on a route between Anchorage and Nome, Alaska. It originated in 1967 as a short race of 56 mi (90 km). By 1973 it had evolved into the current race, a 1,152-mi (1,855-km) trek roughly tracing an old mail route forged in 1910. The race also commemorates an emergency mission to get medical supplies to Nome during a 1925 diphtheria epidemic. It typically takes 9–14 days to complete. See also DOGSLED RACING.

idol Image or statue of a deity used as an object of worship. In Judaism, the making of any representation of God is strictly forbidden, as is the fashioning of any "graven image." Islam has also adhered to this rule. In Christianity, there has been a general acceptance of pictorial or sculpted images of Jesus and the saints and, on occasion, God, and Christianity has thus always faced the danger that such representations could be venerated superstitiously as idols. In Jainism, Hinduism, and Buddhism images of gods and saints are common; they are often the object of veneration. In Hinduism, a statue may be treated as a god as an act of devotion but loses its special status when the act of devotion is finished (see DURGA-PUJA, PUJA).

Idris I \id-ˈrēs\ *in full* **Sidi Muhammad Idris al-Mahdi al-Sanusi** (1890–1983) King of Libya (1951–69). He succeeded his father in 1902 as leader of CYRENAICA but did not rule in his own name until 1916. Negotiations with Italy, which held the Libyan coast, resulted in agreements that confirmed Idris's authority (1917) and established a parliament (1919). His refusal to disarm his tribal supporters led to Italy's invasion of Tripolitania in 1922, and Idris went into exile until after World War II. In 1949 Cyrenaica and the other two Libyan provinces united under a constitutional monarchy headed by Idris. Independence was declared in 1951. He was overthrown by Col. MUAMMAR AL-QADDAFI in a military coup in 1969. He died in exile in Egypt.

Idrisid dynasty \ˈid-ri-sid\ Arab Muslim dynasty that ruled BERBER areas of Morocco 788–921. The founder, Idris I, was a descendant of ALI and established the sharifian tradition in Morocco, by which the claim to descent from MUHAMMAD was established as the principle for monarchic rule. His son Idris II (ruled 803–28) founded Fez (modern FÈS) in 808. The dynasty was the first to incorporate both Berbers and ARABS. It broke up into rival principalities, paving the way for another Berber dynasty, the ALMORAVID DYNASTY.

idyll *or* **idyl** \ˈī-dəl, ˈi-dəl\ Literary term with varying meanings. An idyll may be a short descriptive poem usually dealing with pastoral or rural life (see ECLOGUE); a simple descriptive work (either poetry or prose) that deals with rustic life or pastoral scenes or merely suggests a mood of peace and contentment; or a narrative poem (such as ALFRED TENNYSON's *Idylls of the King*) that treats an epic, romantic, or tragic theme.

Ifat \i-ˈfät\ Muslim state (1285–1415), central ETHIOPIA. Flourishing in the fertile uplands, it was established through the conquests of a 13th-century ruler known as Walashma. It served as a buffer between the pagan kingdom of Damot and the Christian kingdom of Ethiopia. Ifat was conquered by the Ethiopian king Amda Tseyon in 1328 and made tributary to Ethiopia. After a long series of revolts, it was destroyed in 1415 when it was annexed to Ethiopia.

Ifni \ˈif-nē\ Region, southwestern MOROCCO. Located on the Atlantic Coast, it has an area of 580 sq mi (1500 sq km). It was first settled in 1476 by Diego García de Herrera, lord of the Canaries, as a Spanish fishing, slaving, and trading locality. Abandoned in 1524 because of disease and Moorish hostility, it was reclaimed following a Spanish–Moroccan treaty in 1860. Effective Spanish reoccupation began in 1934, and it became part of Spanish West Africa in 1946. Ifni was ceded to Morocco in 1969.

IG Farben World's largest chemical CARTEL from its founding in Germany until its dissolution by the Allies after World War II. It grew out of a complex merger of German manufacturers of chemicals, pharmaceuticals, and dyestuffs *(Farben).* Its major members were the companies known today as BASF AG, BAYER AG, Hoechst AG, Agfa-Gevaert Group, and Cassella AG. They formed a loose association in 1916 and were formally united in 1925, with headquarters in Frankfurt. IG Farben expanded internationally in the late 1920s and the 1930s. During World War II, it established a synthetic oil and rubber plant at AUSCHWITZ to take advantage of slave labor by the death camp's inmates, on whom it also conducted drug experiments. After the war, several company officials were convicted of WAR CRIMES, and IG Farben was broken up into three independent companies.

Igbo \ˈig-bō\ *or* **Ibo** \ˈē-bō\ People of southeastern Nigeria who speak dialects of Igbo, a BENUE-CONGO LANGUAGE of the NIGER-CONGO family. Before European colonization the Igbo lived in autonomous local communities, but by the mid-20th century a sense of ethnic identity was strongly developed. During conflicts in 1966, many Igbo in northern Nigeria were killed or forced into their traditional homelands in the east. In 1967 the eastern region tried to secede from Nigeria as the independent nation of BIAFRA; hundreds of thousands of Igbo were killed or died of starvation. Today they number about 18.6 million. Many are farmers, but trading, crafts, and wage labor are also important, and many have become civil servants and business entrepreneurs.

igloo Temporary dome-shaped winter home or hunting-ground dwelling of Canadian and Greenland Inuit (ESKIMOS), made from blocks of snow. The builder chooses a deep snowdrift of fine-grained, compact snow and cuts it into blocks. After a row of blocks has been laid in a circle, their top surfaces are shaved off in a sloping angle to form the first rung of a spiral. Additional blocks are added to the spiral to draw it inward until a dome is completed, leaving a ventilation hole at the top.

Ignarro, Louis J(oseph) (born 1941) U.S. pharmacologist. He earned a PhD from the University of Minnesota. Along with R.F. FURCHGOTT and FERID MURAD, Ignarro was awarded a 1998 Nobel Prize for the discovery that NITRIC OXIDE acts as a signaling molecule in the cardiovascular system. Ignarro concluded that the factor that Furchgott had named endothelium-derived relaxing factor was nitric oxide. This work uncovered an entirely new mechanism by which blood vessels in the body relax and widen. It was the first discovery that a gas could act as a signaling molecule in a living organism. The principle behind the drug VIAGRA, used to treat impotence, was based upon this research.

Ignatius of Antioch \ig-'nā-shəs\, **St.** (died 107?) Early Christian martyr. Probably of Syrian origin, he may have been a pagan who persecuted Christians before his conversion. He succeeded St. PETER THE APOSTLE as bishop of Antioch. During the reign of TRAJAN, Roman authorities arrested Ignatius and sent him to Rome, where he was tried and executed. He wrote a series of famous letters on the journey to Rome, attempting to encourage his fellow Christians during their persecution. The letters condemn two sets of heretics: the Judaizers, who insisted that Christians continue to follow Jewish law; and the Docetists, who maintained that Jesus only appeared to suffer and die on the cross.

Ignatyev \ig-'nät-yif\, **Nikolay (Pavlovich), Count** (1832–1908) Russian politician and diplomat under ALEXANDER II. A career diplomat, he concluded a treaty with China in 1860 that allowed Russia to construct the city of Vladivostok and become a major power in the northern Pacific. Appointed head of the foreign ministry's Asian department, he gained jurisdiction over Russia's relations with the Ottoman empire as well, and in 1864 he became ambassador to Constantinople. An advocate of PAN-SLAVISM, he encouraged Serbia and Bulgaria in a revolt that proved unsuccessful. In 1878, after Russia's victory in the RUSSO–TURKISH WAR, he negotiated the favorable Treaty of SAN STEFANO. The Western European powers replaced it with the Treaty of Berlin, far less favorable to Russia, and he was forced to resign.

igneous rock Any of various crystalline or glassy noncrystalline rocks formed by the cooling and solidification of molten earth material (magma). Igneous rocks comprise one of the three principal classes of rocks, the others being METAMORPHIC and SEDIMENTARY rocks. Though they vary widely in composition, most igneous rocks consist of quartz, feldspars, pyroxenes, amphiboles, micas, olivines, nepheline, leucite, and apatite. They may be classified as INTRUSIVE or EXTRUSIVE rocks.

ignition system In a GASOLINE ENGINE, the means used for producing an electric spark to ignite the fuel-air mixture in the cylinders to produce the motive force. The ignition system consists of a storage BATTERY recharged by a generator, an induction coil, a device to produce timed high-voltage discharges from the induction coil, a distributor, and a set of SPARK PLUGS. The battery provides an electric current of low voltage, usually 12 volts, that is converted by the system to some 40,000 volts. The distributor routes the successive bursts of high-voltage current to each spark plug in the proper firing order.

iguana \i-'gwä-nə\ Any of about 13 of the larger members of the LIZARD family Iguanidae. Best known is the common iguana *(Iguana iguana),* which ranges from Mexico southward to Brazil. It reaches a maximum length of 6 ft (1.8 m). It lives in trees, especially trees overhanging water, into which it will plunge if disturbed. It is greenish, with brown bands that form regular rings on the tail. It primarily eats tender leaves and fruits but will also eat small birds and crustaceans. Species of the southwestern U.S. and Mexico include the chuckwalla *(Sauromalus obesus)* and desert iguana *(Dipsosaurus dorsalis).*

Iguazú Falls *or* **Iguaçu Falls** \ˌē-gwə-'sü\ *formerly* **Victoria Falls** Cataract on the IGUAZÚ RIVER near the Argentina–Brazil border. The horseshoe-shaped falls were discovered by Á. ALVAR NUNEZ CABEZA DE VACA in 1541. They are 269 ft (82 m) high and 2.5 mi (4 km) wide (four times the width of NIAGARA FALLS), and are divided into 275 waterfalls or cataracts. The scenic beauty and wildlife of the falls are protected by two separate national parks—Iguaçu National Park in Brazil and Iguazú National Park in Argentina, both established in the early 20th century. See photograph opposite.

Iguazú River *or* **Iguaçu River** River, southern Brazil and northeastern Argentina. It winds westward for 820 mi (1,320 km) before joining the PARANÁ RIVER at the point where Argentina, Brazil, and Paraguay meet. Although sections of the river are navigable, it is known chiefly for IGUAZÚ FALLS. Near the falls a major portion of the river tumbles into a chasm called the Garganta del Diablo ("Devil's Throat"), which has been described as "an ocean plunging into an abyss."

Iguvine tables \ī-'gü-vīn\ Set of seven inscribed bronze tables written in the UMBRIAN LANGUAGE and found in 1444 at Iguvium (modern Gubbio, Italy). Some are written in the Umbrian script and others in Latin characters; they probably date from the 3rd–1st century BC. The tables record liturgy, sacred rites, and regulations of the Fratres Atiedii, a brotherhood of priests, and are of great value for the study of ancient ITALIC LANGUAGE and religion.

Ihara Saikaku \ē-'hä-rä-'sī-ˌkä-kü\ *or* **Ibara Saikaku** \ē-'bä-rä\ *known as* **Saikaku** *originally probably* **Hirayama Togo** (1642–1693) Japanese poet and novelist, a brilliant figure of the 17th-century revival in Japanese literature. He first won fame for his speed in composing haikai (humorous linked-verse poems), once producing 23,500 in a day. He is best known for his novels, including *The Life of an Amorous Man* (1682) and *Five Women Who Loved Love* (1686). in which he enchanted readers with racy accounts of the amorous and financial affairs of the merchant class and the demimonde.

Ii Naosuke \'ē-ē-nä-'ōs-kā\ (1815–1860) Japanese DAIMYO and statesman who made the last attempt to reassert the traditional political role of the shogunate. In response to Commodore MATTHEW PERRY's demand that Japan end its centuries-old policy of isolation, Ii favored developing relations. The TOKUGAWA SHOGUNATE signed the Perry Convention, which opened two ports to U.S. ships, exposing the country to Western influence, and began negotiations with TOWNSEND HARRIS over trade. In an unusual move, the shogunate had sought the emperor's consent to the treaty; when antitreaty forces blocked approval, Ii, as head of the shogunal governing body, authorized the signing. This outraged many daimyo; when Ii silenced them, he was beheaded by assassins. See also MEIJI RESTORATION.

IJssel River \'ā-səl, *Engl* 'ī-səl\ River, Netherlands. An important distributary of the RHINE RIVER, it leaves the Lower Rhine (Neder Rijn) just southeast of Arnhem and flows northeastward for 70 mi (113 km) to enter the IJSSELMEER. Zutphen, Deventer, and Zwolle are important cities along its course.

IJsselmeer \'ā-səl-ˌmer\ *English* **Lake Ijssel** Shallow freshwater lake, northern and central Netherlands. Fed by the IJSSEL RIVER, it was formed from the southern part of the former ZUIDER ZEE by a dam, which separates it from both the Wadden Zee and the North Sea. Its total area (1,328 sq mi, or 3,440 sq km) has been reduced by reclamation projects that have increased the land area of the Netherlands by 626 sq mi (1,620 sq km). Regulated by sluices, the formerly brackish water has been replaced by fresh water from the IJssel River, and eel fisheries have been established.

ijtihad \ˌij-tē-'had\ In Islamic law, the analysis of problems not covered precisely in the QURAN, the HADITH, or the scholarly consensus called the *ijma.* In the early Muslim scholarly community, every jurist had the right to exercise such original thinking, but the growth of legal schools prompted SUNNI Muslim authorities to declare that the principal legal issues had been settled by the 10th century. SHIITE Muslims have always recognized ijtihad, and jurists considered learned enough for this kind of analysis have great authority. In the 20th century, an attempt was made to restore ijtihad among Sunnis to help Islam adapt to the modern world.

Iguazú Falls on the Iguazú River at the Argentina-Brazil border.
© R. MANLEY/SUPERSTOCK

H I J K

Ike no Taiga \'ē-ke-nō-'tī-gä\ *orig.* **Matajiro** (1723–1776) Japanese painter. From an early age he was taught calligraphy and the Chinese classics. He helped establish the *bunjin-ga* style of painting (see Literati), originally a Chinese style. His works consist of landscapes and portraits, including the screen pictures *The Five Hundred Disciples of Buddha* and a series of illustrations for *Juben jugicho* (1771), albums based on the poems of Li Liweng of the Qing dynasty (1644–1911). Ike became one of the leading calligraphers of the Edo period.

ikebana \ˌi-kā-'bä-nə\ Japanese art of flower arranging. It was introduced in Japan in the 6th cent by Chinese Buddhist missionaries, who had formalized the ritual of offering flowers to the Buddha. The first school of flower arranging in Japan was founded in the early 7th century. The art is based on harmony of simple linear construction and appreciation of the subtle beauty of flowers and natural material (branches, stems). Several major schools, with differing histories and theories of artistic style, exist to this day. In its highest form, ikebana is spiritual and philosophical in nature, but in modern Japan it is more often practiced as a sign of refinement by marriageable young women or older matrons.

Ikhwan \ik-'wän\ (Arabic: "Brethren") Religious and military brotherhood that helped Ibn Saud unite the Arabian Peninsula. First organized in 1912, its members were settled in colonies around oases in an effort to break down tribal loyalties and force the Bedouin to abandon their nomadic way of life. They also embraced the arch-traditionalist Islamic principles of Ibn Abd al-Wahhab. From 1919 they won many victories in Arabia and Iraq, with conquests including Mecca and Medina. By 1926 the Ikhwan were becoming uncontrollable, attacking Ibn Saud for innovations such as telephones and automobiles. They staged a bloody revolt, which was not put down until 1930, and then only with British help. Members who had remained loyal were eventually absorbed into the National Guard.

Ikhwan al-Safa \ik-'wän-ás-sa-'fa\ Secret Arab brotherhood founded in Basra, Iraq, in the 10th century. The beliefs of the group diverged sharply from orthodox Islam, incorporating elements of Neoplatonism, Gnosticism, astrology, and the occult sciences. The brotherhood is best known for having produced a philosophical and religious encyclopedia, *Epistles of the Brethren of Purity and Loyal Friends,* whose purpose was to provide enlightenment that would purify the soul and provide happiness in the next life.

ikki \'ik-ē\ Peasant uprisings in Japan from the time of the Ashikaga shogunate through the Tokugawa shogunate. Though the welfare of the city dweller improved during the Edo period, the welfare of poor peasants worsened: excessive taxation and rising numbers of famines drove them first to peaceful and then to violent demonstrations. They sometimes received redress for particular hardships, but their spokesmen would forfeit their lives for their audacity.

Il Rosso See Giovanni Battista Rosso

ilang-ilang See ylang-ylang

ileitis \ˌi-lē-'ī-təs\ Chronic inflammation of part of the small or large intestine (strictly, of the ileum). A more serious type, regional ileitis (Crohn's disease), involves both small and large intestines. Ileitis symptoms include chronic or intermittent, sometimes bloody, diarrhea and abdominal cramps. Fever, weight loss, and anemia may occur and in Crohn's disease can cause progressive deterioration. Obstructions or abnormal connections between coils of intestine may develop. Simple ileitis has short-term causes, and many patients recover completely. In Crohn's disease, which may result from an autoimmune defect, remissions and relapses continue for years, causing the intestine's wall to thicken, its channel to narrow, and its lining to ulcerate. X-ray films showing these features are diagnostic. Drug treatment may help, but there is no known cure, and the disease often requires removal of part of the intestine.

ileum \'i-lē-əm\ Final and longest segment of the small intestine, site of absorption of vitamin B12 (see vitamin B complex) and reabsorption of about 90% of conjugated bile salts. It extends about 13 ft (4 m), from the jejunum (middle section of the small intestine) to the ileocecal valve, where it joins the large intestine. Disorders produce B12 deficiency and extensive diarrhea (since bile salts in the large intestine interfere with water absorption).

Iliamna Lake \ˌi-lē-'am-nə\ Lake, Alaska. The largest lake in Alaska, and the second-largest freshwater lake entirely within the U.S., it is 80 mi (129 km) long and 25 mi (40 km) wide, and covers an area of 1,000 sq mi (2,600 sq km). Located west of Cook Inlet in southwestern Alaska, it drains southwest into Bristol Bay and the Bering Sea. The active Iliamna Volcano, 10,016 ft (3,053 m) high, lies northeast of the lake. It was named by Tanaina Indians, whose mythology held that it was inhabited by a giant blackfish capable of biting holes in canoes.

Ilium See Troy

Illinois State (population 1997 est.: 11,896,000), midwestern U.S. It covers 56,400 sq mi (146,076 sq km); its capital is Springfield. The Mississippi River forms the state's western boundary, the Ohio and Wabash rivers form its southeastern border, and the Illinois River traverses it. Located on its northeastern border is Chicago, the nation's third largest city. Indian settlement dates from 8000 BC. The Mississippian culture was centered at Cahokia c. AD 1300; all the tribes inhabiting the area at the time of European settlement were of Algonquian stock. The French explorers Jacques Marquette and Louis Jolliet entered the territory in 1673. France controlled it until 1763, when it passed to Britain after the French and Indian War. It became part of the Northwest Territory in 1783, and part of Indiana Territory in 1800; Illinois Territory was formed in 1809 and it became the 21st state in 1818. Although politically divided during the American Civil War , Illinois remained part of the Union. In the 20th century intense rivalry between Republicans and Democrats, and its large electoral vote made it a major battleground in presidential elections. It is one of the largest U.S. industrial centers, and a top manufacturer of nonelectrical machinery. It is also a major insurance center.

Illinois, University of State system of higher education consisting of a main campus at Urbana-Champaign (founded 1867) and a second campus in Chicago (1946). Both campuses are teaching and research institutions with land-grant standing and a full range of undergraduate, graduate, and professional degree programs, including schools of law and medicine. Facilities at the main campus include the Aviation Research Laboratory and the National Center for Supercomputing Applications. The Chicago campus is home to the Jane Addams School for Social Work. The main library is the third-largest academic collection in the U.S. Total enrollment is about 62,000.

Illinois Central Gulf Railroad Co. (IC) U.S. railroad formed by the merger of the Illinois Central Railroad Co. and the Gulf, Mobile, and Ohio Railroad Co. The Illinois Central was chartered in 1851, and its first line was built from Galena to Cairo, Ill. A spur line to Chicago was built as part of the acquisition of a federal land grant. It eventually absorbed more than 100 smaller railroads across the Midwest and south to the Gulf of Mexico. After merging with the Gulf, Mobile, and Ohio in 1972, the railroad operated in 13 states. In 1985 it sold its line extending from Chicago to Iowa and Nebraska. The IC ships freight and operates passenger trains for Amtrak. It is a subsidiary of IC Industries, Inc., a holding company formed in 1962 that merged with Canadian National (CN) in 1999.

Illinois River River, northeastern Illinois. Formed by the junction of the Des Plaines and Kankakee rivers in Illinois, it flows southwest across the state, joining the Mississippi River after a course of 273 mi (440 km). It drains an area of 25,000 sq mi (65,000 sq km) and occasionally broadens into wide expanses, such as Peoria Lake.

illuminated manuscript Handwritten book decorated with gold or silver, brilliant colors, elaborate designs, or miniature paintings. "Illumination" originally denoted embellishment of text with gold or silver, which gave the impression that the page had been literally illuminated. In the Middle Ages, those who "historiated" (illustrated texts with paintings) were differentiated from

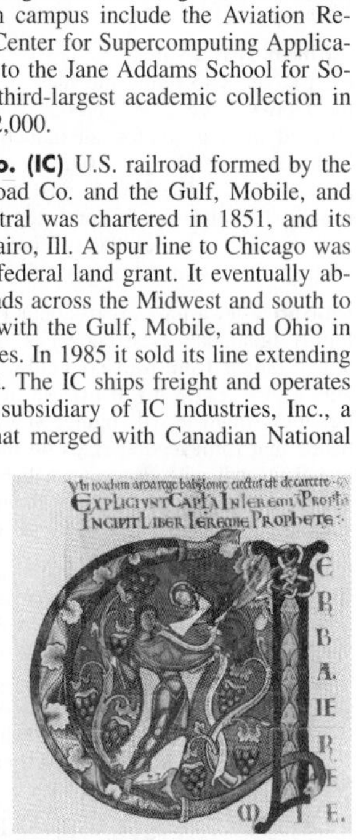

Illuminated initial "U" for "Uerba" (*i.e.,* "Verba") in the book of Jeremiah, from the Winchester Bible, English, 12th century; in the Cathedral Library, Winchester, England (MS. 17, fol. 148R).

those who "illuminated" (embellished the initial capital letters with gold leaf or powder). Today the term denotes the illustration and decoration of early manuscripts in general, whether or not with gold. With the development of printing in Europe in the 15th century, illumination was superseded by printed illustrations.

Illustrated London News Picture magazine of news and the arts, published in London. Founded in 1842 as a weekly, it became a monthly in 1971. A pioneer in the use of various graphic arts, it was London's first illustrated periodical, the first periodical to make extensive use of woodcuts and engravings, and the first to use photographs. In 1912 it became the first periodical using rotogravure to publish an integrated picture and text section. Initially focused mainly on English social life, it later broadened its scope to embrace general news and cultural activities.

illuviation Accumulation of dissolved or suspended soil materials in one area or layer as a result of leaching (percolation) from another. Usually CLAY, iron, or HUMUS wash out and form a line with a different consistency and color. These lines are important for studying the composition and ages of rock strata.

Illyria \ə-'lir-ē-ə\ Ancient country, northwestern BALKAN PENINSULA. It was inhabited from the 10th century BC by the Illyrians, an Indo-European people who later practiced piracy on Roman shipping. After a series of wars with Rome, it was defeated in 168 BC and established as the Roman province of Illyricum. When the Roman empire was divided in AD 395, Illyria east of the DRINA RIVER became part of the Eastern Empire. It was occupied by the Slavs from the 6th century, and its name changed in the 8th–11th century to Arbëri and, finally, to Albania.

Illyrian Provinces \ə-'lir-ē-ən\ Former territory, Dalmatian coast. When the French victory in 1809 compelled Austria to cede part of its southern Slav lands to France, Napoleon combined CARNIOLA, West Carinthia, Görz, ISTRIA, and parts of CROATIA, DALMATIA, and Ragusa to form the Illyrian Provinces, which he incorporated into his empire. The end of the French administration in 1814 returned them to the Austrian empire.

ilm al-hadith \'ilm-âl-hâ-'dēth\ Form of analysis established by 9th-century Muslim traditionalists to verify the merits of the HADITH. Of the many accounts of Muhammad's statements and actions that constituted the Hadith, some were thought to be forgeries or of doubtful reliability. Scholars judged their merit by scrutinizing the ISNADS that detailed the chain of authority through which the story had been handed down.

Ilmen \'il^y-mən^y\, **Lake** Lake, northwestern Russia. It occupies the center of the Ilmen Plain, a glacial lowland drained by nearly 50 rivers, including the Msta, Pola, and Lovat, that flow into the lake; the lake in turn provides the headwaters of the Volkhov River. Its area, 283–807 sq mi (733–2,090 sq km), varies according to river flow. The lake is navigable in summer and has an average depth of 33 ft (10 m).

ilmenite \'il-mə-ˌnīt\ Iron-black, heavy, metallic OXIDE MINERAL, composed of iron and titanium oxide ($FeTiO_3$), which is the major source of TITANIUM. It is found disseminated or in veins in GABBRO, DIORITE, or ANORTHOSITE, as in Quebec, New York state, and Norway. It also forms large masses, as in Iron Mtn., Wyo., and in the Ilmen Mtns., Russia, from which it derives its name. Smaller quantities are present in copper-ore veins, pegmatites, black beach sands, and placer deposits.

Iloilo \ˌē-lō-'ē-lō\ City (pop., 1994 est.: 302,000), PANAY island, Philippines. Pre-Spanish settlement was extensive, but the seaport remained small until 1855, when it was opened to foreign trade. For a time it rivaled CEBU City as the main port of the Visayan islands. It is a major fishing port, and known also for its raw-silk and pineapple-fiber fabrics.

Ilorin \ē-'lō-rēn\ City (pop., 1996 est.: 476,000), western Nigeria. It is located on a minor tributary of the NIGER RIVER. Founded by the YORUBA in the late 18th century, and the capital of a Yoruba kingdom c. 1800, it passed to Britain in 1897. Surrounded by a mud wall, and mainly inhabited by Muslim Yoruba people, it is an industrial, commercial, and educational center.

Ilumquh \i-'lùm-kü\ Arabian god of the moon. Deemed superior to the gods associated with the sun and Venus, he was the protector of cities and patron god of the capital cities of southern Arabia. Pilgrimages were made to his temples, where worshipers often sought divine guidance from oracles. He had many different names and epithets, including Wadd, Amm, and Sin.

image processing Set of computational techniques for analyzing, enhancing, compressing, and reconstructing images. Its main components are importing, in which an image is captured through scanning or digital photography; analysis and manipulation of the image, accomplished using various specialized software applications; and output (e.g., to a printer or monitor). Image processing has extensive applications in many areas, including astronomy, medicine, industrial ROBOTICS, and remote sensing by satellites. See also PATTERN RECOGNITION.

imaginary number Any number of the form $a + bi$ where a and b are real numbers, i is the square root of -1, and b is not zero. If a is zero, the number is called a pure imaginary number. See also COMPLEX NUMBER.

Imagism \'im-i-ˌjiz-əm\ Movement in U.S. and English poetry characterized by the use of concrete language and figures of speech, modern subject matter, metrical freedom, and avoidance of romantic or mystical themes. It grew out of the SYMBOLIST MOVEMENT and was initially led by EZRA POUND, who, inspired by the criticism of T. E. Hulme (1883–1917), formulated its credo c. 1912; HILDA DOOLITTLE was also among the founders. Around 1914 AMY LOWELL largely took over leadership of the group. Imagism influenced the works of CONRAD AIKEN, T. S. ELIOT, MARIANNE MOORE, D. H. LAWRENCE, WALLACE STEVENS, and others.

imam \i-'mäm\ Head of the Muslim community. In SUNNI Islam the imam was identical with the CALIPH, designating the political successor of MUHAMMAD. The Sunnis held the imam to be a man capable of error but deserving obedience provided he maintained the ordinances of Islam. In SHIITE Islam the imam became a figure of absolute religious authority, possessed of unique insights into the Quran, divinely appointed and preserved from sin. With the historical disappearance of the last imam, there arose a belief in the hidden imam, who is identified with the MAHDI. The term imam is also given to Muslims who lead prayers in mosques and is an honorary title.

Imam Bondjol \'bōn-jəl\ (1772–1864) Leader in a religious war that divided the MINANGKABAU people of Sumatra. A convert to reformist Wahhabi Islam, known in Sumatra as the Padri sect, he established the fortified community of Bondjol, from which he took his name, as a center from which to wage holy war. The secular government called on the Dutch to help, but the Dutch were preoccupied with the Java War (1825–30), and Imam Bondjol's forces expanded the area under their control. When the Dutch turned their attention to the Padris, the latter were defeated, he surrendered (1837), and the Minangkabau territory was added to the Dutch colonial holdings.

imamis See ITHNA ASHARIYA

IMF See INTERNATIONAL MONETARY FUND

Imhotep \im-'hō-ˌtep\ *Greek* **Imouthes** (fl. 27th century BC) Egyptian sage and astrologer, later worshiped as the god of medicine. In Greece he was identified with ASCLEPIUS. Imhotep was chief minister to the Egyptian king Djoser and is remembered as a skilled physician as well as the architect of the step-pyramid at SAQQARA in Memphis. Deified around the time of the Persian conquest in 525 BC, he was said to be the son of PTAH and the war goddess Sekhmet. The cult of Imhotep reached its zenith in Greco-Roman times, when sick people slept in his temples with the hope that the god would reveal remedies to them in dreams.

Immaculate Conception In ROMAN CATHOLICISM, the dogma that MARY was not tainted by ORIGINAL SIN. Early exponents included St. JUSTIN MARTYR and St. IRENAEUS; St. BONAVENTURE and St. THOMAS AQUINAS were among those who opposed it. In 1439 the Council of BASEL stated that the belief was in accordance with Catholic faith, and in 1709 Pope Clement XI made the feast of the Immaculate Conception a holy day of obligation. In 1854 PIUS IX issued a papal bull making it official church dogma. See also VIRGIN BIRTH.

immune system Cells, cell products, organs, and structures of the body involved in the detection and destruction of foreign invaders, such as bacteria, viruses, and cancer cells. IMMUNITY is based on the system's ability to launch a defense against such invaders. For the system to function properly, it must be able to distinguish between the material of its own body (self) and material that originates outside of it (nonself). Failure to make this distinction can result in AUTOIMMUNE DISEASES. An exaggerated or inappropriate response by the immune system to nonharmful substances (e.g., pollen, animal dander) can result in ALLERGIES. The system's principal cells include LYMPHOCYTES that recognize ANTIGENS, and related accessory cells (such as phagocytic macrophages, which engulf and destroy foreign material). Lymphocytes arise in the BONE MARROW from stem cells with T lymphocytes (T CELLS) migrating to the THYMUS to mature and B lymphocytes (B CELLS) maturing in the bone marrow. Mature lymphocytes enter the bloodstream, and many become lodged, along with accessory cells, in various body tissues, including the SPLEEN, LYMPH NODES, TONSILS, and intestinal lining. Organs or tissues containing such concentrations are termed lymphoid. Within these organs and tissues the lymphocytes are confined within a delicate network of connective tissue that channels them so they come into contact with antigens. T cells and B cells can mature and multiply further in LYMPHOID TISSUE when suitably stimulated. Fluid (LYMPH) draining from lymphoid tissues is conveyed to the blood through lymphatic vessels. Lymph nodes distributed along these vessels filter the lymph, exposing macrophages and lymphocytes contained within to any antigen present. The spleen plays a similar role, sampling the blood for the presence of antigens. The capability of lymphocytes to pass between lymphoid tissue, the blood, and lymph is an important element in the system's functioning. See also IMMUNODEFICIENCY, IMMUNOLOGY.

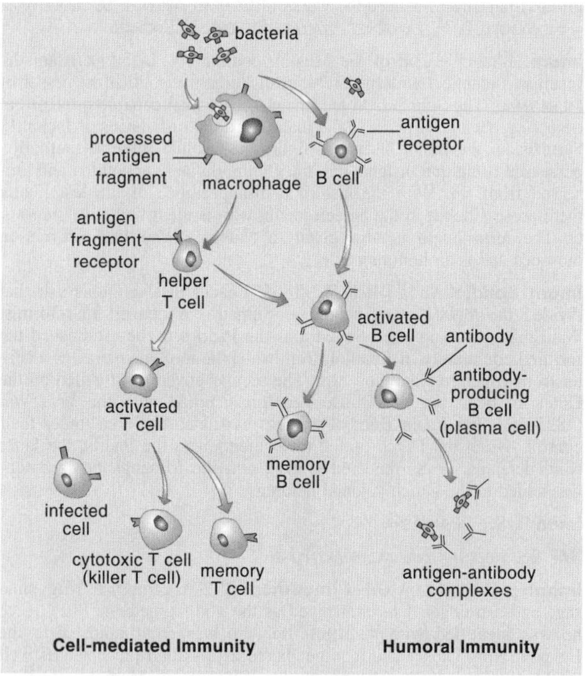

Acquired immunity depends on the activities of T and B lymphocytes (T and B cells). One part of acquired immunity, humoral immunity, involves the production of antibodies by B cells. The other part, cell-mediated immunity, involves the actions of T cells. When an antigen (such as a bacterium) enters the body, it is attacked and engulfed by macrophages, which process and display parts of it on their cell surface. A helper T cell, recognizing the antigen displayed, initiates maturation and proliferation of other T cells. Cytotoxic (killer) T cells develop and attack foreign and infected cells. B cells stimulated by the presence of antigen are activated by helper T cells to divide and form antibody-producing cells (plasma cells). Released antibody binds to antigen, marking the cell for destruction. Helper T cells also induce the development of memory T and B cells needed to mount future immune responses on reinfection with the same pathogen.

immunity Ability to resist attack or overcome infection by invading microbes or larger parasites. Immunity is based on the proper functioning of the body's IMMUNE SYSTEM. In natural or innate immunity, immune mechanisms present at birth work against a wide variety of microbes whether or not they have been encountered before. Acquired immune responses, tailored to act against a specific microbe or its products, are stimulated by the prior presence of that microbe. Previous infection with a particular pathogen, as well as VACCINES, produce this type of immunity. The mechanisms of innate immunity include physical barriers (including the skin) and chemical barriers (such as bactericidal enzymes present in saliva). Microbes that penetrate the body's natural barriers encounter substances (such as interferon) that inhibit their growth or reproduction. Phagocytes (particle-engulfing cells), surround and destroy invading microbes, and natural killer cells pierce the microbe's outer membrane. Innate immunity does not confer lasting resistance, or immunity, to the body. Acquired immunity is based on the recognition of ANTIGEN by B and T CELLS and is activated when innate mechanisms are insufficient to stem further invasion by pathogens. Killer or cytotoxic T cells destroy infected and foreign cells. Helper T cells induce B cells stimulated by the presence of antigen to proliferate into antibody-secreting cells, or plasma cells. ANTIBODIES produced by plasma cells bind to antigen-bearing cells, marking them for destruction. Acquired immunity relies on the long-term survival of sensitized T and B memory cells, which can proliferate quickly upon reinfection by the same pathogen. See also IMMUNODEFICIENCY, IMMUNOLOGY, LEUKOCYTE, RETICULOENDOTHELIAL SYSTEM.

immunity In law, exemption or freedom from liability. Under international treaty, a diplomatic representative is exempt from local laws, both civil and criminal. In many countries, judges, legislators, and government officials, including the heads of state, enjoy limited or absolute immunity at home to protect them from personal liability for wrongful acts or omissions that arise from the performance of their duties. A public prosecutor may grant immunity from prosecution to a witness who is suspected of criminal activity in return for testimony against other suspected criminals.

immunodeficiency Defect in IMMUNITY that impairs the body's ability to resist infection. The IMMUNE SYSTEM may fail to function for many reasons. Immune disorders caused by a genetic defect are usually evident early in life. Others can be acquired at any age through infections (e.g., AIDS) or IMMUNOSUPPRESSION. Aspects of the immune response that may be affected include LYMPHOCYTES, other LEUKOCYTES, ANTIBODIES, and COMPLEMENT. Severe combined immunodeficiency (SCID), which arises from several different genetic defects, disrupts all of these. Depending on the cause, treatment for immunodeficiency may be administration of immunoglobulins, bone-marrow transplant, or therapy for the underlying disease.

immunology Science dealing with the body's defenses against disease-causing microorganisms and disorders of those defenses. Starting with EDWARD JENNER's use of a VACCINE against SMALLPOX in 1796, immunology has arrived at a comprehensive and sophisticated understanding of the role of microorganisms in disease and of the formation, mobilization, action, and interaction of ANTIBODIES and antigen-reactive cells. It covers treatment of ALLERGIES, IMMUNOSUPPRESSION after organ TRANSPLANTS to prevent rejection, and study of AUTOIMMUNE DISEASES and IMMUNODEFICIENCIES. AIDS has stimulated intensive research in the last of these.

immunosuppression Suppression of IMMUNITY with drugs, usually to prevent rejection of an organ TRANSPLANT. Its aim is to allow the recipient to accept the organ permanently with no unpleasant side effects. In some cases the dosage can be reduced or even stopped without causing rejection. Other uses are in the treatment of certain AUTOIMMUNE DISEASES and for prevention of ERYTHROBLASTOSIS FETALIS. Its main drawback is the increased risk of infection for the duration of treatment and of LYMPHOMA in the case of long-term immunosuppression.

impact test Test of the ability of a material to withstand impact, used by engineers to predict its behavior under actual conditions. Many materials fail suddenly under impact, at flaws, cracks, or notches. The most common impact tests use a swinging pendulum to strike a notched bar; heights before and after impact are used to compute the energy required to FRACTURE the bar (see STRENGTH OF MATERIALS). In the Charpy test, the test piece is held horizontally between two vertical bars, much like the lintel over a door. In the Izod test, the specimen stands erect, like a fence post. See also TESTING MACHINE.

impala \im-ˈpa-lə\ Swift-running, graceful ANTELOPE *(Aepyceros melampus)* found in large herds, usually near water, on the savannas and open woodlands of central and southern Africa. Impalas are noted for their jumping ability; when alarmed, they bound off in leaps up to 30 ft (9 m) long and 10 ft (3 m) high. Lightly built, the impala stands 30–40 in. (75–100 cm) high at the shoulder. It has a golden to reddish brown coat, white underparts, a vertical black stripe on each thigh, and a black tuft behind each hind hoof. The male has long, lyre-shaped horns.

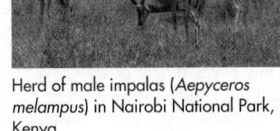

Herd of male impalas (*Aepyceros melampus*) in Nairobi National Park, Kenya.
JAMES P. ROWAN

impatiens \im-ˈpā-shəns\ Any of about 900 species of herbaceous plants in the genus *Impatiens* (BALSAM family), so named because the seedpod bursts when slightly touched. Garden balsam *(I. balsamina),* native to the tropics of Asia, is a favorite showy annual in U.S. gardens; its flowers are irregular, single or clustered, and of almost every color but blue. Familiar related weeds in eastern North America are spotted jewelweed *(I. biflora* or *I. capensis)* and pale TOUCH-ME-NOT. Most impatiens have weak, hollow stems and require high moisture. Close relatives are GERANIUMS and NASTURTIUMS.

impeachment Criminal proceeding instituted against a public official by a legislative body. In the U.S., the president, vice president, and other federal officers, including judges, may be impeached by the U.S. House of Representatives. The House draws up articles of impeachment that itemize the charges and their factual bases. Once approved by a majority of House members, the articles are submitted to the Senate, which holds a trial. At its conclusion, each member votes for or against conviction on each article; conviction requires a two-thirds majority. A convicted official can be removed from office. The U.S. CONSTITUTION specifies that an officer is to be impeached for "high crimes and misdemeanors"; experts agree that impeachment is permitted for noncriminal misconduct (e.g., violation of the Constitution). Two U.S. presidents, ANDREW JOHNSON and WILLIAM JEFFERSON CLINTON, have been impeached but acquitted. Articles of impeachment were drawn up against Pres. RICHARD NIXON in 1974, who resigned before formal proceedings could begin. In Britain, where the House of COMMONS prosecutes and the House of LORDS judges impeachment proceedings, impeachment was formerly a means by which Parliament could get rid of unpopular ministers, usually court favorites protected by the monarch. The procedure fell into disuse in the early 19th century, when cabinet ministers became responsible to Parliament rather than to the sovereign.

Imperial Chemical Industries PLC (ICI) Major British chemical corporation. It was founded in 1926 as Imperial Chemical Industries Ltd. to amalgamate four major British chemical companies. Between World Wars I and II, ICI was a major competitor of IG FARBEN. Today it produces industrial chemicals, paints, and explosives; its drug, pesticide, and specialty chemical concerns were split off into a new corporation, Zeneca Group PLC, in 1993. ICI's headquarters are in London.

Imperial Conferences Periodic meetings held between 1907 and 1937 by the dominions within the British empire and later the COMMONWEALTH. Convened to discuss mutual defense and economic issues, they passed nonbinding resolutions. However, the Statute of WESTMINSTER implemented decisions made at the 1926 and 1930 conferences that described the self-governing dominions (Canada, Australia, New Zealand, South Africa, Ireland, and Newfoundland) as "autonomous communities within the British empire." After World War II, meetings between the countries' prime ministers replaced the conferences.

Imperial Valley Valley extending from southeastern California to Mexico. It forms part of the Colorado Desert. Intensive irrigation began in 1901 with the opening of the Imperial Canal, which diverted water from the COLORADO RIVER. Floodwaters in 1905–7 destroyed the irrigation channels and created the SALTON SEA. The valley is now watered by the HOOVER DAM and the All-American Canal. With 3,000 mi (4,800 km) of irrigation canals, it contains 500,000 acres (200,000 hectares) of cultivated land.

imperialism State policy, practice, or advocacy of extending power and dominion, especially by direct territorial acquisition or by gaining political and economic control of other areas. Because it always involves the use of power, whether military force or some subtler form, imperialism has often been considered morally reprehensible, and the term was often used in the 20th century to denounce and discredit an opponent's foreign policy. Economists have debated whether imperialism is profitable and who benefits from it. Theories such as those of NICCOLO MACHIAVELLI and ADOLF HITLER asserted that nations endowed with superior qualities are destined to rule over others. Arguments relating to strategy describe imperialism as a consequence of the quest for security. After World War II, imperialism through direct conquest gave way to so-called political, economic, and cultural imperialism. See also COLONIALISM, SPHERE OF INFLUENCE.

impetigo \im-pə-ˈtī-ˌgō, im-pə-ˈtē-ˌgō\ Bacterial inflammatory skin disease, the most common skin infection in children. Initial blisters rupture, drying to a crust. Caused by STAPHYLOCOCCUS or STREPTOCOCCUS, it is very contagious in newborns, becoming less so with age. Poor hygiene, crowding, and humid, hot weather may promote its spread. A broad-spectrum antibiotic applied to the blisters can treat simple impetigo; more extensive cases, especially in infants, may require a systemic antibiotic.

Imphal \ˈimp-ˌhəl\ City (pop., 1991: 199,000), capital of MANIPUR state, northeastern India. Located east-northeast of KOLKATA (Calcutta), it lies in the Manipur River valley at an altitude of 2,500 feet (760 meters). It was the seat of the kings of Manipur before the region came under British rule. In 1944 it was the site of a victory for the Anglo-Indian forces over the Japanese on the Burmese front. Imphal is a major trade center, noted for its weaving, brassware, and bronzeware.

implication In LOGIC, a relation that holds between two propositions when they are linked as antecedent and consequent of a true conditional proposition. Logicians distinguish two main types of implication, material and strict. Proposition p materially implies proposition q if and only if the material conditional $p \supset q$ (read "if p then q") is true. A proposition of the form $p \supset q$ is false whenever p is true and q is false; it is true in the other three possible cases (i.e., p true and q true; p false and q true; p false and q false). It follows that whenever p is false, $p \supset q$ is automatically true: this is a peculiarity that makes the material conditional inadequate as an interpretation of the meaning of conditional sentences in ordinary English. On the other hand, proposition p strictly implies proposition q if and only if it is *impossible* for p to be true without q also being true (i.e., if the conjunction of p and not-q is impossible).

impotence \ˈim-pə-təns\ Inability to achieve or maintain erection of the PENIS; hence, inability to participate fully in SEXUAL INTERCOURSE. Erectile impotence (failure to achieve erection) may have either physical causes (e.g., alcoholism, endocrine disease) or psychological ones (e.g., anxiety, hostility toward the partner). Ejaculatory impotence (inability to reach orgasm, sometimes with an erection maintained for a long time) nearly always has an emotional cause. See also VIAGRA.

Impressionism Movement in art that developed in France in the late 19th century. In painting it included works produced c. 1867–86 by a group of artists who shared approaches, techniques, and discontent with academic teaching, originally including CLAUDE MONET, AUGUSTE RENOIR, CAMILLE PISSARRO, ALFRED SISLEY, and BERTHE MORISOT. Later EDOUARD MANET, whose earlier style had strongly influenced several of them, MARY CASSATT, and others adopted the Impressionist style. The identifying feature of their work was an attempt to record the visual reality of a landscape or a scene from modern urban life accurately and objectively, capturing the transient effects of light on color and texture. To this end they abandoned the traditional muted browns, grays, and greens in favor of a lighter, more brilliant palette; stopped using grays and blacks for shadows; and built up forms out of discrete flecks and dabs of color. They adopted EUGENE BOUDIN's practice of direct observation, painting entirely out of doors. As the French Academy's SALON consistently rejected most of their works, they held their own exhibition in 1874; seven others followed. A critic described them derisively as "impressionists," and they adopted the name as an accurate description of their intent. Before dissolving in the late 1880s, the group had revolutionized Western painting. See also POSTIMPRESSIONISM, SALON DES INDÉPENDANTS.

Impressionism Term used for music written in a style initiated by C. DEBUSSY at the end of the 19th century. Introduced by analogy with contemporaneous French painting, the musical term (disliked by Debussy himself) is a somewhat vague one. Elements often termed impressionistic include static harmony, emphasis on instrumental timbres that creates a shimmering interplay of "colors," melodies that lack directed motion, surface ornamentation that obscures or substitutes for melody, and an avoidance of traditional musical form. Impressionism can be seen as a reaction against the rhetoric of Romanticism, disrupting the forward motion of standard harmonic progressions. The other composer most often associated with Impressionism is M. Ravel. Impressionistic passages are common in earlier music by F. Chopin, F. Liszt, and Richard Wagner, and in music by such later composers as C. Ives, Bela Bartok, and George Gershwin.

impressment Enforcement of military or naval service on unwilling men. Until the early 19th century, it flourished in port towns everywhere, as "recruiters" searched through waterfront boardinghouses, brothels, and taverns. They often chose vagabonds or prisoners. Impressed men were forced into service through violence or coercion and were held to their duty by brutal discipline. In the early 19th century, Royal Navy ships halting U.S. vessels to search for British deserters frequently impressed naturalized U.S. citizens, one cause of the War of 1812. Impressment declined in the 19th century as states adopted more systematic recruiting methods. See also conscription.

imprinting Form of learning wherein a very young animal fixes its attention on the first object with which it has visual, auditory, or tactile experience and thereafter follows that object. In nature, the object is almost always a parent; in experiments, other animals and inanimate objects have been used. Imprinting has been studied extensively only in birds, but a comparable form of learning apparently takes place among many mammals and some fishes and insects. Ducklings and chicks, which can imprint in a few hours, lose receptivity to imprinting stimuli within 30 hours of hatching.

improvisation Creation of music in real time. Improvisation usually involves some preparation beforehand, particularly when there is more than one performer. Despite the central place of notated music in the Western tradition, improvisation has often played a role, from the earliest organum through the realization of figured bass. It has taken such forms as creation of a melody over a bass line for dancing, elaborate ornamentation added to a repeated section in an aria, keyboard variations on popular songs, concerto cadenzas, and free solo fantasias. Perhaps at its lowest ebb in the 19th century, improvisation returned to concert music in "experimental" compositions and in "authentic" performances of older music. Its most important contemporary form is jazz.

in vitro fertilization (IVF) \in-'vē-trō\ *or* **test-tube conception** Procedure, used to overcome infertility, in which eggs are removed from a woman, fertilized with sperm outside the body, and inserted into the uterus of the same or another woman. The first child thus conceived was born in 1978. IVF includes extraction of eggs, collection of sperm, fertilization in culture, and introduction into the uterus at the eight-cell stage. In a successful procedure, the embryo is implanted in the uterine wall, and pregnancy begins. The most common problem is failed implantation. IVF has been a source of moral, ethical, and religious controversy since its development.

Inari \ē-'nä-rē\ In Japanese mythology, the patron god of rice cultivation and prosperity. He was worshiped especially by merchants and tradesmen, and he also served as patron deity of swordsmiths, brothels, and entertainers. Inari was variously depicted as a bearded old man riding a fox or as a woman with long hair carrying sheaves of rice. The fox is sometimes identified as his messenger. The god's most popular shrine is the Fushimi Inari Shrine near Kyoto.

Inari, wood figurine, Tokugawa period (1603–1867); in the Musée Guimet, Paris.

BY COURTESY OF THE MUSEE GUIMET, PARIS

inbreeding Mating of closely related individuals. The opposite is outbreeding, the mating of unrelated organisms. Inbreeding is useful in keeping desirable characteristics or eliminating undesirable ones, but it often results in decreased vigor, size, and fertility of the offspring because of the combined effect of harmful genes that were recessive in both parents (see recessiveness). The closest type of inbreeding is self-fertilization. In linebreeding, mates are selected on the basis of their relationships to a certain superior ancestor. The backcross (crossing a first-generation hybrid with one of the parental types) is a common method of inbreeding.

incandescent lamp Any of various devices that produce light by heating a suitable material to a high temperature. In an electric incandescent lamp, or lightbulb, a filament is enclosed in a glass shell that is either evacuated or filled with an inert gas. The filament gives off light when heated by an electric current. The first practical electric incandescent lamps were independently produced in the late 1870s by Joseph Swan and Thomas Alva Edison. Edison has received the major credit because of his development of the power lines and other equipment needed for a lighting system. Inefficient in comparison with fluorescent lamps and electric discharge lamps, incandescent lighting is today reserved mainly for domestic use. See also halogen lamp.

Incarnation Central Christian doctrine that God became man in the form of Jesus, the son of God and the second person of the Holy Trinity. In Jesus the divine and human nature are joined but neither is changed or diminished. This difficult doctrine gave rise to a variety of heresies, some denying Jesus's divine nature, others his human nature. For orthodox believers the conflict was settled at the Councils of Nicaea (AD 325) and Chalcedon (AD 451).

Incas Group of South American Indians who ruled a territory that extended along the Pacific coast and Andean highlands from what is now northern Ecuador to central Chile. According to tradition (the Incas left no written records), the founder of the Inca dynasty led the tribe to Cuzco, which became their capital. Under the fourth emperor, they began to expand, and under the eighth they began a program of permanent conquest by establishing garrisons among the conquered. Under Topa Inca Yupanqui and his successor, the empire reached its southernmost and northernmost extent. By the early 16th cent the Incas controlled an empire of 12 million subjects. They constructed a vast network of roads, which in the end facilitated the Spanish conquest in 1532. Their architecture was highly developed, and the remains of their irrigation systems, palaces, temples, and fortifications are still in evidence throughout the Andes. Inca society was highly stratified and featured an aristocratic bureaucracy. Their pantheon, worshiped in a highly organized state religion, included a sun god, a creator god, and a rain god. The Incas' descendants are the Quechua-speaking peasants of the Andes (see Quechua). In Peru about 45% of the population are of Inca descent. They are primarily farmers and herders living in close-knit communities. Their Roman Catholicism is infused with belief in pagan spirits and divinities. See also Andean civilization, Atahuallpa, Aymará, Chimu, Francisco Pizarro.

incense Grains of resins (sometimes mixed with spices) that burn with a fragrant odor, widely used as religious offerings. Historically, the chief substances used as incense have been resins such as frankincense and myrrh, along with fragrant wood and bark, seeds, roots, and flowers.

incest Sexual relations between persons who, because of the nature of their kinship ties, are prohibited by law or custom from intermarrying. The incest taboo is generally universal, although it is imposed differently in different societies. Usually, the closer the genetic relationship between two people, the stronger and more highly charged is the taboo prohibiting or discouraging sexual relations. Some sociobiologists consider that inbred populations have diminished reproductive success and become gene pools for hereditary disorders. Some cultural anthropologists argue instead that the incest prohibition, with the corresponding rules of exogamy, acts to require males to seek sexual and marital partners outside the group, thereby establishing useful alliances. Other theories emphasize the need to control sexual jealousies within the family or to prepare children to function with restraint in adult society. No single explanation seems satisfactory, causing some to question whether incest should be treated as a unitary subject. Most cases of incest that come before criminal courts concern sexual intercourse between fathers and relatively young daughters (see child abuse).

inch Unit of measure equal to 1/36 yard, and since 1959 defined officially as 2.54 cm (see meter). David I of Scotland (c. 1150) defined the inch as the breadth of a man's thumb at the base of the nail; usually the thumb breadths of three men—one small, one medium, and one large—were added and then divided by three. During the reign of England's Edward II, the inch was defined as "three grains of barley, dry and round, placed end to end lengthwise." At various times it has also been defined as the combined lengths of 12 poppyseeds. See also FOOT, INTERNATIONAL SYSTEM OF UNITS, MEASUREMENT, METRIC SYSTEM.

Inchon \'in-ˌchän\ *formerly* **Jinsen** \'jin-ˌsen\ *or* **Chemulpo** \jə-'mül-pō\ Seaport city (pop., 2000 prelim.: 2,476,000), South Korea, near SEOUL. A fishing port since the 14th century, it was a Korean treaty port in 1883 and developed as an international commercial port before the Japanese occupation (1910–45). During the KOREAN WAR, it was the site of a successful U.N. troop landing in 1950. It now has special city (provincial) status. Its industries produce iron and steel, glass, chemicals, and lumber.

inchworm See LOOPER

incidental music Music composed to accompany a play. The practice dates back to ritualistic Greek drama, and is thus connected to the use of music in other kinds of ritual. Sometimes limited to the role of introduction or interlude (setting a mood or a historical period, for example), it may also accompany spoken dialogue (see MELODRAMA). Film and television music may be considered incidental music.

Inclán, Ramón María del Valle- See R. M. del VALLE-INCLÁN

income statement In accounting, the activity-oriented financial statement issued by businesses. Covering a specified time, such as three months or one year, the income statement is a summary of revenues and expenses. It also lists gains and losses from other transactions, such as the sale of assets or the repayment of debt. Standard accounting rules govern the procedures for recording each item.

income tax Levy imposed by public authority on the incomes of persons or corporations within its jurisdiction. In nations with an advanced system of private enterprise, income tax is the chief source of government revenue. Income tax levied on individuals or family units is known as personal income tax. In 1799 Britain enacted a general income tax to finance the Napoleonic Wars. In the U.S. an income tax was first tried during the Civil War; the Supreme Court held it constitutional in 1881 but declared another income tax unconstitutional in 1894. In 1913 the 16th Amendment to the Constitution made the personal income tax permanent. The fairness of personal income taxation is based on the premise that one's income is the best single index of one's ability to contribute to the support of the government; most personal income taxes are conceived on the theory that when people's financial circumstances differ, their tax liabilities should also differ. Thus U.S. income taxes are PROGRESSIVE TAXES, falling more heavily on those who earn more money, and individual income-tax deductions are allowed for items such as interest paid on home mortgage debt, unusual medical expenses, philanthropic contributions, and state and local income and property taxes. Enforcement has been facilitated by withholding the tax from wages and salaries. See also CAPITAL-GAINS TAX, CAPITAL LEVY, CORPORATE INCOME TAX, REGRESSIVE TAX, SALES TAX, value-added tax.

incomes policy Collective governmental effort to control the incomes of LABOR and CAPITAL, usually by limiting increases in wages and PRICES. The term often refers to policies directed at the control of INFLATION, but it may also indicate efforts to alter the distribution of income among workers, industries, locations, or occupational groups. See also WAGE-PRICE CONTROL.

incontinence Inability to control EXCRETION. Starting and stopping URINATION relies on normal function in pelvic and abdominal muscles, diaphragm, and control nerves. Babies' nervous systems are too immature for urinary control. Later incontinence may reflect disorders (e.g., NEURAL TUBE DEFECT causing "neurogenic bladder"), paralysis of URINARY SYSTEM muscles, long-term bladder distension, or certain urogenital malformations. Weak pelvic muscles can allow small urine losses on coughing or sneezing ("stress incontinence"). Uncontrolled DEFECATION can result from spinal or bodily injuries, old age, extreme fear, or severe DIARRHEA. See also ENURESIS.

incubus and succubus Demons (male and female, respectively) who seek to have sexual intercourse with sleeping humans. In medieval Europe some believed that union with an incubus resulted in the birth of witches, demons, and deformed human offspring. MERLIN was said to have been fathered by an incubus.

incunabulum \ˌin-kyə-'nab-yə-ləm\ Book printed before 1501. The date, though convenient, is arbitrary and unconnected to any development in the printing art. The term was probably first applied to early printing in general c. 1650. The total number of editions produced by 15th-century European presses is generally estimated at above 35,000, excluding ephemeral literature (e.g., single sheets, ballads, and devotional tracts) that is now lost or exists only in fragments in places such as binding linings.

Indépendants, Salon des See SALON DES INDÉPENDANTS

Independence City (pop., 1996 est.: 110,000), western Missouri. Settled in 1827, it served as the starting point for the SANTA FE TRAIL and the OREGON TRAIL, and was a rendezvous for wagon trains during the California GOLD RUSH. Home of a MORMON colony 1831–33, it is now the world headquarters of the Reorganized Church of Jesus Christ of Latter-day Saints. It was occupied by Union troops during the AMERICAN CIVIL WAR and was the scene of two skirmishes with Confederates. The hometown of Pres. HARRY TRUMAN, it is the site of the Harry S. Truman Library and Museum.

Independence, Declaration of See DECLARATION OF INDEPENDENCE

Independence Day *or* **Fourth of July** Anniversary of the adoption of the DECLARATION OF INDEPENDENCE by the Second CONTINENTAL CONGRESS (July 4, 1776). It is the greatest secular holiday in the U.S. Celebrating the day became common only after the War of 1812. Thereafter, civic-minded groups worked to link the ideals of democracy and citizenship to the patriotic spirit of the day.

independent counsel *formerly* **special prosecutor** Official appointed by the court at the request of the U.S. attorney general to investigate and prosecute criminal violations by high government officials, members of Congress, or directors of a presidential election campaign after an investigation by the attorney general finds evidence that a crime may have been committed. The counsel is intended to ensure an impartial investigation in situations in which the attorney general would face a conflict of interest. The law establishing the office was passed after the firing of Archibald Cox by Pres. RICHARD NIXON during the WATERGATE SCANDAL. Independent counsels played a prominent role in the IRAN-CONTRA AFFAIR and the Whitewater investigation. In 1999, in the wake of controversy over perceived abuses of the office during the MONICA LEWINSKY scandal, Congress declined to renew the independent-counsel law.

independent school See PUBLIC SCHOOL (BRITISH)

Independent States, Commonwealth of See COMMONWEALTH OF INDEPENDENT STATES

indeterminacy principle See UNCERTAINTY PRINCIPLE

Index librorum prohibitorum \'in-deks-lī-'brō-rəm-prō-ˌhi-bə-'tō-rəm\ (Latin: "Index of Forbidden Books") List of books once forbidden by Roman Catholic church authority as dangerous to the faith or morals of Catholics. Compiled by official censors, the *Index* was never a complete catalog of forbidden reading; it contained only works that ecclesiastical authority was asked to act on. Though the church's concern over books is much older, the first catalog of banned books to be called an index was published in 1559. Publication of the list ceased in 1966, and it was relegated to the status of a historic document.

indexation Comparison of PRICE levels over time. In fiscal policy, indexation is used as a means of offsetting the effect of INFLATION or DEFLATION on social-security payments and taxes by measuring the real value of money from a fixed point of reference, usually a PRICE INDEX. Without indexing, recipients of social-security benefits, for example, would suffer during times of inflation if their benefits remained at a fixed rate. Indexation is used in some countries to offset "bracket creep," which occurs in any PROGRESSIVE TAX system when inflation pushes taxpayers into higher tax brackets. Indexation may also refer to the linking of wage rates and financial instruments to a price index. The GDP (see GROSS DOMESTIC PRODUCT) deflator is used to adjust for inflation the measure of real output in the economy.

India *officially* **Republic of India** *Hindi* **Bharat** \'bər-ət\ Republic, South Asia. It fronts the Bay of BENGAL on the southeast and the ARABIAN SEA on the southwest. Area: 1,222,559 sq mi (3,166,414 sq km). Population (2002 est.): 1,047,671,000. Capital: NEW DELHI. The peoples of India comprise widely varying mixtures of ethnic strains drawn from peoples settled in the subcontinent before the dawn of history or from invaders. Languages: Hindi, English (both official); many other languages, including Bengali, Kashmiri, Marathi, and Urdu; DRAVIDIAN LANGUAGES; hundreds from several other language families. Religions: Hinduism, Buddhism, Jainism, Sikhism, Islam, Christianity. Currency: rupee. India has three major geographic regions: the HIMALAYAS which form its northern border; the Indo-GANGETIC PLAIN, formed by the alluvial deposits of three great river systems, including the GANGES (Ganga); and the southern region, noted for the DECCAN plateau. Agricultural products include rice, wheat, cotton, sugarcane, coconut, spices, jute, tobacco, tea, coffee, and rubber. Its manufacturing sector is highly diversified and includes both heavy and high-technology industries. It is a republic with two legislative houses; its chief of state is the president, and the head of government is the prime minister. India has been inhabited for thousands of years. Agriculture in India dates back to the 7th millennium BC, and an urban civilization, that of the INDUS valley, was established by 2600 BC. BUDDHISM and JAINISM arose in the 6th century BC in reaction to the caste-based society created by the VEDIC RELIGION and its successor, Hinduism. Muslim invasions began c. AD 1000, establishing the long-lived DELHI SULTANATE in 1206 and the MUGHAL DYNASTY in 1526. VASCO DA GAMA's voyage to India in 1498 initiated several centuries of commercial rivalry among the Portuguese, Dutch, English, and French. British conquests in the 18th and 19th centuries led to the rule of the British EAST INDIA CO. and direct administration by the BRITISH EMPIRE began in 1858. After MOHANDAS K. GANDHI helped end British rule in 1947, JAWAHARLAL NEHRU became its first prime minister and he, his daughter INDIRA GANDHI, and grandson RAJIV GANDHI guided the nation's destiny for all but a few years until 1991. The subcontinent was partitioned into two countries—India, with a Hindu majority, and Pakistan, with a Muslim majority in 1947. A later clash with Pakistan resulted in the creation of Bangladesh in 1971. In the 1980s and '90s, Sikhs sought to establish an independent state in PUNJAB. Ethnic and religious conflicts have occurred in other parts of the country as well.

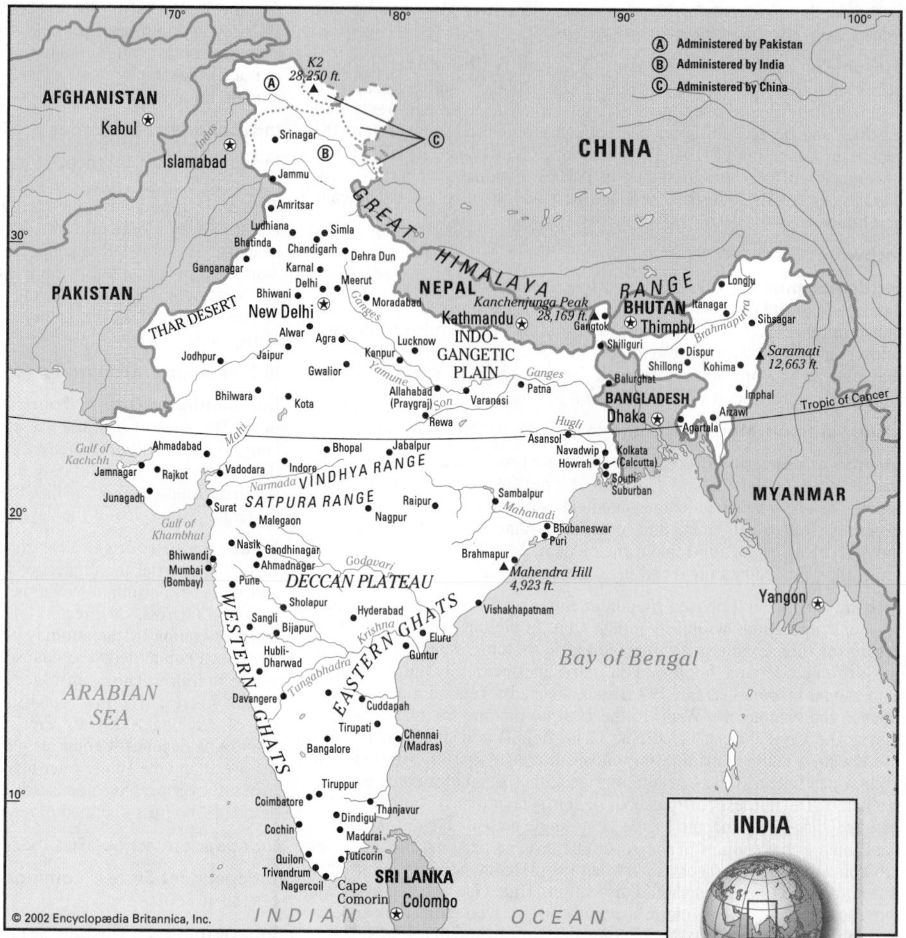

India rubber plant
See RUBBER PLANT

Indian Affairs, Bureau of
(BIA) Agency of the U.S. Department of the INTERIOR that serves as the principal link between federally recognized American Indian populations and the U.S. government. It is responsible for administering about 54 million acres of land held in trust. It also provides various economic development, educational, and natural-resource management services to help promote Indian self-determination and well-being.

Indian architecture
Building traditions of the Indian subcontinent, dating back to at least the 2nd millennium BC. Indian architecture has traditionally been primarily religious. The earliest Indian buildings were Buddhist and Hindu temples made of wood and then brick. By the 4th century BC, stone had become popular, and successive cultures acquired great skill in carving and construction. Large STUPAS were built, along with cave temples and monasteries carved out of solid rock. The Gupta period (4th–6th century AD) saw the rapid development of temple architecture, often decorated with bands of elaborate carving. northern India's most characteristic structure, a temple with a heavily decorated tower (see SIKHARA), reached its stylistic height in the 7th–11th century. The extension of Islam into India in the 11th–12th century introduced typical Muslim architectural forms (e.g., the dome and pointed arch) and decoration. Such masterworks as the TAJ MAHAL resulted from the rule of the Muslim MUGHAL DYNASTY in the 16th–18th century (see MUGHAL ARCHITECTURE). European colonization and British rule introduced European building styles.

Indian buffalo
See WATER BUFFALO

Indian law
Legal practices and institutions of India. Indian law draws on a number of sources, beginning with the customs of the ancient VEDAS and later accretions of Hindu law, which largely concern social matters such as marriage and succession. After the Arab invasions of the 8th century, Islamic law (see SHARIA) was introduced in some areas, particularly in the north. English COMMON LAW became the residual law in jurisdictions under British colonial control, while the Portuguese and French used their own laws in their colonies. Since independence (1947), India has aimed at developing a unified civil code and updating its criminal code.

Indian licorice
See ROSARY PEA

Indian music
Music of the Indian subcontinent. Despite India's vast area and many cultures, its musical traditions are linked by distinctive central threads. Because of early advances of music theory in India, the tradition has had continuity, and because India was the birthplace of Buddhism, its musical influence has spread to other countries. The earliest source is a 5th-century book on theater that includes sections on music and dance. A system of 22 divisions of the octave, from which two basic seven-tone scales derive, was by then already in place. Any tone in both scales could serve as the first tone, making 14 scales in all. The treatise also emphasizes the emotional character of different scales. Cen-

tral to Indian music is the concept of modes known as RAGAS. Rhythm in Indian music, like the construction of scales, is additive. Whereas rhythm in Western music is understood within the context of meter, Indian rhythm is built up from smaller building blocks into larger structures, a concept that has been influential on 20th-cent Western composers. Its basic rhythmic patterns are called talas. Indian music is basically monodic, consisting essentially of a single melody against a drone, though the drum part may virtually constitute another voice. Music is generally for entertainment, but is nevertheless closely linked to Hinduism. Though Indian music has an elaborate theory and employs notation, its tradition is oral and the only authoritative transmission is from master to disciple. The voice is central to traditional Indian music. Indian stringed instruments include the SITAR, sarod, tambura, and vina; the most important percussion instrument is perhaps the TABLA; wind instruments play a lesser role than in Western music.

Indian Mutiny *or* **Sepoy Mutiny** (1857–58) Widespread rebellion against British rule in India begun by Indian troops (sepoys) in the service of the English EAST INDIA CO. The mutiny began when sepoys refused to bite off the ends of new rifle cartridges that may have been lubricated with grease containing a mixture of pigs' and cows' lard. They were shackled and imprisoned; their outraged comrades then shot their British officers and marched to Delhi. The ensuing fight was ferocious on both sides and ended in defeat for the Indians. Its immediate result was abolishment of the East India Co. in favor of direct rule of India by the British government, as well as the beginning of a British policy of consultation with Indians. British-imposed social measures that had antagonized Hindu society (e.g., the introduction of a bill to remove legal obstacles to the remarriage of Hindu women) were halted.

Indian National Congress *or* **Congress Party** Broadly based political party of India, founded in 1885. The Congress Party was a moderate reform party until 1917, when it was taken over by its "extremist" Home Rule wing (see BAL GANGADHAR TILAK). In the 1920s and '30s, under MOHANDAS K. GANDHI, it promoted noncooperation to protest the feebleness of the constitutional reforms of 1919. During World War II, the party announced that India would not support the war until granted complete independence. In 1947 an Indian independence bill became law, and in 1950 the constitution took effect. JAWAHARLAL NEHRU dominated the party from 1951 to 1964. The Indian National Congress has formed most of India's governments since independence was achieved; however, at the end of the 20th century a coalition led by the Hindu nationalist BHARATIYA JANATA PARTY formed the government.

Indian Ocean Body of salt water stretching between Africa in the west, Australia in the east, Asia in the north, and Antarctica in the south. With an area of 28,360,000 sq mi (73,440,000 sq km), it covers approximately one-seventh of the earth's surface, and is the smallest of the world's three major oceans (see ATLANTIC OCEAN, PACIFIC OCEAN). Its greatest depth (24,442 ft or 7,450 m) is in the Java Trench. Its chief marginal seas include the RED SEA, ARABIAN SEA, PERSIAN GULF, Andaman Sea, Bay of BENGAL, and the Great Australian Bight. Its major islands and island groups include MADAGASCAR, SRI LANKA, and the Mascarenes.

Indian paintbrush *or* **paintbrush** Any plant of the genus *Castilleja* (SNAPDRAGON FAMILY), which contains about 200 species of partially or wholly parasitic wildflowers that obtain nourishment from the roots of other plants. The small, tubular, two-lipped flowers are surrounded by brightly colored upper leaves, giving the plant the appearance of having been dipped in a pot of red, orange, yellow, pink, or white paint.

Indian philosophy Any of the numerous philosophical systems developed on the Indian subcontinent, including both orthodox *(astika)* systems, namely, the NYAYA, VAISHESHIKA, SAMKHYA, YOGA, MIMAMSA, and VEDANTA schools of philosophy, and unorthodox *(nastika)* systems, such as BUDDHISM and JAINISM. The history of Indian philosophy may be divided into three periods: the prelogical (to the beginning of the Christian era), the logical (1st–11th century), and the ultralogical (11th–18th century). What Dasgupta calls the prelogical stage covers the pre-Mauryan and the Mauryan periods (c. 321–185 BC) in Indian history. The logical period begins roughly with the Kusanas (1st–2nd century AD) and finds its highest development in the Gupta era (3rd–5th century) and the age of imperial Kanauj (7th century).

Indian pipe Nongreen herbaceous plant *(Monotropa uniflora)* that is saprophytic (living on the remains of dead plants). Clusters grow in moist, shady, wooded areas of North America and Asia. The entire plant is white or grayish, occasionally pink, and turns black as it dries out. A single odorless, cup-shaped flower droops from the tip of a stalk 6–10 in. (15–25 cm) tall. The leaves, which lack CHLOROPHYLL and do not perform PHOTOSYNTHESIS, are small scales. The name reflects the resemblance of this plant to a miniature Indian peace pipe with its stem stuck in the ground.

Indian Removal Act (May 28, 1830) First major legislation that reversed the U.S. policy of respecting the rights of American Indians. The act granted tribes unsettled western prairie land in exchange for their territories within state borders, mainly in the Southeast. Some tribes refused to trade their land, and U.S. troops forced such tribes as the CHEROKEE to march westward along the TRAIL OF TEARS (1838–39). In Florida the SEMINOLES fought resettlement in the SEMINOLE WARS (1835–42).

Indian Reorganization Act (June 18, 1934) Measure enacted by the U.S. Congress to decrease federal control of American Indians and to increase tribal self-government. The act sought to strengthen tribal structure by encouraging written constitutions and to undo the damage caused by the DAWES GENERAL ALLOTMENT ACT by returning surplus lands to the tribes rather than homesteaders. It gave Indians the power to manage their internal affairs and established a revolving credit fund for tribal land purchases and educational assistance. It remains the basic legislation concerning Indian affairs.

Indian sculpture Sculptural traditions, forms, and styles of the civilizations of the Indian subcontinent. Figures, invariably of abstract human forms, were used to instruct people in the truths of HINDUISM, BUDDHISM, and JAINISM. Individuality was suppressed in favor of shapes more perfect and definitive than anything in the transitory appearance of human models. The tradition dates from the INDUS CIVILIZATION of 2500–1800 BC, which produced small terra-cotta figurines. A wide range of styles and traditions flourished over the centuries, but by the 9th–10th century AD sculpture had reached a form that has lasted with little change to the present. From the 10th century it was used mainly for architectural decoration, and numerous small figures were produced for this purpose. See also AMARAVATI SCULPTURE, BHARHUT SCULPTURE, MATHURA ART, SOUTH ASIAN ART, WEST INDIAN BRONZE.

Indian Territory Former territory, U.S. West, including most of modern Oklahoma. The CHOCTAW, CREEK, SEMINOLE, CHEROKEE, and CHICKASAW tribes were forcibly moved to this area between 1830 and 1843, and an 1834 act set aside the land as Indian country. In 1866 its western half was ceded to the U.S.; this portion was opened to white settlers in 1889 and became the Territory of Oklahoma in 1890. The two territories were united and admitted to the Union as the state of Oklahoma in 1907.

Indiana State (population 2000: 6,080,485) midwestern U.S. It covers 36,291 sq mi (93,994 sq km); its capital is INDIANAPOLIS. The WABASH RIVER and the OHIO RIVER define its southern eastern and western borders, respectively. Indiana was originally inhabited by Algonquian-speaking Indians, including the MIAMI, Potawatomi, and DELAWARE. R.-R. LA SALLE explored the region in 1679 and claimed it for France. It passed to Britain in 1763 and then to the U.S. in 1783, and became a territory in 1800. In 1811 U.S. forces won a final victory over the Indians at the Battle of TIPPECANOE. After it was admitted to the Union as the 19th state in 1816, its population began to grow. From 1850 its agriculture expanded, as did industrialization after the AMERICAN CIVIL WAR. For much of the 20th century, steelmaking (see GARY) was important economically.

Indiana, Robert *orig.* **Robert Clark** (born 1928) U.S. painter, sculptor, and graphic artist. Born in New Castle, Ind., he studied at the Art Institute of Chicago. He settled in New York and became a leading exponent of POP ART. He achieved wide recognition for paintings and graphics featuring geometric shapes emblazoned with lettering and vivid colors. In 1964 he collaborated with ANDY WARHOL on the film *Eat* and was commissioned to produce an *EAT* sign for the New York pavilion at the New York World's Fair that year. His most famous image, *LOVE*, first painted on canvas in 1965, became a universal symbol for the Pop generation.

Indiana Dunes State park and national lakeshore, southern shore of Lake MICHIGAN, northern Indiana. The state park (founded 1925) comprises 2,182 acres (883 hectares) of shoreline, marshland, dunes, and forests. At the Big Blowout in the eastern end of the park, lake winds drift sands over a wooded area, creating a "graveyard of trees"; the dunes may reach heights of 200 ft (60 m). The national lakeshore (founded 1966) encloses the state park on three sides. Now covering more than 12,857 acres (5,205 hectares), it includes beaches and wooded ravines.

Indiana University State system of higher education consisting of a main campus in Bloomington (founded 1820) and several other campuses or schools, some operated in cooperation with PURDUE UNIV. All campuses offer undergraduate programs, most offer master's degree programs, and the Bloomington and Indianapolis campuses award doctoral degrees. The medical school is in Indianapolis, the business and law schools in Bloomington. The Bloomington campus has a strong reputation in music and the fine arts and is one of the principal centers for folklore research in the U.S. Campus facilities include the Kinsey Institute for Research in Sex, Gender, and Reproduction. Total enrollment is approx. 86,000.

Indianapolis City (pop., 1996: 747,000) and capital of Indiana. Located on the White River near the center of the state, it was founded in 1821 and made the state capital in 1825. It is a hub of road, rail, and air transportation. It is a leading grain market and an industrial center, with manufactures including pharmaceuticals, machinery, and transportation and electrical equipment. The annual INDIANAPOLIS 500 automobile race is an international event; the Speedway Hall of Fame Museum is located there. It is the site of several colleges and universities.

Indianapolis 500 U.S. automobile race held annually from 1911 at the Indianapolis Motor Speedway, a 2.5-mi (4-km) asphalt oval with banked quarter-mile turns. The "Indy 500" is a 500-mi (805-km) race for top international competitors using specially designed Formula cars (open-wheel, open-cockpit, rear-engine vehicles). Traditionally held on or near Memorial Day, the race is one of the most prestigious on the international racing circuit, drawing large crowds (about 300,000) and offering substantial prizes (over $1.5 million).

Indic writing systems Set of several dozen scripts used now or in the past to write many South and Southeast Asian languages. Aside from the Kharoshthi (Kharosthi) script, used c. 4th century BC–3rd century AD, all extant writing of the region descends from the Brahmi script, first attested in the Middle Indo-Aryan rock inscriptions of ASHOKA (3rd century BC). In the first six centuries after Asoka, Brahmi appears to have diversified into northern and southern variants. The northern types gave rise to the so-called Gupta scripts (4th–5th century), which are ultimately the progenitors of the Devanagari script (now used to write SANSKRIT, HINDI, Marathi, and Nepali), the BENGALI and Oriya scripts, and Gurmukhi, the script of the SIKH scriptures, used also for modern Punjabi in India. The southern types gave rise to the Sinhalese, TELUGU, and Kannada scripts on the one hand, and to the Pallava script on the other. The latter formed the basis of numerous other scripts, including those of the TAMIL and MALAYALAM languages, a host of S.East Asian scripts (e.g., those used to write Mon, Burmese, KHMER, Thai, and Lao), and a number of AUSTRONESIAN LANGUAGES.

indicator, economic See ECONOMIC INDICATOR

indictment In criminal law, a formal written accusation of a crime affirmed by a GRAND JURY and handed up to the court for trial of the accused. In the U.S., the indictment is one of three principal methods of charging offenses, the others being the information (a written accusation resembling an indictment, prepared and presented to the court by a prosecuting official) and, for petty offenses, a complaint by the aggrieved party or by a police officer. An indictment may contain several counts.

Indies, Laws of the Entire body of law promulgated by the Spanish crown in the 16th–18th century for the governance of its colonies. It consists of a compendium of decrees on church government and education, upper and lower courts, political and military administration, Indians, finance, navigation, and commerce. A summary promulgated in 1681 contained 6,377 laws; though criticized for its inconsistencies, for excessive attention to unenforceable details, and for depriving colonists of a responsible role in government, it was the most comprehensive law code ever instituted for a colonial empire, and it set forth humane (if often ignored) principles for treatment of Indians.

indigenismo \ēn-ˌdē-hā-ˈnēs-mō\ Latin American movement pressing for a dominant social and political role for Indians in countries where they constitute most of the population. Its adherents draw a sharp distinction between Indians and people of European ancestry, who have dominated the Indian majorities since the 16th-century Spanish and Portuguese conquest. The movement became very influential in Mexico with the revolution of 1910–20; it was particularly strong during the presidency of LAZARO CARDENAS (1934–40), who made serious efforts to reconstitute the nation in accordance with its Indian heritage. In Peru it is associated with the APRA movement.

indigo \ˈin-di-ˌgō\ Blue vat DYE, obtained until about 1900 entirely from some species of the INDIGO PLANT. Extraction of the dye was important to the economy of colonial American and remained so in India until the early 20th century. Synthetic indigo has replaced the natural dye; chemically it is reduced to the soluble yello leucoindigo, in which form it is applied to textile fibers and reoxidized to indigo.

indigo plant Any shrub or herb in the genus *Indigofera* of the pea family (see LEGUME). Most occur in warm climates and are silky or hairy. The leaves are usually divided into smaller leaflets. Small rose, purple, or white flowers are borne in spikes or clusters. The fruit is a pod. Some species, particularly *I. sumatrana* and *I. arrecta,* were once an important source of indigo dye, a deep navy blue.

indigo snake Nonvenomous snake (*Drymarchon corais,* family Colubridae) found from the southeastern U.S. to Brazil. The largest snake in the U.S., it has a record length of 9.2 ft (2.8 m). In the U.S. it is blue-black; southward it may have brown foreparts, and in the tropics it is often called brown snake. It kills small vertebrates, including venomous snakes, by crushing with its jaws and the weight of its coils, but is not a constrictor. In defense it hisses and vibrates its tail but rarely strikes. It may share a burrow with a gopher tortoise, for which it is often called gopher snake. It has been listed as an endangered species since the 1970s.

Indigo snake (*Drymarchon corais*).
LEONARD LEE RUE III

indiscernibles, identity of See IDENTITY OF INDISCERNIBLES

individualism Political and social philosophy that values individual freedom highly. Modern individualism emerged in Britain with the ideas of ADAM SMITH and JEREMY BENTHAM, and the concept was described by A. DE TOCQUEVILLE as fundamental to the American temper. It is expressed through a value system, a theory of human nature, and a belief in certain political, economic, social, and religious arrangements. All individualist values are people-centered; the individual is of supreme value, and all are morally equal. Individualism opposes authority without consent and views government as an institution whose power should be largely limited to maintaining law and order; society is seen as only a collection of individuals. Individuals are held to have the right to live their lives as they choose and do with their property as they see fit, without unwarranted state interference. Individualistic ideas lost ground in the later 19th and early 20th century, when directly opposing ideas arose, some of which took the form of COMMUNISM and FASCISM, but they gained dominance again later in the 20th century with the near-universal appeal of representative democracy. See also LIBERTARIANISM.

individuation Determination that an individual identified in one way is numerically identical with or distinct from an individual identified in another way (e.g., Venus, known as "the morning star" in the morning and "the evening star" in the evening). Since the concept of an individual seems to require that it be recognizable as such in several possible situations, the problem of individuation is of great importance in ONTOLOGY and LOGIC. The problem of identifying an individual existing at two different times (transtemporal identity) is one of many forms that the problem of individuation can take: What makes that caterpillar identical with this butterfly? What makes the person you are now identical with the person you were a decade ago? In MODAL LOGIC, the problem of transworld individuation (or transworld identity) is of importance because the standard model of theoretic semantics for systems of modal logic assumes that it makes sense to speak of the same individual existing in more than one POSSIBLE WORLD.

Indo-Aryan languages *or* **Indic languages** Major subgroup of the Indo-Iranian branch of the INDO-EUROPEAN LANGUAGE family. Indo-Aryan languages are spoken by over 800 million people, principally in India, Nepal, Pakistan, Bangladesh, and Sri Lanka. The Old Indo-Aryan period is represented by SANSKRIT. Middle Indo-Aryan (c. 600 BC–AD 1000) consists principally of the Prakrit dialects, including PALI. Modern Indo-Aryan speech is largely a single dialect continuum spread over an undivided geographical space, so demarcations between languages and dialects are somewhat artificial. Complicating the situation are competing distinctions between languages with an old literary tradition, local language identification by native speakers (as in censuses), supraregional languages such as Modern Standard HINDI and URDU, and labels introduced by linguists, particularly GEORGE ABRAHAM GRIERSON. In the center of the Indo-Aryan speech area (the "Hindi zone"), covering northern India and extending south as far as Madhya Pradesh, the most common language of administration and education is Modern Standard Hindi. Important regional languages in the northern Indian plain are Haryanvi, Kauravi, Braj, Awadhi, Chhattisgarhi, Bhojpuri, Magahi, and Maithili. Regional languages in Rajasthan include Marwari, Dhundhari, Harauti, and Malvi. In the Himalayan foothills of Himachal Pradesh are Grierson's Pahari languages. Surrounding the Hindi zone, the most significant languages are, moving clockwise, Nepali (East Pahari), Assamese, BENGALI, Oriya, Marathi, Gujarati, Sindhi, the speech of southern, northwestern, and northern Punjab province in Pakistan (called West Punjabi or Lahnda by Grierson), PUNJABI, and Dogri. In JAMMU AND KASHMIR and the far north of Pakistan are the Dardic languages; the most important are Kashmiri, Kohistani, Shina and Khowar. The Nuristani (formerly Kafiri) languages of northwestern Afghanistan are sometimes considered a separate branch of Indo-Iranian. Sinhalese (spoken in Sri Lanka), Divehi (spoken in the Maldive Islands), and ROMANY are also Indo-Aryan languages.

Indo-European languages Family of languages with the greatest number of speakers, spoken in most of Europe and areas of European settlement and in much of southwestern and southern Asia. They are descended from a single unrecorded language believed to have been spoken more than 5,000 years ago in the steppe regions north of the Black Sea and to have split into a number of dialects by 3000 BC. Carried by migrating tribes to Europe and Asia, these developed over time into separate languages. The main branches are ANATOLIAN, Indo-Iranian (including INDO-ARYAN and IRANIAN), GREEK, ITALIC, GERMANIC, ARMENIAN, CELTIC, ALBANIAN, the extinct TOCHARIAN LANGUAGES, BALTIC, and SLAVIC. The study of Indo-European began in 1786 with Sir WILLIAM JONES's proposal that Greek, Latin, Sanskrit, Germanic, and Celtic were all derived from a "common source." In the 19th century, linguists added other languages to the Indo-European family, and scholars such as RASMUS RASK established a system of sound correspondences. Proto-Indo-European has since been partially reconstructed via identification of roots common to its descendants and analysis of shared grammatical patterns.

Indo-Gangetic Plain See GANGETIC PLAIN

Indochina SE peninsula of Asia, occupied by Myanmar, Thailand, Laos, Cambodia, Vietnam, and West Malaysia. The term *Indochina* refers to the intermingling of Indian and Chinese influences in the culture of the region. The French gained control of the eastern part of the peninsula after 1858 and established a colonial empire (see FRENCH INDOCHINA). The western and southern parts were controlled by the British. In World War II parts of the region were occupied by the Japanese (1940–45). See also above-named countries.

Indochina wars 20th-century conflicts in Vietnam, Laos, and Cambodia. The French Indochina War (or First Indochina War) involved France, which had ruled Vietnam as its colony, and the newly independent Democratic Republic of Vietnam under HO CHI MINH; the war ended in Vietnamese victory in 1954. Vietnam was then divided into the communist-dominated north and the U.S.-supported south; war soon broke out between the two. North Vietnam won the Second Indochina War, or VIETNAM WAR, despite heavy U.S. involvement, and the country was reunited in 1976. Cambodia experienced its own civil war between communists and noncommunists during this period, which was won by the communist KHMER ROUGE in 1975. After several years that saw horrifying atrocities under POL POT, the Vietnamese invaded in 1979 and installed a puppet government. Fighting between the Khmer Rouge and the Vietnamese continued throughout the 1980s; Vietnam had withdrawn most of its troops by 1989. In 1993 U.N.-mediated elections established an interim government, and Cambodia's monarchy was reestablished. In Laos, North Vietnam's victory over South Vietnam brought the communist Pathet Lao complete control of Laos.

Indonesia *officially* **Republic of Indonesia** *formerly* **Netherlands Indies** Archipelago nation, located off the coast of mainland Southeast Asia. It comprises about 13,670 islands, of which more than 7,000 are uninhabited. Area: 742,308 sq mi (1,922,570 sq km). Population (2002 est.): 211,023,000. Capital: JAKARTA (on JAVA) It has more than 300 different ethnic groups which fall into three broad divisions: the Muslim rice growers of Java and neighboring islands; the Muslim coastal peoples, including the MALAYS of Sumatra; and the DAYAK and other ethnic groups. Language: Bahasa Indonesia (official); some 250 languages from different ethnic groups. Religions: monotheism (official); Islam (more than four-fifths); Hinduism; Buddhism. Currency: rupiah. Indonesia stretches 3,200 mi (5,100 km) from SUMATRA in the west to NEW GUINEA in the east. Other major islands include Java (with more than half of Indonesia's population), BALI, LOMBOK, SUMBAWA, the western half of TIMOR, BORNEO (part), Celebes (SULAWESI), and the northern MOLUCCAS. The islands are characterized by rugged volcanic mountains and tropical rainforests. Geologically unstable, Indonesia has frequent earthquakes and 220 active volcanoes, including KRAKATAU. Only one-tenth of its land is arable, and rice is the staple crop. Oil, natural gas, timber products, garments, and rubber are the country's major exports. It is a republic with two legislative houses; its head of state and government is the president. Proto-Malay peoples migrated to Indonesia from mainland Asia before 1000 BC. Commercial relations were established with China in about the 1st century AD, and Hindu and Buddhist cultural influences from India began to take hold. Indian traders brought Islam to the islands in the 13th century; it spread throughout the islands, except for BALI, which retained its Hindu religion and culture. European influence began in the 16th century, and the Dutch ruled Indonesia from the late 17th century until 1942, when the Japanese invaded. SUKARNO declared Indonesia's independence in 1945, which the Dutch granted, with nominal union to the Netherlands, in 1949; Indonesia dissolved this union in 1954. The suppression of an alleged coup attempt in 1965 resulted in the deaths of more than 300,000 people the government claimed to be communists, and by 1968 Gen. SUHARTO had taken power. His government forcibly incorporated EAST TIMOR into Indonesia in 1975–76, with much loss of life. In the 1990s the country was beset by political, economic, and environmental problems, and Suharto was deposed in 1998; he was replaced by his vice president, B.J. Habibie. In 1999 the people of East Timor voted for independence from Indonesia, which was granted. Muslim leader Abdurrahman Wahid was elected president that same year but was removed from office in 2001 after being implicated in scandals. He was replaced by his vice president, Megawati Sukarnoputri, the eldest daughter of Sukarno. The rise of communal conflict and secessionist pressures after Suharto's downfall led to speculation about Indonesia's possible breakup. See map on following page.

Indonesian language See MALAY LANGUAGE

Indore \in-'dōr\ City (metro. area pop., 2001 prelim.: 1,639,044), western MADHYA PRADESH state, central India. Located northeast of MUMBAI (Bombay), it was founded in 1715 as a trade market by local landowners, who erected Indreshwar Temple, from which the city's name is derived. It became the capital of the princely state of Indore belonging to the Maratha Holkars. Under the British, it served as the headquarters of the British Central India Agency. The largest city in the state, it is an important commercial and industrial center.

Indra In the ancient VEDIC RELIGION of India, chief of the gods and patron of warriors. Armed with lightning and thunderbolts and strengthened by drinking the elixir SOMA, he vanquished demonic enemies and killed the dragon that kept the monsoon rains from breaking. In later Hinduism Indra was demoted to a rain god and regent of the heavens. He was father to ARJUNA, hero of the *MAHABHARATA*. Indra also appears in Buddhist and Jain mythologies.

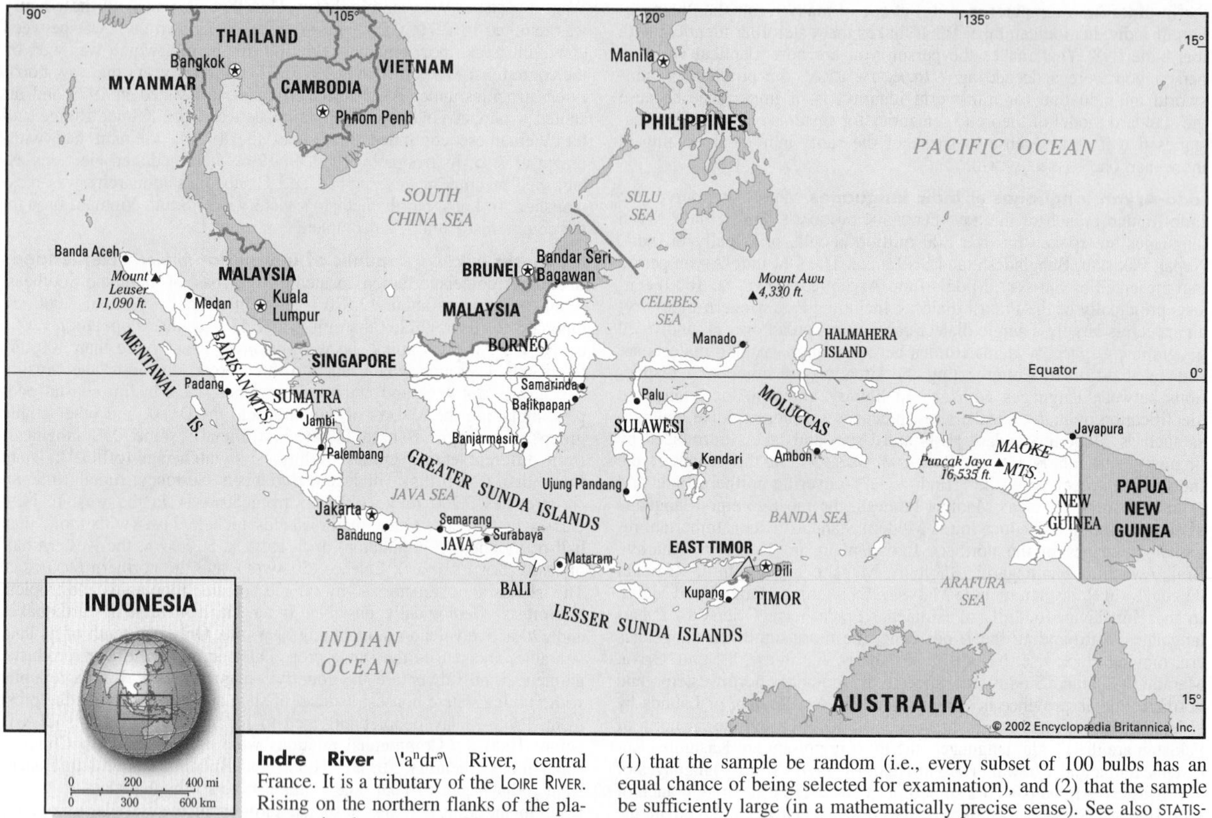

Indre River \'a^{n}dr^{ə}\ River, central France. It is a tributary of the LOIRE RIVER. Rising on the northern flanks of the plateau region known as the MASSIF CENTRAL, it flows northwest through agricultural lands and joins the Loire after a total course of 165 mi (265 km).

inductance Property of a CONDUCTOR, sometimes in the shape of a coil, that is measured by the size of the ELECTROMOTIVE FORCE (emf), or voltage, induced in it, compared with the rate of change of the ELECTRIC CURRENT that produces the voltage. A steadily changing electric current produces a varying MAGNETIC FIELD, which induces an emf in a conductor that is present in the field. The magnitude of this voltage is proportional to the rate of change of the current. The inductance is the proportionality factor. The unit of inductance is the henry, named after JOSEPH HENRY; one henry is equivalent to one volt divided by one ampere per second.

induction In LOGIC, the method of reasoning from a part to a whole, from particulars to generals, from the individual to the universal, or from the characteristics of a sample to the characteristics of the entire population from which it is selected. Logicians traditionally distinguished between deductive logic (see DEDUCTION) and inductive logic, but the problems earlier subsumed under induction are considered to be concerns of the methodology of the natural sciences, and "logic" is generally taken to mean deductive logic. See also problem of INDUCTION, JOHN STUART MILL, SCIENTIFIC METHOD.

induction See ELECTROMAGNETIC INDUCTION, ELECTROSTATIC INDUCTION

induction, problem of Problem of justifying the inference from the characteristics of observed instances of a general concept to unobserved instances of the same concept. For example, if all emeralds I have ever seen have been green, what entitles me to draw the inference that all emeralds are green, given that my past observations do not strictly entail (or deductively imply) that all emeralds are green? May we infer that the characteristics of a sample taken from a population are characteristics of the entire population? A quality-control engineer who looks at a sample of 100 lightbulbs produced by a particular manufacturing process and finds that five are defective may conclude that 5% of all bulbs that have been and will be produced by the process are defective. For the engineer's inference to be justified, two criteria that must be met are (1) that the sample be random (i.e., every subset of 100 bulbs has an equal chance of being selected for examination), and (2) that the sample be sufficiently large (in a mathematically precise sense). See also STATISTICS.

induction heating Method of raising the temperature of an electrically conductive material by subjecting it to an alternating ELECTROMAGNETIC FIELD. Energy in the ELECTRIC CURRENTS induced in the object is dissipated as HEAT. Induction heating is used in metalworking to heat METALS for soldering, tempering, and annealing, and in induction furnaces for melting and processing metals. The principle of the induction-heating process resembles that of the transformer. A water-cooled coil (inductor), acting as the primary winding of a transformer, surrounds the material to be heated (the workpiece), which acts as the secondary winding. Alternating current flowing in the primary coil induces eddy currents in the workpiece, causing it to become heated. The depth to which the eddy currents penetrate, and therefore the distribution of heat within the object, depend on the frequency of the primary alternating current and the magnetic permeability, as well as the resistivity, of the material.

indulgence In ROMAN CATHOLICISM, the remission of temporal punishment for SINS that have been forgiven through the SACRAMENT of penance. The theology of indulgences is based on the concept that, even though the crime of sin and its eternal punishment are forgiven through penance, divine justice demands that the sinner pay for his crime either in this life or in PURGATORY. The first indulgences were intended to shorten times of penance by substituting periods of FASTING, private prayers, almsgiving, and payments of money for religious purposes. After the 12th century they were more widely used, and abuses became common as indulgences were put up for sale to earn money for the church or to enrich unscrupulous clerics. JAN HUS opposed them, and MARTIN LUTHER'S NINETY-FIVE THESES (1517) were in part a protest against indulgences. The Council of TRENT put an end to the abuses in 1562 but not to the doctrine itself.

Indus civilization (c. 2500–c. 1700 BC) Earliest known urban culture of the Indian subcontinent and the most extensive of the world's three earliest civilizations, stretching from near the present-day Iran–Pakistan border on the Arabian Sea in the west to near Delhi in the east, and 500 mi (800 km) to the south and 1,000 mi (1,600 km) to the northeast. It is known to have included two large cities, Harappa and MOHENJO DARO (in what is now Pakistan), whose large size suggests centralization in two large states or one state with two capitals. Alternatively, Harappa may have succeeded Mohenjo Daro. It was a literate civilization; the language has been tentatively identified as Dravidian. Wheat and barley were grown, many animals (including cats, dogs, and cattle) were domesticated, and cotton was cultivated. The best-known artifacts are seals depicting real and imaginary animals. How and when the civilization came to an end is unclear; Mohenjo-daro was attacked and destroyed in the mid-2nd millennium BC, but in the south there was continuity between the Indus civilization and the Copper Age civilizations of central and western India.

Indus River Trans-Himalayan river of southern Asia. It is one of the world's longest rivers, with a length of 1,800 mi (2,900 km). Its annual flow of 272 billion cu yards (207 billion cu m) is twice that of the NILE. It rises in southwestern Tibet and flows northwest along the slopes of the HIMALAYAS. After crossing the western Kashmir border it turns south to enter Pakistan. Swelled by tributaries from the PUNJAB, including the JHELUM, CHENAB, RAVI, BEAS, and SUTLEJ rivers, it widens and flows more slowly. It has supplied water for irrigation on the plains of Pakistan since early times.

industrial and organizational relations *or* **organizational relations** Study of human behavior in the workplace, focusing especially on the influence such relations have on an organization's PRODUCTIVITY. CLASSICAL ECONOMICS viewed workers as instruments of production, subject to the laws of SUPPLY AND DEMAND. Industrial relations did not become the subject of scholarly attention until the late 1920s, when Elton Mayo (1880–1949) studied productivity at Western Electric Co.'s Hawthorne Works. Concluding that merely being chosen to participate in the study improved workers' productivity (the "Hawthorne effect"), Mayo became the first scholar to show workers responding to psychosocial stimuli. Other aspects of industrial and organizational relations include human resources management, which involves the development of job descriptions and organizational structures; recruiting, training, and general oversight of employees; negotiating terms of employment, planning for the future, and the study of managerial styles.

industrial design Design of products made by large-scale industry for mass distribution. Among the considerations for such products are structure, operation, appearance, and conformance to production, distribution, and selling procedures; appearance is the principal consideration in industrial design. The International Council of Societies of Industrial Design was founded in London in 1957 and within 25 years had members in more than 40 countries. Two significant trends have persisted: streamlining, a design principle pioneered by RAYMOND LOEWY and others in the 1930s; and planned obsolescence, design changes that tempt owners to replace goods with new purchases more frequently than would normally be necessary.

industrial ecology Discipline that traces the flow of energy and materials from their natural resources through manufacture, the use of products, and their final recycling or disposal. Research in industrial ecology began in the early 1990s. Life-cycle analysis traces the flow of materials; design for the environment works to minimize energy use, pollution, and waste. Industrial ecologists aim to create industries in which every waste is a raw material for another product.

industrial engineering Application of ENGINEERING principles and techniques of scientific management to the maintenance of high levels of productivity at optimum cost in industrial enterprises. FRED W. TAYLOR pioneered in the scientific measurement of work, and Frank (1868–1924) and Lillian (1878–1972) Gilbreth refined it with TIME-AND-MOTION STUDIES. As a result, production processes were simplified, enabling workers to increase production. The industrial engineer selects tools and materials for production that are most efficient and least costly to the company. The engineer may also determine the sequence of production and the design of plant facilities or factories. See also HUMAN-FACTORS ENGINEERING.

industrial espionage Acquisition of trade secrets from business competitors. Industrial spying is a reaction to the efforts of many businesses to keep secret their designs, formulas, manufacturing processes, research, and future plans. Trade secrets may find their way into the open market through disloyal employees or through various other means. Penalties against those found guilty range from an injunction against further use of the knowledge to substantial damages. See also PATENT.

industrial medicine *or* **occupational medicine** Branch of medicine dealing with workers' health and prevention and treatment of diseases and injuries in the workplace. Workplace hazards include exposure to dangerous materials including asbestos and coal dust, radiation exposure, and machinery capable of causing injuries ranging from minor to life-threatening. Industrial medical programs mandate protective devices around machines' moving parts, proper ventilation of work areas, use of less toxic materials, containment of production processes, and protective equipment and clothing. Good industrial medical programs improve labor-management relations, increase workers' overall health and productivity, and reduce insurance costs.

industrial melanism \'me-lə-ˌni-zəm\ Darkness of the skin, feathers, or fur developed by a population of animals living in an industrial region where the environment is soot-darkened. The melanization of a population increases the probability that its members will survive and reproduce because it offers protection in the form of camouflage; it takes place over the course of many generations as the result of NATURAL SELECTION of the lighter, more conspicuous animals by predators.

industrial-organizational psychology *or* **I-O psychology** Application of the concepts and methods of EXPERIMENTAL, CLINICAL, and SOCIAL psychology to the workplace. I-O psychologists are concerned with such matters as personnel evaluation and placement, job analysis, worker-management relations (including morale and job satisfaction), workforce training and development (including leadership training), and productivity improvement. They may work closely with business managers, industrial engineers, and human-resources professionals.

Industrial Revolution Process of change from an agrarian, handicraft economy to one dominated by industry and machine manufacture. It began in England in the 18th century. Technological changes included the use of iron and steel, new energy sources, invention of new machines that increased production (including the SPINNING JENNY), development of the factory system, and important developments in transportation and communication (including the STEAM ENGINE and TELEGRAPH). Other changes included agricultural improvements, a wider distribution of wealth, political changes reflecting the shift in economic power, and sweeping social changes. The Industrial Revolution was largely confined to Britain from 1760 to 1830, then spread to Belgium and France. Other nations lagged behind, but once Germany, the U.S., and Japan achieved industrial power they outstripped Britain's initial successes. Eastern European countries lagged into the 20th century, and not until the mid-20th century did the Industrial Revolution spread to such countries as China and India. Many analysts saw evidence of a second, or new, industrial revolution in the later 20th century, with the use of new materials and energy sources, automated factories, new ownership of the means of production, and a shift away from LAISSEZ-FAIRE government.

Industrial Workers of the World (IWW) *known as* **the Wobblies** Radical labor organization founded in Chicago in 1905. The founders, who opposed moderate policies of the AFL, included WILLIAM HAYWOOD of the Western Federation of Miners, DANIEL DE LEON of the Socialist Labor Party, and EUGENE V. DEBS. In 1908 the IWW split, and a militant group led by Haywood prevailed. To reach its goal of workers controlling the means of production, it advocated general strikes, boycotts, and sabotage. Its tactics led to arrests and adverse publicity, though it made gains through strikes in the mining and lumber industries. It opposed U.S. participation in World War I, and some of its leaders were prosecuted. By the 1920s membership had dwindled greatly.

industrialization Process of converting to a socioeconomic order in which INDUSTRY is dominant. The changes that took place in Britain during the INDUSTRIAL REVOLUTION of the late 18th and 19th century led the way for the early industrializing nations of Western Europe and North America. Industrialization entailed both TECHNOLOGY and profound social developments. The freeing of laborers from feudal and customary obligations created a free market in labor, with a pivotal role for the entrepreneur. Cities attracted large numbers of people, massing workers in new industrial towns and FACTORIES. Later industrializers attempted to manipulate some of the elements: the Soviet Union eliminated the entrepreneur; Japan stimulated and sustained the entrepreneur's role; Denmark and New Zealand industrialized primarily by commercializing and mechanizing agriculture.

industry Group of productive organizations that produce or supply goods, services, or sources of income. In economics, industries are customarily classified as primary, secondary, and tertiary; secondary industries are further classified as heavy and light. Primary industry includes agriculture, forestry, fishing, mining, quarrying, and extracting minerals. Secondary or MANUFACTURING industry processes the raw materials supplied by primary industries into consumer goods, or further processes goods from other secondary industries, or builds capital goods used to manufacture consumer and nonconsumer goods; secondary industry also includes energy-producing industries and the construction industry. Tertiary or SERVICE INDUSTRY includes banking, finance, insurance, investment, and real estate services; wholesale, retail, and resale trade; transportation, information, and communications services; professional, consulting, legal, and personal services; tourism, hotels, restaurants, and entertainment; repair and maintenance services; education and teaching; and health, social welfare, administrative, police, security, and defense services.

Indy \aⁿ-'dē\, **(Paul Marie Theodore) Vincent d'** (1851–1931) French composer and teacher. Trained in organ and composition, he rejected the prevailing French style as frivolous by comparison with the German musical tradition. He wrote several important stage works, including *Fervaal* (1895) and *Le légende de Saint Christophe* (1915), but such orchestral works as *Symphony on a French Mountain Air* (1886), *Summer Day in the Mountains* (1905), and *Istar* (1896) remain better known. In 1894 he cofounded the music academy called the Schola Cantorum in Paris, where many of France's foremost composers and musicians would be trained.

inequality In mathematics, a statement of an order relationship—greater than, greater than or equal to, less than, or less than or equal to—between two numbers or algebraic expressions. Inequalities can be posed either as questions, much like EQUATIONS, and solved by similar techniques, or as statements of fact in the form of THEOREMS. For example, the triangle inequality states that the sum of the lengths of any two sides of a triangle is greater than or equal to the length of the remaining side. Mathematical ANALYSIS relies on many such inequalities (e.g., the SCHWARZ INEQUALITY) in the proofs of its most important theorems.

inert gas See NOBLE GAS

inertia \i-'nər-shə\ Inherent property of a body that makes it oppose any force that would cause a change in its motion. A body at rest and a body in motion both oppose forces that might cause ACCELERATION. The inertia of a body can be measured by its MASS, which governs its resistance to the action of a force, or by its moment of inertia about a specified axis, which measures its resistance to the action of a TORQUE about the same axis.

inertia, moment of Quantitative measure of the rotational INERTIA of a body. As a rotating body spins about an external or internal axis (either fixed or unfixed), it opposes any change in the body's speed of rotation that may be caused by a TORQUE. It is defined as the sum of the products obtained by multiplying the mass of each particle of matter in a given body by the square of its distance from the axis of rotation.

infancy Among humans, the period of life between birth and the acquisition of language usually one to two years later. The average newborn infant weighs 7.5 lbs (3.4 kg) and is about 20 in (51 cm) long. At birth, infants display a set of inherited reflexes involving such acts as sucking, blinking, and grasping. They are sensitive to light–dark visual contrasts and movements, and show a noticeable preference for gazing at the human face; they also early begin to recognize the human voice. By four months most babies are able to sit up, and most begin crawling in 7–10 months; by 12 months most are able to start walking. Virtually all infants begin to comprehend some words several months before they themselves speak their first meaningful words.

infanticide Killing of the newborn. Infanticide has often been interpreted as a primitive method of BIRTH CONTROL and a means of ridding a group of its weak or undesirable children; but most societies actively welcome children and put them to death (or allow them to die) only under exceptional circumstances—e.g., when there is little or no likelihood of being able to provide support. As late as the 18th century in European countries unwanted infants were disposed of by abandonment and exposure. Firstborn SACRIFICE, or the offering of one's most precious possession to the deities, is known from the Bible and from the histories of Egypt, Greece, Rome, and India.

infantile paralysis See POLIOMYELITIS

infantry Troops who fight on foot. The term applies both to soldiers armed with hand weapons such as the spear and sword in ancient times and to troops armed with automatic rifles and rocket launchers in modern times. Their objective has always been to seize and hold ground and, when necessary, to occupy enemy territory. Apart from the temporary dominance of CAVALRY in the feudal period, it has been the largest single element in Western armies since ancient times.

infection Invasion of the body by various agents—including BACTERIA, fungi (see FUNGUS), PROTOZOANS, VIRUSES, and WORMS—and its reaction to them or their TOXINS. Infections are called subclinical until they perceptibly affect health, when they become infectious diseases. Infection can be local (e.g., an ABSCESS), confined to one body system (e.g., PNEUMONIA in the lungs), or generalized (e.g., SEPTICEMIA). Infectious agents can enter the body by inhalation, ingestion, sexual transmission, passage to a fetus during pregnancy or birth, wound contamination, or animal or insect bites. The body responds with an attack on the invader by LEUKOCYTES, production of ANTIBODIES or ANTITOXINS, and often a rise in temperature. The antibodies may result in short-term or lifelong IMMUNITY. Despite significant progress in preventing and treating infectious diseases, they remain a major cause of illness and death, particularly in regions of poor sanitation, poor nutrition, and crowding.

inferiority complex Acute sense of personal inferiority, often resulting in either timidity or (through overcompensation) exaggerated aggressiveness. Though once a standard psychological concept, particularly among followers of ALFRED ADLER, it has lost much of its usefulness through imprecise popular misuse.

infertility Inability of a couple to conceive and reproduce, defined as failure to conceive after one year of regular intercourse without CONTRACEPTION. Inability to conceive when desired can result from a defect at any of the stages required for FERTILITY (see REPRODUCTIVE SYSTEM). About one in every eight couples is infertile. Most cases involve the female partner, 30–40% involve the male, and 10% are caused by unknown factors. In women, causes include ovulation or hormone problems, fallopian-tube disorders, and a chemical balance that is hostile to SPERM; in men, causes include IMPOTENCE, low sperm count, and sperm abnormalities. Either partner can have a blockage of the pathways the sperm must travel, often treatable by surgery. Emotional factors may contribute; return of normal fertility may require only counseling. Fertility drugs can stimulate the release of EGGS (often more than one, leading to MULTIPLE BIRTHS). Low sperm count may be overcome by limiting intercourse to the time of ovulation, the most fertile period. If these methods are unsuccessful, couples may try ARTIFICIAL INSEMINATION, IN VITRO FERTILIZATION, or SURROGATE MOTHERHOOD, or choose ADOPTION instead.

infinite series In mathematics, the sum of infinitely many numbers, whose relationship can typically be expressed as a formula or a FUNCTION. An infinite series that results in a finite sum is said to converge (see CONVERGENCE). One that does not, diverges. Mathematical ANALYSIS is largely taken up with studying the conditions under which a given function will result in a convergent infinite series. Such series (e.g., the FOURIER SERIES) are particularly useful in solving DIFFERENTIAL EQUATIONS.

infinity In mathematics, the useful concept of a process with no end. As represented by the symbol ∞, it is often mistakenly thought to be the largest number or a place on the real number line. Instead, it is the idea of a limit, as in the expression $x \to \infty$, which suggests that the variable x increases without bound. For example, the function $f(x) = 1/x$, or the reciprocal of x, tends toward 0 as x approaches infinity as a limit. This process of approaching is crucial to the definition of the DERIVATIVE and the INTEGRAL in calculus, as well as to many other concepts of mathematical ANALYSIS.

inflammation Local reaction of living tissues to injury or illness, including burns, pneumonia, leprosy, tuberculosis, and rheumatoid arthritis. Its major signs are heat, redness, swelling, and pain. The process begins with brief contraction of nearby arterioles (see ARTERIES). Dilation follows, flushing the CAPILLARIES with blood, from which fluid, PLASMA proteins, and LEUKOCYTES pass into the injured tissues, causing swelling as they attack the cause of injury. Initial acute inflammation can have any of four outcomes: resolution (return to normal), organization (new tissue buildup; see SCAR), suppuration (pus formation; see ABSCESS), or chronic inflammation. Sometimes treatment—including ANTIBIOTICS for bacteria, or surgical removal of an irritating foreign body—can eliminate the

H I J K

cause. If not, anti-inflammatory drugs (e.g., CORTISONE or ASPIRIN) may be given, or simple remedies (e.g., hot or cold compresses) may be applied.

inflation In astronomy, a hypothesized period of exponential expansion of the universe, shortly after the BIG BANG, which may account for some of the universe's observed properties, such as the distribution of energy and matter. GRAND UNIFIED THEORIES of the forces of nature suggest that inflation could have occurred during the first 10^{-32} of a second after the universe began, when the STRONG FORCE was decoupling from the WEAK and ELECTROMAGNETIC forces. During this time, the universe would have expanded by more than 100 orders of magnitude. Inflation is an effect of general RELATIVITY when the universe is trapped in a state of nonzero energy density (false vacuum).

inflation In economics, increases in the level of PRICES. Inflation is generally thought of as an inordinate rise in the general level of prices. Four theories are commonly used to explain inflation. The first and oldest, the quantity theory, promoted in the 18th century by DAVID HUME, assumes that prices will rise as the supply of money increases. MILTON FRIEDMAN refined the quantity theory in the mid-20th century, arguing that the prescription for stable prices is to increase the money supply at a rate equal to that at which the economy is expanding. A second approach is JOHN MAYNARD KEYNES's theory of income determination, which assumes that inflation occurs when the demand for goods and services is greater than the supply. It calls for the government to control inflation by adjusting levels of spending and taxation and by raising or lowering interest rates. A third approach is the cost-push theory. It traces inflation to a phenomenon known as the price-wage spiral, in which workers' demands for wage increases lead employers to increase prices to reflect their higher costs, thereby sowing the seeds of a further round of wage demands. A fourth approach is the structural theory, which emphasizes structural maladjustments in the economy, as when in developing countries imports tend to increase faster than exports, pushing down the international value of the developing country's currency and causing prices to rise internally. See also DEFLATION, PRICE INDEX.

inflorescence \ˌin-flə-ˈre-sᵊns\ Cluster of flowers on one or a series of branches, which together make a large showy blossom. Categories depend on the arrangement of flowers on an elongated main axis (peduncle) or on sub-branches from the main axis, and on the timing and position of flowering. In determinate inflorescences, the youngest flowers are at the bottom or outside (e.g., ONION flowers). In indeterminate inflorescences, the youngest flowers are at the top or in the center (e.g., SNAPDRAGON, LILY OF THE VALLEY, and *Astilbe* flowers). Other indeterminate inflorescences are the dangling male and female CATKINS of OAK trees, the spike of BARLEY, and the flat head (capitulum) of the DANDELION.

influenza *or* **flu** *or* **grippe** Acute viral INFECTION of the upper or lower respiratory tract. Influenza VIRUSES A (the most common), B, and C produce similar symptoms, but infection with or vaccination against one does not give immunity against the others. Chills, fatigue, and muscle aches begin abruptly. The temperature soon reaches 101–104°F (38–40°C). Head, muscle, abdominal, and joint aches may be accompanied by sore throat. Recovery starts in three to four days, and respiratory symptoms become more prominent. Bed rest, high fluid intake, and aspirin or other anti-fever drugs are standard treatment. Influenza A and B occur in two-to-three-year and four-to-five-year cycles and spread in wavelike epidemics throughout the world. Mortality is usually low, but in rare outbreaks (see INFLUENZA EPIDEMIC OF 1918–19) it reaches immense proportions. Most deaths result from PNEUMONIA or BRONCHITIS.

Influenza Epidemic of 1918–19 *or* **Spanish Influenza Epidemic** Most severe INFLUENZA outbreak of the 20th century. Flu pandemics occur every 30–40 years, but this one was unusually severe and spread very rapidly. It apparently started as a fairly mild strain in a U.S. army camp in early March 1918. Troops sent to fight in World War I spread the virus to Western Europe, where a more lethal strain emerged. Outbreaks occurred in nearly every inhabited part of the world, spreading from ports to cities along transportation routes. PNEUMONIA often developed quickly and killed within two days. Perhaps the most deadly epidemic in history, it left an estimated 30 million dead; unusually, half the deaths were among 20- to 40-year-olds.

information processing Acquisition, recording, organization, retrieval, display, and dissemination of information. Today the term usually refers to computer-based operations. Information processing consists of locating and capturing information, using software to manipulate it into a desired form, and outputting the data. An Internet SEARCH ENGINE is an example of an information-processing tool, as is any sophisticated INFORMATION-RETRIEVAL system. See also DATA PROCESSING.

information retrieval Recovery of information, especially in a DATABASE stored in a computer. Two main approaches are matching words in the query against the database index (keyword searching) and traversing the database using HYPERTEXT or hypermedia links. Keyword searching has been the dominant approach to text retrieval since the early 1960s; hypertext has so far been confined largely to personal or corporate information-retrieval applications. Evolving information-retrieval techniques, exemplified by developments with modern Internet SEARCH ENGINES, combine natural language, hyperlinks, and keyword searching. Other techniques that seek higher levels of retrieval precision are studied by researchers involved with ARTIFICIAL INTELLIGENCE.

information science Discipline that deals with the processes of storing and transferring information. It attempts to bring together concepts and methods from such varied disciplines as library science, computer science and engineering, linguistics, and psychology to develop techniques and devices to aid in the handling of information. In its early stages in the 1960s, information science was concerned primarily with applying the then-new computer technology to the processing and managing of documents. The applied computer technologies and theoretical studies of information science have since permeated many other disciplines. Computer science and engineering still tend to absorb its theory- and technology-oriented subjects, and management science tends to absorb information-systems subjects.

information theory See COMMUNICATION THEORY

infrared astronomy \ˌin-frə-ˈred\ Study of astronomical objects by observing the INFRARED RADIATION they emit. Its techniques enable investigators to examine many celestial objects that give off energy at wavelengths in the infrared region of the ELECTROMAGNETIC SPECTRUM but that cannot otherwise be seen from earth because their temperature is too low to emit much optical light or the light they emit at optical wavelengths is blocked by dust particles. Infrared astronomy originated in the early 19th century with the work of HERSCHEL FAMILY, who discovered infrared radiation while studying sunlight. The first systematic infrared observations of stellar objects were made in the 1920s; modern techniques, such as the use of interference filters for ground-based telescopes, were introduced in the early 1960s. Because water vapor in the atmosphere absorbs infrared rays, observations from spacecraft are more effective. Infrared astronomy has made possible the discovery of solid debris around certain stars, suggesting planetary systems, and BROWN DWARFS.

infrared radiation Portion of the ELECTROMAGNETIC SPECTRUM that extends from the MICROWAVE range to the red end of the visible light range. Its wavelengths vary from about 0.7 to 1,000 micrometers. Most of the radiation emitted by a moderately heated surface is infrared, and it forms a continuous spectrum. Molecular excitation produces extensive infrared radiation but in a discrete spectrum of lines or bands. Infrared wavelengths are useful for night-vision equipment, heat-seeking missiles, molecular SPECTROSCOPY, and INFRARED ASTRONOMY, among other things. The trapping of infrared radiation by atmospheric gases is also the basis of the GREENHOUSE EFFECT.

Inge \ˈinj\, **William (Motter)** (1913–1973) U.S. playwright and screenwriter. Born in Independence, Kan., he worked as a schoolteacher (1937–49) and moonlighted as drama editor of the St. Louis *Star-Times* (1943–46). His first play, *Farther Off from Heaven* (1947), was revised for Broadway as *The Dark at the Top of the Stairs* (1957; film, 1960). He is best known for his plays *Come Back, Little Sheba* (1950; film, 1952), *Picnic* (1953, Pulitzer Prize; film, 1956), and *Bus Stop* (1955; film, 1956), and for his original screenplay for *Splendor in the Grass* (1961, Academy Award). He was one of the first dramatists to explore small-town life in the Midwest.

Inglewood City (pop., 1996 est.: 111,000), southwestern California, situated southwest of LOS ANGELES. Settled by Daniel Freeman in 1873, it was laid out by the Centinela-Inglewood Land Co. in 1887 and incorporated in 1908. It developed along with the Los Angeles metropolitan area and is the site of Hollywood Park racetrack.

ingot \'iŋ-gət\ Mass of METAL cast into a size and shape such as a bar, plate, or sheet convenient to store, transport, and work into a semifinished or finished product. The term also refers to a MOLD in which metal is so cast. Steel ingots range in size from small rectangular blocks weighing a few pounds (or kilograms) to huge, tapered, octagonal masses weighing more than 500 tons (450 metric tons).

Ingres \'aⁿgrᵊ\, **Jean-Auguste-Dominique** (1780–1867) French painter. He studied with J.-L. DAVID in Paris before attending the École des Beaux-Arts (1799–1801), where he won a Prix de Rome scholarship. Critics condemned one of his first public works, the awe-inspiring portrait *Napoleon on His Imperial Throne* (1806), as stiff and archaic, but its style was one he developed intentionally. In Italy (1806–24) he prospered with portraits and history paintings. His small-scale portrait drawings are meticulously rendered. Back in Paris he received critical acclaim at last and won admission to the Academy with *The Vow of Louis XIII* (1824). In 1825 he succeeded David as the leader of French Neoclassical painting and opened a teaching studio. It became one of the largest in Paris, and by the mid-1840s he was France's most sought-after society portraitist. Some of his most notable later works are female nudes. None of his many students attained distinction, but his influence is seen in the work of EDGAR DEGAS, AUGUSTE RENOIR, and PABLO PICASSO.

inhalation therapy See RESPIRATORY THERAPY

inheritance Devolution of property on an heir or heirs upon the death of its owner. In civil-law jurisdictions it is called succession. The concept depends on a common acceptance of the notion of private ownership of goods and property. Under some systems, land is considered communal property and rights to it are redistributed, rather than bequeathed, on the death of a community member. In many countries, a minimum portion of the decedent's estate must be assigned to the surviving spouse and often to the progeny as well. Intestacy laws, which govern the INHERITANCE of estates whose distribution is not directed by a WILL, universally view kinship between the decedent and the beneficiary as a primary consideration. Inheritance usually entails payment of an inheritance tax. See also INTESTATE SUCCESSION, PROBATE.

inheritance tax Levy on the property accruing to each beneficiary of the estate of a deceased person. Inheritance tax may be more difficult to administer than ESTATE TAX because the value passing to each beneficiary must be fixed, and this often requires complex actuarial calculations. Inheritance taxes date back to the Roman Empire. In the U.S. inheritance taxes have always been collected by the individual states, while the federal government has imposed an estate tax. The first state inheritance tax was imposed by Pennsylvania in 1826.

inhibition In enzymology, a phenomenon in which a compound (an inhibitor), usually similar in structure to the substance on which an ENZYME acts (substrate), interacts with the enzyme so that the resulting complex cannot undergo the usual reaction or cannot form the usual product. The inhibitor may function by combining with the enzyme at the site at which the reaction usually occurs (competitive inhibition) or at another site (noncompetitive inhibition). See also ALLOSTERIC CONTROL, FEEDBACK INHIBITION, REPRESSION.

inhibition In psychology, the conscious or unconscious suppression of free or spontaneous thought or behavior through the operation of psychological impediments, including internalized social controls. Inhibition serves such useful social functions as protecting oneself and others from harm and enabling the delay of gratification from pleasurable activities. Both extreme lack of inhibition and excessive inhibition can be personally destructive. Inhibition also plays an important role in LEARNING, since an organism must learn to restrain certain instinctual behaviors or previously learned patterns in order to master new patterns. In PHYSIOLOGICAL PSYCHOLOGY, inhibition refers to the suppression of neural electrical activity.

initiation See rite of PASSAGE, SECRET SOCIETY

injunction In civil proceedings, a court order compelling a party to do or refrain from doing a specified act. It is an equitable remedy for harm for which no adequate remedy exists in law. Thus it is used to prevent a future harmful action (e.g., disclosing confidential information, instituting a national labor strike, or violating a group's civil rights) rather than to compensate for an injury that has already occurred. It also provides relief from harm for which an award of money damages is not a satisfactory solution. A defendant who violates an injunction may be cited for contempt. See also EQUITY.

ink Fluid or paste of various colors (usually black or dark blue) used for writing and PRINTING, composed of a PIGMENT or DYE in a liquid "vehicle." Early inks used lampblack (a form of CARBON) or colored juices, extracts, or suspensions. Modern writing inks usually contain ferrous sulfate (see IRON) with a small amount of an acid; on paper, they darken and bond, becoming permanent. Colored and washable inks usually contain soluble synthetic dyes. Printing inks, with a base of quick-drying SOLVENT, are formulated for various requirements (including color, opacity, fade resistance, pliability, and odorlessness) for uses in OFFSET, LETTERPRESS, screen, ink-jet, laser, and other printing.

Inkatha Freedom Party \in-'kä-tə\ Political party in South Africa consisting largely of the ZULU. It originated in 1924 as a cultural movement under King Dinizulu. His grandson, MANGOSUTHU G. BUTHELEZI, revived it in 1974 as a political party after breaking with the AFRICAN NATIONAL CONGRESS (ANC). Under Buthelezi, Inkatha advocated a struggle against APARTHEID but a willingness to accept power-sharing arrangements short of majority rule. From the late 1980s, Inkatha and ANC followers were regularly involved in bloody clashes with strong tribal (Zulu vs. non-Zulu) overtones. In 1991 the white South African government admitted that it had secretly subsidized Inkatha.

Inland Passage See INSIDE PASSAGE

Inn River Major tributary of the DANUBE RIVER. It rises in Switzerland and flows 317 mi (510 km) northeast across western Austria and southern Germany. Its Swiss section is called the Engadin. In Austria it travels past INNSBRUCK and along the Bavarian ALPS, entering Germany in BAVARIA, where it flows northeast. It forms part of the Austro–German border as it joins the Danube at Passau.

inner ear *or* **labyrinth of the ear** Part of the EAR containing organs of HEARING and equilibrium. The bony labyrinth has three sections (semicircular canals, vestibule, and cochlea); within each structure is a corresponding part of the membranous labyrinth (semicircular ducts, two saclike structures in the vestibule, and cochlear duct). Sound vibrations are transmitted from the middle ear through the membrane-covered oval window to fluid in the snail-shell-shaped cochlea, whose motion stimulates hair cells in the cochlea. The hair cells trigger nerve impulses that travel to the brain, which interprets them as sound. The vestibule and semicircular canals also have organs with hair cells. Those in the vestibule indicate the head's position with respect to the rest of the body (see PROPRIOCEPTION). The three semicircular canals, at right angles to each other, signal motion of the head in three-dimensional space. Continued stimulation after motion stops causes a mismatch with visual input, experienced as dizziness or MOTION SICKNESS.

Inner Mongolia See NEI MONGGOL

inner product space In mathematics, a VECTOR SPACE or function space in which an operation for combining two vectors or FUNCTIONS (whose result is called an inner product) is defined and has certain properties. Such spaces, an essential tool of FUNCTIONAL ANALYSIS and vector theory, allow analysis of classes of functions rather than individual functions. In mathematical ANALYSIS, an inner product space of particular importance is a Hilbert space, a generalization of ordinary space to an infinite number of dimensions. A point in a Hilbert space can be represented as an infinite sequence of coordinates or as a vector with infinitely many components. The inner product of two such vectors is the sum of the products of corresponding coordinates. When such an inner product is zero, the vectors are said to be orthogonal (see ORTHOGONALITY). Hilbert spaces are an essential tool of MATHEMATICAL PHYSICS. See also DAVID HILBERT.

Innes, Michael See J.I.M. STEWART

Inness, George (1825–1894) U.S. landscape painter. Born in Newburgh, N.Y., he was largely self-taught. His early paintings were influenced by the HUDSON RIVER SCHOOL. He spent much time in Europe studying the works of the BARBIZON SCHOOL, and from c. 1855 to 1874 he developed the luminous, atmospheric quality for which his landscapes are known. The influence of CAMILLE COROT is evident in his intimately rendered images of far-reaching expanses. His later works, such as *Autumn Oaks* (c. 1875), are marked by the ascendancy of color over form. His sense of mysticism intensified over time, and the pictures tended to dissolve into shimmering color with no outlines or formal construction. See also LUMINISM.

Innocent III *orig.* **Lothair of Segni** (c. 1160–1216) Pope (1198–1216). He brought the medieval papacy to the height of its prestige and power. He crowned OTTO IV as Holy Roman Emperor, but Otto's determination to unite Germany and Sicily angered him, and in 1212 he gave his support to FREDERICK II. After he excommunicated King JOHN of England for refusing to recognize STEPHEN LANGTON as archbishop of Canterbury, John was obliged to submit and to declare England a fief of the Holy See (1213). Innocent launched the Fourth CRUSADE and the ALBIGENSIAN CRUSADE, approved the Mendicant orders founded by St. DOMINIC and ST. FRANCIS, and convoked the fourth LATERAN COUNCIL, which defined the doctrine of TRANSUBSTANTIATION.

Innocent IV *orig.* **Sinibaldo Fieschi** (died 1254) Pope (1243–54). His clash with Holy Roman Emperor FREDERICK II formed an important chapter in the conflict between papacy and empire. Frederick wanted the newly elected pope to lift his excommunication, but Innocent interrupted the negotiations and fled Rome for France (1244); he later condemned Frederick and urged the election of a new emperor. Concerned with the evangelization of the East, he persuaded LOUIS IX to lead a crusade and sent a mission to the Mongols. He returned to Rome in 1253 and gave the Sicilian throne to Edmund, son of HENRY III of England, but the papal army was defeated by MANFRED, Frederick's illegitimate son, in 1254.

innovation In TECHNOLOGY, an improvement to something already existing. Distinguishing an element of novelty in an invention remains a concern of PATENT law. The Renaissance was a period of unusual innovation: Leonardo da Vinci produced ingenious designs for submarines, airplanes, and helicopters and drawings of elaborate trains of gears and of the patterns of flow in liquids. Technology provided science with instruments that greatly enhanced its powers, such as Galileo's telescope. New sciences have also contributed to technology, as in the theoretical preparation for the invention of the steam engine. In the 20th century, innovations in semiconductor technology increased the performance and decreased the cost of electronic materials and devices by a factor of a million, an achievement unparalleled in the history of any technology.

Inns of Court Four societies of British students and practitioners of law that have the exclusive right to admit people to practice. The four are Lincoln's Inn, Gray's Inn, Inner Temple, and Middle Temple. All are located in London and trace their origins to the Middle Ages. Until the 17th century, when the Inn of Chancery developed (for training in the framing of writs and other legal documents used in the courts of chancery, or EQUITY courts), the Inns of Court had a monopoly over legal education. By the 19th century, modern law schools had emerged.

Innsbruck City (pop., 2001: 113,826) on the INN RIVER in western Austria, southwest of SALZBURG. A small market town in the 12th century, it was located beside a bridge (Brücke) over the Inn. It was chartered in 1239, passed to the HABSBURGS in 1363, and in 1420 became the capital of TIROL. Napoleon gave the city to BAVARIA in 1806, and in 1809 it was the site of an uprising of Tirolian patriots against the Bavarians and the French. The old town has narrow streets lined with medieval houses and arcades. A winter sports center, it was the site of the Winter OLYMPIC GAMES in 1964 and 1976.

Inönü \i-nœ-'nue\, **Ismet** (1884–1973) Turkish army officer and statesman. On the surrender of the Ottoman empire (1918), he was undersecretary of war. He became prime minister in 1923, and president and permanent chairman of his party in 1938 on MUSTAFA KEMAL ATATURK's death. In 1950 he was replaced as president by Celâl Bayar and led the opposition, assuming the role of defender of democracy. Following a 1960 coup d'état, he formed three coalition governments, but in the 1965 and 1969 elections his party suffered overwhelming defeats.

inorganic compound Any substance in which two or more chemical ELEMENTS other than CARBON are combined, nearly always in definite proportions (see BONDING), as well as some COMPOUNDS containing carbon but lacking carbon-carbon bonds (e.g., CARBONATES, CYANIDES). Inorganic compounds may be classified by the elements or groups they contain. (e.g., oxides, SULFATES). The major classes of inorganic POLYMERS are SILICONES, SILANES, silicates, and borates (including BORAX). Coordination compounds (or complexes), an important subclass of inorganic compounds, consist of a central METAL atom (usually a TRANSITION ELEMENT) bonded to one or more nonmetallic LIGANDS (inorganic, organic, or both) and are often intensely colored. See also ORGANIC COMPOUND.

inosilicate \ˌin-ō-'si-lə-kət, ˌī-nō-'si-lə-kət\ *or* **chain silicate** Any of a class of inorganic compounds that have structures characterized by silicate tetrahedrons (a central silicon atom surrounded by four oxygen atoms at the corners of a tetrahedron) arranged in chains. Two of the oxygen atoms of each tetrahedron are shared with other tetrahedrons, forming a chain that is potentially infinite in length. Mineral examples include the PYROXENES and the AMPHIBOLES.

Inoue Enryo \ē-'nō-ü-e-'en-'ryō\ (1858–1919) Japanese philosopher. After studying at the main temple of the Pure Land sect, he earned a degree in philosophy at Tokyo Imperial University. He opposed the Westernization of Japan and the conversion of officials to Christianity. He founded the Philosophical Institute in 1887 to promote the study of Buddhism. As part of his campaign to rid Japan of superstitions associated with folklore and mythology, he established the Ghost Lore Institute in Tokyo.

input-output analysis Economic analysis developed by WASSILY LEONTIEF, in which the interdependence of an economy's various productive sectors is observed by viewing the product of each industry both as a commodity for CONSUMPTION and as a factor in the production of itself and other goods. For example, input-output analysis will break down a nation's total production of trucks, showing that some trucks are used in the production of more trucks, some in farming, some in the production of houses, and so on. An input-output analysis is usually summarized in a gridlike table showing what various industries buy from and sell to one another.

Inquisition In the MIDDLE AGES a judicial procedure that was used to combat HERESY, and in early modern times a formal Roman Catholic judicial institution. *Inquisitio*, a Latin term meaning investigation or inquest, was a legal procedure that involved the assemblage of evidence and the prosecution of a criminal trial. Use of the procedure against the heresies of the CATHARI and WALDENSES was approved by Pope GREGORY IX in 1231. Suspected heretics were arrested, interrogated, and tried; the use of torture was approved by INNOCENT IV in 1252. Penalties ranged from prayer and fasting to imprisonment; convicted heretics who refused to recant could be executed by lay authorities. Medieval inquisitors functioned widely in northern Italy and southern France. The Spanish Inquisition was authorized by SIXTUS IV in 1478; the pope later tried to limit its powers, but was opposed by the Spanish crown. The auto-da-fé, the public ceremony at which sentences were pronounced, was an elaborate celebration, and the grand inquisitor TOMAS DE TORQUEMADA was responsible for burning about 2,000 heretics at the stake. The Spanish Inquisition was also introduced into Mexico, Peru, Sicily (1517), and the Netherlands (1522), and it was not entirely suppressed in Spain until the early 19th century.

insanity In criminal law, a disease, defect, or condition of the mind that renders one unable to understand the nature of a criminal act or the fact that it is wrong. Tests of insanity are not intended as medical diagnoses but serve only as determinations of whether a person may be held criminally responsible for his or her actions. The most enduring definition of insanity in Anglo-American law was that proposed by ALEXANDER COCKBURN (1843). Many U.S. states and several courts have adopted the test proposed by the American Law Institute's Model Penal Code, under which the accused must lack "substantial capacity either to appreciate the criminality of his conduct or to conform his conduct to the requirements of the law." Some states have abolished the insanity plea; others allow a finding of "guilty but mentally ill." See also DIMINISHED CAPACITY.

insect Any member of the class Insecta, the largest ARTHROPOD class, including nearly 1 million known species (about three-fourths of all animals) and an estimated 5–10 million undescribed species. Insect bodies have three segments: head, thorax (which bears three pairs of legs and usually two pairs of wings), and many-segmented abdomen. Many species undergo complete METAMORPHOSIS. There are two subclasses: Apterygota (primitive, wingless forms, including SILVERFISH and bristletails) and Pterygota (more advanced, winged or secondarily wingless forms). The approximately 27 orders of Pterygota are generally classified by wing form: e.g., Coleoptera (BEETLES), Diptera (DIPTERANS), Heteroptera (BUGS). Insects are found in almost all terrestrial and freshwater and some marine habitats. See illustration on following page.

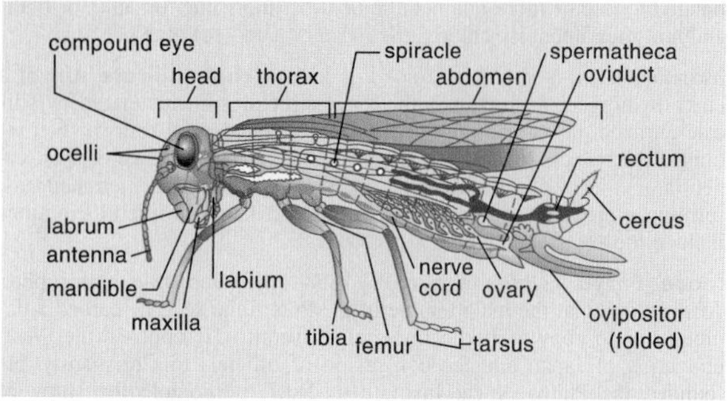

Body plan of a generalized insect. The body is usually divided into a head, thorax, and abdomen. The head bears appendages modified into mouthparts and antennae bearing sense organs. Mouthparts include the toothed mandibles and bladelike maxillae found behind the "upper lip" or labrum. A second pair of maxillae, partly fused, form the "lower lip" or labium. An adult usually has both simple eyes (ocelli) and more complex faceted compound eyes, as well as a pair of wings on the thorax. The tarsal segment of the jointed leg often has claws with adhesive pads, enabling the insect to hold onto smooth surfaces. In some insects (incl. crickets and cockroaches), a pair of feelers (cerci) bearing sense organs are located at the rear of the abdomen. Tiny openings (spiracles) on the thorax and abdomen allow passage of oxygen to and release of carbon dioxide from internal air-filled tubules or tracheae. Sperm from the male is stored in the female's spermatheca until an egg released from the ovary passes through the oviduct. The female may have an ovipositor for depositing eggs.

insecticide Any substance used to kill INSECTS. Such substances are used mainly to control pests that infest cultivated plants and crops or to eliminate disease-carrying insects in specific areas. Inorganic insecticides include ARSENIC, LEAD, and COPPER compounds. Organic insecticides may be natural, like rotenone, pyrethrins, and NICOTINE (see TOXIN), or synthetic, like chlorinated HYDROCARBONS (e.g., DDT, dieldrin, lindane); carbamates, related to UREA (e.g., carbaryl, carbofuran); and parathions, organic PHOSPHORUS ESTERS. Insect HORMONES may be considered a separate class. Insecticides may affect the NERVOUS SYSTEM, inhibit essential ENZYMES, or prevent LARVAE from maturing (e.g., juvenile hormone). Some are stomach POISONS, some inhalation poisons, and others contact poisons. Agents like dormant oils act mechanically, simply blocking the breathing pores. Insecticides vary widely not only in effectiveness against target insects (which may develop resistance) but also in toxicity to nontarget species (including humans) and environmental effects; the worst (e.g., DDT) have been banned.

insectivore \in-'sek-tə-ˌvōr\ Any member of the mammalian order (Insectivora) that includes the HEDGEHOGS, MOLES, and sometimes SHREWS (some of which are considered PRIMATES by some authorities), or, more generally, any animal that eats mainly insects. The mammalian insectivores are generally small, active, and nocturnal. They are found in most parts of the world except Antarctica, Australia, and South America. Most species are solitary (except during the breeding season) and short-lived.

insei (Japanese: "cloistered government") Rule by retired emperors who have taken Buddhist vows and retired to cloisters. During the late 11th century and 12th century, governmental control of Japan passed from the FUJIWARA FAMILY, which had maintained power through marriages to the imperial family, to cloistered emperors. By abdicating, these emperors escaped the control of Fujiwara regents and chancellors; they then retired to cloisters where they surrounded themselves with capable non-Fujiwara aristocrats. It was the edicts of the cloistered emperor, not the reigning one, that were obeyed, insofar as any orders were obeyed in a period of increasing collapse of central authority. See also SHOEN.

inside contracting System of manufacturing intermediate between the putting-out system and full factory production. A factory proprietor supplies to an artisan who then hires the workers needed to make a particular part under a contract with the proprietor. Inside contracting was used extensively in the U.S. in the 19th century.

Inside Passage *or* **Inland Passage** Natural sheltered sea route from SEATTLE to Skagway, Alaska. Extending northwest for more than 1,000 mi (1,600 km), it comprises channels and straits between the mainland and islands (including VANCOUVER ISLAND) that protect it from Pacific storms. It is the favored route for coastal shipping to Alaska. Ports in British Columbia include VICTORIA, VANCOUVER, and Prince Rupert; in Alaska, Ketchikan, Wrangell, and JUNEAU.

insider trading Illegal use of insider information for profit in financial trading. Since 1934, the SECURITIES AND EXCHANGE COMMISSION has prohibited trading while in possession of material nonpublic information. See also ARBITRAGE, MICHAEL R. MILKEN.

insolvency Condition in which liabilities exceed assets so that creditors cannot be paid. It is a financial condition that often precedes BANKRUPTCY. In the context of equity, insolvency is the inability to pay debts as they become due; insolvency under the balance-sheet approach means that total liabilities exceed total assets.

insomnia Inability to sleep adequately. The causes may include poor sleeping conditions, circulatory or brain disorders, breathing disorders (e.g., sleep apnea), mental distress (e.g., tension or depression), or physical discomfort. Mild insomnia may be treated by improving sleeping conditions or through traditional remedies such as warm baths, milk, or systematic relaxation. Apnea and its associated insomnia may be treated surgically or mechanically with breathing apparatus. Severe or chronic insomnia may necessitate the temporary use of barbiturates or tranquilizers, but such drugs are often addictive and may be decreasingly effective as the body builds up tolerance. Other methods of treatment include PSYCHOTHERAPY and HYPNOSIS.

instinct Involuntary response by an animal, resulting in a predictable and relatively fixed behavior pattern. Instinctive behavior is an inherited mechanism that serves to promote the survival of an animal or species. It is most apparent in fighting and sexual activity. The simplest form is the REFLEX. All animals have instinct, but, in general, the higher the animal form, the more flexible the behavior. Among mammals, learned behavior often prevails over instinctive behavior.

Institut Canadien \a^{n}-stē-'tw̅ē-kȧ-nȧd-'ya^{n}\ Literary and scientific society that came into conflict with the Catholic Church in 19th-century French Canada. It was founded in Montreal in 1844 as a discussion forum and free library, and established branches throughout French-speaking Canada. It criticized the institutionalism of the church in Quebec and displayed books considered undesirable. Church leaders, including Ignace Bourget, bishop of Montreal 1840–76, attacked the institute, which appealed to Rome for support. In 1869 the church condemned the movement, and most members withdrew.

institutional economics School of economics that flourished in the U.S. in the 1920s and '30s, which viewed the evolution of economic institutions as part of the broader process of cultural development. THORSTEIN VEBLEN laid the foundation for institutionalism with his criticism of traditional economic theory. He tried to replace the concept of people as the makers of economic decisions with a more realistic image of people as influenced by changing customs and institutions. JOHN R. COMMONS emphasized the collective action of various groups in the economy, viewed within a system of continually evolving institutions and laws. Other U.S. institutional economists include REXFORD TUGWELL and WESLEY C. MITCHELL. See also CLASSICAL ECONOMICS, GERMAN HISTORICAL SCHOOL OF ECONOMICS.

Institutional Revolutionary Party (PRI) Political party that dominated Mexico's political life for 71 years, from the party's founding in 1929 until 2000. It was established as a result of a shift of power from political-military chieftains to state party units following the MEXICAN REVOLUTION of 1910–20. Until the late 1990s, nomination to public office by the PRI virtually guaranteed election, but in 1997 Mexico City elected its first non-PRI mayor. At the national level, the president, as leader of the party, typically selected the party's next presidential candidate—thus effectively choosing his own successor. Pres. ERNESTO ZEDILLO broke from that tradition in 1999, and the following year Vicente Fox, candidate of the National Action Party (PAN), won the presidency, although the PRI maintained control of several state governments.

instrumentalism *or* **experimentalism** Philosophy advanced by JOHN DEWEY holding that what is most important in a thing or idea is its value as an instrument of action and that the truth of an idea lies in its usefulness. Dewey favored these terms over the term PRAGMATISM to label the philosophy on which his views of education rested. His school claimed that cognition has evolved not for speculative or metaphysical purposes but for the practical purpose of successful adjustment. Ideas are conceived as instruments for transforming the uneasiness arising from facing a problem into the satisfaction of solving it.

instrumentation In TECHNOLOGY, the development and use of precise measuring, analysis, and control equipment. Among the oldest known instruments of measurement was the armillary sphere, an astronomical instrument used in ancient China and Greece. The COMPASS was a striking advance in navigational instrumentation made about the 11th century. Theodolites made accurate determination of locations possible in the 18th century. Instrumentation developed rapidly in the INDUSTRIAL REVOLUTION. Manufacturing required precision instruments, such as the screw MICROMETER, which could measure 0.0001 in. (0.0025 mm). The industrial application of electricity required instruments to measure current, voltage, and resistance. Today most manufacturing processes rely on instrumentation for monitoring chemical, physical, and environmental properties. Instruments used in medicine and biomedical research are just as varied as those in industry. See also ANALYSIS.

insulator Substance that blocks or retards the flow of ELECTRIC CURRENT or heat. An insulator is a poor CONDUCTOR because it has a high RESISTANCE to such flow. Electrical insulators are commonly used to hold conductors in place, separating them from one another and from surrounding structures to form a barrier between energized parts of an electric circuit and confine the flow of current to wires or other conducting paths. Electrical insulators include rubber, plastic, porcelain, and mica. Thermal insulators. which break up the heat-flow path by absorbing radiant heat, include fiberglass, cork, and rock wool.

insulin Polypeptide HORMONE (see PEPTIDE) that regulates blood GLUCOSE levels. Secreted by the islets of LANGERHANS in the PANCREAS when blood glucose rises, as after a meal, it helps transfer the glucose into the body's cells to be oxidized (see OXIDATION-REDUCTION) for energy or converted and stored as FATTY ACIDS (mainly palmitic and oleic acids) or GLYCOGEN. When blood glucose falls, insulin secretion stops and the liver releases more glucose into the blood. Insulin has various related functions in the liver, muscles, and other tissues, controlling the balance of glucose with related compounds. Insulin-related disorders include DIABETES MELLITUS and HYPOGLYCEMIA. FREDERICK BANTING and J. J. R. MACLEOD won a Nobel Prize in 1923 for discovering insulin, and FREDERICK SANGER won one in 1958 for determining its amino acid sequence.

Insull \'in-səl\, **Samuel** (1859–1938) British-U.S. public-utilities magnate. Born in London, he moved to the U.S. in 1881 to become the private secretary of THOMAS ALVA EDISON, and rose to become president of the Chicago Edison Co. in 1892. By 1907 he had taken control of Chicago's transit system. By 1912 his vast electric power system, enlarged by various mergers, was operating several hundred power plants. He vigorously promoted the stock of his holding companies. When they collapsed in 1932, he fled to Europe; extradited in 1934, he was tried three times for fraud, violation of bankruptcy laws, and embezzlement, but acquitted each time.

insurance Contract that, by redistributing RISK among a large number of people, reduces losses from accidents incurred by an individual. In return for a specified payment (premium), the insurer undertakes to pay the insured or his beneficiary a specified amount of money in the event that the insured suffers loss through the occurrence of an event covered by the insurance contract (policy). By pooling both the financial contributions and the risks of a large number of policyholders, the insurer is typically able to absorb losses incurred over any given period much more easily than would the uninsured individual. Insurers may offer insurance to any individual able to pay, or may contract with members of a group (e.g., employees of a firm) to offer special rates for group insurance. Marine insurance, covering ships and voyages, is the oldest form of insurance; it originated in ancient times with loans to shipowners that were repayable only on safe completion of a voyage, and it was formalized in medieval Europe. Fire insurance arose in the 17th century, and other forms of property insurance became common with the spread of industrialization in the 19th century. It is now possible to insure almost any kind of property, including homes, businesses, motor vehicles, and goods in transit. See also CASUALTY INSURANCE, HEALTH INSURANCE, LIABILITY INSURANCE, LIFE INSURANCE.

intaglio \in-'tal-yō\ Engraved or incised work on gemstones, glass, ceramics, stone, or similar material in which the design is sunk beneath the surface, the opposite of CAMEO and RELIEF. It is the most ancient form of gem engraving; the earliest known Babylonian cylinder seals date from c. 4000 BC. The term intaglio is also used to describe printmaking processes in which the design is cut, scratched, or etched into a printing surface of copper, zinc, or aluminum; ink is then rubbed into the incisions or grooves, the surface is wiped clean, and the paper is embossed into the incised lines with pressure from a roller press. Intaglio processes are the most versatile of printmaking methods, as they can produce a wide range of effects.

intarsia \in-'tär-sē-ə\ Form of wood inlaying. Italian intarsia, or inlaid mosaic of wood, which probably derived from Oriental ivory and wood inlay, found its richest expression during the Renaissance in Italy (c. 1400–1600). It was often used in panels over the backs of choir stalls and in private studies and chapels of princes.

integer Whole-valued positive or negative number or 0. The integers are generated from the set of counting numbers 1, 2, 3, . . . and the operation of subtraction. When a counting number is subtracted from itself, the result is zero. When a larger number is subtracted from a smaller number, the result is a negative whole number. In this way, every integer can be derived from the counting numbers, resulting in a set of numbers closed under the operation of subtraction (see GROUP THEORY).

integral Fundamental concept of CALCULUS related to areas and other quantities modeled by FUNCTIONS. A definite integral gives the area between the graph of a function and the horizontal axis between vertical lines at the endpoints of an interval. It also calculates the net change in a system over an interval, and thus leads to formulas for the work done by a varying force or the distance traveled by an object moving at varying speeds. According to the fundamental theorem of CALCULUS, a definite integral can be calculated using the indefinite integral, or antiderivative, of the function. Integrals extend to higher dimensions through MULTIPLE INTEGRALS. The process of finding either a definite or an indefinite integral is called INTEGRATION. See also LINE INTEGRAL, SURFACE INTEGRAL.

integral, line See LINE INTEGRAL

integral, surface See SURFACE INTEGRAL

integral calculus Branch of CALCULUS concerned with the theory and applications of INTEGRALS. While DIFFERENTIAL CALCULUS focuses on rates of change in a process, integral calculus deals with the total amount of change in the process over a prescribed interval. Integrating a velocity function yields the distance traveled by an object over an interval of time, for example. The two branches are connected by the fundamental theorem of CALCULUS, which shows how a definite integral is calculated by using antiderivatives. As a result, much of integral calculus deals with the derivation of formulas for finding antiderivatives (indefinite integrals). Its applications include finding exact values for AREAS, lengths, and volumes defined by curves and probabilities associated with RANDOM VARIABLES (see DENSITY FUNCTION).

integral equation In mathematics, an equation with an unknown function within an integral. An example is

$$f(x) = \int_{-\infty}^{\infty} \cos(xt)\varphi(t)dt$$

where $f(x)$ is known and $\varphi(t)$ is to be found, given certain conditions on f. Such equations are useful in solving DIFFERENTIAL EQUATIONS.

integral transform In mathematics, a function that results when a given function is multiplied by a so-called kernel function, and the product is integrated (see INTEGRATION) between suitable limits. Its value lies in its ability to simplify intractable differential equations (subject to particular boundary conditions) by transforming the DERIVATIVES and boundary conditions into terms of an ALGEBRAIC EQUATION that may easily be solved. The solution yielded must be converted to the final solution using an inverse transformation. Several integral transforms are named for the mathematicians who introduced them (FOURIER TRANSFORM, LAPLACE TRANSFORM).

integrated circuit (IC) *or* **microcircuit** *or* **chip** *or* **microchip** Assembly of microscopic electronic components (TRANSISTORS, DIODES, capacitors, and resistors) and their interconnections fabricated as a single unit on a wafer of semiconducting material, and especially on a silicon COMPUTER CHIP, with no external connecting wires. Early ICs of the late 1950s consisted of about 10 components on a chip 0.12 in. (3 mm)

H I J K

square. Very large-scale integration (VLSI) vastly increased circuit density, giving rise to the MICROPROCESSOR. The first commercially successful IC chip (Intel, 1974) had 4,800 transistors; Intel's Pentium (1993) had 3.2 million; and over a billion are now achievable.

Integrated Services Digital Network See ISDN

integration In CALCULUS, the process of finding a FUNCTION whose DERIVATIVE is a given function. The term, sometimes used interchangeably with "antidifferentiation," is indicated symbolically with the integral sign $\int$. (The DIFFERENTIAL dx usually follows to indicate x as the VARIABLE.) The basic rules of integration are: (1) $\int(f + g)dx = \int f\,dx + \int g\,dx$ (where f and g are functions of the variable x), (2) $\int kf\,dx = k\int f\,dx$ (k is a constant), and (3) $\int x^n dx = \left(\frac{1}{n+1}\right)x^{n+1} + C$ (C is a constant). Note that any constant value may be added onto an indefinite integral without changing its derivative. Thus, the indefinite integral of $2x$ is $x^2 + C$, where C can be any real number. A definite integral is an indefinite integral evaluated over an interval. The result is not affected by the choice for the value of C. See also DIFFERENTIATION.

integument \in-'teg-yü-mənt\ Covering of the body, which protects it from the outside world and from drying out. In mammals it consists of the SKIN (including outer epidermis and inner dermis) and its related structures, including HAIR, NAILS, and SEBACEOUS and SWEAT glands.

Intel Corp. U.S. manufacturer of semiconductor computer circuits. Intel was founded in 1968 as N M Electronics by ROBERT N. NOYCE and Gordon Moore, inventors of the integrated circuit, to manufacture large-scale integrated (LSI) circuits. In the early 1970s it introduced the most powerful semiconductor chips then known, which soon replaced the magnetic cores previously used in computer memories. IBM chose to use Intel's 8088 MICROPROCESSOR (introduced 1978) in its first PERSONAL COMPUTER (the IBM PC), and Intel microprocessors became standard for all PC-type machines. Intel later developed faster, more powerful microprocessors, notably the Pentium chip (1993), which could execute more than 100 million instructions per second.

intellectual property Property that derives from the work of the mind or intellect. The notion that an artist's work is legally protected intellectual property assumes a conception of authorship but extends beyond it. Early COPYRIGHT law aimed to protect the economic interests of book publishers rather than the intellectual rights of authors. Current copyright law protects the labor of elaborating an idea, not the idea itself. The concept of discovery also plays a role in intellectual property rights: PATENTS are awarded to those who can demonstrate that they have invented something not previously known. The GENERAL AGREEMENT ON TARIFFS AND TRADE goes further in its rules for intellectual property than had the World Intellectual Property Organization. See also TRADEMARK.

intelligence In government and military operations, evaluated information concerning the strength, activities, and probable courses of action of international actors that are usually, though not always, enemies or opponents. The term also refers to the collection, analysis, and distribution of such information and to the secret intervention in the political or economic affairs of other countries, an activity commonly known as "covert action." Intelligence is an important component of national power and a fundamental element in decision making regarding national security, defense, and foreign policies. It is conducted on three levels: strategic, tactical, and counterintelligence. Despite the public image of intelligence operatives as cloak-and-dagger secret agents, much intelligence work involves an undramatic search of "open" sources, such as radio broadcasts and various publications. Among covert sources of intelligence are imagery intelligence, which includes aerial and space reconnaissance, signals intelligence, which includes electronic eavesdropping and code breaking, and human intelligence, which involves the secret agent working at the classic spy trade. Leading national intelligence organizations are the CENTRAL INTELLIGENCE AGENCY (CIA) in the U.S.; the Federal Security Service in Russia; MI-5 and MI-6 in Britain; and the MOSSAD in Israel.

intelligence In psychology, the ability to learn or understand or to deal with new or trying situations. In psychology, the term may more specifically denote the ability to apply knowledge to manipulate one's environment or to think abstractly as measured by objective criteria (such as the IQ test). Intelligence is usually thought of as deriving from a combination of inherited characteristics and environmental (developmental and social) factors. The subject remains hotly debated, and many have tried to show that either biology (especially genes) or environment (especially conditions reflecting socioeconomic class) are more or less exclusively responsible for producing differences in intelligence. Particularly contested have been studies purporting to show links between RACE and intelligence, most of which have not been accepted in the scientific community. General intelligence is often said to comprise various specific abilities (verbal ability, ability to apply logic in solving problems, etc.), but critics contend that such compartments fail to reflect the nature of cognition and that other models, perhaps based on INFORMATION PROCESSING, are needed. High intelligence (as measured by tests) is sometimes shown to correlate with social achievement, but most experts believe other factors are important and that intelligence is no guarantor of success (and its lack is no guarantor of failure). See also ARTIFICIAL INTELLIGENCE, CREATIVITY.

intelligence quotient See IQ

intensive care unit *or* **critical care unit** Hospital facility for care of critically ill patients at a more intensive level than is needed by other patients. Staffed by specialized personnel, the intensive care unit contains a complex assortment of monitors and life-support equipment that can sustain life in once-fatal situations, including adult RESPIRATORY DISTRESS SYNDROME, KIDNEY FAILURE, multiple organ failure, and sepsis (see SEPTICEMIA).

intention In Scholastic logic and psychology, a mode of being or relation between a mind and an object. In knowing, the mind is said to "intend" or "tend toward" its object, and a thing as known, or in the knowing mind, has "intentional being," as with squaring the circle, which, though impossible, can be an object of intention. In ACTION THEORY, intention is taken in a different but related sense, as in acting with the intention of accomplishing a specific purpose.

intentionality Property of being directed toward an object. Intentionality is exhibited in various mental phenomena. Thus, if a person experiences an emotion toward an object, he has an intentional attitude toward it. Other examples of intentional attitudes toward an object are looking for, believing in, and thinking about. Intentional attitudes also include PROPOSITIONAL ATTITUDES. One characteristic of intentionality is "inexistence": A person may be intentionally related to an object that does not exist. Thus, what a person looks for (and intentionally seeks) may not exist, and an event he or she believes to occur may not occur at all. Another characteristic is referential opacity: A sentence truly ascribing an intentional state to a person will become false when some alternative description of the object of that state is substituted for it. Suppose that my pen is the millionth pen produced this year, so that "my pen" and "the millionth pen produced this year" have the same reference. I may be in the intentional state of searching for it as my pen but not in a state of searching for the millionth pen produced this year.

Inter-American Development Bank (IDB) International organization founded in 1959 by 27 New World governments to finance economic and social development in the Western Hemisphere. It is the oldest and largest institution for regional multilateral development. The largest charter subscribers were Argentina, Brazil, Mexico, Venezuela, the U.S., and Canada; they were later joined by three other New World countries, two Asian nations, and 14 European countries. The IDB group also includes the Inter-American Investment Corp. and the Multilateral Investment Fund.

interaction, fundamental See FUNDAMENTAL INTERACTION

interactionism In sociology, a theoretical perspective that derives social processes (such as conflict, cooperation, identity formation) from human interaction. It was GEORG SIMMEL who first stated that "society is merely the name for a number of individuals connected by interaction." In the U.S., JOHN DEWEY, Charles H. Cooley, and especially GEORGE HERBERT MEAD developed symbolic interactionism, the theory that mind and self are not part of the innate human equipment but arise through social interaction—i.e., communication with others using SYMBOLS. For symbolic interactionists, the individual is always engaged in socialization or the modification of his or her mind, role, and behavior through contact with others. Other theorists, such as ALFRED SCHUTZ, drew on PHENOMENOLOGY to extend interactionism, an effort that led to the creation of such fields as SOCIOLINGUISTICS and ethnomethodology, the study of people's sense-making activities. See also ERVING GOFFMAN.

interactionism In philosophy of MIND, a species of mind–body DUALISM that holds that mind and body, though separate and distinct substances, causally interact. Interactionists assert that a mental event (as when somebody decides to kick a brick wall) can be the cause of a physical action (her foot moving into the wall). Conversely, the physical event (her foot hitting the wall) can be the cause of a mental event (her feeling a sharp pain). RENE DESCARTES gave interactionism its classical formulation, but could not satisfactory explain how the interaction takes place, aside from the speculation that it occurs in the pineal gland. This problem led directly to the OCCASIONALISM of NICOLAS DE MALEBRANCHE and ARNOLD GEULINCX and to various other accounts of the mind–body relation, including G. W. LEIBNIZ's theory of a preestablished harmony between mind and body and BENEDICT DE SPINOZA's monistic theory of mind and body as attributes of one underlying substance. See also DUALISM, MIND–BODY PROBLEM.

interchangeable parts Identical components that can substitute one for another, particularly important in MANUFACTURING. MASS PRODUCTION, which transformed the organization of work, came about by the development of the MACHINE-TOOL industry by a series of 19th-century innovators. With precision equipment, large numbers of identical parts could be produced at low cost and with a small workforce. See also AMERICAN SYSTEM OF MANUFACTURE, ARMORY PRACTICE, AUTOMOBILE industry, FACTORY, HENRY FORD, HENRY LELAND.

intercolumniation In architecture, the space between columns that support an ARCH or ENTABLATURE. Classical, Renaissance, and baroque architecture used a system codified by VITRUVIUS in which the measurement is expressed in terms of the columns' diameters (e.g., two columns might be described as being 3 diameters apart). The system conveniently expressed the measurement of a unit of space, whose size varied from building to building according to the Classical ORDER used.

intercontinental ballistic missile See ICBM

interest Price paid for the use of CREDIT or MONEY. It is usually figured as a percentage of the money borrowed and is computed annually. Interest is charged by the lender as payment for the loss of his or her money for a period of time. The interest rate reflects the risk of lending and is higher for loans that are considered higher-risk, a relationship known as the risk/return tradeoff. Like the prices of goods and services, interest rates are responsive to SUPPLY AND DEMAND. Theories explaining the need for interest include the time-preference theory, according to which interest is the inducement to engage in time-consuming but more productive activities, and the LIQUIDITY-PREFERENCE theory of JOHN MAYNARD KEYNES, according to which interest is the inducement to sacrifice a desired degree of liquidity for a nonliquid contractual obligation. Interest rates may also be used as a tool for implementing MONETARY POLICY (see DISCOUNT RATE). High interest rates may dampen the economy by making it difficult for consumers, businesses, and home buyers to secure loans, while lower rates tend to stimulate the economy and encourage both INVESTMENT and CONSUMPTION.

interference In physics, the net effect of combining two or more WAVE trains moving on intersecting or coincident paths. Constructive interference occurs if two components have the same FREQUENCY and PHASE; the wave amplitudes are reinforced. Destructive interference occurs when the two waves are out of phase by one-half period (see PERIODIC MOTION); if the waves are of equal amplitude, they cancel each other. Two waves moving in the same direction but having slightly different frequencies interfere constructively at regular intervals, resulting in a pulsating frequency called a BEAT. Two waves traveling in opposite directions but having equal frequencies interfere constructively in some places and destructively in others, resulting in a standing wave.

interferon \ˌin-tər-ˈfir-ˌän\ Any of several related PROTEINS produced by all VERTEBRATES and possibly some invertebrates. They play an important role in resistance to infection. The body's most rapidly produced and important defense against VIRUSES, they can also combat BACTERIA and parasites (see PARASITISM), inhibit cell division, and promote or impede cell differentiation. Interferon's effect is indirect—it reacts with susceptible cells, which then resist virus multiplication—in contrast to ANTIBODIES, which act by combining directly with a specific virus. Various types of interferons are distinguished by their characteristics as proteins and by which cells produce them. Some are now produced by GENETIC ENGINEERING. Initial hopes that interferon would be a wonder drug for a wide variety of diseases were deflated by its serious side effects, but a few rare conditions respond to it.

Interior, U.S. Department of the Federal executive division responsible for most of the nation's federally owned lands and natural resources, as well as reservation communities for American Indians. Created in 1849, it encompasses the Bureau of LAND MANAGEMENT, the Bureau of INDIAN AFFAIRS, the Minerals Management Service, the Office of Surface Mining, the Bureau of Reclamation, the U.S. Fish and Wildlife Service, the National Park Service, and the U.S. Geological Survey.

interior design Design of interior spaces, closely related to architecture and sometimes including interior decoration. The designer's goal is to produce a coordinated and harmonious whole in which the architecture, site, function, and visual aspects of the interior are unified, pleasing to mind and body, and appropriate to the activities to be pursued there. Design criteria include harmony of color, texture, lighting, scale, and proportion. Furnishings must be in proportion to the space they occupy and to the needs and lifestyles of the residents. The design of such nonresidential spaces as offices, hospitals, stores, and schools places clear organization of functions ahead of purely aesthetic concerns.

interleukin \ˌin-tər-ˈlü-kən\ Any of a class of naturally occurring PROTEINS important in regulation of LYMPHOCYTE function. Several known types are recognized as crucial constituents of the body's immune system (see IMMUNITY). ANTIGENS and microbes stimulate production of interleukins, which induce production of various types of lymphocytes in a complex series of reactions that ensure a plentiful supply of T CELLS that fight specific infectious agents.

intermediate goods See PRODUCER GOODS

intermediate-range nuclear weapons Class of NUCLEAR WEAPONS with a range of 620–3,400 mi (1,000–5,500 km). Some multiple warheads developed by the Soviet Union could strike several targets anywhere in Western Europe in less than 10 minutes. The U.S. could send a single nuclear warhead from central Europe to Moscow in less than 10 minutes. Both were regarded as offensive, first-strike weapons. U.S.–Soviet arms-control negotiations (1980–87) led to the intermediate nuclear forces (INF) treaty, signed by MIKHAIL GORBACHEV and RONALD REAGAN, to completely remove and dismantle these and shorter-range weapons.

internal-combustion engine Any ENGINE in which a fuel-air mixture is burned in the engine proper so that the hot gaseous products of com-

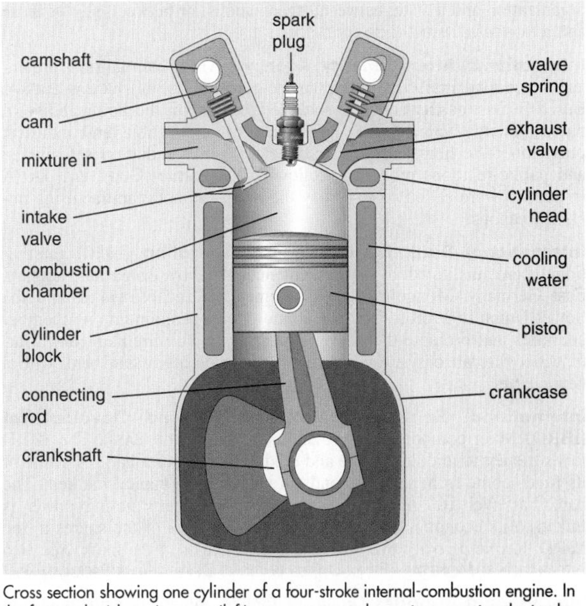

Cross section showing one cylinder of a four-stroke internal-combustion engine. In the first stroke (shown), a cam (left) compresses a valve spring, opening the intake valve to admit the fuel-air mixture to the cylinder. Both valves then close, the mixture is compressed by the piston, and current is sent to the spark plug. Ignited by the spark plug, the burning mixture forces the piston down, producing power to turn the crankshaft and run the car. Another cam (right) opens the exhaust valve and the burned exhaust gases exit.

H I J K

bustion act directly on the surfaces of its moving parts, such as those of pistons (see PISTON AND CYLINDER) or TURBINE rotor blades. Internal-combustion engines include GASOLINE ENGINES, DIESEL ENGINES, gas turbine engines, pure JET ENGINES, and ROCKET engines, and are one class of heat engines. They are commonly divided into continuous-combustion engines and intermittent-combustion engines. In the first type (e.g., jet engines) fuel and air flow steadily into the engine, where a stable flame is maintained for continuous combustion. In the second (e.g., gasoline–reciprocating-piston engines), discrete quantities of fuel and air are periodically ignited. See also AUTOMOBILE industry, MACHINE, STEAM ENGINE.

internal medicine Medical specialty dealing with the entire patient rather than a particular organ system, covering DIAGNOSIS and medical (rather than surgical) treatment in adults. Its development began in the 17th century with THOMAS SYDENHAM's concept of disease, but until disease-specific therapies were developed in the 20th century, internists could do little to treat diseases. As more specific treatments became available, medical knowledge increased, and subspecialties in specific organ systems were defined, internal medicine became recognized as a specialty.

internal reflection, total See TOTAL INTERNAL REFLECTION

Internal Revenue Service (IRS) Agency of the U.S. Department of the TREASURY charged with administering and enforcing federal tax laws, except those relating to alcohol, tobacco, firearms, and explosives. It issues rulings and regulations to supplement the provisions of the Internal Revenue Code; determines, assesses, and collects internal revenue taxes; and determines exempt organization status.

International, Communist See FIRST INTERNATIONAL, SECOND INTERNATIONAL, COMINTERN

international agreement Instrument by which nation-states and international organizations regulate matters of concern. They are governed by INTERNATIONAL LAW, and their purposes include the development and codification of international law, the creation of international bodies, and the resolution of actual and potential international conflict. The most comprehensive agreement is a TREATY; others, including conventions (e.g., the GENEVA CONVENTIONS), charters (e.g., the U.N. charter), and pacts (e.g., the KELLOGG-BRIAND PACT), are less formal and rely primarily on goodwill. Agreements may be negotiated between states, between an organization and a state, between organizations, or between any of those and a NONGOVERNMENTAL ORGANIZATION.

International Atomic Energy Agency (IAEA) International organization founded in 1957 to promote the peaceful use of NUCLEAR ENERGY. Based in Vienna, its activities include research on the applicability of nuclear energy to medicine, agriculture, water location, and industry; provision of technical assistance; development of radiation safeguards; and public-relations programs. Following the PERSIAN GULF WAR, IAEA inspectors were called on to certify that Iraq was not manufacturing nuclear weapons.

International Bank for Economic Cooperation (IBEC) International bank instituted by an agreement signed by Bulgaria, Hungary, East Germany, Mongolia, Poland, Romania, Czechoslovakia, and the Soviet Union in 1963 to facilitate economic cooperation among member countries and promote their development. Cuba and Vietnam joined later. After the fall of the Soviet Union it became a Russian bank with a new charter.

International Bank for Reconstruction and Development (IBRD) Main component organization of the WORLD BANK. The IBRD lends money to middle-income and creditworthy poorer nations. Most of its funds come from sales of bonds in international capital markets. The bank has over 160 member nations. Each member's voting power is linked to its economic strength; the U.S., with 17% of the shares in the IBRD, has veto power over any proposed changes to the bank. See also INTERNATIONAL MONETARY FUND, UNITED NATIONS DEVELOPMENT PROGRAMME.

International Brigades Groups of foreign volunteers who fought on the Republican side against the Nationalist forces in the SPANISH CIVIL WAR (1936–39). So-called because their members initially came from some 50 countries, the International Brigades were recruited, organized, and directed by the COMINTERN, with headquarters in Paris. The U.S. contingent called itself the Abraham Lincoln Batallion. Many of the mostly young recruits were communists before they became involved in the conflict; more joined the party during the course of the war. The total number of volunteers reached about 60,000. The brigades were formally withdrawn from Spain late in 1938.

"The Internationals—United with the Spaniards We Fight the Invader," poster by Parrilla, published by the International Brigades, 1936–37.

BY COURTESY OF THE ABRAHAM LINCOLN BRIGADE ARCHIVES, BRANDEIS UNIVERSITY LIBRARY

International Court of Justice *or* **World Court** Principal judicial body of the UNITED NATIONS, located at The Hague. Its predecessor organization was the Permanent Court of International Justice, the LEAGUE OF NATIONS' judicial body. Its first session was held in 1946. Its jurisdiction is limited to disputes between states willing to accept its authority on matters of INTERNATIONAL LAW. Its decisions are binding, but it has no enforcement power; appeals must be made to the U.N. Security Council. Its 15-member body of judges, each of whom serves a nine-year term, is elected by nations party to the statute founding it, and no two judges may come from the same country. See also EUROPEAN COURT OF JUSTICE.

International Criminal Court (ICC) Permanent judicial body established by the Rome Statute of the International Criminal Court (1998) to prosecute individuals accused of genocide, war crimes, and crimes against humanity. The court began work on July 1, 2002, after the requisite number of countries (60) ratified the agreement (some 140 countries signed the agreement). The ICC was established as a court of last resort to prosecute the most heinous offenses in cases where national courts fail to act. It is headquartered in The Hague.

International Date Line Imaginary line from the North Pole to the South Pole that arbitrarily separates each calendar day from the next. It corresponds along most of its length to the 180th meridian of longitude but deviates to the east through the Bering Strait to avoid dividing Siberia and then deviates to the west to include the Aleutian Islands with Alaska. South of the equator, another eastward deviation allows certain island groups to have the same day as New Zealand. The date line is a consequence of the worldwide use of timekeeping systems arranged so that local noon corresponds approximately to the time at which the sun crosses the local meridian of longitude. See also STANDARD TIME.

international exchange See FOREIGN EXCHANGE

International Harvester Co. See NAVISTAR INTERNATIONAL CORP.

International Herald Tribune Daily newspaper published in Paris. It has long been the staple source of English-language news for American expatriates, tourists, and businesspeople in Europe. Its roots are in the *Paris Herald* (established 1887); a merger in 1924 between its parent, the *New York Herald,* and the *New York Tribune* created the *New York Herald-Tribune* and the *Paris Herald Tribune.* The Paris edition, which was faring well at the time of its parent's demise in 1966, was rescued by a joint venture of the *New York Times*, the *Washington Post*, and Whitney Communications and given its present name.

International Labor Organization Specialized agency of the U.N. system. It was first set up through the Treaty of VERSAILLES as an agency of the LEAGUE OF NATIONS with a mandate to improve the world's living standards by focusing on working conditions. In 1946 it became the first specialized agency affiliated with the U.N. Its activities include compilation of labor statistics, protection of international migrants, and safeguarding of trade-union rights. Its delegates come from member governments (50%), labor (25%), and employers (25%). About 150 nations are represented today. The ILO received the Nobel Peace Prize in 1969.

International Ladies' Garment Workers' Union (ILGWU) Former industrial union in the U.S. and Canada that represented workers in the women's clothing industry. When it was formed in 1900, most of its members were Jewish immigrants working in sweatshops. Successful ILGWU strikes in New York in 1909–10 secured higher wages and shorter hours. Under the leadership of DAVID DUBINSKY (president 1932–66), the union grew from 45,000 members to almost half a million. Active in the effort to organize mass-production industries, it was expelled from the AFL in 1937 but returned in 1940. From the 1970s, membership shrank as U.S. firms moved garment production overseas, and in 1995 the ILGWU merged with the Amalgamated Clothing and Textile Workers' Union to form the Union of Needletrades, Industrial and Textile Employees. See also AFL-CIO.

international law Body of laws, rules, or legal principles that are based on custom, treaties, or legislation and that control or affect the rights and duties of nations in relation to each other. Important elements of international law include SOVEREIGNTY, recognition (which allows a country to honor the claims of another), consent (which allows for modifications in international agreements to fit the customs of a country), freedom of the HIGH SEAS, self-defense (which ensures that measures may be taken against illegal acts committed against a sovereign nation), freedom of commerce, and protection of nationals abroad. International courts, such as the INTERNATIONAL COURT OF JUSTICE, resolve disputes on these and other matters, including WAR CRIMES. See also ASYLUM, IMMUNITY.

International Monetary Fund (IMF) Specialized agency of the U.N. system. It was conceived at the BRETTON WOODS CONFERENCE (1944) and officially founded in 1945 as a voluntary cooperative institution to help ensure the smooth international buying and selling of currency. It provides temporary financial assistance to countries with balance-of-payments problems, but is not a DEVELOPMENT BANK. It currently has over 180 member countries. Members contribute operating funds and receive voting rights according to their volume of international trade, national income, and international reserve holdings; the U.S. holds over 18% of the voting rights, more than twice the percentage of any other member. The IMF has no coercive power over member nations, but it can refuse to lend money to members that refuse to adhere to its policies and, as a last resort, can ask members to withdraw from the organization. See also INTERNATIONAL BANK FOR RECONSTRUCTION AND DEVELOPMENT, WORLD BANK.

international organization Institution whose membership includes two or more sovereign states that maintain continuous relations within it. Only a few existed before 1850; several thousand were active by 2000. Some are intergovernmental (e.g., the UNITED NATIONS), some nongovernmental (e.g., AMNESTY INTERNATIONAL). Some have worldwide or regional multiple purposes (e.g., the EUROPEAN UNION), and some have single purposes. One effect of their proliferation is a stronger sense of interdependence, which in turn has stimulated recognition of the need for systematic international cooperation to avoid international dangers, solve international problems, and exploit international opportunities.

International Organization for Standardization (ISO) Organization concerned with determining standards in most technical and nontechnical fields. Founded in Geneva in 1947, its membership includes more than 100 countries. The ISO publishes the results of its work as "International Standards" (IS), which are reviewed every five years.

international payment Payment made between countries, whether in settlement of a trade debt, as a unilateral transfer of funds, for capital investment, or for some other purpose. The reasons for such payments and the methods of making them and accounting for them are matters of concern to economists and national governments. International debts are settled either from accumulated balances of foreign CURRENCY or claims on foreign currency, or by loans from creditor to debtor, or by drawing on the INTERNATIONAL MONETARY FUND, or by movements of gold. How a country balances its international accounts is one of the most important decisions for its BALANCE OF PAYMENTS.

International Phonetic Alphabet (IPA) Set of symbols intended as a universal system for transcribing speech sounds. The promulgation and updating of the IPA has been a principal aim of the International Phonetic Association (Association Phonétique Internationale), founded in Paris in 1886. The first IPA chart was published in 1888. IPA symbols are based on an extended version of the LATIN ALPHABET, with modifications of some letters and the use of additional symbols, some of which which had been used in earlier phonetic ALPHABETS. Diacritics are used primarily to show various kinds of secondary ARTICULATION.

international relations Study of the relations of states with each other and with international organizations and certain subnational entities (e.g., bureaucracies and political parties). It is related to a number of other academic disciplines, including political science, geography, history, economics, law, sociology, psychology, and philosophy. The field emerged at the beginning of the 20th century largely in the West and particularly in the U.S., as that country grew in power and influence. The study of international relations has always been heavily influenced by normative considerations. For example, scholars have attempted to find alternatives to armed conflict and to understand the basis for international cooperation. At the beginning of the 21st century, research focused on issues such as terrorism, religious and ethnic conflict, the emergence of substate and nonstate entities, the spread of weapons of mass destruction and efforts to counter nuclear proliferation, and the development of international institutions.

International Space Station (ISS) Space station built in earth orbit largely by the U.S. and Russia, with assistance and components from a multinational consortium. The project, which began solely as an American effort, was long delayed by funding and technical problems. Originally called *Freedom* in the 1980s by Pres. Ronald Reagan, it was redesigned in the 1990s to reduce costs and expand international involvement, at which time it was renamed. In-orbit construction started in late 1998 with the launches of the Russian control module Zarya and the U.S.-built Unity connecting node, which were linked in orbit by space shuttle astronauts. In mid-2000 the module Zvezda, a habitat and control center, was added, and later in the year the ISS received its first resident crew, comprising two Russians and an American. Other elements were subsequently joined to the station, with the overall plan calling for the assembly of a complex of laboratories and habitats crossed by a long truss supporting four large solar power arrays. The station would ultimately involve at least 16 countries, including Canada, Japan, Brazil, and 11 members of the European Space Agency. Much of the early work aboard the ISS would focus on long-term life-sciences and material-sciences research in the weightless environment, and it was expected to serve as the basis for human operations in earth orbit for at least the first quarter of the 21st century.

International Standard Book Number (ISBN) 10-digit number assigned before publication to a book or edition thereof, identifying the work's national, geographic, language, or other convenient group, and its publisher, title, edition, and volume number. The ISBN is part of the International Standard Bibliographic Description (ISBD), which was prescribed by the International Organization for Standardization; delegates adopted the numbering system in 1969. The numbers are assigned by publishers and administered by designated national standard book numbering agencies such as the R. R. Bowker Co. in the U.S. and the Standard Book Numbering Agency Ltd. in Britain.

International Style Architectural style that developed in Europe and the U.S. in the 1920s and '30s and dominated Western architecture in the mid-20th century. The term was first used in 1932 by Henry-Russell Hitchcock and PHILIP JOHNSON in their essay *The International Style: Architecture Since 1922*. The style's most common characteristics are rectilinear forms, open interior spaces, large expanses of glass, steel and REINFORCED-CONCRETE construction, and light, taut plane surfaces devoid of

Savoye House, Poissy, Fr., an International Style residence by Le Corbusier, 1929–30.

PIERRE BELZEAUX—RAPHO/PHOTO RESEARCHERS

applied ornamentation. WALTER GROPIUS, LUDWIG MIES VAN DER ROHE, and LE CORBUSIER are among the architects most clearly associated with the style. See also BAUHAUS.

International System of Units *or* **Système International d'Unités** \sēs-'tem-a^{n}-ter-nȧ-syȯ-'nȧl-dü̅-nē-'tā\ *or* **SI system** International decimal system of weights and measures derived from and extending the METRIC SYSTEM of units. Adopted by the 11th General Conference on Weights and Measures in 1960, it was developed to eliminate overlapping but different systems of units of measures fostered by rapid advances in science and technology in the 19th–20th century. Its fundamental units include the meter (m) for length, the kilogram (kg) for mass, and the second (s) for time. Derived units include those for force (newton, N), energy (joule, J), and power (watt, W). See table below.

International Telecommunication Union (ITU) U.N. agency headquartered in Geneva. Its roots can be traced to 1865, when the International Telegraph Union was established to coordinate international development of the telegraph. It acquired its present name in 1934 and became a U.N. specialized agency in 1947. Its activities include regulating allocation of radio frequencies, setting standards on technical and operational matters, and assisting countries in developing their own telecommunications systems.

International Telephone and Telegraph Corp. (ITT) Former U.S. telecommunications company. It was founded in 1920 by Sosthenes and Hernand Behn as a HOLDING COMPANY for their Caribbean-based telephone and telegraph companies. It expanded into the European market and became a major telecommunications manufacturer. In the 1960s and '70s ITT became a conglomerate, acquiring firms including the Sheraton Corp. and the Hartford Fire Insurance Co. It divested its telecommunications businesses in 1987, and in 1995 it split into three companies: ITT Hartford Group Inc. (insurance); ITT Industries Inc. (defense electronics and auto parts); and a "new" ITT Corp., which merged with Starwood Lodgings in 1997.

International System of Units*
(Basic Units)

LENGTH

Unit	*Abbreviation*	*Number of Meters*	*Approximate U.S. Equivalent*
kilometer	km	1,000	0.62 mile
hectometer	hm	100	328.08 feet
dekameter	dam	10	32.81 feet
meter	m	1	39.37 inches
decimeter	dm	0.1	3.94 inches
centimeter	cm	0.01	0.39 inch
millimeter	mm	0.001	0.039 inch
micrometer	μm	0.000001	0.000039 inch

AREA

Unit	*Abbreviation*	*Number of Square Meters*	*Approximate U.S. Equivalent*
square kilometer	sq km *or* km^2	1,000,000	0.3861 square miles
hectare	ha	10,000	2.47 acres
are	a	100	119.60 square yards
square centimeter	sq cm *or* cm^2	0.0001	0.155 square inch

VOLUME

Unit	*Abbreviation*	*Number of Cubic Meters*	*Approximate U.S. Equivalent*
cubic meter	m^3	1	1.307 cubic yards
cubic decimeter	dm^3	0.001	61.023 cubic inches
cubic centimeter	cu cm *or* cm^3 *also* cc	0.000001	0.061 cubic inch

CAPACITY

Unit	*Abbreviation*	*Number of Liters*	*Approximate U.S. Equivalent*		
			cubic	*dry*	*liquid*
kiloliter	kl	1,000	1.31 cubic yards		
hectoliter	hl	100	3.53 cubic feet	2.84 bushels	
dekaliter	dal	10	0.35 cubic foot	1.14 pecks	2.64 gallons
liter	l	1	61.02 cubic inches	0.908 quart	1.057 quarts
cubic decimeter	dm^3	1	61.02 cubic inches	0.908 quart	1.057 quarts
deciliter	dl	0.10	6.1 cubic inches	0.18 pint	0.21 pint
centiliter	cl	0.01	0.61 cubic inch		0.338 fluid ounce
milliliter	ml	0.001	0.061 cubic inch		0.27 fluid dram
microliter	μl	0.000001	0.000061 cubic inch		0.00027 fluid dram

MASS AND WEIGHT

Unit	*Abbreviation*	*Number of Grams*	*Approximate U.S. Equivalent*
metric ton	t	1,000,000	1.102 short tons
kilogram	kg	1,000	2.2046 pounds
hectogram	hg	100	3.527 ounces
dekagram	dag	10	0.353 ounce
gram	g	1	0.035 ounce
decigram	dg	0.10	1.543 grains
centigram	cg	0.01	0.154 grain
milligram	mg	0.001	0.015 grain
microgram	μg	0.000001	0.000015 grain

*For metric equivalents of U.S. units, see Weights and Measurements table

international unit Any of several precision standards used in measuring physical quantities, such as mass, length, and time (see INTERNATIONAL SYSTEM OF UNITS), and also lighting systems, radiation processes, and pharmacology. The luminous intensity or candlepower of a light is expressed in candelas. The second is based on the frequency of radiation emitted by cesium-133 atoms. In radioactive decay, the international unit is the number of disintegrations per second in a sample. In pharmacology, the international unit is the quantity of a substance (vitamin, hormone, or toxin) that produces a specified effect when tested according to an internationally accepted procedure.

International Whaling Commission (IWC) An intergovernmental organization created in 1946 to control the rapid escalation of whaling. The original purpose of the IWC was to preserve whale stocks for commercial whalers. Whale populations, however, continued to decline, and in 1986 the IWC instituted a moratorium on commercial whaling that remains in effect. At the beginning of the 21st century, 40 countries belonged to the commission, but membership has fluctuated over the years. The commission's success has been limited by governments leaving the IWC, ignoring its policies, or breaching regulations.

Internet Publicly accessible computer NETWORK connecting many smaller networks from around the world. It grew out of a U.S. Defense Department program called ARPANET (Advanced Research Projects Agency Network), established in 1969 with connections between computers at UCLA, Stanford Research Institute, UC–Santa Barbara, and the University of Utah. ARPANET's purpose was to conduct research into computer networking in order to provide a secure and survivable communications system in case of war. As the network quickly expanded, academics and researchers in other fields began to use it as well. In 1971 the first program for sending E-MAIL over a distributed network was developed; by 1973, the year international connections to ARPANET were made (from Britain and Norway), E-mail represented most of the traffic on ARPANET. The 1970s also saw the development of mailing lists, NEWSGROUPS and BULLETIN-BOARD SYSTEMS, and the TCP/IP communications PROTOCOLS, which were adopted as standard protocols for ARPANET in 1982–83, leading to the widespread use of the term Internet. In 1984 the DOMAIN NAME addressing system was introduced. In 1986 the National Science Foundation established the NSFNET, a distributed network of networks capable of handling far greater traffic, and within a year more than 10,000 hosts were connected to the Internet. In 1988 real-time conversation over the network became possible with the development of Internet Relay Chat protocols (see CHAT). In 1990 ARPANET ceased to exist, leaving behind the NSFNET, and the first commercial dial-up access to the Internet became available. In 1991 the WORLD WIDE WEB was released to the public (via FTP). The Mosaic BROWSER was released in 1993, and its popularity led to the proliferation of World Wide Web sites and users. In 1995 the NSFNET reverted to the role of a research network, leaving Internet traffic to be routed through network providers rather than NSF supercomputers. That year the Web became the most popular part of the Internet, surpassing the FTP protocols in traffic volume. By 1997 there were over 10 million hosts on the Internet and over 1 million registered domain names. Internet access can now be gained via radio signals, cable-television lines, satellites, and fiber-optic connections, though most traffic still uses a part of the public telecommunications (telephone) network. The Internet is widely regarded as a development of vast significance that will affect nearly every aspect of human culture and commerce in ways still only dimly discernible.

Internet Protocol address See IP ADDRESS

Internet service provider (ISP) Company that provides INTERNET connections and services to individuals and organizations. For a monthly fee, ISPs provide computer users with a connection to their site (see DATA TRANSMISSION), as well as a log-in name and password. They may also provide software packages (such as BROWSERS), E-MAIL accounts, and a personal WEB SITE or home page. ISPs can host Web sites for businesses and can also build the Web sites themselves. ISPs are all connected to each other through network access points (NAPs), public network facilities on the Internet backbone.

Interpol *officially* **International Criminal Police Organization** International organization whose purpose is to fight international crime by promoting cooperation of its members' police forces and developing means of controlling ordinary crime. It was founded in Austria in 1923 with 20 member nations; after World War II its headquarters moved to Paris, and today it has over 175 members. It hunts criminals who operate in more than one country (e.g., smugglers), those who stay home but whose crimes affect other countries (e.g., counterfeiters of foreign currency), and those who commit a crime in one country and flee to another.

interpolation In mathematics, ESTIMATION of a value between two known data points. A simple example is calculating the mean (see MEAN, MEDIAN, AND MODE) of two population counts made 10 years apart to estimate the population in the fifth year. Estimating outside the data points (e.g., predicting the population five years after the second population count) is called extrapolation. If more than two data points are available, a curve may fit the data better than a line. The simplest curve that fits is a POLYNOMIAL curve. Exactly one polynomial of any given degree—an interpolating polynomial—passes through any number of data points.

interrogation In CRIMINAL LAW, process of formally and systematically questioning a suspect in order to elicit incriminating responses. The process is largely outside the governance of law, though in the U.S. relatively elaborate safeguards have been placed on police interrogatory powers in order to protect the rights of the ACCUSED.

Interstate Commerce Commission (ICC) (1887–1995) First REGULATORY AGENCY established in the U.S. and a prototype for independent government regulatory bodies. An agency of the U.S. Department of TRANSPORTATION, it was responsible for the economic regulation of interstate surface transportation, including railroads, trucking companies, and buslines. It certified carriers, regulated rates, oversaw mergers, and approved railroad construction. The ICC was dissolved in 1995; its rail and nonrail functions were assigned to the new Surface Transportation Board, and its licensing and certain nonlicensing motor-carrier functions were transferred to the Federal Highway Administration.

interstellar medium Content of the region between the stars, including vast, diffuse clouds of gases and minute solid particles. Such tenuous matter in the MILKY WAY's interstellar medium accounts for about 5% of the galaxy's total mass. By no means a complete vacuum, the interstellar medium contains mainly hydrogen gas, with a smaller amount of helium and sizable quantities of dust particles of uncertain composition. Primary COSMIC RAYS also travel through interstellar space, and magnetic fields extend across much of it. Most interstellar matter occurs in cloudlike concentrations, which can condense to form STARS. Stars, in turn, continually lose mass through stellar winds (see SOLAR WIND). SUPERNOVAS and planetary nebulae (see PLANETARY NEBULA) also feed mass back to the interstellar medium, where it mixes with matter that has not yet formed stars (see POPULATIONS I AND II).

interval In music, two tones heard in relation to one other, and specifically their distance in musical space. In Western music, intervals are generally named according to the number of scale-steps within a given KEY that they embrace; thus, the ascent from C to G (C–D–E–F–G) is called a 5th since the interval embraces five scale degrees (inclusive of those at both ends). The CHORD C–E–G is made up of two intervals, the 5th C–G and the 3rd C–E. An interval with a simple numerical designation will also have a more precise name; thus, C–E is a major 3rd (since it consists of four semitones), C-sharp–E is a minor 3rd (three semitones), C–E-flat is also a minor 3rd (three semitones), C–E-sharp is an augmented 3rd (five semitones), and C-sharp–E-flat is a diminished 3rd (two semitones). 2nds and 6ths are classified like 3rds, whereas 4ths and 5ths are classified instead as perfect (a perfect 4th consisting of five semitones, a perfect 5th of seven semitones), augmented (when expanded by a semitone), or diminished (when contracted by a semitone).

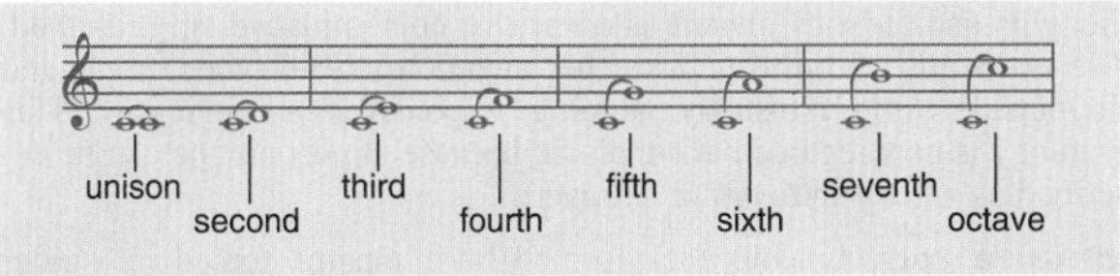

Examples of simple musical intervals.

intestate succession In the law of INHERITANCE, transmission of property or property interests of a decedent as provided by statute, as distinguished from transfer according to the decedent's WILL. Modern laws of intestacy, though they vary widely, share the common principle that the estate should devolve upon persons standing in some kinship relation with the decedent; modern practice tends to favor the rights of the surviving spouse.

intestinal gas Volatile material (mostly swallowed air, partly digestive by-products) in the digestive tract, which normally contains 150–500 cc of gas. Air in the stomach is either belched out or passed to the intestines. Some of its oxygen is absorbed into the blood along the way. Carbon dioxide produced by DIGESTION is added. Nitrogen, the major component, is inert and usually passed on. Obstructions in the small intestine can trap gas in distended pockets, causing severe pain. In the large intestine, bacterial fermentation products are added—mostly hydrogen, but also methane, hydrogen sulfide, ammonia, and sulfur-containing mercaptans. Excess gas in the colon is eventually expelled from the body.

intestinal obstruction Blockage of the SMALL or LARGE intestine, resulting from either lack of PERISTALSIS or mechanical obstruction (e.g., by narrowing, foreign objects, or HERNIA). Obstruction near the start of the small intestine often causes VOMITING. Near the end or in the large intestine, backed-up waste and swallowed air cause intestinal distention; the resulting pressure may cause necrosis (death of intestinal wall tissue). Waste products may escape into the bloodstream. Symptoms and treatment depend on the obstruction's nature and location.

intestine See LARGE INTESTINE, SMALL INTESTINE

intifada \ˌin-ti-ˈfä-də\ (Arabic: "shaking off") Palestinian revolt in 1987–93 against the Israeli occupation in the GAZA STRIP and WEST BANK. Initially a spontaneous reaction to 20 years of occupation and worsening economic conditions, it was soon taken over by the PALESTINE LIBERATION ORGANIZATION (PLO). Its tactics included strikes, boycotts, and confrontations with Israeli troops. The International Red Cross estimated that 800 Palestinians, more than 200 under the age of 16, were killed by Israeli security forces by 1990. Intifada pressure is credited with helping make possible the 1993 Israeli-PLO agreement on Palestinian self-rule. A breakdown in further negotiations in late 2000 led to another outburst of violence, which quickly became known as the Aqsa intifada, named for the Aqsa mosque in Jerusalem where the fighting first began. See also YASIR ARAFAT, FATAH, HAMAS.

Intolerable Acts *or* **Coercive Acts** (1774) Four punitive measures enacted by the British Parliament against the American colonies. Boston's harbor was closed until restitution was made for the tea destroyed in the BOSTON TEA PARTY; the Massachusetts colony's charter was annulled and a military governor installed; British officials charged with capital offenses could go to England for trial; and arrangement for housing British troops in American houses was revived. The QUEBEC ACT added to these oppressive measures. The acts, called "intolerable" by the colonists, led to a convening of the CONTINENTAL CONGRESS.

intonation In PHONETICS, the melodic pattern of an utterance. Intonation is primarily a matter of variation in the pitch level of the voice (see TONE), but in languages such as English, stress and rhythm are also involved. Intonation conveys differences of expressive meaning (e.g., surprise, doubtfulness). In many languages, including English, intonation serves a grammatical function, distinguishing one type of phrase or sentence from another. Thus, "it's gone" is an assertion when spoken with a drop in pitch at the end, but a question when spoken with a rise in pitch at the end.

introvert and extrovert Basic personality types, according to the theories of CARL GUSTAV JUNG. The introvert, who directs his or her thoughts and feelings inward, is often shy, contemplative, and reserved. The extrovert, who directs his or her attention toward other people and the outside world, is usually outgoing, responsive, and aggressive. This typology is now regarded as simplistic because almost no one can be described as wholly introvert or extrovert.

intrusive rock Igneous rock formed from magma forced into older rocks at depths within the earth's crust, which then slowly solidifies below the earth's surface, though it may later be exposed by erosion. Igneous intrusions form a variety of rock types. See also EXTRUSIVE ROCK.

intuition In philosophy, the power of obtaining knowledge that is not or cannot be acquired either by inference or observation. As such, intuition is thought of as an original, independent source of knowledge, since it is designed to account for just those kinds of knowledge that other sources do not provide. Knowledge of some necessary truths and basic moral principles is sometimes explained in this way. A technical sense of intuition, deriving from IMMANUEL KANT, refers to immediate acquaintance with individual entities; intuition *(Anschauung)* in this sense may be empirical (e.g., consciousness of sense-data) or pure (e.g., consciousness of space and time a priori as forms of all empirical intuitions). As conceived by BENEDICT DE SPINOZA and HENRI BERGSON, intuition is taken to be concrete knowledge of the world as an interconnected whole, as contrasted with the piecemeal, "abstract" knowledge obtained by science and observation.

intuitionism School of mathematical thought introduced by the Dutch mathematician Luitzen Egbertus Jan Brouwer (1881–1966). It contends that the primary objects of mathematical discourse are mental constructions. Intuitionists have challenged many of the oldest principles of mathematics as being nonconstructive and hence mathematically meaningless. For example, intuitionists do not admit the use of the law of excluded middle (see laws of THOUGHT) in mathematical proofs in which all members of an infinite class are involved. In metaethics (see ETHICS), intuitionism is a form of COGNITIVISM that maintains that there are objective moral truths that can be known by a kind of rational intuition akin to that by which we recognize self-evident truths in mathematics. RALPH CUDWORTH, Henry More (1614–1687), and Samuel Clarke (1675–1729) asserted that moral distinctions arise from an intellectual intuition of "fitness or unfitness" between circumstances and actions. Ethical intuitionism attracted the support of a line of distinguished thinkers, including Richard Price (1723–1791); in the 20th century, it was associated with the work of Harold Arthur Prichard (1871–1947) and W. D. ROSS.

Inuit See ESKIMO

Invar Trademark name for an ALLOY of IRON (64% iron, 36% nickel) that expands very little when heated. Invar was formerly used for absolute standards of length measurement and is now used for surveying tapes and in watches and various other temperature-sensitive devices. The name expresses the invariability of its dimensions. It was developed by Charles-Édouard Guillaume (1861–1938), winner of the 1920 Nobel Prize for Physics.

inventory In business, any item of property held in stock by a firm, including finished goods held for sale, goods in the process of production, raw materials, and items that will be consumed in the process of producing salable goods. Inventories appear on a company's BALANCE SHEET as assets. Inventory turnover, which indicates the rate at which goods are converted into cash, is a key factor in appraising a firm's financial condition. For financial statements, inventories may be priced either at cost or at market value.

Inverness \ˌin-vər-ˈnes\ City (pop., 1991 est.: 63,000), northwestern Scotland. Located on the River Ness and the Caledonian Canal in northwestern Scotland, it has long been the center of the Scots Highland region, and is the headquarters for the Highlands administrative region. In the 6th century it was the capital of the Pictish kingdom of King Brude. By the 12th century it had become a burgh near the castle of MALCOLM III CANMORE. It is now an educational and tourist center, and its manufacturing is expanding as the offshore oil industry develops.

inverse function Mathematical FUNCTION that undoes the effect of another function. For example, the inverse function of the formula that converts Celsius temperature to Fahrenheit temperature is the formula that converts Fahrenheit to Celsius. Applying one formula and then the other yields the original temperature. Inverse procedures are essential to solving EQUATIONS because they allow mathematical operations to be reversed (e.g. LOGARITHMS, the inverses of EXPONENTIAL FUNCTIONS, are used to solve exponential equations). Whenever a mathematical procedure is introduced, one of the most important questions is how to invert it. Thus, for example, the TRIGONOMETRIC FUNCTIONS gave rise to the inverse trigonometric functions.

invertebrate Any animal that lacks a vertebral column, or backbone. They include the PROTOZOANS, ANNELIDS, CNIDARIANS, ECHINODERMS, FLATWORMS, NEMATODES, MOLLUSKS, and ARTHROPODS. More than 90% of living animals are invertebrates. Worldwide in distribution, they range in size from minute protozoans to giant squids. Apart from the absence of a vertebral column, invertebrates have little in common. They are generally soft-bodied and have an external skeleton for muscle attachment and protection. See also VERTEBRATE.

Investiture Controversy Struggle between the papacy and the Holy Roman Emperor over the ruler's presentation of the symbols of office to churchmen. Pope GREGORY VII condemned lay investiture in 1075 as an unjustified assertion of secular authority over the church; the issue was pivotal in his dispute with the emperor HENRY IV and in the larger struggle between papal and imperial power. HENRY I of England renounced lay investiture (1106) in return for the guarantee that homage would be paid to the king before consecration, and the Concordat of WORMS (1122) forged a similar compromise between Henry V and CALIXTUS II.

investment Process of exchanging income for an asset that is expected to produce earnings at a later time. An investor refrains from CONSUMPTION in the present in hopes of a greater return in the future. In the history of CAPITALISM, investment has been primarily the function of private business, though in the 20th century governments in planned economies and developing countries became important investors. Investment may be influenced by rates of INTEREST, with the rate of investment rising as interest rates fall, but other factors more difficult to measure may also be important—for example, businessmen's expectations about future demand and profit, technical changes in production methods, and expected relative costs of LABOR and CAPITAL. Investment cannot occur without SAVING, which provides funding. Because investment increases an economy's capacity to produce, it is the factor responsible for economic growth.

investment bank Firm that originates, underwrites, and distributes new security issues of corporations and government agencies. The Banking Act of 1933 required the separation of investment banking and COMMERCIAL BANKING functions. Investment banks operate by purchasing all the new security issue from a corporation at one price and selling the issue in smaller units to the investing public at a price high enough to cover the expense of the sale and leave a profit. The investment bank, which can assess interest rates and probable demand, is responsible for setting the public offering price. A syndicate of investment-banking firms underwrites and distributes most security issues in order to divide the RISK. See also BANK, CENTRAL BANK, SAVINGS BANK, SECURITY.

investment casting Precision CASTING for forming METAL shapes with minutely precise details. Casting BRONZE or precious metals typically involves several steps, including forming a MOLD around the sculptured form; detaching the mold (in two or more sections); coating its inside with WAX; forming a second mold, of heat-resisting clay, around the wax shell, and filling the interior with a clay core; baking the assembly (hardening the clay and melting the wax, which escapes through openings in the outer mold); pouring molten bronze into the space vacated by the wax; and breaking the mold to expose the cast form. In modern foundries, plastics, or occasionally frozen mercury, are used instead of wax. See also LOST-WAX CASTING, DIE CASTING.

investment credit Tax incentive that permits businesses to deduct a specified percentage of certain investment costs from their tax liability, in addition to the normal allowances for DEPRECIATION. Investment credits are similar to investment allowances, which permit businesses to deduct a specified percentage of certain capital costs from their taxable income. Both investment credits and investment allowances differ from accelerated depreciation by offering a percentage deduction at the time an asset is purchased. In effect, they are SUBSIDIES for investment. Investment credits and investment allowances were adopted by the U.S. in 1962 in order to protect domestic business from foreign competition, but they were eliminated in the Tax Reform Act of 1969 in an attempt to counteract rising INFLATION.

investment trust *or* **closed-end trust** Financial organization that pools the funds of its shareholders and invests them in a diversified portfolio of SECURITIES. It differs from a MUTUAL FUND, which issues units representing diversified holdings rather than shares in the company itself. Investment trusts have a fixed number of shares for sale; their price depends on the market value of the underlying securities and on the demand for and supply of shares. The first modern investment trusts were formed in England and Scotland as early as 1860. Many early U.S. investment trusts failed with the collapse of the stock market in 1929, but others have since prospered under stricter federal regulation.

Io \ˈī-ō\ In GREEK MYTHOLOGY, the daughter of the river god Argos, who drew HERA's jealousy when ZEUS fell in love with her. Zeus changed her into a white heifer to protect her. Hera set the many-eyed creature Argus to watch over the heifer, but Zeus sent HERMES to lull Argus to sleep and kill him. Hera then sent a gadfly to pursue Io, who fled across Europe and crossed the bodies of water later named the Ionian Sea and the BOSPORUS ("Ford of the Cow") in her honor. When she arrived in Egypt she resumed her original form. She was later identified with the Egyptian goddess ISIS.

iodine Nonmetallic chemical ELEMENT, chemical symbol I, atomic number 53. The heaviest nonradioactive HALOGEN, it is a nearly black crystalline solid (diatomic molecule I_2) that sublimes (see SUBLIMATION) to a deep violet, irritating vapor. It is never found in nature uncombined. Its sources (mostly in brines and seaweeds) and compounds are usually iodides; iodates (small amounts in saltpeter) and periodates also occur. Dietary iodine is essential for THYROID GLAND function, so table SALT usually has potassium iodide (chemical formula KI) added to prevent IODINE DEFICIENCY. Elemental iodine is used in medicine, in synthesizing some organic chemicals, in manufacturing dyes, in analytical chemistry (see ANALYSIS) to measure FAT SATURATION (see HYDROGENATION) and to detect STARCH, and in photography. The radioactive ISOTOPE I-131 (see RADIOACTIVITY), with an eight-day HALF-LIFE, is very useful in medicine (see NUCLEAR MEDICINE, THYROID FUNCTION TEST) and other applications.

iodine deficiency Inadequate intake or metabolism of IODINE. It directly affects THYROID secretions, which influence heart action, nerve response, growth rate, and metabolism. Simple GOITER, the most frequent result, is most common in areas without access to salt water and is rare along seacoasts. Severe, prolonged deficiency can cause hypothyroidism. Lack of iodine during infancy may cause CRETINISM. Eating seafood regularly or using iodized table salt will prevent iodine deficiency. Some countries have made dietary iodine additives mandatory.

ion ATOM or group of atoms with one or more positive (CATION) or negative (ANION) ELECTRIC CHARGES. Ions are formed when ELECTRONS are added to or removed from neutral MOLECULES or other ions, as sodium (Na) and chlorine (Cl) atoms react to form Na^+ and Cl^-; when ions combine with other particles, as hydrogen cation (H^+) and ammonia (NH_3) combine to form ammonium cation (NH_4^+); and when a COVALENT BOND between two atoms is ruptured in such a way that the resulting particles are charged, as water (H_2O) dissociates (see DISSOCIATION) into hydrogen and hydroxide ions (H^+ and OH^-). Many crystalline substances (see CRYSTAL) are composed of ions held in regular geometric patterns by the attraction of the oppositely charged particles for each other. Ions migrate to the electrode of opposite charge in an ELECTRIC FIELD and are the conductors of current in electrolytic cells (see ELECTROLYSIS). Compounds that form ions are called ELECTROLYTES. Ions are also formed in gases when an electrical discharge passes through them.

ion-exchange resin Any of a wide variety of synthetic POLYMERS containing positively or negatively charged sites that can interact with or bind to an ION of opposite charge from a surrounding solution. Light, porous solids in granules, beads, or sheets, they absorb the solution and swell as they attract the target ions; when exhausted, they are removed from it and regenerated by an inexpensive brine or carbonate solution. A solid support of styrene-divinylbenzene copolymer is often attached to sulfonic or carboxylic acid groups and used to attract CATIONS. Quaternary ammonium groups on the solid matrix are used to attract ANIONS. Industrially, these resins are used to soften HARD WATER, purify SUGAR, and concentrate valuable elements (gold, silver, uranium) from their ORES. In the laboratory, they are used to separate and concentrate substances and sometimes as catalysts. ZEOLITES are minerals with ion-exchange properties.

Ionesco \yò-nes-ˈkō\, **Eugène** *orig.* **Eugen Ionescu** (1909–1994) Romanian-French playwright. He studied in Bucharest and Paris, where he lived from 1945. His first one-act "antiplay," *The Bald Soprano* (1950), inspired a revolution in dramatic techniques and helped inaugurate the theater of the ABSURD. He followed it with other one-act plays in which illogical events create an atmosphere both comic and grotesque, including *The Lesson* (1951), *The Chairs* (1952), and *The New Tenant* (1955). His most popular full-length play, *Rhinoceros* (1959), concerns a provincial French town in which all the citizens are metamorphosing into rhinoceroses. Other plays include *Exit the King* (1962) and *A Stroll in the*

Air (1963). He was elected to the Académie Française in 1970.

Eugène Ionesco, 1959.
MARK GERSON

Ionia \ī-'ō-nyə\ Ancient region, western coast of Asia Minor (modern Turkey) bordering on the Aegean Sea. It consisted of a coastal strip that extended from the mouth of the Hermus River to the Halicarnassus Peninsula, a distance of 100 mi (160 km). In the 8th century BC there were 12 major Greek cities in the region, including Phocaea, Erythrae, Colophon, and Miletus on the mainland, and the islands Chios and Samos. It was very prosperous, and until 500 BC Ionic philosophy and architecture and the Ionic dialect were highly influential in Greece. In the mid-6th century BC, it fell to Lydia and then to the Persians. After a brief period of independence beginning 334 BC, it became part of the Seleucid kingdom. In 133 BC it passed to the Romans and became part of the Roman province of Asia. It was devastated during the Turkish conquest of Asia Minor.

Ionian Islands \ī-'ō-nē-ən\ *ancient* **Heptanesos** Group of seven Greek islands (pop., 1991: 191,000) in the Ionian Sea. They include Corfu, Cephalonia, Zacynthus, Leucas, Ithaca, Cythera, and Paxos and have a combined land area of 891 sq mi (2,307 sq km). Controlled by Venice in the 15th–16th century, they were taken by Russian and Turkish forces in 1799. In 1815 the Treaty of Paris placed them under the control of Britain; the British ceded them to Greece in 1864.

Ionian revolt Uprising (499–494 BC) of some of the Ionian cities of Asia Minor against their Persian overlords. The cities deposed their own tyrants and, with help from Athens, tried unsuccessfully to throw off Persian domination. Darius I of Persia used Athens's involvement as a pretext for his invasion of Greece in 490, initiating the Persian Wars, which resulted in a stronger Athenian influence in western Anatolia.

Ionian school School of Greek philosophers of the 6th–5th century BC, including Thales, Anaximander, Anaximenes, Heracleitus, Anaxagoras, Diogenes of Apollonia, Archelaus, and Hippon. Though Ionia was the original center of their activity, they differed so greatly from one another in their conclusions that they cannot truly be said to represent a specific school of philosophy, but their common concern to explain phenomena in terms of matter or physical forces distinguished them from later thinkers.

Ionian Sea Part of the Mediterranean Sea lying between Greece, Sicily, and Italy. Though once considered part of the Adriatic Sea, to which it connects by the Strait of Otranto, it is now considered a separate body. The Mediterranean reaches its greatest depth (16,000 ft or 4,900 m) in the Ionian south of Greece. Along its eastern shore are the Ionian Islands.

Ionians Ancient Greek inhabitants of Ionia, from the collapse of Mycenaean civilization. Ionian cities colonized southern Italy and opened up the Black Sea from c. 700 BC. Their contributions to Greek culture included the epics of Homer and the earliest elegiac and iambic poetry. They began the study of geography, philosophy, and historiography in the 6th century. After Alexander the Great their literary language was the basis of koine, or "common speech," the language of practically all Greek writing to the present day.

ionic bond Electrostatic attraction among oppositely charged ions in which an electron is transferred from one neutral atom (usually a metal, which becomes the cation) to another (a nonmetallic element or a group, which becomes the anion). The two types of ion are held together by electrostatic forces in a solid that does not contain molecules as such; rather, each ion has neighbors of the opposite charge in an ordered overall structure. When, for example, common salt (NaCl) is dissolved in water, it dissociates (see dissociation) into the two ions, in this case cations of sodium (Na^+) and anions of chloride (Cl^-). See also bonding, covalent bond.

ionization Process by which electrically neutral atoms or molecules are converted to electrically charged atoms or molecules (ions) by the removal or addition of negatively charged electrons. It is one of the principal ways in which radiation transfers energy to matter, and hence of detecting radiation. In general, ionization occurs whenever sufficiently energetic charged particles or radiant energy travels through gases, liquids, or solids. A certain minimal level of ionization is present in the earth's atmosphere because of continuous absorption of cosmic rays from space and ultraviolet radiation from the sun.

ionization potential *or* **ionization energy** Amount of energy required to remove an electron from an isolated atom or molecule. There is an ionization potential for each successive electron removed, though that associated with removing the first (most loosely held) electron is most commonly used. The ionization potential of an element is a measure of its ability to enter into chemical reactions requiring ion formation or donation of electrons and is related to the nature of the chemical bonding in the compounds formed by elements. See also binding energy, ionization.

ionosphere \ī-'än-ə-ˌsfir\ Region of the earth's atmosphere in which the number of ions, or electrically charged particles, is large enough to affect the propagation of radio waves. The ionosphere begins at an altitude of about 30 mi (50 km) but is most distinct above about 50 mi (80 km). The ionization is caused mainly by solar radiation at X-ray and ultraviolet wavelengths. The ionosphere is responsible for the long-distance propagation, by reflection, of radio signals in the shortwave and broadcast bands.

Iowa State (population 1997 est.: 2,852,000), midwestern U.S. It covers 56,275 sq mi (145,752 sq km); its capital is Des Moines. The Des Moines River flows across the state from northwest to southeast. The Mississippi River forms its eastern boundary, while the Missouri and the Big Sioux rivers define portions of its western boundary. The Sauk, Fox, Iowa, and Sioux Indians lived in the region when French explorers Louis Jolliet and Jacques Marquette arrived in 1673. The U.S. acquired Iowa as part of the Louisiana Purchase in 1803. Following the Black Hawk War and purchase of eastern Iowa from the Sauk and Fox Indians in the 1830s, white settlement advanced rapidly. It became a territory in 1838 and was made the 29th state in 1846. After the Civil War, railroad expansion drew large waves of immigrants from the east and from Europe. After World War I population growth slowed. Its economy is based on agriculture, and Iowa is a leader in the U.S. production of livestock.

Iowa, University of Public university in Iowa City. Founded in 1847, it was the first public university in the U.S. to admit men and women on an equal basis and the first to award advanced degrees in the creative arts. It comprises colleges of liberal arts, business administration, dentistry, law, medicine, nursing, pharmacy, education, and engineering, and schools of journalism, music, and social work. The campus is home to the renowned Writer's Workshop and International Writing Program. Total enrollment is about 28,000.

Iowa State University Public university in Ames, Iowa. Founded in 1858, it was the first state institution to establish a veterinary school. It comprises colleges of agriculture, business, design, education, engineering, family and consumer sciences, liberal arts and sciences, and veterinary medicine. Campus facilities include several important agricultural research centers. Total enrollment is about 25,000.

IP address *in full* **Internet Protocol address** Number that uniquely identifies a host computer on the Internet. The host communicates with other host computers using the Internet Protocol (see TCP/IP), which specifies how to break up data messages into packets and route them to the destination address on the network. See also domain name, URL.

ipecac \'i-pi-ˌkak\ *or* **ipecacuanha** \ˌi-pi-ˌka-kyə-'wä-nə\ Dried rhizome and roots of either of two tropical New World plants *(Cephaelis acuminata* and *C. ipecacuanha)* of the madder family. It has been used since ancient times especially as a source of a drug to treat poisoning by inducing nausea and vomiting. The name also refers to the drug itself.

Iphigeneia \ˌi-fə-jə-'nī-ə\ In Greek mythology, the eldest daughter of Agamemnon and Clytemnestra and sister of Electra and Orestes. When the Achaean fleet was becalmed at Aulis, her father sacrificed her to Artemis in order to secure favorable winds to carry the ships to Troy. Her mother later avenged her death by murdering Agamemnon. Iphigeneia's story is treated in plays by Aeschylus, Sophocles, and Euripides. According to Euripides, she did not die but was saved by Artemis; she went to the land of Tauris, where she became a priestess, and she saved Orestes from madness and death when he fled there after killing their mother.

Ipoh \'ē-pō\ City (pop., 2000 prelim.: 566,211), western Malaysia. Its name comes from a local tree, whose poisonous resin was once used by aborigines for hunting. The modern city dates from the 1890s, when British tin-mining companies were set up. Immigrant Chinese were brought in to work the tin deposits, and their descendants now dominate the city. It is the nation's mining capital.

Ipsus, Battle of (301 BC) Battle marking the defeat at Ipsus, Phrygia, of Antigonus I Monophthalmus and his son Demetrius I Poliorcetes at the hands of Lysimachus of Thrace, Seleucus I Nicator of Babylon, Ptolemy I Soter of Egypt, and Cassander of Macedonia. Antigonus was killed and his Asian territory lost, but Demetrius kept territory in Greece and Macedonia. The battle was part of the struggle for control of territories that formerly comprised Alexander the Great's empire.

Ipswich Town (pop., 1998 est.: 113,900), county seat of Suffolk, England. Located northeast of London, it was chartered in 1200. It prospered as a port for the export of East Anglian textiles from medieval times to the 17th century. It is now an agricultural market for the region. Its landmarks include the 16th-century Christchurch mansion and the Great White Horse coaching inn mentioned in Charles Dickens's *Pickwick Papers*. It was the birthplace of Thomas, Cardinal Wolsey.

IQ *in full* **intelligence quotient** Number intended to represent a measure of relative intelligence as determined by the subject's responses to a series of test problems. The IQ was originally computed as the ratio of a person's mental age to his or her chronological (physical) age, multiplied by 100, but use of the concept of mental age has been largely discontinued, and IQ is now generally assessed on the basis of the statistical distribution of scores. The most widely used intelligence tests are the Stanford-Binet test (1916), for children, and the Wechsler test (1939), originally for adults but now also for children. A score above 130 is considered to reflect "giftedness," while a score below 70 is considered to reflect mental impairment or mental retardation. Intelligence tests have provoked great controversy, particularly about what kinds of mental ability constitute intelligence and whether IQ adequately represents these abilities, and about cultural and class bias in test construction and standardization procedures.

Iqaluit \ē-'kä-lü-it\ *formerly* **Frobisher Bay** Town (pop., 2001: 5,236), capital of Nunavut territory, Canada. Situated on southeastern Baffin Island, it is the largest community in the eastern Canadian Arctic. It was established as a trading post in 1914 and became an air base during World War II. It later was the site of construction camps for the DEW (Distant Early Warning) line of radar stations. It is the site of a meteorological station and a hospital. It became Nunavut's capital in 1999.

Iqbal \'ik-,bäl\, **Muhammad** *later* **Sir Muhammad** (1877–1938) Indian poet and philosopher. He first won fame for his poetry, which was written in the classical style for public recitation and became known even among the illiterate. His perspective grew increasingly Pan-Islamic, as revealed in the long poem *The Secrets of the Self* (1915), which he wrote in Persian in order to address a broader Muslim audience. Calling for a revitalization of Islam, he advocated the separate Muslim state that would eventually be realized with the founding of Pakistan in 1947, and he was acclaimed after his death as the father of that country. His poetic masterpiece is *The Song of Eternity* (1932). He is considered the greatest 20th-century poet to write in Urdu.

iqta \ik-'tä\ In the Islamic Empire of the caliphate, land-revenue rights granted to army officials for limited periods in lieu of a regular wage. It was established in the 9th century to relieve the state treasury when insufficient revenues made it difficult for the government to pay army salaries. The land originally belonged to non-Muslims, who were required to pay a special property tax; army officers were granted rights to the tax revenue, while the land itself remained in the hands of its owners. The system evolved in differing ways under the Seljuqs and the Il-Khans in Iran (r. 1256–1353) and in Ayyubid Egypt.

IRA See Irish Republican Army

Iran *officially* **Islamic Republic of Iran** *formerly* **Persia** Country, Middle East. Area: 629,315 sq mi (1,629,918 sq km). Population (2002 est.): 65,457,000. Capital: Tehran. Persians constitute 45% of its popula-

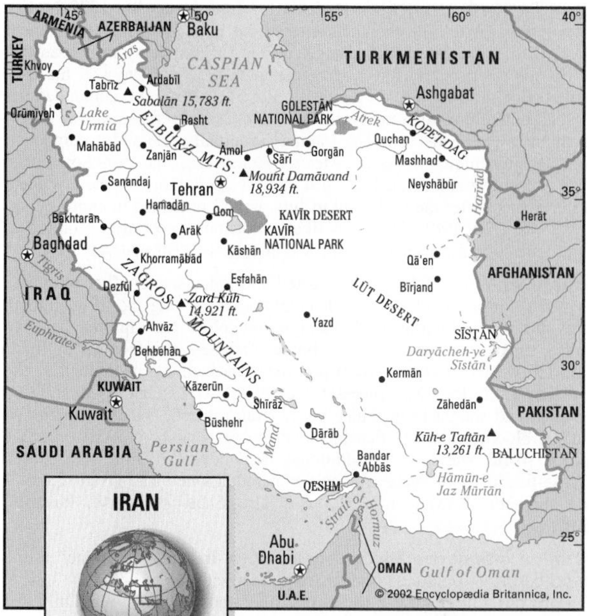

tion; other ethnic groups include the Kurds, the Lurs, the Bakhtyari, and the Balochi. Language: Persian (Farsi: official). Religion: Islam (official); most are Shiites. Currency: rial. Iran occupies a high plateau more than 1,500 ft (460 m) above sea level and is surrounded by mountains. More than half of its surface area consists of salt deserts and other wasteland. About one-tenth of its land is arable, and another one-fourth is suitable for grazing. Iran's rich petroleum reserves account for about 9% of world reserves and are the basis of its economy. It is an Islamic republic with one legislative house but several oversight bodies dominated by the clergy. The head of state and government is the president, but supreme authority rests with the leader (*rahbar*), a ranking cleric. Habitation in Iran dates to c. 100,000 BC, but recorded history began with the Elamites c. 3000 BC. The Medes flourished from c. 728 BC but were overthrown (550 BC) by the Persians, who were in turn conquered by Alexander the Great in the 4th century BC. The Parthians (see Parthia) created a Greek-speaking empire that lasted from 247 BC to AD 226, when control passed to the Sasanians. Various Muslim dynasties ruled from the 7th century. In 1502 the Safavids established a dynasty that lasted until 1736. The Qajars ruled from 1779, but in the 19th century the country was economically controlled by the Russian and British empires. Reza Khan (see R. Shah Pahlavi) seized power in a coup (1921). His son Mohammad Reza Shah Pahlavi alienated religious leaders with a program of modernization and westernization and was overthrown in 1979; Shiite cleric Ruhollah Khomeini then set up an Islamic republic, and Western influence was suppressed. The destructive Iran-Iraq War of the 1980s ended in a stalemate. During the 1990s the government gradually moved to a more liberal conduct of state affairs.

Iran-Contra Affair U.S. political scandal in the mid-1980s involving secret weapons transactions. In 1985 Robert McFarlane, head of the National Security Council, authorized sales of weapons to Iran in an attempt to secure release of U.S. hostages held in Lebanon by pro-Iranian terrorist groups. The deal contravened stated policy regarding both dealings with terrorists and military aid to Iran. Part of the $48 million paid by Iran for the arms was diverted to the Nicaraguan contras with the assistance of Rear Adm. John Poindexter and Oliver North, directly violating a 1984 law banning aid to the contras. A Senate investigation resulted in convictions of North and others (later overturned because of immunity agreements). The affair, which dominated news coverage for months, significantly damaged Ronald Reagan's administration.

Iran hostage crisis (1979–81) Political crisis involving Iran's detention of U.S. diplomats. Anti-American sentiment in Iran—fueled in part by close ties between the U.S. and the unpopular leader Mohammad Reza

Shah Pahlavi—peaked when Pahlavi fled Iran during the 1979 Iranian Revolution. When the monarch entered the U.S. for medical treatment later that year, Islamic militants seized the U.S. embassy in Tehran and took 66 Americans hostage. The hostage-takers, who enjoyed the tacit support of the new Iranian regime of Ruhollah Khomeini, demanded the shah's extradition to Iran, but Pres. Jimmy Carter refused and froze all Iranian assets in the U.S. The Iranians eventually released a number of hostages, including females, African Americans, and non-Americans, but a rescue attempt failed in April 1980. Negotiations for the hostages' return began after the shah died in July, but 52 remained in captivity until January 20, 1981. The crisis likely contributed to Carter's failure to win reelection for a second term. See also Iran-Contra Affair.

Iran-Iraq War (1980–90) Protracted and indecisive conflict prompted by Iraq's invasion of its eastern neighbor. Following the 1979 Iranian Revolution, the Iraqi leadership sought to exploit Iran's military and political chaos in order to resolve border disputes, gain control of Iran's oil-rich western (largely Arab) province, and achieve hegemony in the Persian Gulf. Iraq was successful early (1980–82) but began to lose ground and sought to negotiate peace. Iran refused, and the war turned into a bloody stalemate that included the first use of chemical warfare since World War I. After additional Iraqi advances, Iran agreed to a cease-fire in 1988. Peace was only concluded when Iraq invaded another neighbor, Kuwait, in 1990. See also Saddam Hussein, Ruhollah Khomeini.

Iranian languages Major subgroup of the Indo-Iranian branch of the Indo-European language family. Iranian languages are probably spoken by over 80 million people in southwestern and southern Asia. Only two Old Iranian languages are known, Avestan and Old Persian. A greater number of Middle Iranian languages (c. 300 BC–AD 950) are known; these are divided into a western and an eastern group. Modern Iranian languages have been divided into four groups. The southwestern group includes Modern Persian (Farsi), Dari (in northern Afghanistan), Tajiki (in Tajikistan and other Central Asian republics); Luri and Bakhtiari (in southwestern Iran); and Tat. The northwestern group includes Kurdish (spoken in Kurdistan) and Baluchi (in southwestern Pakistan, southeastern Iran, and southern Afghanistan). The southeastern group includes Pashto (in Afghanistan and northwestern Pakistan) and the 10 or so Pamir languages (in eastern Tajikistan and adjacent parts of Afghanistan and China). The northeastern group includes Ossetic, spoken by the Ossetes in the central Caucasus Mountains, and Yaghnobi, formerly spoken in a single valley of the Pamirs. Nearly all the Modern Iranian languages have been written—if at all—in adaptations of the Arabic alphabet.

Iranian religions Ancient religions of the peoples of the Iranian plateau. The Medes and Persians were dominated by a powerful priestly tribe, the magi. The magi were responsible for chanting accounts of the origin and descent of the gods, and they were probably the source of the dualism that later characterized Zoroastrianism, the best known of the Iranian religions. The chief god of the pre-Zoroastrian pantheon was Ahura Mazda, the creator of the universe and the one who maintains the cosmic and social order. Mithra was the second most important deity and the protector of covenants. Other major deities included Anahita, the war goddess; Rashnu, the god of justice; and astral deities such as Tishtrya, identified with the star Sirius. The ancient Iranians did not build temples or make images of their gods, preferring to worship in the open. The central ritual was the *yazna,* which consisted of a festive meal at which the worshipers made animal sacrifices and invited the deity to attend as a guest. Fire was regarded as a sacred element. The sacred drink *hauma,* which contained a mind-altering drug, was used to inspire worshipers with insight into truth and to stimulate warriors going into battle.

Iraq *officially* **Republic of Iraq** Middle Eastern country, northwest of the Persian Gulf. Area: 167,975 sq mi (435,052 sq km). Population (2002 est.): 24,002,000. Capital: Baghdad. The population consists mainly of an Arab majority and a Kurd minority. Language: Arabic (official). Religion: Islam (official); 60% Shiites, 30% Sunni, who dominate the government. Currency: dinar. The country can be divided into four major regions: the Tigris-Euphrates river basin in central and southeastern Iraq; Al-Jazirah, an upland region in the north between the Tigris and the Euphrates rivers; deserts in the west and south, covering about two-fifths of the country; and highlands in the northeast. Iraq has the world's second-largest proven reserves of petroleum; it also has substantial reserves of natural gas. Agriculture employs one-eighth of the labor force. It is a republic with one legislative house; its head of state is the president. Called Mesopotamia in classical times, the region gave rise to the world's earliest civilizations, including those of Sumer, Akkad, and Babylon. Conquered by Alexander the Great in 330 BC, the area later became a battleground between Romans and Parthians, then between Sasanians and the Byzantines. Arab Muslims conquered it in the 7th century AD, and various Muslim dynasties ruled until the Mongols took over in 1258. The Ottomans took control in the 16th century and ruled until 1917. The British occupied the country during World War I and created the kingdom of Iraq in 1921. The British occupied Iraq again during World War II. A king was restored following the war, but a revolution ended the monarchy in 1958. Following a series of military coups, the socialist Baath Party, led by Saddam Hussein, took control and established totalitarian rule in 1968. The Iran-Iraq War and the Persian Gulf War caused extensive death and destruction, and the economy languished under a UN economic embargo in the 1990s, pending proof that Iraq had divested itself of all weapons of mass destruction. The embargo began to erode in the early 21st century.

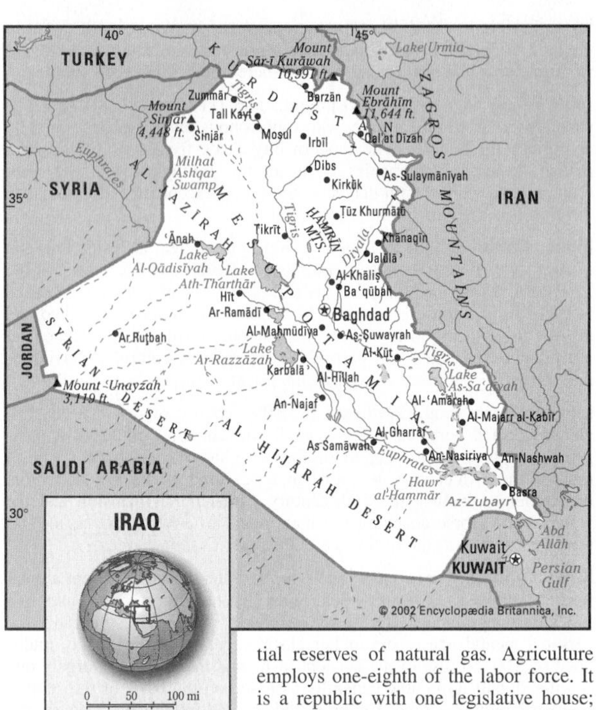

Irbid Town (pop., 1994: 208,329), northern Jordan. Built on Early Bronze Age settlements, it may have been the biblical city of Beth Arbel and the Arbila of the ancient Decapolis. Modern Irbid is one of Jordan's industrial areas and agricultural centers. The many springs in the area, in addition to the Yarmuk River, provide water for irrigation. It is the seat of Yarmuk University.

Iredell \ˈīr-ˌdel\, **James** (1751–1799) U.S. (British-born) jurist. His family emigrated to North Carolina, where he was appointed comptroller of the customhouse at 17. He helped draft and revise the laws of the new state of North Carolina and served as state attorney general (1779–81). He led the state's Federalists in supporting ratification of the U.S. Constitution, and his letters in its defense (signed "Marcus") are said to have prompted Pres. George Washington to appoint him to the U.S. Supreme Court (1790). He wrote several notable dissents, including those for *Chisholm vs. Georgia* (1793; affirming the subordination of the states to the federal government) and *Ware vs. Hylton* (1796; upholding the primacy of U.S. treaties over state statutes). His opinion in *Calder vs. Bull* (1798) helped establish the principle of judicial review five years before it was tested in *Marbury vs. Madison.* He served until 1799.

Ireland *Irish* **Éire** \ˈer-ə\ Republic, occupying the greater part of an island west of England. The republic's only neighbor is Northern Ireland, which occupies the northeastern portion of the island. Area: 27,133 sq mi (70,273 sq km). Population (2001 est.): 3,823,000. Capital: Dublin.

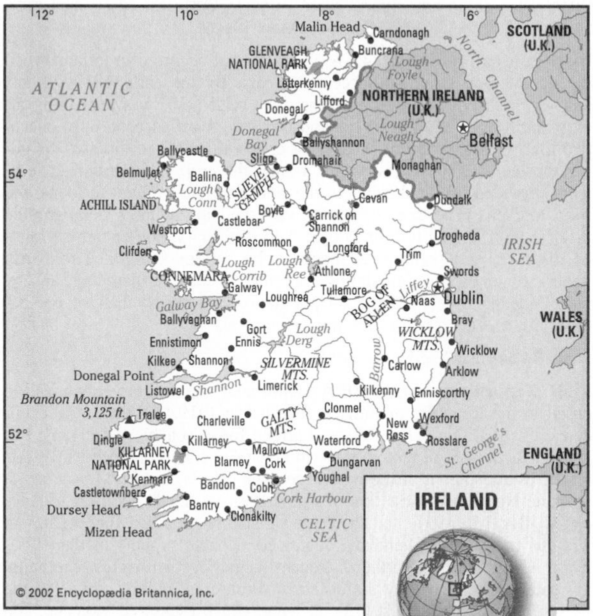

Although it has been invaded and colonized by Celts, Norsemen, Normans, English, and Scots, racial and ethnic distinctions are nonexistent. Languages: Irish, English (both official). Religions: Roman Catholicism (95%), Church of Ireland Episcopalianism, Presbyterianism, Methodism, Judaism. Monetary unit: euro. Ireland's topography consists largely of broad lowlands drained by rivers that include the SHANNON; its coasts are fringed with mountains. Almost three-fifths of the population is urban, and agriculture only employs a small percentage of the workforce. Mining, manufacturing, construction, public utilities, high technology, and tourism are important industries. It is a republic with two legislative houses; its chief of state is the president, and the head of government is the prime minister. Human settlement in Ireland began c. 6000 BC, and Celtic migration dates from c. 300 BC. ST. PATRICK is credited with Christianizing the country in the 5th century. Norse domination began in 795 and ended in 1014, when the Norse were defeated by BRIAN BORU. Gaelic Ireland's independence ended in 1171 when English king HENRY II proclaimed himself overlord of the island. Beginning in the 16th century, Irish Catholic landowners fled religious persecution by the English and were replaced by English and Scottish Protestant migrants. The United Kingdom of Great Britain and Ireland was established in 1801. The Great Famine of the 1840s led over 2 million people to emigrate and built momentum for Irish HOME RULE. The EASTER RISING (1916) was followed by civil war (1919–21) between the Catholic majority in southern Ireland, who favored complete independence, and the Protestant majority in the north, who preferred continued union with Britain. Southern Ireland was granted dominion status and became the Irish Free State in 1921, and in 1937 it adopted the name Éire and became a sovereign independent nation. It remained neutral during World War II. Britain recognized the status of Ireland in 1949 but declared that cession of the northern six counties (see NORTHERN IRELAND) could not occur without the consent of the Parliament of Northern Ireland. In 1973 it joined the European Economic Community (later the EUROPEAN COMMUNITY) and is now a member of the EUROPEAN UNION. The late 20th century was dominated by sectarian hostilities between Catholics and Protestants.

Ireland, Northern Division of the United Kingdom of Great Britain and Northern Ireland occupying the northeastern portion of the island of Ireland. It is bounded by the republic of Ireland, the Irish Sea, the North Channel, and the Atlantic Ocean. Northern Ireland is often referred to as the province of Ulster. Area: 5,452 sq mi (14,120 sq km). Population (2001 est.): 1,705,000. Capital: BELFAST. The people are descended from indigenous Irish and those who emigrated from England and Scotland. Language: English (official). Religions: Protestantism (the majority) and Roman Catholicism (a minority). Currency: pound sterling. Northern Ireland's industries include engineering, shipbuilding, auto manufacturing, textiles, food and beverage processing, and clothing. The service industry employs about two-thirds of the workers; manufacturing, less than one-fifth. Agriculture is important, with most farm income derived from livestock. Northern Ireland shares most of its history with the republic of IRELAND, though Protestant English and Scots immigrating in the 16th–17th century tended to settle in Ulster. In 1801 the Act of Union created the United Kingdom, which united Great Britain and Ireland. In response to mounting Irish sentiment in favor of HOME RULE, the Government of Ireland Act was adopted in 1920, providing for two partially self-governing units in Ireland: the northern six counties constituting Northern Ireland, and the southern counties now making up the Republic of Ireland. In 1968 civil-rights protests by Roman Catholics sparked violent conflicts with Protestants and led to the occupation of the province by British troops in the early 1970s. The IRISH REPUBLICAN ARMY (IRA) mounted a prolonged terrorist campaign in an effort to force the withdrawal of British troops as a prelude to Northern Ireland's unification with Ireland. In 1972 Northern Ireland's constitution and parliament were suspended, bringing it under direct rule by the British. Violence continued for three decades, dropping off in the mid-1990s. In 1998 talks between the British government and the IRA resulted in a peace agreement that provided for extensive home rule in the province. In 1999 power was devolved to an elected assembly. Sporadic sectarian strife continued, at a reduced rate in the 21st century, as the IRA gradually went about decommissioning (disarming).

Irenaeus \ˌī-rə-ˈnē-əs, ˌī-rə-ˈnā-əs\, **St.** (c. 120/40–c. 200) Bishop and theologian. Born of Greek parents in Asia Minor, he was a missionary to Gaul before being named bishop of Lugdunum (modern Lyon, France). All his major works, including *Against Heresies,* were written in opposition to Gnosticism. To counteract Gnostic influence, he promoted the development of an authoritative canon of the New Testament. His defense of the belief that the Christian God and the God of the Old Testament were identical led to the development of the Apostles' Creed. His writings have proved a valuable source of information on the Gnostics, because he gave accurate summaries of their beliefs before refuting them.

H I J K

Ireton \ˈīr-tᵊn\, **Henry** (1611–1651) English politician, leader of the Parliamentary cause in the ENGLISH CIVIL WARS. Joining the Parliamentary army at the outbreak of war, he was involved in many victories. He was elected to Parliament in 1645 and married OLIVER CROMWELL's daughter in 1646. In 1647 he proposed a scheme for a constitutional monarchy; after its rejection by CHARLES I, Ireton provided the ideological foundations for the assault on the monarchy. He helped bring Charles to trial and was one of the signers of his death warrant. As lord deputy of Ireland and commander in chief (1650), he fought against the Roman Catholic rebels and died after the siege of Limerick.

Irgun Zvai Leumi \ir-ˈgün-tsvə-ˈē-lə-ü-ˈmē\ (Hebrew: "National Military Organization") Jewish right-wing underground movement that advocated force in the establishment of a Jewish state on both sides of the Jordan River. It opposed the British and the Arabs; its activities included a 1946 attack on the King David Hotel, leaving 91 dead, and a 1947 raid on an Arab village in which all 254 inhabitants were killed. In 1943 MENACHEM BEGIN became its leader. With Israeli independence its units disbanded. Israel's Herut Party is its political reincarnation. See also LIKUD.

Irian See NEW GUINEA

Irian Jaya Province (pop., 1990: 1,650,000), Indonesia, now called West Papua. It occupies the western half of the island of NEW GUINEA and its offshore islands, and the Schouten and Raja Ampat island groups. The Maoke Mountains rise to 16,503 ft (5,030 m) at Puncak Jaya. First sighted by the Portuguese in 1511, it was claimed by the Dutch in 1828. Transferred to Indonesia in 1963, it was made a province in 1969, with its capital at Jayapura. Rebels led a separatist movement there in the late 1990s.

iridium \i-ˈri-dē-əm\ Metallic chemical ELEMENT, one of the TRANSITION ELEMENTS, chemical symbol Ir, atomic number 77. A very rare, precious, silvery-white, hard, brittle METAL that even resists most ACIDS, it is one of the densest substances known on earth. It probably does not occur uncombined in nature but is found in natural ALLOYS with other noble (i.e., chemically inactive or inert) metals. The pure metal is too hard to work with to have any significant uses; alloys with platinum are used in jewelry, pen points, surgical pins and pivots, electrical contacts and sparking points, and extrusion dies. The international primary standards (see WEIGHTS AND MEASURES) for weight and length are 90% platinum, 10% iridium. The discovery of abnormally high amounts of iridium in rocks dating to between the CRETACEOUS and TERTIARY periods has given rise to a controversial hypothesis that an iridium-containing METEORITE crashing into the earth led to a catastrophic chain of events including extinction of DINOSAURS and many other forms of life.

Irigaray \ē-rē-gà-'rä, *Engl* 'ir-i-ˌgar-ē\, **Luce** (born 1932?) French feminist psychoanalyst and philosopher. She has examined the uses and misuses of language in relation to women in such works as *Speculum of the Other Woman* (1974), which argues that history and culture are written in patriarchal language and centered on men, and that the thinking of SIGMUND FREUD was based in misogyny. Among her other works are *An Ethics of Sexual Differences* (1984) and *Je, tu, nous* (1990).

Irigoyen \ˌir-i-'gō-yen\, **Hipólito** *or* **Hipólito Yrigoyen** (1852–1933) Argentine statesman and president (1916–22, 1928–30). A lawyer, teacher, rancher, and politician, he became leader of the Radical Party in 1896. Working relentlessly for electoral reform, he succeeded in 1912 in securing a secret-ballot vote. Elected president in 1916, he passed measures regulating labor conditions but failed to enforce them, and a serious strike was violently broken in1919. Corruption and failure to implement democratic reforms cost him support after his return to power in 1928, and he was further weakened by the Great Depression. A nearly bloodless military coup ended his career.

iris family Family Iridaceae, composed of about 1,700 species of perennial herbaceous plants, as well as a few shrubs, in some 80 genera. It is known for ornamentals such as irises (genus *Iris*), gladioli (see GLADIOLUS), CROCUSES, and FREESIAS. Irises have swordlike, smooth leaves and bear showy flowers in a great variety of colors and sizes on a smooth stem. Most abundant and diverse in Africa, they are found nearly worldwide across temperate, subtropical, and tropical zones. The underground stems may be RHIZOMES (e.g., New World *Iris* species), BULBS (e.g., southwestern European *Iris* species), or CORMS (e.g., *Gladiolus*).

Irish elk Any member of a genus *(Megaloceros)* of extinct giant DEER commonly found as fossils in Pleistocene deposits (1.6 million–10,000 years ago) in Europe and Asia. About the size of a modern MOOSE, the Irish elk had the largest antlers of any form of deer known, in some specimens about 13 ft (4 m) across. It may have survived until c. 700–500 BC.

Irish Free State See IRELAND

Irish Home Rule See Irish HOME RULE

Irish language *or* **Irish Gaelic language** CELTIC LANGUAGE of Ireland, written in the LATIN ALPHABET introduced with Christianity in the 5th century. Irish is conventionally divided into three periods: Old Irish (7th century–c. 950), Middle Irish (c. 950–1200), and Modern Irish (from c. 1200). OGAM WRITING predates Old Irish. Old and Middle Irish are the vehicles of a rich literature of prose tales and verse. Classical Modern Irish was the exclusive literary medium in Ireland and Scottish Gaeldom into modern times (see SCOTTISH GAELIC LANGUAGE). Literacy in Irish declined under English rule; by 1800 it was all but an unwritten language. The deaths and emigration resulting from the IRISH POTATO FAMINE and a massive shift to English afterward drastically reduced the number of Irish-speakers. Irish was revived as a literary language in the late 19th and early 20th century, and with Irish independence (1921) it was made official. Though it is a true community language only for a small number of people on Ireland's western coast, hundreds of thousands of Irish citizens and people of Irish descent have partial to complete competence in Irish. Its value as a token of cultural identity most likely ensures its survival well into the 21st century.

Irish Literary Renaissance Flowering of Irish literary talent in the late 19th and early 20th century, closely allied with a strong political nationalism and a revival of interest in Ireland's Gaelic heritage. It was given impetus by the GAELIC REVIVAL, the retelling of ancient heroic legends in books such as Standish O'Grady's *History of Ireland* (1878, 1880) and Douglas Hyde's *A Literary History of Ireland* (1899), and the Gaelic League, formed in 1893 to revive the Irish language and culture. It developed into a vigorous literary force centered on WILLIAM BUTLER YEATS; other important figures were AUGUSTA GREGORY, JOHN MILLINGTON SYNGE, and SEAN O'CASEY. See also ABBEY THEATRE.

Irish Potato Famine (1845–49) Famine that occurred in Ireland when the potato crop failed in successive years. By the early 1840s almost half the Irish population, particularly the rural poor, was depending almost entirely on the potato for nourishment. A reliance on only one or two high-yielding varieties made the crop vulnerable to disease, including the late blight fungus, which ruined the crop. The British government provided minimal relief to the starving Irish, limited to loans and soup kitchens. The famine was a watershed in Ireland's demographic history: more than a million people died from starvation or famine-related diseases, and perhaps as many as 1.5 million emigrated to North America and Britain. Population continued to decline thereafter, and by independence in 1921 the Irish population was barely half of the 8.4 million it had been before the famine.

Irish Rebellion See EASTER RISING

Irish Republican Army (IRA) Unofficial semimilitary organization based in the Republic of Ireland, founded in 1919 to fight for independence from Britain. The IRA used armed force to achieve the same objectives as SINN FÉIN, though the two always operated independently. After the establishment of the Irish Free State (1922), it refused to accept a separate Northern IRELAND, and the violence continued. The IRA was declared illegal in 1931, and the Irish legislature provided for internment without trial for its members. It gained popular support in the 1960s when Catholics in Northern Ireland began a civil-rights campaign against discrimination by the dominant Protestant majority. In 1969 the IRA split into the Marxist Official wing, which eschewed violence, and the Provisionals (Provos), Ulster Catholics committed to the use of terror tactics against Ulster Protestants and British military, tactics that included the 1979 assassination of LOUIS MOUNTBATTEN and the killing of over 3,000 before the 1994 cease-fire.

Irish Sea Arm of the North Atlantic Ocean that separates Ireland from Great Britain. Connected with the Atlantic by North Channel and by St. George's Channel, it is about 130 mi (210 km) long and 150 mi (240 km) wide. Its total area is about 40,000 sq mi (100,000 sq km). Its greatest depth measures about 576 ft (175 m). The Isle of MAN and ANGLESEY are its two principal islands.

Irish terrier Breed of TERRIER developed in Ireland, one of the oldest terrier breeds. It stands 16–18 in. (41.5–46 cm) high, weighs 22–26 lbs (10–12 kg), and has a wiry golden-red to reddish brown coat. Nicknamed the daredevil, it is reputedly adaptable, loyal, spirited, and recklessly courageous. It served as a messenger and sentinel in World War I, and has been used to hunt and to retrieve game.

Irish terrier.
SALLY ANNE THOMPSON

Irish wolfhound Tallest of all dog breeds, a keen-sighted HOUND used in Ireland to hunt wolves and other game and noted for its speed and strength. An ancient breed, first mentioned about the 2nd century AD, it is similar in build to the GREYHOUND but far more powerful. The female, substantially smaller than the male, stands at least 30 in. (76 cm) high and weighs 100 lbs (50 kg) or more. The rough coat is long on the brows and underjaw; colors include gray, brindle, red-brown, black, and white. The dog is valued as a gentle, even-tempered companion.

Irkutsk \ir-'kütsk\ City (pop., 1995 est.: 585,000), eastern central Russia. Located on the Angara River, it was founded as a wintering camp in 1652. It soon became a commercial center for the fur trade and a base on the Russian trade route to China and Mongolia. Its importance grew after the opening of the TRANS-SIBERIAN RAILROAD in 1898. It is now an industrial and cultural center for Eastern Siberia and the Russian Far East. It is the seat of Irkutsk State University and the Siberian branch of the Academy of Sciences.

iron Metallic chemical ELEMENT, one of the TRANSITION ELEMENTS, chemical symbol Fe, atomic number 26. Iron is the most used and cheapest METAL, the second most abundant metal and fourth most abundant element in the earth's crust. It occurs rarely as the free metal, occasionally in ALLOYS (especially in meteorites), and in hundreds of minerals and ores, including HEMATITE, MAGNETITE, LIMONITE, and SIDERITE. The human body contains 4.5 g of iron, mostly as HEMOGLOBIN and its precursors; iron in the diet is essential to health. Iron is ferromagnetic at ordinary temperatures and the only metal that can be tempered (see TEMPERING). Its uses in STEELS of various types, as well as in CAST and WROUGHT iron (collectively, "ferrous metals"), are numerous. Alteration of its properties by impurities, especially carbon, is the basis of steelmaking. Iron in compounds usually has VALENCE 2 (ferrous) or 3 (ferric). Ferrous and ferric oxides are used as pigments and the latter as jewelers' rouge. Rust is ferric oxide containing water; ferrites, made from an intermediate oxide, are widely used in computer memories and magnetic tapes. Ferrous and ferric sulfates and chlorides are all of industrial importance, as mordants, reducing agents, flocculating agents, or raw materials and in inks and fertilizers.

Iron Act (1750) Measure by the British Parliament to restrict the American colonial iron industry. Pig iron and iron bar could be exported to England duty-free to meet British needs. Further development of colonial manufacturing to produce finished iron goods was prohibited, as was the export of iron to other countries.

Iron Age Final technological and cultural stage in the Stone–Bronze–Iron-Age sequence (or Three-Age System) in which IRON largely replaced BRONZE in implements and weapons. The start of the Iron Age varied geographically, beginning in the Middle East and southeastern Europe c. 1200 BC but in China not until c. 600 BC. Though the large-scale production of iron implements brought new patterns of more permanent settlement, use of iron for weapons put arms in the hands of the masses for the first time and set off a series of large-scale movements and conquests that did not end for 2,000 years and that changed the face of Europe and Asia. See also BRONZE AGE.

Iron Curtain Political, military, and ideological barrier erected by the Soviet Union after World War II to seal off itself and its dependent Eastern European allies from open contact with the West and other noncommunist areas. WINSTON CHURCHILL employed the term in a speech in Fulton, Mo., about the division of Europe in 1946. The restrictions and the rigidity of the Iron Curtain eased slightly after JOSEPH STALIN's death in 1953, though the construction of the BERLIN WALL in 1961 restored them. The Iron Curtain largely ceased to exist in 1989–90 with the communists' abandonment of one-party rule in Eastern Europe.

iron-deficiency anemia Most common type of ANEMIA, which may develop in times of high iron loss and depletion of iron stores (e.g., rapid growth, pregnancy, menstruation) or in settings of low dietary iron intake or inefficient iron uptake (due to, e.g., starvation, intestinal parasites, GASTRECTOMY). In the U.S., up to 20% of young children and 5–10% of women ages 15–45 may have iron-deficiency anemia. Symptoms include low energy level and sometimes paleness, shortness of breath, cold extremities, sore tongue, or dry skin. In advanced cases, red blood cells are small, pale, and low in HEMOGLOBIN, blood iron levels are reduced, and body iron stores are depleted. Treatment with iron usually brings quick improvement.

iron ore, bog See BOG IRON ORE

iron pyrite See PYRITE

ironclad Type of warship developed in Europe and the U.S. in the mid-19th century, characterized by the iron armor that protected the hull. In the Crimean War (1853–56) the French and British successfully attacked Russian fortifications with "floating batteries," ironclad barges mounting heavy guns. In 1859 the French completed the first iron warship, the *Gloire*; its iron plates, 4.5 in. (11 cm) thick, were backed by heavy timber. Britain and the U.S. soon followed. Union forces launched armored gunboats on the Mississippi at the start of the American Civil War, and a flotilla captured Fort Henry (1862). The first battle between ironclads was the Battle of the *MONITOR* AND *MERRIMACK* (1862). Later refinements led to the BATTLESHIP. See also MONITOR. See photograph opposite.

Irons, Jeremy (born 1948) British actor. He made his London stage debut in *Godspell* (1973) and appeared on Broadway in *The Real Thing* (1984, Tony award). After his screen debut in *Nijinsky* (1980), he won notice for *The French Lieutenant's Woman* (1981) and became widely popular in the hit television series *Brideshead Revisited* (1980–81). His later films include *Dead Ringers* (1988), *Reversal of Fortune* (1990, Academy Award), *Waterland* (1992), and *Lolita* (1997).

Ironside, William Edmund *later* **Baron Ironside** (1880–1959) British field marshal. After serving in the SOUTH AFRICAN WAR, he commanded Allied forces in World War I in northern Russia (1918) and later in northern Persia (1920). He subsequently commanded forces in India (1928–31) and in the Middle East. At the beginning of World War II he was chief of the imperial general staff (1939–40); he was promoted to field marshal in 1940 and commanded the home defense forces.

ironweed Any of about 500 species of perennial plants constituting the genus *Vernonia* (family Asteraceae). Small herbaceous (nonwoody) species are found throughout the world; shrubs and trees are found primarily in tropical regions. Ironweed species have lance-shaped, toothed leaves that alternate along the stem; clusters of flower heads composed only of disk flowers (no ray flowers); and a ring of overlapping BRACTS below the flower heads. Some autumn-blooming species are cultivated as border plants for their attractive white, purple, or pink flower clusters.

Western ironweed (*Vernonia fasciculata*).
DAN MORRILL

ironwood Any of numerous trees and shrubs, found worldwide, that have exceptionally tough or hard wood useful for timber, fence posts, and tool handles. Species include the eastern, or American, hop hornbeam *(Ostrya virginiana)*, a small tree of northern Iran *(Parrotia persica)*, and Ceylon ironwood *(Mesua ferrea)*. Though these trees belong to different plant orders, all have bright yellow to orange and scarlet autumn foliage.

irony Language device in which the real intent is concealed or contradicted by the literal meaning of words or a situation. Verbal irony, either spoken or written, arises from an awareness of contrast between what is and what ought to be. Dramatic irony, an incongruity in a theatrical work between what is expected and what occurs, depends on the structure of a play rather than its use of words, and is often created by the audience's awareness of a fate in store for the characters that they themselves do not suspect. See also FIGURE OF SPEECH.

Iroquoian languages \ˈir-ə-ˌkwȯi-ən\ Family of about 16 North American Indian languages aboriginally spoken around the eastern Great Lakes and in parts of the Middle Atlantic states and the South. Aside from the languages of the Iroquois Confederacy (Mohawk, Oneida, Onondaga, Cayuga, and Seneca, all originally spoken in New York, along with Tuscarora, originally spoken in North Carolina) and Cherokee (originally spoken in the southern Appalachians), the Iroquoian languages are extinct, and with the exception of Huron and Wyandot, the extinct languages are poorly documented. Iroquoian languages are re-

French ironclad *Gloire*, engraving by Smythe after a painting by A.W. Weedon.
BY COURTESY OF THE TRUSTEES OF THE BRITISH MUSEUM; PHOTOGRAPH, J.R. FREEMAN & CO. LTD.

H I J K

markable for their grammatical intricacy. Much of a sentence's semantic content is bound around a verbal base, so a single very long word may constitute a fairly complex utterance.

Iroquois \'ir-ə-ˌkwȯi\ Any member of the IROQUOIS CONFEDERACY or, more broadly, any speaker of IROQUOIAN LANGUAGES. Iroquoian-speaking peoples were semisendentary, practiced agriculture, palisaded their villages, and dwelled in LONGHOUSES that lodged many families. Women worked the fields and, in matrilineal groups, helped determine the makeup of village councils. Men built houses, hunted, fished, and made war. Iroquoian mythology was largely preoccupied with supernatural aggression and cruelty, sorcery, torture, and cannibalism. Their formal religion consisted of agricultural festivals. Warfare was ingrained in Iroquois society, and war captives were often tortured for days or made permanent slaves. Today the various Iroquois tribes include about 20,000 members.

Iroquois Confederacy *or* **League of the Iroquois** Confederation of five (later six) Indian tribes across upper New York that in the 17th–18th century played a strategic role in the struggle between the French and British for supremacy in North America. The five original nations were the MOHAWK, ONEIDA, Onondaga, Cayuga, and SENECA; the Tuscarora joined in 1722. According to tradition, the confederacy was founded between 1570 and 1600 by Dekanawidah, born a Huron, carrying out the earlier ideas of HIAWATHA, an Onondaga. Cemented mainly by their desire to stand together against invasion, the tribes united in a common council composed of 50 sachems; each tribe had one vote, and unanimity was the rule. At first the confederacy barely withstood attacks from the HURON and MAHICAN, but by 1628 the Mohawk had defeated the Mahican and established themselves as region's dominant tribe. When the Iroquois destroyed the Huron in 1648–50, they were attacked by the Huron's French allies. During the AMERICAN REVOLUTION, the Oneida and Tuscarora sided with the Americans while the rest of the league, led by JOSEPH BRANT, fought for the British. The Loyalist Iroquois were defeated in 1779 near Elmira, N.Y., and the confederacy came to an end.

irrational number Among the REAL NUMBERS, any of those that cannot be represented as quotients of integers. In decimal form, irrational numbers are represented by nonterminating, nonrepeating decimals. Examples include square roots of prime numbers and such TRANSCENDENTAL NUMBERS as π and e.

Irrawaddy River \ˌir-ä-'wä-dē\ River, Myanmar. It flows 1,350 mi (2,170 km) across the center of the country and empties into the Bay of BENGAL. The country's most important commercial waterway, it is formed by the confluence of the Nmai and the Mali rivers; in the central dry zone it is joined by its major tributary, the CHINDWIN RIVER. Chief ports are MANDALAY, Chauk, Prome (Pyè), and Henzada.

irrigation Artificial supply of water to land, to maintain or increase yields of food crops, a critical element of modern agriculture. Irrigation can compensate for the naturally variable rate and volume of rain. Water is pumped from natural ponds, lakes, streams, and wells; basin systems and dams hold back larger streams and annual floods. Below the dam, gates to concrete-lined canals are opened, conveying the water over the land through gravity flow. More elaborate, expensive canals flow from huge constructed reservoirs, which hold a year-round water supply. Today portable irrigation systems of lightweight aluminum pipe are in wide use. Drip irrigation, a newer method, uses narrow tubing to supply water directly to the base of each plant. Agricultural irrigation, water towers, and machines invented to lift and distribute water are ancient innovations. Early Egyptians were irrigating with Nile River water by 5000 BC, and such other ancient civilizations as Babylon and China seem to have developed largely as a result of irrigation-based agriculture.

irritable bowel syndrome Chronic disorder characterized by abdominal pain, intestinal gas, and diarrhea, constipation, or both. Other symptoms may include abdominal pain that is relieved after defecation or a sensation of incomplete rectal evacuation. IBS is caused by a motility disturbance of the intestines that may result from increased intestinal sensitivity to distension. Stress or the consumption of fatty foods, milk products, certain fruits or vegetables (e.g., broccoli and cabbage), alcohol, or caffeine may cause similar symptoms. Treatment includes relaxation, exercise, and avoidance of aggravating foods. Antidiarrheal medications or fiber supplements may help lessen symptoms. Although IBS may cause discomfort and emotional distress, the disorder does not result in any permanent intestinal damage.

Irtysh River \ir-'təsh\ *Kazak* **Ertis** \er-'tis\ River rising in the ALTAY SHAN in XINJIANG, China. It flows west across the Chinese border and then northwest across KAZAKHSTAN into Russian Siberia, where it becomes the largest tributary of the OB RIVER. It is 2,640 mi (4,248 km) long and is navigable for most of its course. Its main ports include Tobolsk, Tara, Omsk, Pavlodar, Semey, and Öskemen.

Irvine Royal burgh and seaport (pop., 1990: 155,000), on the Atlantic coast of Scotland, STRATHCLYDE region. The last of Scotland's five new towns, it was designated in 1967 to house overflow population from GLASGOW and provide a focus for the economic and industrial rehabilitation of the area. It had declined in the 18th–19th century because of competition from other towns and the silting of the harbor. Today it is an industrial center that produces chemicals, engineering, electrical goods, and clothing.

Irving City (pop., 2000: 191,615), northeastern Texas. Established in 1903 and incorporated in 1914, the city developed into an industrial hub during the 1950s. A suburb of DALLAS, it is the site of the University of Dallas and the DeVry Institute of Technology as well as of Texas Stadium, home of the Dallas Cowboys professional football team.

Irving, Henry *later* **Sir Henry** *orig.* **John Henry Brodribb** (1838–1905) British actor. He toured for 10 years with a stock company before making his London debut in 1866. With his success in *The Bells* (1871), he became a leading actor in H. L. Bateman's company (1871–77). As actor-manager of the Lyceum Theatre (from 1878), he made it London's most successful theater. He formed a celebrated acting partnership with ELLEN TERRY that lasted until the company dissolved in 1902. They were noted for their Shakespearean roles and drew large audiences in England and the U.S.

Irving, John (Winslow) (born 1942) U.S. novelist. Born in Exeter, N.H., he taught at several universities before beginning to write full-time in the late 1970s. Three early novels, including *Setting Free the Bears* (1969), led to the best-selling *The World According to Garp* (1978; film, 1982), notable, like his other works, for its engaging story line, colorful characterizations, macabre humor, and examination of contemporary issues. Later novels include *The Hotel New Hampshire* (1981; film, 1984), *The Cider House Rules* (1985; film, 1999), *A Son of the Circus* (1994), and *A Widow for One Year* (1999).

Irving, Washington (1783–1859) U.S. author, called the "first American man of letters." Born in New York City, he began his career as a lawyer but soon became a leader of the group that published *Salmagundi* (1807–8), a periodical containing whimsical essays and poems. After his comic *A History of New York . . . by Diedrich Knickerbocker* (1809), he wrote little until his very successful *The Sketch Book* (1819–20), containing his best-known stories, "The Legend of Sleepy Hollow" and "Rip Van Winkle." It was followed by a sequel, *Bracebridge Hall* (1822). He held diplomatic positions in Madrid, where his writings (including *The Alhambra,* 1832) reflected his interest in Spain's past, then spent most of his later life at his Hudson River home, "Sunnyside."

Washington Irving, oil painting by J.W. Jarvis, 1809; in the Historic Hudson Valley collection.

COURTESY OF HISTORIC HUDSON VALLEY

Isaac II Angelus (c. 1135–1204) Byzantine emperor (1185–95). Proclaimed emperor by the Constantinople mob that murdered his cousin, ANDRONICUS I COMNENUS, he drove the Normans out of Greece (1185) but failed to regain Cyprus from rebels. He was forced to help FREDERICK I BARBAROSSA in the Third CRUSADE. He defeated the Serbians (1190), but before he could carry out a planned expedition against the Bulgarians, he was overthrown by his brother, who imprisoned and blinded him (1195). His son Alexius diverted the Fourth Crusade to restore him to power (1203), and father and son briefly ruled as co-emperors before being dethroned and killed in a revolution.

Isaac of Stella (c. 1100–1169?) Monk, philosopher, and theologian. Isaac joined the CISTERCIANS during the reforms carried out by St. BERnard de Clairvaux. His scholarly works make use of logical argumentation and are influenced by the Neoplatonism of St. Augustine. His principal work, *Epistola de anima ad Alcherum* (1162; "Letter to Alcher on the Soul"), integrates Aristotelian and Neoplatonic psychological theories with Christian mysticism. A leader of humanism in his day, he suggests that the intellect enables humans to grasp eternal ideas in time and that intelligence allows humans to intuit the reality of God.

Isaac the Elder See Isaac ben Solomon Israeli

Isabela Island Island, Galápagos Islands. The largest in the group, it is located west of Ecuador in the eastern Pacific Ocean. It has an area of 2,249 sq mi (5,825 sq km), and its northern tip, Albemarle, is crossed by the equator. It has unique species of flightless cormorants and penguins as well as large numbers of iguanas and a flamingo colony.

Isabella I *known as* **Isabella the Catholic** *Spanish* **Isabel la Católica** (1451–1504) Queen of Castile (1474–1504) and of Aragon (1479–1504). Daughter of John II of Castile and León, she married Ferdinand V in 1469. Her reign began with civil war over her succession (1474–79), but in 1479 the kingdoms of Castile and Aragon came together in the persons of their rulers, though they remained separately governed. In a long campaign (1482–92), Isabella and Ferdinand succeeded in conquering Granada, the last Muslim stronghold in Spain. In 1492 Isabella approved support of Christopher Columbus's journey to the New World. That same year she was involved in the expulsion of the Jews under the Inquisition. Along with her spiritual advisers, she reformed the Spanish churches.

Isabella I, portrait by an unknown artist; in the Real Academia de la Historia, Madrid.

ARCHIVO MAS, BARCELONA

Isabella II *Spanish* **Isabel** \ē-sä-'bel\ (1830–1904) Queen of Spain (1833–68). She was the daughter of Ferdinand VII, and the issue of her succession to the throne precipitated the First Carlist War (see Carlism). During her minority (1833–43), her mother and Baldomero Espartero acted as regents; in 1843 Espartero was deposed by military officers and Isabella was declared of age. Liberal opposition to the regime's authoritarianism, scandalous reports about her private life, and her arbitrary political interference led to the Revolution of 1868, which drove her into exile. She abdicated in favor of her son, Alfonso XII.

Isabella Farnese See Elizabeth Farnese

Isaiah \ī-'zā-ə\ (fl. 8th century BC) Prophet of ancient Israel after whom the biblical Book of Isaiah is named. He is believed to have written only some of the book's first 39 chapters; the rest are by one or more unknown authors. Isaiah's call to prophesy came c. 742 BC, when Assyria was beginning the westward expansion that later overran Israel. A contemporary of Amos, Isaiah denounced economic and social injustice among the Israelites and urged them to obey the Law or risk cancellation of God's covenant. He correctly predicted the destruction of Samaria, or northern Israel, in 722 BC, and he declared the Assyrians to be the instrument of God's wrath. The Christian Gospels lean more heavily on the Book of Isaiah than on any other prophetic text, and its "swords-into-plowshares" passage has universal appeal.

ISBN See International Standard Book Number

ischemic heart disease See coronary heart disease

Ischia \'is-kē-ə\ Island, southern Italy. Located in the Tyrrhenian Sea between the Gulf of Gaeta and the Bay of Naples, it has a circumference of 21 mi (34 km) and an area of 18 sq mi (47 sq km) and consists almost entirely of volcanic rock. It rises to 2,585 ft (788 m) at Monte Epomeo, an extinct volcano, which gives its name to the island's famous wine. Known for its mild climate and mineral springs, it is a popular resort area. The chief towns, including Ischia, are located in the north.

ISDN *in full* **Integrated Services Digital Network** Digital telecommunications network that operates over standard copper telephone wires or other media. ISDN connections are used to provide a variety of digital services to customers, including digital voice telephone, fax, e-mail, digital video, and access to the Internet. A wide range of data transfer rates are available, with speeds up to about 128 kilobits per second (kbps). ISDN is faster than an ordinary dial-up connection (at about 56 kbps), but much slower than cable modem or DSL connections (which typically exceed one megabit per second).

Ise Shrine *or* **Grand Shrine of Ise** \'ē-se *Engl* 'ē-sā\ Foremost Shinto shrine in Japan, at Ise, in southern Honshu. The Inner Shrine (traditionally founded 4 BC) is dedicated to the sun goddess Amaterasu. The Outer Shrine (5th century), 4 mi (6 km) away, is dedicated to Toyuke Okami, god of food, clothing, and housing. At both shrines the main building is a thatched hut built in the ancient Japanese style of unpainted Japanese cypress *(hinoki)*. A distinctive feature of Shinto architecture is the *chigi*, a scissor-shaped finial at the front and rear of the roof. Since the 7th century the buildings have been reconstructed every 20 years or 21 years.

Iseo \ē-'zā-ō\, **Lake** Lake, northern Italy. Situated at the southern foot of the Alps, it is fed by the Oglio River, which enters the northern end near Lovere and leaves the southern end at Sarnico. It is 15.5 mi (25 km) long, with a surface area of 24 sq mi (62 sq km). Monte Isola, a large island in the center of the lake, is crowned by a chapel.

Isère River \ē-'zer\ River, southwestern France. Originating in the Savoy Alps on the Italian frontier, it flows 180 mi (290 km) southwest to its confluence with the Rhône River above Valence. It is unnavigable but used for hydroelectric power.

Isfahan See Esfahan

Isherwood, Christopher *orig.* **Christopher William Bradshaw-** (1904–1986) British-U.S. writer. Educated at Cambridge Univ., he became close friends with W. H. Auden, with whom he traveled and collaborated on three verse dramas, including *The Ascent of F6* (1936). He lived in Berlin 1929–33; his two novels about this period, later published together as *The Berlin Stories* (1946), inspired the play *I Am a Camera* (1951; film, 1955) and the musical *Cabaret* (1966; film, 1972). A pacifist, he moved to southern California at the beginning of World War II, where he taught and wrote screenplays. His later fiction and memoirs reflect his homosexuality. A follower of Swami Prabhavananda, he wrote and translated works on Indian Vedanta.

Ishikari River \,ē-shē-'kä-rē\ River, Hokkaido, Japan. Rising near the center of the Kitami Mtns., it flows southwest to empty into Ishikari Bay of the Sea of Japan. At 275 mi (442 km) long, it is the second longest river in Japan. Its name is derived from the Ainu term *ishikaribetsu* ("greatly meandering river").

Ishim River \i-'shim\ *or Kazakh* **Esil** \'es-il\ River, northern central Kazakhstan and the Tyumen and Omsk provinces of southern central Russia. A tributary of the Irtysh River, it rises in the Niyaz Hills in the north of the Kazakh Uplands, flowing northwest before entering the Irtysh at Ust-Ishim. It is 1,522 mi (2,450 km) long.

Ishmael ben Elisha \'ish-mā-əl-,ben-i-'lī-shə\ (fl. 2nd century AD) Jewish scholar. Born into a wealthy priestly family, he was taken captive by the Roman legions that sacked Jerusalem in AD 70, but was ransomed by his former teacher and sent back to Palestine to study. Ishmael founded a rabbinic school and wrote commentaries on the Torah, developing thirteen rules of exegesis based on the seven rules of Hillel. Known for his simple, literal approach to biblical scholarship, he sought to relieve hardship for observant Jews in the interpretation of the Law. He is often portrayed in dispute with Akiba ben Joseph for what he saw as the latter's excessive interpretations of superficial biblical words or phrases.

Ishtar In Mesopotamian religion, the goddess of war and sexual love. Known as Ishtar in Akkadia, she was called Astarte by western Semitic peoples and was identified with Inanna in Sumeria. In early Sumeria she was the goddess of the storehouse as well as of rain and thunderstorms. Once a fertility goddess, she evolved into a deity of contradictory qualities, of joy and sorrow, fair play and enmity. In Akkadia she was associated with the planet Venus and was the patroness of prostitutes and alehouses. Her popularity became universal in the ancient Middle East, and she was called Queen of the Universe. See photograph on following page.

Ishtar, with her cult-animal the lion, and a worshipper, modern impression from a cylinder seal, c. 2300 BC; in the Oriental Institute, University of Chicago.
BY COURTESY OF THE ORIENTAL INSTITUTE, UNIVERSITY OF CHICAGO

Ishtar Gate Enormous burnt-brick double entryway built in the ancient city of BABYLON c. 575 BC. The gate was more than 38 ft (12 m) high and was decorated with glazed brick reliefs. Through the gatehouse ran the stone- and brick-paved Processional Way. Some 120 brick lions lined the street and some 575 dragons and bulls, in 13 rows, adorned the gate.

Isidore of Seville, St. (c. 560–636) Spanish prelate and scholar, last of the Western Fathers of the Church. He became archbishop of Seville c. 600 and presided over several councils that shaped church policy, including the fourth Council of TOLEDO (633). He also promoted the conversion of the Visigoths from Arianism to orthodox Christianity. His best-known work was *Etymologies,* an encyclopedia that became a standard reference work in the Middle Ages. He also wrote theological works, biographies, and treatises on natural science, cosmology, and history. He was canonized in 1598 and declared a Doctor of the Church in 1722.

isinglass See MUSCOVITE

Isis \'ī-səs\ One of the major goddesses of ancient Egypt, the wife of OSIRIS. When Osiris was killed by SETH, she gathered up the pieces of his body, mourned for him, and brought him back to life. She hid their son HORUS from Seth until Horus was fully grown and could avenge his father. Worshiped as a goddess of protection, she had great magical powers and was invoked to heal the sick or protect the dead. By Greco-Roman times she was dominant among Egyptian goddesses, and her cult reached much of the Roman world as a MYSTERY RELIGION.

ISKCON See HARE KRISHNA MOVEMENT

Isla de Pasqua See EASTER ISLAND

Islam Major world religion founded by MUHAMMAD in Arabia in the early 7th century AD. The word *islam* means "submission"—specifically, submission to the will of the one God, called ALLAH in Arabic. Islam is a strictly monotheistic religion, and its adherents, called Muslims, regard the Prophet Muhammad as the last and most perfect of God's messengers, who include ADAM, ABRAHAM, MOSES, JESUS, and others. The sacred scripture of Islam is the QURAN, which contains God's revelations to Muhammad. The sayings and deeds of the Prophet recounted in the SUNNA are also an important source of belief and practice in Islam. The religious obligations of all Muslims are summed up in the Five Pillars of ISLAM. The fundamental concept in Islam is the SHARIA, or Law, which embraces the total way of life commanded by God. Observant Muslims pray five times a day and join in community worship on Fridays at the MOSQUE, where worship is led by an IMAM. Every believer is required to make a pilgrimage to MECCA, the holiest city, at least once in a lifetime, barring poverty or physical incapacity. The month of RAMADAN is set aside for fasting. Alcohol and pork are always forbidden, as are gambling, usury, fraud, slander, and the making of images. In addition to celebrating the breaking of the fast of Ramadan, Muslims celebrate Muhammad's birthday (see MAWLID) and his ascension into heaven (see MIRAJ). The Id al-Adha festival inaugurates the season of pilgrimage to Mecca. Muslims are enjoined to defend Islam against unbelievers through JIHAD. Divisions occurred early in Islam, brought about by disputes over the succession to the caliphate (see CALIPH). About 90% of Muslims belong to the SUNNI branch. The SHIITES broke away in the 7th century and later gave rise to other sects, including the ISMAILIS. Another significant element in Islam is the mysticism known as SUFISM. From the 19th century, the concept of the Islamic community inspired Muslim peoples to cast off Western colonial rule, and in the late 20th century fundamentalist movements (see Islamic FUNDAMENTALISM) threatened or toppled a number of secular Middle Eastern governments.

Islam, Nation of *or* **Black Muslims** African-American religious movement that mingles elements of ISLAM and BLACK NATIONALISM. It was founded in 1931 by Wallace D. Fard (1877?–1934?), who claimed to have been born a Muslim in Mecca and who established its first mosque in Detroit. After Fard's mysterious disappearance in 1934, it was taken over by his assistant ELIJAH MUHAMMAD, who founded a second temple in Chicago. He asserted the moral and cultural superiority of Africans over whites and urged American blacks to renounce Christianity as a tool of the oppressors. The Nation of Islam grew quickly after World War II, and in the early 1960s it achieved national prominence through the work of MALCOLM X. Leadership disputes led to Malcolm's forming a separate organization and finally to his assassination in 1965. In the 1970s Elijah Muhammad was succeeded by his son, Wallace D. Muhammad (born 1933), who renamed the organization the American Muslim Mission. In 1985 he dissolved the Mission, urging its members to become orthodox Muslims. A splinter group headed by LOUIS FARRAKHAN retains the movement's original name and principles.

Islam, Pillars of Five duties imposed on every Muslim. The first is the profession of faith in ALLAH as the one God and in MUHAMMAD as his Prophet. The others are: prayer five times a day; the giving of alms to the poor; fasting during the month of RAMADAN; and the HAJJ.

Islamabad \is-'lä-mə-ˌbäd\ Capital (pop., 1981: 204,000) of Pakistan, located northeast of RAWALPINDI. Established in 1959 to replace KARACHI as the capital, it was designed to blend modern and traditional Islamic architecture. The city itself is small, with an area of 25 sq mi (65 sq km), but the planned capital area is a 350-sq-mi (910-sq-km) expanse of natural terraces and meadows surrounding the city. It is the seat of the University of Islamabad (founded 1965).

Islambuli \ˌis-lam-'bü-lē\, **Khalid al-** (1958–1982) Egyptian radical, assassin of ANWAR AL-SADAT. Born into a family of rural notables, he attended Egypt's military academy and was assigned to the artillery corps as a lieutenant. Furious at the arrest of his brother, leader of the Islamist opposition to Sadat, he joined the radical al-Jihad group, and determined to assassinate Sadat during a parade in 1981 commemorating the 1973 Arab–Israeli war. After a public trial, he was executed in 1982.

Islamic architecture Building traditions of Muslim populations of the Middle East and elsewhere from the 7th century on. Islamic architecture finds its highest expression in religious buildings such as the MOSQUE and MADRASAH. Early Islamic religious architecture, exemplified by Jerusalem's DOME OF THE ROCK (AD 691) and the Great Mosque (705) in Damascus drew on Christian architectural features such as domes, columnar arches, and mosaics, but also included large courts for congregational prayer and a MIHRAB. From early times, the characteristic semicircular horseshoe arch and rich, nonrepresentational decoration of surfaces were employed. Religious architecture came into its own with the creation of the hypostyle mosque (see HYPOSTYLE HALL) in Iraq and Egypt. In Iran a mosque plan consisting of four *eyvans* (vaulted halls) opening onto a central court was used. These brick-built mosques also incorporated domes and decorated squinches (see BYZANTINE ARCHITECTURE) across the corners of the rooms. Persian architectural features spread to India, where they are found in the TAJ MAHAL and Mughal palaces. Ottoman architecture, derived from Islamic and Byzantine traditions, is exemplified by the Selimiye Mosque (1575) at Edirne, Turkey, with its great central dome and slender minarets. One of the greatest examples of secular Islamic architecture is the ALHAMBRA.

Islamic arts Visual, literary, and musical arts of the populations that adopted ISLAM from the 7th century. Islamic visual arts are decorative, colorful, and, in religious art, nonrepresentational; the characteristic Islamic decoration is the ARABESQUE. From AD 750 to the mid-11th century, ceramics, glass, metalwork, textiles, illuminated manuscripts, and woodwork flourished; LUSTERED GLASS became the greatest Islamic contribution to ceramics. Manuscript illumination became an important and greatly respected art, and miniature painting flourished in Iran after the Mongol invasions (1220–60). Calligraphy, an essential aspect of written ARABIC, developed in manuscripts and architectural decoration. Islamic poetry and prose are written in Arabic, Persian, Turkish, and Urdu, Arabic retaining the greatest prestige and importance. Islamic music is monophonic, devoid of harmony, and characterized by distinctive systems of rhythms and melodies; microtones are used for ornamentation. It is usually performed by a singer and a small ensemble of percussion, wind, and bowed and plucked stringed instruments, of which the most characteristic is the UD. See also ISLAMIC ARCHITECTURE.

Islamic calendar See Muslim CALENDAR

Islamic caste Any one of several units of social stratification among Muslims in India and Pakistan. Their development can be traced to the CASTE system of Hinduism and the tendency of Muslim converts from Hinduism to maintain social differences. The highest status is reserved for Muslim Arab immigrants, called ashraf. This level is itself divided into subgroups. The highest subgroup claims descent from MUHAMMAD through his daughter, FATIMA. The non-ashraf Muslim castes consist of three levels: converts from high Hindu castes, artisan castes, and the UNTOUCHABLES.

Islamic law See SHARIA

Islamic philosophy See ARABIC PHILOSOPHY

Islamic Salvation Front (FIS) Algerian religious-political group whose leaders include ALI BELHADJ, A. Haddam, and ABBASI AL-MADANI. The party won a majority of the seats contested in local elections in 1990 and most of the seats in the National Assembly in the first round of balloting in 1991. The government canceled the second round and arrested many of the group's leaders. Since then, FIS and more extreme Islamist groups have waged civil war, in which atrocities by both sides have been charged. FIS was blamed for the assassination of Pres. MUHAMMAD BOUDIAF, but others dispute the claim. See also GROUPE ISLAMIQUE ARMÉE, LIAMINE ZEROUAL.

island Any area of land smaller than a continent and entirely surrounded by water. Islands may occur in oceans, seas, lakes, or rivers. A group of islands is called an archipelago. Continental islands are simply unsubmerged parts of a continental mass that are entirely surrounded by water; Greenland, the world's largest island, is of the continental type. Oceanic islands are produced by volcanic activity, when lava accumulates to enormous thickness until it finally protrudes above the ocean surface. The piles of lava that form Hawaii rise as high as 32,000 ft (9,700 m) above the ocean floor.

island arc Long, curved chain of oceanic ISLANDS associated with intense volcanic and seismic activity and mountain-building processes. Examples include the Aleutian-Alaska Arc and the Kuril-Kamchatka Arc. Most island arcs consist of two parallel rows of islands. The inner row is a string of volcanoes, and the outer row is made up of nonvolcanic islands. In the case of single arcs, many of the islands are volcanically active. An island arc typically has a landmass or a partially enclosed, unusually shallow sea on its concave side. Along the convex side there usually exists a long, narrow DEEP-SEA TRENCH.

Islands, Bay of Inlet, South Pacific Ocean, on the northeastern coast of NORTH ISLAND, New Zealand. Formed when the sea flooded an old river valley system, it has a 500-mi (800-km) shoreline and about 150 islands. It opens to the ocean through a passage between Brett Cape and Wiwiki Cape. The first European to enter the bay was Capt. JAMES COOK in 1769. The bay was the site of the 1840 signing of the Treaty of Waitangi between Britain and native MAORIS. It is now a popular resort area.

Islas Baleares See BALEARIC ISLANDS

Isle of Man See Isle of MAN

Isle of Wight See Isle of WIGHT

Isle Royale National Park Island national park located in northwestern Lake SUPERIOR, northwestern Michigan. Established in 1931, it has an area of 571,790 acres (231,575 hectares) and includes Isle Royale, the largest island in Lake Superior, measuring 45 mi (72 km) long and 9 mi (14 km) across. Its forested wilderness, with streams and inland lakes, contains more than 200 species of birds. Travel is possible only on foot or by canoe, and ferry service is available from mainland Michigan and Minnesota.

islets of Langerhans See islets of LANGERHANS

Ismail I \is-'mä-ˌel\ (1487–1524) Shah of Iran (1501–24) and founder of the SAFAVID DYNASTY. Born into a Shiite family, he became head of a Shiite military force at 14. He captured Tabriz in 1501 and proclaimed himself shah of Iran, bringing the whole country and portions of modern-day Iraq under his control. In 1510 his troops defeated the Uzbek Sunnis despite being outnumbered. He proclaimed Shia the established religion, which provoked the Ottoman Turks to invade in 1514. Ismail lost the battle, but mutiny among the Ottoman troops forced their withdrawal. The conflict between the Safavids and their Sunni neighbors would continue for over a century.

Ismail Pasha \is-'mä-ˌel-pä-'shä\ (1830–1895) Viceroy of Egypt (1863–79). After an education in Paris and diplomatic missions in Europe, he was appointed viceroy and became involved with work on the SUEZ CANAL (1859–69). His plan to unify the Nile valley through creation of a new southern Egyptian province failed but became an important element of nationalist feeling. The sultan dismissed him after the national debt increased by a factor of more than 10.

Ismaili \ˌis-mä-'ē-lē\ Member of a sect of the SHIITE branch of Islam. It came into existence after the death of the sixth IMAM, JAFAR IBN MUHAMMAD, in 765. His son Ismail was accepted as successor only by a minority, who became known as Ismailis. Their doctrine, formulated in the late 8th and early 9th century, made a distinction between ordinary Muslim believers and the elect, who shared a secret wisdom. Subsects arose over the issue of the descent of the caliph. The Qaramita subsect was popular in Iraq, Yemen, and Bahrain in the 9th–11th century, and the Fatimid subsect conquered Egypt in 969 and established the FATIMID DYNASTY. A subgroup of the Fatimids was the Nizaris, who gained control of fortresses in Iran and Syria in the late 11th century and were known as ASSASSINS. The major Nizari line survived into modern times under the leadership of the AGA KHAN, moving from Iran to India in 1840. The DRUZE separated from the Ismailis early in the 11th century and formed a closed society of their own.

Ismay \'iz-mā\, **Hastings Lionel** *later* **Baron Ismay (of Wormington)** (1887–1965) British soldier. A career army officer, he served in India and Africa. As WINSTON CHURCHILL's chief of staff (1940–46) and closest military adviser, he participated in most major policy decisions of the Allied powers, particularly in the decision to make Germany the Allies' first-priority target and in planning for the invasion of France in 1944. After the war he served as secretary-general of NATO 1952–57.

isnad \is-'nad\ In Islam, a list of authorities who have transmitted accounts of the teachings or actions of MUHAMMAD, his family, or the COMPANIONS OF THE PROPHET. Each of these accounts, known as HADITH, includes an isnad that gives the chain of authorities by which it has been handed down, using the form, "It has been related to me by A on the authority of B on the authority of C on the authority of D that Muhammad said . . . ." See also ILM AL-HADITH.

ISO See INTERNATIONAL ORGANIZATION FOR STANDARDIZATION

Isocrates \ī-'sä-krə-ˌtēz\ (436–338 BC) Athenian author, rhetorician, and teacher. His school, unlike PLATO's more philosophical Academy, provided an education for the practical needs of society; it was given over almost entirely to RHETORIC. He promoted Greek political unity and cultural superiority based on monarchy and advocated a unified Greek attack on Persia under PHILIP II of Macedonia to secure unity and peace in Greece. When Greece lost its independence after the Battle of CHAERONEA, Isocrates, in despair, starved himself to death.

isolationism National policy of avoiding political or economic entanglements with other countries. Though isolationism is a recurrent force in American history, the term is most often applied to the sentiment that gripped the U.S. in the 1930s. The failure of Pres. WOODROW WILSON's internationalism, liberal opposition to warfare, and the rigors of the GREAT DEPRESSION were among the reasons for Americans' reluctance to concern themselves with the growth of FASCISM abroad. The Johnson Act (1934) and the Neutrality acts (1935) effectively prevented economic or military aid to any country involved in the European disputes that were to escalate into World War II. U.S. isolationism reinforced British APPEASEMENT and French paralysis in response to Nazi Germany's aggression, but did not ultimately prevent the U.S. from taking steps in the 1930s to mobilize the Western Hemisphere to fight the Depression and resist German encroachments. See also NEUTRALITY.

Isole Eolie See LIPARI ISLANDS

isoleucine \ˌī-sō-ˈlü-ˌsēn\ One of the essential AMINO ACIDS, present in most common PROTEINS. It was first isolated in 1904 from fibrin, a protein involved in COAGULATION. It is used in medicine and biochemical research and as a nutritional supplement.

isomer \ˈī-sə-mər\ One of two or more substances with identical molecular formulas but different CONFIGURATIONS, differing only in the arrangement of their component atoms. It usually refers to stereoisomers (rather than constitutional isomers or tautomers; see ISOMERISM, TAUTOMERISM), of which there are two types. Optical isomers, or enantiomers (see OPTICAL ACTIVITY), occur in mirror-image pairs. Geometric isomers are often the result of rigidity in the molecular structure; in organic compounds, this is usually due to a double bond (see BONDING) or a ring structure. In the case of a double bond between two carbon atoms, if each has two other groups bonded to it and all are rigidly in the same plane, the corresponding groups can be on the same side *(cis)* of the C=C bond or across the C=C bond *(trans)* from each other. An analogous distinction can be made for ring structures that are all in a plane, between isomers whose substituent groups are on the same side and isomers whose substituent groups are on both sides of the plane. Diastereomers that are not enantiomers also fall into this category. Most *cis-trans* isomers are organic compounds.

isomerism \ī-ˈsä-mə-ˌri-zəm\ Existence of sets of two or more substances with identical molecular formulas (see chemical FORMULA) but different CONFIGURATIONS and hence different properties. JONS JACOB BERZELIUS was the first to recognize and name it (1830). In constitutional (structural) isomerism, the molecular formula and molecular weight are the same, but the BONDING differs. For example, C_2H_6O is the molecular formula for both ETHANOL (CH_3CH_2OH) and methyl ETHER (CH_3OCH_3). Constitutional isomers that can be readily converted from one to another are called tautomers (see TAUTOMERISM). In the second type, stereoisomerism, substances with the same atoms are bonded in the same ways but different in their three-dimensional CONFIGURATIONS. See also ISOMER.

Isonzo \ē-ˈzōnt-sō\, **Battles of the** (1915–17) Twelve battles along the Isonzo River on the eastern sector of the Italian front in WORLD WAR I. The Isonzo River, running just inside Austria, is flanked by rugged peaks that the Austrians had fortified before Italy's entry into the war in 1915. Luigi Cadorna (1850–1928) led all the attacks against Austria, but the Italians could not penetrate the formidable natural barriers. Finally they struck with 51 divisions and dislodged the Austrians, but the Germans sent reinforcements and took the offensive, ending in the Battle of CAPORETTO.

isoprenoid \ˌī-sə-ˈprē-ˌnȯid\ *or* **terpene** Class of organic compounds made up of two or more isoprene units. Isoprene is a five-carbon HYDROCARBON with a branched-chain structure and two double bonds (see BONDING). Isoprenoids play a wide variety of roles in plant and animal physiological processes. ESSENTIAL OILS with flavors and fragrances such as geraniol (from geranium oil), a contributor to rose perfumes, menthol (from peppermint oil), citral (from lemongrass oil), and limonene (from lemon and orange oils), as well as pinene (from TURPENTINE) and CAMPHOR have two isoprene units. Examples with more units include phytol, a precursor of CHLOROPHYLL; squalene, a precursor of STEROIDS and triterpenes; lycopene, the red pigment in tomatoes and an important phytochemical; and CAROTENE, the pigment in carrots and a precursor of VITAMIN A. Natural RUBBER and the related gutta-percha are polyisoprenes with many thousands of isoprene units.

isospin \ˈī-sə-ˌspin\ *or* **isobaric spin** *or* **isotopic spin** Property characteristic of families of related SUBATOMIC PARTICLES differing mainly in the values of their ELECTRIC CHARGE. The families are known as isospin multiplets. The components of atomic nuclei, the NEUTRON and the PROTON, form an isospin doublet since they differ only in electric charge and subsidiary properties. They are considered different versions of the same object, called a nucleon. The isospin of a nucleon has a value of ½.

isostasy \ī-ˈsäs-tə-sē\ Theory describing the mass balance in the earth's CRUST, which treats all large portions of the crust as though they were floating on a denser underlying layer, about 70 mi (110 km) below the surface. In this theory, a mass above sea level is supported below sea level, so high mountains must be regions where the crust is very thick, with deep roots extending into the MANTLE. This is analogous to an iceberg floating on water, in which the greater part of the iceberg is under water.

isotope \ˈī-sə-ˌtōp\ One of two or more species of ATOMS of a chemical ELEMENT having nuclei with the same number of PROTONS but different numbers of NEUTRONS. They have the same ATOMIC NUMBER and hence nearly identical chemical behavior but different atomic MASSES. Most elements found in nature are mixtures of several isotopes; tin, for example, has 10 isotopes. In most cases, only stable isotopes of elements are found in nature. The radioactive forms break down spontaneously into different elements (see RADIOACTIVITY). Isotopes of all elements heavier than bismuth are radioactive; some occur naturally because they have long HALF-LIVES.

Isozaki \ˌē-sō-ˈzä-kē\, **Arata** (born 1931) Japanese avant-garde architect. He studied at the University of Tokyo and opened his own studio in 1963. His first notable building is the Oita Prefectural Library (1966), which shows the influence of the METABOLIST school. Later works, which often synthesize Eastern and Western elements, use bold geometric forms and frequently make historical allusions. Among his innovative structures are the Los Angeles Museum of Contemporary Art (1986) and Art Tower in Mito, Japan (1990).

ISP See INTERNET SERVICE PROVIDER

Israel *officially* **State of Israel** Republic, at the eastern end of the Mediterranean Sea. Area: 7,886 sq mi (20,425 sq km). Population (2002 est.): 6,394,000 (includes population of GOLAN HEIGHTS and East Jerusalem; excludes population of the WEST BANK and GAZA STRIP). Capital: JERUSALEM (see below). Jews constitute some four-fifths of the population, and Arabs about one-fifth. Languages: Hebrew, Arabic (both official). Religions: Judaism, Islam (mainly Sunnite), Christianity. Currency: New

Israeli Sheqel (NIS). Israel can be divided into four major regions: the Mediterranean coastal plain in the west; a hill region extending from the northern border into central Israel; the GREAT RIFT VALLEY, containing the JORDAN RIVER, in the east; and the arid NEGEV, occupying nearly the entire southern half of the country. Its major drainage system is the interior basin formed by the Jordan River; the Sea of GALILEE provides water to almost half of the country's agricultural land. It has a mixed economy based largely on services and manufacturing; exports include machinery and electronics, diamonds, chemicals, citrus fruits, vegetables, and textiles. Its population is nine-tenths urban and is concentrated largely in the Mediterranean coastal plain and around Jerusalem. It is a republic with one legislative house, the KNESSET; its head of state is the president, and the head of government is the prime minister. The record of human habitation in Israel (Palestine) is at least 100,000 years old (see PALESTINE for history). Efforts by Jews to establish a national state there began in the late 19th century. Britain supported ZIONISM, and in 1923 assumed political responsibility for what was then Palestine. Migration of Jews there, which increased during the period of NAZI persecution, led to deteriorating relations with Arabs. In 1947 the U.N. voted to partition the region into separate Jewish and Arab states. The State of Israel was proclaimed in 1948, and Egypt, Transjordan, Syria, Lebanon, and Iraq immediately declared war on it. Israel won this war (see ARAB-ISRAELI WARS) as well as the 1967 SIX-DAY WAR, in which it occupied the West Bank, Gaza Strip, and east Jerusalem. (Subsequent claims of Jerusalem as Israel's capital have not received wide international recognition.) Another war with its Arab neighbors followed in 1973, but the CAMP DAVID ACCORDS led to a peace treaty between Israel and Egypt in 1979. Israel invaded Lebanon in 1982 to expel the PALESTINE LIBERATION ORGANIZATION (PLO) from that country, and in late 1987 an uprising broke out among Palestinians of the occupied territories of the West Bank and Gaza Strip (see INTIFADA). Peace negotiations between Israel and the Arab states and Palestinians began in 1992. Israel and the PLO agreed in 1993 to a five-year plan to extend self-government to the Palestinians of the occupied territories. Israel signed a full peace treaty with Jordan in 1994. Israeli soldiers and a Lebanese militia, HIZBULLAH, clashed repeatedly throughout the 1990s. Israeli troops abruptly withdrew from Lebanon in 2000. In late 2000 further negotiations between Israel and the Palestinians broke down amid violence that claimed hundreds of lives.

Israel, tribes of In the Bible, the 12 tribes of the ancient Hebrew people, 10 of which were named for sons of JACOB (Reuben, Simeon, Judah, Issachar, Zebulun, Gad, Asher, Dan, Naphtali, and Benjamin) and two of which were named for sons of Jacob's son JOSEPH (Ephraim and Manasseh). Another of Jacob's sons was LEVI, who headed a clan of religious functionaries; unlike the 12 tribes, the Levites did not receive a territory of their own in CANAAN. In Israel's later history, the tribes of Judah and Benjamin formed a southern kingdom called JUDAH, while the 10 northern tribes formed the kingdom of Israel. After being conquered by Assyria in 721 BC, the northern tribes vanished from history and became known as the 10 lost tribes of Israel. Only Judah and Benjamin remained; they became the source of modern JUDAISM.

Israel Labour Party Israeli political party founded in 1968 as the union of three socialist-labor parties. The Labour Party and its predecessors led governing coalitions uninterruptedly from 1948 to 1977; since 1977 it has competed with the conservative LIKUD party. Its principal figures have included DAVID BEN-GURION, MOSHE DAYAN, GOLDA MEIR, SHIMON PERES, and YITZHAK RABIN.

Israeli, Isaac ben Solomon *or* **Isaac the Elder** (832/855–932/955) Egyptian Jewish physician and philosopher. He began his medical career as an oculist in Cairo and later became court physician to al-Mahdi, founder of the FATIMID DYNASTY in northern Africa. He wrote several medical treatises in Arabic that were later translated into Latin and circulated in Europe. Schooled in classical learning, he wrote philosophical works, including his *Book of Definitions,* that mingled Judaism with Neoplatonic mysticism.

Israeli law Legal practices and institutions of modern Israel. The ancient people of Israel created the law of the TORAH and the MISHNA (the latter was later incorporated into the TALMUD). In the 20th century Israeli law reflects a dual legal heritage: it is based on historic Jewish law and the laws of countries in which the Jews had for generations been living. Modern Israeli law is derived from Ottoman and British legislation and precedents, religious court opinion, and Israeli parliamentary enactments. Courts are composed of professional judges only; juries are not used. Religious courts apply Jewish law in certain matters of personal status; civil courts also apply it when called on to deal with such matters concerning Jews.

Israelite In early Jewish history, a member of the 12 tribes of ISRAEL. After the establishment (930 BC) of two Jewish kingdoms (Israel and Judah) in Palestine, only the ten northern tribes constituting the kingdom of Israel were known as Israelites. When Israel was conquered by the Assyrians (721 BC), its population was absorbed by other peoples, and the term Israelite came to refer to those who were still distinctively Jewish—the descendants of the kingdom of Judah. In liturgical usage, an Israelite is a Jew who is neither a COHEN nor a Levite (see LEVI).

Issus, Battle of (333 BC) Battle on the Issus plain near the Gulf of Iskenderun (in present-day southern Turkey) in which ALEXANDER THE GREAT, on the offensive, defeated Darius III, ruler of the Persian ACHAEMENIAN empire. The Macedonians were said to have lost only 450 men. Darius escaped, but the victory led to Alexander's victories over Phoenicia and Egypt.

Issyk-Kul \ˌi-sik-ˈkəl\ Lake, northeastern Kyrgyzstan. Situated in the northern TIAN SHAN, it is one of the largest mountain lakes in the world, having a surface area of 2,425 sq mi (6,280 sq km) and reaching 2,303 ft (702 m) in depth. Its name (from the Kyrgyz word for "hot lake") refers to the fact that it does not freeze over during the winter. To conserve the lake's wildlife, the Issyk-Kul Preserve was founded in 1948.

Istanbul *formerly* **Constantinople** *ancient* **Byzantium** City and seaport (pop., 1997: 8,260,438), Turkey. Situated on a peninsula at the entrance to the BLACK SEA, and Turkey's largest city, it lies on either side of the BOSPORUS and thus is located in both Europe and Asia. Byzantium was founded as a Greek colony in the 8th century BC. Passing to the Persian empire in 512 BC and then to ALEXANDER THE GREAT, it became a free city under the Romans in the 1st century AD. CONSTANTINE I made the city the seat of the eastern Roman empire in 330, later naming it Constantinople. It remained the capital of the BYZANTINE EMPIRE after the fall of Rome in the late 5th century. In the 6th–13th century it was frequently besieged by Persians, Arabs, Bulgars, and Russians. It was captured by the Fourth CRUSADE (1203) and turned over to Latin Christian rule. It was returned to Byzantine rule in 1261. In 1453 it was made the capital of the OTTOMAN EMPIRE and dubbed Istanbul. The Turkish capital was moved to ANKARA in 1923, and Constantinople was officially renamed Istanbul in 1930. Many of the city's historic sites are located in the medieval walled city (Stamboul). Among its architectural treasures are the HAGIA SOPHIA, the Mosque of Süleyman (1550–57), and the Blue Mosque. Its educational institutions include the University of Istanbul (founded 1453), Turkey's oldest university.

Isthmian Games \ˈis-mē-ən\ In ancient Greece, a festival of athletic and musical competitions in honor of the sea god POSEIDON. It was held in the spring of the second and fourth years of each Olympiad at Poseidon's legendary sanctuary on the Isthmus of Corinth. It died out when Christianity became dominant in the 4th century AD.

Istria Peninsula, extending into the northeastern Adriatic Sea. It has an area of 1,220 sq mi (3,160 sq km). Its northern portion is part of Slovenia, while the central and southern parts belong to Croatia. A tiny strip of coast in the northwest is the site of TRIESTE and belongs to Italy. Istria's ancient Illyrian inhabitants were overthrown by Romans in 177 BC, and Slavic peoples settled there from the 7th century AD. It passed through the hands of various Mediterranean powers until Austria gained control in 1797 and developed Trieste as a port. Istria was seized by Italy in 1919; Yugoslavia occupied most of the peninsula in 1947. Yugoslavian Istria became part of Croatia and Slovenia at those states' independence in 1991.

Itagaki Taisuke \ē-tä-ˈgä-kē-ˈtī-ske\ (1837–1919) Founder of Japan's first political party, the Liberal Party. In the 1860s he became military leader of the domain of TOSA, and under his command Tosa's troops participated in the MEIJI RESTORATION. He served sporadically in the new government, but discontent led him to found first a political club and then a national "Society of Patriots" in support of greater democracy. In 1881 he formed the Liberal Party (Jiyuto). Though he retired in 1900, he remained its symbolic leader. See also ITO HIROBUMI, MEIJI CONSTITUTION, MEIJI PERIOD.

Italian Communist Party See DEMOCRATIC PARTY OF THE LEFT

Italian language ROMANCE LANGUAGE spoken in Italy (including Sicily and Sardinia) and in parts of Switzerland and France (including Corsica). Its 66 million speakers worldwide include many immigrants and their descendants in the Americas. Written Italian dates from the 10th century. The standard literary form is based on the dialect of Florence, but many Italians do not speak it, instead using regional dialects. These include Upper Italian (Gallo-Italian); Venetian in northeastern Italy; Tuscan; the dialects of Marche, Umbria, and Rome; of Abruzzi, Puglia, Naples, Campania, and Lucania; and of Calabria, Otranto, and Sicily. Italian has a sound system similar to that of Latin and Spanish and a grammar with noun-adjective agreement, masculine and feminine genders, and an elaborate system of perfect and progressive verb tenses. See also Italic languages.

Italian Liberal Party (PLI) Moderately conservative political party that dominated Italian politics in the decades after unification (1861) and was a minor party after World War II. It was formed as a parliamentary group in 1848 by Camillo Cavour; his followers favored a centralized government, restricted suffrage, regressive taxation, and free trade. Left Liberals gained control of the party in 1876. Its strength declined after World War I, but in 1944 it reemerged as a minor partner in most of the Christian Democratic coalition governments.

Italian Popular Party (PPI) Centrist political party whose several factions are united by their Roman Catholicism and anticommunism. They advocate programs ranging from social reform to the defense of free enterprise. The original party was founded in 1919 and quickly won popularity, but in 1926 the Fascists banned all political parties. After Italy's surrender in World War II, former party leaders, along with Catholic organizations, founded the Christian Democratic Party. In 1993 the struggling party reverted to its original name, but in the 1994 parliamentary elections it fell from power and was reduced to a minor party.

Italian Socialist Party (PSI) One of the first Italian parties with a national scope and a modern democratic organization. It was founded in 1893 by trade unions and socialists. In the early 20th century the left wing fought for control over the reformists and broke away to form the Italian Communist Party (1921). The PSI formed an alliance with the communists from 1934 until the mid-1950s, when it denounced the Soviet Union after its invasion of Hungary. From 1963 it joined or supported center-left governments. In 1983 Bettino Craxi became the first Socialist premier, but after political scandals in the 1990s the PSI was reduced to a minor party.

Italian Somaliland Former Italian colony, eastern Africa. It extended south from Cape Asir to the boundary of Kenya, occupying an area of 178,218 sq mi (461,585 sq km). Italy obtained control of it in 1889 and it was incorporated as a state in Italian East Africa in 1936. Britain invaded in 1941 and retained control until it became a U.N. trust territory under Italian administration in 1950. In 1960 it was united with British Somaliland to form the independent Republic of Somalia.

Italian Wars (1494–1559) Series of violent wars for control of Italy. Largely fought by France and Spain, but involving much of Europe, they resulted in Italy's domination by the Spanish Habsburgs and shifted power from Italy to northwestern Europe and its Atlantic world. The wars began with the invasion of Italy by the French king Charles VIII in 1494. He took Naples, but an alliance between Maximilian I, Spain, and the pope drove him out of Italy. In 1499 Louis XII invaded Italy and took Milan, Genoa, and Naples, but was driven out of Naples in 1503 by Spain under Ferdinand V. Pope Julius II organized the League of Cambrai (1508) to attack Venice, then organized the Holy League (1511) to drive Louis out of Milan. In 1515 Francis I was victorious at the battle of Marignano, and in 1516 a peace was concluded by which France held onto Milan and Spain kept Naples. Fighting began in 1521 between Emperor Charles V and Francis I. Francis was captured and forced to sign the Treaty of Madrid (1526), renouncing all claims in Italy, but once freed he repudiated the treaty and formed a new alliance with Henry VIII of England, Pope Clement VII, Venice, and Florence. Charles sacked Rome in 1527 and forced the pope to come to terms, and Francis gave up all claims to Italy in the Treaty of Cambrai (1529). By the Treaty of Cateau-Cambrésis (1559), the wars finally ended.

Italic languages \i-'ta-lik\ Indo-European languages spoken in the Apennine Peninsula (Italy) during the 1st millennium BC, after which only Latin survived. Traditionally thought to be a subfamily of related languages, these languages actually may represent three independent members of the Indo-European family: Latin, Osco-Umbrian, and Venetic. Latin, the language of Latium and Rome, began to emerge as the predominant language as early as the 3rd century BC. By AD 100 it had replaced all dialects (except Greek) between Sicily and the Alps. Until then, Oscan dialects were most widely spoken; Umbrian, in central Italy, was closely related to Oscan. Venetic was spoken in the region of Venice. These languages were written in various alphabets, including the Greek and Latin alphabets and modified versions of the Etruscan.

Italic War See Social War

Italo-Turkish War (1911–12) War undertaken by Italy to gain colonies in North Africa by conquering the Turkish provinces of Tripolitana and Cyrenaica (modern Libya). The conflict upset the precarious international balance of power just before World War I by revealing the weakness of Turkey and, within Italy, unleashed the nationalist-expansionist sentiment that guided government policy in the following decades. Turkey conceded its rights to the contested provinces in the peace terms.

Italy *officially* **Italian Republic** *Italian* **Italia** Country, southern Europe. It comprises the boot-shaped peninsula extending into the Mediterranean Sea as well as Sicily, Sardinia, and a number of smaller islands. Area: 116,324 sq mi (301,277 sq km). Population (2000 est.): 57,723,000. Capital: Rome. Despite internal migration, there are regional variations, particularly between the north and the south. Language: Italian (official). Religion: Roman Catholicism. Monetary unit: euro. More than three-quarters of Italy is mountainous or highland country. The Alps stretch from east to west along Italy's northern boundary, and the Apennines stretch southward the length of the peninsula. Most of the country's lowlands lie in the valley of its major river, the Po. Three tectonic plates converge in southern Italy and Sicily, creating intense geologic activity; southern Italy's four active volcanoes include Mount Vesuvius and Mount Etna. The economy is based largely on services and manufacturing; exports include machinery and transport equipment, chemicals, textiles, clothing and shoes, and food products (olive oil, wine,

fruit, and tomatoes). It is a republic with two legislative houses. The chief of state is the president, and the head of government is the prime minister. Italy has been inhabited since Paleolithic times. The Etruscan civilization arose in the 9th century BC and was overthrown by the Romans in the 4th–3rd century BC (see Roman Republic and Empire). Barbarian invasions of the 4th–5th century AD destroyed the western Roman empire. Italy's political fragmentation lasted for centuries but did not diminish its impact on European culture, notably during the Renaissance. From the 15th to the 18th century, Italian lands were ruled by France, the Holy Roman Empire, Spain, and Austria. When Napoleonic rule ended in 1815, Italy was again a grouping of independent states. The Risorgimento successfully united most of Italy, including Sicily and Sardinia by 1861, and the unification of peninsular Italy was completed by 1870. Italy joined the Allies during World War I, but social unrest in the 1920s brought to power the Fascist movement of Benito Mussolini's, and Italy allied itself with Nazi Germany in World War II. Defeated by the Allies in 1943, Italy proclaimed itself a republic in 1946. It was a charter member of NATO (1949) and of the European Community. It completed the process of setting up regional legislatures with limited autonomy in 1970. Since World War II it has experienced rapid changes of government but has remained socially stable. It has worked with other European countries to establish the EUROPEAN UNION.

Itami \ē-'tä-mē\, **Juzo** *orig.* **Yoshihiro Ikeuchi** (1933–1997) Japanese film director and screenwriter. He had a successful 20-year career as an actor in such films as *55 Days at Peking* (1963) before venturing into directing. His directorial debut, *The Funeral* (1984), was acclaimed for its satire of social conventions, a novelty in Japanese cinema. He became an international success with his artful and entertaining *Tampopo* (1986) and *A Taxing Woman* (1987). His satire on Japan's crime syndicate, *The Gangster's Moll* (1992), provoked a near-deadly attack on him by gangsters. He took his own life.

Itanagar \ˌē-tə-'nə-gər\ Capital of ARUNACHAL PRADESH state, northeastern India, situated west of the BRAHMAPUTRA RIVER. The state government has established an industrial estate in the city in order to foster industrial development. It is the seat of Arunachal University.

Itasca \ī-'tas-kə\, **Lake** Lake, northwestern Minnesota. Occupying an area of 1.8 sq mi (4.7 sq km), it is located 1,475 ft (450 m) above sea level. HENRY ROWE SCHOOLCRAFT's theory that Lake Itasca is the source of the MISSISSIPPI RIVER has been widely accepted. He is generally credited with originating the name Itasca, but Indian legend mentions I-tesk-ka, the daughter of HIAWATHA, whose tears of anguish at being spirited away to the netherworld were the source of the Mississippi.

itching *or* **pruritus** \prü-'rīt-əs\ Stimulation of nerve endings in the skin, usually incited by HISTAMINE, that evokes a desire to scratch. It is often transient and easily relieved. Pathological itching with skin changes usually signals dermatologic disease. Generalized itching without skin changes can occur in systemic diseases (e.g., metabolic and endocrine conditions, cancer, drug reactions, and kidney, blood, and liver diseases). Dry skin often itches. Treatment depends on cause.

Iténez River See GUAPORÉ RIVER

Ithna Ashariya \ˌith-na-ȧ-shȧ-'rē-ə\ *or* **imamis** *English* **Twelvers** Largest branch of SHIITE Islam, believing in a succession of 12 IMAMS beginning with ALI IBN ABI TALIB, the fourth caliph and son-in-law of MUHAMMAD. Last of the 12 was Muhammad al-Mahdi al-Hujjah, who disappeared in 873 and is thought to be alive and in hiding, ready to return at the Last Judgment. The Twelvers believe that the world cannot exist without an imam, and pilgrimages to the tombs of the imams secure special rewards. This sect became the state religion of Iran under the SAFAVID DYNASTY (1501–1736). Twelvers also constitute a majority in Iraq and Bahrain, with sizable minorities in other Muslim countries.

Ito Hirobumi \'ē-tō-hē-'rō-bu̇-mē\ (1841–1909) Japanese statesman, prime minister, and writer of the MEIJI CONSTITUTION. He played a minor role in the MEIJI RESTORATION, through which he came in contact with KIDO TAKAYOSHI and OKUBO TOSHIMICHI. When Okubo was assassinated in 1878, Ito succeeded him as home minister. He persuaded the government to adopt a constitution, then traveled abroad to research constitutions. In 1889 the emperor promulgated the resultant document. Later, as prime minister, Ito negotiated an end to extraterritoriality with Britain; other Western nations followed suit, signaling that the West was beginning to treat Japan as an equal. Frustrated with political parties' ability to impede passage of government programs in the Diet, in 1900 Ito founded his own party, the RIKKEN SEIYUKAI. This foray cost him control of the GENRO but made cooperation between high-ranking bureaucrats and party politicians acceptable. In 1906 Ito became resident general in Korea, where he was assassinated in 1909 by a Korean nationalist.

Ito Jinsai \'ē-tō-'jēn-ˌsī\ (1627–1705) Japanese Confucian scholar. The son of a lumberman, he devoted himself to scholarship. He opposed the authoritarian NEO-CONFUCIANISM of the TOKUGAWA SHOGUNATE and advocated a return to the authentic teachings of CONFUCIUS and MENCIUS. He helped establish the Kogaku school of Neo-Confucianism, and with his son founded the Kogi-do academy in Kyoto, which was run by his descendants until 1904. His writings include *Gomojigi* (1683), a commentary on Confucianism that tried to develop a rational basis for morality and the pursuit of happiness.

ITT See INTERNATIONAL TELEPHONE AND TELEGRAPH CORP.

Iturbide \ˌē-tu̇r-'bē-t͟hā\, **Agustín de** *or* **Agustín I** (1783–1824) Leader of the conservative factions in the Mexican independence movement and, briefly, emperor of Mexico (1822–23). An army officer when the independence movement emerged in 1810, he fought for the royalists, but in 1820, in reaction to a liberal coup in Spain, the conservatives did an about-face and advocated immediate independence. Iturbide joined forces with the insurgents and won Mexico's independence in 1821. In 1822 he crowned himself emperor, but his arbitrary and extravagant ways cost him support. His abdication in 1823 did not save him from execution. To Mexico's conservatives he remains the principal hero of Mexican independence.

Ivan III \'ī-vən\ *known as* **Ivan the Great** (1440–1505) Grand prince of Moscow (1462–1505). Determined to enlarge the territory he inherited from his father, Ivan led successful military campaigns against the TATARS in the south (1458) and east (1467–69). He subdued Novgorod (1478) and gained control of most of the remainder of Great Russia by 1485. He also renounced Moscow's subjection to the khan of the GOLDEN HORDE (1480) and won a final victory over the khan's sons in 1502. Stripping the BOYARS of much of their authority, he laid the administrative foundations of a centralized Russian state. IVAN IV the Terrible was his grandson.

Ivan IV *Russian* **Ivan Vasilyevich** *known as* **Ivan the Terrible** (1530–1584) Grand prince of Moscow (1533–84) and first CZAR of Russia (1547–84). Crowned czar in 1547 after a long regency (1533–46), he embarked on wide-ranging reforms, including a centralized administration, church councils that systematized the church's affairs, and the first national assembly (1549). He also instituted reforms to limit the powers of the BOYARS. After conquering KAZAN (1552) and ASTRAKHAN (1556), he engaged in an unsuccessful war to control LIVONIA, fighting against Sweden and Poland (1558–83). After the defeat and the suspected treason of several Russian boyars, Ivan formed an *oprichnina*, a territory separate from the rest of the state and under his personal control. With a large bodyguard, he withdrew into his own entourage and left Russia's management to others. At the same time, he instituted a reign of terror, executing thousands of boyars and ravaging the city of Novgorod. During the 1570s he married five wives in nine years, and in a fit of rage he murdered his son Ivan in 1581.

Ivan IV, icon, late 16th century; in the Nationalmuseet, Copenhagen.

Ivan V *Russian* **Ivan Alekseyevich** (1666–1696) Nominal czar of Russia (1682–96). Though he was a chronic invalid and mentally deficient, when his brother Czar FYODOR III died Ivan was proclaimed coruler with his half brother PETER I, with Ivan's sister SOPHIA as regent. After Sophia's overthrow in 1689, Ivan was allowed to retain his official position, though he never participated in governmental affairs.

Ivan VI *Russian* **Ivan Antonovich** (1740–1764) Infant emperor of Russia (1740–41). The grand-nephew of Empress ANNA, Ivan was proclaimed her heir and then emperor when only eight weeks old, with his mother as regent. In 1741 they were deposed by ELIZABETH, daughter of PETER I, and for the next 20 years he remained in solitary confinement in various prisons. In 1764, when an army officer tried to free Ivan to restore him to power and remove CATHERINE II, who had seized the throne in 1762, Ivan was assassinated by his jailers.

Ivan Asen II \ȧ-'sän\ (died 1241) Czar of the Second Bulgarian empire (1218–41). He took the throne after overthrowing and blinding his cousin Boril. A good soldier and administrator, Ivan restored order, controlled the BOYARS, and acquired much of Albania, Serbia, Macedonia, and Epirus (1230). He forged alliances through the marriages of his daughters, but a treaty to make him regent of the Latin empire was repudiated by Latins fearful of Bulgaria's growing power, and he afterwards separated the Bulgarian church from Rome.

Ivanov \i-'vȧ-nəf\, **Lev (Ivanovich)** (1834–1901) Russian dancer and choreographer. He joined the Imperial Ballet in St. Petersburg in 1852, becoming lead dancer in 1869. In 1885 he was appointed assistant ballet master under MARIUS PETIPA. He is best known for his choreography of

The Nutcracker (1892) and parts of *Swan Lake* (1895), which he based closely on the music rather than emphasizing virtuoso technique.

Ivanov \i-ˈvȧ-nəf\, **Vyacheslav Ivanovich** (1866–1949) Russian philosopher, scholar, and poet. He studied in Berlin and spent much of his life abroad, especially in Italy, where he converted to Roman Catholicism. His first volume of lyric poetry, *Pilot Stars* (1903), immediately established him as a key figure in the Russian Symbolist movement, a position strengthened by later works, including the important *Cor Ardens* (1911). He also produced poetic dramas, essays, criticism, and translations.

Ives, Burl (Icle Ivanhoe) (1909–1995) U.S. singer and actor. Born in Illinois, Ives began performing at 4 and learned Scottish, English, and Irish ballads from his grandmother. He left college to hitchhike around the U.S., collecting songs from hoboes and drifters. Soon after his postwar concert debut in New York, he was hailed by Carl Sandburg as "the mightiest ballad singer of this or any other century." He recorded over 100 albums and had hits with "I Know an Old Lady (Who Swallowed a Fly)," "The Blue Tail Fly," "Big Rock Candy Mountain," "Frosty the Snowman," and "A Little Bitty Tear." He appeared in many films, including *East of Eden* (1955), *Desire Under the Elms* (1958), and *The Big Country* (1958, Academy Award), and appeared in 13 Broadway productions, including *Cat on a Hot Tin Roof* (1955; film, 1958).

Ives, Charles E(dward) (1874–1954) U.S. composer. Born in Danbury, Conn., Ives claimed to be the product of training by his father, George, a highly imaginative former Union Army bandmaster. He received a solid classical grounding and began composing and performing at an early age. At Yale University he studied with Horatio Parker (1863–1919) and composed his first symphony. Under the influence of Transcendentalism, he decided to forgo a music career, and in 1907 he founded a successful insurance firm. With music as a "sideline," he felt free to pursue his unusual interests, though he suffered from his amateur status and a lack of intelligent critiques. A heart attack in 1918 curtailed all activities, and he stopped composing c. 1926. His music is tonal despite much dissonance, atmospheric, and nostalgic, and runs the gamut from sentimental or quirkily humorous songs to exciting tone poems (*The Fourth of July,* 1913) and weighty meditations (*Concord Sonata,* 1915). He apparently made many remarkable tonal innovations, though questions have been raised about whether he later predated his works to give a misleading impression. His music was rediscovered late in his life; the third of his four symphonies won a Pulitzer Prize in 1947.

IVF See In vitro fertilization

ivory Hard white substance, a variety of dentin, that makes up the tusks of such animals as elephants, walruses, and preserved mammoths. It is prized for its beauty, durability, and suitability for carving. In ancient times it was treasured as highly as gold and precious stones. Most ivory used commercially once came from Africa; sales of ivory declined in the 20th century as the populations of African elephants shrank, and worldwide concern about endangered elephant populations have led to bans on the export and import of ivory. The once-thriving markets of Europe have shifted to South Asia, where skilled artisans, often trading illegally, carve ivory into figurines and other objects.

Ivory, James (Francis) (born 1928) U.S. film director. Born in Berkeley, Cal., he met a local producer, Ismail N. Merchant (born 1936), while directing a documentary on India in the 1960s, beginning cinema's longest-lasting partnership. They made several films written by Ivory and Ruth Prawer Jhabvala before their first international success, *Shakespeare Wallah* (1965). It was followed by a series of high-quality, well-acted films noted for their lush cinematography, including *The Europeans* (1979), *The Bostonians* (1984), *A Room with a View* (1986, Academy Award), *Maurice* (1987), *Howards End* (1992), *The Remains of the Day* (1993), and *Surviving Picasso* (1996).

ivory-billed woodpecker Black-and-white woodpecker *(Campephilus principalis)* with a flaring crest (red on the male) and a long whitish bill. The largest North American woodpecker, it is thought to be extinct, though there were unconfirmed sightings of the bird in the southern United States in the late 1990s; a small population on Cuba was last seen in the late 1980s. Its decline coincided with the logging of virgin forest, where it subsisted on deadwood insects. A subspecies, the Cuban ivory-billed woodpecker, is also believed to be extinct. A related species, the imperial woodpecker of Mexico, is critically endangered. All these birds appear to have required large trees and isolation from disturbance.

Ivory-billed woodpeckers (*Campephilus principalis*).

KENNETH W. FINK FROM ROOT RESOURCES—EB INC.

ivory carving Carving of ivory into decorative or utilitarian objects. It has flourished since prehistoric times. Most Stone Age carvings have been found in southern France, in the forms of small nude female figures and animals. A masterpiece of early Egyptian carving is an ivory statuette of Khufu, builder of the Great Pyramid. In China ivory carvings have been found in the tombs of the Shang dynasty (18th–12th century BC). The major artistic use of ivory in Japan was for netsukes, toggles used as fasteners on men's clothing. The early Inuit (Eskimos) produced such utilitarian objects as harpoon shafts and bucket handles out of ivory and often etched them with geometric or curving patterns. See also scrimshaw.

Ivory Coast See Côte d'Ivoire

"An Elopement" (sometimes called "Lancelot and Guinevere"), ivory mirror case, French Gothic, 14th century.

BY COURTESY OF THE LIVERPOOL MUSEUM, ENGLAND

ivy Any of about five species of evergreen woody vines (rarely shrubs) that make up the genus *Hedera* in the ginseng family, commonly grown as ground covers and on stone walls, especially English ivy *(H. helix),* which climbs by aerial roots with adhering disks that develop on the stems. The tough, dark-green leaves of English ivy have three to five lobes and tend to droop horizontally from the stem. Unrelated plants called ivies include Boston ivy *(Parthenocissus,* or *Ampelopsis, tricuspidata),* a clinging woody vine in the grape family whose leaves turn bright scarlet in autumn, and poison ivy.

Ivy League Group of eight universities in the northeastern U.S., high in academic and social prestige, that are members of an athletic conference for intercollegiate football dating to the 1870s. It consists of Harvard, Yale, Princeton, Columbia, Brown, and Cornell universities, the University of Pennsylvania, and Dartmouth College.

Iwo Jima Island, the middle of the three Volcano Islands, Japan. Situated in the western Pacific, it is about 5 mi (8 km) long, 800 yards to 2.5 mi (730 m–4 km) wide, and has an area of 8 sq mi (20 sq km). It was under Japanese control until 1945, when it was the scene of one of the severest campaigns of World War II. After extensive bombing by U.S. planes (December 1944–February 1945), it was invaded by U.S. marines and was finally completely taken by mid-March; it became a strategic base for U.S. planes en route to Japan. In 1968 it was returned to Japan.

U.S. marines raising the American flag over Mount Suribachi, Iwo Jima, in February 1945.

JOE ROSENTHAL—AP/WIDE WORLD

IWW See Industrial Workers of the World

Izabal \ˌē-sä-ˈbäl\, **Lake** Lake, Guatemala. The country's largest lake, it occupies the lowlands in northeastern Guatemala. Fed by the Polochic

River, it drains through the Dulce River into the Caribbean Sea. It lies only 26 ft (8 m) above sea level and has an area of 228 sq mi (590 sq km). The main settlement on the shores is El Estor, which originated as a trading outpost of the UNITED FRUIT CO.

Izanagi and Izanami \ē-'zä-,nä-gē...ē-'zä-,nä-mē\ Brother and sister gods in the Japanese creation myth. They created the first land mass, and their sexual union produced many islands and deities. In giving birth to the fire god, Izanami was burned to death and went to the land of darkness. Izanagi tried to rescue her, but she had eaten the food of the place and could not leave; in disgust he left her rotting corpse and divorced her. As he bathed to purify himself afterwards, other deities were born from him, including the sun goddess AMATERASU, the moon god Tsukiyomi, and the storm god Susanoo. His bath is the basis for SHINTO purification rites.

Izmir \iz-'mir\ *formerly* **Smyrna** City (pop., 1995 est.: 2,018,000), western Turkey. On the Aegean seacoast, it is one of Turkey's largest ports and its third largest city. Founded as early as 3000 BC, it was settled by the Greeks before 1000 BC. It was captured by the Lydians in c. 600 BC, and it ceased to exist until it was refounded by ALEXANDER THE GREAT in the 4th century BC. It became one of the principal cities of ASIA MINOR. After being conquered in turn by the Crusaders and by TIMUR (Tamerlane), it was annexed to the Ottoman empire c. 1425. It has grown rapidly since 1945. It has a large industrial economy and a growing tourist trade.

Izrail \,iz-rä-'ēl\ In ISLAM, the angel of death. One of the four archangels (with JIBRIL, MIKAL, and Israfil), he is of cosmic size, with 4,000 wings and a body formed from innumerable eyes and tongues. He was the only angel brave enough to go down to earth and face IBLIS in order to bring God the materials to create man. For this service he was made the angel of death and given a register of all mankind, which lists the blessed and the damned.

Izu Peninsula \'ē-zü\ Peninsula, southern central HONSHU, Japan. It extends 37 mi (60 km) into the Pacific Ocean and consists largely of volcanic rock and highly eroded volcanoes. It is part of a national park, and its hot springs and warm winter climate attract tourists.

Izumo shrine \'ē-zù-mò, *Engl* ē-'zü-mō\ Oldest SHINTO shrine in Japan (the present building is said to date from 1346), located northwest of Izumo on the island of Honshu. The temple complex covers 40 acres and contains a valuable art collection. Enclosed by hills on three sides, it is approached through an avenue of pines. Most of its present buildings were constructed in the 19th century.

Izvestiya \iz-'ves-tē-ə\ *formerly in full* **Izvestiya Sovetov Deputatov Trudyashchikhsya SSSR** (Russian: "News of the Councils of Working People's Deputies of the U.S.S.R.") Russian daily newspaper published in Moscow, the official national publication of the Soviet government until 1991. Founded in 1917, it grew rapidly in circulation. Restrictions during World War II and under JOSEPH STALIN slowed its growth, but it was transformed into a lively, readable daily under the editorship of Alexei Adzhubei, NIKITA KHRUSHCHEV's son-in-law, while remaining an instrument of the state. Following the Soviet Union's breakup, it became an independent, employee-owned publication whose liberal editorial policy often put it at odds with both unreconstructed communists and Russian nationalists.

Izvolsky \iz-'vòl-skē\, **Aleksandr (Petrovich), Count** (1856–1919) Russian diplomat. A career diplomat, he became minister of foreign affairs in 1906. In 1908 he secured Austria's support for the right of Russian warships to use the Dardanelles strait in return for his reluctant support of Austria's annexation of Bosnia and Herzegovina. While Austria succeeded in its annexation (see BOSNIAN CRISIS), Russia failed to gain access to the Dardanelles; Izvolsky's responsibility for Russia's diplomatic defeat increased tensions with Austria-Hungary prior to World War I. Dismissed in 1910, he served as ambassador to France until 1917.

Jabotinsky \ˌyab-ə-ˈtin-skē\, **Vladimir** (1880–1940) Russian Zionist leader. Born in Odessa, he became a popular journalist and editorialist. By 1903 he was expounding ZIONISM. In 1920 he organized and led the Jewish Palestinian self-defense movement HAGANA, angering the British. A Revisionist Zionist, he passionately advocated a Jewish state extending east of the Jordan River. See also IRGUN ZVAI LEUMI.

Jabrail See JIBRIL

jacaranda \ˌja-kə-ˈran-də\ Any plant of the genus *Jacaranda* (family Bignoniaceae), especially the two ornamental trees *J. mimosifolia* and *J. cuspidifolia*. Jacarandas are grown widely in warm parts of the world and in greenhouses for their showy blue or violet flowers and attractive, oppositely paired, compound leaves. The genus includes about 50 species native to Central and South America and the West Indies. The name is also applied to several tree species of the genera *Machaerium* and *Dalbergia* in the pea family (see LEGUME), the sources of commercial rosewood.

jack In practical MECHANICS, portable hand-operated device for raising heavy weights through short distances, exerting great pressures, or holding assembled work firmly in position. The ratio of the load to the amount of force applied to the handle can be made quite high by using a GEAR or SCREW to regulate the upward extension. A RATCHET allows a heavy weight to be raised in short successive stages. Though limited by the requirements of portability and ease of manual operation, jacks may lift, or exert a force of, several tons. A familiar example is the automobile jack, used to raise one end of a car to change a tire.

jack Any of more than 150 species of fishes (family Carangidae, order Perciformes) found in temperate and tropical portions of the Atlantic, Pacific, and Indian oceans and occasionally in fresh or brackish water. Though body size and shape vary greatly, many species have small scales that create a smooth appearance, a laterally compressed body, rows of large spiky scales along the side near the tail fin, and a deeply forked tail. Many have a bluish green, silvery, or yellowish sheen. Jacks are important commercially and are favored sport fishes. See also AMBERJACK.

jack-in-the-pulpit North American plant *(Arisaema triphyllum)* of the ARUM FAMILY, noted for the unusual shape of its flower. One of the best-known perennial wildflowers of late spring in the eastern U.S. and Canada, it grows in wet woodlands and thickets from Nova Scotia to Minnesota and south to Florida and Texas. Three-part leaves on each of two long stalks overshadow the flower, which consists of a conspicuous green- and purple-striped structure called a spathe ("pulpit") that rises on a separate stalk. The spathe curves in a hood over a club-shaped spadix ("jack") that, at its base, bears minute flowers. In late summer the plant produces a cluster of brilliant red berries that are poisonous to humans but are eaten by many wild animals.

Jack the Ripper Pseudonymous murderer of at least seven women, all prostitutes, in or near London's Whitechapel district, from August 7 to November 10, 1888. Each victim had her throat cut, and usually the body was mutilated in a manner indicating the murderer had considerable knowledge of human anatomy. Authorities received a series of taunting notes from a person calling himself Jack the Ripper and purporting to be the murderer. Though strenuous efforts were made to identify and trap the killer, he remained unknown. The unsolved case retained its hold on the popular imagination, becoming the subject of motion pictures and over 100 books.

jackal Any of three CANINE species of the genus *Canis*. They inhabit open country and live alone, in pairs, or in packs. They hunt at night, feeding on small animals, plant material, or carrion. A pack can bring down larger prey. The golden, or Asiatic, jackal (yellowish) is found from eastern Europe and North Africa to South Asia. The black-backed jackal (rusty red with a black back) and side-striped jackal (grayish with a white-tipped tail and an indistinct stripe on each side) are found in southern and eastern Africa. Jackals are 34–37 in. (85–95 cm) long, including the 12–14-in. (30–35-cm) tail, and weigh 15–24 lbs (7–11 kg).

Black-backed jackal (*Canis mesomelas*).

LEONARD LEE RUE III

jackdaw *or* **daw** Crowlike black bird *(Corvus monedula)* with gray nape and pearly eyes. About 13 in. (33 cm) long, jackdaws breed in colonies in treeholes and on cliffs and tall buildings; their flocks fly in formation around the site. Their cry sounds like their name: "chak." The species ranges from the British Isles to central Asia. See also CROW, GRACKLE.

jackrabbit Any of several large, common North American species of HARES (e.g., *Lepus townsendii*, *L. californicus*). Jackrabbits have very long ears and long hind legs. They are widespread, particularly in the West, but are found most often in prairie and plains environments.

Jackson City (pop., 1996 est.: 193,000) and capital, Mississippi. It lies along the PEARL RIVER in the western central part of the state. Settled in 1792 by Louis Le Fleur, a French-Canadian trader, it was a trading post called Le Fleur's Bluff until settlers began arriving in 1820. It was made the state capital in 1822 and was named for ANDREW JACKSON. During the AMERICAN CIVIL WAR it was burned by Union forces (1863). The state's largest city, it is a railroad and distribution center. It is the seat of Jackson State University (1877) and other educational institutions.

Jackson, A(lexander) Y(oung) (1882–1974) Canadian landscape painter. Born in Montreal, he traveled to every region of Canada, including the Arctic; from 1921 on, he returned every spring to a favorite spot on the St. Lawrence River, where he produced sketches that he later executed in paint (e.g., *Early Spring, Quebec*, 1926; *Laurentian Hills, Early Spring*, 1931). Over a long career he became a leading artistic figure in his country; his easy style, featuring rolling rhythms and rich, full color, exerted a strong influence on Canadian landscape painting.

Jackson, Andrew (1767–1845) Seventh president of the U.S. (1829–37). Born in Waxhaw, S.C., he fought briefly in the American Revolution near his frontier home, where his family was killed. He studied law and in 1788 was appointed prosecuting attorney for western North Carolina. When the region became the state of Tennessee, he was elected to the U.S. House of Representatives (1796–97) and Senate (1797–98). He served on the state supreme court (1798–1804) and in 1802 was elected major general of the Tennessee militia. When the WAR OF 1812 began, he offered the U.S. the services of his 50,000-volunteer militia. He was sent to fight the Creek Indians allied with the British in Mississippi Territory. After a lengthy battle (1813–14), he defeated them at the Battle of Horseshoe Bend. After capturing Pensacola, Fla., from the British-allied Spanish, he marched overland to engage the British in Louisiana. A decisive victory at the Battle of NEW ORLEANS made him a national hero, dubbed "Old Hickory" by the press. After U.S. acquisition of Florida, he was named governor of the territory (1821). One of four candidates in the 1824 presidential election, he won an electoral-votes plurality but the House gave the election to JOHN QUINCY ADAMS. In 1828 Jackson defeated Adams after a fierce campaign and became the first president elected from west of the Appalachian Mountains. His election was considered a triumph of political democracy. He replaced many federal officeholders with his supporters, a process that became known as the SPOILS SYSTEM. He pursued a policy of moving Indians westward with the INDIAN REMOVAL ACTS. He split with his vice president, JOHN C. CALHOUN, over the NULLIFICATION movement. His reelec-

Andrew Jackson, detail of an oil painting by John Wesley Jarvis, c. 1819; in the Metropolitan Museum of Art, New York City.

BY COURTESY OF THE METROPOLITAN MUSEUM OF ART, NEW YORK CITY, HARRIS BRISBANE DICK FUND, 1964

tion in 1832 was due in part to support for his anticapitalistic fiscal policies and a controversial veto that affected the BANK OF THE U.S. (see BANK WAR). His popularity continued to build throughout his presidency. During his tenure a strong DEMOCRATIC PARTY developed that led to a vigorous two-party system.

Jackson, Charles Thomas (1805–1880) U.S. physician, chemist, geologist, and mineralogist. Born in Plymouth, Mass., he graduated from Harvard Medical School in 1829. Known for his tendency to contention and litigiousness, he took credit for the first demonstration of surgical anesthesia with ether by a dental surgeon he had advised on it, and claimed to have told SAMUEL F. B. MORSE the basic principles of the telegraph. His worked many years as a geologist for the U.S. Geological Survey.

Jackson, Glenda (born 1936) British stage and film actress. Discovered by PETER BROOK, she was cast in his theater-of-CRUELTY revue, and soon appeared as the mad Charlotte Corday in his celebrated production of PETER WEISS's *Marat/Sade* (1964; film, 1967). She became known for her tense portrayals of complex women, gaining international acclaim in the film *Women in Love* (1969, Academy Award) and such later successes as *Sunday Bloody Sunday* (1971), *A Touch of Class* (1973, Academy Award), and the television series *Elizabeth R*. Her screen career continued until 1992, when she won a seat in the House of Commons.

Jackson, Jesse (Louis) *orig.* **Jesse Louis Burns** (born 1941) U.S. civil-rights leader. Born in Greenville, S.C., he took his adoptive father's name. He became involved with the CIVIL RIGHTS MOVEMENT as a college student. In 1965 he went to Selma, Ala., to march with MARTIN LUTHER KING, then worked for the SOUTHERN CHRISTIAN LEADERSHIP CONFERENCE (SCLC). In 1966 he helped found the Chicago branch of Operation Breadbasket, the SCLC's economic arm, and was its national director 1967–71. He was ordained a Baptist minister in 1968. In 1971 he founded Operation PUSH. A leading spokesman and advocate for blacks, he led a 1983 voter-registration drive in Chicago that helped elect the city's first black mayor, HAROLD WASHINGTON. Jackson became the first black man to run for president by entering the Democratic primaries in 1984 and 1988; he won 6.7 million votes in 1988. In 1989 he moved to Washington, D.C., and was elected the city's unpaid "statehood senator" to lobby Congress for statehood.

Jesse Jackson, 1988.
© DENNIS BRACK/BLACK STAR

Jackson, Joe *orig.* **Joseph Jefferson** *known as* **Shoeless Joe Jackson** (1889–1951) U.S. baseball player. Born in Pickens Co., S.C., he started his career in 1908 and became an outfielder with the Chicago White Sox. An outstanding hitter, he achieved the third-highest career batting average in baseball history. He was involved in the BLACK SOX SCANDAL; though acquitted in 1921, he was banned from baseball for life by KENESAW MOUNTAIN LANDIS.

Jackson, John Hughlings (1835–1911) British neurologist. He showed that most right-handed persons with aphasia had disease on the left side of the brain, confirming PAUL BROCA's findings. In 1863 he discovered Jacksonian epilepsy (spasms progressing through the body), tracing it to motor region damage. Electroencephalography has confirmed his 1873 definition of epilepsy as "a sudden, excessive, and rapid discharge" of electricity by brain cells.

Jackson, Mahalia (1911–1972) U.S. gospel singer. As a child, Jackson sang in the choir of the New Orleans church where her father preached. She learned sacred songs but was also exposed to blues recordings by BESSIE SMITH and Ida Cox. In Chicago she worked at odd jobs while singing with a touring gospel quintet, and opened several small businesses. Her warm, powerful voice first came to wide public attention in the 1930s, when she participated in a cross-country tour singing such songs as "He's Got the Whole World in His Hands." Closely associated with THOMAS DORSEY, she sang many of his songs. "Move on up a Little Higher" (1948) sold over a million copies, and she became one of the best-selling singers of the 1950s and '60s. She first appeared at Carnegie Hall in 1950. Active in the civil-rights movement from 1955, she sang at the epochal 1963 civil-rights march on Washington. See also GOSPEL MUSIC.

Mahalia Jackson, 1961.
THE BETTMANN ARCHIVE

Jackson, Michael (Joseph) (born 1958) U.S. singer and songwriter. Born in Gary, Ind., the 9-year-old Jackson became the lead singer of The Jackson Five, a family group formed by his father. Their hits on the MOTOWN label included "I Want You Back" and "ABC." They played on their own TV series in the 1970s and were also the subject of a cartoon series. Though Michael remained a member of the Jacksons until 1984, he began recording under his own name in 1971. His album *Off the Wall* (1979) sold millions throughout the world. His next album, *Thriller* (1982), sold more than 40 million copies, more than any other album in history. He outbid PAUL MCCARTNEY and Yoko Ono for publishing rights to more than 250 songs composed by McCartney and JOHN LENNON. He later released the albums *Bad* (1987), *Dangerous* (1991), and *HIStory* (1995). A child-molestation lawsuit was dropped in 1994 when he settled with the parents of a 14-year-old boy. Several of his siblings, notably his sister Janet (born 1966), have also enjoyed solo success.

Jackson, Reggie *orig.* **Reginald Martinez** (born 1946) U.S. baseball player. Born in Wyncote, Pa., he excelled in track, football, and baseball in high school. In the major leagues, batting left-handed and playing outfield, he helped three teams (Oakland Athletics, 1968–75; New York Yankees, 1976–81; California Angels, 1982–87) win five World Series, six pennant races, and 10 divisional play-offs. Noted for his home-run hitting, he was nicknamed "Mr. October" for his reliable prowess in play-off and World Series games. He hit a career total of 563 home runs, placing him sixth-highest of all time.

Jackson, Robert H(oughwout) (1892–1954) U.S. jurist. Born in Spring Creek, Pa., he pleaded his first case while still a minor and was a lawyer by age 21. He became corporation counsel for Jamestown, N.Y. As general counsel for the U.S. Bureau of Internal Revenue (1934), he successfully prosecuted ANDREW W. MELLON for income-tax evasion. He served as U.S. solicitor general (1938–39), and attorney general (1940–41). In 1941 he was appointed by Pres. FRANKLIN ROOSEVELT to the U.S. Supreme Court, where he served until 1954. He infused his well-worded opinions with a blend of liberalism and nationalism. In 1945–46 he served as chief U.S. prosecutor in the NUREMBERG TRIALS.

Jackson, Shirley (Hardie) (1916–1965) U.S. novelist and short-story writer. Born in San Francisco, she is best known for her story "The Lottery" (1948), a chilling tale that provoked outrage when first published, and *The Haunting of Hill House* (1959; films, 1963, 1999). These and her other five novels, including *We Have Always Lived in the Castle* (1962), confirmed her reputation as a master of gothic horror and psychological suspense.

Jackson, Stonewall *orig.* **Thomas Jonathan** (1824–1863) U.S. and Confederate army officer. Born in Clarksburg, Va., he had little education but secured an appointment to West Point. He served with distinction in the Mexican War. At the start of the Civil War, he organized Virginia volunteers into an effective brigade. At the first Battle of BULL RUN he stationed his brigade in a strong line and withstood a Union assault, earning the nickname "Stonewall" and promotion to major general. In 1862 he won campaigns in the Shenandoah Valley and later in the Seven Days' Battles. ROBERT E. LEE used Jackson's troops to encircle the Union forces to win the second Battle of Bull Run, and Jackson assisted Lee at Antietam and Fredericksburg. In April 1863 he moved his troops around the flank of the Union army at CHANCELLORSVILLE, but was accidentally shot and mortally wounded by his own men.

Jackson, William Henry (1843–1942) U.S. photographer. Born in Keesville, N.Y., he worked as a boy for a photographic studio in Troy, N.Y. After the Civil War he went west and opened a studio in Omaha. He was the official photographer for the U.S. Geological and Geographical Survey of the Territories (1870–78), and his photographs were instrumental in the establishment of three national parks: YELLOWSTONE, GRAND TETON, and MESA VERDE.

Jacksonville City (pop., 1996 est.: 680,000), northeastern Florida. It is the site of Florida's first European (French Huguenot) settlement there in 1564. Named for ANDREW JACKSON, it was laid out in 1822 and incorporated in 1832. It was largely destroyed by fire in 1901. In 1968 it was consolidated with most of Duval Co.; it covers 841 sq mi (2,178 sq km), making it one of the largest U.S. cities in terms of land area. A deepwater port with major shipyards, it is Florida's chief transportation and commercial center. It is the site of Jacksonville Univ., University of North Florida, and Jones College.

Jacob Hebrew PATRIARCH, son of Isaac and grandson of ABRAHAM, and the traditional ancestor of the people of Israel. His story is told in the Book of GENESIS. The younger twin brother of Esau, he used trickery to gain Isaac's blessing and Esau's birthright. On a journey to CANAAN he wrestled all night with an angel, who blessed him and gave him the name Israel. Jacob had 13 children, 10 of whom founded tribes of ISRAEL. His favorite son, JOSEPH, was sold into slavery in Egypt by his brothers, but the family was later reunited when a famine forced the brothers to go to Egypt to seek grain.

Jacob \zhȧ-'kȯb\, **François** (born 1920) French biologist. After receiving his doctorate he went to work at the Pasteur Institute in Paris. Beginning in 1958, he worked with JACQUES MONOD studying the regulation of bacterial enzyme synthesis. They discovered regulator genes, so called because they control the activities of other genes. Jacob and Monod also proposed the existence of an RNA messenger, a partial copy of DNA that carries genetic information to other parts of the cell. The two men shared a 1965 Nobel Prize with André Lwoff.

Jacob ben Asher (1269?–1340?) Jewish legal scholar. Probably born in Cologne, he emigrated to Spain with his family in 1303, and his father became chief rabbi in Toledo. Jacob is believed to have made his living as a moneylender. He divided Jewish law into categories by subject, producing a codification known as *Tur,* which became a popular Jewish theological work of the 15th century. The basis for many rabbinic decisions, it was considered standard until superseded by the work of JOSEPH BEN EPHRAIM KARO in the 16th century.

Jacobean age \ˌja-kə-'bē-ən\ Period in the visual and literary arts during the reign of JAMES I (Latin, *Jacobus*) of England (r.1603–25). Jacobean architecture combines motifs from the late Gothic period with classical details and Tudor pointed arches and interior paneling. Jacobean furniture, made of oak, featured heavy forms and bulbous legs. INIGO JONES, following the theories and works of ANDREA PALLADIO, introduced the classical style of Renaissance architecture into England. Most Jacobean portraitists and sculptors were foreign-born or foreign-influenced, and their efforts faded when such Flemish painters as PETER PAUL RUBENS and ANTHONY VAN DYCK worked in England for James's successor, CHARLES I. See also JACOBEAN LITERATURE.

Jacobean literature \ˌja-kə-'bē-ən\ Body of works written during the reign of JAMES I of England (1603–25). The successor to ELIZABETHAN LITERATURE, Jacobean literature was often dark in its questioning of the stability of the social order; some of WILLIAM SHAKESPEARE's greatest tragedies may date from the beginning of the period, and other dramatists, including JOHN WEBSTER, were often preoccupied with the problem of evil. The era's comedy included the acid satire of BEN JONSON and the varied works of FRANCIS BEAUMONT and John Fletcher. Jacobean poetry included the graceful verse of Jonson and the CAVALIER POETS, but also the intellectual complexity of the METAPHYSICAL POETRY of JOHN DONNE and others. In prose, writers such as FRANCIS BACON and ROBERT BURTON showed a new toughness and flexibility of style. The era's monumental prose achievement was the King James Version of the Bible (1611).

Jacobin Club \'ja-kə-bən\ *or* **Jacobins** Political group of the FRENCH REVOLUTION identified with extreme radicalism and violence. Formed in 1789 as the Society of the Friends of the Constitution, it was known as the Jacobin Club because it met in a former convent of the Dominicans (known in Paris as Jacobins). It was originally formed by deputies of the National Assembly to protect the Revolution's gains against a possible aristocratic reaction. Though it did not have a direct role in overthrowing the monarchy in 1792, the club later changed its name to Society of the Jacobins, Friends of Liberty and Equality. It admitted leftist MONTAGNARD deputies of the NATIONAL CONVENTION and agitated for the king's execution and the overthrow of the GIRONDINS. In 1793, with about 8,000 clubs and 500,000 members, the Jacobins became instruments of the REIGN OF TERROR. The Parisian club supported MAXIMILIEN ROBESPIERRE, but it closed after his fall in 1794. Though officially banned, some local clubs lasted until 1800.

Jacobite In British history, a supporter of the exiled Stuart king JAMES II (Latin, *Jacobus*) and his descendants after the GLORIOUS REVOLUTION of 1688. The movement was strong in Scotland, Wales, and Ireland and included Catholics and Anglican Tories. The Jacobites, especially under WILLIAM III and Queen ANNE, could offer a feasible alternative title to the crown, and several attempts were made to restore the Stuarts. In 1689 James II landed in Ireland, but his army was defeated at the Battle of the BOYNE. In the Fifteen Rebellion (1715), led by John Erskine, 6th earl of Mar (1675–1732), Jacobites tried to seize the crown for JAMES EDWARD STUART, the Old Pretender. In the Forty-five Rebellion (1745) CHARLES EDWARD STUART, the Young Pretender, took Scotland, but the Jacobite army was crushed at the Battle of CULLODEN (1746).

Jacobs, Helen Hull (1908–1997) U.S. tennis player.Jacobs was the national junior tennis champion in 1924–25. She was first defeated by HELEN WILLS, who would prove to be her longtime rival, in the 1928 finals at Forest Hills, N.Y. Though Wills was virtually always victorious, Jacobs was a popular favourite. Her only victory over Wills came by default. Though often in Wills's shadow, Jacobs won four U.S. Open singles (1932–35), three doubles (1932 and 1934–35), and mixed doubles (1934) championships. She was ranked in the world's top 10 from 1928 to 1940. In 1933 she became the first woman to break with tradition by wearing man-tailored shorts at Wimbledon. Her autobiography, *Beyond the Game*, appeared in 1936.

Jacobs, Jane *orig.* **Jane Butzner** (born 1916) U.S.-Canadian urbanologist. Born in Scranton, Pa., she became active in urban community work while living in New York City with her architect husband. For 10 years she was an editor at *Architectural Forum.* Her highly influential *Death and Life of Great American Cities* (1961) is a brash, passionate, and highly original reinterpretation of the multiple needs of modern urban places. *The Economy of Cities* (1969) discussed the importance of diversity to a city's prospects. Later works include *Cities and the Wealth of Nations* (1984) and *Edge of Empire* (1996). See also URBAN PLANNING.

Jacopo da Pontormo See Jacopo da PONTORMO

Jacopo della Quercia \'yä-kō-pō-dāl-lä-'kwer-chä\ *orig.* **Jacopo di Piero di Angelo** (c. 1374–1438) Italian sculptor active in Siena. He was the son of a goldsmith and wood carver. His earliest major work is the tomb of Ilaria del Carretto in Lucca Cathedral (c. 1406–8). His most important commission for Siena was the fountain known as Fonte Gaia (1408–19) in the Piazza del Campo. He worked with DONATELLO and LORENZO GHIBERTI on reliefs for the baptismal font in the Baptistery in Siena (1417–30). His last and greatest work was the sculptural reliefs around the portal of San Petronio in Bologna (1425–30). In 1435 he was appointed supervising architect of Siena Cathedral. He elevated Sienese sculpture to a place of prominence and influenced subsequent Sienese painters. The greatest non-Florentine sculptor of the 15th century, he was a major influence on the young MICHELANGELO.

Jacquard \zha-'kär, *Engl* 'ja-ˌkärd\, **Joseph-Marie** (1752–1834) French inventor. In 1801 he demonstrated an automatic loom incorporating revolutionary new technology; it was declared public property in 1806, and Jacquard was rewarded with a pension and a royalty on each machine. His loom utilized interchangeable punched cards that controlled the weaving of the cloth so that any desired pattern could be obtained automatically. The Jacquard loom's technology became the basis of the modern automatic loom and a precursor of the modern computer. His punched cards were adapted by CHARLES BABBAGE as in input-output medium for his proposed analytical engine and by HERMAN HOLLERITH to feed data to his census machine, and punched cards were used for inputting data into early digital computers.

Jacquard loom \'ja-ˌkärd\ LOOM incorporating a special device to control individual warp YARNS. It enabled production of fabrics with intricate

H I J K

woven patterns such as TAPESTRY, BROCADE, and damask, and has also been adapted to the production of patterned knitted fabrics. Developed in France by J.-M. JACQUARD in 1804–5, it used interchangeable punched cards that controlled the weaving of the cloth so that any desired pattern could be obtained automatically. It aroused bitter hostility among weavers, who feared that its labor-saving capabilities would deprive them of jobs; the weavers of Lyon not only burned the machines but attacked Jacquard as well. Eventually the loom's advantages led to its general acceptance, and by 1812 there were 11,000 in use in France. Use of the loom spread to England in the 1820s, and from there virtually worldwide.

Jacuí River \zhá-ˈkwē\ River, southern Brazil. It rises in the hills east of Passo Fundo and flows southward and eastward for 280 mi (450 km). At Pôrto Alegre it receives four other rivers and forms the Guaíba River, a shallow estuary that empties on the Atlantic coast. Navigable as far upstream as Cachoeira do Sul, it has one of the most heavily used river barge systems in Brazil.

jade Either of two tough, compact, typically green gemstones that take a high polish. Both have been carved into jewelry, ornaments, small sculptures, and utilitarian objects from earliest recorded times. The more highly prized of the two jadestones is JADEITE; the other is NEPHRITE. Both types may be white or colorless, but colors such as red, green, and gray may occur.

Dragon among clouds, carved jade medallion or button, Ch'ing dynasty, probably late 18th century (reign of Ch'ien-lung); in the Victoria and Albert Museum, London.

BY COURTESY OF THE BOARD OF TRUSTEES OF THE VICTORIA AND ALBERT MUSEUM, LONDON, WELLS LEGACY

jadeite \ˈjād-ˌīt\ Gem-quality SILICATE MINERAL in the PYROXENE family that is one of the two forms of JADE. Jadeite (imperial jade), sodium aluminum silicate ($NaAlSi_2O_6$), may contain impurities that give it a variety of colors: white, green, red, brown, and blue. The most highly prized variety is emerald green. Jadeite occurs only in metamorphic rocks, most often in those that have been subjected to the high pressures deep below the earth's surface. The area around the city of Mogaung in northern Myanmar has long been the main source of gem-quality jadeite.

Uncut (left) and cut jadeite.

RUNK/SCHOENBERGER–GRANT HEILMAN

jaeger \ˈyā-gər\ Any of three species (genus *Stercorarius,* family Stercorariidae) of seabirds resembling dark GULLS with a forward-set black cap and projecting central tail feathers. Jaegers have two color phases: all brown, or (more commonly) brown above and white below. They nest in the Arctic tundra and then go to sea, many as far as Australia and New Zealand. At sea they catch fish on their own, but while nesting along coasts they force TERNS and KITTIWAKES to disgorge their food, destroy the eggs and young of other seabirds, and capture land birds and rodents. The species range from 14 to 20 in. (35–50 cm) long. In Britain, jaegers are called SKUAS.

Long-tailed jaeger (*Stercorarius longicaudus*).

© ALAN WILLIAMS/NHPA

Jafar ibn Muhammad \ˈjä-fär-ˌi-bən-mu̇-ˈhá-məd\ (c. 700–765) Sixth IMAM of the Shiite branch of Islam and the last to be recognized by all the Shiite sects. He was the great-grandson of ALI. As a possible claimant to the caliphate, Jafar was viewed as a threat to both the UMAYYAD and ABBASID dynasties. He traveled to Baghdad in 762 to prove to the caliph that he was not seeking power, then returned to his native Medina, where his pupils included ABU HANIFAH. After his death the Shiites began to splinter. One sect, the ISMAILIS, became followers of his son, Ismail. Another, the ITHNA ASHARIYA, traced a succession from Jafar to the twelfth imam awaited at the Last Judgment.

Jaffa See TEL AVIV–JAFFA

Jagannatha \ˈjə-gə-ˌnät-ə\ *or* **Jagannath** Form under which KRISHNA is worshiped at Puri, Orissa, a famous religious center of India. His temple at Puri dates from the 12th century. The Rathayatra, or Chariot Festival, is held in his honor each year in June or July. An image of the god is placed on a cart so heavy that it takes thousands of devotees several days to move it to the god's temple outside the city. According to legend, pilgrims sometimes throw themselves under the wagon in hopes of attaining instant salvation, a practice that gave rise to the English word juggernaut.

Jagiello I See WLADISLAW II JAGIELLO

Jagiellon dynasty \yäg-ˈye-lōn\ Family of monarchs of Poland-Lithuania, Bohemia, and Hungary that became one of the most powerful in E-central Europe in the 15th–16th century. It was founded by Jogaila, grand duke of Lithuania, who became WLADYSLAW II JAGIELLO of Poland after marriage to Queen Jadwiga (1373?–1399) in 1386. Wladyslaw III (1424–1444) extended the dynasty by also assuming the throne of Hungary (1440). He was succeeded by CASIMIR IV, who placed his son on the thrones of Bohemia (1471) and Hungary. During the reigns of Casimir's sons John Albert (1459–1501) and Alexander (1461–1506), the Jagiellon rulers lost much of their power in Poland to the nobility. When SIGISMUND I succeeded Alexander in 1506, he strengthened the government and saw the TEUTONIC ORDER convert its lands into the secular Duchy of Prussia (1525), a Polish fief. In 1526 the death of Louis II ended Jagiellon rule in Bohemia and Hungary. In 1561 SIGISMUND II AUGUSTUS incorporated Livonia into Poland, but when he died, leaving no heirs, the Jagiellon dynasty ended (1572).

jagirdar system \jə-ˈgir-ˌdär\ Form of land tenancy introduced in India by the early sultans of Delhi in the early 13th century, in which land, its revenues, and the power to govern it was assigned to an official of the state. The land reverted to the government on the official's death, but heirs could renew the land assignment by paying a fee. Feudalistic in character, the jagirdar system tended to enfeeble the central government by setting up quasi-independent baronies. Periodically abolished, it was always renewed. After Indian independence, measures were taken to abolish absentee landownership.

jaguar Largest New World CAT. Once found in wooded regions from the U.S.-Mexican border south to Patagonia, the jaguar *(Panthera onca)* survives, in reduced numbers, only in remote areas of Central and South America; the largest known population is in the Amazon rain forest. The male is 5.5–9 ft (1.7–2.7 m), including the 23–35-in. (60–90-cm) tail, and weighs 220–350 lbs (100–160 kg). The coat is typically orange-tan with black spots arranged in rosettes with a black spot in the center. A solitary predator, the jaguar usually hunts rodents, deer, birds, and fish; it will also take cattle, horses, and dogs.

Jaguaribe River \ˌzhá-gwá-ˈrē-bē\ River, northeastern Brazil. Formed by the junction of the Carapateiro and Trici rivers, it flows northeastward for 350 mi (560 km) to enter the Atlantic Ocean at Aracati. Long periods of drought, during which much of the river is dry, are followed by catastrophic floods that inundate the towns along its lower course.

Jahangir *or* **Jehangir** \jə-ˈhän-gēr\ (1569–1627) Mughal emperor of India (1605–27). Though designated heir apparent, the impatient Jahangir revolted in 1599; his father, AKBAR, nevertheless confirmed him as his successor. Like Akbar, Jahangir managed diplomatic relations on the Indian subcontinent adroitly, was tolerant of non-Muslims, and was a great patron of the arts. He encouraged Persian culture in Mughal India. During the middle portion of his reign, politics were dominated by his Persian wife (Nur Jahan), her father, and Jahangir's son Prince Khurram (the future SHAH JAHAN).

Jahn \ˈyän\, **Friedrich Ludwig** (1778–1852) German educator who founded the Turnverein (gymnastic club) movement in Germany. As a teacher in Berlin from 1809, he began a program of outdoor exercise for students. He invented the parallel bars, rings, balance beam, horse, and horizontal bar, all of which have become standard equipment for GYMNASTICS. In 1819 he came under suspicion for his fervent nationalism and strong influence on youth. He was arrested and imprisoned for almost a year; his gymnastic club closed, and a national ban was placed on gymnastics (lifted in 1842).

jahrzeit See YAHRZEIT

jai alai \'hī-,lī, ,hī-ə-'lī\ (Basque: "merry festival") Court game resembling HANDBALL, played between two or four players with a ball, and a hurling device, a long, curved wicker basket, strapped to the wrist. Of BASQUE origin, it developed from PELOTA and was given its present name when it was imported to Cuba in 1900. The hurling device, called a cesta, permits the ball to reach speeds up to 150 mph (240 kph). The court, 53.3 m (58.3 yards) long, is three-walled; the object is to bounce the ball off the front wall with such speed and English (spin) as to defeat an opponent's attempt to return it. PARI-MUTUEL betting is permitted in the U.S.

Jaina vrata \'jī-nə-'vrə-tə\ In JAINISM, any of the vows taken by monks, nuns, and lay members. The first five are the *mahavratas*, or "great vows": nonviolence, truthfulness, not stealing, sexual purity, and renunciation of possessions. These are interpreted more moderately for lay members than for monks; for example, lay members need only remain sexually faithful to their spouses, while monks must practice celibacy. The remaining vows are designed to help in keeping the first five. The final vow is the promise to die in meditation during self-starvation when observance of the other vows is no longer possible.

Jainism \'jī-,ni-zəm\ Religion of India established in the 6th century BC by Vardhamana, who was called MAHAVIRA. Jainism's core belief is AHIMSA, or noninjury to all living things. It was founded as a reaction against the VEDIC RELIGION, which required animal sacrifices. Jainism has no belief in a creator god, though there are a number of lesser deities for various aspects of life. Jains believe their religion is eternal and hold that it was revealed in stages by a number of Conquerors, of whom Mahavira was the 24th. Living as an ascetic, Mahavira preached the need for rigorous penance and self-denial as the means of perfecting human nature, escaping the cycle of rebirth, and attaining MOKSHA, or liberation. Jains view KARMA as an invisible material substance that interferes with liberation and can only be dissolved through asceticism. By the end of the 1st century AD the Jains had split into two sects, each of which later developed its own canon of sacred writings: the Digambaras, who held that an adherent should own nothing, not even clothes, and that women must be reborn as men before they can attain moksha; and the more moderate Svetambaras. In keeping with their principle of reverence for life, Jains are known for their charitable works, including building shelters for animals. Jainism preaches universal tolerance and does not seek to make converts.

Jaipur \'jī-,pu̇r\ Capital (pop., 2001 prelim.: 2,324,319) of RAJASTHAN state, northwestern India. A walled town surrounded by hills (except to the south), it was founded in 1727 by Maharaja Sawai Jai Singh to replace Amber as the capital of the princely state of Jaipur. The city, known for its beauty, is unique in its straight-line planning; its buildings are mostly rose-colored, and it is sometimes called the "pink city." It is a popular tourist destination; its historic structures include the city palace, the Hall of Winds, Ram Bagh palace, and Nahargarh, or Tiger Fort.

Jakarta *formerly (1949–72)* **Djakarta** \jə-'kär-tə\ Capital (pop., 1999 est.: 9,604,900) and largest city of Indonesia. Located on the northwestern coast of JAVA, it was founded in 1527 after the sultan of BANTAM defeated the Portuguese on the site. The Dutch took control in 1619, renaming it Batavia and establishing it as the headquarters of the Dutch EAST INDIA CO. In 1949 the city was renamed and made Indonesia's capital. A major trade, industrial, and financial center, it is also the seat of several universities.

Jakobson \'yä-kəb-sən\, **Roman (Osipovich)** (1896–1982) Russian-U.S. linguist. Born and educated in Moscow, Jakobson moved to Prague in 1920; the European political situation forced him to flee to Scandinavia in 1938, and to the U.S. in 1941. He taught at Harvard University 1949–67. His interests ranged from folk epics and the cultural history of the Slavs to general PHONOLOGY, the MORPHOLOGY of the Slavic languages, and speech acquisition. His preoccupation with contrast and opposition is reflected in his analysis of the Russian case system (1938), a brilliant analysis of the Russian verbal system (1948), and preeminently in his work on distinctive features in phonology.

Jalal ad-Din ar-Rumi See Jalal ad-Din ar-RUMI

Jalapa (Enríquez) \hä-'lä-pä\ City (pop., 2000 est.: 375,000), capital of VERACRUZ state, eastern central Mexico. It is located in the SIERRA MADRE Oriental, at 4,681 ft (1,427 m) above sea level. A market city for locally grown coffee and tobacco, it was famous in colonial days for its annual fair, held to dispose of the goods brought from CÁDIZ by the returning Spanish silver fleet. The massive Spanish-Moorish architecture of the city is reminiscent of viceregal days.

Jalisco \hä-'lēs-kō\ State (pop., 2000: 6,322,002), western central Mexico. It has an area of 31,211 sq mi (80,836 sq km); its capital is GUADALAJARA. The SIERRA MADRE Occidental mountain range traverses the state, separating the Pacific coast from a high plateau region. The Sierra region is largely volcanic, and earthquakes are frequent. The state's many lakes include CHAPALA, Mexico's largest. First invaded by Spaniards in 1526, Jalisco was incorporated into Nueva Galicia. In 1889 its area was much reduced by the separation of the territory of Tepic (now NAYARIT state) from its coastal zone. Its economy is based on agriculture, livestock-raising, forest products, and mining.

jam See JELLY AND JAM

Jamaica Island nation, West Indies. Located south of Cuba, it is 146 mi (235 km) long and 35 mi (56 km) wide, the third largest island in the Caribbean. Area: 4,244 sq mi (10,991 sq km). Population (2001 est.): 2,624,000. Capital: KINGSTON. The population consists mostly of descendents of African slaves. Languages: English (official), CREOLE. Religions: Christianity; spiritual sects, RASTAFARIAN. Currency: Jamaica dollar. Jamaica has three major regions: the coastal lowlands, which encircle the island and are heavily cultivated; a limestone plateau, which covers half the island; and the interior highlands, with forested mountain ranges, including the BLUE MTNS. Agriculture employs one-fourth of the workforce,

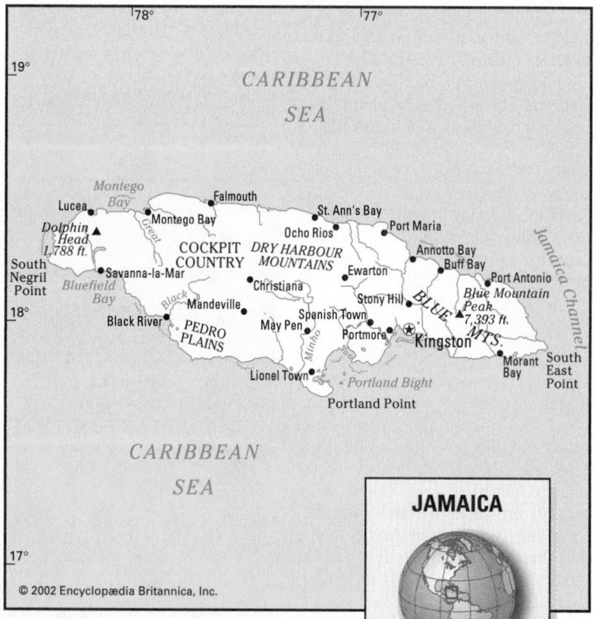

and the major agricultural export is raw sugar, with molasses and rum as by-products. Industry focuses on the production of bauxite and alumina, and on the garment industry. Tourism is very important, and half of the population is employed in services. It is a constitutional monarchy with two legislative houses. Its chief of state is the British monarch, represented by the governor-general, and its head of government is the prime minister. The island was settled by Arawak Indians c. AD 600. It was sighted by CHRISTOPHER COLUMBUS in 1494; Spain colonized it in the early 16th century but neglected it because it lacked gold reserves. Britain gained control in 1655, and by the end of the 18th century it had become a prized colonial possession due to the volume of sugar produced by slave laborers. Slavery was abolished in the late 1830s, and the plantation system collapsed. Jamaica gained full internal self-government in 1959 and became an independent country within the British COMMONWEALTH in 1962. In the late 20th century, the government, led by MICHAEL MANLEY, nationalized many businesses.

Jamaica Bay Inlet of the Atlantic Ocean. It occupies about 20 sq mi (50 sq km) along the southwestern shore of LONG ISLAND, in southeastern New York. Part of the Port of New York, it is sheltered on the south by Rockaway Peninsula, and connects with the ocean through Rockaway Inlet. Near the entrance channel is CONEY ISLAND. On the northeastern shore, at Idlewild, is the John F. Kennedy International Airport.

Jamal al-Din al-Afghani \jə-'mäl-äl-'dēn-äl-af-'gá-nē\ (1838–1897) Muslim politician and journalist. He is thought to have adopted the name Afghani to conceal the fact that he was of Persian Shiite origin. He lived in Afghanistan from 1866, and a year later he became counselor to the khan. Displaced after a change of rulers, he went to Istanbul and then to Cairo in 1871. After becoming known as a rabble-rouser and heretic, he was deported from Egypt in 1879. By 1883 he was in Paris, where he championed Islamic civilization in the face of European domination. In Russia (1887–89) he seems to have worked as an anti-British agitator. His next stop was Iran, from which he was deported as a heretic in 1892; four years later he avenged himself by instigating the shah's murder. He died in Istanbul after failing to interest the sultan in his pan-Islamic ideas.

James, C(yril) L(ionel) R(obert) (1901–1989) Trinidadian writer and political activist. As a young man he moved to Britain, where his first work, *The Life of Captain Cipriani,* was published in 1929. His study of TOUSSAINT-LOUVERTURE, *The Black Jacobins* (1938), was a seminal work. During his first stay in the U.S. (1938–53), he became friends with P. ROBESON. Eventually deported to Britain because of his Marxism and labor activism, James wrote on cricket for the *Guardian.* His *Beyond the Boundary* (1963) mixes autobiography with commentary on politics and sports. He returned to the U.S. in 1970 but eventually settled permanently in Britain.

James, Harry (Haag) (1916–1983) U.S. trumpeter and leader of one of the most popular big bands of the SWING era. Born in Albany, Ga., he joined BENNY GOODMAN's band in 1937, becoming one of its principal soloists before forming his own group in late 1938. The band achieved commercial success through recordings featuring F. SINATRA, virtuoso set pieces, and ballads performed with James's trademark wide vibrato. He married actress BETTY GRABLE in 1943 and appeared in several films. An accomplished and technically brilliant improviser, his music from the late 1940s reflected his renewed interest in jazz, and he continued to perform with his band for over 40 years.

James, Henry (1843–1916) U.S.-British novelist. Born in New York City to a distinguished family, the brother of WILLIAM JAMES, he was privately educated. He traveled frequently to Europe from childhood on; after 1876 he lived primarily in England. His fundamental theme was to be the innocence and exuberance of the New World in conflict with the corruption and wisdom of the Old. *Daisy Miller* (1879) won him international renown; it was followed by *The Europeans* (1879), *Washington Square* (1880), and *The Portrait of a Lady* (1881). In *The Bostonians* (1886) and *The Princess Casamassima* (1886), his subjects were social reformers and revolutionaries. In *The Spoils of Poynton* (1897), *What Maisie Knew* (1897), and *The Turn of the Screw* (1898), he made use of complex moral and psychological ambiguity. *The Wings of the Dove* (1902), *The Ambassadors* (1903), and *The Golden Bowl* (1904) were his great final novels. His intense concern with the novel as an art form is reflected in the essay *The Art of Fiction* (1884), his prefaces to the volumes of his collected works, and his many literary essays. Perhaps his chief technical innovation was his strong focus on the individual consciousness of his central characters, which reflected his sense of the decline of public and collective values in his time.

Henry James, 1905.

SMITH COLLEGE ARCHIVES/PHOTOGRAPH BY KATHERINE E. MCCLELLAN

James, Jesse (Woodson) (1847–1882) U.S. outlaw. Born near Centerville (now Kearny), Mo., Jesse and his brother Frank (1843–1915) were Confederate guerrillas during the Civil War. In 1866 they assembled a gang to rob banks, and they soon took up robbing trains and stagecoaches as well. In 1876 Jesse led a failed attempt on a bank in Northfield, Minn.; the brothers escaped, but the rest of the gang was killed or captured. In 1881 Missouri's governor offered a $10,000 reward for their capture, and in 1882 Jesse was shot in the back of the head by a member of his gang while adjusting a picture on the wall in his home. Frank was subsequently tried and acquitted three times and retired quietly to the family farm. The exploits of the James brothers were romanticized by pulp-fiction writers and in movies.

James, St. *or* **James the Great** (died c. AD 44) One of the 12 APOSTLES of JESUS. He and his brother John (see St. JOHN THE APOSTLE) were fishermen on the Sea of Galilee and were among the first disciples to be called. As a member of the inner circle of disciples, he witnessed the major events in the ministry of Jesus, including the Transfiguration and the agony in the Garden of GETHSEMANE. He was beheaded in AD 44 by order of Herod Agrippa. By tradition, his body was taken to SANTIAGO DE COMPOSTELA, Spain, where his shrine has long been a place of pilgrimage.

James, William (1842–1910) U.S. philosopher and psychologist. Son of the philosophical writer Henry James (1811–1882) and brother of HENRY JAMES, he was born in New York City and studied medicine at Harvard, where he taught from 1872. His first major work, *The Principles of Psychology* (1890), treated thinking and knowledge as instruments in the struggle to live. His most famous work is *The Varieties of Religious Experience* (1902). In *Pragmatism* (1907), he generalized the PRAGMATISM of CHARLES SANDERS PEIRCE by asserting that the meaning of any idea must be analyzed in terms of the succession of experiential consequences it leads to; that truth and error depend solely on these consequences. He applied pragmatism to the analysis of change and chance, freedom, variety, PLURALISM, and novelty. Pragmatism was also the basis for his polemic against MONISM, the "block universe," the idealistic doctrine of internal relations, and all views that presented reality as a static whole. He was also a leader of the psychological movement of FUNCTIONALISM.

William James.

BY COURTESY OF THE HARVARD UNIVERSITY NEWS SERVICE

James I *Spanish* **Jaime** *known as* **James the Conqueror** (1208–1276) King of ARAGON and CATALONIA (1214–76). The most renowned of the medieval kings of Aragon, he was educated by the Knights TEMPLAR, and his great-uncle ruled as regent until 1218. James helped to subdue rebellious nobles and took over the government of his kingdoms in 1227. He reconquered the Balearic Islands (1229–35) and Valencia (1233–38) but renounced his claims to lands in southern France. He also helped ALFONSO X to suppress a Moorish rebellion in Murcia (1266), and he undertook an unsuccessful crusade to the Holy Land (1269).

James I (1566–1625) King of Scotland, as James VI (1567–1625), and first Stuart king of England (1603–25). Son of MARY, QUEEN OF SCOTS, and Lord DARNLEY, at age 1 James succeeded his mother to the Scottish throne. Controlled by a succession of regents, he became the puppet of contending intriguers—both Roman Catholics, who sought to bring his mother back to the throne, and Protestants. In 1583 he began to pursue his own policies as king, allying himself with England. He succeeded to the English throne on the death of ELIZABETH I, as great-great-grandson of HENRY VII. He quickly achieved peace and prosperity by ending England's war with Spain (1604). He presided over the Hampton Court Conference (1604), rejecting most of the Puritans' demands for reform of the Church of England but permitting preparation of a new translation of the Bible, the King James Version. His policies toward Catholics led to the Gunpowder Plot. His growing belief in royal absolutism and his conflicts with an increasingly self-assertive Parliament led to his dissolution of Parliament from 1611 to 1621. With the death of Robert Cecil, he came under the influence of incompetent favorites.

James I (1394–1437) King of the Scots (1406–37). The son and heir of Robert III, he was captured by the English in 1406 and held prisoner in London until 1424. During the 13 years in which he truly ruled Scotland (1424–37), he established the first strong monarchy the Scots had known in nearly a century. He weakened the nobility but did not entirely subdue the Highland lords, and he greatly improved the administration of justice for the common people. His murder in a Dominican friary by a group of rival nobles led to a popular uprising in favor of his widow and 6-year-old son, who succeeded him as James II.

James II *Spanish* **Jaime** *known as* **James the Just** (1264?–1327) King of Aragon (1295–1327) and king of Sicily (as James I, 1285–95). He inherited the Sicilian crown on the death of his father (1285); when his brother died (1291) he inherited Aragon. He resigned Sicily (1295) and married the daughter of the king of Naples in order to make peace with the Angevins. Sardinia and Corsica were given to him in compensation for Sicily, but he was able to occupy only Sardinia (1324).

James II (1633–1701) King of Great Britain (1685–88). He was brother and successor to Charles II. In the English Civil Wars he escaped to the Netherlands (1648). After the Restoration (1660), he returned to England and became lord high admiral in the Anglo–Dutch Wars. He converted to Catholicism c. 1668, and resigned in 1673 rather than take the Test Act oath. By 1678 his Catholicism had created a climate of hysteria about a Popish Plot to assassinate Charles and put James on the throne, and successive Parliaments sought to exclude him from succession. By the time Charles died (1685), James came to the throne with little opposition and strong support from the Anglicans. Rebellions caused him to fill the army and high offices with Roman Catholics and suspend a hostile Parliament. The birth of his son, a possible Catholic heir, brought about the Glorious Revolution in 1688, and he fled to France. In 1689 he landed in Ireland to regain his throne, but his army was defeated at the Battle of the Boyne, and he returned to exile in France.

James II (1430–1460) King of Scotland (1437–60). He succeeded to the throne on the assassination of his father, James I of Scotland. Because he was so young, the strong central authority his father had established quickly collapsed, and his first adult task was the restoration of monarchical authority. He strove to dominate the powerful Douglas family, and in 1452 he stabbed to death William, Earl of Douglas, at Stirling Castle. He established a strong central government and improved the administration of justice. Turning his attention to the English, who had renewed their claims to rule Scotland, he attacked English outposts in Scotland and was killed during a siege of Roxburgh Castle.

James III (1452–1488) King of Scotland (1460–88). He succeeded his father, James II. Unlike the latter, he was unable to restore strong central government after his long minority. A weak monarch, he was confronted with two major rebellions. He evidently offended his nobles by his interest in the arts and by taking artists for his favorites. In 1488 two powerful border families raised a rebellion and won to their cause his son, the future James IV; James III was captured and killed at 36.

James IV (1473–1513) King of Scotland (1488–1513). He unified his country, gaining control over all northern and western Scotland by 1493. He fought border skirmishes with England (1495–97) in support of a pretender to the English throne. His marriage (1503) to Margaret Tudor, daughter of Henry VII, helped stabilize relations between the two countries, but in 1512 he allied with France against England. He invaded England in support of the French in 1513; his army was defeated at the Battle of Flodden, and James was killed.

James Bay Extension of Hudson Bay, located between northern Ontario and Quebec. Generally less than 200 ft (60 m) deep, it is 275 mi (443 km) long and 135 mi (217 km) wide. It contains numerous islands, of which the largest is Akimiski Island. The many rivers that empty into the bay, including the Moose, are the cause of its low salinity. Visited by Henry Hudson in 1610, it is named for Capt. Thomas James, who explored it in 1631.

James River *or* **Dakota River** River rising in central North Dakota and flowing southeast across South Dakota. It joins the Missouri River about 5 mi (8 km) below Yankton after a course of 710 mi (1,140 km). Major cities along the river include Jamestown, N.D., and Huron, S.D.

James River River, Virginia. Formed by the junction of the Jackson and Cowpasture rivers, it flows east across the Blue Ridge Mtns. and past Richmond, then southeast to enter Chesapeake Bay through Hampton Roads after a course of 340 mi (550 km). The historic settlement of Jamestown lies on its lower course.

James the Conqueror See James I (Aragon)

Jameson, Leander Starr *later* **Sir Leander** (1853–1917) British administrator in southern Africa. As Cecil Rhodes's representative, Jameson successfully negotiated mineral concessions in Matabeleland and Mashonaland (present-day Zimbabwe) before becoming the first administrator of the new colony of Rhodesia in 1893. In 1895 Rhodes and Jameson plotted with Uitlander (British) leaders in the Transvaal to overthrow the Boer government of Paul Kruger; the original plan was postponed, but Jameson carried out his own invasion and was quickly captured with all his men. After imprisonment in England, he returned to participate in South African politics.

Jamestown Site of the first permanent British settlement in North America. It was founded in May 1607, on the Jamestown Island peninsula in Virginia's James River. Named after King James I, it initiated the cultivation of tobacco and established the continent's first representative government (1619). When Williamsburg replaced it as the capital of Virginia in 1699, it fell into decline. By the mid-19th century, erosion had transformed the peninsula into an island. In 1936 it was incorporated into the Colonial National Historical Park.

Jami \ˈjō-ˌmē\ *orig.* **Mowlana Nur od-Din 'Abd or-Rahman ebn Ahmad** (1414–1492) Persian scholar, mystic, and poet. Despite offers of patronage by many Islamic rulers, he led a simple life, mostly in Herat. His prose ranges from Qur'anic commentaries to treatises on Sufism and music. His poetry expresses ethical and philosophical views in fresh, graceful language. His best known poetry collection is *The Seven Thrones* (or *Ursa Major*). He is often called the last great mystical poet of Iran.

Jamison \ˈjā-mə-sən\, **Judith** (born 1943) U.S. dancer and choreographer. Born in Philadelphia, she joined Alvin Ailey's American Dance Theater in 1965, where she remained until 1980; she became celebrated for her energetic grace and riveting stage presence and inspired many of Ailey's new dances. She starred in the Broadway musical *Sophisticated Ladies* (1980). She toured worldwide in the 1980s and choreographed for various companies. In 1988 she founded her own troupe, the Jamison Project. In 1989 she returned to the Ailey troupe as artistic director.

Jammu \ˈjə-mü\ City (pop., 2001 prelim.: 378,431) and winter capital of Jammu and Kashmir state, northwestern India. It lies along the Tawi River, south of Srinagar. Once the capital of the Dogra Rajput dynasty, it became part of Ranjit Singh's domain in the 19th century. It is now a railroad and manufacturing center. Sites of interest include a fort, a palace of the rajas, and the University of Jammu (founded 1969).

Jammu and Kashmir *or* **Kashmir** State (pop., 2001 prelim.: 10,069,917), northwestern India. With an area of 39,146 sq mi (101,387 sq km), it occupies the southern portion of the Kashmir region of the northwestern Indian subcontinent. The land is predominantly mountainous and includes segments of the Karakoram and Himalaya ranges. Much of Kashmir's Ladakh region is included in the state. There are two major lowland areas: the Jammu plain and the fertile and heavily populated Vale of Kashmir. The majority of the state's people are Muslims, although Hindus predominate in the southeastern Jammu area, and northeastern Ladakh is largely Buddhist. Formerly a princely state created in the 1840s, Jammu and Kashmir became an Indian state in 1947, even as India and Pakistan were fighting for control of the entire Kashmir region. A cease-fire line, established in 1949, has since served as the state's boundary with the Pakistani-administered area. Tension has remained high in the region, and there have been periodic outbreaks of border fighting.

Janáček \ˈyä-nə-ˌchek\, **Leoš** *orig.* **Leo Eugen** (1854–1928) Czech (Moravian) composer. Son of a church musician, until age 40 he worked as a teacher and choral conductor. When his marriage broke up (1887), he began his first opera and spent the next year collecting folk songs. In 1894 he began his first mature opera, *Jenufa*, in a folk-influenced style; completed nearly a decade later, it had a successful premiere in Brno (1904), and he retired to compose full-time, becoming music's most extraordinary late bloomer. Major works of his last two decades include the *Glagolitic Mass* (1927) and the operas *Kát'a Kabanová* (1921), *The Cunning Little Vixen* (1924), *The Makropulos Affair* (1925), and *From the House of the Dead* (1928). A late love affair inspired the "Kreutzer" and "Intimate Pages" string quartets (1923, 1928).

Janáček.
EASTFOTO

Janissary *or* **Janizary** \'ja-nə-ˌser-ē, 'ja-nə-ˌzer-ē\ Elite corps of the OTTOMAN EMPIRE's army from the late 14th century to 1826. Its original soldiers were Balkan Christians who were converted to Islam upon conscription. Strict early rules, later abandoned, included celibacy. In 1826 they rebelled rather than accept Westernization of the army, and all of them were killed when the sultan, Mahmud II, bombed their barracks and executed the survivors.

Jansen \'yän-sən, *Engl* 'jan-sən\, **Cornelius Otto** (1585–1638) Dutch leader of the Roman Catholic reform movement known as JANSENISM. He studied at the University of Louvain, where he absorbed the teachings of St. AUGUSTINE, especially those concerning original sin and the need for grace. He spent 1611–14 in Bayonne, France, where he directed the episcopal college. After studying theology three more years, he returned to Louvain. He became rector of the university in 1635 and a year later was appointed bishop of Ypres. In 1638 he died of the plague. His major work, the *Augustinus,* was published in 1640; in 1642 Pope Urban VIII forbade the reading of the book.

Jansenism Roman Catholic reform movement inspired by the writings of CORNELIUS JANSEN. Influenced by the works of St. AUGUSTINE and especially by Augustine's attacks on PELAGIANISM and the doctrine of free will, Jansen adopted Augustine's doctrines of PREDESTINATION and the necessity of God's GRACE, a stance considered uncomfortably close to CALVINISM by Roman Catholic authorities, who banned his book the *Augustinus* in 1642. After Jansen's death in 1638, his followers made their base at the abbey in Port-Royal, France. BLAISE PASCAL, the most famous Jansenist, defended their teachings in his *Provincial Letters* (1656–57). In 1709 LOUIS XIV ordered the Port Royal abbey demolished. Followers of Jansen started a Jansenist Church in 1723, which endured into the late 20th century.

Jansky, Karl (Guthe) (1905–1950) U.S. engineer. Born in Red Bank, N.J., he graduated from the University of Wisconsin and went to work for Bell Telephone Laboratories. Assigned to track down static that interfered with telephone calls, he discovered (1931) the first extraterrestrial source of radio waves, emanating from the constellation Sagittarius. The discovery proved that celestial bodies could emit radio waves and marked the beginning of radio astronomy.

Janus \'jā-nəs\ Roman god of doorways and archways, after whom the month of January is named. Often depicted as a double-faced head, he was a deity of beginnings. The worship of Janus dated back to the earliest years of Rome, and the city had many freestanding ceremonial gateways called *jani,* used for symbolically auspicious entrances or exits. The most famous was the Janus Geminus, whose double doors were left open in time of war and closed when Rome was at peace. The festival of Janus, the Agonium, took place on January 9.

The god Janus, beardless, Roman coin; in the Bibliothèque Nationale, Paris.
LAROUSSE

Japan *Japanese* **Nippon** \ni-'pȯn\ *or* **Nihon** \nē-'hȯn\ Island country, lying off the eastern coast of Asia in the western Pacific Ocean. It consists of four main islands—HOKKAIDO, HONSHU, SHIKOKU, and KYUSHU. It is separated from China by the CHINA SEA and from South Korea, North Korea, and Russia by the Sea of JAPAN. Area: 145,883 sq mi (377,835 sq km). Population (1997 est.): 126,110,000. Capital: TOKYO. The Japanese overwhelmingly are a single Asian ethnic group. Language: Japanese (official). Religions: SHINTO, BUDDHISM, and Christianity. Currency: yen. Situated in one of the earth's most geologically active zones, Japan experiences volcanic eruptions and earthquakes. Mountain ranges cover more than four-fifths of Japan's land surface; the country's highest mountain is Mount FUJI. The nation's economy, one of the world's biggest, is based largely on manufacturing and services; exports include electronic and electrical equipment, motor vehicles, chemicals, and iron and steel products. The government's involvement in banking results in unique cooperation between the public and private sectors. It is also one of the world's principal seagoing nations, with an important marine fishing industry. It is a constitutional monarchy with two legislative houses; its chief of state is the emperor, and the head of government is the prime minister. Japan's history began with the accession of the legendary first emperor, JIMMU, in 660 BC. The Yamato court established the first unified Japanese state in the 4th–5th century AD; during this period, Buddhism arrived in Japan by way of Korea. For centuries Japan borrowed heavily from Chinese culture, but it began to sever its links with the mainland by the 9th century. The FUJIWARA FAMILY held sway through the 11th century. In 1192 MINAMOTO YORITOMO established Japan's first BAKUFU, or shogunate (see KAMAKURA SHOGUNATE). The ASHIKAGA SHOGUNATE (1338–1573) was marked by warfare among powerful families. Unification was achieved in the late 1500s under the leadership of ODA NOBUNAGA, TOYOTOMI HIDEYOSHI, and TOKUGAWA IEYASU. During the TOKUGAWA SHOGUNATE, beginning in 1603, the government imposed a policy of isolation. Under the leadership of Emperor MEIJI (1868–1912), it adopted a constitution (1889) and began a program of modernization and Westernization. Japanese imperialism led to war with China (1894–95) and Russia (1904–5) as well as to the annexation of Korea (1910) and Manchuria (1931). During WORLD WAR II Japan attacked U.S. forces in Hawaii and the Philippines (December 1941) and occupied European colonial possessions in South Asia. In 1945 the U.S. dropped ATOMIC BOMBS on HIROSHIMA and NAGASAKI, and Japan surrendered to Allied powers. U.S. postwar occupation of Japan led to a new democratic constitution in 1947. In rebuilding Japan's ruined industrial plant, new technology was used in every major industry. A tremendous economic recovery followed, and it was able to maintain a favorable balance of trade into the 1990s. See map on following page.

Japan, Sea of, *or* **East Sea** Branch of the western Pacific Ocean, bounded by Japan, the island of SAKHALIN, and by Russia and Korea on the Asian mainland. It has a surface area of about 377,600 sq mi (978,000 sq km), a mean depth of 5,748 ft (1,752 m), and a maximum depth of 12,276 ft (3,742 m). Its relatively warm waters contribute greatly to the mild climate of Japan. The growing trade among East Asian countries has increased its use as a commercial waterway.

Japanese architecture Building traditions of Japan. Early building types were the grass-roofed pit house, raised thatched-roof granary (c. 400 BC), and mound tomb *(kofun).* Buddhist temples were first modeled on the Chinese and Korean form, a symmetrical complex bordered by a continuous roofed cloister usually containing a PAGODA, Golden Hall *(kondo),* belfry, and living quarters. Roof tiles, stone, and wood were the essential materials. Structures relied on wood pillars placed on stone bases; horizontal elements were added in varying degrees of complexity. With HORYU-JI finally appeared the distinctive Japanese approach: asymmetrical layouts following the contours of the land. Domestic architecture became marked by unpretentiously rustic buildings, meticulously designed viewing gardens, verandas, and sliding panels offering vistas on nature. The need for a place of contemplation led to the evolution of both the tea room and study room *(tsuke shoin).* The late 19th century saw a rapid assimilation of Western technology, with brick, stone, and reinforced concrete displacing wood. Postwar Japan's finest architectural achievements are in contemporary interpretations of traditional forms. See also SHINDEN-ZUKURI, SHOIN-ZUKURI, SUKIYA STYLE.

Japanese art Painting, sculpture, architecture, calligraphy, and other fine and decorative arts produced in Japan. Characterized by their vibrancy, life, and color, they have been strongly influenced by Chinese visual arts and Buddhist iconography. The Chinese style of monochrome ink painting and calligraphy greatly influenced the development of Japanese painting. A fascination with abstraction from nature is most notable in screen and panel paintings of the 16th–18th century and in the polychrome woodcut, which evolved into the popular UKIYO-E print. Early Japanese sculpture featured small clay figures and carved wooden statues of Buddhist subjects. The Chinese post-and-beam style overshadowed most indigenous forms of architecture (see CHINESE ARCHITECTURE). The Japanese are renowned for their pottery, cloisonné, lacquerwork, and other decorative arts; despite influence by continental styles, a distinctive indigenous pottery developed. See also FUJIWARA STYLE, HIROSHIGE ANDO, HOKUSAI, IKE NO TAIGA, IKEBANA, JOCHO, JOGAN STYLE, KAIKEI, OGATA KENZAN, OKUMURA MASANOBU, PAPER FOLDING, SCROLL PAINTING, TEMPYO STYLE, TORI STYLE, UNKEI, UTAMARO.

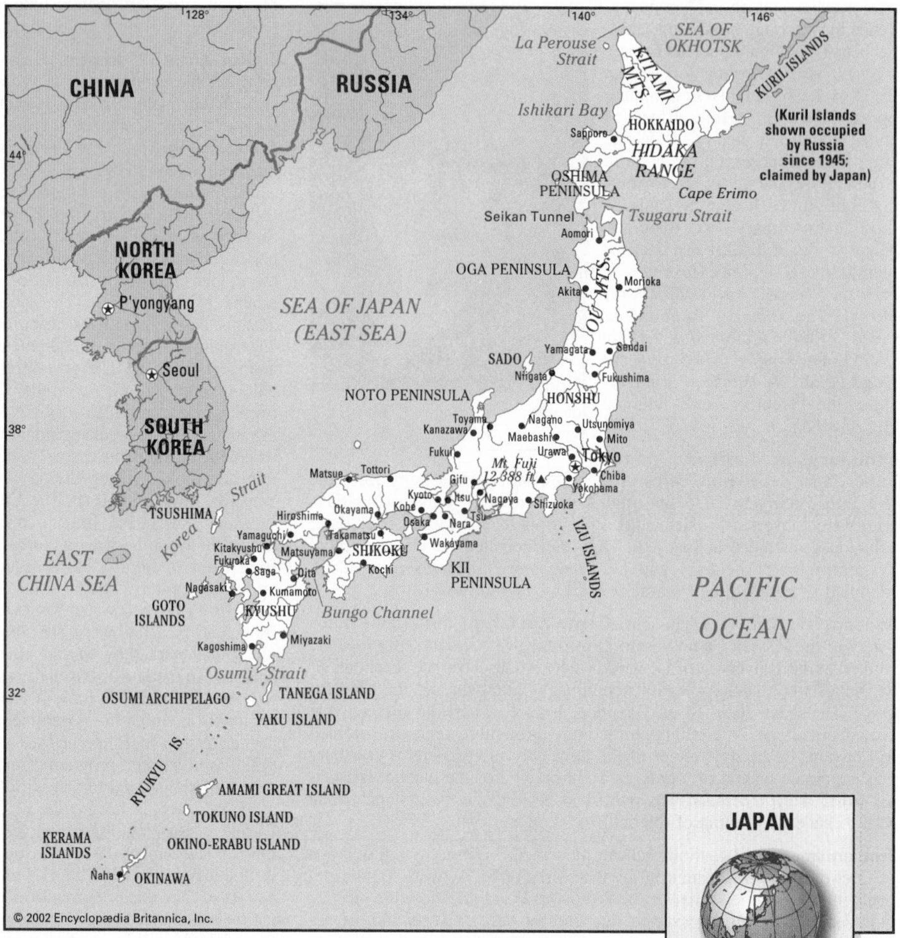

Japanese beetle SCARAB BEETLE (Popillia japonica) that is a major PEST of plants. Introduced accidentally from Japan into the U.S. in 1916, Japanese beetles are known to feed on more than 200 species of plant. Their larvae feed underground on roots; adults feed on flowers, fruit, and foliage. They range from Maine to South Carolina, and infestations have occurred in other parts of North America. The adult, about 0.4 in. (10 mm) long, is bright metallic green with coppery-brown wing covers. Control efforts include the use of poisonous sprays and a disease-inducing bacterium and introduction of the beetle's natural enemies (certain parasitic wasp and fly species).

Japanese crab See KING CRAB

Japanese language Language spoken by about 125 million people on the islands of Japan, including the Ryukyus. The only other language of the Japanese archipelago is Ainu (see AINU), now spoken by only a handful of people on Hokkaido, though once much more widespread. Japanese is not closely related to any other language, though a distant genetic kinship to KOREAN is now thought probable by some scholars, and an even more remote relationship to the ALTAIC LANGUAGES possible. Japanese is first attested in the 8th century AD, when Middle CHINESE characters were utilized solely for their phonetic value to write native Japanese words. Japanese retains a huge stock of loanwords from Middle Chinese, long adapted to native phonetics. Typologically, Japanese is an agglutinative language with basic subject-object-verb word order; modifiers regularly precede what they modify.

Japanese law Law as it has developed in Japan. In the 8th century Japan borrowed and adapted TANG-DYNASTY China's legal system. With the rise of the warrior class, clan codes governing the behavior and actions of warrior families were developed. After the MEIJI RESTORATION (1868), Japan began to borrow heavily from European legal systems, particularly the GERMAN CIVIL CODE. After World War II, Japan melded aspects of the U.S. legal system, including various civil procedures and elements of labor and business law, with its own. Today traditional extralegal dispute-resolution methods remain strong, and litigation plays a less pervasive role than in the U.S.

Japanese music Traditional music of Japan. Absorbing the influences of China, of India (by way of Buddhism), and the West, Japan has concentrated and refined them into something distinct during its periods of withdrawal from outside contact. The earliest music in Japan was apparently religious; by the 6th century this had been codified into a body of music associated with SHINTO called *mikagura*. Once the imperial state was established, a period of receptivity to outside influence ensued, during which GAGAKU was imported from China by way of Korea (612). *Heike-biwa*, a narrative form of singing by minstrel-like figures (often blind) accompanying themselves on the *biwa* (lute), grew in importance as court music declined with the power of the court. When central government was reestablished in the EDO PERIOD (1615–1868), the popularity of such narrative forms was transferred to theatrical forms. A new merchant class supported popular entertainments such as KABUKI and BUNRAKU, while NO DRAMA, though evolved from similar popular sources, was supported by the nobility. During this period, genres associated with certain solo instruments (as in CHINESE MUSIC) also arose, particularly for the SHAKUHACHI, KOTO, and samisen (a three-stringed lute). With Japan's reopening in the 19th century, Western influences became predominant and almost displaced traditional forms, though the resurgent nationalism of the early 20th century fostered their preservation.

Japanese philosophy Conceptual expression of Japanese culture since early 6th century AD. Japanese philosophy is not generally indigenous; Japanese thinkers have always skillfully assimilated alien philosophical categories in developing their own systems. One of the two principal schools of Japanese thought arose from BUDDHISM and was highly tinged with a religious and often somewhat metaphysical character. The second school arose from CONFUCIANISM and was essentially a system of moral philosophy. Since the MEIJI RESTORATION (1868), Western philosophy has been abundantly introduced into Japan. At first British and American philosophies predominated, but in the 20th century the influence of German philosophy became increasingly strong; leading Japanese philosophers were especially influenced by German IDEALISM, PHENOMENOLOGY, and EXISTENTIALISM. To distinguish Western philosophy from Buddhist and Chinese thought, the term *tetsugaku* ("wise learning") was coined and has come into common use.

Japanese writing system System of modified Chinese characters used for writing the JAPANESE LANGUAGE. The Japanese developed a mixed system, partly logographic (based on the CHINESE WRITING SYSTEM) and partly syllabic. In the 9th or 10th century two sets of syllabic signs evolved: *hiragana*, simplified cursive versions of Chinese characters; and *katakana,* based on elements of Chinese characters. Modern Japanese is written with the two syllabaries and Chinese characters.

Japurá River \ˌzhä-pü-ˈrä\ River, northwestern South America. After rising in the Cordillera Central of southwestern Colombia as the Caquetá River, and flowing through southeastern Colombia, it is joined by the Apaporis River at the Brazilian border, where it takes the name Japurá and flows eastward to join the AMAZON RIVER. Its total length, including the Caquetá, is about 1,750 mi (2,820 km). It has a strong current and is navigable by small boats in Brazil.

Jaques-Dalcroze \ˈzhäk-ˌdal-ˈkrōz\, **Émile** (1865–1950) Swiss music educator and composer. He studied composition with A. BRUCKNER, G. FAURE, and L. DELIBES, and in 1892 became professor of harmony at the Geneva Conservatory. In the early 20th century, he experimented with new methods of music education, which evolved into EURYTHMICS. In 1914, having left the conservatory, he founded the Institut Jaques-Dalcroze in Geneva to teach and promulgate his new method.

Jari River *or* **Jary River** \zhȧ-ˈrē\ River, northern Brazil. It flows southeast for about 350 mi (560 km) to join the AMAZON RIVER at Bôca do Jari. The Jari forms the border between Pará and Amapá states, and its lower course is navigable. Since the late 1960s the river's valley has been the focus of large-scale development for lumber production.

Jarmusch \ˈjär-mu̇sh\, **Jim** (born 1953) U.S. film director and screenwriter. Born in Akron, Ohio, he studied at Columbia University and NYU Film School. His first film, *Stranger Than Paradise* (1984), established his reputation as a new voice in independent film. His later films include the offbeat comedies *Down by Law* (1986), *Mystery Train* (1989), and *Night on Earth* (1992). His later films include *Year of the Horse* (1997), a rock-concert documentary, *Dead Man* (1995), and *Ghost Dog* (1999).

Jarrell \ja-ˈrel\, **Randall** (1914–1965) U.S. poet and critic. Born in Nashville, Tenn., he taught at the University of North Carolina (Greensboro) from 1947 until his death. As a critic, he revitalized the reputations of ROBERT FROST, WALT WHITMAN, and WILLIAM CARLOS WILLIAMS in the 1950s; his criticism is collected in *Poetry and the Age* (1953), *A Sad Heart at the Supermarket* (1962), and the posthumous *Third Book of Criticism* (1969). His poems appeared in *Little Friend, Little Friend* (1945) and *Losses* (1948), both drawing on his wartime experiences, and such later collections as *The Seven-League Crutches* (1951) and *The Woman at the Washington Zoo* (1960). He was killed when he stepped in front of a moving car.

Jarrett, Keith (born 1945) U.S. pianist, composer, and bandleader. Born in Allentown, Pa., he played with ART BLAKEY (1965–66) and with M. Davis's jazz-rock group (1970–71) before making a series of solo recordings that won him broad popularity. His trio (from 1966) with bassist Charlie Haden (born 1937) and drummer Paul Motian (born 1931), later expanded to a quartet (1971–76), was highly regarded as well. After releasing acclaimed albums in the 1970s, he has published fully composed works and has recorded classical works as well.

Jarry \zhȧ-ˈrē\, **Alfred** (1873–1907) French writer. He went to Paris to live on his inheritance at 18; after exhausting it, he led a life of calculated buffoonery. His farce *Ubu Roi* (1896), considered a forerunner of theater of the ABSURD and of SURREALISM, featured the grotesque Père Ubu, who becomes king of Poland. Jarry followed it with two sequels, one of which was published posthumously. The brilliant imagery and wit of his stories, novels, and poems usually lapse into incoherence and unintelligible symbolism. A heavy drinker, he died at 34.

Jaruzelski \ˌyär-ü-ˈzel-skē\, **Wojciech (Witold)** (born 1923) Polish army general and chief of state (1981–89) and president (1989–90) of Poland. He rose through the ranks of the army and the Communist Party to be elected premier and first secretary of the party in 1981 as Poland came under increasing pressure from the SOLIDARITY movement. He declared martial law (1981–83), carrying out mass arrests of dissidents. Unable to restore Poland's stagnant economy, in 1988 he began negotiations with Solidarity, which culminated in agreements for reforms in Poland's political system. Elected president in 1989, he resigned his posts in the Communist Party. In 1990 LECH WALESA was elected president and Jaruzelski relinquished the last of communist power in Poland.

jasmine \ˈjaz-mən\ Any of about 300 tropical and subtropical species of fragrant, flowering, woody, climbing shrubs that make up the genus *Jasminum* of the OLIVE family, native to all continents except North America. The jasmine used in perfumery and aromatherapy comes from the fragrant white flowers of common, or poet's, jasmine *(J. officinale),* native to Iran. The dried flowers of Arabian jasmine *(J. sambac)* make jasmine tea. Many fragrant-flowered plants from other families are also commonly called jasmine.

Winter jasmine (*Jasminum nudiflorum*).
VALERIE FINNIS

Jason In Greek legend, the leader of the ARGONAUTS. He was the son of Aeson, king of Iolcos in Thessaly. Raised by CHIRON after his father's half-brother Pelias seized Iolcos, he returned as a young man and was promised his inheritance if he could bring back the Golden Fleece. After an adventurous voyage, he won the fleece with the help of MEDEA. He married her, and the two returned to Iolcos, where Medea murdered Pelias. Driven out by Pelias's son, they sought refuge with King Creon of Corinth. When Jason deserted Medea for Creon's daughter, Medea killed her own children by Jason.

jasper Opaque, fine-grained or dense variety of the SILICA MINERAL CHERT that exhibits various colors, but chiefly brick red to brownish red. Long used for jewelry and ornamentation, it has a dull luster but takes a fine polish; its physical properties are those of QUARTZ. Jasper is common and widely distributed, occurring in the Ural Mtns., North Africa, Sicily, Germany, and elsewhere. For thousands of years, black jasper was used to test gold-silver alloys for their gold content. Rubbing the alloys on the stone, called a touchstone, produces a streak the color of which determines the gold content within 1 part in 100.

Jasper National Park National park, western Alberta. Located on the eastern slopes of the ROCKY MTNS., it was established in 1907. It occupies 4,200 sq mi (10,878 sq km), including the ATHABASCA RIVER valley and the surrounding mountains. It encompasses part of the great Columbia Icefield, whose meltwaters feed rivers that flow to the Atlantic, Pacific, and Arctic oceans. The park's wildlife includes bear, elk, moose, caribou, and cougar.

Jaspers \ˈyäs-pərs\, **Karl (Theodor)** (1883–1969) German-Swiss philosopher and psychiatrist. As a research psychiatrist, he helped establish psychopathology on a rigorous, scientifically descriptive basis, especially in his *General Psychopathology* (1913). He taught philosophy at the University of Heidelberg from 1921 until 1937, when the Nazi regime forbade him to work. From 1948 he lived in Switzerland, teaching at the University of Basel. In his magnum opus, *Philosophy* (3 vols., 1969), he expounds his view that the aim of philosophy is practical; its purpose is the fulfillment of human existence (*Existenz*). For Jaspers, philosophical illumination is achieved in the experience of limit situations that define the human condition—conflict, guilt, suffering, and death—and in mankind's confrontation with these extremes it achieves its existential humanity. One of the most important existentialists, he approached the subject from mankind's direct concern with its own existence.

Jassy See IASI

H
I
J
K

Jassy \'yä-sē\, **Treaty of** (January 9, 1792) Pact signed at Jassy in Moldavia (modern Iasi, Romania), at the conclusion of the RUSSO-TURKISH WAR. The treaty confirmed Russian dominance in the Black Sea by advancing the Russian frontier to the Dniester River. It also restored Bessarabia, Moldavia, and Walachia to the Ottoman Turks.

jaundice Excess BILE pigments (bilirubin) in the bloodstream and tissues, causing a yellow to orange—even greenish—color in the skin, the whites of the eyes, and the mucous membranes. Bilirubin may be overproduced or inadequately removed (retention jaundice) by the LIVER or leak into the bloodstream after removal (regurgitation jaundice); jaundice may also be due to impaired bile flow (obstructive jaundice). Causes include ANEMIA, PNEUMONIA, and liver disorders (e.g., infection or CIRRHOSIS). While bilirubin excess usually does no harm, retention jaundice signals severe liver malfunction.

Jaurès \zhō-'res\, **(Auguste-Marie-Joseph-) Jean** (1859–1914) French socialist leader. He served in the Chamber of Deputies (1885–89, 1893–98, 1902–14) and at first adopted the ideas of ALEXANDRE MILLERAND. After 1899 the socialists split into two groups, and Jaurès headed the FRENCH SOCIALIST PARTY, advocating reconciliation with the state. In the newspaper *L'Humanité*, which he cofounded in 1904, he espoused democratic socialism, but when the SECOND INTERNATIONAL (1904) rejected his position he acquiesced. In 1905 the two French socialist parties united, and his authority continued to grow. On the eve of World War I, he espoused peace through arbitration and championed Franco-German rapprochement, which earned him the hatred of French nationalists, and he was assassinated in 1914 by a young nationalist fanatic. He wrote several books, including the influential *Socialist History of the French Revolution* (1901–7).

Jaurès.
H. ROGER-VIOLLET

Java *Indonesian* **Djawa** \'jä-vä\ Island (pop., 1999 est.: 121,193,000), Indonesia. Lying southeast of Malaysia and Sumatra, it is Indonesia's fourth largest island and contains more than half of the republic's population. Its area, including offshore Madura Island, is 49,228 sq mi (127,499 sq km). The capital of Java and of the republic is JAKARTA. The island's highest point is Mount Semeru, an active volcano measuring 12,060 ft (3,676 m) high. It is inhabited by three major ethnic groups: the Javanese (who constitute 70% of the population), the Sundanese, and the Madurese. The fossilized remains of *HOMO ERECTUS*, or "Java man," indicate that the island was occupied 800,000 years ago. Indian traders began arriving in the 1st century AD, bringing Hindu influences. The Majapahit dynasty was founded in eastern Java in 1293; it fell early in the 16th century when Muslim kingdoms arose. In 1619 the Dutch EAST INDIA CO. took control of Batavia (Jakarta), and extended its influence. Ruled by the Dutch until the 1940s when it was occupied by Japan, it became part of the newly independent Republic of Indonesia in 1950.

Java Modular OBJECT-ORIENTED PROGRAMMING LANGUAGE developed by Sun Microsystems in 1995 specifically for the INTERNET. Java is based on the idea that the same SOFTWARE should run on many different kinds of computers, consumer gadgets, and other devices; its code is translated according to the needs of the machine on which it is running. The most visible examples of Java software are the interactive programs called "applets" that animate sites on the WORLD WIDE WEB, where Java is a standard creative tool. Java provides an interface to HTML.

Java man Common name of fossilized *HOMO ERECTUS* remains found in 1891 at Trinil, Java. They represent the first known fossils of *H. erectus* (though originally assigned to *Pithecanthropus erectus*) and, together with numerous other finds along the Solo River, suggest that *H. erectus* was present in eastern Asia c. 1 million years ago and persisted there for at least 500,000 years and possibly as long as 800,000 years. Java man predates the finds at ZHOUKOUDIAN (Peking Man) in China and is considered somewhat more primitive.

Java Sea Part of the western Pacific Ocean between JAVA and BORNEO islands. Measuring 900 mi (1,450 km) long by 260 mi (420 km) wide, it occupies a total area of 167,000 sq mi (433,000 sq km). A shallow sea, it has a mean depth of 151 ft (46 m). It was the scene of a World War II naval battle (1942) that resulted in an Allied defeat and Japan's invasion of Java.

Javanese Largest ethnic group on the island of JAVA, Indonesia. The Javanese are Muslim, though relatively few are strictly observant. Traditional Javanese social organization varied in structure from relatively egalitarian villages to the highly stratified society of the cities; these differences find expression in the many Javanese styles of speech still in use. Javanese villages are compact groups of single-family houses, generally built of bamboo, surrounding a central square. Rice is the main food crop. The growth of large cities in Java has produced an urban proletariat who live in makeshift huts in enclosed neighborhoods.

JavaScript Computer PROGRAMMING LANGUAGE developed by Netscape in 1995 for use in HTML pages. JavaScript is a scripting language (or interpreted language), which is not as fast as compiled languages (such as JAVA or C++) but easier to learn and use. It is only loosely related to Java, and is not a true object-oriented language (see OBJECT-ORIENTED PROGRAMMING). JavaScript can be quickly added to a pure HTML page to provide dynamic features, such as automatically calculating the current date or activating an action. The JavaScript code must be interpreted and executed by a BROWSER as it reads the Web page or by a Web server before it delivers the page to the browser.

javelin See PECCARY

javelin throw TRACK-AND-FIELD sport of throwing a wooden or metal spear for distance. It is hurled after a short run and must land point first. Included in the ancient Greek Olympic Games as part of the PENTATHLON, it has been part of the modern Olympic program since its inception in 1896. A women's event was added in 1932. See also DECATHLON, HEPTATHLON.

jaw Either of two bones that frame the MOUTH: a movable lower jaw (mandible) and a fixed upper jaw (maxilla). These hold the teeth (see TOOTH) and are used for biting and chewing and in speech. Vertical portions at the back of the lower jaw form hinge joints at the temples. The front of its arch thickens to form the chin. The upper jaw is attached to bones at the bridge of the nose, in the eye sockets and roof of the mouth, and the cheekbones. It contains the large maxillary SINUS.

Jawlensky \yəv-'lān-skē\, **Alexey** *orig.* **Aleksei Iavlenskii** (1864–1941) Russian-German painter. He gave up a military career to study painting, and in 1896 he moved to Munich, where he became affiliated with Der BLAUE REITER. In France in 1905 he worked with HENRI MATISSE. Back in Munich he produced such works as *Mme. Turandot* (1912), featuring flat areas of vibrant Fauve color outlined with simple, thick contours. In Switzerland during World War I he painted a series of "variations" on the view from his window. Their meditative mood culminated in such semiabstract faces as *Looking Within Night* (1923), whose mystical intensity is reminiscent of Russian icon painting. In 1924 he joined VASSILY KANDINSKY, PAUL KLEE, and LYONEL FEININGER to form Der Blaue Vier ("The Blue Four"); they exhibited together until arthritis forced Jawlensky to abandon painting.

Jaworski \jə-'wȯr-skē\, **Leon** (1905–1982) U.S. lawyer. Born in Waco, Texas, he became a prominent attorney, and was a prosecutor in the Nuremberg Trials (1945–46). He reached national prominence in 1973, when he was chosen as special prosecutor to investigate the WATERGATE SCANDAL. He argued successfully before the U.S. Supreme Court that Pres. RICHARD NIXON was obligated to obey a subpoena for 64 White House tape recordings. In response to criticism for not prosecuting Nixon, he said he felt Nixon could not receive a fair trial.

jay Any of 35–40 bird species (family Corvidae) that inhabit woodlands and are known for their bold, raucous manner. Most are found in the New World, but several are Eurasian. Jays are nearly omnivores; some steal eggs, and many store seeds and nuts for winter use. They make a twiggy, cuplike nest in trees. The 12-in. (30-cm) blue jay, blue and white with a narrow black neckline, is found in North America east of the Rockies; westward it is replaced by the dark-blue, black-crested

Steller's jay. Another abundant species is the scrub jay, found throughout western North America and in Florida.

Blue jay (*Cyanocitta cristata*).
JOHN H. GERARD

Jay, John (1745–1829) U.S. jurist, first chief justice of the U.S. Supreme Court. Born in New York City, he practiced law there. He initially favored reconciliation with Britain, but soon became a staunch supporter of independence. He was elected New York's first chief justice in 1777 and was chosen president of the Continental Congress. He helped Benjamin Franklin negotiate terms for a peace treaty with Britain and then served as secretary for foreign affairs (1784–90). Convinced of the need for a stronger centralized government, he urged ratification of the U.S. Constitution. Under the pseudonym Publius, he joined with James Madison and Alexander Hamilton to write essays for *The Federalist* explaining the Constitution's importance. In 1789 he was appointed the first chief justice of the U.S. Supreme Court, where he set legal precedent in affirming subordination of the states to the federal government. In 1794 he was sent to Britain to negotiate a treaty dealing with numerous commercial disputes. The Jay Treaty helped avert war, but Jeffersonian Republicans criticized it as too pro-British. Jay resigned from the court in 1795 and was elected governor of New York (1795–1801).

Jaya, Puncak *or* **Mount Jaya** *formerly* **Mount Sukarno** Peak, Irian Jaya, Indonesia. Located on New Guinea, the 16,500-ft (5,030-m) peak is the highest in the South Pacific and the highest island peak in the world.

Jayavarman VII \jä-yä-'vär-män\ (c. 1120–c. 1215) King of the Khmer (Cambodian) empire of Angkor (r.1181–1215?). Born into the royal family of Angkor, he settled in the Champa kingdom (present-day central Vietnam) in his young adulthood and engaged in military campaigns. In his late fifties he led his people in a struggle for independence after their subjugation by the Cham. He was crowned king of a reconstituted Khmer empire at 61. He ruled more than 30 years and brought the empire to its zenith in terms both of territorial extent and of royal architecture and construction. Champa, southern Laos, and portions of the Malay Peninsula and Burma came under his control. He built temples, hospitals, and rest houses, and rebuilt the city of Angkor (now called Angkor Thom). His dedication to both the spiritual and physical needs of the people has made him a national hero to modern Cambodians.

Jayewardene \ˌjä-ye-'wär-di-nə\, **J(unius) R(ichard)** (1906–1996) Prime minister (1977–78) and president (1978–89) of Sri Lanka. The son of a Supreme Court judge, he became minister of finance in 1948, when Ceylon (from 1972, Sri Lanka) became independent. As prime minister, he amended the constitution to give Sri Lanka an executive presidency and became the first elected president in 1978. His administration steered the nation away from socialism, revitalizing the private sector and reducing government bureaucracy. When ethnic conflict erupted between the island's Sinhalese Buddhist majority and its Tamil Hindu minority, he was unable to end the violence, which continued after his retirement and death.

Jazairi, Abdelqadir al- See Abdelqadir al-Jazairi

Jazari, al- See al-Jazari

Jazirah, Al- See Gezira

jazz Music developed in the U.S. usually incorporating improvisation and syncopated rhythmic momentum. Though its specific origins are not known, the music developed principally as an amalgam in the late-19th- and early-20th-century musical culture of New Orleans. Elements of the blues and ragtime in particular combined to form harmonic and rhythmic structures upon which to improvise. Social functions of music played a role in this convergence: whether for dancing or marching, celebration or ceremony, music was tailored to suit the occasion. Instrumental technique combined Western tonal values with emulation of the human voice. Emerging from the collective routines of New Orleans jazz (see Dixieland), Louis Armstrong became the first great soloist in jazz; the music thereafter became primarily a vehicle for profoundly personal expression through improvisation and composition. Elaboration of the role of the soloist in both small and large ensembles occurred during the swing era, c. 1930–45, the music of Duke Ellington in particular demonstrating the combination of composed and improvised elements. In the mid-1940s Charlie Parker pioneered the technical complexities of bebop as an outgrowth of the refinement of swing: his extremes of tempo and harmonic sophistication challenged both performer and listener. Miles Davis led groups that established the relaxed aesthetic and lyrical phrasing that came to be known as cool jazz in the 1950s, later incorporating modal and electronic elements. John Coltrane's music explored many of the directions jazz would take in the 1960s, including the extension of bebop's chord progressions and experimental free improvisation.

Jeans, James (Hopwood) *later* **Sir James** (1877–1946) British physicist and mathematician. After teaching at Cambridge and Princeton universities, he worked as a research associate at the Mount Wilson Observatory (1923–44). He proposed that matter was continuously created throughout the universe (see steady-state theory). He wrote on a wide variety of phenomena, but is perhaps best known as a writer of popular books about astronomy.

Jeddah See Jidda

jeep Outstanding light vehicle of World War II, developed by the U.S. Army Quartermaster Corps. It weighed 1¼ tons, had a four-cylinder engine, and could climb 60° grades and operate on rough terrain thanks to its four-wheel drive and high clearance. Its name came from its military designation: "vehicle, GP" (i.e., general-purpose). After the war it became widely used in civilian life.

Jeffers, (John) Robinson (1887–1962) U.S. poet. Born to a wealthy family in Pittsburgh, he was educated in literature, medicine, and forestry. His lyrics express contempt for humanity and love of the harsh, eternal beauties of nature, notably the California coast near Carmel, where he moved in 1916. His third book, *Tamar and Other Poems* (1924), brought him fame and revealed the unique style and eccentric ideas later developed in *Cawdor* (1928), *Thurso's Landing* (1932), and *Be Angry at the Sun* (1941). He made a theatrically successful adaptation of Euripides' *Medea* (1946).

Jefferson, Thomas (1743–1826) Third president of the U.S. (1801–9). Born in Shadwell, Virginia, he was a planter and lawyer from 1767, as well as a slaveholder who opposed slavery. While a member of the House of Burgesses (1769–75), he initiated the Committee of Correspondence (1773) with Richard Henry Lee and Patrick Henry. In 1774 he wrote the influential *Summary View of the Rights of British America*, stating that the British Parliament had no authority to legislate for the colonies. A delegate to the second Continental Congress, he was appointed to the committee to draft the Declaration of Independence and became its primary author. He was elected governor of Virginia (1779–81) but was unable to organize effective opposition when British forces invaded the colony (1780–81). Criticized for his conduct, he retired, vowing to remain a private citizen. Again a member of the Continental Congress (1783–85), he proposed territorial provisions later incorporated in the Northwest Ordinances. He traveled in Europe on diplomatic missions and became U.S. minister to France (1785–89). George Washington made him secretary of state (1790–93). He soon became embroiled in conflict with Alexander Hamilton over their opposing interpretations of the Constitution. This led to the rise of factions and political parties, with Jefferson representing the Democratic-Republicans. He served as vice president (1797–1801) but opposed the Alien and Sedition Acts enacted under President John Adams. As part of this opposition, Jefferson drafted one of the Virginia and Kentucky Resolutions. In 1801 he became president after an electoral-vote tie with Aaron Burr was settled by the U.S. House of Representatives. Jefferson initiated frugal fiscal policies and simplicity in the ceremonial role of the president. He also sought to pay off the national debt. He oversaw the Louisiana Purchase and authorized the Lewis and Clark Expedition. He sought to avoid involvement in the Napoleonic Wars by signing the Embargo Act. He retired to his plantation, Monticello, where he pursued his many interests in science, philosophy, and architecture. He served as president of the American Philosophical Society 1797–1815, and in 1819 founded and designed the University of VIRGINIA. In January 2000, the Thomas Jefferson Memorial Foundation accepted the conclusion, supported by DNA evidence, that Jefferson had fathered at least one, and perhaps as many as six, children with Sally Hemings, one of his house slaves. After a long estrangement, he and Adams became reconciled in 1813 and exchanged views on national issues that illuminated much of the founders' philosophies. They both died on July 4, 1826, the 50th anniversary of the signing of the Declaration of Independence.

Jefferson City Capital (pop., 1994 est.: 37,000), Missouri. Located on the Missouri River near the center of the state, it was selected as the site of the state capital in 1821. Named for THOMAS JEFFERSON, it was incorporated as a town in 1825 and as a city in 1839. Loyalties were divided during the AMERICAN CIVIL WAR, but it remained in the Union. The Capitol, completed in 1918, contains murals by THOMAS HART BENTON. It is the trading center for surrounding farmlands and has diversified manufacturing. Lincoln University was founded there by black Union Army veterans in 1866.

Jeffreys, Harold *later* **Sir Harold** (1891–1989) British astronomer and geophysicist. In astronomy, he established that the four large outer planets (Jupiter, Saturn, Uranus, and Neptune) are very cold, devised models of their planetary structure, and studied the origin of the solar system and the theory of latitude. In geophysics, he investigated the thermal history of the earth, was coauthor (1940) of the standard tables of travel times for earthquake waves, and was the first to hypothesize that the earth's core is liquid. He explained the origin of monsoons and sea breezes and showed how cyclones are vital to the general circulation of the atmosphere. Jeffreys also worked on probability theory and on methods of general mathematical physics.

Jehangir See JAHANGIR

Jehovah's Witness Member of an international religious movement founded in Pittsburgh, Pa., by CHARLES T. RUSSELL in 1872. The movement was originally known as the International Bible Students Association, but its name was changed by Russell's successor, Joseph Franklin Rutherford (1869–1942). The Witnesses are a millennialist group whose beliefs are based primarily on the apocalyptic sections of the BIBLE, notably Daniel and the Book of REVELATION. They refuse to perform military service or salute the flag, actions which have brought them into direct conflict with governments around the world. They are famous for their door-to-door evangelizing and for refusing blood transfusions; they believe there is scriptural justification for all their actions and beliefs. Their goal is the establishment of God's kingdom on earth, and they hold that JESUS—who is believed to be God's first creation rather than one person in a trinity—is God's agent in this plan. Their national headquarters is in Brooklyn, N.Y.; their major publications, the *Watchtower* and *Awake!*, are published in about 80 languages. See also MILLENNIALISM.

Jekyll, Gertrude (1842–1932) British landscape architect. She pursued her main interest in painting until 1891, when she turned to garden design. She helped the landscape designer William Robinson (1838–1935) in his writings about the natural garden, and wrote several successful books on her own, including *Wood and Garden* (1899) and *Home and Garden* (1900). She later worked closely with EDWIN LUTYENS, developing a modern, informal style of garden marked by rhythmic use of color and form.

Jellicoe, John Rushworth *later* **Earl Jellicoe** (1859–1935) British admiral. He entered the Royal Navy in 1872 and rose through the ranks to become commander of the fleet during World War I (1914–16). He won a crucial victory in the Battle of JUTLAND (1916), and was promoted to first sea lord of the admiralty (1916–17) and admiral of the fleet (1919). He served as governor of New Zealand 1920–24.

Jellinek \'je-li-ˌnek\, **Elvin M(orton)** (1890–1963) U.S. physiologist. Born in New York City, he studied at the University of Leipzig and worked in Budapest, Sierra Leone, and Honduras before returning to the U.S., where he studied ALCOHOLISM. He was an early proponent of the disease theory, arguing with great persuasiveness that alcoholics should be treated as sick people. He gathered and summarized his and others' research in the authoritative *Alcohol Explored* (1942) and *The Disease Concept of Alcoholism* (1960).

jelly and jam Semitransparent confections consisting of the strained juice of various fruits or vegetables, singly or in combination, sweetened, boiled, slowly simmered, and congealed, often with the aid of PECTIN or GELATIN. Jam differs from jelly in its inclusion of fruit pulp or whole fruit; whole-fruit jam is sometimes called preserve. Fruit and berry jellies and jams are eaten on breakfast breads and in sandwiches and accompany the scones and other baked goods of the British tea meal. Vegetable and herb jellies traditionally complement lamb and other meat dishes.

jellyfish Any of about 200 described species of marine CNIDARIANS (in the classes Scyphozoa and Cubozoa), many of which have a bell-shaped body. The term is also frequently applied to other similar cnidarians (e.g., PORTUGUESE MAN-OF-WAR) and some unrelated forms (e.g., CTENOPHORES and salps). In scyphozoan jellyfish, the free-swimming MEDUSA form is the dominant stage with the sessile POLYP form found only during larval development. Free-swimming jellyfish live in all oceans and include the familiar disk-shaped animals (e.g., CRUSTACEANS) that are often found drifting along the shoreline. Most species are 1–16 in. (2–40 cm) in diameter; some are 6 ft (1.8 m) in diameter. Though some jellyfish simply filter feed, most feed on small animals (e.g., crustaceans) that they catch in their tentacles, whose stinging cells immobilize the animals; contact can be irritating and sometimes dangerous to humans. The cubozoan jellyfish comprise 50 species of box jellies (the rather spherical body is squared off at the edges), which are usually 1–2 in. (2–4 cm) in diameter.

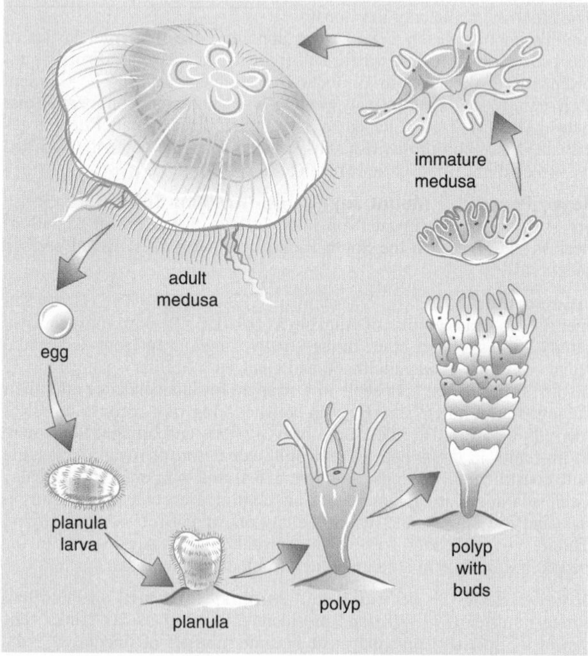

Life cycle of the common jellyfish *Aurelia*. Eggs released by females pass out through the mouth and become lodged in pits on the tentacles. Sperm released from male jellyfish fertilize the eggs, which remain on the tentacles during early development. A fertilized egg develops into a ciliated larva, or planula, which settles on and attaches to a substrate (such as a rock) and develops into a polyp with a mouth and tentacles. The polyp reproduces asexually by budding off saucer-shaped immature medusae, which develop into mature sexually reproducing forms.

Jemison, Mae (Carol) (born 1956) U.S. physician and astronaut. Born in Decatur, Ala., she received an MD from Cornell University and then served in the Peace Corps in Africa. In 1988 she was accepted to NASA's astronaut program and became the first black female astronaut. In 1992 she spent more than a week aboard the space shuttle *Endeavor.* Since 1993 she has taught environmental studies at Dartmouth College.

jen See REN

Jena and Auerstedt \'yä-nə...'au̇-ər-ˌshtet\, **Battles of** (1806) Military engagement of the NAPOLEONIC WARS, fought between French troops and Prussians and Saxons. In 1806 FREDERICK WILLIAM III of Prussia signed a secret alliance with Russia and joined the Third Coalition against NAPOLEON. As the Prussian army moved through Saxony to meet its Russian allies, it was forced to face a French attack from the rear. The Prussians split their forces between Auerstedt and Jena, and on October 14 Napoleon swept the Prussian troops off the field at Jena. At the same time, a secondary French force under LOUIS DAVOUT defeated a Prussian army more than twice its size at Auerstedt. Napoleon completed his conquest of Prussia in six weeks.

Jenkins, Fergie *orig.* **Ferguson Arthur** (born 1943) Canadian-U.S. baseball pitcher. Born in Chatham, Ontario, he excelled in amateur baseball, basketball, and hockey. He played for the Chicago Cubs (1966–73, 1982–84) as well as the Texas Rangers and Boston Red Sox (1974–81), winning at least 20 games in each of six consecutive seasons (1967–72) and setting several season records. He was awarded the Cy Young award in 1971 for his 24–13 won-lost record and 2.77 earned run average.

Jenkins, Roy (Harris) *later* **Baron Jenkins** (of Hillhead) (born 1920) British politician. Elected to Parliament in 1948, he served in Labour Party governments 1964–70 and 1974–76. A strong supporter of NATO and the European Community, he was president of the executive branch of the latter (1976–81). He resigned from the Labour Party and with other dissidents formed the Social Democratic Party in 1981, which he led 1982–83. After accepting a life peerage (1987), he became leader of the Social and Liberal Democratic Party in the House of Lords.

Jenkins' Ear, War of War between Britain and Spain that began in 1739 and eventually merged into the War of the AUSTRIAN SUCCESSION. In 1738 Capt. Robert Jenkins appeared before a committee of the House of Commons and exhibited his own amputated ear, which he alleged was cut off by Spanish coast guards who boarded his ship in the West Indies in 1731. Public opinion had already been aroused by other Spanish outrages on British ships, and the incident was exploited by members of Parliament who opposed the government of ROBERT WALPOLE.

Jenks, Joseph (1602–1683) British-U.S. inventor. A skilled ironworker, he emigrated to America in 1642 to help establish the first American ironworks (see SAUGUS IRON WORKS). He cut the dies for the first coins minted in Boston (1652) and built the first American fire engine (1654). The scythe he designed in 1655 has remained basically unchanged to the present.

Jenner, Edward (1749–1823) English surgeon, discoverer of the smallpox vaccine. He was apprenticed to a surgeon at 13, and at 21 became the house pupil of JOHN HUNTER, who gave him further training and stressed the need for experimentation and observation. Jenner had noticed as a youth that people who had been sick with the relatively harmless disease cowpox did not contract smallpox. In 1796 he inoculated a young boy with matter taken from a dairymaid's fresh cowpox lesions. The boy caught cowpox and, when subsequently inoculated with smallpox, did not contract it. Despite early difficulties, the procedure spread and the death rate from smallpox fell. Jenner received worldwide recognition (though he was also subject to attacks and slander). He retired from public life in 1815 after the death of his wife.

Edward Jenner, detail of an oil painting by James Northcote, 1803; in the National Portrait Gallery, London.
COURTESY OF THE NATIONAL PORTRAIT GALLERY, LONDON

Jensen \'yen-sən\, **Georg** (1866–1935) Danish silversmith and designer. At 14 he was apprenticed to a goldsmith and in 1904 he opened his own workshop in Copenhagen. Exhibiting his silverware and jewelry at major foreign exhibitions, he quickly built a reputation as an outstanding and original silversmith. He was the first to realize a profit from the manufacture of modern silverware and among the first to fashion steel into handsome, serviceable cutlery. By 1935 his firm had stores all over the world and carried more than 3,000 patterns. After his death the business was continued by his son, Søren Georg Jensen (born 1917).

Jensen \'yen-sən\, **Johannes V(ilhelm)** (1873–1950) Danish novelist, poet, and essayist. He initially studied medicine, but later turned to writing. He first made an impression as a writer of tales, including more than 100 published under the recurring title *Myter* ("Myths"). His early writings also include a historical trilogy, *The Fall of the King* (1900–1), about CHRISTIAN II of Denmark. His best-known work is *The Long Journey* (1908–22), a series of six novels that chronicles humanity's rise from primitive times to CHRISTOPHER COLUMBUS's arrival in the Americas. He received the Nobel Prize in 1944.

Jephtha \'jef-thə\ One of the judges in ancient Israel. According to the Book of Judges, he was the son of a Gileadite and a prostitute. After being cast out by his father's legitimate sons, he joined a band of brigands. When the Gileadites were oppressed by an Ammonite army, they asked Jephtha to aid them. He led them to victory, having first promised God a sacrifice of whatever he first saw when he left his house; his first sight happened to be his daughter. His significance in the Book of Judges is as an exemplar of Israel's fidelity to God.

Jeremiah (c. 650 BC–c. 570 BC) Hebrew PROPHET and reformer, author of the Old Testament Book of Jeremiah. Born into a priestly family in a village near Jerusalem, he began to preach c. 627 BC, charging his fellow citizens with injustice and false worship and calling on them to reform. He accurately predicted the destruction of JUDAH by Babylonia. After Jerusalem fell in 586 BC and much of its population was carried into exile, he remained behind under the protection of its new governor. When the governor was assassinated, Jeremiah was taken to Egypt by Jews who feared reprisals, and he remained there until he died. His most significant prophecy looked to a time when God would make a new covenant with Israel.

Jeremiah, detail from a fresco by Michelangelo in the Sistine Chapel, Rome, c. 1512.
ALINARI–ART RESOURCE/EB INC.

Jericho *Arabic* **Ariha** Town (pop., 1997: 14,674), West Bank of the JORDAN RIVER. Inhabited since c. 9000 BC, it is famous in biblical tradition as the first town attacked by the Israelites under Joshua after they crossed the Jordan River. It was several times abandoned or destroyed and rebuilt in the same area. Captured by the British in 1918, it became part of the British mandate of PALESTINE. Incorporated into Jordan in 1950, it became the site of two huge camps of Arab refugees from Israel. In the SIX-DAY WAR (1967) the town was occupied by Israel, and much of the refugee population was dispersed. In 1994 it was turned over to Palestinian rule under the Israeli-Palestinian self-rule agreement.

Jerome, Chauncey (1793–1868) U.S. inventor and clockmaker. Born in Canaan, Conn., in 1824 he designed a popular bronze looking-glass clock, and he formed a company that soon became the leading U.S. clockmaker. He invented the one-day brass movement, an improvement over the wood clock. Applying mass-production techniques, he flooded the U.S. with low-priced brass clocks, which quickly spread to Europe and so astonished the English that "Yankee ingenuity" became a byword.

Jerome, St. (c. AD 347–419/420) Church Father and translator. Born into a wealthy Christian family in Dalmatia, he was educated there and in Rome. Baptized c. 366, he spent most of the next 20 years in travel. He lived two years as a hermit in the desert of Chalcis. From 377 to 379 Jerome was in Antioch, where he studied biblical texts and translated the works of ORIGEN and EUSEBIUS. He lived in Rome 382–85, but theological controversy and opposition to his ascetic views led him to depart for the Holy Land, and he settled in Bethlehem, where he lived until his death. Traditionally regarded as the most learned of the Latin Fathers, he wrote numerous biblical commentaries and theological tracts on PELAGIANISM and other heresies. In 406 he completed his translation of the Bible into Latin, including his own translation of the Old Testament from Hebrew; Jerome's Latin Bible is known as the Vulgate.

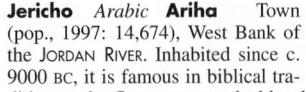

Jersey Largest and southernmost island (pop., 2002 est.: 87,400) of the English CHANNEL ISLANDS. It occupies an area of 45 sq mi (116 sq km); its capital is St. Helier (pop., 1996: 27,523). Separated from NORMANDY in 1204, it kept its Norman law and local customs but was administered for the British king by a warden. It was given legislative authority in 1771. It is now governed by a popularly elected assembly, which is presided over by a royally appointed bailiff. Jersey fabric and JERSEY cattle take their names from the island.

Jersey Breed of small, short-horned dairy CATTLE that originated on Jersey in the English Channel, believed to have descended from French cattle. They are usually fawn- or cream-colored, but darker shades are common. They were introduced in large numbers into England c. 1811 and into the U.S. in 1850. Adaptable to a wide range of conditions, the Jersey is found worldwide. Its milk is remarkably high in butterfat, and it is an important breed wherever butter is produced.

Jersey City City (pop., 2000: 240,055), northeastern New Jersey. It lies opposite NEW YORK CITY. First settled by Dutch trappers (1618) and known as Paulus Hook, it was purchased from the Delaware Indians and established as a permanent settlement by 1660. In 1779, during the AMERICAN REVOLUTION, Gen. HENRY LEE won a victory there over the British. Renamed Jersey City in 1836, it is a manufacturing center.

Jerusalem *Hebrew* **Yerushalayim** \ye-ˌrü-shä-ˈlī-im\ *Arabic* **Al-Quds** \äl-ˈküts\ City (pop., 1999 est.: 633,700) of the Middle East and capital of ISRAEL (see below). Located in the heart of historic PALESTINE, it is nestled between the WEST BANK and ISRAEL. The Old City is a typical, walled Middle Eastern enclosure; the modern city is an urban agglomeration of high-rises and housing complexes. It is holy to Judaism as the site of the TEMPLE OF JERUSALEM; to Christianity because of its association with JESUS; and to Islam because of its connection with the MIRAJ. Jewish shrines include the WESTERN WALL; Islamic holy places include the DOME OF THE ROCK. In 1000 BC DAVID made it the capital of Israel. Razed by the Babylonians in the 6th century BC, it thereafter enjoyed only brief periods of independence. The Romans devastated it in the 1st and 2nd centuries AD, banishing the population. From 637 it was ruled by various Muslim dynasties, except for short periods during the CRUSADES. Rule by the OTTOMAN EMPIRE ended in 1917, and the city became the capital of the British mandate of Palestine. It was thereafter the subject of competing Zionist and Palestinian national aspirations. Israel claimed the city as its capital after the ARAB-ISRAELI WAR in 1948 and took the entire city during the SIX-DAY WAR of 1967. Its status as Israel's capital has remained a point of contention: official recognition by the international community has largely been withheld pending final settlement of territorial rights.

Jerusalem, Council of Conference of the Christian APOSTLES at Jerusalem c. AD 50, which decreed that Gentile Christians did not have to observe the Mosaic law of the Jews. It was occasioned by the controversy over whether CIRCUMCISION was necessary for Gentile converts to Christianity. Led by Sts. PETER THE APOSTLE and JAMES, the council decided the issue in favor of St. PAUL and the Gentile Christians, thus helping to separate early Christianity from Judaism.

Jerusalem, Temple of Either of two temples that were at the center of worship and national identity in ancient Israel. When DAVID captured Jerusalem, he moved the ARK OF THE COVENANT there. As the site for a temple, he selected Mount Moriah, or the Temple Mount, where it was believed that ABRAHAM had built his altar to sacrifice Isaac. The First Temple was constructed under David's son SOLOMON and was completed in 957 BC. It contained three rooms: a vestibule, the main room for religious services, and the HOLY OF HOLIES. From the time of JOSIAH, it was designated as the only place for sacrifice in JUDAH. It was destroyed during the Babylonian conquest in 586 BC. When the Jews returned from exile in 538, they built the Second Temple (finished 515). Its desecration by ANTIOCHUS IV in 167 BC set off the MACCABEES' revolt, after which it was cleansed and rededicated. In 54 BC MARCUS LICINIUS CRASSUS plundered the Temple. It was rebuilt and enlarged by HEROD THE GREAT; construction lasted 46 years. The Jewish rebellion in AD 66 led to its destruction by Roman legions in AD 70. All that remains is part of the WESTERN WALL, a site of pilgrimage. The Temple Mount is now occupied by a Muslim mosque, Al-Aqsa, and the DOME OF THE ROCK.

Jerusalem artichoke SUNFLOWER (Helianthus tuberosus) native to North America and grown for its edible TUBERS. The aboveground part of the plant is a coarse, usually multibranched, frost-tender perennial, 7–10 ft (2–3 m) tall. The numerous showy flower heads have yellow ray flowers and yellow, brownish, or purplish disk flowers. The underground tubers vary in shape, size, and color. The Jerusalem artichoke is popular as a cooked vegetable in Europe and has long been cultivated in France as a stock feed.

Jervis Bay Inlet of the South Pacific, NEW SOUTH WALES, Australia. It occupies an area of 28 sq mi (73 sq km). It was discovered in 1770 and named Long Nose by Capt. JAMES COOK, but in 1791 it was renamed for Adm. John Jervis. In 1915 it was transferred from the jurisdiction of New South Wales to the Australian Commonwealth to provide the AUSTRALIAN CAPITAL TERRITORY with access to the sea. The bay is a resort area and the site of the Royal Australian Naval College (founded 1915).

Jespersen \ˈyes-pər-sən\, **(Jens) Otto (Harry)** (1860–1943) Danish linguist. He led a movement for basing foreign-language teaching on conversational speech rather than textbook study of grammar and vocabulary, helping to revolutionize language teaching in Europe. An authority on English grammar, Jespersen contributed greatly to the advancement of phonetics and linguistic theory. His many published works include *Modern English Grammar* (7 vols., 1909–49), *Language: Its Nature, Development, and Origin* (1922), and *The Philosophy of Grammar* (1924). He originated Novial, an international language.

Jesuit \ˈje-zü-ət\ Member of the Roman Catholic order of religious men called the Society of Jesus. First organized by St. Ignatius of LOYOLA in 1534 at the University of Paris, the order was approved by Pope Paul III in 1540. It discontinued many practices of medieval religious life, such as obligatory penances and fasts and a common uniform, and instead focused on military-style mobility and adaptability. Its organization was characterized by centralized authority, probation lasting many years before final vows, and special obedience to the pope. The Jesuits served as a preaching, teaching, and missionary society, actively promoting the COUNTER-REFORMATION, and by the time of Ignatius's death in 1556 their efforts were already worldwide. The success of their enterprise and their championship of the pope earned them much hostility from both religious and political foes. Under pressure from France, Spain, and Portugal, Pope Clement XIV abolished the order in 1773, but it was restored by Pius VII in 1814. The Jesuits have since become the largest male religious order.

Jesuit Estates Controversy Canadian dispute between Protestants and Roman Catholics after reestablishment of the JESUIT order. After the pope suppressed the Jesuits in 1773, their landholdings in Canada were transferred to the British government. The pope restored the order in 1814, and some Jesuits returned to Canada in 1842. Restitution for their land was discussed, and the Jesuits' Estates Act (1888) gave $400,000 in compensation.

Jesus In CHRISTIANITY, the son of God and the second person of the Holy TRINITY. Christian doctrine holds that by his CRUCIFIXION and resurrection he paid for the sins of all mankind. His life and ministry are recounted in the four GOSPELS of the NEW TESTAMENT. He was born a Jew in Bethlehem before the death of HEROD THE GREAT in 4 BC, and he died while Pontius Pilate was Roman governor of Judaea (AD 28–30). His mother, MARY, was married to Joseph, a carpenter of Nazareth (see St. JOSEPH). Of his childhood after the birth narratives in Matthew and Luke, nothing is known, except for one visit to Jerusalem with his parents. He began his ministry about age 30, becoming a preacher, teacher, and healer. He gathered disciples in the region of GALILEE, including the 12 APOSTLES, and preached the imminent arrival of the KINGDOM OF GOD. His moral teachings, outlined in the SERMON ON THE MOUNT, and his reported miracles won him a growing number of followers, who believed that he was the promised MESSIAH. On Passover he entered Jerusalem on a donkey, where he shared the Last Supper with his disciples and was betrayed to the Roman authorities by JUDAS ISCARIOT. Arrested and tried, he was condemned to death as a political agitator and was crucified and buried. Three days later visitors to his tomb found it empty. According to the Gospels, he appeared several times to his disciples before ascending into heaven.

jet engine Any of a class of INTERNAL-COMBUSTION ENGINES that propel aircraft by means of the rearward discharge of a jet of fluid, usually hot exhaust gases generated by burning fuel with air drawn in from the atmosphere. Jets rely on the third of NEWTON'S LAWS OF MOTION (action and reaction are equal and opposite). The first jet-powered airplane was introduced in 1939 in Germany. The jet engine, consisting of a gas-turbine system, significantly simplified propulsion and enabled substantial increases in aircraft speed, size, and operating altitudes. Modern types of jet engines include TURBOJETS, turbofans, TURBOPROPS, turboshafts, and RAMJETS. See also DRAG, GASOLINE ENGINE, LIFT.

jet lag Period of adjustment of BIOLOGICAL RHYTHM after moving from one time zone to another, experienced as fatigue and lowered efficiency. It reflects a delay in the synchronization of changes in the level of blood cortisol, the major STEROID produced by the adrenal cortex (due to, see ADRENAL GLAND), with the local day-night cycle. Duration and severity depend on how much distance is covered in how little time. Travel by jet, after which the phenomenon may persist for some days, first made it noticeable, accounting for the name.

jet stream Any of several long, narrow, high-speed air currents that flow eastward in a generally horizontal zone in the STRATOSPHERE or upper TROPOSPHERE. Jet streams are characterized by wind motions that generate strong vertical shearing action, considered largely responsible for the clear-air turbulence experienced by aircraft. They also have an effect on weather patterns. Jet streams circle the earth in meandering paths, shifting position as well as speed with the seasons. In the winter they are nearer the equator and their speeds are higher than in the summer. There are often two, sometimes three, jet-stream systems in each hemisphere.

Jew Any person whose religion is JUDAISM. In a wider sense the term refers to any member of a worldwide ethnic and cultural group descended from the ancient Hebrews who traditionally practiced the Jewish religion. The Hebrew term *Yehudi,* translated as *Judaeus* in Latin and *Jew* in English, originally referred to a member of the tribe of JUDAH. In Jewish tradition, any child born of a Jewish mother is considered a Jew; in REFORM JUDAISM a child is considered a Jew if either parent is Jewish.

Jewel Cave National Monument National monument, southwestern South Dakota. Established in 1908, it occupies an area of 2 sq mi (5 sq km). It is noted for its limestone caverns, a series of chambers joined by narrow passages, which extend for at least 77 mi (124 km).

jewelry Objects designed for the adornment of the body, usually made of gold, silver, or platinum, often with precious or semiprecious stones. Jewelry evolved from shells, animal teeth, and other objects used as adornment in prehistoric times. Over the centuries it came to be a sign of social or religious rank. In Renaissance Italy, jewelry making reached the status of a fine art; many Italian sculptors trained as goldsmiths. From the 17th century the decorative function of jewelry again came to the fore, overshadowing its symbolic significance. By the 19th century, industrialization brought jewelry within the reach of the middle class. Firms opened by such jewelers as CARL FABERGE and LOUIS COMFORT TIFFANY achieved great success by making fine jewelry for the wealthy. It has played an important role in world history: in the 16th century the Spaniards established an empire to acquire the gold and jeweled objects of pre-Columbian Mexico and Peru.

Jewett, (Theodora) Sarah Orne (1849–1909) U.S. writer. Born in South Berwick, Me., the daughter of a doctor, she virtually never left the state. Concerned to capture the folkways of a vanishing culture, she wrote realistic sketches of aging Maine natives, whose manners, idioms, and pithiness she recorded with pungency and humor. Outstanding among her 20 volumes are *Deephaven* (1877), *A White Heron* (1886), and *The Country of the Pointed Firs* (1896).

jewfish Any of several large fishes of the SEA BASS family (Serranidae), especially *Epinephelus itajara,* found on the Atlantic coast of the New World tropics. They may reach a length of 8 ft (2.4 m) and a weight of about 700 lbs (320 kg). The adult is dull olive-brown with faint spots and bands and is usually solitary. The South Pacific jewfish *(E. lanceolatus)* may exceed 12 ft (3.7 m) in length. The Warsaw GROUPER *(E. nigritus)* and giant sea bass *(Stereolepis gigas)* are both occasionally called jewfish, and three Australian species in the genera *Johnius* and *Glaucosoma* are called jewfish.

Jewish calendar See Jewish CALENDAR

Jewish philosophy Any of various kinds of reflective thought engaged in by those identified as being Jews. In the Middle Ages, this meant any methodical and disciplined thought pursued by Jews, whether on specifically Judaic themes or not; in modern times, philosophers who do not discuss Judaism are not ordinarily classified as Jewish philosophers. Philosophy arose in Judaism under Greek influence, though a philosophical approach may be discerned in early Jewish religious works apparently uninfluenced by the Greeks. From the Bible, the books of Job and Ecclesiastes were favorite works of medieval philosophers; the book of Proverbs introduces the concept of Wisdom *(Hokhma),* which was to have primordial significance for Jewish philosophical thought; and the Wisdom of Solomon had considerable influence on Christian theology. Major figures of Jewish philosophy include PHILO JUDAEUS, SAADIA BEN JOSEPH, MOSES MAIMONIDES, and BENEDICT DE SPINOZA.

Jezebel \'je-zə-,bel\ (died c. 843 BC) In the Old Testament, the wife of King AHAB of Israel. The daughter of the priest-king Ethbaal of Tyre and Sidon, she persuaded Ahab to introduce the worship of the Tyrian god Baal-Melkart into Israel, thus interfering with the exclusive worship of Yahweh. The Book of 1 Kings tells how she was opposed by ELIJAH. After Ahab's death Jezebel's son Jehoram became king of Israel, but ELISHA encouraged a general, Jehu, to revolt. Jehoram was killed, and Jezebel was thrown from a window to her death. Dogs consumed most of her body, fulfilling a prophecy by Elijah. In history and literature she became the archetype of the wicked woman.

Jhabvala \'jäb-vä-lə\, **Ruth Prawer** *orig.* **Ruth Prawer** (born 1927) German-British-U.S. novelist and screenwriter. Born to a family of Polish Jews in Germany, she emigrated to England with her family in 1939. After receiving a master's degree, she married an Indian architect and moved to India, where she lived until 1975, when she moved to New York. Many of her novels, including *Heat and Dust* (1975, Booker Prize), are set in India. She has written original screenplays for such films as *Shakespeare Wallah* (1965) and film adaptations of such novels as *The Bostonians* (1984), *A Room With a View* (1985), and *Howards End* (1992). Later novels include *Poet and Dancer* (1993) and *Shards of Memory* (1995).

Jharkhand State (pop., 2001: 26,909,428), northeastern India. It occupies 28,833 sq mi (74,677 sq km); its capital is Ranchi. The state lies mainly on the Chota Nagapur Plateau, a series of plateaus, hills, and valleys. Many aboriginal peoples live there. The area now constituting Jharkhand was a part of BIHAR state after Indian independence in 1947 until it was made into a separate state in 2000. It is rich in minerals (notably copper), although most of the population is engaged in agriculture.

Jhelum River \'jā-ləm\ River, India and Pakistan. The westernmost of the "Five Rivers" of the PUNJAB, it rises in the HIMALAYAS in the Indian state of JAMMU AND KASHMIR. It meanders northwest in the Pakistani-held sector of Jammu and Kashmir. Bending southward, it joins the CHENAB RIVER, having traveled a course of 450 mi (725 km). It is believed to be the Hydaspes mentioned by Arrian, ALEXANDER THE GREAT's historian, and the Bidaspes mentioned by PTOLEMY.

Jhering \'yā-riŋ\, **Rudolf von** (1818–1892) German legal scholar. Born in Hanover, he taught law at the Univs. of Vienna (1868–72) and Göttingen (1872–92). He examined the relationship between law and social change in *Geist des römischen Rechts* (1852–65; "The Spirit of Roman Law") and between individual and social interests in *Der Zweck im Recht* (1877–83; "Law as a Means to an End"). He is sometimes called the father of sociological JURISPRUDENCE.

Jiang Jieshi See CHIANG KAI-SHEK

Jiang Jinguo See CHIANG CHING-KUO

Jiang Qing *or* **Chiang Ch'ing** \jē-'äŋ-'chiŋ\ (1914?–1991) Third wife of MAO ZEDONG and member of the radical GANG OF FOUR. Jiang married Mao in the 1930s but entered politics only in the 1960s. As first deputy head of the CULTURAL REVOLUTION, Jiang acquired far-reaching powers over China's cultural life and oversaw the total suppression of a wide variety of traditional cultural activities. Arrested after Mao's death and accused of fomenting the widespread civil unrest that characterized the Cultural Revolution, she refused to confess guilt and received a suspended death sentence that was commuted to life imprisonment. Her death was a suicide.

Jiang Zemin \jē-'äŋ-zə-'min\ (born 1926) General secretary of the CHINESE COMMUNIST PARTY (CCP) since 1989 and president of China since 1993. He started his career in Shanghai as an engineer, received training abroad, and gradually rose through the ranks of the CCP. He was named mayor of Shanghai in 1985 and chairman of China's Central Military

Commission in 1989. Jiang's support of the government's forcible suppression of the pro-democracy student demonstrations of 1989 won him the support of China's leaders at the time, DENG XIAOPING and Li Peng. He has combined a commitment to continued free-market reform with a determination to preserve the CCP's monopoly on political power.

Jiangsu *or* **Kiangsu** \jē-'äŋ-'sü\ Province (pop., 2000 est.: 74,380,000), eastern China. Its capital is NANJING. It occupies a wide alluvial plain that is divided into two sections by the estuary of the CHANG (Yangtze) River. One of the smallest and most densely populated provinces of China, it is also one of the richest. Once a part of the ancient state of Wu, the region was part of the Nanking province under the MING dynasty (1368–1644). It became a separate province in 1667 and served as the headquarters (1853–64) for the TAIPING REBELLION. It was an important base for China's Nationalist Party, which made Nanking the nation's capital 1928–37 and again 1946–49. The province was occupied by Japan during the SINO-JAPANESE WAR (1937–45) and came under Communist control in 1949. It is an important agricultural producer, and has factories producing steel and electronics.

Jiangxi *or* **Kiangsi** \jē-'äŋ-'shē\ Province (pop., 2000 est.: 41,400,000), southern central China. Its capital is NANCHANG. Located in the drainage basin of the GAN RIVER, it is one of China's richest agricultural provinces, and is also renowned for its porcelain industry, which dates from the 11th century. The opening of the GRAND CANAL under the TANG DYNASTY (618–907) set it on the main trade route between northern and southern China. During the MONGOL dynasty (1206–1368) it included part of Guangdong; its current boundaries were established in the MING DYNASTY. It was taken in 1926 by CHIANG KAI-SHEK, and was fought over by the Nationalists and the Communists. Occupied by the Japanese 1938–45, it came under Communist control in 1949. Agricultural production, as well as a thriving timber industry contribute to the economy.

Jibril *or* **Jabrail** \ji-'brēl\ In Islam, the archangel who acts as intermediary between God and mankind who bore divine revelations to MUHAMMAD and previous prophets. His biblical counterpart is GABRIEL. Jibril aided Muhammad in times of crisis and guided him during his ascent into heaven. Muslim legend holds that Jibril appeared to ADAM after his expulsion from Paradise to show him how to write, raise wheat, and work iron, and also aided MOSES in delivering the Israelites from Egypt.

jícama \'hē-kə-mə\ Leguminous vine *(Pachyrhizus erosus*, or *P. tuberosus),* also called yam bean. A native of Mexico and Central and South America, it is grown for its edible root. The irregularly globular, brown-skinned tubers are white-fleshed, crisp, and juicy. There are two varieties, those with clear juice and those with milky juice. Both have a mild flavor and are eaten raw or cooked. Sometimes very young seedpods of the plant are eaten, but the mature seeds are highly toxic.

Jidda *or* **Jeddah** City (pop., 1992: 2,046,251), western Saudi Arabia. Located on the Red Sea, it is a major port and the nation's diplomatic capital. It takes its name (which means "ancestress" or "grandmother") from the reputed tomb of Eve, located there until it was destroyed by the Saudi government in 1928. Jidda has long been a point of entry for Muslim pilgrims journeying to the holy cities of MECCA and MEDINA. It belonged to Turkey until 1916, when it yielded to British forces. It was captured by the Muslim leader IBN SAUD in 1925 and was incorporated into Saudi Arabia in 1927.

jigs and fixtures Components of MACHINE-TOOL installations, specially designed in each case to position the workpiece, hold it firmly in place, and guide the motion of the power tool (e.g., a PUNCH PRESS). Jigs can also be guides for tools or templates, as in the furniture industry. Special cramping jigs that ensure squareness are set up so that, for example, a wardrobe can be glued up in one operation by power-driven rams. See also ASSEMBLY LINE, INTERCHANGEABLE PARTS, MASS PRODUCTION.

jihad \ji-'häd\ In ISLAM, the central doctrine that calls on believers to combat the enemies of their religion. According to the QURAN and the HADITH, jihad is a duty that may be fulfilled in four ways: by the heart, the tongue, the hand, and the sword. The first way (known in SUFISM as the "greater jihad") involves struggling against evil desires. The ways of the tongue and hand call for verbal defense and right actions. The jihad of the sword involves waging war against enemies of Islam. Believers who die in combat become martyrs and are guaranteed a place in paradise. In the 20th century the concept of jihad has sometimes been used as an ideological weapon in the effort to combat Western influences and secular governments and establish an ideal Islamic society.

Jili \jē-'lē\, **al-** (1365–c. 1424) Islamic mystic. Little is known of his life, though he is believed to have visited India in 1387 and to have studied in Yemen 1393–1403. Influenced by IBN AL-ARABI, he developed his doctrine of the "perfect man," which he outlined in his *Studies in Islamic Mysticism.* He asserted that the perfectly moral individual can attain unity with God, a unity already experienced by MUHAMMAD and the other prophets, and then becomes a channel by which the whole community can enjoy contact with the divine being.

Jilin \'je-'lin\ *or* **Kirin** \'kē-rin\ Province (population 2000 est.: 27,280,000), northeastern China. It is China's most urbanized province; its capital is CHANGCHUN, and its second largest city is Jilin. Its major river is the Sungari River, a tributary of the AMUR. It was made a province in 1907. Occupied by the Japanese army in 1931, it became part of the puppet state of MANCHUGUO (1932–45). Chinese communist forces seized the province from the Nationalists in 1948. Industrialization since the late 20th century has been rapid.

Jim Crow laws Laws that enforced racial segregation in the U.S. South between 1877 and the 1950s. The term, taken from a minstrel-show routine, became a derogatory epithet for blacks. After RECONSTRUCTION, Southern legislatures passed laws requiring segregation of whites and "persons of color" on public transportation. These later extended to schools, restaurants, and other public places. In 1954 the U.S. Supreme Court declared segregation in public schools unconstitutional in *BROWN VS. BOARD OF EDUCATION*; later rulings struck down other Jim Crow laws.

Jiménez \k̲ē-'mā-nās, *Engl* hē-'mā-nəs\, **Juan Ramón** (1881–1958) Spanish poet. His early poetry reflects the influence of RUBEN DARIO; this highly emotional style gave way to a more austere tone c. 1917. He achieved popularity in America with *Platero and I* (1917), a prose story of a man and his donkey. During the Spanish Civil War (1936–39) he allied himself with Republican forces; after their defeat he moved to Puerto Rico, where he spent most of the rest of his life. His poetic output was immense. He was awarded the Nobel Prize in 1956.

Jiménez de Quesada \k̲ē-'mā-nās-t̲h̲ā-kā-'sä-t̲h̲ä\, **Gonzalo** (c. 1495–1579) Spanish conquistador. He went to the New World as a colonial chief magistrate, then in 1536 led an expedition of 900 men up the Magdalena River into the central plain of New Granada (modern Colombia), defeating the CHIBCHA Indians to win the land for Spain. In 1538 two rival conquistadores challenged his claim of conquest; the case was submitted to the crown in Madrid and was inconclusively settled, but Jiménez became the most influential person in New Granada. In 1569 he set out in search of the mythical EL DORADO with 500 men; he returned in 1571 with only 25 of his original company.

Jimmu \'jēm-,mü\ Legendary first emperor of Japan and founder of the imperial dynasty. He is credited with establishing his state in 660 BC on the plains of Yamato. (An actual state on the Yamato plains dates from the 3rd century AD.) Jimmu was believed to be a descendant of Ninigi, who was in turn the grandson of the sun goddess AMATERASU.

Jin dynasty *or* **Chin dynasty** \'jin\ First of two major Chinese dynasties to bear the name Jin. The dynasty had two distinct phases: the Western Jin (AD 265–317) and the Eastern Jin (AD 317–420). The latter is considered one of the SIX DYNASTIES that ruled China between the fall of the HAN (AD 220) and the establishment of the SUI (581). China was reunited under Sima Yan (Ssu-ma Yen), first of the Jin emperors, but after his death the empire rapidly crumbled. The XIONGNU nomads of the north overran the Jin capital of Luoyang and later defeated the Jin again at CHANGAN. For the next two centuries China was divided into two societies, northern (plagued by barbarian invasions) and southern. The Eastern Jin, founded by another Sima prince at Nanjing, suffered revolts, court intrigues, and frontier wars, but also saw the flourishing of Buddhism in China and the birth of China's first great painter, Gu Kaizhi (344–406?). See also JUCHEN DYNASTY.

Jina See TIRTHANKARA

Jinan *or* **Tsinan** \'jē-'nän\ City (pop., 1990: 1,481,000), capital of SHANDONG province, northeastern China. It dates at least from the ZHOU period (c. 11th century–3rd century BC), and has been an administrative center since the 8th century BC. Nearby Mount Tai was one of China's greatest holy mountains; many Buddhist cave temples were built in the hills south of the city in the 4th–7th century AD. It was made the capital of Shandong under the MING DYNASTY (1368–1644). Opened to foreign commerce in 1904, it developed further after becoming a railroad junction in 1912. It is now a major administrative and industrial center and Shandong's chief cultural center, with agricultural, medical, and engineering colleges and a large university (1926).

jinja In the SHINTO religion, a place where a god is enshrined or to which it is summoned. Originally rural sites of great natural beauty, they now include urban shrines. They vary in size from small roadside places of prayer to large building complexes such as the Grand ISE SHRINE. There are more than 97,000 such shrines in Japan.

Jinnah, Mohammed Ali (1876–1948) Indian Muslim politician, founder and first governor-general of Pakistan (1947–48). He was educated in Bombay (now Mumbai) and London, where he became a lawyer at 19. After returning to India, he practiced law and was elected to India's Imperial Legislative Council in 1910. Committed to home rule for India and to maintaining Hindu-Muslim unity, he joined the Muslim League in 1913 and worked to ensure the collaboration of the INDIAN NATIONAL CONGRESS and the MUSLIM LEAGUE. He was opposed to MOHANDAS K. GANDHI's noncooperation movement and withdrew from the Congress and the Muslim League. In the late 1920s and early 1930s, he was seen as too moderate by some Muslims but too Muslim by the Congress Party. From 1937, when the Congress Party refused to form coalition governments with the Muslim League in the provinces, Jinnah began to work for the partitioning of India and the creation of a Muslim state. Pakistan emerged as an independent country in 1947, and Jinnah became its first head of state. He died in 1948, revered as the father of the nation.

jinni *or* **genie** In Arabic mythology, any of the supernatural spirits less powerful than angels or devils. Evil spirits of air or fire, they could take animal or human form and could dwell in inanimate objects or under the earth. They had the bodily needs of human beings and could be killed, but were otherwise free of physical restraints. Jinn delighted in punishing humans for any harm done to them, but people who knew the proper magical procedure could exploit them to their own advantage. The jinn were popular subjects for folklore, notably in the tale of ALADDIN in *The THOUSAND AND ONE NIGHTS.*

Jinsha River, *or* **Kinsha River,** *or* **Chin-sha River** \'jin-'shä\ River, China. The westernmost major headwater stream of the YANGTZE RIVER (Chang Jiang), it rises in western QINGHAI province south of the KUNLUN MOUNTAINS. and flows south to form the western border of SICHUAN province for some 250 mi (400 km). It then flows into YUNNAN province, and swings northeast to join the MIN RIVER at Yibin and form the Yangtze.

jito \'jē-tō\ In feudal Japan, a land steward appointed by the central military government to each of the estates (SHOEN) into which the countryside was divided. The jito collected taxes and maintained the peace; he was also entitled to a portion of the taxes collected. The position, created by MINAMOTO YORITOMO, came to be hereditary. As time went by, the jito came to have closer ties with local leaders than with the central government, which contributed to the weakening of the KAMAKURA SHOGUNATE.

jitterbug Dance variation of the two-step in which couples swing, balance, and twirl in standardized patterns to syncopated music in 4/4 time. It originally included acrobatic lifts and swings, but became modified in ballroom versions. It originated in the U.S. in the mid-1930s and became internationally popular in the 1940s. Its step patterns varied, and could include the lindy hop and the jive.

Jiulong See KOWLOON

jiva \'jē-və\ In JAINISM, the SOUL or living spirit. Jivas are believed to be eternal and infinite in number. Many are bound to earthly existence by KARMA that requires them to move through the cycle of rebirth in successive bodies. Eventually a jiva may obtain release, whereupon a replacement is promoted from the lowest class of jivas, the tiny invisible souls called *nigoda*s that fill the whole space of the world.

jizya *or* **jizyah** \'jiz-yə\ Poll tax that early Islamic rulers demanded from their non-Muslim subjects. This tax applied especially to followers of Judaism, Christianity, and Zoroastrianism, who were tolerated in the practice of their religion because they were "peoples of the book." Originally intended to be used for charitable purposes, the revenues from the jizya were paid into the private treasuries of rulers, and the Ottoman sultans used the proceeds to pay military expenses. Many converted to Islam in order to escape the tax.

Joachim \ˌyō-ä-'kēm\, **Joseph** (1831–1907) Austro-Hungarian violinist. A prodigy, he began study as a child in Pest, continuing later in Vienna and Leipzig, where he was associated with F. MENDELSSOHN. He was concertmaster at Weimar under F. LISZT (1850–52), but their tastes in music diverged radically. He became close to J. BRAHMS, who sought Joachim's advice about his violin concerto. Joachim wrote cadenzas that are still used for a number of concertos. As the longtime head of Berlin's Hochschule (1868–1905), he developed it into a first-rank conservatory.

Joachim of Fiore \yō-'ä-kēm...'fyō-rā\ (c. 1130–1201/02) Italian mystic, theologian, and philosopher of history. After a pilgrimage to the Holy Land, he became a Cistercian monk, and by 1177 he was abbot at Corazzo, Sicily. He retired into the mountains to follow a contemplative life in 1191, and in 1196 he founded the order of San Giovanni in Fiore. His *Book of Harmony of the New and Old Testaments* outlined a theory of history and traced correspondences in the Old and New Testaments. In his *Exposition of the Apocalypse* he examined the symbols of the Antichrist, and in *Psaltery of Ten Strings* he expounded his doctrine of the Holy Trinity. A man of vivid imagination, he was both acclaimed as a prophet and denounced as a heretic.

Joan, Pope Legendary female pontiff who supposedly reigned, as Pope John VIII, for about 25 months from 855 to 858. The tale held that she was an Englishwoman who fell in love with a Benedictine monk, disguised herself as a man, and joined his order. After acquiring great learning she moved to Rome, where she became cardinal and then pope. In the earliest version of the story, she was pregnant at the time of her election and gave birth during the procession to the Lateran, whereupon she was dragged out of Rome and stoned to death. The legend, regarded as fact until the 17th century, has since been proved to be apocryphal.

Joan I *or* **Joanna I** *Italian* **Giovanna** (1326–1382) Countess of Provence and queen of Naples (1343–82). She belonged to the house of Anjou, and her marriage to the brother of the king of Hungary was intended to reconcile Hungarian and Angevin claims on Naples. Suspected of her husband's murder, she fled to Avignon (1348). She sold Avignon to the papacy in return for being cleared of the crime, then went back to Naples in 1352. She recognized the antipope Clement VII in 1378, and Pope URBAN VI crowned Charles of Durazzo king of Naples in 1381. When Charles captured Naples, he imprisoned Joanna and had her killed.

Joan of Arc, St. *French* **Jeanne d'Arc** \zhän-'dårk\ (1412?–1431) French military heroine. She was a peasant girl who from an early age believed she heard the voices of Sts. Michael, Catherine, and Margaret. When she was about 16, her voices began urging her to aid France's Dauphin (crown prince) and save France from the English attempt at conquest in the HUNDRED YEARS' WAR. Dressed in men's clothes, she visited the Dauphin and convinced him, his advisers, and the church authorities to support her. With her inspiring conviction, she rallied the French troops and raised the English siege of Orléans in 1429. She soon defeated the English again at Patay. The Dauphin was crowned king at Reims as Charles VII, with Joan beside him. Her siege of Paris was unsuccessful, and in 1430 she was captured by the Burgundians and sold to the English. Abandoned by Charles, she was turned over to the ecclesiastical court at Rouen, controlled by French clerics who supported the English, and tried for witchcraft and heresy (1431). She fiercely defended herself, but finally recanted and was sentenced to life imprisonment; when she again asserted that she had been divinely inspired, she was burned at the stake. She was not canonized until 1920.

Job \'jōb\ Central character of the Book of Job in the OLD TESTAMENT, known for his faithfulness to God despite his many afflictions. At the beginning, Job is a wealthy man with a large family. Satan challenges God to allow him to take away Job's blessings as a test of his faith. Soon Job is desolate, covered with boils, his wealth gone and his family dead. Three friends arrive to comfort him; he disputes with them, denying he has done anything to deserve this misery but maintaining his faith in God. At the end, in a confrontation with God, the power and mystery of the deity are memorably reasserted, but the problem of why the innocent suffer is left unresolved. The book dates from the 6th–4th century BC.

Jobim \zhō-ˈbi^n\, **Antonio Carlos** (1927–1994) Brazilian songwriter and composer. He performed on guitar and piano in Rio de Janeiro clubs before becoming music director of Odeon Records. In 1959 he and Luís Bonfá composed the "Manha de Carnaval" for the film *Black Orpheus*, and his worldwide success soon followed. He transformed samba music into bossa nova ("new wrinkle" or "new wave"), whose fusion of understated samba pulse (quiet percussion, unamplified guitars playing subtly complex rhythms), gentle singing, and the melodic and sophisticated harmonies of cool jazz found a long-lasting niche in U.S. popular music. He collaborated with F. SINATRA, STAN GETZ, and Astrud Gilberto, and he also composed classical works and film scores. His more than 400 songs include "The Girl from Ipanema."

Jobs, Steven P(aul) (born 1955) U.S. businessman. He dropped out of Reed College and went to work for Atari Corp. designing video games. In 1976 he cofounded (with STEPHEN WOZNIAK) Apple Computer, Inc. The first Apple computer, created when Jobs was only 21, changed the public's idea of a computer from a huge machine for scientific use to a home appliance. Apple's Macintosh computer, which appeared in 1984, introduced a GRAPHICAL USER INTERFACE and MOUSE technology that became the standard for all applications interfaces. In 1980 Apple made an initial public offering, and Jobs became the company's chairman. Management conflicts led him to leave Apple in 1985 to form NeXT Computer Inc., but he returned to Apple in 1996 and became CEO in 1997; the striking new iMac computer (1998) revived the company's flagging fortunes.

Jocho \ˈjō-ˌchō\ (died 1057) Japanese Buddhist sculptor. The son and pupil of a sculptor, he worked primarily for the FUJIWARA FAMILY. He was awarded unprecedented honors for sculptures executed for Kyoto's Hojo Temple and for the Fujiwara family temple in Nara. He was instrumental in improving the social standing of Buddhist sculptors by organizing a guild, and he perfected the so-called *kiyoseho,* or joined-wood technique. His only extant work is a carved Amida (Buddha) figure (c. 1053) in the Byodo Temple at Uji.

Joel Second of the 12 Minor Prophets in the OLD TESTAMENT, author of the Book of Joel. (His prophecy is part of a larger book, The Twelve, in the Jewish canon.) He lived sometime during the period of the Second Temple of JERSUSALEM (516 BC–AD 70), but nothing is known of his life. He opens his prophecy by describing a plague of locusts, an allegory of the disasters to come upon a faithless people. His message is simple: salvation will come to Judah only when the people truly turn to Yahweh.

Joffre \ˈzhȯfr^ə\, **Joseph (-Jacques-Césaire)** (1852–1931) French commander in chief on the Western Front in World War I. He was responsible for the calamitous campaign with which the French army began operations in 1914 against Germany, but he shifted his forces and created a new French army under his direct command that won a great victory in the First Battle of the MARNE (1914). As commander in chief (1915–16), he ordered the French armies to burst through the German positions, at ruinous cost. His prestige waned, and because of the lack of French preparation for the Battle of VERDUN (1916) he was stripped of his direct command and resigned. He was created a marshal of France in 1916.

Joffre, detail of a portrait by H. Jacquier, 1915.

H. ROGER-VIOLLET

Joffrey, Robert *orig.* **Abdullah Jaffa Bey Khan** (1930–1988) U.S. dancer and choreographer, founder-director of the Joffrey Ballet. Born in Seattle to an Afghan father, he studied dance there and later in New York. He opened a ballet school in 1953 and formed the first of several groups. In 1956 he founded the Robert Joffrey (later simply Joffrey) Ballet with Gerald Arpino (born 1928). The company gained international fame and toured widely. In 1965 it became affiliated with the New York City Center. After Joffrey's death, Arpino became director; in 1995 he moved the company to Chicago, renaming it the Joffrey Ballet of Chicago.

Jogan style \ˈjō-ˌgän\ Japanese sculptural style of the early HEIAN PERIOD, seen primarily but not exclusively in Buddhist sculptures. The massive figures, carved from single blocks of wood, are columnar, erect, and symmetrical, with large round faces, large lips, wide noses, and wide eyes, almost geometrically simplified. The drapery, composed of alternating series of small and large waves, is its most distinguishing feature. The technique was first seen on the drapery of the colossal image of the Buddha at Bamian, Afghanistan; Chinese and Japanese pilgrims brought back holy images and used them as prototypes.

jogging Aerobic exercise involving running at an easy pace. *Jogging* (1967) by Bill Bowerman and W. E. Harris boosted jogging's popularity for fitness, weight loss, and stress relief. Many medical authorities endorse jogging, but others warn of risks to feet, shins, knees, and backs.

Johanan ben Zakkai \jō-ˈha-nən-ben-ˈza-kā-ˌī\ (fl. 1st century AD) Palestinian Jewish sage. A leading representative of the PHARISEES, he helped preserve and develop Judaism in the years after the destruction of the Second Temple of Jerusalem (AD 70). He is said to have visited the Roman camp and persuaded the future emperor VESPASIAN to allow him to set up an academy at Jamnia near the Judaean coast. He established an authoritative rabbinic body there and was revered as a great teacher and scholar.

Johannesburg City (metro. area population, 1996: 1,480,530), northeastern Republic of South Africa. One of the country's largest cities, it lies on the southern slopes of the highland region called the Witwatersrand. It was founded in 1886 after the discovery of gold nearby and was occupied by the British during the SOUTH AFRICAN WAR in 1900. It was a legally segregated city until 1991, with nonwhites restricted to living in outlying areas called townships, including SOWETO. Greater Johannesburg extends over more than 200 sq mi (500 sq km) and includes more than 500 suburbs and townships. It is a leading industrial and financial center. Its cultural and educational institutions include the Johannesburg Art Gallery, the Civic Theatre, the University of Witwatersrand, and Rand Afrikaans Univ.

Johannsen, Wilhelm Ludvig (1857–1927) Danish botanist and geneticist. He supported HUGO DE VRIES's discovery that variation in genotype can occur by mutation; the new character, while independent of natural selection in its initial occurrence, is then subject to natural selection. Johannsen's *Elements of Heredity* (1909) became an influential text, and his terms phenotype and genotype are now a part of the language of genetics.

Johansson, Carl E(dvard) (1864–1943) Swedish mechanical engineer. He began work on the problem of precision measurement needed in mass production while working at a rifle factory. He devised the principle of standard gauge blocks and devised manufacturing techniques for making them. Johansson's system, adopted at the Cadillac automobile factory in 1910 and subsequently by HENRY FORD, became a fundamental component of 20th-century mass-production technique.

Johansson, (Per) Christian (1817–1903) Swedish-born ballet dancer and teacher. Johansson trained at the ballet school of the Royal Opera in Stockholm and later under AUGUST BOURNONVILLE. He was engaged at the Imperial Russian Ballet in 1841. In his prime his innate nobility and grace were unsurpassed. In 1860 he turned his attention to teaching at the Imperial Ballet School. Over the next four decades he brought a new polish to the Russian style, providing it with a firm base in the French method that he had learned from Bournonville.

John *known as* **John Lackland** (1167–1216) King of England (1199–1216). The youngest son of HENRY II, he joined his brother Richard (later RICHARD I) in a rebellion against Henry (1189). John became lord of Ireland, and when Richard was imprisoned in Germany on his way back from the Third CRUSADE, he tried to seize control of England (1193). On Richard's return John was banished (1194), but the two were later reconciled. Crowned king in 1199, John lost Normandy (1204) and most of his other French lands in a war with PHILIP II AUGUSTUS. After INNOCENT III excommunicated him for refusing to recognize STEPHEN LANGTON as archbishop of Canterbury, John was obliged to declare England a fief of the Holy See (1213). He launched a military campaign against France in 1214 but made no lasting gains. His heavy taxes and aggressive assertion of feudal privileges led to the outbreak of civil war (1215). The barons forced him to sign the MAGNA CARTA, but the civil war continued until his death.

John *or* **John de Balliol** (c. 1250–1313) King of Scotland (1292–96). He was one of 13 claimants to the throne but won by primogeniture. John paid homage to EDWARD I of England but soon refused his request for military aid in Gascony and instead signed a treaty with the French. When Edward invaded Gascony in 1296, the Scots raided northern England. Within months Edward's army had captured strategic castles in Scotland, and John was forced to resign his kingdom to Edward. He was held in the Tower of London until 1299.

John, Augustus (Edwin) (1878–1961) Welsh painter, portraitist, muralist, and draftsman. By the age of 20 he had won a reputation for his brilliant drawing technique. A colorful personality, he roamed Britain, living with Gypsies and learning their customs and language; the painting *Encampment on Dartmoor* (1906) is based on these experiences. His most significant portraits include those of JAMES JOYCE and GEORGE BERNARD SHAW.

John, Elton (Hercules) *orig.* **Reginald Kenneth Dwight** *later* **Sir Elton** (born 1947) British rock singer, pianist, and songwriter. He played piano by ear as a child, winning a scholarship to the Royal Academy of Music at 11. In the late 1960s he began the extraordinarily successful partnership with lyricist Bernie Taupin (born 1950) that would produce such hit albums as *Goodbye Yellow Brick Road* (1973) and such songs as "Rocket Man," "Bennie and the Jets," and "Philadelphia Freedom." The two returned with more hits in the early 1980s, including "I Guess That's Why They Call It the Blues." In 1997 John performed a new version of 1973's "Candle In the Wind" at the funeral of his friend DIANA, PRINCESS OF WALES; his recording immediately became the best-selling single of all time.

John, St. See St. JOHN THE APOSTLE

John I *Portuguese* **João** *known as* **John of Aviz** \ə-'vēzh\ (1357–1433) King of Portugal (1385–1433) and founder of the Aviz dynasty. The illegitimate son of Pedro I, he was elected king in 1385 despite the rivalry of Castilian candidates. He fought off a Castilian invasion (1385) and preserved Portugal's independence. He made an alliance with England (1386), but a joint invasion of León was unsuccessful. John signed a 10-year truce with Castile in 1389, but frontier warfare was intermittent until 1411. He and his sons (including the youngest, later HENRY THE NAVIGATOR) captured Ceuta in Morocco in 1415, thus beginning the era of Portuguese expansion.

John II *French* **Jean** *known as* **John the Good** (1319–1364) King of France (1350–64). At odds with England and Navarre, he tried to make peace with the Navarrese king CHARLES II, then had him imprisoned in 1356. EDWARD THE BLACK PRINCE, son of EDWARD III of England, led an invasion of southern France, defeating and capturing John at the Battle of POITIERS (1356). John was forced to sign the treaties of BRÉTIGNY and Calais (1360), which fixed an extravagant ransom and surrendered most of southwestern France to the English. See also HUNDRED YEARS' WAR.

John II Comnenus \käm-'nē-nəs\ (1088–1143) Byzantine emperor (1118–43). The son of ALEXIUS I COMNENUS, he made it his mission to reconquer Byzantine territory lost to the Arabs, Turks, and crusaders. He sought to strengthen Byzantine finances by ending Venetian trading privileges in the empire but was forced to restore them after an unsuccessful war (1122). John allied himself with the German emperor against ROGER II of Sicily (1130). He reconquered Cilicia (1137) and won homage from Antioch, but he failed to defeat the Syrian Turks.

John III Ducas Vatatzes \'dyü-kəs-və-'tat-sēz\ (1193–1254) Emperor of NICAEA (1222–54). He succeeded THEODORE I LASCARIS and defeated rivals for the imperial throne in 1223. Two years later he triumphed over Latin forces loyal to his rivals and gained control of Asia Minor. He allied with IVAN ASEN II against Epirus (1230) and besieged Constantinople (1235), prompting Asen to go to war with him (1235–37). He acquired territory in Bulgaria (1241) and Epirus (1242) and supported a cultural revival from his capital at Nicaea, paving the way for the eventual reestablishment of the Byzantine Empire. Venerated by his people, he was canonized in the Eastern Church.

John III Sobieski \sòb-'yā-skē\ *Polish* **Jan Sobieski** (1629–1696) Elective king of Poland (1674–96). Named commander in chief of the Polish army (1668), he distinguished himself by victories over the Cossacks and Turks. His reputation was so great that he was elected king in preference to the Habsburgs' candidate. In 1683 he concluded a treaty with Emperor LEOPOLD I against the Ottoman Turks. When a Turkish army approached Vienna later that year, he rushed there with troops, took command of the entire relief force, and achieved a brilliant victory, briefly restoring the kingdom of Poland-Lithuania to greatness for the last time. He was unsuccessful in a Hungarian campaign (1683–91) to liberate Moldavia and Walachia from Ottoman rule. Later, rebellion within his own family, with nobles fighting each other rather than the Turks, led finally to Poland's downfall in the 18th century.

John III Sobieski, engraving by Carel Allardt.

BY COURTESY OF THE TRUSTEES OF THE BRITISH MUSEUM; PHOTOGRAPH, J.R. FREEMAN & CO. LTD.

John V Palaeologus \ˌpā-lē-'ä-lə-gəs\ (1332–1391) Byzantine emperor (1341–91). The son of ANDRONICUS III PALAEOLOGUS, he inherited the throne at age 9; JOHN VI CANTACUZENUS served as his regent and co-emperor (1347–54). John V offered to end the schism between the Byzantine and Latin churches in return for Western help against the Ottoman Turks (1354), but no military aid was given. Impoverished by war, he was arrested as a debtor when he visited Venice (1369). In 1371 he was forced to recognize Turkish overlords, who later helped him to regain the throne (1379) after he was deposed by his son.

John VI Cantacuzenus \ˌkan-tə-kyü-'zē-nəs\ (1292–1383) Byzantine emperor (1347–54). As chief adviser (1328–41) to ANDRONICUS III PALAEOLOGUS, he directed both domestic and foreign policy. He fought to serve as regent for the young JOHN V PALAEOLOGUS, triumphing over John's mother, Anna of Savoy, only by enlisting Turkish aid. From 1347 he ruled as co-emperor with John V, but in 1354 he crowned his own son co-emperor. With Venetian aid, John V then forced him to abdicate, and he retired to a monastery, where he wrote his memoirs.

John VIII Palaeologus \ˌpā-lē-'ä-lə-gəs\ (1390–1448) Byzantine emperor (1421–48). The son of MANUEL II PALAEOLOGUS, he was crowned co-emperor with his father in 1421. Of the diminished and fragmented empire, he ruled only Constantinople and the surrounding area. The city was besieged by the Ottoman Turks (1422), and when Thessaloniki fell to Turkish forces (1430), John appealed to the West for help. He united the Byzantine and Latin churches (1439), but joint efforts against the Turks failed, and the Byzantines refused to submit to the pope. John died amid intrigues over succession.

John XXII *orig.* **Jacques Duèse** (died 1334) Second Avignon pope (1316–34). The successor to CLEMENT V, he established the papal court at Avignon on a permanent basis (see AVIGNON PAPACY). He condemned the Spiritual FRANCISCANS' interpretation of the poverty of Christ and his apostles and upheld papal authority over imperial elections against the opposition of the emperor, LOUIS IV. When John excommunicated Louis, the emperor retaliated by declaring him deposed (1328) and sponsoring the election of an ANTIPOPE. John's views on the Beatific Vision provoked accusations of heresy (1331–32). He is remembered for centralizing church administration and adding to the body of canon law.

John XXIII *orig.* **Angelo Giuseppe Roncalli** (1881–1963) Pope (1958–63). He studied theology in Rome, was ordained a priest in 1904, and held a variety of church offices. In 1944 he was named papal nuncio to newly liberated France, where he successfully revived sympathy for the Vatican. Made a cardinal in 1953, he was

John XXIII, 1963.

KEYSTONE

elected pope after the death of PIUS XII in 1958. Because of his advanced age, he was expected to be little more than a caretaker in the office, but instead he became the major reforming pope of the century. Eager to lead the church into the modern era, he called the Second VATICAN COUNCIL in 1962 and invited Eastern Orthodox and Protestant observers to join Catholic delegates. He also sought to repair relations with the Jews. Though John died before the end of the council, it went on to make major reforms in Catholic liturgy and administration. An advocate of world peace, John was one of the most popular popes in history.

John Birch Society Organization founded in 1958 by Robert H. Welch, Jr. (1899–1985), a retired candymaker, to combat communism and promote ultraconservative causes. It was named for an American missionary and army intelligence officer killed by Chinese Communists in 1945, considered by the society the first hero of the COLD WAR. Its membership reached over 70,000 in the 1960s. Its many publications warned of communist infiltration of the U.S. government and called for the impeachment of such officials as EARL WARREN. *The New American* is the organization's biweekly magazine.

John Day Fossil Beds National Monument National monument, northern central Oregon. With an area of 14,014 acres (5,676 hectares), it is located along the John Day River (named after a Virginian scout of the 1811 Astor overland expedition). Features include fossils more than 30 million years old that provide a paleontological record of five epochs of the Cenozoic era.

John de Balliol See JOHN (SCOTLAND)

John Lackland See JOHN (ENGLAND)

John Maurice of Nassau *Dutch* **Johan Maurits van Nassau** (1604–1679) Dutch colonial governor and military commander. He fought in the campaigns of his cousin FREDERICK HENRY, prince of Orange, against Spain after 1621. As colonial governor in Brazil, recently conquered from Portugal, he secured control of vast areas for the Dutch West India Co. in the years 1636–44, bringing the Dutch empire in Latin America to the peak of its power. He also sponsored the seizure of Angola (1641) and of several key ports on the western African coast to supply slaves for Brazilian plantations, and he led a Dutch army in 1665 in the ANGLO-DUTCH WARS.

John of Brienne \brē-'en\ (1148?–1237) Count of Brienne (in northeastern France), and later king of Jerusalem (1210–29) and Latin emperor of Constantinople (1231–37). He was the penniless younger son of a French count and, with the support of Phillip II Augustus, married the queen of the crusader state of Jerusalem and after her death became regent for their infant daughter. He arranged a truce with Egypt (1212) and participated in the unsuccessful Fifth CRUSADE. In 1228 he became regent and co-emperor of Constantinople, and he was crowned emperor three years later. He fended off attacks by IVAN ASEN II and JOHN III DUCAS VATATZES.

John of Damascus, St. *or* **St. John Damascene** (c. 675–749) Monk and theological doctor of the Greek and Latin churches. As a writer of hymns and theology, he had great influence in the Eastern and Western churches, especially through *De fide orthodoxa* ("The Orthodox Faith"), a summary of the teachings of the Greek fathers. He also wrote against the iconoclasts (see ICONOCLASM).

John of Gaunt *later* **Duke of Lancaster** (1340–1399) English prince. The fourth son of EDWARD III, John's additional name "Gaunt" (a corruption of his birthplace, Ghent) was never used after he was 3 years old; it became the popularly accepted form of his name through its use in WILLIAM SHAKESPEARE's play *Richard II*. John served as a commander in the Hundred Years' War against France then returned to become an important influence in his father's last years as king and in the reign of his nephew RICHARD II. Through his first wife, John acquired the duchy of Lancaster in 1362, and he was the immediate ancestor of the 15th-century monarchs HENRY IV, HENRY V, and HENRY VI.

John of Paris *or* **Jean de Paris** \'zhä^n-də-pȧ-'rē\ *or* **John the Deaf** *or* **John Quidort** \kē-'dȯr\ (c. 1255–1306) Dominican monk and disciple of St. THOMAS AQUINAS. A lecturer at the University of Paris, he wrote on the separation of church and state and the limits of papal authority. His controversial view on the nature of the EUCHARIST (1304) was censured, and he was sentenced to perpetual silence; he died before his appeal could be decided.

John of Salisbury \'sȯlz-ˌber-ē\ (1115/20–1180) English prelate and scholar. A noted Latinist, he served as secretary to Theobald and ST. THOMAS BECKET, archbishops of Canterbury. He wrote *Historia pontificalis* (1163?) and the *Policraticus* and the *Metalogicon* (both 1159) His willingness to champion ecclesiastical independence led HENRY II to exile him to France (1163). He returned to England after the reconciliation of Henry and Becket and was in Canterbury Cathedral when Becket was assassinated. As bishop of Chartres (from 1176) he was active in the third LATERAN COUNCIL.

John of the Cross, St. *Spanish* **San Juan de la Cruz** *orig.* **Juan de Yepes y Álvarez** (1542–1591) Spanish mystic, poet, Doctor of the Church, and reformer of monasticism. He became a Carmelite monk at Medina del Campo and was ordained a priest in 1567. Joining St. TERESA OF ÁVILA in her effort to restore the Carmelites to their original austerity, he cofounded the Discalced Carmelite order in 1568. He opened the first Discalced Carmelite monastery at Duruelo a year later, but reform caused friction within the order and led to his imprisonment at Toledo. He escaped in 1578 and later won high office in the order. In his great mystical poetry, including "The Dark Night of the Soul," he traced the steps of the soul's ascent to union with God.

John o'Groat's Village, Scotland. Near DUNNET HEAD, it was settled in 1793 by John de Groat and his two brothers. It was once considered Britain's most northerly point, giving rise to the expression "from LAND'S END to John o'Groat's."

John Paul II *orig.* **Karol Wojtyla** (born 1920) Pope (from 1978), the bishop of Rome and head of the Roman Catholic church, the first non-Italian pope in 455 years and the first ever from a Slavic country. Born in Kraków, Poland, he studied for the priesthood at an underground seminary in Kraków during World War II and was ordained in 1946. He earned a doctorate in philosophy in Rome (1948) and returned home to serve in a parish, earning a second doctorate (also 1948), in sacred theology, from the Jagellonian University. He became archbishop of Kraków in 1964 and cardinal in 1967. Elected pope after the brief term of John Paul I (1912–1978), he became known for his energy, charisma, and intellect as well as for his conservative theological views and fervent anticommunism. In 1981 John Paul was shot in St. Peter's Square by a Turkish terrorist, but he recovered, resumed his work, and forgave his would-be assassin. Some of his trips abroad attracted some of the largest crowds ever assembled. His nonviolent activism spurred movements that contributed to the peaceful dissolution of the Soviet Union in 1989. He championed economic and political justice in developing nations. In naming 44 cardinals from five continents (February 2001), John Paul reached out to cultures around the world. He also canonized more saints, from more parts of the world, than had any other pope. His ecumenical efforts included meetings with Jewish, Muslim, and Orthodox religious leaders. Although afflicted with Parkinson's disease since the early 1990s, John Paul remained active and made a historic trip to Jerusalem in March 2000, during which he sought to improve relations between the church and Jews.

John Paul II, 1979.
LOCHON-FRANCOLON-SIMON—GAMMA-LIAISON AGENCY

John the Apostle, St. *or* **St. John the Evangelist** *or* **St. John the Divine** (fl. 1st century AD) One of the original 12 APOSTLES of JESUS, traditionally credited with writing the fourth GOSPEL and three New Testament epistles. The Book of REVELATION was also traditionally assigned to him. His father was a Galilean fisherman. John and his brother James (see St. JAMES) were among the first disciples called by Jesus, and John appears to have held a position of authority in the early church after the resurrection. Later accounts of his life are based on legend. He is said to have died in EPHESUS, and his tomb became a site of pilgrimage. John's Gospel, unlike the other three, presents a well-developed theological point of view, on a level with the letters of St. Paul. After a prologue in which he identifies God with the Word (logos), he offers selected episodes from Jesus' life and ministry. His explications of theological issues such as the significance of the Son of God greatly influenced the development of Christian doctrine.

John the Baptist, St. (fl. early 1st century AD) Jewish prophet revered in Christianity as the forerunner of Jesus. Sources for his life are the four Gospels, the Acts of the Apostles, and the historian Josephus. His mother, Elizabeth, was perhaps a relative of Mary; his father was the priest Zechariah. As a young man John lived in the Judaean desert, either as a hermit or as part of a Jewish monastic community such as the Essenes. He attracted much public notice c. AD 28 as a prophet in the Jordan Valley. He preached the imminent wrathful judgment of God and called on his hearers to repent and be baptized. Jesus himself came to be baptized by John and shortly afterward began his own mission. John was imprisoned for criticizing the illegal marriage of Herod Antipas, and was executed after Herod's stepdaughter, Salome, demanded his head as a reward for dancing for the king's guests.

John the Good See John II (France)

Johns, Jasper (born 1930) U.S. painter, sculptor, and printmaker. Born in Augusta, Ga., he began his career as a commercial artist, producing displays for New York shop windows. In 1958 he had his first one-man exhibition, a rousing success. With his friend Robert Rauschenberg, he is considered largely responsible for the vogue for Pop art. His images depict commonplace two-dimensional objects (e.g., flags, maps, targets, numbers, letters of the alphabet) in simple colors. His banal subject matter and rejection of emotional expression departed radically from the Abstract Expressionism that then dominated the U.S. art scene. Among his best-known works is *Painted Bronze* (1960), a cast sculpture of two Ballantine Ale cans. From 1961 he began to attach real objects to his canvases. In the 1970s he produced paintings composed of clusters of parallel lines that he called "crosshatchings." He is one of the most successful living artists.

Johns Hopkins University Private university in Baltimore, Md. It was founded as a graduate school in 1876 through an endowment supplied by the Baltimore merchant Johns Hopkins (1795–1873). It became coeducational after a group of women, in 1893, provided funds for the creation of a medical school. Today its school of medicine and the affiliated Johns Hopkins Hospital constitute one of the nation's leading medical research centers. Besides medicine, the university has schools of arts and sciences, engineering, public health, nursing, music, international studies, and continuing education. Total enrollment is about 6,000.

Johnson, Andrew (1808–1875) 17th president of the U.S. (1865–69). Born in Raleigh, N.C., and reared in Tennessee, he was self-educated and initially worked as a tailor. He organized a workingman's party and was elected to the state legislature (1835–43), where he became a spokesman for small farmers. He served in the U.S. House of Representatives (1843–53) and as governor of Tennessee (1853–57). Elected to the U.S. Senate (1857–62), he opposed antislavery agitation, but in 1860 he opposed Southern secession, even after Tennessee seceded in 1861, and during the Civil War he was the only Southern senator who refused to join the Confederacy. In 1862 he was appointed military governor of Tennessee, then under Union control. In 1864 he was selected to run for vice president with Pres. Abraham Lincoln; he assumed the presidency after Lincoln's assassination. During Reconstruction he favored a moderate policy that readmitted former Confederate states to the Union with few provisions for reform or civil rights for freedmen. In 1867 the Radical Republicans in Congress passed civil-rights legislation and established the Freedmen's Bureau. His veto angered Congress, which passed the Tenure of Office Act. In 1868 in defiance of the act, Johnson dismissed secretary of war Edwin M. Stanton, an ally of the Radicals. The House responded by impeaching the president for the first time in U.S. history. In the subsequent Senate trial, the charges proved weak and the necessary two-thirds vote needed for conviction failed by one vote. Johnson remained in office until 1869, but his effectiveness had ended. He returned to Tennessee, where he won reelection to the Senate shortly before he died.

Andrew Johnson.

BY COURTESY OF THE LIBRARY OF CONGRESS, WASHINGTON, D.C.

Johnson \'yōn-sȯn\, **Eyvind** (1900–1976) Swedish novelist. He endured a grim boyhood of hard labor. His early novels evince feelings of frustration; *Bobinack* (1932) is an exposé of the machinations of modern capitalism, and *Rain at Daybreak* (1933) is an attack on modern office drudgery. *Return to Ithaca* (1946) and *The Days of His Grace* (1960) have been widely translated. Johnson's working-class novels brought new themes to Swedish literature and experimented with new forms and techniques. He shared the 1974 Nobel Prize with Harry Martinson.

Johnson, Frank (Minis), Jr. (1918–1999) U.S. judge. Born in Haleyville, Ala., he earned a law degree at the University of Alabama and served in the army during World War II. After the war he became a district attorney. As a federal district court judge (1955–79), he became legendary for his decisions supporting the civil rights movement, notably in the cases of Rosa Parks (1955) and of the Selma, Ala., voting-rights marchers (1965). He desegregated Alabama's schools and public facilities, and he became the first federal judge to dictate legislative reapportionment. He served on the U.S. District Court of Appeals 1979–92. In 1995 he received the Presidential Medal of Freedom.

Johnson, Jack *orig.* **John Arthur** (1878–1946) U.S. heavyweight boxing champion, the first black to hold the title. Born in Galveston, Texas, his career was marked from the beginning by racial discrimination. He won the national heavyweight crown in 1908 by knocking out Tommy Burns and kept it until 1915, when he was knocked out in Havana by Jess Willard in 26 rounds. After he became champion, a cry for a "Great White Hope" to defeat him produced numerous opponents. He was excoriated by the press for twice marrying white women. In 1912 he was convicted of violating the Mann Act for transporting his fiancée across state lines. He fled to Canada and then to Europe, continuing to fight as a fugitive before surrendering in 1920 to serve a one-year sentence. He died in a car crash. He won 80 of his 114 bouts.

Jack Johnson.

UPI COMPIX

Johnson, James P(rice) (1894–1955) U.S. pianist and composer, a chief figure in the transition of ragtime to jazz. Born in New Jersey, Johnson was performing in saloons and at parties in New York's black community while still in his teens. He created the stride piano technique, a development of ragtime that used two-beat left-hand rhythms to accompany wide-ranging right-hand lines, in such pieces as "Carolina Shout" and "Harlem Strut." He composed and orchestrated music for stage revues, including *Keep Shufflin'* (1928) with his student Fats Waller. His songs include "The Charleston" (largely responsible for the 1920s dance craze) and "Old Fashioned Love." His large-scale works include the *Harlem Symphony* (1932).

Johnson, James Weldon (1871–1938) U.S. writer. He practiced law in Florida before moving to New York with his brother, the composer J. Rosamond Johnson (1873–1954), where the two collaborated on some 200 songs for the Broadway stage. He held diplomatic posts in Venezuela and Nicaragua and served as executive secretary of the NAACP 1920–30. From 1930 he taught at Fisk University. His writings include the novel *Autobiography of an Ex-Colored Man* (1912), *Fifty Years and Other Poems* (1917), and his best-known work, *God's Trombones* (1927), black-dialect sermons in verse. The brothers collaborated on the pioneering anthologies *Book of American Negro Poetry* (1922) and *American Negro Spirituals* (1925, 1926). Their most famous original song, "Lift Every Voice and Sing," became an anthem of the civil-rights movement.

Johnson \'jän-sən\, **John H(arold)** (born 1918) U.S. magazine and book publisher. Born in Arkansas City, Ark., he moved to Chicago with his family and decided on journalism as a career. He introduced *Negro Digest*, a periodical for blacks, in 1942. Three years later he launched *Ebony,* which he modeled on *Life;* by the 1990s the magazine had a circulation of about 2 million. Through Johnson Publishing Co., he has also published black-oriented books and other magazines, and he later moved into radio broadcasting, insurance, and cosmetics manufacturing.

Johnson, Lyndon B(aines) (1908–1973) 36th president of the U.S. (1963–69). Born in Gillespie Co., Texas, he taught school in Houston before going to Washington, D.C., in 1932 as a congressional aide. There he was befriended by Sam Rayburn and his political career blossomed. He won a seat in the U.S. House of Representatives (1937–49) as the New Deal was under conservative attack. His loyalty impressed Pres. Franklin Roosevelt, who made Johnson a protégé. He won election to the U.S. Senate in 1949 in a vicious campaign that saw fraud on both sides. As Democratic whip (1951–55) and majority leader (1955–61), he developed a talent for consensus building among dissident factions with methods both tactful and ruthless. He was largely responsible for passage of the civil-rights bills of 1957 and 1960, the first in the 20th century. In 1960 he was elected vice president; he became president after the assassination of John F. Kennedy. In his first few months in office he won from Congress passage of a huge quantity of important civil-rights, tax-reduction, antipoverty, and conservation legislation. He defeated Barry Goldwater in the 1964 election by the largest popular majority to that time and announced his Great Society program. He was diverted from overseeing its enactment by the escalation of U.S. involvement in the Vietnam War, beginning with the Gulf of Tonkin Resolution. He pursued strategies criticized on both the left and the right. His approval ratings diminished markedly and led to his decision not to seek reelection in 1968. He retired to his Texas ranch.

Johnson, Magic *orig.* **Earvin** (born 1959) U.S. basketball player. Born in Lansing, Mich., he led Michigan State University to the NCAA championship in 1981. He led the Los Angeles Lakers to five championships in the 1980s. Standing 6 ft. 9 in., he was an all-around player equally adept at shooting, rebounding, and defense who brought a new vitality to the game and became one of the sport's first international stars. His no-look passes helped him become the NBA's all-time leader in assists (10,141, a mark later surpassed by John Stockton). His announcement of his infection with HIV in 1991 and consequent retirement was greeted with shock. Johnson subsequently served briefly (1994) as head coach of the Lakers, but has devoted much of his retirement to youth and AIDS work.

Johnson, Michael (Duane) (born 1967) U.S. sprinter. Born in Dallas, he broke the 200-m indoor record in 1989 while attending Baylor University. For much of the 1990s he was virtually unbeaten in the 200-m and 400-m races. He shared an Olympic gold medal in 1992 on the world-record-setting 4 × 400-m relay team, and at the 1996 Olympics he became the first man to win gold medals in both the 200-m and 400-m, setting a world record of 19.32 seconds in the 200-m. In 1999 he set a new world record of 43.18 seconds in the 400-m. In the 2000 Olympics he again won two gold medals.

Johnson, Philip (Cortelyou) (born 1906) U.S. architect and critic. Born in Cleveland, he studied philosophy and architecture at Harvard University. As coauthor of *The International Style: Architecture Since 1922* (1932) and director of the architecture department at the Museum of Modern Art (1932–34, 1946–57), he did much to familiarize Americans with modern European architecture. He gained fame with his own "Glass House" (1949), which struck a balance between the influence of Ludwig Mies van der Rohe (later his collaborator on the Seagram Building) and Classical allusion. His style took a striking turn with the AT&T headquarters, New York (1982), a controversial postmodernist landmark. Johnson was the first recipient of the Pritzker Architecture Prize, in 1979.

Johnson, Rafer (Lewis) (born 1935) U.S. decathloner. Born in Hillsboro, Texas, he won the decathlon gold medal in the Pan-American Games in 1955 while a student at UCLA. He won the gold medal at the 1960 Olympic Games by only 58 points, and was the first black athlete to carry the U.S. flag in the Olympic procession. See photograph above.

Rafer Johnson, putting the shot in the Olympic decathlon, 1960.

AP/WIDE WORLD PHOTOS

Johnson, Richard M(entor) (1780–1850) U.S. politician. Born near Louisville, Va. (now in Kentucky), he practiced law in Kentucky before being elected to the U.S. House of Representatives (1807–19, 1829–37). As a colonel in the War of 1812, he was wounded in the Battle of the Thames, where he reputedly killed Tecumseh. He returned to his congressional seat and later was elected to the Senate (1819–29). He was a loyal supporter of Pres. Andrew Jackson, who picked him as Martin Van Buren's running mate in the 1836 election. None of the four vice-presidential candidates won an electoral-vote majority; the outcome was decided by the Senate, the only such occurrence in U.S. history, and Johnson served one term in the office.

Johnson, Robert (1911?–1938) U.S. blues guitarist, singer, and songwriter. Born in Hazlehurst, Miss., to a sharecropping family, he learned harmonica and guitar, probably influenced by personal contact with such Delta bluesmen as Eddie "Son" House and Charley Patton. He traveled widely throughout the South and as far north as Chicago and New York, playing at house parties, juke joints, and lumber camps. In 1936–37 he recorded songs by House and others, as well as such originals as "Me and the Devil Blues," "Hellhound on My Trail," and "Love in Vain." He is said to have died, at 27, after drinking strychnine-laced whiskey (possibly the work of a jealous husband) in a juke joint. His eerie falsetto and masterly slide guitar influenced many later blues and rock musicians.

Johnson, Robert Wood (1845–1910) U.S. manufacturer. Born in Carbondale, Pa., he began his career as a pharmacist and drug broker. In 1885 he founded Johnson & Johnson with his brothers, and he served as its president until his death. An early proponent of the teachings of Joseph Lister, Johnson worked to make his products as germ-free as possible, and the firm's high-quality and inexpensive medical supplies, including antiseptic bandages and dressings, proved of great value to surgery. The Robert Wood Johnson Foundation is a major philanthropic institution.

Johnson, Samuel *known as* **Dr. Johnson** (1709–1784) British man of letters, one of the outstanding figures of 18th-century England. The son of a poor bookseller, he briefly attended Oxford University. He moved to London after the failure of a school he and his wife had started. He wrote for periodicals and was hired to catalogue the great library of the earl of Oxford. In 1755, after eight years of labor, he produced his monumental *Dictionary of the English Language* (1755), the first great English dictionary, which brought him fame. He continued to write for such periodicals as *The Gentleman's Magazine* and *The Universal Chronicle*, and almost single-handedly wrote and edited the biweekly *The Rambler* (1750–52). He also wrote plays, none of which succeeded on the stage. In 1765 he produced a critical edition of William Shakespeare with a famous preface that did much to establish Shakespeare as the center of the literary canon. His travel writings include *A Journey to the Western Islands of Scotland* (1775). His *Lives of the Most Eminent English Poets* (10 vols., 1779–81) was a significant critical work. Other important works include the long poem *The Vanity of Human Wishes* (1749) and the philosophical tale *Rasselas* (1759). A brilliant conversationalist, he helped found the Literary Club (c. 1763), which became famous for its members of distinction, including David Garrick, Edmund Burke, Oliver Goldsmith, and Joshua Reynolds. His aphorisms helped make him one of the most frequently quoted of English writers. His companion James Boswell wrote Johnson's biography, one of the most admired biographies of all time.

Johnson, Virginia See William Masters and Virginia Johnson

Johnson, Walter (Perry) (1887–1946) U.S. baseball pitcher. Born in Humboldt, Kan., he developed perhaps the most effective fastball ever; he holds the all-time record for most shutouts (110), ranks second to CY YOUNG in wins (416), and established the record for his time for most strikeouts (3,508; broken in 1983). He played for the Washington Senators 1907–27, and subsequently became a baseball manager. He was nicknamed "Big Train" for his overpowering delivery.

Walter Johnson.

UPI/EB INC.

Johnson, William *later* **Sir William** (1715–1774) British colonial official. In 1737 he emigrated from Ireland and settled in New York's Mohawk Valley, becoming one of the largest landholders in British North America. He fostered friendly relations with the Indians and in 1746 was appointed colonel of the IROQUOIS CONFEDERACY. In the FRENCH AND INDIAN WAR he defeated French forces at Lake George, N.Y. (1755), and captured Fort Niagara (1759). He was appointed superintendent of the Six Iroquois Nations (1756–74), helped subdue the Indian uprising called Pontiac's War (1763–64), and negotiated the first Treaty of FORT STANWIX (1768).

Johnston, Joseph E(ggleston) (1807–1891) U.S. army officer. Born near Farmville, Va., he graduated from West Point and served in the Mexican War. At the start of the Civil War he resigned to serve the Confederacy. Appointed brigadier general, he won the first Confederate victory at the Battle of BULL RUN. He was promoted to general but remained at odds with JEFFERSON DAVIS. He defended Richmond in the Peninsular Campaign and was badly wounded at the Battle of Fair Oaks (1862). In 1863 he was sent to conduct the VICKSBURG CAMPAIGN. His order to evacuate the city was countermanded by Davis, but Johnston was blamed for its fall. As commander of the Army of the Tennessee, he avoided defeat as the Union advanced toward Atlanta, but was removed for failing to defeat the invaders. Restored to duty in 1865, he was forced to surrender to WILLIAM T. SHERMAN.

Johnstown Flood Disastrous flood (1889) in the town of Johnstown, Pa. Johnstown lies at the confluence of the Conemaugh River and Stony Creek; at the time of the flood it was a leading U.S. steelmaking center. At 3:10 p.m. on May 31, the South Fork Dam, a poorly maintained earthfill dam holding a major upstream reservoir, collapsed after heavy rains, sending a wall of water rushing down the Conemaugh Valley at speeds of 20–40 mph (30–60 kph). A 30-ft (9-m) wall of water smashed into Johnstown at 4:07 p.m., killing 2,209 people.

Johore Strait \jə-'hōr\ Northern arm of the Singapore Strait between the Republic of Singapore and the southern tip of the MALAY PENINSULA. It is 30 mi (50 km) long and .75 mi (1.2 km) wide. Its eastern portion has a deepwater access channel to Changi naval base on Singapore's northeastern coast. It was the scene of heavy fighting in 1942 during the Japanese drive to conquer Singapore.

joint In geology, a brittle fracture surface in rocks along which little or no displacement has occurred. Present in nearly all surface rocks, joints extend in various directions, generally more vertical than horizontal. Joints may have smooth, clean surfaces, or they may be scarred by slickensides, or striations. Jointing does not extend very far into the earth's crust, because at about 7.5 mi (12 km) even rigid rocks tend to flow plastically in response to stress.

joint Structure connecting two or more BONES. Most joints, including synovial (fluid-containing) joints and those between vertebrae, which incorporate a disk, can move. Immovable joints include the sutures of the SKULL (see FONTANEL). LIGAMENTS connect the bones of a joint, but MUSCLES keep them in place. Joint disorders include various forms of ARTHRITIS, injuries (e.g., sprains, FRACTURES, and DISLOCATIONS), CONGENITAL DISORDERS, and VITAMIN deficiencies. See illustration opposite.

joints and joinery In architecture, the connection of construction materials. All joints are carefully detailed by the architect with concern for strength, movement, penetration by the elements, and incompatibilities. The term joinery refers especially to carpentry. Common types of joints include the dovetail, used for interlocking two flat members at right angles, as in the sides of a drawer; the doweled joint, in which doweling is employed for mechanical strength; and the mortise and tenon, in which a projecting piece fits into a groove, used to join a horizontal member with the vertical member of a frame. See illustration on following page.

Joinville \zhwa^n-'vēl\, **Jean, Sire de** (1224?–1317) French chronicler. A member of the lesser nobility of Champagne, Joinville became friends with LOUIS IX while taking part in the Seventh Crusade (1248–54). His famous *Histoire de Saint Louis*, completed c. 1309, is a prose chronicle that provides a supreme account of the Crusade, including vivid descriptions of the financial hardships, the dangers of sea voyages, the ravages of disease, the confusion and lack of discipline in the crusading army, and Muslim customs. On his return he was made seneschal of Champagne and divided his time between the royal court and his fief of Joinville.

Joliba River See NIGER RIVER

Joliot-Curie \zhȯl-yȯ-kǖ-'rē\, **(Jean-) Frédéric** *orig.* **Jean-Frédéric Joliot** (1897–1956) French physical chemist. In 1926 he married Irene Curie (1900–1958), daughter of Pierre and MARIE CURIE; he would eventually append her name to his. In 1932 he first observed production of an electron-positron pair. The two are remembered for their discovery of new radioactive isotopes prepared artificially, for which they were jointly awarded a 1935 Nobel Prize. Frédéric served in the Resistance during World War II and became a member of the Communist Party; in the postwar years he served as the highest government official in the realm of atomic energy, but was dismissed for his political beliefs. From 1946 to 1956 Irene directed the Radium Institute, where she had first worked in 1918; Frédéric succeeded her in the post. Both died of conditions caused by their long exposure to radioactivity.

Jolliet \zhȯl-'yā\, **Louis** (1645–1700) French-Canadian explorer. Born near Quebec, he led an expedition in the Great Lakes region in 1669. He was appointed to explore the Mississippi River with JACQUES MARQUETTE and five others. In 1673 they set out in birchbark canoes across Lake Michigan, following the Fox and Wisconsin rivers to the Mississippi, then down the Mississippi to its confluence with the Arkansas, concluding that the river flowed south to the Gulf of Mexico and not, as hoped, into the Pacific Ocean. After their return, Jolliet explored areas of Hudson Bay and the Labrador coast.

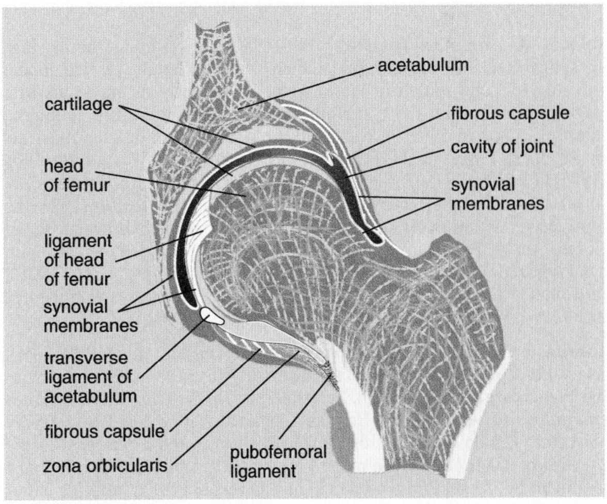

Section through a hip joint. The hip joint, a synovial joint, is of the ball-and-socket type, the head of the femur articulating with the cup-shaped acetabulum. The joint cavity is enclosed by a fibrous capsule lined with a type of connective tissue (synovial membrane) that produces a fluid (synovial fluid) which lubricates the cartilage-covered opposing surfaces of bone. The fibrous capsule is made up of internal circular fibers (zona orbicularis) and external longitudinal fibers, strengthened by ligaments, and covered by muscles.

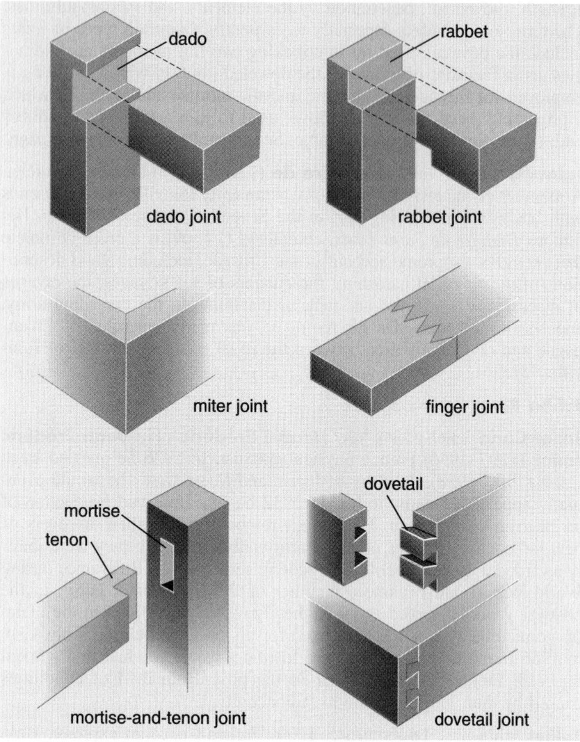

Some common woodworking joints. The dado joint is made by inserting the end of one piece into a rectangular groove (dado) in another. The rabbet joint involves joining pieces along a channel or notch (rabbet) along an edge of one or both members. The miter joint is formed by butting two ends cut at an angle. The finger joint is used to lengthen a board by interlacing fingerlike projections. The mortise-and-tenon joint is made by inserting a projection (tenon) on one piece into a notch or hole (mortise) in the other. The dovetail joint consists of one or more fan-shaped tenons fitting tightly into corresponding mortises.

Jolson, Al *orig.* **Asa Yoelson** (1886–1950) U.S. (Russian-born) singer, songwriter, and blackface comedian. Jolson's family arrived in the U.S. in 1893 and settled in Washington, D.C., where he made his first stage appearance in 1899, performing in vaudeville before joining a minstrel troupe in 1909. In New York he was featured in such musicals as *La Belle Paree* (1911), *Honeymoon Express* (1913), and *Big Boy* (1925). In *Sinbad* (1918) he transformed the unsuccessful GEORGE GERSHWIN song "Swanee" into his trademark number. In *Bombo* (1921) he introduced "My Mammy," "Toot, Toot, Tootsie," and "California, Here I Come." In 1927 he starred in *The Jazz Singer,* the first feature film with synchronized speech. Later films include *The Singing Fool* (1928), *Mammy* (1930), and *Swanee River* (1940). His life story was filmed in *The Jolson Story* (1946) and *Jolson Sings Again* (1949).

Jomini \ˌzhō-mə-ˈnē\, **(Antoine-) Henri, baron de** (1779–1869) Swiss-French general and military theorist. After a volunteer stint with the French army (1798–1800), he wrote his *Treatise on Grand Military Operations* (5 vols., 1805). He was appointed staff colonel in 1805 by NAPOLEON I, who had read his book. He was created a baron after the Treaties of Tilsit (1807). He rose to the post of chief of staff, but unjust treatment by his superiors prompted him to resign (1813), and thereafter he fought for France's enemy, Russia. Of his numerous later works on military history and strategy, the best known are *Principles of Strategy* (1818) and *Summary of the Art of War* (1838). He was the first to fix divisions between STRATEGY, TACTICS, and LOGISTICS, and his systematic attempt to define the principles of warfare made him a founder of modern military thought.

Jomon culture \ˈjō-ˌmän\ (before 5,000–c. 250 BC) MESOLITHIC culture characterized by pottery decorated with cord patterns *(jomon).* Jomon artifacts have been found from Hokkaido to the Ryukyu Islands. The Jomon people lived in sunken pit dwellings and subsisted primarily by hunting, fishing, and gathering. They used chipped-stone and later polished-stone tools and made clothing of bark. Though their pottery was technically primitive, it demonstrated diverse forms and imaginative designs and decorations. See also YAYOI CULTURE.

Jonah (fl. c. 785 BC) One of the 12 Minor Prophets in the OLD TESTAMENT, whose story is told in the Book of Jonah. (His narrative is part of a larger book, The Twelve, in the Jewish canon.) God orders Jonah to prophesy against the wickedness of NINEVEH, but Jonah refuses to believe that the people of this hated foreign city deserve salvation, and he sails away on a ship in the opposite direction. When a great storm threatens to destroy the ship, he confesses his fault and asks the crew to throw him overboard. A great fish swallows him, but he prays for deliverance and the fish spews him out on dry ground. He goes on to Nineveh and preaches God's message, and its sinful people repent. The book was probably written in the 5th or 4th century BC.

Jonathan (c. 10th century BC) In the Old Testament, the eldest son of King SAUL and friend of DAVID. A warrior in the Israelite army, he is first mentioned as victor over the Philistines at Geba. After David joined Saul's household, he and Jonathan became close friends. Saul became jealous of David's popularity and sought to kill him, but Jonathan prevented him. When the two met for the last time, they planned that David would be the next king of Israel and Jonathan his prime minister, but Saul and Jonathan were killed in battle at Mount Gilboa.

Jones, Bill T. *orig.* **William Tass** (born 1952) U.S. dancer and choreographer. Born in Bunnell, Fla., he trained in dance and theater at SUNY. In 1982, with his companion Arnie Zane (1948–1988), he cofounded the Bill T. Jones/Arnie Zane Dance Co. All his performances have been in works he has choreographed alone or with a collaborator; they include *Runner Dreams* (1978) and *Open Spaces* (1980). His works often make explicit reference to social issues; his controversial *Still/Here* (1995) dealt with the sufferings caused by AIDS, with which Jones is infected and which was the cause of Zane's death.

Jones, Bobby *orig.* **Robert Tyre** (1902–1971) U.S. golfer. Born in Atlanta, he won 13 major championships between 1923 and 1930, a feat unequaled until 1973. In 1930 he became the first golfer to achieve the Grand Slam of his time, winning the British and U.S. Open and Amateur championships, after which he retired from competitive golf at age 28, having never become a professional. Jones helped establish the MASTERS TOURNAMENT.

Bobby Jones.

Jones, Chuck *orig.* **Charles M.** (1912–2002) U.S. animator. Born in Spokane, Wash., he became a cartoonist for Warner Brothers (1933–62), where he helped develop such characters as Bugs Bunny, Road Runner, and Wile E. Coyote. Three of his cartoon films, noted for their speed and action, won Academy Awards. He was head of animation for MGM in the 1960s, then formed his own company and directed such animated features as *The Phantom Tollbooth* (1971) and specials for television. He received an Academy Award for lifetime achievement in 1996.

Jones, Deacon *orig.* **David** (born 1938) U.S. football player. Born in Eatonville, Fla., he stood 6 ft 5 in. (1.96 m) tall and weighed 250 lbs (113 kg) and could run the 100-yard dash in 9.7 seconds. He excelled at tackling the quarterback behind the line of scrimmage (for which he coined the term *sack*). As a defensive end for the Los Angeles Rams (1961–1972), he was regarded as one of the sport's premier defensemen and was named all-NFL six consecutive times (1965–70). He later played for the San Diego Chargers (1972–73) and Washington Redskins (1974).

Jones, (Alfred) Ernest (1879–1958) Welsh psychoanalyst. After he became a member of London's Royal College of Physicians, his interest gradually shifted to psychiatry. With Carl Gustav Jung he organized the first psychoanalytic conference (Salzburg, 1908), where he met Sigmund Freud. Jones was instrumental in introducing psychoanalysis to Britain and North America; in 1919 he founded the British Psycho-Analytical Institute, and in 1920 he founded the *International Journal of Psycho-Analysis,* which he edited until 1939. After the Nazi takeover of Austria, he helped the ailing Freud and his family to escape to London. His biography of Freud (3 vols., 1953–57) was for many years the standard biography.

Jones, George (Glenn) (born 1931) U.S. country-music singer and songwriter. He was born in Saratoga, Texas, to an impoverished family, which moved to Beaumont when he was 11. He sang on the streets as a youngster, and he began recording in the early 1950s. His first hit, "Why, Baby, Why" (1955), was followed by "She Thinks I Still Care," "He Stopped Loving Her Today," and many others. In 1957 he joined the Grand Ole Opry. He continued to have hits into the 1980s, including many with his former wife Tammy Wynette. His rocky personal life and career have only increased his fans' enduring affection.

Jones, Inigo (1573–1652) British painter, architect, and designer. The son of a clothworker, he studied painting in Italy and attracted the patronage of the king of Denmark, for whom he apparently designed two palaces, before returning to England. Beginning in 1605, he designed the scenes and costumes for masques by Ben Jonson and others. From 1615 to 1642, he was the King's Surveyor of Works. His first important undertaking was the Queen's House at Greenwich (begun 1616), England's first Palladian-style building. His greatest achievement, the Banqueting House at Whitehall (1619–22), consists of one great raised chamber with colonnades set against the walls, which support a flat, beamed ceiling. For his design for Covent Garden (1630), London's first square, Jones is credited with the introduction of town planning in England.

Jones, James Earl (born 1931) U.S. actor. Born in Arkabutla, Miss., he studied acting in New York and made his Broadway debut in 1957. He was praised for his performance in *Othello* (1964) and in roles with the New York Shakespeare Festival (1961–73). He starred as the black boxer in *The Great White Hope* (1969, Tony award; film, 1970). After returning to Broadway in *Paul Robeson* (1978) and *Fences* (1985, Tony award), he starred in the television series *Paris* (1979–80) and *Gabriel's Fire* (1990–91, Emmy award). He has appeared in numerous films; his sonorous voice lent gravity to *Star Wars* (1977) and its sequels, *The Lion King* (1994), and *Merlin* (1998).

Jones, Jennifer *orig.* **Phyllis Isley** (born 1919) U.S. film actress. Born in Tulsa, she played leads in minor films from 1939 before coming to the notice of David O. Selznick, who cast her in *The Song of Bernadette* (1943, Academy Award). Selznick continued to choose her roles, and she starred in such films as *Love Letters* (1945), *Duel in the Sun* (1946), and *Love Is a Many-Splendored Thing* (1955). She married Selznick in 1949 and appeared in films into the 1960s. After his death in 1965, she married the industrialist Norton Simon.

Jones, Jim *orig.* **James Warren Jones** (1931–1978) U.S. leader of a New Religious Movement. Born near Lynn, Ind., he became a preacher in Indianapolis. He established the People's Temple, which was affiliated with the Disciples of Christ and opposed racism and poverty. The group moved to San Francisco in 1971. Accused of defrauding church members, Jones led his group to Guyana in 1977 and set up the agricultural commune of Jonestown, using threats and force to control his followers. In 1978 Congressman Leo Ryan went to Jonestown to investigate allegations against Jones; upon his departure, Ryan and four others were killed. In the aftermath, most of the residents, in a mass rite of murder-suicide, were shot or poisoned; Jones died of a gunshot wound. The death toll was 913, including many children.

Jones, John Paul *orig.* **John Paul** (1747–1792) Scottish-American naval hero. He went to sea at 12 and became a ship's master at 21. He joined his brother in Virginia in 1775. When the American Revolution began, he joined the new Continental Navy under Esek Hopkins. In 1776 he sailed the *Providence* along the Atlantic coast, capturing eight ships and sinking eight more. In 1777–78 he sailed for France with orders to attack British ships, capturing several prizes. In 1779 he commanded the *Bonhomme Richard* and intercepted a merchant fleet. He engaged an escort ship, the *Serapis,* and, though outgunned, forced its surrender after a fierce battle, answering its challenge to surrender with "I have not yet begun to fight!" His ship sank soon after, and he sailed two British prizes to the Netherlands. He retired to France in 1790 in ill health and died at 45.

John Paul Jones, portrait by Charles Willson Peale, 1781.

BY COURTESY OF THE INDEPENDENCE NATIONAL HISTORICAL PARK COLLECTION, PHILADELPHIA

Jones, Mary Harris *orig.* **Mary Harris** *known as* **Mother Jones** (1830–1930) U.S. labor organizer. Born in Ireland, she was brought to the U.S. in 1835. In 1867 she lost her children and husband (an iron worker) in a yellow-fever epidemic in Memphis; four years later she lost all her possessions in the great Chicago fire. She turned for assistance to the Knights of Labor, which led to her becoming a highly visible figure in the U.S. labor movement. She traveled across the country, organizing for the United Mine Workers and supporting strikes wherever they were being held. At 93 she was still working among striking coal miners in West Virginia. She actively supported legislation to prohibit child labor. She was a founder of the Social Democratic Party (1898) and the Industrial Workers of the World (1905). Her autobiography was published in 1925. She died at the age of 100.

Jones, Quincy *orig.* **Quincy Delight Jones, Jr.** (born 1933) U.S. composer, bandleader, and producer. Born in Chicago, Jones joined a combo with his friend Ray Charles in his early teens, and later studied music in Seattle and Boston. In the early 1950s he played trumpet with Lionel Hampton. He became an arranger for Dizzy Gillespie and others, and ultimately formed his own big band and worked with such figures as Count Basie, Sarah Vaughan, and Dinah Washington. Since the early 1960s he has written scores for dozens of films, including *Walk Don't Run* (1966), *In Cold Blood* (1967), and *The Color Purple* (1985). From the mid-1970s he has principally worked as a producer; as founder of Qwest Productions he has produced enormously successful albums for Mahalia Jackson, F. Sinatra, and others. He founded the music magazine *Vibe.*

Jones, Spike *orig.* **Lindley Armstrong** (1911–1965) U.S. bandleader known for his novelty recordings. Born in Long Beach, Cal., Jones played drums in radio bands in the late 1930s, and soon became known for adding anarchically comical sounds such as car horns, cowbells, and anvils to his percussion. In 1942 he formed Spike Jones and His City Slickers, and the band soon had a hit recording with "Der Fuehrer's Face." Jones's comic hits continued into the 1950s, when he also had his own TV show. Later switching from comedy to dixieland, the band continued to record into the 1960s.

Jones, William *later* **Sir William** (1746–1794) British orientalist, linguist, and jurist. He completed an authoritative *Grammar of the Persian Language* in 1771. For financial reasons he then turned to the study and practice of law. His *Moallakât*, a translation of seven famous Arabic odes, was published in 1782, and the following year he was knighted and sailed for Calcutta (now Kolkata) as judge of the Supreme Court. He founded the Asiatic Society of Bengal to encourage Asian studies and published scholarly works on Hindu and Muslim law. His proposition (1786) that there was a common source for languages ranging from Celtic to Sanskrit led to recognition of the Indo-European language family.

jongleur \zhō^{n}-'glœr, *Engl* 'jäŋ-glər\ Professional storyteller or public entertainer in medieval France. His roles included those of musician, juggler, acrobat, and reciter of literary works. Jongleurs performed in marketplaces on public holidays, in abbeys, and in castles of nobles, who sometimes retained them in permanent employment. Jongleurs were most important in the 13th century; in the 14th century, the various facets of their role were taken over by other performers. See also goliard, trouvère.

jonquil Popular garden flower *(Narcissus jonquilla),* a Mediterranean perennial bulbous herb of the amaryllis family. Bearing long linear leaves, it is widely cultivated for its yellow or white, fragrant, short-tubed, clustered flowers. An oil from jonquil flowers is used in perfumes. See also NARCISSUS.

Jonson, Ben(jamin) (1572–1637) British playwright, poet, and critic. After learning stagecraft as a strolling player, he wrote plays for PHILIP HENSLOWE's theaters. In 1598 his comedy *Every Man in His Humour* established his reputation. He wrote several MASQUES for the court of James I and created the "antimasque" to precede the masque proper. His classic plays *Volpone* (1605–6), *The Alchemist* (1610), and *Bartholomew Fair* (1614) use satire to expose the follies and vices of his age, attacking greed, charlatanism, and religious hypocrisy as well as mocking the fools who fall victim to them. Regarded as the era's leading dramatist after WILLIAM SHAKESPEARE, Jonson influenced later playwrights, notably in the dramatic characterization of Restoration comedies (see RESTORATION LITERATURE). He was also a lyric poet whose works include two famous elegies for his son and daughter.

Jooss \'yōs\, **Kurt** (1901–1979) German dancer, teacher, and choreographer whose dance dramas combined modern dance with ballet technique. After studying dance with RUDOLF LABAN (1920-24), he established a school and company. He became ballet master at the Essen Opera House in 1930, where he choreographed his signature ballet, *The Green Table* (1932). Forced to leave Germany, he moved his school and company to England in 1934, and his renamed Ballets Jooss toured worldwide until disbanding in 1947. He returned in 1949 to Essen, where he continued to choreograph works that combined ballet and modern dance in an Expressionist style.

Jooss in *The Green Table*, c. 1935.
H. ROGER-VIOLLET

Joplin, Janis (Lyn) (1943–1970) U.S. rock and blues singer. Born to a middle-class family in Port Arthur, Texas, she ran away from home at 17 and began singing in Austin and later Los Angeles. She joined the band Big Brother and the Holding Company in San Francisco in 1966, and soon became famous for her raw, powerful, emotional blues style. The album *Cheap Thrills* (1968) contains some of her best-known recordings. Leaving the band, she continued to record hit songs, including "Me and Bobby McGee." Joplin died from an overdose of heroin at age 27.

Joplin, Scott (1868–1917) U.S. pianist and composer, the outstanding exponent of RAGTIME music. Born in Texas, Joplin was a classically trained pianist and composer. His compositions, including "Maple Leaf Rag" (1899), ragtime's first hit, and "The Entertainer" (1902), show an acute logic that transcends the sometimes mechanical dimension of the genre. He also wrote a ballet and two operas, including *Treemonisha* (1911), as well as several didactic works. He suffered a nervous collapse in 1911 and was institutionalized in 1916.

Jordaens \'yȯr-ˌdäns\, **Jacob** (1593–1678) Flemish painter active in Antwerp. He was admitted to the painters' guild in 1615 and by the 1620s had a flourishing studio with many students. After the death of PETER PAUL RUBENS, to whose style he was indebted, he became the leading painter in Flanders. His paintings, crowded with robust figures, are noted for strong contrasts of light and shade and an air of sensual vitality bordering on coarseness. He also produced religious paintings and portraits. His most important commissions were two enormous murals for the royal residence called the Huis ten Bosch, near The Hague. His later works tend to be mediocre and were frequently executed by assistants.

Jordan *officially* **Hashemite Kingdom of Jordan** *Arabic* **Al-Urdun** \äl-'ùr-dùn\ Arab state of the Middle East, lying east of the JORDAN RIVER. It is bordered by Syria, Iraq, Saudi Arabia, Israel, and the WEST BANK. Jordan has 12 miles (19 km) of coastline on the Gulf of AQABA. Area: 34,495 sq mi (89,342 sq km). Population (2002 est.): 5,260,000. Capital: AMMAN. The vast majority of the population are Arabs, about 60% of whom are Palestinian Arabs who fled to Jordan from Israel and the West Bank as a result of the ARAB-ISRAELI WARS. Language: Arabic (official). Religion: Islam (official), with more than 90% of the population Sunnite. Currency: Jordan dinar. Four-fifths of Jordan is occupied by desert, and less than one-tenth of the country's land is arable. The country's highest point, Mount Ramm (5,755 ft, or 1,754 m), lies in the uplands region on the east bank of the Jordan River. The Jordan Valley region contains the DEAD SEA. Jordan's economy is based largely on manufacturing and services (including tourism); exports include phosphate, potash, pharmaceuticals, fruits and vegetables, and fertilizers. It is a constitutional monarchy with two legislative houses; the head of state and government is the king, assisted by the prime minister. Jordan shares much of its history with ISRAEL, since both occupied parts of the area known historically as PALESTINE. Much of present-day eastern Jordan was incorporated into Israel under DAVID and SOLOMON c. 1000 BC. It fell to the Seleucids in 330 BC and to Muslim Arabs in the 7th century AD. The Crusaders extended the kingdom of Jerusalem east of the Jordan River in 1099. Jordan submitted to the OTTOMAN EMPIRE during the 16th century. In 1920 the area comprising Jordan (then known as the Transjordan) was established within the British mandate of Palestine. Transjordan became an independent state in 1927, although the British mandate did not end until 1948. After hostilities with the new state of Israel ceased in 1949, Jordan annexed the West Bank and east JERUSALEM, administering the territory until Israel gained control of them in the SIX-DAY WAR of 1967. In 1970–71 Jordan was wracked by fighting between the government and guerrillas of the PALESTINE LIBERATION ORGANIZATION (PLO), a struggle that ended in the expulsion of the PLO from Jordan. In 1988 King HUSSEIN renounced all Jordanian claims to the West Bank in favor of the PLO. In 1994 Jordan and Israel signed a full peace agreement.

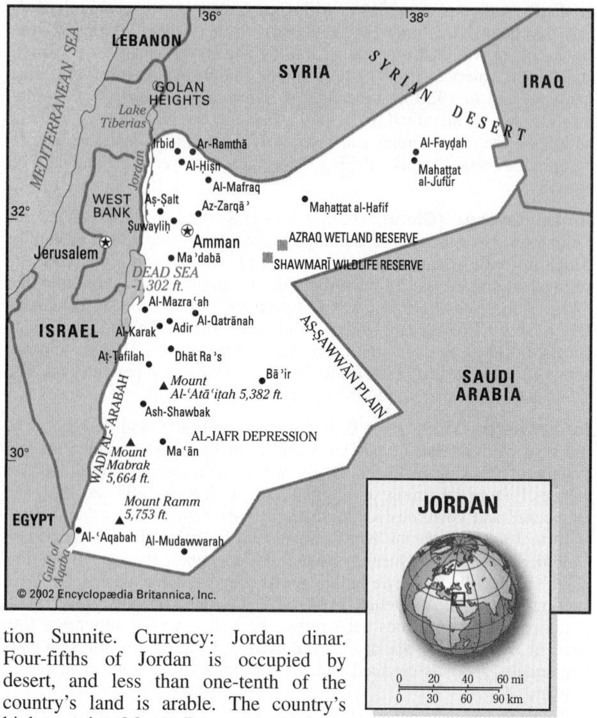

Jordan, Barbara C(harline) (1936–1996) U.S. lawyer and politician. Born in Houston, she earned a law degree in 1959, served in the Texas senate (1966–72), then won election to the U.S. House of Representatives (1973–79), the first black woman to be elected from the Deep South. She became nationally prominent during the 1974 hearings on the impeachment of RICHARD NIXON arising from the WATERGATE SCANDAL. Her keynote address at the 1976 Democratic National Convention confirmed her reputation as an orator. She retired from the House to teach at the University of Texas.

Jordan, David Starr (1851–1931) U.S. educator and ichthyologist. Born near Gainesville, N.Y., he studied at Cornell University and taught at universities in Indiana until 1885, when he became president of INDIANA UNIV. In 1891 he became the first president of STANFORD UNIV., and served until 1913. His extensive field trips led to his naming 1,085 genera and more than 2,500 species of fishes. He was coauthor (with B.

H I J K

W. Evermann) of *The Fishes of North and Middle America* (1896–1900) and author of *Manual of the Vertebrates of the Northern United States* (13 editions, 1876–1929). He devoted his later career mainly to the cause of international peace, acting as chief director of the World Peace Foundation.

Jordan, Jim *orig.* **James Edward and Marian** *orig.* **Marian I. Driscoll** (1896–1988, 1898–1961) U.S. radio comedians. Both were born near Peoria, Ill.; they met at church. Married in 1918, they performed in vaudeville, then adapted their comedy act for radio in 1924. Their success on a local station led to collaboration with the writer Don Quinn to produce a comedy series that evolved into *Fibber McGee and Molly* (1935–57), a weekly show that delighted a national audience with its running gags in skits involving the McGees and their neighbors. The show was one of the most popular of the 1940s.

Jordan, Michael (Jeffrey) (born 1963) U.S. basketball player, considered the greatest all-around player in basketball history. Born in Brooklyn, N.Y., he grew up in North Carolina and attended the University of North Carolina, where as a freshman he scored the winning basket in the NCAA tournament championship game. Drafted by the Chicago Bulls in 1984, he made his professional debut with the team later that year. As a Bull he won 10 scoring titles and 5 Most Valuable Player awards. In 1987 he became the second player (after WILT CHAMBERLAIN) to score 3,000 points in a single season. Nicknamed "Air Jordan" for his extraordinary leaping ability and the acrobatic maneuvers with which he evaded defenders while approaching the basket, he led the Bulls to six championships (1991–93, 1996–98) and led the 1984 and 1992 U.S. Olympic basketball teams to gold medals. He retired briefly in 1993, hoping to play professional baseball, but returned to play with the Bulls from 1995 until his retirement in 1999, by which time he was the most famous athlete in America and an international icon. In 2000 he bought a share of the NBA Washington Wizards and was later appointed president of basketball operations for the club. Before the start of the 2001–02 season, however, Jordan announced that he was returning to professional play as a member of the Wizards, and he renounced his ownership and management positions with the team.

Jordan, Neil (born 1950) Irish film director and screenwriter. He was a novelist and short-story writer when he was hired by JOHN BOORMAN as a script consultant, an experience he turned into a documentary film. He won acclaim for his first feature film, *Angel* (1982), and for *The Company of Wolves* (1984) and *Mona Lisa* (1986). *The Crying Game* (1992), which he based on one of his own short stories, brought him international renown. He is also the director of *Interview with the Vampire* (1994), *Michael Collins* (1996), and *The Butcher Boy* (1998).

Jordan River River, South Asia. It rises in Syria, flows through the Sea of GALILEE, and then receives its main tributary, the YARMUK RIVER. It drains into the DEAD SEA at a depth of 1,312 ft (400 m) below sea level, after a total course of 223 mi (360 km). Revered in many religions, in Christianity it is known as the place where JESUS baptized JOHN THE BAPTIST.

joruri See BUNRAKU

José Bonifácio See Jose Bonifacio de ANDRADA E SILVA

Joseph In the OLD TESTAMENT, the son of the patriarch JACOB and his wife, RACHEL. He was favored by his father, and his brothers became bitterly jealous when he was given a resplendent "coat of many colors" (literally, coat with flowing sleeves). They sold him into slavery in Egypt, telling Jacob he had been killed by a wild beast. In Egypt Joseph gained favor with the pharaoh and rose to high office, owing to his ability to interpret dreams, and his acquisition of grain supplies enabled Egypt to withstand a famine. When famine forced Jacob to send his sons to Egypt to buy grain, the family was reconciled with Joseph and settled there. The story of Joseph, told in GENESIS 37–50, depicts the preservation of Israel and begins the history of the Israelites in Egypt that is continued in EXODUS.

Joseph, Chief (1840–1904) NEZ PERCÉ chief. In 1877 the U.S. attempted to force the Nez Percé to move to a reservation in Idaho. Chief Joseph at first agreed, but finally decided instead to lead his followers on a trek to Canada. During the three-month, 1,000-mile journey, he outmaneuvered and outfought federal troops and won the admiration of many whites by his humane conduct. His group was finally surrounded near the Canadian border and subsequently removed to Indian Territory (Oklahoma). In 1885 they were relocated to a reservation in Washington.

Joseph, Father *orig.* **François-Joseph le Clerc du Tremblay** (1577–1638) French mystic and religious reformer. He joined the Capuchins in 1599. His fervent ambition to convert European Protestants to Roman Catholicism coincided with Cardinal de RICHELIEU's plans for French domination of Europe, and he became Richelieu's secretary in 1611. He became known as the "Gray Eminence" (for his gray Capuchin cloak), and his close collaboration with Richelieu (the "Red Eminence") gave him powers akin to those of a foreign minister, especially during Richelieu's campaign to finance France's participation in the THIRTY YEARS' WAR, which Joseph's policies did much to bring about.

Joseph, St. (fl. 1st century BC–1st century AD) In the NEW TESTAMENT, the husband of MARY and the earthly father of JESUS. Descended from the house of DAVID, he was a carpenter in Nazareth. He was betrothed to Mary, and when he found her already pregnant an angel appeared to him in a vision and told him the expected child was the son of God. He and Mary journeyed to Bethlehem to be counted in the Roman census, and while they were there the child was born. The last mention of Joseph occurs in the Gospel of Luke when he and Mary take the 12-year-old Jesus to Jerusalem.

Joseph II (1741–1790) Holy Roman emperor (1765–90). He succeeded his father, FRANCIS I, and initially coruled with his mother, MARIA THERESA (1765–80). After her death he tried to continue her work of reform. An advocate of ENLIGHTENED DESPOTISM, he abolished serfdom, established religious equality before the law, granted freedom of the press, and emancipated the Jews. He came into conflict with the Roman Catholic Church by attempting to impose state controls over it, and traditional countries such as the Austrian Netherlands and Hungary resisted his far-reaching reforms. His foreign policies were generally failures; he tried to exchange the Austrian Netherlands for Bavaria but was stopped by Prussia. An alliance with CATHERINE II of Russia engaged Austrian troops in a war with Turkey, but Joseph had to return home to head off revolutionary unrest in Hungary and the Austrian Netherlands.

Joseph II, Holy Roman emperor, detail of a painting by Pompeo Batoni, 1769; in the Kunsthistorisches Museum, Vienna.

BY COURTESY OF THE KUNSTHISTORISCHES MUSEUM, VIENNA

Joseph Bonaparte Gulf Inlet of the Timor Sea, northern Australia. It spans 225 mi (360 km) east to west, and it indents the Australian coast for 100 mi (160 km). Entered by a Dutch navigator in 1644, it was visited in 1803 by Nicolas Baudin, a Frenchman who named it after NAPOLEON's brother JOSEPH BONAPARTE.

Joséphine *orig.* **Marie-Josèphe-Rose Tascher de la Pagerie** (1763–1814) Consort of NAPOLEON and empress of the French. Born in Martinique, she married an army officer, Alexandre, vicomte de Beauharnais (1760–1794), in 1779. He was guillotined during the French Revolution, and Joséphine was imprisoned briefly. A leader of Paris society, she married Napoleon in a civil ceremony in 1796. She was an indifferent and extravagant wife, but during the Consulate she used her social position to advance her husband's political fortunes. After he became emperor (1804), she persuaded him to marry her again, with religious rites. In

Joséphine, detail of an oil painting by François Gérard; in the Musée National de Malmaison, Paris.

GIRAUDON—ART RESOURCE/EB INC.

H I J K

1810 he arranged for their marriage to be nullified so that he could make a politically convenient marriage with MARIE-LOUISE.

Josephson, Brian (David) (born 1940) British physicist. He received his PhD from Cambridge University and began building on earlier work done by LEO ESAKI of IBM and Ivar Giaever (born 1929) of General Electric. His contribution was the discovery of what is now called the JOSEPHSON EFFECT. He was elected a fellow of the Royal Society in 1970 and was named a professor at Cambridge in 1974. He has studied the possible relevance of Eastern mysticism to scientific understanding. He shared a Nobel Prize with Esaki and Giaever in 1973.

Josephson effect Flow of electric current between two pieces of superconducting material (see SUPERCONDUCTIVITY) separated by a thin layer of insulating material. This flow was predicted by BRIAN JOSEPHSON in 1962, based on the BCS theory (see JOHN BARDEEN). According to Josephson, pairs of ELECTRONS can move from one superconductor to the other across the insulating layer (tunneling). The locus of this action is called a Josephson junction. The Josephson current flows only if no battery is connected across the two conductors. A major application of this discovery is in superfast switching devices used in computers, which can be 100 times faster than ordinary semiconducting circuits.

Josephus \jō-ˈsē-fəs\, **Flavius** *orig.* **Joseph Ben Matthias** (AD 37/38–c. 100) Jewish priest, scholar, and historian. Born of a priestly family in Jerusalem, Josephus joined the PHARISEES. While on a diplomatic mission he was impressed by the culture and sophistication of Rome, and in the Jewish revolt of AD 66–70 he eventually attached himself to the Roman cause. Favored in the courts of emperors VESPASIAN, TITUS, and DOMITIAN, he wrote valuable historical works. His *History of the Jewish War* (79) is the principal source on the revolt and includes much on Roman tactics and strategy. *The Antiquities of the Jews* (93), his greatest work, traces Judaism from creation up to the revolt. *Against Apion* defends Judaism against Hellenism.

Joshua Leader of the Israelite tribes after the death of MOSES. According to the Old Testament Book of Joshua, Joshua led the people of Israel westward across the Jordan River to invade CANAAN. Under his leadership the Israelites conquered the Canaanites and gained control of the Promised Land. The book begins by recounting the battles, including the famous demolition of the walls of JERICHO. Joshua then divides Canaan among the 12 tribes of ISRAEL, makes his farewell speech, and dies. The book was compiled much later than the events described, perhaps during the BABYLONIAN EXILE in the 6th century BC.

Joshua Tree National Park National park, southeastern California. Situated on the border between the MOJAVE and Colorado deserts, it has an area of 1,241 sq mi (3,214 sq km). It was designated a national monument in 1936 and a national park in 1994. It is noted for its variety of desert plant life, including the Joshua tree, creosote bush, and Mojave yucca. Its fauna include coyotes, bobcats, and tarantulas.

Josiah \jō-ˈsī-ə\ (c. 640–609 BC) King of JUDAH and religious reformer. He became king at 8 after the assassination of his father, Amon. As the Assyrian empire crumbled, Judah gained a measure of independence, and in 621 BC Josiah began a program of national renewal. He drove out foreign cults, abolished local sanctuaries, and centered the worship of Yahweh (God) in the Temple of JERUSALEM. As his reforms were under way, parts of the Book of Deuteronomy were discovered in the Temple, giving added impetus to his efforts to revive observance of Mosaic law. Josiah hoped to reunify Judah and Israel, but he was killed in a battle against the Egyptians.

Jospin, Lionel (born 1937) FRENCH SOCIALIST PARTY politician who was prime minister in 1997–2002. Born in Meudon, he was educated at the elite École Nationale d'Administration. He joined the foreign service and later taught economics at the University Institute of Technology of Paris-Sceaux. He was elected to the National Assembly in 1977 and later was appointed head of the party by President FRANÇOIS MITTERRAND. He served as minister of education and narrowly lost the presidential election in 1995 to JACQUES CHIRAC. After the Socialists and their allies won a majority in the National Assembly in 1997, he was appointed prime minister by Chirac in a cohabitation government. He resigned in 2002 after an unsuccessful presidential bid.

Josquin des Prez \zhōs-ˈka^{n}-de-ˈprā\ (c. 1440–1521) Northern French composer. Perhaps a student of J. OCKEGHEM, he spent his life working as a singer, moving from post to post in Italy, including the Milan Cathedral (1459–72) and the Papal Chapel (1486–94), before returning to Condé in 1504, where he would spend the rest of his life. Josquin was able to balance complexity of imitative counterpoint with an inexhaustible melodic gift. He left over 60 motets (including *Absalon, fili mi*), some 18 complete masses (including *Missa Pange lingua*), and many superb secular songs in the chordal "Italian" style (including "El grillo"). The first music printer, Ottaviano Petrucci (1466–1539), devoted an entire volume to Josquin's works, an honor accorded to no other composer. His posthumous reputation, as attested by MARTIN LUTHER and others, was the greatest of any composer up to his time, and his works were closely imitated throughout the 16th century.

Jotunheim Mountains \ˈyō-t^{ə}n-ˌhām\ Mountain range, southern central Norway. Extending for 80 mi (130 km), it is the highest range in Scandinavia; its tallest peaks are Glitter Mountain (8,045 ft, or 2,452 m) and Galdhø Mountain (8,100 ft, or 2,470 m). The mountains are mentioned in early Norse sagas, but they were not fully explored until the early 19th century.

Joule \ˈjül\, **James (Prescott)** (1818–1889) English physicist. After studying under JOHN DALTON, in 1840 he described "Joule's law," which stated that the heat produced in a wire by an electric current is proportional to the product of the resistance of the wire and the square of the current. In 1843 he published his value for the amount of work required to produce a unit of heat, called the mechanical equivalent of heat, and established that heat is a form of energy. He established that the various forms of energy are basically the same and can be changed from one into another, a discovery that formed the basis of the law of conservation of energy, the first law of thermodynamics. In his honor, the value of the mechanical equivalent of heat is usually represented by the letter *J*, and a standard unit of work is called the joule.

journalism Collection, preparation, and distribution of news and related commentary and feature materials through such media as pamphlets, newsletters, newspapers, magazines, radio, film, television, and books. The term was originally applied to the reportage of current events in printed form, specifically newspapers, but in the late 20th century it came to include electronic media as well. It is sometimes used to refer to writing characterized by a direct presentation of facts or description of events without an attempt at interpretation. Colleges and universities confer degrees in journalism.

jousting Medieval Western European mock battle between two horsemen who charged at each other with leveled lances in an attempt to unseat the other. It probably originated in France in the 11th century, superseding the mêlée, in which mock battles were held between two bodies of armed horsemen, and it flourished in much of Europe in the 12th–15th century. Though the lances were blunted, knights were often seriously wounded or killed. Tournaments were mounted only by royalty and nobility; ladies of the court would sponsor individual knights, for whom jousting became a ritual of COURTLY LOVE. Characterized by striking panoply and pageantry, jousting tournaments represented the preeminent display of CHIVALRY.

Jove See JUPITER

Joyce, James (Augustine Aloysius) (1882–1941) Irish novelist. Educated at a Jesuit school (though he soon rejected Catholicism) and at University College, Dublin, he decided early to become a writer. In 1902 he moved to Paris, which would become his principal home after years spent in Trieste and Zurich. His life henceforth would be a difficult one, marked by financial troubles, chronic eye diseases that occasionally left him totally blind, censorship problems, and his daughter Lucia's mental illness. The remarkable story collection *The Dubliners* (1914) and the autobiographical novel *Portrait of the Artist as a Young Man* (1916) brought new techniques to the English novel and short story which he would lat-

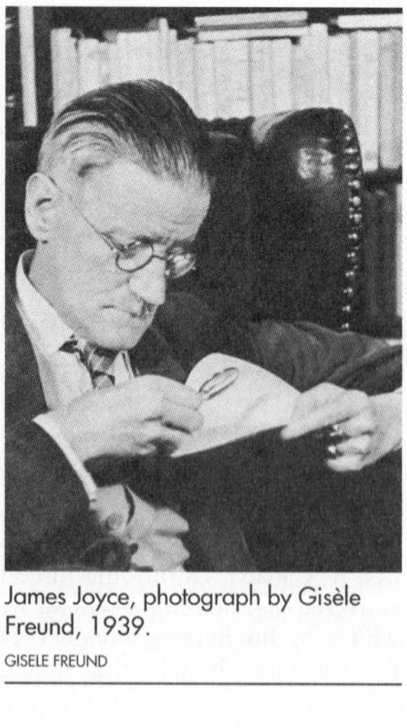

James Joyce, photograph by Gisèle Freund, 1939.
GISELE FREUND

er develop much further. With financial help from friends and supporters, including EZRA POUND and Harriet Shaw Weaver, he spent seven years writing *Ulysses* (1922), the controversial masterpiece (initially banned in the U.S. and Britain) now widely regarded as the greatest 20th-century English-language novel. It embodies a highly experimental use of language and exploration of such new literary methods as interior monologues and stream-of-consciousness narrative. He spent 17 years on his final work, the extraordinary *Finnegans Wake* (1939), famous for its complex and demanding linguistic virtuosity. He also published three poetry collections—*Chamber Music* (1907), *Pomes Penyeach* (1927), and *Collected Poems* (1937)—and the play *Exiles* (1918).

Joyner, Florence Griffith See Florence GRIFFITH JOYNER

Joyner-Kersee, Jackie *orig.* **Jacqueline Joyner** (born 1962) U.S. athlete, considered by some the greatest female athlete ever. Born in East St. Louis, Ill., she won four consecutive National Junior Heptathlon championships and starred in basketball and track and field at UCLA. In 1986 she became the first HEPTATHLON competitor ever to score 7,000 points. She broke that barrier six times, four times establishing a new world record. She won heptathlon gold medals at the 1988 and 1992 Olympics, becoming the first heptathlete ever to achieve consecutive Olympic wins. Her best events were the long jump (world record, 1987; Olympic gold medal, 1988), 100-m hurdles, 200-m run, and high jump.

JPEG \'jā-ˌpeg\ *in full* **Joint Photographic Experts Group.** Standard computer file format for storing graphic images in a compressed form for general use. JPEG images are compressed using a mathematical ALGORITHM. A variety of encoding processes can be used, depending on whether the user's goal is the highest quality of image or smallest file size. The JPEG and GIF formats are the most commonly used graphics formats on the Internet.

Juan Carlos I (born 1938) King of Spain from 1975. The grandson of ALFONSO XIII, he lived in exile until 1947. After FRANCISCO FRANCO abolished the republic and declared Spain a representative monarchy, he prepared Juan Carlos for his future role, paying particular attention to his military education. In 1969 Juan Carlos was designated prince; he acceded to the Spanish throne two days after Franco's death. Though he had sworn loyalty to Franco's National Movement, he proved to be relatively liberal and helped restore parliamentary democracy. In 1981 he deflated a potential military coup and preserved the democracy. He became the first Spanish king to visit the Americas and was the first crowned monarch to make an official visit to China.

Juan de Austria \ˌhwän-thā-'au̇s-trē-ä\ (1547–1578) Illegitimate son of Emperor CHARLES V and half brother of PHILIP II. After Charles's death, Philip gave him the name Don Juan de Austria (1559). He served as a Spanish military commander, and in 1571 was appointed head of naval forces of the HOLY LEAGUE against the Ottoman Turks, achieving victory in the Battle of LEPANTO. In 1576 he was appointed governor-general of the Netherlands, then in open revolt against Spanish authority. When his attempts at diplomacy failed, he resumed the war.

Juan de Fuca Strait \ˌhwän-də-'fyü-kə\ Strait, North Pacific Ocean. Located between the Olympic Peninsula of Washington and Canada's VANCOUVER ISLAND, it is 11–17 mi (18–27 km) wide and 80–100 mi (130–160 km) long. It is named for a Greek who sailed in the service of Spain and who may have visited the passage in 1592. It is used by ships bound for VANCOUVER and SEATTLE. Settlements along its banks include VICTORIA, British Columbia, and Port Angeles, Wash.

Juan Fernández Islands Island group, South Pacific Ocean. Located 400 mi (650 km) west of Chile, it consists of two islands and an islet. They were discovered in 1563 by Spanish navigator Juan Fernández. In 1704 Alexander Selkirk, a Scottish seaman, arrived and remained there alone until 1709; his adventures are believed to have inspired DANIEL DEFOE's *Robinson Crusoe*. Possessions of Chile since the early 19th century, they have since often been used as penal settlements.

Juan José de Austria \ˌhwän-hō-'sā\ (1629–1679) Spanish nobleman, most famous of the illegitimate children of PHILIP IV. He served as a military commander from 1647, and in 1651 he led the royal forces besieging Barcelona. He served as governor of the Netherlands 1656–58. After 1665 he played an active part in the political intrigues surrounding the new king, his half brother CHARLES II, and served as Charles's chief minister 1677–79.

Juárez *or* **Ciudad Juárez** \ˌsyü-'thäth-'hwär-ˌes\ City (pop., 1990: 789,000), northern CHIHUAHUA, Mexico. Located on the RIO GRANDE opposite EL PASO, Texas, it was formerly known as El Paso del Norte, and was renamed in 1888 for BENITO JUAREZ, who headquartered there in 1865. Today it is an important border city and functions as the marketing center for a cotton-growing area. It contains the Guadalupe mission, built in 1659.

Juárez \'hwär-əs\, **Benito (Pablo)** (1806–1872) National hero and president (1861–72) of Mexico. A ZAPOTEC Indian, Juárez initially studied for the priesthood but later took a law degree and became a legislator, a judge, and a cabinet minister. He led La REFORMA, and in 1855, when liberal forces took control of the national government, he was able to put his ideas into practice. An 1856 LAND-REFORM law broke up large landed estates and forced the Roman Catholic Church to sell its land. In 1857 a liberal constitution was promulgated. Conservatives ousted the president in 1858, but Juárez succeeded in restoring the liberal government. He was elected president in 1861 and twice reelected. The French under NAPOLEON III invaded and occupied Mexico, putting MAXIMILIAN of Austria in power, but when Napoleon withdrew his troops Juárez again prevailed, and he had Maximilian executed. His final years were marred by a loss of popular support and personal tragedy. He died in office.

Juárez.

BY COURTESY OF THE LIBRARY OF CONGRESS, WASHINGTON, D.C.

Jubayl See BYBLOS

Jubba River \'jü-bä\ River, Somalia. Originating in southern Ethiopia, it flows south 545 mi (875 km) to the Indian Ocean just north of Kismaayo, one of Somalia's three main ports. It is the only river in the region that is reliably navigable.

Juchen dynasty \'zhü-'jen\ *or* **Jin dynasty** (1115–1234) Dynasty that ruled an empire formed by the Tungus Juchen tribes of Manchuria. It covered much of Inner Asia and all of northern China. Like the LIAO, an earlier Inner Asian dynasty, the Juchen maintained a Chinese-style bureaucracy to rule over the southern part of their conquests and a tribal state to rule in Inner Asia. Very conscious of preserving their ethnic identity, they maintained their language, developed their own script, and banned Chinese clothes and customs from their army.

Judaea *or* **Judea** \jü-'dē-ə\ Southern division of ancient PALESTINE successively under Persian, Greek, and Roman rule. It was bounded on the north by Samaria and on the west by the Mediterranan Sea. It succeeded the kingdom of JUDAH, which was destroyed by the Babylonians. The revived kingdom of Judaea was established by the MACCABEES, who resisted the suppression of Judaism under Roman rule. Family disputes led to Roman intervention in 63 BC. Under Roman control, HEROD was made king of Judaea in 37 BC. After Herod's death the country was ruled alternately by his descendants and by Roman procurators. As a result of the Jewish revolt in AD 66, the city of Jerusalem was destroyed (AD 70). The name *Judaea* is still used to describe approximately the same area in modern Israel.

Judah One of the 12 tribes of ISRAEL, descended from Judah, the fourth son of JACOB. The tribe of Judah entered CANAAN with the other Israelites after the escape from Egypt and settled in the region south of Jerusalem. It eventually became the most powerful tribe, producing the kings DAVID and SOLOMON, and it was prophesied that the MESSIAH would come from among its members. After the 10 northern tribes were dispersed by the Assyrian conquest of 721 BC, the tribes of Judah and Benjamin were left as the sole inheritors of the Mosaic covenant. Judah flourished until 586 BC, when it was overrun by the Babylonians and many of its people were carried into exile. CYRUS THE GREAT allowed them to return in 538 BC, and the Temple of JERUSALEM was rebuilt. The history of Judah from that time forward is the history of the JEWS and JUDAISM. The kingdom of Judah was succeeded by JUDAEA.

Judah ben Samuel (died 1217) Jewish mystic and scholar. He was a member of the Kalonymos family, which provided medieval Germany with many Jewish mystics and spiritual leaders. Around 1195 he settled in Regensburg, where he founded a yeshiva and gathered disciples such as ELEAZAR ben Judah of Worms. He was the founder of 12th-century German Hasidism, an ultrapious movement not directly related to 18th-century HASIDISM. His *Book of the Pious,* a compilation of the writings of Judah, his father, and Eleazar of Worms, offers a detailed manual of conduct for observant Jews; it is one of the most important documents of medieval Judaism.

Judah ha-Nasi \'jü-də-,hä-nä-'sē\ (c. 135–c. 220 AD) Palestinian Jewish scholar. A descendant of the great sage HILLEL, he was patriarch of the Jewish community in Palestine and head of its Sanhedrin, and he became an important figure in early RABBINIC JUDAISM. He spent over 50 years studying the oral law and is said to have compiled it into six sections divided by subject matter, thus creating the MISHNA. His exact role in the Mishna's redaction is not known; other scholars such as MEÏR and AKIBA BEN JOSEPH were probably also involved.

Judaism \'jü-də-,i-zəm, 'jü-dē-,i-zəm\ Religious beliefs and practices of the JEWS. One of the three great monotheistic world religions, Judaism began as the faith of the ancient Hebrews, and its sacred text is the Hebrew BIBLE, particularly the TORAH. Fundamental to Judaism is the belief that the people of Israel are God's chosen people, who must serve as a light for other nations. God made a COVENANT first with ABRAHAM, then renewed it with Isaac, JACOB, and MOSES. The worship of Yahweh (God) was centered in Jerusalem from the time of DAVID. The destruction of the First Temple of JERUSALEM by the Babylonians (586 BC) and the subsequent exile of the Jews led to hopes for national restoration under the leadership of a MESSIAH. The Jews were later allowed to return by the Persians, but an unsuccessful rebellion against Roman rule led to the destruction of the Second Temple in AD 70 and the Jews' dispersal throughout the world in the Jewish DIASPORA. RABBINIC JUDAISM emerged to replace the temple cult at Jerusalem, as the Jews carried on their culture and religion through a tradition of scholarship and strict observance. The great body of oral law and commentaries were committed to writing in the TALMUD and MISHNA. The religion was maintained despite severe persecutions in many nations. Two branches of Judaism emerged in the Middle Ages: the SEPHARDI, centered in Spain and culturally linked with the Babylonian Jews; and the ASHKENAZI, centered in France and Germany and linked with the Jewish culture of PALESTINE and Rome. Elements of mysticism also appeared, notably the esoteric writings of the KABBALA and, in the 18th century, the movement known as HASIDISM. The 18th century was also the time of the Jewish Enlightenment, or HASKALA. CONSERVATIVE and REFORM Judaism emerged in 19th-century Germany as an effort to modify the strictness of ORTHODOX JUDAISM. By the end of the 19th century ZIONISM had appeared as an outgrowth of reform. European Judaism suffered terribly during the HOLOCAUST, when millions were put to death by the Nazis, and the rising flow of Jewish emigrants to Palestine led to declaration of the State of Israel in 1948.

Jewish Festivals

Tishri (Sept.–Oct.)	1–2	Rosh Hashanah (New Year)
	3	Fast of Gedaliah
	10	Yom Kippur (Day of Atonement)
	15–21	Sukkot (Tabernacles)
	22	Shemini Atzereth (Eighth Day of Solemn Assembly)
	23	Simhath Torah (Rejoicing of the Law)
Kislev (Nov.–Dec.)	25	Hanukkah (Festival of Lights) begins
Tebet (Dec.–Jan.)	2 or 3	Hanukkah ends
	10	Fast
Shebat (Jan.–Feb.)	15	New Year for Trees
Adar (Feb.–Mar.)	13	Fast of Esther
	14–15	Purim (Feast of Lots)
Second Adar (Adar Sheni) or Veadar (intercalated month); Adar holidays fall in Veadar during leap years.		
Nisan (Mar.–Apr.)	15–22	Pesach (Passover)
Iyar (Apr.–May)	5	Israel Independence Day
	18	Lag b'Omer (33rd Day of the Omer Counting)
Sivan (May–June)	6–7	Shabuoth (Feast of Weeks, or Pentecost)
Tammuz (June–July)	17	Fast
Ab (July–Aug.)	9	Fast

Judas Iscariot (died c. AD 30) Disciple who betrayed JESUS. He was one of the original 12 disciples. Judas made a deal with the Jewish authorities to betray Jesus into their custody; in return for 30 pieces of silver, he brought the armed guard to the Garden of GETHSEMANE and identified Jesus with a kiss. He later regretted his deed and committed suicide; according to Matthew 27, he returned the money to the priests before hanging himself. His surname may mean "man of Kerioth," or it may link him to the Sicarii, a band of radical Jewish terrorists.

Judas Maccabaeus \,ma-kə-'bē-əs\ (died 161/160 BC) Leader of a Jewish rebellion against the Syrians. Son of an aged priest who took to the mountains in rebellion when ANTIOCHUS IV EPHIPHANES tried to impose the Greek religion on the Jews, Judas became leader of the rebels on his father's death and won a series of victories over the Syrians in 166–164 BC. In 166 he purified the Temple of JERUSALEM, an event celebrated at HANUKKAH. On Antiochus' death in 164, the Seleucids offered the Jews freedom of worship, but Judas continued the war, hoping to gain political freedom. He was killed soon thereafter, but his brothers carried on the struggle. The history of the dynasty is told in the two books of MACCABEES in the APOCRYPHA.

Judd, Donald (1928–1994) U.S. sculptor. Born in Excelsior Springs, Mo., he studied at Columbia University and the Art Students League. He had his first one-man exhibition in 1957. In 1959 he began writing reviews for *Art News* and *Arts Magazine*. In 1960–62 he made the transition from painting to sculpture, and became a leading exponent of MINIMALISM. Much of his work consists of simple cubes or other geometric units, in stainless steel or metal and plexiglass, sometimes painted, which stand on the floor or are cantilevered from the wall, often in stacks or horizontal progressions.

judge Public official vested with the authority to hear, determine, and preside over legal matters brought in court. In JURY cases, the judge presides over the selection of the panel and instructs it concerning pertinent law. The judge may also rule on motions made before or during a trial. In the U.S., judges are elected or appointed. Most federal judges are appointed for life by the president with the advice and consent of the SENATE. The highest-ranking judge in the U.S. legal system is the CHIEF JUSTICE of the SUPREME COURT. See also JUDGMENT, JUDICIARY, MAGISTRATE'S COURT, MISSOURI PLAN.

judgment In law, a formal decision or determination on a matter or case by a court. Judgments are classified as *in personam, in rem,* and *quasi in rem.* A judgment in personam determines the rights and liabilities of a particular person. A judgment in rem affects the status of a particular thing (e.g., an item of property). The designation quasi in rem describes a judgment in which a person's property is subject to court control to satisfy a claim against the person. The court has at its disposal the power to punish for CONTEMPT any party that does not adhere to its orders. See also APPEAL, DECLARATORY JUDGMENT, DEMURRER.

Judgment, Day of In Christianity, the final judgment of God on all people at the end of history. It will occur at the second coming of Christ, when the dead are resurrected. It is especially important in millennialist denominations (see MILLENNIALISM). In Islam, the Day of Judgment is described in the QURAN and the HADITH. Religions that include REINCARNATION (e.g., HINDUISM) lack a Day of Judgment; the determination of how an individual is to be reborn being a particular judgment on the merit of the life just lived (see KARMA).

judgment tale See DILEMMA TALE

judicial review Examination by a country's courts of the actions of the legislative, executive, and administrative branches of government to ensure that those actions conform to the provisions of the constitution. Actions that do not conform are unconstitutional and therefore null and void. The practice is usually considered to have begun with the U.S. Supreme Court's ruling in *MARBURY VS. MADISON* (1803). Several constitutions drafted in Europe and Asia after World War II incorporated judicial review. Especially subject to scrutiny in the U.S. have been actions bearing on civil rights (or CIVIL LIBERTY), DUE PROCESS of law, EQUAL PROTECTION under the law, freedom of religion, FREEDOM OF SPEECH, and rights of PRIVACY. See also CHECKS AND BALANCES.

judiciary Branch of government in which judicial power is vested. The principal work of any judiciary is the adjudication of disputes or controversies. Regulations govern what parties are allowed before a judicial assembly, or court, what evidence will be admitted, what trial procedure will be followed, and what types of judgments may be rendered. Typically present in court are the presiding judge, the parties to the matter (sometimes called litigants), the lawyers representing the parties, and other individuals including witnesses, clerks, bailiffs, and jurors when the proceeding involves a jury. Though the courts' stated function is to administer justice according to rules enacted by the legislative branch, courts also unavoidably make law. In deciding, for example, how legislative provisions are to be applied to specific cases, the courts in effect make law by laying down rules for future cases; this is known as the doctrine of precedent.

Judith Legendary Jewish heroine, the central character in the Book of Judith in the APOCRYPHA. (The book is excluded from the Hebrew Bible.) A beautiful Jewish widow whose city is besieged by the Assyrians under their general, Holofernes, Judith leaves the city in pretended flight and foretells victory to Holofernes. Invited into his tent, she cuts off his head as he lies in a drunken sleep, and the Jews defeat the leaderless Assyrians. Probably fictional, the story may have been written in the 2nd century BC, after the end of the Maccabean revolt.

judo MARTIAL ART that emphasizes the use of quick movement and leverage to throw an opponent. Its techniques are generally intended to turn an opponent's force to one's own advantage rather than to oppose it directly. The opponent must be thrown cleanly, pinned, or mastered through the application of pressure to arm joints or the neck. Judo is now practiced primarily as sport. It became an Olympic sport in 1964; women's judo was added in 1992. The sport evolved out of JUJITSU in late-19th-century Japan.

juge d'instruction \'zhu̅e̅zh-da^{n}-strü̅e̅k-syō^{n}\ (French: "judge of inquiry") In France, a magistrate responsible for conducting the investigative hearing that precedes a criminal trial. In this hearing the major evidence is presented, witnesses are heard, and depositions are taken. If at the end the magistrate is not convinced that the evidence of guilt is sufficient to warrant a trial, no trial will occur. This process differs from the GRAND JURY hearing in the Anglo-American system.

Jugendstil \'yü-gənt-ˌshtēl\ Artistic style that arose near the end of the 19th century in Germany and Austria. Its name was derived from the Munich magazine *Die Jugend* ("Youth"), founded in 1896, which featured Art Nouveau designs. Its early phase, primarily floral in character, was rooted in English Art Nouveau and Japanese prints; a more abstract phase emerged after 1900. Primarily a style in architecture and the decorative arts, it also included the great Austrian painter GUSTAV KLIMT.

juggler Entertainer who keeps several plates, knives, balls, or other objects in the air at once by tossing and catching them. The art of juggling has been practiced since antiquity. Through the 18th century jugglers performed at fairs and marketplaces, and in the 19th century they found larger audiences in CIRCUSES and MUSIC HALLS. In these training grounds the art advanced in technical perfection, producing such outstanding performers as Enrico Rastelli, who could juggle 10 balls. Modern jugglers have introduced such variations as performing while blindfolded on horseback, on a high wire, or on a unicycle.

Jugurtha \jü-'gər-thə\ (c. 160–104 BC) Ruler of the North African kingdom of NUMIDIA under the Romans (118–105 BC). After the death of his uncle Micipsa, then ruler of Numidia, Jugurtha shared rule with his cousins. He had one killed and captured the capital city of the other. Rome intervened with troops, which Jugurtha successfully outwitted until he was captured in 105 BC. See also Gaius MARIUS, Lucius Cornelius SULLA Felix.

Juilliard School \'jü-lē-ˌärd\ Internationally renowned school of the performing arts in New York City. It has its roots in the Institute of Musical Art (founded 1905) and a graduate school (1924) founded through an endowment from the financier Augustus D. Juilliard (1840–1919). It is now the professional educational arm of the LINCOLN CENTER FOR THE PERFORMING ARTS. It offers bachelor's degrees in music, dance, and drama and postgraduate degrees in music. The Juilliard String Quartet (founded 1946) was important to the development of chamber music in the U.S. Total enrollment is about 900.

jujitsu \jü-'jit-sü\ MARTIAL ART that employs holds, throws, and paralyzing blows to subdue or disable an opponent. It evolved among the SAMURAI warrior class in Japan from about the 17th century. A ruthless form of fighting, its techniques included the use of hard or tough parts of the body (e.g., knuckles, fists, elbows, and knees) against an enemy's vulnerable points. Jujitsu declined in the mid-19th century, but many of its concepts and methods were incorporated into JUDO, KARATE, and AIKIDO.

Julia (39 BC–AD 14) Only daughter of AUGUSTUS. She briefly wed MARCELLUS (25–23 BC), then AGRIPPA (21), Augustus' chief lieutenant. Their two eldest sons became Augustus' heirs (17). When Agrippa died (12), Augustus' wife persuaded him to favor her sons, TIBERIUS and Drusus, as heirs. Augustus forced Tiberius to divorce his wife and marry Julia (11). The unhappy Julia became promiscuous, and Tiberius went into self-imposed exile. When Augustus discovered Julia's behavior, he banished her to an island off Campania (2 BC), then to Rhegium. On becoming emperor, Tiberius withheld her allowance, and she starved to death.

Julian *or* **Julian the Apostate** *Latin* **Julianus Apostata** *orig.* **Flavius Claudius Julianus** (AD 331/332–363) Last pagan Roman emperor (361–63). The nephew of CONSTANTINE I, he was raised a Christian but converted to mystical paganism. As caesar (subemperor) in the west, he restored the Rhine frontier and was proclaimed augustus (senior emperor) by his armies. Though Constantius II initially objected to Julian as his successor, he accepted him on his deathbed. At Constantinople, Julian proclaimed freedom of worship for pagans and Christians in 361; he nevertheless promoted paganism over Christianity, against which he committed acts of violence and persecution. He introduced austerity to government, reducing imperial staff and overhauling imperial finances. To reassert Roman power in the east he attacked Persia; the effort failed, and he was killed in a retreat near Baghdad.

Julian the Apostate, detail of a marble statue; in the Louvre, Paris.
GIRAUDON—ART RESOURCE

Julian, George W(ashington) (1817–1899) U.S. politician. Born in Wayne Co., Ind., he practiced law and wrote antislavery articles before being elected to the U.S. House of Representatives (1849–51). He was the FREE SOIL PARTY's vice-presidential candidate in 1852, and in 1856 helped form the REPUBLICAN PARTY. Again elected to the House (1861–71), he made emancipation a war aim in the Civil War. In 1867 he helped prepare articles of impeachment against Pres. ANDREW JOHNSON. He later wrote books and articles on reform causes, including women's suffrage.

Julian Alps Range of the eastern ALPS. It extends southeast from the Carnic Alps in northeastern Italy to the city of LJUBLJANA in Slovenia. The highest peak is Triglav (9,396 ft, or 2,864 m), also the highest point in Slovenia.

Julian of Norwich *or* **Juliana of Norwich** (1342–after 1416) English mystic. After being healed of a serious illness (1373), she wrote two accounts of her visions; her *Revelations of Divine Love* is remarkable for its clarity, beauty, and profundity. She spent her later life as a recluse in Norwich.

Juliana (Louise Emma Marie Wilhelmina) (born 1909) Queen of the Netherlands (1948–80). During World War II she took refuge in Ottawa, while her husband, Prince BERNHARD, remained with Queen WILHELMINA's London government. Returning to the Netherlands in 1945, Juliana acted as regent during her mother's illness and became queen when Wilhelmina abdicated. In 1980 she abdicated in favor of her daughter BEATRIX.

Julio-Claudian dynasty (AD 14–68) Successors of AUGUSTUS, the first Roman emperor: TIBERIUS, CALIGULA, CLAUDIUS, and NERO. It was a loosely defined set of kin relations rather than a direct bloodline. Tiberius' rule was competent, with notable accomplishments, but ended in cruel tyranny. The insane Caligula was wild and capricious. Under Claudius Rome experienced marked development. Under Nero the empire prospered, but he was given to excesses, and his reign ended amid rebellion and civil war.

Julius II *orig.* **Giuliano della Rovere** (1443–1513) Pope (1503–13). The nephew of SIXTUS IV, he fled Rome in 1494 to escape assassination by Alexander VI. Elected pope in 1503, Julius set out to restore the Papal States, subjugating Perugia and Bologna (1508) and defeating Venice (1509) with the aid of the League of Cambrai. His first effort to expel the French from northern Italy failed, but a popular revolt drove them out in 1512, and Parma and Piacenza were added to the Papal States. The greatest art patron of all the popes, Julius was a close friend of Michelangelo, from whom he commissioned the sculpture of Moses and the paintings in the Sistine Chapel. He also commissioned Raphael's Vatican frescoes.

Julius Caesar See Julius Caesar

July Days (1917) Period in the Russian Revolution of 1917 during which Petrograd workers and soldiers staged armed demonstrations against the provisional government that resulted in a temporary decline of Bolshevik influence and in the formation of a new provisional government headed by Aleksandr Kerensky. To undermine Bolshevik popularity, the government produced evidence that Vladimir Ilich Lenin had ties with the German government. The public reacted against the Bolsheviks, Lenin fled to Finland, and Leon Trotsky and other leaders were jailed. The reorganized government was overthrown by the Bolsheviks in October.

July monarchy In French history, the reign of Louis-Philippe (1830–48), brought about by the July Revolution. Also known as the "bourgeois monarchy," the new regime rested on a broad social base centered on the wealthy bourgeoisie. Two factions emerged in the Chamber of Deputies. The right-center faction, led by Francois Guizot, shared the king's political doctrines; the left-center faction, led by Adolphe Thiers, favored restricting the king's role. The 1830s were politically unstable, marked by challenges to the regime by the legitimists and republicans, as well as attempts to assassinate the king. There were several labor uprisings, and Louis-Napoléon (later Napoleon III) made two unsuccessful attempts to take the crown. A period of remarkable stability began c. 1840. Guizot, devoted to the king and preservation of the status quo, became the key figure in the ministry. He imposed high protective tariffs that resulted in an economic boom, beginning France's transformation to an industrial society. In foreign affairs, the regime maintained friendly relations with Britain and supported Belgian independence. However, in 1848 general unrest led to the February Revolution and the end of the July monarchy.

July Plot *or* **Rastenburg Assassination Plot** Abortive attempt on July 20, 1944, by German military leaders to assassinate Adolf Hitler, seize control of the government, and seek more favorable peace terms from the Allies. According to plan, Col. Claus von Stauffenberg (1907–1944) left a bomb in a briefcase in a conference room at the field headquarters at Rastenburg, East Prussia, where Hitler was meeting with top military aides. But the briefcase was pushed behind a table support, and Hitler survived the blast with minor injuries. Meanwhile, the other conspirators in Berlin failed to act. The chief conspirators, including Stauffenberg, Gen. Ludwig Beck, Gen. Erwin Rommel, and other top officers, were promptly shot or forced to commit suicide. In subsequent days, Hitler's police rounded up about 200 conspirators, who were shot, hanged, or viciously strangled.

July Revolution (1830) Insurrection that brought Louis-Philippe to the throne of France. It was precipitated on July 26 by Charles X's publication of restrictive ordinances contrary to the spirit of the Charter of 1814. Demonstrations were followed by three days of fighting (July 27–29), Charles's abdication, and the proclamation of Louis-Philippe as king. The bourgeoisie secured a political and social ascendancy that was to characterize the subsequent July monarchy.

jump rope *or* **skip rope** Children's game in which players hold a rope (jump rope) at each end and twirl it in a circle, while one or more players jump over it each time it reaches its lowest point. Dating from the 19th century, it is traditionally a girl's sidewalk or playground game that usually involves the chanting of a counting rhyme (e.g., "One, two, touch my shoe"). There are many types of jumps, including single, double, and backward; in "double Dutch," two ropes are twirled simultaneously in opposite directions. Single-rope jumping, or rope skipping, is popular with boxers to develop the lungs and legs and improve coordination and footwork.

Junayd \jü-ˈnīd\, **Shaykh** (c. 1430–1460) Fourth head of the Safavid order of Sufi mystics. He became head of the order on his father's death in 1447 and set out to turn a society known for piety and learning into a political force. The arming of his followers led to a conflict with Jahan Shah (died 1467), ruler of Iranian Azerbaijan, and resulted in the expulsion of Junayd and his followers from Ardabil, the traditional center of the Safavid order, in 1448. He continued his military adventurism in the lands of present-day Syria and Turkey and was finally killed in battle against a force of Christian Circassians. His policies were carried on by his son, Haydar, and eventually culminated in the founding of the Safavid dynasty under Junayd's grandson, Ismail I, assuring the dominance of Shiite Islam in Iran.

junco Any of several species of finchlike birds (genus *Junco,* family Fringillidae), about 6 in. (15 cm) long, of Canada and the U.S. Juncos are usually a shade of gray; they have white outer tail feathers that are flashed in flight to the accompaniment of snapping or twittering calls. They are common winter birds. Their favored habitat is mixed or coniferous forest, though they are often found in fields, thickets, and city parks.

Dark-eyed junco (*Junco hyemalis*).
STEVE AND DAVE MASLOWSKI

June beetle *or* **May beetle** *or* **June bug** Any insect of the genus *Phyllophaga,* belonging to a widely distributed, plant-feeding scarab beetle subfamily (Melolonthinae). These red-brown beetles commonly appear in the Northern Hemisphere on warm spring evenings and are attracted to lights. Heavy-bodied, they are 0.5–1 in. (1.2–2.5 cm) long and have shiny wing covers. They feed on foliage and flowers at night, sometimes causing considerable damage. The larvae live in the soil, and can destroy crops and kill lawns and pastures by severing the grasses from their roots; they are considered excellent fish bait.

June beetle (*Phyllophaga rugosa*).
HARRY ROGERS

June Days (June 23–26, 1848) In French history, a brief and bloody civil uprising in Paris in the early days of the Second Republic. The new government instituted numerous radical reforms; but the new assembly, composed mainly of moderate and conservative candidates, was determined to cut costs and end such risky experiments as public-works programs to provide for the unemployed. In Paris, thousands of workers suddenly cut off from the state payroll were joined by radical sympathizers and took to the streets in spontaneous protest. The assembly gave Gen. Louis Eugene Cavaignac authority to suppress the uprising, and he brought up artillery against the protesters' barricades. At least 1,500 rebels were killed, 12,000 were arrested, and many were exiled to Algeria. See also Revolutions of 1848.

Juneau \ˈjü-nō\ City (pop., 1995 est.: 30,000), capital of Alaska. Located in southeastern Alaska, it was settled in 1880 when Joe Juneau and Richard Harris discovered gold nearby. Mining was important until the Alaska-Juneau gold mine closed in 1944. Juneau was made the state capital in 1959. Fishing, forestry, and government activities are important, as is tourism. In 1970 Juneau merged with Douglas, on an island across the channel, to form the largest U.S. city in area (3,108 sq mi, or 8,050 sq km).

Jung \ˈyu̇ŋ\, **Carl Gustav** (1875–1961) Swiss psychiatrist. As a youth he read widely in philosophy and theology. After taking his medical degree (1902), he worked in Zurich with Eugen Bleuler on studies of mental illness. From this research emerged Jung's notion of the complex, or cluster of emotionally charged (and largely unconscious) associations. Between 1907 and 1912 he was Sigmund Freud's close collaborator and most likely successor, but he broke with Freud over the latter's insistence on the sexual basis of neuroses. In the succeeding years he founded the field of analytic psychology, a response to Freud's psychoanalysis. Jung advanced the concepts of the introvert and extrovert personality, archetypes, and the collective unconscious (the pool of human experience passed from generation to generation). He went on to formulate new psychotherapeutic techniques designed to reacquaint the person with his or her unique "myth" or place in the collective unconscious, as expressed in dream and imagination. Sometimes criticized as disguised religion and for its lack of verifiability, his work has been influential in religion and literature as well as psychiatry. His important works include *The Psychology of the Unconscious* (1912; revised as *Symbols of Transformation*), *Psychological Types* (1921), *Psychology and Religion* (1938), and *Memories, Dreams, Reflections* (1962).

jungle fowl Any of four species of Asian birds (genus *Gallus*) that differ from other species in the PHEASANT family in having, in the male, a fleshy comb, lobed wattles hanging below the bill, and a high-arched tail. The red jungle fowl is the ancestor of the CHICKEN. The cock has shining silky plumage, red on the head and back and green-black elsewhere; the hen is rusty brown with speckled neck and minimal comb.

junior college See COMMUNITY COLLEGE

juniper Any of about 60–70 species of aromatic evergreen trees or shrubs that make up the genus *Juniperus* of the CYPRESS family, found throughout the Northern Hemisphere. Juvenile leaves are needlelike; mature leaves are awl-shaped, spreading, and arranged in pairs or in whorls of three. Common juniper *(J. communis)* is a sprawling shrub whose fragrant, spicy-smelling berries are used to flavor foods and alcoholic beverages, particularly GIN. The fragrant wood of eastern red cedar *(J. virginiana)* is made into cabinets, fence posts, and pencils. *J. horizontalis* is a popular U.S. ornamental creeping juniper, and wood of the Mediterranean Phoenician juniper *(J. phoenicea)* is burned as incense.

Juniper berry (*Juniperus communis*).
INGMAR HOLMASEN

junk Classic Chinese sailing vessel of ancient unknown origin, still in wide use. High-sterned, with a projecting bow, the junk carries up to five masts on which are set square sails consisting of panels of linen or matting flattened by bamboo strips. Each sail can be spread or closed at a pull, like a venetian blind. The massive rudder takes the place of a keel. Chinese junks were sailing to Indonesian and Indian waters by the early Middle Ages.

Modern junk with traditional matting sails and a European-type jib.
BBC HULTON PICTURE LIBRARY

junk bond BOND with a rating below BBB. Though the risk of default for junk bonds is great, they offer higher rates of interest than more secure bonds. Junk bonds are considered too risky by the large institutional investors (savings and loan associations, pension funds, insurance companies, and MUTUAL FUNDS) that provide U.S. corporations with much of their investment capital. Such bonds are often issued by smaller, newer companies.

Juno In ROMAN RELIGION, the chief goddess and female counterpart of JUPITER. She was identified with the Greek goddess HERA. With Jupiter and MINERVA she was a member of the Capitoline triad of deities traditionally introduced into Rome by the ETRUSCANS. She was connected with all aspects of the lives of women, particularly marriage. Individualized, she became a female guardian spirit; as every man had his GENIUS, so every woman had her juno. Her temple in Rome eventually housed the Roman mint, and she was invoked as the savior of the state. Her sacred bird was the peacock. See photograph opposite.

Jupiter *or* **Jove** Chief god of ancient Rome and Italy. Like his Greek counterpart, ZEUS, he was worshiped as a sky god. With JUNO and MINERVA he was a member of the triad of deities traditionally believed to have been introduced into Rome by the ETRUSCANS. Jupiter was associated with treaties, alliances, and oaths; he was the protecting deity of the republic and later of the reigning emperor. His oldest temple was on the Capitoline Hill in Rome. He was worshiped on the summits of hills throughout Italy, and all places struck by lightning became his property. His sacred tree was the oak.

Jupiter Fifth PLANET from the sun, the largest nonstellar object in the SOLAR SYSTEM. It has 318 times the mass and over 1,400 times the volume of earth. Its enormous mass gives it nearly 2.5 times the gravity of earth at the top of its atmosphere and exerts strong effects on other members of the solar system. It is responsible for the KIRKWOOD GAPS in the asteroid belt and changes in the orbits of COMETS; it may act as a "sweeper," pulling in bodies that might otherwise collide with other planets. Jupiter has at least 39 moons (see GALILEAN SATELLITE) and a diffuse ring system discovered in 1979 by the VOYAGER spacecraft. The planet is a gas giant, composed mainly of hydrogen and helium in proportions near those of the sun, which it orbits every 11.9 years at an average distance of 484 million mi (778 million km). Its rapid rotation (9 hours, 55.5 minutes) acts on electric currents to give it the largest magnetic field of any of the planets and causes intense storms, including one that has lasted hundreds of years (the GREAT RED SPOT). Little is known of its interior, but it is presumed to have a deep layer of metallic hydrogen and a dense core. Its central temperature is estimated to be 45,000°F (25,000°C); it radiates twice as much heat as it receives from the sun, probably largely heat left over from its formation.

Jupiter Dolichenus \ˌdō-li-ˈkā-nəs\ God of a Roman mystery cult. He was originally a Hittite-Hurrian god of fertility and thunder worshiped at Doliche in Anatolia. He also became identified with the Zoroastrian god AHURA MAZDA as a lord of the universe. Returning legions carried his cult to Rome, where it became popular in the 2nd–3rd century AD. In Roman MYSTERY RELIGION he was believed to control military success and safety. He was usually represented standing on a bull holding a double ax and thunderbolt.

Jura Mountain range, central Europe. It extends 143 mi (230 km) along the boundary of France and Switzerland. Its highest peak is Mount Neige, 5,652 ft (1,723 m) high, located in France. Its western slopes are the source of the DOUBS and Ain rivers in France.

Jurassic period Interval of geologic time, 206–144 million years ago, that is one of the three major divisions of the MESOZOIC ERA, preceded by the TRIASSIC PERIOD and followed by the CRETACEOUS. During the Jurassic, PANGAEA began to break up into the continents we know today. Marine invertebrates flourished, and large reptiles dominated many marine habitats. On land, FERNS, MOSSES, CYCADS, and CONIFERS thrived, some developing flowerlike structures in place of cones. The DINOSAURS rose to supremacy on land, and by the end of the Jurassic the largest species had evolved. ARCHAEOPTERYX, the first primitive bird, appeared before the end of the period. Early mammals, tiny shrewlike creatures that appeared near the close of the preceding Triassic, managed to survive and evolve.

Juno, classical sculpture; in the Museo Archeologico Nazionale, Naples.
ALINARI–ART RESOURCE

Jurchen dynasty See JUCHEN DYNASTY

jurisdiction Authority of a court to hear and determine cases. This authority is constitutionally based. Examples of judicial jurisdiction are: appellate jurisdiction, in which a superior court has power to correct legal errors made in a lower court; concurrent jurisdiction, in which a suit might be brought to any of two or more courts; and federal jurisdiction. A court may also have authority to operate within a certain territory. Summary jurisdiction, in which a magistrate or judge has power to conduct proceedings resulting in a conviction without jury trial, is limited in the U.S. to petty offenses.

H
I
J
K

jurisprudence Science or philosophy of law. Jurisprudence may be divided into three branches: analytical, sociological, and theoretical. The analytical branch articulates axioms, defines terms, and prescribes the methods that best enable one to view the legal order as an internally consistent, logical system. The sociological branch examines the actual effects of the law within society and the influence of social phenomena on the substantive and procedural aspects of law. The theoretical branch evaluates and criticizes law in terms of the ideals or goals postulated for it.

jury In law, a body of individuals selected and sworn to inquire into a question of fact and to render a verdict according to the evidence. Modern juries may deal with questions of law in addition to questions of fact, though federal juries in the U.S. are usually limited to dealing with questions of fact. The modern jury can vary in size depending on the proceeding, but usually has either six or 12 members. By U.S. law, federal grand and petit juries must be "selected at random from a fair cross-section of the community in the district or division wherein the court convenes." State jury selection varies somewhat. The U.S. Supreme Court has stated in a series of decisions that a jury is to be composed of "peers and equals" and that systematic exclusion from a jury of a particular class (e.g., on the basis of sex, race, or ancestry) violates the EQUAL-PROTECTION clause and the defendant's right to a jury trial. A defendant is not, however, entitled to a jury of any particular composition. See also GRAND JURY, PETIT JURY, VOIR DIRE.

just compensation Compensation for property taken under EMINENT DOMAIN that places a property owner in the same position as before the property was taken. It is usually the fair market value of the property taken. Attorney's fees or expenses are usually excluded.

just-in-time manufacturing (JIT) Production-control system, developed by TOYOTA MOTOR CORP. and imported to the West, that has revolutionized MANUFACTURING methods in some industries. By relying on daily deliveries of most supplies, it eliminates waste due to overproduction and lowers warehousing costs. Supplies are closely monitored and quickly altered to meet changing demands, and small and accurate resupply deliveries must be made just as they are needed. Because there are no spares, the components must be free of defects. Plants wholly dedicated to the JIT concept require a logistics staff to schedule production, balancing product demand with plant capacity and availability of inputs. JIT has worked most effectively for large automobile manufacturers, which may have several thousand suppliers feeding parts into 100 factories that assemble components for 20 assembly lines.

just war theory Medieval European concept that a ruler, by proper declaration and with proper motives, might employ armed force outside his normal jurisdiction to defend rights, rectify wrongs, and punish crimes. The concept developed as early as St. AUGUSTINE in the 4th century and was still accepted by HUGO GROTIUS in the 17th century. Its popularity thereafter declined, though in the 20th century it enjoyed a revival in new form, with the idea that a nation might resort to armed force in self-defense or in executing collective international peacekeeping obligations.

justice In philosophy, the concept of a proper proportion between a person's deserts (what is merited) and the good and bad things that befall or are allotted to him or her. ARISTOTLE's discussion of the virtue of justice has been the starting point for almost all Western accounts. For him, the key element of justice is treating like cases alike, an idea that has set later thinkers the task of working out which similarities (need, desert, talent) are relevant. Aristotle distinguishes between justice in the distribution of wealth or other goods (distributive justice) and justice in reparation, as, for example, in punishing someone for a wrong he has done (retributive justice). The notion of justice is also essential in that of the just state, a central concept in POLITICAL PHILOSOPHY. See also LAW.

Justice, U.S. Department of Federal executive division responsible for law enforcement. Headed by the U.S. attorney general, it investigates and prosecutes cases under federal antitrust, civil-rights, criminal, tax, and environmental laws. It controls the FEDERAL BUREAU of Investigation, the Bureau of Prisons, the DRUG ENFORCEMENT ADMINISTRATION, the Office of Justice Programs, the Immigration and Naturalization Service, the U.S. Marshals Service, and the U.S. representative bureau in INTERPOL.

justice of the peace In Anglo-American legal systems, a local magistrate empowered chiefly to administer justice in minor cases. In the U.S., justices of the peace are elected or appointed and hear minor civil matters and petty criminal cases. They may also officiate at weddings, issue arrest warrants, deal with traffic offenses, and hold inquests.

justification In Christian theology, the passage of an individual from SIN to a state of GRACE. Some theologians use the term to refer to the act of God in extending grace to the sinner, while others use it to define the change in the condition of a sinner who has received grace. St. PAUL used the term to explain how people moved from sin to grace through the death and resurrection of JESUS and not through any human effort. St. AUGUSTINE saw it as an act of God that makes sinners righteous, while MARTIN LUTHER stressed justification through faith alone.

Justin II (died 578) Byzantine emperor (565–78). He tolerated the MONOPHYSITE HERESY until 571, then began to persecute its followers. Despite an alliance with the Franks, Justin lost parts of Italy to the Lombards after 568. He also suffered defeats at the hands of the AVARS, to whom he promised to pay tribute (574), and the Western Turks, who seized lands in the Crimea. He invaded Persia in 572, but the Persians repulsed his army and invaded Byzantine territory, capturing Dara in 573. He became insane, and his general Tiberius (his adopted son) was effective ruler of the empire after 574.

Justin Martyr, St. (c. 100–c. 165) Early Christian theologian. A pagan born in Palestine, he studied philosophy before becoming a Christian in 132, probably at Ephesus. He then spent years as an itinerant preacher and teacher. One of the first APOLOGISTS for Christianity, he was the first to blend Greek philosophy and Christian doctrine. He wrote two *Apologies* addressed to Roman emperors, which asserted that Christian faith can be in harmony with human reason and that Christianity is a purer form of the truth glimpsed in pagan philosophy. In his *Dialogue with Trypho* he tried to prove the truth of Christianity to a scholarly Jew named Trypho. While living in Rome he was denounced as subversive and condemned to death.

Justinian, Code of Collections of laws and legal interpretations developed under the sponsorship of the Byzantine emperor JUSTINIAN I from 529 to 565. Strictly speaking, they did not constitute a new legal code. Rather, Justinian's committees of jurists provided basically two reference works that contained collections of past laws and extracts of the opinions of the great Roman jurists. Also included were an elementary outline of the law and a collection of Justinian's new laws.

Justinian I *orig.* **Petrus Sabbatius** (483–565) Byzantine emperor (527–65). Determined to regain former Roman provinces lost to barbarian invaders, Justinian conquered the VANDALS in northern Africa (534) and defeated the OSTROGOTHS in Italy (540). He did not gain control of the whole of Italy until 562, and he was unable to prevent Bulgars, Slavs, HUNS, and AVARS from carrying out raids along the empire's northern frontier. He also carried on an intermittent war with Persia until 561. He reorganized the imperial government and sponsored a body of laws known as the Code of JUSTINIAN. His efforts to root out corruption triggered an abortive revolt in Constantinople in 532; his wife, THEODORA, helped him put down the revolt. Among his public works was the church of HAGIA SOPHIA.

Justinian I, detail of a mosaic, 6th century; in the Basilica of San Vitale, Ravenna.

ALINARI—GIRAUDON FROM ART RESOURCE

jute Either of two herbaceous annuals *(Corchorus capsularis* and *C. olitorius)* in the LINDEN family, or their fiber. The plants grow 10–12 ft (3–4 m) high and have long, serrated, tapered, light-green leaves and small yellow flowers. Jute has been grown and processed in the Bengal area of India (and of present-day Bangladesh) since ancient times. Its biggest use is in burlap sacks and bags, which are used to ship and store many agricultural products. High-quality jute cloths are used as backing for tufted carpets and hooked rugs. Coarser jute fibers are made into twines, rough cordage, and doormats.

Jutland *Danish* **Jylland** \'yu̅e̅-ˌlän\ Peninsula, northern Europe. Forming the Danish mainland and the German state of SCHLESWIG-HOLSTEIN, it is bounded to the west and north by the North Sea. Politically, its name applies only to the mainland of DENMARK. It has an area of 11,496 sq mi (29,775 sq km) and is divided into seven administrative regions. In World War I, the Battle of JUTLAND was fought off its coast.

Jutland, Battle of (May 31–June 1, 1916) Only major encounter between the British and German fleets in WORLD WAR I, fought in the Skagerrak, an arm of the North Sea off the coast of Jutland (Denmark). The battle came to an indecisive end, and both sides claimed victory. Germany destroyed and crippled more ships and men, but Britain retained control of the North Sea. The tactics of the British admiral JOHN R. JELLICOE were criticized at the time, but his strategic victory left the German high-seas fleet ineffective for the rest of the war.

Jutra \zhu̅e̅-'trä\, **Claude** (1930–1986) Canadian film director. Born in Montreal, he worked as a television writer before joining the National Film Board in 1954. After making a feature-length documentary, he directed the acclaimed *Take It All* (1964, Canadian Film Award). His next film, *Mon oncle Antoine* (1971, Canadian Film Award), was considered his masterpiece. His later films were less successful. Diagnosed with Alzheimer's disease, he drowned himself in the St. Lawrence River.

Juvenal \'jü-və-nəl\ *Latin* **Decimus Junius Juvenalis** (c. AD 55–130) Roman poet. He probably came from a well-to-do family, became an army officer, and grew embittered by failure to receive a promotion. He is chiefly known for his 16 *Satires,* indignant attacks on human brutality and folly, particularly the corruption of Roman society under DOMITIAN and his more humane successors NERVA, TRAJAN, and HADRIAN. His verses are technically fine, vivid, and often ruthless, and have been admired and imitated since the 5th century, and many of his phrases and epigrams ("bread and circuses," "who will guard the guards themselves?" etc.) have entered common parlance.

juvenile court Special court handling problems of delinquent, neglected, or abused children. Two types of cases are processed by a juvenile court: civil matters, often concerning care of an abandoned or impoverished child; and criminal matters arising from antisocial behavior by the child. Most statutes provide that all persons under a given age (often 18 years) must first be processed by the juvenile court, which can then, at its discretion, assign the case to an ordinary court. The first juvenile court was established in 1889 in Chicago, and the movement spread rapidly throughout the world.

K2 *or* **Dapsang** \ˌdäp-'säng\ Mountain in the Karakoram Range. The world's second-highest peak, it reaches 28,251 ft (8,611 m); it lies partly in China and partly in the Pakistani portion of the Kashmir region. It was discovered and measured in 1856 by Col. T. G. Montgomerie and was given the symbol K2 because it was the second peak measured in the Karakoram Range. In 1954 the Italians Achille Compagnoni and Lino Lacedelli became the first climbers to reach its summit.

Kaaba Most sacred Muslim shrine, located near the center of the Great Mosque in Mecca. All Muslims face toward it in their daily prayers. The cube-shaped structure, made of gray stone and marble, has its corners roughly oriented to the points of the compass; the interior contains only pillars and silver and gold lamps. Pilgrims to Mecca walk around the Kaaba seven times and touch the Black Stone of Mecca on its eastern side, which may date from the pre-Islamic religion of the Arabs. Tradition holds that the Kaaba was built by Abraham and Ishmael. In 630 Muhammad purged the place of its pagan idols and rededicated it to Islam.

Kabalega National Park \ˌkä-bä-'lā-gä\ National park, northwestern Uganda. Established in 1952, it occupies 1,483 sq mi (3,840 sq km) of rolling grassland. Its central feature is the Kabalega Falls on the lower Victoria Nile River. The falls are about 20 ft (6 m) wide and drop 130 ft (40 m) in the first of three cascades.

Kabbala *or* **Cabbala** \kä-'bä-lə\ Jewish mysticism as it developed in the 12th century and after. Essentially an oral tradition, it laid claim to secret wisdom of the unwritten Torah communicated by God to Adam and Moses. It provided Jews with a direct approach to God, a notion regarded as heretical and pantheistic by Orthodox Judaism. A major text was the 12th-century *Book of Brightness,* which introduced the doctrine of transmigration of souls to Judaism and provided Kabbala with extensive mythical symbolism. In 13th-century Spain the tradition included the *Book of the Image,* which asserted that each cycle of history had its own Torah, and the *Book of Splendor,* which dealt with the mystery of creation. In the 16th century the center of Kabbala was Safed, Galilee, where it was based on the esoteric teachings of the greatest of all Kabbalists, Isaac ben Solomon Luria. The doctrines of Lurianic Kabbala, which called for Jews to achieve a cosmic restoration *(tiqqun)* through an intense mystical life and an unceasing struggle against evil, were influential in the development of modern Hasidism.

Kabila \kə-'bē-lə\, **Laurent (Désiré)** (1939–2001) Rebel Leader and president (1997–2001) of Congo (Zaire). He attended schools abroad, including military school in China, before participating in several Marxist-inspired uprisings in Zaire in the 1960s and '70s. He later became a trader in precious minerals and ivory. In the Rwandan civil war, Kabila collaborated with Paul Kagame in attacking Hutu guerrilla groups in Zaire as well as Zairean government forces. His troops ousted Mobutu Sese Seko in 1997, and Kabila proclaimed himself president and renamed the country. His repressive policies soon led to a new and larger war, in which many African states sent troops and aid to both sides. His assassination was apparently engineered by his own officers; his son Joseph (born 1971) succeeded him.

Kabir \kə-'bir\ (1440–1518) Indian mystic and poet. A weaver who lived in Benares, he preached the essential oneness of all religions and was critical of both Hinduism and Islam for meaningless rites and mindless repetition. From Hinduism he accepted the ideas of reincarnation and the law of karma, but rejected idolatry, asceticism, and the caste system. From Islam he accepted the idea of one God and the equality of all men. Revered by both Hindus and Muslims, he is also considered a forerunner of Sikhism, and some of his poetry was incorporated into the Adi Granth. His ideas led to the founding of several sects, including the Kabir Panth, which regards Kabir as its principal guru or as a divinity.

kabuki \kä-'bü-kē\ Popular Japanese entertainment that combines music, dance, and mime in highly stylized performance. The word is formed of three Japanese characters—*ka* (song), *bu* (dance), and *ki* (skill). Kabuki dates from the end of the 16th century, when it developed from the nobility's No drama and became the theater of townspeople. In its early years it had a licentious reputation, its actors often being prostitutes; women and young boys were consequently forbidden to perform, and kabuki is today performed by an adult all-male cast. Its texts, unlike No texts, are easily understood by its audience. The lyrical but fast-moving and even acrobatic plays, noted for their spectacular staging and elaborate costumes and with striking makeup in place of masks, are vehicles in which the actors demonstrate a wide range of skills. Kabuki employs two musical ensembles, one onstage and the other offstage. It shares much of its repertoire with bunraku.

Kabul \'kä-bəl\ City (population 1994 est.: 700,000), capital of Afghanistan. Located on the Kabul River in a valley strategically located between mountain passes, it has existed for 3,500 years. It became the capital of the Mughal dynasty's empire in the 16th century, and it remained under Mughal rule until 1738, when Iran gained control. Kabul has been the capital of Afghanistan since 1776. The Soviet Union invaded the country in 1979 and established a military command in Kabul. After the Soviet withdrawal in 1989, factional fighting among Afghan guerrillas continued intermittently and the city suffered widespread destruction. In 1996 the Taliban captured Kabul and imposed Islamic fundamentalist rule.

Kabul River River in eastern Afghanistan and northwestern Pakistan. Rising west of Kabul city, it flows east into Pakistan and, after a course of 435 mi (700 km), joins the Indus River northwest of Islamabad. The Kabul River valley is a natural route for travel between Afghanistan and Pakistan; Alexander the Great used it to invade India in the 4th century BC. Much of the Kabul's course is tapped for irrigation.

Kabyle \kə-'bīl\ Berber people of Algeria. Most are Muslim, the rest Christian. They are predominantly agricultural, growing grains and olives and herding goats. Village government is run by an assembly of adult males. Villages are divided into clans, and the society is organized into castes. The current population is about 2 million. See also Rif.

Kachchh, Rann of *or* **Rann of Kutch** \'kəch\ Large salt marsh, western central India and southern Pakistan. The northern portion, Great Rann, occupies an area of 7,000 sq mi (18,000 sq km) in Gujarat state, India. The eastern section, Little Rann, occupies 2,000 sq mi (5,100 sq km) of Gujarat state. Originally an extension of the Arabian Sea, it has been closed off by centuries of silting. A 1965 dispute over the India–Pakistan boundary line of Great Rann ended when an international tribunal awarded 10% of the border area to Pakistan and 90% to India.

Kachin \kä-'chin\ Tribal peoples occupying parts of northeastern Myanmar and contiguous areas of India (Arunachal Pradesh and Nagaland) and China (Yunnan). Numbering over 700,000, they speak a variety of languages of the Tibeto-Burman group. Traditional Kachin society largely subsisted on the shifting cultivation of hill rice, supplemented by the proceeds of banditry and feudal warfare. The traditional Kachin religion is a form of animistic ancestor cult entailing animal sacrifice. About 10% of the Kachin are Christian.

kachina \kə-'chē-nə\ Ancestral spirit of the Pueblo Indians. There are more than 500 of these spirits, who act as intermediaries between humans and the gods. Each tribe has its own kachinas, which are believed to reside with a tribe for half of each year. They can be seen by the community if men properly perform a ritual while wearing kachina masks. The spirit depicted on the

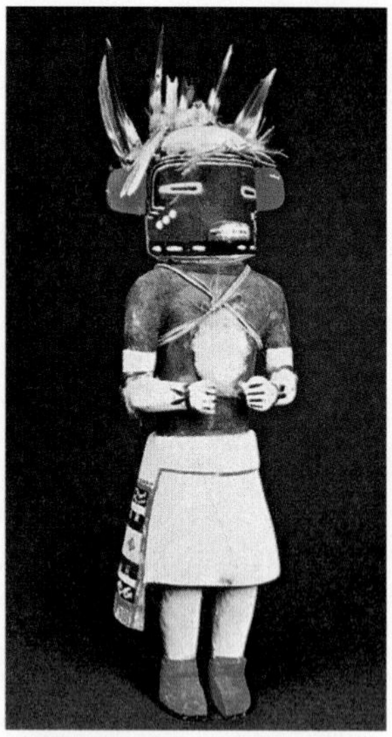

Hopi kachina of *laqán,* or squirrel spirit, c. 1950; in the Museum of the American Indian, Heye Foundation, New York City.

mask is thought to be actually present with the performer, temporarily transforming him. Kachinas are also represented by small wooden dolls, carved and decorated by the men of the tribe.

Kaczynski \kə-ˈzin-skē\, **Theodore** *known as* **the Unabomber** (born 1942) U.S. criminal. Born in Evergreen Park, Ill., he attended Harvard University and earned a doctorate in mathematics from the University of Michigan. He taught at UC–Berkeley (1967–69), then abruptly left to become a hermit in a tiny, isolated shack in rural Montana. Over 17 years, he sent mail bombs to people he perceived as enemies of humanity, most of them professors and researchers in science and technology, killing three people and injuring 23. His manifesto excoriating industrial society was published widely in 1995. Arrested in 1996 on a tip from his younger brother, he was sentenced to life in prison.

Kádár \ˈkä-ˌdär\, **János** *orig.* **János Czermanik** (1912–1989) Premier of Hungary (1956–58, 1961–65) and first secretary (1956–88) of Hungary's Communist Party. He joined the then-illegal Communist Party in 1931 and entered the Hungarian Politburo in 1945. In 1950 he came into conflict with the Stalinists and was expelled from the party and jailed (1951–53). Rehabilitated in 1954, he joined IMRE NAGY's short-lived government. After Soviet troops took over the country in 1956, Kádár formed a new government with Soviet backing and quelled a popular revolt. He later convinced the Soviet Union to withdraw its troops and allow Hungary a modicum of internal independence.

Kadare, Ismail (b. 1936) Albanian novelist and poet. The son of a post-office worker, Kadare became a journalist. Unhappy with the political environment in Albania, he eventually made his home in Paris. Among his better-known works are the novels *The General of the Dead Army* (1963), about post-World War II Albania, and *The Castle* (1970), which explores Albanian nationalism. The stories in *Elegy for Kosovo* (1999) concern a 14th-century battle between Balkan leaders and the Ottoman Empire. He was the only Albanian writer to have an international following in the 20th century.

Kaddish \ˈkä-dish\ Jewish prayer of mourners, recited for a period of 11 months and one day after the death of a parent or close relative. Spoken in the ARAMAIC LANGUAGE rather than in Hebrew, it is a hymn of praise to God and a prayer for the speedy coming of the MESSIAH. Originally recited in the rabbinical academies, it later became a regular feature of the synagogue service. The association of the arrival of the messiah and the resurrection of the dead led to its becoming the prayer of mourners.

Kadesh \ˈkā-ˌdesh\ Ancient city, western Syria. Located just southwest of modern HOMS, it was seized by the Egyptian king THUTMOSE III in the 15th century BC. It remained an outpost of Egypt until it came under HITTITE rule in the mid-14th century BC. The Egyptian king Seti I captured the city, and in 1275 BC it was the scene of a battle between RAMSES II and the Hittite Muwatallis. After invasion by the Sea Peoples c. 1185 BC, Kadesh disappeared from history.

Kadesh-barnea *or* **Kadesh** City of ancient PALESTINE. Its precise location is unknown, but it was situated in the country of the Amalekites, southwest of the DEAD SEA and on the western edge of the Wilderness of Zin. It was twice the scene of encampments of Israelites.

Kadet See CONSTITUTIONAL DEMOCRATIC PARTY

Kaduna River \kä-ˈdü-nä\ River, central Nigeria. The main tributary of the NIGER RIVER, it rises on the Jos Plateau, flowing northwest and then southwest before completing its 340-mi (550-km) course at the Niger in Mureji. The Kaduna (meaning "crocodiles" in the HAUSA LANGUAGE) is navigable only part of the year.

Kael \ˈkāl\, **Pauline** (1919–2001) U.S. film critic. Born in Petaluma, Cal., she managed an art-film theater in Berkeley (1955–60) while writing film reviews for magazines and broadcasting her reviews on network radio. After a collection of her reviews and essays, *I Lost It at the Movies* (1965), gained her national attention, she moved to New York and became film critic for *The New Yorker* (1968–91). Her witty, biting, highly opinionated, and sharply focused reviews (of which five more collections were eventually published) made her the most influential film critic of the time.

Kafka \ˈkäf-kä\, **Franz** (1883–1924) Czech writer who wrote in German. Born into a middle-class Jewish family in Prague (then part of Austria-Hungary), he earned a doctorate and then worked successfully but unhappily at a government insurance office from 1907 until he was forced to retire in 1922 by tuberculosis, which would cause his death at age 40. Hypersensitive and neurotic, he reluctantly published only a few works in his lifetime, including the symbolic story *The Metamorphosis* (1915), the allegorical fantasy *In the Penal Colony* (1919), and the story collection *A Country Doctor* (1919). His unfinished novels *The Trial* (1925), *The Castle* (1926), and *Amerika* (1927), published posthumously against Kafka's wishes, express the anxieties and alienation of 20th-century humanity. His tales, with their inscrutable mixture of the normal and the fantastic, have provoked a wealth of interpretations. Kafka's posthumous reputation and influence have been enormous, and he is regarded as one of the great European writers of the 20th century.

Kafka.

ARCHIV FUR KUNST UND GESCHICHTE, BERLIN

Kafue National Park \kä-ˈfü-ā\ National park, southern central Zambia. Located west of LUSAKA, it was established in 1950. It occupies an area of 8,650 sq mi (22,400 sq km) and consists of a vast plateau, situated along the middle reaches of the KAFUE RIVER. The park is noted for its lush vegetation and abundant wildlife, including hippopotamus, zebra, elephant, black rhinoceros, and lion. Safaris are conducted on foot.

Kafue River River rising on the Zaire-Zambia border. It meanders south then flows southeast to join the ZAMBEZI RIVER near Chirundu, Zimbabwe, after a course of 600 mi (960 km). It cuts through the plateau of central Zambia, and its basin contains the KAFUE NATIONAL PARK. It is one of Zambia's major rivers, and its waters are used for irrigation and hydroelectric power.

Kagame, Paul (born 1957) President of RWANDA from 2000. An ethnic TUTSI, Kagame grew up in exile in Uganda, where in 1986 he helped overthrow MILTON OBOTE in favor of Yoweri Museveni. In 1990 he helped direct an unsuccessful coup in Rwanda, and following the 1994 genocide that left almost one million Rwandans dead (most of them Tutsi), he assumed control of the joint Tutsi-Hutu opposition forces that soon controlled all of Rwanda. In July 1994 he was named vice president and minister of defense under HUTU president Pasteur Bizimungu. After Bizimungu resigned in 2000, Kagame was named president. In 1997 he was instrumental in the overthrow of MOBUTU SESE SEKO in neighboring Zaire (CONGO) and the installation of LAURENT KABILA as president.

Kaganovich \kə-gə-ˈnò-vich\, **Lazar (Moiseyevich)** (1893–1991) Soviet political leader. He joined the BOLSHEVIKS in 1911 and became head of the Soviet government of Tashkent in 1920. As head of the Moscow party organization (1930–35), he brought it firmly under JOSEPH STALIN's control and with VYACHESLAV MOLOTOV formed the core of Stalin's "post-Purge" Politburo. Until 1953 he was largely responsible for heavy industry in the Soviet Union. Under NIKITA KHRUSHCHEV, he held administrative posts, but he opposed de-Stalinization and joined the unsuccessful attempt to depose Khrushchev in 1957, as a result of which he lost all his offices.

Kagera River \kä-ˈgā-rä\ River, northwestern Tanzania. The longest headstream of the NILE RIVER and the largest tributary of Lake VICTORIA, it rises in Burundi near the northern tip of Lake TANGANYIKA and flows north, constituting the boundary between Tanzania and Rwanda. Turning east, it forms the boundary between Tanzania and Uganda before emptying into Lake Victoria. It is 429 mi (690 km) long.

kagura \ˈkä-gü-ˌrä\ In SHINTO, a traditional style of music and dancing used in religious ceremonies. Kagura dances dedicated to native deities are a reenactment of the propitiatory dance that lured the sun goddess AMATERASU from her cave in ancient myth. Largely unchanged for the past 1,500 years, the dances are performed to the accompaniment of chants, drums, brass gongs, and flutes. The music is of two types: one to praise the spirits or seek their aid, the other to entertain the gods.

Kahlo (y Calderón de Rivera) \'kä-lō\, **(Magdalena Carmen) Frida** (1907–1954) Mexican painter. The daughter of a German-Jewish photographer, she had polio as a child and at 18 suffered a serious bus accident. She subsequently underwent some 35 operations; during her recovery, she taught herself to paint. Her marriage to Diego Rivera (from 1929) was tumultuous but artistically rewarding. She is noted for her intense, bizarre, brilliantly colored self-portraits, many reflecting her physical ordeal, which incorporate primitivistic elements but are executed with a fine technique. The Surrealists Andre Breton and Marcel Duchamp helped arrange exhibits of her work in the U.S. and Europe, and though she denied the connection, she is often identified as a Surrealist. She died at 47. Her house in Coyoacán is now the Frida Kahlo Museum.

"Diego and I," oil on masonite, self-portrait (with forehead portrait of Diego Rivera) by Frida Kahlo, 1949; in the gallery of Mary-Anne Martin/Fine Art, New York City.

COURTESY MARY-ANNE MARTIN/FINE ART, NEW YORK CITY

Kahn, Albert (1869–1942) U.S. (German-born) industrial architect. In 1904 he received a commission for the Packard Motor Car Co. auto factory; his design, with its reinforced concrete frame, represented an innovative departure from traditional masonry factory construction. He originated the prototypical modern factory building, a rapidly and inexpensively built steel-frame structure with an unobstructed floor plan and large windows and skylights where all production takes place on one floor. For 30 years he was the principal architect for the major U.S. auto companies, and by 1937 his firm was producing a fifth of all architect-designed industrial buildings in the U.S.

Kahn, Herman (1922–1983) U.S. physicist and strategist. Born in Bayonne, N.J., he studied at Caltech and joined the RAND Corp., where he studied the application to military strategy of new analytic techniques such as game theory, operations research, and systems analysis. He won public notice with *On Thermonuclear War* (1960), in which he contended that thermonuclear war differs only in degree from conventional war and ought to be analyzed and planned in the same way. In 1961 he established the Hudson Institute for research into matters of national security and public policy.

Kahn, Louis I(sadore) (1901–1974) U.S. (Estonian-born) architect. He came to the U.S. as a child and graduated from the University of Pennsylvania. One of the century's most original architects, Kahn turned from the International Style to a timeless, elegant Brutalism evocative of ancient ruins. His Richards Medical Research Building at the university (1960–65) isolated "servant" spaces (stairwells, elevators, vents, and pipes) in four towers distinct from "served" spaces (laboratories and offices). His fortresslike National Assembly Building in Dhaka, Bangladesh (1962–74), utilized geometric shapes to admit light to its inner domed mosque. Like R. Buckminster Fuller, Kahn was concerned about wasteful use of natural resources; his urban-planning schemes proposed geodesic skyscrapers and huge car "silos." He taught at Yale University (1947–57) and the University of Pennsylvania (1957–74), where his intellect elevated him to cult status.

Kaibara Ekiken \'kī-bä-rä-e-'kē-ˌken\ (1630–1714) Japanese philosopher, travel writer, and pioneer botanist. Trained as a physician, he left the medical profession in 1657 to study the Neo-Confucian writings of Zhu Xi. He wrote about 100 philosophical works, which stressed the hierarchical nature of society and translated Confucian doctrine into terms understood by Japanese of all social classes. His writings include *The Great Learning for Women,* a tract on obedience long considered the most important ethical text for Japanese women. He is regarded as the father of botany in Japan.

Kaieteur Falls \'kī-ə-ˌtu̇r\ Cataract on the Potaro River, western central Guyana. After a sheer drop of 741 ft (226 m), the falls pass into a gorge 5 mi (8 km) long, which descends another 81 ft (25 m). The falls are 300 to 350 ft (90 to 105 m) wide at the top and are the central feature of the Kaieteur National Park (established 1930).

Kaifeng *or* **K'ai-feng** \'kī-'fəŋ\ City (pop., 1990: 508,000), northern Henan province, China. In the 4th century BC it became the capital of the state of Wei, and the first of its canals was built. It was destroyed by the Qin dynasty in the late 3rd century BC, and until the 5th century AD it was only a market town. It became an important commercial center in the 7th century, enriched by traffic along the Grand Canal, and it was the capital of the Five Dynasties and the Song dynasty. Kaifeng was the site of China's only large Jewish community (12th–15th century).

Kaikei \'kī-ˌkā\ (1183–1223) Japanese sculptor who helped establish the traditional pattern of Buddhist sculpture. His technique, know as the Anami style, is noted for its gentleness and grace. Together with his teacher, Kokei, and his colleague Unkei, he made statues for the temples of Kofuku and Todai in Nara, Japan's ancient capital. He later became a monk and assumed the name Anami Butsu.

Kairouan \ker-'wän\ Town (pop., 1994: 103,000), northeastern Tunisia. A holy city of Islam, it was founded in 670 by the Arab general Sidi Okba and became the first Arab center in the Maghreb. It was chosen as the Maghreb capital by the Aghlabid dynasty c. 800. It served as an administrative, commercial, religious, and intellectual center under the Fatimid and Zirid dynasties. The rise of Tunis, the new capital, led to Kairouan's decline and its devastation by Bedouins in the 11th century. It is the site of the 9th-century Great Mosque of the Qayrawan, one of the city's 150 mosques.

Kaiser \'kī-zər\, **Henry J(ohn)** (1882–1967) U.S. industrialist. Born in Sprout Brook, N.Y., he undertook his first public-works projects beginning in 1914, eventually building dams in California, levees on the Mississippi River, and highways in Cuba. Between 1931 and 1945, he organized combinations of construction companies to build the Hoover, Bonneville, and Grand Coulee dams and other large public projects. During World War II he ran seven shipyards, making steel in his own integrated steel mill and using assembly-line production to build ships in less than five days. He established the first health maintenance organization, the Kaiser plan, for his shipyard employees; it served more than a million people and became a model for later federal programs. In the postwar era he dealt profitably in aluminum, steel, and automobiles.

Kakinomoto no Hitomaro \'kä-kē-nō-ˌmō-tō-nō-'hē-tō-ˌmä-rō\ *known as* **Hitomaro** (died 708) Japanese poet. He entered the service of the imperial court and later became a provincial official. Japan's first great literary figure, he lived when Japan was moving from a preliterate to a literate, civilized society. His writings, on a wide range of subjects, balance the homely qualities of primitive song with sophisticated interests and literary techniques. All 77 poems accepted as indisputably his, and many others attributed to him, appear in the *Man'yoshu,* the first and largest of Japan's anthologies of native poetry.

Kalacuri dynasty \ˌkä-lə-'kü-rē\ Any of several dynasties in Indian history. Apart from the dynastic name and perhaps a belief in common ancestry, there is little in known sources to connect them. The earliest known Kalacuri family ruled c. 550–620 in central and western India; its power ended with the rise of one branch of the Calukyas. The rise of another Kalacuri dynasty (1156–81) centered in Karnataka coincided with the rise of the Lingayat, or Virashaiva, Hindu sect. The best known Kalacuri family ruled in central India with its base at the ancient city of Tripuri (Tewar); it originated in the 8th century, expanded significantly in the 11th century, and declined in the 12th–13th century.

Kalahari Desert \ˌkä-lä-'hä-rē\ Desert region, southern Africa. It covers an area of 360,000 sq mi (930,000 sq km) and lies mostly in Botswana but also occupies portions of Namibia and South Africa. It was crossed by the British explorers David Livingstone and William C. Oswell in 1849. Although the region has no permanent surface water apart from the Boteti River, it supports trees, low scrub, and grasses as well as abundant wildlife. It includes the Kalahari Gemsbok National Park and the Gemsbok National Park.

Kalahari Gemsbok National Park \'gemz-ˌbäk\ National park in the Kalahari Desert, South Africa. Established in 1931, it lies between Namibia and Botswana and adjoins the Gemsbok National Park of Botswana. It occupies an area of 3,703 sq mi (9,591 sq. km). Its wildlife includes gnu, lions, jackals, cheetahs, and ostriches.

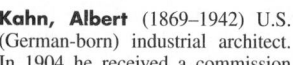

kalam \kə-'läm\ Islamic speculative theology. It arose during the UMAYYAD DYNASTY over varying interpretations of the QURAN and over questions the Quran provoked, including those on predestination, free will, and the nature of God. The most prominent early school was the 8th-century MUTAZILA, which asserted the supremacy of reason, championed free will, and rejected an anthropomorphic characterization of God. The 10th-century school of ASHARIYA displaced Mutazila and moved kalam back toward traditional faith, accepting, for example, the eternal, uncreated nature of the Quran and its literal truth.

Kalamukha See KAPALIKA AND KALAMUKHA

kalanchoe \ˌka-lən-'kō-ē\ Any of several species of SUCCULENT plants that make up the genus *Kalanchoe* in the stonecrop family (Crassulaceae), popular for their easy indoor culture. Potted *K. blossfeldiana* plants are marketed widely for their winter-blooming bright red and orange flowers, which may remain fresh for as long as eight weeks. As succulents, kalanchoes require little care, needing only considerable direct sunlight (or at least bright indirect light) and occasional watering. On some species, young plants grow in notches on the leaves of parent plants, then drop to the soil below and begin root growth.

Kalaupapa Peninsula \kä-ˌlä-ü-'pä-pä\ Promontory on the northern shore of Molokai island, Hawaii. Occupying a 10-sq-mi (26-sq-km) plateau, it is isolated from the rest of the island by 2,000-ft (600-m) cliffs. Kalawao village, now abandoned, was the site of the original leper colony (see LEPROSY) established by King Kamehameha V in 1866; Father DAMIEN ministered to the lepers there 1873–89. The entire peninsula is now the state leprosarium, administered by Hawaii's health department.

Kalb \kälp, *Engl* 'kalb\, **Johann** (1721–1780) German army officer. He served in a German regiment of the French infantry from 1743. In 1768 the French sent him on a secret mission to the American colonies to determine their attitude toward Britain. In 1776 he obtained a commission in the Continental Army and served with GEORGE WASHINGTON at Valley Forge. He joined Gen. HORATIO GATES at Camden, S.C., in an abortive attack on British forces. After Gates was driven from the field, Kalb fought on and was mortally wounded.

kale Loose-leafed, edible plant *(Brassica oleracea* 'acephala') derived from the CABBAGE, in the MUSTARD FAMILY. Common (or Scotch) and Buda kale have stems up to 2 ft (60 cm) long, carrying a rosette of elongated, dark-bluish-green, wavy or frilled leaves. Grown mainly for autumn and winter harvest because cold improves the eating quality of this hardy vegetable, kale is usually served cooked. It is highly nutritious. See also COLLARD.

kaleidoscope Telescope-like visual toy. Its tube contains loose bits of colored material (such as glass or plastic) between two flat plates and two plane mirrors so placed that changes of position of the bits (through rotation or shaking) are reflected in an endless variety of striking and colorful patterns. It was invented by Sir David Brewster c. 1816.

Kalevala \'kä-lā-ˌvä-lä\ Finnish national epic. It was compiled by ELIAS LONNROT from the songs and ballads of Finland's oral tradition and published in complete form in 1849. Kalevala, the dwelling place for the poem's chief characters, is also a poetic name for Finland, meaning "land of heroes." The epic contains a creation story and adventures of legendary heroes. The main character is Väinämöinen, a musician and seer of supernatural origins. Other characters include Ilmarinen, a smith who forged the lids of heaven; Lemminkäinen, a warrior-adventurer and charmer of women; and Louhi, the female ruler of a land in the north. Though the *Kalevala* depicts conditions during the pre-Christian era, it also seems to foretell the decline of the old religions.

Kalf \'kälf\, **Willem** *or* **Willem Kalff** (1619–1693) Dutch painter. He is among the best-known Dutch painters of still lifes, a choice of subject matter influenced by a stay in Paris. His early works depict kitchen interiors, with such elements as gourds and pots strewn on the floor. His later paintings feature luxurious, expensive objects such as Venetian glass and Chinese porcelain, painted with restraint and richness of texture. Works such as *Still Life with a Nautilus Cup* (c. 1660) were popular among Amsterdam's wealthy.

Kali Destructive and devouring Hindu goddess. She is a terrifying aspect of DEVI, who in other forms appears as peaceful and benevolent. Kali is commonly associated with death, violence, sexuality, and, paradoxically, with motherly love. She is usually depicted as a hideous, black-faced hag smeared with blood. In her four hands she holds a sword, a shield, the severed head of a giant, and a noose for strangling. Nearly naked, she wears a garland of skulls and a girdle of severed hands. She is often shown standing or dancing on her husband, SHIVA. Kali developed her taste for blood from killing the demon Raktavija. Until the 19th century the thugs of India worshiped Kali and offered their victims to her.

Kali, sandstone relief from Bheraghat, near Jabalpur, Madhya Pradesh state, India, 10th century AD.
PRAMOD CHANDRA

Kalidasa \ˌkä-lē-'dä-sä\ (fl. c. 5th century) Indian poet and dramatist. Little is known about him; his poems suggest that he was a Brahman (priest). Many works are traditionally ascribed to him, but scholars have identified only six as genuine and one more as likely. The Sanskrit drama *The Recognition of Sakuntala,* his most famous creation, is traditionally judged the major Indian literary effort of any period, and Kalidasa is regarded as perhaps the greatest of all Indian writers.

Kalinga Ancient and medieval kingdom, northeastern India. It corresponds to the area of modern northern ANDHRA PRADESH, most of ORISSA, and a portion of MADHYA PRADESH. It was conquered by Mahapadma, the founder of the NANDA DYNASTY, in the 4th century BC. Beginning in the mid-11th century AD, the Eastern GANGA DYNASTY assumed control. The temple of the sun-god at Konarak was built in the 13th century by Narasimha I. The dynasty collapsed when the sultan of Delhi invaded Kalinga from the south in 1324.

Kalinin \kə-'lē-nyən\, **Mikhail (Ivanovich)** (1875–1946) Russian communist leader and statesman. An early supporter of the BOLSHEVIKS, he participated in the RUSSIAN REVOLUTION OF 1905 and cofounded *PRAVDA*. After the RUSSIAN REVOLUTION OF 1917 he served as mayor of Petrograd (St. Petersburg). In 1919 he became chair of the central executive committee of the All-Russian Congress of Soviets, and thus titular head of the Soviet state, a position he kept until his death. From 1925 he was a member of the Politburo and supported JOSEPH STALIN in crucial votes, thus retaining his high party office.

Kaliningrad \kə-'lē-nin-ˌgråt\ *formerly* **Königsberg** \'kœ-niks-ˌberk\ City (pop., 1992 est.: 411,000), western Russia, situated on the Pregolya River. Founded in 1255 as Königsberg, it was the capital of the dukes of Prussia and later the capital of East Prussia. In 1724 it absorbed the nearby cities of Löbenicht and Kneiphof. Virtually destroyed by the Soviets during World War II, it came under the sovereignty of the U.S.S.R. and was rebuilt in 1946 as Kaliningrad. It is the seat of the University of Kaliningrad and the birthplace of IMMANUEL KANT.

Kalliope See CALLIOPE

Kalmar \'käl-ˌmär\, **Union of** (1397–1523) Scandinavian union that joined the kingdoms of Norway, Sweden, and Denmark under the rule of a single monarch. Margaret I became ruler of the three kingdoms in 1387; she chose her grandson Erik of Pomerania to become their king, and he was crowned at Kalmar, Sweden, in 1397. Each country kept its own laws, customs, and administration. Sweden rebelled and claimed independence under GUSTAV I VASA in 1523, and Norway became a Danish province in 1536.

Kaloyan *or* **Kalojan** \'kå-lò-yån\ (died 1207) Czar of Bulgaria (1197–1207). Having received his crown from the pope, he led a Bulgarian-Greek uprising in the Balkan Peninsula that defeated the Latin crusaders at Adrianople (1205) and took BALDWIN I, the Latin emperor, prisoner. Kaloyan's alliance with the Greeks fell apart, and he died besieging Thessaloniki.

Kama In Indian mythology, the god of love. In the Vedic age he personified cosmic desire or the creative impulse, and he was called the first-born of primeval chaos. He was later often depicted as a handsome youth attended by heavenly nymphs, who shot love-producing flower arrows from a sugarcane bow. He was once killed by SHIVA, who was enraged when Kama disturbed his meditation on a mountaintop, but the great god later relented and brought Kama back to life.

Kama River River, western central Russia. The largest tributary of the VOLGA, it rises in Udmurtiya and flows for 1,122 mi (1,805 km) until it enters the Volga below Kazan. Navigation is possible for about 955 mi (1,535 km). It is one of the most important rivers of Russia, historically as the route to the Urals and Siberia and economically as part of the vast Volga system of waterways.

Kamakura shogunate \ˌkä-mä-'ku̇r-ä\ (1192–1333) Military government of Japan from the city of Kamakura. The Kamakura shogunate was established by MINAMOTO YORITOMO after his 1185 defeat of a rival warrior family, the Taira (see TAIRA KIYOMORI). To assert his authority, Yoritomo had JITO (stewards) assigned to all the estates (SHOEN) in the land to collect taxes, and *shugo* (protectors) assigned to one or more provinces to lead them in times of war. This system was improved by the HOJO FAMILY, which took control of the shogunate upon Yoritomo's death. The creation of the Kamakura shogunate marks the start of Japan's medieval or feudal period, characterized by a warrior ethic of duty, loyalty, and stoicism. Much of what Westerners associate with Japan, including ZEN Buddhism, SAMURAI, SEPPUKU, and the TEA CEREMONY, dates from this period. The True Pure Land and NICHIREN sects of Buddhism, which emphasized salvation through faith alone, provided solace to the masses, while tales of warrior exploits provided them with entertainment. See also BUSHIDO.

Kamchatka \kəm-'chät-kə\ Peninsula, eastern Russia. It lies between the Sea of Okhotsk on the west and the Pacific Ocean and BERING SEA on the east. It is 750 mi (1,200 km) long and 300 mi (480 km) across at its widest point, and has an area of 140,000 sq mi (370,000 sq km). Mountain ranges extend along it, with 22 active volcanoes, including Klyuchevskaya Volcano (15,584 ft, or 4,750 m), the highest peak in SIBERIA.

Kamehameha I \kä-'mā-hä-'mā-hä\ *orig.* **Paiea** *known as* **Kamehameha the Great** (1758?–1819) Hawaiian conqueror and king who united all the Hawaiian islands. His birth came soon after the appearance of Halley's Comet, whose appearance led seers to prophesy the coming of a great conqueror. As a young man he fought his cousin over control of the island of Hawaii; by 1795 he had defeated his cousin and conquered all but two of the Hawaiian islands, and in 1810 the remaining islands were ceded to him. He retained the harsh traditional legal system but protected the common people from the brutality of powerful chiefs and outlawed human sacrifice. He enriched his kingdom through a government monopoly on the sandalwood trade and through port duties imposed on visiting ships, and maintained its independence throughout the difficult period of European discovery and exploration of the islands. He founded the most enduring and best-documented line of HAWAIIAN rulers.

Kamehameha I, detail of a coloured lithograph by D. Veelward, 1822, after an engraving by Louis Choris, 1816.
BERNICE PAUAHI BISHOP MUSEUM, HONOLULU

Kamehameha IV, c. 1862–1863.
BERNICE PAUAHI BISHOP MUSEUM, HONOLULU; PHOTOGRAPH, H.L. CHASE

Kamehameha IV *orig.* **Alexander Liholiho** (1834–1863) Hawaiian ruler (1855–63). Adopted as a child by his uncle, Kamehameha III (1813–1854), he was educated by Protestant missionaries. As king, he sought to curb the power of the U.S. missionaries. He expanded trade with other countries and, to offset U.S. influence, invited the Church of England to establish itself in the islands. A popular and benevolent ruler, he improved harbors to accommodate Hawaii's growing whaling industry and provided free medical care for Hawaiians.

Kamenev \'kä-myə-ˌnyef\, **Lev (Borisovich)** *orig.* **Lev Borisovich Rosenfeld** (1883–1936) Russian political leader. A member of the Bolsheviks from 1903, he worked with VLADIMIR ILICH LENIN in Europe 1909–14, then returned to Russia, where he was arrested and sent to Siberia. After the Russian Revolution of 1917, he served as head of the Moscow soviet 1919–25. When Lenin became seriously ill in 1922, Kamenev joined JOSEPH STALIN and GRIGORY Y. ZINOVYEV to form the ruling triumvirate, attacking LEON TROTSKY. In 1925 Stalin shifted his attack to Kamenev and Zinovyev, and removed Kamenev as Moscow party head. In 1926 he was expelled from the party after conspiring with Zinovyev and Trotsky against Stalin. In 1936 he was tried in the first of the PURGE TRIALS and confessed to fabricated charges, hoping to save his family. He was executed, and his wife, Trotsky's sister, perished in the GULAG.

Kamerlingh Onnes \ˌkä-mər-liŋ-'ō-nəs\, **Heike** (1853–1926) Dutch physicist. He taught at the University of Leiden 1882–1923, and in 1884 founded the Cryogenic Laboratory (now known by his name) that established Leiden as the world's principal research center for low-temperature physics. He was the first to produce liquid helium (1908), and he discovered superconductivity. He also investigated the equations describing the states of matter and the general thermodynamic properties of fluids over a wide range of temperatures and pressures. He was awarded the 1913 Nobel Prize for Physics.

kamikaze \ˌkä-mi-'kä-zē\ Any of the Japanese pilots in World War II who made deliberate suicidal crashes into enemy targets, usually ships. The word means "divine wind," a reference to a typhoon that dispersed a Mongol invasion fleet threatening Japan from the west in 1281. The practice was most prevalent in the final year of the war. Most kamikaze planes were ordinary FIGHTER AIRCRAFT or light bombers, usually loaded with bombs or extra gasoline tanks before their suicidal dive. Such attacks sank 34 ships and damaged hundreds of others; at Okinawa they inflicted the greatest losses ever suffered by the U.S. Navy in a single battle, killing almost 5,000 men. See also ZERO.

Kammu \'kä-mü\ (737–806) Emperor of Japan (781–806). To curb the power of the Buddhist temples located in Nara, he moved the capital from Heijo (Nara) to Nagaoka in 784 and then to the city of Heian (Kyoto) in 794. The establishment of the capital in Heian marked the start of the HEIAN PERIOD.

Kamo no Chomei \'kä-mō-nō-'chō-mā\ (1155–1216) Japanese poet and critic. He is best known for *An Account of My Hut* (1212), a poetic diary describing his life in seclusion written after he left a court office to take Buddhist orders and become a hermit. His poetry is representative of the best of an age that produced many poets of the first rank. His *Mumyosho* (1208/9; "Nameless Notes") is an extremely valuable collection of critical comments and poetic lore.

Kampala \käm-'pä-lä\ City (pop., 1991: 774,000), capital of Uganda. The country's largest city, it is in southern Uganda, north of Lake VICTORIA. It was selected in 1890 by Capt. Frederick Lugard as the headquarters of the British East Africa Co. Lugard's fort on Old Kampala Hill remained the Ugandan colonial administrative headquarters until 1905, when it was moved to Entebbe. In 1962 Kampala became the capital of independent Uganda. It is the headquarters for most of Uganda's large firms and the site of Makerere University and the Uganda Museum.

Kampuchea See CAMBODIA

Kampuchean See KHMER

Kan River See GAN RIVER

Kanarese language See KANNADA LANGUAGE

Kanawa, Kiri Te See Kiri TE KANAWA

Kanawha River \kə-'nȯ-wə\ River, West Virginia. Formed by the confluence of the New and Gauley rivers, it flows northwest for 97 mi (156 km), to enter the OHIO RIVER at Point Pleasant. It has dams and locks and is navigable to Kanawha Falls, located 30 mi (48 km) above Charleston, W.V. The Kanawha River valley has extensive deposits of salt brines and natural gas and oil wells.

Kanchenjunga \ˌkən-chən-'jəŋ-gə\ Peak in the HIMALAYAS. The world's third-highest mountain, it reaches 28,169 ft (8,586 m). It is located on the Nepalese border with Sikkim, India, northwest of Darjeeling. Rinzin Namgyal, a 19th-century explorer, made the first map of the peak. In 1955 a British expedition led by Charles Evans made the first successful climb.

Kandel, Eric (born 1929) U.S. neurobiologist. Born in Austria, he received his MD from New York University. Kandel's research revealed the role of synaptic transmission in learning and memory. He showed that weak stimuli give rise to certain chemical changes in synapses, forming the the basis for short-term memory, and that stronger stimuli cause different synaptic changes, which result in a form of long-term memory. Along with PAUL GREENGARD and ARVID CARLSSON, Kandel was awarded a Nobel Prize in 2000. The findings of the three men resulted in the development of new drugs for PARKINSONISM and other disorders.

Kander, John (born 1927) U.S. songwriter. He was born in Kansas City, studied music at Oberlin College and Columbia Univ., and later wrote arrangements for plays. With lyricist Fred Ebb (born 1932), a native New Yorker who also studied at Columbia and wrote lyrics for revues, he scored some of Broadway's most successful musicals, including *Cabaret* (1966; film, 1972), *Zorba* (1968), *Chicago* (1975), and *Kiss of the Spider Woman* (1992), and films such as *Funny Lady* (1975) and *New York, New York* (1977).

Kandinsky \kan-'din-skē\, **Vasily (Vasilievich)** (1866–1944) Russian painter, a pioneer of pure abstraction in modern painting. Trained in the law and offered a law professorship, he chose painting instead and set out for Germany. After art studies in Munich, he achieved moderate success, most importantly with his series of *Compositions, Improvisations,* and *Impressions* (1909–14). In 1911 he and FRANZ MARC founded the influential BLAUE REITER group. In 1914 he returned to Russia. After the Bolshevik revolution he was lionized by the Soviet government, but in 1921, when the government abandoned abstraction for Socialist Realism, he returned to Germany. He taught at the BAUHAUS in Weimar 1921–33, then emigrated to Paris when the Nazis closed the Bauhaus. Through the years, Kandinsky's work evolved from fluid organic forms to geometric and finally pictographic forms. His late Paris works seem to synthesize the organic manner of the Munich period with the geometric manner of the Bauhaus period. His book *Concerning the Spiritual in Art* (1912) explains his theories on the expressiveness of forms and color, which he likened to qualities of sound (e.g., comparing yellow to a blaring trumpet, and blue to a pipe organ). His influence on 20th-century art was profound.

Kändler \'ken-dler\, **Johann Joachim** (1706–1775) German baroque sculptor. In 1731 he was engaged to reorganize the modeling department of the porcelain factory at Meissen; he held the position of chief modeler there from 1733 until his death. It was largely through Kändler's genius that MEISSEN PORCELAIN gained world renown. Among his best-known works are his commedia dell'arte figurines, largely done between 1736 and 1744.

Harlequin, Meissen hard-paste porcelain figure from the commedia dell'arte modeled by Johann Joachim Kändler, c. 1738; in the Victoria and Albert Museum, London.

BY COURTESY OF THE VICTORIA AND ALBERT MUSEUM, LONDON; PHOTOGRAPH, EB INC.

Kandy Important independent monarchy in Ceylon (Sri Lanka) at the end of the 15th century and the last Sinhalese kingdom to be subjugated by a colonial power. Kandy survived the predations of the Portuguese by allying with the Dutch and survived the Dutch by seeking British aid; when the British took over Ceylon in 1796, Kandy was left on its own. The first British attack on Kandy in 1803 failed; in 1815 Kandyan chiefs invited the British to overthrow a tyrannical king, and in 1818 those chiefs' rebellion against the British was suppressed.

Kane, Paul (1810–1871) Canadian (Irish-born) painter. His family emigrated to Canada in 1819. He worked mainly in Toronto, but traveled as far as the Pacific coast depicting landscapes, American Indian subjects, fur traders, and missionaries; he published an account of his adventures in *Wanderings of an Artist* (1859). Half of his paintings are portraits, works of great historical value in which he recorded the dress and ornaments of his subjects in accurate detail. He excelled at composing large figurative groups in a style similar to contemporary European genre painting.

Kanem-Bornu \'kä-ˌnem-'bōr-nü\ Former African empire around Lake CHAD. It was ruled by the Sef dynasty in the 9th–19th century. Its territory at various times included what is now southern Chad, northern Cameroon, northeastern Nigeria, eastern Niger, and southern Libya. Probably founded in the mid-9th century, it became an Islamic state at the end of the 11th century. Its location made it a trading hub between North Africa, the Nile Valley, and the sub-Saharan region. From the 16th century Kanem-Bornu, sometimes called simply Bornu, was extended and consolidated. The Sef dynasty died out in 1846.

Kang Youwei *or* **K'ang Yu-wei** \'käŋ-'yō-'wā\ (1858–1927) Chinese scholar, a key figure in the intellectual development of modern China. In 1895 Kang led hundreds of provincial graduates to protest the humiliating terms of China's treaty with Japan after the SINO-JAPANESE WAR and to petition for reforms to strengthen the nation. In 1898 the Qing emperor launched a reform program that included streamlining the government, strengthening the armed services, promoting local self-government, and opening Beijing University. The empress CIXI annulled the reforms and had six reform leaders executed, and Kang had to flee the country. In exile, he opposed revolution; he favored rebuilding China through science, technology, and industry. He returned in 1914 and participated in an abortive restoration of the emperor; his fears of a divided country led him to oppose the government of SUN YAT-SEN in southern China. Kang is also known for his reappraisal of Confucius, whom he saw as a reformer.

kangaroo Most broadly defined as any of about 54 species (family Macropodidae) of Australasian MARSUPIALS. Most are terrestrial and all are herbivores; most graze on the Australian plains. They generally have long, powerful hind legs and feet and a long tail, thickened at the base. The hind legs enable their spectacular leaps and are also useful for self-defense; the tail is used for balance. The head is small, the ears large and rounded, and the fur soft and woolly. Females have one young (called a joey) annually; it is suckled in its mother's pouch for six months, and later often returns to be carried in the pouch as well. The gray kangaroo, the best-known and second-largest species, can leap more than 30 ft (9 m). The red kangaroo is the largest species; the male may stand 6 ft (1.8 m) tall and weigh 200 lbs (90 kg). Tree kangaroos are arboreal; they climb trees and leap from branch to branch. Millions are killed annually for their meat and hides and because they compete for forage with livestock. See also WALLABY, WALLAROO.

Gray kangaroo (*Macropus canguru*).

WARREN GARST—TOM STACK AND ASSOCIATES

Kangaroo Island Island (pop., 2001 prelim: 4,259), South Australia. Located at the entrance to the Gulf St. Vincent, southwest of ADELAIDE, it is 90 mi (145 km) long and occupies an area of 1,680 sq mi (4,350 sq km). Visited in 1802 by the English explorer MATTHEW FLINDERS, it was named for its many kangaroos. Nepean Bay was the site of the state's first settlement in 1836.

kangaroo rat Any of about 25 species (genus *Dipodomys,* family Heteromyidae) of RODENTS that leap about on their hind legs; found in dry regions of North America. They have large heads, large eyes, short forelimbs, long hind limbs, and fur-lined external cheek pouches that open alongside the mouth. They are 4–6.5 in. (10–16 cm) long without

H I J K

the long tail, which usually ends in a furry tuft. They are pale buff to brown above and white below, with a white stripe on each hip. They forage by night for seeds, leaves, and other vegetation, carrying food in their cheek pouches to store in their burrows, but seldom drink water.

Kangaroo rat (*Dipodomys*).
ANTHONY MERCIECA FROM ROOT RESOURCES

KaNgwane \käŋ-'gwä-nä\ Former black enclave, eastern Transvaal, South Africa. It was created under the APARTHEID system in 1977 as a homeland for those SWAZI people not residing in Swaziland. The 1994 constitution of South Africa abolished the black enclaves created under the apartheid system, and it is now part of Mpumalanga province.

Kangxi emperor *or* **K'ang-hsi emperor** \'käŋ-'shē\ (1654–1722) Second emperor of the QING DYNASTY. His personal name was Xuanye. One of China's most capable rulers, Kangxi reigned 1661–1722 and laid the foundation for a long period of political stability and prosperity. Under his reign, the Treaty of NERCHINSK was signed with Russia, parts of Outer Mongolia were added to China's territory, and control was extended over Tibet. Domestically, Kangxi's reign oversaw public works such as the repairing of the GRAND CANAL to permit transportation of rice to feed the northern population, and the dredging and banking of the Huang (Yellow) River to prevent destructive flooding. Kangxi reduced taxes many times and opened four ports to foreign ships for trade. Though an ardent proponent of NEO-CONFUCIANISM, he also welcomed Jesuit missionaries, whose accomplishments led him to permit the propagation of Roman Catholicism in China. He commissioned many books, including the Kangxi dictionary and a history of the MING DYNASTY. See also DGA'L-DAN MANCHU, QIANLONG EMPEROR.

Kaniska \kə-'nish-kə\ (fl. 1st century AD) Greatest king of the Kushan dynasty that ruled over the northern part of the Indian subcontinent, Afghanistan, and possibly regions north of Kashmir in Central Asia. He is thought to have taken the throne between AD 78 and 144 and to have ruled for 23 years. Kaniska is noted for having convened a Buddhist council that marked the beginnings of MAHAYANA Buddhism. He was a tolerant king who honored the Zoroastrian, Greek, and Brahmanic deities as well as Buddha. During his reign there was a significant increase in trade with the Roman empire, and contact between him and the Chinese in Central Asia may have inspired the transmission of Buddhism to China.

Kannada language \'kä-nə-də\ *formerly* **Kanarese language** \,ka-nə-'rēz\ DRAVIDIAN LANGUAGE, the official language of the Indian state of KARNATAKA. It is spoken by over 33 million people in Karnataka; an additional 11 million Indians may speak it as a second language.The earliest inscriptional records in Kannada are from the 6th century. Kannada script is closely akin to Telugu script in origin. Like other major Dravidian languages, Kannada has a number of regional and social dialects and marked distinctions in formal and informal usage.

Kannon See AVALOKITESVARA

Kano \'kä-nō\ City (pop., 1996 est.: 674,000), northern Nigeria. Its traditional founder was Kano, a blacksmith of the Gaya tribe who in ancient times came to Dalla Hill in search of iron. It became the capital of the Hausa state of Kano in the early 12th century. It was the capital of an emirate in the 19th century before being captured by the British in 1903. Modern Kano is a major commercial and industrial center. The old city is enclosed by a massive city wall dating from the 15th century; the central mosque is Nigeria's largest.

Kano school (fl. 15th–19th century) Family of Japanese artists that served the shoguns of the ASHIKAGA SHOGUNATE and also ODA NOBUNAGA, TOYOTOMI HIDEYOSHI, and the shoguns of the TOKUGAWA SHOGUNATE. Bold, large-scale designs were executed on the folding screens and sliding panels that acted as space dividers in the castles of the day. Chinese-style ink painting was blended with polychromatic *yamato-e* ("Japanese painting"); some artists used a background of gold leaf for even more gorgeous effects.

Kanphata Yogi Member of an order of religious ascetics that venerate the Hindu god SHIVA. They are followers of Gorakhnath, a master yogi of the 12th century or earlier. Their ideology incorporates elements of magic, mysticism, and alchemy absorbed from both Hindu and Buddhist esoteric systems. Members focus on acquiring supernatural powers rather than following the more orthodox practices of meditation and devotion. They are distinguished by large earrings worn in the hollow of the ear.

Kanpur \'kän-,pu̇r\ *or* **Cawnpore** City (pop., 1991: 1,874,000), UTTAR PRADESH, northern India. The British acquired it in 1801 and made it one of their frontier stations. In 1857, during the INDIAN MUTINY, it was the site of the massacre of British troops and civilians by native forces. One of the largest cities in India, it is a hub of road and rail transportation and a major commercial and industrial center. Its educational institutions include a university and the Indian Institute of Technology.

Kansas State (pop., 1997 est.: 2,595,000), central U.S. It covers 82,277 sq mi (213,097 sq km); its capital is TOPEKA. It is part of the GREAT PLAINS, rising more than 3,000 ft (915 m) from its eastern prairies to the high plains of the west. The region was occupied by the Kansa, OSAGE, PAWNEE, and Wichita Indians before European settlement. The first European explorer was FRANCISCO VAZQUEZ DE CORONADO, who came from Mexico in 1541 in search of gold. R.-R. LA SALLE claimed the region for France in 1682. Kansas was acquired by the U.S. as part of the LOUISIANA PURCHASE in 1803. In the early 19th century the federal government relocated displaced eastern Indians to Kansas. The KANSAS-NEBRASKA ACT of 1854 created Kansas Territory and opened it to white settlement. It was the site of conflicts over slavery, including one spurred by JOHN BROWN (see BLEEDING KANSAS). It entered the Union as the 34th state in 1861. After the Civil War, the coming of the railroads promoted the growth of cow towns; Texas cattlemen drove herds to WICHITA and ABILENE to reach the railheads. Agriculture became important as farmers worked on the Great Plains. During and following World War II, airplane production expanded, and farm products remained strong.

Kansas, Bleeding See BLEEDING KANSAS

Kansas, University of Public university founded in 1866 in Lawrence. It includes a college of liberal arts and sciences and schools offering study in such areas as law, engineering, business, architecture, and pharmacy. Its medical center is in Kansas City. Research facilities include centers for life-span studies, child research, environmental health, oil recovery, and space technology. Total enrollment is about 28,000.

Kansas City City (pop., 1996 est.: 441,000), western Missouri, on the MISSOURI RIVER. The city is contiguous with Kansas City, Kan. First settled by French fur traders in 1821, it was known as Westport Landing, prospering as a river port and as the terminus for the SANTA FE TRAIL and the OREGON TRAIL. Chartered in 1850 as the town of Kansas and as a city in 1853, it became Kansas City in 1889 to distinguish it from the territory. The state's second-largest city, it is a railroad center with stockyards, packing-houses, and grain-storage facilities. It is the seat of the University of Missouri at Kansas City, and the world headquarters for the Church of the Nazarene.

Kansas-Nebraska Act (1854) Legislation that organized the territories of Kansas and Nebraska according to the doctrine of POPULAR SOVEREIGNTY. Introduced by Sen. STEPHEN A. DOUGLAS to stop the sectional division over slavery, the act was criticized by antislavery groups as a capitulation to proslavery advocates. Groups on both sides rushed to settle Kansas Territory with their adherents, leading to the chaotic BLEEDING KANSAS period. Passage of the act led to the formation of the REPUBLICAN PARTY as a political organization opposed to the expansion of slavery to any U.S. territory.

Kansas River *or* **Kaw River** River, northeastern Kansas. It flows east and empties into the MISSOURI RIVER at KANSAS CITY. It is 169 mi (272 km) long, and it drains an area of 61,300 sq mi (158,770 sq km), including northern Kansas and parts of southern Nebraska and eastern Colorado.

Kansu See GANSU

Kant \'känt\, **Immanuel** (1724–1804) German philosopher, the foremost thinker of the ENLIGHTENMENT. Son of a saddler, he was born in Königsberg (now Kaliningrad, Russia), studied at its university, and taught there from 1755 to 1797. His life was uneventful. Much of Kant's work was devoted to arguing that METAPHYSICS, understood as knowledge of things supersensible, is an impossibility. Yet he held that metaphysics, understood as the study of the presuppositions of experience, could be put on "the sure path of science"; it is also possible, and indeed necessary, to hold certain beliefs about God, freedom, and immortality. But however well founded these beliefs may be, they in no sense amount to knowledge: to know about the intelligible world is entirely beyond human capacity. Though the Ideas of God, freedom, and immortality are dismissed in his great *Critique of Pure Reason* (1781) as objects that humans can never know because they transcend human sense experience, he argued in *The Critique of Practical Reason* (1788) that they are essential postulates for the moral life. His *Groundwork of the Metaphysics of Morals* (1785) is among the most important and influential ethical treatises ever written. His last great work was *The Critique of Judgment* (1790). Kant was one of the greatest philosophers of all time; he synthesized new trends that had begun with the RATIONALISM of RENE DESCARTES and the EMPIRICISM of FRANCIS BACON. His comprehensive and systematic work in epistemology, ethics, and aesthetics greatly influenced all subsequent philosophy, especially the various German schools of KANTIANISM and IDEALISM. See also ANALYTIC–SYNTHETIC DISTINCTION, DEONTOLOGICAL ETHICS.

Kantianism \'kan-tē-ə-ˌni-zəm, kän-tē-ə-ˌni-zəm\ System of critical philosophy created by IMMANUEL KANT and the philosophies that have arisen from the study of his writings. Kantianism comprises diverse philosophies that share Kant's concern to explore the nature and limits of human knowledge in the hope of raising philosophy to the level of a science. Each submovement of Kantianism has tended to focus on its own selection and reading of Kant's many concerns. In the 1790s, there emerged in Germany the so-called semi-Kantians, who altered features of Kant's system they viewed as inadequate, unclear, or even wrong; its members included FRIEDRICH SCHILLER, Friedrich Bouterwek (1766–1828), and Jakob Friedrich Fries (1773–1843). The period 1790–1835 was the age of the post-Kantian idealists (see IDEALISM). A major revival of interest in Kantian philosophy began c. 1860. See also JOHANN GOTTLIEB FICHTE, G. W. F. HEGEL, NEO-KANTIANISM, F. W. SCHELLING.

Kantorovich \ˌkän-tə-'rò-vich\, **Leonid (Vitalyevich)** (1912–1986) Soviet mathematician and economist. A professor at Leningrad State University (1934–60), he developed the LINEAR PROGRAMMING model as a tool of economic planning. He used mathematical techniques to show how decentralization of decision making in a planned economy ultimately depends on a system in which prices are based on the relative scarcity of resources. His nondogmatic critical analyses of Soviet economic policy often clashed with the views of his orthodox Marxist colleagues. His most notable work is *The Best Use of Economic Resources* (1959). In 1975 he and Tjalling Koopmans (1910–1985) shared the Nobel Prize for their work on optimal allocation of scarce resources.

Kanuri \kə-'nùr-ē\ African people, the dominant population (4 million) of Borno state in northeastern Nigeria, also found in large numbers in southeastern Niger. Kanuri is one of the NILO-SAHARAN LANGUAGES. The Kanuri developed the powerful empire of BORNU, which reached its peak in the 16th century. They have been Muslims since the 11th century. The Kanuri economy is based on millet agriculture and trade with the FULANI and Arab herders.

Kao-hsiung \'kaù-'shyùŋ\ Port city (pop., 1997 est.: 1,435,000), southwestern Taiwan. It is Taiwan's leading port and a major industrial center. Settled late in the MING DYNASTY, it became a treaty port in 1863 and a customs station in 1864. It grew in importance during the Japanese occupation (1895–1945) and served as the southern terminus of the main north-south railway line. The city was named Takao by the Japanese and made a municipality in 1920. It came under Chinese rule in 1945.

kaolinite \'kā-ə-lə-ˌnīt\ Group of common CLAY MINERALS that are hydrous aluminum silicates and constitute the principal ingredients of kaolin (china clay). The group includes kaolinite, dickite, nacrite, halloysite, and allophane. They are natural alteration products of feldspars, feldspathoids, and other silicates.

Kapalika and Kalamukha \kä-'pä-li-kə...'kä-lä-ˌmù-kə\ Members of either of two groups of extreme Hindu ascetics, prominent in India in the 8th–13th century. They were an offshoot of the Shaivites (see SHAIVISM), who worshiped SHIVA, and their notorious practices included human sacrifice. After sacrificing a BRAHMAN or other high-ranking person, they embraced a 12-year vow of self-abnegation that included eating and drinking from the skull of the sacrificed person and following tantric practices such as going about naked, eating the flesh of the dead, and smearing themselves with the ashes of corpses. Their modern successors are the Aghoris, or Aghorapanthis.

Kapila \'kə-pē-lə\ (fl. 6th century BC) Founder of the SAMKHYA school of Vedic philosophy in India. Legend says he was a descendant of MANU, the primal human being, and a grandson of the creator god, BRAHMA. He has also been thought of as an incarnation of VISHNU. In Buddhist sources he was a well-known philosopher whose students built Kapilavastu, the birthplace of BUDDHA Gautama. He lived as a hermit, and his ascetic regimen was said to have given him an inner store of such intense heat that he was capable of reducing 60,000 men to ashes.

Kaplan, Mordecai Menahem (1881–1983) U.S. (Lithuanian-born) theologian. He came to the U.S. with his family in 1889. Ordained at the Jewish Theological Seminary, he later taught there for 50 years. In 1916 he organized the Jewish Center in New York as a secular community organization with a synagogue as its nucleus. In 1922 he founded the Society for the Advancement of Judaism, which became the core of RECONSTRUCTIONISM. Denying the literal accuracy of the Bible, he called for a new conception of God in an attempt to adapt Judaism to the modern world. He founded the journal *The Reconstructionist* in 1935; his books include *Judaism as a Civilization* (1934) and *Judaism without Superstition* (1958).

kapok \'kā-ˌpäk\ Fiber obtained from the large, tropical silk cotton, or kapok, tree (*Ceiba pentandra,* family Bombacaceae), which bears hundreds of seedpods filled with fibrous seeds. The tree is grown chiefly in Asia and Indonesia. Sometimes called silk cotton or Java cotton, this moisture-resistant, quick-drying, resilient, buoyant fiber is used in life preservers and other water-safety equipment. Kapok is also used to stuff pillows, mattresses, and upholstery, as insulation, and as a cotton substitute in surgery. However, it is highly flammable, and the fibers are too brittle for spinning. Its importance has decreased with the development of foam rubber, plastics, and man-made fibers.

Kapoor, Raj (1924–1988) Indian film actor and director. In the 1930s Kapoor worked as a clapper boy for Bombay Talkies and as an actor for Prithvi Theatres, two companies owned by his father. Kapoor's first major screen role was in *Aag* (1948; "Fire"), which he also produced and directed. In 1950 he formed his own Bombay (now Mumbai) film studio, RK, and the next year he achieved romantic stardom in *Awara* (1951; "The Vagabond"). He wrote, produced, directed, and starred in many successful films. Although he portrayed romantic leads in his early movies, his best-known characters were based on CHARLIE CHAPLIN's tramp. His use of sexual imagery often challenged traditionally strict Indian film standards, and many of his film songs became musical hits.

Kaposi's sarcoma \'ka-pə-sēz\ Usually lethal CANCER appearing as red-purple or blue-brown spots on the skin and other organs. It has been linked to one of the herpes viruses, and there is considerable debate about how it should be classified. When described in 1872 by Moritz Kaposi, it was extremely rare, confined to specific Mediterranean and African populations. Since c. 1980, it has become common in AIDS patients. More homosexual male HIV patients (about 25%) have developed it than heterosexual intravenous-drug-using HIV patients (3%). Remissions have occurred, but there is no known cure.

Kapp Putsch \'käp-'pùch\ (1920) In Germany, a coup d'état that attempted to overthrow the fledgling WEIMAR REPUBLIC. Its immediate cause was the government's attempt to demobilize two FREIKORPS brigades. One of the brigades took Berlin, with the cooperation of the Berlin army-district commander. Wolfgang Kapp (1858–1922), a reactionary member of the Reichstag, formed a government with ERICH LUDENDORFF, and the legitimate republican regime fled to southern Germany. Within four days, a general strike by labor unions and the refusal by civil servants to follow Kapp's orders led to the coup's collapse.

Kara Koyunlu *or* **Qara Qoyunlu** \'kä-rä-ˌkò-yùn-'lü\ Turkmen tribal federation that ruled Azerbaijan and Iraq (c. 1375–1468). Their second leader, Kara Yusuf (r.1390–1400, 1406–20), secured their independence by seizing the Jalayirid capital of Tabriz. He was beaten back by the armies of TIMUR, but regained Tabriz in 1406. He captured Baghdad in 1410. His successor, Jihan Shah, died in battle against a rival Turkmen federation, the Ak Koyunlu, in 1466, and the empire fell in 1468.

Karachi \kä-'rä-chē\ City (pop., 1981: 5,210,000), Pakistan. Located in southern Pakistan on the Arabian Sea northwest of the mouth of the INDUS RIVER, it was a small fishing village when traders arrived in the early

18th century. It was captured by the British in 1839 and was a major port of the British empire by 1914. The provincial capital of Sind from 1936, it was also the capital of Pakistan 1947–59. It is Pakistan's principal seaport and a major industrial and commercial center. It is the seat of the University of Karachi and the terminus of Pakistan's railway system.

Karadžić \kä-'rä-jēt^y^, *Engl* kä-'rad-zich\, **Radovan** (born 1945) Bosnian Serb politician. He trained as a psychiatrist and also wrote poetry and children's books. In 1990 he helped found the Serbian Democratic Party of Bosnia and Herzegovina. In 1992, when the Bosnian Serbs declared an independent state, he became its president. With the support of Yugoslav president SLOBODAN MILOSEVIC and with Bosnian Serb military leader Gen. Ratko Mladic, Karadžić undertook a campaign of "ethnic cleansing" in Bosnia to purge it of non-Serb peoples. In 1995 he was indicted by a U.N. war-crimes tribunal. He was pressured into signing the Dayton peace accords and forced to resign as state president and party head in 1996. However, he continued to influence the Serb-controlled part of Bosnia and Herzegovina from a mountain hideaway outside Sarajevo.

Karadžić \kä-'rä-jēt^y^, *Engl* kä-'rad-zich\, **Vuk Stefanović** (1787–1864) Serbian language scholar and folklorist. He was a largely self-taught writer. After the failure of a Serb revolt against Turkish rule, he left for Vienna (1813), where he was introduced to formal scholarship by the Slavist Jernej Kopitar. In 1814 he published a grammar of Serbian (see SERBIAN AND CROATIAN LANGUAGE), and in 1818 a dictionary; both promulgated a reformed CYRILLIC ALPHABET and a new literary language based on colloquial Serbian rather than the prevailing literary language, which mixed archaic Serbian with Russian Church Slavic (see OLD CHURCH SLAVIC LANGUAGE). After decades of resistance and polemicizing, the renascent Serbian state accepted his reforms, which also had a strong influence on the standardization of literary Croatian.

H I J K

Karaganda *or* **Qaraghandy** \ˌkä-rə-'gän-də\ City (pop., 1995 est.: 574,000), central Kazakhstan. The first settlement appeared in 1856, and small-scale coal mining began the next year. Mining expanded rapidly in the early 1930s, and the town was made a city in 1934. Kazakhstan's second-largest city, it consists of the old town, which grew up haphazardly around more than 20 mining settlements, and the new town, the cultural and administrative center, which includes a university and medical and polytechnic institutes.

Karageorgevic dynasty \ˌkar-ə-'jōr-jə-ˌvich\ *Serbo-Croatian*, Karadordevic. Rulers descended from the Serbian rebel leader Karageorge (1762–1817). It rivaled the OBRENOVICH DYNASTY for control of Serbia during the 19th century and ruled that country and its successor state, the Kingdom of SERBS, CROATS, AND SLOVENES (later Yugoslavia), in 1842–58 and 1903–45. See also ALEXANDER I, PETER I, PETER II.

Karaism *or* **Qaraism** \'kar-ə-ˌi-zəm\ Jewish religious movement that denied the authenticity of the oral law and defended the Hebrew Bible as the only basis of doctrine and practice. It originated in 8th-century Persia, where its members were called Ananites after Anan ben David, who worked out a code of life independent of the TALMUD. Members later adopted the name Karaites from the Hebrew *qara* ("to read"), emphasizing their reliance on a personal reading of the Bible. The movement spread through Egypt and Syria, winning only small numbers of followers and enduring many schisms. It still has about 10,000 members in Israel.

Karajan \'kär-ə-ˌyän\, **Herbert von** (1908–1989) Austrian conductor. Born in Salzburg, he attended its Mozarteum, then continued his studies in Vienna. A prodigious pianist, he took his first conducting post in Ulm in 1929. In 1933 he joined the Nazi Party, and under the Third Reich his reputation grew swiftly. After World War II he initially was not allowed to conduct, but in 1947 he began recording with the Vienna Philharmonic, the start of a legacy of some 800 recordings. His U.S. debut in 1955 was attended by controversy over his Nazi-era activities. That same year he became W. FURTWANGLER's successor at the Berlin Philharmonic, and he headed the Salzburg Festival from 1964 until his death.

Karak See KAYA

Karakoram Range Mountain system, Central Asia. Extending 300 mi (480 km) from eastern Afghanistan to the KASHMIR region, it is one of the highest mountain systems in the world; its loftiest peak is K2. Surrounded by other steep mountain ranges, the Karakorams are virtually inaccessible, although the completion of the Karakoram Highway in 1978 improved transportation in the region. Owing to the harshness of the environment, the mountain population is very sparse.

Karakorum \ˌkä-rä-'kōr-əm\ Ancient capital, MONGOL empire. Its ruins lie on the upper Orhon River in northern central Mongolia. It was first settled c. 750; GENGHIS KHAN established his headquarters there in 1220. In 1235 his son and successor, Ögödei, enclosed the city with walls and built a palace. MARCO POLO visited it c. 1225. Chinese forces invaded Mongolia and destroyed Karakorum in 1388. It was later partially rebuilt but was abandoned by the 16th century.

karakul \'kar-ə-kəl\ Breed of SHEEP that originated in central or western Asia, raised chiefly for the skins of very young lambs, which have a glossy, tightly curled black coat (the "Persian lamb" of the fur trade). The wool of mature karakul sheep, classified as carpet wool, is a mixture of coarse and fine fibers, 6–10 in. (15–25 cm) long, and varies from black to brown and gray.

Karakum Desert *or* **Kara-Kum Desert** \ˌkär-ə-'küm\ Desert area, central Asia. Located in TURKMENISTAN, it is bordered on the east by the AMU DARYA valley. It can be divided into three major regions: the elevated and wind-eroded Trans-Unguz in the north; the low-lying central plain; and salt marshes of the southeast. It is populated by formerly nomadic Turkmens, who live by fishing in the CASPIAN SEA or raising livestock.

Karamanlis \ˌkär-ə-män-'lēs\, **Konstantinos** *or* **Constantine Caramanlis** (1907–1998) Greek prime minister (1955–63, 1974–80) and president (1980–85, 1990–95). In various cabinet posts after World War II (1946–55), he helped rebuild Greece's war-torn economy. Chosen prime minister in 1955, he formed a government and a new conservative party, the National Radical Union. In 1960 he established an independent republic on Cyprus to ease tensions with Britain and Turkey over the island. He resigned in 1963 and lived in exile in Paris until 1974. Recalled as prime minister, he subordinated the military to civilian authority to restore democracy, averted war with Turkey over Cyprus, and oversaw the adoption of a new constitution that strengthened the presidency. In 1975 he held a referendum that resulted in the abolition of the monarchy. In 1980 he resigned as prime minister and was elected president. He helped effect Greece's entry into the European Economic Community in 1981. He resigned in 1985, then was reelected president in 1990.

karaoke \ˌkar-ē-'ō-kē\ Device that plays instrumental accompaniments to songs with the vocal tracks removed, permitting the user to sing the lead; also, the practice of singing to karaoke accompaniment. Karaoke (Japanese: "empty orchestra") apparently first appeared in the amusement quarter of Kobe, Japan, where it became popular among businessmen in the late 1970s. It gained widespread popularity in the U.S. in the late 1980s. It is usually featured at bars, where patrons can perform on a stage and sing popular hits by reading lyrics electronically displayed on a monitor. A video film often accompanies the music.

karate MARTIAL ART in which an attacker is disabled by crippling kicks and punches. Emphasis is on concentration of as much of the body's power as possible at the point and instant of impact. Striking surfaces include hands (particularly the knuckles and the outer edge), ball of the foot, heel, forearm, knee, and elbow. In sporting matches (usually lasting about three minutes) and in sparring, blows and kicks are stopped short. Performances are scored by a panel of judges. Developed from older forms, karate was first systematized in Okinawa in the 17th century. It was imported into Japan in the 1920s and spread from there to other countries. See also TAE KWON DO.

Karbala \ˌkär-bȧ-'lȧ\, **Battle of** (680) Battle between forces of the second Umayyad caliph, YAZID I, and HUSAYN IBN ALI. Husayn was on his way to Kufah, where he had been invited to be proclaimed caliph, when he was attacked and killed in the town of Karbala, Iraq, by an army sent by the Umayyad governor of Basra. Shiites regard the battle's date as a holy day of mourning and Husayn's tomb as the holiest place in the world. See also ALI, FITNAH, al-MUAWIYAH I.

Kardelj \'kär-ˌdel^y^\, **Edvard** (1910–1979) Yugoslav revolutionary and administrator. He joined the outlawed Communist Party in 1926, was imprisoned 1930–32, and fled to the Soviet Union in 1934. Returning to Yugoslavia in 1937, he helped organize resistance to the German occupation in World War II and joined TITO in much of the Partisans' fighting. In 1946 he drew up the Soviet-inspired constitution after Tito became premier, and directed the creation of all succeeding constitutions. He was the main architect of socialist self-management, which distinguished Yugoslavia's political and economic system from the Soviet system. In foreign affairs, he pioneered the concept of Yugoslav nonalignment.

Karen \kə-ˈren\ Variety of tribal peoples of southern Myanmar. The Karen are not a unitary group in any ethnic sense, differing linguistically, religiously, and economically. Rather, they have defined themselves in terms of their common distrust of political domination by Myanmar (in which they are the second-largest minority), which has persisted since the country attained independence in 1948.

Karisimbi \ˌkä-rē-ˈsim-bē\, **Mt.** Peak, VIRUNGA MTNS., eastern central Africa. The highest peak in the Virungas at a height of 14,787 ft (4,507 m), it lies on the boundary between Rwanda and the Democratic Republic of the Congo (Zaire), in the VIRUNGA NATIONAL PARK. It is the habitat of gorillas and is known for its exotic plants.

Karkar *or* **Qarqar** \ˈkär-ˌkär\ Ancient fortress on the ORONTES RIVER, western Syria. A strategic outpost, it was attacked by the Assyrians in 853 BC. It was defended by ARAMAEANS led by Ben-hadad I of Damascus and their allies, including King AHAB of Israel. In 720 BC it was the scene of a battle in which SARGON II of Assyria captured and burned it.

Karl Franz Josef See CHARLES I (AUSTRIA)

Karl-Marx-Stadt See CHEMNITZ

Karlfeldt \ˈkärl-felt\, **Erik Axel** (1864–1931) Swedish poet. His strong ties to the peasant culture of his rural homeland remained a dominant influence on his writing all his life. His essentially regional, tradition-bound poems, some published in English in *Arcadia Borealis* (1938), were very popular. He was elected to the Swedish Academy in 1904 and made its permanent secretary in 1912. He refused the Nobel Prize in 1918, but was awarded it posthumously in 1931.

Karloff, Boris *orig.* **William Henry Pratt** (1887–1969) British-U.S. actor. He emigrated to Canada from England in 1909 and acted with touring companies before moving to Hollywood, where he played minor roles in films from 1919. His performance in Hollywood's first important monster film, James Whale's *Frankenstein* (1931), brought him fame. He acted in over 100 films, specializing in such horror pictures as *The Mummy* (1932), *The Mask of Fu Manchu* (1932), *Bride of Frankenstein* (1935), and *Son of Frankenstein* (1939), and his name became synonymous with the horror genre. He returned to the stage for highly acclaimed performances on Broadway in *Arsenic and Old Lace* (1941) and as Captain Hook in *Peter Pan* (1950).

Boris Karloff.
AP/WIDE WORLD PHOTOS

Karlovy Vary \ˈkär-lȯ-vē-ˈvär-ē\ *German* **Karlsbad** *or* **Carlsbad** \ˈkärls-ˌbät\ City (pop., 1991: 56,000), western Czech Republic. A health resort with sulfur springs, it was developed in 1358 by the Holy Roman emperor CHARLES IV. The CARLSBAD DECREES were drawn up there in 1819.

Karlowitz \ˈkär-lə-ˌvits\, **Treaty of** (1699) Peace settlement that ended hostilities (1683–99) between the Ottoman empire and the Holy League (Austria, Poland, Venice, and Russia). Signed at Karlowitz (now Sremski Karlovci), near Belgrade, it significantly diminished Turkish influence in Eastern Europe and made Austria the dominant power there. Austria received most of Hungary, Transylvania, Croatia, and Slovenia. Venice acquired most of Dalmatia, and Poland regained Podolia and part of Ukraine. The Russians concluded a two-year armistice at Karlowitz, signing a treaty in 1700 that gave Azov to Russia, though the Turks regained Azov in 1711.

karma In Indian philosophy, the influence of an individual's past actions on his future lives or REINCARNATIONS. It is based on the conviction that the present life is only one in a chain of lives (see SAMSARA). The accumulated moral energy of a person's life determines his or her character, class status, and disposition in the next life. The process is automatic, and no interference by the gods is possible. In the course of a chain of lives, people can perfect themselves and reach the level of BRAHMA, or they can degrade themselves to the extent that they return to life as animals. The concept of karma, basic to Hinduism, was also incorporated into Buddhism and Jainism.

Karma-pa See DGE-LUGS-PA

Kármán \ˈkär-män\, **Theodore von** (1881–1963) Hungarian-U.S. engineer. After directing the Aeronautical Institute at Aachen, Germany (1912–30), he emigrated to the U.S., where he taught at the California Institute of Technology (1930–44) and later headed NATO's Advisory Group for Aeronautical Research and Development (1951–63). His pioneering work in aeronautics and astronautics included important contributions to fluid mechanics, turbulence theory, supersonic flight, mathematics in engineering, and aircraft structures. His jet-assisted takeoff (JATO) ROCKET provided the prototype for engines used in present-day long-range missiles. He contributed to the first assisted takeoff of U.S. aircraft with solid- and liquid-propellant rockets, the flight of aircraft with rocket propulsion alone, and the development of spontaneously igniting liquid propellants (later used in the APOLLO modules). In 1963 he was awarded the first National Medal of Science.

Von Kármán.
BY COURTESY OF THE CALIFORNIA INSTITUTE OF TECHNOLOGY, PASADENA

Karnak Village in Upper Egypt, which has given its name to the northern half of the ruins of THEBES (c. 3200 BC) on the Nile's eastern bank. Among its many religious buildings stood the largest of all Egyptian temples, the Temple of AMON. Itself a complex of temples, added to and altered many times, it reflects the fluctuating fortunes of the Egyptian empire. There are no fewer than 10 PYLONS, separated by courts and halls. The most striking feature is the vast HYPOSTYLE HALL built by Ramses I (14th century BC), with an area of 52,000 sq ft (4,850 sq m). Fourteen enormous columns, 78 ft (24 m) high, raised the roofing slabs of the central aisle to produce a CLERESTORY.

Karnali River See GHAGHARA RIVER

Karnataka \kär-ˈnä-tə-kə\ *formerly* **Mysore** \mī-ˈsōr\ State (pop., 1994 est.: 48,150,000), southwestern India. Bordering the Arabian Sea, it occupies the plateau region of the southern DECCAN and the hill region of the Western GHATS. It has an area of 74,051 sq mi (191,791 sq km); its capital is BANGALORE. The area was ruled by a series of Hindu dynasties before coming under British control in 1831. Mysore returned to native rule in 1881 as a princely state. Its name was changed to Karnataka ("lofty land") in 1973. About 80% of the population is engaged in agriculture. Rice and sugarcane are cultivated on the coastal plain, and coffee and tea are grown in the hill region. The population is largely Dravidian, and the KANNADA LANGUAGE is widely spoken.

Karo \ˈkä-rō\, **Joseph ben Ephraim** (1488–1575) Spanish-born Jewish scholar. When the Jews were expelled from Spain in 1492, he and his parents settled in Turkey. Around 1536 he emigrated to Safed in Palestine, where he studied the Talmud and systematized the vast body of material produced by post-Talmudic writers. He was the author of the last great codification of Jewish law, the *House of Joseph,* which was later condensed as *The Well-Laid Table* and is still authoritative for Orthodox Judaism.

Károlyi \ˈkä-rȯl-yē\, **Mihály, Count** (1875–1955) Hungarian statesman. A member of one of the wealthiest families of the Hungarian aristocracy, he entered parliament in 1910 and tried to advance radical ideas in a conservative state, advocating universal suffrage, concessions to Hungary's non-Magyar subjects, and a policy of friendship with states other than Germany. After World War I he served as prime minister 1918–19, and tried unsuccessfully to gain a favorable peace settlement from the Allies. After two months as president of the short-lived Hungarian republic in 1919, he resigned and was replaced by Bela Kun. He fled abroad but returned to Hungary in 1946 and served as ambassador to Paris 1947–49.

Karpov \'kär-ˌpȯf\, **Anatoly (Yevgenyevich)** (born 1951) Russian chess master. A child prodigy, he learned chess at age four. He became world champion in 1975 when Bobby Fischer declined to meet him in tournament play. He defended his title (48-game draw) in 1984–85 against Garry Kasparov but lost to Kasparov later in 1985. He regained the championship in 1993 after Kasparov was stripped of the title for organizing a new chess federation. In 1999 Karpov refused to defend his title in a world championship knockout tournament in Las Vegas, Nev., which was won by Alexander Khalifman of Russia.

Karsavina \kär-'sä-və-nə\, **Tamara (Platonovna)** (1885–1978) Russian-British dancer best known as the leading ballerina in the Ballets Russes from 1909 to 1922. She trained at the Imperial Ballet school in St. Petersburg and joined the Mariinsky Theater company in 1902. She joined the Ballets Russes at its formation in 1909; dancing with Vaslav Nijinsky until 1913, she created most of the leading roles in Michel Fokine's neo-Romantic repertoire, including *Les sylphides, Carnaval, Le spectre de la rose, The Firebird,* and *Daphnis and Chloe.* She settled in London, where she helped found the Royal Academy of Dancing in 1920 and the Camargo Society in 1930, and later coached Margot Fonteyn.

Karsh, Yousuf (1908–2002) Turkish-Canadian photographer. As an Armenian in Turkey, he endured persecution before emigrating at 16 to Canada, where he joined his photographer uncle. He worked for a Boston portrait photographer (1928–31), then returned to Canada and soon opened his own studio in Ottawa. In 1935 he was appointed official portrait photographer of the Canadian government. His portrait of Winston Churchill (1941) brought him international fame. "Karsh of Ottawa" went on to photograph hundreds of the world's most prominent figures, including royalty, statesmen, artists, and writers, employing his dramatic lighting to produce idealized likenesses.

Karsh, self-portrait, 1988.
© 1988 KARSH OF OTTAWA/WOODFIN CAMP & ASSOC.

Karter *or* **Kartir** (fl. 3rd century AD) Persian high priest of Zoroastrianism. Under the protection of a series of Persian kings, he restored the purity of Zoroastrianism and tried to purge the kingdom of all other religions. His chief rival was the prophet Mani, founder of Manichaeism. At Karter's instigation, Mani was put in prison, where he eventually died. After Karter's death a degree of religious tolerance returned to Persia.

karting Driving and racing miniature, skeleton-frame, rear-engine automobiles called karts or GoKarts. The sport originated in the U.S. in the 1950s after the first kart had been assembled from unwanted lawn-mower parts. It thereafter developed into an international sport in Europe. Speeds of 100 mph (160 kph) are not uncommon.

Karun River \kä-'rün\ River, southwestern Iran. A tributary of the Shatt al-Arab, it rises in the Bakhtiari Mountains and flows through mountains for 515 mi (829 km). The Haffar Channel, dug in 986, changed its course, causing frontier disputes between Iran and the Ottoman empire; Iran gained the right to the waterway by treaty in 1847.

Dam on the Karun River, Iran.
DENNIS BRISKIN—TOM STACK & ASSOCIATES

Kasai River \kȧ-'sī\ River, central Africa. It is the chief southern tributary of the Congo River, measuring 1,338 mi (2,153 km) from its source in Angola to its confluence with the Congo. It runs east for its first 250 mi (400 km), then turns north to form the border between Angola and the Democratic Republic of the Congo (Zaire). It is unnavigable in the north, but water traffic is heavy from Kinshasa to Ilebo. After the Kasai is joined by the Kwango River, it is known as the Kwa.

Kasanje \kä-'sän-jā\ Historical African kingdom, on the upper Kwango River in what is now Angola. Founded in 1620 by a group from Lunda, its people became known as the Imbangala. By the mid-17th cent., it had a thriving trade with the states of the interior and with Portuguese traders. Its monopoly of inland Portuguese-African trade lasted until 1850, when Ovimbundu opened alternative routes and markets. Occupied by the Portuguese, it was incorporated into Portuguese Angola in 1910–11.

Kasavubu \kȧ-sȧ-'vü-bü\, **Joseph** (c. 1910–1969) First president of the independent Congo republic (later Zaire), 1960–65. He held a variety of administrative posts before agreeing to serve as president in Patrice Lumumba's government. When Katanga province under Moise Tshombe seceded a few days after independence, Kasavubu threw his support to Tshombe and, together with Col. J. Mobutu (see Mobutu Sese Seko), ousted Lumumba. Four years later a split between Kasavubu and Tshombe enabled Mobutu to seize control.

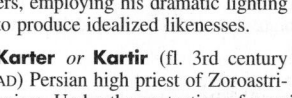

Kasavubu.
AP/WIDE WORLD PHOTOS

Kashmir Region of the northwestern Indian subcontinent. It is bounded to the northeast and east by China, to the south by India, to the west by Pakistan, and to the northwest by Afghanistan. The land is predominantly mountainous and includes K2 and other peaks of the Karakoram Range. India and Pakistan have disputed over the region since India's partition in 1947. Pakistan occupies the northern and western portions, and India administers the largest area, in the south and southeast, organized as the state of Jammu and Kashmir. In addition, China has held portions of the northeastern section since 1962.

kashruth \kä-'shrüt, 'kä-shrůth\ In Judaism, the rules forbidding the eating of certain foods and requiring that other foods be prepared in a specific way. These rules determine which foods can be called kosher. Most information regarding kashruth is found in the Hebrew Bible in the books of Leviticus, Deuteronomy, Genesis, and Exodus. Jews observing kashruth may eat only fish with scales and fins and animals that chew the cud and have cloven feet; shellfish and pork are thus forbidden. Animals and birds must be slaughtered according to ritual and with prayer. Meat and dairy products must be strictly separated; they may not be eaten at the same meal or from the same set of dishes. No restrictions apply to the use of fruits and vegetables. During Passover, bread and other baked goods must be made without leaven.

Kaskaskia River \kas-'kas-kē-ə\ River, Illinois. Rising near Urbana, it flows southwest to enter the Mississippi River after a course of 320 mi (515 km). The village of Kaskaskia, located near the junction of the river with the Mississippi, is near the site of a town founded by Jesuit missionaries in 1703. It was the capital of Illinois Territory (1809) and of the state (1818–20). It was severely damaged by floods several times.

Kasparov \kas-'pär-ȯf\, **Garry** (born 1963) Russian chess master. He was born in Baku, Azerbaijan, and by age 17 he was an international grandmaster. After failing to beat the reigning champion, Anatoly Karpov, in a 48-game draw in 1984–85, he returned later in 1985 to take the title, becoming the youngest champion in the history of the game. The International Chess Federation stripped him of his title in 1993 when he left it to form a new federation. In 1996 he defeated the powerful IBM custom-built chess computer Deep Blue in a match that attracted worldwide attention. In a 1997 rematch, an upgraded Deep Blue prevailed. In 2000 Kasparov lost a 16-game championship match to Vladimir Kramnik of Russia.

Katagum \kə-'tä-gəm\ Traditional emirate, northern Nigeria. The emirate became part of Katagum province under British rule in 1903. Its seat, also named Katagum, was transferred to Azare in 1916. The emirate became part of Bauchi state in 1926.

Kathiawar \ˌkä-tē-ə-'wär\ Peninsula, southwestern GUJARAT state, western central India. Occupying an area of 23,000 sq mi (60,000 sq km), it is bounded by the Arabian Sea on the southwest. It was first settled by Stone Age peoples, then in the 3nd–2nd millennium BC by Harappan peoples. It was ruled by many great dynasties beginning with the MAURYAN EMPIRE in the 3rd century BC. The area came under Muslim rule in the 13th century and became part of the MUGHAL empire in the 16th century. Many of its small princely states came under British protection after 1820. Made a part of Gujarat state in 1960, it is the site of a national park that contains the last wild Indian lions.

Kathmandu *or* **Katmandu** \ˌkat-man-'dü\ City (pop., 2000 est.: 701,499), capital of Nepal. Situated near the confluence of the Baghmati and Vishnumati rivers at an elevation of 4,344 ft (1,324 m), it was founded in 723. Its name refers to a temple (*kath*, "wood"; *mandir*, "temple") said to have been built from the wood of a single tree in 1596. The seat of the ruling Shah family of the Gurkha people since 1768, it is Nepal's most important business and commercial center and the site of Tribhuvan Univ.

Katmai National Park and Preserve \'kat-ˌmī\ National park, southwestern Alaska, at the head of the ALASKA PENINSULA. Occupying an area of 4,090,000 acres (1,655,000 hectares), it was proclaimed a national monument in 1918 after the eruption of Novarupta in 1912. The eruption converted the valley into a wasteland known as the Valley of TEN THOUSAND SMOKES, and the volcanic crater later became a lake. The park abounds in wildlife, including large numbers of brown and grizzly bears.

Katowice \ˌkä-tȯ-'vēt-sə\ City (pop., 1999 est.: 345,934), southern central Poland. Located in the midst of the coalfields of Upper Silesia, it was settled by 1598. It became a city in 1865, when coal mining began in the region. It became part of Poland in 1922 and has since incorporated surrounding villages. It is a center of mining and heavy industry and an important rail junction.

Katsina \'kät-sē-nä\ City (pop., 1996 est.: 207,000), northern Nigeria. Probably founded c. 1100, it was the capital of the kingdom of Katsina, one of the earliest HAUSA states, and an ancient center of learning. The city's Fulani emirs retain traditional and advisory roles. It is a market for local agricultural products as well as a center for traditional crafts and industry.

Katsura Imperial Villa \'kät-sü-rä\ Estate constructed 1620–24 on the southwestern edge of Kyoto, Japan. It was an outstanding attempt to integrate the styles of the HEIAN PERIOD with the architectural innovations spurred by the development of the tea ceremony. Carefully planned meandering paths lead to and from the central structures and through gardens dotted with small pavilions and tea huts offering orchestrated views. The main buildings, set into a landscape created for them, include three attached structures in a typical SHOIN-ZUKURI style.

Kattegat Arm of the NORTH SEA, between Sweden and JUTLAND, Denmark. Its maximum width is 88 mi (142 km). It is connected with both the North and BALTIC seas. Chief ports on its shores are GÖTEBORG and Halmstad in Sweden, and ÅRHUS in Denmark. It is an important commercial navigation passage and a popular summer vacation area.

katydid Any of numerous species in several subfamilies of the long-horned GRASSHOPPER family (Tettigoniidae). Generally green with long wings, katydids live on trees, bushes, or grasses, and many species resemble leaves. They are powerful jumpers; many species do not fly but merely flutter their wings during leaps. They feed chiefly on plant matter, though some also eat other insects. The true katydids of eastern North America are considered great singers; each species has its own repetitive song, which is produced only at night.

Fork-tailed bush katydid (*Scudderia furcata*).

E.S. ROSS

Katyn Massacre \ka-'tin\ Mass execution of Polish military officers by the Soviet Union in WORLD WAR II. After the GERMAN–SOVIET NONAGGRESSION PACT (1939) and Germany's defeat of Poland, Soviet forces occupied eastern Poland and interned thousands of Polish military personnel. After the German invasion of the Soviet Union (1941), the Polish government-in-exile agreed to cooperate with the Soviets against Germany, and the Polish general forming the new army asked to have the Polish prisoners placed under his command, but they could not be located. In 1943 the Germans discovered mass graves in the Katyn forest in western Russia. Over 4,000 corpses were recovered, later identified as Polish officers. Russia claimed the invading German army had killed them, but refused Polish requests to have the Red Cross investigate, and diplomatic relations were severed. In 1992 the government released documents proving the the Soviet secret police were responsible for the executions.

Kauffmann \'kau̇f-ˌmän\, **(Maria Anna) Angelica (Catharina)** (1741–1807). Swiss-Italian painter. She began studying art in Italy as a child, showing great precocity, and in 1766 her friend JOSHUA REYNOLDS brought her to London. There she became known for her decorative work with such architects as ROBERT ADAM. Her pastoral compositions incorporate delicate and graceful depictions of gods and goddesses; though her paintings are Rococo in tone and approach, her figures are Neoclassical. Her portraits of female sitters are among her finest works. After marrying the painter Antonio Zucchi (1726–1795), she returned to Italy in 1781.

Self-portrait, painting on canvas by Angelica Kauffmann; in the Staatliche Museen Preussischer Kulturbesitz, Berlin.

BY COURTESY OF THE STAATLICHE MUSEEN PREUSSISCHER KULTURBESITZ GEMALDEGALERIE, BERLIN—ART RESOURCE

Kaufman, George S(imon) (1889–1961) U.S. playwright and director. Born in Pittsburgh, he was drama critic for the *New York Times* 1917–30. Known for his wit and satirical eye, he collaborated with other writers on numerous plays. With MARC CONNELLY he wrote *Dulcy* (1921), *Merton of the Movies* (1922), and *Beggar on Horseback* (1924). With Morrie Ryskind (1895–1985) he wrote the book for GEORGE GERSHWIN's musical *Of Thee I Sing* (1931, Pulitzer Prize). He wrote *The Royal Family* (1927), *Dinner at Eight* (1932), and *The Land Is Bright* (1941) with EDNA FERBER, and *Once in a Lifetime* (1930), *You Can't Take It with You* (1936, Pulitzer Prize), and *The Man Who Came to Dinner* (1939) with MOSS HART. The MARX BROTHERS films *The Cocoanuts* (1929) and *Animal Crackers* (1930) were based on plays on which he collaborated.

Kaunas \'kau̇-nəs\ *Russian* **Kovno** \'kȯv-nō\ City (pop., 1996 est.: 411,000), southern Lithuania. Founded as a fortress in 1030, it passed to Russia in 1795 after the third Partition of POLAND. It was the capital of independent Lithuania 1920–40, then it was annexed by the U.S.S.R. Many historic buildings survive in the Old Town. In addition to being an important industrial center, it is an educational and cultural center, with polytechnic, medical, and agricultural institutes.

Kaunda \kä-'ün-də\, **Kenneth (David)** (born 1924) Politician who led Zambia to independence and served as its president for 30 years (1961–91). He came to prominence in 1959–60 in the movement to stop Britain from establishing a federation of North and South Rhodesia and Nyasaland. Elected the first president of independent Zambia, he helped avert a civil war in the late 1960s, but ended up imposing single-party rule. From the 1970s he led other southern African na-

Kaunda.

CAMERA PRESS

H I J K

tions in confronting the white-minority governments of Rhodesia and South Africa. He increased Zambia's dependence on copper exports and on foreign aid, allowing agriculture, education, and social services to languish and poverty and unemployment to increase. Several attempted coups in the early 1980s were crushed; in 1990 he was forced to legalize opposition parties, and in 1991 he was voted out of office.

Kaunitz \'kaů-nits\, **Wenzel Anton von** *later* **Fürst (Prince) von Kaunitz -Rietberg** (1711–1794) Austrian state chancellor (1753–92). He entered the Austrian foreign service in 1740 and was responsible for the foreign policy of the Habsburg monarchy, serving MARIA THERESA and her successors. He represented Austria at the 1748 Aix-la-Chapelle peace conference and was ambassador to Paris 1750–52. A lifelong enemy of Prussia, he managed to reverse Austria's alliances during the SEVEN YEARS' WAR, bringing France and Russia into the Habsburg orbit and isolating Prussia. The French Revolution terminated the system of alliances he had created, and he resigned in 1792.

Kautsky \'kaůt-skē\, **Karl** (1854–1938) German Marxist theorist and leader. He was the author of the Erfurt Program adopted by Germany's Social Democrat Party in 1891, which committed the party to an evolutionary form of Marxism that rejected both the radicalism of ROSA LUXEMBURG and the evolutionary socialism of EDUARD BERNSTEIN. He founded the Marxist review *Neue Zeit* in 1883, which he edited in various European cities until 1917, and wrote several books about Marx's doctrines and about ST. THOMAS MORE. He joined the Independent Social Democrats in opposing World War I.

kava *or* **kava kava** \'kä-və\ Nonalcoholic, yellow-green, somewhat bitter beverage made from the root of the PEPPER plant (mainly *Piper methysticum*) in most South Pacific islands. It is traditionally consumed in the kava ceremony, which includes the ritual making and drinking of kava and a ceremonial feast. It is taken to relieve stress and anxiety and as a mood elevator.

Kavaratti Island \,kə-və-'rə-tē\ Island of the Laccadive island group. Located in the Arabian Sea, off the coast of Kerala in southern India, it is 3.5 miles (5.6 km) long and has a maximum width of 0.75 mi (1.2 km). Its only town, Kavaratti (pop., 1991: 9,000), is the administrative center of the Indian territory of LAKSHADWEEP. The town is noted for the ornately carved pillars and roofs of its mosques.

Kaveri River \'kä-və-rē\ *or* **Cauvery River** \'kȯ-və-rē\ River, southern India. Rising in northern KERALA, it flows southeast 475 mi (764 km) to enter the Bay of BENGAL. On the border of KARNATAKA it forms the island of Sivasamudram, on either side of which are the Kaveri (Cauvery) Falls, which descend about 320 ft (515 m). The river is the source for an extensive irrigation system. It is considered one of India's sacred rivers.

Kaw River See KANSAS RIVER

Kawabata \'kä-wä-,bä-tä\, **Yasunari** (1899–1972) Japanese novelist. His writing echoes ancient Japanese forms in prose influenced by post–World War I French literary currents such as Dadaism (see DADA) and EXPRESSIONISM. His best-known novel is *Snow Country* (1948), the story of a forlorn geisha. His other major works (published together in 1952) are *A Thousand Cranes* and *The Sound of the Mountain.* The loneliness and preoccupation with death in many of his mature works may derive from his losing all his near relatives while he was young. He was awarded the Nobel Prize in 1968. He died a suicide.

Kawasaki \,kä-wä-'sä-kē\ City (pop., 1995: 1,202,820) and port, Honshu, Japan. It lies on Tokyo Bay, between TOKYO and YOKOHAMA. Almost completely destroyed in World War II, it has since been rebuilt. It is a major industrial center for machinery and chemicals, as well as having shipbuilding facilities. It is the site of a 12th-century Buddhist temple.

Kawatake Mokuami \,kä-wä-'tä-kä-,mō-kü-'ä-mē\ *orig.* **Yoshimura Yoshisaburo** (1816–1893) Japanese playwright. He apprenticed with the KABUKI playwright Tsuruya Namboku V and became chief playwright of the Kawarasaki Theatre (1843). He was noted for domestic plays that featured ordinary townspeople and picaresque plays that portrayed the lives of thieves. After 1868 he wrote historical plays that emphasized factual accuracy and pioneered the production of domestic plays that described the modernization and Westernization of early MEIJI–PERIOD society. He retired in 1881 but continued to write dance dramas. He wrote over 360 plays, and his works account for half the current kabuki repertory.

Kay, Alan (born 1940) U.S. computer scientist. Born in Springfield, Mass., he received his PhD from the University of Utah. In 1972 he joined Xerox's Palo Alto Research Center and continued work on the first OBJECT-ORIENTED PROGRAMMING language (Smalltalk) for educational applications. He contributed to the development of ETHERNET, laser printing, and CLIENT-SERVER ARCHITECTURE. He left Xerox in 1983 and became a fellow at Apple Computer in 1984. His design of a GRAPHICAL USER INTERFACE was used in Apple's Macintosh and later in Microsoft's Windows operating system.

Kay, John (1704–1764?) British machinist and engineer. In 1733 he received a patent for a "New Engine or Machine for Opening and Dressing Wool" that incorporated his FLYING SHUTTLE, an important step toward automatic WEAVING. Kay's invention so increased yarn consumption that it spurred the invention of spinning machines (including the SPINNING JENNY and SPINNING MULE), but its true importance lay in its adaptation in power LOOMS.

Kay, Ulysses (Simpson) (1917–1995) U.S. composer. Born in Tucson, Ariz., a nephew of KING OLIVER, he was an all-around musician from childhood. At the University of Arizona he was urged to become a composer by W.G. STILL, and he went on to study at the Eastman School and with P. HINDEMITH at Yale. He taught principally at the City University of New York, earning a reputation as a distinguished teacher. His music—neoclassical in style but characterized by verve and warmth—received many awards; mostly orchestral or choral, it includes five operas and several film and television scores.

Kaya *or* **Karak** \'kä-räk\ *Japanese* **Mimana** Tribal league formed sometime before the 3rd century AD in southern Korea and lasting until its subjugation to SILLA in the 6th century. The people of Kaya are thought to have been closely related to the tribes that crossed over from Korea to Japan a century or two earlier, and Kaya often enlisted Japan in its feuds with neighboring Silla and PAEKCHE. The Kaya people invented a unique 12-stringed zither, the *kayagum.*

kayak \'kī-,ak\ Type of CANOE covered by a deck except for a cockpit in which the paddler sits. It has a pointed bow and stern and no keel; the paddler faces forward, grasping a double-bladed paddle and dipping the blades alternately on either side. Usually built for one occupant, it can be designed for two or three. Kayaks were traditionally used for fishing and hunting by ESKIMOS, who stretched seal or other animal skins over a driftwood or whalebone frame and rubbed the skins with animal fat for waterproofing. The paddler wore an overlapping shield to allow the kayak to be righted without taking on water if it rolled over. Now often made of molded plastic or fiberglass, kayaks are widely used for recreation.

Kaye, Danny *orig.* **David Daniel Kaminski** (1913–1987) U.S. actor and comedian. Born in New York City, he worked as a comic busboy in Catskills resorts from age 13 and later worked in vaudeville and nightclubs, developing his trademark pantomimes, rapid-fire nonsense songs, and physical antics. He was a success on Broadway in *The Straw Hat Revue* (1939) and *Lady in the Dark* (1940). His movie debut in *Up in Arms* (1944) was followed by starring roles in *The Secret Life of Walter Mitty* (1947), *The Inspector General* (1949), *Hans Christian Andersen* (1952), and *White Christmas* (1954). He starred on television in *The Danny Kaye Show* (1963–67). Much of his comedy material was written by his wife, Sylvia Fine.

Kaysone Phomvihan \kā-'sō-ne-'pȯm-vē-hän\ (1920–1992) Laotian revolutionary, prime minister (1975–91) and president (1991–92). Son of a Lao mother and a Vietnamese father, Kaysone met HO CHI MINH while studying law in Hanoi and returned to Laos to become the leader of the Pathet Lao, an anti-French revolutionary movement. In 1975 the Pathet Lao overthrew Laos's 600-year-old monarchy, and Kaysone became prime minister of the Lao People's Democratic Republic. He kept the country closely allied with Vietnam and isolated from Western influence until the end of the Cold War, when he first looked to France and Japan for financial aid. As president, he relaxed some government controls and released most political prisoners.

Kazakhstan *or* **Kazakstan** \kə-,zäk-'stän\ *officially* **Republic of Kazakhstan** Country, western central Asia. Area: 1,052,100 sq mi (2,724,900 sq km). Population (1999): 14,952,420. Capital: ASTANA. Kazakhs, a Turkic-speaking people, the original inhabitants, make up less than one-half the population; an equal number of Russians live there

with small minorities of Germans and Ukrainians. Language: Kazakh (official), Russian. Religion: Islam (Sunnite). Currency: tenge. From the steppe and desert lands of western and central Kazakhstan, the country rises to high mountains in the southeast along the border with Kyrgyzstan and China. Its highest point is Mount Khan-Tengri, at 22,949 ft (6,995 m) high. It is intensively agriculturally developed, but much of the country's land area is used for pasture, with sheep and goats as the main livestock. Manufacturing includes cast iron and rolled steel; mining and oil drilling are also important. It is a republic with a parliament consisting of two chambers; its head of state and government is the president, assisted by the prime minister. Named for its earliest inhabitants, the Kazakhs, the area came under Mongol rule in the 13th century. The Kazakhs consolidated a nomadic empire in the 15th–16th century. Under Russian rule by the mid-19th century, it became part of the Kirgiz Autonomous Republic formed by the Soviets in 1920, and in 1925 its name was changed to the Kazakh Autonomous Soviet Socialist Republic. Kazakhstan obtained its independence from the Soviet Union in 1991, and during the 1990s was attempting to stabilize its economy.

Kazan \kə-'zänʸ\ City (pop., 1996 est.: 1,100,000), capital of the Tatarstan republic, western Russia. Located at the confluence of the VOLGA and Kazanka rivers, it was founded in the 13th century by Mongols of the GOLDEN HORDE, and became the capital of an independent khanate in the 15th century. In 1552 IVAN IV captured Kazan and subjugated the khanate. The city was burned in a revolt (1773–74), but after its reconstruction it grew in importance as a trading center, and by 1900 it was one of the chief manufacturing cities of Russia.

Kazan \kə-'zan\, **Elia** *orig.* **Elia Kazanjoglous** (born 1909) U.S. (Greek-born) stage and film director. At age 4 he emigrated to the U.S. with his family. An actor with the GROUP THEATRE in 1932–39, he became a noted Broadway director with such plays as *The Skin of Our Teeth* (1942), *All My Sons* (1947), *A Streetcar Named Desire* (1947; film, 1951), *Death of a Salesman* (1949), *Cat on a Hot Tin Roof* (1952), *J.B.* (1958, Tony award), and *Sweet Bird of Youth* (1959). In 1947 he cofounded the ACTORS STUDIO. He was praised for his naturalistic style in such movies as *A Tree Grows in Brooklyn* (1945), *Gentleman's Agreement* (1947, Academy Award), *On the Waterfront* (1954, Academy Award), and *East of Eden* (1955). Though bitterly attacked for his cooperation with the House Un-American Activities Committee in the early 1950s, he received an honorary Academy Award for lifetime achievement in 1999.

Kazan River \kə-'zan\ River, central Canada. Rising in NUNAVUT, it flows through several lakes to empty into Baker Lake after a course of 455 mi (732 km). It is one of the main streams of the Barren Grounds, an area northwest of HUDSON BAY that has treeless plains marked by many swamps and lakes.

Kazantzákis \kä-zänt-'zä-kēs\, **Níkos** (1885–1957) Greek writer. Educated in law and philosophy, he traveled widely before settling on the island of Aegina before World War II. He is best known for his widely translated novels, including *Zorba the Greek* (1946; film, 1964), *The Greek Passion* (1954), and *The Last Temptation of Christ* (1955; film, 1988). His works also include essays, travel books, tragedies, and translations of such classics as DANTE's *Divine Comedy* and JOHANN W. VON GOETHE's *Faust.* He also wrote lyric poetry and the poetic epic *Odyssey* (1938), a sequel to the Homeric epic.

Kazembe \kä-'zem-bē\ Largest and most organized kingdom of the Lunda empire (see LUBA-LUNDA STATES) in central Africa. At the height of its power (c. 1800), Kazembe occupied the territory now included in the Shaba region of the Democratic Republic of the Congo (Zaire) and in northern Zambia. Created c. 1740 by explorers from western Lunda, it grew more powerful by annexing neighboring states and became an important center of trade between the African interior and the Portuguese and Arabs on the eastern coast. Civil war began in 1850, and the kingdom was destroyed c. 1890.

Kazin \'kā-zən\, **Alfred** (1915–1998) U.S. literary critic. Born in Brooklyn, N.Y., he attended CCNY. His sweeping historical study of modern American literature, *On Native Grounds* (1942), won him instant recognition. Much of his criticism appeared in *Partisan Review, The New Republic,* and *The New Yorker*. His books include *Starting Out in the Thirties* (1965), *Bright Book of Life* (1973), *New York Jew* (1978), *An American Procession* (1984), *A Writer's America* (1988), and *God and the American Writer* (1997).

Kazvin See QAZVIN

kea \'kē-ə\ Large, stocky PARROT (*Nestor notabilis,* subfamily Nestorinae) of New Zealand. The kea occasionally attacks sheep to get at the fat around the kidneys. It lives in mountain habitats and is known for its curious and playful character.

Kean, Edmund (1789–1833) British actor. He acted with a touring stage company from 1805, and in 1814 he won acclaim in London with his innovative portrayal of Shylock in *The Merchant of Venice.* He went on to specialize in other Shakespearean villains, including Richard III, Iago, and Macbeth. He also excelled at playing Othello and Hamlet, as well as Barabas in *The Jew of Malta.* Though praised for his passionate and sensational stage portrayals, he became unpopular for his ungovernable behavior offstage, marked by excessive drinking and a suit for adultery (1825). His son Charles (1811–1868) was an actor-manager noted for his revivals of Shakespearean plays.

Edmund Kean, detail of a pencil drawing by Samuel Cousins, 1814; in the National Portrait Gallery, London.

BY COURTESY OF THE NATIONAL PORTRAIT GALLERY, LONDON

Kearny \'kär-nē\, **Stephen Watts** (1794–1848) U.S. Army officer. Born in Newark, N.J., he served in the War of 1812 and later on the western frontier. At the outbreak of the MEXICAN WAR, he was ordered to seize New Mexico and California. Using diplomacy to persuade Mexican troops to withdraw, he marched unopposed to Santa Fe, where in 1846 he proclaimed a civil government for the province. He left for California, where ROBERT F. STOCKTON and JOHN C. FREMONT had already assumed command. Their forces combined to defeat Mexican rebels in 1847 and, after initial opposition by Frémont, established a stable government. Sent to Mexico, Kearney died of yellow fever.

Keaton, Buster *orig.* **Joseph Francis** (1895–1966) U.S. film actor and director. Born in Pickway, Kan., he acted with his parents in vaudeville (1899–1917), where he developed his mastery of comic falls and subtle timing and his trademark never-smiling face. His film debut in *The Butcher Boy* (1917) was followed by several short films (1917–19) with Fatty Arbuckle. As head of his own production company (1920–28) he directed and starred in such classic silent movies as *The Navigator* (1924), *Sherlock, Jr.* (1924), *The General* (1927), and *Steamboat Bill, Jr.* (1928). For MGM he made *The Cameraman* (1928), but he was denied artistic control over his films and his career declined. He later appeared in *Sunset Boulevard* (1950) and *Limelight* (1952). From the late 1940s his comedies were gradually revived, and he is now regarded as one of the greatest silent comedy stars.

Keaton, Diane *orig.* **Diane Hall** (born 1946) U.S. film actress. Born in Santa Ana, Cal., she acted on Broadway in *Hair* (1968) and with WOODY ALLEN in *Play It Again, Sam* (1969), reprising her role in the movie version (1972). She played a supporting role in *The Godfather* (1972) and its sequels. She starred in such Allen movies as *Sleeper* (1973), *Annie Hall* (1977, Academy Award), *Interiors* (1978), and *Manhattan* (1979). Her other films include *Looking for Mr. Goodbar* (1977), *Reds* (1981), *Mrs. Soffel* (1984), and *First Wives Club* (1996).

Keats, John (1795–1821) English Romantic poet. The son of a livery-stable manager, his formal education was limited. He worked as a surgeon's apprentice and assistant for several years before devoting himself entirely to poetry at 21. His first mature work was the sonnet "On First Looking into Chapman's Homer" (1816). His long *Endymion* appeared in the same year (1818) as the tuberculosis that would kill him at 25. During a few intense months of 1819 he produced many of his greatest works: several great odes (including "Ode on a Grecian Urn," "Ode to a Nightingale," and "To Autumn"), two unfinished versions of the story of the titan Hyperion, and "La Belle Dame Sans Merci." Most were published in the landmark collection *Lamia, Isabella, The Eve of St. Agnes, and Other Poems* (1820). Marked by vivid imagery, great sensuous appeal, and a yearning for the lost glories of the classical world, his finest works are among the greatest of the English tradition. His letters are among the best by any English poet.

Keats, detail of an oil painting by Joseph Severn, 1821; in the National Portrait Gallery, London.

Keb See GEB

Kediri \kä-'dir-ē\ City (pop., 1995 est.: 261,000), eastern JAVA, Indonesia. It is located in the valley of the Brantas River, southwest of Surabaya. In the 11th–13th century it lay at the heart of a powerful Hindu kingdom, also named Kediri; after 1830 it became the capital of a residency under Dutch administration. The modern city is a trading center for local agricultural products, including sugar, coffee, and rice.

Keeling Islands See COCOS ISLANDS

Keen, William (Williams) (1837–1932) First U.S. brain surgeon. Born in Philadelphia, he received his MD from Jefferson Medical College. He was one of the first to successfully remove a brain tumor (1888) and assisted in the removal of Pres. GROVER CLEVELAND's left upper jaw (1893), which contained a malignant tumor. In addition to his teaching and medical work, he edited *Surgery: Its Principles and Practice* (8 vols., 1906–13).

keep See DONJON

Kegon \'kā-gōn\ Buddhist philosophy introduced into Japan from China in the 8th century. The name Kegon ("flower ornament") is a translation of the Sanskrit *avatamsaka,* after the school's chief text, the AVATAMSAKA-SUTRA, which deals with the buddha VAIROCANA. The school was founded in China as Huayan in the late 6th century and reached Japan c. 740. Kegon taught that all living things are interdependent and that the universe is self-creating, with Vairocana at its center. Though the Kegon school is no longer an active faith teaching a separate doctrine, it continues to administer the famous TODAI TEMPLE monastery at Nara.

Keillor \'kē-lər\, **Garrison (Edward)** (born 1942) U.S. radio entertainer and writer. Born in Anoka, Minn., he began writing for *The New Yorker* in college and worked as a staff writer there until 1992. In 1974 he created and hosted the public-radio humor and variety show *A Prairie Home Companion,* about the fictional Minnesota town Lake Wobegon. He revived it after replacing it for several years with *The American Radio Company* (1987–91). His books include the best-selling *Lake Wobegon Days* (1985), *Leaving Home* (1987), *The Sandy Bottom Orchestra* (1996), and *Me* (1999).

Keino \'kā-nō\, **Kip** *orig.* **Hezekiah Kipchoge** (born 1940) Kenyan distance runner. He was originally a goatherd, who trained for distance running in the hill country. At the high-altitude 1968 Olympics in Mexico City, he won a silver medal in the 5,000-m race and, in one of running's greatest upsets, a gold medal in the 1,500-m race, beating Jim Ryun of the U.S. At the 1972 Olympics, Keino won a silver medal in the 1,500-m and a gold in the 3,000-m steeplechase.

Keita \'kā-tä\, **Modibo** (1915–1977) First president of Mali (1960–68). He was instrumental in obtaining independence for Mali (then called French Sudan) from France (1960). As president, Keita nationalized key sectors of the economy and established close ties with communist countries. During an economic crisis in 1967 he launched an unpopular Maoist-inspired cultural revolution, and in 1968 he was overthrown and imprisoned for life.

Keitel \kī-'tel\, **Harvey** (born 1941) U.S. film actor. Born in Brooklyn, N.Y., he served in the Marine Corps and then studied at the Actors Studio. He made his film debut in *Who's That Knocking at My Door?* (1968) under MARTIN SCORSESE, with whom he often worked thereafter. Known for the intensity of his performances, he has played supporting or starring roles in such films as *Mean Streets* (1973), *Taxi Driver* (1976), *Bad Timing* (1980), *Bugsy* (1991), *Thelma and Louise* (1991), *Reservoir Dogs* (1991), and *The Piano* (1993).

Keitel \'kī-tᵊl\, **Wilhelm** (1882–1946) German field marshal. After serving in World War I, he held administrative posts 1918–33, then became minister of war in 1935 and head of the German armed forces high command in 1938. Though one of ADOLF HITLER's most trusted lieutenants, he was generally regarded as a weak officer and served chiefly as Hitler's lackey. He signed the act of Germany's military surrender in 1945. After the war he was convicted at the NUREMBERG TRIALS and executed as a war criminal.

Keizan Jokin \'kā-zän-'jō-kēn\ (1268–1325) Japanese Buddhist priest and founder of the Soji Temple, one of the two head temples of the Soto sect of Zen Buddhism. He joined the priesthood at 12, and after completing his studies he taught the Soto doctrine for 10 years. He was named head priest at Shogaku Temple, which he affiliated with the Soto sect in 1321. It was destroyed by fire in 1898 and later rebuilt on its present site at Yokohama. Keizan devoted himself to building temples and spreading Soto teachings to all parts of Japan. Now called Taiso ("Great Master"), he is revered as the restorer of the Soto sect.

Kekri \'ke-krē\ In ancient Finnish religion, a feast day marking the end of the agricultural season and coinciding with the time when cattle were brought in from pasture for the winter. It originally fell on September 29 but was later moved to November 1, or ALL SAINTS' DAY. It was a time when the ancestor spirits visited their former homes and the living held feasts honoring the dead. Usually a family celebration, it was sometimes marked by a communal sacrifice of a sheep.

Kekule von Stradonitz \'kā-kü-lā-fȯn-'shträ-dō-nits\, **(Friedrich) August** *orig.* **(Friedrich) August Kekule** (1829–1896) German chemist who laid the groundwork for modern structural theory in organic chemistry. His early training in architecture may have helped him conceive his theories. In 1858 he showed that CARBON has VALENCE 4 and that its atoms can link together to form long chains. He is said to have dreamed in 1865 of a BENZENE molecule as a snake biting its own tail and thus conceptualized the six-carbon benzene ring; the facts of organic chemistry known up to that time then fell into place. He also did valuable work on mercury compounds, unsaturated acids, and thio acids and wrote a four-volume textbook.

Keller, Helen (Adams) (1880–1968) U.S. author and educator. Deprived by illness of sight and hearing at the age of 19 months, Keller soon became mute as well. Five years later she began to be instructed by Anne Sullivan (1866–1936), who taught her the names of objects by pressing the manual alphabet into her palm. Eventually Keller learned to read and write in Braille. She wrote several books, including *The Story of My Life* (1902). Her childhood was dramatized in William Gibson's play *The Miracle Worker* (1959; film, 1962).

Helen Keller at 66.

BY COURTESY OF THE AMERICAN FOUNDATION FOR THE BLIND

Kellogg, Frank B(illings) (1856–1937) U.S. lawyer and diplomat. Born in Potsdam, N.Y., he represented the U.S. government in antitrust cases before serving in the U.S. Senate (1917–23) and as ambassador to Britain (1923–25). Appointed U.S. secretary of state (1925–29) by Calvin Coolidge, he negotiated the multinational Kellogg-Briand Pact and was awarded the Nobel Peace Prize in 1929. He served on the Permanent Court of International Justice 1930–35.

Kellogg, John Harvey and W(ill) K(eith) (1852–1943, 1860–1951) U.S. cereal manufacturers. John, born in Tyrone, Mich., was a physician and vegetarian who in 1876 helped found a Seventh-Day Adventist sanitarium in Battle Creek, Mich. There he developed various nut and vegetable products, including a flaked-wheat cereal, to serve to patients, one of whom was C.W. Post. John's younger brother, W. K., born in Battle Creek, founded the W. K. Kellogg Co. in 1906 to manufacture dry breakfast cereals, cornflakes being its sole product in the early years. It soon became a leading U.S. producer of these and other convenience foods; its current annual sales exceed $7 billion. The W. K. Kellogg Foundation is one of the country's largest philanthropic institutions.

Kellogg-Briand Pact \'kel-ˌäg-brē-'än\ *or* **Pact of Paris** (1928) International agreement not to use war as an instrument of national policy. It was conceived by Aristide Briand, who hoped to engage the U.S. in a system of protective alliances to guard against aggression from a resurgent Germany. The U.S. secretary of state, Frank Kellogg, proposed a general multilateral treaty, and the French agreed. Most states signed the treaty, but its lack of enforceability and exceptions to its pacifist pledges rendered it useless. See also Pact of Locarno.

Kells, Book of Illuminated manuscript version of the four Gospels, c. late 8th–early 9th century. A masterpiece of the ornate Hiberno-Saxon style, it features geometric design rather than naturalistic representation, flat areas of color, and complex interlaced patterns. The illumination was probably begun at the Irish monastery on the Scottish island of Iona; the book was apparently taken to the monastery of Kells in Co. Meath, Ireland, after a Viking raid, and may have been completed there. See also Lindisfarne Gospels.

Kelly, Ellsworth (born 1923) U.S. painter and sculptor. Born in Newburgh, N.Y., in the 1960s he became a leading exponent of the hard-edge style of painting, in which abstract contours are sharply and precisely defined. He rejected illusionism in his paintings, which typically consist of adjacent rectangular panels of flat, uninflected primary colors. Influenced by the biomorphic abstractions of Jean Arp and the paper cutouts of Henri Matisse, he used the clean geometric lines of his paintings in his painted, cut-out sheet-metal sculptures.

Kelly, Gene *orig.* **Eugene Curran** (1912–1996) U.S. dancer, choreographer, actor, and movie director. After training at his mother's dance school in his native Pittsburgh, he moved to New York in 1938 and danced in Broadway musicals, creating the title role in *Pal Joey* in 1940. Beginning in 1942, his athletic style and carefree acting—exemplified in the popular *Anchors Aweigh* (1945), *On the Town* (1949), *An American in Paris* (1951), and *Singin' in the Rain* (1952), which he also helped choreograph and direct—became hallmarks of the movie musical. His achievements earned him a special Academy Award in 1951. He later choreographed and directed numerous other movies and created a ballet for the Paris Opera (1960).

Kelly, George *orig.* **George Kelly Barnes, Jr.** *known as* **Machine Gun Kelly** (1895–1954) U.S. gangster. Born in Memphis, he gained notoriety for a series of robberies and slayings in the Midwest. In 1933 he kidnapped the millionaire Charles F. Urschel; arrested soon afterward, he spent the rest of his life in prison. Though designated "Public Enemy No. 1," he was by no means the most dangerous criminal of his day.

Kelly, Grace *later* **Princess Grace of Monaco** (1929–1982) U.S. film actress. Born into a wealthy Philadelphia family, she studied acting and made her Broadway debut in 1949. Her movie debut in *Fourteen Hours* (1951) was followed by roles in *High Noon* (1952), *Mogambo* (1953), and *The Country Girl* (1954, Academy Award). Noted for her stately beauty and alluring reserve, she starred in Alfred Hitchcock's *Dial M for Murder* (1954), *Rear Window* (1954), and *To Catch a Thief* (1955). She made her last movie, *High Society* (1956), before marrying Prince Rainier of Monaco. She died in a car accident after suffering a stroke on a winding mountain road in the Côte d'Azur.

Kelly, Walt(er Crawford) (1913–1973) U.S. cartoonist. Born in Philadelphia, from 1935 he produced animation drawings for Walt Disney Productions, and in the 1940s he worked as a commercial artist in New York. His best-known character, the opossum Pogo, first appeared in a comic book c. 1943. In 1948 *Pogo* began to be published as a daily comic strip in the *New York Star*, and it was soon appearing in many other newspapers. Skillfully drawn, with witty and literate text, it featured Pogo and his winning animal friends in Okefenokee Swamp, characters Keely often used to satirize prominent political figures.

Kelly, William (1811–1888) U.S. ironmaster. Born in Pittsburgh, he purchased ironworks in Eddyville, Ky., and began experiments with an air blast to prepare pig for conversion to wrought iron. Because of the similarity of his apparatus to the first form of Bessemer converter (see Bessemer process), he was awarded a U.S. patent on the pneumatic steel process. There is no evidence that he made steel in any of his trials.

kelp Any of about 30 genera of large seaweeds that make up the order Laminariales (brown algae), found in colder seas. *Laminaria,* abundant along the Pacific coasts and the British Isles, is a source of commercial iodine. Its stipe (stemlike structure) is 3–10 ft (1–3 m) long. The largest known kelp, *Macrocystis*, grows up to 215 ft (65 m) long. Its body, which has a large rootlike holdfast, a hollow stipe, and branching blades with hollow gas bladders, resembles that of higher plants. It is rich in minerals and algin, a complex carbohydrate used as an emulsifier to prevent crystal formation in ice cream. Species of kelp are widely eaten in East Asia.

Kelvin (of Largs), Baron *orig.* **William Thomson** *known as* **Lord Kelvin** (1824–1907) British physicist. Born in Belfast, he entered the University of Glasgow at 10, published two papers by 17, and graduated from Cambridge University at 21. The next year he was awarded the chair of natural philosophy at the University of Glasgow, where he remained until retiring in 1899. He helped develop the second law of thermodynamics, and in 1848 he invented the absolute temperature scale named after him (see absolute zero). He served as chief consultant for the laying of the first Atlantic cable (1857–58). His patent for a mirror galvanometer for receiving telegraph signals (1858) made him wealthy. His work in electricity and magnetism led ultimately to James Clerk Maxwell's theory of electromagnetism. He also contributed to the determination of the age of earth and the study of hydrodynamics. He was raised to the peerage in 1892. He published over 600 scientific papers and received dozens of honorary degrees.

Kemal, Yashar (b. 1922) Turkish novelist of Kurdish descent. At age five Kemal saw his father murdered in a mosque and was himself blinded in one eye. He was arrested several times for his political activism. He is best known for his stories of village life and for his outspoken advocacy on behalf of the dispossessed. His novel *Memed, My Hawk* was translated into 20 languages and was filmed in 1983.

Kemeny \'kem-ə-nē\, **John G(eorge)** (1926–1992) U.S. (Hungarian-born) mathematician and computer scientist. He emigrated to the U.S. with his family at 14. He took a year off from his undergraduate studies at Princeton University to work on the Manhattan Project, and was later a research assistant to Albert Einstein. He received his PhD in 1949 and joined the Dartmouth College faculty in 1953, where he worked to develop the mathematics department. In the mid-1960s he and Thomas E. Kurtz (born 1928) developed the BASIC computer programming language. He was a pioneer in the promotion of "new math" and the use of computers in education. He served as president of Dartmouth 1970–91.

Kemp, Jack (French) (born 1935) U.S. politician. Born in Los Angeles, he played professional football with the Buffalo (N.Y.) Bills. In the U.S. House of Representatives (1971–89), he supported conservative policies but also civil-rights measures. As secretary of housing and urban development (1989–93), he restored confidence in the scandal-ridden agency. As the Republican vice-presidential nominee in 1996, he shared the ticket with ROBERT DOLE.

Kempe \'kemp\, **Margery** (1373?–1440?) English mystic. She had 14 children before beginning a series of pilgrimages to Jerusalem, Rome, Germany, and Spain in 1414. Apparently illiterate, she dictated her autobiography, *Book of Margery Kempe*, describing her travels and her religious ecstasies in an unaffected style (c. 1432–36). It is one of the earliest autobiographies in English literature.

Kempton, (James) Murray (1917–1997) U.S. journalist. Born in Baltimore and educated at Johns Hopkins, he was a reporter and then columnist with the *New York Post* from the 1940s. His political and social commentaries, noted for their uniquely rich and elegant style, moral insight, and sense of fair play, touched on many subjects, especially current affairs. Excepting two periods when he left the *Post,* he continued there until 1981; thereafter he wrote for *Newsday,* winning a Pulitzer Prize in 1985. His books include *Part of Our Time* (1955), on 1930s radical movements in the U.S.; and *The Briar Patch* (1973, National Book Award), on New York's prosecution of the Black Panthers.

Kenai Fjords National Park \'kē-ˌnī\ National park, southern Alaska. Located on the southern coast of the Kenai Peninsula, and established as a national monument in 1978, it became a national park in 1980. Its area of 670,000 acres (271,100 hectares) includes the Harding Icefield and its outflowing glaciers as well as coastal fjords. The park's wildlife includes sea otters, seals, and seabirds.

kendo Japanese sport of fencing with bamboo swords. Derived from the fighting methods of the ancient SAMURAI, it was introduced in the 18th century. Contestants wear traditional protective garments, and the sword (shinai) is held with both hands. Points are awarded for blows delivered to various parts of the upper body. The first combatant to score two points wins the match.

Kendrew, John Cowdery *later* **Sir John** (1917–1997) British biochemist. He received his PhD from Cambridge Univ., and as a Cambridge fellow (1947–75) went on to study the structure of proteins. He determined the structure of the muscle protein myoglobin, which stores oxygen for use by the muscles. Using X-ray diffraction techniques and computers, he devised a three-dimensional model of the arrangement of the its amino-acid units, an achievement for which he shared a 1962 Nobel Prize with MAX FERDINAND PERUTZ.

Kennan, George F(rost) (born 1904) U.S. diplomat and historian. Born in Milwaukee, he graduated from Princeton University and entered the U.S. foreign service (1925), studied Russian language and culture at the University of Berlin (1929–31), and was assigned to the U.S. embassy in Moscow (1933–35). He served in Vienna, Prague, Berlin, and Lisbon, returning to Moscow during and after World War II. His concept of CONTAINMENT, published in an anonymous article in 1947, became the basis of U.S. policy toward the Soviet Union. After serving as an adviser to the State Department, he joined the Institute of Advanced Study at Princeton as professor of historical studies (1956–74). He won simultaneous Pulitzer Prizes and National Book Awards for *Russia Leaves the War* (1956) and *Memoirs, 1925–50* (1967).

Kennebec River River, western central Maine. It rises from Moosehead Lake and flows south for about 150 mi (240 km) to the Atlantic Ocean. It was explored by SAMUEL DE CHAMPLAIN 1604–5. With its main tributary, the Androscoggin River, it forms Merrymeeting Bay, which extends 16 mi (26 km) to the Atlantic.

Kennedy, Anthony M(cLeod) (born 1936) U.S. jurist. Born in Sacramento, Cal., he graduated from Harvard Law School and practiced in San Francisco and Sacramento before being appointed to the U.S. Circuit Court of Appeals in 1975. Nominated to the U.S. Supreme Court in 1988 by Pres. RONALD REAGAN, his record has reflected his conservative outlook, and he has consistently voted against such policies as AFFIRMATIVE ACTION and abortion rights.

Kennedy, Edward M(oore) *known as* **Ted Kennedy** (born 1932) U.S. senator (from 1963). Born in Brookline, Mass., the son of JOSEPH P. KENNEDY and the brother of JOHN F. KENNEDY and ROBERT F. KENNEDY, he was elected to the U.S. Senate in 1962, where he served for decades as an unswerving advocate for liberal causes and social-welfare legislation. In 1969 his car plunged off a Chappaquiddick (Martha's Vineyard), Mass., bridge at night and a young woman in it drowned, an incident that probably cost him his party's presidential nomination.

Kennedy, John F(itzgerald) (1917–1963) 35th president of the U.S. (1961–63). He was born in Brookline, Massachusetts, the son of JOSEPH P. KENNEDY. He graduated from Harvard University and joined the navy in World War II, where he earned medals for heroism. Elected to the U.S. House of Representatives (1947–53) and the Senate (1953–60), he supported social legislation and became increasingly committed to civil rights legislation. He supported the policies of HARRY TRUMAN but accused the State Department of trying to force CHIANG KAI-SHEK into a coalition with MAO ZEDONG. In 1960 he won the Democratic nomination for president; after a vigorous campaign, managed by his brother ROBERT F. KENNEDY and aided financially by his father, he narrowly defeated RICHARD NIXON. He was the youngest person and the first Roman Catholic elected president. In his inaugural address he called on Americans to "ask not what your country can do for you, ask what you can do for your country." He proposed tax-reform and civil rights legislation but received little congressional support. He established the PEACE CORPS and the ALLIANCE FOR PROGRESS. His foreign policy began with the abortive BAY OF PIGS INVASION (1961), which emboldened the Soviet Union to move missiles to Cuba, sparking the CUBAN MISSILE CRISIS. In 1963 he successfully concluded the NUCLEAR TEST-BAN TREATY. In November 1963 he was assassinated while riding in a motorcade in Dallas by a sniper, allegedly LEE HARVEY OSWALD. The killing is considered the most notorious political murder of the 20th century. Kennedy's youth, energy, and charming family brought him world adulation and sparked the idealism of a generation, for whom the Kennedy White House became known as "Camelot." Details about his powerful family and personal life, especially concerning his extramarital affairs, tainted his image in later years.

John F. Kennedy, 1961.
AP/WIDE WORLD

Kennedy, Joseph P(atrick) (1888–1969) U.S. businessman and financier. Born in Boston, he graduated from Harvard and was a bank president by 25 and a millionaire at 30. He acquired a large fortune by speculating in the stock market and was a heavy contributor to the Democratic Party. As chairman of the Securities and Exchange Commission (1934–35), he outlawed the speculative practices that had made him rich. He was the first Irish-American to serve as ambassador to Britain (1937–40). With his wife, Rose, he encouraged his children—including JOHN F. KENNEDY, ROBERT F. KENNEDY, and EDWARD KENNEDY—to strive competitively for public leadership.

Kennedy, Robert F(rancis) (1925–1968) U.S. politician. Born in Brookline, Mass., the son of JOSEPH P. KENNEDY, he served in World War II, earned a law degree (1951), and managed his brother JOHN F. KENNEDY's successful 1952 campaign for the U.S. Senate. He was chief counsel (1957–60) to the Senate committee investigating labor racketeering. He managed his brother's 1960 presidential campaign and was appointed U.S. attorney general (1961–64). He led a drive against organized crime that convicted JIMMY HOFFA. After his brother's assassination, he resigned his cabinet post and was elected to the Senate from New York (1965). He became a spokesman for liberal Democrats and a critic of LYNDON B. JOHNSON's Vietnam War policy. In 1968 he was campaigning for the Democratic presidential nomination in Los Angeles when he was assassinated by Sirhan Sirhan, a Palestinian immigrant.

Kennedy, William (born 1928) U.S. novelist and journalist. He worked as a journalist in New York and Puerto Rico before returning in 1963 to his native Albany, N.Y., which he considers the source of his literary inspiration. His novels set in Albany include *The Ink Truck* (1969), *Legs* (1975), *Billy Phelan's Greatest Game* (1978), and *Ironweed* (1983, Pulitzer Prize). He also wrote the screenplays for *The Cotton Club* (1984) and *Ironweed* (1987).

Kennedy Center for the Performing Arts Huge cultural complex (opened 1971) in Washington, D.C., with a total of six stages, designed by EDWARD DURELL STONE. The complex, surfaced in marble, makes use of the ornamental facade screens for which the architect was known. The three main theaters are entered from the Grand Foyer, which faces the Potomac River. The Concert Hall, the largest auditorium, has been designated a national monument; its acoustics are considered exceptional, and its embossed ceiling and crystal chandeliers have been much admired.

Kenneth I *or* **Kenneth MacAlpin** (died 858?) First king of the united Scots of Dalriada and the PICTS. He inherited (834?) the Scottish kingdom of Dalriada from his father, Alpin, who is thought to have been killed by the Picts. He also gained control over Pictavia, and from 843 the two kingdoms were gradually joined, an important step in the making of a unified SCOTLAND. The union was probably accomplished both by intermarriage and by conquest.

Kent County (population 1995 est.: 1,551,000), southeastern England. It lies along the ENGLISH CHANNEL; the county seat is MAIDSTONE. The Romans ruled the area from AD 43, using CANTERBURY as a base. It was invaded by Jutes and Saxons in the 5th century; it became one of the seven kingdoms of Anglo-Saxon Britain. The king of Kent welcomed St. AUGUSTINE's Christian mission in 587; ST. THOMAS BECKET was murdered in Canterbury cathedral in 1170. It has long been known as the "Garden of England," and such crops as apples, cherries, barley, and wheat are widely grown.

Kent, Earl of See ODO OF BAYEUX

Kent, James (1763–1847) U.S. jurist who helped shape COMMON LAW in the U.S. He was born in Fredericksburgh, N.Y., and practiced law from 1785. He taught law at Columbia University (1793–98, 1823–26) and served as chief justice of the New York Supreme Court (1804–14) and chancellor of the Court of Chancery, then the state's highest judicial office (1814–23). As chancellor, he is said to have made U.S. equity JURISPRUDENCE effective for the first time. His *Commentaries on American Law* (1826–30) proved influential both in the U.S. and in England.

Kent, Rockwell (1882–1971) U.S. painter and illustrator. Born in Tarrytown Heights, N.Y., he studied architecture at Columbia Univ., but later chose to study painting with WILLIAM MERRITT CHASE and ROBERT HENRI. He worked variously as an architectural draftsman, lobsterman, and ship's carpenter in Maine, and traveled in Tierra del Fuego, Newfoundland, Alaska, and Greenland, gathering material for his paintings and travel books. His dramatic pen-and-ink drawings, strongly resembling woodcuts, appeared in many books by contemporary and classic writers and made him one of the most popular artists in the U.S., despite harassment for his radical leftist politics.

Kenton, Stan(ley Newcombe) (1912–1979) U.S. pianist, composer, arranger, and leader of one of the most popular and controversial big bands in jazz. Born in Wichita, Kan., Kenton formed his first band in 1941. The group exhibited the influence of JIMMY LUNCEFORD's precise brass and gained a reputation for a bombastic orchestral approach, often playing arrangements by Pete Rugolo. His players included saxophonist Art Pepper, trumpeter MAYNARD FERGUSON, drummer Shelly Manne, and singers Anita O'Day and June Christy. His efforts to organize the training of student musicians represent some of the earliest instances of formal jazz education.

Kentucky State (population 1997 est.: 3,908,000), southeastern central U.S. It covers 40,395 sq mi (104,623 sq km); its capital is FRANKFORT. Among its geographical features are the APPALACHIAN MTNS. of the east, the interior lowlands, including the BLUEGRASS REGION, and the rich lowlands along the MISSISSIPPI RIVER. Before the arrival of white settlers, the region was a hunting ground for Indian tribes, including the SHAWNEE, IROQUOIS, and CHEROKEE. DANIEL BOONE, among the first white settlers, arrived in 1769; a wave of immigration followed the AMERICAN REVOLUTION. Settlements began as part of a district of Virginia, but in 1792 Kentucky entered the Union as the 15th state. It was a border state during the AMERICAN CIVIL WAR, remaining in the Union but providing troops to both sides. The opening of rail lines into the eastern coal country and the introduction of a tobacco economy spurred growth in the late 19th century. In the 1970s a nationwide energy shortage created a demand for coal, from which Kentucky prospered, but demand dropped in the 1980s and many jobs were lost. Manufacturing is the leading source of income, while tobacco is the chief crop. Kentucky is known for its bourbon whiskey and thoroughbred horses; the KENTUCKY DERBY is run annually at Churchill Downs.

Kentucky, University of Public university in Lexington, Ky., chartered in 1865 as a land-grant institution. It is the principal campus of the University of Kentucky System, which includes a medical center and 14 community colleges. Its colleges offer instruction in such fields as agriculture, business and economics, engineering, and law. Research facilities include a center for robotics, an equine research center, and a particle accelerator. Enrollment at the main campus is about 24,000.

Kentucky Derby One of the classic U.S. Thoroughbred horse races, established in 1875 and run annually on the first Saturday in May at Churchill Downs track in Louisville. With the PREAKNESS and the BELMONT STAKES, it makes up U.S. racing's coveted TRIPLE CROWN. The field is limited to 3-year-olds. The track distance is 1.25 mi (2,000 m).

Kentucky Lake Reservoir, western Kentucky and western Tennessee. One of the world's largest manmade lakes, it is 184 mi (296 km) long and has more than 2,300 mi (3,700 km) of shoreline. It was created in 1944 when the Kentucky Dam was built on the TENNESSEE RIVER. The dam is the largest in the TENNESSEE VALLEY AUTHORITY system, and it regulates the flow from the Tennessee River into the OHIO RIVER.

Kentucky River Tributary of the OHIO RIVER in northern central Kentucky. It is formed by the confluence of North, Middle, and South forks, which originate in the Cumberland Mountains. It is navigable along its 259-mi (417-km) course by means of locks. It empties into the Ohio River at Carrollton.

Kenya *officially* **Republic of Kenya** Republic, eastern Africa. It is bounded by Ethiopia, Sudan, Somalia, the Indian Ocean, Tanzania, and Uganda. Area: 224,961 sq mi (582,646 sq km). Population (1997 est.): 28,803,000. Capital: NAIROBI. With a small group of European settlers' descendents, there are 30–40 ethnic groups, including the KIKUYU, Luhya, Luo, Kamba, Kalenjin, and MASAI. Languages: Swahili, English (both official); others belonging to the Bantu,

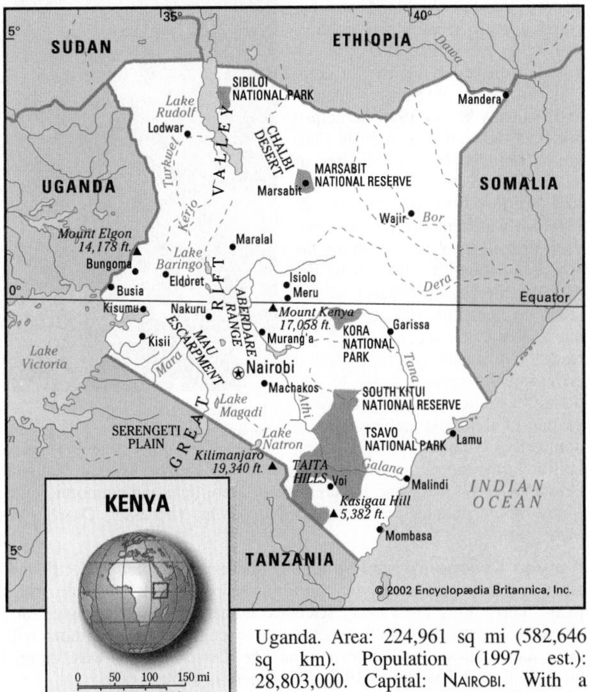

Nilotic, and Cushitic language groups. Religions: Christianity, animism, Islam, Hinduism. Currency: shilling. Kenya can be divided into five regions: the Lake Victoria basin in the southwestern corner; the vast plateau of eastern Kenya; the 250-mi (400-km) coastal belt along the Indian Ocean; the highlands of the Mau Escarpment on the western side of the Great Rift Valley in western Kenya; and the highlands and mountains of the Aberdare Range on the eastern side of the Rift Valley, including Mount Kenya. It is noted for such wildlife as lion, leopard, elephant, buffalo, rhinoceros, zebra, hippopotamus, and crocodile. Only about 4% of the land is arable, and about 7% of the land is used for grazing cattle, goats, and sheep. Agriculture employs four-fifths of the workforce, and tea and coffee are the leading exports. It is a republic with one legislative house; its head of state and government is the president. The coastal region was dominated by Arabs until it was seized by the Portuguese in the 16th century. The Masai people held sway in the north and moved into central Kenya in the 18th century, while the Kikuyu expanded from their home region in southern central Kenya. The interior was explored by European missionaries in the 19th century. After the British took control, Kenya was established as a British protectorate (1890) and a crown colony (1920). The Mau Mau rebellion of the 1950s was directed against European colonialism. In 1963 the country became fully independent, and a year later a republican government under Jomo Kenyatta was elected. In 1992 Kenyan president Daniel arap Moi allowed the country's first multiparty elections in three decades, though the elections were marred by violence and fraud. Political turmoil occurred over the next years.

Kenya, Mt. *Swahili* **Kirinyaga** Extinct volcano, central Kenya. Lying just south of the equator, it is the highest mountain in Kenya, and rises to 17,058 ft (5,199 m). The first European to discover the mountain was Johann Ludwig Krapf in 1849. Mount Kenya National Park, occupying an area of 277 sq mi (718 sq km), contains a variety of big game, including elephant and buffalo. Nanyuki lies at the mountain's northwestern foot and is the chief base for ascents.

Kenyatta \ken-'yä-tə\, **Jomo** (1894?–1978) First prime minister (1963–64) and then president (1964–78) of independent Kenya. Of Kikuyu descent, Kenyatta left the eastern African highlands to become a civil servant and political activist in Nairobi c. 1920. He opposed a union of the British colonial territories of Kenya, Uganda, and Tanganyika. In 1945 he helped organize the sixth Pan-African Congress, attended by such figures as W. E. B. Du Bois and Kwame Nkrumah (see Pan-African movement). In 1953 he was sentenced to a seven-year prison term for directing the Mau Mau rebellion, though he denied the charges. In 1962 he negotiated the constitutional terms leading to Kenya's independence. As its leader he headed a strong central government, rejected calls to nationalize property, and made Kenya one of the most stable and economically dynamic African states. Critics complained of the dominance of his Kenya African National Union (KANU) party and the creation of a political and economic elite. Many of his policies were continued under his successor, Daniel arap Moi.

Kenyatta.

JOHN MOSS—BLACK STAR

Kenyon College Private liberal-arts college in Gambier, Ohio. Founded in 1824, it is affiliated with the Episcopal church. It offers programs in the performing arts, social sciences, humanities, and biological and physical sciences, as well as cooperative engineering programs with three universities. The literary journal *The Kenyon Review* was founded by John Crowe Ransom in 1939. Enrollment is about 1,600.

Keokuk \'kē-ə-,kək\ (1790?–1848?) Sauk Indian orator and politician. Born near present-day Rock Island, Ill., he engaged in a lifelong struggle for power with Black Hawk, who advocated resistance to white settlement on tribal lands. For his refusal to fight U.S. forces, the government named Keokuk leader of the Sauk nation in 1837. He continued to give away land until the Sauk and Fox had to settle on a Kansas reservation. Though wealthy and powerful, he died in disgrace among his people.

Kepler, Johannes (1571–1630) German astronomer. Born into a poor family, he received a scholarship to the University of Tübingen. He received an MA in 1594, after which he became a mathematics teacher in Austria. He developed a mystical theory that the cosmos was constructed of the five regular polyhedrons, enclosed in a sphere, with a planet between each pair. He sent his paper on the subject to Tycho Brahe, who invited Kepler to join his research staff. In attempting to understand atmospheric refraction of light, he became the first to explain accurately how the eye sees, how eyeglasses improve vision, and what happens to light in a telescope. In 1609 he published his finding that the orbit of Mars was an ellipse and not the perfect circle hitherto presumed to be the orbit of all celestial bodies. This fact became the basis of the first of Kepler's laws of planetary motion. He also determined that planets move faster as they near the sun, and in 1619 he showed that a simple mathematical formula related the planets' orbital periods to their distance from the sun. In 1620 he defended his mother from charges of witchcraft, thereby preserving his own reputation as well.

Kerala \'ker-ə-lə\ State (pop., 1994 est.: 30,555,000), southwestern India. Bordering the Arabia Sea, it occupies an area of 15,005 sq mi (38,863 sq km); its capital is Trivandrum. During the 3rd century BC, it was an independent Dravidian kingdom known as Keralaputra. The Kulashekhara dynasty ruled the region in the 9th–12th century, when the regional Malayalam language took hold; it is still the dominant language. Portuguese intervention from 1498 was followed by Dutch rule in the 17th century. The Dutch were ousted in 1741 by the princely state of Travancore, which itself in the 1790s came under British protectorate status. It was given its present name in 1956. Kerala is India's most densely populated state.

keratin \'ker-ə-tən\ Fibrous structural protein of hair, nails, hooves, wool, feathers, and skin. A quarter of the amino acids in keratin are cystine, whose ability to form strong bridging (disulfide) bonds with other cystine units accounts for keratin's great stability. Keratin does not dissolve in cold or hot water and does not easily undergo proteolysis. Its fibers are 10–12% longer at maximum water content (about 16%) than when dry. The sulfurous smell of burning keratin is distinctive.

keratitis \,ker-ə-'tī-təs\ Inflammation of the cornea (see eye). The conjunctiva may also be inflamed (keratoconjunctivitis). Depending on the cause, including dryness of the eye (from low tear production or inability to close the eye), chemical or physical injury, or certain diseases, it may or may not cause pain, visual-field defects (including blindness), and damage to the eye.

Kerensky \'ke-ryən-skē, *Engl* ker-'en-skē\, **Aleksandr (Fyodorovich)** (1881–1970) Russian political leader. A prominent lawyer, he joined the Socialist Revolutionary Party and was elected to the fourth Duma (1912), where he became a noted orator. After the start of the Russian Revolution of 1917, he held posts in both the Petrograd soviet and the provisional government and became a popular figure. In May he became minister of war, and in July prime minister. A moderate socialist, he sought to unify the factions but lost the support of the moderates and officers by dismissing the army commander in chief, Lavr Kornilov, and of the left by refusing to implement their radical programs. When the Bolsheviks seized power in October, he was unable to gather forces to defend his government. He went into hiding, then emigrated to Western Europe in 1918. In 1940 he moved to the U.S., where he lectured at universities and wrote books on the revolution.

Kerguelen Islands \'kər-gə-lən\ Archipelago, southern Indian Ocean. It consists of the island of Kerguelen (also called Desolation Island) and about 300 islets, which together cover about 2,400 sq mi (6,200 sq km). Kerguelen Island, about 100 mi (160 km) long, has active glaciers and peaks up to 6,445 ft (1,965 m). Discovered in 1772 by the French navigator Yves-Joseph de Kerguélen-Trémarec, the archipelago was annexed to France in 1893 and became part of French Southern and Antarctic Territories in 1955. Port-aux-Français is a scientific base on the main island.

Kermadec Islands \kər-'mä-dek\ Volcanic island group, South Pacific Ocean. Located northeast of Auckland, New Zealand, it includes Raoul,

Macauley, and Curtis islands and l'Esperance Rock, and has a total land area of 13 sq mi (34 sq km). Explored in the late 18th century by the British and the French, the islands were annexed to New Zealand in 1887. A meteorological-communications station was built on Raoul, the largest island, in 1937, but permanent settlement is discouraged.

Kern, Jerome (David) (1885–1945) U.S. composer, one of the major U.S. creators of the MUSICAL. Kern studied music in his native New York and in Heidelberg, Germany, and later gained theatrical experience in London. Returning to New York, he worked as a pianist and salesman for music publishers and wrote new numbers for European operettas. In 1912 he composed *The Red Petticoat,* the first musical containing only his own music; its success was surpassed by *Very Good Eddie* (1915). Subsequent musicals included *Oh, Boy!* (1917), *Sally* (1920), and *Sunny* (1925). In 1927 his *Show Boat,* based on Edna Ferber's novel and with lyrics by O. HAMMERSTEIN, became the first American musical with a serious plot drawn from a literary source; it represents a landmark in the history of musical theater. It was followed by *The Cat and the Fiddle* (1931), *Music in the Air* (1932), and *Roberta* (1933). After 1933 he composed for Hollywood. Kern's classic songs include "The Song Is You," "All the Things You Are," "Smoke Gets in Your Eyes," and "Ol' Man River."

kerogen *or* **kerogen shales** \'ker-ə-jən\ *or* **kerogenites** \'ker-ə-jə-ˌnīts\ Complex mixture of compounds with large molecules containing mainly hydrogen and carbon but also oxygen, nitrogen, and sulfur. Kerogen is the organic component of OIL SHALES. It is waxy and insoluble in water; upon heating, it breaks down into recoverable gaseous and liquid substances resembling petroleum. It consists of compacted organic material, such as algae and other low plant forms, pollen, spores and spore coats, and insects.

kerosene *or* **kerosine** Organic compound, a clear, oily, highly flammable liquid with a strong odor, distilled from PETROLEUM (10–25% of total volume). It is a mixture of about 10 different types of fairly simple HYDROCARBONS, depending on its source. It is less volatile than gasoline, boiling at 285–610°F (140–320°C). It is burned in lamps, heaters, and furnaces and used as a fuel or fuel component for diesel and tractor engines, jet engines, and rockets and as a solvent for greases and insecticides.

Kerouac \'ker-ə-ˌwak\, **Jack** *orig.* **Jean-Louis Lebris de** (1922–1969) U.S. poet and novelist. Born to a French-Canadian family in Lowell, Mass., he attended Columbia Univ., served as a merchant seaman, and roamed the U.S. and Mexico before his first book appeared. At Columbia he met ALLEN GINSBERG and other kindred spirits, and he became a spokesman of what would be dubbed the BEAT MOVEMENT (a term he coined). He celebrated its code of poverty and freedom in *On the Road* (1957); his best-known novel, and the first written in the nonstop, unedited style that he advocated, it enjoyed a huge success among young people, for whom Kerouac became a romantic hero. All his novels, including *The Dharma Bums* (1958), *The Subterraneans* (1958), and *Desolation Angels* (1965), are autobiographical. His death at 47 resulted from alcoholism.

Kerr \'kär, 'kər\, **Deborah** *orig.* **Deborah Jane Kerr-Trimmer** (born 1921) Scottish actress. After performing in such British films as *Major Barbara* (1940) and *Black Narcissus* (1947), she moved to Hollywood, where she was often cast in prim roles, though her part in *From Here to Eternity* (1953) was a departure from her ladylike image. Her later films include *The King and I* (1956), *Tea and Sympathy* (1956), *Heaven Knows, Mr. Allison* (1957), *Separate Tables* (1958), *The Sundowners* (1960), and *The Night of the Iguana* (1964). She retired from the screen in 1969. She received a special Academy Award in 1994.

Kertanagara \ˌker-tə-'nä-gə-rə\ Last king (1268–92) of Tumapel (or Singhasari) in Java. His birth reunited two halves of the Javanese kingdom, and his name means "order in the realm." To bolster his kingdom against KUBLAI KHAN, he expanded it, marrying a princess of Champa (central Vietnam), sending envoys to Malayu (Sumatra), and conquering Bali. He refused to pay homage to Kublai Khan, but was killed by a vassal before the Khan's armed forces arrived to punish him. Two early Javanese chronicles give contradictory pictures of the king: one describes him as drunken and incompetent; the other depicts him as a wise king and zealous follower of Tantric Buddhism. He is still venerated as one of Java's greatest rulers. See photograph above.

Stone sculpture thought to be Kertanagara in the form of *hari-hara ardhanari,* c. early 14th century; acquired by the Museum für Völker Kunde, Berlin, in 1865.

Kertész \ker-'tesh\, **André** (1894–1985) Hungarian-U.S. photographer and photojournalist. He moved from Budapest to Paris in 1925 in search of opportunity, and became a major contributor to European illustrated periodicals. He arrived in New York in 1936 intending to work for a commercial studio for a year, but stayed on, doing largely fashion photography for major U.S. magazines. He returned to his creative style c. 1962, and in 1964 the Museum of Modern Art gave an exhibition of his works. His spontaneous, unposed pictures exerted a strong influence on magazine photography.

kerygma and catechesis \kə-'rig-mə, 'kir-ig-mə...ˌka-tə-'kē-səs\ In Christian theology, literally, preaching and teaching. Kerygma means the proclamation of the GOSPEL, especially by the APOSTLES as recorded in the NEW TESTAMENT. In the early church, catechesis referred to the oral instruction (geared to the general absence of literacy) given before BAPTISM to those who had accepted the message of salvation. As the practice of infant baptism spread, a shift took place to teaching the already baptized in preparation for full adult membership, and churches developed statements of basic doctrine called CATECHISMS.

Kesey \'kē-zē\, **Ken (Elton)** (1935–2001) U.S. writer. Born in La Junta, Colorado, he attended Stanford University and later served as an experimental subject and aide in a hospital, an experience that led to his novel *One Flew over the Cuckoo's Nest* (1962; film, 1975), which became one of the most widely read countercultural texts of the 1960s. It was followed by *Sometimes a Great Notion* (1964) and *Sailor Song* (1992). His entourage, the Merry Pranksters, toured the United States in a brightly painted bus from the 1960s and were the subject of TOM WOLFE's *Electric Kool-Aid Acid Test* (1968).

Kesselring, Albert (1885–1960) German field marshal. He became chief of the German air staff in 1936, and commanded early air attacks on Poland, France, Britain, and the Soviet Union. In 1941 he was appointed commander in chief, south, to bolster Italy's efforts in North Africa and against Malta. He codirected the Axis campaign in North Africa with ERWIN ROMMEL. After the Allied invasions of Sicily and Italy in 1943, he fought an effective defensive action that prevented an Allied victory in that theater until 1944. Appointed commander in chief, west, in 1945, he was unable to stop the Allies' drive into Germany and surrendered the southern half of the German forces in May 1945. He was imprisoned for war crimes 1947–52.

kestrel \'kes-trəl\ Any of several BIRDS OF PREY (genus *Falco*) known for hovering while hunting. Kestrels prey on large insects, birds, and small mammals. The male is more colorful than the female. Kestrels are mainly Old World birds, but one species, the American kestrel *(F. sparverius),* often called SPARROW HAWK in the U.S., is common throughout North and South America. It is about 12 in. (30 cm) long, white or yellowish below, and red-

Male common kestrel (*Falco tinnunculus*).

WERNER LAYER—BRUCE COLEMAN LTD.

dish brown and slate- gray above with colorful markings on the head. The common kestrel *(F. tinnunculus)* of the Old World is larger and less colorful. See also FALCON.

Ket See SIBERIAN PEOPLES

ketone \'kē-ˌtōn\ Any of a class of organic compounds containing a carbonyl group (—C=O; see FUNCTIONAL GROUP) bonded to two CARBON atoms. Ketones can participate in many CHEMICAL REACTIONS, though to a lesser extent than the related ALDEHYDES. Many more complex organic compounds have ketones as building blocks. Their chief industrial use is as solvents and in the manufacture of explosives, lacquers, paints, and textiles. ACETONE is the most important ketone; several SUGARS and some natural and synthetic STEROIDS are ketones. In ketosis, ketones produced by LIPID METABOLISM accumulate in the blood and urine in abnormal amounts, usually because of starvation or a metabolic disease such as DIABETES MELLITUS.

Kettering, Charles F(ranklin) (1876–1958) U.S. engineer. Born near Loudonville, Ohio, in 1904 he developed the first electric cash register. With Edward Deeds he founded Delco c. 1910; in 1916 Delco became a subsidiary of General Motors Corp., and Kettering served as vice president and director of research for GM 1920–47. Many of his inventions were instrumental in the evolution of the modern automobile, including the first electric starter (1912), antiknock fuels, leaded gasoline, quick-drying lacquer finishes (with THOMAS JR. MIDGLEY), the high-speed, two-cycle diesel engine, and a revolutionary high-compression engine (1951). He later cofounded the Sloan-Kettering Institute for Cancer Research in New York City.

kettledrums See TIMPANI

Kevlar Trademarked name of poly-*para*-phenylene terephthalamide, a nylonlike POLYMER first produced by Du Pont in 1971. Kevlar can be made into strong, tough, stiff, high-melting fibers, five times stronger per weight than steel; they are used in radial tires, heat- or flame-resistant fabrics, bulletproof clothing, and fiber-reinforced composite materials for aircraft panels, boat hulls, golf-club shafts, and lightweight bicycles.

Kevorkian, Jack (born 1928) U.S. pathologist, advocate and practitioner of physician-assisted suicide. Born in Pontiac, Mich., he expressed early interest in experimentation on death-row inmates who had been rendered unconscious rather than executed; his ideas negatively affected his medical career. In the 1980s he devised his "suicide machine," with which a person could commit suicide by merely pushing a button, and in the 1990s he assisted in the deaths of over 100 terminally ill persons. His actions provoked furious controversy and led to legislation and referenda; he was tried, convicted twice, and jailed, and his medical license was revoked. In 1998 he was convicted of murder for administering a lethal injection himself and was sentenced to 10–25 years in jail.

Kew Gardens *officially* **Royal Botanic Gardens, Kew** Botanic garden located at Kew, site of a former royal estate in the London borough of Richmond upon Thames. In 1759 Augusta, dowager princess of Wales and mother of George III, laid out a portion of her estate as a botanic garden. It became an eminent scientific institution under the unofficial directorship of JOSEPH BANKS. In 1840 the gardens were donated to the nation. Under Sir William Jackson Hooker (1785–1865), they became the world's leading botanical institution. Today they are home to 50,000 different types of plants, a HERBARIUM of more than 5 million dried specimens, and a library of more than 130,000 volumes. The three museums at Kew are devoted largely to economic plant products and a laboratory of plant genetics and classification.

key System of PITCHES and HARMONIES generated from a scale of seven tones, one of which is predominantly important. Keys are a basic element of TONALITY, and represent an outgrowth of modal music (see church mode). When a given piece is "in C," C is its "tonic," or central tone. In Western music after c. 1600, most music has been written either in a major or a minor key. The major scale consists of the interval pattern *tone-tone-semitone-tone-tone-tone-semitone.* The minor scale consistently differs from it by beginning with the pattern *tone-semitone-tone,* producing a minor 3rd rather than a major 3rd above the tonic.

key, cryptographic Secret value used by a computer together with a complex ALGORITHM to encrypt and decrypt messages. Since confidential messages might be intercepted during transmission or travel over public networks, they require encryption so that they will be meaningless to third parties in order to maintain confidentiality. The intended recipient, and only the recipient, must also be able to decrypt them. If someone encrypts a message with a key, only someone else with a matching key should be able to decrypt the message. See also DATA ENCRYPTION.

Key, David M(cKendree) (1824–1900) U.S. politician. Born in Greene Co., Tenn., he practiced law and was active in Democratic politics. He opposed secession but served in the Confederate army during the Civil War. He served in the U.S. Senate 1875–77. Pres. RUTHERFORD B. HAYES made him U.S. postmaster general in fulfillment of a campaign pledge in the disputed 1876 election to appoint a Southerner to his cabinet (see ELECTORAL COMMISSION). From 1880 to 1894 he was a U.S. district judge in Tennessee.

Key, Francis Scott (1779–1843) U.S. lawyer, author of "The Star-Spangled Banner." Born in Frederick Co., Md. he practiced law from 1802. After the burning of Washington D.C., in the WAR OF 1812, he was sent to secure the release of a friend from a British ship in Chesapeake Bay. He watched the British shelling of Fort McHenry during the night of September 13–14, 1814; when he saw the U.S. flag still flying the next morning, he wrote the poem "Defense of Fort M'Henry." Published in the *Baltimore Patriot,* it was later set to the tune of an English drinking song, "To Anacreon in Heaven." It was adopted as the U.S. national anthem in 1931.

Key West City (pop., 1996 est.: 25,000), southwestern Florida. The southernmost city of the continental U.S., it lies on an island about 4 mi (6.5 km) long and 1.5 mi (2.4 km) wide in the western Florida Keys. The name is an English corruption of Cayo Hueso ("Bone Islet"), as it was called by Spanish explorers who found human bones there. In 1822 a U.S. naval depot was set up on Key West as a base of operations against pirates. Now a winter resort, it is also a tourist destination. Many writers and artists have lived there, and the homes of ERNEST HEMINGWAY and JOHN JAMES AUDUBON have been preserved.

Keynes \'kānz\, **John Maynard** *later* **Baron Keynes (of Tilton)** (1883–1946) British economist, known for his revolutionary theories on the causes of prolonged unemployment. He was the son of the distinguished economist John Neville Keynes (1852–1949). He served in the British treasury during World War I and attended the Versailles Peace Conference. He resigned in protest over the Treaty of VERSAILLES, denouncing its provisions in *The Economic Consequences of the Peace* (1919), and returned to teaching at Cambridge University. The international economic crisis of the 1920s and '30s prompted him to write *The General Theory of Employment, Interest and Money* (1935–36), the most influential economic treatise of the 20th century. It refuted laissez-faire economic theories, arguing that the treatment for depression was either to enlarge private investment or to create public substitutes for private investment. In mild economic downturns, MONETARY POLICY in the shape of easier CREDIT and lower interest rates might stimulate investment. More severe crises called for deliberate public deficits (see DEFICIT FINANCING) either in the shape of public works or subsidies to the poor and unemployed. Keynes's theories were put into practice by many Western democracies, notably by the U.S. in the NEW DEAL. Interested in the design of new international financial institutions at the end of World War II, Keynes was active at the BRETTON WOODS CONFERENCE in 1944.

John Maynard Keynes, detail of a watercolour by Gwen Raverat; in the National Portrait Gallery, London.

BY COURTESY OF THE NATIONAL PORTRAIT GALLERY, LONDON

KGB *Russian* **Komitet Gosudarstvennoy Bezopasnosti** ("Committee for State Security") Soviet agency responsible for intelligence, counterintelligence, and internal security. It was the descendant of earlier agencies. The Cheka was established in 1917 to investigate counterrevolution and sabotage. Its successor, the GPU (later OGPU), was the new Soviet Union's first secret-police agency (1923); it also administered corrective labor camps and oversaw the forcible collectivization of Russia's farms. By 1931 it had its own army and its spies and informers were ubiquitous. In 1934 it was absorbed into the NKVD, which carried out extensive purges. In 1941 the state-security and espionage functions were combined in the MGB. In 1954 the KGB was created. At its peak, it was the world's largest secret-police and espionage organization. It lost power under MIKHAIL GORBACHEV, especially after leading a failed coup d'état (1991). It was renamed after the dissolution of the Soviet Union, and its internal-security functions were segregated from its espionage and counterespionage operations.

Khabur River \'kä-ˌbu̇r\ River, southeastern Turkey and northeastern Syria. It rises in the mountains of southeastern Turkey and flows southeast to Syria, where it is joined by the Jaghjaghah River; it then meanders south and empties into the EUPHRATES after a course of 200 mi (320 km). It is an important irrigation source for northeastern Syria.

Khachaturian \ˌkä-chə-'tu̇r-ē-ən\, **Aram (Ilyich)** (1903–1978) Soviet (Armenian) composer. Born in Tbilisi (Tiflis), Georgia, he studied with Reinhold Glière (1875–1956) and Nikolai Myaskovsky (1881–1950). He gained international notice when S. PROKOFIEV recommended a piece for a Paris concert. Active in the composer's union, Khachaturian (along with D. SHOSTAKOVICH and Prokofiev) was criticized by the government in 1948 for "formalist tendencies," though his music was in fact always conservative and accessible. After JOSEPH STALIN's death (1953), he published a call for greater artistic freedom. His ballet scores include *Masquerade* (1944) and *Spartacus* (1954); *Gayane* (1943) contains the well-known "Sabre Dance." Other popular pieces include his piano and violin concertos.

Khadafy, Muammar al- See Muammar al-QADDAFI

Khafaje See TUTUB

Khalkís \k̲äl-'kēs\ *or* **Chalcis** \'kal-səs\ *formerly* **Euripus** \'e-vrē-pəs\ City (pop., 1991: 51,000), on the island of EUBOEA, Greece. It is situated off the EVRIPOS STRAIT, which separates Euboea from the Greek mainland. The city was important as a commercial center as early as the 7th century BC. It established colonies in Macedonia, Italy, and Sicily and was a base for campaigns against Athens until 411 BC. ARISTOTLE died there in 322 BC. The city became part of Greece in 1830.

Khama III (1837?–1923) South African chief. In 1885 he had Bechuanaland (now Botswana) declared a protectorate of the British Empire. He lent reinforcements to the British expedition that crushed LOBENGULA in 1893. His grandson Sir Seretse Khama (1921–1980) was the first president of independent Botswana (r.1966–80).

Khambhat \'kəm-bət\, **Gulf of** *or* **Gulf of Cambay** \kam-'bā\ Inlet, ARABIAN SEA, on the northwestern coast of India, southeast of KATHIAWAR peninsula. It is 120 mi (190 km) wide at its widest but rapidly narrows. It receives many rivers, including the Tapi and Mahi. Its orientation to the southwestern monsoon winds accounts for its high tidal range. All its ports have suffered from silting caused by tides and flood torrents. On its eastern side are Bharuch, one of India's oldest ports, and SURAT. At the gulf's head is the city of Khambhat (pop., 1991: 77,000), which was mentioned by MARCO POLO as one of India's most important seaports.

khan Historically, the ruler or monarch of a Mongol tribe. Early on, a distinction was made between the title of khan and that of *khakan*, or Great Khan. Later, the term khan was adopted by the SELJUQ and KHWAREZM-SHAH dynasties as a title for the highest nobility. Gradually it became an affix to the name of any Muslim property owner; today it is often used as a surname.

Khanka \'kän-kə\, **Lake** *Chinese* **Xingkai Hu** *or* **Hsing-K'ai Hu** \'shiŋ-'kī-'hü\ Lake on the boundary between Siberia and China. Most of the lake is in Russian territory while the northern shore is in China's HEILONGJIANG province. It varies in area from 1,500 to 1,700 sq mi (4,000 to 4,400 sq km), and much of its shore is swampland. Its outlet is a tributary of the USSURI RIVER.

Khanty See SIBERIAN PEOPLES

kharaj \k̲á-'räj\ Tax imposed on recent Islamic converts in the 7th–8th century. In Islamic territories, Jews, Christians, and Zoroastrians who did not convert to Islam were required to pay a tax called the JIZYA. Many people converted to Islam to avoid this tax or to escape the ban on non-Muslims owning land. As financial problems mounted for the Umayyad rulers, authorities imposed the kharaj as a property tax for recent converts. Popular opposition to the tax led to a revolt in 747 and precipitated the downfall of the UMAYYAD DYNASTY.

Kharijite \'k̲är-i-ˌjīt\ Member of the earliest Islamic sect, which emerged in the mid-7th century during conflicts over the succession of the caliphate (see CALIPH). The Kharijites ("separatists") took sides against ALI, the Prophet's son-in-law (whose followers later made up the SHIITE branch of Islam), and led a series of uprisings, assassinating Ali and harassing his rival al-MUAWIYAH. They later caused further disruptions for the Umayyad caliphs. Their constant attacks on Muslim governments were based on their belief that the caliph should be chosen democratically by the entire Muslim community. They called for a literal interpretation of the QURAN and were harsh and puritanical in the exercise of their religion. The movement's Ibadiyah subsect survived into the 20th century in North Africa, Oman, and Zanzibar.

Kharj, Al See AL KHARJ

Kharkiv \'k̲är-kəf\ City (pop., 1996 est.: 1,555,000), northeastern Ukraine. Founded in 1655 as a military stronghold to protect Russia's southern borderlands, it became a seat of provincial government in 1732. It served as the capital of the Ukrainian S.S.R. (1921–34). The second-largest city in Ukraine, it is a heavy industry center, manufacturing agricultural machinery and electrical equipment.

Khartoum \kär-'tüm\ City (pop., 1993: 925,000), capital of the Sudan. Located just south of the confluence of the Blue and White NILE rivers, it was originally an Egyptian army camp (1821). The Mahdists besieged and destroyed the town in 1885, killing CHARLES GEORGE GORDON, the British governor-general. Reoccupied by the British in 1898, it served as the seat of the Anglo-Egyptian government until 1956, when it became the capital of the independent republic of the Sudan. A major trade and communications center, it is the seat of several universities.

khat \'kät\ Slender, straight, East African tree (*Catha edulis;* family Celastraceae). Reaching a height of 80 ft (25 m), the khat tree has large, oval, finely toothed, bitter-tasting leaves. Its best-known relatives are the ornamentals EUONYMUS and BITTERSWEET. Khat leaves are chewed for the stimulants they contain, and the drug is central to social life in some countries.

Khatami \k̲ä-tä-'mē\, **Muhammad al-** (born 1943) President of Iran (from 1997). After graduating from Qom Theology School (1961), he began political activities while studying philosophy at Esfahan University. He headed an Islamic center in Germany during the Ira-nian Revolution (1979) and returned home to seek election to the Majlis (parliament) in 1980. He served in government posts during the IRAN-IRAQ WAR and as cultural adviser to Pres. Rafsanjani and head of the National Library (1992–97) before winning the presidency as a moderate, with 69% of the vote.

Khayr al-Din See BARBAROSSA

Khayyam, Omar See OMAR KHAYYAM

Khazars \kə-'zärz\ Confederation of Turkic-speaking tribes that established a commercial empire in European Russia in the late 6th century. A people of the northern Caucasus region, the Khazars allied with the Byzantines against the Persians in the 7th century and warred with the Arabs until the mid-8th century. Their empire extended westward along the Black Sea, and they controlled trade routes and exacted tribute from their neighbors. The ruling class adopted Judaism and maintained close relations with the Byzantine emperors. The Khazar empire began to decline in the 10th century and was crushed by Kiev in 965.

Khensu See KHONS

Khidr \'k̲i-dər\, **al-** Legendary Islamic figure endowed with immortality who became a popular saint, especially among sailors and Sufi mystics. His legend is based on a narrative from the Quran, which tells how a "man of God" helps Musa (MOSES) search for a fish and at the same time performs seemingly senseless actions such as sinking a boat and killing a young man. By questioning him, Musa forfeits his patronage. Arab commentators embellished the story, giving him the name Khidr ("green") and claiming that he turned green upon diving into the spring of life. In Pakistan he is identified with a water deity who protects mariners and river travelers.

Khíos See CHIOS

Khitan See LIAO DYNASTY

Khmelnytsky \k͟myel-ˈnit-skē\, **Bohdan (Zinoviy Mykhaylovych)** (c. 1595–1657) Ukrainian Cossack leader (1648–57). Though he was educated in Poland and served with the Polish military, he fled to the fortress of the Zaporozhian Cossacks in 1648 and organized a rebellion among them. After winning support from dissatisfied Ukrainian peasants and townspeople, he marched against Poland. After years of war, he sought aid from the Russians in 1654, and they subsequently invaded Poland, achieving the transfer of Ukrainian lands from Polish to Russian control. His attempts to secure autonomy for his Cossack followers resulted only in their later subjection to Russian rule.

Khmer \kə-ˈmer\ *or* **Cambodian** *or* **Kampuchean** Ethnolinguistic group that constitutes most of the population of Cambodia. Smaller numbers of Khmer also live in southeastern Thailand and the Mekong River delta of southern Vietnam. Traditional Khmer are a predominantly agricultural people, subsisting on rice and fish and living in villages. Their crafts include weaving, pottery making, and metalworking. They follow THERAVADA Buddhism, which coexists with pre-Buddhist animistic beliefs. Indian culture has historically been a strong influence on Khmer culture.

Khmer language *or* **Cambodian language** MON-KHMER LANGUAGE spoken by over 7 million people in Cambodia (where it is the national language), southern Vietnam, and parts of Thailand. Khmer is written in a distinctive script, which, like the writing systems of Burmese, Thai, and Lao, is descended from the South Asian Pallava script (see INDIC WRITING SYSTEMS); the earliest inscription in Old Khmer is from the 7th century. During the ANGKOR period (9th–15th century), Khmer lent many words to Thai, Lao, and other languages of the region (see TAI LANGUAGES). Khmer itself has borrowed many learned words from SANSKRIT and PALI.

Khmer Rouge \kə-ˈmer-ˈrüzh\ (French: "Red Khmer") Radical communist movement that ruled Cambodia 1975–79. The Khmer Rouge, under the leadership of POL POT, opposed the government of the popular NORODOM SIHANOUK. They gained support after Sihanouk was toppled by LON NOL (1970) and after U.S. forces bombed the countryside in the early 1970s. In 1975 the Khmer Rouge ousted Lon Nol. Their extraordinarily brutal regime led to deaths from starvation, hardship, and executions that may have reached 2 million. Overthrown in 1979 by the Vietnamese, they retreated to remote areas and continued their struggle for power in Cambodia. The last Khmer Rouge guerrillas surrendered in 1998.

Khnum \ˈk͟nüm\ *or* **Khnemu** \ˈk͟ne-mü\ Ancient Egyptian god of fertility, associated with water and procreation. Worshiped as early as 2800 BC, he was represented as a ram with twisting horns or as a man with a ram's head. He was believed to have created humankind from clay like a potter. His main temple was at Elephantine, near present-day Aswan, and he formed a triad of deities with the goddesses Satis and Anukis. Khnum also had an important cult at Esna, south of Thebes.

Khoikhoi \ˈkȯi-ˌkȯi\ *or* **Khoikhoin** *formerly* **Hottentots** Group of peoples speaking closely related KHOISAN LANGUAGES who were among the first indigenous southern Africans encountered by Europeans. The pre-contact Khoikhoi were pastoralists who tended large herds of cattle and sheep. By 1800 Khoikhoi societies south of the Orange River in Cape Colony had been largely destroyed by disease and warfare, with the remnants either serving as bonded laborers for white farmers or blending into mixed-race frontier communities, such as the Griquas. North of the Orange River in Namibia, the Nama are the largest extant Khoikhoi ethnic group, numbering about 145,000.

Khoisan languages \ˈkȯi-ˌsän\ Group of more than 20 languages presently spoken by perhaps several hundred thousand KHOIKHOI and SAN peoples of southern Africa; the Cape Khoikhoi dialects are extinct, and a number of San languages are now either extinct or spoken by very few people. A remarkable feature of all Khoisan languages is their use of suction sounds known as CLICKS. Though clicks function as interjections in many languages, Khoisan languages, as well as adjacent BANTU LANGUAGES such as Xhosa and Zulu, completely integrate clicks into their consonant systems. The genetic unity of the Khoisan languages remains disputed.

Khomeini \k͟ō-ˈmā-nē\, **Ruhollah** *orig.* **Ruhollah Musawi** (1900–1989) Iranian cleric and revolutionary. After receiving a religious education, he settled in Qom in the early 1920s, where he became known as a Shiite scholar and opponent of Iran's ruler, MOHAMMAD REZA SHAH PAHLAVI. Acclaimed a grand AYATOLLAH in the early 1960s, he was imprisoned and then exiled (1964) for his outspoken criticism of the government. He settled in Iraq; when forced out in 1978, he settled near Paris. From exile he sent tape-recorded messages to his followers to foment revolutionary feeling. Iranian unrest increased until the shah fled in 1979; Khomeini returned two weeks later to be named Iran's political and religious leader for life. His extremely conservative domestic policies were based on a fundamentalist interpretation of Islam, and his foreign policies were both anti-Western and anticommunist. The first years of his rule saw the taking of 66 U.S. hostages (1979–81), a move that greatly angered the U.S., and the commencement of the devastating IRAN–IRAQ WAR (1980–90). He maintained power until his death, unswerving in his ideology.

Khons \ˈkȯns\ *or* **Khensu** \ˈken-sü\ *or* **Chons** \ˈkȯns\ Ancient Egyptian moon god. He was the son of the god AMON and the goddess MUT. He was usually depicted as a young man wearing a lunar disk and a rearing cobra on his head. He was also associated with baboons and was sometimes equated with THOTH, another moon god. In the late New Kingdom (c. 1100 BC) a major temple was built for Khons in the Karnak complex at Thebes.

Khorana \kō-ˈrä-nə\, **Har Gobind** (born 1922) Indian-U.S. biochemist. Born into a poor Indian family, he received his PhD from the University of Liverpool. He later taught in Canada and the U.S., from 1970 at MIT. He shared a 1968 Nobel Prize with MARSHALL WARREN NIRENBERG and ROBERT WILLIAM HOLLEY for research that helped show how the genetic components of the cell nucleus control the synthesis of proteins. His contribution was to synthesize small nucleic-acid molecules whose exact structure was known. Combined with the proper materials, his synthetic nucleic acids caused protein synthesis, just as in the cell; comparing these proteins with the nucleic acid showed which portions of the nucleic acid were the codes for each part of the protein. In 1970 he prepared the first artificial copy of a yeast gene.

Khorasan \ˌk͟ȯr-ä-ˈsän\ *or* **Khurasan** \ˌk͟ür-ä-ˈsän\ Province (pop., 1986: 5,280,000), northeastern Iran. Its capital is MASHHAD. Under Arab rule in early times, it encompassed a vast territory including what is now southern Turkmenistan and northern Afghanistan. It was overrun by Muslims c. 650. It was conquered c. 1220 by GENGHIS KHAN and c. 1380 by TIMUR. Its current frontiers were defined in 1881, and it now occupies an area of 121,887 sq mi (315,687 sq km). Its population is composed of many racial groups as a result of numerous invasions over the centuries. The languages spoken are Turkish, Persian, and Kurdish. The province gives its name to the handcrafted Khorasan carpet.

Khorram-dinan \k͟ȯr-ˌram-dē-ˈnän\ *or* **Khorramiyeh** \k͟ȯr-ˌra-mē-ˈyeh\ Islamic sect that flourished in the 9th–11th century. Though they were Muslims, some members of this sect believed in transmigration of souls and in the Zoroastrian DUALISM of good and evil deities. Like the SHIITES, they were partisans of ALI in the succession of the caliphate, and they held that Islam should be led by descendants of MUHAMMAD. They differed from the Shiites in insisting that the leadership should be hereditary in the person of ABU MUSLIM. Claiming to be a descendant of Abu, their leader Babak led a rebellion against the Abbasid caliphate of Baghdad, which ended with his capture and execution in 838. The sect died out in the 11th century.

Khosrow I \k͟ȯs-ˈrau̇\ *or* **Khosrow Anushirvan** (died 579) Persian king (r.531–79) of the Sasanian empire (see SASANIAN DYNASTY). He reformed taxation, reorganized the army, and launched military campaigns against the Hephthalites (a Central Asian people) and in Armenia, the Caucasus, and Yemen. He is said to have had Sanskrit texts imported for translation. Chess was introduced from India, and astronomy and astrology flourished. Almost any pre-Islamic structure in Iran whose origin is unknown is credited to him.

Khosrow II *or* **Khosrow Parviz** (died 628) Sasanian king (r.590–628) of Persia whose military exploits extended the empire to its maximum. He came to the throne in troubled times, assisted by Byzantium. When a new Byzantine emperor took the throne, Khosrow launched a war against the BYZANTINE EMPIRE, taking Armenia and central Asia Minor. In 613 he took Damascus; Jerusalem fell in 614. His fortunes suffered a reverse when Byzantine forces recaptured lost ground and his ablest generals were killed. Revolution within the royal family followed, and Khosrow was executed. Under his reign, silver-work and carpet weaving reached a peak and there is evidence of a renaissance in rock sculpture. After his death the empire rapidly declined, falling to the Arabs in 640. See also SASANIAN DYNASTY.

Khrushchev \krůsh-'chȯf, *Engl* 'krüsh-chef\, **Nikita (Sergeyevich)** (1894–1971) Soviet leader. Son of a miner, he joined the Communist Party in 1918. In 1934 he was elected to its Central Committee, and in 1935 he became first secretary of the Moscow party organization. He participated in JOSEPH STALIN's purges of party leaders. In 1938 he became head of the Ukrainian party and in 1939 was made a member of the Politburo. After Stalin's death in 1953, he emerged from a bitter power struggle as the party's first secretary, and NIKOLAY A. BULGANIN became premier. In 1955, on his first trip outside the Soviet Union, Khrushchev showed his flexibility and the brash, extroverted style of diplomacy that would become his trademark. At the party's TWENTIETH CONGRESS in 1956, he delivered a secret speech denouncing Stalin for his "intolerance, his brutality, his abuse of power." Thousands of political prisoners were released. Poland and Hungary used de-Stalinization to reform their regimes; Khrushchev allowed the Poles relative freedom, but he crushed the HUNGARIAN REVOLUTION by force (1956) when IMRE NAGY attempted to withdraw from the WARSAW PACT. Opposition within the party crystallized in 1957, but Khrushchev secured the dismissal of his enemies and in 1958 assumed the premiership himself. Asserting a doctrine of peaceful coexistence with capitalist nations, he toured the U.S. in 1959, but a planned Paris summit with DWIGHT D. EISENHOWER in 1960 was canceled after the U-2 AFFAIR. In 1962 he attempted to place Soviet missiles in Cuba; in the ensuing CUBAN MISSILE CRISIS, he retreated. Ideological differences and the signing of the NUCLEAR TEST-BAN TREATY (1963) led to a split with the Chinese. Agricultural failures that necessitated importation of wheat from the West, the China quarrel, and his often arbitrary administrative methods led to his forced retirement in 1964.

Khrushchev, 1960.
WERNER WOLF—BLACK STAR

Khuddaka Nikaya \'kù-də-kə-'nē-kə-yə\ (Pali: "Short Collection") Collection of Buddhist texts. It constitutes the fifth and last section of the Pali-language SUTTA PITAKA, one of the sacred texts of THERAVADA Buddhism. Written between 500 BC and the 1st century AD, its contents include sermons and doctrinal and ethical discourses attributed to the BUDDHA. It also contains all the major poetic works of the Pali canon (see TRIPITAKA).

Khulna \'k̲ùl-nə\ City (pop., 1991: 731,000), southwestern Bangladesh. Located northeast of KOLKATA (Calcutta), India, it is an important river port and trade center and is connected by road and rail to the major cities of the southern GANGES DELTA. It became a municipality in 1884 and is the seat of a university.

Khurasan See KHORASAN

Khuriya Muriya \k̲ù-'rē-yä-mù-'rē-yä\, **Jazair** *or* **Kuria Muria Islands** \'kùr-ē-ə-'mùr-ē-ə\ Island group, Oman. Located in the Arabian Sea, off the country's southeastern coast, it is comprised of five mainly uninhabited islands, with a total land area of 28 sq mi (73 sq km). Al-Hallaniyah, the largest, is sparsely inhabited. The sultan of Oman ceded the islands to Britain in 1854, and they became part of the British colony of Aden in 1937. Britain ceded the islands to Oman in 1967.

Khwarezm-Shah dynasty \'k̲wä-ˌrez-ᵊm-'shä\ (c. 1077–1231) Central Asian and Persian dynasty that first ruled as vassals of the SELJUQ DYNASTY and then independently. It was founded by a kitchen slave, Anustegin Gharachai, who was a Seljuq appointee. At its height the dynasty's territory extended from India to Anatolia. It fell to GENGHIS KHAN in 1231.

Khwarizm \'k̲wä-ˌriz-ᵊm\ *or* **Khwarezm** \'k̲wä-ˌrez-ᵊm\ Historic region along the AMU DARYA, in modern Turkmenistan and Uzbekistan. It formed part of the empire of Achaemenian Persia in the 6th–4th century BC. The Arabs conquered it in the 7th century AD. In the following centuries it was ruled by many, including the MONGOLS and Timurids, until the early 16th century, when it became the center of the khanate of Khiva. In 1873 Russia conquered it and made it a protectorate. After the RUSSIAN REVOLUTION OF 1917, the khanate was replaced by a Soviet republic, which was later dissolved and incorporated into the U.S.S.R.

Khwarizmi, al- See AL-KHWARIZMI

Khyber Pass \'kī-bər\ Pass in the Safed Koh Range on the border between Afghanistan and Pakistan. About 33 mi (53 km) long, it has historically been the gateway for invasions of the Indian subcontinent from the northwest; it was traversed by Persians, Greeks, Mughals, Afghans, and the British. The Pashtun Afridi people of the Khyber area long resisted foreign control, but during the Second Anglo–Afghan War in 1879, the Khyber tribes came under British rule. It is now controlled by Pakistan.

Kiangsi See JIANGXI

Kiangsu See JIANGSU

Kiarostami, Abbas (born 1940) Iranian director. Kiarostami was hired in 1969 by the Institute for the Intellectual Develpment of Children and Young Adults to establish its film division. The institute produced his first film as a director, the lyrical short *Nan va kucheh* (1970; "Bread and Alley"), which featured elements that define his work: improvised performances, documentary textures, and real-life rhythms. His first feature, *Mosafer* (1974; "The Traveler"), is a portrait of a troubled adolescent. In the 1980s Kiarostami created documentaries examining the lives of Iranian schoolchildren. Kiarostami explored the overlap between film and reality throughout the 1990s in films such as *Namay-e nazdik* (1990; "Close-Up"). His film *Badkonake sefid* (1995; "The White Balloon"), a look at life in Tehran through the eyes of a seven-year-old girl, garnered international critical acclaim.

kibbutz \ki-'bùts\ Israeli communal settlement in which all wealth is held in common and profits are reinvested in the settlement. The first kibbutz was founded in 1909; currently there are some 200, with a total population exceeding 100,000. Adults live in private quarters; children are generally housed and cared for as a group. Meals are prepared and eaten communally. Members have regular meetings to discuss business and to take votes on matters requiring decisions. Jobs may be assigned by rotation, by choice, or by skill. The kibbutz movement has declined in recent decades. See also MOSHAV.

Kiche See QUICHE

Kickapoo ALGONQUIAN-speaking North American Indian people related to the SAUK and FOX and formerly inhabiting what is now southern central Wisconsin. The Kickapoo were formidable warriors, whose raids took them as far as the southern and northeastern U.S. About 1765, after dispatching the Illinois Indians, they settled near Peoria, Ill., but later moved under pressure from advancing whites to Missouri, Kansas, Oklahoma, Texas, and Mexico. By the 19th century, central tribal authority had broken down and chiefs of the various bands had become autonomous. The Kickapoo resisted acculturation and sought to retain their old ways. Today the remaining Kickapoo (numbering 2,500) live on reservations in northern Mexico, Oklahoma, and Kansas.

Kidd, Michael *orig.* **Milton Gruenwald** (born 1919) U.S. dancer, choreographer, and director. Born in Brooklyn, N.Y., he studied at the School of American Ballet, dancing with that company in 1937 and later with American Ballet Theatre, for which he choreographed *On Stage I* (1945). He has choreographed many Broadway musicals, including four that won successive Tony awards: *Guys and Dolls* (1951), *Can-Can* (1953), *Li'l Abner* (1956), and *Destry Rides Again* (1959). His film credits include *The Bandwagon* (1953), *Seven Brides for Seven Brothers* (1954), and *Hello, Dolly!* (1969).

Kidd, William *known as* **Captain Kidd** (1645?–1701) British privateer and pirate. He was sailing as a legitimate privateer for Britain when he was commissioned in 1695 to apprehend pirates who molested the ships of the East India Co. He himself turned pirate on the voyage, took several ships, and mortally wounded his gunner, William Moore. He surrendered in New York in 1699, having been promised a pardon. Sent to England for trial, he was found guilty of Moore's murder and five piracy counts, and was hanged. Some of his treasure was recovered from

Gardiners Island (off Long Island), but much has apparently never been found. After his death he attained semilegendary status and was romanticized as a dashing swashbuckler.

Kidder, Alfred V(incent) (1885–1963) U.S. archaeologist, the foremost archaeologist of the American Southwest and Mesoamerica of his day. Born in Marquette, Mich., Kidder received his PhD from Harvard University (1914) for developing the first effective pottery typology relating to the prehistory of the southwestern U.S. He later extended these interests to a classic study (1924) of the development of the PUEBLO cultures and to the creation (1927) of a widely used archaeological classification system (the Pecos system) for the Southwest. He also organized (1929) an interdisciplinary program that resulted in a far-reaching survey of cultural history in the Old and New Maya empires of Mexico and Central America. He taught at Phillips (Andover) Academy (1915–35) and at Harvard University (1939–50) and oversaw various programs at the Carnegie Institution (1927–50).

kiddush \'ki-dəsh, ki-'düsh\ Jewish prayer or blessing recited over a cup of wine immediately before the meal on the eve of the SABBATH or a major festival, acknowledging the sanctity of the day that is beginning. It is usually performed by the head of the household, but it may involve all family members. After the recitation, each person sips wine from the cup. In the ASHKENAZI tradition, two loaves of bread on the table signify the manna gathered by the Israelites during their years of wandering in the wilderness.

Kiderlen-Wächter \'kē-dər-lən-'vek-tər\, **Alfred von** (1852–1912) German diplomat. A career diplomat, he became foreign secretary in 1910 and pursued a belligerent foreign policy, working to establish Germany as the leading power in Europe through the TRIPLE ALLIANCE. In the second of the MOROCCAN CRISES (1911) he refused conciliatory offers by the French government and excluded Britain from negotiations. Though German expansionists denounced the peace treaty as too lenient, Kiderlen's brusque and forceful posturing during the crisis significantly aggravated the international tensions that led to World War I.

kidnapping Crime of seizing, confining, abducting, or carrying away a person by force or fraud, often to subject him or her to involuntary servitude, in an attempt to demand a ransom, or in furtherance of another crime. Most countries consider it a grave offense punishable by a long prison sentence or death.

kidney One of a pair of organs that maintain water balance and expel metabolic wastes. Human kidneys are bean-shaped organs about 4 in. (10 cm) long, in the small of the back. They filter the entire 5-quart (about 4.5-liter) water content of the blood every 45 minutes. Glucose, minerals, and needed water are returned to the blood by reabsorption. The remaining fluid and wastes pass into collecting ducts, flowing to the ureter and bladder as urine. Each kidney has over 1 million functional units (NEPHRONS) involved in the process of filtration and reabsorption. The kidneys also secrete renin, an enzyme involved in blood pressure regulation. Disorders include KIDNEY FAILURE, KIDNEY STONES, and NEPHRITIS. See also URINARY SYSTEM. See illustration opposite.

kidney failure *or* **renal failure** Partial or complete loss of KIDNEY function. Acute failure causes reduced URINE output and blood chemical imbalance, including UREMIA. Most patients recover within six weeks. Damage to various kidney structures can result from chemical exposure, major blood loss, CRUSH INJURY, HYPERTENSION, severe BURNS, severe kidney infections, DIABETES MELLITUS, renal artery or urinary tract blockage, and liver diseases. Complications include HEART FAILURE, pulmonary edema, and high potassium levels. Chronic failure usually results from long-term kidney diseases. The blood becomes too acidic, bones can lose calcium, and nerves can degenerate. The kidneys can sustain life until they lose about 90% of their function. If one is removed, the other increases in size and function to compensate. Failure of both usually requires DIALYSIS or KIDNEY TRANSPLANT.

kidney stone *or* **renal calculus** Mass of minerals and organic matter that may form in a KIDNEY. URINE contains many SALTS in solution, and low fluid volume or high mineral concentration can cause these salts to precipitate and grow, forming stones. Large stones can block urine flow, be a focus for infection, or cause renal colic (painful spasms). They can obstruct the URINARY SYSTEM at various points. Treatment deals with any underlying problem (e.g., infection or obstruction), tries to dissolve stones with drugs or ULTRASOUND (lithotripsy), or removes large ones surgically.

kidney transplant *or* **renal transplant** Replacement of a diseased or damaged KIDNEY with one from a living relative or a legally dead donor. The former's tissue type is more likely to match, reducing the chance of rejection, and gives the patient more time for DIALYSIS before surgery to control existing disease; but removal puts the donor at risk, and a kidney from a dead donor is more likely to be available. The new kidney is implanted and its blood vessels and ureter sewn in place. A near-normal life may be resumed within two months, but the drugs that prevent rejection leave the patient vulnerable to infection. See also TRANSPLANT.

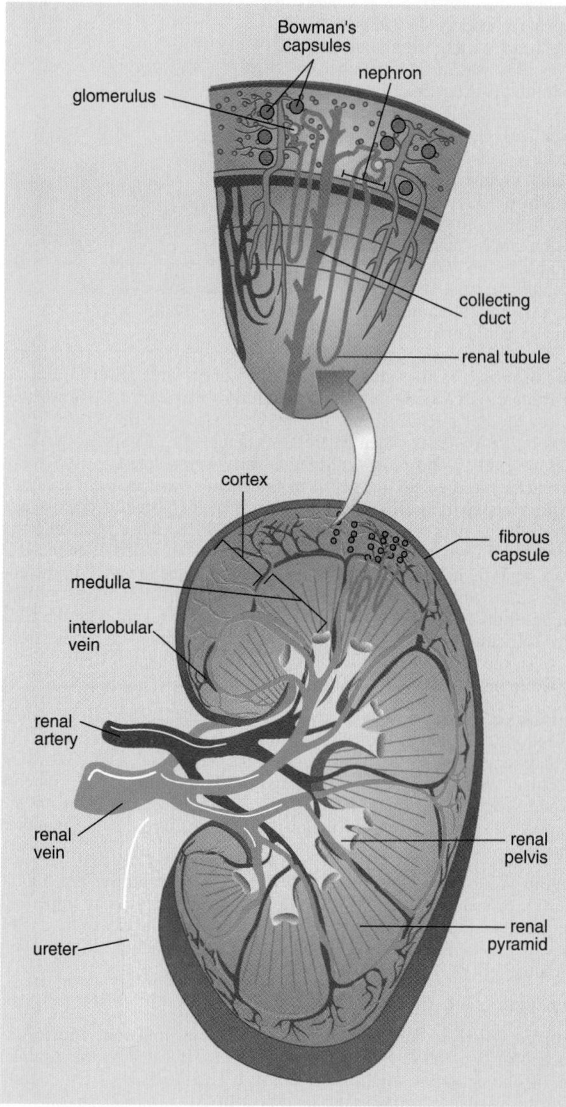

Cross section of a kidney. The kidney is made up of an outermost cortex, a middle medulla, and an inner pelvis. Blood enters via the renal artery, which branches into smaller vessels, each of which terminates in a tuft of capillaries (glomerulus). Fluids from the blood are forced out of the glomerulus into the surrounding Bowman's capsule during filtration. The glomerulus, Bowman's capsule, and associated renal tubule make up the nephron. Any important substances filtered from the blood (incl. glucose, minerals, and much of the water) are returned to it by reabsorption in the renal tubule. The medulla is divided into triangular masses of tissue (renal pyramids) that contain the collecting ducts for the fluid (urine) not reabsorbed into the blood. Water is further removed from the urine as it passes through the collecting ducts into the funnel-shaped renal pelvis, which leads to the ureter.

Kido Takayoshi \'kē-dō-ˌtä-kä-'yō-shē\ *or* **Kido Koin** \'kō-ēn\ (1833–1877) With Saigo Takamori and Okubo Toshimichi, one of the three giants of the Meiji Restoration of 1868. He became head of the government of the han (domain) of Choshu and in that capacity plotted with Saigo and Okubo of Satsuma to overthrow the Tokugawa shogunate. In the new government, Kido was responsible for transferring the capital from Kyoto to Edo (renamed Tokyo) and for persuading the heads of the large han to return their domains to the emperor. He visited Europe in 1871 and on returning helped block a plan to invade Korea. In the late 1870s he worked for the establishment of a Western-style constitution.

Kiefer \'kē-fər\, **Anselm** (born 1945) German painter. In 1970 he studied under the conceptual artist Joseph Beuys. In such huge paintings as *Germany's Spiritual Heroes* (1973) he used visual symbols, somber colors, and naive drawing to comment with irony and sarcasm on Germany's tragic past. In the 1980s his colossal paintings acquired an intense physical presence by means of perspectival devices and unusual textures. He is one of the most prominent figures in late-20th-century Neo-Expressionism.

Kiel \'kēl\ City (pop., 1999 est.: 235,500), capital of Schleswig-Holstein state, northern Germany. A port at the eastern end of the Kiel Canal, it was founded in 1242. It entered the Hanseatic League in 1284; in 1773 it became part of Denmark. Schleswig-Holstein passed to Prussia in 1866, and Kiel became its capital in 1917. An important naval base, it was the target of Allied bombing during World War II. It is the site of St. Nicholas Church (c. 1240), a ducal palace (c. 1280), and the Christian-Albrechts University of Kiel (founded 1665).

Kienholz \'kēn-ˌhȯlts\, **Edward** (1927–1994) U.S. sculptor. Born in Fairfield, Wash., he pursued painting until he moved to Los Angeles and began producing large wooden reliefs for walls (1954). His controversial environmental sculptures, begun in the late 1950s, were elaborately detailed three-dimensional assemblages that harshly indicted U.S. society. His most famous walk-in scenes include *Roxy's*, a replica of a 1943 Los Angeles bordello, and *The Beanery*, a reproduction of a decrepit bar with 17 figures, piped-in smells, jukebox music, and background conversation. Critics labeled some of his images repulsive or pornographic.

Kieran the Younger See St. Ciaran of Clonmacnoise

Kierkegaard \'kir-kə-ˌgärd\, **Søren (Aabye)** (1813–1855) Danish religious philosopher, regarded as the founder of existentialism. He studied theology at the University of Copenhagen. He is famous for his critique of systematic rational philosophy. He attacked G. W. F. Hegel's attempt to systematize the whole of existence, declaring that a system of existence cannot be constructed, since existence is incomplete and constantly developing. In *Concluding Unscientific Postscript* (1846), he proposed that "the objective uncertainty maintained in the most passionate spirit of dedication is truth, the highest truth for one existing"—that is, that subjectivity is truth. With this stance, he intended to clear the ground for an adequate consideration of faith and religion, specifically Christianity. His most famous works include *Either/Or* (1843), *Fear and Trembling* (1843), and *The Sickness unto Death* (1849). He insistently attacked the organized church in his later years; exhausted by the strain, he died at 42. His greatest influence was felt in the 20th century, on such thinkers as Karl Barth, Karl Jaspers, Martin Heidegger, and Martin Buber.

Kierkegaard, drawing by Christian Kierkegaard, c. 1840; in a private collection.

BY COURTESY OF THE ROYAL DANISH MINISTRY OF FOREIGN AFFAIRS

kieselguhr See diatomaceous earth

Kiev \'kē-ef\ *Ukrainian* **Kyyiv** \'kyiv\ City (pop., 1999 est.: 2,620,900), capital of Ukraine. Located along the Dnieper River, it was founded in the 8th century, and by the late 9th century its princes had expanded their territory to establish the state of Kievan Rus. In 1240 it was destroyed by the Tatars of the Golden Horde; after being rebuilt it came successively under Lithuanian, Polish, and Cossack rule. It was incorporated into Russia in 1793, and in 1934 it became the capital of the Ukrainian S.S.R. It remained the capital on Ukraine independence in 1991. An important industrial city, it is also an educational and cultural center; it is the seat of a state university and the Academy of Sciences of Ukraine.

Kievan Rus \'kē-vən-'rüs\ First eastern Slavic state. It was founded by the Viking Oleg, ruler of Novgorod from c. 879, who seized Smolensk and Kiev (882), which became the capital of Kievan Rus. Extending his rule, he united local Slavic and Finnish tribes, defeated the Khazars, and in 911 arranged trade agreements with Constantinople. Kievan Rus peaked in the 10th–11th century under Vladimir I and Yaroslav, when Kiev became eastern Europe's chief political and cultural center. At Yaroslav's death in 1054, his sons divided the empire into warring factions. The 13th-century Mongol conquest decisively ended its power.

Kigali \kē-'gä-lē\ City (pop., 1996 est.: 356,000), capital of Rwanda. Located in the middle of the country, it was a trading center during the German colonial administration (after 1895), and a regional center during the Belgian colonial period (1919–62). It became the capital of independent Rwanda in 1962. The fast-growing city was adversely affected by the country's political turmoil in the 1990s.

Kikuyu \ki-'kü-yü\ Bantu-speaking people who live in the highland area of southern central Kenya, near Mount Kenya. Numbering over 6 million, they are the largest ethnic group in Kenya. They traditionally lived in separate domestic family homesteads, but during the Mau Mau rebellion the British colonial government moved them into villages for security purposes, and this arrangement became permanent. Their traditional economy rested on intensive hoe cultivation of millet and other crops; the main modern cash crops are coffee, corn, and fruits and vegetables. Many Kikuyu serve in government posts.

Kilauea \ˌkē-lau̇-'ā-ə\ Crater, eastern side of Mauna Loa, Hawaii Volcanoes National Park. The world's largest active volcanic crater, it is about 3 mi (5 km) long, 2 mi (3.2 km) wide, and 500 ft (150 m) deep, and is at an altitude of 4,090 ft (1.250 m). In its floor is the vent known as Halemaumau Pit, legendary home of the fire goddess Pele. Its frequent eruptions are usually contained within the vent as a boiling lake of lava, but occasionally the lava escapes; since 1983 a series of eruptions produced lava that reached the sea 30 mi (48 km) away.

Kilburn, Thomas (born 1921) British computer scientist. His book *A Storage System for Use with Binary Digital Computing Machines* (1947) influenced several U.S. and Russian organizations to adopt his techniques. With Frederic C. Williams (1911–1977) he designed the Ferranti Mark I, one of the earliest stored-program computers produced in England (1951) and the first commercial computer. In 1964 he formed Britain's first computer-science department and became its first professor.

Kilby, Jack (St. Clair) (born 1923) U.S. inventor. Born in Jefferson City, Mo., he studied at the University of Wisconsin. In 1958 he joined Texas Instruments; there he envisioned all of a circuit's components made from silicon and integrated on a single surface, which led to the invention of the computer chip. He also coinvented a handheld calculator with a thermal printer that is used in portable data terminals. The owner of more than 60 patents, he has received the National Medal of Science (1970), the Kyoto Prize (1993), and the Nobel Prize for Physics (2000), shared with Hervert Kroemer (born 1928) and Zhores Alferov (born 1930).

kilim \kē-'lēm\ Pileless floor covering handwoven by tapestry techniques in Anatolia, the Balkans, and parts of Iran. The name is also given to a variety of brocaded, embroidered, warp-faced, and other flat-woven rugs and bags. A common characteristic is a slit that occurs wherever two colors meet along a vertical line in the pattern. The finest examples are silk 16th–17th-century pieces from Kashan, Iran. The largest kilims are produced in Turkey, as are smaller examples and prayer kilims (prayer rugs); Turkish weavers often use cotton for the white areas, and small details may be brocaded. The kilims of the southern Balkans, originally copies of Turkish types, gradually developed individual styles. Kilims become progressively less Oriental in color and pattern as the distance from Turkey increases.

Kilimanjaro \ˌki-lə-mən-ˈjä-rō\ Volcanic mountain, northeastern Tanzania. Situated in Kilimanjaro National Park (established 1973), it includes the peaks of three extinct volcanoes: Kibo, Mawensi, and Shira. Its highest peak is Kibo, which rises to 19,340 ft (5,895 m) and is the highest point in Africa. The first Europeans to see Kilimanjaro were German missionaries (1848). Kibo was first scaled in 1889 and Mawensi (16,896 ft, or 5,150 m tall) in 1912.

Crater rim of Kilimanjaro at dawn.
GERALD CUBITT

killdeer Bird *(Charadrius,* sometimes *Oxyechus, vociferus)* that frequents grassy mudflats, pastures, and fields. Its name is suggestive of its loud, insistent whistle. It is about 10 in. (25 cm) long and has a brown back, a white belly, and two black breast bands. Killdeers breed throughout North America and in northwestern South America. They migrate only to escape snow, returning before most songbirds. They eat beetles, grasshoppers, dragonflies, and other insects. To protect their young from predators, killdeers will feign injury and flutter awkwardly away from the nest, luring predators with the promise of an easy kill.

killer whale *or* **orca** TOOTHED WHALE *(Orcinus orca)* found in all seas from the Arctic to the Antarctic, the largest of the oceanic DOLPHINS. The male may be 30 ft (9 m) long and weigh over 10,000 lbs (4,500 kg). The killer whale is black, with white on the underparts, above each eye, and on each flank. The snout is blunt, and the strong jaws have 40–50 large, sharp, conical teeth. Killer whales live in groups of a few to about 50 individuals. They feed on fishes, cephalopods, penguins, and marine mammals; though they are fierce predators of seals and even other whales, there is no recorded instance of a killer whale attacking a human. They are often kept in captivity and trained as performers in marine shows.

Killer whale (*Orcinus orca*).
MIAMI SEAQUARIUM

killifish Any of a few hundred species of egg-laying topminnows (see GUPPY) in the family Cyprinodontidae, found worldwide in brackish, salt, and freshwater, including desert hot springs. Some species grow to 6 in. (15 cm) long. Killifish eat plant or animal material at the surface. Many species (e.g., the lyretail) are attractively colored and are kept in home aquariums. Killifish are also valuable as bait and in mosquito control. Pupfish *(Cyprinodon)* inhabit California coasts and certain western salt-lake shores. Some pupfish are listed as endangered; the Tecopa pupfish (*C. nevadensis;* 1.5 in., or 0.6 cm, long) was declared extinct in 1981.

Killifish (*Fundulus chrysotus*).
GENE WOLFSHEIMER

Killy \kē-ˈlē\, **Jean-Claude** (born 1943) French skier. Born in Saint-Cloud, he was reared in an Alpine ski resort. He became the European champion in 1965, and in 1966 he won the world-combined championship (downhill, slalom, and giant slalom). In 1967 he won the first World Cup for men, repeating this triumph in 1968. In the 1968 Winter Olympics he became the second skier in history to sweep the Alpine events (after Austria's Toni Sailer in 1956). He retired in 1968 but returned as a professional in 1972.

kiln \ˈkiln, ˈkil\ Technique for separating constituents of an ore, metal, or alloy by partial melting. When the material is heated to a temperature where one of the constituents melts and the other remains solid, the liquid constituent can be drained off. It was formerly used for extracting antimony minerals from ore, separating silver from copper with the use of lead as a solvent, and refining tin.

kilt Knee-length, skirtlike garment worn by men as part of the traditional national garb, or Highland dress, of Scotland. It is made of permanently pleated wool and wrapped around the wearer's waist so that the pleats are in the back and the flat ends overlap in front. It is usually worn with the plaid, a rectangular length of cloth draped over the left shoulder. Both kilt and plaid are woven with a TARTAN pattern. The ensemble, which developed in the 17th century, is worn for ordinary purposes as well as for special occasions. Highland dress is the uniform of Scottish regiments in the British army; kilts were worn into battle as recently as World War II.

Kilwa (Kisiwani) \ˈkēl-wä\ Former Islamic city-state, located on an island off the coast of modern southern Tanzania. Founded in the late 10th century by settlers from Arabia and Iran, it became one of the most active commercial centers on the eastern coast of Africa. After being held by the Portuguese in the 16th century, it declined in importance and was abandoned. Extensive ruins remain, including mosques, a Portuguese fort, and a 13th–14th century palace. The modern town of Kilwa on the Tanzanian coast was probably founded in the early 19th century by settlers from the island.

Kim Chong Il \ˈkim-ˈchəŋ-ˈil\ (born 1941) Son of KIM IL-SUNG. He was designated his father's successor in 1980 and became North Korea's de facto leader on his father's death in 1994. Known in North Korea as the Dear Leader, he makes few public appearances, and facts about him difficult to verify. Severe food shortages have plagued North Korea under his administration.

Kim Dae Jung \ˈkim-ˈdī-ˈjəŋ\ (born 1925) South Korean politician and first opposition leader to become president. He first entered politics in 1954, opposing the policies of Syngman RHEE, but did not win a seat in government until 1961. After several arrests in the 1970s, Kim was sentenced to death on charges of sedition and conspiracy; that sentence was commuted to 20 years in prison. In 1985, after a brief exile in the U.S., he resumed his role as a leader of the political opposition. In 1997 he was elected president of South Korea. In 2000 he received the Nobel Peace Prize.

Kim Il-sung \ˈkim-ˈil-ˈsu̇ŋ\ (1912–1994) Communist leader of North Korea from 1948 until his death. When Korea was effectively divided between a Soviet-occupied northern half and a U.S.-supported southern half at the end of World War II, Kim Il-sung helped establish a communist provisional government and became its first premier. He invaded South Korea in an attempt to reunify the country, but the subsequent KOREAN WAR ended without reunification. After the war, Kim introduced a philosophy of self-reliance under which North Korea tried to develop its economy with little help from foreign countries. His omnipresent personality cult enabled him to rule unchallenged for 46 years in one of the world's most isolated and repressive societies. See also NORTH KOREA.

Kim Young Sam \ˈkim-ˈyəŋ-ˈsam\ (born 1927) South Korean moderate opposition leader who served as president (1993–98) after his party merged with the ruling party. First elected to South Korea's National Assembly in 1954, he served there until his expulsion in 1979 by Pres. Park Chung Hee, which touched off riots and demonstrations that preceded Park's assassination. The military takeover of Gen. Chun Doo Hwan in 1980 led to Kim's being put under house arrest until 1983. In 1990 he merged his party with the ruling Democratic Justice Party, a move that helped him win the presidency in 1992. He enacted reforms to end political corruption, and his term was one of rising prosperity for Korea until 1997, when Korea became caught up in an Asian financial crisis.

Kimberley City (pop., urban area, 1996: 170,432), South Africa. Founded in 1871 shortly after the discovery of diamonds in the area, it was the capital of Griqualand West (1873–80) before it became part of Cape Colony. It was besieged by the Boers for four months (1899–1900) during the SOUTH AFRICAN WAR. It is still a diamond-mining center; its outskirts are marked by immense pits and heaps of earth, the aftermath of mining operations. The DE BEERS and Kimberley mines are nearby.

kimberlite *or* **blue ground** Dark, heavy, often fragmented igneous rock that may contain DIAMONDS in the rock matrix. Kimberlite is a MICA peridotite, an ultrabasic rock type with a complex and often highly altered mineral composition. It occurs in the Kimberley district of South Africa and the Kimberley and Lake Argyle regions of Australia, as well as near Ithaca, N.Y.

kimono Garment worn by Japanese men and women from the Early Nara period (645–724) to the present. The essential kimono is an ankle-length gown with long, full sleeves and a V-neck. It is lapped left over right across the chest and secured at the waist by a broad sash known as an obi. The contemporary wide obi dates only from the 18th century. Though the kimono is originally of Chinese origin, its great beauty is attributable to 17th- and 18th-century Japanese designers.

kindergarten School or class for children aged 4–6, a prominent part of PRESCHOOL EDUCATION. The kindergarten originated in the early 19th century as an outgrowth of the ideas and practices of ROBERT OWEN in Britain, JOHANN HEINRICH PESTALOZZI in Switzerland and his pupil FRIEDRICH FROEBEL in Germany (who coined the term), and MARIA MONTESSORI in Italy. Kindergartens generally stress the social and emotional growth of the child, encouraging self-understanding through play activities and greater freedom rather than the imposition of adult ideas.

Kindi, al- *in full* **Yakub ibn Ishaq al-Sabah al-Kindi** (died c. 870) First prominent Islamic philosopher. He worked in Iraq under the caliphs al-MAMUN and al-Mutasim. One of the first Arab students of the Greek philosophers, he translated important Greek works into Arabic and tried to combine the views of PLATO and ARISTOTLE into a new system. His short treatises considered the philosophical questions set forth by NEOPLATONISM. He also wrote over 270 scientific treatises on such subjects as astrology, Indian arithmetic, sword manufacturing, and cooking.

kinematics \ˌki-nə-ˈma-tiks\ Branch of physics concerned with the geometrically possible motion of a body or system of bodies, without consideration of the forces involved. It describes the spatial position of bodies or systems, their VELOCITIES, and their ACCELERATION. See also DYNAMICS.

kinesiology \ki-ˌnē-zē-ˈä-lə-jē\ Study of the mechanics and anatomy of human movement and their roles in promoting health and reducing disease. Kinesiology has direct applications to fitness and health, including developing exercise programs for people with and without disabilities, preserving the independence of older people, preventing disease due to trauma and neglect, and rehabilitating people after disease or injury. Kinesiologists also develop more accessible furniture and environments for people with limited movement and find ways to enhance individual and team efficiency. Kinesiology research encompasses the biochemistry of muscle contraction and tissue fluids, bone mineralization, responses to exercise, how physical skills are developed, work efficiency, and the anthropology of play.

kinetic energy \kə-ˈnet-ik\ Form of energy that an object has by reason of its motion. The kind of motion may be translation (motion along a path from one place to another), rotation about an axis, vibration, or any combination of motions. The total kinetic energy of a body or system is equal to the sum of the kinetic energies resulting from each type of motion. The kinetic energy of an object depends on its MASS and VELOCITY. For instance, the amount of kinetic energy KE of an object in translational motion is equal to one-half the product of its mass m and the square of its velocity v, or $KE = \frac{1}{2}mv^2$, provided the speed is low relative to the speed of light. At higher speeds, RELATIVITY changes the relationship.

kinetic sculpture Sculpture in which movement (as of a motor-driven part or a changing electronic image) is a basic element. Actual movement became an important aspect of sculpture in the 20th century. Pioneers such as NAUM GABO, MARCEL DUCHAMP, LASZLO MOHOLY-NAGY, and ALEXANDER CALDER produced movement by such means as water, mechanical devices, and air currents (as in Calder's MOBILES). Neo-Dadaist works such as JEAN TINGUELY's self-destructing *Homage to New York* (1960) embody the concept of a sculpture that functions as both an object and an event—a "happening."

kinetic theory of gases Theory based on a simple description of a gas, from which many properties of gases can be derived. Established primarily by JAMES CLERK MAXWELL and LUDWIG BOLTZMANN, the theory is one of the most important concepts in modern science. The simplest kinetic model is based on the assumptions that (1) a gas is composed of a large number of identical MOLECULES moving in random directions, separated by distances that are large compared to their size; (2) the molecules undergo perfectly elastic (no energy loss) collisions with each other and with the walls of the container; and (3) the transfer of KINETIC ENERGY between molecules is heat. This model describes a PERFECT GAS but is a reasonable approximation to a real gas. Using the kinetic theory, scientists can relate the independent motion of molecules of gases to their pressure, volume, temperature, viscosity, and heat conductivity.

king Male sovereign over a nation or territory, of higher rank than any other ruler except an EMPEROR. A king's female counterpart is a queen. Some kings have been elected, as in medieval Germany, but most inherit the position. The community may concentrate all spiritual and political power in the sovereign, or power may be shared constitutionally with other government institutions. Some kings are heads of state but not heads of government. In the past, some were regarded as semidivine representatives of God on earth; others were gods in their own right or supernatural beings who became gods after death (see DIVINE KINGSHIP). Since the 17th century, the power held by monarchs has been widely regarded as deriving from the people. See also CONSTITUTIONAL MONARCHY, CZAR, KHAN, MONARCHY, PHARAOH.

King, B. B. *orig.* **Riley B.** (born 1925) U.S. BLUES guitarist. Born in Itta Bena, Miss., and reared in the Mississippi Delta, he was influenced early by gospel music. He worked for a time as a disc jockey in Memphis, where he acquired the nickname B. B. (for Blues Boy). His first hit, "Three O'Clock Blues" (1951), was followed by a long succession of others, including "Every Day I Have the Blues" and "The Thrill Is Gone." To his own impassioned vocal calls, King plays single-string guitar responses with a distinctive vibrato, in a style influenced by Delta blues guitarists and DJANGO REINHARDT. By the late 1960s rock guitarists were acknowledging his influence and introducing King and his guitar, Lucille, to the white public. He remains the most successful bluesman of all time.

B.B. King, 1972.
BY COURTESY OF SIDNEY A. SEIDENBERG, INC.

King, Billie Jean *orig.* **Billie Jean Moffitt** (born 1943) U.S. tennis player. Born in Long Beach, Cal., she learned to play tennis on public courts. When she won her first Wimbledon doubles championship in 1961, she was part of the youngest team to do so. She went on to capture a record 20 Wimbledon titles (singles, women's doubles, and mixed doubles) from the mid-1960s to the mid-1970s. She also won several U.S. singles titles (1967, 1971–72, 1974) and the Australian (1968) and French (1972) titles. She was ranked no. 1 in the U.S. seven times and no. 1 in the world five times. In 1973 she defeated the 55-year-old former men's champion Bobby Riggs in a hugely publicized "battle of the sexes." She was cofounder and first president (1974) of the Women's Tennis Assn., and in 1974, with her husband, Larry King, she also founded World TeamTennis, of which she has served as director. She wrote two autobiographies (with cowriters) and a history of women's tennis, and she cofounded the magazine *Womensport*.

Billie Jean King.
COLORSPORT

King, Larry *orig.* **Lawrence Harvey Zeiger** (born 1933) U.S. talk-show host. Born in Brooklyn, N.Y., he worked in Miami as a radio disc jockey, talk-show host, and freelance broadcaster and writer (1957–78). He hosted the popular national radio talk show *The Larry King Show* (1978–94), and, since 1985, the television talk show *Larry King Live* on CNN. By 2000 he had conducted over 30,000 interviews on his two shows.

King, Martin Luther, Jr. *orig.* **Michael Luther King, Jr.** (1929–1968) U.S. civil-rights leader. Born in Atlanta, he became an adherent of nonviolence philosophies while in college. Ordained a Baptist minister in 1954, he became pastor of a church in Montgomery, Ala. He received his doctorate from Boston University in 1955. He was selected to head the Montgomery Improvement Assn., whose efforts soon ended the city's public-transport segregation policies. In 1957 he formed the SOUTHERN CHRISTIAN LEADERSHIP CONFERENCE and began lecturing nationwide, urging active nonviolence to achieve civil rights for blacks. In 1960 he returned to Atlanta to become copastor with his father of Ebenezer Baptist Church. He was arrested for protesting segregation at a lunch counter and jailed; the case drew national attention, and presidential candidate JOHN F. KENNEDY interceded to obtain his release. In 1963 King helped organize the March on Washington, an assembly of more than 200,000 protestors at which he made his famous "I have a dream" speech. The march influenced the passage of the 1964 CIVIL RIGHTS ACT, and King was awarded the 1964 Nobel Peace Prize. In 1965 he was criticized from within the civil-rights movement for yielding to state troopers at a march in Selma, Ala., and failing in the effort to change Chicago's housing segregation policies. He broadened his advocacy to address the plight of the poor of all races and oppose the Vietnam War. In 1968 he went to Memphis, Tenn., to support a strike by sanitation workers; there on April 4, he was assassinated by JAMES EARL RAY. King's doctorate became a subject of controversy in 1989–90, when evidence surfaced that showed King had plagiarized his dissertation. A U.S. national holiday is celebrated in King's honor on the third Monday in January.

Martin Luther King, Jr.
JULIAN WASSER

King, Rufus (1755–1827) U.S. diplomat. Born in Scarborough, Mass., he was a delegate to the Continental Congress (1784–87), where he called for a new constitution. He helped frame the U.S. Constitution and effected its ratification by Massachusetts. In 1788 he moved to New York, where he was elected one of its first U.S. senators (1789–96, 1813–25). He became a strong Federalist leader and introduced the antislavery provision of the 1787 document that formed part of the NORTHWEST ORDINANCES. He served as ambassador to Britain 1796–1803 and 1825–26.

King, Stephen (Edwin) (born 1947) U.S. writer. Born in Portland, Me., and educated at the University of Maine, he has continued to live a quiet life in the state. His enormously popular books, which have made him one of the world's best-selling writers, blend horror, the macabre, fantasy, and science fiction. *Carrie* (1974), his first published novel and an immediate success, was followed by *Salem's Lot* (1975), *The Shining* (1977), *The Stand* (1978), *The Dead Zone* (1979), *Firestarter* (1980), *Cujo* (1981), *It* (1986), *Misery* (1987), *The Dark Half* (1989), the series *The Dark Tower* (1992–97), *Rose Madder* (1996), the series *The Green Mile* (1996), and *Bag of Bones* (1998), among many others. Many have become highly successful films.

King, W(illiam) L(yon) Mackenzie (1874–1950) Prime minister of Canada (1921–26, 1926–30, 1935–48). Born in Berlin, Ontario, the grandson of WILLIAM L. MACKENZIE, he was deputy minister of labor (1900–8), then was appointed Canada's first minister of labor (1909–11). Reelected to the Canadian Parliament (1919), he became leader of the Liberal Party. As prime minister, he led the government with support from an alliance of Liberals and Progressives. He effected a more independent relationship between the Commonwealth nations and Britain. During and after World War II he unified a country often divided between English and French constituents.

King, William Rufus de Vane (1786–1853) U.S. politician. Born in Sampson Co., N.C., he served in the U.S. House of Representatives 1811–16. He moved to Alabama and became one of its first U.S. senators (1819–44, 1848–52). He was appointed minister to France (1844–46), where he convinced the government not to interfere with U.S. annexation of Texas from Mexico. In 1852 he was elected U.S. vice president under FRANKLIN PIERCE, but died before taking office.

King Cotton Phrase used before the AMERICAN CIVIL WAR to denote the economic supremacy of Southern cotton production. The concept first appeared in the book *Cotton Is King* (1855) and was echoed by Southern politicians, who believed that cotton's economic and political power would bring victory if secession led to war. The South expected support from Britain, a major cotton importer, but Britain instead developed alternative sources of cotton within its empire. Dependence on a one-crop economy contributed to the South's weak position after the Civil War.

king crab *or* **Alaskan king crab** *or* **Japanese crab** Marine DECAPOD *(Paralithodes camtschatica),* an edible CRAB. It is found in the shallow waters off Japan and along the Alaska coast; it also inhabits the Bering Sea. One of the largest crabs, it often weighs 10 lbs (4.5 kg) or more. Its size and tasty flesh make it a valued food, and large numbers are fished commercially each year.

King George Sound Inlet of the Indian Ocean, southern coast of Western Australia. With an area of 35 sq mi (91 sq km), its harbors are Oyster Harbor and Princess Royal Harbor (port of the city of Albany). It was charted in 1791 by Capt. GEORGE VANCOUVER and was first used as a whaling base.

King George's War (1744–48) Inconclusive struggle between France and Britain for mastery of North America. Also called the American phase of the War of the AUSTRIAN SUCCESSION, the war involved disputes over boundaries of Nova Scotia and northern New England and control of the Ohio Valley. After bloody border raids by both sides, aided by their Indian allies, they signed the Treaty of AIX-LA-CHAPELLE (1748), which restored conquered territory but failed to resolve colonial issues. See also FRENCH AND INDIAN WAR.

King Philip's War (1675–76) Bloodiest conflict between American colonists and Indians in 17th-century New England. By 1660 colonial settlers, no longer dependent on Indians for survival, had pushed into Indian territory in Massachusetts, Connecticut, and Rhode Island. To protect their lands, the Wampanoag chief King Philip (METACOM) organized a federation of tribes, which in 1675 destroyed several frontier settlements. In retaliation the colonial militia burned Indian villages and crops. After Philip's death in 1676, Indian resistance collapsed. An estimated 600 settlers and 3,000 Indians were killed in the conflict.

king salmon See CHINOOK SALMON

king snake Any of seven species of SNAKE (genus *Lampropeltis,* family Colubridae) found in numerous habitats from southeastern Canada to Ecuador. They kill by constriction; named for their practice of eating other snakes, they also take small mammals, amphibians, birds, and birds' eggs. They are mainly terrestrial and relatively slow-moving. Strikingly marked and smooth-scaled, they have a small head and are usually less than 4 ft (1.2 m) long, though some specimens may approach 7 ft (2 m). The common king snake, found throughout the U.S. and in northern Mexico, is usually black or dark brown, variously blotched, ringed, or speckled with yellow or white.

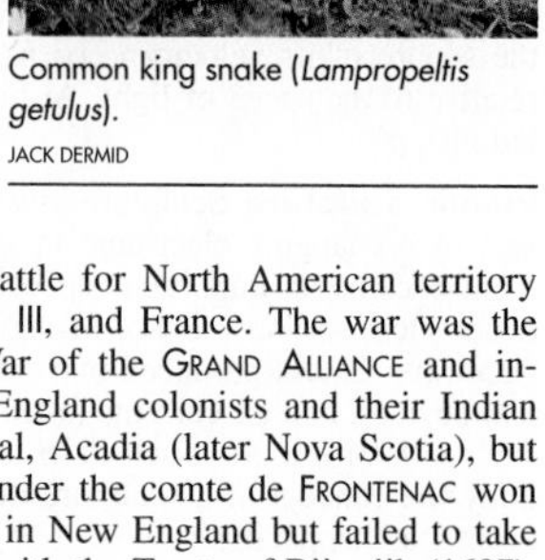
Common king snake (*Lampropeltis getulus*).
JACK DERMID

King William's War (1689–97) Battle for North American territory between Britain, under King WILLIAM III, and France. The war was the North American extension of the War of the GRAND ALLIANCE and involved French Canadians and New England colonists and their Indian allies. The British captured Port Royal, Acadia (later Nova Scotia), but failed to take Quebec. The French under the comte de FRONTENAC won skirmishes at Schenectady, N.Y., and in New England but failed to take Boston. The inconclusive war ended with the Treaty of Rijswijk (1697). See also FRENCH AND INDIAN WAR.

Kingdom of God *or* **Kingdom of Heaven** In CHRISTIANITY, the spiritual realm over which God reigns as king, or the eventual fulfillment of God's will on earth. The term is often used in the NEW TESTAMENT, and it was a central theme in the preaching of JOHN THE BAPTIST and JESUS. Theologians differ as to whether Jesus implied that the kingdom had arrived in his person or whether it was expected as a future event. Christian orthodoxy now holds that the kingdom has been partially realized by the presence of the church in the world, and that it will be fully realized after the Last Judgment.

kingfish Any of various fishes, among them certain species of MACKEREL and a DRUM. The king mackerel, or kingfish *(Scomberomorus cavalla),* is a western Atlantic fish about 67 in. (170 cm) long and weighing 79 lbs (36 kg) or more. The kingfish, or whiting *(Menticirrhus saxatilis),* of the Atlantic, is notable among drums in that it lacks an air bladder.

kingfisher Any of about 90 species of birds (family Alcedinidae), many of which fish for their food. Solitary birds, kingfishers are found worldwide but are chiefly tropical. They have a large head, long and usually narrow bill, compact body, small feet, and usually a short or medium-length tail. Species range from 4 to 18 in. (10–45 cm) long; most have bright, boldly patterned plumage, and many are crested. They utter rattling or piping calls, and they plunge into the water for small fish and other aquatic animals. The only widespread North American species, the belted kingfisher *(Megaceryle alcyon),* is bluish gray above and white below. The forest kingfishers (e.g., KOOKABURRA) have a broader bill.

Kings, Valley of the Defile, western THEBES, Egypt. It is the burial site of nearly all of the pharaohs of the 18th–20th dynasties (1539–1075 BC), from Thutmose I to Ramses XI. The valley contains 60 tombs, virtually all of which have been robbed. Only the tomb of TUTANKHAMEN escaped pillage, and its treasures now reside in the Egyptian Museum in CAIRO. The longest tomb belongs to Queen HATSHEPSUT, whose burial chamber is nearly 700 ft (215 m) from the entrance. The largest tomb, built for the sons of RAMSES II, contains 67 burial chambers.

Kings Canyon National Park National park, SIERRA NEVADAS, southern central California. Occupying an area of 722 sq mi (1,870 sq km), it is administered along with the adjacent SEQUOIA NATIONAL PARK. Established in 1940, it contains giant sequoia trees. Its most spectacular feature is Kings Canyon on the Kings River, which was carved by glacial action.

Kings Mountain, Battle of (October 7, 1780) Battle in the AMERICAN REVOLUTION between American revolutionaries and LOYALISTS. About 2,000 frontiersmen were assembled to resist the British advance into North Carolina; they surrounded the 1,100 soldiers, mainly Loyalists from New York and South Carolina, on Kings Mtn., S.C., near the border with North Carolina. The frontiersmen killed or captured almost the entire Loyalist force, and the battle marked the beginning of the war's turn against the British.

kingship, divine See DIVINE KINGSHIP

Kingsley, Charles (1819–1875) English clergyman and novelist. After studies at Cambridge, he became a parish priest and later chaplain to Queen Victoria, professor of modern history at Cambridge, and canon of Westminster. An enthusiastic advocate of CHRISTIAN SOCIALISM, he published several novels about social problems before writing the very successful historical novels *Hypatia* (1853), *Westward Ho!* (1855), and *Hereward the Wake* (1866). Fearing the Anglican church's trend in the direction of Catholicism, he engaged in a famous controversy with JOHN HENRY NEWMAN. His wholehearted acceptance of CHARLES DARWIN's theory of evolution inspired his popular children's book *The Water-Babies* (1863).

Kingston City (pop., 1991: 104,000; metro. area pop.: 588,000), capital and chief port of JAMAICA. Located on the southeastern coast of the island, it was founded in 1692 after Port Royal was destroyed by an earthquake. It soon became the commercial center of Jamaica, and was made the political capital in 1872. Historic buildings include a 17th-century church, a moated fortress, and the 18th-century Headquarters House. It is the seat of the University of the West Indies.

Kingston, Maxine Hong *orig.* **Maxine Hong** (born 1940) U.S. writer. Born to an immigrant family in Stockton, Cal., she has taught at various schools and universities. Her novels and nonfiction works explore the myths, realities, and cultural identities of Chinese and American families and the role of women in Chinese culture. Her widely admired *The Woman Warrior* (1976) and *China Men* (1980) blend fact and fantasy to tell aspects of her family's history; *Tripmaster Monkey* (1988) concerns a young Chinese-American man.

Kingstown Capital (pop., 1995: 16,000), chief port of ST. VINCENT AND THE GRENADINES, West Indies. Located on the southwestern end of the St. Vincent island, it overlooks Kingstown Harbor. Its sites of interest include the Botanic Gardens (founded 1763), the oldest of its kind in the western Hemisphere; Capt. WILLIAM BLIGH made his 1787 voyage on the *Bounty* to obtain breadfruit trees from TAHITI for this garden.

Kinnock, Neil (Gordon) (born 1942) British politician. Elected to Parliament in 1970, he rose in the Labour Party ranks and was named to its national executive committee in 1978. After the party suffered its heaviest defeat in 48 years in 1983, he was elected party leader, the youngest in its history. By 1989 he had persuaded the party to abandon its radical policies on disarmament and large-scale nationalization. Though the party increased its numbers in Parliament, it lost the 1992 general election to the Conservatives, and Kinnock resigned as party leader.

Kinsey \'kin-zē\, **Alfred (Charles)** (1894–1956) U.S. zoologist and expert on human sexual behavior. After earning a Ph.D. from Harvard University in 1920, he taught zoology at Indiana Univ., where he became the founder-director of the university's Institute for Sex Research in 1942. His inquiries into human sexuality led him to publish *Sexual Behavior in the Human Male* (1948) and *Sexual Behavior in the Human Female* (1953). These reports, based on 18,500 personal interviews, received extraordinary publicity for their revelations about contemporary sexual mores and behavior, but have been criticized because of irregularities in statistical sampling.

Kinsha River See JINSHA RIVER

Kinshasa \kin-'shä-sə\ *formerly* **Léopoldville** Capital and largest city (pop., 1994 est.: 4,655,000), Democratic Republic of the Congo (Zaire). Situated on the southern bank of the CONGO RIVER, it was founded as Léopoldville in 1881 by HENRY MORTON STANLEY. It became the capital of the Belgian Congo in the 1920s. After World War II it emerged as the largest city in sub-Saharan Africa, and it became the capital of the independent republic in 1960. It was given its present name in 1966. A major river port and a commercial center, it is the seat of the University of Kinshasa.

kinship Socially recognized relationship between people who are or are held to be biologically related or who are given the status of relatives by MARRIAGE, adoption, or other ritual. Kinship is the broad term for all the relationships that people are born into or create later in life that are considered binding in the eyes of society. Every person belongs to a FAMILY of orientation (e.g., mother, father, brothers, and sisters); most adults also belong to a family of procreation (which includes a spouse or spouses and children). Familial bonds of DESCENT and marriage may be traced through a genealogy, a written or oral statement of the names of individuals and their kin relations to one another. INHERITANCE and succession (the transmission of power and position in society) usually follow kinship lines. See also EXOGAMY AND ENDOGAMY, INCEST.

kiosk \'kē-äsk\ Originally, in Islamic architecture, an open circular pavilion consisting of a roof supported by pillars. The word has been applied to a Turkish summer garden pavilion and a type of early Persian mosque. Today the term refers to any small urban booth that dispenses newspapers, information, or tickets.

Kiowa \'kī-ə-,wò\ North American Indian people of Kiowa-Tanoan language stock who lived on the southern Great Plains, one of the last Plains tribes to capitulate to the U.S. They hunted buffalo on horseback and lived in large three-poled TEPEES. They had warrior societies, the members of which attained rank according to their exploits in war. They believed that dreams and visions gave them supernatural power, and participated in the SUN DANCE ceremony. They were also noted for their pictographic portrayals, or "calendar histories," of important tribal events. About 5,000 Kiowa live today on an Oklahoma reservation shared with the COMANCHE.

Kipling, (Joseph) Rudyard (1865–1936) British novelist, short-story writer, and poet. Born in India, the son of a museum curator, he was reared in England but returned to India as a journalist. He soon became famous for volumes of stories, beginning with *Plain Tales from the Hills* (1888; including "The Man Who Would Be King"), and later for the poetry collection *Barrack-Room Ballads* (1892; including "Gunga Din" and "Mandalay"). During a residence in the U.S., he published *The Light That Failed* (1890); the two *Jungle Books* (1894, 1895), stories of the wild boy Mowgli in the Indian jungle that have become children's classics; the adventure story *Captains Courageous* (1897); and *Kim* (1901), one of the great novels of India. He wrote six other volumes of short stories and several other verse collections. His children's books include the famous *Just So Stories* (1902) and the fairy-tale collection *Puck of Pook's Hill* (1906). *Stalky & Co.* (1899) is a fictionalized account of his boarding-school education. His poems, often strongly rhythmic, are frequently narrative ballads. He was awarded the Nobel Prize in 1907. His extraordinary popularity in his own time declined as his reputation suffered after World War I because of his widespread image as a jingoistic imperialist.

Kipling.
ELLIOTT AND FRY

Kirchhoff \'kirk-hȯf\, **Gustav Robert** (1824–1887) German physicist. Kirchhoff's laws (1845) allow calculation of the currents, voltages, and resistances of electrical networks (he was the first to show that current flows through a conductor at the speed of LIGHT) and generalized the equations describing current flow to three dimensions. With ROBERT BUNSEN, he demonstrated that every ELEMENT emits colored light when heated at WAVELENGTHS specific to it, a fact that is the basis of spectrum analysis. They used this new research tool to discover CESIUM (1860) and rubidium (1861), and began a new era in astronomy when they applied it to the SPECTRUM of the sun.

Kirchhoff's circuit rules \'kir-ˌkȯfs\ *or* **Kirchhoff's laws** Two statements, developed by GUSTAV KIRCHHOFF, about complex CIRCUITS that embody the laws of conservation (see CONSERVATION LAW) of ELECTRIC CHARGE and energy. They are used to determine the value of the ELECTRIC CURRENT in each branch of the circuit. The first law states that the sum of the currents into a junction in the circuit equals the sum of the currents out of the junction. The second law states that around each loop in an electric circuit, the sum of the ELECTROMOTIVE FORCE is equal to the sum of all the potential drops (changes in voltage) across components in the loop. Using these rules, algebraic equations can be formulated to determine the value of currents in different loops in a circuit.

Kirchner \'kirk-nər\, **Ernst Ludwig** (1880–1938) German painter, printmaker, and sculptor. He was among the founders of the Expressionist group Die BRÜCKE. Kirchner's highly personal style, influenced by ALBRECHT DURER, EDVARD MUNCH, and African and Polynesian art, was noted for its psychological tension and eroticism. He used simple, powerfully drawn forms and often garish colors to create intense, sometimes threatening works, such as his two versions of *Street, Berlin* (1907, 1913). Highly strung and often depressed, he took his own life when the Nazis declared his work "degenerate."

"Street, Berlin," oil on canvas by Ernst Ludwig Kirchner, 1913; in the Museum of Modern Art, New York City.
BY COURTESY OF THE MUSEUM OF MODERN ART, NEW YORK CITY

Kiribati \ˌkir-ə-'bä-tē, ˌkir-i-'bas, 'kir-i-ˌbas\ *officially* **Republic of Kiribati** Independent nation, consisting of 33 islands, central Pacific Ocean. The three major island groups are the GILBERT, PHOENIX, and LINE ISLANDS (excluding the three Line islands that are U.S. territories); Kiribati also includes Banaba Island, the former capital of the GILBERT AND ELLICE ISLANDS colony. Area (land): 313 sq mi (811 sq km). Population (1997 est.): 82,000. Capital: BAIRIKI, on TARAWA atoll. The native people are mostly Micronesians. Languages: English (official), Gilbertese. Religions: Roman Catholicism, Protestantism, Baha'i. Currency: Australian dollar. With the exception of Banaba (which is a coral island and higher in elevation), all the islands of Kiribati are low-lying coral atolls built on a submerged volcanic chain and encircled by reefs. Only about 20 of the islands are inhabited; more than 95% of the population of Kiribati live in the Gilbert Islands. The economy is based on subsistence farming and fishing. It is a republic with one legislative house; its head of state and government is the president. The islands were settled by Austronesian-speaking peoples before the 1st cent AD. Fijians and Tongans arrived c. 14th century. In 1765 the British commodore John Bryon discovered the island of Nikunau; the first permanent European settler arrived in 1837. In 1916 the Gilbert and Ellice islands and Banaba became a crown colony of Britain; the Phoenix Islands joined the colony in 1937. Most of the Line Islands joined the colony in 1972, but in 1976 the Ellice Islands were separated to form the country of Tuvalu. The colony became self-governing in 1977, and in 1979 it became the nation of Kiribati. It caused controversy among neighboring islands when, in 1995, it moved its calculation of the INTERNATIONAL DATE LINE in order to be the first country to reach midnight, December 31, 1999.

Kirin See JILIN

Kiriwina Islands See TROBRIAND ISLANDS

Kirkland, (Joseph) Lane (1922–1999) U.S. labor-union leader. Born in Camden, S.C., he served as an officer in the U.S. merchant marine and joined the AFL as a staff researcher in 1948. He was elected secretary-treasurer of the AFL-CIO in 1969 and succeeded GEORGE MEANY as president in 1979. During Kirkland's tenure (1979–95), the AFL-CIO's membership and political influence waned, owing to shrinking employment in the U.S. manufacturing sector.

Kirkland, Samuel (1741–1808) American clergyman. Born in Norwich, Conn., he became a Congregational missionary to Indian tribes of the Iroquois Confederacy and learned several Indian languages. In the American Revolution he served as chaplain to colonial troops and secured an alliance with the Oneida. He was rewarded with a land grant in New York state, where he founded the Hamilton Oneida Academy for Indian and white students (later HAMILTON COLLEGE).

Kirkuk \kir-'kük\ City (pop., 1987: 419,000), northeastern Iraq. Situated north of BAGHDAD, it was in one of the first Arab areas where oil was discovered in the 20th century. The city was seized by Arab forces in 1941 during World War II; it was retaken by the British. Kirkuk is a trade and export center as well as a center of Iraq's petroleum industry, with oil pipeline connections to Tripoli and to Yumurtalik on the Turkish coast.

Kirkwall Town (pop., 1995 est.: 7,000), headquarters of Orkney administrative region, which covers the ORKNEY ISLANDS. Located on Pomona Island off the northern tip of Scotland, it has evidence of Norse influence persisting as late as the building of the Cathedral of St. Magnus in the 12th century. A service center for the Orkney Islands, it is the seat of the islands' area council. The exploitation of North Sea oil has led to development of offshore servicing and supply for the oil industry.

Kirkwood gaps Interruptions in the distribution of ASTEROIDS that appear where any of these small bodies' orbital periods would be a simple fraction of Jupiter's. Several zones of low density in the asteroid belt were noticed c. 1860 by Daniel Kirkwood (1814–1895), who explained the gaps as resulting from perturbations by Jupiter. Any object that revolved in one of these locations would be disturbed regularly by the planet's gravitational pull and eventually be moved to another orbit.

Kirov \'kē-rȯf\, **Sergey (Mironovich)** *orig.* **Sergey Mironovich Kostrikov** (1886–1934) Soviet political leader. After joining the Bolsheviks, he extended the Communist Party's control in Transcaucasia, and in 1926 JOSEPH STALIN appointed him head of the Leningrad party organization (1926). He modernized the city's industries, was elected to the Politburo (1930), and acquired power that nearly rivaled Stalin's. In 1934 he was assassinated by a young party member, Leonid Nikolayev, who was later shot, along with 13 suspected accomplices. Stalin, claiming that a widespread conspiracy of anti-Stalinist communists planned to assassinate the entire Soviet leadership, used the assassination as a pretext to institute the PURGE TRIALS. In 1956 NIKITA KHRUSHCHEV suggested that Stalin had engineered Kirov's assassination.

Kirov Theater See MARIINSKY THEATER

Kirovabad See Gäncä

Kirstein \'kir-,stēn\, **Lincoln (Edward)** (1907–1996) U.S. dance authority, impresario, and writer. Born in Rochester, N.Y., he graduated from Harvard, where he founded the literary magazine *Hound & Horn.* Financially independent, he focused his artistic interests on ballet and in 1933 persuaded George Balanchine to come to the U.S. to found a ballet school and company. The School of American Ballet opened in 1934; Kirstein was its director from 1940 to 1989. He and Balanchine jointly established a series of ballet companies, culminating in the New York City Ballet (1948), which he served as general director until 1989. He wrote seven books on ballet, including the classic history *Dance* (1935). His influence on the growth of ballet in the U.S. remains unmatched.

Kisangani \,kē-sän-'gä-nē\ *formerly (until 1966)* **Stanleyville** City (pop., 1994 est.: 418,000), northeastern Democratic Republic of the Congo (Zaire). The nation's major inland port after Kinshasa, it is located on the Congo River, below Boyoma Falls. The city was founded in 1883 by Europeans and was known first as Falls Station and then as Stanleyville (for Henry Morton Stanley). It has been the major center of the northern Congo since the late 1800s. It is the seat of the University of Kisangani (1963) and other institutions of higher education.

Kish Ancient Mesopotamian city-state located east of Babylon in what is now southern central Iraq. It lay on the Euphrates before the course of the river changed. City ruins date back to the 4th millennium BC and the Sumerian culture; archaeological evidence of the palace of Sargon I and the temple of Nebuchadnezzar II has also been found.

Kishinev See Chisinau

Kishon River See Qishon River

Kissinger \'ki-sᵊn-jər\, **Henry A(lfred)** (born 1923) U.S. (German-born) foreign-policy adviser (1969–76). He emigrated with his family to the U.S. in 1938. He taught at Harvard Univ., where he directed the Defense Studies Program 1959–69. In 1968 he was appointed assistant for national security affairs by Pres. Richard Nixon and served as head of the National Security Council (1969–75) and later as secretary of state (1973–77). He developed a policy of détente toward the Soviet Union, which led to the SALT agreements. He also developed the first official U.S. contact with Communist China. He negotiated the cease-fire agreement that ended the Vietnam War, for which he shared the Nobel Peace Prize in 1973 with Le Duc Tho (who refused it). He later became an international consultant, lecturer, and writer.

Kit-Cat Club Association of early-18th-cent Whig leaders that met in London. Members included the writers Richard Steele, Joseph Addison, and William Congreve and such political figures as Robert Walpole and the duke of Marlborough. They first met in the tavern of Christopher Cat, whose mutton pies were called kit-cats. Portraits of the 42 members were painted by Godfrey Kneller (1646–1723), and the specific size of the canvas (36" x 28") used for the portraits became known as a kit-cat.

Kitaj \ki-'tī\, **R(onald) B(rooks)** (born 1932) U.S.-British painter. Born in Cleveland, he studied in New York, Vienna, Oxford, and London. In the 1960s he was a prominent member of the Pop art movement in Britain, though he had little interest in the culture of mass media. Deriving inspiration from the pastels of Edgar Degas, he developed an evocative pictorial language of figurative imagery filled with references to historical, artistic, and literary topics executed in a brightly colored, semiabstract style. He has exhibited internationally and has taught at various British art schools.

Kitakami Mountains \kē-'tä-kä-mē\ Mountain range, northeastern Honshu, Japan. It parallels the Pacific coast and extends for about 155 mi (250 km) to the Ojika Peninsula. Its highest peak rises to 6,280 ft (1,914 m). Often referred to as the "Tibet of Japan," the Kitakami Range is the most culturally isolated region of Honshu. Until the mid-20th century relics of old agricultural practices survived, including the serf system known as Nago.

Kitakyushu \kē-'tä-,kyü-shü\ City (pop., 1995: 1,020,000), Kyushu, Japan. It was created in 1963 by the amalgamation of several cities. Part of its long coastline is included in the Inland Sea National Park. It is one of Japan's leading manufacturing centers. Undersea tunnels link the city with Shimonoseki, Honshu.

Kitami Mountains \kē-'tä-mē\ Mountain range, northeastern Hokkaido, Japan. Extending 180 mi (290 km) along the coast of the Sea of Okhotsk, its elevations range generally from 2,500 to 3,100 ft (750 to 950 m), but the highest reaches 6,500 ft (1,980 m).

Kitchener City (pop., 1991: 168,000), southeastern Ontario. It is situated in the Grand River valley, southwest of Toronto. Founded by Bishop Benjamin Eby and settled by German immigrants c. 1807, it was incorporated as a city in 1912. It was known successively as Sand Hill, Ebytown, and Berlin before being renamed in honor of H. H. Kitchener in 1916. The boyhood home of W.L. Mackenzie King is now preserved in Woodside National Historic Park.

Kitchener, H(oratio) H(erbert) *later* **Earl Kitchener (of Khartoum and of Broome)** (1850–1916) British field marshal and imperial administrator. Trained as a military engineer, Kitchener served in posts in the Middle East and Sudan before being appointed commander in chief of the Egyptian army in 1892. In 1898 he crushed the rebellious Mahdist movement in the Battle of Omdurman and forced concessions from France in the Fashoda Incident. In 1899 he entered the South African War as chief of staff, becoming commander in chief a year later. In the last 18 months of the war, he resorted to brutal methods, burning Boer farms and herding Boer women and children into concentration camps. He was later sent to India to reorganize the army there. A clash with Lord Curzon led to the latter's resignation in 1905. In 1911 he returned to Khartoum as proconsul of Egypt and the Sudan. As secretary of state for war during World War I, he organized armies on a scale unprecedented in British history and became a symbol of the national will to victory. He died on a mission to Russia when his ship was sunk by a German mine.

kite Light frame covered with paper or cloth, often provided with a balancing tail, and designed to be flown in the air at the end of a long string; it is held aloft by wind. Its name comes from the kite, a member of the hawk family. Kites have been in use in Asia from time immemorial, and religious significance is still connected to some ceremonial kite-flying there. In a famous experiment in 1752, Benjamin Franklin hung a metal key from a kite line during a storm to attract electricity. Kites were used to carry weather-recording devices aloft before the advent of balloons and airplanes. Types of kite commonly in use today include the hexagonal (or three-sticker), the malay (modified diamond), and the box kite, invented in the 1890s. Newer wing-like kites, with pairs of controlling strings for superior maneuverability, are also flown.

kite Any of numerous lightly built birds of prey that have a small head, partly bare face, short beak, and long, narrow wings and tail. They are found worldwide in warm regions. Some live on insects; others are primarily scavengers but also eat rodents and reptiles; a few eat only snails. In flight, kites slowly flap and then glide with wings angled back. Kites belong to three subfamilies of the family Accipitridae: Milvinae (true kites and snail kites), Elaninae (including the white-tailed kite, one of the few North American raptors increasing in number), and Perninae (including the swallow-tailed kite of the New World). See also hawk.

Swallow-tailed kite (*Elanoides forficatus*).

JAMES A. KERN

kithara \'ki-thə-rə\ Large lyre of classical antiquity, the principal stringed instrument of the Greeks and later of the Romans. It had a box-shaped resonating body from which extended two parallel arms connected by a crossbar to which 3–12 strings were attached. It was held vertically and plucked with a plectrum; the left hand was used to stop and damp the strings. It was played by singers of the Greek epics, as well as by later professional accompanists and soloists.

kittiwake *or* **black-legged kittiwake** White oceanic gull *(Rissa tridactyla)* with pearl-gray mantle, black-tipped wings, black feet, and yellow bill. Kittiwakes nest on narrow cliff ledges along the North and South Atlantic coasts. The red-legged kittiwake *(R. brevirostris)* is found in the Bering Sea region.

kiva \'kē-və\ Underground chamber of the PUEBLO INDIAN villages of the southwestern U.S., notable for the murals that decorate its walls. A small hole in its floor, the *sípapu,* serves as the symbolic place of origin of the tribe. Though the kiva's primary purpose is for ritual ceremonies, men also use it for political meetings or casual gatherings. Women are almost always excluded from the kiva. The traditional round slope of the earliest kiva, in contrast to the otherwise square or rectangular Pueblo architecture, recalls the circular pit houses of the prehistoric basket-weaving culture from which these tribes, primarily HOPI and ZUNI, descend.

Kivu \kē-vü\, **Lake** Lake, central East Africa. Located between Rwanda and the Democratic Republic of the Congo (Zaire), it occupies 1,040 sq mi (2,700 sq km), is 55 mi (90 km) long and 30 mi (48 km) wide, and has a maximum depth of 1,558 ft (475 m). Containing many islands, it was part of a larger body of water until volcanic outpourings along its northern shore created a dam that separated it from Lake EDWARD.

kiwi Any of three species (genus *Apteryx*) of chicken-sized, grayish brown RATITE birds, found in New Zealand. Their Maori name refers to the male's shrill call. Kiwis have vestigial wings hidden within the plumage; nostrils at the tip (rather than the base) of the long flexible bill; soft, hairlike feathers; and stout, muscular legs. Each of the four toes has a large claw. Kiwis live in forests, where they sleep by day and forage for worms, insects and their larvae, and berries at night. They run swiftly and use their claws in defense when cornered.

Common kiwi (*Apteryx australis*).
PICTORIAL PARADE

kiwi fruit Edible fruit of the vine *Actinidia chinensis* (family Actinidiaceae), native to China and Taiwan and grown commercially in New Zealand and California. It became popular in the NOUVELLE CUISINE of the 1970s. It has a slightly acid taste and is high in vitamin C. Kiwi can be eaten raw or cooked, and the juice is sometimes used as a meat tenderizer.

Kiyomori See TAIRA KIYOMORI

Kizil Irmak \ki-'zil-'ir-ˌmäk\ River, central and north central Turkey. The longest river wholly within Turkey and the largest in ASIA MINOR, it rises in northern central Turkey and flows southwest. It turns north and empties into the Black Sea after a total course of 734 mi (1,182 km). Unsuitable for navigation, it is a source of irrigation and hydroelectricity for the region.

KKK See KU KLUX KLAN

Klaipeda \'klī-pə-də\ *German* **Memel** \'mā-məl\ City (pop., 1996 est.: 202,000) and port, Lithuania. It lies on the channel that connects the NEMAN RIVER with the Baltic Sea. A fortress built on the site in the early 13th century was destroyed in 1252 by the TEUTONIC ORDER, who built a new fortress called Memelburg. It came under Prussian control in the 17th century, and the town (Memel) was settled by Germans. In 1923 Memel became part of Lithuania and was renamed Klaipeda. Seized by Germany in 1939, it passed to the U.S.S.R. in 1945. In 1991 it became part of the newly independent Lithuania. The modern city has major shipbuilding yards and is the base for a large deep-sea fishing fleet.

Klamath \'kla-məth\ PLATEAU INDIAN people of Penutian stock whose territory lay in a great trough in the southern Cascade Range of present-day southern Oregon. They were primarily fishers and hunters of waterfowl. The Klamath were divided into relatively autonomous villages, each with its own leaders and MEDICINE MAN; the villages would ally for war, and members of different villages often intermarried. Families lived in earth-covered lodges in winter and domed houses of poles and matting in summer. SWEAT LODGES doubled as community centers for religious activities. The Klamath's closely related neighbors were the MODOC.

Klamath River \'kla-məth\ River, southern Oregon and northwestern California. Rising in Upper Klamath Lake just above Klamath Falls, Oregon, it flows south and southwest for 250 mi (400 km) through the Klamath Mountains in California, and empties into the Pacific Ocean.

Klausenburg See CLUJ-NAPOCA

klebsiella \ˌkleb-zē-'e-lə\ Any of the rod-shaped BACTERIA that make up the genus *Klebsiella.* They are gram-negative (see GRAM STAIN), thrive better without oxygen than with it, and do not move. *K. pneumoniae,* also called Friedländer's BACILLUS, can infect the human respiratory tract and cause pneumonia and, along with some other species, human urinary-tract and wound infections.

Klee \'klā\, **Paul** (1879–1940) Swiss painter. After studies in Germany and Italy, he settled in Munich, where he became associated with Der BLAUE REITER (1911). He taught at the BAUHAUS (1920–31), then at the Düsseldorf Academy. He lost his post when the Nazis came to power in 1933, and returned to Switzerland. One of the foremost artists of the 20th century, he belonged to no movement, yet he assimilated and even anticipated some of the major artistic tendencies of his time. Using both representational and abstract approaches, he produced some 9,000 paintings, drawings, and watercolors in a great variety of styles. His works, which tend to be small in scale, are remarkable for their delicate nuances of line, color, and tonality. In Klee's highly sophisticated art, irony and a sense of the absurd are joined to an intense evocation of the mystery and beauty of nature. His late paintings, anticipating his approaching death, are among his most memorable.

Klee, 1939.
AUFNAHME FOTOPRESS

Kleiber \'klī-bər\, **Erich** (1890–1956) Austro-Hungarian conductor. After his Prague debut in 1911, he held a series of posts that led him to the Berlin State Opera, where he was music director 1923–34. There he premiered such important works as A. BERG's *Wozzeck* (1925) and L. JANACEK's *Jenufa.* When the Nazis forbade the premiere of Berg's *Lulu* (1934), he managed to program the suite from the opera for his last concert. Moving to Buenos Aires, he was head of the German Opera at the Teatro Colón 1937–49. His son Carlos (born 1930) also became an internationally celebrated conductor, especially of opera, with a reputation for perfectionism equal to his father's.

Klein, Calvin (Richard) (born 1942) U.S. fashion designer. Born in New York City, he attended the Fashion Institute of Technology. He opened his own company in 1968, when casual, hippie-style clothing was in fashion, but took a different direction by designing simple, understated, elegant clothing. The first designer to win three consecutive Coty Awards for womenswear (1973–75), he is known for his clothing, cosmetics, linens, and other designer collections, as well as for his erotic advertising photographs, some of which have drawn public protest.

Klein, Melanie *orig.* **Melanie Reizes** (1882–1960) Austrian-British psychoanalyst. Born in Vienna, she married at 21 and had three children before undergoing psychoanalysis with SANDOR FERENCZI in Budapest before World War I. She studied the psychoanalysis of young children, joining the Berlin Psychoanalytic Institute (1921–26), and later moving to London. In works such as *The Psychoanalysis of Children* (1932) and *Narrative of a Child Analysis* (1961), she asserted that children's play was a symbolic way of controlling anxiety and that observation of free play with toys could serve as a means of determining early psychological impulses.

Klein, Yves (1928–1962) French painter, sculptor, and performance artist. With no formal artistic training, he began in the mid-1950s to exhibit nonobjective paintings in which a canvas was uniformly covered in a single color, usually blue; he also used the technique for sculptural figures and reliefs. In 1958 he produced a near-riot with an "exhibition of emptiness," an empty gallery painted white, titled *Le vide* ("The Void"). He used a variety of unorthodox methods to produce pictures, such as imprints of the human body on paper or canvas (*anthropométries*). His work was deliberately extreme and experimental. A member of FLUXUS, he greatly influenced the development of MINIMALISM.

Kleist \'klīst\, **(Bernd) Heinrich (Wilhelm von)** (1777–1811) German writer. He served seven years in the Prussian army, and his work first attracted attention when he was in prison accused as a spy. The grim and intense drama *Penthesilea* (1808) contains some of his most powerful poetry, and *The Broken Pitcher* (1808) is a masterpiece of dramatic comedy; they were followed by *Katherine of Heilbronn* (1810), *Die Hermannsschlacht* (1821), and *The Prince of Homburg* (1821). In 1811 he published a collection of eight masterly novellas, including *Michael Kohlhaas, The Earthquake in Chile,* and *The Marquise of O.* Embittered by a lack of recognition, he ended his unhappy life in a joint suicide with a young woman at 34. He is now considered the first of the great 19th-century German dramatists, and his disturbing and densely written fictions are widely admired by writers.

Kleitias See CLEITIAS

Klemperer, Otto (1885–1973) German conductor. After studying composition with Hans Pfitzner (1869–1949), in 1905 he met G. MAHLER, who recommended him for several positions, including chief conductor at the Hamburg Opera (1910). At the short-lived Kroll Opera (1927–31) he conducted the Berlin premieres of many important works by contemporary composers. In 1933 he fled Germany for the U.S., conducting in Los Angeles (1933–39) and studying with Schoenberg. A brain tumor in 1939 left him partly paralyzed. From the 1950s, though seated on the podium, he created a much-admired recorded legacy with London's Philharmonia Orchestra.

Kleophrades Painter See CLEOPHRADES PAINTER

klezmer music Traditional music played in the Jewish and German ghettos of Eastern Europe, especially for weddings and other ceremonies. The klezmer tradition centered around Odessa, Russia. The Yiddish term means basically "professional musican," and the music played by such musicians has included liturgical music as well as boisterous dance music. Klezmer ensembles have varied considerably; today in the U.S., where a klezmer revival began in the 1980s, a typical band will usually specialize in dance music and might consist of four to six musicians playing clarinet, trumpet, trombone, tuba, and percussion.

Klimt, Gustav (1862–1918) Austrian painter. In 1897, after a period as an academic muralist, his mature style emerged. Revolting against academic art in favor of a decorative style similar to ART NOUVEAU, he founded the Vienna SEZESSION. His later murals are characterized by precisely linear drawing and flat, decorative patterns of color. His most successful works include *The Kiss* (1908) and a series of portraits, in which he treats the human figure without shadow, conveying the sensuality of skin by surrounding it with areas of flat, highly ornamental areas of decoration. He greatly influenced OSKAR KOKOSCHKA and EGON SCHIELE. See also JUGENDSTIL.

Kline, Franz (1910–1962) U.S. painter. Born in Wilkes-Barre, Pa., he studied art in London before settling in New York City. He became one of the leading artists of the ABSTRACT EXPRESSIONISM movement, known for his use of inexpensive commercial paints and large house-painter's brushes to build graphic networks of rough bars of black paint on white backgrounds. He achieved a sense of majesty and power in such large-scale works as *Mahoning* (1956). In the late 1950s he introduced color into his paintings.

Klinefelter's syndrome Chromosomal disorder that occurs in one out of 500 males. With an extra X CHROMOSOME in each cell (XXY), patients look male, with firm, small TESTES, but produce no sperm and may have enlarged breasts and buttocks and very long legs. TESTOSTERONE is low and pituitary reproductive hormones high. Intelligence is usually normal, but social adjustment can be difficult. Rarer variants cause additional abnormalities, including mental retardation. In the XX male syndrome, Y chromosome material has been transferred to another chromosome, causing changes typical of Klinefelter's syndrome. All variants are treated with ANDROGENS.

Klinger, Max (1857–1920) German painter, sculptor, and printmaker. He is known for his use of symbol, fantasy, and dreamlike situations, reflecting a late-19th-century awareness of psychological depths. His vivid, frequently morbid imaginings and his interest in the gruesome and grotesque can be seen in his Goyaesque etchings. He had a deep influence on many artists, including EDVARD MUNCH, KATHE KOLLWITZ, MAX ERNST, and GIORGIO DE CHIRICO.

Klondike gold rush Canadian gold rush of the late 1890s. Gold was discovered on August 17, 1896, near the confluence of the Klondike and YUKON rivers in western Yukon Territory. The news spread quickly, and by late 1898 more than 30,000 prospectors had arrived. Annual production peaked at $22 million worth of gold in 1900, and soon prospectors began moving on to Alaska. By the time mining ended in 1966, the area had yielded $250 million in gold.

Kluane National Park \klü-'ō-nē\ National park, southwestern Yukon. Located on the Alaskan border, and established in 1972, it encompasses some 5,440,000 acres (2,203,000 hectares). Its focal point is Mount LOGAN, the highest peak in Canada. Kluane also has a large glacier system and abundant wildlife.

Kmart Corp. *formerly (until 1977)* **S. S. Kresge Co.** Major U.S. retail chain, marketing general merchandise primarily through discount and variety stores. It originated with a pair of five- and ten-cent stores established in 1897 by S.S. KRESGE and a partner. Kresge's at first restricted the price of its merchandise to not more than 10 cents, but eventually to not more than one dollar. In 1962 Kresge's entered the large-scale discount retail market with construction of the first Kmart outside Detroit. With its success, the company expanded aggressively, erecting an average of 85 discount stores per year over the next two decades. In 1977 it became the second-largest U.S. retailer. It declared bankruptcy, however, in 2002 after years of competition with the world's largest retailer, Wal-Mart Stores, Inc. (see SAM WALTON), and other discount stores. See also SEARS, ROEBUCK AND CO., WOOLWORTH CO.

Knesset \kə-'nes-ət\ (Hebrew: "Assembly") Unicameral national LEGISLATURE of Israel. The first Knesset opened in 1949. Its name and the number of its seats (120) are based on the Jewish assembly of biblical times; its traditions and organization are based on the Zionist Congress, the political system of the Jewish community in pre-Israel Palestine, and more loosely the British House of COMMONS. Its members are elected by proportional representation for four-year terms; candidates are chosen by their parties.

knight *French* **chevalier** \shə-'val-ˌyā\ *German* **Ritter** In the European Middle Ages, a formally professed cavalryman, generally a vassal holding land as a FIEF from the lord he served (see FEUDALISM). At about 7 a boy bound for knighthood became a page, then at 12 a damoiseau ("lordling"), varlet, or valet, and subsequently a shieldbearer or esquire. When judged ready, he was dubbed knight by his lord in a solemn ceremony. The Christian ideal of knightly behavior (see CHIVALRY) required devotion to the church, loyalty to military and feudal superiors, and preservation of personal honor. By the 16th century knighthood had become honorific rather than feudal or military.

Knight, Frank H(yneman) (1885–1972) U.S. economist. Born in McLean Co., Ill., he received his PhD from Cornell University in 1916. He taught at the University of Chicago 1927–52; MILTON FRIEDMAN was one of the many students he influenced. His book *Risk, Uncertainty and Profit* (1921) distinguished between insurable and uninsurable RISKS and asserted that profit was the reward entrepreneurs earned for bearing uninsurable risk. His monograph *Economic Organization* is a classic exposition of MICROECONOMIC THEORY. He is considered the founder of the Chicago school of economics.

Knight Templar See TEMPLAR

Knights of Labor U.S. labor organization. Founded in 1869 by URIAH SMITH STEPHENS as the Noble Order of the Knights of Labor, it included both skilled and unskilled workers, and it proposed a system of workers' cooperatives to replace capitalism. To protect its members from employers' reprisals, it originally maintained secrecy. Under TERENCE V. POWDERLY (1879–93) it favored open arbitration with management and discouraged strikes. National membership reached 700,000 in 1886. Strikes by militant groups and the HAYMARKET RIOT caused an antiunion reaction that rapidly reduced the organization's influence. A splinter group left to form the AFL (later AFL-CIO).

Knights of Malta *or* **Hospitallers** \'häs-ˌpi-tᵊl-ərz\ *in full (since 1961)* **Sovereign Military Hospitaller Order of St. John of Jerusalem, of Rhodes and of Malta** Religious order founded at Jerusalem in the 11th century to care for sick pilgrims. Recognized by the pope in 1113, the order built hostels along the routes to the Holy Land. The Hospitallers acquired wealth and lands and began to combine the task of tending the sick with waging war on Islam, eventually becoming a major military force in the CRUSADES. After the fall of the crusader states, they moved their headquarters to Cyprus and later to Rhodes (1309). They ruled Rhodes until it fell to the Turks in 1523; thereupon they moved to Malta, where they ruled until their defeat by NAPOLEON I in 1798. In 1834 they moved to their present headquarters in Rome.

knitting machine Machine for TEXTILE and garment production. Flatbed machines may be hand-operated or power-driven, and, by selection of color, type of stitch, cam design, and Jacquard device (see JACQUARD LOOM), almost unlimited variety is possible. Modern circular machines may have 100 feeders, allowing each needle to pick up 100 threads per revolution. Both spring (invented c. 1589) and latch (invented 1847) needles are used, with the latter more common. Small bladelike units (sinkers) are inserted between every two needles to engage and hold the completed fabric. Machines may have pattern wheels controlling needle action to produce special stitches, and also a Jacquard mechanism. See also WILLIAM LEE.

Knopf \kə-'nəpf, kə-'nȯpf\, **Alfred A.** (1892–1984) U.S. publisher. Born in New York City, he worked a short time in publishing before he and his wife, Blanche, founded their own firm, Alfred A. Knopf, Inc., in 1915. His appreciation of contemporary literature and his literary contacts helped make the firm renowned for publishing works of high literary quality. By the time of his death, authors published by the firm had won 16 Nobel and 27 Pulitzer prizes. In 1966 it became a subsidiary of RANDOM HOUSE, Inc. Knopf also published the *American Mercury* (1924–34), an influential periodical he cofounded with H.L. MENCKEN and George Jean Nathan.

Knossos \'nä-səs\ Ancient royal city, CRETE. It was King MINOS' capital and the center of the MINOAN civilization. Settled by migrants from ASIA MINOR in the 7th millennium BC, it gave rise to a sophisticated BRONZE AGE culture. Two great palaces were built in the Middle Minoan period, the second c. 1720 BC after an earthquake leveled the city. About 1580 BC Minoan culture began to extend to mainland Greece, where it greatly influenced the MYCENAEAN culture. After its palace was destroyed by fire c. 1400 BC, it was reduced to town status, and Aegean political focus shifted to MYCENAE. Knossos was the site of the legendary labyrinth of DAEDALUS.

knot In cording, the interlacement of parts of one or more ropes, cords, or other pliable materials, commonly used to bind objects together. Knots have existed from the time humans first used vines and cordlike fibers to bind stone heads to wood in primitive axes, and were also used in the making of nets and traps. Knot making became sophisticated when it began to be used in the ropes, or rigging, that controlled the sails of early sailing vessels, and thus became the province of sailors. Knots are still depended on by campers and hikers, mountaineers, fishermen, and weavers, among others.

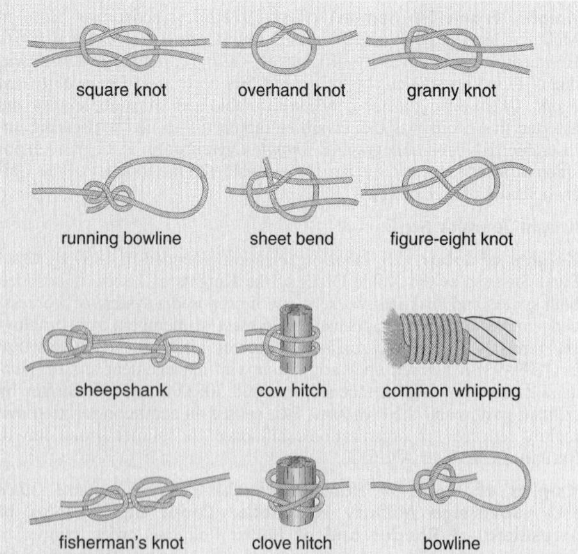

Examples of common knots.

Know-Nothing Party *or* **American Party** U.S. political party of the 1850s. Developed from the anti-immigrant and anti-Roman Catholic movement of the 1840s, the secret Order of the Star-Spangled Banner was formed in New York in 1849, and lodges were soon established in other major cities. Members were instructed to reply to queries about their group with "I know nothing." The group, which officially became the American Party, called for restrictions on immigration and naturalized citizenship. Many local and state candidates won offices in the 1852 election, and by 1855 there were 43 Know-Nothing congressmen. At its 1856 convention the party split over the slavery issue; proslavery advocates left to join the Democrats and antislavery adherents joined the Republicans. By 1859 the party's influence was limited to the border states.

Knowles \'nōlz\, **John** (1926–2001) U.S. author. Born in Fairmont, W.V., and educated at Yale Univ., he gained prominence for his first novel, *A Separate Peace* (1959), about the competitive friendship of two private-school students. Most of his novels, which include *Indian Summer* (1966), *Spreading Fires* (1974), and *Peace Breaks Out* (1981), are psychological examinations of characters caught in conflict between the wild and the pragmatic sides of their personalities.

Knox, Henry (1750–1806) American Revolutionary officer. Born in Boston, he became active in the colonial militia. After joining the Continental Army, he was sent by GEORGE WASHINGTON to transport British artillery captured in the Battle of TICONDEROGA. In mid-winter, he oversaw the transport of 120,000 lbs (55,000 kg) of artillery by oxen and horses over snow and ice 300 mi (480 km) to Boston. Promoted to general, he commanded the artillery in the battles of Monmouth and Yorktown, and in 1783 he succeeded Washington as commander of the army. He was secretary of war under the Articles of Confederation (1785–89) and was appointed the first U.S. secretary of war (1789–95).

Knox, John (c. 1514–1572) Scottish clergyman, leader of the Scottish Reformation and founder of Scottish PRESBYTERIANISM. Probably trained for the priesthood at the University of St. Andrews, he was ordained in 1540. He joined a group of Protestants who fortified St. Andrews Castle, but they were captured by French Catholics and carried away into slavery in 1547. Released through English intervention in 1549, he spent four years preaching in England, where he influenced developments in the Church of England. With the accession of the Catholic MARY I, he fled to the Continent. He served as pastor at Frankfurt am Main and Geneva until his return to Scotland in 1559. In England, ELIZABETH I made common cause with the Scottish Presbyterians, lest the French gain control of Scotland to support its Catholic monarch, MARY, QUEEN OF SCOTS. Knox survived conflicts with Mary and spent the rest of his life in setting up the Presbyterian church.

John Knox, engraving from *Icones*, by T. Beza, 1580.

Knox, Philander Chase (1853–1921) U.S. lawyer and politician. Born in Brownsville, Pa., he worked as a corporation lawyer, and helped organize the U.S. STEEL CORP. He was appointed attorney general (1901–4) and at Pres. THEODORE ROOSEVELT's direction instituted several antitrust lawsuits. He served in the U.S. Senate (1904–9), then was appointed secretary of state (1909–13) by Pres. WILLIAM H. TAFT and helped form the foreign policy of expanded U.S. investment criticized as DOLLAR DIPLOMACY. Reelected to the Senate (1917–21), he opposed the League of Nations.

Knoxville City (pop., 2000: 173,890), eastern Tennessee. In 1785 a treaty with the CHEROKEE Indians opened the region to settlers, and Capt.

James White established a frontier outpost called White's Fort. In 1791 it was renamed Knoxville after HENRY KNOX. It served as the capital of the state of Tennessee 1796–1812, 1817–19. During the AMERICAN CIVIL WAR, it was occupied by the Confederates until 1863. It is the seat of the University of TENNESSEE and Knoxville College as well as the headquarters of the TENNESSEE VALLEY AUTHORITY.

Knudsen \'knüd-sən, 'nüd-sən\, **William Signius** *orig.* **Signius Wilhelm Poul** (1879–1948) Danish-U.S. industrialist. He emigrated to the U.S. in 1900. In 1914 he began supervising FORD MOTOR CO. assembly plants, and directed the firm's construction of submarine patrol boats and other war matériel in World War I. He joined GENERAL MOTORS CORP. in 1922 and became president in 1937. He was appointed director of industrial production for the National Defense Research Committee, and directed production of war matériel as head of the U.S. Office of Production Management.

Knut See CANUTE THE GREAT

Knuth \kə-'nüth\, **Donald E(rvin)** (born 1938) U.S. computer scientist. Born in Milwaukee, he studied mathematics at Case Institute of Technology (now Case Western Reserve), where he first encountered computers. He earned a PhD in 1963 from the California Institute of Technology. A pioneer in computer science, he applied his knowledge of mathematics and programming to typeface design and typesetting to develop a document-preparation system that gave computers their first ability to control text layouts typographically and to print with typeset quality. His system of programs, which he chose not to copyright, has been called the most important achievement in publishing since the invention of the printing press. He has received many awards and honors, including the Kyoto Prize (1996), the Turing Award (1974), and the National Medal of Science (1979). His ongoing multivolume series *The Art of Computer Programming* has been widely acclaimed.

Ko Hung See GE HONG

koala Tree-dwelling MARSUPIAL *(Phascolarctos cinereus)* of coastal eastern Australia. About 24–33 in. (60–85 cm) long and tailless, the koala has a stout, pale gray or yellowish body; broad face; big, round, leathery nose; small, yellow eyes; and fluffy ears. Its feet have strong claws and some opposable digits. The koala feeds only on EUCALYPTUS leaves. The offspring (one born at a time) remains in the rearward-opening pouch for up to seven months. Koala populations have dwindled seriously, formerly because they were killed for their fur and attacked by disease and now because of loss of habitat and the continued spread of disease.

Koala (*Phascolarctos cinereus*).

ANTHONY MERCIECA FROM THE NATIONAL AUDUBON SOCIETY COLLECTION/PHOTO RESEARCHERS

koan \'kō-,än\ In ZEN Buddhism, a brief paradoxical statement or question used as a discipline in MEDITATION. The effort to solve a koan is designed to exhaust the analytic intellect and the will, leaving the mind open for response on an intuitive level. There are about 1,700 traditional koans, which are based on anecdotes from ancient Zen masters. They include the well-known example "When both hands are clapped a sound is produced; listen to the sound of one hand clapping."

kobdas \'gō-aù-,dēs\ Drum used for inducing trances and for DIVINATION by Sami SHAMANS. It consisted of a wooden frame over which a reindeer hide was stretched; the hide was covered with designs representing spirits or deities. In divination, the drum was beaten with a hammer made of reindeer antler, causing a triangular piece of bone or metal called an *arpa* to move along its surface. From these movements the shaman divined the nature of an illness or learned the location of lost or stolen objects.

Kobe \'kō-bā\ City (pop., 1995: 1,424,000), southern central HONSHU, Japan. It is situated on Osaka Bay and occupies a narrow shelf of land between mountains and the sea. With neighboring cities OSAKA and KYOTO, it is the center of an industrial zone. Until the MEIJI RESTORATION it was only a fishing village, but it grew rapidly in the late 19th century. It was severely bombed during World War II and was entirely rebuilt after 1945. It suffered a major earthquake in 1995. Kobe is an important Japanese port and a center of shipbuilding and steel production; it is the seat of Kobe Univ.

Koblenz *or* **Coblenz** \'kō-,blents\ *ancient* **Confluentes** City (pop., 1999 est.: 108,700), western Germany. Situated at the junction of the RHINE and MOSELLE rivers, it was founded by the Romans in 9 BC. It was a Frankish royal seat in the 6th century AD, and was chartered as a city in 1214. The French occupied it in 1794; it passed to Prussia in 1815. After World War I, it was the seat of the Inter-Allied Control Commission for the Rhineland (1919–29). Devastated in World War II, it has since been restored. It is a center for the German wine trade; other industries include tourism and the manufacture of furniture, clothing, and chemicals.

Kobo Daishi See KUKAI

Kobuk Valley National Park \kō-'bùk\ National park, northwestern Alaska. Located north of the Arctic Circle, it was made a national monument in 1978 and a national park in 1980. Occupying an area of 1,750,421 acres (708,920 hectares), it preserves the Kobuk River valley, including the Kobuk and Salmon rivers, forest lands, and the Great Kobuk Sand Dunes. Archaeological sites reveal more than 10,000 years of human occupation. It protects caribou migration routes; other wildlife include grizzly and black bears, fox, moose, and wolves.

Koch \'käch\, **Ed(ward Irving)** (born 1924) U.S. politician. Born in New York City, he served in the army during World War II. A graduate of NYU Law School, he was elected to the U.S. Congress in 1968. In 1978 he was elected to the first of three terms as mayor of New York. He is credited with bringing fiscal stability to the insolvent city and with instituting merit selection of city judges. His brash forthrightness made him an entertaining and popular figure, but his manner and rhetoric increasingly came to be seen as unkind and divisive and eventually resulted in his defeat, after which he became a columnist and talk-show host.

Koch \'kȯk, *Engl* 'kȯk\, **(Heinrich Hermann) Robert** (1843–1910) German physician. As the first to isolate the ANTHRAX bacillus, observe its life cycle, and develop a preventive inoculation for it, he first proved a causal relation between a bacillus and a disease. He perfected pure-culture techniques, based on LOUIS PASTEUR's concept. He isolated the TUBERCULOSIS organism and established its role in the disease (1882). In 1883 he discovered the causal organism for CHOLERA and how it is transmitted, and also developed a vaccination for RINDERPEST. Koch's postulates remain fundamental to pathology: the organism should always be found in sick animals and never in healthy ones; it must be grown in pure culture; the cultured organism must make a healthy animal sick; and it must be reisolated from the newly sick animal and recultured and still be the same. Awarded a Nobel Prize in 1905, he is considered a founder of bacteriology.

Köchel \'kœk-əl, *Engl* 'kər-shəl\, **Ludwig (Alois Ferdinand) von** (1800–1877) Austrian scholar and musicologist. After gaining a law degree, he tutored children of wealthy families and traveled, researching books on a number of different topics, including botany, mineralogy, and music. He is best known for his 1862 thematic catalog of Mozart's works (which are still identified by their "K numbers"), a monument of music scholarship. He also edited LUDWIG VAN BEETHOVEN's letters.

Kocher \'kȯ-kər\, **Emil Theodor** (1841–1917) Swiss surgeon. He was the first surgeon to remove the thyroid gland to treat GOITER (1876). He later found that total removal could cause a state resembling CRETINISM, but that leaving part of the gland in place made this temporary. He introduced a surgical method for reducing shoulder dislocations, as well as many new surgical techniques, instruments, and appliances. A type of forceps and a gallbladder surgery incision named for him are still used. He adopted JOSEPH LISTER's principles of complete asepsis in surgery. In 1909 he won a Nobel Prize.

Kodak Co., Eastman See EASTMAN KODAK CO.

Kodály \'kō-,dī\, **Zoltán** (1882–1967) Hungarian composer, ethnomusicologist, and music educator. He played various instruments as a child, and studied simultaneously at the university and the Budapest Academy of Music, earning diplomas in composition and teaching and a doctorate in Hungarian folk song. With BELA BARTOK, a lifelong friend, he compiled the important *Hungarian Folk Songs* (1906), and he continued to make field recordings until World War I made it impossible. He came to international attention with his *Psalmus hungaricus* (1923) and the opera *Háry János* (1926). His works, based on folk music, are strongly marked by such progressive influences as C. DEBUSSY. He devoted much of his energy to developing a school music curriculum that would develop children's musicality, and the "Kodály method" remains in wide use today.

Kodiak Island Island (pop., 1990: 13,000), in the Gulf of ALASKA. It is 100 mi (160 km) long and 10–60 mi (16–96 km) wide, and has an area of 3,588 sq mi (9,293 sq km). The Kodiak National Wildlife Refuge covers 75% of the island and is the habitat of the Kodiak bear. Discovered in 1763 by a Russian fur trader, the island, known as Kikhtak, became the site in 1784 of the first Russian colony in America. Russian control ended in 1867; the island was renamed Kodiak in 1901. In 1964 a destructive earthquake lowered the island by 5–6 ft (1.5–1.8 m).

Koehler, Ted See Harold ARLEN

Koestler \'kest-lər\, **Arthur** (1905–1983) Hungarian-British novelist, journalist, and critic. He is best known for *Darkness at Noon (*1940); a political novel examining the moral danger in a totalitarian system that sacrifices means to an end, it reflects the events leading to his break with the Communist Party and his experience as a correspondent imprisoned by the fascists in the Spanish Civil War. He also wrote of his disillusionment with communism in the essay collection *The God That Failed* (1949). His later works, mostly concerning science and philosophy, include *The Act of Creation* (1964) and *The Ghost in the Machine* (1967). He died with his wife in a suicide pact.

Koguryo \ˌkō-gu̇r-'yō\ Largest of the three kingdoms into which ancient Korea was divided until 668. Tradition sets its founding at 37 BC, but modern historians believe the tribal state was formed in the 2nd century BC. Eventually the northern half of the Korean peninsula, the Liaodong Peninsula, and much of Manchuria were under Koguryo's rule. Buddhism, Confucianism, and Taoism all influenced the kingdom, which fell to the allied forces of China's TANG DYNASTY and the southern Korean kingdom of SILLA in 668. Numerous surviving tomb paintings give a good picture of the life, ideology, and character of Koguryo's forceful, horse-riding northern people. See also PARHAE.

Koh-i-noor \'kō-ə-ˌnu̇r\ Famous Indian diamond with a history dating perhaps as far back as the 14th century. Originally a 191-carat stone that lacked fire (flashes of color), it was recut to 109 carats in 1852 in an attempt to enhance its fire and brilliance. The Koh-i-noor (Hindi for "mountain of light") was acquired by the British in 1849 and became part of the CROWN JEWELS of Queen Victoria. It was incorporated into the state crown fashioned for Queen Elizabeth, consort of George VI, at her coronation in 1937.

kohen See COHEN

Kohl \'kōl\, **Helmut** (born 1930) Chancellor of West Germany (1982–90) and of the reunified Germany (1990–98). After earning a doctorate at the University of Heidelberg, he was elected to the Rhineland-Palatinate legislature and became the state's minister president (1969). In 1973 he was elected chair of the Christian Democratic Union, and in 1982 became German chancellor of a coalition government. Kohl's centrist policies included modest cuts in government spending and strong support for West German commitments to NATO. After the fall of the Berlin Wall in 1989, Kohl concluded a treaty with East Germany that unified the two countries' economic systems. Absorption of the moribund East German economy proved difficult, and Kohl's government had to increase taxes and cut government spending after unification. In 1998 his coalition government was defeated by the Social Democrats under GERHARD SCHRODER. Revelations of serious financial irregularities during Kohl's chancellorship soon emerged, tainting his reputation and weakening his party.

Köhler \'kœ-lər\, **Wolfgang** (1887–1967) German psychologist. His studies of problem solving by chimpanzees (*The Mentality of Apes,* 1917), in which he examined learning and perception as structured wholes, led to a radical revision of existing theory, and Köhler became a key figure in the development of Gestalt psychology. He continued his research during the 1920s and early '30s at the University of Berlin, publishing *Gestalt Psychology* (1929, rev. 1947), but emigrated to the U.S. after the Nazi takeover and taught at Swarthmore College 1935–55. His other writings include *Dynamics in Psychology* (1940), *The Place of Values in a World of Facts* (1938), and *The Task of Gestalt Psychology* (1969).

kohlrabi \kōl-'rä-bē\ Form of CABBAGE *(Brassica oleracea),* of the MUSTARD FAMILY, which originated in Europe. Its most distinctive feature is the greatly enlarged, globular to slightly flattened stem that grows just above the soil. Its flesh resembles that of a turnip but is sweeter and milder. Low in calories, kohlrabi is an excellent source of ascorbic acid, minerals, and dietary bulk. Though not widely grown commercially, it is popular in some regions as a kitchen vegetable. The young tender leaves may be eaten as greens; the thickened stem is served raw or cooked.

Kohlrabi (*Brassica oleracea*).
W.H. HODGE

koine \kȯi-'nā\ Newly formed compromise language that usually arises from a leveling of features distinguishing dialects of a common base language, or of features distinguishing several closely related languages. The new language is hence deregionalized and does not reflect social or political dominance of any one group of speakers. The classical example of a koine (as well as the source of the term) is Hellenistic GREEK, which developed from Attic Greek through replacement of the most distinctively Attic features by features of Ionic or other dialects. A koine may serve as a LINGUA FRANCA and often forms the basis of a new standard language.

Koizumi Junichiro (born 1942) Third-generation Japanese politician who became prime minister in 2001. Both Koizumi's father and grandfather served in the Diet (parliament). He graduated with a degree in economics from Keio University, Tokyo, in 1967 and then attended the London School of Economics. He ran unsuccessfully for his father's seat upon the latter's death in 1969, but in 1971 he ran again and was elected. In 1992–93 he was minister of posts and telecommunications and in 1988–89 and 1996–98 minister of health and welfare. He ran unsuccessfully for the presidency of the dominant Liberal-Democratic Party (LDP) in 1995 and 1998; upon the resignation of Mori Yoshiro in April 2001 Koizumi ran for the post once more and won, and he was soon confirmed as prime minister. An unconventional advocate of reform, Koizumi enjoyed widespread popular appeal. He appointed a cabinet that slighted traditional party factions and included a record five women, among them Tanaka Makiko as foreign minister. His economic policies included privatization of the country's postal savings system, a reduction in government spending, and an end to the practice of supporting failing businesses.

Kokand See QUQON

Koko Nor See QINGHAI (LAKE)

Kokoschka \kə-'kȯsh-kə\, **Oskar** (1886–1980) Austrian painter and writer. He studied and taught at the Vienna School of Arts and Crafts but was dissatisfied because the school omitted study of the human figure, his primary artistic interest. His early paintings were rendered in delicate, agitated lines and relatively naturalistic colors. After c. 1912 he became a leading exponent of EXPRESSIONISM; his portraits came to be painted with increasingly broader strokes of more varied color and heavier outlines. While recovering from a wound received in World War I, he wrote, produced, and staged three plays; his *Orpheus and Eurydice* (1918) became an opera by E. KRENEK (1926). The landscapes he produced during 10 years of teaching and travel mark the second peak of his career. Shortly before World War II he fled to London, where his paintings became increasingly political and antifascist. He continued his political art after moving to Switzerland in 1953.

Kol Nidre \'kȯl-'ni-drā\ Prayer sung in Jewish synagogues at the start of services on the eve of YOM KIPPUR. The prayer begins with an expression of repentance for all unfulfilled vows, oaths, and promises to God during the previous year. It was in use as early as the 8th century, perhaps as a means of annulling oaths forced on Jews by their Christian persecutors. The melody used by Ashkenazi Jews became famous when the composer M. BRUCH used it in his *Kol Nidre* (1880).

kola nut *or* **cola nut** Caffeine-containing NUT of two evergreen trees *(Cola acuminata* and *C. nitida)* of the cocoa family (Sterculiaceae), native to tropical Africa and cultivated extensively in the New World tropics. The trees grow to 60 ft (18.3 m) in height and have oblong leathery leaves, yellow flowers, and star-shaped fruit. The nut has been used in medicines and in soft drinks, though American "colas" today instead use synthetic flavorings that mimic its taste. Kola nuts are also used where grown as a medium of exchange or are chewed to diminish sensations of hunger and fatigue, to aid digestion, and to combat intoxication, hangover, and diarrhea.

Kola nut (*Cola nitida*).

W.H. HODGE

Kola Peninsula Promontory, northern Russia. It separates the WHITE and BARENTS seas; it occupies 40,000 sq mi (100,000 sq km) and extends across the Arctic Circle. It consists of rock more than 570 million years old. The winter climate is severe; the largest town is the ice-free port of MURMANSK on the northern coast. It has the world's largest deposits of apatite, used for fertilizer production.

Kolbe \'kȯl-bə\, **St. Maksymilian Maria** *orig.* **Rajmund Kolbe** (1894–1941) Polish Franciscan priest martyred by the Nazis. Ordained in 1918, he founded the City of Mary Immaculate religious center (1927) and became its superior, as well as director of Poland's chief Roman Catholic publishing complex. He was arrested by the Gestapo in 1939 and again in 1941 on charges of aiding Jews and the Polish underground. He was imprisoned at Warsaw, then shipped to Auschwitz, where he volunteered his life in place of that of a condemned inmate. Kolbe was canonized in 1982.

Kolchak \kȯl-'chäk\, **Aleksandr (Vasilyevich)** (1874–1920) Russian naval officer and political leader. In 1917 he was forced to resign as commander of the fleet in the Black Sea after the RUSSIAN REVOLUTION began. After a coup d'état in Omsk in 1918, he gained power among the counterrevolutionary White Russians, and in 1919 he was recognized by them as supreme ruler of Russia. After initial successes against the Red Army, his armies were routed in 1919; the next year he was captured and executed by the Bolsheviks.

Kolkata *formerly* **Calcutta** City (metro. area pop., 2001 prelim.: 13,216,546), northeastern India. Capital of WEST BENGAL state, former capital (1772–1912) of British India, and India's second-largest metropolitan area, it is located on the HUGLI RIVER, about 90 miles (145 km) from the river's mouth. Established as an English trading center in 1690, it became the seat of the BENGAL presidency in 1707. It was captured by the nawab of Bengal, who in 1756 imprisoned the English there (in a prison that was later known as the Black Hole); the city was retaken by the British under ROBERT CLIVE. It was an extremely busy 19th-century commercial center then began a decline with the removal of the capital to DELHI in 1912. The decline was furthered by the province's partition between India and Pakistan in 1947 and the creation of Bangladesh in 1971. The flood of refugees from these political upheavals significantly added to widespread poverty in the city. Kolkata was dealt a major blow in September 2000 when floodwaters inundated the city and left hundreds dead and tens of thousands homeless. Despite its problems, the city remains a dominant urban area of eastern India and a major educational and cultural center.

Kollontay \,kä-lən-'tī\, **Aleksandra (Mikhaylovna)** *orig.* **Aleksandra Mikhaylovna Domontovich** (1872–1952) Russian administrator and diplomat. As the first commissar for public welfare in the Bolshevik government (1917), she advocated simplifying marriage and divorce procedures and improving the status of women. She became the first woman to serve as an accredited minister to a foreign country when she was named minister to Norway (1923–25, 1927–30); she later served as minister to Mexico (1926–27) and Sweden (1930–45). In 1944 she conducted the negotiations that ended Soviet–Finnish hostilities in World War II.

Kollwitz \'kȯl-,vits, *Engl* 'kȯl-,wits\, **Käthe** *orig.* **Käthe Schmidt** (1867–1945) German graphic artist and sculptor. She studied painting in Berlin and Munich but devoted herself primarily to etchings, drawings, lithographs, and woodcuts. She gained firsthand knowledge of the miserable conditions of the urban poor when her physician husband opened a clinic in Berlin. She became the last great practitioner of German EXPRESSIONISM and an outstanding artist of social protest. Two early series of prints, *Weavers' Revolt* (1895–98) and *Peasants' War* (1902–8), portray the plight of the oppressed with the powerfully simplified, boldly accentuated forms that became her trademark. After her son died in World War I, she created a cycle of prints dedicated to the theme of a mother's love. She was the first woman elected to the Prussian Academy of Arts, where she was head of the Master Studio for Graphic Arts (1928–33). The Nazis banned her works from exhibition. The bombing of her home and studio in World War II destroyed much of her work.

"Self-Portrait with Hand on Forehead," etching by Käthe Kollwitz, 1910; in the National Gallery of Art, Washington, D.C.

B-7792 "SELF-PORTRAIT WITH HAND ON FOREHEAD," KATHE KOLLWITZ, NATIONAL GALLERY OF ART, WASHINGTON, D.C., ROSENWALD COLLECTION

Kölreuter \'kœl-,rȯi-tər\, **Josef Gottlieb** (1733–1806) German botanist. A pioneer in the study of plant hybrids, he was the first to develop a scientific application of the discovery (made in 1694 by RUDOLPH CAMERARIUS) of sex in plants. Cultivating plants in order to study their fertilization and development, he performed experiments, particularly with the tobacco plant, that included artificial fertilization and the production of fertile hybrids between plants of different species. His results foreshadowed the work of GREGOR MENDEL. Kölreuter recognized the importance of insects and wind as agents of pollen transfer. He applied CAROLUS LINNAEUS's sexual system of classification to lower plant forms. His work was not recognized until long after his death.

Kolyma River \,kä-li-'mä\ River, northeastern SIBERIA, eastern Russia. Rising in the Kolyma Mountains and emptying in the East Siberian Sea, it is 1,323 mi (2,129 km) long. It is navigable upstream to Verkhne-Kolymsk but is ice-free only from June to September. Under JOSEPH STALIN the goldfields of the upper Kolyma River valley held labor camps where more than one million prisoners died (1932–54).

Komarov \kə-mə-'rȯf\, **Vladimir (Mikhaylovich)** (1927–1967) Soviet cosmonaut. He joined the Soviet Air Force at 15, became a pilot in 1949, and piloted Voskhod 1, the first craft to carry more than one human into space, in 1964. He became the first Russian to make two spaceflights on his 1967 flight in SOYUZ 1. During the 18th orbit he attempted a landing; he died when the spacecraft reportedly became entangled in its main parachute at an altitude of several miles and fell back to earth.

Komodo dragon \kə-'mō-dō\ Largest living LIZARD *(Varanus komodoensis),* of the MONITOR LIZARD family Varanidae. They live on Komodo Island and a few neighboring islands in Indonesia. Driven almost to extinction, they are now protected. Komodos grow to 10 ft (3 m) long, weigh up to 300 lbs (135 kg), and may live up to 100 years. They dig a

Komodo dragon (*Varanus komodoensis*).

JAMES A. KERN

burrow as deep as 30 ft (9 m). Carrion is their main diet, but adults may eat smaller Komodos. They can run swiftly and occasionally attack and kill humans.

Komsomol \'käm-sə-ˌmäl\ Organization in the former Soviet Union for young people aged 14–28 that was primarily a political organ for spreading Communist teachings and preparing future members of the COMMUNIST PARTY. It was organized in 1918. Members participated in health, sports, education, and publishing activities and various industrial projects. They were frequently favored over nonmembers for employment, scholarships, and the like. Its membership reached its height, about 40 million, in the 1970s and early 1980s. It disbanded with the collapse of Soviet communism in the early 1990s.

Konbaung dynasty See ALAUNGPAYA DYNASTY

Kondratev \kən-'drät-yəf\, **Nikolay (Dmitriyevich)** (1892–1938?) Russian economist and statistician. In the 1920s he helped develop the first Soviet FIVE-YEAR PLAN, for which he analyzed factors that would stimulate Soviet economic growth. After criticizing JOSEPH STALIN's plan for the total collectivization of agriculture, he was dismissed from his post as director of the Institute for the Study of Business Activity in 1928. He was arrested in 1930 and sentenced to prison; his sentence was reviewed in 1938, and he received the death penalty, which was likely carried out the same year. He is noted for his theory of 50-year BUSINESS CYCLES known as Kondratev's waves. See also GOSPLAN.

Konev \'kȯ-nyəf\, **Ivan (Stepanovich)** (1897–1973) Soviet general in World War II. When the Germans invaded the Soviet Union in 1941, Konev led the first counterattack of the war. He defeated HEINZ GUDERIAN's advance on Moscow and halted large German forces in 1942 and 1943. In 1944 his army was the first to march onto German soil; with the forces of GEORGY K. ZHUKOV, it captured Berlin. After the war he served as commander in chief of Soviet ground forces (1946–50) and later of WARSAW PACT forces (1955–60).

Kong River River, Laos and Cambodia. Rising in central Vietnam southwest of Hue, it flows southwest for 300 mi (480 km), passing through southern Laos. It enters Cambodia east of the MEKONG RIVER and continues southwest across the northern Cambodian plateau to later join the Mekong.

Kongo *or* **Bakongo** Bantu-speaking peoples living along the Atlantic coast in Congo (Zaire), Congo (Brazzaville), and Angola. They engage in subsistence agriculture and cash cropping (including coffee, cacao, and bananas); many live and work in towns. Descent is matrilineal, and most villages are independent of their neighbors. A Kongo kingdom existed from the 14th century; its wealth came from trade in ivory, hides, slaves, and a shell currency. It broke up into warring chiefdoms in 1665.

Königgrätz \'kœ̄-nik-ˌgrets\, **Battle of** *or* **Battle of Sadowa** \'sä-dō-ˌvä\ (July 3, 1866) Decisive battle in the SEVEN WEEKS' WAR between Prussia and Austria, fought at Sadowa, near Königgrätz, Bohemia (now Hradec Králové, Czech Republic). The Austrians, equipped with muzzle-loading rifles and relying heavily on the bayonet charge, were led by Ludwig von Benedek (1804–1881). The Prussians, led by HELMUTH VON MOLTKE, were armed with breech-loading needle guns; they used railroad transport to move their troops, a first in European warfare. The Prussian victory led to Austria's exclusion from a Prussian-dominated Germany.

Königsberg See KALININGRAD

Konkouré River \ˌkȯŋ-kü-'rā\ River, western central Guinea, West Africa. Flowing west for 188 mi (303 km) to empty into the Atlantic Ocean, it is a source of hydroelectric power. Once a major hindrance to transportation between CONAKRY and the towns of Boffa and Boké, it is now bridged at Ouassou.

Konoe Fumimaro \kə-'nȯ-ā-ˌfü-mē-'mä-rō\ (1891–1945) Political leader and prime minister of Japan (1937–39, 1940–41), who tried unsuccessfully to restrict the power of the military and to keep Japan's war with China from widening into a world conflict. In 1941 he signed a nonaggression pact with the Soviet Union and participated in U.S.-mediated negotiations to try to resolve the conflict with China. Later that year he resigned over differences with TOJO HIDEKI. During the war he was forced to leave the center of politics; afterward he was a deputy minister in the Higashikuni Cabinet. He committed suicide after being served an arrest warrant on suspicion of being a war criminal.

Konya \'kȯn-yä\ *ancient* **Iconium** City (pop., 1995 est.: 585,000), central Turkey. First settled in the 3rd millennium BC, it is one of the oldest urban centers in the world. Influenced by Greek culture from the 3rd century BC, Iconium came under Roman rule by 25 BC. It was taken by the Seljuq Turks c. 1072. Renamed Konya, it was a major cultural center in the 13th century and was home to the mystics known as "whirling DERVISHES." Later ruled by the Mongols, it was annexed to the Ottoman empire c. 1467. It declined during Ottoman rule but revived after the Istanbul–Baghdad railway opened in 1896. An important industrial center, it is also a trade center for the agricultural area surrounding it.

kookaburra *or* **laughing jackass** Eastern Australian species *(Dacelo gigas)* of forest KINGFISHER (subfamily Daceloninae). Its call, which sounds like fiendish laughter, can be heard very early in the morning and just after sunset. A gray-brown, woodland-dwelling bird, it reaches a length of 17 in. (43 cm), with a 3.2–4-in. (8–10-cm) beak. In its native habitat it eats invertebrates and small vertebrates, including venomous snakes. In western Australia and New Zealand, where it has been introduced, it has been known to attack chickens and ducklings.

Kookaburra (*Dacelo gigas*).

BUCKY REEVES FROM THE NATIONAL AUDUBON SOCIETY COLLECTION/PHOTO RESEARCHERS

Koolhaas \'kōl-ˌhäs\, **Rem** (born 1944) Dutch architect. He studied architecture in London and worked in New York, then opened his own firm (1975) in Rotterdam and London. He first achieved recognition with his book *Delirious New York* (1978), which profiled Manhattan's architectural development, suggesting that it was an organic process created through a variety of cultural forces. His best-known projects are large-scale structures, including the Kunsthal in Rotterdam, the Grand Palais exhibition hall in Lille (France), and a master plan for the MCA/Universal Studios site in Los Angeles. His book *S, M, L, XL* (1996) addressed the theme of size. In 1998 he won the design competition for a new campus center at the Illinois Institute of Technology. In 2000 he was awarded the Pritzker Architecture Prize.

Kooning, Willem de See Willem DE KOONING

Kootenay National Park National park, southeastern British Columbia. Centered around the KOOTENAY RIVER, the park occupies the western slopes of the ROCKY MTNS., adjacent to BANFF and YOHO national parks. Established as a national park in 1920, it covers 543 sq mi (1,406 sq km). From prehistoric times, the area was a major north–south travel route. Pictographs indicate that humans settled near the hot springs 11,000–12,000 years ago. The park's scenery is characterized by snow-capped peaks, glaciers, cascades, canyons, and verdant valleys. Wildlife includes wapiti (elk), moose, deer, bighorn sheep, and mountain goats.

Kootenay River \'kü-tᵊn-ˌā\ River, western North America. Rising in the ROCKY MTNS. in Alberta, Canada, it flows south through British Columbia. It continues into Montana and then turns north into Idaho and back into British Columbia, where it joins the COLUMBIA RIVER, having traveled a course of 485 mi (780 km).

Koppel, Ted *orig.* **Edward James** (born 1940) U.S. (British-born) television broadcaster. He emigrated to the U.S. in 1953, worked as a correspondent for ABC from 1963, and was its chief diplomatic correspondent 1971–80. As anchor of the late-night live interview show *Nightline* since 1980, he has won several Emmy and other awards.

Köprülü \kœ̄-prœ̄-'lœ̄\, **Fazil Ahmed Pasa** (1635–1676) Grand VIZIER (1661–76) under the Ottoman sultan Mehmed IV. He started his career as a scholar but entered the civil service when his father became grand vizier. Having made the army more efficient, he campaigned successfully against the Austrians (1663), in Crete (1669), and in Poland. He died during his last campaign from the effects of exhaustion and too much wine.

Koraïs \kȯ-'rä-ēs\, **Adamántios** (1748–1833) Greek scholar. He studied medicine in France, but left it to pursue a literary career in Paris for most of his life. His advocacy of a revived classicism, with the goal of awakening national aspirations and an awareness of their heritage in modern Greeks in order to stimulate a new strength and unity, had a great influence on Greek language and culture. His anthologies include the *Library of Greek Literature* (17 vols., 1805–26) and the *Parerga* (9 vols., 1809–27). Largely through his *Atakta* (composed 1828–35), the first Modern Greek dictionary, he created a new Greek literary language by combining elements of vernacular (Demotic) and Classical Greek.

Koran See QURAN

Korbut, Olga (Valentinovna) (born 1956) Soviet gymnast. Born in Grodno, Belarus, she first competed in the 1969 championships at the age of 13. Appealingly diminutive, with a captivating smile, she was the first person ever to do a backward somersault on the balance beam. In the 1972 Olympic Games she won three gold medals (balance beam, floor exercises, and as a member of the winning USSR team) and a silver medal (uneven parallel bars). In the 1976 Olympics she won a team gold medal and a silver for the balance beam.

Korda, Alexander *orig.* **Sándor Laszlo Kellner** *later* **Sir Alexander** (1893–1956) Hungarian-British film director and producer. He worked as a journalist in Budapest, where he founded a film magazine and, in 1917, became manager of the Corvin movie studio. He left Hungary in 1919 to make several films in Berlin, then went to Hollywood, where he directed such movies as *The Private Life of Helen of Troy* (1927). After moving to England in 1931, he founded London Film Productions. He helped develop Britain's film industry, directing and producing such successful films as *The Private Life of Henry VIII* (1933), *Catherine the Great* (1934), *The Scarlet Pimpernel* (1934), and *Rembrandt* (1936), and producing *The Third Man* (1949), *Summertime* (1955), and *Richard III* (1955).

Kordofan \ˌkȯr-də-ˈfan\ *or* **Kurdufan** \ˌku̇r-du̇-ˈfän\ Region, central Sudan. Lying west of the White NILE RIVER, it was originally inhabited by Nubian-speaking peoples. Controlled by the Christian Tungur dynasty 900–1200 AD, it was later taken by Arabs, and in the 17th century a sultanate was established. Egyptian rule began in the 1820s. The slave trade played an important part in the region's economy until its eradication in 1878 by CHARLES GEORGE GORDON. Egyptian rule was ended by a revolt in 1882 led by AL-MAHDI. It became a province of the Sudan in 1899.

kore \ˈkȯ-rā\ Type of freestanding statue of a maiden (the female counterpart of the KOUROS) that appeared with the beginning of Greek monumental sculpture (c. 700 BC) and remained to the end of the Archaic period (c. 500 BC). Carved from marble and originally painted, the kore is a draped female figure standing erect with feet together or one foot slightly advanced. One arm is often extended, holding an offering; the other is lowered, usually clasping a fold of drapery. As in all Greek art, the kore evolved from a highly stylized form to a more naturalistic one. Its prototypes are found in Egyptian and Mesopotamian art.

Korea *Korean* **Choson** \ˈchō-sȯn\ Former kingdom, a peninsula (Korean Peninsula) on the eastern coast of Asia. In 1948 it was partitioned into two republics, North Korea and South Korea. According to tradition, the ancient kingdom of Choson was established in the northern part of the peninsula probably by peoples from northern China in the 3rd millennium BC. Conquered by China in 108 BC, it later developed into the Three Kingdoms of SILLA, KOGURYO, and PAEKCHE. Silla conquered the other two in the 7th century AD, and ruled until 935, when the Paekche dynasty became prominent. Invaded by the Mongols in 1231, the Kingdom of Choson, with its capital at SEOUL, was ruled by the Yi dynasty (see YI SONG-GYE) from 1392 to 1910. From c. 1637 it shut out foreign contacts, but was forced in 1876 to open ports to Japan. Rivalry over Korea brought on the RUSSO-JAPANESE WAR, after which Korea became a Japanese protectorate. Formally annexed to Japan in 1910, it was freed from Japanese control in 1945. After World War II, it was divided into two zones of occupation, Russian in the north and U.S. in the south. In 1948 the two republics were established. For Korea's later history, see NORTH KOREA and SOUTH KOREA; see also KOREAN WAR.

Korea, North *officially* **Democratic People's Republic of Korea** Country, occupying the northern half of the Korean Peninsula, East Asia. Area: 47,399 sq mi (122,762 sq km). Population (1997 est.): 24,317,000. Capital: PYONGYANG. Ethnically, the population is almost completely Korean. Language: Korean (official). Religions: Confucianism, Buddhism, shamanism (formerly prevalent, now suppressed), CH'ONDOGYO. Foreign missionaries were expelled during World War II. Currency: won. Four-fifths of North Korea's land area consists of mountain ranges and uplands; its highest peak is the volcanic Mount Paektu (9,022 ft, or 2,750 m). North Korea has a centrally planned economy based on heavy industry (iron and steel, machinery, chemicals, and textiles) and agriculture. Cooperative farms raise crops such as rice, corn, barley, and vegetables. The country is also rich in mineral resources, including coal, iron ore, and magnesite. It is a republic with one legislature; the chief of state is the Head of State and the head of state and government is the premier. For early history, see KOREA. After the Japanese defeat in World War II, the Soviet Union occupied Korea north of latitude 38° N, while the U.S. occupied the area south of it. The Democratic People's Republic of Korea was established as a communist state in 1948. Seeking to unify the peninsula by force, North Korea launched an invasion of South Korea in 1950, initiating the KOREAN WAR. U.N. troops intervened on the side of South Korea, and Chinese soldiers reinforced the North Korean army in the war, which ended with an armistice in 1953. Under KIM IL-SUNG, North Korea became one of the most harshly regimented societies in the world, with a state-owned economy that failed to produce adequate supplies of food and consumer goods for its citizens. In the late 1990s, under Kim Il-sung's successor KIM CHONG IL, the country endured a serious famine; as many as a million Koreans may have died. In 2000, 50 years after the start of the Korean War, a summit between the leaders of North and South Korea raised hopes for an end to North Korea's long isolation.

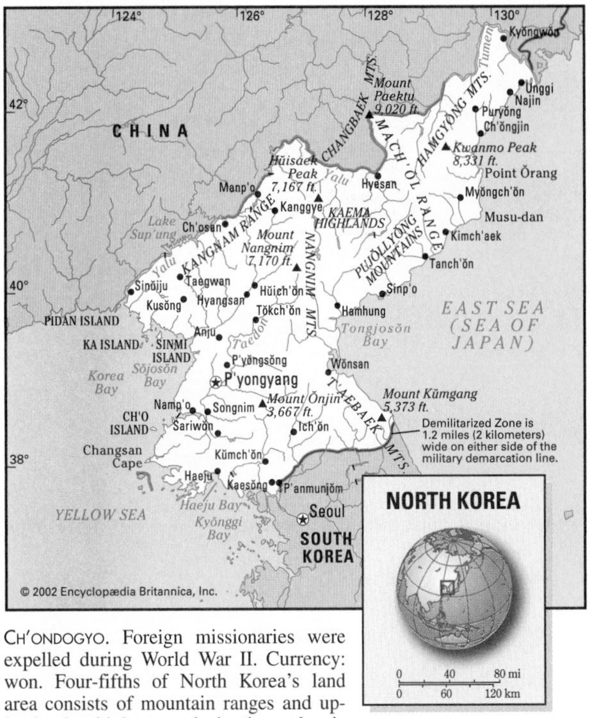

Korea, South *officially* **Republic of Korea** Country, occupying the southern half of the Korean peninsula, East Asia. It is located northwest of Japan and includes Cheju Island, located about 60 mi (97 km) south of the peninsula. Area: 38,330 sq mi (99,274 sq km). Population (1997 est.): 45,628,000. Capital: SEOUL. The population is almost entirely ethnically Korean. Language: Korean (official). Religions: Buddhism, Protestant Christianity, Confucianism (widespread); CH'ONDOGYO. Currency: won. Nearly three-fourths of the total land area of South Korea consists of mountains and uplands; the densely populated lowlands are heavily cultivated for wet rice. The Naktong and HAN are the country's principal rivers. South Korea's economy is based largely on services and industry (including petrochemicals, electronic goods, and steel). It is a republic with one legislative house; its head of state and government is the president, assisted by the prime minister. For early history, see KOREA. The Republic of Korea was established in 1948 in the southern portion of the Korean peninsula, which had been occupied by the U.S. after World War II. In 1950 North Korean troops invaded South Korea, precipitating the

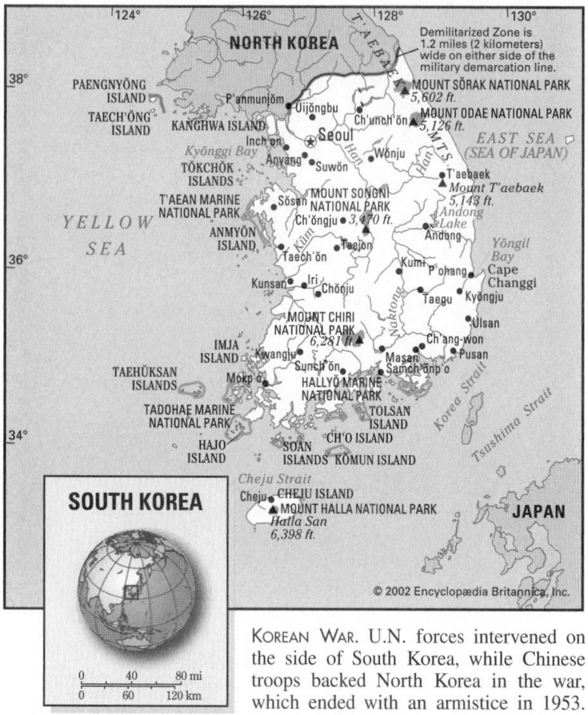

Korean War. U.N. forces intervened on the side of South Korea, while Chinese troops backed North Korea in the war, which ended with an armistice in 1953. The devastated country was rebuilt with U.S. aid, and South Korea prospered in the postwar era, developing a strong export-oriented economy. It experienced an economic downturn in the mid-1990s that affected many economies in the area. In 2000 the leaders of North and South Korea held a summit that revived hopes for reunification.

Korea Strait Channel between South Korea and southwestern Japan. Connecting the East China Sea with the Sea of Japan, it is 120 mi (195 km) wide and is divided by Tsushima island at its center. Its passage to the east is known as Tsushima Strait, site of the Battle of Tsushima (1905); to the west it is called the Western Channel.

Korean art Visual art produced on the Korean peninsula and traditionally characterized by simplicity, spontaneity, and naturalism. Artifacts indicate the early influence of China, beginning with the establishment in 108 BC of Chinese colonies in North Korea. Buddhism, introduced from China in AD 372, resulted in a flowering of the arts and remained the major source of inspiration until the 15th century. During the Koguryo (37 BC–AD 668), Paekche (18 BC–AD 660), and Silla (57 BC–AD 668) kingdoms, Korean art featured granite pagodas, decorative jewelry, unglazed stoneware, and sculpture. The subsequent Koryo period (918–1392) is noted for porcelain with a celadon glaze. A renewal of the arts during the Choson (Yi) period (1392–1910), spurred by the spread of Confucianism, is characterized by a spontaneous decorative sense. Near the end of the Choson period, Western and Japanese influences are evident, attributable to the Japanese occupation of Korea (1910–45).

Korean language Official language of North and South Korea, spoken by over 75 million people, including substantial communities of ethnic Koreans elsewhere. Korean is not closely related to any other language, though a distant genetic kinship to Japanese is now thought probable by some scholars, and an even more remote relationship to the Altaic languages possible. Korean was written with Chinese characters to stand in various ways for Korean meanings and sounds as early as the 12th century, though substantial documentation is not evident until the invention of a unique phonetic script for it in 1443. This script, now called hangul, represents syllables by arranging simple symbols for each phoneme into a square form like that of a Chinese character. Grammatically, Korean has a basic subject-object-verb word order and places modifiers before the element they modify.

Korean War (1950–53) Conflict arising after the post-World War II division of Korea at lat. 38° into North Korea and South Korea. At the end of the war, Soviet forces accepted surrender of Japanese forces north of that line while U.S. forces accepted surrender south of it. Negotiations failed to reunify the two halves, the northern half being a Soviet client state and the southern half being backed by the U.S. In 1950 North Korea invaded South Korea. The U.N. Security Council, minus the absent Soviet delegate, passed a resolution calling for the assistance of all U.N. members in halting the invasion, and Pres. Harry Truman ordered U.S. troops to the assistance of South Korea. At first the North Korean forces drove the South Korean and U.N. forces down to the southern tip of the Korean peninsula, but a brilliant amphibious landing at Inch'on conceived by Gen. Douglas MacArthur turned the tide in favor of the U.N. troops, who advanced to near the border of North Korea and China. The Chinese then entered the war and drove the U.N. forces back south; the front line stabilized at the 38th parallel. MacArthur insisted on voicing his objections to U.S. war aims in a public manner and was relieved of his command by Truman. Pres. Dwight D. Eisenhower participated in the conclusion of an armistice that accepted the front line as the de facto boundary between the two Koreas. The war resulted in the deaths of approximately 2 million Koreans, 600,000 Chinese, 37,000 Americans, and 3,000 Turks, Britons, and other nationals in the U.N. forces.

Kornberg, Arthur (born 1918) U.S. biochemist and physician. Born in Brooklyn, N.Y., he studied at the University of Rochester. In 1959 he joined the faculty at Stanford University. While studying how living organisms manufacture nucleotides, his research led him to the problem of how nucleotides are strung together to form DNA molecules. Adding radioactive nucleotides to an enzyme mixture prepared from cultures of *E. coli*, he found evidence of a reaction catalyzed by the enzyme that adds nucleotides to a preexisting DNA chain. He was the first to accomplish the cell-free synthesis of DNA. He shared a 1959 Nobel Prize with Severo Ochoa.

Korngold, Erich Wolfgang (1897–1957) Austrian-U.S. composer. Son of a music critic, he had his childhood compositions praised by G. Mahler and A. Schnabel. He solidified his reputation with his operatic masterpiece, *Die tote Stadt* (1920). In 1934 he moved to Hollywood, and he became best known for his film scores, his broadly Romantic style proving very suitable to such swashbuckling stories as *Anthony Adverse* (1936, Academy Award) and *The Adventures of Robin Hood* (1938, Academy Award), as well as 17 others. His violin concerto (1946) has been frequently recorded.

Kornilov \kȯr-'nyē-lȯf\, **Lavr (Georgiyevich)** (1870–1918) Imperial Russian general. A career army officer, he was a divisional commander in World War I. After the Russian Revolution of 1917 he was appointed army commander in chief by Aleksandr Kerensky. Conflicts developed because of their opposing views on politics and the role of the army, and when Kornilov sent troops toward Petrograd, Kerensky interpreted the move as an attempted coup and dismissed him. Arrested, he escaped to command an anti-Bolshevik White army and was killed in battle.

Korolyov \kə-rəl-'yȯf\, **Sergey (Pavlovich)** (1907–1966) Soviet designer of guided missiles, rockets, and spacecraft. In 1933 he and F. A. Tsander launched the Soviet Union's first liquid-propellant rocket. During World War II Korolyov designed and tested liquid-fuel rocket boosters for military aircraft. After the war he modified the German V-2 missile and supervised test firing of captured missiles. His work led to the Soviet Union's first intercontinental ballistic missile (ICBM). He directed systems engineering for Soviet launch vehicles and spacecraft, including design, testing, construction, and launching of manned and unmanned spacecraft, and was the guiding genius behind the Soviet spaceflight program.

Koror \'kȯr-ˌȯr\ Island (pop., 1990: 10,000) and town of the same name, capital of Palau, western Pacific Ocean. Lying southwest of Babelthuap Island, it has a land area of 3 sq mi (8 sq km). It was the administrative capital of all Japanese mandated islands in the Pacific 1921–45. Devastated during World War II, it was later developed as a commercial and tourist center.

Korsakoff's syndrome *or* **Korsakoff's psychosis** *or* **Korsakoff's disease** Neurological disorder marked by severe amnesia despite clear perception and full consciousness, resulting from chronic alcoholism, head injury, brain illness, or thiamine deficiency. Sufferers typically cannot remember events in the recent or even immediate past; some retain memories only a few seconds. Longer periods—up to 20 years—may also be forgotten. Confabulation (recounting detailed, convincing "memories" of events that never happened) sometimes coexists with the syndrome, which may be transient or chronic.

Korsakov, Nicolai Rimsky- See Nicolai RIMSKY-KORSAKOV

Koryo \'kȯr-yō\ Korean kingdom ruled by a dynasty of the same name from 935 to 1392. During this period Korea began to form a distinctively Korean cultural tradition. The dynasty was formed by Gen. Wang Kon of Later Koguryo and defeated the kingdoms of SILLA and of Later Paekche to create a unified Korean peninsula in 936. In the late 10th century, a centralized bureaucratic system replaced the old aristocratic tribal system. The kingdom saw a flowering of the arts, particularly ceramics (Koryo celadon), and Buddhism and Confucianism were influential. In the 13th century Koryo suffered a series of Mongol invasions, and in 1392 YI SONG-GYE overthrew the shaky dynasty and founded the CHOSON dynasty.

Kosala \'kō-sə-lə\ Ancient kingdom, northern India. Roughly corresponding to the historical region of OUDH, in what is now southern central UTTAR PRADESH state, it extended into present-day Nepal. In the 6th century BC it rose to become one of the dominant states in northern India. MAGADHA conquered Kosala c. 490 BC, and it became known as Northern Kosala to distinguish it from a larger kingdom to the south known variously as Kosala, Southern Kosala, or Great Kosala. The BUDDHA was born there.

Kosciusko \ˌkä-zē-'əs-kō\, **Mt.** Peak, in the Snowy Mtns., AUSTRALIAN ALPS, southeastern NEW SOUTH WALES, Australia. The highest mountain in mainland Australia, it reaches 7,310 ft (2,228 m). It is located in Kosciusko National Park, which has an area of 2,498 sq mi (6,469 sq km); it is near Mounts Townsend, Twynam, North Ramshead, and Carruthers, whose melting snows feed the rivers and reservoirs that make up the Snowy Mountains Hydroelectric Scheme. The mountain was named in 1840 in honor of TADEUSZ KOSCIUSZKO.

Kosciuszko \kȯsh-'chu̇sh-kō, *Engl* ˌkä-sē-'əs-kō\, **Tadeusz** (1746–1817) Polish patriot who fought in the AMERICAN REVOLUTION. He studied military engineering in Paris and went to America in 1776, where he joined the colonial army. He helped build fortifications in Philadelphia and at West Point, N.Y. As chief of engineers, he twice rescued Gen. NATHANAEL GREENE's army by directing river crossings. He also directed the blockade of Charleston, S.C. At the war's end he was awarded U.S. citizenship and made a brigadier general. He returned to Poland in 1784 and became a major general in the Polish army. In 1794 he led a rebellion against occupying Russian and Prussian forces, during which he defended Warsaw for two months, directing residents to build earthworks. He was jailed in Russia 1794–96, returned to the U.S. in 1797, then left for France, where he continued efforts to secure Polish independence.

kosher See KASHRUTH

Kosi River \'kō-sē\ River, Nepal and northern India. Rising from several tributaries in eastern Nepal, it runs south through the great plain of northern India. It empties into the GANGES RIVER after a course of 450 mi (724 km).

Košice \'kȯ-shēt-sə\ City (pop., 1996 est.: 241,000), eastern Slovakia. Settled in the 9th century and chartered in 1241, it served as a trading settlement during the late Middle Ages. It developed rapidly after becoming part of Czechoslovakia in 1920. Occupied in 1938 by Hungary, it was liberated in 1945 and became the first seat of the postwar Czechoslovakian government. A part of independent Slovakia since 1992, it is the political, economic, and cultural center of southeastern Slovakia.

Kosinski \kō-'sin-skē\, **Jerzy (Nikodem)** (1933–1991) Polish-U.S. writer. He claimed that his horrific experiences as a Jew in World War II Poland and Russia caused him to be mute for much of his childhood. He studied political science and became a professor of sociology before emigrating to the U.S. in 1957. His novel *The Painted Bird* (1965) is a graphic, surrealistic tale of the horrors surrounding the war. Other successful novels were *Steps* (1968) and the satiric fable *Being There* (1970; film, 1979). After his suicide, it was revealed that much of his past had been fabricated.

Kosovo \'kȯ-sȯ-ˌvȯ\ Autonomous province (pop., 1991: 1,950,000), within the republic of SERBIA, Yugoslavia. It occupies an area of 4,203 sq mi (10,887 sq km); its capital is PRISTINA. Before 1999, ethnic Albanians, most of whom are Muslims, made up nine-tenths of its population, with Serbs (mostly Christian) accounting for the remainder. In the late 1980s the Albanians protested when Serbia took control of Kosovo's administration, and in 1992 they voted to secede from Yugoslavia. Serbia responded by tightening its control of Kosovo, which led to the KOSOVO CONFLICT.

Kosovo \'kō-sə-ˌvō\, **Battle of** Name of two battles fought in the Serbian province of KOSOVO. The first (June 13, 1389), between the Serbs and the Ottoman Turks led by their sultan, Murad I, ended in the collapse of Serbia and the encirclement of the crumbling Byzantine empire by Turkish armies, despite the assassination of Murad by subterfuge. The battle, which led to three centuries of Serbian vassaldom, has remained a central event to Serbian nationalists. In the second battle (October 17–20, 1448), between the Ottomans and a Hungarian-Walachian coalition, halted the last major effort by Christian crusaders to free the Balkans from Ottoman rule. See also OTTOMAN EMPIRE.

Kosovo conflict (1998–99) Ethnic war in KOSOVO, Yugoslavia. In 1989 the Serbian president SLOBODAN MILOSEVIC abrogated Kosovo's constitutional autonomy and began systematic oppression of its ethnic Albanians, who constitute some 90% of its population. The Kosovars set up a shadow government and began a campaign of nonviolent resistance. Growing tensions led in 1998 to armed clashes, involving both the police and the Kosovo Liberation Army (KLA). The Contact Group (U.S., Britain, Germany, France, Italy, and Russia) proposed a unified policy, demanding cessation of fighting, unconditional withdrawal of Serbian special police and army forces, return of refugees, and unlimited access for international monitors. Milošević agreed to meet most of the demands, but did not. The U.N. Security Council condemned excessive use of force by Serbian police forces, including so-called ethnic cleansing (killing and expulsion), and imposed a comprehensive arms embargo, but the violence increased. During diplomatic negotiations at Rambouillet, France, Milošević massed troops and tanks for a new offensive. When talks broke down, Serbia launched military forces in a renewed assault, and NATO forces began bombing to prevent a humanitarian catastrophe. Refugees fled to Albania, Macedonia, and Montenegro amid reports of extensive Serbian atrocities. An 11-week NATO bombing campaign extended to Belgrade and significantly damaged Serbia's infrastructure. The bombing halted after NATO and Yugoslavia signed an accord in June 1999 outlining Serbian troop withdrawal and the return of nearly a million ethnic Albanian refugees as well as 500,000 displaced within the province.

Kossuth \'kȯ-ˌshu̇t, *Engl* 'kä-ˌsüth\, **Lajos** (1802–1894) Hungarian patriot. A lawyer from a noble family, he was sent to the national Diet (1832), where he developed his radical political and social philosophy. Imprisoned on political charges 1837–40, he later wrote for a reform journal and gained a devoted following. Reelected to the Diet (1847–49), he led the "national opposition," and after the FEBRUARY REVOLUTION (1848) he persuaded the delegates to vote for independence from Austria. Appointed provisional governor, he became virtual dictator of Hungary. In 1849 Russian armies intervened on behalf of Austria, forcing Kossuth to resign. He fled to Turkey, where he was interned for two years. After his release, he lectured in the U.S. and England, and later, from his home in Turin, watched Hungary reconcile itself with the Austrian monarchy. After the COMPROMISE OF 1867 he retired from political life.

Kossuth, lithograph, 1856.

BY COURTESY OF THE TRUSTEES OF THE BRITISH MUSEUM; PHOTOGRAPH, J.R. FREEMAN & CO. LTD.

Kosygin \kə-'sē-gən\, **Aleksey (Nikolayevich)** (1904–1980) Soviet statesman, premier of the Soviet Union (1964–80). He joined the Communist Party in 1927, and by 1939 was a member of the Central Committee. After 1957 he worked closely with NIKITA KHRUSHCHEV on economic matters, and in 1964, after Khrushchev's forced resignation, he replaced him as chair of the Council of Ministers, becoming head of the

Soviet government. A competent and pragmatic economic administrator, he introduced reforms designed to modernize the Soviet economy. In the late 1960s and early 1970s he shared power with LEONID BREZHNEV and NIKOLAY PODGORNY, but his role decreased as Brezhnev's authority increased, and he retired in 1980.

koto Japanese musical instrument, a long zither with movable bridges and usually 13 strings. It lies on the ground or a low table, and the strings are plucked by plectra on the right hand's fingers while the left hand alters the pitch or ornaments the sound of individual strings by pressing or manipulating them on the other side of each bridge. It is played solo, in chamber ensembles (especially with the SHAKUHACHI and samisen), and in GAGAKU music. The koto is Japan's national instrument.

Kotzebue \'kȯt-sə-ˌbü\, **August (Friedrich Ferdinand) von** (1761–1819) German playwright. He helped popularize poetic drama, which he infused with melodramatic sensationalism and sentimental philosophizing. Prolific (he wrote more than 200 plays) and facile, he is known for such works as the dramas *The Stranger* (1789) and *The Indian Exiles* (1790) and the comedies *Der Wildfang* (1798; "The Trapping of Game") and *Die deutschen Kleinstädter* (1803; "The German Small-towner"). He was denounced by political radicals as a spy and stabbed to death.

Kou Qianzhi *or* **K'ou Ch'ien-chih** \'kō-'chyen-'jə\ (died 448) Chinese Taoist reformer. He probably began his career as a Taoist physician. In 415 he had a vision telling him that Taoism had been perverted by false teachings. He began to curb the orgiastic practices and mercenary spirit that had become associated with Taoism and to emphasize hygienic ritual and good works. His efforts won notice from the emperor and led to the establishment of Taoism as the state religion of China's Northern Wei dynasty. He also succeeded in having Buddhism proscribed and its adherents subjected to persecution. His reforms proved transitory, however, and Buddhism soon experienced a resurgence.

Koufax \'kō-ˌfaks\, **Sandy** (*orig.* Sanford) (born 1935) U.S. baseball player. Born in New York City, he joined the Brooklyn (later Los Angeles) Dodgers in 1955 as a left-handed thrower with a blazing fastball and a sharp breaking curveball. He set several season records for strikeouts (including 382 in 1965), and his career average of one strikeout per inning is a rare accomplishment. In 1965 he pitched his fourth no-hit game, until 1981 a major-league record; the fourth no-hitter was also a perfect game (no player reached first). Despite his early retirement in 1966 because of arthritis, he is regarded as one of baseball's greatest pitchers.

Koufax, 1966.
AP/WIDE WORLD PHOTOS

kouros \'kü-ˌrȯs\ Archaic Greek statue representing a standing male youth. These large stone figures began to appear in Greece c. 700 BC and closely followed the Egyptian style of geometrical, rigid figures. Later forms reflect the Greeks' increased understanding of human anatomy and are more naturalistic. Kouroi sometimes represented the god Apollo, but more commonly served as votive offerings or grave markers. See also KORE.

Koussevitzky \ˌkü-sə-'vit-skē\, **Sergey (Alexandrovich)** (1874–1951) Russian-U.S. conductor. A virtuoso double-bass player, he was self-taught as a conductor. With his father-in-law's financial help, he debuted with the Berlin Philharmonic in 1908. In the following years he founded his own orchestra, which toured the Volga by riverboat. Leaving the Soviet Union in 1920, he established the Concerts Koussevitzky series in Paris before becoming permanent conductor of the Boston Symphony Orchestra (1924–49). He gave about 100 premieres there, including such commissioned works as I. STRAVINSKY's *Symphony of Psalms*, and many works by U.S. composers, inspiring his musicians to legendary performances by the force of his personality. The Tanglewood Music Center in Lenox, Mass., was established during his tenure in Boston.

Kovacs, Ernie *orig.* **Ernest Edward** (1919–1962) U.S. television comedian. Born in Trenton, N.J., he created the television comedy variety show *The Ernie Kovacs Show* (1952–53, 1956) and became noted for his zany slapstick sketches. He later hosted the quiz show *Take a Good Look* (1959–61) and acted in such films as *Operation Mad Ball* (1957) and *Our Man in Havana* (1960) before his death in an auto accident.

Kovno See KAUNAS

Kowloon \'kau̇-'lün\ *or* **Jiulong** \'jyō-'lu̇ŋ\ Peninsula on the Chinese mainland, north of HONG KONG. It is 3 sq mi (8 sq km) in area. An industrial and tourist center, it is administratively part of Hong Kong. The city of Kowloon (pop., 1991: 1,975,000) extends north into the New Territories and includes New Kowloon and Kowloon City. An important commercial center, much of it is of modern development.

Koxinga See ZHENG CHENGGONG

Koyukuk River \'kȯi-ə-ˌkək\ River, central Alaska. It rises on the southern slope of the Brooks Range and flows southwest for 500 mi (800 km) to join the YUKON RIVER, of which it is a major tributary. It was named for the Koyukon, a local Indian tribe.

Kpelle \kə-'pel-ə\ People occupying central Liberia and part of Guinea. Numbering about 400,000, the Kpelle speak a MANDE LANGUAGE of the NIGER-CONGO LANGUAGES. They are primarily rice farmers; cash crops include peanuts, sugarcane, and kola nuts. They are known for their elaborate SECRET SOCIETIES (*poro* for men, *sande* for women), which serve a variety of social and political functions.

kraal \'krȯl, 'kräl\ In southern Africa, an enclosure or group of houses surrounding an enclosure for livestock, or the social unit that inhabits these structures. The term has been more broadly used to describe the associated way of life. Among some ZULUS, the traditional kraal consists of a number of huts arranged in a circle around a cattle corral. Where polygyny is practiced, each wife often has her own hut. The word kraal has also been applied to the temporary encampments of the MASAI of eastern Africa.

Kraepelin \ˌkrep-ə-'lēn\, **Emil** (1856–1926) German psychiatrist. He taught at the Univs. of Heidelberg and Munich, where he developed an influential classification system for mental illness, the *Psychiatric Compendium* (nine eds., 1883–1926). He was the first to distinguish (in 1899) between manic-depressive psychosis (BIPOLAR DISORDER) and dementia praecox (SCHIZOPHRENIA), and the first to distinguish three clinical varieties of the latter: catatonia, hebephrenia, and paranoia.

Krafft-Ebing \'kräft-'ā-biŋ\, **Richard, Freiherr (Baron) von** (1840–1902) German neuropsychiatrist. Educated in Germany and Switzerland, he taught psychiatry at Strasbourg, Graz, and Vienna, and pursued studies that ranged from epilepsy and syphilis to genetic functions in insanity and sexual deviation. He also performed experiments in hypnosis. He is best remembered today for his *Psychopathia sexualis* (1886), a groundbreaking examination of sexual aberrations.

Kraft Foods, Inc. U.S. manufacturer and marketer of food products. It grew out of a wholesale cheese-delivery business established in Chicago in 1903 by James L. Kraft. Incorporated as J. L. Kraft Bros. & Co. in 1909, it prospered by selling processed cheese to the U.S. Army during World War I. Held by various owners since 1930, Kraft was acquired in 1988 by PHILIP MORRIS COS., which also purchased Nabisco Holdings in 2000. Nabisco's business was integrated into Kraft's operations.

kraft process Chemical method for producing WOOD pulp using CAUSTIC SODA and sodium sulfide as the liquor in which the pulpwood is cooked to loosen the fibers. The process (from German *kraft*, "strong") produces particularly strong and durable PAPER; another advantage is its capability of digesting pine chips; RESINS dissolve in the alkaline liquor and are recovered as tall oil, a valuable by-product. Recovery of sodium compounds is important in the economy of the process. In modern kraft mills, operations are completely contained; waste streams are recycled and reused, eliminating water pollution.

Krakatau \ˌkra-kə-'tau̇\ *or* **Krakatoa** \ˌkra-kə-'tō-ə\ Island volcano in the center of the SUNDA STRAIT, between JAVA and SUMATRA, Indonesia. Its eruption in 1883 was one of the most catastrophic in history. Its explosions were heard in Australia, Japan, and the Philippines, and large quantities of ash fell over 300,000 sq mi (800,000 sq km). It caused a tidal wave 120 ft (36 m) high that took 36,000 lives in Java and Sumatra. It erupted again in 1927 and is still active.

Kraków *or* **Cracow** \'krä-ˌküf, *Engl* 'kra-ˌkau̇\ City (pop., 1999 est.: 740,666), southern Poland. Located on both sides of the upper VISTULA RIVER, it was the capital of a principality in 1138. After surviving a Mongol invasion in 1241, it was made the capital of a reunited Poland in 1320. Its importance diminished after the capital was moved to WARSAW in 1609. In 1846 it came under Austrian rule. Returned to Poland in 1918, it was held by Germany during World War II. Rebuilt since the war, it is an industrial center with a giant steelworks on the city's outskirts. Also a cultural center, its university was founded in 1364.

Kramer, Jack *orig.* **John Albert** (born 1921) U.S. tennis player and promoter. Born in Las Vegas, he was selected to play on the U.S. Davis Cup team in 1939. He won the Wimbledon singles (1947) and men's doubles (1946–47), the U.S. singles (1946–47), men's doubles (1940–41, 1943, 1947), and mixed doubles (1941), and was on the winning Davis Cup team in 1946. He played professional tennis from 1947 to 1952, and was instrumental in promoting open tennis, in which amateurs and professionals could compete in major tournaments. He helped establish the Association of Tennis Professionals.

Kramnik, Vladimir (born 1975) Russian international chess grandmaster who won the world championship in 2000 from his countryman GARRY KASPAROV. Kramnik learned to play when he was four years old from his father and began taking instruction at the local Pioneers (a Soviet youth organization) at the age of five. At age 11 he became a "candidate" master. Kramnik had success during his early years, winning the World Under 18 Championship in 1991 and a gold medal for his performance at the 1992 Men's Chess Olympiad. The years from 1992 to 2000 saw Kramnik move into the world's elite by winning numerous international chess tournaments.

Krasner, Lee *orig.* **Lenore Krassner** (1908–1984) U.S. painter. Born in New York City to Russian immigrants, in 1937 she began to study with the painter HANS HOFMANN, who exposed her to the work of PABLO PICASSO and HENRI MATISSE. Synthesizing these European influences, Krasner developed her own style of geometric abstraction, which she grounded in floral motifs and rhythmic gesture. In 1940 she began exhibiting her work with that of other American artists who became known as ABSTRACT EXPRESSIONISTS. After her 1945 marriage to painter JACKSON POLLOCK, Krasner and Pollock both produced a large body of work, each under the other's influence. Krasner continued to paint throughout the 1970s.

Krasnoyarsk City (pop., 1995 est.: 869,000), northern central Russia. Located on the upper YENISEY RIVER, it was founded by COSSACKS in 1628. In the late 17th century, it was often attacked by the Tatars and Kirghiz. The TRANS-SIBERIAN RAILROAD brought a period of rapid growth in the 1890s. The site of one of the world's largest hydroelectric stations, built in the 1960s, it is now a commercial and industrial center.

Kraus \'krau̇s\, **Karl** (1874–1936) Austrian journalist, critic, playwright, and poet. In 1899 he founded *Die Fackel,* a literary and political review, and by 1911 he had become its sole author; he continued to publish it until the year of his death. Believing that language was of great moral and aesthetic importance, he wrote with masterly precision, and his writings exercised wide influence. His works, which are almost untranslatably idiomatic, include *Morality and Criminality* (an essay collection, 1908), *Proverbs and Contradictions* (a collection of aphorisms, 1909), and *The Last Days of Humanity* (a lengthy satirical drama, 1922).

Krebs, Edwin (Gerhard) (born 1918) U.S. biochemist. Born in Lansing, Iowa, he received his medical degree from Washington University. With Edmond H. Fischer (born 1920), he won a 1992 Nobel Prize for the discovery of reversible protein phosphorylation, a biochemical process that regulates the activities of proteins in cells and governs countless processes necessary for life. Errors in protein phosphorylation have been implicated in such diseases as diabetes, cancer, and Alzheimer's disease.

Krebs, Hans Adolf *later* **Sir Hans** (1900–1981) German-British biochemist. He fled Nazi Germany for England in 1933, where he taught at Sheffield and Oxford universities. He was the first to describe the UREA cycle (1932). He and Fritz Lipmann (1899–1986) received a 1953 Nobel Prize for their discovery in living organisms of the series of chemical reactions known as the TRICARBOXYLIC ACID CYCLE (also called the citric-acid cycle, or Krebs cycle), a discovery of vital importance to a basic understanding of cell metabolism and molecular biology.

Krebs cycle See TRICARBOXYLIC ACID CYCLE

Kreisler \'krīs-lər\, **Fritz** *orig.* **Friedrich** (1875–1962) Austrian violinist and composer. He entered the Vienna Conservatory at 7 and finished his musical studies by 12. After touring internationally as a teenager, he quit performing to study medicine. Returning to the violin, he scored successes in Berlin and Vienna (1898). He toured Europe and the U.S. until the start of World War I, premiering E. ELGAR's violin concerto in 1910. After recovering from a war wound, he resumed touring (1919–50). His charming light works, including *Tambourin chinois* and *Liebesfreud*, are still played as encores.

kremlin Central fortress in medieval Russian cities, usually located at a strategic point along a river and separated from the surrounding parts of the city by a wall with ramparts, moat, towers, and battlements. Several capitals of principalities were built around old kremlins, which generally contained cathedrals, palaces, governmental offices, and munitions stores. The Moscow Kremlin (established 1156) served as the center of Russian government until 1712 and again after 1918. Its crenellated brick walls and 20 towers were built in the 15th century by Italian architects. The palaces, cathedrals, and government buildings within the walls encompass a variety of styles, including Byzantine, Russian baroque, and Classical.

Krenek, Ernst (1900–1991) Austrian-U.S. composer. He studied composition from age 16 with Franz Schreker (1878–1934) and first gained attention with his atonal Second Symphony (1923). After a brief neoclassical phase, he reestablished his radical credentials with the jazz-influenced satiric opera *Jonny spielt auf* (1926), which created a sensation. Intrigued by A. SCHOENBERG's twelve-tone method, he devised his own version—which involved "rotation" of the set's order—for the opera *Karl V* (1933), the first twelve-tone opera. He emigrated to the U.S. in 1937 and taught at several institutions, but his large body of work remained more highly esteemed in Europe.

Kresge \'krez-gē\, **S(ebastian) S(pering)** (1867–1966) U.S. merchant. Born in Bald Mount, Pa., he worked as a traveling salesman before becoming a partner in five-and-ten-cent stores in Memphis and Detroit in 1897. He opened several others in major Midwest cities, founding the S. S. Kresge Co. in 1907 (incorporated 1912). After World War II the firm expanded into large discount stores in the U.S., Puerto Rico, and Canada, which eventually numbered nearly 1,000. Kresge established a major charitable foundation in 1924. See also KMART CORP.

Krieghoff \'krēg-hôf\, **Cornelius** (1815–1872) Dutch-Canadian painter. After studying in Düsseldorf, he emigrated to New York around 1837, and later moved to Canada. Working in Montreal and Quebec, he produced over 2,000 images of American Indian and French-Canadian life and colorful landscapes in a detailed, romanticized, anecdotal style that was unsurpassed by contemporary artists. He became very popular, and his work was much imitated and forged.

Kriemhild \'krēm-ˌhilt\ *or* **Gudrun** In the *NIBELUNGENLIED*, the gentle princess courted by SIEGFRIED. Her grief at Siegfried's death transforms her into a "she-devil"; she exacts revenge by marrying ATTILA the Hun and killing her brother (who ordered Siegfried's death). She herself is also killed. In Norse legend, as Gudrun, she appears in tales of revenge. Kriemhild's story may have originated in confusion over events in the life of the historical Attila.

krill Any member of the CRUSTACEAN suborder Euphausiacea, comprising shrimplike animals that live in the open sea. The name also refers to the genus *Euphausia* within the suborder and sometimes to a single species, *E. superba.* The described species, numbering more than 80, range in size from about 0.25 to 2 in. (8–60 mm). Most have bioluminescent organs on the lower side, making them visible at night. They are an important source of food for various fishes, birds, and whales, particularly BLUE and FIN whales. Krill may occur in vast swarms at the ocean surface, where they feed at night, and at depths greater than about 6,000 ft (2,000 m). Because of their vast numbers and nutritive qualities (they are an especially rich source of vitamin A), krill have been regarded as a potential source of food for humans.

Krishna One of the most widely venerated Hindu gods, worshiped as the eighth incarnation of VISHNU and as the supreme deity. Many Krishna legends are drawn from the *MAHABHARATA* and the PURANAS. A prophecy foretold that he would destroy the wicked king of Mathura, and to escape the king's wrath his parents had him smuggled to Gokula, where he was raised by a cowherd. As a child Krishna was beloved for his pranks; he also performed miracles and slew demons. As a youth he was famous as a lover. He returned to Mathura and killed the wicked king, then set up his court at Dvaraka, marrying the princess Rukmini and taking other wives as well. He was killed when a huntsman mistook him for a deer and shot him in the heel, his one vulnerable spot. In art Krishna is often depicted with blue-black skin, wearing a loincloth and a crown of peacock feathers. As a divine lover he is shown playing the flute surrounded by adoring females.

Krishna River *formerly* **Kistna River** River, southern India. Rising in MAHARASHTRA state, it flows southeast and east across KARNATAKA and crosses ANDHRA PRADESH state before entering the Bay of BENGAL after a course of 800 mi (1,290 km).

Krishnamurti \ˌkrish-nə-ˈmu̇r-tē\, **Jiddu** (1895–1986) Indian spiritual leader and theosophist. He was educated in theosophy by ANNIE BESANT, who proclaimed him the coming "World Teacher," a messiah-like figure who would bring about world enlightenment. He became a teacher and writer, and from the 1920s he spent much time in the U.S. and Europe. He broke with formal theosophy in 1929 and renounced any claims to being a World Teacher, but he continued to be a popular lecturer. His desire, he said, was to set people free, a goal that could only be achieved through unflinching self-awareness. He established a number of Krishnamurti foundations in the U.S., Britain, and India to further his aims. His books include *The Songs of Life* (1931) and *Commentaries on Living* (1956–60).

Kristallnacht \krēs-ˈtäl-ˌnäḵt\ *or* **Crystal Night** *or* **Night of Broken Glass** Night of violence against Jews carried out by members of the German NAZI PARTY on November 9–10, 1938, so called from the broken glass left in its aftermath. The violence, instigated by JOSEPH GOEBBELS, left 91 Jews dead and hundreds seriously injured. About 7,500 Jewish businesses were gutted and some 177 synagogues demolished. The GESTAPO arrested 30,000 wealthy Jews, offering to release them only if they emigrated and surrendered their wealth. The incident marked a major escalation in the Nazi program of Jewish persecution, foreshadowing the HOLOCAUST.

Kristeva \krē-stā-ˈvȧ, *Engl* kri-ˈstā-və\, **Julia** (born 1941) Bulgarian-French psychoanalyst, critic, and educator. Professor of linguistics at the University of Paris VII, she is known for her writings in structuralist linguistics (see STRUCTURALISM), psychoanalysis, SEMIOTICS, and feminism. A protégé of ROLAND BARTHES, her theories synthesize elements from such thinkers as JACQUES LACAN, MICHEL FOUCAULT, and MIKHAIL BAKHTIN. Her novels include *The Samurai* (1990) and *The Old Man and the Wolves* (1991).

Kritios See CRITIUS AND NESIOTES

Krivoy Rog See KRYVYY RIH

Kroc, Ray (mond Albert) (1902–1984) U.S. restaurateur, a pioneer of the fast-food industry. Born in Chicago, he was working as a blender salesman when he discovered a restaurant in San Bernardino, Cal., owned by Maurice and Richard McDonald, who used an assembly-line format to prepare and sell a large volume of hamburgers, french fries, and milk shakes. Beginning in 1955 Kroc opened his first McDonald's drive-in restaurant in Des Plaines, Ill., paying the brothers a percentage of the receipts. He soon began selling franchises for new restaurants, and he instituted a training program for owner-managers that emphasized automation and standardization. At the time of his death there were some 7,500 McDonald's restaurants worldwide; today, with more than 25,000 restaurants, McDonald's is the world's largest food-service retailer.

Ray Kroc.
SYGMA

Kroeber \ˈkrō-bər\, **A(lfred) L(ouis)** (1876–1960) U.S. anthropologist who made valuable contributions to American Indian ethnology, New World archaeology, and the study of linguistics, folklore, kinship, and culture. Trained under FRANZ BOAS (PhD, 1901), he later taught at the University of California at Berkeley. Kroeber's career nearly coincided with the emergence of academic, professionalized anthropology in the U.S. and contributed significantly to its development. His most influential books are considered to be *Anthropology* (1923) and *The Nature of Culture* (1952).

Kroemer, Herbert (b. 1928) German physicist. He was born in Weimar, Germany, and received a Ph.D. (1952) from Georg August University in Göttingen. He later moved to the U.S., where he taught at several institutions. In 1957 he carried out theoretical calculations showing that a heterostructure transistor, which is made from several materials, would be superior to a conventional transistor, which is made from only one kind of material. His theory was later confirmed and led to the development of numerous electronic components that had a significant impact on communications technology and computers. He shared the 2000 Nobel Prize for Physics with ZHORES ALFEROV and JACK S. KILBY.

Kronos See CRONUS

Kronshtadt Rebellion \ˈkrōn-ˌshtät\ (1921) Internal uprising against Soviet rule in Russia after the RUSSIAN CIVIL WAR, conducted by sailors from the Kronshtadt naval base. The sailors had supported the Bolsheviks in the RUSSIAN REVOLUTION OF 1917, but disillusionment with the government and inadequate food supplies after the Civil War led them to demand economic and labor reform and political freedoms. The rebels were crushed by a force led by LEON TROTSKY and MIKHAYL TUKHACHEVSKY, and the survivors were shot or imprisoned. By dramatically demonstrating popular dissatisfaction with communist policies, the rebellion, along with several other major internal uprisings, led to the adoption of the NEW ECONOMIC POLICY.

Kronstadt See BRASOV

Kropotkin \krə-ˈpȯt-kən\, **Peter (Alekseyevich)** (1842–1921) Russian revolutionary and geographer, foremost theorist of ANARCHISM. The son of a prince, in 1871 he renounced his aristocratic heritage. Though he achieved renown in such fields as geography, zoology, sociology, and history, he shunned material success for the life of a revolutionist. He was imprisoned on political charges (1874–76) but escaped and fled to Western Europe. In France, he was imprisoned on trumped-up charges of sedition (1883–86), and in 1886 he settled in England, where he remained until the RUSSIAN REVOLUTION OF 1917 allowed him to return home. While in exile, he wrote several influential books, including *Memoirs of a Revolutionist* (1899) and *Mutual Aid* (1902), in which he attempted to put anarchism on a scientific basis and argued that cooperation rather than conflict is the chief factor in the evolution of species. On his return to Russia he was bitterly disappointed that the Bolsheviks had made their revolution by authoritarian rather than libertarian methods, and he retired from politics.

Kropotkin.
BROWN BROTHERS

Kru Group of peoples of Liberia and the Ivory Coast, including the Bassa, Krahn, Grebo, Klao (Kru), Bakwe, and Bete, who speak Kru languages of the NIGER-CONGO LANGUAGES. Members of Kru ethnic groups, especially Klao, Grebo, and Bassa, are known as stevedores and fishermen all along the western coast of Africa and have established colonies in most ports from Dakar to Douala, the largest being in Monrovia.

Kruger, Paul *orig.* **Stephanus Johannes Paulus** (1825–1904) South African soldier and statesman, noted as the builder of the AFRIKANER nation. As a boy of 10, Kruger took part in the GREAT TREK and was impressed by the Boer emigrants' ability to defend themselves against hostile tribes and establish an orderly government. When the British annexed the TRANSVAAL in 1877, Kruger became the recognized champion of his people in the struggle to regain independence. After leading a series of armed attacks, he succeeded in obtaining limited independence and was elected president of the restored republic (1883–1902). In 1895 he fended off an attempt by CECIL RHODES and LEANDER STARR JAMESON to end Boer control of the republic. During the SOUTH AFRICAN WAR he was forced to flee to the Netherlands; he died in Switzerland.

Kruger National Park National park, South Africa. Located in the northeastern part of the country on the Mozambique border, it was created as a game sanctuary in 1898 and became a national park in 1926, named for PAUL KRUGER. It covers an area of 7,523 sq mi (19,485 sq km) and contains six rivers. It has a wide variety of wildlife, including elephant, lion, and cheetah.

Krupa, Gene (1909–1973) U.S. bandleader and the first great drum soloist in jazz. Krupa had worked with Eddie Condon in his native Chicago before moving to New York in 1929, joining BENNY GOODMAN's big band in 1935. He quickly became the best-known drummer of his day, famous for the showmanship and technique displayed on extended drum solos such as "Sing, Sing, Sing." He formed his own successful band in 1938, featuring trumpeter ROY ELDRIDGE and singer Anita O'Day. Krupa's energetic playing became the model for many drummers of the SWING era.

Krupp family \'krüp\ German steel-manufacturing dynasty. Friedrich Krupp (1787–1826) founded a steel factory in Essen in 1811. On his death his son Alfred (1812–1887) took full charge of the faltering concern at age 14. He made a fortune supplying steel to the railways and manufacturing cannons; the performance of Krupp guns in the Franco-German War of 1870–71 led to the firm's being called "the Arsenal of the Reich." At Alfred's death he had armed 46 nations. The rise of the German navy and the need for armor plates further enriched the company under his son Friedrich Alfred (1854–1902). By the time Friedrich Alfred's elder daughter, Bertha (1886–1957), inherited control of the firm, it employed more than 40,000 people. Her husband, Gustav von Bohlen (1870–1950), affixed Krupp to the beginning of his name; an ardent Nazi, he ran the Krupp empire until 1943, when he was succeeded by their son Alfried Krupp (1907–1967). The Krupp works used slave labor during World War II and were a major part of the Nazi war machine; Alfried was later convicted of war crimes at Nuremberg. An Allied order to break up the company in 1953 languished for lack of a buyer, and Alfried eventually restored the Krupp fortune. See also THYSSEN KRUPP STAHL.

Krupp GmbH See THYSSEN KRUPP STAHL

Krupskaya \'krüp-skə-yə\, **Nadezhda (Konstantinovna)** (1869–1939) Russian revolutionary, wife of VLADIMIR ILICH LENIN. A Marxist activist from the 1890s, she met Lenin c. 1894. Sentenced to three years in exile in 1898, she obtained permission to spend her term with Lenin in Siberia, where they were married. After 1901 she lived with Lenin in several European cities and helped found the BOLSHEVIK party faction. She returned to Russia in 1917 to spread Bolshevik propaganda after the revolution began, and later served in several posts in the educational bureaucracy. After Lenin's death (1924), she remained aloof from intraparty struggles.

krypton \'krip-ˌtän\ Chemical ELEMENT, chemical symbol Kr, atomic number 36. One of the NOBLE GASES, it is colorless, odorless, tasteless, and relatively inert, combining only with FLUORINE under very rigorous conditions. Krypton occurs in slight traces in the atmosphere and in rocks and is obtained by fractional distillation of liquefied air. It is used in luminescent tubes, flash lamps, lasers, and tracer studies.

Kryvyy Rih \kri-'vi-'rik\ *Russian* **Krivoy Rog** \kri-'vȯi-'rȯk\ City (pop., 1998 est.: 715,400), southeastern central Ukraine. Founded as a village by Cossacks in the 17th century, it grew slowly until a railway was constructed to the DONETS BASIN in 1884; it soon became a significant iron-mining city. It was seized by Germany in 1941 and retaken by the U.S.S.R. in 1944. Terny, which was annexed to the city in 1969, has a major uranium mine. The city is now a center of industry as well as mining, with metallurgical plants, foundries, mills, and chemical works.

Kshatriya *or* **Ksatriya** \'kshə-trē-ə\ In Hindu India, the second-highest of the four VARNAS, or social classes, traditionally the military or ruling class. In ancient times before the CASTE system was completely defined, they were considered first in rank, placed higher than the BRAHMANS, or priestly class. The legend that they were degraded by an incarnation of VISHNU as a punishment for their tyranny may reflect a historical struggle for supremacy between priests and rulers. In modern times the Kshatriya varna includes members from a variety of castes, united by their status in government or the military or their land ownership.

Ksitigarbha \'kshi-ti-'gər-bə\ Buddhist BODHISATTVA widely revered in China and Japan. Known in India from the 4th century BC, he became popular in China as Dicang and in Japan as Jizo. He is the patron of the oppressed or dying, and he seeks to save the souls of the dead condemned to hell. In China he is the overlord of hell, and in Japan he is known for his kindness to the departed, particularly to dead children. Usually depicted as a monk with a nimbus around his shaved head, he carries a staff to force open the gates of hell and a flaming pearl to light up the darkness.

Ktesibios of Alexandria \te-'sib-ē-ˌōs\ *or* **Ctesibius of Alexandria** \te-'sib-ē-əs\ (fl. c. 270 BC) Greek physicist and inventor. He was the first great figure of the ancient engineering tradition of Alexandria, Egypt, which culminated with HERO OF ALEXANDRIA and Philo of Byzantium. He discovered the ELASTICITY of air, and invented several devices using compressed air, including force PUMPS and an air-powered CATAPULT; an improvement of the WATER CLOCK, in which water dripping at a constant rate raised a float with a pointer; and a hydraulus (water organ), in which the weight of water forced air through the organ pipes. His writings have not survived, and his inventions are known only from references to them.

Ku Klux Klan (KKK) Either of two U.S. terrorist groups. The first was organized by veterans of the Confederate Army, first as a social club and then as a secret means of resistance to RECONSTRUCTION, with the goal of restoring white domination over newly enfranchised blacks. Dressed in robes and sheets, Klansmen whipped and killed freedmen and their white supporters in nighttime raids. It had largely accomplished its goals by the 1870s, and gradually faded away. The second KKK arose in 1915, partly out of nostalgia for the Old South and partly out of fear of the Russian Revolution and the changing ethnic character of U.S. society. It counted Catholics, Jews, foreigners, and labor unions among its enemies. Its membership peaked in the 1920s, with over 4 million members, but declined during the GREAT DEPRESSION. It became active again during the CIVIL-RIGHTS MOVEMENT, with bombings, whippings, and shootings attributed to it, but growing racial tolerance and a government crackdown reduced its numbers to a few thousand.

Kuala Lumpur \'kwä-lə-'lùm-ˌpùr\ City (pop., 2000 prelim.: 1,297,526), capital of MALAYSIA. Founded as a tin-mining camp in 1857, it was made capital of the Federated Malay States in 1895, of the independent Federation of Malaya in 1957, and of Malaysia in 1963. It was designated a municipality in 1972. The most important Malay city on the MALAY PENINSULA, it is a commercial center. It is the site of the world's tallest buildings, the PETRONAS TOWERS. Its educational institutions include the University of Malaya and Universiti Kebangsaan.

Kuan Han-ch'ing See GUAN HANQING

Kuan-yin See AVALOKITESVARA

Kuan Yü See GUAN YU

Kuang-chou See GUANGZHOU

Kuang-wu ti See GUANGWUDI

Kuban River \kü-'banʸ\ River, southwestern Russia. Rising on Mount ELBRUS, in the Republic of Georgia, it flows north then west to enter the Sea of AZOV. It is 563 mi (906 km) long. Much of its water is diverted for irrigation.

Kubitschek (de Oliveira) \'kü-bə-ˌchek\, **Juscelino** (1902–1976) President of Brazil (1956–61). He studied medicine but entered politics, becoming mayor of Belo Horizonte and later winning election to Congress. As president he promoted rapid development of the hydroelectric, steel, and other heavy industries and built 11,000 mi (18,000 km) of roads. He moved the government from Rio de Janeiro to BRASÍLIA, 600 mi (1,000 km) inland, to accelerate the settlement of Brazil's vast interior. One price of his ambitious development was rapid and persistent inflation, exacerbated by the need to spend large sums to aid the drought-stricken northeastern region. The military government revoked his political rights in 1965.

Kublai Khan \'kü-blə-'kän\ (1215–1294) Grandson of GENGHIS KHAN who conquered China and established the YUAN, or Mongol, dynasty. His personal name was Shizu. When Kublai was in his 30s, his brother, the emperor MÖNGKE, gave him the task of conquering and administering SONG-DYNASTY China. Recognizing the superiority of Chinese thought, he gathered around himself Confucian advisers who convinced him of the importance of clemency toward the conquered. In subduing China and establishing himself there, he alienated other Mongol princes; his claim to the title of khan was also disputed. Though he could no longer control the steppe aristocracy effectively, he succeeded in reunifying China, subduing first the North and then the South by 1279. To restore China's prestige, Kublai engaged in wars on its periphery with Burma, Java, Japan, and the nations of Indochina, suffering some disastrous defeats. At home, he set up a four-tiered society, with the Mongols and other Central Asian peoples forming the top two tiers, the inhabitants of northern China ranking next, and those of southern China on the bottom. Posts of importance were allotted to foreigners, including MARCO POLO. Kublai repaired the GRAND CANAL and public granaries and made BUDDHISM the state religion. Although his reign was one of brilliant prosperity, his politics were pursued less successfully by his followers.

Kublai Khan; in the National Palace Museum, Taipei.

Kubrick \'kyü-brik\, **Stanley** (1928–1999) U.S. film director. Born in New York City, he began his career as a photographer for *Look* magazine (1945–50). He directed two documentary films before his first feature film, *Fear and Desire* (1953). He won fame with *Paths of Glory* (1957), *Spartacus* (1960), *Lolita* (1962), *Dr. Strangelove* (1964), and the internationally acclaimed *2001: A Space Odyssey* (1968). His later movies include *A Clockwork Orange* (1971), *Barry Lyndon* (1975), *The Shining* (1980), *Full Metal Jacket* (1987), and *Eyes Wide Shut* (1999). His films are characterized by a cool visual style, meticulous attention to detail, and a detached, often ironic pessimism. He lived in England from 1961 until his death.

Kuchuk Kainarji \kü-'chük-,kī-när-'jē\, **Treaty of** (1774) Pact signed after the RUSSO-TURKISH WAR of 1768–74, in Kuchuk Kainarji (now Kaynardzha), Bulgaria, ending undisputed Ottoman control of the Black Sea. The treaty extended the Russian frontier to the southern Bug River and allowed Russia to navigate freely in Ottoman waters through the Bosporus Strait and the Dardanelles. Most far-reaching was a religious stipulation allowing Russia to represent Eastern Orthodox Christians in several regions, which Russia later interpreted as the right to intervene to protect Eastern Orthodox Christians anywhere in the Ottoman empire.

kudu Slender African ANTELOPES of the genus *Tragelaphus*. The greater kudu lives in small groups in hilly bush country or open woods. It stands about 51 in. (1.3 m) high at the shoulder and has a fringe on the throat and a crest of hair on the neck and back. It is reddish brown to blue-gray, with a white mark between the eyes and narrow vertical white stripes on the body. The male has long, corkscrewlike horns. The lesser kudu lives in pairs or small groups in open bush country; it stands about 40 in. (1 m) high, has more tightly spiraled horns, and has two white patches on the throat and no throat fringe. Both species browse on shrubs and leaves.

kudzu vine \'küd-,zü\ Fast-growing, twining, perennial, woody vine *(Pueraria lobata,* or *P. thunbergiana)* belonging to the pea family (see LEGUME). Transplanted from its native China and Japan to North America in the 1870s as an attractive ornamental that could be planted on steep soil banks to prevent erosion, kudzu has become a rampant weed in much of the southeastern U.S, where it readily spreads to form great canopies over trees, shrubs, and exposed soil. Roots survive even northern winters, and the hairy vine grows to a length of 60 ft (18 m) in one season. It has large leaves, late-blooming reddish-purple flowers, and flat, hairy seedpods. In its native range kudzu is grown for its edible, starchy roots and for a fiber made from its stems. It is also useful as a fodder or cover crop.

Kuei-chou See GUIZHOU

Kuei-yang See GUIYANG

Kuhn \'kün\, **Thomas (Samuel)** (1922–1996) U.S. historian and philosopher of science. Born in Cincinnati, he taught at Berkeley (1956–64), Princeton (1964–79), and MIT (1979–91). In his highly influential *The Structure of Scientific Revolutions* (1962), he questioned the previously accepted view of scientific progress as a gradual accumulation of knowledge based on universally valid experimental methods and results, claiming that progress was often achieved by far-reaching "paradigm shifts." His other works include *The Copernican Revolution* (1957), *The Essential Tension* (1977), and *Black-Body Theory and the Quantum Discontinuity* (1978).

Kuiper belt \'kī-pər\ *or* **Edgeworth-Kuiper belt** Disk-shaped belt of billions of small, icy bodies orbiting the sun beyond the orbit of NEPTUNE, mostly at distances 30–50 times the earth's distance from the sun. Gerard Peter Kuiper (1905–1973) proposed the existence of this large flattened distribution of objects in 1951 in connection with his theory of the origin of the solar system (see SOLAR NEBULA). Kenneth Edgeworth (1880–1972) independently had made similar proposals in 1943 and 1949. Whether the belt extends thinly as far as the OORT CLOUD is not known. Gravitational disturbances by Neptune of objects in the belt are thought to be the origin of most short-period comets. The first Kuiper belt object was discovered in 1992, but the orbit, icy composition, and diminutive size of PLUTO appear to qualify this body, traditionally considered a planet, as a giant Kuiper belt object.

Kukai \'kü-,kī\ *or* **Kobo Daishi** (774–835) Japanese Buddhist saint and founder of the SHINGON school. Born into an aristocratic family, Kukai was given a Confucian education but soon converted to Buddhism. After studying in China (804–6) with Huiguo (746–805), he returned home to spread his doctrines, which emphasized magic formulas, ceremonials, and services for the dead. In 816 he built a temple on Mount Koya, and he helped to establish the Shingon sect as one of the most popular forms of Japanese Buddhism. His major work, *Ten Stages of Consciousness,* traces the development of Confucianism, Taoism, and Buddhism, representing Shingon as the highest stage. He was also a gifted poet, artist, and calligrapher.

kulak (Russian: "fist") Wealthy or prosperous landed peasant in Russia. Before the RUSSIAN REVOLUTION OF 1917, kulaks were major figures in peasant villages, often lending money and playing central roles in social and administrative affairs. In the WAR COMMUNISM period (1918–21), the Soviet government undermined the kulaks' position by organizing poor peasants to administer the villages and requisition grain from richer peasants. The kulaks regained their position under the NEW ECONOMIC POLICY, but in 1929 the government began a drive for rapid collectivization of agriculture and "liquidation of the kulaks as a class" (dekulakization). By 1934 most kulaks had been deported to remote regions or arrested and their land and property confiscated.

Kulturkampf \kül-'tür-,kämpf\ (German: "culture struggle") Bitter struggle by OTTO VON BISMARCK to subject the Roman Catholic church to state controls. Bismarck, a staunch Protestant, doubted the loyalty of Catholics in his new German empire and became concerned by the Vatican Council's 1870 proclamation concerning papal infallibility. In 1872 the state dissolved the JESUIT order in Germany. The May, or Falk, Laws of 1873 (applying only to Prussia) limited church powers, and in 1875 the state mandated civil marriage services. Bismarck retreated in the face of strong Catholic resistance, especially by the Center Party. By 1887, with many anti-Catholic laws repealed, Pope LEO XIII declared the conflict over.

Kumasi \kü-'mä-sē\ *formerly* **Coomassie** \kü-'ma-sē\ City (pop., 1988 est.: 385,000), southern central Ghana. A 17th-century ASHANTI king chose the site for his capital and conducted land negotiations under a kum tree, which gave the town its name. Located on north–south trade routes, it became a major commercial center. The British gained control of the city in 1874. Called the "Garden City of West Africa," it remains the seat of Ashanti kings. Its central market is one of the largest in west-

H I J K

ern Africa. Its educational institutions include a university of science and technology.

Kumazawa Banzan \'kü-mä-ˌzä-wä-'bän-ˌzän\ (1619–1691) Japanese political philosopher. Born a RONIN, he was taken into service by the feudal lord of Okayama at 15. Largely self-taught, he became a disciple of the Chinese Neo-Confucianist WANG YANGMING. As chief minister of Okayama from 1647, he tried to put into practice the Confucian teachings on governance. Forced to resign in 1656, he spent the rest of his life studying and writing. He called for advancement in the government bureaucracy based on merit, not heredity, and advocated more government responsibility in economic life and less control by feudal lords. His ideas so infuriated the government that he was kept in custody or under surveillance the rest of his life.

Kumin \'kyü-min\, **Maxine** *orig.* **Maxine Winokur** (born 1925) U.S. poet. Born in Philadelphia, she studied at Radcliffe College. Her poetry, written primarily in traditional forms, deals with loss, fragility, family, and the cycles of life and nature. Her New Hampshire farm inspired *Up Country* (1972, Pulitzer Prize); later collections include the acclaimed *The Retrieval System* (1978), *Our Ground Time Here Will Be Brief* (1982), *Nurture* (1989), and *Connecting the Dots* (1996). She has written numerous children's books, some with ANNE SEXTON, as well as novels and short stories.

kumquat \'kəm-ˌkwät\ Any of several evergreen shrubs or small trees of the genus *Fortunella* (RUE, or citrus, family), or their fruit. Native to eastern Asia, kumquats are cultivated throughout the subtropics. The mainly thornless branches bear dark green, glossy leaves and white, orangelike flowers. The small, bright orange-yellow, round or oval fruit has mildly acid, juicy pulp and a sweet, edible, pulpy skin. Kumquats may be eaten fresh, preserved, or candied, or made into jams and jellies. In the U.S., hybrids have been produced with other CITRUS fruits.

Kun \'kün\, **Béla** (1886–1939?) Hungarian communist leader. He fought in the Austrian army in World War I, was captured by the Russians, and became a Bolshevik. Returning to Hungary in 1918, he founded the Hungarian Communist Party. When MIHALY, COUNT KAROLYI resigned in March 1919, Kun headed the new Hungarian Soviet Republic. He created a Red Army that reconquered much of the territory lost to Czechoslovaks and Romanians and eliminated moderate elements in the government. In August the regime collapsed, and Kun fled to Vienna and then Russia. As a leader of the COMINTERN, he tried to foment revolution in Germany and Austria in the 1920s. Eventually accused of "Trotskyism," he fell victim to JOSEPH STALIN'S PURGE TRIALS.

Béla Kun, drawing by Béla Uitz, 1930; in the Legújabbkori Történeti Múzeum, Budapest.

BY COURTESY OF THE LEGUJABBKORI TORTENETI MUZEUM, BUDAPEST

kundalini \ˌkůn-də-'lē-nē\ In some tantric forms of YOGA, the cosmic energy believed to be within everyone. It is pictured as a coiled serpent lying at the base of the spine. Through a series of exercises involving posture, meditation, and breathing, a practitioner can force this energy up through the body to the top of the head. This brings about a sensation of bliss, as the ordinary self is dissolved into its eternal essence, ATMAN.

Kundera \'kün-de-rä\, **Milan** (born 1929) Czech-French writer. He worked as a jazz musician and taught at Prague's film academy, but gradually turned to writing. Though a member of the Communist Party for years, his works were banned after he participated in Czechoslovakia's short-lived liberalization movement (1967–68), and he was fired from his teaching positions. He emigrated to France in 1975. His works combine erotic comedy with political criticism. *The Joke* (1967), his first novel, describes life under Stalin. *The Book of Laughter and Forgetting* (1979), a series of wittily ironic meditations on the modern state, and the novel *The Unbearable Lightness of Being* (1984; film, 1988) were banned in his homeland until 1989. His later books include *Immortality* (1990) and *Slowness* (1994).

Kunene River See CUNENE RIVER

kung fu *pinyin* **gongfu** Chinese MARTIAL ART that is simultaneously a spiritual and a physical discipline. It has been practiced at least since the Zhou dynasty (1111–255 BC). Its prescribed stances and actions are based on keen observations of human skeletal and muscular anatomy and physiology, and many of its movements are imitations of the fighting styles of animals. Its combative techniques resemble those used in KARATE and TAE KWON DO. Self-discipline is emphasized. Kung fu performed as exercise resembles T'AI CHI CH'UAN.

Kunitz \'kyü-nits\, **Stanley (Jasspon)** (born 1905) U.S. poet. Born in Worcester, Mass., he worked as an editor while contributing verse to magazines; much of it was collected in such volumes as *Selected Poems 1928–1958* (1958, Pulitzer Prize). With *The Testing-Tree* (1971), he began to write shorter, looser, more emotional poetry. Among his later collections, noted for their subtle craftsmanship and treatment of complex themes, are *The Coat Without a Seam* (1974), *The Lincoln Relics* (1978), *Next-to-Last Things* (1985), and *Passing Through* (1995). In 2000 he was named U.S. poet laureate.

Kunlun Mountains *or* **K'un-lun Mountains** \'kün-'lün\ Mountain system, western Asia. It extends for 1,250 mi (2,000 km) through the western regions of China. From the PAMIRS of Tajikistan, it runs east along the border between XINJIANG UYGUR and Tibet to the Sino-Tibetan ranges in the province of QINGHAI. It divides the northern limit of the Plateau of Tibet from the interior plains of central Asia. Its highest peak measures 25,348 ft (7,726 m).

Kunming *or* **K'un-ming** \'kůn-'miŋ\ City (pop., 1999 est.: 1,350,640), capital of YUNNAN province, southern China. Situated on the northern shore of DIAN LAKE, it has long been a commercial center at the junction of major trading routes. Originally known as Tuodong in the 8th–9th century AD and a part of the independent state of Nanzhao, it came under Chinese control with the Mongol invasion of 1253; it became the provincial capital of Yunnan in 1276 and was visited by MARCO POLO. It became a municipality in 1935 and was transformed into a modern city in 1937 during the SINO-JAPANESE WAR, when Chinese evacuees from the north brought industrial plants and universities to Kunming.

Kunstler, William (Moses) (1919–1995) U.S. radical lawyer. Born in New York City, he graduated from Yale University. In World War II he earned a Bronze Star for service in the Pacific. He later attended Columbia Law School. In the 1950s and '60s he became involved with the AMERICAN CIVIL LIBERTIES UNION and with such clients as MARTIN LUTHER KING. Later he represented the black activists Stokely Carmichael and Bobby Seale and prisoners accused in the aftermath of the 1971 riot at the Attica (N.Y.) state prison. Among his many notorious clients was Sheikh Omar Abdel Rahman, accused of conspiring to blow up the World Trade Center in 1993.

Kuo Hsiang See GUO XIANG

Kuo Mo-jo See GUO MORUO

Kuomintang See NATIONALIST PARTY

Kura River \kə-'rä, 'kůr-ə\ *ancient* **Cyrus** River in Turkey, Georgia, and Azerbaijan. It rises in eastern Turkey and flows north. After entering Georgia, it turns east and flows southeast to enter the CASPIAN SEA. It is 848 mi (1,364 km) long and used in places for irrigation.

Kurath \ků-'räth\, **Hans** (1891–1992) Austrian-U.S. linguist. He emigrated to the U.S. in 1907. He is best known as the chief editor of the *Linguistic Atlas of New England* (3 vols., 1939–43), the first linguistic atlas of a region of the U.S. His other works include *A Word Geography of the Eastern United States* (1949) and *The Pronunciation of English in the Atlantic States* (1961). Kurath was later editor in chief (1946–62) of the *Middle English Dictionary*.

Kurdistan Mountainous region with indefinite boundaries forming a nonpolitical region in southeastern Turkey, and in adjoining areas of northwestern Iran, northeastern Iraq, and northeastern Syria. It covers about 74,000 sq mi (191,660 sq km), and its chief towns are Diyarbakir, Bitlis, and VAN in Turkey, MOSUL and KIRKUK in Iraq, and Kermanshah in Iran. Since early times the region has been the home of the KURDS, a people whose ethnic origins are uncertain. The Treaty of SÈVRES, signed in 1920, provided for the recognition of the Kurdistan state, but this treaty was never ratified.

Kurdistan Workers Party (PKK) Leftist political party founded in Turkish Kurdistan in 1978 and led by Abdullah Öcalan, who was sentenced to death by Turkey in 1999. The party seeks to establish an independent Kurdish state in southeastern Turkey. It attacks Turkish interests and those of Kurdish collaborators from bases in Iraq and Syria. It claims 5,000–10,000 members. See also KURDS.

Kurds Stateless ethnic and linguistic group numbering over 15 million people and living primarily in Iran, Iraq, and Turkey (see KURDISTAN). Ethnically, they are close to the Iranians. Traditionally nomadic, they were forced into farming by the redrawing of national borders after World War I. Most Kurds are Sunni Muslims; some are Sufis or adhere to other sects. Plans for a Kurdish state, promised by the Treaty of SÈVRES (1920), which dissolved the Ottoman empire, were never realized. Kurds in Turkey, Iran, and Iraq have been variously persecuted and pressured to assimilate; Iraqi attacks were particularly severe during the IRAN-IRAQ WAR and the PERSIAN GULF WAR. See also KURDISTAN WORKERS' PARTY.

Kurdufan See KORDOFAN

Kuria Muria Islands See Jazair KHURIYA MURIYA

Kuril Islands \'kyu̇r-,ēl\ Archipelago, eastern Russia. It extends for 750 mi (1,200 km) from the southern tip of Russia's KAMCHATKA peninsula to the northeastern coast of Japan's HOKKAIDO island. The 56 islands cover 6,000 sq mi (15,600 sq km) and together with SAKHALIN form an administrative region (pop., 1995: 648,000) of Russia. The Kurils were originally settled by the Russians in the 17th–18th century. Japan seized the southern islands and in 1875 obtained the entire chain. After World War II, they were ceded to the Soviet Union, and the Japanese population was repatriated and replaced by Soviets. Japan still claims historical rights to the southern islands and has tried repeatedly to regain them.

Kuropatkin \kü-rə-'pät-kin\, **Aleksey (Nikolayevich)** (1848–1925) Russian general. He was chief of staff during the RUSSO-TURKISH WAR, commander in chief in Caucasia in 1897, and minister of war 1898–1904. In the RUSSO-JAPANESE WAR he commanded the Russian troops in Manchuria; he resigned after the Russian defeat in the MUKDEN INCIDENT.

Kurosawa \,ku̇r-ə-'sau̇-ə\, **Akira** (1910–1998) Japanese film director. He studied painting before becoming an assistant director and scenarist at PCL (later Toho) movie studio (1936–43). He wrote and directed his first film, *Sanshiro Sugata,* in 1943, won notice with *Drunken Angel* (1948), starring TOSHIRO MIFUNE, and was internationally acclaimed for *Rashomon* (1950). His later classic films include *Seven Samurai* (1954), *Throne of Blood* (1957), *The Hidden Fortress* (1958), *Kagemusha* (1980), and *Ran* (1985). His ability to combine Japanese aesthetic and cultural elements with a Western sense of action and drama made him, in Western eyes, the foremost Japanese filmmaker. He received an honorary Academy Award for lifetime achievement in 1990.

Kursk, Battle of (July 5–August 23, 1943) Unsuccessful German assault on the Soviet salient around Kursk, in western Russia, in WORLD WAR II. The salient was a bulge in the Soviet lines that protruded 100 mi (160 km) westward into the German lines. The Germans planned a surprise attack to trap the Soviet forces but encountered Russian-laid minefields and antitank defenses. At the height of the assault the Soviets counterattacked and forced a German withdrawal. The largest tank battle in history, it involved some 6,000 tanks, 2 million troops, and 4,000 aircraft. It marked the decisive end of the German offensive on the Eastern Front and cleared the way for the great Soviet offensives of 1944–45.

Kurskiy Zaliv \'ku̇r-skē-'zä-lif\ *or* **Courland Lagoon** \'ku̇r-lənd\ Inlet of the BALTIC SEA at the mouth of the NEMAN RIVER. Its northern portion is in Lithuania and its southern portion lies in Kaliningrad province, Russia. With an area of 625 sq mi (1,619 sq km), it is connected to the Baltic by a navigable strait, on which is the Lithuanian port of KLAIPEDA.

Kuryłowicz \,ku̇r-ə-'lō-vich\, **Jerzy** (1895–1978) Polish historical linguist. His identification of the HITTITE medial *h* in 1927 substantiated the existence of laryngeals, the Indo-European speech sounds postulated by FERDINAND DE SAUSSURE, and stimulated much research in Indo-European PHONOLOGY. His books include *Apophony in Indo-European* (1956) and *The Inflectional Categories of Indo-European* (1964).

Kush See CUSH

Kushan art *or* **Kusana art** Art produced during the Kushan dynasty (late 1st–3rd century AD), in an area that now includes parts of Central Asia, northern India, Pakistan, and Afghanistan. There are two major stylistic divisions among artifacts of the period: the imperial art of Iranian derivation, and the Buddhist art of mixed Greco-Roman and Indian sources. The former is exemplified by stiff, frontal portraits (including those on coins) emphasizing the individual's power and wealth. The second, more realistic, style is typified by the schools of GANDHARA and MATHURA art.

Kushner, Tony (born 1956) U.S. dramatist. Born in New York City, he grew up in Lake Charles, La., and attended Columbia University and NYU. His early plays include *Yes, Yes, No, No* (1985). His major work, *Angels in America,* consists of two lengthy plays that deal with political issues and the catastrophe of AIDS in the 1980s. The first part, *Millennium Approaches* (1991), won a Pulitzer Prize. Later works include *Slavs* (1995) and *Henry Box Brown* (1997).

Kutaisi \,kü-tä-'ē-sē\ City (pop., 1994 est.: 241,000), western central Republic of Georgia. One of the oldest cities of Transcaucasia, it served as the capital of successive kingdoms in Georgia: COLCHIS, Iberia (Kartli), Abkhazia, and Imeretia. It was often caught in wars between Persians, Mongols, Turks, and Russians. Russians occupied it in the 19th century and made it a provincial seat. It is a major regional industrial and trade center.

Kutch, Rann of See Rann of KACHCHH

Kutuzov \kə-'tü-zȯf\, **Mikhail (Illarionovich)** *later* **Prince Kutuzov** *orig.* **Mikhail Illarionovich Golenishchev-Kutuzov** (1745–1813) Russian army commander. A career army officer, in 1805 he was given command of the joint Russian-Austrian army that opposed the French advance on Vienna. Following Austria's defeat in the Battle of ULM, he retreated and preserved his army intact, but ALEXANDER I engaged the French at the Battle of AUSTERLITZ (1805), for which disaster Kutuzov was partly blamed. After NAPOLEON's army entered Russia in 1812, public pressure made Alexander appoint Kutuzov commander in chief. After waging minor engagements, he was forced to fight the inconclusive Battle of BORODINO. When Napoleon led his troops in retreat from Moscow, Kutuzov forced the French army to leave Russia along the path it had devastated when it entered the country. He pursued the French into Prussia, destroying his opponent without fighting another major battle. Considered the finest Russian commander of his day, he appears as a major character in LEO TOLSTOY's *War and Peace.*

Kuusinen \'kü-si-nən\, **Otto V(ilhelm)** (1881–1964) Finnish-Soviet politician. He joined the Social Democratic Party in Finland in 1905 and held various party posts. After Finland's short-lived socialist regime was overthrown in 1918, he fled to Russia, where he cofounded the Finnish Communist Party. He remained in exile to become secretary of the COMINTERN. In the Soviet–Finnish "Winter War" (1939–40) he was head of the pro-Soviet puppet Finnish government, and he later became president of the supreme soviet of the Karelo-Finnish Soviet Socialist Republic (1940–56). He was secretary of the Russian Communist Party's Central Committee 1946–53 and 1957–64.

Kuwait *officially* **State of Kuwait** Country, northwestern coast of the PERSIAN GULF. Area: 6,880 sq mi (17,818 sq km). Population (1997 est.): 1,809,000. Capital: KUWAIT city. Its population is overwhelmingly Arab. Languages: Arabic (official), Persian, English. Religion: Islam (official). Currency: dinar. Except for Al-Jahrah Oasis, at the western end of Kuwait Bay, and a few fertile patches in the southeastern and coastal areas, it is largely desert; annual precipitation totals 1–7 in (25–180 mm). One-twelfth of the country serves as pastureland for livestock, including sheep and goats. Kuwait has almost no agricultural soil; its extensive petroleum and natural-gas deposits are the basis of its economy. Its estimated reserves of petroleum represent 10% of global reserves, ranking Kuwait third only to Iraq and Saudi Arabia. It is a constitutional monarchy with one legislative body; the head of state and government is the emir, assisted by the prime minister. Faylakah island, in Kuwait Bay, had a civilization dating back to the 3rd millennium BC. It flourished until 1200 BC, when it disappeared from the historical record. Greek colonists again settled the island in the 4th century BC. The nomadic Anizah tribe of central Arabia founded Kuwait city in 1710, and Abd Rahim of the SABAH DYNASTY became sheikh in 1756, the first of a family that con-

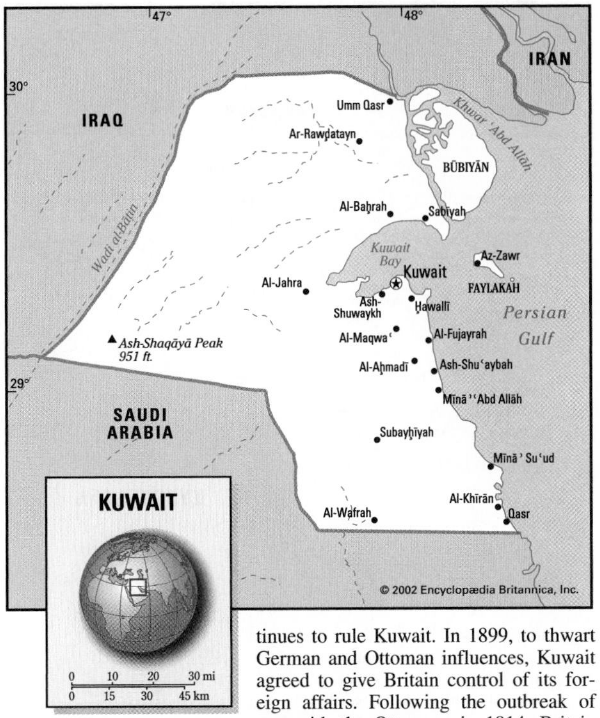

tinues to rule Kuwait. In 1899, to thwart German and Ottoman influences, Kuwait agreed to give Britain control of its foreign affairs. Following the outbreak of war with the Ottomans in 1914, Britain established a protectorate there. In 1961, after Kuwait gained full independence from Britain, Iraq laid claim to Kuwait. British troops were sent to defend Kuwait; the ARAB LEAGUE recognized its independence, and Iraq dropped its claim. During the IRAN–IRAQ WAR of the 1980s, Kuwait made large loans to Iraq. After talks on the repayment of war debts broke down, Iraqi forces invaded and occupied Kuwait in 1990. A U.S.-led military coalition drove the Iraqi army out of Kuwait in 1991 (see PERSIAN GULF WAR). The destruction of nearly half of Kuwait's 1,300 oil wells complicated reconstruction efforts.

Kuwait *or* **Kuwait City** City (pop., 1995: 29,000), capital of Kuwait. Located at the head of the PERSIAN GULF, it was founded in the 18th century, and was a trading city relying on sea and caravan traffic. Until 1957 it was enclosed by a mud wall separating it from the desert and was only 5 sq mi (13 sq km) in area. The development of the country's oil industry after World War II transformed the city into a modern metropolis. Almost all of the country's population is concentrated near the capital. The city was heavily damaged in 1990–91 during the Iraqi occupation and the PERSIAN GULF WAR.

Kuybyshev See SAMARA

Kuyper \'kœi-pər\, **Abraham** (1837–1920) Dutch theologian and politician. After serving as a pastor (1863–74), he founded a Calvinist-oriented newspaper (1872) and was elected to the national assembly (1874). He formed the Anti-Revolutionary Party, the first organized Dutch political party, and built up a lower-middle-class following with a program that combined orthodox religious positions and a progressive social agenda. To provide Calvinist training for pastors, he founded the Free University at Amsterdam (1880), and in 1892 he founded the Reformed Churches in the Netherlands. As prime minister of the Netherlands (1901–5), he advocated a wider franchise and broader social benefits.

Kuznets \'kəz-nets\, **Simon (Smith)** (1901–1985) Russian-U.S. economist and statistician. He emigrated to the U.S. in 1922 and joined the National Bureau of Economic Research in 1927; he later taught at the University of Pennsylvania (1930–54), Johns Hopkins (1954–60), and Harvard (1960–71). His work emphasized the complexity of underlying data in the construction of economic models, stressing the need for information on population structure, technology, labor quality, government structure, trade, and markets. He also described the existence of cyclical variations in growth rates (now called "Kuznets cycles") and their links with underlying factors such as population. In 1971 he received the Nobel Prize.

Kvasir \'kvä-sir\ In Norse mythology, the wisest of all men. He was born from the saliva from two rival groups of gods, the AESIR and the VANIR. As a teacher, he never failed to answer a question correctly. Two dwarfs, Fjalar and Galar, became tired of his great learning, and they killed him and distilled his blood in a magic cauldron. His blood, when mixed with honey by the giant Sattung, formed the mead that gave wisdom and poetic inspiration to those who drank it. Kvasir's story is told in the Edda *Braga Raedur.*

Kwa languages Branch of the NIGER-CONGO family of African languages. Kwa languages are spoken by more than 14 million people. Important languages and language groups include Anyi and Baule in the Ivory Coast, Akan (including Asante, Fante, and Brong) and Ga-Dangme in Ghana, and Gbe (including Ewe, Fon, and Anlo) in southeastern Ghana, Togo, and Benin.

Kwa Ndebele \,kwän-dā-'bā-lā\ Former black enclave, central TRANSVAAL province, South Africa. It was a self-governing "national state" for Transvaal NDEBELE people, although it was never internationally recognized. Situated northeast of JOHANNESBURG, it was founded in 1979, when many Transvaal Ndebele were expelled from Bophuthatswana. In 1994, after the abolition of APARTHEID, Kwa Ndebele became part of the new East Transvaal province, which was subsequently renamed Mpumalanga.

Kwakiutl \,kwä-kē-'yü-tᵊl\ NORTHWEST COAST INDIAN people who live along the shores of Vancouver Island and the mainland opposite. They speak a Wakashan language. Traditionally, the Kwakiutl subsisted mainly by fishing. They had a technology based largely on woodworking. Their society was stratified by rank, determined primarily by inheritance. The POTLATCH was elaborately developed and was often combined with dances and songs dramatizing ancestral experiences with supernatural beings. They continue to be known for their highly stylized art, which includes TOTEM POLES. Today they number about 4,000.

Kwando River River, southern Africa. Rising in central Angola, it flows southeast, forming part of the boundary between Angola and Zambia. It continues east along the northeastern border of Botswana and empties into the ZAMBEZI RIVER just above VICTORIA FALLS. Its total length is 457 mi (731 km).

Kwangju \'gwȯŋ-'jü\ *formerly* **Koshu** City (pop., 1995: 1,256,000), southwestern South Korea. It occupies an area of 193 sq mi (501 sq km) and constitutes a special city (province) by itself. It has been a center of trade and local administration since the Three Kingdoms (c. 57 BC); its modern industrial development began with a railway connection to SEOUL in 1914. It was the site of an armed uprising between civilians and the government in 1980. It is the seat of Choson University (founded 1946).

Kwangsi Chuang See GUANGXI

Kwangtung See GUANGDONG

Kwanzaa *or* **Kwanza** \'kwän-zə\ African-American holiday celebrated from December 26 to January 1 and patterned after African harvest festivals. It was created in 1966 by Maulana Karenga, a black-studies professor at California State University at Long Beach, as a nonreligious celebration of family and community. The name was taken from the Swahili phrase *matunda ya kwanzaa* ("first fruits"). Each day is dedicated to one of seven principles: unity, self-determination, collective responsibility, cooperative economics, purpose, creativity, and faith. Each evening, family members gather to light one of the candles in the *kinara,* a seven-branched candelabra; often gifts are exchanged. On December 31 community members gather for a feast, the *karamu.* Kwanzaa is now observed by more than 15 million people.

kwashiorkor \,kwä-shē-'ȯr-kər\ Condition caused by severe PROTEIN deficiency. It is common in tropical and subtropical regions in young children weaned on a diet chiefly of starchy foods such as grains, cassava, plantain, and sweet potato. It causes potbelly, EDEMA, weakness, irritability, dry skin with rash, reddish-orange hair discoloration, DIARRHEA, ANEMIA, and fat deposits in the liver. Mental development may be stunted. Adults who had the disease in childhood may be at risk of diseases such as CIRRHOSIS. Treatment is protein supplementation, often in the form of dried skim milk. For long-term prevention, development of high-protein plant mixtures based on local food preferences and availability is encouraged. Nondietary causes include inadequate absorption of nutrients by the intestines, chronic alcoholism, kidney disease, and trauma (e.g., infection, burns) causing abnormal protein loss.

Kweichow See Guizhou

Kworra River See Niger River

kyanite \ˈkī-ə-ˌnīt\ *or* **cyanite** \ˈsī-ə-ˌnīt\ *or* **disthene** \ˈdis-ˌthēn\ Silicate mineral, one of several phases in the aluminum silicate (Al_2SiO_5) system. Its color ranges from gray-green to black or blue, with blue and blue-gray being most common. It occurs in Switzerland, Italy, the Ural Mtns., and New England (U.S.). Kyanite is a raw material in the manufacture of spark plugs. A clear, deep-blue variety is sometimes cut as a gemstone.

Kyd \ˈkid\, **Thomas** (1558–1594) English dramatist. With *The Spanish Tragedie* (1592), he initiated the revenge tragedy, a favorite dramatic form in the Elizabethan and Jacobean eras. One of the most popular plays of its time, it prepared the way for William Shakespeare's *Hamlet* and other plays. The only other play certainly by Kyd is *Cornelia* (1594). He was arrested and tortured in 1593 after "atheistical" documents were found in his room; he claimed the papers belonged to Christopher Marlowe, with whom he had shared lodgings. His reputation ruined, he died the next year at 36.

Kynewulf See Cynewulf

Kyoga Lake Lake, southern central Uganda. It is formed by the Victoria Nile, which flows through it. It has a maximum depth of 25 ft (8 m), restricting navigation to shallow-draft vessels. About 80 mi (129 km) long, it has an area of 1,710 sq mi (4,429 sq km).

Kyoto City (pop., 1995: 1,464,000), western central Honshu, Japan. Situated northeast of Osaka, and the center of Japanese culture and Japanese Buddhism, Kyoto ("Capital City") was the capital of Japan and the site of the imperial family residence for more than 1,000 years (794–1868). The modern city has theaters that present No drama and kabuki. Many small workshops produce textiles and porcelain. Buddhist temples and Shinto shrines are found throughout the city and surrounding area. Part of an industrial area, it is also a manufacturing center. Its educational institutions include Kyoto University (founded 1897) and Doshisha University (1875).

Kyrgyzstan \ˌkir-giz-ˈstan\ *officially* **Kyrgyz Republic** Country, central Asia. On the southeast, the Kok Shaal-Tau Range, part of the Tian Shan, forms the border with China. Area: 76,600 sq mi (198,500 sq km). Population (1997 est.): 4,595,000. Capital: Bishkek. The Kyrgyz make up about one-half of the population; the remainder consists of Russians and Uzbecks, and Ukrainians and Germans deported from western Russia in 1941. Languages: Kyrgyz, Russian (both official). Religion: Islam (Sunnite). Currency: som. Kyrgyzstan is a largely mountainous country. At its eastern edge rises Victory (Pobedy) Peak, which at 24,406 ft (7,439 m) is the country's highest peak. The country's valleys and plains, occupying only one-seventh of the total area, are home to most of its people. The economy is based largely on agriculture, including livestock raising and the cultivation of cereals, potatoes, cotton, and sugar beets. Coal mining and industries such as food processing and the production of machinery are also important. It is a republic with two legislative houses; its head of state and government is the president, assisted by the prime minister. The Kyrgyz, a nomadic people of central Asia, settled in the Tian Shan region in ancient times. They were conquered by Genghis Khan's son Jöchi in 1207. The area became part of the Qing empire of China in the mid-18th century. The region came under Russian control in the 19th century, and its rebellion against the Soviet Union in 1916 resulted in a long period of brutal repression. Kirgiziya became an autonomous province of the Soviet Union in 1924 and was made the Kirgiz Soviet Socialist Republic in 1936. Kyrgyzstan gained independence in 1991. In the 1990s it struggled with its democratization process and with establishing a thriving economy.

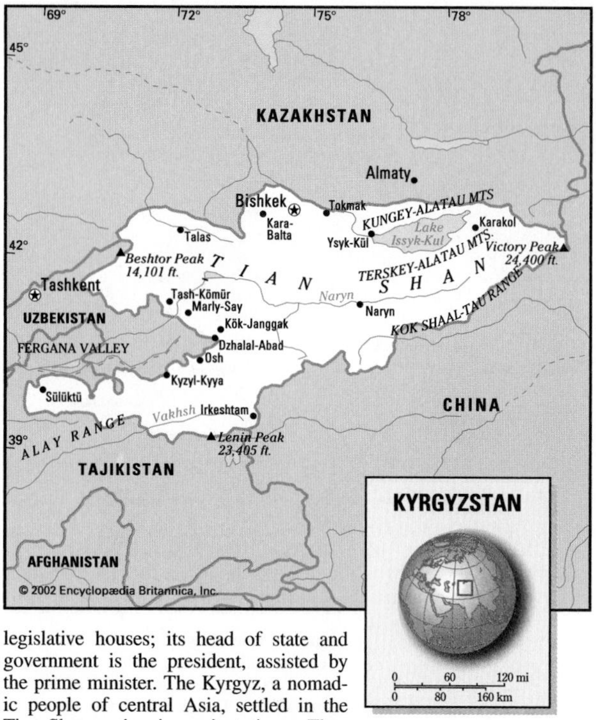

Kyushu Island (pop., 1995: 13,420,000), southernmost of Japan's four main islands. Located off the eastern coast of Asia, it is separated from Honshu to the north by the Shimonoseki Strait and from Shikoku to the east by the Bungo Strait. The island, with an area of 14,177 sq mi (36,719 sq km), is mountainous with several famous peaks ranging from 5,000–6,000 ft (1,525–1,980 m), including Mount Aso. Its chief cities include Fukuoka and Kitakyushu. It was the first part of the Japanese empire opened to foreigners in the 19th century.

Kyzil Kum \ki-ˈzil-ˈküm\ Desert in Kazakhstan and Uzbekistan. Occupying 115,000 sq mi (300,000 sq km), it lies between the Syr Darya and the Amu Darya rivers, southeast of the Aral Sea. Desert plants grow on its sand ridges, serving as pasture for sheep, horses, and camels; there are several small oasis settlements. Its resources include natural gas deposits and gold.

L-dopa See DOPA

La Brea Tar Pits \lə-ˈbrā-ə\ Fossil field in Hancock Park (formerly Rancho La Brea), LOS ANGELES. It is the site of "pitch springs" oozing crude oil, discovered by Gaspar de Portolá's expedition in 1769. The tar pits contain the fossilized bones of PLEISTOCENE mammals that became entrapped there; they include MAMMOTHS, MASTODONS, and SABER-TOOTHED cats. The George C. Page Museum contains more than one million prehistoric specimens exhumed from the pits.

La Bruyère \lä-brūē-ˈyer\, **Jean de** (1645–1696) French satiric moralist. As a tutor and librarian in a royal household, he observed aristocratic idleness, fads, and fashions. His *The Characters, or Manners of the Age, with the Characters of Theophrastus* (1688) was appended to his translation of Theophrastus and written in the latter's style. A masterpiece of French literature, it was an indictment of the vanity and pretensions around him. Eight editions of *Characters,* with expanded character sketches and topical allusions, appeared through 1694.

La Coruña \ˌlä-kō-ˈrü-nyä\ City (pop., 1991: 247,000), northwestern Spain. A seaport on the Atlantic Ocean, it is believed to antedate Roman times. It was part of the caliphate of CORDOBA. The point of departure for the SPANISH ARMADA in 1588, it was sacked by FRANCIS DRAKE in 1589. In the PENINSULAR WARS, it was the site of a notable victory by the English over the French. Today, it is one of northern Spain's most important shipping ports and a large fishing center.

La Follette \lə-ˈfäl-ət\, **Robert M(arion)** (1855–1925) U.S. politician. Born in Primrose, Wis., he served as county district attorney (1880–84) and in the U.S. House of Representatives (1885–91). He returned to Wisconsin, where his progressive reforms won him the governorship (1901–6). In the U.S. Senate (1906–24), he sponsored bills to restrict the railroads' power. He founded *La Follette's Weekly* (1909) to broaden his reform movement, and led Republican opposition to the policies of Pres. WILLIAM H. TAFT. He opposed U.S. entrance into World War I and policies of Pres. WOODROW WILSON that favored big business, and he vigorously exposed postwar corruption, including the TEAPOT DOME SCANDAL. As the PROGRESSIVE PARTY's presidential candidate in the 1924 election, he won 5 million votes, one-sixth of the total. He died the next year; his son Robert (1895–1953) held his Senate seat from 1925 until 1947, when he was defeated by JOSEPH MCCARTHY.

La Fontaine \lä-fōⁿ-ˈten\, **Jean de** (1621–1695) French poet. He made important contacts in Paris, where he was able to attract patrons and spent his most productive years as a writer. He is best known for his *Fables* (1668–94), which rank among the masterpieces of French literature. Comprising some 240 poems, they include timeless tales about simple countryfolk, heroes of Greek mythology, and the familiar animals of FABLES. Their chief theme is the everyday moral experience of humankind. His many lesser works include *The Loves of Cupid and Psyche* (1669) and the often licentious *Tales and Novels in Verse*. He was elected to the ACADÉMIE FRANÇAISE in 1683.

La Galissonnière \lä-gä-lē-sòn-ˈyer\, **Marquis de** *orig.* **Roland-Michel Barrin** (1693–1756) French naval officer. While serving in the French navy (1710–36), he made several supply trips to New France and held various commands in the Atlantic. As commandant general of NEW FRANCE (1747–49), he sought unsuccessfully to fortify a link along the Ohio River between French Canada and the Louisiana settlements and to establish French settlements in Detroit and the Illinois country.

La Guardia \lə-ˈgwär-dē-ə\, **Fiorello H(enry)** (1882–1947) U.S. politician, mayor of New York (1933–45). Born in New York City, he practiced law there from 1910 before serving in the U.S. House of Representatives (1917, 1918–21, 1923–33). A progressive Republican, he cosponsored a bill that restricted the courts' power to ban strikes, boycotts, and picketing by organized labor, opposed Prohibition, and supported women's suffrage and child-labor laws. As New York's mayor, he fought Tammany Hall corruption and introduced reform programs for civic improvement through low-cost housing, social-welfare services, and new roads and bridges. A colorful figure with a flair for the dramatic, he enjoyed enormous popularity for his fearless forthrightness and lack of pretension. In 1945 he declined to run for a fourth term as mayor.

La Harpe \lä-ˈärp\, **Frédéric-César de** (1754–1838) Swiss political leader. From 1784 he was tutor to the future Russian czar ALEXANDER I. He returned to Switzerland in 1794, then went to Paris to obtain French military support to secure independence for his native Vaud canton. In 1798 France invaded to establish the Helvetic Republic. A member of its Directory, La Harpe sought dictatorial powers, but was deposed in 1800. He fled to France, then in 1814 secured from Alexander a promise of Vaudois independence.

La Hontan \lä-ōⁿ-ˈtäⁿ\, **Baron de** *orig.* **Louis-Armand de Lom d'Arce** (1666–1715) French army officer and explorer. He served in NEW FRANCE (1683–93), commanded Ft.-St.-Joseph (now Niles, Mich.), and explored territory along the Wisconsin and Mississippi rivers (1688–89). After political difficulties during a stop in Newfoundland (1692–1693), he fled to Europe. In 1703 he published *New Voyages to North-America,* considered the best 17th-century work on New France and an influence on the works of C.-L. MONTESQUIEU, VOLTAIRE, and JONATHAN SWIFT.

La Niña Cyclic counterpart to EL NIÑO, consisting of a cooling of surface waters of the Pacific Ocean along the western coast of South America. While its local effects on weather and climate are generally the opposite of those associated with El Niño, its global effects can be more complex. La Niña events often follow El Niños, which occur at irregular intervals of about 5–10 years.

La Paz (de Ayacucho) \lä-ˈpäs\ City (pop., 1993 est.: 785,000), administrative capital of Bolivia. Located in western central Bolivia, it is the world's highest capital, built at over 12,000 ft (3,650 m) above sea level. The city center lies in a canyon formed by the La Paz River. Founded in 1548 by the Spanish on the site of an Inca village, it was originally called Nuestra Señora de La Paz ("Our Lady of Peace"). In 1835 it was renamed La Paz de Ayacucho to commemorate the decisive battle in the colony's wars of independence. Since 1898 it has been the administrative capital of Bolivia, though SUCRE remains the legal capital. It is Bolivia's principal industrial center, and also the site of the University of San Andrés and the national museums of art and archaeology.

La Paz City (pop., 1990: 138,000), capital of BAJA CALIFORNIA SUR state, northwestern Mexico. Situated on La Paz Bay of the Gulf of CALIFORNIA, it is a popular resort and the largest urban center in the state. The bay was discovered by the Spanish in 1596; the town was established in the early 1800s and served as the capital of Baja California 1828–87. When the peninsula was divided between the U.S. and Mexico (1887), La Paz then became the capital of the Mexican region.

La Plata City (metro. area pop., 1991: 643,000), Argentina. After BUENOS AIRES became the national capital, La Plata was chosen (1882) as the new provincial seat and modeled after Washington, D.C. It was renamed Eva Perón in 1952, but after the overthrow of Pres. JUAN PERON in 1955, it resumed its original name. Located near the Río de la PLATA estuary, it is a seaport with a large artificial harbor. Its industries include meatpacking and oil refining.

La Plata River River, eastern central Puerto Rico. It flows about 45 mi (70 km) northwest and north, to empty into the Atlantic Ocean. Part of it is dammed to create a lake which provides hydroelectric power.

La Rioja \ˌlä-rē-ˈō-hä\ Autonomous community (pop., 1996 est.: 265,000), province, and historical region, northern central Spain. Covering 1,944 sq mi (5,035 sq km), it was known until 1980 as Logroño; its capital is LOGROÑO (city). Historically belonging to old CASTILE, it is watered by the EBRO RIVER and most of its population is concentrated around the river. Upper Rioja produces some of Spain's finest wines. Through lower Rioja runs the highway linking BILBAO, SARAGOSSA, and BARCELONA.

La Rochefoucauld \lä-ròsh-fü-ˈkō\, **François, duc (duke) de** (1613–1680) French writer. Of a noble family, he joined the army at an early age and was wounded several times. He later played a leading part in the FRONDE, but gradually won his way back into royal favor. He turned his energies to intellectual pursuits and became the leading exponent of the *maxime*, a French form of EPIGRAM that concisely expresses a harsh or paradoxical truth. *Maximes* (five eds., 1665–78), his principal achievement, consists of 500 reflections on human behavior. His *Mémoires* (1664) recount the plots and campaigns of mutinous nobles during the Fronde.

La Salle \lə-'säl\, **René-Robert Cavelier, Sieur (Lord) de** (1643–1687) French explorer. In 1666 he left France for North America and was granted land near Montreal. He explored the Ohio River region (1669), then worked with the comte de FRONTENAC to extend French influence and helped establish Fort Frontenac on Lake Ontario, where as seigneur he controlled the fur trade. He obtained authority from Louis XIV to explore the western frontier of New France and build new forts. He sailed down the Illinois River and with Henri de Tonty (1650?–1704) canoed down the Mississippi River to the Gulf of Mexico. There in 1682 La Salle claimed the entire Mississippi Basin for France, naming it Louisiana after Louis XIV. Back in France, he received authority to build a fort at the mouth of the Mississippi. Beset by losses of men and ships, he mistakenly landed at Matagorda Bay, Texas. After fruitless attempts to locate the Mississippi, he was killed by mutineers.

La Scala Opera house in Milan, Italy. It was built in 1778 to replace the Regio Ducal Teatro, which burned down in 1776, on the former site of the church Santa Maria della Scala. With the works of G. ROSSINI, Italian opera regained international attention, and La Scala, as the site of many of Rossini's premieres, had by the 1830s become the opera landmark it has remained ever since.

La Tène \lä-'ten\ (French: "The Shallows") Archaeological site at the eastern end of Lake Neuchâtel, Switzerland. The name by extension applies to a Late IRON AGE culture of European CELTS. La Tène culture originated in the mid–5th century BC, when the Celts came into contact with Greeks and ETRUSCANS. It passed through several phases and regional variations during the next 400 years, as the Celts populated northern Europe and the British Isles, and ended in the mid–1st century BC when most of the Celts came under Roman control. Objects of the early period are characterized by ornamental S-shapes, spirals, and round patterns. The middle period is notable for long iron swords, heavy knives, and burial in coffins or under stone heaps; later-middle-period findings include decorated scabbards, broad-bladed spearheads, and wooden shields with iron supports. The final period, showing Roman influence, is distinguished by peasant's implements, such as iron sickles, scythes, axes, saws, and ploughshares.

Gold disk found at Auvers, La Tène culture, 5th century BC.

BY COURTESY OF THE BIBLIOTHEQUE NATIONALE, PARIS

La Tour \lə-'tu̇r\, **Georges de** (1593–1653) French painter. He was well known in his lifetime, especially for his depictions of candlelit subjects, then was forgotten until the 20th century, when the identification of works previously misattributed established his reputation as a giant of French painting. His early works were painted in a realistic manner and influenced by the dramatic chiaroscuro of CARAVAGGIO; his later work is more geometric and simplified, as in *St. Joseph the Carpenter* (1645). Little is known of his life, and only four or five of his paintings are dated. The chronology and authenticity of some works attributed to him are still debated.

"St. Joseph the Carpenter," oil on canvas by Georges de La Tour, c. 1645; in the Louvre, Paris.

GIRAUDON—ART RESOURCE/EB INC.

La Vérendrye \lä-ˌver-ən-'drē\, **Pierre Gaultier de Varennes et de** (1685–1749) French-Canadian explorer. Born in Trois-Rivières, New France, he served in the French army before becoming a fur trader north of Lake Superior (1726). From the Indians he heard of a river that might lead to the Pacific Ocean, and with his sons he built a string of fur-trading posts from Ontario to Manitoba (1731–38). Two sons sent farther west became the first Europeans to explore areas of present-day Nebraska, Montana, and Wyoming, and they claimed South Dakota for France. The 30,000 beaver pelts La Vérendrye annually sent to Quebec broke the monopoly of the HUDSON'S BAY CO. Little appreciated in his lifetime, he was later considered one of the greatest explorers of the Canadian West.

Laâyoune See EL AAIÚN

Laban \'lä-bän\, **Rudolf (von)** (1879–1958) Hungarian modern-dance teacher, inventor of the Labanotation system of DANCE NOTATION. After studying dance in Paris, he opened his Choreographic Institute in Zurich in 1915 and later founded branches in Italy, France, and central Europe. He worked in Germany 1919–37, and was ballet director of the Berlin State Opera 1930–34. In 1928 he published his method for recording all forms of human motion, which enabled choreographers to record the dancer's steps and other body movements, including their rhythm. In 1938 he joined his former pupil KURT JOOSS teaching dance in England, where he later formed the Art of Movement Studio. His system was further developed and maintained at centers in Essen (Germany) and New York.

Labdah See LEPTIS MAGNA

labor In economics, the general body of wage earners. In CLASSICAL ECONOMICS, labor is one of the three factors of production, along with CAPITAL and LAND. Labor can also be used to describe work performed, including any valuable service rendered by a human agent in the production of wealth, other than accumulating and providing capital. Labor is performed for the sake of its product or, in modern economic life, for the sake of a share of the aggregate product of the community's industry. The price per unit of time, or wage rate, commanded by a particular kind of labor in the MARKET depends not only on the technical efficiency of the laborer but also on the demand for his services and on the supply of other workers. Other variables include the training, skill, and intelligence of workers and the social status, prospects for advancement, and relative difficulty of the work. All these factors make it impossible for economists to assign a standard value to labor performed. Instead, they often compare different uses of the available supply of labor with reference to the quantity and value of the product they yield.

labor See PARTURITION

Labor, Knights of See KNIGHTS OF LABOR

Labor, U.S. Department of Federal executive division responsible for enforcing labor statutes and promoting the general welfare of U.S. wage earners. Established in 1913, it controls the Employment Standards Administration, the Occupational Safety and Health Administration (OSHA), the Pension and Welfare Benefits Administration, and numerous other agencies involved in administration of programs concerning employment and training, trade adjustment assistance, unemployment insurance, veterans and senior citizens, and mine safety.

Labor Day Annual holiday devoted to the recognition of working people's contribution to society. It is observed on the first Monday in September in the U.S. and Canada. It was first celebrated in New York on September 5, 1882, under the sponsorship of the KNIGHTS OF LABOR. Various U.S. states observed the holiday before 1894, when Congress passed a bill making Labor Day a national holiday. In most other countries, workers are honored on MAY DAY.

labor economics Study of how workers are allocated among jobs, how their rates of pay are determined, and how their efficiency is affected by various factors. The labor force of a country includes all those who work for gain in any capacity as well as those who are unemployed but seeking work. A multitude of factors influence how workers are utilized and how much they are paid, including qualities of the labor force itself (such as health, level of education, distribution of special training and skills, and degree of mobility), structural characteristics of the economy (e.g., proportions of heavy manufacturing, high-technology, and service industries), and institutional factors (including the extent and power of LABOR UNIONS and employers' associations and the presence of minimum-wage laws). Miscellaneous factors such as custom and variations in the BUSINESS CYCLE are also considered. Certain general trends are widely accepted by labor economists; for instance, wage levels tend to be higher in industries that require higher levels of education or training, in economies that have high proportions of such industries, and in industries that are heavily unionized.

labor law Body of law applied to employment, wages, conditions of work, LABOR UNIONS, labor-management relations, and so on. Laws intended to protect workers, including children, from abusive employment practices did not emerge in force until the late 19th century in Europe and slightly later in the U.S. In Asia and Africa labor issues did not arise until the 1940s and '50s. Employment laws cover such matters as hiring, training, advancement, and UNEMPLOYMENT compensation. Wage laws cover the forms and methods of payment, pay rates, SOCIAL SECURITY, PENSIONS, and other matters. Legislation on working conditions regulates hours, rest periods, vacations, CHILD LABOR, EQUALITY in the workplace, and health and safety. Laws on trade unions and labor-management relations deal with the status of unions, the rights and obligations of workers' and employers' organizations, COLLECTIVE-BARGAINING agreements, and rules for settling STRIKES and other disputes. See also ARBITRATION, MEDIATION.

Labor Relations Act, National See WAGNER ACT

labor union Association of workers in a particular trade, industry, or plant, formed to obtain improvements in pay, benefits, and working conditions through collective action. The first fraternal and self-help associations of laborers appeared in Britain in the 18th century, and the era of modern labor unions began in Britain, Europe, and the U.S. in the 19th century. The movement met with hostility from employers and governments, and union organizers were regularly prosecuted. British unionism received its legal foundation in the Trade-Union Act of 1871. In the U.S. the same effect was achieved more slowly through a series of court decisions that whittled away at the use of injunctions and conspiracy laws against unions. The founding of the American Federation of Labor (AFL) in 1886 marked the beginning of a successful, large-scale labor movement in the U.S. The unions brought together in the AFL were craft unions, which represented workers skilled in a particular craft or trade. Only a few early labor organizers argued in favor of industrial unions, which would represent all workers, skilled or unskilled, in a single industry. The Congress of Industrial Organizations (CIO) was founded by unions expelled from the AFL for attempting to organize unskilled workers, and by 1941 it had assured the success of industrial unionism by organizing the steel and automobile industries (see AFL-CIO). The use of COLLECTIVE BARGAINING to settle wages, working conditions, and disputes is standard in all noncommunist industrial countries, though union organization varies from country to country. In Britain, labor unions displayed a strong inclination to political activity that culminated in the formation of the LABOUR PARTY in 1906. In France, too, the major unions are highly politicized; the Confédération Générale du Travail (formed in 1895) was allied with the Communist Party for many years, while the Confédération Française Démocratique du Travail is more moderate politically. Japan developed a form of union organization known as enterprise unionism, which represents workers in a single plant or multiplant enterprise rather than within a craft or industry.

laboratory Place where scientific RESEARCH AND DEVELOPMENT is conducted and analyses performed, in contrast with the field or factory. Most laboratories are characterized by controlled uniformity of conditions (constant temperature, humidity, cleanliness). Modern laboratories use a vast number of instruments and procedures to study, systematize, or quantify the objects of their attention. Procedures often include sampling, pretreatment and treatment, measurement, calculation, and presentation of results; each may be carried out by techniques ranging from having an unaided person use crude tools to running an automated analysis system with computer controls, data storage, and elaborate readouts.

Labour Party British political party whose historic links with trade unions have led it to promote an active role for the state in the creation of economic prosperity and the provision of social services. In opposition to the CONSERVATIVE PARTY, it has been Britain's major democratic socialist party since the early 20th century. In 1900 the Trades Union Congress and the Independent Labour Party (founded 1893) established the Labour Representation Committee, which took the name Labour Party in 1906. In 1918 it became a socialist party with a democratic constitution, and by 1922 it had supplanted the LIBERAL PARTY as the official opposition party. In 1924 JAMES RAMSAY MACDONALD formed the first Labour government, with Liberal support. The party was out of power from 1935 until a spectacular recovery in 1945 brought in CLEMENT R. ATTLEE's government (until 1951), which introduced a system of social welfare, including a NATIONAL HEALTH SERVICE, and extensive nationalization of industry. Labour regained power under HAROLD WILSON (1964–70) and later JAMES CALLAGHAN (1974–79), but foundered because of economic problems and worsening relations with its trade-union allies. In 1983 MICHAEL FOOT's radical program resulted in a massive Labour defeat. Neil Kinnock (born 1942) moved the party toward the center, but only in 1997 did TONY BLAIR and his "New Labour" agenda succeed in returning Labour to power.

Labov \lə-ˈbȯv\, **William** (born 1927) U.S. linguist. Born in Rutherford, N.J., Labov began his graduate work in 1961 after a career as an industrial chemist, focusing on regional and class differences in English pronunciation on Martha's Vineyard, Mass., and in New York City, and ways to assess phonetic change and variation quantitatively. Most of his later research dealt with the same issues in increasingly sophisticated ways, culminating in his monumental *Principles of Linguistic Change* (1994). The discovery that American English pronunciation was becoming regionally more rather than less divergent countered popular belief and attracted attention outside linguistics.

Labrador Large peninsula, northeastern Canada. It is divided between the provinces of Quebec and Newfoundland and Labrador and occupies an area of about 625,000 sq mi (1,620,000 sq km). Its highest mountains are over 5,000 ft (1,520 m), and its coast is lined with islands. It forms the easternmost portion of the plateau known as the CANADIAN SHIELD. Politically, Labrador refers to the Newfoundland and Labrador portion of the peninsula; the Quebec portion is UNGAVA PENINSULA. Political control of the region was disputed by the two provinces until the Quebec–Newfoundland border was established in 1927.

Labrador Current Surface oceanic current flowing southward along the western side of the Labrador Sea. Originating at the Davis Strait, the current is a combination of the West Greenland Current, the Baffin Island Current, and inflow from Hudson Bay. It maintains temperatures of less than 32°F (0°C) and has a low salinity. The current is limited to the CONTINENTAL SHELF and reaches depths only slightly greater than 2,000 ft (600 m). It carries several thousand ICEBERGS southward each year.

labradorite \ˈla-brə-ˌdȯr-ˌīt\ Type of FELDSPAR mineral in the PLAGIOCLASE series that is often valued as a gemstone and as ornamental material for its red, blue, or green iridescence. The mineral is usually gray or brown to black and need not be iridescent. Labradorite is named for its occurrence on the coast of Labrador, Canada.

labyrinth *or* **maze** System of intricate passageways and blind alleys. Labyrinth was the name given by the ancient Greeks and Romans to buildings, entirely or partly underground, containing a number of chambers and passages that made egress difficult. From the European Renaissance on, labyrinths or mazes consisting of intricate paths separated by high hedges were a feature of formal gardens.

Lacan \lȧ-ˈkäⁿ\, **Jacques (Marie Émile)** (1901–1981) French psychoanalyst. A practicing psychiatrist in Paris for much of his career, Lacan emphasized the primacy of language as the mirror of the unconscious mind and introduced the study of language into psychoanalytic theory. His major achievement was his reinterpretation of SIGMUND FREUD's work in terms of structural LINGUISTICS. He became a celebrity in France with *Écrits* (1966; *The Language of the Self*) and in the 1970s was a dominant figure in French cultural life as well as a strong influence on American psychoanalytic and literary theory.

Lacandon \ˌlä-kän-ˈdōn\ MAYA Indians who live in a rich tropical rain forest on the Mexico–Guatemala border. Largely isolated, they maintained a primitive way of life until recently. They fish, hunt, and grow vegetables and fruits. They spin fibers and weave cloth, tan leather, and make pottery, flutes, dugout canoes, and nets. They have preserved their traditional beliefs. They were swept up into the 1994 Chiapas revolt. Their total number is less than 600 and declining.

lace Ornamental openwork fabric formed by the looping, interlacing, braiding, or twisting of threads, originally primarily of linen. Almost all high-quality artistic lace is made by one of two techniques: needle lace involves a difficult technique that originated in Italy; bobbin lace is a more widespread craft that originated in Flanders. The art of lace is a

European achievement. Fully developed lace did not appear before the Renaissance. By 1600 lace had become a fabric of luxury and an important article of commerce. The Industrial Revolution in the 19th century led to the use of machines to produce less-expensive lace made of cotton, and lace gradually disappeared from both men's and women's fashions. By 1920 the industry was dying. Fine handmade lace is still made in Belgium, Slovenia, and elsewhere, but chiefly as souvenirs.

Lacedaemon See SPARTA

lacemaking Methods of producing LACE. The popularity of handmade laces led to the invention of lacemaking MACHINES in the 19th century (see JOHN HEATHCOAT). Early models required intricate engineering mechanisms. Later improvements included Nottingham-lace machines, primarily for coarse lace, and Barmens machines. Schiffli lace, a type of embroidery, is made by modern machines, evolved from a hand version, using needles with points at each end. Many types of machine-made laces are made, frequently with geometrically shaped nets forming their backgrounds. The high strength and comparatively low cost of man-made fiber yarns has made sheer laces widely available

lacewing Any of many species of insects in the order Neuroptera, especially those in the green lacewing and brown lacewing families. The green lacewing has long, delicate antennae, a slender greenish body, golden- or copper-colored eyes, and two pairs of veined wings. It is found worldwide and flies near grasses and shrubs. It is also known as a stinkfly because it emits a disagreeable odor. The larva, with prominent sucking mouthparts, drains body fluids from aphids and other soft-bodied insects. The brown lacewing resembles the green lacewing but is smaller and brown.

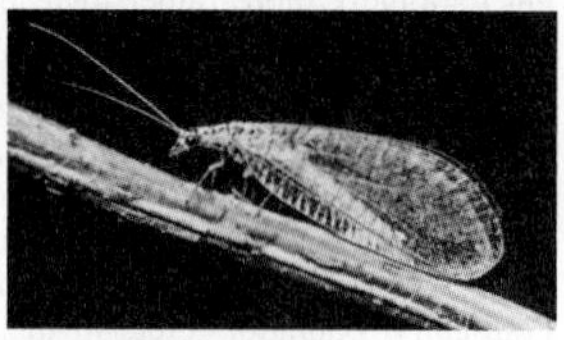

Lacewing (*Chrysopa*).

A.E.MC.R. PEARCE—BRUCE COLEMAN LTD.

Lachaise \lä-'shez\, **Gaston** (1882–1935) French-born U.S. sculptor. Son of a cabinetmaker, he was trained in the decorative arts and studied sculpture at the École des Beaux-Arts (1898–1904). He was a designer of Art Nouveau decorative objects for RENE LALIQUE before emigrating to the U.S. in 1906. His most famous work, *Standing Woman* (1912–27), a female nude with enormous breasts and thighs and sinuous, tapered limbs, typifies the image he worked and reworked throughout his career. He is also known for his portrait busts of JOHN MARIN, MARIANNE MOORE, E.E. CUMMINGS, and others.

Standing Woman, bronze sculpture by Gaston Lachaise, 1932; in the Museum of Modern Art, New York City.

BY COURTESY OF THE MUSEUM OF MODERN ART, NEW YORK, MRS. SIMON GUGGENHEIM FUND

Lachlan River \'lä-klən\ Chief tributary of the MURRUMBIDGEE RIVER, central NEW SOUTH WALES, Australia. Rising in the GREAT DIVIDING RANGE, it flows northwest and turns southwest, joining the Murrumbidgee after a course of 930 mi (1,500 km). Though usually perennial, it may run dry in severe drought years. It was explored in 1815 by George W. Evans and was named after Lachlan Macquarie, governor of New South Wales.

lachrymal duct and gland See TEAR DUCT AND GLAND

Lackland, John See JOHN (England)

Laclos \lä-'klō\, **Pierre (-Ambroise-François) Choderlos de** (1741–1803) French writer. He chose an army career, but soon left it to become a writer. He is chiefly remembered for *Les liaisons dangereuses* (1782; *Dangerous Liaisons*), one of the earliest psychological novels. The epistolary novel of a noble seducer and his female accomplice who take unscrupulous delight in their victims' misery, it caused an immediate sensation and was banned for years. Laclos later returned to the army and ultimately rose to the rank of general under Napoleon.

Laconia \lə-'kō-nē-ə\, **Gulf of** Inlet, southern IONIAN SEA southern coast of the PELOPONNESE, Greece. Cape Maléa, which divides the gulf from the Aegean Sea, was once feared by sailors for its treacherous winds and harborless coast. The major stream entering the gulf is the non-navigable Evrótas River.

Lacoste \lä-'kȯst\, **(Jean-) René** (1904–1996) French tennis player and sportswear entrepreneur. Born in Paris, he became noted for a methodical game in which he tried to outlast his opponents. He won the Wimbledon (1925, 1928) and French (1925, 1927, 1929) singles, and became the first foreigner to win the U.S. championship twice (1926, 1927), the second time beating BILL TILDEN. He also won various doubles matches. Nicknamed "the crocodile," he retired in 1929 to form a sportswear company that featured a crocodile (later alligator) emblem on its clothes.

lacquerwork Any of a variety of decorative objects or surfaces, usually of wood, to which a colored, highly polished, and opaque type of varnish called lacquer has been applied. True lacquerwork is Chinese or Japanese in origin. The technique was copied in Europe, where it was known as "japanning," but European lacquerwork lacks the hardness and brilliance of Asian lacquer. True lacquer is the purified and dehydrated sap of the *Rhus vernicifera* tree, native to China and cultivated in Japan. Lacquer becomes extremely hard but not brittle on exposure to air, and takes a high polish. Many thin layers are applied, allowed to dry, and smoothed before the surface is ready for decoration by carving, engraving, or inlay.

lacrosse (Canadian French *la crosse,* "the crosier") Outdoor team sport in which players use a long-handled stick that has a triangular head with a mesh pouch for catching, carrying, and throwing a hard rubber ball with the object of slinging it into an opponent's goal (for one point). French settlers in Canada adapted the modern game from an ancient American Indian event (baggataway) that was at once sport, combat training, and mystical ceremony. It became an organized sport in the late 19th century. Modern teams have 10 players. The game is divided into four periods of 15 minutes each. Lacrosse is especially popular as a collegiate sport and is played by both men and women. See illustration on following page.

lactation Production of milk by female mammals after giving birth. The milk is discharged by the MAMMARY GLANDS in the breasts. Hormones triggered by delivery of the placenta and by nursing stimulate milk production. Colostrum (milk that the mother produces in the first few days after giving birth) has more proteins, minerals, and antibodies and fewer calories and fats than the mature milk that develops later. Mature milk supplies nutrients, hormones, and substances that provide the infant with IMMUNITY against infectious agents. The American Academy of Pediatrics recommends that babies be fed mother's milk exclusively for the first six months and that nursing continue through the first year. As the child is weaned, lactation tapers off; while nursing continues, FERTILITY is reduced. Problems with lactation may involve hormones, suckling pattern, physical difficulties, or emotional factors. Mothers taking certain drugs or with some diseases (e.g., AIDS) should not nurse, because of risks to the baby.

lactic acid CARBOXYLIC ACID found in certain plant juices, in blood and muscle, and in soil. In blood it occurs as SALTS (lactates) break down products of GLYCOGEN in muscle; it can be reconverted to glycogen in the liver. Stiffness and soreness after prolonged heavy exercise are due to accumulated lactic acid in the muscles. The end product of bacterial FERMENTATION, lactic acid is the commonest acidic constituent of fermented milk products (e.g., sour milk and cream, cheese, buttermilk, yogurt). It is used in other foods as a flavoring or preservative and industrially in tanning leather and dyeing wool and as a raw material or CATALYST in many chemical processes.

lactobacillus \,lak-tō-bə-'si-ləs\ Any of the rod-shaped, gram-positive (see GRAM STAIN) bacteria that make up the genus *Lactobacillus,* widely distributed in animal feeds, manure, and milk and milk products. Various species are used commercially in the production of sour milks, cheeses, and yogurt. Lactobacilli also play an important role in the manufacture of fermented vegetables (pickles and sauerkraut), beverages (beer, wine, and juices), sourdough breads, and some sausages. They inhabit but do not damage animal and human intestinal tracts. Commercial preparations of lactobacilli are used to restore normal intestinal flora after antibiotic therapy.

lactose Slightly sweet SUGAR (disaccharide) composed of two MONOSACCHARIDES, GLUCOSE and GALACTOSE, linked together. Lactose-intolerant adults, and more rarely infants, cannot digest lactose because they lack the ENZYME (lactase) that splits it into simpler sugars and suffer DIARRHEA and bloating when they eat foods containing it. Lactose, which makes up 2–8% of the milk of mammals, is the only common sugar of animal origin. Commercial lactose is obtained from whey, a liquid by-product of cheese. It is used in foods, in pharmaceuticals, and in nutrient broths used to produce penicillin, yeast, and riboflavin, and other products.

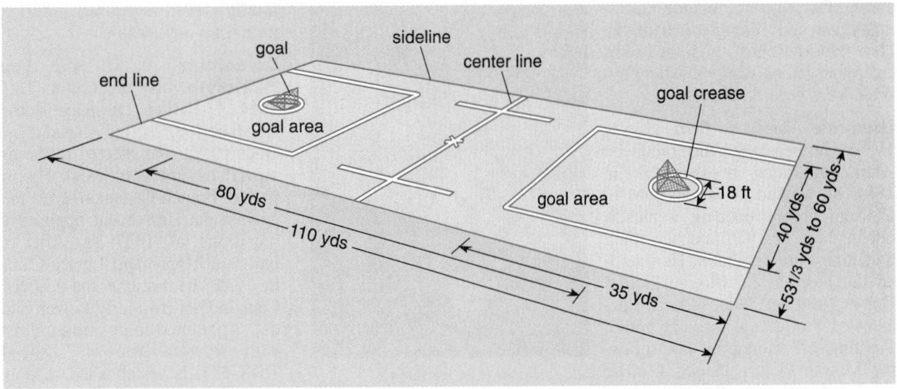

A typical men's lacrosse field. The women's game is often played on a larger field (120 x 82 yards), with the goals 100 yards apart, and usually without the outside boundary lines marked. The ball is put into play by a face-off at the middle of the field, and play is continuous except for goals, fouls, and time-outs. Players may kick the ball, but only the goalie may use his hands.

Ladakh \lə-'däk\ Region, eastern KASHMIR region, northwestern Indian subcontinent. It covers about 45,000 sq mi (117,000 sq km) and includes the western Himalayan Ladakh Range (see HIMALAYAS), the KARAKORAM RANGE, and the upper INDUS RIVER valley. Its capital is Leh. India and Pakistan fought over it before peace negotiations in 1949 gave its southern portion to India (which is part of the Indian state of JAMMU AND KASHMIR) and the rest to Pakistan. In the Sino–Indian War of 1962 China gained a portion of northeastern Ladakh. The region's boundaries are still in dispute.

Ladd-Franklin, Christine *orig.* **Christine Ladd** (1847–1930) U.S. scientist and logician. Born in Windsor, Conn., she fulfilled PhD requirements at Johns Hopkins Univ in the 1880s, but because women candidates were not recognized, was not awarded her degree until 1926. In symbolic logic, she reduced syllogistic reasoning to an inconsistent triad with the introduction of the antilogism, a form that made the testing of deductions easier. The Ladd-Franklin theory of color vision stressed increasing color differentiation with evolution and assumed a photochemical model for the visual system. Her principal works are *The Algebra of Logic* (1883), *The Nature of Color Sensation* (1925), and *Color and Color Theories* (1929).

Ladies' Home Journal U.S. monthly magazine, one of the oldest in the country and long the trendsetter among women's magazines. Founded in 1883 as a supplement to the *Tribune and Farmer* (1879–85), it began an independent publication in 1884. Under the editorship (1889–1919) of EDWARD BOK, it became an outstanding success, with a circulation surpassing that of any other U.S. publication. Bok revolutionized the women's-magazine field by offering high-quality fiction and nonfiction, establishing service departments that answered letters from readers, and conveying a sense of intimacy. After the mid-20th century it was overtaken in circulation by its rival, *McCall's*.

ladino \lə-'dē-nō\ Central American whose primary language is Spanish and who wears modern dress. Genetically ladinos may be Indians, MESTIZOS, or persons of African descent. An Indian may become a ladino by abandoning the Indian dress and customs. Many rural ladinos practice subsistence agriculture much like that of their Indian neighbors, but they tend to put more stress on cash crops and to use modern farming techniques, which the Indians shun. In small towns ladinos commonly engage in commerce as well as farming. In the cities they engage in all occupations, from day laborer to university professor.

Ladino language \lə-'dē-nō\ *or* **Sephardic language** ROMANCE LANGUAGE spoken by Sephardic Jews in the Balkans, the Middle East, North Africa, Greece, and Turkey, though nearly extinct in many of these areas. Ladino is a very archaic form of Castilian SPANISH, mixed with HEBREW elements. It originated in Spain and was carried to its present speech areas by descendants of the Spanish Jews exiled from Spain after 1492. It preserves many words and grammatical usages that have been lost in modern Spanish, and it also has a more conservative sound system. Ladino is usually written in Hebrew characters.

Ladislas I *or* **St. Ladislas** \'lä-dē-ˌsläs\ (1040–1095) King of Hungary (1077–95). He greatly expanded the boundaries of the kingdom, gaining land in Transylvania and occupying Croatia (1091). In the INVESTITURE CONTROVERSY he sided with the pope. Ladislas introduced Roman Catholicism to Croatia and persecuted pagans in his dominions. He also promulgated a legal code that brought order and prosperity to Hungary. He died while preparing for the First CRUSADE and was canonized in 1192.

Lado Enclave \'lä-dō\ Region, central Africa. It was located north of Lake ALBERT on the west bank of the Upper NILE RIVER, in what is now northern Uganda and southeastern Sudan. It was first explored by Europeans in 1841–42 and became a station for ivory and slave traders. Britain claimed the Upper Nile region in 1894 and leased to LEOPOLD II of Belgium the area known as the Lado Enclave. It was incorporated into the Anglo-Egyptian Sudan in 1910.

Ladoga \'lá-də-gə\, **Lake** Lake, western Russia. The largest lake in Europe, it covers an area of 6,700 sq mi (17,600 sq km). It is 136 mi (219 km) long, and has an average width of 51 mi (82 km); its greatest depth is 754 ft (230 m). It contains 660 islands of more than 2.5 acres (1 hectare) in area. Its outlet is the NEVA RIVER, in the southwestern corner. Formerly divided between the U.S.S.R. and Finland, it now lies entirely within Russia. During the Siege of LENINGRAD (1941–43) in World War II, the lake was the lifeline that connected the city with the rest of the Soviet Union.

Ladrone Islands See MARIANA ISLANDS

ladybug *or* **ladybird beetle** Any of the approximately 5,000 widely distributed BEETLES of the family Coccinellidae. The name originated in the Middle Ages, when the beetle was dedicated to the Virgin Mary and called "beetle of Our Lady." Ladybugs are hemispheric and are usually 0.3–0.4 in. (8–10 mm) long. They have short legs and are usually brightly colored with black, yellow, or reddish markings. Several generations are produced each summer. Ladybugs are often used to control such insect pests as APHIDS, SCALES, and MITES, which they eat. Several species feed on plants.

ladyfish *or* **tenpounder** Species (*Elops saurus,* family Elopidae) of primarily tropical coastal marine fish. The ladyfish is slender and covered with fine silver scales; the dorsal and anal fins can be depressed into grooves. A predatory fish, it has small, sharp teeth and a bony throat plate between its mandibles. It is up to 35 in. (90 cm) long and weighs up to 30 lbs (14 kg). The young are transparent and eel-like.

lady's slipper Any member of several genera of ORCHIDS in which the lip of the flower is slipper-shaped. The genus *Cypripedium* has about 50 temperate and subtropical species. Two well-known species, the yellow lady's slipper *(C. calceolus)* and the pink lady's slipper, or moccasin flower *(C. acaule),* are found in temperate coniferous woods in early spring. Other genera include *Phragmipedium* and *Selenipedium* of the New World tropics, and the tropical Asian *Paphiopedilum.* Many hybrids have been developed.

Lady's slipper (*Cypripedium*).
GRANT HEILMAN

Laemmle \'lem-lē\, **Carl** (1867–1939) German-U.S. film producer. After emigrating to the U.S. in 1884, he worked at various jobs in Chicago before opening a nickelodeon there in 1906 and becoming a leading film distributor. He founded the Independent Motion Picture Co. in 1909 and induced such stars as MARY PICKFORD to join his studio. Fighting off monopoly control by the Motion Picture Patents Co., he produced 100 short films by 1910. In 1912 he merged with smaller companies to form UNIVERSAL PICTURES, and in 1915 he opened its 230-acre studio. Financial setbacks forced him to sell the company in 1935.

Laetoli footprints \lī-'tō-lē\ Several trails of bipedal footprints, possibly those of *AUSTRALOPITHECUS afarensis,* preserved in volcanic ash at Laetoli in northern Tanzania and dated to 3.6 million years ago. They were discovered in 1976 by a team led by LEAKEY FAMILY. They indicate that the mechanism of weight and force transference through the early HOMINID foot was virtually identical to that of modern humans, and suggest that two of the individuals, one larger and one smaller, walked together in stride and were close enough to have been touching. See also LUCY.

Laetus \'lī-təs\, **Julius Pomponius** *Italian* **Giulio Pomponio Leto** (1428–1497) Italian humanist. As a youth he decided to dedicate his life to the study of the ancient world. In Rome he gathered other humanists around him in a semisecret society, the Academia Romana. Their celebration of ancient Roman rites aroused the suspicions of Pope Paul II, who briefly dissolved the Academia and imprisoned Laetus and his associates. Laetus' lack of rigor and critical spirit have led modern scholars to treat his scholarly works with caution.

Lafayette, marquis de *orig.* **Marie-Joseph-Paul-Yves-Roch-Gilbert du Motier** (1757–1834) French military leader. Born to an ancient noble family of great wealth, he was a courtier at the court of LOUIS XVI but sought glory as a soldier. In 1777 he went to Philadelphia, was appointed a major general, became a close friend of GEORGE WASHINGTON, and fought with distinction at the Battle of the BRANDYWINE. He returned to France in 1779, persuaded Louis to send a 6,000-man force to aid the colonists, and returned to America in 1780 to command an army in Virginia and help win the Siege of YORKTOWN. Hailed as "the Hero of Two Worlds," he returned to France in 1782, became a leader of liberal aristocrats, and was elected to the Estates General in 1789. He presented the DECLARATION OF THE RIGHTS OF MAN AND OF THE CITIZEN to the National Assembly. Elected commander of the national guard of Paris, he favored a constitutional monarchy. When his guards fired on a crowd of petitioners in the Champ de Mars (1791), he lost popularity and resigned his position. He commanded the army against Austria (1792), then defected to the Austrians, who held him captive until 1797. In the BOURBON RESTORATION, he served in the Chamber of Deputies (1814–24) and commanded the national guard in the JULY REVOLUTION (1830).

Laffite \lə-'fēt\, **Jean** (1780?–1825?) French pirate. He led a band of privateers that preyed on Spanish ships and smuggled goods and slaves through New Orleans, where the group lived on islands south of the city. In the War of 1812 the British offered Laffite $30,000 for his allegiance in their planned attack on the city. He warned Louisiana officials of the attack but was not believed. He then offered his aid to Gen. ANDREW JACKSON, who accepted Laffite's help in the Battle of NEW ORLEANS. After the war Laffite returned to privateering against the Spanish.

Laffitte \lä-'fēt\, **Jacques** (1767–1844) French banker and politician. He became a partner in a Perregaux banking house in 1800 and head of the firm in 1804. As governor of the Bank of France (1814–19), he raised large sums of money for the provisional government in 1814 and for LOUIS XVIII during the HUNDRED DAYS. He saved Paris from a financial crisis in 1818. An early partisan of a constitutional monarchy under LOUIS-PHILIPPE, he helped secure Louis-Philippe's accession to the throne, and briefly served as premier (1830–31) in the JULY MONARCHY.

Jacques Laffitte, drawing by A. Devéria; in the Bibliothèque Nationale, Paris.
BY COURTESY OF THE BIBLIOTHEQUE NATIONALE, PARIS

LaFontaine \lä-fōⁿ-'tan\, **Louis Hippolyte** *later* **Sir Louis** (1807–1864) Canadian statesman. Born in Boucherville, Lower Canada (now Quebec), he was elected to the provincial assembly in 1830. He supported French-Canadian grievances against the British but opposed the rebellions of 1837–38. After the union of Upper and Lower Canada in 1841, he became the leader of Canada East (formerly Lower Canada). Appointed joint prime minister with ROBERT BALDWIN (1842–43, 1848–51), he established responsible (i.e., representative) government for Canada. He passed the Rebellion Losses Bill to compensate property owners for damages in 1837–38, which provoked riots in Montreal but affirmed the strength of the government.

Lagash \'lā-ˌgash\ *modern* **Telloh** \'tel-ō\ Ancient capital in SUMER. It was located midway between the TIGRIS and EUPHRATES rivers in BABYLONIA, now modern southeastern Iraq. Excavations have uncovered palace and temple ruins as well as CUNEIFORM texts that provide knowledge of Sumer in the 3rd millennium BC. Founded in the Ubaid Period (c. 5200–c. 3500 BC), it came under the control of SARGON of Akkad. It later prospered under Gudea, a governor nominally subject to the Guti. It was occupied as late as the Parthian era (247 BC–AD 224).

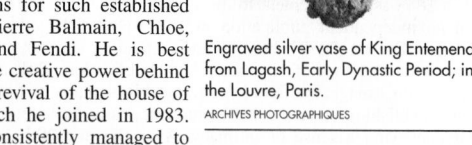

Engraved silver vase of King Entemena, from Lagash, Early Dynastic Period; in the Louvre, Paris.
ARCHIVES PHOTOGRAPHIQUES

Lågen River \'lò-gən\ River, southeastern Norway. Rising in the Hardanger Plateau, it flows south to empty into the Skagerrak, an arm of the NORTH SEA. With a length of 209 mi (337 km), it is the third longest river in the country.

Lagerfeld, Karl (born 1938) German fashion designer. After moving to Paris at age 14, he went on to create designs for such established labels as Pierre Balmain, Chloe, Valentino, and Fendi. He is best known as the creative power behind the modern revival of the house of Chanel, which he joined in 1983. Lagerfeld consistently managed to merge the spirit of the times with the chic, timeless identity established by the house's founder, GABRIELLE "COCO" CHANEL, making Chanel one of the most coveted and influential labels in late 20th-century fashion.

Lagerkvist \'lä-gər-ˌkvēst\, **Pär (Fabian)** (1891–1974) Swedish novelist, poet, and dramatist. He was involved early in life with socialism, and soon began to support literary and artistic radicalism. Though his early works are characterized by extreme pessimism, he declared his faith in humanity with his great prose monologue *The Triumph over Life* (1927). In the 1930s and '40s his writings protested fascism and brutality. The novel *The Dwarf* (1944) was his first best-seller and his first undisputed critical success. He won world recognition with the novel *Barabbas* (1950). He was awarded the Nobel Prize in 1951.

Lagerlöf \'lä-gər-ˌlœf\, **Selma (Ottiliana Lovisa)** (1858–1940) Swedish novelist. She was working as a schoolmistress when she wrote her first novel, *Gösta Berlings saga* (1891), a chronicle of life in her native Värmland. Later works include *Jerusalem* (1901–2), which established her as Sweden's foremost novelist, and *The Wonderful Adventures of*

Nils and its sequel (1906–7), a geography reader for children in fantasy form. A naturally gifted storyteller, she rooted her work in legend and saga. In 1909 she became the first woman and the first Swedish writer to win the Nobel Prize for Literature.

Laghouat \lä-'gwät\ Town (pop., 1987: 67,000) and oasis, northern central Algeria. At the southern edge of the ATLAS MTNS., it was built on two hills that are extensions of Mount Tizigarine. It was settled in the 11th century and came under Moroccan and Turkish control. Seized by the French in 1852, it reverted to Algeria in 1962.

lagoon Area of relatively shallow, quiet water with access to the sea but separated from it by sandbars, barrier islands, or coral reefs. Coastal lagoons have low to moderate tides and constitute about 13% of the world's coastline. Their water is colder than the sea in winter and warmer in summer. In warm regions, evaporation may more than balance any freshwater input and may result in hypersaline water and even the build-up of thick salt deposits. Coral-reef lagoons occur on marginal reefs such as the Great Barrier Reef, but the most spectacular examples, some more than 30 mi (50 km) across, are associated with Pacific ATOLLS.

Lagos \'lā-ˌgäs, 'lä-gəs\ City (pop., 1996 est.: 1,518,000) and chief port, Nigeria. It is Nigeria's largest city, built on four main islands: Lagos, Iddo, Ikoyi, and Victoria, which are connected to each other and to the mainland by bridges. Its population is centered on Lagos Island, on the Bight of Benin. Settled by Yoruba fishers and hunters in the 15th century, it was dominated by Benin in the 16th–19th century. The Portuguese established a slave trade there in 1472. It was ceded to Britain in 1861, became a crown colony, and was governed from Sierra Leone (1866–74) and as part of the Gold Coast colony (1874–86). Joined with the protectorate of Southern Nigeria in 1906, it was made the capital of the colony of Nigeria in 1914. It was the capital (1960–91) of independent Nigeria, until ABUJA became the new capital. It is a major trade and industrial center.

Lagrange \lä-'grä^{n}zh\, **Joseph-Louis** *later* **comte (Count) de L'Empire** (1736–1813) Italian-French mathematician who made important contributions to NUMBER THEORY and to classical and celestial mechanics. By age 25 he was recognized as one of the greatest living mathematicians because of his papers on wave propagation (see WAVE motion) and maxima and minima (see MAXIMUM, MINIMUM) of curves. His prodigious output included his textbook *Mécanique analytique* (1788; "Analytical Mechanics"), the basis for all later work in this field. His remarkable discoveries included the Lagrangian, a DIFFERENTIAL OPERATOR characterizing a system's physical state, and the Lagrangian points, points in space where a small body in the gravitational fields of two large ones remains relatively stable.

Laguna de Bay See Laguna de BAY

Laguna Madre See Laguna MADRE

Lahn River River, western Germany. A tributary of the RHINE RIVER, it rises in western Germany and after a southerly course reaches the Rhine at Lahnstein. It is 152 mi (245 km) long. Small barges are able to navigate to Giessen on the partly canalized river.

Lahore \lə-'hōr\ City (pop., 1981: 2,950,000), capital of PUNJAB province, northeastern Pakistan. The second largest city of Pakistan, it lies in the upper Indus plain on the RAVI RIVER. An ancient city, it became prominent with the coming of the Mughals in the 11th–12th century. It was captured by BABUR's troops in 1524, and was later under AKBAR, and Jahangir. Ruled by Sikhs in the early 19th century, it passed to the British in 1849. After Indian independence, Lahore passed to Pakistan in 1947. It is the site of the mosque of Wazir Khan (1634); a mosque built by AURANGZEB; and the Shalimar gardens, laid out in 1641. It is the seat of Pakistan's oldest university, University of the Punjab (founded 1882).

Lahr, Bert *orig.* **Irving Lahrheim** (1895–1967) U.S. comic actor. Born in New York, he began his career in vaudeville and burlesque, and became a Broadway star with his clowning in *Hold Everything!* (1928). He later appeared in *Two on the Aisle* (1951), SAMUEL BECKETT's *Waiting for Godot* (1956), and *Romanoff and Juliet* (1959), and in 1960 he toured as Bottom in *A Midsummer Night's Dream.* He is perhaps best remembered as the Cowardly Lion in the film *The Wizard of Oz* (1939).

Laibach \'lī-bäk\, **Congress of** (January 26–May 12, 1821) Meeting of the HOLY ALLIANCE powers that set the conditions for Austrian intervention in and occupation of the Kingdom of the Two Sicilies in action against the Neapolitan revolution (1820). The congress proclaimed its hostility to revolutionary regimes, agreed to abolish the Neapolitan constitution, and authorized the Austrian army to restore the absolutist monarchy. The British and French protested the decision.

Laing \'laŋ\, **R(onald) D(avid)** (1927–1989) Scottish psychiatrist. In his widely read and highly controversial book *The Divided Self* (1960), his analysis of SCHIZOPHRENIA led him to theorize that insecurity about one's existence prompts a defensive reaction in which the self splits into separate components, generating psychotic symptoms, and he opposed standard schizophrenia treatments such as hospitalization and electroshock. He even opposed the concept of mental illness, viewing it as induced by family relationships and society, and radically reconceived the role of the psychiatrist. He later modified some of his controversial positions.

laissez-faire \ˌle-sā-'fer\ (French: "allow to do") Policy dictating a minimum of governmental interference in the economic affairs of individuals and society. It was promoted by the PHYSIOCRATS and strongly supported by Adam SMITH and JOHN STUART MILL. Widely accepted in the 19th century, laissez-faire assumed that the individual who pursues his own desires contributes most successfully to society as a whole. The function of the state is to maintain order and avoid interfering with individual initiative. The popularity of the laissez-faire doctrine waned in the late 19th century, when it proved inadequate to deal with the social and economic problems caused by INDUSTRIALIZATION. See also CLASSICAL ECONOMICS.

lake Relatively large body of slow-moving or standing water that occupies an inland basin. Lakes are most abundant in high northern latitudes and in mountain regions, particularly those that were covered by GLACIERS in recent geologic times. The primary sources of lake water are melting ice and snow, springs, rivers, runoff from the land surface, and direct precipitation. In the upper part of lakes there is a good supply of light, heat, oxygen, and nutrients, well distributed by currents and turbulence. As a result, a large number of diverse aquatic organisms can be found there. The most abundant forms are PLANKTON (chiefly DIATOMS), ALGAE, and flagellates. In the lower levels and in the sediments, the main forms of life are bacteria. See also LIMNOLOGY.

Lake Clark National Park National park, southern Alaska. Located on the western shore of Cook Inlet, it was proclaimed a national monument in 1978 and a national park in 1980. Its total area is 3,653,000 acres (1,478,900 hectares). Lake Clark, more than 40 mi (65 km) long, is the largest of its glacial lakes; it feeds rivers that provide the most important spawning ground for red salmon in North America. The park includes glaciers, waterfalls, and active volcanoes.

Lake District Mountainous region, Cumbria, northwestern England. Roughly coextensive with Lake District National Park, the country's largest, it occupies an area of 866 sq mi (2,243 sq km). It contains numerous lakes, including Grasmere, WINDERMERE, and Coniston Water, as well as the country's highest mountains, such as Scafell Pike (3,210 ft or 978 m). It was home to several English poets, including WILLIAM WORDSWORTH, ROBERT SOUTHEY, and SAMUEL TAYLOR COLERIDGE, who celebrated its landscape. The district became a national park in 1951.

Lake Dwellings Remains of various pre- and post-BRONZE AGE settlements within the margins of lakes in southern Germany, Switzerland, France, and Italy. The dwellings appear to have been built on platforms supported by piles above the water surface or above swampy areas along the water's edge. The platforms supported one- or two-room rectangular huts with beaten clay floors. Cattle and sheep were raised in some of the structures. Most dwellings seem to have burned, either by accident or by attack. Because the Lake Dwellers usually rebuilt new villages on the remains of the old, archaeologists were able to work out a cultural sequence confirming that the Bronze Age immediately followed the STONE AGE. See also CRANNOG.

Lake of the Ozarks See Lake of the OZARKS

Lake of the Woods See Lake of the WOODS

Lake Placid Village (pop., 1990: 2,500), northeastern New York, on Mirror Lake and Lake Placid, in the ADIRONDACK MTNS. The site was settled in 1800 but it was abandoned after crop failures. Resettled during the 1840s, it was promoted in 1850 as a summer resort, and MELVIL DEWEY founded the Lake Placid Club there in 1895. It is a year-round recreational area with numerous hotels, golf courses, ski resorts, and mountain scenery. It was the scene of the OLYMPIC GAMES in 1932 and 1980.

lake trout *or* **Mackinaw trout** *or* **Great Lakes trout** *or* **salmon trout** Large, voracious CHAR *(Salvelinus namaycush)* found widely from northern Canada and Alaska to New England and the Great Lakes, usually in deep, cool lakes. They are greenish gray and covered with pale spots. In spring, 5-lb (2.3-kg) lake trout are caught in shallow water; in summer, fish of up to 100 lbs (45 kg) are trolled in deep water. Lake trout were virtually eliminated from the Great Lakes by the sea LAMPREY, which entered through the Welland Canal in the 1930s. They have been introduced in the western U.S., South America, Europe, and New Zealand.

Lake Turkana remains Collection of HOMINID fossils found along the shores of Lake TURKANA in northwestern Kenya. The Koobi Fora site, excavated by LEAKEY FAMILY and others, has proved to be the richest fund of hominid remains found anywhere in the world, yielding fossils that represent perhaps 230 individuals, including members of *HOMO HABILIS*, *HOMO ERECTUS*, and *AUSTRALOPITHECUS*. On the western shore was found a remarkably well preserved skeleton of an 11-year-old boy (the "Turkana Boy") later classified as *Homo ergaster* and dated to c. 1.8 million years ago. This surprisingly human specimen suggests that *H. ergaster* may have been the direct ancestor of the hominids that left Africa for Eurasia c. 1 million years ago. See also HUMAN EVOLUTION.

Lakewood Township (pop., 1994 est.: 47,000), eastern New Jersey. Located southwest of Asbury Park, it was settled by the Dutch and English in 1800, and it was known successively as Three Partners' Mill, Washington's Furnace, Bergen Iron Works, and Bricksburg. Now a popular resort and recreation area, its population nearly doubled in the 1980s.

Lakshadweep \lək-'shäd-,wēp\ Union territory (pop., 1994 est.: 56,000) of India. Located in the Arabian Sea off India's southwestern coast, it includes 27 islands (10 of which are inhabited), with a total land area of 12 sq mi (32 sq km). The capital is KAVARATTI. Once ruled by the Hindu Kulashekhara dynasty, it became part of an Islamic dominion in the 12th century. Britain gained sovereignty over it in the 18th century and assumed direct administration in 1908. It passed to India in 1947 and became the nation's smallest union territory in 1956. Coconut palms are the agricultural mainstay, while fishing is the chief industry.

Lakshmi *or* **Laksmi** \'lək-shmē\ Hindu and Jain goddess of wealth and good fortune. The consort of VISHNU, she is said to have taken different forms to be with him in each of his incarnations. She is a principal object of worship during DIVALI, when her presence is sought in homes, temples, and businesses for the whole of the year to come.

Lalique \lȧ-'lēk\, **René (Jules)** (1860–1945) French jeweler and glassmaker. Trained in Paris and London, he opened his own firm in Paris in 1885 and soon acquired such clients as SARAH BERNHARDT. Reacting against machine-produced jewelry featuring precious gems, he designed elegant and fantastic jewelry with less conventional gemstones (tourmaline, cornelian, etc.) and such materials as horn. His designs contributed significantly to the ART NOUVEAU movement and later the ART DECO movement. His interest in architectural glass led him to develop the style of molded glass for which he is famous, characterized by iced surfaces, elaborate patterns in relief, and occasionally applied or inlaid color.

Enamel, glass, and topaz hair ornament and brooch by Lalique, 1900; in the Victoria and Albert Museum, London.
BY COURTESY OF THE VICTORIA AND ALBERT MUSEUM, LONDON

lama In TIBETAN BUDDHISM, a spiritual leader. Some lamas are considered to be reincarnations of their predecessors; others have won respect for their high level of spiritual development. The most honored of the reincarnate lamas is the DALAI LAMA; second in spiritual authority is the PANCHEN LAMA. The process of discovering the new incarnation of a lama, especially the Dalai Lama, is elaborate and exacting. Oracular messages, unusual signs during the lama's death or during a birth thereafter, and examinations of candidates identify a successor. The child thus identified as the lama's incarnation is given extensive monastic training from an early age.

Lamar \lə-'mär\, **Mirabeau Buonaparte** (1798–1859) U.S. politician. Born in Louisville, Ga., he moved to Texas, where he became involved in the independence struggle against Mexico. As a cavalry commander, he helped win the Battle of San Jacinto (1836) and was appointed secretary of war in the provisional Texas government. He was elected vice president of the Republic of Texas under SAM HOUSTON, whom he succeeded as president (1838–41). He initially opposed annexation to the U.S., but after 1844 advocated statehood to ensure the continuation of slavery.

Lamarck \lə-'märk\, **Jean-Baptiste de Monet, chevalier (knight) de** (1744–1829) French biologist. He is credited with the first use of the word *biology* (1802). He was one of the originators of the modern concept of the museum collection, an array of objects whose arrangement constitutes a classification under institutional sponsorship, maintained and kept up to date by knowledgeable specialists. He seems to have been the first to relate fossils to the living organisms to which they corresponded most closely. His notion that acquired traits could be inherited (called Lamarckism) was discredited after the 1930s by most geneticists except in the Soviet Union, where it dominated Russian genetics until the 1960s (see TROFIM LYSENKO). See also CHARLES DARWIN, DARWINISM.

Lamartine \lȧ-mȧr-'tēn\, **Alphonse de** (1790–1869) French poet and statesman. After brief military service under LOUIS XVIII, he turned to literature, writing verse tragedies and elegies. He is chiefly remembered for his very successful first collection of poetry, the musical, evocative *Méditations poétiques* (1820), which established him as a key figure in French ROMANTICISM. From 1830 he was active in politics, speaking for the working classes. After France's SECOND REPUBLIC was proclaimed in 1848, he briefly headed the provisional government until the revolution was crushed. In later years he published novels, poetry, and historical works in a vain struggle against bankruptcy.

Lamashtu \lä-'mäsh-tü\ In MESOPOTAMIAN RELIGION, the most terrible of all female demons. The daughter of the sky god ANU, Lamashtu killed children, consumed human flesh and blood, blighted plants, spoiled rivers and streams, sent nightmares, caused miscarriages, and brought disease. She had seven names and was often described in incantations as "seven witches." She was portrayed on amulets as a lion- or bird-headed female figure kneeling on an ass, holding a double-headed serpent in each hand and suckling dogs or pigs at her breasts.

lamb Live SHEEP before the age of one year, and the flesh of such animals. The flesh of the mature ram or ewe at least one year old is called mutton; the meat of sheep 12–20 months old may be called yearling mutton. The meat of sheep 6–10 weeks old is usually sold as baby lamb, and spring lamb comes from sheep 5–6 months old. The primary lamb- and mutton-consuming countries (on a per capita basis) are New Zealand and Australia.

Lamb, Charles (1775–1834) English essayist and critic. Lamb was employed as a clerk at India House 1792–1825. From 1796 he was guardian of his sister, the writer Mary Lamb (1764–1847), who in a fit of madness (which proved recurrent) had killed their mother. He is best known for the often autobiographical essays he wrote under the pseudonym Elia for *London Magazine,* collected in *Essays of Elia* (1823) and *The Last Essays of Elia* (1833). Among the greatest of English letter writers, he included some of his most perceptive literary criticism, often

L
M
N

in the form of marginalia, in letters. He collaborated with Mary on *Tales from Shakespear* (1807), a highly popular retelling of the plays for children.

Lamb, William See Viscount MELBOURNE

lambkill See SHEEP LAUREL

lamb's ears *or* **lamb's ear** Widely cultivated perennial herb *(Stachys byzantina,* or *S. olympica)* of the MINT family, native to South Asia. Covered with densely matted hairs, its silver-green leaves, which provide a pleasing contrast to green leaves and to bright- or soft-colored flowers, make lamb's ears a hardy favorite in perennial gardens of the northeastern U.S.

lamella roof \lə-'me-lə\ Vaulted roof consisting of a crisscrossing pattern of parallel arches skewed with respect to the sides of the covered space, composed of relatively short members (lamellae) hinged together to form an interlocking network in a diamond pattern. It was used for the first two great covered sports stadiums built in the U.S. since the 1960s: the Houston Astrodome (1962–64), with a span of 642 ft (196 m), and the New Orleans Superdome (1973), 678 ft (207 m) in diameter.

Lamennais \läm-'ne\, **(Hugues-) Félicité (-Robert de)** (1782–1854) French priest and philosopher. With his brother Jean, he sketched a program of church reform in *Reflections on the State of the Church* (1808) and in 1814 produced a defense of ultramontanism (papal authority). Ordained a priest in 1816, he wrote the acclaimed *Essay on Indifference Toward Religion* (1817–23), which argued for the necessity of religion. After the JULY REVOLUTION (1830), he cofounded the journal *L'Avenir* to advocate democratic principles and church–state separation. Its principles were condemned by the pope in 1832. Lamennais's *The Words of a Believer* (1834), written in response, provoked another papal encyclical and led to Lamennais's severance from the church. Thereafter he wrote in the cause of republicanism and socialism.

Lamerie \läm-'rē\, **Paul de** (1688–1751) Dutch-born British silversmith. His Huguenot parents had left France in the early 1680s and settled in England by 1691. After an apprenticeship with a London goldsmith, he registered his mark and opened a shop in 1713. Early in his career he made simple vessels such as tankards and teapots in an unadorned Queen Anne style; later he used more ornamentation. By the 1730s he had established his own version of the Rococo style, seen in a 1737 cup with handles in the form of snakes.

laminar flow Fluid flow in which the fluid travels smoothly or in regular paths. The VELOCITY, PRESSURE, and other flow properties at each point in the fluid remain constant. Laminar flow over a horizontal surface may be thought of as consisting of thin layers, all parallel to each other, that slide over each other. It is common only where the flow channel is relatively small, the fluid is moving slowly, and its VISCOSITY is relatively high. Examples include the flow of oil through a thin tube and blood flow through capillaries. See also TURBULENT FLOW.

L'Amour \lä-'mòr-, lä-'mùr\, **Louis** *orig.* **Louis Dearborn LaMoore** (1908–1988) U.S. author of westerns. Born in Jamestown, N.D., he left school at 15 and traveled the world before beginning his writing career in the 1940s. He used pseudonyms, including Tex Burns and Jim Mayo, until *Hondo* (1953) became a successful film. His more than 100 works, mostly formula westerns that convincingly portray frontier life, have sold 200 million copies in 20 languages, and more than 30—including *Kilkenny* (1954), *The Burning Hills* (1956), *Guns of the Timberland* (1955), and *How the West Was Won* (1963)—were the basis of films.

lamprey \'lam-prē, 'lam-,prā\ Any of about 22 species of primitive, jawless fishes (with HAGFISHES in class Agnatha). Lampreys live in coastal and freshwater in temperate regions worldwide except Africa. Eel-like, scaleless animals, they are 6–40 in. (15–100 cm) long. Lampreys have well-developed eyes, a single nostril on top of the head, a cartilaginous skeleton, and a sucking mouth with horny teeth surrounding the round opening. They spend years as burrowing larvae; adults of most species move into the sea. They attach to fish with their mouth and feed on their host's blood and tissues. Some species will remain in freshwater, notably the sea lamprey, which entered the Great Lakes and nearly eliminated LAKE TROUT and other commercially important fishes there. See photograph opposite.

Lampsacus \'lamp-sə-kəs\ Ancient Greek colony on the Asian shore of the Hellespont. It was famous for its wines and was the chief seat of the worship of PRIAPUS. Colonized in 654 BC by Ionian Phocaea, it took part in the Ionian revolt against Persia in 499 and later joined the DELIAN LEAGUE. When Athens fell in 405, it came under Persian control until ALEXANDER THE GREAT freed it in 334. It was the home of the philosopher Strato of Lampsacus.

LAN See LOCAL AREA NETWORK

Lan-chou See LANZHOU

Lan Na One of the first major TAI kingdoms in Thai history. It was founded by Mangrai (r.c. 1259–1317) in the northern region of present-day Thailand; its capital was the city of Chiang Mai. Lan Na was a powerful state and a center for the spread of THERAVADA Buddhism. Under Tilokaracha (r.1441–87), it was famous for its Buddhist scholarship and literature. It remained independent until it was conquered by Myanmar in the 16th century. The Siamese did not reassert control over the area until the 19th century.

Lan Sang \'län-'säŋ\ *or* **Lan Xang** \'län-'shäŋ\ *or* **Lan Chang** \'län-'chäŋ\ Laotian kingdom that flourished from the 14th century until it was split into two separate kingdoms in the 18th century. Conflict with its neighbors forced Lan Sang's rulers to move the capital from Luang Prabang to Vientiane in 1563, but the kingdom maintained its power.

Lan-Ts'ang Chiang See MEKONG RIVER

Lanao \lä-'naù\, **Lake** Lake, MINDANAO, Philippines. It is located in a plateau region north of a range of active volcanoes. The second largest lake in the Philippines, it occupies an area of 131 sq mi (340 sq km). It is 22 mi (35 km) long and has a maximum width of 16 mi (26 km).

Lancang Jiang See MEKONG RIVER

Lancashire \'laŋ-kə-,shir\ County (population 1995 est.: 1,426,000), northwestern England. Its county seat is PRESTON. In the early Middle Ages it was a province of the Anglo-Saxon kingdom of NORTHUMBRIA. The region included the ancestral lands of the House of LANCASTER. In the Industrial Revolution it became an important manufacturing region and a center of the textile industry. Lancaster and Preston are its major market and industrial cities; it also has resort towns, including Blackpool, on the Irish Sea.

Lancaster, Burt(on Stephen) (1913–1994) U.S. film actor. Born in New York City, he toured with circuses as an acrobat in the 1930s and served in North Africa and Italy during World War II. His movie debut in *The Killers* (1946) made him a star, and he became noted for his portrayals of physically tough, emotionally sensitive characters. His many films include *Come Back, Little Sheba* (1952), *From Here to Eternity* (1953), *The Rose Tattoo* (1955), *Sweet Smell of Success* (1957), *Elmer Gantry* (1960, Academy Award), *The Birdman of Alcatraz* (1962), *The Leopard* (1963), *The Swimmer* (1968), *Atlantic City* (1981), *Local Hero* (1983), and *Field of Dreams* (1989).

Lancaster, House of Cadet branch of the House of PLANTAGENET that provided three kings of England in the 15th century. (HENRY IV, HENRY V, HENRY VI). The family name first appeared in 1267, when the title earl of Lancaster was granted to HENRY III's son Edmund (1245–1296). Edmund's grandson Henry (died 1361) became the 1st duke of Lancaster,

Lamprey (*Lampetra*) on rainbow trout.

OXFORD SCIENTIFIC FILMS—BRUCE COLEMAN LTD.

L M N

and the inheritance fell to his youngest daughter, Blanche, and to her husband, John of Gaunt. His son, Henry of Lancaster, became King Henry IV, and the duchy of Lancaster was merged in the crown. The Lancaster dynasty ended after the defeat of Henry VI by Edward IV of the House of York (see Wars of the Roses), and the Lancaster claims were passed on to the House of Tudor.

lancelet See amphioxus

Lancelot *or* **Launcelot** \'lan-sə-ˌlät, 'lan-sə-ˌlət\ One of the greatest knights in Arthurian legend, the lover of Guinevere and the father of Galahad. He first appeared in a 12th-century romance by Chrétien de Troyes, and he is a major character in Sir Thomas Malory's *Morte Darthur*. His full name, Sir Lancelot du Lac, refers to his upbringing by the Lady of the Lake, the enchantress who carried him off in infancy and trained him to be a model of chivalry before sending him to Arthur's court. There he became the favorite of King Arthur and the lover of Queen Guinevere. His adultery with Guinevere caused him to fail in the quest for the grail and set in motion the events that led to the destruction of Camelot. He was displaced as the model knight by Galahad, his son by the grailkeeper's daughter Elaine.

Lancet, The British medical journal established in 1823, published weekly from New York and London. Its founder and first editor, Thomas Wakley, considered at the time a radical reformer, stated that the intent of the new journal was to report on hospital lectures and describe important cases of the day. It has since played a significant role in medical and hospital reform movements in Britain and has become a highly prestigious medical journal around the world.

Lanchester \'lan-chəs-tər\, **Frederick William** (1868–1946) British automobile and aeronautics pioneer. Lanchester produced the first British automobile, a one-cylinder, five-horsepower model, in 1896. After he successfully produced improved models, financial backing enabled him to produce several hundred cars over the next few years, vehicles notable for a relative freedom from vibration, a graceful appearance, and a luggage rack. He published an important paper (1897) on the principles of heavier-than-air flight, and later major texts on aeronautics.

Lancisi \län-'chē-zē\, **Giovanni Maria** (1654–1720) Italian anatomist and epidemiologist. He related the prevalence of malaria in swampy areas to the presence of mosquitoes and recommended swamp drainage to prevent it. He linked an increase in sudden deaths in Rome to causes such as hemorrhagic stroke, cardiac enlargement and dilation, and growths on heart valves and explored causes of heart enlargement. He also provided the first description of syphilitic aneurysms.

land In economics, the resource that encompasses the natural resources used in production. In classical economics, the three factors of production are land, labor, and capital. Land was considered to be the "original and inexhaustible gift of nature." In modern economics, it is broadly defined to include all that nature provides, including minerals, forest products, and water and land resources. While many of these are renewable resources, no one considers them "inexhaustible." The payment to land is called rent. Like land, its definition has been broadened over time to include payment to any productive resource with a relatively fixed supply.

Land, Edwin (Herbert) (1909–1991) U.S. inventor and physicist. Born in Bridgeport, Conn., he briefly attended Harvard University and cofounded the Land-Wheelwright Laboratories in Boston in 1932. Interested in light polarization, in 1932 he developed the polarizer (which he called the Polaroid J sheet), for which he envisioned numerous uses. By 1936, Land began to use types of Polaroid material in sunglasses and other optical devices. It was later used in camera filters and other optical equipment. In 1937 Land founded the Polaroid Corp. in Cambridge, Mass. In 1947 he demonstrated the revolutionary Polaroid Land Camera, which produced a finished print in 60 seconds; he introduced color Polaroid film in 1963. His interest in light and color resulted in a new theory of color perception. He received more than 500 patents.

land grant college See Morrill Act of 1862

Land Management, Bureau of Agency of the U.S. Department of the Interior. Established in 1946, it is responsible for managing 262 million acres of public land, including such resources as timber, minerals, oil and gas, geothermal energy, wildlife habitats, endangered plant and animal species, recreation areas, lands with cultural importance, wild and scenic rivers, designated conservation and wilderness areas, and open-space lands.

land mine Explosive charge buried just below the surface of the earth, used in military operations against troops and vehicles. It may be fired by the weight of vehicles or troops on it, the passage of time, or remote control. Though improvised land mines (buried artillery shells) were used in World War I, they only became important in warfare during World War II and have been widely used since. Most early mines had metal cases; later models were sometimes made of other materials to prevent magnetic detection. They are typically used to disrupt or prevent the massed attack of tanks or infantry, but in post–World War II conflicts they have also been used to render land useless to enemy civilian populations. A treaty banning land mines—not signed by the U.S., Russia, and China—went into effect in 1997. See also submarine mine.

land reform Deliberate change in the way agricultural land is held or owned, the methods of its cultivation, or the relation of agriculture to the rest of the economy. The most common political objective of land reform is to abolish feudal or colonial forms of landownership, often by taking land away from large landowners and redistributing it to landless peasants. Other goals include improving the social status of peasants and coordinating agricultural production with industrialization programs. The earliest record of land reform is from 6th-century-BC Athens, where Solon abolished the debt system that forced peasants to mortgage their land and labor. The concentration of land in the hands of large landowners became the rule in the ancient world, however, and remained so through the Middle Ages and the Renaissance. The French Revolution brought land reform to France and established the small family farm as the cornerstone of French democracy. Serfdom was abolished throughout most of Europe in the 19th century. The Russian serfs were emancipated in 1861, and the Russian Revolution of 1917 introduced collectivization of agriculture, attended by loss of capital and devastating famines. Land reform was instituted in a number of other countries where communists came to power, notably China. It remains a potent political issue in many parts of the world. See also absentee ownership.

land tenure, feudal See feudal land tenure

Landau \län-'dau̇\, **Lev (Davidovich)** (1908–1968) Soviet physicist. After graduating from Leningrad State Univ., he studied at Niels Bohr's institute in Copenhagen. He is known for his work in low-temperature physics, atomic and nuclear physics, and solid-state, stellar-energy, and plasma physics. For explaining the phenomenon of liquid helium, he was awarded a 1962 Nobel Prize. For his work in many areas of physics, his name is applied to Landau diamagnetism, Landau levels, Landau damping, the Landau energy spectrum, Landau cuts, and the Landau Institute for Theoretical Physics in Moscow.

Landers, Ann *orig.* **Esther Friedman** (1918–2002) U.S. newspaper columnist. Born in Sioux City, Iowa, she took over an advice column in the *Chicago Sun-Times* in 1955, adopting her now-familiar pseudonym, and made it into the most widely syndicated advice column in the U.S. In 1956 her twin sister Pauline began the equally well-known "Dear Abby" advice column, from 1987 written by her daughter Jeanne Phillips.

Landini \län-'dē-nē\, **Francesco** *or* **Francesco Landino** (c. 1325–1397) Italian composer, organist, and poet. Blinded by smallpox as a child, he took up the study of music and the organ. He later became an organ builder, as well as a composer, lyricist, and performer of more than 150 beautifully melodic two- and three-part songs. Landini's works represent about a quarter of the music that survives from the Italian Ars Nova (14th century).

Landis, 1928.
UPI—EB INC.

Landis, Kenesaw Mountain (1866–1944) U.S. federal judge and first commissioner of professional baseball. Born in Millville, Ohio, he was named for a Georgia mountain where his father had been wounded as a Civil War soldier. He practiced law in Chicago (1891–1905) before being appointed a U.S. district judge (1905–22). In 1907 he presided over a famous case in which Standard Oil Co. was found guilty of granting unlawful freight rebates and fined $29 million (his decision was later reversed). He was named baseball commissioner in 1920 in the aftermath of the Black Sox scandal, and became noted for his uncompromising measures to preserve the game's integrity. Though widely disliked for his stern, autocratic rule, he kept the post until his death.

ländler \ˈlent-lər\ Traditional couple dance of Austria and Bavaria. A gliding and turning dance to music in 3/4 time, it was popular in the 18th–19th century in Vienna, and influenced the later development of the waltz. Such composers as W.A. Mozart, F. Schubert, A. Bruckner, and G. Mahler wrote ländlers and ländler-inspired works.

landlord and tenant Parties to the leasing of real estate, whose relationship is bound by contract. The landlord, or lessor, is the owner; the tenant, or lessee, supplies payment in order to enjoy possession and use of the property for a specified period. Important forms of tenancy include tenancy for a fixed period, periodic (seasonal) tenancy, tenancy at will, and holdover tenancy (whereby a tenant remains after the contract has ended). See also real and personal property, rent.

Landon, Alf(red) M(ossman) (1887–1987) U.S. politician. Born in West Middlesex, Pa., he entered the oil business in Kansas (1912) and became active in Progressive Party politics. He was elected governor of Kansas in 1932 and again in 1934, the only incumbent Republican governor to succeed that year. He was the Republican presidential nominee in 1936; though he won almost 17 million votes, he lost to Franklin Roosevelt in an electoral landslide.

Landon, Michael *orig.* **Eugene Maurice Orowitz** (1936–1991) U.S. television actor and producer. Born in Forest Hills, N.Y., he starred as Little Joe Cartwright in the hit western series *Bonanza* (1959–73), for which he wrote and directed individual episodes. He created and starred in the popular series *Little House on the Prairie* (1974–82), again writing and directing many episodes. He created, directed, and starred in the series *Highway to Heaven* (1984–88) and produced and directed several television movies.

Landor, Walter Savage (1775–1864) British writer. He was educated at Rugby School and Oxford, but left both over disagreements with the authorities. A classicist, he originally wrote many of his works in Latin. Though he wrote lyrics, plays, and heroic poems, he is best remembered for his multivolume *Imaginary Conversations,* prose dialogues between historical personages (1824–53). He spent much of his life in France and Italy, and died in Florence.

Landowska \lan-ˈdȯf-skə\, **Wanda** *orig.* **Alexandra** (1879–1959) Polish-U.S. harpsichordist and pianist. After establishing herself as a pianist and devoting much energy to musicological research, she had a harpsichord made for her by Pleyel in Paris, and first performed on it at the Breslau Bach Festival in 1912, thus beginning the 20th-century revival of the instrument and sparking a new international interest in authentic performance practice. Her many recordings included the first recording of J.S. Bach's *Goldberg Variations*, and she commissioned such works as M. de Falla's harpsichord concerto and F. Poulenc's *Concert champêtre*. As a Jew she was forced to flee the Nazis, and after 1940 she lived and taught in the U.S.

Landrum-Griffin Act (1959) Legislation designed to counter labor-union corruption. Officially called the Labor-Management Reporting and Disclosure Act, it instituted federal penalties for labor officials who misused union funds or prevented union members from exercising their legal rights. The legislation was passed in response to U.S. Senate hearings that showed connections between labor and organized crime.

Land's End Westernmost peninsula, Cornwall, England. Its tip is the southwesternmost point of England and lies about 870 mi (1,400 km) from John o' Groats, traditionally considered the northernmost point of Britain. Off its coast lie dangerous reefs, one group of which, a mile from the mainland, is marked by the Longships lighthouse.

Landsat *officially* **Earth Resources Technology Satellites** Any of a series of unmanned U.S. scientific satellites. The first three were launched in 1972, 1975, and 1978. They were designed mainly to collect information about earth's natural resources. They were also equipped to monitor atmospheric and oceanic conditions and to detect variations in pollution levels and other ecological changes. Four more Landsat satellites were launched (in 1982, 1984, 1993, and 1999), but radio communication with Landsat 6 was lost immediately after its launch.

landscape gardening Process of arranging land, plants, and objects for human use and enjoyment, usually with long and close-up views. Cyclical growth and seasonal changes provide a continuous sense of time and natural rhythms that is absent in buildings and sculptures. Gardens and designed landscapes fill in the open areas in cities and create continuity between urban structures and open rural lands beyond. Landscape-gardening areas may be of any size, from small urban courtyards and suburban gardens to many thousands of acres in regional, state, or national parks. Every landscape garden reflects attitudes toward nature and humans, revealing much about a culture and a period.

Landseer, Edwin (Henry) *later* **Sir Edwin** (1802–1873) British painter and sculptor. He studied with his father, an engraver and writer, and at the Royal Academy. He specialized in animals and developed great skill in depicting animal anatomy, but humanized his subjects to the point of sentimentality or moralizing (e.g., *Dignity and Impudence*, 1839). He achieved great professional and social success, and was a favorite painter of Queen Victoria. He was elected to the Royal Academy in 1831 and knighted in 1850. As a sculptor he is best known for his bronze lions at the base of Nelson's Column in Trafalgar Square (unveiled 1867).

Lane, Burton *orig.* **Burton Levy** (1912–1997) U.S. songwriter. Born in New York City, Lane worked in Tin Pan Alley, where he came to the attention of George Gershwin. His tunes were featured on Broadway from the early 1930s and later heard in films, including *Babes on Broadway* (1942). His greatest success came with *Finian's Rainbow* (1947; film, 1968); his lyricist was E.Y. Harburg. He collaborated with A.J. Lerner on the film *Royal Wedding* (1951), in which Fred Astaire dances on the ceiling to "Too Late Now." Another joint effort with Lerner, *On a Clear Day You Can See Forever* (1965; film, 1970), gave Lane his last notable success.

Lanfranc \ˈlan-ˌfraŋk\ (c. 1005–1089) Archbishop of Canterbury (1070–89). An Italian scholar who settled in Normandy, he joined the Benedictine monastery of Bec and was made its prior. He became a trusted adviser of William I the Conqueror, who nominated him as archbishop of Canterbury after the Norman Conquest. Lanfranc reformed and reorganized the English church, ensuring its independence from the crown. He uncovered a conspiracy against the king (1075), and he secured the succession for William II against Robert II (1087).

Lanfranco \län-ˈfräŋ-kō\, **Giovanni** (1582–1647) Italian painter. Born in Parma, he studied with Agostino Carracci. In 1602 he went to Rome to work with Annibale Carracci in the Farnese Palace. After Annibale's death, he became the leading fresco painter in Rome. His work shows the influence of Correggio's dynamic illusionism. His masterpiece is the *Assumption of the Virgin* in the dome of Sant'Andrea della Valle (1625–27), which he took over from his rival, Domenichino; with its vigorously painted figures floating in the clouds over the viewer, it is a pivotal work of the baroque era. He worked in Naples 1633–46; his best-known work there is the dome of the chapel of San Gennaro in the cathedral (1641–46).

Lang, Fritz (1890–1976) Austrian-U.S. film director. He studied architecture in Vienna and served in the Austrian army in World War I. While recovering from war wounds, he began to write screenplays. He found work at a movie studio in Berlin, where he later directed such successful films as *Between Two Worlds* (1921), *Dr. Mabuse* (1922), the two-part *The Nibelungen* (1924), the expressionistic *Metropolis* (1926), and *M* (1931). After making the anti-Nazi film *The Last Will of Dr. Mabuse* (1933), he left Germany for Paris and later Hollywood. His U.S. films, which equal his German films in their intensity, pessimism, and visual mastery, include *Fury* (1936), *You Only Live Once* (1937), *Ministry of Fear* (1944), *Rancho Notorious* (1952), and *The Big Heat* (1953).

Langdell \ˈlaŋ-dᵊl\, **Christopher Columbus** (1826–1906) U.S. legal educator. Born in New Boston, N.H., he was a schoolteacher before he became a lawyer, after which he practiced law in New York City (1854–70). He was a professor and later dean at Harvard Law School (1870–

95). His case method of teaching law, in which students read and discussed original authorities and derived for themselves the principles of the law, eventually became dominant in U.S. law schools.

Lange \ˈlaŋ\, **Dorothea** (1895–1965) U.S. documentary photographer. Born in Hoboken, N.J., she studied photography and opened a portrait studio in San Francisco in 1919. During the Great Depression, her photos of homeless men led to her employment by a federal agency to bring the plight of the poor to public attention. Her photographs were so effective that the government established camps for migrants. Her *Migrant Mother* (1936) was the most widely reproduced of all Farm Security Administration pictures. She produced several other photo essays, including one documenting the World War II internment of Japanese-Americans.

Lange, Jessica (born 1949) U.S. film actress. Born in Cloquet, Minn., she studied mime in Paris and working as a model in New York before making her movie debut in *King Kong* (1976). She appeared in *All That Jazz* (1979) and *The Postman Always Rings Twice* (1981) and became a star with *Frances* (1982) and *Tootsie* (1982, Academy Award). She won praise for her roles in *Country* (1984), *Sweet Dreams* (1985), and *Music Box* (1989) and in the televised versions of *Cat on a Hot Tin Roof* (1984) and *O Pioneers!* (1992). Later films include *Blue Sky* (1994, Academy Award), *Rob Roy* (1995), *A Thousand Acres* (1997), and *Titus* (1999).

Langer, Susanne K(nauth) (1895–1985) U.S. philosopher. Born in New York City, she taught at Harvard University (1927–42) and other institutions. In *Philosophy in a New Key* (1942), she presented a novel interpretation of the meaning of art. Her *Feeling and Form* (1953) proposed that art, especially music, is a highly articulated form of expression symbolizing intuitive knowledge of life patterns that ordinary language cannot convey. Her *Mind: An Essay on Human Feeling* (3 vols., 1967–82) traced the development of the mind.

Langerhans, islets of *or* **islands of Langerhans** Irregularly shaped patches of endocrine tissue in the PANCREAS, which contains about 1 million of them. Beta cells, the most common type, produce INSULIN to regulate blood glucose. Inadequate production causes DIABETES MELLITUS. Alpha cells produce an opposing hormone, glucagon, which releases glucose from the liver and fatty acids from fat tissue; these favor insulin release and inhibit glucagon secretion. Delta cells produce somatostatin, which inhibits somatotropin (a major pituitary hormone), insulin, and glucagon; its metabolic role is not clear. Small numbers of F cells secrete pancreatic polypeptide, which slows down nutrient absorption. See also ENDOCRINE SYSTEM.

Langland, William (c. 1330–c. 1400) Presumed author of the poem known as *Piers Plowman*. Little is known of his life, though he clearly had a deep knowledge of theology and was interested in the asceticism of St. BERNARD DE CLAIRVAUX. One of the greatest Middle English alliterative poems, *Piers Plowman* is an allegorical work in the form of a series of dream visions with a complex variety of religious themes; written in simple, colloquial language, it contains powerful imagery.

Langley, Samuel (Pierpont) (1834–1906) U.S. astronomer and aeronautics pioneer. Born in Roxbury, Mass., he taught for many years at the future University of Pittsburgh. He studied the effect of solar activity on weather and invented the bolometer (1878), a radiant-heat detector sensitive to extremely small temperature differences. He began conducting experiments on lift and drag of wings by building flying machines, and in 1896 one of his heavier-than-air machines became the first to achieve sustained unmanned flight, flying 3,000 ft (900 m) along the Potomac River.

Langmuir \ˈlaŋ-ˌmyu̇r\, **Irving** (1881–1957) U.S. physical chemist. Born in Brooklyn, N.Y., he received his PhD from the University of Göttingen. As a researcher for General Electric (1909–50), he investigated electrical discharges in gases, electron emission, and the high-temperature surface chemistry of tungsten, making possible a great extension in the life of tungsten-filament lightbulbs. He developed a vacuum pump and the high-vacuum tubes used in radio broadcasting. He formulated theories of atomic structure and chemical bond formation, introducing the term covalence. He received a Nobel Prize in 1932.

Langton, Stephen (died 1228) English cardinal and archbishop of Canterbury (1207–28). Langton was living at Rome when INNOCENT III nominated him as archbishop of Canterbury (1207) to settle a disputed election. When King JOHN refused to allow him into England, the pope excommunicated John (1209). John finally submitted and received Langton in 1213. The new archbishop encouraged baronial opposition to the king but opposed violence. He was present at the signing of the MAGNA CARTA (1215) and influenced its provisions on ecclesiastical liberties.

Langtry, Lillie *orig.* **Emilie Charlotte Le Breton** (1853–1929) British actress. Born on the Isle of Jersey (and later known as the "Jersey Lily"), she married the socially prominent Edward Langtry in 1874. A famous beauty, she caused a sensation when she became the first society woman to go on the stage, starring in *She Stoops to Conquer* (1881). She played to enthusiastic audiences in England and the U.S., notably in *As You Like It*. Her lovers included the Prince of Wales (later EDWARD VII). After her husband died, she married Hugo de Bathe (1899), and she later remodeled and managed the Imperial Theatre (1901–17).

Lillie Langtry.
MANSELL COLLECTION

language System of conventional spoken or written symbols used by people in a shared culture to communicate with each other. A language both reflects and affects a culture's way of thinking, and changes in a culture influence the development of its language. Related languages become more differentiated when their speakers are isolated from each other. When speech communities come into contact (e.g., through trade or conquest), their languages influence each other. Most existing languages are grouped with other languages descended "genetically" from a common ancestral language (see historical LINGUISTICS). The broadest grouping of languages is the language family. For example, all the ROMANCE LANGUAGES are derived from Latin, which in turn belongs to the Italic branch of the INDO-EUROPEAN LANGUAGE family, descended from the ancient parent language, Proto-Indo-European. Other major families include, in Asia, SINO-TIBETAN, AUSTRONESIAN, DRAVIDIAN, ALTAIC, and AUSTROASIATIC; in Africa, NIGER-CONGO, AFRO-ASIATIC, and NILO-SAHARAN; and in the Americas, UTO-AZTECAN, MAYAN, OTOMANGUEAN, and TUPIAN. Relationships between languages are traced by comparing GRAMMAR and SYNTAX and especially by looking for cognates (related words) in different languages. Language has a complex structure that can be analyzed and systematically presented (see LINGUISTICS). All languages begin as SPEECH, and many go on to develop WRITING systems. All can employ different sentence structures to convey MOOD. They use their resources differently for this but seem to be equally flexible structurally. The principal resources are word order, word form, syntactic structure, and, in speech, INTONATION. Different languages keep indicators of number, person, GENDER, TENSE, mood, and other categories separate from the root word or attach them to it. The innate human capacity to learn language fades with age, and languages learned after about age 10 are usually not spoken as well as those learned earlier. See also DIALECT.

language, philosophy of Branch of philosophy whose primary goal is to articulate the form and requirements of a theory of MEANING and reference for natural LANGUAGES. It has historically been associated with the view that philosophical perplexities arise from a misunderstanding or misuse of language. However, not all philosophers of language believe the logical analysis of language to be an appropriate method, let alone the only method, for resolving philosophical problems. See also LINGUISTICS, PRAGMATICS.

Languedoc \lä^{n}g-ˈdȯk\ Historical region, southern central France. Languedoc's name is derived from the traditional language of southern France, in which the word *oc* means "yes" (see OCCITAN LANGUAGE). From 121 BC the region was part of the Roman province of Gallia Narbonensis. With the fall of the Roman empire, it was controlled by the Visigoths in the 5th century. During the Middle Ages it came under the counts of Toulouse. Religious wars (see ALBIGENSIAN CRUSADE) in the 13th century brought it under the French crown. In the 16th–18th century it was the scene of Protestant persecution which culminated in the war of the CAMISARDS. Protestant revolt led to its division into departments.

Lanier \lə-'nir\, **Willie (Edward)** (born 1945) U.S. football player. Born in Clover, Va., he was selected to the Little All-America Team while at Morgan State University. An outstanding defensive player, he played middle linebacker for the Kansas City Chiefs (1967–77). He helped the Chiefs defeat the favored Minnesota Vikings in Super Bowl IV (1970) and was selected to eight consecutive Pro Bowls.

Lansbury, George (1859–1940) British politician. As a member of the House of Commons (1910–12, 1922–40), he became known as a socialist and poor-law reformer, and he led the British Labour Party 1931–35. Pacifist in his leanings, he was unwilling to call for economic sanctions against Italy for its aggression in Ethiopia (1935), fearing it might lead to war, and lost his party leadership post. In 1937 he visited ADOLF HITLER and BENITO MUSSOLINI in the vain hope that his personal influence could stop the movement toward war.

Lansdowne, Marquess of *orig.* **Henry Charles Keith Petty-Fitzmaurice** (1845–1927) Irish nobleman and British diplomat. He inherited his father's title and wealth in 1866 and served in WILLIAM E. GLADSTONE's Liberal administration. As governor-general of Canada (1883–88), he helped settle the RIEL rebellion. As viceroy of India (1888–94) under a Conservative government, he reorganized the police, reconstituted legislative councils, closed Indian mints to the free coinage of silver, and extended railway and irrigation works. As secretary of war (1895–1900), he was blamed for British unpreparedness in the SOUTH AFRICAN WAR. As foreign secretary (1900–6), he concluded the ENTENTE CORDIALE.

L'Anse aux Meadows \ˌlans-ō-'me-ˌdōz\ Site on the northern tip of Newfoundland where Norse settlers established as many as three settlements near the end of the 10th century. After initially fighting each other, the Norse settlers and the Inuit (whom the Norse called Skraeling) established a regular trade relationship. The settlements were soon abandoned, probably as the Norse withdrew from Greenland.

Lansing City (pop., 2000: 119,128), capital of Michigan. Located on the Grand River at its junction with the Red Cedar River, it was a recently settled site when the state capital was moved there from DETROIT in 1847. Originally called Michigan, it adopted the name Lansing in 1848. It became a center of auto manufacturing in the late 19th century. Now a major automobile production center, it is the site of the first U.S. agricultural college, MICHIGAN STATE UNIV. (now in East Lansing).

Lansky, Meyer *orig.* **Maier Suchowljansky** (1902–1983) U.S. (Russian-born) gangster. His family emigrated to New York in 1911. As a young man he joined BUGSY SIEGEL in auto theft, burglary, and liquor smuggling. In 1931 he allegedly organized the murder of crime boss Joe Masseria and joined LUCKY LUCIANO in forming a national crime syndicate. By 1936 he had developed gambling operations in Cuba and the U.S., putting Siegel in charge of Las Vegas. In the 1960s he extended his gambling empire to the Bahamas and elsewhere in the Caribbean, while continuing to run narcotics-smuggling, prostitution, labor-racketeering, and extortion rackets. His holdings in 1970 were estimated at $300 million. Though convicted of income-tax evasion in 1973, he remained free on appeals.

lantana \lan-'tä-nə\ Any of more than 150 shrubs that make up the genus *Lantana* in the VERBENA family, native to the New World and African tropics. They are cultivated for their ornamental foliage, fragrant clusters of flowers, and colorful blue-black fruits. Common lantana *(L. camara),* a weed in the New World tropics, is much used as a garden plant elsewhere. It grows to 10 ft (3 m) and blooms almost continuously with yellow, orange, pink, or white flower heads. The aromatic leaves are rough and oval.

lanthanide \'lan-thə-ˌnīd\ Any of the series of 15 consecutive chemical ELEMENTS in the PERIODIC TABLE from lanthanum to lutetium (atomic numbers 57–71). With scandium and yttrium, they make up the RARE EARTH METALS. Their atoms have similar configurations and similar physical and chemical behavior; the most usual VALENCES are 3 and 4.

Lanzhou *or* **Lan-chou** \'län-'jō\ City (pop., 1999 est.: 1,429,673), capital of GANSU province, northern central China. Situated on the upper HUANG HE (Yellow River), it became part of the territory of Qin in the 6th century BC and later developed as a major trade center on the SILK ROAD. It became the seat of Lanzhou prefecture under the Sui dynasty (581–618 AD) and the capital of Gansu province in 1666. It was badly damaged during the Muslim uprisings in 1864–75. A center of Soviet influence in northwestern China in the early 20th century, it was the terminus of the 2,000-mi (3,200-km) Chinese–Soviet highway that was used during the SINO–JAPANESE WAR for the transport of Soviet supplies. It developed as an industrial and cultural center after World War II. It is the seat of Lanzhou University.

Lao She \'laủ-'shə\ *orig.* **Shu Qingchun** *or* **Shu Sheyou** (1899–1966) Chinese writer. He worked as an educator before going to England in 1924, and was inspired to write his first novel while reading the works of CHARLES DICKENS to improve his English. He originally championed strong, hard-working individuals, but later expressed the futility of the individual's struggle against society, as in *Luotuo Xiangzi* (1936), the tragic story of a ricksha puller; *Rickshaw Boy*, an unauthorized translation with a happy ending (1945), became a U.S. best-seller. After the onset of the SINO-JAPANESE WAR, he wrote lesser patriotic and propagandistic plays and novels. In 1966 he fell victim to the CULTURAL REVOLUTION.

Laocoön \'lā-'ä-kō-ˌän\ In Greek legend, a seer and priest of APOLLO. He was the son of Agenor of Troy or the brother of AENEAS's father Anchises. Laocoön offended Apollo by breaking his priestly vow of celibacy and begetting children, and by warning the Trojans not to accept the wooden horse presented by the Greeks. While preparing to offer a sacrifice to POSEIDON, he and his two sons were crushed to death by sea serpents sent by Apollo.

Laos \'lä-ōs, 'laủs\ *officially* **Lao People's Democratic Republic** Country, S.East Asia. Area: 91,429 sq mi (236,800 sq km). Population (2002 est.): 5,777,000. Capital: VIENTIANE. Laos's major ethnic groups include the Lao-Lum (valley Lao), who make up two-thirds of the population; the Lao-Tai, a highland tribal people; the Lao-Theung (Mon-Khmer), descendants of the region's earliest inhabitants; and the Lao-Soung group, including the HMONG and Man. Languages: Lao (official),

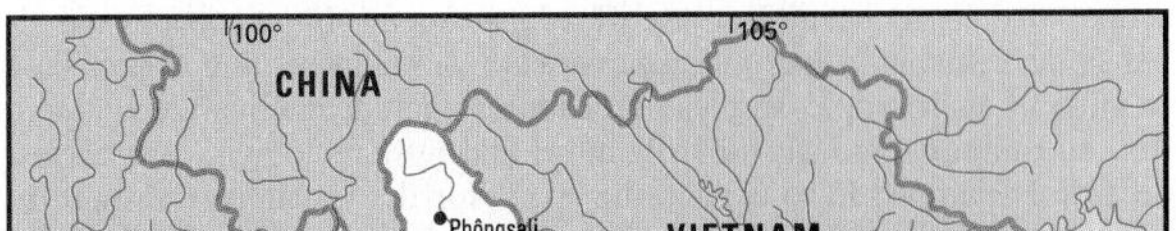

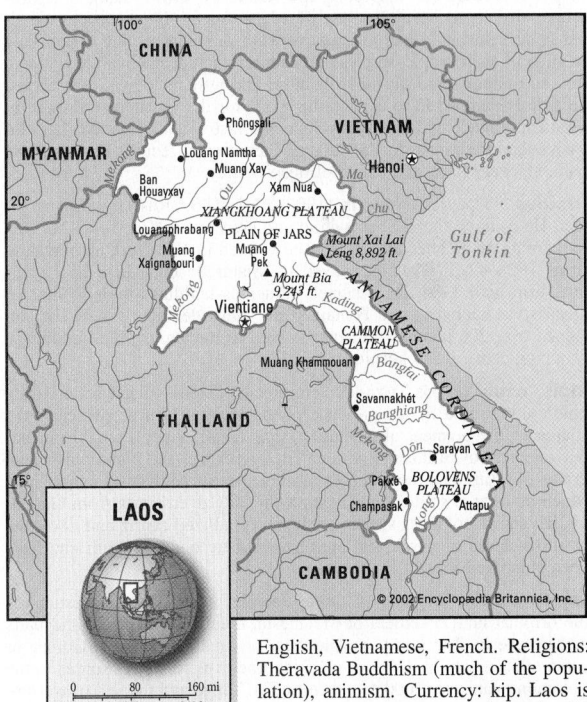

English, Vietnamese, French. Religions: Theravada Buddhism (much of the population), animism. Currency: kip. Laos is largely mountainous, especially in the north; its highest point is Mount Bia (9,245 ft, or 2,818 m). Tropical forests cover more than half of the country's total land area; only 4% of its total area is suitable for agriculture. The floodplains of the MEKONG RIVER provide the country's only lowlands and its major wet-rice fields. Laos has a centrally planned economy based primarily on agriculture (including rice, sweet potatoes, sugarcane, cassava, and opium) and international aid. It is a people's republic with one legislative house; its chief of state is the president and its head of government is the prime minister. The Lao people migrated into Laos from southern China after the 8th century AD, displacing indigenous tribes now known as the Kha. In the 14th century Fa Ngum founded the first Laotian state, Lan Xang. Except for a period of rule by Burma (1574–1637), the Lan Xang kingdom ruled Laos until 1713, when it split into three kingdoms—Vientiane, Champassak, and Luang Prabang. During the 18th century the rulers of the three Laotian kingdoms became vassals of Siam. France gained control of the region in 1893, and Laos became a French protectorate. In 1945 Japan seized control and declared Laos independent. The area reverted to French rule after World War II. By the end of the First INDOCHINA WAR, the leftist Pathet Lao movement controlled two provinces of the country. The Geneva Conference of 1954 unified and granted independence to Laos. Pathet Lao forces fought the Laotian government and took control in 1975, establishing the Lao People's Democratic Republic; about one-tenth of the population fled into neighboring Thailand. Laos held its first election in 1989 and promulgated a new constitution in 1991. Although its economy was adversely affected by the mid-1990s Asian monetary crises, it realized a longtime goal in 1997 when it joined the ASSOCIATION OF SOUTHEAST ASIAN NATIONS.

Laozi *or* **Lao-tzu** \'lau̇-'dzə\ (fl. c. 6th century BC) First philosopher of Chinese TAOISM. He is traditionally named as the author of the *TAO-TE CHING*, though modern scholars hold that the work had more than one author. Legends about his life abound, but little or no certain information survives. The historical Laozi, if he existed, may have been a scholar and caretaker of sacred books at the royal court of the ZHOU DYNASTY. According to legend, he was carried 72 years in his mother's womb, and he met CONFUCIUS as a young man. He is venerated as a philosopher by the Confucianists; as a saint or god by the common people of China; and as a divinity and the representative of the tao by Taoists.

laparoscopy \ˌla-pə-'räs-kə-pē\ *or* **peritoneoscopy** \ˌper-ət-ᵊn-ˌē-'äs-kə-pē\ Procedure for inspecting the ABDOMINAL CAVITY using a laparoscope; also surgery requiring use of a laparoscope. Laparoscopes use fiber-optic lights and small video cameras to show tissues and organs on a monitor. Laparoscopic surgical procedures include gallbladder, appendix, and tumor removal; tubal ligation; and hysterectomy. After carbon dioxide is pumped in to expand the space for the instruments, small incisions are made and the laparoscope and instruments inserted. Less invasive than traditional (open) surgery, laparoscopy reduces postoperative pain, recovery time, and length of hospital stay.

Lapidus \lə-'pē-dəs\, **Morris** (1902–2001) U.S. (Russian-born) architect. He came to the U.S. as a child and grew up in New York City. After earning an architectural degree, he worked in New York architectural firms 1928–42. In 1942 he moved to Miami Beach, where he ran his own firm until 1986. He designed numerous buildings there in the Art Deco style, including the Fontainebleau and Eden Roc hotels. He designed over 200 hotels worldwide as well as numerous office buildings, shopping centers, and hospitals.

lapis lazuli \ˌla-pəs-'la-zə-lē\ Semiprecious stone valued for its deep blue color caused by the presence of the mineral lazurite, which is the source of the pigment ultramarine. Lapis lazuli is not a single mineral but an intergrowth lazurite with calcite, pyroxene, and commonly small grains of PYRITE. The most important mines are in Afghanistan and Chile. Much of what is sold as lapis is an artificially dyed JASPER from Germany that shows colorless specks of clear, crystallized quartz and never the goldlike flecks of pyrite that are characteristic of lapis lazuli and have been compared to stars in the sky.

Lapita culture \lä-'pē-tə\ Cultural complex of what were presumably the original human settlers of Melanesia, much of Polynesia, and parts of Micronesia. The Lapita people were originally from New Guinea or some other region of Austronesia. Seaborne explorers, they spread to the Solomon Islands (c. 1600 BC), then to Fiji, Tonga and the rest of western Polynesia (c. 1000 BC), and finally to Micronesia (c. 500 BC). They are known principally on the basis of the remains of their fired pottery, which was first extensively investigated at the site of Lapita in New Caledonia. They appear to have subsisted largely by fishing but may also have practiced some domestic agriculture and animal husbandry.

Laplace \lə-'pläs\, **Pierre-Simon, marquis de** (1749–1827) French mathematician, astronomer, and physicist. He is best known for his investigations into the stability of the solar system and the theory of magnetic, electrical, and heat wave propagation. In his major lifework he applied Newtonian gravitational theory to the solar system to explain deviations of the planets from the orbits predicted by the theory (1773). NEWTON believed that only divine intervention could explain the solar system's equilibrium, but Laplace established a mathematical basis for it, the most important advance in physical astronomy since Newton. He continued to work on elucidating planetary perturbations through the 1780s. A work published in 1796 included his nebular hypothesis, which attributed the origin of the solar system to the cooling and contracting of a gaseous nebula, a theory that strongly influenced future thought on planetary origins. See also LAPLACE TRANSFORM, LAPLACE'S EQUATION.

Laplace transform In mathematics, an INTEGRAL TRANSFORM useful in solving DIFFERENTIAL EQUATIONS. The Laplace transform of a function is found by integrating the product of that function and the EXPONENTIAL FUNCTION e^{-pt} over the interval from zero to INFINITY. The Laplace transform's applications include solving linear differential equations with constant coefficients and solving boundary value problems, which arise in calculations relating to physical systems.

Laplace's equation In mathematics, a PARTIAL DIFFERENTIAL EQUATION whose solutions (harmonic functions) are useful in investigating physical problems in three dimensions involving gravitational, electrical, and magnetic fields, and certain types of fluid motion. Named for PIERRE-SIMON LAPLACE, the equation states that the sum of the second partial derivatives (the Laplace operator, or Laplacian) of an unknown function is zero. It can apply to functions of two or three variables, and can be written in terms of a differential operator as $\Delta f = 0$, where Δ is the Laplace operator.

Lapland Region (pop., 1992 est.: 113,000), northern Europe. Located within the Arctic Circle, it stretches across northern Norway, Sweden, and Finland, and into Russia's KOLA PENINSULA. Occupying an area of 150,000 sq mi (389,000 sq km), it is bounded by the Norwegian Sea, the BARENTS SEA, and the White Sea. Since it straddles several national borders, it does not exist as any unified administrative entity. It is named for the SAMI (Lapp) people, who have inhabited the region for several thousand years. Those who still practice reindeer herding have liberty of movement across national boundaries. Industries include mining and fishing.

Sami (Lapps) outside their reindeer-skin tent in Finnish Lapland.

© THE NATIONAL GEOGRAPHIC SOCIETY; PHOTOGRAPH, JEAN AND FRANC SHOR

lapwing Any of numerous bird species of the PLOVER family (Charadriidae), especially the Eurasian lapwing *(Vanellus vanellus)* of farmlands and grassy plains. Lapwings are about 12 in. (30 cm) long and have broad, rounded wings. Several species have crests, and some have wing spurs (sharp projections at the bend of the wing). The Eurasian lapwing is green-glossed black above with white cheeks, black throat and breast, white belly, and white tail with a black band. About 24 other species are found in South America, Africa, southern Asia, Malaya, and Australia.

Eurasian lapwing (*Vanellus vanellus*).

INGMAR HOLMASEN

L'Aquila \'lä-kwē-lä\ City (pop., 1991: 67,000), capital of the ABRUZZI region, central Italy. The area was settled by the Sabini, an ancient Italic tribe, and the city was founded c. 1240. After being ruled by the kingdom of Naples, it became part of the kingdom of Italy in 1861. Located near the mountains of Gran Sasso d'Italia, it is a skiing center and summer resort. Historic sites include a 14th-century cathedral and a 16th-century castle.

Laramide orogeny \'lar-ə-ˌmīd-ȯ-'rä-jə-nē\ Series of mountain-building events that affected much of western North America in Late CRETA-

CEOUS and Early TERTIARY time (c. 65 million years ago). The Laramide orogeny originally was believed to mark the Cretaceous-Tertiary boundary. It is now considered to have consisted of many separate pulses of deformation that varied in intensity and age from place to place. Laramide rocks, however, were generally created around the Cretaceous-Tertiary time boundary.

larceny See THEFT

larch Any of about 10–12 species of coniferous trees that make up the genus *Larix* of the PINE family, native to cool temperate and sub-Arctic regions of the Northern Hemisphere. Though the larch has the pyramid shape typical of CONIFERS, it sheds its short, light-green, needlelike leaves in autumn. The most widespread North American larch, the tamarack, or eastern larch (*L. laricina*), matures in 100–200 years, may grow 40–100 ft (12–30 m) tall, and has gray to reddish-brown bark. Coarse-grained, strong, hard, and heavy, larch wood is useful in ship construction and for telephone poles, mine timbers, and railroad ties.

Lardner, Ring(gold Wilmer) (1885–1933) U.S. writer. Born in Niles, Mich., he worked as a newspaper reporter, sportswriter, and columnist before he began publishing fiction. He won popular success with comic stories about a baseball player, some collected in *You Know Me, Al* (1916). Later collections, noted for their satire, narrative skill, and convincing vernacular language, include *How to Write Short Stories* (1924) and *The Love Nest* (1926). He collaborated on the Broadway plays *Elmer the Great* (1928; with GEORGE M. COHAN) and *June Moon* (1929; with GEORGE S. KAUFMAN). His son, the screenwriter Ring Lardner, Jr., was one of the HOLLYWOOD TEN, and later wrote such hit movies as *M*A*S*H* (1970).

Laredo \lə-ˈrā-dō\ City (pop., 1996 est.: 165,000), southern Texas. Located on the RIO GRANDE opposite Nuevo Laredo, Mexico, it was established in 1755 by the Spanish and was named for Laredo, Spain. After the Texas revolt against Mexican rule in 1836, it was without a country and became the seat of the Republic of the Rio Grande (1839–41). Occupied by the Texas Rangers in 1846, it was incorporated as a city in 1852. A rapidly growing city, its manufacturing includes electronic components and oil refining.

Lares \ˈlar-ˌēz\ In ROMAN RELIGION, guardian deities. Originally gods of cultivated fields, Lares were later worshiped in association with the PENATES, the gods of the household. The household Lar, considered the center of the family cult, was often represented as a youthful figure holding a drinking horn and cup. Two Lares might be portrayed standing on either side of VESTA or some other deity. A prayer was said to the Lar or Lares every morning, and offerings were made at family festivals. Public Lares presided over local districts marked by a crossroad; state Lares *(praestites),* guardians of Rome, were worshiped in a temple on the Via Sacra.

large intestine End section of the intestine, about 5 ft (1.5 m) long, wider than the SMALL INTESTINE, with a smooth inner wall. In the first half, ENZYMES from the small intestine complete digestion, and bacteria produce many B vitamins and vitamin K. Over 24–30 hours, churning movements break down tough cellulose fibers and expose CHYME to the COLON's walls, which absorb water and electrolytes; absorption is its main function, along with storing fecal matter for expulsion. The more vigorous "mass movement" (gastrocolic reflex) occurs only two or three times a day to propel waste material toward the ANAL CANAL. Common afflictions include COLITIS, diverticulosis (see DIVERTICULUM), POLYPS, and TUMORS.

Largo Caballero \ˈlär-gō-ˌkä-bäl-ˈyār-ō\, **Francisco** (1869–1946) Spanish socialist leader and prime minister (1936–37). He joined the Socialist Party in 1894 and rose to become head of the party's trade-union federation in 1925. He cooperated with the dictatorship of MIGUEL PRIMO DE RIVERA, then served in the Second Republic as labor minister (1931–33). After the electoral victory of the POPULAR FRONT (1936), he became prime minister and tried to unify the leftist parties; but an extreme-left uprising in Barcelona in 1937 during the Spanish Civil War caused a cabinet crisis and he was forced to resign. He went into exile in France, and was interned by the Germans in World War II (1942–45).

Laristan \ˌlar-ə-ˈstan\ Region, southern Iran. Located on the Persian Gulf, it is a former province; its chief town is Lar. The region was ruled by the Muzaffarid dynasty of Kerman until it was conquered by TIMUR. After his death in 1405, it was ruled by local chiefs under the Safavid dynasty. The last chief was put to death by ABBAS I the Great, who ruled 1587–1629.

lark Any of about 75 species of songbirds (family Alaudidae) found throughout the continental Old World. Only the horned, or shore, lark *(Eremophila alpestris)* is native to the New World. The bill may be small and narrowly conical or long and downward-curving, and the hind claw is long and sometimes straight. The plumage is plain or streaked, closely matching the soil in color. Its body is 5–9 in. (13–23 cm) long. Flocks of larks forage for insects and seeds on the ground. All species have a high, thin, melodious voice. See also SKYLARK.

Horned lark (*Eremophila alpestris*).
HERBERT CLARKE

Larkin, Philip (Arthur) (1922–1985) English poet. Educated at Oxford, Larkin became a librarian at the University of Hull, Yorkshire, in 1955, he would remain a librarian the rest of his life. He wrote two novels before becoming well known with his third volume of verse, *The Less Deceived* (1955), which expressed the antiromantic sensibility prevalent in English verse of his time. Later poetry volumes are *The Whitsun Weddings* (1964), *High Windows* (1974), and *Aubade* (1980). *All What Jazz* (1970) contains essays he wrote as a jazz critic for *The Daily Telegraph* (1961–71).

larkspur *or* **delphinium** Any of about 300 species of herbaceous plants that make up the genus *Delphinium* in the BUTTERCUP family, many of which are grown for their showy flower stalks. Annual larkspurs (sometimes separated as the genus *Consolida*) include the common rocket larkspur *(D. ajacis,* or *C. ambigua)* and its varieties, up to 2 ft (60 cm) tall, with bright blue, pink, or white flowers on branching stalks. Perennial larkspurs, often with blue flowers, include species that grow to 4.5 ft (1.4 m).

Dwarf larkspur (*Delphinium tricorne*).
LOUISE K. BROMAN FROM ROOT RESOURCES—EB INC.

Larne \ˈlärn\ Town (pop., 1991 est.: 18,000), Northern Ireland, on the Irish Sea north of BELFAST. Edward Bruce landed nearby on his journey to accept the Irish throne in 1315. It developed as a holiday resort after 1900. It is the capital of Larne district (pop., 1995 est.: 30,000), which in addition to tourism, has some agricultural production. The Antrim Coast Road, one of the greatest tourist attractions in Northern Ireland, begins at Larne.

Larousse \lə-ˈrüs\, **Pierre (Athanase)** (1817–1875) French publisher, lexicographer, and encyclopedist. Son of a blacksmith, he received a scholarship to study in Versailles. He founded his publishing house, Librairie Larousse, in Paris in 1852. It published textbooks, grammar books, and dictionaries, but his major work, reflecting his desire "to teach everyone about everything," was the combined dictionary and encyclopedia *Grand dictionnaire universel du XIXe siècle* (17 vols., 1866–76). Librairie Larousse continues to publish a multivolume encyclopedia as well as dictionaries and smaller encyclopedias.

Larsa *biblical* **Ellasar.** Ancient capital of BABYLONIA, located on the EUPHRATES RIVER in present-day southern Iraq. It was founded in prehistoric times, and it flourished in a period of Sumerian decline, c. 2000–c. 1760 B.C., when long-distance trade connected the Euphrates with the Indus valley. HAMMURABI of Babylon gained control of the area in 1763 BC.

Larsen Ice Shelf Ice shelf in the northwestern Weddell Sea, adjoining the eastern coast of the Antarctic Peninsula. It is named for Capt. Carl A. Larsen, who explored the ice front by boat in 1893. It covers an area of 33,000 sq mi (86,000 sq km), excluding the numerous small islands within the ice shelf.

Lartigue \lär-'tēg\, **Jacques-Henri (-Charles-Auguste)** (1894–1986) French painter and photographer. Born into a prosperous family, he was given a Brownie camera at 7. From the beginning, his photographs were invariably informal shots of everyday subjects. When his work was discovered in the 1960s, he was acclaimed for his departure from formal, posed portraits and for the ingenuous charm and beguiling spontaneity, freshness, and joyful humor of his boyhood photos of family and friends, and even his documentation of World War I.

larva Active, feeding stage in the development of many animals, occurring after birth or hatching and before the adult form is reached. Larvae are structurally different from adults and often are adapted to a different environment. Some species have free-living larvae but sessile (affixed) adults, the moving larvae thus helping to spread the species; others have aquatic larvae but terrestrial adults. Most larvae are tiny; many are dispersed by entering a host's body, where the adult form of the parasite emerges. Many INVERTEBRATES (e.g., CNIDARIANS) have simple larvae. FLUKES have several larval stages, and ANNELIDS, MOLLUSKS, and CRUSTACEANS have various larval forms. Insect larvae are called CATERPILLARS, grubs, maggots, or worms; the larval stage of many insects may last much longer than the adult stage (e.g., some CICADAS live 17 years as larvae and a week as adults). ECHINODERMS also have larval forms. The larvae of FROGS and TOADS are called TADPOLES. See also METAMORPHOSIS, PUPA.

laryngeal cancer \lə-'rin-jəl\ Malignant tumor of the LARYNX. The larynx is affected by both benign and malignant tumors. Squamous-cell carcinoma, the most common laryngeal malignancy, is associated with smoking and alcohol consumption; it is more common in men. Prolonged hoarseness without pain is the major symptom and should always be investigated. Radiation therapy or surgery may be used to treat tumors.

laryngitis \,lar-ən-'jī-təs\ INFLAMMATION of the LARYNX, causing hoarseness. Simple laryngitis usually occurs with infections such as the common COLD. Other causes include inhalation of irritants. The larynx's lining becomes swollen and secretes mucus. In chronic laryngitis, caused by excessive smoking, drinking, or vocal-cord use, the larynx is dry and has POLYPS. Other types are caused by DIPHTHERIA spreading from the upper throat, TUBERCULOSIS bacteria spreading from the lungs, and advanced SYPHILIS. The last can produce severe scarring and permanent hoarseness.

larynx \'lar-inks\ *or* **voice box** Hollow, tubular structure connecting the PHARYNX with the TRACHEA, through which air passes on the way to the lungs. The larynx consists of a framework of cartilage plates, with a ridge in front (Adam's apple); the epiglottis, a flaplike projection up into the throat that covers the airway during swallowing to keep food and liquid from entering; and the vocal cords, whose vibration produces the sound of the voice (see SPEECH). See illustration opposite.

Las Casas, Bartolomé de (1474–1566) Spanish historian and missionary, called the Apostle of the Indies. He sailed on CHRISTOPHER COLUMBUS's third voyage (1498) and later became a planter on Hispaniola (1502). In 1510 he became the first priest ordained in the Americas. He devoted his life to protesting the mistreatment of the Indians, with whom he worked in Guatemala, Peru, Cuba, Nicaragua, and Mexico. His call for an end to the ENCOMIENDA system aroused implacable opposition. His proposed and quickly regretted solution, the importation of slaves from Africa, was adopted, but the servitude of the Indians had already been irreversibly established. His *Brief Report on the Destruction of the Indians* (1552) and his unfinished *History of the Indians* inspired SIMON BOLIVAR and other revolutionary heroes. See also BLACK LEGEND.

Las Navas de Tolosa \läs-'nä-väs-thā-tō-'lō-sä\, **Battle of** *or* **Battle of Al-'Uqab** \,äl-ù-'käb\ (July 16, 1212) Major battle of the Christian reconquest of Spain. It occurred during a Christian crusade against the Muslim ALMOHAD DYNASTY. Led by King Alfonso VIII, the combined armies of León, Castile, Aragon, Navarre, and Portugal found a secret route through a mountain pass in Andalusia (S Spain) and surprised and defeated the Almohads at a site about 40 mi (65 km) north of Jaén.

Las Palmas (de Gran Canaria) Seaport city (metro. area pop., 1995 est.: 374,000), northeastern Grand Canary Island, Spain. The largest city and chief port of the CANARY ISLANDS, it was founded in 1478 and served as a base for the Spanish conquest of Tenerife and La Palma islands. It grew after the port was constructed in 1883. It is a year-round resort; historic sites include a 15th-century cathedral and the house of CHRISTOPHER COLUMBUS.

Las Vegas City (pop., 1996 est.: 377,000), southeastern Nevada. It is famous for its luxury hotels, casinos, and nightclubs, located in the downtown area known as "The Strip." Mormons from Utah settled the site in 1855 and abandoned it in 1857. It became a railroad town in 1905 and was incorporated in 1911. Gambling was legalized in 1931, and Las Vegas expanded rapidly after 1940. Its connections to crime syndicates began in 1946, when BUGSY SIEGEL opened the Flamingo Hotel. By the late 20th century it was one of the country's fastest-growing metropolitan areas, attracting a year-round population as well as tourists.

Lascaux Grotto \lä-'skō\ Cave near Montignac, France, that contains perhaps the most outstanding known display of prehistoric art. Discovered in 1940, it consists of a main cavern and several steep galleries, all magnificently decorated with engraved, drawn, and painted animals, some of them portrayed in a "twisted perspective." Among the most notable images are four great auroch bulls, a curious unicorn-type animal that may represent a mythical creature, and a rare narrative composition involving a bird-man figure and a speared bison. About 1,500 bone engravings have also been found at the site, which has been dated to the late AURIGNACIAN period (c.15,000 BC). Because of heavy tourist traffic, the cave was closed to the public in 1963, but a full-scale facsimile, Lascaux II, was opened in 1983. See also ROCK ART.

laser Device that produces an intense beam of coherent light (light composed of waves having a constant difference in PHASE). Its name, an acronym derived from "light amplification by stimulated emission of radiation," describes how its beam is produced. The first laser, constructed in 1960 by Theodore Maiman (born 1927) based on earlier work by CHARLES H. TOWNES, used a rod of ruby. Light of a suitable WAVELENGTH from a flashlight excited (see EXCITATION) the ruby ATOMS to higher energy levels. The excited atoms decayed swiftly to slightly lower energies (through PHONON reactions) and then fell more slowly to the ground state, emitting light at a specific wavelength. The light tended to bounce back and forth between the polished ends of the rod, stimulating further emission. The laser has found valuable applications in microsurgery, compact-disc players, communications, and holography, as well as for drilling holes in hard materials, alignment in tunnel drilling, long-distance measurement, and mapping fine details.

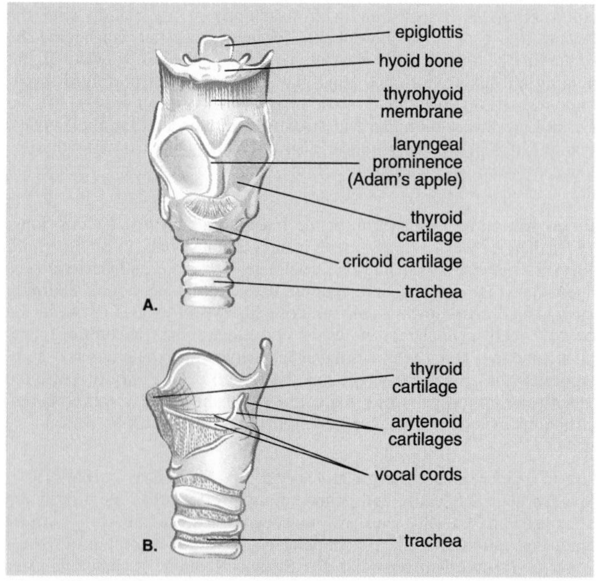

A. Frontal view. The larynx is composed of cartilage plates that are joined together by muscles and ligaments. The thyroid cartilage, the largest, forms a prominence in front called the Adam's apple. The leaf-shaped epiglottis, attached to the upper part of the thyroid cartilage, closes during swallowing. B. Cutaway side view. The vocal cords in the cavity of the larynx are large folds in the mucous membrane lining the larynx. They stretch between the thyroid cartilage in front and the arytenoid cartilages in the back. As air passes between them, they vibrate to emit sound.

Lashley, Karl S(pencer) (1890–1958) U.S. psychologist. Born in Davis, W.V., he taught at the Univs. of Minnesota (1920–29) and Chicago (1929–35) and at Harvard University (1935–55). In *Brain Mechanisms and Intelligence* (1929), he demonstrated that certain types of learning are mediated by the cerebral cortex as a whole, refuting the view that every psychological function is localized at a specific place on the cortex, and showed that some parts of the brain system (e.g., the visual system) can take over the functions of other parts. He also studied the cortical basis of motor activities and the relation between brain mass and learning ability. His paper "The Problem of Serial Order in Behavior" (1951) played a major supporting role in the revolt against simple associative psychology.

Lasker, Emanuel (1868–1941) German chess master. He first won the world championship in 1894 and retained the title until his defeat by JOSE CAPABLANCA in 1921; his term remains the longest reign as world champion in chess history. As the first chess master to demand high fees, he helped strengthen the financial status of chess professionals. He wrote the classic *Common Sense in Chess* (1896) as well as books on mathematics and philosophy. He was forced to leave Nazi Germany in 1933 as a Jew. He returned to chess at age 66 with impressive success.

Laski, Harold J(oseph) (1893–1950) British political scientist, educator, and political leader. After an education at Oxford Univ., he taught at McGill University and Harvard University before returning to Britain to work for the LABOUR PARTY. He later taught at the London School of Economics (1926–50). In the 1930s he argued in such works as *The State in Theory and Practice* (1935) that the economic difficulties of capitalism might lead to the destruction of political democracy, and he came to view socialism as the only available alternative to fascism. He was an assistant to CLEMENT R. ATTLEE during World War II.

Lassalle \lä-ˈsäl\, **Ferdinand** *orig.* **Ferdinand Lasal** (1825–1864) German socialist, a founder of the German labor movement. He took part in the revolution of 1848–49 and established contact with KARL MARX and FRIEDRICH ENGELS. In 1859 he settled in Berlin and became a political journalist. His advocacy of an evolutionary approach to socialism through a democratic constitutional state based on universal suffrage led to his gradual estrangement from Marx. He helped form the General German Workers' Association (1863) and was elected president, but associates rebelled against his authoritarian leadership. In 1864 he went to Switzerland for a rest, fell passionately in love, and was killed in a duel with the woman's former fiancé at 39.

Lassalle, c. 1860.
ARCHIV FUR KUNST UND GESCHICHTE, BERLIN

Lassen Peak *or* **Mount Lassen** Volcano, southern end of the CASCADE RANGE, northeastern California. It erupted on May 30, 1914, and intermittently thereafter until 1921. The peak is 10,457 ft (3,187 m) high and is the principal attraction of Lassen Volcanic National Park, which occupies an area of 106,372 acres (43,081 hectares). In 1821 Luis Argüello, a Spanish officer, became the first European to discover the peak. It is named for Peter Lassen, an explorer who guided settlers through the area.

Lassus \ˈlä-sūs\, **Orlande de** *or* **Orlando di Lasso** \ˈlä-sō\ (1532–1594) Flemish composer. He began as a choirboy (with such a beautiful voice that he is said to have been kidnapped to sing elsewhere), and his first known position was in service to the Gonzaga family in Italy (1544). After 1556 he was based in Munich as chapel master to the duke of Bavaria, but pursued an international career, traveling in Italy, Germany, Flanders, and France. He wrote more than 1,200 works, in every contemporary style and genre, sacred (including some 60 masses and 500 motets) and secular (including hundreds of madrigals and chansons), his attention to the correspondence of music and words being especially remarkable. Because of his range of styles (he always kept up with fashion) and because his works were printed widely during and after his lifetime, he influenced many composers and is regarded as one of the greatest masters of his century.

Last Mountain Lake Lake, southern central Saskatchewan. Draining southward into the QU'APPELLE RIVER, and with an average width of 2 mi (3.2 km) and a length of 60 mi (96 km), it occupies an area of 89 sq mi (231 sq km). It is a popular fishing and resort area.

Lat, al- Northern Arabian goddess of pre-Islamic times. A stone cube near Mecca was held sacred as part of her cult. Two other northern Arabian goddesses, Manat and al-Uzza, are associated with al-Lat in the QURAN. MUHAMMAD once recognized these three as goddesses, but a new revelation led him to abandon his attempt to placate Meccan pagans, and he ordered the sanctuaries of al-Lat and the other two goddesses destroyed. The goddesses were worshiped by Arab tribes located as far away as Palmyra, Syria.

Late Baroque See ROCOCO STYLE

latent heat Characteristic amount of energy absorbed or released by a substance during a change in physical state that occurs without a change in temperature. Heat of fusion is the latent heat associated with melting a solid or freezing a liquid. Heat of VAPORIZATION is the latent heat associated with vaporizing a liquid or condensing (see CONDENSATION) a vapor. For example, when water reaches its BOILING POINT and is kept boiling, it remains at that temperature until it has all evaporated; all the heat added to the water is absorbed as latent heat of vaporization and is carried away by the escaping vapor molecules.

Later Le dynasty \ˈlē\ (1428–1788) Greatest and longest-lasting dynasty of traditional Vietnam. Its founder, LE LOI, drove the Chinese out of Vietnam and began the process of recovering the southern portion of the Indochinese peninsula from the kingdom of CHAMPA. In 1471 the dynasty's greatest ruler, Le Thanh Tong (died 1497), completed that work. He divided the country into provinces patterned on the Chinese model and established a triennial Confucian civil-service examination. After 1533 the Le rulers were only theoretically supreme, real power being held by the Trinh and Nguyen families. In 1771 a peasant uprising toppled the dynasty.

laterality *or* **hemispheric asymmetry** Characteristic of the human BRAIN in which certain functions (such as language comprehension) are localized on one side in preference to the other. One example is handedness (the tendency to use one hand or the other to perform activities): Since the left and right cerebral hemispheres control the right and left sides of the body, respectively, right-handed people are left-dominant in terms of hemispheric control of various motor functions and ordinarily also with respect to seeing (right-eyed) and language comprehension as well. PAUL BROCA first identified the brain center for articulate SPEECH in what is now called Broca's area. Later researchers discovered that functions involving logical or sequential analysis generally reside in the left hemisphere, while the right hemisphere seems to control processing of spatio-visual information and musical relations. More left-handers than right-handers display a reversal of hemispheric specialization or a more even distribution of functions between the two hemispheres. There is no general agreement about whether laterality is genetically transmitted, developed during gestation, or learned.

Lateran Council Any of five ecumenical councils of the Roman Catholic church held in the Lateran Palace in Rome. The First Lateran Council (1123), held during the papacy of CALIXTUS II, reiterated decrees of earlier ecumenical councils (condemning SIMONY, forbidding clergymen to marry, etc.). The Second Lateran Council (1139) was called by Innocent II to end the schism created by the election of a rival pope. The Third Lateran Council (1179), held during the papacy of ALEXANDER III, established a two-thirds majority of the College of Cardinals as a requirement for papal election and condemned the heresies of the CATHARI. INNOCENT III called the Fourth Lateran Council (1215) in an effort to reform the church; its decrees obliged Catholics to make a yearly CONFESSION, sanctioned the doctrine of TRANSUBSTANTIATION, and made preparations for a new CRUSADE. The Fifth Lateran Council (1512–17), convoked by JULIUS II, affirmed the immortality of the soul and restored peace among warring Christian rulers.

Lateran Treaty *or* **Lateran Pact of 1929** Pact of mutual recognition between Italy and the Vatican, signed in the Lateran Palace, Rome. The Vatican agreed to recognize the state of Italy, with Rome as its capital, in return for, among other provisions, formalizing ROMAN CATHOLICISM as the state religion, instituting religious instruction in the public schools, banning divorce, and recognizing papal sovereignty over Vatican City and full independence for the pope. A concordat signed in 1985 ended Catholicism's status as the state religion and compulsory religious education.

laterite \'la-tə-ˌrīt\ Soil layer rich in IRON oxide and sometimes ALUMINUM, derived from a wide variety of rocks by LEACHING. It forms in tropical and subtropical regions where the climate is humid. Laterite is blackish brown to reddish and has been used as an iron ore and, in Cuba, as a source of nickel.

latex Any of several natural or synthetic colloidal suspensions (see COLLOID). Some latexes occur naturally in the cells of plants such as chicle and RUBBER TREES. They are complex mixtures of organic compounds, including various gum RESINS, FATS, or WAXES and, in some instances, poisonous compounds, suspended in a watery medium with dissolved salts, sugars, tannins, alkaloids, enzymes, and other substances from which the latex (or natural RUBBER, the only available rubber until 1926) can be concentrated, coagulated, and vulcanized. Synthetic latexes (e.g., NEOPRENE), made by EMULSION POLYMERIZATION from styrene–butadiene copolymer, acrylate resins, polyvinyl acetate, or other materials, are used as paints and coatings; the PLASTIC, dispersed in the water, forms films by fusion as the water evaporates.

lathe \'lāth\ MACHINE TOOL that performs turning operations in which unwanted material is removed from a workpiece rotated against a cutting tool. Lathes are among the oldest and most important machine tools, used in France from 1569 and important in the INDUSTRIAL REVOLUTION in England, when they were adapted for metal cutting (see HENRY MAUDSLAY). Lathes (usually called engine lathes) today have a power-driven, variable-speed horizontal spindle to which the workholding device is attached. Operations include turning straight or tapered cylindrical shapes, grooves, shoulders, and screw threads and facing flat surfaces on the ends of cylindrical parts. Internal cylindrical operations include most of the common hole-machining operations, such as drilling, boring, reaming, counterboring, countersinking, and threading with a single-point tool or tap. See also BORING MACHINE.

Latimer, Hugh (c. 1485–1555) English Protestant martyr. The son of a prosperous yeoman farmer, he was educated at Cambridge Univ., where he came into contact with the doctrines of MARTIN LUTHER and converted to Protestantism. He supported HENRY VIII's attempt to obtain a marriage annulment, but was later excommunicated for refusing to accept the existence of purgatory or the need to venerate saints. He made a complete submission, and briefly served as bishop of Worcester (1535–39). Again imprisoned on suspicion of heresy, he was freed with the accession of EDWARD VI, during whose brief reign he preached extensively. On MARY I's accession and the subsequent reversion to Catholicism, he was arrested for treason and burned at the stake.

Latin alphabet *or* **Roman alphabet** Most widely used ALPHABET, the standard script of most languages that originated in Europe. It developed before 600 BC from the Etruscan alphabet (in turn derived from the North Semitic alphabet by way of the Phoenician and GREEK alphabets). The earliest known Latin inscriptions date from the 7th–6th cent BC. The classical Latin alphabet had 23 letters, 21 derived from the Etruscan. In medieval times the letter J became differentiated from I, and U and W became differentiated from V, producing the 26-letter alphabet of modern English. In ancient Roman times there were two types of Latin script, capital letters and cursive. Uncial script, mixing both types, developed in the 3rd century AD.

Latin America Countries of SOUTH AMERICA and NORTH AMERICA (including CENTRAL AMERICA and the islands of the CARIBBEAN SEA) south of the U.S.; the term is often restricted to countries where either Spanish or Portuguese is spoken. The colonial era in Latin America began in the 15th–16th century with voyages of discovery to the New World by explorers, including CHRISTOPHER COLUMBUS and AMERICO VESPUCCI. The CONQUISTADORS, including HERNAN CORTES and FRANCISCO PIZARRO, who followed, brought Spanish rule to much of the region. In 1532 the first Portuguese settlement was made in Brazil. The Roman Catholic Church soon established many missions in Latin America; ROMAN CATHOLICISM is still the chief religion in most Latin American countries. Spanish and Portuguese colonists arrived in increasing numbers; they enslaved the native Indian population, which was soon decimated by ill treatment and disease, and then imported African slaves to replace them. A series of movements for independence, led by JOSE DE SAN MARTIN, SIMON BOLIVAR, and others, swept Latin America in the early 19th century. Federal republics were promulgated across the region, but many of the new countries collapsed into political chaos and were taken over by dictators, a situation that persisted into the 20th century. In the 1990s a trend toward democratic rule reemerged; in socialist-run countries many state-owned industries were privatized, and efforts toward regional economic integration were accelerated.

Latin American Free Trade Association (LAFTA) International association of Latin American nations founded in 1960 to improve its members' economic well-being through free trade. It originally comprised Argentina, Brazil, Chile, Mexico, Paraguay, Peru, and Uruguay; by 1970 Ecuador, Colombia, Venezuela, and Bolivia had joined. LAFTA aimed to remove all trade barriers over 12 years, but its members' geographic and economic diversity made that impossible. It was superseded in 1980 by the Latin American Integration Assn., which established bilateral trading agreements between the members, divided into three groups according to their level of economic development. Cuba was admitted with observer status in 1986. See also INTER-AMERICAN DEVELOPMENT BANK.

Latin American music Music of Central and South America and the Caribbean. It combines three basic traditions: indigenous, Spanish-Portuguese ("Iberian"), and African. Indigenous music was as varied as the lives of the indigenous people, which ranged from rural herding and farming to highly urbanized civilizations. Information about indigenous urban music comes mostly from descriptions by Europeans during initial contact; of indigenous rural music, elements have survived in isolated areas, though mixed with European influences. The main instruments seem to have been rattles or shakers (e.g., maracas) and flutes of numerous kinds, including PANPIPES. Under European influence, harps, violins, and guitars were adopted (see MARIACHI). Indigenous scales were three- or five-tone, and choral singing in parallel lines was common in some areas. Spanish and Portuguese music contributed verse forms and self-accompanied solo singing. Iberian dance rhythms are important elements in hybrid forms, as are such dance features as hand clapping and the use of scarves and handkerchiefs. European seven-tone scales and harmonies, especially the common alternation of tonic and dominant chords, are of Iberian origin, as is the use of ground-bass patterns, especially those descending by step from tonic to dominant. African influences on rhythm have included the use of repetitive patterns to accompany extended improvisation, and the prevalence of two- and four-beat patterns, particularly in Caribbean music. The African tradition can also be seen in the use of drums and of syncopation. Another African influence has been the practice of vocal improvisation involving elaborate wordplay.

Latin language INDO-EUROPEAN LANGUAGE of the ITALIC group; ancestor of the modern ROMANCE LANGUAGES. Originally spoken by small groups of people living along the lower TIBER RIVER, Latin spread with the growth of Roman political power, first throughout Italy and then through most of western and southern Europe and the central and western Mediterranean coastal regions of Africa. The earliest known Latin inscriptions date from the 7th century BC; Latin literature dates from the 3rd century BC. A gap soon appeared between literary (classical) Latin and the popular spoken language, Vulgar Latin. The Romance languages developed from DIALECTS of the latter. During the Middle Ages and much of the Renaissance, Latin was the language most widely employed in the West for scholarly and literary purposes. Until the latter part of the 20th century, its use was required in the liturgy of the Roman Catholic church. Latin has a complex system of noun declensions and verb conjugations, with masculine, feminine, and neuter genders.

latite \'lā-ˌtīt\ *or* **trachyandesite** \trā-kē-'an-də-ˌzīt\ Type of igneous rock that is abundant in western North America. Usually white, yellowish, pinkish, or gray, it is the volcanic equivalent of MONZONITE. Latites contain plagioclase FELDSPAR (andesine or oligoclase) as large, single crystals (phenocrysts) in a fine-grained matrix of orthoclase feldspar and augite.

latitude and longitude Coordinate system by which the position or location of any place on the earth's surface can be determined and described. Latitude is a measurement of location north or south of the equator. Lines of latitude are known as parallels, or parallels of latitude. Longitude is a measurement of location east or west of the prime meridian, which passes through Greenwich, England. The combination of meridians of longitude and parallels of latitude establishes a grid by which exact positions can be determined: for example, a point described as 40°N, 30°W is located 40° of arc north of the equator and 30° of arc west of the Greenwich meridian.

Latium \'lā-shē-əm\ Ancient area, western central Italy, on the Tyrrhenian Sea. The Latins (or Latini) came from Indo-European tribes that settled in the Italian peninsula during the 2nd millennium BC. By 500 BC the cities of Latium had formed the Latin League. War broke out between Rome and the Latins in 340 BC and ended in 338 BC with the defeat of the Latins and the dissolution of the league.

Latreille \lȧ-'trāy\, **Pierre-André** (1762–1833) French zoologist, regarded as the father of entomology. An ordained priest, in 1796 he published his *Summary of the Generic Characteristics of Insects, Arranged in a Natural Order,* which led to his becoming head of entomology at the National Museum of Natural History. His principal later work was his *Comprehensive Natural History of Crustaceans and Insects* (14 vols., 1802–5). The two works, representing the first detailed classification of insects and crustaceans, mark the beginnings of modern entomology. In 1829 he took the professorial chair vacated by J.-B. de Monet de Lamarck.

Latrobe \lə-'trōb\, **Benjamin Henry** (1764–1820) British-U.S. architect and civil engineer. He emigrated to the U.S. in 1795. His first important building was the State Penitentiary in Richmond, Va. In 1798, in Philadelphia, he designed the Bank of Pennsylvania, considered the first U.S. monument of the Greek Revival. Pres. Thomas Jefferson appointed him surveyor of public buildings. Latrobe inherited the task of completing the U.S. Capitol, and later rebuilt it after its destruction by the British. In Baltimore he designed the country's first cathedral (1818). He was active as an engineer, especially in the design of waterworks. He is widely regarded as having established architecture as a profession in the U.S.

Latter-day Saints, Church of Jesus Christ of See Mormon

lattice, crystal See crystal lattice

Lattre de Tassigny \'lȧ-trᵊ-də-tȧ-sēn-'yē\, **Jean (-Marie-Gabriel) de** (1889–1952) French military leader. After service in World War I and later in Morocco, he was promoted to general in 1939. An infantry division commander in World War II, he was imprisoned by the Germans 1940–43, but escaped to North Africa. In 1944 he led the French army in the Allied landing operations in southern France and in the drive across France into southern Germany and Austria. He represented France at the signing of the German capitulation (1945). In 1950–51 he commanded French troops in the First Indochina War against the Viet Minh. He was made a marshal of France posthumously.

Latvia *officially* **Republic of Latvia** Country, northeastern Europe, along the shores of the Baltic Sea and the Gulf of Riga. Area: 24,946 sq mi (64,610 sq km). Population (1997 est.): 2,472,000. Capital: Riga. Just over half of the population are Latvians, or Letts, who speak Latvian, one of two surviving Baltic languages. Ethnic Russians make up about one-third of the population. Languages: Latvian (official), Russian. Religions: Lutheranism, Roman Catholicism, Orthodoxy. Currency: lats. Latvia is an undulating plain, with fairly flat lowlands alternating with hills. It is a fully industrialized nation; its leading manufacturing activities are machine building and metal fabrication. Other manufactured goods include ships, transportation equipment, motors, agricultural implements, and textiles. It is a republic with one legislative body; its chief of state is the president, and the head of government is the prime minister. Latvia was settled by the Balts in ancient times. They came under the overlordship of the Varangians, or Vikings, in the 9th century and were later dominated by their German-speaking neighbors to the west, who Christianized Latvia in the 12th–13th century. The Knights of the Sword conquered Latvia by 1230 and established German rule. From the mid-16th to the early 18th century, the region was split between Poland and Sweden, but by the end of the 18th century all of Latvia had been annexed by Russia. Latvia declared its independence after the Russian Revolution of 1917. In 1939 it was forced to grant military bases to the Soviet Union, and in 1940 the Soviet Red Army invaded. Held by Nazi Germany 1941–44, the country was recaptured by the Soviets and incorporated into the Soviet Union (the U.S. did not recognize this takeover). With the Soviet Union breakup, Latvia gained its independence in 1991; throughout the 1990s it sought to privatize the economy and build ties with Western Europe.

Latvian language *or* **Lettish language** East Baltic language spoken by close to 2 million people in the Republic of Latvia and in diaspora communities, including about 85,000 speakers in North America. Like Lithuanian, it is sparsely attested until the first printed books in Latvian appear in 1585–86. The essentials of the present orthography, which employs the Latin alphabet with a number of diacritics, were adopted in 1908. Literary Latvian is based on the dialect spoken in Riga, Latvia's capital, though in recent years there has been a resurgence of literature in High Latvian (Latgalian), the dialect of eastern Latvia. Relative to Lithuanian, Latvian has undergone a number of striking sound changes, though the grammatical structures of the two languages are similar.

Laud, William (1573–1645) Archbishop of Canterbury (1633–45) and religious adviser to Charles I. He became a privy councillor in 1627 and bishop of London in 1628, devoting himself to combating Puritanism and enforcing strict Anglican ritual. By the time he became archbishop of Canterbury he had extended his authority over the whole country. He attacked the Puritan practice of preaching as dangerous, and had Puritan writers such as William Prynne mutilated and imprisoned. Aided by his close ally Thomas Wentworth, he used his influence over the king to influence government social policy. By 1637, opposition to Laudian suppression had grown, and Laud's attempts to impose Anglican forms of worship in Scotland provoked fierce resistance. In 1640 the Long Parliament met, and Laud was accused of high treason. His trial, managed by Prynne, began in 1644, and resulted in Laud's conviction and beheading.

Lauder \'lȯ-dər\, **Estée** *orig.* **Esther Mentzer** (born 1910?) U.S. entrepreneur. Born in New York City, she founded Estée Lauder, Inc., with her husband Joseph in 1946. Their innovative martketing techniques led to huge success in the 1960s and '70s. The company's fragrance and cosmetics products, including Clinique cosmetics and Aramis men's products, are now sold through department and specialty stores in more than 70 countries.

Laue \'lau̇-ə\, **Max (Theodor Felix) von** (1879–1960) German physicist. He taught at the University of Berlin 1919–43. He was the first to use a crystal to diffract X rays, demonstrating that X rays are electromagnetic radiation similar to light and that the molecular structure of crystals is a regularly repeating arrangement. For his work in crystallography he received a 1914 Nobel Prize. He championed Albert Einstein's theory of relativity and studied the quantum theory, the Compton effect, and the disintegration of atoms.

Lauenburg \'lau̇-ən-ˌbu̇rk\ Region and former duchy, northern Germany. It was established as a duchy under the Ascanian dynasty in the 13th century. In 1728 George Louis, elector of HANOVER, became its ruler, thereby attaching it to Hanover. It came under Prussia after the Danish–Prussian War of 1864. The duchy was abolished in 1918, and the region has been part of the state of SCHLESWIG-HOLSTEIN since 1946.

laughing gas See NITROUS OXIDE

laughing jackass See KOOKABURRA

Laughlin \'läk-lin\, **James** (1914–1997) U.S. publisher and poet. Born to a wealthy family in Pittsburgh, Laughlin founded New Directions press in 1936 after graduating from Harvard, initially to publish ignored yet influential writers, including WILLIAM CARLOS WILLIAMS and EZRA POUND, a friend and major influence on his life and work. Its later editions of such authors as DYLAN THOMAS, TENNESSEE WILLIAMS, and HERMANN HESSE (one of the many foreign authors it published in translation) eventually made the house, despite its small size, perhaps the most distinguished literary publisher in the U.S. Laughlin's own poetry is noted for its warmth and biographical frankness.

Laughton \'lȯ-tᵊn\, **Charles** (1899–1962) British-U.S. actor. He made his London stage debut in 1926 and acted in plays such as *The Government Inspector, Three Sisters, Medea,* and *Payment Deferred,* in which he made his New York debut in 1931. He acted in movies from 1929 and earned international acclaim in *The Private Life of Henry VIII* (1933, Academy Award). He was noted for his wide diversity of character roles in such films as *Mutiny on the Bounty* (1935), *Ruggles of Red Gap* (1935), *The Hunchback of Notre Dame* (1939), *Witness for the Prosecution* (1957), and *Advise and Consent* (1962). He directed the memorable *The Night of the Hunter* (1955).

lauma \'lau̇-mä\ In Baltic folklore, a fairy who appeared as a beautiful naked maiden with long blond hair. Laumas lived in the forest near water or stones. They yearned for children, and as they were unable to give birth, they often kidnapped babies to rear as their own. Sometimes they married mortal men and became excellent wives, perfectly skilled in domestic work. Highly temperamental, laumas were seen as benevolent, motherly beings, helpful to orphans and poor girls but extremely vindictive when angered, particularly by disrespectful men. In Latvia and Lithuania in recent centuries, lauma has come to refer to a witch or hag.

Launcelot See LANCELOT

Launceston \'lȯn-sə-stən\ *formerly* **Patersonia** City (pop., 1991: 62,000) and port, northeastern TASMANIA, Australia. Patersonia developed during the 1830s as a whaling port and market center. It is now the largest population and commercial center in northern Tasmania. An export center for a fertile agricultural region, it also has industries, including machine-making factories. One of the world's first hydroelectric stations (built in 1895) lies within the city on the South Esk River.

launch vehicle ROCKET system that boosts a SPACECRAFT into earth orbit or beyond earth's gravitational pull. A wide variety of launch vehicles have been used to lift payloads ranging from a few pounds (or kilograms) to the giant Skylab and Soyuz SPACE STATIONS. Many early launch vehicles were originally developed as intercontinental ballistic missiles (see ICBM). The Saturn V, which carried spacecraft to the moon (see APOLLO program), had three stages. The U.S. SPACE SHUTTLE system (from 1981) represents a significant technical advance, in that the space shuttle can make more than one flight, since most of its principal components can be recovered and refurbished.

"Eleonora of Aragon," portrait bust by Francesco Laurana; in the National Archaeological Museum, Palermo, Sicily.

ALINARI—ART RESOURCE

Laurana \lau̇-'rä-nä\, **Francesco** (c. 1430–1502) Italian (Croatian-born) sculptor and medalist. His early life is obscure. In 1453 he was commissioned to work on the Castel Nuovo in Naples. From 1461 to 1466 he was in Provence at the court of the duke of Anjou, for whom he executed a series of medals. His other documented works include Madonnas and bas-reliefs in Italy (chiefly Sicily and Naples) and France, as well as tombs and architectural sculptures in France. He is best known for his portrait busts of women, characterized by serene, detached dignity and aristocratic elegance.

Laurasia Northern subcontinent of PANGAEA. Formed in the late PALEOZOIC era by the merger of Laurussia with several Asian landmasses, it remained part of Pangaea until its separation from GONDWANA in the early MESOZOIC ERA. During the rest of the Mesozoic era and the early CENOZOIC ERA, it slowly fragmented into the present landmasses of North America, Europe, and Asia (except peninsular India).

Laurel and Hardy U.S. film comedians. Stan (originally Arthur Stanley Jefferson) Laurel (1890–1965) was born in Britain and per formed in circuses and vaudeville before settling in the U.S. in 1910, where he began appearing in silent movies. Oliver Norvell Hardy, Jr. (1892–1957), son of a Georgia lawyer, owned a movie house and acted in silent comedy films from 1913. They joined HAL ROACH's studio in 1926 and began performing together in early short films such as *Putting Pants on Philip* (1927). They made over 100 comedies, including *Leave 'em Laughing* (1928), *The Music Box* (1932), *Sons of the Desert* (1933), and *Way Out West* (1937), and are considered Hollywood's first great comedy team. The skinny Laurel played the bumbling and innocent foil to the fat, pompous Hardy as they converted simple, everyday situations into disastrous tangles of stupidity.

laurel family Family Lauraceae, composed of about 2,200 species of often aromatic and evergreen flowering plants in 45 genera. Included in this family are ornamentals and plants that produce cooking herbs, food fruits, and medicinal extracts. The genus *Laurus* includes bay laurel *(L. nobilis),* native to the Mediterranean, which provides bay leaves for cooking, essential oils for perfumery, and the wreaths that crowned victorious heroes and athletes in ancient Greece. Another genus, *Cinnamomum,* includes the CAMPHOR tree and CINNAMON. Also included in this family are the AVOCADO, MOUNTAIN LAUREL, and SASSAFRAS.

Lauren, Ralph *orig.* **Ralph Lifshitz** (born 1939) U.S. fashion designer. Born in New York, he studied business at night school while working as a department-store salesman. He joined Beau Brummel Neckwear in 1967 and designed the Polo styles for men, later branching into womenswear and then into household goods. He became one of the principal early designers whose names were attached to mass-market fashions, and is famous for the casual elegance of such styles as the "prairie look."

Laurence, Margaret *orig.* **Jean Margaret Wemyss** (1926–1987) Canadian writer. Born in Neepawa, Manitoba, she lived in Africa with her engineer husband in the 1950s; her experiences there provided material for her early works. She is best known for depicting the lives of women struggling for self-realization in the male-dominated world of western Canada. Her works include the novels *The Stone Angel* (1964), *A Jest of God* (1966), and *The Fire-Dwellers* (1969) and the stories collected in *A Bird in the House* (1970) and *The Diviners* (1974). In the 1970s she turned to writing children's books.

Laurence, St. See St. LAWRENCE

Laurentian Mountains \lȯ-'ren-chən\ Range forming the Quebec portion of the CANADIAN SHIELD, bounded by the Ottawa, ST. LAWRENCE, and Saguenay rivers. One of the oldest mountain ranges in the world, it consists of PRECAMBRIAN rocks over 540 million years old. It has greatly eroded over time, and its highest peak measures only 3,905 ft (1,190 m). Two provincial parks there are popular vacation areas.

Laurentide Ice Sheet Principal glacial cover of North America during the PLEISTOCENE EPOCH (1.6 million–10,000 years ago). At its maximum extent it spread as far south as latitude 37°N and covered an area of more than 5 million sq mi (13 million sq km). In some areas its thickness reached 8,000–10,000 ft (2,400–3,000 m) or more.

Laurier \'lȯr-ē-ˌā\, **Wilfrid** *later* **Sir Wilfrid** (1841–1919) Prime minister of Canada (1896–1911). Born in St.-Lin, Canada East (now Quebec), he studied law at McGill Univ., where he was a leading member of the liberal Institut Canadien. He served in the Quebec legislature (1871–74) and the Canadian House of Commons (1874–1919), where in 1885 he delivered a plea for clemency for LOUIS RIEL. He led the Liberal Party to victory in the 1896 election and became prime minister, the first French Canadian and Roman Catholic to hold that office. He advocated unity between English and French Canadians, development of the western territories, protection of Canadian industry, and an expanded transportation system. He championed Canadian autonomy and helped shape the British Commonwealth of independent states. His support for a reciprocity treaty with the U.S. contributed to his government's defeat in 1911. Laurier is remembered as one of Canada's most outstanding statesmen.

Lausanne \lō-'zän\, **Treaty of** (1923) Final treaty concluding WORLD WAR I, between Turkey (successor to the Ottoman empire) and the Allies. Signed in Lausanne, Switzerland, it replaced the Treaty of SÈVRES (1920). It recognized the boundaries of the modern state of Turkey, as well as British possession of Cyprus and Italian possession of the Dodecanese, and the Turkish straits between the Aegean and Black seas were declared open to all shipping.

Lautrec, Henri de Toulouse- See Henri de TOULOUSE-LAUTREC

lava Molten rock originating as MAGMA in the earth's MANTLE that pours out onto the earth's surface through volcanic vents (see VOLCANO) at temperatures of about 1,300–2,200°F (700–1,200°C). MAFIC lavas, such as BASALT, form flows known by the Hawaiian names *pahoehoe* and *aa*. Pahoehoe is smooth and gently undulating; the lava moves through natural pipes known as lava tubes. Aa is very rough, covered with a layer of loose, irregular fragments called clinker, and flows in open channels. Lava that starts out as pahoehoe may turn into aa as it cools. Lavas of intermediate composition form a block lava flow, which also has a top consisting largely of loose rubble, but the fragments are fairly regular in shape, mostly polygons with relatively smooth sides. See also BOMB, NUÉE ARDENTE.

Lava Beds National Monument Region, northern California. It features recent lava flows and related volcanic formations, including deep chasms, chimneys, and cinder cones that rise to 300 ft (90 m) in height. The main battle sites of the MODOC Indian war (1872–73) are located within the monument, which occupies an area of 72 sq mi (186 sq km). It was dedicated as a national monument in 1925.

Laval \lə-'väl\ City (pop., 1996: 330,343), southern Quebec. It occupies the whole of Jesus Island, 20 mi (32 km) long and 8 mi (12 km) wide, and is located north of MONTREAL. First settled in 1681, it was granted to the Society of Jesus (JESUITS) in 1699 and named for François de Laval, the first Roman Catholic Canadian bishop. Development of Jesus Island's Montreal suburbs began after 1945; in 1965 they were merged to form Laval. Development has been rapid with the opening of industrial parks there.

Laval \lä-'väl\, **Carl Gustaf Patrik de** (1845–1913) Swedish scientist, engineer, and inventor. Laval built his first impulse steam TURBINE in 1882. Further advances followed, including a reversible turbine for marine use. A Laval reaction turbine attained a speed of 42,000 revolutions per minute. By 1896 he was operating a complete power plant using an initial steam pressure of 3,400 lbs per sq in. He invented and developed the divergent nozzle to deliver steam to the turbine blades. His flexible shaft and double-helical gear formed the foundation for most subsequent steam turbine development.

Laval \lá-'väl\, **Pierre** (1883–1945) French politician. A member of the Chamber of Deputies (1914–19, 1924–27) and later the Senate (from 1927), he also held a number of cabinet posts, and was premier of France 1931–32 and 1935–36, during which he developed the widely denounced HOARE-LAVAL PACT. In 1940, as minister of state in PHILIPPE PETAIN's government (see VICHY FRANCE), he began negotiations with the Germans on his own initiative, which aroused suspicion. Pétain soon dismissed him, but in 1942 he returned as head of the government. He agreed to provide French laborers for German industries, and announced in a speech that he desired a German victory. In 1945 he was tried and executed as a traitor to France.

Laval University French-language university in Quebec City. Its predecessor institution, the Seminary of Quebec (founded 1663), is considered Canada's first institution of higher learning. The seminary was granted a university charter in 1852 and reorganized in 1970. Today the university has undergraduate and graduate degree programs in numerous fields. Total enrollment is about 36,000.

lavender Any of about 20 species of evergreen shrubs that make up the genus *Lavandula* in the MINT family, the leaves and flowers of which contain scented oil glands. The spikes of flowers are purple, less commonly pink or white. Native to the Mediterranean, lavender is cultivated widely. Several species yield essential oil for fine perfumes and cosmetics. The narrow fragrant leaves and flowers are dried for use in sachets and potpourris. Lavender is widely used in aromatherapy for its clean, fresh scent.

Spanish lavender (*Lavandula stoechas*).

W.H. HODGE

Laver, Rod(ney George) (born 1938) Australian tennis player. Born in Rockhampton, Queensland, he joined Australia's Davis Cup team when he was 18 and remained on the squad until 1962. Nicknamed "Rocket," he became the second male player (after DON BUDGE) to win the Grand Slam (1962) and the first to repeat the feat (1969). He retired in 1971. Having turned professional in 1963, he had become tennis's all-time leading money winner by the time of his retirement.

Lavoisier \lə-'vwä-zē-ˌā\, **Antoine (-Laurent)** (1743–1794) French chemist, regarded as the father of modern chemistry. His work on combustion, oxidation (see OXIDATION-REDUCTION), and GASES (especially those in AIR) overthrew the phlogiston doctrine, which held that a component of matter (phlogiston) was given off by a substance in the process of combustion. That theory had held sway for a century. He formulated the principle of the conservation of MASS (i.e., that the weights of the reactants must add up to the weights of the products) in CHEMICAL REACTIONS, clarified the distinction between ELEMENTS and COMPOUNDS, and was instrumental in devising the modern system of chemical nomenclature (naming oxygen, hydrogen, and carbon). He was among the first to use quantitative procedures in chemical investigations, and his experimental ingenuity, exact methods, and cogent reasoning, along with the resultant discoveries, revolutionized chemistry. He also worked on physical problems, especially heat, and on fermentation, respiration, and animals. Independently wealthy, he had a simultaneous career as a public servant of remarkable versatility in areas including finance, economics, agriculture, education, and social welfare. A reformer and political liberal, he was active in the FRENCH REVOLUTION, but came under increasing attack from extremists and was guillotined.

Lavrovsky \läv-'rȯf-skē\, **Leonid (Mikailovich)** (1905–1967) Russian dancer, choreographer, teacher, and BOLSHOI BALLET director. He studied ballet in St. Petersburg until 1922 and soon was dancing leading roles with the Kirov Ballet, of which he became artistic director in 1938. During 1944–56 and 1960–64 he was chief choreographer of the Bolshoi Ballet, and he became director of its school in 1964. His choreographic work included *Fadetta* (1934), *Romeo and Juliet* (1940), *Giselle* (1944), *The Stone Flower* (1954), and *Night City* (1961).

law Discipline and profession concerned with the customs, practices, and rules of conduct that are recognized as binding by the community. Enforcement of the body of rules is through a controlling authority, such as a group of elders, a regent, a court, or a judiciary. Comparative law is the study of the differences, similarities, and interrelationships of different systems of law. Important areas in the study and practice of law include ADMINISTRATIVE LAW, ANTITRUST LAW, BUSINESS LAW, constitutional law, CRIMINAL LAW, environmental law, family law, health law, immigration law, intellectual property law, INTERNATIONAL LAW, LABOR LAW, MARITIME LAW, PROCEDURAL LAW, property law, public-interest law, tax law, TRUSTS and estates, and TORTS. See also ANGLO-SAXON LAW, CANON LAW, CIVIL LAW, COMMON LAW, EQUITY, GERMANIC LAW, INDIAN LAW, Islamic law (SHARIA), ISRAELI LAW, JAPANESE LAW, JURISPRUDENCE, MILITARY LAW, ROMAN LAW, SCOTTISH LAW, SOVIET LAW.

Law, (Andrew) Bonar (1858–1923) Prime minister of Britain (1922–23), the first born in a British overseas possession. Born in Canada, he was reared in Scotland. He was elected to the House of Commons in 1900 and became leader of the Conservative Party in 1911. He served as colonial secretary 1915–16, and as chancellor of the Exchequer 1916–18, and was leader of the House of Commons 1916–21. After DAVID

L
M
N

LLOYD GEORGE's resignation in 1922, Law formed a Conservative government as prime minister, but resigned seven months later because of ill health.

Law, John (1671?–1729) Scottish monetary reformer. In 1705 he published the banking reform plan *Money and Trade Considered*, in which, unlike other mercantilists, he proposed a central bank as an agency for manufacturing money, as banknotes rather than as gold and silver. France agreed to try his plan in 1716, and he founded the Banque Générale, which was authorized to issue notes. He soon combined it with a company empowered to develop France's North American territories, particularly the lower Mississippi valley. His plan foundered; held responsible for the "Mississippi Bubble" speculative disaster, he fled to France and died in poverty in Venice.

law, philosophy of See JURISPRUDENCE

law code Systematic compilation of law or legal principles. The oldest extant fragments of a code are tablets from the ancient city of Ebla dating to c. 2400 BC. The best-known ancient code is that of HAMMURABI. Roman legal records began in the 5th century BC, but the first formal codification was ordered by JUSTINIAN I in the 6th century AD. In the Middle Ages and into the modern era, only local or provincial compilations were attempted. The first major national code was the NAPOLEONIC CODE, followed by the German, Swiss, and Japanese codes. In COMMON-LAW countries such as England and the U.S., law codes have traditionally been less important than the record of judicial decisions, or precedents, but in the 20th century major codifications have been completed (e.g., the *U.S. Code,* the *Uniform Commercial Code*). See also CIVIL LAW.

Law of the Sea See Law of the SEA

law report In COMMON LAW, a published record of a judicial decision that is cited by lawyers and judges as legal precedent in arguing and deciding cases. The report contains the title of the case, a statement of the facts, a brief case history, the opinion of the court, and the judgment rendered. It often contains a headnote, or analytical summary stating the points decided. The findings of trial courts are not ordinarily reported, but those of appellate courts are.

Lawamon See LAYAMON

Lawes, Henry and William (1596–1662, 1602–1645) English composers. Both brothers served at the court of CHARLES I. Henry became the leading English songwriter of his time; some 435 of his songs survive. His theatrical music included that to JOHN MILTON's masque *Comus* (1634). William wrote a large quantity of instrumental music, mostly for string consorts, and his music for some 25 dramatic productions, including works by BEN JONSON and WILLIAM DAVENANT, made him the principal English theatrical composer before H. PURCELL. He died fighting for his king against OLIVER CROMWELL.

lawn Fine-textured expanse of grass that is kept mowed. A common landscape design element of Western-style gardens and parks, lawns aid in giving a sense of scale and proportion. Made popular in the 18th century by Capability BROWN, the lawn is the antithesis of the French PARTERRE. In the 20th century the lawn became a ubiquitous feature of the gardens of U.S. single-family detached houses, serving to denote ownership and provide a buffer zone between street and private space.

lawn bowls See BOWLS

Lawrence, D(avid) H(erbert) (1885–1930) English novelist, short-story writer, poet, and essayist. The son of a Midlands coal miner and an educated mother, he began to write in 1905 and earned a teaching certificate in 1908. FORD MADOX FORD published much of Lawrence's early work in the *English Review* and helped place his first novel, *The White Peacock* (1911). He often drew his themes from his early life history or from his relationship with his German wife, Frieda, whom he married in 1914. The object of hostility and suspicion during World War I because of his pacifism and her origins, the couple lived in various countries after 1919, never returning to England. *Sons and Lovers* (1913) is an autobiographical novel about working-class family life. *The Rainbow* (1915) and its sequel, *Women in Love* (1920), trace the sickness of modern civilization to the effects of industrialization upon the human psyche. *Kangaroo* (1923) describes the persecution he experienced during the war. *The Plumed Serpent* (1926) was inspired by his fascination with Aztec culture. Lawrence's writing is notable for its intensity and its erotic sensuality; several of his works, including *Lady Chatterley's Lover* (1928), were banned as obscene. He died of the tuberculosis that had plagued him from an early age.

Lawrence, Ernest O(rlando) (1901–1958) U.S. physicist. Born in Canton, S.D., he earned a PhD at Yale University and taught physics at UC–Berkeley from 1929, where he built and directed (from 1936) its radiation laboratory. In 1929 he developed the CYCLOTRON, with which he accelerated protons to speeds high enough to cause nuclear disintegration. He later produced radioactive isotopes for medical use, instituted the use of neutron beams to treat cancer, and invented a color-television picture tube. He worked with the Manhattan Project, converting the Berkeley cyclotron to separate uranium-235 by mass spectrometry. For his invention of the cyclotron, he was awarded a 1939 Nobel Prize, and in 1957 he received the Enrico Fermi Award. Lawrence Berkeley Laboratory and Lawrence Livermore National Laboratory were named in his honor, as was element 103, lawrencium.

Lawrence, Gertrude *orig.* **Gertrude Alexandra Dagmar Klasen** (1898–1952) British actress. She began appearing on stage as a child, and she starred in musical revues in London and New York such as NOEL COWARD's *London Calling* (1923) and GEORGE GERSHWIN's *Oh, Kay!* (1926). A longtime friend of Coward's, she was noted for her performances in many of his comedies, including *Private Lives* (1930) and *Tonight at 8:30* (1936). She was also acclaimed for her roles in the musicals *Lady in the Dark* (1941) and *The King and I* (1951).

Gertrude Lawrence.
CECIL BEATON

Lawrence, Jacob (1917–2000) U.S. painter. Born in Atlantic City, N.J., he moved with his family at 13 to New York's Harlem. Art classes sponsored by the WORKS PROGRESS ADMINISTRATION in 1932 developed his talent. His works portray scenes of African-American life and history with vivid, stylized realism. His best-known works are his series on historical and social themes, such as *Life in Harlem* (1942) and *War* (1947). Gouache and tempera are his characteristic mediums. From 1971 he taught at the University of Washington.

Lawrence, James (1781–1813) U.S. naval officer. Born in Burlington, N.J., he served under STEPHEN DECATUR in the Tripolitan War. In the WAR OF 1812 he commanded the USS *Hornet* in the capture of the British *Peacock.* Promoted to captain of the USS *Chesapeake,* in 1813 he accepted the challenge to a sea fight by the British *Shannon* off the coast of Boston. The *Chesapeake* was defeated in less than an hour, and Lawrence was mortally wounded; his last words, "Don't give up the ship," became one of the U.S. Navy's most cherished traditions.

Lawrence, John (Laird Mair) *later* **Baron Lawrence (of the Punjab and of Grately)** (1811–1879) British viceroy and governor-general of India (1864–69). He worked in Delhi as an assistant judge, magistrate, and tax collector. After the First SIKH WAR (1845–46) he was made commissioner of the newly annexed district of Jullundur, where he subdued the hill chiefs, established courts and police posts, and curbed female infanticide and suttee. On the Punjab board of administration he abolished internal duties, introduced a uniform currency, and encouraged road and canal construction. As viceroy and governor-general from 1864, he promoted increased educational opportunities for Indians but resisted their appointment to high civil-service posts. He avoided entanglements in the affairs of Arabia, the Persian Gulf, and Afghanistan.

Lawrence, St. *or* **St. Laurence** (died 258) Roman martyr. He was one of seven deacons in Rome during the papacy of Sixtus II. When the pope was executed during the persecution of Christians under Valerian, the authorities asked Lawrence to surrender the churches' treasures to the state, and he responded by distributing the money to the poor, for which he was condemned to death. His fearless behavior at his execution was responsible for many conversions; according to one legend, he

L
M
N

was roasted to death on a gridiron, remarking to his torturers, "I am cooked on that side; turn me over, and eat."

Lawrence, T(homas) E(dward) *known as* **Lawrence of Arabia** (1888–1935) British scholar, military strategist, and author. He studied at Oxford, submitting a thesis on crusader castles. He learned Arabic on an archaeological expedition. During World War I he conceived the plan of supporting Arab rebellion against the Turks as a way of undermining Turkey, Germany's ally, and led Arab forces in a guerrilla campaign behind Turkish lines that kept Turkish troops tied up. In 1917 his forces had their first major victory, capturing Aqaba. He was captured later that year, but escaped. His troops reached Damascus in 1918, but Arab factionalism and Anglo-French decisions to divide the area into British- and French-controlled mandates prevented the Arabs from forming a unified nation despite their victory. Lawrence retired, declining royal decorations. Under the name Ross, and later Shaw, he enlisted in the Royal Air Force (and briefly the Royal Tank Corps). He finished his autobiography, *The Seven Pillars of Wisdom,* in 1926. He was eventually posted to India; his experiences provided grist for his semifictional *The Mint*. He died at 46 in a motorcycle accident three months after his discharge.

laws, conflict of Opposition or contradiction in the applicable laws of different states or jurisdictions regarding the rights of the parties in a case. Rules have been created to help determine which set of laws is applicable in a given case, which judicial system is most appropriate for trying the case, and the extent to which other jurisdictions are expected to honor or enforce the outcome of the trial.

lawyer *or* **attorney** Person whose profession is to advise clients as to legal rights and obligations and to represent clients in legal proceedings. Legal practice varies from country to country. In Britain, lawyers are divided into BARRISTERS and SOLICITORS. In the U.S., attorneys often specialize in limited areas of the law (e.g., CRIMINAL LAW, DIVORCE, PROBATE). In France, the most important type of legal professional is the *avocat,* roughly comparable to the English barrister. In Germany, the chief distinction is between lawyers and notaries.

laxative Substance that promotes DEFECATION. These include irritants (stimulants) such as cascara sagrada and castor oil, bulk formers such as bran and psyllium, saline laxatives such as Epsom salts or milk of magnesia, glycerin, lubricants such as mineral oil and some vegetable oils, and stool softeners. A high-fiber diet is more important than laxatives in correcting simple intestinal constipation.

Laxness \'läks-nes\, **Halldór** *orig.* **Halldór Kiljan Guthdjónsson** (1902–1998) Icelandic novelist. He converted to Roman Catholicism while traveling in Europe as a young man, but later dissociated himself from Christianity and turned to socialism, an ideology reflected in his novels from the 1930s and '40s. Works exploring the social issues of Iceland include *Salka Valka* (1936), which deals with the plight of working people in a fishing village; *Independent People* (1935), the story of an impoverished farmer's struggle for economic independence; and the nationalist trilogy *Íslandsklukkan* (1943–46; "Iceland's Bell"). His later works were more lyrical and introspective. He received the Nobel Prize in 1955.

Layamon \'lā-ə-mən\ *or* **Lawamon** \'lò-mən\ (fl. 12th century) Middle English poet. A priest who lived in Worcestershire, he is the author of the romance-chronicle the *Brut* (c. 1200), the outstanding product of the 12th-century English literary revival and the first work in English to treat the ARTHURIAN LEGEND. His source was WACE's *Roman de Brut*. In some 16,000 long alliterative lines, the *Brut* tells of Britain from the landing of Brutus, great-grandson of the Trojan AENEAS, to the final Saxon victory over the Britons in 689.

layering *or* **layerage** Method of propagation in which plants are induced to regenerate missing parts from parts that are still attached to the parent plant. It occurs naturally for drooping black RASPBERRY or FORSYTHIA stems, whose trailing tips root where they come in contact with the soil. They then send up new shoots from the newly rooted portion of the plant. For soil layering, lower stems are bent to the ground and covered with moist soil of good quality. For air layering, a branch is deeply slit and the wound is covered with a ball of earth or moss and kept moist until roots develop; the branch is then severed and transplanted. Layering was practiced by the ancient Egyptians and Greeks. See also CUTTING.

Lazarus In the Gospel of JOHN THE APOSTLE, the man whom JESUS raised from the dead. When Jesus visited Bethany, near Jerusalem, Lazarus' sister Mary lamented that if only Jesus had been there four days earlier, surely he could have prevented her brother from dying. Jesus went to the cave where Lazarus was entombed and commanded him to "come forth," and he did. The miracle inspired many Jews to accept Jesus as the MESSIAH.

Lazarus, Emma (1849–1887) U.S. writer. Born in New York City, she learned languages and the classics at an early age. Her first book (1867) caught the attention of RALPH WALDO EMERSON, with whom she corresponded thereafter. She wrote a prose romance and translated HEINRICH HEINE's poems and ballads. Herself a Jew, she took up the defense of persecuted Jews c. 1881 and began working for the relief of new immigrants to the U.S. The famous closing lines to her poem "The New Colossus" (1883) were inscribed on the base of the Statue of Liberty, dedicated in 1886.

Lazio \'lät-sē-ō\ Autonomous region (pop., 1996 est.: 5,202,000), western central Italy, fronting the Tyrrhenian Sea. Established in 1948, its capital is ROME. In the east are the central APENNINES, and in the west lies a coastal plain. Until the late 19th century, most of its lowlands were marshy and malarial, but in the early 20th century these lands were drained and repopulated. Situated in the region previously known as LATIUM, it supports light industry, but the area is dominated by Rome.

LCD See LIQUID CRYSTAL DISPLAY

LDP See LIBERAL-DEMOCRATIC PARTY

Le Bon \lə-'bōⁿ\, **Gustave** (1841–1931) French social psychologist. After receiving a doctorate in medicine, he traveled and wrote books on anthropology, but his interests later shifted to social psychology. In *The Crowd* (1895) he argued that the personality of the individual in a crowd becomes submerged and that the collective crowd mind comes to dominate.

Le Brun \lə-'brœⁿ\, **Charles** (1619–1690) French painter and designer. After study in Paris and Rome, he received large decorative and religious commissions that made his reputation. Possessing extraordinary organizational as well as technical skills, as the first painter to LOUIS XIV he created or supervised the production of most of the paintings, sculptures, and decorative objects commissioned by the French government for three decades, notably for the Palace of VERSAILLES. As director of the Academy of Painting and Sculpture and organizer of the French Academy at Rome, he was instrumental in establishing the characteristic homogeneity of French art in the 17th century.

Le Carré \lə-kä-'rā\, **John** *orig.* **David John Moore Cornwell** (born 1931) British novelist As a member of the foreign service in West Germany from 1959, he acquired firsthand knowledge of international espionage. He began to write full-time after the success of his third novel, the realistic, suspenseful *The Spy Who Came in from the Cold* (1963; film, 1965). The trilogy of *Tinker, Tailor, Soldier, Spy* (1974), *The Honourable Schoolboy* (1977), and *Smiley's People* (1980) centers on the intelligence agent George Smiley. Other novels include *The Little Drummer Girl* (1983; film, 1984) and *The Russia House* (1989; film, 1990).

Le Châtelier \lə-shä-təl-'yā\, **Henry-Louis** (1850–1936) French chemist. A professor at the Collège de France and the Sorbonne, he is best known for the principle of Le Châtelier, which makes it possible to predict the effect that a change in conditions (TEMPERATURE, PRESSURE, or concentration of components) will have on a CHEMICAL REACTION. The principle, invaluable in the chemical industry in developing the most efficient and profitable chemical processes, may be stated thus: A system at EQUILIBRIUM, when subjected to a perturbation, responds in a way that tends to minimize its effect. Le Châtelier was also an authority on metallurgy, cements, glasses, fuels, explosives, and heat.

Le Corbusier \lə-kòr-bū̄s-'yā\ *orig.* **Charles-Édouard Jeanneret** (1887–1965) Swiss-French architect and city planner. At 13 he began studying enameling and engraving of watch faces; his teacher encouraged him to become an architect. He developed many of his ideas during his travels through Europe (1907–11). After settling in Paris, Le Corbusier (his assumed name, from the surname of an ancestor) and the painter Amédée Ozenfant (1886–1966) formulated the ideas of Purism, with an aesthetic based on modern technology. His early work included theoretical plans for skyscraper cities and mass-produced housing; he

L
M
N

declared that "a house is a machine for living in." The Villa Savoye at Poissy (1929–30), with its structure raised on slender pillars, open floor plan, long strip windows, and roof terrace, embodied his principles of modern housing. Later works include the Unité d'Habitation and the lyrical chapel of Notre-Dame-du-Haut at Ronchamp (1950–55). His government buildings at Chandigarh, India (begun 1950), with their enormous concrete sunshades, sculptural facades, and swooping rooflines, represent the first large-scale application of his city-planning principles. Le Corbusier's many writings gave a firm foundation to the worldwide avant-garde architectural movement he created.

Le Guin \lə-'gwin\, **Ursula K(roeber)** *orig.* **Ursula Kroeber** (born 1929) U.S. writer of science fiction and fantasy. Born in Berkeley, Cal., the daughter of Alfred L. Kroeber, and educated at Radcliffe College, she was influenced by the methods of anthropology and has often included highly detailed descriptions of alien societies in her works. Among her novels are *The Left Hand of Darkness* (1969), *The Word for World Is Forest* (1972), *The Dispossessed* (1974), and *Always Coming Home* (1985) and the Earthsea series.

Le Havre \lə-'hävrᵊ\ Seaport city (pop., 1990: 197,000), northern France. It lies along the English Channel and the Seine River estuary, northwest of Paris. The second port of France after Marseille, it serves as a base for exports; it is also an important industrial center. It was only a fishing village until 1517, when Francis I had a harbor built there. Enlarged and fortified in the 17th century under Richelieu and Louis XIV, it was adapted to accommodate bigger vessels in the late 18th century. Most of the city was destroyed during World War II. Later rebuilt, the city's 17th-century Church of Notre-Dame is one of the few surviving old buildings.

Le Loi \'lā-'lȯi\ *or* **Binh Dinh Vuong** \'bin-'din-'vwȯŋ\ *or* **Thuan Thien** \'twän-'tyen\ (fl. 1428–43) Vietnamese general and emperor who won back independence for Vietnam from China. A wealthy landowner, he was affected by the social conditions of the common people, who suffered under the Chinese and the Vietnamese aristocracy. His series of revolts, begun in 1418, drove the Chinese out. From then on he maintained diplomatic relations with the Chinese Ming dynasty, even sending tribute; the Ming acknowledged his kingdom in 1428. He founded the Later Le dynasty, which lasted for nearly 360 years. Among his achievements were land reforms to help the peasants. He is the most honored Vietnamese hero of the medieval period.

Le Mans \lə-'mäⁿ\, **(Grand Prix d'Endurance)** Automobile race, perhaps the best known in the world, run annually with few exceptions since 1923 at the Sarthe road-racing circuit, near Le Mans, France. The winner is the car that travels the greatest distance in a 24-hour period. The racing circuit is 8.3 mi (13.4 km) long, and the race is open only to sports cars (see sports-car racing).

Le Moyne de Bienville, Jean-Baptiste See Jean-Baptiste Le Moyne de Bienville

Le Moyne d'Iberville, Pierre See Pierre Le Moyne d'Iberville

Le Nain brothers \lə-'naⁿ\ French painters. By 1630 the three brothers—Antoine (c. 1600–1648), Louis (c. 1600–1648), and Mathieu (c. 1607–1677)—had established a workshop together in Paris. They are said to have worked in harmony, often collaborating on the same picture. Most notable of their works are the dignified and sympathetic genre paintings of peasant life. Their realism is unique in 17th-century French art. None of the brothers' works bears more than a surname, and today they are treated as a single painter.

Le Nôtre \lə-'nō-trᵊ\, **André** (1613–1700) French landscape architect. In 1637 he succeeded his father as master gardener to Louis XIII at the Tuileries Palace; he redesigned its gardens and extended the main avenue that later became the Champs-Élysées. Louis XIV placed Le Nôtre in charge of planning the gardens at the Palace of Versailles, which he transformed from a muddy swamp to a park of splendid vistas. He designed numerous other parks and gardens, including St.-Germain-en-Laye, St. Cloud, and Fontainebleau, and probably designed St. James's Park in London. His designs later influenced P.-C. L'Enfant.

Le Pen, Jean-Marie (born 1928) French nationalist politician whose National Front party constituted the main right-wing opposition to the country's mainstream conservative parties from the 1970s through the turn of the 21st century. He was elected in 1956 to the National Assembly as its youngest member. Le Pen helped to found the National Front in 1972, becoming the party's leader later that year. The party emphasized the threat to France posed by immigration, particularly of Arabs from France's former North African colonies. The party also opposed European integration, favored the reintroduction of capital punishment, and sought prohibitions on the building of additional mosques in France. Le Pen ran several times for the presidency; though he captured less than 1 percent of the vote in 1974, in 1988 and 1995 he won some 15 percent. In the presidential election of 2002 Le Pen finished second in the first round of voting, winning 18 percent, though he was easily defeated in the second round. Le Pen was widely regarded as the leader of French neofascism.

leaching Loss of soluble substances and colloids from the top layer of soil by percolating precipitation. The materials are carried downward and are generally redeposited in a lower layer. This transport results in a porous and open top layer and a dense, compact lower layer. In areas of extensive leaching, the remaining quartz and hydroxides of iron, manganese, and aluminum form laterite. In such areas rapid bacterial action results in the absence of humus in the soil, because fallen plant material is oxidized and the products are leached away.

Leacock, Stephen (Butler) (1869–1944) Canadian (British-born) writer and lecturer. He emigrated to Canada with his parents at age 6. Though he taught economics and political science at McGill University (1903–36) and wrote extensively on history and political economy, his true calling was humor. His fame rests on his many books of lighthearted sketches and essays, beginning with *Literary Lapses* (1910) and *Nonsense Novels* (1911). His humor is typically based on a comic perception of social foibles and the incongruity between appearance and reality in human conduct.

Leacock, photograph by Yousuf Karsh.

lead Metallic chemical element, chemical symbol Pb, atomic number 82. Lead is a soft, silvery-white or grayish, malleable, ductile, dense metal that conducts electricity poorly. Its stable isotopes are all end products of radioactive decay of uranium and other heavy elements. Known since ancient times, lead is so durable and resistant to corrosion that Roman lead pipes are still usable. Lead is used in roofing, as cable coverings, and in pipes, conduits, and structures. Other uses are in storage batteries, ammunition, and low-melting-point alloys (e.g., solder, pewter) and as shielding against sound, vibrations, and radiation. Lead is rarely found free in nature; its major ore is the sulfide, galena. Because it and its compounds are poisons (see lead poisoning), lead-based paints and gasoline additives have been banned. Lead in compounds has valence 2 and 4; an oxide (litharge) is the most widely used. Lead compounds are added to lead crystal (see glass), glazes, and ceramics and used as pigments, drying agents for paints and varnishes, insecticides and herbicides, and fireproofing agents and in matches, explosives, and pyrotechnics. Almost half of all lead is recovered from recycled scrap. The "lead" in pencils is graphite.

lead-210 dating Method of age determination that makes use of the ratio of the amount of the radioactive lead isotope lead-210 to that of the stable isotope lead-206. The method has been applied to the ores of uranium. Lead-210 dating is particularly useful for determining the ages of relatively recent marine sediments and so has been applied to studies concerned with the impact of human activity on the aquatic environment.

lead glance See galena

lead poisoning *or* **plumbism** Poisoning by accumulation of lead in the body. Large doses cause gastroenteritis in adults and brain disorders in children. Anemia, constipation and abdominal spasm, confusion, a progressive paralysis, and sometimes brain cancer result from chronic exposure. Children are particularly susceptible to nerve and brain damage; sensitive tests show that even low levels of lead can harm children and are linked to behavioral problems. Sources in the home include lead-based paint, lead drinking-water pipes, and lead-glazed tableware. Babies, who put things in their mouths, are at highest risk. Working where lead is used and exposure to some insecticides are other risk factors. The U.S. phaseout of lead in gasoline was completed in 1996; similar bans are being implemented worldwide. Treatment involves giving ANTIDOTES that bind (see CHELATE) the lead in the tissues.

Leadbelly *orig.* **Huddie (William) Ledbetter** (1885–1949) U.S. folk-blues singer and songwriter. As a child in Mooringsport, La., he learned to play many instruments; he later worked as an itinerant musician with Blind Lemon Jefferson. In 1918 he was imprisoned for murder; he was pardoned in 1925 by the governor of Texas, who had visited the prison and heard him sing. Resuming a life of drifting, he was imprisoned for attempted murder in 1930; he was discovered in 1933 by JOHN LOMAX, who secured his release. Under their guidance he embarked on a concert tour, published 48 songs with commentary about Depression-era conditions of blacks (1936), and recorded extensively. He worked with W. GUTHRIE in the group the Headline Singers. Leadbelly died penniless, but several of his songs, including "Goodnight, Irene," "The Midnight Special," and "Rock Island Line" soon became standards.

leaf Any flattened, green outgrowth from the stem of a VASCULAR PLANT. Leaves manufacture oxygen and GLUCOSE, which nourishes and sustains both plants and animals. Leaves and stem tissue grow from the same apical BUD. A typical leaf has a broad, expanded blade (lamina), attached to the stem by a stalklike petiole. The leaf may be simple (a single blade), compound (separate leaflets), or reduced to a spine or scale. The edge (margin) may be smooth or jagged. Veins transport materials to and from the leaf tissues, radiating from the petiole through the blade. They are arranged in a netlike pattern in dicot leaves and are parallel in monocot leaves (see COTYLEDON). The leaf's outer layer (epidermis) protects the interior (mesophyll), whose soft-walled, unspecialized green cells (parenchyma) produce carbohydrate food by PHOTOSYNTHESIS. In autumn the green CHLOROPHYLL pigments of deciduous leaves break down, revealing other pigment colors (yellow to red), and the leaves drop off the tree. Leaf scars that form during wound healing after the leaves drop are useful for identifying winter twigs. In CONIFERS, evergreen needles, which are a type of leaf, persist for two or three years.

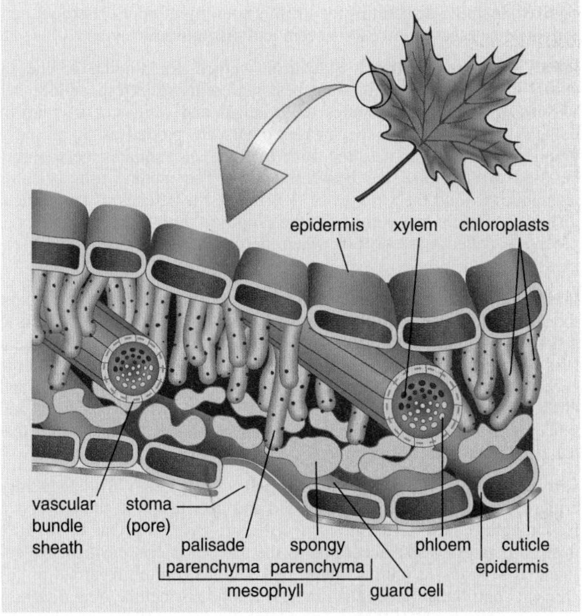

Structures of a leaf. The epidermis is often covered with a waxy protective cuticle that helps prevent water loss from inside the leaf. Oxygen, carbon dioxide, and water enter and exit the leaf through pores (stomata) scattered mostly along the lower epidermis. The vascular or conducting tissues are known as xylem and phloem; water and minerals travel up to the leaves from the roots through the xylem, and sugars made by photosynthesis are transported to other parts of the plant through the phloem. Photosynthesis occurs within the chloroplast-containing mesophyll layer.

leaf-footed bug See SQUASH BUG

leaf insect *or* **walking leaf** Any of about 25 species of flat green insects (family Phylliidae) with a leaflike appearance. Leaf insects, which range from India to the Fiji Islands, are about 2.3 in. (60 mm) long. The female has large leathery forewings (tegmina) that lie edge to edge on the abdomen and resemble, in their vein pattern, the midrib and veins in a leaf. The hind wings have no function. The male has small tegmina and ample, non-leaflike, functional hind wings. The newly hatched young are reddish, but become green after feeding on leaves.

leaf miner Any of various insect larvae that live and feed within a leaf, including CATERPILLARS, SAWFLY larvae, BEETLE and WEEVIL grubs, and DIPTERAN maggots. Most leaf-miner burrows or tunnels are either thin, winding, whitish trails or broad, whitish or brownish blotches. Though leaf miners do not usually cause injury, they mar the appearance of ornamental trees and shrubs. One method of control is to remove and burn infested leaves; spraying with nicotine solutions or dusting with insecticides is effective only when the adults are emerging.

leafhopper Any of the small, slender, often beautifully colored and marked sapsucking insects of the large family Cicadellidae. There is a leafhopper species for almost every type of plant. Most are less than 0.5 in. (12 mm) long. Leafhoppers can be serious economic pests. Their feeding may remove sap, destroy chlorophyll, transmit disease, or curl leaves; they also puncture the host plant while laying eggs. Hopperburn is a diseased condition caused by their injection of a toxin into the plant as they feed.

Red-banded leafhopper (*Graphocephala*).

STEPHEN COLLINS—PHOTO RESEARCHERS/EB INC.

League of Arab States See ARAB LEAGUE

League of Nations Organization for international cooperation established by the ALLIED POWERS at the end of WORLD WAR I. A league covenant, embodying the principles of collective security and providing for an assembly, a council, and a secretariat, was formulated at the PARIS PEACE CONFERENCE (1919) and contained in the Treaty of VERSAILLES. The covenant also set up a system of colonial mandates. Headquartered at Geneva, the League was weakened by the nonadherence of the U.S., which had not ratified the Treaty of Versailles. Discredited by its failure to prevent Japanese expansion in Manchuria and China, Italy's conquest of Ethiopia, and Germany's seizure of Austria, the League ceased its activities during World War II. It was replaced in 1946 by the UNITED NATIONS.

Leahy \'lā-hē\, **William D(aniel)** (1875–1959) U.S. naval officer. Born in Hampton, Iowa, he graduated from Annapolis and served in the Spanish-American War, the Philippine insurrection, and the Boxer Rebellion. He commanded a navy transport in World War I, when he began a friendship with FRANKLIN ROOSEVELT, then assistant secretary of the navy. He became chief of naval operations in 1937–39, was appointed governor of Puerto Rico (1939) and U.S. ambassador to France (1940), and served as Roosevelt's chief of staff during World War II, continuing in that post under HARRY TRUMAN. He was made a fleet admiral in 1944.

Leakey family Family of archaeologists and paleoanthropologists known for their discoveries of HOMINID and other fossil remains in eastern Africa. Louis S. B. Leakey (1903–1972), born of British missionary parents, grew up in Kenya, was educated at Cambridge Univ., and eventually (1931) came to do field research at OLDUVAI GORGE in Tanzania. He was joined there by his wife, Mary D. Leakey (1913–1996), who in 1959 uncovered remains of a form of *AUSTRALOPITHECUS*. The couple later uncovered the first known remains of *HOMO HABILIS*, as well as those of *Proconsul*, a common ancestor of both humans and apes (lived c. 25 million years ago), and *Kenyapithecus*, another ape–human link (lived c. 14 million years ago). L. S. B. Leakey persuaded both JANE GOODALL and DIAN FOSSEY to undertake their pioneering studies of chimpanzees and gorillas. Mary Leakey continued to make important discoveries, including the LAETOLI FOOTPRINTS, after her husband's death. Their son, Richard Leakey (born 1944), is known for his work at the Koobi Fora site on the shores of LAKE TURKANA in Kenya, where he uncovered evidence of *H. habilis* in Africa as early as 2.5 million years ago.

Leal, Juan de Valdés See Juan de VALDES LEAL

Lean, David *later* **Sir David** (1908–1991) British film director. He worked at Gaumont Studios from 1928, becoming head film editor. He codirected *In Which We Serve* (1942) with NOEL COWARD and was sole director of Coward's *Blithe Spirit* (1945) and *Brief Encounter* (1945). He directed film adaptations of *Great Expectations* (1946) and *Oliver Twist* (1948). He won wide acclaim for *The Bridge on the River Kwai* (1957, Academy Award) and later for *Lawrence of Arabia* (1962, Academy Award), *Dr. Zhivago* (1965), and *A Passage to India* (1984).

Leaning Tower of Pisa White marble CAMPANILE in Pisa, Italy, famous for the uneven SETTLING of its foundation, which caused it to lean 5.5 degrees (about 15 ft [4.5 m]) from the perpendicular. Begun in 1173 as the third and final structure of the city's cathedral complex, it was designed to stand 185 ft (56 m) high. Work was suspended several times as engineers sought solutions; the tower, still leaning, was completed in the 14th century. Subsiding at the rate of 0.03 in (1.2 mm) a year, the structure was in danger of collapse, and in 1990 it was closed as engineers undertook a strengthening project that decreased the lean by 17 in (44 cm) to about 13.5 ft (4.1 m). The work was completed in May 2001.

Lear, Edward (1812–1888) English painter and comic poet. From age 15 he earned his living by drawing. Employed to illustrate the earl of Derby's private menagerie in the 1830s, he later produced *Book of Nonsense* (1846) for the earl's grandchildren. Later volumes include *Nonsense Songs, Stories, Botany and Alphabets* (1871), containing "The Owl and the Pussy-Cat," and *Laughable Lyrics* (1877). He is best known for popularizing the LIMERICK. He also published volumes of bird and animal drawings and seven illustrated travel books. Epileptic, homosexual, and depressive, he lived mainly abroad after 1837.

Edward Lear, drawing by William Holman Hunt, 1857; in the Walker Art Gallery, Liverpool.

BY COURTESY OF THE WALKER ART GALLERY, LIVERPOOL

Lear, Norman (Milton) (born 1922) U.S. television producer, writer, and director. Born in New Haven, Conn., he worked in public relations and later in television as a comedy writer and director (1950–59). He wrote and produced such movies as *Come Blow Your Horn* (1963), *Divorce American Style* (1967), and *Cold Turkey* (1971) before returning to television to create and produce such hit series as *All in the Family* (1971–83), for which he received four Emmy awards; *Maude* (1972–78); *Sanford and Son* (1972–77); and *The Jeffersons* (1975–85). He founded the progressive activist group People for the American Way.

Lear, William Powell (1902–1978) U.S. electrical engineer and industrialist. Born in Hannibal, Mo., he founded the Lear Avia Corp. to make radio and navigational devices for aircraft. In World War II, the company manufactured cowl-flap motors and other precision devices for Allied aircraft. After the war, Lear, Inc., introduced a miniaturized autopilot that could be used on small fighter aircraft. In 1963 Lear formed Lear Jet, Inc., whose jets became among the world's most popular private jet aircraft.

learned helplessness In psychology, a mental state in which a laboratory subject forced to bear aversive stimuli becomes unable or unwilling to avoid subsequent applications, even if "escapable," presumably through having learned that situational control is generally out of his or her hands. Experiments, first on dogs and later on humans, have led some researchers, including Martin E. P. Seligman (born 1942) in *Helplessness* (1975), to believe that chronic failure, depression, and similar conditions are forms of learned helplessness. Critics have argued that different conclusions can be drawn from such tests and that broad generalizations are unwarranted.

learning Process of acquiring modifications in existing knowledge, skills, habits, or tendencies through experience, practice, or exercise. Learning includes associative processes (see ASSOCIATION, CONDITIONING), discrimination of SENSE-DATA, psychomotor and perceptual learning (see PERCEPTION), imitation, CONCEPT FORMATION, PROBLEM SOLVING, and insight learning. Animal learning has been studied by ethologists and comparative psychologists, the latter often drawing explicit parallels to human learning (see COMPARATIVE PSYCHOLOGY, ETHOLOGY). The first experiments concerning associative learning were conducted by IVAN PAVLOV in Russia and EDWARD L. THORNDIKE in the U.S. Critics of the early stimulus-response (S-R) theories, such as EDWARD C. TOLMAN, claimed they were overly reductive and ignored a subject's inner activities. GESTALT-PSYCHOLOGY researchers drew attention to the importance of pattern and form in perception and learning, while structural linguists argued that language learning was grounded in a genetically inherited "grammar." Developmental psychologists, such as JEAN PIAGET, highlighted stages of growth in learning. More recently, cognitive scientists have explored learning as a form of INFORMATION PROCESSING, while some brain researchers, such as GERALD MAURICE EDELMAN, have proposed that thinking and learning involve an ongoing process of cerebral pathway building. Related topics of research include ATTENTION, COMPREHENSION, MOTIVATION, and transfer of TRAINING. See also BEHAVIOR GENETICS, BEHAVIORISM, EDUCATIONAL PSYCHOLOGY, IMPRINTING, INSTINCT, INTELLIGENCE.

learning disabilities Chronic difficulties in learning to read, write, spell, or calculate, which are believed to have a neurological origin. Though their causes and nature are still not fully understood, it is widely agreed that the presence of a learning disability does not indicate subnormal intelligence. Rather it is thought that the learning-disabled have a neurologically based difficulty in processing language or figures, which must be compensated for with special learning strategies or with extra effort and tutoring. Examples of learning disabilities include difficulty in reading (DYSLEXIA), writing (dysgraphia), and mathematics (dyscalcula). Learning disabilities may be diagnosed through testing, and children may be enrolled in programs offering special help; left unrecognized, learning disabilities may result not only in poor classroom performance but also in low self-esteem and disruptive behavior.

least squares method Statistical method for finding a line or curve—the line of best fit—that best represents a correspondence between two measured quantities (e.g., height and weight of a group of college students). When the measurements are plotted as points on a graph and seem to fall near the same line, the least squares method may be used to determine the best-fitting line. The method uses calculus techniques to find the MINIMUM of the sum of the squares of the vertical distances of each data point from the proposed line. More generally, the process is called REGRESSION or, when the fitted curve is a line, linear regression.

leather Animal skins and hides treated to preserve them and make them suitable for use. TANNING converts the otherwise perishable skin to a stable and nondecaying material. Though the skins of such diverse animals as ostrich, lizard, eel, and kangaroo have been used, the more common leathers come from cattle, including calf and ox; sheep and lamb; goat and kid; horse, mule, and zebra; buffalo; pig and hog; and seal, walrus, whale, and alligator. Leather making is an ancient art that has been practiced for more than 7,000 years. See also PARCHMENT.

Leavis \'lē-vəs\, **F(rank) R(aymond)** (1895–1978) British literary critic. Born in Cambridge, he attended and later taught at the university. He brought a new seriousness to criticism, believing that the critic's duty is to assess works according to the author's moral position. He cofounded *Scrutiny*, a journal (published 1932–53) often regarded as his greatest contribution to English letters. His books include *New Bearings in English Poetry* (1932) and *The Great Tradition* (1948), in which he reassessed the English novel.

Lebanese civil war (1975–91) Conflict resulting from the presence in Lebanon in the 1970s of the PALESTINE LIBERATION ORGANIZATION (PLO) and exacerbated by tensions among Lebanon's Christian and Muslim populations. In 1975 Lebanon's Muslims supported the PLO and sought more political power; its Christians, seeking to maintain their political dominance, opposed the PLO. The factions fought fiercely through early 1976, and Lebanon became effectively partitioned, with the Christians in power in the north and Muslims in the south. Israel invaded southern Lebanon in 1982 to destroy Palestinian bases; PLO leaders and troops were driven out of Beirut, and by 1985 Israel had withdrawn from most of Lebanon, which by then was split internally over whether to accept Syria's leadership. In 1989 the Christian leader Gen. Michel Aoun attempted to drive Syria from Lebanon but was defeated, and the Arab League mediated a peace deal; his removal from power in 1990 eliminated the largest obstacle to implementing the 1989 peace. In southern Lebanon, fighting between Israeli and Hizbullah forces continued through the 1990s.

Lebanese National Pact Power-sharing arrangement established in 1943 between Lebanese Christians and Muslims whereby the president is always a Christian and the prime minister a Sunni Muslim. The speaker of the National Assembly must be a Shiite Muslim. Amendments made following the Lebanese civil war transferred many presidential powers to a half-Christian, half-Muslim cabinet.

Lebanon *officially* **Republic of Lebanon** Country, eastern shore of the Mediterranean Sea. It is bounded by Syria and Israel. Area: 3,950 sq mi (10,230 sq km). Population (1997 est.): 3,112,000. Capital: Beirut. The Lebanese are ethnically a mixture of Phoenician, Greek, Armenian, and Arab elements. Languages: Arabic (official), French, English. Religions: Islam (Sunnite and Shiite), Christianity (Maronite, Greek Orthodox). Currency: Lebanese pound. Its mountains include the Lebanon Mtns. in the central region and the Anti-Lebanon and Mount Hermon ranges along the eastern border; a low coastal plain stretches along the Mediterranean. The Litani River flows southward through the fertile Bekaa Valley. Originally much of the country was forested (the cedars of Lebanon were famous), but forests now cover only about 8% of the ter-

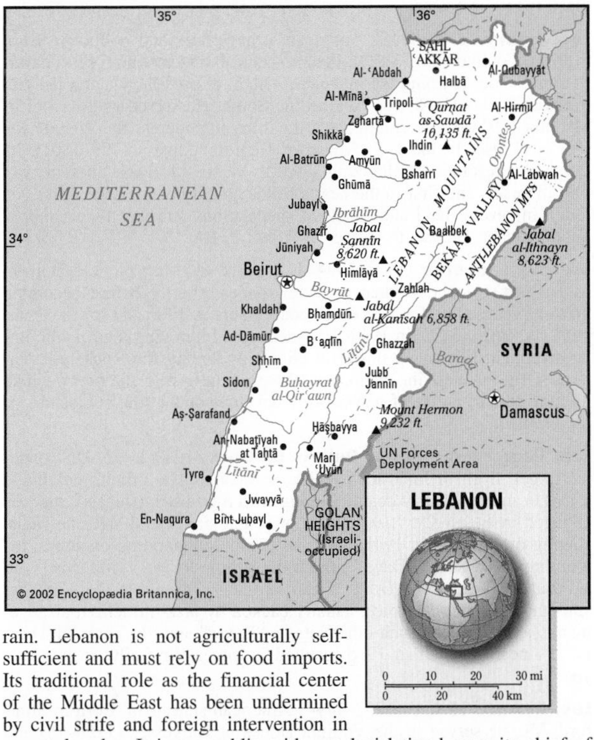

rain. Lebanon is not agriculturally self-sufficient and must rely on food imports. Its traditional role as the financial center of the Middle East has been undermined by civil strife and foreign intervention in recent decades. It is a republic with one legislative house; its chief of state is the president, and the head of government is the prime minister. Much of present-day Lebanon corresponds to ancient Phoenicia, which was settled c. 3000 BC. In the 6th century AD, Christians fleeing Syrian persecution settled in northern Lebanon and founded the Maronite Church. Arab tribesmen settled in southern Lebanon and by the 11th century had founded the Druze faith. Part of the medieval crusader states, Lebanon was later ruled by the Mamluks. In 1516 the Ottoman Turks seized control; the Turks ended the local rule of the Druze Shihab princes in 1842. Poor relations between religious groups resulted in the massacre of Maronites by Druze in 1860. France intervened, forcing the Ottomans to form an autonomous province for the Christian area known as Mount Lebanon. Following World War I, it was administered by the French military, but by 1946 it was fully independent. After the Arab–Israeli War of 1948–49, over 200,000 Palestinian refugees settled in southern Lebanon. In 1970 the Palestine Liberation Organization (PLO) moved its headquarters to Lebanon and began raids into northern Israel. The Christian-dominated Lebanese government tried to curb them, and in response the PLO sided with Lebanon's Muslims in their conflict with Christians, sparking a civil war by 1975. In 1976–82 Syrian and U.N. troops tried to maintain a cease-fire. In 1982 Israeli forces invaded in an effort to drive Palestinian forces out of southern Lebanon; Israeli troops withdrew in 1985, leaving the conflict unresolved. Israeli troops returned, but a cease-fire was agreed to in 1996. It was broken when Israeli soldiers and Lebanon's Hizbullah forces clashed in 1997. Following numerous contentious talks between Lebanon and Israel, Israeli troops abruptly withdrew from Lebanon in 2000.

Lebanon Mountains *Arabic* **Jabal Lubnan** \'ja-bəl-,lüb-'nän\ *ancient* **Libanus.** Mountain range, Lebanon. Running parallel to the Mediterranean coast, they are about 100 mi (160 km) long. The northern section is the highest part of the range and includes the tallest peak, Qurnet al-Sauda, at 10,131 ft (8,088 m) high. On the western flanks are the remaining groves of the Cedars of Lebanon. The snowy peaks may have given Lebanon its name in antiquity; *laban* is Aramaic for "white."

Lebowa \le-'bō-wə\ Former nonindependent black state, northern Transvaal, South Africa. It was designated by the South African government as the national territory for northern Sotho people, including the Pedi, Lovedu, and Kanga-Kone. It was granted self-government in 1972 and held its first election in 1973. After the abolition of apartheid in 1994, it became part of the new Northern province.

Lebrun \lə-'brœⁿ\, **Albert** (1871–1950) French statesman and last president (1932–40) of France's Third Republic. Trained as a mining engineer, he served in the Chamber of Deputies (1900–20) and Senate (1920–32). He was elected president as a compromise candidate and served as a mediator and symbol of unity, rarely influencing policy. In 1940 he complied with the cabinet's decision to seek an armistice with Germany and to his replacement by the Vichy France government. He was interned by the Germans 1943–44. In 1944 he acknowledged Charles de Gaulle as head of the provisional government.

Lebrun, Elisabeth Vigée- See Elisabeth Vigee-Lebrun

Lechfeld \'lek-,felt\, **Battle of** (955) Battle in which the German king Otto I decisively defeated an invasion by the Magyars. Fought on the Lechfeld, a plain near present-day Augsburg, Germany, it marked the last Hungarian effort to invade Germany.

lecithin \'le-sə-thən\ Any of a class of phospholipids (also called phosphatidyl cholines) important in cell structure and metabolism. They are composed of phosphate, choline, glycerol (as the ester), and two fatty acids. Various fatty acids pairs distinguish the various lecithins. Commercial lecithin, a wetting and emulsifying agent used in animal feeds, baking products and mixes, chocolate, cosmetics and soap, insecticides, paint, and plastics, is a mixture of lecithins and other phospholipids in an edible oil.

Leclerc \lə-'kler\, **Jacques-Philippe** *orig.* **Philippe-Marie, vicomte (Viscount) de Hauteclocque** (1902–1947) French general in World War II. He was captured by the Germans in 1939, but escaped to England, where he took the pseudonym Leclerc to protect his family and joined the Free French forces of Charles de Gaulle. He achieved a number of military victories in French Equatorial Africa and North Africa, and in 1944 he commanded a French division in the Normandy invasion. On August 25 he received the surrender of the German commander in Paris. He died in an airplane accident and was named marshal of France posthumously.

lectisternium \,lek-tə-'stər-nē-əm\ (from Latin *lectum sternere,* "to spread a couch") Ancient Greek and Roman rite in which a meal was offered to gods and goddesses whose images were laid on a couch placed in the street. When it originated in Greece, couches were prepared for three pairs of gods: Apollo and Latona, Heracles and Diana, and Mercury and Neptune. During the feast, which lasted seven or eight days, citizens kept open house, debtors and prisoners were released, and every effort was made to banish sorrow. Other gods were later honored

L M N

with the same rite. In Christian times, the word was used for a feast in memory of the dead.

LED See LIGHT-EMITTING DIODE

Leda \'lē-də\ In Greek legend, the daughter of King Thestius of Aetolia and wife of King Tyndareus of Lacedaemon. Visited by ZEUS in the form of a swan, she conceived HELEN of Troy. Zeus was also sometimes said to be the father of her son Pollux, while Leda's own husband, Tyndareus, was held to be the father of his twin, Castor (see DIOSCURI). Tyndareus was also the father of Leda's daughter Clytemnestra, who married AGAMEMNON.

Lederberg \'lā-dər-ˌberg\, **Joshua** (born 1925) U.S. geneticist. Born in Montclair, N.J., he earned a PhD at Yale University. With his student NORTON ZINDER, Lederberg discovered that certain viruses were capable of carrying a bacterial gene from one bacterium to another, a discovery that made bacteria as important a tool of genetic research as drosophila and the bread mold *Neurospora.* He also developed ingenious breeding techniques for bacterial genetics. In 1958 he shared the Nobel Prize with GEORGE WELLS BEADLE and EDWARD L. TATUM for discovery of the mechanisms of genetic recombination in bacteria.

Ledo Road See STILWELL ROAD

Ledoux \lə-'dü\, **Claude-Nicolas** (1736–1806) French architect. In the 1760s and early 1770s he designed private houses in an innovative Neoclassical style, among them Madame du Barry's famous château at Louveciennes (1771–73). In the mid-1770s he planned a new saltworks and surrounding town at the Salines de Chaux, Arc-et-Senans; the design, in which rings of workers' dwellings enclosed a central factory, both facilitated production and ensured healthy conditions for workers. His theater at Besançon (1771–73) was revolutionary in its provision of seats for the ordinary public as well as the upper classes. The elaborate *barrières* (tollhouses) he designed for Paris (1785–89) were ruinously expensive, and Ledoux was removed from the project. Arrested during the French Revolution, he did not practice after his release.

Ledru-Rollin \lə-'drü̅-ró-'lan\, **Alexandre-Auguste** (1807–1874) French radical politician. He was elected to the Chamber of Deputies in 1839, but his insistence on republican government isolated him from other leftists. Following the FEBRUARY REVOLUTION, through his influence as minister of the interior in the provisional government (1848), elections for a new legislature were held for the first time under universal manhood suffrage. In 1849 he demanded the impeachment of Louis-Napoléon (later NAPOLEON III) and led an unsuccessful insurrection. He fled to England, but returned to France after the amnesty of 1870.

Lee, Ang (born 1954) Taiwanese-U.S. film director. He moved to the U.S. in 1978, where he initially worked writing screenplays. He wrote and directed *Pushing Hands* (1992) and later the offbeat comedies *The Wedding Banquet* (1993) and *Eat Drink Man Woman* (1994), which were acclaimed internationally, directed the well-received *Sense and Sensibility* (1995), wrote and directed *The Ice Storm* (1997), and directed the martial-arts epic *Crouching Tiger, Hidden Dragon* (2000).

Lee, Ann (1736–1784) British-American religious leader. A factory worker in her youth in Manchester, England, she joined the SHAKERS in 1758 and was acknowledged as their leader in 1770. Persecuted by the English authorities and commanded by a vision, she emigrated to America in 1774. With a band of followers, she founded a settlement at Niskeyuna (present-day Watervliet), N.Y., in 1776, whence the movement spread rapidly. Mother Ann, as she came to be known, is said to have performed miracles, including healing the sick by touch. She was imprisoned briefly for treason because of her pacifist doctrines and refusal to sign an oath of allegiance.

Lee, Bruce *orig.* **Lee Yuen Kam** (1940–1973) U.S. film actor. Born in San Francisco, the son of a touring Chinese opera star, he spent his childhood in Hong Kong, where he acted in several movies. In the early 1970s he became the very popular star of martial-arts action films, including *The Chinese Connection* (*Fist of Fury,* 1972) and *Enter the Dragon* (1973), which gained an international cult following. His career was cut short by his sudden death at 33 from a brain edema. His son Brandon Lee (1965–1993) was emerging as an action-movie star when he died in a shooting accident on a movie set.

Lee, Gypsy Rose *orig.* **Rose Louise Hovick** (1914–1970) U.S. striptease artist. Born in Seattle, she appeared in a vaudeville act with her sister from 1919 and made her debut in burlesque in 1929. She became the headliner at Billy Minsky's Republic Theatre on Broadway (1931) and appeared in the *Ziegfeld Follies* (1936). Noted for her grace and style, she became the most famous stripper of all time. After retiring from burlesque (1937), she appeared in nightclubs and on television. Her autobiography *Gypsy* (1957) was the basis for a successful 1959 musical (film, 1962).

Gypsy Rose Lee, 1944.

BY COURTESY OF UNITED ARTISTS CORPORATION; PHOTOGRAPH, FROM THE MUSEUM OF MODERN ART FILM STILLS ARCHIVE, NEW YORK

Lee, Harper (b. 1926) American novelist. The daughter of a lawyer, Lee attended the University of Alabama but left for New York City before obtaining her own law degree. An editor helped her transform a series of short stories into the novel *To Kill a Mockingbird* (1960). The only novel that Lee was to publish, it was nationally acclaimed, winning a Pulitzer Prize in 1961. It became a memorable film in 1962. The novel's hero is the lawyer Atticus Finch, whose just and compassionate acts include an unpopular defense of a black man falsely accused of raping a white girl.

Lee, Henry (1756–1818) American army officer and politician. Born in Prince William Co., Va., in the AMERICAN REVOLUTION he rose to cavalry commander (earning the nickname "Light-Horse Harry") and led victories at Paulus Hook, N.J., and in the South. He served as governor of Virginia 1791–94. He commanded the army to suppress the WHISKEY REBELLION (1794). In the U.S. House of Representatives (1799–1801), he wrote the resolution eulogizing GEORGE WASHINGTON as "first in war, first in peace, and first in the hearts of his countrymen." After 1800 Lee failed in several land and financial speculations and was twice imprisoned for debt. He was the father of ROBERT E. LEE.

Lee, Ivy Ledbetter (1877–1934) U.S. PUBLIC-RELATIONS pioneer. Born in Cedartown, Ga., he worked as a newspaper reporter before becoming press representative for a group of coal miners in 1906 and for the PENNSYLVANIA RAILROAD CO. in 1912. His success in improving their public images brought him many powerful clients, including the Rockefeller interests. His greatest innovation was his frankness with the press, which he took care to notify of newsworthy developments at the companies he represented.

Lee, Peggy *orig.* **Norma Deloris Egstrom** (1920–2002) U.S. popular singer. Born in Jamestown, N.D., she endured a difficult childhood after her mother's early death. Singing with a group in Chicago, she was engaged by BENNY GOODMAN as his principal singer in 1941. She began singing on her own in 1943, and also began collaborating on songs, often with her husband, Dave Barbour, including "Fever," "Mañana," and several songs for WALT DISNEY's *Lady and the Tramp* (1955). With her smooth, lightly husky voice, usually backed by jazz-influenced arrangements, she produced such other hits as "Lover" and "Is That All There Is?" A near-fatal fall in 1976 resulted in increasing frailty in her later years.

Lee, Richard Henry (1732–1794) American statesman. Born in Stratford, Va., he served in the Virginia House of Burgesses (1758–75) and opposed the Stamp Act and the Townshend Acts. He helped initiate the COMMITTEES of Correspondence and was active in the Continental Congress. On June 7, 1776, he introduced a resolution calling for independence from Britain. It was adopted and led to the Declaration of Independence, which he signed, as he did the Articles of Confederation. He served in the Congress 1784–89 and as its president 1784–85. He opposed ratification of the U.S. Constitution because it lacked a bill of rights but later served in the first U.S. Senate (1789–92).

Lee, Robert E(dward) (1807–1870) U.S. and Confederate military leader. Born in Stratford, Va., the son of HENRY LEE, he graduated from

West Point, then served in the engineering corps and in the Mexican War under WINFIELD SCOTT. He transferred to the cavalry in 1855 and commanded frontier forces in Texas 1856–57. In 1859 he led U.S. troops to suppress JOHN BROWN's insurgents at Harpers Ferry. In 1861 he was offered command of U.S. troops to force the seceded Southern states back into the Union. Though opposed to secession, he refused. After his home state of Virginia seceded, he became commander of Virginia's forces in the AMERICAN CIVIL WAR and adviser to JEFFERSON DAVIS. After JOSEPH JOHNSTON was wounded, Lee was given command of the Army of Northern Virginia (1862) and repulsed the Union forces in the SEVEN DAYS' BATTLES. He won victories at BULL RUN, FREDERICKSBURG, and CHANCELLORSVILLE. His attempts to draw Union forces out of Virginia by invading the North resulted in failures at ANTIETAM and GETTYSBURG. In 1864–65 he conducted defensive campaigns against Union forces under ULYSSES S. GRANT that caused heavy casualties. Lee ended his retreat behind the fortifications built at Petersburg and Richmond (see PETERSBURG CAMPAIGN). By April 1865 dwindling forces and supplies forced Lee, now general of all Confederate armies, to surrender at APPOMATTOX. He remained a hero to the South, and accepted the post of president of Washington College (later WASHINGTON AND LEE UNIV.), where he served until his death.

Robert E. Lee, 1865.
BY COURTESY OF THE LIBRARY OF CONGRESS, WASHINGTON, D.C.

Lee, Spike *orig.* **Shelton Jackson** (born 1957) U.S. film director. Born in Atlanta, Ga., he grew up in Brooklyn, N.Y., and earned a master's degree in film at NYU, where he began writing, directing, producing, and acting in his movies about African-American life. *She's Gotta Have It* (1986) brought him attention; it was followed by *School Daze* (1988), and later the highly successful *Do the Right Thing* (1989), *Mo' Better Blues* (1990), *Jungle Fever* (1991), the epic *Malcolm X* (1992), *Crooklyn* (1994), *Clockers* (1995), *He Got Game* (1998), and *Summer of Sam* (1999), confirming his reputation as the foremost black American film director.

Lee, William (1550?–1610?) British inventor of the first KNITTING MACHINE. Lee's model (1589) was the only one employed for centuries, and its principle of operation remains in use. Elizabeth I twice denied him a patent because of her concern for the kingdom's hand knitters. With support from Henry IV of France, Lee later made hosiery in Rouen.

Lee Kuan Yew (born 1923) Prime minister of Singapore (1959–90). Born to a wealthy Chinese family, Lee studied at Cambridge University and became a lawyer and a socialist. He won election to Singapore's legislative council in 1955, while the country was still a British crown colony. He helped Singapore achieve self-government and, running as an anticolonialist and anticommunist, was elected prime minister in 1959. His numerous reforms included the emancipation of women. He briefly entered Singapore in the Federation of Malaysia (1963–65); on its withdrawal, Singapore became a sovereign state. Lee industrialized the country and made Singapore the most prosperous nation in S.East Asia. He achieved both labor peace and a rising standard of living for workers, though his mildly authoritarian government at times infringed on civil liberties.

Lee Kuan Yew.
KEYSTONE

Lee Teng-hui \'lē-'dəŋ-'hwē\ (born 1923) First Taiwan-born president (1988–2000) of the Republic of China (TAIWAN). He became president in 1988 after the death of CHIANG CHING-KUO. He was reelected in 1990 and won a landslide victory in 1996 in the first direct presidential election. Lee favored a policy of "flexible diplomacy" in dealing with the People's Republic of China. His successor, Chen Shui-bian (Ch'en Shui-pian) was the first president not from the NATIONALIST PARTY.

leech Any ANNELID of the class Hirudinea (about 300 known species), with a small sucker containing the mouth at the front end and a large sucker at the back end. Species range from tiny to about 8 in. (20 cm) long. Leeches live primarily in freshwater or on land. Some species are predators, some eat organic debris, and others are parasitic. Aquatic leeches may feed on the blood of fishes, amphibians, birds, and mammals, or they may eat snails, insect larvae, and worms. True land leeches feed only on the blood of mammals. Substances in the leech's saliva anesthetize the wound area, dilate the blood vessels, and prevent the blood from clotting. Some species have been used by doctors to drain off blood for centuries. Hirudin, extracted from the European medicinal leech, is used medically as an anticoagulant.

European medicinal leech (*Hirudo medicinalis*).
JACQUES SIX

Leech, John (1817–1864) British caricaturist. He gave up the study of medicine to produce comic sketches and etchings for magazines, notably *Punch*. He collaborated with GEORGE CRUIKSHANK but later departed from the horrific and satirical elements of traditional English caricature to develop his own style of comfortable, warmly humorous middle-class urbanity, underlining character by emphatic contrasts of stock types. With JOHN TENNIEL he created the image of John Bull, a jovial, foursquare Englishman, sometimes in a Union Jack waistcoat, with a bulldog at heel.

Leeds City (metro. area pop., 1995 est.: 725,000), WEST YORKSHIRE, England. It lies along the River Aire, northeast of MANCHESTER. It originated as an Anglo-Saxon township and was incorporated as a city in 1626, becoming an early center of the woolen industry. The completion in 1816 of the Leeds and Liverpool Canal stimulated its growth, and the end of the century saw rapid expansion in the factory production of ready-made clothing. It is the seat of the University of Leeds.

Leek (*Allium porrum*).
G.R. ROBERTS

leek Hardy, vigorous, biennial plant *(Allium porrum)* of the LILY FAMILY, native to the eastern Mediterranean and the Middle East. It has a mild, sweet, onionlike flavor. It is widely used in European soups and stews, and is cooked whole as a vegetable. It became the national emblem of Wales following an ancient victory by an army of Welshmen who wore leeks as a distinguishing sign. The long, narrow leaves and nearly cylindrical bulb of the first season are replaced in the second season by a tall solid stalk bearing leaves and a large umbel with many flowers.

Leeuwenhoek \'lā-vən-,hu̇k\, **Antonie van** (1632–1723) Dutch microscopist. In his youth he was apprenticed to a draper in Delft; a later civil position allowed him to devote time to his hobby: grinding lenses and using them to study tiny

Leeuwenhoek, detail of a portrait by Jan Verkolje; in the Rijksmuseum, Amsterdam.
BY COURTESY OF THE RIJKSMUSEUM, AMSTERDAM

L
M
N

objects. With his simple microscopes he observed protozoa in rainwater and pond and well water, and bacteria in the human mouth and intestine. He also discovered blood corpuscles, capillaries, and the structure of muscles and nerves, and in 1677 he first described the spermatozoa of insects, dogs, and humans. How he enhanced the power of his lenses sufficiently to achieve such results remains a secret. His research on lower animals argued against the doctrine of spontaneous generation, and his observations helped lay the foundations for the sciences of bacteriology and protozoology.

Leeward Islands \'lü-ərd, 'lē-wərd\ Arc of West Indian islands that constitute the most westerly and northerly of the Lesser ANTILLES, northeastern Caribbean Sea. The major islands are, from north to south, the VIRGIN ISLANDS OF THE U.S. and the British VIRGIN ISLANDS, ANGUILLA, ST. MARTIN, ST. KITTS–NEVIS, ANTIGUA AND BARBUDA, MONTSERRAT, and GUADELOUPE. Just south of this chain is DOMINICA, sometimes classified as part of the Leeward Islands but usually designated as part of the WINDWARD ISLANDS.

Lefèvre d'Étaples \lə-'fevrᵊ-dā-'tàplᵊ\, **Jacques** (c. 1455–1536) French humanist, theologian, and translator. Ordained a priest, he taught philosophy in Paris (1490–1507), after which he worked with the abbey of St.-Germain-des-Prés. When suspected of Protestant heresy, he moved temporarily to Strasbourg and later to Nérac, where he was protected by the queen of Navarre. Casting off the influence of medieval Scholasticism, he promoted scriptural studies on the eve of the Reformation. He translated the Bible into French and wrote commentaries on St. PAUL as well as philosophical and mystical works.

Lefkosía See NICOSIA

left In political science, the portion of the political spectrum associated with SOCIALISM. The term derives from the seating arrangement of the French revolutionary parliament in the 1790s, where the socialistic representatives sat to the presiding officer's left. Those who associate themselves with the left favor greater popular sovereignty and democratic control over political, social, and economic life, and regard social welfare as the most important goal of government. Modern liberalism may shade off into socialism, the standard ideology of the left in most countries of the world; COMMUNISM is a more radical and sharply defined leftist ideology.

leg Lower limb of a biped, jointed at the knee, supporting the body and used for walking and running. Its bones are the femur (thighbone), longest bone in the human body; patella (kneecap); tibia (shin); and fibula. The biceps muscle of the thigh bends the leg; the quadriceps straightens it.

legal medicine See MEDICAL JURISPRUDENCE

legend Traditional story or group of stories told about a particular person or place. Formerly the term referred to a tale about a saint. Legends resemble folktales in content; they may include supernatural beings, elements of mythology, or explanations of natural phenomena, but they are associated with a particular locality or person. They are handed down from the past and are popularly regarded as historical though they are not entirely verifiable.

Léger \lā-'zhā\, **Fernand** (1881–1955) French painter. Born to a peasant family in Normandy, he worked as an architectural draftsman in Paris before studying art. Influenced by PAUL CEZANNE and the early Cubists, he developed a painting style that combined bold colors with geometric and cylindrical forms arranged in highly disciplined compositions. His best-known works celebrated modern industrial technology by emphasizing shapes derived from machine parts. Though he was seriously injured in World War I, his art continued to affirm his faith in modern life and popular culture. In 1924 he conceived and directed *Ballet mécanique,* a nonnarrative film with photography by MAN RAY.

Léger, photograph by Arnold Newman, 1941.

Leghorn See LIVORNO

leghorn \'leg-ˌhȯrn, 'le-gərn\ Breed of CHICKEN that originated in Italy; the only Mediterranean breed of importance today. Of the 12 varieties, the single-comb white leghorn is more popular than all the other leghorns combined; the leading egg producer of the world, it lays white eggs and is kept in large numbers in England, Canada, Australia, and the U.S.

Legio Maria See MARIA LEGIO

legion Military organization, originally the largest permanent unit in the Roman army. It was the basis of the military system by which imperial Rome conquered and ruled its empire. The early Roman Republic found the Greek PHALANX too unwieldy for fragmented fighting in the hills and valleys of central Italy. To replace it the Romans evolved a new tactical system based on small and flexible infantry units called maniples. These were grouped in larger units called cohorts, which ranged from 360 to 600 men, depending on the era. Ten cohorts made up a legion, which moved into battle with four cohorts in the first line and three each in the second and third lines. See also FOREIGN LEGION.

Legion of Honor *officially* **Order of the Legion of Honor** Highest-ranking order and decoration of the French republic. It was created by NAPOLEON in 1802 as a general military and civil order of merit. Membership is open to men and women, French citizens and foreigners, irrespective of rank, birth, or religion. Admission into the Legion requires 20 years of civil achievement in peacetime or extraordinary military bravery and service in times of war.

Legion of Mary Church See MARIA LEGIO

Legionnaires' disease Type of PNEUMONIA first identified in American Legion conventioneers in 1976, 29 of whom died. The cause was identified as a previously unknown bacterium, *Legionella pneumophila,* later revealed as causing earlier mysterious outbreaks at widely separated places. Usually, malaise and headache are followed by high fever and often chills, dry cough, shortness of breath, and pain, occasionally with mental confusion. Contaminated water (e.g., in water-distribution systems, humidifiers, and whirlpool spas) is usually suspected as the source. The disease is treated with antibiotics.

legislative apportionment *or* **legislative delimitation** Process by which representation is distributed among the constituencies of a representative assembly. In ancient Athens, every citizen represented himself, but throughout most of history representation has been restricted to certain social classes. With the growth of democracy, the extension of suffrage, and the rise of political parties, apportionment had to be methodically and mathematically arranged to ensure that the distribution of legislative seats would most accurately reflect the electorate's will. Territorial apportionment is currently the most common form. See also GERRYMANDERING, PROPORTIONAL REPRESENTATION.

legislature Lawmaking branch of a government. Before the advent of legislatures, monarchs dictated the law. Early European legislatures include the English PARLIAMENT and the Icelandic Althing (founded c. 930). Legislatures may be unicameral or bicameral (see BICAMERAL SYSTEM). Their powers may include passing laws, establishing the government's budget, confirming executive appointments, ratifying treaties, investigating the EXECUTIVE branch, impeaching and removing from office members of the executive and JUDICIARY, and redressing constituents' grievances. Members may be appointed or directly or indirectly elected; they may represent the people as a whole, particular groups, or territorial subdistricts. In presidential systems, the executive and legislative branches are clearly separated; in parliamentary systems, members of the executive branch are chosen from the legislative membership. See also BUNDESTAG, CONGRESS OF THE U.S., DIET, DUMA, EUROPEAN PARLIAMENT, KNESSET, Canadian PARLIAMENT.

legume \'le-ˌgyüm\ Any of about 18,000 species in about 650 genera of flowering plants that make up the order Fabales, consisting of the single family Leguminosae, or Fabaceae (the pea family). The term also refers to their characteristic fruit, also called a pod. Legumes are widespread on all habitable continents. Leaves of many members appear feathery, and flowers are almost universally showy. In economic importance, this order is surpassed only by the GRASS and SEDGE order (Cyperales). In the production of food, the legume family is the most important of any family. The pods are part of the diet of nearly all humans and supply most

L
M
N

dietary protein in regions of high population density. In addition, legumes perform the invaluable act of NITROGEN FIXATION. Because they contain many of the essential AMINO ACIDS, legume seeds can balance the deficiencies of CEREAL protein. Legumes also provide edible oils, GUMS, fibers, and raw material for plastics, and some are ornamentals. Included in this family are ACACIA, ALFALFA, BEANS, BROOM, CAROB, CLOVER, COWPEA, LUPINE, MIMOSA, PEAS, PEANUTS, SOYBEANS, TAMARIND, and VETCH.

Lehár \'lā-ˌhär\, **Franz (Christian)** *orig.* **Ferencz Christian Lehár** (1870–1948) Austro-Hungarian composer. Born in Hungary, he began study of the violin at 12 in Prague. In the 1890s he was a military bandmaster like his father; by the end of the decade he had moved to Vienna, where he became a popular composer of marches and waltzes. After 1901 he concentrated on orchestra conducting and on composing, especially of 40 witty and melodic operettas that embody the prewar Viennese spirit, including the popular *The Merry Widow* (1905), *The Countess of Luxembourg* (1909), and *The Land of Smiles* (1929).

Lehigh University \'lē-ˌhī\ Private university in Bethlehem, Pa., on the Lehigh River. It was founded in 1865. Women were admitted as undergraduates in 1971. It comprises colleges of arts and sciences, business and economics, education, engineering and applied science, and a graduate school. Research facilities include a center for advanced technology development, a marine station (in New Jersey), and an accelerator. Total enrollment is about 6,500.

Lehmbruck \'lām-brük\, **Wilhelm** (1881–1919) German sculptor, painter and printmaker. His youthful work was academically realistic, but he grew to admire the works of AUGUSTE RODIN, and in 1910 he moved to Paris, where he produced paintings and lithographs as well as sculptures. He became one of the most important German Expressionist sculptors, best known for his elongated nudes, such as *Kneeling Woman* (1911), which suggests a resigned pessimism. He returned to Germany at the outbreak of World War I and tended wounded soldiers in a hospital. *Seated Youth* (1917) reveals his profound depression; he committed suicide two years later.

Leiber \'lē-bər\, **Jerry** (born 1933) U.S. songwriter and producer. He was born in Baltimore but his family settled in Los Angeles, where he met Mike Stoller (born 1933), who had moved there from New York. In 1950, while still in their teens, Leiber and Stoller became a songwriting and production team, among the first to produce recordings that combined pop music with rhythm and blues. Their first successful collaboration came with "Hound Dog," recorded by Big Mama Thornton (1953) and later by E. PRESLEY, who would record more than 20 of their songs. They wrote numerous songs for the Coasters, including "Yakety-Yak." Other hits included "There Goes My Baby," "Stand By Me," and "Is That All There Is?" Their songs have been recorded by the BEATLES, A. FRANKLIN, JAMES BROWN, and B.B. KING, among many others.

Leibniz \'līb-nəts, *Ger* 'līp-nits\, **Gottfried Wilhelm** *later* **Freiherr (baron) von Leibniz** (1646–1716) German philosopher and mathematician. Born in Leipzig, the son of a professor, he obtained a doctorate in law at 20. In *De arte combinatoria* (1666) he set forth the fundamental concepts of the computer. In 1667 he began working for the elector of Mainz, in which position he codified the laws of Mainz, among other important tasks. He served the dukes of Braunschweig-Lüneburg as librarian and councillor (1676–1716). He invented the differential and integral calculus simultaneously with ISAAC NEWTON; though principal credit for the invention has long been disputed, Leibniz's work was published three years earlier (1684) and his notation was universally adopted. He also made important contributions to optics and mechanics. In 1700 he helped found the German Academy of Sciences in Berlin and became its first president. His *Theodicy* (1710) expressed an optimistic faith in reason and became an important text of the Enlightenment. He worked energetically to reconcile the Protestant churches in several countries. He conceived a vast history of the world but never completed it. He was one of the most original philosophers of the early modern period; his chief philosophical contributions were in the fields of logic and metaphysics, in which he provided an alternative to the rationalism of BENEDICT DE SPINOZA and RENE DESCARTES. In metaphysics he espoused PLURALISM (as opposed to Descartes's DUALISM and Spinoza's MONISM). His universal mind and astonishing achievements make him one of the most extraordinary figures of Western civilization.

Leibovitz, Annie *orig.* **Anna-Lou Leibovitz** (born 1949) U.S. photographer. Born in Westbury, Connecticut, Leibovitz enrolled in the San Francisco Art Institute in 1967. In 1970, while still a student, she was given her first commercial assignment for *Rolling Stone* magazine. Leibovitz became the publication's chief photographer in 1973, and over the subsequent decade she created images of the major personalities of contemporary rock music. In 1983 she moved to *Vanity Fair* magazine, which broadened her pool of subjects to include film stars, athletes, and political figures, and in 1986 she began to pursue advertising photography. Many successful monographs of her photographs have been published.

Leicester \'les-tər\ City (metro. area pop., 1999 est.: 270,493), seat of LEICESTERSHIRE, central England. Located on the River Soar, it was settled by Romans. A considerable community by Norman times, it was the site of a Norman castle and abbey built in 1143, the ruins of which still stand. It was where King RICHARD III spent the night before he was killed in the Battle of BOSWORTH FIELD. It was incorporated in 1589, and became an industrial center after the arrival of the railway in 1832. The University of Leicester (founded 1957) is nearby.

Leicester, Earl of See Simon de MONTFORT

Leicester \'les-tər\, **Earl of** *orig.* **Robert Dudley** (1532?–1588) English courtier and favorite of ELIZABETH I. Sentenced to death in 1553 for aiding the attempt by his father, the duke of NORTHUMBERLAND, to put Lady Jane GREY on the throne, he was released in 1554. Handsome and ambitious, he soon won the queen's affection and was made a privy councillor in 1559. When his wife died in 1560, it was rumored that he had murdered her in order to marry Elizabeth. Dudley became an active suitor of Elizabeth; he failed to win the queen's hand but they remained close friends. In 1585 he was sent in command of an English force to assist the Netherlands in its revolt against Spain; he proved incompetent and was recalled (1587).

Leicestershire \'les-tər-ˌshir\ County (population 1999 est.: 606,800), central England. It is located in the East Midlands region; the county seat is LEICESTER. The Soar River crosses the county from south to north on its way to join the TRENT RIVER. East of the Soar Valley lies a territory famous for its fox hunts. In addition to its pastoral agricultural tradition, and its noted production of Stilton cheese, its industrial centers, including Leicester, are manufacturing centers.

Leiden *or* **Leyden** \'līd-ᵊn, *Dutch* 'lā-də\ Commune (pop., 1999 est.: 117,389), western Netherlands. First mentioned in 922 as a possession of Utrecht diocese, it was governed by the court of Holland until 1420. It became a printing center after the ELZEVIR FAMILY set up their press there c. 1581. The University of Leiden was founded in 1575, and the town became a center of theology, science, and art. It was the birthplace of painters REMBRANDT van Rijn and JAN VAN GOYEN. It was the residence of the PILGRIMS for 11 years before they sailed to America in 1620.

Leif Eriksson the Lucky *Norwegian* **Leiv Eriksson den Hepne** (11th century) Icelandic explorer, possibly the first European to reach North America. The second son of ERIK THE RED, he was on his way back from Norway to Greenland, where he had been sent by OLAF I TRYGGVASON to Christianize the natives (c. 1000), when he sailed off course and landed probably at Nova Scotia, which he called VINLAND. This standard account comes from the Icelandic *Eiríks saga*. Another account, the *Groenlendinga saga* ("Tale of the Greenlanders"), says he learned of Vinland from a man who had been there 14 years earlier and that Leif reached North America after 1000.

Leigh \'lē\, **Mike** (*orig.* Michael) (born 1943) British film director and playwright. His first play, *The Box Play* (1965), began the process of improvisation and collaboration with his actors that became the basis of his works for stage, television, and film, which usually depict lower- and working-class life with sharp humor and pathos. After making his film debut with *Bleak Moments* (1971), he later directed such offbeat movies as *High Hopes* (1988), *Life Is Sweet* (1991), and *Naked* (1993). The internationally acclaimed *Secrets and Lies* (1996) was followed by *Career Girls* (1997) and *Topsy-Turvy* (1999).

Leigh, Vivien *orig.* **Vivian Mary Hartley** (1913–1967) British actress. She made her film debut in 1934 and her London stage debut in *The Mask of Virtue* (1935). She was chosen after a well-publicized search for the role of Scarlett in *Gone with the Wind* (1939, Academy Award), which brought her great fame. Noted for her delicate beauty, she later starred in *Waterloo Bridge* (1940), *That Hamilton Woman* (1941), *Anna Karenina* (1948), and *A Streetcar Named Desire* (1951,

Academy Award). From 1940 to 1960 she was married to LAURENCE OLIVIER, with whom she appeared in a number of successful London stage productions.

Leighton \'lā-tᵊn\, **Margaret** (1922–1976) British actress. A member of the Old Vic company, she made her London debut in 1944 and her Broadway debut in 1946. She was acclaimed for her wide range of roles in such plays as *The Cocktail Party* (1950) and *The Applecart* (1953). She received Tony awards for her Broadway appearances in *Separate Tables* (1956) and *The Night of the Iguana* (1962). Her most notable film roles were in *The Winslow Boy* (1948), *The Sound and the Fury* (1959), and *The Go-Between* (1971).

Leinster \'len-stər\ Province (pop., 1991: 1,383,000), eastern Ireland. One of the early provinces, its northern part, Meathe, was a separate kingdom in the 2d century AD. Its disparate parts maintained independence variously to the 12th century, and to the 16th century. Its counties include Carlow, Dublin, Kildare, Kilkenny, Laoighis, Longforth, Louth, Meath, Offaly, Westmeath, Wexford and Wicklow.

Leipzig \'līp-sik̲, 'līp-sig\ City (pop., 1996 est.: 471,000), eastern central Germany. Situated in western SAXONY state, it was, in the 11th century, a fortified town known as Urbs Libzi. It was granted municipal status by 1170, and its location on the principal trade routes of central Europe made it an important commercial center. Several battles of the THIRTY YEARS' WAR were fought near the city, which was also the site of the Battle of LEIPZIG (1813). Massive demonstrations in Leipzig in 1989 helped end the communist regime in East Germany. Historic features include the University of Leipzig (1409), the 13th-century Church of St. Thomas, and the annual Leipzig Fair.

Leipzig, Battle of *or* **Battle of the Nations** (October 16–19, 1813) Decisive defeat for NAPOLEON at Leipzig, resulting in the destruction of what was left of French power in Germany and Poland. Surrounded in the city, Napoleon's army was able only to thwart the allied attacks. As it began to retreat over the single bridge westward from the city, a frightened corporal blew up the bridge, leaving 30,000 French troops trapped in Leipzig to be taken prisoner. The battle was one of the most severe of the NAPOLEONIC WARS; the French lost 38,000 men killed and wounded, and the allies lost 55,000.

Leipzig, University of State-supported university in Leipzig, Germany, founded in 1409. In the 1500s it was a center of Reformation thought, and in the 18th and 19th century it became one of Europe's leading literary and cultural centers, attracting such students as G. W. LEIBNIZ, JOHANN W. VON GOETHE, JOHANN GOTTLIEB FICHTE, and RICHARD WAGNER. Between 1953 and 1990 it was named Karl Marx University of Leipzig. Enrollment is about 21,000.

L M N

leishmaniasis \ˌlēsh-mə-'nī-ə-səs\ Human protozoal infection spread by the bite of a bloodsucking sandfly. It occurs worldwide but is especially prevalent in tropical areas. It is caused by various species of the flagellate protozoan Leishmania, which infect rodents and canines. Visceral leishmaniasis, or kala-azar, occurs throughout the world but is especially prevalent in the Mediterranean area, Africa, Asia, and Latin America; it affects the liver, spleen, and bone marrow and is usually fatal if not treated. Cutaneous leishmaniasis, or Oriental sore, is endemic in areas around the Mediterranean, in central and North Africa, and in southern and western Asia; it is also found in Central and South America and parts of the southern U.S. It is characterized by lesions on the skin of the legs, feet, hands, and face, most of which heal spontaneously after many months.

Leisler \'līs-lər\, **Jacob** (1640–1691) German-American insurrectionist. He emigrated to New York in 1660 and became a wealthy merchant. Objecting to the British unification of New York and New England (1685–89), he led the revolt called Leisler's Rebellion, established himself as lieutenant governor of the province (1689–91), and called the first intercolonial congress (1690) to plan action against the French and Indians. When he reluctantly surrendered to a new British governor, he was charged with treason and hanged.

leitmotiv \'līt-mō-ˌtēf\ In music, a melodic idea associated with a character or an important dramatic element. It is associated particularly with the operas of RICHARD WAGNER, most of which rely on a dense web of associative leitmotifs. Most composers after Wagner (and some of his immediate predecessors) continued to use this musico-dramatic principle, but few as rigorously as he did.

Leizhou Peninsula \'lā-'jō\ *formerly* **Luichow Peninsula** \'lwē-'chau̇\ Peninsula off the southwestern coast of GUANGDONG province, southeastern China. Separated from HAINAN Island by the Hainan Strait, it includes Kwangchowan, a territory leased by France 1898–1945. Occupied by Japan in World War II, it was returned to Chinese control in 1946.

Leland \'lē-lənd\, **Henry Martyn** (1843–1932) U.S. engineer and manufacturer. Born in Danville, Vt., and trained as a machinist, he founded Leland & Faulconer Manufacturing Co. in Detroit in 1890 to build engines for automobile makers. In 1904 he merged the company into his newly founded Cadillac Motor Car Co., where he created the successful Model A Cadillac. In 1917 he founded the Lincoln Motor Co., which was purchased by HENRY FORD in 1922. He was known for his rigorous standards; his innovations included the V-8 engine and adoption of the electric starter.

Lelang See NANGNANG

Lemaître \lə-'me-trᵊ\, **Georges** (1894–1966) Belgian astronomer and cosmologist. He served in the Belgian Army during World War I, then entered a seminary and became a priest. In 1927 he became a professor of astrophysics at the University of London and proposed the modern BIG-BANG model of the formation of the universe. Lemaître's theory, as modified by GEORGE GAMOW, has become the leading theory of the universe's origin. Lemaître also studied COSMIC RAYS and the three-body problem, which concerns the mathematical description of the motion of three mutually attracting bodies in space.

LeMay, Curtis E(merson) (1906–1990) U.S. Air Force officer. Born in Columbus, Ohio, he joined the Army Air Corps in 1928. In World War II he developed advanced strategic bombardment techniques, including pattern bombing, and led bomber commands in Europe and the Pacific, where he launched fire-bombing raids on Japanese cities. As commander of U.S. air forces in Europe (1945–48), he directed the Berlin airlift (see BERLIN BLOCKADE AND AIRLIFT). As head of the U.S. Strategic Air Command (1948–57) he built it into a global strike force. He was chief of staff of the U.S. Air Force (1961–65). In 1968 he was the vice-presidential candidate on the third-party ticket headed by GEORGE WALLACE.

Lemieux \lə-'myü\, **Mario** (born 1965) Canadian hockey player. Born in Montreal, he started skating at about 3 and played his first game when he was 6. In 1984 he made his professional debut as a member of the Pittsburgh Penguins. He quickly became one of the sport's leading offensive threats, earning the nickname "Super Mario." Despite serious back injuries, he led his team to two STANLEY CUP victories (1991–92). In 1992 he was found to have Hodgkin's disease, but after surgery and radiation he returned to lead his team on a 17-game winning streak, an NHL record. He retired after the 1995–96 season with 613 goals and 881 assists. In 1999 he headed a group of investors that purchased the Penguins. Lemieux returned to professional play in 2001, becoming the first owner-player in the history of modern sports.

lemming Any of several species of small RODENTS belonging to the family Cricetidae and found primarily in northern temperate and polar regions of North America and Eurasia. Lemmings have short legs, small ears, and long, soft fur. They are 4–7 in. (10–18 cm) long, including the stumpy tail, and are grayish or reddish brown above, paler below. They feed on roots, shoots, and grasses and live in burrows or rock crevices. They are noted for regular population fluctuations, and for their periodic migrations in spring and fall. Those of the Norway lemming *(Lemmus lemmus)* are the most dramatic, because many of the migrants drown in the sea. However, lemmings are hesitant to enter water and, contrary to legend, do not plunge into the sea in a deliberate death march.

Lemmon, Jack *orig.* **John Uhler** (1925–2001) U.S. actor. Born in Boston, he attended Harvard University and acted in radio and television dramas before making his Broadway debut in 1953. He established his movie career in *Mister Roberts* (1955, Academy Award), and became noted for his character portrayals, often playing excitable, baffled individuals in such movies as *Some Like It Hot* (1959), *The Apartment* (1960), *The Odd Couple* (1968), and *The Out-of-Towners* (1970). His many other films included *Save the Tiger* (1973, Academy Award), *The China Syndrome* (1979), *Missing* (1982), and *Glengarry Glen Ross* (1992). He received an Emmy Award for his portrayal of a dying college professor in the television film *Tuesdays with Morrie* (1999).

lemon Small thorny tree or spreading bush *(Citrus limon)* of the RUE (OR CITRUS) FAMILY, and its edible fruit. Under the yellow outer rind or peel is the white, spongy inner peel, the source of commercial PECTIN. The juicy pulp is acidic and rich in vitamin C, and contains smaller amounts of B vitamins. The climates of coastal Italy and California are especially favorable for the cultivation of lemon trees, which in these regions produce fruit 6–10 times a year. Lemon juice enhances many dishes, and lemonade is a popular warm-weather beverage. Lemon by-products are used in beverages (citric acid), fruit jellies (pectin), and furniture polish (lemon oil).

Lemon (*Citrus limon*).
J. HORACE MCFARLAND CO.

lemon balm See BALM

lemur \'lē-mər\ In general, any of the prosimian PRIMATES (including GALAGOS), all of which have a naked, moist tip to their muzzle; comblike, forward-directed lower front teeth; and clawlike nails on the second toes of the feet. More strictly, the name refers to the typical lemurs (the nine species in the family Lemuridae), found only on Madagascar and the Comoro Islands, which have large eyes; a foxlike face; a slender, monkeylike body; and long hind limbs. All lemurs are docile and gregarious. Species range from 5 in. (13 cm) to about 2 ft (60 cm) long. The bushy tail may be longer than the body, and the woolly fur is reddish, gray, brown, or black. Most are active at night and spend most of their time in trees, eating fruits, leaves, buds, insects, and small birds and birds' eggs. A number of species are listed as endangered.

Lena River \'lē-nə, 'lā-nə\ River, eastern central Russia, one of the longest rivers in the world. From its source in a Siberian mountain lake west of Lake BAIKAL, it flows 2,734 mi (4,400 km) north across Russia to enter the Arctic Ocean. Its basin covers an area of 961,000 sq mi (2,490,000 sq km), and it has many tributaries, including the Vitim and Olekma rivers. The land along its upper course and tributaries is rich in minerals, including gold and coal. Explorers first reached its delta on the Laptev Sea in the early 1630s.

lend-lease System promulgated by Pres. FRANKLIN ROOSEVELT to give aid to U.S. allies in WORLD WAR II. Faced with Britain's inability to pay cash for war materials and food, as required by U.S. law, Roosevelt asked Congress to allow repayment "in kind or property" from countries vital to U.S. defense. The Lend-Lease Act was passed in March 1941, despite arguments that it led the U.S. closer to war. Much of the $49 billion in aid went to British Commonwealth countries; the Soviet Union, China, and 40 other countries also received assistance. U.S. troops stationed abroad received about $8 billion in aid from the Allies.

L'Enfant \lä^{n}-'fä^{n}, *Engl* 'län-ˌfänt\, **Pierre Charles** (1754–1825) French-U.S. engineer, architect, and urban planner. After studies in Paris, he volunteered as a soldier and engineer in the American Revolutionary Army. Congress made him major of engineers in 1783. In 1791 GEORGE WASHINGTON had him prepare a plan for a federal capital on the Potomac River. He designed a gridiron of blocks on which broad diagonal avenues were superimposed; focusing on the Capitol and presidential mansion, the plan incorporated green spaces and provided vistas of street intersections where monuments and fountains could be placed. Though he was dismissed in 1792 for his imperious attitude and died in poverty, his plan was later generally followed.

L'Engle \'leŋ-gəl\, **Madeleine** *orig.* **Madeleine Camp** (born 1918) U.S. author of children's books. Born in New York City, she pursued a career in theater before publishing her first book, *The Small Rain* (1945). In *A Wrinkle in Time* (1962), she introduced a group of children who engage in a cosmic battle against a great evil; their adventures continue in *A Swiftly Tilting Planet* (1978) and other books. Her works often explore such themes as the conflict of good and evil, the nature of God, individual responsibility, and family life. She also has written adult fiction, poetry, and autobiography.

length, area, and volume Dimensional measures of one-, two-, and three-dimensional geometric objects. All three are magnitudes, representing the "size" of an object. Length is the size of a LINE segment (see DISTANCE FORMULAS), area is the size of a closed region in a plane, and volume is the size of a solid. Formulas for area and volume are based on lengths. For example, the area of a CIRCLE equals π times the square of the length of its radius, and the volume of a rectangular box is the product of its three linear dimensions: length, width, and height.

length of a curve Geometrical concept addressed by INTEGRAL CALCULUS. Methods for calculating exact lengths of line segments and arcs of circles have been known since ancient times. ANALYTIC GEOMETRY allowed them to be stated as formulas involving coordinates (see COORDINATE SYSTEMS) of points and measurements of angles. CALCULUS provided a way to find the length of a curve by breaking it into smaller and smaller line segments or arcs of circles. The exact value of a curve's length is found by combining such a process with the idea of a LIMIT. The entire procedure is summarized by a formula involving the INTEGRAL of the function describing the curve.

Lenin, Vladimir (Ilich) *orig.* **Vladimir Ilich Ulyanov** (1870–1924) Founder of the Russian Communist Party, leader of the RUSSIAN REVOLUTION OF 1917, and architect and builder of the Soviet state. Born to a middle-class family, he was strongly influenced by his eldest brother, Aleksandr, who was hanged in 1887 for conspiring to assassinate the czar. He studied law and became a Marxist in 1889 while practicing law. He was arrested as a subversive in 1895 and exiled to Siberia, where he married NADEZHDA KRUPSKAYA. They lived in Western Europe after 1900. At the 1903 meeting in London of the RUSSIAN SOCIAL-DEMOCRATIC WORKERS' PARTY, he emerged as the leader of the BOLSHEVIK faction. In several revolutionary newspapers that he founded and edited, he put forth his theory of the party as the vanguard of the proletariat, a centralized body organized around a core of professional revolutionaries; his ideas, later known as LENINISM, would be joined with KARL MARX's theories to form MARXISM-Leninism, which became the communist worldview. With the outbreak of the RUSSIAN REVOLUTION OF 1905, he returned to Russia, but he resumed his exile in 1907 and continued his energetic agitation for the next 10 years. He saw World War I as an opportunity to turn a war of nations into a war of classes, and he returned to Russia with the RUSSIAN REVOLUTION OF 1917 to lead the Bolshevik coup that overthrew the provisional government of ALEKSANDR KERENSKY. As revolutionary dictator of the Soviet state, he signed the Treaty of BREST-LITOVSK with Germany (1918) and repulsed counterrevolutionary threats in the RUSSIAN CIVIL WAR. He founded the COMINTERN in 1919. His policy of WAR COMMUNISM prevailed until 1921, and to forestall economic disaster he launched the NEW ECONOMIC POLICY. In ill health from 1922, he died of a stroke in 1924.

Leningrad See SAINT PETERSBURG

Leningrad, Siege of (September 8, 1941–January 27, 1944) Prolonged siege of the city of Leningrad (now St. Petersburg) by German forces in World War II. German forces invaded the Soviet Union in June 1941 and approached Leningrad from the west and south while Germany's Finnish allies came from the north. By November 1941 the city was almost completely encircled and its supply lines to the Soviet interior cut off. In 1942 alone, over 650,000 Leningrad citizens died from starvation, disease, and shelling from distant German artillery. Sparse food and fuel supplies reached the city by barge in the summer and by sled in winter across Lake Ladoga. The supplies kept the city's arms factories operating and its 2 million inhabitants barely alive, while another 1 million children, sick, and elderly were evacuated. Soviet offensives in 1943 partially broke the German encirclement and were followed in January 1944 by a successful Soviet attack that drove the Germans westward from the city's outskirts, ending the siege.

Leninism Principles expounded by VLADIMIR ILICH LENIN to guide the transition of society from CAPITALISM to COMMUNISM. The tenets of MARXISM, which Lenin embraced, provided no concrete guidelines for the transition. Lenin believed that a small, disciplined, professional group of revolutionaries was needed to violently overthrow the capitalist system, and that a "dictatorship of the PROLETARIAT" must guide society until the day when the state would wither away. That day never came, and Leninism in practice meant state control of all aspects of life by the COMMUNIST PARTY and the creation of the first modern totalitarian state. See also BOLSHEVIK, STALINISM, TOTALITARIANISM.

Lenni Lenape See DELAWARE

Lennon, John (Winston) (1940–1980) British singer and songwriter. Born in Liverpool, he wanted to be a sailor like his father, but decided to be a musician after hearing E. Presley's recordings. In 1957 he formed the band that became the Beatles, and in the 1960s he enjoyed enormous success performing with the group and writing songs with Paul McCartney. In the mid-1960s he began working on side projects in film and music, notably with the Japanese-U.S. avant-garde artist Yoko Ono (born 1933), whom he married in 1969. Their political activism and social ideals were reflected in much of Lennon's early solo work, including the hit "Imagine," and attracted the attention of the U.S. government, which sought to have him deported. After 1975 he withdrew from public life; he and Ono returned with the album *Double Fantasy* shortly before his murder by a deranged fan. His sons Julian (born 1963) and Sean (born 1975) have also enjoyed recording success.

Leno \'le-nō\, **Jay** *orig.* **James Douglas** (born 1950) U.S. comedian and television talk-show host. Born in New Rochelle, N.Y., he began his career as a stand-up comedian in nightclubs and on television, noted for his pleasant-tempered topical and political humor. From 1987 he was the regular guest host on NBC's *Tonight Show*, and he succeeded Johnny Carson as its host in 1992.

lens Piece of glass or other transparent substance that is used to form an image of an object by converging or diverging rays of light from the object. Because of the curvature of its surface, different rays of light are refracted (see refraction) through different angles. A convex lens causes rays to converge on a single point, the focal point. A concave lens causes rays to diverge as though they are coming from a focal point. Both types cause the rays to form a visual image of the object. The image may be real—inverted and photographable or visible on a screen—or it may be virtual—erect and visible only by looking through the lens.

Lent In the Christian church, a period of penitential preparation for Easter, observed since apostolic times. Western churches once provided for a 40-day fast (excluding Sundays), in imitation of Jesus' fasting in the wilderness; one meal a day was allowed in the evening, and meat, fish, eggs, and butter were forbidden. These rules have gradually been relaxed, and only Ash Wednesday—the first day of Lent in Western Christianity, when the penitent traditionally have their foreheads marked with ashes—and Good Friday are now kept as Lenten fast days. Rules of fasting are stricter in the Eastern churches.

lentil Small annual legume *(Lens esculenta)* and its lens-shaped, protein-rich, edible seed. One of the most ancient of cultivated foods, it is a good source of vitamin B, iron, and phosphorus. Of unknown origin, the lentil is widely cultivated throughout Europe, Asia, and North Africa; though little grown in the Western Hemisphere, its inclusion in the U.S. diet is increasing. Growing 6–18 in. (15–45 cm) high, the plant has compound leaves and pale blue flowers. Animals are fed the stalks and leaves as fodder.

Lenya, Lotte *orig.* **Karoline Blamauer** (1898–1981) Austrian-U.S. actress-singer. Born into poverty, Lenya worked as a dancer and actress in Zurich and later Berlin. She married K. Weill in 1926 and began appearing in such Bertolt Brecht-Weill works as *Mahagonny* (1927) and *The Threepenny Opera* (1928; film, 1930). They fled Nazi Germany for Paris, where she sang in Brecht and Weill's *Seven Deadly Sins* (1933). After moving to New York in 1935, Lenya made her U.S. debut in *The Eternal Road* (1937). After Weill's death, she lent her inimitably husky voice to revivals throughout the 1950s, including a long-running production of *The Threepenny Opera,* and later in *Brecht on Brecht* (1962), *Mother Courage and Her Children* (1965), and *Cabaret* (1966), as well as in films.

Leo (Latin: "Lion") In astronomy, the constellation lying between Cancer and Virgo; in astrology, the fifth sign of the zodiac, governing approximately the period July 23–August 22. Its symbol, a lion, has been associated with the Nemean lion slain by Heracles. The Nemean lion was considered invulnerable because its skin was impervious to arrows, but Heracles battered it to death with a club. Zeus put the lion in the sky as a constellation.

Leo I, St. *known as* **Leo the Great** (c. 400–461) Pope (440–61). He was a champion of orthodoxy and a doctor of the church. When the monk Eutyches of Constantinople asserted that Jesus Christ had only a single divine nature, Leo wrote the *Tome,* which established the coexistence of Christ's human and divine natures. Leo's teachings were embraced by the Council of Chalcedon (451), which also accepted his teaching as the "voice of Peter." Leo dealt capably with the invasions of barbaric tribes, persuading the Huns not to attack Rome (452) and the Vandals not to sack the city (455).

Leo III *known as* **Leo the Isaurian** \ī-'sȯr-ē-ən\ (c. 675–741) Byzantine emperor (717–41), founder of the Isaurian dynasty. A high-ranking military commander, he seized the throne with the help of Arab armies who hoped to subjugate the Byzantine Empire. He then successfully defended Constantinople against the Arabs (717–18). Having crowned his son Constantine V co-emperor (720), Leo used his son's marriage to cement an alliance with the Khazars. Victory over the Arabs at Akroïnos (740) was crucial in preventing their conquest of Asia Minor. He issued an important legal code, the *Ecloga* (726). His policy of iconoclasm (730), which banned the use of sacred images in churches, engendered a century of conflict within the empire.

Leo IX, St. *orig.* **Bruno, Graf (Count) von Egisheim und Dagsburg** (1002–1054). Pope (1049–54). Born in Alsace, he was consecrated bishop of Toul in 1027. He was named pope by Emperor Henry III but insisted on election by the clergy and people of Rome. He strengthened the papacy and instituted reforms, seeking to eradicate clerical marriage and simony. His assertion of papal primacy and his military campaign against the Normans in Sicily (1053) alienated the Eastern Church. His representatives excommunicated the patriarch of Constantinople. Though Leo had already died, their act triggered the Schism of 1054.

Leo X *orig.* **Giovanni de' Medici** (1475–1521) Pope (1513–21), one of the most extravagant of the Renaissance pontiffs. The second son of Lorenzo de'Medici, he was educated at his father's court in Florence and at the University of Pisa. He was named a cardinal in 1492, and in 1494 he was exiled from Florence by the revolt of Girolamo Savonarola. He returned in 1500 and soon consolidated Medici control of the city. As pope, he became a patron of the arts, accelerating construction of St. Peter's Basilica. He strengthened the papacy's political power in Europe, but his lavish spending depleted his treasury. He discouraged reforms at the fifth Lateran Council, and he responded inadequately to the Reformation, excommunicating Martin Luther in 1521 and failing to address the need for change, a lapse that signaled the end of the unified Western church.

Leo XIII *orig.* **Vincenzo Gioacchino Pecci** (1810–1903) Pope (1878–1903). Born into the Italian nobility, he was ordained a priest in 1837 and entered the diplomatic service of the Papal States. He was appointed bishop of Perugia in 1846 and was named a cardinal in 1853. He was elected pope in 1878, and despite his advanced age and frail health he directed the church for a quarter of a century. Like his predecessor, Pius IX, he opposed Freemasonry and secular liberalism, but he brought a new spirit to the papacy by adopting a conciliatory attitude toward civil governments and taking a more positive view of scientific progress.

Leo XIII, 1878.

THE BETTMANN ARCHIVE

Leochares \lē-'ä-kə-ˌrēz\ (fl. mid-4th century BC) Greek sculptor to whom the *Apollo Belvedere* is often attributed. He worked for Philip II of Macedonia and his son, Alexander the Great, and was commissioned to produce gold and ivory statues of the royal family. He is said to have worked with Scopas on the Mausoleum at Halicarnassus, one of the Seven Wonders of the World, c. 350 BC.

León \lā-'ōn\ City (metro. area pop., 1995 est.: 148,000), northwestern Spain. The city began as the camp of a Roman legion; its name is derived from the Latin *legio.* Held by the Goths during the 6th–7th century, it then fell to the Moors, who ruled it until 850. In the 10th century, it became the capital of the kingdom of Leon. An industrial as well as a tourist center, its site includes medieval churches.

León City (pop., 1995 : 124,000), western Nicaragua. The second largest city in Nicaragua, it is the country's political and intellectual center.

It was founded by the Spanish on the edge of Lake Managua in 1524; it was later destroyed by an earthquake and rebuilt in 1610 near the Pacific coast, northwest of MANAGUA. It was the capital of Nicaragua until 1855; it has had a long political and commercial rivalry with the city of GRANADA. The seat of the University of León, it is the burial place of RUBEN DARIO

León Medieval kingdom, northwestern Spain. It began as a Christian kingdom in the early 10th century when García I established his court on a former Roman legion campsite. Its rulers lost ground to the Moors during the 10th century but reconquered much territory in the 11th century. It was united with the kingdom of CASTILE in 1037–1157, then regained its independence and was ruled by its own kings. It was permanently reunited with Castile in 1230. The modern autonomous community of CASTILLA Y LEÓN covers roughly the same area.

Léon, Arthur Saint- See Arthur SAINT-LÉON

Leonard, Buck *orig.* **Walter Fenner** (1907–1997) U.S. baseball player. Born in Rocky Mount, N.C., he began his full professional baseball career in the NEGRO LEAGUES in 1933. With his teammate Josh Gibson, he led the Homestead (Pa.) Grays to nine consecutive championships from 1937 through 1945. Known as a formidable home-run hitter and an outstanding first baseman, he was selected to the East-West All-Star game a record 11 times.

Leonard, Sugar Ray *orig.* **Ray Charles** (born 1956) U.S. welterweight and middleweight boxer. Born in Rocky Mount, N.C., he was an outstanding amateur, winning 145 of 150 bouts, including a 1976 Olympic championship. He gained the world welterweight title in 1979 by defeating Wilfred Benítez, lost it to Roberto Duran in 1980, but recaptured it from him later that year. He retired in the early 1980s with a detached retina, but made a comeback in 1984. In 1987 he went into the ring as a middleweight to defeat MARVIN HAGLER in one of boxing's great matches. He retired again in 1991. He was resoundingly defeated in a final comeback attempt in 1997. Known for his agility and finesse, he won 36 of his 39 professional matches. He later became a television commentator.

Leonardo da Vinci \'vin-chē\ (1452–1519) Renaissance painter, sculptor, draftsman, architect, engineer, and scientist. The son of a landowner and a peasant, he was born and raised in the town of Vinci, near Florence. He received training in painting, sculpture, and mechanical arts as an apprentice to ANDREA DEL VERROCCHIO. In 1482, having made a name for himself in Florence, he entered the service of the duke of Milan as "painter and engineer." In Milan his artistic and creative genius unfolded. Around 1490 he began his project of writing treatises on the "science of painting," architecture, mechanics, and anatomy. His theories were based on the belief that the painter, with his powers of perception and ability to pictorialize his observations, was uniquely qualified to probe nature's secrets. His numerous surviving manuscripts are noted for being written in a backward script that requires a mirror to be read. In 1502–3, as military architect and engineer for CESARE BORGIA, he helped lay the groundwork for modern cartography. After five years of painting and scientific study back in Florence (1503–8), he returned to Milan, where his scientific work flourished. In 1516, after an interlude under MEDICI patronage in Rome, he entered the service of FRANCIS I of France; he never returned to Italy. Though only some 15 completed paintings survive, they are universally seen as masterpieces. The power of *The Last Supper* (1495–97) comes in part from its masterly composition. In the *Mona Lisa* (c. 1503–6) the features and symbolic overtones of the subject achieve a complete synthesis, as did art and science in the unparalleled achievement of Leonardo's career.

Leoncavallo \lā-ˌōn-kä-'väl-lō\, **Ruggero** (1857–1919) Italian composer. After attending Naples Conservatory and earning a doctorate in literature, he toured as a pianist while writing operas, including their libretti. His first, *Chatterton* (1878), was produced with little success, but its libretto attracted the interest of the publisher Ricordi. GIACOMO PUCCINI's rejection of Leoncavallo's help with *Manon Lescaut* and Ricordi's rejection of his own projects caused him in anger to write the verismo one-act opera *I pagliacci* (1892) for a rival. Though he wrote several other operas and operettas, *Pagliacci* was his only enduring success.

Leone \lā-'ō-nā\, **Sergio** (1921?–1989) Italian film director. After working as an assistant to Italian and U.S. directors, he made his directing debut with *The Colossus of Rhodes* (1961). He won a wide audience with *A Fistful of Dollars* (1964), the first of the violent Italian-made "spaghetti westerns"; the equally popular *For a Few Dollars More* (1965) and *The Good, the Bad, and the Ugly* (1966) also starred CLINT EASTWOOD. Among his other films are the epics *Once upon a Time in the West* (1968) and *Once upon a Time in America* (1984).

Leonidas \lē-'ä-nə-dəs\ (died 480) King of SPARTA (c. 490–480 BC). He is noted for his heroic stand against the Persians at the Battle of THERMOPYLAE in 480. Seeing the hopelessness of the situation, he sent most of his troops in retreat, and with his 300-man royal guard withstood the Persian army for two days, battling valiantly to the last man. He became the object of a hero cult at Sparta, and he stands as the epitome of bravery against overwhelming odds. The legend that Spartans never surrender derived from this episode.

Leonov \lē-'ä-nəf\, **Aleksey (Arkhipovich)** (born 1934) Soviet cosmonaut. He joined the Soviet Air Force in 1953 and was selected for cosmonaut training in 1959. In 1965 he became the first person to perform a space walk. After exiting the spacecraft (Voskhod 2) and while tethered to the ship, Leonov made observations, took motion pictures, and practiced maneuvering in free fall before reentering the ship. A decade later, he commanded the Russian Soyuz craft that linked in orbit with the U.S. APOLLO craft in July 1975.

Leontief \lē-'än-tē-ˌef\, **Wassily** (1906–1999) Russian-U.S. economist. After studying at the Univs. of Leningrad (1921–25) and Berlin (1925–28), he emigrated to the U.S. in 1931. At Harvard University (1931–75) he articulated his INPUT-OUTPUT ANALYSIS. He also described what is known as the Leontief paradox: that capital rather than labor is the scarce factor of production in the U.S. He was awarded the 1973 Nobel Prize. From 1975 until his death he taught at New York Univ.

leopard *or* **panther** Big CAT *(Leo,* sometimes *Panthera, pardus)* of the bush and forest, found throughout sub-Saharan Africa, in North Africa, and in Asia. The average leopard weighs 110–200 lbs (50–90 kg) and is about 6 ft (210 cm) long, excluding the 35-in. (90-cm) tail, and 24–28 in. (60–70 cm) high at the shoulder. The background color is typically yellowish above and white below. The dark spots arranged in rosettes over much of the body lack a central spot, unlike those of the JAGUAR. The leopard is solitary and mainly nocturnal. An agile climber, it frequently stores the remains of its kills in tree branches. It generally preys on antelope and deer. It also hunts dogs and, in Africa, baboons. It sometimes takes livestock and may attack humans. Several leopard races are listed as endangered. See also CHEETAH, COUGAR, SNOW LEOPARD.

Leopard (*Panthera pardus*).
LEONARD LEE RUE III

leopard seal *or* **sea leopard** Species *(Hydrurga leptonyx)* of generally solitary earless SEAL (family Phocidae) found in Antarctic and sub-Antarctic regions. It is the only seal that feeds on penguins, young seals, and other warm-blooded prey. It is slender and has a long head and long three-cusped cheek teeth. Named for its black-spotted gray coat, it attains a maximum length and weight (greater in the female) of about 12 ft (3.5 m) and 840 lbs (380 kg). It has a reputation for ferocity but is not known to make unprovoked attacks on humans.

Leopold, (Rand) Aldo (1886–1948) U.S. environmentalist. Born in Burlington, Iowa, he attended Yale University and worked for the U.S. Forest Service 1909–28, mainly in the Southwest. In 1924 the first national wilderness area (Gila Wilderness Area in New Mexico) was created at Leopold's urging. He taught at the University of Wisconsin 1933–48. A fervent campaigner for the preservation of wildlife and wilderness areas, he was a director of the AUDUBON SOCIETY from 1935 and became a founder of the Wilderness Society that same year. His *Game Management* (1933) was followed in 1949 by the posthumous *A Sand County Almanac*, which eloquently called for the preservation of ecosystems; read by millions, it had an important influence on the budding environmental movement.

Leopold I *orig.* **Léopold-Georges-Chrétien-Frédéric** (1790–1865) First king of the Belgians (1831–65). The son of Francis, duke of Saxe-Coburg-Saalfeld, he married Charlotte, daughter of the future English king GEORGE IV in 1816. After her death in 1817 Leopold continued to live in England until elected king of the newly formed Belgium. He helped strengthen the nation's new parliamentary system and scrupulously maintained Belgian neutrality. Highly influential in European diplomacy, he used marriages to strengthen his ties. In 1832 he married the daughter of LOUIS-PHILIPPE. In 1840 he helped arrange the marriage of his niece, VICTORIA, to his nephew, Prince ALBERT of Saxe-Coburg-Gotha. In 1857 he arranged the marriage of his daughter to MAXIMILIAN, archduke of Austria.

Leopold I (1640–1705) Holy Roman emperor. Son of FERDINAND III, Leopold was a devout Catholic destined for the church, but when his elder brother died unexpectedly (1654) he became heir apparent to the Austrian Habsburg lands. He was crowned successively king of Hungary (1655) and of Bohemia (1656), and with his father's death, Leopold became emperor in 1658. During his lengthy reign Austria emerged from a series of struggles to become a great European power.In 1683 the Turks besieged Vienna and were repulsed, but war continued until the Turks were defeated and ceded control of Hungary in the Treaty of KARLOWITZ (1699). Leopold also entered into the War of the GRAND ALLIANCE, but the unfavorable peace treaty ceded Strasbourg to France. He was drawn into the War of the SPANISH SUCCESSION, but died before its end. His third marriage, to Eleonore of Palatinate-Neuburg, was a happy union that produced 10 children, including the future emperors Joseph I and CHARLES VI.

Leopold II *orig.* **Léopold-Louis-Philippe-Marie-Victor** (1835–1909) King of the Belgians (1865–1909). Succeeding his father, LEOPOLD I, he led the first European efforts to develop the Congo River basin. In 1876 he founded an association to explore the Congo area, with HENRY MORTON STANLEY as his main agent. Leopold formed the Congo Free State in 1885 and ruled as its sovereign. Under Leopold, the Congo became the scene of barbarous cruelty by the colonial masters; when news of the conditions there broke c. 1905, it provoked an international scandal. Under British and U.S. pressure, the region was removed from Leopold's personal rule and annexed to Belgium in 1908 as the Belgian Congo. Leopold was succeeded by his nephew, ALBERT I.

Leopold II (1747–1792) Holy Roman emperor (1790–92). Son of MARIA THERESA and Emperor FRANCIS I, he became duke of Tuscany in 1765. A practitioner of ENLIGHTENED DESPOTISM, he built an efficient state government and encouraged representative institutions. In 1790 he succeeded his brother JOSEPH II as emperor and retained many of Joseph's reforms. In 1792 he allied with Prussia against revolutionary France, precipitating the FRENCH REVOLUTIONARY WARS.

Leopold III *orig.* **Léopold-Philippe-Charles-Albert-Meinrad-Hubertus-Marie-Miguel** (1901–1983) King of the Belgians (1934–51). He succeeded his father, ALBERT I, and favored an independent foreign policy but not strict neutrality. In World War II he assumed command of the Belgian army, but surrendered his encircled forces 18 days after the German invasion in May 1940. The Belgian government repudiated his decision to surrender and remain with his forces, rather than join the government-in-exile in London. Under house arrest through the war, he later went to Switzerland (1945–50) to await resolution of the controversy. Though 58% of voters voted for his return to the throne, he abdicated in 1951 in favor of his son BAUDOUIN.

Leopold of Hohenzollern-Sigmaringen \ˌhō-ənt-ˈsȯl-ərn-ˈzē̱k-mä-ˌriŋ-ən\, **Prince** (1835–1905) Prussian candidate for the Spanish throne. He was a member of the Swabian line of the HOHENZOLLERN DYNASTY and the brother of CAROL I of Romania. Chancellor OTTO VON BISMARCK and Spain's de facto leader, Juan Prim (1814–1870), persuaded the reluctant Leopold to accept the Spanish throne, left vacant in 1868. Under French diplomatic pressure, Leopold's candidacy was withdrawn, but Prussia refused to bow to French demands that it never be renewed. The EMS TELEGRAM provoked the French into declaring war (see FRANCO-PRUSSIAN WAR).

Leopardi \ˌlā-ō-ˈpär-dē\, **Giacomo** (1798–1837) Italian poet, scholar, and philosopher. Congenitally deformed, he suffered throughout his life from chronic ailments and frustrated hopes. His usually pessimistic poetry is admired for its brilliance, intensity, and effortless musicality. His verse collections include *Canzoni* (1824), *Versi* (1826), and *I canti* (1831). His finest poems are probably the lyrics called "Idillii." *Operette morali* (1827; "Minor Moral Works") is an influential philosophical exposition, mainly in dialogue form, of his doctrine of despair. He is considered among the great Italian writers of the 19th century.

Léopoldville See KINSHASA

Lepanto \lē-ˈpän-tō\, **Battle of** (October 7, 1571) Naval engagement between allied Christian forces (Venice, the pope, and Spain) and the Ottoman Turks during an Ottoman campaign to acquire the Venetian island of Cyprus. After four hours of fighting off the coast of Lepanto, Greece, the allies, under JUAN DE AUSTRIA, were victorious, capturing 117 galleys and thousands of men. The battle was of little practical value, since Venice would surrender Cyprus to the Turks in 1573, but it had a great impact on European morale and was the subject of paintings by TITIAN, TINTORETTO, and VERONESE.

lepidopteran \ˌle-pə-ˈdäp-tə-rən\ Any of the more than 100,000 species constituting the order Lepidoptera (Greek: "scaly wing"): BUTTERFLIES, MOTHS, and SKIPPERS. The name refers to the dusting of minute scales that covers the wings and bodies of these INSECTS. A slender proboscis is used for sucking. Nearly all lepidopterans are plant eaters, and species are found on every continent except Antarctica. Females may lay from a few to a thousand or more eggs at a time. All lepidopterans undergo complete METAMORPHOSIS. Many types move from one region to another, sometimes crossing thousands of miles of ocean, but the only species that truly migrates—the same individuals making a two-way flight—is the MONARCH BUTTERFLY.

Lepidus \ˈle-pə-dəs\, **Marcus Aemilius** (died 13/12 BC) Roman CONSUL (46, 42 BC) and triumvir (43–36). After the death of Julius CAESAR, Lepidus controlled parts of Gaul, Spain, and Africa and wielded great influence. He and Mark ANTONY opposed republican conspirators and in 43 formed the Second TRIUMVIRATE with Octavian (later AUGUSTUS). He acquired a second Spanish province but lost Spain and Gaul to Antony and Octavian, keeping only Africa. After helping defeat Sextus POMPEIUS (36), he challenged Octavian, but his soldiers defected, and he was forced to retire.

Lepontine Alps \li-ˈpän-ˌtīn\ Segment of the central ALPS along the Italian–Swiss border. It is bordered by the Pennine Alps in the west and southwest, and the Italian lake district in the south; its highest peak, Mount Leone (11,657 ft, or 3,553 m), lies at its western end. Important passes include SIMPLON, ST. GOTTHARD, Lukmanier, and SAN BERNARDINO.

leprechaun \ˈlep-rə-ˌkän\ In Irish folklore, a FAIRY in the form of a tiny old man wearing a cocked hat and leather apron. Solitary by nature, leprechauns lived in remote places and worked as shoemakers. Each was believed to possess a hidden crock of gold. If captured and threatened, a leprechaun might reveal the gold's hiding place, provided his captor never took his eyes off him. Usually the captor was tricked into glancing away, and the lepre-

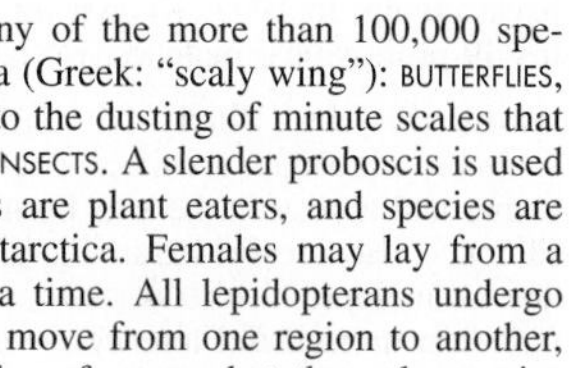

Leprechaun, from the *Irish Fairy Book*, by Alfred Perceval Crave, 1909.

BY COURTESY OF THE FOLKLORE SOCIETY LIBRARY, UNIVERSITY COLLEGE, LONDON; PHOTOGRAPH, R.B. FLEMING

chaun vanished. The word derives from the Old Irish *luchorpan* ("little body").

leprosy *or* **Hansen's disease** Chronic disease of the skin and superficial nerves, caused by the bacterium *Mycobacterium leprae.* In the lepromatous (cutaneous) type, grainy masses infiltrate inflamed tissue under the skin, in the lining of the upper respiratory tract, and in the testes; untreated, the outlook is poor. The tuberculoid type, marked by spots having raised, reddish borders and patches that spread and lose feeling, may not progress or may improve. Long-term SULFA-DRUG therapy usually helps; rehabilitation is usually also needed. Leprosy has a long history, but the disease seen today may not be the same one known in antiquity. A variety of infectious diseases that reached Europe from the East, especially with the returning Crusaders, led to the creation of leper colonies, where the ill were segregated and cared for. How it spreads is still unclear; prolonged close contact with an infected person usually precedes infection. Prevention depends on recognizing cases for isolation and treatment.

Leptis Magna *modern* **Labdah** Largest city of ancient TRIPOLIS, located near modern al-Khums, Libya. Founded by the Phoenicians in the 6th century BC., it passed to Numidia in 202 BC but broke away in 111 BC to become an ally of Rome. TRAJAN made it a Roman colony. The waning of the Roman empire caused its decline, and it was largely abandoned after the Arab conquest of 642. It has some of the best-preserved Roman ruins in North Africa.

lepton \'lep-tän\ Any member of a class of FERMIONS that respond only to electromagnetic, weak, and gravitational forces and do not take part in strong interactions. Leptons have a half-integral SPIN and obey the PAULI EXCLUSION PRINCIPLE. They can either carry one unit of ELECTRIC CHARGE or be neutral. The charged leptons are the electrons, muons, and taus. Each has a negative charge and a distinct MASS. Each charged lepton has an associated neutral partner, or NEUTRINO, which has no electric charge and very little if any mass.

Lerma River River, western central Mexico. It rises southeast of Toluca and flows northwest and then south for 350 mi (560 km) to empty into Lake CHAPALA. The Río Grande de Santiago, which leads from Lake Chapala to the Pacific Ocean, is sometimes considered an extension of the Lerma. With its major tributaries, it constitutes Mexico's largest river system.

Lermontov \'lʸer-mən-təf\, **Mikhail (Yuryevich)** (1814–1841) Russian poet and novelist. His first volume of verse, *Vesna* ("Spring"), was published in 1830, the year he entered Moscow Univ., which he left two years later to enter cadet school. A guards officer after graduating in 1834, he was twice exiled to regiments in the Caucasus because of his passionately libertarian verse. He became popular for having suffered for his poetry, which combined civic and philosophical themes with deeply personal motifs. His mature poems include *Mtsyri* (1840) and *Demon* (1841). His novel *A Hero of Our Time* (1840), a reflection on contemporary society and the fortunes of his generation, is written in superb prose, and the portrait of its alienated hero profoundly influenced later Russian writers. Like ALEKSANDR PUSHKIN, to whom he is often compared, he died in a duel. He is remembered as his country's leading Romantic poet.

Lerner, Alan Jay (1918–1986) U.S. librettist and lyricist. Born in New York City to a prosperous retailing family, he studied at Juilliard and Harvard. He wrote more than 500 radio scripts between 1940 and 1942, the year he met F. LOEWE. Their first Broadway success came with *Brigadoon* (1947; film, 1954). It was followed by *Paint Your Wagon* (1951; film, 1969). *My Fair Lady* (1956) was an unprecedented triumph, setting a record for the longest original run of any musical; the film version (1964) won seven Academy Awards. Their film musical *Gigi* (1958) received nine Academy Awards. *Camelot* followed in 1960 (film, 1967). Lerner also collaborated with K. WEILL (*Love Life*, 1948) and BURTON LANE (*On a Clear Day You Can See Forever,* 1965; film, 1970), among others. His film scripts included *An American in Paris* (1951, Academy Award).

Lerwick Town (pop., 1991 est.: 8,000), administrative center of the SHETLAND ISLANDS, northern Scotland. It is on the eastern coast of the island of Mainland. Britain's northernmost town, it originated as a fishing village and is notable for its herring catch. The North Sea oil boom of the 1970s increased port traffic, and Lerwick became an oil supply and service base. It is the seat of the Shetland Islands Area Council.

Les Six See LES SIX

Les Vingt See LES VINGT

Lesage, Alain-René *or* **Le Sage** \lə-'säzh\ (1668–1747) French novelist and playwright. He studied law in Paris but later abandoned his clerkship to devote himself to literature. His classic *The Adventures of Gil Blas of Santillane* (1715–1735), one of the earliest realistic novels, was influential in making the PICARESQUE NOVEL a European literary fashion. A prolific satirical dramatist, he adapted Spanish models for his early plays, including the highly successful comedy *Crispin, Rival of His Master* (1707). He also composed more than 100 *comédies-vaudevilles* in the tradition of MOLIÈRE.

Lesage \lə-'säzh\, **Jean** (1912–1980) Canadian politician. Born in Montreal, he served as Canadian minister of resources and development 1953–57. In 1958 he became leader of Quebec's Liberal Party; it won the 1960 provincial elections and he became premier. He called for social and cultural reform, appointing the first minister of education and modernizing the school system and civil service. He developed close cultural ties with France. After the Liberals were defeated in 1966, he served as opposition leader until 1970.

lesbianism *also called* **sapphism** *or* **female homosexuality,** the quality or state of intense emotional and usually erotic attraction of a woman to another woman. First used in the late 16th century, the word "lesbian" referred to the Greek island of LESBOS. The connotation of female homosexuality was added in the late 19th century, when an association was made with the poetry of Lesbian poet SAPPHO (c. 610–c. 580 BC). At the turn of the 21st century, issues of concern to lesbians in Europe and North America included legal recognition for same-sex unions, child-rearing rights, women's health-care, taxes, inheritance, and the sharing of medical benefits with a partner.

Lesbos \'lez-ˌbäs\ *or* **Mytilene** \ˌmit-ᵊl-'ē-nē\ *or* **Mitilíni** \ˌmē-tē-'lē-nē\ Third largest island (pop., 1991 est.: 104,000) in the Aegean Sea. It occupies an area of 630 sq mi (1,640 sq km), and with two other islands forms a Greek department. Its main town is Mytilene. It was the birthplace of the poet SAPPHO, and thus is the source of the term "lesbian." Inhabited since c. 3000 BC, it was settled in c. 1050 BC by the Aetolians. After being under Persian rule (527–479 BC) it joined the DELIAN LEAGUE. In the PELOPONNESIAN WAR, it fell to SPARTA (405 BC), then was recovered for ATHENS (389 BC). It later flourished under Byzantium. It was ruled by the Turks 1462–1911, then was annexed by Greece. Fishing is important economically, as is the export of olives.

Leschetizky \ˌle-shə-'tit-skē\, **Theodor** *orig.* **Teodor Leszetycki** (1830–1915) Polish pianist and teacher. A prodigy, he studied in Vienna with KARL CZERNY and Simon Sechter (1788–1867) from age 10, and was already a teacher by 14. In addition to performing, he became the most celebrated piano teacher of his time, first at the conservatory in St. Petersburg (1852–78) and thereafter in Vienna. His students included many of the most renowned pianists of their era, including I. PADEREWSKI and A. SCHNABEL.

leshy \'lʸe-shəy\ In Slavic mythology, a forest spirit. The leshy is an antic spirit who enjoys playing tricks on people, though when angered he can be treacherous. He is seldom seen, but his voice can be heard in the forest laughing, whistling, or singing. He often takes the shape of a man, but his eyebrows, eyelashes, and right ear are missing, his head is pointed, and he lacks a hat and belt. In his native forest, the leshy is as tall as the trees, but the moment he steps beyond it, he shrinks to the size of grass. The leshy is familiar to most Slavs living in heavily forested areas.

Leslie, Frank *orig.* **Henry Carter** (1821–1880) British-U.S. illustrator and journalist. The *Illustrated London News* published his early sketches. He moved to the U.S. in 1848. There he founded numerous newspapers and journals, including the *New York Journal* (1854), *Frank Leslie's Illustrated Newspaper* (1855)—having changed his name in 1857—and the *Boys' and Girls' Weekly.* His illustrations from Civil War battlefields earned him his greatest profits. His second wife, Miriam Florence Leslie (1836?–1914), continued his business after his death, twice rescuing it from debt.

Lesniewski \lesh-'nyef-skē\, **Stanislaw** *or* **Stanislaw Leshniewski** (1886–1939) Polish logician and mathematician. As a professor at the University of Warsaw (1919–39), he became a cofounder and leading representative of the Warsaw school of logic. His distinctive contribution was the construction of three interrelated FORMAL SYSTEMS, to which he gave the Greek-derived names of protothetic, ontology, and MEREOLOGY.

Lesotho \lə-'sü-ˌtü, lə-'sō-ˌtō\ *officially* **Kingdom of Lesotho** *formerly* **Basutoland** Independent kingdom, southern Africa, an enclave lying within the Republic of South Africa. Area: 11,720 sq mi (30,355 sq km). Population (1997 est.): 2,008,000. Capital: MASERU. Almost all of its population belong to the SOTHO, a Bantu-speaking people. Languages: Sotho, English (both official), Africaans, Zulu, Xhosa, French. Religions: Christianity (official), including Roman Catholicism, Lesotho Evangelical Church, Anglicanism. Currency: loti. About two-thirds of Lesotho's total area is mountainous; its highest point is Mount Ntlenyana (11,424 ft, or 3,482 m). The Maloti Mountains in the central northwest are the source of two of South Africa's largest rivers, the TUGELA and the ORANGE. It has scant mineral resources. Agriculture employs two-thirds of the workforce; its chief farm products are corn, sorghum, and wheat. Livestock provide exports (cattle, wool, and mohair). Industries include food processing, textiles and apparel, and furniture. It is a republic with two legislative houses; its chief of state is the king, and the head of government is the prime minister. Bantu-speaking farmers began to settle the area in the 16th century, and a number of chiefdoms arose. The most powerful organized the Basotho in 1824, and obtained British protection in 1843, as tension between the Basotho and the South African Boers increased. It became a British territory in 1868 and was annexed to the Cape Colony in 1871. The colony's effort to disarm the Basotho resulted in revolt in 1880, and four years later it separated from the colony and became a British High Commission Territory. In 1964 it declared its independence as a constitutional monarchy. A new constitution, effective 1993, ended seven years of military rule. In the late 20th century, Lesotho suffered from internal political problems and a deteriorating economy.

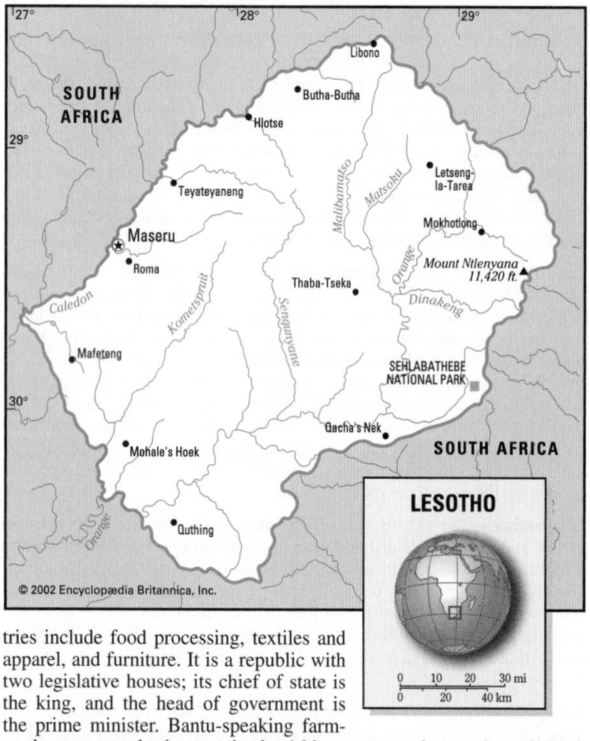

Lesse River \'les, 'le-sə\ River, southeastern Belgium. It rises in the Ardennes and meanders northwest for 52 mi (84 km), emptying into the MEUSE RIVER. It flows underground for about a mile at Han-sur-Lesse through the Grottoes of Han, renowned for their stalactites and stalagmites.

Lesseps \'le-səps\, **Ferdinand (-Marie), vicomte (Viscount) de** (1805–1894) French diplomat, builder of the SUEZ CANAL. A career diplomat, he held posts in Egypt and elsewhere until 1849. In 1854 he was authorized by the viceroy of Egypt to build a canal across the isthmus of the Suez. He organized a company in 1858, with half its capital from the French people, and construction began at Port Said in 1859. The Suez Canal was officially inaugurated in 1869. In 1879 Lesseps organized another company to build a Panama canal, but gave up the project because of political and economic difficulties. He was prosecuted but cleared of misappropriating funds, though French government members were accused of bribe taking.

Lesseps.
CULVER PICTURES

Lesser Armenia See LITTLE ARMENIA

Lesser Slave Lake Lake, central Alberta. Located northwest of EDMONTON and south of GREAT SLAVE LAKE, it occupies an area of 451 sq mi (1,168 sq km) and drains into the ATHABASCA RIVER by the Lesser Slave River. Its name refers to the Slave (Dogrib) Indians, who once inhabited its shores.

Lessing, Doris (May) *orig.* **Doris May Tayler** (born 1919) British novelist and short-story writer. Born in Iran, she lived on a farm in Southern Rhodesia (now Zimbabwe) 1924–49 before settling in England and beginning her writing career. Her works, which have often reflected her leftist political activism, are largely concerned with people caught in social and political upheavals. *Children of Violence* (1952–69), a semi-autobiographical five-novel series featuring Martha Quest, reflects her African experience and is generally considered her most substantial work. *The Golden Notebook* (1962), her most widely read novel, is regarded as a feminist classic. A master of the short story, she has published several collections. She also has written a science-fiction novel sequence and autobiographical works including *Under My Skin* (1994).

Lessing, Gotthold (Ephraim) (1729–1781) German playwright and critic. After writing several light comedies, he became a theater critic in Berlin in 1748. His play *Miss Sara Sampson* (1755) was the first German domestic tragedy. After studying philosophy and aesthetics in Breslau, he wrote the influential treatise *Laocoön:An Essay on the Limits of Painting and Poetry* (1766). *Minna von Barnhelm* (1767), his finest play, marks the beginning of classical German comedy. He was adviser to the first Hamburg national theater and published his reviews as essays on the principles of drama in *Hamburg Dramaturgy* (1767–69). His *Wolfenbüttel Fragments* (1774–78) attacked orthodox Christianity, arousing great controversy. He also wrote the tragedy *Emilia Galotti* (1772) and the famous dramatic poem *Nathan the Wise* (1779).

Lethe \'lē-thē\ Ancient Greek personification of oblivion. She was the daughter of ERIS (Strife). Her name was also applied to a river or plain in the realm of the dead. In the Orphic mysteries it was believed that the newly dead who drank from the River Lethe would lose all memory of their past existence. The initiated were taught to drink instead from Mnemosyne, the river of Memory.

Leto \'lē-tō\ In classical mythology, the mother of APOLLO and ARTEMIS. She was made pregnant by ZEUS, and she wandered in search of a place to give birth until she found the barren island of DELOS. The island was a floating rock borne about by the waves, but it was fixed to the bottom of the sea for the birth of Apollo and Artemis. In some versions, Leto's wanderings are ascribed to the jealousy of Zeus's wife, HERA.

Letterman, David (born 1947) U.S. television talk-show host. Born in Indianapolis, he began his career as a stand-up comedian and was a guest host of JOHNNY CARSON's *Tonight Show* from 1979. He hosted NBC's post-midnight *Late Night with David Letterman* 1982–93, winning six Emmy awards and great popularity with his ironic, abrasive, flippant style of interviewing, which critics viewed as a parody of talk shows. Since 1993 he has hosted *The Late Show with David Letterman* on CBS in the earlier time slot.

letterpress printing *or* **relief printing** *or* **typographic printing** In commercial PRINTING, process by which many copies are produced by repeated direct impression of an inked, raised surface against sheets or a continuous roll of PAPER. Letterpress is the oldest traditional printing technique, the only important one from the time of JOHANNES GUTENBERG (c. 1450) until LITHOGRAPHY (late 18th century) and especially OFFSET PRINTING (early 20th century). The ink-bearing surface for a page of text was originally assembled letter by letter and line by line. The Monotype and LINOTYPE were the first keyboard-activated TYPESETTING machines. Letterpress can produce high-quality work at high speed, but requires much time to prepare and adjust the press. For the sake of speed, newspapers are now printed by the offset process.

Lettish language See LATVIAN LANGUAGE

lettre de cachet \'letrᵊ-də-kà-'shā\ (French: "letter with a seal") Letter bearing an official seal, signed by the king and countersigned by a secretary of state, used primarily to authorize someone's imprisonment without trial. An important instrument of administration under the ANCIEN RÉGIME in France, lettres de cachet were greatly abused in the 17th–18th century. Their use was abolished in 1790.

lettuce Cultivated annual salad plant *(Lactuca sativa)* that produces clusters of crisp, water-filled leaves. The best-known varieties are head, or cabbage, lettuce (variety *capitata*); leaf, or curled, lettuce (variety *crispa*); cos, or romaine, lettuce (variety *longifolia*); and asparagus lettuce (variety *asparagina*). Head lettuce is further divided into butter heads and crisp heads (e.g., iceberg lettuce). In the U.S, large-scale farms grow mainly crisp-head varieties, shipping them nationwide. Small-scale, local farmers raise leaf and butter-head varieties. Lettuce is an early annual crop that grows best in cool weather and with ample water. Though usually consumed in salads, it may also be cooked.

Lettuce (*Lactuca sativa*, variety *capitata*).
DEREK FELL

leucine \'lü-,sēn\ One of the essential AMINO ACIDS, present in most common PROTEINS and particularly abundant in HEMOGLOBIN. One of the first amino acids discovered (1819), it is used in biochemical research and as a nutritional supplement.

leucite \'lü-,sīt\ One of the most common FELDSPATHOID minerals, potassium aluminosilicate ($KAlSi_2O_6$). It occurs only in IGNEOUS ROCKS, particularly potassium-rich, silica-poor, recent lavas. Some important localities include Rome, Italy; Uganda; and Wyoming's Leucite Hills. Leucite is used as a fertilizer in Italy (because of its high potassium content) and as a source of commercial alum.

Leucothea \lü-'kä-thē-ə\ In GREEK MYTHOLOGY, a sea goddess. She is first mentioned in the *Odyssey,* in which she rescued ODYSSEUS from drowning. She was traditionally identified with Ino, daughter of CADMUS, who incurred the wrath of HERA by caring for the infant DIONYSUS, ZEUS's son by SEMELE. Hera drove Ino and her son Melicertes mad, and they leaped into the sea, where they were changed into marine deities—Ino into Leucothea, Melicertes into Palaemon. A dolphin carried Melicertes' body to the Isthmus of Corinth, and the ISTHMIAN GAMES were instituted in his honor.

Leucothea giving Dionysus a drink from the Horn of Plenty, antique bas-relief; in the Lateran Museum, Rome.
ALINARI—ART RESOURCE

leukemia CANCER of blood-forming tissues with high levels of LEUKOCYTES. Radiation exposure and hereditary susceptibility are factors in some cases. In acute leukemias, ANEMIA, fever, bleeding, and lymph-node swelling develop rapidly. Acute lymphocytic leukemia, found mostly in children, was once over 90% fatal in six months. Drug therapy can now cure more than half these children. Acute myelogenous (granulocytic) leukemia, found mostly in adults, has frequent remissions and recurrences, and few patients survive long. Chronic myelogenous leukemia most often begins in the 40s; weight loss, low fever, weakness, and other symptoms may not develop immediately. CHEMOTHERAPY helps the symptoms but may not prolong life. Chronic lymphocytic leukemia, mostly in the elderly, may be inactive for years. Survival rates are better than in myelogenous leukemia; most deaths are caused by infection or hemorrhage.

leukocyte \'lü-kə-,sīt\ *or* **white blood cell** *or* **white corpuscle** Any of several types of blood cells that help defend the body from INFECTION. The different mature forms—granulocytes, including neutrophils (heterophils), basophils, and eosinophils; monocytes, including macrophages; and LYMPHOCYTES—have different functions, including ingesting BACTERIA, PROTOZOANS, or infected or dead body cells; producing ANTIBODIES; and regulating the action of other leukocytes. They act mostly in the tissues and are in the bloodstream only for transport. Blood normally contains 5,000–10,000 leukocytes per cu mm.

leukoderma See VITILIGO

Levant \lə-'vänt\ Historical name for the countries along the shores of the eastern MEDITERRANEAN SEA. It was applied to the coastlands of ASIA MINOR and Syria, sometimes extending from Greece to Egypt. The term was often associated with Venetian trading ventures. It was also used as a synonym for the Middle or Near East. In the 16th–17th century, the term High Levant referred to the Far East. The name Levant States was given to the French mandate of Syria and Lebanon after World War I.

level Device for establishing a horizontal plane. It consists of a small, sealed glass tube containing liquid and an air bubble; the tube is fixed horizontally in a block or frame with a smooth lower surface. When the bubble is in the middle of the glass tube, the device is on a level surface; adjustment to the horizontal is indicated by movement of the bubble. The glass tube is slightly bowed, and the level's sensitivity is proportional to the radius of curvature.

Leveler Member of a republican faction in England during the ENGLISH CIVIL WARS and Commonwealth. The name was coined by the movement's enemies to suggest that its supporters wished to "level men's estates." The movement began in 1645–46 and demanded that sovereignty rest with the House of Commons (to the exclusion of king and lords), believing that manhood suffrage would make Parliament truly representative. The Levelers dominated the NEW MODEL ARMY, but the Putney debates in the army council discussing the Levelers' new social contract (1647) ended in deadlock. The generals restored army discipline by force, ending the Levelers' political power.

Leven \'lē-vən\, **Loch** Lake, eastern central Scotland. Roughly 3 mi (5 km) in diameter, it is one of the shallowest of the Scottish lochs, having an average depth of 15 ft (4.5 m). It contains a subspecies of BROWN TROUT known as Loch Leven trout. Castle Island, one of the lake's seven islands, has the ruins of a 14th-cent castle where MARY, QUEEN OF SCOTS, was imprisoned (1567–68).

lever Simple MACHINE used to amplify physical FORCE. All early people used the lever in some form, for moving heavy stones or as digging sticks for land cultivation. Balance beams for weighing were probably used in Egypt c. 5000 BC; they consist of a bar pivoted at its center with weights on one end balancing the object on the other. As early as 1500 BC people were raising water and lifting soldiers over battlements using the swape or shadoof, a long lever pivoted near one end with a platform or container hanging from the short arm and counterweights attached to the long arm.

Lever Bros. \'lē-vər\ British soap and detergent manufacturer. Lever Bros. was founded in 1885 by William Hesketh Lever, later Viscount Leverhulme (1851–1925), and his brother, James Darcy Lever, to make and sell soap. The first company to market wrapped bars of soap made from vegetable oil instead of tallow, Lever Bros. expanded internationally with the help of energetic advertising slogans. It built a model industrial village at Port Sunlight in 1888 and offered employee benefits such as profit sharing and free insurance. William was elected to Parliament in 1906 and became a viscount in 1922. In 1929, Lever Bros. joined an association of European companies to form UNILEVER.

Levertov, Denise (1923–1997) English-born American poet, essayist, and political activist. The daughter of an immigrant Russian Jew (who converted to Christianity) and a Welsh woman, Levertov became a civilian nurse during World War II. She married an American writer after the war and moved to the United States, where she was associated with the Black Mountain group, which included the poets Charles Olson and Robert Duncan. Influenced by the deliberate simplicity of WILLIAM CARLOS WILLIAMS's poetry, she wrote deceptively matter-of-fact verse on both personal and political themes. Among her poetry collections are *Here and Now* (1957), *The Sorrow Dance* (1967), and *The Freeing of the Dust* (1975). Levertov taught at Stanford University from 1981 to 1994.

Lévesque \lā-'vek\, **René** (1922–1987) Canadian politician. Born in Carlisle, Quebec, he joined the Canadian Broadcasting Corp. in 1946 and was a TV commentator 1956–59. In 1960 he was elected to the Quebec legislature and served in JEAN LESAGE's administration (1960–66). In 1967 he cofounded a separatist group that combined with others to form the PARTI QUÉBÉCOIS. In 1976 his party won control of the Quebec assembly, and he became premier. He proposed an independent Quebec in economic union with the rest of Canada, which he called "sovereignty-association." In 1980 the plan was rejected by the Quebec electorate. He resigned in 1985 due to failing health.

Levi \'lē-,vī\ In ancient Israel, the third son of the patriarch JACOB. Levi became head of the clans of religious functionaries known as Levites. Unlike the 12 tribes of ISRAEL, the Levites were given no allotment of land when CANAAN was conquered. They are thought to have performed subordinate services associated with public worship, serving as musicians, guardians, Temple officials, judges, and craftsmen.

Levi \'lā-vē\, **Primo** (1919–1987) Italian writer and chemist. Two years after obtaining a degree in chemistry, Levi, a Jew, was captured by the Nazis and sent to Auschwitz as a slave laborer. His autobiographical works—*If This Is a Man*, or *Survival in Auschwitz* (1947), *The Reawakening* (1963), and *The Drowned and the Saved* (1986)—are restrained and moving accounts of and reflections on survival in the Nazi camps. His best-known work, *The Periodic Table* (1975), is a collection of 21 meditations, each named for a chemical element. The lingering effects of his wartime trauma may have led to his suicide.

Lévi \lā-'vē\, **Sylvain** (1863–1935) French scholar of Eastern religion, literature, and history. He taught at the Sorbonne (1889–94) and later for many years at the Collège de France (1894–1935). In 1929, with Takakusu Junjiro, he published a classic dictionary of Buddhism. His other writings include the standard treatise *The Indian Theater* (1890), *Nepal* (1905–8), and *India and the World* (1926); he also carried out pioneering studies of the Tocharian languages.

Lévi-Strauss \'lā-vē-'straủs\, **Claude** (born 1908) Belgian-French social anthropologist and leading exponent of STRUCTURALISM. Lévi-Strauss originally studied philosophy at the University of Paris (1927–32) but went on to teach sociology at the University of São Paulo (1934–37) and to conduct field research on the Indians of Brazil. At the New School for Social Research in New York City (1941–45) he came under the influence of the linguist ROMAN JAKOBSON; he came to view CULTURE as a system of communication, analogous to a language. His work is an effort to identify universal structures of the mind as reflected in MYTHS, cultural SYMBOLS, and social organization. From 1950 to 1974 he was director of studies at the École Pratique des Hautes Études, and in 1959 he joined the faculty of the Collège de France. Among his major works are *The Elementary Structures of Kinship* (1949), *Tristes Tropiques* (1955), *Structural Anthropology* (1961), and the four-volume *Mythologiques* (1964–71).

Lévi-Strauss.
AP/WIDE WORLD PHOTOS

Levi Strauss & Co. World's largest maker of pants, noted especially for its blue-denim jeans. The company traces its origin to Levi Strauss (1829–1902), a Bavarian immigrant who sold dry goods to miners during the California GOLD RUSH. Hearing of the miners' need for durable pants, he hired a tailor to make garments out of tent canvas, later substituting DENIM. In 1873, he and an associate received a patent for the copper riveting they used to strengthen their pants. The company's most spectacular growth occurred after 1946, when it decided to concentrate wholly on manufacturing clothing under its own label. In 1959 it began exporting, and during the 1960s jeans became enormously popular worldwide. The company went public in 1971 and was returned to private control (by Strauss's descendants) in 1985.

Levine \lə-'vīn\, **James (Lawrence)** (born 1943) U.S. conductor. Born in Cincinnati, he debuted as a pianist at 10 with the Cincinnati Symphony Orchestra. At Juilliard he studied piano with Rosina Lhévinne (1880–1976) and conducting with Jean Morel (1903–1975). He was assistant conductor of the Cleveland Orchestra 1964–70. A guest appearance conducting *Tosca* (1971) led to his appointment as principal conductor (1973) and later music director (1975) and artistic director (1986) of the Metropolitan Opera. He built the flagging Met orchestra into a virtuoso ensemble and became recognized as one of the world's greatest conductors. He served as director of Chicago's Ravinia Festival 1973–93.

Levinson, Barry (born 1942) U.S. film director. Born in Baltimore, he worked as a comedy writer for CAROL BURNETT and MEL BROOKS in the 1970s, then made his directorial debut with *Diner* (1982), the first of several movies set in his native city. He followed it with *The Natural* (1984), *Young Sherlock Holmes* (1985), *Tin Men* (1987), and *Good Morning, Vietnam* (1987), the highly popular *Rain Man* (1988, Academy Award), *Avalon* (1990), *Bugsy* (1991), *Sleepers* (1996), and *Wag the Dog* (1997).

levirate and sororate \'le-və-rət...'sȯr-ə-rət\ Customs or laws regulating MARRIAGE following the death of a spouse, or in some cases during the lifetime of the spouse. The levirate decrees a dead man's brother to be the widow's preferred marriage partner. In ancient Hebrew society, this practice served to perpetuate the line of a man who died childless. Often, the brother who marries his sister-in-law is a proxy for the deceased and no new marriage is contracted, since all progeny are acknowledged as the seed of the dead man. The sororate decrees the marriage of a man to his deceased wife's sister or, under so-called sororal polygyny, to the wife's younger sisters as they come of age. The latter was practiced by some American Indian tribes in the 19th century and continues among the Australian ABORIGINES.

Leviticus Rabbah \li-'vi-ti-kəs-rä-'bä\ (c. AD 450) Compilation of 37 compositions on topics suggested by the Old Testament Book of Leviticus. Their message is that the laws of history focus on the holy life of Israel (the Jewish people). If the Jews obey the laws of society aimed at Israel's sanctification, then the foreordained history will unfold as Israel hopes. Israel, for its part, can affect its own destiny. Thus salvation at the end of history depends on sanctification in the here and now.

Levitt, Helen (born 1913) U.S. photographer. Born in New York City, Levitt began her career in photography at age 18. Her first show, "Photographs of Children," was held at the Museum of Modern Art in New York in 1943. It featured the subject matter—children, especially the underprivileged—and humanity that characterizes much of her work. In the mid-1940s Levitt collaborated with the novelist JAMES AGEE, filmmaker Sidney Meyers, and painter Janice Loeb on *The Quiet One*, a prizewinning documentary about a young African American boy. For most of the 1960s she concentrated on film editing and directing. Levitt resumed her pursuit of photography in the 1970s.

Levittown Extensive suburban housing development in Hempstead, Long Island, N.Y. Developed 1946–51 by the firm of Levitt and Sons, Inc., it was an early example of a completely preplanned and mass-produced housing complex. It contained thousands of low-cost homes (with accompanying shopping centers, playgrounds, swimming pools, community halls, and schools). Levitt repeated the formula in Bucks County, Pa. (1951–55). The name Levittown became equated with similar developments built across the country in the postwar building boom. Though once widely deplored, his towns differ from other, usually monotonous, middle-class speculative developments in their meandering roads and lush plantings.

levodopa See DOPA

levulose See FRUCTOSE

Lewes \ˈlü-əs\ Town (pop., 1991: 15,376), seat of EAST SUSSEX, England. It lies on the Ouse River 6 mi (10 km) north of the ENGLISH CHANNEL. In 1264 SIMON DE MONTFORT vanquished HENRY III at the Battle of Lewes. Historic sites include the ruins of an 11th-century castle and the 16th-century Barbican House (home of ANNE OF CLEVES). An administrative center, it has some light industry. Glyndebourne, a renowned opera center, is nearby.

Lewin, Kurt (1890–1947) German-U.S. social psychologist. After training and teaching in Berlin, he emigrated to the U.S., where he taught at the State University of Iowa (1935–45) and later became director of a group dynamics research center at MIT (1945–47). He is best known for his field theory of behavior, which holds that human behavior is a function of an individual's psychological environment. To fully understand and predict human behavior, according to Lewin, one must view the totality of events in a person's psychological field, or "lifespace." His works include *A Dynamic Theory of Personality* (1935) and *Field Theory in Social Science* (1951).

Lewis, (Frederick) Carl(ton) (born 1961) U.S. track-and-field athlete. Born in Birmingham, Ala., he qualified for the 1980 Olympics but did not participate because of the U.S. boycott of the Moscow games. At the 1984 Olympics he won the 100-m and 200-m races, the long jump, and the 4×100 relay. At the 1988 Olympics he won the long jump (becoming the first athlete ever to win that event consecutively) and the 100-m race and received a silver medal in the 200-m. In 1992 he again won the long jump and anchored the winning U.S. 4×100-relay team, and in 1996 he astounded observers by winning a fourth consecutive long-jump title. He retired from competition in 1997.

Lewis, C(larence) I(rving) (1883–1964) U.S. philosopher. Born in Stoneham, Mass., he taught primarily at Harvard University (1920–53). His best-known works are *Mind and the World Order* (1929), *Symbolic Logic* (1932), *An Analysis of Knowledge and Valuation* (1947), and *The Ground and Nature of the Right* (1955). He maintained that knowledge is possible only where there is also a possibility of error. His position in epistemology represents a synthesis of EMPIRICISM and PRAGMATISM.

Lewis, C(live) S(taples) (1898–1963) British scholar and writer. Lewis taught first at Oxford (1925–54) and later at Cambridge (1954–63). Many of his books embrace Christian APOLOGETICS, the best known being *The Screwtape Letters* (1942), a satirical epistolary novel in which an experienced devil instructs his young charge in the art of temptation. Also well known are *The Chronicles of Narnia* (1950–56), a series of seven children's stories (including *The Lion, the Witch, and the Wardrobe*) that have become classics of fantasy; and a science-fiction trilogy beginning with *Out of the Silent Planet* (1938). The critical *Allegory of Love* (1936), on medieval and Renaissance literature, is often considered his greatest work.

Lewis, Edward B. (born 1918) U.S. geneticist. Born in Wilkes-Barre, Pa., he received a PhD in genetics from Caltech. By crossbreeding thousands of fruit flies, he showed that genes are arranged on the chromosome in the order corresponding to body segments, an orderliness now known as the colinearity principle. Lewis's work helped explain mechanisms of general biological development, including the causes of deformities present at birth in humans. With Christiane Nüsslein-Volhard (born 1942) and Eric F. Wieschaus (born 1947), he was awarded a 1995 Nobel Prize.

Lewis, Jerry *orig.* **Joseph Levitch** (born 1926) U.S. actor, director, and producer. Born in Newark, N.J., he joined his parents' Borscht Belt act in the Catskills resorts and was an experienced comic by 18. In 1946 he developed a nightclub comedy routine with Dean Martin (1917–1995), who played the suave, romantic singer to Lewis's zany clown, and they appeared together in 16 movies, including *My Friend Irma* (1949), *Jumping Jacks* (1952), and *Pardners* (1956), before ending their partnership in 1956. Lewis then directed, produced, and acted in such movies as *The Bellboy* (1960), *The Nutty Professor* (1963), and *The Big Mouth* (1967). His 1983 film *The King of Comedy* shows the actor in a serious role. Since 1966 he has hosted the U.S. annual Muscular Dystrophy Telethon.

Lewis, Jerry Lee (born 1935) U.S. rock-and-roll musician. Born in Ferriday, La., he began playing piano in his childhood, influenced by blues and gospel musicians. The cousin of singer Mickey Gilley and evangelist Jimmy Swaggart, he attended Bible school in Texas, but was expelled. Returning to Louisiana, he played in several bands, perfecting his signature "pumping" piano technique. His first hits came in 1957 with "Whole Lotta Shakin' Goin' On" and "Great Balls of Fire." In 1958 it was discovered that he had married a 13-year-old relative, and his record sales dropped. Though he had a few more hits, he concentrated on his famously energetic and uninhibited live performances. His career continued to be plagued by controversy, including the deaths of two wives.

Lewis, John L(lewellyn) (1880–1969) U.S. labor leader. Born near Lucas, Iowa, the son of Welsh immigrants, he became a coal miner at 15. He rose through the ranks of the UNITED MINE WORKERS OF AMERICA (UMWA) and from 1911 was also an organizer of the American Federation of Labor (AFL), with which the miners' union was affiliated. As president of the UMWA (1920–60), Lewis joined several other AFL union leaders in forming the Committee for Industrial Organization (1935) to organize workers in mass-production industries. On breaking with the AFL, Lewis and other dissident union heads founded the Congress of Industrial Organizations (see AFL-CIO). As its president (1936–40), Lewis presided over the often-violent struggle to introduce unionism into previously unorganized industries such as steel and automobiles. See also WILLIAM GREEN, LABOR UNION, PHILIP MURRAY.

John L. Lewis, 1963.
AP/WIDE WORLD PHOTOS

Lewis, Lennox *in full* **Lennox Claudius Lewis** (born 1965) British boxer. His professional career began in 1989 in England. He won the World Boxing Council (WBC) heavyweight title in 1992, lost it in 1994, and recaptured it in 1997. In 1999 he faced American EVANDER HOLYFIELD, who held the heavyweight titles of the World Boxing Association (WBA) and the International Boxing Federation (IBF). In a controversial decision, the fight was called a draw. In the rematch Lewis emerged as the undisputed champ, thereby unifying the heavyweight title. In his 2002 bout with American MIKE TYSON, Lewis knocked Tyson out in the eighth round.

Lewis, Matthew Gregory (1775–1818) English novelist and dramatist. The sensational success of his gothic novel *The Monk* (1796) earned him the nickname "Monk" Lewis. Its horror, violence, and eroticism made it avidly read though universally condemned. Lewis also wrote a popular music drama in the same vein, *The Castle Spectre* (1798). After inheriting a large fortune in Jamaica in 1812, he sailed twice to the island to inquire about the treatment of slaves on his estates there, and he died at sea. *Journal of a West India Proprietor* (1834) attests to his humane and liberal attitudes.

Lewis, Meriwether (1774–1809) U.S. explorer. Born near Charlottesville, Va., he served in the army and in 1801 became private secretary to Pres. THOMAS JEFFERSON, who selected him to lead the first overland expedition to the Pacific Northwest, including the area of the LOUISIANA PURCHASE. At Lewis's request, WILLIAM CLARK was appointed to share the command. The success of the LEWIS AND CLARK EXPEDITION (1804–6) was greatly due to Lewis's preparation and skill. At its conclusion, he and Clark each received 1,600 acres of land as a reward. Lewis was named governor of Louisiana Territory in 1808. His death in an inn while en route to Washington was either a murder or a suicide.

Lewis, (Harry) Sinclair (1885–1951) U.S. novelist and social critic. Born in Sauk Center, Minn., he worked as a reporter and magazine writer before making his literary reputation with *Main Street* (1920), a portrayal of Midwestern provincialism. Among his other popular satirical novels puncturing middle-class complacency are *Babbitt* (1922), a scathing study of a conformist businessman; *Arrowsmith* (1925), a look at the medical profession; *Elmer Gantry* (1927), an indictment of fundamentalist religion; and *Dodsworth* (1929), the story of a rich American couple in Europe. He won the 1930 Nobel Prize for Literature, the first given to an American. His later novels include *Cass Timberlaine* (1945). Lewis's reputation declined in later years, and he lived abroad much of the time. He was married to DOROTHY THOMPSON 1928–42.

Sinclair Lewis.
THE GRANGER COLLECTION

Lewis, (Percy) Wyndham (1882–1957) English artist and writer. The founder and principal exponent of VORTICISM, Lewis began a short-lived Vorticist review titled *Blast* in 1914. His first novel, *Tarr,* appeared in 1918. *The Childermass* (1928) was followed by the huge satirical novel *The Apes of God* (1930) and *The Revenge for Love* (1937). In the 1930s he produced some of his most noted paintings, including "The Surrender of Barcelona" (1936). He also wrote essays, short stories, and two admired memoirs. Notorious in the 1930s for championing fascism, he later recanted those beliefs.

Lewis and Clark Expedition (1804–6) First overland expedition to the U.S. Pacific coast and back, led by MERIWETHER LEWIS and WILLIAM CLARK. Initiated by Pres. THOMAS JEFFERSON, the expedition set out to find an overland route to the Pacific, documenting its exploration through the new LOUISIANA PURCHASE. About 40 men, skilled in various trades, left St. Louis in 1804. They traveled up the Missouri River into present-day North Dakota, where they built Fort Mandan (later Bismarck) and wintered among the Mandan Sioux. They left the next spring, hiring Toussaint Charbonneau and his Indian wife, SACAGAWEA, who served as guide and interpreter. They traveled through Montana and by horse over the Continental Divide to the headwaters of the Clearwater River. They built canoes to carry them to the Snake River and thence to the mouth of the Columbia River, where they built Fort Clatsop (later Astoria, Ore.) and wintered over. After the group divided, then reunited to canoe down the Missouri to St. Louis, arriving to great acclaim in September 1806. Only one member had died. The journals kept by Lewis and others documented the Indian tribes, wildlife, and geography and did much to dispel the myth of an easy water route to the Pacific.

Lexington City (pop., 1996 est.: 240,000), northern central Kentucky. Named in 1775 for Lexington, Mass. after the Battles of LEXINGTON AND CONCORD, it was chartered in 1782 and was the site of the first session of the Kentucky legislature (1792). Incorporated as a city in 1832, it merged with Fayette Co. in 1974 to create an urban county government. It is the seat of Transylvania University (founded 1780) and the University of KENTUCKY, and also the headquarters of the American Thoroughbred Breeders Association.

Lexington and Concord, Battles of (April 19, 1775) Initial skirmishes between British soldiers and American colonists that marked the beginning of the AMERICAN REVOLUTION. En route from Boston to seize the colonists' military stores at Concord, Mass., the British force of 700 was met at Lexington by 77 local minutemen (see MINUTEMAN) alerted by PAUL REVERE and others. Who fired the first shot is unclear, and resistance soon ended. The British moved on to nearby Concord, where they were met by over 300 American patriots and were forced to withdraw. On their march back to Boston, they were continually harried by colonists firing from behind barns, trees, and roadside walls. Losses totaled 273 British and 95 Americans.

Leyden See LEIDEN

Leyden, Lucas van See LUCAS VAN LEYDEN

Leyster \'lā-stər\, **Judith** (1609–1660) Dutch painter. A brewer's daughter, she had gained membership in the Haarlem painters' guild by age 24. Many of her known works, primarily portraits, genre paintings, and still lifes, were formerly attributed to her male contemporaries. Though the influence of FRANS HALS is clear, she was also interested in the style of the UTRECHT SCHOOL. She embraced a greater range of subjects than other Dutch painters of the era, and was one of the first to depict domestic scenes.

Leyte \'lā-tē\ Island (pop., 1990: 1,810,000) of the VISAYAN group, eastern Philippines. Occupying an area of 2,785 sq mi (7,214 sq km), it lies southwest of SAMAR Island, with which it is linked by a 7,093-ft (2,162-m) bridge. Known to 16th-century Spanish explorers as Tandaya, it was under Spanish rule until the late 19th century. Under U.S. control in the early 20th century, its population grew rapidly. During World War II it was occupied by the Japanese, who were ousted by U.S. forces in the Battle of LEYTE GULF. It has two major cities, Ormoc and Tacloban.

Leyte Gulf, Battle of (October 23–26, 1944) Decisive air and sea battle of WORLD WAR II that gave the Allies control of the Pacific. After the U.S. amphibious landing on the Philippine island of Leyte (October 20), the Japanese reacted with a plan to decoy the U.S. fleet north while moving three attack forces into Leyte Gulf. The U.S. preempted the plan by discovering one of the forces, which set off three days of continuous surface and air clashes. In the largest naval battle of the war, U.S. forces crippled the Japanese fleet and forced it to withdraw, allowing the U.S. to complete its invasion.

Lezama Lima \lā-'zä-mä-'lē-mä\, **José** (1910–1976) Cuban poet, novelist, and essayist. After studying law in Havana, Lezama was associated with several literary reviews and later with a literary group that published the work of young poets who revolutionized Cuban letters. Among his works are the poetry volumes *Muerte de Narciso* (1937) and *La fijeza* (1949) and the essay collections *Analecta del reloj* (1953) and *La expresión americana* (1957). The novel *Paradiso* (1966), considered his masterpiece, reaffirms his faith in his art and his own aestheticism in the face of the 1959 revolution, of which he largely disapproved.

Lhasa \'lä-sə\ Capital (pop., 1990 est.: 107,000), Tibet autonomous region, China. It is located at an elevation of 11,975 ft (3,650 m) in the Tibetan HIMALAYAS near the Lhasa River. It has served as the religious center of Tibet since at least the 9th cent AD. It became independent Tibet's capital in 1642 and remained so until the Chinese occupied the city (1951) and took over the government (1959). The 7th-century temple of Gtsug-lag-khang is considered the holiest in Tibet. Other landmarks include the temple of Klu-khang; the POTALA PALACE, the DALAI LAMA's former winter residence; and monasteries. It is sometimes known as the "Forbidden City" because of its inaccessibility and the traditional hostility of its religious leaders toward outsiders.

Lhasa apso \'lä-sə-'äp-sō\ Breed of dog from Tibet. The Lhasa apso is hardy, intelligent, and watchful. Longer than it is tall, it stands 10–11 in. (25–28 cm) high and weighs 13–15 lbs (6–7 kg). It has a heavily haired tail that curls over its back and a long, profuse coat that covers its eyes. Its coat may be of various colors, but most breeders prefer golden-brown shades.

Lhasa apso.
SALLY ANNE THOMPSON—EB INC.

L'Hôpital's rule \,lō-pē-'tälz\ Procedure of DIFFERENTIAL CALCULUS for evaluating indeterminate forms such as 0/0 and ∞/∞ when they result from attempting to find a LIMIT. It states that when the limit of $f(x)/g(x)$ is indeterminate, under certain conditions it can be obtained by evaluating the limit of the quotient of the derivatives of f and g (i.e., $f'(x)/g'(x)$). If this result is indeterminate, the procedure can be repeated. It is named for the French mathematician Guillaume de L'Hôpital (1661–1704), who purchased the formula from his teacher the Swiss mathematician Johann BERNOULLI (1667–1748).

Lhotse \'lōt-'sā\ Peak in the Himalayas. Located on the Nepal–Tibet boundary and reaching 27,890 ft (8,501 m), it is one of the world's highest mountains. It is sometimes considered part of Mount EVEREST's massif because it is joined to that peak by a 25,000-ft (7,600-m) ridge. The Swiss climbers Fritz Luchsinger and Ernest Reiss made the first ascent of the mountain in 1956. Lhotse is Tibetan for "south peak." E^1 was its original survey symbol, denoting Everest-1, given it by the Survey of India in 1931.

Li Ao \'lē-'au̇\ (died 844?) Chinese scholar and high official of the Tang dynasty, who helped reinvigorate Confucianism at a time when it was severely challenged by Buddhism and Taoism. Little is known of Li's life, though he is believed to have known HAN YU. He was much influenced by Buddhism, and he helped integrate many Buddhist ideas into Confucianism. He anticipated the ideas of Neo-Confucianism by asserting that human nature and human destiny were central to Confucianism, and he helped establish MENCIUS as a figure almost equal to Confucius in the eyes of Neo-Confucians.

Li Bo *or* **Li Po** \'lē-'bō\ *or* **Li Taibo** \'lē-'tī-'bō\ (701–762) Chinese poet. A student of Taoism, he spent long periods wandering and served as an unofficial court poet. His lyrics are celebrated for their exquisite imagery, rich language, allusions, and cadence. A romantic, he was a famous wine drinker and wrote of the joys of drinking, as well as about friendship, solitude, nature, and the passage of time. Popular legend says that he drowned when, sitting drunk in a boat, he tried to seize the moon's reflection in the water. He rivals DU FU for the title of China's greatest poet.

Li Dazhao *or* **Li Ta-chao** \'lē-'dä-'jau̇\ (1888–1927) Cofounder with CHEN DUXIU of the CHINESE COMMUNIST PARTY. Chief librarian and professor of history at Beijing Univ., Li became inspired by the success of the Russian Revolution and began to study and lecture on Marxism. In 1921 the study groups Li had created formally became the Chinese Communist Party. Li helped the new party carry out the policy of the Communist International (see COMINTERN) and cooperated with the Nationalist Party of SUN YAT-SEN (see GUOMINDANG). His career was cut short when he was seized and hanged by the warlord ZHANG ZUOLIN, but his ideas of a revolution of the impoverished peasantry were brought to fruition by MAO ZEDONG.

Li Hongzhang *or* **Li Hung-chang** \'lē-'hu̇ŋ-'jäŋ\ (1823–1901) Chinese statesman who represented China in the series of humiliating negotiations at the end of the SINO-FRENCH WAR (1883–85), SINO-JAPANESE WAR (1894–95), and BOXER REBELLION (1900). Much earlier in his career, Li had helped with the suppression of the TAIPING REBELLION (1850–64) and had put down the NIAN REBELLION (c. 1852–68). At that time, he came in contact with Westerners (notably England's CHARLES GEORGE GORDON) and Western weapons and became convinced that China needed Western-style firepower if it wanted to protect its sovereignty. In 1870, when Li was appointed governor-general of the capital province, Zhili, he was able to build arsenals, found a military academy, establish two modern naval bases, purchase warships, and undertake other "self-strengthening" measures. Through modernization he hoped to preserve traditional China, but within traditional China Li's innovations could not develop fully, and he was fatally hampered by the system he was trying to protect.

Li Shaozhun \'lē-'shau̇-'ju̇en\ (fl. 2nd century BC) Chinese alchemist. He was the first person to assert that the Taoist's ultimate goal was to achieve the status of *xian,* immortal sage, and he was responsible for much of the mystical content of popular Taoist thought. Claiming to be several centuries old, he gained the confidence of the great Han emperor WUDI and persuaded him that he could become immortal by praying to Zao Jun, a mythical Chinese figure who produced gold dinnerware that conferred immortality, and by eating from a vessel that had been transmuted into gold. Because of Li's influence, prayers to Zao Jun became established in Taoist ritual and Zao Jun came to be considered the first great Taoist divinity.

Li Si *or* **Li Ssu** \'lē-'sü\ (280?–208 BC) Minister of the QIN DYNASTY in China who utilized the ideas of HANFEIZI to make the Qin the first centralized Chinese empire. His ordering of the "Qin bibliocaust"—the burning of all books—earned him the opprobrium of future generations of Confucian scholars.

Li Zicheng *or* **Li Tzu-ch'eng** \'lē-'dzü-'chəŋ\ (1605?–1645) Rebel leader who brought about the fall of China's MING DYNASTY (1368–1644). A former postal worker, he joined the rebel cause in 1631 following a great famine in the northern part of the country. In 1644 he proclaimed himself the first emperor of a new dynasty and marched on Beijing, which he took easily. His victory was short-lived; WU SANGUI, a general loyal to the Ming, called on the MANCHU tribes to drive him out, and he fled north, where he was probably killed by local villagers. See also DORGON.

liability, limited See LIMITED LIABILITY

liability insurance Insurance against claims of loss or damage for which a policyholder might have to compensate another party. The policy covers losses resulting from acts or omissions that are legally deemed to be negligent and that result in damage to the person, property, or legitimate interests of others. It was principally the introduction of the automobile that spurred the rapid growth of this form of insurance, which now extends to a great many activities in addition to driving, including MALPRACTICE insurance for doctors and other professionals, marine liability for boat owners and operators, and product liability for manufacturers of consumer goods. See also CASUALTY INSURANCE, CONSUMER PROTECTION.

liana \lē-'ä-nə\ *or* **liane** \lē-'än\ Any of various long-stemmed, woody VINES, especially of tropical rain forests, that are rooted in the soil and climb or twine around other plants as they grow upward. Lianas often form a tangled network, up to 330 ft (100 m) high, around and among the trees that support them.

Liao dynasty \'lyau̇\ (907–1125) Dynasty formed by the nomadic Khitan tribes in much of present-day Manchuria, Mongolia, and the northeastern corner of China proper. The Chinese portion of the empire was governed on the TANG pattern, while the northern part was set up on a tribal basis. After the establishment of the SONG DYNASTY (960–1279), the Liao carried out a border war for control of northern China. Eventually the Song agreed to pay the Liao an annual tribute. The JUCHEN, former subjects of the Liao, destroyed the dynasty in 1125 but adopted most of its governmental system. The name "Cathay" for China derives from Khitay, another name for the Khitan.

Liao River \'lyau̇\ River, LIAONING province and NEI MONGGOL autonomous region, China. The eastern Liao rises in the eastern mountains of the northeast and the western Liao in southeastern Nei Monggol. They merge and flow southwest to empty into the Gulf of Liaodong, after a course of 836 mi (1,345 km). The river's drainage basin occupies 83,000 sq mi (215,000 sq km). It is navigable for small boats for about 400 mi (645 km) from its mouth.

Liaodong Peninsula *or* **Liao-tung Peninsula** \'lyau̇-'du̇ŋ\ Peninsula, extending from the southern coastline of LIAONING province, northeastern China. It partly separates the BO HAI on the west from Korea Bay on the east. It forms part of a mountain belt that continues in the Changbai Mts.; on the peninsula, the range is known as the Qian Mountains. Near the southern tip of the peninsula lies the port of DALIAN.

Liaoning \'lyau̇-'niŋ\ *formerly (1903–28)* **Fengtien** \'fəŋ-'tyen\ Province (pop., 1996 est.: 40,920,000), northeastern China, southernmost of the three provinces that form the region of MANCHURIA. It has four main topographical regions: the central plains, the LIAODONG PENINSULA, the western highlands, and the eastern mountain zone. The area was known as Sheng-ching in Manchu times (1644–1911); see QING DYNASTY. In 1932–45 it was part of the Japanese puppet state of MANCHUKUO. SHENYANG, the capital, fell to the Chinese Communists in 1948. Liaoning is China's most industrialized province, producing steel, cement, crude oil, and electrical power.

liar paradox Paradox derived from the statement attributed to the Cretan prophet Epimenides (6th century BC) that all Cretans are liars. If Epimenides' statement is taken to imply that all statements made by Cretans are false, then since Epimenides was a Cretan, his statement is false (i.e., not all Cretans are liars). The paradox's simplest form arises from considering the sentence "This sentence is false." If it is true, then it is false, and if it is false, then it is true. Consideration of such semantic PARADOXES led logicians to distinguish between object language and METALANGUAGE and to conclude that no language can consistently contain a complete semantic theory for its own sentences.

Liard River \'lē-ərd\ River, northwestern Canada. Rising in the Yukon Territory, it flows southeast through British Columbia. It then turns northeast and empties into the MACKENZIE RIVER in the Northwest Territories, after a course of 693 mi (1,115 km). Its upper course has rapids and canyons; its lower course is navigable for small boats. It is named for the liards (poplar trees) along its course.

Libby, Willard (Frank) (1908–1980) U.S. chemist. Born in Grand Valley, Col., he studied at Berkeley and later taught there and at the University of Chicago and UCLA. With the MANHATTAN PROJECT, he helped develop a method for separating URANIUM ISOTOPES and showed that TRITIUM is a product of cosmic radiation. In 1947 he and his students developed CARBON-14 DATING, which proved an extremely valuable tool for archaeology, anthropology, and earth science, and earned him a 1960 Nobel Prize.

libel See DEFAMATION

Liber Augustalis See Constitutions of MELFI

Liberace \ˌlib-ə-ˈrä-chē\ *orig.* **Wladziu Valentino Liberace** (1919–1987) U.S. pianist. Born to Polish and Italian immigrants in West Allis, Wis., he appeared as a soloist with the Chicago Symphony Orchestra at 16. He began giving concerts in flamboyant costumes with ornate pianos and candelabra, and though he occasionally performed with symphony orchestras, he built his career playing primarily popular music. Hugely successful, he hosted his own television variety series *The Liberace Show* (1952–55, 1969) and appeared in films such as *Sincerely Yours* (1955). In later years he performed frequently in Las Vegas. His death resulted from AIDS.

liberal arts College or university curriculum aimed at imparting general knowledge and developing general intellectual capacities, in contrast to a professional, vocational, or technical curriculum. In classical antiquity the term designated the education proper to a freeman (Latin, *liber:* "free") as opposed to a slave. In the medieval Western university, the seven liberal arts were grammar, rhetoric, and logic (the *trivium*) and geometry, arithmetic, music, and astronomy (the *quadrivium*). In modern colleges and universities, the liberal arts include the study of literature, languages, philosophy, history, mathematics, and science as the basis of a general, or liberal, education.

Liberal-Democratic Party (LDP) Japan's largest political party, which held power almost continuously from its formation in 1955 until 1993. It was created through the amalgamation and transformation of various factions of the prewar RIKKEN SEIYUKAI and Minseito parties. The conservative LDP appeared threatened in the 1970s but survived; the end of the 1980s boom years (the "bubble economy"), financial crises, and political scandals finally caused the party to lose its majority in the Diet in 1993. It came back to power in a coalition government in 1994, and the late 1990s, though unstable, saw two LDP prime ministers, Hashimoto Ryutaro and KEIZO OBUCHI.

Liberal Party British political party that emerged in the mid-19th century as the successor to the WHIGS. It was the major party in opposition to the CONSERVATIVES until 1918, after which it was supplanted by the LABOUR PARTY. It was initially supported by the middle class that was enfranchised by the REFORM BILL OF 1832. Earl RUSSELL's administration in 1846 is sometimes regarded as the first Liberal government, but the first unequivocally Liberal government was formed in 1868 by WILLIAM E. GLADSTONE. Under Gladstone, until 1894, the party's hallmark was reform; after 1884, it espoused Irish HOME RULE. It championed individualism, private enterprise, human rights, and promotion of social justice; wary of imperial expansion, it was pacific and internationalist. During World War I it split into two camps, centered on H. H. ASQUITH and DAVID LLOYD GEORGE. It continued as a minor party until 1988, when it merged with the Social Democratic Party to form the Liberal Democratic Party.

Liberal Party Minor U.S. political party in New York state. It was founded in 1944 by the moderates of the AMERICAN LABOR PARTY in opposition to the alleged infiltration of that party by communists. It helped carry New York for FRANKLIN ROOSEVELT in the 1944 election, and later generally continued to support Democratic candidates. Its largest membership was in New York City, where it has especially influenced mayoral elections.

Liberal Party of Canada One of the two major Canadian political parties. The party was formed by principles of the REFORM PARTY and the CLEAR GRITS liberals. It advocated the concept of "responsible government" and pressed for parliamentary representation. The first Liberal government was headed by ALEXANDER MACKENZIE (1873–78). The party regained power under WILFRED LAURIER (1896–1911) and was the ruling party for much of the 20th century under such prime ministers as W.L. MACKENZIE KING, LOUIS SAINT LAURENT, LESTER PEARSON, PIERRE TRUDEAU, and JEAN CHRETIEN

liberalism Political philosophy that favors maximizing individual liberties. Liberals believe the state's primary function is to protect the rights of its citizens. They may believe that freedom is a matter for the individual alone and that the state should be uninvolved (a position that tends toward ANARCHISM), or that freedom is a matter of the state and that the state should actively promote it (a position that tends toward SOCIALISM). The ideology of liberalism is a product of the ENLIGHTENMENT; JOHN LOCKE laid the philosophical foundations of British liberalism, and ADAM SMITH expounded economic liberalism (LAISSEZ-FAIRE liberalism). The U.S. Constitution is a product of classical liberalism. Economic liberalism in the U.S. today, which endorses unregulated markets, is generally embraced by those who call themselves conservatives; those who call themselves liberals usually believe in restrictions on corporate freedom, as well as in civil liberties, social-welfare supports, consumer protection, and environmental conservation. See also CONSERVATISM, INDIVIDUALISM, LIBERAL PARTY.

liberalism, theological School of religious thought characterized by concern with inner motivation as opposed to external controls. It was set in motion in the 17th century by RENE DESCARTES, who expressed faith in human reason, and it was influenced by such philosophers as BENEDICT DE SPINOZA, G. W. LEIBNIZ, and JOHN LOCKE. Its second stage, which coincided with the Romantic movement of the late 18th and 19th century, was marked by an appreciation of individual creativity, expressed in the writings of philosophers such as J.-J. ROUSSEAU and IMMANUEL KANT as well as of the theologian FRIEDRICH SCHLEIERMACHER. The third stage, from the mid-19th century through the 1920s, emphasized the idea of progress. Stimulated by the INDUSTRIAL REVOLUTION and by CHARLES DARWIN's *Origin of Species* (1859), thinkers such as T.H. HUXLEY and HERBERT SPENCER in England and WILLIAM JAMES and JOHN DEWEY in the U.S. focused on the psychological study of religious experience, the sociological study of religious institutions, and philosophical inquiry into religious values.

liberation theology Roman Catholic movement that originated in the late 20th century in Latin America and seeks to express religious faith by helping the poor and working for political and social change. It began in 1968, when bishops attending the Latin American Bishops' Conference in Medellín, Colombia, affirmed the rights of the poor and asserted that industrialized nations were enriching themselves at the expense of the Third World. The movement's central text, *A Theology of Liberation* (1971), was written by the Peruvian priest Gustavo Gutiérrez (born 1928). Liberation theologians have sometimes been criticized as purveyors of MARXISM, and the Vatican has sought to curb their influence by appointing more conservative prelates.

Liberation Tigers of Tamil Eelam *or* **Tamil Tigers** Guerrilla organization seeking to establish an independent Tamil state in northern and eastern Sri Lanka. Formed in 1972, it is considered one of the world's most sophisticated and tightly organized insurgent groups. By 1985 it controlled the port of Jaffna and most of the Jaffna Peninsula in northern Sri Lanka. After losing control of Jaffna in 1987, it carried out several attacks, including the assassinations of the Sri Lankan president and the former Indian prime minister (though it denied involvement in the latter killing) and a suicide bombing that killed 100 people in the capital of Colombo. Negotiations between the Tigers and the government broke down in the mid-1990s. Fighting intensified in the late 1990s and continued into the 21st century despite efforts to revive peace talks.

Liberia *officially* **Republic of Liberia** Republic, western Africa. Area: 38,250 sq mi (99,067 sq km). Population (1997 est.): 2,602.000. Capital: MONROVIA. Liberia's ethnic groups include the Americo-Liberians, descendants of the black freedmen who emigrated from the U.S. in the 19th century; and indigenous peoples, including the Mande, Kwa, and Mel. Languages: English (official), native languages. Religions: Christianity, Islam, traditional beliefs. Currency: Liberian dollar. Liberia has coastal lowlands extending 350 mi (560 km) along the Atlantic; farther inland are hills and low mountains. Roughly one-fifth of Liberia consists of tropical rain forest. Less than 4 percent of Liberia is considered arable, but the country has rich iron-ore reserves, which are a major source of exports. The principal cash crops are rubber, coffee, and cacao; the staple crops are rice and cassava. It is a republic with two legislative houses; its head of state and government is the president, assisted by the state minister for presidential affairs. Africa's oldest republic, Liberia was established on land bought from local tribes as a home for freed U.S. slaves under the American Colonization Society, which founded a colony at Cape Mesurado in 1821. In 1822 Jehudi Ashmun, a Methodist minister, became the director of the settlement and Liberia's real founder. In 1824 it was named Liberia, and its main settlement was named Monrovia. Joseph Jenkins Roberts, Liberia's first nonwhite governor, proclaimed Liberian independence in 1847 and expanded its

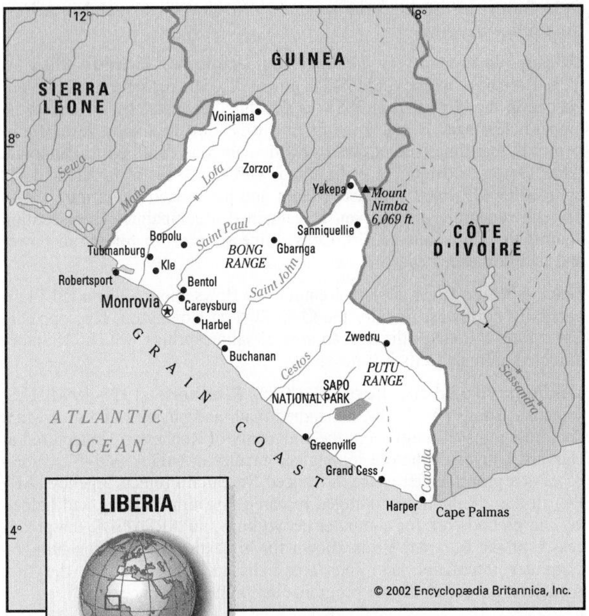

boundaries. Border disputes with the French and British lasted until 1892, when its boundaries were officially established. In 1980 a coup led by Gen. SAMUEL K. DOE marked the end of the Americo-Liberians' long political dominance over the indigenous Africans. A rebellion in 1989 escalated into a destructive civil war in the 1990s. A peace agreement was reached in 1996, and elections were held in 1997, but conflict continued to flare up.

libertarianism Political philosophy that stresses the principles of personal liberty. Libertarians believe that individuals should have complete freedom of action, provided their actions do not infringe on the freedom of others. Libertarianism's distrust of government reveals its roots in 19th-century ANARCHISM. Libertarians not only oppose such government impositions as income tax but also programs usually seen as beneficial, such as social security and the postal service. Their views often cross traditional party boundaries (e.g., they oppose gun control and support legalization of prohibited drugs). Such varied thinkers as HENRY DAVID THOREAU and AYN RAND are embraced by libertarians. The U.S. Libertarian Party was formed in 1971; in 1980 its presidential candidate was on the ballot in all 50 states.

Liberty, Sons of Organization of American colonists formed in 1765 to oppose the STAMP ACT. The name was taken from a speech by Isaac Barré in the British Parliament that referred to American colonials who opposed unjust British measures as "sons of liberty." The group agitated for colonial resistance and helped prevent enforcement of the Stamp Act. After the act's repeal, the organization continued to oppose British measures against the colonists.

Liberty Party (1840–48) U.S. political party formed by a splinter group of abolitionists. It was created by ARTHUR TAPPAN and THEODORE WELD in opposition to WILLIAM LLOYD GARRISON, who scorned political action as a futile way to end slavery. At its first party convention in 1840, JAMES BIRNEY was nominated for U.S. president. By 1844 the party had influenced undecided legislators in many local elections to adopt antislavery stands. In 1848 it dissolved when many of its members joined the Barnburners (see HUNKERS AND BARNBURNERS) to form the FREE SOIL PARTY.

libido \lə-ˈbē-dō\ Physiological and emotional energy associated with the sex drive. The concept was originated by SIGMUND FREUD, who saw the libido as linked not only with sexual desire but with all constructive human activity. He believed that psychiatric illnesses were the result of misdirecting or suppressing the libido. CARL GUSTAV JUNG used the term more broadly to encompass all life processes in all species.

Libra (Latin: "Scales") In astronomy, the constellation lying between Scorpio and Virgo; in ASTROLOGY, the seventh sign of the ZODIAC, governing approximately the period September 22–October 23. Its symbol is either a woman holding a balance scale or the scale alone. The woman is sometimes identified with Astraea, the Roman goddess of justice.

library Collection of information resources in print or in other forms that is organized and made accessible for reading or study. The word derives from the Latin *liber* ("book"). The origin of libraries lies in the keeping of written records, a practice that dates at least to the 3rd millennium BC in Babylonia. The first libraries as repositories of books were those of the Greek temples and those established in conjunction with the Greek schools of philosophy in the 4th century BC. Today's libraries frequently contain periodicals, microfilms, tapes, videos, compact discs, and other materials in addition to books. The growth of online communications networks has enabled library users to search electronically linked databases worldwide. See also LIBRARY SCIENCE.

library classification System of arrangement adopted by a library to enable patrons to locate its materials quickly and easily. Classifications may be natural (e.g., by subject), artificial (e.g., by alphabet, form, or numerical order), or accidental (e.g., chronological or geographic). They also vary in degree; some have minute subdivisions while others are broader. Widely used systems include the DEWEY DECIMAL CLASSIFICATION, the Library of Congress Classification, the Bliss Classification, and the Colon Classification; special libraries may devise their own unique systems.

Library of Alexandria See Library of ALEXANDRIA

library science Principles and practices of library operation and administration, and their study. It emerged as a separate field of study in the second half of the 19th century. The first training program for librarians in the U.S. was established by MELVIL DEWEY in 1887. In the 20th century, library science was gradually subsumed under the more general field of INFORMATION SCIENCE. Today's graduate programs in library and information science are accredited by the American Library Association (founded 1876) and prepare students for professional positions in other areas of the information industry as well.

Libreville \ˈlē-brə-ˌvil\ City (pop., 1993: 362,000), capital of GABON, located on the northern shore of the Gabon Estuary. Pongoue people first settled the region after the 16th century, followed by the Fang in the 19th century. The French built a fort on the estuary's northern bank in 1843, and in 1849 a settlement of freed slaves and a group of Pongoue villages were given the name Libreville. In 1850 France abandoned its fort and resettled on the plateau, now the commercial and administrative center of the city. It is well industrialized and is Gabon's educational center. Libreville was the capital of French Equatorial Africa 1888–1904.

Libya *officially* **Socialist People's Libyan Arab Jamahiriya** \ˌja-mə-hi-ˈrē-yə\ Country, North Africa. Area: 678,400 sq mi (1,757,000 sq km). Population (2001): 5,241,000. Capital: TRIPOLI. Berbers, once the major ethnic group, have been assimilated into the Arab culture. Italians, Greeks, Jews, and black Africans are among the other ethnic groups. Languages: Arabic (official), Hamitic (Berbers). Religions: Islam (official), small percentage Christianity. Currency: dinar. All but two tiny fractions of Libya are covered by the SAHARA desert: Tripolitania, in the northwestern corner, and Cyrenaica in the northeast. Tripolitania is Libya's most important agricultural region and its most populated area. The production and export of petroleum are the basis of Libya's economy; other resources include natural gas, manganese, and gypsum. The rearing of livestock, including sheep and goats, is important in the north. It is a socialist state with one policy-making body; the chief of state is MUAMMAR AL-QADDAFI (de facto), and the head of government is the prime minister. For early history, see CYRENAICA, FEZZAN, TRIPOLITANIA. In the 16th century the Ottoman Turks combined Fezzan, Cyrenaica, and Tripolitania under one regency in Tripoli. In 1911 Italy claimed control of Libya, and by the outbreak of World War II 150,000 Italians had immigrated there. The scene of much fighting in the war, it became an independent state in 1951 and a member of the ARAB LEAGUE in 1953. The discovery of oil in 1959 brought wealth to Libya. A decade later a group of army officers led by Qaddafi deposed the king and made the country an Islamic republic. Under Qaddafi's rule it supported the PALESTINIAN LIBERATION ORGANIZATION (PLO) and terrorist groups, bringing protests from many countries, particularly the U.S. Intermittent warfare

L
M
N

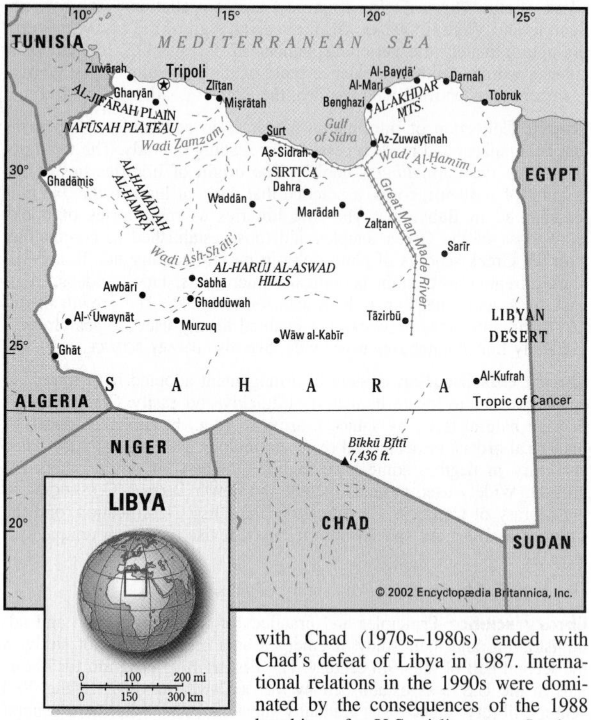

with Chad (1970s–1980s) ended with Chad's defeat of Libya in 1987. International relations in the 1990s were dominated by the consequences of the 1988 bombing of a U.S. airliner over Lockerbie, Scotland; the U.S. accused Libyan nationalists of the deed and imposed a trade embargo on Libya, endorsed by the U.N. in 1992.

Libyan Desert NE portion of the SAHARA desert, extending from eastern Libya through southwestern Egypt into northwestern Sudan. The highest point is Mount Al-Uwaynat (6,345 ft, or 1,934 m), located where the three countries meet. Harsh and arid, it is characterized by bare rocky plateaus and sandy plains.

Licchavi era \ˈlich-ə-vē\ (c. 300–879) In Nepal, the period of rule by the Licchavi dynasty. The dynasty originated in India, used Sanskrit as a court language, and issued Indian-style coins. It maintained close ties to India and also had economic and political relations with Tibet, becoming a cultural center linking Central and southern Asia. The era ended with Amsuvarman's founding of the Thakuri dynasty in AD 879.

lichee See LITCHI

lichen \ˈlī-kən\ Any of about 15,000 species of small, colorful, scaly plants that consist of a symbiotic association of ALGAE (usually green) and fungi (see FUNGUS). These extremely hardy, slow growers often are pioneer species in sparse environments such as mountaintops and the far North. Fungal cells, anchored to the substrate with hairlike growths (rhizines), form the base. In the body (THALLUS), numerous algal cells are distributed among fewer fungal cells. Through PHOTOSYNTHESIS the algal cells provide simple sugars and vitamins for both partners in this symbiotic association. The fungal cells protect the algal cells from environmental extremes. Lichens may form a thin, crustlike, tightly bound covering over their substrate (e.g., cracks in rocks), or they may be small and leafy, with loose attachments to the substrate. Their colors range from brown to bright orange or yellow. In far northern Europe and Asia, lichens provide two-thirds of caribou and reindeer food. They have been the source of medicines and dyes.

Lichtenstein \ˈlik-tən-ˌstīn, ˈlik-tən-ˌstēn\, **Roy** (1923–1997) U.S. painter, sculptor, and graphic artist. Born in New York, he at first embraced Abstract Expressionism, but in the 1960s he turned to the Pop art for which he is best known. Especially popular are his brilliantly colored paintings in the style of large-scale comic strips, such as *Whaam* (1963). In the mid-1960s he turned to making Pop versions of well-known paintings by such artists as CLAUDE MONET, PABLO PICASSO, and HENRI MATISSE. In the 1970s he also made sculptures, in which he reproduced ART DECO forms. In the 1980s he painted a five-story-high mural in a New York office building.

Licinius \lə-ˈsi-nē-əs\ *in full* **Valerius Licinianus Licinius** (died AD 325) Roman emperor (308–24). Born of Illyrian peasant stock, he advanced in the army and in 308 was appointed augustus by his friend the emperor GALERIUS. Because the empire was split up among several emperors at that time (see TETRARCH), his domain was confined to Pannonia. After GALERIUS' death (311) he allied with CONSTANTINE I, defeated his competitor Maximinus in Asia Minor, and partitioned the empire (313). Though reputedly a Christian, he launched a campaign of persecution against the Christians c. 320. Constantine soon drove him from power and had him executed.

Licking River River, eastern Kentucky. It flows about 320 mi (515 km) generally northwest to enter the OHIO RIVER at Covington, Ky., opposite CINCINNATI. It courses through an area of saline springs, which originally attracted animals to its salt licks.

Licklider \ˈlik-ˌlid-ər\, **J(oseph) C(arl) R(obnett)** (1915–1990) U.S. scientist. Born in St. Louis, he studied math and physics, and received a doctorate in psychology from the University of Rochester. He lectured at Harvard University before joining the faculty at MIT (1949–57, 1966–85). As a group leader at the Advanced Research Projects Agency (ARPA) in the 1960s, he encouraged research into time-sharing and helped lay the groundwork for computer networking and ARPANET, the predecessor of the INTERNET. He is known for his extensive work on human–computer interaction and interfaces. His influence lead to the first American advanced-degree programs in computer science.

licorice \ˈli-krish\ Perennial herb *(Glycyrrhiza glabra)* of the pea family (see LEGUME), and the flavoring, confection, and medicine made from its roots. Native to southern Europe, the plant is cultivated around the Mediterranean and in parts of the U.S. It grows to 3 ft (1 m) and bears graceful compound leaves, blue-violet flower clusters, and flat, flexible seedpods 3–4 in. (7–10 cm) long. It is 42 times sweeter than table sugar, and its flavor, similar to ANISE, can mask unpleasant medicinal tastes.

Liddell Hart \ˌlid-ᵊl-ˈhärt\, **Basil (Henry)** *later* **Sir Basil** (1895–1970) British military historian and strategist. He left Cambridge University to join the British army at the outbreak of World War I, and retired as a captain in 1927. He was an early advocate of air power and mechanized tank warfare. He wrote for London newspapers 1925–45. His writings on strategy, which emphasized the elements of mobility and surprise, were more influential in Germany than in France or England; his "expanding torrent" theory of attack became the basis for German BLITZKRIEG warfare in 1939–41. The author of more than 30 books, he was knighted in 1966.

Lie \ˈlē\, **Jonas (Lauritz Idemil)** (1833–1908) Norwegian novelist. He wrote his first novel, *The Visionary or Pictures from Nordland* (1870), with his wife's collaboration. Later novels include *The Barque "Future"* (1872), *One of Life's Slaves* (1883), and the classic *The Family at Gilje* (1883), which deals with the position of women. He sought to reflect in his writings the nature, folk life, and social spirit of his country. With HENRIK IBSEN, BJORNSTJERNE BJORNSON, and Alexander Kielland (1849–1906), he is considered one of "the four great ones" of 19th-century Norwegian literature.

Lie \ˈlē\, **Trygve** (1896–1968) First secretary-general of the UNITED NATIONS (1946–52). Educated in law at the University of Kristiania (Oslo), Lie was active in the Norwegian Labor Party before being appointed foreign minister of Norway's government-in-exile during World War II. As a member of the Norwegian delegation to the U.N. Conference on International Organization (1945), he helped draft the provisions for the UNITED NATIONS SECURITY COUNCIL. As secretary-general, he helped coax Soviet troops out of Iran and dealt with the first ARAB–ISRAELI WAR and the India–Pakistan conflict over Kashmir. The Soviet Union stopped cooperating with him when he supported U.N. intervention in the KOREAN WAR, and his effectiveness was further hampered by the strident anticommunism of the postwar U.S. He resigned in 1952.

lie detector *or* **polygraph** Instrument for recording physiological phenomena (including BLOOD PRESSURE, PULSE rate, and RESPIRATION) of a human subject as he or she answers questions asked by an operator. These data (recorded as graphs) are used as the basis for judging whether the subject is lying. The phenomena usually chosen for recording are those not easily controlled voluntarily. The types of questions asked, their wording, and the mode of presentation have a tremendous effect on the results and their reliability. Used in police interrogation and investigation since 1924, the lie detector is still controversial among psychologists and not always accepted as evidence in courts.

Liebermann \'lē-bər-ˌmän\, **Max** (1847–1935) German painter and etcher. The realism and simplicity of his first exhibited painting, *Women Plucking Geese* (1872), were in striking contrast to the romantic, idealized art then in vogue. A summer in France, where he became acquainted with the BARBIZON SCHOOL, brightened his palette. As a supporter of such academically unpopular styles as IMPRESSIONISM and ART NOUVEAU, he founded the Berlin SEZESSION (1899), but later became president of the conservative Berlin Academy.

Liebig \'lē-bik\, **Justus von** *later* **Freiherr (Baron) von Liebig** (1803–1873) German chemist. He made many important contributions to the early systematization of organic chemistry and to biochemistry, chemical education, and agricultural chemistry. He was the first to demonstrate the existence of FREE RADICALS and did much to clarify the properties of ACIDS. He developed simple analytical methods (see ANALYSIS) that greatly aided his work, analyzed many tissues and body fluids, and showed that plants use carbon dioxide, water, and ammonia. In later years his reputation became so great that he was regarded as the final authority in chemical matters, and he was often involved in scientific controversies.

Liebknecht \'lēp-ˌknekt\, **Karl** (1871–1919) German socialist leader. Son of WILHELM LIEBKNECHT, he became a lawyer and a Marxist. In 1912 he entered the Reichstag and led the opposition to Germany's pre–World War I policy. In 1916 he was expelled from the SOCIAL DEMOCRATIC PARTY for opposing its leadership and came into close alliance with ROSA LUXEMBURG, with whom he founded the SPARTACISTS. He was imprisoned 1916–18 for advocating the overthrow of the government. In 1918 he played a leading role in forming the German Communist Party. A series of bloody clashes culminated in the January 1919 putsch in which Liebknecht resorted to force; he was shot on the pretext that he was attempting to escape arrest.

Karl Liebknecht, 1913.
INTERFOTO-FRIEDRICH RAUCH, MUNICH

Liebknecht, Wilhelm (1826–1900) German socialist, cofounder of the German SOCIAL DEMOCRATIC PARTY. Imprisoned for participating in the REVOLUTIONS OF 1848, he lived in exile in England 1849–62, working closely with KARL MARX and FRIEDRICH ENGELS. Prussia granted him amnesty in 1862, but OTTO VON BISMARCK had him expelled again in 1865. In Leipzig he and AUGUST BEBEL organized the Social Democratic Labor Party in 1869. He was imprisoned 1872–74 for his writings against the Franco-Prussian War. Bismarck's repression of the socialists brought about a merger with the followers of FERDINAND LASSALLE in 1875. With the expiration of the Anti-Socialist Law (1878–90), this party became known as the German Social Democratic Party. Liebknecht continued as a leading spokesman, primarily as a writer for the party's newspaper, *Vorwärts*.

Wilhelm Liebknecht, c. 1890.
ARCHIV FUR KUNST UND GESCHICHTE, BERLIN

Liechtenstein \'lik-tən-ˌshtīn\ *officially* **Principality of Liechtenstein** Principality, western Europe. It is located between Switzerland and Austria. Area: 62 sq mi (160 sq km). Population (1997 est.): 31,000. Capital: VADUZ. The Liechtensteiners are descended from the Alemanni tribe that came into the region after AD 500. Languages: German (official), Alemanni dialect, Walser dialect. Religion: Roman Catholicism. Currency: Swiss franc. The eastern two-thirds of Liechtenstein's small territory is composed of the foothills of the Rhätikon Massif, part of the central ALPS. The western section of the country is occupied by the RHINE RIVER floodplain. It has no natural resources of commercial value, and virtually all raw materials, including wood, have to be imported. Manufacturing includes metalworking, pharmaceuticals, optical lenses, electronics, and food processing. Liechtenstein, a tourist center, is also a center of banking because of its stable political situation and its absolute bank secrecy. It is a constitutional monarchy with one legislative house; its chief of state is the prince, and the head of government is the prime minister. The Rhine plain was occupied for centuries by two independent lordships of the HOLY ROMAN EMPIRE, Vaduz and Schellenberg. The principality of Liechtenstein, consisting of these two lordships, was founded in 1719 and remained part of the Holy Roman Empire. It was included in the GERMAN CONFEDERATION (1815–66). In 1866 it became independent, recognizing the regions of Vaduz and Schellenberg as unique regions forming separate electoral districts. In 1921 it adopted Swiss currency, and in 1923 joined the Swiss customs union. An almost 60-year ruling coalition dissolved in 1997, and the prince urged adoption of constitutional reforms.

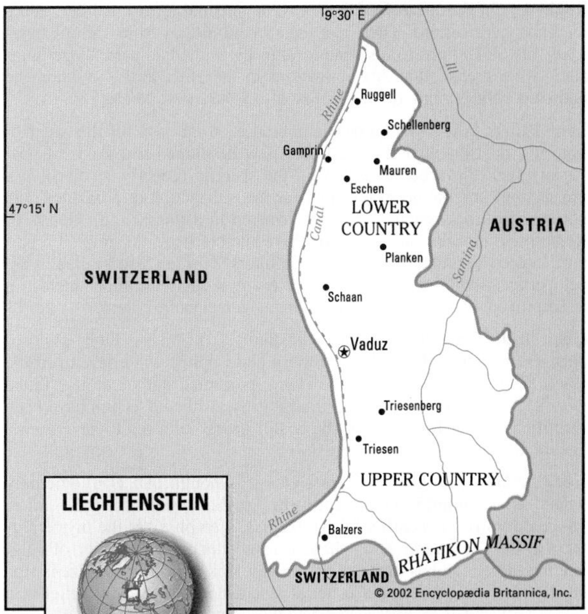

lied \'lēt\ German song, particularly an art song for voice and piano of the late 18th or 19th century. The Romantic movement fostered serious popular poetry by such poets as JOHANN W. VON GOETHE, HEINRICH HEINE, JOSEPH EICHENDORFF, and EDUARD MÖRIKE. Composers often set such poetry to folk-influenced music, but lieder could also be highly sophisticated and even experimental. At first generally performed at private social gatherings, they eventually moved into the concert-hall repertoire. The most influential and prolific lieder composer was F. SCHUBERT, who wrote over 600; R. SCHUMANN, F. MENDELSSOHN, J. BRAHMS, H. WOLF, G. MAHLER, and R. STRAUSS are most prominent in the lied's subsequent history.

Liège \'lyezh\ *Flemish* **Luik** \'lòik\ City (pop., 1996 est.: 191,000), eastern Belgium. Located at the confluence of the MEUSE and Ourthe rivers, it was inhabited in prehistoric times and was known to the Romans as Leodium. It became a town when St. Hubert transferred his see there in 721, and it was noted as a center of learning in the Middle Ages. Annexed to France in 1795, it was later assigned with the rest of Belgium to the Netherlands in 1815. A center of the successful revolt for Belgian independence in 1830, it is now an industrial research center and a major port.

L
M
N

liege \lēj\ In European feudal society, an unconditional bond between a man and his overlord. Thus, if a tenant held estates from various overlords, his obligations to his liege lord, to whom he had paid "liege homage," were greater than his obligations to the other lords, to whom he had paid only "simple homage." See also FEUDAL LAND TENURE.

lien \lēn\ In law, a charge or encumbrance on PROPERTY for the satisfaction of a debt or other duty. COMMON LAW developed two kinds of possessory lien: the specific (a lien on the specific property involved in a transaction) and the general (a lien for the satisfaction of a balance due, not confined to a specific property involved in a transaction). Courts of EQUITY may, through the device of the equitable lien, recognize a creditor's interest in a debtor's property. Statutory liens are also available; developers and building contractors, for example, may use their interest in an improved site as security for payment (a mechanic's lien).

Liezi *or* **Lieh-tzu** \'lye-'dzə\ (fl. 4th century BC) Chinese Taoist philosopher. He was one of the three primary philosophers who developed the tenets of Taoist thought, and he is the presumed author of the Taoist work *LIEZI*. Many of the writings traditionally attributed to him have been identified as later forgeries, but he is still widely believed to have been a historical figure.

Liezi *or* **Lieh-tzu** Chinese Taoist classic. Though LIEZI is traditionally named as its author, in its present form it probably dates from the 3rd or 4th century AD. Like earlier Taoist classics, it emphasizes the mysterious TAO (way). The "Yang Zhu" chapter acknowledges the futility of challenging the tao and asserts that all we can look forward to in life is sex, music, physical beauty, and material abundance—a fatalistic belief in a life of radical self-interest was a new development in TAOISM.

Lifar \'lē-ˌfär\, **Serge** (1905–1986) Russian-French dancer, choreographer, and ballet master. In 1923 he joined the BALLETS RUSSES, becoming lead dancer in 1925 and creating title roles in several of GEORGE BALANCHINE's ballets. He worked at the Paris Opera Ballet as lead dancer and ballet master (1929–45, 1947–58), choreographing over 50 works, including *Prométhée* (1929), *Icare* (1935), *Les mirages* (1947), and *Les noces fantastiques* (1955). He rebuilt the company as a separate performing group, emphasizing the importance of male dancers. He retired as a dancer in 1956 but continued to choreograph for various European companies.

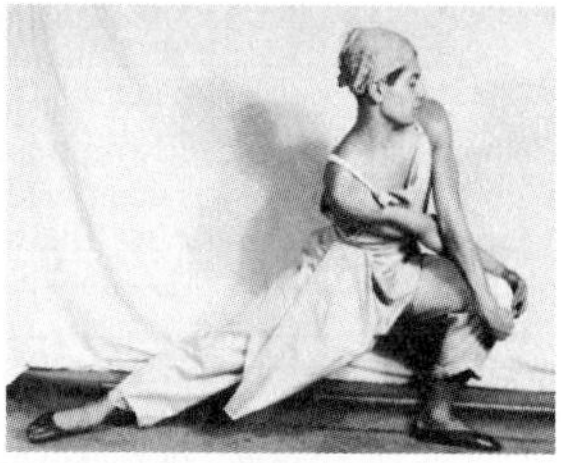

Lifar in *Night*, 1930.

BBC HULTON PICTURE LIBRARY

life State characterized by the ability to metabolize nutrients (process materials for energy and tissue building), grow, reproduce, and respond and adapt to environmental stimuli. Fossil evidence suggests that earth's first living organisms, BACTERIA and CYANOBACTERIA, arose about 3.5 billion years ago. All known life-forms possess either DNA or RNA. VIRUSES, which possess DNA and RNA, cannot reproduce without a host cell and do not metabolize nutrients, and it is uncertain whether they should be classified as living or nonliving. Scientists disagree on the likelihood of extraterrestrial life. See also DRAKE EQUATION.

Life Weekly picture magazine (1936–72) published in New York City. One of the most popular and widely imitated of U.S. magazines, it was founded by HENRY R. LUCE and quickly became a cornerstone of Time-Life Publications. From the start it emphasized photography, with gripping, superbly chosen news photographs, photo features, and photo essays by the best photographers; gradually more writing was added. Its war coverage was notably vivid, authentic, and moving. It ceased publication largely because its costs outstripped revenues. It reappeared in special issues and then, in 1978, on a reduced scale as a monthly.

life insurance Method by which large groups of individuals equalize the burden of financial loss from death by distributing funds to the beneficiaries of those who die. Life insurance is most developed in wealthy countries, where it has become a major channel of saving and investing. There are three basic types of life-insurance contract. Term insurance is issued for a specified number of years; protection expires at the end of the period and there is no cash value remaining. Whole-life contracts run for the whole of the insured's life and also accumulate a cash value, which is paid when the contract matures or is surrendered; the cash value is less than the policy's face value. Endowment contracts run for a specified time period and pay their full face value at the end of the period.

life-safety system Any interior building element designed to protect and evacuate the building population in emergencies, including fires and earthquakes, and less critical events, such as power failures. Fire-detection systems include electronic heat and smoke detectors that can activate audible alarms and automatically notify local fire departments. For fire suppression, hand-operated fire extinguishers and, often, building sprinkler systems are provided. Smoke is as dangerous as fire, so protective measures include the automatic shutdown of ventilating systems and elevators and the division of the building into smokeproof compartments. Occupants evacuate through protected exits (which include exit corridors and stairways in smokeproof enclosures in multistory buildings) leading to the exterior. See also FIRE ESCAPE, FIREPROOFING.

life span Time between birth and death. It ranges from a mayfly's day to certain trees' thousands of years. Its limit appears to depend on heredity, but such factors as (in humans) disease, natural disasters, war, diet, and habits such as smoking reduce it. Maximum life span is theoretical; more meaningful is average life span, which life-insurance companies and actuaries analyze and tabulate. Long-lived progenitors tend to beget long-lived descendants. A very-low-calorie diet appears to prolong life. Reduced infant mortality and improved sanitation and nutrition account for much of the increase since c. 1800—from about 35 to over 70 years in most industrialized countries. The oldest well-documented age reached by a human is 122 years.

Liffey River River, Ireland. Rising southwest of DUBLIN, it flows northwest, then runs west in the Kildare lowland. It crosses east through Dublin, where it is channeled into canals, and empties into Dublin Bay, an arm of the Irish Sea, after a course of 50 mi (81 km). The river is personified as Anna Livia Plurabelle in JAMES JOYCE's *Finnegans Wake*.

lift Upward-acting FORCE on an aircraft wing or AIRFOIL. An aircraft in flight experiences an upward lift force, as well as the thrust of the engine, the force of its own weight, and a DRAG force. The lift force arises because the speed at which the displaced air moves over the top of the airfoil (and over the top of the attached BOUNDARY LAYER) is greater than the speed at which it moves over the bottom and because the pressure acting on the airfoil from below is therefore greater than the pressure from above.

lift-slab construction Technique whereby concrete floor slabs are poured on the ground, one on top of the other, and then lifted into place on top of columns by hydraulic jacks. Used for very tall multistory buildings, this method offers substantial savings in FORMWORK.

ligament Tough fibrous band of CONNECTIVE TISSUE that supports internal organs and holds bones together properly in JOINTS. It is composed of dense bundles of fibers and spindle-shaped cells (fibroblasts), with little ground substance. White ligament is rich in sturdy, inelastic COLLAGEN fibers; yellow ligament is rich in tough elastic fibers, which allow more movement. See also TENDON.

ligand \'li-gənd, 'lī-gənd\ ATOM or MOLECULE attached to a central atom, usually of a TRANSITION ELEMENT, in a coordination COMPOUND, or complex ion (see BONDING). It is almost always the electron-pair donor (NUCLEOPHILE) in a COVALENT BOND. Common ligands include the neutral molecules WATER (H_2O), ammonia (NH_3), and carbon monoxide (CO) and the ANIONS cyanide (CN^-), chloride (Cl^-), and hydroxide (OH^-). Rarely, ligands are CATIONS and electron-pair acceptors (ELECTROPHILES). Organic ligands include EDTA and nitrilotriacetic acid. Biological systems rely on ligands such as the porphyrin in HEMOGLOBIN and CHLOROPHYLL, and numerous COFACTORS are ligands. In CHELATES, the ligand attaches at more than one point, sharing more than one electron pair, and is called "bidentate" or "polydentate"—having two or many "teeth." The ligands in a complex may be the same or different.

Ligeti \lē-'gā-tē\, **György (Sándor)** (born 1923) Hungarian (Transylvanian) composer. By 1950 he was teaching at the Budapest Academy, but not until he met K. STOCKHAUSEN and others in Vienna in 1956 did he find his compositional path. After a brief interest in electronic music, he gained international recognition for pieces composed in his characteristic "planes" of sound (which tend to avoid reliance on traditional pitch and rhythm) but using traditional instruments. His most famous work, *Atmosphères* (1961), was used in the film *2001*. The opera *Le grand macabre* (1978) has been widely performed in Europe.

light Any ELECTROMAGNETIC RADIATION, but especially that portion of the SPECTRUM visible to the human eye. It is a form of energy that travels through empty space at a speed of about 186,000 miles per second (300,000 km/s). In the early 19th century, light was described in terms of waves, but experiments later showed that it exhibits properties of particles as well. Light is the basis for the sensation of sight, and for the perception of COLOR. The eye distinguishes the color of an object as the color of light which the object reflects or transmits. See also OPTICS, WAVE-PARTICLE DUALITY.

light-emitting diode (LED) SEMICONDUCTOR DIODE that produces visible or infrared light when subjected to an electric current, as a result of electroluminescence. Visible-light LEDs are used in many electronic devices as indicator lamps (e.g., an on/off indicator) and, when arranged in a matrix, to spell out letter or numbers on alphanumeric displays. Infrared LEDs are used in optoelectronics (e.g., in auto-focus cameras and television remote controls) and as light sources in some long-range fiber-optic communications systems. LEDs are formed by the so-called III-V compound semiconductors related to gallium arsenide. They consume little power and are long-lasting and inexpensive.

light fixture See LUMINAIRE

light-frame construction System of construction using many small and closely spaced members that can be assembled by nailing. It is the standard for U.S. suburban housing. The balloon-frame house with wood cladding, invented in Chicago in the 1840s, aided the rapid settlement of the western U.S. In North America, with its abundant softwood forests, the framed building enjoyed an extensive revival after World War II in the form of platform frames. In platform framing, each floor is framed separately, as contrasted with balloon framing, in which the studs (vertical members) extend the full height of the building. Freed from the heavy timbers of the POST-AND-BEAM SYSTEM, this system offers ease of construction. Carpenters first fabricate a floor, which consists of wood joists and subflooring. The floor often serves as a working platform on which the stud wall frames are fabricated in sections and then lifted into place. On top of this is placed a second floor or the roof. The roof is formed of rafters (sloping joists) or wood TRUSSES. The standard interior wall sheathing is gypsum board (drywall), which provides fire-resistance, stability, and a surface ready for finishing.

light quantum See PHOTON

light-year Distance traveled by LIGHT moving in a vacuum in one year. At its speed of 186,282 mi/second (298,051 km/second), it equals about 5.88×10^{12} mi (9.46×10^{12} km), 63,240 ASTRONOMICAL UNITS, or 0.307 PARSECS.

Lightfoot, Gordon (born 1938) Canadian singer and songwriter. Born in Orillia, Ontario, Lightfoot began writing folk-oriented pop singles in the mid-1960s, including "Early Morning Rain" and "Ribbon of Darkness." His later hits included "If You Could Read My Mind" and "Sundown." His songs have been covered by singers ranging from BARBRA STREISAND to JERRY LEE LEWIS.

lighthouse Structure, usually with a tower, built onshore or on the seabed to signal danger or provide aid to seafarers. The first known lighthouse was the Pharos of Alexandria. The modern lighthouse dates only from the early 18th century. Initially made of wood, these towers were often washed away in severe storms. The first lighthouse made of interlocking masonry blocks was built on the treacherous Eddystone Rocks reef, off Plymouth, England (1759). Interlocking masonry blocks remained the principal material of lighthouse construction until they were replaced by concrete and steel in the 20th century. Modern construction methods have facilitated the building of offshore lighthouses. The most common illuminant is the electric-filament lamp. Refinements in lenses (e.g., the Fresnel lens) and reflectors made it possible to substantially increase the light's intensity. Radio and satellite-based navigation systems have greatly reduced the need for large lighthouses in sighting land.

lighting Use of an artificial source of light for illumination. It is a key element of architecture and interior design. Residential lighting uses mainly either INCANDESCENT LAMPS or FLUORESCENT LAMPS and often depends heavily on movable fixtures plugged into outlets; built-in lighting is typically found in kitchens, bathrooms, and corridors and in the form of hanging pendants in dining rooms and sometimes recessed fixtures in living rooms. Lighting in nonresidential buildings is predominantly fluorescent. High-pressure sodium-vapor lamps (see ELECTRIC DISCHARGE LAMP) have higher efficiency and are used in industrial applications. HALOGEN LAMPS have residential, industrial, and photographic applications. Depending on their fixtures, lamps (bulbs) produce a variety of lighting conditions. Incandescent lamps placed in translucent glass globes create diffuse effects; in recessed ceiling-mounted fixtures with reflectors, they can light walls or floors evenly. Fluorescent fixtures are typically recessed and rectangular, with prismatic lenses, but other types including indirect cove lights (see COVING) and luminous ceilings, in which lamps are placed above suspended translucent panels. Mercury-vapor and high-pressure sodium-vapor lamps are placed in simple reflectors in industrial spaces, in pole-mounted streetlight fixtures, and in indirect up-lighting fixtures for commercial applications.

lightning Visible discharge of electricity when part of the atmosphere acquires enough electrical charge to overcome the resistance of the air. During a thunderstorm, lightning flashes can occur within clouds, between clouds, between clouds and air, or from clouds to the ground. Lightning is usually associated with cumulonimbus CLOUDS (thunderclouds) but also occurs in nimbostratus clouds, in snowstorms and dust storms, and sometimes in the dust and gases emitted by a volcano. A typical lightning flash involves a potential difference between cloud and ground of several hundred million volts. Temperatures in the lightning channel are on the order of 30,000K (50,000°F). A cloud-to-ground flash comprises at least two strokes: a pale leader stroke that strikes the ground and a highly luminous return stroke. The leader stroke reaches the ground in about 20 milliseconds; the return stroke reaches the cloud in about 70 microseconds. The thunder associated with lightning is caused by rapid heating of air along the length of the lightning channel. The heated air expands at supersonic speeds. The shock wave decays within a meter or two into a sound wave which, modified by the intervening air and topography, produces a series of rumbles and claps. See also THUNDERSTORM.

lightning bug See FIREFLY

lignin \'lig-nən\ Complex oxygen-containing organic compound, a mixture of POLYMERS of poorly known structure. After CELLULOSE, it is the most abundant organic material on earth, making up a quarter to a third of the dry weight of wood. Removed from wood pulp in the manufacture of PAPER, it is used as a binder in particleboard and similar products and as a soil conditioner, filler in certain plastics, adhesive for linoleum, and raw material for chemicals including DMSO and vanillin.

lignite Brown to black COAL that has been formed from PEAT under moderate pressure; it is one of the first products of coalification and is intermediate between peat and subbituminous coal. Dry lignite contains about 60–75% carbon. About 45% of the world's total coal reserves are lignitic, but these reserves have not been exploited to any great extent because lignite is inferior to higher-rank coals (e.g., BITUMINOUS COAL) in heating value, storage stability, and other properties. In some areas, however, the scarcity of fuel has led to extensive developments.

Liguria Autonomous region (pop., 1996 est.: 1,659,000), northwestern Italy. Located on the Ligurian Sea between France and Tuscany, its capital is GENOA. Under Roman rule from the 1st century BC, the region was briefly controlled by the Lombards and FRANKS during the Middle Ages. The city of Genoa emerged as a leading power as early as the 11th century, and by 1400 the entire region benefited from its maritime and commercial powers. In 1815 the Congress of VIENNA gave Liguria to the kingdom of Piedmont-Sardinia. It contributed significantly to the union of Italy in 1861. Its economy is based on agriculture, tourism, and industries centered on its major cities, including Genoa. La Spezia is a major naval base.

likelihood *or* **chance** In mathematics, a subjective assessment of possibility that, when assigned a numerical value on a scale between impossibility (0) and absolute certainty (1), becomes a probability (see PROBABILITY THEORY). Thus, the numerical assignment of a probability depends on the notion of likelihood. If, for example, an experiment (e.g., a die toss) can result in six equally likely possible outcomes, the probability of each is $\frac{1}{6}$.

Likud \li-'küd\ Coalition of Israeli right-wing political parties. It was created by the 1973 merger of the Herut Party (1948) and the Liberal Party (1961), which itself was a merger of the General Zionists and the Progressives. From the late 1970s it alternated in power with the ISRAEL LABOUR PARTY. The party generally was skeptical of the Israeli-Palestinian peace process, opposing the formation of a Palestinian state and supporting continued Jewish settlement of occupied territories. Party leaders have included MENACHEM BEGIN, YITZHAK SHAMIR, and ARIEL SHARON. See also ARAB–ISRAELI WARS, IRGUN ZVAI LEUMI, VLADIMIR JABOTINSKY, LEBANESE CIVIL WAR.

lilac Any of about 30 species of fragrant northern spring-flowering garden shrubs and small trees that make up the genus *Syringa* in the OLIVE family, native to eastern Europe and temperate Asia. Lilacs have deep green leaves and large, oval clusters of compound blooms colored deep purple, lavender, blue, red, pink, white, or creamy yellow; they are often highly fragrant. The common lilac *(S. vulgaris)* reaches 20 ft (6 m) in height and produces many suckers (shoots from the stem or root). The name syringa was formerly used for the mock orange of the SAXIFRAGE family, and the butterfly bush (see BUDDLEIA) is commonly called "summer lilac."

Lilburne, John (1614?–1657) English revolutionary. A Separatist, he joined the Puritan opposition to CHARLES I and helped smuggle Puritan pamphlets into England, for which he was imprisoned 1638–40. He became an officer in the Parliamentary army but resigned in 1645 rather than subscribe to the SOLEMN LEAGUE AND COVENANT. He became a master propagandist for the LEVELERS and criticized Parliament for failing to meet their demands. He was imprisoned 1645–47 but remained very popular with Londoners and was twice acquitted of treason.

Lilith In Jewish folklore, a female DEMON. In rabbinic literature she is depicted either as Adam's first wife or as the mother of his demonic offspring after he separated from Eve outside Paradise (see ADAM AND EVE). The evil that Lilith directed against children could be counteracted by wearing an amulet bearing the names of the three angels who opposed her. A cult associated with Lilith survived into the 7th century AD.

Liliuokalani \li-ˌlē-ə-wō-kə-'lä-nē\ *orig.* **Lydia Kamakaeha** (1838–1917) Hawaiian queen, the last Hawaiian monarch to govern the islands (1891–93). Born in Honolulu, she succeeded her brother, David Kalakaua, to the throne and tried to restore the traditional monarchy. She opposed the reciprocity treaty giving commercial concessions to the U.S. In 1893 she was declared deposed by SANFORD B. DOLE and the Missionary Party, which favored annexation by the U.S. An uprising in her name was suppressed and the rebels jailed. To win pardons for her supporters, she formally abdicated in 1895. A talented musician, she composed the song "Aloha Oe."

Queen Liliuokalani.
BY COURTESY OF THE BERNICE P. BISHOP MUSEUM

Lille \'lēl\ City (pop., 1990: 178,000), northern France, situated on the Deûle River. Fortified in the 11th century, it changed hands several times during the Middle Ages. LOUIS XIV besieged and captured the city in 1667. It was taken by the duke of MARLBOROUGH in 1708 and ceded to France in 1713. It was occupied by the Germans during both World Wars. With Tourcoing and Roubaix, it now forms one of the nation's largest conurbations. It is traditionally France's textile center; other industries include machinery manufacturing and chemical plants. Its museum has a rich art collection.

Lillie, Beatrice (Gladys) (1894–1989) Canadian-British comedienne. Born in Toronto, she made her London stage debut as a singer in 1914 and developed her comic genius in revues produced by André Charlot. She made her New York debut in 1924 and established an international reputation as a high-spirited star of sophisticated comedy. She appeared in revues until 1939 and later starred in *Inside U.S.A.* (1948–50). She toured worldwide in *An Evening with Beatrice Lillie* (1952–56) and later starred in London in *Auntie Mame* (1958) and in New York in *High Spirits* (1964).

Beatrice Lillie.
BROWN BROTHERS

Lilongwe \li-'lȯŋ-gwā\ Capital and second-largest city (metro. area pop., 1994 est.: 396,000), MALAWI. It is located on an inland plain 50 mi (80 km) west of the southern end of Lake MALAWI. An agricultural market center for the fertile Central Region Plateau, it replaced Zomba as the national capital in 1975. The old part of the city functions as a service and commercial center, while the newer district of Capital Hill houses government buildings and embassies.

Lily, William (1468?–1522?) English Renaissance scholar and classical grammarian. Having made a pilgrimage to Jerusalem and visited Greece and Italy, he became a pioneer of Greek learning in England and was appointed master of the school of St. Paul's in 1510. His grammar, which actually consisted of two books, one in English and the other in Latin, first appeared about 18 years after his death. Its use by royal order in all English grammar schools won it the name "the King's Grammar." With corrections and revisions, it continued to be used as late as the 19th century, and influenced generations of English people's views of all languages, including English.

lily family Family Liliaceae (order Liliales), which contains about 4,000 species of flowering herbs and shrubs in 280 genera. The genus *Lilium* includes the true lilies. Native primarily to temperate and subtropical regions, these monocots (see COTYLEDON) usually have six-segmented flowers, three-chambered capsular fruits, and leaves with parallel veins. Among the oldest cultivated plants, true lilies are erect perennials with leafy stems, scaly bulbs, usually narrow leaves, and solitary or clustered flowers, some quite fragrant, in a variety of colors. Most species store nutrients underground in a bulb, corm, or tuber. Important garden ornamentals and houseplants in the family include ALOE, BLUEBELL, CROCUS, DAY LILY, HOSTA, SOLOMON'S SEAL, and TULIP. Food-producing members include ONION, GARLIC, and ASPARAGUS.

lily of the valley Fragrant perennial herb and sole species *(Convallaria majalis)* of the genus *Convallaria* (LILY FAMILY), native to Eurasia and eastern North America. White, bell-shaped flowers droop in a row from one side of a leafless stalk, which bears usually two glossy leaves at its base. The fruit is a single red berry. Lily of the valley is cultivated in shaded garden areas in many temperate parts of the world.

Lima \'lē-mə\ City (metro. area pop., 1993: 5,706,000), capital of PERU, located inland from the Pacific port of CALLAO, near the ANDES. Its nickname, El Pulpo ("The Octopus"), refers to its sprawling metropolitan area of 1,506 sq mi (3,900 sq km). It was founded by FRANCISCO PIZARRO in 1535 on the feast of the EPIPHANY, prompting the name Ciudad de los Reyes ("City of Kings"), but the name never took. It later became the capital of the new viceroyalty of PERU. It was destroyed by an earthquake in 1746 but was rebuilt. Growing rapidly during the 20th century, it now accounts for about one-third of Peru's total population, and is the country's economic and cultural center. Historic sites include the cathedral (begun in the 16th century), and the National University of San Marcos (founded 1551).

Lima, José Lezama See Jose LEZAMA LIMA

Liman von Sanders \'lē-män-fȯn-'zän-dərs\, **Otto** (1855–1929) German general. He entered the German army in 1874 and rose to lieutenant general. He reorganized the Turkish army and made it an effective fighting force in World War I. In command of the Turkish army at Gallipoli, he and the Turkish commanders forced the Allies to end the DARDANELLES CAMPAIGN and prevented the seizure of Constantinople.

Limavady \ˌli-mə-'va-dē\ Town (pop., 1981: 8,000), seat of Limavady district, Northern Ireland. The town is on the River Roe east of the old city of Londonderry. It dates from the Plantation of Ulster in the early

17th century; it was later settled by Protestant Scots. The district (pop., 1995 est.: 31,000), is primarily agricultural.

limb darkening In astrophysics, the gradual decrease in observed brightness of the disk of a star from its center to its edge (limb). This phenomenon, readily apparent in photographs of the sun, occurs because the solar atmosphere's temperature increases with depth. Looking at the center, an observer sees the deepest, hottest layers, which emit the most light. At the limb, only the upper, cooler layers, which produce less light, are visible. Observations of solar limb darkening are used to determine the temperature structure of the sun's atmosphere.

Limbaugh \'lim-,bȯ\, **Rush** *orig.* **Rush Hudson Limbaugh III** (born 1951) U.S. talk-show host and writer. Born in Cape Girardeau, Mo., he began his career as a disc jockey in 1971 and became a top radio host in Sacramento (1985–88), known for his sarcastic right-wing political commentary and his combative replies to listeners' call-in comments. He began the national broadcast of *The Rush Limbaugh Show* from New York in 1988; by 1993 it was the most popular and influential talk show in the U.S., reaching an estimated 20 million listeners daily, and had spawned numerous similar conservative shows nationwide. He hosted a television spin-off show from 1992 and wrote best-selling books such as *The Way Things Ought to Be* (1992) and *See, I Told You So* (1993).

limbo In ROMAN CATHOLICISM, a region between HEAVEN and HELL, the dwelling place of SOULS not condemned to punishment but deprived of the joy of existence with God in heaven. The concept probably developed in the Middle Ages. Two distinct kinds of limbo were proposed: the *limbus patrum* ("fathers' limbo"), where Old Testament saints were confined until liberated by JESUS in his "descent into hell"; and the *limbus infantum* or *limbus puerorum* ("children's limbo"), the abode of those who died without actual sin but whose original sin had not been washed away by BAPTISM or whose free will was restricted by mental deficiency. Today the Catholic church downplays the notion of limbo, and it is not an official part of church doctrine.

Limbourg brothers *or* **Limburg brothers** \'lim-,bürk\ (fl. c. 1400–1416) Flemish illuminators. Sons of a sculptor, the three brothers—Pol, Herman, and Jehanequin de Limbourg—learned the goldsmith's art in Paris and entered the service of the duc (duke) de Berry, for whom they produced one of the most famous of all ILLUMINATED MANUSCRIPTS, a book of hours (private prayer book) known as the "Très riches heures du duc de Berry" (c. 1410–16). Since the brothers worked together, it is difficult to distinguish individual styles. They synthesized the achievements of their contemporaries into a style characterized by tall, aristocratic figures with lavish, curvilinear draperies, and by highly naturalistic seasonal landscapes and scenes of peasant life. Their art did much to determine the course of EARLY NETHERLANDISH ART. Their deaths in the same year suggest that they died of plague.

lime Small shrublike tree *(Citrus aurantifolia)* widely grown in tropical and subtropical areas, and its edible acid fruits. Stiff branches and twigs leave the thorny stem at irregular intervals, and end in green leaves. Clusters of small white flowers produce small oval fruits with a thin, pale greenish-yellow rind. The juicy pulp is more acidic and sweet than that of the LEMON. Limes are used to flavor many foods. High in vitamin C, they were formerly used in the British Navy to prevent SCURVY; hence the nickname "Limey" for British sailors.

Lime (*Citrus aurantifolia*).
GRANT HEILMAN

lime *or* **quicklime** Inorganic compound, white or grayish lumps, chemical formula CaO, made by roasting LIMESTONE (calcium carbonate, $CaCO_3$) until all the carbon dioxide (CO_2) is driven off. One of the four most important basic chemical commodities, it is used as a REFRACTORY, as a flux in steel manufacture, as a CO_2 absorbent, to remove sulfur dioxide from stack gases, to neutralize various acids, in pulp and paper, in insecticides and fungicides, in poultry feeds, for dehairing of hides, in sugar refining, in sewage treatment, and in the manufacture of glass, calcium carbide, and sodium carbonate. Adding water to lime yields calcium hydroxide (slaked lime, calcium hydrate, hydrated lime, or caustic lime), which has uses in mortar, plasters, cements, whitewash, hide dehairing, ammonia recovery, water softening, sugar purification, petrochemicals, poultry feeds, and foods and as a soil conditioner, disinfectant, accelerator in rubber compounds, and source of other calcium salts.

limelight Early form of theatrical lighting. The incandescent calcium light invented by Thomas Drummond in 1816 was first employed in a theater in 1837 and was being widely used by the 1860s. Its soft, brilliant light enabled it to be focused for spotlighting and to create effects such as sunlight and moonlight. The expression "in the limelight" referred to the most desirable acting area on the stage, the front and center, which was illuminated by limelights. Electric lighting replaced limelight in the late 19th century.

limerick Popular form of short, humorous verse, often nonsensical and frequently ribald. It consists of five lines, rhyming *aabba,* and the dominant meter is anapestic, with two feet in the third and fourth lines and three feet in the others. The origin of the term is obscure, but a group of poets in Co. Limerick, Ireland, wrote limericks in Irish in the 18th century. The first collections in English date from c. 1820. Among the most famous are those in EDWARD LEAR's *Book of Nonsense* (1846).

limes \'lē-mās\ (Latin: "path") In ancient Rome, a strip of fortifications along a road that could serve either as a barrier against attack or a path along which troops could advance at the frontier. An example was the continuous system of fortifications and barriers extending 345 mi (552 km) along the Roman frontier in Germany and RAETIA. HADRIAN'S WALL also served as a *limes.* Though not impenetrable, the *limites* allowed the Romans to control communications along frontiers and deterred raiding parties. In the eastern and southern empire, *limites* were often used to guard caravan routes.

limestone Sedimentary rock composed mainly of CALCIUM carbonate ($CaCO_3$), usually in the form of CALCITE and, less commonly, ARAGONITE. It may contain considerable amounts of magnesium carbonate (DOLOMITE) as well. Most limestones have a granular texture; in many cases, the grains are tiny fragments of fossil animal shells. Much knowledge of the earth's history has been derived from the study of FOSSILS embedded in limestone and other carbonate rocks. Limestone is used as a soil conditioner, in the manufacture of glass, and in agriculture. Ornamental varieties are used for flooring, exterior and interior facings of buildings, and monuments.

Limfjorden \'lēm-,fyȯr-dən\ Strait across northern Jutland, Denmark, connecting the North Sea and the Kattegat. It is 110 mi (180 km) long and is actually a series of fjords dotted with islands. In 1825 the North Sea broke through the western part, and the Thyborøn Kanal was cut to keep the outlet open.

limit Mathematical concept based on the idea of closeness, used mainly in studying the behavior of FUNCTIONS close to values at which they are undefined. For example, the function $1/x$ is not defined at $x = 0$. For positive values of x, as x is chosen closer and closer to 0, the value of $1/x$ begins to grow rapidly, approaching INFINITY as a limit. This interplay of action and reaction as the independent VARIABLE moves closer to a given value is the essence of the idea of a limit. Limits provide the means of defining the DERIVATIVE and INTEGRAL of a function.

limitations, statute of Legislative act restricting the time within which legal proceedings may be brought, usually to a fixed period after the occurrence of the events that gave rise to the cause of action. Such statutes are enacted to protect persons against claims made after evidence has been lost, memories have faded, or witnesses have disappeared. The periods prescribed for different actions in different jurisdictions vary considerably.

limited liability Condition under which the loss that an owner (shareholder) of a business may incur is limited to the capital invested in the business and does not extend to personal assets. The forerunners of limited-liability companies were limited partnerships, which were common in Europe and the U.S. in the 18th and early 19th century. In limited partnerships, one partner is entirely liable for losses and the other partners are liable only for the amounts they invested in the business. After the Joint-Stock Companies Act (1844) in England made incorporation easier, joint-stock companies with limited liability for all members be-

L
M
N

came widespread. The development of the limited-liability company was crucial to the rise of large-scale industry in the late 19th and 20th century, since it enabled businesses to mobilize capital from a variety of investors who were unwilling to risk their entire personal fortunes in their INVESTMENTS. See also RISK.

limited obligation bond See REVENUE BOND

limnology \lim-ˈnä-lə-jē\ Subdiscipline of HYDROLOGY that concerns the study of fresh waters, specifically lakes and ponds (both natural and manmade), including their biological, physical, and chemical aspects. François-Alphonse Forel (1841–1912) established the field with his studies of Lake Geneva. Limnology traditionally is closely related to hydrobiology, which is concerned with the application of the principles and methods of physics, chemistry, geology, and geography to ecological problems.

Limoges painted enamel \lē-ˈmōzh\ ENAMELWORK made in Limoges, France, generally considered the finest painted enamelware produced in Europe in the 16th century. The earliest examples show religious scenes in the late Gothic style, but Italian Renaissance motifs appeared c. 1520. Painting in grisaille was later introduced. By the late 16th cent, the quality of the enamelware had degenerated. See also LEONARD LIMOSIN.

Limoges ware PORCELAIN, largely serviceware, produced in Limoges, France, from the 18th century. FAIENCE of undistinguished quality was produced there from 1736, but the manufacture of hard-paste, or true, porcelain dates only from 1771. In 1784 the factory was acquired as an adjunct of the royal factory at Sèvres (see SÈVRES PORCELAIN), and the decorations of the two wares became similar. After 1858 Limoges became a mass exporter of porcelain to the U.S. under the name Haviland.

Limón \li-ˈmōn\, **José (Arcadio)** (1908–1972) U.S. modern dancer, choreographer, and founder-director of the José Limón Dance Co. Born in Mexico, he moved to the U.S. at age 7. He studied with DORIS HUMPHREY and CHARLES WEIDMAN and danced with their company 1930–40. He established his own company in 1947, with Humphrey as artistic director. His choreography conveyed modern-dance expression within a well-defined structure, as exemplified by such works as *The Moor's Pavane* (1949) and *Missa Brevis* (1958). The company toured worldwide during Limón's life and has remained active since his death.

Limón, 1965.
MARTHA SWOPE

limonite \ˈlī-mə-ˌnīt\ One of the major IRON minerals, a hydrous ferric oxide of variable composition. Often brown and earthy, it is formed by alteration of other iron minerals, such as the hydration of HEMATITE or the oxidation and hydration of SIDERITE or PYRITE.

Limonite (left) from Ironwood, Mich., and (right) from Montgomery, Pa.
BY COURTESY OF THE FIELD MUSEUM OF NATURAL HISTORY, CHICAGO; PHOTOGRAPH, JOHN H. GERARD—EB INC.

Limosin \lē-mō-ˈzaⁿ\, **Léonard** *or* **Léonard Limousin** \ˈlē-mü-ˈzaⁿ\ (c. 1505–1575/77) French painter. The most accomplished member of a prominent Limoges family of enamelers, he is known for the revealing realism of the portraits he painted on LIMOGES WARE. His earliest authenticated work is his *Passion of the Lord* (1532), a series of 18 enamel plaques after prints by ALBRECHT DURER. He was later influenced by the Italian Mannerists who worked at FONTAINEBLEAU for FRANCIS I, whom he served as court painter. He was also an accomplished painter in oils.

Limousin \ˌli-mə-ˈzēn, *French* ˌlē-mə-ˈzeⁿ\ Historical region, central France. Originally inhabited by the ancient Gallic tribe of Lemovices, it was conquered by Rome c. 50 BC. Under the CAROLINGIANS, it was part of AQUITAINE. On ELEANOR OF AQUITAINE's marriage to the English king HENRY II in 1152, it passed to English control. Subsequently fought over by England and France, it was finally annexed to the French crown under the French king HENRY IV.

limpet \ˈlim-pət\ Any of various species of SNAILS that have a flattened shell. Most marine species (subclass Prosobranchia) cling to rocks near shore. A common U.S. species is the Atlantic plate limpet *(Acmaea testudinalis)* of cold waters. Keyhole limpets have a slit or hole at the apex of the shell. Some limpets (subclass Pulmonata) live in brackish water and freshwater. See also MOLLUSK.

European limpets (*Patella vulgata*) with acorn barnacles (*Balanus balanoides*).
NEVILLE FOX-DAVIES—BRUCE COLEMAN INC./EB INC.

Limpopo River River, South Africa. Rising as the Crocodile (Krokodil) River in the Witwatersrand, South Africa, it flows northeast along the border of South Africa and southeast across Mozambique to empty into the Indian Ocean. Along its middle course it divides South Africa from Botswana and Zimbabwe. It is 1,100 mi (1,800 km) long but is navigable only 130 mi (208 km) from the coast. The first European to visit it was VASCO DA GAMA, who named its mouth the Espíritu Santo River in 1498.

Lin, Maya (born 1959) U.S. architect and sculptor. Born in Athens, Ohio, she achieved fame when her class assignment at Yale University won the nationwide VIETNAM VETERANS MEMORIAL competition in 1981. Her subsequent, vastly different designs include the major commissions for the Civil Rights Memorial, Montgomery, Ala. (1989), and The Women's Table at Yale (1993), as well as an earth sculpture for the University of Michigan (1994) and an extraordinary translucent clock, *Eclipsed Time,* installed in the ceiling of New York's Pennsylvania Station (1994).

Lin Biao *or* **Lin Piao** \ˈlin-bē-ˈau̇\ (1907–1971?) Chinese military leader who played a prominent role in the CULTURAL REVOLUTION. He joined the Socialist Youth League in 1925 and CHIANG KAI-SHEK's NORTHERN EXPEDITION in 1926. When Chiang turned on the Communists in 1927, Lin fled to join Mao. During the LONG MARCH Lin became legendary for never losing a battle, and he prevailed against the Japanese in the 1930s and the Nationalists in the 1940s. In the early 1960s his reformation and indoctrination of the army in accordance with Mao's teachings became a model for the rest of society, and during the Cultural Revolution he was designated Mao's successor. It is speculated that Mao feared the power Lin had amassed and that Lin plotted a coup in a desperate move to avoid being purged. The government claimed he died in a 1971 plane crash in Mongolia in an attempt to flee China, but Mongolian officals found no proof of his presence on the plane.

Lin Yutang *or* **Lin Yü-t'ang** (1895–1976) Chinese writer. The son of a Presbyterian minister, he studied in the U.S. and Europe. In 1932 he established a highly successful Western-style satirical magazine of a type totally new to China; soon he introduced two other publications. A prolific writer of works in Chinese and English, he produced his first English-language book, *My Country and My People,* in 1935. From 1936 he lived chiefly in the U.S. His other works include *The Wisdom of China and India* (1942), books on Chinese history and philosophy, and highly acclaimed English translations of Chinese literary masterpieces.

Lin Zexu *or* **Lin Tse-hsü** \ˈlin-ˈdzə-ˈshü\ (1785–1850) Leading Chinese scholar and official of the QING DYNASTY, accepted as a national hero for his stance against the British before the Anglo-Chinese OPIUM WAR (1839–42). Lin passed the highest examination in the Chinese examination system and entered the HANLIN ACADEMY and government. Having suggested to the emperor ways to suppress the opium trade, Lin found himself appointed imperial commissioner and dispatched to Canton to deal with the problem directly. He was so successful that, in retaliation for his destruction of their opium stocks, the British ravaged large parts of southern China, and Lin was quickly dismissed. He served loyally at his post of exile and was soon called back to important service. He died on his way to help suppress the TAIPING REBELLION.

linac See LINEAR ACCELERATOR

Linacre \ˈli-ni-kər\, **Thomas** (c. 1460–1524) English physician and classical scholar. Elected a fellow at Oxford in 1484, he became one of the first propagators of the humanist "New Learning" in England; his students included DESIDERIUS ERASMUS and ST. THOMAS MORE. Many prominent Londoners were his medical patients, including HENRY VIII, whose approval he obtained in 1518 to found the Royal College of Physicians, which decided who should practice medicine in greater London and licensed physicians throughout the kingdom, ending the indiscriminate practice of medicine by barbers, clergymen, and others.

Lincoln *ancient* **Lindum** City (pop., 1991: 82,000), seat of LINCOLNSHIRE, eastern England. Lindum served as a Roman fortress, and by AD 71 it had become a settlement for retired soldiers. It later came under Danish rule, and in the Middle Ages was one of England's major towns. HENRY II gave the city its first charter in 1154. It is a market center for an agricultural region, and also possesses some manufacturing. It has many medieval buildings, including the cathedral (begun c. 1075).

Lincoln cathedral, Lincolnshire.
RAY MANLEY–SHOSTAL

Lincoln City (pop., 1996 est.: 209,000), capital of Nebraska. Laid out in 1859 and called Lancaster, it was renamed for ABRAHAM LINCOLN when it was chosen as the capital in 1867. The town was incorporated in 1869 and was the home of the politician WILLIAM JENNINGS BRYAN 1887–1921. It is a railroad junction and commercial center serving the surrounding agricultural region. Its institutions of higher education include the University of NEBRASKA, Union College, and Nebraska Wesleyan Univ.

Lincoln, Abraham (1809–1865) 16th president of the U.S. (1861–65). Born in a log cabin in Hodgenville, Ky., he moved to Indiana in 1816 and to Illinois in 1830. He worked as a storekeeper, rail-splitter, postmaster, and surveyor, then enlisted as a volunteer in the Black Hawk War and became a captain. Though largely self-taught, he practiced law in Springfield, Ill., and served in the state legislature (1834–40). He was elected as a Whig to the U.S. House of Representatives (1847–49). As a circuit-riding lawyer from 1849, he became one of the state's most successful lawyers, noted for his shrewdness, common sense, and honesty (earning the nickname "Honest Abe"). In 1856 he joined the Republican Party, which nominated him as its candidate in the 1858 Senate election. In a series of seven debates with STEPHEN A. DOUGLAS (the LINCOLN-DOUGLAS DEBATES), he argued against the extension of slavery into the territories, though not against slavery itself. Although morally opposed to slavery, he was not an abolitionist. During the campaign, he attempted to rebut Douglas' charge that he was a dangerous radical by reassuring audiences that he did not favor political equality for blacks. Despite his loss in the election, the debates brought him national attention. He again ran against Douglas in the 1860 presidential election, which he won by a large margin. But the South opposed his position on slavery in the territories, and before his inauguration seven Southern states had seceeded from the Union. The ensuing AMERICAN CIVIL WAR completely consumed Lincoln's administration. He excelled as a wartime leader, creating a high command for directing all the country's energies and resources toward the war effort and combining statecraft and overall command of the armies with what some have called military genius. However, his abrogation of some civil liberties, especially the writ of HABEAS CORPUS, and the closing of several newspapers by his generals disturbed both Democrats and Republicans, including some members of his own cabinet. To unite the North and influence foreign opinion, he issued the EMANCIPATION PROCLAMATION (1863); his GETTYSBURG ADDRESS (1863) further ennobled the war's purpose. The continuing war affected some Northerners' resolve and his reelection was not assured, but strategic battle victories turned the tide and he easily defeated GEORGE B. MCCLELLAN in 1864. His platform included passage of the 13th Amendment outlawing slavery (ratified 1865). At his second inaugural, with victory in sight, he spoke of moderation in reconstructing the South and building a harmonious Union. On April 14, five days after the war ended, he was shot by JOHN WILKES BOOTH.

Lincoln, Benjamin (1733–1810) American Revolutionary officer. Born in Hingham, Mass., he served in the Massachusetts militia (1755–76), then was appointed major general in the Continental Army. As commander of forces in the South in 1780, he was forced to surrender with 7,000 troops after the British victory at Charleston, S.C. Released in a prisoner exchange, he served in the Yorktown campaign (1781). He was appointed secretary of war (1781–83). He commanded the militia forces that suppressed SHAYS' REBELLION (1787) and later was collector for the port of Boston (1789–1809).

Lincoln Center for the Performing Arts Travertine-clad cultural complex on the western side of Manhattan (1962–68), built by a board of architects headed by Wallace K. Harrison (1895–1981). The buildings, situated around a plaza with a fountain, are the home of the METROPOLITAN OPERA, the New York City Opera, the New York Philharmonic, the NEW YORK CITY BALLET, and the JUILLIARD SCHOOL. Harrison himself designed the Metropolitan Opera building, and EERO SAARINEN designed the Vivian Beaumont Theater. PHILIP JOHNSON's New York State Theater incorporates a Classical facade and a four-story lobby. Johnson also rebuilt Avery Fisher Hall (home of the New York Philharmonic), originally designed by Max Abramovitz, to correct acoustic deficiencies and improve the lobby spaces.

Lincoln-Douglas Debates Series of seven debates between Republican candidate ABRAHAM LINCOLN and Democratic Sen. STEPHEN A. DOUGLAS in the 1858 Illinois senatorial campaign. They focused on slavery and its extension into the western territories. Lincoln criticized Douglas for his support of POPULAR SOVEREIGNTY and the KANSAS-NEBRASKA ACT, while Douglas accused Lincoln of advocating racial equality and disruption of the Union. Douglas won reelection, but Lincoln's antislavery position and oratorical brilliance made him a national figure in the young REPUBLICAN PARTY.

Lincolnshire \'liŋ-kən-ˌshir\ County (pop., 1995 est.: 612,000), eastern England. It lies along the North Sea from the Humber Estuary to The Wash; the county seat is LINCOLN. Inhabited in prehistoric times, it developed as an area of Roman settlement. Anglo-Saxons later established the kingdom of Lindsey. Danish influence was also widespread through villages established by Danes. Geographically isolated, it remains primarily an agricultural region. Along the coast, tourism has grown.

Lind, James (1716–1794) Scottish naval surgeon and physician. Having observed thousands of SCURVY, TYPHUS, and DYSENTERY cases and the shipboard conditions that caused them, he published *A Treatise on Scurvy* in 1754, a time when scurvy killed more British sailors than combat. He recommended giving citrus fruits and juices (sources of VITAMIN C) to sailors on long voyages, a practice known to the Dutch for nearly two centuries. When the practice was fully instituted in 1795, scurvy disappeared from the ranks "as if by magic." Lind also suggested shipboard delousing and use of hospital ships, and arranged for distillation of seawater for drinking.

Lind, Jenny *orig.* **Johanna Maria** (1820–1887) Swedish soprano. She became prima donna at the Royal Opera in Stockholm at 18. Study with Manuel García (1805–1906) in 1841 averted damage from vocal strain. Her career expanded to Germany, then to Vienna and London, where she created a sensation. Her European fame caught the eye of P. T. BARNUM, who arranged a U.S. tour (dubbing her "the Swedish Nightingale") that launched many modern publicity techniques. She left Barnum in 1851, and resumed singing in Europe, though much less frequently. In her later years she lived and taught in England.

Lindbergh, Charles A(ugustus) (1902–1974) U.S. aviator who made the first nonstop solo flight across the Atlantic Ocean. Born in Detroit, he left college to enroll in army flying schools and became an airmail pilot in 1926. He obtained backing from St. Louis businessmen to compete for a prize for flying from New York to Paris, and in 1927 in the monoplane *Spirit of St. Louis* he made the flight in 33½ hours, becoming an instant hero in the U.S. and Europe. In 1929 he married the writer Anne Morrow, who would later serve as his copilot and navigator. In 1932 their child

Lindbergh, 1927.
BY COURTESY OF THE LIBRARY OF CONGRESS, WASHINGTON, D.C.

L
M
N

was kidnapped and murdered, a crime that received worldwide attention. They moved to England to escape the publicity, returning to the U.S. in 1940 to criticism over his speeches calling for U.S. neutrality in World War II. During the war Lindbergh was an adviser to Ford Motor Co. and United Aircraft Corp. After the war he was a consultant to Pan American Airways and the U.S. Department of Defense and served on many aeronautical boards and committees. In 1953 he wrote the Pulitzer Prize–winning *The Spirit of St. Louis*.

linden Any of about 30 species of trees that make up the genus *Tilia* (family Tiliaceae), native to the Northern Hemisphere. A few are outstanding deciduous ornamental and shade trees, with heart-shaped, coarsely toothed leaves, fragrant cream-colored flowers, and small globular fruit. The American linden (*T. americana*), also called BASSWOOD or whitewood, grows as high as 130 ft (40 m). Its wood is used for beehives, crating, furniture, and packing material; like other linden species, it is also a popular bee tree, yielding a distinctive, pale, fragrant honey.

Lindisfarne *or* **Holy Island** Historic small island 2 mi (3 km) from the English Northumbrian coast. It became a religious center in 635, when St. AIDAN established a monastery and church there. It was abandoned in 875 because of the threat of Danish raids, but the monastery was refounded in 1082 and survived until the dissolution of the monasteries (1536–40) under HENRY VIII. The manuscript of the Lindisfarne Gospels (c. 696–98) is one of the finest surviving illuminated manuscripts of the period. Lindisfarne's present-day parish church may occupy the site of St. Aidan's original monastery.

Lindisfarne Gospels ILLUMINATED MANUSCRIPT version of the four Gospels, produced in the late 7th century for the Northumbrian island monastery of LINDISFARNE. The book was designed and executed by Eadfrith, who became bishop of Lindisfarne in 698. Illuminated in the HIBERNO-SAXON STYLE, the Lindisfarne Gospels (now in the British Library) show the fusion of Irish, classical, and Byzantine elements. See also Book of KELLS.

Lindsay, Howard (1889–1968) U.S. playwright and producer known for his collaboration with Russel Crouse (1893–1966). Born in Waterford, N.Y., Lindsay began his career as an actor, director, and playwright, and Crouse, born in Findlay, Ohio, was a journalist before they were paired by producer Vinton Freedley to write librettos for the successful C. PORTER musicals *Anything Goes* (1934) and *Red, Hot and Blue* (1936). Their most popular play, *Life with Father* (1939), ran for over seven years and starred Lindsay as Father. They produced *Arsenic and Old Lace* (1940) and later wrote librettos for such musicals as *State of the Union* (1945, Pulitzer Prize), *Call Me Madam* (1950), and *The Sound of Music* (1959).

Lindsay, (Nicholas) Vachel (1879–1931) U.S. poet. Born in Springfield, Ill., Lindsay in his youth began traveling the country reciting his poems in return for food and shelter, in an attempt to revive poetry as an oral art form of the common people. He first received widespread recognition for "General William Booth Enters into Heaven" (1913), about the founder of the Salvation Army. His works are full of powerful rhythms, vivid imagery, and bold rhymes and express an ardent patriotism, a passion for progressive democracy, and a romantic view of nature. His collections include *Rhymes to Be Traded for Bread* (1912), *The Congo* (1914), and *The Chinese Nightingale* (1917). He was responsible for discovering the work of LANGSTON HUGHES. Depressed and unstable in later years, he committed suicide by drinking poison.

line Basic element of EUCLIDEAN GEOMETRY. EUCLID defined a line as an interval between two points and claimed it could be extended indefinitely in either direction. Such an extension in both directions is now thought of as a line, while Euclid's original definition is considered a line segment. A ray is part of a line extending indefinitely from a point on the line in only one direction. In a COORDINATE SYSTEM on a plane, a line can be represented by the linear EQUATION $ax + by + c = 0$. This is often written in the slope-intercept form as $y = mx + b$, in which m is the SLOPE and b is the value where the line crosses the y-axis. Because geometrical objects whose edges are line segments are completely understood, mathematicians frequently try to reduce more complex structures into simpler ones made up of connected line segments.

line integral In mathematics, the INTEGRAL of a FUNCTION of several VARIABLES defined on a LINE or curve that has been expressed in terms of arc length (see LENGTH OF A CURVE). An ordinary definite integral is defined over a line segment, whereas a line integral may use a more general path, such as a parabola or a circle. Line integrals are used extensively in the theory of functions of a COMPLEX VARIABLE.

Line Islands Chain of islands (pop., 1990: 5,000), central Pacific Ocean, south of the Hawaiian Islands. It extends 1,600 mi (2,600 km) and has a land area of 193 sq mi (500 sq km). Of the northern group, Teraina (Washington) Island and Tabuaeran (Fanning) and Kiritimati (Christmas) atolls belong to the Republic of KIRIBATI, while Kingman Reef, Palmyra Atoll, and Jarvis Island are U.S. territories. Kiribati also holds the central group (Malden and Starbuck islands) and the southern group (Vostok and Flint islands and Caroline Atoll).

Linear A and Linear B Linear forms of WRITING used by AEGEAN CIVILIZATIONS during the 2nd millennium BC. Examples of Linear A, a syllabary (see ALPHABET) written from left to right, date from 1850 BC to 1400 BC. The language written in Linear A remains unknown. Linear B, adapted from Linear A, was borrowed from the MINOAN civilization by the MYCENAEAN Greeks, probably c. 1600 BC, and used to write the Mycenaean Greek dialect. Examples of Linear B script have been found on clay tablets and vases from c. 1400–1200 BC. These texts represent the oldest known form of Greek. Linear B was deciphered as Greek in 1952 by MICHAEL VENTRIS.

linear accelerator *or* **linac** Type of PARTICLE ACCELERATOR that imparts a series of relatively small increases in energy to subatomic particles as they pass through a sequence of alternating electric fields set up in a linear structure. The small accelerations add together to give the particles a greater energy than could be achieved by the voltage used in one section alone. One of the world's longest linacs is the 2-mi (3.2-km) machine at the Stanford Linear Accelerator Center, which can accelerate electrons to energies of 50 billion electron volts. Much smaller linacs, both proton and electron types, have important practical applications in medicine and industry.

linear algebra Branch of ALGEBRA concerned with methods of solving systems of linear EQUATIONS; more generally, the mathematics of LINEAR TRANSFORMATIONS and VECTOR SPACES. "Linear" refers to the form of the equations involved—in two dimensions, $ax + by = c$. Geometrically, this represents a line. If the variables are replaced by VECTORS, FUNCTIONS, or DERIVATIVES, the equation becomes a linear transformation. A SYSTEM OF EQUATIONS of this type is a system of linear transformations. Because it shows when such a system has a solution and how to find it, linear algebra is essential to the theory of mathematical ANALYSIS and DIFFERENTIAL EQUATIONS. Its applications extend beyond the physical sciences into, for example, biology and economics.

linear approximation In mathematics, the process of finding a line that closely fits a curve, if only locally. Expressed as the linear equation $y = ax + b$ the values of a and b must be chosen so that (1) the function and line have the same value at a chosen value of x, and (2) the first DERIVATIVE of the function at x coincides with the SLOPE of the line. For most curves, linear approximations are good only very close to x. Yet much of the theory of CALCULUS, including the fundamental theorem of CALCULUS and the MEAN-VALUE THEOREM for derivatives, is based on such approximations.

linear programming Mathematical modeling technique useful for guiding quantitative decisions in business, industrial engineering, and to a lesser extent the social and physical sciences. Solving a linear programming problem can be reduced to finding the optimum value (see OPTIMIZATION) of a linear equation (called an objective FUNCTION), subject to a set of constraints expressed as INEQUALITIES. The number of inequalities and VARIABLES depends on the complexity of the problem, whose solution is found by solving the system of inequalities like a SYSTEM OF EQUATIONS. The extensive use of linear programming during World War II to deal with transportation, scheduling and allocations of resources under constraints like cost and priority gave the subject an impetus that carried it into the postwar era. The number of equations and variables needed to model real-life situations accurately is large, and the solution process can be time-consuming even with computers. See also SIMPLEX METHOD.

linear transformation In mathematics, a rule for changing one geometric figure (or MATRIX or VECTOR) into another using a formula with a specified format. The format must be a linear combination, in which the original components (e.g., the x and y coordinates of each point of the original figure) are changed via the formula $ax + by$ to produce the coordinates of the transformed figure. Examples include flipping the figure over the x or y axis, stretching or compressing it, and rotating it. Every such transformation has an inverse, which undoes its effect.

linen Fiber, YARN, and fabric made from the FLAX plant. Flax is one of the oldest TEXTILE fibers used by humans; evidence of its use has been found in Switzerland's prehistoric lake dwellings. Fine linen fabrics have been discovered in ancient Egyptian tombs. The fiber is obtained by subjecting plant stalks to a series of operations, including retting (a fermentation process), drying, crushing, and beating. Linen is stronger than COTTON, dries more quickly, and is more slowly affected by exposure to sunlight. Low elasticity, imparting a hard, smooth texture, makes linen subject to wrinkling. Because linen absorbs and releases moisture quickly and is a good conductor of heat, linen garments feel cool to wearers. Fine grades of linen are made into woven fabrics and laces for apparel and household furnishings. Leading producers include some nations of the former Soviet Union, Poland, and Romania.

linga *or* **lingam** In HINDUISM, the phallus, symbol of the god SHIVA and of generative power. Fashioned from wood, gems, metal, or stone, lingas are the main objects of worship in temples to Shiva and family shrines throughout India. Linga worship dates from at least the 1st–2nd century AD. The YONI, symbol of the female sex organ, often forms the base of the erect linga, a reminder that the male and female principles together represent the totality of existence. The linga is worshiped with offerings of flowers, water, fruit, leaves, and rice; the purity of the materials and the cleanliness of the worshiper are particularly stressed.

Sandstone *linga*, c. 900; in the British Museum.

REPRODUCED BY COURTESY OF THE TRUSTEES OF THE BRITISH MUSEUM

Lingayat \'liŋ-gə-yət\ Member of a Hindu sect that worships SHIVA as the only deity. It has a wide following in southern India. Its followers take their name ("linga-wearers") from the small LINGAS that both men and women wear on a cord around the neck. The Lingayats' belief in a single deity and their concept of BHAKTI (devotion) as an intuitive and loving knowledge of God show the influence of RAMANUJA. They reject BRAHMA and the authority of the VEDAS; their opposition to child marriage and the ill-treatment of widows anticipated the social reform movements of the 19th century.

Lingayen Gulf \ˌliŋ-gä-'yen\ Inlet, South China Sea, northwestern coast of LUZON, Philippines. It is 26 mi (42 km) wide at its entrance and 36 mi (56 km) long. It has several islands; on Pangasinan are Dagupan, the principal commercial center, and Lingayen, the provincial capital. It was the scene of Japanese and U.S. landing operations during World War II.

lingcod Commercially popular fish species *(Ophiodon elongatus)* that is strictly marine, found along the Pacific coast of North America. It is a voracious predator with a large mouth and caninelike teeth. Lingcods are popular game and commercial fish that may reach a length of 5 ft (1.5 m). They have well-developed fins and tails. The meat, though greenish, is considered highly edible.

lingonberry Fruit of a small creeping plant *(Vaccinium vitis-idaea)* of the HEATH FAMILY, related to the BLUEBERRY and CRANBERRY. Also known as cowberry, foxberry, and mountain, or rock, cranberry, the lingonberry is a wild plant used for jelly and juice by northern Europeans and by Scandinavians in the U.S. The plants grow densely in the forest understory, and, like cranberries, can be harvested by raking.

lingua franca \'liŋ-gwə-'fraŋ-kə\ Language used for communication between two or more groups that have different native languages. It may be a standard language—for example, English and French are often used for international diplomacy, and SWAHILI is used by speakers of the many different local languages of eastern Africa. A lingua franca may also be a PIDGIN, like Melanesian Pidgin, widely used in the southern Pacific. The term lingua franca (Latin: "Frankish language") was first applied to a pidgin based on French and Italian developed in the Mediterranean. See also CREOLE.

linguistics Study of the nature and structure of language. Linguists use a synchronic (describing a language as it exists at a given time) or a diachronic (tracing a language's development through its history) approach to language study. Greek philosophers in the 5th century BC who debated the origins of human language were the first in the West to be concerned with linguistic theory. The first complete Greek GRAMMAR, written by Dionysus Thrax in the 1st century BC, was a model for Roman grammarians, whose work led to the medieval and Renaissance vernacular grammars. With the rise of historical LINGUISTICS in the 19th century, linguistics became a science. In the late 19th and early 20th century, FERDINAND DE SAUSSURE established the structuralist school of linguistics, which analyzed actual speech to learn about the underlying structure of language. In the 1950s, NOAM CHOMSKY challenged the structuralist approach, arguing that linguistics should study native speakers' unconscious knowledge of their own language (competence), not their actual production of language (performance), and developed GENERATIVE GRAMMAR.

linguistics, historical Branch of linguistics concerned with examining changes in PHONOLOGY, GRAMMAR, and SEMANTICS during a language's evolution, reconstructing earlier stages, and uncovering evidence of the influence of other languages. Its roots are in classical and medieval writings on etymology and in the comparative study of Greek and Latin during the Renaissance. Only in the 19th century did more scientific language-analysis methods lead to the development of historical linguistics as a scholarly discipline. The Neogrammarians, a group of German linguists who formulated sound correspondences in the INDO-EUROPEAN LANGUAGES, were especially influential. In the 20th century the methods of historical linguistics were extended to other language groups.

linkage In mechanical engineering, a system of solid, usually metallic, links (bars) connected to two or more other links by pin joints (hinges), sliding joints, or ball-and-socket joints to form a closed chain or a series of closed chains. When one link is fixed, the possible movements of the other links relative to the fixed link and to one another depend on the number of links and the number and types of joints. With four pin-connected links, for example, the links all move in parallel planes, and regardless of which link is fixed, the others move in a fixed way relative to the fixed link. With various relative lengths of the links, this four-bar linkage becomes a useful mechanism for converting uniform rotary to non-uniform rotary motion or continuous rotary to oscillatory motion. It is the most commonly used linkage mechanism in machine construction.

linkage group All the GENES on a single CHROMOSOME. They are inherited as a group; during cell division they act and move as a unit rather than independently. Variations in linkage groups can occur if a chromosome breaks, and the sections join with the partner chromosome if it has broken in the same places. This exchange of genes between chromosomes, called crossing-over, usually occurs during MEIOSIS. Sex linkage is the tendency of a characteristic to be linked to one sex; sex-linked traits in humans include red-green color blindness and hemophilia.

Linkletter, Art(hur Gordon) (born 1912) Canadian-U.S. broadcasting host. Born in Moose Jaw, Saskatchewan, he became host of the variety show *House Party* (1943–67), which involved the audience in spontaneous contests and activities; he created the show's popular segment "Kids Say the Darndest Things." He hosted another audience-participation show, *People Are Funny*, on radio (1943–59) and television (1954–61). He wrote over 20 books, including the best-selling *Kids Say the Darndest Things* (1957), *I Wish I'd Said That* (1968), and *Old Age Is Not for Sissies* (1988).

Linnaeus \lə-ˈnē-əs\, **Carolus** *Swedish* **Carl von Linné** (1707–1778) Swedish botanist and explorer. He studied botany at Uppsala University and explored Swedish Lapland before going to Holland to study medicine (1735). There he became the first to develop principles for defining genera and species of organisms and to create a uniform system for naming them, BINOMIAL NOMENCLATURE. Linnaeus's system was based mainly on flower parts, which tend to remain unchanged during evolution. Though artificial, such a system was valuable in that it enabled students to place a plant rapidly in a named category. Linnaeus not only systematized the plant and animal kingdoms, but also classified the mineral kingdom and wrote a study of the diseases known in his day. His manuscripts, herbarium, and collections are preserved by London's Linnaean Society. His works include *Systema Naturae* (1735), *Fundamenta Botanica* (1736), and *Species Plantarum* (1753).

Linnaeus, detail of a portrait by A. Roslin, 1775; in the Svenska Porträttarkivet, Stockholm.
BY COURTESY OF THE SVENSKA PORTRATTARKIVET, STOCKHOLM

linoleum Smooth-surfaced floor covering made from a mixture of oxidized linseed oil, resins, and other substances such as binder, fillers, and pigments, applied to a felt or canvas backing. Linoleum is flexible, warm, and unaffected by ordinary floor temperatures, and it does not readily burn. It is specially hardened to resist indentation and is not susceptible to damage from fats, oils, greases, or organic solvents.

Linotype \ˈlī-nə-ˌtīp\ Trademark name for a TYPESETTING machine by which characters are cast in type metal as a complete line, rather than as individual characters (as on the Monotype typesetting machine). It was patented in 1884 by OTTMAR MERGENTHALER. It has now been almost entirely supplanted by photocomposition. In Linotype, a keyboard is manipulated to compose each line of text. The slugs produced by the machine are rectangular solids of type metal (an alloy of lead, antimony, and tin) with raised characters that are a mirror image of the desired printed line. After hot-metal CASTING, the slug of type, air-cooled briefly, is placed in a "stick" for insertion in the proper position into the press form being made up. See also LETTERPRESS PRINTING, PRINTING.

Linux \ˈli-nəks\ Nonproprietary OPERATING SYSTEM for digital computers. Developed by Linus Torvalds of Finland (for whom it is named) and modified by hundreds of developers around the world, the Linux core program was first released in 1994. A true multiuser, multitasking system, Linux contains features consistent with UNIX-type systems (e.g., virtual memory, shared libraries, memory management, and TCP/IP networking). It has a reputation as a reliable, fast-performing system with good security features. It can be installed on personal computers as well as more powerful machines. Its source code is freely available to anyone; however, several companies sell prepackaged Linux products. Though often mentioned as an alternative to WINDOWS, Linux has instead been gaining popularity as an operating system for business applications and Web servers.

Linz \ˈlints\ *ancient* **Lentia** City (pop., 1991: 203,000), northern central Austria. Located on the DANUBE RIVER west of VIENNA, and on the direct rail route between the Baltic and Adriatic seas, it originated as a Roman fortress. An important medieval trading center, it was noted for its fairs in the 15th century. It was badly damaged in World War II. It is now a cultural center and the seat of Johannes Kepler Univ.

Linz, Juan J. (born 1926) Spanish-U.S. political scientist. Born in Germany to Spanish parents, he obtained his law degree from the University of Madrid and his PhD from Columbia University. He has taught in Spain and elsewhere in Europe; in recent years he has taught at Yale University. His analysis of authoritarianism and democratic transitions has increased attention to the potential fragility of post-totalitarian and post-authoritarian democratic systems.

lion Large, powerfully built CAT *(Panthera leo),* the proverbial "king of beasts." It is now found mainly in parts of sub-Saharan Africa, though about two hundred constitute an Asiatic race living under strict protection in India. Lions inhabit grassy plains and open savanna. The male is 6–7 ft (1.8–2.1 m) long, excluding the 3-ft (1-m) tail, stands about 4 ft (1.2 m) high at the shoulder, and weighs 370–500 lbs (170–230 kg). The female, or lioness, is considerably smaller. The male's coat is usually buff yellow or orange-brown; lionesses are more consistently tawny or sandy. The male's outstanding characteristic is his mane. Lions are unique among cats in that they live in a group, or pride, often consisting of about 15 individuals. Lionesses are the chief hunters. They prey on animals of all sizes, including hippopotamuses, but prefer wildebeests, antelopes, and zebras. After eating, a lion may rest for a week.

Male lion (*Panthera leo*).
R.I.M. CAMPBELL/BRUCE COLEMAN LTD.

Lion, Gulf of Gulf of the Mediterranean Sea, extending along the coast of southern France from the Spanish border to Toulon. Major ports along the gulf are MARSEILLE and Sète.

lionfish Any of several species of showy Indo-Pacific fish of the SCORPIONFISH family (Scorpaenidae), noted for their venomous fin spines, which can inflict painful, though rarely fatal, puncture wounds. Lionfish have enlarged pectoral fins and elongated dorsal fin spines, and each species bears a particular pattern of bold stripes. When disturbed, the fish spread and display their fins, and, if further pressed, present and attack with the dorsal spines. *Pterois volitans,* sometimes kept by fish fanciers, is striped with red, brown, and white and grows to about 12 in. (30 cm) long. Several smaller Indo-Pacific species of the genus *Dendrochirus* are also known as lionfish.

Lions Clubs, International Association of U.S. civilian service club. The nation's largest service-club organization, it was founded in 1917 to foster a spirit of "generous consideration" among peoples of the world and promote good government, good citizenship, and an active interest in civic welfare. Its activities include general community welfare projects, aid to the blind, and promotion of knowledge and support of the U.N. Lions Clubs operate in over 150 countries.

Lipari Islands \ˈli-pə-rē\ *Italian* **Isole Eolie** \ˈē-zō-ˌlā-ā-ˈō-lē-ˌä\ Volcanic island group, Tyrrhenian Sea. Located off the northern coast of SICILY, there are seven major islands and several islets, with a total land area of 34 sq mi (88 sq km). The main islands are Alicudi, Stromboli, Vulcano, Lipari (the largest, at 13 sq mi, or 34 sq km), Salina, Filicudi, and Panarea. Vulcano and Stromboli are active volcanoes. The Greeks believed the islands to be the home of the god Aeolus, who kept the winds confined in one of their caves. They have been inhabited since NEOLITHIC times and were held successively by the Greeks, Carthaginians, Romans, Saracens, Normans, and Aragonese.

Lipchitz \ˈlip-shits\, **(Chaim) Jacques** (1891–1973) Lithuanian-French-U.S. sculptor. Trained as an engineer in Vilnius, he turned to sculpture after moving to Paris in 1909. His early style was Cubist in style. Around 1925 he began producing a series of works known as "transparents," open-spaced, curvilinear bronzes, such as *Harpist* (1928), which would greatly influence the course of sculpture in the following quarter-century. After settling near New York City in 1941, he produced such massive works as *The Prayer* (1943) and *Bellerophon Taming Pegasus* (1966).

lipid \ˈlip-əd\ Any of a diverse class of organic compounds, found in all living things, that are greasy and insoluble in water. Of the three large classes of substances in foods and living cells, lipids contain more than twice as much energy (CALORIES) per unit of weight as the other two, PROTEINS and CARBOHYDRATES. They include the FATS and edible OILS (e.g., butter, olive oil, corn oil), which are primarily TRIGLYCERIDES; phospholipids (e.g., LECITHIN, CHOLINE); WAXES of animal or plant origin; and sphingolipids, complex substances that are components of cell membranes. Since insolubility is the defining characteristic, CHOLESTEROL and related STEROIDS, carotenoids (see CAROTENE), PROSTAGLANDINS, and various other compounds are also classifiable as lipids.

lipid storage disease Any of a group of relatively rare hereditary disorders of FAT METABOLISM in which ENZYME defects cause distinctive types of LIPIDS to accumulate. They include TAY-SACHS DISEASE, Gaucher's disease, Niemann-Pick disease, and Fabry's disease. Several are untreatable and cause death before age 5; others occur in adulthood.

Lipizzaner *or* **Lippizaner** \ˌli-pət-ˈsä-nər\ Breed of light HORSE named for the Austrian imperial stud at Lipizza, near Trieste, formerly part of Austria-Hungary. The founding of the breed, which has six strains, dates to 1580. Lipizzaners have a long back and a short, thick neck, average 15–16 hands (about 60–64 in., or 152–164 cm) in height and 1,000–1,300 lbs (450–585 kg) in weight, and are usually gray. Some are found in countries that were originally part of Austria-Hungary; a few have been exported to the U.S. The best known are those trained at Vienna's Spanish Riding School.

lipoprotein \ˌlī-pə-ˈprō-ˌtēn\ Any of a class of organic compounds that contain both LIPID (FAT) and PROTEIN. They may be soluble (those in egg yolk and blood plasma) or insoluble (those in cell membranes) in water and water solutions. Lipoproteins in blood plasma are the mode of transport for CHOLESTEROL, insoluble by itself. Low-density lipoproteins (LDLs) carry cholesterol from the liver, where it is made, to the cells, where it is used; high-density lipoproteins (HDLs) may carry excess cholesterol back to the liver for breakdown and excretion. LDL-bound cholesterol is primarily responsible for deposits in arteries (see ARTERIOSCLEROSIS) that can lead to CORONARY HEART DISEASE, ANGINA PECTORIS, MYOCARDIAL INFARCTION, or STROKE. HDL does not form such deposits and may actually retard or reduce their buildup.

Lippe \ˈli-pə\ Former German state. It lay between the TEUTOBURG FOREST and the WESER RIVER, and its capital was Detmold. A lordship in medieval times, it became a county in the 16th century. Dynastic divisions in the early 17th century resulted in two counties, Lippe and SCHAUMBURG-LIPPE. In 1720 it was made a principality. A member of the GERMAN CONFEDERATION in 1815, it became part of the German empire in 1871 and of the WEIMAR REPUBLIC in 1918. In 1947 it was incorporated into North Rhine-Westphalia.

Lippe River River, western Germany. Rising on the western edge of the TEUTOBURG FOREST, it follows a westerly course of 155 mi (250 km) and enters the RHINE RIVER near Wesel. Once used for the transport of coal, timber, and agricultural produce, it now supplies water to the RUHR region canal system.

Lippi, Filippino (c. 1457–1504) Italian painter. After the death of his father, FRA FILIPPO LIPPI, when Filippino was 12, he entered the workshop of SANDRO BOTTICELLI and absorbed many aspects of his style. One of his most important assignments was the completion of the frescoes in the Brancacci Chapel in Florence's Santa Maria del Carmine (c. 1485–87), left unfinished when MASACCIO died. His most popular painting is the *Vision of St. Bernard* altarpiece (c. 1480). His highly decorative frescoes in the Carafa Chapel in Santa Maria sopra Minerva, Rome (1488–93), and those in the Strozzi Chapel in Santa Maria Novella, Florence (completed 1502), anticipated Tuscan Mannerism of the 16th century.

"The Madonna and Child with Two Angels," by Fra Filippo Lippi, c. 1465; in the Uffizi, Florence.
ALINARI—ART RESOURCE/EB INC.

Lippi, Fra Filippo (c. 1406–1469) Italian painter. In 1421 he became a Carmelite monk at Santa Maria del Carmine in Florence, where MASACCIO was soon decorating the Brancacci Chapel with frescoes. Lippi himself painted frescoes in the church, much influenced by Masaccio's, then disappeared from the monastery in 1432. In 1434 he was in Padua, but in 1437 he returned to Florence under the protection of the MEDICI FAMILY and was commissioned to execute several works for convents and churches. His *Madonna and Child* (1437) and *Annunciation* (c. 1442) show a maturing style characterized by warm coloring and attention to decorative effects. In 1456, while painting in a convent in Prato, he fled with one of the nuns, Lucrezia Buti. The couple were later released from their vows and permitted to marry, and from that union was born the illustrious FILIPPINO LIPPI. The former friar returned often to Prato, and his frescoes in the cathedral there stand among his finest achievements.

Lippmann, Walter (1889–1974) U.S. newspaper commentator and author. Born in New York City and educated at Harvard, he became an editor at the fledgling *NEW REPUBLIC* (1914–17). His thinking influenced WOODROW WILSON, and he took part in the negotiations that culminated in the Treaty of Versailles. After writing for and editing the reformist *World*, he moved to the *New York Herald-Tribune*, where he began his "Today and Tomorrow" column in 1931; eventually widely syndicated, it would win two Pulitzer Prizes (1958, 1962), and Lippmann would become one of the most respected political columnists in the world. His books include *A Preface to Politics* (1913); *Public Opinion* (1922), perhaps his most influential work; *The Phantom Public* (1925); and *The Good Society* (1937).

Lipset, Seymour Martin (born 1922) U.S. sociologist and political scientist. Born in New York City, he graduated from CCNY and obtained his PhD from Columbia Univ., where he later taught (1950–56). While teaching at UC–Berkeley (1956–66), he also served as director of its Institute of International Studies (1962–66). Since then he has taught at Harvard Univ., Stanford Univ., and George Mason University. His many books about class structure, elite behavior, and political parties have significantly shaped the study of comparative politics.

Lipton, Thomas J(ohnstone) *later* **Sir Thomas** (1850–1931) British merchant who built the Lipton tea empire. Born in Scotland of Irish parents, he opened a small grocery in Glasgow, which grew into a chain of retail shops throughout Britain. To supply his shops cheaply, Lipton bought tea, coffee, and cocoa plantations in Ceylon as well as English fruit farms, jam factories, and bakeries. In 1898 his business was organized into Lipton, Ltd.; he was knighted the same year and made a baronet in 1902. A keen yachtsman, he raced his "Shamrock" yachts five times unsuccessfully for the AMERICA'S CUP.

liquation \lī-ˈkwā-shən\ Technique for separating constituents of an ore, metal, or alloy by partial melting. When the material is heated to a temperature where one of the constituents melts and the other remains solid, the liquid constituent can be drained off. It was formerly used for extracting antimony minerals from ore, separating silver from copper with the use of lead as a solvent, and refining tin.

liqueur \li-ˈkər\ DISTILLED LIQUOR produced by combining a base spirit, usually BRANDY, with fruits or herbs and sweetened with sugar syrup. Alcohol content is 24–60% by volume. Liqueurs were probably first produced commercially by medieval monks and alchemists. Sweet in flavor and containing ingredients that promote digestion, they are popular as after-dinner drinks and are also used in mixed drinks and dessert dishes. Varieties include apricot liquor, crème de menthe (mint-flavored), curaçao (flavored with green orange peel, from Curaçao), and proprietary brands such as Benedictine (a plant liquor), Grand Marnier (a Curaçao from France's Cognac region), Irish Mist (flavored with Irish whiskey and honey), and Kahlúa (coffee-flavored).

liquid One of the three principal states of matter, intermediate between a gas and a solid. A liquid has neither the orderliness of a solid nor the randomness of a gas. Liquids have the ability to flow under the action of very small shear STRESSES. Liquids in contact with their own vapor or air have a SURFACE TENSION that causes the interface to assume the configuration of minimum area (i.e., spherical). Surfaces between liquids and solids have interfacial tensions that determine whether the liquid will wet the other material. With the exception of liquid metals, molten salts, and solutions of salts, the electrical conductivities of liquids are small.

liquid crystal Substance that flows like a liquid but maintains some of the ordered structure characteristic of a CRYSTAL. Some organic substances do not melt directly when heated but instead turn from a crystalline solid to a liquid crystalline state. When heated further, a true liquid is formed. Liquid crystals have unique properties. The structures are easily

L
M
N

affected by changes in mechanical STRESS, ELECTROMAGNETIC FIELDS, temperature, and chemical environment. See also LIQUID CRYSTAL DISPLAY.

liquid crystal display (LCD) Optoelectronic device used in displays for watches, calculators, notebook computers, and other electronic devices. Current passed through specific portions of the LIQUID CRYSTAL solution causes the crystals to align, blocking the passage of light. Doing so in a controlled and organized manner produces visual images on the display screen. The advantage of LCDs is that they are much lighter and consume less power than other display technologies (e.g., CATHODE-RAY TUBES). These characteristics make them an ideal choice for flat-panel displays, as in portable laptop and notebook computers.

liquidity preference In economics, the premium that holders of wealth demand for exchanging ready money or bank deposits for safe, nonliquid assets such as government BONDS. As first used by JOHN MAYNARD KEYNES, liquidity preference referred to the demand for money as an asset. He hypothesized that the amount of money held for this purpose would vary inversely with the rate of INTEREST. Post-Keynesian analysis of liquidity preference has identified other factors that influence the demand for money, including income levels and the yields of various forms of wealth.

liquor See DISTILLED LIQUOR

Liri River \'lē-rē\ River, central Italy. It rises near Cappadocia and flows south and southeast through the APENNINES. Joined by other rivers, it turns southwest to empty into the Tyrrhenian Sea near Minturno. It is 98 mi (158 km) long. During World War II, the Liri valley was invaded by Allies as part of their advance on Rome.

Lisbon *Portuguese* **Lisboa** City (pop., 1991: 677,790), capital of Portugal. The country's chief seaport and largest city, it lies on the TAGUS RIVER near the river's entrance into the Atlantic Ocean. It was under Rome from 205 BC; JULIUS CAESAR made it a municipium called Felicitas Julia. Ruled by a series of barbarian tribes from the 5th century, it was taken by Moors in the 8th century. The Crusaders under AFONSO I gained control of it in 1147, and it became the national capital in 1256. It flourished as a leading European trading city in the 14th–16th century. One of the greatest earthquakes ever recorded struck Lisbon in 1755, killing 30,000. Urban renewal following the earthquake was unrivaled in scope until Lisbon was named host of the World's Fair (Expo '98). It is a major commercial, administrative, educational, and manufacturing center. It was the birthplace of LUIS CAMÕES.

Lisburn Town (pop., 1991: 42,000), seat of Lisburn district (pop., 1995 est.: 106,000), Northern Ireland. Located on the River Lagan southwest of BELFAST, it was a small village known as Lisnagarvey before English, Scots, and Welsh settled there in the 1620s as part of the Plantation of Ulster scheme. It later attracted French linen workers who introduced Dutch looms and reorganized the Ulster linen industry; the town is still an important linen manufacturing center. The district was created in 1973.

LISP \'lisp\ Powerful computer PROGRAMMING LANGUAGE designed for manipulating lists of data or symbols rather than processing numerical data, used extensively in ARTIFICIAL-INTELLIGENCE applications. It was developed in the late 1950s and early 1960s by a group headed by JOHN MCCARTHY at MIT. Its name derives from "list processor." Radically different from such other programming languages as ALGOL, C, C++, FORTRAN, and PASCAL, it requires large memory space and is slow in executing programs.

Lissitzky, El *or* **El Lissitsky** *orig.* **Lazar Markovich Lisitskii** (1890–1941) Russian painter, typographer, and designer. As a teacher at MARC CHAGALL's revolutionary art school in Vitebsk, he met KAZIMIR MALEVICH, whose influence is seen in a series of abstract paintings that were Lissitzky's major contribution to CONSTRUCTIVISM. In 1922, after the Soviet government turned against modern art, he went to Germany. There THEO VAN DOESBURG and LASZLO MOHOLY-NAGY transmitted his ideas to the West through their teaching at the BAUHAUS. In 1925 he returned to Russia and devoted himself to devising new techniques of printing, photomontage, and architecture.

List, (Georg) Friedrich (1789–1846) German–U.S. economist. He first gained prominence as the founder of an association of German industrialists that favored abolishing tariff barriers between the German states. Exiled in 1825 for his liberal views, he went to the U.S. In his *Outlines of American Political Economy* (1827) he maintained that a national economy in an early stage of industrialization required tariff protection to stimulate development. After becoming a U.S. citizen, he returned to Germany as U.S. consul at Baden (1831–34) and Leipzig (1834–37). His best-known work was *The National System of Political Economy* (1841). Financial and other difficulties eventually drove him to suicide.

Lister, Joseph *later* **Baron Lister (of Lyme Regis)** (1827–1912) British surgeon and medical scientist. He received a medical degree from Oxford in 1852 and became an assistant to James Syme, the greatest surgical teacher of the day. In 1861 he was appointed surgeon to the Glasgow Royal Infirmary, where he observed that 45–50% of amputation patients died from sepsis (infection). Initially he theorized that airborne dust might cause sepsis, but in 1865 he learned of LOUIS PASTEUR's theory that microorganisms caused infection. Using PHENOL as an antiseptic, Lister reduced mortality in his ward to 15% within four years. Most surgeons were unconvinced until a widely publicized operation under antiseptic conditions was successful. By the time of his retirement in 1893, he had seen his principle accepted almost universally. He is regarded as the founder of antiseptic medicine.

Joseph Lister, 1857.
BY COURTESY OF THE WELLCOME TRUSTEES, LONDON

Lister, Samuel Cunliffe *later* **Baron Masham (of Swinton)** (1815–1906) British inventor. His wool-combing machine (1845) helped lower the price of clothing and contributed greatly to the development of Australian sheep farming. Another invention (c. 1865) permitted the use of silk waste to make goods that could compete with those manufactured from the perfect cocoon, goods that could be sold at many times the cost of production. His velvet loom for making pile fabrics (c. 1878) was another important innovation.

Liszt \'list\, **Franz** *orig.* **Franciscus** (1811–1886) Hungarian-French composer and pianist. His devout father named him for St. Francis, and Liszt inherited his father's musical and spiritual sides. KARL CZERNY recognized Liszt's talent at age 8, and Liszt studied with Czerny and A. SALIERI in Vienna, making his debut there in 1822. After an 1823 Paris success, he toured Europe, but his father's early death (1828) and a disastrous love affair led to a desire to give up music for the priesthood. Hearing N. PAGANINI in 1832, he was inspired to develop his technique to the utmost and compose his first mature pieces, including the *Transcendental Études* (1837) and *Paganini Études* (1839). An affair with Countess Marie d'Agoult resulted in the birth of his daughter, Cosima (1837–1930), who would marry his friend RICHARD WAGNER. Liszt's touring led to their breakup, for the 1840s were the height of "Lisztomania," the unprecedented frenzy of his audiences sparked by his blazing technique and dashing style. Seeing himself as a messenger of the future, he ceased concertizing in the late 1840s to devote himself to composition and furthering the work of progressive composers. In the 1850s he wrote many of his most ambitious works, including *A Faust Symphony* (1854) and the piano sonata in B minor (1853). In 1865, abandoning hope that Princess Caroline de Sayn-Wittgenstein would marry him, he took minor church orders. His later output is remarkable in anticipating many 20th-century developments.

Liszt, lithograph by Joseph Kriehuber, 1846.
BY COURTESY OF THE MUSEO TEATRALE ALLA SCALA, MILAN

Litani River \li-'tä-nē\ River, southern Lebanon. Rising west of BAALBEK, it flows southwest between the Lebanon and ANTI-LEBANON MOUNTAINS to enter the Mediterranean Sea south of Sidon. Its lower course is known as Qasimiyah. Although only 90 mi (145 km) long, the river irrigates one of Lebanon's most extensive farming regions, the BEKAA VALLEY.

litchi *or* **lichee** *or* **lychee** \'lē-chē, 'lī-chē\ Fruit of the tree *Litchi chinensis* (family Sapindaceae), believed to be native to southern China and adjacent regions, but now also cultivated elsewhere. It has been a favorite fruit of the Cantonese Chinese since ancient times and is a popular dessert in U.S. Chinese restaurants. The fresh pulp tastes musky; when dried, it is acidic and very sweet. The handsome tree develops a compact crown of foliage, with compound leaves that are bright green year-round. Clusters of small, inconspicuous flowers form small, oval red fruits.

literacy Ability to read and write. The term may also refer to familiarity with literature and to a basic level of education obtained through the written word. In ancient civilizations such as those of the Sumerians and Babylonians, literacy was the province of an elite group of scholars and priests. Though more prevalent in classical Greece and Rome, it was often limited to members of the upper classes. The spread of literacy in Europe in the Middle Ages was evidenced by the use of writing for functions once conducted orally, such as the indenture of servants and the notation of evidence at trials. The rise of literacy in Europe was closely tied to great social transformations, notably the Protestant Reformation, which brought individual study of the Bible, and the development of modern science. The spread of literacy during the Reformation and the Renaissance was greatly facilitated by the development of PRINTING from movable type and by the adoption of vernacular languages in place of Latin. Compulsory schooling, established in Britain, Europe, and the U.S. in the 19th century, has led to high rates of literacy in the modern industrialized world.

literary criticism Discipline concerned with philosophical, descriptive, and evaluative inquiries about literature, including what literature is, what it does, and what it is worth. The Western critical tradition began with PLATO's *Republic* (4th century BC). A generation later, ARISTOTLE, in his *Poetics,* developed a set of principles of composition that had a lasting influence. European criticism since the Renaissance has primarily focused on the moral worth of literature and the nature of its relationship to reality. At the end of the 16th century, SIR PHILIP SIDNEY argued that it is the special property of literature to offer an imagined world that is in some respects superior to the real one. A century later, JOHN DRYDEN proposed the less idealistic view that literature must primarily offer an accurate representation of the world for "the delight and instruction of mankind," an assumption that underlies the great critical works of ALEXANDER POPE and SAMUEL JOHNSON. A departure from these ideas appeared in the criticism of the Romantic period, epitomized by WILLIAM WORDSWORTH's assertion that the object of poetry is "truth . . . carried alive into the heart by passion." The later 19th century saw two divergent developments: an aesthetic theory of "art for art's sake," and the view (expressed by MATTHEW ARNOLD) that literature must assume the moral and philosophical functions previously filled by religion. The volume of literary criticism increased greatly in the 20th century, and its later years saw a radical reappraisal of traditional critical modes and the development of a multiplicity of critical factions (see STRUCTURALISM, POST-STRUCTURALISM, DECONSTRUCTION).

literati Scholars in China and Japan whose poetry, calligraphy, and paintings were supposed primarily to reveal their cultivation and express their personal feelings rather than demonstrate professional skill. The concept of literati painters was first formulated in China in the Northern SONG DYNASTY but was enduringly codified in the MING DYNASTY by DONG QICHANG. In the 18th–19th century, literati painting became popular with the Japanese, who exaggerated elements of Chinese composition and brushwork. See also IKE NO TAIGA.

lithification Complex process whereby loose grains of sediment are converted into ROCK. Lithification may occur at the time a sediment is deposited or later. CEMENTATION is one of the main processes involved, particularly for sandstones and conglomerates. In addition, reactions take place within a sediment between various minerals and between minerals and the fluids trapped in the pores; these reactions may form new minerals or add to others already present in the sediment.

lithium Chemical ELEMENT, lightest alkali METAL, chemical symbol Li, atomic number 3. It is soft, white, lustrous, and very reactive, forming compounds in which it has VALENCE 1. The metal is used in certain ALLOYS, as a coolant in nuclear reactors, and (because of its reactivity) as a reagent, scavenger, and rocket fuel. Lithium HYDRIDE is used as a source of hydrogen; lithium hydroxide is used as an additive in storage BATTERIES and to absorb carbon dioxide. Halides (see HALOGEN) of lithium are used as moisture absorbents, and lithium SOAPS are used as thickeners in lubricating greases. Lithium carbonate is an important drug for treating DEPRESSION and BIPOLAR DISORDER.

litho-offset See OFFSET PRINTING

lithography \li-'thä-grə-fē\ PRINTING process that makes use of the immiscibility of grease and water. Aloys Senefelder of Prague (1771–1834) exploited the properties of a stone with a calcium carbonate base and a fine, porous surface, and perfected his printing process in 1798. In Senefelder's process, the stone, with a design drawn on it with crayon or greasy ink, was wetted with water; after various etching and protecting steps, it was brushed with oily ink; it retained the ink only on the design. This inked surface was then printed—either directly on paper, by a special press (as in most fine-art PRINTMAKING), or onto a rubber cylinder and thence onto paper (as in commercial printing). The method of preparing stones for hand printing, still the lithographic method preferred by artists, has hardly changed. Commercial lithographic printing on a modern rotary OFFSET PRINTING press can produce high-quality, finely detailed impressions at high speed, reproducing any material that can be photographed in the platemaking process. It now accounts for more than 40% of all printing, packaging, and publishing, more than twice the percentage produced by any other single printing process.

lithosphere Rigid, rocky outer layer of the earth, consisting of the CRUST and the solid outermost layer of the upper MANTLE. It extends to a depth of about 60 mi (100 km). It is broken into about a dozen separate rigid blocks, or plates (see PLATE TECTONICS). Slow convection currents deep within the mantle, generated by radioactive heating of the interior, are believed to cause the lateral movements of the plates (and the continents that rest on top of them) at a rate of several inches per year.

Lithuania *officially* **Republic of Lithuania** Nation, northeastern Europe. Area: 25,213 sq mi (65,301 sq km). Population (1997 est.): 3,710,000. Capital: VILNIUS. Ethnic Lithuanians make up about four-fifths

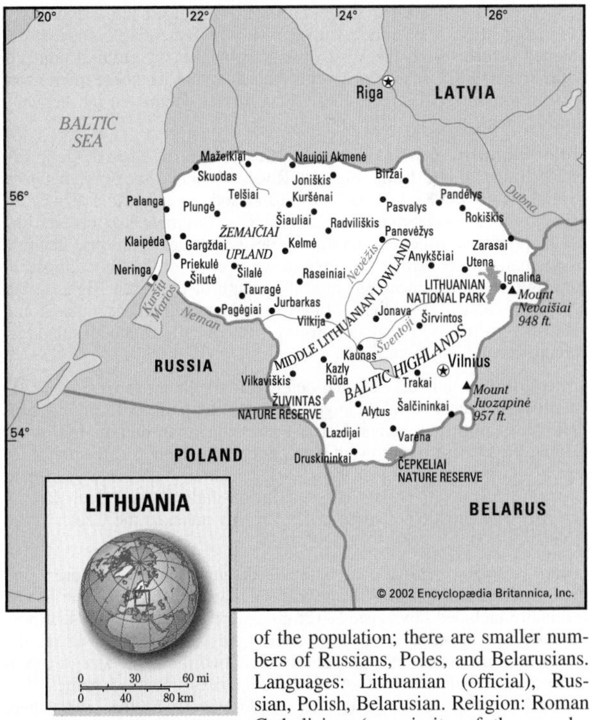

of the population; there are smaller numbers of Russians, Poles, and Belarusians. Languages: Lithuanian (official), Russian, Polish, Belarusian. Religion: Roman Catholicism (a majority of the population). Currency: litas. The country consists of low-lying plains alternating with hilly uplands, watered by rivers that meander westward to the Baltic Sea. Manufacturing, including metalworking, woodworking, and textile production, is the most important sector of the economy, especially in the east and south. Agriculture focuses on livestock breeding, especially dairy farming and pigs, and the cultivation of cereals, flax, sugar beets, potatoes, and fodder crops. It is a republic with one legislative house; its head of state is the president, and the head of government is the prime minister. Lithuanian tribes united in the mid-13th cent to oppose the TEUTONIC knights. Gediminas, one of the grand dukes, expanded Lithuania into an empire that dominated much of eastern Europe in the 14th–16th century. In 1386 the Lithuanian grand duke became the king of Poland, and the two countries remained closely associated for the next 400 years. It was acquired by Russia in the Third Partition of POLAND in 1795 and joined in the Polish revolt in 1863. Occupied by Germany during World War I, it declared its independence in 1918. In 1940 the Soviet Red Army gained control of Lithuania, which was soon incorporated into the Soviet Union as the Lithuanian S.S.R. Germany occupied Lithuania again in 1941–44, but the Red Army regained control in 1944. With the breakup of the U.S.S.R., Lithuania declared its independence in 1990 and gained full independence in 1991. During the 1990s it sought economic stability and hoped to join the EUROPEAN COMMUNITY. It signed a border-treaty with Russia in 1997.

Lithuanian language East BALTIC LANGUAGE spoken by over 4 million people in the Republic of Lithuania and in diaspora communities, with perhaps 70,000 speakers in North America. Lithuanian is sparsely attested until 1547, when the first book in the language was printed. Efforts to develop a standard language in the late 19th century were dominated by speakers of the West High dialect spoken in German-ruled East Prussia. Among them was Jonas Jablonskis, whose orthography (based on the LATIN ALPHABET with numerous diacritics) and grammar (1901) won official acceptance when Lithuania became independent. Lithuanian is renowned for its archaism among living INDO-EUROPEAN LANGUAGES.

litmus \'lit-məs\ Mixture of colored organic compounds obtained from several species of LICHEN. In water solution or as litmus paper, it is the oldest and most used indicator of whether a substance is an ACID or a BASE. It turns red or pink in acid solutions and blue or purple-blue in alkaline solutions.

Little Armenia *or* **Lesser Armenia** Kingdom, southeastern coast of ASIA MINOR. Established in CILICIA by the Armenian Rubenid dynasty in the 12th century, after initial struggles with the Byzantine empire, it developed contacts with the West. It was influenced by cultural contacts with Frankish Crusaders and with Venetian and Genoese merchants passing it along trade routes to the East. It was conquered by the Muslim Mamluks in 1375.

Little Bighorn, Battle of the *or* **Custer's Last Stand** (June 25, 1876) Battle at the Little Bighorn River, Montana Territory, between federal troops led by Col. GEORGE CUSTER and a band of Eastern SIOUX and Northern CHEYENNE Indians. The U.S. government had ordered the northern Plains tribes to return to designated reservations, sending troops under Gen. Alfred H. Terry to enforce the order. Terry hoped to surround an Indian encampment at the mouth of the Little Bighorn, but a party of some 200 soldiers led by Custer launched an early attack and was slaughtered. Government troops subsequently flooded the area, forcing the Indians to surrender.

Little Entente \län-'tänt\ Mutual defense arrangement formed in 1920–21 between Czechoslovakia, Yugoslavia, and Romania, with French support. It was directed against German and Hungarian domination in the Danube River basin and toward protection of its members' territorial integrity. It was successful in the 1920s, but after ADOLF HITLER's rise to power (1933) its members adopted increasingly independent foreign policies. The entente collapsed after Germany annexed the Czech Sudetenland (1938).

Little League International baseball organization for children and youth, started in 1939 in Williamsport, Pa., by Carl E. Stotz. The league originally included boys aged 8–12; girls were admitted in 1974. It now includes two upper divisions for youths aged 13–15 and 16–18. In the junior division the game is played on a field two-thirds the size of a professional baseball diamond. A season comprises about 15 games. The organization expanded rapidly after World War II; by the 1990s there were about 2.5 million players in some 30 countries. The Little League World Series is held in Williamsport each year in August.

little magazine Any of various small, usually avant-garde periodicals devoted to serious literary writings. The name signifies most of all a usually noncommercial manner of editing, managing, and financing. They were published from c. 1880 through much of the 20th century and flourished in the U.S. and England, though French and German writers also benefited from them. Foremost among them were two U.S. periodicals, POETRY and the more erratic and often more sensational *Little Review* (1914–29); the English *Egoist* (1914–19) and *Blast* (1914–15); and the French *transition* (1927–38).

Little Missouri River River, northwestern U.S. It rises in northeastern Wyoming and flows northeast across the southeastern corner of Montana and the northwestern corner of South Dakota. It continues north into North Dakota, turning east to empty into the MISSOURI RIVER after a course of 560 mi (900 km). The THEODORE ROOSEVELT NATIONAL PARK lies along its shores in North Dakota.

Little Richard *orig.* **Richard Wayne Penniman** (born 1932) U.S. RHYTHM-AND-BLUES singer and pianist. Born into a strict religious family in Macon, Ga., he sang and played piano in church, but was later ejected from his home by his father, reportedly for homosexual behavior. He performed in nightclubs, traveled with a medicine show, and recorded as a blues artist from the early 1950s. His first big hit came with "Tutti Frutti" (1956), an energetic performance that, with his penchant for the outrageous, set a standard for the emerging rock idiom. Similar hits followed, including "Long Tall Sally," "Lucille," and "Good Golly, Miss Molly." In 1957 he underwent a religious conversion, and was later ordained a minister. He soon returned to music, becoming a regular attraction in Las Vegas, and has continued to tour and appear in films with much success. He was an original inductee into the Rock and Roll Hall of Fame.

Little Rock City (pop., 2000: 183,133), capital of Arkansas, located on the ARKANSAS RIVER. In 1722 Bernard de la Harpe, a French explorer, named the site La Petite Roche for a rock formation on the riverbank. It became the capital of Arkansas in 1821. It was strongly anti-Union at the outbreak of the AMERICAN CIVIL WAR; Federal troops occupied the city in 1863. It grew as the commercial center of a farming region and as a hub of railway and river transportation. In 1957 federal troops were sent there to prevent state authorities from interfering with desegregation at Central High School. The state's largest city, it has many institutions of higher learning, including the University of Arkansas at Little Rock (1927).

Little St. Bernard Pass Mountain pass, Savoy ALPS. Situated southwest of the Italian border in southeastern France, it connects Bourg-St.-Maurice, France, with La Thuile, Italy. HANNIBAL probably led the Carthaginian army over the pass on his way toward Rome in 218 BC. It was the principal route across the Alps into Gallia Comata, a province of Gaul, until Montgenèvre Pass was opened in 77 BC. Beside the pass is a hospice founded in the 11th century by St. Bernard of Menthon.

little theater Any of the experimental drama centers that emerged from an early-20th-century movement in the U.S. Young dramatists, stage designers, and actors influenced by the vital European theater of the late 19th century, especially by the theories of MAX REINHARDT, established such community playhouses as the Little Theater, New York (1912), the Little Theater, Chicago (1912), and the Toy Theater, Boston (1912). A few became important commercial producers; the Washington Square Players (1915), for example, later became the Theater Guild (1918). Such playwrights as EUGENE O'NEILL, GEORGE S. KAUFMAN, and MAXWELL ANDERSON found their early opportunities in the little theaters.

Little Turtle (1752–1812) American Indian leader. Born near Fort Wayne, Ind., he became chief of the MIAMI tribe and led raids on settlements in the Northwest Territory in the early 1790s. Defeated by Gen. ANTHONY WAYNE at the Battle of FALLEN TIMBERS (1794), he was obliged to sign the Treaty of Greenville (1795), which ceded to the U.S. much of Ohio and parts of Illinois, Indiana, and Michigan. He then advocated peace and kept the Miami from joining the Shawnee confederacy of TECUMSEH.

Littleton, Thomas *later* **Sir Thomas** (1422–1481) British jurist. In a turbulent period he held several high offices, including judge of the Court of COMMON PLEAS (from 1466). His *Littleton on Tenures,* a complete view of English land law, was the earliest treatise on English law ever printed (1481 or 1482). The text formed part of legal education for more than three centuries and was the basis of SIR EDWARD COKE's *Institutes of the Lawes of England.*

liturgical drama Play acted in or near the church in the Middle Ages. The form probably dated from the 10th century, when the "Quem quaeritis" ("Whom do you seek") section of the Easter mass was performed as a small scene in the service. The plays gradually increased in length, with themes derived from biblical stories (particularly those of Easter and Christmas), and they flourished in the 12th–13th century. Their Latin dialogue was frequently chanted to simple melodies. They continued to be written into the 16th century, but the connection with the church eventually ended as the plays came under secular sponsorship and were acted in the vernacular. See also MIRACLE PLAY, MORALITY PLAY, MYSTERY PLAY.

Liturgical Movement 19th- and 20th-century effort to encourage the active participation of the laity in the liturgy of the Christian churches by creating simpler rites more attuned to early Christian traditions and more relevant to modern life. The movement began in the Roman Catholic church in the mid-19th century and spread to other Christian churches in Europe and the U.S. The Second VATICAN COUNCIL (1962–65) called for translation of Latin liturgies into the vernaculars of individual countries and the reform of all sacramental rites. The Lutheran Church revised the *Lutheran Book of Worship* in 1978, and the Episcopal Church adopted a revised *Book of* COMMON PRAYER in 1979.

Litvinov \lyit-'vē-nôf\, **Maksim (Maksimovich)** *orig.* **Meir Walach** (1876–1951) Soviet diplomat and commissar of foreign affairs (1930–39). He joined the RUSSIAN SOCIAL DEMOCRATIC WORKERS' PARTY (1898), was arrested for revolutionary activity (1901), and fled to Britain. In 1917–18 he represented the Soviet government in London, then returned to Russia, where he joined the Commissariat for Foreign Affairs and led Soviet delegations to disarmament conferences. As commissar for foreign affairs, he established diplomatic relations with the U.S. (1934), negotiated anti-German treaties with France and Czechoslovakia (1935), and urged the League of Nations to resist Germany (1934–38). He was dismissed before the signing of the German–Soviet Nonaggression Pact (1939). He served as ambassador to the U.S. 1941–43.

Liu Bang *or* **Liu Pang** \lē-'ü-'bäŋ\ *or* **Han Gaozu** \'hän-'gaù-'dzü\ (256–195 BC) Man of peasant background who rose to become the founder of China's HAN DYNASTY (206 BC–AD 220). When the first emperor of the QIN DYNASTY (221–206 BC) died, Liu joined rebels led by XIANG YU in an effort to overthrow the Qin. Xiang Yu triumphed and rewarded Liu with the kingdom of Han in western China, but the two allies subsequently turned against each other. Liu's pragmatic shrewdness triumphed over Xiang Yu's aristocratic naiveté, and he became the Han dynasty's first ruler.

Liu Shaoqi *or* **Liu Shao-ch'i** \lē-'ü-'shaù-'chē\ (1898–1969) Chairman of the People's Republic of China (1959–68) and chief theoretician of the CHINESE COMMUNIST PARTY. An activist Communist background from the 1920s helped Liu's rise within the CCP in the 1930s and '40s, while his excellent education and studies in the Soviet Union made him an effective spokesman for the new government in China. When Mao resigned as chairman after the failure of his GREAT LEAP FORWARD, Liu assumed the title. His policies for revitalizing agriculture by permitting peasants to cultivate private plots and giving them monetary incentives were ones to which Mao later strongly objected. In 1969 Liu was purged from power for being a "capitalist roader" and LIN BIAO was appointed Mao's successor. Not until 1974 was Liu's death in 1969 made public.

live oak Any of several North American ornamental and timber trees in the red-oak group of the genus *Quercus* in the BEECH family. The southern live oak *(Q. virginiana)* is a massive (50 ft, or 15 m, tall), durable evergreen tree. The trunk divides near the ground into several limbs that extend horizontally as much as two to three times the height of the tree. The elliptical leaves are dark green and glossy above, whitish and hairy below. A valuable timber tree, the southern live oak is also planted as a shade and avenue tree in the southern U.S. The oldest trees are 200–300 years old.

liver Largest GLAND in the body, with several lobes. It secretes BILE; metabolizes PROTEINS, CARBOHYDRATES, and FATS; stores GLYCOGEN, VITAMINS, and other substances; synthesizes COAGULATION factors; removes wastes and toxic matter from the blood; regulates blood volume; and destroys old red blood cells. The portal vein carries blood from the gastrointestinal tract, gallbladder, pancreas, and spleen to the liver to be processed. A duct system carries bile from the liver to the duodenum and the GALLBLADDER. Liver tissue consists of a mass of cells tunneled with bile ducts and blood vessels. About 60% are hepatic cells, which have more metabolic functions than any other cells. A second type, Kupffer cells, play a role in BLOOD-CELL FORMATION, ANTIBODY production, and ingestion of foreign particles and cell debris. The liver manufactures plasma proteins, including ALBUMIN and clotting factors, and synthesizes enzymes that modify substances such as nutrients and toxins, filtered from the blood. Liver disorders include JAUNDICE, HEPATITIS, CIRRHOSIS, TUMORS, vascular obstruction, ABSCESS, and GLYCOGEN-STORAGE DISEASES.

liver function test Laboratory procedure that measures some aspect of liver function. More than 100 tests have been devised to assess metabolism of proteins, fats, carbohydrates, and bile and removal of drugs and toxic chemicals. Since most metabolic substances (e.g., AMINO ACIDS, bilirubin, ENZYMES) enter the SYSTEMIC CIRCULATION, their blood levels can give valuable information about the liver. URINE levels can support these findings. Tests of detoxifying capacity measure how well the liver clears test substances. Other tests include X-ray films with contrast medium, biopsy, and mapping of the distribution of a radioactive compound.

Liverpool City (pop., 1995 est.: 471,000) and seat of MERSEYSIDE, northwestern England, on the estuary of the MERSEY RIVER. King JOHN granted its charter in 1207. Its growth was slow until the 18th century, when it expanded rapidly as a result of trade with the Americas and the West Indies, becoming Britain's most important port after LONDON. The Liverpool and Manchester Railway (opened 1830) was the first in England to link two major cities. Heavily damaged in World War II, it declined in importance as a port and an industrial center in the postwar era. The birthplace of the BEATLES, it is also the seat of the University of Liverpool (1903).

Liverpool, Earl of *orig.* **Robert Banks Jenkinson** (1770–1828) British prime minister (1812–27). He entered the House of Commons in 1790 and became a leading Tory, serving as foreign secretary (1801–4), home secretary (1804–6, 1807–9), and secretary for war and the colonies (1809–1812). The War of 1812 with the U.S. and the final campaigns of the Napoleonic Wars were fought during his premiership. He urged abolition of the slave trade at the Congress of Vienna (1814–15). Though sometimes overshadowed by his colleagues and by the duke of WELLINGTON's military prowess, he conducted a sound administration.

liverwort Any of more than 8,000 species of small, nonvascular, spore-producing land plants that make up the class Hepatopsida (or Hepaticae) of BRYOPHYTES, found worldwide but mostly in the tropics. Thallose liverworts commonly grow on moist soil or damp rocks; leafy liverworts are found in similar habitats and on tree trunks in damp woods. Sexual (GAMETOPHYTE) and asexual (SPOROPHYTE) generations alternate in the life cycle (see ALTERNATION OF GENERATIONS). The THALLUS of thallose liverworts, resembling a lobed liver, gives liverworts their name. Though not economically important to humans, liverworts provide food for animals, facilitate the decay of logs, and aid in the disintegration of rocks by their ability to retain moisture.

livestock Farm animals, with the exception of poultry. In Western countries the category encompasses primarily CATTLE, SHEEP, PIGS, GOATS, HORSES, DONKEYS, and MULES; other animals (e.g., BUFFALO, OXEN, or CAMELS) may predominate in other areas. See also ASS, COW, DAIRY FARMING.

Living Theater (1951–1970) Theatrical avant-garde repertory company. It was formed in New York in 1947 by Julian Beck (1925–1985) and Judith Malina (born 1926) to produce experimental plays, often on radical themes. Its first big success was Jack Gelber's *The Connection* (1959), a drama of drug addiction. Its next, Kenneth Brown's *The Brig* (1963), depicted military discipline as dehumanizing. After problems with U.S. tax authorities, it moved to Europe (1965–68). It returned to New York to present the confrontational *Paradise Now* (1968), a production intended to spark revolution.

living will Document specifying medical measures to be taken or withheld in the event the writer is disabled. Advances in medical technology now allow the body to be kept alive in circumstances that would normally result in death (e.g., inability to eat, breathe, or maintain the heartbeat), but many people do not want to be kept alive if there is no chance of recovery. Because it is impossible to express one's wishes when in a vegetative state, a living will allows them to be stated in advance. Such a document usually specifies conditions under which a do-not-resuscitate (DNR) order is to take effect and authorizes another person to make decisions on the patient's behalf.

Livingston, Robert R. (1746–1813) American lawyer and diplomat. Born in New York City, he served in the Continental Congress and helped draft the DECLARATION OF INDEPENDENCE. As New York's first chancellor (1777–1801), he administered the oath of office to GEORGE WASHINGTON (1789). He was U.S. secretary of foreign affairs (1781–83) and secured diplomatic recognition of American representatives. As minister to France (1801–4) he helped effect the LOUISIANA PURCHASE. He later formed a partnership with ROBERT FULTON and received a steamboat monopoly for New York waters; the first vessel to operate on the Hudson River (1807) was named the *Clermont,* after his ancestral home.

Robert R. Livingston, portrait by Charles Willson Peale, c. 1782; in Independence National Historical Park, Philadelphia.

BY COURTESY OF THE INDEPENDENCE NATIONAL HISTORICAL PARK COLLECTION, PHILADELPHIA

Livingston, William (1723–1790) American politician. Born in Albany, N.Y., he served in the New York legislature (1759–60), wrote political pamphlets and newspaper articles, and helped prepared a digest of New York laws for the period 1691–1756. He moved to New Jersey in 1772 and represented the colony in the Continental Congress (1774–76). As New Jersey's first governor (1776–90), he was a delegate to the Constitutional Convention and led his state to an early ratification of the U.S. Constitution.

Livingstone, David (1813–1873) Scottish missionary and explorer in Africa. Of working-class origins, Livingstone studied theology and medicine in Glasgow before being ordained (1840) and deciding to work in Africa to open up the interior for colonization, extend the Gospel, and abolish the slave trade. By 1842 he had already penetrated farther north of the Cape Colony frontier than any other white man. He was the first European to reach Lake NGAMI (1849) and the first to reach LUANDA from the interior (1854). He discovered VICTORIA FALLS (1855), journeyed across the continent to eastern Mozambique (1856, 1862), explored the Lake MALAWI region (1861–63), discovered Lakes MWERU and BANGWEULU (1867), and penetrated to points farther east of Lake Tanganyika than any previous expedition had managed (1871). His attempt to find the source of the Nile (1867–71) failed. When found by HENRY MORTON STANLEY in 1871, his health was failing; he refused to leave, and in 1873 was found dead by African aides. Livingstone produced a complex body of knowledge—geographic, technical, medical, and social—that took decades to mine. In his lifetime he stirred the imagination of English-speaking peoples everywhere and was celebrated as one of the great figures of British civilization.

David Livingstone, oil painting by F. Havill after photographs; in the National Portrait Gallery, London.

BY COURTESY OF THE NATIONAL PORTRAIT GALLERY, LONDON

Livonia Region, eastern coast of Baltic Sea, north of Lithuania. Originally inhabited by the Livs, a Finno-Ugric people, it eventually expanded to include nearly all of modern Latvia and Estonia. In the 13th century it was conquered and Christianized by the Order of the Brothers of the Sword and organized into the Livonian confederation. A Russian invasion set off the Livonian War (1558–82), in which Russia, Poland, and Sweden seized portions of it. Sweden eventually gained control of most of it but ceded the region to Russia in 1721. In 1918 the northern portion became part of independent Estonia and the southern portion joined independent Latvia.

Livorno *English* **Leghorn** City (pop., 1996: 165,000), TUSCANY region, central Italy, on the Ligurian Sea. Originally a fishing village, it came under Florentine rule in 1421. Cosimo de' MEDICI began construction of the Medici Harbor in the 16th century, and under Ferdinand I of Tuscany (1549–1609) the city became a haven for refugees. In the 18th century Leopold II enlarged the harbor and gave privileges to foreign merchants. Livorno became part of Italy in 1860. One of Italy's largest ports, it has extensive commercial activities and a large shipbuilding yard. Historic sites include a cathedral and a 16th-century fort.

Livy \'li-vē\ *Latin* **Titus Livius** (59/64 BC–AD 17) Roman historian. Little is known of his life, most of which must have been spent in Rome. His lifework was a history of the city, written in 142 books; Books 11–20 and 46–142 have been lost, and those after Book 45 are known only from fragments and later summaries. Unlike earlier Roman historians, Livy played no part in politics, and as a result he presented history not as partisan politics but in terms of character and morality. The Latin prose style he developed was well fashioned for the subject matter. His history, a classic in his lifetime, profoundly influenced the style and philosophy of historical writing down to the 18th century.

lizard Any of about 3,000 species of four-legged REPTILES (suborder Sauria), most diverse and abundant in the tropics but found from the Arctic Circle to southern Africa, South America, and Australia. Like SNAKES, lizards have scales, paired male copulatory organs, and a flexible skull. Typical lizards have a moderately cylindrical body, well-developed legs, a tail slightly longer than the head and body combined, and movable lower eyelids. They range in size from 1-in. (3-cm) GECKOS to the 10-ft (3-m) KOMODO DRAGON, but most are about 12 in. (30 cm) long. Ornamentation includes crests on the head, back, or tail; spines; brightly colored throat fans; and throat frills. Most species feed on insects and rodents, but some, such as the IGUANA, eat plants. See also GILA MONSTER, HORNED TOAD.

Ljubljana \lē-ˌü-blē-'ä-nə\ City (pop., 1996 est.: 270,000), capital of SLOVENIA. Located on the Ljubljanica River, it is surrounded by the northern Dinaric ALPS. The site of the Roman city of Emona in the 1st century BC., it was destroyed in the 5th century AD. and rebuilt by the Slavs as Luvigana. It passed to Carniola in the 12th century and came under HABSBURG rule in 1277. Taken by the French in 1809, it was the administrative seat of the ILLYRIAN PROVINCES until 1813 and the capital of the kingdom of Illyria 1816–49. The center of Slovene nationalism under Austrian rule, in 1918 it became part of what would be Yugoslavia. It remained the Slovenian capital after Slovenia's independence in 1992. A railroad and commercial center, it is the site of the University of Ljubljana (founded 1595).

llama \'lä-mə\ Domesticated South American lamoid (see ALPACA), maintained in herds in Bolivia, Peru, Ecuador, Chile, and Argentina. The llama *(Lama glama)* is used primarily as a pack animal but also as a source of food, wool, hides, tallow for candles, and dried dung for fuel. A 250-lb (113-kg) llama can carry a load of 100–130 lbs (45–60 kg) and travel 15–20 mi (25–30 km) a day. It has a high thirst tolerance and can subsist on a wide variety of plant materials. Though usually white, it may be solid black or brown, or white with black or brown markings. It is usually gentle, but when overloaded or mistreated it will lie down, hiss, spit and kick, and refuse to move. Not known to exist in the wild state, it appears to have been bred from GUANACOS during or before the INCA civilization.

Llandridod Wells \hlan-'drin-ˌdäd\ Town, seat of Powys Co., eastern Wales. Its medicinal waters were first discovered c. 1696, and in the 19th century it became a popular spa. The spa declined after World War II and closed in the 1960s, but reopened in 1983. To the northwest lie the remains of a Roman fort.

Llano Estacado \'la-nō-ˌes-tə-'kä-dō\ *or* **Staked Plain** Plateau, southeastern New Mexico, western Texas, and northwestern Oklahoma. Occupying an area of about 30,000 sq mi (78,000 sq km), it is a semiarid plain with occasional pools filled by rainwater. Its soil supports grazing, dryland farming of grains, and irrigated cotton production. Production of petroleum and natural gas is also important. LUBBOCK and AMARILLO, Tex., are its most important cities.

Llanquihue \läŋ-'kē-wə\, **Lake** Lake, southern central Chile. The largest Chilean lake, it has an area of 330 sq mi (860 sq km); it is 22 mi (35 km) long and 25 mi (40 km) wide. In the distance stand volcanoes and beyond them, on the Argentine border, Mount Tronador (11,660 ft, or 3,554 m). Popular resort towns are located on its shores.

Llosa, Mario Vargas See Mario VARGAS LLOSA

Lloyd, Chris Evert See Chris EVERT

Lloyd, Harold (1893–1971) U.S. film comedian. Born in Burchard, Neb., he began to appear in one-reel comedies in 1913, mastering the comic chase scene as a member of MACK SENNETT's troupe. He joined HAL ROACH's company and created his Lonesome Luke character in popular movies such as *Just Nuts* (1915). He developed his trademark white-faced character in round glasses in 1918. Noted for his use of physical danger as a source of laughter, he performed his own daring stunts, hanging from the hands of a clock far above the street in *Safety Last* (1923) and standing in for a football tackling-dummy in *The Freshman* (1925). He received a special Academy Award in 1952.

Lloyd George, David *later* **Earl Lloyd-George of Dwyfor** (1863–1945) British prime minister (1916–22). Born in Manchester to Welsh parents, he was raised in Wales. He entered Parliament in 1890 as a Liberal and retained his seat for 55 years. He served as president of the Board of Trade 1905–8, then as chancellor of the exchequer 1908–15. Rejection of his controversial "People's Budget" (to raise taxes for social programs) in 1909 by the House of Lords led to a constitutional crisis and passage of the PARLIAMENT ACT OF 1911. He devised the National Insurance Act of 1911, which laid the foundation of the British WELFARE STATE. As minister of munitions (1915–16), he used unorthodox methods to ensure that war supplies were forthcoming. He replaced H. H. ASQUITH as prime minister in 1916, with Conservative support in his coalition government. His small war cabinet ensured speedy decisions. Distrustful of the competence of the British high command, he was constantly at odds with Gen. DOUGLAS HAIG. In the 1918 elections his decision to continue a coalition government further split the Liberals. He was one of the three great statesmen responsible for the Treaty of VERSAILLES at the PARIS PEACE CONFERENCE. He began the negotiations that culminated in the Anglo–Irish treaty of 1921. He resigned in 1922 and headed an ailing Liberal Party 1926–31.

Lloyd Webber, Andrew *later* **Baron Lloyd-Webber** (born 1948) British composer whose eclectic, rock-based works helped revitalize musical theater. Born in London, he studied at Oxford and at the Royal College of Music, which his father directed. His first collaboration with lyricist Tim Rice (born 1944), *Joseph and the Amazing Technicolor Dreamcoat* (1968), was followed by the "rock opera" *Jesus Christ Superstar* (1971), which blended classical forms with rock music. Their last major collaboration was *Evita* (1978): *Cats* (1981), on poems by T. S. ELIOT, became the longest-running musical ever in both London and New York. He later collaborated on *Starlight Express* (1984), *Phantom of the Opera* (1986), *Aspects of Love* (1989), and *Sunset Boulevard* (1993), among other stage works. He was knighted in 1992 and ennobled in 1996.

Lloyd's of London Insurance marketing association in London, specializing in high-risk insurance services. Its history dates to 1688, when Edward Lloyd kept a London coffeehouse where merchants, seafarers, and marine-insurance underwriters met to transact business. The underwriters at Lloyd's eventually formed a marine-insurance association (incorporated 1871); it expanded to include other forms of insurance in 1911. After a series of financial scandals, the corporation was reorganized under the Lloyd's Act of 1982. Today Lloyd's consists of more than 20,000 individual members organized in several hundred syndicates, which are represented at Lloyd's by underwriting agents. Individual syndicate members, rather than the corporation, are liable for losses. Until record losses in the 1980s and '90s bankrupted some syndicate members, they had unlimited liability for business transacted for them; in 1993 that liability was limited. See also INSURANCE, LIABILITY INSURANCE.

Llull \'lyül\\, **Ramon** *English* **Raymond Lully** (1232/33–1315/16) Spanish (Catalan) mystic, poet, and missionary. He was reared at the court of Majorca, where he wrote lyrical troubadour poetry. He later traveled widely, attempting to convert Muslims to Christianity; he is said to have been stoned to death at Bejaïa. As a philosopher, he is best known as the inventor of an "art of finding truth"; primarily intended to support the Church in its missionary work, it was also designed to unify all branches of knowledge. In his principal work, *Ars magna* (1305–8), he tried to relate all forms of knowledge, including theology, philosophy, and the natural sciences, as mutually analogous and manifestations of the godhead in the universe. His writings influenced Neoplatonic mysticism throughout medieval and 17th-century Europe. In Catalan culture, his allegorical novels *Blanquerna* (c. 1284) and *Felix* (c. 1288) enjoy wide popularity; he is also known for his treatise on chivalry, his animal fables, and an encyclopedia of medieval thought.

Llyr \'hlir\ In CELTIC RELIGION, the leader of one of the two warring families of the gods. According to one interpretation, the Children of Llyr were the powers of darkness, constantly in conflict with the Children of Dôn, the powers of light. In Welsh tradition, Llyr and his son Manawydan were associated with the sea. Llyr's other children included BRÂN, Creidylad, and Branwen, wife of the sun god Matholwch, king of Ireland.

Llywelyn ap Gruffudd \hlə-'we-lin-ap-'gri-fith\ (died 1282) Prince of Wales (1258–77). As prince of GWYNEDD in northern Wales from 1255, he sought to extend his rule throughout his native country, and he proclaimed himself prince of Wales in 1258. He fought the English lords of southern Wales (1262) and allied himself with HENRY III's opponent, SIMON DE MONTFORT. After Montfort's death, however, he signed a treaty recognizing Henry as overlord (1267). Llywelyn rebelled against EDWARD I but was defeated by him in 1277. He was killed in a final rebellion in 1282, and Wales soon fell entirely under English rule.

Llywelyn ap Iorwerth \hlə-'we-lin-ap-'yòr-werth\ *known as* **Llywelyn the Great** (died 1240) Welsh prince. The grandson of a powerful Welsh prince, he was exiled as a child from GWYNEDD in northern Wales but returned in 1194 and deposed his uncle, gaining control of most of northern Wales by 1202. Though he married King JOHN's daughter, the English king invaded Wales when Llywelyn's authority reached too far (1211). Llywelyn soon recovered his lands and allied with John's baronial opponents. HENRY III acknowledged his rule in most of Wales (1218), but by 1223 Llywelyn was forced to withdraw to the north.

Lo-lang See NANGNANG

load-bearing wall See BEARING WALL

loam Rich, friable (crumbly) soil with nearly equal parts of sand and silt, and somewhat less clay. The term is sometimes used imprecisely to mean earth or soil in general. Loam in subsoil receives varied minerals and amounts of clay by leaching (percolation) from the topsoil above.

Loanda See LUANDA

Lobachevsky \,lō-bə-'chev-skē\, **Nikolay (Ivanovich)** (1792–1856) Russian mathematician. His entire life centered around the University of Kazan, where he studied and later (from 1816) taught. In 1829 he published his groundbreaking theory, a geometry that rejected EUCLID's PARALLEL POSTULATE. It was the final solution to a problem that had baffled mathematicians for 2,000 years. Lobachevsky also did distinguished work in the theory of infinite series, especially trigonometric series, as well as in INTEGRAL CALCULUS, ALGEBRA, and PROBABILITY. He was largely ignored during his lifetime; acceptance of his new geometry came a decade after his death, though much of the credit went to others. With János Bolyai of Hungary (1802–1860), Lobachevsky is considered the founder of NON-EUCLIDEAN GEOMETRY.

Lobamba Town (pop., 1995 est.: 10,000), legislative capital of Swaziland. Located near MBABANE, it is in a densely populated rural area. It is, according to traditional SWAZI customs, the residence of the Queen Mother, and thereby, the spiritual home of the Swazi nation. It is the site of parliamentary buildings and an official residence of the king.

lobbying Any attempt by a group or individual to influence the decisions of government. The term originated in 19th-century efforts to influence the votes of legislators, generally in the lobby outside a legislative chamber. The effort may be a direct appeal to a decision maker in either the executive or legislative branches, or it may be indirect (e.g., through attempts to influence public opinion). It may include oral or written efforts of persuasion, campaign contributions, public-relations campaigns, research supplied to legislative committees, and formal testimony before such committees. A lobbyist may be a member of a special-interest group, a professional willing to represent any group, or a private individual. In the U.S., the Federal Regulation of Lobbying Act

(1946) requires that lobbyists and the groups they represent register and report contributions and expenditures.

lobelia family \lō-'bēl-yə\ Family Lobeliaceae, which contains about 750 species of flowering plants in 25 genera. Some are grown for their attractive, two-lipped flowers. Postlike and shaggy-tree forms are found on mountains in Africa. The family includes the CARDINAL FLOWER, great blue lobelia *(L. siphilitica),* and Indian tobacco *(L. inflata).* Once used for smoking and for the vomit-inducing ALKALOID in its roots, lobelia is now regarded as poisonous.

Lobengula \ˌlō-beŋ-'gyü-lə\ (1836?–1894) Second and last king of the southern African NDEBELE nation. Son of the founder of the Ndebele kingdom, Mzilikazi, Lobengula succeeded to the throne in 1870 after a period of civil war. He attempted to form an alliance with the British, granting them first farming (1886) and then mineral (1888) concessions. Not satisfied, the British South Africa Co. under CECIL RHODES undertook a military expedition that destroyed the Ndebele kingdom in 1893. See also KHAMA III.

lobotomy \lə-'bä-tə-mē\ Operation to cut nerve pathways linking one or more lobes to the rest of the BRAIN. Introduced in 1935 by ANTONIO EGAS MONIZ and Almeida Lima, it came to be used as a radical measure to help grossly disturbed patients, Favored for patients who did not respond to SHOCK THERAPY, it did reduce agitation, but often caused increased apathy and passivity, inability to concentrate, and decreased emotional response. It was widely performed until c. 1956, when drugs that were more effective in calming patients became available. Lobotomies are now widely disapproved of and performed only rarely.

lobster Any of numerous species of marine shrimplike DECAPODS that are bottom-dwellers and mostly nocturnal. Lobsters scavenge for dead animals but also eat live fish, small mollusks and other bottom-dwelling invertebrates, and seaweed. One or more pairs of legs are often modified into pincers, usually larger on one side than the other. True lobsters have a distinct snout on the upper body shell. The American lobster *(Homarus americanus)* and SCAMPI are the most commercially important, being highly prized as food. The American lobster, found from Labrador to North Carolina, weighs about 1 lb (0.5 kg) and is about 10 in. (25 cm) long when caught in shallow water. Most deepwater specimens weigh about 5.5 lbs (2.5 kg); some may weigh 40 lbs (20 kg). See also SHELLFISH.

American lobster (*Homarus americanus*).

JOHN H. GERARD

local area network (LAN) Communications network consisting of many computers within a local area, such as a single building or company complex. Individual users can share data or files on a LAN as if the data or files resided on their respective computers; a central computer used for this purpose is called a SERVER. Laser printers and other peripheral equipment can be connected to a LAN for common use. COAXIAL and FIBER-OPTIC cables are popular communication lines for LANs because they provide fast data transmission and are easy to install. See also computer NETWORK.

Local Group Group of about 40 galaxies to which the MILKY WAY GALAXY belongs. Nearly half are dwarf elliptical GALAXIES, but the six largest are spiral or irregular galaxies. They are probably kept from separating by mutual gravitational attraction. The Milky Way system is near one end of the group; the great ANDROMEDA GALAXY is near the other end, about 2 million light-years away.

Locarno, Pact of (1925) Multilateral treaty signed in Locarno, Switzerland, intended to guarantee peace in Western Europe. Its signatories were Belgium, Britain, France, Germany, and Italy. Germany's borders with France and Belgium as set by the Treaty of VERSAILLES were decreed inviolable, but its eastern borders were not. Britain promised to defend Belgium and France, but not Poland and Czechoslovakia. Other provisions included mutual defense pacts between France and Poland and between France and Czechoslovakia. The treaty led to the Allied troops' departure from the RHINELAND by 1930, five years ahead of schedule. See also KELLOGG-BRIAND PACT.

Loch Leven See Loch LEVEN

Loch Lomond See Loch LOMOND

Loch Ness See Loch NESS

Lochner \'lȯk-nər\, **Stefan** (c. 1400–1451) German painter. Nothing is known of his early life, but he may have studied in the Netherlands before settling in Cologne c. 1430, for Flemish influence is evident in his attention to minute details. JAN VAN EYCK's influence is seen in *The Adoration of the Magi,* his altarpiece for Cologne's great cathedral, but Lochner adds his own naturalistic observation and masterly sense of color and design. Known for his highly mystical religious paintings, he is considered the greatest representative of the school of Cologne.

"Madonna of the Rose Bower," painting on wood by Stefan Lochner; in the Wallraf-Richartz-Museum, Cologne.

BY COURTESY OF THE WALLRAF-RICHARTZ-MUSEUM, COLOGNE

Lochner v. New York U.S. Supreme Court decision (1905) that struck down a New York law setting 10 hours of labor a day as the legal maximum in the baking trade. Justice Rufus W. Peckham, writing for the Court, declared that the 14th Amendment prohibited states from curtailing employers' freedom to make their own economic arrangements with employees. The opinion drew a stinging rebuke from OLIVER WENDELL HOLMES, JR., whose dissent became the prevailing interpretation of the 14th Amendment by the 1930s, when maximum-hours laws were held constitutional.

lock Mechanical or electronic device for securing a door or receptacle so that it cannot be opened except by a key or a code. The lock originated in the Middle East; the oldest known example was found near Nineveh. Possibly 4,000 years old, it is of the pin tumbler type, otherwise known as an Egyptian lock. The Romans were the first to use metal locks and to make small keys for them. They also invented wards, projections in the keyhole that prevent a key from turning unless it has slots that avoid the projections. Probably the most familiar lock today is the cylinder lock, a pin tumbler lock opened by a flat key with a serrated edge; the serrations raise pins in the cylinder to the proper heights, al-

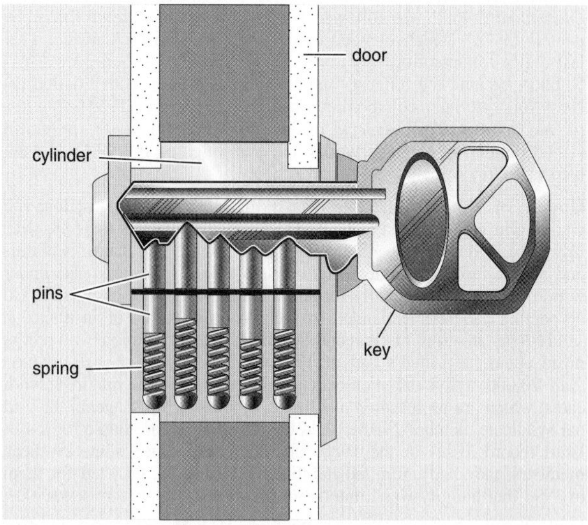

A cylinder lock's tumbler consists of a series of pins arranged in pairs. The pins are spring-loaded to press against the contours of the inserted key. A wrong key will cause one or more of the pins to block the cylinder from turning; only when the tops of all the lower pins line up with the edge of the cylinder can the cylinder turn.

lowing the cylinder to turn. Also common are the unit lock, housed within a rectangular notch cut into the edge of a door, and the mortise lock, housed in a mortise cut into the door edge, the lock mechanism being covered on both sides. Other types include lever and combination locks. Electronic locks that open with a magnetic card key are popular for banks, hotel rooms, and offices.

Locke, John (1632–1704) English philosopher. Educated at Oxford, principally in medicine and science, he later became physician and adviser to the future 3rd Earl of SHAFTESBURY (1667–72). He moved to France, but after Shaftesbury's fall in 1683 he fled to the Netherlands, where he supported the future WILLIAM III, returning to England after the Glorious Revolution to become commissioner of appeals, a post he held till his death. His most famous work is his *Essay Concerning Human Understanding* (1690). He rejected the rationalist view that a thinker could work out by reason alone the truth about the universe, arguing that knowledge of the world could only be gained by experience. In EPISTEMOLOGY, Locke laid the foundations of British EMPIRICISM and of PRAGMATISM. His most important work of political philosophy is *Two Treatises of Government* (1690), which refutes ABSOLUTISM and the divine right of monarchs. Locke's classic expression of LIBERALISM in the treatises was to inspire the leaders of the American and French Revolutions and the authors of the U.S. Constitution. An initiator of the ENLIGHTENMENT in England and France, Locke was also a strong influence on DAVID HUME, GEORGE BERKELEY, and many other 18th-century figures.

Lockheed Martin Corp. U.S. diversified company that is one of the world's largest aerospace manufacturers. It was established in 1995 through the merger of Lockheed Corp. (formed 1926 as Lockheed Aircraft Co.) and Martin Marietta Corp. (formed 1961 from the merger of Martin Co. and American-Marietta Co.). During World War II, Lockheed established a secret division ("Skunk Works") that became the leading U.S. developer of military aircraft (e.g., F-104 fighter, U-2 and SR-71 spy planes, and F-117A stealth fighter). In the early 1970s its financially troubled production of the L-1011 TriStar commercial jetliner necessitated its rescue from bankruptcy by massive U.S. government aid. Lockheed's work in missile development resulted in the Polaris, Poseidon, and TRIDENT submarine-launched ballistic missile systems; in the space sector its activities included the construction and systems integration of the HUBBLE SPACE TELESCOPE. In the early 1990s, in partnership with BOEING CO., it contracted to build the F-22 Raptor stealth fighter (first flown 1997). Martin Co.'s major business after World War II was the development of rockets (e.g., TITAN) and electronics systems for the U.S. government. Later, as Martin Marietta, it constructed the VIKING Mars landers and the Magellan spacecraft to Venus and designed and produced the external fuel tank for the SPACE SHUTTLE. In the mid-1990s Lockheed Martin formed a joint venture, International Launch Services, with the Russian firms ENERGIA and Khrunichev to market commercial space launch services.

lockjaw See TETANUS

lockout Tactic used by employers in labor disputes, in which employees are locked out of the workplace or otherwise denied employment. In the 1880s and '90s factory owners often used lockouts against the KNIGHTS OF LABOR, which was struggling to organize industries such as meatpacking and cigar making. The lockout has been used only rarely in modern times, usually as part of a pact among members of employers' associations to frustrate LABOR UNIONS by closing work facilities in response to STRIKES.

Locofoco Party \ˌlō-kō-ˈfō-kō\ Radical wing of the DEMOCRATIC PARTY organized in New York City in 1835. It included former members of the WORKINGMEN'S PARTY opposed to state banks, monopolies, tariffs, and special interests. Its name derived from the self-igniting friction matches *(locofocos)* that its members used to light candles after TAMMANY HALL regulars turned off the gas lights at the nominating convention. Formally called the Equal Rights Party, it ousted several Tammany candidates and accomplished a separation of government and banking with passage of the Independent Treasury Act (1840). It was reabsorbed into the Democratic Party in the 1840s.

locomotion Any of various animal movements that result in progression from one place to another. Locomotion is classified as either appendicular (accomplished by special appendages) or axial (achieved by changing the body shape). Aquatic protozoans move by ciliary or flagellar appendages or by pseudopods, footlike appendages. Other forms of aquatic locomotion include walking on legs (some ARTHROPODS), crawling (by contracting the body muscles, anchoring to the substrate, and extending), and swimming by either hydraulic propulsion (e.g., JELLYFISH) or undulation (FISHES). Terrestrial arthropods and VERTEBRATES move by means of jointed appendages, the legs. Snakes and other limbless vertebrates crawl by means of muscular thrusts against the substrate. Flight is achieved by the forward thrust of WINGS.

locomotive Self-propelled vehicle used for hauling railroad cars on tracks. Early experimental steam locomotives were built in Wales and England by RICHARD TREVITHICK from 1803. The first practical steam locomotive, the *Rocket,* was developed in 1829 by GEORGE STEPHENSON, in whose "steam blast" system the steam from a multitube boiler drove pistons connected to a pair of flanged driving wheels. The first U.S. steam locomotive was built by JOHN STEVENS in 1825, and the first commercially usable locomotive, the *Tom Thumb,* by PETER COOPER in Baltimore in 1830. Later improvements enabled a locomotive to move up to 200 freight cars at 75 mph (120 kph). Steam from wood or coal fuel was the main source of power until the mid-20th century, though electric power had been used from the early 20th century, especially in Europe. After World War II DIESEL power replaced steam because of its higher efficiency and lower cost, though diesel-electric and gas turbine-electric combinations were also used.

locoweed Any of several species of poisonous plants of the genera *Astragalus* and *Oxytropis,* in the pea family (see LEGUME), native to the prairies of northern central and western North America. These low-growing plants (up to 1.5 ft, or 45 cm, high), have variably hairy, fernlike leaves and spikes of pealike flowers. They pose a danger to grazing animals because they contain a toxin that affects muscle control, producing frenzied behavior, impaired vision, and sometimes death. Because they taste bad, livestock usually eat them only when other forage is scarce. Decaying locoweeds release toxins into the soil that are sometimes absorbed by otherwise harmless forage crops.

Locri Epizephyrii \ˈlō-ˌkrī-ˌe-pi-zə-ˈfir-ē-ˌī\ Ancient city in MAGNA GRAECIA, on the eastern coast of Italy's southwestern extremity. Founded by Greeks c. 680 BC, it was the first Greek community to have a written code of laws, the Locrian code (c. 660 BC). It founded colonies and resisted Athenian intervention during the PELOPONNESIAN WAR. Fickle in its allegiance, it was captured by Rome in 205 BC and destroyed by Sicilian Muslims in 915.

locust In botany, any of about 20 species of trees in the genus *Robinia* of the pea family (see LEGUME), all occurring in eastern North America and Mexico. Best known is the black locust *(R. pseudoacacia),* often called false acacia, or yellow locust. Widely cultivated in Europe as an ornamental, it grows to 80 ft (24 m) high and bears long, compound leaves. The fragrant white flowers hang in loose clusters. There are many varieties, some thornless. The black locust has long been used for erosion control and as a timber tree. The so-called honey locust *(Gleditsia triacanthos),* also of the pea family, is a North American tree commonly used as an ornamental and often found in hedges.

Black locust (*Robinia pseudoacacia*).
JOHN H. GERARD—EB INC.

locust Species (family Acrididae) of short-horned GRASSHOPPER that often increases greatly in number and migrates long distances in destructive swarms. In North America the names locust and grasshopper are used for any acridid; a CICADA may also be called a locust. In Europe, locust refers to large species and grasshopper to small ones. Locusts are found on all continents. Sporadic appearances of locust swarms may be explained by the theory that the swarming species has a solitary phase (the normal state) and a gregarious phase. Nymphs that mature in the presence of many other locusts develop into the gregarious type; thus migratory swarms form only when overcrowding results in a scarcity of resources. Swarms may be almost unimaginably large; in 1889 a Red Sea swarm was estimated to cover 2,000 sq mi (5,000 sq km), and swarms may form huge towers 5,000 ft (1,500 m) high. Locust plagues can be extremely destructive of crops.

lodestone See MAGNETITE

lodge Originally an insubstantial dwelling, or one erected for a temporary occupational purpose (e.g., woodcutting or masonry) or for use during the hunting season. The lodge became a more permanent type of house as the lands around European mansions were developed as parks. The lodge was often the cottage of the gamekeeper, caretaker, gatekeeper, or gardener, or it could be a larger building for occupation by a higher-ranking person. Today the word suggests a rustic dwelling or inn in a natural setting, often one used seasonally (e.g., a ski lodge).

Lodge, Henry Cabot (1850–1924) U.S. politician. Born in Boston, he received the first PhD in political science from Harvard University. He served in the U.S. House of Representatives (1887–93) and Senate (1893–1924). He supported U.S. entry into World War I but opposed participation in the League of Nations; as chairman of the Senate's foreign relations committee he delayed action on the adoption of the Treaty of Versailles with its covenant establishing the League. He proposed amendments (the Lodge reservations) that would require Senate approval before the U.S. would accept certain League decisions. WOODROW WILSON refused to accept the amendments, and the Senate rejected the treaty.

Lodge, Henry Cabot (1902–1985) U.S. politician and diplomat. Born in Nahant, Mass., the grandson of Sen. HENRY C. LODGE, he served in the U.S. Senate (1937–44, 1947–52) and as U.S. representative to the U.N. (1953–60). In 1960 he was the Republican vice-presidential candidate under RICHARD NIXON. He was ambassador to South Vietnam during the critical years 1963–64 and 1965–67, ambassador to West Germany (1968–69), and special envoy to the Vatican (1970–77).

Lodi \'lȯ-dē\, **Peace of** (1454) Treaty between Venice and Milan ending the war of succession to the Milanese duchy in favor of FRANCESCO SFORZA. It recognized Sforza as ruler of Milan and restored Venice's territories in northern Italy, including Brescia and Bergamo. It also provided for a 25-year mutual defensive pact to maintain existing boundaries and established an Italian League. The treaty created a balance of power among Venice, Milan, Naples, Florence, and the Papal States, and it began a 40-year period of relative peace.

Łódź \'wüch, *Engl* 'lōdz\ City (pop., 1996 est.: 826,000), central Poland. Located southwest of WARSAW, it was a village in the 14th century and gained municipal rights in 1798. The Russian-ruled Congress Kingdom of Poland established it as a center of the textile industry in 1820, and by the late 19th century it was Poland's leader in the production of cotton textiles. It was occupied by the Germans during World Wars I and II. It is now a cultural center and Poland's second largest city.

loess \'les, 'lō-əs\ Unstratified, geologically recent deposit of silty or loamy material that is usually buff or yellowish brown and is deposited chiefly by the wind. Loess is a sedimentary deposit composed largely of silt-sized grains that are loosely cemented by calcium carbonate. It is usually homogeneous and highly porous and is traversed by vertical capillaries that permit the sediment to fracture and form vertical bluffs.

Loesser \'le-sər\, **Frank (Henry)** (1910–1969) U.S. composer, librettist, and lyricist. The son of a New York piano teacher, he moved to Hollywood in 1936, where he worked with BURTON LANE, J. STYNE, J. MCHUGH, and H. CARMICHAEL. His wartime songs included "Praise the Lord and Pass the Ammunition" and "What Do You Do in the Infantry?"; postwar hits included "On a Slow Boat to China" and "Baby It's Cold Outside" (Academy Award). His first Broadway musical was *Where's Charley?* (1948; film, 1952). In 1950 he produced *Guys and Dolls* (film, 1955), one of the greatest American musicals. It was followed by *The Most Happy Fella* (1956) and *How to Succeed in Business Without Really Trying* (1962, Pulitzer Prize). His work for film includes the score for *Hans Christian Andersen* (1952).

Loewe \'lō\, **Frederick** (1904–1988) Austrian-U.S. songwriter. Son of a tenor, Loewe was a piano prodigy; at 13 he became the youngest soloist ever to appear with the Berlin Philharmonic Orchestra. He studied with F. BUSONI and Eugène d'Albert. His song "Katrina," written at 15, sold more than a million copies. Arriving in the U.S. in 1924, he contributed music to Broadway revues. In 1942 he met A.J. LERNER; their 18-year collaboration would produce five classic musicals. Personal differences ended their partnership after *Camelot,* but they reunited to adapt *Gigi* for the stage (1973) and write songs for the film *The Little Prince* (1974).

Loewy \'lō-ē\, **Raymond (Fernand)** (1893–1986) French-U.S. industrial designer. After obtaining an advanced degree in electrical engineering, he emigrated in 1919 in New York, where he worked as a fashion illustrator and designer of department-store window displays. He opened his own design firm in 1929, and in the 1930s and '40s he designed a variety of household products with rounded corners and simplified, "streamlined" outlines. A refrigerator designed for Sears, Roebuck & Co. (1934) won first prize at the 1937 Paris International Exposition. In later years his highly functional designs for everything from locomotives to soda dispensers helped shape U.S. industrial design.

Löffler \'lœf-lər\, **Friedrich (August Johannes)** (1852–1915) German bacteriologist. In 1884, with Edwin Klebs (1834–1913), he discovered the organism that causes DIPHTHERIA. Simultaneously with Émile Roux (1853–1933) and Alexandre Yersin (1863–1943), he indicated the existence of a diphtheria toxin. His demonstration that some animals are immune to diphtheria was basic to Emil von Behring's work in developing antitoxins. Löffler also discovered the cause of some swine diseases and identified, with Wilhelm Schütz, the organism that causes the horse disease glanders. With Paul Frosch he found that foot-and-mouth disease is caused by a virus (the first time a virus was found to be the agent of an animal disease) and developed a serum against it.

loft Upper space within a building, often open on one side, used for storage or other purposes (e.g., sleeping loft, hayloft). The term also refers to one of the upper floors in a factory or warehouse, typically undivided by partitions and now often converted to other uses, such as residences or artists' studios. In churches the rood loft is a display gallery above the rood screen (see CATHEDRAL), and a choir or organ loft is a gallery reserved for church singers and musicians. In theaters, the loft is the area above and behind the PROSCENIUM.

Lofting, Hugh (John) (1886–1947) British-U.S. author and illustrator. He lived principally in the U.S. from 1912. He is known for his classic children's books about Doctor Dolittle, a chubby, gentle, eccentric physician to animals who learns their language the better to treat them. He originally created the character to entertain his children in letters he sent from the front during World War I. *The Story of Dr. Dolittle* (1920) won instant success; it was followed by *The Voyages of Dr. Dolittle* (1922, Newbery Medal), *Dr. Dolittle in the Moon* (1928), and *Dr. Dolittle's Return* (1933), among many other volumes.

log cabin Small, one-room house built of logs notched at the ends and laid one upon another with the spaces filled with plaster, moss, mortar, mud, or dried manure. In North America they were built by early settlers, hunters, loggers, and other wilderness dwellers. They have also been built in Europe, particularly Scandinavia. Though designs vary, a common style features a sloping, single-gabled timbered roof and small windows. Modern summer cottages may be built of logs (or given log-cabin siding) to achieve a rustic effect.

Log cabin, Abraham Lincoln's boyhood home, Knob Creek, Ky., originally built early 19th century.

WETTACH—SHOSTAL/EB INC.

Logan, James *orig.* **Tah-gah-jute** (1725?–1780) American Indian leader. He was born in Pennsylvania, the son of the ONEIDA chief Shikellamy, who was a friend of the secretary of the Pennsylvania colony, James Logan (1674–1751). He moved to the Ohio River valley, where he became friendly with Indians and white settlers. After his family was massacred by a frontier trader in 1774, he led Indian raids on white settlements in LORD DUNMORE'S WAR. He refused to participate in peace negotiations, sending his grievances in a message known as "Logan's Lament." He was allied with the British in the American Revolution.

Logan, Mt. Peak, ST. ELIAS MTNS., southwestern Yukon Territory, near the Alaskan boundary. Reaching 19,524 ft (5,951 m), it is the highest mountain in Canada and is second in North America only to Mount MCKINLEY. It is located in Kluane National Park, which occupies 8,500 sq mi (22,000 sq km). The summit was first reached in 1925. The peak was named for William Logan, founder of the Geological Survey of Canada.

loganberry BRAMBLE plant (Rubus loganobaccus) of the ROSE family. It originated in Santa Cruz, Cal., in 1881, apparently as a natural hybrid between the wild BLACKBERRY of the Pacific coast and the red RASPBERRY. It is grown in large quantities in Oregon and Washington and cultivated in Britain and Tasmania. The loganberry is a vigorous, nearly trailing, blackberry-like plant with compound leaves and prickly canes. Its wine-red, tart berries are canned, frozen for preserve or pie stock, or made into wine.

logarithm In mathematics, the power to which a base must be raised to yield a given number (e.g., the logarithm to the base 3 of 9, or $\log_3 9$, is 2, because $3^2 = 9$). A common logarithm is a logarithm to the base 10. Thus, the common logarithm of 100 (log 100) is 2, because $10^2 = 100$. Logarithms to the base *e*, in which $e = 2.71828...$, called natural logarithms (ln), are especially useful in calculus. Logarithms were invented to simplify cumbersome calculations, since exponents can be added or subtracted to multiply or divide their bases. These processes have been further simplified by the incorporation of logarithmic functions into digital calculators and computers. See also JOHN NAPIER.

loggia \'lō-jē-ə\ Hall, gallery, or porch open to the air on one or more sides. It evolved in the Mediterranean region as an open sitting room with protection from the sun. It is often a roofed, arcaded open gallery on an upper story overlooking a court, though it can also be a separate arcaded or colonnaded structure. In medieval and Renaissance Italy, it was often used in conjunction with a public square, as in Florence's Loggia dei Lanzi (begun 1376).

logic Study of inference and argument. In logic, an argument consists of a set of statements (the premises) whose truth is claimed to be sufficient for the truth of a further statement (the conclusion of the argument). Logic may be divided into deductive logic, inductive logic, and the study of what are often called informal fallacies (see DEDUCTION, INDUCTION, FALLACY). Modern formal logic takes as its main subject matter propositions and deductive arguments, and it abstracts from their content the logical forms they embody. The logician uses a symbolic notation to express these logical forms and to facilitate inference and tests of validity. The logical constants include (1) such propositional connectives as "not" (symbolized as $\neg$), "and" (symbolized as $\wedge$), "or" (symbolized as $\vee$), and "if-then" (symbolized as $\supset$), and (2) the existential and universal quantifiers "$(\exists x)$" (which may be read: "For at least one individual, call it x, it is true that") and "$(\forall x)$" ("For each individual, call it x, it is true that"). Furthermore, (3) the concept of identity (expressed by =) and (4) some notion of predication belong to logic. When the logical constants in (1) alone are studied, the field is called PROPOSITIONAL CALCULUS. When (1), (2), and (4) are considered, the field is first-order PREDICATE CALCULUS. If the absence of (3) is stressed, the epithet "without identity" is added. Logic is fundamental to the fields of philosophy and mathematics. See also DEONTIC LOGIC, MODAL LOGIC.

logic, many-valued FORMAL SYSTEM in which the well-formed formulae are interpreted as being able to take on values other than the two classical values of truth or falsity. The number of values possible for well-formed formulae in systems of many-valued logic ranges from three to uncountably many.

logic, philosophy of General philosophical questions about the nature and scope of LOGIC. Examples of questions raised in the philosophy of logic are: "In virtue of what features of reality are the laws of logic true?"; "How do we know the truths of logic?"; and "Could the laws of logic ever be falsified by experience?" The subject matter of logic has been variously characterized as the laws of THOUGHT, "the rules of right reasoning," "the principles of valid argumentation," "the use of certain words called logical constants," "truths based solely on the meanings of the terms they contain," and so on.

logic design Basic organization of the circuitry of a DIGITAL COMPUTER. All digital computers are based on a two-valued logic system—1/0, on/off, yes/no (see BINARY CODE). Computers perform calculations using components called logic gates, which are made up of INTEGRATED CIRCUITS that receive an input signal, process it, and change it into an output signal. The components of the gates pass or block a clock pulse as it travels through them, and the output bits of the gates control other gates or output the result. There are three basic kinds of logic gates, called "and," "or," and "not." By connecting logic gates together, a device can be constructed that can perform basic arithmetic functions.

logical positivism Early form of ANALYTIC PHILOSOPHY, inspired by DAVID HUME, the logic of BERTRAND RUSSELL and ALFRED NORTH WHITEHEAD, and LUDWIG WITTGENSTEIN's *Tractatus* (1921). The school, formally instituted at the University of Vienna in a seminar of Moritz Schlick (1882–1936) in 1922, continued there as the VIENNA CIRCLE until 1938. It proposed several revolutionary theses: (1) All meaningful discourse consists either of (a) the formal sentences of logic and mathematics or (b) the factual propositions of the special sciences; (2) Any assertion that claims to be factual has meaning only if it is possible to say how it might be verified; (3) Metaphysical assertions, coming under neither of the two classes of (1), are meaningless; and (4) All statements about moral, aesthetic, or religious values are scientifically unverifiable and meaningless. See also A. J. AYER, RUDOLF CARNAP, EMOTIVISM, VERIFIABILITY PRINCIPLE.

logicism \'lä-ji-ˌsi-zəm\ In the philosophy of MATHEMATICS, the thesis that mathematics is derivable from LOGIC. As early as 1666, G. W. LEIBNIZ had conceived of logic as a universal science embracing the principles underlying all others. J. W. R. Dedekind in 1888, and especially GOTTLOB FREGE in 1884 and 1893, derived arithmetic from logic. BERTRAND RUSSELL propounded the thesis that all of mathematics is reducible to logic alone.

logistic system See FORMAL SYSTEM

logistics \lō-'jis-tiks, lə-'jis-tiks\ In military science, all the activities of armed-force units in support of combat units, including transport, supply, communications, and medical aid. The term, first used by HENRI JOMINI, ALFRED THAYER MAHAN, and others, was adopted by the U.S. military in World War I and gained currency in other nations in World War II. Its importance grew in the 20th century with the increasing complexity of modern warfare. The ability to mobilize large populations has escalated military demands for supplies and provisions, and sophisticated technology has added to the cost and intricacy of weapons, communications systems, and medical care, creating the need for a vast network of support systems. In World War II, for instance, only about three in 10 U.S. soldiers served in a combat role.

Logone River \lō-'gōn\ River, North Africa. The chief tributary of the CHARI RIVER of the Lake Chad basin in equatorial Africa, it drains northeastern Cameroon and Chad. It flows 240 mi (390 km) northwest to join the Chari at N'DJAMENA, Chad. It is seasonally navigable below Bongor.

logos (Greek: "word," "reason," "plan") In Greek philosophy and theology, the divine reason that orders the cosmos and gives it form and meaning. The concept is found in the writings of HERACLEITUS (6th century BC) and in Persian, Indian, and Egyptian philosophical and theological systems as well. It is particularly significant in Christian theology, where it is used to describe the role of JESUS as the principle of God active in the creation and ordering of the cosmos and in the revelation of the divine plan of salvation. This is most clearly stated in the Gospel of JOHN the Apostle, which identifies Christ as the Word (Logos) made flesh.

Logroño \lə-'grō-nyō\ City (metro. area pop., 1995 est.: 125,000), capital of LA RIOJA autonomous community, Spain. Originating in Roman times, it owed its growth during the Middle Ages to its position on the pilgrimage route to SANTIAGO DE COMPOSTELA. An ancient walled town, it is a trade center in an agricultural region and is known for its Rioja wine.

Lohengrin \'lō-ən-ˌgrēn, *Engl* 'lō-ən-ˌgrin\ Hero-knight of medieval Germanic legends. He was called the knight of the swan because he arrived in a boat drawn by a swan to help a noble lady in distress. He married her but forbade her to ask his origin; when she forgot this promise, he left her, never to return. The first version of his legend appeared c. 1210 in WOLFRAM VON ESCHENBACH's *Parzival,* in which the swan knight was the son and heir of Parzival (PERCEVAL). The anonymous 15th-century epic *Lorengel* provided the basis for RICHARD WAGNER's opera *Lohengrin* (1850).

Loire River \'lwär\ River, southeastern France. The longest river in France, it flows north and west for 634 mi (1,020 km) to the Bay of BISCAY, which it enters through a wide estuary below St.-Nazaire. Embankments were built as early as the 12th century, and in subsequent centuries it was used extensively for the transport of goods. A canal system built in the 17th–18th century is inadequate for modern vessels.

L
M
N

loka \'lō-kə\ In HINDUISM, the universe or any particular division of it. The most common division of the universe is the *tri-loka,* or three worlds (heaven, earth, and atmosphere, or heaven, world, and netherworld), each of which is divided into seven regions. Sometimes, instead of the *tri-loka,* 14 worlds are envisioned, seven above the earth and seven below. Whatever the division, it illustrates the basic Hindu concept of hierarchically ordered worlds.

Loki \'lō-kē\ In Norse mythology, a trickster who was able to change his shape and sex. His father was the giant Fárbauti, but he was included among the AESIR, a tribe of the gods. A companion of the great gods ODIN and THOR, Loki helped them with his clever plans but sometimes embarrassed them. He also appeared as the enemy of the gods, entering their banquets uninvited and demanding drink. After causing the death of the god BALDER, he was punished by being bound to a rock. Loki created a female, Angerboda, with whom he produced three evil progeny: HEL, the goddess of death; Jörmungand, the evil serpent surrounding the world; and FENRIR, the wolf.

Lollards Followers of JOHN WYCLIFFE in late-medieval England. The pejorative name (from Middle Dutch, *lollaert:* "mumbler") had been applied earlier to European groups suspected of heresy. The first Lollard group centered on some of Wycliffe's colleagues at Oxford led by Nicholas of Hereford. In 1382 the archbishop of Canterbury forced some of the Oxford Lollards to renounce their views, but the sect continued to multiply. The accession of HENRY IV in 1399 signaled a wave of repression. In 1414 a Lollard rising was quickly defeated by HENRY V; it brought severe reprisals and marked the end of the Lollards' overt political influence. A Lollard revival began c. 1500, and by 1530 the old Lollard and the new Protestant forces had begun to merge. The Lollard tradition predisposed opinion in favor of HENRY VIII's anticlerical legislation. The Lollards were responsible for a translation of the Bible by Nicholas of Hereford.

Lomax \'lō-ˌmaks\, **John** (1867–1948) U.S. ethnomusicologist. Born in Goodman, Miss., he attended Harvard University and soon thereafter began publishing collections of cowboy songs. In the 1930s he and his teenage son Alan (born 1915) collected folk songs of the Southwest and Midwest. JELLY-ROLL MORTON, LEADBELLY, and M. WATERS were perhaps the most significant of their many important discoveries; the Lomaxes' archive of Morton's performance and storytelling was of particular significance. Both men did important work at the Library of Congress's Archive of Folk Music. Their many books and anthologies spurred the folk-music revival of the 1950s and '60s.

Lombard, Carole *orig.* **Jane Alice Peters** (1908–1942) U.S. film actress. Born in Fort Wayne, Ind., she made her screen debut in *A Perfect Crime* (1921) and appeared in comedy shorts from 1925. After starring in *Twentieth Century* (1934), she appeared in a series of popular screwball comedies, including *My Man Godfrey* (1936), *Nothing Sacred* (1937), *Mr. and Mrs. Smith* (1941), and *To Be or Not to Be* (1942). She married CLARK GABLE in 1939. She died in a plane crash while on tour to sell war bonds.

Lombard, Peter See PETER LOMBARD

Lombard League Italian league that resisted attempts by the Holy Roman emperors to curtail the liberties of the communes of Lombardy in northern Italy in the 12th–13th century. Founded in 1167, it was backed by Pope ALEXANDER III, who saw it as an ally against Emperor FREDERICK I BARBAROSSA. After several military setbacks at the hands of the league, Frederick was forced to grant the Lombard cities communal liberties and jurisdiction under the Peace of Constance. The league again was renewed in 1226 and resisted FREDERICK II's attempt to reassert imperial power in northern Italy.

Lombardi, Vince(nt Thomas) (1913–1970) U.S. football coach. Born in Brooklyn, N.Y., he attended Fordham Univ., where he played on the famous line known as the "Seven Blocks of Granite." As head coach and general manager of the Green Bay Packers (1959–67), he imposed a strenuous regimen on the disheartened players and led them to five NFL championships (1961, 1962, 1965, 1966, 1967) and to victories in Super Bowls I and II (1967, 1968). As coach, general manager, and part owner of the Washington Redskins in 1969, he led that team to its first winning season in 14 years. His career was cut short a year later by cancer.

Lombardo, Guy (Albert) (1902–1977) Canadian-U.S. bandleader. Born in London, Ontario, he trained as a violinist. In 1917 he formed his band the Royal Canadians. They began broadcasting nationally from Chicago in 1927, and from 1929 he was the winter attraction at New York's Roosevelt Grill, a booking repeated for more than 30 years. He later moved to the Waldorf-Astoria Hotel, continuing the famous New Year's Eve broadcasts, begun in 1954, that climaxed with "Auld Lang Syne." Though derided by critics as the "king of corn," Lombardo gained long-lasting popularity by conducting what was billed as "the sweetest music this side of heaven."

Lombards Germanic people who from 568 to 774 ruled a kingdom in the region of LOMBARDY. Originally a pastoral tribe from northwestern Germany, the Lombards migrated southward and adopted an imperial military system. In the 6th century they moved into northern Italy, conquering the cities that had been left defenseless after the overthrow of the OSTROGOTHS by the BYZANTINE EMPIRE. In the 8th century Liudprand, probably the greatest of the Lombard kings, steadily reduced the area of Italy still under Byzantine rule. When the Lombard kings invaded papal territories, Pope Adrian I sought aid from CHARLEMAGNE. In 773 the Franks besieged the Lombard capital, capturing Desiderius, the Lombard king; Charlemagne became king of the Lombards as well as of the Franks, and Lombard rule in Italy ended.

Lombardy \'läm-bər-dē\ Autonomous region (pop., 1996 est.: 8,925,000), northern Italy. Bounded on the north by Switzerland, it contains many alpine peaks as well as the fertile valley of the PO RIVER. Its capital is MILAN. Inhabited by Celtic peoples from the 5th century BC, it was conquered by Rome after the Second PUNIC WAR and became part of Cisalpine Gaul. In AD 568–774 it was the center of the kingdom of the Lombards. During the Middle Ages several of its towns became self-governing municipalities; they formed the LOMBARD LEAGUE in the 12th century and won autonomy by defeating FREDERICK I BARBAROSSA in 1176. The area was later ruled by Spain (1535–1713), Austria (1713–96), and France (1796–1814). In 1859 Lombardy joined the newly unified Italy. Italy's most populous region, it includes part of the country's northern industrial triangle, including GENOA, TURIN, and MILAN.

Lombok \'lȯm-ˌbȯk\ Island (pop., 1980: 1,960,000), Indonesia. It is one of the Lesser SUNDA ISLANDS, separated from BALI by the Lombok Strait and from SUMBAWA by the Alas Strait. It is 70 mi (115 km) long and 50 mi (80 km) wide and occupies an area of 2,098 sq mi (5,435 sq km). Divided by two mountain chains, its northern range includes Mount Rindjani (12,224 ft, or 3,726 m), Indonesia's tallest mountain. It was ruled by the sultan of Makasar in 1640. The Balinese later seized control and established four kingdoms there; the Dutch ruled the kingdom of Mataram from 1843 and gained control of the entire island by the late 19th century. Following World War II, it became part of Indonesia.

Lomé \lō-'mā\ City (metro. area pop., 1990 est.: 513,000), capital of Togo. Located on the Gulf of GUINEA in southwestern Togo, it was chosen as the capital of German Togoland in 1897 and developed as an administrative and commercial center. Its port was modernized in the 1960s, and its deepwater harbor is a major shipping center. An oil refinery was opened in 1978. It is the site of the University of Bénin (1965).

Loménie de Brienne \lō-mā-'nē-də-brē-'en\, **Étienne Charles de** (1727–1794) French ecclesiastic and minister of finance (1787–88) before the FRENCH REVOLUTION. Unable to cope with the worsening financial crisis, he resigned in favor of JACQUES NECKER. Made archbishop of Sens and then cardinal (1788), he was one of the few prelates who took the oath to the CIVIL CONSTITUTION OF THE CLERGY (1790). He died in prison during the REIGN OF TERROR.

Lomond \'lō-mənd\, **Loch** Lake, Scotland. The country's largest lake, and located at the southern edge of the Highlands, it is 24 mi (39 km) long and 0.75 to 5 mi (1.2 to 8 km) wide, and occupies an area of 27 sq mi (70 sq km). It drains by the short River Leven into the Firth of CLYDE at Dumbarton. Its eastern shore near Ben Lomond is the region made famous by the outlaw ROB ROY.

Lomonosov \lə-ˌmə-'nȯ-səf\, **Mikhail Vasilyevich** (1711–1765) Russian scientist, poet, and grammarian, considered the first great Russian linguistic reformer. Educated in Russia and Germany, he established what became the standards for Russian verse in the *Letter Concerning the Rules of Russian Versification.* In 1745 he joined the faculty at the St. Petersburg Imperial Academy of Sciences, where he made substantial contributions to the physical sciences. He later wrote a Russian grammar and worked to systematize the Russian literary language, which had been an amalgam of church Slavic and Russian vernacular. He also reorganized the academy, founded Moscow State University (which now bears his name), and created the first colored-glass mosaics in Russia.

Lon Nol (1913–1985) Cambodian military and political leader. A magistrate in the French colonial service, he became successively head of the national police (1951), later army chief of staff (1955), and commander in chief (1960). He was twice premier (1966–67, 1969–70) under Norodom Sihanouk. In 1970 he was the chief architect of the U.S.-supported coup that deposed Sihanouk. He abandoned Sihanouk's policy of neutrality in the Vietnam War and threw Cambodia's support behind the U.S. and South Vietnam. In 1972 he assumed total power in Cambodia; he fled to the U.S. in 1975 when the Khmer Rouge takeover was imminent.

London Capital and largest city (metro. area pop., 1999: 7,285,000), United Kingdom, situated in southeastern England on the River Thames. Inner London includes the original City of London and 13 of London's 33 boroughs; Greater London, includes all 33 boroughs. Founded by the Romans as Londinium in the 1st century AD, it passed to the Saxons in the 6th century. City fortifications were destroyed by the Danes, who invaded England in 865, but were later rebuilt. William I the Conqueror established the central stronghold of the fortress known as the Tower of London. Norman kings selected Westminster as their seat of government, and Edward the Confessor built the church known as Westminster Abbey. The largest city in Europe north of the Alps by 1085, it was struck by the Black Death in 1348–49. In the mid-16th century it saw important growth in trade, fueled by the establishment of Britain's overseas empire. In 1664–65 the plague killed about 70,000 Londoners, and in 1666 the Great Fire of London consumed five-sixths of the City; it was afterwards rebuilt (see Christopher Wren). It was the center of world trade from the late 18th century to 1914. It opened the world's first electric underground railway in 1890. It was severely damaged by German bombs in the Battle of Britain during World War II. Among its sites of interest are Buckingham Palace, the Tate Gallery, the National Gallery, the British Museum, and the Victoria and Albert Museum.

London City (metro. area pop., 2001: 432,451), southeastern Ontario. It lies on the Thames River, near several of the Great Lakes. Its name and site were chosen in 1792 for the location of a capital of Upper Canada, but the plans failed to materialize. First settled in 1826, it was incorporated as a city in 1855. It became an important transportation and industrial center as a result of its interlake location. It is the seat of the University of Western Ontario.

London, Great Fire of See Great Fire of London

London, Great Plague of See Great Plague of London

London, Jack *orig.* **John Griffith Chaney** (1876–1916) U.S. novelist and short-story writer. Born to poverty and illegitimacy in San Francisco, the largely self-educated London became a sailor, hobo, Alaskan gold miner, and militant socialist. He gained a wide audience with his first book, *The Son of the Wolf* (1900), and the story "To Build a Fire" (1908). Thereafter he wrote steadily; his 50 books of fiction and nonfiction, including many romantic depictions of elemental struggles for survival as well as socialist tracts, include *The Call of the Wild* (1903), *The Sea-Wolf* (1904), *White Fang* (1906), *The Iron Heel* (1907), *Martin Eden* (1909), and *Burning Daylight* (1910). Though his work brought him wealth and fame, his suicide at 40 was the result of alcoholism and mounting debt.

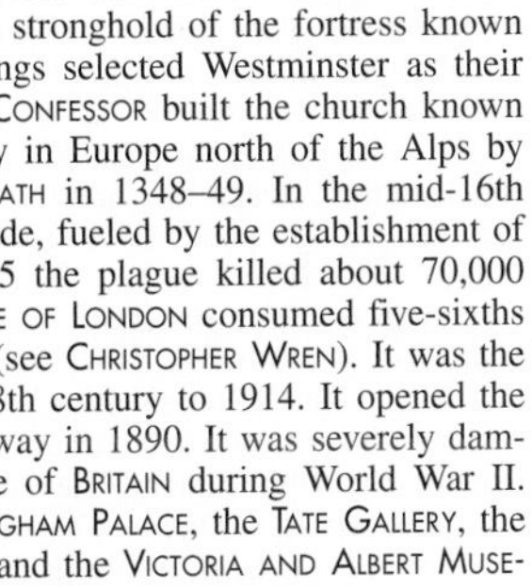

Jack London writing *The Sea Wolf*, 1903.
JACK LONDON STATE HISTORIC PARK

London, Treaty of (April 1915) Secret treaty between neutral Italy and the Allied forces of France, Britain, and Russia to bring Italy into World War I. The Allies wanted Italy's participation because of its border with Austria. Italy was promised Trieste, southern Tyrol, northern Dalmatia, and other territories in return for a pledge to enter the war within a month. Despite the opposition of most Italians, who favored neutrality, Italy joined the war against Austria-Hungary in May.

London, University of Federation of more than 50 British institutions of higher learning, located primarily in London. It was established by liberals and religious dissenters in 1828, and accepted for enrollment Roman Catholics, Jews, and other non-Anglicans. The first two colleges were University College and King's College. From 1849 a student enrolled in any university in the British Empire could be awarded a University of London degree after examination. By the early 20th century many institutions had become affiliated with the university, including Bedford College, the first British university to grant degrees to women; the London School of Economics and Political Science, now an internationally renowned center for the social sciences; and three other institutions that later became the Imperial College of Science and Technology. Total enrollment is about 95,000.

London Bridge Any of several successive structures spanning the River Thames. The Old London Bridge of nursery-rhyme fame was built by Peter of Colechurch between 1176 and 1209, replacing an earlier timber bridge. Because of obstructions encountered in building the cofferdams, the arch spans varied from 15 to 34 ft (4.6–10.4 m); the uneven construction resulted in frequent need for repair, but the bridge survived more than 600 years. Its roadway was loaded with a jumble of houses and shops, many projecting out over the river. It was demolished and replaced in the 1820s by New London Bridge, designed and built by John Rennie, Sr. (1761–1821), and his son John Rennie, Jr. (1794–1874). In the 1960s it was again replaced; the old masonry facing was dismantled and reerected at Lake Havasu City, Ariz., as a tourist attraction.

London Co. British trading company chartered by James I in 1606 to colonize the eastern American coast. Its shareholders were London men. Three ships with 120 colonists, led by John Smith, reached Virginia in 1607 and founded Jamestown. The company expanded its territory with new charters (1609, 1612) and authorized a two-part legislature (1619), including a House of Burgesses. Though the colony prospered, the company was divided by internal disputes and was dissolved in 1624, whereupon Virginia became a royal colony. See also Plymouth Co.

London Naval Conference (January 21–April 22, 1930) Conference held in London to discuss naval disarmament and review the treaties of the Washington Conference. Representatives of Britain, the U.S., France, Italy, and Japan agreed to regulate submarine warfare and to place limits on new construction of cruisers, destroyers, submarines, and other warships. A treaty limiting battleship size was not signed, and the treaties renewed in 1935 were canceled on the outbreak of World War II.

London Stock Exchange London marketplace for securities. It was formed in 1773 by a group of stockbrokers who had been doing business informally in local coffeehouses. In 1801 its members raised money for construction of a building in Bartholomew Lane; they established rules for the exchange the following year. In 1973 the London Stock Exchange merged with several regional British stock exchanges. It is governed by a council of its members and is not subject to government regulation.

Londonderry See Derry (district), Derry (town)

Long, Huey (Pierce) (1893–1935) U.S. politician. Born near Winnfield, La., he practiced law and became railroad commissioner at 25. His call for state regulation of utilities and attacks on Standard Oil Co. won him widespread popularity. Elected governor (1928–31), he became known for his fiery oratory and unconventional behavior, and was nicknamed "Kingfish." He implemented public-works projects and education reform, but used autocratic methods to control state government, including state appointments to educational, police,

Huey Long.
UPI

and fire jobs as well as the state militia, judiciary, and election and tax-assessing apparatus. Elected to the U.S. Senate (1932–35), he sought national power with a Share-the-Wealth program at the height of the GREAT DEPRESSION. In 1935 he was assassinated by Carl A. Weiss, whose father Long had vilified. His brother Earl K. Long (1895–1960) later served as governor (1939–40, 1948–52, 1956–60).

Long Beach City (pop., 2000: 461,522), southwestern California. Originally an Indian trading camp, the site was part of Spanish ranches in the 18th century. Laid out as Willmore City in 1881 and incorporated in 1888, it was renamed for its 8.5-mi (13.5-km) beach. The discovery of oil nearby in 1921 led to rapid growth. An earthquake in 1933 caused extensive damage. Connected to the LOS ANGELES harbor by the Cerritos Channel, it is the site of a U.S. naval station and shipyard. The British ocean liner *Queen Mary* has been moored in the harbor since 1969.

long-distance running In TRACK AND FIELD (athletics), foot races ranging from 5,000 m through 10,000, 20,000, 25,000, and 30,000 m and up to the MARATHON, as well as CROSS-COUNTRY RUNNING. Women rarely ran in races beyond 3,000 m until recent decades, but became frequent marathon competitors from the 1970s.

Long Island Island (pop., 2000: 7,448,618), southeastern New York, lying between LONG ISLAND SOUND and the Atlantic Ocean. It has four counties: Kings, Queens, Nassau, and Suffolk. Kings Co. (the borough of BROOKLYN) and Queens Co. (the borough of QUEENS) form part of NEW YORK CITY. At its western end it is separated from the BRONX and MANHATTAN by the EAST RIVER and from STATEN ISLAND by the Narrows. It is 118 mi (190 km) long, 12-23 mi (19-37 km) wide, and has an area of 1,401 sq mi (3,629 sq km). Its eastern portion has many beaches; it serves as a recreation area for New York City. Its southern shore, lined by sand spits (see FIRE ISLAND) shelters several bays, including JAMAICA BAY. Originally inhabited by Indians (mostly Delaware), it was included in a grant to the PLYMOUTH CO. It was settled by Dutch and English, but the whole island became part of the British colony of New York in 1664. It was the site of the Battle of Long Island (August 27, 1776), an American defeat in the AMERICAN REVOLUTION.

Long Island Sound Body of water between the southern shore of Connecticut and the northern shore of LONG ISLAND, New York. It connects with the East River and with Block Island Sound. Covering 1,180 sq mi (3,056 sq km), it is 90 mi (145 km) long and 3-20 mi (5-32 km) wide. Its shores have many residential communities and summer resorts.

long jump *or* **broad jump** TRACK-AND-FIELD sport consisting of a horizontal jump for distance. It was formerly performed from both standing and running starts, as separate events, but the standing long jump is no longer included in major competitions. The running long jump was an event in the OLYMPIC GAMES of 708 BC and in the modern Games from 1896. In 1935 JESSE OWENS set a record of 8.13 m (26.6 ft) that was not broken until 1960, and Bob Beamon of the U.S. held the record of 8.90 m (29.2 ft) from 1968 until 1991. In 1948 the women's long jump became an Olympic event.

Long March (1934–35) Trek of 6,000 mi (10,000 km) by Chinese Communists, resulting in the relocation of their revolutionary base from southeastern China to northwestern China and the emergence of MAO ZEDONG as their undisputed leader. Having withstood four of CHIANG KAI-SHEK's campaigns against their base area, the Communists were nearly defeated by his fifth attack. The remaining 85,000 troops broke through Nationalist lines and fled first westward under ZHU DE and then north under Mao. By the time Mao arrived at Shaanxi, he was followed by only about 8,000 survivors, most of the rest having been killed by fighting, disease, and starvation (among the casualties were Mao's two children and a brother). At their new base the Communists were able to build up their strength at a safe remove from the Nationalists in preparation for their eventual victory in 1949.

Long Parliament Session of the English Parliament summoned in November 1640 by CHARLES I, so named to distinguish it from the Short Parliament of April–May 1640. Charles called the session to raise the money needed for his war against the Scots. Resistant to Charles's demands, the Parliament caused the king's advisers to resign and passed an act forbidding its own dissolution without its members' consent. Tension between the king and Parliament increased until the ENGLISH CIVIL WAR broke out in 1642. After the king's defeat (1646), the army, led by THOMAS PRIDE, exercised political power and in 1648 expelled all but 60 members of the Long Parliament. The remaining group, called the Rump, brought Charles to trial and execution (1649); it was forcibly ejected in 1653. After OLIVER CROMWELL's protectorate, the Parliament was reestablished in 1659 and, with those excluded in 1648 restored to membership, it dissolved itself in 1660.

longbow Leading missile weapon of the English from the 14th century into the 16th century. Probably of Welsh origin, it was usually 6 ft (2 m) tall and shot arrows more than a yard long. The best were made of YEW, might require a force of 100 lbs (45 kg) to draw, and had an effective range of 200 yards (180 m). English archers used longbows in the HUNDRED YEARS' WAR, and the weapon played an important role in the battles of CRÉCY, Poitiers, and AGINCOURT. See also BOW AND ARROW, CROSSBOW.

Longfellow, Henry Wadsworth (1807–1882) U.S. poet. Born in Portland, Mass. (now in Maine), Longfellow graduated from Bowdoin College and traveled in Europe before joining the modern-language faculties of Bowdoin (1829–35) and Harvard (1836–54). His *Voices of the Night* (1839), containing "The Psalm of Life" and "The Light of the Stars," first won him popularity. *Ballads and Other Poems* (1841), including "The Wreck of the Hesperus" and "The Village Blacksmith," swept the nation, as did his long poem *Evangeline* (1847). With *Hiawatha* (1855), *The Courtship of Miles Standish* (1858), and *Tales of a Wayside Inn* (1863), including "Paul Revere's Ride," he became the best-loved American poet of the 19th century. He later translated DANTE's *Divine Comedy* (1867) and published his intended masterpiece, *Christus*, a trilogy on Christianity (1872). The hallmarks of his verse are gentleness, simplicity, and an idealized vision of the world.

Longfellow.
HISTORICAL PICTURES SERVICE, CHICAGO

longhair Generic term for any member of breeds of DOMESTIC CATS noted for their long, soft, flowing coat. Longhair breeds include Balinese, Birman, Cymric, Himalayan, Javanese, Norwegian forest cat, MAINE COON CAT, PERSIAN, Ragdoll, Somali, and TURKISH ANGORA. Though considered more lethargic than shorthair cats, longhairs are, like shorthairs, noted for playfulness, affection, and the ability to defend themselves if necessary.

Longhi \ˈlōŋ-gē\, **Pietro** *orig.* **Pietro Falca** (1700/02–1785) Italian painter. Son of a Venetian goldsmith, he studied painting in Bologna and thereafter became known for his scenes of everyday life among Venice's upper class and bourgeoisie. Popular for their charm, these genre paintings manifest the interest in social observation characteristic of the Enlightenment. He also painted landscapes and portraits.

longhouse Traditional communal dwelling of the IROQUOIS Indians until the 19th century. The longhouse was a rectangular box built out of poles, with doors at each end and saplings stretched over the top to form the roof, the whole structure being covered with bark. It was about 20 ft (6 m) wide and could be more than 200 ft (60 m) in length, depending on the number of families living in it. Down the middle of the house were fires, which were shared by families on either side. The term is also applied today to an Iroquois building designated as church and meeting hall, though its form is entirely different. See also POLE CONSTRUCTION.

longitude See LATITUDE AND LONGITUDE

Longmen caves *or* **Lung-men caves** Series of Chinese cave temples carved into the rock of a high riverbank south of Luoyang, in HENAN province. Construction began late in the NORTHERN WEI DYNASTY (AD 386–535) and continued sporadically through the 6th century and the TANG DYNASTY. Delicately crafted to create ethereal effects in stone, the temples contain images of the BUDDHA clothed as a Chinese scholar. Work at Longmen culminated in 672–75 with the construction of a monumental shrine known as Fengxian Si, which includes a seated Buddha more than 35 ft. (10.7 m) high.

Longshan culture *or* **Lung-shan culture** (2500–1900 BC) Neolithic culture of China's Huang (Yellow) River valley. Large sites with rammed-earth walls have been found. Characteristic Longshan pottery has thin walls and is well crafted; there are tall-stemmed black cups with eggshell-thin walls as well as polished black beakers. Oracle bones were used for divination. There is evidence of differentiation in social status, and jade artifacts and traces of metallurgy have been found.

longship *or* **Viking ship** Sail-and-oar vessel widely used in northern Europe for more than 1,500 years. It was a 45–75-ft (14–23-m) GALLEY with up to 10 oars on a side, a square sail, and a 50–60-man capacity. Double-ended and built with overlapped planks, it was exceptionally sturdy in high seas. Examples have been found from as early as 300 BC. It carried the Vikings on their piratical raids of the 9th century and bore LEIF ERIKSSON to America in 1000. Dutch, French, English, and German merchants and warriors also used it.

Longstreet, James (1821–1904) U.S. army officer. Born in Edgefield District, S.C., he graduated from West Point but resigned from the U.S. Army when South Carolina seceded. Appointed brigadier general in the Confederate army, he fought in the battles of Bull Run, Antietam, and Fredericksburg. He was second in command to ROBERT E. LEE at the Battle of GETTYSBURG, where his delay in attacking contributed to the Confederate defeat. He directed the attack at Chickamauga and was badly wounded in the Battle of the Wilderness but later resumed command. He surrendered with Lee at Appomattox. He later served as U.S. minister to Turkey (1880–81) and commissioner of Pacific railways (1898–1904).

Lönnrot \'lœn-rüt\, **Elias** (1802–1884) Finnish folklorist and philologist. While serving as a medical officer for 20 years in a remote part of eastern Finland, Lönnrot collected linguistic information and folk poetry from the region's inhabitants. Believing that the short poems were fragments of a continuous epic, he added connective material of his own and assembled them into the *KALEVALA* (1835, enlarged 1849), which became the Finnish national epic. He also published *Kanteletar* (1840–41; "Old Songs and Ballads of the Finnish People") and other collections.

Lonsdale, Kathleen *orig.* **Kathleen Yardley** *later* **Dame Kathleen** (1903–1971) British crystallographer. In 1929 her X-ray crystallography techniques established the regular hexagonal arrangement of carbon atoms in molecules of benzene compounds. She developed a technique with which she measured (to seven figures) the distance between carbon atoms in diamond. She also applied crystallographic techniques to medical problems, in particular the study of bladder stones and certain drugs. In 1945 she became the first woman elected to the Royal Society of London, and in 1956 she was created Dame of the British Empire.

loofah *or* **luffa** \'lü-fə\ Any of six species of annual climbing vines, also called vegetable sponge or sponge gourd, that make up the genus *Luffa* in the GOURD family, native to the Old World tropics. Two species cultivated in temperate areas *(L. acutangula* and *L. aegyptiaca)* produce 1-ft (30-cm) cucumber-shaped fruits. Edible and greenish when young, these fruits become straw-colored with age. On removal of the skin, pulp, and seeds, there remains a complex of closely netted vascular bundles (food- and water-carrying tubes) that resembles a sponge in texture. This spongelike product is used for bathing, for washing dishes, and as an industrial fiber.

loom Machine for WEAVING cloth. The earliest looms date from the 5th millennium BC and consist of bars or beams forming a frame to hold a number of parallel threads in two alternating sets. By raising one set of these threads (which together formed the warp), it was possible to run a cross thread (a weft, or filling) between them. A SHUTTLE carried the filling strand through the warp. The fundamental operation of the loom remained unchanged, but over centuries many improvements were introduced in both Asia and Europe. The drawloom, probably invented in Asia for SILK weaving, provided a means for raising warp threads in groups as required by a pattern. In the 18th century, JACQUES DE VAUCANSON and J.-M. JACQUARD mechanized this function by the ingenious use of punched cards; the cards programmed the mechanical drawboy, saving labor and eliminating errors (see JACQUARD LOOM). In England the inventions of JOHN KAY (FLYING SHUTTLE), EDMUND CARTWRIGHT (power drive), and others contributed to the INDUSTRIAL REVOLUTION, in which the loom and other TEXTILE machinery played a central role. See illustration above.

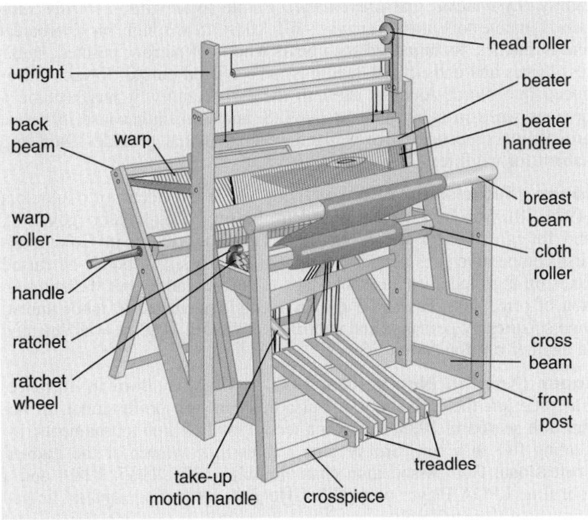

Principal parts of a traditional hand loom.

loon *or* **diver** Any of four species (genus *Gavia*) of diving birds of North America and Eurasia. Loons range in length from 2 to 3 ft (60–90 cm). They have small pointed wings, webs between the front three toes, legs placed far back on the body, making walking awkward, and thick plumage that is mainly black or gray above and white below. They feed mainly on fishes, crustaceans, and insects. Almost wholly aquatic, they can swim long distances underwater and can dive to a depth of 200 ft (60 m). They are generally found singly or in pairs, but some species winter or migrate in flocks. They are known for their eerie, "laughing" cries.

Common loon, or great northern diver (*Gavia immer*).

WAYNE LANKINEN–BRUCE COLEMAN LTD.

looper *or* **cankerworm** *or* **inchworm** LARVA of any member of a large, widespread group (mostly in the family Geometridae, with some in the family Noctuidae) of MOTHS. Loopers move in a characteristic "inching" or "looping" gait by extending the front part of the body and bringing the rear up to meet it. Resembling twigs or leaf stems, they feed on foliage, and can seriously damage or destroy trees.

Loos \'lōs\, **Adolf** (1870–1933) Austrian architect. Born in Moravia and educated in Dresden, he practiced in Vienna, though he spent extended periods in the U.S. and Paris. Opposed to both Art Nouveau and Beaux-Arts historicism, he announced as early as 1898 his intention to avoid the use of unnecessary ornament. His Steiner House, Vienna (1910), is a skillful composition of austere Cubistic forms. His best-known large structure is the Goldman and Salatsch Building (1910), in which a little Classical detail is offset by large areas of blank, polished marble.

Loos, Anita (1893–1981) U.S. novelist and screenwriter. Born in Sissons, Cal., she began as a child actress. She wrote many scenarios for silent films; her later screenwriting credits included *Blossoms in the Dust* (1941) and *I Married an Angel* (1942). *Gentlemen Prefer Blondes* (1925) brought fame to Loos and her central character, the naive gold digger Lorelei Lee; a musical version (1949) starred Carol Channing (born 1921), and a film (1953) starred MARILYN MONROE. Loos also wrote two memoirs, *A Girl Like I* (1966) and *Kiss Hollywood Good-Bye* (1974).

loosestrife Any ornamental plant of the family Lythraceae, especially in the genera *Lythrum* and *Decodon,* and two genera of the PRIMROSE family *(Lysimachia* and *Steironema).* Purple loosestrife *(Lythrum salicaria),* native to Eurasia, grows 2–6 ft (0.6–1.8 m) high on riverbanks and in ditches. Its branched stem bears whorls of narrow, pointed, stalkless leaves and ends in tall, tapering spikes of red-purple flowers. Introduced into North America early in the 19th century, it has become a noxious weed in many parts of the U.S. and Canada because its dense growth outcompetes native wetland vegetation that provides food and habitat for wildlife.

López (Michelsen), Alfonso (born 1913) President of Colombia (1974–78). Son of a former president, he served as senator, governor, and foreign minister before his 1974 landslide victory in Colombia's first competitive presidential election in 16 years. A liberal, he raised taxes on high incomes and took steps to curb inflation, but the elimination of price subsidies and a rise in unemployment led to labor unrest, land seizures by peasants, and guerrilla activity. In 1982 he was defeated in another run for the presidency.

Lopez (Knight), Nancy (born 1957) U.S. golfer. Born in Torrance, Cal., she left the University of Tulsa early to turn professional. In her first full season in 1978, she won a record total of nine tournaments, including five in a row. She became a three-time winner of the Ladies' Professional Golf Association championship (1978, 1985, 1989) and a four-time LPGA Player of the Year. Her success and personality helped rejuvenate women's golf.

López Portillo (y Pacheco) \'lō-ˌpez-pȯr-'tē-yō\, **José** (born 1920) President of Mexico (1976–82). He was a professor before joining the governments of Gustavo Díaz Ordaz (1911–1979) and Luis Echeverría (born 1922). As president, he emphasized foreign investment, tax concessions to stimulate industrial development, creation of nonagricultural jobs, and exploitation of oil and natural gas. His most significant political reform was to increase participation of minority parties, facilitating later challenges to the INSTITUTIONAL REVOLUTIONARY PARTY. Most of the wealth that flowed from expanded oil exports was squandered or pocketed by government and union officials. His administration was discredited by the huge foreign debt it amassed and charges of corruption. See also PEMEX.

loquat \'lō-ˌkwät\ Subtropical evergreen tree *(Eriobotrya japonica)* of the ROSE family, related to the APPLE and other well-known fruit trees of the temperate zone. Usually less than 33 ft (10 m) tall, it is common in parks and gardens, often trained to ornamental flatttened shapes by ESPALIER. Dense, fragrant, white flowers grow beyond clusters of leaves with serrated edges. The small yellow-orange fruits have a pleasant, mildly acid taste; they are eaten fresh, stewed, or as jelly or liqueur. The loquat is grown commercially (usually on a small scale) in many subtropical regions.

Loquat (*Eriobotrya japonica*).
G.R. ROBERTS

Lorca, Federico García See Federico GARCÍA LORCA

lord See FEUDALISM

Lord Chamberlain's Men See CHAMBERLAIN'S MEN

lord chancellor British official who heads the judiciary and presides over the House of LORDS. Until the 14th century the chancellor served as royal chaplain and king's secretary. The office acquired a more judicial character in the reign of Edward III (1327–77). Most of the office's power, exemplified in the administrations of ST. THOMAS BECKET (died 1170) and THOMAS, CARDINAL WOLSEY (died 1530), ceased to exist centuries ago. The judicial work of contemporary chancellors is confined to the House of Lords and the PRIVY COUNCIL. As speaker of the House of Lords, the chancellor states the question and takes part in debates.

Lord Dunmore's War (1774) Attack by Virginia militia on the SHAWNEE in Kentucky. The militiamen seized Fort Pitt on the western border, renaming it after their royal governor, Lord Dunmore, who had ordered attacks against the Shawnee, seen as a threat to white settlers then spreading into the Indian hunting grounds. Defeated at the Battle of Point Pleasant, the Shawnee signed a treaty giving up their hunting grounds. The war was probably started to divert Virginians from disagreements with royal administrators; as such, it has been called the first battle of the AMERICAN REVOLUTION.

Lorde \'lȯrd\, **Audre (Geraldine)** (1934–1992) U.S. poet and essayist. Born in New York City to West Indian parents, she worked as a librarian until 1968, when she began to write full-time. She is best known for her passionate writings on lesbian feminism and racial issues, including *Cables to Rage* (1970), *New York Head Shop and Museum* (1974), and *The Black Unicorn* (1978), often called her finest work. Her battle with cancer inspired *The Cancer Journals* (1980) and *A Burst of Light* (1988, National Book Award).

Lords, House of Upper house of Britain's bicameral PARLIAMENT. From the 13th–14th century it was the house of the aristocracy. Until 1999, its membership included clergy, hereditary peers, life peers (peers appointed by the prime minister since 1958), and the judges of the Supreme Court of Judicature (Britain's final court of appeal). Though it predates the House of COMMONS and dominated it for centuries, its power gradually diminished. Its powers to affect revenue bills were constrained by the PARLIAMENT ACT OF 1911, and the Parliament Act of 1949 revoked its power to delay enactment of any bill passed by the Commons by more than a year. In 1999 the hereditary peers lost their right to sit in the House of Lords, though an interim reform retains their voice in a more limited fashion. The body's chief value has been to provide additional consideration to bills that may be insufficiently formulated.

Lord's Prayer Prayer taught by JESUS to his disciples and used by all Christians as the basic prayer in common worship. It appears in two forms in the New Testament: a shorter version in Luke 11:2–4, and a longer version, part of the SERMON ON THE MOUNT, in Matthew 6:9–13. In both contexts it is offered as a model of how to pray. It is sometimes called the Pater Noster (Latin: "Our Father") for its first two words.

Lorelei \'lȯr-ə-ˌlī\ Rock on the bank of the RHINE RIVER near Sankt Goarshausen in Germany. It produces an echo and is associated with the legend of a beautiful maiden who drowned herself over a faithless lover. She was transformed into a SIREN who lured fishermen to their death. CLEMENS BRENTANO claimed to have invented the essentials of the legend. HEINRICH HEINE's poem on the Lorelei has been set to music by more than 25 composers.

Loren \lȯ-'ren\, **Sophia** *orig.* **Sofia Scicolone** (born 1934) Italian film actress. After a poverty-stricken childhood in war-torn Naples, she became a model and movie extra in Rome. Coached by the producer Carlo Ponti (later her husband), she acted in Italian movies from 1950, including *The Gold of Naples* (1954). Her later films, in which she became noted for her statuesque beauty and earthy femininity, include *The Black Orchid* (1959), *El Cid* (1961), *Two Women* (1961, Academy Award), *Boccaccio '70* (1962), *Yesterday, Today, and Tomorrow* (1964), *Marriage Italian Style* (1964), and *A Special Day* (1977).

Sophia Loren in *Boccaccio '70* (1962).
BROWN BROTHERS

Lorentz \'lōr-ˌents\, **Hendrik Antoon** (1853–1928) Dutch physicist. He taught at the University of Leiden 1878–1912, and later directed Haarlem's Teyler Institute. In 1875 he refined JAMES CLERK MAXWELL's theory of electromagnetic radiation so that it explained the reflection and refraction of light. Aiming to devise a single theory to explain the relationship of electricity, magnetism, and light, he later suggested that atoms might consist of charged particles that oscillate and produce light. In 1896 his student Pieter Zeeman (1865–1943) demonstrated this phenomenon (see ZEEMAN EFFECT), and in 1902 the two men were awarded the second Nobel Prize for Physics. In 1904 Lorentz developed the Lorentz transformations (including the so-called Fitzgerald-Lorentz contraction), mathematical formulas that relate space and time measurements of one observer to those of a second observer moving relative to the first. These formed the basis of ALBERT EINSTEIN's special theory of RELATIVITY.

Lorentz-FitzGerald contraction *or* **space contraction** In RELATIVITY physics, the shortening of an object along the direction of its motion relative to an observer. Dimensions in other directions are not contracted. This concept was proposed by the Irish physicist George F. FitzGerald (1851–1901) in 1889 and later independently developed by HENDRIK ANTOON LORENTZ. Significant at speeds approaching that of LIGHT, the contraction results from the properties of space and time, not from compression, cooling, or any similar physical disturbance. See also TIME DILATION.

Lorentz transformations Set of equations in RELATIVITY physics that relate the space and time coordinates of two systems moving at a constant speed relative to each other, developed in 1904 by HENDRIK ANTOON LORENTZ. Required to describe phenomena approaching the speed of LIGHT, these transformations express the concepts that space and time are not absolute; that length, time, and mass depend on the observer's relative motion; and that the speed of light in a vacuum is constant and independent of the motion of the observer or the source.

Lorenz, Edward (Norton) (born 1917) U.S. meteorologist. Born in West Hartford, Conn., he studied at Dartmouth and Harvard colleges and began teaching at MIT in 1946. In the 1960s he discovered that long-range weather forecasting is impossible. He showed that a simple model of heat convection possesses intrinsic unpredictability, a circumstance he called the butterfly effect, suggesting that the mere flapping of a butterfly's wing can change the weather. His ideas became basic to the emerging field of CHAOS THEORY.

Lorenz \'lōr-ents\, **Konrad (Zacharias)** (1903–1989) Austrian zoologist and founder (with NIKOLAAS TINBERGEN) of modern ETHOLOGY. While still a schoolboy he nursed sick animals from the nearby zoo. In 1935 he first elucidated and demonstrated the phenomenon of IMPRINTING in ducklings and goslings. He later examined the roots of human aggression (in the best-selling *On Aggression*, 1963) and the nature of human thought. His other popular works include *King Solomon's Ring* (1949) and *Man Meets Dog* (1950). He shared a 1973 Nobel Prize with Tinbergen and KARL VON FRISCH.

Lorenzetti \ˌlō-rānt-'set-tē\, **Pietro and Ambrogio** (fl. c. 1306–1345, c. 1317–1348) Italian painters. Both brothers were possibly pupils of DUCCIO di Buoninsegna, whose influence is seen in Pietro's altarpiece in the Pieve di Santa Maria at Arezzo and in Ambrogio's early works. Ambrogio's works reveal an individualistic realism and preoccupation with three-dimensional space and form, most evident in his fresco series in Siena's Palazzo Pubblico (1338–39). These most important of Sienese frescoes reveal him to be an explorer of perspective and a political and moral philosopher. His dramatic frescoes in the lower church of San Francesco at Assisi (c. 1315) show his relation to the art of GIOTTO, though he departs from Giotto in his attention to detail. His *Birth of the Virgin* and Ambrogio's *Presentation in the Temple,* for Siena Cathedral (1342), are notable for their handling of perspective. With SIMONE MARTINI, the brothers were the principal exponents of Sienese art in the years before the BLACK DEATH, in which both presumably died.

Lorenzo Monaco \lō-'rent-sō-'mō-nä-kō\ *orig.* **Piero di Giovanni** (c. 1370/75–c. 1425) Italian painter. He took the vows of the Camaldolese order in Florence in 1391 (Monaco means "Monk"), but in 1402 he was enrolled in the painters' guild there under his lay name and living outside the monastery. His work combined the graceful lines and decorative feeling of the Sienese school with the traditions of the Florentine school. His *Coronation of the Virgin* (1413) reveals his predilection for swirling draperies and rhythmic, curvilinear forms and his understanding of light. His late frescoes in the Bartolini Chapel of Santa Trinità in Florence establish him as a master of Gothic art.

Lorenzo the Magnificent See Lorenzo de' MEDICI

Lorestan Bronze See LURISTAN BRONZE

loris Any of three species of nocturnal, arboreal PRIMATES in the family Lorisidae. Lorises have soft gray or brown fur, huge eyes encircled by dark patches, and no tail. They move slowly and often hang by their feet, leaving their hands free to grasp branches or food. The slender loris *(Loris tardigradus)* of India and Sri Lanka is 8–10 in. (20–25 cm) long; it eats insects and small animals. The slow lorises (genus *Nycticebus)* of South Asia and the Malay Peninsula eat insects, small animals, fruit, and vegetation. *Nycticebus pygmaeus* is about 8 in. (20 cm) long; *N. coucang* is 10.5–15 in. (27–38 cm) long. Habitat degradation and hunting have seriously depleted loris populations.

Loris-Melikov \'lȯr-is-'myāl-i-kȯf\, **Mikhail (Tariyelovich), Count** (1826–1888) Russian military officer and statesman. He commanded an army corps to notable victories in the RUSSO-TURKISH WAR of 1877–78, for which he was made a count. As governor-general of the central Russian provinces (1879), he recommended administrative and economic reforms to alleviate social discontent. Impressed, ALEXANDER II appointed him minister of the interior (1880) and approved his efforts to liberalize the Russian autocracy, but the czar was assassinated before the reforms were enacted. Loris-Melikov resigned when ALEXANDER III rejected his reforms.

Lorrain, Claude See CLAUDE LORRAIN

Lorraine Duchy, western Europe. Originally known as Upper Lorraine, and later simply as Lorraine, it was formed by the division of LORRAINE (Lotharingia) into two duchies in 959. Upper Lorraine, in the region of the MEUSE and MOSELLE rivers, was ruled by one ducal family from the 11th century. METZ, Toul, and Verdun, outside the dukes' control, were seized by France in 1552. It came permanently under the French crown in 1766 and was divided into departments in 1790. After the FRANCO-PRUSSIAN WAR, part of it was ceded to Germany as part of ALSACE-LORRAINE.

Lorraine *or* **Lotharingia** \ˌlō-thə-'rin-jə\ Medieval region, present-day northeastern France. By the Treaty of VERDUN (843), it became part of the realm of LOTHAIR I. Inherited by his son Lothair, it became the kingdom of Lotharingia. After his death, it was contested by Germany and France, and came under German control in 925.

Lorre \'lȯr-ē\, **Peter** *orig.* **Laszlo Loewenstein** (1904–1964) Hungarian-U.S. film actor. He played bit parts with a German theatrical troupe before earning international fame as the psychotic murderer in the German film *M* (1931). He left Germany in 1933 and made his English-language debut in *The Man Who Knew Too Much* (1934). He went to Hollywood, where he played malevolent characters in such movies as *Mad Love* (1935), *The Maltese Falcon* (1941), *Casablanca* (1942), and *The Beast with Five Fingers* (1946). He also starred in the eight Mr. Moto detective movies (1937–39). He later directed and starred in the German film *The Lost One* (1951).

Los Alamos Town (pop., 2000: 11,909), northern central New Mexico. It lies on the Pajarito plateau of the Jemez Mtns., northwest of SANTA FE. The site was chosen by the U.S. government in 1942 as the location for the MANHATTAN PROJECT, which developed the first ATOMIC BOMB. After World War II, the Los Alamos Scientific Laboratory developed the first NUCLEAR FUSION bomb. The town was built to house laboratory employees; it is still the site of a major nuclear research facility.

Los Angeles City (pop., 2000: 3,694,820), southern California. The second largest city in the U.S., it is situated between the San Gabriel Mountains and the Pacific Ocean. Bisected by the Santa Monica Mtns., which separate the neighborhoods of HOLLYWOOD, BEVERLY HILLS, and Pacific Palisades from the SAN FERNANDO VALLEY, it is near the SAN ANDREAS FAULT and earthquakes are frequent. It began in 1771 as a Spanish mission; the city was established as El Pueblo de la Reyna de los Angeles (the Town of the Queen of the Angels) in 1781. Taken by U.S. forces in the MEXICAN WAR, it prospered in the wake of the 1849 GOLD RUSH. Incorporated in 1850, the city grew rapidly after the arrival of the railroads in 1876 and 1885. In 1913 an aqueduct was built to supply it with water from the slopes of the SIERRA NEVADA. It was struck by a major earthquake in 1994. Sites of interest include early Spanish missions, the GETTY MUSEUM, the Los Angeles Co. Museum of Art, and the Museum of Contemporary Art. Educational institutions include the University of SOUTHERN CALIFORNIA, OCCIDENTAL COLLEGE, and the University of CALIFORNIA at Los Angeles.

Los Angeles Times Morning daily newspaper. Established in 1881, it was purchased and incorporated in 1884 by Harrison Gray Otis (1837–1917) under The Times-Mirror Co. It prospered and became a power in conservative politics in California. It was long dominated by the Chandler family, beginning with Otis's son-in-law, Harry Chandler, in 1917. After Otis Chandler became publisher in 1960, its editorial policies changed; it developed from an ultraconservative regional paper into a model of balanced, fair, and comprehensive journalism and was recognized as one of the world's great newspapers.

Los Glaciares National Park \,lòs-glä-'syär-rās\ National park, southwestern Argentina. Located in the ANDES at the Chilean border, it was established in 1937, and has an area of 625 sq mi (1,618 sq km). It has two distinct regions: forests and grassy plains in the east, and peaks, lakes, and glaciers in the west. Its highest point is Mount Fitzroy (11,073 ft, or 3,375 m).

Lost Generation Group of U.S. writers who came of age during World War I and established their reputations in the 1920s; more broadly, the entire post–World War I American generation. The term was coined by GERTRUDE STEIN in a remark to ERNEST HEMINGWAY. The writers considered themselves "lost" because their inherited values could not operate in the postwar world and they felt spiritually alienated from a country they considered hopelessly provincial and emotionally barren. The term embraces Hemingway, F. SCOTT FITZGERALD, JOHN DOS PASSOS, E.E. CUMMINGS, ARCHIBALD MACLEISH, and HART CRANE, among others.

lost-wax casting Traditional method of producing MOLDS for METAL SCULPTURE and other CASTINGS. It requires a positive, a core made of refractory material and an outer layer of wax. The positive can be produced either by direct modeling in wax over a prepared core (direct lost-wax casting), or by casting in a piece mold or flexible mold taken from a master cast. The wax positive is invested with a mold made of refractory materials and heated to melt the wax, leaving a narrow cavity between the core and the investment. Molten metal is poured into this cavity. When the metal has solidified, the investment and core are broken away. See also INVESTMENT CASTING.

Lot Nephew of ABRAHAM. He emigrated with Abraham from Ur to CANAAN and settled in Sodom, a city so evil that God decided to destroy it. Warned by angels of the coming disaster, Lot fled the city with his family. His wife disobeyed God's orders by looking back at the burning city and was turned into a pillar of salt. Lot later had children by his own daughters, and they became the founders of the Moabite and Ammonite nations, enemies of Israel. See also SODOM AND GOMORRAH.

Lot River River, southern France. It flows 300 mi (480 km) west to join the GARONNE RIVER near Aiguillon, and in its course passes Cahors, the old capital of QUERCY. It is navigable for part of its course, but has little boat traffic.

Lothair I \'lō-tär\ *German* **Lothar** (795–855) Frankish emperor. The eldest son of LOUIS I THE PIOUS, he was crowned king in Bavaria (814) and coemperor with Louis (817). He led a revolt against his father and deposed him (833), but Louis was restored to power the next year, and Lothair's rule was restricted to Italy. On his father's death (840) he attempted to gain sole control over the Frankish territories, but his brothers, Louis the German and CHARLES II THE BALD, defeated him (841). The Treaty of VERDUN gave Lothair the middle realm, or heartland, of the Frankish dominions, from the North Sea to Italy, and the imperial title.

Lothair I, miniature from his psalter, 9th century; in the British Library (MS. Add. 37768).

Lothair II *German* **Lothar** (1075–1137) German king (1125–37) and Holy Roman Emperor (1133–37). The most powerful noble in Saxony, he took part in revolts (1112–15) against the German king Henry V. Elected king on Henry's death, he fought a war against the HOHENSTAUFENS who claimed the throne (1125–29); his victory was a triumph for elective monarchy over hereditary succession. Lothair was crowned emperor as a reward for supporting Pope Innocent II (1133). He made peace with the Hohenstaufens (1135) but attacked ROGER II of Sicily, driving him out of southern Italy (1136–37) for a time.

Lotharingia See LORRAINE

Loti \lō-'tē\, **Pierre** *orig.* **Louis-Marie-Julien Viaud** (1850–1923) French novelist. As a naval officer, Loti visited the Middle East and East Asia, which later provided the exotic settings of his novels and reminiscences. His first novel, *Aziyadé* (1879), won him critical and popular success. Other novels include *An Iceland Fisherman* (1886), *Japan: Madam Chrysanthemum* (1887), and *Disenchanted* (1906). Among his recurring motifs are love, death, and despair at the passing of sensuous life. He reveals his compassion in such works as *The Book of Pity and of Death* (1890). His themes anticipated some of the preoccupations of French literature between the world wars.

lottery Drawing of lots in which prizes are distributed to the winners among persons buying a chance. A form of GAMBLING, lottery in its modern form may be traced to 15th-century Europe. The Continental Congress in 1776 voted to establish a lottery to raise funds for the American Revolution. By the mid-19th century, in the wake of abuses by private organizers, U.S. states began passing antilottery laws. An 1878 Supreme Court opinion held that lotteries had "a demoralizing influence upon the people," and by the 1890s most had been eliminated. A revival began in the mid-1960s; many state governments seeking revenues instituted officially sanctioned, independently audited lotteries. In most such operations, the bettor buys a numbered receipt or writes down his or her number choices, a drawing is held, and the winners identify themselves. The value of the prizes is the amount remaining after expenses and the state's share are deducted from the pool. Winnings are usually subject to taxes. The top prize can grow into the tens of millions, usually causing a buying frenzy as it increases, but the odds against winning remain astronomical.

Lotto, Lorenzo (c. 1480–1556) Italian painter. Born in Venice, he worked in several other cities as well and developed an idiosyncratic style. His work exhibits a preference for opulent colors and a faculty for narrative painting. His nervous temperament is evident in such works as the *Crucifixion* in Monte San Giusto (c. 1530), with its highly charged mysticism and crowded composition. Toward the end of his life (1554), he became a lay brother at the Santa Casa in Loreto to escape his critics and his debts. Though primarily a religious painter, he is best known today for his psychologically acute portraits.

lotus Any of several different plants. The lotus of the Greeks was *Ziziphus lotus* (family Rhamnaceae), a shrub native to southern Europe; wine made from its fruit was thought to produce contentment and forgetfulness. The Egyptian lotus is a white WATER LILY *(Nymphaea lotus)*. The sacred lotus of the Hindus is an aquatic plant *(Nelumbo nucifera)* with white or delicate pink flowers; the lotus of eastern North America is *Nelumbo pentapetala,* a similar plant with yellow blossoms. *Lotus* is also a genus of the pea family (see LEGUME), containing about 100 species found in temperate regions of Europe, Asia, Africa, and North America; the 20 or more species in North America are grazed by animals. The lotus is a common ornament in architecture, and since ancient times it has symbolized fertility, purity, sexuality, birth, and rebirth of the dead.

Lotus Sutra Text central to the Japanese Tendai (Chinese TIANTAI) and NICHIREN sects of MAHAYANA Buddhism. It represents the BUDDHA as divine and eternal, having attained perfect enlightenment eons ago. All beings are invited to become fully enlightened Buddhas through the grace of innumerable BODHISATTVAS. Composed largely in verse, the sutra contains many charms and MANTRAS. First translated into Chinese in the 3rd century AD, it was extremely popular in China and Japan, where the simple act of chanting it was thought to bring salvation.

Lou Gehrig's disease See AMYOTROPHIC LATERAL SCLEROSIS

loudspeaker *or* **speaker** In SOUND reproduction, device for converting electrical energy into acoustical (sound) signal energy that is radiated into a room or open air (see ACOUSTICS). The part of the speaker that converts electrical into mechanical energy is frequently called the motor, or voice coil. The motor vibrates a diaphragm that vibrates the air in immediate contact with it, producing a sound wave corresponding to the pattern of the original speech, music, or other acoustic signal. See illustration opposite on following page.

Louganis \lü-'gā-nəs\, **Greg(ory Efthimios)** (born 1960) U.S. diver, considered the greatest diver in history. Born in San Diego, he was trained early in dancing, tumbling, and acrobatics. During his diving career, he won an unprecedented 47 national and 13 world championships, including two Olympic gold medals (1984) and one silver (1976). In 1982 he became the first diver ever to earn a perfect score of 10, and the following year he received 99 points in springboard competition. He was known for his graceful, effortless style. In 1994 he revealed that he was gay and the following year announced that he had AIDS.

Lough Erne See Lough ERNE

Lough Neagh See Lough NEAGH

Louis, Joe *orig.* **Joseph Louis Barrow** (1914–1981) U.S. heavyweight boxing champion. He was born into a sharecropper's family in Lexington, Ala. He began boxing after his family moved to Detroit. He won the U.S. Amateur Athletic Union title in 1934 and turned professional that year. On the road to his first title bout he defeated six previous or subsequent champions, including Max Baer, Jack Sharkey, James J. Braddock, Max Schmeling, and Jersey Joe Walcott. Nicknamed "the Brown Bomber," he gained the title by defeating Braddock in 1937, and held it until 1949. He lost to Schmeling in 1936 but defeated him in one round in 1938. He successfully defended his title 25 times (21 by knockout) before retiring in 1949. He made unsuccessful comeback attempts against Ezzard Charles in 1950 and ROCKY MARCIANO in 1951.

Louis, Morris *orig.* **Morris Louis Bernstein** (1912–1962) U.S. painter. Born in Baltimore, he studied painting at the Maryland Institute and worked as an easel painter for the WPA FEDERAL ART PROJECT. Inspired by HELEN FRANKENTHALER's color stain technique, in 1954 he began a series of paintings titled *Veils*, featuring stained vertical waves of color; the desired effects were an impersonal, nonpainterly quality and isolated visual elements of color. His later work featured diagonal parallel streams of color that flowed across the bottom corners of the picture plane. In his last series, *Stripes*, bunched, straight vertical bands of color are surrounded by empty canvas.

Louis I \'lü-ē\ *known as* **Louis the Pious** (778–840) Frankish emperor (814–40). The son of CHARLEMAGNE, he was crowned coemperor with his father in 813 and became emperor in 814 on his father's death. By dividing his lands among his nephew Bernard and his four sons—Lothair (later LOTHAIR I), Pepin, Louis the German, and Charles (CHARLES THE BALD)—he only increased their appetite for power, manifested in a series of revolts beginning in 817. Twice deposed by his sons, he recovered the throne each time (830, 834), but at his death the Carolingian empire was in disarray.

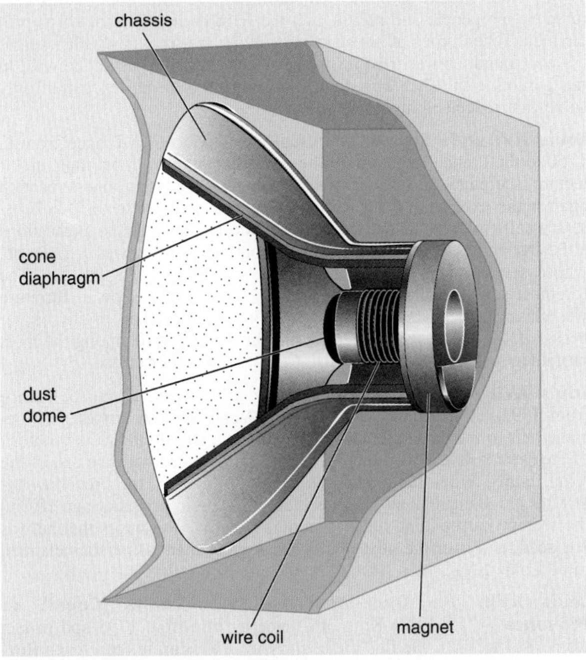

Components of a loudspeaker. Electrical signals sent through the coil cause it to act as an electromagnet, which is alternately repelled by or attracted to the permanent magnet. This movement causes the cone diaphragm to vibrate, creating sound waves.

Louis IV *or* **Ludwig IV** *known as* **Louis the Bavarian** (1283?–1347) German king (1314–47) and uncrowned Holy Roman Emperor (1328–47). As the Luxembourg candidate for emperor, he was opposed by the Habsburg candidate Frederick III of Austria. Both men were elected and crowned king in 1314, and Louis' forces defeated Frederick's army in 1322. A conflict with Pope JOHN XXII over the appointment of the imperial vicar in Italy led to his excommunication (1324). To placate his opponents Louis agreed to corule with Frederick, an arrangement that continued until Frederick's death (1330). He accepted the imperial crown from the Roman people instead of from the pope (1328) and backed the appointment of an ANTIPOPE. In 1346 Pope CLEMENT VI secured the election of a rival king, Charles of Moravia, and Louis died of a heart attack before finishing his preparations for war.

Louis VI *known as* **Louis the Fat** (1081–1137) King of France (1108–37). He was effective ruler of France well before the death of his father, Philip I, in 1108, and he spent much time in subduing the unruly French barons. He fought HENRY I of England (1104–13, 1116–20) and prevented a threatened invasion by Emperor Henry V (1124). He died a month after arranging his son's marriage to ELEANOR OF AQUITAINE, whereupon his son succeeded him as LOUIS VII.

Louis VII *known as* **Louis the Younger** (c. 1120–1180) King of France (1137–80). One of the CAPETIAN kings, he married ELEANOR OF AQUITAINE in 1137, thus temporarily extending his kingdom to the Pyrenees. Doubtful of her fidelity, he had the marriage annulled in 1152, and she married HENRY II of England. Henry then took control of Aquitaine, and Louis carried on a long rivalry with him (1152–74) marked by recurrent warfare and constant intrigue. Louis was joined by CONRAD III in leading the Second CRUSADE against the Turks (1147–49).

Louis IX *or* **St. Louis** (1214–1270) King of France (1226–70). He inherited the throne at age 12. His mother served as regent until 1234, helping to subdue rebellious barons and Albigensian heretics. Louis led the Seventh CRUSADE (1248–50) in hopes of regaining Jerusalem and Damascus, but his troops were badly defeated by the Egyptians. On his return he reorganized the royal administrative system and standardized coinage. He built the extraordinary Sainte-Chapelle to house a religious relic. He made peace with the English in the Treaty of PARIS (1259), allowing HENRY III to keep Aquitaine and neighboring lands but obliging him to declare himself Louis's vassal. He died of plague in Tunisia during a crusade. The most popular of the CAPETIAN kings, his reputation for justness and piety led the French to venerate him as a saint even before his canonization in 1297.

Louis XI (1423–1483) King of France (1461–83). He plotted against his father, Charles VII, and was exiled to DAUPHINÉ (1445), which he ruled as a sovereign state until Charles approached its borders with an army (1456). Louis then fled to the Netherlands, returning to France to become king on his father's death in 1461. He fought rebellious French princes (1465) and made concessions to CHARLES THE BOLD (1468). Seeking to strengthen and unify France, he destroyed the power of the Burgundians in 1477. He regained control of Boulonnais, Picardy, and Burgundy, took possession of Franche-Comté and Artois (1482), annexed Anjou (1471), and inherited Maine and Provence (1481).

Louis XII (1462–1515) King of France (1498–1515). He became king on the death of his cousin CHARLES VIII. He annulled his marriage to marry Charles's widow, ANNE OF BRITTANY, and reinforce the union of her duchy with France. He continued France's part in the ITALIAN WARS, often with disastrous results. He conquered Milan in 1499, then lost it, but was later recognized as duke of Milan by Emperor MAXIMILIAN I. He concluded a treaty with FERDINAND V that partitioned Naples (1500), but the two kings went to war and Louis lost all of Naples (1504). In 1508 he consolidated the League of CAMBRAI, but when the league fell apart in 1510 its members joined England in a Holy League against France, invading it several times. Despite his failures, Louis was highly popular with the French, who called him the "Father of the People."

Louis XIII (1601–1643) King of France (1610–43). He was the son of HENRY IV and MARIE DE MÉDICIS. His mother was regent until 1614 but continued to govern until 1617; she arranged Louis's marriage to the Spanish ANNE OF AUSTRIA in 1615. Resentful of his mother's power, Louis exiled her, but Cardinal de RICHELIEU, her principal adviser, reconciled them in 1620. In 1624 Louis made Richelieu his principal minister; and the two cooperated closely to make France a leading European power, consolidating royal authority in France and fighting to break the dominant rule of the Spanish and Austrian Habsburgs in the THIRTY YEARS' WAR. Pro-Spanish Catholic zealots led by Marie de Médicis appealed to Louis to reject Richelieu's policy of supporting the Protestant states, but Louis stood by his minister and his mother withdrew into exile. France declared war on Spain in 1635, and had won substantial victories by the time Richelieu died in 1642. Louis was succeeded by his son LOUIS XIV.

Louis XIII style Style of the visual arts produced in France during the reign of LOUIS XIII, including the regency of his mother, MARIE DE MÉDICIS, who introduced much of the art of her native Italy. The MANNERISM of Italy and Flanders was so influential that a true French style did not develop until the mid-17th cent, when the influence of CARAVAGGIO was assimilated by GEORGES DE LA TOUR and the LE NAIN BROTHERS, and the influence of the CARRACCI brothers was extended by SIMON VOUET, who trained the academic painters of the next generation. The sculpture of the period was undistinguished. The most prolific area of the arts was architecture. Here, too, the Italian influence is seen, as in the Palais de Justice at Rennes and the Luxembourg Palace in Paris, both designed by Salomon de Brosse, and the Church of the Sorbonne in Paris, designed by Jacques Lemercier. The furniture of the period is typically massive and solidly built, and commonly decorated with cherubs, ornate scrollwork, fruit-and-flower swags, and grotesque masks.

Louis XIV *known as* **the Sun King** (1638–1715) King of France (1643–1715), ruler during one of France's most brilliant periods and the symbol of absolute monarchy of the classical age. He succeeded his father, LOUIS XIII, at age 4, under the regency of his mother, ANNE OF AUSTRIA. In 1648 the nobles and the Paris Parlement, who hated the prime minister, Cardinal MAZARIN, rose against the crown and started the FRONDE. In 1653, victorious over the rebels, Mazarin gained absolute power, though the king was of age. In 1660 Louis married Marie-Thérèse of Austria (1638–1683), daughter of PHILIP IV of Spain. When Mazarin died in 1661, Louis astonished his ministers by informing them that he intended to assume responsibility for ruling the kingdom. A believer in dictatorship by divine right, he viewed himself as God's representative on earth. He was assisted by his able ministers, JEAN-BAPTISTE COLBERT and the marquis de LOUVOIS. Louis weakened the nobles' power by making them dependent on the crown. A patron of the arts, he protected writers and devoted himself to building splendid palaces, including the extravagant VERSAILLES, where he kept most of the nobility under his watchful eye. In 1667 he invaded the Spanish Netherlands in the War of DEVOLUTION (1667–68) and again in 1672 in the Third Dutch War. The Sun King was at his zenith; he had extended France's northern and eastern borders and was adored at his court. In 1680, a scandal involving his mistress, the marquise de Montespan (1641–1707), made him fearful for his reputation and he openly renounced pleasure. The queen died in 1683, and he secretly married the pious MARQUISE DE MAINTENON. After trying to convert French Protestants by force, he revoked the Edict of NANTES in 1685. Fear of his expansionism led to alliances against France during the War of the GRAND ALLIANCE (1688–97) and the War of the SPANISH SUCCESSION (1701–14). Louis died at 77 at the end of the longest reign in European history.

Louis XIV style Style of the visual arts produced in France during the reign of LOUIS XIV. In 1648 CHARLES LE BRUN founded the Royal Academy of Painting and Sculpture, which rigidly dictated styles for the rest of the reign. The most influential painter was NICOLAS POUSSIN, who forged the way for French Classicism (see CLASSICISM AND NEOCLASSICISM). Sculpture reached a new zenith with the works of FRANCOIS GIRARDON and PIERRE PUGET. A national style in the decorative arts evolved through the Gobelin factory (see GOBELIN FAMILY). Furniture was veneered, inlaid, and heavily gilded, commonly decorated with shells, satyrs, garlands, mythological heroes, and dolphins; the style is particularly associated with ANDRE-CHARLES BOULLE. In architecture, JEAN-BAPTISTE COLBERT rigidly controlled the renovation of the Palace of VERSAILLES, with landscaping by ANDRE LE NOTRE

Louis XV (1710–1774) King of France (1715–74). An orphan from age 3, Louis succeeded to the throne on the death of his great-grandfather LOUIS XIV (1715), under the regency of Philippe II, duc d'Orléans (1674–1723). His marriage to Princess Marie Leszczynska of Poland (1703–1768) in 1725 led to France's involvement in the War of the POLISH SUCCESSION (1733–38). He chose ANDRE-HERCULE DE FLEURY as his chief minister in 1726, and his own influence became perceptible only after Fleury's death in 1744. Louis's mistresses, particularly Madame de POMPADOUR, held considerable political influence. Louis brought France into the War of the AUSTRIAN SUCCESSION (1740–48) and the SEVEN YEARS' WAR (1756–63), by which France lost to Britain almost all its colonial possessions. As the crown's moral and political authority declined, the Parlements gained in power, preventing fiscal reform. The king died hated by his subjects.

Louis XV style ROCOCO STYLE of French decorative arts during the reign of LOUIS XV, when artists produced exquisite decor for the homes of royalty and nobility. Emphasis was laid on the ensemble, so that paintings and sculptures became part of the decorative arts. The full range of richness in decorative techniques was represented—superb carving, ornamentation of all types of metal, inlay work in exotic woods, metal, mother-of-pearl, and ivory, and exquisite lacquered chinoiserie that rivaled products from the Far East. Fantasy joined nature and Oriental themes in providing decorative motifs. Notable artists and designers include J.-H. FRAGONARD, FRANCOIS BOUCHER, and J.-B. OUDRY.

Louis XVI (1754–1793) Last king of France (1774–92) in the Bourbon line preceding the FRENCH REVOLUTION. In 1770 he married MARIE-ANTOINETTE, and in 1774 he succeeded to the throne on the death of his grandfather, LOUIS XV. Immature and lacking in strength of character, he was unable to give the necessary support to his ministers, including ANNE ROBERT JACQUES TURGOT and JACQUES NECKER, in their efforts to stabilize France's tottering finances. Restoration of the Parlements in 1774 shifted power to the aristocracy. Aristocratic opposition to the economic reforms of CHARLES-A. DE CALONNE forced the king to summon the Estates General in 1788, setting the Revolution in motion. Dominated by the reactionary court faction, he defended the privileges of the clergy and nobility. He dismissed Necker in 1789 and refused to sanction the achievements of the NATIONAL ASSEMBLY. His resistance to popular demands was one cause for the royal family's forcible transfer from Versailles to the Tuileries palace in Paris. He lost credibility further when he attempted to escape the capital in 1791 and was caught at Varennes and returned to Paris. Thereafter he was dominated by the queen, who encouraged him to a policy of subterfuge instead of implementing the CONSTITUTION OF 1791, which he had sworn to maintain. In 1792 the Tuileries was captured by the people and militia, and the First French Republic was proclaimed. When proof of his counterrevolutionary intrigues with foreigners was found, he was tried for treason. Condemned to death, he went to the guillotine in 1793. His dignity during his trial and execution only somewhat redeemed his reputation.

Louis XVI style Style of the visual arts produced in France from c. 1760 to the French Revolution. The predominant style in painting, architecture, sculpture, and the decorative arts was Neoclassicism—a reaction against the excesses of the Rococo style and a response to J.-J. ROUSSEAU's call for "natural" virtue, as well as a response to the excavations at POMPEII and HERCULANEUM. The most prominent painter was J.-L. DAVID, whose severe compositions recalled the style of NICOLAS POUSSIN. The foremost sculptor of the day was J.-A. HOUDON. The style in furniture was classical, yet workmanship was more complex than in any earlier period. J.-H. RIESENER and other German craftsmen were among the most prominent cabinetmakers. See also CLASSICISM AND NEOCLASSICISM.

Louis XVII *orig.* **Louis-Charles** (1785–1795) Titular king of France from 1793. The second son of LOUIS XVI and MARIE-ANTOINETTE, he became heir to the throne on his brother's death, shortly after the outbreak of the FRENCH REVOLUTION. In 1792 he was imprisoned with the rest of the royal family. When his father was beheaded in 1793, the French ÉMIGRÉ NOBILITY proclaimed Louis-Charles king. He died in prison at age 10, but the secrecy surrounding his last months gave rise to rumors that he was not dead, and over the next few decades more than 30 persons claimed to be Louis XVII.

Louis XVIII *orig.* **Louis-Stanislas-Xavier, comte (Count) de Provence** (1755–1824) King of France by title from 1795 and in fact from 1814 to 1824. He fled the country in 1791, during the French Revolution, and issued counterrevolutionary manifestos and organized ÉMIGRÉ-NOBILITY associations. He became regent for his nephew LOUIS XVII after the 1793 execution of LOUIS XVI, and at the dauphin's death in 1795 he proclaimed himself king. When the allied armies entered Paris in 1814, CHARLES MAURICE DE TALLEYRAND negotiated the BOURBON RESTORATION and Louis was received with jubilation. He promised a constitutional monarchy, and the CHARTER OF 1814 was adopted; after the interruption of the HUNDRED DAYS, when NAPOLEON returned from Elba, he resumed his constitutional monarchy. The legislature included a strong right-wing majority, and though Louis opposed the extremism of the ULTRAS, they exercised increasing control and thwarted his attempts to heal the wounds left by the Revolution. He was succeeded at his death by his brother, CHARLES X.

Louis-Napoléon See NAPOLEON III

Louis-Philippe *known as* **the Citizen King** (1773–1850) King of the French (1830–48). Eldest son of the duc d'ORLÉANS, he supported the new government at the outbreak of the French Revolution and joined the Revolutionary army in 1792, but deserted during the war with Austria (1793) and lived in exile in Switzerland, the U.S., and England. He returned to France on the restoration of LOUIS XVIII and joined the liberal opposition. Following the JULY REVOLUTION (1830) and CHARLES X's abdication, he was proclaimed the "citizen king" by ADOLPHE THIERS and elected by the legislature. During the JULY MONARCHY, he consolidated his power by steering a middle course between the right-wing monarchists and the socialists and other republicans, but resorted to repressive measures because of numerous rebellions and attempts on his life. He strengthened France's position in Europe and cooperated with the British in forcing the Dutch to recognize Belgian independence. Mounting middle-class opposition to his arbitrary rule and his inability to win allegiance from the new industrial classes caused his abdication during the FEBRUARY REVOLUTION of 1848.

Louis the Bavarian See LOUIS IV

Louis the Fat See LOUIS VI

Louis the Pious See LOUIS I

Louis the Younger See LOUIS VII

Louisiade Archipelago \lü-ˌē-zē-ˈäd\ Island group (pop., 1987 est.: 16,000), Papua New Guinea, southeast of NEW GUINEA. Stretching for more than 100 mi (160 km), it occupies 10,000 sq mi (26,000 sq km) of the South Pacific. It has nearly 100 islands; the largest are Misima, Tagula, and Rossel. It was visited by the Spanish in 1606 and was named after LOUIS XV of France in 1768. Occupied by Japanese forces in 1942, the islands are near the site of the Battle of the CORAL SEA.

Louisiana State (pop., 1997 est.: 4,352,000), southern U.S. It covers 48,523 sq mi (125,674 sq km); its capital is BATON ROUGE. It can be divided physically into the MISSISSIPPI RIVER flood plain and delta, and the low hills of the Gulf of Mexico coastal plain. It is the only U.S. state to be governed under the NAPOLEONIC CODE. Indian occupancy in the area probably spanned 16,000 years; at the time of European settlement the region was inhabited by CADDO and CHOCTAW Indians. French explorer R.-R. LA SALLE descended the Mississippi River in 1682 and claimed the entire river basin for France. The city of NEW ORLEANS was founded in 1718, and Louisiana became a French crown colony in 1731. Colonization increased in the 1760s with the arrival of French-speaking Acadians (CAJUNS) from Nova Scotia. Spain controlled the territory 1762–1800; then it passed back to the French. The lands that constitute modern Louisiana were acquired by the U.S. as part of the LOUISIANA PURCHASE in 1803 and became the Territory of Orleans in 1804. Louisiana became the 18th U.S. state in 1812. It seceded from the Union in 1861 at the start of the AMERICAN CIVIL WAR and was readmitted in 1868. The plantation economy continued with the farmer class denied ownership, which contributed to the rise of the populist HUEY LONG in the 1920s. After World War II Louisiana experienced more rapid development with the rise of offshore oil and gas drilling. Major agricultural products are soybeans and cotton; tree farming and shrimp fishing are also important. Petroleum and natural gas are the chief mineral resources.

Louisiana Purchase Territory purchased by the U.S. from France in 1803, for $15 million. It extended from the MISSISSIPPI RIVER to the ROCKY MTNS. and from the Gulf of Mexico to British America (Canada). In 1762 France had ceded Louisiana west of the Mississippi River to Spain, but Spain returned it to French control in 1800. Alarmed by this potential increase in French power, Pres. THOMAS JEFFERSON threatened to form an alliance with Britain. NAPOLEON then sold the U.S. the entire Louisiana Territory, although its boundaries remained unclear; its northwestern and southwestern limits were not established until 1818–19. The purchase doubled the area of the U.S.

Louisiana State University State university system with eight universities on 10 campuses in five cities, the main institution being Louisiana State University and Agricultural and Mechanical College in Baton Rouge. There are about 28,000 students at the main university and 57,000 in the entire system. The university began with a series of U.S. government grants (the first in 1806) to create a seminary. It was officially authorized in 1853 and opened in 1860. It operates some 800 sponsored research projects and includes a Center for Coastal, Energy, and Environmental Resources. ROBERT PENN WARREN and others founded *The Southern Review* there in 1935.

Louisville \ˈlü-i-ˌvil\ City (pop., 1996 est.: 261,000), northern central Kentucky, located on the OHIO RIVER. Settled in 1778 on Corn Island, it expanded the next year when the settlers moved ashore. Named for LOUIS XVI of France, it became an important river trading center and was chartered as a city in 1828. During the AMERICAN CIVIL WAR it served as a Union military headquarters and supply depot. The largest city in Kentucky, it is a leading producer of bonded bourbon whiskey and cigarettes. It is home to the University of Louisville (founded 1798) and Churchill Downs, the site of the KENTUCKY DERBY.

Loup River \ˈlüp\ River, eastern central Nebraska. It flows east to join the PLATTE RIVER. It is 300 mi (485 km) long, and is harnessed to produce hydroelectric power. Its name is derived from the French name (meaning "wolf") for the Skidi Indians.

Lourdes PILGRIMAGE site in southwestern France, situated southwest of Toulouse at the foot of the Pyrenees. The town and its fortress formed a strategic stronghold in medieval times, but its modern significance dates from 1858, when a 14-year-old girl had repeated visions of the Virgin MARY (see BERNADETTE OF LOURDES). The visions were declared authentic by Pope PIUS IX in 1862. The underground spring in the grotto where Bernadette had her visions was declared to have miraculous qualities, and Lourdes has since become one of the foremost destinations for Roman Catholic pilgrims. Nearly 3 million visit annually, many of them sick or disabled people hoping to be healed. A basilica was built above the grotto in 1876, and a vast underground church was added in 1958.

Lourenço Marques See MAPUTO

louse Any member of one of some 3,300 species of small, wingless, parasitic insects of the order Phthiraptera, which consists mainly of biting, or chewing, lice (parasites of birds and mammals) and the sucking lice (see SUCKING LOUSE). The louse's body is flattened. The eggs, or nits, are cemented to the hair or plumage of the host, and most species spend their entire lives on the body of host animals. Heavy infestations cause much irritation and may lead to secondary infections. In moving from host to host, lice may spread many diseases, including tapeworm infestation in dogs and murine typhus in rats. See also human LOUSE.

louse, human Any of three types of SUCKING LOUSE that infest humans. The body louse (mainly *Pediculus humanus humanus,* also called human louse or cootie) and head louse (*P. h. capitis*) are spread by person-to-person contact and through shared clothing, bedding, combs, and other personal items. Body lice carry the organisms that cause relapsing fever, trench fever, and TYPHUS. Head lice may cause IMPETIGO. Both are readily spread under conditions of overcrowding, especially among children. The crab louse, or pubic louse (*Phthirus pubis*) infests primarily the pubic region and occasionally other hairy regions. Its first pair of legs is smaller than the other two pairs, making it look like a crab. Crab lice are transmitted primarily through sexual intercourse. Lice infestations can be quickly cured with shampoos, soaps, and lo-

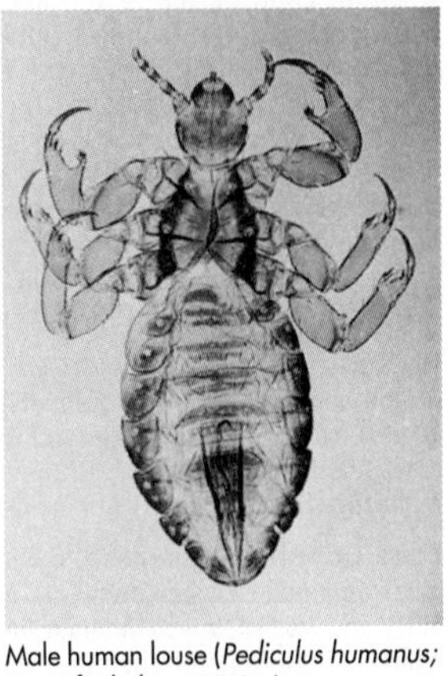

Male human louse (*Pediculus humanus;* magnified about 15½ ×).
WILLIAM E. FERGUSON

L M N

tions containing benzene hexachloride, along with the thorough washing of bedding and clothing.

lousewort Any of about 500 species of herbaceous plants that make up the genus *Pedicularis* in the SNAPDRAGON FAMILY, found throughout the Northern Hemisphere but especially on the mountains of central and eastern Asia. The bilaterally symmetrical flowers sometimes have very unusual shapes. The flowers of the little elephant *(P. groenlandica),* for example, resemble the head, trunk, and ears of an elephant. Louseworts are semiparasitic on the roots of other plants.

Lousewort (*Pedicularis lanceolata*).
KITTY KOHOUT FROM ROOT RESOURCES—EB INC.

Louvain \lü-'va^{n}\, **Catholic University of** Either of two Belgian universities established in 1970, both descended from a renowned university founded in 1425 in Louvain. The original university included on its faculty in the early 1500s DESIDERIUS ERASMUS, J. Lipsius, and GERARDUS MERCATOR. The modern university was reorganized into separate units following student riots and government upheavals in 1969. At the Katholieke Universiteit te Leuven, the language of instruction is Dutch; enrollment is about 27,000. At the Université Catholique de Louvain, located in Louvain-la-Neuve, instruction is in French; enrollment is about 22,000.

louver \'lü-vər\ Arrangement of parallel, horizontal blades or slats of glass, wood, or other material designed to regulate airflow or light penetration. Louvers are often used in windows or doors to allow air or light in while keeping the elements out. They may be either movable or fixed. The term also refers to metal blades covering the intake and exhaust outlets of ventilation and air-conditioning units.

Louvois \lüv-'wä\, **marquis de** *orig.* **François-Michel Le Tellier** \lə-tāl-'yā\ (1639–1691) French secretary of state for war under LOUIS XIV and his most influential minister 1677–91. The son of Michel Le Tellier (1603–1685), one of the most powerful officials in France, he was groomed by his father to replace him as war secretary. A brilliant administrator, Louvois brought his father's military reforms to fruition, making the French army one of the most formidable in Europe. He was complicit in the military policy that led up to the revocation of the Edict of NANTES (1685), and was also responsible for the destruction of the Palatinate (1688), which led to the War of the GRAND ALLIANCE.

Louvre Museum \'lüvr^{ə}\ National museum and art gallery of France, in Paris. It was built as a royal residence, begun under FRANCIS I in 1546 on the site of a 12th-century fortress. It ceased to be used as a palace when the court moved to Versailles in 1682, and plans were made in the 18th century to turn it into a public museum. In 1793 the revolutionary government opened the Grand Gallery; Napoleon built the northern wing; and two major western wings were completed and opened by Napoleon III. The completed Louvre included a vast complex of buildings forming two main quadrilaterals and enclosing two large courtyards. A controversial steel-and-glass pyramid entrance designed by I. M. PEI opened in 1989. The painting collection is one of the richest in the world, representing all periods of European art up to Impressionism; its collection of French 15th–19th-century paintings is unsurpassed.

lovage \'lə-vij\ Herb *(Levisticum officinale)* of the PARSLEY family, native to southern Europe. It is cultivated for its stalks and foliage, which are used for tea, as a vegetable, and to flavor foods. Its RHIZOMES are used as a carminative, and the seeds are used for flavoring desserts. Oil obtained from the flowers is used in perfumery.

Love Canal Neighborhood in NIAGARA FALLS, N.Y., the site of the worst environmental disaster involving chemical wastes in U.S. history. Originally the site of an abandoned canal, it became a dumping ground for nearly 22,000 tons of chemical waste in the 1940s and 1950s. The canal was later filled in, and housing was built on it. The leakage of toxic chemicals into these homes was detected in 1978, and residents were discovered to have a high incidence of chromosomal damage. After their evacuation, 1,300 former residents obtained a $20 million settlement from the dumping company and the city. In the early 1990s New York state ended its cleanup and declared parts of the area safe for residence.

lovebird Any of nine species of small PARROTS (genus *Agapornis,* subfamily Psittacinae) of Africa and Madagascar. Popular as pets for their pretty colors and the seemingly affectionate closeness of pairs, lovebirds are 4–6 in. (10–16 cm) long, chunky, and short-tailed. Most have a red bill and prominent eye ring. The two sexes look alike. Large flocks forage in woods and scrublands for seeds and may damage crops. Hardy and long-lived, they are combative toward other birds and have a loud, squawky voice. Though not easy to tame, they can be taught to perform tricks and mimic human speech to a limited extent.

Lovebirds (*Agapornis personata*).
TONI ANGERMAYER

Lovejoy, Elijah P(arish) (1802–1837) U.S. newspaper editor and abolitionist. Born in Albion, Me., he moved to St. Louis in 1827, and in 1833 became editor of the *St. Louis Observer*, a Presbyterian weekly in which he wrote articles strongly condemning slavery. Under threat of mob violence (1836), he moved his paper from the slave state of Missouri across the river to Alton, in the free state of Illinois. There mobs repeatedly destroyed his presses; he was shot and killed while defending his building against a mob attack. News of his death strengthened abolitionist sentiment.

Lovelace, (Augusta) Ada King, Countess of *orig.* **Lady Augusta Ada Byron** (1815–1852) English mathematician. Her father was the poet Lord BYRON, though she never knew him personally. In 1835 she married William King, 8th Baron King; when he was created an earl in 1838, she became a countess. She became interested in CHARLES BABBAGE's analytical machines as early as 1833, and in 1843 she translated and annotated an article about them by Luigi Federico Menabrea. For creating a program for Babbage's prototype of a digital computer, she has been called the first female computer programmer. The programming language ADA is named for her.

Lovell \'lə-vəl\, **(Alfred Charles) Bernard** *later* **Sir Bernard** (born 1913) British radio astronomer. He received his PhD from the University of Bristol, worked for the Air Ministry during World War II, and lectured at the University of Manchester after the war. He built the first giant RADIO TELESCOPE (1957) at Jodrell Bank, near Manchester; its bowl diameter is 250 ft (76 m).

low blood pressure See HYPOTENSION

Low Countries Coastal region, northwestern Europe, consisting of BELGIUM, the NETHERLANDS, and LUXEMBOURG. Known as the Low Countries because much of the land along the North Sea is below or at sea level, they are often called the BENELUX countries, from the initial letters of their names.

low relief See BAS-RELIEF

Lowell City (pop., 2000: 105,167), northeastern Massachusetts. Settled in 1653 as East Chelmsford, it became a major center of cotton-textile manufacturing in the 19th century. It was renamed for industrialist FRANCIS LOWELL, and was incorporated as a city in 1836. In the 20th century it began losing textile manufacturing to southern states, and it diversified into other industries. The Lowell National Historical Park (established 1978) commemorates the Industrial Revolution in the U.S. It is the birthplace of the artist JAMES M. WHISTLER and the seat of the University of Massachusetts–Lowell.

Lowell, Amy (1874–1925) U.S. critic and poet. Born into the prominent Lowell family of Boston, she devoted herself to poetry at age 28 but published nothing until 1910. Her first volume, *A Dome of Many-Coloured Glass* (1912), was succeeded by *Sword Blades and Poppy Seed* (1914), which included her first poems in free verse and what she called "polyphonic prose." She became a leader of IMAGISM and was noted for her vivid and powerful personality and her scorn of conventional behavior. Her other works include *Six French Poets* (1915), *Tendencies in Modern American Poetry* (1917), and *John Keats* (2 vols., 1925).

Lowell, Francis Cabot (1775–1817) U.S. businessman. Born into a prominent Massachusetts family in Newburyport, Mass., Lowell closely studied the British textile industry while visiting Britain. With PAUL MOODY he devised an efficient power LOOM and spinning apparatus. His Boston Manufacturing Co. in Waltham (1812–14) was apparently the world's first mill in which were performed all operations converting raw COTTON into finished cloth. His example greatly stimulated the growth of New England industry. Lowell, Mass., is named for him.

Lowell, James Russell (1819–1891) U.S. poet, critic, editor, and diplomat. Born in Cambridge, Mass., he received a law degree from Harvard but chose not to practice. In the 1840s he wrote extensively against slavery, including the *Biglow Papers* (1848), satirical verses in Yankee dialect. His other most important works are *The Vision of Sir Launfal* (1848), a long poem on the brotherhood of mankind; and *A Fable for Critics* (1848), a witty evaluation of contemporary authors. After his wife's death in 1853 he wrote mainly essays on literature, history, and politics. A highly influential man of letters in his day, he taught at Harvard, edited *The Atlantic Monthly* and *The North American Review,* and served as minister to Spain and ambassador to Britain.

James Russell Lowell.
BY COURTESY OF THE LIBRARY OF CONGRESS, WASHINGTON, D.C.

Lowell, Percival (1855–1916) U.S. astronomer. He was born into a distinguished Boston family. In the 1890s he built a private observatory in Flagstaff, Ariz., to study Mars. He championed the now-abandoned theory that intelligent inhabitants of a dying Mars had constructed a planetwide system of irrigation. He thought that the so-called canals of MARS were bands of cultivated vegetation dependent on this irrigation. Lowell's theory, long vigorously opposed, was finally put to rest by information received from the U.S. Mariner spacecraft. His prediction of a planet beyond Neptune was vindicated when Pluto was discovered in 1930.

Lowell, Robert *orig.* **Robert Traill Spence Lowell, Jr.** (1917–1977) U.S. poet. Born in Boston, Lowell was a descendant of a distinguished family that included JAMES RUSSELL LOWELL and AMY LOWELL. Though he turned away from his Puritan heritage, it forms the subject of much of his poetry. His first major work, *Lord Weary's Castle* (1946, Pulitzer Prize), contains "The Quaker Graveyard in Nantucket." *Life Studies* (1959) contains an autobiographical essay and 15 complex, confessional poems largely based on his family history and disturbed personal life, which included time in mental institutions. His activities in liberal causes in the 1960s influenced his next three volumes, including *For the Union Dead* (1964). His later collections include *The Dolphin* (1973, Pulitzer Prize).

Lower Canada See CANADA EAST

Lowry \'laü-rē\, **(Clarence) Malcolm** (1909–1957) British novelist, short-story writer, and poet. In his youth Lowry rebelled against his conventional upbringing and shipped to China as a cabin boy; he later lived in France, the U.S., Mexico, Canada, and Italy. His reputation rests on the novel *Under the Volcano* (1947), about the last desperate day of a dispirited alcoholic and former British consul in Mexico. Its juxtaposition of images of social decay and self-destructiveness was seen as a symbolic vision of Europe on the verge of World War II. Though critically praised, it received popular recognition only after Lowry's death at 47, probably the result of alcoholism.

Loy, Myrna *orig.* **Myrna Williams** (1905–1993) U.S. film actress. Born in Radersburg, Mont., she played bit parts in Hollywood movies before being cast as the exotic mistress in *Ben Hur* (1926), establishing her early film persona as a foreign vamp. She earned praise as the wittily sophisticated Nora Charles in *The Thin Man* (1934) and its sequels, and in other movies such as *The Best Years of Our Lives* (1946), *Mr. Blandings Builds His Dream House* (1948), *Cheaper by the Dozen* (1950), and *Lonelyhearts* (1958). She worked for the American Red Cross in World War II and later for UNESCO.

Loyalists American colonists loyal to Britain in the AMERICAN REVOLUTION. About one-third of American colonists were Loyalists, including officeholders who served the British crown, large landholders, wealthy merchants, Anglican clergy and their parishioners, and Quakers. Loyalists were most numerous in the South, New York, and Pennsylvania but did not constitute a majority in any colony. At first they urged moderation in the struggle for colonial rights; when denounced by radical patriots, they became active partisans. Some joined the British army, including 23,000 from New York; when captured in battle, they were treated as traitors. All states passed laws against them, confiscating or heavily taxing their property. Beginning in 1776 about 100,000 Loyalists fled into exile, many to Canada. Public sentiment against them diminished after 1789, and punitive state laws were repealed by 1814.

Loyola, St. Ignatius of *orig.* **Iñigo de Oñaz y Loyola** (1491–1556) Spanish founder of the Society of Jesus (JESUITS). Born into the nobility, he began his career as a soldier. While convalescing from wounds inflicted by a French cannonball in 1521, he experienced a religious conversion. After a pilgrimage to Jerusalem, he pursued religious studies in Spain and France. In Paris he gathered about him the companions (including ST. FRANCIS XAVIER) who were to join him in founding the Jesuits. Ordained a priest in 1537, he established the Society of Jesus in 1539. The new order received papal approval in 1540, and Loyola served as its general until his death, by which time it had branches in Italy, Spain, Germany, France, Portugal, India, and Brazil. Loyola described his mystical vision of prayer in *The Spiritual Exercises*. In his last years he laid the foundations of a system of Jesuit schools.

Loyola University Chicago Private university in Chicago. Affiliated with the JESUITS, it is one of the largest Roman Catholic universities in the U.S., with a total enrollment of about 14,000. It was founded in 1870 as St. Ignatius College and assumed its current name in 1923. In addition to two Chicago campuses, it has campuses in the suburbs of Wilmette and Maywood and an overseas campus in Rome. It offers doctoral degrees in more than 30 fields and several professional degrees. Its medical center pioneered open-heart surgery and was the first to establish a cardiac intensive-care unit.

Lozi \'lō-zē\ *or* **Barotse** \bə-'rät-sə\ Complex of 25 Bantu-speaking peoples divided into six cultural groups centering on the area formerly known as Barotseland in western Zambia. Numbering about 700,000, the Lozi move between two sets of villages in response to annual flooding. Their economy is based on agriculture, animal husbandry, and fishing. Their stratified society consists of aristocrats, commoners, and serfs.

LSD *in full* **lysergic acid diethylamide** Highly potent HALLUCINOGEN. An organic compound, LSD can be derived from the ALKALOIDS ergotamine and ergonovine, found in the ERGOT fungus, but most LSD is produced synthetically. It can block the action of the NEUROTRANSMITTER SEROTONIN and produces marked deviations from normal perceptions and behavior lasting 8–10 hours or longer. Mood shifts, time and space distortions, and impulsive behavior may progress to suspicions of the intentions and motives of other people and aggression against them. Flashbacks to LSD-induced hallucinations can occur years later. LSD is not an approved drug, and no clinically valuable uses have been found for it.

Lu Vassal state of ancient China that originated during the Western ZHOU and came to prominence in the WARRING STATES PERIOD of the Eastern Zhou. It is known as the birthplace of CONFUCIUS. The *CHUNQIU* ("Spring and Autumn Annals"), one of the Confucian Classics, records the major events at the court of Lu between 722 and 481 BC.

Lü-ta See DALIAN

Lu Xiangshan *or* **Lu Hsiang-shan** \'lü-'shyäŋ-'shän\ *or* **Lu Jiuyuan** \'lü-'jyō-'ywän\ (1139–1193) Chinese Neo-Confucian philosopher of the Southern SONG DYNASTY. A government official and a teacher, he was the rival of the great Neo-Confucian rationalist ZHU XI. Lu taught that the highest knowledge of the way (TAO) comes from constant inner reflection and self-examination. In this process, one develops or recovers the fundamental goodness of one's nature. Lu's writings were published af-

L
M
N

ter his death, and his thought was revised three centuries later by WANG YANGMING, who established the Xin Xue school of NEO-CONFUCIANISM, often called the Lu-Wang school.

Lu Xun *or* **Lu Hsün** \'lü-'shu̅e̅n\ *orig.* **Zhou Shuren** (1881–1936) Chinese writer. He became associated with the nascent Chinese literary movement in 1918 (part of the larger May Fourth Movement), when he published his short story "Kuangren riji" ("Diary of a Madman"), a condemnation of traditional Confucian culture and the first Western-style story written wholly in Chinese. Though best known for his fiction, he was also a master of the prose essay, a vehicle he used especially late in life. He never joined the Communist Party himself, but he recruited many of his countrymen to communism and came to be considered a revolutionary hero.

Lualaba River \,lü-ä-'lä-bä\ River, central Africa. The headstream of the CONGO RIVER, its 1,100-mi (1,800-km) course lies entirely within the Democratic Republic of the Congo (Zaire). It is harnessed in places for hydroelectric power.

Luan River \lu̇-'wän\ River, HEBEI province, northeastern China. It rises in eastern NEI MONGGOL province and flows north, then curves to the southeast. It passes through the GREAT WALL and divides into a number of smaller rivers, discharging into BO HAI after a course of 545 mi (877 km). The river is navigable below Chengde.

Luanda \lu̇-'än-də\ *or* **Loanda** \lō-'än-də\ City (pop., 1999 est.: 2,555,000), capital of Angola. Situated on the Atlantic coast, it is Angola's largest city and its second busiest seaport. Founded in 1576 by Paulo Dias de Novais, it became the administrative center for the colony of Angola in 1627. It was a major outlet for slave traffic to Brazil until the 19th century. Many Mbundu live in the city, and there is a sizable Cuban community. It is a commercial and industrial area, with oil-refining capacity. It is the seat of the University of Luanda; the old fortress of São Miguel lies beyond the port.

Luang Pradist Manudharm See PRIDI PHANOMYONG

Luba *or* **Baluba** Cluster of Bantu-speaking peoples who share a common political history surrounding the Luba empires (see LUBA-LUNDA STATES). They are savanna and forest dwellers who hunt and gather, engage in agriculture, and keep livestock; they also fish intensively in the Congo and its tributaries. They have associations for hunting, magic, and medicine and a well-developed literature that includes epic cycles.

Female Luba ancestral statue of carved wood; in the Musée de l'Homme, Paris.

BY COURTESY OF THE MUSEE DE L'HOMME, PARIS

Luba-Lunda states \'lü-bə-'lün-də\ Complex of kingdoms that flourished in Central Africa in the 16th–19th century. In the late 15th century a small group of ivory hunters founded a kingdom around which a number of satellites proliferated, spreading by the 17th century into the southern Congo Basin, western Angola, and Zambia. The northeastern portion was inhabited by the Luba; the southwestern portion by the Lunda. The kingdom traded slaves and ivory to the Portuguese for cloth and other goods. In the 18th century, migrants founded the Kazembe kingdom farther southeast; it flourished until late in the 19th century, when it was colonized by the British.

Lubbock \'lə-bək\ City (pop., 2000: 199,564), northwestern Texas. Located south of AMARILLO, it was named for Tom S. Lubbock, a signer of the Texas declaration of independence. Formed in 1890 from Old Lubbock and Monterey, it developed as a ranching center and was incorporated in 1909. A tornado in 1970 caused widespread damage. It is one of the nation's leading cotton markets and the center of a diversified agricultural and industrial region. It is the seat of Texas Tech University (1923).

Lübeck \'lu̅e̅-,bek\ City (population 1999 est.: 213,800), northern Germany. Founded on the site of a Slavic settlement in 1143, it developed as a trading post. It became a free city in 1226 and the seat of the HANSEATIC LEAGUE in 1358. It declined after the 16th century, and its trade was ruined during the NAPOLEONIC WARS. It revived after the Elbe–Lübeck canal was built in 1900. Its status as a self-governing entity ended in 1937, when the Nazis made it part of the Prussian province of SCHLESWIG-HOLSTEIN. It is one of Germany's largest Baltic ports. Historic sites include a 12th-century cathedral and several Gothic churches.

Lubitsch \'lü-bich\, **Ernst** (1892–1947) German-U.S. film director. He acted with MAX REINHARDT's German stage company (1911–14) and in short film comedies, then turned to directing costume dramas which were the first German films shown abroad, including *Passion* (1919), *Deception* (1920), and *The Loves of Pharaoh* (1921), as well as such comedies as *The Doll* (1919) and *The Oyster Princess* (1919). He moved to Hollywood in 1923 and developed a style of sophisticated wit and unerring narrative timing—the famous "Lubitsch touch"—in such successful comedies as *The Marriage Circle* (1924), *The Love Parade* (1929), *Trouble in Paradise* (1932), *Ninotchka* (1939), *The Shop Around the Corner* (1940), *To Be or Not to Be* (1942), and *Heaven Can Wait* (1943).

Lublin \'lü-blin\ City (pop., 1999 est.: 356,251), eastern Poland, situated on the Bystrzyca River. Founded as a stronghold in the late 9th century, the settlement received town rights in 1317. In 1795 it passed to Austria and in 1815 to Russia. The first independent temporary Polish government was proclaimed there in 1918. In World War II the Nazi CONCENTRATION CAMP Majdanek was established in one of its suburbs. After the war Lublin served briefly as the seat of the national government. It is now an industrial and cultural center for southeastern Poland.

lubrication Introduction of any of various substances between sliding surfaces to reduce wear and FRICTION. Lubricants may secondarily control corrosion, regulate temperature, electrically insulate, remove contaminants, or damp shock. Prehistoric peoples used mud and reeds to lubricate sledges, timbers, or rocks. Animal fat lubricated the axles of the first wagons and continued in wide use until crude OIL became the chief source of lubricants. Crude oil has been the basis of products designed for the specific lubricating needs of automobiles, aircraft, locomotives, turbojets, and all other power machinery. There are three basic varieties of lubrication: fluid-film (in which a fluid film completely separates sliding surfaces), boundary (in which the friction between surfaces is determined by the properties of the surfaces and properties of the lubricant other than VISCOSITY), and solid (used when liquid lubricants lack adequate resistance to load or temperature extremes). The principal lubricants are liquid, oily materials (petroleum-based or synthetic, and including greases); solids (such as graphite, molybdenum disulfide, soft metals, waxes, and plastics); and gases.

Lubumbashi \,lü-büm-'bä-shē\ *formerly (until 1966)* **Elisabethville** City (pop., 1994 est.: 851,000), Democratic Republic of the Congo (Zaire). Near the border with Zambia, it was established by Belgian colonists in 1910 and grew to become the site of one of the world's largest copper mining and smelting operations. It was the center of Katanga province's secession movement in the early 1960s.

Luca da Cortona See Luca SIGNORELLI

Lucas, George (born 1944) U.S. film director and producer. Born in Modesto, Cal., he studied filmmaking at USC and later worked with FRANCIS FORD COPPOLA. His first feature film, *THX 1138* (1971), was followed by the surprise success *American Graffiti* (1973). He wrote and directed the immensely popular science-fiction movie *Star Wars* (1977), which made innovative use of computerized special effects. He formed the production company Lucasfilms (1978) and its special-effects division Industrial Light and Magic. He produced the *Star Wars* sequels, *The Empire Strikes Back* (1980) and *The Return of the Jedi* (1993), as well as STEVEN SPIELBERG's *Raiders of the Lost Ark* (1981) and its sequels. He returned to directing with the first *Star Wars* "prequel," *The Phantom Menace* (1999). Others followed.

Lucas, Robert E., Jr. (born 1937) U.S. economist. Born in Yakima, Wash., he studied at the University of Chicago, and has taught there

L
M
N

since 1975. He questioned the influence of JOHN MAYNARD KEYNES in MACROECONOMICS and the efficacy of government intervention in domestic affairs. He criticized the PHILLIPS CURVE for failing to provide for the dampened expectations of companies and workers in an inflationary economy. His theory of rational expectations, which suggests that individuals may alter the expected results of national fiscal policy by making private economic decisions based on anticipated results, won him the 1995 Nobel Prize. See also ECONOMETRICS, INFLATION.

Lucas (Huyghszoon) van Leyden \'lūē-käs-vän-'lī-dən\ or (c. 1494–1533) Netherlandish painter and engraver. Born in Leiden, he was trained by his father, a painter, but his great talent was as an engraver. Even such youthful prints as *Muhammad and the Monk Sergius* (1508) show great technical skill. In 1510, under the influence of ALBRECHT DURER, he produced two masterpieces of engraving, *The Milkmaid* and *Ecce Homo,* the latter much admired by REMBRANDT. He is thought to have developed the technique of etching on copper (instead of iron) plates; the softness of copper permitted him to combine etching and line engraving in the same print. He was also among the first to employ AERIAL PERSPECTIVE in prints. Though his paintings seldom attain the power of his engravings, he was an outstanding Netherlandish painter of his period; *The Last Judgment* (1526–27) is his most celebrated painting.

Luce, Clare Boothe *orig.* **Clare Boothe** (1903–1987) U.S. politician and dramatist. She worked as an editor at fashion magazines before marrying HENRY R. LUCE in 1935. Three of her witty plays were adapted into films: *The Women* (1936), *Kiss the Boys Goodbye* (1938), and *Margin for Error* (1939). As a member of the House of Representatives 1943–47, she became influential in Republican Party politics. She served as ambassador to Italy 1953–56. In 1983 she was awarded the Presidential Medal of Freedom.

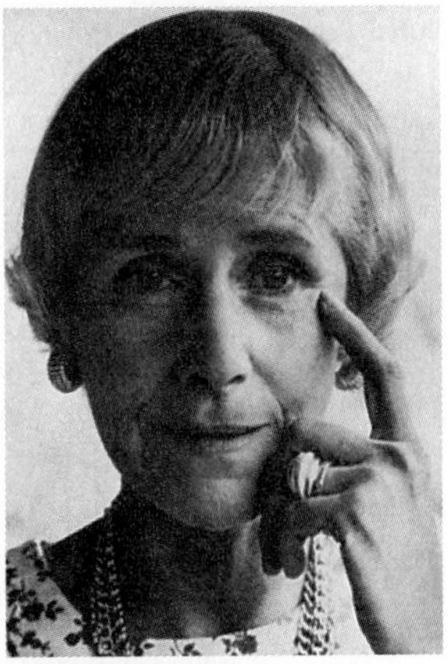
Clare Boothe Luce.
CAMERA PRESS

Luce, Henry R(obinson) (1898–1967) U.S. (Chinese-born) magazine publisher. Born to missionary parents, Luce graduated from Yale University in 1920. While at Yale he met Briton Hadden, with whom he launched *TIME* in 1923. He added to his publishing empire with the business magazine *Fortune,* begun in 1929, and *LIFE*, begun in 1936. Among other Luce magazines were *House & Home*, established in 1952, and *Sports Illustrated*, launched in 1954. His publications, founded as means of educating what Luce considered a poorly informed U.S. public, had many imitators, and Luce became one of the most powerful figures in the history of U.S. journalism. Both he and his wife, CLARE BOOTHE LUCE, had a major influence on the Republican Party and on national affairs.

Lucerne \lü-'sərn\ *German* **Luzern** \lüt-'sern\ City (pop., 1998 est.: 57,193), central Switzerland. Located southwest of ZURICH, on a river outlet of Lake LUCERNE, it developed around an 8th-century monastery. It joined the Swiss Confederation in 1332. A stronghold of Catholicism during the REFORMATION, it later took part in the SONDERBUND war. It is a tourist center, with its medieval walls, towers, and covered bridges. Among its many monuments is the famous "Lion of Lucerne," carved in rock, and commemorating the Swiss Guards slain while defending the Tuileries Palace in PARIS in 1792.

Lucerne, Lake *or* **Lake of the Four Forest Cantons** *German* **Vierwaldstätter See** \'fēr-vält-,shtet-ər-'zā\ Lake, central Switzerland. It is 24 mi (39 km) long and 0.5-2 mi (0.8-3 km) wide, with an area of 44 sq mi (114 sq km). It has a maximum depth of 702 ft (214 m). The "Cross of Lucerne" is formed by its four main basins, which are joined by narrow channels. Named after the city of LUCERNE at its western end, it is in a region of resorts and tourist attractions.

Luchow See HEFEI

Lucian \'lü-shən\ *Greek* **Lucianos** *Latin* **Lucianus** (c. AD 120–after 180) Ancient Greek rhetorician, pamphleteer, and satirist. As a young man he acquired a Greek literary education while traveling through western Asia Minor. He became a public speaker before turning to writing essays. His works, outstanding for their mordant wit, are a sophisticated critique of the shams and follies of the literature, philosophy, and intellectual life of his day. In such works as *Charon, Dialogues of the Dead, True History,* and *Nigrinus,* he satirized nearly every aspect of human behavior. His best work of literary criticism is *How to Write History*.

Luciano \lü-'chä-nō\, **Lucky** *orig.* **Salvatore Lucania** *later* **Charles Luciano** (1896–1962) U.S. (Italian-born) gangster. He emigrated with his family to New York in 1906, and was soon involved in crime. In 1916 he joined Frank Costello and MEYER LANSKY, earning the nickname "Lucky" by evading arrest and winning at craps. He joined crime boss Joe Masseria in 1920, and was soon directing Masseria's bootlegging, narcotics, and prostitution rackets. In 1931 he planned the assassinations of both Masseria and rival boss Salvatore Maranzano, and began developing a national crime syndicate. Jailed for extortion in 1936, he continued to direct crime operations from his prison cell. In 1946 his sentence was commuted and he was deported to Italy, where he continued to direct drug traffic and the smuggling of aliens into the U.S.

Lucifer In classical mythology, the morning star (the planet VENUS at dawn), personified as a male figure. Lucifer (Latin: "Light-Bearer") carried a torch and served as herald of the dawn. In Christian times, Lucifer came to be regarded as the name of Satan before his fall; it was thus used by JOHN MILTON in *Paradise Lost*.

Lucite *or* **Plexiglas** *or* **Perspex** Trademark names of the organic compound polymethyl methacrylate, a synthetic POLYMER of methyl methacrylate. Colorless and highly transparent, it has high dimensional stability and good resistance to weathering and shock. It is used in aircraft canopies and windows, boat windshields, and the like. An object made of Lucite has the unusual property of keeping a beam of light reflected within its surfaces and thus carrying the beam around bends and corners; Lucite is therefore used in devices for illuminating interior organs during surgery, as well as for ornaments, medallions, and lenses.

Lucknow \'lək-,naù\ City (metro. area pop., 1995: 2,029,000) and capital, UTTAR PRADESH state, northern India, on the Gomati River southeast of DELHI. It was captured by the Mughal ruler BABUR in 1528 and under his grandson AKBAR became part of OUDH province. In 1775 it became the capital of Oudh. It is now an important rail center with paper factories and other industrial development. Notable sites include the Great Imambara (tomb) of one of the nabobs of Oudh, the Residency where the British were besieged during the INDIAN MUTINY of 1857, and the University of Lucknow.

Lucretius \lü-'krē-shəs\ *in full* **Titus Lucretius Carus** (96?–c. 55 BC) Latin poet and philosopher. He is known for his long poem *On the Nature of Things,* the fullest extant statement of the physical theory of EPICURUS. In it he established the main principles of ATOMISM and refuted the rival theories of HERACLEITUS, EMPEDOCLES, and ANAXAGORAS; demonstrated the mortality of the soul, employing a sermon on the theme "Death is nothing to us"; described the mechanics of sense perception, thought, and certain bodily functions and condemned sexual passion; and described the creation and working of this world and the celestial bodies and the evolution of life and human society.

Lucullus \lü-'kə-ləs\, **Lucius Licinius** (117?–58/56 BC) Roman general who served as CONSUL 74 BC. He fought alongside SULLA and was the only officer to take part in Sulla's march on Rome. After Sulla's death, Lucullus maintained his power through intrigue. He commanded the legions that drove MITHRADATES from Bithynia and Pontus to Armenia, and later invaded Armenia and defeated its king, Tigranes. Mutinies prevented complete victory, and Lucullus was replaced by POMPEY, whom he opposed in the Senate. His legendary hedonism and extravagance made "Lucullan" a synonym of "lavish."

Lucy Nickname for a remarkably complete (40% intact) HOMINID skeleton found by Donald Johanson at HADAR, Ethiopia, in 1974 and dated to 3.2 million years ago. The specimen is usually classed as *AUSTRALOPITHECUS afarensis,* and suggests—by virtue of its long arms, short legs, apelike chest and jaw, small brain, but relatively human pelvis—that bipedal locomotion preceded the development of a larger (humanlike) brain

L
M
N

in hominid evolution. Lucy stood about 3 ft 7 in. (109 cm) and weighed about 60 lbs (27 kg). See also LAETOLI FOOTPRINTS, STERKFONTEIN.

lud \'lüd\ Among the Votyak and Zyryan peoples of Russia, a sacred grove, usually consisting of fir trees, where sacrifices were performed. Enclosed by a high fence, the lud contained a place for a fire and tables for the sacrificial meal. It was forbidden to break even a branch from a tree in the grove, which was watched over by a hereditary guardian. The annual sacrificial rite generally centered on an ancient tree dedicated to a deity. All food had to be consumed at the site, and the hides of sacrificed animals were hung from the trees. Groves were sacred in most other FINNO-UGRIC RELIGIONS as well.

Luda See DALIAN

Luddite Member of organized groups of early-19th-century English craftsmen who surreptitiously destroyed the textile machinery that was replacing them. The movement began in Nottingham in 1811 and spread to other areas in 1812. The Luddites, or "Ludds," were named after a probably mythical leader, Ned Ludd. Harsh repressive measures by the government included a mass trial at York in 1813 that resulted in many hangings and banishments. The term Luddite was later used to describe anyone opposed to technological change.

Ludendorff \'lü-dᵊn-ˌdȯrf\, **Erich** (1865–1937) German general. In 1908 he joined the German army general staff and worked under HELMUTH VON MOLTKE in revising the SCHLIEFFEN PLAN. In World War I he was appointed chief of staff to PAUL VON HINDENBURG, and the two won a spectacular victory at the Battle of TANNENBERG. In 1917 Ludendorff approved unrestricted submarine warfare against the British, which led to the U.S.'s entry into the war. In 1918 his offensive on the Western Front failed and he demanded an armistice, but then insisted the war continue when he realized the severity of the ARMISTICE conditions. Political leaders opposed him, and he resigned his post. Ludendorff insisted he had been betrayed, and for the next 20 years he led reactionary political movements and took part in the KAPP PUTSCH (1920) and BEER HALL PUTSCH (1923). He served in Parliament as a National Socialist (1924–28) and believed that "supranational powers"—Jewry, Christianity, Freemasonry—had deprived him and Germany of victory in World War I.

Ludendorff, c. 1930.
ARCHIV FUR KUNST UND GESCHICHTE, BERLIN

Ludlum, Robert (1927–2001) U.S. author of spy thrillers. Born in New York City, he worked in the theater as an actor and a successful producer and acted for television before turning to writing. Among his best-sellers were *The Scarlatti Inheritance* (1971), *The Osterman Weekend* (1972; film, 1983), *The Matarese Circle* (1979), and *The Bourne Identity* (1980; film, 1988). Though critics often found his plots unlikely and his prose uninspired, his fast-paced combination of international espionage, conspiracy, and mayhem proved enormously popular.

Ludwig, Carl F(riedrich) W(ilhelm) (1816–1895) German physician. He invented devices to record arterial blood-pressure changes, measure blood flow, and separate gases from blood (which established their role in blood purification). He was the first to keep animal organs alive outside the body. His paper on urine secretion in 1844 hypothesized a filtering role for the kidney. Nearly 200 of Ludwig's students became prominent scientists, and he is regarded as the founder of the physicochemical school of physiology.

Ludwig I \'lüt-vik\ *or* **Louis I** (1786–1868) King of Bavaria (1825–48). The son of MAXIMILIAN I, Ludwig won early acclaim as a liberal and a German nationalist, but after his accession he feuded with the Diet and came to distrust all democratic institutions. By 1837 the reactionary Bavarian government had begun to erode the liberal constitution of 1818 that Ludwig had worked to establish. An outstanding patron of the arts, he collected the art works that fill Munich's museums and transformed Munich into the artistic center of Germany. His planning created the city's present layout and classic style. He caused scandal by his affair with L. MONTEZ, and at the outbreak of the REVOLUTIONS OF 1848 he abdicated in favor of his son MAXIMILIAN II.

Ludwig II *or* **Louis II** *known as* **Mad King Ludwig** (1845–1886) King of Bavaria (1864–86). The son of MAXIMILIAN II of Bavaria, he supported Prussia in the FRANCO-PRUSSIAN WAR (1870–71). He brought his territories into the newly founded German empire in 1871 but concerned himself only intermittently with affairs of state, preferring a life of increasingly morbid seclusion. He developed a mania for extravagant building projects; the most fantastic, NEUSCHWANSTEIN, was a fairy-tale castle decorated with scenes from operas by RICHARD WAGNER. Formally declared insane, he drowned himself three days later.

Ludwig IV See LOUIS IV

Lueger \'lü̅-gər\, **Karl** (1844–1910) Austrian politician. He was elected to the Vienna city council (1875) and to the Austrian parliament (1885), and cofounded the Christian Social Party (1889). He effectively used the prevalent anti-Semitic and German nationalist currents in Vienna to advance his political objectives. He was elected mayor of Vienna in 1895 and transformed the Austrian capital into a modern city, bringing streetcars, electricity, and gas under city government control. He also developed parks, schools, and hospitals. He was instrumental in introducing universal suffrage in Austria (1907).

luffa See LOOFAH

Lufthansa *in full* **Deutsche Lufthansa AG** Leading air passenger, cargo, and airline services company with headquarters in Cologne, Germany. As of 2002 it had more than 300 destinations in 90 countries.

Lugano \lü-'gä-nō\, **Lake** *or* **Lago Ceresio** \che-'res-yō\ Lake in Switzerland and Italy, located between MAGGIORE and COMO lakes. Straddling the border of the two countries, it has an area of 19 sq mi (49 sq km) and a maximum depth of 945 ft (288 m). Between Melide and Bissone, the lake is so shallow that a stone dam across it carries the St. Gotthard railway. The resort town of Lugano (pop., 1998 est.: 25,771), on its shores in Switzerland, is Italian in appearance.

Lake Lugano, near Lugano, Switz.
R.G. EVERTS—RAPHO/PHOTO RESEARCHERS

Lugard \lü-'gärd\, **F(rederick) (John) D(ealtry)** *later* **Baron Lugard (of Abinger)** (1858–1945) British colonial administrator. In Nigeria he served as high commissioner (1900–6) and governor and governor-general (1912–19). He fought as an officer in British campaigns in Asia and North Africa before accepting posts with the British East Africa Co., the Royal Niger Co., and other private enterprises. He succeeded, in advance of the French, in establishing trade routes centered at BUGANDA, the Middle Niger, and Bechuanaland. As the chief government administrator in Nigeria, he succeeded in uniting the disparate northern and southern districts and greatly influenced British colonial policy by exercising control centrally through native rulers and respecting native legal systems and customs.

Lugdunensis \ˌləg-də-ˈnen-sis\ Roman province, one of the three administrative divisions of GAUL. It extended northwest from its capital at Lugdunum (modern LYON) and included the land between the SEINE and LOIRE rivers up to BRITTANY and the Atlantic coast. It was conquered by Julius CAESAR during the GALLIC WARS and became a Roman province in 27 BC under AUGUSTUS.

lugeing \ˈlü-zhiŋ\ Sled-racing using a small sled (luge) that is ridden in a supine position and steered with the feet and a hand rope. Dating back to the 16th century, lugeing is a traditional winter sport in Austria and is also practiced in other countries. The course used is similar to that employed in BOBSLEDDING, and speeds above 60 mph (100 kph) are not uncommon. Lugeing became a Winter Olympics sport in 1964.

Lugones \lü-ˈgō-nās\, **Leopoldo** (1874–1938) Argentine poet, critic, and cultural ambassador. He initially worked as a socialist journalist, but thought of himself primarily as a poet. His early verse, collected in such volumes as *Las montañas del oro* (1897; "Mountains of Gold"), reveals his affinity with MODERNISMO. Later he embraced political conservatism, and his poetry and prose treated national themes in a realistic style. He was director of the National Council of Education 1914–38, and also produced histories of Argentina and studies and translations of classical Greek literature. He strongly influenced such younger writers as JORGE LUIS BORGES.

Lugosi \lə-ˈgō-sē\, **Bela** *orig.* **Béla Ferenc Dezsö Blaskó** (1882–1956) Hungarian-U.S. film actor. He acted with the National Theater in Budapest (1913–19) and appeared in German films before coming to the U.S. in 1921. He directed and starred in the play *Dracula* in New York in 1927; he reprised the role, which was ideally suited for his aristocratic manner and heavy accent, in the movie *Dracula* (1931). His other horror movies included *The Black Cat* (1934), *Mark of the Vampire* (1935), *Son of Frankenstein* (1939), and *The Ape Man* (1943). He died while making the low-budget *Plan 9 from Outer Space* (1956).

Lugosi as Count Dracula.
CULVER PICTURES

Lugus \ˈlü-gəs\ *or* **Lug** Major god of the CELTIC RELIGION. In Irish tradition, Lug Lámfota ("Lug of the Long Arm") was the sole survivor of triplet brothers. In Wales, as Lleu Llaw Gyffes ("Lleu of the Dexterous Hand"), he was said to be the son of the virgin goddess Aranrhod. His mother sought to destroy him, but his uncle Gwydion raised him and kept him safe. When his mother denied him a wife, Gwydion created a woman for him from flowers. His name is an element in such European and British place-names as Lyon, Leiden, and Carlisle.

Luhya *or* **Luyia** \ˈlü-yə\ Cluster of several closely related Bantu-speaking peoples of western Kenya. They emerged as a coherent group only c. 1945, when it was found to be politically advantageous to possess a supertribal identity. Today, numbering 3.5 million, the Luhya are the second-largest ethnic group in Kenya. They grow corn, cotton, and sugarcane as cash crops, and millet, sorghum, and vegetables as staples, and also keep livestock. Many have moved to urban areas seeking work.

Luichow Peninsula See LEIZHOU PENINSULA

Luini \lü-ˈē-nē\, **Bernardino** (c. 1480/85–1532) Italian painter active in Milan. Little is known of his life. His earliest surviving works are a polyptych in a church near Como (c. 1510) and a fresco *Madonna and Child* (1512) at the Cistercian monastery of Chiravalle, near Milan. He was a prominent follower of LEONARDO DA VINCI in Lombardy; many of his frescoes and altarpieces are in Lombard churches. He also painted mythological subjects, most notably a *Europa* and a *Cephalus and Procris* (c. 1520), originally for a Milanese palace.

Lukács \ˈlü-ˌkäch\, **György** (1885–1971) Hungarian philosopher and critic. Born into a wealthy Jewish family, he joined the Hungarian Communist Party in 1918. In *History and Class Consciousness* (1923), he developed a Marxist philosophy of history and laid the basis for his literary criticism by linking the development of form in art with the history of the class struggle. A major figure during the 1956 Hungarian uprising, he was deported but was allowed to return in 1957. His works include the essay collection *Soul and Form* (1911) and *The Historical Novel* (1955). His earlier work, especially *Theory of the Novel* (1920) and *History and Class Consciousness* (1923), is now considered superior to his later Stalinist-influenced criticism, which celebrated the official Soviet policy of Socialist Realism.

Luke, St. (fl. 1st century AD) In Christian tradition, the author of the third GOSPEL and the Acts of the Apostles. He wrote in Greek and is considered the most literary of the NEW TESTAMENT writers. By his own account, he was not an eyewitness to the ministry of JESUS. He was a companion to St. PAUL, who called him the "beloved physician," and he is believed to have accompanied Paul on missionary journeys to Macedonia and Rome. Though little is known of his life, tradition holds that he was a gentile and a native of Antioch in Syria, and that he died a martyr.

Lula See Luis SILVA

Lully \lü-ˈlē\, **Jean-Baptiste** *orig.* **Giovanni Battista Lulli** (1632–1687) French (Italian-born) composer. Born in Florence, he was made a ward of the court after his mother died, and was sent to a noble French household at age 13 as valet. There he learned guitar, organ, violin, and dancing, and came to know the composer Michel Lambert (1610–1696), who introduced him to society and later became his father-in-law. Lully became a dancer and musician for the king and at 30 was put in charge of all royal music. In the 1660s he composed the incidental music for MOLIÈRE's plays as well as those of France's great tragedians. In the early 1670s he obtained the sole patent to present opera and produced the series of "lyric tragedies," most with librettos by Philippe Quinault (1635–1688), for which he is known, including *Alceste* (1674), *Atys* (1676), and *Armide* (1686). The orchestra he developed was an important forerunner of the modern orchestra. A self-inflicted injury to his toe with his heavy conducting stick led to his death. His style prevailed in France for many decades after his death.

Lully, Raymond See Ramon LLULL

lumber Collective term for harvested wood, whether cut into logs, heavy timbers, or members used in light-frame construction. Lumber is classified as hardwood or softwood (see WOOD). The term often refers specifically to the products derived from logs in a sawmill. Conversion of logs to sawed lumber involves debarking, sawing into boards or slabs, resawing into thinner boards of varying sizes, edging, crosscutting to square the ends and remove defects, grading according to strength and appearance, and drying in the open air or in kilns. Drying below the fiber-saturation point results in shrinkage and generally greater strength, stiffness, and density and better prepares the wood for finishing. Preservatives are often applied to protect the wood from deterioration and decay.

Lumet \ˈlu̇-mət\, **Sidney** (born 1924) U.S. television and film director. Born in Philadelphia, he worked a child actor in the Yiddish theater and on Broadway. After serving in World War II, he directed plays and taught acting. He directed over 200 television dramas for CBS (1951–57), including *Playhouse 90* and *Studio One* productions, before making his debut as a movie director with the acclaimed *Twelve Angry Men* (1957). He showed himself a master of psychological drama with such films as *The Fugitive Kind* (1960), *Fail Safe* (1964), *The Pawnbroker* (1965), *Serpico* (1973), *Dog Day Afternoon* (1975), *Network* (1976), *Prince of the City* (1981), *The Verdict* (1982), and *Night Falls on Manhattan* (1997).

Auguste Lumière.
BOYER–H. ROGER-VIOLLET

Lumière \lu̇e-ˈmyer\, **Auguste and Louis** (1862–1954, 1864–1948) French inventors. In 1882 Louis developed a method of making photographic plates, and by

1894 the brothers' factory was producing 15 million plates a year. They worked on improving THOMAS ALVA EDISON's Kinetoscope and patented their combination movie camera and projector, the Cinématographe, in 1895. Their film "Workers Leaving the Lumière Factory," which they showed to a paying audience in Paris in 1895, is considered the first movie. In 1896 the brothers, led by Louis, made over 40 films recording everyday French life. They made the first newsreels, sending crews all over the world to shoot new material and show their films. In addition to the films he directed, Louis served as producer for some 2,000 films. The brothers also made basic innovations in color photography.

luminaire *or* **light fixture** Complete lighting unit, consisting of one or more lamps (bulbs or tubes that emit light), along with the socket and other parts that hold the lamp in place and protect it, wiring that connects the lamp to a power source, and a reflector that helps direct and distribute the light. Fluorescent fixtures usually have lenses or louvers to shield the lamp (thus reducing glare) and redirect the light emitted. Luminaires include both portable and ceiling- or wall-mounted fixtures.

luminescence Process by which an excited material emits light in a process not caused solely by a rise in temperature. The EXCITATION is usually achieved with ULTRAVIOLET RADIATION, X RAYS, ELECTRONS, alpha particles, ELECTRIC FIELDS, or CHEMICAL ENERGY. The color, or wavelength, of the light emitted is determined by the material, while the intensity depends on both the material and the input energy. Examples of luminescence include light emissions from neon lamps, luminescent watch dials, television and computer screens, fluorescent lamps, and fireflies. See also BIOLUMINESCENCE, FLUORESCENCE, PHOSPHORESCENCE.

Luminism Painting style that emphasizes a particular clarity of light. It is characteristic of the works of a group of U.S. painters of the later 19th century, influenced by the HUDSON RIVER SCHOOL. Typically landscapes or seascapes, with sky occupying nearly half of the composition, Luminist works are distinguished by cool, clear colors and meticulously detailed objects modeled by light. The most prominent Luminist painters were MARTIN JOHNSON HEADE and FitzHugh Lane.

Lumumba \lə-'mùm-bə\, **Patrice (Hemery)** (1925–1961) African nationalist leader, first prime minister of the Democratic Republic of the CONGO (June–September 1960). Lumumba worked as a trade-union organizer before founding the Mouvement National Congolais, Congo's first nationwide political party, in 1958. That same year his militant nationalism at a major PAN-AFRICAN conference in Accra brought him to prominence. During negotiations in Belgium in 1960, he was asked to form the first independent Congolese government. His rival MOISE TSHOMBE immediately announced the secession of Katanga province. When Belgian troops arrived to sustain the secession, Lumumba appealed first to the U.N. and then to the Soviet Union. He was dismissed by Pres. JOSEPH KASAVUBU and, a short time later, assassinated by Tshombe loyalists. His death caused a scandal throughout Africa, where he was looked on as a leader of Pan-Africanism.

Lumumba.
AGENCE DALMAS

Luna See SELENE

Luna Any of a series of 24 unmanned Soviet lunar probes, launched between 1959 and 1976, responsible for various lunar "firsts." Luna 2 (1959) was the first spacecraft to strike the MOON; Luna 3 (1959) was the first to circle the moon and took the first photographs of its far side. Luna 9 (1966) made the first successful lunar soft landing. Luna 16 (1970) was the first unmanned spacecraft to carry lunar soil samples back to earth. Luna 17 (1970) soft-landed a robot vehicle for exploration; it also contained television equipment and sent live pictures of several miles of the moon's surface. See also PIONEER, RANGER, SURVEYOR.

luna moth Species *(Actias luna)* of SATURNIID MOTH of eastern North America. Lunas are pale green and have a wingspread of 4 in. (10 cm). The wings have a thin brown border, and each hind wing has a long tail-like projection. The larvae feed on the leaves of many kinds of trees and shrubs. See also MOTH.

Lunacharsky, Anatoly (Vasilyevich) (1875–1933) Russian politician and writer. Deported in 1898 for his revolutionary activities, he joined the Bolsheviks in 1904 and disseminated propaganda to Russian students and political refugees in foreign countries. He joined VLADIMIR ILICH LENIN in Russia in 1917 and was appointed commissar for education, and in this role did much to ensure the preservation of works of art during the Russian Civil War. He encouraged innovation in the theater and in education, and published plays of his own.

Lunceford \'ləns-fərd\, **Jimmy** *orig.* **James Melvin** (1902–1947) U.S. musician and arranger, leader of one of the most original and popular big bands of the SWING era. Born in Fulton, Mo., Lunceford was a well-schooled musician who played saxophone and taught music before forming a band in 1929. Trumpeter and arranger Sy Oliver joined in 1933, bringing a crisp ensemble sound to the two-beat rhythmic approach of the band. Lunceford's band gained national attention after succeeding CAB CALLOWAY at the Cotton Club in Harlem in 1934, and was thereafter counted among the finest big bands in jazz, rivaling DUKE ELLINGTON and COUNT BASIE in popularity.

Lunda empire See LUBA-LUNDA STATES

Lundy, Benjamin (1789–1839) U.S. abolitionist and publisher. Born in Sussex Co., N.J., he worked in Virginia and Ohio, where he organized the Union Humane Society (1815), one of the first antislavery societies. He founded and edited the *Genius of Universal Emancipation* (1821–35), then founded the *National Enquirer* (later the *Pennsylvania Freeman*) in Philadelphia (1836–38). He traveled in search of places for former slaves to settle, including Canada and Haiti.

lung Either of two light, spongy, elastic organs in the chest, used for breathing. Each is enclosed in a membrane (pleura). Contraction of the DIAPHRAGM and the muscles between the ribs draw air into the lungs through the TRACHEA, which splits into two primary bronchi, one per lung. Each bronchus branches into secondary bronchi (one per lobe of lung), tertiary bronchi (one per segment of lung), and many bronchioles leading to the PULMONARY ALVEOLI. There, oxygen in the inspired gas is exchanged for carbon dioxide from the blood in the surrounding CAPILLARIES (see PULMONARY CIRCULATION). Adequate tissue oxygen supply depends on sufficient distribution of air (ventilation) and blood (perfusion) in the lungs. Lung injuries or diseases (e.g., EMPHYSEMA, EMBOLISM, PNEUMONIA) can affect either or both.

lung cancer Malignant tumor of the LUNG, the leading cause of CANCER-related death in the U.S. Four major types (squamous-cell carcinoma, adenocarcinoma, large-cell carcinoma, and small-cell carcinoma) have roughly equal prevalence. Most cases are due to long-term cigarette SMOKING. Heavy smoking and starting smoking earlier in life increase the risk. Passive inhalation ("secondhand smoke") is linked to lung cancer in nonsmokers. Other risk factors include exposure to RADON or ASBESTOS. Symptoms, including coughing (sometimes with blood), chest pain, and shortness of breath, seldom appear until lung cancer is advanced, when treatment with surgery, chemotherapy, and radiation or some combination of the three is less effective. Most patients die within a year of diagnosis.

lung collapse See ATELECTASIS

lung congestion Distention of blood vessels in the lungs and filling of the PULMONARY ALVEOLI with blood. It results from infection, HYPERTENSION, or inadequate heart function (e.g., left-sided HEART FAILURE, MITRAL STENOSIS). Congestion seriously impairs gas exchange, leading to breathing difficulty, bloody discharge in sputum, and bluish skin tint.

lung infarction Death of lung tissue due to inadequate blood supply. It is usually caused by obstruction of a pulmonary blood vessel by either EMBOLISM or THROMBOSIS, most often in an impaired lung. If it extends to the lung's surface, fluids and blood can seep out and distend the pleura, making breathing difficult and occasionally painful. Other symptoms include spitting up blood, coughing, and fever. Blood analysis shows a high white-cell count and red-cell sedimentation rate. The dead tissue (infarct) is replaced by scar tissue.

Lung-men caves See LONGMEN CAVES

Lung-shan culture See LONGSHAN CULTURE

Luni River \'lü-nē\ River, RAJASTHAN state, western India. Rising in the western Aravalli Range, where it is known as the Sagarmati, it flows southwest and enters a patch of desert before dissipating into the Rann of KACHCHH, after a total course of 330 mi (530 km). Its Sanskrit name is Lavanavari ("Salt River"), referring to its high salinity. The major river in the region, it serves as a source of irrigation.

Lunt, Alfred and Lynn Fontanne *orig.* **Lillie Louise** (1892–1977, 1887–1983) U.S. acting team. Born in Milwaukee, Lunt made his acting debut in Boston in 1912 and starred in *Clarence* on Broadway (1919). Fontanne, born in England, made her acting debut in London in 1909 and in New York in 1910. She and Lunt married in 1922 and performed with the THEATRE GUILD in 1924–29. They acted together in more than 25 plays, including *The Guardsmen* (1924), *Arms and the Man* (1925), *Elizabeth the Queen* (1930), *Design for Living* (1933), *Idiots Delight* (1936), *The Pirate* (1942), *O Mistress Mine* (1946), and *The Visit* (1958). Considered the foremost acting couple of the U.S. theater, they were acclaimed for the subtlety and effortless cooperation of their performances, especially in comedies by GEORGE BERNARD SHAW and NOEL COWARD.

Lunyu \'lün-'yü\ *English* ***Analects*** One of four Confucian texts that, when published together in 1190 by ZHU XI, made up the FOUR BOOKS. Scholars consider *Lunyu* the most reliable source of the doctrine of CONFUCIUS. It covers almost all the basic ethical concepts of CONFUCIANISM—for example, REN (benevolence), *junzi* (the superior man), TIAN (Heaven), *zhong yong* (doctrine of the mean), *li* (proper conduct), and *zheng ming* (rectification of names). It also contains many direct quotations from Confucius and personal glimpses of the sage as recorded by his disciples. See also NEO-CONFUCIANISM, ZHONG YONG.

Luo \lə-'wō\ People of the flat country near Lake Victoria in western Kenya and northern Uganda who speak a language of the NILO-SAHARAN family. Numbering 3.2 million, the Luo are the third-largest ethnic group in Kenya. They are settled agriculturalists who also keep cattle; many work as agricultural laborers and in urban occupations. Most are Christians. See also NILOTES.

Lupercalia \,lü-pər-'kā-lē-ə\ Ancient Roman festival held each February 15. Its origins are uncertain, but the likely derivation of its name from *lupus* (Latin: "wolf") may signal a connection with a primitive deity who protected herds from wolves or with the legendary she-wolf who nursed ROMULUS AND REMUS. Each Lupercalia began with the sacrifice of goats and a dog; two of its priests (Luperci) were then led to the altar and their foreheads were anointed with blood. After all had feasted, the Luperci cut thongs from the skins of the sacrificed animals and ran around the Palatine hill, striking at any woman who came near them; a blow from the thong was supposed to bestow fertility.

lupine *or* **lupin** \'lü-pən\ Any of about 200 species of herbaceous and partly woody plants that make up the genus *Lupinus* in the pea family (see LEGUME), found throughout the Mediterranean and especially on the prairies of western North America. Many are grown in the U.S. as ornamentals, and a few species are useful as cover or forage crops. Herbaceous lupines, which grow up to 4 ft (1.25 m) tall, have low, divided leaves and an upright flower spike, and many are hybridized for gardens. The name comes from the Latin for "wolf" because these plants were once thought to deplete, or "wolf," minerals from the soil; in actuality some species aid soil fertility through NITROGEN FIXATION.

Lupino family \lü-'pē-nō\ Celebrated British theatrical family. The earliest member, Signor Luppino, flourished probably in Italy c. 1610. His descendant George William Luppino (1632–1693), a puppet master, emigrated to England as a political refugee. A later descendant, the scenic artist and dancer Thomas Frederick Lupino (1749–1845), spelled the family name Lupino. Another family member, George Hook Lupino (1820–1902), had 16 children, 10 of whom were dancers. His eldest son George Lupino (1853–1932) was a famous clown; George's son Barry Lupino (1884–1962) excelled in pantomime and musical comedy; another son, Stanley Lupino (1894–1942), performed in comedy revues. Stanley's nephew Henry Lupino (1892–1959), a cockney comedian known as Lupino Lane, created the "Lambeth walk" dance in the musical *Me and My Girl* (1937). Stanley's daughter Ida Lupino (1916–1995) moved to the U.S. in 1934, where she starred in such movies as *They Drive by Night* (1940), *The Sea Wolf* (1941), and *The Hard Way* (1942). One of the first women film directors, she was noted for *The Hitch-Hiker* (1953) and *The Bigamist* (1953), and also directed several dramas for television.

lupus erythematosus \'lü-pəs-,er-ə-,thē-mə-'tō-səs\ Either of two inflammatory AUTOIMMUNE DISEASES, both more common in women. In the discoid type, a skin disease, red patches with grayish brown scales appear on the upper cheeks and nose (often in a butterfly pattern), scalp, lips, and/or inner cheeks. Sunlight worsens it. Antimalarial drugs may help. The second type, systemic (disseminated) lupus erythematosus (SLE), may affect any organ or structure, especially the skin (with marks like those of the discoid type), kidneys, heart, nervous system, serous (moisture-forming) membranes (e.g., in synovial joints or lining the abdomen), and lymph nodes, with acute episodes and remissions. Symptoms vary widely. Kidney and central-nervous-system involvement can be life-threatening. Treatment includes pain relief, control of inflammation, and trying to limit damage to vital organs.

Luria, A(leksandr) R(omanovich) (1902–1977) Soviet neuropsychologist. After earning degrees in psychology, education, and medicine, he became professor of psychology at Moscow State University and later head of its department of neuropsychology. Influenced by his former teacher L.S. VYGOTSKY, he studied language disorders and the role of speech in mental development and retardation. During World War II Luria made advances in brain surgery and in the restoration of brain functions after trauma. He also developed theories concerning the functioning of the frontal lobe and the existence of zones of brain cells working in concert. His books include *Higher Cortical Functions in Man* (1966), *The Working Brain* (1973), and *Basic Problems of Neurolinguistics* (1976).

Luria \'lür-yä\, **Isaac ben Solomon** (1534–1572) Jewish mystic and founder of a school of KABBALA. He was born in Jerusalem and brought up in Egypt, where he pursued rabbinic studies. He dedicated himself to the study of the Kabbala with messianic fervor, and in 1570 he journeyed to a center of the movement in Galilee. He died two years later in an epidemic, having written little. The Lurianic Kabbala, a collection of Luria's doctrines recorded after his death by a pupil, had great influence on later Jewish mysticism and on HASIDISM. It propounds a theory of the creation and later degeneration of the world and calls for restoration of the original harmony through ritual meditation and secret combinations of words.

Luria \'lür-ē-ə\, **Salvador (Edward)** (1912–1991) Italian-U.S. biologist. He fled Italy for France in 1938, arriving in the U.S. in 1940. In 1942 he obtained an electron micrograph of phage particles that confirmed earlier descriptions of them as consisting of a round head and a thin tail. In 1943 he and MAX DELBRUCK showed that viruses can undergo permanent changes in their hereditary material. He also proved that the simultaneous existence of phage-resistant bacteria with phage-sensitive bacteria in the same culture was a result of the selection of spontaneous bacterial mutants. In 1945 he and A. D. HERSHEY demonstrated the existence not only of such bacterial mutants but also of spontaneous phage mutants. The three men shared a 1969 Nobel Prize.

Luristan Bronze \'lür-ə-,stan\ *or* **Lorestan Bronze** \'lōr-ə-,stan\ Objects excavated since the late 1920s in the valleys of the Zagros Mountains in the Luristan region of western Iran. Dating from c. 1500 to c. 500 BC, they consist of utensils, weapons, jewelry, horse trappings, belt buckles, and ritual and votive objects. They are believed to have been produced either by the CIMMERIANS or by Indo-European peoples of MEDIA or PERSIA.

Lusaka \lü-'sä-kä\ City (pop., 1990: 982,000; 1999 est., metropolitan area pop.: 1,577,000), capital of ZAMBIA. In the 1890s the area was taken by the British South Africa Co. during the formation of Northern RHODESIA; it became the capital in 1935. After the federation of Northern and Southern Rhodesia in 1953, it was a center of the civil-disobedience movement that led to the creation of the independent state of Zambia in 1960, with Lusaka as its capital. Possessing some light industry, it is also a commercial center for the surrounding agricultural region. The University of Zambia (founded 1965) is located nearby.

Lüshun *or* **Lü-shun** \'lü-'shün\ *formerly* **Port Arthur** Town, LIAONING province, northeastern China. Situated at the southern tip of the LIAODONG PENINSULA, near DALIAN, it was used as a staging post as early as the 2nd century BC. Fortified under the MING DYNASTY, it was captured by the MANCHUS in 1633 and served as the seat of a defense unit under the

QING DYNASTY. In 1878 it became the chief base for China's first modern naval force. Leased to Russia in 1898, it was captured by Japan (1905) in the RUSSO–JAPANESE WAR and made the seat of a provincial government. Under a 1945 treaty it became a Sino-Soviet military base; the Soviet forces withdrew in 1955.

Lusitania British ocean liner sunk by a German submarine off the coast of Ireland on May 7, 1915. The British Admiralty had warned the *Lusitania* to avoid the area and to use the evasive tactic of zigzagging, but the crew ignored these recommendations. Though unarmed, the ship was carrying munitions for the Allies, and the Germans had circulated warnings that the ship would be sunk. The loss of life—1,198 people drowned, including 128 U.S. citizens—outraged public opinion. The U.S. protested Germany's action, and it limited its submarine campaign against Britain. When Germany renewed unrestricted submarine warfare, the U.S. entered World War I in April 1917.

Lussac, Joseph Gay- See Joseph GAY-LUSSAC

luster In mineralogy, the appearance of a mineral surface in terms of its light-reflecting qualities. Luster depends on a mineral's refractivity (see REFRACTION), transparency, and structure. Variations in these properties produce different kinds of luster, from metallic (e.g., gold) to dull (e.g., chalk).

lustered glass *or* **lustred glass** Art glass of the ART NOUVEAU style, delicately iridescent with rich colors, mimicking the iridescent sheen produced by the corrosion of ancient buried glassware. In 1893 LOUIS COMFORT TIFFANY founded the Stourbridge Glass Co. to produce lustered drinking glasses, bowls, vases, lamps, and jewelry. His lustered glass, produced by metallic pigments applied to opaque glass, produced a pearl-like sheen, whereas that produced in Europe in the 1870s used transparent glass, which resulted in a mirrorlike surface. Tiffany's wares were so popular that he made thousands of pieces annually until 1933.

lute Plucked STRINGED INSTRUMENT popular in 16th–17th-century Europe. It originated from the Arab UD, which reached Europe in the 13th century. Like the ud, the lute has a deep pear-shaped body with an ornamental soundhole, a fretted neck with a bent-back pegbox, and strings hitched to a bridge glued to the instrument's belly. In later years it acquired several unstopped bass strings. It became the preferred instrument for cultivated amateur musicians and acquired an extensive literature of song accompaniments and solo and consort music.

Angel playing a lute, from "Presentation in the Temple," painted altarpiece by Vittore Carpaccio, 1510; in the Accademia, Venice.

SCALA–ART RESOURCE

Luther, Martin (1483–1546) German priest who sparked the REFORMATION. The son of a miner, he studied philosophy and law before entering an Augustinian monastery in 1505. He was ordained two years later and continued his theological studies at the University of Wittenberg, where he became a professor of biblical theology. He was shocked by the corruption of the clergy on a trip to Rome in 1510, and was later troubled by doubts centering on fear of divine retributive justice. His spiritual crisis was resolved when he hit on the idea of JUSTIFICATION by faith, the doctrine that salvation is granted as a gift through God's grace. He urged reform of the Roman Catholic church, protesting the sale of INDULGENCES and other abuses, and in 1517 he distributed to the archbishop of Mainz and several friends his NINETY-FIVE THESES (according to legend, Luther nailed these theses to the door of the castle church in Wittenberg); the theses questioned Roman Catholic teaching and called for reform. In 1521 he was excommunicated by POPE LEO IX and declared an outlaw at the DIET OF WORMS. Under the protection of the elector of Saxony, Luther took refuge in the Wartburg. There he translated the Bible into German; his superbly vigorous translation has long been regarded as the greatest landmark in the history of the GERMAN LANGUAGE. He later returned to Wittenberg, and in 1525 he married the former nun, Katherina von Bora, with whom he raised six children. Though his preaching was the principal spark that set off the PEASANTS' WAR (1524–26), his vehement denunciation of the peasants contributed to their defeat. His break with Rome led to the founding of the Lutheran Church (see LUTHERANISM); the Lutheran confession of faith or AUGSBURG CONFESSION was produced with Luther's sanction by PHILIPP MELANCHTHON in 1530. Luther's writings included hymns, a liturgy, and many theological works.

Lutheranism Protestant movement founded on the principles of MARTIN LUTHER. Lutheranism arose at the start of the REFORMATION, after Luther posted his NINETY-FIVE THESES in Wittenberg. It spread through much of Germany and into Scandinavia, where it was established by law. It was brought to the New World by the colonists of New Netherland and NEW SWEDEN and spread through the U.S. Middle Atlantic states in the 18th century and the Midwest in the 19th century. Its doctrines are contained in the catechisms of Luther and in the AUGSBURG CONFESSION. Lutheran doctrine emphasizes SALVATION by faith alone and the primacy of the BIBLE as the church's authority. The Lutheran World Federation is based in Geneva. See also PIETISM.

lutite \'lü-,tīt\ Any fine-grained sedimentary rock consisting of clay- or silt-sized particles (less than 0.0025 in., or 0.06 mm, in diameter) that are derived principally from nonmarine (continental) rocks. Laminated lutites and lutites that split easily into thin layers are usually called SHALES. Other lutites may be called claystones, siltstones, or mudstones.

Lutoslawski \,lü-tə-'släv-skē\, **Witold** (1913–1994) Polish composer. Born in Warsaw and trained there, he initially became known as a pianist. His international reputation was secured by the premiere of his *Concerto for Orchestra* (1954), full of color and based on folk elements, and later the *Funeral Music* for string orchestra (1958). From the late 1950s his works incorporate limited aleatory, often using it as a contrast to traditional genres, such as fugue. His four symphonies, particularly the second (1967) and third (1983), are widely admired, as are his *Livre pour orchestra* (1968) and his string quartet (1964).

Lutuli \lə-'tü-lē\, **Albert (John Mvumbi)** (1898–1967) ZULU chief and president of the AFRICAN NATIONAL CONGRESS (1952–60). Trained at a mission school, Lutuli taught and served a small community as chief before being elected ANC president. He was frequently imprisoned for his anti-apartheid activities. He set forth his views in *Let My People Go* (1962). In 1960 he became the first African to be awarded a Nobel Peace Prize.

Lutyens \'lə-chənz\, **Edwin L(andseer)** *later* **Sir Edwin** (1869–1944) British architect. The house at Munstead Wood, Godalming, Surrey (1896), designed for GERTRUDE JEKYLL, established his reputation. In the series of country houses that followed, many designed in collaboration with Jekyll, Lutyens adapted past styles to contemporary domestic life in delightful and original ways. For the new Indian capital at Delhi, he devised a plan based on a series of hexagons separated by broad avenues; his most important building there, the Viceroy's House (1912–30), combined aspects of Classical architecture with Indian motifs. After World War I he became architect to the Imperial War Graves Commission, for which he designed the Cenotaph in London (1919–20) and other memorials.

Luxembourg \'lu̇k-səm-,bürk, *Engl* 'lək-səm-,bərg\ *officially* **Grand Duchy of Luxembourg** Country, western Europe. Area: 998 sq mi (2,586 sq km). Population (2001 est.): 444,000. Capital: LUXEMBOURG. Most of the population is ethnically French or German. Languages: Luxembourgian, French, German. Religions: Roman Catholicism, Protestantism (Lutheranism), Judaism (a small minority). Monetary unit: euro. At 51 mi (82 km) long and 35 mi (56 km) wide, it is divided into two regions: the Oesling, an extension of the Ardennes Mountains in the northern third of the country consisting of a high plateau dissected by river valleys; and the Bon Pays, or Gutland, a rolling plateau that occupies the rest of the country. Luxembourg's economy is largely based on heavy industry and international trade and banking, and its per capita income is the second highest in the world (after Switzerland). It is a constitutional monarchy with two legislative houses; its chief of state is the Grand Duke, and the head of government is the prime minister. At the time of Roman conquest (57–50 BC), the Luxembourg area was inhabited by a Belgic tribe, the Treveri. After AD 400, Germanic tribes invaded the region. It later came under CHARLEMAGNE's empire. Made a duchy in 1354, it was ceded to the house of BURGUNDY in 1441 and to the HABSBURGS in 1477. In the mid-16th century it became part of the Spanish Netherlands. The CONGRESS OF VIENNA in 1815 made it a grand duchy

and awarded it to the Netherlands. After an uprising in 1830, its western portion became part of Belgium, while the remainder was held by the Netherlands. In 1867 the European powers guaranteed the neutrality and independence of Luxembourg. In the late 19th century it built a great steel industry by exploiting its extensive iron-ore deposits. It was invaded and occupied by Germany in both world wars. Following World War II, it abandoned its neutrality by joining NATO in 1949. It joined the Benelux Economic Union in 1944 and the European Economic Community in 1957. A member of the European Union, its economy has continued to expand.

Luxembourg City (pop., 1997 est.: 78,000), capital of Luxembourg. A rocky promontory along the Alzette River was the site of a Roman fortress and later of a Frankish castle, around which the medieval town developed. Siegfried, count of Ardennes, purchased this castle and made the duchy of Luxembourg independent in 963. The strongest in Europe after Gibraltar, the castle was garrisoned by the Prussians as a bulwark of the German Confederation 1815–66; it was dismantled by treaty in 1867. Long an important road and railway focus, the city is also an important industrial and financial center. It is the seat of the European Court of Justice and several administrative offices of the European Community.

Luxembourgian Dialect of German spoken exclusively in Luxembourg. A Moselle-Franconian dialect of the West Middle German group, enriched by many French words and phrases, Luxemburgian is spoken by all classes. Luxembourg's population is generally bilingual or trilingual. Luxemburgian is mostly used orally, French in government and the courts, and German in newspapers; all three languages are used in the schools.

Rosa Luxemburg.
INTERFOTO—FRIEDRICH RAUCH, MUNICH

Luxemburg \'lu̇k-səm-ˌbu̇rk, *Engl* 'lək-səm-ˌbərg\, **Rosa** (1871–1919) Polish-German political radical, intellectual, and author. As a Jew in Russian-controlled Poland, she was drawn early into underground political activism. In 1889 she fled to Zurich, where she obtained her doctorate. Having become involved in the international socialist movement, in 1892 she cofounded what would become the Polish Communist Party. The Russian Revolution of 1905 convinced her that the world revolution would originate in Russia. An advocate of the mass strike as the proletariat's most important tool, she was imprisoned in Warsaw for agitation, then moved to Berlin to teach and write (1907–14). Early in World War I, she cofounded the Spartacus League (see Spartacists), and in 1918 she oversaw its transformation into the German Communist Party; she was assassinated less than a month later. She believed in a democratic path to socialism after a world revolution to overthrow capitalism, and opposed what she recognized as Vladimir Ilich Lenin's emerging dictatorship.

Luxor \'lək-ˌsȯr, 'lu̇k-ˌsȯr\ Town (pop., 1991 est.: 142,000), Upper Egypt. Its name has been given to the southern half of the ruins of Thebes. It is centered on the Great Temple of Amon, which was built on the eastern bank of the Nile River by King Amenhotep III in the 14th century BC. Tutankhamen and Horemheb completed the temple, and Ramses II added to it. Ruins include pillars and courts of the original temple as well as the remains of Coptic churches and a mosque. The town serves as a tourist center and as the market center for an agricultural district. See also Karnak.

luxury tax Excise levy on goods or services considered to be luxuries rather than necessities (e.g., jewelry and perfume). Luxury taxes may be levied with the intent of taxing the rich or in a deliberate effort to alter consumption patterns, either for moral reasons or in times of national emergency. Today revenue productivity generally overshadows the moral argument.

Luyia See Luhya

Luzon \lü-'zän\ Island (pop., 1990: 30,660,000), Philippines. The country's largest island, with an area of 40,420 sq mi (104,688 sq km), it is the site of Quezon City and Manila, the nation's capital. Located in the northern Philippine archipelago, it is bounded by the Philippine Sea, the Sibuyan Sea, and the China Sea, and is separated from Taiwan by the Luzon Strait. It represents 35% of the nation's land area and 50% of its population. It is largely mountainous; in 1991 the eruption of Mount Pinatubo altered the island's geography. It is the nation's leader in both industry and agriculture.

Luzon Strait Passage between northern Luzon, Philippines, and southern Taiwan. Connecting the China Sea on the west with the Philippine Sea on the east, and extending 200 mi (320 km), it is part of an important shipping route. A series of channels, it is dotted with the islands of the Batan and Babuyan island groups.

Lviv \lə-'vē-ü, *Engl* lə-'vēf\ *or* **Lvov** \lə-'vȯf\ City (pop., 1991 est.: 802,000), western Ukraine. Founded c. 1256 by Prince Daniel of Galicia, it came under Polish rule in 1349. It became one of the great medieval trading towns and changed hands many times. It was taken by the Cossacks in 1648 and by the Swedes in 1704. Given to Austria in 1772, it became the capital of the Austrian province of Galicia. It passed to Poland in 1919, after an unsuccessful attempt by Ukrainians to set up a republic (1918). It was seized by the Soviet Union in 1939 and, after German occupation, annexed by the Soviets in 1945. It is now a center for Ukrainian culture and the seat of a university (founded 1661).

Lvov \lə-'vȯf\, **Georgy (Yevgenyevich), Prince** (1861–1925) Russian politician, first head of the provisional government established during the Russian Revolution of 1917. In 1905 he joined the liberal Constitutional Democratic Party and was elected to the first Duma (1906). He became chairman of the All-Russian Union of Zemstvos (1914) and won the respect of political liberals and army commanders. In March 1917 he became premier but was unable to satisfy the increasingly radical demands of the populace. He resigned in July, after a major left-wing demonstration, in favor of Aleksandr Kerensky. Arrested when the Bolsheviks seized power, he escaped and settled in Paris.

Lyallpur See Faisalabad

Lyautey \lyō-'tā\, **Louis-Herbert-Gonzalve** (1854–1934) French soldier and first colonial administrator in Morocco under the Protectorate (1912–56). Early in his career he served in Indo-china, Madagascar, and Algeria. As resident general in Morocco (1912–24), he pacified the colony and advocated the principle of indirect rule.

Lycaonia \ˌlī-kā-ˈō-nē-ə\ Ancient region, southern Asia Minor, in present-day Turkey. Situated north of the Taurus Mtns., and bounded by Caria and Pamphylia, it was ruled by Alexander the Great, the Seleucids, the Attalids, and, finally, the Romans. Under Rome it was attached to Galatia and Cappadocia. From Seleucid times on, Iconium served as its capital. It was visited by St. Paul and by the 4th century had an organized ecclesiastical system.

lyceum movement \lī-ˈsē-əm\ Form of adult education popular in the U.S. during the mid-19th century. The lyceums were voluntary local associations that sponsored lectures and debates on topics of current interest. The first was founded in 1826, and by 1834 there were approx. 3,000 in the Northeast and Midwest. They attracted such speakers as Ralph Waldo Emerson, Frederick Douglass, Henry David Thoreau, Daniel Webster, Nathaniel Hawthorne, and Susan B. Anthony. The movement began to decline with the outbreak of the Civil War, and eventually blended into the postbellum Chautauqua movement. In their heyday the lyceums contributed to the broadening of the school curricula and the development of local museums and libraries.

lychee See litchi

Lycia \ˈli-shə\ Ancient district, southwestern Asia Minor, in present-day Turkey. Located along the Mediterranean coast between Caria and Pamphylia, by the 8th century BC it was a thriving maritime country. It later fell to Cyrus, to Achaemenian Persia, and finally to Rome. Annexed to Roman Pamphylia in AD 43, it later became a separate Roman province after the 4th century.

Lycurgus \lī-ˈkər-gəs\ (fl. 7th century BC?) Legendary founder of the legal institutions of ancient Sparta. Because sources give differing accounts of his career, some scholars conclude that he never existed, but many believe that a man named Lycurgus instituted drastic reforms in Sparta after the revolt of the helots in the 7th century BC. He is thought to have devised the militarized communal system that made Sparta unique among Greek city-states and to have determined the powers of the council and the assembly.

Lycurgus of Athens (c. 390–324? BC) Athenian orator and statesman. He supported Demosthenes' policy of opposition to Macedonia. As controller of state finances (338–326), he was noted for his efficient administration and vigorous prosecution of corrupt officials. He reconstituted the army and remodeled the fleet, carried on a major building program that included reconstruction of the theater of Dionysus, produced the official edition of the dramas of Aeschylus, Sophocles, and Euripides, and worked to restore Athenian cults and festivals.

Lydia Ancient land, western Asia Minor, in present-day Turkey. Bounded on the west by the Aegean Sea, it profoundly influenced the Ionian Greeks in the 7th century–6th century BC, through such economic developments as metallic coinage and permanent retail shops. It was conquered by the Persians under Cyrus the Great in 546 BC. It later passed to Syria and Pergamum, and under the Romans it became part of the province of Asia.

lye Alkaline (see alkali) liquid extracted by soaking wood ashes in water, commonly used for washing and in making soap. More generally, lye is any strong alkaline solution or solid, such as sodium hydroxide (caustic soda) or potassium hydroxide (caustic potash).

Lyell, detail of a replica in oil by L. Dickinson, 1883; in the National Portrait Gallery, London.

BY COURTESY OF THE NATIONAL PORTRAIT GALLERY, LONDON

Lyell \ˈlī-əl\, **Charles** *later* **Sir Charles** (1797–1875) Scottish geologist. While studying law at Oxford Univ., he became interested in geology and later met such notable geologists as Alexander von Humboldt and Georges Cuvier. Lyell came to believe that there were natural (as opposed to supernatural) explanations for all geologic phenomena, a position he supported with many examples in his three-volume *Principles of Geology* (1830–33). A recognized leader in his field, he gained the friendship of other well-known men of science, including Herschel family and Charles Darwin, whose *Origin of Species* (1859) persuaded Lyell to accept evolution. Lyell was largely responsible for the general acceptance of the concept of uniformitarianism in geology.

Lyly \ˈli-lē\, **John** (1554?–1606) English writer. Educated at Oxford, Lyly gained fame in London with two prose romances, *Euphues* (1578) and *Euphues and His England* (1580). The novels inspired "euphuism," an elegant, extravagant Elizabethan literary style, and made Lyly the first English prose stylist to leave an enduring impression on the language. As a dramatist he also contributed to the development of prose dialogue in English comedy, a genre to which he devoted himself almost exclusively after 1580. *Endimion* (performed 1588) is considered his finest play.

Lyme disease Tick-borne bacterial disease identified in 1975, named for Old Lyme, Conn. It is caused by a spirochete, *Borrelia burgdorferi,* transmitted by ticks, which pick it up in the blood of infected animals, mostly deer. Humans can be bitten by ticks in tall grass or fallen leaves. Lyme disease has three stages: a target-shaped rash, often with flulike symptoms; migrating arthritic pain and neurological symptoms (disturbances to memory, vision, or locomotion); and crippling arthritis, with symptoms like those of multiple sclerosis, and sometimes facial paralysis, meningitis, or memory loss. Most cases do not progress beyond the first stage, but those that do reach the third within two years. Prevention involves avoiding tick bites. Diagnosis can be difficult, especially if the initial rash is not noticed. Early antibiotic treatment can prevent progression. Advanced cases need more powerful antibiotics, and symptoms may recur.

lymph Pale fluid that bathes tissues, maintaining fluid balance and removing bacteria. It enters the blood system at a vein under the collarbone that it reaches via channels and ducts, being driven through them mainly by surrounding muscle activity. The lymphatic organs (spleen and thymus) and lymph nodes filter out bacteria and other particles the lymph takes up from body tissues. Lymph contains lymphocytes and macrophages, the primary cells of the immune system. See also lymphatic system.

lymph node Small, rounded mass of lymphoid tissue contained in connective tissue. They occur all along lymphatic vessels, with clusters in certain areas (e.g., neck, groin, armpits). They filter bacteria and other foreign materials out of lymph and expose them to lymphocytes and macrophages that can engulf them; these cells multiply in response to accumulation of such materials, which is why lymph nodes swell during infections. The nodes also produce lymphocytes and antibodies, to be carried by lymph throughout the lymphatic system. In Hodgkin's disease and other lymphomas, malignant lymph cells proliferate, causing lymph-node enlargement. Other cancers often invade lymphatic vessels, which can carry cells from the tumor to lymph nodes, where they are trapped and grow into secondary tumors. Lymph nodes are therefore removed in cancer surgery to detect or prevent tumor spread.

lymphatic system System of lymph nodes, vessels, and nodules, and lymphoid tissue, including the thymus, spleen, tonsils, and bone marrow, through which lymph circulates and is filtered. Its primary function is to return proteins, waste products, and fluids to the blood; molecules too big to enter the capillaries pass through the more permeable walls of lymphatic vessels. Valves keep lymph flowing in one direction, more slowly than blood and at a lower pressure. The lymphatic system also has a role in the immune system. Nodes filter bacteria and foreign matter from lymph. Smaller nodules, which often produce lymphocytes, form in areas more exposed to such materials. They can merge and become permanent, as in the tonsils. Blockage of a lymph vessel may cause fluid to collect in the tissues, producing lymphedema (tissue swelling). Other lymphatic-system disorders include lymphocytic leukemias and lymphoma. See also reticuloendothelial system.

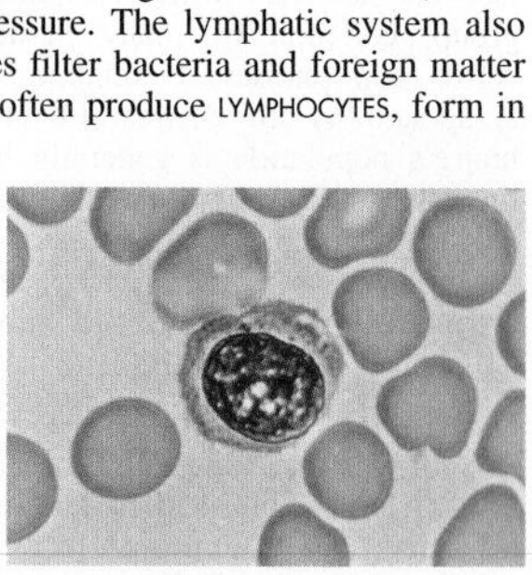

Human lymphocyte (phase-contrast microphotograph).

MANFRED KAGE—PETER ARNOLD

lymphocyte Type of leukocyte fundamental to the immune system, regulating and participating in acquired immunity. Each has receptor molecules on its surface that bind to a specific ANTIGEN. The two primary types, B and T CELLS, originate from stem cells in BONE MARROW and travel to LYMPHOID TISSUES. When a B cell binds to an antigen, it multiplies to form a clone of identical cells. Some of these, acted on by helper T cells, differentiate into plasma cells that produce ANTIBODIES against the antigen. Others (memory cells) multiply, providing long-term IMMUNITY to the antigen.

lymphoid tissue Cells, tissues, and organs composing the IMMUNE SYSTEM, including the BONE MARROW, THYMUS, SPLEEN, and LYMPH NODES. The most highly organized components are the thymus and lymph nodes, and the least organized are the cells that wander in the loose CONNECTIVE-TISSUE spaces under membranes lining most body systems, where they can establish lymph nodules (local LYMPHOCYTE production centers) in response to ANTIGENS. The most common lymphoid tissue cell is the lymphocyte. Others are macrophages, which engulf foreign materials and probably alter them to initiate the immune response, and reticular cells, which produce and maintain thin networks of fibers as a framework for most lymphoid organs. See also IMMUNITY, LYMPHATIC SYSTEM.

lymphoma \lim-'fō-mə\ Any of a group of malignant diseases (see CANCER) that usually start in the LYMPH NODES or LYMPHOID TISSUES. The two major types, HODGKIN'S DISEASE and non-Hodgkin's lymphoma, each have several subtypes. Diagnosis of either type requires BIOPSY, usually from the lymph nodes. Non-Hodgkin's lymphomas may be diffuse (widespread) or nodular (concentrated in nodules); nodular lymphomas generally develop more slowly.

lymphoreticuloma See HODGKIN'S DISEASE

Lynch, David (born 1946) U.S. film director. Born in Missoula, Mont., and trained as an artist, in 1977 he made his first feature, *Eraserhead,* a grotesque and nightmarish film that became a cult favorite. He directed the critically acclaimed *The Elephant Man* (1980), the science-fiction *Dune* (1984), and the bizarre mystery *Blue Velvet* (1986); his later films include *Wild at Heart* (1990), *Lost Highway* (1997), and *The Straight Story* (1999). He also created the offbeat television series *Twin Peaks* (1990–91).

lynching Execution of a presumed offender by a mob without trial, under the pretense of administering justice. It sometimes involves torturing the victim and mutilating the body. Lynching has often occurred under unsettled conditions. The term derives from the name of Charles Lynch, a Virginian who headed an irregular court to persecute Loyalists during the American Revolution. In the U.S., lynching was widely used in the post-Reconstruction South against blacks, often to intimidate other blacks from exercising their civil rights.

Lynd \'lind\, **Robert (Staughton) and Helen** *orig.* **Helen Merrell** (1892–1970, 1894–1982) U.S. sociologists. Husband and wife (born respectively in New Albany, Ind., and La Grange, Ill.), the Lynds taught for several decades at Columbia University and Sarah Lawrence College, respectively. In their collaboration on the studies *Middletown* (1929) and *Middletown in Transition* (1937), classics of sociological literature as well as popular successes, they became the first scholars to apply the methods of CULTURAL ANTHROPOLOGY to the study of a modern Western city (Muncie, Ind.).

Lynn, Loretta *orig.* **Loretta Webb** (born 1935) U.S. COUNTRY-MUSIC singer. Born in a coalminer's shack in Butcher Hollow, Ky., Lynn married at 13 and bore the first of six children the next year. In 1960 she released her first single, "Honky Tonk Girl," which became a hit. In 1962 she joined the GRAND OLE OPRY, and by the mid-1960s such hits as "Don't Come Home A-Drinkin'" made her one of country's biggest stars. In 1970 she released her signature song, "Coal Miner's Daughter"; it provided the title of a bestselling autobiography and a popular film (1980). Her half-sister, Crystal Gayle (born 1951), has also had a successful recording career.

Lynn Canal Deep fjord, southeastern Alaska. An important gateway to the Klondike region, it is 80 mi (129 km) long and 6 mi (10 km) wide. The northernmost fjord to penetrate the Coast Mtns., it was named in 1794 by Capt. George Vancouver for his birthplace, King's Lynn, England.

lynx Short-tailed forest CAT *(Felis lynx)* of Europe, Asia, and northern North America. The Canada lynx is sometimes regarded as a distinct species *(Felis canadensis).* The lynx has long legs, large paws, tufted ears, hairy soles, and a broad, short head. Its coat, which forms a bushy ruff on the neck, is tawny to cream-colored and mottled with brown and black. Its dense, soft winter fur has been used for trimming garments. Lynx are approximately 30–40 in. (80–100 cm) long, without the 4–8-in. (10–20-cm) tail, and stand about 24 in. (60 cm) high at the shoulder. They weigh 20–45 lbs (10–20 kg). Nocturnal and silent except during mating season, lynx live alone or in small groups. They climb and swim well, and feed on birds, small mammals, and occasionally deer. Some races are considered endangered.

Lyon \'lyō^{n}\ *English* **Lyons** \'lyō^{n}, 'lī-ənz\ City (pop., 1990: 422,000), eastern central France. Located at the confluence of the RHÔNE and SAÔNE rivers, it was founded as the Roman military colony Lugdunum in 43 BC (see LORRAINE), and became a principal city of Gaul. It was incorporated into the Holy Roman Empire in 1032 and into the kingdom of France in 1312. It flourished economically in the 15th century, and by the 17th century was the silk-manufacturing center of Europe. It was a center of the French RESISTANCE movement during World War II. A major river port, it has a diversified economy, including textile, metallurgical, and printing industries. Its many ancient buildings include a Roman theater, a 12th-century Gothic cathedral, and a 15th-century palace.

Lyon, Councils of 13th and 14th ecumenical councils of the Roman Catholic Church. The First Council of Lyon was convened by Pope INNOCENT IV in 1245 after he fled to Lyon from the besieged city of Rome; the pope deposed the emperor, FREDERICK II, and urged support for Louis IX on the Seventh CRUSADE. At the Second Council in 1274, Pope GREGORY X nominally reunited the Eastern and Western churches, but the Greek clergy soon repudiated the union.

Lyon, Mary (Mason) (1797–1849) U.S. pioneer in higher education for women. Born in Buckland, Mass., she studied at various academies, supporting herself from age 17 by teaching. Her success as a teacher and administrator, and the demand for the young women she had trained, led to her plan for a permanent instructional institution for women. The school she founded in South Hadley, Mass., opened in 1837 as the Mount Holyoke Female Seminary (the forerunner of MOUNT HOLYOKE COLLEGE), and she served as its principal until her death.

lyre Stringed musical instrument consisting of a resonating body with two arms and a crossbar to which the strings extending from the resonator are attached. Lyrelike instruments existed in Sumer before 2000 BC. Greek lyres were of two types, the KITHARA and the lyra. The latter had a rounded body and a curved back—often a tortoiseshell—and a skin belly. It was the instrument of the amateur; professionals used the more elaborate kithara. In ancient Greece the lyre was an attribute of APOLLO.

East African bowl lyre; in the Pitt Rivers Museum, Oxford.

BY COURTESY OF THE PITT RIVERS MUSEUM, OXFORD

lyrebird Either of two species of insectivorous suboscine PASSERINES (family Menuridae) named for the shape of their extremely long tail when spread in courtship display. Found in forests in southeastern Australia, lyrebirds are ground dwellers with chickenlike bodies. About 40 in. (1 m) in total length, the male superb lyrebird is the longest of the passerines. He displays in a small clearing, bringing his tail forward so that the beautiful white plumes form a canopy over his head and the lyrelike feathers stand out to the side. In this position, while prancing in rhythm, he sings far-carrying melodious notes interspersed with perfect mimicry of other creatures and even of mechanical sounds.

lyric Verse or poem that can, or supposedly can, be sung to musical accompaniment (in ancient times, usually a lyre) or that expresses intense personal emotion in a manner suggestive of a song. Lyric poetry expresses the thoughts and feelings of the poet and is sometimes contrasted with narrative poetry and verse drama, which relate events in the form of a story. The ELEGY, ODE, and SONNET are important forms of lyric poetry.

Lysander \lī-ˈsan-dər\ (died 395 BC) Spartan leader in the PELOPONNESIAN WAR. In his first year as admiral he won the support of the Persian king Cyrus the Younger and defeated the Athenian fleet at Notium (406), causing the dismissal of ALCIBIADES. He destroyed the Athenian fleet at the Battle of AEGOSPOTAMI (405), closing Athens's grain route and starving the city into surrender. He installed the THIRTY TYRANTS, and made his friends governors of Athens's former empire. He suffered a defeat when Sparta allowed the restoration of democracy in Athens (403). He helped AGESILAUS II become king (399). Having led his forces into Boeotia, he was killed while attacking Haliartus.

Lysenko \lə-ˈseŋ-kō**, Trofim (Denisovich)** (1898–1976) Russian biologist and agronomist. During the Soviet famines of the 1930s he proposed imaginative techniques for the enhancement of crop yields, rejecting orthodox Mendelian GENETICS on the basis of unconfirmed experiments, and gained a large popular following. As director of the Soviet Academy of Sciences' Institute of Genetics (1940–65), he became the controversial "dictator" of Stalinist biology. He promised greater, more rapid, and less costly increases in crop yields than other biologists believed possible, claiming, among other things, that wheat plants raised in the appropriate environment would produce seeds of rye. Eventually his "grassland" system of crop rotation was abandoned in favor of cultivation with mineral fertilizers, and a hybrid-corn program based on the U.S. example was pursued. In 1964 Lysenko's doctrines were officially discredited, and intensive efforts were made toward reestablishing orthodox genetics in the Soviet Union.

Lysenko, 1938.
SOVFOTO

Lysias \ˈli-sē-əs\ (c. 445–after 380 BC) Greek orator. As a METIC in Athens, he was forbidden to speak for himself; all his speeches were delivered by others. He and his brother were seized by the ruling oligarchy in 404 as disaffected aliens; his brother was killed but Lysias escaped. He ranks with ANTIPHON as a writer of clear, simple prose of great effectiveness; many of his writings survive.

lysine \ˈlī-ˌsēn\ One of the essential AMINO ACIDS, present in many common PROTEINS. Its proportion in the proteins of some important food plants (including wheat and corn) is so small that populations dependent on these grains as the sole source of dietary protein suffer from lysine deficiency, affecting growth in children and general well-being in adults. It is used in biochemical and nutritional research, in pharmaceuticals, in fortified foods, and as a nutritional supplement and feed additive.

Lysippus *or* **Lysippos** \lī-ˈsi-pəs\ (fl. c. 370–300 BC) Greek sculptor. He was famous for the new and slender proportions of his figures and for their lifelike naturalism. He reportedly made more than 1,500 works, most in bronze. None survive, but some copies may be reliably ascribed to him, including *Apoxyomenos,* a young athlete scraping oil from his skin. Another key work is the colossal Heracles at Sikyon. He made many portrait busts of ALEXANDER THE GREAT from boyhood on; it was said that Alexander would have no other sculptor portray him.

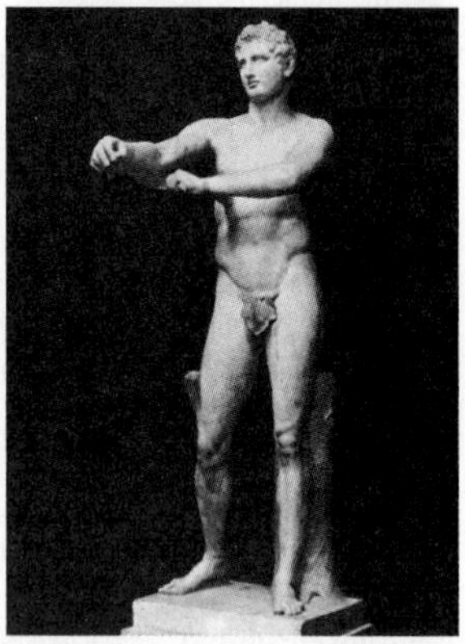

"Apoxyomenos," Roman marble copy of Greek bronze by Lysippus, c. 310 BC; in the Vatican Museum.
ANDERSON—ALINARI FROM ART RESOURCE

lysogeny \lī-ˈsä-jə-nē\ Type of life cycle that takes place in a BACTERIOPHAGE after it infects certain types of bacteria. The bacteriophage's genome (entire collection of genes) enters the chromosome of the host bacterium and replicates together with it. No offspring viruses are produced; instead, the infecting virus lies dormant within the host's chromosome until the host is exposed to certain stimuli, such as ultraviolet light. At that point, the virus genome is removed from the host chromosome and begins to multiply, forming new viruses. Finally, the bacterial host is destroyed (lysed), releasing virus particles into the environment to infect new bacterial cells.

lysosome \ˈlī-sə-ˌsōm\ Membrane-enclosed organelle found in all eukaryotic cells (see EUKARYOTE) that is responsible for the cell's digestion of macromolecules, old cell parts, and microorganisms. Lysosomes contain a wide variety of enzymes that break down macromolecules such as nucleic acids, proteins, and polysaccharides. Many of the products of lysosomal digestion, including amino acids and nucleotides, are recycled back to the cell for use in synthesizing new cellular components.

M16 rifle *or* **AR-15** ASSAULT RIFLE adopted as a standard weapon by the U.S. Army in 1967. The M16, which superseded the M14, has both semiautomatic and fully automatic capabilities. It weighs less than 8 lbs (3.6 kg), is equipped with a 20-round or 30-round magazine, is 39 in. (99 cm) long, and fires .22-caliber ammunition at the rate of 700–950 rounds per minute. It was used in the Vietnam War and the Persian Gulf War and in Kosovo in 1999. The M4/M4A1 is gradually replacing it. See also SPRINGFIELD RIFLE, AK-47.

M31 See ANDROMEDA GALAXY

Ma, Yo-Yo (born 1955) U.S. (French-born) cellist. Born to Chinese parents in Paris, he made his cello debut when he was 5. He attended Harvard University. His huge repertoire includes much contemporary music and many works written especially for him. He is known for his many recordings with the pianist Emanuel Ax (born 1949), for his collaborations with an unusual range of other musicians and artists, and for his energetic work on behalf of music programs for young people and a variety of international causes.

Ma-fa-mu-ts'o See MAPAM YUMCO

maa-alused \'mä-'ä-lü-ˌsed\ In Estonian folk religion, mysterious elves living under the earth. These small folk had suitably tiny possessions, and their world was differently oriented from the mortal world above them (up was down and right was left). People came in contact with them either by chance or at the elves' wish. Legends tell of distraught elves seeking help from humans in cases of difficult childbirth or illness. A human could marry an elf, but such marriages eventually dissolved. In Finland, such elves were called *maahiset.*

Maasai See MASAI

Maastricht Treaty \mä-'strikt, *Engl* 'mä-strikt\ *officially* **Treaty on European Union.** Agreement that established the EUROPEAN UNION (EU) as successor to the EUROPEAN COMMUNITY. It bestowed EU citizenship on every national of its member states, provided for the introduction of a central banking system and a common currency (see EURO), and committed the member states to work toward a common foreign and security policy. Signed in 1991, it was ratified and took effect in 1993. See also EUROPEAN COURT OF JUSTICE, EUROPEAN PARLIAMENT, Treaties of ROME.

Maat \'mä-ˌät\ In ancient Egyptian religion, the personification of truth, justice, and the cosmic order. Maat was the daughter of RE, the sun god, and she stood at the head of his bark as it traveled through the sky and the underworld. She was also associated with THOTH, god of wisdom. The judgment of the dead was believed to be determined by the weighing of the heart of the deceased in a scale she balanced. In its abstract sense, maat was the divine order established at creation and reaffirmed at the accession of each new king of Egypt.

Mabinogion \mȧ-bē-'nȯg-yən, *Engl* ˌma-bə-'nō-gē-ən\ Collection of 11 medieval Welsh tales based on mythology, folklore, and heroic legends. The tales have multiple authors and are versions of stories told and retold through the centuries. Among the finest are four stories known as "The Four Branches of the Mabinogi," written in the late 11th century. Some show Celtic, Norman, and French influence; "Peredur Son of Efrawg," for example, parallels CHRÉTIEN DE TROYES's *Perceval.* Four other tales show little continental influence: "Kulhwch and Olwen," "Lludd and Llefelys," "The Dream of Macsen," and "The Dream of Rhonabwy."

Mabuse See Jan GOSSART

Mac ind Óg See MAPONOS

Mac-Mahon \mȧk-mȧ-'ōⁿ\, **(Marie-Edme-Patrice-) Maurice, comte (Count) de** *later* **duc (Duke) de Magenta** (1808–1893) French soldier and second president (1873–79) of the THIRD REPUBLIC. Descended from an Irish Jacobite family, he began his army career in 1827 and distinguished himself in the Crimean War and in the Italian campaign at the Battle of MAGENTA (1859), after which he was made a marshal of France and duc de Magenta. He was governor-general of Algeria 1864–70, and later a commander in the Franco–Prussian War. He was appointed head of the Versailles Army, which defeated the PARIS COMMUNE in 1871. He was elected president after the resignation of ADOLPHE THIERS. During his term the CONSTITUTIONAL LAWS OF 1875 were promulgated. Mac-Mahon resigned following a constitutional crisis that was resolved in favor of parliamentary control of the government. Thereafter in the Third Republic, the office of president became largely honorific.

macadam \mə-'ka-dəm\ Form of PAVEMENT invented by JOHN MCADAM. McAdam's road cross-section consisted of a compacted subgrade of crushed granite or greenstone designed to support the load, covered by a surface of light stone to absorb wear and tear and shed water to the drainage ditches. In modern macadam construction, crushed stone or gravel is placed on the compacted base course and bound together with ASPHALT cement or hot tar. A third layer to fill the spaces is then added and rolled. Cement-sand slurry is sometimes used as the binder.

macadamia \ˌma-kə-'dā-mē-ə\ Any of about 10 species of ornamental evergreen trees in the family Proteaceae, and their edible, richly flavored dessert NUTS. Macadamias originated in the coastal rain forests and scrubs of northeastern Australia. Those grown commercially in Hawaii and Australia are principally of two species, the smooth-shelled *Macadamia integrifolia* and the rough-shelled *M. tetraphylla.* Macadamias are grown in quantity also in parts of Africa and South and Central America. Hard to propagate and slow to bear, the trees grow only in rich, well-drained soil with 50 in. (130 cm) of rain annually. Fragrant pink or white flower clusters on trees with large, shiny, leathery leaves produce bunches of 1–20 fruits. The nuts contain much fat but are a good source of minerals and vitamin B.

MacAlpin, Kenneth See KENNETH I

Macao \mə-'kau̇\ *Portuguese* **Macau** \mə-'kau̇\ *Chinese* **Aomen** \'au̇-'mən\ Former Portuguese territory (pop., 1996 est.: 433,000), southern coast of China. It consists of a small peninsula projecting from GUANGDONG province and two small islands, about 40 mi (64 km) west of HONG KONG. It occupies a total land area of 6.5 sq mi (17 sq km); Macao city (pop., 1995 est.: 424,000) is the administrative center. Portuguese traders first arrived in 1513, and it soon became the chief market center for the trade between China and Japan. It was declared a Portuguese colony in 1849 and an overseas territory in 1951. In December 1999 Portugal returned it to Chinese rule. Tourism and gambling are the mainstay of its economy.

macaque \mə-'kak\ Any of about 12 primarily Asian species of omnivorous, diurnal MONKEYS (genus *Macaca*) with cheek pouches for carrying food. Some species have long tails, some have short tails, and some have none. Males are 15–30 in. (40–70 cm) long (excluding the tail) and weigh 8–40 lbs (3.5–18 kg). Troops live in mountains and lowlands and along shores. Some species, including the RHESUS monkey, are important to humans. Malays train pigtailed macaques *(M. nemestrina)* to pick coconuts. See also BARBARY APE, BONNET monkey, CELEBES BLACK APE.

MacArthur, Charles (Gordon) (1895–1956) U.S. playwright and screenwriter. Born in Scranton, Pa., he worked as a reporter in Chicago and New York (1914–26) before collaborating with Edward Shelden on the play *Lulu Belle* (1926). With BEN HECHT he wrote the Broadway hits *The Front Page* (1928; film, 1931) and *Twentieth Century* (1932; film, 1934) and several later plays noted for his graphic, crisp dialogue. Their screenplays included the film adaptations of their own plays and *Wuthering Heights* (1939), and they wrote and directed such movies as *Crime Without Passion* (1934), *The Scoundrel* (1935), and *Soak the Rich* (1936). He was married to HELEN HAYES.

MacArthur, Douglas (1880–1964) U.S. general. Born in Little Rock, Ark., son of Gen. Arthur MacArthur (1845–1912), he graduated from West Point, of which he became superintendent (1919–22). He rose through the ranks to become general and army chief of staff (1930–35). In 1932 he commanded the troops that evicted the BONUS ARMY. In 1937 he took over command of the Philippine military. He was recalled to active duty when World War II broke out. He led the combined Philippine-

U.S. forces in the Philippines until it was overrun by the Japanese (1942). From Australia, he commanded U.S. forces in the South Pacific and directed the recapture of strategic islands, returning as promised ("I shall return") to liberate the Philippines in 1944. Promoted to general of the army, he received Japan's surrender on September 2, 1945. As Allied commander of the postwar OCCUPATION of Japan (1945–51), he directed the restoration of its economy and the drafting of a democratic constitution. When the KOREAN WAR began in 1950, he was selected to command U.N. forces and stemmed the advance of North Korean troops. His desire to bomb China was rejected by Pres. H. Truman; when MacArthur made the dispute public, Truman relieved him of his command for insubordination. He returned to the U.S. to a hero's welcome, though many deplored his egoism. He was twice (1948, 1952) seriously considered for the Republican nomination for president.

MacArthur-Forrest process See CYANIDE PROCESS

Macassar See UJUNG PANDANG

Macaulay \mə-'kȯ-lē\, **Thomas Babington** *later* **Baron Macaulay of Rothley** (1800–1859) English politician, historian, and poet. While a fellow at Cambridge Univ., Macaulay published the first of his essays, on JOHN MILTON (1825), and gained immediate fame. After entering Parliament in 1830, he became known as a leading orator. From 1834 he served on the Supreme Council in India, supporting the equality of Europeans and Indians before the law and inaugurating a national educational system. He reentered Parliament on returning to England in 1838. He published *Lays of Ancient Rome* (1842) and *Critical and Historical Essays* (1843) before retiring into private life and beginning his brilliant *History of England* (5 vols., 1849–61); covering the period 1688–1702, it established a WHIG interpretation of English history that influenced generations.

Thomas Macaulay, detail of an oil painting by J. Partridge, 1840; in the National Portrait Gallery, London.

BY COURTESY OF THE NATIONAL PORTRAIT GALLERY, LONDON

macaw \mə-'kȯ\ Any of about 18 species of large tropical New World PARROTS (subfamily Psittacinae) with very long tails and big sickle-shaped beaks. Macaws eat fruits and nuts. They are easily tamed and often kept as pets; some learn to mimic human speech, but most only screech. A few have lived 65 years. Best known is the scarlet macaw *(Ara macao),* found from Mexico to Brazil, a 36-in. (90-cm) bright-red bird with blue and yellow wings, blue and red tail, and white face.

MacBride, Seán (1904–1988) Irish statesman. Born to Irish patriots—his mother was WILLIAM BUTLER YEATS's beloved Maud Gonne (1866–1953), and his father was Maj. John MacBride, executed for his part in the 1916 Easter Rising—he became chief of staff of the IRISH REPUBLICAN ARMY at 24, but eventually accepted the fact of partition and the futility of warfare. In 1936 he founded the Irish Republican Party; he served in the Irish legislature 1947–58, and as minister of external affairs 1948–51. He was the first chairman of AMNESTY INTERNATIONAL (1961–75). He also served as U.N. assistant secretary-general for S.West Africa and Namibia (1973–77). In 1974 he was awarded the Nobel Peace Prize for his efforts on behalf of human rights.

Maccabees \'ma-kə-ˌbēz\ (fl. 2nd century BC) Priestly family of Jews who organized a successful rebellion against ANTIOCHUS IV EPIPHANES in Palestine and reconsecrated the defiled Temple of JERUSALEM. The rebellion began under the leadership of the Jewish priest Mattathias after Antiochus sought to stamp out Judaism by forbidding all Jewish practices and desecrating the temple (167 BC). When Mattathias died (c. 166 BC), his son JUDAS MACCABAEUS recaptured Jerusalem and reconsecrated the temple. After Judas's death, the war continued intermittently under his brothers Jonathan and Simon. The Maccabees formed the HASMONEAN DYNASTY.

Macchiaioli \ˌmäk-kē-ˌī-'ō-lē\ Group of 19th-century Tuscan painters who reacted against the rule-bound art academies and looked to nature for instruction. Like the French Impressionists, the Macchiaioli considered patches or spots *(macchie)* of color the most important aspect of painting, but they put even greater emphasis on color structure. The effect of a painting on the spectator was to derive from the painted surface itself rather than from any ideological message; however, being active during the RISORGIMENTO, the Macchiaioli did have strong nationalist sentiments.

MacDiarmid, Alan G. (b. 1927) U.S. chemist. Born in Masterson, New Zealand, he earned Ph.D.'s in chemistry at the University of Wisconsin at Madison (1953) and the University of Cambridge (1955). He then began teaching at the University of Pennsylvania, becoming Blanchard Professor of Chemistry there in 1988. With ALAN J. HEEGER and HIDEKI SHIRAKAWA, he demonstrated that certain plastics can be chemically altered to be almost as conductive as metals. The discovery led scientists to uncover other conductive polymers, which contributed to the growing field of molecular electronics. In 2000 he received the Nobel Prize for Chemistry with Heeger and Shirakawa.

MacDiarmid \mək-'dər-məd\, **Hugh** *orig.* **Christopher Murray Grieve** (1892–1978) Scottish poet. In 1922 he founded the monthly *Scottish Chapbook,* in which he published his lyrics and sparked the Scottish literary renaissance. A radical leftist, he rejected English as a medium and scrutinized modern society in verse written in "synthetic Scots," an amalgam of various dialects. A noted work is the extended rhapsody *A Drunk Man Looks at the Thistle* (1926). He later returned to standard English in such volumes as *A Kist of Whistles* (1947) and *In Memoriam James Joyce* (1955). He is regarded as Scotland's preeminent poet of the early 20th century.

Macdonald, Dwight (1906–1982) U.S. writer and film critic. Born in New York City, he graduated from Yale University. During World War II he founded the magazine *Politics,* which featured the work of such figures as ANDRE GIDE, ALBERT CAMUS, and MARIANNE MOORE. One of the first serious film critics, he was a staff writer for *The New Yorker* 1951–71, and reviewed films for *Esquire* magazine 1960–66. Politically, he moved from Stalinism through Trotskyism and anarchism to pacifism. During the Vietnam War, he urged young men to defy the draft. His best-known collection is *Against the American Grain* (1963).

Macdonald, John (Alexander) *later* **Sir John** (1815–1891) Canadian (Scottish-born) politician, first prime minister of the Dominion of Canada (1867–73, 1878–91). He emigrated to Canada as a child and practiced law in Kingston, Upper Canada (now Ontario), from 1836. He served in the Province of Canada's assembly 1844–54, and advocated the unification of Canada. He cofounded the Liberal-Conservative Party (see PROGRESSIVE CONSERVATIVE PARTY OF CANADA) and became premier of the province in 1857. He worked for confederation and helped secure passage of the BRITISH NORTH AMERICA ACT, which created the Dominion of Canada (1867). As prime minister, he supported trade protectionism, aided completion of the Pacific railway, and advocated Canadian unity, loyalty to the British Commonwealth, and independence from the U.S.

MacDonald, (James) Ramsay (1866–1937) British politician, first LABOUR PARTY prime minister of Britain (1924, 1929–31, 1931–35). He joined the precursor of the Labour Party in 1894 and was its secretary 1900–11. He served in the House of Commons 1906–18, and as leader of the Labour Party 1911–14, but was forced to resign after opposing Britain's participation in World War I. Reelected to Parliament in 1922, he led the Labour opposition. He became prime minister in 1924 with Liberal Party support, but was forced to resign later that year when Conservatives regained a majority. In 1929 Labour won a majority and he returned as prime minister. In 1931 he offered his resignation during the Great Depression but decided instead to remain in office as head of a national coalition until 1935, when STANLEY BALDWIN became prime minister. MacDonald remained in the government as lord president of the council until 1937.

Macdonnell Ranges Mountain system, southern central Northern Territory, Australia. Extending east and west of the town of ALICE SPRINGS for 230 mi (380 km), its highest peak is Mount Ziel (4,954 ft, or 1,510 m). The mountains were first explored in 1860 by John McDouall Stuart and were named after Richard Macdonnell, governor of South Australia.

Macdonough \mək-'dä-nə\, **Thomas** (1783–1825) U.S. naval officer. Born in The Trap, Del., he joined the navy in 1800 and served with STEPHEN DECATUR in the Tripolitan War. In the WAR OF 1812 he was ordered to cruise the lakes between Canada and the U.S. When British troops threatened Plattsburg, N.Y., site of U.S. Army headquarters on the northern frontier, he sailed his 14-ship fleet to meet the British 16-ship squadron on Lake Champlain. His victory there (September 11, 1814) saved New York and Vermont from invasion.

MacDowell, Edward (Alexander) *orig.* **Edward Alexander McDowell** (1860–1908) U.S. composer. Born in New York City, he started piano lessons at 8. In Germany for further study, he impressed the composer Joachim Raff (1822–1882), who urged him to write a piano concerto (1882), then brought it to F. LISZT, who assisted MacDowell with performances and publication. In 1888 he returned to the U.S. with his wife, and in 1896 he became Columbia Univ.'s first professor of music. Paresis made him unable to perform or compose after 1904, and he lapsed into insanity and died at 47. His farm in Peterborough, N.H., became the MacDowell Colony for artists after his death. His most popular works are the Second Piano Concerto (1886), the Second Orchestral ("Indian") Suite (1895), and such piano sets as *Woodland Sketches* (1896) and *Sea Pieces* (1898).

Macedonia *officially* **Republic of Macedonia** Country, southeastern Europe, southern Balkans region. Area: 9,928 sq mi (25,713 sq km). Population (2000 est.): 2,041,000. Capital: SKOPJE. Two-thirds of the population are Slavic Macedonians and about one-fifth are Albanians. Languages: Macedonian (official). Religions: Serbian Orthodoxy, Islam. Currency: denar. Located on a high plateau studded with mountains, Macedonia has few mineral resources and is one of the poorest countries in Europe. Agriculture is central to its economy, and includes the production of tobacco, rice, fruit, vegetables, and wine; sheep herding and dairy farming are also important. It is a republic with one legislative

house; its head of state is the president, and the head of government, the prime minister. Macedonia has been inhabited since before 7000 BC. Under Roman rule, part of the region was incorporated into the province of MOESIA in AD 29. It was settled by Slavic tribes by the mid-6th century AD and was Christianized during the 9th century. Seized by the Bulgarians in 1185, it was ruled by the Ottoman empire 1371–1912. The north and center of the region were annexed by Serbia in 1913 and became part of the Kingdom of Serbs, Croats, and Slovenes (later YUGOSLAVIA) in 1918. When Yugoslavia was partitioned by the AXIS POWERS in 1941, Yugoslav Macedonia was occupied principally by Bulgaria. Macedonia once again became a republic of Yugoslavia in 1946. After Croatia and Slovenia seceded from Yugoslavia, fear of Serbian dominance drove Macedonia to declare its independence in 1991. In order to appease Greece, which has an area traditionally known as Macedonia, it adopted as its formal title Former Yugoslav Republic of Macedonia, and normalized relations with Greece in 1995. In 2001 ethnic strife endangered national stability as pro-Albanian rebel forces in the north, near the KOSOVO border, led guerilla attacks on government forces.

Macedonian language See BULGARIAN LANGUAGE

Macedonian Wars Three wars fought by PHILIP V of Macedonia and his successor, PERSEUS, against Rome (215–205 BC, 200–197, 171–167). The first war, fought by Rome in the context of the Second PUNIC WAR, ended favorably for the Macedonians. Rome was victorious in the next two wars. The Macedonian forces were assisted by CARTHAGE and the SELEUCIDS, Rome by the AETOLIAN LEAGUE and PERGAMUM. After Rome's victory at the Battle of PYDNA (168), Macedonian territory was divided into four republics. Another conflict, fought in 149–148, may be considered a fourth Macedonian War; it resulted in a decisive Roman victory, and in its aftermath Macedonia became the empire's first province.

Macfadden, Bernarr *orig.* **Bernard Adolphus** (1868–1955) U.S. publisher and champion of physical health. Born in Mill Spring, Mo., in 1898 he began publishing *Physical Culture* magazine, in which he promoted his ideas of exercise, diet, and fasting. In later decades he built up a publishing empire, bringing out the first confession magazine, *True Story* (1919), followed by *True Romances* (1923), *True Detective Mystery Magazine* (1925), and other periodicals. His bids for the presidency, U.S. Senate, and governorship of Florida all failed. Physically fit into old age, he parachuted into Paris on his 84th birthday.

Mach \'mäk, *Engl* 'mäk\, **Ernst** (1838–1916) Austrian physicist and philosopher. After earning a doctorate in physics in 1860, he taught at the Univs. of Vienna and Graz as well as Charles University in Prague. Interested in the psychology and physiology of sensation, in the 1860s he discovered the physiological phenomenon known as Mach's bands, the tendency of the human eye to see bright or dark bands near the boundaries between areas of sharply differing illumination. He later studied movement and acceleration and developed optical and photographic techniques for measuring sound waves and wave propagation. In 1887 he established the principles of supersonics and the Mach number, the ratio of the velocity of an object to the velocity of sound. He also proposed the theory of inertia known as Mach's principle. In *Contributions to the Analysis of the Sensations* (1886), he asserted that all knowledge is derived from sensory experience or observation.

Machado de Assis \mä-'shä-dō-dē-ä-'sēs\, **Joaquim Maria** (1839–1908) Brazilian poet, novelist, and short-story writer. Machado began to write in his spare time while working as a printer's apprentice. By 1869 he was a successful man of letters. His witty, pessimistic works, rooted in European cultural traditions, include the eccentric first-person narrative *Epitaph of a Small Winner* (1881) and the novels *Philosopher or Dog?* (1891) and *Dom Casmurro* (1899), his masterpiece. Considered the classic master of Brazilian literature, he became the first president of the Brazilian Academy of Letters in 1896.

Machaut \mä-'shō\, **Guillaume de** (c. 1300–1377) French poet and composer. After possibly receiving a university education and taking holy orders, he traveled throughout

Machaut, detail of a miniature from *Oeuvres de Guillaume de Machaut*, c. 1370–80; in the Bibliothèque Nationale (Ms. Fr. 1584).

BY COURTESY OF THE BIBLIOTHEQUE NATIONALE, PARIS

Europe as secretary to the king of Bohemia. From 1340 he settled in Reims, supported by several royal patrons, including the duc de BERRY, and King CHARLES V. Beside 14 narrative poems incorporating short lyrics, he wrote more than 400 separate lyric poems. His musical output numbers dozens each of the genres of FORMES FIXES, as well as the first complete setting of the mass for four voices, and he was the outstanding figure of the ARS NOVA. His poetry was a source for GEOFFREY CHAUCER.

Machiavelli \ˌmä-kē-ə-ˈvel-ē\, **Niccolò** (1469–1527) Italian statesman, historian, and political theorist. Born in Florence, he rose to power after the overthrow of GIROLAMO SAVONAROLA in 1498. Working as a diplomat for 14 years, he came in contact with the most powerful figures in Europe. Dismissed when the MEDICI FAMILY returned to power in 1512, he was arrested and tortured for conspiracy the next year; though soon released, he was not permitted to return to public office. His famous treatise *The Prince* (1513, published 1532), is a handbook for rulers; though dedicated to the Medici, it failed to win him their favor. He viewed *The Prince* as objective description of political reality; because he viewed human nature as venal, grasping, and thoroughly self-serving, he suggested that ruthless cunning is appropriate to the conduct of government. Though admired for its incisive brilliance, the book has long been widely condemned as cynical and amoral, and "Machiavellian" has come to mean deceitful, unscrupulous, and manipulative. His other works include a set of discourses on LIVY (completed c. 1518), the comedy *Mandragola* (completed c. 1518), and *The Art of War* (published 1521)

Machiavelli, detail of an oil painting by Santi di Tito; in the Palazzo Vecchio, Florence.

ALINARI–ART RESOURCE

machine Device that amplifies or replaces human or animal effort to accomplish a physical task. A machine may be further defined as a device consisting of two or more parts that transmit or modify force and motion in order to do work. The five simple machines are the LEVER, the WEDGE, the WHEEL and AXLE, the PULLEY, and the SCREW; all complex machines are combinations of these basic devices. The operation of a machine may involve the transformation of chemical, thermal, electrical, or nuclear ENERGY into mechanical energy, or vice versa. All machines have an input, an output, and a transforming or modifying and transmitting device. Machines that receive their input energy from a natural source (such as air currents, moving water, coal, petroleum, or uranium) and transform it into mechanical energy are known as prime movers; examples include WINDMILLS, WATERWHEELS, TURBINES, STEAM ENGINES, and INTERNAL-COMBUSTION ENGINES.

machine gun Automatic weapon of small caliber capable of rapid, sustained fire, usually 500–1,000 rounds per minute. Developed in the late 19th century, it profoundly altered modern warfare. Hand-cranked machine guns, notably the GATLING GUN, were used in the American Civil War. The invention of smokeless GUNPOWDER in the 1880s was followed by the development of a truly automatic weapon, primarily because smokeless powder's even combustion made it possible for HIRAM MAXIM to harness the recoil. The World War I battlefield was dominated by the belt-fed machine gun, which remained little changed into World War II. See also SUBMACHINE GUN.

machine language *or* **machine code** Elemental language of computers, consisting of a string of 0's and 1's. Because machine language is the lowest-level computer language and the only language that computers directly understand, a program written in a more sophisticated language (e.g., C, PASCAL) must be converted to machine language prior to execution. This is done via a compiler or assembler. The resulting binary file (also called an executable file) can then be executed by the CPU. See also ASSEMBLY LANGUAGE.

machine tool Stationary, power-driven machine used to cut, shape, or form materials such as metal and wood. Machine tools date from the invention of the STEAM ENGINE in the 18th century; most common machine tools were designed by the middle of the 19th century. Today dozens of different machine tools are used in the workshops of home and industry. They are frequently classified into seven types: turning machines such as LATHES; SHAPERS and PLANERS; power DRILLS or DRILL PRESSES; MILLING machines; GRINDING MACHINES; power SAWS; and presses (e.g., PUNCH PRESSES).

machismo \mä-ˈchēz-mō\ Exaggerated pride in masculinity, perceived as power, often coupled with a minimal sense of responsibility and disregard of consequences. In machismo there is supreme valuation of characteristics culturally associated with the masculine and denigration of characteristics associated with the feminine. It has for centuries been a strong current in Latin American politics and society. CAUDILLOS, prominent in the history of Latin America, have typified machismo with their bold and authoritarian approach to government and their willingness to employ violence to achieve their ends.

Mach's principle \ˈmäks\ Hypothesis that the inertial forces acting on a body in accelerated motion are determined by the quantity and distribution of MATTER in the universe. ALBERT EINSTEIN found its suggested connection between geometry and matter helpful in formulating his theory of general RELATIVITY; unaware that GEORGE BERKELEY had proposed similar views in the 18th century, he attributed the idea to ERNST MACH. He abandoned the principle when he realized that INERTIA is assumed in the geodesic equation of motion (see GEODESY) and need not depend on the existence of matter elsewhere in the universe.

Machu Picchu \ˈmä-chü-ˈpēk-chü\ Ancient fortress city of the INCAS in the ANDES, southern central Peru, northwest of CUZCO. Perched in a narrow saddle between two sharp peaks, at an altitude of 7,710 ft (2,350 m), it escaped detection by the Spaniards and was discovered only in 1911 by U.S. explorer Hiram Bingham. One of the few pre-Columbian urban centers found nearly intact, it is about 5 sq mi (13 sq km) in area, and includes a temple and a citadel. The period of occupancy is uncertain.

Machu Picchu.

MAYES–FPG

MacIver \mə-ˈkē-vər\, **Robert M(orrison)** (1882–1970) Scottish-U.S. sociologist and political scientist. Educated at Edinburgh and Oxford, he taught at the University of Aberdeen and later at Canadian and U.S. universities, principally Columbia (1915–26). He believed in the compatibility of individualism and social organization, and saw societies as evolving from highly communal states to states in which individual functions and group affiliations were extremely specialized. His works included *The Modern State* (1926), *Leviathan and the People* (1939), and *The Web of Government* (1947).

Mack, Connie *orig.* **Cornelius (Alexander) McGillicuddy** (1862–1956) U.S. baseball manager and team executive. Born in East Brookfield, Mass., he played professional baseball 1886–96, usually as a catcher, before becoming manager of the Milwaukee Brewers (1897–1900) and the Philadelphia Athletics (1901–50). He was president of the Athletics 1937–53. His teams won 3,776 games and lost 4,025, both all-time records. He helped establish the AMERICAN LEAGUE as a major league.

Mackenzie Former administrative district, Canada. Occupying an area of 527,490 sq mi (1,366,199 sq km), it included the greater part of the northern mainland of Canada between YUKON TERRITORY and Keewatin district, as well as most of the MACKENZIE RIVER valley, GREAT BEAR LAKE, and GREAT SLAVE LAKE. Created in 1895, it was administered from EDMONTON; it ceased to exist in 1979.

Mackenzie, Alexander *later* **Sir Alexander** (1755?–1820) Scottish-Canadian explorer. Emigrating to Canada as a young man, he entered a fur-trading firm in 1779. In 1788 he set up a trading post, Fort Chipewyan, on Lake Athabasca. There began his 1789 expedition, which followed the Mackenzie River from Great Slave Lake to the Arctic Ocean. In 1793 he journeyed from Fort Chipewyan to the Pacific coast, crossing the Rocky Mtns., becoming the first European to reach the Pacific after crossing the Rockies.

Mackenzie \mə-'ken-zē\, **Alexander** (1822–1892) Scottish-Canadian politician, first Liberal prime minister of Canada (1873–78). He emigrated to Canada West (now Ontario) in 1842. In 1852 he became editor of a local Liberal newspaper and befriended GEORGE BROWN, leader of the Reform Party. When the Dominion of Canada was created in 1867, Mackenzie was elected to the House of Commons, where he led the Liberal opposition. As prime minister, his efforts at renewed reciprocity with the U.S. failed to address economic concerns, and his government was defeated in 1878. He resigned as leader of the opposition but held a seat in Parliament until his death.

Mackenzie, (Edward Montague) Compton *later* **Sir Edward** (1883–1972) British novelist and playwright. Educated at Oxford Univ., he gave up legal studies to finish his first play, *The Gentleman in Grey* (1906). During World War I he directed the Aegean Intelligence Service in Syria; when he wrote about those experiences in *Greek Memories* (1932), he was prosecuted under Britain's Official Secrets Act. He founded *Gramophone* magazine in 1923 and edited it until 1962. He served as rector of Glasgow University (1931–34) and as literary critic for the London *Daily Mail;* his more than 100 novels, plays, and biographies include ten volumes of memoirs.

Mackenzie, James *later* **Sir James** (1853–1925) Scottish cardiologist. He received his MD from the University of Edinburgh and practiced medicine in Lancashire for 25 years before moving to London. His classic *The Study of the Pulse* (1902) described an instrument called a polygraph, which simultaneously recorded arterial and venous pulses so that they could be correlated with the heartbeat to distinguish harmless from dangerous irregularities. A pioneer in the study of cardiac arrhythmia, he also proved the efficacy of digitalis for its treatment.

Mackenzie, William Lyon (1795–1861) Scottish-Canadian insurgent leader. He emigrated to Canada in 1820 and became a merchant in Upper Canada (later Ontario). He founded the *Colonial Advocate,* in which he assailed the administration (1824–34). Elected to the province's assembly (1828–36), he was expelled six times by the conservative majority for his editorial invective against the government. A list of Canadian grievances against British colonial rule that he published led to the recall of the province's governor. In 1837 he led 800 followers in an unsuccessful attempt to overthrow the provincial government. He tried to rally his forces on Navy Island in the Niagara River, N.Y., and was jailed for breaking U.S. neutrality laws. He returned to Canada in 1849 and served in the Canadian Parliament 1851–58.

Mackenzie River River system, Northwest Territories. It flows northward from GREAT SLAVE LAKE into the Beaufort Sea of the Arctic Ocean. Its basin, with an area of 697,000 sq mi (1,805,200 sq km), is the largest in Canada. It is 1,025 mi (1,650 km) long and 1–2 mi (1.5–3 km) wide. With the Finlay River, its farthest headstream, the entire system is 2,635 mi (4,241 km) long, making it the second longest river in North America. It was discovered by the explorer ALEXANDER MACKENZIE in 1789.

mackerel Swift-moving, carnivorous, torpedo-shaped food and sport fishes of temperate and tropical seas worldwide. Mackerels (family Scombridae, order Perciformes) are 1–5.5 ft (30–170 cm) long. The common mackerel *(Scomber scombrus)* of the North Atlantic and the chub mackerel *(S. colias)* of California and the Atlantic are economically important, as are the Indian mackerels (genus *Rastrelliger*) and the frigate mackerels (genus *Auxis*). Other species (genus *Scomberomorus*) are favorite game fish. The name mackerel also refers to certain shark species (see MACKEREL SHARK), TUNA, and BONITO.

Mackerel shark (*Lamna nasus*).
PAINTING BY RICHARD ELLIS

mackerel shark Any of several temperate-water SHARKS (genus *Lamna*) in a family (Isuridae) that also includes the GREAT WHITE SHARK and the MAKO shark group. The swift, active mackerel sharks have a crescent-shaped tail and slender teeth. They are gray or blue-gray above and paler below and about 10 ft (3 m) long. They eat fishes such as herring, mackerel, and salmon, sometimes taking fishermen's catches and damaging nets. They are fished commercially for food. Common species include the Atlantic mackerel shark, or porbeagle *(L. nasus),* and the Pacific mackerel shark, or salmon shark *(L ditropis).*

Mackinac \'ma-kə-ˌnȯ\, **Straits of** Channel connecting Lake MICHIGAN with Lake HURON. Forming an important waterway between the Upper and Lower peninsulas of Michigan, the straits are 30 mi (48 km) long and 4 mi (6 km) wide at their narrowest point. They are spanned by the Mackinac Bridge, a 3,800-ft (1,158-m) suspension bridge built in 1957.

Mackinac Island Island in the Straits of MACKINAC, southeastern Upper Peninsula of Michigan. It is 3 mi (5 km) long. It was an ancient Indian burial ground called Michilimackinac when the British built a fort there in 1780. After the U.S. took possession in 1783, it became the headquarters of the AMERICAN FUR CO. Occupied by the British during the WAR OF 1812, the island returned to U.S. control in 1815. It has been a state park since 1895; automobiles are banned from the island.

Mackinaw trout See LAKE TROUT

Mackintosh, Charles Rennie (1868–1928) Scottish architect, furniture designer, and artist. A giant of the ARTS AND CRAFTS MOVEMENT, he is especially revered for his glass-and-stone studio building at the Glasgow School of Art (1896–1909), where he had attended classes. In the 1890s he achieved an international reputation creating unorthodox posters, craftwork, and furniture. Considered Britain's first designer of true ART NOUVEAU architecture, he produced work of an unrivaled lightness, elegance, and originality, as exemplified by four remarkable tearooms he designed in Glasgow (1896–1904). By 1914 he was dedicating all his energies to watercolor painting. The late 20th century saw a revival of interest in his work and the manufacture of reproductions of his chairs and settees, with their starkly simple geometric lines.

MacLaine, Shirley *orig.* **Shirley MacLean Beaty** (born 1934) U.S. film actress. Born in Richmond, Va., the sister of WARREN BEATTY, she worked as a dancer on Broadway. After replacing the injured star in *The Pajama Game* (1954), she made her movie debut in *The Trouble with Harry* (1955) and went on to play comic and dramatic roles in *Some Came Running* (1959), *The Apartment* (1960), *Irma La Douce* (1963), *Sweet Charity* (1969), *The Turning Point* (1977), *Terms of Endearment* (1983, Academy Award), and *Madame Sousatzka* (1988). She wrote several best-selling books, often about her mystical experiences, including *Out on a Limb* (1983) and *Going Within* (1989).

Maclean, Donald See Guy BURGESS

Maclean's \mə-'klānz\ Weekly newsmagazine published in Toronto, the leading Canadian magazine. It provides coverage of Canadian affairs and world news from a Canadian perspective. Founded in 1905 in a large-page format, it presented feature articles and fiction reflecting a conservative view of Canadian life and values and developed a reputation for outstanding photography. In the 1970s its page size was reduced and its format revised.

MacLeish \mə-'klēsh\, **Archibald** (1892–1982) U.S. poet, playwright, teacher, and public official. Born in Glencoe, Ill., he practiced law before leaving for France in 1923 to perfect his poetic craft. His early poems include "Ars Poetica" (1926) and "You, Andrew Marvell" (1930). He later expressed his concern for democratic ideals in such "public" verse as *Conquistador* (1932, Pulitzer Prize) and *Public Speech* (1936). Other works include the radio verse play *Air Raid* (1938), *Collected Poems* (1952, Pulitzer Prize), and the verse drama *J.B.* (1958, Pulitzer Prize). He served as librarian of Congress (1939–44) and assistant secretary of state (1944–45) and later taught at Harvard (1949–62).

MacLennan \mə-'klen-ən\, **(John) Hugh** (1907–1990) Canadian novelist and essayist. Born in Glace Bay, Nova Scotia, he was a Rhodes scholar at Oxford University and earned a doctorate at Princeton, then taught at McGill University 1951–81. His novels include *Barometer Rising* (1941), *Two Solitudes* (1945), *The Watch That Ends the Night* (1959), and *Voices in Time* (1980). He won five Governor-General's awards for his fiction and nonfiction. He is regarded as the first major English-speaking novelist to use Canadian themes.

Macleod \mə-'klau̇d\, **J(ohn) J(ames) R(ickard)** (1876–1935) Scottish physiologist. He taught in U.S., Canadian, and Scottish universities, becoming noted for his work on carbohydrate metabolism. With FREDERICK BANTING and CHARLES BEST he discovered insulin, an achievement for which he and Banting shared a Nobel Prize in 1923.

Macmillan, Daniel and Alexander (1813–1857, 1818–1896) Scottish booksellers and publishers. Apprenticed to a bookseller in Scotland at 11, Daniel worked for London booksellers 1837–43. In 1843 he and his brother Alexander founded Macmillan & Co., a successful bookshop in Cambridge that began publishing textbooks in 1844 and novels in 1855. After Daniel's death, Alexander expanded the firm's list and founded *Macmillan's Magazine* (1859–1907), a literary periodical, and *Nature* (1869–), a leading scientific journal. He established offices abroad and published many important Victorian writers. Long led by Daniel's descendants, the company grew into one of the largest publishing firms in the world.

Macmillan, (Maurice) Harold *later* **Earl of Stockton** (1894–1986) British prime minister (1957–63). He served in the House of Commons 1924–29 and 1931–64, and held posts in WINSTON CHURCHILL's wartime coalition government. After the war he served as minister of housing (1951–54), minister of defense (1954), foreign secretary (1955), and chancellor of the exchequer (1955–57). In 1957 he became prime minister and leader of the CONSERVATIVE PARTY. He worked to improve relations with the U.S. and visited NIKITA KHRUSHCHEV in 1959. Domestically, Macmillan supported Britain's postwar social programs. His government began to lose popularity in 1961 because of a wage freeze and other deflationary measures and a Soviet espionage scandal involving John Profumo, secretary of state for war. In 1963 CHARLES DE GAULLE vetoed British entry into the EUROPEAN ECONOMIC COMMUNITY. Demands for a new party leader led to his resignation in 1963. He wrote a series of memoirs (1966–75) and served as chair (1963–74) of his family's publishing house, Macmillan & Co.

MacMillan, Kenneth *later* **Sir Kenneth** (1929–1992) British dancer, choreographer, and director of the ROYAL BALLET. After studies at the Sadler's Wells ballet school, he danced with its ballet companies from 1946. He choreographed his first work, *Somnambulism,* in 1953, followed by *Danses concertantes* (1955). His ballet *Romeo and Juliet* (1965) made an international impact. He was ballet director of the German Opera in Berlin (1966–69). In 1970 he was appointed director of the Royal Ballet; in 1977 he resigned to become its principal choreographer. His other successful ballets included *Anastasia* (1971), *Manon* (1974), and *Isadora* (1981).

L M N

MacNeice, Louis (1907–1963) British poet and playwright. He published his first book of poetry, *Blind Fireworks* (1929), while studying at Oxford. In the 1930s he became known as one of a group of socially committed young poets that included W. H. AUDEN, C. DAY-LEWIS, and STEPHEN SPENDER. His volumes include *Autumn Journal* (1939) and *The Burning Perch* (1963). He wrote and produced radio verse plays for the BBC, notably *The Dark Tower* (1947), with music by BENJAMIN BRITTEN. Among his prose works are the *Letters from Iceland* (1937; with Auden) and *The Poetry of W.B. Yeats* (1941).

MacNeice.
CAMERA PRESS

MacNelly, Jeff(rey Kenneth) (1947–2000) U.S. cartoonist. Born in New York and educated at the University of North Carolina, he was known for the highly entertaining style of his political cartoons. In 1972 he became the youngest person ever to win a Pulitzer Prize for editorial cartooning; he won it again in 1978 and 1985. In his widely syndicated comic strip "Shoe" (1977), all the characters were birds.

Macon \'mā-kən\ City (pop., 1996 est.: 113,000), central Georgia. A fort was built near the site, and in 1806 a settlement grew up around it. Macon was laid out across the river in 1823, and it annexed the settlement in 1829; the town was named for NATHANIEL MACON. During the AMERICAN CIVIL WAR, it was a Confederate supply depot. A distribution center in an agricultural region, it is the site of several institutions of higher learning and Robins Air Force Base, as well as the birthplace of the poet Sidney Lanier (1842–1881).

Macon, Dave *orig.* **David Harrison** (1870–1952) U.S. COUNTRY-MUSIC singer and banjo player, first star of the GRAND OLE OPRY. Born in Smart Station, Tenn., he grew up in Nashville, where his parents ran a hotel that catered to traveling performers. He was in the mule business for 20 years; after the trucking industry put him out of business, he became a professional musician. Performing as Uncle Dave Macon, his jovial folk tunes, such as "Go Long Mule," and energetic showmanship soon made him a star. He was an Opry regular from the mid-1920s until his death at 81.

Macon, Nathaniel (1758–1837) U.S. politician. Born in Edgecombe, N.C., he fought in the American Revolution and served in the North Carolina legislature 1781–85. Elected to the U.S. House of Representatives (1791–1815), he became speaker (1801–7) and was a leading ANTI-FEDERALIST. In the Senate (1815–28), he continued to advocate states' rights and opposed legislation that strengthened the central government.

Macphail, Agnes Campbell (1890–1954) Canadian politician. Born in Grey Co., Ontario, she became a schoolteacher and entered politics to represent the region's farmers. In 1921, the first year women could vote in national elections, she was elected to the Canadian House of Commons as its first female member, and served until 1940. She advocated prison reform and women's rights as well as a protective tariff. She was the first female Canadian delegate to the League of Nations. Elected to the Ontario legislature (1943–45, 1948–51), she sponsored Ontario's first equal-pay legislation.

Macquarie \mə-'kwar-ē\, **Lachlan** (1761–1824) British soldier and colonial governor. He served with the British army in North America, Europe, the West Indies, and India before being appointed governor of New South Wales, Australia, in 1809. There he replaced the corrupt military corps that had overthrown the previous governor, WILLIAM BLIGH. He began a program of public-works construction and town planning that gave opportunities to Emancipists (freed convicts), established the colony's currency, and encouraged exploration and settlement. His policy favoring Emancipist agriculture angered the large landowners and sheep farmers (Exclusionists), and he was recalled in 1821.

Macquarie Harbour \mə-'kwar-ē\ Inlet of the Indian Ocean, western TASMANIA, Australia. It is 20 mi (32 km) long and 5 mi (8 km) wide. Visited in 1815 by Capt. James Kelly, it was named after Lachlan Macquarie, governor of New South Wales. Its coast was the site of a penal colony 1821–33.

Macready \mə-'krē-dē\, **William (Charles)** (1793–1873) English actor-manager. He made his debut in 1810, and by 1820 he was famous for his performances as Hamlet, Lear, and Macbeth. As theater manager of London's COVENT GARDEN (1837–39) and DRURY LANE (1841–43), he introduced such reforms as full rehearsals, historically accurate costumes and sets, and a reversion to the original Shakespeare texts. He toured the U.S. in 1826, 1843, and 1848–49; his last tour ended with the Astor Place riot, caused by partisans of EDWIN FORREST. He retired from the stage in 1851. His diary provides a view of 19th-century theatrical life.

macrobiotics Dietary practice based on the Chinese philosophy of balancing yin and yang (see YIN-YANG). It stresses avoiding foods that are classified as strongly yin (e.g., ALCOHOLIC BEVERAGES) or yang (e.g. MEAT) and relying mainly on near-neutral foods such as grains. In addition, foods that grow naturally in one's climate should be the mainstay of the diet. Macrobiotics was first articulated in Asia in the 1930s and swept Europe and the U.S. in the late 1960s. Adherents maintain that not only can one's quality of life be enhanced, but that serious ailments such as cancer can be healed; critics counter that uninformed attempts to practice such a diet can lead to MALNUTRITION.

macroeconomics Study of the entire economy in terms of the total amount of goods and services produced, total income earned, level of employment of productive resources, and general behavior of prices. Until the 1930s, most economic analysis focused on specific firms and industries. With the GREAT DEPRESSION and the development of national income and product statistics, the field of macroeconomics began to expand. The goals of macroeconomic policy include economic growth, price stability, and full employment. See also MICROECONOMICS.

macromolecule Any very large MOLECULE, composed of much larger numbers (hundreds or thousands) of ATOMS than ordinary molecules. Some macromolecules are individual entities that cannot be subdivided without losing their identity (e.g., certain PROTEINS, with MOLECULAR WEIGHTS into the millions). Others (POLYMERS) are multiples of a repeating building block (MONOMER) in chains or networks (e.g., PLASTICS, CELLULOSE). Most macromolecules are in the size range typical of COLLOIDS.

macrophage system See RETICULOENDOTHELIAL SYSTEM

macular degeneration Degeneration of the macula (central part of the RETINA), with corresponding VISUAL-FIELD DEFECT. It is the leading cause of BLINDNESS in old age. Probably due to reduced blood circulation, it is now known to have a genetic component. It is twice as common in smokers as in nonsmokers, and it is also correlated with lifelong sun exposure. Peripheral vision usually remains, but loss of central visual acuity makes reading or fine work difficult or impossible, even with special magnifying eyeglasses. Some forms of macular degeneration can be halted (but not reversed) by laser surgery.

Macumba \mə-ˈküm-bə\ Afro-Brazilian religion characterized by the syncretism of traditional AFRICAN RELIGIONS, Brazilian SPIRITUALISM, and ROMAN CATHOLICISM. Of the several Macumba sects in Brazil, the most important are CANDOMBLÉ and Umbanda. African elements include an outdoor ceremonial site, the sacrifice of animals (e.g., cocks), spirit offerings (e.g., candles and flowers), and dances. Macumba rites are led by mediums, who fall prostrate in trances and communicate with holy spirits. Roman Catholic elements include the cross and the worship of saints, who are given African names.

Macy and Co. *in full* **R. H. Macy and Co., Inc.** Major U.S. DEPARTMENT-STORE chain. Its main outlet, the 11-story store that occupies a city block in New York's Herald Square, was for many years the largest single store in the country. Rowland H. Macy (1822?–1877) established the business in 1858; its red star trademark was derived from a tattoo he bore. STRAUS FAMILY acquired part interest in the company in 1887 and took full control in 1896, whereupon they began purchasing or building branch stores around the country. Forced into bankruptcy in 1992, Macy's agreed to a merger with Federated Department Stores Inc. in 1994.

mad cow disease *or* **bovine spongiform encephalopathy (BSE)** \ˈspən-ji-ˌfȯrm-in-ˌ-sef-ə-ˈläp-ə-thē\ Fatal neurodegenerative disease of cattle. Symptoms include behavioral changes (e.g., agitation), gradual loss of coordination and locomotive function, and, in advanced stages, weight loss, fine muscular contractions, and abnormal gait. Brain tissue becomes pitted with holes and spongy. Death usually follows within a year. The disease is similar to the neurodegenerative disease of sheep called scrapie. No treatment is known. A BSE epidemic in Britain that began in the mid-1980s is believed to have been caused by the use of cattle feed containing supplements made from ruminant carcasses and trimmings. Hundreds of thousands of infected cattle were slaughtered and the use of animal-derived protein supplements ended. The cause of both BSE and scrapie is attributed to an infectious aberrant protein called a PRION. The unusual occurrence of CREUTZFELDT-JAKOB DISEASE, another prion-related illness, in young people beginning in the mid-1990s may be linked to eating meat from cattle with BSE.

Madagascar *officially* **Republic of Madagascar** Nation, occupying the island of Madagascar, off the southeastern coast of Africa. The island of Madagascar, the world's fourth-largest island, is about 976 mi (1,570 km) long and 355 mi (571 km) wide. It is separated from the African coast by the Mozambique Channel. Area: 226,658 sq mi (587,041 sq km). Population (1997 est.): 14,062,000. Capital: ANTANANARIVO. Almost all the population belongs to about 20 Malayo-Indonesian groups. Languages: Malagasy, French (both official). Religions: Traditional animism; Christianity (Roman Catholicism, Protestantism), Islam. Currency: Malagasy franc. Madagascar's high central plateau rises to 9,436 ft (2,876 m) at the volcanic Tsaratanana massif; the island was once heavily forested, and forests still cover one-fourth of the land area. Agriculture dominates the economy, with staple crops, including rice and cassava, and cash crops, including coffee, cloves, and vanilla. It is a republic with one legislative house; its chief of state is the president, and the head of government is the prime minister. Indonesians migrated to Madagascar c. AD 700. The first European to visit the island was Portuguese navigator Diogo Dias in 1500. Trade in arms and slaves allowed the development of Malagasy kingdoms at the beginning of the 17th century. In the 18th century the Merina kingdom became dominant; with

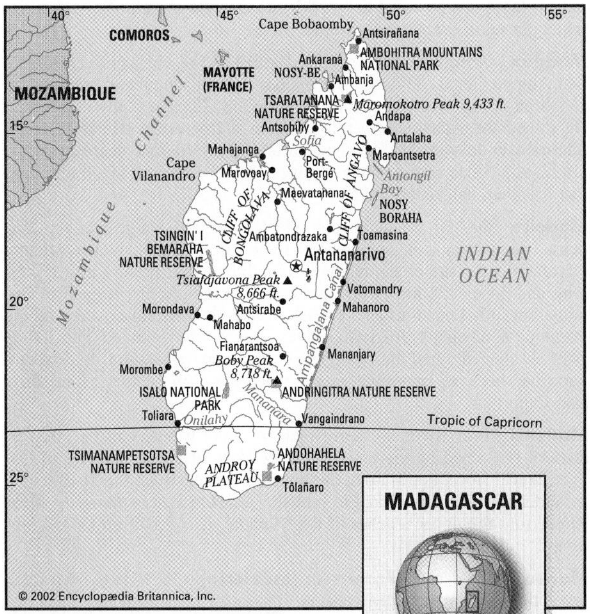

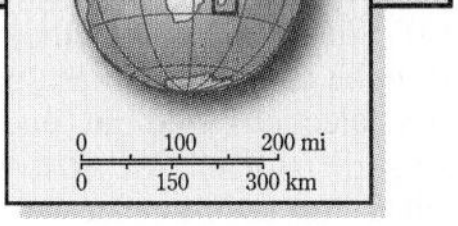

British assistance, it gained control of a large part of Madagascar in the early 19th century. In 1868 Merina signed a treaty granting France control over the northwestern coast, and in 1895 French troops took the island. Madagascar became a French overseas territory in 1946. In 1958 France agreed to let the territory decide its own fate; as the Malagasy Republic, it gained independence in 1960. It severed ties with France in the 1970s, taking its present name in 1975. A new constitution was adopted in 1992. The country has since been both politically and economically unstable.

Madani \ˈmȧ-dȧ-nē\, **Abbasi al-** (born 1931) Cofounder, with ALI BELHADJ, of the Algerian ISLAMIC SALVATION FRONT (FIS). After earning a doctorate in London, he returned to Algeria to teach at the University of Algiers, where he became a leader of religious students. He traveled with other itinerant preachers around the country, exchanging ideas and preaching the outlines of a religious political movement. He was arrested after the first round of voting in the 1991–92 legislative elections. In 1999 he endorsed a peace agreement put forward by Algeria's president, Abdelaziz Bouteflika, between the FIS and the Algerian government.

Madariaga y Rojo \ˌmä-də-rē-ˈä-gə-ē-ˈrō-hō\, **Salvador de** (1886–1978) Spanish writer, diplomat, and historian. Abandoning an engineering career for journalism, he joined the League of Nations Secretariat in 1921 as a press member, served as ambassador to the U.S. and France, and was Spain's permanent delegate to the League 1931–36. When the Spanish Civil War broke out in 1936, he moved to England, returning only after FRANCISCO FRANCO's death. He wrote prolifically in English, German, French, and Spanish, his works including *Englishmen, Frenchmen, Spaniards* (1928), *Spain* (1942), *The Rise and Fall of the Spanish American Empire* (1945), and novels based on Latin-American history.

madder family Family Rubiaceae, composed of about 6,500 species of herbs, shrubs, and trees in 500 genera. The leaves usually are large and evergreen in tropical species, deciduous in temperate species, and needlelike or scalelike in desert species. The plants may bear a single flower or many small flowers clustered together. Economically important products of the family include COFFEE, QUININE, IPECAC, the red dye alizarin (from the roots of common madder, *Rubia tinctorum,* and of *R. cordifolia*), and ornamentals including GARDENIAS.

Madderakka \ˈmäd-dä-ˌräh-kä\ Among the SAMI, the goddess of childbirth. She was assisted by three of her daughters—Sarakka, the cleaving woman; Uksakka, the door woman; and Juksakka, the bow woman—who watched over the child from conception through early childhood. Madderakka was believed to receive the soul of a child from Veralden-

L
M
N

radien, the god who ruled the world; she then gave it a body, which Sarakka placed in the mother's womb.

Maddux, Greg(ory Alan) (born 1966) U.S. baseball player. Born in San Angelo, Texas, he was a star pitcher in high school and was drafted and brought up to the major leagues by the Chicago Cubs (1986–92). He joined the Atlanta Braves in 1993 as a free agent. He is the only pitcher ever to win the Cy Young pitching award four years in a row (1992–95). Since coming to the Braves he has won over 100 games and lost less than half that number.

Madeira \mä-'dār-ə\ Island (pop., 1991: 265,000), largest of the Madeira Island group, an autonomous region of Portugal, North Atlantic Ocean. It is the site of the region's capital, FUNCHAL. It is 34 mi (55 km) long and 14 mi (22 km) wide, and has deep ravines and rugged mountains. Possibly known to ancient PHOENICIANS, it was rediscovered by the Portuguese navigator João Gonçalves Zarco, who founded Funchal in 1421. It allegedly had the world's first sugarcane plantation. Its Madeira wine has been an important export since the 17th century. Tourism is also important.

Madeira River River, western Brazil. A major tributary of the AMAZON RIVER, it is formed by the junction of the MAMORÉ and BENI rivers in Bolivia, and it flows north along the border between Bolivia and Brazil. It meanders northeast in Brazil to join the Amazon east of MANAUS. Measured from the upper reaches of the Mamoré, it is 2,082 mi (3,352 km) long.

Madero \mə-'der-ō\, **Francisco (Indalecio)** (1873–1913) Mexican revolutionary and president (1911–13). Son of a wealthy landowner, in 1908 he called for honest, participatory elections and an end to the long dictatorship of PORFIRIO DIAZ. Jailed for sedition but released on bail, he incited an armed insurrection that led to Díaz's resignation. He was elected president in 1911. Handicapped by political inexperience and excessive idealism, he was quickly overwhelmed by conflicting pressures from conservatives and revolutionaries, and his administration ended in personal and national disaster when he was assassinated in 1913. See also MEXICAN REVOLUTION, PANCHO VILLA, EMILIANO ZAPATA.

Madero, c. 1910.
ARCHIVO CASASOLA

Madhya Pradesh \'mä-dyə-prə-'dāsh\ State (pop., 2001 prelim.: 60,385,118), central India. Occupying an area of 119,016 sq mi (308,252 sq km), it is India's second largest state. Its capital is BHOPAL. It is the source of some of the most important rivers of India, including the NARMADA, the TAPI, the Mahanadi, and the Wainganga. It was part of the Mauryan empire of the 4th–3rd century BC and was ruled by numerous other dynasties. Under Islamic control from the 11th century, it was annexed by the Mughal empire in the 16th century. It was under Maratha rule by 1760 and passed to the British early in the 19th century. The state was formed after India gained its independence in 1947; its boundaries were altered in 1956. In 2000 the eastern portion of the state was made into the new state of CHHATTISGARH. Though Madhya Pradesh is rich in mineral resources, its economic mainstay is agriculture.

Madhyamika \mäd-'yə-mi-kə\ School in the MAHAYANA Buddhist tradition. Its name means "middle" and derives from its middle position between the realism of the SARVASTIVADA school and the idealism of the YOGACARA school. The most renowned Madhyamika thinker was NAGARJUNA.

Madison City (pop., 2000: 208,054), capital of Wisconsin. It is located in the southern central part of the state, on an isthmus between lakes Mendota and Monona. Founded in 1836 and named for JAMES MADISON, it became the capital of Wisconsin Territory the same year. It was incorporated as a village in 1846 and as a city in 1856. Steady development followed the 1854 arrival of the railroad. Noted for its parks and wooded lakeshore, it is the commercial center of an agricultural region. Educational and governmental services are economically important; it is the seat of the University of WISCONSIN's main campus.

Madison, James (1751–1836) Fourth president of the U.S. (1809–17). Born in Port Conway, Va., he served in the state legislature (1776–80, 1784–86). At the Constitutional Convention (1787), his active participation and his careful notes on the debates earned him the title "father of the Constitution." To promote ratification, he collaborated with ALEXANDER HAMILTON and JOHN JAY on *The FEDERALIST*. In the U.S. House of Representatives (1789–97), he sponsored the Bill of Rights, was a leading Jeffersonian Republican, and split with Hamilton over funding state war debts. In reaction to the ALIEN AND SEDITION ACTS, he drafted one of the VIRGINIA AND KENTUCKY RESOLUTIONS (1798). He was appointed secretary of state (1801–9) by THOMAS JEFFERSON, with whom he developed U.S. foreign policy. Elected president in 1808, he was occupied by the trade and shipping embargo problems caused by France and Britain that led to the WAR OF 1812. He was reelected in 1812; his second term was marked principally by the war, during which he reinvigorated the U.S. Army, and also saw approval of the charter of the Second BANK OF THE U.S. and the first U.S. protective tariff. He retired to his Virginia estate, Montpelier, with his wife, Dolley (1768–1849), whose political acumen he had long prized. He continued to write articles and letters and served as rector of the University of Virginia (1826–36).

Madonna In Christian art, a depiction of the Virgin MARY. Though often shown with the infant JESUS, the Madonna (Italian: "My lady") may also be represented alone. Byzantine art was the first to develop a set of Madonna types—the Madonna and child enthroned, the Madonna as intercessor, the Madonna nursing the child, and so on. Western art adapted and added to the Byzantine types during the Middle Ages, producing images of the Virgin that sought to inspire piety through beauty and tenderness. In the Renaissance and Baroque periods, the most popular image of the Madonna foreshadowed the CRUCIFIXION, showing the Virgin looking gravely away from the playful child.

"The Grand-Duke's Madonna," oil painting by Raphael, 1505; in the Pitti Palace, Florence.
SCALA—ART RESOURCE

Madonna *orig.* **Madonna Louise Ciccone** (born 1958) U.S. pop singer, songwriter, and actress. Born in Bay City, Mich., she studied dance at the University of Michigan and later with MARTHA GRAHAM and ALVIN AILEY. Her first hit single, "Holiday" (1983), forged an upbeat dance-club sound that sold 70 million albums by 1991, including *Like a Virgin* (1984). In music videos and in concert, she captivated fans and scandalized critics with provocatively sexual showmanship. Ever atop the latest trend, she incorporated TECHNO in *Music* (2000). Her films include *Desperately Seeking Susan* (1985) and *Evita* (1996). Few female entertainers have attained her levels of power and control in the pop music industry.

Madras See TAMIL NADU

Madras See CHENNAI

madrasah \'mad-rə-sə\ (Arabic: "school") Islamic theological seminary and law school attached to a MOSQUE. The residential madrasah was a newer building form than the mosque, flourishing in most Muslim cities by the end of the 12th century. The Syrian madrasahs in Damascus tended to follow a standardized plan: An elaborate facade led into a domed hallway and then into a courtyard where instruction took place, with at least one *eyvan* (vaulted hall) opening onto it. The madrasah at the Qalaun Mosque in Cairo (1283–85) has a unique cruciform *eyvan* on the richly carved *qibla* (wall facing Mecca) side and a smaller *eyvan* opposite. Residential cells for scholars occupy the other two sides.

Madre, Laguna Long narrow inlet of the Gulf of Mexico along the shore of southern Texas and northeastern Mexico. Sheltered from the gulf by barrier islands, including PADRE ISLAND, it is divided into two sections by the delta of the RIO GRANDE; the U.S. portion extends south for 120 mi (190 km) from Corpus Christi Bay, and the Mexican portion extends north for 100 mi (160 km) from the mouth of the Soto la Marina River. The GULF INTRACOASTAL WATERWAY runs through it.

Madre de Dios River River, southeastern Peru and northwestern Bolivia. Rising in the easternmost range of the ANDES, in Peru, it flows east to the Bolivian border. There it turns northeast and crosses the tropical rain forest of northwestern Bolivia, joining the BENI RIVER after a course of 700 mi (1,100 km). A tributary of the AMAZON RIVER, it is navigable in its upper course and again below the Peru–Bolivia border.

Madrid City (pop., 1996: 2,867,000), capital of Spain, and of MADRID autonomous community. Located on the central plateau of the Iberian Peninsula, at 2,100 ft (635 m) above sea level, it is one of Europe's highest capitals. The original town grew up around the Moorish alcazar (castle), overlooking the Manzanares River. King ALFONSO VI captured the town from the Muslims in 1083. PHILIP II moved the Spanish court to Madrid in 1561, and in 1607 PHILIP III made it the official capital. It was occupied by French troops during the NAPOLEONIC WARS but returned to Spanish control in 1812. During the SPANISH CIVIL WAR, it was held by the Loyalists 1936–39. Spain's principal transportation center for the interior provinces, it is an important commercial, industrial, and cultural center. Major institutions include the PRADO MUSEUM and the University of Madrid.

Madrid \mä-'thrēth, *Engl* mə-'drid\ Autonomous community (pop., 1996 est.: 5,022,000), central Spain. It occupies an area of 3,087 sq mi (7,995 sq km), and its capital is MADRID. The province extends across the southern slopes of the Guadarrama Mountains and roughly coincides with the region drained by the Jarama, Henares, and Manzanares rivers. It was the scene of several decisive battles during the SPANISH CIVIL WAR (1936–39). All the national railways converge in the province. The Somo Mountain Pass provides access to the northeast through the central mountains.

madrigal Form of vocal chamber music, usually polyphonic and unaccompanied, of the 16th–17th century. It originated and developed in Italy, under the influence of the French CHANSON and the Italian frottola. Usually written for three to six voices, madrigals came to be sung widely as a social activity by cultivated amateurs, male and female. The texts were almost always about love; most prominent among the poets whose works were set are PETRARCH, TORQUATO TASSO, and BATTISTA GUARINI. ORLANDE DE LASSUS, L. MARENZIO, C. GESUALDO, and C. MONTEVERDI were among the greatest of the Italian madrigalists; T. MORLEY, THOMAS WEELKES, and JOHN WILBYE created a distinguished body of English madrigals.

Madura *Dutch* **Madoera** \mä-'du̇r-ə\ Island (pop., 1980: 2,690,000), Jawa Timur province, Indonesia, off northeastern JAVA. Its capital is Pamekasan. With an area of 2,042 sq mi (5,290 sq km), it has a hilly terrain rising to more than 1,400 ft (430 m) in the east. Dutch influence was established in the late 17th century. Madura was attached to Java as a residency in 1885 and became part of Indonesia in 1949. Bull races, usually held in September, attract huge crowds.

Maeander River See MENDERES RIVER

Maecenas \mī-'sē-nəs\, **Gaius (Cilnius)** (c. 70–8 BC) Roman diplomat and literary patron. He claimed descent from Etruscan kings. Though highly influential in the state, he held no title, nor did he wish to be a senator. From 43 on, he helped Octavian (later AUGUSTUS) diplomatically and domestically, administering Rome and Italy while Octavian was fighting POMPEIUS in 36 and Mark ANTONY in 31. He is best remembered as the generous patron of such writers as VIRGIL, HORACE, and PROPERTIUS; he used the work of such literati to glorify Augustus' regime. In 23, after the discovery of his brother-in-law's conspiracy against Augustus, he was forced to retire.

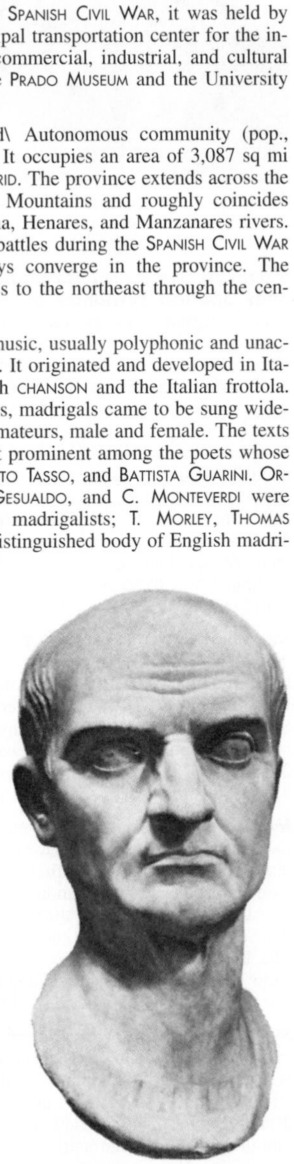

Gaius Maecenas, marble bust; in the Palazzo dei Conservatori, Rome.
ALINARI—ART RESOURCE/EB INC.

Maekawa \ˌmä-ā-'kä-wä\, **Kunio** (1905–1986) Japanese architect. Maekawa worked as a drafter for LE CORBUSIER in Paris and for ANTONIN RAYMOND in Tokyo. His community centers influenced KENZO TANGE, who started out in Maekawa's office. His works, large Brutalist masses teeming with activity, reflect an effort to use concrete in a manner appropriate to the material. The Harumi Flats, Tokyo (1959), the Setagaya Community Center, Tokyo (1959), and the Saitama Cultural Center (1966) provide fine examples.

maenads and bacchantes \'mē-ˌnadz...bə-'känts, bə-kän-tēz\ Female followers of the Greek wine-god DIONYSUS. The word maenad comes from the Greek, meaning "mad" or "demented." During the orgiastic rites of Dionysus, maenads roamed the mountains and forests performing frenzied, ecstatic dances, and were believed to be possessed by the god. While under his influence they were supposed to have unusual strength; it was said they could tear animals or people to pieces (the fate met by ORPHEUS). As bacchantes they were named for Bacchus, the Roman counterpart of Dionysus.

Maes \'mȧs\, **Nicolaes** (1634–1693) Dutch painter. A native of Dordrecht, he went to Amsterdam c. 1650 to study with REMBRANDT. Before his return to Dordrecht in 1653 he painted a few life-size Rembrandtesque genre scenes. From 1655 to 1660 he painted smaller domestic scenes, usually of women spinning, eavesdropping, reading the Bible, or cooking. In 1673 he moved permanently to Amsterdam and devoted himself to portraiture, abandoning intimacy and the deep glowing colors characteristic of Rembrandt for elegance and cooler tones reminiscent of ANTHONY VAN DYCK. He was a prolific painter and his portraits enjoyed great success.

Maeterlinck \'mā-tər-ˌliŋk\, **Maurice** *later* **comte (Count) Maeterlinck** (1862–1949) Belgian playwright and poet. He studied law in Ghent but soon turned to writing poems and plays. His *Pelléas et Mélisande* (1892), considered the masterpiece of Symbolist drama, was the basis of C. DEBUSSY's opera (1902) and works by other composers. He wrote a collection of Symbolist poems, *Hothouse Blooms* (1899), and plays such as *Monna Vanna* (1902), *The Blue Bird* (1908), and *The Burgomaster of Stilmonde* (1918). He was also noted for his popular treatments of scientific subjects, including *The Life of the Bee* (1901) and *The Intelligence of Flowers* (1907). He was awarded the Nobel Prize in 1911.

Maffei I and II \mä-'fā\ Two GALAXIES relatively close to the Milky Way galaxy, first detected in the late 1960s by the Italian astronomer Paolo Maffei. Maffei I is a large elliptical galaxy, while Maffei II is a spiral galaxy. Though they are large and nearby, they were not discovered earlier because they were hidden in the Milky Way's zone of AVOIDANCE. At a distance of about 10 million light-years, they appear to be major members of one of the nearest galaxy groups outside the LOCAL GROUP.

Mafia Society of criminals of primarily Italian or Sicilian origin, and criminal organizations in Sicily and the U.S. The Mafia arose in Sicily in the late Middle Ages, possibly as a secret organization to overthrow the rule of foreign conquerors. It drew its members from the small private armies, or *mafie,* hired by landlords to protect their estates. By 1900 the Mafia "families" of western Sicily controlled the economies of their localities. In the 1920s BENITO MUSSOLINI jailed most of the members, but they were released by the Allies after World War II and resumed their activities. In the 1970s their control of the heroin trade led to fierce rivalry among the clans, followed in the 1980s by renewed governmental efforts to imprison the Mafia leadership. In the U.S., Sicilian immigrants included former Mafia members who set up similar criminal operations. Their operations expanded from bootlegging in the 1920s to gambling, narcotics, and prostitution, and the Mafia, or Cosa Nostra, became the largest U.S. syndicated crime organizations. About 24 Mafia groups or "families" controlled operations in the U.S.; the heads (or "dons") of the largest families formed a commission whose main function was judicial, it being able to override a don's authority. In the late 20th century the Mafia's power was greatly diminished through convictions of top officials, defections, and murderous internal disputes. See also ORGANIZED crime.

mafic rock \'ma-fik\ In geology, any IGNEOUS ROCK dominated by the silicates pyroxene, amphibole, olivine, and mica. These minerals are high in magnesium and ferrous iron, and their presence gives mafic rock its characteristic dark color. It is usually contrasted with FELSIC ROCK. Common mafic rocks include BASALT and GABBRO.

Mafikeng \'ma-fə-ˌkiŋ\, **Siege of** Boer siege of a British military outpost in the SOUTH AFRICAN WAR at the town of Mafikeng (Mafeking) in northwestern South Africa in 1899–1900. The garrison, under the command of Col. ROBERT S. BADEN-POWELL, held out against the larger Boer force for 217 days until reinforcements could arrive. The rejoicing in British cities on news of the rescue produced the word *mafficking.*

Magadha \'mə-gə-də\ Ancient kingdom, India, situated in present-day BIHAR state, northeastern India. An important kingdom in the 7th century BC, it absorbed the kingdom of Anga in the 6th century BC. Pataliputra (PATNA) was its capital. Its strength grew under the NANDA DYNASTY; under the MAURYAN dynasty (4th–2nd century BC), it comprised nearly the entire Indian subcontinent. It afterwards declined. Revived in the 4th century AD under the GUPTA DYNASTY, it was conquered by the Muslims in the late 12th century. It was the scene of many events in the life of BUDDHA.

Magadi \mä-'gä-dē\, **Lake** Lake, GREAT RIFT VALLEY, southern Kenya, east of Lake VICTORIA. Occupying an area of 240 sq mi (622 sq km), it is 20 mi (32 km) long and 2 mi (3 km) wide. Its bed consists almost entirely of soda deposits, which dye the waters a vivid pink.

magazine *or* **periodical** Printed collection of texts (essays, articles, stories, poems), often illustrated, that is produced at regular intervals. Modern magazines have roots in early printed pamphlets, broadsides, chapbooks, and almanacs. One of the first magazines was the German *Erbauliche Monaths-Unterredungen* ("Edifying Monthly Discussions"), issued 1663–68. In the early 18th century, JOSEPH ADDISON and RICHARD STEELE brought out the influential periodicals *The Tatler* and *The SPECTATOR*; other critical reviews began in the mid-1700s. By the 19th century, magazines catering to less learned audiences had developed, including the women's weekly, the religious and missionary review, and the illustrated magazine. One of the greatest benefits to magazine publishing in the late 19th and 20th century was the addition of advertisements as a means of financial support. Subsequent developments included more illustrations and vastly greater specialization.

Magdalen Islands \'mag-də-lən\ *French* **Îles de la Madeleine** \ˌēl-də-lə-måd-'len\ Island group (pop., 1991: 14,000) of eastern Quebec. Located in the Gulf of ST. LAWRENCE between Prince Edward Island and Newfoundland, the group comprises several islands and islets, with a total area of 88 sq mi (228 sq km). The largest include Havre-Aubert (Amherst) and Cap aux Meules (Grindstone). Discovered by JACQUES CARTIER in 1534, the islands are inhabited mainly by French Canadians.

Magdalena River \ˌmag-də-'lā-nə\ River, southern central and northern Colombia. It rises on the eastern slopes of the ANDES in southern Colombia and flows northward for 930 mi (1,497 km) to empty into the Caribbean Sea near Barranquilla. Navigable for 930 mi (1,496 km), it has been a major commercial artery since the Spanish conquest.

Magdalenian culture \ˌmag-də-'lē-nē-ən\ STONE-TOOL INDUSTRY and artistic tradition of Upper PALEOLITHIC Europe, named after the type-site La Madeleine in southwestern France. The Magdalenians lived some 11,000–17,000 years ago, at a time when reindeer, wild horses, and bison formed large herds; they appear to have lived a semisettled life surrounded by abundant food. They killed animals with spears, snares, and traps and lived in caves, rock shelters, and tents. Magdalenian stone tools include blades, burins, scrapers, borers, and projectile points. Their bone tools—often engraved with animal images—include adzes, hammers, spearheads, harpoons, and eyed needles. Cave art in the early period is characterized by coarse black drawings, while that of the later period includes beautifully rendered realistic figures in polychrome, such as those at ALTAMIRA. Magdalenian culture disappeared as the climate warmed at the end of the Fourth (Würm) Glacial Period (c. 10,000 BC) and herd animals became scarce.

Magdeburg \'mäg-də-ˌbu̇rk\ City (pop., 1996 est.: 258,000), capital of Saxony-Anhalt state, eastern central Germany. Located on the ELBE RIVER, it was a trading settlement as early as the 9th century, and a leading member of the HANSEATIC LEAGUE by the 13th century. It embraced the REFORMATION in 1524 and was governed by Protestant titular archbishops. In 1631, during the THIRTY YEARS' WAR, it was burned and sacked. Captured by the French during the NAPOLEONIC WARS, it soon passed to the Prussians, and in 1815 it became the capital of the province of SAXONY. It was heavily bombed during World War II. One of Germany's most important inland ports, it is also a railroad junction. The composer G.P. TELEMANN was born there.

The cathedral at Magdeburg, Ger.
W. KRAMMISCH—BRUCE COLEMAN INC./EB INC.

Magellan \mə-'jel-ən\, **Ferdinand** *Portuguese* **Fernão de Magalhães** ***Spanish*** **Fernando de Magallanes** (c. 1480–1521) Portuguese navigator and explorer. Born to the nobility, from 1505 Magellan served in expeditions to the East Indies and Africa. Having twice asked King MANUEL I for a higher rank and been refused, he went to Spain in 1517 and offered his services to King Charles I (later Emperor CHARLES V), proposing to sail west to the Moluccas (Spice Islands) to prove that they lay in Spanish rather than Portuguese territory. In 1519 he left Seville with five ships and 270 men. He sailed around South America, quelling a mutiny on the way, and discovered the Strait of Magellan. With three ships left, he crossed the "Sea of the South," which he later called the Pacific Ocean because of their calm crossing. He was killed by natives in the Philippines, but two of his ships reached the Moluccas, and one, the *Victoria*, commanded by Juan de Elcano (1476?–1526), continued west to Spain, accomplishing the first circumnavigation of the world in 1522.

Magellan, Strait of *Spanish* **Estrecho de Magallanes** \ā-'strā-chō-t͟hā-ˌmä-gä-'lyä-nās\ Strait linking the Atlantic and Pacific oceans, between the southern tip of South America and TIERRA DEL FUEGO. It extends westward from the Atlantic between Cape Vírgenes and Cape Espíritu Santo, and curves northwest at Froward Cape to reach the Pacific. Lying mostly within Chilean territorial waters, it is 350 mi (560 km) long and 2–20 mi (3–32 km) wide. Discovered in 1520 by FERDINAND MAGELLAN, it was an important route before the building of the PANAMA CANAL.

Magellanic Cloud \ˌma-jə-'la-nik\ Either of two irregular companion GALAXIES of the Milky Way, named for FERDINAND MAGELLAN, whose crew discovered them during the first voyage around the world. They share a gaseous envelope and lie about 22° apart in the sky near the southern celestial pole (see CELESTIAL SPHERE). They are visible to the unaided eye in the Southern Hemisphere but cannot be seen from northern latitudes. The Large Magellanic Cloud is more than 150,000 light-years from earth; the Small Magellanic Cloud is roughly 200,000 light-years away. They are excellent laboratories for the study of the evolution of STARS.

Magenta \mə-'jen-tə\, **Battle of** (June 4, 1859) Battle fought during the Franco–Piedmontese war against the Austrians (second War of Italian Independence) in Lombardy, northern Italy. The narrow French victory over the Austrians was an important step toward Italian independence, leading many districts and cities to throw off Austrian rule and join the cause of Italian unity.

Maggiore \mä-'jō-rā\, **Lake** *ancient* **Lacus Verbanus.** Lake, northern Italy and southern Switzerland, bordered on the north by the Swiss ALPS. Occupying an area of 82 sq mi (212 sq km), it is Italy's second largest lake. It is 34 mi (54 km) long, with a maximum width of 7 mi (11 km) and a maximum depth of 1,220 ft (372 m). Traversed from north to south by the TICINO RIVER, it is also fed by the Tresa River from Lake LUGANO on the east. It is a popular resort area.

Magherafelt \ˌma-krə-ˈfelt\ District (pop., 1995 est.: 37,000), central Northern Ireland. It is bounded by the River BANN, Lake Neaghon, and the Sperrin Mountains. It was formerly part of Co. Londonderry (see DERRY) but was organized as a separate district in 1973. The town of Magherafelt (pop., 1991: 7,000), originally settled as an English company (Plantation of Ulster) town, is the seat of the district and its marketing center.

Maghreb \ˈmə-grəb\ Region of North Africa bordering the Mediterranean Sea. Comprising the coastal plain of Morocco, Algeria, Tunisia, and Libya, it was known to the ancients as Africa Minor. It later included Moorish Spain. It resisted Punic, Roman, and Christian invasions but was conquered by the Arabs and absorbed into Muslim civilization in the 7th–8th century.

Magi \ˈmā-ˌjī\ In Christian tradition, wise men from the East who came to pay homage to the infant JESUS. According to Matthew 2:1–12, they followed a miraculous guiding star to BETHLEHEM and brought gifts of "gold and frankincense and myrrh." HEROD asked them to report the location of Jesus' birth on their return journey, but an angel warned them of his evil intentions. In later Christian tradition they were said to be kings and were given the names Melchior, Balthasar, and Gaspar. Their visit was seen as evidence that the Gentiles as well as the Jews would worship Jesus, and it is celebrated in the feast of Ephiphany. See also MAGUS.

"The Adoration of the Magi," oil painting by Albrecht Dürer, 1504; in the Uffizi, Florence.

SCALA–ART RESOURCE/EB INC.

magic Use of means (such as charms or spells) believed to have supernatural power over natural forces. It constitutes the core of many religious systems and plays a central social role in many nonliterate cultures. Magic is often distinguished from RELIGION as being more impersonal and mechanical and emphasizing technique. Its techniques are usually regarded as means to specific ends (an enemy's defeat, rainfall, etc.), although another view ascribes a more symbolic, expressive character to such activity. Thus, a rainmaking ritual may both elicit rainfall and stress the symbolic importance of rain and the agricultural activities associated with it. Both the magician and the magical rite are typically surrounded by TABOOS, purification procedures, and other activities that draw the participants into the magical sphere. Strains of magic in Western tradition, formerly associated with heretics, alchemists, witches, and sorcerers, persist in modern times in the activities of satanists and others. The art of entertaining by performing apparently magical feats (sometimes called conjuring) relies on the use of sleight of hand and other means. See also SHAMAN, VODUN, WITCHCRAFT AND SORCERY.

magic realism *or* **magical realism** Latin-American literary phenomenon characterized by the matter-of-fact incorporation of fantastic or mythical elements into otherwise realistic fiction. The term was first applied to literature in the 1940s by the Cuban novelist Alejo Carpentier (1904–1980), who recognized the tendency of his region's contemporary storytellers as well as contemporary novelists to illuminate the mundane by means of the fabulous. Prominent practitioners include GABRIEL GARCIA MARQUEZ, JORGE AMADO, JORGE LUIS BORGES, MIGUEL ANGEL ASTURIAS, JULIO CORTAZAR, and Isabel Allende (born 1942). The term has been applied to literature and art outside of Latin America as well.

magic show See CONJURING

Maginot \má-zhē-ˈnō\, **André (-Louis-René)** (1877–1932) French politician. He was elected to the French Chamber of Deputies (1910) and fought in World War I, where he was severely wounded. He served as France's minister of war 1922–24 and 1929–31, and was a strong advocate of military preparedness against Germany. He directed the beginning of construction of the defensive barrier in northeastern France that was later named the MAGINOT LINE in his honor.

Maginot Line \ˈma-zhə-ˌnō\ Elaborate defensive barrier in northeastern France built in the 1930s. Named after its principal creator, ANDRE MAGINOT, it was an ultramodern defensive fortification along the French-German frontier. Made of thick concrete and supplied with heavy guns, it had living quarters, supply storehouses, and underground rail lines. However, it ended at the French-Belgian frontier, which German forces crossed in May 1940. They invaded Belgium (May 10), crossed the Somme River, struck at the northern end of the line (May 12), and continued around to its rear, making it useless.

magistrates' court In England and Wales, any of the inferior courts with primarily criminal jurisdiction covering a wide range of offenses, from minor traffic violations and public-health nuisances to somewhat more serious crimes, such as petty theft or assault. Magistrates' courts with similar jurisdictions, including jurisdiction over small civil claims, may be found in certain large U.S. municipalities.

magma Molten or partially molten rock from which IGNEOUS ROCKS form, usually consisting of silicate liquid. Magma migrates either at depth or to the earth's surface, where it is ejected as LAVA. The interactions of several physical properties, including chemical composition, viscosity, content of dissolved gases, and temperature, determine the characteristics of magma. Numerous events that can occur during crystallization influence the resulting rock: separation of early crystals from liquid prevents reaction between them; magma can cool too rapidly for reaction to occur; and loss of volatiles may remove some components from the magma.

Magna Carta (Latin: "Great Charter") Document guaranteeing English political liberties, drafted at Runnymede, a meadow by the Thames, and signed by King JOHN in 1215 under pressure from his rebellious barons. Resentful of the king's high taxes and aware of his waning power, the barons were encouraged by the archbishop of Canterbury, STEPHEN LANGTON, to demand a solemn grant of their rights. Among the charter's provisions were clauses providing for a free church, reforming law and justice, and controlling the behavior of royal officials. It was reissued with alterations in 1216, 1217, and 1225. Though it reflects the feudal order rather than democracy, the Magna Carta is traditionally regarded as the foundation of British constitutionalism.

Magna Graecia \ˈmag-nə-ˈgrē-shə\ Group of ancient Greek cities along the coast of southern Italy. Euboeans founded the first colonies, including CUMAE, c. 750 BC, and subsequently Spartans settled at Tarentum (TARANTO); Achaeans at Metapontum, SYBARIS, and Croton; Locrians at LOCRI EPIZEPHYRII; and Chalcidians at Rhegium (REGGIO DI CALABRIA). It was a busy commercial center as well as the seat of the PYTHAGOREAN and ELEATIC systems of philosophy. After the 5th century BC, most of the cities declined in importance.

Magnani \män-ˈyä-nē\, **Anna** (1908–1973) Italian film actress. An illegitimate child brought up in poverty, she became a nightclub singer noted for her bawdy street songs. After acting in a touring company, she made her film debut in *The Blind Woman of Sorrento* (1934). She earned international fame for her role in ROBERTO ROSSELLINI's *Open City*

L
M
N

(1945). She became known for her forceful portrayals of earthy lower-class women in such films as *The Miracle* (1948), *Bellissima* (1951), *The Rose Tattoo* (1955, Academy Award), *The Fugitive Kind* (1960), and *Mamma Roma* (1962).

Magnes \'mag-nəs\, **Judah Leon** (1877–1948) U.S.-Israeli educator and religious leader. Born in San Francisco, he was ordained as a rabbi in 1900 and earned a doctorate at the University of Heidelberg in 1902. Serving as rabbi for three congregations in New York, he moved from Reform to Orthodox Judaism and became a Zionist. He drifted away from Zionism during World War I, preferring relief efforts for Jews in Palestine over political activism. After the war he became the principal founder and first president (1935–48) of the HEBREW UNIVERSITY OF JERUSALEM, working to advance Arab-Jewish reconciliation and advocating a binational Arab-Jewish state.

Magnesia ad Sipylum \mag-'nē-zhə-ad-'si-pi-ləm\ Ancient city, LYDIA, near modern Manisa, Turkey. Dating back to the 5th century BC., it was located near the regions associated with NIOBE and TANTALUS. It was the site of a famous battle during the winter of 190–189 BC, when the Romans under Lucius SCIPIO defeated the Syrians under ANTIOCHUS the Great, forcing them back across the TAURUS range. It suffered severe earthquakes, notably in AD 17, and there are few archaeological remains.

magnesium Chemical ELEMENT, one of the ALKALINE EARTH METALS, chemical symbol Mg, atomic number 12. The silvery-white METAL does not occur free in nature, but compounds such as the SULFATE (Epsom salts), OXIDE (magnesia), and CARBONATE (magnesite) have long been known. The metal is used in photographic flash devices, bombs, flares, and pyrotechnics and in lightweight alloys for aircraft, spacecraft, cars, machinery, and tools. The compounds, in which it has VALENCE 2, are used as insulators and REFRACTORIES, in fertilizers, cement, rubber, and plastics and in foods and pharmaceuticals (antacids, purgatives, LAXATIVES). Magnesium is an essential element in human nutrition; it is the COFACTOR in ENZYMES of carbohydrate METABOLISM and in CHLOROPHYLL.

magnet Any material capable of attracting IRON and producing a MAGNETIC FIELD outside itself. By the end of the 19th century, all known elements and many compounds had been tested for MAGNETISM, and all were found to have some magnetic property. However, only three elements—iron, NICKEL, and COBALT—exhibit FERROMAGNETISM. See also COMPASS, ELECTROMAGNET. See illustration opposite.

magnetic dipole Tiny magnet with subatomic dimensions, equivalent to the flow of ELECTRIC CHARGE around a loop. Examples include ELECTRONS circulating around atomic nuclei, rotating atomic nuclei, and single SUBATOMIC PARTICLES with SPIN. On a large scale, these effects may add together as in iron atoms, to make magnetic compass needles and bar magnets, which are macroscopic magnetic dipoles. The strength of a magnetic dipole, its magnetic moment, is a measure of its ability to turn itself into alignment with a given external MAGNETIC FIELD. When free to rotate, dipoles align themselves so that their moments point predominantly in the direction of the magnetic field. The SI unit for dipole moment is the ampere–square meter.

magnetic field Region around a magnet, ELECTRIC CURRENT, or changing ELECTRIC FIELD in which MAGNETIC FORCES are observable. The field around a permanent magnet or wire carrying a steady DIRECT CURRENT is stationary, while that around an ALTERNATING CURRENT or changing direct current is continuously changing. Magnetic fields are commonly represented by continuous lines of force, or magnetic flux, that emerge from north-seeking magnetic poles and enter south-seeking poles. The density of the lines indicates the magnitude of the field, the lines being crowded together where the magnetic field is strong. The SI unit for magnetic flux is the weber.

magnetic force Attraction or repulsion that arises between electrically charged particles that are in motion. While only electric forces exist among stationary ELECTRIC CHARGES, both electric and magnetic forces exist among moving electric charges. The magnetic force between two moving charges is the force exerted on one charge by a MAGNETIC FIELD created by the other. This force is zero if the second charge is traveling in the direction of the magnetic field due to the first and is greatest if it travels at right angles to the magnetic field. Magnetic force is responsible for the action of electric motors and the attraction between magnets and iron.

magnetic permeability Relative increase or decrease in the MAGNETIC FIELD inside a material compared with the magnetic field in which the material is located. In empty space the magnetic permeability is 1, because there is no matter to modify the field. Materials may be classified by the value of their magnetic permeability. Diamagnetic materials (see DIAMAGNETISM) have constant relative permeabilities of slightly less than 1. Paramagnetic materials (see PARAMAGNETISM) have constant relative permeabilities of slightly more than 1. The relative permeability of ferromagnetic materials (see FERROMAGNETISM) increases as the magnetizing field increases, reaches a maximum, and then decreases. Pure iron and some alloys have relative permeabilities of 100,000 or more.

magnetic resonance Absorption or emission of ELECTROMAGNETIC RADIATION by electrons or atomic nuclei in response to certain MAGNETIC FIELDS. The principles of magnetic resonance are used to study the atomic and nuclear properties of matter; two common laboratory techniques are NUCLEAR MAGNETIC RESONANCE and ELECTRON SPIN RESONANCE. In medicine, MAGNETIC RESONANCE IMAGING is used to produce images of human tissue.

magnetic resonance imaging (MRI) Computer production of images from MAGNETIC RESONANCE. The structural and biochemical information it provides is helpful in the diagnosis of abnormalities without the possibly harmful effects of X RAYS or GAMMA RAYS. It is invaluable in detecting and delineating tumors and in providing images of the brain, the heart, and other soft-tissue organs. MRI may produce anxiety because the patient must often lie quietly inside a narrow tube. Another disadvantage is that it requires a longer scanning time than other computer-assisted forms of scanning, which makes it more sensitive to motion and of less value in scanning the chest or abdomen. However, MRI images provide better contrast between normal and diseased tissue than those produced by other computer-assisted imagery.

magnetism Phenomenon associated with MAGNETIC FIELDS, the effects of such fields, and the motion of ELECTRIC CHARGES. Some types of magnetism are DIAMAGNETISM, PARAMAGNETISM, FERROMAGNETISM, and FERRIMAGNETISM. Magnetic fields exert forces on moving ELECTRIC CHARGES. The ef-

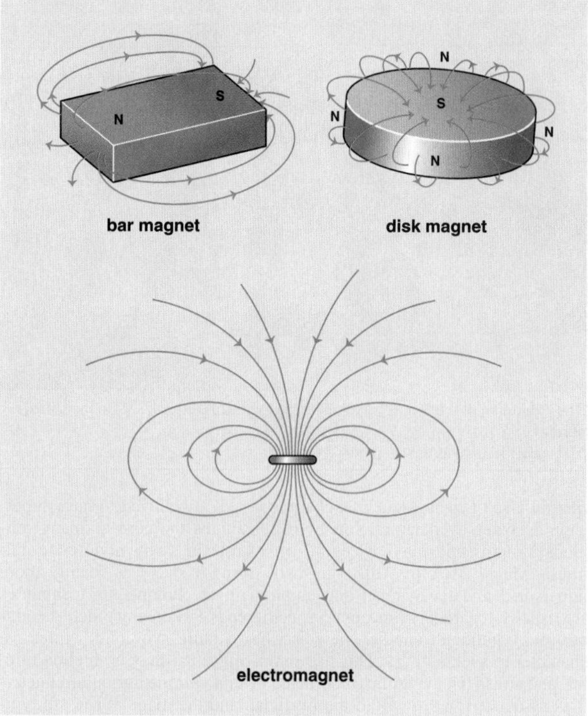

Magnets and their associated magnetic field lines. A permanent magnet (such as a bar or disk magnet) possesses a magnetic field by virtue of the alignment of all the magnetic particles it is composed of. An electromagnet is generated by a current flowing through a wire loop at the center of the field.

fects of such forces are evident in the deflection of an electron beam in a CATHODE-RAY TUBE and the motor force on a current-carrying CONDUCTOR. Other applications of magnetism range from the simple magnetic door catch to medical imaging devices and electromagnets used in high-energy PARTICLE ACCELERATORS.

magnetite *or* **lodestone** *or* **magnetic iron ore** Iron OXIDE MINERAL (Fe_3O_4), the chief member of one of the series of the spinel group. Minerals in this series form black to brownish, metallic, moderately hard octahedrons and masses in igneous and metamorphic rocks and in granite pegmatites, stony meteorites, and high-temperature sulfide veins. Magnetite, as the name implies, is strongly attracted to a magnet. It is a common constituent of iron ores. Magnetite with an intrinsic magnetic field (a natural magnet) is known as lodestone.

magneto \mag-'nē-tō\ Permanent-magnet alternating generator used mainly to produce electrical current for the IGNITION SYSTEM in various types of INTERNAL-COMBUSTION ENGINES, such as aircraft, marine, tractor, and motorcycle engines. The main parts of a magneto are a permanent-magnet rotor, a primary winding of a small number of turns of coarse wire, a secondary winding with a large number of turns of fine wire, a cam-type circuit breaker, and a capacitor. As the rotor turns, it produces a current in the primary winding, charging the capacitor. The cam breaks the circuit, and the magnetic field around the primary winding collapses. The capacitor releases its stored current into the primary winding, causing a reversed magnetic field. The collapse and reversal of the magnetic field produce a current in the secondary winding that is sent to the SPARK PLUGS.

magnetosphere Region around a PLANET where magnetic phenomena and the high atmospheric conductivity caused by IONIZATION strongly influence the behavior of charged particles (see ELECTRIC CHARGE). A planet's MAGNETIC FIELD, like its gravitational field, becomes weaker with distance from the planet. The SOLAR WIND sweeps the magnetosphere out away from the sun in a "tail" trailing well beyond the planet.

magnitude In astronomy, the measure of the brightness of a star or other celestial body. The brighter the object, the lower the number assigned as a magnitude. In ancient times, six magnitude classes were used, the first containing the brightest stars (see HIPPARCHUS). In the present system, a difference of one magnitude is defined as a ratio of brightness of 2.512 times. Thus, a difference of five magnitudes corresponds to a brightness ratio of 100 to 1. Apparent magnitude is an object's brightness as seen from earth (e.g., –26.7 for the sun, about –11 for the moon). Absolute magnitude is an object's brightness as it would be seen at a distance of 10 PARSECS (32.6 light-years; e.g., 4.8 for the sun). See also ALBEDO, PHOTOMETRY.

magnolia Any of about 80 species of trees and shrubs in the genus *Magnolia,* native to North and Central America, the Himalayas, and East Asia. They are valued for their fragrant flowers and handsome leaves. *Magnolia* is one of 12 genera in the family Magnoliaceae, which contains 210 species. Magnolias are among the most primitive of flowering plants; their primitive features include long floral axes, spiral arrangement of flower parts, and simple water-conducting cells.

Magnus effect Generation of a sidewise FORCE on a spinning cylindrical or spherical solid immersed in a fluid (liquid or gas) when there is relative motion between the spinning body and the fluid. Named after Heinrich Gustav Magnus (1802–1870), who first investigated the effect experimentally in 1853, it is responsible for the curved trajectory of a tennis or golf ball and affects the path of an artillery shell.

Magnus Eriksson (1316–1374) King of Sweden (1319–63, as Magnus II) and Norway (1319–55, as Magnus VII). Grandson of Norway's Haakon V, and nephew of the Swedish king, Magnus became ruler of both countries. Since he spent almost all his time in Sweden, Norwegian nobles arranged for his son Haakon's succession, and Magnus abdicated in 1355. He antagonized many Swedish nobles, raising taxes and curbing the economic power of the church and nobility. In 1356 he was forced to cede half his Swedish kingdom to his son Erik, and he began making concessions to the nobility. When he renewed his efforts to control the Swedish nobles, they deposed him.

Magnus Pius, Sextus Pompeius See Sextus POMPEIUS MAGNUS PIUS

magpie Any of several genera of long-tailed songbirds of the CROW family (Corvidae). The black-billed magpie *(Pica pica)* is 18 in. (45 cm) long and strikingly pied (black-and-white), with an iridescent blue-green tail. It is found in North Africa, across Eurasia, and in western North America. A bird of farmlands and tree-studded open country, it eats insects, seeds, small vertebrates, the eggs and young of other birds, and fresh carrion. It makes a large, round nest of twigs cemented with mud, and is known for hoarding small, bright objects. Other species (in the genera *Cyanopica, Cissa,* and *Urocissa*) include the brilliant blue or green magpies of Asia.

Magritte \mȧ-'grēt\, **René (-François-Ghislain)** (1898–1967) Belgian painter. After study at the Belgian Academy of Fine Arts (1916–18), he designed wallpaper and did advertising sketches until the support of a Brussels art gallery enabled him to become a full-time painter. His early works were in the Cubist and Futurist styles, but in 1922 he discovered the work of GIORGIO DE CHIRICO and embraced SURREALISM with *The Menaced Assassin* (1927). Certain images appear over and over again in Magritte's works—the sea, wide skies, the female torso, the bourgeois "little man" in a bowler hat, rocks that hover overhead—and dislocations of space, time, and scale were common elements in his enigmatic and illogical paintings.

Magsaysay \mäg-'sī-ˌsī\, **Ramon** (1907–1957) President of the Philippines (1953–57). Son of a Malay artisan, he was a schoolteacher before becoming a guerrilla leader during World War II. In 1950, as secretary of defense, he launched one of the most successful antiguerrilla campaigns in modern history against insurgents of the HUKBALAHAP REBELLION. He deprived them of popular support by offering peasants land and tools and insisting that the army treat them with respect. By 1953 the Huks were no longer a threat, and Magsaysay was elected president. His efforts at reform were frustrated by a conservative Congress.

maguey See CENTURY PLANT

magus \'mā-gəs\ Member of an ancient Persian clan specializing in cultic activities. The magi were a priestly caste during the SELEUCID, Parthian, and SASANIAN dynasties, and parts of the AVESTA are probably derived from them. Their PRIESTHOOD is believed to have served several religions, including ZOROASTRIANISM. From the 1st century AD onward, the word magus in its Syriac form *(magusai)* was applied to magicians and soothsayers, chiefly from BABYLONIA. As long as the Persian empire lasted there was a distinction between the Persian magi, credited with profound religious knowledge, and the Babylonian magi, often considered outright imposters. See also MAGI.

Magyars \'mag-ˌyärz, 'mä-ˌjärz\ People who form the dominant ethnic group in Hungary. Speakers of a FINNO-UGRIC LANGUAGE, they migrated from their early home in the region of present-day Bashkortostan in eastern European Russia across the southern Russian and Ukrainian steppes into the northern Balkans in the 9th century. After collisions with neighboring peoples, the Magyars crossed the Carpathians and settled in the middle basin of the Danube River in the late 9th century, subjugating Slavs and other peoples there. They adopted Christianity in the 11th century.

Mah-jongg \ˌmä-'zhäŋ\ Game of Chinese origin usually played by four persons with 144 domino-like tiles that are drawn and discarded until one player secures a winning hand. The object of play is similar to that of the RUMMY card games. It is probably of 19th-century origin. The name was coined by J. P. Babcock, who introduced the game to the West after World War I. The mah-jongg set includes a pair of dice, a quantity of tokens or chips used for scorekeeping, and a rack for keeping tiles upright and keeping their faces hidden from other players.

Mahabharata \mə-ˌhä-'bä-rə-tə\ One of the two major SANSKRIT epics of India, valued for its literary merit and its religious inspiration. It tells of the struggle for supremacy between two groups of cousins, the Kauravas and the Pandavas. Many myths and legends are woven into the poem, along with didactic material on topics such as the proper conduct of a warrior and the way to attain emancipation from rebirth. Together with the second major epic, the *RAMAYANA,* it is an important source of information about the evolution of HINDUISM. Contained within the *Mahabharata* is the BHAGAVADGITA, Hinduism's single most important religious text. The sage Vyasa (fl. c. 5th century BC) is traditionally named as the *Mahabharata*'s author, but he probably compiled existing material. The poem reached its present form c. AD 400.

Mahan \mə-'han\, **Alfred Thayer** (1840–1914) U.S. naval officer and historian. Born in West Point, N.Y., he studied at the U.S. Naval Academy. His nearly 40 years of active naval duty included fighting in the American Civil War. He was president of the Naval War College in Newport, R.I. (1886–89). His classic analysis *The Influence of Sea Power upon History, 1660–1783* (1890) argued that sea power was decisive in determining national supremacy. In *The Influence of Sea Power upon the French Revolution and Empire, 1793–1812* (1892), he stressed the interdependence of military and commercial control of the sea. Avidly read in Britain and Germany, both books greatly influenced the buildup of naval forces before World War I.

Alfred Thayer Mahan, 1897.

BY COURTESY OF THE LIBRARY OF CONGRESS, WASHINGTON, D.C.

Maharashtra \ˌmä-hə-ˈräsh-trə\ State (pop., 2001 prelim.: 96,752,247), western central India. It is bounded by the Arabian Sea; its capital is MUMBAI (Bombay). Occupying an area of 118,800 square miles (307,690 square km), it covers much of the DECCAN plateau, containing the valleys of the KRISHNA, BHIMA, and GODAVARI rivers. The population is a mixture of ethnic groups; Marathi is the state language. The region was divided into Hindu kingdoms in the 8th–13th century; they were followed by a series of Muslim dynasties. A MARATHA kingdom ruled by 1674, and by the 18th century a Maratha empire had been established. The British gained control early in the 19th century. When India won independence in 1947, the area was known as Bombay state; it was divided on linguistic lines in 1960, creating GUJARAT in the north and Maharashtra in the south. Its economy is primarily agricultural; industries include oil-refining and cotton textiles.

Maharishi Mahesh Yogi *orig.* **Mahad Prasad Varma** (born 1911?) Indian religious leader, founder of TRANSCENDENTAL MEDITATION (TM). He took a degree in physics before going to the Himalayas to study the ADVAITA school of VEDANTA religious thought with the yogi Guru Dev for 13 years. He arrived in the U.S. in 1959, preaching the virtues of TM; in the 1960s the BEATLES were perhaps his most celebrated followers. The Maharishi (the title means "great sage") returned to India in the late 1970s and moved to the Netherlands in 1990. His organization, which includes real-estate holdings, schools, and clinics, was worth more than $3 billion in the late 1990s.

Mahasanghika \mə-ˌhä-ˈsəŋ-gi-kə\ Early Buddhist school in India that anticipated the MAHAYANA tradition. Its emergence in the 4th century BC, about 100 years after the BUDDHA's death, represented the first major schism in the Buddhist community. Though accounts of the second Buddhist council attribute the split to a dispute over rules, later texts emphasize differences between the Mahasanghikas and the Theravadins (see THERAVADA) regarding the nature of the Buddha and sainthood. The Mahasanghikas believed in a plurality of buddhas and held that the Buddha in his earthly existence was only an apparition.

Mahathir bin Mohamad \mä-ˈhä-tēr-bin-mō-ˈhä-məd\ *in full* **Datuk (Headman) Seri Mahathir bin Mohamad** (born 1925) Malaysian politician, prime minister from 1981. Son of a schoolmaster, Mahathir studied medicine and worked as a government medical officer before entering Parliament in 1964, where he became a forceful advocate of policies to ensure ethnic Malay economic success. Once prime minister, he was reelected repeatedly; under his leadership Malaysia acquired one of the most prosperous economies in S.East Asia, rising literacy rates, and increased life expectancies. The economy's fortune plunged in the late 1990s, and Mahathir's dismissal of his deputy prime minister, Anwar Ibrahim, in 1998 led to a wave of demonstrations calling for Mahathir's resignation.

Mahavira \mə-ˌhä-ˈvē-rə\ *orig.* **Vardhamana** (599?–527 BC) Indian reformer of the Jaina monastic community, last of the 24 TIRTHANKARAS, or saints, who founded JAINISM. Born into the warrior caste, he renounced the world at 30 for a life of extreme asceticism. He had no possessions, not even rags to cover his body or a bowl for alms or food, and after 12 years he attained *kevala,* the highest stage of perception. An advocate of nonviolence and vegetarianism, he revived and reorganized Jaina doctrine and established rules for its monastic order. His followers made five vows of renunciation (see JAINA VRATA).

Mahavira enthroned, miniature from the *Kalpa-sutra,* 15th-century western Indian school; in the Freer Gallery of Art, Washington, D.C.

BY COURTESY OF THE SMITHSONIAN INSTITUTION, FREER GALLERY OF ART, WASHINGTON, D.C.

Mahayana \mə-ˌhä-ˈyä-nə\ One of the three major Buddhist traditions. It arose in the 1st century AD and is widely followed today in China, Korea, and Japan, and Tibet. Mahayanists distinguish themselves from the more conservative THERAVADA Buddhists of Sri Lanka, Burma, Thailand, Laos, and Cambodia. Whereas the Theravadins view the historical Buddha as a (merely) human teacher of the truth, Mahayanists see him as an earthly manifestation of a celestial Buddha. Mahayanists revere BODHISATTVAS, key figures in universal salvation. Compassion, the chief virtue of the bodhisattva, is valued as highly as wisdom, the virtue emphasized by the ancient Buddhists. Within Mahayana Buddhism, some branches emphasize esoteric practices (e.g., SHINGON, TIBETAN BUDDHISM). See also KEGON, NICHIREN BUDDHISM, PURE LAND BUDDHISM, TIANTAI, ZEN.

mahdi (Arabic: "divinely guided one") In Islamic eschatology, a messianic deliverer who will bring justice to the earth, restore true religion, and usher in a short golden age before the end of the world. Though the mahdi is not mentioned in the QURAN and is questioned by SUNNI theologians, he is important in SHIITE doctrine. The doctrine of the mahdi gained currency during the religious and political upheavals of early ISLAM (7th–8th century) and received new emphasis in periods of crisis (e.g., after most of Spain was conquered by Christians in 1212, and during Napoleon's invasion of Egypt). The title has been claimed by Islamic revolutionaries, notably in North Africa (see al-MAHDI, MAHDIST movement).

Mahdi, al- *orig.* **Muhammad Ahmad ibn al-Sayyid Abd Allah** (1844–1885) Sudanese religious and political leader. The son of a shipbuilder in Nubia, he was brought up near KHARTOUM. After orthodox religious study, he turned to a mystical interpretation of Islam in the Sufi tradition, joined a religious brotherhood, and in 1870 moved to a hermitage with his disciples. In 1881 he proclaimed a divine mission to purify Islam and the governments that defiled it, targeting the Turkish ruler of Egypt and its dependency, Sudan. He defeated CHARLES GEORGE GORDON to capture Khartoum in 1885, and established a theocratic state, but died the same year, probably of typhus. See also MAHDI, MAHDIST MOVEMENT, SUFISM.

Mahdist movement \ˈmä-dəst\ Religious and political movement founded by the Sudanese prophet al-MAHDI. He adopted the name al-Mahdi (meaning "Divinely Inspired One") because of his conviction that he had been divinely chosen to lead a holy war (JIHAD) against Sudan's Egyptian ruling class, which he believed had deserted the Islamic faith. His uprising began in 1881, and within four years he had conquered almost all the territory formerly occupied by Egypt, his crowning victory being the capture of KHARTOUM from Gen. CHARLES GEORGE GORDON in 1885. Establishing a new capital at OMDURMAN, he became head of an armed theocracy. When he died from illness, his disciple ABD ALLAH succeeded him. Following initial victories, Abd Allah's forces were gradually hunted down by Anglo-Egyptian armies under H. H. KITCHENER and almost entirely destroyed in the Battle of OMDURMAN. The movement sustained a small following through the next century, but its political import had been destroyed.

Mahfouz \mä-ˈfüz\, **Naguib** (born 1911) Egyptian writer. He worked in the cultural section of the Egyptian civil service 1934–71. His major work, the *Cairo Trilogy* (1956–57)—including the novels *Palace Walk, Palace of Desire,* and *Sukkariyah*—represents a penetrating overview of 20th-century Egyptian society. Subsequent works offer critical views of the Egyptian monarchy, colonialism, and contemporary Egypt. Other well-known novels include *Midaq Alley* (1947), *Children of Gebelawi* (1959), and *Miramar* (1967). He has also written short-story collections, more than 30 screenplays, and several stage plays. In 1988 he became the first Arabic writer to win the Nobel Prize.

Mahican \mə-ˈhē-kən\ *or* **Mohican** \mō-ˈhē-kən\ ALGONQUIAN-speaking Indian people of the upper Hudson River Valley above the Catskill Mtns. The Mahican consisted of five major divisions governed by hereditary sachems (chiefs) assisted by elected counselors. They lived in strongholds of 20–30 houses situated on hills or in woodlands. In 1664 they were forced by the MOHAWK to move to what is now Stockbridge, Mass., where they became known as the Stockbridge Indians. Later they moved to Wisconsin, where they now number about 1,000. JAMES FENIMORE COOPER drew a romanticized portrait of the declining Mahican in *The Last of the Mohicans* (1826).

Mahilyow *or* **Mogilev** \mə-gi-ˈlyȯf\ City (pop., 1996 est.: 367,000), eastern central Belarus, on the DNIEPER RIVER. It was founded in 1267 as a fortress and became a town in 1526 while under Lithuanian rule. Later passing to Poland, it became Russian in the First Partition of POLAND in 1772. In 1812 a major battle between NAPOLEON's troops and Russian forces was fought outside the town. It was severely damaged in World War II but rebuilt; it is now a major industrial city.

Mahler, Gustav (1860–1911) Austro-Hungarian composer and conductor. Born in Bohemia, he attended the Vienna Conservatory, studying piano with Julius Epstein (1832–1926), who encouraged him despite his temperament and arrogance. He wrote his first large work, *Das klagende Lied* (1880), on his own text, as he was eking out an existence by giving lessons. In 1880 he decided to become a conductor, and though his dictatorial manner put people off and critics found his interpretations extreme, by 1886 he had achieved success in Prague. He also began the first of his ten symphonies (1888–1910), his main compositional legacy. In 1897 he was named director of the Vienna Opera; his stormy reign there was acknowledged as an artistic success. He moved to the Metropolitan Opera in 1908 and the New York Philharmonic in 1909–10. Ill with heart disease and mourning his daughter's death, he wrote the masterly orchestral song cycle *Das Lied von der Erde* (1908–9) and his ninth symphony. His orchestral songs *Des Knaben Wunderhorn* (1892–98) and *Kindertotenlieder* (1904) are frequently performed. His emotionally charged and subtly orchestrated music waited decades to be widely accepted.

Mahmud of Ghazna \mä-ˈmüd\ (971–1030) Son of the founder of the GHAZNAVID dynasty, Sebüktigin. After ascending the throne in 998, he gave nominal allegiance to the ABBASID caliph and in return was granted autonomy. He expanded his kingdom through some 17 invasions of the Punjab and northeastern India, carrying with him the banner of Islam. With the treasures he amassed, he transformed the city of Ghazna into a brilliant cultural center. At his court were the scholar al-BIRUNI and the poet FERDOWSI.

mahogany family Family Meliaceae (order Sapindales), composed of 575 species of trees and (rarely) shrubs in 51 genera, native to tropical and subtropical regions. Trees of the genus *Swietenia* and *Entandrophragma*, commonly called mahogany, and of the genus *Cedrela* (especially the cigar-box cedar, *C. odorata*) are economically important timber trees. The China tree *(Melia azedarach),* also called chinaberry, bead tree, and Persian lilac, is an ornamental Asian tree with fragrant, lilac-colored flowers and attractive but poisonous round yellow fruits, often cultivated in tropical and warm temperate areas. Most members of the family have large compound leaves and branched flower clusters. A few have edible fruits.

Mahone \mə-ˈhōn\, **William** (1826–1895) U.S. politician and railroad magnate. Born in Southampton Co., Va., he became president of Norfolk–Petersburg Railroad in 1861. In the Civil War he was appointed quartermaster general of the Confederacy but served with the army of northern Virginia, rising to major general. After the war he resumed railroading, becoming president of the Atlantic, Mississippi, and Ohio (later Norfolk & Western) Railroad (1867). He built a political base through railroad patronage but lost control of the railroad in the 1870s. Unable to win the Democratic nomination for governor (1877), he organized a coalition of blacks and poor whites to form a political party, the Readjusters (1879), which succeeded in enacting reforms. He served as a Republican in the U.S. Senate 1880–87.

Mahre \ˈmär\, **Phil(ip)** (born 1957) U.S. Alpine skier. Born in Yakima, Wash., he was named to the U.S. Ski Team at 15. In 1981 he became the first American to win the WORLD CUP championship. He repeated his World Cup victory in 1982 and 1983, becoming one of only three male skiers to achieve three consecutive wins. He won a silver medal in slalom at the 1980 Olympic Games and a gold medal in 1984. The silver medal in 1984 was won by his twin brother, Steve.

Maiano, Benedetto da See BENEDETTO DA MAIANO

Maidstone Town (pop., 1994 est.: 139,000), seat of KENT, southeastern England. Situated on the River Medway, southeast of LONDON, its name is derived from one given it in the DOMESDAY BOOK. A residence of the Norman archbishops of CANTERBURY until the REFORMATION, it grew as a market town. Still an agricultural center, it is located in England's largest hops-growing area, and brewing is important to its economy. Among many sites of architectural interest is the medieval archbishop's palace.

mail, chain See CHAIN MAIL

mail-order business See DIRECT-MAIL MARKETING

Mailer, Norman (born 1923) U.S. novelist. Born in Long Branch, N.J., he studied at Harvard University. He drew on his wartime service in the Pacific for his celebrated novel *The Naked and the Dead* (1948), which established him as one of the major Jewish-American writers of the postwar decades. A flamboyant and controversial figure who has often enjoyed antagonizing critics and readers, he has since commanded less respect for his fiction—which also includes the novels *An American Dream* (1965) and *Why Are We in Vietnam?* (1967)—than for journalistic works that convey actual events with the richness of novels, including *The Armies of the Night* (1968, Pulitzer Prize); *Miami and the Siege of Chicago* (1968); *Of a Fire on the Moon* (1970), and *The Executioner's Song* (1979, Pulitzer Prize), about the execution of a murderer.

Mailer, 1968.

NEWSWEEK PHOTO BY BERNARD GOTFRYD, COPYRIGHT NEWSWEEK, 1968

Maillol \mȧ-ˈyȯl\, **Aristide** (1861–1944) French sculptor, painter, and printmaker. He was a painter and tapestry designer until he was almost 40, when eyestrain persuaded him to turn to sculpture. He rejected the highly emotional style of AUGUSTE RODIN and attempted to preserve and purify the classical sculpture of Greece and Rome. Most of his works depict the mature female form, and are characterized by emotional restraint, clear composition, and serene surfaces. After 1910 he was internationally famous and never lacked for commissions. He resumed painting later in life, and produced excellent woodcut illustrations for fine editions of Latin poets, but he remained preeminently a sculptor.

Maimon \ˈmī-mȯn\, **Salomon** *orig.* **Salomon ben Joshua** (c. 1754–1800) Polish Jewish philosopher. As a young man he pursued Hebrew and rabbinic studies, adopting the name Maimon out of admiration for MOSES MAIMONIDES. His unorthodox commentaries on Maimonides earned him the enmity of other Jews, and he left Poland at 25 to wander through Europe as a scholar and tutor. A skeptic who emphasized the limits of pure thought, he is best known for his *Search for the Transcendental Philosophy* (1790), a major critique of Kantian philosophy. His other writings include *Philosophical Dictionary* (1791) and *Critical Investigations of the Human Spirit* (1797).

Maimonides \mī-ˈmä-nə-ˌdēz\, **Moses** *orig.* **Moses ben Maimon** (1135–1204) Jewish philosopher, jurist, and physician. Born in Córdoba, Spain, he was obliged to practice his faith secretly under Islamic rule. To gain religious freedom he settled in Egypt (1165), where he won fame for his medical skill and became court physician to the sultan SALADIN. Maimonides' first major work, begun at age 23 and completed 10 years later, was an Arabic commentary on the MISHNA. His other writings included a monumental code of Jewish law called the MISHNE TORAH (in Hebrew) and a classic work of religious philosophy, *The Guide of the Perplexed* (in Arabic), which called for a more rational approach to

Judaism and sought to reconcile science, philosophy, and religion. He is considered the greatest intellectual figure of medieval Judaism.

Main River \'mīn\ River, central Germany. Rising in northern Bavaria, and flowing west, it passes through FRANKFURT before emptying into the RHINE RIVER; it is 326 mi (524 km) long. It forms part of the Main-Danube Canal, which links the Rhine and DANUBE rivers to create a 2,200-mi (3,500-km) waterway from the North Sea to the Black Sea.

Maine \'men\ Historical region, northwestern France. A hereditary countship in the 10th century, it was united with ANJOU in 1126 and came under English rule in 1154. With Anjou and NORMANDY, it fell to France early in the 13th century. After alternating between English and French rule, it reverted to the French crown in 1481 and was made a duchy under LOUIS XIV.

Maine State (pop., 1997 est.: 1,242,000), northeastern U.S. One of the NEW ENGLAND states, it covers 33,265 sq mi (86,156 sq km); its capital is AUGUSTA. The APPALACHIAN MTNS. cross the state, rising to 5,268 ft (1,606 m) at Mount Katahdin; Maine's upland region has many lakes and valleys, and its Atlantic coast is rocky and scenic. Algonquian Indians were the earliest-known inhabitants of the area. European settlers found the Penobscot and Passamaquoddy tribes living along the river valleys and coasts. The French included Maine as part of the province of ACADIA in 1603, and Britain included it in territory granted to the PLYMOUTH CO. in 1606. During the 17th century Britain established scattered settlements, but the area was a constant battleground until the British conquered the French in eastern Canada in 1763. Maine was governed as a district of MASSACHUSETTS from 1652 until it was admitted as the 23rd state of the Union under the MISSOURI COMPROMISE in 1820. Its Canadian boundary was established in 1842. The AMERICAN CIVIL WAR and the INDUSTRIAL REVOLUTION diverted workers and capital from Maine in the 19th century. In the 20th century it has seen slow but steady economic gains, especially in the southwestern coastal region. Its economy is based on agriculture and natural resources. Chief products include timber and wood products, potatoes, and lobsters. Tourism is also an important source of income.

Maine, destruction of the (February 15, 1898) Incident preceding the SPANISH-AMERICAN WAR in which a mysterious explosion sank the U.S. battleship *Maine* in the harbor of Havana, Cuba, killing 260 sailors. The U.S. had sent the *Maine* to Havana in January 1898 to protect U.S. citizens and property after riots in Cuba's struggle for independence from Spain. U.S. anti-Spanish sentiment was inflamed by newspapers proclaiming "Remember the *Maine,* to hell with Spain!" and armed intervention followed in April. It is now believed that the explosion was caused internally.

Maine, Henry (James Sumner) *later* **Sir Henry** (1822–1888) British jurist and legal historian. Born in Scotland, he taught civil law at Cambridge University (1847–54) and lectured on Roman law at the Inns of Court. These lectures became the basis of his *Ancient Law* (1861) and *Early History of Institutions* (1875), which influenced both political theory and anthropology. He served as legal adviser on the governor-general's council in India (1863–69), shaping plans for the codification of INDIAN LAW.

Maine, University of Public university system. A land-grant and sea-grant university based in Orono, it was established in 1865 and took its current name in 1897. Its Farmington campus was Maine's first institution of higher education. There are now seven campuses; enrollment at both the Orono campus and the University of Southern Maine, in Portland, exceeds 10,000. The College of Natural Resources, Forestry, and Agriculture is one of the largest of its kind.

Maine coon cat North America's only native breed of longhaired DOMESTIC CAT. Though its origins are unknown, it was first shown in Boston in 1878. Maines are large, muscular, and heavy-boned; they may have been named for their raccoon-like tail. Excellent mousers, they are known for their gentleness, intelligence, and kind disposition, and are especially good with children and dogs. Most are brown tabbies.

mainframe DIGITAL COMPUTER designed for high-speed data processing with heavy use of input/output units such as large-capacity disks and printers. They have been used for such applications as payroll computations, accounting, business transactions, information retrieval, airline seat reservations, and scientific and engineering computations. Mainframe systems, with remote "dumb" terminals, have been displaced in many applications by CLIENT-SERVER ARCHITECTURE.

Maintenon \ma^n-tə-'nō^n\, **marquise de** *orig.* **Françoise d'Aubigné** *known as* **Madame de Maintenon** (1635–1719) Second wife of LOUIS XIV of France. After an impoverished childhood, in 1652 she married the poet PAUL SCARRON, 25 years her senior. She presided over his literary salon, where she was intellectually formed. Widowed in 1660, she was left penniless, but with the help of influential friends she became governess in 1668 to the king's children born to his mistress, the marquise de Montespan (1641–1707). In 1675 Louis bestowed the title of the Château de Maintenon and lands on her, and after the queen's death in 1683 he secretly married her, either in 1683 or 1697. Though she was blamed for being a bad influence on Louis politically, she maintained a climate of decency, dignity, and piety around him.

Mainz \'mīnts\ *French* **Mayence** \mȧ-'yä^{n}s\ City (pop., 1992 est.: 183,000), western central Germany. Situated on the RHINE RIVER opposite the mouth of the MAIN RIVER, it was established as a Roman military camp c. 14 BC on the site of an earlier Celtic settlement. It became an archbishopric in AD 775, a free city in 1244, and the head of the Rhenish League in 1254. It was under French rule 1797–1816, then passed to Hesse-Darmstadt. It served as a fortress of the GERMAN CONFEDERATION and later of the German empire until 1918. Severely damaged during World War II, it was rebuilt. The birthplace of JOHANNES GUTENBERG, it is the seat of Johannes Gutenberg Univ.

Maipuran languages See ARAWAKAN LANGUAGES

Maistre \'mestr^ə\, **Joseph de** (1753–1821) French polemical writer and diplomat. A member of the Savoy senate, he moved to Switzerland after the French invasion of Savoy in 1792. He served under the king of Sardinia as envoy to Russia 1803–17, then settled in Turin as chief magistrate and minister of state of the Sardinian kingdom. He was an exponent of the absolutist, conservative tradition and opposed the progress of science and liberal beliefs in such works as *Du pape* (1819) and *Les soirées de Saint-Petersbourg* (1821).

Maitland, Frederic William (1850–1906) British legal historian. He practiced law in London before joining the faculty of Cambridge University (1888). With FREDERICK POLLOCK he wrote *History of English Law Before the Time of Edward I* (1895), which became a standard authority on the subject. He helped found the Selden Society (1887) for the study of English law.

Maitland (of Lethington), William (1528?–1573) Scottish statesman. As secretary to MARY, QUEEN OF SCOTS (1560), he sought to unite the realms of England and Scotland by securing Mary recognition as the successor to ELIZABETH I. With that aim, he supported the murders of DAVID RICCIO and Lord DARNLEY, and joined a coalition of Protestant and Catholic nobles. After Mary fled to England in 1568, Maitland tried to restore her to power and broke with the supporters of the infant king James VI (later JAMES I). In the ensuing civil war, he held Edinburgh Castle until forced to surrender; he died in prison.

Maitreya \mī-'trā-yə\ In Buddhist tradition, the future Buddha who will descend to earth to preach again the DHARMA (law) when the teachings of the BUDDHA Gautama have completely decayed. Until then, Maitreya is believed to be a BODHISATTVA residing in the Tusita heaven. Mentioned in scriptures from the 3rd century AD, he is the earliest bodhisattva around whom a cult developed and is still the only one generally honored by the THERAVADA tradition. His images, found throughout the Buddhist world, convey an air of expectancy and promise.

Miroku (Maitreya) in meditation, gilt bronze figure, Japanese, Asuka period, 7th century; in the Cleveland Museum of Art.

THE CLEVELAND MUSEUM OF ART, JOHN L. SEVERANCE FUND, 50.86

maize See CORN

Majapahit empire \,mä-jä-'pä-hit\ (13th–16th century) Last Indianized kingdom in Indonesia, based in eastern Java. It was founded by Vijaya, a prince of Singhasari who collaborated with the invading Mongol troops of KUBLAI KHAN (see

KERTANAGARA) to defeat a rival and then drove the Mongols out. Some scholars believe that Majapahit territory included present-day Indonesia and part of Malaysia; others maintain that it was confined to eastern Java and Bali. It reached its height in the mid-14th century under King Hayam Wuruk and his prime minister GAJAH MADA. The rise of the Islamic states along the northern Java coast brought the empire to an end.

majolica \mə-ˈjä-li-kə\ *Italian* **maiolica** \mə-ˈyä-li-kə\ Tin-glazed EARTHENWARE introduced from Moorish Spain by way of the island of Majorca and produced in Italy from the 14th century. Majolica is usually restricted to five colors: cobalt blue, antimony yellow, iron red, copper green, and manganese purple; the purple and blue were used, at various periods, mainly for outline. White tin enamel was used also for highlights or alone on the white tin glaze. The most common shape of the pottery was a display dish, decorated in the *istoriato* style, a 16th-century Italian narrative style that uses the pottery body solely as support for a purely pictorial effect. See also DELFTWARE, FAENZA majolica, FAIENCE, URBINO majolica.

Major, John (born 1943) British politician and prime minister (1990–97). He was elected to the House of Commons as a Conservative in 1979 and rose quickly through the party ranks. In 1989 MARGARET THATCHER appointed him foreign secretary and then chancellor of the exchequer. He won the party leadership after Thatcher's resignation in 1990 and in 1992 won in the general election. Major's first years in office coincided with a long economic recession (1990–93). His government became increasingly unpopular, and Major himself was perceived as a colorless and indecisive leader. In 1997 the Conservatives lost by a landslide to the Labour Party, and Major was succeeded by TONY BLAIR.

Majorca \mä-ˈjȯr-kə, mä-ˈyȯr-kə\ *Spanish* **Mallorca** \mä-ˈlyȯr-kə\ *ancient* **Balearis Major** Island (pop., 1994 est.: 737,000) and autonomous community, Spain; its capital is PALMA. The largest of the BALEARIC ISLANDS, it lies in the western Mediterranean Sea and occupies an area of 1,405 sq mi (3,640 sq km). The kingdom of Majorca was established by JAMES I of Aragon in the 13th century and was united to ARAGON in the 14th century. During the SPANISH CIVIL WAR (1936–39), it was a base for Italian aid to the Nationalists. Now a popular tourist center, it was a favorite haunt of F. CHOPIN.

Majorelle \mȧ-yȯ-ˈrel\, **Louis** (1859–1926) French artist, cabinetmaker, and furniture designer. The son of a cabinetmaker in Nancy, he was trained as a painter and studied under J.-F. MILLET at the École des Beaux-Arts. After his father's death in 1879, he returned home to take charge of the family workshop. He moved from 18th-century reproductions to the developing ART NOUVEAU style and became one of its leading exponents. His style incorporated a flowing line with polished woods, highlighted by Art Nouveau bronze mounts.

Majuro \mä-ˈjü-rō\ Atoll (pop., 1988: 20,000), southeastern MARSHALL ISLANDS, western Pacific Ocean. It comprises 64 islets on a 25-mi (40-km) reef and has a total land area of 4 sq mi (10 sq km). It has the largest population of any of the Marshall Islands; its main settlement, Majuro, situated on the three islands of Dalap, Uliga, and Darrit connected by landfills, is the capital of the republic.

majuscule \ˈma-jəs-ˌkyül, mə-ˈjəs-ˌkyül\ Uppercase, capital, or large letter in CALLIGRAPHY, in contrast to the MINUSCULE, lowercase, or small letter. All the letters in a majuscule script are contained between a single pair of real or theoretical horizontal lines. The earliest known Roman majuscule letters are in the style known as square capitals, distinguished by downstrokes that are heavier than upstrokes and by serifs (short strokes at right angles to the top and bottom of a letter). Square capitals were used mainly in inscriptions on Roman imperial monuments. Rustic capitals, used in books and official documents, formed a freer, more elliptical script. Roman cursive capitals, a running-hand script used for notes and letters, were a forerunner of the minuscule scripts that appeared later.

Makalu \ˈmə-kə-ˌlü\ Peak in the HIMALAYAS, on the Nepalese–Tibetan border. Located east-southeast of Mount EVEREST, it reaches 27,766 ft (8,463 m), making it one of the world's highest mountains. Attempts to ascend its steep, glacier-covered sides did not begin until 1954. On May 15, 1955, two French climbers—Jean Couzy and Lionel Terray—reached the summit, and seven more members of their party arrived within two days.

Makarios III \mä-ˈkär-ē-ˌōs\ *orig.* **Mikhai Khristodolou Mouskos** (1913–1977) Archbishop and primate of the Orthodox Church of Cyprus. Son of a poor shepherd, he was ordained in 1946; he became bishop in 1948 and archbishop in 1950. A supporter of Cyprus's union with Greece, opposing both independence and partition, he negotiated with the British governor of Cyprus (1955–56), but was arrested for sedition and exiled. In 1959 he accepted independence for Cyprus and was elected president, with a Turkish vice president. Twice reelected, he weathered an attempted coup by the Greek Cypriot National Guard and increasing separatism on the part of Turkish Cypriots.

Makarios III.
CAMERA PRESS

Makarova \mȧ-ˈkär-ə-və\, **Natalia (Romanovna)** (born 1940) Russian ballerina, considered one of the greatest of classical dancers. She trained in Leningrad (St. Petersburg), joining the Kirov Ballet in 1959 to become a leading ballerina. She defected while on tour in London in 1970, and soon joined the AMERICAN BALLET THEATRE. She has performed as a guest artist with the Royal Ballet and other companies, and is best known for her leading role in *Giselle*.

Makassar Strait \mə-ˈka-sər\ Narrow passage of the western central Pacific Ocean, Indonesia. Located between BORNEO and SULAWESI, it connects the Celebes Sea to the Java Sea. It is 500 mi (800 km) long and 80-230 mi (130-370 km) wide. It contains numerous islands, the largest of which are Laut and Sebuku. In 1942, during World War II, it was the scene of naval and air battles as the Allies tried to prevent the Japanese from occupying BORNEO.

makeup In the performing arts, material used by actors for cosmetic purposes and to help create the characters they play. Not needed in Greek and Roman theater because of the use of masks, makeup was used in the religious plays of medieval Europe, in which the angels' faces were painted red and those of God and Christ white or gold. In Elizabethan England, crude makeup methods included powdering the face with chalk (to play ghosts and murderers) or blackening it with burnt cork (to play Moors). As stage lighting improved in the 19th century, theatrical makeup became more artistic; stick greasepaint, invented by Ludwig Leichner in the 1860s, enabled actors to create more subtle characterizations. Stage makeup proved too heavy for motion pictures; in 1910 Max Factor created semiliquid greasepaint makeup suitable for early filmmaking, and in 1928 he created panchromatic makeup to keep pace with the development of incandescent lighting and more sensitive film. Makeup was later further modified for color filmmaking and for television. See also COSMETICS.

mako shark \ˈmä-kō\ Any of certain potentially dangerous SHARKS (genus *Isurus*) in the MACKEREL SHARK family (Isuridae). Two species are generally recognized: the Atlantic *I. oxyrinchus* and the Indo-Pacific *I.*

Mako shark (*Isurus glaucus*).
PAINTING BY RICHARD ELLIS

L
M
N

glaucus. Makos range throughout tropical and temperate seas. Blue-gray, with a white belly, they are about 13 ft (4 m) long and weigh about 1,000 lbs (450 kg). They prey on fishes such as herring, mackerel, and swordfish. Outstanding game fish, they are prized for their fighting qualities and their spectacular repeated leaps out of the water.

Maktum \mák-'tüm\ Ruling family of Dubayy. One of the two members of the al Bu Falasah family to emigrate from Abu Dhabi to Dubayy in 1833 was Bhutti bin Suhail, father of Maktum bin Bhutti, the first ruler of Dubayy (r.1833–52). The current ruler, Maktum bin Rashid, who is also vice president of the UNITED ARAB EMIRATES, is the ninth of the dynasty. The Maktum are a branch of the same Bani Yas confederation that includes the NAHYAN, rulers of Abu Dhabi.

Malabar Coast \'ma-lə-ˌbär\ Region, southwestern coast of India, stretching from the Western GHATS to the Arabian Sea. It now includes most of KERALA state and the coastal region of KARNATAKA state. It has sometimes been used to refer to the entire western coast of peninsular India. A large part of it was within the ancient kingdom of Keralaputra. The Portuguese established trading posts there; they were followed by the Dutch in the 17th century and the French in the 18th century. The British gained control of the region in the late 18th century.

Malabo \mä-'lä-bō\ *formerly (until 1973)* **Santa Isabel** City (pop., 1991 est.: 58,000), capital of EQUATORIAL GUINEA. Located on the northern edge of the island of BIOKO, it is the republic's commercial and financial center. The main activity of its harbor is the export of cocoa, timber, and coffee. Its European population declined after 1969 riots there, and after its Nigerian contract workers returned to Nigeria in the mid-1970s.

Malacca \mə-'lä-kə\, **Strait of** Channel connecting the Indian Ocean and the CHINA SEA. It lies between SUMATRA and the MALAY PENINSULA. It is 500 mi (800 km) long and is funnel-shaped; only 40 mi (65 km) wide in the south, it broadens in the north to 155 mi (249 km). Numerous islets hinder passage at its southern entrance. The shortest sea route between India and China, it is one of the most heavily traveled shipping channels in the world.

Malacca, sultanate of (1403?–1511) Malay dynasty that ruled the great entrepôt of Malacca (Melaka) and its dependencies. Malacca, which commanded the main sea route between India and China, was founded by Paramesvara (died 1424), who converted to Islam and took the title Sultan Iskandar Shah in 1414. It benefited from the rearoused desire of MING-DYNASTY China to trade with the West. By the mid-1430s it had become a major commercial emporium; by the mid-15th century it was an important territorial power as well. The wealthy state encouraged literature, learning, and a lively political and religious life; the period of its ascendancy is considered the golden age of Malay history. The city fell to the Portuguese in 1511.

Malachi \'ma-lə-ˌkī\ (5th century BC) One of the 12 Minor Prophets in the OLD TESTAMENT. (His prophecy is part of a larger book, The Twelve, in the Jewish canon.) His name comes from a Hebrew word meaning "my messenger," suggesting that the author's real name is unknown. The book consists of dialogues in question-and-answer form, in which the prophet defends the justice of God to a community doubtful because its expectations of salvation for Israel are unfulfilled. Malachi calls for faithfulness to God's covenant and promises that the day of judgment will soon arrive. The book was probably written in the 5th century BC.

malachite \'ma-lə-ˌkīt\ Widespread CARBONATE MINERAL of copper, a hydrous copper carbonate, $Cu_2CO_3(OH)_2$. Because of its distinctive bright green color and its presence in the weathered zone of nearly all copper deposits, malachite serves as a prospecting guide. It is found in Siberia, France, Namibia, and Arizona in the U.S. Malachite has been used as an ornamental stone and as a gemstone.

Malachy \'ma-lə-kē\, **St.** (1094–1148) Irish archbishop and religious reformer. He studied at Armagh and was ordained a priest in 1119. While serving as vicar to the archbishop of Armagh, he persuaded the Irish church to accept reforms being promoted by Pope GREGORY VII, and he introduced the Roman liturgy into Ireland. He served as bishop in Cos. Down and Connor before being named abbot of Iveragh. He became archbishop of Armagh in 1129, but resigned in 1137. In 1142 he introduced the Cistercians into Ireland. In 1190 he became the first Irish Catholic to be canonized.

Málaga \'mä-lä-gä\ Port city (metro. area pop., 1995 est.: 532,000), southern Spain. It lies on a bay of the Mediterranean Sea at the mouth of the Guadalmedina River. It was founded by the PHOENICIANS in the 12th century BC and was later conquered by the Romans and the Visigoths. Under Moorish rule from 711 AD, it became one of the chief cities of ANDALUSIA. It fell to Spanish rulers FERDINAND II and ISABELLA I in 1487. It is the foremost Spanish Mediterranean port after BARCELONA; among its exports are fruit and Malaga wine. It was the birthplace of PABLO PICASSO.

Malagasy peoples \ˌma-lə-'ga-sē\ Complex of about 20 ethnic groups in Madagascar who speak Malagasy, an AUSTRONESIAN LANGUAGE. The largest group is the Merina ("Elevated People"), who primarily inhabit the central plateau. Written Malagasy is a standardized version of the Merina dialect. The second-largest is the Betsimisaraka, who live generally in the east. The third is the Betsileo, who inhabit the plateau around Fianarantsoa. Others include the Tsimihety, the Sakalava, the Antandroy, the Tanala, the Antaimoro, and the Bara. Most Malagasy peoples live in rural areas and grow rice, cassava, and other crops. About half are Christian, while the rest practice their traditional religion based on ancestor worship.

Malaita \mä-'lā-tä\ Volcanic island, SOLOMON ISLANDS, South Pacific Ocean. Located northeast of GUADALCANAL, it is about 115 mi (185 km) long and 22 mi (35 km) across at its widest point, and has an area of 1,870 sq mi (4,843 sq km). It is mountainous and covered with dense forests, and its interior has not yet been extensively explored.

Malamatiya \ˌmȧ-lȧ-mȧ-'tē-ə\ Muslim mystic group in the Sufi tradition that flourished in Iran during the 8th century. The name, derived from the Arabic *lama* ("to be wicked"), refers to the group's focus on their own failings and misdeeds. The Malamatiyas saw self-blame as conducive to detachment from worldly things and disinterested service to God. To avoid praise and respect, they hid their knowledge and piety, and they made known their faults as a reminder of the need for self-improvement, while remaining tolerant and forgiving toward others. See also SUFISM.

Malamud \'ma-lə-ˌməd\, **Bernard** (1914–1986) U.S. novelist and short-story writer. Born to Russian-Jewish immigrants in Brooklyn, N.Y., he was educated at CCNY and Columbia Univ., and later taught principally at Bennington College. His novels, which often make parables out of Jewish immigrant life, include *The Natural* (1952), about a baseball hero; *The Assistant* (1957), about a Jewish grocer and a Gentile hoodlum; and *The Fixer* (1966, Pulitzer Prize), often considered his finest novel. His genius is most apparent in his stories, collected in *The Magic Barrel* (1958), *Idiots First* (1963), *Pictures of Fidelman* (1969), and *Rembrandt's Hat* (1973).

malamute, Alaskan See ALASKAN MALAMUTE

Malan \mə-'lan\, **Daniel F(rançois)** (1874–1959) South African politician. Malan obtained a doctorate in divinity (1905) and became a Dutch Reformed minister before entering parliament (1918). He joined J.B.M. HERTZOG's cabinet (1924–33), but broke with Hertzog to form the Purified Nationalist Party (1934). Reconciled with Hertzog in 1939, he assumed leadership of the NATIONAL PARTY after Hertzog withdrew (1940). His party won the 1948 elections by appealing to AFRIKANER racial sentiments, and he formed South Africa's first exclusively Afrikaner government (1948–54) and instituted APARTHEID.

Mälaren \'mā-ˌlär-ən\ Lake, eastern Sweden. Located just west of STOCKHOLM, it has an area of 440 sq mi (1,140 sq km) and a length of 75 mi (120 km); it is the country's third largest lake. Connected with the Baltic Sea by navigable channels, it has more than 1,200 islands.

malaria PROTOZOAL DISEASE, a serious, relapsing infection caused by protozoa of the genus *Plasmodium* (see PLASMODIUM), transmitted by the bite of *Anopheles* MOSQUITOES. Known since before the 5th century BC, it occurs in tropical and subtropical regions near swamps. The roles of the mosquito and the parasite were not proven until the early 20th century. Annual cases worldwide are estimated at 250 million and deaths at 2 million. Malaria from different *Plasmodium* species differs in severity, mortality, and geographic distribution. The parasites have an extremely complex life cycle; in one stage they develop synchronously inside red blood cells. Their mass fissions at 48- or 72-hour intervals cause attacks lasting 4–10 hours. Shaking and chills are followed by fever of up to 105°F (40.6°C), with severe headache, and then profuse sweating as temperature returns to normal. Patients often have anemia, spleen enlargement, and general weakness. Complications can be fatal. Malaria is diagnosed by detecting the parasites in blood. QUININE was long used to alleviate the fevers. Synthetic drugs, such as chloroquine, destroy the parasites in blood cells, but many strains are now resistant. Carriers of a gene for a HEMOGLOBINOPATHY have natural resistance. Malaria prevention requires preventing mosquito bites by eliminating mosquito breeding places and using insecticides or natural predators, window screens, netting, and insect repellent.

Malawi \mä-'lä-wē\ *officially* **Republic of Malawi** *formerly* **Nyasaland** \nī-'a-sə-,land\ Country, South Africa. Area: 45,747 sq mi (118,484 sq km). Population (2002 est.): 10,520,000. Capital: LILONGWE. Almost the entire population consists of BANTU-speaking black Africans. Languages: English (official), Chewa, Lomwe. Religions: Protestantism, Roman Catholicism, Islam, animism. Currency: kwacha. Malawi's terrain is characterized by dramatic highlands and extensive lakes, with forests occupying about two-fifths of the total land area. The GREAT RIFT VALLEY runs north–south and contains Lake MALAWI. Agriculture employs four-fifths of the workforce; staple crops include corn, peanuts, beans, and peas, and cash crops include tobacco, tea, sugarcane, and cotton. Coal mining and the quarrying of limestone also contribute to the economy. Major industrial products are sugar, beer, cigarettes, soap, chemicals, and textiles. It is a republic with one legislative house; its head of state and government is the president. Inhabited since 8000 BC, the region was settled by Bantu-speaking peoples between the

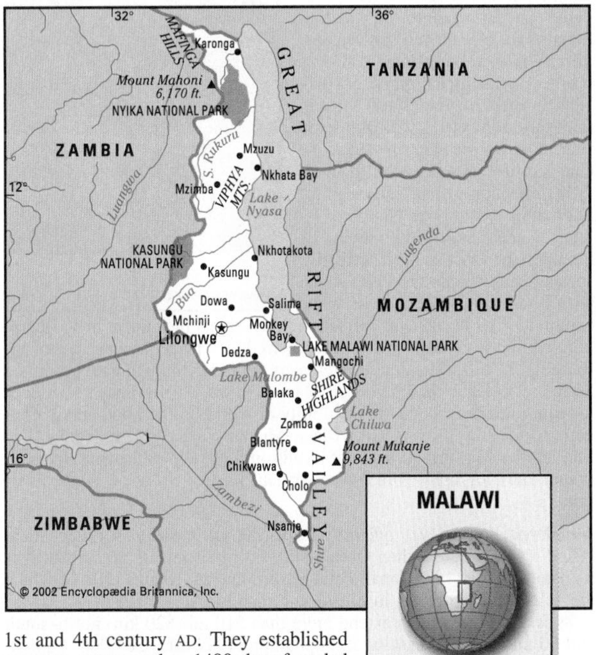

1st and 4th century AD. They established separate states, and c. 1480 they founded the Maravi Confederacy, which encompassed most of central and southern Malawi. In northern Malawi the Ngonde people established a kingdom c. 1600, and in the 18th century the Chikulamayembe state was founded. The slave trade flourished during the 18th–19th century, the same era in which Islam and Christianity arrived in the region. Britain established colonial authority in 1891, creating the Nyasaland Districts Protectorate. It became the British Central Africa Protectorate in 1893 and Nyasaland in 1907. The colonies of Northern and Southern Rhodesia and Nyasaland formed a federation (1951–53), which was dissolved in 1963. The next year Malawi achieved independence as a member of the British COMMONWEALTH. In 1966 it became a republic, with HASTINGS BANDA as president. In 1971 he was designated president for life, and he ruled for three decades before being defeated in multiparty presidential elections in 1994. A new constitution was adopted in 1995.

Malawi, Lake *or* **Lake Nyasa** \nī-'a-sə\ Lake, South Africa, bounded on the west and south by Malawi, on the east by Mozambique, and on the north by Tanzania. It is the southernmost and third-largest of the GREAT RIFT VALLEY lakes. It is about 360 mi (580 km) long with an average width of 25 mi (40 km); it covers an area of 11,430 sq mi (29,604 sq km). It contains Likoma Island, site of an Anglican cathedral completed in 1911. On the heavily populated Malawi shore there are several government stations. Fed by 14 rivers, its sole outlet is the SHIRE RIVER. There are about 200 recorded species of fish in the lake.

Malay Archipelago Largest group of islands in the world, located off the southeastern coast of Asia between the Indian and Pacific oceans. It consists of the more than 13,000 islands of INDONESIA and some 7,000 islands of the PHILIPPINES. Sometimes called the East Indies, the archipelago extends along the equator for more than 3,800 mi (6,100 km). Principal islands include the Greater SUNDAS (SUMATRA, JAVA, BORNEO, and SULAWESI), the Lesser Sundas, the MOLUCCAS, NEW GUINEA, LUZON, MINDANAO, and the VISAYAN ISLANDS.

Malay language \mə-'lā, 'mā-,lā\ AUSTRONESIAN LANGUAGE with perhaps over 33 million first-language speakers in the Malay Peninsula, Sumatra, Borneo, and other parts of Indonesia and Malaysia. Because Malay was spoken on both sides of the Strait of Malacca, a crucial trade route between India and China, Malay-speaking groups were drawn into international commerce centuries before European penetration of the region, and Malay became a LINGUA FRANCA in Indonesian ports, giving rise to a range of PIDGINS and CREOLES known as Bazaar Malay (Melayu Pasar). In 20th-century Indonesia, a standardized form of Malay was adopted as the national language, Indonesian; written in Latin letters, it is now spoken or understood by about 70% of the population. Similar standardizations of Malay comprise the national languages of Malaysia and Brunei. The oldest known Malay texts are 7th-century inscriptions from southern Sumatra in an Indic script (see INDIC WRITING SYSTEM); a continuous Malay literary tradition did not begin until the Islamicization of the Malay Peninsula in the 14th century.

Malay Peninsula Peninsula, southeast Asia. Comprising MALAYSIA, southwestern THAILAND, and SINGAPORE, it occupies an area of 70,000 sq mi (181,300 sq km), has a width of 200 mi (322 km) and extends south for 700 mi (1,127 km) to Cape Balai, the southernmost point of the Asian continent. Its central mountain range, rising to 7,175 ft (2,187 m) at Mount Tahan, divides the peninsula lengthwise and is the source of many rivers. Both its western and eastern coast are exposed to monsoons. It has large tracts of tropical rain forest and is a major producer of rubber and tin.

Malayalam language \,mä-lə-'yä-ləm\ DRAVIDIAN LANGUAGE spoken by more than 36 million people mainly in the Indian state of KERALA. Malayalam is closely related to TAMIL, from which it is estimated to have separated around the 10th century AD. The earliest literary composition in the language is from the 13th century. Like other major Dravidian languages, Malayalam has a number of regional dialects, social dialects that reflect differences in caste and religion, and marked distinctions in formal and informal usage. Literacy among Malayalam-speakers is believed to be higher than literacy among speakers of any other Indian language.

Malayan Emergency (1948–60) Twelve-year period of unrest following the creation of the Federation of Malaya (precursor of Malaysia) in 1948. The Communist Party of Malaya, which was mostly Chinese, was alarmed at the special guarantees of Malay rights, including the position of sultans, and began a guerrilla insurgency, which was supported by only a minority of the Chinese. British efforts to suppress the insurgency militarily were unpopular, especially their relocation of rural Chinese into tightly controlled "New Villages"; when the British addressed political and economic grievances, the rebels became more and more isolated, and the emergency ended. See also Tunku ABDUL RAHMAN PUTRA AL-HAJ, MALAYAN PEOPLE'S ANTI-JAPANESE ARMY.

Malayan People's Anti-Japanese Army (MPAJA) Guerrilla movement formed to oppose the Japanese occupation of Malaya (Peninsular Malaysia) during World War II. The British military, foreseeing a Japanese invasion, trained small groups of Malayans as guerrilla troops; these became the MPAJA. Members of the MPAJA, who were primarily Chinese communists, emerged as heroes from the war and attempted to seize power before the British military returned. Its leadership then went underground until the uprising of 1948. See also MALAYAN EMERGENCY.

L M N

Malayo-Polynesian languages See AUSTRONESIAN LANGUAGES

Malays \mə-ˈlā, ˈmā-ˌlā\ Members of an ethnic group that probably originated in Borneo and expanded into Sumatra and the Malay Peninsula. They constitute more than half the population of Peninsular Malaysia. They are mainly a rural people, growing rice for food and rubber as a cash crop. Heavily influenced by India, they were Hinduized before converting to Islam in the 15th century. Their culture has also been influenced by the cultures of the Siamese, Javanese, and Sumatrans. Malay society has traditionally been somewhat feudal; class distinctions are still marked, and marriages have traditionally been arranged by parents and are governed by Islamic law.

Malaysia Country, S.East Asia. It is composed of two regions—Peninsular or West Malaysia and East Malaysia—separated by 400 mi (650 km) of the CHINA SEA. West Malaysia occupies the southern half of the MALAY PENINSULA, and is bordered on the north by Thailand. East Malaysia occupies the northwestern part of the island of BORNEO and consists of the states of Sarawak and Sabah. Area: 127,584 sq mi (330,442 sq km). Population (1997 est.): 21,770,000. Capital: KUALA LUMPUR. Because it lies on the heavily traveled Strait of MALACCA, the country's population is a very diverse mix, in which ethnic Malays and Chinese form the largest groups. Smaller ethnic groups include Indians, Pakistanis, and Tamils. Languages: Malay (official), Chinese, Indo-European languages. Religions: Islam (official), Buddhism, Taoism, Confucianism, Hinduism. Currency: ringgit. West Malaysia is largely mountainous; East Malaysia has coastal plains rising to hills and then to a mountainous core. Much

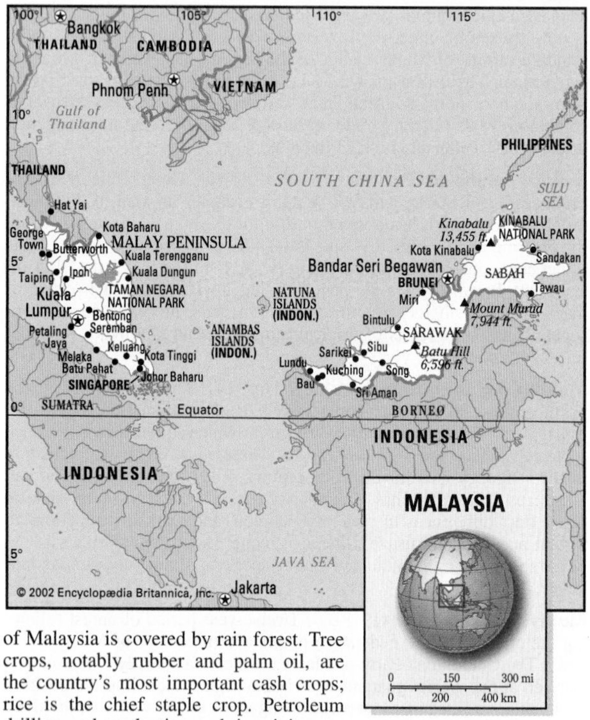

of Malaysia is covered by rain forest. Tree crops, notably rubber and palm oil, are the country's most important cash crops; rice is the chief staple crop. Petroleum drilling and production and tin mining are important, as is the manufacture of rubber goods, cement, and iron and steel products. It is a constitutional monarchy with two legislative houses; the chief of state is the Paramount Ruler, and the head of government is the prime minister. Malaya has been inhabited for 6,000–8,000 years, and small kingdoms existed in the 2nd–3rd century AD, when adventurers from India first arrived. Sumatran exiles founded the city-state of Malacca c. 1400, and it flourished as a trading and Islamic religious center until its capture by the Portuguese in 1511. Malacca passed to the Dutch in 1641. The British founded a settlement on SINGAPORE island in 1819, and by 1867 they had established the STRAITS SETTLEMENTS, including Malacca, Singapore, and PENANG island. During the late 19th century Chinese began to migrate to Malaya. Japan invaded Malaya in 1941 and captured Singapore in 1942. Opposition to British rule led to the creation of the United Malaya National Organization (UMNO) in 1946, and in 1948 the peninsula was federated with Penang. Malaya gained independence from Britain in 1957, and the federation of Malaysia was established in 1963. Its economy expanded greatly from the late 1970s, but it suffered from the economic slump that struck the area in the mid-1990s.

Malcolm II (954?–1034) King of Scotland (1005–34). He acquired the throne after killing Kenneth III and defeating a Northumbrian army at Carham (c. 1016). He became the first king to reign over territory roughly equivalent to modern SCOTLAND. He tried to eliminate rivals to his grandson DUNCAN I, but Macbeth survived to challenge the succession.

Malcolm III Canmore (1031?–1093) King of Scotland (1058–93). The son of King DUNCAN I, he lived in exile in England after Macbeth murdered his father. He defeated and killed Macbeth in 1057 and was crowned king, founding a dynasty that consolidated royal power in Scotland. He gave refuge to the Anglo-Saxon prince EDGAR THE AETHELING in 1066. Though he recognized WILLIAM I as overlord in 1072, Malcolm made five raids into England, during the last of which he was killed.

Malcolm X *orig.* **Malcolm Little** ***later*** **El-Hajj Malik El-Shabazz** (1925–1965) U.S. black militant leader. Born in Omaha, Neb., he was raised in Michigan, where the family house was burned by the Ku Klux Klan; his father was later murdered and his mother was institutionalized. He moved to Boston, drifted into petty crime, and was sent to prison for burglary in 1946. He converted to the Black Muslim faith (Nation of ISLAM) the same year. On his release in 1952, he changed his last name to X to signify his rejection of his "slave name." Soon after meeting the Nation of Islam's leader, ELIJAH MUHAMMAD, he became the sect's most effective speaker and organizer. He spoke with bitter eloquence against white exploitation of blacks and derided the civil rights movement and integration, calling instead for black separatism, black pride, and the use of violence for self-protection. Differences with E. Muhammad prompted Malcolm to leave the Nation of Islam in 1964. A pilgrimage to Mecca led him to acknowledge the possibility of world brotherhood and to convert to orthodox Islam. Rival Black Muslims made threats against his life, and he was shot to death at a rally in a Harlem ballroom. His celebrated autobiography (1965) was written by ALEX HALEY on the basis of interviews.

Malcolm X.
AP/WIDE WORLD PHOTOS

Maldives \ˈmȯl-ˌdēvz\ *officially* **Republic of Maldives** Independent island nation in the Indian Ocean, situated southwest of Sri Lanka. It is a chain of about 1,300 small coral islands and sandbanks (202 of which are inhabited), grouped in clusters, or atolls. Area (land): 115 sq mi (298 sq km); the islands extend more than 510 mi (820 km) north–south and 80 mi (130 km) east–west. Population (1997 est.): 267,000. Capital: MALE. The population is ethnically mixed; ancestors include Dravidian and Sinhalese peoples as well as Arabs, Chinese, and others from surrounding Asian areas. Languages: Divehi (official), Arabic, Hindi, English. Religion: Islam (official). Currency: rufiyaa. All of the islands are low-lying, none rising to more than 6 ft (1.8 m) above sea level. The atolls have sandy beaches, lagoons, and a luxuriant growth of coconut palms, together with breadfruit trees and tropical bushes. One of the world's poorest countries, the Maldives has a developing economy based on fishing, tourism, boatbuilding, and boat repairing. It is a republic with one legislative house; its head of state and government is the president. The archipelago was settled in the 5th century BC by Buddhists from Sri Lanka and southern India, and Islam was adopted in 1153. The Portuguese held sway in Male in 1558–73. The islands were a sultanate under the Dutch rulers of Ceylon (now Sri Lanka) during the 17th century. After the British gained control of Ceylon in 1796, the area became a British protectorate, a status formalized in 1887. The islands won full

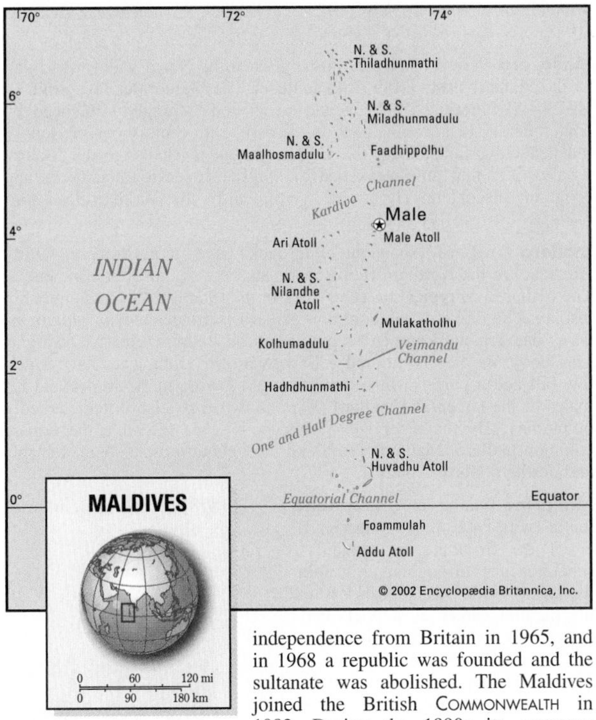

independence from Britain in 1965, and in 1968 a republic was founded and the sultanate was abolished. The Maldives joined the British COMMONWEALTH in 1982. During the 1990s its economy gradually improved.

Maldon \'mȯl-dən\, **Battle of** (991) Conflict fought between SAXONS and victorious VIKING raiders. The battle was commemorated in an Old English heroic poem, which described the war parties aligned on either side of a stream in Essex. It recorded the names of English deserters as well as those who stood fast against the Vikings.

Male \'mä-lē\ Chief island (pop., 1995: 63,000) and capital of MALDIVES. Located in the center of the Maldives, it comprises two groups of islets: North Male, which is 32 mi (51 km) by 23 mi (37 km); and South Male, which is 20 mi (32 km) by 12 mi (19 km). It has central courts, a government hospital, an international airport, and public and private schools. It is a trade and tourist center.

Malebranche \mȧl-'bräⁿsh\, **Nicolas de** (1638–1715) French priest, theologian, and philosopher. His philosophy sought to synthesize CARTESIANISM with the thought of St. AUGUSTINE and with NEOPLATONISM. Central to Malebranche's metaphysics is his doctrine that "we see all things in God." What are commonly called "causes" are merely "occasions" on which God acts to produce effects. This view, known as OCCASIONALISM, was developed by Malebranche to render Cartesian dualism compatible with orthodox Catholicism. His principal work is *Search After Truth* (3 vols., 1674–75).

Malenkov \mə-'len-ˌkȯf\, **Georgy (Maksimilianovich)** (1902–1988) Soviet politician and prime minister (1953–55). He joined the Communist Party in 1920 and rose swiftly through the ranks as a close associate of JOSEPH STALIN. In 1946 he became a full member of the Politburo and deputy prime minister. After Stalin's death (1953), he was forced to yield his post as senior party secretary to NIKITA KHRUSHCHEV, but as prime minister Malenkov worked to reduce arms appropriations, increase the production of consumer goods, and provide more incentives for collective farm workers. His programs were opposed by other party leaders and he was forced to resign as prime minister (1955). Involved in the unsuccessful effort to depose Khrushchev, he was expelled from his other posts (1957) and from the party (1961) and was exiled to central Asia to manage a hydroelectric plant.

Malesherbes \mȧl-'erb\, **Chrétien Guillaume de Lamoignon de** (1721–1794) French royal administrator. A lawyer, he was made a counselor in the Parlement (high court) of Paris in 1744. As director of the press (1750–63), he allowed publication of many works by the PHILOSOPHES, including DENIS DIDEROT's *Encyclopédie*. In 1775 he became secretary of state for the royal household and instituted prison and legal reforms, including ending the misuse of LETTRES DE CACHET, and supported the economic reforms of the comptroller general, ANNE ROBERT JACQUES TURGOT. He failed to win the king's support for his projects and resigned in 1776. In the FRENCH REVOLUTION, he helped conduct the defense of LOUIS XVI (1792). He was arrested in 1793, tried for treason, and guillotined.

Malevich \mə-'lyā-vich\, **Kazimir (Severinovich)** (1878–1935) Russian painter and designer. He discovered Cubism on a trip to Paris in 1912 and returned to lead the Russian Cubist movement. In 1915 he exhibited paintings more abstractly geometrical than any seen before, consisting of simple geometrical forms painted in a limited palette, a style he called SUPREMATISM. In 1917–18 he created his well-known *White on White* series, austere, unearthly images of a white square floating on a white background. In 1919 he joined MARC CHAGALL at his revolutionary art school in Vitebsk, where he exerted strong influence on EL LISSITZKY. In the 1920s he returned to representational painting but could not accede to the government's demand for SOCIALIST REALISM. Though his career was doomed, he greatly influenced Western art and design.

Malherbe \mə-'ler-bə\, **François de** (1555–1628) French poet and theoretician. He converted to Roman Catholicism after receiving a Protestant education. In 1577 he became secretary to the governor of Provence, Henri d'Angoulême. His ode to the new queen, MARIE DE MÉDICIS, made his name widely known, and he became court poet in 1605. His 200-odd surviving letters provide a picture of court life, and his commentary on the poetry of Philippe Desportes (1546–1606) reveal his conviction that poetry must demonstrate verbal harmony, propriety, and intelligibility.

Mali *officially* **Republic of Mali** Country, West Africa. Area: 482,077 sq mi (1,248,574 sq km). Population (1997 est.): 9,940,000. Capital: BAMAKO. The BAMBARA constitute about one-third of the country's total population. Other ethnic groups include the FULANI, the BERBERS, and the MOORS. Languages: French (official), indigenous languages and dialects,

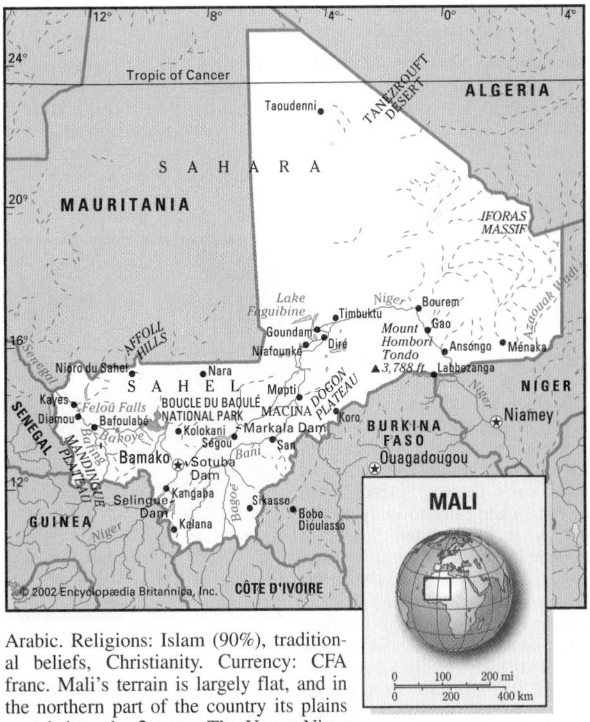

Arabic. Religions: Islam (90%), traditional beliefs, Christianity. Currency: CFA franc. Mali's terrain is largely flat, and in the northern part of the country its plains stretch into the SAHARA. The Upper Niger River basin is situated in the south, and nearly one-third of the total length of the NIGER RIVER flows through Mali. Only about 2% of Mali's total land area is considered arable. Its mineral reserves, which are largely unexploited, include iron ore, bauxite, petroleum, gold, nickel, and copper. Agriculture is the largest industry; staple crops include millet, sorghum, corn (maize), and rice; cash crops include cotton and peanuts. It is a republic with one legislative house; its head of state is the president, and the head of government is the prime minister. Inhabited since prehistoric times, the region was situated on a caravan route across the Sahara. In the 12th century the MALINKE empire of Mali was founded on the Upper and Middle Niger. In the 15th century the SONGHAI EMPIRE in the Timbuktu-Gao region gained control. In 1591 Morocco invaded the area, and Timbuktu (now TOMBOUCTOU) remained under the Moors for two centuries. In the mid-19th century the French conquered the area, which became part of French West Africa. In 1946 the area, known as the French Sudan, became an overseas territory of the French Union. In 1958 it was proclaimed the Sudanese Republic, and joined with Senegal (1959–60) to form the Mali Federation. Senegal seceded, and in 1960 the independent Republic of Mali was formed. The government was overthrown by military coups in 1968 and 1991. During the 1990s elections were held twice, and economic problems did not stop elections in 2002.

Mali empire Trading empire that flourished in West Africa in the 13th–16th century. It developed from the state of Kangaba, on the Upper NIGER RIVER, and was probably founded before AD 1000. The MALINKE inhabitants of Kangaba acted as middlemen in the gold trade in ancient GHANA. Growing in the 13th century, it continued to expand in the 14th century and absorbed Gao and Timbuktu (now TOMBOUCTOU). Its boundaries extended to the HAUSA people in the east and to FULANI and Tukulor peoples in the west. It eventually outgrew its political and military strength, and many of its subject areas revolted. By c. 1550 it had ceased to be an important political entity.

Malinke \mə-'liŋ-kē\ *or* **Mandinka** *or* **Mandingo** Cluster of peoples occupying parts of Mali, Guinea, Ivory Coast, Senegal, Gambia, and Guinea-Bissau. They speak a MANDE LANGUAGE of the NIGER-CONGO family. Numbering 4.7 million, they are divided into numerous independent groups dominated by a hereditary nobility. One group, the Kangaba, has one of the world's most ancient dynasties; its rule has been virtually continuous since the 7th-century founding of the MALI EMPIRE. Most contemporary Malinke grow millet and sorghum and tend cattle. In religion they are divided among Islam and indigenous faiths.

Malinovsky, Rodion (Yakovlevich) (1898–1967) Soviet marshal prominent in World War II. A corps commander in 1941, he rose to army-group commands and played an important role in the Battle of STALINGRAD, then commanded the Soviet drives into Romania (1944) and Austria (1945). After the war he held command positions in the Soviet Far East (1945–55). As minister of defense (1957–67), he oversaw a buildup of Soviet military power.

Malinowski \ˌma-lə-'nȯf-skē\, **Bronislaw (Kasper)** (1884–1942) Polish-British anthropologist generally regarded as the founder of modern, fieldwork-based social anthropology in Britain. He is principally associated with studies of the peoples of Oceania and with the school of thought known as FUNCTIONALISM. After taking degrees in philosophy, physics, and mathematics in Poland, Malinowski happened upon JAMES GEORGE FRAZER's *Golden Bough* and came to study anthropology at the London School of Economics and Political Science (1910–16). Doing research in the Trobriand Islands, he lived in a tent among the people (see TROBRIANDERS), spoke the vernacular fluently, recorded "texts" freely on the scene as well as in set interviews, and observed reactions with an acute clinical eye. He was thus able to present a dynamic picture of social institutions that clearly separated ideal norms from actual behavior, and in doing so laid much of the basis for modern anthropological field research. He taught at the London School of Economics (1922–38) and Yale University (1938–42). Among his works are *Argonauts of the Western Pacific* (1922), *Crime and Custom in Savage Society* (1926), *Sex and Repression in Savage Society* (1927), and *Magic, Science and Religion* (1948).

Malinowski.
BY COURTESY OF THE POLISH LIBRARY, LONDON

Malla era Period of Nepal's history when the Nepal valley was ruled by the Malla dynasty (10th–18th century). The Malla ruler Jaya Sthiti (r. 1382?–95) introduced a legal and social code strongly influenced by contemporary Hindu principles. In the early 18th century one of Nepal's independent principalities, the Gurkha, began to challenge the Mallas, who were at that time weakened by familial dissension and social and economic discontent. They were overthrown by the Gurkha ruler PRITHVI NARAYAN SHAH in 1769. See also NEWAR.

mallard \'mal-ərd\ Abundant "wild duck" (*Anas platyrhynchos,* family Anatidae) of the Northern Hemisphere, ancestor of most domestic DUCKS. The mallard is a typical DABBLING duck in its general habits and courtship display. The drake of the common mallard (subspecies *A. p. platyrhynchos*) has a metallic green or purplish head, reddish breast, and light-gray body; the hen is mottled yellowish brown. Both sexes have a yellow bill and a purplish blue, white-bordered wing mark. Males and females of the Greenland mallard *(A. p. conboschas)* also differ markedly in plumage. In the other subspecies, both sexes resemble the female common mallard. Mallards are found throughout most of Asia, Europe, and northern North America.

Mallarmé \mà-làr-'mā\, **Stéphane** (1842–1898) French poet, an originator (with PAUL VERLAINE) and leader of the SYMBOLIST MOVEMENT. A schoolteacher throughout his life, Mallarmé made steady progress in his parallel career as a poet. Perhaps partly owing to tragedies in his life, most of his verse expresses an intellectual longing to transcend reality and find refuge in an ideal world, as in the dramatic poems *Hérodiade* (1869) and *L'après-midi d'un faune* (1876; "The Afternoon of a Faun"), which inspired CLAUDE DEBUSSY's famous prelude, and the typographically innovative *Un coup de dés* (1897). After 1868 he devoted himself to writing complex, exquisitely wrought, and extraordinarily difficult poems about the nature of imagination itself. The poems were intended for what he called his *Grand oeuvre*, which he never completed.

Mallarmé, 1891.
ARCHIVES PHOTOGRAPHIQUES

Malle \'mál\, **Louis** (1932–1995) French film director. He made his first feature film, *Frantic,* in 1957, and gained commercial success with *The Lovers* (1958), starring JEANNE MOREAU, becoming a leading figure in the French NEW WAVE. In *The Fire Within* (1963), *Thief of Paris* (1967), *Murmur of the Heart* (1971), and *Lacombe, Lucien* (1973), he achieved emotional realism and stylistic simplicity. In 1975 he moved to the U.S., where he directed such admired films as *Pretty Baby* (1978), *Atlantic City* (1980), *My Dinner with André* (1981), *Au revoir les enfants* (1987), and *Vanya on 42nd Street* (1994).

Mallet, Robert (1810–1881) Irish civil engineer and scientific investigator. Born in Dublin to a foundry owner, he studied at Trinity College and in 1831 took charge of his father's Victoria foundry, which he expanded into the dominant foundry in Ireland. His commissions included the construction of railroad terminals, the Nore viaduct, the Fastnet Rock lighthouse, and several swivel bridges over the Shannon. His major innovation in bridge technology was buckled-plate flooring. He built an early form of seismograph, and advanced the technique of making large castings of iron, such as heavy cannon.

Mallorca See MAJORCA

mallow family Family Malvaceae (order Malvales), which contains about 95 genera of herbs, shrubs, and small trees. Mallow species occur in all but the coldest parts of the world, but they are most numerous in the tropics. Hairs that branch into starlike patterns commonly cover some or most vegetative (nonflower) parts of these plants. The flowers are regular and often showy. COTTON is the most important member of the family economically. The green fruits of OKRA are edible. Many species are valued as ornamentals, including HOLLYHOCK and ROSE OF SHARON.

Malmö \'mäl-ˌmœ\ Port city (metro. area pop., 2000 est.: 257,574), southern Sweden, located across from COPENHAGEN. Originally known as Malmhaug, it was chartered in the late 13th century. Following its union with Sweden in 1658, it suffered an economic decline, owing in part to the loss of trade. The building of the harbor in 1775 and the arrival of the railroad after 1800 stimulated economic development. Sweden's third largest city, it is an important commercial center. Its economy is based on export products, shipbuilding, and textile manufactures. Its historic buildings include a 16th-century fortress, the town hall, and the 14th-century St. Peter's Church.

malnutrition Condition resulting from inadequate diet or from inability to absorb or metabolize nutrients because of disease. Food intake may be insufficient to supply CALORIES or PROTEIN (see KWASHIORKOR), or deficient in one or more essential VITAMINS or minerals. The latter case can lead to specific nutritional-deficiency diseases (including BERIBERI, PELLAGRA, RICKETS, and SCURVY). Metabolic defects, especially of the digestive system, LIVER, KIDNEYS, or ERYTHROCYTES, prevent proper DIGESTION, absorption, and metabolism of nutrients. See also NUTRITION.

Malory, Sir Thomas (fl. c. 1470) English author of *Le morte darthur* ("The Death of Arthur"). Even in the 16th century Malory's identity was unknown, but he is tentatively identified as a Welshman and knight who was imprisoned at various times. *Le morte darthur* (completed c. 1470) was the first account of ARTHURIAN LEGEND in English prose. Though based on French romances, it differs from its models in its emphasis on the brotherhood of the knights rather than on courtly love, and on the conflicts of loyalty that destroy the fellowship. Only one extant manuscript predates its printing by WILLIAM CAXTON in 1485.

Malpighi \mal-'pē-gē\, **Marcello** (1628–1694) Italian physician and biologist. In 1661 he identified the pulmonary capillary network, proving WILLIAM HARVEY's theory on blood circulation. He discovered the taste buds and was the first to see red blood cells and realize that they gave blood its color. He studied subdivisions of the liver, brain, spleen, kidneys, bone, and deeper skin layers (Malpighian layers), concluding that even the largest organs are composed of minute glands. Malpighi also studied insect larvae (especially the silkworm), chick embryology, and plant anatomy, seeing an analogy between plant and animal organization. He is regarded as the founder of microscopic anatomy and may be regarded as the first histologist.

malpractice NEGLIGENCE, misconduct, lack of ordinary skill, or breach of duty in the performance of a professional service (e.g., in medicine) that results in injury or loss. The plaintiff must usually demonstrate a failure by the professional to perform according to the field's accepted standards. Physicians, lawyers, accountants, and other professionals became increasingly subject to malpractice suits in the U.S. in the late 20th century.

Malraux \mål-'rō\, **André (-Georges)** (1901–1976) French novelist, art historian, and statesman. Imprisoned at 21 by French colonial authorities while on an archaeological expedition in Cambodia, Malraux became a fervent anticolonialist and advocate for social change. He became involved with revolutionary movements in Indochina and later fought in the Spanish Civil War and with the French Resistance during World War II. He was CHARLES DE GAULLE's minister of cultural affairs 1958–68. His novels, which often draw on his experiences, include *The Conquerors* (1928); *Man's Fate* (1933, Prix Goncourt), his masterpiece; and *Man's Hope* (1937). After 1945 he abandoned fiction for art history and criticism; *The Voices of Silence* (1951) is his major work of the period.

malt Grain product used in beverages and foods as a basis for FERMENTATION and to add flavor and nutrients. Malt is made by steeping grain, usually BARLEY, in water and allowing partial GERMINATION to occur. The flavor of BEER primarily results from the malt from which it is made. The enzymes produced within the barley seed during germination break down STARCH into malt sugar, or maltose, which is then fermented by YEAST to yield alcohol and carbon dioxide. WHISKEY likewise is made with malt.

Malta Independent state, located on a small archipelago, south of Sicily in the Mediterranean Sea. It consists of three inhabited islands, Malta (the largest), Gozo, and Comino, and two uninhabited islets, Comminotto and Filfla. Area: 122 sq mi (316 sq km). Population (2002 est.): 386,000. Capital: VALLETTA. Malta's population, nearly all native-born, has a mixture of Italian, Arab, British, and Phoenician heritages. Languages: Maltese, English (both official). Religion: Roman Catholicism (official). Currency: Maltese lira. Although two-fifths of the total land area is arable, it imports most of its food; tourism is its major industry. It is a republic with one legislative house; its chief of state is the president, and its head of government is the prime minister. Inhabited as early as 3800 BC, it was ruled by the Carthaginians c. 8th–7th century BC. It came under Roman control in 218 BC. In AD 60 the apostle PAUL was shipwrecked on the island and converted the inhabitants to Christianity. It was under Byzantine rule until the Arabs seized control in 870. In 1091 the Normans defeated the Arabs, and it was ruled by a succession of feudal lords until the early 16th century. In 1530 it came under the KNIGHTS OF MALTA; NAPOLEON seized control in 1798, and the British took it in 1800. The 1802 Treaty of Amiens returned the islands to the Knights. The Maltese protested and acknowledged the British as sovereign; this arrangement was ratified in the 1814 Treaty of Paris. It became self-governing in 1921 but reverted to a colonial regime in 1936. Malta was severely bombed by Germany and Italy during World War II, and in 1942 it received Britain's George Cross for "heroism and devotion," the first time that this medal was conferred upon other than an individual. In 1964 it gained independence within the Commonwealth, and in 1974 became a republic. When its alliance with Britain ended in 1979, Malta proclaimed its neutral status.

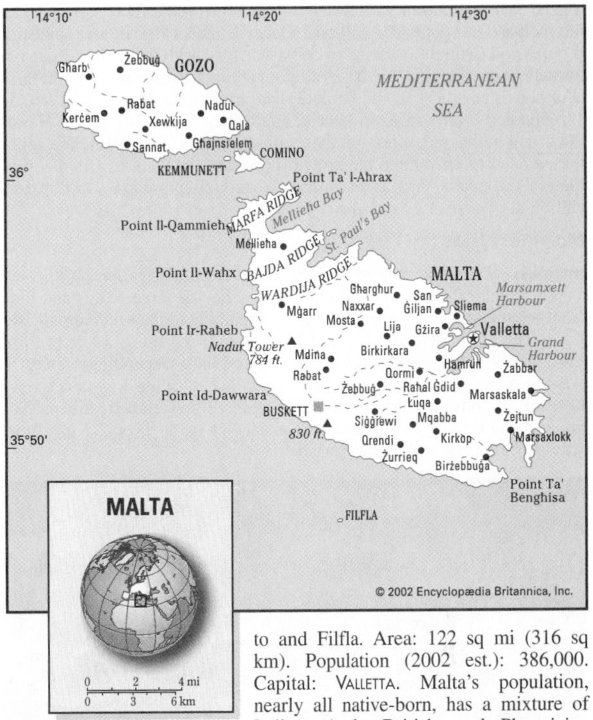

Malta, Knights of See KNIGHTS OF MALTA

Maltese Breed of TOY DOG named for the island of Malta, where it may have originated about 2,800 years ago. Delicate-looking but vigorous, affectionate, and lively, it was once the valued pet of the wealthy and aristocratic. It has a long, silky, pure-white coat, hanging ears, a compact body, and a plumed tail that curves over its back. It stands about 5 in. (13 cm) and weighs up to 7 lbs (3 kg).

Maltese language Principal language of Malta, developed from a DIALECT of ARABIC closely related to the western Arabic dialects of Algeria and Tunisia. It has been strongly influenced by the Romance languages, especially Italian. Maltese is the only form of Arabic written in the LATIN ALPHABET.

Malthus \'mal-thəs\, **Thomas Robert** (1766–1834) British economist and demographer. Born into a prosperous family, he studied at Cambridge University and was elected a fellow of Jesus College in 1793. In 1798 he published *An Essay on the Principle of Population*, in which he argued that population will always tend to outrun the food supply—that the increase of population will take place, if unchecked, in a geometrical progression, while the means of subsistence will increase only in an arithmetical progression. He believed population would expand to the limit of subsistence and would be held there by famine, war, and ill health. He enlarged on his ideas in later editions of his work (to 1826). He argued that relief measures for the poor should be strictly limited since they tended to encourage the growth of excess population. His theories, though erroneous, had great influence on contemporary social policy and on such economists as DAVID RICARDO.

Malvinas, Islas See FALKLAND ISLANDS

mamba \'mäm-bə\ Any of four or five species of slender, agile ELAPID snakes (genus *Dendroaspis,* or *Dendraspis)* having large scales and long front teeth. They inhabit sub-Saharan Africa, where they hunt small animals. The aggressive black mamba *(D. polylepis),* up to 14 ft (4.2 m) long, may be dull gray, greenish brown, or black, depending on age. It dens in rocky open country. It rears up to strike, biting a person's head or trunk. Its bite is nearly always fatal without antivenin treatment. The green mamba (e.g., *D. angusticeps*) is smaller (to 9 ft, or 2.7 m), more strongly arboreal, and less aggressive.

Green mamba (*Dendroaspis angusticeps*).
E.S. ROSS

Mamet \'mam-it\, **David (Alan)** (born 1947) U.S. playwright and screenwriter. Born in Chicago, he founded the St. Nicholas Theatre Co. there in 1973, which first performed his plays. He won wider notice with *Sexual Perversity in Chicago* (1976) and followed it with such works as *American Buffalo* (1977), *A Life in the Theater* (1977), and *Glengarry Glen Ross* (1983, Pulitzer Prize). He became known for rapid-fire dialogue studded with obscenities and for his preoccupation with power relationships and corporate corruption. His later plays include *Speed-the-Plow* (1987), *Oleanna* (1992), and *The Cryptogram* (1994). He wrote screenplays for such movies as *The Verdict* (1980), *The Untouchables* (1986), *The Edge* (1994), and *Wag the Dog* (1997) and directed *House of Games* (1987), *Things Change* (1988), and *Homicide* (1991).

Mamluk regime \'mam-,lük\ *or* **Mameluke regime** \'mam-ə-,lük\ (1250–1517) Rule of Syria and Egypt that originated from the ranks of slave soldiers during the AYYUBID DYNASTY. The term is an Arabic word for slave. Slave soldiers had been used in the Islamic world since the 9th century; they often exploited the military power vested in them to seize control from the legitimate political authorities. Mamluk generals seized the throne on the death of the Ayyubid sultan Al-Malik al-Salih Ayyub (r.1240–49). The Mamluks revived the caliphate in 1258 and patronized the rulers of Mecca and Medina. Under Mamluk rule the remaining crusaders were expelled from the eastern Mediterranean coast and the Mongols were driven back from Palestine and Syria. Culturally, they oversaw achievement in historical writing (see IBN KHALDUN) and architecture. A shift in their ethnic makeup from Turkish to Circassian corresponded with their slow decline; their failure to adopt field artillery as weapons except in siege warfare permitted their defeat by the Ottomans in 1517 (see OTTOMAN EMPIRE). From then on, though they remained intact as a class and continued to exercise political power, they were only one of several forces influencing Egyptian political life. See also BAYBARS I.

mammal Any member of a class (Mammalia) of warm-blooded VERTEBRATES having four limbs (except for some aquatic species) and distinguished from other CHORDATE classes by the female's milk-secreting glands and the presence of hair at some stage of development. Other unique characteristics include a jaw hinged directly to the skull, hearing through bones in the middle ear, a muscular diaphragm separating the pectoral and abdominal cavities, and nonnucleated mature red blood cells. Mammals range in size from the tiny SHREW to the enormous BLUE WHALE. MONOTREMES (PLATYPUS and ECHIDNA) lay eggs; all other mammals bear live young. MARSUPIAL newborns complete their development outside the womb, sometimes in a pouchlike structure. Placental mammals (see PLACENTA) are born at a relatively advanced stage of development. The earliest mammals date from the late TRIASSIC PERIOD (ended 206 million years ago); their immediate ancestors were the reptilian therapsids. For 70 million years mammals have been the dominant animals in terrestrial ecosystems, a consequence of two principal factors: the great behavioral adaptability provided by the ability of mammalian young to learn from their elders (a consequence of their dependence on their mothers for nourishment), and the physical adaptability to a wide range of climates and conditions provided by their warm-bloodedness. See also CARNIVORE, CETACEAN, HERBIVORE, INSECTIVORE, OMNIVORE, PRIMATE, RODENT.

mammary gland \'mam-ə-rē\ Milk-producing GLAND of female mammals, usually present but undeveloped and nonfunctional in males. Regulated by the ENDOCRINE SYSTEM, it is derived from a modification of SWEAT GLANDS. The mammary gland of a woman who has not borne children consists of a conical disk of glandular tissue, encased in fat that gives the breast its shape. The gland is made up of lobes drained by separate ducts that meet at the nipple. Pregnancy causes the cells lining the lobes to multiply, and LACTATION begins in response to hormones released starting at the time of birth. At the end of lactation, the glands return almost to their state before pregnancy. After MENOPAUSE, they atrophy and are largely replaced by connective tissue and fat.

mammoth Any of several species of extinct ELEPHANT (genus *Mammuthus*) whose fossils have been found in Pleistocene deposits (beginning 1.6 million years ago) on every continent except Australia and South America. The woolly, Northern, or Siberian mammoth *(M. primigenius)* is the best-known species because the Siberian permafrost preserved numerous carcasses intact. Most species were about the size of modern elephants; some were much smaller. The North American imperial mammoth *(M. imperator)* grew to a shoulder height of 14 ft (4 m). Many species had a short, woolly undercoat and a long, coarse outer coat. Mammoths had a high, domelike skull and small ears. Their long, downward-pointing tusks sometimes curved over each other. Cave paintings show them traveling in herds. Mammoths survived until about 10,000 years ago; hunting by humans may have been a cause of their extinction. See also MASTODON.

Mammoth Cave National Park National park, southwestern central Kentucky. The park, authorized in 1926 and established in 1941, occupies a surface area of 82 sq mi (212 sq km) that covers a system of limestone caverns. In 1972 a passage was discovered linking the Mammoth Cave and the Flint Ridge Cave System; the explored underground passages have a combined length of some 329 mi (530 km). The caves are inhabited by various animals that have undergone evolutionary adaptation to the dark, including cave crickets, blindfish, and blind crayfish. Mummified Indian bodies, possibly of pre-Columbian origin, have been found in the caves.

Mamoré River \,mä-mō-'rā\ River, northern central Bolivia. It rises in Andean cordilleras, and in its upper course it is sometimes known as Río Grande. It flows north to the Brazilian border, where it is joined by the GUAPORÉ RIVER; it forms the Bolivia-Brazil boundary as far north as Villa Bella, where it joins the BENI RIVER to form the MADEIRA RIVER, after a total course of 1,200 mi (1,900 km). It is navigable to Guajará-Mirim, Brazil.

Mamoulian \mə-'mü-lē-ən\, **Rouben** (1897–1987) Russian-U.S. director. After training as an actor at the Moscow Art Theatre, he moved to London in 1918, where he directed operettas and musicals. After emigrating to the U.S. in 1923, he worked for the Theatre Guild and directed the play *Porgy* (1927); he later directed the original production of its musical adaptation, *Porgy and Bess* (1935), and later such musicals as *Oklahoma!* (1943) and *Carousel* (1945). Invited to direct the film musical *Applause* (1929), he won acclaim for his innovative camera work;

Mamoulian.
UPI

his later films include *City Streets* (1931), *Queen Christina* (1933) with GRETA GARBO, *Becky Sharp* (1935), *The Gay Desperado* (1936), *Blood and Sand* (1941), and *Silk Stockings* (1957).

Mamun \mȧ-'mün\, **al-** (786–833) Son of HARUN AL-RASHID. He bested his brother in a civil war after their father's death (809) and became the seventh ABBASID caliph (813). Attempting to reconcile Sunni and Shiite Muslims, he designated as his heir a Shiite, to whom he married his daughter; the move, which failed to satisfy Shiite extremists and angered Sunnis, was nullified by the heir's death. He became a supporter of the MUTAZILA movement, which proposed a created rather than eternal nature for the QURAN, but failed to impose Mutazili doctrine on his people. His sponsorship of translations of Greek philosophical and scientific works and his building of observatories proved a more lasting legacy.

Man, Isle of Island (pop., 1995 est.: 69,600), in the IRISH SEA, off northwestern coast of England. It is a self-governing crown possession of Britain, with its own legislature. Its capital is Douglas (pop., 1991: 22,000). It is about 30 mi (48 km) long and 10 mi (16 km) wide, with an area of 221 sq mi (572 sq km). The MANX breed of tailless cats is believed to have originated there. The isle was home to Irish missionaries beginning in the 5th century AD. It was held by the Norse (9th–13th century), Scots (13th–14th century), and English settlers (from the 14th century). It was made a crown possession in 1828.

Man, Paul de See Paul DE MAN

man-eater Term that usually refers to either of two species of dangerous SHARKS: the GREAT WHITE SHARK or the Lake Nicaragua shark (family Carcharhinidae). The name has also been given to large felines (including lions and tigers) that have acquired a habit of eating human flesh. See also TIGER SHARK.

Man o' War U.S. Thoroughbred racehorse. In two seasons (1919–20), he won 20 of 21 races, including the Preakness and Belmont stakes. (He did not run in the Kentucky Derby.) He sired 64 stakes horses, including War Admiral, a TRIPLE CROWN winner (1937). In a 1950 Associated Press poll, Man o' War was voted the greatest horse of the first half of the 20th century.

man-o'-war bird See FRIGATE BIRD

Man Ray See Man RAY

mana \'mä-nə\ Among Polynesian and Melanesian peoples, a supernatural force or power that may be ascribed to persons, spirits, or inanimate objects. Mana may be either good or evil, beneficial or dangerous, but it is not impersonal; it is never spoken of except in connection with powerful beings or things. The term was first used in the 19th century in the West in connection with RELIGION, but mana is now regarded as a symbolic way of expressing the special qualities attributed to persons of status in a hierarchical society, of providing sanction for their actions, and of explaining their failures. See also ANIMISM.

Management and Budget, Office of See OFFICE OF MANAGEMENT AND BUDGET

managerial economics Application of economic principles to decision making in business firms or other management units. The basic concepts are drawn from MICROECONOMIC theory, but new tools of analysis have been added. Statistical methods, for example, are increasingly important in estimating current and future demand for products. The methods of operations research and programming provide scientific criteria for maximizing PROFIT, minimizing COST, and selecting the most profitable combination of products. Decision-making theory and GAME THEORY, which recognize the conditions of uncertainty and imperfect knowledge under which business managers operate, have contributed to systematic methods of assessing investment opportunities.

Managua \mä-'nä-gwä\ City (pop., 1995: 864,201), capital of NICARAGUA, on southern shore of Lake MANAGUA. Of minor importance during Spanish colonial times, it was selected as the nation's capital in 1857 when a choice between León and Granada could not be settled. It was devastated by earthquake and fire in 1931 and by another major earthquake in 1972. It was the scene of fighting in 1978–79 during the civil war. The largest city and commercial center of Nicaragua, it has several institutions of higher education, including the University of Managua, now part of the National University of Nicaragua. Sites of interest include Darío Park, with its monument to RUBEN DARIO

Managua, Lake Lake, western Nicaragua. Occupying an area of 400 sq mi (1,035 sq km), it is 36 mi (58 km) long and 16 mi (25 km) wide. Located north of MANAGUA, it is fed by numerous streams rising in the central highlands and is drained by the Tipitapa River, which flows into Lake NICARAGUA. The lake is also known by its Indian name, Xolotlán. Momotombo Volcano (4,199 ft, or 1,280 m) is on the northwestern shore.

Manala \'mä-nä-ˌlä\ In Finnish mythology, the realm of the dead. Manala is ruled by the goddess Louhi, a fierce haglike creature. It is reached by crossing a fiery stream, the river of death, either over a narrow bridge or on a boat brought by a denizen of the other world. Though dark and gloomy, it is not a place of everlasting torment like the Christian HELL.

Manama \mȧ-'nȧ-mə\ *or* **Al-Manamah** City (pop., 1995 est.: 148,000), capital of BAHRAIN. Situated at the northeastern tip of Bahrain island, it is Bahrain's largest city, with about one-third of the emirate's population, and is one of the PERSIAN GULF's most important ports. A commercial and financial center enriched by Bahrain's oil wealth, it is linked by causeway with the island city of Muharraq. First mentioned in Islamic chronicles c. 1345, it was taken by the Portuguese in 1521 and by the Persians in 1602. It has been held, with brief interruptions, by the Al Khalifah dynasty since 1783. It was the seat of the British political resident for the Persian Gulf 1946–71, then it became the capital of independent Bahrain.

Manapouri Lake \ˌmä-nä-'pu̇r-ē\ Lake, southwestern SOUTH ISLAND, New Zealand. With a maximum depth of 1,455 ft (444 m), it is the deepest lake in the country. It is one of the Southern Lakes, located in FIORDLAND NATIONAL PARK. Its name derives from a Maori word meaning "lake of the sorrowing heart," and legend holds that its waters are the tears of dying sisters. It has an area of 55 sq mi (142 sq km) and drains a basin of 1,785 sq mi (4,623 sq km).

Manasarowar See MAPAM YUMCO

Manasseh ben Israel \mə-'na-sə-ben-'iz-rē-əl\ *orig.* **Manoel Dias Soeiro** (1604–1657) Portuguese-Dutch Hebrew scholar and Jewish leader. He was born to a family of marranos, whom persecution drove to Amsterdam. A brilliant theology student, he became rabbi of a Portuguese congregation in Amsterdam in 1622. In the belief that the messiah would come only when the Jews were dispersed throughout the world, he lobbied the English government to allow Jews to live in England and wrote *Vindication of the Jews* (1656). His efforts led to unofficial English acceptance of Jewish settlement and to the granting of an official charter of protection to the Jews of England in 1664, after Manasseh's death.

manatee Any of three species (family Trichechidae) of slow-moving, shallow-water herbivorous mammals. Manatees have a tapered body ending in a rounded flipper, no hind flippers, and foreflippers near the head. The Caribbean manatee *(Trichechus manatus)* lives along coasts of the southeastern U.S. and northern South America; the Amazonian manatee *(T. inunguis)* and the West African manatee *(T. senegalensis)* inhabit rivers and estuaries. Adults are 8–15 ft (2.5–4.5 m) long and weigh up to 1,500 lbs (700 kg). Manatees live singly or in small herds and are protected by law in most areas. The manatee or its relative, the DUGONG, may have given rise to the folklore of mermaids. See also SEA COW.

Manaus \mȧ-'nau̇s\ City (metro. area pop., 2000 prelim.: 1,394,724), northwestern Brazil. Located in the heart of the Amazon rain forest, it lies along the northern bank of the NEGRO RIVER above its junction with the AMAZON RIVER. The first European settlement was a small fort built in 1669. The village, called Villa da Barra, became the capital of the Rio Negro captaincy general in 1809. It prospered in 1890–1920 as the

L
M
N

world's only supplier of rubber, after which it declined. Though 1,000 mi (1,600 km) from the sea, it is again a major inland port and commercial center, having revived economically in the mid–20th century. Notable features include botanical gardens (c. 1669), an opera house, and University of the Amazon.

Manawatu River \ˌmä-nä-ˈwä-tü\ River, southern central NORTH ISLAND, New Zealand. It flows northwest to pass between the Ruahine and Tararua ranges. It then runs southwest past Palmerston North to enter the South Taranaki Bight of the TASMAN SEA. It is 113 mi (182 km) long.

Mance \ˈmäⁿs\, **Jeanne** (1606–1673) French founder of the first hospital in Montreal. She was a member of a French association that planned a utopian colony at Montreal. She sailed with the first settlers in 1641 and founded the Hôtel-Dieu de Montréal in 1644. After a trip to France (1657), she returned with Sisters Hospitallers to staff the hospital.

Mancha, La See CASTILLA-LA MANCHA

Manche, La See ENGLISH CHANNEL

Manchester City (pop., 1999: 431,100), seat of GREATER MANCHESTER, northwestern England. Lying northwest of LONDON and east of LIVERPOOL, it was the site of a Roman fort AD 78–86 but was abandoned after the 4th century. By 919 the town of Manchester had sprung up nearby. In the 16th century it was important in the wool trade, and with the onset of the INDUSTRIAL REVOLUTION in the 18th century it became an important manufacturing city known for its textile production. The world's first modern railroad, the Liverpool and Manchester, opened in 1830. Beset by urban and industrial problems, it now is undergoing redevelopment. Its many educational institutions include the University of Manchester.

Manchester City (pop., 2000: 107,006), southern New Hampshire. Located on the MERRIMACK RIVER, it is the state's largest city. It was settled in 1722–23 and incorporated as the town of Derryfield in 1751. One of America's first textile mills was built there in 1805, beginning a period of rapid industrial growth. Renamed Manchester in 1810, it was incorporated as a city in 1846. Canal systems built in the early 19th century opened navigation to BOSTON. The textile industry's decline in the 1930s spurred industrial diversification. It is the seat of St. Anselm College, Notre Dame College, and New Hampshire College.

Manchester, (Victoria) University of Public university in Manchester, England. It has its origins in a nonsectarian college for men founded in 1851. It became a university in 1880, having established colleges in Leeds and Liverpool which later (1903) became universities in their own right. ERNEST RUTHERFORD conducted important research on atomic physics at Manchester, and one of the first modern computers was built there in the late 1940s. The university grants undergraduate and advanced academic and professional degrees in a broad range of subjects. Total enrollment is about 18,000.

Manchester school Political and economic school of thought led by RICHARD COBDEN and JOHN BRIGHT that originated in meetings of the Manchester Chamber of Commerce in 1820 and dominated the British LIBERAL PARTY in the mid-19th century. Its followers believed in LAISSEZ-FAIRE economic policies, including free trade, free competition, and freedom of contract, and were isolationist in foreign affairs. Its adherents tended to be businessmen, not theorists.

Manchu People, many of JUCHEN ancestry, who acquired a Manchu identity in the 17th century before conquering China and forming the QING DYNASTY (1644–1911/12). Though official policy aimed to maintain the Manchus as a distinct people, this did not prevent considerable intermarriage and adoption of Chinese customs in areas of maximum contact with Chinese. China today recognizes the Manchu as a distinct ethnic group with over 10 million members living mainly in northeastern China.

Manchu dynasty See QING DYNASTY

Manchu-Tungus languages \ˌman-ˈchü-tůŋ-ˈgüz\ *or* **Tungusic languages** Family of about 10 ALTAIC LANGUAGES spoken by fewer than 55,000 people in Siberia, Mongolia, and northern China. All the languages have been losing ground for centuries as their speakers switch to the languages of surrounding populations—Russian and Yakut in Siberia, and Chinese, Turkic, and Mongolian languages in China. Evenki has about 10,000 speakers in Siberia and far northeastern China. Even has fewer than 6,000 speakers in northeastern Siberia and the Kamchatka Peninsula. Nanai has fewer than 7,000 speakers near the lower Amur River. Juchen, the tribal language of the founders of the JUCHEN DYNASTY, is now extinct, and Manchu is spoken by fewer than 100 people, though close to 10 million inhabitants of northeastern China count themselves as ethnically MANCHU. Effectively a dialect of Manchu is Xibe (Xibo, Shibe), spoken by 10,000 descendants of Manchu-speaking soldiers garrisoned at 18th-century military outposts.

Manchuguo *or* **Manchukuo** \ˈman-ˈchü-ˈgwō\ Puppet state created in 1932 by Japan out of the three historic Manchurian provinces. After the RUSSO-JAPANESE WAR, Japan gained control of the Russian-built South Manchurian Railway and its army established a presence in the area; expansion in Manchuria was seen as necessary for Japan's status as an emerging world power. In 1931 the Japanese army created an excuse to attack Chinese troops there, and in 1932 Manchuguo was proclaimed an independent state. The last Qing emperor was brought out of retirement and made Manchuguo's ruler, but the state was actually rigidly controlled by the Japanese, who used it as their base for expansion into Asia. An underground guerrilla movement composed of Manchurian soldiers, armed civilians, and Chinese Communists opposed the occupying Japanese, many of whom had come over to settle in the new colony. After Japan's defeat in 1945 the settlers were repatriated.

Manchuria \man-ˈchůr-ē-ə\ *Chinese* **Dongbei** *or* **Tung-Pei** \ˈdůŋ-ˈbā\ Historical region, northeastern China. It consists of the modern provinces of LIAONING, JILIN, and HEILONGJIANG; the northeastern portion of NEI MONGGOL is sometimes also included. Throughout the early Chinese dynasties, China had only limited control over Manchuria. In 1211 GENGHIS KHAN invaded and occupied Manchuria. Chinese rebellions overthrew the YUAN DYNASTY of the Mongols in 1368, and established the MING DYNASTY. The QING (MANCHU) DYNASTY originated there in the early 17th century and eventually spread over China. Russia and Japan fought each other for a foothold there in the RUSSO–JAPANESE WAR of 1904–5; after its defeat, Russia ceded southern Manchuria to Japan. The Japanese occupied all of Manchuria in 1931 and created the puppet state of MANCHUGUO in 1932. The Soviets captured Manchuria in 1945, and Chinese Communist guerrillas soon came to power. In 1953 Beijing divided Manchuria into its three current provinces. It is now one of China's most important industrial areas.

Mancini, Henry (1924–1994) U.S. composer. Born in Cleveland, he briefly attended graduate school at Juilliard, then worked as pianist and arranger with the postwar Glenn Miller Band. He first gained wide attention with his jazz-inflected music for the television series *Peter Gunn* (1958), but he is perhaps best known for his humorous scores for the *Pink Panther* movies. Other scores include *The Glenn Miller Story* (1954), *Touch of Evil* (1958), *Breakfast at Tiffany's* (1961; with the song "Moon River"), *Days of Wine and Roses* (1962), and *Victor/Victoria* (1982). He contributed music to some 200 films, won four Academy Awards, and conducted and played piano on some 80 albums.

Mancini family \män-ˈchē-nē\ Family of Italian sisters, noblewomen noted for their great beauty. Nieces of Cardinal JULES MAZARIN, they moved to France at an early age. Laure Mancini, duchesse de Mercoeur (1636–1657), married Louis de Vendôme, duc de Mercoeur and grandson of King HENRY IV. Olympe Mancini, comtesse de Soissons (1639–1708), was a mistress of LOUIS XIV. She was involved with her sister, Marie Anne, in the notorious "Affair of the Poisons" and was also accused of poisoning her husband; she was the mother of Prince EUGENE OF SAVOY. Marie Mancini, princesse de Colonna (1640–1715), was also a mistress of Louis XIV; Mazarin intrigued to prevent their marriage, and she spent most of her life in Spain. Hortense Mancini, duchesse de Mazarin (1646–1699), married Armand Charles de la Porté, who assumed the Mazarin title. After leaving her husband, she became a famous beauty at the English court of CHARLES II. Marie Anne Mancini, duchesse de Bouillon (1649–1714), was known for her literary salon, but was banished in 1680 for the alleged poisoning of the sorceress La Voisin (Catherine Monvoisin).

Mandaeanism \man-ˈdē-ə-ˌni-zəm\ Ancient Middle Eastern Gnostic sect surviving in Iraq and southwestern Iran. Like other dualistic systems, it stresses salvation of the soul through esoteric knowledge, or gnosis, of its divine origin. (Its name derives from *mandayya,* "having knowledge.") In its cosmology, evil ARCHONS obstruct the soul's ascent through the heavenly spheres to reunion with the supreme deity. Unlike many Gnostic systems, Mandaeanism supports marriage and forbids sexual license. It is also characterized by elaborate cultic rituals, particularly for baptism. Mandaeans view JESUS as a false messiah but revere JOHN THE BAPTIST, whose life is chronicled in their sacred writings. See also DUALISM, GNOSTICISM.

mandala \'mən-də-lə\ In tantric Hinduism and Buddhism (see VAJRAYANA), a diagram representing the universe, used in sacred rites and as an instrument of MEDITATION. The mandala serves as a collection point for universal forces. By mentally "entering" the mandala and moving toward its center, one is guided through the cosmic processes of disintegration and reintegration. Mandalas may be painted on paper or cloth, drawn on the ground, or fashioned of bronze or stone. Two types of mandalas represent different aspects of the universe: the *garbha-dhatu* ("womb world"), in which the movement is from one to the many; and the *vajra-dhatu* ("diamond world"), from the many into one.

Mandalay City (pop., 1983: 533,000), central Myanmar, situated on the IRRAWADDY RIVER. It is the nation's second largest city, after YANGÔN. It was built in 1857 by King Mindon to replace Amarapura as his capital. The last capital of the Myanmar kingdom, it fell to Britain in 1885. It was nearly destroyed during the Japanese occupation in World War II. An important Buddhist religious center, it is the site of the famous Mahamuni pagoda and of 730 pagodas that house marble tablets inscribed with Buddhist scriptures.

Mandan \'man-ˌdan\ PLAINS INDIAN people of SIOUAN LANGUAGE stock who lived along the Missouri River in what is now southwestern North Dakota. They lived in dome-shaped, earth-covered lodges clustered in stockaded villages; planted corn, beans, pumpkins, and sunflowers, hunted buffalo, and made pottery and baskets. They held elaborate ceremonies, including the SUN DANCE and the bear ceremony, a healing and war-preparation rite. They had age-graded warrior societies as well as shamanistic and women's societies. Artists depicted heroic deeds on buffalo robes. GEORGE CATLIN portrayed Mandan life and people in a series of paintings. By the mid-19th century the Mandan, reduced by smallpox, were removed to a North Dakota reservation, where today they number about 1,000.

Mandarin In imperial China, a public official drawn from the ranks of the lesser officeholders who had achieved success in the CHINESE EXAMINATION SYSTEM. The word comes from the Portuguese version of the Malay term for a minister of state. It has come to mean a pedantic official, a bureaucrat, or a person of position and influence (and usually a traditionalist or reactionary mindset) in intellectual or literary circles. The Mandarin language is the most widely spoken of the CHINESE LANGUAGES.

Mande languages \'män-ˌdā, män-'dā\ Branch of the NIGER-CONGO family of African languages. Mande comprises more than 25 languages of West Africa with over 10 million speakers. The most significant subgroup is the Mandekan complex, a continuum of languages and dialects, including Malinke, Maninka, Bambara, and Dyula (see BAMBARA, MALINKE), spoken from Senegambia and Guinea east through Mali to Burkina Faso. Other major Mande languages are Soninke in Mali, Kpelle in Liberia, Susu in Guinea, and Mende in Sierra Leone.

Mandeb, Strait of See BAB EL-MANDEB

Mandel \mäⁿ-'del\, **Georges** *orig.* **Louis-Georges Rothschild** (1885–1944) French political leader. A member of a prosperous Jewish family, he served as a personal aide to GEORGES CLEMENCEAU (1906–9, 1917–20), in the National Assembly (1919–24, 1928–40), and in cabinet posts (1934–40). As minister of the interior (1940), he supported PAUL REYNAUD's refusal to accept an armistice with Germany. Mandel was arrested in 1940, imprisoned in France and Germany, then returned to Paris in 1944, where he was shot on orders of the Vichy police chief.

Mandela \man-'del-ə\, **Nelson** (born 1918) South African black nationalist leader and statesman. The son of a XHOSA chief, Mandela qualified in law at the University of Witwatersrand in 1942 and joined the AFRICAN NATIONAL CONGRESS (ANC) in 1944. After the Sharpeville massacre (1960), he abandoned his nonviolent stance and helped found the "Spear of the Nation," the ANC's military wing. Arrested in 1962, he was sentenced to life imprisonment. He retained wide support among South Africa's black population and became an international cause célèbre. Released by Pres. F.W. DE KLERK in 1990, he replaced OLIVER TAMBO as president of the ANC in 1991. In 1993 Mandela and de Klerk were awarded the Nobel Peace Prize for their efforts to end APARTHEID and bring about the transition to nonracial democracy. In 1994 he was elected president in the country's first all-race elections; by the time he stepped down in 1999, Mandela was the most universally respected figure of postcolonial Africa.

Nelson Mandela, 1990.

Mandelbrot \'man-dəl-ˌbrȯt\, **Benoit B.** (born 1924) Polish-U.S. mathematician. He received his doctorate in Paris and emigrated to the U.S. in 1958. He is best known for his work with fractals (a term he coined; see FRACTAL GEOMETRY), which, he showed, can occur in many different places in mathematics and in nature. He was influenced by Gaston Maurice Julia (1893–1978), whose 1918 paper on dynamical systems theory received the Grand Prix de l'Académie des Sciences. Julia's work was forgotten until the 1970s, when Mandelbrot's fundamental computer experiments and use of computer graphics breathed new life into it. The Mandelbrot set is a mathematical set of imaginary numbers generated from a simple equation. It appears infinitely complex when graphed on a computer.

Mandelstam \mən-dyil-'shtȧm\, **Osip (Emilyevich)** (1891–1938) Russian poet and critic. He published his first poems in 1910. A leader of the Acmeist poets, who rejected the mysticism and abstraction of Russian Symbolism, he wrote intellectually demanding, apolitical verse in such volumes as *Tristia* (1922). In 1934 he was arrested for an epigram about JOSEPH STALIN. While suffering from mental illness, he composed the *Voronezh Notebooks,* which contain some of his finest lyrics. Arrested again in 1938, he died in custody at 47. Most of his works went unpublished in the Soviet Union until after Stalin's death and were almost unknown in other countries until the mid-1960s.

Mander \'män-dər\, **Karel van** (1548–1606) Dutch painter, poet, and writer. Born of a noble family, after much wandering he settled in Haarlem in 1583 and founded a successful academy of painting with HENDRIK GOLTZIUS and Cornelis Cornelisz (1562–1638). He is best known for his *Het Schilderboeck* (*The Book of Painters,* 1604), which contains about 175 biographies of Dutch, Flemish, and German painters of the 15th–16th century, and became for the northern countries what GIORGIO VASARI's *Lives of the Painters* had been for Italy.

Mandeville \'man-də-ˌvil\, **Sir John** (fl. 14th century) Purported author of *The Voyage and Travels of Sir John Mandeville, Knight,* a Middle English collection of traveler's tales. The book originated in French c. 1356–57; an English version appeared c. 1375. The narrator declares that he is writing of his travels in the years 1322–56. Because most of the material was available in contemporary encyclopedias and travel books, it is not clear whether the author ever traveled at all, but his literary skill and imagination have kept the book popular and highly readable.

Sir John Mandeville, detail from a manuscript, early 15th century; in the British Library (MS. Add. 24,189).

Mandingo See MALINKE

Mandinka See MALINKE

mandolin \ˌman-də-'lin\ Small STRINGED INSTRUMENT related to the LUTE. It evolved in the 17th century in Italy, but its present form owes principally to the 19th-century maker Pasquale Vinaccia (1806–1882). It has a pear-shaped body with a deeply vaulted back, a short fretted fingerboard, and four pairs of steel strings. (The American folk mandolin is a shallow, flat-backed version.) It is

L M N

played with a plectrum; each pair of strings is strummed rapidly back and forth to produce a characteristic tremolo.

mandrake Any of six plant species of the genus *Mandragora* (NIGHTSHADE FAMILY), native to the Mediterranean and the Himalayas. The best-known species, *M. officinarum,* has a short stem bearing a tuft of ovate flowers, with a thick, fleshy, often forked root. The mandrake has long been known for its poisonous properties. In ancient times it was used as a narcotic and an aphrodisiac, and it was believed to have magical powers. When pulled from the ground, its forked root, supposed to resemble the human form, was said to utter a shriek that killed or drove mad anyone who heard it. Once pulled, however, the plant was said to provide soothing sleep, heal wounds, induce love, and facilitate pregnancy. In North America, the name "mandrake" is often used for the mayapple *(Podophyllum peltatum),* a spring forest wildflower.

mandrill Diurnal MONKEY (family Cercopithecidae, usually genus *Mandrillus*) of equatorial African rain forests, known for its striking coloring. The stout-bodied, primarily terrestrial mandrill has a short tail, prominent brow ridges, and small, close-set, sunken eyes. The ribbed bare skin on the adult male's cheeks is bright blue, with scarlet on the nose; the buttock pads are pink to crimson, shading to bluish; the beard and neck are yellow. The adult male is about 3 ft (90 cm) long and weighs about 45 lbs (20 kg); the female is duller and smaller. Mandrills eat fruit, roots, insects, and small reptiles and amphibians.

Mandrill (*Mandrillus sphinx*).
RUSS KINNE—PHOTO RESEARCHERS

Manes See MANI

Manet \mȧ-ˈnā\, **Édouard** (1832–1883) French painter and printmaker. His father, a prosperous civil servant, intended him for a naval career, but he was a poor student interested only in drawing. In 1856, after six years of study, he opened a studio. The Salon rejected his first submission, *The Absinthe Drinker* (1859), but in 1861 it exhibited his *Spanish Singer* (1860). When it rejected his *Déjeuner sur l'herbe* (*Luncheon on the Grass*) in 1863, he exhibited it at the SALON DES REFUSÉS. It aroused critical hostility and the enthusiasm of a group of young painters who later formed the nucleus of the Impressionists. Manet uncomfortably found himself a leader of the avant-garde, though he continued to seek the Salon's approval. In 1868 it welcomed his portrait of É. ZOLA and in 1869 *The Balcony,* whose model was his future sister-in-law, BERTHE MORISOT. His *Olympia* (1863) caused a scandal at the Salon of 1865.

"A Bar at the Folies-Bergère," oil on canvas by Édouard Manet, 1882; in the Courtauld Institute Galleries, London.
COURTAULD INSTITUTE GALLERIES, LONDON (COURTAULD COLLECTION)

His friendship with CLAUDE MONET led to his luminous open-air painting *Boating* (1874). His last great work, *A Bar at the Folies Bergère* (1882), appeared at the Salon. Manet broke new ground in choosing subjects from his own time and in stressing the definition of painting as the arrangement of paint areas on a canvas over and above its function as representation.

Manfred *Italian* **Manfredi** (1232?–1266) King of Sicily (1258–66). The illegitimate son of FREDERICK II, he was made vicar of Italy and Sicily for his half brother Conrad IV, but following Conrad's death, he soon began seeking the Sicilian crown for himself. He resisted Pope Alexander IV's efforts to assign the throne to an English rival, and after fighting off a papal army, Manfred was crowned king in 1258. He became a defender of the Ghibellines in northern Italy (see GUELPHS AND GHIBELLINES). Pope Urban IV declared Charles of Anjou (later CHARLES I) king of Sicily, and Manfred fell in battle against Charles's army.

mangal-kavya \ˈməŋ-gəl-ˈkä-vyə\ Type of verse in honor of a god or goddess in BENGAL. Most mangal-kavyas tell how a local deity established his or her worship on earth. They are often recited at the festivals of the deities they praise. Some have become so popular that performers sing them to entertain village audiences. Many variants exist, since each singer is free to change the verses. Most are written in a simple couplet form, using earthy imagery drawn from village, field, and river.

manganese \ˈmaŋ-gə-ˌnēz\ Metallic chemical ELEMENT, one of the TRANSITION ELEMENTS, chemical symbol Mn, atomic number 25. It is a silvery white, hard, brittle METAL, widely distributed in the earth's crust in combination with other elements. NODULES rich in manganese occur in huge quantities on the sea floor, but no economical way to exploit them has been devised. More than 95% of the manganese produced is used in iron and steel alloys and much of the rest in nonferrous aluminum and magnesium alloys, to improve their corrosion resistance and mechanical properties. Manganese compounds, in which it has various VALENCES, are used in fertilizers and textile printing and as reagents and raw materials. Potassium permanganate is used for disinfecting, deodorizing, and bleaching and as a reagent in ANALYSIS. Manganese is essential to plants for growth and to higher animals to promote the action of many ENZYMES.

mango Evergreen tree and fruit *(Mangifera indica)* of the SUMAC, or cashew, family, one of the most important and widely cultivated fruits of the tropical world. The yellow to orange fruit is juicy, distinctively spicy, and a rich source of vitamins A, C, and D. Mango fruit varies in shape, color, and size from ovoid to long, from vividly red and yellow to dull green, and from plum- to melon-sized. It is used in Theravada Buddhist ceremonies. The long-lived tree reaches 50–60 ft (15–18 m) and has long, lance-shaped leaves and clusters of small, pinkish, fragrant flowers.

mangrove Any of certain shrubs and trees of the families Rhizophoraceae, Verbenaceae, Sonneratiaceae, and Arecaceae (PALM) that grow in dense thickets or forests along tidal estuaries, in salt marshes, and on muddy coasts. The term also applies to the thickets and forests of such plants. Mangroves characteristically have prop roots (exposed, supporting roots). In addition, in many species respiratory, or knee, roots project above the mud and have small openings through which air enters, passing through the soft, spongy tissue to the roots beneath the mud. Mangrove fruits put out an embryonic root before they fall from the tree; the root may fix itself in the mud before the fruit separates from the parent. Likewise, branches and trunks put out adventitious roots which, once they are secure in the mud, send up new shoots. The common mangrove *(Rhizophora mangle)* grows to about 30 ft (9 m) tall and bears short, thick, leathery leaves on short stems, and pale-yellow flowers. Its fruit is sweet and wholesome.

Mangu See MÖNGKE

Manhae See HAN YONGUN

Manhattan Borough (pop., 2000: 1,537,195) of NEW YORK CITY, southeastern New York. It includes all of Manhattan island and three smaller islands in the EAST RIVER. Bounded by the HUDSON RIVER, Harlem River, East River, and Upper New York Bay, it is said to have been purchased by PETER MINUIT in 1626 from the Manhattan Indians with trinkets valued at 60 guilders. Incorporated as New Amsterdam in 1653, it was obtained by Britain in 1664 and renamed New York City. In 1898 Manhattan was chartered as one of five boroughs comprising Greater New York. It is one of the world's great commercial, financial, and cultural centers.

L M N

Among its many points of interest are CENTRAL PARK, the EMPIRE STATE BUILDING, the site of the former WORLD TRADE CENTER, the UNITED NATIONS headquarters, WALL ST., the METROPOLITAN MUSEUM, the MUSEUM OF MODERN ART, LINCOLN CENTER for the Performing Arts, CARNEGIE HALL, COLUMBIA UNIV., the JUILLIARD SCHOOL, and NEW YORK UNIV.

Manhattan Project (1942–45) U.S. government research project that produced the first ATOMIC BOMB. In 1939 U.S. scientists urged Pres. FRANKLIN ROOSEVELT to establish a program to study the potential military use of fission, and $6,000 was appropriated. By 1942 the project was code-named Manhattan, after the site of Columbia University, where much of the early research was done. Research was also carried out at the Universities of California and Chicago. In 1943 a laboratory to construct the bomb was established at LOS ALAMOS, N.M., and staffed by scientists headed by J. ROBERT OPPENHEIMER. Production was also carried out at Oak Ridge, Tenn., and Hanford, Wash. The first bomb was exploded in a test at Alamogordo air base in southern New Mexico. By its end the project had cost some $2 billion and involved 125,000 people.

Mani \mȧ-ˈnē\ *or* **Manes** \mȧ-ˈnē, ˈmā-nēz\ *or* **Manichaeus** \ˌma-nə-ˈkē-əs\ (AD 216–274?) Persian founder of MANICHAEISM. Born in southern Babylonia, he had his first vision of an angel in his boyhood. When he was 24 the angel reappeared and called him to preach a new religion. He traveled to India and made converts there. The Persian king Shapur I permitted him to preach in the Persian empire, but during the reign of Bahram I he was attacked by Zoroastrian priests. After a 26-day trial he was sentenced to prison, where he died.

manic-depressive psychosis See BIPOLAR DISORDER

Manichaeism \ˈma-nə-ˌkē-ˌi-zəm, ˌma-nə-ˈkē-ˌi-zəm\ Dualistic religion founded by MANI in Persia in the 3rd century AD. Inspired by a vision of an angel, Mani viewed himself as the last in a line of prophets that included ADAM, BUDDHA, ZOROASTER, and JESUS. His writings, now mostly lost, formed the Manichaean scriptures. Manichaeism held that the world was a fusion of spirit and matter, the original principles of good and evil, and that the fallen soul was trapped in the evil, material world and could reach the transcendent world only by way of the spirit. Zealous missionaries spread its doctrine through the Roman empire and the East. Vigorously attacked by both the Christian church and the Roman state, it disappeared almost entirely from Western Europe by the end of the 5th century but survived in Asia until the 14th century. See also DUALISM.

Manicouagan River \ˌma-ni-ˈkwä-gən\ River, eastern Quebec province. Rising near the Labrador border, it flows south to empty into the ST. LAWRENCE RIVER near its mouth. From its remotest headstream it is more than 340 mi (550 km) long. The region's dense forests are the source of its Indian name, meaning "where there is bark." The Daniel-Johnson Dam, one of the world's largest multiarch dams, generates hydroelectric power.

Manifest Destiny Concept of U.S. territorial expansion westward to the Pacific Ocean. The phrase was coined in 1845 by the editor John L. O'Sullivan, who described the U.S. annexation of Texas and, by extension, the occupation of the rest of the continent as a divine right of the American people. The term was used to justify the U.S. annexation of Oregon, New Mexico, and California and later U.S. involvement in Alaska, Hawaii, and the Philippines.

manifold In mathematics, a topological space (see TOPOLOGY) with a family of local COORDINATE SYSTEMS related to each other by certain classes of coordinate TRANSFORMATIONS. Manifolds occur in ALGEBRAIC GEOMETRY, DIFFERENTIAL EQUATIONS, and classical DYNAMICS. They are studied for their global properties by the methods of ALGEBRA and ALGEBRAIC TOPOLOGY and form a natural domain for the global ANALYSIS of differential equations. See also TENSOR ANALYSIS.

Manila City (metro. area pop., 2000: 9,932,560), capital of the PHILIPPINES. Located on LUZON island on the eastern shore of MANILA BAY, it is the chief port and the economic, political, and cultural center of the Philippines. The walled Muslim settlement originally built on the site was destroyed by Spanish CONQUISTADORS, who founded the fortress city of Intramuros in 1571. It was briefly held by the British (1762–63) during the SEVEN YEARS' WAR. During the SPANISH–AMERICAN WAR, U.S. forces gained control of Manila in 1898. Occupied by the Japanese in 1942, it was widely damaged during the fight for its recapture by U.S. forces in 1945. In 1946 it became the capital of the newly independent Republic of the Philippines, and was rebuilt. QUEZON CITY became the capital in 1948, but Manila regained that position in 1976. In addition to its diversified industries, including shipbuilding and food processing, it is the seat of several universities.

Manila Bay Inlet of the CHINA SEA extending into southwestern LUZON island, Philippines. Considered one of the world's great harbors, it forms a nearly landlocked body of water with an area of 770 sq mi (2,000 sq km). It measures 36 mi (58 km) across at its widest point. The decisive Battle of MANILA BAY, in the SPANISH-AMERICAN WAR, took place there in 1898. The Japanese gained control of the bay in 1942, but it was recaptured by U.S. forces in 1945. Corregidor Island, the scene of intense fighting in World War II, divides the bay's entrance into the South Channel and the North Channel.

Manila Bay, Battle of (May 1, 1898) Naval engagement in the SPANISH-AMERICAN WAR. The U.S. Asiatic squadron under GEORGE DEWEY was ordered to sail from its Hong Kong base to destroy the Spanish fleet then in the Philippines. In one morning the U.S. destroyed the Spanish ships anchored in Manila Bay; Spanish casualties totaled 381; the U.S. suffered fewer than 10. Manila later surrendered and was occupied by U.S. troops in August. The battle established the U.S. as a major naval power.

Manin \mä-ˈnēn**, Daniele** (1804–1857) Italian leader of the RISORGIMENTO in Venice. A lawyer in the Austrian province of Venitia, Manin became a proponent of home rule and was imprisoned in 1848. He was freed following the rebellion that year and became president of the Venetian republic, reluctantly accepting union with the kingdom of Piedmont-Sardinia in the name of Italian unification. He led a heroic defense of Venice against an Austrian siege, but was forced to surrender in 1849. Banished, he lived in Paris the rest of his life, but in 1868 his body was returned to liberated Venice for a state funeral.

manioc See CASSAVA

Manipur \ˈmə-ni-ˌpu̇r\ State (pop., 2001 prelim.: 2,388,634), northeastern India. Occupying an area of 8,621 sq mi (22,327 sq km), it is bounded by Myanmar; its capital is IMPHAL. Its two main physical features are the Manipur River valley and the western mountainous region. In 1762 and 1824 Manipur requested British assistance in repelling Burmese invasions. The British administered the area in the 1890s, but in 1907 a local government took over; a tribal uprising in 1917 led to a new government administered from ASSAM. In 1947 Manipur acceded to the Indian Union; it was ruled as a union territory until it became a state in 1972. Agriculture and forestry are economic mainstays.

Manitoba \ˌma-ni-ˈtō-bə\ Province (pop., 2001: 1,119,583), central Canada. It is bounded by Nunavut, Hudson Bay, Ontario, Saskatchewan, and by Minnesota and North Dakota; its capital is WINNIPEG. Three-fifths of its territory is covered by the CANADIAN SHIELD, an area of rocks, forests, and rivers. The region was first inhabited by the Inuit (ESKIMO) and by the CREE, ASSINIBOIN, and OJIBWA Indians. The HUDSON'S BAY CO. opened Manitoba to European influence, and the region became a focus of French and British competition for Canadian fur trade dominance; it was ceded by France to Britain in 1763. The Métis rebellion led to the passage of the Manitoba Act in 1870, making it the fifth province of the Dominion of Canada. Steamboat and rail transportation opened the province to settlers from Europe in the late 19th century. Though much of the economy is based on farming, lumbering, and mining, heavy industry has become important to an expanding Winnipeg.

Manitoba, Lake Lake, southern central MANITOBA. Located northwest of WINNIPEG, it drains into Lake WINNIPEG. It is more than 125 mi (200 km) long and up to 28 mi (45 km) wide, with an area of 1,785 sq mi (4,624 sq km). It was discovered in 1738 by PIERRE LA VERENDRYE, who named it Lac des Prairies. The name Manitoba is believed to come from the ALGONQUIAN word *manito-bau* or *manito-wapau* ("strait of the spirit").

Manitoba, University of Public university in Winnipeg, Manitoba, founded in 1877. It has faculties of agricultural and food sciences, architecture, arts and sciences, education, engineering, law, graduate studies, management, medicine, human ecology, and social work, among other fields. Campus facilities include centers for the study of aging, defense and security, and diabetes. Total enrollment is about 25,000.

Manizales \ˌmä-nē-ˈsä-läs\ City (pop., 1999 est.: 337,580), central Colombia. It is situated on a ridge of the Cordillera Central of the ANDES, 6,975 ft (2,126 m) above sea level; its cathedral is visible for miles in all directions. Founded in 1848, it is the commercial center of Colombia's most important coffee-growing district. It is connected by highway and railroad with CALI and by aerial cableway with Mariquita. It is the seat of the University of Caldas.

Manjusri \ˌmən-ˈjü-shrē\ In MAHAYANA Buddhism, the BODHISATTVA personifying supreme wisdom. He is usually considered a celestial being, though some traditions give him a human history. SUTRAS were composed in his honor by AD 250, and he appears in Buddhist art by AD 400. He is often shown wearing princely ornaments and holding aloft the sword of wisdom, and he is sometimes seated on a lion or a blue lotus. His cult spread widely in China in the 8th century, and Mount Wutai in Shanxi province, which is dedicated to him, is covered with his temples.

Manjusri, basalt figure from Java, 1343; formerly in the Museum für Indische Kunst, Staatliche Museen, Berlin (missing from 1945).

BY COURTESY OF THE MUSEUM FUR INDISCHE KUNST, STAATLICHE MUSEEN, BERLIN

Mankiewicz \ˈman-ki-ˌwits\, **Joseph L(eo)** (1909–1993) U.S. film director, producer, and screenwriter. Born in Wilkes-Barre, Pa., he wrote scripts for Paramount from 1929 and later produced such movies as *Fury* (1936), *The Philadelphia Story* (1940), and *Woman of the Year* (1942). He wrote and directed such films as *Dragonwyck* (1946), *A Letter to Three Wives* (1949, Academy Awards for best director and screenplay), *All About Eve* (1950, Academy Awards for best picture, director, and screenplay), *The Barefoot Contessa* (1954), *Guys and Dolls* (1955), *The Quiet American* (1958), and directed *Julius Caesar* (1953), *Suddenly Last Summer* (1959), and the disastrously expensive *Cleopatra* (1963). His older brother, Herman (1897–1953), was a screenwriter and a famous wit, best remembered as the principal author of *Citizen Kane* (1941, Academy Award).

Manley, Michael (Norman) (1924–1997) Jamaican political leader. Son of a prime minister of Jamaica and a sculptor, Manley become a leader of the People's National Party and the National Worker's Union before becoming prime minister in 1972. His leftist government made significant improvements in housing, education, and health care, but a dramatic rise in oil prices precipitated an economic crisis. Much of the middle class fled the country, unemployment rose to 30%, and violence broke out in the run-up to the 1980 election, in which he was defeated. He was reelected in 1989, this time as a moderate; he stepped down in 1992 for health reasons.

Mann, Horace (1796–1859) U.S. educator, the first great American advocate of public education. Raised in poverty, Mann educated himself at the Franklin, Mass., town library and gained admission to Brown University. He later studied law and was elected to the state legislature. As state secretary of education he vigorously espoused educational reform, arguing that in a democratic society education should be free and universal, nonsectarian, and reliant on well-trained, professional teachers. In his later years he served in the U.S. congress (1849–53) and as first president of ANTIOCH COLLEGE (1853–59), and worked resolutely to end slavery.

Horace Mann.

BY COURTESY OF ANTIOCH COLLEGE, YELLOW SPRINGS, OHIO

Mann \ˈmän\, **Thomas** (1875–1955) German novelist and essayist, considered the greatest German novelist of the 20th century. After a brief period of office work, Mann devoted himself to writing, as had his elder brother Heinrich (1871–1950). *Buddenbrooks* (1901), his first novel, was an elegy for old bourgeois virtues. In the novella *Death in Venice* (1912), a somber masterpiece, he took up the tragic dilemma of the artist in a collapsing society. Though ardently patriotic at the start of World War I, after 1919 he slowly revised his views of the authoritarian German state. His great novel *The Magic Mountain* (1924) clarified his growing espousal of Enlightenment principles as one strand of a complex and multifaceted whole. An outspoken opponent of Nazism, he fled to Switzerland on ADOLF HITLER's accession; he settled in the U.S. in 1938, but returned to Switzerland in 1952. His tetralogy *Joseph and His Brothers* (1933–43) concerns the biblical Joseph. *Doctor Faustus* (1947), his most directly political novel, analyzes the darker aspects of the German soul. The often hilarious *Felix Krull, Confidence Man* (1954) remained unfinished. He is noted for his finely wrought style enriched by humor, irony, and parody and for his subtle, many-layered narratives of vast intellectual scope. His essays examined such figures as LEO TOLSTOY, SIGMUND FREUD, JOHANN W. VON GOETHE, FRIEDRICH NIETZSCHE, ANTON CHEKHOV, and FRIEDRICH SCHILLER. He received the Nobel Prize in 1929.

Mannerheim \ˈmä-nər-ˌhām\, **Carl Gustaf (Emil), Baron** (1867–1951) Finnish soldier and president of Finland (1944–46). A career officer in the Russian imperial army (1889–1917), he commanded the anti-Bolshevik forces (1918) in the Finnish Civil War and expelled the Soviet forces. He served as regent of Finland (1918–19) until the new republic was declared. As chairman of the national defense council (1931–39) he oversaw construction of the Mannerheim line of fortifications across the Karelian Isthmus. As commander in chief of Finnish forces (1939–40, 1941–44), he won initial successes against greatly superior Soviet forces in the RUSSO-FINNISH WAR (1939–40). Named president of the Finnish republic in 1944, he negotiated a peace agreement with the Soviets.

Mannerism Artistic style that predominated in Italy from the end of the High Renaissance in the 1520s to the beginnings of the baroque period c. 1590. Mannerism originated in Florence and Rome but ultimately spread as far as central and northern Europe. A reaction to the harmonious classicism and idealized naturalism of High Renaissance art, Mannerism was concerned with solving intricate artistic problems, such as portraying nudes in complex poses. It is characterized by artificiality, a self-conscious cultivation of technical facility, and a sophisticated indulgence in the bizarre. After being superseded by the baroque style, it was seen as decadent and degenerative. By the 20th century, it was appreciated anew for its technical bravura and elegance.

Mannheim City (pop., 1999 est.: 308,400), southwestern Germany. One of Europe's largest inland ports, it is situated on the RHINE RIVER at the mouth of the NECKAR RIVER. It was a village in the 8th century, fortified by Elector Frederick IV, and chartered in 1607. The town was twice destroyed in wars during the 17th century, and was rebuilt when the Palatine electors (see PALATINATE) moved their residence there in 1720. Destroyed again in 1795, the city was rebuilt and became a center of the revolutionary movement in 1848. Today it is an industrial center, manufacturing chemicals, textiles, and fertilizers.

Mannheim \ˈmän-ˌhīm\, **Karl** (1893–1947) Hungarian sociologist. Mannheim taught in Germany (University of Heidelberg, 1926–30; Frankfurt am Main, 1930–33) and England (University of London, 1933–47). He helped found the sociology of knowledge, the study of how knowledge is produced and maintained in societies. He emphasized the role that IDEOLOGY played in shaping knowledge. His major work was *Ideology and Utopia* (1929).

Manning, Henry Edward *known as* **Cardinal Manning** (1808–1892) British Roman Catholic cardinal. The son of a banker and member of Parliament, he was ordained a priest of the Church of England in 1833. A member of the OXFORD MOVEMENT, he became a Catholic in 1851 and was ordained a priest later that year. He rose rapidly, being appointed archbishop of Westminster in 1865 and cardinal in 1875. He favored the centralization of authority in the church (Ultramontanism) and supported stronger wording on PAPAL INFALLIBILITY than was eventually adopted by the First Vatican Council. He established many schools and was highly regarded for his concern for social welfare.

L
M
N

manorialism *or* **seignorialism** \sān-'yōr-ē-əl-i-zəm\ Political, economic, and social system by which the peasants of medieval Europe were tied to their land and their lord through SERFDOM. The basic unit was the manor, a self-sufficient landed estate, or FIEF, under the control of a lord. Free tenants paid rent or provided military service in exchange for the use of the land. Peasants farmed small plots of land and owed rent and labor to their lord, and most were not free to leave the estate. The manorial system was flourishing in Western Europe by the 8th century and had begun to decline by the 13th century, while in Eastern Europe it achieved its greatest strength after the 15th century.

Mansa Musa See MUSA

Mansfield, Earl of *orig.* **William Murray** (1705–1793) British jurist. Born in Scotland, he gained a wide reputation in 1737 when he eloquently supported before the House of Commons a merchants' petition to stop Spanish assaults on their ships. As chief justice of the King's Bench (1756–88), he conducted several scrupulously fair trials of persons accused of treason and seditious libel. He reduced an unwieldy mass of outmoded commercial law to a coherent body of rules, refined the law of contracts, and made major contributions to MARITIME LAW. THOMAS B. MACAULAY called him the "father of modern toryism."

Mansfield, Katherine *orig.* **Kathleen Mansfield Beauchamp** (1888–1923) New Zealand–British writer. After moving to England at 19, she secured her reputation with the story collection *Bliss* (1920). She reached the height of her powers in the collection *The Garden Party* (1922). Her delicate stories, which focus on psychological conflicts, are written in a distinctive prose style with poetic overtones that shows the influence of ANTON CHEKHOV. Her last five years were shadowed by tuberculosis, of which she died at 34.

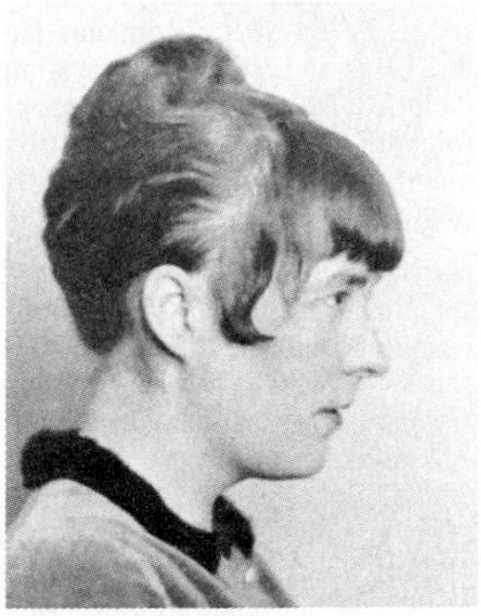

Katherine Mansfield.
BBC HULTON PICTURE LIBRARY

Mansfield, Mike *orig.* **Michael Joseph** (1903–2001) U.S. politician who was the longest-serving majority leader (1961–77) in the Senate. Born in New York City, he worked in Montana copper mines and later taught history at Montana State University. He served in the U.S. House of Representatives 1943–53 and in the Senate 1953–77. An outspoken critic of U.S. involvement in the Vietnam War, he sponsored a 1971 bill calling for a cease-fire and phased withdrawal. He was a persistent critic of Pres. RICHARD NIXON, especially during the Watergate investigation. After retiring, he served as U.S. ambassador to Japan (1977–88).

Mansi See SIBERIAN PEOPLES

manslaughter See HOMICIDE

Manson, Charles (born 1934) U.S. cult leader. Born in Cincinnati, he was a criminal from an early age. In 1967 he formed a communal cult, the Manson Family. He tried to become a pop musician in Los Angeles, but when the producer Terry Melcher failed to help him, Manson decided to launch a racial war by murdering prominent white people, for which he believed blacks would be blamed. In 1969 he sent cult members to Melcher's house, which was rented to the actress Sharon Tate and ROMAN POLANSKI; they murdered Tate and five friends and elsewhere killed three others. In 1971 Manson and his followers were sentenced to death; when California abolished the death penalty (1972), the sentences were commuted to life imprisonment.

manta ray *or* **devil ray** *or* **devilfish** Any of several genera of warm-water marine RAYS, constituting the family Mobulidae, that are wider than they are long. Extensions of the pectoral fins project from the front of the head, looking like devils' horns; these sweep plankton and small fishes into their mouths. The long, whiplike tail may have one or more stinging spines. Mantas swim near the surface by flapping their pectoral fins. The largest species, the powerful but inoffensive Atlantic manta, or giant devil, ray *(Manta birostris),* may grow to over 23 ft (7 m) wide; contrary to old tales, it does not envelop and eat divers.

Mantegna \män-'tān-yə\, **Andrea** (1431?–1506) Italian painter. The son of a woodworker, he was adopted by Francesco Squarcione, a tailor-turned-painter; Mantegna was one of several pupils who later sued him for exploitation. At about 17 he established his own workshop and received an important commission for an altarpiece, now lost. His frescoes in Padua's Eremitani Church (1448–57), with their monumental figures and detailed treatment of classical architecture, show that he had fully mastered perspective and foreshortening and was successfully experimenting with illusionistic effects, best seen in his frescoes of the GONZAGA family (completed 1474) in the Palazzo Ducale's Camera degli Sposi (Bridal Chamber) in Mantua, which transform the small interior room into an open-air pavilion. He married BELLINI FAMILY's daughter in 1453, but did not join Bellini's studio. He later became court painter to Ludovico Gonzaga. His humanistic approach to antiquity and his spatial illusionism were to have far-reaching influence.

Mantinea \ˌman-tə-'nī-ə\ Ancient Greek city of ARCADIA, situated north of modern TRIPOLIS. At the first Battle of Mantinea in 418, SPARTA defeated the coalition of Mantinea, Elis, Argos, and Athens. In 362 the Theban army defeated Spartan troops in an encounter nearby. In 207 BC Philopoemen, Greek general of the ACHAEAN LEAGUE, defeated the Spartans there. In the later Roman empire, Mantinea had dwindled to a mere village, and it finally disappeared under Ottoman rule.

mantis *or* **praying mantis** Any of over 1,500 species of the INSECT suborder Mantodea (order Orthoptera). The long-bodied, slow-moving mantis (or mantid) eats only living insects, using its large forelimbs to capture and hold its struggling prey. The female is likely to eat the male after mating. The European *Mantis religiosa* and the Chinese mantis *(Tenodera aridifolia sinensis)* have been introduced to North America. The latter grows to 3–8 in. (7–10 cm) long. The name mantis ("diviner") reflect an ancient Greek belief in its supernatural powers.

mantle That part of the earth that lies beneath the CRUST and above the central CORE. On average, the mantle begins about 22 mi (35 km) below the surface and ends at a depth of about 1,800 mi (2,900 km). Predominant in the rock material are OLIVINES, PYROXENES, and the silicate perovskite, a dense form of ENSTATITE.

Mantle, Mickey (Charles) (1931–1995) U.S. baseball player. Born in Spavinaw, Okla., he had to play with his legs heavily taped for much of his career because of injuries to his ankles and knees. He joined the New York Yankees in 1951 and became a powerful switch-hitting outfielder and first baseman. Between 1954 and 1961 "the Mick" led the American League four times in home runs, six times in runs, and once in RBIs, the latter occurring in the year (1956) that he won the triple crown for home runs, RBI, and batting average (.353). In 1961 he hit 54 home runs, finishing second in the home-run race behind his teammate ROGER MARIS, who broke BABE RUTH's season record that same year. He retired in 1968 with a lifetime total of 536 home runs.

mantra In HINDUISM and BUDDHISM, a sacred utterance (syllable, word, or verse) believed to possess mystical or spiritual power. Mantras may be spoken aloud or uttered in thought, and they may be either repeated or sounded only once. Most have no apparent verbal meaning, but they are thought to have profound significance and to serve as distillations of spiritual wisdom. Repetition of a mantra can induce a trancelike state and can lead the participant to a higher level of spiritual awareness. Widely used mantras include OM in Hinduism and *om mani padme hum* in TIBETAN BUDDHISM.

Manu \'mə-nü\ In the mythology of India, the first man and the legendary author of the *MANU-SMRTI*. Manu appears in the VEDAS as the performer of the first sacrifice. He is also known as the first king, and most rulers of medieval India claimed him as an ancestor. In the story of the great flood, Manu combines the characteristics of NOAH and ADAM. He built a boat after being warned of the flood by a fish. His boat came to rest on a mountaintop, and as the flood receded Manu poured out an oblation of milk and butter. A year later a woman calling herself the "daughter of Manu" was born from the waters, and these two became the parents of a new human race to replenish the earth.

Manu-smrti \'mə-nü-'smri-tē\ *officially* **Manava-dharma-shastra** Most authoritative of the books of the Hindu law code *(Dharma-shastra).* It is attributed to the legendary first man and lawgiver, MANU. In its present form it dates from the 1st century BC. It prescribes the DHARMA of each Hindu, stating the obligations attached to his or her social class and stage of life. Making no distinction between religious and secular law, it deals with cosmogony, SACRAMENTS, and other religious topics as well as with marriage, hospitality, dietary restrictions, the conduct of women, and the law of kings.

Manual of Discipline *or* **Rule of the Community** Major document produced by the ESSENE community of Jews. The manual, written on scrolls found in 1947 in caves at QUMRAN (see DEAD SEA SCROLLS), explains the sect's religious and moral ideals and describes its admission ceremony, mystical doctrines, and organizational and disciplinary statutes.

Manuel I \mən-'wel\ *known as* **Manuel the Fortunate** (1469–1521) King of Portugal (1495–1521). He opened trade with India and Brazil, sending PEDRO ALVARES CABRAL on a voyage to the Orient (1500), and gained riches from VASCO DA GAMA's voyage around Africa. Manuel's claims to the newly discovered lands were confirmed by the pope and recognized by Spain. In order to marry the daughter of FERDINAND V and Isabella, he agreed to expel Jews and Muslims from Portugal (1496). His reign saw the founding of Portuguese outposts in India and the Malay Peninsula, and his explorers reached China in 1513. Manuel also centralized Portuguese administration, reformed the courts, and revised the legal code.

Manuel I Comnenus \'man-yù-əl...käm-'nē-nəs\ (1122?–1180) Byzantine emperor (1143–80). The son of JOHN II COMNENUS, he renewed alliances in the West against the Normans in Sicily and Antioch. He took Apulia briefly (1155) but was defeated at Brindisi (1156) by a joint force of Germans, Venetians, and Normans, ending Byzantine influence in Italy. He reasserted his authority over the crusader states (1158–59) and extended his influence among the Hungarians and Serbs, adding Dalmatia, Croatia, and Bosnia to the empire in 1167. He launched a campaign against the Seljuq Turks (1176), and his defeat showed the waning of Byzantine power and ended his plan of restoring the Roman empire.

Manuel II Palaeologus \'man-yù-əl...,pā-lē-'ä-lə-gəs\ (1350–1425) Byzantine emperor (1391–1425). He was crowned co-emperor with his father, JOHN V PALAEOLOGUS, in 1373; his brother Andronicus IV seized the throne in 1376, but Manuel and his father regained it with Turkish aid in 1379. They were obliged to pay tribute to the sultan, who later helped them quash a rebellion by Andronicus's son (1390). Manuel was forced to live as a vassal at the Turkish court but escaped after his father's death (1391). A treaty in 1403 kept peace with the Turks until 1421, when Manuel's son and co-emperor JOHN VIII meddled in Turkish affairs. After the Turks besieged Constantinople (1422) and took southern Greece (1423), Manuel signed a humiliating treaty and entered a monastery.

manufacturing Any INDUSTRY that makes products from raw materials by the use of manual labor or machines and that is usually carried out systematically with a division of labor. In a more limited sense, manufacturing is the fabrication or assembly of components into finished products on a fairly large scale. Among the most important manufacturing industries are those that produce aircraft, automobiles, chemicals, clothing, computers, consumer electronics, electrical equipment, furniture, heavy machinery, refined petroleum products, ships, steel, and tools. See also FACTORY, MASS PRODUCTION.

manure Organic material that is used to fertilize land, usually consisting of the feces and urine of domestic LIVESTOCK, with or without litter such as straw, hay, or bedding. Some countries also use human excrement ("night soil"). Though livestock manure is less rich in nitrogen, phosphorus, and potash than synthetic FERTILIZERS and therefore must be applied in much greater quantities, it is rich in organic matter, or HUMUS, and thus improves the capacity of the soil to absorb and store water, thereby preventing erosion. Because manure must be carefully stored and spread in order to derive the most benefit, some farmers decline to expend the necessary time and effort. Manufactured chemical fertilizers, though more concentrated and efficient, are also more costly and more likely to cause excess runoff and pollution. See also GREEN MANURE.

Manutius \mə-'nü-shəs\, **Aldus, the Elder** *Italian* **Aldo Manuzio il Vecchio** (1449–1515) Italian printer, the leading figure of his time in printing, publishing, and typography. In 1490 he settled in Venice and gathered around him a group of compositors and Greek scholars. He produced the first printed editions of many Greek and Latin classics and is particularly associated with the production of small, excellently edited pocket-size books printed in inexpensive editions. The *Hypnerotomachia Poliphili* (1499) of Francesco Colonna, with outstanding woodcuts, was his most famous book. After his death, the Aldine Press was taken over by members of his family, who probably printed 1,000 editions between 1495 and 1595.

Manx cat Breed of DOMESTIC CAT believed to have come from the Isle of Man. Affectionate, loyal, and courageous, the compact Manx is distinguished by its taillessness and hopping gait. The rump is distinctly higher than the shoulders because the hind legs are longer than the forelegs. The Manx may be born with a tail, but ideally it should be tailless. The double coat may be any color.

Manzanar Relocation Center \'man-zə-,när\ Internment facility for Japanese-Americans during WORLD WAR II. Fear that Japan would invade the western U.S. with the aid of spies living in the U.S. led the government to force Japanese-Americans in western states to relocate to one of ten camps, of which Manzanar, in California, was the first to be established and the best known. During its operation, over 11,000 people were confined there.

Manzikert, Battle of (1071) Battle near the town of Manzikert (present-day Malazgirt, Turkey), in which the Seljuq Turks (see SELJUQ DYNASTY) under Sultan ALP-ARSLAN defeated the Byzantines under ROMANUS IV DIOGENES. Romanus had assembled a large army to confront the Turks and end their forays into Byzantine-ruled Anatolia. His troops included Turkmen mercenaries who deserted to the enemy the night before the battle; the Turks destroyed the Byzantine army and took Romanus prisoner. The battle was followed by the Seljuq conquest of most of Anatolia.

Manzoni, Alessandro (1785–1873) Italian novelist and poet. After spending much of his childhood in religious schools, Manzoni wrote a series of religious poems, *Sacred Hymns* (1815), and later two historical tragedies influenced by WILLIAM SHAKESPEARE, *Il conte di Carmagnola* (1820) and *Adelchi* (performed 1822). He is best known for the novel *The Betrothed* (3 vols., 1827), a masterpiece of world literature and the most famous Italian novel of its century, in which, prompted by a patriotic urge to forge a language accessible to a wide readership, he employed a clear, expressive prose that became a model for many subsequent Italian writers. Manzoni's advocacy of a united Italy made him a hero of the RISORGIMENTO; his death prompted G. VERDI's great *Requiem*.

Manzoni, oil painting by Francesco Hayez; in the Brera Gallery, Milan.
ALINARI—ART RESOURCE

Manzù \'mänd-zü\, **Giacomo** *orig.* **Giacomo Manzoni** (1908–1991) Italian sculptor. Apprenticed at an early age, he learned to work in wood, metal, and stone. In 1950, after making a name for himself with sculptures of more than 50 Roman Catholic cardinals and a series of female nudes, he was commissioned to create sculptural bronze doors for ST. PETER'S BASILICA. His sober realism and extremely delicate modeling achieved both severity and sensuousness of form.

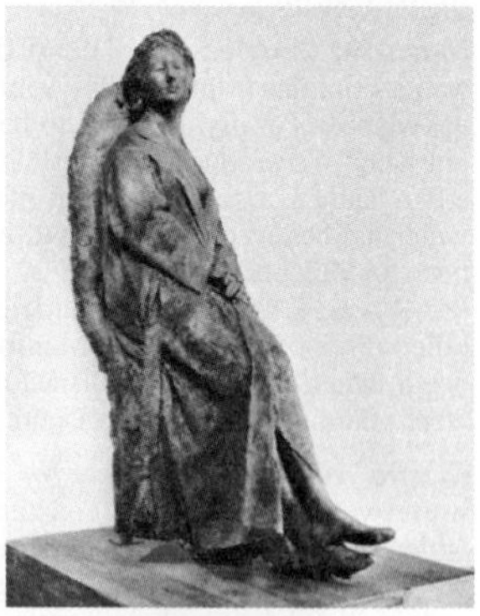

"Portrait of a Lady," bronze sculpture by Giacomo Manzù, 1946; in the Museum of Modern Art, New York City.
BY COURTESY OF THE MUSEUM OF MODERN ART, NEW YORK; A. CONGER GOODYEAR FUND

Mao Dun *or* **Mao Tun** \'maù-'dùn\ *orig.* **Shen Dehong** *or* **Shen Yanbing** (1896–1981) Chinese author and editor. A founder of the League of Left-Wing Writers in 1930, he served as minister of culture after the Communist government was established (1949–64). Many Western critics consider his trilogy of novellas *Shi* (1930; "The Canker") to be his masterpiece, though it was attacked by Marxists. English translations of his works include *Spring Silkworms and Other Stories* (1956) and the novel *Rainbow* (1992). He is generally considered China's greatest novelist of REALISM.

Mao Shan \'maù-'shän\ Sacred mountain in Jiangsu province in China, the focus of Taoist revelations to the visionary Yang Xi (AD 364–70). Yang Xi was visited by a group of perfected immortals *(zhenren)* from the heaven of Shangqing (Supreme Purity), who gave him a new set of scriptures and instructions on the coming apocalypse, during which the good were to take refuge in luminous caverns beneath such sacred mountains as Mao Shan. The Mao Shan revelations incorporated elements of BUDDHISM into Taoist thought and proposed reforms of TAOISM, including rejection of its sexual rites in favor of a spiritualized union with a celestial partner.

Mao Zedong *or* **Mao Tse-tung** \'maù-dzə-'dùŋ\ (1893–1976) Chinese Marxist theorist, soldier, and statesman who led China's communist revolution and served as chairman of the People's Republic of China (1949–59) and chairman of the CHINESE COMMUNIST PARTY (1931–76). The son of a peasant, Mao joined the revolutionary army that overthrew the QING DYNASTY but after six months as a soldier left to acquire more education. At Beijing University he met LI DAZHAO and CHEN DUXIU, founders of the Chinese Communist Party, and in 1921 he committed himself to MARXISM. At that time, Marxist thought held that revolution lay in the hands of urban workers, but in 1925 Mao concluded that in China it was the peasantry, not the urban proletariat, that had to be mobilized. He became chairman of a Chinese Soviet Republic formed in rural Jiangxi; its Red Army withstood repeated attacks from CHIANG KAI-SHEK's Nationalist army but at last undertook the LONG MARCH to a more secure position in northwestern China. Here Mao became the undisputed head of the Communist Party. Guerrilla-warfare tactics, appeals to the local population's nationalist sentiments, and Mao's agrarian policies gained the party military advantages against their Nationalist and Japanese enemies and broad support among the peasantry. Mao's agrarian Marxism did not sit well with the Soviet Union, but when the Communists succeeded in taking power in 1949, the Soviet Union agreed to provide the new communist state with technical assistance. It took Mao's GREAT LEAP FORWARD and his criticism of "new bourgeois elements" in the Soviet Union and China to alienate the Soviet Union irrevocably. Soviet aid was withdrawn in 1960. Mao clung to his vision, following the failed Great Leap Forward with the equally disastrous CULTURAL REVOLUTION, but more moderate forces helped mitigate their effects. After Mao's death, DENG XIAOPING introduced social and economic reforms and the cult of Mao was greatly diminished. See also JIANG QING, LIU SHAOQI, MAOISM.

Maoism \'maù-,i-zəm\ Variation of MARXISM and LENINISM developed by MAO ZEDONG. It diverged from its antecedents in its agrarian focus: Mao substituted the dormant power of the peasantry (discounted by traditional Marxists) for the urban PROLETARIAT that China largely lacked. The Maoist faith in revolutionary enthusiasm and the positive value of the peasants' lack of sophistication as opposed to technological or intellectual elites fueled the GREAT LEAP FORWARD of the 1950s and the CULTURAL REVOLUTION of the 1960s and '70s. The disastrous consequences of both upheavals led Mao's successors to abandon Maoism as counterproductive to economic growth and social order. Maoism was embraced by insurgent guerrilla groups worldwide; under the KHMER ROUGE it became Cambodia's national ideology.

Maori \'maù-rē\ Polynesian people of New Zealand. Maori traditional history describes their origins in terms of waves of migration from a mythical land between the 12th and 14th century, but archaeologists have dated habitations in New Zealand back to at least AD 800. Their first European contact was with ABEL JANSZOON TASMAN (1642), who did battle with a group of Maori. Later Europeans were initially welcomed, but the arrival of muskets, disease, Western agricultural methods, and missionaries corroded Maori culture and social structure, and conflicts arose. The British assumed formal control of New Zealand in 1840; war over land broke out repeatedly over the next three decades. By 1872 all fighting had ended and great tracts of Maori land had been confiscated. Today, about 9% of New Zealanders are classified as Maori; nearly all have some European ancestry. Though largely integrated into modern urban life, many Maori keep alive traditional cultural practices and struggle to retain control of their ancestral lands.

map Graphic representation, drawn to scale and usually on a flat surface, of features—usually geographic, geologic, or geopolitical—of an area of the earth or of any celestial body. Globes are maps represented on the surface of a sphere. Cartography is the art and science of making maps and charts. Major types of maps include topographic maps, showing features of the earth's land surface; nautical charts, representing coastal and marine areas; hydrographic charts, which detail ocean depths and currents; and aeronautical charts, which detail surface features and air routes.

Mapam Yumco \'mä-,päm-'yùm-kō\ *or* **Manasarowar** \,mä-nä-sä-'rō-,wär\ *or* **Ma-fa-mu-ts'o** \'ma-,fä-'mü-tsō\ Lake in the HIMALAYAS, southwestern Tibet, China. Lying nearly 15,000 ft (4,570 m) above sea level, it is generally recognized as the highest body of fresh water in the world. It is prominent in Hindu mythology and is one of the most sacred places of pilgrimage for Hindus.

maple family Family Aceraceae, composed of about 200 species (in the genera *Dipteronia* in China and *Acer* across the Northern Hemisphere) of ornamental, shade, and timber trees. Maples are important ornamentals for lawns, along streets, and in parks. They offer a great variety of form, size, and foliage; many display striking autumn color. The red maple *(A. rubrum)* is one of the most common trees in its native eastern North America, where it tolerates compact, wet soils and city pollution. Box elder *(A. negundo)* grows quickly to 30–50 ft (9–15 m) and resists drought, so early prairie settlers planted many for shade and for wood to make crates, furniture, paper pulp, and charcoal. The watery, sweet sap of the sugar maple *(A. saccharum)* is boiled down for syrup and sugar; the wood of certain sugar maples is used for furniture.

mapmaking See CARTOGRAPHY

Maponos \mä-'pō-nōs\ *or* **Mac ind Óg** \'mȧ-kən-'dōg\ *or* **Oenghus** \'ē-nəs, 'òin-gəs\ In CELTIC RELIGION, a god similar to APOLLO who is often associated with healing. He appears in Welsh mythology as Mabon, who was carried off from his divine mother when he was three nights old. In Irish mythology he is said to be the son of DAGDA and of Boann, the personified sacred river of Irish tradition. He lived in the great Neolithic (and therefore pre-Celtic) passage grave of Newgrange.

Mapplethorpe \'mā-pəl-,thòrp\, **Robert** (1946–1989) U.S. photographer. Born in New York City, he attended Pratt Institute (1963–70) and soon became noted for his austere black-and-white photographs of flowers, celebrities, and male nudes. The explicit homoeroticism of some of his nudes aroused controversy, though their beauty was widely recognized. His death resulted from AIDS. A retrospective exhibition of his work in 1990, funded partly by the NATIONAL ENDOWMENT FOR THE ARTS (NEA), stirred a debate about government subsidies of "obscene" art and provoked Congress to enact restrictions on future NEA grants.

mappo \'mäp-,pō\ In Japanese Buddhism, the age in which the BUDDHA's law will degenerate. The period following the death of the Buddha is divided into three ages: the age of the true law, the age of the copied law, and the age of the latter law or degeneration of the law. A new period, in which true faith will again flower, will then be ushered in by the BODHISATTVA MAITREYA (Japanese, Miroku). Japanese Buddhists calculate that the age of mappo began in AD 1052. Since it is expected to continue for 10,000 years, the current era of human history continues to be the age of mappo.

Mapuche \mä-'pü-chē\ Most numerous group of Araucanian-speaking South American Indians (see ARAUCANIANS), who live in the central valley of Chile. They are noted for their 350-year struggle against Spanish and Chilean domination. In the 16th–18th century they learned to use horses in battle and united over great distances to fight Spanish incursions. After Chile gained independence in the 19th century, the government settled them on reservations. In the 1980s the reservation land was transferred to individuals, but their hold on their land is endangered by indebtedness to support their nonintensive agriculture.

Maputo \mä-'pü-tō\ *formerly (until 1976)* **Lourenço Marques** \lō-'rā^{n}-sü-'mär-kish\ Port city (pop., 1991 est.: 932,000), capital of MOZAMBIQUE. It lies on the northern bank of Espírito Santo Estuary of DELAGOA BAY, an inlet of the Indian Ocean. It derived its former name from the Portuguese trader who first explored the region in 1544. The town developed around a Portuguese fortress completed in 1787. Created a city town in 1887, it superseded Moçambique as the capital of Portuguese East Africa in 1907. Since the nation's independence in 1975, the collapse of tourism and reduced access to foreign trade have damaged the city's economy.

maqam \mȧ-'käm\ Spiritual stage that serves as a milestone on the path followed by Muslim mystics (Sufis) as they strive to reach the vision of and union with God. The Sufi progresses through his own spiritual efforts and through the guidance of SHEIKHS. In each maqam the Sufi strives to purify himself of all worldly inclinations and prepare himself to attain an ever higher spiritual level. Most Sufis identify seven major maqams: repentance, fear of the Lord, renunciation, poverty, patience, trust, and satisfaction. See also SUFISM.

Maqtul, al- See al-SUHRAWARDI

Mar del Plata Coastal city (pop., 1999: 579,483), eastern central Argentina. It was the site of a Spanish mission 1746–51. In 1856 Portuguese explorer Jose Coelho Mierelles founded the fishing village La Peregrina. Mar del Plata was established in 1874 and promoted as a seaside resort; it became a city in 1907. It is famous for its luxurious casino, one of the largest in the world. In addition to tourism, its economy is based on construction, textiles, and commercial fishing and canning. It is the seat of the National University of Mar del Plata.

Mara Buddhist Lord of the Senses, who repeatedly tempted the BUDDHA Gautama. When Gautama seated himself under the BODHI TREE to await enlightenment, the evil Mara appeared in the guise of a messenger claiming that a rival had usurped the family throne. After sending a storm of rain, rocks, ashes, and darkness to frighten away the gods who had gathered, he challenged Gautama's right to sit beneath the tree and sent forth his three daughters, Trsna, Rati, and Raga (thirst, desire, and delight), to seduce Gautama, but to no avail. After the Buddha had achieved enlightenment, Mara pressed him to abandon any attempt to preach, but the gods successfully persuaded him to preach the law.

marabou \'mär-ə-ˌbü\ African STORK *(Leptoptilos crumeniferus)*. At 5 ft (1.5 m) tall, with a wingspread of 8.5 ft (2.6 m), the marabou is the largest of all storks. Mainly gray and white, it has a naked pinkish head and neck; a reddish, inflatable throat pouch; and a straight, heavy bill. Marabous eat carrion, often feeding with VULTURES, which they dominate.

Maracaibo \ˌmä-rä-'kī-bō\ City (pop., 2000 est.: 1,764,038), northwestern Venezuela, situated on the channel connecting Lake MARACAIBO with the Gulf of Venezuela. It is Venezuela's second-largest city. Founded in 1571 as Nueva Zamora, it became a center for inland trade after Gibraltar, at the head of the lake, was destroyed in 1669. It changed hands several times during Venezuela's struggle for independence from Spain. Within a decade of the discovery of oil in 1917, it became the oil metropolis of Venezuela and South America.

Maracaibo, Lake Inlet of the CARIBBEAN SEA, northwestern Venezuela. The largest natural lake in South America, it occupies an area of 5,130 sq mi (13,280 sq km), extending southward for 130 mi (210 km) from the Gulf of Venezuela and reaching a width of 75 mi (121 km). Many rivers flow into the lake, notably the CATATUMBO RIVER. It is in one of the world's richest oil-producing regions; it supplies about two-thirds of Venezuela's total petroleum output. Its oil fields are located along the eastern shore, extending 20 mi (32 km) into the lake.

Maradona, Diego Armando (born 1960) Argentine football (soccer) player. A midfielder renowned for his ability to create scoring chances for himself and others, he led club teams to championships in Argentina, Italy, and Spain. He starred for the Argentine national team that won the 1986 World Cup. His performance included two memorable goals against England, one scored with his hand (the referee mistakenly thought the ball struck his head) and now remembered as the "Hand of God," and another that saw him dribble through a pack of defenders. He was twice suspended for use of banned substances. An Internet poll conducted by the Fédération Internationale de Football Association named Maradona the top player of the 20th century.

Marajó \ˌmȧ-rȧ-'zhō\ Island in the AMAZON RIVER delta, Brazil. The world's largest fluvial island, it is 183 mi (295 km) long and 124 mi (200 km) wide, with an area of 15,500 sq mi (40,100 sq km). The main flow of the Amazon passes north of Marajó, but numerous narrow channels direct part of its water into the PARÁ RIVER, an estuary that separates the island from the mainland to the south. Archaeological remains in the eastern savanna are similar to those of pre-Columbian Andean cultures.

Marañón River \ˌmä-rä-'nyōn\ River, central Peru. Rising in the ANDES, it is part of the headwaters of the AMAZON RIVER. It flows northwest at elevations of 12,000 ft (3,650 m) and descends through jungles in unnavigable rapids and falls; emerging from the most spectacular of these rapids, the Pongo de Manseriche, it is only 575 ft (175 m) above sea level. For the rest of its 879-mi (1,415-km) course, it meanders eastward, receiving the HUALLAGA RIVER and then joining the UCAYALI RIVER to form the Amazon.

Marat \mȧ-'rȧ\, **Jean-Paul** (1743–1793) French politician and a leader of the radical MONTAGNARD faction in the FRENCH REVOLUTION. He was a well-known doctor in London in the 1770s. Returning to France in 1777, he was appointed physician at the court of LOUIS XVI's brother, the comte d'Artois (later CHARLES X). Marat wrote scientific publications as well as political pamphlets. From 1789, as editor of the newspaper *L'Ami du Peuple*, he became an influential voice for radical measures against the aristocrats. He criticized moderate revolutionary leaders and warned against the ÉMIGRÉ NOBILITY, then advocated the execution of counterrevolutionaries. One of the most influential members of the NATIONAL CONVENTION (1792), he was actively supported by Parisians in street demonstrations. In April 1793 the GIRONDINS brought him before a Revolutionary tribunal, but he was acquitted. In July a young Girondin supporter, CHARLOTTE CORDAY, gained admittance to his room and stabbed him to death in his bath, making him a martyr to the people's cause.

Marat, detail of a portrait by J. Boze, 1793; in the Museum of the History of Paris.

GIRAUDON—ART RESOURCE

Maratha confederacy \mä-rə-'tä\ Maratha alliance formed in the 18th century in western India after SIVAJI's Maratha kingdom collapsed under Mughal pressure. Under Sivaji's grandson, power fell to peshwas (chief ministers) from leading Maratha families, who ruled effectively in the early 18th century but quarreled as the century waned. The confederacy fell to the British in 1818.

Maratha Wars (1775–82, 1803–5, 1817–18) Three conflicts between the British and the MARATHA CONFEDERACY. At the time, the confederacy controlled large portions of the DECCAN and the western coast of the Indian peninsula. The British lost the first conflict, in which they supported one contender's bid for the office of peshwa (chief minister). They won the second, defeating members of the confederacy who challenged their restoration of an ousted peshwa. The third war was caused by the British invasion of Maratha territory in pursuit of robber bands. When Maratha forces rose against the British, they were defeated, Maratha territory was annexed, and British supremacy in India became complete.

marathon Long-distance footrace run on an open course of 26 miles 385 yards (42.2 km). First held at the revived Olympic Games in 1896, it commemorates the legendary feat of a Greek soldier who is said to have run from Marathon to Athens in 490 BC, a distance of about 25 mi (40 km), to report the Greek victory at the Battle of MARATHON, after which he dropped dead. Marathons today are usually open events for both men and women, often run by thousands of participants, including the venerable Boston Marathon (established 1897) and the New York Marathon. Women's marathons became an Olympic event in 1984.

Marathon, Battle of (490 BC) Decisive battle on the plain of Marathon outside Athens in the PERSIAN WARS. DARIUS I led his enormous army against a much smaller Athenian force led by MILTIADES. The Athenians attacked with great speed, while the Persian cavalry was absent, devastating the Persian line and resulting in Darius' departure from Greece. The victory was overwhelming: 6,400 Persians but only 192 Athenians died. It is said that a messenger ran about 25 miles (40 km) back to Athens, where he announced the victory before dying of exhaustion (see MARATHON). In another version, an Athenian runner was sent to Sparta before the battle to ask for help, running 150 mi (240 km) in two days; Sparta refused, so Athens fought with help only from PLATAEA.

Maravi confederacy \'mä-rə-vē\ Centralized system of government established in southern Africa c. 1480. It was created by members of related ethnolinguistic groups who had migrated from the north into what is now central and southern MALAWI. Its seat was southwest of Lake MALAWI, and at its peak in the 17th century it ruled an area stretching from the Zambezi River to the Mozambique coast. Its leaders traded with the Portuguese and Arabs in ivory, slaves, and iron. By 1720 it split into several autonomous factions.

marble Granular LIMESTONE or DOLOMITE that has recrystallized under the influence of heat, pressure, and aqueous solutions. The main mineral in marble is CALCITE. Commercially, "marble" includes all decorative calcium-rich rocks that can be polished, as well as some SERPENTINES. Marbles are used principally for buildings and monuments, interior decoration, statuary, tabletops, and novelties. Color and appearance are their most important qualities. Statuary marble, the most valuable variety, must be pure white and of uniform grain size.

Marblehead Town (pop., 2000: 20,377), northeastern Massachusetts. Its harbor is sheltered by Marblehead Neck, a promontory about 1.5 mi (2.5 km) long. Settled in 1629 as a part of Salem, it was incorporated as a town in 1649 and developed as a fishing and shipbuilding center. The port declined after the WAR OF 1812. It is now a resort center.

Marbury v. Madison First U.S. Supreme Court decision to declare an act of Congress unconstitutional (1803), thus establishing the doctrine of JUDICIAL REVIEW. The case, involving a man appointed justice of the peace by an outgoing administration whose appointment was not honored by the incoming administration, hinged on authority granted by the Judiciary Act of 1789. Chief Justice JOHN MARSHALL, writing for the Court, held that a section of the act contravened the Constitution and was thus invalid, declaring that the Constitution must always take precedence in any conflict between it and a law passed by Congress.

Marc, Franz (1880–1916) German painter. His early works were academic, but exposure to IMPRESSIONISM and JUGENDSTIL lightened his style, and in 1911, with VASSILY KANDINSKY and other abstract painters, he became a founding member of the BLAUE REITER group. He believed that spiritual essence is best revealed through abstraction, and was passionately interested in the art of primitive peoples, children, and the mentally ill. His own work consisted primarily of animal studies, since he believed nonhuman forms of life to be the most expressive manifestation of the vital force of nature. He was killed in action in World War I.

marcasite \'mär-kə-ˌsīt\ Iron SULFIDE MINERAL that forms pale bronze-yellow crystals; the name cockscomb marcasite refers to the shape of a common form of its crystals. Marcasite has the same chemical formula as PYRITE (FeS_2) but a different internal (atomic) structure. It is less stable than pyrite, being easily decomposed, and is much less common.

Marceau \mȧr-'sō\, **Marcel** (born 1923) French MIME. After serving in World War II, he studied with the pantomimist Étienne Decroux and had his first success in the role of Arlequin in *Baptiste*. He formed a mime troupe (1948–64) and earned worldwide acclaim in the 1950s with his production of the "mimodrama" of NIKOLAY GOGOL's *Overcoat.* In 1978 he founded a school of mimodrama in Paris. He is noted for his eloquent, deceptively simple portrayals, including his celebrated white-faced character Bip, reminiscent of Pierrot and of CHARLIE CHAPLIN's tramp.

Marcel, Gabriel (-Honoré) (1889–1973) French philosopher, dramatist, and critic. His philosophical works explore aspects of human existence (e.g., trust, fidelity, hope, and despair) which had traditionally been dismissed as not amenable to philosophical consideration. To do so, he undertakes a phenomenological description of the mind, actions, and attitudes of the faithful, hopeful, or trusting person. His use of PHENOMENOLOGY was independent of the work of EDMUND HUSSERL. Marcel is considered the first French proponent of EXISTENTIALISM.

Gabriel Marcel, 1951.
H. ROGER-VIOLLET

Marcellus, Marcus Claudius (268?–208 BC) Roman general. Elected CONSUL in 222, he fought in Gaul and won the *spolia opima* ("spoils of honor"), awarded for killing an enemy chief in single combat, for the third and last time in Roman history. He was consul again in 215 and 214. Serving in Sicily (214–211) in the Second PUNIC WAR, he took Syracuse after a two-year siege; his troops sacked the city and carried its art treasures to Rome. He served again as consul in 210 and 208. While fighting HANNIBAL near Venusia, he was caught in an ambush and killed.

Marcellus \mär-'se-ləs\, **Marcus Claudius** (42–23 BC) Roman leader. Son of AUGUSTUS' sister Octavia, he was Augustus' presumed heir. He married Augustus' daughter JULIA in 25 BC and later that year served with Augustus in Spain. Great hopes had rested with him, and his unexpected death led to problems of succession.

march Musical form with an even meter with strongly accented beats to facilitate military marching. Development of the European march may have been stimulated by the Ottoman invasions of the 14th–16th century. Marches were not notated until the late 16th century; until then, time was generally kept by percussion alone, often with improvised fife embellishment. With the extensive development of BRASS INSTRUMENTS especially in the 19th century, marches became widely popular and were often elaborately orchestrated. Such composers as W.A. MOZART, LUDWIG VAN BEETHOVEN, JOHANN, JR. STRAUSS, and G. MAHLER wrote marches, often incorporating them into their operas, sonatas, or symphonies. The later popularity of J.P. SOUSA's band marches was unmatched.

March, Frederic *orig.* **Frederick McIntyre Bickel** (1897–1975) U.S. actor. Born in Racine, Wis., he made his screen debut in *The Dummy* (1929). He subsequently appeared in over 65 films, including *The Royal Family of Broadway* (1931), *Dr. Jekyll and Mr. Hyde* (1932, Academy Award), *A Star Is Born* (1937), *The Best Years of Our Lives* (1946, Academy Award), *Death of a Salesman* (1951), and *Inherit the Wind* (1960). He starred on the stage, often with his wife, Florence Eldridge, in such plays as *The Skin of Our Teeth* (1942), *The Autumn Garden* (1951), and *Long Day's Journey into Night* (1956, Tony award).

Marchand \mȧr-'shäⁿ\, **Jean** (1918–1988) Canadian politician. Born in Champlain, Quebec, he served as president of the Confederation of National Trade Unions (1961–65). He was elected to the Canadian House of Commons (1965) and served in the cabinet of LESTER PEARSON until 1968, then continued in various cabinet posts under PIERRE TRUDEAU (1968–76). Elected to the Canadian Senate in 1976, he was speaker 1980–83.

Marche \'märsh\ Historical region, central France. Once part of Limousin, it was made a separate frontier countship (march) in the 10th century. During 12th–13th century it was divided into western and eastern halves. It was held by the Bourbons 1342–1435 and by the Armagnacs 1435–77. Confiscated by FRANCIS I in 1527, it was granted to the widows of French kings 1574–1643. It was a province of France until the FRENCH REVOLUTION.

Marche \'mär-kā\ Autonomous region (pop., 2000 est.: 1,460,989), central Italy. Situated between the Adriatic Sea and the region of UMBRIA, it is crossed by the APENNINES; its only level land is along its river valleys and on the Adriatic shore near ANCONA, its capital. Originally inhabited by Gauls and Picenes, it came under Roman rule by AD 292. During the early Middle Ages the southern part was ruled by the Lombards and the northern part by the Byzantines. Conflicts arose in 12th–13th century with powerful feudal families and the attempt of the popes to reestablish their temporal authority; this culminated in 1631, when the duchy of Urbino was incorporated into the PAPAL STATES. Marche joined the kingdom of Italy in 1860. An agricultural area, it has some industrial development.

Marciano \ˌmär-shē-'ä-nō\, **Rocky** *orig.* **Rocco Francis Marchegiano** (1923–1969) U.S. world heavyweight boxing champion. Born in Brockton, Mass., he began boxing in the army in World War II. An unscientific but hard-punching and exceptionally durable fighter, he won the championship title in 1952 by defeating Jersey Joe Walcott and relinquished it on retiring in 1956. He was undefeated in 49 professional fights, scoring 43 knockouts.

Marco Polo See Marco POLO

Marco Polo Bridge Incident Conflict in 1937 between Chinese and Japanese troops near the Marco Polo Bridge outside Beijing. The inci-

L
M
N

dent expanded into a general war between Japan and China, with Japan concerned to protect its interests in Manchuria and China intent on ending Japanese territorial aggression. See also MANCHUGUO.

Marconi, Guglielmo (1874–1937) Italian physicist and inventor. He began experimenting with radio waves in 1894. In 1896 he went to England, where he developed a successful system of radio telegraphy. His work on the development of shortwave wireless communication constitutes the basis of nearly all modern radio broadcasting. His improved aerials greatly extended the range of radio signaling. In 1899 he established communication across the English Channel. In 1900 he established the American Marconi Co. In 1901 he sent signals across the Atlantic for the first time. He acquired numerous patents, though probably his most famous one, No. 7777, for an apparatus that enabled several stations to operate on different wavelengths without interference, was later overturned. In his later years he worked on developing shortwave wireless communication. Marconi shared the 1909 Nobel Prize for Physics with K. Ferdinand Braun (1850–1918). He was made a marquis and nominated to the Italian senate (1929), and he was elected president of the Royal Italian Academy (1930).

Marconi, c. 1908.
BY COURTESY OF THE LIBRARY OF CONGRESS, WASHINGTON, D.C.

Marcos, Ferdinand (Edralin) (1917–1989) Philippine head of state (1966–86). Son of a politician, he practiced as a trial lawyer before serving under MANUEL ROXAS, first president of the independent Philippines. He was himself elected president in 1966. In his first term he made progress in agriculture, industry, and education, but in 1972 he imposed martial law, and his later years in power were noted for rampant government corruption, economic stagnation, political repression, and the steady growth of a communist insurgency. Following public outcry over the assassination of the opposition leader Benigno Aquino (1932–1983) and Marcos's apparently fraudulent electoral victory over Aquino's widow, CORAZON AQUINO, Marcos was forced into exile in Hawaii, where he and his wife, Imelda, were indicted on racketeering charges relating to embezzlement of billions of dollars from the Philippine economy. After his death, she returned to the Philippines, where she was tried and sentenced to 18 years in prison.

Marcus, Rudolph A. (born 1923) Canadian-U.S. chemist. Born in Montreal and educated at McGill Univ., he worked at the Polytechnic Institute of Brooklyn (from 1951), the University of Illinois (from 1964), and Caltech (from 1978). He studied electron transfer in redox reactions in the 1950s and '60s, finding that subtle changes in the molecular structures of the reactants and the solvent molecules around them influence the ability of electrons to move between the molecules. He also discovered the parabolic relationship between the driving force of an electron-transfer reaction and the reaction's rate. His work, which has shed light on fundamental phenomena such as photosynthesis, cell metabolism, and simple corrosion, won him a 1992 Nobel Prize.

Marcus Aurelius, bas-relief depicting his triumphal entry into Rome in a *quadriga;* in the Palazzo dei Conservatori, Rome.
ALINARI–ART RESOURCE

Marcus Aurelius \ˌmär-kəs-ȯ-ˈrēl-yəs\ *in full* **Caesar Marcus Aurelius Antoninus Augustus** *orig.* **Marcus Annius Verus** (AD 121–180) Roman emperor (161–80). He was born into a wealthy and prominent family, and HADRIAN arranged that he and Lucius Verus be adopted by the designated future emperor ANTONINUS PIUS, who dutifully groomed Marcus as his heir. On his accession, Marcus nevertheless shared power with his adoptive brother as coemperor, though he himself remained the more dominant. His reign was marked by numerous military crises, all the major frontiers being threatened by invasion. Struggles against the Parthians (162–66) were successful, but returning troops brought a devastating plague to Rome. With a concurrent German invasion, Roman morale declined; the Germans were repulsed, but Verus died during the campaign (169). Marcus made his son COMMODUS coemperor in 177. Though a man of gentle character and wide learning, Marcus opposed Christianity and supported persecution of its adherents. His *Meditations* on STOICISM, considered one of the great books of all times, gives a full picture of his religious and moral values. His reign is often thought to mark the Golden Age of Rome.

Marcuse \mär-ˈkü-zə\, **Herbert** (1898–1979) German-U.S. political philosopher. A member of the FRANKFURT SCHOOL, he fled Germany in 1933. After working in U.S. intelligence in World War II, he taught at several universities, principally UC–San Diego (1965–76). His major writings include *Eros and Civilization* (1955), *One-Dimensional Man* (1964), and *Counterrevolution and Revolt* (1972). He believed that Western society was unfree and repressive, that its technology had bought the complacency of the masses with material goods, and that it had kept them intellectually and spiritually captive. He was also hostile to the Soviet system. His Marxist philosophy and Freudian analyses of 20th-century Western society were popular among student leftists, especially after the 1968 rebellions at Columbia University and the Sorbonne.

Marcy, William L(earned) (1786–1857) U.S. politician. Born in Southbridge, Mass., he became a leading member of the New York state Democratic group known as the Albany Regency and was the state's comptroller (1823–29) and a justice of the supreme court (1829–31). In the U.S. Senate (1831–33), he championed the SPOILS system, remarking "To the victor belong the spoils of the enemy." He served as governor 1833–39, as U.S. secretary of war 1845–49, and as secretary of state 1853–57.

Mardi Gras \ˈmär-dē-ˌgrä\ (French: "Fat Tuesday") CARNIVAL celebrated on or culminating on Shrove Tuesday, the day before Ash Wednesday, the start of LENT. Traditionally, households consumed all the remaining foods that would be forbidden during Lent (e.g., eggs) on that day. It is a one-day event in France, but in the U.S. it lasts several days in New Orleans, where it is marked by parades, street celebrations, and extravagant costumes.

Marduk \ˈmär-ˌdük\ *or* **Bel** In Mesopotamian religion, the chief god of the city of BABYLON and the national god of BABYLONIA. He began as a god of thunderstorms, and according to legend he became lord of all the gods after conquering the monster of primeval chaos, TIAMAT. Marduk's star was the planet Jupiter, and his sacred animals were horses, dogs, and a dragon with a forked tongue, representations of which adorned Babylon's walls.

mare \ˈmär-ā\ Any flat, low, dark plain on the MOON. Maria are huge lava flows marked by ridges, depressions (graben), and faults; though mare means "sea" in Latin, they lack water. The best known is probably Mare Tranquillitatis ("Sea of Tranquility"), the site of the APOLLO 11 moon landing. All 14 maria are on the side of the moon that always faces earth; they are its largest surface features and can be seen from earth with the unaided eye. The features of the "man in the moon" are maria.

Mare, Walter De la See Walter DE LA MARE

Marengo \mə-ˈreŋ-gō\, **Battle of** (June 14, 1800) Narrow victory for NAPOLEON against Austria in the NAPOLEONIC WARS, fought on the Marengo Plain in northern Italy. The initial French force was overpowered, but when the Austrian commander gave up command to a subordinate in the belief that victory was secured, French reinforcements forced the Austrians into retreat. The victory resulted in the French occupation of Lombardy and secured Napoleon's military and civilian authority in Paris.

Marenzio \mä-ˈrents-yō\, **Luca** (1553?–1599) Italian composer. Little is known of his early life or training. He moved to Rome in the mid-1570s to work for Cardinal Luigi d'Este, whose patronage enabled the publication in the 1580s of the first 10 of his 25 books of MADRIGALS, the works for which he is best known and whose style became influential in Italy and England. His later madrigals, more serious in tone, use dissonance and chromaticism to reflect their texts, and are sometimes linked into cycles. He also composed some 75 sacred motets.

Marfan's syndrome Rare hereditary CONNECTIVE-TISSUE disorder. Patients are tall, with long, thin limbs and spiderlike fingers (arachnodactyly). The lens of the eye is dislocated, and many patients have GLAUCOMA or DETACHED retina. Heart-muscle abnormalities and various malfunctions and malformations occur; rupture of the AORTA is the commonest cause of death. Severity varies; affected individuals may die young or live essentially normal lives. The underlying abnormality cannot be cured, but some of the defects can be surgically corrected.

Margaret of Angoulême \ä^{n}-gü-'lem\ *or* **Margaret of Navarre** *French* **Marguerite d'Angoulême** (1492–1549) Queen consort of Henry II of Navarre and an outstanding figure of the French Renaissance. She was the daughter of the comte d'Angoulême, and when her brother FRANCIS I acceded to the crown in 1515 she became highly influential in his court. After her first husband died, she married Henry in 1525. She was noted as a patron of humanists and reformers and of such writers as FRANCOIS RABELAIS. She was a writer and poet herself; her most important work was the *Heptaméron*, 72 tales modeled on BOCCACCIO's *Decameron*, that was published in 1558–59.

Margaret of Antioch, St. *or* **St. Marina** (fl. 3rd or 4th century AD) Early Christian martyr. Tradition held that she was a virgin of Antioch in Syria during the reign of DIOCLETIAN. When she refused to marry the Roman prefect of Antioch, she was tortured and beheaded. Her designation as patron saint of expectant mothers (especially those in difficult labor) was based on the story that during her trials she was swallowed by Satan in the form of a dragon and later disgorged unharmed. Widely venerated in the Middle Ages, she is now thought to have been fictitious.

Margaret of Austria (1480–1530) Habsburg ruler who was regent of the Netherlands (1507–15, 1519–30) for her nephew, the future emperor CHARLES V. In 1497 she married the infante John, heir to the Spanish kingdoms, who died a few months later. In 1501 she married Philibert II, duke of Savoy, who died in 1504. Appointed regent by her father, the emperor MAXIMILIAN I, she pursued a pro-English foreign policy. In the 1520s she extended the Habsburg dominion in the northeastern Netherlands and negotiated the Treaty of CAMBRAI (1529), called the "Ladies' Peace," with Louise of Savoy (1494–1547), regent for FRANCIS I.

Margaret of Austria, detail of a painting attributed to Bernard van Orley, c. 1505; in Windsor Castle, Berkshire.

Margaret of Parma (1522–1586) Duchess of Parma, Habsburg regent, and governor-general of the Netherlands (1559–67). The illegitimate daughter of Emperor CHARLES V, she was married first (1536) to ALESSANDRO DE'MEDICI, who was murdered in 1537, and then (1538) to Ottavio Farnese, duke of Parma. Appointed to govern the Netherlands by her half brother, PHILIP II of Spain, Margaret tried to appease the nobility with more moderate treatment of Protestants, but she brought in an army in 1567 after Calvinist extremists attacked Catholic churches. Philip then sent the duke of ALBA, who assembled a Spanish army and enforced stern measures against dissident Protestants, precipitating open revolt. Margaret resigned when Alba assumed power.

Margaret of Scotland, St. (1045?–1093) Patron saint of Scotland. Sister of EDGAR THE AETHELING, she married MALCOLM III CANMORE, and three of their sons succeeded to Scotland's throne. She founded abbeys, worked for justice, improved conditions for the poor, and persuaded Malcolm to initiate a series of ecclesiastical reforms that transformed Scotland's religious and cultural life.

Margaret of Valois \väl-'wä\ *or* **Margaret of France** *French* **Marguerite** *known as* **Queen Margot** \mår-'gō\ (1553–1615) Queen consort of Navarre who played a secondary part in the Wars of RELIGION (1562–98). The daughter of HENRY II of France, her relations with her brothers CHARLES IX and the future HENRY III were strained, and she had an early affair with Henri, duc de GUISE, leader of the extremist Catholic party. She was married in 1572 to the Protestant king of Navarre, the future HENRY IV of France, to seal the peace between Catholics and Protestants, but days later the SAINT BARTHOLOMEW'S DAY MASSACRE began. Aware of her involvement in conspiracies, Henry III banished her to the castle at Usson in 1586. She granted her husband an annulment in 1600 and lived out her life in Paris. She was known for her beauty, learning, and licentious life; her *Mémoires* provide a vivid picture of contemporary France.

Margaret Tudor (1489–1541) Queen consort of King JAMES IV of Scotland (1503–13). The daughter of HENRY VII of England, she was married to James to improve relations between England and Scotland. After her husband's death (1513), she became regent for her son, James V (1512–1542). When she married the pro-English earl of Angus (1514), she was forced to give up the regency, but she played a key role in the conflict between the pro-French and pro-English factions in Scotland, shifting her allegiances to suit her financial interests. She obtained an annulment from Angus (1527) to marry Henry Stewart, Baron Methven, who became James's chief adviser.

margarine Food made from one or more vegetable or animal fats or oils mixed with milk and other ingredients. It is used in cooking and as a spread as a substitute for BUTTER. It was developed by the French chemist H. Mège-Mouriès in the late 1860s. The fats used have varied widely; polyunsaturated oils such as corn and sunflower oil, considered more healthful than saturated fats, are common today.

Margherita Peak \,mär-ge-'rē-tə\ Highest summit of the Ruwenzori Range in East Africa. It is situated on the border between Uganda and the Democratic Republic of the Congo (Zaire). The higher of the two peaks on Mount Stanley, the central mountain of the Ruwenzori, it rises to 16,795 ft (5,119 m) between Lake ALBERT and Lake EDWARD. First climbed in 1906 by an Italian expedition, it was named for Queen Margherita of Italy. It is the third-highest mountain in Africa, after KILIMANJARO and Mount KENYA.

margin In finance, the amount by which the value of collateral pledged as security for a loan exceeds the amount of the loan. This excess provides the lender a "margin" of safety over and above the collateral offered and thus makes extending a loan a more attractive proposition. The size of the margin varies with the type of collateral, the stability of its market price, and the credit standing of the borrower. The term *margin* is used especially with reference to transactions in SECURITIES and commodity FUTURES. When securities are purchased "on margin," the buyer supplies a percentage of the purchase price in cash and borrows the remainder from his broker, pledging the security as collateral. The U.S. Federal Reserve Board (see FEDERAL RESERVE SYSTEM) sets minimum margin requirements on loans made for the purpose of buying securities, so as to prevent excessive use of credit for speculation in STOCKS, as happened before the stock-market crash of 1929. Dealings on margin are not allowed on British stock exchanges.

marginal-cost pricing In economics, the practice of setting a product's price equal to the additional (marginal) cost of producing one more unit of output. The producer charges an amount equal to the cost of the additional economic resources. The policy is used to maintain a low selling price or to keep a business operating during a period of poor sales. Because fixed costs such as rent and building maintenance must be paid whether a company produces or not, a firm experiencing temporary difficulties may decide to remain in production and sell the product at marginal cost, since its losses will be no greater than if it ceased production.

marginal productivity theory In economics, the theory that firms will pay a productive agent only what he adds to the financial success of the firm. Developed by writers such as John Bates Clark and Philip Henry Wicksteed at the end of the 19th century, marginal productivity theory holds that it is unprofitable to buy, for example, a man-hour of labor if it adds less to its buyer's income than it costs. The amount in excess of COSTS that a productive input yields is the value of its marginal product; every type of input should be paid the value of its marginal product.

marginal utility In economics, the additional satisfaction or benefit (utility) that a consumer derives from buying an additional unit of a commodity or service. The law of diminishing utility implies that utility or benefit is inversely related to the number of units already owned. For example, the marginal utility of one slice of bread offered to a family that has five slices will be great, since the family will be less hungry and the difference between five and six is proportionally significant. An extra slice offered to a family that has 30 slices will have less marginal utility, since the difference between 30 and 31 is proportionally smaller and the family's appetite may be satisfied by what it already has. The concept grew out of attempts by 19th-century economists to explain the fundamental economic reality of PRICE.

marguerite \ˌmär-gə-ˈrēt\ Any of several genera of golden daisylike flowers in the COMPOSITE FAMILY. Yellow or white ray flowers and yellow disk flowers are borne in the compact flower heads. Marguerites are cultivated as garden ornamentals, especially golden marguerite, also called yellow chamomile *(Anthemis tinctoria)*. See also CHAMOMILE, DAISY.

Maria Legio \mə-ˈrē-ə-ˈlā-gē-ˌō\ *or* **Legio Maria** *or* **Legion of Mary Church** Independent African church influenced by ROMAN CATHOLICISM. It originated in Kenya in 1963 when two Catholics of the LUO group, Simeon Ondeto and Gaundencia Aoko, claimed to have undergone prophetic experiences. The church, which offers healing by prayer and exorcism of evil spirits, adds features of PENTECOSTALISM to Catholic worship and hierarchy. In its first year it gained about 90,000 adherents, but membership had dropped to 50,000 by the end of the decade. It rejects Western and traditional medicines, alcohol, tobacco, and dancing but accepts polygamy and is strongly nationalistic.

Maria Theresa \tə-ˈrā-sə\ *German* **Maria Theresia** (1717–1780) Archduchess of Austria and queen of Hungary and Bohemia (1740–80). She was the eldest daughter of Emperor CHARLES VI, who promulgated the PRAGMATIC SANCTION to allow her to succeed to the Habsburg domains. Opposition to her succession led in 1740 to the War of the AUSTRIAN SUCCESSION. After Emperor CHARLES VII died (1745), she obtained the imperial crown for her husband, who became FRANCIS I. She helped initiate financial and educational reforms, promoted commerce and the development of agriculture and reorganized the army, all of which strengthened Austria's resources. Continued conflict with Prussia led to the SEVEN YEARS' WAR and later to the War of the BAVARIAN SUCCESSION. After her husband's death (1765), her son became emperor as JOSEPH II. She criticized many of his actions but agreed to the Partition of POLAND (1772). A key figure in the power politics of 18th-century Europe, Maria Theresa brought unity to the Habsburg monarchy and was considered one of its most capable rulers. Her 16 children also included MARIE-ANTOINETTE and LEOPOLD II.

mariachi \ˌmär-ē-ˈä-chē\ Traditional Mexican street ensemble. In the 19th century, mariachis consisted solely of stringed instruments, including violin, guitar, guitarrón, vihuela, mandolin, and double bass; since the 1920s they have generally included trumpets and often other wind instruments as well. The mariachi repertoire includes songs and lively dance music.

Mariam, Mengistu Haile See MENGISTU HAILE MARIAM

Mariana Islands \ˌmar-ē-ˈa-nə\ *formerly* **Ladrone Islands** \lə-ˈdrōn\ Island group, western Pacific Ocean. Located east of the Philippines, it comprises 15 islands and is divided politically into GUAM and the NORTHERN MARIANA ISLANDS. The population is descended from the pre-Spanish Chamorro people and Spanish, Mexican, German, Philippine, and Japanese settlers. Spanish cultural traditions are strong. After FERDINAND MAGELLAN became the first European to discover them in 1521, they were visited frequently but were not colonized until 1668, at which time Jesuit missionaries changed their name to honor Mariana of Austria, regent of Spain.

Mariana Trench Submarine trench in the floor of the western Pacific Ocean. It is the deepest known depression on the surface of the earth, with a maximum depth of 36,198 ft (11,033 m). The trench extends from southeast of GUAM to northwest of the MARIANA ISLANDS, a distance of over 1,580 mi (2,550 km), and has a mean width of 43 mi (69 km).

Mariátegui \ˌmä-rē-ˈä-tā-gē\, **José Carlos** (1895–1930) Peruvian political leader and essayist. In 1919 he was sent to study in Italy, where he met leading socialists of the day, including MAXIM GORKY. At first a strong supporter of APRA, he split with that movement to form the Peruvian Communist Party in 1928. While emphasizing the economic aspects of Marxism in his writings, he recognized the value of religion and myth in his treatment of the Indians and advocated a greater social and political role for them. His influence is seen in the Maoist SHINING PATH revolutionary movement.

Marib \ˈmar-ib\ Ancient city ruins, northern central YEMEN. The ancient fortified city of Marib was the center of the pre-Islamic state of Saba (950–115 BC). It was located on one of the caravan routes between the Mediterranean world and the Arabian Peninsula, and it prospered through its trading monopoly on frankincense and myrrh. The ancient Marib Dam was built c. 7th cent BC to regulate the waters of the Wadi Sadd; about 1,800 ft (550 m) long, it irrigated more than 4,000 acres (1,600 hectares) and supported a densely settled agricultural region. The dam was destroyed in the 6th century AD.

mariculture See AQUACULTURE

Marie-Antoinette (-Josèphe-Jeanne d'Autriche-Lorraine) (1755–1793) Queen consort of LOUIS XVI of France. The daughter of Emperor FRANCIS I and MARIA THERESA, she was married in 1770 to the French dauphin. After he became king (1774), she was criticized for her extravagance and frivolous circle of court favorites. She was unjustly implicated in the Affair of the DIAMOND NECKLACE (1786), which discredited the monarchy. After the FRENCH REVOLUTION began, she influenced Louis to resist attempts by the NATIONAL ASSEMBLY to restrict the royal prerogative. She became the target of agitators, who attributed to her the celebrated remark, after being told the people had no bread, "Let them eat cake!" She tried to save the crown by negotiating secretly with monarchist factions and with her brother, Emperor LEOPOLD II. News of her intrigues further enraged the French and led to the overthrow of the monarchy (1792). After a year in prison, she was tried and guillotined in 1793.

Marie-Antoinette, detail of a portrait by Élisabeth Vigée-Lebrun; in the Château de Versailles.

CLICHE MUSEES NATIONAUX

Marie de France (fl. late 12th century) French poet, the earliest known woman poet of France. She wrote verse narratives on romantic and magical themes and may have inspired the musical lais of the later TROUBADOURS. She probably wrote in England and may have based her fables on an English source; her verses were dedicated to a "noble" king, either HENRY II of England or his son. She also wrote fables called *Ysopets*.

Marie de Médicis \də-mā-dē-ˈsēs\ *Italian* **Maria de' Medici** (1573–1642) Queen consort of HENRY IV of France. The daughter of Francesco de' Medici, of the noted MEDICI FAMILY, she was married in 1600 to Henry as his second wife. On his assassination in 1610, she became regent for their son, LOUIS XIII. Guided by the unscrupulous marquis d'Ancre, she squandered state revenues and bought the loyalty of rebellious nobles. After Ancre was assassinated, Louis assumed the throne (1617) and exiled Marie to Blois. She tried to raise a revolt and won favorable peace terms through her adviser, the future Cardinal de RICHELIEU. Restored to the king's council (1622), she obtained a cardinal's hat for Richelieu and persuaded Louis to make him chief minister. Richelieu gradually withdrew from Marie's influence and by 1628 was opposing her policies. She attempted to have him dismissed, but Louis rejected her plot and banished Marie from court. In 1631 she fled to Brussels, where she later died in poverty.

Marie-Louise *German* **Maria-Luise** (1791–1847) Austrian archduchess and second wife of NAPOLEON. The eldest daughter of Emperor FRAN-

CIS II, she was married to Napoleon (1810) and gave birth to his long-desired heir, the future NAPOLEON II, in 1811. When Napoleon abdicated (1814), Marie-Louise returned to Vienna with her son. She ignored Napoleon's entreaties to join him in exile and again after his return to France (1815). Made duchess of Parma, Piacenza, and Guastalla (1816), she ruled in accordance with Austrian prescriptions. After Napoleon's death (1821), she contracted morganatic marriages with Adam Adalbert, count von Neipperg, who died in 1829, and in 1834 with Charles René, count de Bombelles.

Marie-Louise, detail of a portrait by Joseph Franque; in the Château de Versailles.
ALINARI—ART RESOURCE

marigold Any of about 30 species of annual herbaceous plants that make up the genus *Tagetes* in the COMPOSITE FAMILY, native to southwestern North America. The name also refers to the pot marigold (CALENDULA) and unrelated plants of several families. Marigolds include popular garden ornamentals such as African marigold *(T. erecta)* and French marigold *(T. patula),* which have solitary or clustered red, orange, and yellow flowers and usually finely cut leaves. Because the strongly scented leaves discourage insect pests, marigolds are often planted among vegetable crops.

French marigold (*Tagetes patula*).
ROBERT BORNEMANN—PHOTO RESEARCHERS

Mariinsky Theater \mär-'yin-skē\ *formerly* **Kirov Theater** Russian imperial theater in St. Petersburg. The theater opened in 1860 and was named for Maria Aleksandrovna, wife of the reigning czar. Ballet was not presented there until 1880, and regularly only after 1889. The theater housed the ballet company whose dancers had been trained at the affiliated Imperial Ballet school. The theater's name was changed to the State Academic Theater (1917–35) and later to the Kirov (for SERGEY KIROV) State Academic Theater for Opera and Ballet (1935–91); it reverted to its original name in 1991. Its resident ballet company, the celebrated Kirov (or Mariinsky) Ballet, tours worldwide.

marijuana \,mar-ə-'wä-nə\ Indian HEMP plant (*Cannabis sativa*), or the crude drug made of its dried and crushed leaves or flowers. The active ingredient is tetrahydrocannabinol (THC). Also called pot, grass, and weed, the drug has long been used as a sedative or analgesic; it was in use in China by the 3rd millennium BC, and had reached Europe by AD 500. Today it is used worldwide, though it has been generally illegal at least since the International Opium Convention of 1925. Its psychological and physical effects, including mild euphoria and alterations in vision and judgment, vary with strength and amount consumed, the setting, and the user's experience. Chronic use is not physically habit-forming but may be mildly psychologically habit-forming. Marijuana has been shown to be medically therapeutic for patients suffering from glaucoma, AIDS, and the side effects of CHEMOTHERAPY. Supporters of legalization claim that it is a more benign drug than alcohol; opponents contend that it is addictive and leads to use of more serious drugs. A resin from the plant is the source of HASHISH.

marimba XYLOPHONE with resonators under each bar. The original African instrument uses tuned calabash resonators. In Mexico and Central America, where it was brought by African slaves, the wooden bars may be affixed to a frame supported by legs or hung at the player's waist. The orchestral marimba uses long metal tubes as resonators.

Marin \'mar-ən\, **John** (1870–1953) U.S. painter and printmaker. Born in Rutherford, N.J., he worked as an architectural draftsman before studying painting. After exposure to Cubism and German Expressionism, he developed a personal form of expressionism, consisting of semi-abstract images based on objective reality. While watercolor usually produces delicate, transparent effects, Marin's command of the medium allowed him to use it to render the monumental power of New York City (e.g., *Lower Manhattan,* 1922) and the relentless surge of the sea (e.g., *Maine Islands,* 1922).

"Maine Islands," watercolour by John Marin, 1922; in the Phillips Collection, Washington, D.C.
BY COURTESY OF THE PHILLIPS COLLECTION, WASHINGTON, D.C.

Marín, Luis Muñoz See Luis MUNOZ MARIN

Marina See ESPÍRITO SANTO

Marina, St. See St. MARGARET OF ANTIOCH

marine Member of a military force trained for service at sea and in land operations related to naval campaigns. They existed as far back as the 5th century BC, when the Greek fleets were manned by *epibatai,* or heavily armed sea soldiers. In the Middle Ages ordinary soldiers were often assigned to shipboard duty; not until the naval wars of the 17th century was the distinct role of marines rediscovered almost simultaneously by the British and the Dutch, who raised the first two modern marine corps, the Royal Marine (1664) and the Koninklijke Nederlandse Corps Mariniers (1665). See also U.S. MARINE CORPS.

marine biology Science that deals with the animals and plants of the sea and estuaries and with airborne and terrestrial organisms that depend directly on bodies of saltwater for food and other necessities. Marine biologists study the relations between ocean phenomena and the distribution and adaptations of organisms. Of particular interest are adaptations to the chemical and physical properties of seawater, the movements and currents of the ocean, the availability of light at various depths, and the composition of the sea floor. Other important areas of study are marine food chains, the distribution of economically important fish and crustaceans, and the effects of pollution. In the later 19th century, the emphasis was on collecting and cataloging marine organisms, for which special nets, dredges, and trawls were developed. In the 20th century, improved diving equipment, submersible craft, and underwater cameras and television have made direct observation possible.

marine geology *or* **geologic oceanography** Scientific discipline concerned with all geologic aspects of the CONTINENTAL SHELVES and slopes and the ocean basins. Marine geology originally focused on marine sedimentation and the interpretation of bottom samples. The advent of the concept of SEAFLOOR SPREADING, however, broadened its scope. Many investigations of the OCEANIC RIDGE system, the magnetism of rocks on the seafloor, geochemical analyses of deep brine pools, and seafloor spreading and CONTINENTAL DRIFT may be considered within the general realm of marine geology.

marine geophysics Subdiscipline of GEOPHYSICS that is concerned with ocean phenomena. The main techniques and areas of study include heat-flow data, seismic reflection and refraction techniques, geomagnetics, and gravity studies. The principal concepts in marine geophysics are SEAFLOOR SPREADING, CONTINENTAL DRIFT, and PLATE tectonics.

marine sediment Any deposit of insoluble material, primarily rock and soil particles, transported from land areas to the ocean by wind, ice, and rivers, as well as the remains of marine organisms, products of submarine volcanic activity, and chemical precipitates from seawater that accumulate on the seafloor.

Mariner \'mar-ə-nər\ Any of a series of 10 unmanned U.S. space probes sent near VENUS, MARS, and MERCURY. Mariners 2 (1962) and 5 (1967) passed Venus within 22,000 mi (35,000 km) and 2,500 mi (4,000 km), respectively, and made measurements of temperature and atmospheric density. Mariners 4 (1965), 6 and 7 (1969), 9 (1971–72), and 10 (1973–75) obtained striking photographs of the surface of Mars and analyzed its atmosphere and magnetic field. Mariner 10 is the only spacecraft ever to have visited Mercury (1974–75).

Marinetti \ˌmä-rē-'nāt-tē\, **Filippo Tommaso (Emilio)** (1876–1944) Italian-French writer, the ideological founder of FUTURISM. In early poetry such as *Destruction* (1904), he showed the vigor and anarchic experimentation with form that would characterize his later work. Futurism officially began with the 1909 publication of his manifesto in the Paris newspaper *Le Figaro*. His ideas were quickly adopted in Italy, and he later elaborated on his theory in a novel and several dramatic works. Arguing that FASCISM was Futurism's natural extension, he became an active fascist and lost most of his following in the 1920s.

Marini, Marino (1901–1980) Italian sculptor and painter. Working primarily in bronze, he concentrated on two major images: the earthbound woman and the horse and rider. His sensitivity to form and surface owes much to Etruscan and Roman works, but the inner tension of his bold, straining figures reflects an expressionist sensibility. His portrait busts, as of I. STRAVINSKY (1950), capture the spiritual substratum of his subjects. In the 1940s he turned to painting nearly abstract works.

Marinid dynasty \'mar-i-ˌnid\ BERBER dynasty that followed the ALMOHAD DYNASTY in North Africa in the 13th–15th century. The Marinids were a tribe of the Zanatah group, which was allied to the Umayyads in Córdoba. In 1248 Abu Yahya captured Fès and made it the Marinid capital. The capture of Marrakech (1269) made the Marinids masters of Morocco. They waged inconclusive war in Spain and Africa that gradually depleted their resources, reducing the realm to anarchy in the 15th century. Sadi sharifs captured Fès in 1554.

Marino, Dan *orig.* **Daniel Constantine Marino, Jr.** (born 1961) U.S. football quarterback. Born in Pittsburgh, he played football in high school and at the University of Pittsburgh. Chosen by the Miami Dolphins in the first round of the 1983 NFL draft, he set all-time career records for passes completed (4,453 in 7,452 attempts), yards passing (55,416), and touchdown passes (385), and in 21 other categories. In 1984 he became the first quarterback to pass for more than 5,000 yards in a single season (5,084) and the first to complete over 40 touchdown passes (48) in a season.

Marino, Giambattista (1569–1625) Italian poet, founder of the school of Marinism (later *secentismo*), which dominated 17th-century Italian poetry. Trained for the law, Marino chose not to practice and instead found immense success with poetry that he managed to get published despite censorship. His most important work, a labor of 20 years, is *Adonis* (1623), an enormous poem (45,000 lines) that relates, with many digressions, the love story of Venus and Adonis. His work, praised throughout Europe, far surpassed that of his imitators, who carried his complicated wordplay and elaborate conceits and metaphors to such extremes that Marinism became a pejorative term.

Mariology \ˌmar-ē-'ä-lə-jē\ Study of doctrines concerning MARY, the mother of JESUS, or the content of those doctrines. The New Testament contains little information about Mary, though the tradition that she remained a virgin despite giving birth to Jesus was accepted in the early church. Various feast days in her honor were established in both the Eastern and Western liturgical traditions, and she became an especially important figure in ROMAN CATHOLICISM. PIUS IX proclaimed the doctrine of the IMMACULATE CONCEPTION in 1854. Mary is seen as the spiritual mother and heavenly intercessor of every Catholic and as a partner with Jesus in the redemption of human beings. In 1950 PIUS XII proclaimed the doctrine that at her death Mary was bodily assumed into heaven.

Marion, Francis *known as* **the Swamp Fox** (1732?–1795) American Revolutionary commander. Born in Winyah, S.C., he fought the Cherokee (1759) and later served as a member of the provincial assembly (1775). In the AMERICAN REVOLUTION he commanded troops in South Carolina and escaped after Gen. BENJAMIN LINCOLN's surrender at Charleston. Gathering a band of guerrillas, he harassed British troops with surprise raids, escaping into the region's swamps when pursued. In 1781 he led a daring rescue of American troops surrounded by the British at Parkers Ferry, S.C., and was appointed a brigadier general.

marionette Puppet figure manipulated from above by strings attached to a wooden cross or control. The figure, also called a string puppet, is usually manipulated by nine strings, attached to each leg, hand, shoulder, and ear and at the base of the spine. Additional strings give more sensitive control of movement, and some marionettes can be made to imitate almost every human and animal action. Early marionettes were controlled by an iron rod instead of strings, a form that survived in Sicily. In the 18th century, marionette operas were extremely popular, and they are still performed today in Salzburg to Mozart's music. See also PUPPETRY.

Maris \'mar-əs\, **Roger (Eugene)** (1934–1985) U.S. baseball player. Born in Hibbing, Minn., he excelled in high-school sports in Fargo, N.D., playing American Legion baseball in the summer. An outfielder and left-handed hitter, he played for the Cleveland Indians (1957–59), the New York Yankees (1960–66), and the St. Louis Cardinals (1967–68). In 1961 his one-season total of 61 home runs broke BABE RUTH's long-standing record of 60, edging out his Yankee teammate MICKEY MANTLE. Maris's record stood until 1998, when it was broken by MARK MCGWIRE's 70 and SAMMY SOSA's 66.

Maritain \må-rē-'taⁿ\, **Jacques** (1882–1973) French philosopher. A devout Roman Catholic, his thought was based on Aristotelianism and THOMISM, but incorporated features from other classical and modern philosophers and drew on anthropology, sociology, and psychology. Referring to Thomism as existentialist intellectualism, he emphasized the importance of the individual as well as the Christian community. Among his major works are *Art and Scholasticism* (1920), *The Degrees of Knowledge* (1932), *Art and Poetry* (1935), *Man and the State* (1951), and *Moral Philosophy* (1960).

maritime law *or* **admiralty law** *or* **admiralty** Body of legal rules that governs ships and shipping. One early compilation of maritime regulations is the 6th-century Digest of Justinian. Roman maritime law and the 13th-century Consolat de Mar ("Consulate of the Sea") both brought temporary uniformity of maritime law to the Mediterranean, but nationalism led many countries to develop their own maritime codes. Maritime law deals mainly with the eventualities of loss of a ship (e.g., through collision) or cargo, with insurance and liability relating to those eventualities, and with collision compensation and salvage rights. There is an increasing tendency to make maritime laws uniform; the chief organization overseeing maritime law is the International Maritime Committee, composed of the maritime-law associations of several nations.

Maritime Provinces Canadian provinces of NEW BRUNSWICK, NOVA SCOTIA, and PRINCE EDWARD ISLAND. They are located on the Atlantic Coast and the Gulf of ST. LAWRENCE. With NEWFOUNDLAND they form the Atlantic Provinces. The name ACADIA was applied to much of the region during French colonial rule, until it was ceded to the British in 1713.

Maritsa River \mə-'rēt-sə\ *Greek* **Évros** \'ev-ˌrȯs\ *Turkish* **Meriç** \me-'rēch\ River, southeastern Europe. Rising southeast of SOFIA, Bulgaria, it flows east and southeast across Bulgaria, briefly forms the Bulgaria–Greece border, and then runs along the Greece–Turkey border. At Edirne it changes direction, and flows southwest to enter the AEGEAN SEA after a course of about 300 mi (480 km).

Marius \'mar-ē-əs\, **Gaius** (157?–86 BC) General and consul who redesigned the Roman army. He secured command of the army in Africa (107) and solved the chronic manpower shortage by enlisting landless citizens for the first time. He defeated JUGURTHA in 106. At Rome he held unconstitutional successive consulships (104–100) while it was threatened by the Cimbri and the Teutones, whom he fought and defeated. He held a command during the SOCIAL WAR and was awarded another in 88 to replace SULLA as Asian commander and confront MITHRADATES. When an outraged Sulla marched on Rome, Marius fled for his life. He returned forcibly in 87, was elected consul for the seventh time, and ruthlessly murdered his opponents.

Marivaux \mà-rē-'vō\, **Pierre (Carlet de Chamblain de)** (1688–1763) French playwright. Born into an aristocratic family, he joined Paris salon society, which he described in his journalistic writings. The loss of his fortune in 1720 and the death of his young wife a few years later prompted him to embark on a serious literary career. He wrote his first plays, including the tragedy *Annibal* (1720), for the COMÉDIE-FRANÇAISE, but preferred to write for the Italian COMMEDIA DELL'ARTE theater in Paris, for which he produced *Harlequin Brightened by Love* (1723) and *The Game of Love and Chance* (1730). His nuanced feeling and clever wordplay became known as *marivaudage.* He also wrote the satires *Isle of Slaves* (1725), *Isle of Reason* (1727), and *The New Colony* (1729).

marjoram *or* **sweet marjoram** \'mär-jə-rəm\ Perennial herb *(Majorana hortensis)* of the MINT family, or its fresh or dried leaves and flowering tops. Native to the Mediterranean and western Asia, marjoram is cultivated as an annual where winter temperatures kill the plant. It is used to flavor many foods. Various other aromatic herbs or undershrubs of the genera *Origanum* (see OREGANO) and *Majorana* of the mint family are also called marjoram.

Mark, St. (fl. 1st century AD) Christian evangelist to whom the second GOSPEL is traditionally ascribed. He joined Sts. PAUL and BARNABAS on their first missionary journey but left them at Perga and returned to Jerusalem. He may also have aided St. PETER in Rome, and some scholars believe that his Gospel is based on Peter's account of his experiences as one of the 12 disciples. If this is true, it was probably written shortly after Peter's death c. AD 65. The Egyptian church claims Mark as its founder, and he is patron saint of the Italian cities of Aquileia and Venice. His symbol is the lion.

Mark Antony See Mark ANTONY

market Means by which buyers and sellers are brought into contact with each other and goods and services are exchanged. The term originally referred to a place where products were bought and sold; today a market is any arena, however abstract or far-reaching, in which buyers and sellers make transactions. The COMMODITY EXCHANGES in London and New York, for example, are international markets in which dealers communicate by telephone and computer links as well as through direct contact. Markets trade not only in tangible commodities such as grain and livestock but also in financial instruments such as SECURITIES and CURRENCIES. CLASSICAL ECONOMISTS developed the theory of perfect competition, in which they imagined free markets as places where large numbers of buyers and sellers communicated easily with each other and traded in commodities that were readily transferable; prices in such markets were determined only by SUPPLY AND DEMAND. Since the 1930s, economists have focused more often on the theory of imperfect competition, in which supply and demand are not the only factors that influence the operations of the market. In imperfect competition the number of sellers or buyers is limited, rival products are differentiated (by design, quality, brand name, etc.), and various obstacles hinder new producers' entry into the market.

market research Study of the requirements of specific markets, the acceptability of products, and methods of developing and exploiting new markets. Various strategies are used for market research: past sales may be projected forward; surveys may be made of consumer attitudes and product preferences; and new or altered products may be introduced experimentally into designated test-market areas. Formal market research dates back to the 1920s in Germany and the 1930s in Sweden and France. After World War II, U.S. firms led in the use and refinement of market-research techniques, which spread throughout much of Western Europe and Japan.

marketing Activities that direct the flow of goods and services from producers to consumers. In advanced industrial economies, marketing considerations play a major role in determining corporate policy. Once primarily concerned with increasing sales through ADVERTISING and other promotional techniques, corporate marketing departments now focus on credit policies (see CREDIT), product development, customer support, distribution, and corporate communications. Marketers may look for outlets through which to sell the company's products, including retail stores, DIRECT-MAIL MARKETING, and WHOLESALING. They may make psychological and demographic studies of a potential market, experiment with various marketing strategies, and conduct informal interviews with target audiences. Marketing is used both to increase sales of an existing product and to introduce new products. See also MERCHANDISING.

marketing board Organization set up by a government to regulate the buying and selling of a certain commodity within a specified area. The simplest type of board is designed to carry out MARKET RESEARCH, promote sales, and furnish information; it is usually financed by a fee levied on all sales of the product concerned. Examples include the Tea Propaganda Board of Sri Lanka and the Tobacco Export Promotion Council of Zimbabwe. Other boards are empowered to regulate terms and conditions of sale, usually by establishing packing standards and quality analysis. The primary goal of most marketing boards is to stabilize PRICES, especially of products intended for the export market, where price fluctuations are often violent. The boards may raise average prices through manipulation of commodity flows, with the objective of maintaining reasonably high levels of demand at all times. Marketing boards are also used for products whose perishability requires that outlets be set up in advance. See also CARTEL.

Markham \'mär-kəm\ City (pop., 1991: 154,000), southeastern Ontario. It is situated on the Rouge River, northeast of TORONTO. Settled in 1794, the town was named for William Markham, archbishop of York. It annexed the nearby township of Markham in 1971.

Markham, Beryl *orig.* **Beryl Clutterbuck** (1902–1986) British pilot, adventurer, and writer. Raised in British East Africa, she became a horse trainer and breeder, training several Kenya Derby winners. Turning to aviation, she carried goods, people, and mail to far corners of Africa, and in 1936 she made a historic east-to-west solo flight across the North Atlantic from England to Cape Breton Island. In 1942 she published her celebrated memoir *West with the Night* (1942).

Markham River River, eastern Papua New Guinea. It rises in northeastern mountains and flows southeast for 110 mi (180 km) to enter the Huon Gulf of the Solomon Sea, south of Lae. It is named for Clements Markham of the Royal Geographical Society. During World War II its valleys were the scene of fighting in 1943 between Japan and the Allies. The area around the river suffered severe earthquakes in 1993.

Markova \mär-'kō-və\, **Alicia** *later* **Dame Alicia** *orig.* **Lilian Alicia Marks** (born 1910) British ballerina. She made her debut with the BALLETS RUSSES in 1924 and became a leading ballerina, noted for her ethereal lightness. At the Vic-Wells Ballet (1931–35) she became the first English dancer to dance the lead in *Giselle.* With her frequent partner ANTON DOLIN, she formed and directed several Markova-Dolin companies (1935–38) and London's Festival Ballet (1949–52). She continued to dance as a guest artist with many companies worldwide, admired for her interpretations of roles in *Les sylphides, Pas de quatre,* and *Giselle,* among others. She retired in 1963, and served as director of the Metropolitan Opera Ballet 1963–69.

markup language Standard text-encoding system consisting of a set of symbols inserted in a text document to control its structure, formatting, or the relationship among its parts. The most widely used markup languages are SGML, HTML, and XML. The markup symbols can be interpreted by a device (computer, printer, browser, etc.) to control how a document should look when printed or displayed on a monitor. A marked-up document thus contains two types of text: text to be displayed and markup language on how to display it.

marl Earthy mixture of fine-grained minerals, which range widely in composition. LIME (calcium carbonate) is present as shell fragments of snails and BIVALVES, or as powder mixed with clay and silica-containing silt. Large deposits contain 80–90% calcium carbonate and less than 3% magnesium carbonate. With decreasing amounts of lime, calcium-containing marls are called clays and clayey limestones. Marls rich in POTASH (potassium carbonate), called greensand marls, are used as water softeners. Marls have also been used in the manufacture of insulating material and PORTLAND CEMENT, as liming material, and in making bricks.

Marlborough, Duchess of *orig.* **Sarah Jennings** (1660–1744) Wife of John Churchill, duke of MARLBOROUGH. A childhood friend of Princess (later Queen) ANNE, she entered the household of Anne's father, the duke of York. She married Churchill in 1678 and served as a lady of the bedchamber after Anne's marriage (1683). When Anne acceded to the throne (1694), the Marlboroughs enjoyed great favor at court. Sarah's influence grew until her strong Whig sympathies alienated Anne, who dismissed her in 1711. The Marlboroughs retired to BLENHEIM PALACE, which Sarah completed building after her husband's death in 1722.

Marlborough, Duke of *orig.* **John Churchill** (1650–1722) British military commander. He served with distinction at Maastricht (1673), was promoted rapidly, and advanced at court, in part because his wife (see Duchess of MARLBOROUGH) was a confidant of Princess (later Queen) ANNE. On the accession of JAMES II in 1685, he was made a lieutenant general and effective commander in chief. In 1688 he transferred his allegiance to WILLIAM III, who rewarded him with the earldom of Marlborough and a succession of commands in Flanders and Ireland. His relationship with William deteriorated in the 1690s. Queen Anne appointed him commander of English and Dutch forces in the War of the SPANISH SUCCESSION, and for his successes he was created duke of Marlborough (1702). His victory at the Battle of BLENHEIM (1704) helped change the balance of power in Europe. In gratitude, he was granted a royal manor, where BLENHEIM PALACE was built. His outstanding military tactics continued to produce victories, notably at Ramillies (1706) and Oudenaarde (1708). His influence with Queen Anne and financial backing for the war were undermined by intrigue between Tories and Whigs. After his Whig allies lost the election of 1710, he was dismissed on charges of misuse of public money. He retired from public life, though he was restored to favor by GEORGE I in 1714. Considered one of England's greatest generals, he secured a reputation in Europe that was unrivaled until the rise of Napoleon.

John Churchill, 1st Duke of Marlborough, painting attributed to J. Closterman; in the National Portrait Gallery, London.

BY COURTESY OF THE NATIONAL PORTRAIT GALLERY, LONDON

Marley, Bob *orig.* **Robert Nesta** (1945–1981) Jamaican singer and songwriter. Raised in the Kingston slum known as Trenchtown, Marley apprenticed himself to a welder. In the early 1960s he formed the Wailers with Peter Tosh, Bunny Livingston (later called Bunny Wailer), and others. In the 1970s they became the first international REGGAE stars with such releases as *Catch a Fire* (1973), *Exodus* (1977), and *Uprising* (1980). He died of cancer at 36. Marley's music, an amalgamation of American, African, and Jamaican styles, reflected his RASTAFARIAN beliefs in universal peace, love, equality, and hope and of unification and empowerment for the black race. Since his death he has attained near-legendary stature. His son, Ziggy (born 1968), has also recorded successfully.

marlin Any of four species (genus *Makaira,* family Istiophoridae) of deep-blue to blue-green marine fish with a long body, a long dorsal fin, a rounded spear extending from the snout (which it uses to club the fish it feeds on), and usually pale vertical stripes. They are highly prized for sport and food. Species range in weight from about 100 lbs (45 kg) to more than 1,500 lbs (700 kg). The Indo-Pacific black marlin *(M. nigricans)* has a distinctive, stiff pectoral fin set at an angle.

Marlowe, Christopher (1564–1593) British poet and playwright. The son of a Canterbury shoemaker, he earned a degree from Cambridge University. From 1587 he wrote plays for the London theaters, starting with *Tamburlaine the Great* (published 1590), in which he established dramatic blank verse. *Tamburlaine* was followed by *Dido, Queen of Carthage* (published 1594), cowritten with THOMAS NASHE; *The Massacre at Paris* (c. 1594); and *Edward II* (1594). His *Tragical History of Doctor Faustus* (published 1604) is one of the most admired English dramas of all time. *The Jew of Malta* (published 1633) may have been his final work. His poetry includes the unfinished long poem *Hero and Leander.* Known for leading a disreputable life, he died a violent death at 29 in a tavern brawl, which may have been an assassination for his service as a government spy. His brilliant short career makes him WILLIAM SHAKESPEARE's most important contemporary in English drama.

Marmara \'mär-mə-rə\, **Sea of** Inland sea lying between the Asian and European parts of Turkey. It is connected with the BLACK SEA through the BOSPORUS, and with the AEGEAN SEA through the DARDANELLES. It is 175 mi (280 km) long and nearly 50 mi (80 km) wide, and it occupies an area of 4,382 sq mi (11,350 sq km). The sea has two distinct island groups. The Kizil Islands in the northeast are primarily resort areas. The Marmara Islands in the southwest are rich in granite, slate, and marble, which have been quarried since antiquity.

marmoset Any species of arboreal, diurnal, long-tailed South American MONKEY (family Callitrichidae) classified in two groups: eight species with short tusks (lower canine teeth), called marmosets, and 25 with long tusks, called TAMARINS. Marmosets move in a quick, jerky manner and eat insects and sometimes fruit and small animals. Members of the common marmoset genus *Callithrix* are 6–10 in. (15–25 cm) long, excluding the 10–16-in. (25–40-cm) tail. The dense, silky fur is white, reddish, or blackish; the ears are generally tufted. Marmosets have been kept as pets since the early 17th century.

marmot \'mär-mət\ Any of about 14 species (genus *Marmota*) of stout-bodied, diurnal, terrestrial SQUIRRELS found in North America, Europe, and Asia. Marmots are 12–24 in. (30–60 cm) long, excluding the short tail, and weigh 7–17 lbs (3–7.5 kg). Most species live in burrows or among boulders. They frequently sit upright and emit a whistling alarm call. Marmots live almost entirely on green plants, storing fat for hibernation. The black-and-white hoary marmot *(M. caligata),* of Siberia and northwestern North America, which hibernates for up to nine months, is hunted for food and fur. The yellow-bellied marmot *(M. flaviventris)* inhabits the western U.S. and British Columbia. See also WOODCHUCK.

Olympic marmot (*Marmota olympus*).

E.R. DEGGINGER

Marne, First Battle of the (September 6–12, 1914) Military offensive by French and British troops in WORLD WAR I. After the invading German forces had moved to within 30 mi (50 km) of Paris at the MARNE RIVER, JOSEPH-JACQUES-CESAIRE JOFFRE counterattacked and halted the German advance. French reinforcements were driven to the front by 600 Paris taxis, the first automotive transport of troops. French and British troops forced the Germans to retreat north of the Aisne River, where they dug in to conduct the TRENCH WARFARE of the next three years. The Allied success thwarted Germany's plan for a quick victory on the Western Front.

Marne, Second Battle of the (July 15–18, 1918) Last large German attack in WORLD WAR I. As part of its final offensive to split the French forces, German troops under ERICH LUDENDORFF crossed the Marne River but were met by strong French resistance under FERDINAND FOCH. Allied counterattacks, especially at the Marne salient, forced the Germans to retreat to their former position along the Aisne and Vesle rivers.

Marne River \'märn\ River, northeastern France. It flows northwest into the SEINE RIVER near PARIS. It is navigable for 220 mi (350 km) of its total length of 326 mi (525 km) and has extensive canals. Its valley was the scene of crucial battles in WORLD WAR I (see First Battle of the MARNE, Second Battle of the MARNE).

Maroni River \mä-'rō-nē\ River forming the boundary between FRENCH GUIANA and SURINAME, South America. It rises near the Brazilian border and descends northward to enter the Atlantic Ocean at Point Galibi, Suriname, after a course of 450 mi (725 km). Its upper course is known as the Litani in Suriname, or Itany in French Guiana; its middle course is called the Lawa, or Aoua. Shallow-draft vessels can navigate 60 mi (100 km) upstream from the river's mouth.

Maronite Church \'mar-ə-ˌnīt\ Eastern-rite community centered in LEBANON (see EASTERN RITE CHURCH). It traces its origin to St. Maron, a Syrian hermit of the 4th–5th century AD, and St. John Maron, under whom the invading Byzantine forces were defeated in 684. For several centuries the Maronites were considered heretics, followers of Sergius, patriarch of Constantinople, who taught that Jesus had only a divine will and not a human will. No permanent affiliation with Rome took place until the 16th century. A hardy mountain people, the Maronites preserved their freedom in Lebanon during the Muslim caliphate. In 1860 the Ottoman government incited a massacre of the Maronites by the DRUZE, an event that led to the establishment of Maronite autonomy within the Ottoman empire. The Maronites obtained self-rule under French protection in the early 20th century. Since the establishment of a fully independent Lebanon in 1943, they have constituted a major religious group in the country. Their spiritual leader (after the pope) is the patriarch of Antioch, and the church retains the ancient West Syrian liturgy.

Marot \må-'rō\, **Clément** (1496?–1544) French poet. While imprisoned in 1526 for defying Lenten abstinence regulations, he wrote some of his best-known works, including "L'Enfer" ("The Inferno"), an allegorical satire on justice. He held several court posts; his long service to FRANCIS I was only briefly interrupted. One of the greatest poets of the French Renaissance, he markedly influenced the style of his successors with his use of the forms and imagery of Latin poetry. When not writing official court poems, he spent most of his time translating the Psalms.

Marpa (1012–1096) Tibetan religious leader. According to tradition, he was born to wealthy parents, and to curb his violent nature he was sent to a Tibetan monastery to study Buddhism. He later spent three periods studying under the yogi Naropa in India, returning to Tibet during the intervals and gathering disciples. A major figure in the revival of Buddhism in Tibet, he is known for his translations of Indian VAJRAYANA Buddhist texts and of mystical songs of the Indian tantric tradition.

Marquesas Islands \mär-'kā-səz\ Group (pop., 1988: 7,000) of 10 islands in FRENCH POLYNESIA, central South Pacific Ocean, northeast of Tahiti. The southeastern group includes Hiva Oa, the largest and most populated and the burial place of artist PAUL GAUGUIN; Fatu Hiva and Tahuata; and the uninhabited Motane and Fatu Huku. The northwestern group comprises Nuku Hiva, Ua Pu, Ua Huka, Eiao, and Hatutu. The Spanish explorer Àlvaro de Mendaña de Neira named the islands for the Marquesa de Mendoza in 1595. Annexed by France in 1842, the Marquesas form an administrative division of French Polynesia, with headquarters at Taiohae on Nuku Hiva.

marquess \'mär-kwəs\ *or* **marquis** \mär-'kē\ European title of nobility, ranking in modern times immediately below a DUKE and above a COUNT or earl. The wife of a marquess is a marchioness or marquise. The term originally denoted a count holding a march, or mark (frontier district).

Marquess of Queensberry rules See QUEENSBERRY RULES

marquetry \'mär-kə-trē\ Decorative work in which thin pieces of wood, metal, or organic material, such as shell or mother-of-pearl, are affixed in intricate patterns to the flat surfaces of furniture. Marquetry became popular in late-16th-century France and spread throughout Europe as the demand for luxurious home furnishings rose in the next two centuries. See also A.-C. BOULLE.

Marquette \mär-'ket\, **Jacques** *known as* **Père Marquette** (1637–1675) French missionary and explorer. Ordained a Jesuit priest, he arrived in Quebec in 1666 to preach among the Ottawa. He helped found missions at Sault Ste. Marie (1668) and St. Ignace (1671) (both now in Michigan). In 1673 he accompanied LOUIS JOLLIET on his commission to explore the Mississippi River, traveling south to the mouth of the Arkansas River. They returned via the Illinois River to Green Bay on Lake Michigan, where Marquette remained. In 1674 he set out to found a mission among the Illinois Indians, reaching the site of present-day Chicago. His journal of his voyage with Jolliet was published in 1681.

Márquez, Gabriel García See Gabriel GARCÍA MÁRQUEZ

Marr, Nikolay (Yakovlevich) (1865–1934) Russian linguist, archaeologist, and ethnographer. A specialist in CAUCASIAN LANGUAGES, he published collections of literature in the GEORGIAN and ARMENIAN languages and tried to prove a relationship between the Caucasian and AFRO-ASIATIC LANGUAGES and the BASQUE LANGUAGE. His theory that all languages evolved from one original language and that the creation of language was a class-related phenomenon was adopted as official Soviet linguistic doctrine until 1950, when Stalin denounced it.

Marrakech *or* **Marrakesh** \mə-'rä-kish, ˌmar-ə-'kesh\ City (metro. area pop., 1994: 622,000), southern Morocco. One of the four imperial cities, it lies in the center of the Haouz plain. It was founded in 1062 by Yusuf ibn Tashufin as the African capital of the ALMORAVID DYNASTY. It fell to the ALMOHADS in 1147, passed to the MARINIDS in 1269, and was the capital under the Saadians in the 16th century. In the medieval era, it was one of Islam's great cities. It was captured by the French in 1912 and remained under the French until 1956. Now a popular tourist resort, it has many historical buildings and a well-known souk.

Marrano \mä-'rä-nō\ Spanish Jew who converted to Christianity to escape persecution but continued to practice Judaism secretly. During fierce persecutions in the late 14th century, many Jews died rather than renounce their faith, but at least 100,000 converted to Christianity in order to survive. In time the Marranos came to form a compact society within Spain, growing rich and gaining political power. They were viewed with suspicion, and the name Marrano was originally a term of abuse. Resentment against them led to riots and massacres in 1473. In 1480 the INQUISITION intensified the persecution, and thousands of Marranos lost their lives. In 1492 a royal edict ordered the expulsion of all Jews who refused to renounce their faith. Many Marranos settled in North Africa and Western Europe. By the 18th century, emigration and assimilation had led to the disappearance of the Marranos in Spain.

marriage Legally and socially sanctioned union, usually between a man and one or more women, that accords status to their offspring and is regulated by laws, rules, customs, beliefs, and attitudes that prescribe the rights and duties of the partners. In 2000 The Netherlands became the first country to legalize same-sex marriages. The universality of marriage is attributed to the many basic social and personal functions it performs, such as procreation and provision for sexual gratification and regulation, care of children and their education and socialization, regulation of lines of DESCENT, DIVISION OF LABOR between the sexes, economic production and consumption, and satisfaction of personal needs for SOCIAL STATUS, affection, and companionship. Until modern times, marriage was rarely a matter of free choice. In Western society, love has come to be associated with marriage; historically, however, romantic love has not been a primary motive for matrimony in most eras, and permissible marriage partners have been carefully regulated in most societies. In societies in which the extended FAMILY remains the basic unit, marriages are usually arranged by the family. The assumption is that love between the partners comes after marriage, and much thought is given to the socioeconomic advantages accruing to the larger family from the match. Some form of DOWRY or BRIDEWEALTH is almost universal in societies that use arranged marriages. The rituals and ceremonies surrounding marriage are associated primarily with religion and fertility and validate the importance of marriage for the continuation of a family, CLAN, TRIBE, or society. See also DIVORCE, EXOGAMY AND ENDOGAMY, POLYGAMY.

marriage chest See CASSONE

marriage law Body of legal specifications and requirements and other laws that regulate the initiation, continuation, and validity of marriages. In Western Europe, most marriage law descends from Roman Catholic canon law, but though the Church regarded marriage as a sacred, indissoluble union, modern Western European and U.S. marriage law regards marriage as a civil transaction. It allows only monogamous unions; partners must be above a certain age and not within prohibited degrees of blood relationship, and must be free to marry and give consent to the marriage. DIVORCE is now almost universally allowed. Islamic law regards marriage as a purely civil contract for the "legalization of intercourse and the procreation of children." The practice of POLYGAMY, though historically permitted, has waned; polygamous marriages are permitted under customary laws in many African nations, but there is a growing trend toward monogamy. Marriage law in present-day China and Japan resembles that in the West.

Marriott \'mar-ē-ˌät\, **J(ohn) Willard** (1900–1985) U.S. businessman who founded one of the largest U.S. hotel and restaurant organizations. Born in Marriott, Utah, the son of a Mormon rancher, he opened a root-beer and barbecue stand in Washington, D.C., in 1927. By the end of World War II his chain of Hot Shoppe family restaurants extended over the entire East Coast, and in 1957 he opened his first hotel. His son J. Willard Marriott, Jr., succeeded him as president of the Marriott Corp. in 1964. At the time of the elder Marriott's death, the Marriott Corp. had 140,000 employees in 26 countries and total annual sales of $3.5 billion. He was posthumously awarded the Presidential Medal of Freedom in 1988.

Marryat \'mar-ē-ət\, **Frederick** (1792–1848) English naval officer and novelist. He served in the Royal Navy from age 14 until he retired in 1830 as a captain. He then began a series of adventure novels—including *The King's Own* (1830), *Peter Simple* (1834), and *Poor Jack* (1840)—marked by a lucid, direct narrative style, humor, and incidents drawn from his varied experience at sea. His *Children of the New Forest* (1847), set during the English Civil Wars, is a classic of children's literature.

Mars Ancient Roman god of war and protector of Rome, second only to JUPITER in importance. His festivals occurred in the spring (March) and fall (October). Until the time of AUGUSTUS, Mars had only two temples in Rome. His sacred spears were kept in a sanctuary; on the outbreak of war, the consul had to shake the spears, saying "Mars vigila!" ("Mars, awake!") Under Augustus, Mars became not only the guardian of Rome in its military affairs but the emperor's personal guardian. He was identified with the Greek god ARES.

Mars Fourth PLANET from the sun, named after the Roman god of war. Its mean distance from the sun is 141 million mi (227 million km); its day is 24.6 earth hours and its year about 687 earth days. It has two small moons, Phobos and Deimos. Mars's equatorial diameter is 4,220 mi (6,792 km), about half that of earth, and it is less dense than earth. Its mass is about one-tenth of earth's, and its surface gravity about one-third as strong. No magnetic field has been detected on Mars, suggesting, as does its low density, the absence of a substantial metallic core. Like earth, it has seasons and an atmosphere, but its average daytime surface temperature is only −10°F (−20°C). Mars's thin atmosphere is mainly carbon dioxide, with some nitrogen and argon and traces of water vapor. Spacecraft images show a cratered surface, with volcanoes, lava plains, flood channels, and canyons, many large by earth standards; OLYMPUS MONS, for example, is the largest known volcano in the solar system. Wind is an important element on Mars, sculpting features such as dunes and occasionally causing global dust storms. In the distant past Mars appears to have had a denser, warmer atmosphere and much more water than at present. Images from the Mars Global Surveyor spacecraft suggest that some liquid water may have flowed near the planet's surface in relatively recent times. No life has been detected on the planet.

Mars, canals of Apparent systems of straight-line markings on the surface of MARS, now known to be an illusion caused by the chance alignment of various surface features. Giovanni Virginio Schiaparelli (1835–1910) observed about 100 of what he described as channels. PERCIVAL LOWELL called them canals and believed them to be evidence of intelligent life. Most astronomers could not see them, and many doubted their reality. The controversy was finally resolved when pictures from MARINER spacecraft showed nothing resembling a network of channels.

Mars Pathfinder and Rover First spacecraft to land on MARS since the VIKING 1976 missions. Launched in 1996 by NASA, Pathfinder descended to the Martian surface in July 1997 using parachutes, rockets, and airbags. It then deployed instruments, including Sojourner, a small, wheeled Rover, which explored as far as 1,600 ft (500 m) from the lander and sent pictures back for over a month. The mission's main objective was to show that low-cost Mars landings and exploration are feasible.

Marsalis \mär-'sa-ləs\, **Wynton** (born 1961) U.S. trumpeter and composer, a major figure in the renewal of interest in jazz. Born in New Orleans, Marsalis was a trumpet prodigy and was recognized as an important soloist in both the classical and jazz traditions at an early age. He joined ART BLAKEY's Jazz Messengers (1980–82) before leading his own groups. As a composer he has written ballet and concert works and won the 1997 Pulitzer Prize for his oratorio *Blood on the Fields*.

Marseille *or* **Marseilles** \mär-'sā\ City (pop., 1999: 797,486), southeastern France. One of the Mediterranean's major seaports and the second-largest city in France, it is located on the Gulf of Lion, west of the French RIVIERA. It was settled by Greeks during the 7th century BC and was annexed by the Romans, who called it Massilia, in 49 BC. It declined along with the Roman empire but revived as a commercial port during the CRUSADES era; it passed to the French crown in 1481. The plague of 1720 killed half of its population. In the 19th century the development of France's colonial empire added to the city's importance. Following World War II, rapid industrial growth took place around the the port complex at Fos-sur-Mer and in suburbs such as Marignane and Vitrolles.

marsh Freshwater or marine wetland ecosystem characterized by poorly drained mineral soils and by plant life dominated by grasses. Fewer plant species grow in marshes than on well-watered but not waterlogged land; grasses, sedges, and reeds or rushes are most common. Commercially, rice is by far the most important freshwater marsh plant: it supplies a major portion of the world's grain. Salt marshes are formed on intertidal land by seawater flooding and draining, and salt-marsh grasses will not grow on permanently flooded flats. See also SWAMP.

Marsh, (Edith) Ngaio *later* **Dame Ngaio** (1899–1982) New Zealand writer of detective stories. Originally an artist, she later acted in and produced Shakespearean repertory theater (1938–64). She is known for her mystery stories featuring Inspector Roderick Alleyn of Scotland Yard. Her novels, including *Overture to Death* (1939), *Final Curtain* (1947), *Death of a Fool* (1956), and *Dead Water* (1963), helped make the detective story a respectable literary genre.

Marsh, O(thniel) C(harles) (1831–1899) U.S. paleontologist. Born in Lockport, N.Y., he spent his entire career at Yale University (1866–99) as the first professor of vertebrate paleontology in the U.S. From 1870 he led scientific expeditions to the West; in 1871 his party discovered the first pterodactyl found in the U.S. In 1882 he was placed in charge of the U.S. Geological Survey's work in vertebrate paleontology, aggravating a fierce rivalry between him and EDWARD D. COPE. Credited with discovering more than 1,000 fossil vertebrates and describing at least 500 more, Marsh published major works on toothed birds, gigantic horned mammals, and North American dinosaurs. His books include *Fossil Horses in America* (1874) and *Introduction and Succession of Vertebrate Life in America* (1877).

Marsh, Reginald (1898–1954) U.S. painter and printmaker. Born to American parents in Paris and educated at Yale Univ., from 1922 to 1925 he produced a daily column of drawings of vaudeville acts for the *New York Daily News*. In 1925 he became an original member of the staff of *The New Yorker* magazine, for which he drew humorous illustrations and metropolitan scenes. In 1929 he began painting scenes of city life, including Coney Island crowds and Bowery derelicts. He taught at the Art Students League from 1934 until his death.

marsh gas See METHANE

marsh mallow Perennial herbaceous plant *(Althaea officinalis)* of the MALLOW FAMILY, native to eastern Europe and northern Africa and naturalized in North America. Found usually in marshy areas near the sea, the marsh mallow has strongly veined, heart-shaped or oval leaves and pinkish flowers borne on stalks about 6 ft (1.8 m) tall. The root was formerly processed to make marshmallows.

marsh marigold Perennial herbaceous plant *(Caltha palustris)* of the BUTTERCUP family, native to wetlands in Europe and North America. It is grown in boggy wild gardens. The plant has a hollow stem, heart-shaped or round leaves, and glossy pink, white, or yellow flowers composed solely of sepals (petals are absent). The stems, leaves, and roots are sometimes cooked and eaten as a vegetable, though the fresh plant is poisonous. See also COWSLIP.

Marshall, Alfred (1842–1924) British economist, one of the founders of English neoclassical economics. The first principal of University College, Bristol (1877–81) and a professor at Cambridge University (1885–1908), he reexamined and extended the ideas of classical economists such as ADAM SMITH and DAVID RICARDO. His best-known work, *Principles of Economics* (1890), introduced several influential economic concepts, including elasticity of demand, CONSUMER'S SURPLUS, and the representative firm. His writings on the theory of value proposed time as a factor in analysis and reconciled the classical cost-of-production principle with the theory of MARGINAL UTILITY. See also CLASSICAL ECONOMICS.

Marshall, George C(atlett) (1880–1959) U.S. Army officer and statesman. Born in Uniontown, Pa., he graduated from Virginia Military Institute, and served in the Philippines (1902–3) and in World War I. He was an aide to Gen. JOHN PERSHING (1919–24) and assistant commandant of the army's infantry school (1927–33), where he taught many future World War II commanders. As chief of staff of the U.S. Army (1939–45), he directed army operations throughout World War II. After he retired (1945), Pres. HARRY TRUMAN sent him to mediate the civil war in China (1945–47). As secretary of state (1947–49), Marshall proposed the European aid program known as the MARSHALL PLAN and initiated discussions that led to NATO. He resigned because of ill health but was called back by Truman to become secretary of defense (1950–51) and to prepare the armed forces for the KOREAN WAR. In 1953 he was awarded the Nobel Peace Prize.

Marshall, John (1755–1835) U.S. patriot, politician, and jurist. Born near Germantown, Va., he was the eldest of 15 children. In 1775 he joined a regiment of minutemen; he served as a lieutenant under Gen. GEORGE WASHINGTON in the American Revolution. After his discharge (1781), he served in the Virginia legislature and on Virginia's executive council (1782–95), gaining a reputation as a leading Federalist. He supported ratification of the U.S. Constitution at the state's ratifying convention. He was one of three commissioners sent to France 1797–98 (see XYZ AFFAIR). He served Pres. JOHN ADAMS as secretary of state (1800–1). In 1801 Adams named Marshall chief justice of the U.S. Supreme Court, in which post he would remain until his death. He participated in more than 1,000 decisions, writing 519 himself. During his tenure the Court set forth the main structural lines of the government; its groundbreaking decisions included *MARBURY VS. MADISON*, *MCCULLOCH VS. MARYLAND*, the DARTMOUTH COLLEGE CASE, and *GIBBONS VS. OGDEN*. Marshall is remembered as the principal founder of the U.S. system of constitutional law, including the doctrine of JUDICIAL REVIEW.

Marshall, Paule *orig.* **Paule Burke** (born 1929) U.S. writer. Born in Brooklyn, N.Y., to Barbadian parents, she attended Brooklyn College. Her autobiographical first novel, *Brown Girl, Brownstones* (1959), was acclaimed for its acute rendition of dialogue. Her short story "Reena" (1962) was one of the first pieces of fiction to feature a college-educated, politically active black woman as its protagonist. Her most eloquent statement of her belief in black Americans' need to rediscover their African heritage is the novel *Praisesong for the Widow* (1983).

Marshall, Thomas R(iley) (1854–1925) U.S. politician. Born in North Manchester, Ind., he served as governor of Indiana (1909–13), sponsoring a broad program of social legislation. In 1912 he was elected vice president on a ticket with WOODROW WILSON, and he became the first vice president to serve two terms (1913–21) in almost 100 years. A popular public official, he was heard to remark during a tedious debate, "What this country needs is a really good five-cent cigar."

Marshall, Thurgood (1908–1993) U.S. jurist and civil-rights advocate. Born in Baltimore, he studied law at Howard University. He went to work for the NAACP in 1936 and became its chief counsel in 1940. He won 29 of the 32 cases he argued before the U.S. Supreme Court, including the landmark *BROWN VS. BOARD OF EDUCATION* (1954) and others that established EQUAL PROTECTION for blacks in housing, voting, employment, and graduate study. He served as U.S. solicitor general (1965–67) before becoming the first black Supreme Court justice in 1967. Marshall was a steadfast liberal during his tenure on the Court, championing the rights of the individual, 1st-Amendment freedoms, and AFFIRMATIVE ACTION. He retired in 1991.

Marshall Islands *officially* **Republic of the Marshall Islands** *Marshallese* **Majol** \'mä-jōl\ Independent republic, central Pacific Ocean. It is composed of two parallel chains of low-lying coral atolls: the Ratak, or Sunrise, to the east and the Ralik, or Sunset, to the west. The chains lie 125 mi (200 km) apart and extend some 800 mi (1,290 km) northwest to southeast. The islands and islets number more than 1,200. Area: 70 sq mi (181 sq km). Population (1997 est.): 60,000. Capital: MAJURO. The indigenous people are Micronesian. Languages: Marshallese, English (both official). Religions: Christianity (a majority). Currency: U.S. dollar. The largest atoll is Kwajalein, consisting of about 90 islets, with a total land area of 6 sq mi (16 sq km). Much of Kwajalein is used as a missile-testing range by the U.S. military, which provides a major source of revenue. Subsistence farming, fishing, and the raising of pigs and poultry are the principal economic activities. It is a republic with two legislative houses; its head of state and government is the president. The islands were sighted in 1529 by the Spanish navigator Àlvaro Saavedra. Germany declared the islands a protectorate in 1885 and purchased them from Spain in 1899. Japan seized them in 1914 and after 1919 administered them as a League of Nations mandate. During World War II the U.S. seized Kwajalein and Enewetak, and the Marshall Islands were made part of the U.N. Trust Territory of the Pacific Islands under U.S. jurisdiction in 1947. BIKINI and Enewetak atolls served as testing grounds for U.S. nuclear weapons 1946–58. The country became an internally self-governing republic in 1979. It signed a compact of free association with the U.S. in 1982, which was to last until 2001. It became fully self-governing in 1986.

Marshall Plan (1948–51) U.S.-sponsored program to provide economic aid to European countries after World War II. The idea of a European self-help plan financed by the U.S. was proposed by GEORGE MARSHALL in 1947 and was authorized by Congress as the European Recovery Program. It provided almost $13 billion in grants and loans to 17 countries and was a key factor in reviving their economies and stabilizing their political structures. The plan's concept was extended to less-developed countries under the POINT FOUR PROGRAM.

Marshfield Bay See COOS BAY

Marsic War See SOCIAL WAR

Marsilius of Padua (c. 1280–1343?) Italian political philosopher. He was consultant to the Ghibellines until condemned as a heretic (1327) after writing *Defensor pacis* (1320–24) and fleeing to the court of LOUIS IV of Bavaria. He helped declare Pope JOHN XXII a heretic, install NICHOLAS V as antipope, and crown Louis emperor (1328). In his secular concept of the state, the power of the church is limited and political power lies with the people, a theory that influenced the modern idea of the state.

Marston, John (1576–1634) English dramatist. He began his literary career as a poet in 1598 but soon turned to writing for the theater. One of the most vigorous satirists of his era, he wrote all his plays before taking holy orders in 1609. His best-known work is the tragicomedy *The Malcontent* (1604), which rails at the iniquities of a lascivious court. Also notable is *The Dutch Courtezan* (produced 1603–4), one of the cleverest comedies of its time. Though he satirized and feuded with BEN JONSON, the two collaborated on *Eastward Hoe* (1605; with George Chapman) and *Love's Martyr* (1607).

Marston Moor, Battle of (July 2, 1644) First major Royalist defeat in the ENGLISH CIVIL WAR. Royalist forces under Prince RUPERT relieved the siege of York and pursued the Parliamentary forces to nearby Long Marston. A surprise counterattack by Parliamentary forces under OLIVER CROMWELL caused heavy losses to Royalist troops. With the fall of York, CHARLES I lost control of the north, and Cromwell emerged as the leading Parliamentary general.

marsupial \mär-'sü-pē-əl\ Any MAMMAL of the infraclass Marsupialia, characterized by premature birth and continued development outside the womb. The young remain attached to the mother's teats for a period corresponding to the late stages of fetal development of a placental mammal. More than 170 species (e.g., BANDICOOTS, KANGAROOS, KOALAS, WOMBATS) are found in Australia, New Guinea, and nearby islands. About 65 species of OPOSSUM occur in the Americas and seven species of ratlike marsupials in South America. Many species have a pouch (marsupium), a fold of skin covering the nipples on the mother's lower belly, where the young continue their development.

Marsyas Painter \mär-'sē-əs\ (fl. c. 350–325 BC) Greek painter of the late Classical period, known for two containers, both dated 340–330 BC. Both are painted in the so-called Kerch style, named for the area north of the Black Sea where many such vessels were excavated. Characterized by slender, mannered forms, elaborate decoration, and polychrome effects, the Kerch style is thought to be the last major style of Attic RED-FIGURE POTTERY.

marten Any of several forest-dwelling CARNIVORE species (genus *Martes,* family Mustelidae). Species differ in size and color, but they resemble WEASELS in general proportions, and their fur is valuable.

"Peleus Taming Thetis," pelike by the Marsyas Painter, c. 340–330 BC; in the British Museum.

L M N

Their total length is 20–40 in. (50–100 cm); they may weigh 2–5 lbs (1–2.5 kg) or more. Martens hunt alone, feeding on animals, fruit, and carrion. The fur of the American marten *(M. americana)* of northern North America is sometimes sold as sable. Other species include the pine, baum, or sweet marten *(M. martes)* of Europe and central Asia and the yellow-throated marten, or honey dog (*M. flavigula*), named for its preference for sweet foods, of southern Asia. See also FISHER, POLECAT.

Stone marten (*Martes foina*).
REINHARD/REISER–BAVARIA-VERLAG

Martha's Vineyard Island, Atlantic Ocean, off southeastern coast of Massachusetts. Situated across Vineyard Sound from CAPE COD, it is nearly 20 mi (32 km) long and 2–10 mi (3–16 km) wide. It was first described in 1602 by Bartholomew Gosnold and was named for its wild grapevines. Purchased by Thomas Mayhew in 1641, it was considered part of New York before being ceded to Massachusetts in 1692. It was once a center of the whaling and fishing industries; it is now a popular summer resort.

Martí (y Pérez) \mär-'tē\, **José Julián** (1853–1895) Cuban poet, essayist, and patriot. Involved in an 1868 revolutionary uprising, Martí was deported to Spain, where he received a law degree and continued his political activities and writing. He later lived in various countries, spending most of 1881–95 in New York City. He organized and unified the movement for Cuban independence and died in battle. As a writer, he is noted for his personal prose and deceptively simple verse on themes of a free and united America. His essays, such as those in *Nuestra América* (1881; "Our America"), are often considered his greatest contribution to Latin-American letters. He is the national hero of Cuba.

Martial \'mär-shəl\ *Latin* **Marcus Valerius Martialis** (c. AD 38/41–c. 103) Roman poet. Born in a Roman colony in Spain, Martial went to Rome as a young man. There he associated with such figures as SENECA, Lucan, and JUVENAL and enjoyed the patronage of the emperors TITUS and DOMITIAN. His early poetry, some marred by gross adulation of Titus, was undistinguished. He is renowned for his 12 books of EPIGRAMS (86–102?), a form he virtually created. Pointed and often obscene, they provide a picture of Roman society during the early empire that is remarkable both for its completeness and for its accurate portrayal of human foibles.

martial art Any of several arts of combat and self-defense that are widely practiced as sport. There are armed and unarmed varieties, most based on traditional fighting methods used in East Asia. In modern times, derivatives of armed martial arts include KENDO (fencing) and kyudo (archery). Unarmed varieties include AIKIDO, JUDO, KARATE, KUNG fu, and TAE KWON DO. Because of the influence of Taoism and Zen Buddhism, there is a strong emphasis in all the martial arts on the practitioner's mental and spiritual state. A hierarchy of expertise, ranging from the novice ("white belt") to the master ("black belt"), is usually recognized. See also T'AI CHI CH'UAN, JUJITSU.

martial law Temporary rule of a designated area by military authorities in time of emergency when the civil authorities are deemed unable to function. Under martial law, civil rights are usually suspended and the activities of civil courts restricted or supplanted entirely by military tribunals. Its application is limited primarily by INTERNATIONAL LAW and the conventions of civilized warfare. See also HUMAN RIGHTS, WAR CRIMES.

martin Any of several species of songbirds in the family Hirundinidae. In the U.S., the name refers to the purple martin *(Progne subis)*, at 8 in. (20 cm) long, the largest U.S. SWALLOW. The sand martin, or bank swallow *(Riparia riparia)*, a 5-in. (12-cm) brown-and-white bird, breeds throughout the Northern Hemisphere, nesting in sandbank burrows. The house martin *(Delichon urbica)*, blue-black above and white-rumped, is common in Europe. The African river martin *(Pseudochelidon eurystomina)* of the Congo is black, with red eyes and bill.

Martin, Agnes (born 1912) Canadian-U.S. painter. Born in Saskatchewan, she came to the U.S. in 1932 and became a U.S. citizen in 1940. She studied at Columbia Teachers College and taught at the University of New Mexico, then moved back to New York in 1957 and had her first solo exhibition in 1958. She is a prominent exponent of geometric abstraction; for her, a gray grid of intersecting penciled lines became the ultimate geometric composition. In the 1970s she produced printed equivalents of her paintings; a notable series of silkscreens, *On a Clear Day* (1973), were produced after her mathematically annotated sketches.

Martin, Mary (Virginia) (1913–1990) U.S. singer and actress. She co-owned a dancing school in her native Weatherford, Texas, before moving to New York in 1938, where she won a small part in the musical *Leave It to Me* and became famous with her rendition of "My Heart Belongs to Daddy." She appeared in movies before returning to Broadway to star in *One Touch of Venus* (1943). She originated the role of Nellie Forbush in *South Pacific* (1949–53), and later starred in *Peter Pan* (1954, Tony award; television version, 1955), *The Sound of Music* (1959, Tony award), and *I Do, I Do* (1966).

Martin, Quinn *orig.* **Martin Cohn** (1922–1987) U.S. television producer. Born in New York City, he worked as a film editor and producer before forming the television production company QM Productions (1960–79). He produced 20 television movies and created 16 series, including such crime dramas as *The Untouchables* (1959–63), *The Fugitive* (1963–67), *The F.B.I.* (1965–74), *Cannon* (1971–76), *The Streets of San Francisco* (1972–77), and *Barnaby Jones* (1973–80).

Martin, Steve (born 1945) U.S. comedian and writer. Born in Waco, Texas, he attended the University of California, where he began writing for the Smothers Brothers in 1967. In the 1970s he wrote for and performed on such shows as *Saturday Night Live*. His slapstick and absurdist humor were showcased in *The Jerk* (1979), which he both wrote and starred in. His other film comedies include *All of Me* (1984), *Roxanne* (1987), *Little Shop of Horrors* (1986), *Dirty Rotten Scoundrels* (1988), *Parenthood* (1989), *L.A. Story* (1991), and *Bowfinger* (1999). He wrote the stage play *Picasso at the Lapin Agile* (1995) and has written for such magazines as *The New Yorker.*

Martin V *orig.* **Oddo Colonna** (1368–1431) Pope (1417–31). His election at the Council of Constance marked the end of the Western SCHISM. He condemned conciliar theory (see CONCILIAR MOVEMENT) and any appeals of papal judgment on matters of faith. Martin rejected French efforts to persuade him to live at Avignon (see AVIGNON PAPACY). Instead he returned to Rome (1420), where he helped to rebuild the ruined city. He also tried to recover control of the PAPAL STATES. He mediated in the HUNDRED YEARS' WAR and organized crusades against the HUSSITES, and he asserted the rights of the church against the crown.

Martin du Gard \mår-ta^{n}-dǖ-'går\, **Roger** (1881–1958) French novelist and dramatist. Originally trained as a paleographer and archivist, he brought to his literary works a spirit of objectivity and a scrupulous regard for detail. He first attracted attention with the novel *Jean Barois* (1913), the story of an intellectual torn between the Catholic faith of his childhood and the scientific materialism of his maturity. He is best known for the eight-novel cycle *Les Thibault* (1922–40), the record of a family's development that chronicles the social and moral issues facing the French bourgeoisie in the pre–World War I era. He received the 1937 Nobel Prize.

Martin of Tours \'tür\, **St.** (AD 316–397) Patron saint of France. Born a pagan, he converted to Christianity at 10. He was forced to join the Roman army but asked to be released because service was incompatible with his Christianity. After imprisonment he settled in Poitiers, and from there became a missionary on the Balkan Peninsula. He returned to Poitiers and founded the first monastery in Gaul. In 371 he was made bishop of Tours. A second monastery he founded, at Mormoutier, became a great monastic complex. St. Martin was known as a miracle worker in his own lifetime and was one of the first saints to be revered who was not a martyr.

Martineau \'mär-ti-ˌnō\, **Harriet** (1802–1876) English essayist, novelist, and economic and historical writer. She became prominent among English intellectuals of her time despite deafness, heart disease, and other disabilities. She first gained a large reading public with a series popularizing classical economics, published in several collections (1832–34). Her chief historical work was *The History of the Thirty Years' Peace, A.D. 1816–1846* (1849), a widely read popular treatment. Her most scholarly work is a condensed translation of *The Positive Philosophy of Auguste Comte* (1853). Her best-regarded novel is *Deerbrook* (1839).

Martínez Montañés, Juan See Juan Martínez MONTAÑES

Martini, Simone (c. 1284–1344) Italian painter. An exponent of GOTHIC ART, he did much to spread the influence of Sienese painting. DUCCIO di Buoninsegna influenced his use of harmonious, pure color, but his graceful, decorative lines were inspired by French Gothic art, as can be seen in his *Maestà* fresco (1315), which depicts the Madonna as a Gothic queen holding court beneath a Gothic canopy. His equestrian portrait of Guidoriccio da Fogliano (1328), was an important precedent for Renaissance equestrian portraits.

Martinique \ˌmär-tə-ˈnēk\ Island (pop., 2002 est.: 386,000) of the WINDWARD ISLANDS, WEST INDIES, and overseas department of France. It is 50 mi (80 km) long and 22 mi (35 km) wide and occupies an area of 436 sq mi (1,128 sq km). Largely mountainous, its highest point, Mount PELÉE, is an active volcano. Its capital is FORT-DE-FRANCE. Tourism is the basis of its economy. Carib Indians, who had ousted earlier Arawak inhabitants, resided on the island when CHRISTOPHER COLUMBUS visited it in 1502. In 1635 a Frenchman established a colony there, and in 1674 it passed to the French crown. The British captured and held the island 1762–63, and occupied it again during the NAPOLEONIC WARS, but each time it was returned to France. Made a department of France in 1946, it remained under French rule despite a communist-led independence movement in the 1970s.

Martins, Peter (born 1946) Danish-U.S. dancer, choreographer, and director of the NEW YORK CITY BALLET. He trained at the Royal Danish Ballet School and became a member of its company in 1965. He joined the New York City Ballet in 1969 as a principal dancer, creating roles in JEROME ROBBINS's *Goldberg Variations* and GEORGE BALANCHINE's *Duo concertante.* He began choreographing for the company in 1977 with *Calcium Light Night;* other works include *L'histoire du soldat* and *Symphony No. 1.* After Balanchine's death in 1983 Martins became codirector (until 1990) and then sole director of the company.

Martinson, Harry (Edmund) (1904–1978) Swedish novelist and poet. He spent his childhood in foster homes and his young adulthood as a merchant seaman, laborer, and vagrant. He described his early experiences in two autobiographical novels, *Flowering Nettle* (1935) and *The Way Out* (1936), and in travel sketches. Among his best-known works are the poetry collection *Trade Wind* (1945), the novel *The Road* (1948), and the epic poem *Aniara* (1956). In 1949 he became the first self-taught working-class writer ever elected to the Swedish Academy. He shared the 1974 Nobel Prize with EYVIND JOHNSON.

Martinů \mär-ˈtē-nü\, **Bohuslav (Jan)** (1890–1959) Czech (Bohemian) composer. He started composing at 10, but was expelled from the conservatory for neglecting his studies. His early pieces combined the influences of folk music and C. DEBUSSY. In Paris from 1923, he gained a reputation for his colorful ballet scores, and experimented with neoclassicism, jazz, and ragtime. After World War II he lived in France, Italy, and Switzerland, and his Czech heritage reasserted itself. He wrote much music very quickly, including six symphonies, operas (including *Julietta*, 1938), and large choral works (including *The Epic of Gilgamesh*, 1955), but did little to promote it.

Martov \ˈmär-ˌtȯf\, **L.** *orig.* **Yuly Osipovich Tsederbaum** (1873–1923) Russian revolutionary. He first lived in Vilna, where he belonged to the Bund, a Jewish socialist group. In 1895 he and VLADIMIR ILICH LENIN formed the St. Petersburg Union of Struggle for the Liberation of the Working Class. After his arrest and exile to Siberia (1896–99), he joined Lenin in Switzerland as an editor of *Iskra*. From 1903 Martov supported the MENSHEVIK faction of the RUSSIAN SOCIAL-DEMOCRATIC WORKERS' PARTY and became its leader (1905–7). After the RUSSIAN REVOLUTION OF 1917, he supported the BOLSHEVIK government in the RUSSIAN CIVIL WAR but later opposed many of its dictatorial measures. He left Russia in 1920 and edited the *Socialist Courier* in Berlin.

martyr Person who voluntarily suffers death rather than deny his or her religion. Readiness for martyrdom was a collective ideal in ancient Judaism, notably in the era of the MACCABEES, and its importance has continued into modern times. ROMAN CATHOLICISM sees the suffering of martyrs as a test of their faith. Many SAINTS of the early church underwent martyrdom during the persecutions of the Roman emperors. Martyrs need not perform MIRACLES to be canonized. In Islam, martyrs are thought to comprise two groups of the faithful: those killed in JIHAD and those killed unjustly. In Buddhism, a BODHISATTVA is regarded as a martyr because he voluntarily postpones enlightenment to alleviate the suffering of others.

Marvell \ˈmär-vəl\, **Andrew** (1621–1678) English poet and politician. He was employed as a tutor, including to OLIVER CROMWELL's ward, before becoming an assistant to JOHN MILTON in the foreign office in 1657. From 1659 he held a seat in Parliament. His reputation as one of the finest secular Metaphysical poets (see METAPHYSICAL POETRY) is based on a small body of brilliant lyric verse, including "To His Coy Mistress" (1681) and "The Garden." Among his other works are classical odes, such as "An Horatian Ode upon Cromwell's Return from Ireland" (1650); political verse satires opposing the government after the Restoration, such as *Last Instructions to a Painter* (1667); and prose satires.

Marx, Karl (Heinrich) (1818–1883) German political theorist and revolutionary. He studied humanities at the University of Bonn (1835) and law and philosophy at the University of Berlin (1836–41), where he was exposed to the works of G. W. F. HEGEL. Working as a writer in Cologne and Paris (1842–45), he became active in leftist politics, and he met FRIEDRICH ENGELS, who would become his lifelong collaborator. Expelled from France in 1845, he moved to Brussels, where his political orientation matured and he and Engels made names for themselves through their writings. Marx was invited to join a secret left-wing group in London, for which he and Engels wrote the *COMMUNIST MANIFESTO* (1848). That same year he organized the first Rhineland Democratic Congress in Germany and opposed the king of Prussia when he dissolved the Prussian Assembly. Exiled, he moved to London in 1849, where he would live the rest of his life. For years his family lived in poverty, and two of his children died. He worked part-time as a European correspondent for the *New York Tribune* (1851–62) while writing his major critique of CAPITALISM, *Das Kapital* (3 vols., 1867–94). He was a leading figure in the FIRST INTERNATIONAL from 1864 until the defection of MIKHAIL BAKUNIN in 1872. See also COMMUNISM, DIALECTICAL materialism, MARXISM.

Marx Brothers U.S. comedy team. The original five brothers were Chico (*orig.* Leonard) (1886–1961), Harpo (*orig.* Adolph Arthur) (1888–1964), Groucho (*orig.* Julius Henry) (1890–1977), Gummo (*orig.* Milton) (1893–1977), and Zeppo (*orig.* Herbert) (1901–1979). They formed a vaudeville act with their mother, Minnie, called "The Six Musical Mascots" (1904–18). Gummo left the act early on, and the brothers later became "The Four Marx Brothers." They won fame with their first Broadway play, *I'll Say She Is* (1924), which was followed by *The Cocoanuts* (1925; film, 1929) and *Animal Crackers* (1926; film, 1930). They later starred in *Monkey Business* (1931), *Horse Feathers* (1932), *Duck Soup* (1933), *A Night at the Opera* (1935), and *Room Service* (1938), among other films, developing a skillful blend of visual and verbal humor, with Groucho supplying wisecracks and a running commentary as counterpoint to the frantic, anarchic activities of the silent Harpo

Groucho, Harpo, and Chico Marx.
THE BETTMANN ARCHIVE

and the Italian-accented Chico. Zeppo left the act in 1934, and the brothers disbanded in 1949. Groucho later hosted the successful television quiz program *You Bet Your Life* (1950–61).

Marxism Ideology and socioeconomic theory developed by KARL MARX and FRIEDRICH ENGELS. The fundamental ideology of COMMUNISM, it holds that all people are entitled to enjoy the fruits of their labor but are prevented from doing so in a capitalist economic system, which divides society into two classes: nonowning workers and nonworker owners. Marx called the resulting situation "alienation," and said that when the workers repossessed the fruits of their labor, alienation would be overcome and class divisions would cease. The Marxist theory of history posits class struggle as history's driving force, and sees CAPITALISM as the most recent and most critical historical stage—most critical because at this stage the proletariat will at last arise united. The failure of the 1848 European revolutions and an increasing need to elaborate on Marxist theory, whose orientation is more analytical than practical, led to such adaptations as LENINISM and MAOISM; the collapse of the Soviet Union and China's adoption of many elements of a free-market economy seemed to mark the end of Marxism as an applicable economic or governmental theory, though it retains interest as a critique of market capitalism and a theory of historical change. See also *COMMUNIST MANIFESTO*, DIALECTICAL materialism, SOCIALISM, STALINISM, TROTSKYISM.

Mary *or* **St. Mary** *or* **Virgin Mary** Mother of JESUS. According to the GOSPELS, she was betrothed to St. JOSEPH when the archangel GABRIEL appeared to her to announce the coming birth of Jesus. Other incidents in the Gospels in which she appears include the visit to Elizabeth, mother of JOHN THE BAPTIST; the birth of Jesus and his presentation in the Temple; the coming of the MAGI and the flight to Egypt; the marriage at Cana in Galilee; the attempt to see Jesus while he was teaching; and watching at the cross. Eastern Orthodoxy, Roman Catholicism, and most Protestant denominations hold Jesus to have been divinely conceived and Mary to have remained a virgin. The Roman Catholic church also holds to the doctrine of her IMMACULATE CONCEPTION and her bodily assumption into heaven. Catholics pray to Mary as an intercessor. See also MARIOLOGY.

Mary See MERV

Mary, Queen of Scots *orig.* **Mary Stuart** (1542–1587) Queen of Scotland (1542–67). She became queen when her father, James V (1512–42), died six days after her birth. She was sent by her mother, Mary of GUISE, to be raised at the court of the French king HENRY II and was married in 1558 to his son FRANCIS II. After Francis's brief rule as king (1559–60) ended with his premature death, Mary returned to Scotland (1561), where she was distrusted because of her Catholic upbringing. In 1565 the beautiful, redhaired queen married her ambitious cousin Henry Stewart, Lord DARNLEY, and became a victim of intrigues among the Scottish nobles. Darnley conspired with them to murder her confidant DAVID RICCIO. After the birth of her son James (later JAMES I of England) in 1566, Mary was estranged from Darnley, who was murdered in 1567. Ignoring objections by the jealous Scottish nobility, she married James Hepburn, earl of Bothwell (1535?–1578), a suspect in Darnley's murder. The rebellious nobles deserted her army at Carberry Hill and forced her to abdicate in favor of her son (1567). After failed attempts to win back the throne, she sought refuge in England with her cousin ELIZABETH I, who arranged to keep her in captivity. Several uprisings by English Catholics in Mary's favor convinced Elizabeth to have Mary tried and condemned; she was beheaded at Fotheringhay Castle in 1587.

Mary I *or* **Mary Tudor** (1516–1558) Queen of England (1553–58). The daughter of King HENRY VIII and CATHERINE OF ARAGON, she was declared illegitimate after Henry's divorce and new marriage to ANNE BOLEYN (1533). In 1544 she was restored to court and granted succession to the throne. After becoming queen (1553), she married PHILIP II of Spain, restored Roman Catholicism, and revived the laws against heresy. The resulting persecution of Protestant rebels and the execution of some 300 heretics earned her the hatred of her subjects and the nickname "Bloody Mary." She waged an unsuccessful war against France that in 1558 resulted in the loss of Calais, England's last foothold on the Continent.

Mary II (1662–1694) Queen of England (1689–94). The daughter of King JAMES II, a Catholic convert, she was reared as a Protestant and in 1677 married to her cousin, William of Orange. They lived in Holland until English nobles opposed to James's pro-Catholic policies invited William and Mary to assume the English throne. After William landed with a Dutch force (1688), James fled, and Mary and William (as King WILLIAM III) became corulers of England (1689). Mary enjoyed great popularity, and her Dutch tastes had an influence on English pottery, landscape gardening, and interior design. She died of smallpox at 32.

Mary Magdalene, St. (fl. 1st century AD) Follower of JESUS and the first person to see the resurrected Christ. According to Luke 8:2 and Mark 16:9, Jesus cleansed her of seven demons. She accompanied him in Galilee, and she witnessed his crucifixion and burial. On EASTER morning she went with two other women to anoint the corpse and found the tomb empty. Christ later appeared to her and instructed her to tell the APOSTLES that he was ascending to God. Popular tradition has long associated her with the repentant prostitute who anointed Christ's feet.

Maryinsky Theater See MARIINSKY THEATER

Maryland State (pop., 1997 est.: 5,094,000), eastern U.S. A middle-Atlantic state, it covers 10,460 sq mi (27,091 sq km); its capital is ANNAPOLIS. The state's main geographic regions are the coastal plain along CHESAPEAKE BAY, the rich farming country of the Piedmont plateau, and the APPALACHIAN MTNS. First occupied by late Ice Age hunters c. 10,000 BC, the area was later inhabited by the Nanticoke and Piscataway tribes. Capt. JOHN SMITH charted the Chesapeake Bay region in 1608. Maryland was included in a charter given by the British king to Cecil Calvert, Lord Baltimore. Leonard Calvert, his brother, founded the first settlement in 1634 at St. Marys City. Maryland became the first American colony to establish religious freedom. Its boundary dispute with Pennsylvania was settled in the 1760s with the drawing of the MASON-DIXON LINE. In 1788 Maryland became the 7th state to ratify the U.S. Constitution. The state ceded the DISTRICT OF COLUMBIA as the site for a new federal capital in 1791. It was involved in the WAR OF 1812, (see FORT MCHENRY). The U.S. NAVAL ACADEMY was founded at Annapolis in 1845. Maryland remained in the Union during the AMERICAN CIVIL WAR, but strong Southern sentiments resulted in the imposition of martial law. After the war, it prospered as an important entrepôt for consumer goods to the South and Midwest. During the 20th century its proximity to the national federal government spurred population growth. Its economy is based primarily on government services and manufacturing.

Maryland, University of State university system consisting of 11 campuses in seven cities. It has its origins in the founding in 1807 of a medical college in Baltimore. Reorganized in 1988, the system is an academic and research institution with land- and sea-grant status. The main campus at College Park provides comprehensive undergraduate, graduate, and professional programs and has research facilities that include seven libraries. Enrollment at the main campus is about 34,000.

Masaccio \mə-'zä-chē-ˌō\ *orig.* **Tommaso di Giovanni di Mone Cassai** (1401–1428) Italian painter. Little is known about him until 1422, when he entered the artists' guild in Florence. GIOTTO probably influenced his massive figures and spare composition, but the gestural and emotional expression in his rendering of the human body are closer in spirit to DONATELLO. In his most famous work, the frescoes in the Brancacci Chapel of Florence's Santa Maria del Carmine (c. 1425–28), painted in conjunction with his sometime partner, MASOLINO, his figures are constructed with strongly differentiated areas of light and dark that give them a three-dimensional effect. His *Trinity* fresco (c. 1427–28) in Florence's Santa Maria Novella is the first extant example of the systematic use of one-point PERSPECTIVE in a painting. He went to Rome in 1428 and died there so suddenly that some people suspected he had been poisoned. The rationality, realism, and humanity of the art he created in his brief six years of work inspired the major Florentine painters of the mid-15th century, and ultimately influenced the course of Western painting.

Masada \mə-'sä-də\ Ancient mountaintop fortress, southeastern Israel. It occupies the entire top of a mesa, which is 1,424 ft (434 m) tall and has an area of 18 acres (7 hectares). Its fortifications were built by HEROD the Great in the 1st century BC; it was captured by the Zealots, a Jewish sect, in their revolt against Rome in AD 66. After the fall of JERUSALEM, Masada, the last remnant of Jewish rule in Palestine, refused to surrender. In AD 73, after a lengthy siege, it was finally taken by the Romans, who found that nearly all of the 1,000 Zealots had committed suicide rather than be captured. A symbol of Jewish heroism, it is one of Israel's most popular tourist attractions.

Masai *or* **Maasai** \ma-'sī\ Nomadic herders of southern Kenya and northern Tanzania who speak a language (sometimes called Maa) of the

NILO-SAHARAN family. Numbering about 450,000, the Masai subsist almost entirely on the meat, blood, and milk of their cattle herds. A kraal, consisting of a large circular thornbush fence around a ring of mud-dung houses, holds four to eight families and their herds. POLYGAMY is common among older men. All men are grouped into AGE SETS. Young men traditionally live in isolation in the bush for varying lengths of time in order to develop strength, courage, and endurance. See also NILOTES.

Masamune Okazaki (Goro Nuido) \ˌmä-sä-ˈmu̇-ne-ō-kä-ˈzä-kē\ (fl. 1300) Japanese swordsmith. Masamune was appointed chief swordsmith by Emperor Fushimi in 1287. He founded the Soshu school of Samurai swordmaking, in which blades were made entirely of steel and hardened throughout. It marked an important advance in metallurgical technique, significantly in advance of technique in Europe or elsewhere in Asia.

Masaryk \ˈmä-sə-rik\, **Jan (Garrigue)** (1886–1948) Czech statesman. The son of TOMAS MASARYK, he entered the foreign service of the newly independent Czechoslovakia in 1919 and served as ambassador to Britain 1925–38. During World War II he was foreign minister of the Czechoslovak provisional government in London (1940–45) and later Prague (1945–48). At the request of Pres. EDVARD BENES, he remained at his post after the communist takeover in 1948. Two weeks later he either jumped or was pushed to his death from a window in the foreign office.

Masaryk, Tomàš (Garrigue) (1850–1937) First president of Czechoslovakia (1918–35). After receiving a doctorate from the University of Vienna, he taught philosophy at the Czech University of Prague (1882) and wrote on the Czech Reformation; his most important works were a study of Marxism (1898) and *Russia and Europe* (1913). In the Austrian Reichsrat (1891–93, 1907–14), he supported democratic policies and criticized Austria-Hungary's alliance with Germany. In 1915 he went to Western Europe, where he organized the Czech national council, which in 1918 gained recognition as the de facto government of the future Czechoslovakia. He negotiated its liberation as one of the FOURTEEN POINTS in the projected post–World War I peace settlement. Elected president of the new country (1918–35), he was occupied with settling conflicts between the Czech and Slovak parties.

Masbate \mäs-ˈbā-tā\ Island (population 1990: 600,000) of the VISAYAN group, central Philippines. The V-shaped island occupies an area of 1,262 sq mi (3,269 sq km); its capital is Masbate (pop., 1990: 59,000). Explored by Spain in the late 16th century, it was ruled by the Spanish until the SPANISH-AMERICAN WAR, when the U.S. gained control. It was occupied by the Japanese during World War II but was recovered by the U.S. in 1945. Gold has been mined for centuries near Aroroy in the north.

Mascagni \mäs-ˈkän-yē\, **Pietro** (1863–1945) Italian composer. He began to compose very young. At the Milan Conservatory he studied with Amilcare Ponchielli (1834–1886) and was G. PUCCINI's roommate, but was expelled. Taking conducting jobs with touring opera companies, he started writing operas and won a contest with his one-act *Cavalleria rusticana* (1890), a smash hit from its premiere and his most lasting work. His later operas *L'amico Fritz* (1891), *Iris* (1899), and *Il piccolo Marat* (1921) also enjoyed some success.

Masefield, John (1878–1967) English poet. He went to sea in his youth, then lived precariously several years in the U.S. before settling in London. He is best known for his poems of the sea, *Salt-Water Ballads* (1902, including "Sea Fever" and "Cargoes"), and for his long narrative poems, such as *The Everlasting Mercy* (1911), containing phrases of colloquial coarseness that were unknown in earlier 20th-century English verse. After he became poet laureate in 1930, his poetry became more austere. He also wrote adventure novels, sketches, and works for children.

maser \ˈmā-zər\ Device that produces and amplifies ELECTROMAGNETIC RADIATION in the MICROWAVE range of the spectrum. The first maser was built in 1951 by CHARLES H. TOWNES. Its name is an acronym for "microwave amplification by stimulated emission of radiation." The wavelength produced by a maser is so constant and reproducible that it can be used to control a clock that will gain or lose no more than a second over hundreds of years. Masers have been used to amplify faint signals returned from radar and communications satellites, and have made it possible to measure faint radio waves emitted by Venus, giving an indication of the planet's temperature. The maser was the principal precursor of the LASER.

Maseru \ˈma-zə-ˌrü\ City (metro. area pop., 1995 est.: 297,000), capital of Lesotho. It lies on the Caledon River near the border with Free State province, Republic of South Africa. In 1869 the chief of the Basotho (Sotho) nation, Mshweshwe I, founded the town near his mountain stronghold of Thaba Bosiu. Diamond-mining is important economically. The nation's only urban center, it is the site of government buildings, as well as a technical school, and Lesotho Agricultural College. Roma, to the southeast, is the seat of the National University of Lesotho.

Mashhad \ˈmȧsh-hȧd, mə-ˈshad\ *or* **Meshed** \mə-ˈshed\ City (pop., 1994 est.: 1,964,000), northeastern Iran, situated in the valley of the Kashaf River. For centuries it has been an important trade center along the caravan routes and highways of the Middle East. It was damaged in a Mongol attack in 1220 and was sacked by Turkmen and Uzbeks in the 16th–17th century. NADIR SHAH, who reigned 1736–47, made Mashhad his capital. The city is the burial place of HARUN AL-RASHID and is a site of pilgrimage.

Masinissa \ˌma-sə-ˈni-sə\ (c. 240–148 BC) Ruler of the North African kingdom of NUMIDIA. Originally an ally of CARTHAGE, he switched sides to help Rome after being persuaded by SCIPIO AFRICANUS THE ELDER (206). After winning the Battle of ZAMA (202) he was awarded a larger kingdom. Though displeased with the presence of CATO's army in Africa (149), he remained faithful to Rome and a client of the Scipios until his death.

Masjid-i-Jami \ˈmȧs-jid-i-ˈjä-mē\ *or* **Great Mosque** Complex of buildings, chiefly of the Seljuq period (see SELJUQ DYNASTY), in Esfahan, Iran. The MOSQUE (completed c. 1130) has a central courtyard framed by four huge *eyvans,* or vaulted niches. It is renowned for its fine brickwork, vaulting, and two domed sanctuaries. The brick dome of the main sanctuary (c. 1070–75) is supported by heavy piers. The smaller domed chamber (1088) is known for its beauty of proportion; its dome, resting on a series of arches, is a structural masterpiece. The dome and the four-*eyvan* plan became standard for Seljuq mosques.

Masjid-i-Shah \ˈmȧs-jid-i-ˈshä\ Celebrated 17th-century MOSQUE in Esfahan, Iran. The mosque, part of the rebuilding effort of the Safavid Shah ABBAS I, was located at the center of Esfahan, along a great central mall called the *meydan*. Along with neighboring structures of the period, it is notable for its logically precise vaulting and use of colored tiles.

mask Object worn either to disguise or protect the face or to project the image of another personality or being. Masks have been used in art and religion since the Stone Age. In most primitive societies, their form is dictated by tradition, and they are thought to have supernatural power. Death masks, associated with the return of the spirit to the body, were used in ancient Egypt, Asia, and the Inca civilization, and were sometimes kept as portraits of the dead. Masks worn on holidays such as Halloween and Mardi Gras signal festivity and license. They have also been widely used in the theater, beginning with the Greek drama and continuing through medieval MYSTERY PLAYS, and the Italian COMMEDIA DELL'ARTE, as well as in other theater traditions (e.g., Japanese NO DRAMA).

Maslow \ˈmaz-lō\, **Abraham H(arold)** (1908–1970) U.S. psychologist. Born in New York City, he taught at Brooklyn College (1937–51) and Brandeis University (1951–69). A practitioner of HUMANISTIC PSYCHOLOGY, he is known for his theory of "self-actualization." In *Motivation and Personality* (1954) and *Toward a Psychology of Being* (1962), Maslow argued that each person has a hierarchy of needs that must be satisfied, ranging from basic physiological requirements to love, esteem, and, finally, self-actualization. As each need is satisfied, the next higher level in the emotional hierarchy dominates conscious functioning.

masochism \ˈma-sə-ˌki-zəm, ˈma-zə-ˌki-zəm\ Psychosexual disorder in which an individual achieves erotic release by being subjected to pain or humiliation. The term is derived from the name of Leopold von Sacher-Masoch, a 19th-century Austrian novelist who wrote extensively about the sexual enjoyment he derived from verbal and physical abuse. The amount of pain involved can vary from ritual humiliation with little violence to severe whipping or beating; it is usually sought out and to some degree controlled by the masochist. The traits of masochism and SADISM often occur in the same individual.

Masolino \ˌmä-sō-ˈlē-nō\ *orig.* **Tommaso di Cristoforo Fini** (1383–after 1435) Italian painter. He came from the same district in Tuscany as his younger contemporary MASACCIO, with whom his career is closely linked. The two worked together on frescoes for the Brancacci Chapel in Florence's Santa Maria del Carmine. Masaccio's influence is evident in Masolino's contributions, but upon Masaccio's death Masolino returned to the more decorative Gothic style of his earlier years.

Mason, George (1725–1792) American Revolutionary statesman. Born in Fairfax Co., Va., he owned a large plantation and became active in the effort to promote western expansion. He helped his neighbor GEORGE WASHINGTON draft the Fairfax Resolves (1774), which called for a boycott of English goods. In 1776 he drafted the state constitution and the VIRGINIA DECLARATION OF RIGHTS, which influenced THOMAS JEFFERSON and provided a model for other states. A member of the Virginia House of Delegates (1776–88), he attended the Constitutional Convention but did not sign the U.S. Constitution and opposed Virginia's ratification.

George Mason, detail of an oil painting by L. Guillaume after a portrait by J. Hesselius; in the collection of the Virginia Historical Society.
BY COURTESY OF THE VIRGINIA HISTORICAL SOCIETY

Mason, James (1909–1984) British film actor. After studying architecture at Cambridge Univ., he made his screen debut in *Late Extra* (1935) and soon became a star in British films such as *The Man in Grey* (1943), *The Seventh Veil* (1945), and *Odd Man Out* (1947). He moved to Hollywood in the late 1940s but continued to make films in Britain as well. Noted for his urbane characterizations of flawed individuals, he appeared in more than 100 movies, including *Madame Bovary* (1949), *The Desert Fox* (1951), *A Star Is Born* (1954), *20,000 Leagues Under the Sea* (1954), *North by Northwest* (1959), *Lolita* (1962), *Georgy Girl* (1966), *The Boys from Brazil* (1978), and *The Verdict* (1982).

Mason, James Murray (1798–1871) U.S. politician. A grandson of GEORGE MASON, he practiced law in his native Virginia from 1820. He served in the state legislature (1826, 1828–32), U.S. House of Representatives (1837–39), and U.S. Senate (1847–61). An advocate of secession, he resigned his Senate seat in 1861. Appointed Confederate commissioner to England, he was captured at sea with JOHN SLIDELL aboard the *Trent* and imprisoned for two months (see TRENT AFFAIR). Released in 1862, he remained in England until 1865 but was unable to win support for the Confederate cause.

Mason-Dixon Line Originally, the boundary between Maryland and Pennsylvania. The 233-mi (375-km) line was surveyed by Charles Mason and Jeremiah Dixon in 1765–68 to define the disputed boundaries between the land grants of the Penns, proprietors of Pennsylvania, and the Baltimores, proprietors of Maryland. The term was first used in congressional debates leading to the MISSOURI COMPROMISE (1820) to describe the dividing line between the slave states to its south and the free-soil states to its north. It is still used as the figurative dividing line between the North and South.

masonry Craft of building in stone, BRICK, or block. By 4000 BC, Egypt had developed an elaborate cut-stone technique. In Crete, Italy, and Greece, cyclopean work overcame material weaknesses by using enormous irregularly shaped stones without mortar, thereby reducing the number of joints. African stonemasons also were skilled at mortarless work, and Japanese mortarless castle walls resisted collapse during earthquakes. The Roman inventions of concrete and mortar permitted the development of the ARCH into one of the basic construction forms and gave rise to a number of variations in the facing used for walls: squared stone blocks, concrete studded with rough stones, concrete with diagonal stone courses, brick- and tile-faced concrete, and mixed brick and stone. The Assyrian and Persian empires, which lacked stone outcroppings, used sun-dried clay bricks. Stone and clay were the primary masonry materials in the Middle Ages and later. PRECAST-CONCRETE blocks, often used as infill in modern steel framing, did not effectively compete with brick until the 20th century. Brick and block are often combined or used in CAVITY WALLS. Glass-block walls, which utilize steel rods to reinforce the mortar joints, admit light and afford greater protection against intruders and vandals than ordinary glass. See also ADOBE, building STONE.

Masqat *or* **Muscat** \'məs-ˌkät\ City (pop., 1993: 52,000), capital of OMAN, located on the Gulf of Oman. Situated on a cove surrounded by volcanic mountains, it came under Persian control in the 6th century BC and was converted to Islam in the 7th century AD. The Portuguese gained control in 1508 and made Masqat their Arabian headquarters 1622–48. Held by the Persians 1650–1741, it later became part of the sultanate of Oman. Two 16th-century Portuguese forts overlook the town; the sultan's Indian-style palace is built at the edge of the sea.

masque Short dramatic entertainment performed by masked actors. It originated in the folk ceremony known as mummery (see MUMMING PLAY) and evolved into elaborate court spectacles in the 16th–17th century. A masque presented an allegorical theme using speeches, dances, and songs, in a performance often embellished with rich costumes and spectacular scenery. The genre reached its height in 17th-century England when the court poet, BEN JONSON, collaborating with INIGO JONES on many notable masques (1605–34), gave it literary force. The masque later merged with OPERA, also influencing ballet and pantomime.

mass Quantitative measure of INERTIA, or the resistance of a body to a change in motion. The greater the mass, the smaller is the change produced by an applied force. Unlike WEIGHT, the mass of an object remains constant regardless of its location. Thus, as a satellite moves away from the gravitational pull of earth, its weight decreases but its mass remains the same. In ordinary, classical chemical reactions, mass can be neither created nor destroyed. The sum of the masses of the reactants is always equal to the sum of the masses of the products. For example, the mass of wood and oxygen that disappears in combustion is equal to the mass of water vapor, carbon dioxide, smoke, and ash that appears. However, ALBERT EINSTEIN's special theory of RELATIVITY shows that mass and energy are equivalent, so mass can be converted into energy and vice versa. Mass is converted into energy in NUCLEAR FUSION and NUCLEAR FISSION. In these instances, conservation of mass is seen as a special case of a more general conservation of mass-energy. See also CRITICAL MASS.

mass Celebration of the EUCHARIST in the Roman Catholic church. It is considered a sacramental reenactment of the death and resurrection of JESUS as well as a true sacrifice in which the body and blood of Jesus (the bread and wine) are offered to God. It is also seen as a sacred meal that unifies and nourishes the community of believers. The mass includes readings from Scripture, a sermon, an offertory, a eucharistic prayer, and communion. The rite was greatly changed after the Second VATICAN COUNCIL, notably in the adoption of vernacular languages in place of Latin. See also SACRAMENT, TRANSUBSTANTIATION.

mass action, law of Fundamental law of chemical kinetics (the study of rates of CHEMICAL REACTIONS), formulated in 1864–79 by the Norwegian scientists Cato M. Guldberg (1836–1902) and Peter Waage (1833–1900). The law states that the REACTION RATE of any simple chemical reaction is proportional to the product of the molar concentrations of the reacting substances, each raised to the power corresponding to the number of MOLECULES of that substance in the reaction.

mass-energy equation See EINSTEIN'S MASS-ENERGY RELATION

mass flow *or* **convection** In physiology, the mechanism responsible for movement of air from the atmosphere into the LUNGS and for movement of BLOOD between the lungs and the tissues. It is one of two principal mechanisms of exchange by which oxygen and carbon dioxide move between the environment and the tissues, the other being DIFFUSION. Local flows (e.g., through skeletal muscles during exercise) can be increased selectively, increasing the exchange of gases between tissue cells and the capillaries.

mass movement *or* **mass wasting** Bulk movements of soil and rock debris down slopes, or the sinking of confined areas of the earth's ground surface. The term mass wasting refers only to gravity-driven processes that move large masses of earthen material from one place to another. The term mass movement includes the sinking of confined areas.

mass production Application of the principles of specialization, DIVISION OF LABOR, and standardization of parts to the manufacturing of goods on a large scale. Modern mass-production methods have led to such improvements in the cost, quality, quantity, and variety of goods available that the largest global population in history is now sustained at the highest general standard of living ever. The requirements for mass production of a particular product include the existence of a market large enough to justify a large investment; a product design that can use standardized parts (see INTERCHANGEABLE PARTS) and processes; a physical layout that minimizes materials handling; division of labor into simple, short, repetitive steps (see TIME-AND-MOTION STUDY); continuous flow of work; and tools designed specifically for the tasks to be performed. See also ASSEMBLY LINE.

mass spectrometry *or* **mass spectroscopy** Analytic technique by which chemical substances are identified by sorting gaseous IONS by mass using ELECTRIC and MAGNETIC fields. A mass spectrometer uses electrical means to detect the sorted ions, while a mass spectrograph uses photographic or other nonelectrical means; either device is a mass spectroscope. The process is widely used to measure masses and relative abundances of different ISOTOPES, to analyze products of a separation by liquid or gas CHROMATOGRAPHY, to test vacuum integrity in high-vacuum equipment, and to measure the geological age of minerals.

mass transit Transportation systems, usually publicly but sometimes privately owned and operated, designed to move large numbers of people in various types of vehicles in cities, suburbs, and large metropolitan areas. Modern mass transit is an outgrowth of industrialization and urbanization. In the 1830s early mass transit in New York City included horse-drawn buses, which were soon replaced by fixed-rail horse-drawn trolleys. By 1900 motorized BUSES had appeared in Europe and America. With the advent of electricity, STREETCARS and SUBWAYS were introduced in many large cities. In the 20th century the AUTOMOBILE's increasing popularity undermined mass-transit development; fixed-rail streetcar systems were widely removed to provide space for cars. In the late 20th century, concern over air pollution has revived interest in light-rail transit and led to regional mass transit systems.

Massachusetts *officially* **Commonwealth of Massachusetts** State (pop., 1997 est.: 6,118,000), northeastern U.S. One of the NEW ENGLAND states, it covers 8,284 sq mi (21,456 sq km); its capital is BOSTON. Bounded on the east by the Atlantic Ocean, the state's soils are poor and rocky, and agriculture plays a limited role in the economy, although cranberry farming is important. The region was inhabited by Algonquian Indian tribes when the first English settler, Bartholomew Gosnold, arrived in 1602. PLYMOUTH was settled by the PILGRIMS, who came on the *Mayflower* in 1620. The MASSACHUSETTS BAY COLONY was founded and governed by the Massachusetts Bay Co. spurring Puritan settlement. It joined the NEW ENGLAND CONFEDERATION in 1643 and acquired MAINE in 1652. The southeastern and central state's settlements experienced KING PHILIP'S WAR in 1675. After losing its first charter in 1684, it became part of the Dominion of New England in 1686. Its second charter in 1691 granted the colony jurisdiction over Maine and Plymouth. In the 18th century Massachusetts became a center of resistance to British colonial policy; it was the scene of the BOSTON TEA PARTY, and of uprisings at the Battles of LEXINGTON AND CONCORD that marked the beginning of the AMERICAN REVOLUTION. In 1788, it became the sixth state to ratify the U.S. Constitution. It was in the forefront of the 19th century INDUSTRIAL REVOLUTION and was known for its textile mills. Today its major industries are electronics, high technology, and communications. It is well-known as the location of many institutions of higher learning. Tourism is important especially in the CAPE COD region and the BERKSHIRES.

Massachusetts, University of State university system consisting of campuses at Amherst, Boston, Worcester, Lowell, and North Dartmouth. The main campus at Amherst (founded 1863), in its nine colleges and schools, offers about 80 bachelor's degree programs, 70 master's programs, 40 doctoral programs, and various continuing-education programs. The Worcester campus houses the medical school; the Boston campus includes colleges of public and community service, management, and other fields. Enrollment at the main campus is about 23,000.

Massachusetts Bay Colony Early English colony in MASSACHUSETTS. It was settled in 1630 by a group of 1,000 Puritan refugees from England (see PURITANISM). In 1629 the Massachusetts Bay Co. had obtained an English charter allowing it to trade and colonize in New England. Puritan stockholders envisioned the colony as a refuge from religious persecution in England, and they transferred control of the company to the emigrants in Massachusetts. Led by JOHN WINTHROP, the colonists founded their colony on the CHARLES RIVER at what would become BOSTON. In 1684 England annulled the company's charter and in 1691 established royal government under a new charter, which merged PLYMOUTH colony and Maine into the Massachusetts Bay Colony.

Massachusetts Institute of Technology (MIT) Private university in Cambridge, Mass., famous for its scientific and technological training and research. Founded in 1861, MIT has schools of architecture and planning, engineering, humanities and social sciences, management (the Sloan School), and science, and a college of health sciences and technology. Though it is best known for its programs in engineering and the physical sciences, other areas such as economics, political science, urban studies, linguistics, and philosophy are also strong. Among its facilities are a nuclear reactor, a computation center, geophysical and astrophysical observatories, a linear accelerator, a space research center, supersonic wind tunnels, an artificial-intelligence laboratory, a center for cognitive science, and an international-studies center. Total enrollment is about 10,000.

massage \mə-'säzh\ Systematic, scientific manipulation of body tissues with the hands to relieve pain and reduce swelling, relax muscles, and speed healing after strains and sprains. It has been used for more than 3,000 years by the Chinese. Early in the 19th century, the Swedish physician Per Henrik Ling (1776–1839) devised a massage system for joint and muscle ailments, which was later extended to relieve deformities of arthritis and re-educate muscles following paralysis. Manipulations include light or hard stroking, compression (kneading, squeezing, and friction), and percussion (striking with the edges of the hands in rapid alternation). In ACUPRESSURE, a style of massage derived from China, pressure is exerted on Chinese ACUPUNCTURE points for healing effects. See also PHYSICAL MEDICINE AND REHABILITATION.

Massasoit \ˌmas-ə-'sȯit\ (c. 1590–1661) American Indian chief. Born near present Bristol, R.I., he became the grand sachem (intertribal chief) of the Wampanoag Indians, who inhabited parts of Massachusetts and Rhode Island. In March 1621, several months after the *Mayflower* landed, he journeyed to Plymouth and established peaceful relations with the settlers. Having shared techniques of planting, fishing, and cooking, in 1623 he was nursed back to health from a serious illness by grateful Pilgrims. Peace dissolved after his death; KING PHILIP'S WAR (1675) was led by his son METACOM.

Masséna \mȧ-sā-'nȧ\, **André** *later* **prince d'Essling** (1758–1817) French general. Entering the army in 1775, he served in the Revolutionary government's army and rose to general in 1793. In campaigns against the Austrians in Italy, he became NAPOLEON's most trusted officer; he then commanded the French army in Switzerland, defeating the Russians at Zurich (1799). Sent by Napoleon to restore the demoralized army of Italy, he successfully defended Genoa against Austrian besiegers and enabled the French victory at the Battle of MARENGO. He was made a marshal in 1804 and duc de Rivoli in 1808. He displayed heroism against the Austrians, notably at Aspern-Essling and the Battle of WAGRAM (1809), and Napoleon made him prince d'Essling (1810). In command of the French forces in Portugal and Spain (1810–11), he was defeated by the British under the duke of WELLINGTON. Masséna was relieved of his command and returned to Paris, where he supported the restoration of the monarchy.

Massenet \ˌma-sᵊn-'ā\, **Jules (Émile Frédéric)** (1842–1912). French composer. He attended the Paris Conservatoire from 1851. When his family left Paris in 1854, he ran away to continue his studies, playing piano and drums and teaching to support himself. His hard work paid off when he won the Prix de Rome in 1863, and he began writing operas in 1867. His reputation was established with his oratorio *Marie-Magdeleine* (1873), and his *Le roi de Lahore* was performed at the Paris Opéra in 1877. There followed the series of successes for which he is chiefly known, including *Hérodiade* (1881), *Manon* (1884), *Le Cid* (1885), *Esclarmonde* (1889), *Werther* (1892), and *Thaïs* (1894).

Massey, (Charles) Vincent (1887–1967) Canadian administrator, first Canadian governor-general of Canada (1952–59). Born in Toronto, he taught history at the University of Toronto (1913–15) and was appointed associate secretary of the cabinet war committee in World War I. He operated a farm-machinery business until 1925. An active Liberal, he served in W.L. MACKENZIE KING's cabinet (1925) and was appointed Canada's first minister to the U.S. (1926–30) and high commissioner for Canada in Britain (1935–46). After serving as chancellor of the University of Toronto (1947–52), he was named governor-general. His brother was the actor Raymond Massey (1896–1983).

Massif Central \ma-'sēf-sä^{n}-'träl\ Plateau region, southern central France. It is bordered by the lowlands of AQUITAINE, the Loire Basin, the Rhône-Saône Valley, and the Mediterranean coastlands of LANGUEDOC. Comprising about one-sixth of France, it occupies an area of 35,006 sq mi (90,665 sq km). It consists mainly of plateaus with elevations of 2,000–3,000 ft (600–900 m). Its highest peak is Puy de Sancy, which reaches 6,184 ft (1,885 m). It is the source of many rivers, including the LOIRE, Allier, Cher, and Creuse.

Massine \ma-'sēn\, **Léonide** *orig.* **Leonid Fyodorovich Miassin** (1896–1979) Russian-French dancer, teacher, and choreographer of over 50 ballets. He joined the BALLETS RUSSES in 1914 and produced his first ballet, *Le soleil de nuit,* in 1915; this was followed by *Parade* (1917), *The Three-Cornered Hat* (1919), and *Pulcinella* (1920). He extended MICHEL FOKINE's reforms by enriching the characterization of many roles. During 1932–38 he was principal dancer and choreographer for the BALLET RUSSE DE MONTE CARLO. His ballets *Les présages* (1933), *Choreartium* (1933), and *Rouge et noir* (1939) displayed innovative choreography and set designs and were among the first dances based on symphonies. In 1938–42 he directed his re-formed Ballet Russe de Monte Carlo, and he became artistic director of a new Ballet de Monte Carlo in 1966.

Massinger \'ma-sin-jər\, **Philip** (1583–1639/40) English playwright. After a period during which he collaborated with such playwrights as John Fletcher, Massinger began c. 1620 to write independently. From 1625 he was associated with the theatrical company The King's Men. His 15 surviving solo works are noted for their social realism and satirical power. They include the comedies *A New Way to Pay Old Debts* (c. 1624), his most popular and influential play, and *The City Madam* (c. 1632), both of which probed economic and social issues; and the historical tragedy *The Roman Actor* (c. 1626).

Masson \mȧ-'sō^{n}\, **André (-Aimé-René)** (1896–1987) French painter and graphic artist. After studying painting in Brussels and Paris, he was severely wounded in World War I, and an overriding pessimism penetrated his art. He joined the Surrealist movement in 1924 and became the leading practitioner of AUTOMATISM. In the late 1920s and 1930s he produced turbulent images of violence, psychic pain, eroticism, and physical metamorphosis, using sinuous lines to delineate abstract biomorphic forms. He lived in Spain (1934–36) and later the U.S. (1941–45), where he became an important link between Surrealism and Abstract Expressionism, then returned to France and concentrated on landscape painting.

mastaba \'mas-tə-bə\ (Arabic: "bench") Rectangular superstructure of ancient Egyptian tombs, built of mud brick or, later, stone, with sloping walls and a flat roof. A deep shaft descended to the underground burial chamber. Old Kingdom mastabas were used chiefly for nonroyal burials. Storage chambers were stocked with food and equipment, and walls were often decorated with scenes showing the deceased's expected daily activities. What had earlier been a niche on the side grew into a chapel with an offering table and a false door through which the spirit of the deceased could leave and enter the burial chamber.

mastectomy \ma-'stek-tə-mē\ Surgical removal of a breast, usually because of BREAST CANCER. If the cancer has spread, radical mastectomy may remove surrounding tissue and/or nearby structures, including chest muscles and LYMPH NODES. Modified radical mastectomy leaves at least the main chest muscle, has an equally high survival rate, and makes reconstruction easier. Simple mastectomy is removal of the breast only; lumpectomy is removal of the tumor only.

Edgar Lee Masters.
BY COURTESY OF THE LIBRARY OF CONGRESS, WASHINGTON, D.C.; PHOTOGRAPH, ARNOLD GENTHE

master of the animals See master of the ANIMALS

Masters, Edgar Lee (1869–1950) U.S. poet and novelist. Born in Garnett, Kan., he grew up on his grandfather's Illinois farm and became a lawyer in Chicago. He wrote undistinguished poetry and plays before publishing *Spoon River Anthology* (1915), his major work. Its 245 free-verse epitaphs in the form of monologues are spoken from the grave by the former inhabitants of a fictitious small town, who tell of their bitter, unfulfilled lives in its dreary confines. Among his novels are *Mitch Miller* (1920) and *The Nuptial Flight* (1923).

Masters, William H(owell) and Virginia E(shelman) Johnson *orig.* **Virginia Eshelman** (1915–2001, born 1925) U.S. human-sexuality research team. Masters was born in Cleveland, Johnson in Springfield, Mo. Together (as physician and psychologist, respectively), they founded and codirected the Masters & Johnson Institute in St. Louis. They observed couples having sex under laboratory conditions, using biochemical equipment to record sexual stimulations and reactions. Their book *Human Sexual Response* (1966) was considered the first comprehensive study of the physiology and anatomy of human sexual activity (see SEXUAL RESPONSE). They were married in 1971 and continued to collaborate after their divorce in 1993.

Masters Tournament Invitational golf competition held annually since 1934 at the Augusta National Golf Club, Augusta, Ga. One of the world's most prestigious golf contests, it comprises 72 holes of stroke play (the player with the lowest score wins). The course, famous for its beauty and for the speed and difficulty of its greens, was designed by BOBBY JONES and Alister MacKenzie.

Masterson, Bat *orig.* **Bartholomew** (1853–1921) U.S. (Canadian-born) lawman and gambler. Born in Henryville, Canada East (now Quebec), he grew up on farms in the U.S. In Dodge City, Kan., he worked as a buffalo hunter and Indian scout (1873–75), Ford Co. sheriff (1877–79), and deputy U.S. marshal (1879). In Tombstone, Ariz. (1880–81) he was associated with WYATT EARP and became known as a defender of order on the frontier. He lived a gambler's life in Denver (1887–1902), then moved to New York, where he was a deputy U.S. marshal (1905–7) and a prominent sports editor for the *Morning Telegraph.*

mastication See CHEWING

mastiff Breed of powerful but gentle dog of Europe and Asia dating to 3000 BC. Mastiffs fought bears, lions, tigers, bulls, and gladiators in Roman arenas and were used in English bull- and bear-baiting rings. The mastiff stands 28–30 in. (70–75 cm) tall and weighs 165–185 lbs (75–85 kg). It has a broad head, short dark muzzle, and dark drooping ears. Its short coat is apricot, silver fawn, or brindled. The bullmastiff, a BULLDOG-mastiff crossbreed standing 24–27 in. (61–69 cm) tall and weighing 100–130 lbs (45–59 kg), is used as a police and guard dog.

Mastiff.
SALLY ANNE THOMPSON

mastitis \ma-'stī-təs\ INFLAMMATION of the breast. Acute mastitis, usually caused by BACTERIA, begins almost exclusively in the first three weeks of nursing and can be cured with antibiotics without stopping nursing. The breasts may become swollen, red, hard, and tender; without treatment ABSCESSES may occur. Mastitis can be localized or widespread, and the breast's LYMPHATIC SYSTEM may be involved. Girls may have brief hormone-induced breast inflammation soon after birth and during puberty. Chronic mastitis usually occurs in systemic diseases (e.g., TUBERCULOSIS, SYPHILIS). One rare type is seen mostly in older women with a history of difficult nursing. Some mastitis cases resemble certain cancers.

mastodon \'mas-tə-ˌdän\ Any of several extinct ELEPHANT species (genus *Mastodon*) that lived worldwide 23.7 million–10,000 years ago or later in North America, where they were contemporaneous with historic American Indian groups. Well-preserved remains are quite common. Mastodons ate leaves and had small grinding teeth and long, parallel, upward-curving upper tusks; males also had short lower tusks. Shorter than modern elephants, they had long, heavily built bodies and short, pillarlike legs. Their long hair was reddish brown. The skull was similar to that of modern elephants but lower and flatter, and the ears were small. Human hunting may have played a role in the mastodon's extinction. See also MAMMOTH.

mastoiditis \ˌmas-ˌtȯid-ˈī-təs\ INFLAMMATION of the mastoid process, a bony projection just behind the ear, almost always due to OTITIS media. It may spread into small cavities in the bone, blocking their drainage. Very severe cases infect the whole middle ear cleft. It causes pain behind the ear and on the side of the head. Temperature and pulse rate may rise. Tissues over the bone may swell until an ABSCESS develops, indicating destruction of the bone's outer layer. Complications of inward spread include abscess inside the skull, THROMBOSIS, and INNER-EAR infection; meningitis is a serious danger. Now rare with treatment of otitis media, mastoiditis usually responds to early ANTIBIOTIC treatment; if not, surgical drainage with removal of all diseased bone is necessary.

Mastroianni \mäs-trȯy-ˈä-nē\, **Marcello** (1924–1996) Italian film actor. He made his film debut in 1947 and was a well-known actor in Italy by the mid-1950s. Darkly handsome, with a screen persona alternately winning and morose, he won international fame in such films as LUCHINO VISCONTI's *White Nights* (1957) and FEDERICO FELLINI's *La Dolce Vita* (1960). He acted in over 100 movies, including *La Notte* (1960), *Divorce—Italian Style* (1961), *8½* (1963), *Yesterday, Today, and Tomorrow* (1963), *A Special Day* (1977), *Ginger and Fred* (1985), *Dark Eyes* (1987), and *Everybody's Fine* (1990).

masturbation Erotic stimulation of one's own genital organs, usually to achieve orgasm. Masturbatory behavior is common in infants and adolescents, and is indulged in by many adults as well. Studies indicate that over 90% of U.S. males and 60–80% of U.S. females have masturbated at one time or another. Christian moral teaching condemned masturbation as the sin of Onan, who in the Old Testament was censured for spilling his seed, and the Roman Catholic Church still officially condemns it.

Masurian Lakeland \mə-ˈzu̇r-ē-ən\ Lake district, northeastern Poland, containing more than 2,000 lakes. It extends 180 mi (290 km) eastward from the lower VISTULA RIVER to the Poland–Belarus border, and occupies an area of 20,000 sq mi (52,000 sq km). It was the scene of Russian defeats in 1914–15 during World War I. It came under Russian control in January 1945 but was later granted to Poland by the POTSDAM CONFERENCE.

Mata Hari *orig.* **Margaretha Geertruida Zelle** (1876–1917) Dutch courtesan and alleged spy in World War I. In 1895 she married Campbell MacLeod, a Scottish officer, and lived in Java and Sumatra (1897–1902), after which they returned to Europe and separated. In 1905 she began to dance in Paris, calling herself Mata Hari (a Malay expression for the sun). Beautiful and exotic and willing to dance virtually nude, she soon had numerous lovers, including military officers. Details of her spying activities are unclear, but she apparently spied for Germany from 1916. She was arrested by the French in 1917, tried by a military court, and shot by firing squad.

Mata Hari.
H. ROGER-VIOLLET—HARLINGUE

Matabele See NDEBELE

matador In BULLFIGHTING, the principal performer, who works the capes and attempts to dispatch the bull with a sword thrust between the shoulder blades. Most of the techniques used by modern matadors were established in the 1910s by Juan Belmonte of Spain (1894–1962). The matador's traditional costume, which offers no protection, is known as the "suit of lights." The audience judges the matador according to his skill, grace, and daring. Almost every matador is gored at least once a season with varying degrees of severity, and some have been killed in the ring.

Matamba \mä-ˈtäm-bə\ Historic African kingdom of the MBUNDU people, located northeast of LUANDA, Angola. A strong state in the early 16th century, it came into conflict with the Portuguese colonists of Angola. About 1630 it was conquered by Nzinga, ex-ruler of NDONGO, who strengthened it and stopped Angola's eastward expansion in the 1670s. A 1684 treaty remained in effect until the Portuguese seized part of Matamba's territory in 1744. The rest of it, assigned to Angola by European treaties of 1870–1900, remained a self-governing kingdom until it was occupied by Portuguese troops in the early 20th century.

Matamoros City (pop., 1990: 304,000), northern TAMAULIPAS state, Mexico. It is situated on the southern bank of the RIO GRANDE, across from Brownsville, Texas. Founded in 1824, it was the scene of bitter fighting in the MEXICAN WAR and was occupied by U.S. troops in 1846. It is now one of Mexico's chief ports of entry for tourists, and a trade center.

Matapédia Valley \ˌma-tə-ˈpē-dē-ə\ Valley of the Notre Dame Mtns., GASPÉ PENINSULA, eastern Quebec province. Extending for some 60 mi (100 km), it forms a direct lowland route through the mountains from the ST. LAWRENCE RIVER to the Atlantic coast. It serves as an important transportation route between the MARITIME PROVINCES and the Canadian mainland. It is drained by the Matapédia River, which flows 50 mi (80 km) to join the Restigouche River.

Mataram \mə-ˈtä-rəm\ Historic kingdom, JAVA. Originally a vassal state of Pajang, it became powerful under Senapati, who became its first king in the late 16th century. Its territory expanded in the early 17th century, but the kingdom later began to decline. In the mid-18th century it lost both power and territory to the Dutch EAST INDIA CO., and was a vassal state of the company by 1749. Wars of succession in 1755 led to its division into the regions of Surakarta and Yogyakarta.

matchlock Device for igniting GUNPOWDER, invented in the 15th century. The first mechanical ignition system, it represented a major advance in small-arms manufacture. It consisted of an S-shaped arm, called a serpentine, that held a match, and a trigger device that lowered the serpentine so the lighted match would fire the priming powder in the pan at the side of the barrel. The flash in the pan penetrated a small port in the breech and lit the main charge. Though slow and somewhat clumsy, the matchlock was useful because it protected all the working elements inside the lock and freed the user's hand. Early matchlock guns included the MUSKET.

maté *or* **yerba maté** \ˈmä-tā\ Stimulating tealike beverage, popular in many South American countries, brewed from the dried leaves of an evergreen shrub or tree *(Ilex paraguariensis)* related to HOLLY. It contains caffeine and tannin but is less astringent than tea. To brew maté, the dried leaves *(yerba)* are placed in dried hollow gourds *(matés* or *culhas)* decorated with silver and covered with boiling water and steeped. The tea is sucked from the gourd with a tube, often made of silver, with a strainer at one end to catch leaf particles. Though usually served plain, maté is sometimes flavored with milk, sugar, or lemon juice.

Silver vessel for the preparation and serving of maté; in a private collection.
LIBRAIRIE LAROUSSE

material implication See IMPLICATION

materialism In METAPHYSICS, the doctrine that reality is essentially of the nature of matter. In the philosophy of MIND, materialism typically asserts that states of mind are identical to states of the brain. Supporters of this theory (called central-state materialism) agree that mind and body are conceptually distinct but argue, usually on grounds of ontological economy (see OCKHAM'S RAZOR) that they are identical. What seems to be a state of mind is really a state of the brain, and the mental is thus reduced to the physical. Critics have pointed out that the correlations so far established between mental occurrences and states of the brain are at best incomplete. See also IDENTITY THEORY, MIND–BODY PROBLEM.

materials science Study of the properties of solid materials and how those properties are determined by the material's composition and structure, both macroscopic and microscopic. Materials science grew out of solid-state physics, metallurgy, ceramics, and chemistry, since the numerous properties of materials cannot be understood within the context of any single discipline. With a basic understanding of the origins of properties, materials can be selected or designed for an enormous variety of applications, from structural steels to computer microchips. Materials science is therefore important to many ENGINEERING fields, including electronics, aerospace, telecommunications, information processing, nuclear power, and energy conversion. See also MECHANICS, METALLOGRAPHY, STRENGTH OF MATERIALS, TESTING MACHINE.

mathematical physics Branch of mathematical ANALYSIS that emphasizes tools and techniques of particular use to physicists and engineers. It focuses on VECTOR SPACES, MATRIX algebra, DIFFERENTIAL EQUATIONS (especially for boundary value problems), INTEGRAL EQUATIONS, INTEGRAL TRANSFORMS, INFINITE SERIES, and COMPLEX VARIABLES. Its approach can be tailored to applications in electromagnetism, classical MECHANICS, and QUANTUM MECHANICS.

mathematical programming Theoretical tool of management science and economics in which management operations are described by mathematical equations that can be manipulated for a variety of purposes. It is used for problems for which CALCULUS is unsuitable. If the basic descriptions involved take the form of linear algebraic equations, the technique is identified as LINEAR PROGRAMMING. If more complex forms are required, it is called nonlinear programming. Mathematical programming is used in planning production schedules, in transportation, in military LOGISTICS, and in calculating economic growth.

mathematics Science of structure, order, and relation that has evolved from counting, measuring, and describing the shapes of objects. It deals with logical reasoning and quantitative calculation. Since the 17th century it has been an indispensable adjunct to the physical sciences and technology, to the extent that it is considered the underlying language of science. Among the principal branches of mathematics are ALGEBRA, ANALYSIS, ARITHMETIC, COMBINATORICS, EUCLIDEAN and NON-EUCLIDEAN geometries, GAME THEORY, NUMBER THEORY, NUMERICAL ANALYSIS, OPTIMIZATION, PROBABILITY, SET THEORY, STATISTICS, TOPOLOGY, and TRIGONOMETRY.

mathematics, foundations of Scientific inquiry into the nature of mathematical theories and the scope of mathematical methods. It began with EUCLID's *Elements* as an inquiry into the logical and philosophical basis of mathematics—in essence, whether the AXIOMS of any system (be it EUCLIDEAN GEOMETRY or CALCULUS) can ensure its completeness and consistency. In the modern era, this debate for a time divided into three schools of thought. LOGICISTS supposed that abstract mathematical objects can be entirely developed starting from basic ideas of sets and rational, or logical, thought—a variant known as mathematical PLATONISM views these objects as existing external to and independent of an observer; Formalists believed mathematics to be the manipulation of configurations of symbols according to prescribed rules, a "game" independent of any physical interpretation of the symbols; and INTUITIONISTS rejected certain concepts of logic and the notion that the AXIOMATIC METHOD would suffice to explain all of mathematics, instead seeing mathematics as an intellectual activity dealing with mental constructions (see CONSTRUCTIVISM) independent of language and any external reality. In the 20th century, GÖDEL'S THEOREM ended any hope of finding an axiomatic basis of mathematics that was both complete and free from contradictions.

mathematics, philosophy of Branch of philosophy concerned with the EPISTEMOLOGY and ONTOLOGY of mathematics. Early in the 20th century, three main schools of thought—called LOGICISM, formalism, and INTUITIONISM—arose to account for and resolve the crisis in the foundations of mathematics. Logicism argues that all mathematical notions are reducible to laws of pure thought, or logical principles; a variant known as mathematical PLATONISM holds that mathematical notions are transcendent Ideals, or Forms, independent of human consciousness. Formalism holds that mathematics consists simply of the manipulation of finite configurations of symbols according to prescribed rules; a "game" independent of any physical interpretation of the symbols. Intuitionism is characterized by its rejection of any knowledge- or evidence-transcendent notion of truth. Hence, only objects that can be constructed (see CONSTRUCTIVISM) in a finite number of steps are admitted, while actual infinities and the law of the excluded middle (see laws of THOUGHT) are rejected. These three schools of thought were principally led, respectively, by BERTRAND RUSSELL, DAVID HILBERT, and the Dutch mathematician Luitzen Egbertus Jan Brouwer (1881–1966).

Mather \ˈma-t͟hər\, **Cotton** (1663–1728) American Puritan leader. The son of INCREASE MATHER, he earned a master's degree from Harvard College and was ordained a Congregational minister in 1685, after which he assisted his father at Boston's North Church (1685–1723). He helped work for the ouster of the unpopular British governor of Massachusetts, EDMUND ANDROS (1689). Though his writings on witchcraft fed the hysteria that resulted in the SALEM WITCH TRIALS, he disapproved of the trials and argued against the use of "spectral evidence." His best-known writings include *Magnalia Christi Americana* (1702), a church history of New England, and his *Diary* (1711–12). His *Curiosa Americana* (1712–24) won him membership in the Royal Society of London. He was an early supporter of smallpox inoculation. See also CONGREGATIONALISM, PURITANISM.

Cotton Mather, portrait by Peter Pelham; in the collection of the American Antiquarian Society, Worcester, Mass.

BY COURTESY OF THE AMERICAN ANTIQUARIAN SOCIETY, WORCESTER, MASS.

Mather, Henry See Charles S. and Henry M. GREENE

Mather, Increase (1639–1723) American Puritan leader. The son of a Puritan cleric, he was born in the MASSACHUSETTS BAY COLONY and was educated at Harvard College and at Trinity College, Dublin. He returned to New England and served as minister of Boston's North Church (1661–1723). He and his son COTTON MATHER lobbied successfully for the removal of the hated governor of Massachusetts, EDMUND ANDROS, and obtained a new charter for the colony in 1691. He served as president of Harvard College 1685–1701. His writings include *Case of Conscience Concerning Evil Spirits Personating Men* (1693), which helped end the SALEM WITCH TRIALS. See also PURITANISM.

Mathewson, Christy *orig.* **Christopher** (1880–1925) U.S. baseball pitcher. Born in Factoryville, Pa., he played football and baseball for Bucknell University and was one of the first college men to enter the major leagues. Throwing right-handed for the New York Giants (1900–16), he won more than 20 games in each of 13 seasons, and 30 or more in four of those years. He ranks third in all-time wins (373) and shutouts (80) and fourth in earned run average (2.13). He played for and managed the Cincinnati Reds (1916–18) and later served as president of the Boston Braves (1923–25). He died of tuberculosis at 45.

Mathewson, 1909.

CULVER PICTURES

Mathias \mə-ˈthī-əs\, **Bob** *orig.* **Robert Bruce** (born 1930) U.S. athlete. Born in Tulare, Cal., he suffered from anemia as a child and turned to athletics to gain strength. In 1948, at 17, he won a gold medal in the Olympic DECATHLON, becoming the youngest gold medalist ever to win an Olympic track-and-field event. He won a second decathlon gold medal in 1952; that same year he played fullback on Stanford Univ.'s football team at the Rose Bowl. He won all 11 decathlon competitions he entered in his career. He later served in the U.S. House of Representatives.

Mathura art \'mə-tə-rə\ Buddhist visual art that flourished in the trading and pilgrimage center of Mathura, Uttar Pradesh, India, from the 2nd century BC to the 12th century AD. Standing and seated Buddhas are represented with broad shoulders, large chest, legs apart, and feet firmly planted, conveying a sense of enormous energy. Female figures are frankly sensuous.

A *yaksi* (female nature spirit) holding tray and pitcher, red sandstone relief from Mathura, Uttar Pradesh, India, 2nd century AD; in the Archaeological Museum, Mathura.

P. CHANDRA

Matilda *or* **Maud** (1102–1167) Daughter of HENRY I of England and claimant to the English throne. She married Emperor Henry V in 1114; he died in 1125, and she made a second marriage to Geoffrey Plantagenet. Her brother's death in 1120 left her as Henry I's sole legitimate heir, and Henry named her as his successor in 1127. STEPHEN of Blois seized the throne on Henry's death in 1135, and his army defeated her supporters in 1141. Matilda retired to Normandy in 1148; her son became HENRY II of England.

Matilda of Canossa \kə-'nä-sə\ *Italian* **Matilde** *known as* **Matilda the Great Countess** (1046–1115) Countess of Tuscany. A close friend of Pope GREGORY VII, she backed him in his struggle against the emperor HENRY IV (see INVESTITURE CONTROVERSY), and it was at her castle at Canossa that the emperor performed his barefoot penance before Gregory (1077). After Henry's second excommunication, she was intermittently at war with him until his death (1106), sometimes donning armor to lead her own troops, and she helped finance the pope's military operations and encouraged Henry's son Conrad to rebel against his father (1093). Her unwavering support for the popes of Rome was honored by her reburial in St. Peter's Basilica in 1634.

Matisse \mà-'tēs\, **Henri (-Emile-Benoît)** (1869–1954) French painter, sculptor, and graphic artist. He was a law clerk when he became interested in art. After study with GUSTAVE MOREAU at the École des Beaux-Arts, he exhibited four paintings at the Salon and scored a triumph when the government bought his *Woman Reading* (1895). Self-confident and venturesome, he experimented with pointillism but eventually abandoned it in favor of the swirls of spontaneous brushwork and riots of color that became known as FAUVISM. He remained a Fauve to the end. Though his subjects were largely domestic and figurative, his works exhibit a distinctive Mediterranean verve. He also took up sculpture, and would produce some 60 pieces during his lifetime. The ARMORY SHOW exhibited 13 of his paintings. In 1917 he moved to the French Riviera, where his paintings became less daring but his output remained prodigious. After 1939 he became increasingly active as a graphic artist, and in 1947 published *Jazz*, a book of reflections on art and life with brilliantly colored illustrations made by "drawing with scissors": the motifs were pasted together after being cut out of sheets of colored paper. He was ill during most of his last 13 years; as thanks to the Dominican nuns who cared for him, he designed the magnificent Chapelle du Rosaire at Vence (1948–51). His well-known paintings include *Joy of Life* (1906), *The Red Studio* (1915), *Piano Lesson* (1916), and *The Dance I* and *II* (1931–33).

Matlock Town (pop., 1995 est.: 14,000), seat of DERBYSHIRE, northern central England. It consists of a group of settlements built along the River DERWENT, in a region noted for its beautiful valleys and rugged hills. Between Cromford (site of R. ARKWRIGHT's first waterpowered mill in 1771) and the 16th-century Matlock Bridge, the river runs through a narrow gorge. The town was once famous for its hydropathic treatment.

Mato Grosso \'mä-tü-'grō-sü\ State (pop., 1991 est.: 2,314,000), southwestern Brazil. It occupies an area of 352,400 sq mi (912,716 sq km), and is bounded by Bolivia on the southwest and west. Its capital is Cuiabá (pop., 1991: 401,000), founded in 1719 after the discovery of gold. In 1748 Mato Grosso became an independent captaincy, in 1822 a province of the empire, and in 1889 a state of the federal union. One of the few great frontier regions still in existence, it consists of grassland, dense forest, and highland plains, with some areas that remain largely unexplored.

matriarchy \'mā-trē-,är-kē\ Hypothetical social system in which familial and political authority is wielded by women. Under the influence of CHARLES DARWIN's theories of evolution, and particularly the work of the Swiss anthropologist J. J. Bachofen (1815–1887), some 19th-century scholars believed that matriarchy followed a stage of general promiscuity and preceded male ascendancy (patriarchy) in human society's evolutionary sequence. Like other elements of the evolutionist view of culture, the notion of matriarchy as a universal stage of development is now generally discredited, and the modern consensus is that a strictly matriarchal society has never existed. Nevertheless, in those societies in which matrilineal DESCENT occurs, access to socially powerful positions is mediated through the maternal line of kin. See also SOCIOCULTURAL EVOLUTION.

matrix Set of numbers arranged in rows and columns to form a rectangular array. Matrix elements may also be differential operators, vectors, or functions. Matrices have wide applications in engineering, physics, economics, and statistics, as well as in various branches of mathematics. They are usually first encountered in the study of SYSTEMS OF EQUATIONS represented by matrix equations of the form $Ax = B$, which may be solved by finding the inverse of matrix A or by using an algebraic method based on its DETERMINANT.

matsuri \'mät-sü-,rē\ Civil or religious festival in Japan, especially the shrine festivals of SHINTO. It traditionally has two parts: a solemn ritual of worship and a joyous celebration. The participants first purify themselves (see HARAI) by periods of abstinence and by bathing. The inner doors of the shrine are then opened, a drum or bells are sounded, and the deity or sacred power *(kami)* is called to descend. The ritual continues with offerings, prayers, and ceremonial music and dancing. The celebration usually includes a feast, dancing, theatrical performances, divination, and athletic contests. The *kami* is often taken out in a portable shrine and carried in procession.

Matsushita Electric Industrial Co., Ltd. \mät-'sü-shi-tə\ Major Japanese manufacturer of electric appliances and consumer electronics products. Founded in 1918 by Matsushita Konosuke (1894–1989) to produce electric lamp sockets and plugs, the company was incorporated in 1935. In the 1930s it manufactured a variety of electrical products, including radios and phonographs. In the 1950s it added television sets, tape recorders, and household appliances; a decade later it brought out microwave ovens, air conditioners, and videotape recorders. It markets products under the brand names Panasonic and Quasar. Matsushita is noted for its heavy investment in research and development. Its headquarters are in Kadoma, near Osaka; it has manufacturing and sales subsidiaries in many oversea markets.

Matteotti \,mä-tā-'ȯt-tē\, **Giacomo** (1885–1924) Italian Socialist leader. A lawyer, he joined the Italian Socialist Party and was elected to the Chamber of Deputies in 1919. As head of the Socialists in 1924, he strongly denounced the Fascist Party. Two weeks after his speech, he was kidnapped and murdered by Fascists. The murder created a worldwide scandal, and Mussolini took responsibility as head of the Fascist Party and dared his critics to prosecute him. Opposition was weak, and the Matteotti crisis enabled Mussolini to further consolidate his power.

matter Material substance that constitutes the observable universe and, together with ENERGY, forms the basis of all objective phenomena. ATOMS are the basic building blocks of matter. Every physical entity can be described, physically and mathematically, in terms of interrelated quantities of MASS, INERTIA, and GRAVITATION. Matter in bulk occurs in several states; the most familiar are the gaseous (see GAS), LIQUID, and SOLID states (PLASMAS, GLASSES, and various others are less clearly defined), each with characteristic properties. According to ALBERT EINSTEIN's special theory of

L M N

RELATIVITY, matter and energy are equivalent and interconvertible (see CONSERVATION LAW).

Matterhorn *French* **Mont Cervin** \ˌmōⁿ-ser-ˈveⁿ\ *Italian* **Monte Cervino** \ˈmōn-tā-cher-ˈvē-nō\ Mountain in the ALPS, on the border between Italy and Switzerland. Rising to 14,692 ft (4,478 m), it appears from the Swiss side to be an isolated peak, but it is actually the end of a ridge. The Italian slope is more difficult to climb than the Swiss slope. It was first scaled on July 14, 1865, by British explorer Edward Whymper, who ascended the Swiss side. Three days later Giovanni A. Carrel led an Italian group in the first ascent from the Italian side.

The Matterhorn reflected in one of the Riffel lakes, Switzerland.
EWING GALLOWAY

Matthau \ˈma-thau̇\, **Walter** (1920–2000) U.S. actor. Born in New York City, he began his career as a child actor in Yiddish theater and appeared on Broadway in plays such as *Once More, with Feeling* (1958) and *A Shot in the Dark* (1962). He made his film debut in *The Kentuckian* (1955). He won stardom with his stage role in *The Odd Couple* (1965), which he reprised in the 1968 film version with his frequent costar, JACK LEMMON. His other films include *The Fortune Cookie* (1966, Academy Award), *The Sunshine Boys* (1975), and *I'm Not Rappaport* (1996).

Matthew, St. (fl. 1st century AD) One of the Twelve APOSTLES, traditional author of the first GOSPEL. According to the Gospels, he was a tax collector known as Levi when Jesus called him to be a disciple. Other information about him is scarce. The Gospel of Matthew is directed at a Jewish-Christian audience in a Jewish environment and may have been written originally in Hebrew, but it is now doubted that the Apostle Matthew was its author. Tradition holds that Matthew conducted his ministry in Judaea, after which he served as a missionary to Ethiopia and Persia. Legend differs as to whether he died a martyr's death.

Matthews, Leigh (born 1952) Australian Rules football player. A tenacious forward, he was legendary for his robust play and extraordinary skills. He played for Hawthorn (1969–1985), scoring 915 goals and helping the team to four league titles. He enjoyed subsequent success as a coach at Collingwood (1986–95) and Brisbane (1999–), guiding both teams to league titles. He was inducted into the Australian Football Hall of Fame and elevated to Legend in 1996.

Matthias I *or* **Matthias Corvinus** \mə-ˈthī-əs...kȯr-ˈvī-nəs\ *Hungarian* **Mátyás Corvin** *orig.* **Mátyás Hunyadi** (1443–1490) King of Hungary (1458–90). He spent much of his reign combating the claims of the HABSBURG DYNASTY and attempting to reconstruct the Hungarian state after decades of feudal anarchy. He raised taxes, modernized the army, and codified Hungarian law. After fighting off Turks on Hungary's southern border, Matthias organized a defensive system against them. He gained control of Bosnia (1463) but lost a struggle with Poland for Bohemia. Long a rival of Emperor FREDERICK III, he occupied Vienna and other Habsburg lands.

Matthiessen \ˈmath-ə-sən\, **Peter** (born 1927) U.S. naturalist and writer. Born in New York City, he attended Yale University and worked as a fisherman on Long Island before undertaking his extensive world travels. His nonfiction, much of it inspired by his career as a naturalist, includes *Wildlife in America* (1959), *The Snow Leopard* (1978, National Book Award), and *In the Spirit of Crazy Horse* (1983). His novels include *At Play in the Fields of the Lord* (1965; film, 1991), *Far Tortuga* (1975), and *Killing Mister Watson* (1990).

mattock \ˈma-tək\ Picklike digging implement, one of the oldest tools of agriculture. It resembles the modern hoe but with a stone or wooden blade rather than a metal one, set at right angles to a long wooden handle. Home gardeners and horticulturists may still use mattocks to loosen dirt and to chop weeds.

Maturidiya \mȧ-ˌtu̇r-ē-ˈdē-ə\ Muslim orthodox school of theology named after its founder, Abu Mansur Muhammad al-Maturidi (died 944). It is characterized by reliance on the QURAN with minimal reasoning and little scope for interpretation. On the question of free will, it once emphasized the absolute omnipotence of God and allowed only limited freedom of action, but later stated unequivocally that humans have the utmost freedom to act. The Maturidiya asserted that a Muslim who sincerely performed all religious duties as prescribed in the Quran was assured of a place in heaven.

Mau Mau \ˈmau̇-ˌmau̇\ Militant KIKUYU-led nationalist movement of the 1950s in Kenya. The Mau Mau (the name's origin is uncertain) advocated violent resistance to British domination in Kenya. In response to actions by Mau Mau rebels, the British Kenya government launched a series of military operations between 1952 and 1956. Some 11,000 Kikuyu, 100 Europeans, and 2,000 African loyalists were killed in the fighting; another 20,000 Kikuyu were put into detention camps. Despite their losses, Kikuyu resistance spearheaded the independence movement, and JOMO KENYATTA, jailed as a Mau Mau leader in 1953, became prime minister of independent Kenya in 1963.

Mauchly \ˈmäk-lē\, **John W(illiam)** (1907–1980) U.S. physicist and engineer. Born in Cincinnati, he joined the faculty at the University of Pennsylvania after completing his graduate studies. During World War II he and J. PRESPER ECKERT were asked by the U.S. Army to devise ways to accelerate the recomputation of artillery firing tables, for which they eventually developed ENIAC. The two men formed a computer-manufacturing firm in 1948, and in 1949 produced the Binary Automatic Computer (BINAC), which used magnetic tape instead of punched cards for data storage. Their third computer, the UNIVAC I, was designed to handle business data.

Maud See MATILDA

Maudslay \ˈmȯdz-lē\, **Henry** (1771–1831) British engineer and inventor. The son of a workman, he became the inventor of machines fundamentally important to the INDUSTRIAL REVOLUTION, most outstandingly the metal LATHE. He also invented methods for printing calico cloth and for desalting seawater for ships' boilers, as well as a measuring machine that was accurate to 0.0001 in. (0.00025 cm). See also JOSEPH BRAMAH.

Maugham \ˈmȯm\, **W(illiam) Somerset** (1874–1965) English novelist, playwright, and short-story writer. He abandoned a short career in medicine when his first novel, *Liza of Lambeth* (1897), had some success. His plays, mainly Edwardian social comedies, brought him financial security. His reputation rests primarily on the novels *Of Human Bondage* (1915), *The Moon and Sixpence* (1919), *Cakes and Ale* (1930), and *The Razor's Edge* (1944). His short stories often portray the confusion of Europeans in alien surroundings. His works, regarded less highly today than formerly, are characterized by a clear, unadorned style, cosmopolitan settings, and a shrewd understanding of human nature.

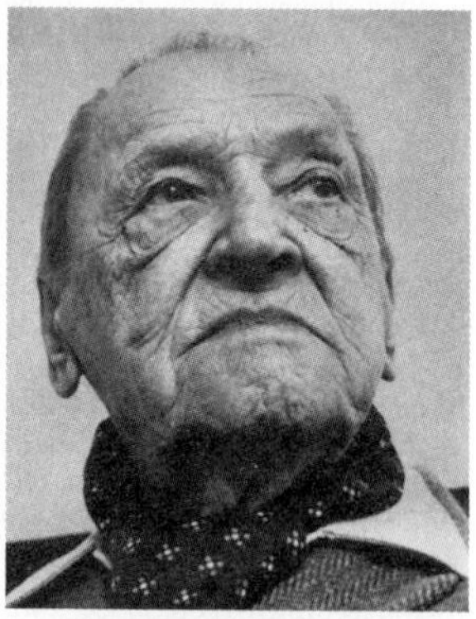

W. Somerset Maugham.
MICHAEL OCHS ARCHIVES/VENICE, CALIF.

Mauldin \'mȯl-din\, **Bill** *orig.* **William Henry** (born 1921) U.S. cartoonist. Born in Mountain Park, N.M., he studied at the Chicago Academy of Fine Arts and worked as a cartoonist before World War II, when he enlisted in the army. His sardonic cartoons for *Stars and Stripes,* featuring Willie and Joe, disheveled enlisted men who managed to retain their humanity between the onslaughts of war and an often fatuous army hierarchy, were widely republished. After the war he became a political cartoonist, first for the *St. Louis Post-Dispatch* and then for the *Chicago Sun-Times*. He won Pulitzer Prizes in 1945 and 1959.

Mauna Kea \ˌmau̇-nä-'kē-ə\ Dormant volcano, northern central HAWAII island, Hawaii. Rising to 13,796 ft (4,205 m), it is the highest point in the state and is the chief feature of a state park occupying 500 acres (202 hectares). Its name means "white mountain," referring to its snow-capped peak. Its dome is 30 mi (48 km) across, and is the site of a major astronomical observatory. Its lava flows have buried the southern slopes of the Kohala Mountains to the northwest, and its own western and southern slopes are covered with lava from its neighbor, MAUNA LOA.

Mauna Loa Volcano, southern central HAWAII island, Hawaii. Located in HAWAII VOLCANOES NATIONAL PARK, it is the world's largest mountain in cubic content. It rises to 13,678 ft (4,169 m) and has a dome 75 mi (120 km) long and 64 mi (103 km) wide. Mokuaweoweo, its pit crater, has an area of nearly 4 sq mi (10 sq km) and a depth of 500–600 ft (150–180 m). It has averaged one eruption every 3 1/2 years since 1832. Many of its eruptions are confined within Mokuaweoweo; others are from fissures and vents. Its lava flows occupy more than 2,000 sq mi (5,120 sq km) of the island. See also KILAUEA.

Maupassant \mō-pȧ-'säⁿ\, **(Henry-René-Albert-) Guy de** (1850–1893) French writer of short stories. His law studies were interrupted by the FRANCO-PRUSSIAN WAR; his experience as a volunteer provided him with material for some of his best works. Later, as a civil-service employee, he became a protégé of GUSTAVE FLAUBERT. He first gained attention with "Boule de Suif" (1880), probably his finest story. In the next 10 years he published some 300 short stories, six novels, and three travel books. Taken together, his stories present a broad, naturalistic picture of French life from 1870 to 1890. His subjects include war, the Norman peasantry, the bureaucracy, life on the banks of the Seine, the emotional problems of the different classes, and, ominously, hallucination. Maupassant was phenomenally promiscuous, and before he was 25 his health was being eroded by syphilis. He attempted suicide in 1892 and was committed to an asylum, where he died at 42. He is generally considered France's greatest master of the short story.

Maupassant, photograph by Nadar (Gaspard-Félix Tournachon), c. 1885.
ARCHIVES PHOTOGRAPHIQUES

Mauretania Ancient region of North Africa corresponding to present-day northern MOROCCO and western and central ALGERIA. It was settled by the Phoenicians and Carthaginians from the 6th century BC. Its later inhabitants were known to the Romans as the Mauri and Massaeyli. It was annexed to Rome c. AD 42, and divided into two provinces. It had become virtually independent in the 5th century, but it was overrun by the VANDALS and Arabs in the 7th century.

Mauriac \mór-'yák\, **François** (1885–1970) French writer. Mauriac grew up in a pious and strict Catholic family, and he subsequently placed at the heart of all his works the soul grappling with the problems of sin, grace, and salvation. He is best known for his austere, psychological novels, including *Young Man in Chains* (1913); *The Kiss to the Leper* (1922); *Thérèse* (1927); *Vipers' Tangle* (1932), often considered his masterpiece; and *A Woman of the Pharisees* (1941). His plays include *Asmodée* (1938). He wrote polemical works against totalitarianism and fascism in the 1930s and worked with the Resistance during World War II. He was awarded the 1952 Nobel Prize

Maurice of Nassau *Dutch* **Maurits, Prins (Prince) van Oranje, Graaf (Count) van Nassau** (1567–1625) The son of WILLIAM I THE SILENT, he was invested in 1585 as stadtholder (chief executive) of the northern provinces of the Netherlands. With political direction from JOHAN VAN OLDENBARNEVELT, Maurice consolidated the power of the provinces against Spain and made them trade and shipping centers. He used military planning and siege warfare to defeat Spanish forces in the north and east but failed to take the southern Netherlands and was forced to conclude a truce with Spain in 1609. His development of military strategy and tactics made the Dutch army the most modern in Europe. In 1618 he consolidated his political power after removing Oldenbarnevelt from office, and as prince of Orange, count of Nassau, he became effectively king of the Netherlands.

Maurier, Daphne du See Daphne DU MAURIER

Maurier, George du See George DU MAURIER

Mauritania *officially* **Islamic Republic of Mauritania** Republic, North Africa. It is bordered by the Atlantic Ocean. Area: 398,000 sq mi (1,030,700 sq km). Population (1997 est.): 2,410,000. Capital: NOUAKCHOTT. The Moors (of mixed Arab-Berber and Sudanic black descent) consitute the great majority of the population. Languages: Arabic (official); Fulani, Soninke, Wolof (all national). Religion: Islam (official). Currency: ouguiya. Most of Mauritania is made up of low-lying desert that forms the westernmost part of the Sahara. Only a tiny fraction of its land is arable, but almost 40% is rangeland or pasture, and the

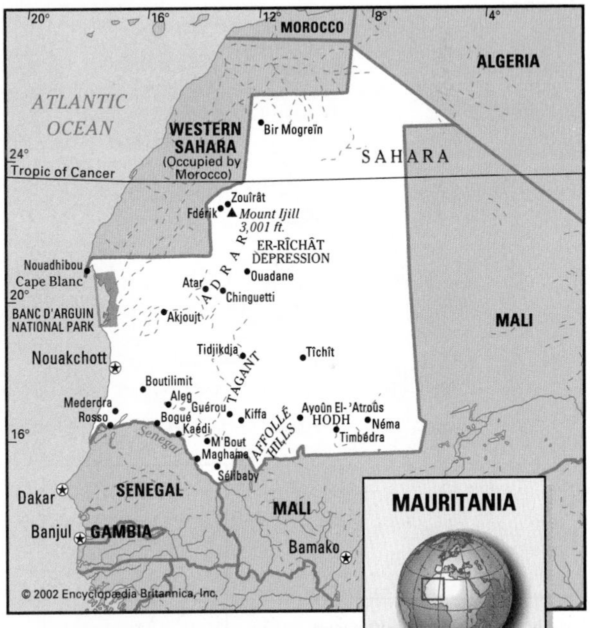

nomadic herding of goats, sheep, and camels occupies a large portion of the population. Ocean fishing and iron-ore production are major sources of revenue. It is a republic with two legislative houses; its head of state and government is the president, assisted by the prime minister. Inhabited in ancient times by Sanhadja BERBERS, in the 11th–12th century it was the center of the Berber ALMORAVID movement, which imposed Islam on many of the neighboring peoples. Arab tribes arrived in the 15th century and formed several powerful confederations: Trarza and Brakna, which dominated the Sénégal River region; Kunta in the east; and Rigaibat in the north. The Portuguese arrived in the 15th century. France gained control of the coastal region in the Senegal treaty of 1817, and in 1903 a formal protectorate was extended over the territory. In 1904 it was added to French West Africa, and in 1920 it became a colony. In 1960 Mauritania achieved independence and left the French Community. The country's first president, Moktar Ould Daddah, was ousted in a coup in 1978, and a military government was established. In 1980 a civilian government was set up and in 1991 a new constitution was adopted. During the 1990s, relations between the government and opposition groups deteriorated, even as there was some success in liberalizing the economy.

Mauritius \mò-'ri-shəs\ *officially* **Republic of Mauritius** Island country, lying east of Madagascar in the Indian Ocean. The central independent island state of the Mascarene group, it extends 38 mi (61 km) north–south and 29 mi (47 km) east–west. Its outlying territories are Rodrigues Island to the east, the Cargados Carajos Shoals to the northeast, and the Agalega Islands to the north. Area: 788 sq mi (2,040 sq km). Population (1997 est.): 1,140,000. Capital: PORT LOUIS. About three-fifths of the population are either Creole or of French descent, and two-fifths are Indian. Languages: English (official), Creole (lingua franca), various ethnic languages. Religions: Hinduism (one-half the population), Christianity (one-third), Islam. Currency: rupee. Volcanic in origin and almost surrounded by coastal reefs, Mauritius rises to 2,711 ft (826 m) at the Petite Rivière-Noire Peak; its chief water source is Lake Vacoas. About half of its land is arable, and sugarcane is the major crop, though the government has sponsored agricultural diversification. The country is

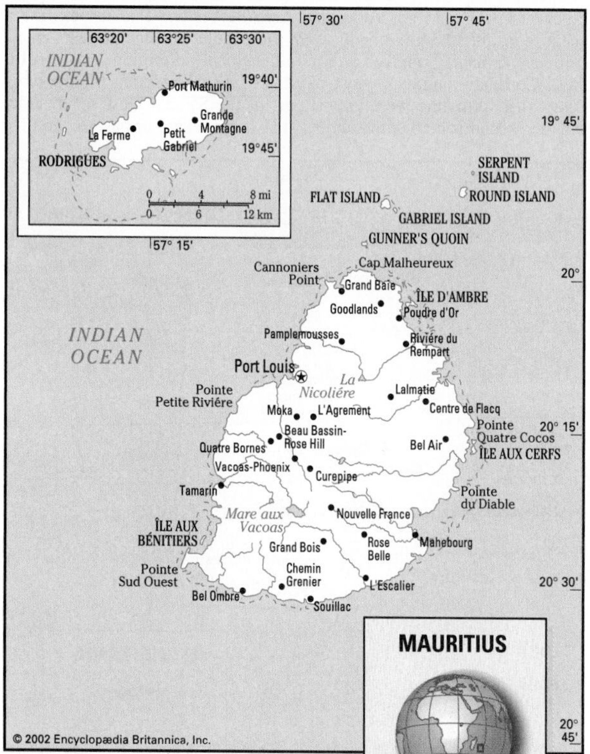

heavily dependent on food imports, mainly rice. The nation's population density is one of the highest in the world. The island was visited, but not settled, by the Portuguese in the early 16th century. The Dutch took possession 1598–1710, called it Mauritius after the governor Maurice of Nassau, and attempted to settle it (1638–58, 1664–1710) before abandoning it to pirates. The French East India Co. occupied it, renamed it Île de France in 1721, and governed it until the French ministry of marine took over its administration in 1767. Sugar planting was the main industry, and the colony prospered. The British captured the island in 1810 and were granted formal control of it under the Treaty of PARIS in 1814; the name Mauritius was reinstated, and slavery was abolished. In the late 19th century competition from beet sugar caused an economic decline, compounded by the opening of the SUEZ CANAL in 1869. After World War II, Mauritius adopted political and economic reforms, and in 1968 it became an independent state within the COMMONWEALTH. In 1992 it became a republic. It experienced political unrest during the 1990s.

Maurois \mōr-'wä\, **André** *orig.* **Émile Herzog** (1885–1967) French writer. An officer in the British army during World War I, Maurois had his first literary success with *The Silences of Colonel Bramble* (1918), a humorous commentary on warfare and the British character. His novels include *Bernard Quesnay* (1926) and *Whatever Gods May Be* (1928). He is best known for biographies with the narrative interest of novels, including those of PERCY B. SHELLEY, Lord BYRON, VICTOR HUGO, and MARCEL PROUST. He also wrote histories of England and the U.S., essays, and children's tales.

Maurras \mò-'räs\, **Charles (-Marie-Photius)** (1868–1952) French writer and political theorist. In 1891 he cofounded a group of poets opposed to the SYMBOLISTS and later known as the *école romane*. An ardent monarchist, he cofounded *L'Action Française* (1899), a review whose "integral nationalism" promoted the idea of the supremacy of the state; it became the party organ of the reactionary ACTION FRANÇAISE. He also wrote philosophical short stories and poetry. During World War II he was a strong supporter of the government of PHILIPPE PETAIN, for which he was imprisoned 1945–52.

Maurya See CANDRA GUPTA

Mauryan empire \'maù-rē-ən\ (321?–185? BC) In ancient India, a state centered at Pataliputra (later Patna) near the junction of the Son and Ganges rivers. After the death of ALEXANDER THE GREAT, CANDRA GUPTA, the dynastic founder, carved out an empire that encompassed most of the subcontinent except for the Tamil south. ASHOKA (r.c. 265–238 BC or c. 273–232 BC), the famous Buddhist emperor, left stone edicts that include some of the oldest deciphered original texts of India. The empire declined after Ashoka's death, but in its heyday it was an efficient and highly organized autocracy. See also GUPTA DYNASTY, NANDA DYNASTY.

mausoleum Large, impressive tomb, especially a stone building with places for entombment of the dead aboveground. The word is derived from MAUSOLUS, whose widow raised a splendid tomb at HALICARNASSUS (c. 353–350 BC). Probably the most ambitious mausoleum is the TAJ MAHAL.

Mausolus \mò-'sō-ləs\ (died 353/352 BC) Satrap (governor) of Caria in South Asia Minor. Nominally under the control of the Persian empire, he took advantage of upheaval in Asia Minor to gain independence. He was influential among the Greek cities of Ionia and instigated the revolt of Athens's allies in 357. He endowed his capital, HALICARNASSUS, with fine buildings. The greatest was his tomb, the Mausoleum, one of the SEVEN WONDERS OF THE WORLD, designed by the Greek architect Pythius and finished by Mausolus' sister and wife, ARTEMISIA.

Mauss \'mōs\, **Marcel** (1872–1950) French sociologist and anthropologist. Mauss was the nephew of É. DURKHEIM, who contributed much to his intellectual formation and with whom he collaborated in such important works as *Suicide* (1897) and *Primitive Classification* (1901–2). His most influential independent work was *The Gift* (1925), a highly original comparative study of the relation between forms of GIFT EXCHANGE and social structure. He taught at the École Pratique des Hautes Études and Collège de France, and cofounded the University of Paris's Institut d'Ethnologie. His views on ethnological theory and method influenced CLAUDE LEVI-STRAUSS, A. R. RADCLIFFE-BROWN, BRONISLAW MALINOWSKI, and EDWARD EVANS-PRITCHARD.

Mawlana See Jalal ad-Din ar-RUMI

mawlid \'maù-lid\ *or* **milad** \,mē-'lad\ In ISLAM, the birthday of a holy figure, especially MUHAMMAD. His birthday is fixed by tradition as the 12th day of the month of Rabi I (actually the day of his death). First celebrated by the Muslim faithful in the 13th century, Muhammad's birthday was preceded by a month of merrymaking, which ended with animal sacrifices and a torchlight procession. The day of the mawlid included a public sermon and a feast. Though mawlid festivities are considered idolatrous by some Islamic fundamentalists, they continue to be widely celebrated throughout the Muslim world and have been extended to popular saints and the founders of Sufi brotherhoods.

Maxim, Hiram (Stevens) *later* **Sir Hiram** (1840–1916) U.S.-British inventor. Son of a Maine farmer, he was apprenticed to a carriage maker. He became chief engineer of the U.S. Electric Lighting Co. (1878–81), for which he introduced carbon filaments for electric lightbulbs. At his lab in London he began working on a fully automatic MACHINE GUN; in 1884 he succeeded with a design that used the recoil of the barrel to eject the spent cartridges and reload the chamber. He also developed his own smokeless GUNPOWDER, cordite. Soon every army was equipped with Maxim guns or adaptations. His other inventions included a hair-curling iron, a pneumatic gun, and an airplane (1894). His Maxim Gun Co. was eventually absorbed into Vickers, Ltd. His son Hiram Percy (1869–1936) invented the Maxim silencer for rifles, which he adapted to mufflers and other technologies, and designed the Columbia electric automobile.

Maximian \mak-'sim-ē-ən\ *Latin in full* **Marcus Aurelius Valerius Maximianus** (died AD 310) Roman emperor with DIOCLETIAN (286–305). Assigned the government of the West, he could not suppress revolts in Gaul and Britain; CONSTANTIUS I CHLORUS took charge of these, leaving him Italy, Spain, and Africa. Though known as a persecutor of Christians, he probably acted on Diocletian's orders. He reluctantly abdicated with Diocletian, but recanted to support his son Maxentius' claim as caesar. He abdicated again and lived at the court of his son-in-law, CONSTANTINE I. After raising a failed revolt against Constantine, he was murdered or committed suicide.

Maximilian *orig.* **Ferdinand Maximilian Joseph** (1832–1867) Archduke of Austria and emperor of Mexico (1864–67). The younger brother of FRANCIS JOSEPH I of Austria-Hungary, he served in the Austrian navy and as governor-general of the Lombardo-Venetian kingdom. He accepted the offer of the Mexican throne, naively believing that the Mexicans had voted him their king. In fact, the offer was a scheme between Mexican conservatives, who wanted to overthrow Pres. BENITO JUAREZ, and NAPOLEON III, who wanted to collect a debt from Mexico and had imperialist ambitions there. Intending to rule with paternal benevolence, Maximilian upheld Juárez's reforms, to the fury of the conservatives. The end of the American Civil War allowed the U.S. to intervene on Juárez's behalf; French forces that had been supporting Maximilian left at the request of the U.S., and Juárez's army retook Mexico City. Refusing to abdicate, Maximilian was defeated and executed.

Maximilian.

BY COURTESY OF THE LIBRARY OF CONGRESS, WASHINGTON, D.C.

Maximilian I (1573–1651) Duke of Bavaria (1597–1651) and elector from 1623. Succeeding his father as duke, he restored the duchy to solvency, revised the law code, and built an effective army. Opposed to the Protestant cause, he established the CATHOLIC LEAGUE (1610). In the THIRTY YEARS' WAR, he gave military aid to Austria against the Palatine elector Frederick V and with military victories by GRAF VON TILLY obtained both territory and the electorship of Bavaria (1623). Threatened by an independent army under ALBRECHT W. E. VON WALLENSTEIN, he forced the general's dismissal in 1630. Maximilian later fought unsuccessfully against France and Sweden and made a separate peace to retain the electorship.

Maximilian I *orig.* **Maximilian Joseph** (1756–1825) First king of Bavaria (1806–25). A member of the House of WITTELSBACH, in 1799 he inherited its territories as Maximilian IV Joseph, elector of Bavaria. Forced by Austria to enter the war against France, he signed a separate peace in 1801. Distrustful of Austria, he supported the French war effort (1805–9) through Bavaria's membership in the CONFEDERATION OF THE RHINE. He received territories by which he crowned himself king of Bavaria (1806). After 1813 he allied with Austria to guarantee the integrity of his kingdom and gave up sections of western Austria in return for territories on the western bank of the Rhine. Aided by his chief minister, Count von Montgelas (1759–1838), Maximilian made Bavaria into an efficient, liberal state under a new constitution (1808) and charter (1818) that established a bicameral parliament.

Maximilian I (1459–1519) German king and Holy Roman Emperor (1493–1519). The eldest son of Emperor FREDERICK III and a member of the HABSBURG DYNASTY, he gained BURGUNDY's lands in the Netherlands by marriage in 1477, but was later forced to give Burgundy to LOUIS XI (1482). He retook most of the Habsburg lands in Austria from the Hungarians by 1490, and after being crowned Holy Roman emperor he drove the Turks from the empire's southeastern borders. He fought a series of wars against the French, helping to force them out of Italy in 1496 but losing Milan to them in 1515. He lost Switzerland as well, but acquired the TIROL peacefully. He acquired Spain for the Habsburgs through his children's marriages, gained influence in Hungary and Bohemia, and built an intricate network of European alliances. A popular monarch, he encouraged culture and the arts.

Maximilian II (1811–1864) King of Bavaria (1848–64). Son of King LUDWIG I, he succeeded to the throne on his father's abdication in 1848. He proposed a league of smaller states as a "third force" in German affairs but was opposed by the dominant states of Austria and Prussia. He successfully introduced liberal reforms in Bavaria, including freedom of the press and ministerial responsibility. He made Munich a center of culture and gave support to such scholars as LEOPOLD RANKE. He was succeeded by his son LUDWIG II.

Maximilian II (1527–1576) Holy Roman emperor (1564–76). Son of the future emperor FERDINAND I, he was a humanist Christian who favored compromise between Catholics and Protestants. He became king of Bohemia in 1562 and succeeded to the imperial throne in 1564. He extended religious tolerance and worked for reform of the Roman Catholic church. He failed to achieve his political goals; an unsuccessful campaign against the Turks ended in a truce in 1568 that compelled him to continue to pay tribute to the sultan.

maximum In mathematics, a point at which a FUNCTION's value is greatest. If the value is greater than or equal to all other function values, it is an absolute maximum. If it is merely greater than any nearby point, it is a relative, or local, maximum. In CALCULUS, the DERIVATIVE equals zero or does not exist at a function's maximum point. Techniques for finding maximum and minimum points motivated the early development of calculus and have made it easier to solve problems such as finding the dimensions of a container that will hold the most for a given amount of material used to make it. See also MINIMUM, OPTIMIZATION.

Maximus the Greek (1480–1556) Greek scholar and linguist. Educated in Paris, Venice, and Florence, he became part of a circle of humanist scholars and was influenced by the Dominican reformer GIROLAMO SAVONAROLA. He became a Greek Orthodox monk and was chosen to translate Greek liturgical and theological texts into Russian, thus making possible the dissemination of Byzantine culture throughout Russia. In Moscow he became involved in a religious controversy when he joined a faction called the Nonpossessors, who advocated renunciation of property ownership by the church. Arrested for heresy in 1525, he was imprisoned for 20 years in a monastery. After his death he was venerated as a saint.

Maxwell, James Clerk (1831–1879) Scottish physicist. Born in Edinburgh, he published his first scientific paper at 14, entered the University of Edinburgh at 16, and graduated from Cambridge University. He taught at Aberdeen Univ., King's College London, and Cambridge (from 1871), where he supervised the building of Cavendish Laboratory. His most revolutionary achievement was his demonstration that light is an electromagnetic wave, and he originated the concept of ELECTROMAGNETIC RADIATION. His field equations (see MAXWELL'S EQUATIONS) paved the way for ALBERT EINSTEIN's special theory of relativity. He established the nature of Saturn's rings, did important work on color perception, and produced the kinetic theory of gases. His ideas formed the basis for QUANTUM MECHANICS and ultimately for the modern theory of the structure of atoms and molecules.

Maxwell, (Ian) Robert *orig.* **Jan Ludvik Hoch** (1923–1991) Czech-British publisher. Of Jewish origin, he lost many family members in the Holocaust but managed to reach Britain and become an army officer. After the war he founded Pergamon Press, which became a major publisher of trade journals and scientific books. In the 1980s he revived the British Printing Corp. and purchased the Mirror Group Newspapers, though his financial practices were officially questioned. Among the U.S. acquisitions of Maxwell Communications were the *New York Daily News* (1991) and the publishing house Macmillan. The revelation of fraudulent financial dealings aimed at bolstering his collapsing empire was followed by his death by drowning from his yacht in the Atlantic, assumed a suicide.

Maxwell, William (1908–2000) American editor and author. Born in Lincoln, Ill., Maxwell taught English at the University of Illinois before joining the staff of *The New Yorker* magazine. In his 40 years there, he edited writers such as JOHN CHEEVER, J.D. SALINGER, EUDORA WELTY, and MAVIS GALLANT. He himself was the author of spare, evocative short stories and novels. Perhaps his best-known work is *The Folded Leaf* (1945), about the friendship of two small-town boys. Among his other works are the novels *The Château* (1961) and *So Long, See You Tomorrow* (1980) and the short-story collection *All the Days and Nights* (1995).

Maxwell's equations Four equations, formulated by JAMES CLERK MAXWELL, that together form a complete description of the production and interrelation of ELECTRIC and MAGNETIC fields. The statements of these four equations are (1) electric field diverges from ELECTRIC CHARGE, (2) there are no isolated magnetic poles, (3) electric fields are produced by changing magnetic fields, and (4) circulating magnetic fields are produced by changing electric fields and by electric currents. Maxwell based his description of ELECTROMAGNETIC FIELDS on these four statements.

May beetle See JUNE BEETLE

May Day In Europe, the day (May 1) for traditional springtime celebrations. It probably originated in pre-Christian agricultural rituals. Celebrations included people carrying trees, green branches, or garlands; a May king and queen, and a Maypole. May Day was designated an international labor day by the International Socialist Congress of 1899, and it remains the standard Labor Day worldwide, with a few exceptions, including Canada and the U.S. A major holiday in the Soviet Union and other communist countries, it was the occasion for important political demonstrations.

May Fourth Movement Chinese intellectual revolution and sociopolitical reform movement (1917–21). In 1915 young intellectuals inspired by CHEN DUXIU began agitating for the reform and strengthening of Chinese society through acceptance of Western science, democracy, and schools of thought, one objective being to make China strong enough to resist Western imperialism. On May 4, 1919, reformist zeal found focus in a protest by Beijing's students against the Versailles Peace Conference's decision to transfer former German concessions in China to Japan. After more than a month of demonstrations, strikes, and boycotts of Japanese goods, the government gave way and refused to sign the peace treaty with Germany. The movement spurred the successful reorganization of the GUOMINDANG and gave birth to the CHINESE COMMUNIST PARTY. See also Treaty of VERSAILLES.

Maya \'mī-ə\ Group of Mesoamerican Indians who between AD 250 and 900 developed one of the Western Hemisphere's greatest civilizations. By AD 200 they had developed cities containing palaces, temples, plazas, and ball courts. They used stone tools to quarry the immense quantities of stone needed for those structures; their sculpture and relief carving were also highly developed. MAYAN HIEROGLYPHIC WRITING survives in books and inscriptions. Mayan mathematics featured positional notation and the use of the zero; Mayan astronomy featured an accurately determined solar year and precise tables of the positions of Venus and the moon. Calendrical accuracy was important for the elaborate rituals and ceremonies of the Mayan religion, which was based on a pantheon of gods. Ritual bloodletting, torture, and human sacrifice were employed to propitiate the gods, ensure fertility, and stave off cosmic chaos. At the height of its Classic period, Mayan civilization included more than 40 cities of 5,000–50,000 people. After 900 the civilization declined rapidly for unknown reasons. Descendants of the Maya are now subsistence farmers in southern Mexico and Guatemala. See also CHICHÉN ITZÁ, COPÁN, LACANDON, MAYA CODICES, MAYAN LANGUAGES, QUICHE, TIKAL, TZELTAL, TZOTZIL, UXMAL.

maya \'mī-ə\ In HINDUISM, a powerful force that creates the cosmic illusion that the phenomenal world is real. The word maya originally referred to the wizardry with which a god can make human beings believe in what turns out to be an illusion, and its philosophical sense is an extension of this meaning. The concept is especially important in the ADVAITA school of the orthodox system of VEDANTA, which sees maya as the cosmic force that presents the infinite BRAHMAN as the finite phenomenal world.

Maya Codices Books in MAYAN HIEROGLYPHIC WRITING that survived the Spanish conquest. They are made of fig-bark paper folded like an accordion, with covers of jaguar skin. Though most Mayan books were destroyed as pagan by Spanish priests, four are known to have survived: the DRESDEN CODEX, probably dating from the 11th or 12th century, a copy of earlier texts of the 5th–9th century; the Madrid Codex, dating from the 15th century; the Paris Codex, slightly older than the Madrid Codex; and the Grolier Codex, discovered in 1971 and dated to the 13th century. They deal with astronomical calculations, divination, and ritual.

Mayakovsky \mə-ˌyə-'kȯf-skē\, **Vladimir (Vladimirovich)** (1893–1930) Russian poet. Repeatedly jailed for subversive activity, he began writing poetry during solitary confinement in 1909. On his release he became the spokesman for Futurism in Russia, and his poetry became conspicuously self-assertive and defiant. He was the leading poet of the Russian Revolution of 1917 and the early Soviet period, producing declamatory works saturated with politics and aimed at mass audiences, including "Ode to Revolution" (1918) and "Left March" (1919) and the drama *Mystery Bouffe* (performed 1921). Disappointed in love, increasingly alienated from Soviet reality, and denied a visa to travel abroad, he committed suicide at 36.

Mayan hieroglyphic writing \'mī-ən\ System of writing used by people of the MAYA civilization from about the 3rd century AD to the 17th century. Of various scripts developed in pre-Columbian Mesoamerica, Mayan writing is by far the most elaborate and abundantly attested: about 800 signs have been inventoried in more than 5,000 instances (see MAYA CODICES). Signs—some representational, some quite abstract—are either logographic, representing words, or syllabic, representing consonant-vowel sequences. Typically, up to five signs are fit into tight square or rectangular clusters, which are further arranged into rows or grids. The language of Classic Period writing (c. AD 250–900) is generally thought to be Cholan, ancestral to several modern MAYAN LANGUAGES; later inscriptions were in Yucatec. By the 1990s, scholars had an accurate grasp of 60–70% of Mayan inscriptions, with some texts almost completely readable and some still quite opaque. Most inscriptions record significant events and dates in the lives of Mayan rulers.

Mayan languages Family of about 30 American Indian languages and language complexes, spoken by more than 3 million people, mainly in southern Mexico and Guatemala. While some have few remaining speakers, Yucatec in Mexico, and K'iche (Quiché), Kaqchikel (Cakchiquel), Mam, and Q'eqchi' (Kekchí) in Guatemala count speakers in the hundreds of thousands. Mayan languages typically have an opposition of glottalized and plain-stop consonants, place the verb in a clause first, and are ergative at least in part (see ERGATIVITY). Mayan languages were recorded in an indigenous script (see MAYA CODICES, MAYAN HIEROGLYPHIC WRITING), as well as in colonial documents in a Spanish-based orthography, including the *POPOL VUH* and the Yucatec prophetic texts known as the *Books of Chilam Balam*.

Mayer, Louis B(urt) *orig.* **Eliezer** *or* **Lazar** (1885–1957) U.S. (Russian-born) film executive. Born in Minsk, he emigrated to Canada and then the U.S. with his family, and worked in his father's scrap-iron business from age 14. He bought a small nickelodeon near Boston in 1907, and by 1918 owned the largest chain of movie theaters in New England. He founded a film production company in Hollywood in 1917 and merged it with other companies to form MGM in 1925. As head of MGM, he made it Hollywood's largest and most prestigious studio, aided by his artistic director, IRVING THALBERG. The creator of the star system, Mayer had under contract many of the outstanding screen stars of the day, including GRETA GARBO, CLARK GABLE, and JUDY GARLAND. He was considered the most powerful Hollywood executive until his forced retirement in 1951. He was the chief founder of the Academy of Motion Picture Arts and Sciences.

Mayer \'mī-ər\, **Maria (Gertrude)** *orig.* **Maria (Gertrude) Goeppert** (1906–1972) German-U.S. physicist. She emigrated to the U.S. in 1930, where she taught at various universities. She worked on the separation of URANIUM ISOTOPES for the MANHATTAN PROJECT. Her work in theoretical physics led to the explanation of properties of atomic nuclei based on a structure of "shells" occupied by protons and neutrons. For her work she was awarded a 1963 Nobel Prize, which she shared with Hans Jensen (1907–1973) and EUGENE P. WIGNER.

Mayerling affair See RUDOLF

Mayfield, Curtis (1942–1999) U.S. singer and songwriter. Born in Chicago, in 1953 he formed a group with Jerry Butler (born 1939) that was a precursor of the Impressions, and after reshufflings and changes of recording label, the two remained the group's nucleus through the 1960s, when Mayfield's songs gained a new social consciousness ("It's All Right," "People Get Ready," "Choice of Colors"). The highpoint of his solo career (from 1970) was the influential soundtrack to *Superfly* (1972). Though paralyzed in 1990 when a lighting tower fell on him, he continued to record.

mayflower See TRAILING ARBUTUS

Mayflower Compact (1620) Document signed by 41 male passengers on the *Mayflower* before landing at Plymouth (MASSACHUSETTS BAY COLONY). Concerned that some members might leave to form their own colonies, WILLIAM BRADFORD and others drafted the compact to bind the group into a political body and pledge members to abide by any laws that would be established. The document adapted a church covenant to a civil situation and was the basis of the colony's government.

mayfly Any INSECT of the order Ephemeroptera, found around streams and ponds. The approximately 2,000 species are up to 1.6 in. (4 cm) long, have triangular membranous forewings, smaller round hind wings, and two or three long, threadlike tails. Wings are held vertically when at rest. Chewing mouthparts in the aquatic larvae are vestigial in the adult, which lives just long enough to mate and reproduce. Males "dance" in large swarms to attract females. The adult's entire life span is usually only a few hours (though at least one species lives as long as two days), and poets have used the mayfly as a symbol of life's ephemeral nature.

mayhem CRIME of willfully and permanently crippling, mutilating, or disfiguring any part of another's body. Some jurisdictions do not distinguish between mayhem and other types of battery. JAPANESE LAW treats all batteries similarly; INDIAN LAW divides bodily harms into "hurts" and "grievous hurts." In most U.S. states mayhem is encompassed by assault and aggravated assault.

Mayhew, Henry (1812–1887) English journalist and sociologist. He studied law but soon turned to journalism. In 1841 he founded the highly successful *PUNCH*. A vivid and voluminous writer, he is best known for *London Labour and the London Poor* (1851–62), an evocation of the sights and sounds of the working-class districts of London, which influenced CHARLES DICKENS and other writers. He also wrote plays, farces, fairy tales, and novels, some in collaboration with his brother Augustus Septimus Mayhew (1826–75).

Henry Mayhew, engraving after a photograph.
BBC HULTON PICTURE LIBRARY

Mayo family Family of U.S. physicians. William Worrall Mayo (1819–1911) was born in England and came to the U.S. in 1845. He opened a surgical practice in Rochester, Minn., in 1863, and in 1889 he opened St. Mary's Hospital with his two sons and the Sisters of St. Francis. The elder son, William James (1861–1939), specialized in surgery of the abdomen, pelvis, and kidney, and served as administrator. Charles Horace (1865–1939), a gifted surgeon in all areas, originated modern procedures in goiter surgery, neurosurgery, and orthopedic surgery. Around 1900 the partnership was changed to a voluntary association of physicians and specialists, later known as the Mayo Clinic. In 1915 the brothers established the Mayo Foundation for Medical Education and Research, which offers graduate training in medicine and related subjects. The clinic currently includes about 500 physicians, treating more than 200,000 patients a year.

Mayon Volcano \mä-'yōn\ *or* **Mount Mayon** Active volcano, southeastern LUZON, Philippines. One of the world's most perfect volcanic cones, it has a base 80 mi (130 km) in circumference and rises to 7,943 ft (2,421 m). It is popular with climbers and campers and is the center of Mayon Volcano National Park, which occupies 21 sq mi (55 sq km). It has erupted more than 30 times since 1616; an eruption in 1993 caused 75 deaths. Its most destructive eruption was in 1814, when the town of Cagsawa was buried.

mayor Political leader of a municipal corporation. Mayors are either appointed or elected for a limited term. In Europe until the mid-19th century, most mayors were appointed by the central government; in France, they are still agents of the central government. In the U.S., they are either directly elected by the populace or chosen by an elected council. Some fulfill only ceremonial functions, executive power being held by a professional manager hired by the legislature. A mayor's powers may include the power to make appointments, veto legislation, administer budgets, and manage administrative functions. See also CITY GOVERNMENT.

Mayotte \mä-'yȯt\ Southeasternmost island (pop., 1991 est.: 86,000) of the COMOROS archipelago, a French overseas territorial collectivity. Located northwest of Madagascar, it occupies an area of 144 sq mi (373 sq km); Mamoutzo is its chief town and capital designate. Dzaoudzi, the current capital, is its other main city and port. Most of its people are of Malagasy origin. Originally inhabited by descendants of BANTU and Malayo-Indonesian peoples, it was converted to Islam by Arab invaders in the 15th century. Taken by a Malagasy tribe from Madagascar at the end of the 18th century, it came under French control in 1843. Together with the other Comoros islands and Madagascar, it became part of a single French overseas territory in the early 20th century. It has been administered separately since 1975, when the three northernmost islands of the Comoros declared independence.

maypole Tall wooden pole garlanded with flowers and greenery and often hung with ribbons that are woven into complex patterns by dancers in a ceremonial folk dance. The custom probably originated in ancient fertility rites that involved dancing around a living tree in the springtime. In many European countries, notably England, the pole is set up on May 1 as part of MAY DAY festivities. Similar ribbon dances were performed in India and in pre-Columbian Latin America.

Mayr \'mīr\, **Ernst (Walter)** (born 1904) German-U.S. biologist. He received his PhD from the University of Berlin and emigrated to the U.S. in 1932. While curator of the American Museum of Natural History (1932–53), he wrote more than 100 papers on avian taxonomy. From 1953 to 1975 he taught at Harvard University. His early studies of speciation and of founder populations made him a leader in the development of the modern synthetic theory of EVOLUTION. In 1940 Mayr proposed a definition of species that won wide acceptance and led to the discovery of some previously unknown species. His influential works include *Systematics and the Origin of Species* (1942) and *The Growth of Biology Thought* (1982).

Ernst Mayr.
BY COURTESY OF THE DEPARTMENT OF LIBRARY SERVICES, THE AMERICAN MUSEUM OF NATURAL HISTORY, NEW YORK CITY, NEG. NO. 334102

Mays, Willie (Howard) (born 1931) U.S. baseball player. Born in Westfield, Ala., he played for the Birmingham Black Barons in the National Negro League when he was only 16. The "Say Hey Kid" later played principally for the New York (later San Francisco) Giants in the major leagues (1951–72). A brilliant centerfielder and a powerful right-handed hitter, he ranks among the all-time top five in home runs (660), runs (2,062), and extra-base hits (1,323) and among the top ten for runs batted in (1,903) and hits (3,283). Mays is considered one of the greatest all-around players in the history of the game.

Mays.
UPI

Maysles \'mā-zəlz\, **Albert and David** (born 1926, 1932–1987)

L M N

U.S. documentary filmmakers. The Maysles brothers were born in Boston, and Albert made his first documentary, *Psychiatry in Russia*, in 1955. The two thereafter collaborated on documentaries in the Cinéma vérité style, which they called "direct cinema," becoming noted for their *Salesman* (1969) and *Gimme Shelter* (1970), both made with Charlotte Zwerin. Their later films include *Christo's Valley Curtain* (1972), *Grey Gardens* (1975), and *Vladimir Horowitz* (1985).

Mazarin \ˌma-zə-ˈraⁿ\, **Jules, Cardinal** *orig.* **Giulio Raimondo Mazarini** (1602–1661) Italian-French cardinal and statesman. A member of the papal diplomatic service (1627–34), he negotiated an end to the War of the Mantuan Succession between France and Spain. He served as papal nuncio to the French court (1634–36), where he admired Cardinal de Richelieu. He worked for French interests in the papal court, then entered the service of France and became a naturalized French citizen (1639) and a cardinal (1641). After the deaths of Richelieu (1642) and Louis XIII (1643), Mazarin was appointed first minister of France by Anne of Austria, regent for Louis XIV, and he directed Louis's education. A highly influential adviser to the young king, he helped train a staff of able administrators. His foreign policy established France's supremacy among the European powers, effecting the Peace of Westphalia (1648) and the Treaty of the Pyrenees (1659). A patron of the arts, Mazarin founded an academy of painting and sculpture and compiled a large library.

Mazarin, detail of a portrait by Philippe de Champaigne; in the Musée Condé, Chantilly, Fr.

Mazatlán \ˌmä-sä-ˈtlän\ Seaport city (pop., 2000 est.: 325,000), southwestern Sinaloa state, northern central Mexico. It occupies a peninsula overlooking Olas Altas Bay, on the Gulf of California. It is Mexico's largest Pacific port, and its island-studded harbor is known for its fine sandy beaches. Lying diagonally across the gulf from the tip of Baja California, it provides a communications link between Baja and the mainland. Mazatlán, called the Pearl of the Pacific, is a fishing center and a popular tourist resort.

Mazda Motor Corp. \ˈmäz-də\ Japanese automotive manufacturer. Mazda is affiliated with the Sumitomo group; its headquarters are in Hiroshima. Founded in 1920 as a cork plant, the firm was called Toyo Kogyo Co. from 1927 until 1984, when it adopted the name Mazda Motor Corp. It began producing trucks in 1931 and supplied the Japanese armed forces during World War II; its factory survived the atomic bombing of Hiroshima because it lay shielded behind a hill. In the 1960s it began manufacturing passenger cars and marketing them in the U.S. After enduring a slump in the 1970s, it became one of the largest auto manufacturers in Japan. Mazda also supplies axles to Ford Motor Co. and ships a ready-to-assemble car that Ford markets.

Mazdakism \ˈmaz-də-ˌki-zəm\ Dualistic religion that arose in Iran in the late 5th cent AD. Its origins are uncertain, and no Mazdakite scriptures survive. It is named for Mazdak, its main Persian proponent in the 5th century, who converted the Sasanid king Kavadh I. It held that there were two original principles, Light (or Good) and Darkness (or Evil), which accidentally became mixed, producing the world. Humans' duty was to strive to release Light in the world through moral conduct. Mazdakism was suppressed in the 6th century by Persian nobles and Zoroastrian clergy who objected to its tenets concerning the common holding of property and women, but it survived in secret until the 8th century. See also Dualism, Zoroastrianism and Parsiism.

maze See Labyrinth

Mazia \ˈmā-zē-ə\, **Daniel** (1912–1996) U.S. cell biologist. Born in Scranton, Pa., he received his PhD from the University of Pennsylvania. His research focused on various aspects of cell reproduction, including mitosis and regulation. He is best known for isolating the structure responsible for cell division, research that he carried out with Katsuma Dan (1905?–1996) in 1951.

Mazowiecki \ˌmä-zō-ˈvyet-skē\, **Tadeusz** (born 1927) Polish politician. After studying law, he cofounded and edited the independent Catholic monthly *Wiez* (1958–81). A principal adviser to the Solidarity labor movement, he was appointed its newspaper editor (1981) by Lech Walesa. After the 1989 national elections, he was appointed prime minister of a coalition government of Solidarity and communist members. He undertook radical economic reforms to develop a free-market economy, which helped stabilize Poland's consumer-goods market and increased exports but caused high unemployment. He lost his bid for president in 1990 and was replaced as prime minister in 1991.

Mazrui \mäz-ˈrü-ē\, **Ali Al Amin** (born 1933) Kenyan-U.S. political scientist. After receiving a doctorate from Oxford Univ., he taught at Uganda's Makerere University (1963–73) and later at the University of Michigan (1974–91). At SUNY–Binghamton he founded and directed the Institute of Global Cultural Studies. He has also taught at many other universities worldwide, has been a consultant to numerous international organizations, and is the author of many books on African politics and society as well as postcolonial patterns of development and underdevelopment. For television he wrote the nine-hour BBC-PBS coproduction *The Africans* (1986).

mazurka \mə-ˈzər-kə\ Polish folk dance in 3/4 time for a circle of couples, characterized by stamping feet and clicking heels, traditionally danced to the music of bagpipes. Originating in Masuria (NE Poland) in the 16th century, it became popular at the Polish court and spread to Russia and Germany, reaching England and France by the 1830s. The 50 piano mazurkas by F. Chopin reflected and extended its popularity. The dance had no set figures and allowed improvisation among its more than 50 different steps.

Mazzini \mät-ˈsē-nē\, **Giuseppe** (1805–1872) Italian patriot and a major figure in the making of modern Italy. A lawyer, he joined the secret independence group Carbonari. After he was imprisoned for its activities, he moved to Marseille (1831), where he founded the patriotic movement Young Italy. He later expanded his plan for a world republican federation and in Switzerland founded Young Europe. In London (1837), he continued his revolutionary activities by correspondence with agents worldwide. He founded the People's International League (1847) and received support from English liberals. In 1848 he returned to Italy to help govern the short-lived Republic of Rome, but returned to England after the pope reestablished control in Rome. Mazzini founded the Friends of Italy (1851) and backed unsuccessful uprisings in Milan, Mantua, and Genoa. An uncompromising republican, he disapproved of the new united Kingdom of Italy (1861). See also Risorgimento.

Mbabane \əm-bä-ˈbä-nā\ Capital and largest town (pop., 1998 est.: 60,000) of Swaziland. Located in western Swaziland, it developed near the cattle kraal of the Swazi king Mbandzeni in the late 19th century. The actual town was founded in 1902, when the British assumed control of Swaziland and set up an administrative headquarters there. A Mozambican railway link near Mbabane was established in 1964, primarily to export iron ore extracted in the region; production of the ore had virtually ceased by the late 1970s.

Mbeki \em-ˈbek-ē\, **Thabo** (born 1942) President of South Africa (from 1999). The son of an anti-apartheid activist, he studied economics at Sussex University in Britain, then received military training in the Soviet Union. He was appointed deputy president by Nelson Mandela following South Africa's first all-race elections in 1994, and soon took control of the government's day-to-day workings. Less charismatic than Mandela, Mbeki has been criticized for his views on the biology of AIDS. He has been particularly involved in South Africa's postapartheid economic-growth strategy.

mbira \em-ˈbir-ə\ *or* **thumb piano** African musical instrument consisting of a set of tuned metal or bamboo tongues attached to a board or resonator. The tongues are depressed and released with the thumbs and fingers to produce melodies and song accompaniments. The mbira dates to at least the 16th century in Africa, and was imported into Latin America by slaves.

Mboya \em-ˈbȯi-ə\, **Tom** *orig.* **Thomas Joseph** (1930–1969) Kenyan political leader. During the Mau Mau rebellion (1952–56) and the period leading up to Kenyan independence (1963), the Oxford-educated Mboya headed the Kenya Federation of Labor. In 1960 he helped found the dominant Kenyan African National Union Party (KANU). Following independence, he served in top administrative posts in JOMO KENYATTA's government. His assassination in 1969 shocked the nation and exacerbated tensions between the dominant KIKUYU and other ethnic groups, especially Mboya's own LUO.

Mbundu \em-'bün-dü\ Group of Bantu-speaking peoples occupying northern central Angola. In the 15th century they founded the Ndongo kingdom, a rival of the KONGO kingdom. It was destroyed by the Portuguese in the late 1600s. In the 1970s the Mbundu provided the main support for the Marxist-oriented Popular Movement for the Liberation of Angola (MPLA), which assumed power in 1976. Today they number about 2.3 million.

Mbuti \em-'bü-tē\ PYGMY people of the Ituri Forest of the Congo (Zaire). Numbering about 7,500, they average under 4 ft 6 in. (137 cm) in height, and differ in blood type from their BANTU and Sudanic neighbors. Probably the earliest inhabitants of the area, they are nomadic hunters and gatherers, have no chiefs or formal councils of elders, believe in a benevolent forest deity, and practice numerous rites of PASSAGE. Their music, complex in rhythm and harmony, is often accompanied by dance or mime.

MCA *in full* **Music Corporation of America** Entertainment conglomerate. It was founded in Chicago in 1924 by Jules Stein as a talent agency. In the 1960s it bought Decca Records and UNIVERSAL PICTURES, and today it produces films, music, and television shows. It was acquired by Matsushita of Japan in 1990.

McAdam, John (Loudon) (1756–1836) Scottish inventor of the MACADAM road surface. He made an early fortune in his uncle's New York countinghouse (1770–83). Back in Scotland, he noted the poor condition of the highways near his estate and undertook experiments in road making. He recommended that roads be raised above the adjacent ground for good drainage and covered, first with larger stones and then with smaller stones, the whole mass to be bound with fine gravel or slag. In 1823 his views were officially adopted, and in 1827 he was appointed Britain's Surveyor General of Metropolitan Roads. Macadamization was quickly adopted in other countries and did much to facilitate travel and communication.

McAdoo \'ma-kə-,dü\, **William G(ibbs)** (1863–1941) U.S. public official. Born near Marietta, Ga., he moved to New York in 1892, where he organized the Hudson and Manhattan Railway companies (later consolidated), which built tunnels under the Hudson River. He supported WOODROW WILSON in the 1912 presidential campaign and was appointed secretary of the treasury (1913–18); he married Wilson's daughter in 1914. In World War I he directed drives that raised $18 billion to finance the war effort. He was director general of U.S. railroads 1917–19, and later U.S. senator from California (1933–38).

McCarthy, Cormac *orig.* **Charles McCarthy, Jr.** (born 1933) U.S. novelist. Born in Providence, R.I., he grew up in Tennessee, and dropped out of the University of Tennessee to join the Air Force. He began writing in 1959. His novels, known for their natural observation, morbid realism, and violence, are in the Southern gothic tradition. They include *The Orchard Keeper* (1965), *Outer Dark* (1968), *Blood Meridian* (1985), and the widely read Border Trilogy (*All the Pretty Little Horses,* 1992; *The Crossing,* 1994; *Cities of the Plain,* 1999).

McCarthy, Eugene J(oseph) (born 1916) U.S. politician. Born in Watkins, Minn., he taught at the College of St. Thomas in St. Paul, Minn., before being elected to the U.S. House of Representatives (1949–59) and later the Senate (1959–71). A liberal Democrat, he became an outspoken critic of the Vietnam War. In 1967 he entered the Democratic primaries for the presidential nomination. His initial successes convinced Pres. LYNDON B. JOHNSON not to seek reelection. McCarthy failed to win the nomination, left the Senate in 1971, and turned to lecturing and writing.

McCarthy, John (born 1927) U.S. computer scientist. Born in Boston, he received his PhD from Princeton University. A pioneer in the field of artificial intelligence, he created LISP in 1958. He also developed ideas about the processing characteristics of trees (as used in computing), as distinct from nets. He is a recipient of the Turing Award (1971), the Kyoto Prize (1988), and the National Medal of Science (1990).

McCarthy, Joseph R(aymond) (1908–1957) U.S. politician. Born near Appleton, Wis., he practiced law before becoming a state circuit judge (1940–42) and serving with the Marines in World War II. He upset ROBERT LA FOLLETTE, Jr., to win election to the U.S. Senate in 1946. He remained little known until 1950, when he charged that communists had infiltrated the U.S. State Department. His anticommunist crusade gained wide popular support. As chairman of the Senate's subcommittee on investigations (1952), he held hearings to question government officials and others about suspected communist activities, in a campaign of persecution and slander that became known as McCarthyism. The 1954 televised hearings on charges of subversion by U.S. Army officers and an exposé by EDWARD R. MURROW revealed McCarthy's irresponsible tactics, and he was censured by the Senate for his conduct that year. A heavy drinker, he died at 48.

McCarthy, Mary (Therese) (1912–1989) U.S. novelist and critic. Born in Seattle, she served on the editorial staff of the *Partisan Review* 1937–48. She began writing fiction at the urging of her second husband, EDMUND WILSON. Her work is noted for bitingly satiric commentaries on marriage, the impotence of intellectuals, and the role of women in contemporary urban America. Her novels include *The Company She Keeps* (1942); *The Group* (1963), her most popular work; *Birds of America* (1971); and *Cannibals and Missionaries* (1979). She also wrote two autobiographies, *Memories of a Catholic Girlhood* (1957) and *How I Grew* (1987).

McCartney, (James) Paul *later* **Sir Paul** (born 1942) British singer and songwriter. Born to a working-class Liverpool family, he learned piano but switched to guitar after hearing American rock-and-roll recordings. In the mid-1950s he met JOHN LENNON, with whom he formed the Quarrymen, which evolved into the BEATLES. He and Lennon cowrote scores of songs, including some of the most popular songs of the 20th century. He released his first solo album in 1970. With his wife, the photographer Linda Eastman (1941–1998), he formed the group Wings; their hit albums included *Band on the Run* (1973) and *Wings at the Speed of Sound* (1976). After the band dissolved, McCartney had a string of hits in the 1980s. In Rio de Janeiro in 1990, he set a world record by performing before a paying audience of over 184,000. He was knighted in 1997.

McCarty, Maclyn (born 1911) U.S. biologist. Born in South Bend, Ind., he received his MD at Johns Hopkins. With OSWALD AVERY and Colin M. MacLeod he provided the first experimental evidence that the genetic material of living cells is composed of DNA. In their classic experiments (1944), the introduction of certain material from one type of pneumococcus bacteria into another type transformed the receiving bacteria into the type from which the material had been taken, results indicating that the substance responsible for the change was DNA.

McClellan, George B(rinton) (1826–1885) U.S. Army officer. Born in Philadelphia, he served in the Mexican War and conducted military engineering surveys, then resigned to become chief of engineering for the Illinois Central Railroad (1857) and president of the Ohio and Mississippi Railroad (1860). In the AMERICAN CIVIL WAR he was named commander of the department of the Ohio. He defeated Confederate forces in western Virginia and helped keep Kentucky in the Union. Appointed general in chief by ABRAHAM LINCOLN (1861), he reorganized the army into an efficient force, but his lack of offensive action led Lincoln to issue his General War Order (1862) calling for forward movement of all armies. McClellan cautiously conducted the Peninsular Campaign but failed to take Richmond, and he fought indecisively in the SEVEN DAYS' BATTLES. At the Battle of ANTIETAM he failed to destroy ROBERT E. LEE's army, and Lincoln removed him from command. In 1864 he was the Democratic candidate for president against Lincoln. He was president of the Atlantic and Great Western Railroad 1872–77.

McClintock, Barbara (1902–1992) U.S. geneticist. Born in Hartford, Conn., she received her doctorate from Cornell University. In the 1940s and '50s, her experiments with variations in the coloration of kernels of corn revealed that genetic information is not stationary. She isolated two control elements in genetic material and found not only that they moved but that the change in position affected the behavior of neighboring genes, and suggested that these elements were responsible for the diversity in cells during an organism's development. Her pioneering research, whose importance was not recognized for many years, eventually resulted in her being awarded a 1983 Nobel Prize.

McClung, Clarence E(rwin) (1870–1946) U.S. zoologist. Born in Clayton, Cal., he received his PhD from the University of Kansas. His study of the mechanisms of heredity led to his hypothesis (1901) that an extra, or accessory, chromosome determined sex. The discovery of the sex-determining chromosome provided some of the earliest evidence that a given chromosome carries a definable set of hereditary traits. McClung also studied how the behavior of chromosomes in the sex cells of different organisms affects their heredity.

McClung, Nellie *orig.* **Nellie Mooney** (1873–1953) Canadian writer. Born in Chatsworth, Ontario, she married in 1896 and became prominent in the temperance movement. Her *Sowing Seeds in Danny*, a 1908 novel about life in a small western town, became a national best-seller. She lectured widely on women's suffrage and other reforms in Canada and the U.S. and served in the Alberta legislature (1921–26). She wrote many articles and short stories and 16 books.

McCormack, John (1884–1945) Irish-U.S. tenor. He toured with Dublin's cathedral choir as a boy, studied voice in Milan, and made his Italian debut in 1906. He debuted the next year in London in *Cavalleria rusticana*, an international operatic career ensued, especially in the U.S., for the next decade. From 1918 he concentrated on recitals and recordings, ranging from German lieder to sentimental popular songs, his Irish songs becoming particularly beloved.

McCormick, Cyrus Hall (1809–1884) U.S. industrialist and inventor. Born in Rockbridge Co., Va., he is generally credited with the development (from 1831) of the mechanical REAPER, which revolutionized the harvesting of grain. By 1850 the McCormick reaper was known throughout the U.S.; its prizes and honors, including the Grand Medal of Honor at the 1855 Paris exposition, made it famous around the world. In 1902 the McCormick Harvesting Co. joined with other companies to form International Harvester Co., with McCormick's son Cyrus, Jr., as its first president.

Cyrus McCormick.
CULVER PICTURES

McCormick, Robert R(utherford) *known as* **Colonel McCormick** (1880–1955) U.S. newspaper editor and publisher. Born in Chicago, he was a grandnephew of CYRUS H. MCCORMICK and grandson of Joseph Medill, editor and publisher of the *CHICAGO TRIBUNE*. He was president of the Chicago Tribune Co. from 1911 and sole editor and publisher of the *Tribune* from 1925. Under his direction the paper achieved the largest circulation among U.S. standard-sized newspapers and led the world in newspaper advertising revenue. His idiosyncratic editorials made him the personification of reactionary journalism in the U.S.

McCrea \mə-'krā\, **Joel (Albert)** (1905–1990) U.S. film actor. Born in Pasadena, Cal., he worked in Hollywood as a stuntman and bit player before getting his first leading role, in *The Silver Horde* (1930). His films—many of them westerns in which he portrayed a dependable, even-tempered man—include *The Most Dangerous Game* (1932), *Wells Fargo* (1937), *Union Pacific* (1939), *Foreign Correspondent* (1940), *Sullivan's Travels* (1941), *The Virginian* (1946), and *Ride the High Country* (1962).

McCullers, Carson *orig.* **Lula Carson Smith** (1917–1967) U.S. novelist and short-story writer. Born in Columbus, Ga., she studied at Columbia University and NYU and eventually settled in New York's Greenwich Village. A series of strokes suffered as a child left her partly paralyzed. She typically set her stories in small Southern communities and depicted the inner lives of lonely people. Her novels include *The Heart Is a Lonely Hunter* (1940; film, 1968), perhaps her finest work; *Reflections in a Golden Eye* (1941; film, 1967); *The Member of the Wedding* (1946; film, 1952), which she adapted into a play (1950; film, 1952); and *The Ballad of the Sad Café* (1951; film, 1991), dramatized by EDWARD ALBEE in 1963.

McCulloch, Hugh (1808–1895) U.S. financier and statesman. Born in Kennebunk, Me., he moved in 1833 to Fort Wayne, Ind., where he practiced law, then turned to banking. Appointed U.S. secretary of the treasury (1865–69), he attempted to return the U.S. to the gold standard by withdrawing paper money from circulation, but was thwarted by public opposition. He served again as secretary of the treasury 1884–85.

Hugh McCulloch.
BY COURTESY OF THE LIBRARY OF CONGRESS, WASHINGTON, D.C.

McCulloch v. Maryland U.S. Supreme Court decision (1819) that affirmed the constitutional doctrine of Congress's implied powers. The case concerned the legitimacy of the authority of a newly created national bank to control the issuance of currency by the states, including Maryland. The unanimous opinion, written by JOHN MARSHALL, established that Congress possesses not only the powers expressly conferred on it by the Constitution but also the authority appropriate to the utilization of such powers, in this case the creation of such a bank. This doctrine, drawn from the "elastic clause" of Article 1, became a powerful force in the steady growth of federal powers. It also bolstered the power of JUDICIAL review established in *MARBURY V. MADISON*.

McDonnell Douglas Corp. U.S. manufacturer of jet fighters, commercial aircraft, and space vehicles. It was formed in the 1967 merger of the McDonnell Aircraft Co. (founded 1939) and the Douglas Co. (1921). During World War II, Douglas contributed 29,000 warplanes, one-sixth of the U.S. airborne fleet. After the war, it dominated commercial air routes with its DC-6 and DC-7. With the development of commercial jets, Douglas began to lag behind BOEING CO. and sought a merger with McDonnell, which had grown quickly during World War II and had continued to be a major defense supplier, designing the first carrier-based jet fighter. After the merger McDonnell Douglas produced widely used jet fighters (including the F-4 Phantom, A-4 Skyhawk, F-15 Eagle, and F-18 Hornet), as well as LAUNCH VEHICLES and CRUISE MISSILES. It was bought by Boeing in 1997. See also LOCKHEED-MARTIN.

McEnroe, John (Patrick), Jr. (born 1959) U.S. tennis player. Born in Wiesbaden, Germany, he grew up in Douglaston, N.Y. In 1978 he helped the U.S. win the Davis Cup. In three consecutive years (1979–81) he won the U.S. Open, winning it a fourth time in 1984. He also won the Wimbledon singles in 1981, 1983, and 1984, as well as several doubles titles. Known for his temper tantrums and invective on court, he became the first player ejected from a Grand Slam match in nearly 30 years.

McFadden, Daniel L. (b.1937) U.S. economist and winner of the 2000 NOBEL PRIZE in Economic Sciences, along with James HECKMAN, for development of methods for analyzing individual or household behaviour. McFadden studied physics (B.S. 1957) and economics (Ph.D. 1962) at the University of Minnesota. He taught economics at the University of California, Berkeley (1963–79 and 1990–), Yale University (1977–78), and the Massachusetts Institute of Technology (1978–91). In 1974 McFadden developed conditional logit analysis—a method for determining how people make choices that maximize the utility of their decisions. His work has helped predict usage rates for MASS TRANSIT, and his statistical methods have been applied to labor-force participation, health care, housing, and the environment.

McGill University Privately endowed but state-supported university in Montreal. It was founded in 1821 through a gift left by the Scottish-Canadian merchant James McGill (1744–1813). It is internationally known for its work in chemistry, medicine, and biology. In addition, it has faculties of agricultural and environmental sciences, arts, dentistry, education, engineering, law, management, music, religious studies, and science. The language of instruction is English, though students may write examinations in French. Total enrollment is about 31,000.

McGillivray \mə-'gil-ə-,vrā\, **Alexander** (1759?–1793) Principal chief of the CREEK Indians in the years following the American Revolution. Of French-Creek descent, he was tutored by whites in Charleston, S.C., before being made a Creek chief. Distrustful of American land speculators, he signed a treaty (1784) with the Spanish in Florida putting the

Creek under Spain's protection. After repeated U.S. entreaties, he agreed to American sovereignty over Creek lands as long as the Creek could remain there free of American encroachments.

McGovern, George S(tanley) (born 1922) U.S. politician. Born in Avon, S.D., he earned a doctorate in history and taught at Dakota Wesleyan University Active in Democratic politics from 1948, he was elected to the U.S. House of Representatives (1957–61) and Senate (1963–81), where he held important hearings on hunger in the U.S. A leading opponent of the Vietnam War, he won the 1972 Democratic presidential nomination but lost to Pres. RICHARD NIXON by a large margin. He failed to win reelection to the Senate in 1980 and returned to teaching, lecturing, and writing.

McGraw, John (Joseph) (1873–1934) U.S. baseball player and manager. Born in Truxton, N.Y., he was a star infielder for the Baltimore National League team in the 1890s. His .391 average in 1899 remains the highest ever for a third baseman. As manager of the New York Giants (1902–32), he led the team to 10 National League championships and three World Series titles (1905, 1921, 1922). For his shrewdness and veneer of harshness, he acquired the nickname "Little Napoleon."

John McGraw, 1910.
THE BETTMANN ARCHIVE

McGrory \mə-ˈgrȯr-ē\, **Mary** (born 1918) U.S. columnist. Born in Boston, she began her newspaper career as a book reviewer for the *Boston Herald* (1942–47) and then for the *Washington Star* (1947–54). At the *Star* she became a feature writer. Starting with the JOSEPH MCCARTHY hearings in 1954, she wrote political commentaries noted for acute observations and pungent analyses that capture the essence of people and events. Her column has been syndicated since 1960, and she won a Pulitzer Prize in 1975. In 1981 she joined the *Washington Post*.

McGuffey, William Holmes (1800–1873) U.S. educator remembered chiefly for his series of elementary readers. McGuffey taught in the Ohio frontier schools and then at MIAMI UNIV. (1826–36). His six readers were published between 1836 and 1857. Collections of didactic tales and excerpts from great books, they reflect McGuffey's view that the proper education of young people required their introduction to a wide variety of topics and practical matters. They became standard texts in nearly all states for the next 50 years and sold over 125 million copies.

McGwire, Mark (David) (born 1963) U.S. baseball player. Born in Pomona, California, he played first base in college, then joined the Oakland Athletics in 1987 and quickly displayed the strength that would become his trademark. His 49 home runs that year set a rookie record, and he was named the American League's Rookie of the Year. In 1989 his .343 postseason batting average guided Oakland to the World Series championship. Injuries plagued him in 1993–95. Traded to the St. Louis Cardinals in 1997, he hit 58 homers. In 1998 he sought to top ROGER MARIS's 37-year-old season record of 61 home runs. He and SAMMY SOSA thrilled fans with their competition, and McGwire achieved the new record with 70; the record was broken in 2001 by BARRY BONDS (73). In 1999 McGwire hit 65 home runs. Following the 2001 season he retired from professional play.

McHugh, Jimmy *orig.* **James Francis** (1896–1969) U.S. song composer. Born in Boston, McHugh became a TIN PAN ALLEY song plugger and began writing songs for Broadway and COTTON CLUB revues. His extensive work for Broadway and Hollywood includes collaborations with F. LOESSER, J. MERCER, and especially D. FIELDS, with whom he wrote "I Can't Give You Anything but Love" and "On the Sunny Side of the Street." In the 1950s he led a band, and he later founded a music-publishing company.

McKay, Claude (1890–1948) Jamaican-U.S. poet and novelist. He published two volumes of Jamaican dialect verse before moving to the U.S. in 1912. With the publication of the poetry volumes *Spring in New Hampshire* (1920) and *Harlem Shadows* (1922), he emerged as the first and most militant voice of the HARLEM RENAISSANCE. An advocate of full civil rights and racial solidarity, in his writings he searched among the common folk for a distinctive black identity. His *Home to Harlem* (1928) was the most popular novel by an American black to that time. He lived abroad in various countries from 1922 to 1934.

McKellen, Ian (Murray) *later* **Sir Ian** (born 1939) British actor. Educated at Cambridge University, he made his professional stage debut in 1961 and won acclaim as Richard II at the Edinburgh Festival in 1969. He cofounded the Actors' Co. in 1971 but left in 1974 to join the Royal Shakespeare Co. A versatile and passionate actor, he has played in a repertory ranging from Elizabethan to contemporary. In 1981 he won a Tony award for *Amadeus*. His films include *Plenty* (1985), *Richard III* (1995), and *Gods and Monsters* (1998), and he played the wizard Gandalf in the film version of J.R.R. TOLKIEN's *Lord of the Rings*. He has been a vocal supporter of gay rights since 1988. He was knighted in 1991.

McKim, Charles Follen (1847–1909) U.S. architect. Born in Chester Co., Pa., he was educated at Harvard University and at the École des Beaux-Arts in Paris. In 1879 he joined William Rutherford Mead and STANFORD WHITE to found McKim, Mead & White, the most successful U.S. architectural firm of its time. Until 1887 the firm excelled at SHINGLE-STYLE residences. In later years it championed the formal Renaissance tradition and its Classical antecedents. Among the widely admired examples of McKim's planning are the Boston Public Library (1887), the Columbia University Library (1893), the Morgan Library (1903), and the magnificent Pennsylvania Railway Station (1904–10; demolished 1963).

McKinley, Mt. *Athabascan* **Denali** \də-ˈnä-lē\ Highest mountain in North America. Located near the center of the Alaska Range, in southern central Alaska, and in DENALI NATIONAL PARK, it rises to 20,320 ft (6,194 m). The northern peak was first scaled in 1910, and in 1913, Hudson Stuck and Harry Karstens ascended the southern peak, the true summit. It was named Densmores Peak in 1889 after a prospector but was renamed in 1896 in honor of Pres. WILLIAM MCKINLEY.

McKinley, William (1843–1901) 25th president of the U.S. (1897–1901). Born in Niles, Ohio, he served in the Civil War as an aide to Col. RUTHERFORD B. HAYES, who later encouraged his political career. He was elected to the U.S. House of Representatives (1877–91), where he favored protective tariffs and sponsored the McKinley Tariff of 1890. With the support of MARK HANNA, he was elected governor of Ohio (1892–96). In 1896 he won the Republican presidential nomination and the general election, defeating WILLIAM JENNINGS BRYAN. He called a special session of Congress to increase customs duties, but was soon involved in events in Cuba and the sinking of the USS *MAINE*, which led to the SPANISH-AMERICAN WAR. At the war's end, he advocated U.S. dependency status for the Philippines, Puerto Rico, and other former Spanish territories. He again defeated Bryan by a large majority in 1900, and began a tour to urge control of trusts and commercial reciprocity to boost foreign trade, issues neglected during the war. In Buffalo, N.Y., on September 6, 1901, he was fatally shot by an anarchist, Leon Czolgosz. He was succeeded by THEODORE ROOSEVELT.

William McKinley.
BY COURTESY OF THE LIBRARY OF CONGRESS, WASHINGTON, D.C.

McLuhan \mək-ˈlü-ən\, **(Herbert) Marshall** (1911–1980) Canadian communications theorist and educator. Born in Edmonton, Alberta, he taught from 1946 at the University of Toronto. His aphorism "the medium is the message" summarized his view of the potent influence of television, computers, and other electronic information disseminators in shaping styles of thinking and thought, whether in sociology, art, science, or religion. He regarded the printed book as fated to disappear. His highly influential works include *The Gutenberg Galaxy* (1962), *Under-*

standing Media (1964), and *The Medium Is the Massage* (*sic*; with Q. Fiore, 1967).

McMahon Line Frontier between Tibet and ASSAM in British India, negotiated between Tibet and Britain at the end of the Simla Conference in 1913–14. It was named after the chief British negotiator, Sir Henry McMahon. China refused to recognize the boundary on the grounds that Tibet, being subordinate to China, could not make treaties. The 1962 Indo-Chinese conflict failed to resolve the border dispute; China still considers the boundary illegal.

McMaster University Privately endowed university in Hamilton, Ontario. It was founded in 1887 through a gift from Sen. William McMaster (1811–1887) . It offers undergraduate and graduate degree programs in the sciences, humanities, social sciences, business, engineering, and other fields. Campus resources include a nuclear reactor, education research facilities, and the BERTRAND RUSSELL Archives. Current enrollment is about 15,000.

McMurdo Sound Inlet of the southwestern Ross Sea. Lying at the edge of ROSS ICE SHELF, the channel is 92 mi (148 km) long and up to 46 mi (74 km) wide; it has been a major center for Antarctic explorations. First discovered in 1841 by Scottish explorer James C. Ross, it served as one of the main access routes to the Antarctic continent. Ross Island was the site of headquarters for British explorers ROBERT FALCON SCOTT and ERNEST SHACKLETON.

McMurtry, Larry (Jeff) (born 1936) U.S. novelist. The son of a rancher, he was born in Wichita Falls, Tex. He is noted for novels set in the American West, often in Texas. *The Last Picture Show* (1966; film, 1971) examines the isolation of small-town life. *Lonesome Dove* (1985, Pulitzer Prize) is part of an epic frontier series that also includes *Streets of Laredo* (1993), *Dead Man's Walk* (1995), and *Comanche Moon* (1997). His other novels include *Horseman, Pass By* (1961; filmed as *Hud,* 1963), *Terms of Endearment* (1975; film, 1983), and *Buffalo Girls* (1990).

McNally, Terrence (born 1939) U.S. dramatist. Born in St. Petersburg, Fla., he worked as a newspaper reporter, as tutor for the children of JOHN STEINBECK, and as stage manager at the Actors Studio. Starting in 1964 his plays were produced in regional, off-Broadway, and Broadway theaters. They include *Bad Habits* (1971), *The Tubs* (1974), *Master Class* (1995), *Love! Valor! Compassion!* (1995; film, 1997), and the controversial *Corpus Christi* (1998). He wrote the book for the musical *Kiss of the Spider Woman* (1993).

McNamara \'mak-nə-mar-ə\, **Robert S(trange)** (born 1916) U.S. secretary of defense (1961–68). Born in San Francisco, he developed logistical and statistical systems for the military during World War II. After the war, he was one of the "Whiz Kids" hired to revitalize the Ford Motor Co., and in 1960 he became the first person not in the Ford family to be named its president. In 1961 he was appointed secretary of defense by JOHN F. KENNEDY and proceeded to revamp Pentagon operations. He initially supported U.S. involvement in the Vietnam War, but by 1967 was seeking peace negotiations. He opposed the bombing of North Vietnam and lost influence with Pres. LYNDON B. JOHNSON. He resigned in 1968 to become president of the World Bank (1968–81).

McNeill, Don (1907–1996) U.S. radio entertainer. Born in Galena, Ill., he entered radio in the 1920s as part of a singing team. In 1933 he took over as host of an NBC morning program in Chicago and created *The Breakfast Club.* Usually unscripted, it relied on listeners' comments, poems, and folksy humor. It was the longest-running show in radio network history when it ended in 1968.

McPhee, John (Angus) (born 1931) U.S. journalist and nonfiction writer. Born in Princeton, N.J., he attended Princeton University. After working as an associate editor at *Time* (1957–64), he became a staff writer at *The New Yorker* in 1965 and has written for it since. His nonfiction covers a wide variety of topics. His first book was on BILL BRADLEY; places he has written about include New Jersey, Alaska, the American West (several books), and Switzerland; other topics include the citrus industry, aeronautical engineering, and nuclear terrorism. He has taught journalism at Princeton since 1975.

McPherson, Aimee Semple *orig.* **Aimee Elizabeth Kennedy** (1890–1944) U.S. (Canadian-born) Pentecostal evangelist. Born on a farm near Ingersoll, Ontario, she began preaching at 17, and in 1908 she went as a missionary to China with her husband, Robert Semple. After his death she came to the U.S., where her second marriage, to Harold McPherson, ended in 1918 when she became an itinerant evangelist and healer. She settled in Los Angeles and founded the International Church of the Foursquare Gospel. For nearly 20 years she preached to large audiences at her Angelus Temple; she also built a radio station, wrote books and pamphlets, and established about 200 missions. In 1926 she disappeared mysteriously for five weeks; her tale of kidnapping on her reappearance was greeted with skepticism. A third marriage ended in divorce, and she faced numerous trials for financial irregularities. She died from an overdose of barbiturates.

McQueen, (Terrence) Steve(n) (1930–1980) U.S. film actor. Born in Beech Grove, Ind., he served time in a reform school and a stint in the U.S. Marines before studying acting in New York. He won notice on Broadway in *A Hatful of Rain* (1955) and made his screen debut in *Somebody up There Likes Me* (1956), then starred in the television series *Wanted: Dead or Alive* (1958–61). He played the heroic loner in such films as *The Great Escape* (1963), *The Sand Pebbles* (1966), *Bullitt* (1968), *The Thomas Crown Affair* (1968), *Papillon* (1973), and *The Towering Inferno* (1974).

McRae, Carmen (1922–1994) U.S. singer and pianist. Born in New York City, McRae was influenced by BILLIE HOLIDAY and SARAH VAUGHAN. She began her career in 1943 singing at Minton's Playhouse in Harlem, absorbing the innovations of the first BEBOP musicians. Working as a soloist from the mid-1950s, McRae became one of the most accomplished scat singers and ballad interpreters in jazz.

Me 109 See MESSERSCHMITT 109

Me Nam River See CHAO PHRAYA River

mead Alcoholic beverage fermented from HONEY and water. It can be light or rich, sweet or dry, or even sparkling. Alcoholic drinks made from honey were common in ancient Scandinavia, Gaul, Teutonic Europe, and Greece; they were particularly common in northern Europe, where grapevines do not flourish. By the 14th century, ale and sweetened wine were surpassing mead in popularity. Today mead is made as a sweet or dry wine of low alcoholic strength. Spiced mead is called metheglin.

Mead, George Herbert (1863–1931) U.S. philosopher, sociologist, and social psychologist prominent in the development of PRAGMATISM. Born in South Hadley, Mass., he studied at Harvard and later taught at the University of Chicago with JOHN DEWEY and CHARLES HORTON COOLEY. Mead's focus was the relationship between the self and society, particularly the emergence of the human self in the process of social interaction. His works include *The Philosophy of the Present* (1932) and *Mind, Self, and Society* (1934). See also INTERACTIONISM.

Mead, Lake Reservoir of the HOOVER DAM, on the Arizona–Nevada border. One of the largest man-made lakes in the world, it was formed by the damming of the COLORADO RIVER. Lake Mead is 115 mi (185 km) long and 1–10 mi (1.6–16 km) wide; it has a capacity of over 31 million acre ft (38 billion cubic m), with a surface area of 229 sq mi (593 sq km). It was named after Elwood Mead, commissioner of reclamation. Lake Mead National Recreation Area (established 1936) has an area of 2,338 sq mi (6,055 sq km) and extends 240 mi (386 km) along the river.

Mead, Margaret (1901–1978) U.S. anthropologist. Born in Philadelphia, she studied under FRANZ BOAS and RUTH BENEDICT at Columbia Univ., and did fieldwork in Samoa before completing her PhD (1929). The first and most famous of her 23 books, *Coming of Age in Samoa* (1928), presents evidence in support of cultural determinism with respect to the formation of personality or TEMPERAMENT. Her other books include *Sex and Temperament in Three Primitive Societies* (1935), *Male and Female* (1949), and *Culture and Commitment* (1970). Her theories were based on observational methods and conclusions that were subsequently questioned by other anthropologists. In her later years, she became a prominent voice on such wide-ranging issues as women's rights and nuclear proliferation, and her great fame owed as much to the force of her personality and her outspokenness as to the quality of her scientific work. She served in curatorial positions at the American Museum of Natural History for over 50 years.

Meade, George G(ordon) (1815–1872) U.S. general in the AMERICAN CIVIL WAR. Born in Cádiz, Spain, to U.S. parents, he graduated from

West Point. In 1861 he was commissioned brigadier general of Pennsylvania volunteers. He fought at Bull Run, Antietam, and Chancellorsville. Three days before the Battle of GETTYSBURG, he replaced JOSEPH HOOKER as commander of the Army of the Potomac. At Gettysburg he repulsed the Confederate attack, turning the tide of the war, but was criticized for failing to pursue ROBERT E. LEE's forces. After 1864 he was subordinate to Gen. ULYSSES S. GRANT, whom he served loyally. After the war he commanded several military departments.

meadowlark Any sharp-billed, plump songbird of the genus *Sturnella* (family Icteridae), 8–11 in. (20–28 cm) long. The two North American species are streaked brown above and have a yellow breast crossed by a black V; the short tail has distinctive white outer feathers. The eastern, or common, meadowlark *(S. magna),* from eastern Canada to Brazil, has a simple four-note whistle; the western meadowlark *(S. neglecta),* from western Canada to Mexico, has an intricate fluting song. Meadowlarks eat insects in summer and seeds in fall and winter. Their nests are grass domes hidden in fields.

mealybug Any insect of the family Pseudococcidae (order Homoptera). Not a true BUG, the mealybug is covered by a white sticky powder resembling cornmeal. The females, about 0.4 in. (1 cm) long, and "crawlers" (the active young) cluster along the veins and undersides of leaves, especially of citrus trees and potted plants; the males are active two-winged fliers. Common species are the citrus mealybug *(Pseudococcus citri)* and the citrophilus mealybug *(P. gahani).*

mean, median, and mode In mathematics, the three principal ways of designating the average value of a list of numbers. The arithmetic mean is found by adding the numbers and dividing the sum by the number of numbers in the list. This is what is most often meant by an average. The median is the middle value in a list ordered from smallest to largest. The mode is the most frequently occurring value on the list. There are other types of means. A geometric mean is found by multiplying all values in a list and then taking the root of that product equal to the number of values (e.g., the square root if there are two numbers). The geometric mean is typically used in cases of exponential growth or decline (see EXPONENTIAL FUNCTION). In STATISTICS, the mean of a RANDOM VARIABLE is its expected value—i. e., the theoretical long-run arithmetic mean of the outcomes of repeated trials, such as a large number of tosses of a die.

mean life In RADIOACTIVITY, the average lifetime of all the nuclei of a particular unstable atomic species. This time interval is the sum of the lifetimes of all the individual unstable nuclei in a sample, divided by the total number of unstable nuclei present. It is the reciprocal of the decay constant. For a given isotope, the mean life is always 1.443 times its HALF-LIFE. For example, lead-209 decays to bismuth-209 with a half-life of 3.25 hours and a mean life of 4.69 hours.

mean-value theorems In mathematics, two theorems, one associated with DIFFERENTIAL CALCULUS and one with INTEGRAL CALCULUS. The first proposes that any differentiable FUNCTION defined on an interval has a mean value, at which a TANGENT LINE is parallel to the line connecting the endpoints of the function's graph on that interval. For example, if a car covers a mile from a dead stop in one minute, it must have been traveling exactly a mile a minute at some point along that mile. In integral calculus, the mean value of a function on an interval is, in essence, the arithmetic mean (see MEAN, MEDIAN AND MODE) of its values over the interval. Because the number of values is infinite, a true arithmetic mean is not possible. The theorem shows how to find the mean value using a definite INTEGRAL. See also ROLLE'S THEOREM.

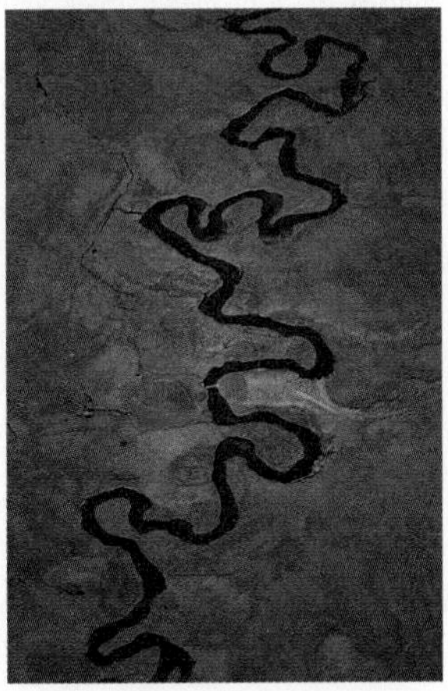

Meanders, Owens River, near Mammoth Lakes, Calif.

meander \mē-ˈan-dər\ Extreme U-bend in a stream, usually occurring in a series, that is caused by flow characteristics of the water. Meanders form in stream-deposited sediments and may stack up upstream of an obstruction, resulting in a gooseneck or extremely bowed meander. A cutoff may form through the gooseneck and allow the former meander bend to be sealed off as an OXBOW LAKE. Silt deposits may eventually fill the lake to form a MARSH or a meander scar.

meaning In philosophy, the sense of an expression (e.g., a word or sentence) by contrast with its reference (i.e., the relation between expressions and what they designate). For example, "the tallest person" means "the person whose height is greater than that of any other," but its reference may be John Doe—or no one, since two or more can be tallest. Thus, it will not do to say that words mean the thing they designate (or make us think of). Further problems beset this referential theory of meaning. Two expressions may have the same referent but not the same meaning (e.g., "the morning star" and "the evening star" denote the same planet, yet do not have exactly the same meaning). Meaningful phrases can also pretend to refer without really doing so (e.g., "the present king of France" is meaningful even though there is no such person). By contrast, semantic theories claim that the notion of meaning is best explained in terms of truth rather than reference, that a word's meaning should be explained in terms of its contribution to the truth conditions of the sentences in which it occurs. Difficulties with semantic theories led to the use theory of meaning, inspired by the work of LUDWIG WITTGENSTEIN and J. L. AUSTIN. It admits that not all words refer to something, and not all utterances are true or false; that what is common to all words and sentences is that people use them in speech (see SPEECH ACT THEORY); and that their meaning may consequently be nothing more than their use, or, alternatively, the rules that govern their employment. See also SEMANTICS.

Meany, George (1894–1980) U.S. labor leader. Born in New York City, a plumber by trade, he joined the United Association of Plumbers and Steam Fitters in 1915 and rose through the ranks as a union official. He was elected secretary-treasurer of the American Federation of Labor (AFL) in 1939 and became its president in 1952. He led the merger of the AFL and CIO in 1955, helping reconcile the two federations despite their competitiveness and long-standing differences. Conservative and anticommunist, as president of the AFL-CIO (1955–79) he steered the U.S. labor movement away from radicalism. Feisty and often dictatorial, he expelled the TEAMSTERS UNION from the AFL-CIO in 1957, and he lost the UNITED AUTOMOBILE WORKERS in 1967 after disputes with WALTER REUTHER. Meany wielded considerable influence in the Democratic Party through the 1970s.

measles *or* **rubeola** \ˌrü-bē-ˈō-lə, rü-ˈbē-ə-lə\ Highly contagious viral childhood disease. It initially resembles a severe cold with red eyes and fever; a blotchy rash and higher fever later develop. After recovery, patients have lifelong immunity. Adult patients tend to have more severe cases. ANTIBIOTICS now prevent death from secondary infections. Measles itself, for which there is no drug, requires only bed rest, eye protection, and steam for bronchial irritation. A vaccine developed in the 1960s proved not to give permanent immunity and is too heat-sensitive for use in tropical areas. The worldwide incidence of measles continues to rise. Research is currently directed toward development of a more stable vaccine. See also RUBELLA.

measurement Association of numbers with physical quantities and natural phenomena by comparing an unknown quantity with a known quantity of the same kind. WEIGHTS and measures are standard quantities with which such comparisons are made. The earliest ones measured mass (weight), volume (liquid or dry measure), length, and area using units mostly based on dimensions of the human body. The cubit, representing the distance from elbow to fingertips, was the most widespread unit of measure in the ancient world. As such units were standardized, more were added, including units of temperature, luminosity, pressure, and electric current. Measurements made by the senses instead of by measurement devices are called estimates (see ESTIMATION).

measure theory In mathematics, a generalization of the concepts of length and area (see LENGTH, AREA, AND VOLUME) to arbitrary sets of points not composed of line segments or rectangles. A measure is any rule for associating a number with a set. The result must be nonnegative and also additive, meaning that the measure of two nonoverlapping sets equals the sum of their individual measures. This is simple enough for sets consisting of line segments or rectangles, but the measure of sets such as curved regions or intervals with missing points requires more abstract methods, including LIMITS and upper and lower bounds.

meat Flesh and other edible parts of animals, particularly MAMMALS, used for food. Not only the MUSCLES and FAT but also such organs as the liver, kidney, and heart are consumed as meat. Meat is valued as a complete-PROTEIN food, containing all the AMINO ACIDS necessary for the human body. It digests slowly, largely because of the presence of fats. BEEF is the most widely consumed meat; PORK is second; mutton and lamb, goat, venison, and rabbit are other common meats. The U.S. produces and consumes about a third of the world's meat, while much of the world's population eats little if any meat, though it is generally prized.

Mecca *Arabic* **al-Makkah** \,ȧl-'mȧ-kə\ City (pop., 1991 est.: 630,000), western Saudi Arabia. The holiest city of ISLAM, it was the birthplace of the Prophet MUHAMMAD. It was his home until AD 622, when he was forced to flee to MEDINA (see also HEGIRA); he returned and captured the city in 630. It came under the control of the Egyptian Mamluks in 1269 and of the Ottoman Turks in 1517. King IBN SAUD occupied it in 1925, and it became part of the Kingdom of Saudi Arabia. It is a religious center to which Muslims must attempt a pilgrimage (see HAJJ) once during a lifetime; only Muslims may reside in Mecca permanently. Facilities related to pilgrimages are the main service industries. It is the site of the Al-Haram Mosque, which contains the KAABA.

mechanical advantage Force-amplifying effectiveness of a simple MACHINE (LEVER, WEDGE, WHEEL and AXLE, PULLEY, or SCREW). The theoretical mechanical advantage of a system is the ratio of the FORCE that performs the useful work to the force applied, assuming there is no friction in the system. In practice, the actual mechanical advantage will be less than the theoretical value by an amount determined by the amount of friction.

mechanical efficiency See EFFICIENCY

mechanical energy Sum of a system's KINETIC ENERGY (KE) and POTENTIAL ENERGY (PE). Mechanical energy is constant in a system that experiences no dissipative forces such as friction or air resistance. For example, a swinging pendulum that experiences only gravitation has greatest KE and least PE at the lowest point on the path of its swing, where its speed is greatest and its height least. It has least KE and greatest PE at the extremities of its swing, where its speed is zero and its height is greatest. As it moves, energy is continuously passing back and forth between the two forms. Neglecting friction and air resistance, the pendulum's mechanical energy is constant.

mechanical engineering Branch of ENGINEERING concerned with the design, manufacture, installation, and operation of ENGINES, MACHINES, and MANUFACTURING processes. Mechanical engineering involves application of the principles of DYNAMICS, control, THERMODYNAMICS and heat transfer, FLUID MECHANICS, STRENGTH OF MATERIALS, MATERIALS SCIENCE, ELECTRONICS, and MATHEMATICS. It is concerned with MACHINE TOOLS, motor vehicles, textile machinery, packaging machines, printing machinery, metalworking machines, welding, air conditioning, refrigerators, agricultural machinery, and many other machines and processes essential to an industrial economy.

mechanical system Any building service using machines. They include PLUMBING, ELEVATORS, ESCALATORS, and HEATING and AIR-CONDITIONING systems. The introduction of mechanization in buildings in the early 20th century brought about major adjustments; the new equipment demanded floor space, and the design team began to include electrical and HVAC (heating, VENTILATING, and air-conditioning) engineers. Heating and cooling changed dramatically. Modern buildings, with their large heat gains, turned central heating into little more than a supplement. Heat removal is a much more serious burden, especially in warm weather. The roofs of high-rises are occupied by cooling towers and mechanical PENTHOUSES; entire floors are often dedicated to the containment of blowers, compressors, water chillers, boilers, pumps, and generators.

mechanics Science of the action of forces on material bodies. It forms a central part of all physical science and engineering. Beginning with NEWTON'S LAWS OF MOTION in the 17th century, the theory has since been modified and expanded by the theories of QUANTUM MECHANICS and RELATIVITY. Newton's theory of mechanics, known as classical mechanics, accurately represented the effects of forces under all conditions known in his time. It can be divided into statics, the study of EQUILIBRIUM, and DYNAMICS, the study of motion caused by forces. Though classical mechanics fails on the scale of ATOMS and molecules, it remains the framework for much of modern science and technology.

mechanism In mechanical construction, the means of transmitting and modifying motion in a MACHINE or an assembly of mechanical parts. The chief characteristic of the mechanism of a machine is that all members have constrained motion; that is, the parts can move only in certain ways in relation to each other. Despite its complexity, the mechanism of a machine can always be analyzed as a group of simple basic mechanisms, each of which contains members that transmit motion from one moving link to another. In general, motion is transmitted in one of three ways: by a wrapping connector such as a CHAIN DRIVE or BELT DRIVE, by direct contact as in a CAM or GEAR, or by a pin-connected LINKAGE.

mechanism Form of MATERIALISM that holds that all natural processes can be explained in terms of laws of matter in motion. Upholders of mechanism were mainly concerned with eliminating from science such unobservables as substantial form and occult qualities that could not be empirically confirmed or mathematically treated. Mechanism advocated the reduction of biological functions to physical and chemical processes, thus paving the way for elimination of mind–body DUALISM. Mechanism opposes the assumption of TELEOLOGY as an explanatory principle in natural science. See also ATOMISM.

mechanization Use of MACHINES, either wholly or in part, to replace human or animal labor. Unlike AUTOMATION, which may not depend at all on a human operator, mechanization requires human participation to provide information or instruction. Mechanization began with human-operated machines to replace the handwork of craftspeople; today computers are frequently used to control mechanized processes.

mechanoreception \,me-kə-nō-ri-'sep-shən\ Ability to detect and respond to mechanical stimuli in one's environment. A slight deformation of a mechanoreceptive NEURON causes an electric charge at its surface, activating a response. Mechanoreceptors in "pain spots" (pressure points) in the skin (probably clusters of nerve endings) vary in sensitivity. They respond to a wide range of stimuli, sometimes with a REFLEX (e.g., a pricked finger pulled away before the brain registers pain). The structures that respond to sound (see EAR), sense orientation with respect to gravity (see INNER EAR), or detect the position and movement of limbs (see PROPRIOCEPTION) are mechanoreceptors. Some animals have mechanoreceptors that detect water motion or air currents. See also SENSE.

Mecherino See Domenico BECCAFUMI

Meckel, Johann Friedrich (1781–1833) German anatomist. He was the first to describe the embryonic cartilage (Meckel's cartilage) that becomes part of the lower jaw in fishes, amphibians, and birds, and also described a congenital pouch (Meckel's diverticulum) of the small intestine. He wrote a treatise on pathological anatomy and an atlas of human abnormalities.

Med fly See MEDITERRANEAN FRUIT FLY

medal Piece of metal struck with a design to commemorate a person, place, or event. Medals can be of various sizes and shapes, ranging from large medallions to small plaques, or plaquettes. Most medals are made of gold, silver, bronze, or lead, the precious metals being used for the finer productions. The art of the medalist began in the mid-15th century with bronze medals of Italian Renaissance rulers and humanists. Some of the most beautiful were made by BENVENUTO CELLINI.

Henry IV and Marie de Medicis portrayed on the obverse side of a bronze-gilt medal by Guillaume Dupré, 1603; in the National Gallery of Art, Washington, D.C.

Medan \mā-'dän\ City (pop., 1990: 1,731,000), northeastern Sumatra. After the introduction of tobacco plantations in 1873, Medan became the commercial center of an agricultural region where cash crops, including tobacco and rubber, were raised for export. It was made a city by the Dutch in 1886. It was occupied by the Japanese during World War II. The sultan of Deli's palace dates to the 19th century. It is the seat of the University of North Sumatra and the Islamic University of North Sumatra.

Medawar \'me-də-wər\, **Peter B(rian)** *later* **Sir Peter** (1915–1987) British (Brazilian-born) zoologist. Educated at Oxford, he began transplant research in 1949. His finding (1953) that adult animals injected with foreign cells early in life accept skin grafts from the original donor or its twin lent support to MACFARLANE BURNET's hypothesis that during and just after birth, cells learn to distinguish "own" from "foreign." He found that nonidentical cattle twins accept skin grafts from each other, proving that antigens "leak" between the embryos' yolk sacs, and showed with mice that each cell contains genetic antigens important to immunity. His work deflected immunology from dealing with the fully developed immunity mechanism to attempting to alter the mechanism itself (e.g., suppression of transplant rejection). He and Burnet shared the 1960 Nobel Prize for Physiology or Medicine.

Medea \mə-'dē-ə\ In GREEK MYTHOLOGY, the daughter of King Aeetes of Colchis. After helping JASON, leader of the ARGONAUTS, to obtain the Golden Fleece from her father, the two were married and she returned with him to Iolcos, where she killed the king who had deprived Jason of his inheritance. Forced into exile, the couple settled in Corinth. In EURIPIDES' tragedy *Medea,* Jason later deserts her for the daughter of King Creon, and Medea takes revenge by killing Creon, his daughter, and her own two children by Jason before fleeing to Athens.

Médecins Sans Frontières See DOCTORS WITHOUT BORDERS

Medellín \,mā-thā-'yēn, *Engl* ,mā-də-'lēn\ City (pop., 1999 est.: 1,861,265), northwestern Colombia. It is the nation's second largest city and is heavily industrialized. Founded in 1675 as a mining town, it grew rapidly after the completion of the PANAMA CANAL and the arrival of the railroad in 1914. It is now noted for its textile mills, clothing factories, and steel mills. It is one of Colombia's largest trading centers for coffee. It became a center for the illegal international distribution of cocaine in the late 20th century.

Media \'mē-dē-ə\ Ancient country, southern Asia. It was situated in modern northwestern Iran and occupied by the Medes, an Iranian people. In 625 BC Cyaxares united the area's tribes into a kingdom. In 614 BC he captured ASHUR; he later defeated the Assyrian empire and seized territory in Iran, northern Assyria, and Armenia. In 550 BC it became part of the new ACHAEMENIAN empire under Persia's CYRUS THE GREAT. ALEXANDER THE GREAT occupied it in 330 BC. In the partition of his empire, southern Media was given to the Macedonians and then to the SELEUCIDS; northern Media became the kingdom of Atropatene, which passed to Parthia, Armenia, and Rome. In 226 BC the whole of Media passed to the SASANIANS.

median See MEAN, MEDIAN, AND MODE

mediation In law, a nonbinding intervention between parties to promote resolution of a grievance, reconciliation, settlement, or compromise. It is used especially in labor disputes. In many industrialized nations, the government provides mediation services in order to protect the public interest. In the U.S., the National Mediation Board functions in this capacity. Mediation is also commonly used in international conflicts. See also ARBITRATION.

medical examiner See CORONER

medical imaging See DIAGNOSTIC IMAGING

medical jurisprudence *or* **legal medicine** Science of applying medical facts to legal problems. Routine tasks include filling out birth and death certificates, deciding insurance eligibility, and reporting infectious disease. Perhaps more significant is medical testimony in court. When merely relating observations, doctors are ordinary witnesses; interpreting facts based on medical knowledge makes them expert witnesses, required to present their opinions without bias toward the side that called them. Conflicts between medicine and law can occur, usually over medical confidentiality. See also FORENSIC MEDICINE.

Medicare and Medicaid U.S. government programs in effect since 1966. Medicare covers most people 65 or older and those with long-term disabilities. Part A, a hospital insurance plan, also pays for home health visits and hospice care. Part B, a supplementary plan, pays for doctors' services, tests, and other services. Requirements and benefits are complex. Patients pay deductibles and copayments. Medicaid, a joint federal-state program, covers low-income people under age 65 and those who have exhausted Medicare benefits. It pays for hospital care, doctors' services, nursing-home care, home health services, family planning, and screening. Participating states must offer Medicaid to all persons on public assistance but decide their own eligibility guidelines. Many physicians refuse to treat Medicaid patients because of low reimbursement levels.

Medici \'me-də-chē\, **Alessandro de'** (1510–1537) First duke of Florence (1532–37). A member of the elder branch of the MEDICI FAMILY, he was probably the illegitimate son of Cardinal Giulio de' Medici (later Pope CLEMENT VII). The pope made Cardinal Passerini regent in Florence for Alessandro, but they were forced to flee when the unpopular regency provoked a revolt in 1527. An agreement between the pope and Emperor CHARLES V restored the Medici in Florence (1530), and Alessandro was declared a hereditary duke (1532). A tyrannical ruler, he sought to solidify his control by marrying Charles V's daughter, MARGARET OF AUSTRIA, in 1536. In an unsuccessful attempt to cause a revolt, a distant cousin, Lorenzino de' Medici (1514–1548), murdered Alessandro in 1537.

Medici \'me-də-,chē\, **Cosimo de'** *known as* **Cosimo the Elder** (1389–1464) Founder of one of the main lines of the MEDICI FAMILY. The son of the Florentine banker Giovanni di Bicci de' Medici (1360–1429), Cosimo represented the Medici bank and handled papal finances, becoming the wealthiest man of his time. Another leading family, the Albizzi, had him imprisoned (1433) and tried to assassinate him, but a year later the Medici regained power in Florence and Cosimo triumphantly returned. He was the architect of the Peace of LODI (1454). An alliance with the SFORZAS of Milan provided him with troops to crush a coup d'état in 1458, after which he created a Senate composed of 100 loyal supporters (the Cento). He was a patron of scholarship and the arts, including such figures as DONATELLO and FILIPPO BRUNELLESCHI.

Medici, Cosimo I de' (1519–1574) Second duke of Florence (1537–74) and first grand duke of Tuscany (1569–74). The son of Giovanni de' MEDICI, Cosimo became head of the Florentine republic in 1537 after the assassination of his distant cousin Alessandro de' MEDICI. He continued Alessandro's tyrannical rule and defeated attempts to oust him with aid from Emperor CHARLES V. Seeking to expand his power, he attacked Siena in 1554 and brought nearly all of Tuscany under his control. He used his despotic power to improve the government's efficiency and to sponsor artistic projects. Far advanced for the time as an administrator, he united all public services into one building, the UFFIZI ("Offices"), designed by GIORGIO VASARI. He promoted the talents of such artists as Il BRONZINO and BARTOLOMMEO AMMANNATI, sponsored archaeological excavations of Etruscan sites, and established the Florentine Academy for linguistic studies. In 1569 he was given the title grand duke of Tuscany.

Medici, Giovanni de' *orig.* **Lodovico** (1498–1526) Italian general. A member of the younger branch of the MEDICI FAMILY, he was the son of Giovanni de' Medici, who died soon after his birth, and Caterina Sforza, of the powerful SFORZA FAMILY of Milan. He took his father's name, trained as a soldier, and fought for a Medici cousin, Pope LEO X, in 1516–17 and 1521. In the service of the French (1522, 1525) he fought with the army of the League of Cognac in 1526, and was mortally wounded in the battle near Mantua. He was known as Giovanni dalle Bande Nere ("of the Black Bands") for the black banners his army (or bands) carried in mourning for Leo X after 1521.

Medici, Giuliano de' (1479–1516) Ruler of Florence (1512–13). A member of the elder branch of the MEDICI FAMILY, he was the son of Lorenzo de' MEDICI. In 1494 his brother, Piero de' Medici, was ousted as ruler of Florence by the republicans, aided by the French. In 1512 Pope JULIUS II demanded that Florence enter his Holy League against France and allow the exiled Medici to return to Florence. Giuliano returned as ruler (Piero having died in 1503), and used harsh measures to suppress a conspiracy. In 1513, after another brother became Pope LEO X, he went to Rome as a cardinal. In 1515 he received the French title duc de Nemours.

Medici, Lorenzo de' *known as* **Lorenzo the Magnificent** (1449–1492) Florentine statesman and patron of arts and letters. The grandson of COSIMO DE'MEDICI, he was the most brilliant of the MEDICI FAMILY. He ruled FLORENCE with his younger brother, Giuliano, from 1469. Giuliano was assassinated in 1478 by the Pazzi, a leading Florentine banking family, which was in league with SIXTUS IV (who did not support the assassination) and the king of Naples. Lorenzo's direct appeal to the king allowed him to regain power in Florence, and he was sole ruler of the city until his death. His 13-year-old son Giovanni was created a cardinal by Pope Innocent VIII and later became pope as LEO X. Lorenzo used the Medici riches to patronize many artists, including SANDRO BOTTICELLI, LEONARDO DA VINCI, and MICHELANGELO, and he remains perhaps the most famous patron of all time. His policies bankrupted the Medici bank, but the political power of the Medici remained strong in Florence and Tuscany.

Lorenzo de' Medici, terra-cotta bust by Andrea del Verrocchio, c. 1485; in the National Gallery of Art, Washington, D.C.

BY COURTESY OF THE NATIONAL GALLERY OF ART, WASHINGTON, D.C., SAMUEL H. KRESS COLLECTION, 1943

Medici family Italian bourgeois family that ruled Florence and later Tuscany from c. 1430 to 1737. The family, noted for its often tyrannical rulers and its beneficent patrons of the arts, also provided the church with four popes (LEO X, CLEMENT VII, Pius IV, and Leo XI) and married into the royal families of Europe, notably in France (CATHERINE DE MÉDICIS and MARIE DE MÉDICIS). The effective founder of the family was Giovanni di Bicci de' Medici (1360–1429), a merchant who amassed great wealth in trade and was the virtual ruler of Florence 1421–29. From his two sons derived the major branches of the family. The so-called elder branch began with Cosimo de' MEDICI. His grandson, Lorenzo de' MEDICI, or Lorenzo the Magnificent, greatly expanded the family's power. His son Giuliano de' MEDICI became duc de Nemours. Another son, Giovanni, became Pope Leo X. Lorenzo's great-granddaughter became CATHERINE DE MÉDICIS. Another of Cosimo's grandsons, Giulio de' Medici (1478–1534) became pope as Clement VII. His probable illegitimate son, Alessandro de' MEDICI, a tyrant, was the last of the direct male line of the elder branch. The so-called younger branch of the family began with Giovanni's younger son Lorenzo de' MEDICI. His son Giovanni married Caterina Sforza of the powerful SFORZA FAMILY, and their son Giovanni de' MEDICI became a noted general. His son Cosimo I de' MEDICI became duke of Florence, and Cosimo's son Francesco de' Medici (1541–1587) was the father of MARIE DE MÉDICIS. Cosimo I's grandson Cosimo II (1590–1621) gave up the family practice of banking and commerce. His grandson Cosimo III (1642–1723) was a weak ruler, under whom Tuscany's power declined. His son Gian Gastone de' Medici (1671–1737), who died without issue, was the last grand duke of Tuscany.

medicinal poisoning *or* **drug poisoning** Harmful effects of medicinal drugs, from overdose or sensitivity to regular doses. Many medicines are dangerous; the margin between dose and overdose is often narrow. A normally safe dose may be toxic in some people, over time, or in combination with certain foods, alcohol, or other drugs. Safeguards to prevent medicinal poisoning include testing in animals, then human volunteers, and then patients. The companies that produce new drugs conduct the tests under supervision by the Food and Drug Administration. Drugs unsafe for self-medication are available only to doctors or by prescription. Pharmacists advise the public on proper use.

medicine Set of scientific fields related to prevention, DIAGNOSIS, and treatment of disease and maintenance of health, practiced in doctors' offices, HEALTH-MAINTENANCE-ORGANIZATION facilities, hospitals, and clinics. In addition to FAMILY PRACTICE, INTERNAL MEDICINE, and specialties for specific body systems, it includes research, PUBLIC HEALTH, EPIDEMIOLOGY, and PHARMACOLOGY. Each country sets its own requirements for medical degrees (MDs) and licenses. Medical boards and councils set standards and oversee medical education. Boards of certification have stringent requirements for physicians seeking to practice a specialty and stress continuing education. Advances in therapy (see THERAPEUTICS) and diagnosis have raised complex legal and moral issues in areas such as ABORTION, EUTHANASIA, and patients' rights. Recent changes include treating patients as partners in their own care and taking cultural factors into consideration.

Medicine Bow Mountains NW section of the Front Range, in the central ROCKY MTNS. Averaging a height of 10,000 ft (3,050 m), the mountains run southeast for about 100 mi (160 km) from Medicine Bow, Wy., to Cameron Pass, Col., just northwest of ROCKY MOUNTAIN NATIONAL PARK. The highest summit, Medicine Bow Peak, reaches 12,014 ft (3,662 m). The name refers to the practices of local Indians, who collected wood for bows in the area and held ceremonial medicine dances.

medicine man Priestly healer or SHAMAN, especially among the American Indians. The medicine man (often a woman in some societies) commonly carries a kit of objects such as feathers, stones, or hallucinogenic plants that have magical associations. The work of healing often involves the extraction—by sucking, pulling, or other means—of offending substances from the patient's body. Singing, recitation of myths, and other ceremonies often accompany the healing rite.

Médicis, Catherine de See CATHERINE DE MÉDICIS

Médicis, Marie de See MARIE DE MÉDICIS

Medill \mə-'dil\, **Joseph** (1823–1899) Canadian-U.S. editor and publisher. Born into a family of shipbuilders near St. John, New Brunswick, he studied law in the U.S. and was admitted to the bar in 1846. He turned to newspaper publishing in 1849. As managing editor of the *Chicago Tribune* (from 1855), he set its antislavery editorial policy. He helped found the Republican Party (1854) and worked for ABRAHAM LINCOLN's nomination. As mayor of Chicago (1871–74), he helped establish the Chicago Public Library (1872–74). In 1874 he resigned and acquired a controlling share in the *Chicago Tribune.* Four of his grandchildren, including ROBERT McCORMICK, also ran newspapers.

Medina *Arabic* **Al-Madinah** \ˌäl-mä-'dē-nə\ *ancient* **Yathrib** City (pop., 1991: 400,000), western Saudi Arabia, north of MECCA. It developed from an oasis settled by Jews c. AD 135. In 622 MUHAMMAD fled from Mecca to Medina (see HEGIRA). It served as capital of the Islamic state until 661. Held by the Ottoman Turks 1517–1804, it then was seized by the WAHHABIS. An Ottoman-Egyptian force retook it in 1812. Ottoman rule ceased during World War I, and in 1925 it fell to IBN SAUD. A sacred city of ISLAM, it is second only to Mecca as a place of Muslim pilgrimage; among its many mosques is the Prophet's Mosque, containing the tomb of MUHAMMAD.

medina worm See GUINEA WORM

meditation Private religious devotion or mental exercise, in which techniques of concentration and contemplation are used to reach a heightened level of spiritual awareness. The practice has existed in all religions since ancient times. In Hinduism it has been systematized in the school of YOGA. One aspect of Yoga, *dhyana* (Sanskrit: "concentrated meditation"), gave rise to a school of its own among the Buddhists, becoming the basis of ZEN. In many religions, meditation involves verbal or mental repetition of a single syllable, word, or text (e.g., a MANTRA). Visual images (e.g., a MANDALA) or mechanical devices such as PRAYER WHEELS or ROSARIES can be useful in focusing concentration. In the 20th century, movements such as TRANSCENDENTAL MEDITATION emerged to teach meditation techniques outside a religious context.

Mediterranean fever See BRUCELLOSIS

Mediterranean fruit fly *or* **Med fly** FRUIT FLY *(Ceratitis capitata)* proven to be particularly destructive to citrus crops, at great economic cost. The Med fly lays up to 500 eggs in citrus fruits (except lemons and sour limes), and the larvae tunnel into the fruit, making it unfit for human consumption. Because of this pest, quarantine laws regulating fruit importation have been enacted worldwide.

Mediterranean Sea Inland sea enclosed by Europe, Africa, and Asia. It measures as much as 2,300 mi (3,700 km) east–west, and occupies an area of about 970,000 sq mi (2,512,000 sq km). It has a maximum depth of 16,896 ft (5150 m). In the west the Strait of GIBRALTAR connects the Mediterranean with the Atlantic Ocean. In the northeast the Sea of MARMARA, the DARDANELLES, and the BOSPORUS link it with the BLACK SEA. The SUEZ CANAL connects it with the RED SEA in the southeast. A submarine ridge between SICILY and Africa divides the sea into eastern and western parts, which are subdivided into the Adriatic, Aegean, Tyrrhenian, Ionian, and Ligurian seas. Its largest islands are MAJORCA, CORSICA, SARDINIA, SICILY, CRETE, CYPRUS, and RHODES. The RHÔNE, PO, and NILE rivers form its only large deltas.

Medusa In GREEK MYTHOLOGY, the most famous of the monsters known as GORGONS. Anyone who looked directly at Medusa turned to stone. She was the only Gorgon who was mortal. The hero PERSEUS, looking only at her reflection in a shield given to him by ATHENA, killed her by cutting off her head. Perseus later gave the severed head to Athena, who placed it in her shield; according to another account, he buried it in the marketplace of ARGOS.

medusa \mi-'dü-sə\ In zoology, one of the two principal CNIDARIAN body forms; the typical form of the JELLYFISH. Its name derives from its tentacles, resembling the snakes borne by MEDUSA in place of hair. The medusoid body is bell- or umbrella-shaped. Hanging downward from the center is a stalklike structure, the manubrium, bearing the mouth at its tip. The mouth opens into the main body cavity, which connects with radial canals extending to the outer rim of the bell. A free-swimming form, the medusa moves by rhythmic muscular contractions of the bell, providing a slow propulsive action against the water. The other principal cnidarian body type is the POLYP.

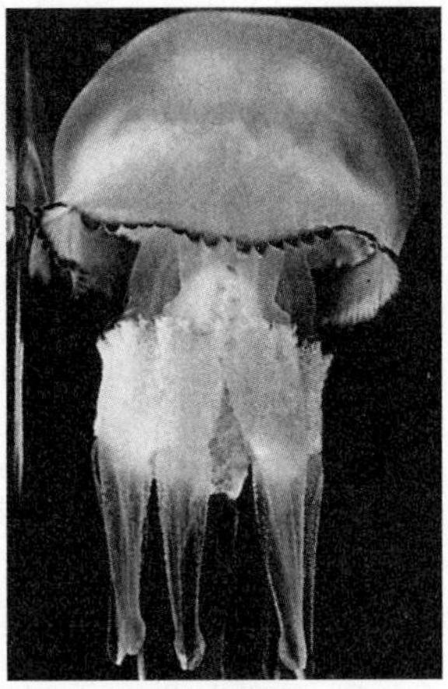

Medusa stage of a jellyfish.
TOM MCHUGH—PHOTO RESEARCHERS

Meegeren \'mā-k̲ə-rə, *Engl* 'mā-gə-rən\, **Han van** *orig.* **Henricus Antonius** (1889–1947) Dutch art forger. He forged at least 14 "old masters" and sold them at enormous profit; critics had hailed his *Christ and the Disciples at Emmaus* as a JOHANNES VERMEER masterpiece. His activities came to light after World War II when a commission was established to restore to their owners artworks collected by Nazi leaders. Discovering a work purportedly by Vermeer among those amassed by HERMANN GORING, the commission traced it to Meegeren. Charged with collaboration, he confessed. He died of a heart attack before his one-year sentence began.

meerkat Certain carnivore species of the CIVET family (Viverridae), specifically the suricate and various MONGOOSE species (in the genera *Mungos, Cynictis,* and others). The colonial, burrowing suricate *(Suricata suricatta),* or slender-tailed meerkat, found in South Africa, differs from mongooses in having four (rather than five) toes on each foot, and the yellow mongoose differs in having four toes on the hind foot. The suricate grows to a total length of 17–24 in. (43–60 cm). Bulbous roots constitute most of its diet, but it also eats meat. It is diurnal and is easily tamed as a pet.

meerschaum \'mir-shəm, 'mir-ˌshóm\ Fibrous hydrated magnesium silicate that is opaque and white, gray, or cream in color. Also called sepiolite, meerschaum (German: "sea foam") is easily fashioned, and has been used in jewelry and for tobacco pipes. It is soft when first extracted, but it hardens on drying. Meerschaum is an alteration product of SERPENTINE. The most important commercial deposit is the plain of Eskishehr, Turkey, where it is found as irregular nodules in alluvial deposits; it also occurs in France, Greece, the Czech Republic, the U.S., and elsewhere.

megalith Huge, often undressed stone used in various types of NEOLITHIC and Early BRONZE AGE monuments. The most ancient form of megalithic construction may be the dolmen, a type of burial chamber consisting of several upright supports and a flat roofing slab. Another form is the menhir, a simple upright stone usually placed with others to form a circle, as at STONEHENGE and Avebury in England, or a straight alignment, as at Carnac in France. The meaning of megalithic monuments remains largely unknown, but all share certain architectural and technical features suggesting that their creators sought to impose a conspicuously human design on the landscape and imbue it with cultural symbols. See also ROCK ART.

Megalópolis \ˌme-gä-'lò-pò-lēs\ Ancient city, central Peloponnese, Greece. Occupying both banks of the Helisson River, it was founded in 371–368 BC by Epaminondas of THEBES as the seat of the ARCADIAN LEAGUE. Attacked several times by SPARTA, it joined the ACHAEAN LEAGUE in 234 BC. It declined rapidly after being plundered by Cleomenes III of Sparta in 223 BC, and by the 2nd cent AD it lay in ruins. The nearby modern town lies in a rich lignite-bearing region that fuels thermal-power stations.

megalopolis \ˌme-gə-'lä-pə-lis\ Highly urbanized region of the U.S., stretching between the metropolitan areas of BOSTON on the northeast to WASHINGTON, D.C. on the southwest. It was given the name, which means "great city," by French geographer Jean Gottmann. The term describes a densely populated social and economic entity encompassing two or more cities and the increasingly urbanized space between them. It also includes the metro areas of NEW YORK, PHILADELPHIA, and BALTIMORE.

Mégara \'me-gə-rə\ Port city (pop., 1991: 26,000), Greece. Situated on the Saronic Gulf, west of Athens, it served as the capital of ancient Megaris. A maritime power, by the 7th century BC it had established colonies in Sicily, Chalcedon, Byzantium, Bithynia, and Crimea. During the PELOPONNESIAN WAR (431–404 BC), it was subjugated by Athens and forced into financial ruin. In the 4th century AD it recovered some prosperity, but in 1500 it was depopulated by the Venetians. It was the birthplace of Eucleides, founder of the MEGARIAN SCHOOL of philosophy.

Megarian school \me-'gar-ē-ən\ *or* **Megarics** School of philosophy founded in Greece in the early 4th century BC by Eucleides of Megara (died c. 380 BC). It is noted more for its criticism of ARISTOTLE and its influence on Stoic logic (see STOICISM) than for its doctrines. Among Eucleides' successors was Eubulides of Miletus, who criticized Aristotle's doctrines of categories, movement, and potentiality. Other Megarians were Diodorus Cronus (fl. 4th century BC) and Stilpo (fl. c. 380–300 BC); Stilpo taught ZENO OF CITIUM, and Menedemus (339?–c. 265 BC). The school died out at the beginning of the 3rd century BC.

megaron \'me-gə-ˌrän\ In ancient Greece and the Middle East, an architectural form consisting of a porch, vestibule, and large hall with a central hearth. The megaron was found in all Mycenaean palaces and also in houses. It probably originated in the Middle East, later attaining the uniquely Aegean aspect of the open porch supported by columns.

Meghalaya \ˌmā-gə-'lā-ə\ State (pop., 1994 est.: 1,960,000), northeastern India. Occupying an area of 8,660 sq mi (22,429 sq km), it is bounded by Bangladesh. Its few urban centers include SHILLONG, its capital. The tribal hill people of Meghalaya trace their origin to pre-Aryan times in India. The area came under nominal British rule in the 19th century; it was included in the state of ASSAM and was made a separate state in 1972. Although it has vast mineral resources, its economy centers on agriculture.

Meghna River \'māg-nə\ River, Bangladesh. It is formed by the SURMA RIVER. Flowing south, it is joined southeast of DHAKA by the Padma River, which is formed from the waters of the GANGES and BRAHMAPUTRA rivers. After a course of about 164 mi (264 km) it empties into the Bay of BENGAL through four mouths. A river of depth and velocity, it is navigable all year but often dangerous. At spring tide the sea rushes upriver in a single 20-ft (6-m) wave.

Megiddo \mi-'gi-dō\ City, ancient Palestine, in present-day northern Israel. It occupied a strategic location at the crossing of military and trade routes; it was also famous as a battlefield and is thought to be the biblical ARMAGEDDON. The first town was built early in the 4th millennium BC. It was captured by the Egyptian king THUTMOSE III c. 1468 BC. It later passed to the Israelites, and King SOLOMON rebuilt it as a military center. British general EDMUND H. H. ALLENBY defeated the Turks near the site in 1918.

Meher Baba \'mā-hər-'bä-bä\ *orig.* **Merwan Sheriar Irani** (1894–1969) Indian spiritual master. Born into a Zoroastrian family of Persian descent, he created a system of spiritual beliefs according to which the goal of life was to realize the oneness of God, from whom the whole universe emanates. Convinced that his calling was to awaken the world to that realization through love, he worked zealously with the poor and the physically and mentally ill. Though he attracted a sizable following in India and abroad, he did not try to establish a religion. For the last 44 years of his life he maintained silence, communicating by means of gestures and an alphabet board. His tomb at Meherabad is a place of pilgrimage.

Mehmed II \me-'met\ (1432–1481) Ottoman sultan. His father, Murad II, abdicated in his favor when Mehmed was 12, but reclaimed the throne two years later in the aftermath of a Christian Crusade. Mehmed regained the throne when his father died (1451) and began to plan the conquest of CONSTANTINOPLE. In 1453 he captured the city, then restored it to a level of grandeur suitable for an imperial capital; within fifty years it was Europe's largest city. In the next 25 years he conquered the Balkans. Under his reign, criminal and civil laws were codified in one code; he collected a library of Greek and Latin works and had eight colleges built.

Meidias Painter \'mā-dē-əs\ (fl. c. 420–400 BC) Greek vase painter known for his theatrical "florid" style. A large hydria (water vessel) with scenes from the rape of the daughters of Leucippus and of Heracles in the garden of the Hesperides, now in the British Museum, is representative of his work.

Meier \'mī-ər\, **Richard (Alan)** (born 1934) U.S. architect. Born in Newark, N.J., and educated at Cornell Univ., Meier's early experience included work with the firm of Skidmore, Owings & Merrill and with MARCEL BREUER. His houses typically feature the interplay between plane and volume, and in their crisp whiteness contrast sharply with the natural setting; the Douglas House, Harbor Springs, Mich. (1973), is a dramatically sited example. His works on a larger scale show his skills at manipulating geometric forms and combining drama and simplicity. The Getty Center in Los Angeles (1992–97), with its terraced gardens, is a resplendent acropolis in travertine stone. Meier received the 1984 Pritzker Architecture Prize.

Meiji Constitution \'mā-jē\ Constitution of Japan from 1890 to 1947. After the MEIJI RESTORATION, Japan's leaders sought to create a constitution that would define Japan as a capable, modern nation deserving of Western respect while preserving their own power. The resultant document called for a bicameral parliament (the DIET) with an elected lower house and a prime minister and cabinet appointed by the emperor. The emperor was granted supreme control of the army and navy. A privy council composed of the Meiji leaders (see GENRO), created prior to the constitution, advised the emperor and wielded actual power. Voting restrictions, which limited the electorate to about 5% of the adult male population, were loosened over the next 25 years, resulting in universal male suffrage. Political parties made the most of their limited power in the 1920s, but in the 1930s the military was able to exert control without violating the constitution. After World War II, a U.S.-approved constitution stating that "sovereign power resides with the people" replaced the Meiji Constitution. See also ITO HIROBUMI, TAISHO DEMOCRACY.

Meiji emperor *orig.* **Mutsuhito** (1852–1912) Emperor of Japan during whose reign (1867–1912) the TOKUGAWA SHOGUNATE was overthrown, Japan was transformed into a world power, and the imperial throne came to the forefront of the political scene after centuries of being overshadowed by shogunal rule. He believed in the need to modernize Japan along Western lines. Under the Meiji emperor the domains (han) and old class system were abolished, a new school system was introduced, and the MEIJI CONSTITUTION was promulgated. His reign also saw the annexation of Taiwan after the SINO-JAPANESE WAR (1894–95), the annexation of Korea (1910), and Japan's defeat of Russia in the RUSSO-JAPANESE WAR (1904–5). See also MEIJI PERIOD, MEIJI RESTORATION.

Meiji period (1868–1912) Period in Japanese history beginning with the restoration of the MEIJI EMPEROR and ending with his death. It was a time of rapid modernization and westernization. Feudal domains were abolished and replaced with prefectures; DAIMYO and SAMURAI were relieved of their special privileges. Not all samurai were happy with the changes, and there were numerous rebellions, notably that of SAIGO TAKAMORI. To secure a strong central government, a national army was formed and universal conscription was enacted. A new agricultural tax was instituted to finance the new government, and a decimal currency was introduced. Eager to encourage economic growth, the government aided the textile industry, established railways and shipping lines, and founded an ironworks. Education was also reformed, and compulsory coeducational elementary schools were introduced. By 1912 the goals of the MEIJI RESTORATION had been largely accomplished: the unequal treaties with Western powers had been revised, the country was developing well economically, and its military power had won the respect of the West. See also CHARTER OATH, MEIJI CONSTITUTION.

Meiji Restoration Overthrow of Japan's TOKUGAWA SHOGUNATE and restoration to power of the MEIJI EMPEROR in 1868. In the 19th century, the Tokugawa shogunate's policy of isolation was challenged by Russia, England, and the U.S., making Japanese feudal leaders aware of Japan's vulnerability to superior Western firepower. After the visit of Commodore MATTHEW PERRY, the country was forced to sign a series of unequal treaties, which, as in China, gave Western nations special privileges in Japan. In response, young SAMURAI from feudal domains historically hostile to the Tokugawa regime took up arms against the government. In January 1868 they announced the restoration of the emperor to power, and in May 1869 the last Tokugawa forces surrendered. The revolutionaries had the emperor issue the CHARTER OATH, which promised a break with the feudal class restrictions of the past and a search for knowledge that could transform Japan into a "rich country with a strong military." The Restoration ushered in the MEIJI PERIOD, a time of rapid modernization and westernization. See also CHOSHU, II NAOSUKE, OKUBO TOSHIMICHI, SAIGO TAKAMORI, SATSUMA, TOSA.

Meillet \me-'ye\, **Antoine** (1866–1936) French linguist. He argued that any attempt to account for linguistic change must recognize that language is a social phenomenon. His *Introduction to the Comparative Study of the Indo-European Languages* (1903) explained the relationships of the INDO-EUROPEAN LANGUAGES to each other and to their parent tongue. Meillet suggested that languages that develop farther from a center of common origin are less disturbed by changes at the point of origin and more likely to retain archaic characteristics. He produced authoritative grammars of classical ARMENIAN and Old Iranian and made notable contributions to Slavic studies.

Meinhof \'mīn-,hôf\, **Carl** (1857–1944) German scholar of African languages. A specialist in the BANTU LANGUAGES who also studied Khoisan and other African language families, he was one of the first to treat African languages in terms of PHONETICS and MORPHOLOGY. His books include *Outline of the Phonetics of the Bantu Languages* (1899) and *Principles of the Comparative Grammar of the Bantu Languages* (1906).

Meinong \'mī-nòŋ\, **Alexius** *later* **Ritter (knight) von Handschuchsheim** (1853–1920) Austrian philosopher and psychologist. He is remembered for his contributions to AXIOLOGY and the theory of objects. He taught at the Univ of Graz 1889–1920. Like his teacher FRANZ BRENTANO, he considered INTENTIONALITY to be the essence of mental states. In *On Assumptions* (1902), he maintained that objects remain objects and have definite properties *(Sosein)* even if they have no being *(Sein),* an aspect of his thought that influenced BERTRAND RUSSELL. His major writings include *On Possibility and Probability* (1915) and *On Emotional Presentation* (1917).

meiosis \mī-'ō-səs\ *or* **reduction division** Division of a gamete-producing cell in which the NUCLEUS splits twice, resulting in four sex cells (gametes, or eggs and sperm), each possessing half the number of CHROMOSOMES of the original cell. Meiosis is characteristic of organisms that reproduce sexually and have a diploid set of nuclear chromosomes (see PLOIDY). Before meiosis, chromosomes replicate and consist of joined sister strands (chromatids). Meiosis begins as homologous paternal and maternal chromosomes line up along the midline of the cell. The chromosomes exchange genetic material by the process of crossing-over (see LINKAGE GROUP), in which chromatid strands from homologous pairs entangle and exchange segments to produce chromatids containing genetic material from both parents. The pairs then separate and are pulled to opposite ends of the cell, which then pinches in half to form two daughter cells, each containing a haploid set (half the usual number) of double-stranded chromosomes. In the second round of meiotic division, the double-stranded chromosomes of each daughter cell are pulled apart, resulting in four haploid gametes. When two gametes unite during fertilization, each contributes its haploid set of chromosomes to the new individual, restoring the diploid number. See also MITOSIS.

Meïr \mā-'ir\ (fl. 2nd century AD) Rabbi and scholar of Palestine. He fled Palestine during the persecutions that followed the BAR KOKHBA revolt in AD 132–35, but later returned and helped reestablish the SANHEDRIN. The patriarch of the Sanhedrin eventually threatened him with excommunication over a question of protocol, and he left for Asia Minor, where he had been born. Known for his great dialectical skill, he is cited repeatedly in the Talmud and is remembered as the greatest of the *tannaim,* a group of masters of the Jewish oral law. Legends of his miraculous powers sprang up during the Middle Ages.

Meir \me-'ir\, **Golda** *orig.* **Goldie Mabovitch** *later* **Goldie Myerson** (1898–1978) U.S.-Israeli (Ukrainian-born) stateswoman, fourth prime minister of Israel (1969–74). Her family emigrated to Milwaukee in 1906, where she became a leader of the Milwaukee Labor Zionist Party. In 1921 she and her husband emigrated to Palestine, where she emerged as a forceful negotiator with British authorities during World War II. A signer of Israel's independence declaration in 1948, she served in the Knesset (1949–74) and held the posts of minister of labor (1949–56) and foreign minister (1956–66). As prime minister, she was sought diplomatic solutions to ease the region's tensions; unable to prevent the Yom Kippur War of 1973 (see Arab–Israeli Wars), she resigned six months later.

Golda Meir.
DENNIS BRACK–BLACK STAR/EB INC.

Meir of Rothenburg *orig.* **Meir ben Baruch** (c. 1215–1293) German Jewish scholar. After studying in France, he served as rabbi in several communities in Germany, notably Rothenburg, where he opened a Talmudic school. He became famous as an authority on rabbinic law, writing notes and commentary on the Talmud and acting for nearly half a century as the supreme court of appeals for Jews of Germany and surrounding countries. Persecution prompted him to flee Germany with a group of followers in 1286, but he was caught and imprisoned for the rest of his life in an Alsatian fortress.

Meissen porcelain \'mī-sᵊn\ German hard-paste, or true, porcelain produced at the Meissen factory, near Dresden in Saxony (now Germany), from 1710 until the present day. It was the first successfully produced true porcelain in Europe and dominated the style of European porcelain until c. 1756. The high point of the Meissen factory was reached after 1731 with the modeling of Johann Joachim Kandler. The onion pattern, introduced c. 1739, was widely copied. Meissen porcelain is marked with crossed blue swords.

Meissen hard-paste porcelain bird, c. 1750; in the Victoria and Albert Museum, London.
BY COURTESY OF THE VICTORIA AND ALBERT MUSEUM, LONDON; PHOTOGRAPH, EB INC.

Meissonier \ˌmā-sᵊn-'yā\, **Juste-Aurèle** (1695–1750) French goldsmith, designer, and architect. Appointed goldsmith and cabinetmaker to Louis XV in 1726, he became a leading originator of the influential Rococo style. His highly inventive work included fantastic grottoes, animated metalwork designs, snuffboxes, watch cases, sword hilts, and tureens. His sketches for interior decoration, furniture, and goldsmith designs became widely known through engravings. Few of his architectural plans were realized.

meistersinger \'mī-stər-ˌsiŋ-ər, 'mī-stər-ˌziŋ-ər\ (German: "master singer") Member of a German guild whose function was to continue the tradition of the minnesinger. In the 14th–16th century, these amateur guilds spread throughout Germany until most towns had one. The guilds held monthly singing contests. Because of their educational aims of fostering morality and religious belief, they came to be instrumental in promulgating the Protestant message during the Reformation, though their music is not regarded as highly distinguished. The most famous meistersinger, Hans Sachs (1494–1576), devoted his art exclusively to the Lutheran cause after 1530.

Meitner \'mīt-nər\, **Lise** (1878–1968) German physicist. She worked at Berlin's Kaiser Wilhelm Institute 1912–1938, also teaching at the University of Berlin 1926–38. At the laboratory she set up with Otto Hahn, the two isolated the radioactive isotope protactinium-231. In the 1930s, with Hahn and Fritz Strassmann (1902–1980), she investigated the products of neutron bombardment of uranium. She left Germany in 1938 for Sweden. After Hahn and Strassmann demonstrated that barium appears in neutron-bombarded uranium, she and her nephew Otto Frisch (1904–1979) explained the physical characteristics of this division and in 1939 proposed the term "fission" for the process. She shared the 1966 Enrico Fermi Award with Hahn and Strassmann. Element 109, meitnerium, is named in her honor.

Mekhilta \mə-'k̲il-tə\ Hebrew commentary on the Book of Exodus. One of the exegetic commentaries known as the Halakhic Midrashim, the *Mekhilta* presents a composite of three kinds of materials concerning the Book of Exodus: exegeses of certain passages, propositional and argumentative essays on theological principles, and topical articles on the written and oral Torah. It was produced by a Talmudic school founded by Ishmael ben Elisha c. AD 300 and known as the House of Ishmael. The name *Mekhilta* (Hebrew: "measure") refers to its use as a rule or norm for conduct. See also Halakhah, Midrash, Talmud.

Meknès \mek-'nes\ City (pop., 1994: 188,000), northern central Morocco. It was one of Morocco's four imperial cities, founded in the 10th century by Berbers. Originally a group of villages among olive groves, it became the Moroccan capital in 1673 under Maulay Isma'il, who built palaces and mosques that earned for Meknès the name "Versailles of Morocco." After his death it declined, and in 1911 it was occupied by the French. It is now a commercial center for agricultural products, fine embroidery, and carpets.

Mekong River \'mā-'kȯŋ\ *Chinese* **Lancang Jiang** *or* **Lan-Ts'ang Chiang** \'län-'tsäŋ-'jē-'äŋ\ Longest river, S.East Asia. Rising in eastern Tibet, China, it flows south across the highlands of Yunnan province. It then forms part of the border between Myanmar and Laos, as well as between Laos and Thailand. It runs through Laos and Cambodia before entering the China Sea in a delta south of Ho Chi Minh City in Vietnam after a course of 2,700 mi (4,350 km). Vientiane and Phnom Penh stand on its banks. Its lower course has about one-third of the combined population of Cambodia, Laos, Thailand, and Vietnam. In 1957 the U.N. initiated the Mekong River Development Project, an international effort to harness the river for hydroelectricity and irrigation.

Melanchthon \mə-'laŋk-thən, *German* mā-'länk̲-tȯn\, **Philipp** *orig.* **Philipp Schwartzerd** (1497–1560) German Protestant reformer. His education in Germany was greatly influenced by humanist learning, and he was named professor of Greek at Wittenberg in 1518. A friend and defender of Martin Luther, Melanchthon was the author of *Loci communes* (1521), the first systematic treatment of the principles of the Reformation, and of the Protestant creed known as the Augsburg Confession (1530). He also reorganized the entire educational system of Germany, founding and reforming several of its universities. His willingness to compromise with Catholics on theological issues in his later years became controversial.

Melanchthon, engraving by Albrecht Dürer, 1526.
BY COURTESY OF THE STAATLICHE MUSEEN KUPERSTICHKABINETT, BERLIN

Melanesia \ˌme-lə-'nē-zhə\ Collective name for the islands in the South Pacific Ocean, northeast of Australia and south of the equator. A subdivision of Oceania, it includes New Guinea, Admiralty Islands, Bismarck and Louisiade archipelagoes, Solomon Islands, Santa Cruz Islands, New Caledonia and the Loyalty Islands, Vanuatu, Fiji, Norfolk Island and numerous others. Two distinct populations and cultures exist in the region. The Papuans, who have inhabited the area for 40,000 years, devised one of the earliest agricultural systems and developed the Papuan languages. Seafaring peoples with an Austronesian language and a Southeast Asian cultural tradition settled in the area about 3,500 years ago.

melanin \'me-lə-nən\ Any of several organic compounds, dark biological pigments that give coloration (shades of yellow to brown) to skin, hair, feathers, scales, eyes, and some internal tissues, notably the substantia nigra in the brain. In humans, melanins help protect the skin against the damaging effects of ultraviolet radiation, but melanoma may arise from cells that produce it. The amount in the skin depends on both genetic and environmental factors. Melanin is produced from the amino acid tyrosine; albinos lack the enzyme that catalyzes that reaction (see albinism).

melanism, industrial See industrial melanism

L
M
N

melanoma \ˌme-lə-ˈnō-mə\ Dark-colored tumor most often derived from MELANIN-pigmented skin cells. Though sometimes derived from other body tissues, they are called melanomas because of their dark color. A melanoma may or may not be malignant. It may develop from irritation of a mole or wart. Melanomas are prone to metastasize (see CANCER) and are associated with the highest death rate of any skin cancer. Removal, together with a collar of surrounding healthy skin, cures melanoma if done early. Melanomas are very rare in persons with dark skin.

melatonin \ˌme-lə-ˈtō-nən\ Only HORMONE secreted by the PINEAL GLAND of most vertebrates. It appears to be important in regulating sleeping cycles; more is produced at night, and test subjects injected with it become sleepy. Melatonin may be involved in SEASONAL AFFECTIVE DISORDER. It also appears to regulate sexual maturation; children produce more melatonin than adults, and those with pineal-gland tumors that decrease melatonin production mature sexually unusually early. In mammals other than humans, melatonin may act as a cue to breeding and mating in season.

Melba, Nellie *later* **Dame Nellie** *orig.* **Helen Porter Mitchell** (1861–1931) Australian soprano. After study with Mathilde Marchesi (1821–1913) in Paris, she debuted in Brussels in *Rigoletto* (1887), and in the next six years was heard in all the major houses of the world. One of the most celebrated coloraturas in the years preceding World War I, she sang mostly at Covent Garden after 1902. Concentrating on a few Italian and French operas, she possessed abundant technique and vocal beauty, though some found her performances cold.

Melbourne \ˈmel-bərn\ City (pop., 1995 est.: 3,218,000), capital of the state of VICTORIA, southeastern Australia. Situated at the head of Port Phillip Bay and the mouth of the Yarra River, the area was discovered by Europeans in 1802 and incorporated into the colony of New South Wales. The first settlement was founded in 1835 by settlers from Tasmania, and in 1837 it was named for the British prime minister, Lord MELBOURNE. Made the capital of Victoria in 1851, it grew rapidly with the gold rush of the early 1850s. It served as the first capital of the Australian commonwealth 1901–27, until CANBERRA became the new capital. Second in size to SYDNEY, it is an industrial, commercial, and financial center, and is the seat of several universities, including the University of MELBOURNE.

Melbourne, University of Public university in Melbourne, Australia. Founded as a liberal-arts college in 1853, in subsequent decades it added schools or faculties of law, engineering, medicine, music, dentistry, agriculture, veterinary medicine, education, architecture, and commerce. It continued to expand rapidly after World War II, adding programs in nuclear science, applied economic research, and South and Southeast Asian studies. Current enrollment is about 30,000.

Melbourne (of Kilmore), Viscount *orig.* **William Lamb** (1779–1848) British prime minister (1834, 1835–41). A lawyer, he entered the House of Commons in 1806 and the House of Lords in 1829. Though a Whig, he served in Tory governments as chief secretary for Ireland (1827–28) and advocated political rights for Roman Catholics. He served as home secretary (1830–34) in Earl GREY's Whig government, reluctantly supporting the REFORM BILL OF 1832. As prime minister (1834), he gained the support of Whigs and moderate Tories and opposed further parliamentary reform and efforts to repeal the CORN LAWS. In his second administration (1835–41), he became the young Queen VICTORIA's valued chief political adviser. His firm stand in foreign policy averted war with France over Syria (1840). His wife, Lady Caroline Lamb (1785–1828), was a minor novelist, famous for her affair with Lord BYRON in 1812–13.

Melchior \ˈmel-kē-ˌȯr\, **Lauritz** *orig.* **Lebrecht Hommel** (1890–1973) Danish-U.S. tenor. He debuted as a baritone in 1913, but further study extended his range upward and he made his tenor debut as Tannhäuser in 1918. Additional training readied him for Bayreuth, where he sang 1924–31, and he remained the preeminent Wagnerian tenor of his time, regularly singing (often opposite K. FLAGSTAD) at Covent Garden (until 1939) and the Metropolitan Opera (1926–50), and making many recordings.

Melchizedek \mel-ˈki-zə-ˌdek\ Canaanite king and priest revered by ABRAHAM. In the Book of Genesis, Abraham rescues his kidnapped nephew, LOT, from the Mesopotamians, and on returning from battle he meets Melchizedek, king of Salem (probably another name for Jerusalem), who gives him bread and wine and blesses him in the name of "God Most High." St. PAUL's Epistle to the Hebrews treats Melchizedek as a foreshadowing of Christ.

Melfi \ˈmel-fē\, **Constitutions of** *or* **Liber Augustalis** (1231) Legal code drawn up by Emperor FREDERICK II for the kingdom of Sicily. Based on Roman and canon law, the constitutions centralized royal administration, established greater efficiency in the courts, and rationalized civil and criminal procedures in the interests of justice.

Méliès \māl-ˈyes\, **Georges** (1861–1938) French filmmaker. He was a professional magician and manager-director of the Théâtre Robert-Houdin in Paris when he saw the first movies made by the LUMIÈRE brothers in 1895. In his film experiments he exploited the basic camera tricks of slow motion, dissolve, and fade-out. From 1899 to 1912 he made over 400 films, which combined illusion, comic burlesque, and pantomime in fantasy productions, including *A Trip to the Moon* (1902). He also filmed reconstructed news events as an early form of newsreel. Overtaken by the commercial growth of the film industry, he was forced to sell his studio in 1913.

Méliès.
RENE DAZY–J.P. ZIOLO

Melilla \mə-ˈlē-yä\ Spanish enclave (population 1996 est.: 60,000), North Africa. A military station and seaport, it constitutes with CEUTA an autonomous community of Spain. Located on Morocco's northern coast, it was successively colonized by the Phoenicians, Greeks, and Romans. It fell as a Berber town to Spain in 1497, and remained Spanish despite a long history of attack and siege. In the early 20th century Spain modernized its port and made it an administrative center for Spanish Morocco. It was the first Spanish town to rise against the Popular Front government in 1936, helping to precipitate the SPANISH CIVIL WAR. It was retained by Spain when Morocco achieved independence in 1956.

Mello, Fernando Collor de See Fernando COLLOR DE MELLO

Mellon, Andrew W(illiam) (1855–1937) U.S. financier. Born in Pittsburgh, he entered his father's banking house in 1874. Over three decades he built up a financial empire by supplying capital for corporations to expand in fields such as aluminum, steel, and oil. He helped found the Aluminum Co. of America (ALCOA) and the GULF OIL CORP., and he joined HENRY CLAY FRICK to found Union Steel Co. and Union Trust Co. By the early 1920s he was one of the richest men in the U.S. As secretary of the Treasury (1921–32) he persuaded Congress to lower taxes in order to encourage business expansion. He was praised for the economic boom of the 1920s but criticized during the GREAT DEPRESSION, and in 1932 he resigned to serve as ambassador to England. A noted art collector and philanthropist, Mellon donated an extensive art collection and $15 million to establish the NATIONAL GALLERY OF ART.

melodrama Sentimental drama marked by extravagant theatricality, subordination of character development to plot, and focus on sensational incidents. It usually has an improbable plot that features such stock characters as the noble hero, the long-suffering heroine, and the hard-hearted villain, and it ends with virtue triumphing over vice. Written by such playwrights as Guilbert de Pixérécourt and DION BOUCICAULT, melodramas were popular in Europe and the U.S. during the 19th century. They often featured spectacular events such as shipwrecks, battles, fires, earthquakes, and horse races. Melodrama died out as a theatrical form in the early 20th century but remained popular in silent film. It can still be seen in contemporary film genres such as the action movie.

melody Rhythmic succession of single tones organized as an aesthetic whole. The melody is often the highest line in a musical composition. Melodies may suggest their own HARMONY or COUNTERPOINT. As fundamental as RHYTHM AND METER (and more so than harmony), melody is common to all musical cultures.

melon Any of the seven groups of *Cucumis melo,* a trailing vine grown for its edible, sweet, musky-scented fruit. Members of the horticulturally diverse GOURD family, melons are frost-tender annuals native to central

Asia but widely grown in many cultivated varieties in warm regions worldwide. They have soft, hairy, trailing stems, large round to lobed leaves, yellow flowers, and large flat seeds. The fruits of the numerous cultivated varieties differ greatly in size, shape, surface texture, flesh color, flavor, and weight. Examples include cantaloupe, honeydew, and casaba. Plants resembling true melons include the WATERMELON, the Chinese watermelon, the melon tree (see PAPAYA), and the melon shrub, or pear melon (*Solanum muricatum*).

Melos \'mē-ˌläs\ *Greek* **Mílos** \'mē-ˌlȯs\ Island (pop., 1991: 4,302) of the CYCLADES, Greece. It is 14 mi (23 km) long and occupies an area of 58 sq mi (151 sq km). Melos (Mílos) is the chief town. On the ancient acropolis of Adamanda the Venus de Milo, now in the LOUVRE MUSEUM, was found in 1820. The settlement of Phylakopi, dating from 1550 BC, was destroyed c. 1100 BC by DORIAN settlers. In 416 BC it was conquered by ATHENS, which killed the entire male population in reprisal for the island's neutrality in the PELOPONNESIAN WAR. LYSANDER later restored the island to the Dorians, but it never recovered its prosperity. Under Frankish rule it formed part of the duchy of NAXOS.

Melqart *or* **Melkarth** Phoenician god, the chief deity of TYRE and of two of its colonies, CARTHAGE and Gadir (CÁDIZ, Spain). Probably a sun god, he was often depicted as a bearded figure wearing a high, rounded hat and a kilt; he held an Egyptian ANKH as a symbol of life and an ax as a symbol of death. His sanctuary in Tyre was the scene of annual winter and spring festivals and is believed to have been the model for SOLOMON's temple in Jerusalem.

meltdown Occurrence in which a huge amount of THERMAL ENERGY and RADIATION is released as a result of an uncontrolled CHAIN REACTION in a NUCLEAR POWER REACTOR. The chain reaction that occurs in the reactor's core must be carefully regulated by control rods, which absorb neutrons, and a moderator, which reduces their energy. If the core becomes too hot, it can melt, releasing large amounts of radiation. See also CHERNOBYL ACCIDENT.

melting point Temperature at which the solid and liquid states of a pure substance can exist in EQUILIBRIUM. As heat is applied to a solid, its temperature increases until it reaches the melting point. At this temperature, additional heat converts the solid into a liquid without a change in temperature. The melting point of solid water (ice) is 32°F (0°C). Though the melting point of a solid is generally considered to be the same as the FREEZING POINT of the corresponding liquid, they may differ because a liquid may freeze into different crystal systems and impurities can lower the freezing point.

Melville, Herman *orig.* **Herman Melvill** (1819–1891) U.S. writer. Born to a wealthy New York family that suffered great financial losses, Melville had little formal schooling and began a period of wanderings at sea in 1839. In 1841 he sailed on a whaler bound for the South Seas; the next year he jumped ship in the Marquesas Islands. His adventures in Polynesia were the basis of his successful first novels, *Typee* (1846) and *Omoo* (1847). After the allegorical fantasy *Mardi* (1849) failed, he quickly wrote *Redburn* (1849) and *White-Jacket* (1850), about the rough life of sailors. *Moby-Dick* (1851), his masterpiece, is both an intense whaling narrative and a symbolic examination of the problems and possibilities of American democracy; it brought him neither acclaim nor reward when published. Increasingly reclusive and despairing, he wrote *Pierre* (1852), which, intended as a piece of domestic "ladies" fiction, became a parody of that popular genre; *Israel Potter* (1855), *The Confidence-Man* (1857), and magazine stories, including "Bartleby the Scrivener" (1853) and "Benito Cereno" (1855). After 1857 he wrote verse. In 1866 a customs-inspector position finally brought him a secure income. He returned to prose for his last work, the novel *Billy Budd, Foretopman*, which remained unpublished until 1924. Neglected for much of his career, Melville came to be regarded by modern critics as one of the greatest American writers.

Melville Island Island in the Timor Sea, off the coast of NORTHERN TERRITORY, Australia. It is 80 miles (130 km) long and 55 mi (88 km) wide, with an area of 2,240 sq mi (5,800 sq km). It was sighted by the Dutch in 1644; the British built Fort Dundas there in 1824. Known to the Tiwi people as Yermalner, it is one of the few areas of Australia still occupied by AUSTRALIAN ABORIGINES according to their ancestral rights. In 1978 the island's ownership passed from the Australian government to the Tiwi Land Council.

Melville Island One of the largest of the Parry Islands, in the Arctic Ocean, Canada. Located north of VICTORIA ISLAND, it is 200 mi (320 km) long and 30–130 mi (50–210 km) wide, with an area of 16,274 sq mi (42,149 sq km). It has no human inhabitants, but it supports MUSK OXEN and has natural-gas deposits. It was discovered in 1819 by William Parry.

Melville Sound See VISCOUNT MELVILLE SOUND

membrane In biology, the thin layer that forms the outer boundary of a living cell or of an internal cell compartment. The outer boundary is the plasma membrane, and the compartments enclosed by internal membranes are called organelles. Biological membranes have a dual function: separation of vital but incompatible metabolic processes conducted in the organelles; and passage of nutrients, wastes, and metabolic products between organelles and between the cell and the outside environment. Membranes consist largely of a double layer of LIPIDS in which are embedded large proteins, many of which transport IONS and water-soluble molecules across the membrane. See also CYTOPLASM, EUKARYOTE.

membrane structure Structure with a thin, flexible surface (membrane) that carries loads primarily through tensile stresses. There are two main types: TENT STRUCTURES and PNEUMATIC STRUCTURES. The Denver International Airport (1995) features a terminal building roofed by a white membrane stretched from steel masts.

Memel See KLAIPEDA

Memel dispute \'mā-məl\ Post–World War I dispute over sovereignty of the former German Prussian territory of Memelland. Located on the Baltic Sea northern of the Memel River, the area was mainly inhabited by Lithuanians. In 1919 at the PARIS PEACE CONFERENCE, the newly formed state of Lithuania requested annexation of the area. A commission recommended formation of a free state, but Lithuanian inhabitants of the region took over the government in 1923. Protests by the Allied Powers resulted in the signing of the Memel Statute to establish Memelland as an autonomous region within Lithuania.

Memling \'mem-liŋ\, **Hans** *or* **Hans Memlinc** \'mem-liŋk\ (c. 1430/40–1494) Flemish painter. He settled in Bruges in 1465 and established a large workshop that became very successful and made him one of the city's wealthiest citizens. Though somewhat derivative of the works of contemporary Flemish painters (JAN VAN EYCK, DIRCK BOUTS, HUGO VAN DER GOES, and particularly ROGIER VAN DER WEYDEN), his art has great charm and a distinctive character. Memling's religious paintings and portraits of wealthy patrons (e.g., *Tommaso Portinari and His Wife*, c. 1468) were, and remain, enormously popular.

Detail of Madonna and Child from Diptych with Madonna and Martin van Nieuwenhove (left wing), oil on panel by Hans Memling, 1487.

BY COURTESY OF THE MEMLING-MUSEUM, BRUGGE, BEL., PHOTOGRAPH, © A.C.L., BRUSSELS

Memminger \'me-mən-jər\, **Christopher G(ustavus)** (1803–1888) German-U.S. public official. He emigrated to the U.S. in his teens and became a successful lawyer in Charleston, S.C. After South Carolina seceded (1860), he helped draft the provisional constitution of the Confederacy and was appointed its treasury secretary (1861–64). To raise money, he issued increasing amounts of paper currency, which depreciated greatly by 1863. Held responsible for the collapse of Confederate credit, he resigned in 1864.

Memnon In GREEK MYTHOLOGY, a king of the Ethiopians. The son of Tithonus (of the Trojan royal house) and Eos (Dawn), he fought bravely for his uncle PRIAM against the Greeks, and was slain by ACHILLES. Moved by the tears of Eos, ZEUS granted him immortality. His companions, changed into birds, came every year to fight and lament over his grave. In Egypt his name was connected with the colossal stone statues of AMENHOTEP III near THEBES; the harplike sounds these statues emitted when touched by the rays of the rising sun were believed to be the voice of Memnon responding to the greeting of his mother, Eos.

memoir History or record composed from personal observation and experience. Closely related to AUTOBIOGRAPHY, a memoir differs chiefly in the degree of emphasis on external events. Unlike writers of autobiography, who are concerned primarily with themselves as subject matter, writers of memoir usually have played roles in, or have closely observed, historical events, and their main purpose is describing or interpreting those events.

Memorial Day *or* **Decoration Day** U.S. holiday. Originally held in commemoration of soldiers killed in the AMERICAN CIVIL WAR (1868), its observance later extended to all U.S. war dead. Most states conform to the federal practice of observing it on the last Monday in May, but some retain the traditional day of celebration, May 30. National observance is marked by the placing of a wreath on the Tomb of the Unknowns in Arlington National Cemetery.

Memorial University of Newfoundland Public university in St. John's, Newfoundland, founded in 1925. It offers undergraduate and graduate programs in the sciences, arts and humanities, social sciences, business administration, education, engineering, medicine, and other fields. Campus facilities include centers for research in ocean resources, maritime history, and political economy. Total enrollment is about 17,000.

memory In DIGITAL COMPUTERS, a physical device used to store such information as data or programs on a temporary or permanent basis. Most digital computer systems have two types of memory, the main memory and one or more auxiliary storage units. In most cases, the main memory is a high-speed RAM. Auxiliary storage units include HARD DISKS, FLOPPY DISKS, and magnetic tape drives. Besides main and auxiliary memories, other forms of memory include ROM and optical storage media such as VIDEODISCS and COMPACT DISCS (see CD-ROM).

memory Power or process of recalling or reproducing what has been learned or experienced. Research indicates that the ability to retain information is fairly uniform among normal individuals; what differs is the degree to which persons learn or take account of something to begin with and the kind and amount of detail that is retained. ATTENTION, MOTIVATION, and especially ASSOCIATION facilitate this process. Visual images are generally better remembered than are other forms of sense-data. Memory prodigies, or people with "photographic" or "eidetic" memories, often draw heavily on visual associations, including mnemonics. Many psychologists distinguish between short- and long-term memory. The former (variously said to last ten seconds to three minutes) is less subject to interference and distortion than the latter. Long-term memory is sometimes divided into episodic (i.e., event-centered) and semantic (i.e., knowledge-centered) memory. Various models of memory have been proposed, from the Enlightenment notion of impressions made on brain tissues (restyled as "memory molecules" or coded "engrams" in the 20th century) to B. F. SKINNER's "black box" to more recent ideas concerning INFORMATION PROCESSING or the formation of neuronal groups. Disorders of or involving memory include ALZHEIMER'S DISEASE, AMNESIA, KORSAKOFF's syndrome, POST-TRAUMATIC STRESS DISORDER, and SENILE DEMENTIA. See also HYPNOSIS.

Memphis Capital of ancient Egypt during the Old Kingdom (c. 2575–c. 2130 BC), located on the western bank of the NILE RIVER, south of CAIRO. The modern town of Mit Rahina now occupies the site. Founded c. 2925 BC by Menes, it was by the 3rd dynasty a flourishing community. Despite the rivalry of Heracleopolis and THEBES, it remained important, particularly in the worship of PTAH. Beginning in the 8th century BC, it fell successively to Nubia, Assyria, Persia, and ALEXANDER THE GREAT. Its importance as a religious center was undermined by the rise of Christianity and then of Islam. It was abandoned after the Muslim conquest of Egypt in AD 640. Its ruins include the great temple of Ptah, royal palaces, and an extensive necropolis. Nearby are the pyramids of SAQQARA and GIZA.

Memphis City (pop., 1996 est.: 597,000), southwestern Tennessee. Situated above the Mississippi River where the borders of Arkansas, Mississippi, and Tennessee meet, it was founded in 1819 on the site of a CHICKASAW Indian village and a U.S. fort. It was incorporated as a city in 1849. A Confederate military center at the start of the AMERICAN CIVIL WAR, it was captured by Union forces in 1862. In the 1870s yellow fever killed 8,000 residents, and the city was forced into bankruptcy. Rechartered in 1893, it was the state's largest city by 1900. Sites of interest include Beale St., made famous by W.C. HANDY as the birthplace of the blues; and Graceland, the mansion of E. PRESLEY. It is the seat of several educational institutions, including Memphis State Univ.

Memphremagog \ˌmem-fri-ˈmā-ˌgäg\, **Lake** Lake that crosses the U.S.–Canadian border. Extending from northern Vermont into southern Quebec, it is 27 mi (43 km) long and only 1–2 mi (1.5–3 km) wide for most of its length. It has several large bays, including Fitch Bay and Sargents Bay. At its northern end the lake drains into the St. Francis River. Its name is an Algonquian term meaning "where there is a big expanse of water."

Menai Strait \ˈmē-ˌnī\ Channel of the IRISH SEA separating the Isle of ANGLESEY from the mainland of northern Wales. It extends 15 mi (24 km) and varies in width from 600 ft (180 m) to 2 mi (3 km). Two famous bridges span the strait: THOMAS TELFORD's suspension road bridge of 1827 and ROBERT STEPHENSON's Britannia tubular railway bridge of 1849.

Menander \mə-ˈnan-dər\ (342?–292? BC) Athenian dramatist, considered by ancient critics the supreme poet of Greek NEW COMEDY. He produced his first play in 321 BC, and in 316 BC he won a prize with *Dyscolus* ("The Misanthrope"), the only one of his plays for which a complete text still exists. By the end of his career he had written over 100 plays and won eight victories at Athenian dramatic festivals. He excelled at presenting such characters as stern fathers, young lovers, and intriguing slaves. As adapted by the Romans PLAUTUS and TERENCE, his plays influenced the later development of Renaissance comedy.

Mencius \ˈmen-shē-əs\ *Chinese* **Mengzi** *or* **Meng-tzu** \ˈməŋ-ˈtsə\ *orig.* **Meng K'o** (372?–289? BC) Chinese philosopher. The book *MENCIUS* records his doings and sayings and contains statements on innate human goodness, a topic warmly debated by Confucianists up to modern times. That the four principles *(si duan)*—the feelings of commiseration, shame, courtesy, and right and wrong—are all inborn in humans was a self-evident truth to Mencius; and the four principles, when properly cultivated, will develop into the four cardinal virtues of REN (benevolence), righteousness, decorum, and wisdom. His development of orthodox CONFUCIANISM earned him the title "second sage," and for the last thousand years he has been revered as the cofounder of Confucianism.

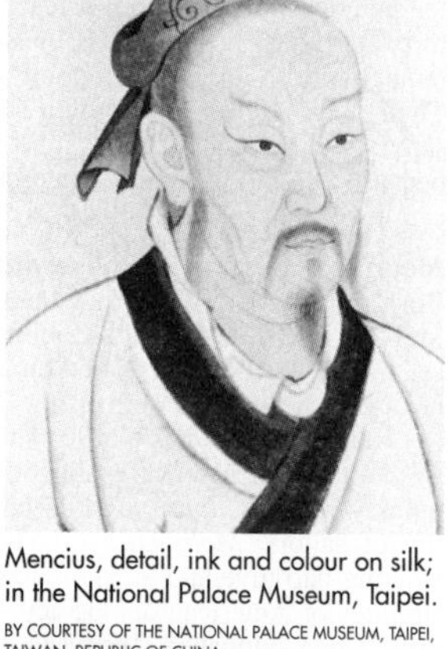

Mencius, detail, ink and colour on silk; in the National Palace Museum, Taipei.

BY COURTESY OF THE NATIONAL PALACE MUSEUM, TAIPEI, TAIWAN, REPUBLIC OF CHINA

Mencius *or* **Mengzi** *or* **Meng-tzu** Chinese Confucian text concerning government, written by MENCIUS. The book maintains that the welfare of the common people comes before every other consideration. When a ruler no longer practices benevolence and righteousness, the mandate of heaven (his right to rule) is withdrawn and he should be removed. *Mencius* did not become a classic until the 12th century, when it was published by ZHU XI together with *DA XUE*, *ZHONG YONG*, and *LUNYU* as the FOUR BOOKS. See also CONFUCIANISM.

Mencken, H(enry) L(ouis) (1880–1956) U.S. controversialist, humorous journalist, and critic. A native of Baltimore, Mencken worked on the staff of the *Baltimore Sun* for much of his life. With George Jean Nathan (1882–1958), he coedited *The Smart Set* (1914–23) and cofounded and edited (1924–33) the *American Mercury*, both important literary magazines.

H.L. Mencken.

BY COURTESY OF THE ENOCH PRATT FREE LIBRARY, BALTIMORE; PHOTOGRAPH, ROBERT KNIESCHE

Probably the most influential U.S. literary critic in the 1920s, he often used criticism to jeer at the nation's social and cultural weaknesses. *Prejudices* (1919–27) collects many of his reviews and essays. In *The American Language* (1919; supplements 1945, 1948), he brought together American expressions and idioms; by the time of his death, he was perhaps the leading authority on the language of his country.

Mendel \'men-dəl\, **Gregor (Johann)** (1822–1884) Austrian botanist and plant experimenter. He became an Augustinian monk in 1843 and later studied at the University of Vienna. In 1856, working in his monastery's garden, he began the experiments that led to his formulation of the basic principle of heredity. He crossed varieties of the garden pea that had maintained constant differences in such single alternative traits as tallness and dwarfishness, flower color, and pod form. He theorized that the occurrence of the visible alternative traits of the plants, in the constant varieties and in their descendants, was due to the occurrence of paired elementary units of heredity, now known as genes. What was new in Mendel's interpretation of his data was his recognition that genes obey simple statistical laws. His system proved to be of general application and is one of the basic principles of biology. He achieved fame only after his death, through the work of CARL ERICH CORRENS, ERICH TSCHERMAK VON SEYSENEGG, and HUGO DE VRIES, who independently obtained similar results and found that both the experimental data and the general theory had been published 34 years previously.

Mendele Moykher Sforim \'men-də-lə-mō-'k̲er-sfä-'rēm\ *or* **Mendele Mokher Sefarim** \ˌsef-ə-'rēm\ **("Mendele the Itinerant Bookseller")** *orig.* **Shalom Jacob Abramovitsh** (1835–1917) Russian author. He lived much of his life in Ukraine, becoming a rabbi and head of a traditional school (Talmud Torah) at Odessa. His stories, written with lively humor and gentle satire, are invaluable in the study of Jewish life in Eastern Europe at the time when its traditional structure was giving way. His greatest work is *The Travels and Adventures of Benjamin the Third* (1875), a panorama of Jewish life in Russia. He is considered the founder of both modern Yiddish and modern Hebrew narrative literature and the creator of modern literary Yiddish.

Mendeleyev \ˌmen-də-'lā-əf\, **Dmitry (Ivanovich)** (1834–1907) Russian chemist. He taught at the University of St. Petersburg (1867–90) and later served as director of Russia's bureau of weights and measures. He made a fundamental contribution to chemistry by establishing in 1869 the principle of periodicity of the ELEMENTS. His first PERIODIC TABLE was based on arranging the elements in ascending order of ATOMIC WEIGHT and grouping them by similarity of properties. Mendeleyev's theory allowed him to predict the existence and atomic weights of several elements not discovered until years later.

Mendelsohn \'men-dəls-ˌzōn\, **Erich** (1887–1953) German architect. While studying architecture in Munich, he was influenced by the BLAUE REITER group of Expressionist artists. Mendelsohn's Einstein Tower, Potsdam (1919–21), a highly sculptured structure, reflects his early preoccupation with science fiction. In the 1920s he designed a number of imaginative structures, including the Schocken stores in Stuttgart (1927) and Chemnitz (1928), notable for their prominent use of glass in strongly horizontal compositions. He fled the Nazis in 1933 and eventually settled in the U.S.; his American works include the Maimonides Hospital, San Francisco (1946).

Mendelssohn (-Bartholdy), (Jakob Ludwig) Felix (1809–1847) German composer. Grandson of MOSES MENDELSSOHN, he grew up in a wealthy Jewish family that had converted to Protestantism. He was exposed early to his mother's glittering salon, and began to compose at 11. At 16 he wrote his first masterpieces, the Octet in E-flat and the overture to *A Midsummer Night's Dream*. In 1829 he conducted the first performance of J.S. BACH's *St. Matthew Passion* in 100 years, greatly contributing to the Bach revival. His "Reformation" (1832) and "Italian" (1833) symphonies date from this period. After serving as music director of the Catholic city of Düsseldorf 1833–35, he took the parallel position in Protestant Leipzig. There he built up the Gewandhaus Orchestra, with which he established the historical concert programming that has remained standard to the present day. His appointment as kapellmeister in Berlin (1841–45) was a source of much frustration. His last decade produced such great works as the "Scottish" Symphony (1842), the violin concerto (1844), and the oratorio *Elijah* (1846). His beloved sister, Fanny Mendelssohn Hensel (1805–1847), had been considered his equal in musical talent as a girl, but was discouraged from composing until her marriage to the painter Wilhelm Hensel (1794–1861), and eventually wrote more than 500 works. Her death was a severe shock to Mendelssohn; years of overwork simultaneously caught up with him, and he died six months after her at 38. His other works include the oratorio *St. Paul*, several concert overtures, the large piano set *Songs Without Words*, and two piano concertos.

Mendelssohn, Moses *orig.* **Moses ben Menachem** (1729–1786) German Jewish philosopher and scholar. The son of an impoverished scribe, he began his career as a tutor but eventually won fame for his philosophical writings, which would become influential among the 19th-century U.S. Transcendentalists. He combined Judaism with the rationalism of the Enlightenment, becoming one of the principal figures in the HASKALA, which helped bring Jews into the mainstream of European culture. His works include *Phädon* (1767), a defense of the immortality of the soul, and *Jerusalem* (1783), on the relationship of religion and the state. His friend GOTTHOLD LESSING based the protagonist of his celebrated drama *Nathan the Wise* on Mendelssohn. He was the grandfather of the composer F. MENDELSSOHN.

Mendenhall Glacier Blue ice sheet, 12 mi (19 km) long, 1.5 mi (2.4 km) wide, and more than 100 ft (30 m) high. It flows from the southern half of the huge Juneau Icefield, which lies in the Boundary Ranges in southeastern Alaska. A relic of the Little Ice Age (1500–1750), it recedes 90 ft (27 m) a year. The adjacent Mendenhall Lake began to form about 1900 and is now 1.5 mi (2.5 km) long and 1 mi (1.6 km) wide.

Menderes \men-'der-əs\, **Adnan** (1899–1961) Turkish prime minister (1950–60). Son of an aristocrat, he entered parliament as a member of MUSTAFA KEMAL ATATURK's party (1930). In 1945 he cofounded the first opposition party, and he won the prime ministership in the 1950, 1954, and 1957 elections. His policies included seeking closer ties with Muslim states, encouraging private enterprise, and lifting restraint on religious expression. Intolerant of critics, he instituted press censorship. In challenging Atatürk's ideals, he earned the enmity of the army and was overthrown and executed.

Menderes River \ˌmen-de-'res\ Name of two rivers in Turkey. The first (also called in Turkish, Büyük Menderes) runs through southwestern Turkey. It empties into the AEGEAN SEA after a course of 363 mi (584 km). It classical name, Maeander, is derived from the winding course of its lower reaches. The second (also called in Turkish, Küçük Menderes) was known in antiquity as the Scamander; it rises in northwestern Turkey and flows 60 mi (97 km) west across the plain of ancient TROY, emptying into the DARDANELLES.

Mendès-France \maⁿ-des-'fräⁿs\, **Pierre** (1907–1982) French politician and premier (1954–55). Born into a Jewish family, he became a lawyer and served in the Chamber of Deputies 1932–40. In World War II he was imprisoned by the Vichy government but escaped to London, where he joined the Free French air force and served in finance posts in CHARLES DE GAULLE's provisional government. As a legislator in postwar France (1946–58), he criticized government policies on economics and the wars in Indochina and North Africa. In 1954 he became premier; he ended France's involvement in Indochina and also helped effect autonomy for Tunisia. His proposed economic reforms led to his defeat in 1955. He sought without success to make the RADICAL-SOCIALIST PARTY the center of the noncommunist left and opposed de Gaulle's presidency.

Menelaus \ˌme-nə-'lā-əs\ In GREEK MYTHOLOGY, the king of SPARTA and the younger son of ATREUS. When his wife, HELEN, was abducted by PARIS, he asked the other Greek kings to join him in an expedition against Troy, thus beginning the TROJAN WAR. He served under his brother AGAMEMNON. At the war's end he recovered Helen and brought her back to Sparta instead of killing her as he had intended. Having forgotten to appease the gods of defeated Troy, he endured a hard voyage home, and many of his ships were lost.

Menem \'me-nem\, **Carlos (Saúl)** (born 1930) President of Argentina (1989–99). The son of Syrian immigrants, he converted to Roman Catholicism and joined the PERONIST movement in 1956. He held typical Peronist views, favoring nationalism, expansion of the government, large raises for wage earners, and tax breaks for businesses. By the time he took office, however, inflation had risen to 28,000% and Argentina was in crisis; he consequently abandoned his party orthodoxy in favor of a fiscally conservative policy and succeeded in stabilizing the economy. A flamboyant figure, he enjoyed great popularity despite his controversial pardoning of convicted human-rights violators connected with the period of military rule. In 2001 Menem was placed under house arrest after he was indicted for illegal arms dealing.

Menéndez de Avilés \mə-'nen-dəs-dā-,ä-və-'lās\, **Pedro** (1519–1574) Spanish conquistador. He ran away to sea at 14 and rose to captain of the Indies fleet (1554–63). He was sent to Florida to establish a colony and remove a potential threat to Spain's American possessions posed by a French settlement on the St. Johns River. In 1565 he entered the bay of St. Augustine, where he built a fort. He attacked the French colony at Fort Caroline and massacred its entire population, calling its members heretics. He then explored the Atlantic coast and built a string of forts, firmly establishing Spain's control of Florida.

Menéndez Pidal \mā-,nān-dāth-pē-'thäl\, **Ramón** (1869–1968) Spanish language scholar. His work on the origins of the SPANISH LANGUAGE and his critical editions of literary texts generated a revival of the study of medieval Spanish poetry and chronicles. His writings include *Manual of Historical Spanish Grammar* (1904), *The Cid and His Spain* (1929), and *The Spaniards in Their History* (1947). He was twice president of the Spanish Academy.

Mengele \'meŋ-gə-lə\, **Josef** (1911–1979) German Nazi doctor. Influenced by the racial ideology of ALFRED ROSENBERG, in 1934 Mengele joined the research staff of the newly founded Institute for Hereditary Biology and Racial Hygiene. An ardent Nazi, he served in World War II as medical officer with the SS. In 1943 he was appointed chief doctor at AUSCHWITZ-Birkenau, where he selected incoming Jews for labor or extermination, becoming known as the "Angel of Death," and conducted medical experiments on inmates in pseudoscientific racial studies. After the war he escaped to South America, where he died in 1979 under the name of Wolfgang Gerhard, a Nazi he befriended in Brazil and whose identity he assumed.

Mengistu Haile Mariam \men-'gis-,tü-'hī-lē-'mär-yäm\ (born 1937) Ethiopian army officer and head of state (1974–91). Mengistu headed a group of rebel soldiers that overthrew HAILE SELASSIE (1974). After assassinating his rivals, he became the new regime's acknowledged strongman. By 1978 he had crushed a major rebellion in Eritrea and, with Soviet and Cuban help, an invasion of the OGADEN region by the Somalis. In the 1980s he faced new rebellions in Eritrea and Tigray, and devastating droughts and famines drew attention to his failed agricultural policies. With the withdrawal of Soviet support in 1991, his power was weakened and he fled to Zimbabwe.

Mengs \'meŋs\, **Anton Raphael** (1728–1779) German painter. After study in Dresden and Rome, he became painter to the Saxon court in Dresden in 1745. Back in Rome in the late 1740s and again in the early 1750s, he developed an enthusiasm for classical antiquity. His fresco *Parnassus* (1760–61) at the Villa Albani helped establish the ascendancy of Neoclassical painting. He also worked extensively for the Spanish court in Madrid. He was regarded as Europe's greatest living painter in his day, but his reputation has since declined.

menhaden \men-'hā-dᵊn\ *or* **pogy** Any of several species of Atlantic coastal fishes (genus *Brevoortia* of the HERRING family), used for oil, fish meal (mainly for animal feed), and fertilizer. Menhaden have a deep body, sharp-edged belly, large head, and tooth-edged scales. Adults are about 15 in. (38 cm) long and weigh 1 lb (0.5 kg) or less. Dense schools of menhaden range from Canada to South America. When feeding, they swim with mouth agape and gill openings widespread to strain out plankton.

menhir \'men-,hir\ Type of ancient megalithic stone monument (see MEGALITH). Menhirs were simple upright stones, sometimes of great size, erected chiefly in Western Europe. Arrangements of menhirs often form vast circles, semicircles, or ellipses. Many were built in Britain, the best-known sites being STONEHENGE and Avebury in Wiltshire. Menhirs were also placed in parallel rows, called alignments, the most famous being the Carnac alignments in northwestern France, with 2,935 menhirs. These were probably used for ritual processions.

Menilek II \'men-ə-,lek\ *orig.* **Sahle Miriam** (1844–1913) King of the semi-independent state of Shewa, or Shoa (1865–89), and emperor of Ethiopia (1889–1913). Captured and imprisoned for 10 years after his father, King Malakot of Shewa, was deposed by TEWODROS II, he escaped in 1865 and returned to Shewa to assume the title of *negus* (king). On the death of Emperor Yohannes IV (r.1872–89), he ascended to the Ethiopian throne, taking his crown name from Menilek I, legendary son of Solomon and the Queen of Sheba. When Italy sought to make Ethiopia a protectorate, Menilek roundly defeated its forces at the Battle of ADOWA (1896). In later years he expanded the empire, initiated modern educational programs, and built up the country's infrastructure.

Menilek II, detail of an oil painting by Paul Buffet, 1897; in the Senate Palace, Paris.

J.E. BULLOZ

Menindee Lakes \mə-'nin-dē\ Series of reservoirs, western NEW SOUTH WALES, Australia. Located near the town of Menindee, they are part of the Darling River Conservation Scheme. The lakes are flooded through creeks linking them with the DARLING RIVER. The total capacity of the Menindee Lakes Storage Scheme is 2 million acre-ft (2.47 billion cubic-m). Menindee is an Aboriginal word meaning "egg yolk."

meninges \mə-'nin-jēz\ Three fibrous membranes that surround the BRAIN and SPINAL CORD to protect the central NERVOUS SYSTEM. The pia mater, a very thin membrane, adheres to the surface of the brain and spinal cord. The subarachnoid space, containing CEREBROSPINAL FLUID, separates the pia mater from a second membrane, the arachnoid. Around the brain, fine filaments connect these two membranes, which are believed to be impermeable to fluid. The third membrane, the dura mater, is strong, thick, and dense. It envelops the arachnoid, covers the inside of the skull, and surrounds and supports the large venous channels carrying blood from the brain. Several septa divide it and support different parts of the brain. In the spine, the dura mater and the arachnoid mater are separated by the subdural space; the arachnoid and pia mater are separated by the subarachnoid space. The extradural space (between the dura mater and the wall of the vertebral canal) is the site of epidural anesthesia (see ANESTHESIOLOGY).

meningitis \,me-nən-'jī-təs\ INFLAMMATION of the MENINGES. Bacteria (including MENINGOCOCCUS, among others), often from infection elsewhere, produce the most dangerous forms. Symptoms develop rapidly: vomiting, then severe bursting headache, then stiff neck, often pulling back the head. Young children may have convulsions. The patient may die within hours. Pus in cerebrospinal fluid can block brain passages and spinal spaces, leading to life-threatening HYDROCEPHALUS. Speedy diagnosis (by lumbar puncture) and treatment (with antibiotics) can prevent brain damage and death. Viral meningitis usually has a short course and requires no therapy.

meningococcus \mə-,niŋ-gə-'kä-kəs\ *Neisseria meningitidis,* the bacterium that causes meningococcal MENINGITIS in humans, the only natural hosts in which it causes disease. Meningococci are spherical, frequently occur in pairs, and are strongly gram-negative (see GRAM STAIN). They enter the nasal passage and may cause no symptoms there (up to 30% of the population may harbor them between epidemics), or they may enter the bloodstream and produce the symptoms of meningitis.

Menninger family \'men-iŋ-ər\ U.S. physicians and pioneers in psychiatric treatment. Charles Frederick Menninger (1862–1953) was born in Tell City, Ind., and began practicing medicine in Topeka, Kan., in 1889. He saw the benefit of group medical practice after visiting the MAYO FAMILY's clinic in 1908. His son Karl (1893–1990) was born in Topeka and received psychiatric training in Boston. In 1920 the two founded the Menninger Diagnostic Clinic for the group practice of general medicine. With Charles's youngest son, William (1899–1966), they established the Menninger Sanitarium and Psychopathic Hospital, to link the understanding of behavior as applied to the treatment of patients and the use of the hospital's social environment as a part of therapy. Their treatment of the mentally ill attracted other scientists, and they made significant strides in establishing psychiatry as a legitimate science. In 1931 the sanitarium became the first training facility for nurses specializing in psychiatric care, and in 1933 it opened a neuropsychiatric residency program for physicians. In 1941 they formed the Menninger Foundation, followed by the Menninger School of Psychiatry, which Karl directed (1946–69).

Menno Simonsz. \'sī-mənz, 'sē-mȯns\ *or* **Menno Simons** *or* **Menno Simonszoon** (1496–1561) Dutch ANABAPTIST leader. Born into a peasant family, he was ordained a Roman Catholic priest, but doubting the doctrine of transubstantiation, he came under the influence of Lutheranism and withdrew from the church in 1536. Convinced that infant baptism was wrong and that only people of mature faith were eligible for membership in the church, he became a leader in the peaceful wing of the Anabaptist movement in 1537. Pronounced a heretic, he was in constant danger of arrest for the rest of his life but continued to organize Anabaptist groups. He wrote and printed many theological works, and his followers founded the MENNONITE Church.

Menno Simonsz., engraving by Christopher van Sichem, 1605–08.

BY COURTESY OF THE MENNONITE LIBRARY AND ARCHIVES, NORTH NEWTON, KANSAS

Mennonite \'me-nə-,nīt\ Member of a Protestant church named for MENNO SIMONSZ. They trace their origins to the Swiss Brethren (established 1525), nonconformists who rejected infant baptism and stressed the separation of church and state. Persecution scattered them across Europe; they found political freedom first in the Netherlands and northern Poland, and from there moved to Ukraine and Russia. They first emigrated to North America in 1663. Many Russian Mennonites emigrated to the U.S. Midwest and to Canada in the 1870s when they lost their exemption from Russian military service. Today Mennonites are found in many parts of the world, especially in North and South America. Their creed stresses the authority of the Scriptures, the example of the early church, and baptism as a confession of faith. They value simplicity of life, and many refuse to swear oaths or serve in the military. The various Mennonite groups include the strictly observant AMISH and HUTTERITES as well as the more moderate Mennonite church.

Menominee \mə-'nä-mə-,nē\ ALGONQUIAN-speaking North American Indian people who lived along the Menominee River at the present-day Wisconsin-Michigan border. They lived in villages of dome-shaped houses and collected wild plants, fished, and hunted to obtain food. Originally organized into CLANS, their social organization changed as a result of the fur trade, when they scattered in mobile BANDS. In 1852 the U.S. government moved most of the tribe to a reservation in Wisconsin. Sporadic uprisings occurred into the early 20th century, and political opposition was renewed in the 1960s and '70s. Today the Menominee number about 3,000.

menopause Final cessation of MENSTRUATION, ending female FERTILITY. It usually begins between ages 45 and 55. A gradual decline in function of the OVARIES reduces ESTROGEN production. Ovulation becomes irregular and gradually ceases. The length of the menstrual cycle and periods may vary; flow may lessen or increase. Adjustment of the ENDOCRINE SYSTEM to estrogen reduction causes hot flashes, often at night, with a warm sensation, flushing, and sweating; other symptoms, such as irritability and headaches, may be related more to reactions to aging. Removal or destruction of the ovaries to treat disease causes artificial menopause, with similar but more sudden effects. Changes in HORMONE balance usually cause no physical or mental disturbances. However, the protective effect of estrogen against OSTEOPOROSIS and atherosclerosis (see ARTERIOSCLEROSIS) is lost, and risk of fracture and CORONARY HEART DISEASE increase. Hormone replacement therapy, once widely prescribed to reduce these risks, may raise the risk of endometrial (see UTERUS) and breast cancer.

menorah \mə-'nōr-ə\ Multibranched candelabra used during HANUKKAH. It holds nine candles (or has nine receptacles for oil). Eight of the candles stand for the eight days of Hanukkah—one is lit the first day, two the second, and so on. The ninth candle, or *shammash* ("servant") light—usually set in the center and raised above the others—is used to light the others. The menorah is an imitation of the seven-branched golden candelabra of the TABERNACLE, which signified the seven days of creation.

Roman soldiers carrying the menorah from the Temple of Jerusalem, AD 70; detail of a relief on the Arch of Titus, Rome, AD 81.

ALINARI–ART RESOURCE

Menotti \mə-'nä-tē\, **Gian Carlo** (born 1911) Italian-U.S. composer, librettist, and stage director. Having written an opera by age 10, he spent his early teens absorbing the repertoire at La Scala. A. TOSCANINI recommended study at the Curtis Institute; there he met S. BARBER, who would become his lifelong companion. In 1939 he produced the radio opera *The Old Maid and the Thief; The Island God* (1942) was an unsuccessful commission for the Metropolitan Opera. *The Medium* (1946) had a Broadway run, and *The Consul* was also successful (1950, Pulitzer Prize). The highly popular *Amahl and the Night Visitors* (1951), for television, was followed by *The Saint of Bleecker Street* (1955, Pulitzer Prize). In 1958 he founded the Festival of Two Worlds in Spoleto, Italy; it enjoyed great success, and in 1977 he founded a New World counterpart in Charleston, S.C.

Menshevik \'men-shə-vik\ Member of the non-Leninist wing of the RUSSIAN SOCIAL-DEMOCRATIC WORKERS' PARTY. The group evolved in 1903 when L. MARTOV called for a mass party modeled after Western European groups, as opposed to VLADIMIR ILICH LENIN's plan to restrict the party to professional revolutionaries. When Lenin's followers obtained a majority on the party central committee, they called themselves BOLSHEVIKS ("those of the majority"), and Martov and his group became the Mensheviks ("those of the minority"). The Mensheviks played active roles in the RUSSIAN REVOLUTION OF 1905 and in the St. Petersburg SOVIET, but they became divided over World War I and later by the RUSSIAN REVOLUTION OF 1917. They attempted to form a legal opposition party but in 1922 were permanently suppressed.

Menshikov \'myen-shi-kȯf\, **Aleksandr (Danilovich)** (1673–1729) Russian soldier and administrator. In 1686 he became an orderly for PETER I THE GREAT and soon was the czar's favorite. Menshikov commanded troops to victories in the Second NORTHERN WAR, including the Battle of POLTAVA, after which he received the title of field marshal (1709). As an administrator from 1714, he was criticized for corrupt practices as he amassed power and wealth. After Peter's death in 1725, he succeeded in having his ally CATHERINE I proclaimed empress, making him the virtual ruler of Russia. After her death in 1727, he arranged to have his daughter marry the young czar PETER II, but his enemies turned Peter against him and forced Menshikov's exile to Siberia.

menstruation Periodic discharge from the VAGINA of blood, secretions, and shed mucous lining of the UTERUS (endometrium). The endometrium prepares to receive a fertilized EGG by thickening and producing secretions. If the egg released by the OVARY is not fertilized, the endometrium breaks down and is expelled by contractions of the uterus. The first menstruation (menarche) occurs after other changes of PUBERTY, usually at 11–13 years of age, apparently triggered by the passing of a weight threshold. Bleeding may be irregular or heavy at first. In adult women, menstrual periods begin at an average interval of 28 days and last about five days; some variation among women and in the same woman is normal. Uterine contractions are felt as cramps. The amount of blood lost is usually less than 1.7 oz (50 ml). Menstruation ends with MENOPAUSE. Menstrual disorders include dysmenorrhea (painful menstruation) and AMENORRHEA (no bleeding), heavy or light bleeding, and UTERINE BLEEDING. See also PREMENSTRUAL SYNDROME.

mental disorder Any illness with a psychological origin, manifested either in symptoms of emotional distress or in abnormal behavior. Most mental disorders can be broadly classified as either psychoses or neuroses (see NEUROSIS, PSYCHOSIS). Psychoses (e.g., SCHIZOPHRENIA and BIPOLAR DISORDER) are major mental illnesses characterized by such severe symptoms as delusions, HALLUCINATIONS, and inability to objectively evaluate reality. Neuroses are less severe and more treatable illnesses, including DEPRESSION, ANXIETY, and PARANOIA as well as OBSESSIVE-COMPULSIVE DISORDERS and POST-TRAUMATIC STRESS DISORDERS. Some mental disorders, such as ALZHEIMER'S DISEASE, are clearly caused by organic disease of the brain, but the causes of most others are either unknown or not yet verified. Schizophrenia appears to be partly caused by inherited genetic factors. Some mood disorders, such as mania and depression, may be caused by imbalances of certain NEUROTRANSMITTERS in the brain; they are treatable by drugs that act to correct these imbalances (see PSYCHOPHARMACOLOGY). Neuroses often appear to be caused by psychological factors such as emotional deprivation, frustration, or abuse during childhood, and they may be treated through PSYCHOTHERAPY. Certain neuroses, particularly the anxiety disorders known as PHOBIAS, may represent maladaptive responses built up into the human equivalent of conditioned reflexes.

mental hygiene Science of maintaining mental health and preventing disorders to help people function at their full mental potential. It includes all measures taken to promote and preserve mental health: rehabilitation of the mentally disturbed, prevention of mental illness, and aid in coping in a stressful world. Community mental health acknowledges the relation between mental health, population pressures, and social unrest. It also deals with social problems, from drug addiction to suicide prevention. Treatment of the mentally ill through the ages has ranged from neglect, ill treatment, and isolation to active treatment and integration into the community, often in response to crusading reformers. Prevention of mental illness includes prenatal care, child-abuse awareness programs, and counseling for crime victims. Treatment includes PSYCHOTHERAPY, drug therapy, and support groups. One of the most important efforts is public education to combat the stigma still attached to mental illness and encourage those affected to seek treatment.

mental retardation Subaverage intellectual ability that is present from birth or infancy and is manifested by abnormal development, learning difficulties, and problems in social adjustment. A standardized INTELLIGENCE test is a common method of identification. Individuals with IQ scores of 53–70 are usually classified as mildly retarded and are able to learn academic and pre-vocational skills with some SPECIAL EDUCATION. Those with scores of 36–52 are classified as moderately retarded and are able to learn functional academic skills and undertake semiskilled work under supervised conditions. Those in the severe (21–35) and profound (below 21) ranges require progressively more supervision or full-time custodial care. Mental retardation can be caused by genetic disorders (such as DOWN'S SYNDROME), infectious diseases (such as MENINGITIS), metabolic disorders, poisoning from lead, radiation, or other toxic agents, injuries to the head, and MALNUTRITION.

menthol Crystalline organic compound of the ISOPRENOID family. It has a strong, minty, cooling odor and taste. It is obtained from the oil of the Japanese MINT and used in cigarettes, cosmetics, chest rubs, cough drops, and flavorings. Of its two optical isomers (see OPTICAL ACTIVITY, ISOMERISM), only *l*-menthol has the desirable cooling effect.

Menuhin \'men-yə-wən\, **Yehudi** *later* **Baron Menuhin** (1916–1999) U.S.-British violinist and conductor. Born in New York and raised in San Francisco, he made his debut at 7. In 1927 he studied with George Enescu (1881–1955) in Paris; he returned to perform to tremendous acclaim in New York the same year, and went on to astound audiences worldwide with his precocious depth and mastery. From 1959 he lived in London. He directed the Bath Festival 1958–68 and the Gstaad Festival from 1956. In 1958 he founded his own chamber orchestra. Often accompanied by his pianist sister, Hephzibah (1920–1981), he also made recordings with the sitarist RAVI SHANKAR. In later years he devoted much energy to the cause of international cooperation and world peace.

Menzies \'men-,zēz\, **Robert (Gordon)** *later* **Sir Robert** (1894–1978) Australian statesman and prime minister (1939–41, 1949–66). A successful lawyer, he served as Australia's attorney general 1934–39. Leader of the United Australia Party, he served as prime minister 1939–41. He organized the Liberal Party in 1944 and again became premier in 1949. In the 1950s he fostered industrial growth in Australia and immigration from Europe. He strengthened military ties with the U.S. and encouraged the ANZUS PACT and Australia's membership in the SOUTHEAST ASIA TREATY ORGANIZATION. He retired in 1966 after the longest ministry in Australian history.

mer \'mer\ Among the Cheremi and Udmurt peoples of Russia, a sacred grove where people of several villages gathered periodically to hold religious festivals and sacrifice animals to nature gods. The groves where the mer festivals were held were not fenced (see LUD) and did not have permanent altars. Mer festivals were infrequent; five years or more might elapse between them.

mercantile agency Specialized organization that supplies information on the creditworthiness and financial strength of business firms. The first such agency, the Mercantile Agency, was founded in New York City in 1841. It provided information to businesses that were expanding nationally and were unable to assess the credit history of prospective customers in distant locations. It changed its name to R. G. Dun & Co. after 1859 and merged with the Bradstreet Co. in 1933 to form Dun & Bradstreet, Inc., the best-known mercantile agency. Mercantile agencies may provide information on all types of business firms or may limit their investigations to firms in a particular line of trade or a particular region. Most agencies provide both general and special reports. General reports, issued periodically on all firms investigated by the agency, assign a rating to the firm's financial statement and creditworthiness. Special reports containing more detailed information are issued to clients of the agency on request. See also CREDIT BUREAU.

mercantile law See BUSINESS LAW

mercantilism Economic theory and policy influential in Europe from the 16th to the 18th century, calling for government regulation of a nation's economy in order to increase its power at the expense of rival nations. Though the theory existed earlier, the term was not coined until the 18th century; it was given currency by ADAM SMITH in his *Wealth of Nations* (1776). Mercantilism's emphasis on the importance of gold and silver holdings as a sign of a nation's wealth and power led to policies designed to obtain precious metals through trade by ensuring "favorable" trade balances (see BALANCE OF TRADE), meaning an excess of exports over imports, especially if a nation did not possess mines or have access to them. In a favorable trade balance, payments for the goods or services had to be made with gold or silver. Colonial possessions were to serve as markets for exports and as suppliers of raw materials to the mother country, a policy that created conflict between the European colonial powers and their colonies, in particular fanning resentment of Britain in the American colonies and helping bring about the American Revolution. Mercantilism favored a large population to supply laborers, purchasers of goods, and soldiers. Thrift and SAVING were emphasized as virtues because they made possible the creation of CAPITAL. Mercantilism provided a favorable climate for the early development of CAPITALISM, but was later severely criticized, especially by advocates of LAISSEZ-FAIRE, who argued that all trade was beneficial and that strict government controls were counterproductive.

Mercator \mər-'kā-tər\, **Gerardus** *orig.* **Gerhard Kremer** (1512–1594) Flemish cartographer. He received a master's degree in 1532 from the University of Louvain (Belgium), where he settled. By 24 he was a skilled engraver, calligrapher, and scientific-instrument maker. He and his colleagues made Louvain a center for construction of maps, globes (terrestrial and celestial), and astronomical instruments. He was appointed court cosmographer to Duke Wilhelm of Cleve in 1564, and in 1569 he perfected what has become known as the Mercator projection, in which parallels and meridians are rendered as straight lines spaced so as to produce at any point an accurate ratio of latitude to longitude. It permitted mariners to steer a course over long distances by plotting straight lines without continually adjusting compass readings. While the meridians are equally spaced parallel vertical lines, the lines of latitude are spaced farther and farther apart as their distance from the equator increases; on world maps the projection greatly enlarges areas distant from the equator.

mercenary \'mər-sᵊn-,er-ē\ Hired professional soldier who fights for any state or nation without regard to political principles. From the earliest days of organized warfare, governments supplemented their military forces with mercenaries. After the Hundred Years' War (1337–1453), Swiss soldiers were hired out all over Europe by their own cantonal governments and won a high reputation. Rulers of the German state of Hesse also hired out their soldiers, and Hessian troops fought for the British in the AMERICAN REVOLUTION. Since the late 18th century, most mercenaries have been individual soldiers of fortune.

Mercer, Johnny *orig.* **John Herndon** (1909–1976) U.S. songwriter. Born in Georgia, Mercer began to write lyrics in New York in the late 1920s, and later joined PAUL WHITEMAN's orchestra as singer and master of ceremonies. In 1939 he joined Benny Goodman's radio show. In 1942 Mercer cofounded Capitol Records. On Broadway, he collaborated with H. Arlen on *St. Louis Woman* (1946) and *Saratoga* (1959), and also provided lyrics for *Seven Brides for Seven Brothers* (1954), *Li'l Abner* (1956), and *Foxy* (1964). His songs for films won four Academy Awards. He collaborated with such composers as H. Carmichael, H. Warren, J. Kern, and J. Van Heusen, and is credited with over 1,000 lyrics, including "Ac-cent-tchu-ate the Positive," "One for My Baby," "Autumn Leaves," and "Moon River."

mercerization \ˌmər-sə-rə-ˈzā-shən\ Chemical treatment applied to cotton fibers or fabrics to make them permanently able to accept dyes and various chemical finishes more easily. The method, patented in 1850 by the English calico printer John Mercer (1791–1866), also gives cotton cloth increased tensile strength and greater absorptive properties. Higher-quality cotton goods are usually mercerized. The treatment consists of dipping the yarn or fiber in a solution of sodium hydroxide and then treating the material with water or acid to neutralize the sodium hydroxide.

merchandising Element of marketing concerned especially with the sale of goods and services to customers. One aspect of merchandising is advertising aimed at capturing the interest of the segment of the population most likely to buy the product. Merchandising also involves product display; companies provide display and promotional materials such as banners and cardboard stands to retailers and negotiate shelf space. The development of sales strategies includes the determination of pricing, discounts, and special offers; the invention of sales pitches; and the identification of avenues for sales, including store-based retailing and alternative means such as direct-mail marketing, telemarketing, commercial websites, vending machines, and door-to-door sales.

Merchant, Ismail See James Ivory

merchant marine Commercial ships of a nation, whether privately or publicly owned, and the personnel who operate such ships, as distinct from the personnel of naval vessels. Merchant ships are used to transport people, raw materials, and manufactured goods. Merchant fleets can be important economic assets for nations with limited natural resources or a small industrial base. By carrying the commerce of other nations on the seas, a merchant fleet contributes to its home nation's foreign-exchange earnings, promotes trade, and provides employment. The U.S. Merchant Marine Academy (founded 1943) is in Kings Point, N.Y.

Mercia \ˈmər-shə\ Ancient Anglican kingdom, central England. One of a group of seven Anglo-Saxon kingdoms, it originally comprised the border areas of modern Staffordshire, Derbyshire, Nottinghamshire, and northern West Midlands and Warwickshire. Offa, who ruled 757–796, created a single state from the Humber to the English Channel. After Offa's death, Mercia declined, overshadowed by Wessex. In 877 the Danes divided Mercia into English and Danish sections. After the reconquest of the Danish lands in the early 10th century, it came under the rule of Wessex.

Mercury In Roman religion, the god of merchants, commonly identified with the Greek messenger of the gods, Hermes. His temple on Rome's Aventine Hill was dedicated in 495 BC. The goddess Maia was identified as his mother, and the two were honored in a festival on May 15. Mercury is sometimes depicted holding a purse, symbolic of his business functions. More often, he is given the attributes of Hermes and portrayed wearing winged sandals or a winged cap and carrying a caduceus.

Mercury Innermost planet of the solar system. Its average distance from the sun is about 36 million mi (58 million km), but its highly elliptical orbit carries it 7.5 million mi (12 million km) nearer to and farther from the sun. It is the second-smallest major planet (after Pluto), having a diameter of about 3,050 mi (4,870 km) and a mass about one-eighteenth of earth's. With the shortest period of revolution (only 88 earth days) and the highest average orbital speed (30 mi/second, or 48 km/second) of any planet, it is aptly named after the fleet-footed Roman messenger god. It rotates very slowly, making one complete rotation relative to the stars every 59 earth days, while its solar day (from one sunrise to the next) is 176 earth days, owing to its revolution around the sun. Its surface is heavily cratered. Its most impressive feature is perhaps the 800-mi (1,300-km) Caloris Basin, formed by a huge meteorite impact. Mercury also has steep cliffs that extend for hundreds of miles. The discovery of a magnetic field in its vicinity suggests it has a large iron core, which would account for a mean density almost as high as earth's. Its atmosphere is negligible; its surface gravity, about one-third that of earth's, holds little more than a thin layer of gases. Temperatures at its surface change dramatically, ranging from a high of about 756°F (402°C) on the side facing the sun to a low of about −279°F (−173°C) at the end of its night.

Mercury First series of U.S. manned spaceflights (1961–63), which began about three weeks after Yury A. Gagarin became the first human in space. In May 1961, Alan B. Shepard rode the first Mercury space capsule, Freedom 7, on a 15-minute, 302-mi (486-km) flight, attaining a maximum altitude of 116 mi (186 km). The first U.S. manned flight in orbit was that of Friendship 7, commanded by John H. Glenn, Jr., in February 1962; it completed three orbits. The last Mercury flight, Faith 7, launched in May 1963, was the longest, making 22 orbits in about 34 hours.

mercury *or* **quicksilver** Metallic chemical element, chemical symbol Hg, atomic number 80. Mercury is the only elemental metal that is liquid at ordinary temperatures, with a freezing point of −38°F (−39°C) and a boiling point of 674°F (356.9°C). Silvery white, dense, toxic (see mercury poisoning), and a good conductor of electricity, mercury is occasionally found free in nature but usually occurs as the sulfide ore, cinnabar. It has many uses, in dental and industrial amalgams, as a catalyst, in electrical and measuring apparatus and instruments, as the cathode in electrolytic cells, in mercury-vapor lamps, and as a coolant and neutron absorber in nuclear power plants. Many of mercury's compounds, in which it has valence 1 or 2, are pigments, pesticides, and medicinals. It is a dangerous pollutant because it concentrates in animal tissues in increasing amounts up the food chain.

mercury poisoning Harmful effects of mercury compounds. Manufacture of paints, various household items, and pesticides uses mercury; the finished product and the waste products released into air and water may contain mercury. The aquatic food chain can concentrate organic mercury compounds in fish and seafood, which, if eaten by humans, can affect the central nervous system, impairing muscle, vision, and cerebral function, leading to paralysis and sometimes death (see Minamata disease). Acute mercury poisoning causes severe digestive-tract inflammation. Mercury accumulates in the kidneys, causing uremia and death. Chronic poisoning, from occupational inhalation or skin absorption, causes metallic taste, oral inflammation, blue gum line, extremity pain and tremor, weight loss, and mental changes (depression and withdrawal). Drugs containing mercury can cause sensitivity reactions, sometimes fatal. In young children, acrodynia (pink disease) is probably caused by an organic mercury compound in house paints.

Meredith, George (1828–1909) English novelist and poet. Though ostensibly launched on a law career at 18, he concentrated instead on writing poems and articles and making translations. Because they brought in little pay, he turned to writing prose. The novel *The Ordeal of Richard Feverel* (1859) is typical of his best work, rich in allusion, metaphor, lyrical prose, witty dialogue, and psychological insight. It failed to make him wealthy, and he was forced to begin reading manuscripts for a publisher. Writing in his spare time, he produced a comedy, *Evan Harrington* (1860), and a volume of poems, *Modern Love* (1862). He finally won fame and fortune with the novels *The Egoist* (1879) and *Diana of the Crossways* (1885). His works are noted for their use of interior monologue and their treatment of women as equals of men.

George Meredith, detail of an oil painting by G.F. Watts, 1893; in the National Portrait Gallery, London.

BY COURTESY OF THE NATIONAL PORTRAIT GALLERY, LONDON

Meredith, James (Howard) (born 1933) U.S. civil-rights leader. Born in Kosciusko, Miss., he grew up in poverty in the most racially segregated state in the U.S. In 1961 he took aim at the system of racial segregation by applying to the all-white University of Mississippi. He won a legal battle to be admitted, but federal troops and Justice Department officials had to be brought in to enforce the court order. While participating in a voter-registration drive after his graduation from "Ole Miss," he was shot and wounded by a white supremacist.

merengue \mə-'reŋ-gā\ Couple dance from the Dominican Republic or Haiti, danced throughout Latin America. Originally a folk dance, it has become a ballroom dance, where it is danced with a limping step, the weight always on the same foot. Varieties include the jaleo and juangomero. Dominican merengue music became widely popular in the late 20th century.

mereology \ˌmir-ē-'ä-lə-jē\ Branch of LOGIC, founded by STANISLAW LESNIEWSKI, that tries to clarify class expressions and theorizes on the relation between parts and wholes. It attempts to explain BERTRAND RUSSELL'S PARADOX of the class of all those classes that are not elements of themselves. Lesniewski claimed that a distinction should be made between the distributive and the collective interpretation of class expressions, because failure to do so makes the presuppositions of Russell's paradox appear to be true, whereas once the distinction is made, some of them are revealed as false on either interpretation.

merganser *or* **fish duck** Any species of the DIVING DUCK genus *Mergus*. Essentially freshwater birds, they are classified as a sea duck (tribe Mergini). Mergansers have a long body and a narrow, serrated, hooked bill for catching fish. The males of all but the common merganser, or goosander *(M. merganser),* are crested. The common merganser, the hooded merganser *(M. cucullatus),* the red-breasted merganser *(M. serrator),* and the smew *(M. albellus),* a small, compact merganser with a short bill, live in northern regions; the only southern species is the Brazilian merganser *(M. octosetaceus)*. Mergansers are called trash ducks because their flesh is rank. See also SHELDUCK.

Mergenthaler \'mər-gən-ˌthä-lər\, **Ottmar** (1854–1899) German-U.S. inventor. He emigrated to the U.S. in 1872. While working in a Baltimore machine shop he began experimenting with type molds, and in 1884 he patented the LINOTYPE typesetting machine. The reduced costs achieved by thus speeding up the typesetting process led to a dramatic expansion of all kinds of publishing.

merger Combination of two or more independent business corporations into a single enterprise, usually involving the absorption of one or more firms by a dominant firm. The dominant firm may purchase the other firm's assets with cash or SECURITIES, purchase the other firm's STOCK, or issue its own stock to the other firm's stockholders in exchange for their shares in the acquired firm (thus acquiring the other company's assets and liabilities). In horizontal mergers, both firms produce the same commodity or service for the same market. In vertical mergers, a firm acquires either a supplier or a customer. If the merged business is not related to that of the acquiring firm, the new corporation is called a conglomerate. The reasons for mergers are various: the acquiring firm may seek to eliminate a competitor, to increase its efficiency, to diversify its products, services, and markets, or to reduce its taxes.

Mergui Archipelago \mər-'gwē\ Group of more than 200 islands in the Andaman Sea off the coast of southeastern Myanmar. The largest island is Mali Kyun (Tavoy Island) at its northern end. Other major islands in the group include Kadan (King), Thayawthadangyi (Elphinstone), Daung (Ross), Saganthit (Sellore), Bentinck, Letsok-aw (Domel), Kanmaw (Kisseraing), Lanbi (Sullivan's), and Zadetkyi (St. Matthew's). Mountainous and jungle-covered, the islands are inhabited chiefly by the Selungs.

Mérida City (pop., 1990: 557,000), capital of YUCATÁN state, southeastern Mexico. It lies near the northwestern tip of the YUCATÁN PENINSULA, south of Progreso; its port is on the Gulf of Mexico. It was founded in 1542 on the site of the ancient MAYA city of T'ho. It is the site of numerous colonial buildings, a 16th-century cathedral, Yucatán Univ., and the Regional Technical Institute of Mérida. It serves as a tourist base for trips to nearby Maya cities, including CHICHÉN ITZÁ, Dzibilchaltún, UXMAL, and Kabáh.

Mérida \'mā-rē-thä\ *ancient* **Emerita Augusta** Town (pop., 1991: 48,000), capital of the autonomous community of EXTREMADURA, western Spain. Situated on the northern bank of the Guadiana River, it was founded by the Romans in 25 BC. It served as the capital of the province of Lusitania and became one of the most important towns in Iberia. Occupied in 713 AD by the Moors, it was recaptured in 1228 by Alfonso IX of Leon, who granted it to the Knights of Santiago. It is known for its Roman ruins, including a bridge, an amphitheater, and an aqueduct. The modern town's economy is based on agricultural trade and tourism.

Mérimée \mā-rē-'mā\, **Prosper** (1803–1870) French short-story writer and dramatist. In youth a student of languages and literatures, he wrote his first play, *Cromwell* (1922), at 19. His passions were mysticism, history, and the unusual. His stories, often mysteries, were inspired mainly by Spanish and Russian sources, notably ALEKSANDR PUSHKIN; they include *Mateo Falcone* (1829), the collection *Mosaïque* (1833), and the novellas *Colomba* (1840) and *Carmen* (1845), the basis of G. BIZET'S opera. He also wrote works of history and archaeology, historical fiction, and literary criticism and carried on correspondences that were published posthumously. He became a senator in 1853.

Merino Breed of medium-sized SHEEP originating in Spain that has become prominent worldwide. It has a white face, white legs, and crimped fine-wool fleece. Known as early as the 12th century, it may have been a Moorish importation. Well adapted to semiarid climates and to nomadic pasturing, it has served as foundation stock for many sheep breeds and strains.

meristem \'mer-ə-ˌstem\ In plants, region of cells capable of division and growth. Meristems are classified by location as apical, or primary (at root and shoot tips), lateral, or secondary (in the vascular CAMBIUM and cork cambium), or intercalary (at internodes, stem regions between the places at which leaves attach, and at leaf bases, especially in certain monocots, e.g., grasses). Apical meristems give rise to the primary plant body. Lateral meristems provide increase in stem girth. Injured tissues can convert other cells to new meristem for wound healing.

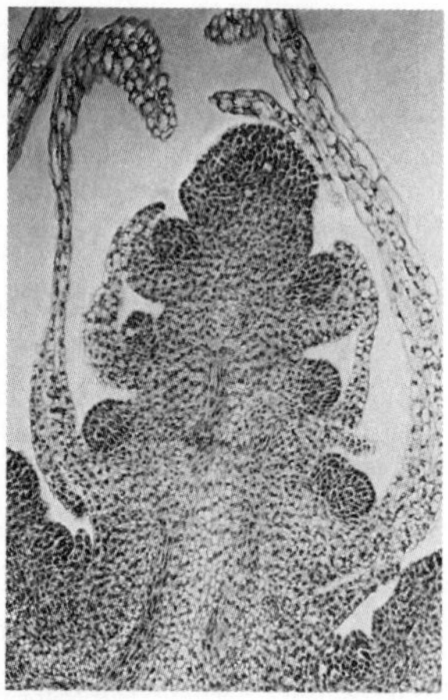
Meristem.
J.M. LANGHAM

Merkabah *or* **Merkava** \ˌmer-kä-'vä\ Throne or chariot of God, as described by EZEKIEL. It became an object of visionary contemplation for Jewish mystics in Palestine in the 1st century AD; in the 7th–11th century, Merkabah mysticism was centered in BABYLONIA. Merkabah mystics courted ecstatic visions that involved a dangerous ascent through celestial hierarchies to the throne of God. Hostile angels guarded the gates to the seven "heavenly dwellings," and a successful journey required magical formulas. The TALMUD warns that of four men who engaged in Merkabah, only one had a true vision; of the others, one died, one went mad, and one became an apostate.

Merleau-Ponty \mer-lō-pō^{n}-'tē\, **Maurice** (1908–1961) French philosopher. With J.-P. SARTRE and SIMONE DE BEAUVOIR he founded the journal *Les Temps Modernes* in 1945. From 1949 he taught at the Sorbonne. One of France's leading exponents of PHENOMENOLOGY, he claimed that perception is the source of knowledge and serves as the ultimate foundation of the constructions of the natural sciences. His most influential work was *The Phenomenology of Perception* (1945). His ardent defense of Soviet Marxism tended to distract attention from his more philosophical writings, which are now required reading in AESTHETICS.

Merlin Magician and wise man in ARTHURIAN LEGEND. In GEOFFREY OF MONMOUTH'S *History of the Kings of England,* Merlin was an adviser to King Arthur, with magical powers that recalled his Celtic origins. Later narratives made him a prophet of the GRAIL and gave him credit for the idea of the Round Table. In SIR THOMAS MALORY'S *Morte Darthur* he brought Arthur to the throne and served as his mentor throughout his reign. His downfall was linked to his infatuation for an enchantress, who imprisoned him after learning the magic arts from him.

merlin *or* **pigeon hawk** Small blue-gray FALCON (*Falco columbarius,* family Falconidae), with a narrowly white-banded tail, found at high latitudes in Canada, the western U.S. south to Colorado, the British Isles, Scandinavia, and Iceland. Most migrate to just south of the breeding range, but some go as far as northern South America. The merlin inhabits wet, open country or conifer and birch woods. It usually lays its eggs on the ground in bushes, but may occupy an old rook or magpie nest in a tree. An aggressive hunter, it was once much used in FALCONRY.

Merlin (*Falco columbarius*).
ERIC HOSKING

Merman, Ethel *orig.* **Ethel Agnes Zimmerman** (1909–1984) U.S. singer and actress. Born in Queens, N.Y., Merman, who had never taken voice lessons, worked as a secretary before her first professional singing engagement in 1929. She made her stage debut in G. and I. Gershwin's *Girl Crazy* (1930) (see GEORGE GERSHWIN, IRA GERSHWIN). Her brassy, ebullient style and powerful voice made her a favored performer for IRVING BERLIN, C. PORTER, and others. In the mid-1930s Merman made her first Hollywood appearance, and she later starred on her own radio show. Her many Broadway successes include *Anything Goes* (1934), *Red, Hot and Blue* (1936), *Annie Get Your Gun* (1946), *Call Me Madam* (1950), and *Gypsy* (1959).

Meroë \'mer-ō-ˌwē\ City of ancient CUSH in North Africa. Situated on the eastern bank of the NILE RIVER, north of modern Kabushiyah, Sudan, it was the southern administrative center for the kingdom of Cush, beginning c. 750 BC. After the sack of Napata c. 590, it became the capital of the kingdom. It included the region between the Nile and Atbara rivers, where the Meroitic language developed. It survived a Roman invasion but fell to Aksumite armies in the 4th century AD. The ruins of its temples and palaces still exist near Kabushiyah.

Merovingian art \ˌmer-ə-'vin-jən\ Visual arts produced under the MEROVINGIAN DYNASTY of the 5th–8th century AD. They consisted mainly of small-scale metalwork, little of which has survived, and several important manuscripts. The style blends Roman classical style with native Germanic-Frankish traditions, which favored abstraction and geometric patterning. The human figure was rarely attempted; artists were concerned primarily with surface design. Though modest, Merovingian art was influential long after the end of the dynasty.

Merovingian dynasty (476–750) Frankish dynasty considered the first French royal house. It was named for Merovech (fl. c. 450), whose son Childeric I (died 482?) ruled a tribe of Salian FRANKS from his capital at Tournai. His son, CLOVIS I, united nearly all of Gaul in the late 5th century except Burgundy and present-day Provence. On his death the realm was divided among his sons, but by 558 it was united under his last surviving son, CHLOTAR I. The pattern of dividing and then reuniting the realm continued for generations. After the reign of DAGOBERT I (623–39), the Merovingian kings were little more than puppets, and the real power lay in the hands of the mayors of the palace. In 750 the last Merovingian king, Childeric III, was deposed by PEPIN III, the first of the CAROLINGIAN DYNASTY. See also BRUNHILD, CHILDEBERT II, CHILPERIC I, SIGEBERT I.

Merrick, David *orig.* **David Margulois** (1912–2000) U.S. theatrical producer. Born in St. Louis, Mo., he practiced law until 1949, when he became a producer in New York. His first independent production, *Clutterbuck* (1949), was followed over the next 40 years by more than 85 other Broadway shows, including *Look Back in Anger* (1957), *The Entertainer* (1958), *Gypsy* (1959), *Becket* (1960), *Oliver!* (1963), *Hello, Dolly!* (1964), *Play It Again, Sam* (1969), and *42nd Street* (1980). Many were critical and commercial successes, and he was known for his skillful use of publicity.

Merrick, Joseph See ELEPHANT MAN

Merrill, Charles E(dward) (1885–1956) U.S. investment banker. Born in Green Cove Springs, Fla., he held a series of jobs before joining a Wall Street firm in 1911. In 1914 he cofounded the investment-banking firm Merrill, Lynch & Co., which soon became the broker for some of the largest chain-store SECURITIES, including S. S. Kresge Co. and J. C. Penney Co. He helped create Safeway Stores in 1926, and founded *Family Circle* magazine six years later. Foreseeing the crash of 1929, he advised many of his clients to lighten their stock holdings. In the 1930s the firm focused on underwriting and investment banking, but in 1940 it returned to brokerage. The company (now Merrill Lynch, Pierce, Fenner & Smith), which had 115 offices in the U.S. at the time of Merrill's death, is today the largest retail brokerage house in the U.S. He was the father of JAMES MERRILL.

Merrill, James (Ingram) (1926–1995) U.S. poet. Son of a founder of the investment firm Merrill Lynch, he was born in New York and attended Amherst College. Inherited wealth enabled him to devote his life to poetry. His lyric and epic poems are known for their fine craftsmanship, erudition, and wit. Many of his later works were stimulated by sessions with a Ouija board. His collections include *Nights and Days* (1966); the trilogy of *Divine Comedies* (1976, Pulitzer Prize), *Mirabell: Books of Number* (1978), and *Scripts for the Pageant* (1980), published together in *The Changing Light at Sandover* (1982); and *A Scattering of Salts* (1995). *A Different Person,* a memoir, was published in 1994.

Merrimack River River, northeastern U.S. Rising in the White Mountains of central New Hampshire, it flows south into Massachusetts, then turns northeast and empties into the Atlantic Ocean after a total course of 110 mi (177 km). The main cities along the river include CONCORD, MANCHESTER, and Nashua, N.H., and LOWELL, Lawrence, and Haverhill, Mass.; they used the river to power their textile mills in the 19th century.

Mersey River \'mər-zē\ River, northern TASMANIA, Australia. Fed by the Dasher and Fisher rivers, it flows 91 mi (146 km) north, east, and again north to enter an estuary at Latrobe and then empty into BASS STRAIT at Devonport. The stream cuts a gorge up to 2,000 ft (600 m) deep; its water is harnessed there for hydroelectric power.

Mersey River River, northwestern England. It flows west through the southern suburbs of MANCHESTER and is joined by the Irwell in its canalized form as the Manchester Ship Canal. The Mersey is itself modified by the canal as far as Warrington, where it becomes tidal. At Runcorn it is joined by the Weaver, and it forms the Mersey Estuary, the harbor of LIVERPOOL. It enters the Irish Sea after a course of 70 mi (110 km).

Merseyside \'mər-zē-ˌsīd\ Metropolitan county (pop., 1995 est.: 1,427,000), northwestern England. Located on the estuary of the MERSEY RIVER, its county seat was LIVERPOOL. In 1986 it lost its administrative functions, which it held from 1974, and now exists in name only. During the 17th century many ships sailing from Liverpool, its main harbor, were engaged in the West Indies slave trade. In the 19th century the area benefited from U.S. cotton imports. Merseyside residents possess a distinctive local dialect, "scouse," that provides the region with a strong identity. It was bombed heavily during World War II. It is famous for its contributions to national popular culture, from the BEATLES to its football teams and its noted golf links.

Merton, Robert K(ing) (born 1910) U.S. sociologist. Born in Philadelphia, he taught at Columbia University (1941–79), where he inspired many students. His diverse interests included deviant behavior, the sociology of science, and mass communications, and he generally advanced a functionalist approach to the study of society. Among his writings are *Mass Persuasion* (1946), *Social Theory and Social Structure* (1949), *On the Shoulders of Giants* (1965), and *The Sociology of Science* (1973). See also BUREAUCRACY, FUNCTIONALISM.

Merton, Thomas *later* **Father M. Louis** (1915–1968) U.S. (French-born) monk and Roman Catholic writer. Educated in England, France, and the U.S., Merton taught English at Columbia University before entering a Trappist order in Kentucky. In 1949 he was ordained a priest. His early works, on spiritual themes, include poetry collections; the autobiographical *Seven Storey Mountain* (1948), which brought him international fame and led many readers to the monastic life; and *The Waters of Siloe* (1949), a history of the Trappists. In the 1960s his writings tended toward social criticism, Oriental philosophy, and mysticism. He was accidentally electrocuted at a monastic convention in Thailand.

Merv *modern* **Mary** \mä-'rē\ Ancient city, central Asia. Lying near the modern town of Mary (formerly Merv) in Turkmenistan, it is mentioned in ancient Persian texts as Mouru and in cuneiform inscriptions as Margu, and was the seat of a satrapy of the Persian empire. Under the Arabs in the 7th century AD, it was rebuilt and served as a base for Muslim expansion into central Asia. A great center of Islamic learning under the ABBASID caliphs, it reached its zenith under the SELJUQ sultan Sanjar (r.1118–59). It was destroyed by the MONGOLS in 1221, then rebuilt in the 17th century. It was occupied by Russia in 1884.

Merwin, W(illiam) S(tanley) (born 1927) U.S. poet and translator. Born in New York City, he attended Princeton University and earned critical acclaim with his first poetry collection, *A Mask for Janus* (1952). He became known for the spare style of his poetry, which often expresses concerns about the natural environment and our relation to it. His volumes include *The Lice* (1967), *The Carrier of Ladders* (1970, Pulitzer Prize), and *Travels* (1993). His translations, often collaborations with others, range from plays of EURIPIDES and FEDERICO GARCIA LORCA to epics to ancient and modern works from Chinese, Sanskrit, and Japanese.

Mesa \ˈmā-sə\ City (pop., 1996 est.: 345,000), southern central Arizona, located near PHOENIX. It was settled in 1878 by MORMONS who used ancient Hohokam Indian canals for irrigation (see HOHOKAM CULTURE); it was incorporated as a town in 1883 and as a city in 1930. A SALT RIVER reclamation project enabled the community to grow fruit and raise other crops. The city grew rapidly through industrialization after World War II. It is the site of Mesa Community College and Mesa Southwest Museum.

mesa \ˈmā-sə\ (Spanish: "table") Flat-topped tableland with one or more steep sides, common in the Colorado Plateau regions of the U.S.; a BUTTE is similar but smaller. Both are formed by erosion; during denudation, or downcutting and stripping, areas of harder rock in a plateau act as flat protective caps for portions of underlying land situated between such places as stream valleys, where erosion is especially active. This results in a table mountain (mesa) or fortress hill.

Mesa Verde National Park \ˈmā-sə-ˈver-dē\ National park, southwestern Colorado. It was established in 1906 to preserve prehistoric Indian cliff dwellings. Occupying a high tableland area of 52,085 acres (21,078 hectares), it contains hundreds of PUEBLO ruins up to 13 centuries old. The most striking are multistoried apartments built under overhanging cliffs. Cliff Palace, the largest, was excavated in 1909 and contains hundreds of rooms, including kivas, the circular ceremonial chambers of the PUEBLO INDIANS.

mescaline \ˈmes-kə-lin\ HALLUCINOGEN, the active principle in the flowering heads of the PEYOTE cactus. An ALKALOID related to EPINEPHRINE and norepinephrine, first isolated in 1896, mescaline is usually extracted from the peyote and purified, but can also be synthesized. Its hallucinogenic effects begin in two to three hours and may last over 12 hours; the hallucinations vary greatly among individuals and from one time to the next, but are usually visual rather than auditory. Side effects include nausea and vomiting.

Meselson \ˈme-səl-sən\, **Matthew Stanley** (born 1930) U.S. molecular biologist. Born in Denver, he received his PhD from Caltech; from 1964 he taught at Harvard University. He conducted imaginative research with FRANKLIN STAHL that showed that, during cell division, DNA splits into its two component strands, each of which acquires a newly synthesized partner strand before passing into one of the daughter cells.

Meshed See MASHHAD

Meslamtaea \ˌmes-lam-ˈtē-ə\ In MESOPOTAMIAN RELIGION, the god of the city of Cuthah in AKKAD. The name of his temple, Emeslam or Meslam ("luxuriant *mesu* tree"), may indicate that he was originally a tree god. Later he was identified as the ruler of the netherworld and the spouse of its queen, ERESHKIGAL. He was the son of Enlil, god of the atmosphere, and Ninlil, goddess of grain, and he often appears in hymns as a warrior. He sometimes visited terrible plagues on his people and their herds.

Mesmer \ˈmez-mər\, **Franz Anton** (1734–1815) German physician. After studying medicine at the University of Vienna, he developed his theory of "animal magnetism," which held that an invisible fluid in the body acted according to the laws of magnetism and that disease was caused by obstacles to the free circulation of this fluid. In Mesmer's view, harmony could be restored by inducing "crises" (trance states often ending in delirium or convulsions). In the 1770s he carried out dramatic demonstrations of his ability to "mesmerize" his patients using magnetized objects. Accused by Viennese physicians of fraud, he left Austria and settled in Paris (1778), where he also came under fire from the medical establishment. Though his theories were eventually discredited, his ability to induce trance states in his patients made him the forerunner of the modern use of HYPNOSIS.

Mesoamerican architecture \ˈme-zō-ə-ˈmer-ə-kən\ Building traditions of the indigenous cultures in parts of Mexico and Central America before the 16th-century Spanish conquest. The idea of constructing temple-pyramids appears to have taken hold early. La Venta, the center of OLMEC culture c. 800–400 BC, contains one of the earliest pyramidal structures, a mound of earth and clay 100 ft (30 m) high. Mesoamerican pyramids were generally earth mounds faced with stone. Typically of stepped form, they were topped by a platform or temple which only privileged community members were allowed to approach. The best-known include the Pyramid of the Sun (rivaling the Great Pyramid of Khufu at GIZA) and Pyramid of the Moon at TEOTIHUACÁN, the Castillo at CHICHÉN ITZÁ, and largest of all, the 177-ft (54-m) Pyramid of Quetzalcoatl at Cholula. The Classic period (AD 100–900) saw the flourishing of Mayan architecture, in which the corbeled vault made its first appearance in the Americas. Ceremonial centers in the Maya Lowlands proliferated, as did inscribed and dated stelae and monuments. TIKAL, UAXACTÚN, Copán, PALENQUE, and UXMAL all attained their glory in these centuries. A common feature at these sites is a *tlachtli,* or ball court. Their raised platforms were often the architectural center of ancient cities. See also MONTE ALBÁN.

Mesoamerican civilization Complex of aboriginal cultures that developed in parts of Mexico and Central America before the Spanish conquest in the 16th century. This civilization and the ANDEAN CIVILIZATION in South America constitute a New World counterpart to those of ancient Egypt, Mesopotamia, and China. Humans have been present in Mesoamerica from as early as 21,000 BC; a shift from hunting and gathering to agriculture, which began c. 7000 BC as the climate warmed with the end of the Ice Age, was completed by c. 1500 BC. The earliest great Mesoamerican civilization, the OLMEC, dates to c. 1150 BC. The Middle Formative period (900–300 BC) saw increased cultural regionalism and the rise of the ZAPOTEC people. Civilizations of the Late Formative and Classic periods (lasting until c. AD 900) include the MAYA and the civilization centered at TEOTIHUACÁN; later societies include the TOLTECS and the AZTECS. See also CHICHÉN ITZÁ, MIXTEC, MONTE ALBÁN, NAHUA, NAHUATL LANGUAGE, TENOCHTITLÁN, TIKAL.

Mesoamerican religions Religions of the pre-Columbian cultures of Mexico and Central America, notably the OLMEC, MAYA, TOLTEC, and AZTEC. All religions of Mesoamerica were polytheistic. The gods had to be constantly propitiated with offerings and sacrifices. The religions also shared a belief in a multilevel universe that had gone through five creations and four destructions by the time of the Spanish conquest. Mesoamerican religions heavily emphasized the astral bodies, particularly the sun, the moon, and Venus, and the observations of their movements by astronomer-priests were extraordinarily detailed and accurate. The Aztecs approached the supernatural through a complex calendar of ceremonies that included songs, dances, acts of self-mortification, and human sacrifices performed by a professional priesthood, in the belief that the welfare of the universe depended on offerings of blood and hearts as nourishment for the sun. The Mayan religion likewise called for human sacrifices, though on a smaller scale. Information on the astronomical calculations, divination, and ritual of the Mayan priests has been gathered from the MAYA CODICES. See also MESOAMERICAN CIVILIZATION.

Mesolithic period \ˌme-zə-ˈli-thik\ ("Middle Stone Age") Ancient technological and cultural stage (c. 8000–2700 BC) between the PALEOLITHIC and NEOLITHIC periods in northwestern Europe. The Mesolithic hunter, using a tool kit of chipped and polished stone together with bone, antler, and wooden tools, achieved a greater efficiency than his predecessors and was able to exploit a wider range of animal and vegetable food sources. Immigrant Neolithic farmers probably absorbed many indigenous Mesolithic hunters and fishers. There is no direct counterpart to the Mesolithic outside Europe, and the term is no longer used to reflect a hypothetical worldwide sequence of SOCIOCULTURAL EVOLUTION.

meson \ˈme-ˌzän\ Any member of a family of SUBATOMIC PARTICLES composed of a QUARK and an antiquark (see ANTIMATTER). Mesons are sensitive to the STRONG FORCE, have integral SPIN, and vary widely in MASS. Though unstable, many mesons last a few billionths of a second, long enough to be observed with particle detectors. They are readily produced in the collisions of high-energy subatomic particles (e.g., in COSMIC RAYS).

Mesopotamia Region between the TIGRIS and EUPHRATES rivers in western Asia, constituting the greater part of modern Iraq. The region's location and fertility gave rise to settlements from c. 10,000 BC, and it became the cradle of some of the world's earliest civilizations. Its seat was the city of Mesopotamia, founded in the 4th millennium BC by the Sumerians. It was ruled by the third dynasty of UR, and later by BABYLON, which gave its name to the southern portion of Mesopotamia. The city declined under the Hurrians and the Kassites 1600–1450 BC. It was conquered by the army of Ashur. Mesopotamia was ruled by SELEUCIDS from c. 312 BC until the middle of the 2nd century BC, when it became part of the Parthian empire. In the 7th century AD the region was conquered by Muslim Arabs. The region's importance declined after the Mongol invasion in 1258. The Ottoman Turks ruled in the 16th–17th century. The area became a British mandate in 1920; the following year Iraq was established there.

Mesopotamian religions \ˌme-sə-pə-ˈtā-mē-ən\ Religious beliefs and practices of the Sumerians and Akkadians, and later of their successors, the Babylonians and Assyrians, who inhabited ancient MESOPOTAMIA. The deities of SUMER were usually associated with aspects of nature, such as fertility of the fields and livestock. The gods of ASSYRIA and BABYLONIA, rather than displacing those of Sumer and AKKAD, were gradually assimilated into the older system. Among the most important of the many Mesopotamian gods were ANU, the god of heaven; Enki, the god of water; and Enlil, the earth god. Deities were often associated with particular cities. Astral deities such as SHAMASH and SIN were also worshiped. The Mesopotamians were skilled astrologers who studied the movements of the heavenly bodies. Priests also determined the will of the gods through the observation of omens, especially by reading the entrails of sacrificed animals. The king functioned as the chief priest, presiding at the new-year festival held in spring, when the kingship was renewed and the triumph of the deity over the powers of chaos was celebrated.

Mesozoic era \ˌme-zə-ˈzō-ik\ Second of the earth's three major geologic eras and the interval during which the continental landmasses as known today were separated from the supercontinents LAURASIA and GONDWANA by CONTINENTAL DRIFT. It lasted from c. 248 to c. 65 million years ago and includes the TRIASSIC, JURASSIC, and CRETACEOUS periods. The Mesozoic saw the evolution of widely diversified and advanced flora and fauna, quite different from those that had developed earlier during the PALEOZOIC era or that would develop later during the CENOZOIC era.

mesquite \mə-ˈskēt\ Any of the spiny, deep-rooted shrubs or small trees that make up the genus *Prosopis* of the pea family (see LEGUME). Mesquites form extensive thickets in areas from South America to the southwestern U.S. Two races occur: one of tall trees (50 ft, or 15 m), the other low and far-reaching, called running mesquite. Water-seeking roots grow to depths of up to 70 ft (20 m). Stems bear compound olive-green to white hairy leaves, then dense, cream-colored CATKINS of flowers, followed by clusters of long, narrow, pale-yellow beans. In warmer parts of the U.S., mesquites are considered pests and are eradicated. Cattle eat the beans, which contain a sweet pulp, and the wood, formerly used in railroad ties, now has value only for unusual furniture and trinkets and as aromatic firewood.

Mesrob \mes-ˈrōp\, **St.** *or* **St. Mesrop Mashtots** \mash-ˈtōts\ (c. 360–440) Armenian theologian and linguist. A scholar of classical languages, he became a monk c. 395 and eventually founded several monasteries, spreading the Gospel in remote areas of Armenia. He systematized or invented the Armenian alphabet and sponsored the first translation of the Bible into Armenian (c. 410). He also wrote biblical commentaries and translated other theological works, and he helped establish Armenia's golden age of Christian literature. See also ARMENIAN LANGUAGE.

Messene \me-ˈsā-nā, mə-ˈsē-nē\ Ancient city, southwestern PELOPONNESE, Greece, located north of the modern city of the same name. Founded c. 369 BC as the site of the new capital of Messenia, it formed a strategic barrier against SPARTA, along with MEGALOPOLIS, MANTINEA, and ARGOS. It survived several Macedonian and Spartan sieges but fell to PHILIP II of Macedonia in 338 BC. Nothing is known of its history after the 2nd century BC.

Messenia \mə-ˈsē-nē-ə\, **Gulf of** Gulf of the Ionian Sea, on the coast of the southwestern PELOPONNESE, Greece. On the west side of the gulf is the port of Koroni, originally settled by Argives after the First Messenian War (c. 735–715 BC), and reoccupied during the Middle Ages by refugees from the north. The French landed at the Gulf of Messenia in 1828 during the War of GREEK INDEPENDENCE to drive the Turks from the Peloponnese.

Messerschmitt, Willy (1898–1978) German aircraft designer. From 1926 he was chief designer and engineer at the Bayerische Flugzeugwerke in Augsburg, Germany, which in 1938 became Messerschmitt AG. In 1939 his first military aircraft, the MESSERSCHMITT 109, set a speed record of 481 mph (775 kph). In World War II his factory produced 35,000 ME 109's for the German air force, as well as the ME 110 bomber, the ME 163 rocket-propelled plane, and the ME 262, the first combat jet. Under a postwar ban on aircraft production, his firm made prefab housing and sewing machines until 1958.

Messerschmitt 109 (Me 109) FIGHTER AIRCRAFT of Nazi Germany. Originally designed in 1934 at the Bavarian Airplane Co. (BFW), it was renamed when its designer, WILLY MESSERSCHMITT, took over production. It was modified after it saw action in the Spanish Civil War. The model used in the Battle of BRITAIN was a single-seat, single-engine monoplane with a top speed of 350 mph (570 kph) and a ceiling of 36,000 ft (11,000 m). Germany's premier fighter, it could dive and climb rapidly but was limited in range by a small fuel capacity. By 1944 improved Allied fighters had outstripped it.

Messiaen \mes-ˈyä^{n}\, **Olivier (Eugène Prosper Charles)** (1908–1992) French composer. At 11 he entered the Paris Conservatory, where he won five first prizes. In 1931 he became principal organist at the church of the Sainte Trinité, where he would remain for 40 years. He wrote his *Quartet for the End of Time* in a German POW camp. After the war, he taught at the Conservatoire (1947–78), where his students included P. BOULEZ, K. STOCKHAUSEN, and I. XENAKIS. His music's main sources of inspiration were his devout Catholic faith and his love of nature, many works being inspired by birdsong. He also was influenced rhythmically by study of Indian music, and he systematically explored nontonal harmonic materials. Major works include *Vingt regards sur l'enfant Jésus* (1944) and *Catalogue d'oiseaux* (1958) for piano, *La nativité du Seigneur* (1935) for organ, the *Turangalîla-symphonie* (1948), *Et expecto resurrectionem mortuorum* (1964), and the opera *Saint François d'Assise* (1983).

Olivier Messiaen.

messiah In JUDAISM, the expected king of the line of DAVID who will deliver the Jews from foreign bondage and restore Israel's golden age. The term used for the messiah in the Greek NEW TESTAMENT, *christos,* was applied to JESUS, who is accepted by Christians as the promised redeemer. Messiah figures also appear in various other religions and cultures; SHIITE Muslims, for example, look for a restorer of the faith known as the MAHDI, and MAITREYA is a redeeming figure in Buddhism.

Messier catalog \mās-ˈyā, *Engl* ˈme-sē-ˌā\ List of about 109 STAR clusters, nebulae (see NEBULA), and GALAXIES compiled by the French astronomer Charles Messier (1730–1817), who discovered many of them. Still a valuable guide to amateur astronomers, it has been superseded by the New General Catalogue (NGC); both NGC numbers and M numbers remain in common use.

Messina *ancient* **Zankle** City (pop., 1991: 272,000), northeastern SICILY, Italy. Founded by Greeks in the 8th century BC, it was destroyed by Carthaginians in 397 BC. The Romans took the city in 264 BC, precipitating the First PUNIC WAR. After the war it became a free city allied with Rome. It was taken successively by the Goths, Byzantines, Arabs, Normans, Spaniards, and finally the Italians in 1860. Heavily bombed during World War II, it was rebuilt. It is now an important Italian port. Sites of interest include the cathedral and the university (founded 1548).

Messina, Antonello da See ANTONELLO DA MESSINA

Messina, Strait of *ancient* **Siculum Fretum** Channel between southern Italy and northeastern Sicily. It is 2.5–12 mi (4–19 km) wide.

The city of MESSINA lies on its bank in SICILY, opposite Reggio di Calabria. Ferry service across the strait links Messina with the Italian mainland.

Mesta River \me-ˈstä\ *or* **Néstos River** River, southwestern Bulgaria and northeastern Greece. It rises in the northwestern RHODOPE MTNS. and flows southeast for 150 mi (240 km) into the northern AEGEAN SEA opposite the island of THÁSOS. As it crosses the Bulgarian frontier into Greece, it divides Macedonia from Thrace.

mestizo \mes-ˈtē-zō\ Any person of mixed blood. In Spanish America, the term denotes a person of combined Indian and European extraction. In some countries, such as Ecuador, it has acquired social and cultural connotations: a pure-blooded Indian who has adopted European dress and customs is called a mestizo (or *cholo*). In Mexico the term's meaning has varied so greatly that it has been abandoned in census reports. In the Philippines it denotes a person of mixed foreign (e.g., Chinese) and native ancestry. See also LADINO.

metabolism \mə-ˈta-bə-ˌli-zəm\ Sum of all the CHEMICAL REACTIONS that take place in every CELL of a living organism, providing energy for the processes of life and synthesizing new cellular material. "Intermediary metabolism" refers to the vast web of interconnected CHEMICAL REACTIONS by which all the cell's constituents, many rarely found outside it, are created and destroyed. Anabolic reactions use energy to build complex MOLECULES from simpler organic compounds (e.g., PROTEINS from AMINO ACIDS, CARBOHYDRATES from SUGARS, FATS from FATTY ACIDS and GLYCEROL); catabolic reactions break complex molecules down into simpler ones, releasing chemical energy. For most organisms, the energy comes ultimately from the sun, whether they obtain it by PHOTOSYNTHESIS and store it in organic compounds or consume those that photosynthesize for the energy stored in their organic compounds. In some BACTERIA in special environments such as DEEP-SEA VENTS, the energy comes from chemical bonds instead. Energy is transferred within the cell and the organism by ATP; anabolic reactions consume it, and catabolic reactions generate it. Every cellular chemical reaction is mediated by a specific ENZYME. The process that breaks down a substance is not usually the reverse of the process that makes it and uses a different enzyme. See also DIGESTION, FERMENTATION, TRICARBOXYLIC ACID CYCLE.

Metabolist school \mə-ˈta-bə-list\ Japanese architectural movement of the 1960s that combined high-tech imagery, BRUTALISM, and an interest in megastructures (multifunctional complexes that verge on self-containment). Tange launched the movement with his Boston Harbor Project design (1959), which included two gigantic A-frames hung with "shelving" for homes and other buildings. Led by ARATA ISOZAKI, KENZO TANGE, Kiyonori Kikutake (born 1928), and Kisho Kurokawa (born 1934), the Metabolists focused on loosely composed, multifunctional projects with broken skylines, rough surfaces, and a dynamic science-fiction quality. The Metabolist manifestos put out at the World Design Conference in 1960 paved the way for such later projects as PAOLO SOLERI's Arcosanti. The use of such devices as artificial land platforms above cities on the ground, which grew out of a desire for economy of land use, revolutionized architectural thinking.

Metacom \ˈme-tə-ˌkäm\ *or* **Metacomet** *or* **King Philip** (1638?–1676) Wampanoag Indian chief who led the most severe Indian war in New England history, known as KING PHILIP'S WAR (1675–76). His father, MASSASOIT, had negotiated peace with the Pilgrims in 1621. Embittered by the subsequent humiliations to which he and his people were continually subjected by whites, Metacom in June 1675 led a group of Wampanoag, Narragansett, ABENAKI, Nipmuck, and MOHAWK warriors into battle. He was killed in the final confrontation. His body was quartered and his head displayed on a pole for 25 years at Plymouth.

metal Any of a class of substances with, to some degree, the following properties: good heat and electricity conduction, malleability, ductility, high light reflectivity, and capacity to form positive IONS in solution and HYDROXIDES rather than ACIDS when their OXIDES meet water. About three-quarters of the ELEMENTS are metals; these are usually fairly hard and strong crystalline (see CRYSTAL) solids with high chemical reactivity that readily form ALLOYS with each other. Metallic properties increase from lighter to heavier elements in each vertical group of the PERIODIC TABLE and from right to left in each row. The most abundant metals are aluminum, iron, calcium, sodium, potassium, and magnesium. The vast majority are found as ORES rather than free. The cohesiveness of metals in a crystalline structure is attributed to metallic BONDING: The ATOMS are packed close together, with their very mobile outermost ELECTRONS all shared throughout the structure. Metals fall into the following classifications (not mutually exclusive and most not rigidly defined): ALKALI METALS, ALKALINE EARTH METALS, TRANSITION ELEMENTS, noble (precious) metals, platinum metals, lanthanide (RARE EARTH) metals, ACTINIDE metals, light metals, and heavy metals. Many have essential roles in NUTRITION or other biochemical functions, often in trace amounts, and many are toxic as both elements and compounds (see MERCURY POISONING, LEAD POISONING).

metal fatigue Weakened condition of METAL parts of MACHINES, vehicles, or structures caused by repeated stresses or loadings, ultimately resulting in FRACTURE under a STRESS much weaker than that necessary to cause fracture in a single application. Fatigue-resistant metals have been developed and their performance improved by surface treatments, and fatigue stresses have been significantly reduced in aircraft and other applications by designing to avoid stress concentrations.

metal point *or* **silverpoint** Method of drawing with a small sharpened metal rod—of lead, copper, gold, or most commonly silver—on specially prepared paper or parchment. Silverpoint produces a fine gray line that oxidizes to a light brown; the technique is best suited for small-scale work. It first appeared in medieval Italy and achieved great popularity in the 15th century. ALBRECHT DURER and LEONARDO DA VINCI were its greatest exponents. It went out of fashion in the 17th century with the rise of the graphite pencil, but was revived in the 18th century by the miniaturists and in the 20th century by Joseph Stella.

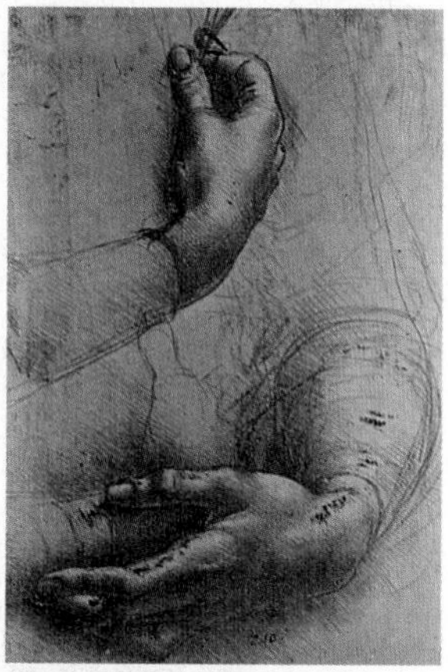

"Study of Hands," silverpoint heightened with white on pink grounded paper by Leonardo da Vinci; in Windsor Castle, Berkshire, Eng.

metalanguage \ˈme-tə-ˌlaŋ-gwij\ In LINGUISTICS and LOGIC, language used to analyze or describe the sentences or elements of the object language (the ordinary language used to talk about things or objects in the world). The concept of metalanguage was developed by such 20th-century logical positivists as Alfred Tarski (1902–1983) and RUDOLF CARNAP.

metallography \ˌme-tᵊl-ˈä-grə-fē\ Study of the structure of METALS and ALLOYS, particularly using microscopic and X-RAY DIFFRACTION techniques. Visual and optical microscopic observation of metal SURFACES and FRACTURES can reveal valuable information about the crystalline, chemical, and mechanical makeup of the material. In electron microscopes a beam of electrons instead of a beam of light is directed onto the specimen. The development of transmission electron microscopes has made it possible to examine internal details of very thin metal foils. X-ray diffraction techniques are used to study phenomena related to the grouping of the atoms themselves. See also MATERIALS SCIENCE, HENRY C. SORBY.

metallurgy \ˈme-tᵊl-ˌər-jē\ Art and science of extracting METALS from their ORES and modifying the metals for use. Metallurgy usually refers to commercial rather than laboratory methods. It also concerns the chemical, physical, and atomic properties and structures of metals and the principles by which metals are combined to form ALLOYS. Metals are extracted from crude ore in two phases, ORE DRESSING and process metallurgy. In ore dressing, the ore is broken down to isolate the desired metallic elements from the crude ore. In process metallurgy, the resulting minerals are reduced to metal, alloyed, and made available for use. See also BLAST FURNACE, POWDER METALLURGY, SMELTING.

metalogic \ˈme-tə-ˌlä-jik\ Study of the syntax and the semantics of formal languages and FORMAL SYSTEMS. It is related to, but does not include, the formal treatment of natural languages (e.g., English, Russian, etc.). Metalogic has led to a great deal of work of a mathematical nature in axiomatic SET THEORY, model theory, and recursion theory (in which functions that are computable in a finite number of steps are studied).

metalwork Useful and decorative objects fashioned of various metals. The oldest technique is hammering. After c. 2500 BC, CASTING was also used, molten metal being poured into a mold and allowed to cool. Various decorative techniques are used. GOLD and SILVER have been worked since ancient times. Gold and silver objects were in such demand in the 12th century that gold- and silversmiths organized guilds. High-quality gold and silver objects were produced in pre-Columbian America. COPPER was worked in ancient Egypt and was widely used for household utensils in 17th–18th-century Europe. Both BRONZE and BRASS were widely used in ancient Greece. PEWTER plates and tankards were made in the Middle Ages and remained popular until they were superseded by cheaper EARTHENWARE and PORCELAIN in the 18th century. WROUGHT IRON has been used for decorative hinges, gates, and railings since the 16th century. LEAD has traditionally been used for roof coverings.

metamorphic rock Any of a class of rocks that result from the alteration of preexisting rocks in response to changing geological conditions, including variations in temperature, pressure, and mechanical stress. The preexisting rocks may be IGNEOUS, SEDIMENTARY, or other metamorphic rocks. The structure and mineralogy reflect the particular type of METAMORPHISM that produced the rock and the composition of the parent rock. Metamorphic rocks are commonly classified by type of facies, predictable mineral assemblages associated with certain temperature and pressure conditions (see, e.g., GRANULITE FACIES).

metamorphism Mineralogic and structural changes in solid rocks caused by physical conditions different from those under which the rocks originally formed. Changes produced by surface conditions such as compaction are usually excluded. The most important agents of metamorphism are temperature (from 300°–2,200°F, or 150°–1200°C), pressure (from 10 to several hundred kilobars, or 150,000 to several million lbs. per sq in.), and stress. Dynamic metamorphism results from mechanical deformation with little long-term temperature change. Contact metamorphism results from increases in temperature with minor differential stress, is highly localized, and may occur relatively quickly. Regional metamorphism results from the general increase, usually correlated, of temperature and pressure over a large area and a long period of time, as in mountain-building processes. See also METAMORPHIC ROCK.

metamorphosis In biology, any striking developmental change of an animal's form or structure, accompanied by physiological, biochemical, and behavioral changes. The best-known examples occur among insects, which may exhibit complete or incomplete metamorphosis (see NYMPH). The complete metamorphosis of butterflies, moths, and some other insects involves four stages: EGG, LARVA (CATERPILLAR), PUPA (chrysalis or cocoon), and adult. The change from TADPOLE to frog is an example of metamorphosis among amphibians; some echinoderms, crustaceans, mollusks, and tunicates also undergo metamorphosis.

metaphor FIGURE OF SPEECH in which a word or phrase denoting one kind of object or action is used in place of another to suggest a likeness or analogy between them (as in "the ship plows the seas" or "a volley of oaths"). A metaphor is an implied comparison (as in "a marble brow"), in contrast to the explicit comparison of the SIMILE ("a brow white as marble"). Metaphor is common at all levels of language and is fundamental in poetry, in which its varied functions range from merely noting a likeness to serving as a central concept and controlling image.

Metaphysical painting *Italian* **Pittura Metafisica** Style of painting that flourished c. 1910–20 in the works of the Italian painters GIORGIO DE CHIRICO and Carlo Carrà (1881–1966). The movement began with Chirico, whose dreamlike works with sharp contrasts of light and shadow often had a vaguely threatening, mysterious quality. Chirico, his younger brother Alberto Savinio, and Carrà formally established the school and its principles in 1917. Their representational but bizarre and incongruous imagery produces disquieting effects and had a strong influence on SURREALISM in the 1920s.

Metaphysical poetry Highly intellectualized poetry written chiefly in 17th-century England. Less concerned with expressing feeling than with analyzing it, Metaphysical poetry is marked by bold and ingenious conceits (e.g., metaphors drawing sometimes forced parallels between apparently dissimilar ideas or things), complex and subtle thought, frequent use of paradox, and a dramatic directness of language, the rhythm of which derives from living speech. JOHN DONNE was the leading Metaphysical poet; others include GEORGE HERBERT, HENRY VAUGHAN, ANDREW MARVELL, and ABRAHAM COWLEY.

metaphysics Branch of philosophy whose object is to determine the real nature of things, to determine the meaning, structure, and principles of whatever is insofar as it is. In the history of Western philosophy, metaphysics has been understood as: (1) an inquiry into what sorts or basic kinds of things (e.g., the mental and the physical) exist; (2) the science of reality, as opposed to appearance; (3) the study of the world as a whole; and (4) a theory of first principles. The term means literally "what comes after physics," and was used to refer to the contents of ARISTOTLE's treatise on what he himself called "first philosophy." Aristotle had distinguished two tasks for the philosopher: to investigate the nature and properties of what exists in the natural, or sensible, world, and to explore the characteristics of "being as such" and inquire into the character of "the substance that is free from movement," the unmoved mover. The first constituted "second philosophy" and was carried out primarily in his *Physics*; the second, which he also called "theology" (because God was the unmoved mover), is discussed in his *Metaphysics*.

metasomatic replacement \ˌme-tə-sō-ˈma-tik\ Process of simultaneous solution and deposition in which one mineral replaces another. It is the method by which wood is petrified (silica replaces the wood fibers), minerals form pseudomorphs (new minerals that preserve the characteristic outward form of the earlier mineral that was replaced), or an ore mineral assemblage takes the place an earlier rock type. Replacement minerals may themselves be replaced, and definite mineral successions have been established. Replacement deposits may be highly valuable ore deposits.

metastable state \ˌme-tə-ˈstā-bəl\ Excited state (see EXCITATION) of an ATOM, NUCLEUS, or other system that has a longer lifetime than the ordinary excited states and generally has a shorter lifetime than the ground state. It can be considered a temporary energy trap or a somewhat stable intermediate stage of a system of which the energy may be lost in discrete amounts. The many photochemical reactions of mercury are a result of the metastable state of mercury atoms, and RADIATION from metastable oxygen atoms accounts for the characteristic green color of the aurora borealis and aurora australis.

Metastasio \ˌmā-tä-ˈstäz-yō\, **Pietro** *orig.* **Antonio Domenico Bonaventura Trapassi** (1698–1782) Italian opera librettist. His name was changed by his adoptive father, who left the youth enough money to embark on a career as a poet. His first libretto, *Didone abbandonata* (1724), was so successful that he was soon known throughout Italy. Such important librettos as *Enzio* (1728) and *Semiramide* (1729) soon followed. He was invited to Vienna as court poet by CHARLES VI. His 27 three-act librettos were set in more than 800 operas in the 18th and early 19th century by such composers as A. VIVALDI, G.F. HANDEL, C.W. GLUCK, F.J. HAYDN, W.A. MOZART, and L. CHERUBINI.

Metaxas \ˌmet-äk-ˈsäs\, **Ioannis** (1871–1941) Greek general and premier (1936–41). He rose in the Greek army to become chief of staff (1913–17). An ardent monarchist, he left Greece when King CONSTANTINE I was deposed in 1917, but returned in 1920. After the monarchy's fall in 1923, he led an opposition ultraroyalist party until the monarchy was restored in 1935. He was appointed premier in 1936 and, with royal authority, established a dictatorship. He suppressed political opposition, carried out some beneficial economic and social reforms, and brought a united country into the Western alliance in World War II.

Élie Metchnikoff.
H. ROGER-VIOLLET

Metcalfe, Ralph (Harold) (1910–1978) U.S. sprinter. Born in Atlanta, he grew up in Chicago and became an outstanding sprinter at Marquette University. In 1932 and 1936 he won Olympic silver medals in the 100-m dash, losing close races to his great rivals Eddie Tolan and JESSE OWENS, and won a gold medal in the 1936 games with the 4×100-m relay team. He later became a U.S. Congressman (1971–79).

Metchnikoff \ˈmech-ni-ˌkȯf\, **Élie** *orig.* **Ilya Ilich Mechnikov** (1845–1916) Russian zoologist and microbiologist. In 1888 LOUIS PAS-

TEUR offered him a post at the Pasteur Institute, and he succeeded Pasteur as director in 1895. Working with starfish, he discovered amoebalike cells in their systems that engulf foreign bodies such as bacteria. He established that phagocytes (as he named these cells, using the Greek for "devouring cells") are the first line of defense against acute infection in most animals. This phenomenon, now known as phagocytosis, is fundamental to immunology. He shared a 1908 Nobel Prize with PAUL EHRLICH.

metempsychosis See REINCARNATION

meteor *or* **shooting star** *or* **falling star** Streak of light in the sky that results when a particle or small chunk of stony or metallic matter enters earth's ATMOSPHERE and is vaporized by FRICTION. The term is sometimes applied to the falling object itself, properly called a meteoroid. Most meteoroids, traveling at five times the speed of sound or more, burn up in the upper atmosphere, but a large one may survive its fiery plunge and reach the surface as a solid body (METEORITE). See also METEOR SHOWER.

meteor shower Entry into earth's atmosphere of multiple meteoroids (see METEOR), traveling in parallel paths, usually spread over several hours or days. Most meteor showers come from matter released during passage of a COMET close to the sun, and recur annually as the earth crosses the comet's orbital path. Meteor showers are usually named for a constellation (e.g., Leonid for Leo) or star in their direction of origin. Most showers are visible as a few dozen meteors per hour, but occasionally the earth crosses an especially dense concentration of meteoroids, as in the great Leonid meteor shower of 1833, in which hundreds of thousands of meteors were seen in one night all over North America.

meteorite Any interplanetary particle or chunk of stony or metallic matter (meteoroid) that survives passage through earth's atmosphere and strikes the ground, or reaches the surface of another planet or moon. The speed of entry—at least 7 mi/second (11 km/second)—generates enough FRICTION with the air to vaporize the meteoroid and produce a streak of light (METEOR). Though vast numbers of meteoroids enter the atmosphere each year, only a few hundred reach the ground.

meteorite crater Depression that results from the impact of a METEORITE with any planetary body. Impact craters have been discovered on the earth, the moon, Mars, and other planets and satellites; they probably occur on unprotected planetary and satellite surfaces throughout the universe. Impact craters are much less common on the earth than on the moon, partly because friction burns up most of the smaller bodies that enter the earth's atmosphere. Thus, any craters formed on the earth's surface tend to be larger than the average size of all entering meteorites.

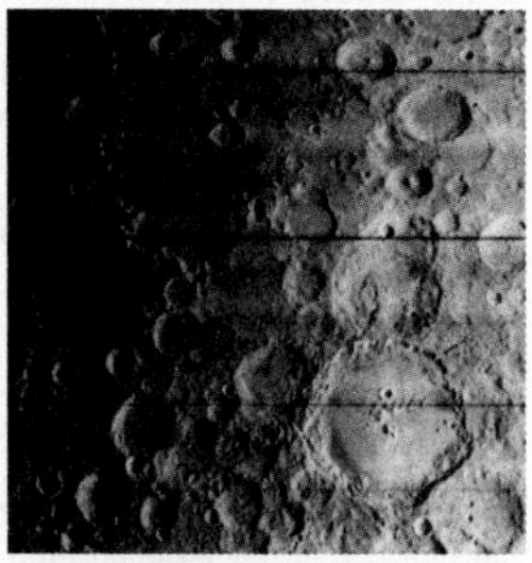

Meteorite craters on the surface of the Moon, photographed by Lunar Orbiter IV.

BY COURTESY OF NATIONAL AERONAUTICS AND SPACE ADMINISTRATION

meteoritics \ˌmē-tē-ə-ˈri-tiks\ Study of the chemistry and mineralogy of METEORITE samples that have been collected on the earth and of METEORS as they pass through the earth's atmosphere. These studies provide information about the age of meteorites, the conditions under which they formed, where they come from, and the geological history of their original planets, including asteroids, Mars, and the moon. The field of study is especially important for understanding the early geological history of the solar system.

meteorology Scientific study of atmospheric phenomena, particularly of the TROPOSPHERE and lower STRATOSPHERE. Meteorology entails the systematic study of weather and its causes, and provides the basis for WEATHER FORECASTING. See also CLIMATOLOGY.

meter In poetry, the rhythmic pattern of a poetic line. Various principles have been devised to organize poetic lines into rhythmic units. Quantitative verse, the meter of classical Greek and Latin poetry, measures the length of time required to pronounce syllables, regardless of their stress; combinations of long and short syllables form the basic rhythmic units. Syllabic verse is most common in languages that are not strongly accented, such as French or Japanese; it is based on a fixed number of syllables within a line. Accentual verse occurs in strongly stressed languages such as the Germanic; only stressed syllables within a line are counted. Accentual-syllabic verse is the usual form in English poetry; it combines syllable counting and stress counting. The most common English meter, iambic pentameter, is a line of 10 syllables, or five iambic feet; each foot contains an unstressed syllable followed by a stressed syllable. FREE VERSE does not follow regular metrical patterns. See also PROSODY.

meter Basic unit of length in the METRIC SYSTEM and the INTERNATIONAL SYSTEM OF UNITS. In 1983 the General Conference on Weights and Measures decided that the accepted value for the speed of light would be exactly 299,792,458 meters per second, so the meter is now defined as the distance traveled by light in a vacuum in 1/299,792,458 second. One meter is equal to about 39.37 in. in U.S. units.

meter See RHYTHM AND METER

methadone \ˈme-thə-ˌdōn\ Organic compound, a potent synthetic NARCOTIC drug, the most effective form of treatment for addiction to HEROIN and other NARCOTICS (see DRUG ADDICTION). It has been widely used in heroin-addiction programs in the U.S. since the 1960s. Though addictive itself, it is easier to stop using than heroin. It also causes no euphoric effects and does not lead to development of tolerance, so increasing doses are not required. A person taking a daily maintenance dose does not experience either heroin withdrawal symptoms or a heroin rush from any attempt to resume heroin, so heroin's psychological hold on the user can be broken.

methanal See FORMALDEHYDE

methane *or* **marsh gas** Organic compound, chemical formula CH_4, colorless, odorless GAS that occurs naturally in NATURAL GAS (called "firedamp" in coal mines) and from bacterial decomposition of vegetation in the absence of oxygen (including in the rumens of cattle and other RUMINANTS). The simplest member of the PARAFFIN HYDROCARBONS, methane burns readily, forming CARBON DIOXIDE and WATER with enough OXYGEN, and CARBON MONOXIDE without it. Mixtures of 5–14% methane in air are explosive and have caused many mine disasters. The chief source of methane is natural gas, but it can also be produced from coal. Abundant, cheap, and clean, methane is used widely as a fuel in homes, commercial establishments, and factories. As a safety measure, it is mixed with trace amounts of an odorant to allow its detection. It is also a raw material for many industrial materials, including fertilizers, explosives, methanol, chloroform, carbon tetrachloride, and carbon black, and is the principal source of METHANOL.

methanol *or* **methyl alcohol** *or* **wood alcohol** Simplest of the ALCOHOLS, chemical formula CH_3OH. Once produced by destructive distillation of wood, it is now usually made from the METHANE in natural gas. Methanol is an important industrial material; its derivatives are used in great quantities for making a vast number of compounds, among them many important synthetic dyes, resins, drugs, and perfumes. It is also used in automotive antifreezes, in rocket fuels, and as a solvent. It is flammable and explosive. A clean-burning fuel, it may substitute (at least in part) for GASOLINE. It is also used for DENATURATION of ETHANOL. A violent poison, it causes blindness and eventually death when drunk.

methionine \mə-ˈthī-ə-ˌnēn\ SULFUR-containing essential AMINO ACID, present in many common PROTEINS, particularly egg ALBUMIN. It is used in pharmaceuticals, in enriched foods, and as a nutritional supplement and feed additive.

Method acting See STANISLAVSKY METHOD

Methodism Protestant religious movement originated by JOHN WESLEY in 18th-century England. Wesley, an Anglican clergyman, underwent an epiphany in 1738 in which he felt an assurance of personal salvation, and he soon began open-air preaching. Methodism began as a movement to revitalize the Church of England and did not formally break with the church until 1795. The Methodists' well-organized system of church government combined a strong central authority with effective local organization and the employment of lay preachers. Especially successful among the working class in industrial areas, the movement expanded rapidly in the 19th century. The Methodist Episcopal Church was founded in the U.S. in 1784, and Methodist circuit riders won many followers on the frontier. British and U.S. missionaries have since spread Methodism throughout the world. Methodist doctrine emphasizes the power of the Holy Spirit, the need for a personal relationship with God, simplicity of worship, and concern for the underprivileged.

Methodius, St. See Sts. CYRIL AND METHODIUS

Methuselah \mə-'thü-zə-lə\ Old Testament patriarch who lived to the age of 969. The son of Enoch, he is mentioned in GENESIS as a descendant of Seth, the son of Adam and Eve begotten after CAIN. He is remembered as the world's oldest human being. He was the father of Lamech and grandfather of NOAH; his later descendants included ABRAHAM, JACOB, and DAVID.

metics \'me-tiks\ (Greek, *metoikos*) Resident foreigners, including freed slaves, in ancient Greece. In Athens they represented one-third of the free population but lacked full citizenship. For a small tax they enjoyed the protection of the law and most of a citizen's duties, including supporting public funds, financing festivals, and serving in the military, but could not marry a citizen or own land. They were found in most states, Sparta being an exception.

Métis \mā-'tēs\ In Canadian history, a person of mixed Indian and French or Scottish ancestry. The first Métis were the offspring of local Indian women and European fur traders in the Red River area of what is now southern Manitoba. For over half a century they cultivated a distinctive way of life and came to think of themselves as a nation. They resisted the Canadian takeover of the Northwest in 1869, established a provisional government under the leadership of LOUIS RIEL, and in 1870 negotiated a union with Canada that resulted in the establishment of the province of Manitoba. Today there are about 100,000 Métis in western Canada.

metric space In mathematics, a set of objects equipped with a concept of distance. The objects can be thought of as points in space, with the distance between points given by a DISTANCE FORMULA, such that: (1) the distance from point A to point B is zero if and only if A and B are identical, (2) the distance from A to B is the same as from B to A, and (3) the distance from A to B plus that from B to C is greater than or equal to the distance from A to C (the triangle inequality). Two- and three-dimensional EUCLIDEAN SPACES are metric spaces, as are INNER PRODUCT SPACES, VECTOR SPACES, and certain topological spaces (see TOPOLOGY).

metric system International decimal system of weights and measures, based on the METER (m) for length and the kilogram (kg) for mass, originally adopted in France in 1795. All other metric units were derived from the meter, including the gram (g) for weight (1 cc of water at its maximum density) and the liter (l, or L) for capacity (0.0001 cu m). In the 20th century, the metric system became the basis for the INTERNATIONAL SYSTEM OF UNITS, which is now used officially almost worldwide.

metrical foot See metrical FOOT

Metro-Goldwyn-Mayer, Inc. See MGM

metrology \me-'trä-lə-jē\ Science of MEASUREMENT. Measuring a quantity means establishing its ratio to another fixed quantity of the same kind, known as the unit of that kind of quantity. A unit is an abstract idea, defined either by reference to a randomly chosen material standard or to a natural phenomenon. For example, the METER, the standard of length in the METRIC SYSTEM, was formerly defined (1889–1960) by the separation of two lines on a particular metal bar, but it is now defined as the distance traveled by light in a vacuum in 1/299,792,458 second. See also INTERNATIONAL SYSTEM OF UNITS.

Metropolitan Museum of Art Most comprehensive collection of art in the U.S. and one of the foremost in the world. It was incorporated in New York City in 1870, and the present building in Central Park on Fifth Avenue was opened in 1880. Much of the medieval collection is housed at The Cloisters in Manhattan's Fort Tryon Park; its building (1938) incorporates parts of medieval monasteries and churches. The Metropolitan was built with the private fortunes of businessmen; today it is owned by the city but supported mainly by private endowment. Its outstanding Egyptian, Mesopotamian, Far and Near Eastern, Greek and Roman, European, pre-Columbian, and U.S. collections include—in addition to paintings, sculpture, and graphic arts—architecture, glass, ceramics, textiles, metalwork, furniture, arms and armor, and musical instruments. It also incorporates a Costume Institute and the Thomas J. Watson Library, one of the world's greatest art and archaeology reference collections.

Metropolitan Opera Oldest opera company in New York, founded in 1883. Started by a group of millionaires who had failed to get boxes at the Academy of Music, the Met soon outlived its frivolous origin, becoming the American equivalent of LA SCALA and second to no opera house in the world in the quality of the singers it attracted. Originally sited at Broadway and 39th Street, it moved into its new home at LINCOLN CENTER FOR THE PERFORMING ARTS in 1966.

Metsys \'met-sīs\, **Quentin** (c. 1465–1530) Flemish artist. According to tradition, Metsys (whose name was also spelled Massys and Matsys) was trained as a blacksmith but studied painting after falling in love with an artist's daughter. He was admitted to the Antwerp artists' guild in 1491. His most celebrated paintings are two large triptych altarpieces, *The Holy Kinship* (1507–9) and *The Entombment of Christ* (1508–11), both of which exhibit strong religious feelings and precision of detail. He painted many notable portraits, including one of DESIDERIUS ERASMUS. He was the first important painter of the Antwerp school, and the first Flemish artist to effect a genuine synthesis of the northern European and Italian Renaissance traditions.

Metternich (-Winneburg-Beilstein) \'me-tər-,nik\, **Klemens (Wenzel Nepomuk Lothar), Fürst (Prince) von** (1773–1859) Austrian statesman. He served in the diplomatic service as Austrian minister in Saxony (1801–3), Berlin (1803–5), and Paris (1806–9). In 1809 FRANCIS I of Austria appointed him minister of foreign affairs, a position he would retain until 1848. He helped promote the marriage of NAPOLEON and Francis's daughter MARIE-LOUISE. By skillful diplomacy and deceit, he kept Austria neutral in the war between France and Russia (1812) and secured its position of power before finally allying with Prussia and Russia (1813). In gratitude for his diplomatic achievements, the emperor created Metternich a hereditary prince. As the organizer of the Congress of VIENNA (1814–15), he was largely responsible for the policy of balance of power in Europe to ensure the stability of European governments. After 1815 he remained firmly opposed to liberal ideas and revolutionary movements. He was forced to resign by the REVOLUTION OF 1848. He is remembered for his role in restoring Austria as a leading European power.

Metz \'metz, *French* 'mes\ City (pop., 1997 est.: 124,000), northeastern France. It derives its name from the Mediomatrici, a Gallic tribe who made it their capital. Fortified by the Romans, it became a bishopric in the 4th century AD. It passed to Frankish rule in the 5th century, becoming the capital of LORRAINE in 843. It prospered as a free town within the HOLY ROMAN EMPIRE. Taken by the French in 1552, it was formally ceded to France in 1648. It fell to German rule in 1871, but was returned to France after World War I. It was the birthplace of PAUL VERLAINE.

Porte des Allemands (Gate of the Germans), Metz, France.
P. SALOU–SHOSTAL

Meuse River \'mœz, *Engl* 'myüz\ *Dutch* **Maas** \'mäs\ River, western Europe. Rising in northeastern France, it flows north into Belgium, where it forms part of the border between Belgium and the Netherlands. It divides at Venlo, the Netherlands, one branch flowing into the Hol-

L
M
N

landsch Canal (an outlet of the North Sea), and another joining the Waal River to become the Merwede, which eventually empties into the North Sea. It is 590 mi (950 km) long and is an important waterway in western Europe. Its valley was the scene of heavy fighting in World War I; the crossing of the Meuse was critical to Germany's invasion of France in 1940 in World War II.

mews Row of stables and coach houses with living quarters above, built behind houses, especially in 17th–18th-century London. Most have been converted into modernized dwellings. The term originally referred to the royal stables in London, built where the king's hawks once stayed at molting ("mew") time.

Mexicali City (pop., 1990: 602,000), capital of BAJA CALIFORNIA (Norte) state, northwestern Mexico. It lies in the Mexicali Valley, an extension of the IMPERIAL VALLEY of the U.S., in northeastern Baja California. It extends across the Mexico–U.S. border to Calexico, Cal. Its name, formed from the first two syllables of Mexico and California, was chosen as a gesture of international friendship. Its economy is chiefly based on tourism and the processing and distribution of cotton, fruits, vegetables, and cereals. It is the seat of the Autonomous University of Baja California.

Mexican process See PATIO PROCESS

Mexican Revolution (1910–20) Lengthy struggle that began with the overthrow of PORFIRIO DIAZ, whose elitist and oligarchic policies had caused widespread dissatisfaction. FRANCISCO MADERO, PANCHO VILLA, Pascual Orozco, and EMILIANO ZAPATA amassed supporters, and in 1911 Madero was declared president, but his slow-paced reforms alienated both former allies and foes. He was deposed by Gen. VICTORIANO HUERTA, whose own drunken and despotic dictatorship quickly fell to Villa, ALVARO OBREGON, and VENUSTIANO CARRANZA. Carranza declared himself president in 1914 over Villa's objections and, after further bloodshed, prevailed. He oversaw the writing of the liberal constitution of 1917 but did little to implement its key provisions; in 1920 he was killed while fleeing a rebellion. With the election of the reform-minded ALVARO OBREGON, the revolutionary period ended, though sporadic clashes continued until LAZARO CARDENAS took office in 1934.

Mexican War *or* **Mexican-American War** War between the U.S. and Mexico, 1846–48. It grew from a border dispute after the U.S. annexed Texas in 1845; Mexico claimed the southern border of Texas was the Nueces River, while the U.S. claimed it was the Rio Grande River. A secret mission by JOHN SLIDELL to negotiate the dispute and purchase New Mexico and California for up to $30 million was aborted when Mexico refused to receive him. In response to the snub, Pres. JAMES POLK sent troops under ZACHARY TAYLOR to occupy the disputed land between the two rivers. In April 1846 Mexican troops crossed the Rio Grande and attacked Taylor's troops; Congress approved a declaration of war in May. Ordered to invade Mexico, Taylor captured Monterrey and defeated a large Mexican force under ANTONIO SANTA ANNA at the Battle of BUENA VISTA in February 1847. Polk then ordered Gen. WINFIELD SCOTT to move his army by sea to Veracruz, capture the city, and march inland to Mexico City. Scott followed the plan, meeting resistance at CERRO GORDO and CONTRERAS, and entered Mexico City in September. Under the Treaty of GUADALUPE HIDALGO, Mexico ceded nearly all of present New Mexico, Utah, Nevada, Arizona, California, Texas, and Colorado. Casualties included about 13,000 American deaths, all but 1,700 of which were caused by disease. The war, which made a national hero of Taylor, reopened the slavery-extension issue supposedly settled by the MISSOURI COMPROMISE.

Mexico *Spanish* **México** \'me-hē-ˌkō\ *officially* **United Mexican States** Republic, southern North America. The RIO GRANDE forms part of its northeastern border with the U.S. Area: 756,066 sq mi (1,958,201 sq km). Population (1997 est.): 94,270,000. Capital: MEXICO CITY. About three-fifths of Mexico's population is MESTIZO, one-third is American Indian, and the rest are of European ancestry. Languages: Spanish (official); more than 50 Indian languages are spoken. Religion: Roman Catholicism. Currency: Mexican peso. Mexico has two major peninsulas, the YUCATÁN in the southeast and BAJA CALIFORNIA in the northwest. The high Mexican Plateau forms the core of the country and is enclosed by mountain ranges: the SIERRA MADRE Occidental, the Sierra Madre Oriental, and the Cordillera Neo-Volcánica. The last has the nation's highest peak, the volcano CITLALTÉPETL. Mexico has a mixed economy based on agriculture, manufacturing, and petroleum extraction. About one-eighth of the land is arable; its major crops include corn, wheat, rice, beans, coffee, cotton, fruits, and vegetables. It is the world's largest producer of silver, bismuth, and celestite, and its crude-oil reserves rank seventh in the world. Manufactures include processed foods, chemicals, transport vehicles, and electrical machinery. It is a republic with two legislative houses; its chief of state and head of government is the president. Inhabited for more than 20,000 years, the area produced great civilizations in AD 100–900, including the OLMEC, TOLTEC, MAYAN, and AZTEC. The Aztec were conquered in 1521 by Spanish explorer HERNAN CORTES, who established Mexico City on the site of the Aztec capital, TENOCHTITLÁN. Francisco de Montejo conquered the remnants of Maya civilization in 1526, and Mexico became part of the viceroyalty of NEW SPAIN. In 1821 rebels negotiated a status quo independence from Spain, and in 1823 a new congress declared Mexico a republic. In 1845 the U.S. voted to annex TEXAS, initiating the MEXICAN WAR. Under the Treaty of GUADALUPE HIDALGO in 1848, it ceded a vast territory in what is now the western and southwestern U.S. The Mexican government endured several rebellions and civil wars in the late 19th and early 20th century (see MEXICAN REVOLUTION). During World War II it declared war on the AXIS POWERS (1942), and in the postwar era it was a founding member of the UNITED NATIONS (1945) and the ORGANIZATION OF AMERICAN STATES (1948). In 1993 it ratified the NORTH AMERICAN FREE TRADE AGREEMENT. The election of Vicente Fox (2000) ended 71 years of rule by the INSTITUTIONAL REVOLUTIONARY PARTY. See map on following page.

Mexican Presidents from 1917

President	Term	President	Term
Venustiano Carranza*	1917–20	Adolfo Ruiz Cortines	1952–58
Adolfo de la Huerta	1920	Adolfo López Mateos	1958–64
Álvaro Obregón	1920–24	Gustavo Díaz Ordaz	1964–70
Plutarco Elías Calles	1924–28	Luis Echeverría Álvarez	1970–76
Emilio Portes Gil	1928–30	José López Portillo	1976–82
Pascual Ortíz Rubio	1930–32	Miguel de la Madrid	1982–88
Abelardo L. Rodríguez	1932–34	Carlos Salinas de Gortari	1988–94
Lázaro Cárdenas	1934–40	Ernesto Zedillo	1994–2000
Manuel Ávila Camacho	1940–46	Vicente Fox	2000–
Miguel Alemán	1946–52		

*Claimed the presidency as early as 1914.

México \'me-hē-ˌkō\ State (pop., 1995 est.: 11,708), central Mexico, almost completely surrounding the Federal District and MEXICO CITY. Its capital is TOLUCA. Occupying an area of 8,245 sq mi (21,355 sq km), it contains many preconquest ruins, including Tenayuca, Malinalco, and TEOTIHUACAN. The state's elevation at more than 10,000 ft (3,000 m) above sea level creates a cool climate; its population density is the highest of any Mexican state. The economy is based on agriculture and manufacturing.

Mexico, Gulf of Gulf, southeastern coast of North America, connected to the Atlantic Ocean by the Straits of Florida and to the Caribbean Sea by the Yucatán Channel. Covering an area of 600,000 sq mi (1,550,000 sq km), it is bounded by the U.S., Mexico, and Cuba. It has a maximum depth, in the Mexico Basin, of 17,070 ft (5,203 m). The GULF STREAM, enters it from the Caribbean Sea and flows out to the Atlantic. The MISSISSIPPI and the RIO GRANDE are the major rivers draining into the gulf. Its major ports are VERACRUZ in Mexico, and GALVESTON, NEW ORLEANS, Pensacola, and TAMPA in the U.S.

Mexico, National Autonomous University of Government-financed university in Mexico City, founded in 1551. The original university building, dating from 1584, was demolished in 1910, and the university was moved to a new campus in 1954. Between 1553 and 1867 the university was controlled by the Roman Catholic Church. After 1867, independent professional schools of law, medicine, engineering, and architecture were established by the government. The university was given administrative autonomy in 1929. It offers a broad range of programs in all major academic and professional subjects. Total enrollment is about 270,000.

Mexico City *officially* **Ciudad de México, D.F.** \ˌsyü-'t͟hät͟h-t͟hā-'me-hē-ˌkō\ Capital (metro. area pop., 1995 est.: 16,560,000) of the Federal District and of Mexico. Located at an elevation of 7,350 ft (2,240 m), and occupying an area of 571 sq mi (1,479 sq km), it is the world's larg-

est city proper and one of the world's fastest-growing metropolitan areas. It generates about one-third of Mexico's industrial production. It lies on an ancient lake bed, the site of the AZTEC capital, TENOCHTITLÁN, which was taken by the Spanish explorer HERNAN CORTES in 1521. It was the seat of the viceroyalty of NEW SPAIN throughout the colonial period. Captured by Mexican revolutionaries under Gen. AGUSTIN DE ITURBIDE in 1821, it was seized by the U.S. in 1847 during the MEXICAN WAR and by the French 1863–67 under MAXIMILIAN. It was greatly improved during the presidency of PORFIRIO DIAZ. In 1985 it was struck by a severe earthquake that killed 9,500 people. The old city center, the Zócalo, has many historic buildings, including the Metropolitan Cathedral (built on the site of an Aztec temple) and the National Palace (built on the ruins of the palace of MONTEZUMA II). Its educational institutions include the National Autonomous University of Mexico (founded 1551), the College of Mexico, and the Ibero-American Univ.

Meyer \ˈmī-ər\, **Adolf** (1866–1950) Swiss-U.S. psychiatrist. He emigrated to the U.S. in 1892, and taught principally at Johns Hopkins University (1910–41). He developed a concept of human behavior—ergasiology, or psychobiology—that sought to integrate psychological and biological study. Meyer emphasized accurate case histories, suggested a role of childhood sexual feelings in mental problems in the years preceding wide recognition of SIGMUND FREUD's theories, and decided that mental illness results essentially from personality dysfunction rather than brain pathology. He became aware of the importance of social environment in mental disorders, and his wife interviewed patients' families in what is considered the first psychiatric social work.

Meyerbeer \ˈmī-ər-ˌbār\, **Giacomo** *orig.* **Jakob Liebmann Meyer Beer** (1791–1864) German-French composer. Brother of the astronomer Wilhelm Beer (1797–1850) and the playwright Michael Beer (1800–1833), he achieved early success as a pianist. After studying vocal writing in Italy, his Italian operas were well received. In Paris from c. 1825, he undertook work on a libretto by E. SCRIBE, and his *Robert le diable*

(1831) was one of opera's greatest triumphs from its premiere. Three later grand operas also became part of the international repertoire: *Les Huguenots* (1836), *Le prophète* (1849), and *L'africaine* (1864). RICHARD WAGNER's criticism of Meyerbeer's "desertion" of German music, tainted by jealousy and anti-Semitism, led to neglect of his music for many years, but Meyerbeer exercised unmistakable influence on both GIUSEPPE VERDI and Wagner himself.

Meyerhof \'mī-ər-ˌhōf\, **Otto** (1884–1951) German biochemist. His work on glycolysis remains a basic contribution to the understanding of muscle action, despite the need for later revision. He shared with Archibald V. Hill (1886–1977) a 1922 Nobel Prize for his research on metabolism in muscle. His chief published work was *The Chemical Dynamics of Life Phenomena* (1924).

Meyerhold \'mī-ər-ˌhōlt\, **Vsevolod (Yemilyevich)** (1874–1940) Russian theatrical producer and director. He acted with the MOSCOW ART THEATRE in 1898 and formulated his avant-garde theories of symbolic theater. Opposed to the naturalism of KONSTANTIN STANISLAVSKY, he directed plays in a nonrepresentational style that became known as biomechanics. After 1908 he staged plays in St. Petersburg that drew on commedia dell'arte and Asian theater. He was noted for his direction of *The Magnificent Cuckold* (1920) and for his controversial production of *The Queen of Spades* (1935). Condemned by Soviet critics for his artistic individuality and opposition to socialist realism, he was arrested and imprisoned in 1939 and was probably executed.

mezzotint \'met-sō-ˌtint\ (from Italian, *mezza tinta:* "halftone") Engraving produced by pricking the surface of a metal plate with innumerable small holes that will hold ink; when the engraving is printed, the ink produces large areas of tone with soft, subtle gradations. Engraved or etched lines are often introduced to give the design greater definition. Mezzotint was invented in Holland by German-born LUDWIG VON SIEGEN in the 17th century but thereafter was practiced primarily in England. Its adaptability to making color prints made it ideal for reproduction of paintings. After the invention of photography it was rarely used. In recent years the technique has been revived, especially by U.S. and Japanese printmakers.

Mfecane \em-fe-'kä-nā\ ("The Crushing") Series of ZULU and other NGUNI wars and forced migrations in the early 19th century that changed the demographic, social, and political configuration of southern and central Africa. Set in motion by the rise of the Zulu military kingdom under SHAKA, it took place in the context of drought, social unrest, and competition for trade. Ethnic group was set against ethnic group in an ever-increasing radius, resulting in the creation of large refugee populations as well as the establishment of new kingdoms under the Basuto, Gaza, NDEBELE, and SWAZI peoples.

MGM *in full* **Metro-Goldwyn-Mayer, Inc.** U.S. corporation and film studio. It was formed when the film distributor Marcus Loew, who bought Metro Pictures in 1920, merged it with the Goldwyn production company in 1924 and with Louis B. Mayer Pictures in 1925. LOUIS B. MAYER was executive head of the studio for 25 years, assisted by production manager IRVING THALBERG. It reached its peak in the 1930s and '40s, when it had most of Hollywood's famous stars under contract. It produced such hits as *Grand Hotel* (1932), *The Good Earth* (1937), *The Philadelphia Story* (1940), *Gaslight* (1944), *The Asphalt Jungle* (1950), *Ben-Hur* (1959), *Doctor Zhivago* (1965), and *2001: A Space Odyssey* (1968). It was especially celebrated for its lavish musicals, including *The Wizard of Oz* (1939), *Easter Parade* (1948), *On the Town* (1949), *An American in Paris* (1951), *Singin' in the Rain* (1952), and *Gigi* (1958). MGM began to decline in the 1950s and sold off many of its assets in the 1970s. It diversified into hotels and casinos and later merged with UNITED ARTISTS CORP. as MGM/UA Entertainment. In 1986 it was bought by TED TURNER, who resold the production and distribution units. Various transfers of ownership led to its purchase in 1992 by Crédit Lyonnais, which restored the name MGM Inc. It was subsequently bought by Tracinda Corp.

MI-5 *in full* **Military Intelligence (Unit 5)** British Security Service. Originally organized in 1909 to counter German espionage, in 1931 it assumed wider responsibility for assessing threats to national security, including international communist subversion and subsequently fascism. Today the Security Service Act (1989) forms its statutory basis. As Britain's domestic-security intelligence agency, its purpose is to protect against such threats as terrorism, espionage, and subversion. Since the passing of the Security Service Act (1996), its role has been expanded to provide support to law-enforcement agencies in the field of organized crime.

Miami ALGONQUIAN-speaking Indian people who lived in various settlements between Wisconsin and Ohio but eventually consolidated in Indiana. The staple of the Miami diet was corn, though bison were hunted. Each village consisted of mat-covered dwellings and a large house in which councils and ceremonies were held. A secret medicine society conducted rites aimed at ensuring tribal welfare. In the 19th century the Miami ceded most of their lands to the U.S., with one band remaining in Indiana and the rest removing to a reservation in Oklahoma. In 1990 there were about 4,500 Miami in the U.S. See also LITTLE TURTLE.

Miami City (pop., 2000: 362,470), southeastern Florida, situated on BISCAYNE BAY at the mouth of the Miami River. The southernmost large city in the continental U.S., it has a beach 7 mi (11 km) long. A Spanish mission was founded near the site in 1567, but permanent settlement did not begin until 1835, when U.S. forces built Fort Dallas for the removal of SEMINOLE Indians to the West. The arrival of the railway in 1896 spurred development, and Miami was incorporated the same year. The city has been damaged by occasional hurricanes, notably in 1926 and 1935. Nearly 300,000 Cuban refugees have arrived since 1959 (see CUBA), establishing "Little Havana" within the city. It is a major resort and retirement center, and its port handles the world's largest number of cruise-ship passengers. It is also a banking center. Educational institutions include the University of MIAMI and Florida International Univ.

Miami, University of Private university in Coral Gables, Fla., founded in 1925. Through its 14 schools and colleges it offers comprehensive undergraduate, graduate, and professional programs, including schools of medicine, law, architecture, and marine and atmospheric science. Research facilities include centers and institutes for the study of aging, vision, international studies, and molecular and cellular evolution. Total enrollment is about 14,000.

Miami Beach City (pop., 2000: 87,933), southeastern Florida. It is situated on an island across BISCAYNE BAY from MIAMI. Until 1912 the site was a mangrove swamp. John S. Collins and Carl F. Fisher pioneered real estate development and built a bridge across the bay; the area was dredged to form an island measuring 7.4 sq mi (19 sq km), with an 8-mi (13-km) beach. The city, incorporated in 1915, is now a luxury resort and convention center. It is connected with Miami by several causeways and is noted for its ART DECO architecture.

Miami University Public university in Oxford, Ohio, founded in 1809 and named for the Miami River. It offers undergraduate and graduate degrees in the liberal arts, sciences, and business management. Two branch campuses award associate's degrees only. The main campus is the site of the McGuffey Museum, a national historic landmark. Total enrollment is about 20,000.

Miao See HMONG

Miao-Yao languages See HMONG-MIEN LANGUAGES

mica \'mī-kə\ Any of a group of hydrous potassium, aluminum SILICATE MINERALS that exhibit a two-dimensional sheet, or layer, structure. A very abundant variety of mica is MUSCOVITE; two other common varieties are BIOTITE and phlogopite. Micas have various industrial uses. The varieties that contain little iron are used as thermal or electrical insulators in appliances and in such electrical devices as capacitors. In ground form, micas are used in the manufacture of wallpaper, roofing paper, and paint. Ground micas also serve as lubricants, absorbents, and packing material.

mica, black See BIOTITE

Micah \'mī-kə\ (late 8th century BC) One of the 12 Minor Prophets in the OLD TESTAMENT, traditional author of the Book of Micah. (His prophecy is part of a larger book, The Twelve, in the Jewish canon.) He probably began to prophesy before the fall of the northern kingdom of Israel in 721 BC. Modern scholars usually attribute the book's first three chapters, which predict judgment from God on idolaters and unjust leaders, to Micah. Much of the rest, which promises the establishment of a kingdom of peace in Zion, probably dates from several centuries later.

Michael In the BIBLE and the QURAN, one of the archangels. The captain of the heavenly hosts, he was invoked by early Christian armies against the heathen. In Christian tradition he is thought to escort the soul into the presence of God at the time of death. In art he is depicted as a warrior, sword in hand, in triumph over a dragon. His feast day, known in England as Michaelmas, is September 29. See also MIKAL.

Michael (born 1921) King of Romania. After his father, the future king CAROL II, had been excluded from the royal succession (1926), Michael was proclaimed king under a three-member regency. Carol reclaimed the throne in 1930, and Michael was reduced to crown prince. With Carol's abdication in 1940, Michael again became king but was in effect a prisoner of the military dictator ION ANTONESCU. In 1944 he helped lead the coup that overthrew the military regime and severed Romania's ties with the Axis powers. He strongly opposed the communists' subsequent rise to power, but was forced to abdicate in 1947. He went into exile in Switzerland and became an executive with a U.S. brokerage firm.

Michael *or* **Michael Romanov** \rō-'mä-nəf, 'rō-mə-ˌnäf\ *Russian* **Mikhail Fyodorovich Romanov** (1596–1645) Czar of Russia (1613–45) and founder of the ROMANOV DYNASTY. A young nobleman elected as czar after the chaotic Time of TROUBLES, he allowed his mother's relatives to direct the government early in his reign. They restored order to Russia and made peace with Sweden (1617) and Poland (1618). In 1619 his father, released from captivity in Poland, returned to Russia and became coruler. Michael's father dominated the government, increasing contact with Western Europe and strengthening central authority and serfdom. After his death in 1633, Michael's maternal relatives once again held sway.

Michael VIII Palaeologus \ˌpā-lē-'äl-ə-gəs\ (1224?–1282) Nicaean emperor (1259–61) and Byzantine emperor (1261–82), founder of the Palaeologan dynasty. Appointed regent for the 6-year-old son of Theodore II (1258), he seized the throne and blinded the rightful heir. He recovered Constantinople from the Latins (1261) and allied with the pope against his rivals, briefly reuniting Greek and Roman churches in 1274 (see Councils of LYON). In 1281 the new pope, Martin IV, excommunicated him and declared Charles of Anjou's planned campaign against Byzantium to be a holy crusade against the schismatic Greeks. The SICILIAN VESPERS prevented Charles's expedition and thus saved Byzantium from a second occupation by the Latins.

Michael Cerularius \ˌker-ü-'lär-ē-əs\ (c. 1000–1059) Greek Orthodox patriarch of Constantinople (1043–58). He thwarted CONSTANTINE IX's efforts to ally the Byzantine and Roman empires against the Normans, and he closed Latin churches in Constantinople that refused to use the Greek language and liturgy (1052). When negotiations broke down between Michael and the papal legates sent by LEO IX, each side excommunicated the other, initiating the SCHISM OF 1054. Michael forced Constantine to support the schism, but in 1058 he was exiled by Constantine's successor.

Michaelis-Menten hypothesis \mi-'kā-ləs-'men-tən\ Explanation of the speed and general mechanism of enzyme-catalyzed reactions. First stated in 1913, it assumes that a complex between an ENZYME and its substrate (the substance on which it acts) forms rapidly and reversibly. In addition, the rate of formation of the product of the enzymatic action is assumed to be proportional to the concentration of the complex. The speed of enzymatic action is greatest when the substrate concentration is very high. These relationships provide the basis for all studies of enzymes and have been applied to studies of the effects of carriers on the transport of substances through cell membranes.

Michaels, Lorne (born 1944) Canadian-U.S. television writer and producer. Born in Toronto, he began his career as a television writer (1968–75). He created and produced the hit late-night comedy show *Saturday Night Live* (1975–80, 1985–), which featured many up-and-coming comedians. He has produced *Late Night with Conan O'Brien*, has cowritten and produced numerous television specials, and has won eight Emmy awards.

Michelangelo (di Lodovico Buonarroti) (1475–1564) Italian sculptor, painter, architect, and poet. Born in Caprese, he served a brief apprenticeship with DOMENICO GHIRLANDAIO in Florence before beginning the first of several sculptures for LORENZO DE'MEDICI. After Lorenzo's death in 1492, he left for Bologna and then for Rome. There his *Bacchus* (1496–97) established his fame and led to a commission for the *Pietà* now in ST. PETER'S BASILICA, the masterpiece of his early years, in which he demonstrated his unique ability to extract two distinct figures from one marble block. His *David* (1501–4), commissioned for the cathedral of Florence, is still considered the prime example of the Renaissance ideal of perfect humanity. On the side he produced several Madonnas for private patrons and his only universally accepted easel painting, *The Holy Family* (known as the *Doni Tondo*). Attracted to ambitious sculptural projects, which he did not always complete, he reluctantly agreed to paint the ceiling of the SISTINE CHAPEL (1508–12). The first scenes, depicting the story of Noah, are relatively stable and on a small scale, but his confidence grew as he proceeded, and the later scenes evince boldness and complexity. His figures for the tombs in Florence's Medici Chapel (1519–33), which he designed, are among his most accomplished creations. He devoted his last 30 years largely to the *Last Judgment* fresco in the Sistine Chapel, to writing poetry (he left more than 300 sonnets and madrigals), and to architecture. He was commissioned to complete St. Peter's Basilica, begun in 1506 and little advanced since 1514. Though it was not quite finished at Michelangelo's death, its exterior owes more to him than to any other architect. He is regarded today as among the most exalted of artists.

Michelet \mēsh-'le\, **Jules** (1798–1874) French nationalist historian. He taught history and philosophy before he was appointed head of the historical section of the Record Office in 1831. His time there provided him with unique resources for his life's work, the 17-volume *Histoire de France* (1833–67). His method, an attempt to resurrect the past by immersing his own personality in his narrative, resulted in a historical synthesis of great dramatic power, though the 11 volumes that appeared in 1855–67 are distorted by his hatred of priests and kings, hasty or abusive treatment of documents, and mania for symbolic interpretation. His other works include the vivid and impassioned *Histoire de la révolution française* (7 vols., 1847–53). In his later years he wrote a series of lyrical books on nature, displaying his superb prose style.

Michelet, detail of an oil painting by Thomas Couture; in the Carnavalet Museum, Paris.
GIRAUDON—ART RESOURCE

Michelin \ˌmē-shə-'laⁿ\ Leading French manufacturer of tires and other rubber products. It was founded in 1888 by the Michelin brothers, André (1853–1931) and Édouard (1859–1940), to manufacture tires for bicycles and horse-drawn carriages. It introduced pneumatic tires for automobiles in the 1890s and soon became one of the major European tire producers. Michelin opened its first foreign plant in Turin in 1906 and today operates plants in many countries; it was reorganized as a HOLDING COMPANY in 1951. It also publishes a famous series of travel guides and road maps. Its headquarters are at Clermont-Ferrand.

Michelson \'mī-kəl-sən\, **A(lbert) A(braham)** (1852–1931) U.S. (Prussian-born) physicist. His family emigrated to the U.S. in 1854. He studied at the U.S. Naval Academy and in Europe, and later taught principally at the University of Chicago (1892–1931), where he headed the physics department. He invented the interferometer, with which he used light to make extremely precise measurements. He is best remembered for the MICHELSON-MORLEY EXPERIMENT, undertaken with Edward W. Morley (1838–1923), which established that the speed of light is a fundamental constant. Using a more refined interferometer, Michelson measured the diameter of the star Betelgeuse, the first substantially accurate determination of the size of a star. In 1907 he became the first American scientist to receive a Nobel Prize.

Michelson-Morley experiment Attempt to detect the VELOCITY of the earth with respect to ether, a hypothetical medium in space formerly proposed to carry light waves. It was first performed in Berlin in 1881 by A. A. MICHELSON and refined in the U.S. in 1887 by Michelson and Edward W. Morley (1838–1923). The procedure assumed that if the speed of light were constant with respect to the ether, the motion of the earth could be detected by comparing the speed of light in the direction of earth's motion and the speed of light at right angles to earth's motion. No difference was found, and the result discredited the ether theory. As

L
M
N

a result, ALBERT EINSTEIN proposed in 1905 that the speed of light is a universal constant.

Michener \'mich-nər\, **James A(lbert)** (1907?–1997) U.S. novelist and short-story writer. Michener was a foundling discovered in Doylestown, Pa., and raised as a Quaker. Initially a teacher, during 1944–46 he was a naval historian in the South Pacific, the area of his early fiction; his *Tales of the South Pacific* (1947, Pulitzer Prize) was adapted as the Broadway musical *South Pacific* (1949; film, 1958). He is best known for epic and detailed novels drawing on extensive research, including *Hawaii* (1959; film, 1966), *Centennial* (1974), *Chesapeake* (1978), *Space* (1982), and *Mexico* (1992).

Michigan State (pop., 1997 est.: 9,774,000), midwestern U.S. Surrounded almost entirely by the GREAT LAKES, it covers 58,527 sq mi (151,585 sq km); its capital is LANSING. Michigan is divided into two large land segments: the Upper and Lower peninsulas. The western region of the Upper Peninsula is a rugged upland rich in minerals, and the remainder of the state consists of lowlands and rolling hills. The area was originally inhabited by ALGONQUIAN-speaking Indians. The French arrived in the 17th century, founding SAULT STE. MARIE in 1668 and DETROIT in 1701; fur trading was their primary activity. The English gained control of Michigan in 1763 following the FRENCH AND INDIAN WAR, and it passed to the U.S. in 1783. It was included in the NORTHWEST TERRITORIES in 1787 and in Indiana Territory in 1800. Michigan Territory was organized on the Lower Peninsula in 1805. Though surrendered to the British in the WAR OF 1812, U.S. rule was restored in 1813 by the victory of OLIVER PERRY at the Battle of Lake Erie. A boundary dispute with Ohio, known as the Toledo War, was settled by Congress, with Michigan receiving the Upper Peninsula and statehood as compensation. In 1837 it became the 26th U.S. state. Throughout the AMERICAN CIVIL WAR, it made major contributions to the Union cause. In the 20th century its economy has been dominated by the automotive industry.

Michigan, Lake Third-largest of the five GREAT LAKES, and the only one lying wholly within the U.S. Bordered by the states of Michigan, Wisconsin, Illinois, and Indiana, it connects with Lake HURON through the Straits of MACKINAC in the north. It is 321 mi (517 km) long and up to 118 mi (190 km) wide, with a maximum depth of 923 ft (281 m); it occupies an area of 22,300 sq mi (57,757 sq km). The first European to discover it was the French explorer JEAN NICOLET in 1634; R.-R. LA SALLE brought the first sailing ship there in 1679. It now attracts international shipping as part of the Great Lakes-St. Lawrence Seaway. The name is derived from the Algonquian word *michigami* or *misschiganin*, meaning "big lake."

Michigan, University of State university with its main campus in Ann Arbor and branch campuses in Flint and Dearborn. It originated as a preparatory school in Detroit in 1817 and moved to Ann Arbor in 1837. Today it is one of the nation's leading research universities, consisting of a college of literature, science, and the arts and numerous graduate and professional schools. Special facilities include a nuclear reactor, a hospital complex, an aerospace engineering laboratory, a Great Lakes research center, and the Gerald R. Ford Presidential Library. Enrollment at the main campus is about 37,000.

Michigan State University Public university in East Lansing. Chartered in 1855, it became the prototype for the land-grant colleges created under the MORRILL ACT of 1862. It offers comprehensive undergraduate, graduate, and professional degree programs. Campus facilities include a plant research laboratory, the National Superconducting Cyclotron laboratory, and centers for international studies, economic development, and environmental toxicology. Total enrollment is about 42,000.

Michizane See SUGAWARA MICHIZANE

Michoacán \,mē-chō-ä-'kän\ State (pop., 1995 est.: 3,871,000), southwestern Mexico. Bounded by the Pacific Ocean, and occupying an area of 23,138 sq mi (59,928 sq km), it rises from a narrow coastal plain to the SIERRA MADRE. Its capital is MORELIA; other important cities are Uruapan, Zamora, and Pátzcuaro. In the 1530s the Dominican Vasco de Quiroga established the first successful missions among the Tarascan Indians around Lake Pátzcuaro. The state lies in an area of great volcanic activity: Mount Jorullo was formed by an eruption in 1759, and PARICUTÍN was created by an eruption that lasted from 1943 to 1952. It produces a wide range of forest products and tropical crops.

Mickey Mouse Famous character of WALT DISNEY's animated cartoons. He was introduced in *Steamboat Willie* (1928), the first animated cartoon with sound. Mickey was created by Disney, who also provided his high-pitched voice, and was usually drawn by the studio's head animator, Ub Iwerks. Noted for his overlarge head and round black ears, he became the star of over 100 cartoon shorts. In 1932 Disney received an honorary Academy Award for his creation.

Mickiewicz \mʸēts-'kʸe-vʸēch\, **Adam (Bernard)** (1798–1855) Polish poet. A lifelong apostle of Polish national freedom and one of Poland's greatest poets, Mickiewicz was deported to Russia for his revolutionary activities in 1823 and later settled in Paris. His *Poezja* (2 vols., 1822–23; "Poetry") was the first major Polish Romantic work; it contained two parts of *Forefathers' Eve,* a cycle combining folklore and mystic patriotism. Other works include the erotic *Sonnets from the Crimea* (1826); *The Books of Our Pilgrimage* (1832), a prose interpretation of the history of the Poles; and his masterpiece, the poetic epic *Master Thaddeus* (1834), which describes the life of the Polish gentry in the early 19th century. He also was a professor, edited a radical newspaper, and undertook missions on behalf of Poland.

Micmac Largest of the Indian tribes of Canada's eastern Maritime Provinces. Early chronicles describe them as fierce and warlike, but they were among the first Indians to accept Jesuit teachings and intermarry with the settlers of New France. The Micmac formed a confederacy of several CLANS. In winter they hunted caribou, moose, and small game; in summer they fished, gathered shellfish, and hunted seals. They were expert canoeists. In the 17th–18th century they were allies of the French against the English. Today their descendants, mixed with whites, number about 15,000.

Micon *or* **Mikon** \'mī-,kän\ (5th century BC) Greek painter and sculptor. A contemporary and pupil of POLYGNOTUS, he joined him in developing the treatment of space and perspective in Greek painting. Mikon is known for the mural painting on the Stoa Poikile (Painted Portico) on the Agora at Athens and for the paintings at the Theseum at Athens. His innovations in spatial elaboration helped initiate the decline of Greek pottery painting.

microbiology Scientific study of microorganisms, a diverse group of simple life-forms including PROTOZOANS, ALGAE, MOLDS, BACTERIA, and VIRUSES. Microbiology is concerned with the structure, function, and classification of these organisms and with ways of controlling and using their activities. Its foundations were established in the later 19th century, with the work of LOUIS PASTEUR and ROBERT KOCH. Since then, many disease-causing microorganisms have been identified and means of controlling their harmful effects have been developed. In addition, means of channeling the activities of various microorganisms to benefit medicine, industry, and agriculture have been discovered. Molds, for example, produce ANTIBIOTICS, notably PENICILLIN. See also BACTERIOLOGY, GENETIC ENGINEERING.

microchip See INTEGRATED CIRCUIT

microcircuit See INTEGRATED CIRCUIT

microclimate Climatic condition in a relatively small area, within a few feet above and below the earth's surface and within canopies of vegetation. Microclimates are affected by such factors as temperature, humidity, wind and turbulence, dew, frost, heat balance, evaporation, the nature of the soil and vegetation, the local topography, latitude, elevation, and season. Weather and climate are sometimes influenced by microclimatic conditions, especially by variations in surface characteristics.

microcline Common FELDSPAR mineral, one form of potassium aluminosilicate ($KAlSi_3O_8$) that occurs in many rock types. Green specimens are called amazonstone and may be used as gems. It is an end-member composition in the alkali feldspar series. See also ORTHOCLASE.

micrococcus \,mī-krō-'kä-kəs\ Any of the spherical BACTERIA that make up the genus *Micrococcus,* which are widespread in nature. These gram-positive (see GRAM STAIN) cocci (see COCCUS) are usually not considered to cause disease. They are normal inhabitants of the human body and may even be essential in keeping the balance among the various microorganisms found on the skin. Some species are found in the dust of the air, in soil, in marine waters, and on the skin of vertebrates. Certain species are found in milk and can result in spoilage.

microcomputer Small DIGITAL COMPUTERS whose CPU is contained on a single integrated SEMICONDUCTOR chip. As large-scale and then very large-scale integration (VLSI) have progressively increased the number of TRANSISTORS that can be placed on one chip, the processing capacity of microcomputers has grown immensely. The PERSONAL COMPUTER is the most common example of a microcomputer, but high-performance microcomputer systems are widely used in business, in engineering, and in "smart" machines in manufacturing. See also INTEGRATED CIRCUIT, MICROPROCESSOR.

microeconomics Study of the economic behavior of individual consumers, firms, and industries and the distribution of total production and income among them. It considers individuals both as suppliers of LAND, LABOR, and CAPITAL and as the ultimate consumers of the final product, and it examines firms both as suppliers of products and as consumers of labor and capital. Microeconomics seeks to analyze the MARKET or other mechanisms that establish relative prices among goods and services and allocate society's resources among their many possible uses. See also MACROECONOMICS.

micrometer (caliper) \mī-'krä-mə-tər\ Instrument for making precise linear measurements of dimensions such as diameters, thicknesses, and lengths of solid bodies. It consists of a C-shaped frame with a movable jaw operated by a screw. The accuracy of the measurements depends on the accuracy of the screw–nut combination.

Micronesia Group of western Pacific islands. A subdivision of OCEANIA, it comprises KIRIBATI, GUAM, NAURU, the Northern MARIANAS, the FEDERATED STATES OF MICRONESIA, the MARSHALL ISLANDS, and PALAU. Located mostly north of the equator, it includes the westernmost of the Pacific Islands. It was first colonized in the 17th century by Spain, which sold the islands to Germany in 1885–99. Japan occupied the islands in 1914 and was granted a mandate to govern them in 1920. The U.S. occupied Micronesia in 1944 and received a trusteeship mandate in 1947. A government on the U.S. model was created in 1968. In 1973–74 the Congress of Micronesia adopted guidelines for independence, but regional differences led to a division of the islands into several constituencies after 1978.

Micronesia, Federated States of Republic, western Pacific Ocean. It comprises the four island states of Yap, Chuuk (Truk), Pohnpei (Ponape), and Kosrae, all in the CAROLINE ISLANDS. Area: 271 sq mi (701 sq km). Population (1999 est.): 116,268. Capital: PALIKIR on the island of Pohnpei, the largest island. The people of the Federated States are Micronesian. Languages: Malayo-Polynesian languages, English. Religions: Christianity (predominant). Currency: U.S. dollar. The islands and atolls extend about 1,750 mi (2,800 km) east–west and about 600 mi (965 km) north–south. U.S. government grants constitute the main source of revenue; subsistence farming and fishing are the principal economic activities. It is a republic in free association with the U.S., and has one legislative house; its head of state and government is the president. The islands were probably settled by people from eastern Melanesia some 3,500 years ago. They were colonized by Spain in the 17th century and came under Japanese rule after World War I. They were captured by U.S. forces during World War II, and in 1947 they became part of the U.N. Trust Territory of the Pacific Islands, administered by the U.S. The islands became an internally self-governing federation in 1979. In 1982 the Federated States signed a compact of free association with the U.S., which is responsible for Micronesia's defense until 2001. In the late 1990s, the republic was struggling to solve its economic difficulties.

microphone Device for converting sound waves into electric power that has wave characteristics essentially similar to those of the sound. By proper design, a microphone may be given directional characteristics so that it will pick up sound primarily from a single direction, from two directions, or more or less uniformly from all directions. In addition to their use in telephone transmitters, microphones are most widely applied in hearing aids, sound-recording systems (principally magnetic and digital tape recorders), dictating machines, and public-address systems. See illustration opposite.

microprocessor Miniature electronic device that contains the arithmetic, logic, and control circuitry needed to function as a DIGITAL COMPUTER's CPU. Microprocessors are INTEGRATED CIRCUITS that can interpret and execute program instructions as well as handle arithmetic operations. Their development in the late 1970s enabled computer engineers to develop MICROCOMPUTERS. Microprocessors led to "intelligent" terminals, such as bank ATMs and point-of-sale devices, and to automatic control of much industrial instrumentation and hospital equipment, programmable microwave ovens, and electronic games. Many automobiles use microprocessor-controlled ignition and fuel systems.

microprogramming Process of writing microcode for a MICROPROCESSOR. Microcode is low-level code that defines how a microprocessor should function when it executes MACHINE-LANGUAGE instructions. Typically, one machine-language instruction translates into several microcode instructions. On some computers, the microcode is stored in ROM and cannot be modified; on some larger computers, it is stored in EPROM and therefore can be replaced with newer versions.

microscope Instrument that produces enlarged images of small objects, allowing them to be viewed at a scale convenient for examination and analysis. Formed by various means, the image is received by direct imaging, electronic processing, or a combination of these methods. The most familiar type of microscope is the optical, or light, microscope, in which LENSES are used to form the image. Other types of microscopes use the wave nature of various physical processes, the most important being the electron microscope (see ELECTRON MICROSCOPY), which uses a beam of ELECTRONS in its image formation. Crude microscopes date to the mid-15th century, but not until 1674 were the powerful microscopes of A. VAN LEEUWENHOEK able to detect phenomena as small as protozoa.

Microsoft Corp. U.S. computer firm, the leading developer of personal-computer software systems and applications. Microsoft, headquartered in Redmond, Wash., also publishes books and multimedia titles and manufactures hardware. It was founded in 1975 by BILL GATES and Paul G. Allen (born 1954), who adapted BASIC for use on PERSONAL COMPUTERS. They licensed versions of it to various companies, developed other programming languages, and in 1981 released MS-DOS for the IBM PC. The subsequent adoption of MS-DOS by most other personal-com-

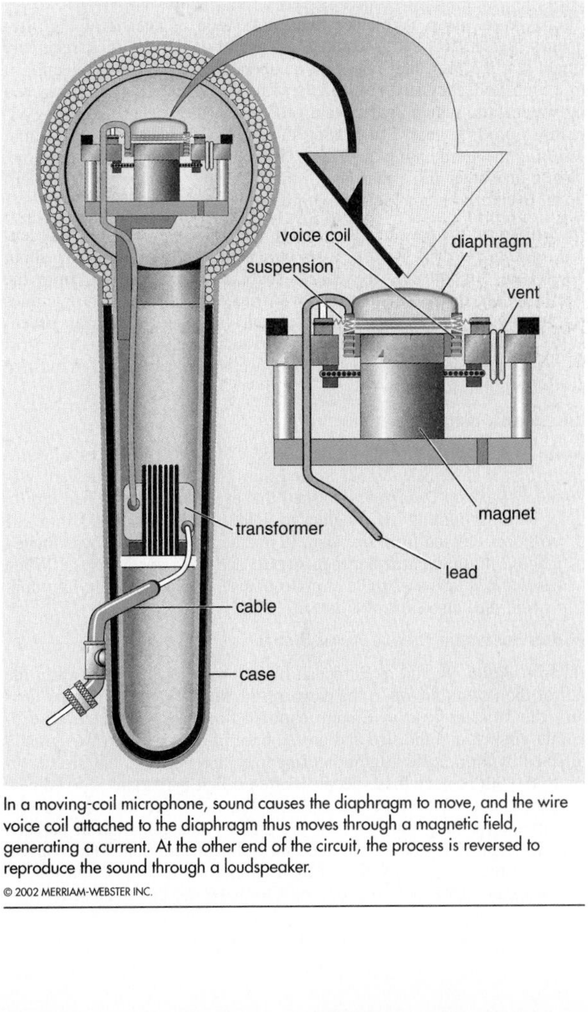

In a moving-coil microphone, sound causes the diaphragm to move, and the wire voice coil attached to the diaphragm thus moves through a magnetic field, generating a current. At the other end of the circuit, the process is reversed to reproduce the sound through a loudspeaker.

puter manufacturers generated vast revenues for Microsoft, which became a publicly owned corporation in 1986. It issued the first version of Microsoft Word, its popular word-processing program, in 1983, and Microsoft Windows, a GRAPHICAL USER INTERFACE for MS-DOS-based computers, in 1985. In 1999, following a trial that lasted 30 months, Microsoft was found in violation of the Sherman Antitrust Act. Microsoft immediately began an appeals process that was expected to reach the U.S. Supreme Court.

microsurgery *or* **micromanipulation** Surgical technique for operating on minute structures, with specialized, tiny precision instruments under observation through a microscope, sometimes equipped with cameras to show the operation on a monitor. Microsurgery permits operations that were once impossible—surgery on the delicate bones of the inner and middle ear, reattachment of severed limbs or digits, repair of the retina, and removal of tumors intricately embedded in vital structures.

microtubule \ˌmī-krō-ˈtü-byül\ Thin tubular structure enclosed by a membrane. Of varying length, microtubules are found within animal and plant cells. They have several functions. They help give shape to many cells and are major components of cilia and flagella, participate in the formation of spindle fibers during cell division (MITOSIS), and assist the flow of materials from the cell bodies of nerve cells toward the ends of those cells' long extensions (axons).

microwave Portion of the spectrum of ELECTROMAGNETIC RADIATION with frequencies between about 1 gigahertz (10^9 Hz) and 1 terahertz (10^{12} Hz). Microwaves are the principal carriers of television, telephone, and data transmissions between stations on earth and between earth and satellites. RADAR beams are short pulses of microwaves used to locate ships and planes, track weather systems, and determine the speeds of moving objects. Objects such as glass and ceramics do not absorb microwaves and are not heated by them; metals, however, reflect microwaves, so metal containers block them out. See also MASER, MICROWAVE OVEN.

microwave oven Appliance that cooks food by means of high-frequency ELECTROMAGNETIC RADIATION. A microwave oven is a relatively small, boxlike oven that raises the temperature of food by subjecting it to a high-frequency ELECTROMAGNETIC FIELD. The microwaves are absorbed by water, fats, sugars, and certain other molecules, whose resulting vibrations produce heat. The heating thus occurs inside the food, without warming the surrounding air. This process greatly reduces cooking time; baking and other tasks that may require an hour or more in a conventional oven can be completed in minutes in a microwave oven.

Mid-Atlantic Ridge Submarine ridge lying along the floor of the central Atlantic Ocean. It is a long mountain chain running for about 10,000 mi (16,000 km) in a north–south direction, curving from the Arctic Ocean to the southern tip of Africa. The mountains sometimes reach above sea level, forming such islands or island groups as Ascension, ST. HELENA, and Tristan da Cunha. Running along its crest is a rift in which molten magma continuously wells up, cools, and is pushed away from the ridge.

mid-ocean ridge See OCEANIC RIDGE

Midas \ˈmī-dəs\ In Greek and Roman legend, a king of PHRYGIA. Midas captured the satyr Silenus but treated him kindly, and as a reward was granted a wish by DIONYSUS. He asked that everything he touched turn to gold; but after turning his daughter to gold when she embraced him, he asked to be released from his wish. In another legend Midas was invited to judge a music contest between APOLLO and the satyr Marsyas. When Midas decided against Apollo, Apollo punished him by giving him donkey's ears. See also SATYR AND SILENUS.

Midas See MISSILE DEFENSE ALARM SYSTEM

Middle Ages Period in European history traditionally dated from the fall of the ROMAN EMPIRE to the dawn of the RENAISSANCE. In the 5th century the Western Roman Empire endured declines in population, economic vitality, and the size and prominence of cities. It also was greatly affected by a dramatic migration of peoples that began in the 3rd century. In the 5th century these peoples, often called barbarians, carved new kingdoms out of the decrepit Western Empire. Over the next several centuries these kingdoms oversaw the gradual amalgamation of barbarian, Christian, and Roman cultural and political traditions. The longest lasting of these kingdoms, that of the Franks, laid the foundation for later European states. It also produced CHARLEMAGNE, the greatest ruler of the Middle Ages, whose reign was a model for centuries to come. The collapse of Charlemagne's empire and a fresh wave of invasions led to a restructuring of medieval society. The 11th through 13th centuries mark the high point of medieval civilization. The church underwent reform that strengthened the place of the pope in church and society but led to clashes between the pope and emperor. Population growth, the flourishing of towns and farms, the emergence of merchant classes, and the development of governmental bureaucracies were part of cultural and economic revival during this period. Meanwhile, thousands of knights followed the call of the church to join the CRUSADES. Medieval civilization reached its apex in the 13th century with the emergence of GOTHIC ARCHITECTURE, the appearance of new religious orders, and the expansion of learning and the university. The church dominated intellectual life, producing the SCHOLASTICISM of St. THOMAS AQUINAS. The decline of the Middle Ages resulted from the break down of medieval national governments, the great papal schism, the critique of medieval theology and philosphy, and economic and population collapse brought on by famine and disease.

Middle Congo See Republic of the CONGO

Middle East *or* **Mideast** Region comprising the countries of South Asia and North Africa. It is an unofficial and imprecise term that now generally encompasses the lands around the southern and eastern shores of the Mediterranean Sea, notably Libya, Egypt, Jordan, Israel, Lebanon, and Syria, as well as Iran, Iraq, and the countries of the Arabian Peninsula. The term was formerly used by Western geographers and historians to describe the region from the Persian Gulf to S.East Asia.

Middle Eastern music Music of the Arabic, Turkish, and Persian Muslim world. Despite three major languages and associated cultural differences, the music can be seen as a single great tradition because of the unifying element of Islam. The fact that Islam has historically found music problematic has resulted in relatively little religious ceremonial music, but has not held back secular music, and has even enriched it with a strong religious strain. Only certain sects, such as SUFISM, have used music (and dance) for worship, music in the mosque having generally been limited to the call to prayer and the chanting of the Quran. Folk music and art music differ less in the Middle East than elsewhere, because folk music, like art music, has long been the province of professionals (including many women), and art music has represented merely the refinement of basic folk elements. Both tend to feature soloists, either alone or accompanied by a small group. Rhythmic treatment is similar, being closely related to principles of PROSODY, and both include characteristic nonmetric improvisations. The modes *(maqam)* are the same in both folk and art music, and how they are used bears some resemblance to the RAGA in INDIAN MUSIC. The main formal principle is an alternation of composed and improvised sections, the composed portions being accompanied by percussion beating one of a number of traditional patterns. Accompanying melodic instruments play in unison with the solo line during the composed parts, and echo it one or two beats behind in the improvised parts. Especially after 1950, the rise of Western-influenced commercial popular music affected Middle Eastern art music, which now employs less improvisation and more strict unison between parts, in shorter pieces. The Middle East has been an important source of musical instruments for other parts of the world, including BAGPIPES, GUITAR, LUTE, OBOE, TAMBOURINE, VIOLS, and ZITHERS.

Middle English Vernacular spoken and written in England c. 1100–1500, the descendant of OLD ENGLISH and the ancestor of Modern English. It can be divided into three periods: Early, Central, and Late. The Central period was marked by the borrowing of many Anglo-Norman words and the rise of the London dialect, used by such poets as JOHN GOWER and GEOFFREY CHAUCER in a 14th-century flowering of English literature. The dialects of Middle English are usually divided into four groups: Southern, East Midland, West Midland, and Northern.

Middle West See MIDWEST

Middlebury College Private liberal-arts college in Middlebury, Vt., founded in 1800. It is known for its curriculum emphasizing modern languages. Middlebury sponsors the Bread Loaf Writers' Conference, an annual gathering for established and aspiring authors. Student enrollment is about 2,100.

Middlesbrough \ˈmi-dᵊlz-brə\ Town (pop., 1994 est.: 147,000), seat of CLEVELAND CO., England. Situated on the southern bank of the TEES RIVER, it was formed in 1830 with the arrival of the railway to the site of a new coal-exporting port. Its development was later fostered by the discovery of ironstone nearby.

Middlesex Former county, southeastern England, situated along the Thames River. Its earliest settlements date from 500 BC; Belgic tribes arrived in the 1st century BC, followed by the Romans, who established outposts along the river. It was colonized by Saxons in the early 5th century AD. Situated between the East and West Saxons, it obtained its name (meaning "middle Saxons") by AD 704. Middlesex was established as an administrative county in 1888. In 1965 Greater London incorporated parts from the former county.

Middleton, Thomas (1570?–1627) British playwright. He studied at Oxford University and had written three books of poetry by 1600. He learned to write plays by collaborating with John Webster and others on works for the producer Philip Henslowe. His tragedies *Women Beware Women* (c. 1621) and *The Changeling* (1622, with William Rowley) are considered his masterpieces. His comedies, which picture a society dazzled by money, included *Michaelmas Terme* (c. 1605), *A Trick to Catch the Old-one* (1608), *A Mad World, My Masters* (1608), *A Chast Mayd in Cheape-side* (c. 1613), and *A Game at Chess* (1625).

middot \mē-ˈdōt\ In Jewish biblical interpretation, the principles used to explicate the meaning of biblical words or passages. The middot are used especially to determine the bearing that a passage has on a new question or situation. The first known middot were compiled by Hillel in the 1st century BC; others were compiled by Ishmael ben Elisha (c. AD 100) and Eliezer ben Yose the Galilaean (c. AD 150). Among the best-known are the *kol wa-homer* ("how much more"), in which the interpreter proceeds from a minor to a major premise, and the *gezera shawa* (comparison of similar expressions or laws), in which an inference is made by analogy.

Midgard In Norse mythology, the dwelling place of humankind. According to legend, it was made from the body of the first created being, the giant Aurgelmir (Ymir). The gods killed him and rolled his body into the central void of the universe, forming the land from his flesh, the oceans from his blood, the mountains from his bones, and so on. Aurgelmir's skull, held up by four dwarfs, became the dome of the heavens. The sun, moon, and stars were made of scattered sparks caught in the skull.

midge Any of a group of tiny dipterans, sometimes called gnats and classified as nonbiting (family Chironomidae), biting (family Ceratopogonidae), or gall (family Cecidomyiidae) midges. Nonbiting midges resemble mosquitoes but are harmless. Humming swarms can be found around water in late afternoon. The often blood-red, aquatic larvae (bloodworms) are important food for aquatic animals. Biting midges (no-see-ums) are the smallest bloodsucking insect (about 0.04 in., or 1 mm, long). Punkies or sand flies (genera *Culicoides* and *Leptoconops*) attack humans but do not transmit disease; many species attack other insects. Gall-midge larvae cause tissue swellings (galls) in plants.

Midge (Chironomidae).
N.A. CALLOW

Midgley, Thomas, Jr. (1889–1944) U.S. engineer and chemist. Born in Beaver Falls, Pa., he studied at Cornell University and later worked as an industrial researcher and administrator. In 1921 he discovered the effectiveness of tetraethyl lead as an antiknock additive for gasoline. He also discovered dichlorodifluoromethane, a refrigerant sold commercially as Freon-12 (see Freon), which with related compounds came into universal use as refrigerants and later as aerosol propellants. Midgley conducted extensive research on natural and synthetic rubbers and discovered one of the first catalysts for "cracking" (breaking down) hydrocarbons.

Midhat Pasa \mid-ˈhät-pä-ˈshä\ (1822–1883) Ottoman grand vizier. As governor of Niš and Baghdad, his successful reforms earned the respect of the sultan Abdülaziz, who appointed him grand vizier in 1872, a post he held only three months. In 1876 he helped depose Abdülaziz and later Murad V; again appointed grand vizier, he was dismissed after six months. He was banished, then recalled and made governor of Smyrna, and then arrested and convicted for Abdülaziz's death. A death sentence was commuted to permanent exile. See also Tanzimat.

MIDI \ˈmi-dē\ *in full* **Musical Instrument Digital Interface** Protocol for transmission of musical data between digital components, such as synthesizers and a computer's sound card. The MIDI uses 8-bit asynchronous serial transmission with a data rate of 31.25 kilobytes per second. The transmitted data do not represent musical sound but specify aspects of i (a given pitch, its loudness, its starting and stopping points in time). The data are then applied to waveforms stored digitally on a computer chip to create a specific sound.

Midler, Bette (born 1945) U.S. actress and singer. Born in Honolulu, she studied drama at the University of Hawaii. Moving to New York, she developed a popular though bawdy nightclub act. Her Broadway show *The Divine Miss M* (1974) won a Tony award as well as a Grammy award for the album. Her successful films include *The Rose* (1979), *Down and Out in Beverly Hills* (1986), *Stella* (1990), and *The First Wives Club* (1996). "The Rose" and "Wind Beneath My Wings" were among her hit singles.

Midrash \mē-ˈdräsh, ˈmi-ˌdräsh\ In Judaism, a large collection of writings that examine the Hebrew Bible in the light of oral tradition. Midrashic activity reached its height in the 2nd century AD with the schools of Ishmael ben Elisha and Akiba ben Joseph. The Midrashim are divided into two groups: Halakhah, which clarify legal issues; and Haggadah, nonlegal writings intended simply to enlighten. The Midrashim are extensively quoted in the Talmud.

Midway *formerly* **Brooks Islands** Unincorporated U.S. territory (no permanent population), central Pacific Ocean. It consists of two coral islands, Eastern and Sand islands, with a total land area of 2 sq mi (5 sq km). Claimed for the U.S. in 1859 by Capt. N. C. Brooks, the islands were formally annexed in 1867. Their location, over 1,300 mi (2,100 km) northwest of Honolulu, gave them strategic importance for U.S. forces during World War II, and in 1941 the U.S. Navy established an air and submarine base there. The Battle of Midway (1942) took place in nearby waters. Midway's importance as a commercial air base later declined, and its airfield was closed in 1993.

Midway, Battle of (June 3–6, 1942) Major World War II naval battle between the U.S. and Japan. Japanese naval forces under Yamamoto Isoroku sought to seize Midway Island by engaging the numerically inferior U.S. Pacific fleet. Since U.S. intelligence had broken the Japanese naval code, the U.S. was prepared for the assault by mobilizing about 115 land-based aircraft as well as three aircraft carriers. On June 3 its bombers began striking Japan's carrier force. Japan was unable to match the U.S. air power and, after heavy losses, abandoned efforts to land on Midway.

Midwest *or* **Middle West** Region, northern and central U.S., lying midway between the Appalachian and Rocky mountains, and north of the Ohio River. As defined by the federal government, it comprises the states of Illinois, Indiana, Iowa, Kansas, Michigan, Minnesota, Missouri, Nebraska, North Dakota, Ohio, South Dakota, and Wisconsin. It includes much of the Great Plains, the region of the Great Lakes, and the upper Mississippi River valley.

midwifery \mid-ˈwif-ər-ē\ Art of attending women in childbirth. It is known to date to ancient biblical, Greek, and Roman times. It declined in the Middle Ages, when childbirth carried high mortality for mothers and infants, but advanced considerably in the 17th–19th century. Later, with advances in obstetrics and gynecology, most women gave birth in hospitals. In the 1960s, the natural childbirth movement, feminism, and other factors renewed interest in the personal care given by midwives. In the U.S., certified nurse-midwives (CNMs)—registered nurses trained in midwifery—accept only low-risk patients. If problems develop, a physician is called. CNMs also provide pre- and postnatal care and reproductive health advice. Lay midwives usually have no formal training, are unlicensed, and deliver (at home) about three-fourths of infants born throughout the world, mostly in developing countries and rural areas of developed nations.

Mies van der Rohe \ˌmēs-ˌvan-də-ˈrō-ə\, **Ludwig** *orig.* **Maria Ludwig Michael Mies** (1886–1969) German-U.S. architect, the undisputed leader of the International Style. Mies learned masonry from his father and later worked in the office of Peter Behrens. His first great work was the Barcelona Pavilion for the 1929 International Exposition, a travertine platform with chromed steel columns and spaces defined by planes of extravagant onyx, marble, and frosted glass. His steel-and-leather Barcelona chair became a 20th-century classic. He directed the Bauhaus 1930–33, first in Dessau and then, during its final months, in Berlin. In 1937 Mies moved to the U.S., where he directed the School of Architecture at Chicago's Armour Institute (now Illinois Institute of Technology). He designed the school's new campus (1939–41). Other projects include Chicago's Lake Shore Drive Apartments (1949–51), the Seagram Building, and Berlin's New National Gallery (1963–68). Steel skeletons sheathed in glass curtain-wall facades, these buildings exemplify Mies's dictum that "less is more." Steel-and-glass office buildings influenced by his work were built all over the world.

The Lake Shore Drive Apartments, Chicago, designed by Mies van der Rohe; photographed in 1955.
EZRA STOLLER © ESTO

Miescher \'mē-shər\, **Johann Friedrich** (1844–1895) Swiss biologist. In 1869 he discovered a substance containing both phosphorus and nitrogen in the nuclei of white blood cells found in pus. The substance, first named nuclein because it seemed to come from cell nuclei, became known as nucleic acid after Miescher separated it into a protein and an acid molecule. He also discovered that it is the carbon dioxide concentration (rather than the oxygen concentration) in the blood that regulates breathing.

Mieszko I \'myesh-kȯ\ (c. 930–992) Prince or duke of Poland (963?–92). He accepted Christianity from Rome (966) to avoid forced conversion by the Germans and the incorporation of Poland into the Holy Roman Empire. He expanded Poland southward into Galicia and northward as far as the Baltic Sea.

Mifune \mi-'fü-nā\, **Toshiro** (1920–1997) Japanese film actor. After serving in the Japanese army in World War II, he made his screen debut in *These Foolish Times* (1947). He followed it with *Drunken Angel* (1948) and achieved international fame in *Rashomon* (1950). He acted in over 100 films and was best known for his portrayals of samurai in those of Akira Kurosawa, including *Seven Samurai* (1954), *The Hidden Fortress* (1958), *Yojimbo* (1961), and *Sanjuro* (1962), which made him Japan's greatest international film star. His other films include *Throne of Blood* (1957), *The Lower Depths* (1957), *Red Beard* (1965), and *Midway* (1976); he also appeared in the TV miniseries *Shogun* (1980).

MiG \'mig\ Any member of a family of Soviet military fighter aircraft produced by a design bureau founded in 1939 by Artem Mikoyan and Mikhail Gurevich. The early MiGs, built in World War II, were propeller-driven. The MiG-15, first flown in 1947, was among the best of the early jet fighters; it saw extensive combat in the Korean War. North Vietnam used the MiG-17 in the Vietnam War. The twin-engine MiG-19, first flown in 1953, was the first supersonic fighter of European manufacture. The MiG-25 (1970) was the fastest combat aircraft ever in active service, registering speeds of Mach 2.7 and 2.8, with an operational ceiling above 80,000 ft (24,000 m).

MiG *officially* **ANPK imeni A.I. Mikoyana** *formerly* **OKB-155** Russian design bureau that is the country's major producer of jet fighters. The company originated in 1939 within another Soviet design bureau as a department under Artem Mikoyan and his deputy, Mikhail Gurevich. Three years later it became the independent bureau OKB-155. Its first design, a single-engine interceptor (first flown 1940), eventually bore the name MiG-1 ("MiG" being an acronym based on "Mikoyan" and "Gurevich"). After World War II it produced the first Soviet jet fighter, the MiG-9 (1946), and followed on with some of the U.S.S.R.'s most notable high-speed aircraft (see MiG [fighter aircraft]). The last major fighters designed under Mikoyan (died 1970) were the variable-wing MiG-23 (entered service 1972), and the MiG-25 (introduced 1970; capable of about Mach 3). The organization later produced several new designs, including the MiG-29 and MiG-31 (both first flown in the 1970s). In the late 1980s its formal name became ANPK imeni A.I. Mikoyana. In the 1990s, after the breakup of the Soviet Union, MiG was consolidated with several other major firms into the giant state-owned aerospace complex VPK MAPO. MiG diversified modestly into the civilian passenger plane market and continued to develop advanced fighter concepts, including the 1.42 (1.44I) multifunctional fifth-generation fighter (first flown 2000).

Mighty Five, The Group of Russian composers that joined together in 1875 to produce a Russian national music. The Five were César Cui (1835–1918), A. Borodin, M. Balakirev, M. Mussorgsky, and N. Rimsky-Korsakov. A somewhat larger group around this core was referred to by a music critic as "the Mighty Handful," and the names have tended to merge.

migmatite \'mig-mə-ˌtīt\ Rock composed of a metamorphic host material that is streaked or veined with granite; the name means "mixed rock." Many migmatites probably represent partial fusion of the metamorphic host; some components of the rock are fused and gather to produce the streaks of granite. Migmatite also can form near large intrusions of granite when some of the magma is injected into neighboring metamorphic rocks.

migraine Recurrent vascular headache, usually on one side of the head. Severe throbbing pain is sometimes accompanied by nausea and vomiting. Some migraine patients have warning symptoms (an "aura") before the headache, including visual disturbance, weakness, numbness, or dizziness. If a stimulus (e.g., a particular food or drink) is found to trigger attacks, avoidance can prevent them. Drugs may be taken as an attack begins (to abort it) or daily by patients with very frequent attacks (to prevent them or reduce their severity).

migrant labor Unskilled workers who move from one region to another offering their services on a temporary, usually seasonal, basis. In North America, migrant labor is generally employed in agriculture, and moves seasonally from south to north following the harvest. In Europe and the Middle East, migrant labor usually involves urban rather than agricultural employment and calls for longer periods of residence. The migrant labor market is often disorganized and exploitative. Many workers are supervised by middlemen such as labor contractors and crew leaders, who recruit and transport them and dispense their pay. Laborers frequently endure long hours, low wages, poor working conditions, and substandard housing. In some countries, notably India, child labor is widespread among migrant laborers, and even in the U.S. those children who do not work often do not go to school, since schools are usually open only to local residents. Workers willing to accept employment on these terms are driven by even worse conditions in their home countries. Labor organizing is made difficult by mobility and by low rates of literacy and political participation, though some migrant laborers in the U.S. have been unionized. See also Cesar Chavez.

migration, human Permanent change of residence by an individual or group, excluding such movements as nomadism and migrant labor. Migrations may be classed as internal or international and as voluntary or forced. Voluntary migration is usually undertaken in search of a better life; forced migrations include expulsions during war and transportation of slaves or prisoners. The earliest humans migrated from Africa to all the continents except Antarctica within about 50,000 years. Modern mass migrations include the Great Atlantic Migration from Europe to North America, a total of 37 million people between 1820 and 1980, and the forced migration of 20 million people from Africa to North America as slaves. War-related forced migrations and refugee flows continue to be very large, as are voluntary migrations from developing nations to industrialized ones. Internal migrations have tended to be from rural areas to urban centers.

mihrab \'mē-rəb\ Semicircular prayer niche in the *qibla* wall (the wall facing Mecca) of a mosque, reserved for the prayer leader *(imam).* The mihrab originated in the reign (705–15) of the Umayyad prince al-Walid I, when the famous mosques at Medina, Jerusalem, and Damascus were built. It was adapted from the prayer niches common in Coptic Christian monasteries. Mihrabs are usually ornately decorated.

Mikal \mi-'käl\ In Islam, the counterpart of the biblical archangel Michael. Mikal is mentioned only once in the Quran, but according to legend he and Jibril were the first angels to obey God's order to worship Adam. The two are credited with purifying Muhammad's heart before his ascension to heaven (see miraj). Mikal is said to have been so shocked at the sight of hell when it was created that he never laughed again. He is also believed to have helped the Muslims win their first significant military victory in Arabia in 624.

Mikan \'mī-kən\, **George (Lawrence)** (born 1924) U.S. basketball player and executive. Born in Joliet, Ill., he was an outstanding center at DePaul Univ., where he also took his law degree. Standing about 6 ft 10 in. (2 m 8 cm), he was the first of the outstanding big men in post–World War II professional basketball. He played for the Minneapolis Lakers 1947–56, leading them to six championships. He was later named first commissioner of the American Basketball Association (1967–69). An Associated Press poll named him the greatest basketball player of the first half of the 20th century.

Mikolajczyk \ˌmē-kȯl-'ī-chik\, **Stanislaw** (1901–1966) Polish statesman. He cofounded the Peasant Party and served as its leader 1931–39. After the German invasion of Poland (1939), he fled to London, where he served in the Polish government-in-exile as prime minister 1943–44. He returned in 1945 and became second deputy premier in the communist-dominated provisional government. He tried to effect a democratic government, but persecution of the noncommunist Peasant Party forced him to flee in 1947 to Britain and then the U.S.

Mikon See MICON

Mikoyan \ˌmē-kō-'yän\, **Anastas (Ivanovich)** (1895–1978) Russian statesman. After joining the Bolsheviks in 1915, he became a party leader in the Caucasus. His support of JOSEPH STALIN earned him a post on the Communist Central Committee (1923). He was commissar of trade from 1926, a member of the Politburo from 1935, and deputy premier 1946–64, directing the country's trade. He supported NIKITA KHRUSHCHEV's rise to power and became his close adviser and a first deputy premier of the Soviet Union. He was chairman of the Presidium of the Supreme Soviet 1964–65.

milad See MAWLID

Milan \mə-'lan, mə-'län\ *Italian* **Milano** \mē-'lä-nō\ Capital (metro. area pop., 1996 est.: 1,306,000), LOMBARDY region, northern Italy. The area was settled by the Gauls c. 600 BC. Known as Mediolanum, it was conquered by the Romans in 222 BC. Attacked in AD 452 by ATTILA and in 539 by the Goths, it fell to CHARLEMAGNE in 774. Its power grew in the 11th century, but it was destroyed by the HOLY ROMAN EMPIRE in 1162. Rebuilt as part of the LOMBARD LEAGUE in 1167 it achieved independence in 1183. In 1450 FRANCESCO SFORZA founded a new dynasty; after 1499 it was ruled alternately by the French and the Sforza family until 1535, when the HABSBURGS obtained it. NAPOLEON took power in 1796, and in 1805 it became the capital of his kingdom of Italy. It was incorporated into Italy in 1860. Milan was heavily damaged during World War II, but was rebuilt. It is Italy's most important economic center, with industrial development and textile manufacturing. It is noted for its fashion industry and electronic goods production, and is Italy's financial center. Its historic sites include the medieval Duomo, Europe's third-largest cathedral; the Palazzo di Brera (1651); the 15th-century monastery that houses LEONARDO DA VINCI's *Last Supper*; and LA SCALA opera house.

Milan Decree (December 17, 1807) Economic policy in the NAPOLEONIC WARS. It was part of the CONTINENTAL SYSTEM invoked by Napoleon to blockade trade with the British. It expanded the blockade of continental ports to those of neutral ships trading with Britain and eventually affected U.S. shipping.

mildew Conspicuous mass of threadlike hyphae (see MYCELIUM) and fruiting structures produced by various fungi (division Mycota; see FUNGUS). Mildew grows on cloth, fibers, leather goods, and plants, using these substances as food for growth and reproduction. Downy mildew and powdery mildew are plant diseases that affect hundreds of species.

mile Any of various units of distance, including the statute mile of 5,280 ft (1.61 km). It originated from the Roman *mille passus*, or "thousand paces," which measured 5,000 Roman ft, or 4,840 English ft (1,475 km). A nautical mile is the length on earth's surface of one minute of arc, or, by international definition, 1,852 m (6,076.12 ft, or 1.1508 statute mi); it remains in universal use in both marine and air transportation. A knot is 1 nautical mile per hour. See also INTERNATIONAL SYSTEM OF UNITS, METRIC SYSTEM.

Miletus \mī-'lē-təs\ Ancient Greek city of western ASIA MINOR. Before 500 BC, it was the greatest Greek city in the east, distinguished as a commercial and colonial power and also for its intellectual figures, including THALES, ANAXIMANDER, ANAXIMENES, and Hecataeus. Ruled by Greek tyrants, it later passed successively to LYDIA and PERSIA. About 499 BC Miletus led the Ionian revolt that sparked the PERSIAN WARS, and it was destroyed by the Persians in 494 BC. After the Greeks defeated the Persians, it joined the DELIAN LEAGUE. It fell to ALEXANDER in 334 BC but retained its commercial importance. By the 6th century AD, its two harbors had silted up, and it was eventually abandoned. Now an archaeological site, it is near the mouth of the MENDERES RIVER.

Milford Sound Inlet of the TASMAN SEA, southwestern coast of South Island, New Zealand. About 2 mi (3 km) wide, it extends inland for 12 mi (19 km). It was named by a whaler in the 1820s for its resemblance to Milford Haven in Wales. It is the northernmost fjord in Fiordland National Park, and the site of Milford Sound town, one of the region's few permanently inhabited places.

Milhaud \mē-'yō\, **Darius** (1892–1974) French composer. He studied at the Paris Conservatoire, then at the Schola Cantorum with V. D'INDY. He accompanied PAUL CLAUDEL to Brazil (1916), and wrote *Saudades do Brazil* (1921) on his return, when he was becoming known as one of Les SIX. The influence of jazz is audible in his best-known work, *La création du monde* (1923). He wrote many ballets, operas, and film scores in the 1920s, culminating in the grand opera *Christophe Colomb* (1928). In 1940 he moved to the U.S. and taught at Mills College; though he returned to Europe in 1947, he taught alternate years at Mills and in Paris. He had a longtime association with the Aspen Music Festival, which he helped found in 1949.

miliaria \ˌmi-lē-'ar-ē-ə\ Inflammatory SKIN disorder, with multiple small sites at sweat pores. Blockage of ducts causes sweat to escape into various levels of the skin and produce different inflammatory reactions. The most common type, known as prickly heat, results when sweat escapes into the epidermis. Pinhead blisters or pimplelike bumps occur mostly on the trunk and limbs and cause itching and burning. It mainly affects infants in tropical climates. See also PERSPIRATION, SWEAT GLAND.

Military Academy, U.S. See UNITED STATES MILITARY ACADEMY

military engineering Art and practice of designing and building military works and of building and maintaining lines of military transport and communications. It includes both tactical support (see TACTICS) on the battlefield, including construction of FORTIFICATIONS and demolition of enemy installations, and strategic support (see STRATEGY) away from the front lines, such as construction or maintenance of airfields, ports, roads, railroads, bridges, and hospitals. Its most notable feat in ancient times was the GREAT WALL of China. The preeminent military engineers of the ancient Western world were the Romans, who maintained their power by constructing not only forts and garrisons but roads, bridges, aqueducts, harbors, and lighthouses. See also CIVIL ENGINEERING.

military government Administration of territory by an occupying power. The definition does not cover military forces stationed in neutral or friendly territory that share administrative responsibilities with local civil authorities. Military government must also be distinguished from MILITARY LAW and MARTIAL LAW. Its control lasts until it either gives up power voluntarily or is overthrown. The term is popularly used for rule of a country by its own military, whether it comes to power through a COUP D'ÉTAT or is the legitimate governing body.

military law Law prescribed by statute for governing the armed forces and their civilian employees. It in no way relieves military personnel of their obligations to their country's civil code or to the codes of INTERNATIONAL LAW. MUTINY, insubordination, desertion, misconduct, and other offenses injurious to military discipline constitute violations of military law; offenders may be subject to COURT-MARTIAL. Lesser offenses may be penalized summarily by a commanding officer (e.g., through the withdrawal of privileges or the cancellation of liberty).

military unit Group of a prescribed size with a specific combat role within a larger military organization. The chief units in the ancient world were the Greek PHALANX and the Roman LEGION. Modern units originated in the 16th–18th century, when professional armies reemerged in Europe after the end of the Middle Ages. Since then the basic units—company BATTALION, BRIGADE, and division—have remained in use. The smallest unit today is the squad, which has 7–14 soldiers and is led by a sergeant. Three or four squads make up a PLATOON, and two or more platoons make up a company, which has 100–250 soldiers and is commanded by a captain or a major. Two or more companies make up a battalion, and several battalions form a brigade. Two or more brigades, along with various specialized battalions, make up a division, which has 7,000–22,000 troops and is commanded by a major general. Two to seven divisions make up an army corps, commanded by a lieutenant general, which with 50,000–300,000 troops is the largest regular army formation, though in wartime two or more corps may be combined to form a field army (commanded by a general), and field armies in turn may be combined to form an army group.

militia \mə-ˈli-shə\ Military organization of citizens with limited military training who are available for emergency service, usually for local defense. In many countries the militia is of ancient origin. The Anglo-Saxons required every able-bodied free male to serve. In colonial America, it was the only defense against hostile Indians when regular British forces were not available. In the AMERICAN REVOLUTION, the militia, called the Minutemen, provided the bulk of the American forces. Militias played a similar role in the WAR OF 1812 and the AMERICAN CIVIL WAR. State-controlled volunteer militias in the U.S. became the National Guard. The U.S. in recent decades has seen a rise in so-called civilian or unorganized militias, paramilitary organizations of uncertain legal status whose members profess to be patriots training to protect the U.S. from threats to its sovereignty from within and without. Many have white-supremacist leanings, and some have been implicated in terrorist attacks (including the 1995 bombing of Oklahoma City's federal building). Some find justification for their actions in perceived persecution by the U.S. government.

milk Liquid secreted by the mammary glands of female mammals to nourish their young. The milk of domesticated animals is also an important food source for humans. Most milk consumed in Western countries is from the cow; sources important elsewhere include the sheep, goat, water buffalo, and camel. Milk is essentially an emulsion of FAT and PROTEIN in water, along with dissolved sugar, minerals (including CALCIUM and PHOSPHORUS), and VITAMINS (particularly VITAMIN B COMPLEX); commercial cow's milk is commonly enriched with vitamins A and D. Many countries require PASTEURIZATION to protect against naturally occurring and artificially introduced microorganisms. Cooling further prevents spoilage (souring and curdling). Fat from whole milk (about 3.5% fat content) can be removed in a separator to produce CREAM and leave low-fat milk (1–2% fat) or skim milk (0.5% fat). Commercially sold milk is usually homogenized, forced under high pressure through small openings to distribute the fat evenly. It may also be condensed or dehydrated for preservation and ease of transport. Other dairy products include BUTTER, CHEESE, and YOGURT.

Milk, Harvey (Bernard) (1930–1978) U.S. political leader. Born in Woodmere (Long Island), N.Y., he settled in San Francisco and soon gained a devoted following as a leader of the city's gay community. In 1977 he was elected to the city's Board of Supervisors, becoming one of the first openly gay elected officials in U.S. history. In 1978 Milk and the city's mayor, George Moscone (1929–1978), were shot and killed in City Hall by Dan White, a conservative former city supervisor. After White was convicted only of voluntary manslaughter, his attorneys having argued that eating junk food had impaired his judgment, riots broke out in the city.

Milken, Michael R. (born 1946) U.S. financier. Born in Encino, Cal., he studied at the University of Pennsylvania's Wharton School and went to work in 1969 for what was to become Drexel Burnham Lambert Inc., an investment-banking company. In 1971 he became head of its bond-trading department. He persuaded many of his clients to invest in JUNK BONDS issued by new or financially troubled companies; the capital he raised financed a new class of "corporate raiders" who carried out numerous mergers, acquisitions, hostile takeovers, and leveraged buyouts in the 1980s. By the end of the decade, the junk-bond market was worth $150 billion, and the firm was a leading financial firm. In 1986 its client Ivan Boesky, convicted of INSIDER TRADING, implicated Milken and the firm in his dealings. Charged with securities fraud and heavily fined, the firm declared bankruptcy in 1990 when the junk-bond market collapsed. Milken pled guilty to securities fraud the same year and was sentenced to 10 years in prison and a $600 million fine; released after 22 months, he has since made a second fortune.

milkweed family Family Asclepiadaceae, composed of about 2,000 species of flowering herbaceous plants or shrubby climbers in more than 280 genera. Most family members have milky juice, podlike fruits, and tufted silky-haired seeds that drift on wind currents to new locations for sprouting. Common milkweed *(Asclepias syriaca)* and bloodflower *(A. curassavica)* often are cultivated as ornamentals. *Hoya carnosa,* commonly called wax plant because of its waxy white flowers, is often grown indoors as a potted plant. The family also includes some SUCCULENTS, some PITCHER PLANTS, and BUTTERFLY WEED.

Milky Way galaxy Large spiral GALAXY (roughly 150,000 light-years in diameter) that contains our SOLAR SYSTEM. It includes the multitude of stars whose light is seen as the Milky Way, the irregular luminous band that encircles the sky defining the plane of the galactic disk. The Milky Way system contains about 100 billion stars and large amounts of interstellar gas and dust. Because the dust obscures our view of many of its stars, large areas could not be studied before the development of INFRARED ASTRONOMY and radio astronomy (see RADIO AND RADAR ASTRONOMY). Its precise constituents, shape, and true size and mass are still not known; it is believed to contain large amounts of DARK MATTER. The sun lies in one of the galaxy's spiral arms, about 27,000 light-years from the center.

Mill, James (1773–1836) Scottish philosopher, historian, and economist. After studying at the University of Edinburgh and teaching, he went to London in 1802, where he met JEREMY BENTHAM and became a major promulgator of Bentham's UTILITARIANISM. He wrote for several journals, including the *Edinburgh Review* (1808–13), and contributed articles on government and education to the *Encyclopaedia Britannica.* He helped found London University in 1825. After completing his *History of British India* (3 vols., 1817), he was appointed an official in India House (1819) and later became head of the examiner's office (1830). His criticism of British rule led to changes in the government of India. His *Elements of Political Economy* (1821) summarized the views of DAVID RICARDO, and his *Analysis of the Phenomena of the Human Mind* (1829) associated psychology with utilitarianism, a doctrine continued by his son, JOHN STUART MILL. Mill is considered the founder of philosophical radicalism.

Mill, John Stuart (1806–1873) British philosopher and economist. He was educated exclusively and exhaustively by his father, JAMES MILL. In *A System of Logic* (2 vols., 1843), he makes a valiant attempt to formulate a logic of the human sciences based on causal explanation. Intended by his father as the philosophical successor to JEREMY BENTHAM, he cofounded the Utilitarian Society with Bentham (1823), though he later significantly modified the UTILITARIANISM he inherited from both men to meet the criticisms it encountered. In 1825 he and Bentham cofounded University College London. In *On Liberty* (1859) Mill eloquently defended individual freedom. His *Utilitarianism* (1863) was a closely reasoned attempt to answer objections to his ethical theory and address misconceptions about it; he was especially insistent that "utility" include the pleasures of the imagination and the gratification of the higher emotions, and that his system include a place for settled rules of conduct. His *The Subjection of Women* (1869) made a strong and controversial call for women's rights. His other works include *Principles of Political Economy* (1848), *Three Essays on Religion* (1874), and an autobiography (1873). Prominent as a publicist in the reforming age of the 19th century, he remains of lasting interest as a logician and ethical theorist. See also MILL'S METHODS.

Millais \ˈmi-ˌlā, mi-ˈlā\, **John Everett** *later* **Sir John** (1829–1896) British painter and illustrator. In 1848 he became a founding member of the PRE-RAPHAELITES. His period of greatest achievement came in the 1850s, with *The Return of the Dove to the Ark* (1851) and one of his greatest public successes, *The Blind Girl* (1856), a tour de force of Victorian sentiment and technical facility. He was popular as a portraitist and also as a book illustrator, notably for the novels of ANTHONY TROLLOPE.

Milland \mi-ˈland\, **Ray** *orig.* **Reginald Truscott-Jones** (1905–1986) British-U.S. actor. Born in Wales, he made his film debut in 1929 and moved to Hollywood in 1930. The debonair romantic leading man in many movies of the 1930s and '40s, he won acclaim for his performance as an alcoholic writer in *The Lost Weekend* (1945, Academy Award) and also played dramatic parts in *The Big Clock* (1948), *Something to Live For* (1952), and *Dial M for Murder* (1954).

Millay, Edna St. Vincent (1892–1950) U.S. poet and dramatist. She was born and raised in Maine, and her work is filled with the imagery of coast and countryside. In the 1920s, when she lived in Greenwich Village, she came to personify the romantic rebellion and bravado of youth. Among her volumes are *Renascence* (1917); *A Few Figs from Thistles* (1920); *The Harp Weaver* (1923, Pulitzer Prize); *The Buck in the Snow* (1928), which introduced a more somber tone; the sonnet sequence *Fatal Interview* (1931); and *Wine from These Grapes* (1934). Other works include three verse plays and the libretto for Deems Taylor's opera *The King's Henchman* (1927).

Mille, Agnes de See Agnes DE MILLE

millefleurs tapestry \mēl-ˈflərz\ (French: "thousand flowers") TAPESTRY characterized by a background motif of many small flowers. Most millefleurs tapestries show secular scenes or allegories. They are thought to have been made first in the Loire district of France in the mid-15th century. As they became popular, they were produced in many parts of France and the Low Countries until the end of the 16th century.

millennialism *or* **millenarianism** Belief in the millennium of Christian prophecy (Rev. 20), the 1,000 years when Christ is to reign on earth, or a religious movement associated with that belief. During the millennium, yearnings for the rule of righteousness on earth will be realized; at its end, Satan will be loosed for a time to deceive the nations, but he will be defeated and the dead will be gathered for the final judgment. Throughout the Christian era, periods of social change or crisis have tended to lead to a resurgence in millennialism; it is now associated especially with such Protestant denominations as the ADVENTISTS, JEHOVAH'S WITNESSES, and MORMONS.

millennium Period of 1,000 years. The GREGORIAN CALENDAR, put forth in 1582 and subsequently adopted by most countries, did not include a year 0 in the transition from BC (years before Christ) to AD (those since his birth). Thus, the 1st millennium is defined as spanning years 1–1000 and the 2nd years 1001–2000. Although numerous popular celebrations marked the start of the year 2000, the 21st century and 3rd millennium AD began on Jan. 1, 2001.

millennium bug See Y2K BUG

miller *or* **owlet moth** Any of the more than 20,000 MOTH species in the LEPIDOPTERAN family Noctuidae, common worldwide. Some species have a 1-ft (30-cm) wingspan, the largest wingspan of any moth, but most species have a wingspan of 1.5 in. (4 cm) or less. The wings are usually dull-colored. Both larvae and adults of most species feed at night. Adults feed on fruits, sap, or nectar. The larvae of many species are agricultural pests (e.g., CUTWORM, BOLLWORM) that feed on foliage and seeds, bore into stems and fruits, and eat or sever roots. A few species prey on SCALE INSECTS.

Miller, Arthur (born 1915) U.S. playwright. Born in New York City, he began writing plays while at the University of Michigan. His first important play, *All My Sons* (1947), was followed by his most famous work, *Death of a Salesman* (1949, Pulitzer Prize), the tragedy of the aging salesman Willy Loman, who is driven to suicide. Noted for combining social awareness with a searching concern for his characters' inner lives, Miller wrote many other plays, including *The Crucible* (1953), *A View from the Bridge* (1955), *After the Fall* (1964), *Incident at Vichy* (1964), *The Price* (1968), *The Archbishop's Ceiling* (1977), and *The Last Yankee* (1992). He also wrote the screenplay for *The Misfits* (1961), which starred his wife MARILYN MONROE.

Miller, George A(rmitage) (born 1920) U.S. psychologist. Born in Charleston, W.V., he taught at Harvard, Rockefeller, and Princeton universities. He is known for his work in cognitive psychology, particularly communication and psycholinguistics. In *Plans and the Structure of Behavior* (with Eugene Galanter and Karl Pribram, 1960), Miller examined how knowledge is accumulated and organized into a practical "image" or plan. His other works, including *Language and Communication* (1951) and *The Science of Words* (1991), focus on the psychology of language and communication. He received the National Medal of Science in 1991.

Miller, (Alton) Glenn (1904–1944) U.S. trombonist and leader of one of the most popular dance bands of the SWING era. Born in Clarinda, Iowa, Miller formed his band in 1937. His music was characterized by the precise execution of arrangements that featured a clarinet leading the saxophone section. Miller disbanded in 1942 to join the war effort leading a military band. Traveling from London to Paris, his plane disappeared over the English Channel and was never recovered.

Miller, Henry (Valentine) (1891–1980) U.S. writer and perennial bohemian. Miller wrote about his Brooklyn childhood in *Black Spring* (1936). *Tropic of Cancer* (1934), a monologue about his life as an impoverished expatriate in Paris, and *Tropic of Capricorn* (1939), which draws on his earlier New York phase, were banned as obscene in the U.S. and Britain until the 1960s. *The Air-Conditioned Nightmare* (1945) is a critical account of a tour of the U.S. He settled on the California coast, where he became the center of a colony of admirers and wrote his *Rosy Crucifixion* trilogy, *Sexus*, *Plexus*, and *Nexus* (U.S. ed., 1965).

Henry Miller.
CAMERA PRESS

Miller, Jonathan (Wolfe) (born 1934) British director, writer, and actor. After earning a medical degree at Cambridge Univ., he made his professional stage debut at the Edinburgh Festival in the hit satirical revue *Beyond the Fringe* (1960). As a director of plays, he gained notoriety for his controversial interpretations of classic works. His innovative opera productions for the English National Opera and other groups have become internationally celebrated. He wrote the BBC medical series *The Body in Question* (1977) and *States of Mind* (1982).

Miller, Neal E(lgar) (born 1909) U.S. psychologist. Born in Milwaukee, he earned his PhD from Yale University and remained at Yale's Institute of Human Relations to continue his experiments on learning. In *Social Learning and Imitation* (1941) and *Personality and Psychotherapy* (1950), he and John Dollard presented a theory of motivation based on the satisfaction of psychosocial drives, combining elements of earlier reinforcement theories of behavior and learning. Miller suggested that behavior patterns were produced through the modification of biologically or socially derived drives by conditioning and reinforcement. He taught at Rockefeller University 1966–81.

Millerand \mēl-ˈrä^{n}\, **Alexandre** (1859–1943) French politician. He was an editor of socialist journals 1883–98 and served from 1885 to 1920 in the Chamber of Deputies. He implemented reforms while serving in various governments as minister of commerce (1899–1901), public works (1909–10), and war (1912–15). He became premier in 1920 and, as leader of a moderate coalition, was elected president of the Republic (1920–24). After advocating a revision of the constitution to strengthen the power of the presidency, he was forced to resign by the CARTEL DES GAUCHES. He served in the Senate 1927–40.

millet Any of various GRASSES (family Poaceae, or Gramineae), that produce small edible seeds used as forage crops and as food CEREALS. Most millets range in height from 1 to 4 ft (0.3 to 1.3 m). Except for pearl millet *(Pennisetum glaucum,* or *P. americanum),* seeds remain enclosed in hulls after threshing. Cultivated in China since at least the 3rd millennium BC, millets are today an important food staple in much of Asia, Russia, and western Africa. High in carbohydrates, they are somewhat strong in taste and cannot be made into leavened bread, so they are consumed mainly in flatbreads and porridges or prepared and eaten much like rice. In the U.S. and western Europe they are used chiefly for pasture or to produce HAY.

millet \mə-ˈlet\ Turkish autonomous religious community under the OTTOMAN EMPIRE (c. 1300–1923). Millets were responsible to the central government for such obligations as taxes and internal security. Each millet also had responsibility for social and administrative functions not provided by the state. Beginning in 1856, a series of secular legal reforms eroded much of their administrative autonomy. See also TANZIMAT.

Millet \mē-ˈyā, *Engl* mi-ˈlā\, **Jean-François** (1814–1875) French painter. Born to a peasant family near Cherbourg, he studied with a painter in Paris, but when one of his two submissions to the Salon was rejected (1840), he returned to Cherbourg, where initially he painted mostly portraits. His first success came with *The Milkmaid* (1844), and in 1848 another peasant scene, *The Winnower,* was shown at the Salon. In 1849 he settled in the village of Barbizon. Because he continued to exhibit peasant scenes that emphasized the labors of rustic life, he was accused of being a socialist, but his aims were not political. His *Angelus* (1859) became one of the most popular paintings of the 19th century. Because he later turned to landscape, he is often linked with the BARBIZON SCHOOL.

Millikan, Robert (Andrews) (1868–1953) U.S. physicist. Born in Morrison, Ill., he received his doctorate from Columbia University and taught physics at the University of Chicago (1896–1921) and Caltech (from 1921). To measure electric charge he devised the MILLIKAN OIL-DROP EXPERIMENT. He verified ALBERT EINSTEIN's photoelectric equation and obtained a precise value for the Planck constant. He was awarded a 1923 Nobel Prize.

Millikan oil-drop experiment \'mil-ə-kən\ First method for direct measurement of the ELECTRIC CHARGE of a single ELECTRON, originally performed in 1909 by ROBERT MILLIKAN. He used a microscope to measure the rate of descent of tiny oil droplets directed through the top of a box. By halting the descent of droplets carrying their own electric charge by means of precisely adjusting the voltage between the box's metal top and bottom, he discovered that the electric charges on the drops were all whole-number multiples of a lowest value, the elementary electric charge itself, and thus that electric charge exists in basic natural units.

milling See FULLING

milling machine MACHINE TOOL that rotates a circular tool with numerous cutting edges arranged symmetrically about its axis, called a milling cutter. The metal workpiece is usually held in a vise clamped to a table that can move in three perpendicular directions. Cutters of many shapes and sizes are available for a wide variety of milling operations. Milling machines cut flat surfaces, grooves, shoulders, inclined surfaces, dovetails, and T-slots. Various form-tooth cutters are used for cutting concave forms and convex grooves, for rounding corners, and for cutting gear teeth.

millipede Any of about 10,000 species of the ARTHROPOD class Diplopoda, found worldwide. Most species live in and eat decaying plant matter. Some injure living plants, and a few are predators and scavengers. Millipedes are 1–11 in. (2.5–28 cm) long and have from 11 to more than 100 diplosomites, double segments formed from the fusion of two segments. The head is legless; the next three segments have one pair of legs each; and the remaining segments have two pairs each. In defense, millipedes do not bite; most species tuck headfirst into a tight coil, and many secrete a pungent, toxic liquid or gas.

Mills, Billy *orig.* **William Mervin** (born 1938) U.S. athlete. Of part Oglala Sioux extraction, he spent his early years on a reservation in Pine Ridge, S.D., and was orphaned at 12. At the University of Kansas he excelled in track. He became the first American to win an Olympic gold medal in the 10,000-m race (1964), in an electrifying upset victory over Ron Clarke. In 1965 he set an outdoor world record in the 6-mi run and U.S. records in the 10,000-m and indoor 3-mi races.

Mills, C(harles) Wright (1916–1962) U.S. sociologist. Born in Waco, Texas, Mills joined the faculty of Columbia Univ.; there he became associated with the theories of MAX WEBER and with issues regarding the role of intellectuals in modern life, and contributed to the development of a critical sociology in the U.S. and abroad. He believed social scientists should shun "abstracted empiricism" and become activists on behalf of social change. His radical analysis of U.S. business and society appeared in *White Collar* (1951) and *The Power Elite* (1956); other works include *The Causes of World War Three* (1958) and *The Sociological Imagination* (1959). A colorful public figure, he wore black leather and rode a motorcycle. His death at 45 resulted from heart disease.

Mill's methods Five methods of experimental reasoning distinguished by JOHN STUART MILL in his *System of Logic* (1843). Suppose one is interested in determining what factors play a role in causing a specific effect, E, under a specific set of circumstances. The method of agreement tells us to look for factors present on all occasions when E occurs. The method of difference tells us to look for some factor present on some occasion when E occurs and absent on an otherwise similar occasion when it does not. The joint method of agreement and difference combines the two previous methods. The method of residues applies when part of E is explicable by reference to known factors, and tells us to attribute the "residue" to the remaining circumstances under which E occurs. The method of concomitant variation is used when E can be present in various degrees; if we identify a factor F, such as temperature, whose variations are positively or negatively correlated with variations in E, for instance, size, then we can infer that F is causally connected with E.

millstone Either of two flat, round stones used for grinding grain to make flour. The stationary bottom stone is carved with shallow grooved channels that radiate from the center. The upper stone rotates horizontally, and has a central hole through which grain is poured. The channels of the bottom stone lead the grain onto the flat grinding section, called the land, and to the edge, where it emerges as flour. The best millstones are made from French buhrstone, quarried near Paris. In the U.S., quartz conglomerate, quartzite, sandstone, or granite is used. Stone-ground flour accounts for only a small proportion of milled flour today.

Milne \'miln\, **A(lan) A(lexander)** (1882–1956) English writer. He joined the staff of *Punch* in 1906, and produced successful light comedies and a memorable detective novel, *The Red House Mystery* (1922), before verses written for his son Christopher Robin grew into the collections *When We Were Very Young* (1924) and *Now We Are Six* (1927), which became beloved classics. Stories about the adventures of Christopher Robin and the toy animals Pooh, Piglet, Kanga, Roo, and Eeyore are told in the immensely popular *Winnie-the-Pooh* (1926) and *The House at Pooh Corner* (1928).

A.A. Milne, pen and ink drawing by P. Evans, c. 1930; in the National Portrait Gallery, London.

Milne Bay Inlet of Papua New Guinea, South Pacific. Located at the southeastern extremity of New Guinea island, it is 30 mi (50 km) long and 6–8 mi (10–13 km) wide. A Spanish explorer charted the bay in 1606; it was named by the British for Adm. Alexander Milne in 1873. European interest in it increased during the 1889–99 gold rush. A Japanese base of operations in World War II, it was the scene of Japan's first major setback in 1942, and it served as an Allied base for the remainder of the war.

Milner, Alfred *later* **Viscount Milner (of St. James's and Cape Town)** (1854–1925) British high commissioner in South Africa (1897–1905). At the crucial Bloemfontein Conference with Pres. PAUL KRUGER (1899), Milner advocated granting full citizenship to the Uitlanders (British residents in the TRANSVAAL) after five years' residence. Kruger opposed the policy, but was prepared to make concessions. Milner was not, claiming that "war has got to come"; Boer forces invaded Natal four months later, marking the beginning of the SOUTH AFRICAN WAR. He later served as secretary for war (1916–19) and colonial secretary (1919–21).

Milon of Croton \'mī-ˌlän\ *or* **Milo of Croton** (fl. late 6th century BC) Ancient Greek athlete. The most renowned wrestler of antiquity, he won numerous Olympic and Pythian Games. His name has long been synonymous with extraordinary strength, and he is said to have carried an ox on his shoulders across the Olympic stadium.

Milošević \mi-'lō-sə-ˌvich\, **Slobodan** (born 1941) Serbian nationalist politician. Born in Serbia, Yugoslavia, he joined the local Communist Party at 18. He later became head of the state-owned gas company and president of a major Belgrade bank. Advised by his wife, a communist ideologue, he became head of the Communist Party in Belgrade (1984) and later in Serbia (1987). He replaced party leaders with his supporters, and in 1989 the Serbian assembly named him president of the republic. His opposition to a confederation with Croatia and Slovenia led to the breakup of Yugoslavia (1991). He supported Serb militias fighting Muslims in Bosnia and Croatia (see BOSNIAN CONFLICT) but later signed a peace agreement on behalf of the Bosnian Serbs. As president of the new Federal Republic of Yugoslavia, he maintained his power by repression and control of the mass media. In 1999 he launched an offensive against insurgents in the ethnically Albanian province of Kosovo (see KOSOVO CONFLICT), which drew a massive retaliatory bombing campaign against Serbian targets by NATO forces. The subsequent ETHNIC CLEANSING of the province by troops under his command drove hundreds of thousands of Albanian Kosovars to other countries as refugees and earned him worldwide loathing as a war criminal. In 2000 he was defeated in national elections. The following year he was arrested and extradited to The Netherlands to stand trial for war crimes and crimes against humanity. He was subsequently charged with GENOCIDE.

Milosz \'mē-lȯsh\, **Czeslaw** (born 1911) Polish-U.S. author, translator, and critic. Milosz was a socialist by the time he published his first book of verse at 21. During the Nazi occupation of Poland, he was active in the resistance. After serving briefly as a diplomat for communist Poland, he emigrated to the U.S., where he taught for decades at the University of California at Berkeley. His poetry, including such collections as *Bells in Winter* (1978), is noted for its classical style and preoccupation with philosophical and political issues. His well-known essay collection *The Captive Mind* (1953) condemned the accommodation of many Polish intellectuals to communism. Critic Helen Vendler wrote that Milosz's *Treatise on Poetry* (1957) seemed to her "the most comprehensive and moving poem" of the latter half of the 20th century. He was awarded the Nobel Prize in 1980.

Milstein \'mil-ˌstīn, 'mil-ˌstēn\, **César** (1927–2002) Argentine-British immunologist. In 1975 Milstein and Georges Köhler (1946–95) fused short-lived, highly specific lymphocytes with the cells of a myeloma, a type of tumor that can reproduce indefinitely. The hybrid cells, like lymphocytes, secreted antibody to a single antigen and, like myeloma cells, perpetuated themselves. This enabled production of large quantities of pure antibodies against single antigenic characteristics (monoclonal antibodies). Milstein, Köhler, and Niels K. Jerne (1911–94) shared a Nobel Prize in 1984.

Miltiades (the Younger) \mil-'tī-ə-ˌdēz\ (554?–489? BC) Athenian general. He was sent by HIPPIAS to strengthen Athenian control of the sea routes from the Black Sea and made himself a petty tyrant there. He fought the Scythians with DARIUS I in 513 and supported the Persians until the IONIAN REVOLT (499–494). When the revolt failed, he fled to Athens and led the Athenian army to victory at the Battle of MARATHON (490). He was put on trial and fined the next year for a failed naval expedition meant to punish Paros for collaborating with Persia; he died in prison soon after from a gangrenous wound.

Milton, John (1608–1674) English poet. A brilliant youth, Milton attended Cambridge University (1625–32), where he wrote poems in Latin, Italian, and English; these included *L'Allegro* and *Il Penseroso,* both published later in *Poems* (1645). During 1632–38 he engaged in private study—writing the masque *Comus* (1637) and the extraordinary elegy "Lycidas" (1638)—and toured Italy. Concerned with the Puritan cause in England, he spent much of 1641–60 pamphleteering for civil and religious liberty and serving in OLIVER CROMWELL's government. His best-known prose is in the pamphlets *Areopagitica* (1644), on freedom of the press, and *Of Education* (1644). He lost his sight c. 1651, and thereafter dictated his works. His disastrous first marriage ended with his wife's death in 1652; two later marriages were more successful. After the Restoration he was arrested as a noted defender of the Commonwealth but was soon released. In *Paradise Lost* (1667), his epic masterpiece on the Fall of Man written in blank verse, he uses his sublime "grand style" with superb power; his characterization of Satan is a supreme achievement. He further expressed his purified faith in God and the regenerative strength of the individual soul in *Paradise Regained* (1671), an epic in which Christ overcomes Satan the tempter, and *Samson Agonistes* (1671), a tragedy in which the Old Testament figure conquers self-pity and despair to become God's champion. Considered second only to WILLIAM SHAKESPEARE in the history of English-language poetry, Milton had an immense influence on later literature; though attacked early in the 20th century, he had regained his place in the Western canon by mid-century.

Milwaukee City (pop., 2000: 596,974) and lake port, southeastern Wisconsin. The state's largest city, it is situated on Lake MICHIGAN. Visited by French missionaries and fur traders in the 17th century, it was called *Mahn-a-waukee Seepe* ("Gathering Place by the River") by local Indian tribes. Although settled in 1800, the town did not develop until the Indians relinquished their claims in 1831–33. Milwaukee was formed in 1839 and incorporated in 1846. It was a center of German immigration until c. 1900. It is a major GREAT LAKES port, shipping especially grain; it also produces electrical machinery. It has several educational institutions, including Marquette University and the University of Wisconsin–Milwaukee.

Milyukov \mʸil-yü-'kȯf\, **Pavel (Nikolayevich)** (1859–1943) Russian politician and historian. He taught history at Moscow University until 1895 and wrote the acclaimed *Outlines of Russian Culture* (3 vols., 1896–1903). A liberal who admired the political values of democratic countries, he cofounded the progressive CONSTITUTIONAL DEMOCRATIC PARTY in 1905 and led the party in the Duma (1907–17). In 1917 he helped form the provisional government under Prince GEORGY Y. LVOV and served briefly as minister of foreign affairs. He tried to form a moderate coalition against the Bolsheviks but was forced to leave Russia and eventually settled in Paris.

Mimamsa \mē-'mäm-sä\ Probably the earliest of the six orthodox systems (DARSHANS) of Indian philosophy. Mimamsa is fundamental to VEDANTA and has deeply influenced Hindu law. Its aim is to give rules for the interpretation of the VEDAS and to provide a philosophical justification for the observance of Vedic ritual. The earliest work of the system, the Mimamsa-sutra of Jaimini (c. 4th century BC), was followed by the writings of a long line of interpreters and teachers, notably Kumarila Bhatta and Prabhakara Mishra (8th century). Kumarila is credited with using Mimamsa to defeat Buddhism in India; Prabhakara was a realist who believed that sense perceptions were true.

Mimana See KAYA

mime and pantomime Dramatic performance in which a story is told solely by expressive body movement. Mime appeared in Greece in the 5th century BC as a comic entertainment that stressed mimetic action but included song and spoken dialogue. A separate Roman form developed from c. 100 BC and centered on crude and licentious subjects. Roman pantomime differed from Roman mime by its loftier themes and its use of masks, which called for expression through posture and hand gestures. Mime was also important in Asian drama from ancient times, and it forms an element in major Chinese and Japanese dramatic forms (e.g., NO DRAMA). The Roman tradition of pantomime was modified in the 16th-century COMMEDIA DELL'ARTE, which in turn influenced the 18th-century French and English comic interludes that developed into 19th-century pantomime, a children's entertainment emphasizing spectacle. Modern Western mime developed into a purely silent art in which meanings are conveyed through gesture, movement, and expression. Famous mimes include Jean-Gaspard Deburau, Étienne Decroux (who developed a systematic language of gesture), and MARCEL MARCEAU. CHARLIE CHAPLIN was an accomplished mime, as were SID CAESAR and the circus clown Emmett Kelly.

Marcel Marceau, French mime, as Bip, a character of his own invention, playing the violin.
RONALD A. WILFORD ASSOCIATES, INC.

mimicry Similarity between organisms that confers a survival advantage on one. In Batesian mimicry, an organism lacking defenses mimics a species that does have defenses. In Müllerian mimicry, all species in a group are similar even though all individually have defenses. In aggressive mimicry, a predatory species mimics a benign species so that it can approach its prey without alarming it, or a parasitic species mimics its host. Some plant species mimic the color patterns and scents of animals for the purposes of pollination and dispersal. Mimicry differs from camouflage in that camouflage hides the organism, whereas mimicry benefits the organism only if the organism is detected.

L M N

Mimir \'mē-mir\ In Norse mythology, the wisest of the gods of the tribe AESIR. He was also believed to be a water spirit. Mimir was sent by the Aesir as a hostage to the rival gods (the VANIR), but he was decapitated and his head was returned to the Aesir. ODIN preserved the head in herbs and gained knowledge from it. Other tales claim that Mimir lived by a well beneath the roots of YGGDRASILL, the world tree, and that he was a smith who taught the hero SIEGFRIED his craft.

mimosa \mə-'mō-sə\ Any member of the more than 450 species that make up the genus *Mimosa* in the family Mimosaceae, native to tropical and subtropical areas throughout both hemispheres. Most are herbaceous plants or undershrubs; some are woody climbers; a few are small trees. They are often prickly. Mimosas are widely cultivated for the beauty of their foliage and for their interesting response to light and mechanical stimuli: the leaves of some species droop in response to darkness and close up their leaflets when touched. The name comes from this "mimicking" of animal sensibility. The roots of some species are poisonous; others contain skin irritants. Many ACACIAS are commonly but incorrectly called mimosas. See also SENSITIVE PLANT.

Min River River, central FUJIAN province, southeastern China. Rising in the mountains near the Fujian–Jiangxi border, it flows southeast to empty into the CHINA SEA after a course of 358 mi (577 km). The arrival of a railway system in 1957 increased its use for navigation, and there are transshipment points along it.

Min River River, SICHUAN province, southern central China. It flows southeast through the Red Basin into the CHANG RIVER at Yibin. At about 350 mi (560 km) long, it is navigable for most of its course.

Minamata disease \,mi-nə-'mä-tə\ Disease first identified in 1956 in Minamata, Japan. A fishing port, Minamata was also the home of Nippon Chisso Hiryo Co., a manufacturer of chemical fertilizer, carbide, and vinyl chloride. Methyl mercury discharged from the factory contaminated fish and shellfish, which in turn caused illness in the local inhabitants who consumed them and birth defects in their children. The sometimes fatal disease was the first whose cause was recognized as industrial pollution of seawater. It aroused worldwide concern and stimulated the development of the environmental movement.

Minamoto Yoritomo \,mē-nä-'mō-tō-,yò-rē-'tō-mō\ (1147–1199) Founder of the KAMAKURA SHOGUNATE. A member of the Minamoto warrior clan, Yoritomo was banished in his youth as a consequence of his father's revolt against the reigning TAIRA family. In exile Yoritomo found support for his cause in Hojo Tokimasa (see HOJO FAMILY), and in 1185 he defeated the Taira. In 1192 the cloistered emperor (see INSEI) granted him the title of SHOGUN, which made him the supreme authority over all military forces in the country. He established his own constables and stewards throughout Japan, thereby creating a governmental infrastructure in competition with, and gradually superseding, that of the imperial court. He was thus able to rule without actually overthrowing the emperor, a pattern that was to be emulated by future shogunates. See also GEMPEI WAR, JITO.

Minamoto Yoshitsune \,mē-nä-'mō-tō-,yò-shēt-'sùn-ā\ (1159–1189) Charismatic half brother of MINAMOTO YORITOMO who helped bring him victory against the TAIRA family. He was raised in a monastery but ran away at 15 to join Yoritomo. On Yoritomo's orders, Yoshitsune seized Kyoto and then attacked and defeated the remaining Taira forces along Japan's Inland Sea. Yoritomo became jealous of Yoshitsune and, though Yoshitsune eluded him for several years, eventually was able to have him killed. Yoshitsune is the epitome of the Japanese underdog hero; many legends, stories, kabuki plays, and even films celebrate his adventures with his faithful follower, the monk Benkei. See also GEMPEI WAR.

Minangkabau \,mē-näŋ-kä-'baù\ Largest ethnic group on the island of SUMATRA, Indonesia. Though Muslim, the Minangkabau are matrilineal. Traditionally, the wife remained with her maternal relatives after marriage; her husband lived with his mother but visited his wife. The domestic unit, a community house, held a head woman, her sisters, their daughters, and their children and visiting husbands. Today, that kinship structure has declined and more men have left their villages to establish their own households with wives and children. Traditional Minangkabau are farmers, and their crafts include wood carving, metalwork, and weaving. Some migrated to Malaya (Peninsular Malaysia) in the 1850s to participate in the rapid expansion of Malayan tin mining; over time immigrants switched to farming, and in the 20th century they came to control most of Malaya's retail trade. The Minangkabau number 2–5 million.

Minas Basin \'mī-nəs\ Eastern inlet of the Bay of FUNDY, into central Nova Scotia. Up to 25 mi (40 km) wide and more than 50 mi (80 km) long, it has some of the highest tides in the world; fluctuations exceeding 50 ft (15 m) have been recorded. SAMUEL DE CHAMPLAIN named it "Le Bassin des Mines" in 1604 after the mineral deposits found along its shores.

Minch Sea channel between the Outer HEBRIDES islands and the northwestern coast of Scotland. It is a variable 25–45 mi (40–70 km) wide and has great depth and a rapid current. Little Minch, its southern extension, lies between the island groups of the Outer and Inner Hebrides.

mind, philosophy of Branch of philosophy that studies the nature of mind and its various manifestations, including intentionality, sensation and sense perception, feeling and emotion, dreams, traits of character and personality, the unconscious, volition, thought, memory, and belief. It is distinguished from empirical studies of the mind (e.g., psychology, biology, physiology, sociology, and anthropology) by its method, which emphasizes the analysis and clarification of concepts.

mind-body problem Metaphysical problem of the relationship between mind and body. The modern problem stems from the thought of RENE DESCARTES, who gave DUALISM its classical formulation. Descartes's INTERACTIONISM had many critics even in his own day. THOMAS HOBBES argued that nothing existed but matter in motion, that there was no such thing as mental substance, only material substance. MATERIALISM of a sort was also supported by Descartes's correspondent Pierre Gassendi (1592–1655). BENEDICT DE SPINOZA posited a single substance of which the mental and the material are attributes; his theory is known as psycho-physical parallelism. Other views that have received much recent discussion are central-state materialism, also known as the IDENTITY THEORY, and DOUBLE ASPECT THEORY.

Mindanao \,min-də-'nä-,ō, ,min-də-'naù\ Island (pop., 1990: 13,230,000), southern Philippines. The second largest island in the Philippines, it has an area of 36,537 sq mi (94,630 sq km); it is 324 mi (521 km) long and 293 mi (471 km) wide. It is mountainous and contains active volcanoes, including Mount APO, the highest peak in the Philippines. The rare monkey-eating eagle is unique to the island. Islam spread throughout Mindanao in the 16th century. It was visited by FERDINAND MAGELLAN in 1521. It was later claimed by Spain, but the resistance of its Muslim inhabitants kept it largely independent of Spanish authority. The autonomous region of Muslim Mindanao, in the western and southwestern portions of the island, was created in 1990.

Mindanao River *formerly* **Cotabato River** \,kō-tä-'bä-tō\ Main river of central MINDANAO, Philippines. It meanders northwest to enter Illana Bay in two tributaries, the Cotabato and Tamentaka, after a 200-mi (320-km) course. The river system waters a fertile basin and is a major inland-transportation artery.

Mindon \'min-'dòn\ (1814–1878) King of Myanmar (r.1853–78). He came to power after the Second ANGLO–BURMESE WAR. He was unable to persuade the British to return Pegu (in southern Myanmar) and was also forced to make large economic concessions. Domestically, his reign saw numerous reforms and great cultural and religious flowering. In 1857 he built the new capital, Mandalay, with palaces and monasteries that are masterpieces of traditional Myanmar architecture. He held the fifth Buddhist Council there in 1871 in an effort to revise and purify the Pali scriptures.

Mindoro Island (pop., 1990: 833,000), western central Philippines. It is separated from LUZON on the north by the Verde Island Passage. It is 80 mi (130 km) long and 50 mi (80 km) wide, with an area of 3,759 sq mi (9,735 sq km). First visited by the Spanish in 1570, it came under U.S. rule in 1901. It was occupied by the Japanese during World War II. The tamaraw, a small water buffalo, is unique to the island.

Mindszenty \mĕnd-'shen-tē\, **József** *orig.* **József Pehm** (1892–1975) Hungarian cardinal who opposed fascism and communism. Ordained a priest in 1915, he was arrested as an enemy of totalitarian governments in 1919 and again in 1944. He was appointed primate of Hungary in 1945 and made a cardinal in 1946. Refusing to permit Hungary's Catholic schools to be secularized by the communists, he was arrested in 1948 and convicted of treason the next year. Sentenced to life imprisonment, he was freed in the Hungarian Revolution (1956). When the communists regained control, he sought asylum in the U.S. embassy in Budapest and lived there for 15 years, refusing Vatican requests to leave Hungary. He relented in 1971, settled in Vienna, and was retired as primate of Hungary in 1974.

mine See LAND MINE, SUBMARINE MINE

Miner, Jack *orig.* **John Thomas** (1865–1944) Canadian naturalist. Born in Dover Center, Ohio, he moved to Canada in 1878. In 1904 he established a bird sanctuary on his farm in Kingsville, Ontario. Banding more than 50,000 ducks between 1910 and 1915, he made the first complete banding records of North American birds. In 1931 his friends established the Jack Miner Migratory Bird Foundation to ensure the continuation of his work. He received the Order of the British Empire in 1943.

mineral Any naturally occurring homogeneous solid that has a definite (but not fixed) chemical composition and a distinctive internal crystal structure. Minerals are usually formed by inorganic processes. Synthetic equivalents of various minerals, such as emeralds and diamonds, are manufactured for commercial purposes. Although most minerals are chemical compounds, a small number (e.g., sulfur, copper, gold) are elements. Minerals combine with each other to form rocks. For example, granite consists of the minerals feldspar, quartz, mica, and amphibole in varying amounts. Rocks are generally, therefore, an intergrowth of various minerals.

mineral processing See ORE DRESSING

mineralogy Scientific study of MINERALS, including their physical properties, chemical composition, internal crystal structure, occurrence and distribution in nature, and origins or conditions of formation. Mineralogic studies range from description and classification of new or rare minerals to analysis of crystal structure and laboratory or industrial synthesis of mineral species. The methods employed include physical and chemical identification tests, determination of crystal symmetry and structure, optical examination, X-ray diffraction, and isotope analysis.

Minerva In ROMAN RELIGION, the goddess of handicrafts, the professions, the arts, and, later, war. She was commonly identified with the Greek ATHENA. Some scholars believe that worship of Minerva began when Athena's cult was introduced at Rome from Etruria. Minerva was one of the Capitoline triad, along with JUPITER and JUNO, and her shrine in Rome was a meeting place for craftsmen's guilds. The worship of Minerva attained its greatest vogue under the emperor DOMITIAN, who claimed her special protection.

minesweeper Naval vessel used to clear SUBMARINE MINES from an expanse of water. In naval warfare, they are used to clear mines from sealanes to protect merchant shipping as well as to clear paths for warships to engage in battle or amphibious warfare. The earliest examples used sweeping wires with sawlike projections to cut the cables anchoring submarine mines and allow them to rise to the surface, where they would be destroyed by gunfire. The wide use of magnetic mines (set off by the magnetic field of steel ships) in the Korean War led to wood-hulled minesweepers.

Ming dynasty (1368–1644) Chinese dynasty that provided an interval of native rule between eras of MONGOL and MANCHU dominance. The Ming extended Chinese influence farther than any other native rulers of China in one of the most stable but autocratic of dynasties. Under the Ming, the capital of China was moved from Nanjing to Beijing and the FORBIDDEN CITY was constructed. Naval expeditions led by ZHENG HE paved the way for trade with S.East Asia, India, and eastern Africa. The era saw the creation of novels in the vernacular, while philosophy benefited from the work of WANG YANGMING in NEO-CONFUCIANISM. Ming monochrome porcelain became famous the world over, with imitations created in Vietnam, Japan, and Europe.

Mingus, Charles (1922–1979) U.S. bassist, composer, and bandleader, one of the most important and colorful figures in modern jazz. Born in Nogales, Ariz., Mingus played in the groups of LIONEL HAMPTON, DUKE ELLINGTON, and Red Norvo, ultimately working with many of the innovators of BEBOP. In 1953 he organized the Jazz Workshop ensemble, which played a spirited combination of loosely arranged passages and improvisation, incorporating elements of the blues and free jazz. As a pioneering bandleader and virtuoso bassist, Mingus remained an uncompromising and innovative force in jazz for the rest of his career.

Minhow See FUZHOU

miniature painting Small, detailed painting, usually a portrait, executed in watercolor on vellum (parchment), prepared card, copper, or ivory that can be held in the hand or worn as a piece of jewelry. The name derives from the *minium,* or red lead, used to emphasize initial letters in medieval illuminated manuscripts. Combining the traditions of illumination and the Renaissance medal, it flourished from the early 16th to the mid-19th century. The earliest datable examples were painted in France by JEAN CLOUET THE YOUNGER at the court of FRANCIS I; in England, H. Holbein the Younger produced masterpieces in miniature under HENRY VIII and inspired a long tradition of the practice, known as "limning." NICHOLAS HILLIARD served as miniature painter to ELIZABETH I for more than 30 years. In the 17th–18th century, painting in enamel on metal became popular in France. In Italy ROSALBA CARRIERA introduced the use of ivory (c. 1700) as a luminous surface for transparent pigments, stimulating a great revival of the medium in the late 18th century. By the mid-19th century, miniature paintings were regarded as luxury items and rendered obsolete by the new medium of photography.

minicomputer Computer that is smaller, less expensive, and less powerful than a MAINFRAME or supercomputer, but more expensive and more powerful than a PERSONAL COMPUTER. Minicomputers are used for scientific and engineering computations, business-transaction processing, file handling, and database management, and are often now referred to as small or midsize SERVERS.

Minimalism 20th-century movements in art and music characterized by extreme simplicity of form and rejection of emotional content. In the visual arts, minimalism originated in New York in the 1950s as a form of abstract art and became a major trend in the 1960s and '70s. The Minimalists believed that a work of art should be entirely self-referential; personal elements were stripped away to reveal the objective, purely visual elements. Leading Minimalist sculptors include CARL ANDRE and DONALD JUDD; Minimalist painters include ELLSWORTH KELLY and AGNES MARTIN. In music, Minimalism was an entirely separate movement that arose in the 1960s. It employs a steady pulsing beat, incessant repetition of tones and chords with only gradual changes in their components, a slow rate of harmonic change, and little or no counterpoint. Its principal antecedents are the musics of India and S.East Asia. Its most important early practitioners included La Monte Young (born 1935), Terry Riley (born 1935), whose *In C* (1964) is perhaps its most seminal work, S. REICH, P. GLASS, and JOHN ADAMS.

minimum In mathematics, a point at which the value of a function is lowest. If the value is less than or equal to all other function values, it is an absolute minimum. If it is merely less than at any nearby point, it is a relative, or local, minimum. In CALCULUS, the DERIVATIVE equals zero or does not exist at a function's minimum point. See also MAXIMUM, OPTIMIZATION.

minimum reserve system See FRACTIONAL RESERVE SYSTEM

minimum wage Wage rate established by COLLECTIVE BARGAINING or by government regulation, specifying the lowest rate at which workers may be employed. A legal minimum wage is one mandated by government for all workers in an economy, with few exceptions. Privately negotiated minimum wages determined by collective bargaining apply to a specific group of workers in the economy, usually in specific trades or industries. The modern minimum wage, combined with compulsory arbitration of labor disputes, first appeared in Australia and New Zealand in the 1890s. In 1909 Britain established trade boards to set minimum wage rates in certain trades and industries. The first minimum wage in the U.S. (which applied only to women) was enacted by Massachusetts in 1912. Minimum-wage laws or agreements now exist in most nations.

mining Excavation of materials from the earth's crust, including those of organic origin, such as coal and petroleum. Modern mining is costly and complicated. First, a mineral vein that can likely produce enough of the desired substance to justify the cost of extraction must be located. Then the size of the vein or deposit is determined, and mining engineers decide the best way to mine it. Excavating a mine and extracting mineral substances involve different combinations of drilling, blasting, hoisting, and hauling. Minerals are usually removed in trains of steel boxes drawn along tracks by an electric locomotive. A vital consideration in mining is how to ventilate the underground tunnels and caverns, to provide fresh air to miners and to disperse harmful gases.

mink Either of two species of nocturnal, semiaquatic carnivores in the WEASEL family (Mustelidae) that are trapped and raised commercially for their pelts. *Mustela vison,* found throughout North America except in arid parts of the southwestern U.S., is 17–29 in. (43–74 cm) long and weighs up to 3.5 lbs. (1.6 kg). The Eurasian species *(M. lutreola)* is slightly smaller. The rich brown coat consists of a dense, soft underfur overlaid with glossy guard hairs. Except for furs in the rare mutant colors produced by crossbreeding, wild mink fur is more valuable than "ranch mink."

Minkowski \miŋ-'kȯf-skē\, **Oskar** (1858–1931) German physiologist and pathologist. While researching DIABETES MELLITUS in 1884, he found that beta-hydroxybutyric acid and a decrease in blood bicarbonate cause diabetic acidosis (low blood pH); and that diabetic coma is accompanied by decreased blood carbon dioxide and can be treated by alkali therapy. Experiments on dogs with Joseph von Mering (1849–1908) led him to propose that the pancreas is the source of an "antidiabetic" substance, now known to be insulin. He also demonstrated that the liver produces bile pigments and uric acid.

Minneapolis City (pop., 1996 est.: 359,000), eastern Minnesota. The state's largest city, it is situated on the MISSISSIPPI RIVER near the mouth of the MINNESOTA RIVER. With ST. PAUL across the river it forms the Twin Cities metropolitan area. First visited by French missionary LOUIS HENNEPIN in 1680, the area developed as a military outpost. On the eastern bank was the village of St. Anthony (incorporated 1855), on the western bank, Minneapolis village (incorporated 1856). In 1872 the two merged as the city of Minneapolis, which developed as a center of the lumber and wheat industries. Still a grain market for the surrounding agricultural region, it is also a manufacturing center. Its educational institutions include the University of MINNESOTA.

Minnelli, Vincente (1910–1986) U.S. film director. Born in Chicago, he was a stage manager and costume designer from age 16, achieved success as a Broadway director c. 1935, and moved to Hollywood in 1940. He combined a daring use of color with imaginative camera work in such films as *Cabin in the Sky* (1943), *Meet Me in St. Louis* (1944), *The Pirate* (1948), *Father of the Bride* (1950), *An American in Paris* (1951), *The Bad and the Beautiful* (1952), *The Band Wagon* (1953), *Brigadoon* (1954), and *Gigi* (1958, Academy Award). He was married to JUDY GARLAND 1945–51. Their daughter, the singer and actress Liza Minnelli (born 1946), won a Tony award while still in her teens in *Flora, the Red Menace* (1965). Her movie roles have included *The Sterile Cuckoo* (1969) and *Cabaret* (1972, Academy Award), and she has won a wide following through her energetic and emotional performances in concert and on television.

minnesinger \'mi-nə-ˌsiŋ-ər, 'mi-nə-ˌziŋ-ər\ (from German, *Minne:* "love") German poet-musician, c. 1150–c. 1325, parallel to the TROUBADOURS and TROUVÈRES. Like their French counterparts, the minnesingers' songs were not limited to love but also commented on politics and ethics. Originally members of the high nobility, minnesingers later came from the emerging middle class and had an economic as well as social interest in singing. WALTHER VON DER VOGELWEIDE, Neidhardt von Reuental (c. 1180–c. 1250), and TANNHÄUSER were among the most famous of the minnesingers.

Minnesota State (pop., 1997 est.: 4,686,000), midwestern U.S. It covers 84,068 sq mi (217,736 sq km); its capital is ST. PAUL. The most northerly of the 48 contiguous U.S. states, it has extensive woodlands, fertile prairies, and numerous lakes. Before European settlement, the region was inhabited by the Ojibwa (Chippewa) and the Dakota (SIOUX) tribes. French explorers arrived in search of the NORTHWEST PASSAGE in the mid-17th century. The northeastern portion passed to the British in 1763 and then to the U.S. in 1783, becoming part of the Northwest Territories in 1787. The southwestern portion was acquired by the U.S. in 1803 as part of the LOUISIANA PURCHASE, and the northwestern portion was ceded to the U.S. by the British by treaty in 1818. The first permanent U.S. settlement was made in 1819, when Fort Snelling was founded. The Minnesota Territory, established in 1849, included present-day Minnesota and the eastern sections of North and South Dakota. Minnesota became the 32nd U.S. state in 1858. The Sioux Uprising in southern Minnesota in 1862 resulted in the death of 500 civilians, soldiers, and Indians. Commercial iron-ore production began in 1884 and after the huge iron reserves of the Mesabi Range were discovered in 1890, the population at DULUTH and Superior grew rapidly. Today agriculture, especially grains, meat, and dairy products, is the basis of the economy. Mineral resources include iron ore, granite, and limestone.

Minnesota, University of State university system consisting of a main campus in the Twin Cities district and three branch campuses. The main campus originated as a preparatory school in 1851 and received land-grant status in 1862. The university offers comprehensive undergraduate, graduate, and professional programs. Its noted undergraduate programs include chemical engineering, medical technology, geography, economics, psychology, and architecture. There are over 100 research facilities, and its library houses about 5 million volumes. Enrollment at the main campus is about 37,000.

Minnesota Mining & Manufacturing Co. (3M) U.S. corporation headquartered in St. Paul, Minn., manufacturing a wide range of products. It was incorporated under its present name in 1902; its first product was sandpaper. It grew steadily, adding the original cellophane tape—Scotch tape—and masking tape to its product line. Today its products include photographic film, videocassettes, computer-synthesized graphics, and health-care products. It is notable among diversified U.S. corporations in that its growth has been primarily by internal means rather than by large-scale acquisitions.

Minnesota River River, southern Minnesota. Rising on the South Dakota–Minnesota boundary, it flows southeast then turns northeast to join the MISSISSIPPI RIVER just south of ST. PAUL, after a course of 332 mi (534 km). Once known as the St. Peter or St. Pierre, it was important to early explorers and fur traders.

minnow Small fishes, especially of the CARP family (Cyprinidae), as well as some ROCKFISH (family Umbridae) and KILLIFISHES (family Cyprinodontidae). The numerous species of North American cyprinid minnows are freshwater fishes, 2.4–12 in. (6–30 cm) long. Many are valuable as food for fishes, birds, and other animals and as live bait. The bluntnose *(Pimephales notatus)* and fathead *(P. promelas)* minnows, the common SHINER, and the American ROACH are good bait species. The term also refers to the young of many large fish species. The minnow of Europe and northern Asia *(Phoxinus phoxinus)* is about 3 in. (7.5 cm) long and varies from golden to green.

Mino da Fiesole \'mē-nō-dä-fyā-'zō-lā\ (1429–1484) Italian sculptor. Probably trained in Florence (near his hometown of Fiesole), he was active both in Florence and Rome, where he created monuments (especially wall tombs) and busts of cardinals and other prominent individuals. Among the earliest Renaissance portrait sculptures, his works were greatly admired in the 19th century but are now considered less inspired than those of DESIDERIO DA SETTIGNANO, Antonio Rossellino (1427–1479), and other eminent contemporaries.

Minoans \mi-'nō-ənz\ Non-Indo-European people who flourished (c. 3000–c. 1100 BC) on the island of Crete during the BRONZE AGE. The sea was the basis of their economy and power. Their sophisticated culture, based at KNOSSOS, was named for the legendary King MINOS. It represented the first high civilization in the Aegean area. The Minoans exerted great influence on the MYCENAEAN culture of the Greek islands and mainland. Minoan culture reached its peak c. 1600 BC and was noted for its cities and palaces, extended trade contacts, and use of writing (see LINEAR A AND LINEAR B). Its art included elaborate seals, pottery, and, notably, the vibrant frescoes decorating palace walls, which depicted both religious and secular scenes, including goddesses reflective of a matriarchal religion. Palace ruins show evidence of paved streets and piped water. Familiar Minoan art motifs are the snake (symbol of the goddess) and the bull and leaping dancer, also of mystical significance.

Minos \'mī-nəs\ In Greek legend, a king of Crete, the son of ZEUS and EUROPA. He gained the throne with the aid of POSEIDON and also became ruler of the Aegean islands. His wife Pasiphaë fell in love with a bull and gave birth to the MINOTAUR, which was imprisoned in the Labyrinth. Minos waged war against Athens and exacted a tribute of youths and maidens to feed the Minotaur until THESEUS killed the monster with the aid of Minos's daughter ARIADNE. Minos was killed in Sicily when boiling water was poured over him as he was taking a bath. Many scholars now consider that Minos was a royal or dynastic title for the priestly rulers of Bronze Age, or MINOAN, civilization in KNOSSOS (Minoan means "of Minos").

Minot \'mī-nət\, **George (Richards)** (1885–1950) U.S. physician. Born in Boston, he received his medical degree from Harvard University. He reversed anemia in dogs (induced by excessive bleeding) with a diet of raw liver; subsequently he and William Murphy (1894–1987) found that eating raw liver reversed pernicious anemia in humans. They shared a Nobel Prize in 1934 with GEORGE WHIPPLE for their treatment of the previously invariably fatal disease. He and EDWIN JOSEPH COHN prepared liver extracts that, taken orally, were the main treatment for pernicious anemia until 1948, when vitamin B_{12} was isolated.

Minotaur \'mi-nə-ˌtȯr\ In GREEK MYTHOLOGY, a monster of Crete with the body of a man and the head of a bull. It was the offspring of Pasiphaë, wife of King MINOS, and a snow-white bull sent by POSEIDON and intended for sacrifice. When Minos kept it instead, the god punished him by making his wife fall in love with the bull. The Minotaur (whose name means "Minos bull") was imprisoned in the Labyrinth built by DAEDALUS. After defeating Athens in a war, Minos forced the Athenians to send human tribute to be devoured by the Minotaur. The third year the tribute was sent, THESEUS volunteered to go, and with the help of ARIADNE he killed the monster.

Minsk Capital (pop., 1996 est.: 1,700,000) and largest city of Belarus. Settled before 1067, it became the seat of a principality in 1101. It passed to Lithuania in the 14th century and later to Poland. Annexed by Russia in the Second Partition of POLAND in 1793, it became a provincial center. It was occupied by French troops in 1812. It grew in importance as an industrial center after the arrival of the railways in 1870. During World War I it was occupied first by the Germans and then by the Poles. It was almost entirely destroyed in World War II, especially during the Soviet advance in 1944. Once the capital of the Belorussian S.S.R., it remained the capital when Belarus gained independence in 1991. It is the country's administrative and industrial center.

Minsky, Marvin (Lee) (born 1927) U.S. computer scientist. Born in New York City, he received his PhD from Princeton University and joined the faculty at MIT, where he has remained for his entire career. His research has contributed to advances in ARTIFICIAL INTELLIGENCE, cognitive psychology, NEURAL NETWORKS (he built the first neural-network simulator in 1951), and the theory of Turing machines. A pioneer in robotics, he built some of the first mechanical hands with tactile sensors, visual scanners, and accompanying software and computer interfaces. He influenced many robotic projects outside MIT and has worked to build into machines the human capacity for commonsense reasoning. In his *The Society of Mind* (1987), 270 interconnected one-page ideas reflect the structure of his theory. He has participated in many studies of advanced technologies for space exploration. He received the Turing Award in 1969.

minstrel Wandering musician of the Middle Ages, often of low status. The term (and equivalents such as Latin *ioculator* and French *jongleur*) was applied in medieval times to people ranging from singing beggars to traveling musicians hired by towns for special occasions to court jesters. The modern folksinger is a descendant. See also MINSTREL SHOW.

minstrel show Form of entertainment popular in the U.S. in the 19th and early 20th century. It originated in the 1830s with the popular white performer Thomas D. Rice, known as "Jim Crow," who wore the stylized makeup called blackface and performed songs and dances in a stereotyped imitation of black Americans. Blackfaced white minstrel troupes were particularly popular in the U.S. and England in 1840–80 and included such groups as the Christy Minstrels, who played on Broadway for 10 years and had songs composed for them by S. FOSTER. Black minstrel troupes also performed after the Civil War. The minstrel show included an opening chorus and frequent exchanges of jokes between the emcee, Mr. Interlocutor, and the end men, Mr. Tambo (who played the tambourine) and Mr. Bones (who rattled the bones), interspersed with ballads, comic songs, and instrumental numbers (usually on the banjo and violin), as well as individual acts, soft-shoe dances, and specialty numbers.

mint In botany, any fragrant, strong-scented herb of the genus *Mentha,* composed of about 25 species of perennial herbs, and certain related genera of the mint family (Lamiaceae, or Labiatae), which contains about 3,500 species of flowering plants in about 160 genera. Mints are important to humans as herb plants useful for flavor, fragrance, and medicinal properties. True mints have square stems, opposite, aromatic leaves, and small flowers usually of a pale purple, pink, or white color arranged in clusters, either forming separate whorls or crowded together in a terminal spike. All *Mentha* species contain volatile oil in resinous dots in the leaves and stems. Included in this genus are PEPPERMINT, SPEARMINT, MARJORAM, ROSEMARY, and THYME; other members of the mint family include LAVENDER, HYSSOP, and CATNIP.

mint In economics, a place where coins are made according to exact compositions, weights, and dimensions, usually specified by law. The first state mint was probably established by the Lydians in the 7th century BC. The art spread through the Aegean Islands into Italy and other Mediterranean countries, as well as to Persia and India. The Romans laid the foundations of modern minting standards. Coining originated independently in China in the 7th century BC and spread to Japan and Korea. In medieval Europe, mints proliferated as every feudal authority—kings, counts, bishops, and free cities—exercised the mint privilege; the wide variation in coinage that resulted often handicapped commerce. Most countries now operate only one mint, though the U.S. has two active mints, in Philadelphia and Denver. Proof sets of coins for coin collectors are minted in San Francisco. Countries not large or prosperous enough to establish a national mint have their coins struck in foreign mints. Many mints perform functions other than minting, notably refining precious metals and manufacturing medals and seals. See also CURRENCY, MONEY.

minuet \ˌmin-yə-'wet\ Dignified couple dance derived from a French folk dance, dominant in European court ballrooms in the 17th–18th century. Using small, slow steps to music in 3/4 time, dancers often performed choreographed figures combined with stylized bows and curtsies. The most popular dance of the 18th-century aristocracy, it fell from favor after the French Revolution in 1789. It was of great importance in art music; commonly incorporated into the SUITE c. 1650–1775, it was the only dance form retained in the SYMPHONY, SONATA, STRING QUARTET, and other multimovement art-music genres up to c. 1800.

Minuit \'min-yə-wət\, **Peter** (1580?–1638) Dutch colonial governor of New Netherland. In 1626 the Dutch West India Co. named him director general of the colony on Manhattan Island. To legitimize the European occupation of the island, he persuaded the Indians to sell it for a few trinkets worth (according to legend) 60 guilders ($24). At the island's southern tip he founded New Amsterdam. He was recalled to Holland (1631) and later was sent to establish the colony of New Sweden on Delaware Bay, where he again purchased land from the Indians and built Fort Christina (later Wilmington, Del.) in 1638.

minuscule \'mi-nəs-ˌkyül, mi-'nəs-ˌkyül\ Lowercase letters in CALLIGRAPHY, in contrast to MAJUSCULE, or uppercase letters. Unlike majuscules, minuscules are not fully contained between two real or hypothetical lines; their stems can go above or below the line. Developed by ALCUIN in the 8th century, it allowed the division of writing into sentences and paragraphs by beginning sentences with capital letters and ending them with periods. The script was originally rounded, but gradually the strokes became heavier until it became what is now known as Gothic or BLACK LETTER SCRIPT.

minuteman Colonial soldier of the AMERICAN REVOLUTION. Minutemen were first organized in Massachusetts in September 1774, when revolutionary leaders sought to eliminate Tories, or British sympathizers, from the militia by replacing all officers. One-third of the members of each new regiment was to be ready for military duty "at a minute's warning." Their first great test was at the Battles of LEXINGTON AND CONCORD. On July 18, the Continental Congress recommended that other colonies organize minuteman units.

Minuteman missile U.S. ICBM first deployed in 1962. Its three generations—the Minuteman I (1962), the Minuteman II (from 1966), and the Minuteman III (from 1970)—constituted most of the land-based nuclear arsenal of the U.S. from the 1960s through the 1980s. They were the first U.S. ICBMs to be based in underground silos. From 1986 they began to be replaced by the Peacekeeper.

Miocene epoch \'mī-ə-ˌsēn\ Major division of the TERTIARY PERIOD, from 23.8 to 5.3 million years ago. The extensive fossil record of terrestrial life during the Miocene provides a fairly complete picture of the development of vertebrates, especially mammals. Miocene mammals were essentially modern, and half of the known modern families are present in the Miocene record. The horse evolved, mainly in North America, and advanced primates, including apes, were present in southern Europe. Some interchange of faunas occurred in the Northern Hemisphere between the Old and New Worlds. Communication between Africa and Eurasia occurred, but South America and Australia remained isolated.

Miquelon See SAINT-PIERRE AND MIQUELON

Mir Russian SPACE STATION consisting of a core module launched in 1986 and five additional modules launched separately over the next decade and attached to the core unit to create a large, versatile space laboratory. The third generation of Russian space stations (see SALYUT), Mir featured six docking ports for modules and other spacecraft, expanded living quarters, more power, and modernized research equipment. It supported human habitation between 1986 and 2000, including an uninterrupted stretch of occupancy of almost 10 years, and it hosted a series of U.S. astronauts in 1995–98 as part of a Mir-SPACE SHUTTLE cooperative endeavor. In 1995, Valery Polyakov (born 1942) set a new world endurance record of nearly 438 days in space aboard Mir. In March 2001 the abandoned station was brought down in a controlled reentry, with the surviving pieces falling into the Pacific Ocean.

Mir Sayyid Ali (fl. 16th century) Persian miniature painter. Born in Tabriz, he went to India about 1545. He and fellow countryman ABD AL-SAMAD instructed the artists of the imperial atelier, most of them Indians, and thereby helped to found the school of MUGHAL PAINTING. He supervised part of the production of the illustrations to the Mughal manuscript *Dastan-e Amir Hamzeh* ("Stories of Amir Hamzeh"). The few paintings by him that have survived reveal that he was a highly gifted painter, wielding a delicate brushstroke and great powers of observation.

Mirabai \'mē-rä-'bä-ē\ (1450?–1547?) Rajput princess and Hindu mystic whose songs are popular in northern India. According to legend, Mirabai dedicated her life to KRISHNA after her husband's death. She received sadhus and pilgrims at her private temple dedicated to Krishna and composed songs of devotion to him. Her poems allude to two attempts on her life, both foiled miraculously. When a delegation of Brahmans sought to return her to her husband's kingdom, she disappeared. Only two poems bearing her signature can be dated before the 18th century, but her story is the most familiar of those of northern Indian saints.

Mirabeau \mē-rȧ-'bō\, **comte (Count) de** *orig.* **Honoré-Gabriel Riqueti** (1749–1791) French politician and orator. Son of the economist Victor Riqueti, he was often imprisoned for intrigues and wild behavior, and he wrote several essays on prison life. In 1789 he was elected to the Estates General from the Third Estate. A skilled orator, he was popular with the people and was influential in the early years of the French Revolution. He advocated a constitutional monarchy and tried to mediate between the absolute monarchists and the revolutionaries. He was elected president of the National Assembly in 1791, but died soon after.

Mirabello Gulf Gulf of the AEGEAN SEA on the northern coast of CRETE, Greece. The gulf is separated by a promontory from the Bay of Sitías on the east. Olonte and Lato are ruined classical settlements; at Gourniá and on the islets of Psíra and Mókhlos are the remains of Late MINOAN (1600–1450 BC) settlements.

miracle Extraordinary event attributed to a supernatural power. Belief in miracles exists in all cultures and nearly all religions. The UPANISHADS assert that the experience of religious insight and transformation is the only "miracle" worth considering, but popular HINDUISM attributes miraculous powers to the ascetic yogis. CONFUCIANISM had little room for miracles; TAOISM, however, mingled with Chinese folk religion to produce a rich crop of miracles. Miracles are taken for granted throughout the OLD TESTAMENT and were fairly common in the Greco-Roman world. Though BUDDHA Gautama deprecated his own miraculous powers as devoid of spiritual significance, accounts of his miraculous birth and life were later woven into his legend and into those of later Buddhist saints. The NEW TESTAMENT records miracles of healing and other wonders performed by JESUS. Miracles also attest to the holiness of Christian saints. MUHAMMAD renounced miracles as a matter of principle (the QURAN was the great miracle), but his life was later invested with miraculous details. Muslim popular religion, particularly under the influence of SUFISM, abounds in miracles and wonder-working saints.

miracle play Type of vernacular drama performed in the Middle Ages, presenting a real or fictitious account of the life, miracles, or martyrdom of a saint. The genre evolved from the LITURGICAL DRAMAS of the 10th–11th century, which were intended to enhance church calendar festivals. By the 13th century the plays were separated from church services and performed at public festivals by amateur actors. Most miracle plays concerned either the Virgin Mary or St. NICHOLAS, both of whom had active cults in the Middle Ages. See also MORALITY PLAY, MYSTERY PLAY.

mirage \mə-'räzh\ In optics, the deceptive appearance of a distant object caused by the bending of light rays (REFRACTION) in layers of air of varying density. Under certain conditions, such as over a stretch of pavement or desert air heated by intense sunshine, the air cools rapidly with elevation and therefore increases in density and refractive power. Sunlight reflected down from the upper portion of an object will be directed through cool air in the normal way; although the light would not be seen ordinarily because of the angle, it curves upward after it enters the rarefied hot air near the ground, thus being refracted to the observer's eye as though it had originated below the heated surface. When the sky is the object of the mirage, the land is mistaken for a body of water.

miraj \'mi-rȧj\ Ascension of MUHAMMAD into heaven. Muhammad was visited by two archangels, who opened his body and purified his heart of all doubt, error, and paganism. He was carried to heaven, where he ascended the seven levels to reach the throne of God. Along the way he and the archangel JIBRIL met the prophets ADAM, Yahya (JOHN THE APOSTLE), Isa (JESUS), Yusuf (JOSEPH), Idris, Harun (AARON), Musa (MOSES), and Ibrahim (ABRAHAM) and visited hell and paradise. He learned that he was more highly regarded by God than all the other prophets. The miraj is popularly celebrated with readings of the legend on the 27th day of Rajab, called the Laylat al-Miraj ("Night of the Ascension").

Miranda \mi-'ran-də\, **Carmen** *orig.* **Maria do Carmo Miranda da Cunha** (1909–1955) Brazilian singer and actress. In the 1930s she was the most popular recording artist in Brazil, where she appeared in five films. Recruited by a Broadway producer, she starred in *The Streets of Paris* (1939), then made her U.S. film debut in *Down Argentine Way* (1940). Typecast as the "Brazilian Bombshell" and given such caricature roles as "The Lady in the Tutti-Frutti Hat" in *The Gang's All Here* (1943), she became the highest-paid female performer in the U.S. during World War II. Her final U.S. film was *Scared Stiff* (1953).

Miranda \mē-'rän-dä\, **Francisco de** (1750–1816) Venezuelan revolutionary who helped pave the way for his country's independence. He joined the Spanish army but fled to the U.S. in 1783, where he met leaders of the AMERICAN REVOLUTION and formed plans for the liberation of South America, which he envisioned ruled by an Incan emperor and a bicameral legislature. He launched an unsuccessful invasion of Venezuela in 1806 and returned at the request of SIMON BOLIVAR to fight again in 1810. He assumed dictatorial powers in 1811 when independence was declared, but succumbed to a Spanish counterattack and signed an armistice. Fellow revolutionaries, viewing his surrender as traitorous, thwarted his attempt to escape. He died in a Spanish prison cell.

Miranda v. Arizona U.S. Supreme Court decision (1966) that specified a code of conduct for police during interrogations of criminal suspects. *Miranda* established that the police are required to inform arrested persons that they have the right to remain silent, that anything they say may be used against them, and that they have the right to an attorney. The case involved a claim by the plaintiff that the state of Arizona, by obtaining a confession from him without having informed him of his right to have a lawyer present, had violated his rights under the 5th Amendment regarding SELF-INCRIMINATION. The 5–4 decision shocked the law-enforcement community; later decisions have served to limit its scope somewhat. See also rights of the ACCUSED.

Mirim \mē-'rēm\, **Lake** *Spanish* **Laguna Merín** \mā-'rēn\ Tidewater lake separating the eastern boundary of Uruguay from the extreme southern tip of Brazil. It is about 118 mi (190 km) long and 30 mi (48 km) across at its widest point, covering an area of 1,542 sq mi (3,994 sq km). A low, marshy bar, 10–35 mi (17–59 km) wide and containing small lagoons, separates it from the Atlantic Ocean.

Miró \mē-'rō\, **Joan** (1893–1983) Spanish (Catalan) artist. Born in Barcelona, from the beginning he sought to express concepts of nature metaphorically. From 1919 on he lived alternately in Spain and Paris, where he came under the influence of Dada and Surrealism. The influence of PAUL KLEE is apparent in his "dream pictures" and "imaginary landscapes" of the late 1920s, in which linear configurations and patches of color look almost as though they had been set down randomly. His mature style evolved from the tension between this fanciful, poetic impulse and his vision of the harshness of modern life. He worked extensively in lithography and produced numerous murals, tapestries, and sculptures for public spaces.

Miró, photograph by Yousuf Karsh, 1966.

MIRV \'mərv\ *in full* **Multiple Independently Targeted Reentry Vehicle** Any of several nuclear warheads carried on the front end of a ballistic missile. The technique allows separately targeted nuclear warheads to be fired independently. The warheads can be released from the missile at different speeds and on different trajectories. MIRV technology was first developed in the U.S.; today all the U.S. and Russian ICBMs and submarine-launched ballistic missiles can be equipped with MIRVs.

miscarriage *or* **spontaneous abortion** Spontaneous expulsion of an EMBRYO or FETUS from the UTERUS before it can live outside the mother. More than 60% are caused by an inherited defect in the fetus, which might result in a fatal abnormality. Other causes may include acute infectious disease, especially if it reduces the fetus's oxygen supply; abnormalities of the uterus that have physical or hormonal origins; and death of the fetus from umbilical-cord knotting. The main sign of impending miscarriage is vaginal bleeding.

misdemeanor See FELONY AND MISDEMEANOR

Mises \'mē-zes\, **Ludwig (Edler) von** (1881–1973) Austrian-U.S. libertarian economist. He taught at the University of Vienna (1913–38) before emigrating to the U.S. and joining the New York University faculty (1945–69). In *The Anti-Capitalistic Mentality* (1956), an examination of U.S. socialism, he dealt with the opposition to the free market of intellectuals, who, in his view, bear an unwarranted resentment toward the necessity of obeying mass demand, which is the basis of prosperity in big business.

Mishima \'mē-shē-mä\, **Yukio** *orig.* **Hiraoka Kimitake** (1925–1970) Japanese writer. Having failed to qualify physically for military service in World War II, Mishima worked in a Tokyo factory and after the war studied law. He won acclaim with his first novel, *Confessions of a Mask* (1949). Many of his characters are obsessed with unattainable ideals and erotic desires, as in *The Temple of the Golden Pavilion* (1956). His epic *The Sea of Fertility* (4 vols., 1965–70) is perhaps his most lasting achievement. Strongly opposed to Japan's imitation of the West in the postwar era, he formed a small private army, hoping to preserve Japan's martial spirit and protect the emperor. After seizing a military headquarters, he died by committing SEPPUKU. He is often considered his nation's most important 20th-century novelist.

Mishna *or* **Mishnah** \mēsh-'nä, 'mish-nə\ Oldest authoritative collection of Jewish oral law, supplementing the written laws in the OLD TESTAMENT. It was compiled by a series of scholars over two centuries and was given final form in the 3rd century AD by JUDAH HA-NASI. Annotations by later scholars in Palestine and Babylonia resulted in the GEMARA; the Mishna and Gemara are usually said to make up the TALMUD. The Mishna has six major sections, on daily prayer and agriculture, SABBATH and other religious ritual, married life, civil and criminal law, the Temple of JERUSALEM, and ritual purification.

Mishne Torah \mēsh-'ne-tō-'rä\ Extensive commentary on the TALMUD, composed in the 12th century by MOSES MAIMONIDES. Its 14 volumes deal with laws covering such subjects as ethical conduct, civil affairs, torts, marriage and divorce, and gifts to the poor. Maimonides intended the Mishne Torah to combine religious law and philosophy and to serve as a vehicle for teaching rather than merely to prescribe conduct.

Miskito Coast See MOSQUITO COAST

Miskolc \'mish-ˌkōlts\ City (pop., 1997 est.: 178,000), northeastern Hungary. It lies on the eastern margin of the Avas Hills. Caves in the limestone hills, inhabited from prehistoric times, now serve as cellars for the wine-making industry. Settled by Germanic tribes, Sarmatians and Avars, the town was conquered by the Hungarians in the 10th century. It was invaded by the Mongols in the 13th century. It became a free city in the 15th century. A major industrial center, it produces iron and steel. Historic buildings include a 13th-century Gothic church.

misrepresentation In law, any false or misleading expression of fact, usually with the intent to deceive or defraud. It most commonly occurs in insurance and real-estate contracts. False advertising may also constitute misrepresentation. Any contract that contains or constitutes a misrepresentation is usually rendered void, and the injured party may insist that the misrepresentation be made good.

missile ROCKET-propelled weapon designed to deliver an explosive warhead with great accuracy at high speed. Missiles vary from small tactical weapons effective out to only a few hundred feet to much larger strategic weapons with ranges of several thousand miles. They were not developed in any significant way until after World War II. Almost all contain some form of guidance and control mechanism and are therefore often called GUIDED MISSILES. An unguided military missile, as well as any launch vehicle used to penetrate the upper atmosphere or place a satellite in space, is usually called a rocket. A propeller-driven underwater missile is called a TORPEDO, and a guided missile powered along a low, level flight path by an air-breathing jet engine is called a CRUISE missile. With the development of ICBMs, missiles became central to COLD WAR strategy. See also ANTIBALLISTIC MISSILE, MINUTEMAN MISSILE, V-1 MISSILE, V-2 MISSILE.

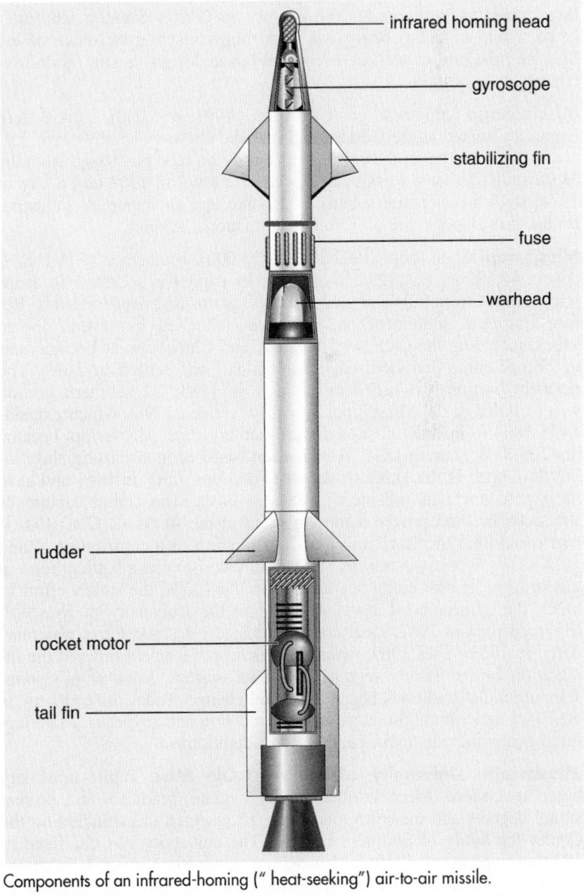

Components of an infrared-homing ("heat-seeking") air-to-air missile.

Missile Defense Alarm System (Midas) Any of a series of unmanned U.S. military satellites developed to provide warning of surprise attacks by Soviet intercontinental ballistic missiles. Midas was the first such warning system in the world. Launched in the early 1960s, the reconnaissance satellites were equipped with infrared sensors capable of detecting the heat of a ballistic missile's rocket exhaust shortly after firing.

mission Organized effort to spread the Christian faith. St. PAUL evangelized much of Asia Minor and Greece, and the new religion spread rapidly along the trade routes of the Roman empire. The advance of Christianity slowed with the disintegration of the Roman empire after 500 and the growth of Arab power in the 7th–8th century, but Celtic and British missionaries continued to spread the faith in western and northern Europe, while missionaries of the Greek church in Constantinople worked in eastern Europe and Russia. Missions to Islamic areas and the Orient began in the medieval period, and when Spain, Portugal, and France established overseas empires in the 16th century, the Roman Catholic church sent missionaries to the Americas and the Philippines. A renewed wave of Roman Catholic missionary work in the 19th century focused on Africa and Asia. Protestant churches were slower to undertake foreign missions, but in the 19th and early 20th century there was a great upsurge in Protestant missionary activity. Missionary work continues today, though it is often discouraged by the governments of former European colonies that have won independence.

Mission style *or* **Spanish Mission style** Style of the missions established by Spanish Franciscans in Florida, Texas, Arizona, New Mexico, and especially California (1769–1823). Their portals were often handsomely ornate, but the overall impression is one of simple geometric volumes of white stucco complemented by sharply incised windows and simplified interior details. Mission style also commonly refers to a style largely created in the early 20th century by GUSTAV STICKLEY, who marketed a line of plain, heavy oak furnishings inspired by those of the Spanish missions, as well as a series of house designs to suit modest incomes.

Mississauga \ˌmi-sə-ˈsȯ-gə\ City (pop., 1991: 463,000), southeastern Ontario. Situated at the western end of Lake ONTARIO, southwest of TORONTO, it was settled in the early 19th century on land purchased from the Mississauga Indians. Mississauga became a town in 1968 and a city in 1974. Both a residential suburb of Toronto and an important industrial center, it is also the site of Toronto International Airport.

Mississippi State (pop., 1997 est.: 2,731,000), southern central U.S. It covers 47,689 sq mi (123,514 sq km); its capital is JACKSON. Its landscape ranges from hills and pine woods to plains and river lowlands. Before European settlement, the area was inhabited by several Indian tribes, including the CHOCTAW, Natchez, and Chickasaw. It became part of French-controlled Louisiana, and Biloxi was settled in 1699. The northern portion was ceded to the U.S. in 1783; the southern portion was included in the Mississippi Territory (created 1798), which expanded in 1804 to include most of the present-day state. Mississippi became the 20th U.S. state in 1817. A plantation-based economy using slave labor developed in the 1820s. It seceded from the Union in 1861 and gave the Confederacy its president, JEFFERSON DAVIS. The Union capture of VICKSBURG in 1863 proved a turning point in the AMERICAN CIVIL WAR. It was readmitted to the Union in 1870 and adopted a constitution aimed at blocking RECONSTRUCTION in 1890. The state became a battleground in the struggle against racial segregation in the 1960s: the state's effort to block the admission of JAMES MEREDITH to the University of MISSISSIPPI triggered riots in 1962; local civil rights leader MEDGAR EVERS was murdered in 1963. After 1969, when the federal government ordered the integration of the state's segregated school system, Mississippi's longstanding racial traditions began a gradual change. Today, its economy is based on agricultural products, including cotton and soybeans. Manufactured goods include textiles and electrical equipment.

Mississippi, University of *known as* **Ole Miss** Public university based in Oxford, Miss. It offers undergraduate, graduate, and professional degrees and manages more than 15 research units, including the Center for Study of Southern Culture. The university was chartered in 1844 and opened in 1848. Its law school, established in 1854, is one of the oldest public law schools in the U.S. Women were first admitted in 1882; racial segregation was forcibly ended in 1962 (see GEORGE WALLACE). WILLIAM FAULKNER attended classes at the university, which now operates his Oxford home as a museum. Enrollment at the main campus exceeds 11,000.

Mississippi River River, central U.S. It rises at Lake ITASCA in Minnesota and flows south, meeting its major tributaries, the MISSOURI and the OHIO rivers, about halfway along its journey to the Gulf of MEXICO. It enters the Gulf southeast of NEW ORLEANS, after a course of 2,350 mi (3,780 km). It is the largest river in North America, and with its tributaries it drains an area of 1.2 million sq mi (3.1 million sq km). Spanish explorer HERNANDO DE SOTO was the first European to discover the river in 1541. French explorers LOUIS JOLLIET and JACQUES MARQUETTE traveled down it in 1673 as far as the ARKANSAS RIVER. French explorer R.-R. LA SALLE, reached the delta in 1682 and claimed the entire Mississippi region for France, as Louisiana. France kept control over the upper river, but the lower portion passed to Spain in 1769. It was designated as the western boundary of the U.S. in 1783. France sold it to the U.S. in 1803 as part of the LOUISIANA PURCHASE. During the AMERICAN CIVIL WAR, Union forces captured VICKSBURG in 1863, breaking the Confederate hold on the river. A powerful river, it was immortalized by MARK TWAIN in *Huckleberry Finn*. As the central river artery of the U.S, it is one of the busiest commercial waterways in the world.

Mississippian culture Last major prehistoric cultural development in North America, c. 800–1550. It spread over much of the Southeast and the mid-continent, especially in the major river valleys. It was based on intensive cultivation of corn, beans, squash, and other crops. Each large town dominated a group of satellite villages. Each had a central ceremonial plaza with one or more pyramidal or oval earthen mounds surmounted by a temple, a pattern indicating a connection to Central America. The immense Cahokia Mounds near present-day Collinsville, Ill., was the culture's largest urban center. Craftwork was executed in copper, shell, stone, wood, and clay. The culture had already begun to decline by the time Europeans first penetrated the Southeast. See also SOUTHEASTERN INDIANS, WOODLAND CULTURES.

Mississippian period In North America, an interval of geologic time roughly equivalent to what is internationally designated the Early CARBONIFEROUS epoch (360–320 million years ago). Because the rocks associated with this period are typified by those in the Mississippi valley, some U.S. geologists prefer the designation Mississippian to the European term Early Carboniferous.

Missouri State (pop., 1997 est.: 5,402,000), midwestern U.S. It covers 69,697 sq mi (180,515 sq km); its capital is JEFFERSON CITY. The MISSOURI RIVER runs from west to east across the state. The area north of it has rolling hills and fertile plains, the area south has deep valleys and swift streams. The region was originally inhabited by different Indian tribes, one of which, the Missouri, gave the state its name. The first permanent European settlement was made in 1735 at Ste. Genevieve by French hunters and lead miners. ST. LOUIS was founded in 1764. The U.S. gained control of the region in 1803 as part of the LOUISIANA PURCHASE. It was part of Louisiana Territory in 1805 and Missouri Territory in 1812. An influx of U.S. settlers occurred after the WAR OF 1812. Missouri became the 24th state in 1821, but only after the MISSOURI COMPROMISE allowed its admission as a slave state. It suffered much tension between slaveholders and abolitionists, evidenced in the DRED SCOTT DECISION in 1857. Missouri remained in the Union during the AMERICAN CIVIL WAR, though its citizens fought on both sides. After the war, its economic growth expanded and was celebrated in the St. Louis Exhibition of 1904. After World War II, its economy shifted from agriculture to manufacturing. It leads the nation in lead production, based mainly in the OZARKS region.

Missouri, University of State university system with campuses in Columbia (main campus), St. Louis, Kansas City, and Rolla. It was founded in Columbia in 1839, and in 1870 was given land-grant status. The Columbia campus provides comprehensive undergraduate, graduate, and professional degree programs and is divided into numerous schools and colleges. The Kansas City branch includes schools of dentistry and pharmacy, a music conservatory, and a telecommunications program. The St. Louis branch is known for its school of optometry and its center for metropolitan studies. Both the Columbia and Kansas City campuses have law and medical schools. Total enrollment exceeds 50,000.

Missouri Compromise (1820) Act passed by the U.S. Congress admitting Missouri to the Union as the 24th state. After the territory requested statehood without slavery restrictions, Northern congressmen tried unsuccessfully to attach amendments restricting further slaveholding. When Maine (originally part of Massachusetts) requested statehood, a compromise led by HENRY CLAY allowed Missouri admission as a slave state and Maine as a free state, with slavery prohibited from then on in territories north of Missouri's southern border. Clay's compromise appeared to settle the slavery-extension issue but highlighted the sectional division.

Missouri Plan Method of selecting judges that originated in the state of Missouri and was later adopted elsewhere. Designed to overcome the weaknesses of the elective system, the plan permits the governor to select a judge from a list of nominees recommended by a special commission, but requires that the judge be approved in a public referendum after serving a period of time.

Missouri River River, central U.S. The longest tributary of the Mississippi River, it is formed in the Rocky Mtns. of southwestern Montana. It flows east to central North Dakota and south across South Dakota, forming sections of the South Dakota–Nebraska boundary, the Nebraska–Iowa boundary, the Nebraska–Missouri boundary, and the Kansas–Missouri boundary. It then meanders east across central Missouri to join the Mississippi River north of St. Louis, after a total course of 2,315 mi (3,726 km). It has been nicknamed "Big Muddy" because of the amount of silt that it carries. The first Europeans to visit its mouth were French explorers Jacques Marquette and Louis Jolliet in 1673. The first exploration of the river from its mouth to its headwaters was made in 1804–5 by the Lewis and Clark Expedition. Since the mid-20th century, programs have been instituted along its banks to check its turbulent flooding and to harness it for irrigation.

Missouri River, Little See Little Missouri River

Misti \'mēs-tē\, **El** *or* **Volcán Misti** Volcano, Andes, southern Peru. It is flanked by Chachani and Pichupichu volcanoes and rises to 19,098 ft (5,821 m) above sea level, towering over the city of Arequipa. Its pristine, snowcapped cone is thought to have had religious significance for the Incas, and it has inspired legends and poetry. Now dormant, it last erupted during an earthquake in 1600.

mistletoe Any of many species of semiparasitic green plants of the families Loranthaceae and Viscaceae, especially those of the genera *Viscum, Phoradendron,* and *Arceuthobium,* all members of the Viscaceae family. *V. album,* the traditional mistletoe of literature and Christmas celebrations, is found throughout Eurasia. This yellowish evergreen bush (2–3 ft, or 0.6–0.9 m, long) droops on the branch of a host tree. The thickly crowded, forking branches bear small leathery leaves and yellowish flowers, which produce waxy-white berries containing poisonous pulp. A modified root penetrates the bark of the host tree and forms tubes through which water and nutrients pass from the host to the slow-growing but persistent parasite. The North American counterpart is *P. serotinum.* Mistletoe was formerly believed to have magical and medicinal powers, and kissing under hanging mistletoe was said to lead inevitably to marriage.

Leaves and berries of American mistletoe (*Phoradendron serotinum*).
JOHN H. GERARD

Mistral \mē-'strȧl\, **Frédéric** (1830–1914) French poet. A leader of the 19th-century revival of Provençal, Mistral cofounded the Félibrige, an influential association for maintaining the customs and language of Provence and later the whole of southern France. He devoted 20 years to creating a scholarly dictionary of Provençal. His literary output includes lyrics; short stories; *Memoirs of Mistral* (1906), his best-known work; and long narrative poems, including *Mireio* (1859) and *The Song of the Rhône* (1897), his two greatest works. He shared the 1904 Nobel Prize with Jose Echegaray.

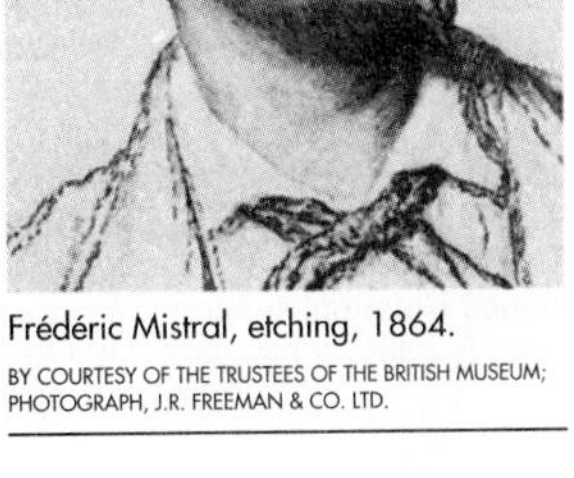

Frédéric Mistral, etching, 1864.
BY COURTESY OF THE TRUSTEES OF THE BRITISH MUSEUM; PHOTOGRAPH, J.R. FREEMAN & CO. LTD.

Mistral \mēs-'träl\, **Gabriela** *orig.* **Lucila Godoy Alcayaga** (1889–1957) Chilean poet. Mistral combined writing with a career as a cultural minister and diplomat, and as a professor in the U.S. Her reputation as a poet was established in 1914 when she won a prize for three "Sonetos de la muerte" ("Sonnets of Death"). Her passionate lyrics, with love of children and of the downtrodden as principal themes, are collected in such volumes as *Desolación* (1922), *Tala* (1938), and *Lagar* (1954). In 1945 she became the first Latin-American woman to win the Nobel Prize.

Gabriela Mistral, 1941.
BY COURTESY OF THE LIBRARY OF CONGRESS, WASHINGTON, D.C.

MIT See Massachusetts Institute of Technology

Mitanni \mi-'ta-nē\ Ancient kingdom of upper Mesopotamia, extending from the Euphrates River nearly to the Tigris River. Founded by Indo-Iranians who settled among the Hurrian peoples of the region, it competed with Egypt for control of Syria. Under King Saustatar in the 15th century BC, the soldiers of Mitanni looted the Assyrian palace in Ashur. In the mid-14th century BC, Wassukkani, its capital, was sacked by the Hittites, and the kingdom became part of the Hittite empire as Hanigalbat. Shortly afterward it was made an Assyrian province.

Mitchell, Arthur (born 1934) U.S. dancer, choreographer, and director of the Dance Theatre of Harlem. Born in New York City, he studied at the High School for the Performing Arts. He began dancing in Broadway musicals, and worked with several companies before joining the New York City Ballet in 1956 as its first black dancer. He created roles in several of George Balanchine's ballets, including *A Midsummer Night's Dream* (1962) and *Agon* (1967), before leaving the company in 1972. In 1968 he cofounded a ballet school, whose company, Dance Theatre of Harlem, made its debut in 1971, and he has continued as its director and choreographer.

Mitchell, Billy *orig.* **William** (1879–1936) U.S. aviator. Born in France to U.S. parents, he enlisted in the army and served in the Spanish-American War. Having learned to fly, he became the top U.S. air commander in World War I, initiating mass-bombing formations and leading an attack involving 1,500 planes. An outspoken advocate for a separate air force, he foresaw that the bomber would replace the battleship. He criticized the military hierarchy for an ill-equipped air service. When a navy dirigible was lost in a storm (1925), he accused the U.S. war and navy departments of incompetence. Charged with insubordination, he was court-martialed and suspended from duty. He resigned in 1926 and continued to champion air power and warned of advances by foreign air forces. In 1948 he was posthumously honored by the new U.S. Air Force with a special medal.

Mitchell, John (Newton) (1913–1988) U.S. public official. Born in Detroit, he became a prominent lawyer in New York and practiced with Richard Nixon after their firms merged in 1967. He managed Nixon's successful 1968 presidential campaign. As U.S. attorney general (1969–72), he was criticized for prosecuting war protesters, approving unauthorized wiretaps, and blocking publication of the Pentagon Papers. He resigned to direct Nixon's reelection campaign and became involved in the Watergate scandal. Convicted of conspiracy, obstructing justice, and perjury, he served 19 months in prison.

Mitchell, Joni *orig.* **Roberta Joan Anderson** (born 1943) Canadian singer and songwriter. Born in Fort Macleod, Alberta, Mitchell studied art in Calgary, where she began to sing in clubs. She eventually settled in Laurel Canyon, Cal. Several early songs, including "Both Sides Now" and "Woodstock," became hits for other artists. While her early recordings, such as *Clouds* (1969) and *Blue* (1971), were folk-oriented and reflected the idealism of the time, later releases, such as *Court and Spark* (1974), *Hejira* (1976), *Mingus* (1979, with Charles Mingus) and *Turbu-*

lent Indigo (1994), were marked by strong pop and jazz influences. Her notably original lyrics and musical settings have made her perhaps the preeminent female songwriter of her time.

Mitchell, Margaret (1900–1949) U.S. writer. Born in Atlanta, Mitchell attended Smith College and then wrote for *The Atlanta Journal* before spending 10 years writing her one book, *Gone with the Wind* (1936, Pulitzer Prize; film, 1939). A story of the American Civil War and Reconstruction from the Southern point of view, it was almost certainly the largest-selling novel in the history of U.S. publishing to that time. She died when she was struck by a car.

Mitchell, Mt. Peak, western North Carolina. The highest U.S. peak east of the Mississippi River, it rises to 6,684 ft (2,037 m). It is situated in North Carolina's Black Mtns., part of the BLUE RIDGE system, within Mount Mitchell State Park and the Pisgah National Forest. Formerly called Black Dome, it was renamed for Elisha Mitchell, who surveyed it as the highest point in the eastern U.S. in 1835; he died on the mountain and is buried at its summit.

Mitchell, Peter Dennis (1920–1992) British chemist. He discovered how the distribution of ENZYMES in mitochondrial membranes helps them use energy from HYDROGEN IONS to convert ADP to ATP, and received a 1978 Nobel Prize for formulating the chemiosmotic theory, which explained how energy is generated in the mitochondria of living cells.

Mitchell, Wesley C(lair) (1874–1948) U.S. economist. Born in Rushville, Ill., and educated at the University of Chicago under THORSTEIN VEBLEN and JOHN DEWEY, he later taught at several universities, including Columbia (1913–19, 1922–44). He helped found the National Bureau of Economic Research in 1920 and was its director of research until 1945. His work greatly influenced the development of quantitative studies of economic behavior in the U.S. and abroad, and he was the foremost expert of his day on BUSINESS CYCLES.

Mitchell River River, northern QUEENSLAND, Australia. Rising in the Eastern Highlands, it flows for 350 mi (560 km) northwest across Cape York Peninsula to the Gulf of CARPENTARIA. Fed by several rivers, it varies seasonally and may be dry for three months each year. It was explored in 1845 by Ludwig Leichhardt and was named for Thomas Mitchell, surveyor general for New South Wales. Crocodiles abound along its banks.

Mitchum, Robert (1917–1997) U.S. film actor. Born in Bridgeport, Conn., he spent his teenage years wandering the country and working odd jobs. After joining an acting company in California, he made his screen debut in 1943, acting in several Hopalong Cassidy westerns. He won praise for his role in *The Story of G.I. Joe* (1945). With his trademark sleepy-eyed, tough-guy appearance, he usually played loners and villains, in such movies (many of them B movies that have grown in critical esteem over time) as *Out of the Past* (1947), *Crossfire* (1947), *The Big Steal* (1949), *The Lusty Men* (1952), *The Night of the Hunter* (1955), *Thunder Road* (1958), *Cape Fear* (1962), *El Dorado* (1967), *The Friends of Eddie Coyle* (1973), *Farewell, My Lovely* (1975), and *The Big Sleep* (1978).

mite Any of about 20,000 species of tiny ARACHNIDS (subclass Acari, sometimes Acarina or Acarida). Species range from microscopic to 0.25 in. (6 mm) long. Mites live in water and soil, on plants, and as plant and animal parasites. Both parasitic and nonparasitic forms transmit plant and animal diseases. Itch mites (family Sarcoptidae), which burrow into the skin of humans and animals, cause the highly contagious disease scabies. A few species transmit tapeworms to cattle. Grain mites (family Glycyphagidae) damage stored products and irritate the skin of those who handle the products. House dust allergy is caused by species of the common genus *Dermatophagoides*. See also CHIGGER.

Red velvet mite (*Dinothrombium*; magnified about five times).

ANTHONY BANNISTER FROM NATURAL HISTORY PHOTOGRAPHIC AGENCY

Mitford, Nancy (1904–1973) British writer. Born into an eccentric, aristocratic family, she became known for her witty satiric novels of upper-class life, including the quasi-autobiographical *The Pursuit of Love* (1945), *Love in a Cold Climate* (1949), *The Blessing* (1951), and *Don't Tell Alfred* (1960). A volume of essays she coedited, *Noblesse Oblige* (1956), popularized the distinction between linguistic usages that are "U" (upper-class) and "non-U." Her sister Jessica (1917–1996) was a noted writer on U.S. society whose best-known book was *The American Way of Death* (1963).

Mithra \mē-'trȧ, 'mith-rə\ In Indo-Iranian myth, the god of light. He was born bearing a torch and armed with a knife, beside a sacred stream and under a sacred tree, a child of the earth itself. He soon rode, and later killed, the life-giving cosmic bull, whose blood fertilizes all vegetation. This deed became the prototype for a bull-slaying fertility ritual. As god of light, Mithra was associated with the Greek HELIOS and the Roman Sol Invictus. The first written reference to Mithra dates to 1400 BC. See also MITHRAISM.

Mithradates VI Eupator \ˌmith-rə-'dā-tēz...'yü-pə-ˌtȯr\ **("Born of a Noble Father")** *known as* **Mithradates the Great** (died 63 BC) King of PONTUS (120–63 BC) and enemy of Rome. As a boy he was coruler with his mother from c. 120 BC, then overthrew her to become sole ruler in 115. He gradually conquered areas along the western and southern regions of the Black Sea. He waged three wars against Rome, called the Mithradatic Wars (88–85, 83–82, 74–63). Though he originally seemed a champion to Greeks seeking relief from the Roman threat, his defeat by SULLA (86) destroyed that hope. When it became necessary, he extorted money and supplies from his Greek territories in Asia Minor. Greek revolts led to cruel reprisals. Greece turned to Rome after 86 but suffered the harsh demands of both until Mithradates' final defeat by POMPEY. He was one of the few leaders successfully to challenge Roman expansion in Asia.

Mithradates VI, bust in the Louvre, Paris.

CLICHE MUSEES NATIONAUX, PARIS

Mithraism \'mith-rə-ˌi-zəm\ Ancient Iranian religion based on the worship of MITHRA, the greatest of Iranian deities before the coming of ZOROASTER in the 6th century BC. It spread from India through Persia and the Hellenic world; in the 3rd–4th century AD, soldiers of the Roman empire carried it as far west as Spain, Britain, and Germany. The most important Mithraic ceremony was the sacrifice of the bull, an event associated with the creation of the world. Mithraic ceremonies were held by torchlight in subterranean caverns. A form of Mithraism in which the old Persian ceremonies were given a Platonic interpretation was popular in the 2nd–3rd century AD in the Roman empire, where Mithra was honored as the patron of loyalty to the emperor. After CONSTANTINE I accepted CHRISTIANITY in the early 4th century, Mithraism rapidly declined.

mitigating circumstance See EXTENUATING CIRCUMSTANCE

Mitilíni See LESBOS

Mitla \'mēt-lä\ Village and archaeological site, OAXACA state, southern Mexico. It lies at an elevation of 4,855 ft (1,480 m), surrounded by the mountains of the SIERRA MADRE del Sur. It was established as a sacred burial site by the ZAPOTECS, who used it until c. AD 900. The Mixtecs moved down from northern Oaxaca 900–1500, and took possession of Mitla. The modern village, composed of thatched huts and adobe houses, serves as a base for the study of the ruins.

Mito \'mē-tō\ Japanese HAN (domain) belonging to one of the three branches of the Tokugawa family from which the SHOGUN was chosen during the EDO PERIOD. During the 19th century, nationalists from Mito adopted the slogan *Sonno joi*, "Honor the emperor and expel the barbarians." Tokugawa Nariaki (1800–1860), DAIMYO of Mito at the time of Commodore MATTHEW PERRY's mission to Japan, called for Japan's continued isolation, supported by greater national unity and military renovation. See also II NAOSUKE, MEIJI RESTORATION, YOSHIDA SHOIN.

mitosis \mī-'tō-səs\ Cell division, or reproduction, in which a cell gives rise to two genetically identical daughter cells. Strictly applied, the term describes the duplication and distribution of CHROMOSOMES. Prior to mitosis, each chromosome is replicated, producing two strands (chromatids) attached at a centromere. During mitosis, the membrane around the cell's nucleus dissolves and the chromatids of each chromosome are separated and pulled to each end of the cell. As the nuclear membrane re-forms around each set of chromosomes, the cytoplasm of the parent cell begins to divide to form two daughter cells. Following mitosis, the cell membrane pinches in to separate the daughter cells. Mitosis is essential to life because it provides new cells for growth and for replacement of worn-out cells. It may take minutes or hours, depending on the kind of cells and species of organisms. It is influenced by time of day, temperature, and chemicals. See also CENTROMERE, MEIOSIS.

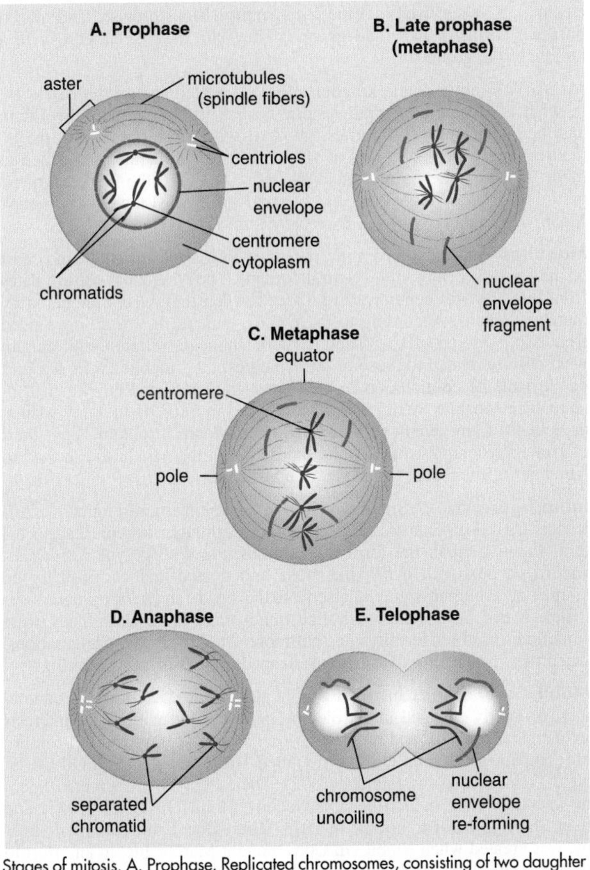

Stages of mitosis. A. Prophase. Replicated chromosomes, consisting of two daughter strands (chromatids) attached by a centromere, coil and contract. Two pairs of specialized organelles (centrioles) begin to move apart, forming a bridge of hollow protein cylinders known as microtubules (spindle fibers) between them. Microtubules also extend in a radial array (aster) from the centrioles to the poles of the cell. B. Late prophase. As the centrioles move apart, the nuclear envelope breaks down and microtubules extend from each centromere to opposite sides or poles of the cell. C. Metaphase. The centromeres align in a plane midway between the poles known as the equator or metaphase plate. During late metaphase, each centromere divides into two, freeing sister chromatids from each other. D. Anaphase. Sister chromatids are drawn to opposite ends as centromeric microtubules shorten and polar microtubules lengthen, causing the poles to move farther apart. E. Telophase. Chromosomes uncoil, microtubules disappear, and the nuclear envelope reforms around each set of daughter chromosomes. The cytoplasm begins to pinch in to create two daughter cells. The process of cytoplasmic division is completed during cytokinesis.

Mitra In Vedic HINDUISM, one of the gods in the category of Adityas, or sovereign principles of the universe. He represents friendship, integrity, harmony, and all other qualities necessary to maintain order in human existence. He is usually paired with Varuna, the guardian of the cosmic order, whose powers he complements as guardian of the human order. As spirit of the day, he is sometimes associated with the sun. His Iranian counterpart is MITHRA.

mitral insufficiency \'mī-trəl\ *or* **mitral regurgitation** Inadequate closure of the HEART's mitral valve, allowing backflow of blood from the left ventricle into the left atrium. The most common cause is scarring from rheumatic heart disease (see RHEUMATIC FEVER); others are congenital defects in the valve or the muscles that close it, and, less often, ENDOCARDITIS and cardiac tumor. Diagnosis is based on a heart murmur and patterns on echocardiography or ELECTROCARDIOGRAPHY. Mitral insufficiency may have no symptoms or may cause easy tiring and difficulty in breathing. The atrium may enlarge, after which left ventricular failure (see HEART FAILURE) eventually develops. It is treated by restricting vigorous exercise, reducing sodium intake and increasing its excretion, and administering anticlotting drugs. Valves with severe defects are surgically replaced.

mitral stenosis \ste-'nō-səs\ Narrowing of the mitral valve between the HEART's left atrium and ventricle, usually resulting from RHEUMATIC FEVER, and more rarely from a congenital disorder. Most common in women under 45, the narrowing causes blood to back up into the atrium and PULMONARY CIRCULATION, where increased pressure may lead to LUNG CONGESTION and EDEMA. Difficulty in breathing and right HEART FAILURE may follow. ATRIAL FIBRILLATION occurs in most patients. Blood clots may form in the atrium and cause EMBOLISM. Diagnosis is based on typical heart sounds and echocardiography or ELECTROCARDIOGRAPHY patterns. Treatment includes limiting exercise, reducing sodium intake and increasing its excretion, and using anticoagulant drugs. Surgical valve replacement may be necessary.

Mitre \'mē-trā\, **Bartolomé** (1821–1906) President of Argentina (1862–68). An exiled critic of the dictator JUAN MANUEL DE ROSAS, he helped defeat Rosas by leading Uruguayan forces against him, then led a successful campaign to make Buenos Aires the capital of a united Argentina. Once elected president, he suppressed the rural CAUDILLOS, extended mail and telegraph service, organized public finances, established new courts, and founded the newspaper *La Nación* (1870) and the Argentine Academy of History. See also JUSTO JOSE DE URQUIZA.

Mitscher \'mich-ər\, **Marc A(ndrew)** (1887–1947) U.S. naval officer. Born in Hillsboro, Wis., he graduated from Annapolis. As a navy pilot, he helped develop naval aviation as a component of the fleet. In World War II he commanded the aircraft carrier *Hornet* in the Battle of MIDWAY. He commanded aircraft-carrier attacks in the battles of the Philippine Sea and LEYTE GULF and at IWO JIMA and OKINAWA. Promoted to admiral in 1946, he became commander in chief of the U.S. Atlantic fleet.

Mitsubishi group Loose consortium of independent Japanese companies. The first Mistsubishi company was a trading and shipping concern established in 1873 by Iwasaki Yataro. Several subsidiaries were created after World War I, and by the 1930s Mitsubishi was Japan's second-largest ZAIBATSU. During World War II it was a major military contractor, its best-known product being the Zero fighter plane. By the end of the war it controlled some 200 companies. The zaibatsu was broken up by U.S. occupation forces, and the stock of the subsidiary firms was sold to the public. After the occupation the independent Mitsubishi companies began to reassociate, but without an overarching holding company. The group today consists of more than a dozen independent companies; its major firms are multinational corporations based in Tokyo.

Mitterrand.

CAMERA PRESS—GLOBE PHOTOS

Mitterrand \mē-tə-'rä^{n}\, **François (-Maurice-Marie)** (1916–1996) President of France (1981–95). After serving in World War II, he was elected to the National Assembly (1946) and held cabinet posts in 11 Fourth Republic governments

(1947–58). Moving to the political left, he opposed CHARLES DE GAULLE's government and ran unsuccessfully against him in 1965 but won 32% of the vote. In 1971 he became secretary of the FRENCH SOCIALIST PARTY and made it the majority party of the left, which led to his election as president in 1981. With a leftist majority in the National Assembly, he introduced radical economic reforms, which were modified when a right-wing majority regained power in 1986. Reelected president in 1988, he strongly promoted the European Union. His domestic policy was less successful, and France experienced high unemployment. In 1991 he appointed Edith Cresson (born 1934) prime minister, the first French woman to hold that office (1991–92). A defeat for the Socialists in the legislative elections of 1993 further moderated Mitterrand's policies.

Mix, Tom *orig.* **Thomas Hezikiah** (1880–1940) U.S. film actor. Born in Mix Run, Pa., he worked as a cowhand and a deputy sheriff, and served in the army and in the Texas Rangers before joining a Wild West show in 1906. He made his screen debut as a roughriding hero in 1910 and soon became a star of silent westerns. Over the years his horse, Tony, became almost as famous as Mix himself. He appeared in more than 200 one- and two-reelers and feature films, many of which he also produced or directed. His career declined with the coming of sound.

Mixco \'mēsh-kō\ City (pop., 1995 est.: 437,000), southern central Guatemala. It is a western suburb of GUATEMALA CITY, and it supplies the capital with produce.

Mixtec \mēs-'tek\ Indian population in southern Mexico. They attained a high degree of civilization in AZTEC and pre-Aztec times, leaving behind written records. Today they are slash-and-burn agriculturists who also hunt, fish, herd, and gather wild foods. Their crafts include ceramics and weaving. Nominally Roman Catholic and active in church brotherhoods (*cofradías*), they blend pre-Christian beliefs and practices with Catholic rituals.

Mizoguchi Kenji \ˌmē-zō-'gü-chē-'ken-jē\ (1898–1956) Japanese film director. After studying painting, he became an actor at the Nikkatsu studio in 1919, and made his debut as a director in 1922. His early films included *Street Sketches* (1925), *Tokyo March* (1929), *Osaka Elegy* (1936), and *The Story of the Last Chrysanthemums* (1939). His pictorially beautiful films, of which he made over 80, often dealt with the conflict between modern and traditional values. He won international acclaim for *Ugetsu monogatari* (1953), an allegorical commentary on postwar Japan. He was also noted for his films about women, including *The Love of Actress Sumako* (1947), *Women of the Night* (1948), and *Street of Shame* (1956).

Mizoram \mi-'zȯ-rəm\ State (pop., 1994 est.: 775,000), northeastern India. Occupying an area of 8,140 sq mi (21,081 sq km), it is bounded by Myanmar and Bangladesh. It is largely mountainous; its capital is AIZAWL. The various ethnic groups of Mizoram are known collectively as the Mizo (Lushai), and they speak a variety of Tibeto-Burman dialects. They were in revolt against India for decades, and the establishment of Mizoram as a union territory in 1972 failed to appease them. The conflict was settled in 1987 with the promotion of Mizoram to statehood and the election of a Mizo-led state government. The economy is based on agriculture.

Mizuno Tadakuni \mē-'zün-ō-ˌtä-dä-'kü-nē\ (1794–1851) Chief adviser to the 12th Tokugawa SHOGUN, Tokugawa Ieyoshi (r.1837–53). In the face of social and economic decline, Mizuno tried to implement a series of reforms that would return late EDO-PERIOD Japan to the martial simplicity of the early days of the TOKUGAWA SHOGUNATE. He enacted sumptuary laws, canceled SAMURAI debts, decreed a price and wage cut, and tried to force unauthorized peasant migrants to leave the cities and return to the countryside. These so-called Tempo Reforms failed, and Mizuno was removed from office.

Mjollnir \'myœl-nir, 'myȯl-nir\ In Norse myth, the hammer of THOR and the symbol of his power. Forged by dwarfs, the hammer never failed Thor as a weapon or as an instrument of sanctification. It had many magical qualities, including the ability to return to Thor's hand after it had been thrown. It was stolen by the giant Thrym, who asked as ransom the hand of FREYJA. When Freyja refused to go to Thrym, Thor, masquerading as Freyja, managed to seize the hammer, which had been brought out to consecrate Freyja as Thrym's bride, and slaughtered Thrym and the other giants.

Mjosa \'mœ̄-sä\, **Lake** Lake, southeastern Norway, situated north of OSLO at the southern end of Gudbrands Valley. The country's largest lake, it serves as a link between the LÅGEN RIVER to the north and the Vorma-Glåma river system to the south. Occupying an area of 142 sq mi (368 sq km), it is 62 mi (100 km) long and 1–9 mi (1.6–14 km) wide. Lillehammer, at its northern end, and Hamar, on its eastern shore, are the largest lakeshore towns.

Mo-tzu See MOZI

moa Any of 13–25 species of extinct RATITE of New Zealand constituting the order Dinornithiformes. Species ranged from turkey-sized to 10 ft (3 m) high. Moas were swift runners that defended themselves by kicking. They were hunted for their flesh (eaten as food), bones (used as weapons and ornaments), and eggs (used for water vessels). The larger moas were probably extinct by the late 17th century; a few smaller species may have survived into the 19th century. Moas browsed and grazed on seeds, fruits, leaves, and grasses. They laid a single large egg in a hollow in the ground.

Moab \'mō-ˌab\ Ancient kingdom, Syria. Located east of the DEAD SEA, in what is present-day southwestern Jordan, it was bounded by Edom and the country of the Amorites. MOABITES were closely related to the Israelites, and were sometimes at war with them and sometimes allied to them. The Moabite Stone, found at DIBON, recorded the 9th century BC victories of the Moab king Mesha, and especially those over Israel. Moab was conquered by the BABYLONIANS in 582 BC.

Moabites \'mō-ə-ˌbīts\ Semitic people who lived in the highlands east of the DEAD SEA (now in W-central Jordan). The Moabites' culture dates from the late 14th century BC to 582 BC, when they were conquered by the Babylonians. According to the Old Testament, they were descended from Moab, a son of LOT. Though their language, religion, and culture were closely related to those of the Israelites, the Moabites were not part of the Israelite community. DAVID's great-grandmother Ruth was a Moabite. The Moabite Stone, a stela discovered in 1868, is the only written document of any length that survives from Moab; it tells of King Omri of Israel's reconquest of Moabite lands, which the Moabites ascribed to the anger of their god, Chemosh. See also DIBON.

moai figure \'mō-ˌī\ Small wooden statue of uncertain religious significance, carved on EASTER ISLAND. The figures, thought to represent ancestors who live on in the form of skeletons, are of two types: *moai kavakava* (male), with a beaklike nose and goatee and occasionally an animal or a human figure incised on the head; and *moai paepae* (female), which have a flat, relieflike quality and large eyes. They were sometimes used for fertility rites but more often for harvest celebrations, when the first picking of fruits was heaped around them as offerings.

Mobil Corp. Former name of one of the largest U.S. holding companies, primarily engaged in petroleum operations but with major interests in chemical products and retailing. Mobil's roots are in two 19th-century oil companies, Vacuum Oil Co. (founded 1866) and Standard Oil Co. of New York (or Socony, founded 1882). Their 1931 merger created Socony-Vacuum Corp., which became Socony Mobil Oil Corp. (1955) and then Mobil Oil Corp. (1966). In 1974 Mobil Corp., the holding company, was created when Mobil Oil Corp. bought Marcor Inc. in an effort to diversify. By 1988 Mobil had sold Marcor's major non-oil-related portions, including MONTGOMERY WARD, to refocus on petroleum products. Mobil Oil Corp. carries on a full range of petroleum operations from exploration to marketing, with major production in the Gulf of Mexico, California, the Atlantic coast, Alaska, the North Sea, and Saudi Arabia. It merged with EXXON CORP. to become Exxon Mobil Corp. in 1999.

Mobile \'mō-ˌbēl, mō-'bēl\ City (pop., 1996 est.: 203,000), southwestern Alabama, situated on MOBILE BAY at the mouth of the Mobile River. The site was explored by Spaniards in 1519. French colonists built a fort near the river's mouth in 1702. It served as the capital of French Louisiana until 1720. It was ceded to the British in 1763. It was captured by the Spanish during the AMERICAN REVOLUTION. Incorporated as a town in 1814 as part of West Florida, it passed to the U.S. with the purchase of Florida from Spain in 1819. During the AMERICAN CIVIL WAR it was an important Confederate port, but Federal forces won the Battle of MOBILE BAY and captured the city. The state's only seaport, it is a major industrial and manufacturing center, and the site of several institutions of higher education.

mobile \'mō-ˌbēl\ Abstract sculpture that has moving parts, driven either by motors or by the natural force of air currents. Its revolving parts create a new visual experience of constantly changing volumes and forms. The term was initially suggested by MARCEL DUCHAMP for a 1932 Paris exhibition of such works by ALEXANDER CALDER, who became the mobile's greatest exponent.

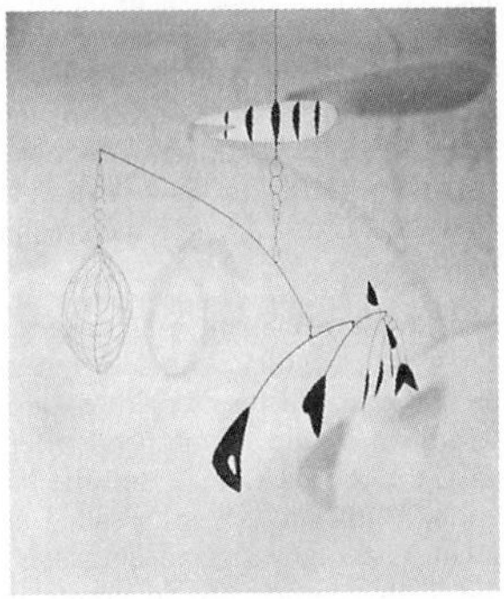

"Lobster Trap and FishTail," mobile of painted steel wire and sheet aluminum by Alexander Calder, 1939; in the Museum of Modern Art, New York.

COLLECTION, THE MUSEUM OF MODERN ART, NEW YORK, GIFT OF THE ADVISORY COMMITTEE

Mobile Bay Inlet of the Gulf of MEXICO, extending 35 mi (56 km) north to the mouth of the Mobile River in southwestern Alabama. It is 8–18 mi (13–29 km) wide and enters the gulf through a dredged channel between Dauphin Island and Mobile Point. During the AMERICAN CIVIL WAR it was the scene of the Battle of MOBILE BAY.

Mobile Bay, Battle of (August 5, 1864) Naval engagement in the AMERICAN CIVIL WAR. The Union fleet under DAVID FARRAGUT sailed into Mobile Bay, Ala., breaching the protective string of mines (torpedoes) and engaging the Confederate ironclad *Tennessee*. After a two-hour battle, the Union fleet won control of the bay. With the surrender of nearby Fort Morgan, the former Confederate port of Mobile was sealed off from Confederate blockade runners.

mobilization Organization of a nation's armed forces for active military service in time of war or other national emergency. It includes recruiting and training, building military bases and training camps, and procuring and distributing weapons, ammunition, uniforms, equipment, and supplies. Full mobilization involves summoning all of a nation's resources to support the military effort; for example, civilians may gather raw materials needed by the military, conserve scarce resources such as gasoline for military use, or sell war bonds to fund the war effort.

Möbius \'mœ-bē-ůs, *Engl* 'mō-bē-əs\, **August Ferdinand** (1790–1868) German mathematician and theoretical astronomer. He began teaching at the University of Leipzig in 1815, and established his reputation with many publications. His mathematical papers are chiefly concerned with geometry. He introduced homogeneous coordinates into analytic geometry and dealt with geometric transformations, in particular projective transformations. He was a pioneer in TOPOLOGY; in a memoir discovered after his death he discussed the properties of one-sided surfaces, including the famous Möbius strip.

Mobutu Sese Seko \mə-'bü-tü-'sā-sā-'sā-kō\ *orig.* **Joseph Mobutu** (1930–1997) President of Zaire (now Congo), 1965–97. Mobutu served in the Belgian Congolese army and as a journalist before joining PATRICE LUMUMBA in independence negotiations in Brussels in 1960. When independence was achieved, the coalition government of Pres. JOSEPH KASAVUBU and Premier Lumumba put Mobutu in charge of defense. In the rift between Kasavubu and Lumumba over the secession of Katanga province under MOISE TSHOMBE, Mobutu helped Kasavubu seize control. Four years later, in a power struggle between Pres. Kasavubu and Premier Tshombe, Mobutu removed Kasavubu in a coup and assumed the presidency. He established single-party rule and put down several attempted coups. He Africanized all European names, changing his own to Mobutu Sese Seko ("All-Powerful Warrior"). His repressive regime failed to spur economic growth; corruption, mismanagement, and neglect led to decline, while Mobutu himself amassed one of the largest personal fortunes in the world. He was overthrown by LAURENT KABILA in 1997, and died in exile in Morocco.

mocambo See QUILOMBO

moccasin Either of two species of PIT VIPER: the WATER MOCCASIN or the Mexican moccasin *(Agkistrodon bilineatus)*. The Mexican moccasin, or cantil, is a dangerous snake of lowland regions from the Rio Grande to Nicaragua. About 3 ft (1 m) long, it is brown or black with narrow, irregular, whitish bars on its back and sides. See also COPPERHEAD.

Moche \'mō-chā\ Dominant civilization on the northern coast of present-day Peru in the 1st–8th century AD. The name comes from the great site of Moche, in the Moche River valley, apparently the capital of the Moche peoples. Their settlements extended along northern Peru's hot, arid coast from the Lambayeque River valley south to the Nepeña River valley. They irrigated extensively, and their agriculture supported many urban centers with stepped pyramids. They were skilled metalworkers and produced sophisticated craft goods, including fine mold-made pottery. The cause of their demise is unknown. See also ANDEAN CIVILIZATION.

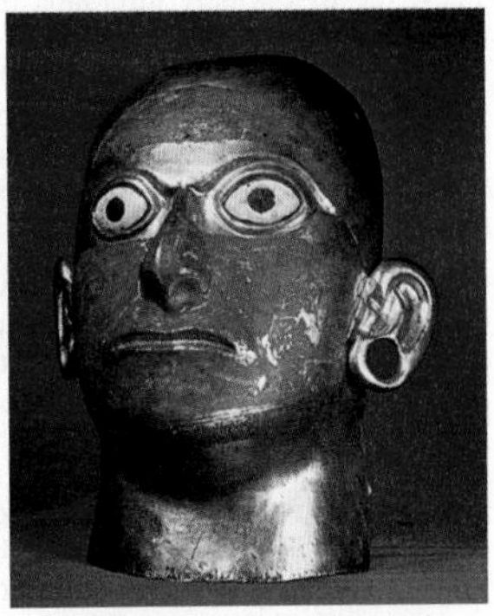

Mask of copper and gold alloy with eyes of shell, found in the Huaca de la Luna, Moche River valley about 400 BC–AD 600; in the Linden-Museum, Stuttgart, Ger.

FERDINAND ANTON

mockingbird Any of several versatile songbirds of a New World family (Mimidae). The common, or northern, mockingbird *(Mimus polyglottos)* can imitate the songs of 20 or more species within 10 minutes. About 10 in. (27 cm) long, it is gray, with darker, white-marked wings and tail. It ranges from the northern U.S. to Brazil; it has been introduced into Hawaii and thrives in suburban areas. It sings from perches, even at night, and vigorously defends its territory. Other *Mimus* species range from Central America to Patagonia, and the blue mockingbird (genus *Melanotis*) inhabits much of Mexico. Various subspecies of the Galápagos mockingbird (genus *Nesomimus*) inhabit the different islands.

Moctezuma II See MONTEZUMA II

modal logic \'mō-dᵊl-\ FORMAL SYSTEMS incorporating MODALITIES such as NECESSITY, possibility, impossibility, contingency, strict IMPLICATION, and certain other closely related concepts. The most straightforward way of constructing a modal logic is to add to some standard nonmodal logical system a new primitive operator intended to represent one of the modalities, to define other modal operators in terms of it, and to add axioms and/or transformation rules involving those modal operators. For example, one may add the symbol L, which means "It is necessary that," to classical PROPOSITIONAL CALCULUS; thus, Lp is read as "It is necessary that p." The possibility operator M ("It is possible that") may be defined in terms of L as $Mp = \neg L \neg p$ (where $\neg$ means "not"). In addition to the axioms and rules of inference of classical propositional logic, such as system might have two axioms and one rule of inference of its own. Some characteristic axioms of modal logic are: (A1) $Lp \supset p$ and (A2) $L(p \supset q) \supset (Lp \supset Lq)$. The new rule of inference in this system is the Rule of Necessitation: If p is a theorem of the system, then so is Lp. Stronger systems of modal logic can be obtained by adding additional axioms. Some add the axiom $Lp \supset LLp$; others add the axiom $Mp \supset LMp$.

modality Properties of propositions such as NECESSITY, contingency, possibility, and impossibility, as opposed to truth and falsity. Thus, the propositions "Some humans may be immortal" and "Humans are necessarily social animals" are modal propositions. Though modal syllogisms were considered by ARISTOTLE, MODAL LOGIC remains today a somewhat controversial field. See also DEONTIC LOGIC.

mode In music, any of a variety of concepts used to classify SCALES and melodies. In Western music, the term is particularly used for the medieval CHURCH MODES. KEYS in tonal music are normally said to be in either major or minor mode, depending particularly on the third degree of the scale. Indian RAGAS can be regarded as modes. The concept of mode may involve much more than simply a classification of scales, extending to embrace an entire vocabulary of melodic formulas and perhaps other aspects of music that traditionally occur in tandem with a given set of formulas. The term mode has also been used for purely rhythmic patterns such as those of the ARS ANTIQUA, which were based on ancient Greek poetic meters.

mode See MEAN, MEDIAN, AND MODE

Model T Automobile built by the FORD MOTOR CO. from 1908 until 1927, the first widely affordable mass-produced car. ASSEMBLY-LINE production methods introduced by HENRY FORD in 1913 enabled the price of this five-seat touring car to drop from $850 in 1908 to $300 in 1925. Over 15 million Model T's were built. The car was offered in several body styles, all mounted on a standard chassis. Various colors were initially available, but after 1913 its sole color was black. It was replaced by the popular Model A in 1928.

modem \'mō-ˌdəm\ Electronic device that converts digital data into analog (modulated-wave) signals suitable for transmission over analog telecommunications circuits (e.g., traditional phone lines), and demodulates received analog signals to recover the digital data transmitted. The "*mo*dulator/*dem*odulator" thus makes it possible for existing communications channels to support a variety of digital communications, including E-MAIL, INTERNET access, and FAX transmissions. An ordinary modem, operating over traditional phone lines, has a data transmission speed limit of about 56 kilobits per second. ISDN lines allow communications at over twice that rate, and CABLE MODEMS and DSL lines have transmission rates of over a million bits per second.

modem, cable See CABLE MODEM

Modena \'mò-dā-nä\ City (pop., 1995 est.: 175,000), EMILIA-ROMAGNA region, northern Italy. It lies between the Secchia and Panaro rivers, northwest of BOLOGNA. An ancient Etruscan city, it was made a Roman colony in 183 BC. It was attacked and pillaged by the Huns under ATTILA and later by the Lombards. It passed to the house of ESTE in 1288. It was taken by France in 1796 and made part of Napoleon's kingdom of Italy in 1805. It reverted to Este rule in 1815, then joined Italy in 1860. The automobile industry is important to its economy; it is also an agricultural market center. Sites of interest include the 11th-century cathedral and the university (founded 1175).

modern art Painting, sculpture, architecture, and graphic arts characteristic of the later 19th century and the 20th century. Modern art embraces a wide variety of movements, theories, and attitudes that tend to reject traditional, historical, or academic forms and conventions. Its origins can be traced to 19th-century French IMPRESSIONISM. POSTIMPRESSIONISM went further in rejecting traditional techniques and subject matter. A succession of movements and styles emerged, including NEO-IMPRESSIONISM, SYMBOLISM, FAUVISM, CUBISM, FUTURISM, EXPRESSIONISM, SUPREMATISM, CONSTRUCTIVISM, METAPHYSICAL PAINTING, DE STIJL, DADA, SURREALISM, SOCIAL REALISM, ABSTRACT EXPRESSIONISM, POP ART, OP ART, MINIMALISM, and NEO-EXPRESSIONISM.

modern dance Theatrical dance that developed in the U.S. and Europe in the 20th century as a reaction to traditional ballet. Precursors included LOIE FULLER and ISADORA DUNCAN. Formal teaching of modern dance began with the establishment of the Denishawn schools by RUTH SAINT DENIS and TED SHAWN in 1915. Many of their students, principally DORIS HUMPHREY and MARTHA GRAHAM, further contributed to modern dance's definition as a technique based on principles of fall and recovery (Humphrey) and of contraction and release (Graham). Movement often stressed the expression of emotional intensity and contemporary subjects rather than focusing on the narrative style and often classical narratives of ballet. Later developments included a revolt against Expressionism in the 1950s led by MERCE CUNNINGHAM, whose choreography included ballet technique and the element of chance. See also AGNES DE MILLE, HANYA HOLM, JOSE LIMON, ALWIN NIKOLAIS, ANNA SOKOLOW, PAUL TAYLOR, TWYLA THARP.

Modern Jazz Quartet (MJQ) U.S. jazz ensemble founded by pianist John Lewis, vibraphonist Milt Jackson, drummer Kenny Clarke, and bassist Ray Brown in 1951. They originally worked together as the rhythm section for DIZZY GILLESPIE's big band in 1946. The quartet established a reserved and subtle approach to the modern jazz innovations of the mid-1940s, incorporating elements of classical chamber music with original compositions and jazz standards. Percy Heath replaced Brown in 1952, and Connie Kay replaced Clarke in 1955; upon Kay's death in 1994, Percy's brother Albert "Tootie" Heath joined the group.

modernism In the arts, experimentation that flouted traditional conventions and aimed to be "new," from the late 19th century to the mid-20th century. Its rise owed greatly to the factors that made the era modern: industrialization, rapid social change, advances in science and the social sciences (e.g., DARWINISM, Freudian theory), and the accompanying sense of alienation. Modernist works tended no longer to speak for a society or a people, but to be either individualistic and idiosyncratic on the one hand (speaking only for the creator) or broadly universal on the other (bypassing nationality or cultural heritage). MODERN ART and MODERN DANCE are manifestations of modernism. In literature, the works of T. S. ELIOT, JAMES JOYCE, and VIRGINIA WOOLF are considered typically modernist; in music, the compositions of A. SCHOENBERG, I. STRAVINSKY, and A. WEBERN; and in architecture, buildings in the BAUHAUS and INTERNATIONAL styles.

Modernismo Spanish-language literary movement of the late 19th and early 20th century, founded by RUBEN DARIO. Reacting against the sentimental romantic writers then popular in Latin American, *modernistas* wrote on exotic themes and often about artificial worlds—the ancient past, the distant Orient, and the lands of childhood fancy and sheer creation. With "art for art's sake" as their creed, they brought about the greatest revitalization of language and poetic technique in Spanish since the 17th century. Its adherents included Peru's José Santos Chocano (1875–1934) and Cuba's JOSE MARTI. Though the movement was over by 1920, its influence continued well into the 20th century.

modernization Transformation from a traditional, rural, agrarian society to a secular, urban, industrial society. It is closely linked with INDUSTRIALIZATION. As societies modernize, increased emphasis falls on the individual, who replaces the family, community, or occupational group as the basic unit of society. Division of labor, characteristic of industrialization, is also applied to institutions, which become more highly specialized. Instead of being governed by tradition or custom, society comes to be governed according to abstract principles formulated for that purpose. Traditional religious or spiritual beliefs often decline in importance, and distinctive cultural traits are often lost.

Modersohn-Becker \'mō-dər-ˌzōn-'be-kər\, **Paula** *orig.* **Paula Becker** (1876–1907) German painter. After studying art in London and Paris, she became one of the first artists to introduce French POSTIMPRESSIONISM into German art. While her early work is meticulously naturalistic, her later paintings, such as *Self-Portrait with a Camellia* (1907), combine a lyrical naturalism with the broad areas of simplified color characteristic of PAUL GAUGUIN and PAUL CEZANNE. Her death at 31 resulted from giving birth to her first child.

"Self-Portrait with a Camellia," oil on canvas by Paula Modersohn-Becker, 1907; in the Museum Folkwang, Essen, Germany.
BY COURTESY OF THE MUSEUM FOLKWANG, ESSEN, GER

Modesto City (pop., 1996 est.: 179,000), central California, east of SAN FRANCISCO. Founded in 1870 by the Central Pacific Railway, it was called Modesto (Spanish: "modest") when W. C. Ralston, a railway director, modestly declined to have the community named in his honor. It was incorporated as a city in 1884. It is a shipping center for the surrounding agricultural region that includes fruit, nut orchards, and wineries.

Modigliani \ˌmō-dēl-'yä-nē\, **Amedeo** (1884–1920) Italian painter and sculptor. After studying art in Italy, he settled in Paris (1906), where he exhibited several paintings at the SALON DES INDÉPENDANTS in 1908. Following the advice of CONSTANTIN BRANCUSI, he studied African sculpture and in 1912 exhibited 12 stone heads whose simplified and elongated forms reflect African influence. When he returned to painting, his portraits and nudes—characterized by asymmetry of composition, elongation of the figure, and a simplification of outline—reflected the style of his sculpture. By almost eliminating chiaroscuro, he achieved a sculptural quality by the strength of his contours and the richness of juxtaposed colors. In 1917 he began painting a series of female nudes that, with their warm, glowing colors and sensuous, rounded forms, are among his best works. His work reflects his lifelong admiration for Italian Renaissance masters, as well as the influence of Paul Cezanne and Brancusi. He died at 35 of tuberculosis.

"Self-Portrait," oil on canvas by Amedeo Modigliani, 1919; in the Museum of Contemporary Art of the University of São Paulo, Brazil.

BY COURTESY OF THE MUSEU DE ARTE CONTEMPORANEA DA UNIVERSIDADE DE SAO PAULO, GIFT OF MR. FRANCISCO M. SOBRINHO AND MRS. YOLANDA

Modigliani \ˌmō-dēl-ˈyä-nē\, **Franco** (born 1918) Italian-U.S. economist. He fled fascist Italy for the U.S. in 1939 and earned a doctorate from the New School for Social Research in 1944. He taught at several universities, including MIT (from 1962). His work on personal savings prompted him to formulate the life-cycle theory, which asserts that individuals build up savings during their younger working lives for use during their own old age and not as an inheritance for their descendants. In order to analyze financial markets, he invented a technique for calculating the value of a company's expected future earnings that became a basic tool in corporate decision-making and finance. He received the Nobel Prize in 1985.

Modoc \ˈmō-ˌdäk\ Plateau Indian people of Penutian language stock from south of the Cascade Range in northern California. Their economy was based on hunting and gathering and they lived much like their closely related neighbors the Klamath. In 1864 the U.S. government forced the Modoc to live on Klamath lands, giving rise to the Modoc War of 1872–73. About 80 families retreated to the California Lava Beds but eventually surrendered and were removed to Oklahoma. Survivors were permitted to return to Oregon in 1909. Today the Modoc number about 500.

modulation In electronics, a technique for impressing information (voice, music, picture, or data) on a radio-frequency carrier wave by varying one or more characteristics of the wave in accordance with the signal. There are various forms of modulation, each designed to alter a particular characteristic of the carrier wave. The most commonly altered characteristics include amplitude (see AM), frequency (see FM), phase, pulse sequence, and pulse duration.

modulation In music, a change of mode or key. In tonal music, the change is almost always temporary. Of the seven lettered pitches in a given key, six are shared with the most closely related keys; modulation to those keys thus requires changing the letter whose pitch is not shared. For example, if "The Star-Spangled Banner" is played in C major, whose fourth step is F, the F-sharp on "-ly" ("dawn's ear*ly* light") creates a fleeting modulation to the key of G major, which differs from C major only in that one note.

module \ˈmä-ˌjül\ In architecture, a unit adopted to regulate the dimensions, proportions, or construction of the parts of a building. Modules based on the diameter of a column were used in Classical architecture. In Japanese architecture, room sizes were determined by combinations of standard rice mats called *tatami.* Both Frank Lloyd Wright and Le Corbusier used modular proportioning systems. Standardized modular design reduces waste, lowers costs, and offers ease of erection, flexible arrangement, and variety of use; however, most architects and producers of building materials continue to use modules based on their own special needs and interests.

modulus, bulk See bulk modulus

modus ponens and modus tollens \ˈmō-dəs-ˈpō-nənz...ˈtò-ləns\ (Latin: "method of affirming" and "method of denying") In logic, two types of inference that can be drawn using a hypothetical proposition—i.e., from a proposition of the form "If p, then q" (symbolically $p \supset q$). Modus ponens refers to inferences of the form $p \supset q$; p, therefore q. Modus tollens refers to inferences of the form $p \supset q$; $\neg q$, therefore, $\neg p$. An example of modus tollens is the following: "If an angle is inscribed in a semicircle, then it is a right angle; this angle is not a right angle; therefore, this angle is not inscribed in a semicircle."

Moeris \ˈmir-əs\, **Lake** Ancient lake, northern Egypt. It occupied the al-Fayyum depression, now the site of the much smaller Lake Qarun. Its waters began falling in Paleolithic times due to silt accumulation from the Nile River. During the Middle Kingdom (c. 2040–1786 BC), access was renewed to the Nile's waters. Land-reclamation projects in the 3rd century BC drained the lake, opening 450 sq mi (1,200 sq km) of alluvial soil that was irrigated by canals. The region declined after the first two centuries of Roman rule.

Moero, Lac See Lake Mweru

Moesia \ˈmē-shə\ Province of the Roman empire, southeastern Europe. Bordered by the Danube River and the Black Sea, it was conquered by Rome 30–28 BC and became a Roman province in AD 15. During the Dacian Wars (AD 85–89), it was divided into two provinces: Moesia Superior and Moesia Inferior. Despite barbarian invasions, it remained part of the eastern Roman empire until the 7th century, when it was occupied by Slavs and Bulgarians.

Mogadishu \ˌmō-gə-ˈdē-shü\ City (pop., 1995 est.: 997,000), capital of Somalia, located north of the equator on the Indian Ocean. Founded in the 10th century by Arab settlers, it carried on trade with the Arab states and later with the Portuguese. It fell under control of the sultan of Zanzibar in 1871. Italy leased the port in 1892 and purchased it in 1905. Subsequently the capital of Italian Somaliland and of the Somalia trust territory, it became the capital of independent Somalia in 1960. In the 1980s and 1990s civil war in Somalia caused widespread destruction in the city.

Mogilev See Mahilyow

Mogollon culture \ˌmō-gə-ˈyōn\ Culture of a group of North American Indians who lived in what is now southeastern Arizona and southwestern New Mexico c. 200 BC–AD 1200. The first pottery in the Southwest was made by the Mogollon; its high quality from the beginning suggests that the craft may have been imported from Mexico. The early economy was based on gathering wild plant foods and hunting small game. Corn cultivation emerged c. AD 500. At this time houses also became more elaborate, being constructed of stone masonry. In the final, or Mimbres, period (1050–1200) new patterns of house design (multilevel pueblos centered around a plaza) and pottery (crisp black-on-white designs of animals or geometric lines) emerged, suggesting contact with the Anasazi peoples to the north. For unknown reasons, Mogollon culture came to an end in the 13th century.

Mogul dynasty See Mughal dynasty

Mohave See Mojave

Mohawk Iroquoian-speaking North American Indian people, the easternmost group of the Iroquois Confederacy. The Mohawk lived near what is now Schenectady, N.Y. They were semisedentary; women practiced corn agriculture while men hunted during the fall and winter and fished during the summer. Related families lived together in longhouses. Most Mohawk sided with the British in both the French and Indian War and the American Revolution, in the latter under Joseph Brant. Today they number about 10,000 and work in various fields, notably the structural steel industry.

Mohawk River River, eastern central New York. The Hudson River's largest tributary, it flows 148 mi (238 km) south and east to join the Hudson at Waterford, north of Troy. The Mohawk Valley (Mohawk Trail) was the historic route of westbound pioneers through the Appalachian Mtns. into the Great Lakes region. The Five Nations of the Iroquois confederacy lived in the valley, which was a major battleground during the French and Indian War and the American Revolution.

Mohegan \mō-ˈhē-gən\ Algonquian-speaking North American Indian people who once inhabited the area of southeastern Connecticut. They later seized land in Massachusetts and Rhode Island from other tribes. Their economy was based on corn cultivation, hunting, and fishing. In the 17th century the Mohegan and the Pequot tribes were ruled jointly by a Pequot chief, but a rebellion led to Mohegan independence and the

L
M
N

destruction of the Pequot. Having made an alliance with the English, the Mohegan were the only important tribe remaining in southern New England after KING PHILIP'S WAR (1675–76). Today there is a remnant (approx. 1,000) near Norwich, Conn.

Mohenjo Daro Ancient city on the bank of the Indus River, in present-day southern Pakistan. At about 3 mi (5 km) in circuit, it was the largest city of the INDUS CIVILIZATION in the 3rd–2nd millennium BC, and it probably served as the capital of an extensive state. It was fortified, and its citadel contained, according to archaeological finds, an elaborate bath, a granary, and two halls of assembly.

Mohican See MAHICAN

Mohism See MOZI

Moho \'mō-ˌhō\ *or* **Mohorovičić discontinuity** \ˌmō-hə-'rō-və-ˌchich\ Boundary between the earth's CRUST and its MANTLE. The Moho lies at a depth of about 22 mi (35 km) below continents and about 4.5 mi (7 km) beneath the oceanic crust. Modern instruments have determined that the velocity of SEISMIC WAVES increases rapidly at this boundary. The Moho was named for ANDRIJA MOHOROVIČIĆ.

Moholy-Nagy \'mȯ-hȯi-'näd^y\, **László** (1895–1946) Hungarian painter, photographer, and art teacher. After studying law in Budapest, he went to Berlin in 1919, and in 1923 he took charge of the metal workshop of the BAUHAUS as well as the *Bauhausbook* series of publications. As a painter and photographer he worked predominantly with light. His "photograms" were composed directly on film, and his "light modulators" (oil paintings on transparent or polished surfaces) included mobile light effects. As an educator, he developed a widely accepted curriculum to develop students' natural visual gifts instead of specialized skills. Fleeing Nazi Germany in 1935, he went to London and then to Chicago, where he organized and headed the New Bauhaus.

Mohorovičić, Andrija (1857–1936) Croatian meteorologist and geophysicist who discovered the boundary between the earth's CRUST and the MANTLE, later named the Mohorovičić discontinuity, or MOHO. A professor at the Main Technical School in Zagreb, he was also director of its meteorological observatory from 1892. From observations of SEISMIC WAVES, he deduced that the solid earth consisted of an outer and inner layer and that between them lay a distinct boundary. He also devised a technique for locating earthquake epicenters and calculated the travel time of seismic waves. He was an early advocate of earthquake-resistant construction.

Mohs hardness \'mōz\ Rough measure of the resistance of a smooth surface to scratching or abrasion, expressed in terms of a scale devised by German mineralogist Friedrich Mohs in 1812. Minerals are ranked in comparison with the Mohs scale, which is made up of 10 minerals that have been given arbitrary hardness values on a scale from 1 (least hard, or talc) to 10 (hardest, or diamond).

Mohs Hardness Table

Mineral	Mohs no.	Other materials	Description
Talc	1		very easily scratched by the fingernail; has a greasy feel
Gypsum	2	~2.2 fingernail	can be scratched by the fingernail
Calcite	3	~3.2 copper penny	very easily scratched with a knife and just scratched with a copper coin
Fluorite	4		very easily scratched with a knife but not as easily as calcite
Apatite	5	~5.1 pocketknife ~5.5 glass plate	scratched with a knife with difficulty
Orthoclase	6	~6.5 steel needle	cannot be scratched with a knife, but scratches glass with difficulty
Quartz	7	~7.0 streak plate	scratches glass easily
Topaz	8		scratches glass very easily
Corundum	9		cuts glass
Diamond	10		used as a glass cutter

Moi \'mȯi\, **Daniel (Toroitich) arap** (born 1924) Five-term president of Kenya (from 1978). Trained as a teacher, Moi served in the cabinet and as vice president (1967–78) under Pres. JOMO KENYATTA before succeeding him as president. Head of the dominant Kenyan African National Union (KANU) party, he governed autocratically, finally permitting multiparty elections only when forced to by international pressure in 1991. His subsequent electoral victories (1992, 1998) led to civil unrest and charges of stealing the elections. During his time in office some sectors of the economy have grown, but critics have attributed this to the strong political patronage system.

Moiseyev \mȯi-'sā-ef\, **Igor (Aleksandrovich)** (born 1906) Russian dancer, choreographer, and founder-director of the State Academic Folk Dance Ensemble, popularly called the Moiseyev Ensemble. He joined the BOLSHOI company in 1924. In 1936 he became head choreographer at Moscow's Theater of Folk Art and later founded Folk Dance Ensemble, in which ballet professionals performed dances from all U.S.S.R. republics. His choreography combined authentic folk-dance steps with theatrical effects, and he created over 170 dances for the ensemble. The ensemble served as a model for other countries in subsequently forming their own folk-dance ensembles.

Mojave *or* **Mohave** \mō-'hä-vē\ YUMAN-speaking Indian farmers of the Mojave Desert along the lower Colorado River. This valley was a patch of green surrounded by barren desert. In addition to farming, the Mojave fished, hunted, and gathered wild plants. The essential social unit was the patrilineal family. There were no settled villages; wherever there was suitable floodland for farming, the Mojave built scattered houses. They believed in a supreme creator and attached great significance to dreams, considered the source of all special powers. About 1,500 Mojave live on or near the Colorado River reservation in Arizona.

Mojave Desert *or* **Mohave Desert** \mō-'hä-vē\ Arid region, southeastern California. Occupying more than 25,000 sq mi (65,000 sq km), it extends from the SIERRA NEVADA to the Colorado Plateau and merges with the Great Basin Desert to the north and the SONORAN DESERT to the south and southeast. It joins the Sonoran, Great Basin, and Chihuahuan deserts in forming the North American Desert. The Mojave Desert receives an average annual rainfall of 5 in (13 cm). It is the location of JOSHUA TREE NATIONAL PARK.

moksha *or* **moksa** \'mōk-shə\ In HINDUISM and JAINISM, the ultimate spiritual goal, the soul's release from the bonds of transmigration. The soul, once entered upon a bodily existence, remains trapped in a chain of successive rebirths until it has attains the perfection or enlightenment that allows it release. The methods by which release is sought and attained differ from one philosophical school to the next, but most schools consider moksha to be the highest purpose of life.

Molcho \'mȯl-ḵō\, **Solomon** *orig.* **Diogo Pires** (c. 1500–1532) Portuguese Jewish martyr. Born into a marrano family, he became royal secretary in a Portuguese high court of justice. When an Arabian adventurer, David Reubeni (died c. 1532), arrived in Portugal, mystic visions convinced Pires that Reubeni was a herald of the messiah. After circumcising himself and changing his name, he preached the coming of the messiah in Turkey, Palestine, and Rome. In 1532 he and Reubeni were imprisoned by CHARLES V and turned over to the Inquisition. Molcho refused to recant his faith and was burned at the stake.

Mold Town (pop., 1995 est.: 9,000), seat of Clwyd Co., northeastern Wales. Situated between the industrial centers of Deeside and Wrexham it grew up around a motte-and-bailey castle built by the Normans in the 12th century. In the area earlier, native Christians had defeated the pagan PICTS and Scots in a battle waged in AD 430. Long a market center, it became the administrative center of Clwyd in 1967.

mold In biology, a conspicuous mass of MYCELIUM and fruiting structures produced by various fungi (division Mycota; see FUNGUS). Molds of the genera *Aspergillus, Penicillium,* and *Rhizopus* are associated with food spoilage and plant diseases, but some have beneficial uses, as in the manufacture of ANTIBIOTICS (e.g., PENICILLIN) and certain cheeses. *Neurospora,* or orange bread mold, has been invaluable in the study of

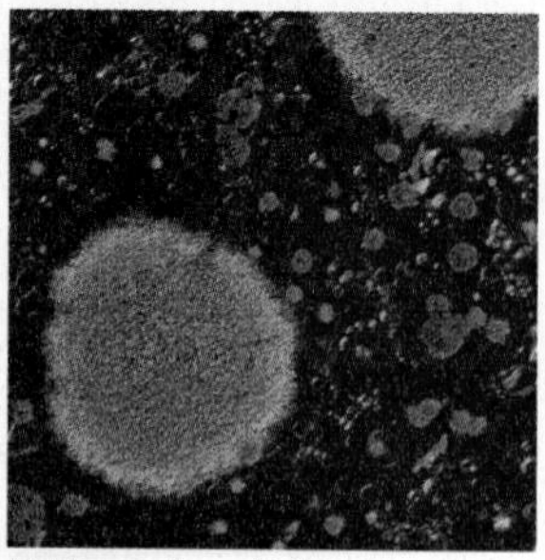

Mold on surface of jelly.
INGMAR HOLMASEN

biochemical genetics. Water molds live in fresh or brackish water or wet soils, absorbing dead or decaying organic matter. See also SLIME MOLD.

mold In manufacturing, a cavity or surface in which a fluid or plastic substance is shaped into a desired finished product. A molten substance, such as metal or plastic, is poured or forced into a mold and allowed to harden. Molds are made of various materials, depending on the application; sand is frequently used for metal CASTING, hardened steel for molds for plastic materials, and plaster for various purposes. See also INGOT, PATTERNMAKING, TOOL AND DIE MAKING.

Moldavia \mäl-ˈdā-vē-ə\ Former principality, southeastern central Europe. Located on the lower DANUBE RIVER, it was founded in the 14th century by the Vlachs, and achieved independence in 1349. In the mid-16th century it was under the OTTOMAN EMPIRE. In 1774 it came under Russian control; it soon lost its northwestern territory, Bukovina, to Austria, and its eastern portion and BESSARABIA to Russia. In 1859 Moldavia and WALACHIA formed the state of ROMANIA. In 1918 the territories earlier ceded by Moldavia joined Romania. That part still under Russian control, east of the Dniester River, within the Ukrainian S.S.R., became in 1924 the Moldavian Autonomous S.S.R. See also MOLDOVA.

molding In architecture and the decorative arts, a defining, transitional, or terminal element that serves to contour or outline edges and surfaces. The surface of a molding may be plain or modeled with recesses and reliefs, which either maintain a constant profile along its length or are set in rhythmically repeated patterns. Types of flat or angular moldings are the FASCIA, chamfer (or bevel), and fillet (narrow band). Single curved moldings include the cavetto (concave, with a quarter-circle profile), scotia (deep concave), flute (grooved), ovolo (convex, with a quarter-circle profile), torus (semicircular convex), roll (rounded convex), and astragal (narrow semicircular convex). Among the most common compound moldings are the projecting, double-curved cyma recta or ogee, often used as a crown molding, and the cyma reversa, used for crown or base. The profiles of moldings are traditionally enhanced by flower or leaf forms, geometric motifs, or spirals.

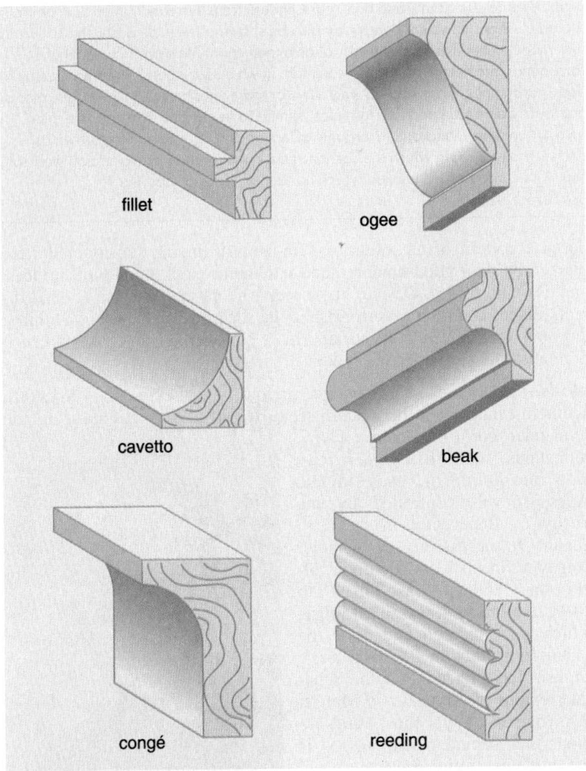

Examples of common molding styles.

Moldova \mȯl-ˈdȯ-və\ *officially* **Republic of Moldova** Republic, northeastern BALKAN region of central Europe. It is bordered by Ukraine and Romania. Area: 13,000 sq mi (33,700 sq km). Population (1997

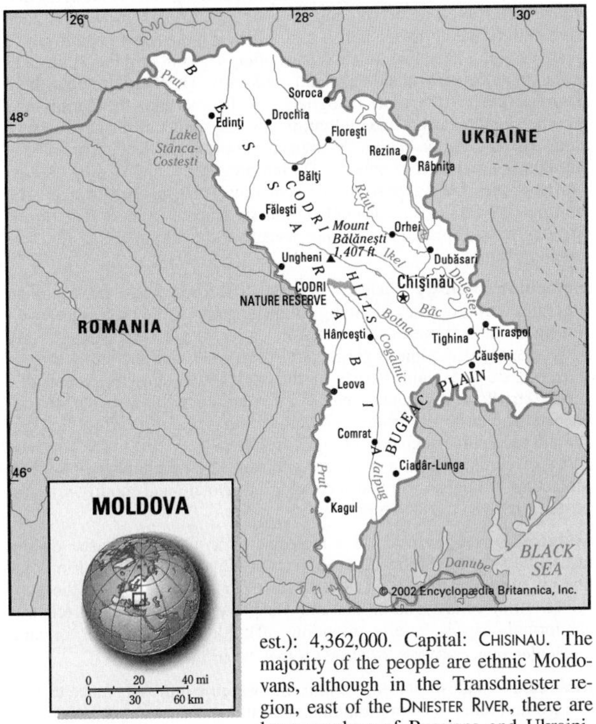

est.): 4,362,000. Capital: CHISINAU. The majority of the people are ethnic Moldovans, although in the Transdniester region, east of the DNIESTER RIVER, there are large numbers of Russians and Ukrainians. Languages: Romanian (official), Russian, Ukrainian. Religion: Eastern Orthodoxy. Currency: leu. Most of Moldova is a fertile region lying between the Dniester and Prut rivers; the northern and central regions of the country are forested. The economy is based on agriculture; the major farm products are grapes, winter wheat, corn, and dairy products. Industry is centered on food processing. It is a republic with one legislative body; its head of state is the president, and the head of government is the prime minister. The area of present-day Moldova consists of that part of the principality of Moldavia lying east of the Prut River (part of Romania before 1940) and, adjoining it on the south, the region of BESSARABIA along the Black Sea coast. (See MOLDAVIA for history prior to 1940.) The two regions were incorporated as the Moldavian S.S.R. in 1940. In 1991 Moldavia declared independence from the Soviet Union. It adopted the Romanian spelling of Moldova and had, earlier, legitimized use of the Roman rather than the Cyrillic alphabet. The republic was admitted to the U.N. in 1992. During the 1990s it struggled to find economic equilibrium.

mole *or* **mol** \ˈmōl\ Standard unit for measuring everyday quantities of such minute entities as ATOMS or MOLECULES. For any substance, the number of atoms or molecules in a mole is AVOGADRO'S NUMBER (6.02×10^{23}) of particles. Defined exactly, it is the amount of pure substance containing the same number of chemical units there are in exactly 12 g of carbon-12. For each substance, a mole is its ATOMIC WEIGHT, MOLECULAR WEIGHT, or FORMULA WEIGHT in GRAMS. The number of moles of a solute in a liter of SOLUTION is its molarity *(M);* the number of moles of solute in 1,000 grams of SOLVENT is its molality *(m).* The two measures differ slightly and have different uses. See also STOICHIOMETRY.

mole Any burrowing, often blind, INSECTIVORE in the families Talpidae (including 22 species of true moles) or Chrysochloridae (11 species of golden moles). Most species have short legs and tail, a pointed head, velvety grayish fur, no external ears, and a strong odor. They range from 3.5 to 8 in. (9–20 cm) long. The forelimbs are rotated and have broad or pointed claws on the toes. Moles are active day and night, digging both surface tunnels in search of earthworms, grubs, and other invertebrates and deep (10-ft, or 3-m) vented burrows (molehills) for occupancy. The star-nosed mole *(Condylura cristata)* of northeastern North America has 22 pink, tentacle-like touch organs radiating from its nose.

mole Pigmented flat or fleshy SKIN mark, made up mostly of cells that produce MELANIN, which gives moles their light to dark brown or black color and, in the dermis, a bluish cast. Thicker moles also contain nerve elements and connective tissue. Moles often begin in childhood, usually as flat spots between the dermis and epidermis. Those that remain there are more likely to become malignant. Most move into the dermis and become slightly raised. In children, moles may undergo changes resembling cancer but are benign. Malignant MELANOMA can begin in moles, but almost never before puberty. During pregnancy, moles may enlarge and new ones may appear. Moles sometimes disappear with age. The term nevus refers to a congenital skin mark, whereas a mole may develop after birth. Epidermal nevi are usually the same color as the surrounding skin.

molecular biology Field of science concerned with the chemical structures and processes of biological phenomena at the molecular level. Having developed out of the related fields of BIOCHEMISTRY, GENETICS, and BIOPHYSICS, the discipline is particularly concerned with the study of PROTEINS, NUCLEIC ACIDS, and ENZYMES. In the early 1950s, growing knowledge of the structure of proteins enabled the structure of DNA to be described. The discovery in the 1970s of certain types of enzymes that can cut and recombine segments of DNA (see RECOMBINATION) in the CHROMOSOMES of certain bacteria made recombinant-DNA technology possible. Molecular biologists use that technology to isolate and modify specific GENES (see GENETIC ENGINEERING).

molecular weight MASS of a molecule of a substance, based on the fact that a MOLE of carbon-12 has a mass of 12 g. It is calculated in practice by summing the ATOMIC WEIGHTS of the atoms making up the substance's molecular formula. The molecular weight of hydrogen (chemical formula H_2) is 2 (after rounding off); for many complex organic molecules (e.g., PROTEINS, POLYMERS) it may be in the millions.

molecule Smallest identifiable unit into which a pure substance can be divided and retain its composition and chemical properties. Division into still smaller parts, eventually ATOMS, involves destroying the BONDING that holds the molecule together. For NOBLE GASES, the molecule is a single atom; all other substances have two (diatomic) or more (polyatomic) atoms in a molecule. The atoms are the same in ELEMENTS, such as hydrogen (H_2), and different in COMPOUNDS, such as glucose ($C_6H_{12}O_6$). Atoms always combine into molecules in fixed proportions. Molecules of different substances can have the same constituent atoms, either in different proportions, as in carbon monoxide (CO) and carbon dioxide (CO_2), or bonded in different ways (see ISOMER). The COVALENT BONDS in molecules give them their shapes and most of their properties. (The concept of molecules has no significance in solids with IONIC BONDS.) ANALYSIS with modern techniques and computers can determine and display the size, shape, and CONFIGURATION of molecules, the positions of their nuclei and electron clouds, the lengths and angles of their bonds, and other details. ELECTRON MICROSCOPY can even produce images of individual molecules and atoms. See also MOLECULAR WEIGHT. See illustration opposite.

Moley, Raymond (Charles) (1886–1975) U.S. educator and political adviser. Born in Berea, Ohio, he taught political science at Columbia University 1923–54. He prepared political and social studies for Gov. FRANKLIN ROOSEVELT, and when Roosevelt was preparing for his 1932 presidential campaign, Moley formed the BRAIN TRUST to advise him on national issues. Moley wrote many of Roosevelt's campaign speeches and coined the term NEW DEAL. He was a *Newsweek* contributing editor 1937–68.

Molière \mȯl-'yer\ *orig.* **Jean-Baptiste Poquelin** (1622–1673) French playwright, actor, and director. The son of a prosperous upholsterer, he left home to become an actor in 1643, joining forces with the BÉJART FAMILY. He cofounded the troupe known as the Illustre Théâtre and toured the French provinces (1645–58), writing plays and acting in them. After his troupe was established in a permanent theater in Paris under the patronage of LOUIS XIV, he won acclaim in the court and among bourgeois audiences for his comedy *The Affected Young Ladies* (1659). His other major plays included *The School for Wives* (1662), *Tartuffe* (1664; initially banned by religious authorities), *The Misanthrope* (1666), *Amphitryon* (1668), *The Miser* (1669), *The Bourgeois Gentleman* (1670), and *The Imaginary Invalid* (1673). His plays composed a portrait of all levels of 17th-century French society, and were marked by their good-humored and intelligent mockery of human vices, vanities, and follies. Despite his success, he never ceased to act and direct. Taken ill during a performance, he died of a hemorrhage within a day and was denied holy burial. He is considered the greatest French dramatist and the father of modern French comedy.

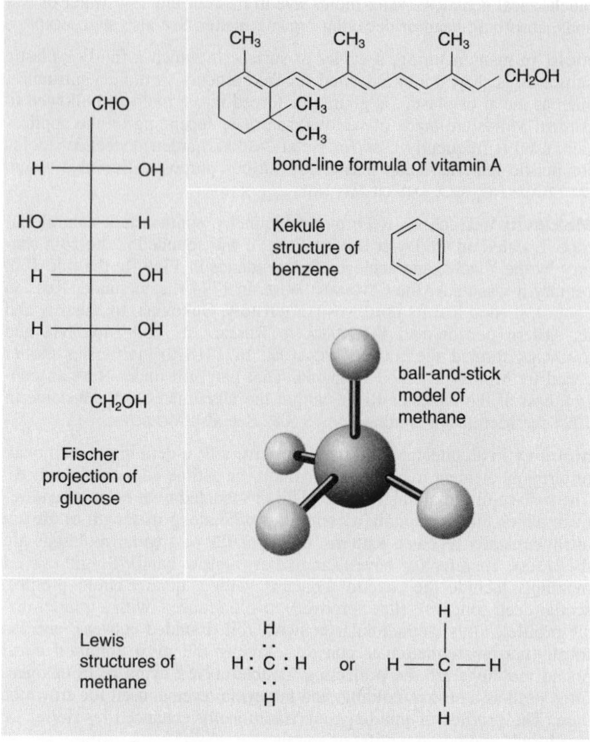

Several methods of representing a molecule's structure. In Lewis structures, element symbols represent atoms, and dots represent electrons surrounding them. A pair of shared electrons (covalent bond) may also be shown as a single dash. The ball-and-stick model better illustrates the spatial arrangement of the atoms. For aromatic compounds, the Kekulé structure is common, in which each bond is represented by a dash, carbon atoms are implied where two or more lines meet, and hydrogen atoms are usually omitted. Bond-line formulas, similar to the Kekulé structure, are often used for complex nonaromatic organic compounds. Sugars are often drawn as Fischer projections, in which the carbon "backbone" is drawn as a straight vertical line, with carbon atoms implied where horizontal lines intersect the vertical one.

Molise \mō-'lē-zā\ Autonomous region (pop., 1996 est.: 331,000), southern central Italy. Its western sector is part of the APENNINES, and the remainder consists mostly of low mountains and hills. Under LOMBARD rule during the early Middle Ages, it was controlled by the duchy of Benevento. In the 13th century it successively came under Angevin, Spanish, and Bourbon rulers. In 1860 it was joined to ABRUZZI, to form Abruzzi e Molise, which was incorporated into the kingdom of Italy. In 1965 Abruzzi e Molise was divided into the separate regions of Abruzzi and Molise. It is one of Italy's most rural regions; its capital, CAMPOBASSO, is the only city of any size.

Mollet.

Mollet \mȯ-'le\, **Guy** (1905–1975) French politician. An English teacher in Arras, he joined the Socialist

Party in 1921 and became head of the Socialist teachers' union in 1939. After serving in World War II, he was elected to the Chamber of Deputies and became secretary-general of the Socialist Party (1946–69). With PIERRE MENDES-FRANCE, he led the Republican Front to victory and became premier (1956–57). Failures in dealing with the Algerian rebellion and the Suez Crisis led to the government's defeat, but Mollet continued to serve as a deputy and as mayor of Arras.

mollusk *or* **mollusc** Any of some 75,000 species of soft-bodied INVERTEBRATE animals (phylum Mollusca), many of which are wholly or partly enclosed in a calcium carbonate shell secreted by the mantle, a soft covering formed from the body wall. Between the mantle and the body is the mantle cavity. Mollusks occur in most habitats from the deep sea to high mountains. Living mollusks are usually grouped into eight classes: Gastropoda (see GASTROPOD), Bivalvia or Pelecypoda (see BIVALVE), Cephalopoda (see CEPHALOPOD), Scaphopoda (tusk shells), Aplacophora (Solenogasters), Caudofoveata (sometimes included in the Aplacophora order), Polyplacophora (chitons), and Monoplacophora. Mollusks are economically important as food, and their shells are widely used in jewelry and decorative items. See illustration opposite.

Molly Maguires (1862–76) Secret organization of U.S. coal miners in Pennsylvania and West Virginia. To protest poor working conditions and employment discrimination in the 1860s, the Irish-American miners formed a group named for an Irish widow who had led antilandlord agitators in Ireland. Acts of sabotage and terrorist murders in the coalfields were blamed on the group, and mine owners hired a Pinkerton detective, James McParlan, to infiltrate the organization. Based on his testimony in the widely publicized trials (1875–77), 10 "Mollies" were convicted of murder and hanged.

Molnár \'mōl-ˌnär\, **Ferenc** (1878–1952) Hungarian writer. He published his first stories at 19 and achieved his first success with the play *The Devil* (1907). Among his other plays, some adapted as films, are *Liliom* (1909), which was also adapted as the musical *Carousel*; *The Swan* (1920); and *The Red Mill* (1923). Some of his stories, especially those in *Muzsika* (1908; "Music"), are masterpieces examining the problems of the poor. Of his many novels, only *The Paul Street Boys* (1907) was a success.

Moloch \'mō-ˌläk, 'mä-lək\ Ancient Middle Eastern deity to whom children were sacrificed. The laws given to MOSES by God expressly forbade the Israelites to sacrifice children to Moloch, as the Egyptians and Canaanites did. A shrine to Moloch outside the walls of Jerusalem was destroyed during the reign of JOSIAH the reformer.

Molotov \'mȯ-lə-ˌtȯf\, **Vyacheslav (Mikhaylovich)** *orig.* **Vyacheslav Mikhaylovich Skryabin** (1890–1986) Soviet political leader. A member of the Bolsheviks from 1906, he worked in provincial Communist Party organizations from 1917. A staunch supporter of JOSEPH STALIN, he became secretary of the Central Committee in 1921. Promoted to the Politburo in 1926, he purged the Moscow party organization of anti-Stalinists (1928–30). He served as prime minister 1930–41, and as foreign minister 1939–49 and 1953–56. He negotiated the GERMAN–SOVIET NONAGGRESSION PACT in 1939, and in World War II he ordered the production of the crude bottle bombs later called "Molotov cocktails." He arranged the alliances with the U.S. and Britain and was the Soviet spokesman at the Allied conferences during and after the war. After being dismissed in 1956 by NIKITA KHRUSHCHEV, Molotov joined an unsuccessful attempt to depose Khrushchev (1957) and lost all his party offices; in 1962 he was expelled from the Communist Party.

molting Shedding or casting off of an animal's outer layer or covering and formation of its replacement. Regulated by hormones, molting occurs throughout the animal kingdom. It includes the shedding and replacement of horns, hair, skin, and feathers and the process by which a nymph or other organism sheds an external skeleton for the purpose of growth or change in shape.

Moltke \'mōlt-kə\, **Helmuth (Karl Bernhard) von** *later* **Graf (Count) von Moltke** (1800–1891) Prussian general. He joined the Prussian army in 1822 and was appointed to its general staff in 1832. After a stint as adviser to the Turkish army (1835–39), he traveled widely and wrote several books on history and travel. In 1855 he served as personal aide to the Prussian prince Frederick William (later FREDERICK III), then was selected as chief of the Prussian general staff (1857–88). Highly intelligent and militarily creative, he reorganized the Prussian army and devised new strategic and tactical command methods for modern mass armies. He directed the strategies that produced victories in the Prussian and German wars against Denmark (1864), against Austria in the SEVEN WEEKS' WAR (1866), and against France in the FRANCO-PRUSSIAN WAR (1870–71). He was created count in 1870 and field marshal in 1871.

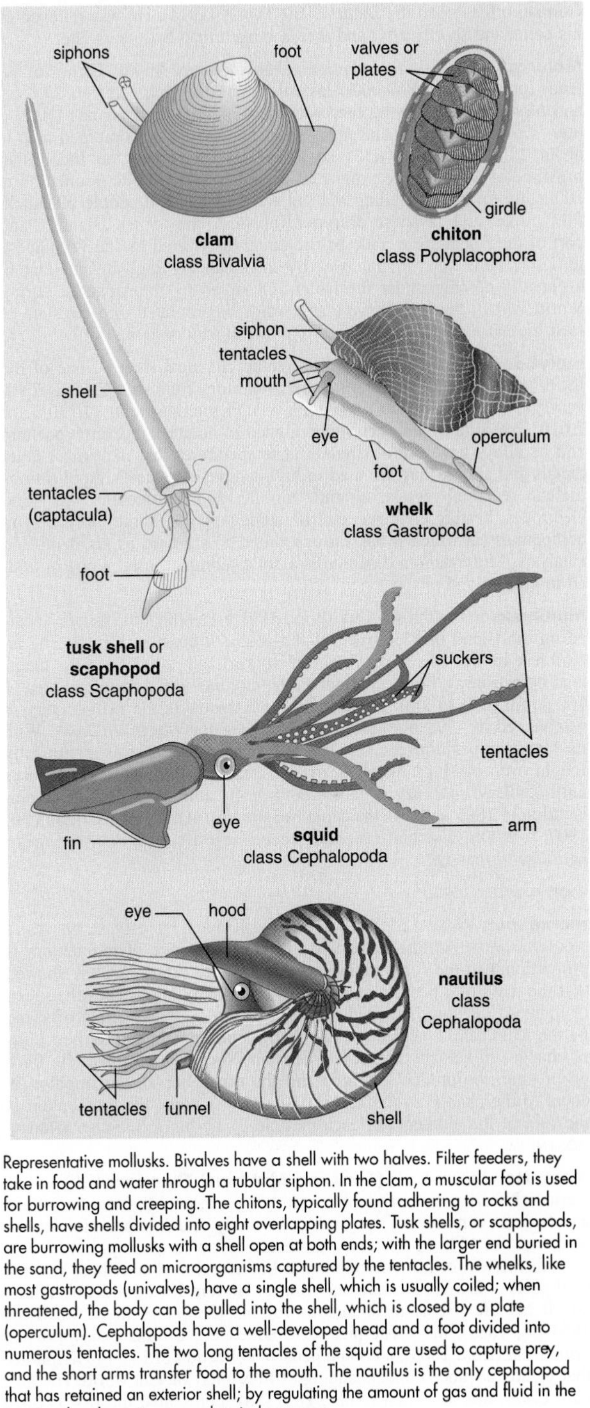

Representative mollusks. Bivalves have a shell with two halves. Filter feeders, they take in food and water through a tubular siphon. In the clam, a muscular foot is used for burrowing and creeping. The chitons, typically found adhering to rocks and shells, have shells divided into eight overlapping plates. Tusk shells, or scaphopods, are burrowing mollusks with a shell open at both ends; with the larger end buried in the sand, they feed on microorganisms captured by the tentacles. The whelks, like most gastropods (univalves), have a single shell, which is usually coiled; when threatened, the body can be pulled into the shell, which is closed by a plate (operculum). Cephalopods have a well-developed head and a foot divided into numerous tentacles. The two long tentacles of the squid are used to capture prey, and the short arms transfer food to the mouth. The nautilus is the only cephalopod that has retained an exterior shell; by regulating the amount of gas and fluid in the interior chambers, it can regulate its buoyancy.

L M N

Moltke, Helmuth (Johannes Ludwig) von (1848–1916) German soldier. A nephew of HELMUTH VON MOLTKE, he rose rapidly in the German army and served as adjutant to his uncle from 1882. He was appointed quartermaster general in 1903 and chief of the German general staff in 1906. At the outbreak of World War I, he applied the SCHLIEFFEN PLAN, devised by his predecessor, but his inability to revise the plan to cope with tactical and command errors contributed to the halt of the German offensive in the Battle of the MARNE (1914). He was relieved of his command shortly after and died a broken man two years later.

Moluccas \mō-'lə-kəz\ *Indonesian* **Maluku** \mä-'lü-kü\ Group of islands (pop., 1990: 1,860,000), eastern Indonesia, lying between SULAWESI and NEW GUINEA. The Moluccas comprise three large islands (HALMAHERA, CERAM, and BURU) and many smaller ones. Their combined area is about 28,767 sq mi (74,505 sq km). They constitute the Indonesian province of Maluku; the provincial capital is AMBON. The population is ethnically diverse, including Malays and Papuans and people of Dutch, Portuguese, and Javanese descent. Known as the "Spice Islands," and part of the Asian spice trade before being discovered by the Portuguese in 1511, they were fought over by the Spanish, English, and Dutch, eventually coming under the Dutch. Occupied by the Japanese during World War II, the islands were afterwards incorporated into the state of East Indonesia and then into the Republic of Indonesia in 1949.

molybdenum \mə-'lib-də-nəm\ Metallic chemical ELEMENT, one of the TRANSITION ELEMENTS, chemical symbol Mo, atomic number 42. It is a silvery gray, relatively rare METAL with a high melting point (4,730°F, or 2,610°C) that does not occur uncombined in nature. Since molybdenum and its alloys have useful strength at temperatures that melt most other metals and alloys, they are used in high-temperature steels. Applications include reaction vessels; aircraft, missile, and automobile parts; and electrodes, heating elements, and filament supports. Some molybdenum compounds (in which it has various VALENCES) are used as pigments and catalysts. Molybdenum disulfide is a solid lubricant, used alone or added to greases and oils.

Mombasa \mōm-'bä-sə\ City (pop., 1991 est.: 600,000), Kenya, located on the island of Mombasa off the southern coast of Kenya. The island has an area of 5.5 sq mi (14.25 sq km) and is linked to the mainland by causeway, bridge, and ferry; the city includes a mainland area of 100 sq mi (259 sq km). Founded by Arab traders in the 11th century, it was visited in 1498 by the Portuguese navigator VASCO DA GAMA. With its strategic position for the Indian Ocean trade, it was continually fought over, passing among the Arabs, Persians, Portuguese, and Turks until 1840, when ZANZIBAR gained control. It came under British administration in 1895 and was the capital of the East Africa Protectorate until 1907. It is Kenya's chief port and second-largest city; it is also a major agricultural market.

moment See TORQUE

momentum Product of the MASS of a particle and its VELOCITY. NEWTON'S SECOND LAW OF MOTION states that the rate of change of momentum is proportional to the force acting on the particle. ALBERT EINSTEIN showed that the mass of a particle increases as its velocity approaches the speed of light. At the speeds treated in classical MECHANICS, the effect of speed on the mass can be neglected, and changes in momentum are the results of changes in velocity alone. If a constant force acts on a particle for a given time, the product of force and the time interval, the impulse, is equal to the change in momentum. For a rigid body, the momentum is the sum of the momenta of each particle in the body. See also ANGULAR MOMENTUM.

Mommsen \'mȯm-zən\, **(Christian Matthias) Theodor** (1817–1903) German historian and writer. After studying law, he did research in Italy and became a master of epigraphy, the study and interpretation of inscriptions. In 1848 he became a professor of law at Leipzig, but he was soon dismissed for his participation in liberal political activities; he later held posts at Zurich, Breslau, and Berlin. He remained politically minded all his life. He is most famous for his *History of Rome* (4 vols., 1854–56, 1885), his masterpiece. He edited the *Corpus Inscriptionum Latinarum* (from 1863), a comprehensive collection of Latin inscriptions that greatly advanced understanding of life in the ancient world. His *Roman Constitutional Law* (3 vols., 1871–88) represented the first codification of Roman law. His lifetime scholarly output was immense, his publications numbering close to 1,000. He received the 1902 Nobel Prize for Literature.

Mon \'mōn\ People thought to have originated in western China and currently living in the eastern delta region of Myanmar and in W-central Thailand. They have lived in their present area for the last 1,200 years and brought Myanmar its writing (Pali) and its religion (Buddhism). Rice and teak are their most important agricultural products. Today they number more than 1.1 million. See also DVARAVATI, MON KINGDOM.

Mon-Khmer languages \'mōn-kə-'mer\ Family of about 130 AUSTROASIATIC LANGUAGES, spoken by more than 80 million people in South and Southeast Asia. VIETNAMESE has far more speakers than all other Austroasiatic languages combined. Other languages with many speakers are Muong, with about a million speakers in northern Vietnam; KHMER; Kuay (Kuy), with perhaps 800,000 speakers; and Mon, spoken by more than 800,000 people in southern Myanmar and parts of Thailand. Of all the Mon-Khmer languages, only Mon, Khmer, and Vietnamese have written traditions dating earlier than the 19th century. Old Mon, which is attested from the 7th century, was written in a script of South Asian origin that was later adapted by the Burmese (see MON KINGDOM, INDIC WRITING SYSTEMS). Typical phonetic features of Mon-Khmer languages are a large vowel inventory, contrast in vowels having plain rather than breathy or creaky register, and lack of TONE distinctions.

Mon kingdom Kingdom of the MON people, who were powerful in Myanmar in the 9th–11th century, the 13th–16th century, and briefly in the mid-18th century. By 825 they had founded their capital city, Thaton, and the city of Pegu. The Mon kingdom was defeated by the Burman kingdom of PAGAN. When Pagan fell to the Mongols (1287), the Mon regained their independence and their former territory. Defeated again in 1539, they reestablished Pegu briefly in the 18th century, but it was destroyed by Alaungpaya (see ALAUNGPAYA DYNASTY) in 1757. See also DVARAVATI.

Monaco \'mä-nə-,kō\ *officially* **Principality of Monaco** Independent principality, on the Mediterranean Sea near the France–Italy border. Area: .73 sq mi (1.9 sq km). Population (1997 est.): 32,000. The majority of Monaco's population is composed of French citizens, with a small minority of Italians. Less than 15% are of Monagesque descent. Language: French (official). Religion: Roman Catholicism. Currency: French franc. Inhabited since prehistoric times, the area was known to the Phoenicians, Greeks, Carthaginians, and Romans. In 1191 the Genoese took possession of it; in 1297 the reign of the Grimaldi family began. The Grimaldis allied themselves with France except for the period 1524–1641, when they were under the protection of Spain. France annexed Monaco in 1793, and it remained under French control until the fall of NAPOLEON, when the Grimaldis returned. In 1815 it was put under the protection of Sardinia. A treaty in 1861 called for the sale of the towns of Menton and Roquebrune to France and the establishment of Monaco's independence. Monaco is one of Europe's most luxurious resorts, known for its MONTE CARLO gambling center, international sports car races, and beaches. In 1997 the 700-year rule of the Grimaldis, now under Prince RAINIER, was celebrated.

Monaco, Lorenzo See LORENZO MONACO

monarch butterfly Species (*Danaus plexippus,* family Danaidae) of milkweed BUTTERFLY, occurring worldwide but mainly in the Americas. It is the only LEPIDOPTERAN species to make a true migration (a two-way flight by the same individual). In North America, thousands of monarchs gather in autumn, migrate southward, sometimes more than 1,800 mi (2,900 km), and return north in spring. The distinctive coloration of the adult's wings (reddish brown, with black veins, a black border, and two rows of spots) warns predators of its bad taste. Several other species derive protection by mimicking its coloration.

monarchy Undivided SOVEREIGNTY or rule by a single person, who is the permanent head of state. The term is now used to refer to countries with hereditary sovereigns. The monarch was the ideal head of the new nation-states of the 16th–17th century; his powers tended toward ABSOLUTISM, though in Britain PARLIAMENT limited that power from early on. The old idea that the monarch represented (within the limits of his dominions) the rule of God over all things culminated in the 17th century in the doctrine of the divine right of KINGS (see DIVINE KINGSHIP), exemplified by LOUIS XIV. Monarchical absolutism adapted to the ENLIGHTENMENT by evolving into "benevolent despotism," as typified by the rule of CATHERINE II of Russia. The French Revolution dealt absolute monarchy a crushing blow, and World War I effectively destroyed what remained of it, the rulers of Russia, Germany, and Austria-Hungary being held responsible for the war and postwar misery.

monarchy, constitutional See CONSTITUTIONAL MONARCHY

monastery Local community or residence of a religious order, particularly an order of monks. Christian monasteries originally developed in Egypt, where the monks first lived as hermits and then in small groups. Walls were built for defense, and monks' cells were later constructed against the walls, leaving a central space for church, chapels, fountain, and dining hall. The *vihara* was an early type of Buddhist monastery, consisting of an open court surrounded by open cells accessible through an entrance porch. Originally built in India to shelter monks during the rainy season, viharas took on a sacred character when small STUPAS and images of the Buddha were installed in the central court. In western India, viharas were often excavated into rock cliffs. See also ABBEY.

monasticism Institutionalized religious movement whose members are bound by vows to an ascetic life of prayer, meditation, or good works. Members of monastic orders (monks) are usually celibate, and they live apart from society either in a community of monks or nuns or as religious recluses. The earliest Christian monastic communities were founded in the deserts of Egypt, most notably by the hermit St. ANTHONY OF EGYPT (251–356). Monasticism spread throughout the BYZANTINE EMPIRE and Western Europe. The BENEDICTINE order, founded by St. BENEDICT OF NURSIA in the 6th century, called for moderation of ascetic practices and established worship services at regular hours. Throughout the Middle Ages, monasticism played a vital role not only in spreading Christianity but also in preserving and adding to literature and learning. It underwent periodic reforms, notably by the CISTERCIANS in the 12th century, and saw the founding of mendicant orders such as the DOMINICANS and FRANCISCANS. Monasticism has also been important in Eastern religions. In early Hindu times (c. 600–200 BC) there were hermits who lived in groups (ASHRAMS), though they did not lead a strictly organized communal life. Jainism may be the first religion to have had an organized monastic life, which was characterized by extreme asceticism. Buddhist monks observe a moderate rule that avoids extremes of self-indulgence and self-mortification.

Monck \'məŋk\, **George** *later* **Duke of Albemarle** (1608–1670) English general. He served with the Dutch army against the Spanish in the Netherlands (1629–38) and later suppressed a rebellion in Ireland (1642–43). He fought in Ireland and Scotland in the ENGLISH CIVIL WARS, then served in Scotland as commander (1650) and governor (1654). Appointed a general at sea (1652) in the ANGLO-DUTCH WARS, he played a leading part in the English naval victories. In 1660 he was the chief architect of the RESTORATION of the Stuart monarchy, for which he was created duke of Albemarle.

Mond, Ludwig (1839–1909) German-British chemist and industrialist. He emigrated to England in 1862. He improved the Solvay process for making sodium carbonate (soda ash) and developed a process for extracting NICKEL from its ores. He was a founder of the important chemical firm Brunner, Mond and Co. and of the Mond Nickel Co.

Mondale, Walter F(rederick) (born 1928) U.S. politician. Born in Ceylon, Minn., he practiced law and became active in Minnesota's Farmer-Labor Party and worked for HUBERT H. HUMPHREY's U.S. Senate campaign in 1948. He was Minnesota's attorney general 1960–64, and served in the U.S. Senate 1964–76 when he won election as vice president with JIMMY CARTER. In 1984 he won the Democratic presidential nomination, but lost to RONALD REAGAN. He resumed his law practice and later served as ambassador to Japan (1993–96).

Monde \'mōⁿd\, **Le** (French: "The World") Daily newspaper published in Paris, one of the most important and widely respected newspapers in the world. It was established in 1944, just after the German army left the city, as an independent organ free of government or private subsidies. Covering national and world news in depth from the start, it soon earned a reputation for accuracy and independence. Its writers present their own views, with the result that the paper reveals no consistent ideological outlook, causing it to earn both praise and criticism from every part of the French political spectrum.

Mondino de' Luzzi \mōn-'dē-nō-dā-'lüt-sē\ *Latin* **Mundinus** (1270?–1326?) Italian physician and anatomist. Mondino reintroduced the systematic teaching of anatomy, abandoned for many centuries, into the medical curriculum and did dissections at public lectures. His *Anathomia Mundini* (1316, printed 1478) was the standard handbook for dissectors until the time of ANDREAS VESALIUS. Though it followed GALEN's teachings slavishly, with sometimes inaccurate descriptions of internal organs, it inaugurated a new era in the dissemination of anatomical knowledge.

Mondrian \'mȯn-drē-ˌän\, **Piet** *orig.* **Pieter Cornelis Mondriaan** (1872–1944) Dutch painter. At the insistence of his father, headmaster of a Calvinist school, he obtained an education degree, but then immediately began taking painting lessons. His first paintings, which followed the prevailing trend of Dutch landscape and still-life painting, were exhibited in 1893. Later he broke away from tradition and became a leading figure in DE STIJL. His mature style emerged around 1920 in "Neoplasticism," intended as a purely objective vision of reality, based on the simplest harmonies of straight line, right angle, and the primary colors plus black, white, and gray (e.g., *Composition in Yellow and Blue,* 1929). He painted in the Neoplastic style for the next 20 years, until he fled war-torn Paris for London and then New York in 1940. Inspired by the city's pulsating life and the new rhythms of U.S. music, he replaced his austere patterns with a series of small squares and rectangles that coalesced into a flow of colorful vertical and horizontal lines. His late masterpieces (e.g., *Broadway Boogie-Woogie,* 1942–43) express this new vivacity. His work exerted a profound influence on 20th-century art, architecture, and graphic design.

moneran See BACTERIA, PROKARYOTE

Monet \mō-'nā\, **Claude** (1840–1926) French Impressionist landscape painter. Monet spent his early years in Le Havre, where his first teacher, EUGENE BOUDIN, taught him to paint in the open air. Moving to Paris, he formed lifelong friendships with other young painters, including AUGUSTE RENOIR, ALFRED SISLEY, and PAUL CEZANNE, who were also to become leading Impressionists. An early Monet canvas, *Impression: soleil levant,* shown at the first Impressionist Exhibition in 1874, gave its name to the movement of which he was the leader. Restless by nature, he painted outdoors around France (often at Argenteuil) and also in England, Venice, Holland, and elsewhere. In his mature works Monet developed his method of producing several studies of the same motif in series, changing canvases with the light or as his interest shifted. These series, including *Haystacks* (1891) and *Rouen Cathedral* (1894), were generally dated and were often exhibited together. In the garden at his home in Giverny, Monet created the water-lily pond that inspired his most famous works, the lyrical *Nymphéas* (water lilies) paintings. His work exerted huge influence internationally, and he is regarded as the emblematic representative of IMPRESSIONISM.

monetarism School of economic thought that maintains that the MONEY SUPPLY is the chief determinant of economic activity. MILTON FRIEDMAN and his followers promoted monetarism as an alternative to Keynesian economics (see JOHN MAYNARD KEYNES); their economic theories became influential in the 1970s and early 1980s. Monetarism holds that a change in the money supply directly affects and determines production, employment, and price levels, though its influence is evident only over a long and often variable period of time. Fundamental to the monetarist approach is the rejection of FISCAL POLICY in favor of "monetary rule." Friedman and others asserted that fiscal measures such as tax-policy changes or increased government spending have little significant effect on the fluctuations of the BUSINESS CYCLE. They argued that government intervention in the economy should be kept to a minimum and asserted that economic conditions would change before specific policy measures designed to address them could take effect. Steady, moderate growth of the money supply, in their view, offered the best hope of assuring a constant rate of economic growth with low inflation. U.S. economic performance in the 1980s cast doubts on monetarism, and the proliferation of new types of bank deposits made it difficult to calculate the money supply.

monetary policy Measures employed by governments to influence economic activity, specifically by manipulating the money supply and interest rates. Monetary and FISCAL policy are two ways in which governments attempt to achieve or maintain high levels of employment, price stability, and economic growth. Monetary policy is directed by a nation's CENTRAL BANK. In the U.S., monetary policy is the responsibility of the FEDERAL RESERVE SYSTEM, which uses three main instruments: OPEN-MARKET OPERATIONS, the DISCOUNT RATE, and reserve requirements (see FRACTIONAL RESERVE SYSTEM). In the post-World War II era, economists reached a consensus that, in the long run, inflation results when the money supply grows at too rapid a rate. See also MONETARISM.

money Commodity accepted by general consent as a medium of economic exchange. It is the medium in which PRICES and values are expressed; it circulates from person to person and country to country, thus facilitating trade. Throughout history various commodities have been used as money, including seashells, beads, and cattle, but since the 17th century the most common forms have been metal coins, paper notes, and bookkeeping entries. In standard economic theory, money is held to have four functions: to serve as a medium of exchange universally accepted in return for goods and services; to act as a measure of value, making possible the operation of the price system and the calculation of COST, PROFIT, and loss; to serve as a standard of deferred payments, the unit in which loans are made and future transactions are fixed; and to provide a means of storing wealth not immediately required for use. Metals, especially gold and silver, have been used for money for at least 4,000 years; standardized coins have been minted for perhaps 2,600 years. In the late 18th and early 19th century, banks began to issue notes redeemable in gold or silver, which became the principal money of industrial economies. Temporarily during World War I and permanently from the 1930s, most nations abandoned the GOLD STANDARD. To most individuals today, money consists of coins, notes, and bank deposits. In terms of the economy, however, the total MONEY SUPPLY is several times as large as the sum total of individual money holdings so defined, since most of the deposits placed in banks are loaned out, thus multiplying the money supply several times over. See also SOFT MONEY.

money, quantity theory of Economic theory relating changes in the price level to changes in the quantity of money. It has often been used to analyze the factors underlying INFLATION and DEFLATION. The quantity theory was developed in the 17th and 18th century by philosophers such as JOHN LOCKE and DAVID HUME and was intended as a weapon against MERCANTILISM. Drawing a distinction between MONEY and wealth, advocates of the quantity theory argued that if the accumulation of money by a nation merely raised prices, the mercantilist emphasis on a favorable BALANCE OF TRADE would only increase the supply of money without increasing wealth. The theory contributed to the ascendancy of FREE TRADE over PROTECTIONISM. In the 19th–20th century it played a part in the analysis of BUSINESS CYCLES and in the theory of rates of FOREIGN EXCHANGE.

money market Set of institutions, conventions, and practices whose aim is to facilitate the lending and borrowing of money on a short-term basis. The money market is, therefore, different from the capital market, which is concerned with medium- and long-term CREDIT. The transactions that occur on the money market involve not only banknotes but assets that can be turned into cash at short notice, such as short-term government SECURITIES and BILLS OF EXCHANGE. Though the details and mechanism of the money market vary greatly from country to country, in all cases its basic function is to enable those with surplus short-term funds to lend and those with the need for short-term credit to borrow. This function is accomplished through middlemen who provide their services for a profit. In most countries the government plays a major role in the money market, acting both as a lender and borrower and often using its position to influence the MONEY SUPPLY and INTEREST rates according to its MONETARY POLICY. The U.S. money market covers financial instruments ranging from bills of exchange and government securities to funds from CLEARINGHOUSES and CERTIFICATES OF DEPOSIT. In addition, the FEDERAL RESERVE SYSTEM provides considerable short-term credit directly to the banking system. The international money market facilitates the borrowing, lending, and exchange of currencies between countries.

money order Certificate requiring the issuer to pay a certain sum of money on demand to a specific person or organization. Money orders provide a fast, safe, and convenient means of transferring small sums of money. They are issued by governments (usually through postal authorities), banks, and other qualified institutions to buyers who pay the issuer the face amount of the money order plus a service charge. Because they are exchangeable for cash on demand, they are a generally accepted means of payment. The AMERICAN EXPRESS CO., which began issuing money orders in 1882, is the largest nonbank issuer; its money orders are used throughout the world. See also CURRENCY.

money supply Liquid assets held by individuals and banks. The money supply includes coins, CURRENCY, and demand deposits (checking accounts). Some economists consider time and savings deposits to be part of the money supply because such deposits can be managed by governmental action and are nearly as liquid as currency and demand deposits. Other economists believe that deposits in mutual savings banks, SAVINGS AND LOAN ASSOCIATIONS, and CREDIT UNIONS should be counted as part of the money supply. CENTRAL BANKS regulate the money supply to stabilize their national economies. See also MONETARY POLICY.

Möngke \'mȯŋ-kā\ (1208–1259) Grandson of GENGHIS KHAN and brother of KUBLAI KHAN. He was elected great khan in 1251. Under Möngke, the MONGOLS conquered Iran, Iraq, and Syria as well as the Thai kingdom of Nan-chao and the area of present-day Vietnam. He died before the Mongols could complete the conquest of China, which happened under the reign of Kublai.

Mongkut \ˌmȯŋ-'küt\ *or* **Phrachomklao** \ˌprä-ˌkȯm-'klau̇\ *or* **Rama IV** (1804–1868) King of Siam (r.1851–68). The 43rd child of King Rama II, he was a Buddhist monk and scholar before he ascended the throne. His reformed Buddhism grew into the Thammayut order, which today occupies the intellectual center of Thai Buddhism. Mongkut's intellectual pursuits also brought him into contact with Western thought. As king, he fully opened Siam to Western commerce and combined tolerance and shrewdness to help ensure its survival as an independent nation. The reminiscences of an English governess employed in his household became the basis for the musical comedy *The King and I.*

Mongo Any of several peoples living in the African equatorial forest, all of whom speak a dialect of a common language, Mongo or Nkundo. The Mongo traditionally cultivated cassava and bananas in addition to hunting, fishing, and gathering. Mongo religion emphasizes ANCESTOR WORSHIP and nature spirits; it also features magic and witchcraft. Their art has been mainly oral, and they have a rich talking-drum and song literature. The Mongo population is declining because of a falling birthrate.

Mongol Member of an Asian people from the Mongolian plateau who share a common language and a nomadic tradition of herding sheep, cattle, goats, and horses. In the 10th–12th century the Khitans (see LIAO DYNASTY), JUCHEN, and TATARS, all Mongol peoples, ruled in Mongolia, but Mongol power was greatest in the 13th century, when GENGHIS KHAN, his sons (including ÖGÖDEI), and his grandsons BATU and KUBLAI KHAN, created one of the world's largest empires. It declined greatly in the 14th century, when China was lost to the MING DYNASTY and the GOLDEN HORDE was taken by Muscovites. Ming incursions effectively ended Mongol unity, and by the 15th–16th century only a loose federation existed. Today the plateau is divided between independent Mongolia and Chinese-controlled NEI MONGGOL. Other Mongols live in Siberia. Tibetan Buddhism is the principal Mongol religion. See also KHAN, TO-WANG.

Mongol dynasty See YUAN DYNASTY

Mongolia *or* **Outer Mongolia** Country (pop., 1997 est.: 2,370,000), northern central Asia, between Russia and China. Area: 604,800 sq mi (1,566,500 sq km). Capital: ULAANBAATAR. Almost four-fifths of the population are Mongols; minorities consist of Kazaks, Russians, and Chinese. Languages: Khalkha Mongolian, Turkic languages, Russian, Chinese. Religions: Tantric Buddhism (Lamaism) 96%; Islam. Currency: tugrik. Mongolia averages an elevation of about 5,200 ft (1,580 m) above sea level. Three mountain ranges stretch across the north and west: the Altai, the Hangayn (Khangai), and the Hentiyn (Khentei). The south and east are occupied by the GOBI DESERT. Livestock raising, especially sheep raising, accounts for about 70% of the total value of agricultural production; wheat is the major crop. Mongolia's rich mineral resources include coal, iron ore, and tin. It is a republic with one legislative house; its chief of state is the president, and the head of government is the prime minister. In Neolithic times it was inhabited by small groups of hunters and nomads. During the 3rd century BC it became the center of the XIONGNU empire. Turks held sway in the 4th–10th century AD. In the early 13th century GENGHIS KHAN united the Mongol tribes and conquered central Asia. His successor, ÖGÖDEI, conquered the JIN (CHIN) DYNASTY of CHINA in 1234. KUBLAI KHAN established the YUAN, OR MONGOL, DYNASTY in China in 1279. After the 14th century, the MING DYNASTY of China confined the Mongols to their original homeland in the steppes. Ligdan Khan (r.1604–34) united Mongol tribes in defense against the MANCHU, but after his death, the Mongols became part of the Chinese QING (CH'ING) DYNASTY. Inner Mongolia was incorporated into China in 1644. After the fall of the Manchu dynasty in 1912, Mongol princes, supported by Russia, declared Mongolia's independence from

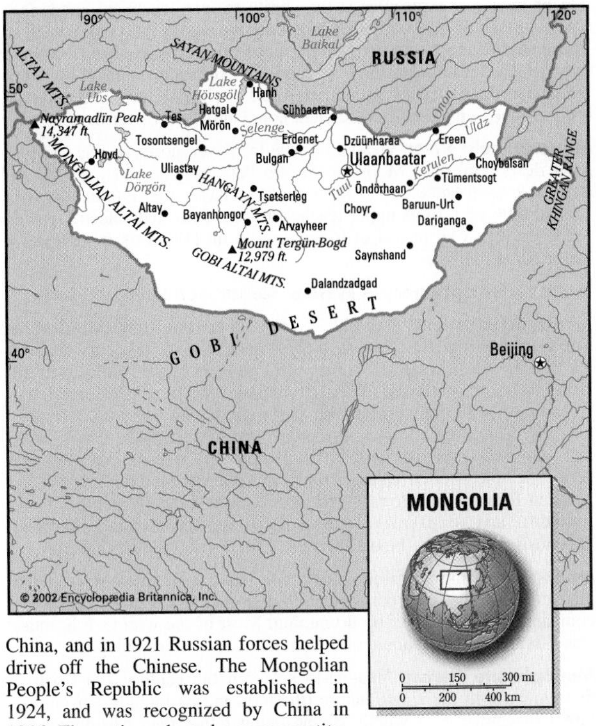

China, and in 1921 Russian forces helped drive off the Chinese. The Mongolian People's Republic was established in 1924, and was recognized by China in 1946. The nation adopted a new constitution in 1992 and shortened its name to Mongolia.

Mongolian languages Family of about eight ALTAIC LANGUAGES spoken by 5–7 million people in central Eurasia. All Mongolian languages are relatively closely related; those languages whose speakers left the core area in Mongolia the earliest tend to be the most divergent. The most remote language is Mogholi (Moghul, Mongol), now spoken by fewer than 200 people in western Afghanistan. Less divergent are the languages of several ethnic groups in northwestern China, eastern Qinghai, and adjacent parts of Gansu and Inner Mongolia, altogether spoken by under a half-million people. The core languages are Mongolian proper, the dominant dialect in the Republic of Mongolia and the basis of Modern Standard Mongolian, and a group of peripheral dialects. The core group of Mongolian-speakers traditionally have used Classical Mongolian as their literary language; it is written in a vertical alphabetic script borrowed from the Uighurs (see TURKIC LANGUAGES). Modern Mongolian was written in this script until 1946, when the People's Republic of Mongolia introduced a script using a modified CYRILLIC ALPHABET. With political democratization in the 1990s, the old script has been revived. In Inner Mongolia it has been in continuous use.

Mongoloid See RACE

mongoose Any of more than 40 species in 15 genera of the CIVET family (Viverridae), carnivores found in Africa, Asia, and southern Europe. RUDYARD KIPLING's famous "Rikki-tikki-tavi" was an Indian, or gray, mongoose *(Herpetes edwardsi).* Species range from 7 to 35 in. (17–90 cm) long, excluding the furry 6–12-in. (15–30-cm) tail. Mongooses have short legs, a pointed nose, and small ears. Most species are diurnal. The gray to brown fur may have light flecks or dark markings. Mongooses live in burrows, alone, in pairs, or in large groups, and eat small mammals, birds, reptiles, eggs, and fruit. A few species are semiaquatic. Though not immune to venom, some species attack and kill poisonous snakes by cracking the skull with a powerful bite. See also MEERKAT.

monism \'mō-ˌni-zəm\ In METAPHYSICS, the doctrine that the world is essentially one substance or contains only one kind of substance. Monism is opposed both to DUALISM and to PLURALISM. Examples of monism include MATERIALISM, PANTHEISM, and metaphysical IDEALISM. See also BENEDICT DE SPINOZA.

monitor IRONCLAD warship originally designed for use in shallow harbors and rivers to blockade the Confederate states in the AMERICAN CIVIL WAR. The original ironclad, built by JOHN ERICSSON, was named *Monitor.* Its innovative design included minimal exposure above the waterline, a heavily armored deck and hull, and a revolving gun turret. The inconclusive Battle of the MONITOR AND MERRIMACK (1862) was the first between ironclad warships. Never seaworthy, the *Monitor* sank during a gale off Cape Hatteras that same year, but the U.S. Navy built many improved monitors during the war. The British navy kept its monitors in service as late as World War II.

Monitor and Merrimack, Battle of (March 9, 1862) Naval engagement in the AMERICAN CIVIL WAR at Hampton Roads, Va. The *Merrimack,* originally a federal frigate, had been salvaged by the Confederates, fitted with iron armor, and renamed the *Virginia.* It sank several wooden Union warships before meeting the Union's *Monitor.* After a four-hour battle both ships were damaged, but each side claimed victory. Both ships were destroyed later in 1862, the *Virginia* by its crew to avoid capture and the *Monitor* in a storm.

monitor lizard Any of about 30 species of LIZARDS (genus *Varanus,* family Varanidae), found in the Old World tropics and subtropics. Most have an elongated head and neck, a heavy body, a long tail, and well-developed legs. The smallest monitor grows to 8 in. (20 cm), but several species (e.g., the KOMODO DRAGON) are very large. The two-banded, or water, monitor *(V. salvator),* of South Asia, grows to 9 ft (2.7 m). The perenty *(V. giganteus),* of Australia, grows to 8 ft (2.4 m). The so-called earless monitor *(Lanthanotus borneensis),* a rare lizard of Borneo and the only species of the family Lanthanotidae, grows to 16 in. (40 cm) long.

monk See MONASTICISM

Monk, Meredith (Jane) (born 1942) U.S. (Peruvian-born) composer. She was raised in Connecticut and New York and attended Sarah Lawrence College. She soon formed her first group, The House (1968), to explore extended vocal techniques (many learned from study of other cultures) in combination with dance, film, theater, and other elements, in such genre-defying works as *Juice* (1969). One of the original creators of performance art, she has remained unique and unclassifiable.

Monk, Thelonious (Sphere) *orig.* **Thelious Junior Monk** (1917–1982) U.S. pianist and composer, one of the most original and influential musicians in modern jazz. Born in Rocky Mount, N.C., Monk grew up in New York City. He worked as the house pianist at Minton's Playhouse in New York (1940–43), where the expanding harmonic vocabulary of BEBOP was developed. He performed with COLEMAN HAWKINS, Cootie Williams, and DIZZY GILLESPIE before making recordings under his own name beginning in 1947. His highly idiosyncratic, percussive playing made frequent use of sharp dissonances and insistent rhythms unusual in jazz. His best-known composition, "'Round Midnight," has become a jazz standard.

monkey Any member of two tropical anthropoid PRIMATE groups: OLD WORLD monkeys and NEW WORLD monkeys. Almost all species are tropical or subtropical, and almost all are diurnal. Most species are arboreal, using all four limbs to leap from tree to tree. They can sit upright and stand erect. Most species run along branches rather than swinging arm over arm like the APES. Monkeys are highly social omnivores, organized in clans as large as several hundred individuals headed by an old male. Sexually mature males of all species are always potent, and all nonpregnant females have a monthly menstrual cycle. Most species bear a single young, which is reared by the mother for years.

monkey puzzle tree Evergreen ornamental and timber CONIFER *(Araucaria araucana)* of the family Araucariaceae, native to the Andes Mountains of South America. The tree may grow to 150 ft (45 m) in height and 5 ft (1.5 m) in diameter. The rigid, overlapping, needle-pointed leaves are spirally arranged on stiff branches, which form a tangled, prickly network that discourages animals from climbing the tree. The NORFOLK ISLAND PINE is a relative.

monkfish Any of 10–12 species of SHARKS (genus *Squatina,* family Squatinidae) having a flattened head and body, with winglike pectoral and pelvic fins that make them resemble RAYS. The tail bears two dorsal fins and a well-developed caudal fin. Behind each eye, on the upper surface of the head, is a prominent spiracle. Monkfish grow up to 6.25 ft (2.5 m) long. They inhabit tropical and warm temperate waters of the continental shelf worldwide. The angelfish, or angel shark *(S. squatina)*, is often caught for food in European and Mediterranean waters.

Monmouth \'män-məth\, **Duke of** *orig.* **James Fitzroy** *or* **James Crofts** *later* **James Scott** (1649–1685) British military leader. The illegitimate son of CHARLES II of England, he lived in Paris with his mother. In 1662 he was brought to England as a favorite of the king, who created him duke of Monmouth. He married the Scottish heiress Anne Scott, duchess of Buccleuch, and took her surname. A member of the king's guard from 1668, he commanded troops in the ANGLO-DUTCH WAR and against Scottish rebels in 1679. He was championed for the royal succession by the anti-Catholic Whigs, but after the unsuccessful RYE HOUSE PLOT he took refuge in the Netherlands (1684). Returning after Charles's death to challenge JAMES II, he and his army of peasants were defeated and he was captured and beheaded.

Duke of Monmouth, oil painting after W. Wissing, c. 1683; in the National Portrait Gallery, London.

BY COURTESY OF THE NATIONAL PORTRAIT GALLERY, LONDON

Monnet \mò-'nā\, **Jean** (1888–1979) French economist and diplomat. Born in Cognac, he managed his family's brandy business before becoming a partner of an investment bank (1925). In World War II he chaired a Franco-British economic committee and proposed a Franco-British union. In 1947 he created and directed the successful Monnet Plan to rebuild and modernize France's economy. In 1950, with ROBERT SCHUMAN, he proposed the plan for the EUROPEAN COAL AND STEEL COMMUNITY, predecessor of the EUROPEAN ECONOMIC COMMUNITY, and served as its first president (1952–55). He was also the founder and president of the action committee for the United States of Europe (1955–75).

monocot See COTYLEDON, FLOWERING PLANT

Monod \mò-'nō\, **Jacques (Lucien)** (1910–1976) French biochemist. In 1961 he and FRANCOIS JACOB proposed the existence of messenger RNA (mRNA), theorizing that the messenger carries the information encoded in the base sequence to the RIBOSOMES, where the sequence of bases of the messenger RNA is translated into the sequence of amino acids of a protein. In advancing the concept of gene complexes that they called OPERONS, they suggested the existence of a class of genes that regulate the function of other genes by regulating the synthesis of mRNA. The two shared a 1965 Nobel Prize with André Lwoff (1902–1994).

monody \'mä-nə-dē\ Accompanied solo song style of the early 17th century. It represented a reaction against the contrapuntal style of the 16th-century MADRIGAL and MOTET and an attempt to emulate ancient Greek music, which was thought to have achieved an ideally expressive musical equivalence for the lyric text. This resulted in a decisive distinction between melody and accompaniment, and coincides with the early appearance of FIGURED BASS. The first collection of monodic songs was published by G. CACCINI in 1602. See also OPERA, RECITATIVE.

monogram Originally a cipher consisting of a single letter, later a design or mark consisting of two or more letters intertwined. The letters thus interlaced may be either all the letters of a name or the initial letters of the given names and surname of a person for use on notepaper, seals, or elsewhere. Many early Greek and Roman coins bear the monograms of rulers or towns. Most famous is the sacred monogram, which is formed by the conjunction of the first two Greek letters of ΧΡΙΣΤΟΣ (Christ), usually with the α (alpha) and ω (omega) of the Apocalypse on each side of it. The Middle Ages were extremely prolific in inventing ciphers for ecclesiastical, artistic, and commercial use. Related devices are the colophons used for identification by publishers and printers, the HALLMARKS of goldsmiths and silversmiths, and the logos adopted by corporations.

monomer \'mä-nə-mər\ MOLECULE of any of a class of mostly organic compounds that can react with other molecules of the same or other compounds to form very large molecules (POLYMERS). The essential feature of monomer molecules is the ability to form chemical bonds (see BONDING) with at least two other monomer molecules (polyfunctionality). Those able to react with two others can form only chainlike polymers; those able to react with three or more can form cross-linked, network polymers. Examples of monomers (and their polymers) are styrene (polystyrene), ethylene (polyethylene), and amino acids (proteins).

Monongahela River \mə-,nän-gə-'hē-lə\ River, northern West Virginia. It flows north past Morgantown into Pennsylvania and joins the ALLEGHENY RIVER at PITTSBURGH to form the OHIO RIVER, after a total course of 128 mi (206 km). In its upper reaches it is used for hydroelectric power. Made navigable by means of locks for 106 mi (170 km), it serves as a major barge route.

mononuclear phagocyte system See RETICULOENDOTHELIAL SYSTEM

mononucleosis \,mä-nō-,nü-klē-'ō-səs\, **infectious** *or* **glandular fever** Common infection, caused by EPSTEIN-BARR VIRUS. It occurs most often at ages 10–35. Infected young children usually have little or no illness but become immune. Popularly called "the kissing disease," it is spread mostly by oral contact with exchange of saliva. It usually lasts 7–14 days. The most common symptoms are malaise, sore throat, fever, and lymph-node enlargement. Liver involvement is usual but rarely severe. The spleen often enlarges and in rare cases ruptures fatally. Less frequent features include rash, PNEUMONIA, ENCEPHALITIS (sometimes fatal), MENINGITIS, and peripheral NEURITIS. Relapse and second attacks are rare. Diagnosis may require blood analysis. There is no specific therapy.

monophony \mə-'nä-fə-nē\ Music consisting of a single unaccompanied melodic line. The concept often also includes melody that is accompanied by a drone of by drumming. Most of the world's folk music was essentially monophonic until contact with Western polyphony.

Monophysite heresy \mə-'nä-fə-,sīt\ (5th–6th century AD) Doctrine that emphasized the single nature (the term means literally "of one nature") of Christ, as a wholly divine being rather than part-divine and part-human. Monophysitism began to appear in the 5th century; though condemned as a heresy at the Council of CHALCEDON (451), it was tolerated by such Byzantine leaders as JUSTIN II, THEODORA, and ZENO, resulting in a full-fledged schism between East and West. Several Monophysite churches, including the COPTIC ORTHODOX CHURCH, were founded in the 6th century.

monopolistic competition Market situation in which many independent buyers and sellers may exist but competition is limited by specific market conditions. The theory was developed almost simultaneously by Edward Hastings Chamberlin in his *Theory of Monopolistic Competition* (1933) and JOAN V. ROBINSON in her *Economics of Imperfect Competition* (1933). It assumes product differentiation, a situation in which each seller's goods have some unique properties, thereby giving the seller some monopoly power. See also MONOPOLY, OLIGOPOLY.

monopoly Exclusive possession of a market by a supplier of a product or service for which there is no substitute. In the absence of competition, the supplier usually restricts output and increases PRICE in order to maximize PROFITS. The concept of pure monopoly is useful for theoretical discussion but is rarely encountered in actuality. In situations where having more than one supplier is inefficient (e.g., for electricity, gas, or water), economists refer to "natural monopoly" (see PUBLIC UTILITY). For monopoly to exist there must be a barrier to the entry of competing firms. In the case of natural monopolies, the government creates that barrier. Either local government provides the service itself, or it awards a franchise to a private company and regulates it. In some cases, the barrier is attributable to an effective PATENT. In other cases, the barrier that eliminates competing firms is technological. Large-scale, integrated operations that increase efficiency and reduce production costs confer a benefit on firms that adopt them and may confer a benefit on consumers if the lower costs lead to lower product prices. In many cases, the barrier is a result of anticompetitive behavior on the part of the firm. Most free-enterprise economies have adopted laws to protect consumers from the abuse of monopoly power. The U.S. ANTITRUST LAWS are the oldest examples of this type of monopoly-control legislation; public-utility law is an outgrowth of the English common law as it pertains to natural monopolies. Antitrust law prohibits MERGERS and acquisitions that lessen competition. The question asked is whether consumers will benefit from increased efficiency or be penalized with a lower output and a higher price. See also OLIGOPOLY.

monopsony \mə-ˈnäp-sə-nē\ In economic theory, market situation in which there is only one buyer. An example of pure monopsony is a firm that is the only buyer of labor in an isolated town, such a firm being able to pay lower wages to its employees than it would if other firms were present. Though cases of pure monopsony are rare, monopsonistic elements are found wherever there are many sellers and few purchasers.

monorail Electric railway that runs on a single rail either above or under the railway cars. The first systems were introduced in the early 20th century; the earliest probably opened in 1901 in Wuppertal, Germany. Short-run monorails have since been built in such cities as Tokyo and Seattle. Because of higher costs and slower speeds than conventional rail systems, the monorail has not gained wide support. High-speed monorail vehicles that use magnetic levitation have been undergoing research for many years.

monosaccharide \ˌmä-nə-ˈsa-kə-ˌrīd\ Any of the simple sugars that serve as building blocks for carbohydrates. They are classified based on their backbone of carbon (C) atoms: Trioses have three carbon atoms, tetroses four, pentoses five, hexoses six, and heptoses seven. The carbon atoms are bonded to hydrogen atoms (—H), hydroxyl groups (—OH; see functional group), and carbonyl groups (—C=O), whose combinations, order, and configurations allow a large number of stereoisomers (see isomer) to exist. Pentoses include xylose, found in woody materials; arabinose, found in gums from conifers; ribose, a component of RNA and several vitamins; and deoxyribose, a component of DNA. Important hexoses include glucose, galactose, and fructose. Monosaccharides combine with each other and other groups to form a variety of disaccharides, polysaccharides, and other carbohydrates.

monosodium glutamate (MSG) White crystalline substance, a sodium salt of the amino acid glutamic acid, used to intensify the natural flavor of meats and vegetables. It elicits a unique taste different from the four basic tastes. Originally derived from seaweed and first used in Japan in 1908, it has become an important ingredient in Chinese and Japanese cooking. MSG in large amounts may have physical effects, including an allergic reaction commonly called "Chinese restaurant syndrome."

monotheism \ˈmä-nə-ˌthē-ˌi-zəm\ Belief in the existence of one god. It is distinguished from polytheism. The earliest known instance of monotheism dates to the reign of Akhenaton of Egypt in the 14th century BC. Monotheism is characteristic of Judaism, Christianity, and Islam, all of which view God as the creator of the world, who oversees and intervenes in human events, and as a beneficent and holy being, the source of the highest good. The monotheism that characterizes Judaism began in ancient Israel with the adoption of Yahweh as the single object of worship and the rejection of the gods of other tribes and nations without, initially, denying their existence. Islam is clear in confessing one, eternal, unbegotten, unequaled God, while Christianity holds that a single God is reflected in the three persons of the Holy Trinity.

monotreme \ˈmä-nə-ˌtrēm\ Any of three living species of egg-laying mammals (order Monotremata): the platypus and two species of echidna. Monotremes are found only in Australia, Tasmania, and New Guinea. Except for their egg laying, they have mammalian characteristics, such as mammary glands, hair, and a complete diaphragm. They lack teats; the young suck milk through pores on the mother's skin. The earliest fossil monotremes, found in Australia, are only about 2 million years old and differ little from present species. Monotremes probably originated from a line of mammal-like reptiles different from the line that gave rise to placental mammals and marsupials.

monotype *or* **monoprint** In art printmaking, a technique prized because of its unique textural qualities. Monotypes are made by drawing with printer's ink or oil paint onto glass or a plate of metal or stone. The drawing is then pressed by hand onto a sheet of absorbent paper or printed on an etching press. The pigment remaining on the plate is usually insufficient to make another print unless the original design is reinforced. Subsequent prints invariably differ from the first, because variations in repainting and printing are inevitable. In the 19th century, William Blake and Edgar Degas experimented with the technique.

Monro family Family of Scottish physicians. Three generations of the family made Edinburgh University an international center of medical teaching, holding the chair of anatomy for 126 years (1720–1846) without interruption. Alexander primus (1697–1767) lectured in anatomy and surgery; his anatomical preparations were outstanding, and, though not a surgeon, he advanced many new ideas for instruments and dressings. His son Alexander secundus (1733–1817) began lecturing in his second year of medical study; of the three, he is judged the greatest teacher and anatomist, and his research also covered pathology and physiology. Alexander tertius (1773–1859) relied largely on the notes handed down to him.

Monroe, Bill *orig.* **William Smith** (1911–1996) U.S. singer, songwriter, and mandolin player, inventor of the bluegrass style. Born in Rosine, Ky., Monroe began to play professionally in 1927, and later toured with his brother Charlie. They made their first recordings in 1936 and recorded 60 songs over the next two years. He formed the Blue Grass Boys in 1939. His bluegrass sound emerged fully in 1945, when banjoist Earl Scruggs and guitarist Lester Flatt joined his band. The Blue Grass Boys established the classic makeup of a bluegrass group—mandolin, fiddle, guitar, banjo, and upright bass—and bequeathed its name to the genre itself. Monroe continued to perform until shortly before his death.

Monroe, Harriet (1860–1936) U.S. editor. A native of Chicago, she worked on various newspapers in the city as an art and drama critic while privately writing verse and verse plays. In 1912 she founded *Poetry* magazine, securing the backing of wealthy patrons and inviting contributions from a wide range of poets. Monroe's open-minded editorial policy and awareness of the importance of the revolution in contemporary poetry made her a major influence in its development.

Monroe, James (1758–1831) Fifth president of the U.S. (1817–25). Born in Westmoreland Co., Va., he fought in the American Revolution and studied law under Thomas Jefferson. He served in the Congress (1783–86) and U.S. Senate (1790–94), where he opposed George Washington's administration. He nevertheless became U.S. minister to France (1794–96), where he misled the French about U.S. politics and was recalled. He served as governor of Virginia 1799–1802. Pres. Jefferson sent him to France, where he helped negotiate the Louisiana Purchase (1803), then named him minister to Britain (1803–7). He returned to Virginia and became governor (1811), but resigned to become U.S. secretary of state (1811–17) and secretary of war (1814–15). He served two terms as president, presiding in a period that became known as the Era of Good Feelings. He oversaw the Seminole War (1817–18) and the acquisition of the Floridas (1819–21), and signed the Missouri Compromise (1820). With secretary of state John Quincy Adams, he developed the principles of U.S. foreign policy later called the Monroe Doctrine.

James Monroe, oil sketch by E.O. Sully, 1836, after a contemporary portrait by Thomas Sully; in Independence National Historical Park, Philadelphia.

BY COURTESY OF THE INDEPENDENCE NATIONAL HISTORICAL PARK COLLECTION, PHILADELPHIA

Monroe, Marilyn *orig.* **Norma Jean Mortenson** (1926–1962) U.S. film actress. Born in Los Angeles, she endured a loveless childhood and a brief teenage marriage. After working as a photographer's model, she made her screen debut in 1948 and won bit parts in *The Asphalt Jungle* (1950) and *All About Eve* (1950). She achieved stardom as a blonde sex symbol in the comedies *Gentlemen Prefer Blondes* (1953), *How to Marry a Millionaire* (1953), and *The Seven Year Itch* (1955). After studying at

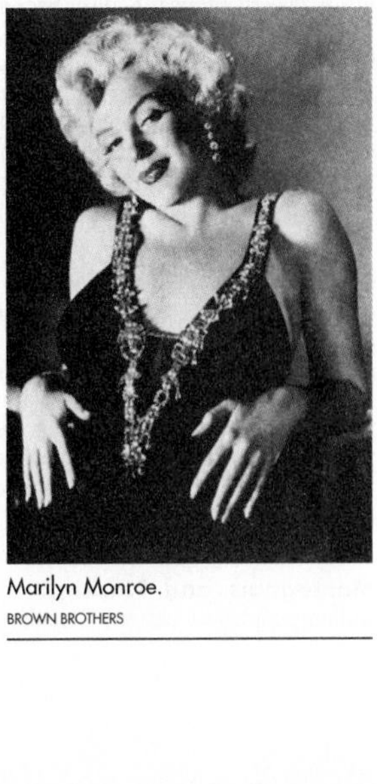

Marilyn Monroe.

BROWN BROTHERS

the ACTORS STUDIO, she starred in more ambitious films, including *Bus Stop* (1956), *Some Like It Hot* (1959), and *The Misfits* (1961). Her private life, which included marriages to JOE DIMAGGIO and ARTHUR MILLER, was widely publicized. She died at 36 of an apparently self-administered barbiturate overdose.

Monroe Doctrine U.S. foreign-policy statement enunciated by Pres. JAMES MONROE on December 2, 1823. Concerned that the European powers would attempt to restore Spain's former colonies, he declared that any attempt by a European power to control any nation in the Western Hemisphere would be viewed as a hostile act against the U.S. It was reiterated in 1845 and 1848 by Pres. JAMES POLK to discourage Spain and Britain from establishing footholds in Oregon, California, or Mexico's Yucatán peninsula. In 1865 the U.S. massed troops on the Rio Grande to back up demands that France withdraw from Mexico. In 1904 Pres. THEODORE ROOSEVELT added the Roosevelt Corollary, stating that in the event of flagrant wrongdoing by a LATIN AMERICAN state, the U.S. had the right to intervene in its internal affairs. As the U.S. became a world power, the Monroe Doctrine came to define the Western Hemisphere as a U.S. sphere of influence. See also GOOD NEIGHBOR POLICY.

Monrovia Port city (metro. area pop., 1999 est.: 479,000), capital of LIBERIA, located on the Atlantic coast. It was founded in 1822 by the American Colonization Society as a settlement for freed U.S. slaves and named for Pres. JAMES MONROE. Bushrod Island contains the artificial harbor and free port of Monrovia, the only such port in West Africa. It is Liberia's largest city and its administrative and commercial center. Many of the city's buildings were damaged during the civil war that began in 1990, and its increased population includes many formerly rural people displaced by the war. It is the seat of the University of Liberia.

Monsarrat \ˌmän-sə-ˈrat\, **Nicholas (John Turney)** (1910–1979) British novelist. Trained in law, he served with the Royal Navy 1940–46, chiefly on dangerous Atlantic convoy runs. He put his experience to account in such books as *H. M. Corvette* (1942) and his best-known work, *The Cruel Sea* (1951), a best-seller that vividly captures life aboard a small ship in wartime. His later work includes *The Story of Esther Costello* (1953) and *Smith and Jones* (1963).

monsoon Major wind system that seasonally reverses its direction (e.g., one that blows for six months from the northeast and six months from the southwest). The most prominent examples occur in Africa and southern Asia. The primary cause of monsoons is the difference between annual temperature trends over land and sea. Seasonal changes in temperature are large over land but small over oceans. A monsoon blows from cold toward warm regions: from sea toward land in summer and from land toward sea in winter. Most summer monsoons produce copious amounts of rain; winter monsoons tend to cause drought.

Mont, Allen Du See Allen B. DU MONT

Mont Blanc See Mont BLANC

Mont-Saint-Michel \mōⁿ-saⁿ-mē-ˈshel\ Rocky, almost circular islet rising out of Mont-Saint-Michel Bay between Brittany and Normandy, northwestern France. It only becomes an island at high tide. Around its base are medieval walls and towers, above which rise the village's clustered buildings, with an ancient ABBEY crowning the mount. Over the centuries it has been a pilgrimage center, fortress, and prison. The fine abbey church has an imposing 11th-century Romanesque nave and an elegant FLAMBOYANT-STYLE Gothic choir. The exterior walls of the Gothic monastery building combine the power of a military fortress and the simplicity of a religious building. Some of the houses bordering the island's narrow, winding streets date back to the 15th century.

montage \män-ˈtäzh\ (French: "mounting") Pictorial technique in which cut-out illustrations, or fragments of them, are arranged together and mounted on a support, producing a composite picture made from several different pictures. It differs from COLLAGE in using only ready-made images chosen for their subject or message. The technique is widely used in advertising. Photomontage uses photographs only. In motion pictures, montage is the sequential assembling of separate pieces of thematically related film by the director, film editor, and visual and sound technicians, who cut and fit each part with the others to produce visual juxtapositions and complex audio patterns.

Montagnais and Naskapi \ˌmän-tən-ˈyā...ˈnas-kə-pē\ Two related Indian peoples of eastern Canada that speak almost identical ALGONQUIAN dialects. The Montagnais, traditionally occupying a large forested area above the northern shores of the Gulf of St. Lawrence, lived in birch-bark wigwams and subsisted on moose, salmon, eel, and seal. The Naskapi, living farther north on the Labrador plateau, hunted caribou and fished. Both groups used canoes in summer and sleds and snowshoes in winter. Religious belief centered on *manitou*, or supernatural power; much importance was attached to nature and animal spirits. The basic social unit was the nomadic BAND. There are some 14,000 Montagnais and 1,100 Naskapi.

Montagnard \mōⁿ-ˌtän-ˈyär\ (French: "Mountain Man") Radical deputy in the NATIONAL CONVENTION during the FRENCH REVOLUTION. The Montagnards were so called because as deputies they sat on the higher benches (the Mountain) above the uncommitted deputies of the PLAIN. The Montagnards emerged in 1792 as opponents of the moderate GIRONDINS and later associated with the radical JACOBINS in the COMMITTEE OF PUBLIC SAFETY. After the THERMIDORIAN REACTION, many Montagnards were executed or purged from the convention, and they became a minority called the *crête* ("crest").

Montagu \ˈmän-tə-ˌgyü\, **Lady Mary Wortley** *orig.* **Lady Mary Pierrepont** (1689–1762) English writer, the most colorful Englishwoman of her time. A prolific letter writer, Montagu is remembered chiefly for 52 superb letters chronicling her time in Constantinople, where her husband was ambassador 1716–18. On their return, they introduced the Near Eastern practice of smallpox vaccination into England. Also a poet, essayist, feminist, and eccentric, she was a friend of JOHN GAY and ALEXANDER POPE, who later turned against and satirized her. Among her writings are six "town eclogues," witty adaptations of VIRGIL; a lively attack on JONATHAN SWIFT (1734); and essays dealing with feminism and the moral cynicism of her time.

Montaigne \mōⁿ-ˈtenʸ, *Engl* män-ˈtān\, **Michel (Eyquem) de** (1533–1592) French courtier and author. Born into the minor nobility, Montaigne received an excellent classical education (speaking only Latin up to age 6) before studying law and serving as counselor at the Bordeaux Parliament. There he met the lawyer Étienne de La Boétie, with whom he formed an extraordinary friendship; the void left by La Boétie's death in 1563 likely led Montaigne to begin his writing career. He retired to his château in 1571 to work on his *Essais* (1580, 1588), a series of short prose reflections on many subjects that form one of the most captivating and intimate self-portraits ever written. At once deeply critical of his time and deeply involved in its struggles, he sought understanding through self-examination, which he developed into a description of the human condition and an ethic of authenticity, self-acceptance, and tolerance. Though most of his later years were devoted to writing, he occasionally served as mediator in episodes of religious conflict in his region and beyond, and served as mayor of Bordeaux during the troubled period 1581–85. See also ESSAY.

Montale \mōn-ˈtä-lā\, **Eugenio** (1896–1981) Italian poet, prose writer, editor, and translator. Montale began his literary activities after World War I, cofounding a journal, writing for other journals, and serving as a library director in Florence. His first book of poems, *Cuttlefish Bones* (1925), expressed the bitter pessimism of the postwar period. He was identified with HERMETICISM in the 1930s and '40s, before his works became progressively introverted and obscure. *The Storm and Other Poems* (1956) and subsequent works showed increasing skill, warmth, and directness. His stories and sketches were collected in *The Butterfly of Dinard* (1956). He received the Nobel Prize in 1975.

Montalembert \mōⁿ-tä-läⁿ-ˈber\, **Charles (-Forbes-René), comte (Count) de** (1810–1870) French politician and historian. He began his political career as a journalist for several Catholic journals, became a leader of the liberal Roman Catholics in the JULY MONARCHY, and was a member of the House of Peers 1835–48. A champion of civil and religious liberties, he opposed NAPOLEON III's policies after 1851. He wrote such historical works as *The Catholic Interest in the 19th Century* (1852), *The Political Future of England* (1856), and *Monks of the West* (1863–77).

Montana State (pop., 2000: 902,195), northwestern U.S. It covers 147,046 sq mi (380,849 sq km); its capital is HELENA. Montana straddles the GREAT PLAINS to the east and the ROCKY MTNS. to the west. Unique among the states, its rivers flow into three of the continent's primary watersheds: the Pacific, the Gulf of Mexico, and Hudson Bay. At the time of European settlement the region was inhabited by various Indian tribes, including the CHEYENNE, BLACKFOOT, NEZ PERCÉ, and CROW. Most of Montana was obtained by the U.S. through the LOUISIANA PURCHASE of 1803. The western part was disputed until 1846, when Britain relinquished its claim to the area. The LEWIS AND CLARK EXPEDITION explored Montana in 1804–6. St. Mary's Mission, established in 1841 by Roman Catholic missionaries, became the first permanent town as Stevensville. Gold was discovered in the early 1860s; cattle and sheep grazing were introduced later that decade, leading to bitter battles with the Indians, whose hunting grounds were destroyed. Montana Territory was established in 1864. Though the U.S. troops of GEORGE CUSTER were defeated and slain at the Battle of the LITTLE BIGHORN in 1876, the Indians ceased fighting in 1877 and were placed on reservations. Montana became the 41st state in 1889. Vast deposits of copper were found in the 1890s, and mining was the economic mainstay for almost a century. The state's economy now emphasizes tourism.

Montana, Joe *orig.* **Joseph Clifford Montana, Jr.** (born 1956) U.S. football quarterback. Born in New Eagle, Pa., he played for the University of Notre Dame. Playing with the San Francisco 49ers from 1979 to 1993, he led the team to Super Bowl championships in 1982, 1985, 1989, and 1990. He maintained one of the highest passing-completion rates in the NFL, with a career average of 63.2. His career totals for passes completed (3,409), yards passing (40,551), and touchdown passes (273) are among the highest on record. He finished his career with the Kansas City Chiefs (1993–95) and was inducted into the Pro Football Hall of Fame in 2000.

Montana, University of Public university system based in Missoula. It offers a variety of associate, undergraduate, graduate, and professional degrees, and is particularly strong in forestry and journalism. It was chartered in 1893, and instruction began in 1895. HAROLD C. UREY is a notable alumnus. Total enrollment is about 12,000.

Montand \mōⁿ-'täⁿ\, **Yves** *orig.* **Ivo Livi** (1921–1991) French (Italian-born) actor and singer. Raised in Marseille, he was sponsored as a singer by E. PIAF in the late 1940s. He married the actress Simone Signoret (1921–1985) in 1951. International renown came with his appearance in the film *Wages of Fear* (1953). In Hollywood he starred opposite MARILYN MONROE in *Let's Make Love* (1960), and their romantic affair was widely publicized. He thereafter divided his time between the U.S. and France; his later films included *Z* (1969), *Jean de Florette,* and *Manon of the Spring* (both 1987). For most of his life he was known as a supporter of left-wing causes, and as a singer he enjoyed great success, especially in France.

Montañés \,mōn-tän-'yās\, **Juan (de) Martínez** (1568–1649) Spanish sculptor. After studying in Granada, he established his studio in Seville and was instrumental in the transition from Mannerism to the baroque. He became known as *el dios de la madera* ("the god of wood") because of his great skill at wood carving, and his output over 50 years was enormous. He is remembered for his wood altars and altar figures covered with polished gold and colored paint, which are realistic yet idealized. His work influenced not only the later sculptors and altar makers of Spain and Latin America but also the Spanish painters of his century.

Montanism \'män-tə-,ni-zəm\ Heretical Christian movement founded in AD 156 by Montanus. Having converted to Christianity, Montanus fell into a trance and began to prophesy. Others joined him, and the movement spread through Asia Minor. The Montanists held that the HOLY SPIRIT was speaking through Montanus and that the Second Coming was imminent. The bishops of Asia Minor excommunicated the Montanists (c. 177), but the movement continued in the East as a separate sect; it also flourished in Carthage, where its most illustrious convert was TERTULLIAN. It had almost died out by the 5th–6th century, though some remnants survived into the 9th century.

Montcalm (de Saint-Véran) \mänt-'kälm\, **Marquis de** *orig.* **Louis-Joseph de Montcalm-Grozon** (1712–1759) French military leader. He joined the French army at 12 and fought in several European conflicts. In 1756 he was placed in command of French troops in North America, but his commission excluded most military resources in Canada. He forced the British to surrender their post at Oswego and captured Fort William Henry (1757). At the Battle of TICONDEROGA (1758), he repulsed an attack by 15,000 British troops with 3,800 French forces. Promoted to lieutenant general, he received authority over military affairs in Canada. In 1759 a British force of 8,500 under Gen. JAMES WOLFE marched on Quebec; in the ensuing Battle of QUEBEC, Montcalm was mortally wounded after fighting with conspicuous gallantry.

Monte Albán \'mōn-tā-äl-'bän\ Ridgetop site of the ruins of the ancient center of ZAPOTEC culture, located near Oaxaca, Mexico. Construction at the site began around the 8th century BC. Monte Albán reached its height AD 250–700. The site contains great plazas, truncated pyramids, a *tlachtli* court for an ancient ballgame, underground passageways, and about 170 tombs, the most elaborate yet uncovered in the New World. The great plaza atop the highest hill is flanked by four platforms; two temples stand on the platform to the south. In its final phase, Monte Albán was inhabited by the MIXTEC.

Monte Carlo Resort (pop., 1990: 15,000), one of the four sections of MONACO. It is situated on the French RIVIERA, northeast of NICE. In 1856 Charles III of Monaco granted a charter allowing a joint stock company to build a casino, which opened in 1861. The district around it, called Monte Carlo, became a luxurious playground for the world's rich. The government took over the casino's operating company in 1967.

Monte Carlo method Numerical method of solving mathematical problems that samples a random subset of a very large set to approximate sampling the whole set. It is useful for numerical integration of functions in many dimensions, where it is more efficient than purely deterministic methods. Because the method is based on random chance, it was named after a gambling resort.

Monte Cassino Principal monastery of the BENEDICTINE order, located in Latium, central Italy. It was founded c. 529 by St. BENEDICT OF NURSIA and reached its peak under Desiderius (later Pope VICTOR III), who was abbot 1058–87. Its buildings were destroyed by the Lombards (c. 581), the Arabs (883), an earthquake (1349), and World War II bombardment (1944), but were rebuilt each time. It was reconsecrated in 1964.

Montego Bay \män-'tē-gō\ Seaport (pop., 1991: 83,000), northwestern Jamaica, located northwest of KINGSTON. It lies on the site of an ARAWAK village visited by CHRISTOPHER COLUMBUS in 1494. The Spanish, ousted by the British after 150 years, destroyed many original buildings. One of Jamaica's largest cities, it is a commercial center and busy port. It is also a popular tourist resort noted for its white sandy beaches.

Montenegro \,mōn-tā-'nā-grō\ *Serbo-Croatian* **Crna Gora** \,tsər-nə-'gōr-ə\ Constituent republic of the Federal Republic of YUGOSLAVIA, comprising about 20% of its land. Area: 5,333 sq mi (13,812 sq km). Population (2001 est.): 674,000. Capital: PODGORICA. The republic's name ("Black Mtn.") refers to Mount Lovcen (5,738 ft, or 1,749 m), its ancient stronghold near the Adriatic Sea. Its landscape ranges from arid hills to forests and fertile valleys. Its economy is based on agriculture, especially the raising of sheep and goats and the cultivation of cereal grains. The majority of its population are Montenegrins who follow the Eastern Orthodox church; there are sizable Muslim and Albanian minorities. Under the Roman empire the region was part of the province of ILLYRIA. Settled by Slavs in the 7th century, it was incorporated in the Serbian empire in the late 12th century. It retained its independence following the Turkish defeat of the Serbians in 1389 (see Battle of KOSOVO). Often at war with the Turks and Albanians, it began an alliance with Russia in 1711. In the BALKAN WARS of 1912–13, it cooperated against Turkey. It supported SERBIA during and after World War I. It was then absorbed into Serbia; the union became part of the Kingdom of Serbs, Croats, and Slovenes (from 1929, Yugoslavia). During World War II it was occupied by the Italians and was the scene of heavy fighting. In 1946 the federal constitution of the new Yugoslavia made Montenegro one of Yugoslavia's six nominally autonomous federated units. Yugoslavia broke up in 1991; one year later Montenegro and Serbia combined as the new Federal Republic of Yugoslavia; and a decade later the two governments chose to be renamed Serbia and Montenegro, despite ongoing agitation for independence within Montenegro. A constitution for the new state was to be approved in the fall of 2002, after which Yugoslavia will formally cease to exist.

Monterrey City (pop., 2000: 1,108,400), capital of NUEVO LEÓN state, northern Mexico. Mexico's fourth-largest city, it lies at an altitude of 1,765 ft (538 m). It was founded in 1579, but its growth was slow until the late 19th century. In 1846 it was taken by U.S. Gen. ZACHARY TAYLOR in the MEXICAN WAR. In 1882 rail connections were established with Laredo, Tex., and in 1930 construction began on the Inter-American Highway, leading to the development of large-scale smelting and heavy-industry enterprises. It has several institutions of higher education.

Montesquieu \,män-təs-'kyü\, *orig.* **C(harles)-L(ouis) de Secondat, baron de (La Brède et de)** (1689–1755) French PHILOSOPHE and satirist. Born into a noble family, he held public office in Bordeaux from 1714. His satirical *Persian Letters* (1721) gave him his first literary success. From 1726 he traveled widely to study social and political institutions. His magnum opus, the huge *L'esprit des lois* (1750; *The Spirit of the Laws*), profoundly influenced European and American political thought; it advocated the separation of the legislative, judicial, and executive powers, and was relied on by the framers of the U.S. Constitution. His other works include *Causes of the Greatness and Decadence of the Romans* (1734).

Montessori \ˌmän-tə-ˈsȯr-ē\, **Maria** (1870–1952) Italian educator. Montessori took a degree in medicine (1894) and worked in a clinic for retarded children before going on to teach at the University of Rome. In 1907 she opened her first children's school, and for the next 40 years she traveled throughout Europe, India, and the U.S. lecturing, writing, and setting up Montessori schools. Today there are hundreds of such schools in the U.S. and Canada alone; their principal focus is on PRESCHOOL EDUCATION, but some provide ELEMENTARY EDUCATION to grade 6. The Montessori system is based on belief in children's creative potential, their drive to learn, and their right to be treated as individuals. It relies on the use of "didactic apparatuses" to cultivate hand-eye coordination, self-directedness, and sensitivity to premathematical and preliterary instruction.

Monteverdi \ˌmän-tə-ˈver-dē\, **Claudio (Giovanni Antonio)** (1567–1643) Italian composer. The first of his nine books of madrigals appeared in 1587, the second in 1590. He visited the court of the Gonzagas in Mantua, and his next book (1592) shows freer use of dissonance and close coordination of music and words. He married in 1599 and settled in Mantua. Attacked in 1600 for the even freer dissonance in his newest works, he replied that music now had two "practices," the stricter first practice for sacred works and the more expressive second practice for secular music. The year 1607 saw the premiere of *L'Orfeo*, his landmark first opera. In 1610 he completed his great *Vespers*. Having long tried to obtain his release from Mantua, he was finally granted it in 1612, and the next year was put in charge of music at ST. MARK'S BASILICA, Venice. After the first opera house opened in Venice (1637), he wrote his last three operas, including *Il ritorno d'Ulisse in patria* (1640) and the remarkable *Incoronazione di Poppea* (1643). Monteverdi is the first great figure of baroque music, a remarkable innovator who synthesized the elements of the new style to create the first baroque masterpieces of both sacred and secular music.

Montevideo \ˌmän-tə-vi-ˈdā-ō\ Port city (pop., 1996: 1,379,000), capital of Uruguay, situated on the northern shore of the Río de la PLATA Estuary. It was founded by the Spanish in 1726 to stem the Portuguese advance into the area from Brazil. From 1807 to 1830 it was alternately occupied by British, Spanish, Argentine, Portuguese, and Brazilian forces. It became the capital of the newly independent Uruguay in 1830. A major seaport of South America, it is the commercial, political, and cultural center of Uruguay. It is the site of Uruguay's only institutions of higher education: the Universidad de la República and the Universidad del Trabajo del Uruguay.

Montez \ˈmän-ˌtez\, **Lola** *orig.* **Marie Eliza Gilbert** (1818–1861) Irish adventuress and dancer, who achieved notoriety as the mistress of King LUDWIG I of Bavaria. After a few dance lessons in Spain, she toured Europe, billing herself as a Spanish dancer. While in Munich in 1846 she became Ludwig's mistress and influenced him toward supporting liberal and anti-Jesuit policies. Her power over the king provoked angry reactions in the government in 1848, forcing her to flee and causing his abdication. After further tours, she settled in New York.

Montezuma II *or* **Moctezuma II** (1466–1520) Ninth emperor of the AZTECS. In 1502 he inherited from his uncle an empire of 5–6 million people that stretched from present-day Mexico to Nicaragua. Aztec belief in the prophesied return of the god QUETZALCÓATL, whose description the conquistador HERNAN CORTES resembled, contributed to his downfall. Cortés, who had made alliances with tribes eager to be rid of Aztec domination, held Montezuma prisoner in TENOCHTITLÁN, and he died in custody.

Montezuma Castle National Monument National monument, central Arizona. Situated in the Verde River Valley, it occupies an area of 842 acres (341 hectares). Declared a national monument in 1906, it is the site of the country's best-preserved pre-Columbian PUEBLO INDIAN cliff dwellings. The "castle" is a 5-story, 20-room adobe brick structure, dating from c. 1100 AD, built into the cliff face about 80 ft (24 m) above the valley floor. To the northeast is Montezuma Well, a large sinkhole rimmed with communal dwellings.

Montfort \mōⁿ-ˈfȯr\, **Simon de** (1165?–1218) French leader of the ALBIGENSIAN CRUSADE. From 1209 he led a crusade against the CATHARI heretics, and he became governor of the lands he conquered in southern France. The fourth LATERAN COUNCIL gave him Toulouse (1215), but RAYMOND VI, count of Toulouse, refused to accept defeat, and Montfort was killed while besieging the city. His eldest son ceded the Montfort lands in southern France to King Louis VIII.

Montfort, Simon de *later* **Earl of Leicester** (c. 1208–1265) The second son of SIMON DE MONTFORT, he gave up Montfort lands in France but revived the family claim to the English earldom of Leicester. His marriage to HENRY III's sister (1238) offended the barons and led to his temporary exile. Simon distinguished himself on a crusade to the Holy Land (1240–42) and joined Henry's failed invasion of France (1242). Sent to pacify Gascony (1248), he was censured for his harsh methods there and recalled. He joined the other leading barons in forcing Henry to accept the Provisions of OXFORD. When Louis IX annulled the Provisions, Simon defeated and captured Henry (1264) and summoned (1265) what became the beginning of the modern Parliament. He governed England for less than a year before being defeated and killed by Henry's son Edward.

Montgolfier \mōⁿ-gȯl-ˈfyā\, **Joseph-Michel and Jacques-Étienne** (1740–1810, 1745–1799) French designers of the hot-air BALLOON. The brothers discovered that heated air collected in a lightweight bag would cause the bag to rise. In 1783 they demonstrated their discovery with a balloon that rose 3,000 ft (1,000 m) and remained aloft 10 minutes. Later that year they sent a sheep, a duck, and a rooster up as passengers, and they followed that experiment with the first manned untethered balloon flight.

Montgomery City (pop., 1996 est.: 196,000), capital of Alabama. The site was inhabited by Indian mound builders in prehistoric times. In 1715 the French built Fort Toulouse on the river above the present site of Montgomery. The city was founded in 1819 and named for Gen. Richard Montgomery; it became the state capital in 1847. In 1861, during the AMERICAN CIVIL WAR, it served briefly as the capital of the Confederacy; it was captured by Union troops in 1865. It was a center of the CIVIL RIGHTS MOVEMENT, notably the protests organized by MARTIN LUTHER KING, Jr. Located southeast of BIRMINGHAM, it serves as the commercial center of an agricultural region, trading in cotton and livestock and producing fertilizer. It is the seat of Alabama State University and several colleges.

Montgomery, Bernard Law *later* **Viscount Montgomery (of Alamein, of Hindhead)** (1887–1976) British general in WORLD WAR II. Educated at Sandhurst, he distinguished himself in World War I and remained in the army, becoming known as a tough and efficient leader. In World War II he commanded the British army in the NORTH AFRICA CAMPAIGN and forced the German retreat from Egypt after the Battle of EL ALAMEIN (1942). He commanded troops in the Allied invasion of Sicily and Italy (1943) and in the NORMANDY CAMPAIGN, leading the British-Canadian army group across northern France and into northern Germany. Promoted to field marshal, he became chief of the imperial staff (1946–48) and later deputy commander of NATO (1951–58). A cautious, thorough strategist, "Monty" often exasperated fellow Allied commanders, including DWIGHT D. EISENHOWER, but his insistence on complete readiness ensured his popularity with his troops.

Montgomery, L(ucy) M(aud) (1874–1942) Canadian novelist. She worked as a teacher and journalist before achieving worldwide success with *Anne of Green Gables* (1908). The sentimental story of a spirited orphan girl, it drew on her childhood experiences and the rural life of her native Prince Edward Island. Six sequels, following Anne through motherhood, were less successful. She also produced another series of juvenile books, several collections of stories, and two books for adults.

Montgomery, Wes *orig.* **John Leslie** (1923–1968) U.S. guitarist, the most influential guitar improviser in modern jazz. He was born in Indianapolis, and his principal early inspiration was CHARLIE CHRISTIAN. He was a member of LIONEL HAMPTON's band (1948–50) before forming a small group with his brothers. His finest recordings are small-group efforts made after 1959, although commercial success came using accompanying orchestras in the 1960s. His unconventional technique, using his thumb rather than a plectrum, made possible his frequent use of octaves and chords in solos.

Montgomery Ward & Co. U.S. retail merchandising company. It was founded in Chicago in 1872 by Aaron Montgomery Ward (1844–1913), who bought merchandise wholesale and sold it directly to farmers. He distributed the world's first mail-order catalog and offered a money-back guarantee. The company opened its first retail stores in 1926, and by 1930 retail sales exceeded catalog sales. In 1968 it merged with Container Corp. of America and formed a holding company, Marcor Inc. In 1976 Marcor merged with MOBIL CORP., but Montgomery Ward was sold by Mobil in 1988. It ended its mail-order business in 1985, and in 1997 it scaled back operations after filing for bankruptcy protection. Another bankruptcy in December 2000 caused the company to close its 250 stores and go out of business the following year. See also DIRECT-MAIL MARKETING, SEARS, ROEBUCK AND CO.

Montherlant \mō^{n}-ter-'lä^{n}\, **Henry (-Marie-Joseph-Millon) de** (1896–1972) French novelist and dramatist. Born into a noble family, he wrote stylistically concise works that reflect his own egocentric and autocratic personality. His major work of fiction is a cycle of four novels (1936–39) translated as *The Girls*, which describes the relationship between a libertine novelist and his adoring female victims. In the 1940s he turned to theater; his best dramatic works include *Malatesta* (1946), *Port-Royal* (1954), and *La guerre civile* (1965).

Monticello \ˌmän-tə-'se-lō, ˌmän-tə-'che-lō\ Home of THOMAS JEFFERSON, located southeast of Charlottesville, Va. Designed by Jefferson and constructed 1768–1809, it is one of the finest examples of the early Classical Revival style in the U.S. Jefferson took the floor plan of the house from an English pattern book; the facade was influenced by the work of ANDREA PALLADIO. The final structure is a three-story brick-and-frame building with 35 differently shaped rooms. An octagonal dome dominates the structure; below it, a balustrade runs around the roof's edge.

Montmorency \mō^{n}-mȯ-rä^{n}-'sē *Engl* ˌmänt-mə-'ren-sē\, **Anne, duc de** (1493–1567) French soldier and Constable of France. Named for his godmother, Queen ANNE OF BRITTANY, he served three kings—FRANCIS I, HENRY II, and CHARLES IX—in war and peace. He fought in numerous wars in northern Italy and southern France against Emperor CHARLES V, and in campaigns against the Huguenots. In 1529 he helped negotiate the Peace of CAMBRAI between France and Charles V. He was created Constable of France in 1538, and became a duke and peer in 1551. Wounded at the Battle of Saint-Denis, he died two days later.

Montpelier \mänt-'pēl-yər\ City (pop., 2000: 8,035), capital of Vermont. Named for MONTPELLIER, France, it commanded the main pass through the GREEN MTNS. and was chartered in 1781 by proprietors from Massachusetts and western Vermont. It became the state capital in 1805 and defeated attempts by other cities, including BURLINGTON, to succeed it as capital. In addition to providing state government services, it bases its economy on financial services and the local ski industry. It is the site of a campus of Norwich Univ./Vermont College and was the birthplace of Adm. GEORGE DEWEY.

Montpellier \mō^{n}-pel-'yā\ City (pop., 1999: 225,392), southern France, situated near the Mediterranean coast. Founded in the 8th century, it later came under control of ARAGON and the king of MAJORCA. It developed as a trading station for spice imports in the 10th century and acquired a charter in 1141. It reverted to France in the 14th century and served as a HUGUENOT stronghold until its capture by LOUIS XIII in 1622. It then became the administrative capital of the LANGUEDOC region. The city's schools of medicine and law date from the 12th century, and the University of Montpellier was founded in 1220. It is a tourist center, and its industries include food processing and electronics. Historic sites include France's oldest botanical gardens (founded 1593), and a 14th-century Gothic cathedral.

Montreal \ˌmän-trē-'ȯl\ City (metro. area pop., 2001: 3,426,350), southeastern Canada. It occupies about one-third of Île de Montréal (Montreal Island), near the confluence of the Ottawa and ST. LAWRENCE rivers. The metropolitan area encompasses Montréal and other islands, as well as both shores of the St. Lawrence. It is built on the slopes of a mountain, Mont-Royal, from which the city's name is derived. English and French are spoken throughout the city, which is the chief center of French-Canadian industry and culture. The site was occupied by the HURON Indian settlement of Hochelaga when visited by French explorer JACQUES CARTIER in 1535. The first European settlement was founded by the French in 1642, and was given the name Ville-Marie de Montréal. Rapid colonization based on the fur trade began in the first half of the 18th century, and the city soon grew beyond its walls. It surrendered to British forces in 1760 and, with all of NEW FRANCE, became part of the British North American empire in 1763. Montreal served as the capital of Canada 1844–49. It is one of Canada's chief ports for both oceangoing and inland shipping. It is Canada's second-largest city and a major cultural center, with a complex of theater and concert halls and several museums. It is the seat of the English-language universities MCGILL UNIV. and Concordia Univ., and of the French-language University de MONTRÉAL and the University du Québec à Montréal.

Montreal, University of Public French-language university founded in 1878. It provides instruction in the arts and sciences, education, law, medicine, theology, architecture, social work, criminology, and other fields. Affiliated schools include a polytechnic school and a school of advanced business studies. Total enrollment is about 50,000.

Montreux \'mȯ^{n}-'trœ\ Resort town (pop., 2001: 22,170), western Switzerland, eastern shore of Lake GENEVA. It was formed by the 1962 merger of the villages of Le Châtelard, Les Planches, and Veytaux. The nearby 13th-century Château de Chillon was made famous by Lord BYRON's poem "Prisoner of Chillon."

Montreux Convention \mō^{n}-'trœ\ (1936) Agreement concerning the Dardanelles strait. In response to Turkey's request to refortify the area, the signers of the Treaty of LAUSANNE and others met in Montreux, Switzerland, and agreed to return the zone to Turkish military control. The convention allowed Turkey to close the straits to all warships when it was at war, and to permit merchant ships free passage. See also STRAITS QUESTION.

Montrose \män-'trōz\, **Marquess of** *orig.* **James Graham** (1612–1650) Scottish general in the ENGLISH CIVIL WARS. He served in the Covenanter army that invaded northern England (1640), but remained a royalist. Appointed lieutenant-general by CHARLES I (1644), he led his royalist army of Highlanders and Irish to victories in major battles in Scotland. After Charles's defeat in 1645, Montrose fled to the European continent. He returned to Scotland in 1650 with 1,200 men, but was defeated, captured, and hanged.

Montserrat Island (pop., 2001 est.: 3,600), British crown colony, West Indies. Situated in the eastern Caribbean Sea, it occupies an area of 40 sq mi (103 sq km); it is 11 mi (18 km) long and 7 mi (11 km) wide. It was visited and named by C. COLUMBUS in 1493 and was colonized by the British and Irish in 1632. France later held it briefly, but from 1783 it remained British. Its colonial economy was based on cotton and sugar plantations that used African slave labor. It was part of the colony of Leeward Islands 1871–1956, and then of the Federation of the West Indies 1958–62. It was rebuilt after a devastating hurricane in 1989. A major eruption of the Soufriere Hills volcano in 1996 led to the evacuation of the southern half of the island and the abandonment of its capital, Plymouth. By 1998 more than two-thirds of its mid-1990s population had left the island.

Monty Python('s Flying Circus) British comedy troupe. The innovative group, formed in the early 1960s, came to prominence in the 1970s, first on TV and later in films. Its members, most of whom met while attending Cambridge Univ., included Graham Chapman (1941–1989) and JOHN CLEESE (coauthors of most of their skits and films) as well as Terry Jones (born 1942), Terry Gilliam (born 1940), Eric Idle (born 1943), and Michael Palin (born 1943). The troupe's parodies of celebrity interviews and their array of absurd characters surprised and delighted international audiences. Their films included *Monty Python and the Holy Grail* (1975) and *Monty Python's Life of Brian* (1979).

Monumentum Ancyranum \ˌmän-yu̇-'men-təm-ˌan-sir-'ā-nəm\ (after AD 14) Latin and Greek inscription on the temple of Rome and Augustus at Ancyra (Ankara, Turkey). Known as the *Res gestae divi Augusti* ("Achievements of the Divine Augustus"), it represents the official account of his reign. It was composed by AUGUSTUS himself, who directed in his will that it be engraved on pillars at his mausoleum in Rome. The originals are missing, the copies at Ancyra being two of many.

monzonite \män-'zō-ˌnīt, 'män-zə-ˌnīt\ Type of IGNEOUS ROCK that contains abundant and approximately equal amounts of plagioclase and potash FELDSPAR, as well as other minerals. The type region is Monzoni, Italy, in the Italian Tirol; similar rocks have been described from Montana, Norway, Sakhalin island, and other localities. Monzonite is not rare, but it generally occurs in rather small, heterogeneous masses mixed with diorites, pyroxenites, or gabbros.

mood *or* **mode** In GRAMMAR, a category that reflects the speaker's view of an event's reality, likelihood, or urgency. Often marked by special verb forms (inflections), moods include the indicative, for factual or neutral situations (e.g., "You did your work"); the imperative, to convey commands or requests ("Do your work"); and the subjunctive. The subjunctive's functions vary widely. It may express doubt, possibility, necessity, desire, or future time. In English it often indicates a condition contrary to fact (e.g., "If he were to work here, he would have to learn to be punctual").

Moody, Dwight L(yman) (1837–1899) U.S. Protestant evangelist. Born in East Northfield, Mass., he was brought up on a farm. He converted to evangelical Christianity in 1856, and he engaged in missionary work with the YMCA 1861–73. He founded Moody Church and preached in the slums, emphasizing literal interpretation of the Bible and the need to prepare for the Second Coming. In 1870 he teamed up with the hymn writer Ira D. Sankey (1840–1908), and they began a series of highly popular revival tours in Britain and the U.S. Moody founded the Northfield School (1879) and the Mount Hermon School (1881) as well as the Chicago Bible Institute (1889, now the Moody Bible Institute).

Moody, Paul (1779–1831) U.S. inventor and mechanic. Born in Byfield, Mass., he worked for years with FRANCIS LOWELL, overseeing his Waltham, Mass., factory. Together they designed the first power LOOM constructed in the U.S. (1814). Moody's numerous other innovations greatly aided the development of the New England textile industry.

moon Sole natural SATELLITE of earth, which it orbits from west to east at a mean distance of about 239,900 mi (384,400 km). It is less than one-third the size of earth (diameter about 2,160 mi, or 3,476 km, at its equator), about one-eightieth as massive, and about two-thirds as dense. Its surface gravity is about one-sixth that of earth, and its gravitational pull is largely responsible for earth's TIDES. The moon shines by reflected sunlight, but its ALBEDO is only 7.3%. It rotates relative to the sun in about 29.5 days, in exactly the time it takes to orbit earth, and therefore always presents the same face to earth. However, that face is lit by the sun at different angles as the moon revolves, causing it to display different phases over the month, from new to full. Most astronomers now believe the moon formed from a cloud of fragments ejected into earth orbit when a MARS-sized body struck the proto-earth early in the solar system's history. Its surface has been studied by telescope since GALILEO first observed it in 1609, and lunar rocks were brought back to earth in the APOLLO program. The dominant process affecting it has been impacts, both from micrometeorite bombardment, which grinds rock fragments into fine dust, and from METEORITE strikes, which produced the craters profusely scattered over its surface mostly early in its history, over 4 billion years ago. The maria (see MARE) are huge, ancient lava flows. In 1998, possible signs of water ice near the moon's poles were found. More generally, a moon is any natural satellite orbiting a planet.

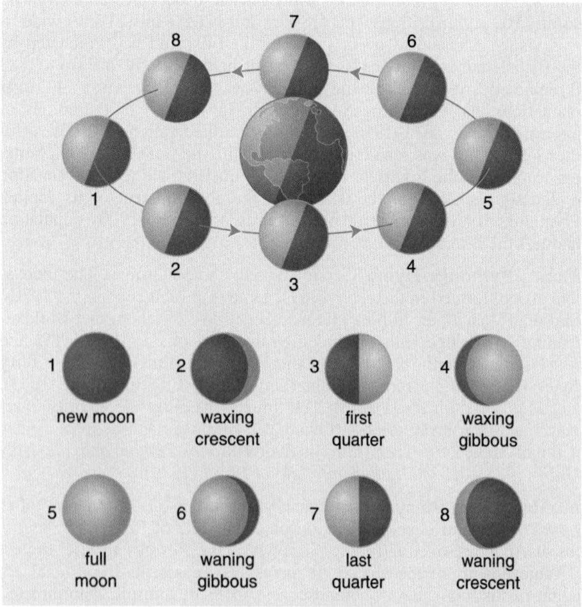

As the moon revolves around the earth, the amount of its illuminated half seen from the earth slowly increases and decreases (waxes and wanes). The cycle takes about 29½ days.

Moon, Sun Myung (born 1920) South Korean religious leader. Convinced that he was designated by God as a successor to JESUS, Moon began to preach a new religion loosely based on Christianity in North Korea in 1946. After being imprisoned by North Korean authorities, he escaped or was released and went to South Korea, where he founded the UNIFICATION CHURCH in 1954 and built a multimillion-dollar business empire. In 1973 he moved his headquarters to Tarrytown, N.Y., where he became the focus of controversies over fund-raising techniques, tax evasion, and the indoctrination of followers (popularly called Moonies). In 1982 Moon was convicted of tax evasion, sentenced to 18 months in prison, and fined $25,000. He has since been accused of extensive sexual misconduct within his organization. In the 1990s he moved to Brazil, where his church's purchase of large tracts of rain forest has been widely criticized.

Moore, Archie *orig.* **Archibald Lee Wright** (1913–1998) U.S. boxer. Born in Benoit, Miss., he began boxing in the 1930s but had difficulty advancing because contending fighters thought him too formidable. In 1952 he defeated Joey Maxim to win the world light-heavyweight championship. He held the crown until 1962, when he was disqualified for failing to meet the leading contender, Harold Johnson. From 1936 to 1963 he fought 229 bouts and won 194 of them, 141 by knockouts. He later became a film actor and youth worker.

Moore, Brian (1921–1999) Irish-Canadian novelist. Moore emigrated to Canada in 1948 and was a writer for the *Montreal Gazette* from 1952. He is best known for his first novel, *The Lonely Passion of Judith Hearne* (1955; film, 1987), about an aging spinster whose pretensions to gentility are gradually dissolved in alcoholism. His later novels include *The Luck of Ginger Coffey* (1960), *The Emperor of Ice Cream* (1965), *The Doctor's Wife* (1976), and *The Magician's Wife* (1998).

Moore, Clement Clarke (1779–1863) U.S. scholar remembered for the ballad that begins "'Twas the night before Christmas." Born in New York City, Moore cofounded General Theological Seminary and taught Oriental and Greek literature there 1821–50. He is said to have composed "A Visit to St. Nicholas" to amuse his children on Christmas 1822, and it was published anonymously in the *Troy* (N.Y.) *Sentinel*, on Dec. 23, 1823. In 2000 it was determined that the poem was probably the work of Henry Livingston, Jr. (1748–1828).

Moore, Ely (1798–1860) U.S. publisher. Born near Belvidere, N.J., he became a printer and newspaper editor. He was elected the first president of New York's federation of craft unions (1833). He became chairman of the National Trades Union, which joined with TAMMANY HALL to elect him to the U.S. House of Representatives (1835–39), where he advocated the 10-hour workday. He resumed his publishing career in New Jersey as editor of the *Warren Journal*.

Moore, G(eorge) E(dward) (1873–1958) British philosopher. While a fellow at Cambridge University (1898–1904), he published his major ethical work, *Principia Ethica* (1903). A friend of BERTRAND RUSSELL, he became a leading figure in the BLOOMSBURY group. He edited the journal *Mind* (1921–47) and taught at Cambridge (1925–39). In part because of his view that "the good" is knowable by direct apprehension, he became known as an ethical intuitionist (see INTUITIONISM). He claimed that efforts to define the term "good" commit the NATURALISTIC FALLACY. His major works, which also included *Philosophical Studies* (1922), *Some Main Problems of Philosophy* (1953), and *Philosophical Papers* (1959), were important in undermining the influence of G. W. F. HEGEL and IMMANUEL KANT on British philosophy.

Moore, Henry (1898–1986) English sculptor and graphic artist. The son of a coal miner, he was enabled to study at the Royal College of Art by a rehabilitation grant after being wounded in World War I. His early works were strongly influenced by the Maya sculpture he saw in a Paris museum. From c. 1931 on he experimented with abstract art, combining abstract shapes with the human figure and at times leaving the human figure behind altogether. When materials grew scarce during World War II, he concentrated on drawings of Londoners sheltering from bombs in Underground stations. Commissions for a *Madonna and Child* and a family group turned his style from abstraction to the more humanistic approach that became the basis of his international reputation. He returned to experimentation in the 1950s with angular, pierced standing figures in bronze. Much of his work is monumental, and he is particularly well known for a series of reclining nudes. Among his major commissions were sculptures for UNESCO's Paris headquarters (1957–58), Lincoln Center (1963–65), and the National Gallery of Art (1978).

Moore, Marianne (Craig) (1887–1972) U.S. poet. Born in St. Louis, she attended Bryn Mawr College and later settled in Brooklyn, N.Y., with her mother. After 1919 she devoted herself to writing, contributing poetry and criticism to many journals. She edited the influential journal *The Dial* 1925–29. Her poetry volumes include *Observations* (1924) and *Collected Poems* (1951; Pulitzer and Bollingen Prizes, National Book Award). In her highly disciplined poems, she distilled moral and intellectual insights from close observation of objective detail, especially in the animal world, often in innovative stanzaic forms. In "Poetry" (1921) she calls for poems presenting "imaginary gardens with real toads in them." In her late years, the winningly eccentric Moore, in her cape and tricornered hat, became an icon of sprightly gentility.

Marianne Moore, 1957.
IMOGEN CUNNINGHAM

Moore, Mary Tyler (born 1936) U.S. television and film actress. Born in Brooklyn, N.Y., she studied dance and appeared in commercials and in minor roles on television before costarring in the hit *Dick Van Dyke Show* (1961–66; two Emmy awards). She achieved even greater success as the star of *The Mary Tyler Moore Show* (1970–77; four Emmy awards), which became the most popular situation comedy of the 1970s. Her films include *Ordinary People* (1980) and *Flirting with Disaster* (1996).

Moore, Stanford (1913–1982) U.S. biochemist. Born in Chicago, he shared a 1972 Nobel Prize with Christian Anfinsen (1916–1995) and William Stein (1911–1980) for research on the molecular structures of PROTEINS. He is best known for his applications of CHROMATOGRAPHY to the analysis of AMINO ACIDS and PEPTIDES obtained from proteins and biological fluids and for the use of those analyses in determining the structure of the ENZYME ribonuclease.

Moore, Thomas (1779–1852) Irish poet, satirist, composer, and singer. Moore graduated from Trinity College and studied law in London, where he became a close friend of Lord BYRON and PERCY B. SHELLEY. His collections *Irish Melodies* and *National Airs* (1807–34) consist of 130 original poems set to folk melodies, including "The Minstrel Boy," "Believe Me, if All Those Endearing Young Charms," and "The Last Rose of Summer." Performed by Moore for London's aristocracy, they aroused sympathy and support for Irish nationalists. His reputation among his contemporaries rivaled that of Byron and WALTER SCOTT. His poem *Lalla Rookh* (1817), a romantic Oriental fantasy, became the most translated poem of its time. In 1824 he was entrusted with Byron's memoirs; he burned them, presumably to protect Byron. He later brought out biographies of Byron and others, as well as a *History of Ireland* (1827).

moorhen *or* **common gallinule** Bird of the migratory GALLINULE species (*Gallinula chloropus,* family Rallidae) of Europe, Africa, and eastern North America. Moorhens are blackish and have a scarlet frontal shield (fleshy plate on the forehead). In North America, the moorhen is sometimes called the Florida gallinule.

Moors Muslim population of Spain, of mixed Arab, Spanish, and Berber origins. North African Muslims (called in Latin *Mauri,* i.e., natives of Roman Mauretania) invaded Spain in the 8th century and, under the UMAYYAD and ALMORAVID dynasties, created the great Arab Andalusian civilization in such cities as Córdoba, Toledo, Granada, and Seville. The Christian reconquest of Spain under ALFONSO VI began in the 11th century; from then until the Moors' final defeat in 1492, and for another century thereafter, many Moors settled as refugees in North Africa. See also MUDEJARS.

moose Largest species *(Alces alces)* in the DEER family (Cervidae) found in northern North America and Eurasia; called ELK in Europe. Moose have long legs, an inflated pendulous muzzle, short neck and tail, and a brown, shaggy, coarse coat. They stand 5–7 ft (1.5–2 m) and weigh up to 1,800 lbs (820 kg). Males have enormous flattened, tined antlers that are shed and regrown annually. Moose wade in forest-edged lakes and streams, eating submerged aquatic plants, and browse on leaves, twigs, and bark. They are usually solitary, but North American moose often assemble in bands in winter. They range throughout the Canada coniferous forests and those of the northern U.S. They have been protected from extermination by regulation of hunting. See also WAPITI.

Bull moose (*Alces alces*) in velvet.
© LEONARD LEE RUE III—PHOTO RESEARCHERS, INC.

Moose River River, northeastern Ontario. It flows northeast for more than 60 mi (100 km) to empty into JAMES BAY. A wide stream, it is actually the estuary for several rivers, including the Abitibi and Mattagami.

moraine \mə-ˈrān\ Accumulation of rock debris (till) carried or deposited by a GLACIER. The material may range in size from blocks or boulders to sand and clay, is unstratified when dropped by the glacier, and shows no sorting or bedding. Several kinds of moraines are recognized, depending on how they are deposited by the glacier; these include lateral moraines along the margins of the glacier and terminal moraines at its leading edge.

Medial moraine of Gornergletscher (Gorner Glacier) in the Pennine Alps near Zermatt, Switz.
JEROME WYCKOFF

moral psychology Study of the psychological development of the moral sense, that is, beliefs about the appropriateness or goodness of what one does, thinks, or feels. The U.S. psychologist Lawrence Kohlberg hypothesized that people's development of moral standards passes through several levels. At the early level, that of preconventional moral reasoning, the child uses external and physical events (such as pleasure or pain) as the source for moral decisions; his standards are based strictly on what will avoid punishment or bring pleasure. At the intermediate level, that of conventional moral reasoning, the child or adolescent views moral standards as a way of maintaining the approval of authority figures, chiefly his parents, and acts in accordance with their precepts. At the third level, that of postconventional moral reasoning, the adult bases his moral standards on principles that he himself has evaluated and accepts as inherently valid, regardless of society's opinion.

Morales \mō-ˈrä-lās\, **Luis de** (c. 1520–1586) Spanish painter. He lived all his life in Badajoz, leaving only for occasional commissions. He is considered Spain's greatest Mannerist painter and is known especially for his emotional religious paintings. He always worked on panels, often depicting such subjects as the Ecce Homo, the Pietà, and the Virgin and Child. His paintings show the influence of LEONARDO DA VINCI and RAPHAEL, and are marked by detailed execution and the anguished asceticism of 16th-century Spain.

"The Virgin and Child," panel by Luis de Morales; in the National Gallery, London.
BY COURTESY OF THE NATIONAL GALLERY, LONDON; PHOTOGRAPH, A.C. COOPER

morality play Allegorical drama of 15th–16th-century Europe. The play's characters personified moral qualities (such as charity or vice) or abstractions (such as death or youth). One of the main types of vernacular drama of its time, it provided a transition from LITURGICAL DRAMA to professional secular drama. The plays were short works, usually performed by semiprofessional acting troupes that relied on public support. *Everyman* (c. 1495), featuring Everyman's summons by Death and his journey to the grave, is considered the greatest morality play. See also MIRACLE PLAY, MYSTERY PLAY.

Morandi \mȯ-ˈrän-dē\, **Giorgio** (1890–1964) Italian painter and etcher. He first exhibited his paintings with the Futurists and he was closely associated with the Metaphysical painters, but he is identified with neither school. His simple, geometric still lifes of bottles, jars, and boxes contributed to the development of 20th-century formalism. His contemplative approach gave his landscapes and still lifes a delicacy of tone and subtlety of design. As instructor of etching at Bologna's Academy of Fine Arts (1930–56), he had a profound influence on Italian graphic artists.

L
M
N

Morava River \ˈmȯ-rä-vä\ *German* **March** \ˈmärk\ River, eastern Czech Republic. It rises in mountains and flows south to enter the DANUBE RIVER just above BRATISLAVA, Slovakia, after a course of 227 mi (365 km). In its lower course it first divides the Czech Republic from Slovakia and then divides Slovakia from Austria. It gives its name to MORAVIA, the area around it.

Morava River River, Serbia, Yugoslavia. Formed by the confluence of the South (Juzna) Morava and West (Zapadna) Morava rivers, it flows north to enter the DANUBE RIVER, after a course of 137 mi (221 km). With an area of 14,457 sq mi (37,444 sq km), the Morava River basin is almost the size of SERBIA.

Moravia \mə-ˈrā-vē-ə\ Region, central Europe. Bounded by Bohemia, Silesia, Slovakia, and northeastern Austria, and crossed by the MORAVA RIVER, it was inhabited from the 4th century BC. Dominated by the Avars in the 6th–7th century AD and later settled by Slavic tribes, in the 9th century it became the state of Great Moravia and included BOHEMIA as well as parts of modern Poland and Hungary. It was destroyed by the MAGYARS in 906. In 1526 it came under HABSBURG rule. After the Revolution of 1848 it became an Austrian crown land with its capital at BRNO. In 1918 it was incorporated into the new state of Czechoslovakia. Germany annexed parts of it in 1938; after World War II they were restored to Czechoslovakia. It was included in the Czech Socialist Republic created in 1968, and in the CZECH REPUBLIC in 1993.

Moravia \mō-ˈräv-yä\, **Alberto** *orig.* **Alberto Pincherle** (1907–1990) Italian journalist, novelist, and short-story writer. He worked as a journalist in Turin and as a foreign correspondent in London. *Time of Indifference* (1929), his first novel, is a scathing study of middle-class moral corruption. His works were censored by BENITO MUSSOLINI's fascists and placed on the *INDEX LIBRORUM PROHIBITORUM*. Later important novels, many of them portrayals of social alienation and loveless sexuality, include *The Conformist* (1951; film, 1971), *Two Women* (1957; film, 1961), and *The Empty Canvas* (1960). His books of short stories include *Roman Tales* (1954) and *More Roman Tales* (1959). He was married to the writer Elsa Morante (1918–1985).

Moravian Church Protestant denomination founded in the 18th century. It traces its origins to the Unity of Brethren, a 15th-century HUSSITE movement in Bohemia and Moravia. The original Brethren movement was eroded by persecution, but it was renewed in 1722 at Herrnhut, a theocratic community established in Saxony. In America the Moravians founded Bethlehem, Pa. (1740), and several other settlements, and carried out missionary work among the Indians. The Moravians ordain bishops but are governed by synods of elected representatives; they are guided by the Bible as their only rule of faith and worship.

moray \mə-ˈrā, ˈmȯr-ˌā\ Any of about 80 species (family Muraenidae) of shallow-water EELS inhabiting all tropical and subtropical seas, where they live among reefs and rocks, hiding in crevices. Their skin is thick, smooth, scaleless, and usually vividly marked or colored. Most species lack pectoral fins. Morays have a wide mouth and strong, sharp teeth for seizing and holding prey (chiefly other fishes). They attack humans only when disturbed. Most species are less than 5 ft (1.5 m) long, but *Thyrsoidea macrurus*, of the Pacific, may grow to more than 11 ft (3.5 m). Morays are sometimes eaten, but their flesh may be toxic and can cause illness or death.

Green moray (*Gymnothorax funebris*).
CARLETON RAY—PHOTO RESEARCHERS

Moray Firth \ˈmər-ē\ Inlet of the NORTH SEA, northeastern Scotland. It extends inland for 39 mi (63 km) and is 16 mi (29 km) wide at its widest point. Its inner reaches are divided by a peninsula, the Black Isle, into two smaller inlets, Cromarty Firth and the Firth of Inverness; the city of INVERNESS lies there.

Mordecai \ˈmȯr-də-ˌkī\ In the Old Testament Book of Esther, the cousin or guardian of ESTHER. Mordecai was a Jew who offended Haman, minister of King Ahasuerus. Haman persuaded the king to order Mordecai's execution and the destruction of all the Jews in the Persian Empire, but Esther, Ahasuerus's beloved Jewish queen, pleaded for him to change his mind, and Ahasuerus ordered Haman hanged and named Mordecai to his position. See also PURIM.

More, St. Thomas (1477–1535) English statesman and humanist. He studied at Oxford and was successful as a lawyer from 1501, after living in a Carthusian monastery to test his vocation for the priesthood. He served as an undersheriff of London (1510–18) and endeared himself to Londoners as a fair judge and consultant. He wrote the notable *History of King Richard III* (1513–18) and the renowned *Utopia* (1516), an immediate success with the humanists, including DESIDERIUS ERASMUS. In 1517 More was named to the king's council, and he became HENRY VIII's secretary and confidant. In 1523 he was elected speaker of the House of Commons. He wrote *A Dialogue Concerning Heresies* (1529) to refute heretical writings. After the fall of Cardinal WOLSEY (1529), More succeeded him as lord chancellor, but he resigned in 1532 when he could not affirm Henry's divorce from Catherine. He also refused to accept the Act of SUPREMACY. In 1534 More was charged with high treason and imprisoned in the Tower, where he wrote his *Dialogue of Comfort Against Tribulation*. In 1535 he was tried and sentenced to death by hanging, which the king commuted to beheading. He was canonized in 1935.

Moreau \mȯ-ˈrō\, **Gustave** (1826–1898) French painter. He developed a distinctive style in the Symbolist mode, becoming known for his erotic paintings of mythological and religious subjects. Such works as *Oedipus and the Sphinx* (1864) and *Dance of Salome* (1876) have often been described as decadent. He made a number of technical experiments, including scraping his canvases; and his nonfigurative paintings, done in a loose manner with thick impasto, have led some to call him a herald of Abstract Expressionism.

Moreau, Jeanne (born 1928) French film actress. At age 20 she became the youngest member of the COMÉDIE-FRANÇAISE. She made her screen debut in *The Last Love* (1949) and won acclaim for her roles in LOUIS MALLE's *Frantic* (1957) and *The Lovers* (1958). Though not conventionally beautiful, she became noted for her sensuality and sophistication. She starred in *Moderato cantabile* (1960), *La Notte* (1961), and *Jules et Jim* (1961), playing a woman loved by two men in the movie that established her as an international star, and later in *The Trial* (1962), *Diary of a Chambermaid* (1964), and *The Bride Wore Black* (1968). She has also directed films, including *Lumière* (1976) and *L'adolescente* (1978).

Morehouse College Private, historically black, men's liberal-arts college in Atlanta. It was founded as the Augusta Institute, a seminary, in 1867 and renamed in 1913 in honor of Henry L. Morehouse, an administrator. It offers programs in business, education, humanities, and physical and natural sciences. It is part of an educational consortium in which six institutions, including SPELMAN COLLEGE, exchange faculty, students, facilities, and curricula. Enrollment is about 3,000.

morel \mə-'rel\ Any of various species of edible MUSHROOMS in the genera *Morchella* and *Verpa*. Morels have a convoluted or pitted head, or cap, vary in shape, and occur in diverse habitats. The edible *M. esculenta*, found in woods during early summer, is among the most highly prized edible fungi. The bell morel *(Verpa)*, an edible mushroom with a bell-shaped cap, is found in woods and in old orchards in early spring. False morels, or lorchels, are represented by the genera *Gyromitra* and *Helvella*. Most species of *Gyromitra* are poisonous.

Morelia \mō-'rāl-yä\ City (pop., 1990: 490,000), capital of MICHOACÁN state, western central Mexico. It was founded in 1541 as Valladolid, at the site of a Tarascan Indian settlement. It replaced Pátzcuaro as the provincial capital in 1582. During the Mexican wars for independence it served briefly as the base of operations for the revolution; in 1828 its name was changed from Valladolid to Morelia in honor of revolutionary leader José María Morelos. It is the commercial center of an agricultural region. Its educational institutions include the University of Michoacán and the Colegio San Nicolás (founded 1540), Mexico's oldest institution of higher learning.

Morelos \mō-'rā-lōs\ State (pop., 1995 est.: 1,443,000), central Mexico. Located on the southern slope of the central Mexican plateau, it occupies an area of 1,911 sq mi (4,950 sq km). Its capital is CUERNAVACA. It is one of the country's most flourishing agricultural states, with valleys that produce a variety of agricultural products. It was named after José María Morelos and was the birthplace of EMILIANO ZAPATA, both heroes of Mexico's war for independence.

Moreton Bay \'mōr-tᵊn\ Inlet of the Pacific Ocean, southeastern coast of QUEENSLAND, Australia. It is 65 mi (105 km) long and 20 mi (32 km) wide, and serves as the gateway to BRISBANE. In 1770 British navigator Capt. JAMES COOK named the bay (misspelling it) after the earl of Morton. The first settlement on the mainland was a penal colony established at Redcliffe in the early 19th century.

Morey, Samuel (1762–1843) U.S. inventor. He was born in Hebron, Conn. With support from ROBERT R. LIVINGSTON, he experimented with steamboats in the 1790s; though none was commercially successful, he later claimed that ROBERT FULTON had stolen his ideas. In 1826 he received the first U.S. patent for an INTERNAL-COMBUSTION ENGINE. His many other patents included his American Water Burner (1818), a precursor of the water-gas process.

Morgan Breed of light HORSE founded by a Vermont horse (foaled 1793, died 1821) named after his owner, Justin Morgan (1747–1797). The "Justin Morgan horse," a blend of THOROUGHBRED, ARABIAN, and other elements, was a compact, heavily muscled, short-legged horse of great style, energy, and endurance. Because he alone founded the breed, he is the world's best example of prepotency (ability to pass one's traits to one's offspring). Modern Morgans are used mostly for riding. They are 14.1–15.2 hands (57–61 in., 145–155 cm) high, weigh 900–1,100 lbs (400–500 kg), and resemble the Arabian in conformation and endurance.

Morgan, Daniel (1736–1802) American Revolutionary army officer. Born in Hunterdon Co., N.J., he was commissioned a captain of Virginia riflemen and fought under BENEDICT ARNOLD in the unsuccessful assault on Quebec (1775). He joined Gen. HORATIO GATES in the Battle of Saratoga (1777). In 1780 he was made brigadier general and fought in the South, defeating a large British force at Cowpens, S.C. In 1794 he led Virginia militiamen to help suppress the WHISKEY REBELLION.

Morgan, Henry *later* **Sir Henry** (1635–1688) British buccaneer. In the second ANGLO-DUTCH WAR, he commanded buccaneers against the Dutch colonies in the Caribbean. After capturing Puerto Príncipe in Cuba and sacking the city of Portobelo, he set out in 1670 with 36 ships and 2,000 buccaneers to capture the major Spanish colonial city of Panamá, defeated a large Spanish force, and sacked and burned the city. On the return journey, he deserted his followers and took most of the booty. In 1674 he was knighted and sent to Jamaica as deputy governor. An exaggerated account of Morgan's exploits created his popular reputation as a bloodthirsty pirate.

Morgan, J(ohn) P(ierpont) (1837–1913) U.S. financier. Born in Hartford, Conn., the son of a financier, he began his career as an accountant in 1857 and became an agent for his father's banking company in 1861. In 1871 he was named a partner in the firm of Drexel, Morgan, which became the chief source of U.S. government financing. In 1895 it became J. P. Morgan and Co. In the 1880s and '90s Morgan reorganized several major railroads, notably the ERIE RAILROAD and the NORTHERN PACIFIC. He was instrumental in achieving railroad rate stability and discouraging overly chaotic competition, and became one of the world's most powerful railroad magnates, controlling about 5,000 mi (8,000 km) of railway by 1902. After the panic of 1893, Morgan formed a syndicate to supply the U.S. Treasury's depleted gold reserves. He led the financial community in averting a general financial collapse following the stock-market panic of 1907. He financed a series of giant industrial consolidations, organizing the mergers that formed GENERAL ELECTRIC, U.S. STEEL CORP., and International Harvester Co. (see NAVISTAR INTERNATIONAL CORP.). A noted art collector, he donated many artworks to the METROPOLITAN MUSEUM OF ART; his book collection and the building that housed it became the Pierpont Morgan Library.

Morgan, J(ohn) P(ierpont), Jr. (1867–1943) U.S. banker and financier. Born in Irvington, N.Y., he joined J. P. Morgan and Co. in 1892 and took control of it in 1913 on the death of his father, J. P. MORGAN. In World War I he served as purchasing agent in the U.S. for the British and French governments and organized the underwriting of more than $1.5 billion in Allied bonds. He pooled funds with other bankers in an unsuccessful attempt to prevent the crash of 1929. The Banking Act of 1933 compelled his firm to separate its investment-banking and commercial-banking activities. Morgan, Stanley and Co. became a new investment-banking firm, while Morgan himself remained head of J. P. Morgan & Co., which was from then on strictly a commercial-banking firm.

Morgan, Joe *orig.* **Joseph Leonard** (born 1943) U.S. baseball player. Born in Bonham, Texas, he was named Rookie of the Year in 1965, his first full season with the Houston Astros. During each of his eight seasons with the Cincinnati Reds (1973–79) he made the All-Star team as second baseman. He was named the National League's Most Valuable Player in 1975 and 1976, when he led the Reds to World Series championships. He broke ROGERS HORNSBY's record for home runs by a second baseman, with 266.

Morgan, John (1735–1789) U.S. medical educator. Born in Philadelphia, he studied medicine in Europe before returning to the American colonies to found their first medical school in 1765 at the University of Pennsylvania. As North America's first professor of medicine, he required a liberal education of his students and separated medicine, surgery, and pharmacology into distinct disciplines, policies widely opposed by colonial physicians. He was made head of the army's medical system in 1775; however, the Continental Congress did not let him organize the system and dismissed him in 1777, holding him responsible for the war's high death rate. Though absolved in 1779, he never recovered and died an impoverished recluse. Morgan was one of the first U.S. physicians to adopt and advocate EDWARD JENNER's smallpox vaccination method.

Morgan, Julia (1872–1957) U.S. architect. Born in San Francisco, she received an engineering degree from UC–Berkeley. The first female architecture student at the École des Beaux-Arts in Paris (1898), she later became California's first licensed woman architect. The San Francisco earthquake of 1906 provided her with the opportunity to design hundreds of buildings in the Bay area. She designed and supervised the building of WILLIAM RANDOLPH HEARST's private castle at SAN SIMEON (1919–38).

Morgan, Lewis Henry (1818–1881) U.S. ethnologist and a principal founder of scientific anthropology. Born near Aurora, N.Y., and trained as an attorney, Morgan developed a deep interest in the American Indians and in 1846 was eventually adopted by the SENECA. His *Systems of Consanguinity and Affinity of the Human Family* (1871) was a world survey of KINSHIP systems that sought to establish connections between cultures and particularly to establish the Asiatic origin of the American Indians. This work led to a comprehensive theory of SOCIOCULTURAL EVOLUTION, set forth in *Ancient Society* (1877). He claimed that advances in social organization arose primarily from changes in food production, and that society had progressed from a hunting-and-gathering stage ("savagery") to one of settled agriculture ("barbarism") to modern "civilization." This theory, with the related theory that society originated in a state of sexual promiscuity and advanced through various forms of family life before culminating in monogamy, is now obsolete. For many years, however, Morgan was the dean of American anthropology, and his pioneering ideas influenced the theories of KARL MARX and FRIEDRICH ENGELS, among others.

Morgan, Thomas Hunt (1866–1945) U.S. zoologist and geneticist. Born in Lexington, Ky., he received his doctorate from Johns Hopkins University. As a professor at Columbia University. (1904–28) and Caltech (1928–45), he conducted important research on HEREDITY. Like many of his contemporaries, Morgan found CHARLES DARWIN's theory of natural selection implausible because it could not be tested experimentally, and objected to Mendelian and chromosome theories, arguing that no single chromosome could carry specific hereditary traits. His opinion changed as a result of his studies of drosophila. He developed the hypothesis of sex-linked traits. He adopted the term *gene,* and concluded that genes were possibly arranged in a linear fashion on chromosomes. He was awarded the Nobel Prize in 1933. See also CALVIN BLACKMAN BRIDGES.

Morgan le Fay ("Morgan the Fairy") Enchantress in ARTHURIAN LEGEND. Skilled in the arts of healing and changing shape, she ruled AVALON, the island where King ARTHUR retreated to be healed of his wounds after his last battle. She had learned her magic powers from books and from MERLIN. In other stories she is Arthur's sister and enemy, and seduces him to produce a son who later kills Arthur.

Morgenthau \'mȯr-gən-ˌthȯ\, **Henry, Jr.** (1891–1967) U.S. public official. Born in New York City, he became the editor of *American Agriculturist* (1922–33) and a close friend of FRANKLIN ROOSEVELT. He served as secretary of the treasury in Roosevelt's cabinet (1934–45) and was responsible for financing the New Deal programs and the enormous expenditures of World War II. Over $370 billion was spent during the period, three times more money than was spent by the 50 previous secretaries of the treasury. He resigned after Roosevelt's death and retired to his farm.

Morghab River See MURGAB RIVER

Mörike \'mœ̄-rē-kə\, **Eduard Friedrich** (1804–1875) German lyric poet. A clergyman, Mörike suffered all his life from psychosomatic illnesses and retired at 39, supplementing his pension by lecturing on literature. His small literary output includes the novel *Maler Nolten* (1832), fairy tales, and *Mozart on the Way to Prague* (1856), a humorous examination of the problems of artists in a world uncongenial to art. His best works are his exquisite lyrics, notably the "Peregrina" poems, which immortalize a youthful love, and sonnets to a onetime betrothed; many were set to music by H. WOLF.

Morison, Samuel Eliot (1887–1976) U.S. biographer and historian. Born in Boston, he taught at Harvard University for 40 years. To give authenticity to his writings on maritime history, he undertook numerous voyages and during wartime served on 12 ships as a commissioned officer in the U.S. Naval Reserve. His works include *Admiral of the Ocean Sea* (1942, Pulitzer Prize), on CHRISTOPHER COLUMBUS; *John Paul Jones* (1959, Pulitzer Prize); the monumental *History of U.S. Naval Operations in World War II* (15 vols., 1947–62); and *The Oxford History of the American People* (1965).

Morison, Stanley (1889–1967) English typographer, scholar, and historian of printing. He attained much of his printing and typographic experience by working for publishing houses. He served as editor of the influential typographic journal *The Fleuron* (1926–30). He worked for *The Times* (London) in various capacities, including editor of *The Times Literary Supplement* (1929–60). He is best known as the designer of Times New Roman, which was adopted as *The Times's* basic typeface in 1932, and went on to become the most successful new typeface of the 20th century.

Morisot \mȯ-rē-'zō\, **Berthe** (1841–1895) French painter and printmaker. Granddaughter of J.-H. FRAGONARD, she studied with CAMILLE COROT, but the major influence over her work was EDOUARD MANET, whose brother she later married. She exhibited regularly with the Impressionists. None of her exhibits proved commercially successful, but she outsold CLAUDE MONET, AUGUSTE RENOIR, and ALFRED SISLEY. Her coloring was delicate and subtle, often with a subdued emerald glow, and her subjects were often members of her family (e.g., *The Artist's Sister Edma and Their Mother,* 1870). She is best known for her extremely loose brushwork, and for the sensitivity she brought to her female subjects.

Morita \mȯ-'rē-tə\, **Akio** (1921–1999) Japanese entrepreneur, cofounder of SONY CORP. The son of an old sake-brewing family, Morita was trained as a physicist. In 1946 he and Ibuka Masaru cofounded the Tokyo Telecommunications Engineering Corp., which changed its name to Sony Corp. in 1958. Primarily responsibly for finances and marketing, Morita adopted U.S. advertising techniques and established Sony's first U.S. plant in 1972. He became chief executive officer in 1971 and chairman of the board in 1976, in which post he served until 1994. Under his direction Sony became a world-renowned manufacturer of consumer electronics.

Morley, John *later* **Viscount Morley (of Blackburn)** (1838–1923) English politician and historian. He worked as a journalist in London from 1860, mainly as editor of the liberal *Fortnightly Review* (1867–82). A supporter of WILLIAM E. GLADSTONE, Morley served in the House of Commons 1883–95 and 1896–1908. As chief secretary for Ireland (1886, 1892–95), he helped prepare the Irish HOME RULE bills. As secretary for India (1905–10), he brought elected Indian representation into the government. He was also wrote acclaimed historical works, including biographies of Gladstone, VOLTAIRE, J.-J. ROUSSEAU, and OLIVER CROMWELL.

Morley, Thomas (1557?–1602) English composer and music theorist. He was educated at Oxford and studied with W. BYRD. Though he composed a number of anthems and Psalms, he is best known for his secular songs, including the *First Booke of Ayres* (1600), and for the treatise *A Plaine and Easie Introduction to Practicall Musick* (1597). By editing and printing several anthologies of Italian music (often reworked), he was instrumental in bringing the Italian madrigal to England. *The Triumphes of Oriana* (1601) was his collection of works by 23 English composers.

Mormon Member of the Church of Jesus Christ of Latter-day Saints or of a sect closely related to it (e.g., the REORGANIZED CHURCH OF JESUS CHRIST OF LATTER-DAY SAINTS). The Mormon religion was founded by JOSEPH SMITH, who received an angelic vision telling him the location of golden plates containing God's revelation; this he published in 1830 as the Book of MORMON. Smith and his followers accepted the Bible as well as the Mormon sacred scriptures but diverged significantly from orthodox Christianity, especially in their assertion that God has evolved from humans and that humans might evolve into gods. Other unique doctrines include the belief in preexisting souls waiting to be born and in salvation of the dead through retroactive baptism. The sect became notorious for its practice of POLYGAMY, though polygamy was only officially sanctioned 1852–90. Smith and his followers migrated from Palmyra, N.Y., to Ohio, Missouri, and finally Illinois, where Smith was killed by a mob in 1844. In 1846–47, under BRIGHAM YOUNG, the Mormons made a 1,100-mi (1,800-km) trek to Utah, where they founded SALT LAKE CITY. Today the church has a worldwide membership of nearly 10 million, swelled yearly by the missionary work usually required (for two years) of all male members. Mormons look forward to the establishment of God's kingdom in America, to be ruled in person by Jesus.

Mormon, Book of Holy scripture of the MORMONS, supplemental to the BIBLE. First published in 1830, it is held by all branches of Mormonism to be a divinely inspired work translated by the founder of their religion, JOSEPH SMITH. It relates the history of a tribe of Hebrews who migrated from Jerusalem to America c. 600 BC. They eventually split into two groups: the Lamanites, who were ancestors of the American Indians; and the Nephites, who were instructed by Jesus before being destroyed by the Lamanites. The prophet Mormon recorded their history on gold tablets, which were buried and remained hidden for centuries. Moroni, Mormon's son, appeared to Smith in angelic form and revealed their location.

morning-glory family Family Convolvulaceae, composed of about 1,400 species of flowering plants in 50 genera, widely cultivated for their colorful, funnel-shaped flowers. Most are twining and erect herbaceous plants; a few are woody vines, trees, or shrubs. The family is widespread in both tropical and temperate areas. Most popular morning glories are of the genus *Ipomoea,* as is the sweet potato. Several species of bindweeds are agricultural pests. The seeds of two species, *Rivea corymbosa* and *I. violacea,* contain hallucinogenic compounds of historical interest.

Morny \mȯr-ˈnē\, **Charles-Auguste-Louis-Joseph** *later* **duc (Duke) de Morny** (1811–1865) French politician. Half brother of Louis-Napoléon (later Napoleon III), Morny devoted himself to Parisian society and to making a fortune before serving in the Chamber of Deputies (1842–48, 1849). Appointed minister of the interior in 1851, he organized the plebiscite that made Louis-Napoléon dictator. As president of the legislature (1856–65) he tried unsuccessfully to persuade Napoleon III to give France more liberty.

Moro, Aldo (1916–1978) Italian politician and premier of Italy (1963–64, 1964–66, 1966–68, 1974–76, 1976). A professor of law at the University of Bari, he was elected to the legislature in 1946. He served in several cabinet posts, then became secretary of the Christian Democrat Party (1959–63). As premier of Italy, he included socialists in his coalition governments. In 1976 he became president of the Christian Democrats and remained influential in Italian politics. In 1978 he was kidnapped in Rome by Red Brigades terrorists; after the government refused to release Brigades members on trial in Turin, he was murdered by his captors.

Moroccan Crises (1905–6, 1911) Two European incidents centering on Germany's attempt to block France's control of Morocco and to restrict French power. While visiting Tangiers in 1905, the German emperor William II issued a statement of support for Moroccan independence, which caused international panic. The crisis was resolved at the Algeciras Conference (1906), which recognized France's special political interests in Morocco. The second crisis occurred in 1911 when a German gunboat arrived in Agadir, ostensibly to protect German economic interests during a local uprising. The French objected and made preparations for war, as did Britain, but a settlement was negotiated that gave France rights to a protectorship over Morocco. In return, Germany acquired part of the French Congo.

Morocco *officially* **Kingdom of Morocco** *Arabic* **Al-Mamlakah al-Maghribiyah** \äl-ˈmäm-lä-kə-äl-ˌmä-grē-ˈbē-yə\ Country, North Africa. Area: 177,117 sq mi (458,730 sq km). Population (1997 est.): 27,220,000. Capital: Rabat. Arabized Berbers are the country's largest ethnolinguistic group; there are French, Spanish, and Bedouin minorities. Languages: Arabic (official), Berber. Religion: Islam (official), mostly Sunni. Currency: dirham. Morocco is a mountainous country with an average elevation of 2,600 ft (800 m) above sea level. The Er Rif runs along the northern coast; the Atlas Mtns. rise in the nation's center, and include Mount Toubkal (13,665 ft, or 4,165 m), the country's highest peak. The area is a zone of severe seismic activity, and earthquakes are frequent. Its fertile lowlands support agriculture; major crops include barley, wheat, and sugar beets. Morocco is the world's largest supplier of phosphate. The nation's industrial center is Casablanca, its largest city. It is a constitutional monarchy with one legislative house; its chief of state and head of government is the king, assisted by the prime minister. The Berbers entered Morocco near the end of the 2nd millennium BC. Phoenicians established trading posts along the Mediterranean during the 12th century BC, and Carthage had settlements along the Atlantic in the 5th century BC. After the fall of Carthage, Morocco became a loyal ally of Rome, and in 46 AD it was annexed by Rome as part of the province of Mauretania. It was invaded by Muslims in the 7th century. The Almoravids conquered it and the Muslim areas of Spain in the mid-11th century; in the 12th century the Almohads overthrew the Almoravids. They in turn were conquered by the Marinids in the 13th century. After the fall of the Marinids in the mid-15th century, the Sa'dis ruled for a

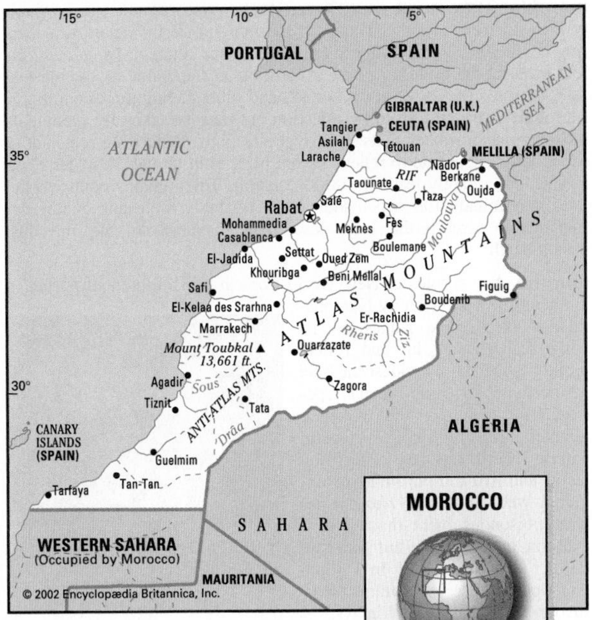

century after 1550. Association with the Barbary Coast states compelled Europeans to enter the area: the French fought Morocco over the Algerian boundary, Britain obtained trading rights in 1856, and the Spanish seized part of Moroccan territory in 1859. It was a French protectorate from 1912 until its independence in 1956. In the late 1970s it reasserted claim to the Spanish Sahara (see Western Sahara), and in 1976 Spanish troops withdrew from the region, leaving behind the Algerian-supported Saharan guerrillas of the Polisario Front. Relations with Mauritania and Algeria deteriorated, and fighting over the region continued into the 1990s. As the decade wore on, the U.N. tried to solve the dispute.

Moroni Town (pop., 1991 est.: 30,000), capital of the Comoros Islands, located on Grande Comore (Njazidja) island in the Indian Ocean. Founded by Arabic-speaking settlers, it is the largest settlement of the Comoros and has served as the capital since 1958. The port of Moroni consists of a small quay in a natural cove. The town retains an Arabic character, and it has several mosques, including Chiounda, a pilgrimage center.

Moros Several Muslim peoples living in the southern Philippines. The Moros, who constitute about 5% of the Philippine population, are not racially different from other Filipinos but, with a separate Islamic faith and local cultures, they have been the object of prejudice and neglect. They have a centuries-long history of conflict with ruling powers; first with Roman Catholic Spanish colonialists (16th–19th century), then with U.S. occupation troops, and finally with the independent Philippine government. The Moro National Liberation Front, which espoused Moro separatism and led a violent insurgency in the late 1960s and 1970s, split into factions at the end of the 1970s, but the insurgency continued. Provisions for the expansion of the Autonomous Region of Muslim Mindanao, established in the late 1980s, were included in a 1996 treaty, but some separatists continue to hold out for complete independence.

morpheme In linguistics, the smallest grammatical unit of speech. It may be an entire word *(cat)* or an element of a word *(re-* and *-ed* in *reappeared).* In so-called isolating languages, like Vietnamese, each word contains a single morpheme; in languages like English, words often contain multiple morphemes. The study of morphemes is included in morphology.

Morpheus In Greek and Roman mythology, the god of dreams. He was one of the sons of Hypnos (Somnus), god of sleep. Morpheus sent human shapes of all kinds to the dreamer, while his brothers Phobetor and Phantasus sent the forms of animals and inanimate objects.

morphine HETEROCYCLIC COMPOUND, NARCOTIC ANALGESIC ALKALOID originally isolated from OPIUM. It is among the most powerful naturally occurring compounds in its ability to reduce pain and distress; its calming effect protects the system against exhaustion in traumatic SHOCK, internal HEMORRHAGE, CONGESTIVE HEART FAILURE, and other debilitating conditions. Morphine is usually given by injection but may be taken by mouth. Its most serious drawback is its addictiveness; many doctors are reluctant to use amounts adequate to relieve severe pain, even though short-term use in such cases rarely leads to DRUG ADDICTION. This remains controversial even in terminal cases, when addiction is arguably irrelevant; another issue in such cases is that large doses depress RESPIRATION and may thus hasten death.

morpho Any species of New World tropical brush-footed BUTTERFLIES in the genus *Morpho* (family Nymphalidae). Microscopic ridges on its wing scales break up and reflect light, producing the iridescent blue of the males of some *Morpho* species. The generally duller-colored females have broader, less graceful wings. The hairy larvae feed on plants and live and pupate in a communal web. Some *Morpho* species have poisonous hairs that cause a rash on human skin, but they are raised commercially in South America for use in jewelry, lampshades, pictures, and tray inlays.

Morpho butterfly (*Morpho nestira*).
APPEL COLOR PHOTOGRAPHY

morphology \mȯr-'fä-lə-jē\ In biology, the study of the size, shape, and structure of organisms in relation to some principle or generalization. Whereas ANATOMY describes the structure of organisms, morphology explains the shapes and arrangement of parts of organisms in terms of such general principles as evolutionary relations, function, and development.

morphology In linguistics, the internal construction system of words and its study. Languages vary widely in the number of MORPHEMES a word can have. English has many words with multiple morphemes (e.g., *replacement* is composed of *re-*, *place*, and *-ment*). Many American Indian languages have a highly complex morphology; other languages, such as Chinese, have a very simple one. Morphology includes the grammatical processes of inflection, marking categories like person, tense, and case (e.g., the *-s* in *jumps* marks the third-person singular in the present tense), and derivation, the formation of new words from existing words (e.g., *acceptable* from *accept*).

Morrill (Land-Grant College) Act of 1862 U.S. congressional enactment that provided grants of land to state colleges specializing in the teaching of "agriculture and the mechanic arts." It was named for its sponsor, Vermont congressman Justin Smith Morrill (1810–1898). Since 1862 some 12 million acres have been distributed, on which some 70 land-grant colleges currently flourish.

Morris, Gouverneur (1752–1816) American statesman and financial expert. Born in New York City, he served in the provincial congress (1775–77) and the Continental Congress (1778–79). He was appointed assistant superintendent of finance (1781–85) and proposed the decimal coinage system that became the basis for U.S. currency. A member of the Constitutional Convention, he helped write the final draft of the U.S. Constitution. He served as minister to France 1792–94 and as a U.S. Senator 1800–3, and was the first chairman of the Erie Canal commission (1810–16).

Morris, Mark (born 1956) U.S. dancer and choreographer. Born in Seattle, he danced with various companies before forming the Mark Morris Dance Group in 1980. The group was the resident company at the Théâtre Royal de la Monnaie in Brussels (1988–91), where Morris served as director of dance. In 1990 he cofounded the White Oak Dance Project with MIKHAIL BARYSHNIKOV. Known for his daring and highly imaginative style, he has choreographed more than 90 works for his own company and has directed and choreographed opera productions and television performances, including a widely seen *Nutcracker*. In 2001 the Mark Morris Dance Center opened in Brooklyn, New York, as the troupe's first permanent home in the United States.

Morris, Robert (1734–1806) American (British-born) financier and politician. He emigrated to join his father in Maryland as a boy and entered a Philadelphia mercantile firm in 1748. As a member of the Continental Congress in the AMERICAN REVOLUTION, he raised money to buy supplies for the Continental Army. He served as U.S. superintendent of finance 1781–84, and established the Bank of North America. He was a delegate to the Annapolis Convention and the Constitutional Convention, then served in the U.S. Senate (1789–95). After investing in western land speculation, he went bankrupt and was confined to debtors' prison 1798–1801.

Morris, Robert (born 1931) U.S. artist. His studies took him from his native Kansas City to San Francisco, where he had a one-man exhibition in 1957, and to New York, where he began in 1960 to produce large monochromatic geometric sculptures. From the late 1960s, he experimented with a wide variety of forms, including the "happening," "dispersal pieces" (in which materials were strewn apparently at random on the gallery floor), and environmental sculpture. He is also a prominent exponent of Minimalism, conceptual art, and performance art.

Morris, William (1834–1896) British painter, designer, craftsman, poet, and social reformer, founder of the ARTS AND CRAFTS MOVEMENT. Born into a wealthy family, he studied medieval architecture at Oxford. He was apprenticed to an architect, but visits to Europe turned him toward painting. In 1861, with DANTE GABRIEL ROSSETTI, EDWARD BURNE-JONES, FORD MADOX BROWN, and others, he founded Morris, Marshall, Faulkner & Co., an association of "fine art workmen" based on the medieval guild. They produced furniture, tapestry, stained glass, fabrics, carpets, and most notably wallpaper designs. In 1891 Morris founded the Kelmscott Press, and over the next seven years produced 53 titles in 66 volumes; its *Works of Geoffrey Chaucer* is one of the greatest examples of the art of the printed book. Though he sought to produce fine art objects for the masses, only the rich could afford his expensive handmade products. A utopian socialist, he did much to develop British socialism; in 1884 he formed the Socialist League. In 1877 he founded the Society for the Protection of Ancient Buildings, one of the world's first preservationist groups. He wrote several volumes of poetry and many prose romances, as well as the four-volume epic *Sigurd the Volsung* (1876). His works and writings revolutionized Victorian taste, and he ranks as one of the largest cultural figures of 19th-century Britain.

William Morris, drawing by C.M. Watts.
THE MANSELL COLLECTION

morris dance Ritual folk dance mainly danced in rural England from about the 15th century. The name, a variant of "Moorish," refers to the dancers' blacking their faces as part of the ritual disguise. It is principally a fertility dance, performed especially in the spring. Danced by groups of men often dressed in white and wearing bells on their legs, the steps are varied and intricate and are maintained in a jog-trot while handkerchiefs are waved in both hands. It calls for such individual characters as a hobbyhorse, a fool, and a blackamoor.

Morris Jesup, Cape Cape, in the Peary Land region, northern GREENLAND, on the Arctic Ocean. Situated 440 mi (710 km) from the NORTH POLE, it is the world's most northerly point of land. ROBERT E. PEARY was the first explorer to reach it in 1900; it was named for Morris K. Jesup, a merchant-banker who financed polar expeditions.

Morrison, Jim *orig.* **James Douglas** (1943–1971) U.S. rock singer and songwriter. Born in Melbourne, Fla., the son of a rear admiral, he studied film at UCLA, where he met Ray Manzarek (born 1935); with Robbie Krieger (born 1946) and John Densmore (born 1945), they formed the psychedelic rock group the Doors, taking their name from ALDOUS HUXLEY's *Doors of Perception.* Morrison's haunted voice made the band one of the most popular of the 1960s, with such hits as "Light My Fire" and "Hello I Love You." His drinking and drug use and outrageous stage behavior led to arrests on a variety of charges, including indecent exposure. In 1971 he left the Doors to write poetry and moved to

Paris, where his death of a heart attack at 27 made him a tragic symbol of 1960s youth culture.

Morrison, Toni *orig.* **Chloe Anthony Wofford** (born 1931) U.S. writer. Born in Lorain, Ohio, she studied at Howard and Cornell Univs., taught at various universities, and worked as an editor before publishing *The Bluest Eye* (1970), a novel dealing with some of the shocking realities of the lives of poor blacks, and *Sula* (1973). The brilliant *Song of Solomon* (1977) brought her national attention. Her later novels include *Tar Baby* (1981), *Beloved* (1987, Pulitzer Prize), *Jazz* (1992), and *Paradise* (1998). The African-American experience, particularly that of women, is the principal theme of her fiction, which is enriched by fantasy, myth, and a poetic style. She was awarded the Nobel Prize in 1993.

Morristown National Historical Park Historical park, Morristown, N.J. In the AMERICAN REVOLUTION, the Continental army under GEORGE WASHINGTON had its main winter campsite here in 1776–77 and 1779–80. Established in 1933, the park covers 1,684 acres (682 hectares). It includes the house that served as Washington's headquarters and other artifacts of the Revolution.

Morrow, Dwight W(hitney) (1873–1931) U.S. lawyer and diplomat. Born in Huntington, W.V., he practiced law in New York City (1905–14), helping draft a workers' compensation law (1911). He became a partner in J. P. Morgan & Co. (1914–27) and organized the Kennecott Copper Corp. In World War I he was an adviser on transportation, and after the war he helped devise a national aviation policy. He served as ambassador to Mexico 1927–30. His daughter Anne married CHARLES A. LINDBERGH.

Morse, Carlton E. (1901–1993) U.S. radio writer and producer. Born in Jennings, La., he worked as a newspaper reporter before joining NBC radio as a writer in 1930. He wrote, directed, and produced many radio programs, including the highly popular soap opera *One's Man's Family* (1932–59; television, 1949–52), the drama *I Love a Mystery* (1939–44, 1949–52), and the soap opera *The Woman in My House* (1951–59).

Morse, Samuel F(inley) B(reese) (1791–1872) U.S. painter and inventor. Born in Charlestown, Mass., the son of a distinguished geographer, he attended Yale University and studied painting in England 1811–15. He returned home to work as an itinerant painter; his portraits still rank among the finest produced in the U.S. He cofounded the National Academy of Design and served as its first president (1826–45). Independent of similar efforts in Europe, he developed an electric TELEGRAPH (1832–35), believing his to be the first. He developed the system of dots and dashes that became known internationally as MORSE CODE (1838). Though denied support from Congress for a transatlantic telegraph line, he received congressional support for the first U.S. telegraph line, from Baltimore to Washington; on its completion in 1844 he sent the message "What hath God wrought!" His patents brought him fame and wealth.

Morse code System for representing letters, numerals, and punctuation marks by a sequence of dots, dashes, and spaces. It is transmitted as electrical pulses of varied lengths or analogous mechanical or visual signals, such as flashing lights. The original system was invented by SAMUEL F. B. MORSE in 1838 for his TELEGRAPH; the International Morse Code, a simpler and more precise variant with codes for letters with diacritic marks, was devised in 1851. With minor changes, this code has remained in use for certain types of radiotelegraphy, including amateur radio.

mortar Short-range ARTILLERY piece with a short barrel and low muzzle velocity that fires an explosive projectile in a high-arched trajectory. Large mortars were used against fortifications and in siege operations from medieval times through World War I. Since 1915, small portable models have been standard infantry weapons, especially for mountain or TRENCH WARFARE. Medium mortars, with a caliber of about 3–4 in. (70–90 mm), a range of up to about 2.5 mi (4 km), and a bomb weight of up to 11 lbs (5 kg), are now widely used.

mortar Material used in building construction to bond brick, stone, tile, or concrete blocks into a structure. The ancient Romans are credited with its invention. Mortar consists of sand mixed with cement and water. The resulting substance must be sufficiently flexible to flex slightly but not collapse under the weight of the masonry units. Before the 19th-century invention of PORTLAND CEMENT, masons used thin joints of lime mortar, which required greater precision than the thicker joints of portland-cement mortar and were not as strong. For tilework, a very thin mortar called grout is used. Pointing is the process of finishing a masonry joint.

mortgage In Anglo-American law, the method by which a debtor (mortgagor) conveys an interest in property to a creditor (mortgagee) as security for the payment of a money debt. The modern mortgage has its roots in medieval Europe. Originally, the mortgagor gave the mortgagee ownership of the land on the condition that the mortgagee would return it once the mortgagor's debt was paid off. Over time, it became the practice to let the mortgagor remain in possession of the land; it then became the mortgagor's right to remain in possession of the land so long as there was no default on the debt.

Morton, Earl of *orig.* **James Douglas** (1516?–1581) Scottish nobleman. Appointed chancellor by MARY, QUEEN OF SCOTS, in 1563, he conspired with other Protestant nobles to murder Mary's adviser DAVID RICCIO and probably was involved in the murder of Lord DARNLEY. He led the nobles that drove Mary's husband, the earl of Bothwell, from Scotland and forced her to abdicate in favor of her infant son, James (later JAMES I of England). He became regent for James in 1572 and restored the rule of law to Scotland. Resented by the other nobles, he was forced to resign in 1578; he was later charged with complicity in Darnley's murder and executed.

Morton, Jelly Roll *orig.* **Ferdinand Joseph La Menthe** (1890–1941) U.S. pianist and the first important composer in jazz. Morton was born in New Orleans and was apparently active as a gambler, pool shark, and procurer in his youth. He toured the country as a pianist from 1904, making his first recordings in Chicago in 1923 with his ensemble the Red Hot Peppers. An exponent of the New Orleans tradition, Morton achieved success integrating elements of ragtime with improvised and arranged ensemble passages, often on his own compositions such as "King Porter Stomp." By the early 1930s, Morton's fame had been overshadowed by that of LOUIS ARMSTRONG and other emerging innovators.

Mosaddeq \'mòs-ad-ˌdek\, **Muhammad** (1880–1967) Iranian opposition leader. After law school in Switzerland, he served in the government until R. Shah PAHLAVI became shah (1925). After Pahlavi was deposed in 1941, he was reelected to the parliament (1944). His popularity forced M. R. Shah PAHLAVI to appoint him premier (1951) following Mosaddeq's successful nationalization of the British-owned Anglo-Iranian Oil Co. Tension between the two led to his dismissal, but the resulting unrest sent the shah into exile until Mosaddeq's U.S.-backed opponents could overthrow him and restore the shah (1953). Convicted of treason, he spent three years in prison and the rest of his life under house arrest.

mosaic Surface decoration of small colored components—such as stone, glass, tile, or shell—closely set into an adhesive ground. Mosaic pieces, or tesserae, are usually small squares, triangles, or other regular shapes. Mosaics cannot create the variations of light and shadow that paintings can, but glass tesserae can achieve a greater brilliance, especially those to which gold and silver foil have been applied. This technique was responsible for the great shimmering mosaics of the Byzantine period. The earliest known mosaics date from the 8th century BC and were made of pebbles, a technique refined by the Greeks in the 5th century. The Romans used mosaics widely, particularly for floors. Pre-Columbian Americans favored mosaics of garnet, turquoise, and mother-of-pearl, which usually encrusted shields, masks, and cult statues.

Mosby \'mōz-bē\, **John Singleton** (1833–1916) U.S. guerrilla leader. Born in Edgemont, Va., he joined the Confederate cavalry in the Civil War and was a scout with JEB STUART's troops. He led guerrilla units, called Mosby's Rangers, on raids on Union outposts in northern Virginia and Maryland, disrupting supply and communication lines. His capture of Gen. E. H. Stoughton behind federal lines (1863) earned him promotion to colonel. After the war he resumed his law practice, and he later served as U.S. consul to Hong Kong (1878–85) and as assistant attorney in the U.S. Justice Department (1904–10).

Mosca \'mō-skä\, **Gaetano** (1858–1941) Italian political theorist. Educated at the University of Palermo, he taught constitutional law there (1885–88) and at the Univs. of Rome (1888–96) and Turin (1896–1908). A member of the Italian chamber of deputies from 1908, he was made senator for life by VICTOR EMMANUEL III in 1919. In works such as *Elementi di scienza politica* (1896; *The Ruling Class*) he argued that society has historically and properly been governed by minorities, whether military, religious, oligarchical, or aristocratic.

Mosconi, Willie *orig.* **William Joseph** (1913–1993) U.S. pocket billiards player. Born in Philadelphia, the son of a billiards parlor owner, he began playing professionally in the early 1930s. Known for his accurate rapid-fire shooting, he was world champion 15 times between 1941 and 1957, and once had a run of 526 consecutive balls.

Moscow \'mäs-kō, 'mäs-kau̇\ *Russian* **Moskva** \mȧs-'kvȧ\ Capital and largest city (pop., 2000 est.: 8,369,200) of Russia and the Russian Republic. It is located on both sides of the MOSKVA RIVER, in western Russia, about 400 mi (640 km) southeast of ST. PETERSBURG and about 600 mi (970 km) east of Poland. Inhabited since Neolithic times, the site was first mentioned as a village in 1147 and became the capital of the principality of Moscow (Muscovy) in the late 13th century. It expanded in the 15th–16th century under its grand dukes IVAN III and IVAN IV and became the capital of a united Russia (1547–1712). In 1812 it was occupied by the French under NAPOLEON and almost entirely destroyed by fire. In 1918 it became the capital of the U.S.S.R. and expanded greatly. It suffered much damage from German bombing in World War II. In 1993 it was the scene of armed conflict between opposing government factions after the dissolution of parliament by BORIS YELTSIN. The spiritual home of the Russian Orthodox Church for more than 600 years, it is a political, industrial, transportation, and cultural center. Its most notable structure is the KREMLIN, a medieval fortress on the Moskva, with Red Square along its eastern wall. The Lenin Mausoleum is nearby, and St. Basil's Cathedral is at the southern end of the square. It is also home to the Bolshoi Theater, MOSCOW STATE UNIV., and many other institutions of higher education.

Moscow Art Theatre Russian theater specializing in naturalism, founded in 1898 by KONSTANTIN STANISLAVSKY (as artistic director) and Vladimir Nemirovich-Danchenko (administrative director) with the goal of replacing old-fashioned histrionic acting and heavy-handed staging with a simpler and truer style. It opened with ALEKSEY K. TOLSTOY's *Tsar Fyodor Ioannovich* and won its first major success with ANTON CHEKHOV's *The Seagull*. Along with other plays by Chekhov, the theater mounted new works by writers such as MAXIM GORKY and MAURICE MAETERLINCK. Its company received acclaim on European and U.S. tours in 1922 and influenced later theatrical development worldwide. Since 1939 it has been known as the Moscow Academic Art Theatre.

Moscow River See MOSKVA RIVER

Moscow school School of late-medieval Russian icon and mural painting. It succeeded the NOVGOROD SCHOOL as the dominant school of painting when Moscow rose to a leading position in the movement to expel the Mongols. The school flowered first under the influence of the painter Theophanes the Greek (c. 1330/40–1405), who moved to Moscow from Novgorod c. 1400 and introduced complexity of composition, subtle color, and almost impressionistic rendering of figures. His most distinguished successor was ANDREI RUBLEV. From 1430 to the end of the century, Moscow grew in prestige and sophistication as the Mongols were driven out of Russia. When Constantinople fell to the Turks in 1453, Moscow became the center of EASTERN ORTHODOXY, and the new prestige of the Russian Orthodox Church led to a new didactic iconography that expounded mysteries, rites, and dogma. By the 17th century, the STROGANOV SCHOOL of Moscow artists assumed the leadership of Russian art.

"The Savior," icon painted on panel by Andrei Rublev, Moscow school, 1411; in the State Tretyakov Gallery, Moscow.
NOVOSTI–SOVFOTO

Moscow State University State-operated university in Moscow. Founded in 1755 by the linguist MIKHAIL LOMONOSOV, it is the oldest, largest, and most prestigious university in Russia. By the later 19th century it had established itself as a major center of scientific research and scholarship. It maintained its preeminence following the Russian Revolution, and continued to expand during the Soviet period. It now has more than 350 laboratories, a number of research institutes, several observatories, and various affiliated museums. Its library is one of the largest in the world (8.5 million vols.). Total enrollment is about 28,000.

Moselle River *or* **Mosel River** \mō-'zel, *German* 'mō-zəl\ River, western Europe, about 340 mi (545 km) long. Rising in northeastern France, it flows north, forming part of the border between Germany and Luxembourg, then northeast into the RHINE RIVER at KOBLENZ. In this part of the valley are the vineyards that produce the famous Moselle wines. The river, which is navigable for most of its course, passes Nancy, METZ, and Thionville in France and Trier in Germany. Among its chief tributaries are the ORNE and the SAAR.

Moser-Proell \'mō-zər-'prōl\, **Annemarie** *orig.* **Annemarie Proell** (born 1953) Austrian downhill skier. She began skiing at age 4. She won downhill and slalom silver medals in the 1972 Winter Olympics and a downhill gold medal in 1980. She holds the all-time record of six women's World Cup championships, including five in succession (1971–75). She established a career record for both men and women in individual World Cup races won (59).

Moses (fl. 13th century BC) Prophet of JUDAISM. According to the Book of EXODUS, he was born in Egypt to Hebrew parents, who set him afloat on the Nile in a reed basket to save him from an edict calling for the death of all newborn Hebrew males. Found by the pharaoh's daughter, he was reared in the Egyptian court. After killing a brutal Egyptian taskmaster, he fled to Midian, where Yahweh (God) revealed himself in a burning bush and called Moses to deliver the Israelites from Egypt. With the help of his brother AARON, Moses pleaded with the pharaoh for the Israelites' release. The pharaoh let them go after God had visited a series of plagues on Egypt, but then sent his army after them. God parted the waters of the Red Sea to allow the Israelites to pass, then drowned the pursuing Egyptians. God made a COVENANT with the Israelites at Mount SINAI and delivered the TEN COMMANDMENTS to Moses, who continued to lead his people through 40 years of wandering in the wilderness until they reached the edge of CANAAN. He died before he could enter the Promised Land. Authorship of the first five books of the Bible (see TORAH) is traditionally ascribed to him.

Moses, Edwin (born 1956) U.S. track-and-field athlete. Born in Dayton, Ohio, he went to Morehouse College on an academic scholarship but starred in track. He won the gold medal for the 400-m hurdle in the 1976 and 1984 Olympics and set four successive world records in the event between 1976 and 1983.

Moses, Grandma *orig.* **Anna Mary Robertson** (1860–1961) U.S. naive painter. Born in Greenwich, N.Y., she began to produce embroidery pictures after her husband died in 1927. When arthritis impaired her embroidering, she turned to painting. She had her first exhibition in a drugstore in 1938 at age 78. She went on to produce more than 1,000 nostalgic scenes of turn-of-the-century rural life (e.g., *Catching the Thanksgiving Turkey*, *Over the River to Grandma's House*). By 1939 her pictures were being exhibited internationally, and from 1946 they were regularly reproduced on holiday greeting cards. She died at 101.

Moses, Robert (1888–1981) U.S. public official. Born in New Haven, Conn., he began his long career in public service in New York City's bureau of municipal research. In 1919 Gov. ALFRED E. SMITH appointed him chief of staff of the New York state reconstruction commission and, in 1924, head of both the New York and Long Island state park commissions. For 40 years in these and related positions, Moses supervised the vast expansion of the park system and the construction of numerous roads, bridges, tunnels, and housing projects in and around the city, reshaping it on a grand scale in often controversial ways.

Moses de León *orig.* **Moses ben Shem Tov** (1250–1305) Reputed author of the *SEFER HA-ZOHAR*, the most important work of Jewish mysticism. Little is known of his life, though he is believed to have lived in Guadalajara (the center for Spanish adherents of the Kabbala) until 1290 and later to have traveled widely. He represented the Zohar as an ancient book that he had discovered, but it is more likely a work of his own authorship.

moshav \mō-'shäv\ (Hebrew: "settlement") Israeli cooperative community that combines privately farmed land and communal marketing, sometimes with light industry as well. The land on a moshav belongs to the state or the Jewish National Fund. The first successful moshavim were organized in the 1920s. New immigrants were directed to these settlements in the early years of the Israeli state. See also KIBBUTZ.

Moshoeshoe \mō-ˈshwā-ˌshwā\ *or* **Mshweshwe** \em-ˈshwā-ˌshwā\ (1786?–1870) Founder and first paramount chief of Sotho (later Basutoland; now Lesotho). In the 1830s and '40s he carefully played off British and Boer interests against one another. Involved in a series of wars, he proved a skillful tactician. In 1868 the British annexed Sotho, and Moshoeshoe's power waned. His descendant Moshoeshoe II (1938–1996) was the first king of independent Lesotho.

Moskva River \mäs-ˈkvä\ *or* **Moscow River** River, flowing through Moscow province and part of Smolensk province, western Russia. It is 315 mi (507 km) long and flows through the city of Moscow to join the Oka River just below Kolomna. The river flows southeast through the Volga basin. It is navigable from Moscow and is an important source of the city's water supply.

Mosley, Sir Oswald (Ernald) (1896–1980) English politician and fascist. He served in the House of Commons (1918–31) as, successively, a Conservative, an Independent, and a Labourite. After a visit to Italy, he founded the British Union of Fascists in 1932. With his followers, he distributed anti-Semitic propaganda, conducted hostile demonstrations in the Jewish sections of eastern London, and wore Nazi-style uniforms. During World War II, he was interned (1940–43) with his wife, Diana Guinness, a sister of Jessica and Nancy Mitford and friend of Adolf Hitler. In 1948 Mosley founded the Union Movement, an amalgam of right-wing book clubs.

mosque Islamic public place of prayer. The *masjid jami,* or "collective mosque," is the center of community worship and the site of Friday prayer services. Though the mosque—originally a sacred plot of ground—has been influenced by local architectural styles, the building has remained essentially an open space, usually roofed, with a minaret sometimes attached. Statues and pictures are not permitted as decoration. The *minbar,* a seat at the top of steps placed at the right of the mihrab, is used by the preacher *(khatib)* as a pulpit. Occasionally there is also a *maqsurah,* a box or wooden screen originally used to shield a worshiping ruler from assassins. The minaret, originally any elevated place but now usually a tower, is used by the muezzin (crier) to proclaim the call to worship five times each day. During prayer, Muslims orient themselves toward the Kaaba. See also Islamic architecture.

Mosque of Omar See Dome of the Rock

mosquito Any of 2,500 dipteran species in the family Culicidae. The females of most species require a blood meal to mature their eggs. Through bloodsucking, females of various species (genera *Aedes, Anopheles,* and *Culex*) transmit human diseases, including dengue fever, encephalitis, filariasis, malaria, yellow fever, and elephantiasis. The adult has a long proboscis, a slender, elongated body, and long, fragile legs. The males (and sometimes the females) feed on plant juices. The female's characteristic sound is made by the vibration of thin membranes on the thorax. The females lay their eggs on the surface of a body of usually stagnant water, and the eggs hatch into aquatic larvae (wrigglers). In the far north larvae pass the winter frozen into ice. The wrigglers are eaten by fishes and aquatic insects, the adults by birds and dragonflies. Control measures have included elimination of breeding sites, application of surface films of oil to clog the larvae's breathing tubes, and use of larvicides.

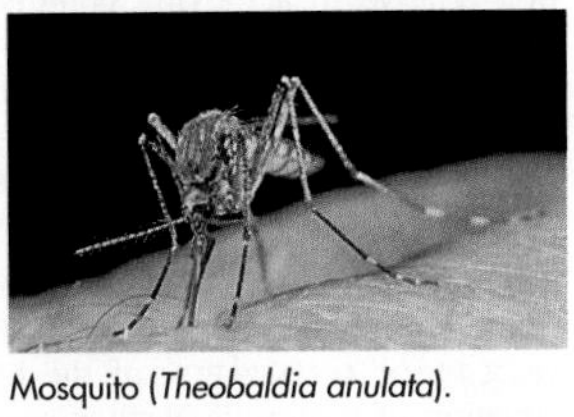
Mosquito (*Theobaldia anulata*).
N.A. CALLOW—EB INC.

Mosquito Coast *or* **Miskito Coast** Region along the coast of eastern Nicaragua and Honduras. It comprises a lowland about 40 mi (65 km) wide that skirts the Caribbean Sea for about 225 mi (360 km). It was visited by Christopher Columbus in 1502, but Europeans had little contact with the area until 1655, when England established a protectorate over the area. It is named for the Miskito Indians. Spain, Nicaragua, and the U.S. disputed England's protectorate until the 1850 Clayton-Bulwer Treaty. In 1894 it was incorporated into Nicaragua, but the northern part was granted to Honduras in 1960 by the International Court of Justice. The chief town is Bluefields, at the mouth of the Escondido River in Nicaragua.

moss Any of at least 10,000 species of small, spore-bearing land plants in the bryophyte division, found worldwide except in salt water since the Permian period (290–248 million years ago). Commonly found in moist, shady locations (e.g., forest floors), mosses may range in size from microscopic forms to plants more than 40 in. (1 m) long. They prevent erosion and release nutrients. The life cycle shows clear alternation of generations between the sexual gametophyte, with stemlike and leaflike structures that produce eggs and swimming sperm, and the sporophyte, a raised stalk that ends in a spore case (sporangium). Mosses also reproduce asexually by branching. The economically important genus *Sphagnum* forms peat. Many so-called mosses are not bryophytes, including Irish moss (a red form of algae); beard moss, Iceland moss, oak moss, and reindeer moss (all lichens); Spanish moss (a name used variously for a lichen or an air plant of the pineapple family); and club moss (an evergreen herb of the family Lycopodiaceae).

Moss, Stirling (born 1929) British Formula One racing driver. He won his first event in 1950 in England and went on to win scores of races, including the British Grand Prix and the Monaco Grand Prix (three times). In 1962 an accident ended his career, and he turned to business, journalism, and broadcasting.

Mossad \mō-ˈsäd\ *Hebrew* **Mossad Merkazi le-Modiin U-letafkidim Meyuhadim ("Central Institute for Intelligence and Security")** Most important of Israel's five major intelligence agencies. It conducts foreign intelligence, espionage, and covert operations abroad; its head reports directly to Israel's prime minister. It enjoys a high international reputation for effectiveness. The secret agents it maintains abroad are credited with the apprehension of Adolf Eichmann, the execution of the killers of Israeli athletes at the 1972 Olympics, and the Israeli success in the Entebbe incident.

Mossi \ˈmō-sē\ People of Burkina Faso and other parts of western Africa who speak Mooré, a Gur language of the Niger-Congo family. Mossi society is organized as in the former Mossi states (c. 1500–1895), being divided into royalty, nobles, commoners, and formerly slaves. The *morho naba* ("big lord") occupies a court in Ouagadougou. In the colonial era the Mossi acted as trading intermediaries between the forest states and the cities of the Niger. Today most of the 5.4 million Mossi are sedentary farmers.

Mossi states Complex of independent western African kingdoms (c. 1500–1895) around the headwaters of the Volta River, within present-day Burkina Faso and Ghana. Though tradition held that their ancestors came from the east, perhaps in the 13th century, the kingdoms' origins are obscure. The Mossi people harassed the empires of Mali and Songhai and vied for control of the Niger River. From c. 1400 the states acted as trading intermediaries between the forest states and the cities of the Niger. They remained independent until the French invasions of the late 19th century.

most-favored-nation treatment Guarantee of same trading opportunities (i.e., tariff concessions) already granted to the most favored nation. It is a method of establishing equal trading opportunities among states by making originally bilateral agreements multilateral. Attempts to guarantee equal trading opportunities were incorporated into commercial treaties as far back as the early 17th century. The Anglo-French treaty signed in 1860 became the model for many later agreements, establishing a set of interlocking tariff concessions (see tariff) later extended worldwide by most-favored-nation treatment. Such treatment has always applied primarily to the duties charged on imports, but specific provisions have extended the principle to other areas of economic contact, including property rights, patents, and copyrights. See also General Agreement on Tariffs and Trade, World Trade Organization.

Mostel \mä-ˈstel\, **Zero** *orig.* **Samuel Joel** (1915–1977) U.S. actor. Born in New York City, he initially worked both on Broadway and in film, but after being blacklisted in Hollywood after 1955, he subsequently worked principally in the New York theater. He gave acclaimed performances in *Ulysses in Nighttown* (1958) and *Rhinoceros* (1961), and had lead roles in the musicals *A Funny Thing Happened on the Way to the Forum* (1962) and *Fiddler on the Roof* (1964). His later films included Mel Brooks's *The Producers* (1968) and *The Front* (1976), a film about the blacklisting era. Mostel was also a serious painter throughout his life.

Mosul \mō-'sül, 'mō-səl\ *Arabic* **Al-Mawsil** \ˌal-maủ-'sēl\ City (pop., 1987: 664,000), northern Iraq. Located across the TIGRIS RIVER from the ruins of ancient NINEVEH, which it succeeded, Mosul prospered until 1258, when it was ravaged by the MONGOLS. It was a center of the OTTOMAN EMPIRE c. 1534–1918. After World War I it was occupied by the British, and in 1926 ceded to Iraq. Iraq's third-largest city and chief commercial center in the northwest, it is a trade center for grain, wool, livestock, and fruit, and has an oil refinery and nearby oil fields. It has many ancient buildings, some dating from the 13th century, including the Great Mosque and the Red Mosque.

Motagua River \mō-'tä-gwä\ River, eastern Guatemala. It is the country's longest river, flowing about 340 mi (550 km) east and northeast into the Gulf of Honduras near the Honduran border. Locally the river is called the Silbapec near its source and the Río Grande farther downstream. It is a major transportation artery for bananas, coffee, and other crops raised in the valleys of its eastern portion.

motel Hotel designed for persons traveling by automobile, with convenient parking space provided (the name blends the words "motor hotel"). Originally usually consisting of a series of separate or attached roadside cabins, motels serve commercial and business travelers and persons attending conventions and business meetings as well as vacationers and tourists. By 1950 the automobile was the principal mode of travel in the U.S., and motels were built near large highways, just as hotels had been built near railroad stations.

motet Latin choral composition, generally in one movement. Its origins are in the 13th century, when words (French, *mots*) began to be added to originally wordless polyphonic lines in settings of plainchant. It grew directly out of the clausula, a polyphonic decoration of a portion of ORGANUM, but soon split off to become a separate composition, while retaining a meaningless fragment of chant text and melody in the tenor part. The upper texts often became a confusing mixture of sacred and secular—and even anticlerical—poems, indicating its intended performance in courtly as well as ecclesiastical settings. The motet was the most important musical genre of the 13th century and an essential vehicle for the development of polyphony. In the Renaissance sacred motets, now employing a single text, were written by such composers as JOSQUIN DES PREZ, ORLANDE DE LASSUS, and W. BYRD, though it remains unclear how often they were performed in church settings. In the 17th–18th century, motets were written by J.-B. LULLY, M.-A. CHARPENTIER, H. SCHUTZ, and J.S. BACH. After c. 1750 the genre declined and its distinguishing characteristics became diffuse.

moth Any of several thousand LEPIDOPTERAN species; found in all but polar habitats. Moths are chiefly nocturnal and have a stouter body, duller coloring, and proportionately smaller wings than BUTTERFLIES. They have distinctive feathery antennae and, when at rest, fold their wings, wrap them around the body, or hold them extended at their sides. Wingspans range from less than an inch to about 1 ft (30 cm). The life cycle has four stages: egg, LARVA (caterpillar, or worm), PUPA (chrysalis), and adult (imago). Both larvae and adults of most species are plant eaters, and many seriously damage forests, agricultural crops, and fabrics. See also BAGWORM MOTH, GYPSY MOTH, HAWK MOTH, LUNA MOTH, MILLER, SATURNIID MOTH, SILKWORM MOTH, TIGER MOTH, TUSSOCK MOTH.

Mother Goose Fictitious old woman, reputedly the source of the body of traditional children's songs and verses known as NURSERY RHYMES. Often pictured as a beak-nosed, sharp-chinned old woman riding on the back of a flying gander, she was first associated with nursery rhymes in *Mother Goose's Melody* (1781), published by the successors of JOHN NEWBERY. The name apparently derived from the title of CHARLES PERRAULT's collection of fairy tales *Ma mère l'oye, or* "My Mother Goose" (1697). The persistent rumor that Mother Goose was an actual Boston woman is false.

Mother Jones See Mary Harris JONES

Mother Lode Country Former gold-rush belt, SIERRA NEVADA foothills, central California. It was about 150 mi (240 km) long, but only a few miles wide. The GOLD RUSH was sparked by the 1848 discovery of placer gold on JOHN SUTTER's property. The term "mother lode" evolved from the miners' concept of one main quartz vein with subsidiary offshoot veins. Exhaustion of the main gold streaks and a government-enforced price structure for gold caused mining operations to cease there in the 1930s. The area is dotted with scores of ghost camps and old mining towns.

Mother's Day and Father's Day U.S. holidays. A nationwide observance of Mother's Day was suggested by Anna Jarvis of Grafton, W.V., and in 1908 formal observances were held in churches in Grafton and Philadelphia. By 1911 every state celebrated the occasion on the second Sunday in May. It was formalized by Congress in 1914. In Britain, Mother's Day is celebrated in mid-Lent as Mothering Sunday. Father's Day was first celebrated in 1910 in Spokane, Wash., through efforts of Sonora Dodd and the YMCA. Celebrated on the third Sunday in June, it was signed into law in 1972.

Motherwell, Robert (1915–1991) U.S. painter, writer, and teacher. Born in Aberdeen, Wash., he received an art scholarship at 11, but he earned degrees from Stanford and Harvard before deciding to become a serious painter. He espoused Abstract Expressionism from the beginning, and his erudite writings were largely responsible for the intellectual tone of the movement. In his *Elegy to the Spanish Republic* series, begun in 1949 and continued over three decades, he developed a limited repertory of simple, serene black forms that were applied to the picture plane in a way that created a sense of slow, solemn movement. Though he worked in various styles, his reputation rests on his pioneering work as a founder and principal exponent of Abstract Expressionism.

Motherwell, photograph by Arnold Newman, 1959.

motion Change in position of a body relative to another body or with respect to a frame of reference or coordinate system. Motion occurs along a definite path, the nature of which determines the character of the motion. Translational motion occurs if all points in a body have similar paths relative to another body. Rotational motion occurs when any line on a body changes its orientation relative to a line on another body. Motion relative to a moving body, such as motion on a moving train, is called relative motion. Indeed, all motions are relative, but motions relative to the earth or to any body fixed to the earth are often assumed to be absolute, as the effects of the earth's motion are usually negligible. See also BROWNIAN MOTION, SIMPLE HARMONIC MOTION, PERIODIC MOTION, SIMPLE MOTION, UNIFORM CIRCULAR MOTION.

motion, equation of Mathematical formula that describes the MOTION of a body relative to a given frame of reference, in terms of the position, VELOCITY, or ACCELERATION of the body. In classical MECHANICS, the basic equation of motion is Newton's second law (see NEWTON'S LAWS OF MOTION), which relates the force on a body to its MASS and ACCELERATION. When the force is described in terms of the time interval over which it is applied, the velocity and position of the body can be derived. Other equations of motion include the position-time equation, the velocity-time equation, and the acceleration-time equation of a moving body.

motion picture *or* **movie** Series of still photographs on film, projected in rapid succession onto a screen. Motion pictures are filmed with a movie camera, which makes rapid exposures of people or objects in motion, and shown with a movie projector, which reproduces sound synchronized with the images. The principal inventors of motion-picture machines were THOMAS ALVA EDISON in the U.S. and the LUMIÈRE brothers in France. Film production was centered in France in the early 20th century, but by 1920 the U.S. had become dominant. As directors and stars moved to HOLLYWOOD, movie studios expanded, reaching their zenith in the 1930s and '40s, when they also typically owned extensive theater chains. Moviemaking was marked by a new internationalism in the 1950s and '60s, which also saw the rise of the independent filmmaker. The sophistication of special effects increased greatly from the 1970s. The U.S. film industry, with its immense technical resources, has continued to dominate the world market to the present day. See also COLUMBIA PICTURES, MGM, PARAMOUNT COMMUNICATIONS, RKO, UNITED ARTISTS, WARNER BROTHERS.

motion sickness Sickness caused by contradiction between external data from the eyes and internal cues from the balance center in the INNER EAR. For example, in seasickness the inner ear senses the ship's motion, but the eyes see the still cabin. This stimulates stress hormones and accelerates stomach-muscle contraction, leading to dizziness, pallor, cold sweat, and nausea and vomiting. Minimizing changes of speed and direction may help, as may reclining, not turning the head, closing the eyes, or focusing on distant objects. Drugs can prevent or relieve motion sickness but may have side effects. Pressing an ACUPUNCTURE point on the wrist helps some people.

motion study See TIME-AND-MOTION STUDY

motivation Factors within a human being or animal that arouse and direct goal-oriented behavior. Motivation has long been a central subject of study in psychology. Early researchers, influenced by CHARLES DARWIN, ascribed much of animal and human behavior to INSTINCT. SIGMUND FREUD believed that much of human behavior was also based on irrational instinctive urges or unconscious motives. WALTER B. CANNON proposed that basic human drives served homeostatic functions by directing energies toward the reduction of physiological tensions. Behavioral psychologists, in contrast, stress the importance of external goals in prompting action, while humanistic psychologists examine the role of felt needs. Cognitive psychologists have found that a motive sensitizes a person to information relating to that motive: a hungry subject, for example, will perceive food stimuli as larger than other stimuli. See also BEHAVIOR GENETICS, HUMAN NATURE, LEARNING.

Motley, Marion (1920–1999) U.S. football player. Born in Leesburg, Ga., he played fullback and linebacker for South Carolina State University and the University of Nevada. In 1946 he helped desegregate professional football by joining the Cleveland Browns as a fullback, establishing himself as a leading rusher and helping the Browns to five consecutive league championships (All-American Football Conference, 1946–49; NFL, 1950).

motocross Form of motorcycle racing in which cyclists compete on a closed course marked out over natural or simulated rough terrain. Courses vary widely but must be 1.5–5 km (1–3 mi) in length, with steep inclines, hairpin turns, and mud. Motorcycles are grouped into classes according to engine displacement (e.g., 125-, 250-, 500-cc). It is probably the most physically demanding motorcycle sport.

Motocross racing.
KINNEY JONES

Motoori Norinaga \,mō-tō-'ō-rē-,nō-rē-'nä-gä\ (1730–1801) Japanese Shinto scholar. Trained as a physician, he came under the influence of the Kokugaku movement, which stressed the importance of Japan's literary heritage. The critical methods he used in his commentaries on Japanese classics provided the theoretical foundation of the modern Shinto revival. Rejecting Buddhist and Confucian interpretations, he traced the genuine spirit of Shinto to Japanese myths and sacred traditions. He reaffirmed the ancient Japanese concept of *musubi* (the mysterious power of all creation and growth), which has become one of the main tenets of modern Shinto.

motorcycle Bicycle or tricycle propelled by an INTERNAL COMBUSTION ENGINE. The first motor tricycle was built in 1884 in England, and the first gasoline-engine motorcycle was built by GOTTLIEB DAIMLER in 1885. Motorcycles were widely used after 1910, especially by the armed forces in World War I. After 1950 a larger, heavier motorcycle was used mainly for touring and sport competitions. The moped, a light, low-speed motor bicycle that can also be pedaled, was developed mainly in Europe, and the sturdier Italian-made motor scooter also became popular for its economy.

motorcycle racing Sport of running motorcycles on tracks, closed circuits, or natural terrain. The main types are (1) road racing, conducted on a course made up wholly or partly of public roads; (2) trials, conducted both on and off the highway; (3) speedway racing, conducted on a short, flat, oval dirt track; (4) drag racing, conducted on a straight quarter-mile strip of pavement; (5) hill climbs, conducted on a large dirt mound; and (6) MOTOCROSS. The first international road race took place in Douran, France, in 1905. The most famous race is the Tourist Trophy, established on Britain's Isle of Man in 1907. Motorcycle racing in North America began in 1903; since 1937 the Daytona 200-mi (320-km) race has been the leading U.S. race.

Motorola, Inc. U.S. manufacturer of wireless communications, electronic systems, and semiconductors. The company, headquartered in Schaumburg, Ill., was founded in 1928 in Chicago by brothers Paul and Joseph Galvin as the Galvin Manufacturing Corp. In 1930 the company began selling a low-cost automobile radio, called the Motorola. In 1947 the company changed its name to Motorola, and the next year it introduced a television set. Motorola licensed the design for transistors from Bell Laboratories in 1952 and began to sell them to other manufacturers in 1956. By 1962 the company had more than 4,000 different electronic components on the market. In 1974 Motorola released its first microprocessor for sale to computer makers. In 1993 the company developed the first consumer RISC (reduced-instruction-set computing) chip, the PowerPC, with IBM Corp. and Apple Computer, Inc. In the market for embedded microprocessors—ubiquitous in such common items as kitchen appliances, pagers, video games, and handheld personal computers—Motorola became the leading manufacturer. Motorola was also a leader in the development of cellular telephone systems. In 1989 the company introduced the MicroTAC flip phone, which quickly became an international status symbol.

Motown First large black-owned music company in the U.S., the originator of a regional variant of black popular music that achieved enormous popularity in the 1960s. It was founded in Detroit in 1959 by the songwriter Berry Gordy, Jr. (born 1929). (Motown, a contraction of "Motortown," refers to Detroit's automotive industry.) It scored its first nationwide hits with "Shop Around" (1960) by the Miracles (see S. ROBINSON) and "Please Mr. Postman" (1961) by the Marvelettes. Its roster soon included the Temptations, the Four Tops, the SUPREMES, Marvin Gaye, and S. WONDER, who, with the songwriting teams Holland-Dozier-Holland (see BRIAN AND EDDIE HOLLAND) and Nick Ashford and Valerie Simpson, helped create the "Motown sound," which typically featured lyrical ballads sung to an infectiously rhythmic accompaniment. Later Motown names included the Isley Brothers, Gladys Knight and the Pips, and, in 1969, the Jackson Five (see MICHAEL JACKSON). Motown continued to produce best-selling recordings by new artists such as Lionel Ritchie into the 1980s. Gordy moved the company headquarters to Los Angeles in 1971, and finally sold the label to MCA in 1988.

Mott, Lucretia *orig.* **Lucretia Coffin** (1793–1880) U.S. social reformer and women's-rights advocate. Born in Nantucket, Mass., she attended a Quaker boarding school near Poughkeepsie, N.Y., where she later taught. In 1811 she married a fellow teacher, James Mott, and she became an official Quaker minister in 1821. The Motts were active in the antislavery campaign, and Lucretia lectured widely on social reform. In 1848 she and ELIZABETH CADY STANTON organized the SENECA FALLS CONVENTION, and she thereafter devoted her attention primarily to women's rights, writing articles and lecturing widely. After the Civil War, she also worked for voting rights for freedmen.

Moultrie \'mül-trē, 'mōl-trē\, **William** (1730–1805) American Revolutionary officer. Born in Charleston, S.C., he served in the provincial assembly (1752–62) and gained military experience fighting the Cherokee. In the American Revolution he took command of a log fort on Sullivan's Island in Charleston harbor, where he repulsed a British attack in 1776. The fort was named in his honor and he was made a brigadier general. He fought the British at Beaufort, S.C. (1779), but surrendered with the fall of Charleston (1780). He later served as governor of South Carolina (1785–87, 1792–94).

Mound Builders See HOPEWELL CULTURE

Mount, William Sidney (1807–1868) U.S. painter. Born in Setauket, Long Island, N.Y., he was apprenticed at 17 to his older brother as a sign painter. After studying drawing at the National Academy of Design, he painted historical subjects, but he later turned to genre painting and achieved immediate success with such works as *Rustic Dance After a Sleigh Ride* (1830). His portrayals of country life, affectionate and humorous without being sentimental, are a valuable record of his time. He was one of the first and most notable U.S. genre painters.

Mount Aspiring National Park Park, southwestern South Island, New Zealand. Established in 1964, it has an area of 1,223 sq mi (3,167 sq km), including much of the Southern Alps and Mount Aspiring (9,932 ft, or 3,027 m). Its southern boundary is Fiordland National Park. Its landscape is varied, including glaciers, mountains, gorges, waterfalls, and passes, and it is the source of headwaters of seven major rivers. Birds common in the park include the tui, bellbird, fantail, and gray warbler.

Mount Cook National Park Park, western central South Island, New Zealand. Established in 1953, it has an area of 270 sq mi (700 sq km) and shares a western boundary with Westland National Park. It extends along the crest of the Southern Alps. There are some 27 peaks higher than 10,000 ft (3,000 m) in the park, including Mount Cook, the highest point in New Zealand at 12,349 ft (3,764 m). More than one-third of the park is covered by permanent snow and glacial ice.

Mount Holyoke College Private liberal-arts college for women in South Hadley, Mass. Founded by Mary Lyon as a female seminary in 1837, it was one of the first institutions of higher education for women in the U.S. Baccalaureate courses are taught in the humanities, science and mathematics, and social sciences. Mount Holyoke is part of an educational exchange program with Amherst, Hampshire, and Smith colleges and the University of Massachusetts. Enrollment is about 2,000.

Mount of Olives See Mount of Olives

Mount Vernon Home and burial place of George Washington. It is located in northern Virginia, on the Potomac River near Washington, D.C. The estate was inherited by Washington in 1751. Near the 18th-century Georgian mansion is a plain brick tomb, built at Washington's direction, that holds his and his wife's remains. After the U.S. government declined to buy it, in 1858 the Mount Vernon Ladies' Association of the Union raised $200,000 and purchased the house and 200 acres (80 hectares) of the estate; the association still maintains the site.

Mount Wilson Observatory Astronomical observatory located atop Mount Wilson, near Pasadena, Cal. Founded in 1904 by George Ellery Hale (1868–1938), it was operated jointly with the Palomar Observatory as the Hale Observatories 1948–80. Its optical telescope, with a diameter of 100 in. (2.5 m), enabled Edwin Hubble and his associates to discover evidence of an expanding universe and to estimate its size.

mountain Landform that rises well above its surroundings, generally exhibiting steep slopes, a relatively confined summit area, and considerable local relief (inequalities of elevation). Mountains are considered larger than hills, but the term has no standardized geologic meaning. Mountains are formed by the folding, faulting, or upwarping of the earth's surface due to the movement of plates (see plate tectonics) or by the emplacement of volcanic rock onto the surface. For example, the Himalayan Mountains where India meets the Eurasian Plate were formed by a collision between plates that caused extreme compressional folding and the uplifting of large areas. The mountain ranges around the Pacific basin are attributed to the sinking of one plate beneath another. See also plateau.

mountain ash Any of several shrubs or trees of the genus *Sorbus*, in the rose family, native to the Northern Hemisphere. They are widely cultivated as ornamentals for their white flower clusters and bright-orange fruits. Most noteworthy are the handsome American mountain ash, or dogberry *(S. americana)*, and European mountain ash *(S. aucuparia)*, also called rowan, or quickbeam. The European species grows to 60 ft (18 m), twice as high as the American species.

mountain goat *or* **Rocky Mountain goat** Ruminant (bovid species *Oreamnos americanus*) of the Yukon to the northern Rockies that is more closely related to antelopes than to goats. Stocky, with a hump at the withers, mountain goats stand about 40 in. (1 m) at the shoulder. Both sexes bear short, hollow, slightly backward-curving, black horns. The shaggy, coarse white hair covers a thick, woolly underfur, and a beard frames the slender muzzle. The hooves are black. Mountain goats are agile climbers and can leap more than 12 ft (3.5 m). They live in small bands above the timberline, eating moss, lichen, and scrub foliage.

Mountain goat (*Oreamnos americanus*).
EARL KUBIS—ROOT RESOURCES

mountain laurel Flowering evergreen shrub *(Kalmia latifolia)* of the heath family, occurring in most mountainous regions of eastern North America. It grows to about 3–18 ft (1–6 m) in height and has oval leaves. The rosy, pink, or white flowers appear in large clusters above the foliage. The shrub is popular in landscape plantings.

mountain lion See cougar

mountain sheep See bighorn

mountaineering *or* **mountain climbing** Sport of scaling mountains. It is a group activity, with each member both supporting and supported by the group's efforts. Its pleasures lie not only in the conquest of the peak but also in the physical and spiritual satisfactions brought about through intense personal effort, ever-increasing proficiency, and contact with natural grandeur. The greater rewards do not come without considerable risk and danger. The first great peak ascended in modern times was Mont Blanc, in 1786. Other Alpine peaks followed, capped by the ascent of the Matterhorn in 1865. By the 1910s, most peaks of the Andes, the Rockies, and other Western Hemisphere ranges had been climbed, including Mount McKinley (1913). Beginning in the 1930s a series of successful ascents of mountains in the Himalayas occurred, culminating in the 1953 ascent of Mount Everest by Edmund Hillary and Tenzing Norgay. In the 1960s mountaineering became an increasingly technical sport, emphasizing the use of specialized anchoring, tethering, and grappling gear in the ascent of vertical rock or ice faces.

Mountbatten, Louis *later* **Earl Mountbatten (of Burma)** *orig.* **Louis Francis Albert Victor Nicholas, Prince of Battenberg** (1900–1979) British statesman and naval commander. Son of Prince Louis of Battenberg and great-grandson of Queen Victoria, he was born in England and entered the Royal Navy in 1913, becoming an aide to the Prince of Wales in 1921. In World War II he was allied commander for S.East Asia (1943–46) and directed the recapture of Burma. Appointed viceroy of India (1947), he administered the transfer of power from Britain to the independent nations of India and Pakistan and served as the first governor-general of India 1947–48. He became first sea lord (1955–59) and chief of the United Kingdom Defense Staff (1959–65). In 1979, while on a sailing visit to Ireland, he was assassinated by Irish terrorists who planted a bomb on his boat.

Mountbatten family See Battenberg family

Mounties See Royal Canadian Mounted Police

mourning dove Species *(Zenaida macroura)* of pigeon (family Columbidae), the common wild pigeon of North America. They have long, pointed tails, and the sides of the neck are violet and pink. Their name comes from their call's haunting, mournful tone. Mourning doves are migratory; the northernmost populations migrate the farthest south. They are popular game birds. See also dove.

Mourning dove (*Zenaida macroura*).
ALVIN E. STAFFAN—THE NATIONAL AUDUBON SOCIETY COLLECTION/PHOTO RESEARCHERS

mouse Any of many species (family Muridae) of small, scampering rodents. They are distinguished from rats principally by their smaller size. Mice are basically Asian in origin, but species have been introduced worldwide. Species in other rodent families (e.g., deer mouse, pocket mouse) are called mice without scientific basis. Mice eat grains, roots, fruit, grass, and insects. They can become pests but are mostly beneficial; they are the main prey of most furbearers and of predators

House mouse (*Mus musculus*).
INGMAR HOLMASEN

that might otherwise take more valuable prey. The white laboratory mouse is a form of HOUSE MOUSE. See also FIELD MOUSE.

mouse Hand-controlled electromechanical device for interacting with a DIGITAL COMPUTER that has a GRAPHICAL USER INTERFACE. The mouse can be moved around on a flat service to control the movement of a cursor on the computer display screen. Equipped with one or more buttons, it can be used to select text, activate programs, or move items around the screen by quickly pressing and releasing one of the buttons ("clicking") or by keeping a button depressed while moving the device ("clicking and dragging").

mouse deer See CHEVROTAIN

Mousterian industry \mü-'stir-ē-ən\ Tool culture traditionally associated with the NEANDERTHALS in Europe, western Asia, and northern Africa during the early Fourth (Würm) Glacial Period (c. 40,000 BC). The Mousterian tool assemblage included small hand axes made from disk-shaped cores; flake tools such as scrapers and points; toothed, sawlike instruments produced by making notches in a flake; and round limestone balls, believed to have served as bolas. Wooden spears were used to hunt large game such as the MAMMOTH and woolly rhinoceros. Mousterian implements disappeared abruptly from Europe with the passing of the Neanderthals.

mouth *or* **oral cavity** *or* **buccal cavity** \'bək-əl\ Orifice through which food and air enter the body. It opens to the outside at the lips and empties into the throat at the rear and is bounded by the lips, cheeks, hard and soft PALATES, and glottis. Its chief structures are the teeth (see TOOTH), TONGUE, and PALATE. It is the site of CHEWING and SPEECH formation. The mouth is lined by mucous membranes containing small GLANDS that, along with the SALIVARY GLANDS, keep it moist and clear of food and other debris.

mouth organ See HARMONICA

mouth-to-mouth resuscitation See ARTIFICIAL RESPIRATION

movie See MOTION PICTURE

Moyers, Bill D(on) (born 1934) U.S. journalist. Born in Hugo, Okla., he originally trained for the ministry. He served as special assistant and press secretary to Pres. LYNDON B. JOHNSON 1963–67. He created and hosted the public-affairs program *Bill Moyers' Journal* on public television (1971–76, 1978–81) and later served as a news analyst for CBS News (1981–86). He formed Public Affairs TV, Inc., in 1987, producing such television specials and series as *A World of Ideas* (1989), *Healing and the Mind* (1990), and *Genesis* (1996), and numerous best-selling books derived from them. He has won more than 30 Emmy awards for his programs, among many other awards.

Moyle District (pop., 1999 est.: 15,400), Northern Ireland. It stretches along the northern coast of Ireland and includes Rathlin Island and part of the Antrim Mountains. A cave on Rathlin Island is said to have been the hiding place of ROBERT I in 1306. BALLYCASTLE is Moyle's administrative seat. The Giant's Causeway, along the coastal cliffs, and five of the nine Glens of Antrim are in Moyle.

Moynihan, Berkeley George Andrew *later* **Baron Moynihan (of Leeds)** (1865–1936) British surgeon and teacher of medicine. He wrote or cowrote authoritative monographs on surgery to treat diseases of various abdominal organs, as well as *Abdominal Operations* (1905), a standard text for two decades, and *Duodenal Ulcer* (1910), which secured his reputation as a clinical scientist. He stressed obtaining medical evidence from living bodies on the operating table rather than from autopsies. He helped found the *British Journal of Surgery* (1913) and organizations to promote nationwide and international communication among surgeons and specialists. He was raised to the peerage in 1929.

Moynihan, Daniel Patrick (born 1927) U.S. scholar and politician. Born in Tulsa, Okla., he grew up in poverty in New York City. He received his doctorate from Tufts University and worked in New York state government in the 1950s and in the U.S. Labor Department 1961–65, where he cowrote a controversial report on the urban American black family. He taught at Harvard 1966–77 and held advisory posts in RICHARD NIXON's administration. He was ambassador to India 1973–75, and U.S. representative to the U.N. 1975–76. As a Democrat in the U.S. Senate (1977–2001), he was a liberal advocate for social reform. In 2000 he received the Presidential Medal of Freedom.

Mozambique \ˌmō-zäm-'bēk\ *officially* **Republic of Mozambique** *formerly* **Portuguese East Africa** Nation, southeastern coast of Africa. Area: 297,846 sq mi (771,421 sq km). Population (2002 est.): 18,082,000. Capital: MAPUTO. About half the people are Bantu-speaking Africans. Ethnolinguistic groups include the Makua, Tsonga, Malawi, Shona, and YAO peoples. Languages: Portuguese (official), BANTU, SWAHILI. Religions: traditional beliefs, Christianity, Islam. Currency: metical. Mozambique may be divided into two broad regions: the lowlands in the south and the highlands in the north, separated by the ZAMBEZI RIVER. It has a centrally planned, developing economy based on agriculture, international trade, and light industries. Several industries were national-

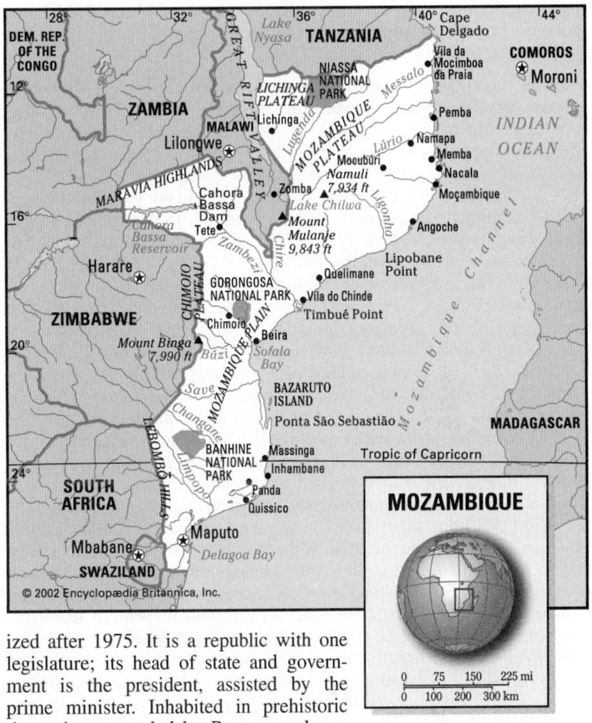

ized after 1975. It is a republic with one legislature; its head of state and government is the president, assisted by the prime minister. Inhabited in prehistoric times, it was settled by Bantu peoples c. 3rd century AD. Arab traders occupied the coastal region from the 14th century, and the Portuguese controlled the area from the early 16th century. The slave trade later became an important part of the economy. Outlawed in the mid-18th century, it continued illegally. In the late 19th century private trading companies began to administer parts of the inland areas. It became an overseas province of Portugal in 1951. An independence movement became active in the 1960s, and after years of war, the country was granted independence in 1975. A single-party state under the Frelimo, or Mozambique Liberation Front party, it was wracked by civil war in the 1970s and 1980s. In 1990 a new constitution ended its Marxist collectivism and introduced privatization, a market economy, and multiparty government. A peace treaty was signed with the rebels in 1992.

Mozambique Channel Strait, western Indian Ocean. Located between Madagascar and Mozambique, it is about 950 mi (1,530 km) long, 250–625 mi (400–1,000 km) wide, and has a maximum depth of 10,000 ft (3,000 m). An important shipping route for eastern Africa, it receives all major Madagascar rivers and fronts the ports of Mahajanga and Toliara in Madagascar. Along the Mozambican coast are the mouth of the ZAMBEZI RIVER and the ports of MAPUTO and BEIRA.

Mozarabic architecture \mō-'zar-ə-bik\ Building style of Christians who stayed in the Iberian Peninsula after the Arab invasion of 711. The style shows the assimilation of such Islamic decorative motifs and forms as the horseshoe-shaped arch and the ribbed dome. Even those who emigrated to non-Islamic areas continued to produce Mozarabic-style art and architecture, thereby helping spread Arabic influences north into Europe. Many churches built in the Mozarabic style by monks who emigrated to northern Spain (9th–11th century) survive. San Miguel de Escalada, near León, the largest surviving example of Mozarabic architecture, was founded by monks from Córdoba and consecrated in 913. See also MOZARABIC ART.

Mozarabic art \mō-ˈzar-ə-bik\ Architecture and religious arts of the Mozarabs, Christians who lived in the Iberian Peninsula after the Arab invasion of 711. Exposure of the conquered Christians to Islamic culture and art forms proved influential, and their art became a synthesis of the two traditions. The subject matter is Christian, but the style shows the assimilation of Islamic decorative motifs and forms. Islamic influence is seen especially in Mozarabic architecture, with its horseshoe-shaped arches and ribbed domes. Through the emigration of Mozarabs, Islamic influence in the arts spread northward into the rest of Europe. See also MOZARABIC ARCHITECTURE.

Mozart \ˈmōt-ˌsärt\, **Wolfgang Amadeus** *orig.* **Joannes Chrysostomus Wolfgangus Theophilus Mozart** (1756–1791) Austrian composer. Son of the violinist and composer Leopold Mozart (1719–1787), he was born the year of the publication of Leopold's best-selling treatise on violin playing. He and his older sister, Maria Anna (1751–1829), were prodigies; by age 4, Wolfgang was playing Nannerl's keyboard lessons without instruction. At 5 he began to compose and gave his first public performance. From 1762 Leopold toured throughout Europe with them, showing off the "miracle that God allowed to be born in Salzburg." The first round of touring (1762–69) took them as far as France and England, where Wolfgang met J.C. BACH and wrote his first symphonies (1764). Tours of Italy followed (1769–74); there he first saw the string quartets of F.J. HAYDN and wrote his own first Italian opera. In 1775–77 he composed his violin concertos and his first piano sonatas. In 1777 he met the Webers, the family of his future wife. His mother died in 1779. He returned to Salzburg as cathedral organist and in 1781 wrote his opera seria *Idomeneo.* Chafing under the archbishop's rule, he was released from his position in 1781 and moved in with the Webers, now in Vienna, to begin his independent career. He married Constanze Weber, gave piano lessons, and wrote *The Abduction from the Seraglio* (1782) and many of his great piano concertos. The later 1780s saw the height of his success, with the string quartets dedicated to Haydn (who called Mozart the greatest living composer), the three great operas on L. DA PONTE's librettos—*The Marriage of Figaro* (1786), *Don Giovanni* (1787), and *Così fan tutte* (1790)—and his superb late symphonies. In his last year he composed the opera *The Magic Flute* and his great *Requiem* (left unfinished). Despite his success, he always lacked money (possibly because of gambling debts and a fondness for fine clothes) and had to borrow heavily from friends. His death at 35 may have resulted from a kidney infection. No other composer left such an extraordinary legacy in so short a lifetime.

Mozi *or* **Mo-tzu** \ˈmō-ˈdzə̄\ (470?–391? BC) Chinese philosopher. Originally a follower of CONFUCIUS, Mozi evolved a doctrine of universal love that gave rise to a religious movement called Mohism. Like Confucius, he spent much of his life traveling from one feudal state to another in search of a prince who would allow him to put his teachings into practice. The *Mozi,* the principal Mohist work, condemned offensive war and urged people to lead a simple life harmful to none. Mohism won a considerable body of followers, but it died out after the 2nd century BC.

MP3 Standard technology and format for the compression of audio signals into very small computer files. For example, sound data from a COMPACT DISK (CD) can be compressed to one-twelfth the original size without sacrificing sound quality. Because of their small file size and ease of production from CD sources, MP3 files have become the most popular type of sound files on the Internet. Recording companies now provide sample songs in MP3 format to promote CD sales, and some musicians bypass recording companies and issue their songs in MP3 format only.

MRI See MAGNETIC RESONANCE IMAGING

MS See MULTIPLE SCLEROSIS

MS-DOS \ˌem-ˌes-ˈdȯs\ *in full* **Microsoft Disk Operating System.** OPERATING SYSTEM for PERSONAL COMPUTERS. MS-DOS was based on DOS, developed in 1980 by Seattle Computer Products. MICROSOFT CORP. bought the rights to DOS in 1981, and released MS-DOS with IBM's PC that year. Thereafter, most manufacturers of personal computers licensed MS-DOS as their operating system; by the early 1990s more than 100 million copies had been sold. WINDOWS, a GRAPHICAL USER INTERFACE program based on MS-DOS, became a popular alternative with the release of Verson 3.0 in 1990; Windows 95 fully integrated the operating system and the graphical interface.

MSG See MONOSODIUM GLUTAMATE

Mshweshwe See MOSHOESHOE

MTV *in full* **Music Television** U.S. cable television network, established in 1980 to present videos of musicians and singers performing new rock music. MTV won a wide following among rock-music fans worldwide and greatly affected the popular-music business. Soon virtually every major pop or rock performer was making videos to be shown on MTV, and the reception of their videos directly affected future sales. MTV is controlled by the media conglomerate Viacom Inc.

Muawiyah I \mu̇-ˈä-wē-yə\, **al-** (602?–680) First CALIPH (661–80) of the UMAYYAD DYNASTY. Born into a clan that rejected MUHAMMAD, he converted only after Muhammad had conquered Mecca. As governor of Damascus he built up the Syrian army until it was strong enough to resist Byzantine attacks. Opposed to ALI's caliphate, he eventually overthrew Ali and, as commander of the largest Muslim military force, became CALIPH. To win the loyalty of non-Syrian Arabs, he introduced methods by which the tribes could keep the caliph informed of their interests. He channeled tribal aggressiveness into anti-Byzantine campaigns, and in North Africa captured Tripolitania and Ifriqiyah. To administer his large empire, he adopted Roman and Byzantine procedures, employing Christians whose families had served in Byzantine governments. By securing his son as his successor, he established hereditary rule. Though disliked by pious Muslim historians for deviating from Muhammad's leadership style and by Shiites for his role in Ali's death, he is praised in Arabic literature as the ideal ruler. See also AMR IBN AL-AS, FITNAH, HUSAYN IBN ALI, Battle of KARBALA.

Hosni Mubarak, 1982.
BARRY IVERSON/GAMMA

Mubarak \mu̇-ˈbä-räk\, **Hosni** (born 1928) President of Egypt (from 1981). He attended a Soviet air academy, and as air-force commander (from 1972) he planned Egypt's opening moves in the 1973 ARAB-ISRAELI WAR. Named vice president in 1975, he became president on ANWAR AL-SADAT's assassination in 1981. He has maintained relations with Israel while working to restore Egypt to its traditional position as the most influential of the Arab states. Islamic fundamentalism in the 1990s weakened his power base.

"Cycles Perfecta," poster by Alphonse Mucha to advertise an English brand of bicycle, 1902.
POSTERS PLEASE, INC.

Mucha \ˈmu̇-k̲ä\, **Alphonse** *orig.* **Alfons Maria** (1860–1939) Czech painter and designer. After study in Prague, Munich, and Paris, he became the principal designer of posters advertising the stage appearances of SARAH BERNHARDT; he designed sets and costumes for her as well. His many opulent posters and magazine illustrations made him one of the foremost designers in the ART NOUVEAU style. In 1922, after Czechoslovakia had become independent, he settled in Prague and designed the new republic's stamps and banknotes.

muckraker Any of a group of U.S. writers identified with pre-

World War I reform and exposé literature. The term, first used derisively, originated in an allusion THEODORE ROOSEVELT made in 1906 to a passage in JOHN BUNYAN's *Pilgrim's Progress* about a man with a muckrake who "could look no way but downward." Later it took on favorable connotations of social concern and exposure of injustice. The movement emerged from the YELLOW JOURNALISM of the 1890s and from popular magazines, such as a 1903 issue of *McClure's Magazine* with articles by LINCOLN STEFFENS, Ray Stannard Baker, and IDA TARBELL on municipal government, labor, and trusts. The best-known muckraking novel is UPTON SINCLAIR's *The Jungle* (1906).

mucoviscidosis See CYSTIC FIBROSIS

mudang \'mü-ˌdäŋ\ In Korean religion, a priestess who effects cures, tells fortunes, soothes spirits of the dead, and wards off evil. Her male counterpart is called a *paksu*. The principal occasion for a performance by a mudang is the *kut,* a trance ritual in which singing and dancing invite happiness and repel evil. The *kut* addresses a series of gods or spirits, such as the gods of childbirth, harvest, and households. After an altar is set on the floor and offerings are made, the mudang goes into a trance, during which the god is said to arrive, to be placated, and then to communicate a message intended for the client.

Mudejars \mu̇-'th̲ā-härz\ (from Arabic *mudajjan:* "permitted to remain") Muslims who remained in Spain after the Christian reconquest of the Iberian Peninsula (11th–15th century). In return for payment of a tax, the Mudejars were a protected minority, allowed to keep their religion, language, and customs. They formed separate communities in larger towns, where they were subject to their own Muslim laws. By the 13th century they had begun to use Spanish, which they wrote in Arabic characters. After 1492 they were forced to leave Spain or convert to Christianity, and by the early 17th century more than 3 million Spanish Muslims had been expelled.

mudflow Flow of water that contains large amounts of suspended particles and silt. Mudflows usually occur on steep slopes where vegetation is too sparse to prevent rapid erosion, but they can also occur on gentle slopes under certain conditions. Factors other than slope include heavy precipitation in a short period and easily erodible material.

Mudge, Thomas (1717–1794) British watchmaker. In 1765 he invented the lever escapement, the most dependable and widely used device for regulating the movement of the spring-driven WATCH. He later worked to improve the marine CHRONOMETER.

mudor suan \mü-'dōr-shü-'än\ Ceremony in which the Votyaks or Udmurts (peoples of the Ural Mtns.) consecrated a new family or clan shrine when the ancestral home was too small to accommodate all its members and a new site had to be blessed. The main ceremony consisted of taking ashes from the hearth of the ancestral shrine *(kuala)* and transferring them to the shrine at the new location, which was then considered a subsidiary of the ancestral *kuala*.

mudra \mu̇-'drä\ In BUDDHISM and HINDUISM, a symbolic gesture of the hands and fingers used in ceremonies, dance, sculpture, and painting. Hundreds of mudras are used in ceremony and dance, often in combination with movements of the wrists, elbows, and shoulders. In ceremonies, especially in Buddhism, a mudra acts as a kind of seal, affirming a mystical or magical vow or utterance, such as a prayer to ward off evil. A mudra often accompanies the utterance of a MANTRA.

mufti \'mu̇f-tē\ Islamic legal authority charged with issuing an opinion *(fatwa)* in answer to an inquiry by a judge or a private individual. Such a judgment requires extensive knowledge of the QURAN and the HADITH as well as of legal precedents. During the Ottoman empire the mufti of Istanbul was Islam's chief legal authority, presiding over the whole judicial and theological hierarchy. The development of modern legal codes in Islamic countries has significantly reduced the authority of mufti, and they now deal only with questions of personal status such as inheritance, marriage, and divorce.

Mugabe \mu̇-'gä-bā**, Robert (Gabriel)** (born 1924) First prime minister (1980–87) and executive president (from 1987) of Zimbabwe. With JOSHUA NKOMO, Mugabe led a Marxist-inspired guerrilla war that forced the white-dominated government of IAN SMITH to accept universal elections, which Mugabe's party, Zimbabwe African National Union (ZANU), easily won. He formed a coalition government with Nkomo's Zimbabwe African People's Union (ZAPU), but removed Nkomo in 1982. In 1984 the two parties were merged as ZANU–Patriotic Front, as Mugabe moved to convert Zimbabwe from a parliamentary democracy into a one-party socialist state. His rule has been marked by a struggle to balance the needs of Zimbabwe's dwindling population of white farmers and businessmen with those of black Zimbabweans, and by a decreasing tolerance of political opposition.

Muggeridge, Malcolm (Thomas) (1903–1990) British writer and social critic. A lecturer in Cairo in the late 1920s, he worked for newspapers in the 1930s before serving in British intelligence during World War II. He then resumed his journalistic career, including a stint as editor of *Punch* (1953–57). An outspoken and controversial iconoclast, he targeted liberalism and other aspects of contemporary life with his stinging wit and elegant prose. He was early an avowed atheist but moved gradually to embrace Roman Catholicism. He wrote some 30 books, including satiric novels and religious accounts, and from the 1950s was a popular interviewer, panelist, and documentarian on British television.

Mughal architecture \'mü-gəl\ Building style that flourished in India under the Mughal emperors from the mid-16th to the late 17th century. The Mughal period marked a striking revival of ISLAMIC ARCHITECTURE in northern India, where Persian, Indian, and various provincial styles were fused to produce works of great refinement. White marble and red sandstone were favored materials. Most of the early Mughal buildings used arches only sparingly, relying on post-and-beam construction. The use of the double dome, a recessed archway inside a rectangular *fronton* (arena), and parklike surroundings are typical of the SHAH JAHAN period (1628–58), when Mughal design reached its zenith. Symmetry and balance between the parts of a building were stressed, as was delicate ornamental detail. Important undertakings include the TAJ MAHAL and the palace-fortress at Delhi (begun 1638).

Mughal dynasty \'mü-gəl\ *or* **Mogul dynasty** \'mō-gəl\ Muslim dynasty that ruled most of northern India from the early 16th to the mid-18th century. The dynasty's rulers, descended from TIMUR and GENGHIS KHAN, included unusually talented rulers over the course of seven generations, and the dynasty was further distinguished by its emperors' efforts to integrate Hindus and Muslims into a united Indian state. Prominent among the Mughal rulers were the founder, BABUR (r.1526–30); his grandson AKBAR (r.1556–1605); and SHAH JAHAN. Under AURANGZEB (r.1658–1707) the empire reached its greatest extent, but his intolerance sowed the seeds for its decline. It broke up under pressure from factional rivalries, dynastic warfare, and the invasion of northern India in 1739 by NADIR SHAH.

Mughal painting Style of painting, confined mainly to book illustrations and miniatures, that evolved in India during the MUGHAL DYNASTY (16th–19th century). In the initial phases, the technique often involved a team of artists: one determined the composition, a second did the actual coloring, and a specialist in portraiture worked on individual faces. Probably the earliest example of Mughal painting is the illustrated folktale *Tuti-nameh* ("Tales of a Parrot"). Essentially a court art, it flourished under the emperors' patronage and declined when they lost interest. See also MUGHAL ARCHITECTURE.

Bird perched on rocks, Mughal painting, c. AD 1610; in the State Museum, Hyderabad, Andhra Pradesh, India.

P. CHANDRA

Mugwumps Reform faction of the REPUBLICAN PARTY. In 1884 the Mugwumps refused to support the Republican presidential candidate, JAMES BLAINE, whom they considered politically corrupt, and campaigned for Democratic nominee GROVER CLEVELAND, whom they saw as a reformer. The term, derived from an Indian word for "war leader," had been used in political slang to mean "kingpin" and was applied to the breakaway group by a New York newspaper. It later came to mean any independent voter.

L M N

Muhammad *or* **Mohammed** (c. 570–632) Arab prophet who established the religion of Islam. He was born in Mecca, the son of a merchant of the ruling tribe, and was orphaned at 6. He married a rich widow, Khadijah, with whom he had six children, including Fa'timah, a daughter. According to tradition, in 610 he was visited by the angel Gabriel, who informed Muhammad that he was the messenger of God (Allah). His revelations and teachings, recorded in the Quran, are the basis of Islam. He began to preach publicly c. 613, urging the rich to give to the poor and calling for the destruction of idols. He gained disciples but also acquired enemies, whose plan to murder Muhammad forced him to flee Mecca for Medina in 622. This flight, known as the Hegira, marks the beginning of the Islamic era. Muhammad's followers defeated a Meccan force in 624; they suffered reverses in 625 but repelled a Meccan siege of Medina in 627. He won control of Mecca by 629 and of all Arabia by 630. He made his last journey to Mecca in 632, establishing the rites of the hajj, or pilgrimage to Mecca. He died later that year and was buried at Medina. His life, teachings, and miracles have been the subjects of Muslim devotion and reflection ever since.

Muhammad, Elijah *orig.* **Elijah Poole** (1897–1975) U.S. black separatist and leader of the Nation of Islam. Born in Sandersville, Ga., the son of sharecroppers and former slaves, he moved to Detroit in 1923. He joined the Nation of Islam and established its second temple in Chicago; on the disappearance of its founder, Wallace D. Fard, in 1934, he became head of the movement. He was jailed for advocating draft evasion during World War II, but he continued to build membership of the Black Muslims in the postwar era. His relentless call for a separate nation for African Americans, whom he declared to be Allah's chosen people, prompted his most famous disciple, Malcolm X, to break with the group in 1964. He moderated his views in his later years.

Muhammad I Askia \mu̇-'hä-mȧd...ȧs-'kē-ə\ *or* **Muhammad Ture** \'tu̇r-ˌā\ (died 1538) West African statesman and military leader who usurped the throne of the Songhai empire (1493) and, in a series of conquests, greatly expanded the empire and strengthened it. After succeeding in wresting power from Sonni Ali's son Sonni Baru, Muhammad created an Islamic state whose civil code was the Koran and whose official writing was Arabic. He set up an exemplary administration, and remained in power until overthrown by his son, Askia Musa, in 1528.

Muhammad V *orig.* **Sidi Muhammad ben Yusuf** (1909–1961) Sultan (1927–59) and king (1957–60) of Morocco. On his father's death, he was appointed sultan of French-ruled Morocco over his two brothers because the French regarded him as more compliant. His nationalist feelings were subtly expressed throughout his rule. He protected Moroccan Jews from the Vichy occupation in World War II. In 1953 the French exiled him for two years, but sustained nationalist pressure forced them to let him return. In 1956 he negotiated independence from France, and in 1957 he took the title of king. See also Hassan II.

Muhammad Ali (1769–1849) Ottoman viceroy of Egypt (1805–48) and founder of the dynasty that ruled Egypt until 1953. He reorganized Egyptian society in the aftermath of the Napoleonic occupation, eliminating the Mamluks, restricting native merchants and artisans, and stamping out peasant rebellions. He nationalized most land, introduced cash crops, and attempted industrialization, but his efforts were undermined by lack of trained workers, excessive taxation, and peasant conscription. He succeeded in securing the hereditary right to rule Egypt and Sudan (1841), which opened the way to eventual independence from Ottoman and British domination. See also Abbas Hilmy I, Ottoman empire.

Muhammad ibn Tughluq \mu̇-'hä-mȧd-ˌi-bən-ˌtəg-'lək\ (c. 1290–1351) Second sultan (r.1325–51) of the Tughluq dynasty, who briefly extended the rule of the Delhi sultanate of northern India over most of the subcontinent. He transferred the capital from Delhi to Deogir in an attempt to consolidate his hold on southern India; the result of the consequent migration of northerners was the spread of the Urdu language. He tried to enlist the services of the *ulama* (Muslim clerics) but was rebuffed; his overtures to the Sufis met a similar fate. His agricultural innovations included crop rotation and state farms as well as improvements in irrigation. Though he desired to create a more equitable social order, his harshness undermined his authority: between 1325 and 1351 he contended with 22 rebellions.

Muhasibi \mu̇-ˌhä-sē-'bē, mu̇-ˌkä-sē-'bē\, **al-** (781?–857) Sufi theologian. Born in Basra, Iraq, he was reared in Baghdad in a prosperous family. He evolved a rationalist theology, advancing his ideas in didactic conversations with his pupils and in books written in the form of dialogues. His principal work minimized asceticism and acts of outward piety in favor of inward self-examination. Near the end of his life, he was persecuted as a heretic, but he was later seen as anticipating the doctrines of Muslim orthodoxy.

Muhlenberg family \'mē-lən-ˌberk, *Engl* 'myü-lən-ˌbərg\ Distinguished U.S. family associated with the state of Pennsylvania and the Lutheran church. Henry Melchior Mühlenberg (1711–1787) emigrated to Pennsylvania from Germany and served as overseer of all the Lutheran churches from New York to Maryland; in 1748 he founded the first Lutheran synod in America. His eldest son, John Peter Gabriel (1746–1807), was a Lutheran minister, a brigadier general in the Continental Army, and a member of Congress. Frederick Augustus Conrad (1750–1801), the second son, was a Lutheran minister who served in the Continental Congress and later became the first Speaker of the House of Representatives. William Augustus (1796–1877), grandson of Frederick Augustus Conrad, became an Episcopal priest and was the founder of St. Paul's College on Long Island and St. Luke's Hospital in New York City. Frederick Augustus Muhlenberg (1818–1901), nephew of the earlier Frederick Augustus, was a Lutheran clergyman and educator who served as the first president of Muhlenberg College in Allentown.

Muir \'myu̇r\, **John** (1838–1914) U.S. naturalist and conservationist. Born in Scotland, Muir emigrated with his family to Wisconsin in 1849. An 1867 accident caused him to abandon an industrial career and devote himself to nature. He began his efforts to establish a federal forest conservation policy in 1876. His writings swung public opinion in favor of Pres. Grover Cleveland's proposal for national forest reservations and influenced Pres. Theodore Roosevelt's conservation program, and he was largely responsible for establishing Sequoia and Yosemite national parks (1890). He was the chief founder and first president of the Sierra Club (1892–1914). In 1908 the U.S. government established the Muir Woods National Monument in Marin Co., California.

John Muir.

BY COURTESY OF THE LIBRARY OF CONGRESS, WASHINGTON, D.C.

Muir Woods National Monument National woodland, northern California. A virgin stand of coastal redwoods, it covers an area of 554 acres (224 hectares) near the Pacific coast, northwest of San Francisco. Some of the trees are more than 300 ft (90 m) high, 15 ft (5 m) in diameter, and 2,000 years old. The park, established in 1908, was named in honor of John Muir.

Muisca See Chibcha

mujahidin \mü-ˌja-hi-'dēn\ (Arabic: "fighters") In Afghanistan, the guerrilla rebel fighters who opposed invading Soviet forces and the Afghan communist government (1979–92). Politically fragmented, their military efforts remained uncoordinated throughout the Afghan War. In 1992 various rebel groups drove the communist president, Mohammad Najibullah, from power. Rival factions fought from 1992 to 1994, when the Taliban emerged. Two years later the Taliban captured Kabul and instituted a strict Islamic state.

Mukden See Shenyang

Mukden Incident \'mu̇k-dən\ (1931) Seizure of the Manchurian city of Mukden (now Shenyang, China). Responding to Russian pressure from the north and to the increasingly successful unification of China by Chiang Kai-shek, the Japanese garrison in Manchuria used the pretext of an explosion along its railway to occupy Mukden. With reinforcements from the Japanese colony of Korea, its army had occupied all of Manchuria within three months. The Chinese withdrew and allowed the Japanese to establish the state of Manchuguo.

mulberry family Family Moraceae, composed of about 1,000 species of deciduous trees or evergreens in about 40 genera, found mostly in tropical and subtropical regions. Plants of the family contain a milky latex and produce multiple fused fruits. Edible fruits grow on the common mulberries (genus *Morus*), FIG (in the largest genus, *Ficus*), and BREADFRUIT. SILKWORMS feed almost exclusively on the leaves of white mulberry *(M. alba)*. Among the ornamentals in the family are paper mulberry and Osage orange *(Maclura pomifera)*. Other species include the India RUBBER TREE of office lobbies and the wide-spreading BANYAN tree.

mule Offspring of a male ASS and a female HORSE. The less common cross of a female ass and a male horse is called a hinny. Most mules are sterile. The mule resembles the horse in height and in shape of neck and croup (rump); it resembles the ass in its long ears, small hooves, and short mane. The coat is usually brown or bay. Mules are 12–17.5 hands (50–70 in., 120–180 cm) high and weigh 600–1,500 lbs (275–700 kg). They have been used as pack animals for at least 3,000 years because of their ability to withstand hardships.

mule deer Large-eared DEER *(Odocoileus hemionus)* of western North America that lives alone or in small groups at high altitudes in summer and lower altitudes in winter. Mule deer stand 3–3.5 ft (90–105 cm) and are yellowish brown in summer, grayish brown in winter. The tail is white with a black tip, except on the black-tailed deer *(O. h. columbianus)*, a Pacific Northwest subspecies. The male's antlers fork twice above a short tine near the base; a mature male normally has five tines on each antler. It is related to the WHITE-TAILED DEER.

mullah \'mə-lə\ Muslim title applied to a scholar or religious leader, especially in the Middle East and the Indian subcontinent. It means "lord" and has also been used in North Africa as an honorific attached to the name of a king, sultan, or member of the nobility. The title is now given to a variety of religious leaders, including teachers in religious schools, scholars of canon law, leaders of prayer in the mosques (IMAMS), or reciters (QURRA) of the scripture (QURAN). The word can also refer to the entire class that upholds the traditional interpretation of Islam.

Muller \'mə-lər\, **Hermann Joseph** (1890–1967) U.S. geneticist. Born in New York City, he attended Columbia University. The possibility of consciously guiding human evolution provided the initial motivation for his research, leading him to work in the Soviet Union's Institute of Genetics. He later assisted the Republican forces in the Spanish Civil War before returning to the U.S. in 1940; he thereafter taught principally at Indiana University. (1945–67). In 1926 he first induced genetic mutations through the use of X rays, and he demonstrated that mutations are the result of breakages in chromosomes and of changes in individual genes. His receipt of the Nobel Prize in 1946 increased his opportunities to publicize the dangers posed by accumulating spontaneous mutations in the human gene pool as a result of industrial processes and radiation, and he devoted much energy to increasing public awareness of the genetic dangers of radiation.

Müller \'mīē-lər\, **Johannes Peter** (1801–1858) German physiologist, comparative anatomist, and natural philosopher. He studied at the Univs. of Bonn and Berlin and later taught at both. His discovery that each sense organ responds to stimuli differently implied that external events are perceived only by the changes they produce in sensory systems. His investigations in physiology, evolution, and comparative anatomy contributed to knowledge of reflexes, the secretion and coagulation processes, the composition of blood and lymph, vision, and hearing. His studies of tumor-cell structure began to establish pathological histology as a branch of science.

mullet Any of fewer than 100 species (family Mugilidae) of abundant, commercially valuable schooling fishes found in brackish or fresh waters throughout tropical and temperate regions. Mullets frequent shallow, inshore areas, searching the sand or mud for microscopic plants and small animals. They are silvery and 1–3 ft (30–90 cm) long, with large scales, a short snout, a cigar-shaped body, a forked tail, and two distinct dorsal fins, the first containing four stiff spines. The common, or striped, mullet *(Mugil cephalus)*, cultivated in some areas, is a well-known species found worldwide.

Mulligan, Gerry *orig.* **Gerald Joseph** (1927–1996) U.S. saxophonist, pianist, composer, arranger, and bandleader, one of the best-known exponents of cool jazz (see BEBOP). Mulligan was born on Long Island, N.Y. He worked as staff arranger for GENE KRUPA's band in 1946, later writing arrangements and playing for the MILES DAVIS nonet's "Birth of the Cool" recordings (1949). He formed a pianoless quartet in Los Angeles featuring trumpeter CHET BAKER in 1952.

Mullis, Kary B(anks) (born 1944) U.S. biochemist. Born in Lenoir, N.C., he received his doctorate from UC–Berkeley. In 1983 he invented the POLYMERASE CHAIN REACTION (PCR), with which scientists can determine the order of nucleotides in a gene, use genetic fingerprinting to identify individuals by their DNA patterns, study evolution, and make medical diagnoses. He did his prizewinning research at Cetus Corp., and later became a freelance consultant. He shared a 1993 Nobel Prize with Michael Smith (born 1932). He is known for his freewheeling personal style and his iconoclastic opinions and writings, including *Dancing Naked in the Mind Field* (1998).

Mulroney \məl-'rü-nē\, **(Martin) Brian** (born 1939) Prime minister of Canada (1984–93). Born in Baie-Comeau, Quebec, he grew up bilingual in English and French. A lawyer in Montreal from 1965, he served on a commission to investigate crime in Quebec's construction industry (1974). He was president of the Iron Ore Co. 1977–83. Elected leader of the Progressive Conservative Party in 1983, he became prime minister when the party won a majority over the Liberals in 1984. He created a coalition of Quebec nationalists and western conservatives and advocated unification while recognizing Quebec as a "distinct society." He sought U.S. cooperation on acid rain and trade policies and helped negotiate the NORTH AMERICAN FREE TRADE AGREEMENT. He retired from politics in 1993.

Mulroney, 1993.
RICK FRIEDMAN/BLACK STAR

Multan \mu̇l-'tän\ City (pop., 1981: 742,000), central Pakistan, near the CHENAB RIVER. An ancient city, it was taken by ALEXANDER THE GREAT in 326 BC. It fell to the Muslims c. AD 712. For three centuries it remained the outpost of ISLAM in what was then India. It was subject to the Delhi sultanate and the Mughal empire and was captured by the Afghans (1779), the Sikhs (1818), and the British (1849–1947). It is a commercial and industrial center, with textile mills, glass factories, and cottage industries, including pottery and camelskin work. It is the site of many Muslim shrines and an ancient Hindu temple.

multimedia Computer-delivered electronic system that allows the user to control, combine, and manipulate different types of media, such as text, sound, video, computer graphics, and animation. The most common multimedia machine consists of a PERSONAL COMPUTER with a sound card, MODEM, digital speaker unit, and CD-ROM. Interactive multimedia systems under commercial development include CABLE TELEVISION services with computer interfaces that enable viewers to interact with TV programs; high-speed interactive audiovisual communications systems that rely on digital data from FIBER-OPTIC lines or digitized wireless transmission; and VIRTUAL-REALITY systems that create small-scale artificial sensory environments.

multinational corporation Any corporation registered and operating in more than one country at a time, usually with its headquarters in a single country. A firm's advantages in establishing itself multinationally include both vertical and horizontal economies of scale (reductions in cost that result from an expanded level of output). Critics usually regard the multinational corporation as destructive of local economies abroad and as prone to monopolistic practices. See also CONGLOMERATE.

multiple birth Birth of more than one child from one pregnancy. Twins are most common, born in one of about every 80 pregnancies. Identical twins develop from a single fertilized egg, which splits into two genetically identical embryos (though physical traits may be modified during their development); they occur randomly but are more likely in older mothers. Incomplete or late division results in CONJOINED TWINS. Fraternal twins develop from two eggs fertilized by two sperm and are no more genetically alike than are other siblings. Most common among persons of African ancestry and least common among those of Asian ancestry, fraternal twins also seem to run in families. Medical and psy-

L
M
N

chological "twin studies" compare fraternal and identical twins to learn about genetic influences on various characteristics and diseases. Other types of multiple births may be identical, fraternal, or a combination. The use of fertility drugs has increased the number of high-order multiple births.

multiple integral In CALCULUS, the INTEGRAL of a FUNCTION of more than one variable. As the integral of a function of one variable over an interval results in an area, the double integral of a function of two variables calculated over a region results in a volume. Functions of three variables have triple integrals, and so on. Like the single integral, such constructions are useful in calculating the net change in a function that results from changes in its input values.

multiple personality disorder *or* **dissociative identity disorder** Rare condition in which two or more independent and distinct PERSONALITY systems develop in the same individual. Each personality may alternately inhabit the person's conscious awareness to the exclusion of the others, but one is usually dominant. The various personalities typically differ from one another in outlook, temperament, and body language, and give themselves different first names. The condition is generally viewed as resulting from dissociative mental processes—that is, the splitting off from conscious awareness and control of thoughts, feelings, memories, and other mental components in response to situations that are painful, disturbing, or somehow unacceptable to the person experiencing them. Treatment is aimed at integrating the disparate personalities back into a single and unified personality.

multiple sclerosis (MS) \sklə-'rō-səs\ Disease of the BRAIN and SPINAL CORD in which gradual, patchy destruction of the myelin sheath of nerve fibers causes interruption or disordered transmission of nerve impulses. Its early symptoms may include limb weakness or trembling, visual problems, sensory disturbances, unsteady walking, and defective bladder control, which come and go irregularly. Attacks grow more severe, and some symptoms become permanent, with eventual complete PARALYSIS. Average survival from onset is about 25 years, but a rare acute form progresses over months. The cause remains uncertain and treatment unsatisfactory. Corticosteroids may ease symptoms. MS may be due to a delayed immune response that attacks the myelin sheaths; suggested causes include various common viruses. Dietary causes have also been suggested.

multiplexing Process of transmitting multiple (but separate) signals simultaneously over a single channel or line. Because the signals are sent in one complex transmission, the receiving end has to separate the individual signals. The two main types of multiplexing methods are time-division multiplexing (TDM) and frequency-division multiplexing (FDM). In TDM (typically used for digital signals), a device is given a specific time slot during which it can use the channel. In FDM (typically used for analog signals), the channel is subdivided into subchannels, each with a different frequency width that is assigned to a specific signal. Optical-fiber networks can use DWDM (dense wavelength-division multiplexing), in which different data signals are sent in different wavelengths of light in the fiber-optic medium.

multiplier In economics, a numerical coefficient showing the effect of a change in one economic variable on another. One macroeconomic multiplier, the autonomous expenditures multiplier, relates the impact of a change in total national investment on the nation's total income; it equals the ratio of the change in total income to the change in investment. If, for example, the total investment in an economy is increased by $1 million, a chain reaction of increases in consumption is set off. Producers of raw materials used in the investment projects and workers employed in the projects gain $1 million in income. If they spend on average three-fifths of that income, $600,000 will be added to the incomes of others. The makers of the goods they buy will in turn spend three-fifths of their new income on consumption. The process continues such that the amount by which total income increases may be computed by an algebraic formula. In this case, the multiplier equals 1/(1-3/5), or 2.5. This means that a $1 million increase in investment creates a $2.5 million increase in total income. Other multipliers include the money multiplier, which measures money creation resulting from a change in MONETARY POLICY; the government spending multiplier, which measures the change in national income resulting from changes in FISCAL POLICY; and the tax multiplier, which measures the changes in national income resulting from a change in taxes. The concept of the multiplier process was popularized in the 1930s by JOHN MAYNARD KEYNES as a means of measuring the effect of government spending.

multiprocessing Mode of computer operation in which two or more processors (see CPU) are connected and are active at the same time. In such a system, each processor is executing a different program or set of instructions, thus increasing computation speed over a system that has only one processor (which means only one program can be executed at a time). Because the processors must sometimes access the same resource (as when two processors must write to the same disk), a system program called the task manager has to coordinate the processors' activities.

multitasking Mode of COMPUTER operation in which the computer works on multiple tasks at the same time. A task is a computer program (or part of a program) that can be run as a separate entity. On a single-processor system, the CPU can perform preemptive (also called time slicing or time sharing) multitasking, where it executes part of one program, then switches to another program, and then returns to the first one. On MULTIPROCESSING systems, each processor can handle a separate task.

Mumbai \'məm-ˌbī\ *formerly* **Bombay** City (metro. area pop., 2001 prelim.: 16,368,084), capital of MAHARASHTRA state, western India. Located partly on Mumbai Island, it is flanked by Mumbai Harbor and the ARABIAN SEA. It is India's principal port on that sea and one of the largest and most densely populated cities in the world. The town was acquired by the Portuguese in 1534. It was ceded to the English as part of the dowry of CATHERINE OF BRAGANZA, who married CHARLES II in 1661. Granted to the British EAST INDIA CO. in 1668, it became the company's headquarters in 1672, and in 1708 it was made the center of British authority in India. After the opening of the SUEZ CANAL in 1869, Mumbai grew to be the largest distributing center in India. It remains India's economic hub and chief financial and commercial center, its cultural and education center, and headquarters of its film industry.

Mumford, Lewis (1895–1990) U.S. architectural critic, urban planner, and cultural historian. Born in Flushing, N.Y., he taught at various universities and wrote for *The New Yorker* and other magazines. In works such as *Technics and Civilization* (1934), *The City in History* (1961), and *The Myth of the Machine* (3 vols., 1967–70), Mumford analyzed the effects of technology and urbanization on human societies, criticizing the dehumanizing tendencies of modern technological society and urged that it be brought into harmony with humanistic goals and aspirations. See also URBAN PLANNING.

mumming play *or* **mummers' play** Traditional dramatic entertainment, still performed in a few villages of England and Northern Ireland, in which a champion is killed in a fight and then restored to life by a doctor. It probably has links with primitive ceremonies marking important stages in the agricultural year. The name has been connected with words such as *mumble* and *mute* and non-English words meaning "mask." Mummers were originally bands of masked persons who during winter festivals in Europe paraded through the streets and entered houses to dance or play dice in silence.

mummy Body embalmed or preserved for burial in the manner of the ancient Egyptians. The process varied from age to age in Egypt, but it always involved removing the internal organs, treating the body with resin, and wrapping it in linen bandages. (In later Egyptian times, the organs were replaced after treatment.) Among the many other peoples who practiced mummification were those of the TORRES STRAIT, near Papua New Guinea, and the INCAS.

mumps *or* **epidemic parotitis** \ˌpar-ə-'tīt-əs\ Acute contagious viral disease with inflammatory swelling of the SALIVARY GLANDS. Epidemics often occur, mostly among 5- to 15-year-olds. Cold symptoms with low fever are followed by swelling and stiffening in front of the ear, often on both sides. This rapidly spreads toward the neck and under the jaw. Pain is seldom severe, with little redness, but chewing and swallowing are difficult. During recovery in patients past puberty, other glands may be affected, but usually not seriously. The testes may atrophy, but sterility is very rare. While inflammation of the brain and MENINGES is fairly common, chances of recovery are good. Mumps needs no special treatment, and patients usually develop immunity. Vaccination can prevent it.

Muna Island \'mü-nə\ Island (pop., 1980: 174,000), SULAWESI, Indonesia. Located in the Flores Sea, it is 63 mi (101 km) long and 35 mi (56 km) wide, and has an area of 1,124 sq mi (2,911 sq km). It has a hilly, forested surface, rising to 1,460 ft (445 m). The Muna, a Muslim people who speak an Austronesian language, practice a simple agriculture, growing rice and tubers. The hoglike babirusa and the marsupial cuscus are found on the island. The main town and principal port is Raha, on the northeastern coast.

Munch \'muŋk\, **Edvard** (1863–1944) Norwegian painter and printmaker. His life and art were marked by the deaths of both parents, his brother, and his sister during his childhood, and the mental illness of another sister. He received little formal training, but the encouragement of a circle of artists in Christiania (now Oslo) and exposure to Impressionism and Postimpressionism helped him develop a highly original style. It was principally through his work of the 1890s, a series of paintings on love and death in which he gave form to mysterious and dangerous psychic forces, that he made crucial contributions to modern art. *The Scream* (1893), his most famous work, is often seen as a symbol of modern humanity's spiritual anguish. His etchings, lithographs, dry point, and woodcuts closely resemble his paintings in style and subject matter. After a nervous breakdown in 1908–9, therapy lent his work a more positive, extroverted tone, but his art never recovered its former intensity.

Edvard Munch, self-portrait, lithograph, 1895; in the Albertina, Vienna.
BY COURTESY OF THE ALBERTINA, VIENNA

Munda \'mən-də\, **Battle of** (45 BC) Conflict that ended the Roman civil war between the forces of POMPEY THE GREAT and Julius CAESAR. The two forces met in Spain, where the late Pompey's sons had seized Córdoba in revolt. Caesar lured the Pompeians from their high ground to do battle; when the rebels maneuvered a contingent to meet a cavalry charge, it was mistaken for a retreat by their army, which broke and fled, and Caesar claimed victory.

Munda languages \'mun-də\ Family of about 17 languages spoken in India, Bangladesh, and Nepal that together with MON-KHMER comprises the AUSTROASIATIC superfamily. Munda languages are spoken by more than 7 million people, all members of tribal groups living mainly in hilly and forested regions. Most significant are Santali, with over 4 million speakers concentrated in northern Orissa, southern and eastern Bihar, northwestern Bengal, and the Nepal-Assam border; Ho, with about 750,000 speakers mainly in Bihar and Orissa; Mundari, with about 850,000 speakers scattered over northeastern India; and Korku, the westernmost Munda language, spoken by about 320,000 in southern Madhya Pradesh and northern Maharashtra. Munda languages differ from all other Austroasiatic languages in complexity of MORPHOLOGY and in having basic subject-object-verb rather than subject-verb-object word order.

Mundell, Robert A(lexander) (b.1932) Canadian-born economist who received the Nobel Prize in Economic Sciences in 1999 for his work on monetary dynamics and optimum currency areas. Mundell earned degrees from the University of British Columbia (B.A., 1953), the University of Washington (M.A., 1954), and the Massachusetts Institute of Technology (Ph.D., 1956). He taught economics at the University of Chicago (1956–57) and Columbia University (1974–). Through research for the INTERNATIONAL MONETARY FUND, Mundell analyzed the effect of EXCHANGE RATES on MONETARY POLICIES. In 1961 he theorized that an economic region characterized by free movement of labor and trade could support a single currency. His theories contributed to the creation of the EURO, the single currency adopted by the EUROPEAN UNION on January 1, 1999.

Munich \'myü-nik\ *German* **München** \'mᵫn-ḵən\ City (pop., 1996 est.: 1,236,000), capital of Bavaria, Germany. Located along the Isar River, it is was founded c. 1158 at the site of an ancient monastery. It became the capital of Bavaria under the ruling WITTELSBACH family. The city developed as a center of music and theater through the 19th century. After World War I, it became a center of right-wing political ferment; it was the site of the 1923 BEER HALL PUTSCH, ADOLF HITLER's attempted rising against the Bavarian government, and subsequent NAZI PARTY activities. It was the site for the signing of the 1938 MUNICH AGREEMENT. In World War II it suffered heavily from Allied bombing. Some medieval structures survived, including the cathedral and town hall. It is a trade, cultural, educational, and industrial center known for its many museums and for manufacturing and beer and ale brewing.

Munich, University of *German* **Ludwig-Maximilians Universität München** Autonomous university supported by the state of Bavaria, Germany. It was founded in Ingolstadt in 1472 and modeled after the University of VIENNA. During the Protestant Reformation it was a center of Roman Catholic opposition to MARTIN LUTHER. In 1799 schools of economics and political science were added, and in 1826 it moved to Munich, where agricultural and technical programs were founded. Current enrollment is about 60,000.

Munich agreement (1938) Settlement reached by Germany, France, Britain, and Italy permitting German annexation of Czechoslovakia's SUDETENLAND. ADOLF HITLER's threats to occupy the German-populated part of Czechoslovakia stemmed from his avowed broader goal of reuniting Europe's German-populated areas. Though Czechoslovakia had defense treaties with France and the Soviet Union, both countries agreed that areas in the Sudetenland with majority German populations should be returned. Hitler demanded that all Czechoslovaks in those areas depart; when Czechoslovakia refused, Britain's NEVILLE CHAMBERLAIN negotiated an agreement permitting Germany to occupy the areas but promising that all future differences would be resolved through consultation. The agreement, which became synonymous with APPEASEMENT, was abrogated when Hitler annexed the rest of Czechoslovakia the next year.

Munich Putsch See BEER HALL PUTSCH

Muñoz Marín \mün-'yōs-mə-'rēn\, **Luis** (1898–1980) Statesman and four-term governor of Puerto Rico (1948–64). Educated in the U.S., he became editor of the newspaper *La Democracia* and was elected to the Puerto Rican senate in 1932. Early in his career he advocated independence from the U.S., but later he worked closely with the U.S.-appointed governor to improve conditions in Puerto Rico. He achieved success with Operation Bootstrap, a program for rapid economic growth. When Puerto Rico received the right to elect its own governor in 1948, he was overwhelmingly elected and repeatedly reelected. He achieved his goal of making Puerto Rico a commonwealth.

Muñoz Rivera \'mün-yōs-rē-'ver-ä\, **Luis** (1859–1916) Puerto Rican statesman, publisher, and patriot. In 1889 he founded the newspaper *La Democracia*, which crusaded for Puerto Rican self-government. He was instrumental in obtaining Puerto Rico's charter of home rule from Spain in 1897. He was president of the first autonomist cabinet, but he resigned after Spain ceded Puerto Rico to the U.S. His son LUIS MUÑOZ MARÍN was governor of Puerto Rico (1949–65).

Munro \mən-'rō\, **Alice** *orig.* **Alice Anne Laidlaw** (born 1931) Canadian writer. Born in Wingham, Ont., she is known for exquisitely drawn short stories, usually set in rural Ontario and peopled by characters of Scotch-Irish stock. Her collections *Dance of the Happy Shades* (1968), *Who Do You Think You Are?* (1978), and *The Progress of Love* (1986) won the Governor General's Literary Award. Her other collections include *Something I've Been Meaning to Tell You* (1974), *The Moons of Jupiter* (1982), *Friend of My Youth* (1986), *Open Secrets* (1994), and *The Love of a Good Woman* (1998).

Munsey, Frank Andrew (1854–1925) U.S. newspaper and magazine publisher. Born in Mercer, Me., he managed a telegraph office before moving to New York City, where he founded *Golden Argosy* (1882), later renamed *Argosy Magazine*; and *Munsey's Magazine* (1889), the first cheap, general-circulation, illustrated magazine in the U.S. He acquired several newspapers in Baltimore and New York, some of which disappeared in profitable mergers. He viewed his publications purely as moneymaking enterprises and maintained colorless editorial policies. Most of his large fortune went to the Metropolitan Museum of Art.

Münster \'mᵫn-stər\ City (pop., 1993 est.: 267,000), western Germany. Founded in 804 as a bishopric, it was named Münster in 1068 and was chartered in 1137. A member of the HANSEATIC LEAGUE from the 13th century, it was seized by the ANABAPTISTS in 1535. The Peace of WESTPHALIA was signed there in 1648, and in 1815 Münster became the capital of Prussian WESTPHALIA. Although it suffered heavy damage in World War II, most of its historic buildings were restored or rebuilt, including the

13th-century cathedral and 14th-century town hall. It is a center of Westphalian culture.

Munster Province (pop., 1991: 790,000), southern Ireland. The area was ruled by a clan in the south, which gradually extended its power over Munster by c. AD 400. In the 10th century Vikings invaded and eventually settled in Waterford and Limerick. After the 12th century Anglo-Norman invasion, it was ruled by the feudal families of Fitzgerald and Butler. It now comprises the counties of Clare, Cork, Kerry, Limerick, Tipperary (North Riding and South Riding), and Waterford.

muntjac \'mənt-ˌjak\ *or* **barking deer** Any of about seven species of solitary, nocturnal DEER, native to Asia and introduced into England and France, that constitute the genus *Muntiacus* (family Cervidae). Named for their cry, most species stand 15–25 in. (40–65 cm) high, weigh 33–77 lbs (15–35 kg), and are grayish, reddish, or brown. Males have tusklike upper canine teeth and short one-branched antlers. Bony ridges extend from the antler base onto the face. The giant muntjac (88–110 lbs, or 40–50 kg) was discovered in northern Vietnam in 1993–94. Fea's muntjac *(M. feae),* of Myanmar and Thailand, is endangered, and other muntjac species are threatened.

Chinese muntjac (*Muntiacus reevesi*).
KENNETH W. FINK–ROOT RESOURCES

Müntzer \'mu̅e̅nt-sər\, **Thomas** *or* **Thomas Munzer** (1489?–1525) German religious reformer. A student of theology and an associate of MARTIN LUTHER, he served as a pastor until his socialism and mystical doctrines led to his removal. His belief in the inner light of the Holy Spirit as opposed to the authority of the Bible alienated the Lutherans. He preached widely, championing the common people, and in 1525 he organized the working classes of Mühlhausen. He led the PEASANTS' REVOLT in Thuringia in 1524–25; after the defeat of his forces, he was tortured, tried, and executed.

muqarnas See STALACTITE WORK

Murad, Ferid (born 1936) U.S. pharmacologist. He received his MD and PhD from Western Reserve University (later Case Western Reserve University). Murad showed that NITROGLYCERIN and related heart drugs induce the formation of NITRIC OXIDE, a gas that increases the diameter of blood vessels. Along with R.F. FURCHGOTT and L.J. IGNARRO, he was awarded a 1998 Nobel Prize for the discovery that nitric oxide acts as a signaling molecule in the cardiovascular system. Their combined work uncovered an entirely new mechanism for how blood vessels relax and widen. This discovery led to the development of the drug VIAGRA, which is used to treat impotence.

mural Painting applied to and made integral with the surface of a wall or ceiling. Its roots can be found in the universal desire that led prehistoric peoples to create cave paintings—the desire to decorate their surroundings and express their ideas and beliefs. The Romans produced large numbers of murals in Pompeii and Ostia, but mural painting (not synonymous with FRESCO) reached its highest degree of creative achievement in Europe with the work of such Renaissance masters as MASACCIO, Fra ANGELICO, LEONARDO DA VINCI, MICHELANGELO, and RAPHAEL. In the 20th century, the mural was embraced by artists of the Cubist and Fauve movements in Paris, revolutionary painters in Mexico (e.g., DIEGO RIVERA, JOSE CLEMENTE OROZCO, DAVID A. SIQUEIROS), and Depression-era artists under the sponsorship of the U.S. government (e.g., BEN SHAHN, THOMAS HART BENTON).

Murasaki Shikibu \mu̇-'rä-sä-kē-'shē-kē-bu̇\ (978?–1014?) Japanese writer. Her real name is unknown, and the primary source of knowledge about her life is a diary she kept 1007–10. Her *Tale of Genji* (completed c. 1010) is a long and complex tale concerned mostly with the loves of Prince Genji and the women in his life. Supremely sensitive to human emotions and the beauties of nature, it provides delightful glimpses of life at the court of the empress Joto mon'in, whom Murasaki served. It is generally considered one of the world's oldest and greatest novels.

Murat \mu̅e̅-'rä\, **Joachim** (1767–1815) French soldier and king of Naples (1808–15). He served in Italy and Egypt as a daring cavalry commander, and later aided NAPOLEON in his coup d'état (1799) and married Napoleon's sister CAROLINE BONAPARTE. He helped win the Battle of MARENGO (1800). Appointed governor of Paris, he was promoted to marshal in 1804. After victories at the Battles of AUSTERLITZ (1805) and JENA (1806), he was made king of Naples (1808), where he carried out administrative and economic reforms and encouraged Italian nationalism. He led troops in Napoleon's Russian campaign at the Battle of BORODINO (1812) but left the army during its retreat from Moscow. He supported Napoleon again during the HUNDRED DAYS in 1815, but was defeated with his Neapolitan forces at the Battle of Tolentino, and was later taken prisoner and shot.

Murat, detail of a drawing by Antoine-Jean Gros; in the École des Beaux-Arts, Paris.
CLICHE MUSEES NATIONAUX, PARIS

Murchison, Ira (born 1933) U.S. track star. Born in Chicago, he was the 1951 Illinois state champion in the 100- and 200-yard dashes. As a member of the 1956 U.S. Olympic 4×100-m relay team, he helped secure a gold medal and set a new world record. That year he also twice jointly held the world 100-m record.

Murchison River River, WESTERN AUSTRALIA, Australia. Sporadically flowing west to the Indian Ocean, it is 440 mi (708 km) long. In 1891 the river's name was given to one of Australia's richest goldfields, and some gold is still mined in the area. Kalbarri National Park is on the lower Murchison, where the river cuts a scenic gorge through the coastal range.

Murcia \'mər-shə\ Autonomous community (pop., 1996 est.: 1,097,000), province, and historical region, southeastern Spain. It covers 4,369 sq mi (11,316 sq km), and its capital is the city of MURCIA. It was an independent Moorish kingdom until its annexation by CASTILE in 1243. The autonomous community was established in 1982. The Segura River flows through its center, irrigating rich farmland and orchards. The ports of CARTAGENA, Mazarrón, and Aguilas have grown with the development of shipping and mining along the coastal plain. Principal crops are grain, olives, grapes, and melons.

Murcia City (metro. area pop., 1995 est.: 345,000), capital of MURCIA, southeastern Spain. The site was settled before the Roman occupation of Spain in the 3rd century BC. It became the Muslim city of Mursiyah in 825 AD, when it was made a provincial capital by the emir of CÓRDOBA. It was the birthplace of IBN AL-ARABI (1165). The Segura River divides the city into older and newer parts. The 14th-century cathedral was restored in the 18th century. It is a communications and agricultural-trade center for surrounding areas. Its silk industry, dating from Moorish times, continues today.

murder See HOMICIDE

Murder, Inc. Popular name for an arm of the U.S. national crime syndicate founded c. 1930 in Brooklyn, N.Y., to threaten, maim, or murder designated victims for a price. Its services were available to any syndicate member anywhere in the country; many of its victims were themselves syndicate members who were killed for "business reasons." Its principal figures were Louis Buchalter, known as Louis Lepke, and Albert Anastasia. Investigated by THOMAS DEWEY, it was exposed in 1940–41 by a former member, Abe "Kid Twist" Reles, who described some 70 murders and suggested hundreds more; he himself died mysteriously in the middle of the investigation.

Murdoch \'mər-ˌdäk\, **(Jean) Iris** *later* **Dame Iris** (1919–1999) British novelist and philosopher. A graduate of Oxford Univ., she worked as a university lecturer while pursuing her writing career. Her first published work was a study of J.-P. SARTRE (1953). Her novels, which typically have convoluted plots featuring philosophical and comic elements, include *The Bell* (1958), *A Severed Head* (1961), *The Black Prince* (1973), *The Sea, The Sea* (1978), and *The Book and the Brotherhood* (1987). Her other philosophical works include *The Sovereignty of Good* (1970) and *Metaphysics as a Guide to Morals* (1992). Her decline under

Alzheimer's disease was chronicled by her husband, the critic John Bayley, in *Elegy for Iris* (1999).

Murdoch, (Keith) Rupert (born 1931) Australian-U.S. newspaper publisher and media entrepreneur. Son of a famous war correspondent and publisher, he inherited two Adelaide newspapers in 1954 and boosted their circulation by emphasizing crime, sex, scandal, sports, and human-interest stories, while taking an outspokenly conservative editorial stance. He used this approach with soaring success with papers bought in Australia, Britain, and the U.S. by his global media holding company, The News Corporation Ltd. He also acquired conventional and respected publications, including *The* TIMES of London. In the 1980s and '90s he expanded into book and electronic publishing, television broadcasting, and film and video production. His holdings include the *New York Post*; Fox, Inc. (see FOX BROADCASTING CO.); HarperCollins Publishers; British Sky Broadcasting; Star TV, a pan-Asian television service; and the Los Angeles Dodgers.

Mures River \'mü-resh\ River, rising in the eastern CARPATHIAN MTNS., eastern central Romania. It flows west across northern Romania and across the Hungarian border to join the TISZA RIVER at Szeged, Hungary; it is about 450 mi (725 km) long. It is the Tisza's most important tributary and a significant traffic route; it is navigable for small boats for more than 200 mi (320 km).

Murgab River \mủr-'gäb\ *or* **Morghab River** \mủr-'gäb\ River, northwestern Afghanistan and southeastern Turkmenistan. It flows generally west and then north into Turkmenistan and is about 600 mi (970 km) long. It forms the border between Turkmenistan and Afghanistan for several miles. North of MARY, it disappears into the sands of the KARAKUM DESERT.

muriatic acid See HYDROCHLORIC ACID

Murillo \mủ-'rē-ō, *Engl* myủ-'ri-lō\, **Bartolomé Esteban** (c. 1618–1682) Spanish painter. The most popular baroque religious painter of 17th-century Spain, he is noted for his idealized figures, most of them painted for religious orders and the confraternities of his native Seville. His early works were executed in the naturalistic style of FRANCISCO ZURBARAN, but with the development of his mature style in the 1650s he soon surpassed the older master in fame and popularity. The softly modeled forms, rich colors, and broad brushwork of the later paintings, such as the *Immaculate Conception* of 1652 (his favorite subject), reveal the influence of 16th-century Venetian and Flemish baroque painters. Murillo's works were copied and imitated throughout Spain and its empire, and he was the first Spanish painter to achieve fame outside the Spanish world.

Murjia \'mủr-jē-ə\ Moderate and liberal sect of ISLAM. It flourished during the 7th–8th century, a period of strife in the Muslim community. Unlike the Khawarij, a militant sect that wanted to oust serious sinners from the community and declare JIHAD against them, the Murjia, who advocated leaving great sinners to ALLAH, claimed that no one who had professed ISLAM could be declared an infidel. When the Khawarij revolted against the UMAYYAD DYNASTY, the Murjia declared that revolt against a Muslim ruler could not be justified under any circumstances.

Murmansk Seaport (pop., 1995 est.: 407,000), northwestern Russia. Situated on the eastern shore of Kola Bay near the BARENTS SEA, it is the world's largest city north of the ARCTIC CIRCLE. Its ice-free harbor makes it Russia's only port with unrestricted access to the Atlantic. Founded in 1915 as a supply port in World War I, it was a base for the British, French, and U.S. forces against the BOLSHEVIKS in 1918; it also served as a major supply base during World War II. In addition to a Russian naval base, it has a large fishing fleet and fish-processing industry.

Murnau \'mủr-ˌnaủ\, **F. W.** *orig.* **Friedrich Wilhelm Plumpe** (1889–1931) German film director. After studying at the University of Heidelberg, he became a protégé of MAX REINHARDT in Berlin. During World War I he served as a combat pilot and made propaganda films. He directed his first feature in 1919 and won international acclaim for *Nosferatu* (1922) and *The Last Laugh* (1924). In 1927 he moved to Hollywood, where he made such films as *Sunrise* (1927), his masterpiece, and *Tabu* (1931; with ROBERT FLAHERTY). He died in a car crash at 41.

Muromachi period See ASHIKAGA SHOGUNATE

Murphy, Audie (Leon) (1924–1971) U.S. war hero and actor. Born near Kingston, Texas, he enlisted in the army in 1942 and became the most decorated U.S. soldier of World War II, killing hundreds of Germans and once jumping onto a burning tank destroyer to turn its machine gun on the enemy troops. In 1945 he received the Medal of Honor. After the war he became a movie actor on the strength of his heroic status, and had starring roles in such films as *The Red Badge of Courage* (1951), *To Hell and Back* (1955), and *The Quiet American* (1958). He died when his private plane crashed.

Murphy, Frank *orig.* **William Francis** (1890–1949) U.S. Supreme Court justice (1940–49). Born in Harbor Beach, Mich., he served as mayor of Detroit 1930–33. He was governor-general (1933–35) and U.S. high commissioner (1935–36) of the Philippines. Elected governor of Michigan (1937–38), he refused to use troops to break sit-down strikes by automobile workers. As U.S. attorney general (1939–40), he established the Justice Department's civil-rights unit. On the Supreme Court, he strongly defended individual civil rights and dissented in a case upholding internment of Japanese-Americans in World War II.

Frank Murphy.

BY COURTESY OF THE LIBRARY OF CONGRESS, WASHINGTON, D.C.

Murphy, Isaac Burns (1861–96) African American jockey, the first jockey to be elected to the National Museum of Racing's Hall of Fame in Saratoga Springs, N.Y. Murphy began racing in 1875 and was one of the first jockeys to pace his mount for a charge down the homestretch—a technique soon described as the "grandstand finish." His win of the Travers Stakes at Saratoga Springs in 1879 catapulted him to national fame. He rode in the Kentucky Derby 11 times and was the first three-time winner, in 1884, 1890, and 1891. In 1884 he won the first American Derby in Chicago, Ill., the most prestigious race of the era. He won this race again in 1885, 1886, and 1888. Murphy's career winning percentage of 34.5 has never been equaled. Even though Murphy rode before jockeys received a share of the winnings, he was the highest-paid athlete in America, earning close to $20,000 a year at his peak in the late 1880s. By the mid-1890s, however, his ongoing battles with weight gain and alcoholism had severely curtailed his career.

Murray, George Redmayne (1865–1939) British physician. After receiving his MD from Cambridge Univ., he became a pioneer in the treatment of endocrine disorders. He was one of the first to use extracts of animal thyroid glands to relieve MYXEDEMA, which was known to be caused by thyroid deficiency.

Murray, James (Augustus Henry) *later* **Sir James** (1837–1915) Scottish lexicographer. He taught in a grammar school 1855–85. His *Dialect of the Southern Counties of Scotland* (1873) and a major article on English for *Encyclopædia Britannica* (1878) established him as a leading philologist. He was hired by the Philological Society as editor of the vast *New English Dictionary on Historical Principles*, later called the OXFORD ENGLISH DICTIONARY, in 1879, and applied himself to the work with legendary energy and resourcefulness. The first volume appeared in 1884, and by his death he had completed about half the dictionary.

Murray, Matthew (1765–1826) British engineer. With little formal education, he went to work for a flax spinner in Leeds, where he introduced innovations in flax-spinning machinery. He established his own factory, and was soon patenting various improvements to the STEAM ENGINE. The LOCOMOTIVES he built for local collieries in 1812 were the first regularly employed for commercial purposes. In 1813 he built an early commercial STEAMBOAT, and he claimed the planing machine as his invention.

Murray, Philip (1886–1952) Scottish-U.S. labor leader. After emigrating to the U.S. in 1902, he became a coal miner in Pennsylvania. He joined the UNITED MINE WORKERS OF AMERICA and rose through the ranks to serve as vice president (1920–42) under JOHN L. LEWIS. When Lewis became president of the newly formed CIO in 1936, he delegated Murray to create an industry-wide steelworkers' union (see UNITED STEEL-

L M N

WORKERS OF AMERICA). Murray succeeded Lewis as CIO president in 1940 and held the post until his death. See also AFL-CIO.

Murray River Principal river of Australia. Rising near Mount KOSCIUSKO, in southeastern NEW SOUTH WALES, it flows across southeastern Australia from the Snowy Mountains to the GREAT AUSTRALIAN BIGHT of the Indian Ocean; it is 1,610 mi (2,590 km) long. It forms the boundary between VICTORIA and NEW SOUTH WALES and then turns south and flows into Encounter Bay through Lake ALEXANDRINA. River shipping was important in the 19th century, but navigation practically ceased with growing competition from railways and the demand for irrigation water. The river valley is of great economic importance, fostering the production of grains, fruit, and wine, and the raising of cattle and sheep.

murre \'mər\ Any of certain black-and-white seabirds (genus *Uria,* family Alcidae) that are about 16 in. (40 cm) long and breed from the Arctic Circle to Nova Scotia, California, Portugal, and Korea. Murres nest in vast numbers on sheer cliffs. When half grown, the single chick enters the sea with its parents to escape gulls and SKUAS. In autumn the birds swim south. See also GUILLEMOT.

Common murres (*Uria aalge*), ringed phase at left.

R.J. TULLOCH—BRUCE COLEMAN INC./EB INC.

Murrow, Edward (Egbert) R(oscoe) (1908–1965) U.S. radio and television broadcaster. Born in Greensboro, N.C., he joined CBS in 1935 and two years later became head of its European Bureau. He became famous for his eyewitness reportage of events leading to and during World War II. After the war, with FRED FRIENDLY, he produced *Hear It Now,* an authoritative radio news digest, and on television the comparable *See It Now*. He also produced *Person to Person* and other television programs. In the 1950s he was an influential force for the free dissemination of information, producing a notable exposé of the tactics of Sen. JOSEPH MCCARTHY.

Murrumbidgee River \,mə-rəm-'bi-jē\ River, southeastern NEW SOUTH WALES, Australia. The major right-bank tributary of the MURRAY RIVER, it flows west from the GREAT DIVIDING RANGE near CANBERRA to join the Murray 140 mi (224 km) from the VICTORIA border; it is 980 mi (1,578 km) long. Small vessels can navigate it for about 500 mi (800 km) in the rainy season. The Murrumbidgee Irrigation Area involves more than 1,000 sq mi (2,600 sq km) of farmland and supports livestock pastures, grapes, citrus fruits, wheat, cotton, and rice.

Musa \'mü-sä\ *or* **Mansa Musa** (died 1332/37?) Emperor *(mansa)* of the western African empire of MALI from 1307 (or 1312). Mansa Musa left a realm notable for its extent and riches (he built the Great Mosque at TOMBOUCTOU), but is best remembered for the splendor of his pilgrimage to Mecca (1324), which awakened the world to Mali's stupendous wealth and stimulated a desire among North Africans and Europeans to locate its source. Under Mansa Musa, Mali became one of the largest empires in the world and Tombouctou grew to be a major commercial city.

Musa al-Sadr \'mü-sä-äl-'sädrᵊ\ (1928–1978?) Iranian-Lebanese Shiite cleric. After graduating from a religious college, he moved to Lebanon in 1960. He became involved in social work among the Shiites, and in 1968–69 he formed the Higher Shia Islamic Council to advocate for the interests of Lebanon's Shiites. In 1975 he formed a militia, Amal, to fight for Shiite interests in the LEBANESE CIVIL WAR. He disappeared on an official trip in Libya, reportedly kidnapped and killed.

Musandam Peninsula \mə-'san-dəm\ Peninsula, northeastern extension of the Arabian Peninsula, Oman. It separates the Gulf of OMAN from the Persian Gulf to form the Strait of HORMUZ to the north. Part of Oman, it is divided from the rest of the country by the United Arab Emirates. It is a mountainous region with a rocky coast hazardous to ships. Fishing is the main industry, and there are reserves of petroleum off the western coast. The oasis town of Diba is on the southeastern coast.

Muscat See MASQAT

Muscat and Oman See OMAN

muscle Contractile tissue that produces motion for functions including body movements, digestion, focusing, circulation, and body warmth. It can be classified as striated, cardiac, and smooth or as phasic and tonic (responding quickly or gradually to stimulation, respectively). Striated muscle, whose fibers appear striped under a microscope, is responsible for voluntary movement. Most of these muscles are phasic. They are attached to the skeleton and move the body by contracting in response to signals from the central NERVOUS SYSTEM; contraction is achieved by the sliding of thin filaments (of ACTIN) between thick ones (of myosin); stretch receptors in the tissue provide feedback, allowing smooth motion and fine motor control. The branched fibers of cardiac muscle give it a netlike structure; contraction originates in the heart's muscle tissue itself with a signal from the natural pacemaker; vagus and sympathetic nerves control heart rate. Smooth muscle, the muscle of internal organs and blood vessels, is generally involuntary and tonic; its cells can operate either collectively or individually (in response to separate nerve endings) and have different shapes. Disorders of voluntary muscle cause weakening, atrophy, pain, and twitching. Some systemic diseases (e.g., dermatomyositis, polymyositis) can cause muscle inflammation. See also ABDOMINAL MUSCLE, EXTENSOR MUSCLE, FLEXOR MUSCLE, MUSCLE TUMOR, MUSCULAR DYSTROPHY, MYASTHENIA GRAVIS.

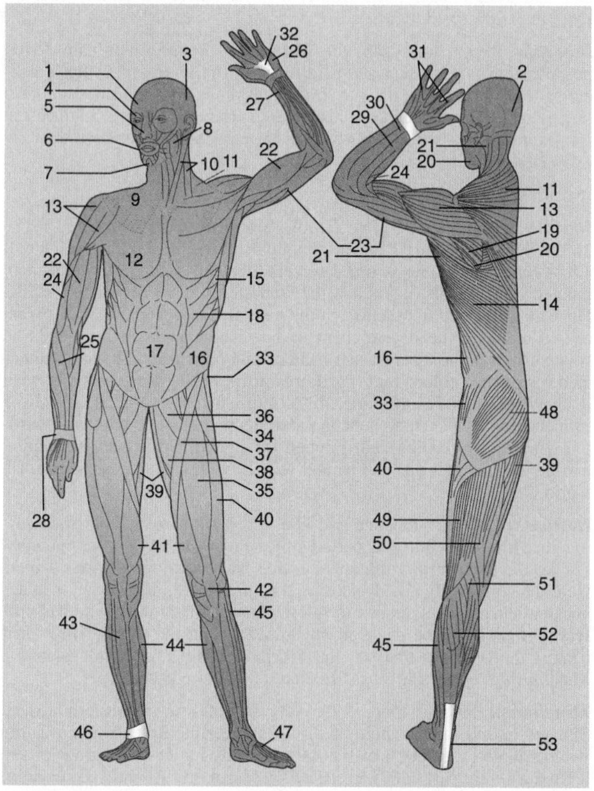

Major muscles of the human body. (1) frontalis, (2) occipitalis, (3) temporalis, (4) orbicularis of eye, (5) nasalis, (6) orbicularis of mouth, (7) mentalis, (8) masseter, (9) platysma, (10) sternocleidomastoid, (11) trapezius, (12) pectoralis major, (13) deltoid, (14) latissimus dorsi, (15) anterior serratus, (16) external oblique, (17) rectus abdominis, (18) internal oblique, (19) infraspinatus, (20) teres minor, (21) teres major, (22) biceps, (23) triceps, (24) brachialis, (25) long radial extensor of wrist, (26) short palmaris, (27) pronator quadratus, (28) annular ligament of the carpus, (29) common extensor of digits, (30) ulnar extensor of wrist, (31) tendons of extensors of digits and wrists, (32) palmar aponeurosis, (33) gluteus medius, (34) tensor of the fascia lata, (35) rectus femoris, (36) pectineus, (37) sartorius, (38) long adductor of thigh, (39) gracilis, (40) vastus lateralis, (41) vastus medialis, (42) patella, (43) anterior tibialis, (44) medial head of gastrocnemius, (45) soleus, (46) annular ligament of ankle, (47) short extensor, (48) gluteus maximus, (49) biceps of thigh, (50) semitendinosus, (51) plantaris, (52) lateral head of gastrocnemius, (53) Achilles' tendon.

Muscle Shoals Former rapids, TENNESSEE RIVER, northwestern Alabama. At about 37 mi (60 km) long, it was a navigation hazard but is now submerged under at least 9 ft (3 m) of water by the Wilson, Wheeler, and Pickwick Landing dams, which completely eliminated the rapids. Manufacturing plants and hydroelectric power facilities are administered by the TENNESSEE VALLEY AUTHORITY (TVA). The city of Muscle Shoals (1990 pop.: 10,000) developed from the TVA complex in the Wilson Dam area.

muscle tumor Abnormal tissue growth in or originating from MUSCLE tissue. There are three major types. Leiomyomas are tumors of smooth muscles, seen most often in the uterus but also in the digestive, urinary, and female genital systems. Part of the tumor may become malignant, but it usually does not spread or recur. Rhabdomyomas occur most often in cardiac muscle. Some forms spread, and it may remain contained in tissue or become diffuse and hard to remove. Rhabdomyomas involving both smooth and striated muscle are often malignant and may grow very large. The several types of rhabdomyosarcoma are rare; they arise in skeletal muscle, usually in the leg or arm, and are extremely malignant.

muscovite \'məs-kə-ˌvīt\ *or* **common mica** *or* **potash mica** *or* **isinglass** Abundant SILICATE mineral that contains potassium and aluminum and has a layered atomic structure. It is the most common member of the MICA group. Because it occurs in thin, transparent sheets, it was used in Russia for window panes and became known as Muscovy glass (isinglass), hence its name. Muscovite is usually colorless but may be light gray, brown, pale green, or rose red. Its low iron content makes it a good electrical and thermal insulator.

muscular dystrophy \'dis-trə-fē\ Inherited disease that causes progressive weakness in the skeletal (and occasionally heart) muscle. Muscle tissue degenerates and regenerates randomly and is replaced by scar tissue and fat. There is no specific treatment. Physical therapy, braces, and corrective surgery may help. Duchenne's muscular dystrophy, the most common, strikes only males. Symptoms, including frequent falls and difficulty in standing up, start in boys 3–7 years old; muscle wasting progresses from the legs to the arms and then the diaphragm. Pulmonary infection or respiratory failure usually causes death before age 20. The gene can now be detected in female carriers and male fetuses. Becker's dystrophy, also sex-linked, is less severe and begins later. Patients remain able to walk and usually survive into their 30s and 40s. Myotonic muscular dystrophy affects adults of both sexes, with MYOTONIA and degeneration two to three years later, along with cataracts, baldness, and gonadal atrophy. Limb-girdle dystrophy affects the pelvic or shoulder muscles in both sexes. Facioscapulohumeral (face, shoulder-blade, and upper-arm) dystrophy starts in childhood or adolescence and affects both sexes; after initial symptoms of difficulty raising the arms, the legs and pelvic muscles can be affected; the main facial effect is difficulty in closing the eyes. Life expectancy is normal.

Muse In Greco-Roman religion and myth, any of a group of sister goddesses, daughters of ZEUS and Mnemosyne (Memory). A festival was held in their honor every four years near Mount Helicon, the center of their cult in Greece. They probably began as the patron goddesses of poets, though later their range was extended to include all the liberal arts and sciences. Nine Muses are usually named: Calliope (heroic or epic poetry), Clio (history), Erato (lyric or love poetry), Euterpe (music or flutes), Melpomene (tragedy), Polyhymnia (sacred poetry or mime), Terpsichore (dancing and choral song), Thalia (comedy), and Urania (astronomy).

museum Public institution dedicated to preserving and interpreting the primary tangible evidence of humans and their environment. Types of museums include general (multidisciplinary) museums, natural-history museums, science and technology museums, history museums, and art museums. In Roman times the word referred to a place devoted to scholarly occupation (see MUSEUM OF ALEXANDRIA). The public museum as it is known today did not develop until the 17th–18th century. The first organized body to receive a private collection, erect a building to house it, and make it publicly available was Oxford Univ.; the resulting Ashmolean Museum opened in 1683. The 18th century saw the opening of such great museums as the BRITISH MUSEUM, LOUVRE, and UFFIZI GALLERY. By the early 19th century the granting of public access to formerly private collections had become common. What followed for the next 100 years was the worldwide founding of museums intended for the public. In the 20th century, museums have broadened their roles as educational facilities, sources of leisure activity, and information centers. Many sites of historical or scientific significance have been developed as museums. Museum attendance has increased greatly, often attracted by "blockbuster" exhibitions, though museums have had to become more financially resourceful due to constraints in public funding.

Museum of Alexandria Ancient center of classical learning at ALEXANDRIA in Egypt. A research institute organized into faculties and headed by a president-priest, the Museum, with its renowned library, was built near the royal palace either by PTOLEMY II PHILADELPHUS c. 280 BC or by his father, PTOLEMY I SOTER. The best surviving description is by STRABO. In AD 270 its buildings were probably destroyed by ZENOBIA, though its educational and research functions seem to have continued until the 5th century.

Museum of Modern Art (MOMA) Museum in New York City, the world's most comprehensive collection of U.S. and European art from the late 19th century to the present. It was founded in 1929 by a group of private collectors. The original building on 53rd St. opened in 1939; a later addition and sculpture garden were designed by PHILIP JOHNSON (1953). A condominium tower and western wing, doubling the exhibition space, were completed in 1984. Its collections of Cubist, Surrealist, and Abstract Expressionist paintings are extensive; other holdings include sculpture, graphic arts, industrial design, architecture, photography, and film. Through its permanent collections, exhibitions, and many publications, it exerts a strong influence on public taste and artistic production.

Museveni \mü-'sə-ven-ˌē\, **Yoweri (Kaguta)** (born 1944) President of Uganda (from 1986). As a university student he led a group allied with African liberation movements. When IDI AMIN came to power in 1971, Museveni went into exile. He founded the Front for National Salvation, which helped topple Amin in 1979. He replaced MILTON OBOTE as president in 1986, winning election to the post in 1996. Though he rejected multiparty democracy, he allowed a free press and private enterprise. He is credited with bringing stability and economic growth to Uganda, though his support for rebels in other African countries has been controversial.

Musgrave, Thea (born 1928) Scottish-U.S. composer. She studied with N. BOULANGER and A. COPLAND, and later taught at UC–Santa Barbara (1970–78) and elsewhere in the U.S. She has written a number of dramatic concertos, some of which reflect her interest in music's spatial dimension, but is best known for her operas, including *The Voice of Ariadne* (1973), *Mary, Queen of Scots* (1977), and *Simon Bolívar* (1995).

Mushet \'məsh-ət\, **Robert Forester** (1811–1891) British steelmaker. He was the son of the ironmaster David Mushet (1772–1847). Robert's discovery in 1868 that adding tungsten to STEEL greatly increases its hardness even after air cooling produced the first commercial steel ALLOY, a material that formed the basis for the development of tool steels for the machining of metals. Mushet also discovered that the addition of manganese to steel produced by the BESSEMER PROCESS improved the steel's ability to withstand rolling and forging at high temperatures.

mushroom Fleshy spore-bearing structure of certain fungi (see FUNGUS), typically of the class Basidiomycetes. It arises from the MYCELIUM, which may live hundreds of years or a few months, depending on its food supply. Some species grow cellular strands (hyphae) in all directions, forming a circular mat with a "fairy ring" of fruiting bodies around the outside. Popularly, "mushroom" refers to the edible sporophores, while "toadstool" refers to inedible or poisonous sporophores, but there is no scientific distinction between the two names. Mushrooms are classified by cap shape. Umbrella-shaped sporophores with spore-shedding gills on the undersurface are found chiefly in the AGARIC family (Agaricaceae). Mushrooms that bear spores in an easily detachable layer on the underside of the cap belong to the family Boletaceae. Together the agarics and boletes include most of the forms known as mushrooms. The highly prized edible CHANTERELLE is a bolete. The MORELS (class Ascomycetes) are popularly included with the true mushrooms because of their shape and fleshy structure. Since some poisonous mushrooms closely resemble edible ones, mushrooms intended for eating must be accurately identified. Mushroom poisoning can cause nausea, diarrhea, vomiting, cramps, hallucinations, coma, and sometimes death. See illustration on following page.

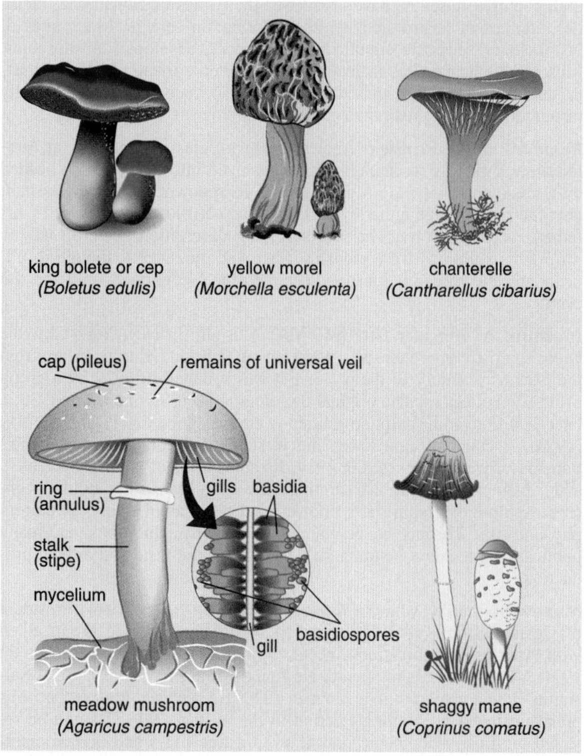

A mushroom typically consists of a stalk (stipe) and a cap (pileus). As the mushroom develops from an underground mycelium and pushes upward, it is protected by a thin membrane (universal veil), which eventually ruptures, leaving fragments on the cap. Another membrane, attaching the cap to the stalk, also ruptures, allowing the cap to expand and leaving a remnant ring (annulus) on the stalk. Radiating rows of gills are found on the cap's undersurface; these bear the club-shaped reproductive structures (basidia) which form minute spores known as basidiospores, of which a single mushroom may produce millions.

mushroom poisoning *or* **toadstool poisoning** Sometimes fatal effect of eating any of the 70–80 species of poisonous MUSHROOMS, or toadstools. Many contain toxic ALKALOIDS. The most deadly, *Amanita phalloides* (death cup), causes violent abdominal pain, vomiting, and bloody diarrhea. Severe liver, kidney, and central-nervous-system damage lead to coma. Over half the victims die. Treatment with thioctic acid, glucose, and penicillin or by filtering the blood with charcoal may be effective. *A. muscaria* causes vomiting, diarrhea, excessive perspiration, and confusion, with recovery within 24 hours. *Gyromitra esculenta* toxin is usually destroyed by cooking, but in susceptible people it affects the central nervous system and breaks down blood cells, causing jaundice. Some poisonous mushrooms resemble harmless ones, so extreme caution is needed in wild-mushroom gathering.

Musial.

PICTORIAL PARADE

Musial \'myü-zē-əl\, **Stan(ley Frank)** (born 1920) U.S. baseball player. Born in Donora, Pa., he played his entire career for the St. Louis Cardinals (1941–63), starting as a pitcher but switching to the outfield and ultimately first base. A left-handed batter, "Stan the Man" became one of the game's great hitters. His lifetime totals of hits (3,630), runs (1,949), and times at bat were second only to those of TY COBB, his total of runs batted in (1,951) was the fourth-highest of all time, and his total of extra-base hits (1,477) was only surpassed later by HANK AARON. Popular among fans for his unfailing graciousness, he became a Cardinals executive after retirement.

music Organization of sound. Music most often implies sounds with distinct PITCHES that are arranged into MELODIES and organized into patterns of RHYTHM AND METER. The melody will usually be in a certain KEY or MODE, and will usually suggest HARMONY that may be made explicit as accompanying CHORDS or COUNTERPOINT. Music is used for such social purposes as worship, coordination of movement, communication, and entertainment.

music box Mechanical musical instrument in which projecting pins on a revolving brass cylinder or disk, encoding a piece of music, pluck tuned steel tongues. It was probably invented c. 1780 in Switzerland. With its modular cylinders or disks, it was a popular domestic instrument until displaced by the player piano and phonograph.

German music box, with disk in playing position, from Leipzig, c. 1900.

BY COURTESY OF THE MUSICAL WONDER HOUSE, WISCASSET, MAINE; PHOTOGRAPH, JOHN SPINKS

music hall and variety theater Popular entertainment that featured successive acts by singers, comedians, dancers, and actors. The form derived from the taproom concerts given in city taverns in 18th–19th-century England. To meet the demand for entertainment for the working class, tavern owners often annexed nearby buildings as music halls, where drinking and smoking were permitted. The originator of the English music hall as such was Charles Morton, who built Morton's Canterbury Hall (1852) and Oxford Hall (1861) in London. Leading performers included LILLIE LANGTRY, Harry Lauder (1870–1950), and GRACIE FIELDS. Music halls evolved into larger, more respectable variety theaters, such as London's Hippodrome and the Coliseum. Variety acts combined music, comedy acts, and one-act plays and featured such celebrities as SARAH BERNHARDT and HERBERT TREE. See also VAUDEVILLE.

musica ficta (Latin: "feigned music") Practice of unnotated CHROMATICISM in performance of polyphonic music of the Middle Ages and Renaissance. According to treatises of the times, it was left to the performers to "correct" certain INTERVALS. Which intervals were to be changed, and how and under what circumstances, varied over time. The highly dissonant interval of the diminished 5th (e.g., B–F), considered the "devil in music," was often required to be made "perfect" by flatting the B, and the interval below the tonic often had to be altered to a semitone.

musical (comedy) Theatrical production, normally sentimental and amusing, with a simple but distinctive plot, that offers music and dancing as well as spoken dialogue. Its roots can be traced to such 18th- and 19th-century genres as BALLAD OPERA, SINGSPIEL, and opéra comique, in which dialogue is mostly spoken. *The Black Crook* (1866), often called the first musical comedy, attracted patrons of opera and serious drama as well as those of BURLESQUE SHOWS. V. HERBERT, R. FRIML, and S. ROMBERG brought a form of OPERETTA to the U.S. that became an essential source. GEORGE M. COHAN ushered in the genre's heyday, and in the 1920s and '30s it entered its richest period with the works of J. KERN, G. and I. Gershwin (see GEORGE GERSHWIN, IRA GERSHWIN), C. PORTER, R. RODGERS, O. HAMMERSTEIN, and H. ARLEN. Kern and Hammerstein's *Show Boat* (1927) was perhaps the first musical to employ music thoroughly integrated with the narrative; later tightly constructed musicals included Rodgers and Hammerstein's *Oklahoma!* (1943) and *South Pacific* (1949). The genre flourished with the works of A.J. LERNER, F. LOEWE, and LEONARD BERNSTEIN, but began to decline in the late 1960s, by which time musicals had begun to diverge in many different directions, as exemplified by Gerome Ragni, James Rado, and Galt MacDermott's rock musical *Hair* (1967), JOHN KANDER and Fred Ebb's *Cabaret* (1966), S. SONDHEIM's *Sweeney Todd* (1979), Stephen Swartz's *Godspell* (1971), ANDREW LLOYD WEBBER and Tim Rice's *Jesus Christ Superstar* (1971), Marvin Hamlisch and Edward Kleban's *A Chorus Line* (1975), Alain Boublil and Claude-Michel Schönberg's *Les Misérables* (1985), and Jonathan Larson's *Rent* (1995).

musical notation System of symbols with which music is written down. There are two basic approaches to notating music. Tablature (seen in guitar chord diagrams) depicts the actions a performer is to take (in particular, showing where to put the fingers to produce a given sound). Symbolic notation describes the sounds themselves, and includes methods that vary from assigning different pitches different letters of the alphabet to representing a given combination of notes by a graphic sign. The Western notation system combines rhythmic notation (the shape of a note indicates its duration) with pitch notation (the line or space on a staff where a note is placed indicates its pitch). Thus, a single symbol shows both pitch and duration, and a string of these symbols notates both melody and rhythm.

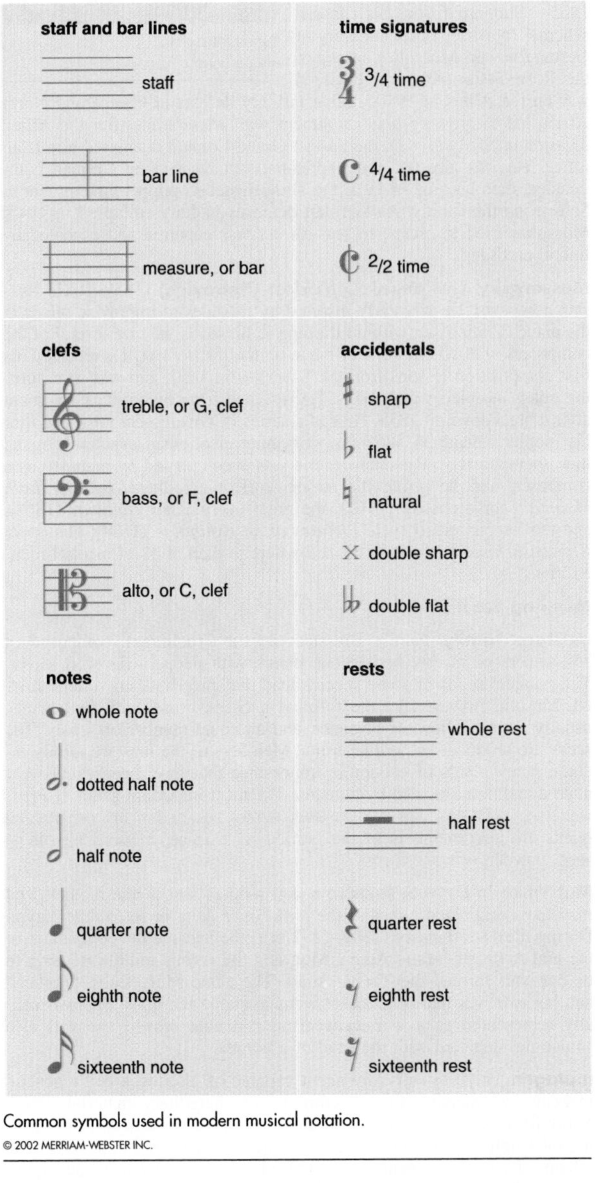

Common symbols used in modern musical notation.

musicology Scholarly study of music. In the late 18th and early 19th century, such study was done by amateurs such as LUDWIG VON KOCHEL. As interest about earlier music grew, greater professionalism was required, including the ability to decipher and assess manuscript sources of both music itself and writing about it. Musicology's first great monument was the first edition of J.S. BACH's complete works (1851–99). Today musicology combines elements of older disciplines, such as music theory, music history, and sociology, and utilizes the latest scientific methods. The best modern performers continue to use the tools musicology puts at their disposal. In recent decades music theory has again became a separate specialization.

musk ox Arctic RUMINANT (BOVID species *Ovibos moschatus*) with a musky odor, large head, and small ears. The neck, legs, and tail are short. Males stand 5 ft (1.5 m) and may weigh almost 900 lbs (400 kg). Both sexes have horns. The broad-based horns of males, up to 2 ft (60 cm) long, start at the middle of the head, dip downward along the sides, and then curve upward. The shaggy, dark-brown coat reaches nearly to the feet. Eskimos make a fine cashmerelike cloth from the thick wool undercoat, which is shed in summer. Musk oxen travel in herds of 20–30, eating grass, lichen, willow, and other low-growing plants.

Musk-oxen (*Ovibos moschatus*).

LEONARD LEE RUE III

muskellunge \'məs-kə-ˌlənj\ Species *(Esox masquinongy)* of somewhat uncommon PIKE valued as a fighting game fish and, to a lesser extent, as a food fish. It inhabits weedy rivers and lakes of the North American Great Lakes region. It averages about 20 lbs (9 kg), but may grow to 6 ft (1.8 m) long and weigh 80 lbs (36 kg) or more, making it the largest fish in the pike family. The lower part of the cheeks and the gill covers are scaleless.

musket Muzzle-loading shoulder firearm developed in 16th-century Spain. Designed as a larger version of the harquebus, muskets were fired with MATCHLOCKS until FLINTLOCKS were developed in the 17th century; flintlocks were replaced by percussion locks in the early 19th century. Early muskets were often handled by two persons and fired from a portable rest. Typically 5.5 ft (1.7 m) long and weighing about 20 lbs (9 kg), they fired a ball about 175 yards (160 m) with little accuracy. Later types were smaller, lighter, and accurate enough to hit a person at 80–100 yards (75–90 m). The musket was replaced in the mid-19th century by the breech-loading RIFLE.

Muskogean languages \məs-'kō-jē-ən\ Family of about eight North American Indian languages spoken or formerly spoken across much of what is now the southeastern U.S. In the 16th century, Koasati (Coushatta) and Alabama were probably spoken in what is now northern Alabama, Creek (Muskogee) and Hitchiti in Alabama and Georgia, and Apalachee in the Florida Panhandle. To the west were Chickasaw in northern Mississippi and western Tennessee and Choctaw in central Mississippi. By the mid-19th century, Apalachee was long extinct, and the forced removals of the 1830s (see TRAIL OF TEARS) had pushed most of the remaining Muskogean-speakers either west of the Mississippi or into Florida, where the SEMINOLES continue to speak a dialect of Creek in central Florida and Mikasuki (Miccosukee) in the Everglades. The extant Muskogean languages continue to be spoken, at least by adults, with Choctaw (in Oklahoma and Mississippi) having the most speakers.

muskrat Either of two semiaquatic, brown RODENT species (family Cricetidae) native to marshes, shallow lakes, and streams of North

America and introduced into Europe. The compact, heavy-bodied muskrat, or musquash *(Ondatra zibethica),* is about 12 in. (30 cm) long, not including the long, scaly, flat tail. The partially webbed hind feet have a stiff, bristly fringe. Anal sacs produce a musky secretion. The commercially valuable fur consists of long, stiff, glossy guard hairs overlying a dense, soft underfur. Muskrats live in either a burrow dug into the bank or a reed-and-rush mound built in the water. They eat sedges, reeds, roots, and an occasional aquatic animal. The round-tailed muskrat, or Florida water rat *(Neofiber alleni),* is smaller.

Muskrat (*Ondatra zibethica*).
JOHN H. GERARD

Muslim Brotherhood *Arabic* **al-Ikhwan al-Muslimun** Religio-political organization founded in Egypt in 1928 by Hasan al-Banna (1906–1949) that promoted the QURAN and HADITH as the proper basis for society. It quickly gained many followers throughout North Africa and the Middle East. It became politicized after 1938, rejecting Westernization, modernization, and secularization. Suppressed in Egypt after a 1954 assassination attempt on GAMAL ABDEL NASSER, it operated clandestinely in the 1960s and '70s. In the late 1980s it experienced an upsurge, competing in legislative elections in Egypt and Jordan.

Muslim calendar See Muslim CALENDAR

Muslim League *orig.* **All India Muslim League** Political group that led the movement calling for a separate Muslim nation to be created out of the partition of British India (1947). It was founded in 1906, and in 1913 it adopted self-government for India as its goal. For several decades it supported Hindu-Muslim unity in an independent India, but in 1940, fearing Hindu domination, the league called for a separate nation for India's Muslims. After the creation of Pakistan in 1947, the Muslim League (as the All Pakistan Muslim League) became Pakistan's dominant political party, but it gradually declined in popularity and by the 1970s had disappeared altogether. See also MOHAMMED ALI JINNAH.

mussel Any of numerous BIVALVE species of either the marine family Mytilidae, found worldwide, or the freshwater superfamily Unionacea, called naiads, found mostly in the U.S. and S.East Asia. Marine mussels are usually wedge-shaped or pear-shaped and 2–6 in. (5–15 cm) long. They may be smooth or ribbed and often have a hairy covering. The shells of many species are dark blue or greenish brown on the outside and pearly on the inside. Mussels attach themselves to solid objects or to one another, often forming dense clusters. Some burrow into soft mud or wood. They are eaten by birds and starfishes, and some species are raised commercially for food.

Atlantic ribbed mussels (*Modiolus demissus*).
WALTER DAWN

Musset \mü̅e̅-'sā\, **(Louis-Charles-) Alfred de** (1810–1857) French poet and playwright. A member of a noble family, Musset came under the influence of Romanticism in adolescence and produced his first work, *Stories of Spain and of Italy*, in 1830. After an early play failed, he published historical tragedies and comedies but refused to let them be performed. He is best remembered for his poetry, including light satirical pieces and poems of dazzling technical virtuosity, as well as passionate, eloquent lyrics such as "La nuit d'octobre" (1837). A fitful love affair with GEORGE SAND inspired some of his finest work.

Mussolini, Benito (Amilcare Andrea) *known as* **Il Duce** \il-'dü-chā\ (1883–1945) Italian dictator (1922–43). An unruly but intelligent youth, he became an ardent socialist and served as editor of the party newspaper, *Avanti!* (1912–14). When he reversed his opposition to World War I, he was ousted by the party. He founded the pro-war *Il Popolo d'Italia,* served with the Italian army 1915–17, then returned to his editorship. Advocating government by dictatorship, he formed a political group in 1919 that marked the beginning of FASCISM. A dynamic and captivating orator at rallies, he organized the March on ROME (1922) to prevent a Socialist-led general strike. After the government fell, he was appointed prime minister, the youngest in Italian history. He obtained a law to establish the Fascists as the majority party and became known as *Il Duce* ("The Leader"). He restored order to the country and introduced social reforms and public-works improvements that won widespread popular support. His dreams of empire led to the invasion of Abyssinia (later Ethiopia) in 1935. Supported in his fascist schemes by ADOLF HITLER but wary of German power, Mussolini agreed to the ROME–BERLIN AXIS and declared war on the Allies in 1940. Italian military defeats in Greece and North Africa led to growing disillusionment with Mussolini. After the Allied invasion of Sicily (1943), the Fascist Grand Council dismissed him from office. He was arrested and imprisoned but rescued by German commandos, then became head of the Hitler-installed puppet government at Salò in northern Italy. As German defenses in Italy collapsed in 1945, Mussolini tried to escape to Austria but was captured and executed by Italian partisans.

Benito Mussolini.
H. ROGER-VIOLLET

Mussorgsky \mu̇-'sȯrg-skē\, **Modest (Petrovich)** (1839–1881) Russian composer. He was early inspired by folktales to improvise music at the piano. Composing without training in his teens, he met several of the composers with whom he later made up the MIGHTY FIVE. He received his first composition lessons from M. BALAKIREV in 1857, and was soon turning out piano pieces and songs. He resigned from his military regiment after a breakdown in 1858. He had a series of government jobs, but after his mother's death in 1865 his worsening alcoholism eventually made him unemployable. Personal decline was accompanied by maturity as a composer, and he wrote his major works, including *Night on Bald Mountain* for orchestra (1867), the great opera *Boris Godunov* (1868), and the famous piano cycle *Pictures at an Exhibition* (1874). His opera *Khovanshchina* was left unfinished when he died at 42 of alcohol-related illnesses.

Mustang See P-51

mustard family Family Brassicaceae (or Cruciferae), composed of 350 genera of mostly herbaceous plants with peppery-flavored leaves. The pungent seeds of some species lead the spice trade in volume traded. Mustard flowers take the form of a Greek cross, with four petals, usually white, yellow, or lavender, and an equal number of sepals. The seeds are produced in podlike fruits. Members of the mustard family include many plants of economic importance that have been extensively altered and domesticated by humans. The most important genus is *Brassica* (see BRASSICA); TURNIPS, RADISHES, RUTABAGAS, and many ornamental plants are also members of the family. As a spice, mustard is sold in seed, powder, or paste form.

Mut \'müt\ In EGYPTIAN RELIGION, a sky goddess and divine mother. Mut may have originated either in the Nile River delta or in Middle Egypt. During the 18th dynasty (1539–1292 BC), she became the companion of the god AMON at THEBES. Amon, Mut, and the young god KHONS (said to be her son) formed the Theban triad. The name Mut means "mother," and her role was that of an older woman among the gods. She was usually represented as a woman wearing a double crown; she was also sometimes depicted with the head of a lioness.

mutagen \'myü-tə-jən\ Any agent capable of altering a cell's genetic makeup by changing the structure of the hereditary material, DNA. Many forms of electromagnetic radiation (e.g., cosmic rays, X rays, ultraviolet light) are mutagenic, as are various chemical compounds. The effects of some mutagens are increased or suppressed in some organisms by the presence of certain other, nonmutagenic substances; oxygen, for example, makes cells more sensitive to the mutagenic effects of X rays.

Mutanabbi \ˌmu̇-tä-'näb-bē\, **(Abu al-Tayyib Ahmad ibn Husayn) al-** (915–965) Poet regarded by many as the greatest in the Arabic language. Born in Iraq, he received an education, unusual for his time and rank, because of his poetic talent. He lived among the Bedouin and,

L
M
N

claiming to be a prophet, led an unsuccessful Muslim revolt in Syria. After two years' imprisonment he became a wandering poet, eventually leaving Syria for Egypt and Iran. He primarily wrote PANEGYRICS in a flowery, bombastic style marked by improbable metaphors. Proud and arrogant in tone, his verse is crafted with consummate skill and artistry.

mutation Alteration in the genetic material of a cell that is transmitted to the cell's offspring. Mutations may be spontaneous or induced by outside factors (MUTAGENS). They take place in the GENES, occurring when one base is substituted for another in the sequence of bases that determines the GENETIC CODE, or when one or more bases are inserted or deleted from a gene. Many mutations are harmless, often masked by the presence of a dominant normal gene (see DOMINANCE). Some have serious consequences; for example, a particular mutation inherited from both parents results in SICKLE-CELL ANEMIA. Only mutations that occur in the sex cells (eggs or sperm) can be transmitted to the individual's offspring. Alterations caused by these mutations are usually harmful. In the rare instances in which a mutation produces a beneficial change, the percentage of organisms with this gene will tend to increase until the mutated gene becomes the norm in the population. In this way, beneficial mutations serve as the raw material of EVOLUTION.

Mutazila \mü-'tä-zi-lə\ In ISLAM, political or religious neutralists. The term also applies to members of a theological school that flourished in BASRA and BAGHDAD in the 8th–10th century. The Mutazila were the first Muslims to use the categories and methods of Hellenistic philosophy to derive their dogma. The tenets of their faith included the oneness of God, free will and responsibility for one's actions, and the justice of God and the consequent inevitability of reward in heaven or punishment in hell. Their doctrine of a created (as opposed to eternal) QURAN held sway 827–49, but was ultimately abandoned. Mutazili beliefs were disavowed by SUNNI Muslims but accepted by SHIITES.

mutiny Any concerted resistance to lawful military authority. Mutiny was formerly regarded as a most serious offense, especially aboard ships at sea. Wide disciplinary powers were given the commanding officer, including the power to inflict CAPITAL PUNISHMENT without a COURT-MARTIAL. With the development of radio communications, the threat diminished and harsh punishment was prohibited in the absence of a court-martial.

Mutsuhito See MEIJI EMPEROR

mutual fund *or* **unit trust** *or* **open-end trust** Company that invests the funds of its subscribers in diversified SECURITIES and issues units representing shares in those holdings. It differs from an INVESTMENT TRUST, which issues shares in the company itself. While investment trusts have a fixed capitalization and a limited number of shares for sale, mutual funds make a continuous offering of new shares at net asset value (plus a sales charge) and redeem their shares on demand at net asset value, determined daily by the market value of the securities they hold.

Muybridge \'mī-ˌbrij\, **Eadweard** *orig.* **Edward James Muggeridge** (1830–1904) British-U.S. photographer. He emigrated to the U.S. from England as a young man, and in 1868 his photos of Yosemite Valley made him famous. Hired by LELAND STANFORD to photograph a trotting horse in motion, to test Stanford's contention that it lifted all four legs simultaneously, he developed a special fast shutter for his battery of 12–24 cameras, and in 1877 was able to prove Stanford right. He lectured widely on animal locomotion, illustrating his lectures with his zoopraxiscope, a predecessor of the movie projector. His extensive photographic studies of human movement (1884–87) have been useful to artists and scientists.

Mwene Matapa \'mwā-nā-mȧ-'tȧ-pə\ Title borne by a line of kings ruling a South African territory between the Zambezi and Limpopo rivers, in what is now Zimbabwe and Mozambique, from the 14th to the 17th century. Their domain, often called Matapa (or Mutapa), is associated with the historical site of ZIMBABWE in southeastern Zimbabwe.

Mweru, Lake \'mwā-rü\ *French* **Lac Moero** \ˌlȧk-mwā-'rō\ Lake, central Africa. It is located on the boundary between southeastern Democratic Republic of the Congo (Zaire) and Zambia, west of the southern tip of Lake TANGANYIKA. Part of the CONGO RIVER system, it is 76 mi (122 km) long and has a surface area of 1,900 sq mi (4,920 sq km). The Luapula River, a headstream of the Congo River, flows through it. The Bangweulu Swamps adjoin the lake.

My Lai incident \'mē-'lī\ (March 16, 1968) Massacre of 502 unarmed villagers by U.S. soldiers in the village of Song My during the VIETNAM WAR. William Calley was the platoon leader who directed the killing in the hamlet of My Lai, where soldiers shot men, women, children, and babies. Many villagers were beaten or raped before being killed. The incident was initially covered up by high-ranking Army officers. Calley was convicted of premeditated murder and originally sentenced to life in prison, but Pres. RICHARD NIXON intervened on his behalf and he was paroled after three years. The massacre and other atrocities revealed during the trial shocked the U.S. public and contributed to opposition to the war.

Myanmar \'myän-ˌmär\ *or* **Burma** *officially* **Union of Myanmar** Nation, S.East Asia, on the Bay of BENGAL and the ANDAMAN SEA. Area: 261,789 sq mi (678,034 sq km). Population (1997 est.): 46,822,000. Capital: YANGON (Rangoon). Inhabitants are chiefly Burman; others include Chin, Shan, and Karen. Languages: Burmese (official), many indigenous languages. Religions: Buddhism (the majority), Christianity, animism, Islam, and Hinduism. Currency: kyat. Myanmar may be divided into four main regions: the northern and western mountains, the central lowlands, and the Shan Plateau in the east. Its major rivers are the IRRAWADDY and the SALWEEN. Myanmar's tropical climate is greatly influenced by the monsoons of southern Asia, and only about one-sixth of its extremely mountainous land is arable. It has a centrally planned, developing economy that is largely nationalized and based on agriculture and trade. Rice is the most important crop and principal export; teak is also

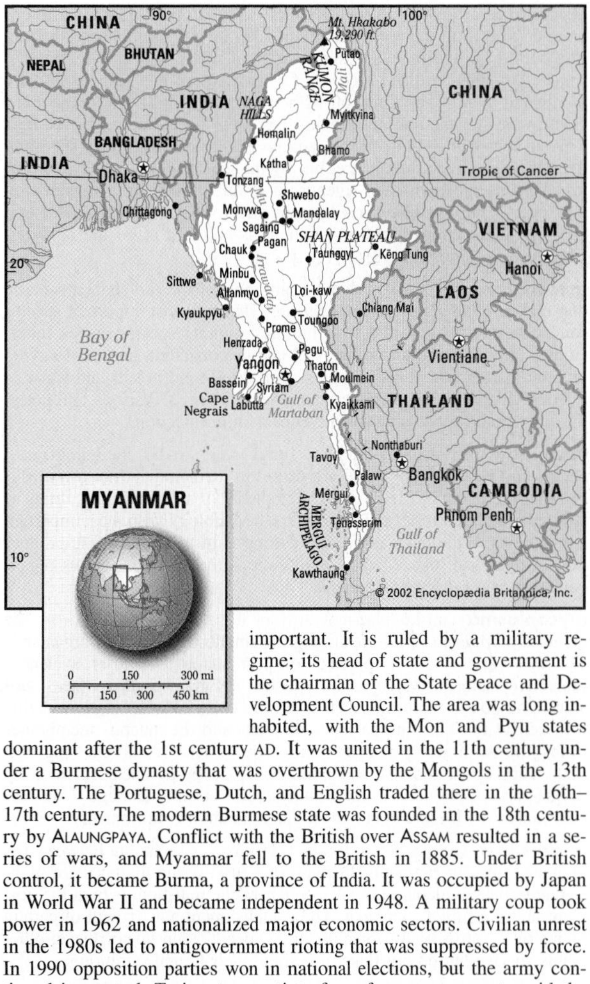

important. It is ruled by a military regime; its head of state and government is the chairman of the State Peace and Development Council. The area was long inhabited, with the Mon and Pyu states dominant after the 1st century AD. It was united in the 11th century under a Burmese dynasty that was overthrown by the Mongols in the 13th century. The Portuguese, Dutch, and English traded there in the 16th–17th century. The modern Burmese state was founded in the 18th century by ALAUNGPAYA. Conflict with the British over ASSAM resulted in a series of wars, and Myanmar fell to the British in 1885. Under British control, it became Burma, a province of India. It was occupied by Japan in World War II and became independent in 1948. A military coup took power in 1962 and nationalized major economic sectors. Civilian unrest in the 1980s led to antigovernment rioting that was suppressed by force. In 1990 opposition parties won in national elections, but the army continued in control. Trying to negotiate for a freer government amid the unrest, AUNG SAN SUU KYI was awarded the Nobel Peace Prize in 1991.

myasthenia gravis \ˌmī-əs-ˈthē-nē-ə-ˈgra-vəs\ Chronic AUTOIMMUNE DISEASE causing MUSCLE weakness. Autoantibodies block the response of muscle cells to ACETYLCHOLINE. Muscles weaken with repeated use but regain their strength after rest. The pattern varies, but usually muscles used in eye movements, facial expressions, chewing, swallowing, and respiration are affected first, then neck, trunk, and limb muscles. Severe cases impede breathing. Anticholinesterase drugs stimulate nerve-impulse transmission, and corticosteroids may help. Removal of the THYMUS has improved severe cases. Remission lasting several years may occur.

mycelium \mī-ˈsē-lē-əm\ Mass of branched, tubular filaments (hyphae) of fungi (see FUNGUS) that penetrate soil, wood, and other organic matter. The mycelium makes up the THALLUS (undifferentiated body) of a typical fungus. The mass may be microscopic in size or developed into visible structures, such as brackets, MUSHROOMS, PUFFBALLS, or TRUFFLES. The mycelium produces SPORES, directly or through special fruiting bodies.

Mycenae \mī-ˈsē-nē\ Prehistoric city, northeastern PELOPONNESE, Greece. A natural rock citadel, it was the legendary capital of AGAMEMNON. It flourished during the BRONZE AGE, building the distinctive MYCENAEAN civilization. It was at its height in the Aegean c. 1400 BC and declined c. 1100 BC with the invasion of the DORIANS from the north. Excavations at Mycenae began in 1840, but the most celebrated discoveries there were those by HEINRICH SCHLIEMANN c. 1876. Ruins include the Lion Gate, acropolis, granary, and several royal BEEHIVE TOMBS and shaft graves.

Mycenaeans \ˌmī-sə-ˈnē-ənz\ Warlike Indo-European peoples who entered Greece from the north starting c. 1900 BC and established a BRONZE AGE culture on the mainland and nearby islands. Their culture was dependent on that of the MINOANS of Crete, who for a time politically dominated them. They threw off Minoan control c. 1400 and were dominant in the Aegean until they themselves were overwhelmed by the next wave of invaders c. 1150. MYCENAE continued to exist as a city-state into the period of Greek dominance, but by the 2nd century AD it was in ruins. Mycenaean myths and legends lived on through oral transmission into later stages of Greek civilization and form the basis of Homeric epic and Greek tragedy. Their language is believed to be the most ancient form of Greek.

mycobacterium \ˌmī-kō-bak-ˈtir-ē-əm\ Any of the rod-shaped BACTERIA that make up the genus *Mycobacterium.* The two most important species cause TUBERCULOSIS and LEPROSY in humans; another species causes tuberculosis in both cattle and humans. Some mycobacteria live on decaying organic matter; others are parasites. Most are found in soil and water in a free-living form, or in diseased tissue of animals. Various antibiotics have had some success against mycobacterium infections.

mycology \mī-ˈkä-lə-jē\ Study of fungi (see FUNGUS), including MUSHROOMS and YEASTS. Many fungi are useful in medicine and industry. Mycological research has led to the development of such antibiotic drugs as PENICILLIN, STREPTOMYCIN, and TETRACYCLINE. Mycology also has important applications in the dairy, wine, and baking industries and in the production of dyes and inks. Medical mycology is the study of fungus organisms that cause disease in humans.

mycoplasma \ˌmī-kō-ˈplaz-mə\ Any of the BACTERIA that make up the genus *Mycoplasma.* They are among the smallest of bacterial organisms. The cell varies from a spherical or pear shape to that of a slender branched filament. Mycoplasma species are gram-negative (see GRAM STAIN) and do not require oxygen. They are colonial microorganisms that lack cell walls. They are parasites of joints and the mucous membranes lining the respiratory, genital, or digestive tracts of cud-chewing animals, carnivores, rodents, and humans. Toxic by-products excreted by the bacteria accumulate in the host's tissues, causing damage. One species causes a widespread but rarely fatal pneumonia in humans.

mycorrhiza \ˌmī-kə-ˈrī-zə\ Product of close association between the branched, tubular filaments (hyphae) of a FUNGUS and the ROOTS of higher plants. The association usually enhances the nutrition of both the host plant and the fungal symbiont. The establishment and growth of certain plants (e.g., citrus plants, orchids, pines) depends on mycorrhizae; other plants survive but do not flourish without their fungal symbionts.

mycoses See FUNGAL DISEASES

mycotoxin TOXIN produced by a FUNGUS. Numerous and varied, mycotoxins can cause hallucinations, skin inflammation, liver damage, hemorrhages, miscarriage, convulsions, neurological disturbances, and/or death in livestock and humans. The best-known mycotoxins are AFLATOXIN, ERGOT toxin, and the agents of MUSHROOM POISONING.

myeloid tissue See BONE MARROW

mynah *or* **myna** \ˈmī-nə\ Any of several Asian songbird species of the STARLING family (Sturnidae). The hill mynah *(Gracula religiosa)* of southern Asia, called the grackle in India, is about 10 in. (25 cm) long and glossy black with white wing patches, yellow wattles, and orange bill and legs. In the wild, it chuckles and shrieks; caged, it learns to imitate human speech far better than its chief rival, the gray PARROT. The common, or Indian, mynah *(Acridotheres tristis)* was introduced into Australia, New Zealand, and Hawaii. The crested mynah *(A. cristatellus),* native to China and Indonesia, was introduced into British Columbia, Canada, but has not spread.

myocardial infarction \ˌmī-ə-ˈkär-dē-əl-in-ˈfärk-shən\ *or* **heart attack** Death of a section of HEART muscle when its blood supply is cut off, usually by a blood clot in a coronary artery narrowed by ARTERIOSCLEROSIS. HYPERTENSION, DIABETES MELLITUS, high CHOLESTEROL, cigarette SMOKING, and CORONARY HEART DISEASE increase the risk. Symptoms include severe chest pain, often radiating to the left arm, and shortness of breath. Up to 20% of victims die before reaching the hospital. Diagnosis is done by ELECTROCARDIOGRAPHY and by analysis for ENZYMES in the blood. Treatment aims to limit the area of tissue death (infarct) and prevent and treat complications. Thrombolytic (clot-dissolving) drugs may be administered. BETA-BLOCKERS alleviate pain and slow the heart rate. ANGIOPLASTY or CORONARY BYPASS restores blood flow to heart muscle. Follow-up may include drugs, exercise programs, and counseling on diet and lifestyle changes.

myositis \ˌmī-ə-ˈsī-təs\ INFLAMMATION of MUSCLE tissue, often from bacterial, viral, or parasitic INFECTION but sometimes of unknown origin. Most types destroy muscle and surrounding tissue. Bacteria may directly infect muscle (usually after injury) or produce substances toxic to it. Some chronic diseases (e.g., TUBERCULOSIS, third-stage SYPHILIS) can involve the muscles. Parasites (e.g., TAPEWORMS, PROTOZOANS) in contaminated food enter the bloodstream from the intestines and lodge in muscle.

myotonia \ˌmī-ə-ˈtō-nē-ə\ Disorder causing difficulty relaxing contracted voluntary MUSCLES. All or only a few may be affected. Myotonia seems to originate in the muscles (myopathy) rather than the NERVOUS SYSTEM. Certain TOXINS can cause it. A hereditary form, myotonia congenita (Thomsen's disease), can affect eyelid and eye motion, swallowing, or talking. Quick movements cause muscle stiffening. There is also a myotonic form of MUSCULAR DYSTROPHY. ANALGESICS, ANESTHETICS, and anticonvulsant drugs can alleviate the symptoms.

Myra \ˈmī-rə\ Ancient city, LYCIA, southern coast of ASIA MINOR, now southwestern Turkey. Ancient ruins dating from the 5th–3rd century BC include an acropolis, a magnificent theater, and several rock-cut tombs that resemble wooden houses and shrines. As a prisoner on his way to Rome in the 1st century AD, St. PAUL changed ships in Myra. St. NICHOLAS was bishop of the city in the 4th century AD. It declined in the 7th century after Arab raids.

Myrdal \ˈmēr-ˌdäl, *Engl* ˈmir-ˌdäl\, **(Karl) Gunnar** (1898–1987) Swedish economist and sociologist. He received his PhD from Stockholm University and taught there from 1933 until 1967. His early work emphasized pure theory, but he later focused on applied economics and social problems. He explored the social and economic problems of blacks in the U.S. (1938–40) and in 1944 published the classic study *An American Dilemma,* in which he presented his theory that poverty breeds poverty. In regard to development economics, he argued that rich and poor countries, rather than converging economically, might well diverge, the poor countries becoming poorer as the rich countries enjoyed economies of scale and the poor ones were forced to rely on primary products. In 1974 he shared the Nobel Prize with FRIEDRICH VON HAYEK. His wife, Alva Myrdal (1902–1986), was a sociologist, diplomat, U.N. administrator, and antiwar activist; she shared the 1982 Nobel Peace Prize with Alfonso García Robles.

Myron \ˈmī-rən\ (c. 480–440 BC) Greek sculptor. An older contemporary of PHIDIAS and POLYCLITUS, he was considered by the ancients one of the most versatile and innovative of all Attic sculptors. He was the first

Greek sculptor to combine a mastery of movement with a gift for harmonious composition. Working almost exclusively in bronze, he is best known for his studies of athletes in action, particularly the *Discobolos* (*Discus Thrower*, c. 450 BC).

"Discobolos," Roman marble copy of Greek bronze by Myron, c. 450 BC; in the National Roman Museum, Rome.
ALINARI—ART RESOURCE

myrtle Any of the evergreen shrubs in the genus *Myrtus* (family Myrtaceae). Authorities differ widely over the number of species included; most occur in South America, while some are found in Australia and New Zealand. Common myrtle *(M. communis)* is native to the Mediterranean and the Middle East and is cultivated in southern England and the warmer portions of North America. Other plants known as myrtle include the MOUNTAIN LAUREL and PERIWINKLE. The family Myrtaceae, commonly called the myrtle family, includes the plants that produce the spices ALLSPICE and CLOVES, and the genus *Eucalyptus*. See also CRAPE MYRTLE.

Mysore See KARNATAKA

Mysore \mī-'sōr\ City (pop., 1991: 607,000), southern KARNATAKA state, southern India. Situated midway between the KAVERI and Kabbani rivers, the site was inhabited before the 3rd century BC. The city was the capital of the princely state of Mysore 1799–1831, then was occupied by the British. The state's second-largest city, it is an important industrial center producing textiles, chemicals, and foodstuffs. Sites of interest include the 17th-century British residency, the maharaja's palace, and the University of Mysore (founded 1916). Nearby Chamundi Hill has a monolith representing Nandi, the sacred bull of the Hindu deity SHIVA.

mystery play Vernacular drama of the Middle Ages. It developed from the LITURGICAL DRAMA, and usually represented a biblical subject. In the 13th century, craft guilds began producing mystery plays at sites removed from the church, adding apocryphal and satirical elements to the dramas. In England groups of 25–50 plays were later organized into lengthy cycles, such as the Chester plays and the Wakefield plays. In England the plays were often performed on moveable pageant wagons, while in France and Italy they were acted on stages with scenery representing heaven, earth, and hell. Technical flourishes such as flying angels and fire-spouting devils kept the spectators' attention. The genre of the mystery play declined by 1600. See also MIRACLE PLAY, MORALITY PLAY.

mystery religions Secret cults of the Greco-Roman world. Derived from primitive tribal ceremonies, mystery religions reached their peak of popularity in Greece in the first three centuries AD. Their members met secretly to share meals and take part in dances and ceremonies, especially initiation rites. The cult of DEMETER produced the most famous of the mystery religions, the ELEUSINIAN MYSTERIES, as well as the ANDANIA MYSTERIES. DIONYSUS was worshiped in festivals that included wine, choral singing, sexual activity, and mime. The Orphic cult, by contrast, based on sacred writings attributed to ORPHEUS, required chastity and abstinence from meat and wine. Mystery cults also attached to ATTIS, ISIS, and JUPITER DOLICHENUS, among others.

mystery story Work of fiction in which the evidence related to a crime or to a mysterious event is so presented that the reader has an opportunity to consider solutions to the problem, the author's solution being the final phase of the piece. The mystery story is an age-old popular genre and is related to several other forms. Elements of mystery may be present in narratives of horror or terror, pseudoscientific fantasies, crime stories, accounts of diplomatic intrigue, affairs of codes and ciphers and secret societies, or any situation involving an enigma. See also DETECTIVE STORY; GOTHIC NOVEL.

mysticism Spiritual quest for union with the divine. Forms of mysticism are found in all major religions. HINDUISM, with its goal of absorption of the soul in the All, is inherently predisposed to mystical experience. BUDDHISM emphasizes MEDITATION as a means of moving toward NIRVANA. In ISLAM, SUFISM employs metaphors of intoxication and of the love between bride and bridegroom to express the desire for union with the divine. In JUDAISM, the foundations of mysticism were laid in the visions of the biblical prophets and were later developed in the KABBALA and in HASIDISM. Mysticism has appeared intermittently in CHRISTIANITY, notably in the writings of St. AUGUSTINE and St. TERESA OF ÁVILA, and in the works of Meister ECKHART and his 14th-century successors.

myth Traditional story of ostensibly historical events that serves to unfold part of the worldview of a people or explain a practice, belief, or natural phenomenon. Myths relate the events, conditions, and deeds of gods or superhuman beings that are outside ordinary human life and yet basic to it. These events are set in a time altogether different from historical time, often at the beginning of creation or at an early stage of prehistory. A people's myths are usually closely related to their religious beliefs and rituals. The modern study of myth arose with early-19th-century ROMANTICISM. Wilhelm Mannhardt, JAMES GEORGE FRAZER, and others later employed a more comparative approach. SIGMUND FREUD viewed myth as an expression of repressed ideas, a view later expanded by CARL GUSTAV JUNG in his theory of the "collective unconscious" and the mythic ARCHETYPES that arise out of it. BRONISLAW MALINOWSKI emphasized how myth fulfills common social functions, providing a model or "charter" for human behavior. CLAUDE LEVI-STRAUSS has discerned underlying structures in the formal relations and patterns of myths throughout the world. MIRCEA ELIADE and RUDOLF OTTO held that myth is to be understood solely as a religious phenomenon. Features of myth are shared by other kinds of literature. Origin tales explain the source or causes of various aspects of nature or human society and life. FAIRY TALES deal with extraordinary beings and events but lack the authority of myth. SAGAS and EPICS claim authority and truth but reflect specific historical settings.

myxedema \‚mik-sə-'dē-mə\ Physiological reaction to low levels of thyroid hormone in adults, either due to THYROID-GLAND removal, lack of function, or atrophy, or secondary to a PITUITARY-GLAND disorder. Gradual changes include enlarged tongue, thick, puffy skin, drowsiness, cardiac enlargement, and slow metabolism. Low thyroid hormone affects levels of other hormones, and may result in low blood sodium and disorders of the reproductive system (including reduced fertility), adrenal glands, and circulatory system. Treatment is with thyroid hormone.

Myxomycetes See SLIME MOLD

myxovirus \‚mik-sō-'vī-rəs\ Any of a group of VIRUSES that are agents of INFLUENZA and can cause the common COLD, MUMPS, and MEASLES in humans, canine DISTEMPER, rinderpest in cattle, and Newcastle disease in fowl. The virus particle is encased in a fatty membrane, variable in shape from spheroidal to threadlike, and studded with spikelike protein projections; it contains RNA. These viruses react with a protein on the surface of red blood cells; many of them cause red blood cells to clump together.

L
M
N

NAACP *in full* **National Association for the Advancement of Colored People** Oldest and largest U.S. civil-rights organization. It was founded in 1909 to secure political, educational, social, and economic equality for blacks; W. E. B. DU BOIS and IDA B. WELLS were among its 60 founders. Its most successful efforts have been lawsuits, political activity, and public-education programs. In 1939 it organized the independent Legal Defense and Education Fund as its legal arm, which sued for school desegregation in *BROWN VS. BOARD OF EDUCATION* (1954). During World War II it pressed for desegregation of the armed forces, which was achieved in 1948. In 1967 its general counsel, THURGOOD MARSHALL, became the U.S. Supreme Court's first black justice.

Naber, John (born 1956) U.S. swimmer. Born in Evanston, Ill., he swam for USC, winning 15 championships. At the 1976 Olympics he won four gold medals and a silver; his world-record times in the 100-m and 200-m backstroke stood for seven years.

Nabis \'nä-bēz\ (from Hebrew, *navi,* "prophet, seer") Group of French artists who paved the way for the development of abstract art in the early 20th century. The Nabis preached that a work of art is the visual expression of an artist's synthesis of nature and his or her personal aesthetic. They were influenced by PAUL GAUGUIN and the PONT-AVEN SCHOOL, as well as by Japanese woodcuts, Symbolist painting, and the Pre-Raphaelites. Paul Sérusier (1865–1927), the group's founder, painted the first Nabi work, *Landscape at the Bois d'Amour at Pont-Aven* (also called *Talisman;* 1888). Original members included PIERRE BONNARD and EDOUARD VUILLARD; a later member was ARISTIDE MAILLOL.

Nabisco See KRAFT FOODS, INC.

Nabokov \nə-'bȯ-kəf, 'na-bə-ˌkȯf\, **Vladimir (Vladimirovich)** (1899–1977) Russian-U.S.-Swiss novelist and critic. Born to an aristocratic family, he had an English-speaking governess. He published two collections of verse before leaving Russia in 1919 for Cambridge Univ., but by 1925 had turned to prose as his main genre. During 1919–40 he lived in England, Germany, and France. His life before coming to the U.S. in 1940 is recalled in his superb autobiography, *Speak, Memory* (1951). Beginning with *King, Queen, Knave* (1928), his writing began to feature intricate stylistic devices. His novels are principally concerned with the problem of art itself, presented in various disguises, as in *Invitation to a Beheading* (1938); parody is frequent in *The Gift* (1937–38) and later works. His novels written in English include the notorious and greatly admired best-seller *Lolita* (1955), which brought him wealth and international fame; *Pale Fire* (1962); and *Ada* (1969). His critical works include a monumental translation of and commentary on ALEKSANDR PUSHKIN's *Eugene Onegin* (4 vols., 1964).

Nabokov, 1968.

© PHILIPPE HALSMAN

Nabu \'nä-ˌbü\ Major god in the Assyrian-Babylonian pantheon, the son of MARDUK. He was patron of the art of writing and a god of vegetation. As the recorder of the fates assigned to humans by the gods, Nabu's symbols were the clay tablet and the stylus. His holy city was Borsippa. Goddesses associated with Nabu were Nana, a Sumerian deity; the Assyrian Nissaba; and the Akkadian Tashmetum.

Nabuco (de Araújo) \nä-'bü-kō\, **Joaquim (Aurelio Barretto)** (1849–1910) Leader of Brazil's abolitionist movement. Both in the national chamber of deputies (from 1878) and in the Brazilian Anti-Slavery Society, which he founded, Nabuco worked tirelessly to end slavery in Brazil. Emancipation was proclaimed in 1888, and in the ensuing economic disruption the emperor PEDRO II was overthrown (1889) and a republic established. A monarchist, Nabuco retired from public life until 1900, when he accepted the republic and entered its service. As ambassador to the U.S. he distinguished himself as an advocate of Pan-Americanism.

Nadar \ná-'dár\ *orig.* **Gaspard-Félix Tournachon** (1820–1910) French photographer, caricaturist, and writer. When his father's bankruptcy forced him to leave medical school in 1838, he settled in Paris and began selling caricatures to humor magazines. By 1853 he had become an expert photographer and had opened a portrait studio. His studies of prominent Parisians such as CHARLES BAUDELAIRE (1855) and EUGENE DELACROIX (1855) were exceptional in their naturalness, in contrast to the stiff formality of most portraits of the time. His studio became a favorite meeting place of the Paris intelligentsia, and was the site of the first Impressionist exhibit. A tireless innovator, in 1855 he patented the idea of using aerial photographs in mapmaking and surveying, and in 1858 he himself made the first successful aerial photograph, from a balloon. He also wrote novels, essays, satires, and autobiographical works.

Nader, Ralph (born 1934) U.S. lawyer and consumer advocate. Born in Winsted, Conn., he attended Princeton University and Harvard Law School. In 1963 he left his private practice in Hartford to hitchhike to Washington, D.C., where he began public-interest work. His concern about unsafe car designs resulted in the best-selling book *Unsafe at Any Speed* (1965), which led directly to the passage of national auto-safety standards. Since then, he and his associates, known as "Nader's Raiders," have performed numerous studies on consumer health, safety, and financial issues and have lobbied for greater government regulation of business and industry in a variety of areas. He was instrumental in the passage of the Freedom of Information Act (1966) and in establishing OSHA, the Consumer Product Safety Commission, and the ENVIRONMENTAL PROTECTION AGENCY. He also founded the consumer organization Public Citizen and the U.S. Public Interest Research Group, an umbrella organization for other public-interest research groups. As the Green Party candidate for president of the U.S., he won 3 percent of the national vote in 2000. His work has had major and lasting effects on many aspects of American life.

Nadir Shah \nä-'dēr-'shä\ (1688–1747) Iranian conqueror and ruler. Originally a bandit, he helped restore Tahmasp II of the SAFAVID DYNASTY, defeating the Ghilzay Afghan usurper Mahmud. He later deposed Tahmasp II to place Tahmasp's infant son on the throne; he made himself regent, then deposed the son and took the throne himself in 1736. He engaged in constant warfare with his neighbors, enlarging his empire from the Indus River to the Caucasus Mountains Suspicious of those around him and capriciously cruel, he was assassinated by his own troops.

NAFTA See NORTH AMERICAN FREE TRADE AGREEMENT

Nag Hammadi \'nág-hám-'ma-dē\ Town in Upper Egypt on the Nile. In 1945 a collection of 13 codices containing 53 Gnostic texts (scriptures and commentaries) was found nearby at the site of an ancient settlement on the river's eastern bank. Written in the Coptic language, the texts were composed in the 2nd or 3rd century and copied in the 4th century. They include accounts of the life of JESUS and his sayings after his resurrection, predictions of the APOCALYPSE, and theological treatises. As the only surviving documents written by Gnostics themselves, they constitute a major source of knowledge about GNOSTICISM.

Nadir Shah, painting by an unknown artist, c. 1740; in the Victoria and Albert Museum, London.

BY COURTESY OF THE VICTORIA AND ALBERT MUSEUM, LONDON

naga \'nä-gə\ In Hindu and Buddhist mythology, a semidivine being, half human and half serpent. Nagas can assume either wholly human or wholly serpentine form. They live in an underground kingdom filled with beautiful palaces that are adorned with gems. Brahma is said to have relegated the nagas to the nether regions and to have commanded them to bite only the truly evil or those destined to die prematurely. They are also associated with waters—rivers, lakes, seas, and wells—and are regarded as guardians of treasure.

Naga Hills Hill region, India and Myanmar. A northern extension of the Arakan Yoma system, the hills reach a height of 12,552 ft (3,826 m) at Mount Saramati on the frontier. The densely forested hills receive heavy monsoon rains. The area is inhabited by villages of Naga tribes.

Nagaland State (pop., 1994 est.: 1,410,000), northeastern India. It borders Myanmar and has an area of 6,366 sq mi (16,488 sq km). Its capital is Kohima. Except for a small area of plain, the entire state is covered with ranges of hills that are part of the Himalayas. Myanmar ruled the region 1819–26, until the British began annexing its hill areas. The Naga people accepted statehood within an independent India in 1963. There are more than 20 major Naga tribes and subtribes, with different dialects and customs. About two-thirds are Christian, and most others, Hindu or Muslim. Agriculture is the mainstay of the economy. Crops include rice, millet, sugarcane, potatoes, and tobacco.

Nagarjuna \nä-'gär-jü-nə\ (c. AD 150–c. AD 250) Indian monk and philosopher, founder of the Madhyamika school of Buddhism. Born into a Brahman family of southern India, he underwent a spiritual conversion when he studied the doctrines of Mahayana Buddhism. His *Fundamentals of the Middle Way* and *Averting the Arguments* are critical analyses of false views about how existence arises, the means of knowledge, and the nature of reality. He established the concept of *sunyata*—emptiness, or the lack of an absolute reality behind the changing forms of existence—as a fundamental tenet of the Madhyamika school.

Nagasaki City (pop., 1995: 439,000), western Kyushu, Japan. It is a seaport and commercial city at the mouth of the Urakami River where it empties into Nagasaki harbor. It was the only Japanese port open to foreign trade 1639–1859. After the Portuguese and English traders were expelled in 1639, only the Dutch, Chinese, and Koreans were allowed into the harbor. In the 19th century it was the winter port of the Russian Asian fleet until 1903. It became a major shipbuilding center in the early 20th century. In 1945 the second atomic bomb was dropped there by the U.S. in World War II, killing about 39,000 people and injuring about 25,000 others. The bomb also destroyed about 40% of its buildings. The city has been rebuilt and is a spiritual center for movements to ban nuclear weapons.

Nagorno-Karabakh Region (pop., 1991 est.: 193,000), southwestern Azerbaijan. It occupies an area of 1,700 sq mi (4,400 square km) on the northeastern flank of the Karabakh Range. Russia annexed the area from Persia in 1813, and in 1923 it was established as an autonomous province of the Azerbaijan S.S.R. In 1988 the region's ethnic Armenian majority demonstrated against Azerbaijani rule, and in 1991, after the breakup of the U.S.S.R. brought independence to Armenia and Azerbaijan, war broke out between the two ethnic groups. Since 1994 it has been held by ethnic Armenians, though officially it remains part of Azerbaijan.

Nagoya City (pop., 1995: 2,152,000), southern Honshu, Japan. Located east of Kyoto, at the head of Ise Bay, it is one of Japan's leading industrial cities. Manufactures include textiles, watches, bicycles, sewing machines, machine tools, chemicals, and ceramics. The city dates from 1610, when a great castle was erected by the Owari branch of the Tokugawa shogunate; the castle was destroyed during World War II and rebuilt in 1959. The city's educational and cultural institutions include Nagoya University and the Tokugawa Art Museum. The Atsuta Shrine and the Ise Shrine located there are the oldest and most highly esteemed Shinto shrines in Japan.

Nagpur \'näg-ˌpu̇r\ City (pop., 1991: 1,625,000), northeastern Maharashtra state, India. It is situated along the Nag River, almost at the geographic center of India. Founded in the 18th century by a Gond prince, it became the capital of members of the Maratha confederacy. In the 19th century it was under British control. The city's products include textiles, iron goods, pharmaceuticals, transport equipment, cotton, and oranges. It is dominated by the former British fort built at its center. It is an educational and cultural center.

nagual \nä-'gwäl\ *or* **nahual** \nä-'wäl\ In some Mesoamerican religions, a personal guardian spirit that resides in an animal. The person who wishes to find his nagual goes to sleep in an isolated spot, and the animal that appears in a dream or that confronts him when he awakens will thereafter be his guardian spirit. Many modern Mesoamerican Indians believe that the first creature to cross over the ashes spread before a newborn baby becomes the child's nagual. In some areas, nagual refers to the animal into which men with magical powers can transform themselves to do evil.

Nagy \'näd^{y}\, **Imre** (1896–1958) Hungarian politician. He fought in World War I, was captured by the Russians, and joined the Red Army. He lived in Moscow 1929–44, then returned to Hungary under the Soviet occupation and held several ministerial posts. An advocate for peasants' rights, he became premier (1953–55) but was ousted for his independent ideas. During the Hungarian Revolution (1956), he again served as premier and sought to establish Hungary's independence from Soviet domination. He made an unsuccessful appeal to the West for help against the invading Soviet troops, but was arrested, tried, and executed.

Nagy, László Moholy- See László Moholy-Nagy

Nahanni National Park \nä-'hä-nē\ National park, southwestern Northwest Territories. Established in 1972, it occupies an area of 1,177,700 acres (476,968 hectares). Its central feature is the South Nahanni River, a tributary of the Liard River; it flows southeast from the Mackenzie Mountains and is 350 mi (563 km) long. The park also contains three large canyons and a variety of birds, wildlife, and flowers.

Nahda \'nä-hə-də\ (Arabic: "Islamic Tendency Movement") Tunisian political party founded in 1981 by Rachid al-Ghannouchi and Abdel Fatah Mourou. Its platform calls for a fairer distribution of economic resources, multiparty democracy, and more religiosity in daily life, all through nonviolence. After 1984 the party was reorganized to operate clandestinely as well as publicly. Though the government of Zine al-Abidine Ben Ali has treated it less harshly than did that of Habib Bourguiba, it remains illegal.

Nahua \'nä-wə\ Indian population of Mexico and Central America, of whom the Aztecs are the best known. Modern-day Nahua are agricultural, using the slash-and-burn technique and cultivating both common and private land. They are skilled weavers, using fibers of the maguey plant, wool, and cotton. Nahua parents and godparents have strong ties in a fictive kin relationship. Though they profess Roman Catholicism, the Nahua believe in witchcraft and recognize a variety of supernatural beings. See also Nahuatl language.

Nahuatl language \'nä-ˌwä-t^{ə}l\ Uto-Aztecan language of Mexico, which continues to be spoken by more than a million modern Mexicans in various markedly divergent dialects. Nahuatl was the language of perhaps the majority of the inhabitants of pre-Conquest central Mexico, including Tenochtitlán (now Mexico City), the capital of the Aztec empire. Soon after the Conquest in the 1520s, Nahuatl began to be written in a Spanish-based orthography, and an abundance of documents survive from the colonial period, including annals, municipal records, poetry, formal addresses, and *The History of the Things of New Spain,* a remarkable compendium of Nahua culture compiled by Indian informants under the direction of the Franciscan friar Bernardino de Sahagún (1499–1590).

Nahuel Huapí \nä-'wel-wä-'pē\, **Lake** Lake, in the eastern foothills of the Andes, southwestern Argentina, near the Chilean border. The largest lake in Argentina's lake district, it has an area of 212 sq mi (549 sq km), and a depth of nearly 1,000 ft (300 m). It is dotted with islands, including Isla Victoria, the site of a forestry research station. The lake region was designated the Nahuel Huapí National Park in 1934.

Nahuel Huapí National Park National park, southwestern Argentina, including Lake Nahuel Huapí. Originating as a reserve in 1903 with a private donation of 18,500 acres (7,500 hectares), it became Argentina's first national park in 1934. The park and adjacent nature reserve include dense forests, rivers, glaciers, and snow-clad peaks, including El Tronador ("the Thunderer") and Mount Catedral.

Nahum \'nā-(h)əm\ (late 7th century BC) One of the 12 Minor Prophets in the Old Testament, traditional author of the Book of Nahum. (His prophecy is part of a larger book, The Twelve, in the Jewish canon.) The prophet Nahum is identified only as a resident of Elkosh. His subject is the collapse of the Assyrian Empire and the fall of its capital, NINEVEH (612 BC), which he views as a demonstration of God's desire to punish the wickedness of the Assyrians, Israel's longtime enemies.

Nahyan dynasty \ˌnȧ-hə-ˈyan\ Ruling family of ABU DHABI. The family were originally BEDOUIN of the Bani Yas confederation of Arabia in the Liwa oasis. The first emir arrived in the late 1770s and established a commercial port on the island. The current emir, Sheikh Zayid bin Sultan al-Nahyan, is also president of the United Arab Emirates. See also al-MAKTUM.

nail In construction and carpentry, a slender metal shaft, pointed at one end and flattened at the other end, used as a FASTENER. Most often used to join pieces of wood, nails are also used with plastic, drywall, masonry, and concrete. They are usually made of steel but can also be made of stainless steel, iron, copper, aluminum, or bronze. The pointed end is called the point, the shaft is called the shank, and the flattened part is called the head.

nail Structure made of KERATIN that grows on the back of the end of each finger and toe. Nails consist of a root, under the skin; a translucent plate, attached to a nail bed beneath; and a free edge. Nail plate (and probably bed) cells are produced at the root and pushed forward as new cells form behind them. They die and turn white as they reach the free edge and lose contact with the richly vascularized nail bed, which supplies them with nutrients. Fingernails grow continuously at about 0.5 mm per week; toenails grow more slowly. They protect the tips of fingers and toes, help the fingers pry, and scratch.

Nain brothers, Le See LE NAIN BROTHERS

Naipaul \ˈnī-ˌpȯl\, **V(idiadhar) S(urajprasad)** *later* **Sir Vidiadhar** (born 1932) Trinidadian novelist. Descended from Hindu Indians who emigrated to Trinidad as indentured servants, Naipaul left Trinidad in 1950 to attend Oxford University. He won critical recognition with *A House for Mr. Biswas* (1961), about an immigrant's attempt to assert his identity and independence. Other novels that explore, in an often harshly critical tone, the disintegration and alienation typical of postcolonial nations include *In a Free State* (1971; Booker Prize), *Guerrillas* (1975), and *A Bend in the River* (1979). He also wrote *The Enigma of Arrival* (1987), *Half a Life* (2001), and nonfictional studies of India. Naipaul was awarded the Nobel Prize for Literature in 2001.

Nairobi \nī-ˈrō-bē\ City (pop., 1999: 2,143,254), capital of Kenya. It is located in southern central Kenya at an elevation of about 5,500 ft (1,680 m). Founded c. 1899 as a colonial railroad site, it became the capital of BRITISH EAST AFRICA in 1905. As a government and trade center, it attracted many settlers from rural Kenya, making it one of the largest cities in Africa. When Kenya gained independence in 1963, it remained the capital, with its area greatly expanded by the new constitution. It is Kenya's principal commercial and industrial city, producing beverages, processed food, cigarettes, and furniture. The city exports many products via the port of MOMBASA. Noted institutions and landmarks include the University of Nairobi and the National Museum of Kenya. The NAIROBI NATIONAL PARK attracts many visitors.

Nairobi National Park National park, Kenya. Located about 15 mi (25 km) south of NAIROBI, it was established in 1946. It has an area of 45 sq mi (117 sq km). It is noted for wildlife, including lion, gazelle, black rhinoceros, giraffe, antelope, zebra, numerous reptiles, and hundreds of bird species.

James Naismith holding a ball and a peach basket, the first basketball equipment.
UPI—EB INC.

Naismith \ˈnā-ˌsmith, ˈnāz-məth\, **James A.** (1861–1939) Canadian-U.S. physical-education instructor, inventor of BASKETBALL. At the YMCA Training School (later Springfield College) in Springfield, Mass. (1890–95), he was asked to devise a new indoor winter sport. His version of basketball called for nine players (later reduced to five) per team and the use of peach baskets (later netted hoops) as goals. He later coached the basketball team at the University of Kansas (1898–1937). He is also credited with inventing the protective helmet for football players. The Naismith Memorial Basketball Hall of Fame was incorporated in Springfield in 1959.

Naivasha \nī-ˈvä-shä\, **Lake** Lake, southwestern central Kenya. Located in the GREAT RIFT VALLEY, at 6,135 ft (1,870 m) above sea level, it is 12 mi (19 km) long and 9 mi (14 km) wide and has an area of 108 sq mi (280 sq km); it has no known outlet. It serves as a weekend resort for residents of NAIROBI, to the southeast.

naive art Work of artists in sophisticated societies who lack or reject formal training. Naive artists create with passion but without formal knowledge of methods. Naive works are often extremely detailed, with a tendency toward the use of brilliant, saturated colors and the absence of perspective, which creates the illusion of figures floating in space. Well-known naive artists include HENRI ROUSSEAU and Grandma MOSES.

Najd See NEJD

Nakae Toju \ˈnä-kä-ˌe-ˈtō-jü\ *orig.* **Gen** (1608–1648) Japanese philosopher. He taught and studied the works of ZHU XI, but eventually he abandoned Zhu's philosophy for the idealist thought of WANG YANGMING. Like Wang, he believed truth was to be discovered through intuition and reflection rather than empirical investigation, and that the universe's unifying principle exists in the human mind, not in the external world. He believed that a concept could be fully understood only when acted upon; this emphasis on action made him popular with 19th- and 20th-century Japanese nationalists.

Nakhon Ratchasima \ˌnä-ˌkȯn-ˌrä-chə-ˈsē-mä\ City (pop., 1999 est.: 181,400), northeastern Thailand. It is the area's transportation, commercial, financial, and governmental center. It grew rapidly during the 1960s and 1970s with the buildup of its Royal Thai Air Force Base, from which U.S. planes operated during the VIETNAM WAR. Nearby are restored 11th-century KHMER temples, a major tourist attraction.

Nakhon Si Thammarat \ˌnä-ˌkȯn-ˌsē-ˌtä-mə-ˈrät\ Town (pop., 1999 est.: 105,176), southern Thailand, on the eastern coast of the MALAY PENINSULA. The walled town, one of Thailand's oldest, was founded more than 1,000 years ago. The capital of a powerful state that controlled the midsection of the peninsula, it was often called Ligor until the early 20th century. It is the area's commercial center and site of the Wat Mahathudu temple complex. It is noted for its NIELLO work in silver.

Nalanda \nä-ˈlən-də\ Buddhist monastic center, often spoken of as a university, in northern Bihar state, India. Though it is traditionally dated to the time of the BUDDHA (6th–5th century BC), archaeological excavations date its foundations to the 5th century AD. It housed a population of several thousand teachers and students. Topics studied covered included logic, grammar, astronomy, and medicine. It continued to flourish through the 12th century and became a center of religious sculpture. It was probably sacked during Muslim raids c. 1200 and never recovered.

Nalchik \ˈnälʸ-chik\ City (pop., 1999 est.: 234,700), southwestern Russia. It lies along the Nal'chik River where the river leaves the Caucasian foothills. Founded as a Russian fortress in 1818, it gained importance after the RUSSIAN REVOLUTION OF 1917. It is a popular vacation and health resort, and has a university and research institute. Industries include footwear, clothing, and furniture.

Namath \ˈnā-məth\, **Joe** *orig.* **Joseph William** (born 1943) U.S. football quarterback. Born in Beaver Falls, Pa., he developed his quarterback skills at the Univ. of Alabama. An exceptional passer, in his third season with the New York Jets (1965–77) he threw for a record 4,007 yards. Though long hampered by knee injuries, by the time of his retirement he had set seasonal and career records for most games with 300 yards or more gained in passing. The nickname "Broadway Joe" reflected his fondness for New York nightlife.

Namatjira, Albert (1902–1959) Australian Aborigine painter. A member of the Aranda tribe, Namatjira learned European watercolor painting techniques at a Lutheran mission school. In 1936 he sold his first painting, and, in 1938, he sold all 41 watercolors on display in his first major solo exhibition in Melbourne. He exhibited his work—generally depictions of the desertlike landscape of central Australia—frequently in the next two decades and became well known in Australia and overseas. One of his paintings was presented to Queen Elizabeth II in 1954.

Nambudiri \nəm-ˈbü-drē\ Dominant caste of the Indian state of Kerala. Rigidly orthodox, its members regard themselves as the representatives of the ancient VEDIC RELIGION and of the traditional Hindu code. They place great emphasis on their priestly status and do not normally engage in business. The chief landowners of Kerala, they derive their wealth from their landholdings.

name One or more words designating an individual entity. The names of certain specific people, places, and things, called proper nouns, are capitalized. Types of names include personal names (Christopher, Nancy), place-names (London, Nairobi), titles of works of art *(Mona Lisa, Paradise Lost),* brand names (Sanka, Vaseline), names of historical events or eras (War of the Roses, Renaissance), and political, artistic, or philosophical movements (Progressivism, Cubism). Personal names may pass from one culture to another, often changing form—Jochanan (Hebrew), Johann (German), John (English), Ian (Scottish), etc. Family names (surnames) are of more recent origin; the conventions that govern them have existed only since the 11th century. Many hereditary family names came from given names—for example, Alfred, the son of John, might be called Alfred Johnson. Others came from place-names or occupations—Henri from the town of Avignon might become Henri d'Avignon, and Robert, a blacksmith, might become Robert Smith.

Namib Desert \ˈnä-mib\ Desert region, along the entire coast of Namibia. It is an almost rainless area, about 800 mi (1,300 km) long and 30–100 mi (50–160 km) wide, traversed by rail lines linking WALVIS BAY with the Republic of South Africa. It is basically a smooth platform of bedrock of various types and ages. In the southern half the platform is covered with sand. The eastern part, the Inner Namib, supports large numbers of antelope. The shore area has a dense population of marine birds, including flamingos, pelicans, and penguins.

Namibia \nə-ˈmi-bē-ə\ *officially* **Republic of Namibia** *formerly (1915–68)* **South-West Africa** Nation, southwestern coast of Africa. Area: 318,580 sq mi (825,118 sq km). Population (1997 est.): 1,727,000. Capital: WINDHOEK. More than half the people are Ovambo. Others include Nama, Kavango, Herero, and San. Languages: English,

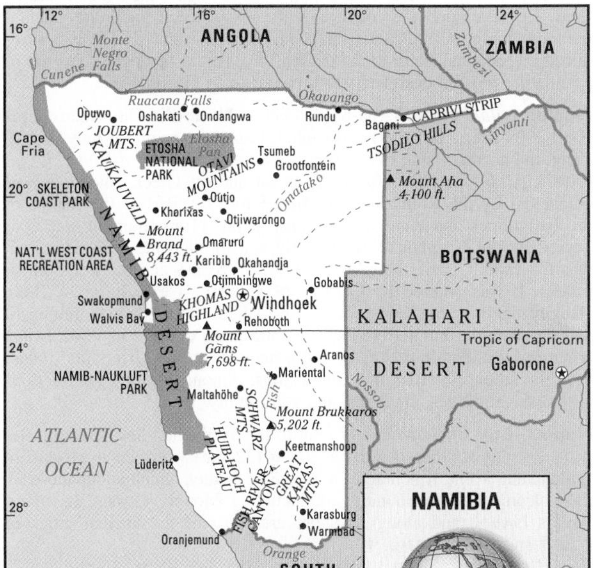

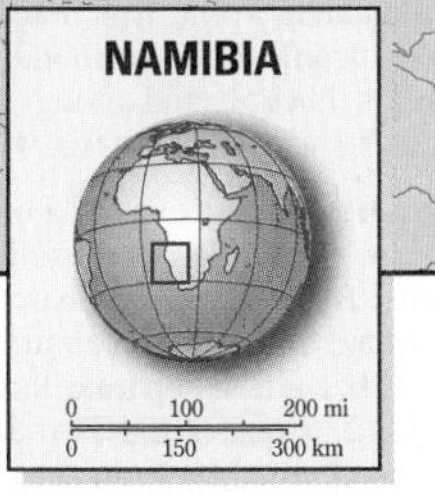

(official), Afrikaans, Bantu, German. Religions: Christianity, animism. Currency: Namibian dollar. Namibia may be divided into three broad regions: the NAMIB DESERT, the Central Plateau, and the KALAHARI DESERT. The economy is based largely on agriculture and on the production and export of diamonds. It is a republic with two legislative houses; its head of state and government is the president. Long inhabited by indigenous peoples, it was explored by the Portuguese in the late 15th century. In 1885 it was annexed by Germany as German Southwest Africa. It was captured in World War I by South Africa, which received it as a mandate from the LEAGUE OF NATIONS in 1918 and refused to give it up after World War II. A U.N. resolution in 1966 ending the mandate was challenged by South Africa in the 1970s and '80s. Through long negotiations involving many factions and interests, it achieved independence in 1990.

Namri Songtsen See GNAM-RI STRONG-BTSAN

Nanak \ˈnä-nək\ (1469–1539) Indian founder of SIKHISM. Born into a Hindu merchant caste, he worked as a storekeeper until a spiritual experience caused him to leave his job and family and begin a 20-year phase of travel. He eventually settled in Kartarpur, a village in Punjab, to which he attracted many disciples, and became the first GURU of the Sikhs. His doctrine stressed the unity and uniqueness of God and offered salvation through disciplined meditation on the divine name. It stipulated that meditation must be inward, and rejected all external aids such as idols, temples, mosques, scriptures, and set prayers. After his death, the stories told of his life were collected in the anthologies called the *Janam-sakhis*.

Nanchang *or* **Nan-ch'ang** City (pop., 1991 est.: 1,350,000), capital of JIANGXI province, southeastern China. An old walled city on the right bank of the GAN RIVER, it was founded in 201 BC. In AD 959 under the TANG regime, it became the southern capital. At the end of the MONGOL period it was a battleground between the founder of the MING DYNASTY and local warlords. In the early 16th century a rebellion was launched against the Ming regime. Nanchang suffered from the TAIPING REBELLION. In 1927 it was the site of revolutionary activities of the Chinese Communist Party. Since 1949 it has become industrialized; its products include textiles, milled rice, and automotive parts.

Nanda dynasty Family that ruled Magadha, in northern India (343?–321? BC). Legends regarding the low-class origins and ruthless conquests of its founder, Mahapadma, are supported by independent evidence. The brief spell of Nanda rule, along with the lengthy tenure of the MAURYAN EMPIRE that succeeded them, represent the political aspect of a great transitional epoch in which settled agriculture and the growing use of iron resulted in production surpluses and the growth of cities. There are references to the wealth of the Nandas, their sizable military, and administrative initiatives such as irrigation projects.

Nanga Parbat \ˈnəŋ-gə-ˈpər-bət\ Peak, western HIMALAYAS. It is located in the region of JAMMU AND KASHMIR under Pakistani control. In 1895 the British climber Albert F. Mummery led the first expedition to the 26,660-ft (8,126-m) summit, but he died in the attempt. Severe weather and frequent avalanches caused the deaths of at least 30 other climbers before the Austrian Hermann Buhl reached the top in 1953.

Nangnang *or* **Lelang** *or* **Lo-lang** Colony of HAN-DYNASTY China in northern Korea, near modern-day Pyongyang, from which the Chinese incorporated southern Korea and parts of Japan into their sphere of influence. The Chinese maintained a commandery there for 400 years. Its presence introduced the local people to wet-rice cultivation, iron technology, and high-fired ceramic technology.

Nanjing *or* **Nan-ching** \ˈnän-ˈjiŋ\ *or* **Nanking** \ˈnan-ˈkiŋ\ City (pop., 1999 est.: 2,388,915), capital of JIANGSU province, eastern central China. Located on the southern bank of the YANGTZE RIVER (Chang Jiang), northwest of SHANGHAI, the site has been inhabited for thousands of years. The present city was founded in 1368 by the MING DYNASTY, which had its capital there 1368–1421. It was taken by the British in the OPIUM WARS of 1842 and was largely destroyed during the TAIPING REBELLION in 1853–64. It was opened as a treaty port in 1899 and was the NATIONALIST capital 1928–37, then was taken by the Japanese. It was the site of the NANJING MASSACRE, in the SINO-JAPANESE WAR. Occupied by communist forces in 1949, it became the provincial capital in 1952. It is a port city and a major industrial and communications center with a university and several colleges. Nearby monuments include mausoleums of SUN YAT-SEN and a Ming emperor.

Nanjing, Treaty of (August 29, 1842) Treaty that ended the first OPIUM WAR, the first of the unequal treaties between China and foreign imperialist powers. China paid the British an indemnity, ceded the territory of Hong Kong, and agreed to establish a "fair and reasonable" tariff. British merchants, who had previously been allowed to trade only at Guangzhou (Canton), were now permitted to trade at five "treaty ports"

L M N

and with whomever they pleased (see CANTON SYSTEM). The treaty was supplemented in 1843 by the British Supplementary Treaty of the Bogue, which allowed British citizens to be tried in British courts and granted Britain any rights in China that China might grant to other nations. See also British EAST INDIA CO., LIN ZEXU.

Nanjing Massacre *or* **Rape of Nanjing** Mass killing and rape of Chinese people in Nanjing by Japanese soldiers during their destruction of the city in the weeks at the end of 1937 and beginning of 1938. Estimates of the number killed range from 100,000 to more than 300,000, and tens of thousands of rapes were committed. Japanese wartime brutality in China kept relations between the two countries cool into the 21st century. See also WAR CRIMES and WORLD WAR II.

Nanna See SIN

Nanni di Banco \'nän-nē-dē-'bäŋ-kō\ (c. 1380/85–1421) Florentine sculptor. Trained by his father, a sculptor who worked on the cathedral of Florence, Nanni received his first important commission from the cathedral, a life-size marble statue of the prophet Isaiah. The classically influenced *Four Crowned Saints* (c. 1411–13) for Or San Michele is considered his masterpiece. He is thought to have been the teacher of DELLA ROBBIA FAMILY. His work exemplifies the stylistic transition from Gothic to Renaissance in early-15th-century Italy.

Nanning *or* **Nan-ning** \'nän-'niŋ\ *formerly (1913–45)* **Yung-ning** \'yu̇ŋ-'niŋ\ City (pop., 1999 est.: 984,061), capital of GUANGXI province, southeastern China. Located on the northern bank of the Yung River, it was the site of a county seat first established in AD 318. A frontier prefecture under the SONG DYNASTY, it was later ruled successively by the MING and QING dynasties. It was opened to foreign trade in 1907. It was occupied by the Japanese during the SINO-JAPANESE WAR, although it was briefly a U.S. air base. It was a supply base for Communist forces during the anti-French war in INDOCHINA and the VIETNAM WAR. Formerly an essentially commercial and administrative center, it has experienced industrial growth.

Nansen \'nän-sən\, **Fridtjof** (1861–1930) Norwegian explorer and statesman. In 1888 he led the first expedition to cross the ice fields of Greenland. On a later expedition, in an attempt to reach the North Pole, in 1895 he reached the farthest northern latitude then attained. He engaged in scientific research 1896–1917, and led oceanographic expeditions in the North Atlantic in 1900 and 1910–14. He undertook diplomatic missions as Norway's first minister to Britain (1906–8) and as head of Norway's delegation to the new League of Nations (1920). He directed the repatriation from Russia of over 400,000 prisoners of war for the League and organized famine relief in Russia for the Red Cross. In 1922 he was awarded the Nobel Peace Prize; he used the prize money for international relief work. In 1931 the Nansen International Office for Refugees was established in Geneva.

Nantahala River \ˌnan-tə-'hā-lə\ River, western North Carolina. It flows 40 mi (64 km) north through the Nantahala National Forest into the Little Tennessee River, and is noted for whitewater rafting and for its scenery. The Nantahala Gorge is the subject of many CHEROKEE legends.

Nantes \'nänt\ *Breton* **Naoned** \'nȧ-ned\ *ancient* **Condivincum** City (metro. area pop., 1999: 268,695), northwestern France. Located on the LOIRE RIVER, west of TOURS, it derives its name from the Namnetes, a Gallic tribe settled there before the Romans conquered GAUL. The Huns, the Normans, and dukes of BRITTANY claimed it before it passed to France in 1499. It rallied to King HENRY IV of France after he signed the Edict of NANTES in 1598. During the FRENCH REVOLUTION its populace suffered many executions. Occupied by German troops in World War II, it was heavily damaged by Allied bombing; it was taken by U.S. troops in 1944. Rebuilt into a major economic center, it has important industrial plants and shipbuilding yards. It also boasts a castle, a cathedral, a university, and a fine art museum.

Nantes, Edict of (April 13, 1598) Law promulgated by HENRY IV of France to grant religious liberty and full civil rights to the Protestant HUGUENOTS. It stipulated that Protestant pastors were to be paid by the state, and public worship was permitted in most of the kingdom, though not in Paris. It also restored Catholicism in all areas where Catholic practice had been interrupted by the Wars of RELIGION. The edict was resented by the Catholic clergy; Cardinal de RICHELIEU annulled its political clauses in 1629, and the full edict was revoked by LOUIS XIV in 1685.

Nantucket Island (pop., 2000: 9,520), Atlantic Ocean, south of CAPE COD, Mass. It is separated from MARTHA'S VINEYARD by the Muskeget Channel. Of glacial origin, it has sandy beaches, a good harbor, and a moderate climate. Purchased from the PLYMOUTH colony in 1641, it became part of New York and was settled in 1659 by Quakers, then ceded to Massachusetts in 1692. It was a whaling center in the 18th century. The summer tourist trade is now its economic mainstay.

naos See CELLA

napalm \'nā-ˌpäm\ Organic compound, the aluminum SOAP or SALT of a mixture of FATTY ACIDS, used to thicken GASOLINE for use as an incendiary in flamethrowers and firebombs. The thickened mixture, itself also called napalm, burns more slowly and can be propelled more accurately and over greater distances than gasoline. When it comes in contact with surfaces, including the human body, it sticks tenaciously and continues to burn. It was developed and first used by the U.S. in World War II. Its use in the Vietnam War became highly controversial.

Napata \'na-pə-tə\ Town in ancient Egypt. Located below the fourth cataract of the NILE RIVER, in the northern part of modern Sudan, it was the capital (c. 750–590 BC) of the NUBIAN kingdom of CUSH and was part of the homeland of the Karmah culture. From the early 18th dynasty it came under Egyptian influence. Ruins in the area include pyramids and temples.

naphthalene \'naf-thə-ˌlēn\ Simplest of the fused (condensed) ring HYDROCARBONS, an AROMATIC COMPOUND composed of two BENZENE rings sharing two adjacent carbon atoms ($C_{10}H_8$). It is a white solid at room temperature, very volatile, with a characteristic odor. Naphthalene is an important raw material in the manufacture of dyes and synthetic resins and has been used as a moth repellent.

Napier \'nā-pər\, **John** (1550–1617) Scottish mathematician and champion of PROTESTANTISM. He divided his life between attacks on the Church of Rome and the pursuit of numerical calculations. On a number of occasions he urged James IV of Scotland to deal firmly with the Catholic threat. From 1594 he worked on developing secret weapons, including a metal chariot with small holes through which shot could be fired. He developed the concept of the LOGARITHM to facilitate calculations involving multiplication, division, roots, and powers. He also introduced the decimal point as a notation for decimal FRACTIONS. The set of calculating rods he designed was a precursor to the slide rule.

Naples *Italian* **Napoli** \'nä-pō-lē\ *ancient* **Neapolis** City (metro. area pop., 2000 est.: 1,002,619) and capital, CAMPANIA, southern Italy. Located on the northern side of the Bay of NAPLES, southeast of Rome, it was founded c. 600 BC by refugees from an ancient Greek colony; it was conquered by the Romans in the 4th century BC. Part of the realms of the Byzantines and then the Saracens, in the 11th century it was conquered by the Norman ruler of Sicily and through the 19th century it was the capital of the kingdom of the Two SICILIES and the kingdom of NAPLES. It was entered by GIUSEPPE DE GARIBALDI's expedition in 1860. Heavily damaged in World War II by Allied and German bombing, it was later rebuilt, but suffered severe earthquake damage in 1980. It is a commercial and cultural center and a major port with diversified industries, including shipbuilding and textiles. Among the city's attractions are medieval castles, churches, and a university.

Naples, Bay of Semicircular inlet of the Tyrrhenian Sea, southern Italy. It extends southeastward for 20 mi (32 km) from Cape Miseno to Campanella Point. It is noted for its scenic beauty, which is enhanced by the volcanic hills surrounding it, including Mount VESUVIUS. Its major port is NAPLES, and along its shore are ruins of the ancient cities of POMPEII and HERCULANEUM.

Naples, Kingdom of Former kingdom comprising the southern portion of the Italian peninsula. The region was held successively by Romans, Byzantines, Lombards, and Saracens before it was conquered by Normans in the 11th century and incorporated into their kingdom of SICILY. It became a separate kingdom in 1282 but was reunited with Sicily in 1442 as one of the Two SICILIES. Again separating from Sicily in 1458, it was claimed by France and then by Spain, which ruled it for two centuries. It was ceded to the Austrian HABSBURGS in 1713 but was conquered in 1734 by the Spanish BOURBONS, who reestablished the kingdom of the Two Sicilies. Napoleon annexed it to France and then made it an independent kingdom 1806–15, after which the Bourbons were restored. In 1860 Naples and Sicily voted for unification with northern Italy.

Napo River \'nä-pō\ River, northeastern Ecuador and northeastern Peru. It rises in Ecuador and flows east across the Peruvian border through dense rain forests for about 700 mi (1,100 km) to empty into the Amazon River. It is an important transport route. Cattle are raised along its banks, and the forests yield rubber, chicle, and timber.

Napoleon *originally Italian* **Napoleone Buonaparte** *French* **Napoléon Bonaparte** (1769–1821) French general and emperor (1804–15). Born in Corsica to parents of Italian ancestry, he was educated in France and became an army officer in 1785. He fought in the French Revolutionary Wars and was promoted to brigadier general in 1793. After victories against the Austrians in northern Italy, he negotiated the Treaty of Campo Formio (1797). He attempted to conquer Egypt (1798–99) but was defeated by the British under Horatio Nelson in the Battle of the Nile. The Coup of 18–19 Brumaire brought him to power in 1799, and he installed a military dictatorship, with himself as First Consul. He introduced numerous reforms in government, including the Napoleonic Code, and reconstructed the French education system. He negotiated the Concordat of 1801 with the pope. After victory against the Austrians at the Battle of Marengo (1800), he embarked on the Napoleonic Wars. The formation of coalitions of European countries against him led Napoleon to declare France a hereditary empire and to crown himself emperor in 1804. He won his greatest military victory at the Battle of Austerlitz against Austria and Russia in 1805. He defeated Prussia at the Battles of Jena and Auerstedt (1806) and Russia at the Battle of Friedland (1807). He then imposed the Treaty of Tilsit on Russia, ending the fourth coalition of countries against France. Despite his loss to Britain at the Battle of Trafalgar, he sought to weaken British commerce and established the Continental System of port blockades. He consolidated his European empire until 1810, but became embroiled in the Peninsular War (1808–14). He led the French army into Austria and defeated the Austrians at the Battle of Wagram (1809), signing the Treaty of Vienna. To enforce the Treaty of Tilsit, he led an army of over 450,000 into Russia in 1812, winning the Battle of Borodino, but was forced to retreat from Moscow with disastrous losses. His army greatly weakened, he was met by a strong coalition of allied powers, who defeated him at the Battle of Leipzig (1813). After Paris was taken by the allied coalition, Napoleon was forced to abdicate in 1814 and was exiled to the island of Elba. In 1815 he mustered a force and returned to France to reestablish himself as emperor for the Hundred Days, but was decisively defeated at the Battle of Waterloo. He was sent into exile on the remote island of St. Helena, where he died six years later. One of the most celebrated figures in history, Napoleon revolutionized military organization and training and brought about reforms that permanently influenced civil institutions in France and throughout Europe.

Napoleon II *or* **Duke of Reichstadt** *orig.* **Napoléon-François-Charles-Joseph Bonaparte** (1811–1832) The only son of Napoleon and Marie-Louise, he was born during Napoleon's reign as emperor and received the title King of Rome. On his father's abdication (1814), he was named his successor, but the Allies refused to accept him. His mother took him to live at the court of her father, Emperor Francis II. Given the Austrian title of duke of Reichstadt, he was controlled by Klemens, Furst von Metternich. In 1830 Bonapartist insurgents attempted to restore Reichstadt as Napoleon II, but he was already ill with the tuberculosis that would kill him.

Napoleon III, detail of a portrait by Hippolyte Flandrin; in the Musée de Versailles.

H. ROGER-VIOLLET

Napoleon III *or* **Louis-Napoléon** *orig.* **Charles-Louis-Napoléon Bonaparte** (1808–1873) Emperor of France (1852–70). The nephew of Napoleon, he spent his youth in exile in Switzerland and Germany (1815–30). With the death in 1832 of Napoleon's son, Napoleon II, he became the claimant to the French throne. After an abortive coup d'état, he was exiled by King Louis-Philippe to the U.S. After another attempted coup (1840), he was arrested, tried, and imprisoned. He escaped to England in 1846 and returned to Paris in 1848, where he was elected to the national assembly. He evoked the legend of Napoleon to win the popular vote as president of the Second Republic. Attempting to expand his power, he staged a coup in 1851 and made himself dictator; in 1852, as Napoleon III, he became emperor of the Second Empire. Seeking to reestablish French power, he led France into the Crimean War and helped negotiate the treaty at the Congress of Paris (1856). He sided with Sicily against Austria (1859) and was victorious at the Battle of Solferino. He aided Italy in achieving unity and annexed Savoy and Nice (1860). He promoted liberalized policies within France, which enjoyed prosperity during much of his reign. In the 1860s he gradually introduced political liberalization. He expected material rewards from his "Latin empire" by installing Maximilian as emperor of Mexico (1864–67), but was disappointed. He kept France neutral in the Austro–Prussian War (1866), but in 1870 Otto von Bismarck contrived to involve France in the disastrous Franco–Prussian War. After leading his troops to defeat in the Battle of Sedan, he surrendered and was deposed as emperor.

Napoleonic Code *French* **Code Civil** French civil code enacted by Napoleon in 1804. It clarified and made uniform the private law of France and followed Roman law in being divided into three books: the law of persons, things, and modes of acquiring ownership of things. In Louisiana, the only civil-law state in the U.S., the civil code of 1825 (revised in 1870 and still in force) is closely connected to the Napoleonic Code. See also law code.

Napoleonic Wars (1799–1815) Series of wars that ranged France against shifting alliances of European powers. Originally an attempt to maintain French strength established by the French Revolutionary Wars, they became efforts by Napoleon to affirm his supremacy in the balance of European power. A victory over Austria at the Battle of Marengo (1800) left France the dominant power on the continent. Only Britain remained strong, and its victory at the Battle of Trafalgar (1805) ended Napoleon's threat to invade England. Napoleon won major victories in the Battles of Ulm and Austerlitz (1805), Jena and Auerstedt (1806), and Friedland (1807) against an alliance of Russia, Austria, and Prussia. The resulting Treaties of Tilsit (1807) and the Treaty of Schönbrunn (1809) left most of Europe from the English Channel to the Russian border either part of the French Empire, controlled by France, or allied to it by treaty. Napoleon's successes resulted from a strategy of moving his army rapidly, attacking quickly, and defeating each of the disconnected enemy units. His enemies' responding strategy was to avoid engagement while withdrawing, forcing Napoleon's supply lines to be overextended; the strategy was successfully used against him by the Duke of Wellington in the Peninsular War and by Mikhail, Prince Barclay de Tolly de Tolly in Russia. In 1813 the Quadruple Alliance formed to oppose Napoleon and amassed armies that outnumbered his. Defeated at the Battle of Leipzig, he was forced to withdraw west of the Rhine River, and after the invasion of France (1814) he abdicated. He rallied a new army to return in the Hundred Days (1815), but a revived Quadruple Alliance opposed him. His final defeat at the Battle of Waterloo was caused by his inability to surprise and to prevent the two armies, led by Wellington and Gebhard von Blucher, from joining forces to defeat him. With his second abdication and exile, the era of the Napoleonic Wars ended.

nappe \'nap\ In geology, a large body or sheet of rock that has been moved by faulting or folding a distance of about 1 mi (1.5 km) or more from its original position. A nappe may be the hanging wall of a low-angle thrust fault (a fracture in the rocks of the earth's crust caused by contraction), or it may be a large recumbent fold (i.e., an undulation in the stratified rocks that have an essentially horizontal axial plane); both processes position older rocks over younger rocks.

Naqada *or* **Naqadah** \nə-'kä-də\ Village (pop., 1986 est.: 17,000), Egypt. Located on the western bank of the Nile River north of Karnak, it is the site of a Neolithic town and burial grounds of the prehistoric period (before 2900 BC). It was first excavated by Flinders Petrie in 1895. The modern town has pottery and silk industries.

Nara period (710–784) Period of Japanese history during which the emperor resided in Nara. The capital city was modeled on the capital of Tang-dynasty China, Changan, from whom the Japanese borrowed extensively in this period. Buddhism, which had entered Japan a little over a century earlier, rose in popularity, and many temples and statues were commissioned. The CHINESE WRITING SYSTEM was introduced and modified by the Japanese (see JAPANESE WRITING SYSTEM), allowing the production of two official histories and the earliest Japanese poetry collections. The Taiho Code, adopted officially in 701, was based on Chinese law, and the Chinese EQUAL-FIELD SYSTEM of land distribution, though no longer rigorously enforced, continued to remain in effect. The imperial state extended its frontiers to include southern Kyushu and northern Honshu.

Narayan(swami) \nə-'rī-ən\, **R(asipuram) K(rishnaswami)** (1906–2001) Indian writer. Narayan briefly worked as a teacher before deciding to write full-time. His first novel, *Swami and Friends* (1935), recounts the adventures of a group of schoolboys. His novels, which typically portray human relationships and the ironies of Indian daily life, in which modern urban existence clashes with ancient tradition, include *The English Teacher* (1945), *The Guide* (1958), *The Man-Eater of Malgudi* (1961), *The Vendor of Sweets* (1967), *A Tiger for Malgudi* (1983), and *The World of Nagaraj* (1990). He also wrote short stories, memoirs, and modern prose versions of Indian epics.

Narayanan, Kocheril Raman (b. 1921) President of India (1997–), the first member of the country's lowest social caste—the group considered to be untouchable—to occupy the office. Raised in poverty he attended the University of Travancore on a scholarship and graduated from the London School of Economics with top academic honors. In 1949 he became a diplomat, despite opposition from upper-caste officials, and was ambassador to several countries, including China and the U.S. After serving as a cabinet minister in parliament, he was named vice president in 1992 and president in 1997.

Narbonensis \ˌnär-bə-'nen-səs\ *or* **Gallia Narbonensis** Ancient Roman province between the Alps, the Mediterranean Sea, and the Cévennes Mtns., comprising what is now southeastern France. Part of Roman Gallia (see GAUL), it was originally called Provincia (see PROVENCE) and was renamed Gallia Narbonensis under AUGUSTUS. It became fully Romanized and was governed by a PROCONSUL. The mild climate attracted many Roman immigrants. Vineyards prospered, olive groves were cultivated, and splendid buildings were erected. The province was also famous for its culture, especially the schools at Massilia (see MARSEILLE).

narcissism \'när-sə-ˌsi-zəm\ Mental disorder characterized by extreme self-absorption, an exaggerated sense of self-importance, and a need for attention and admiration from others. First identified by HAVELOCK ELLIS in 1898, the disorder is named for the mythological NARCISSUS, who fell in love with his own reflection. In addition to an inflated self-image and addiction to fantasy, narcissism is characterized by the tendency to take others for granted or to exploit them and by an unusual coolness and composure, which is shaken only when the narcissistic confidence is threatened. According to SIGMUND FREUD, narcissism is a normal stage in children's development, but it is considered a disorder when it occurs after puberty.

Narcissus \när-'si-səs\ In GREEK MYTHOLOGY, a beautiful youth who fell in love with his own reflection. He was the son of the river god Cephissus and the nymph Leriope. His mother was told by a seer that he would have a long life, provided he never saw his own reflection. His callous rejection of the nymph ECHO or of his lover Ameinias drew upon him the gods' vengeance: he fell in love with his own image in the waters of a spring and wasted away. The NARCISSUS flower sprang up where he died.

narcissus \när-'si-səs\ Any of about 40 species of bulbous, fragrant, ornamental plants that make up the genus *Narcissus* in the AMARYLLIS FAMILY, native mainly to Europe. Popular spring garden flowers include the DAFFODIL, or narcissus *(N. pseudonarcissus),* the JONQUIL *(N. jonquilla),* and poet's narcissus *(N. poeticus).* The stem bears one large blossom. The central crown of each yellow, white, or pink flower ranges in shape from the form of a trumpet, as in the daffodil, to a ringlike cup, as in the poet's narcissus. Rushlike or flattened leaves arise from the base of the plant. Though poisonous, the bulbs were once used in medicines.

narcolepsy SLEEP disorder with sudden, uncontrollable spells of daytime sleep and disturbances of nighttime sleep. It usually begins in youth or early adulthood and is presumably due to dysfunction of certain brain structures. Narcoleptics can fall asleep anywhere and anytime—for instance, while talking, eating, or driving. Sleep usually lasts a moment, rarely over an hour, and the narcoleptic is easily awakened. Sleep paralysis, normal when falling asleep or waking, occurs during full consciousness in narcolepsy, with brief but complete inability to move.

narcotic DRUG that produces analgesia (see ANALGESIC), narcosis (stupor or sleep), and DRUG ADDICTION. In most people narcotics also produce euphoria. Those that occur naturally in the OPIUM POPPY, notably MORPHINE, have been used since ancient Greek times. The main therapeutic use of narcotics is for pain relief. Most countries limit the production, sale, and use of narcotics because of their addictive properties and detrimental effects and the incidence of drug abuse. With the development in the 19th century of the hypodermic needle and of HEROIN, five to 10 times as potent as morphine, the use and abuse of narcotics increased dramatically. A narcotic overdose can cause central nervous system depression, respiratory failure, and death.

Narmada River \nər-'mə-də\ *or* **Nerbudda River** River, central India. Rising in MADHYA PRADESH state, it is 801 mi (1,289 km) long. It flows west into the Gulf of KHAMBHAT, and forms the traditional boundary between Hindustan and the DECCAN. Called Namade by the Greek geographer PTOLEMY in the 2nd century AD, it has always been an important route between the Arabian Sea and the GANGES RIVER valley. It is a pilgrimage route for Hindus who regard it their most sacred river after the Ganges.

Narodnik See POPULIST

Narragansett Bay \ˌnar-ə-'gan-sət\ Inlet of the Atlantic Ocean, southeastern Rhode Island. It extends north for 28 mi (45 km) into the state, almost dividing it into two parts. The bay includes Rhode, Prudence, and Conanicut islands and Mount Hope Bay, which is crossed by one of New England's longest bridges. Since colonial times it has been an active shipping center; its chief ports are PROVIDENCE and NEWPORT. Much of the bay's area is devoted to fishing and recreation.

Narses \'när-ˌsēz\ (c. 480–574) Byzantine general under JUSTINIAN I. A eunuch, he commanded the imperial bodyguard and rose to become grand chamberlain. He helped to quell a riot in 532 and save Justinian's throne. In 538 Narses was sent on a military expedition to retake Italy, but his inability to cooperate with the commander allowed the OSTROGOTHS to triumph. He returned to Italy in 551 and conquered the Ostrogothic kingdom. He held power in Italy until removed by Justinian's successor (567).

narthex Long, narrow porch, usually colonnaded or arcaded, crossing the entire width of a church at its entrance. The narthex is usually separated from the NAVE by columns or a pierced wall. In Byzantine churches the space is divided into two parts: An exonarthex forms the outer entrance to the building and bounds the esonarthex, which opens onto the nave.

narwhal *or* **narwal** \'när-ˌwäl\ *or* **narwhale** \'när-ˌwāl\ TOOTHED WHALE (*Monodon monoceros,* family Monodontidae) of the Arctic, found in groups of 15–20 along coasts and sometimes in rivers. Narwhals are mottled gray, 11.5–16 ft (3.5–5 m) long, and have no dorsal fin. They have only two teeth, at the upper jaw tip. The male's left tooth is a straight, protruding tusk, 8.9 ft (2.7 m) long, that is grooved on the surface in a left-handed spiral. It was prized in medieval times as the uni-

Narwhal (*Monodon monoceros*).
PAINTING BY RICHARD ELLIS

corn horn. The tusk has no known function but is thought to have evolved as a sexual display. Narwhals eat fishes, cephalopods, and crustaceans. They are hunted by humans for their tusks and meat.

NASA *in full* **National Aeronautics and Space Administration** Independent U.S. government agency established in 1958 for research and development of vehicles and activities for aeronautics and space exploration. Its goals include improving our understanding of the universe, the solar system, and earth and establishing a manned SPACE STATION. NASA, previously the National Advisory Committee for Aeronautics (NACA), was created largely in response to Russia's launch of SPUTNIK in 1957. Its organization was well under way in 1961, when Pres. JOHN F. KENNEDY proposed that the U.S. put a man on the moon by the end of the 1960s (see APOLLO). Later unmanned programs (e.g., VIKING, MARINER, VOYAGER, GALILEO) explored other PLANETS, and orbiting observatories (e.g., the HUBBLE SPACE TELESCOPE) have studied the cosmos. NASA also developed and launched various SATELLITES with earth applications, such as LANDSAT and communications and weather satellites. It also planned and developed the SPACE SHUTTLE.

NASDAQ \'naz-dak\ *in full* **National Association of Securities Dealers Automated Quotations** U.S. market for over-the-counter securities. Established in 1971 by the National Association of Securities Dealers, NASDAQ is an automated quotation system that reports on the trading of domestic securities not listed on the regular stock exchanges. It publishes two composite PRICE INDEXES daily as well as bank, insurance, transportation, utilities, and industrial indexes. By the 1990s it had surpassed the AMERICAN STOCK EXCHANGE (AMEX) to become the second-largest U.S. securities market. Members register with the SECURITIES AND EXCHANGE COMMISSION and meet requirements for assets, capital, public shares, and shareholders. In 1999 it merged with AMEX to form the Nasdaq-Amex Market Group. See also OVER-THE-COUNTER MARKET.

Naseby \nāz-bē\, **Battle of** (June 14, 1645) Decisive battle in the ENGLISH CIVIL WARS between the Parliamentary NEW MODEL ARMY and the royalist army of CHARLES I. The two armies met near Naseby, south of Leicester, and deployed along parallel ridges. The 10,000-man royalist force under Prince RUPERT drove back part of the Parliamentary cavalry but then engaged in wild pursuit, leaving the royalist infantry exposed. The more disciplined Parliamentary force under OLIVER CROMWELL regrouped and counterattacked, routing the royalists and taking 4,000 prisoners. With the loss of his best soldiers, Charles could no longer meet the New Model Army in open battle and effectively lost the war.

Nash, John (1752–1835) British architect and city planner. From 1798, Nash was employed by the Prince of Wales. Acquiring considerable wealth, he built for himself East Cowes Castle, Isle of Wight (1798), which had much influence in the GOTHIC REVIVAL period. He subsequently dotted England and Ireland with castles, houses, and cottages in Gothic or Italianate style. Regent's Park (1811) comprises a canal, lake, wooded area, botanical garden, and, on the periphery, shopping arcades and picturesque groupings of residences. Beginning in 1821, he began to reconstruct Buckingham House, London, as a royal palace; dismissed before completing the project, he faced an inquiry into its cost and structural soundness.

Nash, John Forbes (born 1928) U.S. mathematician. He earned a doctorate from Princeton University at 22. He began teaching at MIT in 1951, but left in the late 1950s because of mental illness; thereafter he was informally associated with Princeton. Beginning in the 1950s with his influential thesis "Non-cooperative Games," Nash established the mathematical principles of GAME THEORY. His theory, known as the Nash solution or Nash equilibrium, attempted to explain the dynamics of threat and action among competitors. Despite its practical limitations, it was widely applied by business strategists. He shared the 1994 Nobel Prize in Economics with John C. Harsanyi (born 1920) and Reinhard Selten (born 1930). A film version of his life, *A Beautiful Mind* (2001), won an Academy Award for best picture.

Nash, (Frederic) Ogden (1902–1971) U.S. writer of humorous poetry. Born in Rye, N.Y., Nash sold his first verse in 1930 to the *New Yorker,* on whose staff he worked. In 1931 he published *Hard Lines*, the first of 20 collections that include *The Bad Parents' Garden of Verse* (1936), *I'm a Stranger Here Myself* (1938), and *Everyone but Thee and Me* (1962). His audacious, quotable verse employs delightfully impossible rhymes, puns, and ragged stanzas, often interrupted by digressions. He wrote several children's books and the lyrics for the musicals *One Touch of Venus* (1943) and *Two's Company* (1952).

Nashe \'nash\, **Thomas** (1567–1601?) English pamphleteer, poet, dramatist, and novelist. The first of the English prose eccentrics, Nashe wrote in a vigorous combination of colloquial diction and idiosyncratic coined compounds that was ideal for controversy. Among his works are the satire *Pierce Penilesse His Supplication to the Divell* (1592); the masque *Summers Last Will and Testament* (1592, published 1600); *The Unfortunate Traveller* (1594), the first picaresque novel in English; and *Nashes Lenten Stuffe* (1599). The play *Dido, Queen of Carthage* (1594) was a collaboration with CHRISTOPHER MARLOWE.

Nashville City (pop., 2000: 545,524), capital of Tennessee. It is located on the CUMBERLAND RIVER. Founded in 1779 as Nashborough, it was incorporated as the town of Nashville in 1784. It became a city in 1806 and the state capital in 1843. During the AMERICAN CIVIL WAR, it was occupied by Federal troops (1862). The war's last major battle (1864) took place outside the city. It is a financial and commercial center, producing shoes, clothing, glass, and tires. Important industries include printing, publishing, and recording. Well known for COUNTRY AND WESTERN MUSIC, it is the site of Opryland U.S.A. and the Country Music Hall of Fame and Museum. It is the home of many universities, including VANDERBILT and FISK.

Nashville Convention (1850) Two-session meeting of proslavery U.S. Southerners. In 1849 Mississippi held a convention at the urging of JOHN C. CALHOUN and called for all slave-holding states to send delegates to Nashville, Tenn., to form a united front against perceived Northern aggression. Delegates from nine Southern states met in June 1850; though extremists favored SECESSION, moderate Whigs and Democrats prevailed. The group adopted 28 resolutions defending slavery but was willing to allow an extension of the MISSOURI COMPROMISE line to the Pacific. After the COMPROMISE OF 1850, a smaller group of delegates met in November; dominated by extremists, it denounced the compromise and called again for secession.

Näsijärvi \'na-sē-ˌyar-vē\ *or* **Lake Näsi** Lake, southwestern Finland. About 20 mi (32 km) long and 8 mi (13 km) wide at its widest point, it is the largest of the Pyhä lakes. Its southern banks are flat and barren, but the northern shore is more developed. Ferries have operated on the lake since 1858.

Nasir al-Din Shah \nä-'sēr-ȧl-'dēn-'shä\ (1831–1896) QAJAR DYNASTY shah of Persia (1848–96). He was forced to suppress the riots that ensued on his taking the throne after his father's death. Corrupt and repressive, he was also Western-oriented; he curbed the clergy's secular power, introduced telegraph and postal services, and started Iran's first newspaper. His graft-influenced grants of foreign concessions inspired intense popular resistance that has been regarded as the birth of Iranian nationalism. He was assassinated by a fanatic.

Nasir Hamid Abu Zayd \'na-sir-hȧ-'mēd-ˌab-ü-'zīd\ (born 1943) Egyptian scholar. His research and writings on Quranic exegesis, including his well-known *Critique of Islamic Discourse* (1995), have offended some Islamic conservatives. In 1993 a colleague denounced him in a major Cairo mosque. Islamic radicals successfully sought a nullification of his marriage from an Egyptian family court on the grounds that his writings demonstrated his apostasy. Though the court declined to pass judgment, an appeals court divorced Abu Zayd and his wife, a decision confirmed by the Egyptian Supreme Court. The case has attracted widespread concern among intellectuals and human-rights groups. Since 1995 Abu Zayd and his wife have lived in exile in the Netherlands.

Nasir-i-Khusraw \nȧ-'ser-e-k̲ȯs-'rō\ (1004–1072/77?) Persian poet and theologian. Born into a family of government officials, he attended school only briefly. In 1045 he made a pilgrimage to Mecca and then traveled to Palestine and Egypt. He returned to his homeland in what is now Afghanistan to serve as a missionary for the Ismaili sect, but his efforts aroused Sunni hostility and he was obliged to flee. Considered one of the greatest Persian writers, he is remembered for his didactic and devotional poetry as well as for his *Diary of a Journey Through Syria and Palestine*.

Naskapi See MONTAGNAIS AND NASKAPI

Nasmyth \'nā-ˌsmith\, **James** (1808–1890) Scottish engineer. Son of the artist Alexander Nasmyth (1758–1840), he is known mainly for his invention of the steam hammer (1839), an important metallurgical tool of the Industrial Revolution. He also devised such tools as a planing machine, a steam pile driver, and a hydraulic punching machine, and he manufactured more than 100 steam locomotives. He retired at 48 to devote himself to his hobby, astronomy.

Nassau City (pop., 1990: 172,000), capital of the Bahamas. Located on the northeastern coast of New Providence island, it was settled by the English in the 17th century and became a rendezvous for pirates in the 18th century. Forts were built there to ward off attacks by encroaching Spaniards. During the AMERICAN CIVIL WAR, it became a base for Confederate blockade-runners. It is now a popular resort; its economy is based on tourism.

Nassau Historical region of Germany, former duchy, western part of modern HESSE. It is a thickly forested and hilly area north and east of the Rhine, crossed by the LAHN RIVER and the Taunus Mountains. The title "Count of Nassau" was first assumed in the 12th century. Nassau joined the CONFEDERATION OF THE RHINE and became a duchy in 1806. It was annexed by Prussia in 1866. The descendants of the house of Nassau are royal heads of the Netherlands and Luxembourg to this day.

Nasser, Gamal Abdel *Arabic* **Jamal Abd al-Naser** (1918–1970) Egyptian leader. In his youth, he took part in anti-British demonstrations. As an army officer, he led a coup that deposed the royal family (1952) and installed Gen. Mohammad Naguib as a puppet head of state. In 1954 he deposed Naguib and made himself prime minister. The MUSLIM BROTHERHOOD tried to assassinate him but failed. In 1956 he promulgated a constitution that made Egypt a one-party socialist state with himself as president. In the same year, he nationalized the Suez Canal (see SUEZ CRISIS) and secured Soviet assistance to build the ASWAN HIGH DAM when the U.S. and Britain canceled their offer of aid. He weathered a British-French-Israeli attack on his airfields and the Sinai Peninsula. A charismatic figure, he dreamed of becoming leader of the Muslim world, and succeeded briefly in forming the United Arab Republic with Syria (1958–61). He had tentatively accepted a U.S. peace plan for Egypt and Israel when he died of a heart attack. See also ARAB–ISRAELI WARS, ANWAR AL-SADAT.

Nasser, photograph by Yousuf Karsh.

Nasser, Lake *or in Sudan* **Lake Nubia** Lake, southern Egypt and northern Sudan. It is about 300 mi (483 km) long, and was formed in the 1960s as a result of the construction of the ASWAN HIGH DAM. Its waters, when discharged downstream, have brought 800,000 acres (324,000 hectares) of additional land under irrigation. It has flooded a number of archaeological sites, including ABU SIMBEL.

Nast, Thomas (1840–1902) U.S. (German-born) political cartoonist. He arrived in the U.S. at 6, and from 1862 to 1886 he worked as a cartoonist for *Harper's Weekly.* His cartoons in support of the Northern cause in the Civil War were so effective that ABRAHAM LINCOLN called him "our best recruiting sergeant." Many of his most effective cartoons were attacks on the New York political machine of WILLIAM MARCY TWEED in the 1870s; one led to Tweed's identification and arrest in Spain. Nast originated the Republican Party's elephant and one of the most popular images of Santa Claus, and popularized the Democratic Party's donkey. Left destitute by the failure of a brokerage house, he was appointed U.S. consul in Ecuador, where he died.

Thomas Nast, self-portrait etching, 1892.

nasturtium \nas-'tər-shəm\ Any of various annual plants of the genus *Tropaeolum* (family Tropaeolaceae), native to Mexico, Central America, and northern South America, and cultivated elsewhere as garden plants. Brilliant yellow, orange, or red flowers are funnel-shaped and have a long spur that contains sweet nectar. The peppery-tasting leaves and flowers are sometimes used in salads, and the young flower buds and fruit are sometimes used as seasoning. *Nasturtium* also is a genus of aquatic herbs in the MUSTARD FAMILY (see WATERCRESS).

Natal \nə-'täl\ Seaport city (pop., 1991: 606,000), northeastern Brazil. It is situated near the mouth of the Potengi River, on the Atlantic coast. Founded by the Portuguese in 1597 near the site of a fort, it was given town status in 1611. It is the capital and principal commercial center of the state of Rio Grande do Norte; it is also a busy port and naval base. It is the seat of the State University of Rio Grande do Norte. The Marine Research Institute and the Barreira do Inferno rocket base are located in the vicinity.

Natal \nə-'täl\ Former province, southeastern Republic of South Africa. The area was occupied for centuries by BANTU-speaking peoples. It was given the name Natal by VASCO DA GAMA when he sighted the harbor of Port Natal (now DURBAN) on Christmas Day (Portuguese, *Natal*) in 1497. The first European settlers arrived in 1824. In 1837 AFRIKANERS arrived in the interior and, after they defeated the Zulus there, established the Republic of Natal. Annexed by the British in 1843, it was extended by numerous acquisitions. During the SOUTH AFRICAN WAR, Natal was invaded by Afrikaner forces, which were checked by the British. In 1910 it became a province of the Union of South Africa and in 1961, of the Republic of South Africa. The fragmented, nonindependent black state, or homeland, of KwaZulu was later created within Natal, which was the scene of clashes by rival black factions (see AFRICAN NATIONAL CONGRESS, INKATHA FREEDOM PARTY). After the South African elections of 1994, the region was united to form the province of KwaZulu-Natal.

Nataraja \ˌnə-tə-'rä-jə\ SHIVA in his form as the cosmic dancer. The most common images show him with four arms and flying locks, dancing on a dwarf (a symbol of human ignorance) and encircled by a ring of flames. The Nataraja sculpture shows Shiva as the source of all movement within the cosmos, represented by the arch of flames. The dance's purpose is to release humans from illusion; the place where the god performs it is believed to lie both at the center of the universe and within the human heart.

Nataraja, dancing Shiva, Indian bronze image, 12th–13th century AD; in the Museum of Asiatic Art, Amsterdam.

Natchez Trace Old road, southeastern U.S. It follows an Indian trail (or trace) to the northeast from Natchez, Miss., across northwestern Alabama to Nashville, Tenn. and is more than 500 mi (800 km) long. A wagon road constructed in the early 19th century was used by traders and settlers. Among its historical landmarks are the Emerald and Bynum Indian ceremonial mounds and Chickasaw Village, in Mississippi, and Napier Mine and Metal Ford in Tennessee.

Nathan (fl. 10th century BC) Prophet at the courts of DAVID and SOLOMON in ancient Israel. In II Samuel he rebuked David for taking Bathsheba from her husband. As punishment, David was not allowed to build the Temple at Jerusalem, since Nathan had a vision informing him that its construction must be postponed until Solomon succeeded to the throne. Nathan later anointed the new king.

Nathans, Daniel (1928–1997) U.S. microbiologist. Born in Wilmington, Del., he received a medical degree from Washington University Working principally at Johns Hopkins Univ., he used the restriction enzyme isolated from a bacterium by HAMILTON O. SMITH to investigate the structure of the DNA of a monkey virus (SV40), the simplest virus known to produce cancer. His construction of a genetic map of the virus was the first application of restriction enzymes to the problem of identifying the molecular basis of cancer. He shared a 1978 Nobel Prize with Smith and WERNER ARBER.

nation People whose common identity creates a psychological bond and a political community. Their political identity usually comprises such characteristics as a common language, culture, ethnicity, and history. More than one nation may comprise a state, but the terms nation, state, and country are often used interchangeably. A nation-state is a state populated primarily by the people of one nationality.

Nation, Carry (Amelia) *orig.* **Carry Moore** (1846–1911) U.S. temperance advocate. Born in Garrard Co., Ky., she married in 1867 but soon left her alcoholic husband. In 1877 she married David Nation, a lawyer; he would divorce her for desertion in 1901. After a 1890 U.S. Supreme Court decision weakened the prohibition laws of Kansas, where she was living, she joined the TEMPERANCE MOVEMENT and came to believe that the illegality of saloons meant they could be destroyed with impunity. A tall and heavy woman, she would march alone or with hymn-singing supporters into saloons and proceed to sing, pray, shout, and smash their fixtures and stock with a hatchet. She was jailed many times, paying her fines with proceeds from her lectures and sales of souvenir hatchets.

Carry Nation.
BROWN BROTHERS

Nation, The U.S. weekly journal of opinion, the oldest continuously published U.S. periodical. Founded in 1865 by FREDERICK LAW OLMSTED and Edwin L. Godkin (1831–1902) as a reformist publication, it was sold to the *New York Evening Post* in 1881 and was a weekly edition of the paper until 1914. While Oswald Garrison Villard (1872–1949) was owner and editor (1918–34), it moved decisively to the political left, and has remained there under subsequent owners and editors, as during its outspoken opposition to Sen. JOSEPH MCCARTHY and to U.S. involvement in the Vietnam War. In circulation it is now one of the largest intellectual journals in America.

Nation of Islam See Nation of ISLAM

National Aeronautics and Space Administration See NASA

National Assembly *French* **Assemblée nationale** French parliamentary body. The name was first used during the FRENCH REVOLUTION to designate the revolutionary assembly formed by representatives of the THIRD ESTATE (1789), and then as a short form for the National Constituent Assembly (1789–91). It was used again when the National Assembly of 1871–75 drafted a new constitution. In the THIRD REPUBLIC (1875–1940), the name designated the two houses of parliament, the Senate and the Chamber of Deputies. In the FOURTH REPUBLIC (1946–58) and FIFTH REPUBLIC (from 1958), the name was applied only to the lower house (the former Chamber of Deputies).

National Association for the Advancement of Colored People See NAACP

national bank In the U.S., any COMMERCIAL BANK chartered and supervised by the federal government and operated by private individuals. National banks were created during the Civil War under the National Bank Act of 1863 to combat financial instability caused by state banks and help finance the war effort. When these banks purchased federal BONDS and deposited them with the comptroller of the currency, they were permitted to put into circulation national bank notes, thereby creating a stable, uniform national CURRENCY. After the Civil War, the government began to retire the bonds issued during the war, which reduced the number of national bank notes that could be issued. Concern over the inflexibility of national bank notes led to the formation of the FEDERAL RESERVE SYSTEM in 1913, which all national banks were required to join. The U.S. Treasury assumed the obligation of issuing national bank notes in 1935, effectively ending the issue of money by private commercial banks.

National Basketball Association (NBA) U.S. professional basketball league formed in 1949 by the merger of two rival organizations, the National Basketball League (founded 1937) and the Basketball Association of America (1946). In 1976 the NBA was augmented by the absorption of four teams from the former American Basketball Association (founded 1967). The NBA membership is divided into two conferences, each with two divisions. The Eastern Conference consists of the Atlantic Division (Boston Celtics, Miami Heat, New Jersey Nets, New York Knicks, Orlando Magic, Philadelphia 76ers, and Washington Wizards) and the Central Division (Atlanta Hawks, Chicago Bulls, Cleveland Cavaliers, Detroit Pistons, Indiana Pacers, Milwaukee Bucks, New Orleans Hornets, and Toronto Raptors). The Western Conference consists of the Midwest Division (Dallas Mavericks, Denver Nuggets, Houston Rockets, Memphis Grizzlies, Minnesota Timberwolves, San Antonio Spurs, and Utah Jazz) and the Pacific Division (Golden State Warriors, Los Angeles Clippers, Los Angeles Lakers, Phoenix Suns, Portland Trail Blazers, Sacramento Kings, and Seattle SuperSonics).

National Broadcasting Company See NBC

National Collegiate Athletic Association (NCAA) Organization that administers U.S. intercollegiate athletics. It was formed in 1906, but did not acquire significant powers to enforce its rules until 1942. Headquartered at Indianapolis, Ind., it functions as a general legislative and administrative authority, formulating and enforcing rules of play for various sports and eligibility criteria for athletes. It has about 1,200 member schools and conducts about 80 national championships in a total of about 20 sports.

National Convention *French* **Convention nationale** Governing assembly (1792–95) of the FRENCH REVOLUTION. It comprised 749 deputies elected after the overthrow of the monarchy (1792) to provide a new constitution for France. The struggle between the radical MONTAGNARDS and the moderate GIRONDINS dominated the Convention until the Girondins were purged in 1793. The democratic constitution already approved by the Convention was not put into effect while the Montagnards controlled the assembly (1793–94). After the THERMIDORIAN REACTION (1794), the balance of power in the Convention was held by members of the PLAIN. The Girondins were recalled, and the CONSTITUTION OF 1795 was approved for the DIRECTORY regime that replaced the Convention.

national debt *or* **public debt** Total indebtedness of a government, especially as evidenced by SECURITIES issued to investors. The national debt grows whenever the government operates a budget deficit—that is, when government spending exceeds government revenues in a year. To finance its debt, the government can issue securities such as BONDS or TREASURY BILLS. The level of national debt varies from country to country, from less than 10% of the GROSS DOMESTIC PRODUCT to more than twice the GDP. Public borrowing is thought to have an inflationary effect on the economy and thus is often used during RECESSIONS to stimulate CONSUMPTION, INVESTMENT, and employment. See also DEFICIT FINANCING, JOHN MAYNARD KEYNES.

National Education Association (NEA) Voluntary association of U.S. teachers, administrators, and other educators associated with elementary and secondary schools and colleges and universities. Founded in 1857 as the National Teachers Assn., it is today the world's largest professional organization (approx. 2.7 million members). Operating much like a LABOR UNION, it represents its members through numerous state and local affiliates. It seeks to improve the schools and working conditions, advance the cause of public education, promote federal legislation, and sponsor research. See also AMERICAN FEDERATION OF TEACHERS.

National Endowment for the Arts (NEA) Independent agency of the U.S. government that supports the creation, dissemination, and performance of the arts. It was created by the U.S. Congress in 1965 and funds projects in literature, music, theater, film, dance, fine arts, sculpture, and crafts. Most grants go directly to institutions, such as art museums and symphony orchestras, but some individual artists are funded for specific projects as well. The NEA has often encouraged cultural diversity; opposition by conservative members of Congress to some works it has supported has resulted in a reduction of its funding.

National Endowment for the Humanities (NEH) U.S. independent agency. Founded in 1965, it supports research, education, preserva-

L
M
N

tion, and public programs in the HUMANITIES. It provides grants to museums, libraries, archives, television programs, historic sites, translation and editorial projects by academic presses, educational and research institutions, and individuals.

National Film Board of Canada Canadian department of film production. It was established in 1939 and directed by John Grierson (1898–1972), who developed the studio into a leading producer of documentaries, including the World War II propaganda films *Canada Carries On* and *The World in Action.* The studio also made high-quality animated movies by Norman McLaren (1914–1987) and others, and later expanded to produce feature films, including *The Luck of Ginger Coffey* (1964) and *The Apprenticeship of Duddy Kravitz* (1974).

National Football League (NFL) Major professional football organization in the U.S. It was founded in 1920 at Canton, Ohio; its first president was JIM THORPE. In 1970 it merged with the rival American Football League (founded 1959). Beginning with the 2002 season, it was divided into two conferences, each with four divisions. The National Conference consists of the East Division (Dallas Cowboys, New York Giants, Philadelphia Eagles, and Washington Redskins), the South Division (Atlanta Falcons, Carolina Panthers, New Orleans Saints, and Tampa Bay Buccaneers), the North Division (Chicago Bears, Detroit Lions, Green Bay Packers, and Minnesota Vikings), and the West Division (Arizona Cardinals, St. Louis Rams, San Francisco Forty-Niners, and Seattle Seahawks). The American Conference consists of the East Division (Buffalo Bills, Miami Dolphins, New England Patriots, and New York Jets), the South Division (Houston Texans, Indianapolis Colts, Jacksonville Jaguars, and Tennessee Titans), the North Division (Baltimore Ravens, Cincinnati Bengals, Cleveland Browns, and Pittsburgh Steelers), and the West Division (Denver Broncos, Kansas City Chiefs, Oakland Raiders, and San Diego Chargers). The league season culminates with the SUPER BOWL, the annual championship game between the winners of the National and American conferences.

national forest, U.S. Any of numerous forest areas under federal supervision for the purposes of conserving water, timber, wildlife, fish, and other renewable resources, and providing public recreation areas. Administered by the U.S. Department of AGRICULTURE's Forest Service, the forests numbered 155 in the early 21st century and occupied 352,000 sq mi (911,700 sq km) in 40 states and Puerto Rico. They were founded in 1891 as a system of forest reserves and were renamed national forests in 1907. See also GIFFORD PINCHOT.

L
M
N

National Gallery of Art Museum in Washington, D.C., part of the SMITHSONIAN INSTITUTION. It was founded in 1937 when ANDREW W. MELLON donated his collection of European paintings to the nation. He also donated funds to construct the gallery's neoclassical building, opened in 1941. Now known as the West Building, it is connected by plaza and underground concourse to the East Building, designed by I. M. PEI (completed 1978). The museum houses an extensive collection of U.S. and European paintings, sculpture, decorative arts, and graphic arts from the 12th to the 20th century; especially well represented are works by Italian Renaissance, 17th-century Dutch, and 18th–19th-century French artists.

National Gallery of Canada National art museum founded in Ottawa in 1880. Its holdings include extensive collections of Canadian art as well as important European works. Its nucleus was formed with the donation of diploma works by members of the Royal Canadian Academy. In 1911 the drawing collection was formed with important works by ALBRECHT DURER and REMBRANDT (1913–24), and the photography collection was begun in 1967. A new building opened in 1988; the Canadian Centre for the Visual Arts opened in 1991 and a multimedia learning center in 1996. The museum circulates several hundred exhibitions to other cities throughout the country each year.

National Geographic Society U.S. scientific society founded in 1888 in Washington, D.C., by a small group of eminent explorers and scientists "for the increase and diffusion of geographic knowledge." Today it has more than 9 million members. It has supported more than 7,000 major scientific projects and expeditions, including those of ROBERT E. PEARY, RICHARD E. BYRD, LEAKEY FAMILY, JACQUES-YVES COUSTEAU, JANE GOODALL, and DIAN FOSSEY. It has published numerous books, atlases, and bulletins and has created hundreds of television documentaries. *National Geographic Magazine* is a monthly magazine of geography, archaeology, anthropology, and exploration. It became a leader in reproducing color photographs and printing photographs of undersea life, views from the stratosphere, and animals in their natural habitats. It also became famous for articles containing substantial information on environmental, social, and cultural aspects of the regions covered. See also GILBERT GROSVENOR.

National Guard, U.S. Reserve group organized by the U.S. Army and Air Force. Every state and territory of the U.S. has a National Guard, which can be called on by state governors during emergencies such as riots and natural disasters. Guard units may also be ordered into active duty for up to two years by the U.S. president in the event of a national emergency. Enlistment in the National Guard is voluntary.

National Health Service (NHS) Comprehensive government public-health service in Britain covering virtually the entire population, established in 1946. Financed primarily by general taxes, most services are free. General practitioners and dentists are paid per patient registered with them and may also have private patients. Hospital and specialist services are provided in government hospitals and other facilities by salaried professionals. Local health authority services provide maternity and child welfare, home nursing, and other preventive services. The NHS has provided generally good health care at relatively low cost, but the increasing expense of hospital stays has caused financial strain.

National Hockey League (NHL) Organization of professional North American ice-hockey teams. The league was formed in 1917 by five Canadian teams; the first U.S. team, the Boston Bruins, was added in 1924. It today consists of 30 teams in two conferences and six divisions. The Eastern Conference includes the Atlantic Division (New Jersey Devils, New York Islanders, New York Rangers, Philadelphia Flyers, and Pittsburgh Penguins), the Northeast Division (Boston Bruins, Buffalo Sabres, Montreal Canadiens, Ottawa Senators, and Toronto Maple Leafs), and the Southeast Division (Atlanta Thrashers, Carolina Hurricanes, Florida Panthers, Tampa Bay Lightning, and Washington Capitals). The Western Conference includes the Central Division (Chicago Blackhawks, Columbus Blue Jackets, Detroit Red Wings, Nashville Predators, and St. Louis Blues), the Northwest Division (Calgary Flames, Colorado Avalanche, Edmonton Oilers, Minnesota Wild, and Vancouver Canucks), and the Pacific Division (Mighty Ducks of Anaheim, Dallas Stars, Los Angeles Kings, Phoenix Coyotes, and San Jose Sharks). At the end of the regular winter season, the top teams in each division engage in a play-off for the STANLEY CUP.

national income accounting Set of principles and methods used to measure a country's income and production. There are two ways of measuring national economic activity: the expenditure approach, which measures the money value of the total output of goods and services in a given period (usually a year); and the income approach, which measures the total income derived from economic activity after allowing for capital CONSUMPTION. The most commonly used indicator of national output is the GROSS DOMESTIC PRODUCT (GDP). National income may be derived from gross national product (GNP) by making allowances for certain non-income costs included in the GNP, such as indirect taxes, SUBSIDIES, and DEPRECIATION. National income thus calculated represents the aggregate income of the owners of the factors of production; it is the sum of wages, salaries, PROFITS, INTEREST, DIVIDENDS, RENT, and so on. The data accumulated for calculating the GDP and national income may be manipulated in various ways to show various relationships in the economy. Common uses of the data include breakdowns of GDP according to type of product, breakdowns of national income by type of income, and analyses of the sources of financing (e.g., personal savings, company funds, or national deficits).

National Institutes of Health (NIH) U.S. government agency made up of numerous specialized institutes (e.g., National Cancer Institute; National Heart, Lung, and Blood Institute; National Institute on Aging; National Institute of Child Health and Human Development; and National Institute of Mental Health) that conduct or support biomedical research in their fields. Part of the Department of HEALTH AND HUMAN SERVICES, it also trains health researchers; disseminates information; and maintains other offices and divisions, the National Library of Medicine (foremost source of medical information in the U.S.), and several research centers.

National Labor Relations Act See WAGNER ACT

National Labor Relations Board (NLRB) U.S. government agency charged with administering the National Labor Relations Act (1935), enacted to facilitate the organizing of LABOR UNIONS. The three-member NLRB, appointed by the president, organizes elections to determine whether employees wish to be represented by a union in COLLECTIVE BARGAINING and monitors labor practices by employers and unions. It does not initiate investigations; its involvement must be sought by employers, individuals, or unions. Though it lacks enforcement power for its orders, it can prosecute cases in court.

National League Oldest existing U.S. major-league professional baseball organization. The league was founded in 1876. Its supremacy was challenged by several rival organizations over the years, of which only the AMERICAN LEAGUE has survived; since 1903 the champions of the two leagues have engaged in an annual WORLD SERIES competition. Today the National League consists of 16 teams aligned in three divisions. In the Eastern Division are the Atlanta Braves, Florida Marlins (Miami), Montreal Expos, New York Mets, and Philadelphia Phillies. In the Central Division are the Chicago Cubs, Cincinnati Reds, Houston Astros, Milwaukee Brewers, Pittsburgh Pirates, and St. Louis Cardinals. In the Western Division are the Arizona Diamondbacks (Phoenix), Colorado Rockies (Denver), Los Angeles Dodgers, San Diego Padres, and San Francisco Giants.

National Liberal Party German political party (1871–1918). It began in Prussia (1867) as a moderate faction of the Prussian Liberal Party. In its support of OTTO VON BISMARCK, it constituted a virtual government party (1871–79). After losing many seats in the election of 1879, the party split over the issue of giving the Reichstag (parliament) control over revenues. It formed a coalition with the Conservatives in 1890, but its influence waned thereafter.

National Liberation Front Title used by nationalist, usually socialist, movements in various countries since World War II. In Greece, the National Liberation Front–National Popular Liberation Army was a communist-sponsored resistance group that operated in occupied Greece during the war. In Vietnam, the National Front for the Liberation of the South was formed (1960) to overthrow the South Vietnamese government (see VIET MINH). In Algeria, the National Liberation Front, successor to the body that directed Algeria's war of independence (1954–62), was the only constitutionally legal party from 1962 to 1989. In Uruguay, the leftist guerrilla Tupamaro National Liberation Front (1963) battled police and the army (1967–72); it later became a legal political party. In the Philippines, the Moro National Liberation Front (1968) espoused separatism for the MOROS; its terrorist insurgency (1973–76) left 50,000 dead. The Corsican National Liberation Front (1976), the largest and most violent Corsican nationalist movement, remained active into the 21st century. See also SANDINISTAS.

national monument, U.S. Any of numerous areas reserved by the federal government for the protection of objects or places of historical, scientific, or prehistoric interest. They include natural physical features, remains of Indian cultures, and places of historical importance. In 1906 Pres. THEODORE ROOSEVELT established the first national monument, DEVILS TOWER in Wyoming. They are administered by the National Park Service of the U.S. Department of the INTERIOR.

National Organization for Women (NOW) U.S. women's-rights organization. It was founded in 1966 by BETTY FRIEDAN to challenge sex discrimination in all areas of society, particularly in employment. With about half a million members (both women and men), it addresses, through lobbying and litigation, child care, pregnancy leave, and abortion and pension rights. In the 1970s it focused on the adoption of the EQUAL RIGHTS AMENDMENT to the Constitution, but failed to gain ratification. It has had greater success on the state level, with such issues as equal-pay legislation.

national park Area set aside by a national government for the preservation of its natural environment. Most national parks are kept in their natural state. Those in the U.S. and Canada focus on land and wildlife preservation; those in Britain focus mainly on the land, and those in African nations focus primarily on animals. The world's first national park, YELLOWSTONE, was established in the U.S. by Pres. ULYSSES S. GRANT in 1872. Canada's first national park, BANFF, was established in 1885. Japan and Mexico established their first national parks in the 1930s; Britain's national parks date to 1949. The U.S. National Park Service, established in 1916, now also manages national monuments, preserves, recreation areas, and seashores, as well as lakeshores, historic sites, parkways, scenic trails, and battlefields. See also NATIONAL FOREST.

National Party of South Africa South African political party that ruled the country 1948–94. Its following includes most AFRIKANERS and many English-speaking whites. It was founded in 1914 by J.B.M. HERTZOG to rally Afrikaners against the Anglicizing policies of the government of LOUIS BOTHA and JAN SMUTS. From 1933 to 1939 Hertzog and Smuts joined a coalition government and fused their followings into the United Party. Some Nationalists, led by DANIEL F. MALAN, held out and kept the National Party alive, and in 1939 accepted Hertzog back as their leader. After winning the 1948 elections and enacting a mass of racial legislation, the party named its policy APARTHEID. In 1961 it broke South Africa away from the Commonwealth, making it a republic. In 1982 much of its right wing broke off in opposition to liberalizing policies to form the Conservative Party. Under F.W. DE KLERK, it began to seek repeal of racial laws. It was defeated in South Africa's first multiracial elections in 1994, but participated in a coalition government with its longtime rival, the AFRICAN NATIONAL CONGRESS. With the enactment of a new constitution in 1996, the Nationalists resigned from the government in protest. See also P. W. BOTHA.

National Public Radio (NPR) U.S. public radio network. It was established by the Corporation for Public Broadcasting in 1970 to provide programming to U.S. noncommercial and educational radio stations. While initially providing programs in the arts, after 1983 the network focused largely on news programming. It features the daily programs *Morning Edition* and *All Things Considered,* as well as the interview programs *Fresh Air* and *Talk of the Nation.* Other programs include *Car Talk, NPR Playhouse,* and *Latino USA.*

National Recovery Administration (NRA) (1933–35) U.S. government agency established to stimulate business recovery during the GREAT DEPRESSION. As part of the National Industrial Recovery Act (1933), the NRA established codes to eliminate unfair trade practices, reduce unemployment, and set minimum wages and maximum hours. The U.S. Supreme Court invalidated the act in 1935 because it gave quasi-legislative powers to the executive branch. Many of its provisions appeared in subsequent legislation.

National Republican Party U.S. political party formed after the Jeffersonian Republicans split in 1825. The National Republicans included the followers of JOHN QUINCY ADAMS and HENRY CLAY and the opponents of ANDREW JACKSON. Adams ran as the party's unsuccessful candidate in the 1828 presidential election. Its 1832 presidential nominee was Clay, whose platform favored a high tariff and the BANK OF THE U.S. (see BANK WAR). After losing again to Jackson, the party joined with conservatives and other anti-Jackson forces to form the WHIG PARTY.

National Rifle Association (NRA) Organization for the sport of shooting with rifles and pistols. It was originally founded in Britain in 1860. The U.S. organization was formed in 1871; today it has over 2 million members. It sponsors regional and national shooting competitions and offers gun-safety programs. It promotes the right to bear arms; one of the most powerful political lobbies in the U.S., it has vigorously opposed many legislative proposals for firearms control.

National Security Agency U.S. intelligence agency responsible for cryptographic and communications intelligence and security. Established in 1952 by presidential directive rather than by law, it has remained relatively free from congressional oversight. Its director has always been a general or admiral. Its mission includes the protection and formulation of codes, ciphers, and other cryptology as well as the interception, analysis, and solution of coded transmissions. It conducts research into all forms of electronic transmission, operating listening posts around the world for the interception of signals. A target for penetration by foreign intelligence services, until recently it maintained no contact with the public or the press. Though its budget is secret, it is acknowledged to be far larger than that of the CENTRAL INTELLIGENCE AGENCY.

National Security Council (NSC) U.S. agency that advises the president on domestic, foreign, and military policies related to national security. With the CENTRAL INTELLIGENCE AGENCY, it was established by the 1947 National Security Act. It provides the White House with a foreign-policy-making instrument independent of the State Department. It has four members—the president, vice president, and secretaries of state and defense—and its staff is headed by the national security adviser.

National Socialism *or* **Nazism** Totalitarian movement led by ADOLF HITLER as head of Germany's NAZI PARTY (1920–45). It had its roots in the tradition of Prussian militarism and discipline and German Romanticism, which celebrated a mythic past and proclaimed the rights of the exceptional individual over all rules and laws. Its ideology was shaped by Hitler's beliefs in German superiority and the dangers of communism and need for an enemy. It rejected liberalism, democracy, the rule of law, and human rights, stressing instead the subordination of the individual to the state and the necessity of strict obedience to leaders. It emphasized the inequality of individuals and races and the right of the strong to rule the weak. Politically, National Socialism favored rearmament, reunification of the German areas of Europe, expansion into non-German areas, and the purging of "undesirables," especially Jews. See also FASCISM.

nationalism Loyalty and devotion to one's NATION or country, especially as above loyalty to other groups or individual interests. Before the era of the nation-state, the primary allegiance of most people was to their immediate locality or religious group. The rise of large, centralized states weakened local authority, and society's increasing secularization weakened loyalty to religious groups, though shared religion, along with race, political heritage, and history, is one of the factors that draws people together in nationalist movements. Early nationalist movements in 18th- and early 19th-century Europe were liberal and internationalist, but they gradually became more conservative, parochial, and chauvinistic. Nationalism is seen as a major contributing cause of both world wars and many other wars in the modern era. In Africa and Asia in the 20th century, it often arose in opposition to COLONIALISM. After the fall of the Soviet Union, it made a powerful resurgence in Eastern Europe and the Soviet Union's former republics, contributing (with ethnicity) to increased conflict in territories such as that of the former Yugoslavia.

Nationalist China See TAIWAN

Nationalist Party *or* **Kuomintang** *or* **Guomindang** \'gwō-'min-'däŋ\ Political party that governed all or part of mainland China from 1928 to 1949 and subsequently ruled Taiwan. Founded by Song Jiaoren (1882–1913) and led by SUN YAT-SEN, it evolved from a revolutionary league working to overthrow the QING DYNASTY into a political party. In the early 1920s the party received guidance from the Soviet Bolshevik party; until 1927 it collaborated with the CHINESE COMMUNIST PARTY. Sun's program, which stressed nationalism, democracy, and people's livelihood, was ineffectively implemented by his successor, CHIANG KAI-SHEK, who became increasingly conservative and dictatorial. During World War II, Chiang focused on suppressing the Chinese communists at the expense of defending the nation from the Japanese; in 1949 the Nationalists were driven from the mainland to Taiwan. There they maintained a monopoly on political power until 1989, when the first legal opposition party won seats in the legislature. See also WANG JINGWEI.

nationality Affiliation with a particular NATION or sovereign state. People, business corporations, ships, and aircraft all have nationalities. Nationality is inferior to CITIZENSHIP, insofar as the latter implies a full set of political privileges and the former does not. Countries have limited rights to determine which of their inhabitants will be their nationals. People generally acquire a nationality by birth within a particular country's territory, by inheritance from one or both parents, or by NATURALIZATION. It may change or be augmented or taken away if a country cedes control of the territory where one lives to another country.

Nations, Battle of the See Battle of LEIPZIG

Native American See AMERICAN INDIAN

Native American Church *or* **peyotism** Religious movement among North American Indians involving the drug PEYOTE. Peyote was first used to induce supernatural visions in Mexico in pre-Columbian times; its use extended north into the Great Plains in the 19th century, and peyotism is now practiced among more than 50 tribes. Peyotist beliefs, which combine Indian and Christian elements, vary from tribe to tribe. They involve worship of the Great Spirit, a supreme deity who deals with humans through various other spirits. In many tribes peyote is personified as Peyote Spirit and is associated with JESUS. The rite often begins on Saturday evening and continues through the night. The Peyote Road is a way of life calling for brotherly love, family care, self-support through work, and avoidance of alcohol.

Native Dancer U.S. Thoroughbred racehorse. Foaled in 1950, he won the Preakness and Belmont stakes in 1953 but finished second in the Kentucky Derby. In 1954 he was named Horse of the Year. He won 21 of 22 total starts, achieving widespread popularity as the first horse whose major victories were seen on national television.

native element Any of the 19 chemical elements that occur as MINERALS and are found in nature uncombined with other elements. They are commonly divided into three groups: metals (platinum, iridium, osmium, iron, zinc, tin, gold, silver, copper, mercury, lead, chromium); semimetals (bismuth, antimony, arsenic, tellurium, selenium); and nonmetals (sulfur, carbon). Members of the group of native elements form under widely varying physicochemical conditions and in very different rock types. Many deposits are sufficiently abundant to be commercially important; e.g., native gold and silver are the principal ores of those metals.

NATO *in full* **North Atlantic Treaty Organization** International military alliance created to defend Western Europe from Soviet expansion. A 1948 collective-defense alliance between Britain, France, The Netherlands, Belgium, and Luxembourg was recognized as inadequate to deter potential Soviet aggression, and in 1949 the U.S. and Canada agreed to join their European allies in an enlarged alliance. The North Atlantic Treaty, in its Article 5, stated that an attack on one signatory should be regarded as an attack on the rest. A centralized administrative structure was set up, and three major commands were established, focused on Europe, the Atlantic, and the English Channel. The admission of West Germany in 1955 led to the Soviet Union's creation of the opposing Warsaw Treaty Organization, or WARSAW PACT. France withdrew from military participation in 1966. Since NATO ground forces were smaller than those of the Warsaw Pact, the balance of power was maintained by superior weaponry, including intermediate-range nuclear weapons. After the Warsaw Pact's dissolution in 1991, NATO withdrew its nuclear weapons and attempted to refine its mission in the post-Cold War period. It involved itself in the Balkan conflicts of the 1990s. In 1999 the admission of Poland, Hungary, and the Czech Republic, all former Warsaw Pact members, brought the number of full members to 19. On September 12, 2001, NATO invoked Article 5 for the first time in response to the terrorist SEPTEMBER 11 ATTACKS on the U.S.

Natsume Soseki \ˌnä-tsü-'mā-'sō-ˌse-kē\ *known as* **Soseki** *orig.* **Natsume Kinnosuke** (1867–1916) Japanese novelist. Originally a teacher, Natsume made his literary reputation with two very successful comic novels, *I Am a Cat* (1905–6) and *Botchan* (1906). After 1907 he gave up teaching and produced somber works dealing with attempts to escape from loneliness, including *The Wayfarer* (1912–13), *The Gate* (1910), *Kokoro* (1914), and *Grass on the Wayside* (1915). The first writer of modern realistic novels in Japan, he articulately and persuasively depicted the plight of the alienated modern Japanese intellectual.

natural bridge *or* **natural arch** Naturally created arch formation resembling a bridge. Most are erosion features that occur in sandstone or limestone. Some are formed by the collapse of part of a cavern roof. Others may be produced by entrenched rivers eroding through MEANDER necks to form cutoffs. Still others are produced by exfoliation (separation of successive thin shells) and may be enlarged by wind erosion.

Natural Bridges National Monument National monument, southeastern Utah. Comprising three large natural bridges carved by two winding streams, it was established in 1908. The largest bridge, Sipapu, is 222 ft (68 m) high and spans 261 ft (80 m). Pictographs were carved on another of the bridges, Kachina, by early cliff dwellers.

natural childbirth Any of the systems (e.g., the Lamaze method) of managing birth without drugs or surgery. All begin with classes to teach pregnant women about the birth process, including when to push and what breathing and relaxation techniques to use. The goal is to reduce fear and muscle tension, which can increase the pain of labor, and to make the mother an active participant in the process. The father or another partner usually attends the classes with the mother and coaches her during the birth. See also MIDWIFERY, OBSTETRICS AND GYNECOLOGY.

natural gas Colorless, highly flammable gaseous HYDROCARBON consisting primarily of methane and ethane. It may also contain heavier hydrocarbons, carbon dioxide, hydrogen, hydrogen sulfide, nitrogen, helium, and argon. It commonly occurs in association with crude oil (see PETROLEUM). Natural gas is extracted from wells drilled into the earth. Some natural gas can be used as it comes from the well, without any refining, but most requires processing. It is transported either in its natural gaseous state by pipeline or, after liquefaction by cooling, by tankers. Liquefied natural gas occupies only about 1/600 of the volume of the gas. It has grown steadily as a source of energy since the 1930s.

natural law In philosophy of SCIENCE, a universal statement that describes and/or explains the course of natural events (e.g., NEWTON'S LAWS OF MOTION); in JURISPRUDENCE and POLITICAL PHILOSOPHY, a system of right or justice common to all humankind and derived from nature rather than from the rules of society, or positive law. This concept can be traced back to ARISTOTLE, who held that what was "just by nature" was not always the same as what was "just by law." In one form or another, the existence of natural law was asserted by the Stoics (see STOICISM), CICERO, the Roman jurists, St. PAUL, St. AUGUSTINE, GRATIAN, THOMAS AQUINAS, JOHN DUNS SCOTUS, William of OCKHAM, and FRANCISCO SUAREZ. In the modern period, HUGO GROTIUS and THOMAS HOBBES constructed a system of natural law by deduction from a "state of nature" followed by a SOCIAL CONTRACT. JOHN LOCKE described the state of nature as a state of society based on natural law. J.-J. ROUSSEAU postulated a savage who was virtuous in isolation and actuated by self-preservation and compassion. The DECLARATION OF INDEPENDENCE refers only briefly to "the Laws of Nature" before citing equality and other "unalienable" rights as "self-evident." The French DECLARATION OF THE RIGHTS OF MAN AND OF THE CITIZEN asserts liberty, property, security, and resistance to oppression as "imprescriptible natural rights."

natural selection Process that results in adaptation of an organism to its environment by means of selectively reproducing changes in its GENOTYPE. Variations that increase an organism's chances of survival and procreation are preserved and multiplied from generation to generation at the expense of less advantageous variations. As proposed by CHARLES DARWIN, natural selection is the mechanism by which EVOLUTION occurs. It may arise from differences in survival, fertility, rate of development, mating success, or any other aspect of the life cycle. MUTATION, GENE FLOW, and GENETIC DRIFT, all of which are random processes, also alter GENE abundance. Natural selection moderates the effects of these processes because it multiplies the incidence of beneficial mutations over generations and eliminates harmful ones, since the organisms that carry them leave few or no descendants. See also SELECTION.

naturalism Aesthetic movement of the late 19th to early 20th century inspired by the adaptation of the principles and methods of natural science, especially DARWINISM, to literature and art. In literature it extended the tradition of REALISM, aiming at an even more faithful, pseudoscientific representation of reality, presented without moral judgment. Characters in naturalistic literature typically illustrate the deterministic role of heredity and environment on human life. Naturalism originated in France, where its leading exponent was É. ZOLA. In America the movement is associated with the work of STEPHEN CRANE and THEODORE DREISER. Visual artists associated with naturalism chose themes from life, capturing subjects unposed and not idealized, thus giving their works freshness and immediacy. Following the lead of GUSTAVE COURBET, painters chose themes from contemporary life, and many deserted the studio for the open air, finding subjects among peasants and tradespeople, capturing them as they found them. As a result, finished canvases had the freshness and immediacy of sketches. While naturalism was short-lived as a historical movement, it contributed to art an enrichment of realism, new areas of subject matter, and a formlessness that was closer to life than to art.

naturalism In philosophy, the theory that affirms that all beings and events in the universe are natural and therefore can be fully known by the methods of scientific investigation. While naturalism has often been equated with MATERIALISM, it is much broader in scope. Though materialism is naturalistic, the converse is not necessarily true. Strictly speaking, naturalism has no ontological bias toward any particular set of categories of reality: DUALISM and MONISM, ATHEISM and THEISM, IDEALISM and materialism are all compatible with it. So long as all of reality is natural, no other limitations are imposed. Naturalism's greatest vogue occurred in the 1930s and '40s, chiefly in the U.S. among philosophers such as F. J. E. Woodbridge (1867–1940), Morris R. Cohen (1880–1947), JOHN DEWEY, Ernest Nagel (1901–1985), Sidney Hook (1902–1989), and W. V. O. QUINE.

naturalistic fallacy FALLACY of treating the term "good" (or any equivalent term) as if it were the name of a natural property. In 1903 G. E. MOORE presented in *Principia Ethica* his "open-question argument" against what he called the naturalistic fallacy, with the aim of proving that "good" is the name of a simple, unanalyzable quality, incapable of being defined in terms of some natural quality of the world, whether it be "pleasurable" (JOHN STUART MILL) or "highly evolved" (HERBERT SPENCER). Since Moore's argument applied to any attempt to define good in terms of something else, including something supernatural such as "what God wills," the term "naturalistic fallacy" is not apt. The open-question argument turns any proposed definition of good into a question (e.g., "Good means pleasurable" becomes "Is everything pleasurable good?")—Moore's point being that if the question is meaningful, the proposed definition cannot be correct, since if it were, the question of would be meaningless.

naturalization Process of granting NATIONALITY or CITIZENSHIP to an ALIEN. It may be granted after voluntary application or through legislation, marriage to a citizen, or parental action. Involuntary naturalization occurs when one's home territory is annexed by a foreign state. Qualifications for naturalization may include a minimum residency period, a minimum age, law-abiding character, good health, self-sufficiency, satisfactory knowledge of the new country, and willingness to give up one's former nationality.

Nature Conservancy Nonprofit organization dedicated to environmental conservation and the preservation of biodiversity, founded in 1951, that operates the largest private system of nature sanctuaries in the world. It owns and manages more than 1,500 preserves throughout the U.S., comprising more than 9 million acres (3.8 million hectares) of ecologically significant land, and has expanded into Latin America and the Pacific. Government-administered programs identify the relative abundance of plant and animal species and the habitats they need to survive, and the Conservancy then acquires—through gifts, exchanges, easements, debt-for-nature swaps, purchases, and other nonconfrontational arrangements—areas that are home to threatened species.

nature/nurture controversy See BEHAVIOR GENETICS

Naucratis \'nȯ-krə-təs\ Ancient Greek settlement, Egypt, in the NILE delta. It was founded in the 7th century BC and flourished as a center of trade and cultural relations between Greece and Egypt. It declined after ALEXANDER THE GREAT's conquest of Egypt and the founding of ALEXANDRIA in 332 BC. In 1884 FLINDERS PETRIE discovered the site and helped excavate it.

Nauru \nä-'ü-rü\ *Nauruan* **Naoero** \nä-'ür-ō\ *officially* **Republic of Nauru** Island republic, southeastern MICRONESIA, South Pacific Ocean. Area: 8 sq mi (21 sq km). Population (1997 est.): 10,000. Capital: Yaren. About three-fifths of the population are indigenous Nauruans of Polynesian, Micronesian, and Melanesian ancestry. Language: Nauruan, English. Religion: Christianity (predominantly). Currency: Australian dollar. Nauru is a coral island with a central plateau 100–200 ft (30–60 m) high. A thin strip of fertile land encircling the island is the major zone of human settlement. It lacks harbors, and ships must anchor to buoys beyond a reef. Nauru had the world's largest concentration of phosphate, and its economy was formerly based on its mining and processing; deposits are now depleted, and the economy is being converted to fishing and other ventures. It is a republic with one legislative house; its head of state and government is the president. Nauru was inhabited by Pacific islanders when the first British explorers arrived in 1798 and named it Pleasant Island after their friendly welcome. Annexed by Germany in 1888, it was occupied by Australia at the start of World War I, and in 1919 it was placed under a joint mandate of Britain, Australia, and New Zealand. During World War II it was occupied by the Japanese. Made a U.N. trust territory under Australian administration in 1947, it gained complete independence in 1968 and joined the British Commonwealth in 1969. During the mid-1990s it suffered political unrest.

nausea Discomfort in the pit of the stomach associated with disgust for food and a feeling that VOMITING will follow, as it often does. Nausea results from irritation of nerve endings in the stomach or duodenum, which stimulate brain centers that control nausea and vomiting. Nausea can be a symptom of minor or serious disorders. Common causes include indigestion (from eating too fast or from stress around mealtime), FOOD POISONING, MOTION SICKNESS, and PREGNANCY (morning sickness). Nausea may also arise from any cause of abnormal lack of appetite (e.g., SHOCK, pain, influenza, badly fitting dentures, liver or kidney disease). Simple nausea often is relieved by vomiting.

nautilus \'nȯ-tᵊl-əs\ Either of two genera of CEPHALOPODS. The pearly, or chambered, nautilus (genus *Nautilus*) lives in the outermost chamber of its smooth, coiled, usually 36-chambered shell, about 10 in. (25 cm) in diameter. A connecting tube adjusts the gases in the chambers, allowing the shell to act as a float. Nautiluses search the ocean bottom for shrimp or other prey, which they capture with up to 94 small, suckerless, contractile tentacles. The paper nautilus (genus *Argonauta*) feeds on plankton near the surface of tropical and subtropical seas. The female resembles an OCTOPUS but has a thin, unchambered, coiled shell, 12–16 in. (30–40 cm) in diameter. The much smaller male has no shell.

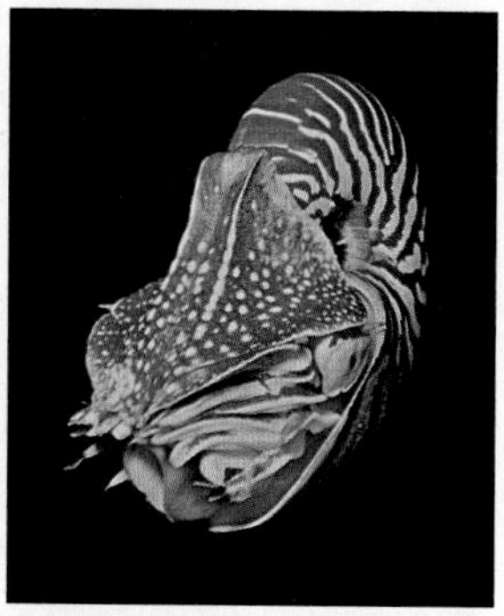

Chambered nautilus (*Nautilus*).
DOUGLAS FAULKNER

Nautilus Any of at least three historic SUBMARINES. ROBERT FULTON built one of the earliest submersible craft in 1800 in France; his *Nautilus* had a collapsible mast and sail for surface propulsion and a hand-turned propeller for power. Andrew Campbell and James Ash of Britain built a *Nautilus* submarine driven by battery-powered electric motors in 1886. The name was also chosen for the world's first nuclear-powered submarine, launched by the U.S. Navy in 1954. Capable of longer submersion than any previous submarine, it made a historic trip under the ice cap of the North Pole from Point Barrow, Alaska, to the Greenland Sea in 1958.

Navajo *or* **Navaho** \'na-və-,hō\ Most populous Indian group in the U.S., with about 200,000 individuals in northwestern New Mexico, Arizona, and southeastern Utah. The Navajo speak an ATHABASKAN language related to that of the APACHE. The Navajo and Apache migrated to the Southwest from Canada c. AD 900–1200, after which the Navajo came under the influence of the PUEBLO INDIANS. Painted pottery and the famous Navajo rugs, as well as SANDPAINTING, are products of this influence. The craft of silversmithing probably came from Mexico in the mid-19th century. Their traditional economy was based on farming, and later herding of sheep, goats, and cattle. The basic social unit was the BAND. Religion focused on the emergence of the first people from worlds beneath the earth's surface. In 1863, the U.S. government ordered Col. KIT CARSON to put an end to Navajo and Apache raiding, his offensives resulting in the incarceration of about 8,000 Navajo and the destruction of crops and herds. Today many Navajo live on or near the Navajo Reservation (24,000 sq mi; 64,000 sq km); thousands earn their living as transient workers. Their language has been tenaciously preserved.

Navajo National Monument National monument, northern Arizona. Covering 360 acres (146 hectares), it comprises three historic cliff dwellings: Betatakin (Navajo: "Ledge House"), Keet Seel ("Broken Pottery"), and Inscription House, among the best-preserved and most elaborate cliff dwellings known. The largest, Keet Seel, was first discovered by whites in 1895; the three sites were made a national monument in 1909. The dwellings were the principal home of the Kayenta ANASAZI c. 1250–1300. The 135 rooms of Betatakin are tucked into a cliffside alcove 452 ft (138 m) high and 370 ft (113 m) wide. Also situated in a cliff alcove are the 160 rooms and 6 kivas (ceremonial houses) of Keet Seel. Inscription House (closed to the public) has 74 rooms.

Navajo weaving Blankets and rugs made by the NAVAJO, considered among the best-made textiles produced by Native Americans of the U.S. By 1500 the Navajo were well established in what is now the southwestern U.S., where they began to practice weaving when they turned from a seminomadic life to agriculture. From the HOPI they learned how to make looms and weave fabrics on a large scale; but whereas the Hopi limited their designs to striped patterns, the Navajo introduced geometric shapes, diamonds, lozenges, and zigzags. Traditionally, Navajo blankets were made of natural-colored wool or wool in dark colors produced by dyes made from roots, herbs, and minerals. After the introduction of aniline dyes in the late 19th century, Navajo weavers began using brighter wools and a broader range of decorative motifs.

Naval Academy, U.S. See UNITED STATES NAVAL ACADEMY

Naval Limitation, International Conference on See WASHINGTON CONFERENCE

naval warfare Military operations conducted on, under, or over the sea and waged against other seagoing vessels or targets on land or in the air. The earliest naval attacks were raids by the armed men of a tribe or town using fishing boats or merchant ships. The first warships were GALLEYS, replaced in the 16th–17th century by sail-driven warships equipped with cannons. The British victory over the Spanish ARMADA (1588) marked a major development: British galleons refused to allow the Spanish ships to get close enough for boarding and hand-to-hand combat and instead pounded them with guns of superior firing capability. SHIPS OF THE LINE and CRUISERS emerged in the 17th–18th century. In the later 19th century, steam replaced sail propulsion, and IRONCLADS offered greater protection against the increasing power of guns. The BATTLESHIP, developed in these years, reigned until World War II, when the Pearl Harbor attack proved that bombers launched from AIRCRAFT CARRIERS could sink any and all surface ships. Since then, naval air power—MISSILES as well as carrier-based planes—has been the primary weapon of the world's fleets. SUBMARINES have also played a major role in 20th-century naval warfare.

navaratri In HINDUISM, a nine-day festival followed on the 10th day by the DURGA-PUJA. It includes feasting, visiting, public concerts, plays, and fairs. Durga's followers are especially numerous in BENGAL and ASSAM; in other parts of India, the 10th day is associated with the victory of RAMA over RAVANA, acted out in a pageant climaxed by the burning of effigies of demons.

Navarino \,nä-vä-'rē-nō\, **Battle of** (October 20, 1827) Naval engagement in the War of GREEK INDEPENDENCE against Turkey. A fleet of British, French, and Russian ships was sent to aid Greece by intercepting supplies to the Egyptian-Turkish fleet anchored in the Navarino Bay in the Peloponnese. Shortly after it entered the harbor, the superior guns of the European fleet sent three-fourths of the larger Egyptian-Turkish fleet to the bottom and forced others aground. The defeat marked the last significant battle between wooden sailing ships and led to Turkey's evacuation from Greece.

Navarra \nä-'vä-rä\ Autonomous community (pop., 1996 est.: 521,000) and province, northern Spain. It is approximately coextensive with the Spanish part of the historical kingdom of NAVARRE. Established in 1982, it has an area of 4,024 sq mi (10,422 sq km) and is bordered by France. The PYRENEES dominate the northern half of the province, and a Mediterranean climate prevails in the south. Manufacturing industries are clustered around the commercial center and capital, PAMPLONA.

Navarre \nə-'vär\ *Spanish* **Navarra** Ancient kingdom, northern Spain, bordered by France, ARAGON, CASTILE, and the BASQUE COUNTRY. It encompassed the modern autonomous community of NAVARRA and part of the modern French department of Basses-Pyrénées. It was conquered by the Romans, then the Visigoths, and CHARLEMAGNE. It became an independent kingdom in the 10th century. A succession of French dynasties ruled Navarre after 1234. Incorporated into Castile in 1515, it was united to the French crown when Henry of Navarre became King HENRY IV of France in 1589.

Navarro \nä-'vä-rō\, **Fats** *orig.* **Theodore** (1923–1950) U.S. jazz trumpeter, one of the primary exponents of BEBOP. Born in Key West, Fla., Navarro replaced DIZZY GILLESPIE in the big band of BILLY ECKSTINE in 1946, acquiring a reputation as a virtuoso player capable of executing complex phrases with rare grace. He participated in the burgeoning jazz milieu based around 52nd St. in New York in the late 1940s, working with such bebop innovators as BUD POWELL, CHARLIE PARKER, and Tadd Dameron. Addiction to heroin curtailed his activity, and he died of tuberculosis at age 26.

Navas de Tolosa, Battle of Las See Battle of LAS NAVAS DE TOLOSA

nave Main part of a Christian church, extending from the entrance (the NARTHEX) to the TRANSEPT or chancel (area around the altar). In a basilican church (see BASILICA), which has side aisles, nave refers only to the central section. Medieval naves were generally divided into many bays, producing the effect of great length. During the Renaissance, the nave format became more flexible, and the nave was divided into fewer compartments, giving a feeling of spaciousness and balanced proportion among the height, length, and width, as in St. Paul's Cathedral.

navigation Science of directing a craft by determining its position, course, and distance traveled. Early mariners followed landmarks visible on shore and studied prevailing winds for clues to direction. The Phoenicians and Polynesians sailed out of sight of land and used the stars to set their course. The compass (first used by the Chinese c. 1100) was the first navigational aid that gave a constant reference point, though its accuracy was limited, especially in heavy seas. Modern compasses are stabilized by gyroscopes and housed in binnacles that compensate for the craft's motion. Ship speed was first calculated by dropping overboard a log attached to a reel of line knotted at regular intervals; the number of knots exposed while the log drifted and a sandglass emptied gave the vessel's speed in knots (nautical mph). Charts are another essential navigational tool. Fixing a position requires charts detailing known locations, together with instruments that calculate a vessel's bearing relative to them. The earliest instrument for determining latitude was the quadrant, which measured the altitude of the polestar or the noonday sun. Other early instruments included the sextant and the astrolabe. Longitude (used for navigation with increasing success in the 17th–18th century) was fixed using chronometers and tables showing positions of celestial bodies throughout the year. In the 20th century, radio beacons and satellite networks allowed aircraft and ships to determine their position. Dead reckoning uses an accurate history of a vessel's headings and speeds drawn from gyroscopes and from computerized measurements of the craft's acceleration. See also Global Positioning System.

Nave, Salisbury Cathedral, England, begun 1220.

A.F. KERSTING

Navigation Acts English laws in the 17th–18th century that required the use of English or colonial ships to carry English trade. The laws were designed to encourage English shipbuilding and restrict trade competition from England's commercial rivals, especially the Dutch. The acts of the 18th century gradually restricted trade by the American colonies and contributed to growing colonial resentment with the imposition of additional duties on sugar, tobacco, and molasses.

Navistar International Corp. Leading U.S. truck manufacturer. It originated as International Harvester Co., which was incorporated in 1902, merging McCormick Harvesting Machine Co. (founded by Cyrus H. McCormick to market his mechanical reaper) with four smaller machinery makers. It became a pioneer in motorized trucks when it introduced its high-wheeled "auto wagons" for farmers. It began producing tractors in the 1930s and soon became a major manufacturer of earth-moving equipment. Facing economic difficulties in the early 1980s, it sold most of its U.S. construction-equipment business and disposed of its farm-equipment line to concentrate almost entirely on trucks, and in 1986 changed its name to Navistar International.

Navratilova \ˌnav-rə-ti-ˈlō-və\, **Martina** (born 1956) Czech-U.S. tennis player. She became the undisputed top-seeded player in the world in 1979 after winning the Wimbledon women's singles and doubles. In 1982 she won 90 of 93 matches, and in 1983 she won 86 of 87 matches. In 1984 she was honored for winning the Grand Slam, but later was denied the title on a technicality. By 1987 she had won 37 individual Grand Slam championships and by her retirement she had 56, ranking her second only to Margaret Smith Court. By 1992 she had accumulated more championships (158) than any other player, male or female, in tennis history, and she retired in 1994 with 167 titles.

navy Warships and craft of every kind maintained by a nation for fighting on, under, or over the sea. A large modern navy includes aircraft carriers, cruisers, destroyers, frigates, submarines, minesweepers and minelayers, gunboats, and various types of support, supply, and repair ships, as well as naval bases and ports. Naval ships are the chief means by which a nation extends sea power. Their two chief functions are to achieve sea control and sea denial. Control of the sea enables a nation and its allies to carry on maritime commerce, amphibious assaults, and other seaborne operations that may be essential in wartime. Denial of the sea deprives enemy merchant vessels and warships of safe navigation. See also U.S. Navy.

Naxos \ˈnak-säs\ Largest island (pop., 1981: 14,000) of the Cyclades, Greece. It is about 22 mi (35 km) long and 16 mi (26 km) wide, with an area of 165 sq mi (427 sq km). The capital and chief port, Náxos, on the western coast, is on the site of the island's ancient and medieval capitals. In ancient times, it was famous for its wines and the worship of Dionysus. In mythology, it is where Theseus abandoned Ariadne. In the 7th–6th century BC, a deep-grained white marble was exported for statuary. It was captured by the Persians in 490 BC and by Athens in 471 BC. A Venetian duchy ruled 1207–1566; it was later ruled by the Turks. In 1830 it joined the Greek kingdom. Ruins of a Mycenaean settlement (see Mycenae) have been found there. Naxos produces white wine, citrus, and emery.

Nayar \ˈnä-yər\ Hindu caste of the Indian state of Kerala. Before the British conquest in 1792, the Nayar caste supplied Kerala's royalty and nobility, militia, and land managers. During British rule, it became prominent in politics, medicine, education, and law. Unlike most Hindus, Nayars traditionally were matrilineal, and fathers had no rights or obligations with regard to their children. Plural marriage, in which both men and women could receive multiple "visiting" spouses, was practiced until the 19th century. Laws passed in the 1930s enforced monogamy and gave children full rights of inheritance from the father.

Nayarit \ˌnī-ə-ˈrēt\ State (pop., 1995 est.: 897,000), western central Mexico. Located on the Pacific Ocean, it has an area of 10,664 sq mi (27,620 sq km). The capital is Tepic. The Sierra Madre cuts the state's terrain into gorges and valleys. The volcanoes Ceboruco and Sangangüey are notable, and the coastal lagoons are well-known bird refuges. The main river, Grande de Santiago, flowing from Lake Chapala, is sometimes considered a continuation of the Lerma River. Nayarit is primarily agricultural.

Nazarenes \ˈna-zə-ˌrēnz\ Members of the Brotherhood of St. Luke, an association formed in 1809 by young German, Swiss, and Austrian painters in reaction against Neoclassicism. It was the first effective anti-academic movement in European painting. They acquired the nickname Nazarenes when four of them visited Rome, because of their biblical style of hair and dress. The Nazarenes believed that all art should serve a moral or religious purpose. They admired medieval and early Renaissance painters and rejected most subsequent painting, believing it abandoned religious ideals in favor of artistic virtuosity. Members lived and worked together in a semimonastic existence, trying to imitate the teaching situation of the medieval workshop. Its leading members were Friedrich Overbeck (1789–1869), Franz Pforr (1788–1812), and Peter von Cornelius (1783–1867).

Nazareth *Hebrew* **Nazerat** \ˌnä-zə-ˈrät\ *Arabic* **En Nasira** \en-ˈnä-sē-ˌrä\ Town (pop., 1992 est.: 50,000), northern Israel, southeast of Haifa. It is Israel's largest Arab city. In the New Testament, it is the childhood home of Jesus. It contains many Christian churches and is a pilgrimage center. It was captured several times during the Crusades. In 1517 it was taken by the Turks. It was part of British-mandate Palestine from 1918 and part of Israel from 1948. Christian Arabs form the majority of the population.

Nazi Party German political party of National Socialism. Founded in 1919 as the German Workers' Party, it changed its name to the National Socialist German Workers' Party when Adolf Hitler became leader (1920–21). The nickname Nazi was taken from the first word of its full name, Nationalsozialistische Deutsche Arbeiter-Partei. The party grew from its home base in Bavaria and attracted members from disaffected elements throughout Germany. It organized strong-arm groups (later the SA) to protect its rallies. Though the failed Beer Hall Putsch diminished the party's influence, the effects of the Great Depression brought millions of new members, and in 1932 the party became the largest bloc in the Reichstag. After Hitler was named chancellor in 1933, he obtained passage of the Enabling Act, and his government declared the Nazi party to be the only political party in Germany and required bureaucrats to become members. The party controlled virtually all activities in Germany until Germany's defeat in World War II (1945), after which the party was banned.

NBA See NATIONAL BASKETBALL ASSN.

NBC *in full* **National Broadcasting Co.** Major U.S. commercial BROADCASTING company. It was formed in 1926 by RCA CORP., GENERAL ELECTRIC CO., and WESTINGHOUSE and was the first U.S. company to operate a broadcast network. Directed by RCA's president DAVID SARNOFF, it became wholly owned by RCA in 1930. NBC was initially divided into the semi-independent Blue Network, based on station WJZ, and the Red Network, based on WEAF, each with links to stations in other cities. By 1938 the Red Network carried 75% of NBC's programs. The Blue Network was sold in 1941 and became the American Broadcasting Co. (ABC). NBC continued to lead the networks with its popular comedy, variety, and drama programs, but in the late 1940s it lost several leading performers to CBS in a talent raid. NBC entered television broadcasting in a weakened position, and by 1952 it trailed CBS in audience ratings, though it gradually regained its leading position. In 1986 RCA was sold to GE; in 1987 NBC sold its radio networks.

NCAA See NATIONAL COLLEGIATE ATHLETIC ASSN.

NCR Corp. U.S. manufacturer of cash registers, computers, and information-processing systems. It was founded in 1884 as National Cash Register Co. by John H. Patterson, who bought a failing maker of cash registers in Dayton, Ohio. He improved the design, sent out an aggressive sales force, and hired repairmen to service his products after sale. The company expanded in the 20th century, introducing accounting machines in the 1920s, electronic products during World War II, computer hardware and software in the 1960s, and microelectronics in the 1970s. In 1991 it was purchased by AT&T CORP. and renamed AT&T Global Information Solutions. When AT&T split into three companies in 1996, NCR Corp. was spun off and resumed its original name.

Ndebele \en-də-'bē-lē\ *or* **Matabele** \ˌmad-ə-'bē-lē\ Bantu-speaking people who live primarily around the city of BULAWAYO, Zimbabwe. They originated early in the 19th century as an offshoot of the NGUNI of Natal, moving first to Basutoland (now LESOTHO) and ultimately to Matabeleland (Zimbabwe). Under LOBENGULA they grew in power, but were defeated by the British in 1893. Today they are a farming and herding people numbering 1.5 million.

N'Djamena \ᵊn-jä-'mā-nä\ *formerly* **Fort-Lamy** \ˌfȯr-lə-'mē\ City (metro. area pop., 1993: 530,965), capital of Chad. It lies adjacent to Cameroon on the eastern bank of the CHARI RIVER where it joins the LOGONE RIVER. Founded in 1900 as Fort-Lamy, it remained a small settlement until after Chad's independence in 1960. In 1973 its name was changed to N'Djamena. It was occupied by Libyan forces in 1980–81 during the civil war that began in the 1960s. It is an important marketplace for cotton, cattle, and fish. It is the site of the nation's only university, the University of Chad (founded 1971).

Ndongo \ᵊn-'dȯŋ-gō\ Historical African kingdom of MBUNDU people. Established c. 1500 in what is now Angola, it instituted trade relations with the Portuguese of SÃO TOMÉ in the 16th century. When Portugal tried to take it over, some 100 years of fighting ensued. It was absorbed into Angola c. 1670.

Ne Win \'nā-'win\, **U** *or* **Shu Maung** \'shü-'mau̇ŋ\ (born 1911) Leader of Burma (Myanmar) from 1962 to 1988. He became involved in the Burmese independence movement in the mid-1930s. During World War II he initially served in the Japanese-sponsored army, but he later helped organize underground resistance to the Japanese. In 1962 he ousted the elected prime minister U NU; his subsequent regime combined military dictatorship with a socialist economic program. Burma became isolated and impoverished under Ne Win, and he resigned in 1988, but continued to exercise power behind the scenes.

NEA See NATIONAL EDUCATION ASSN., NATIONAL ENDOWMENT FOR THE ARTS

Neagh \'nā\, **Lough** Lake, eastern central Northern Ireland. It is the largest lake in the British Isles, with an area of 153 sq mi (396 sq km). It is about 15 mi (24 km) wide and 18 mi (29 km) long, but only about 40 ft (12 m) deep. Ancient deposits in Toome Bay, on its northwestern shore, have yielded the oldest recorded human artifacts in Ireland. In 1959 flood-control works significantly lowered the lake level.

Neanderthal \nē-'an-dər-ˌthȯl, nā-'än-dər-ˌtäl\ Species of the genus *Homo* that inhabited much of Europe and the Mediterranean lands in the late PLEISTOCENE, c. 100,000–35,000 years ago. The name derives from the discovery in 1856 of remains in a cave above Germany's Neander Valley. Some scholars designate the species as *Homo neanderthalensis* and do not consider them direct human ancestors, while others regard them as a late archaic form of *HOMO SAPIENS* that was absorbed into modern human populations in some areas while simply dying out in others. Neanderthals were short, stout, and powerful. Cranial capacity equaled or surpassed that of modern humans, though their braincases were long, low, and wide. Their limbs were heavy, but they seem to have walked fully erect and had hands as capable as those of modern humans. They were cave dwellers who used fire, hunted animals using stone tools and wooden spears, buried their dead, and cared for their sick or injured. They probably used language and may have practiced a primitive form of religion. See also MOUSTERIAN INDUSTRY.

Nebraska State (pop., 2000: 1,711,263), western central U.S. It covers 77,355 sq mi (200,349 sq km); its capital is LINCOLN. The MISSOURI RIVER is on its eastern boundary. The North Platte and South Platte unite in southwestern central Nebraska to form the PLATTE RIVER. Various prehistoric peoples inhabited the area as early as 8000 BC. Indian tribes living in the area include PAWNEE, UTE, and Omaha in the east and SIOUX, ARAPAHO, and COMANCHE in the west. The U.S. bought the territory from France as part of the LOUISIANA PURCHASE in 1803. In 1804 the LEWIS AND CLARK EXPEDITION visited the Nebraska side of the Missouri River. It became part of Nebraska Territory with the KANSAS-NEBRASKA ACT of 1854. Nebraska was admitted to the Union as the 37th state in 1867. Soon after, population increased, and as Indian resistance on the frontier was broken, settlement extended to Nebraska's panhandle. At the turn of the 20th century, it experienced a short but influential POPULIST MOVEMENT. In 1937 it established a unicameral legislature, the only one in the nation. Most of the state is agricultural; its industries include food processing and machinery. Petroleum is the principal mineral resource. In addition to Lincoln, OMAHA is the state's other cultural and industrial center.

Nebraska, University of State university system with campuses in Lincoln, Omaha, and Kearney. It was chartered in 1869 as a land-grant institution. The Lincoln campus has nine colleges, including colleges of architecture, law, and human resources and family sciences, and offers bachelor's, master's, and doctoral programs in numerous fields. The Omaha campus is home to the university medical center. The Kearney campus awards bachelor's degrees only. The university conducts research in such fields as computer science, biochemistry, food processing, and agriculture. Total enrollment is about 51,000.

Nebuchadnezzar II \ˌneb-yə-kəd-'ne-zər\ *or* **Nebuchadrezzar** \ˌneb-yə-kəd-'re-zər\ (c. 630–561? BC) Second and greatest king of the Chaldean dynasty of BABYLONIA. He began his military career as an administrator (c. 610 BC) and ascended the throne on his father's death, just after winning Syria from the Egyptians (605 BC). He attacked Judah, capturing Jerusalem in 597 and recapturing it in 587/6, and deporting prominent citizens to BABYLON. He devoted time and energy to rebuilding Babylon, paving roads, rebuilding temples, and digging canals. At least in folk tradition, he is credited with building the Hanging Gardens of Babylon.

nebula \'neb-yə-lə\ Any of various tenuous clouds of gas and dust in interstellar space. Nebulae constitute only a small percentage of a GALAXY's mass. Dark nebulae (e.g., the COALSACK) are very dense, cold molecular clouds that appear as large, obscure, irregularly shaped areas in the sky. Bright nebulae (e.g., the CRAB NEBULA, PLANETARY NEBULA) appear as faintly luminous, glowing surfaces; they emit their own light or reflect that of stars near them.

nebular hypothesis See SOLAR NEBULA

NEC Corp. Major Japanese telecommunications and computer manufacturer. Nippon Electric Company, Ltd. (officially NEC Corp. in 1983) was founded in 1899 with funding from the WESTERN ELECTRIC CO. INC. of the United States. NEC was the first Japanese joint venture with a foreign company. As Japan's preeminent telecommunications company, NEC contributed to developments in mobile telephony, fiber-optic networks, private-branch exchanges (PBXs), and microwave, digital, and satellite communications systems. Besides mainframe computers, NEC was an early manufacturer of personal computers (PCs). In 1997 NEC merged its North American PC operations with Zenith Data Systems and Packard Bell to form Packard Bell–NEC, Inc.

necessity In LOGIC and METAPHYSICS, a MODALITY of propositions that is dual to the modality of possibility. A necessary proposition may be either necessarily true or necessarily false. A necessarily true proposition is one that could not be false in any POSSIBLE WORLD (e.g., 2 + 2 = 4). A contingently true proposition is one that is true (e.g., "France is a democracy") but would have been false had the world differed in certain ways. A necessarily false proposition is one that is false in every possible world (e.g., 2 + 2 = 5), while a contingently false proposition is one that would have been true had the world differed in certain ways. Necessary propositions therefore include both necessary truths and necessary falsehoods, though the term is often restricted to the class of necessary truths. See also A PRIORI, ANALYTIC–SYNTHETIC DISTINCTION.

Nechako River \ni-'cha-kō\ River, central British Columbia. The major tributary of the FRASER RIVER, it flows east for nearly 150 mi (240 km). The Stuart River, a tributary 258 mi (415 km) long, joins it between Fort Fraser and Prince George, where it parallels the Canadian National Railway. In 1952 the Nechako was bisected by Kenney Dam, which created a reservoir whose overflow generates electricity.

Neckar River \'ne-kär\ River, southwestern Germany. It rises in the BLACK FOREST near the headwaters of the DANUBE RIVER and is 228 mi (367 km) long. It flows north and northeast, passing STUTTGART. Its picturesque valley becomes broader and deeper, passing hills crowned by feudal castles. It flows past HEIDELBERG and enters the RHINE RIVER at MANNHEIM.

Necker \nā-'ker, 'ne-kər\, **Jacques** (1732–1804) Swiss-French financier and director-general of finance under LOUIS XVI. Born in Geneva, he became a banker in Paris. After becoming wealthy from speculating during the Seven Years' War, he was appointed minister of Geneva in Paris (1768). He retired from banking in 1772, and became France's director-general of finance in 1777. Despite his cautious reforms, he was forced to resign in 1781 over opposition to his scheme to help finance the AMERICAN REVOLUTION. He was recalled in 1788 to rescue the almost-bankrupt France, and proposed financial and political reforms that included a limited constitutional monarchy. Opposition from the royal court led to Necker's dismissal on July 11, 1789, an event that provoked the storming of the BASTILLE. After serving again briefly (1789–90), he retired to Geneva. GERMAINE DE STAEL was his daughter.

necropolis \ni-'krä-pə-ləs\ (Greek: "city of the dead") Extensive and elaborate burial place serving an ancient city. The locations of these cemeteries varied. Many in Egypt, such as the necropolis of western Thebes, were situated across the Nile River opposite the cities. In Greece and Rome a necropolis often lined the roads leading out of town. A necropolis was discovered in the 1940s under ST. PETER'S BASILICA in Rome.

necropsy See AUTOPSY

nectarine Smooth-skinned PEACH *(Prunus persica* 'nectarina'), grown throughout warmer temperate regions. They result when some peaches self-pollinate or are crossed so that they express a genetic factor for smooth skin. Nectarines are commonly eaten fresh or cooked in desserts and jams; they are a good source of vitamins A and C.

Nectarine (*Prunus persica* var. *nectarina*).

J.C. ALLEN AND SON

Needham, John Turberville (1713–1781) British naturalist. He was a Roman Catholic priest, whose reading about microscopic organisms led him to study natural history in London and Paris (1746–49). He became a strong supporter of the theory that life arose from inorganic matter (spontaneous generation) and that life processes cannot be explained by the laws of chemistry and physics (vitalism). In 1750 he presented a paper explaining the theory of spontaneous generation and attempting to offer scientific evidence supporting it.

needle Basic implement used in sewing or embroidering and, in variant forms, for knitting and crocheting. The sewing needle is small, slender, and rodlike. One end is sharply pointed to make passing it through fabric easy; the other end has a slot (called an eye) to carry a THREAD. Modern sewing needles are made of steel. Crocheting needles are eyeless and have a hook on one end; they are usually of steel or plastic. Knitting needles are long, made of various materials, and bluntly pointed at one or both ends, sometimes with a knob at the end opposite the point.

needlefish Any of about 60 species (family Belonidae) of primarily marine, edible, carnivorous fishes found throughout temperate and tropical waters. Needlefish are adept jumpers and have a long, slender jaw with sharp teeth. They are long, slim, and silvery, with a blue or green back. The largest species grows to 4 ft (1.2 m) long. The garfish *(Belone belone)* occurs in Europe, and the houndfish *(Tylosurus crocodilus)* is found everywhere in the tropics.

needlepoint Type of embroidery in which the stitches are counted and worked with a needle over the threads, or mesh, of a canvas foundation. It was known as canvas work until the early 19th century. If the canvas has 16 or more mesh holes per linear inch, the embroidery is called petit point; most needlepoint was petit point in the 16th–18th century. Needlepoint as it is known today originated in the 17th century, when the fashion for furniture upholstered with embroidered fabrics prompted the development of a more durable material to serve as the embroidery's foundation. Wool is generally used for needlepoint, silk yarn less often. Needlepoint kits, containing canvas stamped with a design and all the materials needed for the project, were sold as early as the mid-18th century. See also BARGELLO.

Nefertiti \ˌne-fər-'tē-tē\ (14th century BC) Queen of Egypt and wife of AKHENATON (r.1353–1336 BC). She is known from her portrait bust found at TELL EL-AMARNA, the king's new capital. She may have been an Asian princess from Mitanni. She appears with Akhenaton in reliefs at Tell el-Amarna and followed his new cult of the sun god ATON. Of her six daughters, two became queens of Egypt. In the 12th year of Akhenaton's reign, she either retired after losing favor or died.

Nefertiti, painted limestone bust, about 1350 BC; in the Egyptian Museum, Berlin.

BILDARCHIV PREUSSISCHER KULTURBESITZ, AGYPTISCHES MUSEUM, STAATLICHE MUSEEN ZU BERLIN–PREUSSISCHER KULTURBESITZ, BERLIN; PHOTOGRAPH, JURGEN LIEPE

Negev \'ne-ˌgev\ *or* **Ha-Negev** Desert region, southern Israel. Bounded by the SINAI Peninsula and the Jordan Rift Valley, it has an area of about 4,700 sq mi (12,200 sq km). It was a pastoral region in biblical times and an important source of grain for the Roman empire. After the Arab conquest of Palestine (7th century AD), it was left desolate, and for more than 1,200 years it had only a small population of BEDOUIN. Modern agricultural development began with three KIBBUTZIM in 1943; others were founded after World War II, when irrigation projects were initiated. Assigned to Israel in the partition of Palestine in 1948, it was the scene of clashes between Israeli and Egyptian forces in 1948–49. It is the site of many planned Israeli settlements, including the port city of Elat, Israel's outlet to the Red Sea. Beersheba is an important administrative center. The region produces grain, fruit, and vegetables; mineral resources include potash, bromine, and copper.

negligence In law, failure to exercise the degree of care expected of a person of ordinary prudence in protecting others from a risk of harm. It may render one civilly and sometimes criminally liable for resulting injuries. The doctrine of negligence does not require the elimination of all risk, but rather only foreseeable and unreasonable risk. Thus a higher standard applies to explosives manufacturers than to manufacturers of kitchen matches. The plaintiff must ordinarily prove the defendant's negligence with a preponderance of evidence. See also CONTRIBUTORY NEGLIGENCE.

negotiable instrument Transferable document (e.g., a bank note, check, or draft) containing an unconditional promise or order to pay a specified amount to its holder upon demand or at a specified time. In the U.S., the Uniform Commercial Code governs negotiable instruments.

Negritude \nā-grē-'tūēd\ Literary movement of the 1930s, '40s, and '50s that began among French-speaking African and Caribbean writers living in Paris as a protest against French colonial rule and the policy of assimilation. Its leading figures—Leopold Senghor of Senegal, Aime Cesaire of Martinique, and Léon Damas (1912–78) of French Guiana—began to examine Western values critically and to reassess African culture. The group believed that the value and dignity of African traditions and peoples must be asserted, that Africans must look to their own heritage for values and traditions, and that writers should use African subject matter and poetic traditions. The movement faded in the early 1960s after its objectives had been achieved in most African countries.

Negro \'nā-grō\, **Río** *or* **Río Guainía** \'rē-ü-gwī-'nē-ə\ River, northwestern South America. A major tributary of the Amazon River, it rises in the rainforest of eastern Colombia, where it is known as the Guainía, and forms a section of the Colombia–Venezuela boundary. It crosses Brazil and continues into the Amazon at Manaus. It is about 1,400 mi (2,250 km) long and is a major transport artery. Its name comes from its jet-black color, which is caused by the decomposition of organic matter and its low silt content.

Negro, Río River, central Uruguay. It rises in the southern highlands of Brazil. It flows southwest across Uruguay, where a dam creates the Río Negro Reservoir, the largest artificial lake in South America, with an area of 4,000 sq mi (10,400 sq km). The river joins the Uruguay River at Soriano. Although it is 434 mi (698 km) long, it is navigable for only 45 mi (72 km) upstream from its mouth.

Negro Leagues Associations of teams of African American baseball players active largely between 1920 and the late '40s. The principal leagues were the Negro National League, originally organized by Rube Foster in 1920, and the Negro American League, organized in 1937. The most noted teams included the Homestead (Pa.) Grays, who won nine pennants in the years 1937–45 and included the great hitters Cool Papa Bell, Buck Leonard, and Josh Gibson. In the mid-1930s the Pittsburgh Crawfords included Satchel Paige and the clutch-hitter William Julius "Judy" Johnson. The Kansas City Monarchs, after winning four national championships, lost Jackie Robinson to the Brooklyn Dodgers; the breaking of the color barrier in major- and minor-league baseball led to the Negro Leagues' quick decline.

Negroid See Race

Negros \'nā-grōs\ Island (pop., 2000: 3,691,784) in the Visayan group, central Philippines. The fourth-largest island of the archipelago, it is shaped like a boot. It is about 135 mi (217 km) long with an area of 4,907 sq mi (12,710 sq km). It produces about 50% of Philippine sugar and is one of the wealthiest and most politically influential regions in the nation. Its largest city, Bacolod on the northwestern coast, is an important sugar exporter.

Nehemiah \ˌnē-ə-'mī-ə\ (fl. 5th century BC) Jewish leader who supervised the rebuilding of Jerusalem. His story is told in the Old Testament Book of Nehemiah. He was cupbearer to the Persian ruler Artaxerxes I soon after the end of the Babylonian Exile, when the Temple of Jerusalem had been rebuilt but the Jewish community was still weak and fragmented. Around 444 BC he was put in charge of Jerusalem's reconstruction, and he organized the rebuilding of the city walls. He also revived adherence to Mosaic law and forbade intermarriage with non-Jews. His work as a reformer was later continued by Ezra.

Jawaharlal Nehru, photograph by Yousuf Karsh, 1956.

Nehru \'nā-rü\, **Jawaharlal** (1889–1964) First prime minister of independent India (1947–64). Son of the independence advocate Motilal Nehru (1861–1931), Nehru was educated at home and in Britain and became a lawyer in 1912. More interested in politics than law, he was impressed by Mohandas K. Gandhi's approach to Indian independence. His close association with the Indian National Congress began in 1919; in 1929 he became its president, presiding over the historic Lahore session that proclaimed complete independence (rather than dominion status) as India's political goal. He was imprisoned nine times between 1921 and 1945 for his political activity. When India was granted limited self-government in 1935, the Congress Party under Nehru unwisely refused to form coalition governments with the Muslim League in some provinces; the hardening of relations between Hindus and Muslims that followed ultimately led to the partition of India and the creation of Pakistan. Shortly before Gandhi's assassination in 1948, Nehru became the first prime minister of independent India. He attempted a foreign policy of nonalignment during the Cold War, drawing harsh criticism when he strayed into either camp. During his tenure India clashed with Pakistan over Kashmir and with China over the Brahmaputra River valley. He also wrested Goa from the Portuguese. Domestically he promoted democracy, socialism, secularism, and unity, adapting modern values to Indian conditions. His daughter, Indira Gandhi, became prime minister two years after his death.

Nei Monggol \'nā-'mu̇ŋ-'gȯl\ *or* **Nei-meng-ku** \'nā-'məŋ-'gü\ *English* **Inner Mongolia** Autonomous region (pop., 1999 est.: 23,620,000), China. Located in northern and northeastern China, its capital is Hohhot. Mongols and Chinese make up the bulk of the population, most of which is concentrated in the agricultural belt near the Huang River. It is an inland plateau lying at an elevation of about 3,000 ft (900 m), fringed by mountains and valleys. Its northern portion lies within the Gobi Desert, and its southern border is partly marked by the Great Wall. Inner Mongolia was separated from Mongolia (or Outer Mongolia) in 1644. It was established as an autonomous region in 1947. Its harsh climate restricts agriculture; some industrial development has occurred there.

Neilson \'nēl-sən\, **James Beaumont** (1792–1865) Scottish inventor. Working at the Glasgow Gasworks (1817–47), he introduced the use of a hot-air blast for the smelting of iron. It had been believed that a blast of cold air was the most efficient smelting method (see William Fairbairn); Neilson demonstrated that the opposite was true, patenting his idea in 1828. Use of the hot blast tripled iron output per ton of coal, permitted iron to be recovered from lower-grade ores, and made possible the efficient use of raw coal and lower grades of coal instead of coke and the construction of larger smelting furnaces.

Neiman Marcus \ˌnē-mən-'mär-kəs\ Prestigious U.S. department-store chain. It was founded in Dallas in 1907 by Herbert Marcus, his sister Carrie Marcus Neiman, and her husband A. L. Neiman. From the beginning it featured unusual merchandise, particularly extravagant and outlandish gifts (including camels and Chinese junks) intended to appeal to the rich, in addition to a more standard selection for moderate-income customers. In 1999 Neiman Marcus Group, which included the retailer Bergdorf Goodman, became a publicly held company.

Neith \'nēt\ Ancient Egyptian goddess, patroness of the city of Sais, in the Nile River delta. Neith was worshiped in predynastic times (c. 3000 BC), and several queens of the 1st dynasty were named after her. She also became an important goddess in the city of Memphis. She was usually depicted as a woman wearing a red crown, holding crossed arrows and a bow. She was the mother of Sebek, and later of Re.

Nejd \'nezhd\ *or* **Najd** \'nàzhd\ Region of central Saudi Arabia. Comprising a rocky plateau sloping eastward from the mountains of the Hejaz, it is sparsely settled, except for a few fertile oases. It became the center of the Wahhabi, a fundamentalist Islamic movement, in the mid-18th century, which, by 1803 had expanded into Mecca. Nejd was captured by Ibn Saud c. 1905. It was united with the Hejaz and became the independent kingdom of Saudi Arabia in 1932.

Nelson, (John) Byron (born 1912) U.S. golfer. Born in Fort Worth, Texas, "Lord Byron" began as a caddie at age 12 and turned professional in 1932. He won the U.S. Open (1939), the Masters (1937, 1942), and the PGA championship (1940, 1945), setting records in 1945 when he won 18 out of 30 tournaments, 11 in succession.

Nelson, Horatio *later* **Viscount Nelson** *known as* **Lord Nelson** (1758–1805) British naval commander. He entered the navy in 1770 and served in the West Indies 1777–83. In 1793 he was sent to support the British allies against the French in the Mediterranean. After the British victory against the Spanish and French in the Battle of Cape St. Vincent (1797), he was promoted to rear admiral. In 1798 he pursued NAPOLEON's fleet to Egypt, where he won the decisive Battle of the NILE. During a prolonged stay in Naples for his ships' repairs, he pursued a love affair with Emma, Lady HAMILTON. For helping restore the Neapolitan king FERDINAND I to power (1799), he was created duca (Duke) di Bronte. As second in command of an expedition to attack Denmark, he skillfully won the Battle of COPENHAGEN (1801), and was appointed commander in chief of the navy. In 1805 he was sent to the Mediterranean to meet the threat posed by the French fleet in Napoleon's scheme to invade England. In the ensuing Battle of TRAFALGAR, Nelson, aboard his flagship *Victory,* was shot by a French sniper from the *Redoutable* and died just as the British fleet secured its victory. His death was widely mourned, and he became England's most popular hero. His brilliant tactical command assured British naval supremacy for over 100 years.

Nelson, Willie (born 1933) U.S. COUNTRY-MUSIC singer and songwriter. Born in Abbott, Texas, he learned guitar from his grandfather and by 10 was performing at local dances. After working as a disc jockey, in 1961 he moved to Nashville, where he wrote hit songs for dozens of country, rhythm-and-blues, and pop singers, including "Hello Walls," "Night Life," and "Crazy." Returning to Texas, he released the hit album *Red Headed Stranger* (1975); it was followed by *Wanted: The Outlaws,* which outsold every country album that had preceded it, and *Stardust* (1978), with songs by H. CARMICHAEL and IRVING BERLIN. He has recorded with at least 75 other singers, including Waylon Jennings (born 1937). In the 1980s he organized annual Farm Aid festivals to raise money for farmers.

Nelson River River, northern central Manitoba. Flowing out of northern Lake WINNIPEG into HUDSON BAY, it is 400 mi (644 km) long. It was discovered in 1612 by the English explorer Thomas Button, and a trading post of the HUDSON'S BAY CO. was established there c. 1670. Fur traders used the river as an inland route. The Hudson Bay Railway now follows most of the river's course.

Neman River \'ne-mən\ *Lithuanian* **Nemunas** \'ne-mü-ˌnäs\ River, central Europe. Rising in Belarus, south of MINSK, it flows west into Lithuania, and between Lithuania and Kaliningrad province, Russia, to empty into the BALTIC SEA. It is 582 mi (936 km) long and navigable for most of its length. It was known as the Memel River in the former eastern Prussia and as the Russ 22 mi (35 km) from its mouth. It was the scene of many battles between Russian and German forces in World War I.

Nemanja, Stefan See STEFAN NEMANJA

nematode \'ne-mə-ˌtōd\ *or* **roundworm** Any of more than 15,000 named and many more unnamed species of WORMS in the class Nematoda (phylum Aschelminthes). Nematodes include plant and animal parasites and free-living forms found in soil, freshwater, saltwater, and even vinegar and beer malts. They are bilaterally symmetrical and usually tapered at both ends. Some species have separate sexes; others are hermaphroditic. They range from microscopic to about 23 ft (7 m) long. Nematode parasites can occur in almost any body organ but are most common in the digestive, circulatory, or respiratory system. Hookworms, PINWORMS, and EELWORMS are nematodes. See also FILARIAL WORM, GUINEA WORM, TRICHINA.

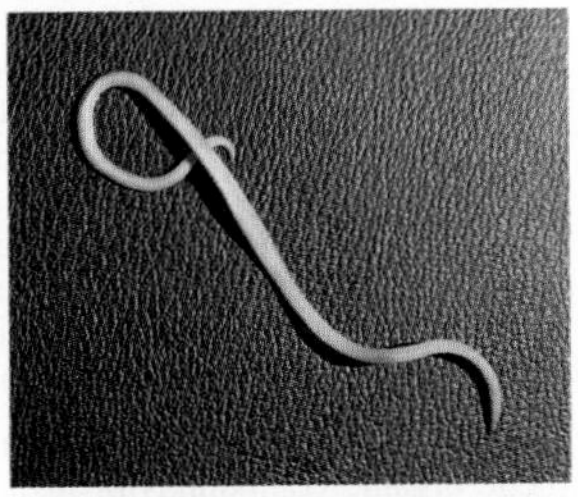
Nematode (*Ascaris lumbricoides*).
JAVIER PALAUS SOLER—OSTMAN AGENCY

Nemea, Battle of \'nē-mē-ə\ (394 BC) Battle in the Corinthian War (395–387 BC). The conflict took place when a coalition of Greek city-states determined to destroy Sparta's ascendancy after its victory in the PELOPONNESIAN WAR. The outnumbered Spartans were victorious, crushing first the Athenians and then the Thebans, Corinthians, and Argives.

Nemerov \'nem-ər-ˌȯf\, **Howard** (1920–1991) U.S. poet. Born in New York City, he attended Harvard University and served as a pilot in World War II before teaching at various colleges, including Bennington. His verse, marked by irony and self-deprecatory wit, is often about nature; it appears in volumes beginning with *The Image and the Law* (1947) and including *Collected Poems* (1977, Pulitzer Prize, National Book Award). His fiction includes *The Homecoming Game* (1957) and *A Commodity of Dreams and Other Stories* (1960). He was poet laureate of the U.S. 1988–90. DIANE ARBUS was his sister.

Nemesis \'ne-mə-səs\ Greek goddess of retribution. In the earliest Greek religion she was worshiped as a fertility goddess. Later legends told how ZEUS, in the form of a swan, coupled with her in the form of a goose. Nemesis then laid the egg from which HELEN of Troy was born (in other versions LEDA was said to be Helen's mother). Nemesis dealt out punishments that expressed gods' disapproval of human presumption. Her cult was also popular in Rome, particularly among soldiers.

Nemi \'nā-mē\, **Lake** *ancient* **Lacus Nemorensis.** Crater lake in the Alban Hills, southeast of Rome, Italy. Its area is about 0.67 sq mi (1.7 sq km), and it is 110 ft (34 m) deep. Nearby were a temple and grove sacred to the goddess DIANA. Two ships from the period of the emperor CALIGULA were raised from the bottom of the lake in the 1920s but were burned by the retreating German army in 1944.

Nen River *formerly* **Nonni River** River, northeastern China, main tributary of the SONGHUA RIVER. It rises on the eastern slopes of Da Hinggan Ling in northern HEILONGJIANG province and flows south, forming part of the border between Heilongjiang and JILIN provinces and watering the fertile northern section of the Manchurian plain. It is about 740 mi (1,190 km) long and is an important route; much of it is navigable.

nene \'nā-ˌnā\ *or* **Hawaiian goose** Species *(Branta sandvicensis)* of GOOSE, the state bird of Hawaii. A close relative of the CANADA GOOSE, the nene is a nonmigratory, nonaquatic species with shortened wings and half-webbed feet. It is about 25 in. (65 cm) long and has a gray-brown barred body and black face. It feeds on berries and grasses on high lava slopes. Predation by introduced mammals (including dogs, cats, pigs, and mongooses) and human hunting had reduced the population to a few small flocks by 1911. It has since been successfully bred in captivity, but flocks released in the wild have failed to form self-sustaining colonies.

Nenni, Pietro (Sandro) (1891–1980) Italian politician. He joined the Italian Socialist Party (PSI) in 1921 and edited its newspaper, *Avanti!* (1922–26). After criticizing the Fascists and BENITO MUSSOLINI, he was arrested and fled to Paris (1926). In the Spanish Civil War, he cofounded the Garibaldi Brigade. He was imprisoned in Germany and Italy in World War II, then became leader of the PSI; he led the left wing in alliance with the Communist Party until 1956. In 1963 he allied the PSI with the Christian Democrats and served as vice premier in three successive cabinets and as foreign minister 1968–69.

Neo-Confucianism In China, a rationalistic revival of CONFUCIANISM in the 11th century AD that influenced Chinese thought for 800 years. The movement sought to reestablish the supremacy of the Confucian heritage over the increasingly popular BUDDHISM and TAOISM. Its two principal schools of thought were the Li Xue (School of Principle), whose chief philosopher was ZHU XI, and the Xin Xue (School of Mind), represented by LU XIANGSHAN and WANG YANGMING. Neo-Confucianism was introduced into Japan by ZEN Buddhists in medieval times and became the guiding philosophy of the TOKUGAWA SHOGUNATE (1603–1867), providing a heavenly sanction for the existing social order. Its emphasis on classical literature led to renewed interest in the Japanese classics and a revival of SHINTO studies.

neo-Darwinism Theory of evolution that represents a synthesis of CHARLES DARWIN's theory in terms of NATURAL SELECTION and modern population genetics. The term was first used after 1896 to describe the theories of August Weismann (1834–1914), who asserted that his germ-plasm theory made impossible the inheritance of acquired characteristics and supported natural selection as the only major process that would account for biological evolution.

Neo-Expressionism Art movement, chiefly of painters, that dominated the European and American art market in the early to mid-1980s. It was controversial both in the quality of its production and in the highly commercialized aspects of its presentation. Its practitioners, including JULIAN SCHNABEL and ANSELM KIEFER, returned to portraying the human body and other recognizable objects, in reaction to the highly intellectualized abstract art of the 1970s. Their art was characterized by a tense yet playful presentation of objects in a primitivist manner, painted in

L
M
N

vivid color harmonies, conveying inner tension and alienation. See also EXPRESSIONISM.

Neo-Impressionism Movement in French painting of the late 19th century, in reaction against the realism of IMPRESSIONISM. The Neo-Impressionists, led by GEORGES SEURAT and PAUL SIGNAC, applied paint to canvas in dots of contrasting pigments, scientifically chosen so that adjacent dots would blend from a distance into a single color. The technique is known as POINTILLISM. Whereas the Impressionists captured the fugitive effects of color and light, the Neo-Impressionists crystallized them into immobile monumentality.

Neo-Kantianism Revival of KANTIANISM in German universities that began c. 1860. At first primarily an epistemological movement, Neo-Kantianism slowly extended over the whole domain of philosophy. The first decisive impetus toward reviving IMMANUEL KANT's ideas came from natural scientists. HERMANN VON HELMHOLTZ applied physiological studies of the senses to the question of the epistemological significance of spatial perception raised by *The Critique of Pure Reason* (1781). Neo-Kantianism reached its apex in the early-20th-century Marburg school, which included Hermann Cohen (1842–1918) and Paul Natorp (1854–1924). They repudiated Helmholtz's NATURALISM and reaffirmed the importance of the transcendental method. ERNST CASSIRER, another Marburg-school figure, brought Kantian principles to bear on the whole realm of cultural phenomena. Wilhelm Windelband (1848–1915) and Heinrich Rickert (1863–1936) introduced Kantianism into the philosophy of HISTORY. Neo-Kantianism also influenced the PHENOMENOLOGY of EDMUND HUSSERL and of the early works of MARTIN HEIDEGGER.

Neo-Paganism Any of several movements that attempt to revive the polytheistic religions of Europe and the Middle East. Largely a product of the 1960s, contemporary Neo-Paganism has flourished particularly in the U.S., Britain, and Scandinavia. Its adherents often have deep ecological concerns and an attachment to nature; many worship an earth-mother goddess and center their rituals on the change of the seasons. Since the late 1970s, Neo-Paganism has also attracted feminists open to female personifications of the deity. Major Neo-Pagan groups include the Church of All Worlds, Feraferia, Pagan Way, the Reformed Druids of North America, the Church of the Eternal Source, and the Viking Brotherhood. See also WICCA.

Neo-Thomism \\,nē-ō-'tä-,mi-zəm\\ Modern revival of the philosophical and theological system developed by THOMAS AQUINAS and his later commentators. Neo-Thomism follows Aquinas in distinguishing between the realms of nature (in which reason and philosophy hold sway) and supernature (in which faith and theology are dominant). Aquinas's thought was analyzed and restated especially by Dominican commentators up through the 16th century. In the 19th–20th century, the study was revived, especially under the influence of the Jesuits and the papacy, as a philosophical basis for answering contemporary problems. Since the mid-20th century, neo-Thomists have tried to develop an adequate philosophy of science, to take account of phenomenological and psychiatric findings, and to evaluate the ONTOLOGIES of EXISTENTIALISM and NATURALISM. See also JACQUES MARITAIN.

Neoclassical architecture Modern classicism (as it was known at the time) of the 18th and early 19th century. The movement concerned itself with the logic of entire Classical volumes, unlike Classical Revivalism (see GREEK REVIVAL), which tended to reuse Classical parts. Neoclassical architecture is characterized by grandeur of scale; simplicity of geometric forms; Greek, especially Doric (see ORDER), or Roman detail; dramatic use of columns; and a preference for blank walls. The new taste for antique simplicity represented a general reaction to the excesses of ROCOCO STYLE. Neoclassicism thrived in the U.S. and Europe, with examples occurring in almost every major city. Russia's CATHERINE II transformed St. Petersburg into an unparalleled collection of Neoclassical buildings as advanced as any contemporary French and English work. By 1800 nearly all new British architecture reflected the Neoclassical spirit (see ROBERT ADAM, JOHN SOANE). France's boldest innovator was C.-N. LEDOUX, who had a central role in the evolution of Neoclassical architecture. In the U.S., Neoclassicism continued to flourish throughout the 19th century.

Neoclassicism See CLASSICISM AND NEOCLASSICISM

neofascism political philosophy and movement that arose in the post-World War II era and, like earlier fascist movements, advocated extreme nationalism and authoritarianism, opposed the liberal individualism of the Enlightenment, attacked Marxist and other left-wing ideologies, indulged in racist and xenophobic scapegoating, posed as a protector of traditional national culture and religion, glorified violence, and promoted populist right-wing economic programs. Unlike earlier fascists, however, neofascists placed more blame for their countries' problems on non-European immigrants than on leftists and Jews, displayed little interest in taking lebensraum (German: "living space") through the military conquest of other states, and made concerted efforts to portray themselves as democratic and "mainstream." Among European movements and parties considered by many to be neofascist: in Italy, the National Alliance (formerly the Italian Social Movement), led by Gianfranco Fini; in Germany, the Republicans, led by former Waffen-SS member Franz Schönhuber; in France, the National Front, led by Jean-Marie Le Pen; in Russia, the Liberal-Democratic Party, led by Vladimir Zhirinovsky; the Serbian Radical Party, led by Vojislav Seselj; and the Croatian Party of Rights, led by Dobroslav Paraga. Neofascist organizations outside Europe include the regime of JUAN PERÓN in Argentina (1946–55; 1973–74); the White Workers Party (formerly the South African Gentile National Socialist Movement) in South Africa; and the regimes of MUAMMAR AL-QADDAFI in Libya and SADDAM HUSSEIN in Iraq.

Neolithic period \\,nē-ə-'li-thik\\ ("New Stone Age") Final stage of technological development or cultural evolution among prehistoric humans, characterized by stone tools shaped by polishing or grinding, domestication of plants or animals, permanent villages, and such crafts as pottery and weaving. The Neolithic followed the PALEOLITHIC period (and in northwestern Europe the MESOLITHIC) and preceded the BRONZE AGE. Its beginning is associated with the villages that emerged in South Asia c. 9000 BC and flourished in the TIGRIS and EUPHRATES river valleys from c. 7000 BC. Farming spread northward throughout Eurasia, not reaching Britain and Scandinavia until after 3000 BC. Neolithic technologies also spread to the Indus River valley of India by 5000 BC and to the Huang (Yellow) River valley of China by c. 3500 BC. The term is not applied to the New World, though Neolithic modes of life were achieved independently there by c. 2500 BC.

neon Chemical ELEMENT, chemical symbol Ne, atomic number 10. One of the NOBLE GASES, neon is colorless, odorless, tasteless, and completely unreactive. It occurs in minute amounts in the atmosphere and is obtained by fractional DISTILLATION of liquefied air. When under low pressure, it glows a bright orange-red if an electric current is passed through it. It was discovered in 1898, and since the 1920s its chief use has been in luminous tubes and bulbs.

neoplasm See TUMOR

Neoplatonism Form of PLATONISM developed by PLOTINUS in the 3rd century AD and modified by his successors. It came to dominate the Greek philosophical schools and remained predominant until the teaching of philosophy by pagans ended in the late 6th century. It postulated an all-sufficient unity, the One, from which emanated the Divine Mind, or LOGOS, and below that, the World Soul. Those transcendent realities were thought to support the visible world. All things emanated from the One, and individual souls could rise to mystical union with the One through contemplation. Though Plotinus's thought resembles GNOSTICISM in some respects, he was a passionate opponent of Gnosticism.

neoprene \\'nē-ə-,prēn\\ Any of a class of elastomers (rubberlike synthetic organic compounds of high molecular weight) made by POLYMERIZATION of the MONOMER 2-chloro-1,3-butadiene and vulcanized (cross-linked, like RUBBER), by sulfur, metallic oxides, or other agents. These synthetic rubbers, discovered in 1931 (see W. H. CAROTHERS), are generally too expensive to use in making tires, but their resistance to chemicals and oxidation (see OXIDATION-REDUCTION) makes them valuable in specialized applications, including shoe soles, hoses, adhesives, gaskets, seals, and foamed articles.

Neorealism *or* **neorealismo** Italian literary movement that flourished especially after World War II and that sought to deal realistically with the events leading up to the war and with their resulting social problems. Rooted in the 1920s, it was similar to the *verismo* ("realism") movement, from which it originated, but differed in that its upsurge resulted from the intense feelings inspired by fascist repression, the Resistance, and the war. Neorealist writers include ITALO CALVINO, ALBERTO MORAVIA, CESARE PAVESE, SALVATORE QUASIMODO, IGNAZIO SILONE, and ELIO VITTORINI. During the fascist years many Neorealist writers went into hiding, were imprisoned or exiled, or joined the Resistance. The movement reemerged after the war in full strength.

Neosho River \nē-ˈō-shō\ *or* **Grand River** River, southeastern Kansas and northeastern Oklahoma. It rises in eastern central Kansas and flows into Oklahoma, where it is also known as the Grand, to join the Arkansas River near Fort Gibson. It flows about 460 mi (740 km). Neosho is an Osage Indian word meaning "clear and abundant water." The crossing of the river at Council Grove was a starting point for the Santa Fe Trail.

Nepal \nə-ˈpȯl\ *officially* **Kingdom of Nepal** Nation, southern Asia. Area: 54,362 sq mi (140,798 sq km). Population (1997 est.): 21,424,000. Capital: Kathmandu. Most of the people are Nepalese of Indo-Aryan ancestry; there is a significant minority of Tibeto-Nepalese peoples. Languages: Nepali (official), Newari. Religion: Hinduism (official); small minority, Buddhism. Currency: Nepalese rupee. Nepal contains some of the most rugged mountainous terrain in the world. The great Himalayas, including Mount Everest, are in its central and northern parts. As a result of its years of geographic and self-imposed isolation, it is one of the least-developed nations of the world. Its market economy is mostly based on agriculture, and it is a major producer of medicinal herbs, which grow on the slopes of the Himalayas. It is a constitutional monarchy with a bicameral parliament; its chief of state is the king, and the head of government is the prime minister. The region developed under early Buddhist influence, and dynastic rule dates from c. 4th century AD. It was formed into a single kingdom in 1769 and fought border wars with China, Tibet, and British India in the 18th–19th century. Its independence was recognized by Britain in 1923. A new constitution in 1990 restricted royal authority, stated basic human and civil rights, and accepted a democratically elected parliamentary government. In its national outreach, it signed trade agreements with India in 1997.

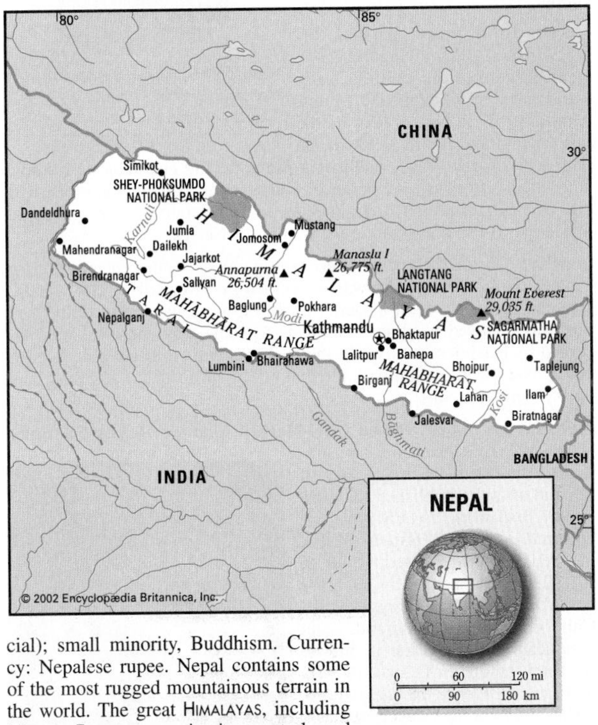

nepheline \ˈne-fə-ˌlēn\ *or* **nephelite** Most common feldspathoid mineral, an aluminosilicate of sodium and potassium ($Na_3KAl_4Si_4O_{16}$). It is sometimes used as a substitute for feldspars in the manufacture of glass and ceramics.

nepheline syenite \ˈsī-ə-ˌnīt\ Medium- to coarse-grained igneous rock, a member of the alkali-syenite group, which consists largely of feldspar and nepheline. Nepheline syenite from Canada is used to replace feldspar in the manufacture of ceramic and glass products.

nephrite \ˈne-ˌfrīt\ Gem-quality, usually green silicate mineral in the tremolite-actinolite-ferrotremolite series of amphiboles. It is the less prized but more common of the two types of jade and may be distinguished from jadeite by its splintery fracture and oily luster. Nephrite occurs in low-grade (formed under low-temperature, low-pressure conditions), regionally metamorphosed rocks. Important deposits occur in China, Siberia, New Zealand, Switzerland, Alaska, and Wyoming.

nephritis \ni-ˈfrī-təs\ Inflammation of the kidneys. There are numerous kinds, involving different kidney tissues. The most common type is Bright's disease. Symptoms vary with the type of nephritis; severe cases can result in kidney failure. Causes include infection, allergy or autoimmune disease, blockage in the urinary system, and hereditary diseases. Treatment addresses the cause where possible.

nephrology \ni-ˈfrä-lə-jē\ Branch of medicine dealing with kidney function and diseases. An understanding of kidney physiology is important not only in treating kidney disease but in knowing the effect of drugs, diet, and hypertension on kidney disease, and vice versa. The first scientific observations of the kidney were made in the mid-17th century by Lorenzo Bellini (1643–1704) and Marcello Malpighi; Carl Ludwig was the first to elaborate on their true physiological function (1844). A key development in nephrology was the permanent arteriovenous shunt (1960), which made repeated hemodialysis feasible, instantly changing the outlook for chronic-renal-disease patients from certain death to 90% survival. See also dialysis, kidney failure, kidney stone, kidney transplant, nephron.

nephron Functional unit of the kidney that removes waste and excess substances from the blood to produce urine. Each of the million or so nephrons in each kidney is a tubule 1.2–2.2 in. (30–55 mm) long. At one end it is closed, expanded, and folded into a double-walled cuplike structure (Bowman's capsule) enclosing a cluster of capillaries (glomerulus). Fluid forced out of the blood through the capillary walls of the glomerulus into Bowman's capsule flows into the adjacent renal tubule, where water and nutrients are selectively reabsorbed from the fluid back into the blood, and electrolytes such as sodium and potassium are balanced in several distinct sections along its length. The final concentrated product is urine. See also urinary system.

Neptune In Roman religion, the god of water. Neptune was originally the god of fresh water, but by 399 BC he was identified with the Greek god Poseidon and thus became a deity of the sea. His female counterpart, Salacia, probably began as a goddess of spring water but was later equated with the Greek goddess Amphitrite. Neptune's festival (Neptunalia) took place in the heat of summer (July 23), when fresh water was scarcest. In art Neptune is often given Poseidon's attributes, the trident and dolphin.

Neptune holding his trident, classical sculpture; in the Lateran Museum, Rome.
ALINARI—ART RESOURCE

Neptune Eighth planet from the sun, discovered in 1846 and named after the Roman god of the sea. It has an average distance of 2.8 billion mi (4.5 billion km) from the sun, taking 165 years to complete one orbit and rotating every 16.11 hours. Neptune has more than 17 times earth's mass, 58 times its volume, and 12% stronger gravity at the top of its atmosphere. It has an equatorial diameter of 30,775 mi (49,528 km). Neptune consists largely of hydrogen and helium. It has no apparent solid surface but may have a frozen, rocky core. Its atmosphere contains substantial amounts of methane gas, whose absorption of red light causes Neptune's deep blue color. The Voyager 2 space probe in 1989 discovered winds of over 700 meters per second, the fastest of any of the sun's planets, and dark spots that may be storms similar to Jupiter's Great Red Spot. Neptune receives little solar radiation, but temperature measurements of about –353°F (–214°C) suggest an internal heat source. Neptune's weak magnetic field traps solar wind and

COSMIC RAYS in a belt around the planet. Neptune has at least four rings, made largely of dust-sized particles, and eight known satellites; the largest is TRITON, almost as big as earth's moon.

Nerbudda River See NARMADA RIVER

Nerchinsk, Treaty of (1689) Peace settlement between Russia and QING-DYNASTY China that checked Russia's eastward expansion. Russia lost easy access to the Sea of Okhotsk but gained the right of passage to Beijing for its trade caravans. The treaty also gained China's implied recognition of Russia as a state of equal status, something other European countries could not accomplish. The Nerchinsk treaty was the basis of Russo-Chinese relations until 1858–60.

Nereid \'nir-ē-əd\ In GREEK MYTHOLOGY, any of the daughters of the sea god NEREUS and of Doris, daughter of Oceanus. The Nereids, who numbered 50 or 100, were depicted as young girls, inhabiting any water, salt or fresh, and benign toward humanity. They were popular figures in Greek literature. The best known were Amphitrite, consort of POSEIDON; THETIS, wife of Peleus (king of the Myrmidons) and mother of ACHILLES; and Galatea, a Sicilian loved by the Cyclops POLYPHEMUS.

Nereus \'nir-ē-əs\ Greek sea god. The son of Pontus (a personification of the sea) and GAEA, he was noted for his gift of prophecy and his ability to change his shape. He lived at the bottom of the sea with his daughters, the NEREIDS. HERACLES wrestled with him in a variety of shapes in order to gain his advice about recovering the golden apples of the Hesperides.

Nereus struggling with Heracles, detail from a Greek water jar found at Vulci, c. 490 BC; in the British Museum.

BY COURTESY OF THE TRUSTEES OF THE BRITISH MUSEUM

Nergal In MESOPOTAMIAN RELIGION, a secondary god of the Sumero-Akkadian pantheon. He was identified with Irra, the god of scorched earth and war, and with Meslamtaea. The city of Cuthah was the center of his cult. In the 1st millennium BC he was described as a benefactor who hears prayers, restores the dead to life, and protects agriculture and flocks. Later he was called a "destroying flame" and was depicted as a god of pestilence, hunger, and devastation. The other sphere of Nergal's power was the underworld, where he ruled as king and where the goddess Ereshkigal was his queen.

Neri \'nā-rē\, **St. Philip** (1515–1595) Roman Catholic mystic. Born in Florence, he went to Rome to pursue religious studies in 1533. In 1548 he cofounded a society of laymen dedicated to the care of pilgrims, the poor, and the sick. After his ordination in 1551 he moved to the community of San Girolamo della Carità in Rome. From 1564 to 1575 he was rector of the church of San Giovanni, and in 1575 GREGORY XIII granted him Santa Maria in Vallicella, where he established his Congregation of the Oratory, a group of priests and clerics engaged in devotion and charitable activities. One of the outstanding mystics of the Counter-Reformation, he was noted for his eloquence as a preacher.

Nernst \'nernst\, **Walther Hermann** (1864–1941) German scientist, one of the founders of modern PHYSICAL CHEMISTRY. He taught at the Univs. of Göttingen and Berlin until forced to retire in 1933 by the Nazi regime. Nernst's researches on the theory of electric cells (see BATTERY), the thermodynamics of chemical EQUILIBRIUM, the properties of vapors at high temperatures and of solids at low temperatures, and the mechanism of photochemistry have had important applications. His formulation of the third law of THERMODYNAMICS gained him a 1920 Nobel Prize. He also invented an improved electric light and an electronically amplified piano.

Nero *in full* **Nero Claudius Caesar Augustus (*or* Drusus) Germanicus** *orig.* **Lucius Domitius Ahenobarbus** (AD 37–68) Roman emperor (54–68). He became CLAUDIUS' adoptive son when the emperor married Nero's mother, AGRIPPINA THE YOUNGER, and took the throne after she had Claudius poisoned. He was guided by his tutor, SENECA, and by Agrippina until he murdered her and broke free of his advisers. By respecting the Senate and leaving imperial administration alone, he became popular in the east, but BOUDICCA's revolt in Britain (61), unemployment, and contempt for his frivolousness and excesses caused dissatisfaction. In 64 a fire, possibly lit at his orders, destroyed much of Rome; he persecuted the Christians as scapegoats and proceeded to build a garish palace, the Domus Aurea. With his reign in decline, he murdered his wife, Octavia, as well as her successor, Poppaea, ordered Seneca to kill himself, and executed senators who criticized him. Revolts in Gaul and Spain were led by GALBA, who was declared emperor by his army. Nero came to be regarded as mad, giving public lyre and theatrical performances to the disgust of his subjects. Condemned by the Senate, he chose suicide over execution.

Nero, portrait bust; in the Roman National Museum, Rome.

ANDERSON—ALINARI FROM ART RESOURCE

Nerses I the Great \'ner-sēz\, **St.** (c. 310–373?) Patriarch of the Armenian church from c. 353. A descendant of St. Gregory the Illuminator (240–332), Nerses became the most important figure in Armenia during his patriarchate, establishing monastic and charitable institutions and schools. He was a supporter of King Pap of Armenia but broke with him over his fostering of religious ties with the court of Constantinople, which led to Pap's instigating the murder of Nerses.

Nerthus \'ner-thůs\ Ancient Germanic goddess. TACITUS refers to her as Mother Earth and says she was worshiped by seven tribes. Her worship centered on a temple in a sacred grove on an island in the Baltic Sea. She was believed to enjoy visiting her people. Her presence was discerned by her priest, and while she was among them her people lived in peace. Her identification with the god NJÖRD suggests that she may have been a hermaphrodite.

Neruda \nā-'rü-thä\, **Pablo** *orig.* **Neftalí Ricardo Reyes Basoalto** (1904–1973) Chilean poet and diplomat. He began writing poetry at 10, and at 20 he published his most widely read work, *Twenty Love Poems and a Song of Despair* (1924), inspired by an unhappy love affair. In 1927 he was named an honorary consul, and he later represented Chile in several Asian and Latin American countries; late in life he was ambassador to France. In Asia he began *Residence on Earth* (1933, 1935, 1947), a verse cycle remarkable for its examination of social decay and personal isolation. In 1945 he was elected senator and joined the Communist Party; he later spent years in exile when the government turned toward the right. *Canto General* (1950), his great epic poem about the American continents, was deeply influenced by WALT WHITMAN and is the culminating expression of his political beliefs. *Elemental Odes* (1954) celebrates common, everyday objects. He was awarded the Nobel Prize in 1971.

Pablo Neruda.

CAMERA PRESS

Nerva \'nər-və\ *in full* **Nerva Caesar Augustus** *orig.* **Marcus Cocceius Nerva** (c. AD 30–98) Roman emperor (96–98), first of the Five Good Emperors. A member of a distinguished senatorial family, Nerva served twice as consul (71, 90). After an undistinguished career, he was chosen to succeed DOMITIAN because of his age, dignity, and lack of children who would succeed him. He rejected Domitian's autocratic tyranny but completed Domitian's building projects and instituted his administrative and financial reforms. He adopted TRAJAN as his heir.

nerve See NEURON

nerve gas Organophosphate that interferes with normal nerve transmission and induces intense and fatal bronchial spasm. A derivative of fluorophosphoric acid, nerve gas has been used as both a weapon and an insecticide. Developed by Germany during World War II but not used, nerve gas was banned from modern warfare by the Geneva Protocol. Gases include VX, soman, tabun, and sarin, which was used in 1995 in a lethal attack in the Tokyo subways by the AUM SHINRIKYO cult.

Nervi \'ner-vē\, **Pier Luigi** (1891–1979) Italian engineer and building contractor. He became internationally renowned for his invention of ferrocement, a type of concrete reinforced with steel mesh, for use in thin shell design. His first significant projects included a series of airplane hangars in Italy (1935–41), conceived as concrete vaults with huge spans. In addition to designing buildings, he succeeded in building a sailboat with a ferroconcrete hull only .5 in (1.25 cm) thick. Ferroconcrete was vital to his complex for the Turin Exhibition (1949–50), a prefabricated, corrugated cylindrical 309-ft (93-m) arch. Nervi worked on the UNESCO headquarters in Paris (1950) with MARCEL BREUER and helped design Italy's first skyscraper, the Pirelli Building in Milan (1955–59).

nervous system System of specialized cells (neurons, or nerve cells) that conduct stimuli from a sensory receptor through a NEURON network to the site (e.g., a gland or muscle) where the response occurs. In humans, it consists of the central and peripheral nervous systems, the former consisting of the BRAIN and SPINAL CORD and the latter of the nerves, which carry impulses to and from the central nervous system. The cranial nerves handle head and neck sensory and motor activities, except the vagus nerve, which conducts signals to visceral organs. Each spinal nerve is attached to the spinal cord by a sensory and a motor root. These exit between the vertebrae and merge to form a large mixed nerve, which branches to supply a defined area of the body. Disorders include AMYOTROPHIC LATERAL SCLEROSIS, CHOREA, EPILEPSY, MYASTHENIA GRAVIS, NEURAL TUBE DEFECT, PARKINSONISM, and POLIOMYELITIS. Effects of disorders range from transient tics and minor personality changes to major personality disruptions, seizures, paralysis, and death.

Nesiotes See CRITIUS AND NESIOTES

Ness, Eliot (1903–1957) U.S. crime fighter. Born in Chicago, he was hired at 26 as a special agent of the U.S. Department of Justice to head its Chicago prohibition bureau, with the express purpose of breaking up AL CAPONE's bootlegging network. He formed a nine-man team of extremely dedicated and unbribable officers, "the Untouchables." Evidence they collected helped send Capone to prison. After the end of Prohibition in 1933, Ness headed the alcohol-tax unit of the U.S. Treasury department (1933–35), was director of public safety in Cleveland (1935–41), and directed a division of the Federal Security Agency (1941–45).

Ness, Loch Lake, INVERNESS district in the Highland region, Scotland. At 788 ft (240 m) deep and about 23 mi (36 km) long, it has the largest volume of fresh water in Britain. It forms part of the Caledonian Canal system developed by THOMAS TELFORD. On its shores are remains of two fortresses. Surface oscillations, or seiches, caused by differential heating, are common. Reports of an aquatic monster inhabiting Loch Ness date back centuries but remain unproved.

Nesselrode \nyis-syilʸ-'ròd-yi, *Engl* 'ne-səl-ˌrōd\, **Karl (Robert Vasilyevich), Count** (1780–1862) Russian statesman. After serving in the Russian diplomatic service, he served as minister of foreign affairs 1822–56, and as chancellor 1845–62. He sought to influence the Ottoman empire with the Treaty of UNKIAR SKELESSI (1833) and the Straits Convention (1841). He supported aid to Austria in suppressing the Hungarian uprising (1848). His policy of promoting Russia's influence in the Balkans helped precipitate the CRIMEAN WAR. He negotiated the subsequent treaty at the Congress of PARIS.

Nest of the American robin.

JEFF FOOTT—BRUCE COLEMAN INC.

nest Structure built by an animal as a permanent home or for bearing and rearing offspring. The social insects build systems of chambers and tunnels, above or below ground. Fishes' nests vary from shallow depressions in sand to enclosed structures constructed of vegetation. Certain frog species build mud-basin nests or floating masses of hardened froth. Alligators use mud and vegetation and cobras use leaves and forest litter to build a nest for their eggs. The most common type of bird nest is a cup-shaped or domed structure of twigs, leaves, mud, and feathers. Many mammals, especially small ones, build nests in trees, on the ground, or in burrows.

Nestlé SA Multinational manufacturer of food products. Headquartered in Vevey, Switzerland, it operates branches and subsidiaries in more than 70 countries. Its products include condensed and powdered milk, baby foods, chocolate, cheese, instant coffee and tea, condiments, and frozen foods. Its history dates to 1866, when two Swiss firms were established, the Anglo-Swiss Condensed Milk Co. and a company founded by Henri Nestlé to manufacture the first infant formula. In 1905 they merged to become the Nestlé and Anglo-Swiss Condensed Milk Co. Nestlé created the first milk chocolate, and in 1937 the first instant coffee, which it produced under the name Nescafé. It acquired various other firms, including Crosse & Blackwell in 1960, Stouffer Corp. in 1973, and Carnation Co. in 1984. The company adopted its present name in 1977. Today it claims to be the world's largest food company.

Nestor In Greek legend, the king of Pylos in Elis. All his brothers were killed by HERACLES, but Nestor survived. In HOMER's *Iliad* he appeared as an elder statesman who entertained the warriors with tales of his youthful exploits. He brought 90 ships to aid the Greeks in their war against Troy. When, at the war's end, the Greeks sailed for home, Nestor went in a different direction and missed the storm ATHENA sent to disperse their ships. In the *Odyssey* Telemachus, son of ODYSSEUS, came to Elis looking for his father, and Nestor entertained him.

Nestorian Member of a Christian sect that originated in Asia Minor and Syria in the 5th century AD., inspired by the views of NESTORIUS. Nestorians stressed the independence of Christ's divine and human natures. Nestorian scholars played a prominent role in the formation of Arab culture after the Arab conquest of Persia; Nestorianism also spread to India, China, Egypt, and Central Asia, where certain tribes were almost entirely converted. Today the Nestorians are represented by the Church of the East, or Persian Church, usually referred to in the West as the Assyrian or Nestorian Church. Most of its 170,000 members live in Iraq, Syria, and Iran.

Nestorius (late 4th century AD–c. 451) Founder of NESTORIAN Christianity. Born of Persian parents, he studied in Antioch and was ordained a priest. As bishop of Constantinople from 428, he aroused controversy when he objected to CYRIL OF ALEXANDRIA's granting MARY the title of Theotokos (God-Bearer), which he believed compromised Christ's full humanity. In 431 the Council of Ephesus condemned his teaching as heresy on the ground that he denied the reality of Christ's incarnation, and Nestorius went into exile, first in the Libyan desert and then in Upper Egypt. His ideas were adopted by the Persian Church, whose members still adhere to it.

Néstos River See MESTA RIVER

Netherlands *officially* **Kingdom of the Netherlands** *Dutch* **Nederland** \'nā-dər-ˌlänt\ Country, northwestern Europe. Area: 16,033 sq mi (41,525 sq km). Population (2000 est.): 15,896,000. Capital: AMSTERDAM; Seat of Government: THE HAGUE. Most of the people are Dutch. Languages: Dutch (official), English. Religions: Roman Catholicism, Protestantism. Monetary unit: euro. The Netherlands' southern and eastern region consists mostly of plains and a few high ridges; its western and northern region is lower and includes the ZUIDER ZEE and the common delta of the RHINE, MEUSE, and SCHELDE rivers. Coastal areas are almost completely below sea level and are protected by dunes and artificial dikes. The country has a developed market economy based largely on financial services, light and heavy industries, and trade. It is a constitutional monarchy with a parliament comprising two legislative houses; its chief of state is the monarch, and the head of government is the prime minister. Celtic and Germanic tribes inhabited the region at the time of the Roman conquest. Under the Romans trade and industry flourished, but by the mid-3rd century AD Roman power had waned, eroded by resurgent German tribes and the encroachment of the sea. A Germanic invasion (406–7) ended Roman control. The MEROVINGIAN DYNASTY followed the Romans but was supplanted in the 7th century by the CAROLINGIAN DYNASTY, which converted the area to Christianity. After

CHARLEMAGNE's death in 814, the area was increasingly the target of VIKING attacks. It became part of the medieval kingdom of Lotharingia (see LORRAINE), which avoided incorporation into the HOLY ROMAN EMPIRE by investing its bishops and abbots with secular powers, leading to the establishment of an Imperial Church. In the 12th–14th centuries large areas of land in the Holland-Utrecht peat-bog plain were made available for agriculture, and dike building occurred on a large scale; FLANDERS developed as a textiles center. The dukes of BURGUNDY gained control in the late 14th century. By the early 16th century the Low Countries were ruled by the Spanish HABSBURGS. The Dutch had taken the lead in fishing, shipbuilding, and beer brewing, laying the basis for Holland's remarkable 17th-century prosperity. Culturally, this was the period of JAN VAN EYCK, THOMAS À KEMPIS, and DESIDERIUS ERASMUS. CALVINISM and the ANABAPTISTS' doctrines attracted many followers. In 1581 the seven northern provinces, led by Calvinists, declared their independence from Spain, and in 1648, following the THIRTY YEARS' WAR, Spain recognized Dutch independence. The 17th century was the golden age of Dutch civilization. BENEDICT DE SPINOZA and RENÉ DESCARTES enjoyed the country's intellectual freedom, and REMBRANDT and JOHANNES VERMEER painted their masterpieces. The DUTCH EAST INDIA COMPANY secured Asian colonies, and the country's standard of living soared. In the 18th century, Dutch maritime power declined; the region was conquered by the French during the FRENCH REVOLUTIONARY WARS and became the kingdom of Holland under NAPOLEON (1806). The Netherlands remained neutral in World War I and declared neutrality in World War II but was occupied by Germany. After the war it lost the Netherlands Indies, which became Indonesia (1949), and Netherlands New Guinea (1962). It joined NATO in 1949 and was a founding member of the EUROPEAN ECONOMIC COMMUNITY (later renamed the European Community). It is a member of the EUROPEAN UNION.

Netherlands, Austrian See AUSTRIAN NETHERLANDS

Netherlands, Republic of the United See DUTCH REPUBLIC

Netherlands, Spanish See SPANISH NETHERLANDS

Netherlands Antilles \an-'ti-lēz\ *formerly* **Curaçao** \ˌkür-ə-'sō, ˌkyür-ə-'saů\ Five islands (pop., 1994 est.: 197,000), in the CARIBBEAN SEA. An autonomous part of the NETHERLANDS since 1954, they have a combined area of 309 sq mi (800 sq km). The Netherlands Antilles consists of two widely separated groups of islands: the northern group (St. Eustatius, the southern section of ST. MARTIN, and SABA) at the northern end of the LEEWARD ISLANDS; and the southern group, about 500 mi (800 km) to the southwest, off the coast of Venezuela (CURAÇAO and Bonaire, ARUBA until 1986). The capital, on Curaçao, is WILLEMSTAD. The islands were sighted by CHRISTOPHER COLUMBUS in 1493 and were claimed for Spain. In the 17th century the Dutch gained control, and in 1845 the islands became the Netherlands Antilles. In 1954 they became an integral part of the Netherlands, with full autonomy in domestic affairs. Aruba seceded from the group in 1986.

Neto \'nā-tü\, **(Antônio) Agostinho** (1922–1979) Poet, physician, and first president of Angola. In 1948 Neto joined a movement aimed at rediscovering indigenous Angolan culture. He studied medicine in Lisbon and returned to Angola in 1959 as a doctor. In 1960 he was arrested in the presence of his patients by colonial authorities, who opened fire when the patients protested. He was imprisoned in Portugal for two years before escaping to join the Marxist Movimento Popular de Libertação de Angola (MPLA), whose president he became in 1962. When Angola became independent in 1975, he was proclaimed president, though he never controlled all the country's territory (see JONAS M. SAVIMBI). His poems were widely recognized in the Portuguese-speaking world.

nettle family Family Urticaceae, composed of about 45 genera of herbaceous plants, shrubs, small trees, and a few vines, found mostly in tropical regions. Many species, especially the nettles *(Urtica)* and Australian nettle trees *(Laportea),* have on their stems and leaves stinging hairs that break the skin and release a fluid that irritates it for hours. Ornamental species include artillery plant *(Pilea microphylla)* and baby tears *(Helxine soleiroli),* both creeping plants. The trumpet tree *(Cecropia peltata),* a species of the New World tropics, has hollow stems that are inhabited by biting ants. Ramie, or China grass *(Boehmeria nivea),* produces a valuable fiber. Some nettles can be cooked and eaten.

network In broadcasting, a radio or television company that produces programs for broadcast to member stations. See ABC, CBS, CNN, NBC, PBS.

network, computer Two or more computers and peripheral equipment (e.g., printers) that are connected with one another for the purpose of exchanging data electronically. Two basic network types are LOCAL AREA NETWORKS (LANs) and wide-area networks. Wide-area networks connect computers and smaller networks to larger networks over greater geographical areas, including different continents. Communications may occur over cables, fiber optics, or satellites, but most computer users access the network via a modem, using telephone lines. The largest wide-area network is the INTERNET. In the 1990s the WORLD WIDE WEB was introduced and became the most popular way to access other Internet sites.

Netzahualcóyotl \nā-ˌtsä-wäl-'kō-ˌyō-tᵊl\ City (pop., 1990: 1,260,000), central Mexico, suburb of MEXICO CITY. It is Mexico's third-largest municipality. Settlement began just after 1900, when Lake TEXCOCO was reduced in size and large areas of land were uncovered along the southern shore. Xochiaca Dam to the north, built in 1946, protects the city from floods.

Neubrandenburg \'nȯi-ˌbrän-dən-ˌbůrk\ City (pop., 1992 est.: 88,000), northeastern Germany, near the northern end of Tollense Lake. It was founded in 1248 as a fortified outpost, became part of Mecklenburg in 1292, and prospered from its weaving industry and as a market center. In the 17th–18th century it was plundered during the THIRTY YEARS' WAR, devastated by fire, and battered by the NAPOLEONIC WARS. Its medieval fortifications are well preserved, but most of its buildings were destroyed by bombing in World War II. Much rebuilt after 1952, it has engineering, food-processing, and chemical industries.

Neuchâtel, Lake \ˌnœ-shä-'tel\ Lake, western Switzerland. With an area of 84 sq mi (218 sq km), it is the largest lake entirely within Switzerland. It is a survivor of a former glacial lake in the lower Aare valley, at the base of the JURA Mountains. On the northern shore is LA TÈNE, a prehistoric site, which dates to the late Iron Age culture.

Neue Sachlichkeit \ˌnȯi-ə-'zäk̲-lik̲-ˌkīt\ (German: "New Objectivity") Movement in German painting of the 1920s and early 1930s reflecting the cynicism and resignation of the post–World War I period. The term was coined in 1925 by Gustav Hartlaub, director of the Mannheim Kunsthalle, for an exhibition including works by GEORGE GROSZ, OTTO DIX, and MAX BECKMANN, the movement's leading exponents. They worked in a realistic style, as opposed to the prevailing styles of abstraction and EXPRESSIONISM, using meticulous detail to portray evil in smooth, cold, and static images derived from Italian METAPHYSICAL PAINTING for the purpose of violent social satire. The movement ended in the 1930s with the rise of Nazism.

Neue Zürcher Zeitung \'nȯi-ə-'tsu̅e̅r-k̲ər-'tsī-tu̇ŋ\ (German: "New Zurich Newspaper") Daily newspaper published in Zurich, Switzerland, generally considered one of the world's great newspapers. Founded as the weekly *Zürcher Zeitung* in 1780, it took its present name in 1821. In 1868 it became a joint-stock company, with shares held by Zurich citizens. Two daily editions were published by 1869, and three by 1894. From its founding it has appealed to readers interested in deep coverage of international news. Austere in demeanor, it is characterized by careful, nonsensational reporting, highly informed and extremely thorough analysis, and background information supplied as context for every major story.

Neuilly \nœ-'yē\, **Treaty of** (November 27, 1919) Peace treaty between Bulgaria and the Allied Powers after WORLD WAR I, signed at Neuilly-sur-Seine, France. Bulgaria was forced to reduce its army to 20,000 men, cede lands to Yugoslavia and Greece that involved the transfer of 300,000 people, and pay reparations to the Allies.

Neumann \'nȯi-ˌmän\, **(Johann) Balthasar** (1687–1753) German architect. Born in Bohemia, Neumann moved to Würzburg in 1711. In 1719 he began work on the prince-bishop's new palace, especially noted for its grand staircase. He was eventually put in charge of all major building projects in Würzburg and Bamberg, including palaces, public buildings, bridges, a water system, and many churches. A master of the ROCOCO STYLE, his best work was the pilgrimage church at Vierzehnheiligen (1743–53), in which he made ingenious use of domes and barrel vaults to create sequences of round and oval spaces whose airy elegance is lit by huge windows; the lively interplay of these elements is accented by lavish use of decorative plasterwork, gilding, statuary, and murals.

Neumann, John von See John VON NEUMANN

neural network Type of parallel computation in which computing elements are modeled on the network of NEURONS that constitute animal NERVOUS SYSTEMS. This model, intended to simulate the way the brain processes information, enables the computer to "learn" to a certain degree. A neural network typically consists of a number of interconnected processors, or nodes. Each handles a designated sphere of knowledge, and has several inputs and one output to the network. Based on the inputs it gets, a node can "learn" about the relationships between sets of data, sometimes using the principles of FUZZY LOGIC. For example, a backgammon program can store and grade results from moves in a game; in the next game, it can play a move based on its stored result and can regrade the stored result if the move is unsuccessful. Neural networks have been used in pattern recognition, speech analysis, oil exploration, weather prediction, and the modeling of thinking and consciousness.

neural tube defect Congenital defect of the BRAIN or SPINAL CORD from abnormal growth of their precursor, the neural tube (see EMBRYOLOGY), usually with spine or skull defects. The tube may fail to close properly, have parts missing, or have a blockage (see HYDROCEPHALUS). In spina bifida, vertebrae are open over the back of the spinal cord, usually at the base. This may not affect function if no further defects (local absence of skin or MENINGES, protrusion of tissue, defect opening into the spinal cord) exist. The more serious forms can cause paralysis and impair bladder and bowel function. In encephalocele, a meningeal sac containing brain tissue protrudes from the skull. The effects depend on the amount of tissue involved. Adequate folic-acid intake by women of childbearing age reduces the risk of neural tube defects. Early surgery can prevent or minimize disability.

neuralgia \nyu̇-'ral-jə\ Pain of unknown cause in the area covered by a peripheral sensory nerve. In trigeminal neuralgia (tic douloureux), brief attacks of severe shooting pain along a branch of the trigeminal nerve (in front of the ear) usually begin after middle age, more often in women. Initially weeks or months apart, they become more frequent and easily triggered by touching the affected area, talking, eating, or cold. Analgesics help, but permanent cure requires surgery. Glossopharyngeal neuralgia causes recurring severe pain, most often in men over 40. Excruciating pains begin in the throat and radiate to the ears or down the neck, with or without a trigger (e.g., sneezing, yawning, chewing). Usually separated by long intervals, attacks subside before analgesics take effect. Surgery may help in extreme cases. See also NEURITIS.

Neurath \'nȯi-rät\, **Konstantin, Freiherr (Baron) von** (1873–1956) German diplomat. He entered the diplomatic service in 1903 and served as minister to Denmark 1919–22, ambassador to Italy 1922–30, and ambassador to Britain 1930–32. As Germany's foreign minister (1932–38), he lent respectability to ADOLF HITLER's expansionist foreign policy. As "protector" of Bohemia and Moravia (1939–41), he was accused of being too lenient and was replaced by REINHARD HEYDRICH. After World War II, he was tried and imprisoned for war crimes (1946–54).

neuritis \nyu̇-'rī-təs\ INFLAMMATION of one or several nerves. The cause may be mechanical, vascular, allergic, toxic, metabolic, or viral. Symptoms—tingling, burning, or stabbing pains with sensory nerves, and anything from muscle weakness to paralysis with motor nerves—are usually confined to the part of the body served by the inflamed nerve. In Bell's palsy, facial nerve inflammation causes a characteristic facial muscle distortion. Analgesics can relieve the pain. Once the underlying cause is treated, recovery is usually rapid but may be incomplete in severe cases, with residual motor and sensory disturbances. See also NEURALGIA.

neurology Medical specialty concerned with NERVOUS-SYSTEM function and disorders. Clinical neurology did not begin to develop until the mid-19th century, when mapping of the functional areas of the brain first began and understanding of the causes of conditions such as EPILEPSY improved. The development of the ELECTROENCEPHALOGRAPH in the 1920s aided in the diagnosis of neurological disease, as did the development of COMPUTED AXIAL TOMOGRAPHY in the 1970s and nuclear MAGNETIC RESONANCE IMAGING in the 1980s. In addition to dealing with physical disorders (e.g., tumors, trauma), neurology is unique among medical specialties in its intersection with PSYCHIATRY. Greater understanding of the brain chemistry of disorders such as SCHIZOPHRENIA and DEPRESSION has led to a wide array of effective drugs that nevertheless work best in conjunction with PSYCHOTHERAPY. Side effects of drug or surgical therapy can be serious, and many nervous-system disorders have no effective treatment.

neuron *or* **nerve cell** Any of the cells of the NERVOUS SYSTEM. Sensory neurons relay information from sense organs, motor neurons carry impulses to muscles and glands, and interneurons transmit impulses between sensory and motor neurons. A typical neuron consists of dendrites (fibers that receive stimuli and conduct them inward), a cell body (a nucleated body that receives input from dendrites), and an axon (a fiber that relays the nerve impulse from the cell body outward to its terminals, the synaptic knobs). Both axons and dendrites may be referred to as nerve fibers. Impulses are conducted by NEUROTRANSMITTER chemicals released by the axon's synaptic knobs across the synapses (junctions be-

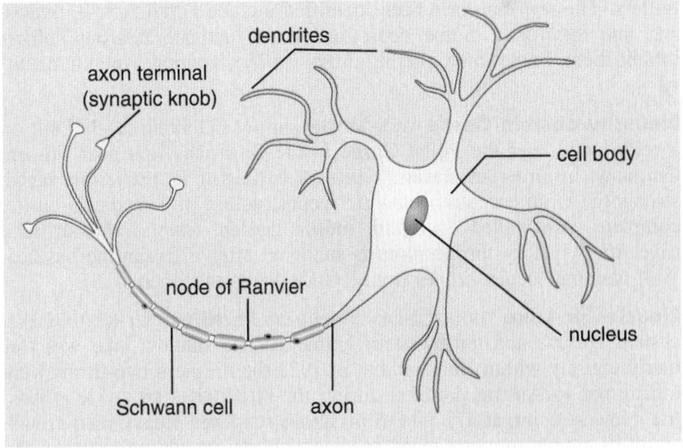

Structure of a neuron. Dendrites, usually branching fibers, receive and conduct impulses to the cell body, which integrates inputs arriving from various dendrites and sends nerve impulses out to the axon. When an impulse reaches the end of the axon, terminals release neurotransmitters into a gap (synapse) between the neuron and a neighboring cell. The neurotransmitter diffuses across the gap to start an impulse in an adjacent neuron or effector cell (as of a muscle or gland). Schwann cells surround the axon, forming an insulating myelin sheath. A space (node of Ranvier) between two Schwann cells serves to conduct the nerve impulse quickly along the axon.

L
M
N

tween neurons, or between a neuron and an effector cell, such as a muscle cell) or, in some cases, pass directly from one neuron to the next. Most neurons are insulated by a myelin sheath formed by cells (Schwann cells) surrounding the axons. Bundles of fibers from neurons held together by CONNECTIVE TISSUE form nerves.

neuropathy \nu̇-'rä-pə-thē\ Disorder of the peripheral NERVOUS SYSTEM. It may be genetic or acquired, progress quickly or slowly, involve motor, sensory, and/or autonomic (see AUTONOMIC NERVOUS SYSTEM) nerves, and affect only certain nerves or all of them. It can cause pain or loss of sensation, weakness, PARALYSIS, loss of REFLEXES, muscle ATROPHY, or, in autonomic neuropathies, disturbances of blood pressure, heart rate, or bladder and bowel control; impotence; and inability to focus the eyes. Some types damage the NEURON itself, others the myelin sheath that insulates it. Examples include CARPAL TUNNEL SYNDROME, AMYOTROPHIC LATERAL SCLEROSIS, POLIOMYELITIS, TABES DORSALIS, SHINGLES, and nerve DEAFNESS. Causes include diseases (e.g., DIABETES MELLITUS, LEPROSY, SYPHILIS), injury, TOXINS, and VITAMIN deficiency (e.g., BERIBERI). See also NEURALGIA, NEURITIS.

neuropsychology Science concerned with the integration of psychological observations on behavior with neurological observations on the central NERVOUS SYSTEM (CNS), including the BRAIN. The field emerged through the work of PAUL BROCA and Carl Wernicke (1848–1905), both of whom identified sites on the CEREBRAL CORTEX involved in the production or comprehension of language. Great strides have since been made in describing neuroanatomical systems and their relation to higher mental processes. The related field of neuropsychiatry addresses itself to such disorders as APHASIA, KORSAKOFF'S SYNDROME, TOURETTE'S SYNDROME, and other CNS abnormalities. See also LATERALITY.

neurosis Mental and emotional disorder that affects only part of the PERSONALITY, is accompanied by a less distorted perception of reality than in a PSYCHOSIS, and is characterized by various physiological and mental disturbances (such as visceral symptoms and impaired concentration). The neuroses include ANXIETY attacks, certain forms of DEPRESSION, HYPOCHONDRIASIS, hysterical reactions, OBSESSIVE-COMPULSIVE DISORDERS, PHOBIAS, various SEXUAL DYSFUNCTIONS, and some TICS. They have traditionally been thought to be based on emotional CONFLICT in which a blocked impulse seeks expression in a disguised response or symptom. Behavioral psychologists regard them as learned, inappropriate responses to stress, which can be unlearned.

neurotransmitter Chemical released by NEURONS to stimulate neighboring neurons, allowing impulses to be passed from one cell to the next throughout the NERVOUS SYSTEM. A nerve impulse arriving at the axon terminal of one neuron stimulates release of a neurotransmitter, which crosses the microscopic gap (see SYNAPSE) in milliseconds to the adjoining neuron's dendrite. Many chemicals are believed to act as neurotransmitters. The few that have been identified include ACETYLCHOLINE, DOPAMINE, and SEROTONIN. Some neurotransmitters activate neurons; others inhibit them. Some mind-altering drugs act by changing synaptic activity.

Neuschwanstein Castle \'nȯi-'shvän-ˌshtīn\ Elaborate castle built on a rock ledge over the Pöllat Gorge in the Bavarian Alps near Füssen, Germany, by order of Bavaria's LUDWIG II. Begun in 1869, this lavish stronghold is an eccentric romantic reconstruction of a medieval castle, complete with walled courtyard, indoor garden, towers, and artificial cave. Its two-story throne room is modeled after a Byzantine basilica. Wall paintings depict scenes from RICHARD WAGNER's operas.

Neusiedler Lake \'nȯi-ˌzēd-lər\ *Hungarian* **Fertö tó** \'fer-tœ-'tō\ Lake, eastern Austria and northwestern Hungary. The shallow lake was formerly entirely within Hungary, but in 1922 the northern two-thirds were transferred to Austria. Formed during the PLEISTOCENE EPOCH, it is Austria's lowest point, at 377 ft (115 m) above sea level. Heavy reed growth along its shores supports many species of birds, which are protected by an international sanctuary and a biological station.

Neustria \'nü-strē-ə\ During the MEROVINGIAN period, the western part of the kingdom of the FRANKS after the 6th century AD conquest by CLOVIS. The eastern kingdom was AUSTRASIA. Neustria corresponded roughly to the area of present-day France west of the MEUSE RIVER and north of the LOIRE RIVER. The name later denoted a much smaller area; by the 11th–12th century it was sometimes used synonymously with NORMANDY.

neutering See CASTRATION

Neutra \'nȯi-trä, *Engl* 'nü-trə\, **Richard (Joseph)** (1892–1970) Austrian-U.S. architect. Educated in Vienna and Zurich, Neutra moved to the U.S. in 1923. He began with white Cubistic forms and moved on to light cages of steel and wood, in harmony with their lush landscaping. He achieved renown with the Lovell House, Los Angeles (1927–29), with glass expanses and cable-suspended balconies in the INTERNATIONAL STYLE. Other memorable works include the Kaufmann Desert House, Palm Springs (1946–47), and the Tremaine House, Santa Barbara (1947–48). He was particularly concerned that a house reflect the owner's way of life. His later works included office buildings, churches, housing projects, and cultural centers. His many writings include *Survival Through Design* (1954).

neutralism See NONALIGNMENT

neutrality Legal status arising from a country's abstention from all participation in a war between other countries, the maintenance of an attitude of impartiality toward the belligerents, and the recognition by the belligerents of this abstention and impartiality. In the past, rights of a neutral country included freedom of its territory from use or occupation by any warring party, maintenance of diplomatic relations with other neutrals and belligerents, freedom of its citizens to go about their business, and respect for its intent to be neutral. In the two world wars, many of the basic concepts of neutrality ceased to be respected; the freedom of the neutral was sharply reduced in the later 20th century.

neutrino \nü-'trē-nō\ Fundamental particle with no ELECTRIC CHARGE, little MASS, and a SPIN value of ½. Neutrinos belong to the LEPTON family of SUBATOMIC PARTICLES. There are three types of neutrino, each associated with a charged lepton: the electron, the muon, and the tau. Neutrinos are the most penetrating of subatomic particles because they react with matter only by the WEAK force. They do not cause IONIZATION, because they are not electrically charged. All types of neutrino have masses much smaller than their charged partners.

neutrino problem \nü-'trē-nō\, **solar** Shortfall in the number of NEUTRINOS produced by the sun that are detected on earth. Early experiments detected only one-third to two-thirds the number of electron-neutrinos expected by theory to arrive from the sun, where they are emitted as a result of NUCLEAR FUSION in the solar core. This discrepancy could be explained if interaction with matter converted some of the electron-neutrinos into tau-neutrinos or muon-neutrinos, which could occur only if neutrinos had mass—a property not established by theory. In 1998 and 2002, detectors in Japan and Canada confirmed that neutrinos do "oscillate" between types, though specific masses have not been confirmed.

neutron One of the constituent particles of every atomic NUCLEUS except ordinary hydrogen. Discovered in 1932 by James Chadwick (1891–1974), it has no ELECTRIC CHARGE and has nearly 1,840 times the mass of the ELECTRON. Free neutrons undergo BETA DECAY with a HALF-LIFE of about 10 minutes. Thus, they are not readily found in nature, except in COSMIC RAYS. They are a penetrating form of radiation. When bombarded with neutrons, various elements undergo NUCLEAR FISSION and release more free neutrons. If enough free neutrons are produced, a CHAIN REACTION can be sustained. This process led to the development of NUCLEAR POWER as well as the ATOMIC BOMB. Neutron beams produced in CYCLOTRONS and nuclear reactors are important probes of matter, revealing details of structure in both organic and inorganic susbtances.

neutron bomb *or* **enhanced radiation warhead** Small thermonuclear weapon that produces minimal blast and heat but releases large amounts of lethal RADIATION. The blast and heat are confined to a radius of only a few hundred yards; within a somewhat larger area, the bomb throws off a massive wave of neutron and gamma radiation, which is extremely destructive to living tissue. Such a bomb could be used with deadly efficiency against tank and infantry formations on the battlefield without endangering towns or cities only a few miles away. It can be carried in a missile or delivered by a howitzer or even an attack aircraft.

neutron star Any of a class of extremely dense, compact STARS thought to be composed mainly of NEUTRONS with a thin outer atmosphere of primarily iron atoms and electrons and protons. Though typically about 12 mi (20 km) in diameter, they have a mass roughly twice the sun's and thus extremely high densities (about a hundred trillion times that of water). Neutron stars have very strong MAGNETIC FIELDS. A solid surface differentiates them from BLACK HOLES. Below it, the pressure is much too high for individual atoms to exist; protons and electrons are compacted together into neutrons. The discovery of PULSARS in 1967 provided the first evidence of the existence of neutron stars, predicted in the early 1930s and believed by most investigators to be formed in SUPERNOVA explosions. See also WHITE DWARF STAR.

Neva River \nye-'vä\ River, northwestern Russia. It flows 46 mi (74 km) from Lake LADOGA west to the Gulf of Finland in the BALTIC SEA. Although it is usually frozen from November to April, it is navigable by large ships. The city of ST. PETERSBURG is at its mouth. Its banks were the scene of a battle in 1240 in which ALEXANDER NEVSKY, prince of NOVGOROD, defeated the Swedes.

Nevada State (pop., 2000: 1,998,257), western U.S. It covers 110,567 sq mi (286,368 sq km); its capital is CARSON CITY. The Black Rock Desert is in the northwest; the COLORADO RIVER forms its extreme southeastern boundary. Human settlement in the area has spanned more than 20,000 years, and evidence of prehistoric inhabitants include dwelling remains and ROCK ART. Early inhabitants included the SHOSHONE and PAIUTE Indians. Spanish missionaries in the 18th century and fur traders in the 1820s arrived before major exploration and mapping were done by J.C. FREMONT and KIT CARSON 1843–45. Nevada was part of the land ceded to the U.S. by Mexico in 1848 and was included in the Utah Territory (1850–61). Settlements increased after the discovery of the Comstock Lode, a rich silver deposit, at Virginia City in 1859. It became the Territory of Nevada in 1861 and the 36th U.S. state in 1864. It began its transition to a modern economy during the GREAT DEPRESSION when gambling was legalized. Construction of the HOOVER DAM aided the economy of southern Nevada. In the 1950s the state became the main testing site for atomic-energy experiments. The traditional bases of its economy, mining and agriculture, are overshadowed by governmental activity and tourism, the latter centered on LAS VEGAS, RENO, and Lake TAHOE.

Nevada, University of Public university with campuses in Reno and Las Vegas. The Reno campus was established as a land-grant university in 1887. Its Mackay School of Mines and Donald W. Reynolds School of Journalism are notable; it also has institutes for desert research and gambling research. The Las Vegas campus, which comprises 12 schools and colleges, was established in 1957. Total enrollment is about 31,000.

Nevelson, Louise *orig.* **Louise Berliavsky** (1899–1988) U.S. (Ukrainian-born) sculptor. Born in Kiev, she moved with her family to Maine in 1905. She studied at New York's Art Students League and with HANS HOFMANN in Munich (1931). Her early figurative sculptures feature blockish, interlocking masses and found objects (e.g., *Ancient Figure,* 1932) that anticipate her mature style. By the 1950s she was working almost exclusively in abstract forms. She is best known for the large, monochromatic abstract sculptures of this period, consisting of open-faced wooden boxes stacked to make freestanding walls. Within the boxes are highly suggestive collections of abstract-shaped objects mingled with pieces of architectural debris and other found objects skillfully arranged to produce a sense of mystery (e.g., *Sky Cathedral,* 1958) and then painted a single color, usually black. She is recognized as one of the foremost sculptors of the 20th century.

Neville, Richard See Earl of WARWICK

Nevins, Allan (1890–1971) U.S. historian. Born in Camp Point, Ill., he taught at Columbia University (1928–58). His best-known works include biographies of U.S. political and industrial figures and his eight-volume history of the American Civil War. In 1948 he inaugurated at Columbia the first oral history program in the U.S.

Nevsky, Alexander See St. ALEXANDER NEVSKY

nevus See MOLE

New Age movement Movement that spread through occult communities in the 1970s and 80s that looked forward to a "New Age" of love and peace and offered a foretaste of the coming era through personal transformation and healing. The movement's strongest supporters were followers of esotericism, a religious perspective based on the acquisition of mystical knowledge. At its height, the movement attracted millions of Americans, who practiced ASTROLOGY, YOGA, and channeling, and used crystals as a healing tool. New Agers sought to bring about global transformation and in 1987 many participated in the Mass Harmonic Convergence, an attempt to accomplish that goal.

New Britain *formerly* **Neu-Pommern** \nȯi-'pȯ-mərn\ Largest island (population 1999 est.: 435,000) in the BISMARCK ARCHIPELAGO, PAPUA NEW GUINEA. It was visited and named by English explorer William Dampier in 1700. After periods under German, Australian, and Japanese rule, it became part of Papua New Guinea in 1975 when that nation attained independence. It is crescent-shaped, heavily forested, and has several volcanoes. Its highest peak, Mount Sinewit, at 7,999 ft (2,438 m), erupted violently in 1937. Commercial products include coconuts, cocoa, and palm oil. Its harbors include Blanche Bay, Talasea, and Jacquinot Bay.

New Brunswick Province (pop., 2001: 729,498), one of the four MARITIME PROVINCES, eastern Canada. Bounded by the Bay of FUNDY, it is connected with Nova Scotia by the Isthmus of Chignecto. Its capital, FREDERICTON, is home to the University of New Brunswick (founded 1785, one of Canada's oldest universities). New Brunswick was part of the original ACADIA; it was colonized by the French in the 18th century, then captured by the British, who expelled the French-speaking Acadians in 1755 and incorporated the area into Nova Scotia. After the AMERICAN REVOLUTION, some 14,000 loyalists from the U.S. settled there. As a result of this large influx, it was separated from Nova Scotia, and the province of New Brunswick was established in 1784. In 1867 it became an original member of the Dominion of Canada. Forests cover 90% of the province, whose major cities include ST. JOHN and Moncton. Forestry and lumbering are the largest industries, followed by commercial fishing.

New Caledonia *French* **Nouvelle Calédonie** \nü-'vel-kȧ-lā-dȯ-'nē\ French overseas territory (pop., 2001 est.: 216,000), South Pacific Ocean. It consists of the islands of New Caledonia and Walpole, the Isle of Pines, and several other island groups; its capital is NOUMÉA. The main island, New Caledonia, has rich deposits of nickel that are among the largest in the world. Excavations indicate an Austronesian presence in the area c. 2000–1000 BC. The islands were visited by Capt. JAMES COOK in 1774 and by various navigators and traders in the 18th–19th century. They were occupied by France in 1853 and were a penal colony 1864–94. New Caledonians joined the FREE FRENCH cause of CHARLES DE GAULLE in 1940; the islands were the site of Allied bases (1942–44). They became part of the French overseas territory in 1946. In 1987 residents voted by referendum to remain part of France.

New Church *or* **Swedenborgians** Church whose members follow the teachings of EMANUEL SWEDENBORG. Swedenborg did not himself found a church, but he believed that his writings would be the basis of a "new church," which he associated with the "new Jerusalem" mentioned in the Book of Revelation. In 1788, soon after his death, a group of his followers established a church in London. The first Swedenborgian society in the U.S. was organized in Baltimore in 1792. Baptism and the Lord's Supper are the two SACRAMENTS of the church, and New Church Day (June 19) is added to the established Christian festivals. There are three New Church groups: the General Conference of the New Church, the General Convention of the New Jerusalem in the U.S.A., and the General Church of the New Jerusalem.

New Comedy Greek drama from c. 320 BC to the mid-3rd century BC that offers a mildly satiric view of contemporary Athenian society. Unlike Old Comedy, which parodies public figures and events (see ARISTOPHANES), New Comedy features fictional average citizens in domestic life. The CHORUS, the representative of forces larger than life, is reduced to a small band of musicians and dancers. Plays usually involve the conventionalized situation of thwarted lovers and contain stock characters. MENANDER introduced the New Comedy and became its most famous exponent; PLAUTUS and TERENCE translated its plays for the Roman stage. New Comedy influenced European drama down to the 18th century.

New Criticism *or* **formalism** Post–World War I school of Anglo-American literary theory that insisted on the intrinsic value of a work of art and focused attention on the individual work alone as an independent unit of meaning. New Critics were opposed to the practice of bringing historical or biographical data to bear on the interpretation of a work. The primary critical technique was analytic (or "close") reading of the text, concentrating on its language, imagery, and emotional or intellectual tensions. Critics associated with the movement include I. A. RICHARDS, WILLIAM EMPSON, JOHN CROWE RANSOM, and R. P. Blackmur (1904–1965).

New Deal U.S. domestic program of Pres. FRANKLIN ROOSEVELT to bring economic relief (1933–39). The term was taken from Roosevelt's speech accepting the 1932 presidential nomination, in which he promised "a new deal for the American people." New Deal legislation was enacted mainly in the first three months of 1933 (Roosevelt's "hundred days") and established such agencies as the Civil Works Administration and the CIVILIAN CONSERVATION CORPS to alleviate unemployment, the NATIONAL RECOVERY ADMINISTRATION to revive industrial production, the FEDERAL DEPOSIT INSURANCE CORP. and the SECURITIES AND EXCHANGE COMMISSION to regulate financial institutions, the AGRICULTURAL ADJUSTMENT ADMINISTRATION to support farm production, and the TENNESSEE VALLEY AUTHORITY to provide public power and flood control. A second period of legislation (1935–36), often called the second New Deal, established the NATIONAL LABOR RELATIONS BOARD, the WORKS PROGRESS ADMINISTRATION, and the SOCIAL SECURITY system. Some legislation was declared unconstitutional by the U.S. Supreme Court, and some programs did not accomplish their aims, but many reforms were continued by later administrations and permanently changed the role of government. See also PUBLIC WORKS ADMINISTRATION.

New Delhi \'de-lē\ City (pop., 2001: 294,783), capital of India, on the western bank of the YAMUNA RIVER, south of Old Delhi in DELHI union territory. Built from 1912 to 1929, it was formally opened in 1931, when it became the capital. In contrast to the convoluted street plan of Old Delhi, New Delhi has an orderly, diagonal pattern and gives a feeling of openness and quiet. The main east-west axis is Central Vista Park, a thoroughfare with government buildings, museums, and research centers.

New Democratic Party Minor Canadian political party. Formed in 1961 from the CO-OPERATIVE COMMONWEALTH FEDERATION, it favored an association with organized labor. The party's base was among the farmers of Manitoba and Saskatchewan and the urban workers of British Columbia and Ontario. With its predecessor, it has formed provincial governments intermittently from the 1940s on.

New Economic Policy (NEP) Economic policy of the Soviet Union, 1921–28. A temporary retreat from the failed WAR COMMUNISM policy of extreme centralization and doctrinaire socialism, the new measures included the return of most agriculture, retail trade, and light industry to private ownership (though the state retained control of heavy industry, banking, transport, and foreign trade) and the reintroduction of money into the economy. The policy allowed the economy to recover from years of war. In 1928 chronic grain shortages prompted JOSEPH STALIN to begin to eliminate private ownership of farmland and to collectivize agriculture under state control, effectively ending the NEP. By 1931 state control was reimposed over all industry and commerce.

New England Region, northeastern U.S. It consists of the states of Maine, New Hampshire, Vermont, Massachusetts, Rhode Island, and Connecticut, and has an area of 66,667 sq mi (172,668 sq km). Named by JOHN SMITH, who explored its shores in 1614, it was later settled by English Puritans (see PURITANISM). The New England colonies, fueled by self-sufficient farmers, evolved representative governments. The area's numerous harbors soon promoted the growth of overseas commerce and a vigorous shipbuilding industry. In the 18th century it became a hotbed of agitation for independence from Britain, and its patriots played leading roles in the AMERICAN REVOLUTION.

New England Confederation *or* **United Colonies of New England** Organization of four American colonies. In 1643 delegates from Massachusetts, Connecticut, New Haven, and Plymouth met to solve trade, boundary, and religious disputes and form a common defense against the French, Dutch, and Indians. They drew up articles of agreement and established a directorate of eight commissioners. The confederation was weakened by its advisory status and by the 1665 merger of Connecticut and New Haven. It was active in KING PHILIP'S WAR but dissolved in 1684 when the Massachusetts charter was revoked.

New England Mountains Mountain range and plateau, northeastern NEW SOUTH WALES, Australia. Part of the GREAT DIVIDING RANGE, it is about 200 mi (320 km) long, creating Australia's largest plateau. The highest peak, Ben Lomond, is 4,877 ft (1,487 m). The New England National Park, on the eastern slope of the mountain range, contains a tropical forest.

New England Renaissance See AMERICAN RENAISSANCE

New France Possessions of France in North America from 1534 to the Treaty of PARIS in 1763. After the first land claim for France by JACQUES CARTIER (1534), the company of New France was established in 1627. With the explorations by SAMUEL DE CHAMPLAIN, JACQUES MARQUETTE, R.-R. LA SALLE, LOUIS JOLLIET, and others, the boundaries of New France expanded beyond the lower ST. LAWRENCE RIVER to include the GREAT LAKES and the Mississippi Valley. From 1689 rivalry between England and France affected their possessions in North America. The FRENCH AND INDIAN WAR (1754–63) resulted in the cession of Canada and the territory east of the MISSISSIPPI RIVER to England and the territory west of the Mississippi to Spain, with France keeping only the islands of St.-Pierre and Miquelon.

New Goa See PANAJI

New Granada Spanish viceroyalty in northwestern South America during colonial times. Conquered and named by the Spaniards in 1537–38, it was subject to the viceroyalty of PERU until 1740. It then became a separate viceroyalty that included the modern countries of Colombia, Panama, Venezuela, and Ecuador. Its capital was Santa Fé (modern BOGOTÁ). It was liberated from Spain in 1823.

New Guinea *Indonesian* **Irian** \,ir-ē-'än\ Island, eastern MALAY ARCHIPELAGO, located in the western Pacific, north of Australia. Divided between IRIAN JAYA in its western half, and PAPUA NEW GUINEA in its eastern half, it is the second-largest island in the world. It is about 1,500 mi (2,400 km) long and 400 mi (650 km) wide at its widest point, with an area of about 309,000 sq mi (800,000 sq km). The terrain ranges from lowland rainforest to fertile highlands and its climate is tropical. Copper and gold are its chief mineral resources. The bulk of the population are subsistence farmers.

New Hampshire State (pop., 2000: 1,235,786), northeastern U.S. One of the NEW ENGLAND states, it covers 9,279 sq mi (24,033 sq km); its capital is CONCORD. The CONNECTICUT RIVER forms its western boundary with Vermont. The White Mountains in its central part, contain Mount WASHINGTON. The region was inhabited by Algonquian Indian tribes (see ALGONQUIAN LANGUAGES) when the first English people settled near Portsmouth in 1623. The area came under the jurisdiction of Massachusetts in 1641 and became a separate crown colony in 1679. It was the first colony to declare its independence from Britain in 1776. Following the nation's establishment, the state grew rapidly. Agriculture flourished and manufacturing developed along the rivers. Portsmouth became a major shipbuilding center. The economy is now based primarily on manufacturing and tourism, although dairy farming and granite quarrying are also important. Because it holds the nation's earliest presidential primary, it has furnished the first testing ground for many candidacies. DARTMOUTH and the University of NEW HAMPSHIRE are two of the state's prominent educational institutions.

New Hampshire, University of Public university based in Durham, N.H. The state's only university, it has land-grant, sea-grant, and space-grant status. It has colleges of liberal arts, life science and agriculture, and engineering and physical sciences; its graduate school comprises the School of Health and Human Services and the Whittemore School of Business and Economics. Total enrollment exceeds 13,000.

New Haven City (pop., 2000: 123,626), southern central Connecticut. A port of entry on Long Island Sound, it was originally settled in 1638 and became part of the colony of Connecticut in 1664. It was the co-capital with HARTFORD until 1875. It was sacked by LOYALIST forces during the AMERICAN REVOLUTION (1779). During the AMERICAN CIVIL WAR it was a center of Abolitionist activity (see ABOLITIONISM). A number of famous inventors made it a center of industrial technology, including CHARLES GOODYEAR, ELI WHITNEY, and SAMUEL F. B. MORSE. It is the home of YALE UNIV. and several other educational and cultural institutions.

New Hebrides See VANUATU

New Ireland *formerly* **Neu-Mecklenburg** \nȯi-'me-klən-,berg\ Island and province (pop., 1999 est.: 111,906), BISMARCK ARCHIPELAGO, Papua New Guinea. The island has an area of 3,340 sq mi (8,651 sq km) and is about 200 mi (320 km) long. The terrain is largely mountainous. The province includes many nearby smaller islands. It was discovered by Dutch navigators in 1616 but was little known before 1884, when it became part of a German protectorate. After World War I it was mandated to Australia. The island was occupied by the Japanese in World War II. When Papua New Guinea gained independence in 1975, it became part of that country. Most of the inhabitants live in the north. Copra production dominates commercial development.

New Jersey State (pop., 1997 est.: 8,053,000), eastern U.S. It covers 7,787 sq mi (20,168 sq km); its capital is TRENTON. The HUDSON RIVER forms its northeastern boundary; the DELAWARE RIVER, its western boundary. Before European colonization, the region was inhabited by DELAWARE Indian tribes. Although it was sighted by GIOVANNI VERRAZZANO and HENRY HUDSON, it was first settled by Dutch and Swedish traders. It was the site of numerous battles during the AMERICAN REVOLUTION, including one led by Gen. GEORGE WASHINGTON in 1776, after crossing the Delaware (see Battles of TRENTON AND PRINCETON). It was the third state to ratify the U.S. Constitution in 1787. Between the Revolutionary and Civil wars, it underwent tremendous industrialization, abetted by the construction of canals and, later, railways. Although known as the "Garden State," a name influenced by its 18th century agricultural fertility, its economy is based primarily on manufacturing, and it has many research facilities and laboratories. Tourism, led by ATLANTIC CITY, is also important. Chief cities include NEWARK, JERSEY CITY, PATERSON, and ELIZABETH.

New Mexico State (pop., 1997 est.: 1,730,000), southwestern U.S. It covers 121,593 sq mi (314,926 sq km); its capital is SANTA FE. In the west, it is crossed north–south by the CONTINENTAL DIVIDE. The RIO GRANDE bisects the state and for a short distance forms the boundary with Texas. Human settlement in the area has probably spanned 10,000 years. Before the NAVAJO and APACHE arrived in the 15th century, an agricultural Indian civilization had developed irrigation systems, PUEBLOS, and CLIFF DWELLINGS whose ruins still dot the state. Spaniards from Mexico claimed the area for Spain in the 16th century, and in 1540 FRANCISCO VAZQUEZ DE CORONADO explored it. The first settlement was at Santa Fe in 1610. Missionaries were active in the 1600s. It became part of Mexico in 1821 and was ceded to the U.S. in 1848 at the end of the MEXICAN WAR. The Territory of New Mexico was established by Congress in 1850. It became the 47th U.S. state in 1912, and retained its frontier image. World War II spurred economic and social change, bringing research facilities, including that at LOS ALAMOS. The economy today is largely dependent on the export of raw materials and on federal government expenditures; oil and natural gas are also important. The University of NEW MEXICO and a fine arts community are in ALBUQUERQUE.

New Mexico, University of Public university in Albuquerque, founded in 1889. It offers a comprehensive array of undergraduate, graduate, and professional degree programs. Academic specialties include Southwest Americana and Latin American studies. Other research areas include meteorites, robotics, ceramics, and lithography (through the Tamarind Institute). There are branch campuses at five other sites. Enrollment is about 27,000.

New Model Army (1645) Army that won the ENGLISH CIVIL WAR for Parliament. It was formed to provide a well-trained force drawn from all parts of England instead of the limited local militias. The new army also replaced the private armies raised by individual generals that lacked a unified command. Under BARON FAIRFAX and OLIVER CROMWELL, the New Model Army won the Battle of NASEBY and effectively ended the first phase of the civil wars.

New Nationalism American political policy espoused by THEODORE ROOSEVELT. Influenced by Herbert Croly's *The Promise of American Life* (1910), Roosevelt used the phrase in a speech to promote social justice and federal regulation of interstate industry. New Nationalism formed the basis of the PROGRESSIVE PARTY platform in Roosevelt's unsuccessful 1912 presidential campaign. See also ROBERT LA FOLLETTE.

New Orleans City (pop., 1996 est. est.: 477,000), southeastern Louisiana. Situated between the MISSISSIPPI RIVER and Lake PONTCHARTRAIN, it is the state's largest city and a major deepwater port. Founded in 1718 by French colonist J.-B. BIENVILLE, it was ceded to Spain in 1763. In 1803 it was ceded back to France and sold to the U.S. by NAPOLEON. Incorporated in 1805, it was the state capital 1812–49. During the AMERICAN CIVIL WAR the city was captured and occupied by Union forces (1862). A notable tourist center, its attractions include the MARDI GRAS and the French Quarter, a popular tourist area noted for its nightclubs and Creole architecture. It is also a medical, industrial, and educational center.

New Orleans, Battle of (1815) U.S. victory over Britain in the WAR OF 1812. Late in 1814 a British fleet of more than 50 ships commanded by Gen. Edward Pakenham (1778–1815) sailed into the Gulf of Mexico and prepared to attack New Orleans. Gen. ANDREW JACKSON, commander of the U.S. Army of the Southwest, which consisted chiefly of militiamen and volunteers, fought the British regulars who stormed their position on January 8, 1815. His troops were so effectively entrenched behind earthworks and the British troops so exposed that the fighting was brief, ending in a decisive U.S. victory and British withdrawal. Gen. Pakenham was killed. The battle was without military value, since the Treaty of Ghent ending the war had been signed in December, but the news had been slow to arrive. The victory nevertheless contributed to national morale, enhancing Jackson's reputation as a hero and preparing his way to the presidency.

New Orleans, Battle of (April 24–25, 1862) Naval action in the AMERICAN CIVIL WAR. A Union squadron of 43 ships led by DAVID FARRAGUT entered the Mississippi River below New Orleans and breached the chain cables stretched across the river as a defense. The 3,000 Confederate troops under Mansfield Lovell withdrew northward and the city fell. The Union army under BENJAMIN BUTLER entered the city on May 1 and began an occupation that lasted until the end of the war. The loss of New Orleans was a major blow to the Confederacy.

New Orleans jazz See DIXIELAND

New Realism Early-20th-century movement in METAPHYSICS and EPISTEMOLOGY that opposed the IDEALISM dominant in British and U.S. universities. Early leaders included WILLIAM JAMES, BERTRAND RUSSELL, and G. E. MOORE, who adopted the term REALISM to signal their opposition to idealism. In 1910 William Pepperel Montague, Ralph Barton Perry, and others signed an article entitled "The Program and First Platform of Six Realists," and followed it with a cooperative volume, *The New Realism* (1912). In defending the independence of known things, New Realism affirmed that in cognition "the content of knowledge, that which lies in or before the mind when knowledge takes place, is numerically identical with the thing known" (a form of direct realism). To some realists, this epistemological MONISM seemed unable to give a satisfactory explanation of the mind's proneness to error.

new religious movement (NRM) Any religion originating in recent centuries having characteristic traits including eclecticism and syncretism, a leader who claims extraordinary powers, and a "countercultural" aspect. Regarded as outside the mainstream of society, NRMs in the West are extremely diverse but include millennialist movements (e.g., the JEHOVAH'S WITNESSES), Westernized Hindu or Buddhist movements (e.g., the HARE KRISHNA MOVEMENT), so-called "scientific" groups (e.g., SCIENTOLOGY), and nature religions (see NEO-PAGANISM). In the East they include China's 19th-century Taiping movement (see TAIPING REBELLION) and present-day FALUN GONG movement, Japan's TENRIKYO and PL KYODAN, and Korea's CH'ONDOGYO and UNIFICATION CHURCH. Some NRMs fade away or meet tragic ends; others, such as the MORMON church, eventually become accepted as mainstream.

New Republic, The Weekly journal of opinion, founded in 1914 by Willard Straight, with Herbert Croly as editor. Long one of the most influential liberal magazines in the U.S., it early reflected the progressive movement and sought reforms in U.S. government and society, declining in the 1920s when liberalism was out of favor but reviving in the 1930s. After initially opposing FRANKLIN ROOSEVELT's administration, it supported Roosevelt's NEW DEAL. After becoming editor in 1946, former vice president HENRY WALLACE moved the magazine further left until he was forced to resign. In the early 1980s, the magazine began to display an array of commentary reflecting the resurgence of conservatism in U.S. politics.

New River River, southwestern Virginia and southern West Virginia. It is formed in North Carolina, and flows north across Virginia into West Virginia where it joins the Gauley River to form the KANAWHA RIVER. It is about 320 mi (515 km) long and is spanned by the longest steel-arch bridge in the world, the River Gorge bridge near Fayetteville, W.Va., whose main span is 1,700 ft (518 m).

New School University *formerly* **New School for Social Research** Private university in New York City. It was established in 1919 as an informal center for adult education and soon became the first American university to specialize in CONTINUING EDUCATION. In 1934 it established a graduate faculty of political and social sciences, staffed mainly by refugee academics from Nazi Germany. It also includes a liberal-arts college, a graduate school of management, the Mannes College of Music, and the Parsons School of Design. Total enrollment is about 7,000.

New Siberian Islands Island group, Arctic Ocean, northeastern Russia, north of eastern SIBERIA. The islands divide the Laptev Sea from the East Siberian Sea. They are separated from the Siberian mainland by Dmitry Laptev Strait. With an area of about 14,500 sq mi (38,000 sq km), they are snow-covered for more than nine months of the year. Arctic fox, northern deer, LEMMING, and many species of birds inhabit the islands.

New South Wales State (pop., 1996: 6,039,000), southeastern Australia. Bounded by the Pacific Ocean, it has an area of 309,433 sq mi (801,428 sq km); the capital is SYDNEY. The dominant geographic feature is the GREAT DIVIDING RANGE. Inhabited from prehistoric times, it was claimed for Britain by Capt. JAMES COOK in 1770. The colony included the entire continent except for Western Australia. The interior was explored throughout the 19th century and colonies set up there, separate from New South Wales. In 1901 it became part of Commonwealth of Australia. The state ceded the area of the AUSTRALIAN CAPITAL TERRITORY beginning in 1911. It is the center of Australia's commercial farming, industry, and culture.

New Spain Former Spanish viceroyalty (1535–1821), principally in North America, including the southwestern U.S., Mexico, Central America north of Panama, much of the West Indies, and the Philippines. MEXICO CITY was the seat of the government, which also had jurisdiction over Spain's Caribbean possessions. The first viceroy sent FRANCISCO VAZQUEZ DE CORONADO on his northern expeditions. The viceroyalty succumbed to the coalition forged by AGUSTIN DE ITURBIDE in 1821.

New Sweden Only Swedish colony in North America, on the DELAWARE RIVER, extending from the site of TRENTON, N.J., to the mouth of the river. It was established by the New Sweden Co. led by PETER MINUIT in 1638, when Fort Christina was built at what is now WILMINGTON, Del. It was captured by the Dutch in 1655 under PETER STUYVESANT. The Swedish colonists were allowed to keep their lands and continue their customs under Dutch rule.

New Testament Second of the two major divisions of the Christian BIBLE. Christians see the New Testament as the fulfillment of the promise of the OLD TESTAMENT. It recounts the life and ministry of JESUS and interprets their meaning for the early church, focusing especially on the new COVENANT created between God and the followers of Jesus. There are 27 books in the New Testament: four GOSPELS, or stories of the life and teachings of Christ; the Acts of the Apostles, a historical narrative of the first years of the Christian church; 21 epistles, or letters of advice and instruction to early Christians; and the Book of REVELATION, a description of the coming APOCALYPSE. Most were written in the later 1st century AD, though none can be dated precisely. Only two authors are known for certain: St. PAUL, credited with 13 epistles; and St. LUKE, writer of the third gospel and the Book of Acts. Attributions of other authors range from highly likely (for the other three gospels) to completely unknown (for the Epistle to the Hebrews). These documents circulated among the early churches and were used as preaching and teaching sources. The earliest known list of the current New Testament canon dates from AD 367 in a work by St. ATHANASIUS. A church council of 382 gave final approval to the list.

New Thought Mind-healing movement that originated in the U.S. in the 19th century. Its earliest proponent, Phineas P. Quimby (1802–1866), was a mesmerist who taught that illness is mental. New Thought was influenced by philosophers ranging from PLATO to EMANUEL SWEDENBORG, G. W. F. HEGEL, and RALPH WALDO EMERSON and in turn influenced MARY BAKER EDDY's CHRISTIAN SCIENCE. The International New Thought Alliance (formed 1914) asserts that sin and illness stem from incorrect thinking. New Thought groups emphasize JESUS as a teacher and healer and proclaim his kingdom as being within each person.

new town Form of urban planning designed to relocate populations away from large cities by grouping homes, hospitals, industry and cultural, recreational, and shopping centers to form entirely new, relatively autonomous communities. The new-town movement was anticipated by the Utopian Ebenezer Howard in the early 20th century (see GARDEN CITY). The first official new towns were proposed in Britain's New Towns Act of 1946. The idea found favor in other countries, especially in the U.S., Western Europe, and Soviet Siberia. New towns outside Britain often failed to incorporate enough of the mixed-use atmosphere that gives a town vitality. A dramatic increase in commuting and use of the car obviated the need for new towns to be so self-contained.

New Wave *French* **nouvelle vague** Group of individualistic French film directors of the late 1950s, including CLAUDE CHABROL, FRANÇOIS TRUFFAUT, J.-L. GODARD, LOUIS MALLE, ERIC ROHMER, ALAIN RESNAIS, and others. Most of the New Wave directors were associated with the important film magazine *Cahiers du Cinéma,* in which they developed the highly influential AUTEUR THEORY, calling for films to express the director's personal vision. Their films were characterized by a brilliance of technique that sometimes overshadowed the subject matter. Among the most important New Wave films were Godard's *Breathless* (1959), Truffaut's *The 400 Blows* (1959), and Resnais's *Hiroshima mon amour* (1959).

New World monkey Any South American MONKEY (platyrrhine) species in either of two families: MARMOSETS (Callitrichidae) or South American monkeys other than marmosets (Cebidae), including CAPUCHINS and SPIDER MONKEYS. Platyrrhines have a broad nose, with a wide septum separating the outwardly directed nostrils, and relatively unopposable thumbs. Most species have a long tail, which in a few species is prehensile. See also OLD WORLD MONKEY.

New Year's Day First day of the new year, celebrated with religious, cultural, and social observances around the world. It is usually marked by rites and ceremonies that symbolize casting off the old year and rejoicing in the new. Judaism, Christianity, and Islam all use different calendars and celebrate the new year on different dates. In the West January 1 is now the accepted date. The Jewish New Year, ROSH HASHANAH, begins on the first day of the month of Tishri, which can fall anytime from September 6 to October 5 in the Western calendar. The Muslim new year falls on the first day of the month of Muharram, which, because Islam uses a lunar calendar, gradually regresses through the Western calendar year. The Chinese New Year falls from late January to early February and is marked by prolonged festivities that include the expulsion of demons (often with the aid of fireworks), theatrical performances, and offerings to ancestors and gods of the hearth.

New York State (pop., 1997 est.: 18,137,000), eastern U.S. It covers 49,576 sq mi (128,402 sq km); its capital is ALBANY. The HUDSON, ST. LAWRENCE, DELAWARE, and NIAGARA rivers all form parts of its boundaries. The ADIRONDACK MTNS. are in the northeast; the CATSKILLS are in the east. Before European colonization, Algonquians (see ALGONQUIAN languages) and IROQUOIS inhabited the area. In 1524 GIOVANNI VERRAZZANO visited New York Bay. The 1609 explorations of HENRY HUDSON and SAMUEL DE CHAMPLAIN led to settlement. In 1664 the Dutch colony, New Netherland, led by PETER STUYVESANT, surrendered to the British and was renamed New York. The FRENCH AND INDIAN WAR resulted in skirmishes in northern and central New York; its conclusion confirmed English dominance in the region. In the AMERICAN REVOLUTION, it was the scene of many battles, including those of TICONDEROGA and SARATOGA, and of BENEDICT ARNOLD's treason at West Point. New York adopted the first state constitution (1777). The capital moved from NEW YORK CITY to Albany in 1797. The opening of the ERIE CANAL in 1825 spurred development of the western part of the state. In the 19th century the growing influence in New York City of TAMMANY HALL caused tension between the city and the state. The economy was once based largely on manufacturing in cities, including BUFFALO, ROCHESTER, and SYRACUSE. It is now dominated by service industries, concentrated in New York City.

New York, State University of (SUNY) Largest university system in the U.S. (total enrollment about 400,000). Founded in 1948, it consists of university centers in Albany, Binghamton, Buffalo, and Stony Brook; colleges of arts and sciences in Brockport, Buffalo, Cortland, Fredonia, Geneseo, New Paltz, Old Westbury, Oneonta, Oswego, Plattsburgh, Potsdam, and Purchase; three medical centers (two in New York City and one in Syracuse); several two-year agricultural and technical colleges; a nonresidential continuing-education program (Empire State College); over 30 community colleges; and various other specialized units.

New York Central Railroad Major U.S. railroad. It was founded in 1853 to consolidate 10 railroads that paralleled the Erie Canal between Albany and Buffalo, the oldest being the Mohawk and Hudson, New York state's first railway (established 1831). CORNELIUS VANDERBILT won control of the New York Central in 1867 and combined it with his New York and Hudson railroads running from Manhattan to Albany. The system grew until it had 10,000 mi (16,000 km) of track linking New York with Boston, Montreal, Chicago, and St. Louis. The New York Central began to decline after World War II, and in 1968 it merged with its chief competitor, the PENNSYLVANIA RAILROAD CO., to form the Penn Central Transportation Co. The merger failed, and the railroad was forced into bankruptcy in 1970. Its passenger services were taken over by AMTRAK in 1971, and its other railroad assets were transferred to CONRAIL in 1976.

New York City City (pop., 2000: 8,008,278), southeastern New York, at the mouth of the HUDSON RIVER. The largest city in the U.S. and an important seaport, it consists of five boroughs: the BRONX, BROOKLYN, MANHATTAN, QUEENS, and STATEN ISLAND. The site of a Dutch trading post on Manhattan Island, it was colonized as New Amsterdam by Dutch director general PETER MINUIT, who bought it from the Indians in 1626. The colony surrendered to the British in 1664 and was renamed New York. It was the capital of the state 1784–97 and of the U.S. 1789–90. The economy grew after the opening of the ERIE CANAL in 1825, and the city expanded rapidly after the AMERICAN CIVIL WAR, developing transportation and communications systems. In 1898 the five boroughs were merged into a single city. Long a magnet for immigrants to the U.S., it is a center of world trade and finance, media, art, entertainment, and fashion. Because of its prominence and its central role in world commerce, the city was a target for acts of TERRORISM. In September 2001, hijackers intentionally flew airliners into the twin towers of the WORLD TRADE CENTER, destroying them and destroying or damaging several adjacent buildings; the attacks killed some 2,800 people. See SEPTEMBER 11 ATTACKS.

New York City Ballet Preeminent U.S. ballet company. The company is descended from the American Ballet, founded by GEORGE BALANCHINE and LINCOLN KIRSTEIN in 1935, which was revived as the Ballet Society in 1946; it assumed its current name in 1948 and moved to its permanent home, the New York State Theater at Lincoln Center, in 1964. Under Balanchine's artistic direction, the company became the leading U.S. ballet troupe, combining European classical ballet with American characterization and innovation and exerting enormous influence on American dance. Later artistic directors JEROME ROBBINS and PETER MARTINS contributed numerous works to its repertoire. Its leading dancers have included MARIA TALLCHIEF, EDWARD VILLELLA, JACQUES D'AMBOISE, and SUZANNE FARRELL.

New York Daily News Morning daily tabloid newspaper published in New York City. It was founded in 1919 by Joseph Medill Patterson and his cousin ROBERT MCCORMICK as a subsidiary of the Tribune Co. of Chicago. The first successful tabloid-format newspaper in the U.S., it quickly attracted a large readership with sensational coverage of crime, scandal, and violence; lurid photographs; and cartoons and other entertainment features. It was an early user of wirephoto services and developed a large staff of photographers. In 1993 it was bought by Mortimer B. Zuckerman.

New York Public Library Largest city public library in the U.S. and one of the great libraries of the world. It was established in 1895, and its central building opened in 1911. Its holdings include more than 10 million books and more than 10 million manuscripts, as well as large collections of pictures, maps, books for the blind, films, and microfilms.

New York school Painters who participated in the development of contemporary art, particularly ABSTRACT EXPRESSIONISM, in or around New York City in the 1940s and '50s. During and after World War II, leadership in avant-garde art shifted from war-torn Europe to New York, and the New York school maintained a dominant position in world art into the 1980s. Abstract Expressionism, MINIMALISM, POP ART, and the new realist styles of the late 1960s, among others, all had their beginnings in New York. See also ACTION PAINTING.

New York Stock Exchange (NYSE) World's largest marketplace for SECURITIES. The exchange began as an informal meeting of 24 men in 1792 on what is now WALL STREET in New York City. It was formally constituted as the New York Stock and Exchange Board in 1817, and its present name was adopted in 1863. Since 1868 membership has been obtained by purchasing a seat from an existing number; membership has been limited to 1,366 since 1953. The exchange provided capital for the industrialization of the U.S. in the 19th century. After the Panic of 1837, it began to demand that companies disclose information about their finances to the public as a condition of offering stock. The stock-market crash of 1929 led to regulation by the SECURITIES AND EXCHANGE COMMISSION. To be listed on the NYSE, a company must earn $2.5 million before taxes, have at least one million shares of stock outstanding, give common stockholders voting rights, and publish periodic financial statements. See also AMERICAN STOCK EXCHANGE, NASDAQ.

New York Times, The Morning daily newspaper, long the U.S. newspaper of record. From its establishment in 1851 it has aimed to avoid sensationalism and to appeal to cultured, intellectual readers. In 1896 it was bought by ADOLPH OCHS, who built it into an internationally respected daily. Its prestige was notably enhanced by its coverage of the sinking of the TITANIC and of the two world wars. In the 1970s it became involved in controversy with its publication of the PENTAGON PAPERS. Later in the decade, under ARTHUR OCHS SULZBERGER, its organization and staff underwent sweeping changes, including the introduction of a national edition printed at regional sites. Today it is perhaps the most respected and influential newspaper in the world. It is the flagship of The New York Times Co., whose interests include other newspapers (including the *BOSTON GLOBE*), magazines, and broadcast and electronic media.

New York University (NYU) Private university in New York City, founded in 1831. It consists of 13 schools, colleges, and divisions at six major centers in Manhattan. Programs are offered in the arts and sciences, graduate studies, business, public administration, education, health, nursing, medicine, dentistry, law, social work, and the fine arts. The Gallatin Division, organized in 1972, offers degrees through innovative study programs. Total enrollment is about 30,000.

New Yorker, The U.S. weekly magazine, famous for its varied literary fare and humor. It was founded in 1925 by HAROLD ROSS, who was its editor until 1951. Initially focused on New York City's amusements and social and cultural life, it gradually acquired a broader scope, encompassing literature, current affairs, and other topics. Aimed at a sophisticated, liberal audience, it became renowned for its short fiction, cartoons, major (occasionally book-length) nonfiction pieces, and detailed reviews in the arts. It was sold in 1985 to Samuel I. Newhouse, Jr. (see NEWHOUSE FAMILY). Since Ross, its editors have been William Shawn (1952–87), Robert Gottlieb (1987–92), Tina Brown (1992–98), and David Remnick (from 1998).

New Zealand Island nation, South Pacific Ocean. Area: 104,454 sq mi (270,534 sq km). Population (2002 est.): 3,893,000. Capital: WELLINGTON. Most of the people are of European origin; about 10% are MAORI, and some are Pacific Islanders and Chinese. Languages: English and

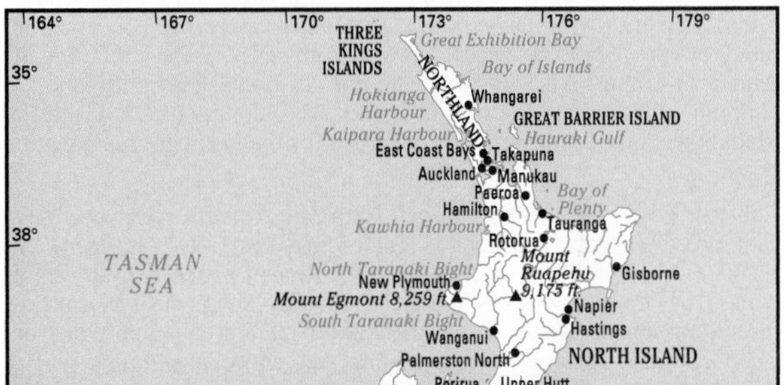

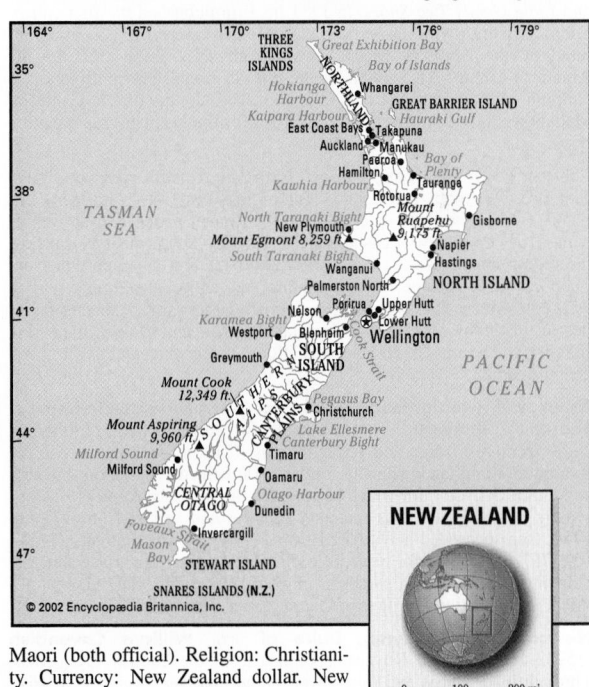

Maori (both official). Religion: Christianity. Currency: New Zealand dollar. New Zealand consists of the NORTH ISLAND and the SOUTH ISLAND, which are separated by COOK STRAIT, and several smaller islands. Both main islands are bisected by mountains in the south and hills in the north. New Zealand has a developed market economy largely based on agriculture, dominated by sheep raising, small-scale industries, and services. It is a constitutional monarchy with one legislative house; its chief of state is the British monarch represented by the governor-general, and the head of government is the prime minister. Polynesian occupation dates to c. AD 1000. First sighted by Dutch explorer ABEL JANSZOON TASMAN in 1642, the main islands were charted by Capt. JAMES COOK in 1769. Named a British crown colony in 1840 at Wellington, the area was the scene of warfare between colonists and native Maori through the 1860s. The capital was moved from AUCKLAND to Wellington in 1865, and in 1907 the colony became the Dominion of New Zealand. It administered Western SAMOA 1919–62 and participated in both world wars. The literacy rate is nearly 100%, and the cultural milieu is predominantly European, although a revival of traditional Maori culture and art is underway. CHRISTCHURCH is the major city on South Island. When Britain joined the EUROPEAN ECONOMIC COMMUNITY in the early 1970s, its influence led New Zealand to expand its export markets and diversify its economy. It has also become more independent in its foreign relations.

Newar \'nä-'wär\ People who make up about half the population of the Kathmandu Valley in Nepal. Most are Hindu, but some practice an Indian form of Buddhism. The Newar have a wide range of occupations; they have traditionally been noted as architects and artisans, the builders of the famous temples and shrines of Kathmandu. Painting and sculpture flourished among them in the 10th–16th century. The Newar population of Nepal is estimated to be about 540,000.

Newark \'nü-ərk\ City (pop., 1996 est.: 269,000) and port of entry, northeastern New Jersey, west of NEW YORK CITY. It was founded in 1666 by Puritans and was chartered as a township in 1693. It was the site of the College of New Jersey (now PRINCETON UNIVERSITY) 1748–56. In 1776 the city served as a supply base for Gen. GEORGE WASHINGTON. It was incorporated as a city in 1836. The largest city in the state, it was the scene of major civil disturbances in 1967. It is a highly diversified industrial, transportation, and insurance center. It was the birthplace of AARON BURR and STEPHEN CRANE.

Newbery, John (1713–1767) English publisher. In 1744 he set up a bookshop and publishing house in London, and it became one of the first to publish children's books, including *A Little Pretty Pocket-Book* and *Little Goody Two-Shoes.* In 1781 his firm published the first collection of nursery rhymes associated with Mother Goose. He is commemorated by the Newbery Medal, awarded annually since 1922 by the American Library Association for the most distinguished contribution to children's literature in the U.S. It is presented along with the Caldecott Medal (see RANDOLPH CALDECOTT), awarded for the best children's picture book.

Newcastle *or* **Newcastle upon Tyne** City (metro. area pop., 1995 est.: 283,000), port, and county seat of TYNE AND WEAR, northern England, on the TYNE RIVER. It dates from the Roman period and derives its name from the NORMAN castle built in 1080 by ROBERT II of Normandy, the oldest son of WILLIAM I THE CONQUEROR. At first an important wool trade center, it became a major mining area and coal-shipping port in the 16th century. It was among the world's largest ship repairing facilities; its economy now rests on associated marine and heavy engineering industries. The city is also an educational center and features a 14th-century church.

Newcastle (-under-Lyme), Duke of *orig.* **Thomas Pelham** *or* **Thomas Pelham-Holles** (1693–1768) British politician. He inherited lands from his father and uncle that by 1714 made him one of the wealthiest Whig landowners in England. He helped bring about the succession of GEORGE I, for which he received the title of duke (1715). Chosen by ROBERT WALPOLE as secretary of state and served from 1724 to 1754, then succeeded his brother HENRY PELHAM as prime minister (1754–56, 1757–62). Noted for his skill in distributing patronage to secure parliamentary support for a particular ministry, Newcastle wielded great political influence in the reigns of George I and GEORGE II.

Newcastle (-upon-Tyne), Duke of *orig.* **William Cavendish** (1593?–1676) British Royalist commander in the ENGLISH CIVIL WARS. Through inheritances and royal favor, he became very wealthy. In 1642 he was given command of the four northern English counties and raised the siege of York (1642). After the Royalist defeat at the Battle of MARSTON MOOR, he left England for France and Holland. He returned at the RESTORATION and regained his estates. A patron of poets and dramatists, he also wrote several comedies.

Newcomen \'nü-kə-mən\, **Thomas** (1663–1729) British engineer. In 1712 he built his atmospheric STEAM ENGINE, a precursor of JAMES WATT's engine. In the Newcomen engine, atmospheric pressure pushed the piston down after the condensation of steam had created a vacuum in the cylinder. Newcomen engines were used for some years in the draining of mines and in raising water to power waterwheels.

Newell, Allen (1927–1992) U.S. cognitive scientist. Born in San Francisco, he taught at Carnegie Mellon University from 1961 until his death. In the late 1950s and early 1960s he collaborated with HERBERT SIMON in constructing an influential model of human problem solving (*Human Problem Solving*, 1972). His later work has concerned artificial intelligence, and he is known for his development of computer models of human cognition and the development of a unified theory of cognition (*Unified Theories of Cognition,* 1990). In 1992 he received the National Medal of Science.

Newfoundland and Labrador \'nü-fənd-lənd\ Province (pop., 1996: 564,000), one of the four Atlantic provinces, Canada. Consisting of the island of Newfoundland and LABRADOR on the mainland, and bounded by Quebec, it extends into the North Atlantic Ocean and is the easternmost part of NORTH AMERICA. Its capital is ST. JOHN'S. It was originally settled by Indians and ESKIMOS. VIKING ruins from c. AD 1000 have been found in the northern part of the island. JOHN CABOT claimed the island for England in 1497; the first colony was established at St. John's in 1583. France and England disputed possession of the area, and though England retained control with the 1713 Peace of UTRECHT, controversies over fishing rights continued through the 19th century. A province since 1949, it includes the GRAND BANKS fishing grounds. Fishing, mainly for cod, was virtually the only industry until the early 20th century, when western Labrador's vast iron reserves began to be exploited.

Newfoundland Dog breed developed in Newfoundland, possibly from crosses between native dogs and the Great Pyrenees dogs that Basque fishermen introduced into North America in the 17th century. Noted for sea rescues, the gentle, patient Newfoundland stands 26–28 in. (66–71 cm) and weighs 110–150 lbs (50–68 kg). Powerful hindquarters, a large lung capacity, large webbed feet, and a heavy, oily coat enable it to swim in cold waters. It has also been used as a watchdog and draft animal. The typical Newfoundland is solid black; the Landseer Newfoundland is usually black and white.

Newfoundland, Memorial University of See MEMORIAL UNIVERSITY OF NEWFOUNDLAND

Newhouse family U.S. family, builders of a huge publishing empire in the U.S. in the later 20th century. The family's fortunes began with Samuel Irving Newhouse (1895–1979), who, as a clerk at 17, made a failing newspaper in Bayonne, N.J., profitable. From the early 1920s he bought and turned around other papers; at his death his company, Advance Publications Inc., owned 31 newspapers, seven magazines, five radio stations, six television stations, and 15 cable television systems. Led by his sons Samuel I. Newhouse, Jr. (born 1928), and Donald E. Newhouse (born 1930), Advance Publications greatly expanded, buying several book publishers, including RANDOM HOUSE, and becoming one of the largest U.S. magazine publishers with such titles as *The* NEW YORKER, *Vanity Fair*, *Vogue*, *Glamour*, *Bride's*, and *Gourmet*.

Newman, Arnold (Abner) (born 1918) U.S. photographer. Born in New York, he studied art at the University of Miami, then worked in the photography studio of a Miami department store. In 1946 he opened his own studio in New York, where he specialized in portraits of well-known people posed in settings associated with their work. His "environmental portraiture" greatly influenced 20th-century portrait photography. His best-known portraits include those of MAX ERNST, ALFRED STIEGLITZ, GEORGIA O'KEEFFE, I. STRAVINSKY, PABLO PICASSO, and JEAN COCTEAU.

Newman, Barnett *orig.* **Baruch** (1905–1970) U.S. painter. Born in New York City to Polish immigrant parents, he studied at the Art Students League and City College. With ROBERT MOTHERWELL and MARK ROTHKO, he cofounded the school called "Subject of the Artist" (1948), which held open sessions and lectures for other artists. He developed a style of mystical abstraction and achieved his breakthrough with *Onement I* (1948), in which a single stripe (or "zip") of orange vertically bisects a field of dark red. This austerely geometric style became his trademark and had a great influence on artists such as AD REINHARDT and FRANK STELLA.

Newman, John Henry *known as* **Cardinal Newman** (1801–1890) English churchman and man of letters. He attended Oxford Univ., where in 1833 he became the leader of the Oxford Movement, which stressed the Catholic elements in the English religious tradition and sought to reform the Church of England. He was received into the Roman Catholic church in 1845, but he came under suspicion among the more rigorous clergy because of his quasi-liberal spirit. A challenge from Charles Kingsley prompted him to write an eloquent exposition of his spiritual history, the widely admired *Apologia pro Vita Sua* (1864). The work assured his place in the church, and in 1879 he became a cardinal-deacon. He also wrote several hymns, including "Lead, Kindly Light," theological works, and religious poetry.

Newman, Paul (born 1925) U.S. film actor. Born in Cleveland, he studied drama at Yale University and the Actors Studio, and first appeared on Broadway in *Picnic* (1953). He began acting in films in 1955 and won favorable notice in *Somebody up There Likes Me* (1956) and *The Long Hot Summer* (1958). His performances in such successful films as *Cat on a Hot Tin Roof* (1958), *The Hustler* (1961), *Hud* (1963), *Cool Hand Luke* (1967), *Butch Cassidy and the Sundance Kid* (1969), *The Sting* (1973), *Absence of Malice* (1981), *The Verdict* (1982), and *The Color of Money* (1986; Academy Award) made him one of the most popular and enduring stars of his time. He directed and produced such films as *Rachel, Rachel* (1968) and *The Glass Menagerie* (1987), both of which starred his wife, Joanne Woodward.

Newport Town (pop., 1995 est.: 22,000) and county seat of the Isle of Wight, in the English Channel. It was probably the Roman settlement of Medina; there is no trace of Saxon settlement. The first charter was granted between 1177 and 1184, and the borough was incorporated in 1608. It is the island's trade and agricultural center.

Newport City (pop., 1994 est.: 24,000) and port of entry, southeastern Rhode Island, at the mouth of Narragansett Bay. Founded in 1639 by colonists from Massachusetts, it became a haven for religious refugees. With Providence, it was the joint capital of the state until 1900. Newport has held many of the America's Cup yacht races, and it is a center for naval education. It also is the site of one of Cornelius Vanderbilt's mansions (The Breakers), and the Touro synagogue, which is the oldest in the U.S.

Newport City (pop., 1991: 130,000) and port, southeastern Wales, at the Bristol Channel mouth of the River Usk. By c. 1126 it was a medieval borough with a castle. The city was chartered in 1385. It was industrialized in the 19th century and was the scene of Chartist riots in 1839 (see Chartism). Industries include coal, steel, and aluminum.

Newport News City (pop., 1996 est.: 176,000) and port of entry, southeastern Virginia, at the mouth of the James River. The site was settled in 1621 by 50 colonists from Ireland. It was incorporated as a city in 1896 and was an important embarkation point in both World Wars. With Norfolk and Portsmouth, it constitutes the Port of Hampton Roads. It is the site of one of the largest shipyards in the world, producing luxury liners, aircraft carriers, and nuclear-powered submarines.

Newry and Mourne District (pop., 1995 est.: 84,000), southeastern Northern Ireland. Bordered by the Irish Sea and the Irish republic, it is divided in two by the Newry Canal, the first major canal in the British Isles, built 1730–41. Limestone and granite are quarried in the Mourne Mountains. The district seat is at Newry.

news agency *or* **news service** *or* **wire service** Organization that gathers, writes, and distributes news to newspapers, periodicals, radio and television broadcasters, government agencies, and other users. It does not publish news itself but supplies news to subscribers, who, by sharing costs, obtain services they could not otherwise afford. All the mass media depend on agencies for the bulk of the news they carry. Some agencies focus on special subjects or on a local area or nation. Many are cooperatives, with members providing news from their area to a pool for general use. The largest news agencies are United Press International, Associated Press, Reuters, and Agence France-Presse.

newscast Radio or television broadcast of news events. News gathering and broadcasting by the radio networks began in the mid-1930s and increased significantly during World War II. The television newscast began in 1948 with 15-minute programs that resembled movie newsreels. The current U.S. format employs a newscaster or anchorperson reading news stories, with interpolated audiotape (for radio) or videotape (for television) and live reports from remote journalists. Noted newscasters have included Edward R. Murrow, Walter Cronkite, and David Brinkley.

Newsday Evening daily tabloid newspaper published in Long Island, N.Y. It was established in 1940, as the residential suburbs in Nassau and Suffolk counties began to expand. Following a liberal-independent policy, it has specialized in reporting serious local news. The newspaper itself has earned three Pulitzer Prizes for meritorious public service, and its writers and reporters have earned many more. It is part of the Times Mirror Co. group, publisher of the *Los Angeles Times*.

newsgroup Internet forum for discussion of specific subjects. Newsgroups are organized into subjects (e.g., automobiles); each typically has several subgroups (e.g., classic cars, Formula One racing cars). A person starts a threaded discussion by "posting" (uploading) an article; the follow-up replies (including replies to replies) comprise the discussion. A newsgroup name usually consists of an abbreviation (e.g., "rec" for the recreation newsgroup) followed by subgroup names separated by dots (e.g., "rec.music.jazz"). Viewing and posting messages requires a news reader, a program that connects the user to an Internet news server. Most newsgroups are connected via Usenet, a worldwide network that uses the Network News Transfer Protocol (NNTP). See also bulletin-board system.

newspaper Publication usually issued daily, weekly, or at other regular times that provides news, views, features, and other information of public interest and often carries advertising. Forerunners of the modern newspaper appeared as early as ancient Rome (see Acta). More or less regular papers printed from movable type appeared in Germany, Italy, and the Netherlands in the early 17th century. The first English daily was *The Daily Courant* (1702–35). Though preceded by official papers, James Franklin's *New-England Courant* (1721) was the first independent newspaper in the English colonies. By 1800 the principles of a free press and a basic formula for both serious and popular papers were taking root in much of Europe and the U.S. In the 19th century the number of U.S. papers and their circulations rose dramatically, owing to wider literacy, broadening appeal, lower prices, and technological advances in typesetting, printing, communications, and transport. By late in the century, newspapers had achieved great power. Competition for readers often led to sensationalism and, in the 20th century, gave rise to the so-called tabloids (see yellow journalism). Since 1900 newspaper publishing worldwide has expanded greatly; in large countries, it has experienced consolidation into chains and the absorption of smaller papers into larger ones.

Newsweek U.S. newsweekly, published in New York City. Founded (as *News-Week*) in 1933 by Thomas J. C. Martyn, a former editor of *Time*, it merged with *Today* magazine in 1937. It initially offered a rather drab survey of the news with columns of analysis. After World War II it grew livelier, especially after its purchase by Philip Graham, publisher of *The Washington Post*, in 1961. It has a strong reputation for accurate, brisk, and vivid reporting, and, like *Time*, presents news in terse summary form, organized by departments.

newt *or* **eft** Any of more than 40 salamander species (family Salamandridae) prevalent in the southeastern U.S. and Mexico and also found in Asia and Great Britain. Aquatic species are called newts; terrestrial species are called efts. Newts have a long, slender body, and the tail is higher than it is wide. They eat earthworms, insects, snails, and other small animals. Both aquatic and terrestrial species breed in ponds. The three species (genus *Triturus*) in Britain are sometimes called tritons. The red eft *(Notophthalmus viridescens)* of eastern North America is bright red during its terrestrial youth, after which it becomes permanently aquatic and dull green.

Warty newt (*Triturus cristatus*).
TONI ANGERMAYER

newton Absolute unit of force, abbreviated N, in the meter-kilogram-second (MKS) system of physical units (see International System of Units). It is defined as the force necessary to provide a mass of 1 kg with an acceleration of 1 m per second per second. One newton is equal to a force of 100,000 dynes in the centimeter-gram-second (CGS) system, or a force of about 0.2248 lb in the foot-pound-second (English or U.S.) system. It is named for ISAAC NEWTON, whose second law of motion describes the changes a force can produce in the motion of a body.

Newton, Huey P(ercy) (1942–1989) U.S. black activist. Born in New Orleans, he graduated from high school illiterate but taught himself to read before attending college. He met Bobby Seale (born 1936) while attending the San Francisco School of Law, and in 1966 they formed the BLACK PANTHER PARTY. In 1974 Newton was accused of murder and fled to Cuba; on his return in 1977, he was freed after two trials ended in hung juries. In 1989 he was sentenced to six months in jail for misusing public funds intended for a Black Panther–founded school; later that year he was found shot dead on a street in Oakland, Cal.

Newton, Isaac *later* **Sir Isaac** (1642–1727) English physicist and mathematician. The son of a yeoman, he was raised by his grandmother. He was educated at Cambridge University (1661–65), where he discovered the work of RENE DESCARTES. His experiments passing sunlight through a prism led to the discovery of the heterogeneous, corpuscular nature of white light and laid the foundation of physical OPTICS. He built the first reflecting telescope in 1668 and became a professor of mathematics at Cambridge in 1669. He worked out the fundamentals of CALCULUS, though this work went unpublished for more than 30 years. His most famous publication, *Principia Mathematica* (1687), grew out of correspondence with EDMOND HALLEY. It describes his works on the laws of motion (see NEWTON'S LAWS OF MOTION), orbital dynamics, tidal theory, and the theory of universal GRAVITATION, and is regarded as the seminal work of modern science. He was elected president of the ROYAL SOCIETY of London in 1703 and became the first scientist ever to be knighted in 1705. During his career he engaged in heated arguments with several of his colleagues, including ROBERT HOOKE (over authorship of the inverse square relation of gravitation) and G. W. LEIBNIZ (over the authorship of calculus). The battle with Leibniz dominated the last 25 years of his life; it is now well established that Newton developed calculus first, but that Leibniz was the first to publish on the subject. Newton is regarded as one of the greatest scientists of all time.

Newton's law of gravitation Statement that any particle of matter in the universe attracts any other with a force (f) that is proportional to the product of their masses (m_1 and m_2) and inversely proportional to the square of the distance (R) between them. In symbols: $f = G(m_1m_2)/R^2$, where G is the gravitational constant. ISAAC NEWTON put forth the law in 1687 and used it to explain the observed motions of the planets and their moons, which had been reduced to mathematical form by JOHANNES KEPLER early in the 17th century.

Newton's laws of motion Relations between the FORCES acting on a body and the MOTION of the body, formulated by ISAAC NEWTON. The laws describe only the motion of a body as a whole and are valid only for motions relative to a reference frame. Usually, the reference frame is the earth. The first law, also called the law of INERTIA, states that if a body is at rest or moving at constant speed in a straight line, it will continue to do so unless it is acted upon by a force. The second law states that the force f acting on a body is equal to the MASS m of the body times its ACCELERATION a, or $f = ma$. The third law, also called the action-reaction law, states that the actions of two bodies on each other are always equal in magnitude and opposite in direction.

Newtown St. Boswells \'nüt-ᵊn-sənt-'bäz-wəlz\ Town, southeastern Scotland. It lies on the Edinburgh–Carlisle railway. Before 1929 its population consisted mainly of railroad employees. The town is now a county and regional administration center for the Borders region. Dryburgh Abbey, founded in 1150, has the tombs of Sir WALTER SCOTT and field marshal DOUGLAS HAIG.

Newtownabbey \ˌnüt-ᵊn-'a-bē\ Town and district (pop., 1995 est.: 79,000), eastern Northern Ireland, established in 1973. The town was formed in 1958 from seven villages and is a residential continuation of BELFAST. It is surrounded by modern industrial complexes that manufacture tires, telephones, and textiles. The district's light agricultural activity is centered around the administrative seat of Ballyclare.

Newtownards \ˌnüt-ᵊn-'ärdz\ Town (pop., 1992: 24,000), district seat of ARDS, Northern Ireland. Settled in 1608 on the site of a ruined monastery, it is located east of BELFAST. It is now a manufacturing center.

Ney, Michel *later* **prince de la Moskowa** (1769–1815) French army officer, best known of NAPOLEON's marshals. He distinguished himself in the FRENCH REVOLUTIONARY WARS and rose to general in 1799. A supporter of Napoleon, he was created marshal of France in 1804 and duke of Elchingen in 1808 after victories in the NAPOLEONIC WARS. He led French forces in the Battle of FRIEDLAND (1807) and at the Battle of BORODINO (1812). In the French retreat from Moscow, he courageously commanded the exposed rear guard and earned Napoleon's praise as "the bravest of the brave." After Napoleon's abdication, Ney favored LOUIS XVIII but rallied to Napoleon's support in the HUNDRED DAYS and commanded troops at the unsuccessful Battle of WATERLOO. After the BOURBON RESTORATION, he was court-martialed and shot by firing squad.

Neyshabur \ˌnā-shä-'bür\ *or* **Nishapur** \ˌnē-shə-'pu̇r\ Town (pop., 1994 est.: 155,000), northeastern Iran. Its name derives from its founder, the SASANIAN king Shapur I (died 272). One of the four great cities of the region of KHORASAN, it was the residence of the 5th-century Sasanian king Yazdegerd II. It declined by the mid-7th century, but flourished again under the Tahirid (821–873) and Samanid dynasties (ended 999). It was the residence of TOGHRÏL BEG in the 11th century, but again declined in the 12th century. The tombs of OMAR KHAYYAM and the poet and mystic Farid od-Din Attar are nearby.

Nez Percé \'nez-'pərs\ Sahaptian-speaking North American Indian people who lived in an area centering on the Snake River in central Idaho, western Oregon, and western Washington. Their culture was primarily that of the PLATEAU INDIANS, with some PLAINS INDIAN influence. Their domestic life centered on small villages near streams with abundant salmon; they also hunted small game and collected wild plant foods. After acquiring horses they began to hunt bison and became more warlike, eventually becoming one of the dominant tribes in the region. Through a series of treaties in the mid-1800s, their traditional territory was severely reduced; the tragic Nez Percé War (1877), led by Chief JOSEPH, was the result. Today some 2,500 Nez Percé remain on a reservation in Idaho.

Nezami \'nez-ˌó-ˌmē\ *or* **Nizami** \'nē-ˌzó-ˌmē\ *in full* **Elyas Yusof Nezami Ganjavi** (1141?–1209) Greatest romantic epic poet in Persian literature. Little is known of his life, which he spent in Ganja, in what is now Azerbaijan. Only a handful of his qasidas (odes) and GHAZELS have survived; his reputation rests on his great *Khamseh* ("The Quintuplet"), a group of five poems totaling 30,000 couplets, in which he brought a colloquial and realistic style to the epic. The fourth, *The Seven Beauties*, is considered his masterpiece.

NFL See NATIONAL FOOTBALL LEAGUE

Ngami \əŋ-'gä-mē\, **Lake** Shallow lake, northwestern Botswana, north of the KALAHARI DESERT. It was a large lake, estimated at more than 170 mi (275 km) in circumference, when the explorer DAVID LIVINGSTONE sighted it in 1849. The lake varies in size with the amount of rainfall, and although it is much smaller today than in Livingstone's time, it is rich in birdlife.

NGO See NONGOVERNMENTAL ORGANIZATION

Ngo Dinh Diem \'ŋō-'din-dē-'em, *Engl* en-'gō-'din-dē-'em\ (1901–1963) President of South Vietnam (1955–63). Of noble birth, Diem was on friendly terms with the Vietnamese imperial family and served as Emperor BAO DAI's minister of the interior (1933), but resigned when the French would not accept his legislative reforms. He turned down an invitation to join HO CHI MINH's forces and lived in self-imposed exile until invited back in 1954 by Bao Dai to serve as prime minister of South Vietnam. In 1955 he ousted the emperor and made himself president. He refused to carry out elections mandated by the Geneva Accords of 1954, ruled autocratically, and showed preference to fellow Roman Catholics in an overwhelmingly Buddhist country. An unpopular leader, Diem was assassinated by his generals in 1963.

Ngonde See NYAKYUSA

Ngugi wa Thiong'o \ᵊŋ-'gü-gē-wä-'t͟hyȯŋ-gō\ *orig.* **James Thiong'o Ngugi** (born 1938) Kenyan novelist. Educated in Uganda and England, he wrote the first major novel in English by an East African; the popular *Weep Not, Child* (1964) is the story of a family drawn into the struggle for Kenyan independence. His other novels include *A Grain of Wheat* (1967) and *Petals of Blood* (1977). As he became more sensitive to the effects of colonialism, he adopted his traditional name and wrote in the language of the Kikuyu people. He also has written plays and numerous essays on literature, culture, and politics.

Nguni \en-'gü-nē\ Cluster of related ethnic groups living in South Africa, Swaziland, and Zimbabwe, including the XHOSA, ZULU, SWAZI, and NDEBELE, who speak very closely related BANTU LANGUAGES. The Nguni were dispersed from their original homeland in what is now eastern Cape province and KwaZulu/Natal by the MFECANE disturbances of the 1820s and the expansion of European power.

Nguyen dynasty \'ŋüē-ən, *Engl* 'nü-ən, en-gī-'en\ (1802–1945) Last Vietnamese dynasty. During the 16th century, while the emperors of the LATER LE DYNASTY were nominally in control, the Nguyen family came to rule southern Vietnam in an essentially independent fashion. Emperor Gia Long (1762–1820), founder of the dynasty, conquered all of Vietnam in 1802; his successors modeled their administration on the Chinese QING dynasty (1644–1911/12). The French invaded in 1858 and eventually took control of the entire country. They retained the Nguyen emperors as rulers of Annam (central Vietnam) and Tonkin (N Vietnam), but not southern Vietnam (called Cochinchina). BAO DAI, the last emperor, abdicated following the Vietnamese Nationalists' proclamation of independence in 1945.

NHL See NATIONAL HOCKEY LEAGUE

niacin \'nī-ə-sən\ *or* **nicotinic acid** \,ni-kə-'tē-nik, ,ni-kə-'ti-nik\ *or* **vitamin B_3** HETEROCYCLIC COMPOUND essential to growth and health in animals, including humans. It is an aromatic CARBOXYLIC ACID in the form of a PYRIDINE ring. It is found in the body only in combined form as a COENZYME, nicotinamide adenine dinucleotide (NAD), which is involved in the METABOLISM of CARBOHYDRATES and the oxidation of SUGAR derivatives and other substances. One of the most stable vitamins (see VITAMIN B COMPLEX), it survives cooking and most preserving processes. It is widely found in dietary sources, especially lean meat. Deficiency causes PELLAGRA. It is used as a drug to raise high-density-LIPOPROTEIN CHOLESTEROL levels.

Niagara Falls Great falls of the NIAGARA RIVER, on the U.S.–Canadian border. They are divided by Goat Island into the Horseshoe (or Canadian) Falls and the American Falls. At the foot of the American Falls is the Cave of the Winds, a large rocky chamber formed by erosion. The river below the falls flows between high cliffs, forming Whirlpool Rapids. Bridges spanning the river include Rainbow Bridge between the U.S. and Canadian cities of Niagara Falls. Indian tribes knew of the falls for years before European settlement. French missionary LOUIS HENNEPIN visited in 1678. Tourism is a major industry, and it is a hydroelectric center.

Niagara River River forming the U.S.–Canada boundary between western New York and southern Ontario. Its high flow and steep descent make it one of the best sources of hydroelectric power in North America. It connects Lake ERIE with Lake ONTARIO, and NIAGARA FALLS lies about halfway along its course. The U.S. and Canadian cities of the same name are on either bank of the river. It is navigable from Lake Erie to the upper rapids.

Niamey \'nyä-mā\ City (pop., 1994 est.: 420,000), capital of Niger, along the NIGER RIVER. Originally an agricultural village of Maouri, Zerma, and FULANI peoples, it became the capital of Niger colony in 1926 and grew rapidly after World War II. At the intersection of trade routes, it has residents from other parts of Niger, as well as YORUBA and HAUSA traders, merchants, officials, and craftsmen from Nigeria, Benin, and Togo. It is a commercial center with a university.

Nian Rebellion *or* **Nien Rebellion** \'nyán\ (c. 1852–68) Rebellion in northern China during the QING DYNASTY. The Nian, a secret society, was probably a reincarnation of the WHITE LOTUS Society; it attracted poor peasants, salt smugglers, and army deserters who used guerrilla hit-and-run tactics to attack the wealthy and redistribute the plundered goods among the needy. They took over local militias and formed their own armies. They were finally crushed by LI HONGZHANG, who defeated them using modern weapons and blockade lines. See also TAIPING REBELLION.

Niarchos \nē-'är-kōs\, **Stavros (Spyros)** (1909–1996) Greek shipping magnate. He first bought ships to transport wheat for his family's flour mill, then established his own shipping firm, Niarchos Group, in 1939. His ships were used by Allied forces in World War II, and after the war he used the insurance money he gained from ships sunk in combat to buy oil tankers. He favored large ships, and many of his supertankers (of which Niarchos Ltd. at its height operated more than 80) set world records for size and carrying capacity. His longtime rivalry with ARISTOTLE ONASSIS was famous.

Nias \'nē-əs\ Island (pop., 1980: 468,000), Indonesia, in the Indian Ocean. It is the largest island in a chain along the western coast of SUMATRA. It is 80 mi (129 km) long and 30 mi (48 km) wide, with an area of 1,569 sq mi (4,064 sq km). Most of the people are animists (see ANIMISM) and speak dialects of the AUSTRONESIAN LANGUAGE family. The chief village is Gunungsitoli on the northeastern coast. Megalithic monuments and wooden sculptures honoring the dead or representing fertility are common on the island.

Nibelungenlied \'nē-bə-,lùŋ-ən-,lēt\ ("Song of the Nibelungs") Middle High German epic poem written c. 1200 by an unknown poet from the Danube region in what is now Austria. It is preserved in three main 13th-century manuscripts. Elements of great antiquity are discernible in the poem, traceable to Old Norse literature, stories in the *Poetic EDDA*, and Scandinavian SAGAS. The principal characters are Prince SIEGFRIED, Queen BRUNHILD, Princess Kriemhild, her brother King Gunther, and his henchman Hagen; the story focuses on deceit, revenge, and slaughter. Many variations and adaptations of the poem appeared in later centuries, including RICHARD WAGNER's opera cycle *Der Ring des Nibelungen* (1853–74).

Nicaea \nī-'sē-ə\ Independent principality (1204–61) of the fragmented BYZANTINE EMPIRE. It was founded in 1204 by THEODORE I LASCARIS. It was the political and cultural center from which a restored Byzantium arose in the mid-13th century under MICHAEL VIII PALAEOLOGUS. It extended from the BLACK SEA coast east of the Sangarius River southwest across western Asia Minor to MILETUS and the Maeander. It became a center of Greek education, especially under Theodore II Lascaris who founded an imperial school. It declined after 1261, when Michael VIII regained Constantinople.

Nicaea \nī-'sē-ə\, **Council of** (AD 325) First ecumenical council of the Christian Church, held at Nicaea (now Iznik, Turkey). Called by Emperor CONSTANTINE I, the council condemned ARIANISM and drew up the NICENE CREED. It failed to set a uniform date for Easter.

Nicaragua *officially* **Republic of Nicaragua** Republic, Central America. Area: 50,464 sq mi (130,700 sq km). Population (2002 est.):

5,024,000. Capital: MANAGUA. Most of the people are MESTIZOS. Languages: Spanish (official), indigenous Indian languages, English. Religion: Roman Catholicism. Currency: córdoba oro. Nicaragua's western half consists of thickly forested mountain ranges and fertile valleys. Parallel to the Pacific coast is a belt of about 40 dormant and active volcanoes. The eastern coastline along the Caribbean is known as the MOSQUITO COAST. Earthquakes are common. Nicaragua has a developing market economy based largely on agriculture, light industries, and trade. It is a republic with one legislative house; its head of state and government is the president. The area has been inhabited for thousands of years, most notably by the MAYA. CHRISTOPHER COLUMBUS arrived in 1502, and Spanish explorers discovered Lake NICARAGUA soon thereafter. Nicaragua was governed by Spain until 1821, when it declared its independence. It was part of Mexico and then the United Provinces of Central America until 1938 when full independence was achieved. The U.S. intervened in political affairs by maintaining troops there 1912–33. Ruled by the dictatorial SOMOZA dynasty 1936–79, it was taken over by the SANDINISTAS after a popular revolt. They were opposed by armed insurgents, the U.S.-backed CONTRAS, from 1981. The Sandinista government nationalized several sectors of the economy but lost the national elections in 1990. The new coalition government returned many economic activities to private control, but unrest between the ruling government and the Sandinistas continued through the 1990s.

Nicaragua, Lake Lake, southwestern Nicaragua. It is 102 mi (164 km) long, with a surface area of about 3,100 sq mi (8,000 sq km). The largest freshwater lake between the U.S. and Peru, it is connected with Lake MANAGUA by the Tipitapa River and is the source of the SAN JUAN RIVER. It is the only freshwater lake containing oceanic animal life, including sharks, swordfish, and tarpon. Its largest island, Ometepe, is the preeminent site in Nicaragua for pre-Columbian archaeological finds.

Nice \'nēs\ *ancient* **Niceaea** City (metro. area pop., 1990: 476,000) southeastern France. It is located on the CÔTE D'AZUR of the Mediterranean Sea, near the Italian border. Founded by Greeks c. 350 BC, it was conquered by Romans in the 1st century AD and became a trading station. It was held by the counts of PROVENCE in the 10th century. In 1388 it passed to the counts of SAVOY. The city was ceded to France in 1860. Sheltered by beautiful hills, Nice has a pleasant climate and is the leading resort of the French RIVIERA.

Nicene Creed \'nī-ˌsēn, nī-'sēn\ Ecumenical Christian statement of faith accepted by the Roman Catholic, Eastern Orthodox, Anglican, and major Protestant churches. Originally written in Greek, it was long thought to have been drafted at the Council of NICAEA (325), but is now believed to have been issued by the Council of CONSTANTINOPLE (381), based on a baptismal creed already in existence.

Nicephorus II Phocas \nī-'se-fə-rəs...'fō-kəs\ (912–969) Byzantine emperor (963–69). A powerful military commander, he fought the Arabs in the east, liberated Crete from its Arab rulers (961), and gained control of the eastern Mediterranean. After the death of Romanus II, Nicephorus cooperated in a plot to seize the throne, accepting the crown (963) and marrying Theophano, the regent of the two legitimate heirs. He continued his exploits against the Arabs but was surrounded by discontent and intrigue at home; he retired to a fortified palace, where he was killed by former friends guided by his wife and his chief lieutenant.

Niche with statue of Apollo, by Jacopo Sansovino, in the Loggetta, Venice, 1540.

ALINARI—ART RESOURCE/EB INC.

niche \'nich\ Smallest unit of a HABITAT that is occupied by an organism. A habitat niche is the physical space occupied by the organism; an ecological niche is the role the organism plays in the community of organisms found in the habitat. The activities of an organism and its relationships to other organisms are determined by its particular structure, physiology, and behavior.

Nichiren \'nē-chē-ˌren\ *orig.* **Zennichi** (1222–1282) Japanese Buddhist prophet, founder of NICHIREN BUDDHISM. The son of a fisherman, he entered a Buddhist monastery at 11. After an exhaustive study of all the major Buddhist schools existing in Japan, he concluded in 1253 that the LOTUS SUTRA was the only doctrine suitable for his age and predicted calamity for Japan if all other sects were not abandoned. This pronouncement caused him to be banished from his monastery. He also claimed that Japan was the chosen country of Buddhism, from which Buddhist salvation would spread to other lands. He was later exiled to an island in the Sea of Japan, where in 1272 he wrote his major work, *The Opening of the Eyes*.

Nichiren Buddhism One of the largest schools of Japanese BUDDHISM, founded by NICHIREN. It believes that the essence of the BUDDHA's teachings are contained in the LOTUS SUTRA and that the beliefs of other Buddhist schools are erroneous. In Nichiren Buddhism, the chanting of the title of the Lotus Sutra can lead to salvation. After Nichiren's death the school split into various subsects, notably Nichiren-shu, which controls the temple founded by Nichiren at Mount Minobu, and Nichiren-shoshu, which is headquartered in a temple at the foot of Mount Fuji. Nichiren-sho-shu has adherents in the U.S.; in Japan its lay organization is the SOKA-GAKKAI.

Nicholas *Russian* **Nikolay Nikolayevich** (1856–1929) Russian grand duke. The nephew of ALEXANDER II, he entered the imperial army (1872) and served in the Russo-Turkish War (1877–78). As inspector general of calvary (1895–1905), he introduced reforms in training and equipment. From 1905 he commanded the St. Petersburg military district, and in 1914 he was appointed head of all Russian forces. A popular commander, he led the army to early successes in World War I but was hampered by shortages. Dismissed in 1915 by NICHOLAS II, he commanded in the Caucasus 1915–17. After the Russian Revolution he moved to France, where he led an organization to unite anticommunist Russian émigrés.

Nicholas, St. *or* **Santa Claus** (fl. 4th century) Minor saint associated with CHRISTMAS. He was probably bishop of Myra in Asia Minor. He is reputed to have provided dowries for three poor girls to save them from prostitution and to have restored to life three children who had been chopped up by a butcher. He became the patron saint of Russia and Greece, of charitable fraternities and guilds, and of children, sailors, unmarried girls, merchants, and pawnbrokers. After the Reformation, his cult disappeared in all the Protestant countries of Europe except Holland, where he was known as Sinterklaas. Dutch colonists brought the tradition to New Amsterdam (now New York City), and English-speaking Americans adopted him as Santa Claus, who lives at the North Pole and brings gifts to children at Christmas.

Nicholas I *Russian* **Nikolay Pavlovich** (1796–1855) Czar of Russia (1825–55). Son of PAUL I, he trained as an army officer. In 1825 he succeeded his brother ALEXANDER I as emperor and suppressed the DECEMBRIST REVOLT. His reign came to represent autocracy, militarism, and bureaucracy. To enforce his policies, he created such agencies as the THIRD SECTION (political police), directed by COUNT ALEKSEY G. ORLOV. In foreign policy, Nicholas quelled an uprising in Poland (1830–31) and aided Austria against a Hungarian uprising (1849). His designs on Constantinople led to war with Turkey (1853) and drew other European powers into the CRIMEAN WAR. He was succeeded by his son ALEXANDER II.

Nicholas II *orig.* **Gerard of Burgundy** (died 1061) Pope (1058–61). Known as an advocate of reform, he was bishop of Florence before being elected pope in opposition to the ANTIPOPE Benedict X. At the LATERAN COUNCIL of 1059 he reformed the process of papal election, eliminating the emperor's role. The German bishops voided his decree (1061), signifying the beginning of the contest between empire and papacy and a diplomatic revolution. Nicholas sought an alliance with the Normans in southern Italy and invested ROBERT GUISCARD as duke of Apulia, Calabria, and Sicily (1059).

Nicholas II *Russian* **Nikolay Aleksandrovich** (1868–1918) Czar of Russia (1894–1917). Son of ALEXANDER III, he received a military education and succeeded his father as czar in 1894. He was an autocratic but indecisive ruler and was devoted to his wife, ALEXANDRA, who strongly influenced his rule. His interest in Asia led to construction of the TRANS-SIBERIAN RAILROAD and also helped cause the disastrous RUSSO-JAPANESE WAR (1904–5). After the RUSSIAN REVOLUTION OF 1905, he agreed reluctantly to a representative DUMA but restricted its powers and made only token efforts to enact its measures. His prime minister, PIOTR STOLYPIN, attempted reforms, but Nicholas, increasingly influenced by Alexandra and GRIGORY RASPUTIN, opposed him. After Russia suffered setbacks in WORLD WAR I, Nicholas ousted the popular grand duke NICHOLAS as commander in chief of Russian forces and assumed command himself, at the bidding of Alexandra and Rasputin. His absence from Moscow and Alexandra's mismanagement of the government caused increasing unrest and culminated in the RUSSIAN REVOLUTION OF 1917. Nicholas abdicated in March 1917 and was detained with his family by GEORGY Y. LVOV's provisional government. Plans for the royal family to be sent to England were overruled by the local Bolsheviks. Sent to the city of Yekaterinburg, the family was executed in a cellar there in July 1918.

Nicholas V *orig.* **Tommaso Parentucelli** (1397–1455) Pope (1447–55). Soon after his election, he ended the schism caused by the rivalry between popes and church councils. He restored peace to the Papal States, won Poland's allegiance, and gained the support of Austria by promising to crown Frederick III as Holy Roman Emperor. Nicholas initiated the Peace of LODI (1455) in order to end strife in Italy. A patron of art and scholarship, he rebuilt many of Rome's architectural treasures and founded the Vatican Library.

Nicholas Brothers U.S. tap dancing duo. Fayard Antonio (born 1914) and his brother Harold Lloyd (1921–2000) developed the "classical tap" form, combining jazz dance, ballet, and acrobatics with tap. They gained fame at a young age while dancing at Harlem's COTTON CLUB (1932–39); they went on to appear in films such as *Stormy Weather* (1943), as well as on Broadway and later on television. They began their careers at a time when opportunities were few and stereotyped roles the norm for black entertainers, but they rose above this marginalization and enhanced the art of tap with their elegance and sensational showmanship.

Nicholas of Cusa (1401–1464) German cardinal, mathematician, scientist, and philosopher. Ordained a priest in 1440, he was made a cardinal in Italy and became bishop in 1450. In *On Catholic Concordance* (1433), he supported the supremacy of the general councils of the church over the papacy's authority. Skilled in nearly every branch of learning, he anticipated the work of COPERNICUS by discerning a movement in the universe that did not center on the earth. He also carried out botanical experiments and collected ancient manuscripts. In his discourse *On Learned Ignorance* (1440), he described the learned man as one who is aware of his own ignorance.

Nicholas of Verdun (fl. 1181–1205) French enamelist and goldsmith, considered the greatest of his day. He was an important figure during the transition from late ROMANESQUE to early GOTHIC style. His best-known work is the altarpiece of the Abbey Church of Klosterneuburg, Austria (1181), which reveals his mastery of metalworking and the technique of champlevé enameling, in which compartments hollowed out from a metal base are filled with vitreous enamel.

Nichols, Mike *orig.* **Michael Igor Peschkowsky** (born 1931) U.S. (German-born) stage and film director. He was born in Berlin to Jewish parents, who fled to the U.S. in 1938. After studying at the ACTORS STUDIO, he formed a comic improvisational group in Chicago. He and Elaine May (born 1932) toured with and recorded a set of brilliant social-satire routines. He later directed several Broadway hits, including *Barefoot in the Park* (1963) and *The Odd Couple* (1965). His first film, *Who's Afraid of Virginia Woolf?* (1966), was followed by *The Graduate* (1967, Academy Award); his later films include *Silkwood* (1983) and *Primary Colors* (1998).

Nicholson, Jack (born 1937) U.S. film actor. Born in Neptune, N.J., he acted in low-budget movies before earning acclaim for his role in *Easy Rider* (1969). He followed it with such successful films as *Five Easy Pieces* (1970), *Chinatown* (1974), and *One Flew over the Cuckoo's Nest* (1975, Academy Award). He won two more Academy Awards in 1983 and 1997. Noted for his devilish grin and his portrayals of unconventional outsiders, he attained iconic status.

Nicias \'ni-shē-əs\ (died 413 BC) Athenian leader. He was renowned for his enormous wealth. Seeking to end the PELOPONNESIAN WAR (431–404 BC), in 421 he negotiated a 50-year alliance (the Peace of Nicias), which held for six years before the ambitions of ALCIBIADES led to renewed warfare. In 415 he reluctantly shared command of a Sicilian expedition with Lamachus and Alcibiades. When Alcibiades was recalled and Lamachus died, Nicias lost the advantage they had achieved in the siege of Syracuse; his troops were overwhelmed and he was captured and executed.

nickel Metallic chemical ELEMENT, one of the TRANSITION ELEMENTS, chemical symbol Ni, atomic number 28. Nickel is silvery white, tough, harder than iron, ferromagnetic (see FERROMAGNETISM), and highly resistant to rusting and corrosion. It occasionally occurs free and is fairly common but not often concentrated in igneous rocks. As pure metal, it is used to coat other metals and as a catalyst. In alloys, it is used in coins, stainless steels, and cutlery. Its compounds, in which it most often has VALENCE 2, have a variety of industrial uses, as CATALYSTS and mordants (see DYE) and in ELECTROPLATING.

nickelodeon Early motion-picture theater, so named because admission typically cost a nickel. Nickelodeons offered continuous showings of one- and two-reel films, lasting from 15 minutes to one hour and accompanied by a piano. The success of the Pittsburgh nickelodeon established in 1905 by Harry Davis made it the model for their rapid proliferation throughout the U.S. By 1910 they numbered 10,000, fueling a huge demand for silent films and projection equipment and providing the impetus for the development of the modern motion-picture industry.

Nicklaus \'nik-ləs\, **Jack (William)** (born 1940) U.S. golfer, a dominating figure in world golf from the 1960s to the 1980s. Born in Columbus, Ohio, he won the U.S. Amateur Championship twice. After turning professional in 1962, he won the U.S. Open four times (1962, 1967, 1972, 1980), the Masters Tournament six times (1963, 1965, 1966, 1972, 1975, 1986), the PGA championship five times (1963, 1971, 1973, 1975, 1980), and the British Open three times (1966, 1970, 1978). By 1986 "the Golden Bear" had played in 100 major championships, finishing in the top three 45 times. His great career was a reflection of his ability to combine skill and power with remarkable concentration and composure under pressure. He is widely regarded as the greatest golfer in the game's history.

Nicklaus, 1982.
FOCUS ON SPORTS INC.

Nicobar Islands See ANDAMAN AND NICOBAR ISLANDS

Nicolet \,ni-kə-'lā\, **Jean** (1598–1642) French explorer in North America. In 1618 he traveled to New France, where he lived with Indian tribes. He learned several Indian languages and became the interpreter for the French colony at Three Rivers (1633). He journeyed into Huron territory, canoeing with several Indians through the Straits of Mackinac to became the first European to see Lake Michigan (1634), and later explored the region of present-day Wisconsin.

Nicolls, Richard (1624–1672) English colonial governor of New York. In 1664 he became the first governor of the English colony of New York by forcibly acquiring it from the Dutch. After the English ships blockaded the city of New Amsterdam, the Dutch surrendered without a fight. Nicolls renamed the province and its main city for his patron, the Duke of York. An efficient administrator, he issued the first legal code of New York (1665). He returned to England in 1668 and resumed his duties as gentleman of the bedchamber to the duke.

Nicopolis (Actia) \nə-'kä-pə-lis\ Ancient city, northwestern Greece. Its ruins lie about 4 mi (6 km) north of Préveza. It was founded in 31 BC by Octavian (later AUGUSTUS) to commemorate his victory over Mark ANTONY and CLEOPATRA at the Battle of ACTIUM. It became the capital of the coastal region, encompassing ACARNANIA and EPIRUS, and was famous for its buildings and for the Actian games. Destroyed in the 4th century AD and rebuilt, it was finally destroyed by Bulgarians in the 11th century. Its ruins include a basilica, a Roman theater, and an aqueduct.

Nicopolis \nə-'kä-pə-ləs\, **Battle of** (September 25, 1396) Turkish victory over an army of European crusaders. When the Ottoman Turks besieged Constantinople (1395), MANUEL II PALAEOLOGUS appealed to Europe for help. The king of Hungary organized a crusade intended to expel the Turks from the Balkans and then march to Jerusalem. The crusaders laid siege to Nicopolis, the main Turkish stronghold on the Danube River, but Turkish forces arrived from Constantinople and slaughtered most of the crusaders. The battle ended international efforts to halt Turkish expansion into the Balkans and central Europe.

Nicosia \ˌni-kə-ˈsē-ə\ *or* **Lefkosía** \ˈlef-kō-ˈsē-ə\ City (metro. area pop., 1994 est.: 186,000), capital of CYPRUS. Lying on the Pedieos River, it is bordered by mountains to the north and south. It was a kingdom in the 7th century BC and has been the capital of the island since the 10th century AD. It came successively under the control of the Byzantines, Venetians, and Turks; the British held it from 1878 until 1960. During the 20th century the city has grown beyond the existing circular Venetian walls. The population in the surrounding area is engaged mainly in agriculture. A U.N. buffer zone has separated the city's Greek and Turkish sectors since 1974.

nicotine Principal ALKALOID of TOBACCO, occurring throughout the plant but mostly in the leaves. It is a HETEROCYCLIC COMPOUND, containing a PYRIDINE ring; its chemical formula is $C_{10}H_{14}N$. Nicotine is the chief addictive ingredient (see DRUG ADDICTION) in cigarettes and cigars and in snuff. It has a unique biphasic effect: Inhaled in short puffs it is a stimulant, but when inhaled slowly and deeply it can be a tranquilizer. In larger doses, nicotine is a highly toxic poison, used as an insecticide, fumigant, and vermifuge.

nicotinic acid See NIACIN

Nicoya \nē-ˈkō-yä\, **Gulf of** Inlet of the Pacific Ocean, northwestern coast of Costa Rica. It extends north for about 50 mi (80 km). The Tempisque, Abangares, and Tárcoles rivers empty into the gulf. It has several islands, including Chira, the largest, and San Lucas. The largest town and port on the shores of the gulf is Puntarenas.

Nicoya Peninsula Peninsula, western Costa Rica. It is bounded on the west and south by the Pacific Ocean, on the northeast by the Cordillera de Guanacaste, and on the southeast by the Gulf of NICOYA. It measures about 85 mi (140 km) northwest–southeast. Descendants of the pre-Columbian Chorotega-Mangues Indians are still found in villages on the peninsula.

Niebuhr \ˈnē-ˌbu̇r\, **Barthold Georg** (1776–1831) German historian. Niebuhr held posts in state service in Denmark and Prussia before resigning to become state historiographer. In 1810 he began a series of lectures at the University of Berlin that were the basis of his great work, the enormously influential *History of Rome* (1811–32). In it he introduced skepticism to historical scholarship, showing how to analyze historical sources, discard worthless material, and lay bare elements from which historical facts could be reconstructed, and thereby initiating a new era in historiography.

Niebuhr \ˈnē-ˌbu̇r\, **Reinhold** (1892–1971) U.S. theologian. Born in Wright City, Mo., the son of an evangelical minister, he studied at Eden Theological Seminary and Yale Divinity School. He was ordained in the Evangelical Synod of North America in 1915 and served as pastor of Bethel Evangelical Church in Detroit until 1928. His years in that industrial city made him a critic of capitalism and an advocate of socialism. From 1928 to 1960 he taught at New York's Union Theological Seminary. His influential writings, which forcefully criticized liberal Protestant thought and emphasized the persistence of evil in human nature and social institutions, include *Moral Man and Immoral Society* (1932), *The Nature and Destiny of Man* (1941–43), and *The Self and the Dramas of History* (1955).

Reinhold Niebuhr, 1963.

BY COURTESY OF THE RARE BOOK DEPARTMENT, UNION THEOLOGICAL SEMINARY LIBRARY, NEW YORK CITY

niello \nē-ˈe-lō\ Black metallic alloy of sulfur with silver, copper, or lead, used to fill designs that have been engraved on the surface of a metal object, usually of silver. The black sulfides are powdered, and after the engraved silver has been moistened, the powder is spread on it. When the metal is heated, the niello melts and runs into the engraved channels. After the excess niello is scraped away, the surface is polished. The contrast of the black niello against the bright surface produces an attractive decorative effect. During the height of its popularity in the Renaissance, the technique was widely used for embellishing liturgical as well as utilitarian objects. Nielli (objects decorated with niello) were produced in ancient Rome and 9th-century England. In Russia niello work is known as Tula work.

Nielsen, Carl (August) (1865–1931) Danish composer. He studied violin and trumpet as a child and began composing by imitating classical models. In 1890 he went to Germany to learn of newer developments and met J. BRAHMS, whose music came to influence his own. His individual style—still following classical forms but using intense chromaticism combined with a lyric, melodic strain—emerged after 1900. The last five of his six symphonies (1902–25) are the core of his work, but he also composed many short orchestra pieces, piano and chamber music, concertos for violin, flute, and clarinet, and a wind quintet.

Nielsen ratings National rating of the popularity of television shows. Developed by A. C. Nielsen in 1950, the system now samples television viewing in about 5,000 homes. A meter attached to each television set records the channel being watched and sends the data to a computer center; individual buttons record which person in each household is watching a given program. Separate surveys are done for many large media market areas.The ratings project each program's total audience; for example, a rating of 20 denotes that 20% of U.S. households tuned in to a particular program. Commercial television networks use the ratings to set advertising rates for each program as well as to determine which programs to continue and to cancel.

Niemeyer (Soares Filho) \ˈnē-ˌmī-ər\, **Oscar** (born 1907) Brazilian architect. Beginning in 1934, he worked in the office of Lúcio Costa, an early exponent of the Modern movement in Brazil. Niemeyer's first major independent project was the plan for Pampulha (1941), a suburb of Belo Horizonte. He is famous for his work on BRASÍLIA (1956–61), a series of rather plain, isolated monuments surrounded by vast space. Active into his nineties, he was commissioned to design the mushroomlike Museum of Contemporary Art in Niterói, Brazil (1991). With its lyrical and sculptural forms, his work is free-flowing and optimistic. Niemeyer received the Pritzker Architecture Prize in 1988.

Niemöller \ˈnē-ˌmœl-ər\, **(Friedrich Gustav Emil) Martin** (1892–1984) German theologian. A war hero as a submarine commander in World War I, he became a minister in 1924. When the Nazis came to power in 1933, he protested their interference in church affairs and helped combat discrimination against Christians of Jewish background. As founder of the anti-Nazi CONFESSING CHURCH, he worked to oppose ADOLF HITLER. Arrested in 1937, he was interned until 1945. After the war he helped rebuild the Evangelical Church. Increasingly disillusioned with prospects for demilitarization, he became a controversial pacifist; for his efforts to extend friendship ties to Eastern-bloc countries, he received the Lenin Peace Prize (1967) and West Germany's Grand Cross of Merit (1971).

Nien Rebellion See NIAN REBELLION

Niepce \ˈnyeps\, **(Joseph-) Nicéphore** (1765–1833) French inventor. In 1807 Niepce and his brother invented an internal-combustion engine (fueled with lycopodium powder). In 1813 he began experiments with lithography. He is best remembered for his experiments with photography, which he called heliography. In 1826–27, using a camera, he made a view from his workroom window on a pewter plate—the first permanently fixed image from nature. In 1829 he began a partnership with L.-J.-M. DAGUERRE to perfect and exploit heliography, but he died before they had achieved any further advance.

Nietzsche \ˈnē-chə, ˈnē-chē\, **Friedrich (Wilhelm)** (1844–1900) German-Swiss philosopher and writer, one of the most influential modern thinkers. The son of a Lutheran pastor, he studied at Bonn and Leipzig and at 24 became professor of classical philology at the University of Basel. He became close to the older RICHARD WAGNER, in whose operas he saw the potential for the revival of Western civilization, but broke with Wagner angrily in 1876. His *Birth of Tragedy* (1872) contained major insights into ancient Greek drama; like *Untimely Meditations* (1873), it is dominated by a Romantic perspective also influenced by ARTHUR SCHOPENHAUER. Mental and physical problems forced him to leave his position in 1878, and he spent 10 years attempting to recover his health in various resorts, while continuing to write prolifically. His works from *Human, All Too Human* (1878) to *The Gay Science* (1882) extol reason and science, experiment with literary genres, and express his emancipation from his earlier Romanticism. His mature writings, particularly *Beyond Good and Evil* (1886), *A Genealogy of Morals* (1887), and *Thus Spake Zarathustra* (1883–92), were preoccupied with the origin and function of values in human life. If, as he believed, life neither possesses nor lacks intrinsic value and yet is always being evaluated, then such evaluations can usefully be read as symptoms of the evaluator's condition. He fulminated against Christianity and announced the death of God. His major breakdown in 1889 marked the virtual end of his productive life. He was revered by ADOLF HITLER for his dislike of democracy and his heroic ideal of the *Übermensch* (Superman), though the Nazis ignored much in Nietzsche's thought that was hostile to their aims. His analyses of the root motives and values that underlie traditional Western religion, morality, and philosophy affected generations of theologians, philosophers, psychologists, poets, novelists, and playwrights.

Niger \'nī-jər, nē-'zher\ *officially* **Republic of Niger** Nation, western Africa, on the southern edge of the SAHARA. Area: 459,073 sq mi (1,188,999 sq km). Population (1997 est.): 9,389,000. Capital: NIAMEY. More than half the people are HAUSA; there are also Songhai-Zerma and Kanuri. Languages: French (official), HAUSA, Arabic. Religions: Islam,

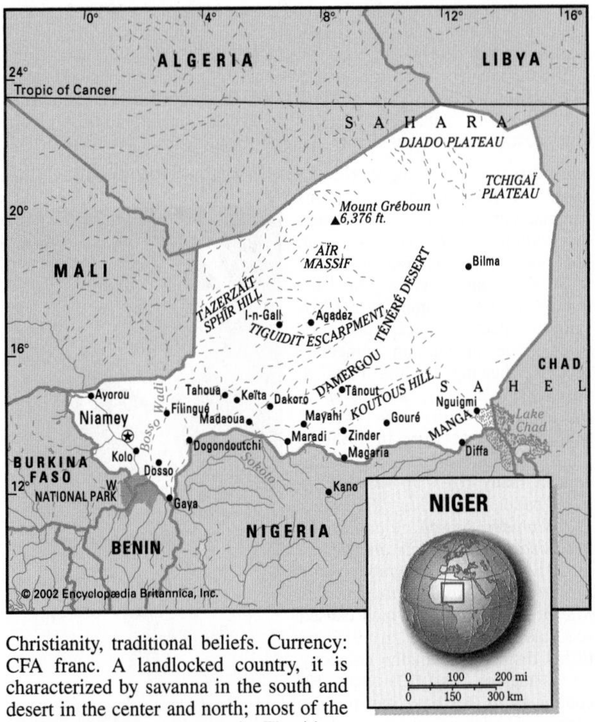

Christianity, traditional beliefs. Currency: CFA franc. A landlocked country, it is characterized by savanna in the south and desert in the center and north; most of the population lives in the south. The NIGER RIVER dominates in the southwest, and the Aïr Massif, a mountainous region, in the northern central part of the country. Niger has a developing economy based largely on agriculture and mining. It is a republic with one legislative body; its head of state and government is the president, assisted by the prime minister. There is evidence of NEOLITHIC culture in the region, and there were several precolonial kingdoms. First explored by Europeans in the late 18th century, it became part of FRENCH WEST AFRICA in 1904. It became an overseas territory of France in 1946 and gained independence in 1960. The first multiparty elections were held in 1993. The leader of a military coup of 1996 promulgated a new constitution that year.

Niger-Congo languages Superfamily of 900–1,300 languages spoken by most of the population of sub-Saharan Africa, from northern Senegal and Kenya in the north to Namibia and Eastern Cape province (South Africa) in the south. The name Niger-Congo was introduced in 1955 by JOSEPH H. GREENBERG. As understood today, Niger-Congo has nine branches: MANDE, Kordofanian, ATLANTIC (formerly West Atlantic), Kru, GUR, KWA, Ijoid, ADAMAWA-UBANGI (formerly Adamawa-Eastern), and BENUE-CONGO. Kordofanian is a family of more than 20 languages whose speakers (numbering under 200,000) live in the Nuba Mountains of southern Kordofan province in Sudan. Kru comprises more than 10 languages and language complexes whose 1–2 million speakers live primarily in southwestern Ivory Coast and southern Liberia. Ijoid is a group of eight closely related groups of dialects spoken by close to 2 million members of the Ijo (Ijaw) and Defaka peoples of the Niger River delta in Nigeria.

Niger River *or* **Joliba** \'jäl-ə-bə\ *or* **Kworra** \'kwȯr-ə\ Principal river of western Africa. The third longest on the continent, it rises in Guinea near the Sierra Leone border and flows into Nigeria and the Gulf of GUINEA. It is 2,600 mi (4,183 sq km) long, and its middle course is navigable for about 1,000 mi (1,600 km). Peoples living along the Niger include the BAMBARA, the MALINKE, and the SONGHAI. It was explored by MUNGO PARK beginning in 1796.

Nigeria *officially* **Federal Republic of Nigeria** Nation, western Africa. Area: 356,669 sq mi (923,773 sq km). Population (1997 est.): 103,460,000. Capital: ABUJA. There are more than 250 ethnic groups, including HAUSA, FULANI, YORUBA, and IGBO (Ibo). Languages: English (official), HAUSA. Religions: Islam, Christianity, animism. Currency: naira. Nigeria consists of plateaus and the lowlands between them, which are major river basins fed especially by the NIGER RIVER. It has a developing, mixed economy based largely on petroleum production and agriculture. Manufacturing remains undeveloped. Services, trade, and transportation employ more than two-fifths of the workforce. Nigeria is governed by a military regime. Inhabited for thousands of years, the region was the

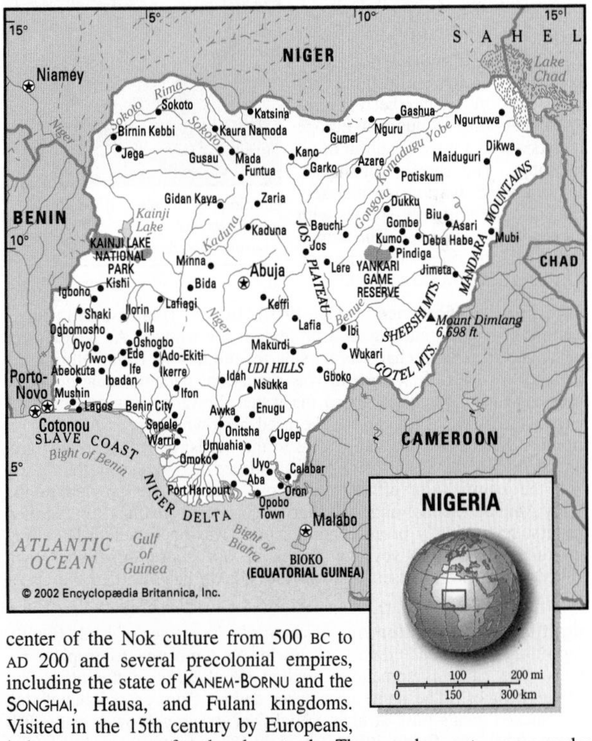

center of the Nok culture from 500 BC to AD 200 and several precolonial empires, including the state of KANEM-BORNU and the SONGHAI, Hausa, and Fulani kingdoms. Visited in the 15th century by Europeans, it became a center for the slave trade. The area began to come under British control in 1861, and was entirely British-controlled by 1906. Nigeria gained independence in 1960 and became a republic in 1963, with NNAMDI AZIKIWE as president. Ethnic strife soon led to military coups, and military groups ruled the country 1966–79 and from 1983 to the present. Civil war between the central government and the former eastern region, Biafra, in 1967–70 ended in Biafra's surrender after the death by starvation of a million Biafrans. In 1991 the capital was moved from Lagos to Abuja. The government's execution of Ken Saro-Wiwa in 1995 led to international sanctions, and civilian rule was finally reestablished in 1999. By far the most populous nation in Africa, Nigeria suffers from rapid population increase, political instability, foreign debt, slow economic growth, a high rate of violent crime, and rampant government corruption.

night fighter Fighter aircraft with special sighting, sensing, and navigating equipment enabling it to function at night. In a day fighter, weight and space are saved by eliminating this special equipment.

Night of the Long Knives (June 30, 1934) Purge of Nazi leaders by Adolf Hitler. Fearing that the paramilitary SA had become too powerful, Hitler ordered his elite SS guards to murder the organization's leaders, including Ernst Rohm. Also killed that night were hundreds of other perceived opponents of Hitler, including Kurt von Schleicher and Gregor Strasser.

nighthawk Any of several species of North and South American birds in the whippoorwill family (Caprimulgidae) that are buff, reddish, or grayish brown, usually with light spots or patches, and 6–14 in. (15–35 cm) long. They fly about at night, especially at evening and dawn, catching flying insects in their mouth. The common nighthawk *(Chordeiles minor),* or bullbat, inhabits most of North America, migrating to South America in winter. It is about 8–12 in. (20–30 cm) long and grayish brown, with a white throat and wing patches. It has a sharp nasal call. During courtship it dives swiftly, creating audible whirring sounds.

nightingale Any of several small Old World thrushes (family Turdidae) renowned for their song. The name refers in particular to the Eurasian nightingale *(Erithacus,* or *Luscinia, megarhynchos),* a brown bird, 6.5 in. (16 cm) long, with a rufous tail. It sings day and night from perches in shubbery. Its strong and varied song, with prominent crescendo effects, has been regarded for centuries throughout Europe and Asia as the most beautiful of all birdsongs. The thrush nightingale, or sprosser *(E. luscinia),* is a closely related, more northerly species with slightly darker plumage. The term is also applied to other birds with rich songs (e.g., the wood thrush).

Eurasian nightingale (*Erithacus megarhynchos*).
H. REINHARD–BRUCE COLEMAN INC.

Nightingale, Florence (1820–1910) British (Italian-born) nurse, founder of trained nursing as a profession for women. As a volunteer nurse, she was put in charge of nursing the military in Turkey during the Crimean War. Her first concern was sanitation: patients' quarters were infested with rats and fleas, and the water allowance was one pint per head per day for all purposes. She used her own finances to purchase supplies. She also spent many hours in the wards; her night rounds giving personal care to the wounded established her image as the "Lady with the Lamp." Her efforts to improve soldiers' welfare led to the Army Medical School and a Sanitary Department in India. She started the first scientifically based nursing school, was instrumental in setting up training for midwives and nurses in workhouse infirmaries, and helped reform workhouses. She was the first woman awarded the Order of Merit (1907).

nightjar *or* **goatsucker** Any of about 60–70 species of birds (family Caprimulgidae) found almost worldwide in temperate to tropical regions. The name is sometimes applied to all birds in the order Caprimulgiformes. (The name goatsucker derives from an old belief that they sucked goat's milk at night.) Nightjars are gray, brown, or reddish brown. They eat flying insects at night. The common nightjar *(Caprimulgus europaeus)* has a flat head; wide, bristle-fringed mouth; large eyes; and soft plumage that results in noiseless flight. It is about 12 in. (30 cm) long. Its North American relatives include the nighthawk and whippoorwill.

nightshade family Family Solanaceae, composed of at least 2,400 species of flowering plants in about 95 genera. Though found worldwide, the nightshades are most abundant in tropical Latin America. Many nightshades are economically important food or medicinal plants. The medicinally significant nightshades are potent sources of such alkaloids as nicotine, atropine, and scopolamine; they include deadly nightshade (belladonna), jimsonweed (Datura stramonium), henbane, and mandrake. The most important nightshades are the potato, eggplant, tomato, garden pepper, tobacco, and many garden ornamentals, including petunias. The genus *Solanum* contains almost half the species in the family. The species usually called nightshade in North America and England is *S. dulcamara,* also called bittersweet and woody nightshade.

nihilism \'nī-ə-ˌli-zəm, 'nē-ə-ˌli-zəm\ Any of various philosophical positions that deny that there are objective foundations for human value systems. In 19th-century Russia, the term was applied to a philosophy of skepticism that negated all forms of aestheticism and advocated utilitarianism and scientific rationalism; it was popularized through the figure of Bazarov in Ivan Turgenev's *Fathers and Sons* (1862). Rejecting the social sciences, classical philosophical systems, and the established social order, nihilism negated all authority exercised by the state, the church, or the family and based its belief on nothing but scientific truth. It gradually became associated with political terror and degenerated into a philosophy of violence.

Nijinska \nə-'zhin-skə\, **Bronislava (Fominitshna)** (1891–1972) Russian-U.S. dancer, choreographer, and teacher. She trained at the Imperial Ballet school in St. Petersburg, and joined the Mariinsky Theater company in 1908. She danced with the Ballets Russes from 1909 and joined the company with her brother, Vaslav Nijinsky, in 1911. She choreographed several ballets for the company, including *Les noces* (1923), *Le train bleu* (1924), and *Les biches* (1924). During the 1920s and 1930s she created works for other companies, including her own (1932–37), including *Hamlet* (1934) and *Les cent baisers* (1935). She moved to Los Angeles in 1938, where she opened a school, and continued to work as a guest choreographer into the early 1960s.

Nijinsky \nə-'zhin-skē\, **Vaslav (Fomich)** (1889–1950) Russian ballet dancer. After early lessons from his parents, famous dancers with their own company, he and his sister, Bronislava Nijinska, trained further in St. Petersburg, and he joined the Mariinsky Theater company in 1907. With his spectacular leaps and unrivaled grace, he was an immediate success, dancing leading roles in *Giselle, Swan Lake,* and *Sleeping Beauty,* often with Anna Pavlova and Tamara Karsavina. In 1909 he joined the new Ballets Russes and created many roles in Michel Fokine's ballets, including *Carnaval, Les sylphides, Le spectre de la rose, Petrushka,* and *Daphnis and Chloe.* In 1912–13 he choreographed *The Afternoon of a Faun, Jeux,* and *The Rite of Spring,* all of which caused scandals. His marriage in 1913 led to his dismissal from the company by his mentor Sergey Diaghilev. He continued to perform but to less success. His intensifying mental illness led to his retirement in 1919, and he lived mostly in mental institutions in Switzerland, France, and England until his death. His legendary reputation is unequaled in the history of dance.

Nijinsky in *Spectre de la rose.*
BY COURTESY OF THE DANCE COLLECTION, THE NEW YORK PUBLIC LIBRARY AT LINCOLN CENTER, ROGER PRYOR DODGE COLLECTION

Nijmegen \'nā-ˌmā-kə\, **Treaties of** (1678–79) Peace treaties that ended the Franco-Dutch War. In the treaty between France and the Dutch Republic, France agreed to return Maastricht and to suspend the anti-Dutch tariff of 1667. In the treaty between France and Spain, Spain gave up regions to France that gave it a protected northeastern border and secured the safety of Paris. By negotiating separate treaties, France gained advantages over its enemies in the war.

Nike \'nī-kē, 'nē-kā\ Greek goddess of victory. She was the daughter of the giant Pallas and the river STYX. Nike was originally an attribute of both ATHENA and ZEUS, represented as a small figure carried in their hand. She gradually came to be recognized as a mediator between gods and mortals, and was frequently shown carrying a palm branch, wreath, or staff as the messenger of victory. When depicted on her own, she was often a winged figure hovering over the victor in a competition. At Rome she was worshiped as Victoria.

Nike, sculpture from a bronze vessel, probably made in a Greek city of southern Italy, c. 490 BC; in the British Museum.

BY COURTESY OF THE TRUSTEES OF THE BRITISH MUSEUM

Nike Inc. U.S. sportswear company. It was founded in 1964 as Blue Ribbon Sports by Bill Bowerman (born 1911), a track-and-field coach at the University of Oregon, and his former student Phil Knight (born 1938). They opened their first retail outlet in 1966, launched the Nike-brand shoe in 1972, and renamed the company Nike Inc. in 1978. In 1979 it claimed 50% of the U.S. running-shoe market. In 1980 the company went public. Part of Nike's success has owed to endorsements by such athletes as JOHN MCENROE and MICHAEL JORDAN. In the 1990s the company suffered from revelations about conditions in its overseas factories.

Nikolais \'nē-kə-lī\, **Alwin** (1910–1993) U.S. dancer, choreographer, composer, and designer. Born in Southington, Conn., he studied modern dance with various teachers, including HANYA HOLM, whose assistant he later became. In 1948 he became director of the Henry Street Playhouse in New York, and in 1951 formed the Nikolais Dance Theater to present his productions of integrated motion, sound, shape, and color. The group toured in the U.S. and Europe. Nikolais directed the Center for Contemporary Dance in Angers, France (1979–81). In 1989 his company merged with another to form Nikolais and Murray Louis Dance Company.

Nikolais.

MARTHA SWOPE

Nikon \'nyē-kən\ *orig.* **Nikita Minin** (1605–1681) Leader of the Russian Orthodox Church. Born a peasant, he rose through the ranks of the priesthood to become patriarch of Moscow and all Russia in 1652. Granted sovereign power during the absence of Czar ALEXIS on military campaigns, he purged Russian religious books and practices of what he considered corruptions and exiled his opponents. His reforms so troubled many believers that they led to a schism in the church (see OLD BELIEVERS) as well as widespread disaffection (see DOUKHOBORS), and his high-handedness alienated Alexis. In 1666 a council of Greek patriarchs convened by Alexis stripped Nikon of all priestly functions but retained his reforms.

Nile, Battle of the (August 1, 1798) Battle between the British fleet under HORATIO NELSON and French Revolutionary forces at Abu Qir Bay, near Alexandria, Egypt. In a plan to constrict British trade routes by invading Egypt, NAPOLEON ordered the French fleet to sail from its port of Toulon to Alexandria. The French eluded the British fleet to reach Abu Qir Bay, where they anchored in a defensive line. Nelson discovered the French at twilight and ordered an immediate attack. In an all-night battle, the British destroyed or captured all but two of the 13 French ships. The decisive victory isolated Napoleon's army in Egypt and secured British control of the Mediterranean.

Nile perch Large food and game fish (family Latidae) found in the Nile and other African rivers and lakes. The Nile perch *(Lates niloticus)* has a large mouth and is greenish or brownish above, silvery below. It grows to about 6 ft (1.8 m) and weighs 300 lbs (140 kg). It has a slender body, a protruding lower jaw, a rounded tail, and two dorsal fins. Other species in the same family are found in African river systems and in Asian and Australian estuaries and coastal waters. The members of the family are sometimes classified with SNOOKS (family Centropomidae).

Nile River *Arabic* **Al-Bahr** \al-'bär\ River, eastern and North Africa. The longest river in the world, it is about 4,160 mi (6,693 km) long from its remotest headstream and 3,473 mi (5,588 km) from Lake VICTORIA to the Mediterranean Sea. It flows generally north from eastern Africa through Uganda, Sudan, and Egypt. It receives major tributaries, including the Blue Nile and the ATBARA RIVER before entering Lake NASSER near the Egypt–Sudan border. After the ASWAN HIGH DAM impounds the lake, it continues northward to its delta near CAIRO, where it empties into the Mediterranean. The first use of the Nile for irrigation in Egypt began when seeds were sown in the mud left after its annual flood waters had subsided. It has supported continuous human settlement for at least 5,000 years, with canals and waterworks built in the 19th century. The Aswan High Dam, built 1959–70, provides protection and hydroelectric power for both crops and humans. The Nile is also a vital waterway for the transport of people and goods.

Nilo-Saharan languages \ˌnī-lō-sə-'hä-rən\ Hypothesized superfamily of perhaps 115 African languages spoken by more than 27 million people from Mali west to Ethiopia and from southernmost Egypt south to Tanzania. The concept of Nilo-Saharan as a single stock combining a number of earlier groupings was introduced in 1963 by JOSEPH H. GREENBERG; most Africanists accept it as a working hypothesis. Greenberg's scheme, largely upheld by later scholars, divided Nilo-Saharan into two large families, Central Sudanic and Eastern Sudanic, and a number of small families and single languages. Among the latter are Songhai, spoken by over 2 million people around the bend of the Niger River in Mali and Niger, and Kanuri, spoken by about 4.5 million in northeastern Nigeria and adjacent Chad and Niger. Central Sudanic comprises languages of southern Chad, southern Sudan, and northeastern Congo (Zaire). Eastern Sudanic includes the Nubian family (including the only Nilo-Saharan language with an ancient written tradition), spoken along the Nile in northern Sudan and southern Egypt, and the Nilotic languages, spoken by about 14 million people (see NILOTES), including the DINKA, NUER, LUO, Turkana, Kalenjin, and MASAI.

Nilotes \'nī-lə-ˌtēz\ Cluster of eastern central African peoples living in southern Sudan, northern Uganda, and western Kenya. The name refers to the region of the Upper Nile and its tributaries, where most of them live. Nilotic languages belong to the eastern Sudanic group of the NILO-SAHARAN family. A notable shared physical characteristic is their average height, men commonly reaching 7 ft (210 cm). The Acholi, DINKA, LUO, MASAI, Nandi, NUER, and Shilluk are classed as Nilotes. Altogether they number about 7 million.

Nilsson, Birgit *orig.* **Märta Birgit Svennsson** (born 1918) Swedish soprano. She made her debut in Stockholm in 1946, and she sang her first Brünnhilde in a complete *Ring* in Munich (1954–55). She went on to sing most of the major Wagnerian soprano roles at Bayreuth between 1959 and 1970, acclaimed as the greatest Wagnerian soprano of her time for the astonishing power and capacities of her steely voice. From 1959 she was a popular fixture at the Metropolitan Opera, as R. STRAUSS's Elektra and Salome, G. PUCCINI's Turandot, and LUDWIG VAN BEETHOVEN's Leonora, in addition to her Wagnerian repertoire, until she retired in 1984.

Nimbarka (fl. 12th or 13th century?) Indian yogi and founder of the devotional sect called Nimbarkas or Nimandi. Little is known of his life except that he was a Brahman and a notable astronomer. Like RAMANUJA, he believed that the creator god and the souls he created were distinct but shared in the same substance, and he stressed devotion to KRISHNA as the only means of liberation from the cycle of rebirth. The Nimanda sect flourished in the 13th–14th century in eastern India.

Nimeiri \nə-'mer-ē\, **Gaafar Mohamed el-** (born 1930) President of Sudan (1971–85). In 1969 he helped overthrow the civilian regime of Ismail al-Azhari. Nimeiri's own government was temporarily ousted in 1971, but he was returned to office following a plebiscite. He granted autonomy to the Southern Sudan in 1972, inaugurated one of the world's largest sugar-refinery projects (1981), and sought to develop agriculture. His attempts to impose Islamic law were resisted by Christians and others in the south, which led to his fall from power.

Nîmes \'nēm\ *ancient* **Nemausus** City (pop., 1990: 134,000), southern France. It was the capital of a Gaulish tribe that submitted to Rome in 121 BC. AUGUSTUS founded a new city there, and for five centuries it was one of the principal cities of Roman GAUL. It was plundered by the VANDALS and VISIGOTHS in the 5th century AD and occupied by the MOORS in the 8th century. It passed to the French crown in 1229. Damaged in 1815 during fighting between royalists and Bonapartists, it returned to prosperity with the coming of the railways in the late 19th century. It is noted for its Roman remains, including an amphitheater, an aqueduct, and the Maison Carée (an ancient temple restored in 1789).

Tour Magne, a ruined Roman tower, Nîmes, Fr.
ART RESOURCE—EB INC.

Nimitz \'ni-mits\, **Chester W(illiam)** (1885–1966) U.S. naval officer. Born in Fredericksburg, Texas, he graduated from Annapolis in 1905 and served in World War I with the U.S. Atlantic submarine force. He rose to become chief of the navy's bureau of navigation in 1939. After the Japanese attack on Pearl Harbor, he was made commander in chief of the Pacific fleet, which won the battles of MIDWAY and the CORAL SEA. He led later naval operations in the Pacific that ended with the Japanese surrender, signed aboard his flagship, the USS *Missouri.* He served as chief of naval operations 1945–47.

Nimrud See CALAH

Nin \'nēn, 'nin\, **Anaïs** (1903–1977) French-U.S. author. Daughter of the Cuban composer Joaquín Nin (1878–1949), she began her literary career in Paris in 1932. In the 1940s she moved to New York, where she published novels and short stories at her own expense. Her writing, including the novel *Cities of the Interior* (5 vols., 1959), shows the influence of Surrealism and psychoanalysis. She won late recognition in 1966 with the publication of the first volume of her personal diaries; seven more volumes followed. Her account of her long incestuous relationship with her father was published posthumously. Though admired by some, her work has been criticized as narcissistic and pretentious.

Niña, La See LA NIÑA

9-11 attacks See SEPTEMBER 11 ATTACKS

Ninety-five Theses Propositions for debate on the question of INDULGENCES, written by MARTIN LUTHER and, according to legend, posted on the door of the Castle Church in Wittenberg, Germany, on October 31, 1517. This event is now seen as the beginning of the Protestant REFORMATION. The theses were written in response to the selling of indulgences to pay for the rebuilding of ST. PETER'S BASILICA in Rome. They represented an implicit criticism of papal policy and stressed the spiritual character of the Christian faith. Widely circulated, they aroused much controversy. In 1518 Luther published a Latin manuscript with explanations of the theses.

Nineveh \'ni-nə-və\ *ancient* **Ninus** Oldest and most populous city of the ancient ASSYRIAN empire, on the eastern bank of the TIGRIS RIVER opposite modern MOSUL, Iraq. Its greatest development was under SENNACHERIB and ASHURBANIPAL in the 7th century BC. It was captured and destroyed by Nabopolassar of BABYLONIA and his allies, the Scythians and Medes, in 612 BC. Excavations by A. H. Layard in 1845 revealed palaces, a library, city walls, and many gates and buildings.

Ningxia (Huizu) *or* **Ningsia (Huisu)** \'niŋ-'shyä\ Autonomous region (pop., 2000 est.: 5,620,000), northern China. It is bounded by GANSU, NEI MONGGOL, and SHANXI. China's GREAT WALL runs along its northeastern boundary. The capital is YINCHUAN. It is nearly coextensive with the ancient kingdom of the TANGUT people, whose capital was captured by GENGHIS KHAN in the early 13th century. The region is mostly desert and is sparsely settled, but the vast plain of the HUANG HE (Yellow River) in the north has been irrigated for centuries; over the years many canals have been built.

Ninhursag \nin-'kůr-,säg\ In MESOPOTAMIAN RELIGION, the city goddess of Adab and of KISH. Worshiped especially by the herders of northern Mesopotamia, she was the goddess of the stony, rocky ground, and she had the power to produce wildlife in the foothills and in the desert. A mother figure, she was the goddess of birth; she also appeared as a sorrowing mother in her lament for her son, a young colt. Her husband was the god Shulpae, and among their children was Mululil, a dying god whose death was mourned in yearly rites.

Niño, El See EL NIÑO

Ninsun \'nin-,sůn\ In MESOPOTAMIAN RELIGION, the city goddess of Kullab. Worshiped especially by herders in southern Mesopotamia, she was originally represented as a cow and was considered to be the divine power behind all the qualities that herders wanted in their cattle. She was also represented in human form and could give birth to human offspring. Her son was the wild bull Dumuzi, whom she lamented in a yearly ritual, and her husband was the legendary hero Lugalbanda. Her Sumerian counterparts included NINHURSAG.

Ninurta \ni-'nůr-tä\ In MESOPOTAMIAN RELIGION, the city god of Girsu. The son of Enlil and Ninlil, he was the god of thunder and of the spring rains and floods as well as the god of the plow. His original name was Imdugud ("Raincloud"), and his earliest form was that of the thundercloud represented as an enormous black bird roaring its thunder cry from a lion's head. Eventually Ninurta was given human form, and his original shape was assigned to his ancient enemy. His festival marked the beginning of the plowing season.

Niobe \nī-'ō-bē\ In GREEK MYTHOLOGY, the prototype of the bereaved mother. The daughter of TANTALUS, she married King Amphion of Thebes and bore him six sons and six daughters. She made the mistake of boasting of her fertility to the Titaness Leto, who had only two children, APOLLO and ARTEMIS. As punishment for her pride, Apollo killed all of Niobe's sons and Artemis all her daughters. Niobe was so overwhelmed with grief that the gods turned her into a rock on Mount Sipylus (near modern Izmir, Turkey), which weeps endlessly as its snow melts.

Apollo and Artemis killing the children of Niobe, red-figure calyx krater by the Niobid Painter, c. 455–450 BC; in the Louvre, Paris.
CLICHE MUSEES NATIONAUX, PARIS

Niobid Painter \nī-'ō-bid\ (fl. c. 475–450 BC) Greek vase painter, named for a calyx krater showing the death of the children of NIOBE. Because the Niobid Painter made a deliberate effort to express space and depth by arranging figures on different levels, the vessel is thought to reflect the innovative technique of the now lost mural paintings of POLYGNOTUS.

Niobrara River \,nī-ə-'brar-ə\ River, Wyoming and Nebraska. Flowing east across Wyoming's high plains and Nebraska's sandhills and low plains, it joins the MISSOURI RIVER at the village of Niobrara, Neb., at the South Dakota line. It is 431 mi (694 km) long. The AGATE FOSSIL BEDS NATIONAL MONUMENT is located on the river, north of Scottsbluff, Neb.

Nipigon \'ni-pi-,gän\, **Lake** Lake, Ontario. Located north of Lake SUPERIOR and northeast of Thunder Bay, it is about 70 mi (110 km) long and 50 mi (80 km) wide and has an area of 1,870 sq mi (4,840 sq km). It lies at an elevation of 1,050 ft (320 m) and has maximum depths of 540 ft (165 m). Its Indian name means "deep, clear water." It is studded with many wooded islands, and large bays characterize its shoreline. Its outlet is the Nipigon River which flows into Lake Superior.

Nipissing \'ni-pə-,siŋ\, **Lake** Lake, southeastern Ontario. Located midway between the OTTAWA RIVER and GEORGIAN BAY, it is 50 mi (80 km) long and 30 mi (48 km) wide, with an area of 321 sq mi (832 sq km). A remnant of glacial Lake Algonquin, it contains many islands. The French River drains the lake as it flows west into Georgian Bay. It was discovered by Étienne Brûlé c. 1610 and was later a fur-trading route linking the Ottawa River with the upper GREAT LAKES.

Nippur \ni-'pùr\ Ancient city of MESOPOTAMIA, now in southeastern Iraq, southeast of the site of BABYLON. It was originally on the EUPHRATES RIVER, whose course later changed. By 2500 BC it was the center of worship of the important Sumerian storm god Enlil (see SUMER). Parthian construction (see PARTHIA) later buried Enlil's sanctuary, and the city fell into decay in the 3rd century AD. It was abandoned in the 12th or 13th century.

Excavations have revealed temples, a ZIGGURAT, and thousands of clay tablets that are a primary source of knowledge of ancient Sumerian civilization. Also uncovered were an Akkadian tomb (see AKKAD) and a large temple to the Mesopotamian goddess of healing.

Female figure, made of gypsum, with a gold mask that stood at a temple altar in Nippur, c. 2700 BC; in the Iraq Museum, Baghdad.

BY COURTESY OF THE IRAQ MUSEUM, BAGHDAD; PHOTOGRAPH, DAVID LEES

Nirenberg \'nir-ən-ˌbərg\, **Marshall Warren** (born 1927) U.S. biochemist. Born in New York City, he received his PhD from the University of Michigan. He demonstrated that each possible triplet (codon) of the four different kinds of nitrogen-containing bases found in DNA and (in some viruses) in RNA (with three exceptions) ultimately causes the incorporation of a specific amino acid into a cell protein. His research earned him a Nobel Prize in 1968, which he shared with ROBERT WILLIAM HOLLEY and HAR GOBIND KHORANA, whose work, like Nirenberg's, helped show how genetic instructions in the cell nucleus control the composition of proteins.

nirvana \nir-'vä-nə\ (Sanskrit: "Extinction") In Indian religious thought, the transcendent state of freedom achieved by the extinction of desire and of individual consciousness. Nirvana is the supreme goal of the disciplines of MEDITATION, particularly in BUDDHISM. Release from desire (and consequent suffering) and the continuous round of rebirths constitutes enlightenment, or the experience of nirvana. THERAVADA Buddhism conceives of nirvana as tranquillity and peace; MAHAYANA Buddhism equates it with *sunyata* (emptiness), *dharma-kaya* (the essence of the Buddha), and *dharma-datu* (ultimate reality).

Nis *or* **Nish** \'nēsh\ *ancient* **Naissus** *or* **Nissa** City (pop., 1991: 175,000), southeast of BELGRADE, Yugoslavia. The ancient Roman city was mentioned by PTOLEMY in the 2nd century AD. It was the birthplace of CONSTANTINE THE GREAT (c. 280), who adorned it with many buildings. Bomb damage in World War II and postwar construction erased much of its Turko-Byzantine style. It was held at various periods by Bulgarians, Hungarians, and Turks. During the Turkish period it became an important station on the route from Istanbul to Hungary. It was ceded to Serbia by the Treaty of Berlin in 1878 and was its capital until 1901. It is a railroad junction and commercial center.

Nishapur See NEYSHABUR

Nissan Motor Co., Ltd. \'nē-'sän\ Japanese automaker and industrial corporation. Headquartered in Tokyo, Nissan manufactures cars, trucks, and buses as well as communications satellites, pleasure boats, and machinery. Formed from the merger of two smaller firms in 1925, it adopted its present name in 1934. In World War II the company produced military vehicles; seized by Allied forces in 1945, it did not return to full production until 1955. Nissan's production and sales grew rapidly after it entered the world market in the 1960s, and it established assembly plants in several countries, including Australia, Germany, Mexico, and the U.S. It declined in the 1990s, and in 1999 the French automaker Renault bought a 37% stake in the company.

NIST See BUREAU OF STANDARDS

niter See SALTPETER

nitrate Any SALT or ESTER of NITRIC ACID (HNO_3). The salts are inorganic compounds with IONIC BONDS, containing the nitrate ION (NO_3^-) and any CATION. Many, particularly ammonium nitrate, are used as agricultural fertilizers (see SALTPETER). Their runoff in surface water and groundwater can cause serious illness in humans. The esters are organic compounds with COVALENT BONDS, having the structure $R—O—NO_2$, in which R represents an organic combining group such as methyl, ethyl, or phenyl.

nitric acid \'nī-trik\ Inorganic compound, colorless, fuming, highly corrosive liquid, chemical formula HNO_3. A common laboratory reagent, it is important in the manufacture of fertilizers and explosives (including NITROGLYCERIN), as well as in organic syntheses, metallurgy, ore flotation, and reprocessing of spent nuclear fuel. A strong ACID, it is toxic and can cause severe burns. It attacks most metals and is used for etching steel and photoengraving.

nitric oxide Colorless, toxic gas (NO), formed from nitrogen and oxygen by the action of electric sparks or high temperatures or, more conveniently, by the action of dilute nitric acid on copper or mercury. First prepared c. 1620 by JAN B. HELMONT, it was first studied in 1772 by JOSEPH PRIESTLEY, who called it "nitrous air." An industrial procedure for the manufacture of hydroxylamine is based on the reaction of nitric oxide with hydrogen in the presence of a catalyst. The formation of nitric oxide from nitric acid and mercury is applied in a volumetric method of analysis for nitric acid or its salts.

nitrifying bacteria \'nī-trə-ˌfī-iŋ\ Small group of oxygen-requiring BACTERIA that use nitrogen as an energy source. These microorganisms are important in the NITROGEN CYCLE as converters of soil AMMONIA to NITRATES, compounds usable by plants. The nitrification process requires two distinct groups: bacteria that convert ammonia to NITRITES, and bacteria that convert nitrites to nitrates. In agriculture, irrigation with dilute solutions of ammonia results in an increase in soil nitrates through the action of nitrifying bacteria. See also DENITRIFYING BACTERIA.

nitrite \'nī-ˌtrīt\ Any SALT or ESTER of nitrous acid (HNO_2). The salts are inorganic compounds with IONIC BONDS, containing the nitrite ION (NO_2^-) and any CATION. The esters are organic compounds with COVALENT BONDS, having the structure R—O—N—O, in which R represents a carbon-containing combining group and the BONDING is from carbon to oxygen. These covalent nitrites are constitutional ISOMERS (see ISOMERISM) of the NITRO COMPOUNDS, NITRIC ACID derivatives ($R—NO_2$), in which the bonding is from carbon to nitrogen. Nitrites are used as food preservatives and color enhancers, though they are so toxic they have caused deaths and combine with AMINES to produce CARCINOGENS. They are used in medicine to dilate blood vessels.

nitro compound \'nī-ˌtrō\ Any of a class of chemical COMPOUNDS in which the nitro group ($—NO_2$) forms part of the molecular structure. The most common examples are organic compounds, ISOMERS of NITRITE esters in which a carbon atom is linked by a COVALENT BOND to the nitro group's nitrogen atom. Many nitro compounds are commercially used as explosives, solvents, or raw materials and chemical intermediates. They are generally made by a reaction between NITRIC ACID and an organic compound.

nitrogen Gaseous chemical ELEMENT, chemical symbol N, atomic number 7. A colorless, odorless, tasteless GAS, it makes up 78% of the earth's atmosphere and is a constituent of all living matter. As the almost inert diatomic molecule N_2, it is useful as an inert atmosphere or to dilute other gases. Nitrogen is commercially produced by DISTILLATION of liquefied air. NITROGEN FIXATION, achieved naturally by soil microbes and industrially by the HABER-BOSCH PROCESS, converts it to water-soluble compounds (including AMMONIA and NITRATES). Ammonia is the starting material for most other nitrogen compounds (especially nitrates and NITRITES), whose main uses are in agricultural fertilizers and explosives. Nitrogen forms several OXIDES: NITROUS OXIDE; NITRIC OXIDE (NO), recently found to play key roles in physiology; and nitrogen dioxide (NO_2) and other forms (including N_2O_3 and N_2O_5) notorious for causing air pollution, especially when acted on by sunlight. Other compounds include the nitrides, exceptionally hard materials made from nitrogen and a metal; CYANIDES; azides, used in detonators and percussion caps; and thousands of organic compounds containing nitrogen in FUNCTIONAL GROUPS or in a linear or ring structure (see HETEROCYCLIC COMPOUND). See also NITROGEN CYCLE.

nitrogen cycle Circulation of NITROGEN in various forms throughout nature. Nitrogen is essential to life, but most is inert and unavailable in AIR. NITROGEN FIXATION by microbes turns this nitrogen into NITRATES and other compounds, which plants or algae assimilate into their tissues. Animals that eat plants in turn incorporate the compounds into their own tissues. Microbes decompose the remains and waste of all living things into AMMONIA (ammonification); the ammonia may leave the soil through vaporization into the air or leaching into water or be converted through nitrogen fixation so that the cycle can start again. Once fixed from the air, nitrogen can go through the cycle repeatedly without reverting to the gaseous state. In waterlogged, oxygen-deficient soils, there are bacteria that convert nitrates into free nitrogen (denitrification).

nitrogen fixation Any natural or industrial process that causes free NITROGEN in the air to combine chemically with other elements to form more reactive nitrogen compounds such as AMMONIA, NITRATES, or NITRITES. Soil microorganisms (e.g., *Rhizobium* bacteria living in root nodules of LEGUMES) are responsible for more than 90% of all nitrogen fixation. Though nitrogen is part of all PROTEINS and essential in both plant and animal METABOLISM, plants and animals cannot use elemental nitrogen such as the nitrogen gas (N_2) that forms 80% of the atmosphere. Symbiotic nitrogen-fixing bacteria invade the root hairs of host plants, where they multiply and stimulate the formation of root nodules, enlargements of plant cells and bacteria in close association. Within the nodules the bacteria convert free nitrogen to nitrates, which the host plant uses for its development. Nitrogen fixation by bacteria associated with legumes is of prime importance in agriculture. Before the use of synthetic FERTILIZERS in the industrial countries, usable nitrogen was supplied as MANURE and by CROP ROTATION that included a legume crop.

nitrogen narcosis *or* **nitrogen euphoria** *or* **raptures of the deep** Effects of breathing nitrogen under increased pressure. In divers breathing compressed air, nitrogen saturates the nervous system, causing an intoxicating light-headed, numb feeling, then slowed reasoning and dexterity, and then emotional instability and irrationality. Severe cases progress to convulsions and blackout. Susceptibility varies, and severity increases with depth, but there are no aftereffects. Physical function remains normal, and divers may be unaware of the growing irrationality that can cause them to rise too fast (see DECOMPRESSION SICKNESS) or let their air supply run out. Helium, which dissolves less easily in body tissues, is substituted for nitrogen for deep dives.

nitroglycerin \ˌnī-trə-ˈgli-sə-rən\ *or* **glyceryl trinitrate** Organic compound, powerful explosive and ingredient of most forms of DYNAMITE. It is a colorless, oily, somewhat toxic liquid with a sweet, burning taste. Its safe use as a blasting explosive became possible after ALFRED P. NOBEL developed dynamite in the 1860s with an inert porous material (moderator) such as charcoal or diatomaceous earth. Nitroglycerin is also used in a mixture in rocket propellants. In medicine, it is used to dilate blood vessels, especially to ease ANGINA PECTORIS.

nitrous oxide \ˈnī-trəs\ *or* **laughing gas** Inorganic compound, one of the OXIDES of NITROGEN. A colorless gas with a pleasantly sweetish odor and taste, it has an ANALGESIC effect when inhaled, and is used as an ANESTHETIC (often called just "gas") in dentistry and surgery. This effect is preceded by mild hysteria, sometimes with laughter, hence the name "laughing gas." It is also used as a propellant in food aerosols and as a leak detector.

Nivernais \ˌnē-vər-ˈnā\ Historical region, central France. Originally part of BURGUNDY, it became a county c. 10th century. FRANCIS I of France made it a duchy in 1539 for Francis of Cleves. In 1659 it was sold to Cardinal MAZARIN. His descendants possessed it until the FRENCH REVOLUTION, when it was the last great FIEF to be reunited to the French crown. During the ANCIEN RÉGIME it was administered from Nevers.

Nixon, Richard M(ilhous) (1913–1994) 37th president of the U.S. (1969–74). Born in Yorba Linda, Cal., he studied law at Duke University and practiced in California 1937–42. After serving in World War II, he was elected to the U.S. House of Representatives in 1947, employing harsh campaign tactics. He came to national attention with the ALGER HISS case and was elected to the Senate in 1950, again following a bitter campaign. He won the vice presidency in 1952 on a Republican ticket with DWIGHT D. EISENHOWER; they were reelected easily in 1956. As presidential candidate in 1960, he lost narrowly to JOHN F. KENNEDY. After failing to win the 1962 California gubernatorial race, he retired from politics and moved to New York to practice law. He reentered politics by running for president in 1968, and he defeated HUBERT H. HUMPHREY with his "southern strategy" of seeking votes from southern and western conservatives in both parties. As president, he began to gradually withdraw U.S. military forces in an effort to end the VIETNAM WAR while ordering the secret bombing of North Vietnamese military centers in Laos and Cambodia. Attacks on North Vietnamese sanctuaries in Cambodia drew widespread protest. Economic problems caused by inflation made the U.S. budget deficit the largest to date, and in 1971 Nixon established unprecedented peacetime controls on wages and prices. He won reelection in 1972 with a landslide victory over GEORGE MCGOVERN. Assisted by HENRY A. KISSINGER, he concluded the Vietnam War. He reopened communications with Communist China and made a state visit there. On his visit to the Soviet Union, the first by a U.S. president, he signed the bilateral SALT agreements. The WATERGATE SCANDAL overshadowed his second term; his complicity in efforts to cover up his involvement and the likelihood of impeachment led to his becoming, in August 1974, the first president to resign from office. Though never convicted of wrongdoing, he was pardoned by his successor, GERALD FORD. He retired to write his memoirs and books on foreign policy.

Nizam al-Mulk \nē-ˈzám-u̇l-ˈmülk\ *orig.* **Abu Ali Hasan ibn Ali** (c. 1018–1092) Persian VIZIER of the Turkish SELJUQ DYNASTY sultans. He worked for the GHAZNAVID DYNASTY before serving ALP-ARSLAN as governor of Khorasan. In 1063 he was made VIZIER, a position he occupied for 30 years, serving Alp-Arslan's son Malik-Shah from the latter's ascension. Believing that a ruler's power should be absolute and that the ruler should preserve the kingdom's stability and traditions, he recorded his views in the *Seyasat-hameh* ("Book of Government"). He is seen as the quintessential vizier. He was assassinated after falling out of favor with Malik-Shah.

Nizami See NEZAMI

Nizam's Dominions See HYDERABAD

Nizhny Novgorod \ˈnizh-nē-ˈnȯv-gə-rət\ *formerly (1932–90)* **Gorky** City (pop., 1996 est.: 1,400,000), central Russia. It is located on the southern bank of the VOLGA RIVER at its confluence with the OKA RIVER. Founded in 1221, it was annexed to MOSCOW in 1392. It was strategically important in the Russian conquest of the Volga through the mid-16th century. In 1932 it was renamed for MAXIM GORKY, who was born there. Under the Soviet regime it was a place of internal exile for ANDREY SAKHAROV. The city has several 16th–17th-century buildings and is one of Russia's major industrial centers.

Njáls saga \ˈnyau̇ls\ *or* ***Njála*** \ˈnyau̇-lä\ *or* ***Burnt Njáll*** \ˈbərnt-ˈnyau̇l\ ICELANDERS' SAGA, one of the longest and perhaps the finest. Set in a society where blood ties impose inescapable obligations and honor demands vengeance for past injuries, it presents the most comprehensive picture of Icelandic life in the heroic age. Its overriding mood is tragic pessimism. Its vividly drawn characters, who range from comic to sinister, include two heroes—Gunnar (Gunther), a brave, guileless, generous youth, and Njál, a wise and prudent man endowed with prophetic gifts.

Njörd \ˈnyȯrd, ˈnyȯrth\ Norse god of the wind and of the sea and its riches. His aid was invoked in seafaring and hunting, and he was the god of prosperity. He was the father of FREYR and FREYJA by his sister. Njörd's tribe, the VANIR, gave him as a hostage to the rival tribe of AESIR, and the giantess Skadi chose him as her husband. The marriage failed because Njörd preferred to live in Nóatún, his home by the sea, whereas Skadi was happier in her father's mountain dwelling place. Several traditions hold that Njörd was a divine ruler of the Swedes.

Nkomo \en-ˈkō-mō\, **Joshua (Mqabuko Nyongolo)** (1917–1999) Zimbabwean (formerly Rhodesian) black nationalist. Nkomo helped lead the guerrilla war against white rule in Rhodesia, but his forces played a less important role than those of ROBERT MUGABE. As leader of the Zimbabwe African People's Union (ZAPU), he became Mugabe's longtime rival. They participated in a coalition government 1980–82, but Nkomo was removed following a breach between them. ZAPU and Mugabe's Zimbabwe African National Union (ZANU) merged in 1987 to form ZANU–Patriotic Front, and Nkomo became a vice president in Mugabe's government in 1990.

Nkrumah \en-ˈkrü-mə\, **Kwame** (1909–1972) Nationalist leader who led the Gold Coast's drive for independence and served as head of the new nation of Ghana. Nkrumah worked as a teacher before going to the U.S. to study literature and socialism (1935–45). In 1949 he formed the Convention People's Party, which advocated nonviolent protests, strikes, and noncooperation with the British authorities. Elected prime minister of the Gold Coast (1952–60) and then president of independent Ghana (1960–66), Nkrumah advanced a policy of Africanization and built new roads, schools, and health facilities. After 1960 he devoted much of his time to the PAN-AFRICAN MOVEMENT, at the expense of Ghana's economy. Following an attempted coup in 1962, he increased authoritarian controls, withdrew from public life, increased contacts with communist countries, and wrote works on political philosophy. With the country facing economic ruin, he was deposed in 1966 while visiting Beijing.

Nkrumah, 1962.
MARC AND EVELYNE BERNHEIM—WOODFIN CAMP AND ASSOCIATES

No drama *or* **Noh drama** Classic Japanese theatrical form. One of the world's oldest extant theatrical forms, No drama has a heroic theme, a chorus, and highly stylized action, costuming, and scenery. Its all-male performers are storytellers who use their visual appearances and movements to suggest their tale rather than enact it. No (meaning "talent" or "skill") developed from ancient forms of dance-drama and became a distinctive form in the 14th century. The five types of No plays are the *kami* ("god") play, which involves a sacred story of a SHINTO shrine; the *shura mono* ("fighting play"), which centers on warriors; the *katsura mono* ("wig play"), which has a female protagonist; the *gendai mono* ("present-day play") or *kyojo mono* ("madwoman play"), which is varied in content; and the *kiri* or *kichiku* ("final" or "demon") play, which features devils and strange beasts. Kanami (1333–1384) and his son Zeami (1363–1443) wrote many of the most beautiful No texts; over 200 remain in the modern No repertoire.

no-till farming *or* **till-less agriculture** Cultivation technique in which the soil is disturbed only along the slit or hole into which seeds are planted. Reserved detritus from previous crops covers and protects the seedbed. Primary benefits are a decreased rate of soil erosion; reduced need for equipment, fuel, and fertilizer; and significantly less time required for tending crops. The method also improves soil-aggregate formation, microbial activity in the soil, and water infiltration and storage. Conventional tillage controls weed growth by plowing and cultivating, but no-till farming selectively uses HERBICIDES to kill weeds and the remains of the previous crop. No-till farming is one of several primitive farming methods revived as conservation measures in the 20th century.

Noah Biblical character from GENESIS. The son of Lamech and ninth in descent from ADAM, he was a man of blameless piety, who was chosen by God to perpetuate the human race after his wicked contemporaries had perished in the flood. On God's instructions, Noah built an ark and took into it one male and one female of each of the world's animals. After the waters receded, God set a rainbow in the sky as a guarantee of his promise never again to curse the earth. Noah was the father of Shem, Ham, and Japheth, from whom the entire human race is supposed to have descended. Noah is also said to have been the originator of vineyard cultivation.

noaide \nō-'ī-dē\ In SAMI religion, a SHAMAN who mediates between his clients and various supernatural beings and forces. To aid people suffering from illness or other serious troubles, the noaide performs a dramatic séance, which includes divination, trance, confrontation of supernatural beings, and the ritual treatment of the patient. The noaides can accomplish both good and evil, and their powers were formerly much feared.

Nobel \,nō-'bel\, **Alfred (Bernhard)** (1833–1896) Swedish chemist, engineer, and industrialist. His attempts to find a safe way to handle NITROGLYCERIN resulted in the invention of DYNAMITE and the blasting cap. He built a network of factories to manufacture dynamite and corporations to produce and market his explosives. He went on to develop more powerful EXPLOSIVES and to construct and perfect detonators for explosives that did not explode on simple firing (e.g., when lit with a match). Nobel registered over 350 patents, many unrelated to explosives (e.g., artificial silk and leather). A complex personality, both dynamic and reclusive, he was a pacifist but was labeled the "merchant of death" for inventing explosives used in war. Perhaps to counter this label, he left most of his immense fortune, from worldwide explosives and oil interests, to establish the NOBEL PRIZES, which would become the most highly regarded of all international awards.

Nobel Prize Any of the prizes awarded annually by four institutions (three Swedish and one Norwegian) from a fund established under the will of ALFRED B. NOBEL. The will specified that awards should be given "to those who, during the preceding year, shall have conferred the greatest benefit on mankind." Since 1901, prizes have been awarded for physics, chemistry, physiology or medicine, literature, and peace; since 1969, a sixth prize, established by the Bank of Sweden, has been awarded in economic sciences. They are regarded as the most prestigious prizes in the world. See tables on following pages.

noble gas *or* **inert gas** Any of the six chemical ELEMENTS that make up the rightmost group of the PERIODIC TABLE as usually arranged: HELIUM, NEON, ARGON, KRYPTON, XENON, and RADON. All are colorless, odorless, and nonflammable and occur in tiny amounts in the atmosphere (though helium is the most plentiful element in the universe). Their stable electronic CONFIGURATIONS; with no unpaired ELECTRONS to share, make them extremely unreactive—hence "noble" (i.e., aloof) or inert—though the three heaviest, with outer electrons held less firmly, can form compounds (mainly with FLUORINE). These gases absorb and give off ELECTROMAGNETIC RADIATION in a much less complex way than other substances, a property exploited in their use in fluorescent lighting devices and discharge lamps: They glow with a characteristic color when confined in a glass tube at low pressure with an electric current passing through it. Their very low boiling and melting points make them useful as refrigerants for low-temperature research.

nocturne 19th-century character piece for piano. The name was first used c. 1812 by the Scottish composer John Field (1782–1837) for works employing a lyrical melody over an accompaniment of broken chords. F. CHOPIN's romantic nocturnes, similar in style, are the most celebrated.

nodule \'nä-jül\ In geology, a rounded mineral concretion that is distinct from, and may be separated from, the formation in which it occurs. Nodules usually are elongated and have a knobby irregular surface; they are generally oriented parallel to the bedding. CHERT AND FLINT, clay ironstone, and PHOSPHORITES commonly occur as nodules. Manganese-rich nodules are found on the ocean floor.

Noel-Baker, Philip John *later* **Baron Noel-Baker (of the City of Derby)** *orig.* **Philip John Baker** (1889–1982) British statesman and advocate of disarmament. He worked for the League of Nations secretariat 1919–22, and taught international relations at London University 1924–29. He served in the House of Commons 1929–31 and 1936–70 and in ministerial posts 1945–61. He helped draft the U.N. charter, and he campaigned widely for peace through multilateral disarmament. An Olympic runner in 1912, 1920, and 1924, he later served as president of UNESCO's International Council on Sport and Physical Recreation (1960–82). In 1959 he was awarded the Nobel Peace Prize.

Nogi Maresuke \'nō-gē-,mä-'rās-kā\ (1849–1912) General in MEIJI-PERIOD Japan. He served as governor of Taiwan and fought in the RUSSO-JAPANESE WAR. On the death of the MEIJI EMPEROR, Nogi and his wife committed the ultimate SAMURAI act of loyalty, following him into death by their own suicide. This action affected such Meiji-period writers as NATSUME SOSEKI and Mori Ogai (1862–1922) and illuminated the contrast between the Japan's feudal past and rapidly modernizing present. See SEPPUKU.

Noguchi \nō-'gü-chē\, **Isamu** (1904–1988) U.S. sculptor and designer. Though born in Los Angeles, he spent his early years in Japan. After premedical studies at Columbia Univ., he became CONSTANTIN BRANCUSI's assistant in Paris. He was influenced as well by ALBERTO GIACOMETTI, ALEXANDER CALDER, PABLO PICASSO, and JOAN MIRO. His premedical training suggested to him the interrelatedness of bone and stone, as seen in *Kouros* (1945). Much of his work, such as *Bird C(MU)* (1953–58), consists of elegantly abstracted, rounded forms in highly polished stone. His long collaboration with MARTHA GRAHAM resulted in stage sets for many ballets, and he also designed many public sculptures, sculptural gardens, and playgrounds, as well as furniture.

noise Undesired sound that is intrinsically objectionable or that interferes with other sounds being listened to. In electronics and information theory, noise refers to those random, unpredictable, and undesirable signals, or changes in signals, that mask the desired information content. In radio, this noise is called static; in television, it is called snow. White

Nobel Prize winners[1]

	physics		chemistry		literature		physiology or medicine		peace		economic science
1901	Wilhelm Röntgen	Ger.	Jacobus van't Hoff	Neth.	Sully Prudhomme; poet	France	Emil von Behring	Ger.	Jean-Henri Dunant Frédéric Passy	Switz. France	prize not awarded until 1969
1902	Hendrik Antoon Lorentz Pieter Zeeman	Neth. Neth.	Emil Fischer	Ger.	Theodor Mommsen; historian	Ger.	Ronald Ross	U.K.	Élie Ducommun Charles-Albert Gobat	Switz. Switz.	
1903	Henri Becquerel Pierre Curie Marie Curie	France France France[2]	Svante Arrhenius	Sweden	Bjørnstjerne Bjørnson; novelist, poet, dramatist	Norway	Niels R. Finsen	Den.	Randal Cremer	U.K.	
1904	Lord Rayleigh	U.K.	Sir William Ramsay	U.K.	Frédéric Mistral; poet José Echegaray y Eizaguirre; dramatist	France Spain	Ivan Pavlov	Russia	Institute of International Law	(founded 1873)	
1905	Philipp Lenard	Ger.	Adolf von Baeyer	Ger.	Henryk Sienkiewicz; novelist	Poland	Robert Koch	Ger.	Bertha von Suttner	Austria	
1906	J.J. Thomson	U.K.	Henri Moissan	France	Giosuè Carducci; poet	Italy	Camillo Golgi Santiago Ramón y Cajal	Italy Spain	Theodore Roosevelt	U.S.	
1907	A.A. Michelson	U.S.[2]	Eduard Buchner	Ger.	Rudyard Kipling; poet, novelist	U.K.	Alphonse Laveran	France	Ernesto Teodoro Moneta Louis Renault	Italy France	
1908	Gabriel Lippmann	France	Ernest Rutherford	U.K.	Rudolf Eucken; philosopher	Ger.	Paul Ehrlich Élie Metchnikoff	Ger. Russia	Klas Pontus Arnoldson Fredrik Bajer	Sweden Den.	
1909	Guglielmo Marconi Ferdinand Braun	Italy Ger.	Wilhelm Ostwald	Ger.	Selma Lagerlöf; novelist	Sweden	Emil Kocher	Switz.	Baron d'Estournelles de Constant Auguste Beernaert	France Belgium	
1910	Johannes van der Waals	Neth.	Otto Wallach	Ger.	Paul von Heyse; poet, novelist, dramatist	Ger.	Albrecht Kossel	Ger.	International Peace Bureau	(founded 1891)	
1911	Wilhelm Wien	Ger.	Marie Curie	France[2]	Maurice Maeterlinck; dramatist	Belgium	Allvar Gullstrand	Sweden	Tobias Asser Alfred Fried	Neth. Austria	
1912	Nils Gustaf Dalén	Sweden	Victor Grignard Paul Sabatier	France France	Gerhart Hauptmann; dramatist	Ger.	Alexis Carrel	France	Elihu Root	U.S.	
1913	Heike Kamerlingh Onnes	Neth.	Alfred Werner	Switz.[2]	Rabindranath Tagore; poet	India	Charles Richet	France	Henri-Marie Lafontaine	Belgium	
1914	Max von Laue	Ger.	Theodore Richards	U.S.	(no award)	—	Robert Bárány	Austria	(no award)	—	
1915	William Bragg Lawrence Bragg	U.K. U.K.	Richard Willstätter	Ger.	Romain Rolland; novelist	France	(no award)	—	(no award)	—	
1916	(no award)	—	(no award)	—	Verner von Heidenstam; poet	Sweden	(no award)	—	(no award)	—	
1917	Charles Barkla	U.K.	(no award)	—	Karl Gjellerup; novelist Henrik Pontoppidan; novelist	Den. Den.	(no award)	—	International Red Cross Committee	(founded 1863)	
1918	Max Planck	Ger.	Fritz Haber	Ger.	Erik Axel Karlfeldt (declined)	Sweden	(no award)	—	(no award)	—	
1919	Johannes Stark	Ger.	(no award)	—	Carl Spitteler; poet, novelist	Switz.	Jules Bordet	Belgium	Woodrow Wilson	U.S.	
1920	Charles Guillaume	Switz.	Walther Nernst	Ger.	Knut Hamsun; novelist	Norway	August Krogh	Den.	Léon Bourgeois	France	
1921	Albert Einstein	Switz.[2]	Frederick Soddy	U.K.	Anatole France; novelist	France	(no award)	—	Karl Branting Christian Lous Lange	Sweden Norway	
1922	Niels Bohr	Den.	Francis Aston	U.K.	Jacinto Benavente y Martínez; dramatist	Spain	A.V. Hill Otto Meyerhof	U.K. Ger.	Fridtjof Nansen	Norway	
1923	Robert Millikan	U.S.	Fritz Pregl	Austria	William Butler Yeats; poet	Ireland	F.G. Banting J.J.R. Macleod	Canada U.K.	(no award)	—	
1924	Manne Siegbahn	Sweden	(no award)	—	Wladyslaw Reymont; novelist	Poland	Willem Einthoven	Neth.	(no award)	—	
1925	James Franck Gustav Hertz	Ger. Ger.	Richard Zsigmondy	Austria	George Bernard Shaw; dramatist	Ireland	(no award)	—	Sir Austen Chamberlain Charles G. Dawes	U.K. U.S.	
1926	Jean Perrin	France	The Svedberg	Sweden	Grazia Deledda; novelist	Italy	Johannes Fibiger	Den.	Aristide Briand Gustav Stresemann	France Ger.	
1927	Arthur Holly Compton C.T.R. Wilson	U.S. U.K.	Heinrich Wieland	Ger.	Henri Bergson; philosopher	France[2]	Julius Wagner-Jauregg	Austria	Ferdinand Buisson Ludwig Quidde	France Ger.	

Nobel Prize winners[1] (continued)

	physics		chemistry		literature		physiology or medicine		peace		economic science
1928	Owen Richardson	U.K.	Adolf Windaus	Ger.	Sigrid Undset; novelist	Norway	Charles Nicolle	France	(no award)	—	
1929	Louis-Victor de Broglie	France	Arthur Harden	U.K.	Thomas Mann; novelist	Ger.	Christiaan Eijkman	Neth.	Frank B. Kellogg	U.S.	
			Hans von Euler-Chelpin	Sweden[2]			Sir Frederick Hopkins	U.K.			
1930	Sir Chandrasekhara Raman	India	Hans Fischer	Ger.	Sinclair Lewis; novelist	U.S.	Karl Landsteiner	U.S.[2]	Nathan Söderblom	Sweden	
1931	(no award)	—	Carl Bosch	Ger.	Erik Axel Karlfeldt; poet (posthumous award)	Sweden	Otto Warburg	Ger.	Jane Addams	U.S.	
			Friedrich Bergius	Ger.					Nicholas Murray Butler	U.S.	
1932	Werner Heisenberg	Ger.	Irving Langmuir	U.S.	John Galsworthy; novelist	U.K.	Edgar D. Adrian	U.K.	(no award)	—	
							Sir Charles Sherrington	U.K.			
1933	P.A.M. Dirac	U.K.	(no award)	—	Ivan Bunin; poet, novelist	U.S.S.R	Thomas Hunt Morgan	U.S.	Sir Norman Angell	U.K.	
	Erwin Schrödinger	Austria									
1934	(no award)	—	Harold Urey	U.S.	Luigi Pirandello; dramatist	Italy	George R. Minot	U.S.	Arthur Henderson	U.K.	
							William P. Murphy	U.S.			
							George H. Whipple	U.S.			
1935	James Chadwick	U.K.	Frédéric Joliot-Curie	France	(no award)	—	Hans Spemann	Ger.	Carl von Ossietzky	Ger.	
			Irène Joliot-Curie	France							
1936	Victor Hess	Austria	Peter Debye	Neth.	Eugene O'Neill; dramatist	U.S.	Sir Henry Dale	U.K.	Carlos Saavedra Lamas	Arg.	
	Carl Anderson	U.S.					Otto Loewi	Ger.			
1937	Clinton Davisson	U.S.	Norman Haworth	U.K.	Roger Martin du Gard; novelist	France	Albert Szent-Györgyi	Hung.	Viscount Cecil of Chelwood	U.K.	
	George Paget Thomson	U.K.	Paul Karrer	Switz.							
1938	Enrico Fermi	Italy	Richard Kuhn (declined)[3]	Ger.	Pearl Buck; novelist	U.S.	Corneille Heymans	Belgium	Nansen International Office for Refugees	(founded 1931)	
1939	Ernest Lawrence	U.S.	Adolf Butenandt (declined)[3]	Ger.	Frans Eemil Sillanpää; novelist	Finland	Gerhard Domagk (declined)[3]	Ger.	(no award)	—	
			Leopold Ruzicka	Switz.[2]							
1943	Otto Stern	U.S.[2]	George de Hevesy	Hung.	(no award)	—	Henrik Dam	Den.	(no award)	—	
							Edward A. Doisy	U.S.			
1944	Isidor Rabi	U.S.[2]	Otto Hahn	Ger.	Johannes V. Jensen; novelist	Den.	Joseph Erlanger	U.S.	International Red Cross Committee	(founded 1863)	
							Herbert S. Gasser	U.S.			
1945	Wolfgang Pauli	Austria	Artturi Virtanen	Finland	Gabriela Mistral; poet	Chile	Sir A. Fleming	U.K.	Cordell Hull	U.S.	
							Ernst Boris Chain	U.K.[2]			
							Sir Howard Florey	Austl.			
1946	P.W. Bridgman	U.S.	James Sumner	U.S.	Hermann Hesse; novelist	Switz.[2]	Hermann J. Muller	U.S.	Emily Greene Balch	U.S.	
			John Northrop	U.S.					John R. Mott	U.S.	
			Wendell Stanley	U.S.							
1947	Sir Edward Appleton	U.K.	Sir Robert Robinson	U.K.	André Gide; novelist, essayist	France	Carl F. Cori	U.S.[2]	American Friends Service Committee	U.S.	
							Gerty T. Cori	U.S.[2]			
							Bernardo Houssay	Arg.	Friends Service Council	U.K.	
1948	Patrick Blackett	U.K.	Arne Tiselius	Sweden	T.S. Eliot; poet, critic	U.K.[2]	Paul Müller	Switz.	(no award)	—	
1949	Yukawa Hideki	Japan	William Giauque	U.S.	William Faulkner; novelist	U.S.	Walter Rudolf Hess	Switz.	Lord Boyd-Orr	U.K.	
							António Egas Moniz	Port.			
1950	Cecil Powell	U.K.	Otto Diels	Ger.	Bertrand Russell; philosopher	U.K.	Philip S. Hench	U.S.	Ralph Bunche	U.S.	
			Kurt Alder	Ger.			Edward C. Kendall	U.S.			
							Tadeus Reichstein	Switz.[2]			
1951	Sir John Cockcroft	U.K.	Edwin McMillan	U.S.	Pär Lagerkvist; novelist	Sweden	Max Theiler	S.Af.	Léon Jouhaux	France	
	E.T.S. Walton	Ireland	Glenn Seaborg	U.S.							
1952	Felix Bloch	U.S.[2]	A.J.P. Martin	U.K.	François Mauriac; poet, novelist, dramatist	France	Selman A. Waksman	U.S.[2]	Albert Schweitzer	Alsace	
	E.M. Purcell	U.S.	R.L.M. Synge	U.K.							
1953	Frits Zernike	Neth.	Hermann Staudinger	Ger.	Sir Winston Churchill; historian, orator	U.K.	Fritz A. Lipmann	U.S.[2]	George C. Marshall	U.S.	
							Hans A. Krebs	U.S.[2]			
1954	Max Born	U.K.[2]	Linus Pauling	U.S.	Ernest Hemingway; novelist	U.S.	John F. Enders	U.S.	Office of the United Nations High Commissioner for Refugees	(founded 1951)	
	Walther Bothe	Ger.					Thomas H. Weller	U.S.			
							Frederick Robbins	U.S.			
1955	Willis Lamb, Jr.	U.S.	Vincent Du Vigneaud	U.S.	Halldór Laxness; novelist	Iceland	Axel Hugo Theorell	Sweden	(no award)	—	
	Polykarp Kusch	U.S.[2]									

Nobel Prize winners[1] (continued)

	physics		chemistry		literature		physiology or medicine		peace		economic science	
1956	William Shockley	U.S.	Nikolay Semyonov	U.S.S.R.	Juan Ramón Jiménez;	Spain	Werner Forssmann	Ger.	(no award)	—		
	John Bardeen	U.S.	Sir Cyril Hinshelwood	U.K.	poet		Dickinson Richards	U.S.				
	Walter H. Brattain	U.S.					André F. Cournand	U.S.[2]				
1957	Tsung-Dao Lee	China	Sir Alexander Todd	U.K.	Albert Camus; novelist,	France	Daniel Bovet	Italy[2]	Lester B. Pearson	Canada		
	Chen Ning Yang	China			dramatist							
1958	Pavel A. Cherenkov	U.S.S.R.	Frederick Sanger	U.K.	Boris Pasternak; novelist,	U.S.S.R	George W. Beadle	U.S.	Dominique Georges Pire	Belgium		
	Ilya M. Frank	U.S.S.R.			poet (declined)		Edward L. Tatum	U.S.				
	Igor Y. Tamm	U.S.S.R.					Joshua Lederberg	U.S.				
1959	Emilio Segrè	U.S.[2]	Jaroslav Heyrovský	Czech.	Salvatore Quasimodo;	Italy	Severo Ochoa	U.S.[2]	Philip Noel-Baker	U.K.		
	Owen Chamberlain	U.S.			poet		Arthur Kornberg	U.S.				
1960	Donald Glaser	U.S.	Willard Libby	U.S.	Saint-John Perse; poet	France	Sir Macfarlane Burnet	Austl.	Albert Lutuli	S.Af.		
							Peter B. Medawar	U.K.				
1961	Robert Hofstadter	U.S.	Melvin Calvin	U.S.	Ivo Andrić; novelist	Yugos.	Georg von Békésy	U.S.[2]	Dag Hammarskjöld	Sweden		
	Rudolf Mössbauer	Ger.										
1962	Lev D. Landau	U.S.S.R.	John C. Kendrew	U.K.	John Steinbeck; novelist	U.S.	Francis H.C. Crick	U.K.	Linus Pauling	U.S.		
			Max F. Perutz	U.K.[2]			James D. Watson	U.S.				
							Maurice Wilkins	U.K.				
1963	J. Hans D. Jensen	Ger.	Giulio Natta	Italy	George Seferis; poet	Greece	Sir John Eccles	Austl.	International Red Cross	(head-		
	Maria Goeppert Mayer	U.S.[2]	Karl Ziegler	Ger.			Alan Lloyd Hodgkin	U.K.	Committee	quarters		
	Eugene Paul Wigner	U.S.[2]					Andrew Huxley	U.K.	League of Red Cross	of both in		
									Societies	Geneva)		
1964	Charles H. Townes	U.S.	Dorothy M.C. Hodgkin	U.K.	Jean-Paul Sartre;	France	Konrad Bloch	U.S.[2]	Martin Luther King, Jr.	U.S.		
	Nikolay G. Basov	U.S.S.R.			philosopher, dramatist		Feodor Lynen	Ger.				
	Aleksandr M. Prokhorov	U.S.S.R.			(declined)							
1965	Julian S. Schwinger	U.S.	R.B. Woodward	U.S.	Mikhail Sholokhov;	U.S.S.R	François Jacob	France	United Nations Children's	(founded		
	Richard P. Feynman	U.S.			novelist		Jacques Monod	France	Fund (UNICEF)	1946)		
	Tomonaga Shin'ichiro	Japan					André Lwoff	France				
1966	Alfred Kastler	France	Robert S. Mulliken	U.S.	Shmuel Yosef Agnon;	Israel[2]	Charles B. Huggins	U.S.[2]	(no award)	—		
					novelist		Francis Peyton Rous	U.S.				
					Nelly Sachs; poet	Sweden[2]						
1967	Hans A. Bethe	U.S.[2]	Manfred Eigen	Ger.	Miguel Ángel Asturias;	Guat.	Haldan Keffer Hartline	U.S.	(no award)	—		
			Ronald G.W. Norrish	U.K.	novelist		George Wald	U.S.				
			George Porter	U.K.			Ragnar A. Granit	Sweden				
1968	Luis W. Alvarez	U.S.	Lars Onsager	U.S.[2]	Kawabata Yasunari;	Japan	Robert W. Holley	U.S.	René Cassin	France		
					novelist		Har Gobind Khorana	U.S.[2]				
							Marshall W. Nirenberg	U.S.				
1969	Murray Gell-Mann	U.S.	Derek H.R. Barton	U.K.	Samuel Beckett; novelist,	Ireland	Max Delbrück	U.S.[2]	International Labour	(founded	Ragnar Frisch	Norway
			Odd Hassel	Norway	dramatist		A.D. Hershey	U.S.	Organisation	1919)	Jan Tinbergen	Neth.
							Salvador E. Luria	U.S.[2]				
1970	Hannes Alfvén	Sweden	Luis F. Leloir	Arg.[2]	Aleksandr Solzhenitsyn;	U.S.S.R	Julius Axelrod	U.S.	Norman E. Borlaug	U.S.	Paul A. Samuelson	U.S.
	Louis Néel	France			novelist		Sir Bernard Katz	U.K.[2]				
							Ulf von Euler	Sweden				
1971	Dennis Gabor	U.K.[2]	Gerhard Herzberg	Canada[2]	Pablo Neruda; poet	Chile	Earl W. Sutherland, Jr.	U.S.	Willy Brandt	Ger.	Simon Kuznets	U.S.[2]
1972	John Bardeen	U.S.	Christian B. Anfinsen	U.S.	Heinrich Böll; novelist	Ger.	Gerald M. Edelman	U.S.	(no award)	—	Sir John Hicks	U.K.
	Leon N. Cooper	U.S.	Stanford Moore	U.S.			Rodney Porter	U.K.			Kenneth J. Arrow	U.S.
	John R. Schrieffer	U.S.	William H. Stein	U.S.								
1973	Leo Esaki	Japan	Ernst Fischer	Ger.	Patrick White; novelist	Austl.	Karl von Frisch	Austria	Henry Kissinger	U.S.	Wassily Leontief	U.S.[2]
	Ivar Giaever	U.S.[2]	Geoffrey Wilkinson	U.K.			Konrad Lorenz	Austria	Le Duc Tho (declined)	North		
	Brian D. Josephson	U.K.					Nikolaas Tinbergen	U.K.[2]		Vietnam		
1974	Sir Martin Ryle	U.K.	Paul J. Flory	U.S.	Eyvind Johnson; novelist	Sweden	Albert Claude	U.S.[2]	Sato Eisaku	Japan	Gunnar Myrdal	Sweden
	Antony Hewish	U.K.			Harry Martinson;	Sweden	Christian R. de Duve	Belgium	Seán MacBride	Ireland	Friedrich von Hayek	U.K.
					novelist, poet		George E. Palade	U.S.[2]				
1975	Aage N. Bohr	Den.	John W. Cornforth	U.K.	Eugenio Montale; poet	Italy	Renato Dulbecco	U.S.[2]	Andrey D. Sakharov	U.S.S.R.	Leonid V. Kantorovich	U.S.S.R.
	Ben R. Mottelson	Den.[2]	Vladimir Prelog	Switz.			Howard M. Temin	U.S.			Tjalling C. Koopmans	U.S.[2]
	L. James Rainwater	U.S.					David Baltimore	U.S.				

Nobel Prize winners[1] (continued)

	physics		chemistry		literature		physiology or medicine		peace		economic science	
1976	Burton Richter	U.S.	William N. Lipscomb	U.S.	Saul Bellow; novelist	U.S.[2]	Baruch S. Blumberg	U.S.	Mairead Corrigan	N.Ire.	Milton Friedman	U.S.
	Samuel C.C. Ting	U.S.					D. Carleton Gajdusek	U.S.	Betty Williams	N.Ire.		
1977	Philip W. Anderson	U.S.	Ilya Prigogine	Belgium	Vicente Aleixandre; poet	Spain	Rosalyn S. Yalow	U.S.	Amnesty International	(founded	Bertil Ohlin	Sweden
	Sir Nevill F. Mott	U.K.					Roger Guillemin	U.S.		1961)	James Meade	U.K.
	John H. Van Vleck	U.S.					Andrew Schally	U.S.				
1978	Pyotr L. Kapitsa	U.S.S.R.	Peter D. Mitchell	U.K.	Isaac Bashevis Singer;	U.S.[2]	Werner Arber	Switz.	Menachem Begin	Israel	Herbert A. Simon	U.S.
	Arno A. Penzias	U.S.[2]			novelist		Daniel Nathans	U.S.	Anwar el-Sadat	Egypt		
	Robert W. Wilson	U.S.					Hamilton O. Smith	U.S.				
1979	Sheldon Glashow	U.S.	Herbert C. Brown	U.S.[2]	Odysseus Elytis; poet	Greece	Allan M. Cormack	U.S.[2]	Mother Teresa of Calcutta	India[2]	Sir W. Arthur Lewis	U.K.
	Abdus Salam	Pak.	Georg Wittig	W.Ger.			Godfrey N. Hounsfield	U.K.			Theodore W. Schultz	U.S.
	Steven Weinberg	U.S.										
1980	James W. Cronin	U.S.	Paul Berg	U.S.	Czeslaw Milosz; poet	U.S.[2]	Baruj Benacerraf	U.S.[2]	Adolfo Pérez Esquivel	Arg.	Lawrence R. Klein	U.S.
	Val Logsdon Fitch	U.S.	Walter Gilbert	U.S.			George D. Snell	U.S.				
			Frederick Sanger	U.K.			Jean Dausset	France				
1981	Kai M. Siegbahn	Sweden	Fukui Kenichi	Japan	Elias Canetti; novelist	Bulg.	Roger W. Sperry	U.S.	Office of the United	(founded	James Tobin	U.S.
	Nicolaas Bloembergen	U.S.[2]	Roald Hoffmann	U.S.[2]	and essayist		Torsten N. Wiesel	Sweden	Nations High Commis-	1951)		
	Arthur L. Schawlow	U.S.					David H. Hubel	U.S.[2]	sioner for Refugees			
1982	Kenneth G. Wilson	U.S.	Aaron Klug	U.K.[2]	Gabriel García	Colom.	Sune K. Bergström	Sweden	Alva Myrdal	Sweden	George Stigler	U.S.
					Márquez; novelist,		Bengt I. Samuelsson	Sweden	Alfonso García Robles	Mexico		
					journalist, social critic		John R. Vane	U.K.				
1983	Subrahmanyan	U.S.	Henry Taube	U.S.	William Golding;	U.K.	Barbara McClintock	U.S.	Lech Walesa	Poland	Gerard Debreu	U.S.
	Chandrasekhar				novelist							
	William A. Fowler	U.S.										
1984	Carlo Rubbia	Italy	Bruce Merrifield	U.S.	Jaroslav Seifert; poet	Czech.	Niels K. Jerne	U.K.-Den.	Desmond Tutu	S.Af.	Sir Richard Stone	U.K.
	Simon van der Meer	Neth.					Georges J.F. Köhler	W.Ger.				
							César Milstein	Arg.				
1985	Klaus von Klitzing	W.Ger.	Herbert A. Hauptman	U.S.	Claude Simon; novelist	France	Michael S. Brown	U.S.	International Physicians	(founded	Franco Modigliani	U.S.
			Jerome Karle	U.S.			Joseph L. Goldstein	U.S.	for the Prevention of	1980)		
									Nuclear War			
1986	Ernst Ruska	W.Ger.	Dudley R. Herschbach	U.S.	Wole Soyinka;	Nigeria	Stanley Cohen	U.S.	Elie Wiesel	U.S.[2]	James M. Buchanan	U.S.
	Gerd Binnig	W.Ger.	Yuan T. Lee	U.S.	playwright and poet		Rita Levi-Montalcini	Italy				
	Heinrich Rohrer	Switz.	John C. Polanyi	Canada								
1987	J. Georg Bednorz	W.Ger.	Donald J. Cram	U.S.	Joseph Brodsky; poet	U.S.[2]	Tonegawa Susumu	Japan	Oscar Arias Sánchez	Costa	Robert M. Solow	U.S.
	K. Alex Müller	Switz.	Charles J. Pedersen	U.S.	and essayist					Rica		
			Jean-Marie Lehn	France								
1988	Leon M. Lederman	U.S.	Johann Deisenhofer	W.Ger.	Naguib Mahfouz;	Egypt	Sir James W. Black	U.K.	United Nations		Maurice Allais	France
	Melvin Schwartz	U.S.	Robert Huber	W.Ger.	novelist		Gertrude B. Elion	U.S.	peacekeeping forces			
	Jack Steinberger	U.S.	Hartmut Michel	W.Ger.			George H. Hitchings	U.S.				
1989	Norman F. Ramsey	U.S.	Sidney Altman	U.S.	Camilo José Cela;	Spain	J. Michael Bishop	U.S.	Dalai Lama	Tibet	Trygve Haavelmo	Norway
	Hans G. Dehmelt	U.S.	Thomas R. Cech	U.S.	novelist		Harold E. Varmus	U.S.				
	Wolfgang Paul	W.Ger.										
1990	Jerome I. Friedman	U.S.	Elias James Corey	U.S.	Octavio Paz; poet and	Mexico	Joseph E. Murray	U.S.	Mikhail Sergeyevich	U.S.S.R.	Harry M. Markowitz	U.S.
	Henry W. Kendall	U.S.			essayist		E. Donnall Thomas	U.S.	Gorbachev		Merton H. Miller	U.S.
	Richard E. Taylor	Canada									William F. Sharpe	U.S.
1991	Pierre-Gilles de Gennes	France	Richard R. Ernst	Switz.	Nadine Gordimer;	S.Af.	Erwin Neher	Ger.	Aung San Suu Kyi	Myanmar	Ronald H. Coase	U.S.
					novelist		Bert Sakmann	Ger.				
1992	Georges Charpak	France	Rudolph A. Marcus	U.S.[2]	Derek Walcott; poet	St. Lucia	Edmond H. Fischer	U.S.	Rigoberta Menchú	Guat.	Gary S. Becker	U.S.
							Edwin G. Krebs	U.S.				
1993	Russell A. Hulse	U.S.	Kary B. Mullis	U.S.	Toni Morrison; novelist	U.S.	Richard J. Roberts	U.K.	F.W. de Klerk	S.Af.	Robert W. Fogel	U.S.
	Joseph H. Taylor, Jr.	U.S.	Michael Smith	Canada			Phillip A. Sharp	U.S.	Nelson Mandela	S.Af.	Douglass C. North	U.S.
1994	Bertram N. Brockhouse	Canada	George A. Olah	U.S.	Oe Kenzaburo; novelist	Japan	Alfred G. Gilman	U.S.	Yasir Arafat	Pales-	John C. Harsanyi	U.S.[2]
	Clifford G. Shull	U.S.					Martin Rodbell	U.S.		tinian	John F. Nash	U.S.
									Shimon Peres	Israel	Reinhard Selten	Ger.
									Yitzhak Rabin	Israel		

Nobel Prize winners[1] (continued)

	physics		chemistry		literature		physiology or medicine		peace		economic science	
1995	Martin L. Perl	U.S.	Paul Crutzen	Neth.	Seamus Heaney; poet	Ireland	Edward B. Lewis	U.S.	Joseph Rotblat	U.K.[2]	Robert E. Lucas, Jr.	U.S.
	Frederick Reines	U.S.	Mario Molina	U.S.[2]			Christiane Nüsslein-Volhard	Ger.	Pugwash Conferences on Science and World Affairs	(founded 1957)		
			F. Sherwood Rowland	U.S.			Eric F. Wieschaus	U.S.				
1996	David M. Lee	U.S.	Robert F. Curl, Jr.	U.S.	Wislawa Szymborska; poet	Poland	Peter C. Doherty	Austl.	Carlos Ximenes Belo	Timorese	James A. Mirrlees	U.K.
	Douglas D. Osheroff	U.S.	Sir Harold W. Kroto	U.K.			Rolf M. Zinkernagel	Switz.	José Ramos-Horta	Timorese	William Vickrey	U.S.
	Robert C. Richardson	U.S.	Richard E. Smalley	U.S.								
1997	Steven Chu	U.S.	Paul Boyer	U.S.	Dario Fo; playwright, actor	Italy	Stanley B. Prusiner	U.S.	International Campaign to Ban Landmines	(founded 1992)	Robert C. Merton	U.S.
	Claude Cohen-Tannoudji	France[2]	Jens C. Skou	Den.								
	William D. Phillips	U.S.	John E. Walker	U.K.					Jody Williams	U.S.	Myron S. Scholes	U.S.
1998	Robert B. Laughlin	U.S.	Walter Kohn	U.S.[2]	José Saramago; novelist	Port.	Robert E. Furchgott	U.S.	John Hume	N.Ire.	Amartya Sen	India
	Horst L. Störmer	U.S.[2]	John A. Pople	U.S.			Louis J. Ignarro	U.S.	David Trimble	N.Ire.		
	Daniel C. Tsui	U.S.[2]					Ferid Murad	U.S.				
1999	Gerardus t'Hooft	Neth.	Ahmed H. Zewail	Egypt/ U.S.	Günter Grass; novelist	Ger.	Günter Blobel	U.S.[2]	Doctors Without Borders	(founded 1971)	Robert A. Mundell	Canada
	Martinus J.G. Veltman	Neth.										
2000	Zhores I. Alferov	Russia	Alan J. Heeger	U.S.	Gao Xingjian; novelist, playwright	France[2]	Arvid Carlsson	Sweden	Kim Dae Jung	S.Kor.	James J. Heckman	U.S.
	Jack S. Kilby	U.S.	Alan G. MacDiarmid	U.S.[2]			Paul Greengard	U.S.			Daniel L McFadden	U.S.
	Herbert Kroemer	Ger.	Shirakawa Hideki	Japan			Eric Kandel	U.S.[2]				
2001	Eric A. Cornell	U.S.	William S. Knowles	U.S.	Sir V.S. Naipaul	Trin.	Leland H. Hartwell	U.S.	United Nations	(founded 1945)	George A. Akerlof	U.S.
	Wolfgang Ketterle	Ger.	Noyori Ryoji	Japan			R. Timothy Hunt	U.K.			A. Michael Spense	U.S.
	Carl E. Wieman	U.S.	K. Barry Sharpless	U.S.			Sir Paul M. Nurse	U.K.	Kofi Annan	Ghana	Joseph E. Stiglitz	U.S.

[1]Nationality given is the citizenship of recipient at the time award was made. [2]Naturalized citizen. [3]Adolf Hitler forbade Germans to accept Nobel prizes (January 1937).
[4]No awards made 1940–42.

noise is a complex signal or sound covering the entire range of component frequencies, or TONES, all of which possess equal intensity.

Nok culture ancient Iron Age culture that existed on the Benue Plateau of Nigeria between about 500 BC and AD 200. First discovered in 1928 in the village of Nok, artifacts having similar features were found over an area that stretched about 300 miles (480 km) east to west and 200 miles (320 km) north to south. The most characteristic of these are hollow, coil-built clay figurines of animals and stylized human beings, usually heads. Other artifacts include iron and stone tools and stone ornaments.

Nolan, Sir Sidney (1917–1992) Australian artist. Early in his career, he created greatly simplified abstractions. In the mid 1940s, he began to paint the local desolate desert landscapes in a more representational style. In his mature work he often applied unusual media—such as polyvinyl acetate—to masonite, glass, or canvas. Apart from his landscapes, most of his works dealt with Australian historical or legendary characters and events—notably, the bushranger Ned Kelly.

Noland, Kenneth (born 1924) U.S. painter of the ABSTRACT EXPRESSIONIST school. Born in Asheville, N.C., he studied at Black Mountain College there. He was one of the first to use the technique of staining the canvas with thinned paints, and he is best known for minimalist works in which he deploys his colors in concentric rings and parallel bands.

Noland, photograph by Arnold Newman, 1967.

Nolde \'nōl-də\, **Emil** *orig.* **Emil Hansen** (1867–1956) German Expressionist artist. Born to a peasant family, he carved wood for a living and came late to painting. Though briefly a member of Die BRÜCKE (1906–7), he was essentially a solitary painter. Fervently religious and racked by a sense of sin, he created works in which the figures' erotic frenzy and demonic faces are rendered with deliberately crude draftsmanship and dissonant colors. After about 1915 he produced brooding landscapes and colorful flowers. As a graphic artist he was noted especially for the stark black-and-white effect of his crudely incised woodcuts.

nomadism Way of life of peoples who do not live continually in the same place but move cyclically or periodically. It is based on temporary centers whose stability depends on the availability of food supply and the technology for exploiting it. HUNTING AND GATHERING SOCIETIES form one class of nomadic group. Pastoral nomads, who depend on domestic livestock, migrate in an established territory to find pasturage for their animals. Tinker or trader nomads, such as the GYPSIES (Rom) and the Irish Tinkers, are associated with a larger society but maintain their mobility. Nomadism has declined in the 20th century as urban centers have expanded and governments have sought to regulate or eliminate it.

Nome Seaport (pop., 2000: 3,505), western Alaska, on the southern side of the SEWARD PENINSULA. Founded as a miner's camp called Anvil City after the discovery of gold at nearby Anvil Creek in 1898, it became a center of the Alaskan gold rush of 1899–1903. Its population had dwindled to 852 by 1920. Gold mining remained the chief occupation until the dredge fields were closed in 1962. The finish line for the IDITAROD trail race, it also serves as a supply center for northwestern Alaska.

non-Euclidean geometry Any theory of the nature of geometric space differing from the traditional view held since EUCLID's time. These geometries arose in the 19th century when several mathematicians working independently explored the possibility of rejecting Euclid's PARALLEL POSTULATE. Different assumptions about how many lines through a point not on a given line could be parallel to that line resulted in HYPERBOLIC GEOMETRY and ELLIPTIC GEOMETRY. Mathematicians were forced to abandon the idea of a single correct geometry; it became their task not to discover mathematical systems but to create them by selecting consistent axioms and studying the theorems that could be derived from them. The development of these alternative geometries had a profound impact on the notion of space and paved the way for the theory of RELATIVITY. See also NIKOLAY LOBACHEVSKY, BERNHARD RIEMANN.

nonalignment *or* **neutralism** Peacetime policy of avoiding political or ideological affiliations with major power blocs. In the 20th century, a policy of nonalignment was adopted primarily by Asian and African states that had once been colonies of the Western powers and were wary of being drawn into a new form of dependence by the West or the communist bloc. The nonaligned movement, founded by JAWAHARLAL NEHRU, GAMAL ABDEL NASSER, and others, held its first official meeting in 1961; it was attended by 25 nations. Meetings have since been held on a three-year schedule. While the Soviet Union existed, the nations tended to seek development assistance from both sides but refrained from forming political or military alliances with either. Though the communist bloc dissolved in 1991, the movement today counts over 110 members, whose current concerns include debt forgiveness and fairer trade relationships. See also THIRD WORLD.

noncognitivism Denial of the characteristic cognitivist thesis that moral sentences are used to express factual statements. Noncognitivists have proposed various alternative theories of meaning for moral sentences. In *Language, Truth and Logic* (1936), A. J. AYER stated the emotivist thesis that moral sentences are not statements at all (see EMOTIVISM). In *The Language of Morals* (1952), Richard M. Hare (born 1919) agreed that in making moral judgments we are not primarily seeking to describe anything, but claimed that neither are we simply expressing our attitudes; instead, he suggested that moral judgments prescribe—that is, are a form of imperative sentence (see PRESCRIPTIVISM).

Nonconformist Any English Protestant who does not conform to the doctrines or practices of the established Church of ENGLAND. The term was first used after the Restoration of the monarchy in 1660 to describe congregations that had separated from the national church. Such congregations, also called Separatists or Dissenters, often rejected Anglican rites and doctrines as being too close to Catholicism. In the late 19th century, Nonconformists of various denominations joined together to form the Free Church Federal Council. In England and Wales the term is generally applied to all Protestant denominations outside Anglicanism, including Baptists, Congregationalists, Unitarians, Presbyterians, Methodists, Quakers, and Churches of Christ.

nondirective psychotherapy *or* **client-centered therapy** Type of PSYCHOTHERAPY in which the counselor refrains from interpretation or explanation but encourages the client to establish a person-to-person relationship with him or her and to talk freely. It originated with CARL R. ROGERS and influenced later individual and GROUP THERAPIES. The goal is to enable the client to see him- or herself more clearly and react more openly with the therapist and others. The client determines the course, speed, and duration of treatment.

nongovernmental organization (NGO) Organization not part of any individual government. NGOs' purposes cover the entire range of human interests, and may be international or domestic in scope. Many are nonprofit organizations. Some fulfill quasi-governmental functions for ethnic groups that lack a state of their own. NGOs may be financed by private donations, international organizations, governments, or a combination of these. In Britain quasi-autonomous nongovernmental organizations, or quangos, are organizations that have nonelected boards and receive public funds which they also disburse.

Nonni River See NEN RIVER

Nono, Luigi (1924–1990) Italian composer. A law student, he also studied music with Gian Francesco Malipiero (1882–1973), Bruno Maderna (1920–1973), and Hermann Scherchen (1891–1966). His early twelve-tone works performed at Darmstadt in 1950 won international notice. In 1955 he married the daughter of A. SCHOENBERG. A communist, his political ideals were reflected in his titles and texts. Interested in neither "total serialism" nor aleatory, he focused on the voice, while increasingly fragmenting language and electronically manipulating the vocal sounds. His best-known work is the opera *Intolleranza* (1961).

nonobjective art See ABSTRACT ART

Nonpartisan League Alliance of U.S. farmers to gain protection from wheat monopolies. Founded in North Dakota in 1915 by Arthur Townley, it demanded that mills, grain elevators, banks, and hail-insurance companies be state owned. In 1916 its candidate, Lynn Frazier, was elected governor of North Dakota, and the state legislature enacted its program in 1919. The league declined after the 1920s and affiliated with the Democrats in 1956.

nonrepresentational art See ABSTRACT ART

nonsense verse Humorous or whimsical verse that features absurd characters and actions and often contains evocative but meaningless words coined for the verse. It is unlike the ritualistic gibberish of children's counting-out rhymes in that it makes such words sound purposeful. It differs from other comic verse in its resistance to any rational or allegorical interpretation. Most nonsense verse has been written for children and is modern, dating from the beginning of the 19th century. Examples include EDWARD LEAR's *Book of Nonsense* (1846), LEWIS CARROLL's "Jabberwocky" (1871), and HILAIRE BELLOC's *Bad Child's Book of Beasts* (1896). See also LIMERICK.

nonsteroidal anti-inflammatory drugs See NSAIDs

Nootka \'nůt-kə\ NORTHWEST COAST INDIAN people of southwestern Vancouver Island and northwestern Washington. Culturally related to the KWAKIUTL, the Nootka were specialized whale hunters. They moved seasonally, returning to their principal homesites during the winter. Local groups were usually socially and politically independent. The most important religious ceremony was the shaman's dance, a reenactment of mythological themes that ended with a POTLATCH. Today the Nootka number about 5,000.

Nootka Sound Controversy (1790) Dispute between Spain and Britain over ship seizures off the western Canadian coast. Spain seized four British trading ships in Nootka Sound, an inlet of Vancouver Island, Canada, in accordance with Spanish claims to the northwestern coast of America. Britain threatened war, maintaining that sovereignty necessitated actual occupation of the land. Spain yielded to British demands and signed an agreement acknowledging the right of each nation to trade and establish settlements on unoccupied land.

Nora Ancient city, southwest of CAGLIARI, SARDINIA. Ruins from the 7th century BC indicate that the site was first settled by PHOENICIANS. It was the capital of Sardinia after the Roman annexation in the 1st century AD. Excavations have revealed a wealthy imperial Roman city with a theater, an aqueduct, a temple of Juno, a nymphaeum, and private villas overlying a typical Phoenician port.

Nordenskiöld \'nür-dən-ˌshœld\, **Adolf Erik** *later* **Frihere (Baron) Nordenskiöld** (1832–1901) Finnish-Swedish geologist, mineralogist, geographer, and explorer. In 1858 he settled in Stockholm and became professor and curator of mineralogy at the Swedish State Museum. He led several expeditions to the Arctic island of Spitsbergen between 1864 and 1873, and in 1870 he led an expedition to western Greenland. In 1878–79, on the steam vessel *Vega,* he sailed from Norway to Alaska on the first expedition to successfully navigate the Northeast Passage. He was created a baron on his return. In 1883 he became the first to break through the great sea ice barrier of the southeastern Greenland coast.

Nordic skiing Skiing techniques and events of Scandinavian origin that include CROSS-COUNTRY SKIING and SKI JUMPING. Nordic events were included in the first Winter Olympics in 1924. See also ALPINE SKIING.

norepinephrine \ˌnȯr-ˌep-ə-'nef-rən\ *or* **noradrenaline** One of two CATECHOLAMINE HORMONES (EPINEPHRINE is the other) secreted by the ADRENAL GLANDS, as well as at nerve endings, as a NEUROTRANSMITTER. It resembles adrenaline chemically and in its actions on the body, which mimic sympathetic NERVOUS SYSTEM stimulation. It constricts most blood vessels, and is given for certain types of SHOCK. Norepinephrine is formed from TYROSINE and converted to epinephrine. It was discovered by Ulf von Euler-Chelpin (1905–1983) in the mid-1940s.

Norfolk \'nȯr-fək\ County (pop., 1995 est.: 772,000), eastern England. Bounded by the North Sea on the north and east, it is low-lying and has reed swamps, including the famous Broads that resulted from medieval peat cutting and a subsequent change in sea level. Paleolithic, Mesolithic, and Neolithic artifacts have been found, including impressive STONE AGE flint mines in Breckland. In the Middle Ages the region's prosperity depended mainly on wool. County towns include the county seat of NORWICH, and Great Yarmouth. The economy is now largely agricultural.

Norfolk City (pop., 1996 est.: 233,000), southeastern Virginia. A port of entry on the Elizabeth River, it is located just south of HAMPTON ROADS. Founded in 1682, it was incorporated as a borough in 1736. It was destroyed by fires in 1776 and 1799. YELLOW FEVER killed 10% of the population in 1855. During the AMERICAN CIVIL WAR the city was occupied by Union troops. Prosperity resumed after 1870 when railroads linked the port to other trade centers. With NEWPORT NEWS and PORTSMOUTH it comprises the Port of Hampton Roads. Shipping, shipbuilding, and light industry are the major economic activities. Norfolk is the headquarters of the U.S. Atlantic Fleet and NATO's Supreme Allied Command, Atlantic.

Norfolk, 2nd Duke of *orig.* **Thomas Howard** (1443–1524) English noble prominent in the reigns of HENRY VII and HENRY VIII. Son of the 1st duke of Norfolk, he was made steward of the royal household and created earl of Surrey in 1483. While fighting for RICHARD III, he was taken prisoner (and his father killed) in the Battle of BOSWORTH FIELD. After his release in 1489, he commanded the defense of the Scottish borders and later defeated the Scots at the Battle of FLODDEN. Norfolk later served as lord treasurer and a privy councillor, and helped arrange the marriage of MARGARET TUDOR to JAMES IV of Scotland. In 1520 he was guardian of England during Henry VIII's absence in France.

Norfolk, 3rd Duke of *orig.* **Thomas Howard** (1473–1554) English noble prominent in the reign of HENRY VIII. Son of the 2nd duke of NORFOLK, he was made lord high admiral in 1513 and helped rout the Scots at the Battle of FLODDEN. Succeeding his father as duke (1524), he led the faction opposed to THOMAS, CARDINAL WOLSEY, whom he replaced as president of the royal council in 1529. He supported the marriage of his niece ANNE BOLEYN to Henry (1533), but later as lord high steward presided over her trial (1536). He skillfully suppressed the PILGRIMAGE OF GRACE rebellion and by 1540 was the most powerful of Henry's councillors. His position weakened after his niece CATHERINE HOWARD was put to death (1542) and his son Henry Howard (1517–1547) was executed for treason. Imprisoned as an accessory to his son, he was released by Queen MARY in 1553.

Norfolk, 4th Duke of *orig.* **Thomas Howard** (1538–1572) English noble executed for his intrigues against Queen ELIZABETH I. He was the grandson of the 3rd duke of NORFOLK, whom he succeeded as duke in 1554. In favor with both Queen MARY and Queen Elizabeth, Norfolk commanded the English forces that invaded Scotland in 1559–60. He led the commission to resolve problems between MARY, QUEEN OF SCOTS, and Scotland's Protestant nobility (1568). He became involved in a plan to free Mary from imprisonment by marrying her, and was arrested after a failed revolt by Catholic nobles (1569). Released in 1570, Norfolk was drawn into another plot to install Mary on the English throne through a Spanish invasion of England; discovery of the plot led to his arrest and execution.

Norfolk Island Southern Pacific island, a territory of Australia. Located midway between New Caledonia and New Zealand, it has an area of 13 sq mi (35 sq km). Discovered by Capt. JAMES COOK in 1774, it became a British penal colony (1788–1814, 1825–55). The population of PITCAIRN ISLAND was moved here in 1856, and many residents are descended from crew members of HMS *BOUNTY*. Of volcanic origin, it has generally rugged terrain with abundant NORFOLK ISLAND PINE. The major industry is tourism.

Norfolk Island pine Evergreen timber and ornamental CONIFER *(Araucaria excelsa,* or *A. heterophylla)* of the family Araucariaceae, native to Norfolk Island in the South Pacific Ocean. In nature this PINE grows to a height of 200 ft (60 m), with a trunk sometimes reaching 10 ft (3 m) in diameter. The wood of large trees is used in construction, furniture, and shipbuilding. The sapling stage is grown worldwide as a houseplant and as an outdoor ornamental in regions with a Mediterranean climate. The MONKEY PUZZLE TREE is a relative.

Noricum Ancient kingdom and Roman province, western central Europe. It was located roughly south of the DANUBE RIVER and north of modern Italy. Originally controlled by a Celtic confederacy, it was annexed by AUGUSTUS c. 15 BC. It had rich iron and gold mines worked by the Romans. Latin inscriptions on coins indicate a Romanized culture. Emperor CLAUDIUS enhanced the significance of several of Noricum's towns and recruited soldiers from the area for the PRAETORIAN GUARD c. AD 50. The FRANKS settled there by the end of the 5th century AD.

Noriega (Morena) \ˌnȯr-ē-ˈā-gə\, **Manuel (Antonio)** (born 1938) Panamanian general who was the actual power behind a civilian president. Born into a poor family, he attended military school in Peru and joined Panama's National Guard on his return. As chief of military intelligence in the 1970s, he cooperated with the CENTRAL INTELLIGENCE AGENCY and negotiated the release of U.S. freighter crews held by Cuba, but was tainted by persistent reports of drug trafficking and brutality. In 1989, as head of the armed forces, he canceled election results that displeased him. The U.S. government then invaded Panama, primarily to capture Noriega. He was brought to trial in the U.S., convicted of racketeering, drug trafficking, and money laundering, and sentenced to 40 years in prison.

normal distribution In statistics, a FREQUENCY DISTRIBUTION in the shape of the classic bell curve. It accurately represents most variations in such attributes as height and weight. Any RANDOM VARIABLE with a normal distribution has a mean (see MEAN, MEDIAN, AND MODE) and a standard deviation that indicates how much the data as a whole deviate from the mean. The standard deviation is smaller for data clustered closely around the mean value and larger for more dispersed data sets.

Norman, Greg(ory John) (born 1955) Australian golfer. After barely losing the 1984 U.S. Open, he won the British Open in 1986 and repeated that victory in 1993. Nicknamed "the Great White Shark" for his light blond hair and his aggressive style, he had compiled 78 career individual victories by 1998. Though he is one of the top PGA career money winners, victory in the most prestigious tournaments has often eluded him.

Norman, Jessye (born 1945) U.S. soprano. Born in Augusta, Ga., she won the Munich International Music Competition in 1968, and debuted in Berlin as Elisabeth in *Tannhäuser* (1969). She appeared at La Scala in 1972 and made recital debuts in London and New York the next year. Having garnered extraordinary praise for years, she made her Metropolitan Opera debut in *Les Troyens* in 1983, confirming her reputation as perhaps the greatest soprano of her generation. An imposing stage presence, her operatic and concert repertoire ranges with equal conviction and musicality across an exceptionally wide range.

Norman Conquest (1066) Military conquest of England by William, duke of Normandy (later WILLIAM I), mainly through his victory over HAROLD II at the Battle of HASTINGS. EDWARD THE CONFESSOR had designated William as his successor in 1051, and when Harold, duke of Wessex, was crowned king of England in 1066 instead, William assembled an invasion force of 5,000 Norman knights. After defeating Harold's army near Hastings and advancing to London, he was crowned king in Westminster Abbey on Christmas Day, 1066. Native revolts continued until 1071, notably in Northumbria. The Norman Conquest brought great social and political changes to England, linking the country more closely with Western Europe, strengthening feudalism, and replacing the old English aristocracy with a Norman aristocracy. The English language was subjected to a long period of influence by Anglo-French, which remained in literary and courtly use until the reign of EDWARD III, and in legal reporting until the 17th century.

Normandy *French* **Normandie** \nȯr-mäⁿ-ˈdē\ Historic region, northwestern France. The capital was ROUEN. Inhabited since PALEOLITHIC times, its Celtic population was conquered by the Romans c. 56 BC, when it became part of the province of LUGDUNENSIS. Invaded by VIKINGS in the mid-9th cent, it was ceded to their chief, ROLLO, in 911 by Charles III the Simple of France. The Vikings became known as Normans, hence the region's name. After the NORMAN CONQUEST (1066), it was united to England by WILLIAM I of Normandy. It became a province of France in 1450 and was divided into several departments after the FRENCH REVOLUTION. It was the site of the World War II Allied invasion of German-occupied France in 1944 (see NORMANDY CAMPAIGN).

Normandy Campaign (June 6, 1944) Allied invasion of northern Europe in WORLD WAR II that began in Normandy, France. Also called Operation Overlord, the largest amphibious landing in history transported 156,000 U.S., British, and Canadian troops across the English Channel in over 5,000 ships and 10,000 planes. Directed by Gen. DWIGHT D. EISENHOWER, the invasion was planned for June 5, but the worst Channel weather in 25 years delayed the famous D-Day until June 6. Preceded by airborne commando units that crippled German communications, the Allied assault forces landed at five beaches on the Normandy coast and soon established beachheads, despite stiff German resistance and heavy losses at the code-named Omaha Beach. Allied air supremacy prevented rapid German reinforcements, and discord between ADOLF HITLER and his generals stalled crucial counterattacks. Though delayed by heavy fighting around Caen and near Cherbourg, the Allied ground troops had begun their rapid advance across France by mid-July.

Normans VIKINGS, or Norsemen, who settled in northern France (or the Frankish kingdom) and their descendants. As pagan pirates from Denmark, Norway, and Iceland, they raided the European coast in the 8th century. They settled in the lower Seine valley by c. 900 and then extended their territory westward. They founded the duchy of Normandy, governed by a line of rulers who called themselves counts or dukes of Normandy. Though the Normans converted to Christianity and adopted the French language, they continued to display the recklessness and appetite for conquest of their Viking ancestors. In the 11th century they seized England in the NORMAN CONQUEST and colonized southern Italy and Sicily.

Norodom \'nȯr-ə-dəm\ *orig.* **Vody** (1834–1904) King of Cambodia (r. 1860–1904). Cambodia had been under the joint vassalage of Vietnam and Siam (Thailand) since 1802. After the death of Norodom's father in 1860, the Siamese asserted sole dominion over Cambodia by refusing to allow the Vietnamese to participate in Norodom's crowning. France opposed Siamese claims on the country and forced Norodom to accept French protection. He was crowned in 1864, and during his reign France dominated Cambodian affairs.

Norodom Sihanouk \ˌsē-ə-'nük\, **King** *in full* **Preah Norodom Sihanouk** (born 1922) Cambodia's king (1941–55 and from 1993); he also held other posts. He abdicated in favor of his father in 1955, becoming his father's prime minister; he became head of state on his father's death in 1960. During the Vietnam War he steered a neutral course between the radical right and left in both his foreign and internal policies. Overthrown by LON NOL in 1970, he campaigned for the KHMER ROUGE but was imprisoned after they came to power, and most of his family was killed. Released in the face of a Vietnamese invasion (1979), he denounced both the Vietnamese and the Khmer Rouge. In 1982 he became president of a fragile coalition of resistance groups. Following U.N.-sponsored elections in 1993, Cambodia's National Assembly voted to restore the monarchy, and Sihanouk again became king.

Norris, (Benjamin) Frank(lin) (1870–1902) U.S. novelist and short-story writer. Born in Chicago, Norris initially worked as an overseas correspondent and in publishing. He became the first important American author to embrace NATURALISM. *McTeague* (1899) is a portrait of an acquisitive society. He adopted a more humanitarian ideal beginning with his masterpiece, *The Octopus* (1901), the first novel of a projected trilogy dealing with the economic and social forces involved in the wheat industry. The second part, *The Pit,* appeared in 1903, but the third was unwritten at his death. Despite romanticizing tendencies, his works present a vivid, authentic picture of life in California in his day.

Norris, George W(illiam) (1861–1944) U.S. politician. Born in Sandusky, Ohio, he served in the U.S. House of Representatives 1903–13. In the U.S. Senate (1913–43), he drafted the 20th Amendment to the Constitution, abolishing the lame-duck session of Congress. He introduced the bill establishing the TENNESSEE VALLEY AUTHORITY and coauthored the Norris-La Guardia Act, which restricted the use of injunctions in labor disputes. An independent Republican, he said he "would rather be right than regular."

Norsemen See VIKINGS

North, Alex (1910–1991) U.S. film composer and conductor. Born in Chester, Pa., North studied at the Curtis Institute and Juilliard. In the early 1930s he traveled to Moscow and became the sole American member of the Union of Soviet Composers. He composed ballet scores for MARTHA GRAHAM and others and later studied and conducted in Mexico City. North's score for *A Streetcar Named Desire* (1951), the first jazz-based film score, brought him to prominence. His dozens of films over 30 years include *Viva Zapata!* (1952), *The Bad Seed* (1956), *Spartacus* (1960), *Who's Afraid of Virginia Woolf?* (1966), and *Prizzi's Honor* (1985).

North (of Kirtling), Frederick *later* **Earl of Guilford** *known as* **Lord North** (1732–1792) English prime minister (1770–82). Elected to Parliament at 22, he served as lord of the treasury 1759–65, and as chancellor of the exchequer 1767–70. As prime minister, he gave vacillating support to both harsh and conciliatory measures toward the American colonies before the American Revolution. Though only a halfhearted supporter of the war, he was a pliant agent of GEORGE III. He resigned on hearing the news of CHARLES CORNWALLIS's defeat at the Siege of Yorktown. In 1783 he formed a brief coalition with his former Whig opponent CHARLES JAMES FOX.

North, Oliver (Laurence) (born 1943) U.S. marine involved in the IRAN-CONTRA AFFAIR. Born in San Antonio, he graduated from the U.S. Naval Academy and served in the Vietnam War. In 1981 he was assigned to the National Security Council, where his work focused on Central America. Embracing the cause of the Nicaraguan contras, he raised private donations for them. In 1986, after Congressional investigation of the Iran-Contra Affair, he was reluctantly dismissed by RONALD REAGAN. In 1988 he was indicted for conspiracy to defraud the government and resigned from the Marine Corps; at his 1989 trial, he was found guilty of obstructing Congress, destroying documents, and accepting an illegal gratuity and was sentenced to two years' probation. In 1991, after a prosecution witness claimed that his testimony had been tainted, all charges against North were dropped. From 1995 he hosted a radio talk show.

North, Simeon (1765–1852) U.S. firearms manufacturer. Born in Berlin, Conn., he supplied pistols and rifles to the U.S. government from 1799. He developed the use of INTERCHANGEABLE PARTS in manufacturing (see ARMORY PRACTICE, MASS PRODUCTION) and the first-known milling machine. In 1825 he built a breech-loading rifle with fully interchangeable parts.

North Africa Campaigns (1940–43) Battles in WORLD WAR II for control of North Africa. After the 1940 victory by Italian troops in Egypt, the Italians were driven back into Libya by British troops. German reinforcements led by ERWIN ROMMEL forced the British to retreat into Egypt after the defense of Tobruk. In 1942 the British under BERNARD LAW MONTGOMERY counterattacked at the Battles of EL ALAMEIN and pushed the Germans west into Tunisia. In November 1942 U.S.and British forces under DWIGHT D. EISENHOWER landed in Algeria and Morocco, then moved east into Tunisia. In May 1943 the Allies, advancing from east and west, defeated the Axis forces and forced the surrender of 250,000 Axis troops.

North America Continent, Western Hemisphere. The third-largest continent on earth, it lies mostly between the ARCTIC CIRCLE and the TROPIC OF CANCER. It is almost completely surrounded by bodies of water, including the Pacific Ocean, the Bering Strait, the Arctic Ocean, the Atlantic Ocean, and the Caribbean Sea and Gulf of Mexico. Area: 9,361,791 sq mi (24,247,039 sq km). Population (2001 est.): 454,225,-000. Shaped like an inverted triangle, North America was apparently the first continent to achieve its current approximate size and shape. Its geologic structure is built around a stable platform of Precambrian rock called the CANADIAN SHIELD. To the southeast are the APPALACHIAN MTNS., and to the west are the younger and much taller Cordilleras. These mountains extend the length of the continent and occupy about one-third of the total land area. The ROCKY MTNS. constitute the eastern Cordillera. The highest point is Mount MCKINLEY. The MISSISSIPPI RIVER basin, including its major tributaries, the MISSOURI and OHIO, occupies more than one-eighth of the continent's total area. Generally temperate climatic conditions prevail. Arable land accounts for about one-eighth of the land area and forests for about one-third. English, the primary language of the U.S., predominates, followed by Spanish; French is spoken in parts of Canada. Most of the continent's population of European descent is found in the U.S. and Canada. Intermarriage between whites and Indians was common in Mexico, and MESTIZOS constitute about three-fifths of the Mexican population. North America has a mixture of developed, partly developed, and developing economies, adequate reserves of most metallic resources, and the world's largest reserves of cadmium, copper, lead, molybdenum, silver, and zinc. It is the world's leading food producer, largely because of mechanized and scientific farming in the U.S. and Canada. Among the continent's democratically governed states are Canada, Mexico, Costa Rica, and the U.S. The nations of North America have sought hemispheric unity as members of the ORGANIZATION OF AMERICAN STATES, which also includes SOUTH AMERICAN countries. The first inhabitants were AMERICAN INDIANS, who migrated from Asia about 20,000 years ago. The greatest pre-Columbian civilizations were in Mesoamerica (see MESOAMERICAN CIVILIZATION) and included the OLMEC, MAYA, TOLTEC, and AZTEC, who were conquered by the Spanish. The continent long remained sparsely settled and undeveloped. Beginning in the 17th century it underwent a profound transformation with the coming of Europeans and the Africans they introduced as slaves. The style of life became Latin American south of the RIO GRANDE and Anglo-American

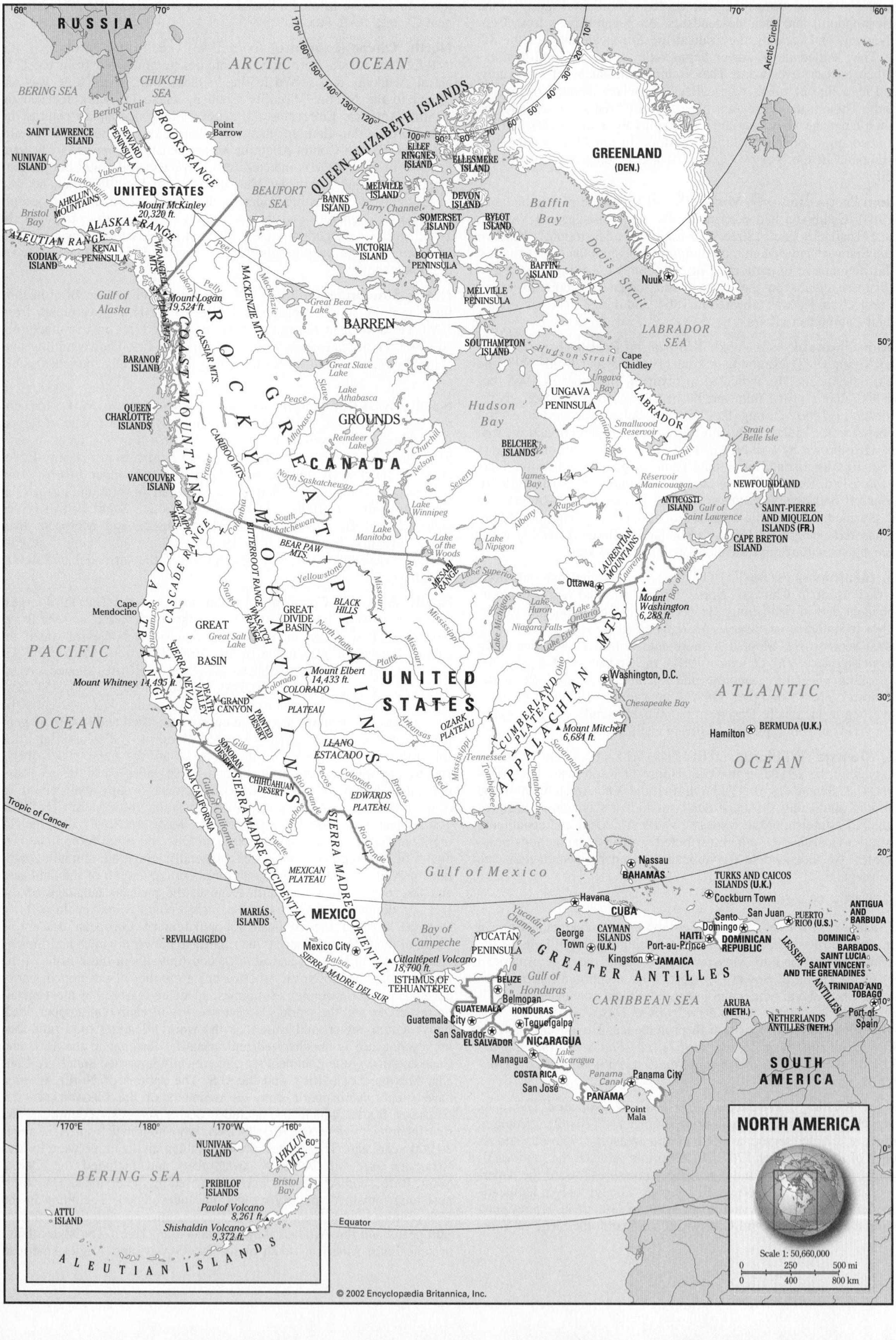
NORTH AMERICA
RUSSIA
ARCTIC OCEAN
BERING SEA
CHUKCHI SEA
Bering Strait
SAINT LAWRENCE ISLAND
SEWARD PENINSULA
BROOKS RANGE
Point Barrow
NUNIVAK ISLAND
Yukon
Kuskokwim
UNITED STATES
AHKLUN MOUNTAINS
Mount McKinley 20,320 ft.
Bristol Bay
ALASKA RANGE
ALEUTIAN RANGE
KENAI PENINSULA
KODIAK ISLAND
WRANGELL MTS.
ST. ELIAS MTS.
Mount Logan 19,524 ft.
Gulf of Alaska
QUEEN ELIZABETH ISLANDS
BEAUFORT SEA
BANKS ISLAND
MELVILLE ISLAND
Parry Channel
ELLEF RINGNES ISLAND
ELLESMERE ISLAND
DEVON ISLAND
SOMERSET ISLAND
BYLOT ISLAND
VICTORIA ISLAND
BOOTHIA PENINSULA
BAFFIN ISLAND
MELVILLE PENINSULA
GREENLAND (DEN.)
Baffin Bay
Davis Strait
Nuuk
Arctic Circle
Peel
Pelly
Mackenzie
MACKENZIE MTS.
Great Bear Lake
BARREN GROUNDS
SOUTHAMPTON ISLAND
Hudson Strait
Cape Chidley
LABRADOR SEA
UNGAVA PENINSULA
Ungava Bay
LABRADOR
Smallwood Reservoir
Churchill
Strait of Belle Isle
BARANOF ISLAND
COAST MOUNTAINS
CASSIAR MTS.
ROCKY MOUNTAINS
GREAT PLAINS
Great Slave Lake
Slave
Peace
Lake Athabasca
Athabasca
Reindeer Lake
Hudson Bay
BELCHER ISLANDS
QUEEN CHARLOTTE ISLANDS
CARIBOO MTS.
Fraser
CANADA
Nelson
North Saskatchewan
South Saskatchewan
Severn
James Bay
Rupert
Réservoir Manicouagan
NEWFOUNDLAND
VANCOUVER ISLAND
OLYMPIC MTS.
Columbia
Lake Winnipeg
Lake Manitoba
Albany
ANTICOSTI ISLAND
Gulf of Saint Lawrence
SAINT-PIERRE AND MIQUELON ISLANDS (FR.)
CAPE BRETON ISLAND
BEAR PAW MTS.
Lake of the Woods
Lake Nipigon
Red
Lake Superior
MESABI RANGE
LAURENTIAN MOUNTAINS
Ottawa
Lawrence
Mount Washington 6,288 ft.
Bay of Fundy
CASCADE RANGE
COAST RANGES
BITTERROOT RANGE
Yellowstone
Missouri
Snake
Cape Mendocino
GREAT BASIN
Great Salt Lake
WASATCH RANGE
GREAT DIVIDE BASIN
BLACK HILLS
North Platte
Platte
Mississippi
Lake Michigan
Lake Huron
Lake Ontario
Lake Erie
Niagara Falls
PACIFIC OCEAN
Sacramento
SIERRA NEVADA
Mount Whitney 14,495 ft.
DEATH VALLEY
Mount Elbert 14,433 ft.
Colorado
COLORADO PLATEAU
GRAND CANYON
PAINTED DESERT
UNITED STATES
Arkansas
OZARK PLATEAU
CUMBERLAND PLATEAU
Ohio
APPALACHIAN MTS.
Washington, D.C.
Chesapeake Bay
Mount Mitchell 6,684 ft.
Savannah
ATLANTIC OCEAN
Hamilton
BERMUDA (U.K.)
Gila
SONORAN DESERT
LLANO ESTACADO
Tennessee
Tombigbee
Chattahoochee
Red
Brazos
Pecos
CHIHUAHUAN DESERT
EDWARDS PLATEAU
Rio Grande
Conchos
BAJA CALIFORNIA
Gulf of California
SIERRA MADRE OCCIDENTAL
SIERRA MADRE ORIENTAL
Fuerte
Tropic of Cancer
Gulf of Mexico
Nassau
BAHAMAS
MEXICAN PLATEAU
TURKS AND CAICOS ISLANDS (U.K.)
Cockburn Town
Havana
CUBA
MARIÁS ISLANDS
MEXICO
Yucatán Channel
Santo Domingo
San Juan
PUERTO RICO (U.S.)
ANTIGUA AND BARBUDA
Bay of Campeche
YUCATÁN PENINSULA
George Town
CAYMAN ISLANDS (U.K.)
HAITI
DOMINICAN REPUBLIC
Port-au-Prince
DOMINICA
BARBADOS
SAINT LUCIA
SAINT VINCENT AND THE GRENADINES
REVILLAGIGEDO
Mexico City
Balsas
Citlaltépetl Volcano 18,700 ft.
Kingston
JAMAICA
GREATER ANTILLES
LESSER ANTILLES
SIERRA MADRE DEL SUR
ISTHMUS OF TEHUANTEPEC
BELIZE
Belmopan
Gulf of Honduras
CARIBBEAN SEA
TRINIDAD AND TOBAGO
GUATEMALA
HONDURAS
Tegucigalpa
Guatemala City
San Salvador
EL SALVADOR
NICARAGUA
ARUBA (NETH.)
NETHERLANDS ANTILLES (NETH.)
Port-of-Spain
Managua
Lake Nicaragua
COSTA RICA
San José
Panama Canal
Panama City
PANAMA
Point Mala
SOUTH AMERICA
BERING SEA
NUNIVAK ISLAND
AHKLUN MTS.
Bristol Bay
PRIBILOF ISLANDS
ATTU ISLAND
Pavlof Volcano 8,261 ft.
Shishaldin Volcano 9,372 ft.
ALEUTIAN ISLANDS
Equator
Scale 1: 50,660,000
0 250 500 mi
0 400 800 km
© 2002 Encyclopædia Britannica, Inc.

L
M
N

to the north, with enclaves of French culture in Canada and Louisiana. Slavery, practiced in the 16th–19th century, added a significant minority culture of African origin, especially in the U.S. and the Caribbean (see WEST INDIES). The huge industrial economy of the U.S., its abundant resources, and its military strength give the continent considerable global influence.

North American Free Trade Agreement (NAFTA) Trade pact signed by Canada, the U.S., and Mexico in 1992, which took effect in 1994. Inspired by the European Community's success in reducing trade barriers among its members, NAFTA created the world's largest free-trade area. It basically extended to Mexico the provisions of a 1988 Canada–U.S. free-trade agreement, calling for elimination of all trade barriers over a 15-year period, granting U.S. and Canadian companies access to certain Mexican markets, and incorporating agreements on labor and the environment. See also GENERAL AGREEMENT ON TARIFFS AND TRADE, WORLD TRADE ORGANIZATION.

North Atlantic Treaty Organization See NATO

North Canadian River River, central Oklahoma. Formed by the junction of Beaver River and Wolf Creek, it is 440 mi (708 km) long and rises in a high plateau in New Mexico. It flows east through the Texas and Oklahoma panhandles past OKLAHOMA CITY, joining the CANADIAN RIVER in the Eufaula Reservoir.

North Carolina State (pop., 1997 est. 7,425,000), U.S., southern Atlantic region. It covers 52,669 sq mi (136,413 sq km); its capital is RALEIGH. Ranges of the APPALACHIAN MTNS., including the GREAT SMOKY MTNS., are in the west; the BLUE RIDGE MTNS. are in the east. Several Indian tribes, including the Algonquians, SIOUX, and IROQUOIS, inhabited the area before Europeans arrived. The coast was explored by GIOVANNI VERRAZZANO in 1524, and the first English settlement in the New World was established at ROANOKE ISLAND in 1585. It formed part of the Carolina grant of 1663. A provincial congress in April 1776 gave the first explicit sanction of independence by an American colony, and it was invaded by British troops in 1780. An original state of the Union, it was the 12th to ratify the Constitution. Its 18th century agricultural economy based on slave labor continued into the 19th century. It seceded from the Union in 1861; in 1865, following the AMERICAN CIVIL WAR, it annulled the secession order and abolished slavery, and it was readmitted to the Union in 1868. In the 1940s its economy was improved as some of the nation's largest military installations, including Fort Bragg were located there. After World War II the long struggle to eliminate racial segregation began. It has a large rural population but is also the leading industrial state of its region, and has an expanding high technology industry in the Raleigh-Durham area. Products include tobacco, corn, and furniture.

North Carolina, Regulators of See REGULATORS of North Carolina

North Carolina, University of State system of higher education, consisting of a main campus in Chapel Hill and branches in five other locations. The Chapel Hill campus, chartered in 1789, is a major research university, with schools of law, medicine, dentistry, and business. Total enrollment is about 24,000. The system also includes North Carolina State University in Raleigh and its various sister institutions, including some two-year colleges. North Carolina State, founded in 1887, operates a large research forest and a college of forest resources, among its other schools and facilities. Enrollment at the Raleigh campus is about 27,000.

North Cascades National Park National park, northwestern Washington. Established in 1968 to preserve mountain snowfields, glaciers, alpine meadows, and lakes in the northern part of the CASCADE RANGE, it covers an area of 504,781 acres (204,436 hectares). The Ross Lake National Recreation Area separates the park into two sections, the northern unit extending to the Canadian border and the southern unit adjoining the Lake Chelan National Recreation Area.

North Dakota State (pop., 1997 est.: 641,000), U.S. Situated in the northern central region, it covers 70,665 sq mi (183,022 sq km); its capital is BISMARCK. The MISSOURI RIVER crosses it; the RED RIVER forms its eastern boundary. There is evidence of prehistoric inhabitation throughout the state. At the time of European contact, it was inhabited by various tribes of PLAINS INDIANS. It became part of the U.S. with the LOUISIANA PURCHASE of 1803. The northeastern corner was added by a treaty with Great Britain in 1818. In 1804–5 the LEWIS AND CLARK EXPEDITION wintered there among the Indians. In 1861 it became part of the Dakota Territory. Separated from South Dakota, it was admitted to the Union in 1889 as the 39th state. In the 20th century North Dakota's history has been marked by the increasing mechanization of agriculture, the enlargement of farms, and the loss of a rural population. In the 1950s it became an oil-producing state, and in the 1960s air bases and missile sites were built there. Its larger cities include FARGO, Grand Forks, and Minot.

North Dakota, University of Public university located in Grand Forks. It includes colleges of arts and sciences, business and public administration, fine arts, nursing, and human-resources development. Its medical and law schools are the state's only sources for medical and legal training. It was established in 1883 and awarded its first graduate degree in 1895. Total enrollment is about 11,000.

North Down District (pop., 1995 est.: 74,000), eastern Northern Ireland. Located on the southern shores of Belfast Lough, it was established in 1973, with BANGOR as its administrative seat. Most of the working population is employed in BELFAST. Tourism flourishes, and Bangor is a popular seaside resort.

North German Confederation (1867–71) Union of the German states north of the Main River, formed after Prussia's victory in the SEVEN WEEKS' WAR. The confederation recognized the individual states' rights but was effectively controlled by Prussia, whose king served as its president and whose chancellor was OTTO VON BISMARCK. Its constitution served as a model for that of the German empire, with which it merged in 1871.

North Island Island (pop., 1991: 2,550,000), New Zealand. The smaller of the nation's two principal islands, it is separated from SOUTH ISLAND by COOK STRAIT. It has an area of 44,297 sq mi (114,729 sq km) and an increasing majority of the national population, concentrated in the cities of WELLINGTON and AUCKLAND.

North Korea See North KOREA

North Platte River River, Colorado, Wyoming, and Nebraska. One of the two main arms of the PLATTE RIVER, it rises in northern Colorado, flows north into Wyoming, then turns east and southeast across the Nebraska border to join the SOUTH PLATTE and form the Platte. It is 680 mi. (1,094 km) long and is part of an irrigation, power, and flood-control project of the MISSOURI RIVER basin. It has large reservoirs and dams.

North Pole Northern end of the earth's geographic axis, located at 90°N latitude, the northern point from which all meridians of longitude start. Lying in the Arctic Ocean and covered with drifting pack ice, it has six months of constant sunlight and six months of total darkness each year. ROBERT E. PEARY claimed to have reached the pole by dogsled in 1909, but that is now in dispute; ROALD AMUNDSEN and possibly RICHARD E. BYRD reached it by air in 1926. The geographic pole does not coincide with the magnetic North Pole, which in 1993 lay at about 78°27′N, 104°24′W, or with the geomagnetic North Pole, which is at about 79°13′N, 71°16′W.

North Sea *ancient* **Mare Germanicum** Arm of the Atlantic Ocean. Extending south from the NORWEGIAN SEA between Norway and the British Isles, it connects the Skagerrak Channel with the ENGLISH CHANNEL. It is about 600 mi (970 km) long and 350 mi (560 km) wide, with an average depth of 308 ft (94 m). Parts of the sea feature deep trenches, while others have excellent fishing, renowned fisheries, and extensive oil and natural gas deposits.

North Star See POLARIS

North West Co. (1783–1821) British-Canadian fur-trading company. Its operations were centered around the Lake Superior region and the valleys of the Red, Assiniboine, and Saskatchewan rivers. It later spread north and west to the Arctic and Pacific oceans. When its competitor, the HUDSON'S BAY CO., established a colony on the Red River (1811–12), North West workers destroyed the colony in the SEVEN OAKS MASSACRE. Hudson's Bay workers retaliated by destroying the North West post at Fort Gibraltar. The British government pressured the two companies to merge in 1821 as the Hudson's Bay Co.

North York City (pop., 1991: 563,000), part of metropolitan TORONTO. It became a borough in 1967 and a city in 1979. Planned industrial and residential development protects more than 4,000 acres (1,620 hectares) of parks and open space. York University and the Black Creek Pioneer Village are among its attractions.

North Yorkshire County (pop., 1995 est.: 556,000), northern England. Its county seat is NORTHALLERTON. Prehistoric sites show evidence of a military Roman occupation. In the Middle Ages, it was a peripheral region of England with numerous castles of the great landowning families. Monastic orders, including the CISTERCIANS, grew wealthy from sheep farming. The area played a significant part in the Wars of the ROSES and the ENGLISH CIVIL WARS. The modern economy is mainly agricultural.

Northallerton Town (pop., 1981: 10,000), county seat of North Yorkshire, England. It was the scene of the Battle of the Standard in 1138, in which English forces defeated Scottish supporters of the Holy Roman Empress MATILDA led by her uncle, King DAVID I of Scotland.

Northampton City (pop., 1994 est.: 188,000), county seat of NORTHAMPTONSHIRE, England. Originating c. 1100 as a walled town with a castle, it was granted its first charter in 1189. In 1460, during the Wars of the ROSES, King HENRY VI was captured here by Yorkists. The town walls survived until the RESTORATION, when they were torn down under King CHARLES II as punishment for supporting the Parliamentarians. Now a retail and marketing center, it also supports light industry.

Northampton, Earl of *orig.* **Henry Howard** (1540–1614) English noble noted for his intrigues in the reigns of ELIZABETH I and JAMES I. Younger brother of the 4th duke of NORFOLK, he was implicated in efforts to free MARY, QUEEN OF SCOTS. He successfully sought favor with the Scottish king James VI, who on his accession as JAMES I of England made Howard a privy councillor (1603) and earl of Northampton (1604). As a judge at the trials of WALTER RALEIGH (1603) and GUY FAWKES (1605), he pressed for conviction.

Northamptonshire \nȯr-'thamp-tən-,shir\ County (pop., 1995 est.: 599,000), eastern Midlands region, England. It has remains of early settlements, including pre-Celtic and Roman. Norman and early English building styles coexist with mansions and country houses from as early as the 13th century. The county was largely pro-Parliament during the ENGLISH CIVIL WARS. It combines traditional rural life with a modern economy of varied industries in such centers as the county seat of NORTHAMPTON, and Corby.

Northcliffe (of Saint Peter), Viscount *orig.* **Alfred Charles William Harmsworth** (1865–1922) British newspaper publisher. After an impoverished childhood and a few attempts to make a quick fortune, he joined his brother, Harold Sidney Harmsworth (1868–1940), in publishing popular periodicals that formed the basis of Amalgamated Press, at the time the world's largest periodical publishing empire. In 1896 he started the *Daily Mail,* one of the first British newspapers to popularize its coverage to appeal to a mass readership. He also founded the *Daily Mirror* (1903) and bought *The* TIMES (1908), transforming it into a modern newspaper. His influence was greatest in shifting the press away from its traditional informative role to that of the commercial exploiter and entertainer of mass publics. He is considered the most successful publisher in the history of the British press.

Northeast Passage Maritime route along the northern coast of Europe and Asia. It lies between the Atlantic and Pacific oceans mainly off northern Russian SIBERIA. Early explorers included Willem Barents, Olivier Brunel, and HENRY HUDSON. In 1778 Capt. JAMES COOK saw both sides of the strait and demonstrated that Asia and North America are two separate continents. The passage was first traversed by Baron ADOLF ERIK NORDENSKIOLD 1878–79. Since the late 1960s it has been kept open in summer by icebreakers.

Northern Dvina River See Northern DVINA RIVER

Northern Expedition (1926–27) Campaign of the Chinese Nationalist army, led by CHIANG KAI-SHEK, that advanced north from Guangzhou (Canton) to the Chang (Yangtze) River battling warlord forces. The Northern Expedition was aided by Soviet arms and advisers and by a propaganda corps that preceded them. After defeating the warlords, the Nationalist army turned on Britain as the chief imperialist power and primary enemy. In response, the British returned their concessions in Hankou and Jiujiang but prepared to defend Shanghai. The alliance between the Communists and the Nationalists fell apart at this point: when Communist-led labor unions captured Shanghai for Chiang he attacked and suppressed them, and when he set up his new government in Nanjing he expelled the Communists from it. See also ZHANG ZUOLIN.

Northern Ireland See Northern IRELAND

Northern Mariana Islands Self-governing commonwealth (pop., 1994 est.: 46,000) in political union with the U.S., in the western Pacific Ocean. Composed of 22 islands north of GUAM, the islands extend 450 mi (720 km) and have an area of 184 sq mi (477 sq km). The capital, Chalan Kanoa, is on SAIPAN. Saipan, Tinian, and Rota are the principal islands and, together with Alamagan and Agrihan, are inhabited. The indigenous people are Micronesian; other inhabitants are Chamorro and Filipino. Pagan was evacuated in 1981 after a volcanic eruption. The islands were discovered by FERDINAND MAGELLAN in 1521. They were colonized by Spain in 1668. Sold by Spain to Germany in 1899, they were occupied by Japan in 1914 and became a Japanese mandate from the LEAGUE OF NATIONS after 1919. They were the scene of fierce fighting in World War II; Tinian was the base for U.S. planes that dropped atomic bombs on HIROSHIMA and NAGASAKI. They were granted to the U.S. in 1947 by the U.N. as a trust territory, became self-governing in 1978, and became a commonwealth under U.S. sovereignty in 1986, when its residents became U.S. citizens. The U.N. trusteeship ended in 1990.

Northern Pacific Railway Co. Major U.S. railroad that operated between St. Paul and Seattle. It was chartered by Congress in 1864 to build a line from Lake Superior to the Pacific coast. Financed by JAY COOKE until 1873, it was later completed with HENRY VILLARD's backing. Financially troubled in the 1890s, it was reorganized by J. P. MORGAN. He shared control of it with JAMES J. HILL, whose Great Northern Railway Co. was a competitor and who sought to combine the two railroads with the Chicago, Burlington and Quincy through the Northern Securities Co. This arrangement was declared a violation of antitrust laws by the Supreme Court in 1904, but the three railroads remained financially linked and in 1970 were permitted to merge as the Burlington Northern, Inc. Burlington Northern acquired the St. Louis-San Francisco Railway Co. in 1980 and the Santa Fe Pacific Corp. in 1995.

Northern Rhodesia See ZAMBIA

Northern Territory Territory (population 1996: 195,000), northern Australia. It covers an area of 519,800 sq mi (1,346,200 sq km). Its capital is DARWIN; the only other sizeable town is ALICE SPRINGS. Most of the people are of European descent; about one-fifth are AUSTRALIAN ABORIGINES. It consists mainly of tableland, with Simpson Desert in the southeast and the ARNHEM LAND plateau in the north. It was inhabited by Aborigines for thousands of years; they held AYERS ROCK as central to their culture. The coast was explored by the Dutch in the 17th century and surveyed in the early 19th century by MATTHEW FLINDERS. First included as part of NEW SOUTH WALES, it was annexed to SOUTH AUSTRALIA in 1863. It reverted to direct control of the Commonwealth in 1911. The northern parts were bombed by the Japanese in World War II and occupied by Allied troops. It was granted self-government within the Commonwealth in 1978. It remains sparsely inhabited; its economy rests on cattle farming, mining, and government services, although tourism was growing in the late 20th century.

Northern War, First (1655–1660) Final stage of the struggle over the Polish–Swedish succession. In 1655 the Swedish king CHARLES X GUSTAV declared war on Poland on the pretext that it refused to recognize him as king. In alliance with Brandenburg, Sweden invaded Poland with initial success, but when Russia, Denmark, and Austria declared war on Sweden, Brandenburg deserted to join the coalition. The Swedes were driven from Poland but later twice invaded Denmark. The war ended with the Polish sovereigns renouncing their claim to the Swedish throne and the Swedes acquiring Skåne from Denmark.

Northern War, Second *or* **Great Northern War** (1700–1721) Military conflict to challenge Sweden's supremacy in the Baltic area. Sweden's expansion in the Baltic Sea coastlands antagonized Russia, Denmark-Norway, and Saxony-Poland, which formed an anti-Swedish coalition in 1698. They attacked Swedish-held regions in 1700, but Sweden's CHARLES XII successfully countered the attacks and restored the status quo. The Russians eventually succeeded in establishing their power on the eastern Baltic coast, and PETER I THE GREAT founded his new capital of St. Petersburg there in 1703. Sweden renewed its attack on Russia in 1707, but was defeated at the Battle of POLTAVA (1709). Despite an alliance with Turkey against Russia (1710–11), Swedish forces suffered defeats in its territories by the revived anti-Swedish coalition, which by then included England and Prussia. Charles opened peace negotiations in 1717, but in 1718 he invaded southeastern Norway, where he was killed. His successor, Frederick I (1676–1751), negotiated peace settlements in 1719–21, including the Treaty of Nystad, which ceded Estonia, Livonia, and other territory to Russia. The war marked the decline of Swedish influence and the emergence of Russia as a major power.

Northern Wei dynasty *or* **Toba dynasty** (AD 386–534/35) Longest-lived and most powerful of the northern Chinese dynasties that ruled after the HAN DYNASTY fell and before the SUI and TANG reunified China. Founded by Toba tribesmen, the Northern Wei defended its territory against other northern nomads and by 439 had unified all of northern China. The Wei lifestyle became more sedentary, and the Toba people, impressed by Chinese culture, began to emulate the Chinese. To bring into cultivation land abandoned during war, hundreds of thousands of peasants were relocated and allocated land under the EQUAL-FIELD SYSTEM of land distribution. The rulers of the Northern Wei were great patrons of Buddhism, and the period is noted for its Buddhist art, particularly at the caves of YUNGANG. The one exception, the emperor Taiwu, persecuted Buddhists and supported Taoism.

Northern Wei sculpture Chinese sculpture, dominated by simple images of the Buddha, dating from the era of the NORTHERN WEI DYNASTY (AD 386–534/535). The art represents the first major influence of BUDDHISM on China, and may be divided into two major periods. The first style (c. 452–494), an amalgam of foreign influences traceable to the Buddhist art of India, is characterized by heavy stylization of blocky volumes. The second style (c. 494–535) clothes the Buddha in the costume of the Chinese scholar and emphasizes a sinuous cascade of drapery falling over an increasingly flattened figure.

Northrop \'nȯr-thrəp\, **John Howard** (1891–1987) U.S. biochemist. Born in Yonkers, N.Y., he worked most of his career on the staff of New York's Rockefeller Institute for Medical Research (1916–62). His early research on FERMENTATION processes led to a study of enzymes essential for DIGESTION, RESPIRATION, and general life processes. He established that enzymes obey the laws of chemical reactions, crystallized PEPSIN, trypsin, and chymotrypsin and their ZYMOGENS. With JAMES B. SUMNER and WENDELL M. STANLEY he shared a 1946 Nobel Prize.

Northumberland County (pop., 1999 est.: 310,100), northern England. It includes several islands, including Lindisfarne (Holy Island), and the ancient Anglo-Saxon kingdom of NORTHUMBRIA. The landscape is varied, with coastal plains in the east, the rugged CHEVIOT HILLS and moors in the west, and industrial areas in the southern TYNE RIVER valley. It was the site of prehistoric settlement before the Roman domination began in AD 122, when HADRIAN'S WALL was built. It was the scene of border warfare with Scotland until the union of Scotland with England in 1603. Good farmland is limited; industrial complexes produce heavy machinery.

Northumberland, Duke of *orig.* **John Dudley** (1502–1553) English politician. After serving as deputy governor of English-occupied Calais (1538) and lord high admiral (1542), he fought in the invasion of Scotland (1544) and captured the French city of Boulogne (1544). He was created earl of Warwick (1546) and in 1547 became a member of the regency council that governed for the young EDWARD VI. After engineering the fall of the duke of SOMERSET, Warwick assumed control of the regency (1550). He made himself duke of Northumberland in 1551 and ordered Somerset's arrest and execution in 1552. He imposed strict conformity to Protestant doctrine in support of the Reformation. In 1553 he persuaded the dying Edward VI to will the crown to Northumberland's daughter-in-law, Lady Jane GREY; thwarted by supporters of Mary Tudor (MARY I), he was arrested and executed for treason.

Northumbria Anglo-Saxon kingdom of Britain. Located between the Humber River and the Firth of Forth, it extended from the Irish Sea to the North Sea. Its religious, artistic, and intellectual achievements in the 7th–8th century were epitomized by such centers as Lindisfarne and the monasteries of Wearmouth and Jarrow. Jarrow, with its fine library, was the home of the Venerable BEDE. After Northumbria's expansion in the 7th century, it became the most powerful of the Anglo-Saxon kingdoms before being destroyed by the Danes, who captured YORK in 866. In 944 the last Scandinavian ruler of York was expelled, and Northumbria became an earldom within the kingdom of England.

Northwest Coast Indians Any of the American Indian peoples who inhabited a narrow but rich belt of coastland and offshore islands from southeastern Alaska to northwestern California. From north to south: TLINGIT, HAIDA, TSIMSHIAN, northern KWAKIUTL (Heiltsuq), Bella Coola, southern KWAKIUTL, NOOTKA, Coast Salish, a series of lesser divisions, and CHINOOK.

Northwest Ordinances (1784, 1785, 1787) Measures enacted by the U.S. Congress for the division and settlement of the Northwest Territory, the frontier region extending north of the Ohio River to the Great Lakes and west of Pennsylvania to the Mississippi River. The original ordinance, written by THOMAS JEFFERSON, divided the territory into self-governing districts and set population requirements for statehood. The final ordinance, written partly by RUFUS KING, set land-grant sizes and prices, provided public land for schools, outlawed slavery, and guaranteed civil liberties. It established the principle of admitting new states on equal terms with the original 13 states.

Northwest Passage Sea passage between the Atlantic and Pacific oceans along the northern coast of America. The search for a commercial sea route around the American land barrier dates from the end of the 15th century and attracted explorers such as JACQUES CARTIER, FRANCIS DRAKE, MARTIN FROBISHER, and Capt. JAMES COOK. The passage was finally navigated successfully in 1906 by ROALD AMUNDSEN. As a modern trade route it has been marginally useful because of the polar ice cap and giant icebergs. Canada and the U.S. have encouraged international commerce over it, which would significantly shorten many international shipping distances.

Northwest Territories Territory (pop., 2001 est.: 40,900), northern Canada. Bounded by the YUKON TERRITORY, HUDSON BAY, and NUNAVUT, it stretches across the roof of the North American continent, reaching into the Arctic Circle. The capital is YELLOWKNIFE. It includes many islands, including VICTORIA ISLAND; the MACKENZIE RIVER; and GREAT BEAR and GREAT SLAVE lakes. More than half the people are Inuits (ESKIMOS) and American Indians. In the 18th century the mainland was explored by Samuel Hearne for the HUDSON'S BAY CO. and by ALEXANDER MACKENZIE. European settlers were mainly whalers, fur traders, and missionaries until the 1920s, when oil was discovered and the territorial administration was formed. Mining is the principal industry and centers on the petroleum and natural gas fields in the western Arctic coastal regions.

Northwestern University Private university in Evanston, Ill., founded in 1851. It is a comprehensive research institution that includes a college of arts and sciences, and schools of music, education, social policy, graduate studies, law, medicine, and dentistry. It also includes the Medill School of Journalism, the McCormick School of Engineering and Applied Science, and the Kellogg Graduate School of Management. Research facilities include centers for the study of learning, urban affairs and policy, and superconductivity. Total enrollment is about 12,000.

Norton, Charles Hotchkiss (1851–1942) U.S. maker of MACHINE TOOLS. Born in Plainville, Conn., he built a powerful GRINDING MACHINE capable of great precision while producing at mass-production speeds; his machine could grind an automobile crankshaft in 15 minutes, a process that previously had required 5 hours. He acquired 150 patents for improvements to a variety of machine tools.

Norton, Edwin (1845–1914) U.S. inventor and manufacturer. Born in Illinois, he began manufacturing tin cans on a small scale in 1868. With his brother, he opened a number of successively larger and more diversified Norton plants. By 1890 he had perfected the first automatic canmaking line. He invented the solder-trimmed cap and the machinery for making it, revolutionizing can manufacturing. He received more than 300 patents. Socially, he was an influential supporter of shorter working hours for laborers.

Norway *officially* **Kingdom of Norway** *Norwegian* **Norge** \'nȯr-gə\ Nation, northwestern Europe. Area: 125,050 sq mi (323,878 sq km). Population (2002 est.): 4,537,000. Capital: OSLO. Most of the people are of Germanic origin; the largest minority group is the Sami (Lapps). Language: Norwegian (official). Religion: Evangelical Lutheranism (official). Currency: Norwegian krone. In the western part of the Scandinavian Peninsula, Norway is Europe's fifth-largest country. It is a mountainous land with extensive plateau regions in its southwestern and central parts. Traditionally a fishing and lumbering country, it has greatly increased its mining and manufacturing activities since World War II. It has a developed economy largely based on services, petroleum and natural gas production, and light and heavy industries. Literacy is virtually 100%. It is a constitutional monarchy with one legislative house; its

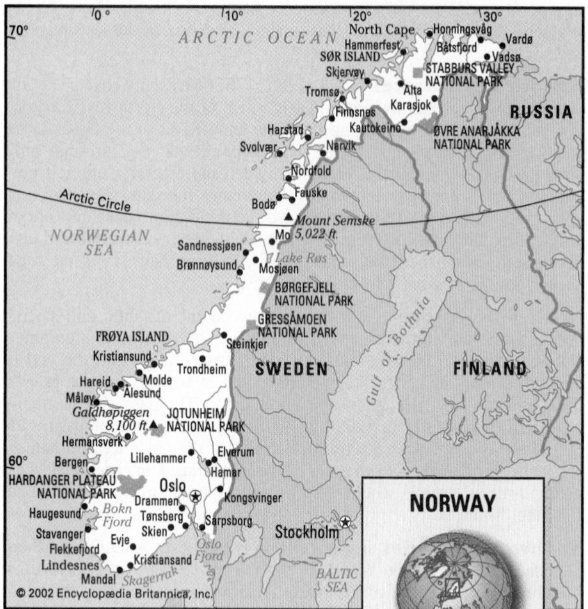

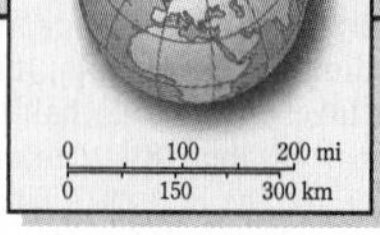

chief of state is the king, and the head of government is the prime minister. Several principalities were united into the kingdom of Norway in the 11th century. From 1380 it had the same king as Denmark until it was ceded to Sweden in 1814. The union with Sweden was dissolved in 1905, and Norway's economy grew rapidly. It remained neutral during World War I, although its shipping industry played a vital role in the conflict. It declared its neutrality in World War II but was invaded and occupied by German troops. Norway maintains a comprehensive welfare system and is a member of NATO. It turned down membership in the European Union in 1994. Its economy has grown consistently during the 1990s.

Norway lobster See scampi

Norwegian language North Germanic language of the West Scandinavian branch, spoken in Norway. Old Norwegian became a separate language by the end of the 12th century. Middle Norwegian became the tongue of most native speakers around the 15th century. Modern Norwegian has two rival forms. Dano-Norwegian (Bokmål, or Riksmål), the more popular, stems from written Danish used during the union of Denmark and Norway (1380–1814; see Union of Kalmar). It is used in national newspapers and most literary works. New Norwegian (Nynorsk), based on western rural dialects, was created by Ivar Aasen in the mid-19th century to carry on the tradition of Old Norse. Both languages are used in government and education. Plans to unite them gradually in a common language, Samnorsk, are controversial.

Norwegian Sea Open sea, northern Hemisphere. It is bordered by Greenland, Iceland, Spitsbergen, and Norway. A submarine ridge linking Greenland, Iceland, the Faeroe Islands, and northern Scotland separates the Norwegian Sea from the Atlantic Ocean. The sea is crossed by the Arctic Circle, but the warm Norway Current that flows northeast off the Norway coast produces generally ice-free conditions. Colder currents mixing with this warm water create excellent fishing grounds.

Norwich \'nȯr-ich\ City (pop., 1994 est.: 128,000), county seat of Norfolk, England. Located on the Wensum River northeast of London, it had become an important market center when it was sacked and occupied by the Danes in the 11th century. It was among the most prosperous English provincial towns for centuries; its economy was fostered by Edward III who induced Flemish weavers to settle there, and by the influx of immigrants during the reign of Elizabeth I. One of England's largest centers of footwear manufacturing, it features a Norman castle and cathedral. It is the traditional regional capital of East Anglia, and the site of a cathedral founded shortly after the Norman Conquest.

nose Prominent structure between and below the eyes. With the complex nasal cavity behind it, it functions for breathing and smelling. Behind the front section (vestibule), which includes the nostrils, it is divided vertically by three convoluted ridges (conchae) into air passages. In the highest one, the olfactory region, a small segment of mucous membrane lining contains neurons covered by a moisture layer, in which microscopic particles in inhaled air dissolve and stimulate the neurons. The rest of the cavity warms and moistens inhaled air and filters particles and bacteria out of it. Sinus cavities in the bone on both sides of the nose drain into the air passages. During swallowing, the soft palate closes off the back of the nose against food.

Nossob River \'nō-ˌsäb\ *or* **Nosop River** \'nō-ˌsäp\ River, South Africa. Rising in central Namibia, it flows southeast through the western Kalahari Desert and forms part of the border between Botswana and South Africa, bisecting the Kalahari Gemsbock National Park. It joins the Auob River before emptying into the Molopo River, which flows into the Atlantic Ocean. It is about 500 mi (800 km) long. Because of irregular rainfall, the lower Nossob's riverbed has contained flowing water only a few times in the 20th century.

nostoc \'nä-ˌstäk\ Any of the cyanobacteria that make up the genus *Nostoc*. The cells are arranged in beadlike chains grouped together in a gelatinous mass. Ranging from microscopic to walnut-sized, nostoc masses may be found on soil and floating in still water. A special thick-walled cell has the ability to withstand drying for long periods of time. After 70 years of dry storage, cells of one species can germinate into filaments when moistened. Like most other cyanobacteria, nostocs contain two pigments and are capable of nitrogen fixation.

Nostradamus \ˌnäs-trə-'dā-məs\ *orig.* **Michel de Notredame** (1503–1566) French astrologer and physician known for his prophecies. He practiced medicine in southern France from 1529, and gained a reputation for his innovative treatment of plague victims in 1546–47. He began making prophecies in 1547, and in 1555 they were published in a book titled *Centuries.* He wrote them in rhymed quatrains, using a cryptic style that mingled French, Latin, Spanish, and Hebrew. Catherine de Médicis invited him to her court as an astrologer, and in 1560 he was appointed physician to Charles IX. His prophecies are still widely read; readers have discovered apparent predictions of such world events as the French Revolution and World War I.

Nostratic hypothesis \nō-'strat-ik\ Proposal of an overarching northern Eurasian language family, still of uncertain validity. Holger Pedersen was the first to suggest that the Indo-European, Uralic, Altaic, Afroasiatic, and other language families might belong in one broad category (Nostratic). In the 1960s Vladislav Illich-Svitych made a detailed case in favor of the hypothesis and added Kartvelian (see Caucasian languages) and Dravidian to the list; he began reconstructing Proto-Nostratic but died in 1966 before finishing. The hypothesis remains highly controversial.

notary public Public officer who certifies and attests to the authenticity of writings (e.g., deeds) and takes affidavits, depositions, and protests of negotiable instruments. The notary is commissioned by the state and may act only within the territory authorized by state statutes. Most states set maximum fees for notarial services and require that a notarial seal or stamp be impressed on documents authenticated by a notary public.

notation, musical See musical notation

Noto Peninsula \'nō-tō\ Peninsula, Honshu, Japan. Jutting north into the Sea of Japan, it encloses Toyama Bay. The largest peninsula on the northern Honshu coast, it extends north for 50 mi (80 km) and has a width of about 19 mi (30 km). The town of Wajima, at the peninsula's northern tip, is known for its women pearl divers and its production of elaborate lacquer ware. Parts of the peninsula were designated national park land in 1968.

Nôtre, André Le See André Le Nôtre

Notre Dame, University of Private university in Notre Dame, near South Bend, Ind. It was founded in 1842 and reorganized in the 1920s; it became coeducational in 1972. It is affiliated with the Roman Catholic church. It has colleges of arts and letters, science, engineering, and business administration. It also has a graduate school and a law school. Total enrollment is about 10,000.

Notre-Dame de Paris \nȯ-tr^{ə}-'dȧm-də-pȧ-'rē\ (1163–c. 1350) Gothic cathedral on the Île de la Cité in Paris. Probably the most famous Gothic cathedral, Notre-Dame is a superb example of the RAYONNANT STYLE. Two massive Early Gothic towers (1210–50) crown the western facade, which is divided into three stories and has doors adorned with Early Gothic carvings and surmounted by a row of figures of Old Testament kings. The single-arch flying buttresses at the eastern end are notable for their boldness and grace. Its three great ROSE WINDOWS, which retain their 13th-century glass, are of awe-inspiring beauty.

Notre-Dame de Paris.
BY COURTESY OF ELECTA, MILANO

Notre-Dame school Composers of ORGANUM at the Cathedral of NÔTRE-DAME DE PARIS in the late 12th and early 13th century. Léonin (c. 1135–1201?) is credited with composing two-voice florid organum characterized by a rhythmically patterned "melisma" (a series of notes sung on one syllable) added to each sustained note of the plainchant (see GREGORIAN CHANT). He may have devised the rhythmic notation (ligatures) that made this possible, or at least codified the important system of rhythmic modes. His younger contemporary Pérotin (fl. c. 1200) is said to have edited, extended, and added parts to Léonin's *Magnus liber organi* ("Great Book of Organum") and created the first three- and four-voice textures known in world music. See also ARS ANTIQUA.

Notte, Gherardo delle See Gerrit VAN HONTHORST

Nottingham \'nä-tiŋ-əm\ City (pop., 1998 est.: 286,800), north-central England. Located on the TRENT RIVER, northeast of BIRMINGHAM, the original Saxon town was held by the Danes in the 9th century and became part of the DANELAW. It was the scene of three parliaments in the 14th century. In 1642, on Standard Hill, King CHARLES I raised his standard at the outbreak of the ENGLISH CIVIL WARS. Nottingham Castle stands on that site. The link between Nottingham and ROBIN HOOD is commemorated by a statue on Castle Green. The city has a distinctive lace quarter. It is the site of the University of Nottingham.

Nottinghamshire \'nä-tiŋ-əm-,shir\ County (pop., 1998 est.: 744,800), north-central England. It has coalfields and railway lines in the west, and in its center, a broad belt of infertile sandstone. Here the medieval forest of Sherwood, the haunt of ROBIN HOOD, stretched north from the city of NOTTINGHAM. Farmland is found in the Vales of Trent and Belvoir, where agriculture includes dairy farming. The chief river is the TRENT, along which there are numerous thermal electric power stations. The southwestern part of the county is densely populated and heavily industrialized.

Nouakchott \nu̇-'äk-,shät\ City (pop., 1995 est.: 735,000), capital of Mauritania. It is on a plateau near the western African Atlantic coast, north-northeast of DAKAR, Senegal. It was a small village until Mauritania was granted full independence from France in 1960. Then the city was developed as the capital of the new nation. It was a major refugee center during the Saharan droughts of the 1970s and grew rapidly. A port facility was built nearby for the export of petroleum and copper.

Nouméa \nü-'mā-ə\ *formerly* **Port-de-France** \,pȯr-də-'frä^{n}s\ Town (pop., 1989: 65,000), port, and capital of NEW CALEDONIA territory. Located on the southwestern coast of New Caledonia Island, it was founded in 1854 as Port-de-France. The city is situated on an excellent deep-water harbor protected by Nou Island and a reef. It has modern buildings, a large public market, and St. Joseph's Cathedral, an old stone structure.

nouvelle cuisine \nü-'vel-kwi-'zēn\ Style in international cuisine developed in France in the 1960s and '70s that stresses freshness, lightness, and clarity of flavor as distinct from the richer and more calorie-laden classic haute cuisine. Dishes commonly include sauces made of vegetable and fruit purees, novel combinations of foods in small quantities, and elegant displays highlighting details of texture and color.

nova Any of a class of STARS whose luminosity temporarily increases by several thousand up to a million times normal. Most appear to be BINARY STARS, one of which is a WHITE DWARF STAR drawing in matter from the other until it becomes unstable, causing an outburst in which the outer layer of material is shed. A nova reaches maximum luminosity within hours after its outburst and may shine intensely for several days or even a few weeks; it then slowly returns to its former level. Stars that become novas are usually too faint to see with the unaided eye until their sudden increase in luminosity, sometimes great enough to make them readily visible in the night sky. To observers, such objects may appear to be new stars; hence their name (Latin for "new"). See also SUPERNOVA.

Nova Scotia \,nō-və-'skō-shə\ Province, (pop., 1996: 948,000), Canada, one of the MARITIME PROVINCES. It comprises the peninsula of Nova Scotia, Cape Breton Island, and a few small adjacent islands, and it is bounded by the Northumberland Strait, the Gulf of St. Lawrence, the Atlantic Ocean, the Bay of Fundy, and New Brunswick. Its capital is HALIFAX. The region was first visited by VIKINGS c. AD 1000 and was inhabited by MICMAC Indians when JOHN CABOT claimed it for England in 1497. French settlers in 1605 adopted the Micmac name ACADIA for the region. English and Scottish colonists arrived by 1621. The conflict between France and England over control of the area was ended by the 1713 Peace of UTRECHT, which awarded it to England. In the 1750s, the British expelled most of the French settlers. Following the AMERICAN REVOLUTION, many Loyalists emigrated there. It joined the Dominion of Canada in 1867 as one of the original members. The province's economic mainstays are fishing, shipbuilding, and transatlantic shipping.

Novalis \nō-'vä-lis\ *orig.* **Friedrich Leopold, Freiherr (baron) von Hardenberg** (1772–1801) German Romantic poet and theorist. Born into a noble family, he took his pseudonym from a former family name. He studied law and then mining, and in 1799 became a mine inspector. His beautiful *Hymns to the Night* (1800) express his grief on the death of his young fiancée. In the years before his own death from tuberculosis at 28, he drafted a philosophical system based on idealism and produced his most significant poetic work. His mythical romance *Heinrich von Ofterdingen* (1802) describes a young poet's mystical and romantic searchings.

Novalis, detail of an engraving by Edouard Eichens, 1845.
BY COURTESY OF THE STAATLICHE MUSEEN ZU BERLIN, GERMANY; PHOTOGRAPH, WALTER STEINKOPF

Novara \nō-'vä-rä\, **Battle of** (March 23, 1849) Battle of the first Italian war of independence at Novara, Italy, near Milan. Austrian troops under JOSEPH RADETZKY defeated a larger Italian force under CHARLES ALBERT, king of Sardinia-Piedmont. The defeat revealed Piedmont's lack of support from the smaller Italian states and led to the abdication of Charles Albert.

Novartis AG See CIBA-GEIGY

novel Fictional prose narrative of considerable length and some complexity that deals imaginatively with human experience through a connected sequence of events involving a group of persons in a specific setting. The genre encompasses a wide range of types and styles, including PICARESQUE, EPISTOLARY, GOTHIC, romantic, realist, and historical novels. Though forerunners of the novel appeared in a number of places, including classical Rome, the European novel is usually said to have begun with MIGUEL DE CERVANTES's *Don Quixote.* The novel was established as a literary form in England in the 18th century through the work of DANIEL DEFOE, SAMUEL RICHARDSON, and HENRY FIELDING. The novel has remained popular because of its capacity for providing a faithful image of everyday reality. In the 20th century, writers seeking to capture elusive qualities of experience stretched the limits of the conventional novel, a process that perhaps culminated in the ANTINOVEL.

novella Story with a compact and pointed plot, often realistic and satiric in tone. Originating in Italy during the Middle Ages, it was often based on local events; individual tales often were gathered into collections. The novella developed into a psychologically subtle and structured short tale, with writers often using a frame story to unify tales around a theme, as in GIOVANNI BOCCACCIO's *Decameron.* The term is also used to describe a work of fiction intermediate in length and complexity between a SHORT STORY and a NOVEL. Examples include FYODOR DOSTOYEVSKY's *Notes from the Underground*, JOSEPH CONRAD's *Heart of Darkness*, THOMAS MANN's *Death in Venice* (1912), and HENRY JAMES's *The Aspern Papers.*

Noverre \nò-'ver\, **Jean-Georges** (1727–1810) French dancer and choreographer. In the 1750s he choreographed ballets in Paris, London, and Stuttgart; in Vienna (1767–74) he collaborated with the composer C.W. GLUCK. His 1760 treatise, *Letters on Dancing and Ballets,* stressed the need for unified dramatic structure by integrating story, music, choreography, and set design, as opposed to the loosely connected episodes of the dance suite that then prevailed. This innovative approach—called *ballet d'action,* or "ballet with a story"—brought major reforms in ballet production. His invention of *ballet d'action* was challenged by GASPARO ANGIOLINI, who had developed a simpler approach to the new form. In 1776 Noverre became ballet master of the Paris Opera. He choreographed over 150 ballets, including *Les fêtes chinoises* (1754), *Médée et Jason* (1763), and *Les petits riens* (1778).

Novgorod \'nòv-gə-rət\ City (pop., 1995 est.: 233,000), northwestern Russia. Located on the Volkhov River north of Lake ILMEN, it is one of the oldest Russian cities. First mentioned in the chronicles of AD 859, it came under RURIK in c. 862. It was of great importance in the 11th–15th cents., when it was the capital of the principality of Novgorod. It prospered by trade with the Orient, Constantinople, and the HANSEATIC LEAGUE. The center of the NOVGOROD SCHOOL of painting, it was ruled by ALEXANDER NEVSKY in the 13th century. It became a rival of MOSCOW, was destroyed by IVAN IV in 1570, and declined with the rise of ST. PETERSBURG. It was held by the Germans in World War II and suffered heavy damage. Many historic buildings were later restored, and it is a center of tourism.

"Miracle of St. George over the Dragon," icon by an anonymous artist of the Novgorod school, egg tempera on panel, beginning of the 15th century; in the State Tretyakov Gallery, Moscow, I.A. Ostroukhov Collection.
NOVOSTI PRESS AGENCY

Novgorod school Important school of Russian medieval icon and mural painting that flourished around NOVGOROD in the 12th–16th century. Novgorod, Russia's cultural center in the 13th–14th century, when most of the rest of the country was occupied by the Mongols, preserved the Byzantine traditions that formed the basis of Russian art, but introduced lighter and brighter colors, flatter forms, softening of facial types, and increasing use of a graceful, rhythmic line to define form. Until the early 14th century, artistic activity was dominated by mural painting. A new artistic impetus was provided by the introduction of the ICONOSTASIS. When icons were displayed together on the iconostasis rather than scattered about the walls of the church, they demanded a coherent overall impression, which was achieved by strong, rhythmic lines and color harmonies. Figures took on the elongated shape that became standard in Russian art. In the 16th century, artistic leadership passed to the MOSCOW SCHOOL.

Novi Sad \'nò-vē-'säd\ *Hungarian* **Újvidék** \'ü-ē-,vē-,dāk\ City (pop., 1991: 180,000), Serbia, northern Yugoslavia. The administrative capital of the autonomous region of VOJVODINA, it is a transit port on the DANUBE RIVER, northwest of BELGRADE. Founded in the 17th century, it was part of Hungary until the formation of Yugoslavia in 1918. The city is an ethnically diverse agricultural center; its economy suffered badly during the 1990s Balkan upheavals.

Novosibirsk \,nō-vò-si-'birsk\ *formerly (1895–1925)* **Novonikolayevsky** City (pop., 1996 est.: 1,400,000), southern central Russia in Asia. The capital of Novosibirsk province, it is the chief city of western SIBERIA and lies on the OB RIVER where the latter is crossed by the TRANS-SIBERIAN RAILROAD. The city began in 1893 and was named for the czar NICHOLAS II in 1895. During World War II many Russian factories from the west were moved there. It is renowned for industry and scientific research. As Siberia's cultural and educational center, it developed the satellite town Akademgorodok with research institutes and a university.

NOW See NATIONAL ORGANIZATION FOR WOMEN

Noyce, Robert (Norton) (1927–1990) U.S. engineer. Born in Burlington, Iowa, he received his PhD from MIT. In 1957 he launched Fairchild Semiconductor, one of the first electronics firms in what came to be called SILICON VALLEY. Simultaneously but independently, he and JACK KILBY invented the INTEGRATED-CIRCUIT COMPUTER CHIP in 1959. With his colleague Gordon Moore, he founded INTEL CORP. in 1968. In 1988 Noyce became president of Sematech, Inc., a research consortium formed and financed jointly by industry and the U.S. government to keep the U.S. semiconductor industry at the forefront of semiconductor manufacturing technology.

Noyes \'nòiz\, **John Humphrey** (1811–1886) U.S. social reformer. Born in Brattleboro, Vt., he studied for the ministry at Yale and declared his belief in "perfectionism," announcing that he had achieved a state of sinlessness. In 1836 he organized a community of "Bible communists" in Putney, Vt., where he advocated free love and "complex" marriage as opposed to "simple" or monogamous marriage. Arrested for adultery in 1846, he fled to Oneida, N.Y., where he established the ONEIDA COMMUNITY, which he led until 1879, when he fled to Canada to avoid legal action. He wrote several books on perfectionism and a history of U.S. utopian communities.

NPR See NATIONAL PUBLIC RADIO

NRA See NATIONAL RECOVERY ADMINISTRATION, NATIONAL RIFLE ASSN.

NSAIDs \'en-,sedz, 'en-,sādz\ *or* **nonsteroidal anti-inflammatory drugs** Drugs that reduce INFLAMMATION and are neither STEROIDS nor opioids (natural and synthetic opiates). They are also effective against pain (see ANALGESIC) and FEVER. Most are available with or without prescription and are usually used for short periods for mild pain. ASPIRIN is technically an NSAID, but the term is generally applied to a newer class of drugs, including IBUPROFEN and similar drugs (e.g., naproxen, ketoprofen) that, like aspirin, inhibit PROSTAGLANDIN synthesis. They act with fewer side effects, but aspirin-sensitive people should not use them.

Nu See NUN

Nu, U *orig.* **Thakin Nu** (1907–1995) Burmese independence leader and prime minister of Myanmar (1948–58, 1960–62). A prominent nationalist activist since his student days, U Nu became the first prime minister of independent Myanmar (then called Burma) in 1948. Though an able statesman, he was plagued by ethnic-minority insurrections and economic difficulties. He resigned in 1958, was reinstated in 1960, and was overthrown and imprisoned by NE WIN in 1962. After his release he organized resistance to Ne Win. He made an unsuccessful bid for power after Ne Win's government fell in 1988.

Nu Gua *or* **Nu Kua** \'nü-'gwä\ In Chinese mythology, the patroness of matchmakers. As wife or sister of the legendary emperor Fu Xi, she helped establish norms for marriage (including the use of go-betweens) and regulated conduct between the sexes. She is represented with a human head and the body of a snake or fish. She repaired the pillars of the heavens and the broken corners of the earth, which the rebel Gong Gong had destroyed in a fit of anger, and her beautiful palace was said to be the prototype for the walled cities of China.

Nu River See SALWEEN RIVER

Nubia Ancient region, Nile Valley, North Africa. It extended north to include ASWAN and, before completion of the Aswan Dam, the first cataract of the Nile in Upper Egypt. Now part of Sudan and Egypt, it contains the NUBIAN DESERT in the northeast. For about 1,800 years in ancient times it was subject to Egypt as a part of Ethiopia. The culture and nation of the CUSH were centered in the southern part. It was the center of a powerful state, with Dongala as its capital, 6th–14th century AD; then it was captured by the Arabs. The region was conquered by Egypt in 1820–22.

Nubia, Lake See Lake NASSER

Nubian Desert Desert, northeastern Sudan. It is separated from the LIBYAN DESERT by the NILE RIVER valley to the west. Rocky and rugged, with some dunes, it is essentially a sandstone plateau interspersed with many wadis (seasonal rivers) that die out before reaching the Nile. Rainfall averages less than 5 in (13 cm) a year.

nuclear energy *or* **atomic energy** Energy released from atomic nuclei in significant amounts. In 1919 ERNEST RUTHERFORD discovered that alpha rays could split the NUCLEUS of an ATOM. This led ultimately to the discovery of the NEUTRON and the release of huge amounts of energy by the process of NUCLEAR FISSION. Nuclear energy is also released as a result of NUCLEAR FUSION. The release of nuclear energy can be controlled or uncontrolled. Nuclear reactors carefully control the release of energy, whereas the energy release of a NUCLEAR WEAPON or resulting from a core MELTDOWN in a nuclear reactor is uncontrolled. See also CHAIN REACTION, NUCLEAR POWER, RADIOACTIVITY.

nuclear fission Division of a heavy atomic NUCLEUS into two fragments of roughly equal MASS, accompanied by the release of a large amount of energy, the BINDING ENERGY of the SUBATOMIC PARTICLES. The energy released in the fission of one uranium nucleus is about 50 million times greater than that released when a carbon atom combines with oxygen atoms in the burning of coal. The energy appears as KINETIC ENERGY of the fragments, which converts to THERMAL ENERGY as the fragments collide in matter and slow down. Fission also releases two or three free NEUTRONS. The free neutrons can bombard other nuclei, leading to a series of fissions called a CHAIN REACTION. The energy released from nuclear fission is used to generate electricity, to propel ships and submarines, and is a source of the vast destructive power of NUCLEAR WEAPONS. See illustration opposite.

nuclear fusion Process by which nuclear reactions between light elements form heavier ones, releasing huge amounts of energy. In 1939 HANS BETHE suggested that the energy output of the sun and other stars is a result of fusion reactions among HYDROGEN nuclei. In the early 1950s American scientists produced the HYDROGEN BOMB by inducing fusion reactions in a mixture of the hydrogen isotopes DEUTERIUM and TRITIUM, forming a heavier helium nucleus. Though fusion is common in the sun and other stars, it is difficult to produce artificially and is very difficult to control. If controlled nuclear fusion is achieved, it might provide an inexpensive energy source because the primary fuel, deuterium, can be extracted from ordinary water, and eight gallons of water could provide the energy equivalent to 2,500 gallons of gasoline. See illustration opposite.

nuclear magnetic resonance (NMR) Selective ABSORPTION of very high-frequency RADIO WAVES by certain atomic nuclei subjected to a strong stationary MAGNETIC FIELD. Nuclei that have at least one unpaired PROTON or NEUTRON act like tiny magnets. When a strong magnetic field acts on such nuclei, it sets them into PRECESSION. When the natural FREQUENCY of the precessing nuclear magnets corresponds to the frequency of a weak external radio wave striking the material, energy is absorbed by the nuclei at a frequency called the resonant frequency. NMR is used to study the molecular structure of various solids and liquids. MAGNETIC RESONANCE IMAGING, or MRI, is a version of NMR used in medicine to view soft tissues of the human body in a hazard-free, noninvasive way.

nuclear medicine Medical specialty using radioactive ELEMENTS or ISOTOPES for diagnosis and treatment of disease. A radioisotope is introduced into the body (usually by injection). The radiation it emits, detected by a scanner and recorded, reflects its distribution in different tissues and can reveal the presence, size, and shape of abnormalities in various organs. The isotopes used have short half-lives and decay before RADIOACTIVITY causes any damage. Different isotopes tend to concentrate in particular organs (e.g., iodine-131 in the thyroid). Radioactive substances are also implanted to treat small, early-stage cancers. This yields a slow, continuous dose that limits damage to normal cells while destroying tumor cells. See also COMPUTED AXIAL TOMOGRAPHY, DIAGNOSTIC IMAGING, POSITRON EMISSION TOMOGRAPHY, RADIATION THERAPY, RADIOLOGY.

Nuclear Nonproliferation Treaty *officially* **Treaty on the Nonproliferation of Nuclear Weapons** International agreement intended to prevent the spread of nuclear technology, signed by the U.S., Brit-

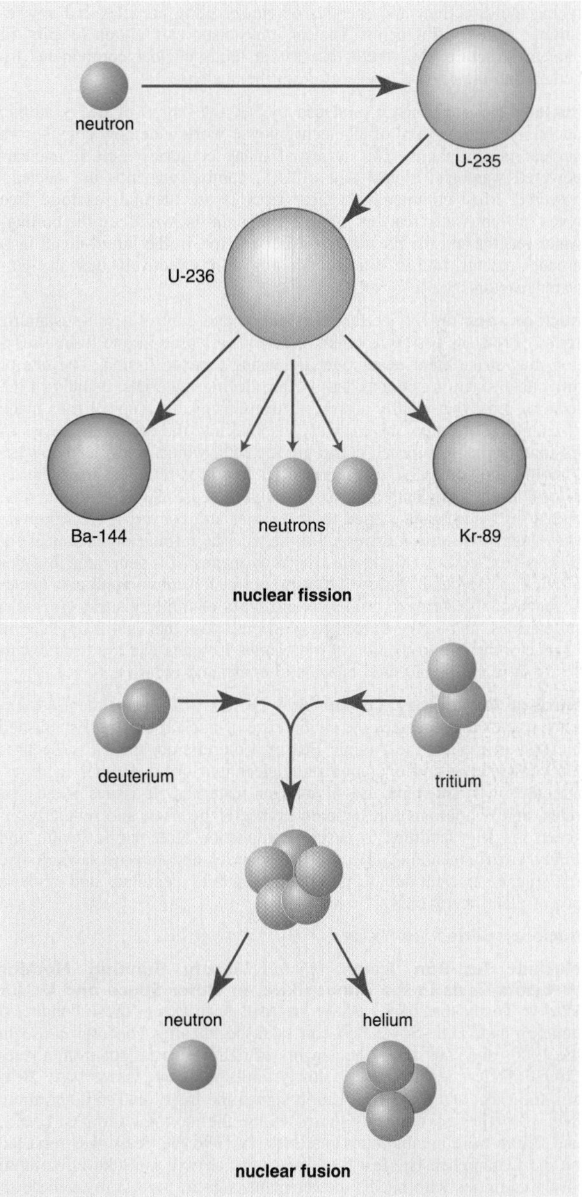

Top: Uranium-235 combines with a neutron to form an unstable intermediate, which quickly splits into barium-144 and krypton-89 plus three neutrons in the process of nuclear fission. Bottom: Deuterium and tritium combine by nuclear fusion to form helium plus a neutron.

ain, the Soviet Union, and 59 other countries in 1968. The three major signatories agreed not to assist states lacking nuclear weapons to obtain or produce them; the nonnuclear signatories agreed not to attempt to develop them, and in exchange were promised assistance in developing nuclear power for peaceful purposes. France and China, both nuclear powers, declined to ratify the treaty until 1992, and some nuclear powers, including Israel and Pakistan, have never signed. In 1995, when the treaty was due to expire, it was extended indefinitely by a consensus vote of 174 countries at the U.N. See also NUCLEAR TEST-BAN TREATY.

nuclear physics Branch of PHYSICS dealing with the structure of the atomic NUCLEUS and RADIATION from unstable nuclei. A principal research tool of nuclear physics is a high-energy beam of particles, such as PROTONS or ELECTRONS, directed as projectiles against nuclear targets. By analyzing the directions and energies of the recoiling particles and any resulting nuclear fragments, nuclear physicists can obtain details of nuclear structure, the STRONG FORCE that binds nuclear components together, and the release of energy from the nucleus.

nuclear power Energy produced by NUCLEAR FISSION of heavy atomic nuclei. About one-third of all electric power worldwide now comes from nuclear power plants. The navies of many countries include nuclear-powered warships; almost half of U.S. combat warships are nuclear-powered. Most commercial nuclear reactors are thermal reactors. Two types of light-water reactors in use throughout the world are the boiling-water reactor and the pressurized-water reactor. In the liquid-metal fast-breeder reactor, fuel is utilized 60 times more effectively than in light-water reactors. See also NUCLEAR ENERGY.

nuclear reactor Device that can initiate and control a self-sustaining series of NUCLEAR-FISSION reactions. Neutrons released in one fission reaction may strike other heavy nuclei, causing them to fission. The rate of this chain reaction is controlled by introducing materials, usually in the form of rods, that readily absorb neutrons. Typically, control rods made of cadmium or boron are gradually inserted into the core if the series of fissions begins to proceed at too great a rate, which could lead to MELTDOWN of the core. The heat released by fission is removed from the reactor core by a coolant circulated through the core. Some of the thermal energy in the coolant is used to heat water and convert it to high-pressure steam. This steam drives a turbine, and the turbine's mechanical energy is then converted into electricity by means of a generator. Besides providing a valuable source of electric power for commercial use, nuclear reactors also serve to propel certain types of military surface vessels, submarines, and some unmanned spacecraft. Another major application of reactors is the production of radioactive isotopes that are used extensively in scientific research, medical therapy, and industry.

Nuclear Regulatory Commission (NRC) U.S. independent REGULATORY AGENCY that oversees the civilian use of nuclear energy. Established in 1974 to replace the Atomic Energy Commission, the NRC licenses the construction and operation of nuclear reactors and other facilities, and the ownership and use of nuclear materials. It issues standards, rules, and regulations for the maintenance of licenses, and regularly inspects nuclear facilities to ensure compliance with public health and safety, environmental quality, national security, and antitrust laws. It also investigates nuclear incidents, conducts public hearings, and reviews power-plant operations.

nuclear species See NUCLIDE

Nuclear Test-Ban Treaty *officially* **Treaty Banning Nuclear Weapons Tests in the Atmosphere, in Outer Space and Under Water** Treaty that bans NUCLEAR WEAPONS tests except those conducted underground. U.S.–Soviet test-ban talks began after concerns arose in the 1940s and '50s about the dangers of radioactive fallout from aboveground nuclear tests, but went slowly until the CUBAN MISSILE CRISIS. Britain, the U.S., and the Soviet Union signed the treaty in 1963, and more than 100 other governments signed within the next few months. France and China were notable nonsignatories. In 1996 the treaty was replaced by the Comprehensive Test-Ban Treaty, which will not take effect until all 44 countries with nuclear-power plants sign it. India refuses to do so on the ground that the treaty lacks disarmament provisions and permits nonexplosive testing. See also NUCLEAR NONPROLIFERATION TREATY.

nuclear weapon *or* **atomic weapon** *or* **thermonuclear weapon** Bomb or other warhead that derives its force from either NUCLEAR FISSION or NUCLEAR FUSION and is delivered by an aircraft, missile, or other strategic delivery system. Nuclear weapons are the most potent explosive devices ever invented. Fission-dependent devices break heavy-element nuclei down into fragments; fusion devices fuse hydrogen nuclei at high temperatures to form helium nuclei. The destructive effects include not only the actual blast but also blinding light, searing heat, and lethal radioactive FALLOUT. See also ATOMIC BOMB, HIROSHIMA, HYDROGEN BOMB, MANHATTAN PROJECT, MIRV, NAGASAKI, NEUTRON BOMB, NUCLEAR TEST-BAN TREATY, START.

nuclear winter Environmental devastation that some scientists contend would probably result from a nuclear war. The basic cause, as hypothesized, would be huge fireballs created by exploding nuclear warheads, which would ignite great fires (firestorms). Smoke, soot, and dust would be lifted to high altitudes and driven by winds to form a uniform belt encircling the Northern Hemisphere. The clouds could block out all but a fraction of the sun's light, and surface temperatures would plunge for as much as several weeks. The semidarkness, killing frosts, and subfreezing temperatures, combined with high doses of RADIATION, would interrupt plant photosynthesis and could thus destroy much of the earth's vegetation and animal life. Other scientists dispute the results of the original calculations, and, though such a nuclear war would undoubtedly be devastating, the degree of damage to life on the earth remains controversial.

nucleic acid \nu̇-ˈklē-ik, nu̇-ˈklā-ik\ Any of the organic compounds making up the genetic material of living cells. Nucleic acids direct the course of PROTEIN synthesis, thereby regulating all cell activities. Their transmission from one generation to the next is the basis of HEREDITY. The two main types, DNA and RNA, are composed of similar materials but differ in structure and function. Both are long chains of repeating NUCLEOTIDES. The sequence of PURINES and PYRIMIDINES (bases)—ADENINE (A), GUANINE (G), and CYTOSINE (C) and THYMINE (T) or URACIL (U)—in the nucleotides, in groups of three (triplets, or codons), constitutes the GENETIC CODE.

nucleophile \ˈnü-klē-ə-ˌfīl\ ATOM or MOLECULE that contains an ELECTRON pair available for BONDING and in CHEMICAL REACTIONS therefore seeks a positive center, such as the NUCLEUS of an atom, or the positive end of a polar molecule (see COVALENT BOND, ELECTRIC DIPOLE). In the Lewis electron theory (see ACID–BASE THEORY), advanced by Gilbert N. Lewis in 1923, nucleophiles are by definition Lewis bases. Examples include the hydroxide ion (OH^-), the halogen ions (Cl^-, Br^-, and I^-), ammonia (NH_3), and water (H_2O). See also BASE, ELECTROPHILE.

nucleoprotein \ˌnü-klē-ō-ˈprō-ˌtēn\ Macromolecular complex consisting of a protein linked to a NUCLEIC ACID, either DNA or RNA. The proteins that combine with DNA are generally of characteristic types called HISTONES and protamines. The resulting nucleoproteins (deoxynucleoproteins) make up the CHROMOSOMES of living cells. Many VIRUSES are little more than organized agglomerations of deoxynucleoproteins. Many specific RNA nucleoproteins are also known; they have diverse cellular functions.

nucleoside \ˈnü-klē-ə-ˌsīd\ Any of a class of organic compounds, including structural subunits of NUCLEIC ACIDS. Each consists of a molecule of a five-carbon SUGAR (RIBOSE in RNA, deoxyribose in DNA) and a nitrogen-containing base, either a PURINE or a PYRIMIDINE. The base URACIL occurs in RNA, THYMINE in DNA, and ADENINE, GUANINE, and CYTOSINE in both, as part of the nucleosides uridine, deoxythymidine, adenosine or deoxyadenosine, guanosine or deoxyguanosine, and cytidine or deoxycytidine. Nucleosides usually have a PHOSPHATE group attached, forming NUCLEOTIDES. Usually obtained by decomposition of nucleic acids, nucleosides are important in physiological and medical research. Those that are not part of nucleic acids include puromycin and certain other ANTIBIOTICS produced by fungi.

nucleosynthesis \ˌnü-klē-ō-ˈsin-thə-səs\ Production on a cosmic scale of all the chemical ELEMENTS from one or perhaps two simple types of atomic nuclei (see NUCLEUS). Elements differ in the number of PROTONS and ISOTOPES of each element by the number of NEUTRONS in their nuclei. One type of nucleus can be transformed into another by adding or removing protons, neutrons, or both, processes that go on in stars. Many of the first 26 elements (up to iron) and their present cosmic abundances can be accounted for by successive NUCLEAR-FUSION reactions, beginning with HYDROGEN. Heavier elements are created by capture of successive neutrons and decay of some of these into protons (with ejection of an ELECTRON and a NEUTRINO each time).

nucleotide \'nü-klē-ə-ˌtīd\ Any of a class of organic compounds, including the structural units of NUCLEIC ACIDS. Each consists of a NUCLEOSIDE and one or more PHOSPHATE groups. In nucleic acids, the phosphate of one nucleotide joins to the sugar of the next to form the backbone. Important nucleotides that are not part of nucleic acids include ATP, cyclic AMP (needed in GLYCOGEN breakdown), and certain COENZYMES.

nucleus Specialized structure occurring in most CELLS (except BACTERIA) and separated from the rest of the cell by the nuclear membrane. This membrane seems to be continuous with the cell's ENDOPLASMIC RETICULUM and has pores that permits the passage of large molecules. The nucleus controls and regulates the cell's activities (e.g., growth and metabolism) and carries the GENES. Nucleoli are small bodies often seen within the nucleus that play an important part in the synthesis of RNA and protein. A cell normally contains only one nucleus.

nucleus Central, positively charged core of an ATOM. It consists of positively charged PROTONS and neutral NEUTRONS, known collectively as nucleons, held together by the STRONG FORCE. The number of nucleons can range from 1 to about 270, depending on the element. ISOTOPES are atoms of the same element that have the same number of protons but different numbers of neutrons. Some nuclei, especially heavier ones, are unstable, or radioactive (see RADIOACTIVITY), emitting energy in the form of alpha rays (see ALPHA DECAY), beta rays (see BETA DECAY), or GAMMA RAYS. The nucleus makes up nearly all the MASS but only a minute fraction of the volume of the atom.

nuclide *or* **nuclear species** Species of ATOM as characterized by the number of PROTONS, NEUTRONS, and the energy state of the NUCLEUS. A nuclide is characterized by its mass number and its ATOMIC NUMBER. To be regarded as distinct, a nuclide must have an energy content sufficient for a measurable lifetime, usually more than 10^{-10} second. Nuclear ISOMERS, which have the same number of protons and neutrons but differ in energy content and RADIOACTIVITY, are also distinct nuclides. Nuclides are associated with radioactive decay and may be stable or unstable. There are about 1,700 known nuclides, of which about 300 are stable and the rest radioactive.

nudibranch \'n(y)ü-də-ˌbraŋk\ *or* **sea slug** Any marine GASTROPOD in the order Nudibranchia. Most nudibranchs lack a shell, mantle cavity (see MOLLUSK), and gills, and breathe through the body surface. The delicately colored body, up to 16 in. (43 cm) long, has bizarre defensive outgrowths, called cerata, that discharge nematocysts ingested from CNIDARIAN prey. Antennalike organs arise from the head. Nudibranchs occur in shallow waters of all oceans, where they feed chiefly on other invertebrates, particularly SEA ANEMONES. Some species can swim; others are bottom creepers. The term sea slug sometimes refers to all members of the subclass Opisthobranchia.

nuée ardente \nü-'ā-är-'dänt\ (French: "fiery or glowing clouds") Highly destructive, incandescent mass of gas-enveloped particles that is associated with volcanic eruptions. These glowing avalanches, as they are sometimes called, can move down even slight inclines at speeds as high as 100 mph (160 kph). The temperature of the gases can reach 1,100–1,300°F (600–700°C). Nuées ardentes are exceedingly destructive, killing all living things in their path. Most occur in the circum-Pacific region known as the Ring of Fire. See also TUFF.

Nuer \'nü-ər\ People of the marsh and savanna on both banks of the Nile River in southern Sudan who speak an eastern Sudanic language of the NILO-SAHARAN family. The Nuer are cattle-raising people who also cultivate millet and spear fish. They spend the rainy season in permanent villages on the higher ground and the dry season in riverside camps. Feuding between clans is common, as is warfare with the DINKA. They number 1.5 million. See also NILOTES.

Nuevo León \'nwā-vō-lā-'ōn\ State (pop., 1995 est.: 3,550,000), northeastern Mexico. It has an area of 25,067 sq mi (64,924 sq km); its capital is MONTERREY. The SIERRA MADRE Oriental crosses the state in a southeastern path. The region became a state in 1824 and was occupied by U.S. troops during the MEXICAN WAR. Its iron and steel industries were the first heavy industry in Latin America; the state also supports agricultural and textile enterprises.

nuisance In law, an act, object, or practice that interferes with another's rights or interests by being offensive, annoying, dangerous, obstructive, or unhealthful. Such activities as obstructing a public road, polluting air and water, operating a house of prostitution, or keeping explosives are public nuisances and constitute criminal violations. A private nuisance is an activity or condition (e.g., excessive noise, disagreeable odor) that interferes with the use and enjoyment of one's property and that may be a cause of action in civil litigation. An attractive nuisance is something on one's property that poses a risk to children or others who may be attracted to it.

Nujoma \nü-'jō-mə\, **Sam (Daniel)** (born 1929) First president (from 1990) of independent Namibia. In the late 1950s Nujoma helped found the Ovamboland People's Organization, forerunner of the SOUTH WEST AFRICA PEOPLE'S ORGANIZATION (SWAPO). He became SWAPO's first president in 1960, and after years of petitioning the U.N. to compel South Africa to release control of S.West Africa, authorized armed resistance (1966). In 1989, after some 30 years in exile, he led SWAPO to victory in the U.N.-supervised elections.

Nuku'alofa \ˌnü-kü-ä-'lō-fə\ Town (pop., 1990 est.: 34,000), capital and chief port of Tonga. Located on the northern shore of Tongatapu Island, in the southern Pacific Ocean, it has a deep-draft harbor that is protected by reefs. Commercial activities center on the export of copra and bananas. Landmarks include the 19th-century royal palace and a chapel and royal tombs.

Nullarbor Plain \'nə-lə-ˌbȯr\ Vast limestone plateau along the coast of southwestern South Australia. The plain extends into southeastern Western Australia and north from the GREAT AUSTRALIAN BIGHT to the Great Victoria Desert. It occupies 100,000 sq mi (260,000 sq km) of generally flat surface in bedrock. The name Nullarbor is derived from the Latin *nullus arbor* ("no tree"). The Nullarbor National Park preserves rare vegetation and fauna. The plain has many limestone caves, including Koonalda Cave, an archaeological site. It is crossed by the world's longest stretch of straight railroad track (300 mi or 530 km).

nullification Doctrine upholding the right of a U.S. state to declare null and void an act of the federal government. First enunciated in the VIRGINIA AND KENTUCKY RESOLUTIONS (1798), it was expanded by JOHN C. CALHOUN in response to the Tariff of 1828. Calhoun maintained that a state "interposition" could block enforcement of a federal law. The South Carolina legislature agreed by passing the Ordinance of Nullification (1832), threatening to secede if the federal government forced collection of the 1828 tariff duties. Pres. ANDREW JACKSON asserted the supremacy of the federal government. The U.S. Congress passed a compromise tariff bill reducing the duties but also passed the Force Bill, which authorized federal enforcement of the law. The South Carolina legislature rescinded its ordinance, but the conflict highlighted the danger of nullification.

number Basic element of mathematics used for counting, measuring, solving equations, and comparing quantities. They fall into several categories. The counting numbers are the familiar 1, 2, 3 . . . ; whole numbers are the counting numbers and ZERO; INTEGERS are the whole numbers and the negative counting numbers; and the RATIONAL NUMBERS are all possible quotients formed by integers, including FRACTIONS. These numbers can be symbolically represented by terminating or repeating decimals. IRRATIONAL NUMBERS cannot be represented by fractions of integers or repeating decimals and must be represented by special symbols such as $\sqrt{2}$, e, and π. Together, the rational and irrational numbers constitute the REAL NUMBERS, which form an algebraic field (see FIELD THEORY), as do the COMPLEX NUMBERS. While the counting numbers and rational numbers come about as the means of counting, calculating, and measuring, the others arose as means of solving equations. See also TRANSCENDENTAL NUMBER.

number system Method of writing numerals to represent numbers. The use of ZERO as a placeholder was the greatest advance in number systems. The most common system is the decimal system, in which 10 symbols (the HINDU-ARABIC NUMERALS) denote multiples of powers of 10 by their position relative to the decimal point. Computers have brought greater awareness of the binary number system, in which two symbols, 0 and 1, represent multiples of powers of 2.

number theory Branch of mathematics concerned with properties of and relations among INTEGERS. It is a popular subject among amateur mathematicians and students because of the wealth of seemingly simple problems that can be posed. Answers are much harder to come up with. It has been said that any unsolved mathematical problem of any interest more than a century old belongs to number theory. One of the best examples, recently solved, is FERMAT'S LAST THEOREM.

numerical analysis Branch of applied mathematics that studies methods for solving complicated equations using arithmetic operations, often so complex that they require a computer, to approximate the processes of ANALYSIS (i.e., CALCULUS). The arithmetic model for such an approximation is called an ALGORITHM, the set of procedures the computer executes is called a PROGRAM, and the commands that carry out the procedures are called CODE. An example is an algorithm for deriving π by calculating the perimeter of a regular polygon as its number of sides becomes very large. Numerical analysis is concerned not just with the numerical result of such a process but with determining whether the ERROR at any stage is within acceptable bounds.

numerical control (NC) Control of a system or device by direct input of data in the form of numbers, letters, symbols, words, or a combination of these forms. It is a principal element of COMPUTER-INTEGRATED MANUFACTURING, particularly for controlling the operation of machine tools. NC is also essential to the operation of modern industrial ROBOTS. The two basic types of NC systems are point-to-point, in which a device is programmed to perform a series of motions with fixed starting and stopping points, and continuous-path, in which a point-to-point programmed device has sufficient memory to be "aware" of its former actions and their results and to act in accordance with this information.

numerology Use of numbers to interpret a person's character or divine the future. It is based on the assertion by PYTHAGORAS that all things can be expressed in numerical terms because they are ultimately reducible to numbers. Using a method analogous to that of the Greek and Hebrew alphabets (in which each letter also represented a number), modern numerology attaches a series of digits to an inquirer's name and uses these, along with the date of birth, to reveal the person's true nature and prospects.

Numidia \nü-'mi-dē-ə\ Ancient country, northern Africa, approximately coextensive with modern Algeria. During the Second PUNIC WAR, its two great tribes divided, one supporting the Romans and the other the Carthaginians. The tribal chief MASINISSA was made king of Numidia after the Roman victory in 201 BC. After the destruction of CARTHAGE, thousands fled to Numidia, which became a Roman province in 46 BC. Its capital was Cirta, and the chief city was Hippo, the see of St. AUGUSTINE. After its conquest by the VANDALS in AD 429, its Roman civilization declined rapidly; native elements revived to outlive the Arab conquest in the 8th century.

numismatics \ˌnü-məz-'ma-tiks\ Systematic accumulation and study of coins, tokens, paper money, and objects of similar form and purpose. During the 15th–16th century, nobles collected coins from Greece and Rome, whose cultures they admired. In the 17th century, catalogs and systematic analysis became more common, and false coins were more easily distinguished. In the 20th century museums have taken over the main task of forming large collections of great detail and range. London is the world's largest numismatic market, serving the interests of public collections and private collectors in many lands. A frequent justification for collecting coins is their investment value. Because the number of a particular coin issue remains static or decreases as coins are worn, damaged, lost, or destroyed, its value generally increases over time, especially if demand by collectors for that issue increases. Coins are also usually worth at least face value for their metal alone.

Nun \'nün\ *or* **Nu** Oldest of the Egyptian gods and father of RE, the sun god. Nun represented the dark, turbulent waters out of which the cosmos was churned. Since it was believed that the primeval ocean continued to surround the ordered cosmos, the creation myth was reenacted each day as the sun rose from the waters. Nun was also thought to exist as subsoil water and as the source of the annual flooding of the NILE.

Nun River \'nün\ River, southern Nigeria. Considered the direct continuation of the NIGER RIVER, it flows southwest to the Gulf of GUINEA, at Akassa. It was a trade route in the 19th century, when the IGBO kingdom controlled commerce. Petroleum was discovered along the Nun in 1963, and oil is piped from the oil fields along the Trans-Niger Pipeline.

Nunavut \'nü-nə-ˌvüt\ Territory (pop., 1998: 25,000), northern central Canada. Nunavut (Inuit for "our land") is the result of Canada's largest land claim settlement, created to give the Inuit (see ESKIMO), representing 85% of its population, a greater voice in Canadian government. Occupying an area of 772,000 sq mi (2 million sq km), or one-fifth of Canada's landmass, it comprises the central and eastern parts of the former NORTHWEST TERRITORIES, including BAFFIN and ELLESMERE islands. Its capital is IQALUIT. The area was settled by Inuits from 4500 BC to AD 1000. Vikings probably visited during the Middle Ages, but the first records of exploration are from MARTIN FROBISHER's 1576 search for the NORTHWEST PASSAGE. The mainland was explored by Englishman Samuel Hearne in 1770–72. After passing through British possession, it was transferred to Canada in 1870. In 1976 a political organization called for the creation of a territory to settle Inuit claims in the Northwest Territories. The proposal was approved by the Canadian government in 1993. Nunavut's first elections were held in February 1999, and the territory was inaugurated on April 1, 1999.

Nur al-Hilmi \'nůr-ȧl-'hil-mē\, **Burhanuddin bin Muhammad** (1911–1969) Malay nationalist leader. After serving the administration of the Japanese occupation during the war, Nur al-Hilmi became a prominent left-wing leader who worked for an independent and multiracial Malaysia. In 1956 he became president of the Pan-Malayan Islamic Party, which became the principal opposition party in Malaysian politics. With its agrarian-populist, anticolonialist platform, the party won a substantial share of the Malay vote.

Nuremberg *German* **Nürnberg** \'nūērn-ˌberk\ City (pop., 1992 est.: 497,000), BAVARIA, southern Germany, on the Pegnitz River. It grew up around a castle in the 11th century, and in 1219 it received its first charter. It became one of the greatest of the German free imperial cities, reaching the height of its power in the 16th century. In 1806 it became part of the kingdom of Bavaria. In the 1930s it was a center of the NAZI PARTY; it was the site of the annual NUREMBERG RALLIES, and in 1935 it gave its name to the anti-Semitic NUREMBERG LAWS. It was severely damaged in World War II. After the war, it was the scene of the NUREMBERG TRIALS. Rebuilt, it is now a commercial and manufacturing center. Its historic sites include the 11th-century royal palace. Its Academy of Arts (founded 1662) is the oldest in Germany. The city was the birthplace of ALBRECHT DURER.

Nuremberg Laws (1935) Two measures designed by ADOLF HITLER and approved by a NAZI PARTY convention at Nuremberg, Germany, on September 15, 1935. The laws deprived Jews of German citizenship and forbade marriage or sexual relations between Jews and "citizens of German or cognate blood." Supplementary decrees defined a Jew as a person with at least one Jewish grandparent and declared that Jews could not vote or hold public office.

Nuremberg Rallies Massive NAZI PARTY rallies held in Nuremberg, Germany, to showcase its power. After smaller rallies at Nazi Party conventions in 1923 and 1927, the first large-scale rally was held in 1929 and featured the nationalistic pageantry that marked subsequent annual rallies (1933–38). Attended by hundreds of thousands of party members, the rallies were carefully staged to reinforce party enthusiasm, with martial songs, massed banners and flags, goose-step marches, torchlight processions, and lengthy orations by ADOLF HITLER and other Nazi leaders.

Nuremberg Trials (1945–46) Trials of former NAZI PARTY leaders held in Nuremberg, Germany. At the end of World War II, the International Military Tribunal was established by the U.S., Britain, France, and the Soviet Union to indict and try former Nazis as war criminals. The tribunal defined the offenses as crimes against peace (planning and waging of war in violation of treaties); crimes against humanity (extermination, deportation, and GENOCIDE); and WAR CRIMES. After 216 court sessions, three of the original 22 defendants were acquitted, four (including KARL DONITZ and ALBERT SPEER) were sentenced to prison for 10–20 years, three (including RUDOLF HESS) were sentenced to life imprisonment, and 12 (including WILHELM KEITEL, JOACHIM VON RIBBENTROP, ALFRED ROSENBERG, ARTHUR SEYSS-INQUART, and JULIUS STREICHER) were sentenced to death by hanging. HERMANN GORING committed suicide before he could be executed, and MARTIN BORMANN was convicted in absentia.

Nureyev \nü-'rā-yef\, **Rudolf (Hametovich)** (1938–1993) Russian ballet dancer of charismatic virtuosity. He studied in Leningrad (1955–58) and joined the Kirov Ballet as a soloist. He defected during the company's tour to Paris in 1961. Thereafter he danced as a guest artist with many companies, especially the Royal Ballet from 1962 to the mid-1970s, where he regularly partnered M. Fonteyn in such ballets as *Giselle, Marguerite and Armand,* and *Swan Lake.* His electrifying performances, combining an intensely romantic sensibility with stunning muscularity and technique, made him a huge international star. He choreographed new versions of *Romeo and Juliet, Manfred,* and *The Nutcracker,* and also performed on television and in movies. From 1983 to 1989 he was artistic director of the Paris Opera Ballet. He continued to dance well after his prime. His death resulted from AIDS. He was widely acclaimed as the greatest ballet virtuoso since Vaslav Nijinsky.

Nureyev and Margot Fonteyn.
KEYSTONE

Nurhachi \'nu̇r-'hä-chē\ (1559–1626) Chieftain of one branch of the Juchen (later called Manchu), whose 1618 attack on China presaged his son Dorgon's conquest. Nurhachi first defeated a rival in his own tribe and then subdued the other four Juchen tribes in his immediate area. During this time, he also established a Manchu state and enlisted the scholar Erdeni to create a Manchu writing system. He organized his troops under the Banner System. In 1616 Nurhachi proclaimed himself khan and called his dynasty Jin, harking back to the Juchen Jin dynasty of the 12th century. In 1626 he was defeated by the Chinese and died of battle wounds. See also Hongtaiji, Qing dynasty.

Nuri al-Said \ˌnu̇r-ē-ȧl-sȧ-'ēd\ (1888–1958) Iraqi soldier and prime minister. He entered the Turkish army in 1909 when Iraq was a province of the Ottoman Empire. Captured by the British during World War I, he joined a British-backed Arab revolt against the Turks. After the war he joined the Iraqi government under the Hashemite king Faisal. Prime minister on 14 different occasions, he was pro-British and supported the Hashemite dynasty. In 1958 he supported union with Jordan, which the army opposed; he was killed by a mob following his overthrow by the military. See also Pan-Arabism.

Nurmi, Paavo (Johannes) (1897–1973) Finnish track athlete. He captured nine gold medals and three silvers in three Olympic Games (1920, 1924, 1928), setting two records at the 1924 games in a little over an hour. He held the world record for the mile run for eight years (1923–31). For his prowess he was nicknamed "the Flying Finn."

Nurmi, 1931.
UPI

nurse shark Only Atlantic species *(Ginglymostoma cirratum)* of 25 carpet shark species (family Orectolobidae). Yellow- or gray-brown, sometimes with dark spots, it may grow to over 13 ft (4 m) long. It may attack swimmers, especially when provoked, but is not related to the dangerous gray nurse *(Odontaspis arenarius),* a sand shark.

nursery Place where plants are grown for transplanting, for use as stocks for budding and grafting, or for sale. Nurseries produce and distribute woody and herbaceous plants, including ornamental trees, shrubs, and bulb crops. While most nursery-grown plants are ornamental, the nursery business also includes fruit plants and certain perennial vegetables used in home gardens (e.g., asparagus, rhubarb). See also floriculture.

nursery rhyme Verse customarily told or sung to small children. Though the oral tradition of nursery rhymes is ancient, the largest number date from the 16th, 17th, and (most frequently) 18th century. Apparently most rhymes were originally composed for adults, many as popular ballads and songs. The earliest known published collection is *Tommy Thumb's (Pretty) Song Book* (London, 1744), including "Little Tom Tucker," "Sing a Song of Sixpence," and "Who Killed Cock Robin?" The most influential collection was *Mother Goose's Melody* (1781), including "Jack and Jill," "Ding Dong Bell," and "Hush-a-bye Baby on the Tree Top."

nursing Health-care profession providing physical and emotional care to the sick and disabled and promoting health in all individuals through activities including research, health education, and patient consultation. Nursing gained recognition in the 19th century with the activities of Florence Nightingale. Many nurses have specialties (e.g., psychiatry, critical care). Nurse-practitioners, clinical nurse specialists, nurse-anesthetists, and nurse-midwives undertake tasks traditionally performed by physicians. The American Nurses Association sets standards, gives examinations, provides continuing education, and promotes legislation. Registered nurses (RNs) earn a degree and pass an exam. Licensed practical nurses (LPNs) complete a year of training and assist RNs. Nursing degrees go as high as the doctorate, and staff positions include administration. In addition to health-care settings, nurses practice in schools, the military, industry, and private homes. Community (public health) nurses educate the public on topics such as nutrition and disease prevention.

nursing home Facility for care (usually long-term) of patients who are not sick enough to need hospital care but are not able to remain at home. Historically, most residents were elderly or ill or had chronic irreversible and disabling disorders, and medical and nursing care was minimal. Today nursing homes have a more active role in health care, helping patients prepare to live at home or with a family member when possible. They help conserve expensive hospital facilities for the acutely ill and improve the prospects of the chronically disabled. However, quality of care varies widely, and the potential for abuse exists.

Nusayri See Alawi

Nut \'nüt\ In Egyptian religion, a goddess of the sky. She represented the vault of the heavens and was often depicted as a woman arched over the earth god Geb. Nut was believed to swallow the sun in the evening and to give birth to it again in the morning. She was sometimes portrayed as a cow, the form she took to carry the sun god, Re, on her back to the sky. On five days preceding the New Year, Nut gave birth successively to the deities Osiris, Horus, Seth, Isis, and Nephthys.

nut Dry, hard, one-seeded fruit consisting of a kernel, usually oily, surrounded by a hard or brittle shell that does not split open at maturity. Nuts include chestnuts, filberts, and walnuts; but other so-called nuts are botanically seeds (Brazil nut, pistachio), legumes (peanut), or drupes (almond and coconut). Most edible nuts are well known as dessert nuts. Some nuts are sources of oil or fat. Not all nuts are edible; some are used for ornament.

nut In technology, a fastening device consisting of a square or hexagonal block, usually of metal, with a hole in the center having internal, or female, threads that fit on the male threads of an associated bolt or screw. Bolts or screws with nuts are widely used for fastening machine and structural components. See also fastener.

nuthatch Any of about 22 species (genus *Sitta,* family Sittidae) of songbirds that are 4–7.5 in. (9.5–19 cm) long and have a short, square tail, short neck, and thin, pointed bill. Most are forest dwellers; some live in rocky areas. Nuthatches search tree trunks and rocks for insects, often descending headfirst. They also eat seeds, which they may store for winter. The nest is a grass- or hair-lined cavity. Nuthatches are most common from Eurasia to Japan and southward; four species occur in North America. Most are bluish above and white or reddish below; there may be a black eye stripe or a cap.

European nuthatch (*Sitta europaea*).
BRUCE COLEMAN LTD.

nutmeg Spice consisting of the seed of a tropical evergreen tree *(Myristica fragrans),* native to the Moluccas in Indonesia. It has a distinctive, pungent fragrance and is used in cooking and sachets and as incense. The tree yields fruit eight years after sowing, reaches its prime in 25 years, and bears fruit for 60 years or longer. The name nutmeg is also applied in different countries to other fruits or seeds, including the Brazilian nutmeg *(Cryptocarya moschata),* the Peruvian nutmeg *(Laurelia aromatica),* and the California nutmeg *(Torreya californica).*

Nutmeg *(Myristica fragrans).*
G.R. ROBERTS

nutria *or* **coypu** Semiaquatic South American RODENT *(Myocastor coypus)* in the hutia family (Capromyidae). The nutria has small ears, a long, rounded, scaly tail, partially webbed hind feet, and broad orange incisors. It is about 40 in. (1 m) long, including the tail, and may weigh 18 lbs (8 kg). Its reddish brown fur consists of coarse guard hairs overlying a soft undercoat. The nutria lives in a shallow burrow along a pond or river and mainly eats aquatic plants. Because their fur is valuable, nutrias were introduced into North America and Europe, and in some places have become pests that damage crops and compete with other wildlife.

Nutria *(Myocastor coypus)* feeding.
DOUGLAS FISHER

nutrition Processes of taking in and utilizing food substances. Food generates energy and supplies materials used in body tissues and processes. CALORIES are supplied by CARBOHYDRATES (SUGARS and STARCHES), FATS, and PROTEINS. Other nutrients include minerals, VITAMINS, and dietary FIBER. Minerals are used in many ways—IRON for HEMOGLOBIN; CALCIUM for bones, teeth, and cellular processes; SODIUM and POTASSIUM to regulate HOMEOSTASIS, IODINE to produce thyroid HORMONES. Trace minerals have less well understood functions. Fiber is not broken down chemically in the body but aids DIGESTION, lowers blood CHOLESTEROL, and may help prevent some CANCERS and HYPERTENSION. Different amounts of these nutrients exist in different foods; a varied diet ensures an adequate supply. Nutritional supplements, required by some people, do not compensate for an unhealthy diet. Sufficient WATER is always essential. Inadequate nutrient intake or absorption leads to MALNUTRITION and disease. The U.S. Food and Drug Administration and other agencies assess nutritional requirements.

Nuuk \'nük\ *or* **Godthåb** \'gȯt-ˌhȯp\ City (pop., 1996 est.: 13,000), capital of GREENLAND. Located on the southwestern coast near the mouth of Godthåb Gulf, it is Greenland's main port. The modern town dates from 1721, when a Norwegian missionary founded a colony near the site of Vesterbygden, a 10th-century Norse settlement. It is the seat of the parliament and supreme court and has foreign consulates, a teachers' college, and research stations. Government administration, hunting, fishing, and farming are the main occupations. Most transportation is by boat or helicopter.

Nyakyusa \nyȧk-'yü-sə\ *or* **Ngonde** \əŋ-'gȯn-dā\ Bantu-speaking people living north of Lake MALAWI in Tanzania, and in Malawi. Traditionally they lived in unique age villages. All the boys of a district aged 11–13 would leave their paternal homes and establish a new hamlet, eventually marrying and bringing their wives there; their native village would die as its founders died in old age. With modern land shortages, this practice has largely stopped. Numbering about 1.6 million, they are primarily hoe cultivators.

nyala \nē-'ä-lə\ Slender ANTELOPE *(Tragelaphus angasi)* of South Africa having a crest of hair along the back from head to tail and standing 3.5 ft (110 cm). The male, which has loosely spiraled horns and a long fringe on the throat and underparts, is dark brown with reddish brown on the lower legs, white on the face and neck, and vertical white stripes on the body. The female is reddish brown with more conspicuous striping. Nyalas live alone or in small groups in forests. The rare mountain nyala *(T. buxtoni)* of central Ethiopia is grayish brown.

Nyasa, Lake See Lake MALAWI

Nyasaland See MALAWI

Nyaya \'nyä-yə\ One of the six DARSHANS (orthodox systems) of Indian philosophy, important for its analysis of logic and epistemology and for its detailed model of the reasoning method of inference. Like other darshans, Nyaya is both a philosophy and a religion; its ultimate concern is to bring an end to human suffering, which results from ignorance of reality. It recognizes four valid means of knowledge: perception, inference, comparison, and testimony.

Nyerere \ni-'rar-ē\, **Julius (Kambarage)** (1922–1999) First prime minister of independent Tanganyika (1961), first president of Tanzania (1964–85), and the major force behind the ORGANIZATION OF AFRICAN UNITY (OAU). He taught in Catholic schools before studying history and economics in Britain. As leader of the Tanganyika African National Union (TANU), he advocated peaceful change, social equality, and ethnic harmony. In elections in 1958–60 TANU won many seats in the legislature. As president he collectivized village farmlands, carried out mass literacy campaigns, and instituted universal education. He sought to make Tanzania economically self-sufficient, an effort that ultimately failed. In 1979 he authorized the invasion of Uganda to overthrow IDI AMIN. Within the OAU he advocated the overthrow of white-supremacist governments in South Africa, Rhodesia, and S.West Africa. After retiring from politics in 1990, Nyerere devoted the rest of his life to farming and diplomacy.

Nyerere, 1981.
HANOS—LIAISON AGENCY

Nyiragongo \ˌnyē-rä-'gȯŋ-gō\, **Mt.** Active volcano, VIRUNGA MTNS., eastern central Africa. It lies in the volcano region of VIRUNGA NATIONAL PARK, eastern Congo (Zaire), near the border with Rwanda. It is 11,385 ft (3,470 m) high, with a main crater 1.3 mi (2 km) wide and 820 ft (250 m) deep containing a liquid lava pool. Some older craters are noted for their plant life.

Nykvist \'nu̇e-kvist, *Engl* 'nī-kvist\, **Sven** (born 1922) Swedish cinematographer. He joined the Swedish movie company Sandrews in 1941, shot his first film in 1945, and his first for INGMAR BERGMAN in 1953. He became Bergman's regular cinematographer at Svensk Filmindustri in 1960. Best known for his subtle, luminous camera work in a long series of Bergman films, he won Academy Awards for *Cries and Whispers* (1972) and *Fanny and Alexander* (1983). With U.S. directors, he has shot such movies as *The Unbearable Lightness of Being* (1988) and *Crimes and Misdemeanors* (1989).

nylon Any synthetic PLASTIC material composed of polyamides of high MOLECULAR WEIGHT and usually, but not always, manufactured as a fiber. Nylons were developed by Du Pont in the 1930s. The successful production of a useful fiber by chemical synthesis from compounds readily available from air, water, and coal or petroleum stimulated expansion of research on POLYMERS, leading to a rapidly growing family of synthetics. Nylon can be made to form fibers, filaments, bristles, or sheets to be manufactured into YARN, TEXTILES, and cordage, and can also be formed into molded products. It has high resistance to wear, heat, and chemicals. Most applications are in the form of filaments in such articles as hosiery, parachutes, and outerwear. See also W. H. CAROTHERS.

nymph In GREEK MYTHOLOGY, any of a large class of minor female divinities. Nymphs were usually associated with features of the natural world, such as trees and water. Though not immortal, they were extremely long-lived, and they tended to be well disposed toward humans. They were grouped according to the sphere of nature with which they were connected.

nymph In entomology, the sexually immature form of insects that undergo incomplete METAMORPHOSIS (e.g., GRASSHOPPERS). The nymph is similar to the adult but differs in body proportions and (in winged species) has only wing buds, which develop into wings after the first few molts (see MOLTING). During each successive growing stage (instar), the nymph begins to resemble the adult more closely. The nymphs of aquatic species (also called naiads), such as DRAGONFLIES, have gills and other modifications for an aquatic existence. At maturity, they float to the surface or crawl out of the water, undergo a final molt, and emerge as winged adults.

nymphaeum \nim-'fē-əm\ Ancient Greek and Roman sanctuary consecrated to water nymphs. Nymphaea also served as reservoirs and assembly chambers for weddings. The name, originally denoting a natural grotto with springs, later referred to an artificial grotto or building filled with plants, sculpture, fountains, and paintings. Nymphaea existed at Corinth, Antioch, and Constantinople, and remains have been found in Rome, Asia Minor, Syria, and northern Africa.

Nymphenburg porcelain German hard-paste, or true, PORCELAIN produced in Bavaria from the mid-18th century to the present day. Its fame rests on its figures, particularly those in the ROCOCO STYLE modeled between 1754 and 1763 by Franz Anton Bustelli (1723–1763). Tableware and vases produced at the factory in Nymphenburg, on the outskirts of Munich, often contain ozier, or basketwork, pattern borders.

Nyoro \'nyȯr-ō\ *or* **Bunyoro** Bantu-speaking people of western central Uganda. Until the 18th century the Bunyoro kingdom included present-day Uganda. It declined in the 18th and 19th century, surrendering its preeminence to the BUGANDA kingdom. It was brought into the Uganda Protectorate by the British. Today the Nyoro, numbering about 600,000, live in scattered settlements and cultivate millet, sorghum, and plantains.

Nystad, Treaty of See Second NORTHERN WAR

NYU See NEW YORK UNIV.

Oahu \ō-'wä-hü\ Island (pop., 1990: 836,000) of Hawaii. Situated between the islands of Kauai and Molokai, it occupies 607 sq mi (1,574 sq km), and is the third-largest and most densely populated of the Hawaiian Islands. Of volcanic origin, it has two parallel mountain groups, the Koolau Range and Waianae Ranges, which are connected by a central plateau. It is the site of Honolulu, Pearl Harbor, and Waikiki. Military installations, tourism, pineapples, and sugar are important to its economy.

oak Any of about 450 species of ornamental and timber trees and shrubs that make up the genus *Quercus* in the beech family, found throughout temperate climates. Oaks are deciduous trees that bear spring catkins (male flowers) and spikes (female flowers) on the same tree. The leaves have lobed, toothed, or smooth margins. The fruit is the acorn. They are hardy and long-lived shade trees. White oaks have smooth leaves and rapidly germinating sweet acorns; red, or black, oaks have bristle-tipped leaves and bitter, hairy acorns. Red- and white-oak lumber is used in construction, flooring, furniture, millwork, barrel making, and the production of crossties, structural timbers, and mine props. The genus includes many ornamentals and natural hybrids.

Oakland City (pop., 1996 est.: 367,000), western California, on the eastern side of San Francisco Bay. Settled by the Spanish in 1820, it was incorporated as a city in 1854. In 1869 it was chosen as the terminus of the first transcontinental railroad, which led to the development of its deep-water port. It suffered damage and loss of life in the earthquake of 1989, which also damaged the Bay Bridge that connects it with San Francisco. Lake Merritt, near the central business district, is a wildfowl refuge surrounded by parkland. Several colleges are located there.

Oakley, Annie *orig.* **Phoebe Anne Oakley Moses** (1860–1926) U.S. sharpshooter. Born in Darke Co., Ohio, to a Quaker family, she won acclaim for her marksmanship as a girl and toured vaudeville circuits with her marksman husband, Frank Butler. In 1885 they joined Buffalo Bill's Wild West Show, where they remained for 17 years. Oakley's famous act included shooting the end off a cigarette held in Butler's lips, hitting the thin edge of a playing card from 30 paces, and shooting distant targets while looking into a mirror.

OAS See Organization of American States

oasis Fertile tract of land that occurs in a desert wherever a permanent supply of fresh water is available. Oases vary in size from about 2.5 acres (1 hectare) around small springs to vast areas of naturally watered or irrigated land. Underground water sources account for most oases; their springs and wells are supplied from sandstone aquifers whose intake areas may be more than 500 mi (800 km) away. Two-thirds of the population of the Sahara live in oases, where the date palm is the main source of food; the palm also provides shade for growing citrus fruits, figs, peaches, apricots, vegetables, and cereal grains.

Oates, Joyce Carol (born 1938) U.S. writer. Born in Lockport, N.Y., Oates has taught at the University of Windsor (1967–78) and Princeton University (from 1978). Beginning with the story collection *By the North Gate* (1963) and the novel *With Shuddering Fall* (1964), she has written prolifically, often portraying people whose intensely experienced lives end in bloodshed and self-destruction owing to forces beyond their control. Her major novels include *A Garden of Earthly Delights* (1967), *Them* (1969), and *Do with Me What You Will* (1973). Also significant is a parodic gothic series including *Bellefleur* (1980), *A Bloodsmoor Romance* (1982), and *Mysteries of Winterthurn* (1984).

Oates, Titus (1649–1705) English fabricator of the Popish Plot. Son of a Baptist preacher, he was ordained in the Church of England. Though jailed for perjury in 1674, in 1677 he became chaplain to the Protestants in the household of the Catholic 6th duke of Norfolk. In 1678, with the fanatically anti-Catholic Israel Tonge, he invented a Jesuit conspiracy to kill Charles II and place his Catholic brother James (later James II) on the throne. Oates's testimony caused some 35 persons to be executed, but inconsistencies in his story emerged, and he was convicted of perjury and imprisoned in 1685; released in 1688, he died in obscurity.

oats Hardy cereal plant *(Avena sativa),* cultivated in temperate regions, that is able to live in poor soil. The edible starchy grain is used primarily as livestock feed, but is also processed into rolled oats and oat flour for human consumption. High in carbohydrates, oats also provide protein, fat, calcium, iron, and B vitamins. Oat straw is used for animal feed and bedding.

OAU See Organization of African Unity

Oaxaca \wä-'hä-kä\ State (pop., 1995 est. : 3,229,000), southern Mexico. Bounded by the Pacific Ocean, it occupies 36,820 sq mi (95,364 sq km) and includes most of the Isthmus of Tehuantepec. The capital is Oaxaca. The Sierra Madre del Sur ends at the isthmus. Remains of pre-Columbian Zapotec and Mixtec structures are found at Mitla and Monte Albán. It has the largest population of Indian descent in Mexico. It is an agricultural and mining area.

Oaxaca (de Juárez) City (pop., 1990: 213,000), capital of Oaxaca state, southern Mexico. It lies in the fertile Oaxaca Valley, 5,085 ft (1,550 m) above sea level. Founded in 1486 as an Aztec garrison and conquered by the Spanish in 1521, it had an important role in Mexican history and was the home of Benito Juarez and Porfirio Diaz. It is noted for its 16th-century architecture and its handicraft market.

Ob River \'öb\ River, western Russia. Flowing across western Siberia northwestward from the Altay Shan of central Asia, it courses through the Gulf of Ob into the Kara Sea of the Arctic Ocean. It is about 2,287 mi (3,680 km) long. Its middle course is through taiga, swampy coniferous forest with expanses of marshland. In the north are vast stretches of icy, treeless tundra. The Ob is an important source of hydroelectric power and one of Siberia's major transportation routes during the six months of the year when it is not frozen.

Obadiah \,ō-bə-'dī-ə\ (between 9th and 6th century BC) One of the 12 Minor Prophets in the Old Testament, traditional author of the Book of Obadiah. The Old Testament's shortest book, it consists of one chapter of 21 verses. (It is part of a larger book, The Twelve, in the Jewish canon.) Nothing is known of Obadiah, whose name means "servant of Yahweh (God)." He castigates Edom for failing to help Israel repel foreign invaders and announces that the Day of Judgment is near for all nations. The final verses predict the restoration of the Jews to their native land.

O'Bail, John See Cornplanter

obelisk Tapered four-sided pillar, originally erected in pairs at the entrance to ancient Egyptian temples. The Egyptian obelisk was carved from a single piece of stone, usually granite, and embellished with hieroglyphics. It was wider at its square or rectangular base than at its pyramidal top, and could be over 100 ft (30 m) high. During the Roman empire, many obelisks were transported from Egypt to Italy. A well-known modern obelisk is the Washington Monument.

Oberammergau See Passion play

Oberlin College Private liberal-arts college in Oberlin, Ohio. Founded in 1833, it was the first U.S. college to admit women and the first to admit black students on an equal footing with whites. In its early years it was a station on the Underground Railroad. It has faculties of science, communications, arts, foreign languages, law, letters, mathematics, psychology, public service, and social sciences, as well as a music conservatory. Enrollment is about 3,000.

obesity Excessive body fat, defined as weight at least 20% more than optimum. It is usually caused by sedentary habits and a diet high in fat, alcohol, or total calories. Calories consumed but not used are stored as fat. Rare causes include glandular defects and excess steroids (see Cushing's syndrome). Obesity raises the risk of heart disease and diabetes mellitus. Treatment, by reducing calorie intake and increasing exercise, is best undertaken with a doctor's advice.

obia *or* **obeah** \'ō-bē-ə\ In West African folklore, a gigantic animal that steals into villages by night to kidnap girls on behalf of witches. In some Caribbean cultures the word is used to refer to overpowering and extremely evil forms of witchcraft and sorcery. Bewitched objects, buried with the intent of causing harm, are sometimes called obia. A person who uses the power of obia is called an obiama or obiaman.

object language See METALANGUAGE

object-oriented programming (OOP) Computer programming that emphasizes the structure of data and their encapsulation with the procedures that operate upon it. It is a departure from traditional or procedural programming. OOP languages incorporate objects that are self-contained collections of computational procedures and DATA STRUCTURES. Programs can be written by assembling sets of these predefined objects in far less time than is possible using conventional procedural languages. OOP has become extremely popular because of its high programming productivity. C++ and Objective-C (early 1980s) are object-oriented versions of C that have gained much popularity. See also JAVA.

oblation In Christianity, the offering up by the faithful of any gift for use usually by the clergy, the church, or the sick or poor. The bread and wine offered for consecration in the EUCHARIST are oblations. In the Middle Ages children dedicated to a monastery and left there to be brought up were called oblates. Later, oblates were laity who lived at or in close connection with a monastery but who did not take religious vows. Members of certain Roman Catholic communities take the title oblate (e.g., the Oblates Regular of St. Benedict).

oboe Double-reed WOODWIND INSTRUMENT. The oboe developed out of the more powerful SHAWM in the early 17th century. Intended (unlike the shawm) for indoor use with stringed instruments, its tone was softer and less brilliant. In its early form it had as few as two keys; today it has about 13. With its sweet but piercing sound, it was by the end of the 17th century the principal wind instrument of the orchestra and military band, and, after the violin, the leading solo instrument of the time. With the decline in popularity of the military band, the oboe likewise declined somewhat in popularity. Today the orchestra generally includes two oboes. The oboe d'amore, an alto oboe with a pear-shaped bell, was especially popular in the 18th cent; the modern alto oboe is the ENGLISH HORN.

Obote \ō-'bō-tā\, **(Apollo) Milton** (born 1924) First prime minister (1962–70) and president (1966–71, 1980–85) of Uganda. Elected to the legislative council in 1958, he led his country to independence in 1962. As prime minister, he accepted a constitution that granted federal status to five traditional kingdoms, including BUGANDA, but in 1966 he sent troops under Gen. IDI AMIN to subdue Buganda's ruler, Mutesa II, and abolished all the kingdoms. He was overthrown in a coup led by Amin in 1971, but returned after Amin was deposed in 1979 to establish a repressive government. Having neglected to quell ethnic strife between northern and southern ethnic groups, despite his own often brutal policies, he was again ousted in 1985.

Obote.
MARION KAPLAN

Obraztsov \ˌò-brəst-'sòf\, **Sergey (Vladimirovich)** (1901–1992) Russian puppeteer. While working as an actor in Moscow (1922–31), he gave independent vaudeville-style puppet shows. In 1931 he was chosen the first director of Moscow's State Central Puppet Theatre. There his performances, displaying technical excellence and stylistic discipline, established puppetry as an art form in the Soviet Union, and on worldwide tours he inspired the formation of several rod-puppet theaters. His notable productions included *Aladdin's Magic Lamp* (1940), *An Unusual Concert* (1946), and *Don Juan* (1976).

Obrecht \'ō-ˌbrekt\, **Jacob** (c. 1450–1505) Flemish composer. Little is known of his origins or education, but by 1475 he was being called the equal of older masters such as G. DUFAY and J. OCKEGHEM. Most outstanding are his 29 masses; he also wrote about 30 motets and some secular music. Despite his contemporary renown, he had little influence on later composers, since his works were not widely distributed and his intellectual but exuberant music came to seem old-fashioned with the advent of JOSQUIN DES PREZ.

Obregón \ˌō-brā-'gōn\, **Álvaro** (1880–1928) President of Mexico (1920–24). A skillful military leader who fought for the moderate presidents FRANCISCO MADERO and VENUSTIANO CARRANZA during the MEXICAN REVOLUTION, he was largely responsible for the liberal constitution of 1917. In response to Carranza's increasingly reactionary policies, Obregón took a leading role in the revolt that deposed him, and was elected president in 1920. He managed to impose relative peace and prosperity on his war-torn country. He was elected again in 1928 but was shot and killed before assuming office.

Obrenovich dynasty \ò-'bren-ə-ˌvēch\ Family that provided Serbia with five rulers between 1815 and 1903. Its founding member, Milos (1780–1860), was prince of Serbia 1815–39 and 1858–60. His elder son, Milan III, reigned only 26 days before dying in 1839. Milos's second son, Michael III, was prince on two occasions (1839–42, 1860–68). A cousin, Milan IV (1854–1901), became prince in 1868 and then king of Serbia 1882–89. His son Alexander (1876–1903) succeeded him as king in 1889, but was assassinated in 1903.

O'Brian, Patrick *orig.* **Richard Patrick Russ** (1914–2000) British-French writer. He was the eighth of nine children; an early marriage ended in divorce, and after World War II he married again, changed his name, and moved to a small, secluded coastal French town near the Spanish border. He received little critical notice until age 54, when he began publishing his 18th-century seafaring series featuring Capt. Jack Aubrey and ship's surgeon Stephen Maturin; it eventually numbered 20 books (1969–99) and was compared with the works of HERMAN MELVILLE, ANTHONY TROLLOPE, and MARCEL PROUST, though the writer O'Brian himself most esteemed was JANE AUSTEN.

O'Brien, Flann *orig.* **Brian Ó Nuallain** (1911–1966) Irish novelist, dramatist, and newspaper columnist. Under the name Myles na gCopaleen, he wrote a column for the *Irish Times* for 26 years. He is most celebrated for the novel *At Swim-Two-Birds* (1939), a literary experiment that combines folklore, legend, humor, poetry, and linguistic games. His other novels include *The Hard Life* (1961) and *The Dalkey Archive* (1964).

O'Brien, Lawrence *in full* **Lawrence Francis O'Brien, Jr.** (1917–1990) U.S. political official. Born in Springfield, Mass., he managed JOHN F. KENNEDY'S successful campaigns for Senate (1952, 1958) and president (1960), then served as Kennedy's special assistant (1961–65), U.S. postmaster general (1965–68), chairman of the Democratic National Committee (1968–69, 1970–73), and commissioner of the National Basketball Association (1975–84).

O'Brien, William Smith (1803–1864) Irish political insurgent. Born in Ireland, he served in the British House of Commons 1828–48, and initially supported the Anglo-Irish legislative union (see Act of UNION). In 1843 he joined the anti-union Repeal ssociation, then broke with DANIEL O'CONNELL in 1846 to lead the radical Young Ireland movement. In 1848 he supported violent revolution and led an abortive insurrection in Co. Tipperary. Convicted of high treason; he received a death sentence that was commuted to exile in Tasmania. He was released in 1854 and pardoned in 1856.

William Smith O'Brien, lithograph by H. O'Neill after a daguerreotype by Glukman, 1848.
BY COURTESY OF THE TRUSTEES OF THE BRITISH MUSEUM; PHOTOGRAPH, J.R. FREEMAN & CO. LTD.

obscenity Act, utterance, or matter that is deeply offending according to contemporary community standards of morality and decency. The U.S. Supreme Court has ruled that materials are obscene if they appeal predominantly to a prurient interest in sexual conduct, depict or describe sexual conduct in a patently offensive way, and lack serious literary, artistic, political, or scientific value. Material deemed obscene by the Court is not protected by the free-speech guarantee of the 1st Amendment. See also FREEDOM OF SPEECH, PORNOGRAPHY.

observatory Structure containing TELESCOPES and secondary instruments for observing celestial objects. Observatories can be classified by the part of the ELECTROMAGNETIC SPECTRUM they can receive. Most are optical, observing in and near the region of the visible spectrum. Some are equipped to detect RADIO WAVES; others (orbiting astronomical observatories) are earth SATELLITES that carry special telescopes and detectors to study celestial sources of high-energy radiation (e.g., GAMMA RAYS, ULTRAVIOLET RADIATION, X RAYS) from above the ATMOSPHERE. STONEHENGE may have been an early optical observatory. Perhaps the first observatory that used instruments to accurately measure the positions of celestial objects was built c. 150 BC by HIPPARCHUS. The first notable premodern European observatory was that at Uraniborg, built for TYCHO BRAHE in 1576. Observatory House, in Slough, England, built and operated by the HERSCHELS, was one of the technical wonders of the 18th century. Today, the world's largest groupings of optical telescopes are atop Mauna Kea, in Hawaii, and Cerro Tuldo, in Chile. Other major observatories include ARECIBO OBSERVATORY, MOUNT WILSON OBSERVATORY, PALOMAR OBSERVATORY, and ROYAL GREENWICH OBSERVATORY.

obsessive-compulsive disorder Mental disorder characterized by recurring obsessions and compulsions. An obsession is a persistent disturbing preoccupation with an unreasonable idea or feeling (such as of being contaminated through shaking hands with someone). A compulsion is an irresistible impulse to perform an irrational act (such as repeatedly washing the hands). The two phenomena are usually, but not always, linked in the obsessive-compulsive person. Onset of the illness has been linked to malregulation of the neurotransmitter SEROTONIN as well as to the ill effects of high STRESS.

obsidian Natural glass of volcanic origin that is formed by the rapid cooling of viscous LAVA. It has a glassy luster and is slightly harder than window glass. It is typically jet black, but the presence of hematite (iron oxide) produces red and brown varieties, and tiny gas bubbles may create a golden sheen. It is sometimes used as a semiprecious stone. Obsidian was used by American Indians and others for weapons, implements, tools, and ornaments, and by the ancient Aztecs and Greeks for mirrors.

obstetrics and gynecology \ˌgī-nə-ˈkä-lə-jē\ Medical and surgical specialty concerned with the management of PREGNANCY and childbirth and with the health of the female REPRODUCTIVE SYSTEM. Obstetrics, first practiced by midwives, developed as a medical discipline in the 17th–19th century, adopting the use of forceps in delivery, anesthetics, and antiseptic methods. The last two made CESAREAN SECTION possible. Obstetricians confirm pregnancy, diagnose ECTOPIC PREGNANCY, conduct prenatal care, perform AMNIOCENTESIS, deliver babies, and perform abortions. In the late 20th century, a backlash against the excessive medicalization of birth led to a revival of MIDWIFERY and encouragement of NATURAL CHILDBIRTH. Gynecologists do routine pelvic exams, take samples for PAP SMEARS, advise on and prescribe birth control, and treat reproductive system disorders (e.g., ENDOMETRIOSIS, hormonal imbalances, problems with MENSTRUATION and MENOPAUSE). They perform surgery to prevent conception (tubal ligation), repair pelvic injuries, and remove cysts and tumors from the UTERUS, cervix, and OVARIES. Both specialties are involved in diagnosis and treatment of INFERTILITY. See also HYSTERECTOMY.

Obuchi \ˈō-bu̇-chē\, **Keizo** (1937–2000) Japanese politician. A graduate of Waseda Univ., he was first elected to the Diet in 1963, where he spent 12 terms, serving as chairman of the finance committee (1976) and minister for foreign affairs (1997). As Japan's prime minister (1998–2000), Obuchi had to deal with Japan's flagging economy and the related Asian economic crisis.

O'Casey, photograph by J. Bown.
CAMERA PRESS

O'Casey, Sean *orig.* **John Casey** (1880–1964) Irish playwright. Born to a poor Protestant family in Dublin, he educated himself and worked from age 14 at manual labor. He embraced the Irish nationalist cause, changed his name to its Irish form, and became active in the labor movement and its paramilitary Irish Citizens Army. By 1915 he had turned from politics to writing realistic tragicomedies about Dublin slum dwellers in war and revolution. The ABBEY THEATRE produced three of his earliest and best plays—*The Shadow of a Gunman* (1923), *Juno and the Paycock* (1924), and *The Plough and the Stars* (1926)—which caused riots by Irish patriots. When his antiwar play *The Silver Tassie* was rejected, O'Casey moved to England, where it was produced in 1929. His later plays include *Within the Gates* (1934), *The Star Turns Red* (1940), and *Red Roses for Me* (1946) and he published a six-volume autobiography (1939–56).

Occam, William of See William of OCKHAM

Occam's razor See OCKHAM'S RAZOR

occasionalism Type of mind–body DUALISM that maintains that apparent interactions between mental and physical events are in reality the result of God's constant causal action. Starting from Descartes's mind–body DUALISM, the occasionalists, whose most prominent exponents were NICOLAS DE MALEBRANCHE and ARNOLD GEULINCX, drew the conclusions that there can be no interaction between mind and body, and that all causality is immanent, within one order or the other, and any appearance of mind affecting body or of body affecting mind must be explained as the result of a special intervention by God, who, on the occasion of changes in one substance, produces corresponding changes in the other.

Occidental College Private liberal-arts college in Los Angeles, founded in 1887. It awards the baccalaureate degree in a number of disciplines as well as a master's degree in teaching. The curriculum emphasizes interdisciplinary and multicultural studies. Enrollment is about 1,600.

Occitan language \ˈäk-sə-ˌtan\ *or* **Provençal language** \ˌprō-ˌvän-ˈsäl, ˌprä-vən-ˈsäl\ ROMANCE LANGUAGE spoken in Occitania, a region of southern France, whose 1.5 million speakers use its dialects in everyday life and FRENCH as their official and cultural language. The term *langue d'oc* is based on the use of the word *oc* for "yes." The name Provençal originally referred to the dialects of the Provence region, used by medieval TROUBADOURS and as a standard and literary language in France and northern Spain in the 12th–14th century. Today's major dialects are those of Limousin, Auvergnat, Provence, and Languedoc. Gascon, spoken in southwestern France and usually classified as an Occitan dialect, is sometimes considered a distinct language. Occitan is closely related to CATALAN and, despite recent French influences, has more in common with Spanish than with French.

occultism Theories, practices, and rituals based on esoteric knowledge of the world of spirits and unknown forces. The wide range of occult beliefs and practices includes ASTROLOGY, ALCHEMY, DIVINATION, MAGIC, and WITCHCRAFT and sorcery. Devotees of occultism seek to explore spiritual mysteries through what they regard as higher powers of the mind. The Western tradition of occultism has its roots in Hellenistic magic and alchemy (especially the HERMETIC WRITINGS ascribed to THOTH) and in the Jewish mysticism associated with the KABBALA.

Occupation (of Japan) (1945–52) Occupation of Japan after its defeat in World War II. Theoretically an international occupation, in fact it was carried out almost entirely by Gen. DOUGLAS MACARTHUR. The Occupation oversaw the repatriation of Japanese soldiers and civilians abroad to Japan, the dismantling of arms industries, and the release of political prisoners. Wartime leaders stood trial for WAR CRIMES and seven were executed. A new constitution, vesting power in the people, replaced the MEIJI CONSTITUTION; in it Japan renounced its right to wage war, the emperor was reduced to ceremonial status, and women were given the right to vote. The Occupation also carried out land reform, reducing the number of farmers who were tenants from 46% to 10%, and began the breakup of the ZAIBATSU. Labor unions were initially encouraged; as fears of leftist organizations grew with the advent of the COLD WAR, stronger governmental control of labor was supported. The education system, seen as elitist, was revised to resemble the U.S. system. Though the U.S. wanted to end the Occupation in 1947, the Soviet Union vetoed a peace treaty; in 1951 a treaty was signed, and the Occupation ended the following year.

occupational disease Illness associated with a particular occupation. The Industrial Revolution's long working hours, dim light, lack of fresh air, and dangerous machinery fostered illness and injury in general, but certain occupations (e.g., mining) carry particular risks (e.g., black lung, a type of PNEUMOCONIOSIS). 20th-century innovations (including use of new chemicals and radioactive materials) have caused an increase in certain cancers (e.g., leukemia and bone cancer in workers exposed to radiation) and injuries. So-called "sick buildings" (in which pathogens grow in air circulation systems) contribute to health problems among office workers. Occupational medicine also covers work-related emotional stresses. See also ASBESTOSIS, INDUSTRIAL MEDICINE.

occupational medicine See INDUSTRIAL MEDICINE

occupational therapy Use of activities to promote health and independence, particularly after the acute phase of illness. Such therapy is often vital for reorienting patients unable to work for long periods. Occupational therapists assess patients' abilities, tailor programs to restore physical function, and devise ways to help those with permanent limitations carry out everyday functions. See also PHYSICAL MEDICINE AND REHABILITATION.

occupational training See EMPLOYEE TRAINING

ocean Large, continuous body of salt water. Ocean covers nearly 71% of the earth's surface and is divided into major oceans and smaller seas. The three principal oceans, the Pacific, Atlantic, and Indian, are largely delimited by land and submarine topographic boundaries. All are connected to what is sometimes called the Southern Ocean, the waters encircling Antarctica. Important marginal seas, primarily in the Northern Hemisphere, are partially enclosed by landmasses or ISLAND ARCS. The largest are the Arctic Ocean and adjacent seas, Caribbean and adjacent waters, Mediterranean, Bering Sea, Sea of Okhotsk, Yellow and China Seas, and Sea of Japan.

ocean current Horizontal and vertical circulation system of ocean waters, produced by gravity, wind friction, and water density variation. CORIOLIS FORCES cause ocean currents to move clockwise in the Northern Hemisphere and counterclockwise in the Southern Hemisphere and deflect them about 45° from the wind direction. This movement creates distinctive currents called gyres. Major ocean currents include the Gulf Stream–N. Atlantic–Norway Current in the Atlantic Ocean, the Peru (Humboldt) Current off South America, and the western Australia Current. See illustration below.

ocean liner Large merchant ship that visits designated ports on a regular schedule, carrying whatever cargo and passengers are available on the date of sailing. The first liners were operated in the North Atlantic, notably by SAMUEL CUNARD of Britain, beginning in 1840. Their heyday lasted from the late 19th to the mid-20th century. Many were extraordinarily luxurious. Among the most famous were Cunarders such as the *Mauretania* and the *Queen Mary;* the German *Vaterland* (later renamed *Leviathan*), for many years the largest ship afloat; the ill-fated TITANIC; and the *United States*. Their reign ended in the 1960s with the rise of jet travel, but liners ranging from cruise ships to refrigerated cargo ships continued to sail.

ocean perch See REDFISH

Oceania \ˌō-shē-ˈa-nē-ə\ Collective name for the islands scattered throughout most of the Pacific Ocean. These are especially islands of the central and southern Pacific, including MICRONESIA, MELANESIA, and POLYNESIA, and sometimes Australia, New Zealand, and the MALAY ARCHIPELAGO. In its most restricted sense, excluding Australia, but including Papua New Guinea, it includes more than 10,000 islands, with an area of about 317,000 sq mi (821,000 sq km) and a population (1990 est.) of 9,400,000. See map on following page.

Oceanic arts \ˌō-shē-ˈa-nik\ Visual arts of the Pacific islands of OCEANIA, including Australia as well as Polynesia, Melanesia, and Micronesia. Their isolation and wide range of environmental conditions led to the development of a rich variety of artistic styles. Throughout Oceania, the supernatural was the inspiration for the principal achievements of the arts. Wood was the main artistic medium; secondary materials included clay, shell, and stone. Extant works include wooden masks, clubs, and religious effigies; carved stone sculptures; feather cloaks and helmets; and bark cloth stenciled with bold, dense geometric designs The most famous monuments of Oceanic art are the gargantuan stone figures of EASTER ISLAND. See also BISJ POLE.

oceanic plateau \ˌō-shē-ˈa-nik\ *or* **submarine plateau** Large submarine elevation rising sharply at least 660 ft (200 m) above the surrounding seafloor and having an extensive, relatively flat or gently tilted summit. Most plateaus are steplike interruptions of the CONTINENTAL SLOPES. Some, however, occur well beyond the continental margins. They stand alone, high above the surrounding seafloor, and are believed to be fragments of continent that were isolated during CONTINENTAL DRIFT and SEAFLOOR SPREADING.

Oceanic religions Non-Christian religions practiced in OCEANIA. Traditional Melanesian religions, which are giving way under the pressures of Christianity and capitalism, hold that ancestral ghosts and other spirits are participants in daily life. Their presence and effects are manifested in dreams, in divination, and in human successes and failures. Magic is widely practiced, and sorcery is seen as the major cause of death and

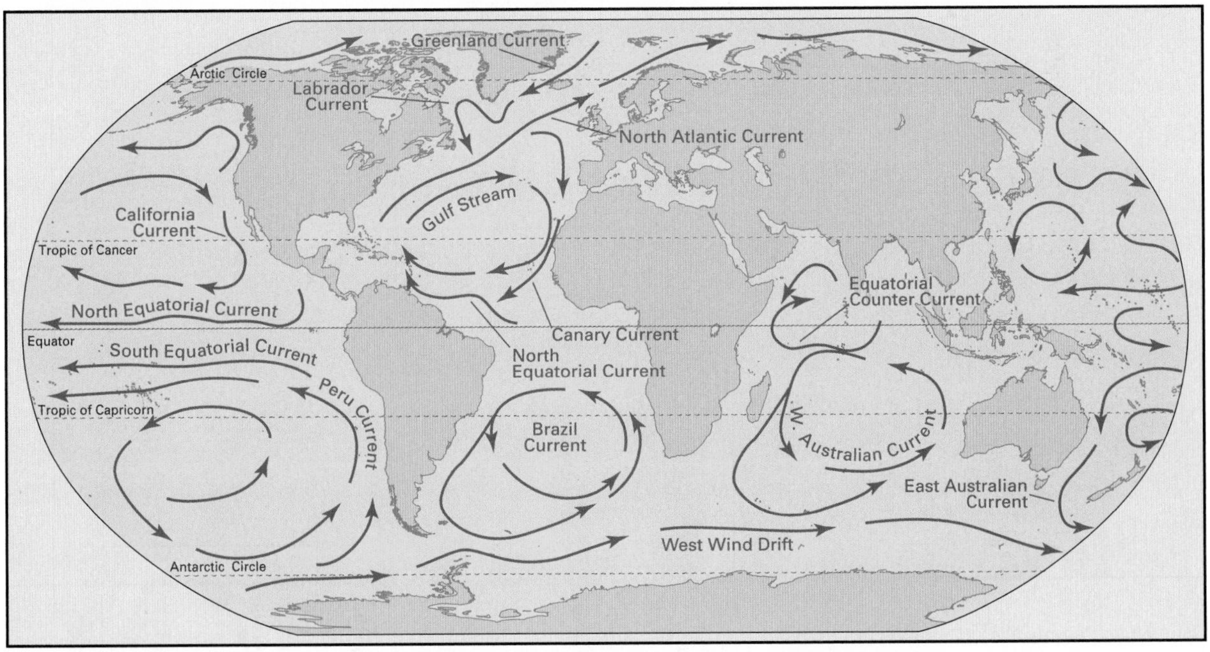

Major surface currents of the world's oceans. Subsurface currents also move vast amounts of water, but are not known in such detail.

O
P
Q
R

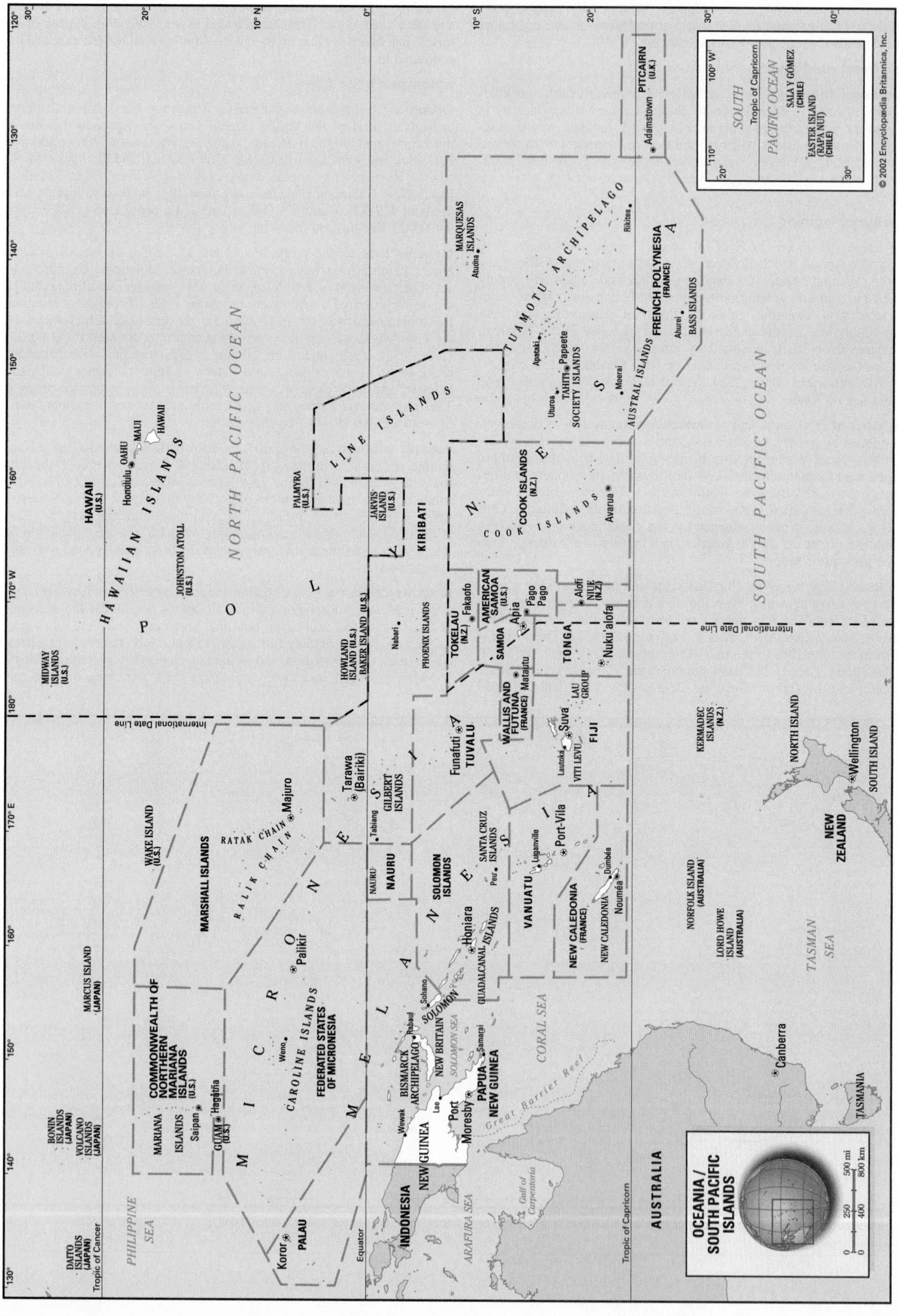
OCEANIA / SOUTH PACIFIC ISLANDS
NORTH PACIFIC OCEAN
SOUTH PACIFIC OCEAN
MICRONESIA
MELANESIA
POLYNESIA
HAWAIIAN ISLANDS
HAWAII (U.S.)
Honolulu
OAHU
MAUI
HAWAII
MIDWAY ISLANDS (U.S.)
JOHNSTON ATOLL (U.S.)
WAKE ISLAND (U.S.)
MARCUS ISLAND (JAPAN)
BONIN ISLANDS (JAPAN)
VOLCANO ISLANDS (JAPAN)
DAITO ISLANDS (JAPAN)
MARIANA ISLANDS
COMMONWEALTH OF NORTHERN MARIANA ISLANDS (U.S.)
Saipan
GUAM (U.S.)
Hagåtña
MARSHALL ISLANDS
RATAK CHAIN
RALIK CHAIN
Majuro
CAROLINE ISLANDS
FEDERATED STATES OF MICRONESIA
Palikir
Weno
PALAU
Koror
PHILIPPINE SEA
INDONESIA
NEW GUINEA
Wewak
Lae
PAPUA NEW GUINEA
Port Moresby
Samarai
BISMARCK ARCHIPELAGO
Rabaul
NEW BRITAIN
SOLOMON SEA
SOLOMON ISLANDS
Sohano
Honiara
GUADALCANAL
SANTA CRUZ ISLANDS
Peu
NAURU
GILBERT ISLANDS
Tabiang
Tarawa (Bairiki)
KIRIBATI
PHOENIX ISLANDS
LINE ISLANDS
PALMYRA (U.S.)
JARVIS ISLAND (U.S.)
HOWLAND ISLAND (U.S.)
BAKER ISLAND (U.S.)
Nabari
TUVALU
Funafuti
TOKELAU (N.Z.)
Fakaofo
SAMOA
Apia
AMERICAN SAMOA (U.S.)
Pago Pago
WALLIS AND FUTUNA (FRANCE)
Mata-Utu
FIJI
VITI LEVU
Lautoka
Suva
LAU GROUP
TONGA
Nuku'alofa
NIUE (N.Z.)
Alofi
COOK ISLANDS (N.Z.)
Avarua
VANUATU
Luganville
Port-Vila
NEW CALEDONIA (FRANCE)
Nouméa
Dumbéa
CORAL SEA
Great Barrier Reef
ARAFURA SEA
Gulf of Carpentaria
AUSTRALIA
Canberra
TASMANIA
TASMAN SEA
NORFOLK ISLAND (AUSTRALIA)
LORD HOWE ISLAND (AUSTRALIA)
KERMADEC ISLANDS (N.Z.)
NEW ZEALAND
NORTH ISLAND
SOUTH ISLAND
Wellington
FRENCH POLYNESIA (FRANCE)
MARQUESAS ISLANDS
Atuona
TUAMOTU ARCHIPELAGO
Apataki
SOCIETY ISLANDS
TAHITI
Papeete
Uturoa
AUSTRAL ISLANDS
Moerai
BASS ISLANDS
Ahurei
Rikitea
PITCAIRN (U.K.)
Adamstown
EASTER ISLAND (RAPA NUI) (CHILE)
SALA Y GÓMEZ (CHILE)
International Date Line
Equator
Tropic of Cancer
Tropic of Capricorn
0 250 500 mi
0 400 800 km
© 2002 Encyclopædia Britannica, Inc.

O
P
Q
R

illness. The traditional religions of Micronesia, which have largely died out, recognized several high gods and many other spirits, including the spirits of ancestors and the dead. Magic played an important role. In Polynesia, each of the gods, whether high or local, had its own ritual requirements, and schools of priests were often required to carry them out. All things were believed to possess MANA, which had to be protected by complicated rules and taboos. The Polynesians often offered human sacrifices on important occasions, such as the formal investiture of a priest or chief. With the introduction of modern goods, the peoples of all these islands became susceptible to CARGO CULTS.

oceanic ridge Continuous submarine mountain chain extending approximately 50,000 mi (80,000 km) through all the world's oceans, separating them into distinct basins. The main ridge extends down the middle of the Atlantic Ocean, passes between Africa and Antarctica, turns north to the Indian Ocean, then continues between Australia, New Zealand, and Antarctica and across the Pacific basin to the mouth of the Gulf of California. Lateral ridges extend from islands on the axis of the oceanic ridge to coasts of adjacent continents. The oceanic ridge system is the largest feature of the earth's surface after the continents and the ocean basins themselves; it is explained by the theory of PLATE TECTONICS as a boundary between diverging plates where molten rock is brought up from deep beneath the earth's crust. See also SUBDUCTION ZONE.

oceanic trench See DEEP-SEA TRENCH

oceanography Scientific discipline concerned with all aspects of the world's oceans and seas, including their physical and chemical properties, origin and geology, and life forms. Research entails sampling seawater and marine life, remote sensing of oceanic processes with aircraft and satellites, and exploration of the seafloor. Oceanography aids in predicting weather and climate, in exploitation of the earth's resources, and in understanding the effects of pollutants. See also MARINE GEOLOGY.

Oceanside City (pop., 1996 est.: 146,000), southwestern California. Located along the Pacific coast on the Gulf of Santa Catalina, north of SAN DIEGO, it is a beach resort. Incorporated in 1888, the city's growth was spurred in 1942 by the opening of a U.S. Marine Corps base, Camp Pendleton, to the north. Nearby is the restored Mission San Luis Rey (founded 1798).

ocelot \'ä-sə-ˌlät\ Species *(Felis,* or *Leopardis, pardalis)* of CAT found in forests, grasslands, and brush-covered regions from Texas to northern Argentina. The ocelot is 36–52 in. (90–130 cm) long, excluding the 12–16-in. (30–40-cm) tail. It stands about 18 in. (45 cm) and weighs 24–35 lbs (11–16 kg). The upper body varies from whitish to tawny yellow to gray. The head, neck, and body are marked by specific patterns of black stripes and spots: spots on the head, two stripes on each cheek, oblong spots arranged in chainlike bands on the body, and bars or blotches on the tail. The ocelot hunts at night for small mammals, birds, reptiles, and fish. It is listed as an endangered species in the U.S.

Ocelot (*Felis*, or *Leopardus*, *pardalis*).
WARREN GARST—TOM STACK AND ASSOCIATES

Ochoa \ō-'chō-ə\, **Severo** (1905–1993) Spanish-U.S. molecular biologist. He received his MD and subsequently studied in Germany and Britain before emigrating to the U.S. in 1941, where he taught principally at New York University. In 1955, while researching high-energy phosphates, he discovered an enzyme in bacteria that enabled him to synthesize RNA. The enzyme normally breaks down RNA, but in a test tube it runs its natural reaction in reverse. It has been valuable in enabling scientists to understand and recreate the process whereby the hereditary information contained in genes is translated into enzymes that determine each cell's functions and character. With ARTHUR KORNBERG he received a 1959 Nobel Prize.

Ochs \'äks\, **Adolph Simon** (1858–1935) U.S. newspaper publisher. Born in Cincinnati, Ochs grew up in Tennessee, where he worked for various newspapers. At 20 he borrowed $250 to become proprietor of the moribund *Chattanooga Times,* which he developed into one of the South's leading newspapers. He gained control of the financially faltering *NEW YORK TIMES* in 1896. Despising YELLOW JOURNALISM, he adopted the slogan "All the News That's Fit to Print" and emphasized comprehensive and trustworthy news gathering. Under his ownership the *Times* became one of the world's outstanding newspapers. From 1900 he was a director of the ASSOCIATED PRESS.

Ockham \'ä-kəm\, **William of** *or* **William of Occam** (c. 1285–1347/49) English Franciscan philosopher, theologian, and political writer. A late Scholastic thinker, he is regarded as the founder of nominalism, which denies that UNIVERSALS have any reality apart from individual things. With his passion for logic, he placed great trust in mankind's natural reason. As a theologian, he stressed the importance of the God of the creed, whose omnipotence determines the gratuitous salvation of humans. He believed that God's GRACE consists in giving without any obligation and is already profusely demonstrated in the creation of nature. See also OCKHAM'S RAZOR

Ockham's razor Methodological principle of parsimony in scientific explanation. Traditionally attributed to William of OCKHAM, the principle prescribes that entities are not to be multiplied beyond necessity. In practice, this means that if a phenomenon can be explained without assuming the existence of an entity, then philosophers and scientists should not assume the entity's existence. The history of science provides many examples of the principle's application (e.g., the rejection by scientists of the hypothesis of a luminiferous ether in response to ALBERT EINSTEIN's Special Theory of Relativity). See also MATERIALISM.

Ockeghem \'ō-kə-gem\, **Johannes** *or* **Jean d'Ockeghem** (c. 1415–1497) Flemish composer and singer. He is first mentioned as a member of an Antwerp choir in 1443. He held a series of posts in the Low Countries and France; he may have been associated with Gilles Binchois (c. 1400–1460) and G. DUFAY, and Antoine Busnois (c. 1430–1492) may have been his student. Though universally admired, his output, over a career of more than 50 years, was small, comprising 14 mass cycles, about 10 motets, and about 20 chansons. His richly sonorous works often reflect intricate structural principles.

Ocoee River \ō-'kō-ē\ River, rising in the BLUE RIDGE MTNS. in northeastern Georgia and southeastern Tennessee. In northern Georgia, where it is called the Toccoa, is the Blue Ridge Dam, forming Lake Toccoa. Three other dams on the river are all in Tennessee. The four dams are run by the TENNESSEE VALLEY AUTHORITY. It is about 70 mi (115 km) long.

O'Connell, Daniel *known as* **the Liberator** (1775–1847) Irish nationalist leader. A lawyer, he gradually became involved in the struggle for CATHOLIC EMANCIPATION, organizing nationwide "aggregate meetings" of Irish Catholics to petition for their legal rights. In 1823 he cofounded the Catholic Association, which won support from Irish political and church leaders. After helping win passage of the 1829 Emancipation Act, which allowed Irish Catholics to serve in the British Parliament, he was elected to the House of Commons. He supported the Whig Party in return for Irish reform measures, but became disenchanted with the administration's inaction. In 1839 he formed the Repeal Association to dissolve the Anglo-Irish Act of UNION. A series of illegal mass meetings in Ireland led to his arrest for sedition in 1843. After his release in 1844, he faced dissension from WILLIAM SMITH O'BRIEN's radical Young Ireland movement.

O'Connor, Feargus Edward (1796?–1855) Irish leader of CHARTISM. Born in Ireland, he practiced law and served in the British Parliament 1832–35. He turned to radical agitation in England and was active in the Chartist movement as a popular public speaker. His journal *Northern Star* (1837) gave his views wide circulation. He became the Chartists' leader in 1841 but was unable to effect passage of the Chartist petition in 1848. After a mental collapse, he was declared insane in 1852.

O'Connor, (Mary) Flannery (1925–1964) U.S. writer. Born in Savannah, she spent most of her life on her mother's farm in Milledgeville, Ga. A devout Roman Catholic, she usually set her works in the rural South and often tried to examine the relationship between the individual and God by putting her characters in grotesque and extreme situations. Her first novel, *Wise Blood* (1952), combines the keen ear for common speech, caustic religious imagination, and flair for the absurd that characterize her later work. With the story collections *A Good Man Is Hard to Find* (1955) and *Everything That Rises Must Converge* (1965), she was acclaimed as a master of the form. Her other work of fiction was the novel *The Violent Bear It Away* (1960). Long crippled by lupus, she died at 39. The Flannery O'Connor Award for Short Fiction is the preeminent American award of its kind.

O'Connor, Frank *orig.* **Michael O'Donovan** (1903–1966) Irish writer. Brought up in poverty, O'Connor became a librarian and a director of Dublin's ABBEY THEATRE. He won popularity in the U.S. for short stories in which apparently trivial incidents illuminate Irish life, appearing in volumes including *Guests of the Nation* (1931) and *Crab Apple Jelly* (1944) and in the *New Yorker* magazine. He also wrote critical studies on Irish life and literature and translations of Gaelic works of the 9th–20th century, including the great 17th-century satire *The Midnight Court* (1945).

O'Connor, Sandra Day *orig.* **Sandra Day** (born 1930) U.S. jurist. Born in El Paso, Texas, she studied law at Stanford Univ., graduating first in her class, and entered private practice in Arizona. She served as an assistant state attorney general (1965–69) before being elected in 1969 to the state senate, where she became the first woman in the U.S. to hold the position of majority leader (1972–74). After serving on the superior court of Maricopa Co. and the state court of appeals, she was nominated in 1981 by Pres. RONALD REAGAN to the U.S. Supreme Court and became the first female justice in the Court's history. She has proved to be a moderate and pragmatic conservative who sometimes sides with the Court's liberal minority on social issues (e.g., abortion rights). She is known for dispassionate and meticulously researched opinions.

OCR *in full* **optical character recognition** Scanning and comparison technique intended to identify printed text or numerical data. It avoids the need to retype already printed material for data entry. OCR software attempts to identify characters by comparing shapes to those stored in the software library. The software tries to identify words using character proximity and will try to reconstruct the original page layout. High accuracy can be obtained by using sharp, clear scans of high-quality originals, but it decreases as the quality of the original declines.

Octavian See Caesar AUGUSTUS

October Manifesto Document issued by Czar NICHOLAS II in October 1905. In response to the unrest caused by the RUSSIAN REVOLUTION OF 1905 and on the advice of his minister SERGEY WITTE, Nicholas promised to guarantee civil liberties and establish a popularly elected DUMA. The manifesto satisfied the moderate revolutionaries, and further unrest was crushed. In 1906 the Fundamental Laws were established to serve as a constitution and to create the Duma. The Duma was in fact given only a limited voice in the government, and the civil rights actually granted were far less substantial than those promised by the manifesto.

October Revolution See RUSSIAN REVOLUTION OF 1917

octopus In general, any eight-armed CEPHALOPOD of the order Octopoda; specifically, members of a large, widely distributed group (genus *Octopus*) of shallow-water species. Species range from about 2 in. (5 cm) to 18 ft (5.5 m) long with an armspan up to 30 ft (9 m). The head is usually only slightly demarcated from the saccular body. Each arm is contractile and bears fleshy suckers. Two sharp beaks and a filelike organ in the mouth drill crustacean shells and rasp away flesh. Most octopuses crawl along the bottom; when alarmed, they may jet-propel themselves backward, and they sometimes eject an inky substance to cloud the water and protect themselves from predators. They can change color rapidly, a reflection of their environment or mood. The common octopus *(O. vulgaris)* is thought to be the most intelligent of all INVERTEBRATES.

Octopus granulatus, a South African species.

ANTHONY BANNISTER FROM THE NATURAL HISTORY PHOTOGRAPHIC AGENCY—EB INC.

oculus \'ä-kyə-ləs\ (Latin: "eye") In architecture, any of several elements resembling an eye, such as a round or oval window or the round opening at the top of some domes (see PANTHEON). The capital of an Ionic column features a disk known as an oculus at the center of each of its spiral scrolls.

Oda Nobunaga \'ō-dä-ˌnō-bü-'nä-gä\ (1534–1582) With TOYOTOMI HIDEYOSHI and TOKUGAWA IEYASU, one of the Three Unifiers of Japan. He brought the domain of his birth, Owari, under his control and followed that success by defeating the huge forces of a neighboring DAIMYO. In 1562 he formed an alliance with Tokugawa Ieyasu and together they captured Kyoto, which Nobunaga controlled from 1573, thereby ending the ASHIKAGA SHOGUNATE. He then turned his attention to crushing the militant Tendai monks of Enryaku-ji, destroying their headquarters in 1571. He spent the next decade fighting the fanatically religious Ikko sect, defeating their fortress-monastery in Osaka in 1580. His efforts to weaken the strength of the Buddhist temples extended to permitting Jesuit missionaries to build a church in Kyoto; his own interest in Christianity was purely political. In 1582 he had conquered central Japan and was attempting to extend his control over western Japan when he was brought down by a discontented general.

ode Ceremonious lyric poem on an occasion of dignity in which personal emotion and universal themes are united. The form is usually marked by exalted feeling and style, varying line length, and complex stanza forms. The term ode derives from a Greek word alluding to a choric song, usually accompanied by a dance. Forms of odes include the PINDARIC ODE, written to celebrate public events such as the Olympic games, and the form associated with HORACE, whose intimate, reflective odes have two- or four-line stanzas and polished meters. Both were revived during the Renaissance and influenced Western lyric poetry into the 20th century. The ode also flourished in pre-Islamic Arabic poetry.

Odense \'ü-ən-zə, *Engl* 'ō-den-sə\ City (metro. area pop., 1996 est. : 184,000), northern central FYN Island, Denmark. Sacred in pagan times as the sanctuary of ODIN, the Norse god of war, it first appears in records c. AD 1000. A bishop's seat from the 10th century, it became a center of pilgrimage to the shrine of CANUTE. It was burned in 1247, but many medieval structures remain. It grew after its port and harbor were built and the Odense Canal was opened in 1804. Denmark's third-largest city, it is a shipbuilding and manufacturing center. The home of HANS CHRISTIAN ANDERSEN, who was born there, is now a museum.

Oder-Neisse Line \'ō-dər-'nī-sə\ Polish–German border along the Oder and Neisse rivers proposed by the Allied Powers at the end of WORLD WAR II. After inconclusive talks at the YALTA CONFERENCE to redraw the Polish–German border so as to grant more territory to Poland, the Soviet Union unilaterally occupied all territory east of its preferred Oder-Neisse line. The U.S. and Britain, dubious about Soviet domination of an enlarged Poland, protested the action but eventually agreed to the provisional border, which was not recognized by West Germany until it signed treaties with the Soviet Union and Poland in 1970.

Oder River \'ō-dər\ *or* **Odra River** \'ò-drä\ *ancient* **Viadua** River, northern Europe. It flows from its source in the Oder Mountains in the Czech Republic north through western Poland, where it forms the boundary between Poland and Germany. As the second-largest river emptying into the BALTIC SEA, it is economically important as a transport route. Navigable for 475 mi (765 km), it is connected by canal with the VISTULA RIVER and with the western European waterway system. It was partially internationalized under the Treaty of VERSAILLES in 1919. Considered German until the 1945 Potsdam settlement, it was formally recognized as the Polish–German border in 1950 by East Germany and in 1970 by West Germany.

Odessa City (pop., 1996 est.: 1,046,000), southwestern Ukraine. A Tatar fortress was established there in the 14th century. The city was ceded to Russia in 1791 and became its second most important port after ST. PETERSBURG, with grain as its principal export. It was a center of revolutionary activity in 1905 (see RUSSIAN REVOLUTION OF 1905). It suffered heavy damage in World War II but remains a major seaport and industrial center, with shipbuilding, engineering, and oil refineries. It is also a cultural center, with a university, museums, and theaters.

Odets \ō-'dets\, **Clifford** (1906–1963) U.S. playwright. He acted with repertory companies 1923–28 and joined the GROUP THEATRE in 1931. His first play, the social-protest drama *Waiting for Lefty* (1935), helped establish his and the company's reputation. He followed it with *Awake and Sing!* (1935) and *Golden Boy* (1937). He moved to Hollywood in the late 1930s, where he wrote screenplays and directed the movies *None but the Lonely Heart* (1944) and *The Story on Page One* (1959). His later plays included *The Big Knife* (1949), *The Country Girl* (1950), and *The Flowering Peach* (1954).

odeum \ō-'dē-əm\ Comparatively small, often semicircular roofed theater of ancient Greece and Rome used for musical performances. One still in use was built by Herodes Atticus at the base of the Athenian Acropolis (AD 161). Odea were constructed in most cities of the Roman empire for use as assembly halls as well as for performances. See also AMPHITHEATER.

Odin \'ō-din\ *or* **Wotan** \'vō-,tän\ One of the principal Norse gods. A war god from earliest times, Odin appeared in Scandinavian heroic literature as the protector of heroes. Fallen warriors were believed to join him in VALHALLA. Odin was the great magician among the gods and was associated with RUNIC WRITING. His eight-legged horse, Sleipnir, could gallop through the air and over the sea. Odin was usually depicted as a tall old man with a flowing beard and only one eye (the other he gave in exchange for wisdom); he wore a cloak and a wide-brimmed hat and carried a spear. The wolf and the raven were dedicated to him.

Odo of Bayeux \'ō-dō...bá-'yœ\ *or* **Earl of Kent** (1036?–1097) Bishop of Bayeux, Normandy, and half brother of WILLIAM I THE CONQUEROR. He fought in the Battle of HASTINGS and probably commissioned the BAYEUX TAPESTRY. Made earl of Kent in 1067, he guarded southeastern England and ruled (with others) in William's absence. William imprisoned him (1082–87) for raising troops without royal permission, and he later joined a rebellion in support of ROBERT II. He helped organize the First CRUSADE and died on his way to the Holy Land.

Odoacer \,ō-dō-'ā-sər\ *or* **Odovacar** \,ō-dō-'vā-kər\ (433?–493) First barbarian king of Italy (476–93). A German warrior in the Roman army, he led a revolt against the usurper Orestes (475). He was proclaimed king by his troops in 476, the date that traditionally marks the end of the Western Roman Empire. Odoacer paid homage to the Eastern emperor, ZENO, but asserted his own right to rule Italy. He conquered Dalmatia (482), defeated the Rugi (487–88), and retook Sicily from the Vandals. By attacking the Eastern Empire he alienated Zeno, who encouraged the Ostrogothic king THEODORIC to invade Italy (489). Theodoric captured almost the entire peninsula and killed Odoacer after inviting him to a banquet.

O'Donnell, Guillermo (born 1936) Argentine political scientist. He earned a law degree in Argentina and a PhD from Yale University. He has taught at universities in South America, Europe, and the U.S. (principally Notre Dame), and has written many books on Latin American authoritarianism and democracy and the transition from one to the other. His pathbreaking analysis of "bureaucratic authoritarianism" as a specific type of military rule found especially in Latin America from the 1960s to the 1980s contributed greatly to the understanding of comparative politics.

Odum, Howard W(ashington) (1884–1954) U.S. sociologist. Born in Bethlehem, Ga., he was educated at Clark University and Columbia University. He joined the faculty of the University. of North Carolina in 1920, where he established its departments of sociology and public welfare and founded the journal *Social Forces* (1922). His scholarly focus was folk sociology, particularly of southern blacks, for whom he urged equal opportunity. His books include *Southern Regions of the United States* (1936), *American Regionalism* (1938, with Harry Moore), and *Understanding Society* (1947).

Odysseus \ō-'di-sē-əs\ *Roman* **Ulysses** \yü-'li-sēz\ Hero of HOMER's *Odyssey*. According to Homer, Odysseus was the king of Ithaca. His shrewdness, resourcefulness, and endurance enabled him to capture TROY (through the device of the Trojan horse) and endure nine years of wandering and adventures before reaching his home in Ithaca, where his wife, Penelope, and son, Telemachus, awaited him. Classical opinion was divided on whether he was an unscrupulous politician or a wise and honorable statesman. Odysseus has been one of the most frequently portrayed figures in literature, treated by numerous Greek and Roman poets and by such later writers as WILLIAM SHAKESPEARE *(Troilus and Cressida)*, NIKOS KAZANTZAKIS *(The Odyssey: A Modern Sequel)*, and (metaphorically) by JAMES JOYCE *(Ulysses)* and DEREK WALCOTT *(Omeros)*.

Odysseus slaying the suitors, detail of a red-figure skyphos fromTarquinii, c. 450 BC; in the Staatliche Museen zu Berlin, Ger.

BY COURTESY OF THE STAATLICHE MUSEEN ZU BERLIN, GER

Oe \'ō-e\, **Kenzaburo** (born 1935) Japanese novelist. Oe first attracted attention on the literary scene while still a student at the University of Tokyo. His works, written in a rough prose style that at times nearly violates the natural rhythms of Japanese, reflect his life and epitomize the rebellion of the post–World War II generation. They include *A Personal Matter* (1964), which uses the birth of an abnormal baby to investigate the problem of culturally disinherited youth; *Hiroshima Notes* (1965); and *The Silent Cry* (1967). He received the Nobel Prize in 1994.

OECD See Organization for ECONOMIC COOPERATION AND DEVELOPMENT

Oedipus \'e-də-pəs, 'ē-də-pəs\ In GREEK MYTHOLOGY, a king of THEBES who unwittingly killed his father and married his mother. In the most familiar version of the story, Laius, king of Thebes, was warned by an oracle that his son would slay him. When his wife, Jocasta, bore a son, he exposed the baby on a mountainside, but the infant Oedipus was saved by a shepherd and adopted by the king of Corinth. In early manhood, as Oedipus traveled toward Thebes, he met Laius, who provoked a quarrel; in the ensuing fracas, Oedipus killed him. He then rid Thebes of the destructive SPHINX by answering her riddle, and as a reward was given the throne of Thebes and the hand of the widowed queen—his mother. They had four children, including ANTIGONE. When at last they learned the truth, Jocasta committed suicide and Oedipus blinded himself and went into exile. Oedipus has served as the hero of many tragedies, most notably Sophocles' *Oedipus Rex* and *Oedipus at Colonus*.

Oedipus complex In psychoanalytic theory, a desire for sexual involvement with the parent of the opposite sex and a sense of rivalry with the parent of the same sex. The term was introduced by SIGMUND FREUD in his *Interpretation of Dreams* (1899) and is derived from the mythological OEDIPUS, who killed his father and married his mother; its female analogue is the Electra complex. Considered a normal stage in the development of children ages 3–5, it ends when the child identifies with the parent of the same sex and represses its sexual instincts. Freud believed that the process of overcoming the Oedipus complex gave rise to the SUPEREGO.

Oehlenschläger \'œ-lens-,leg-ər\, **Adam Gottlob** (1779–1850) Danish poet and dramatist, considered the national poet of Denmark. He became the leader of Romanticism in Danish literature with his poem *The Golden Horns* (1802). Important collections of his poetry, with several lyrical dramas, appeared in 1802 and 1805. His plays drawing on Nordic history and mythology include *Earl Haakon the Great* (1807). His most significant later work is the poetic epic *The Gods of the North* (1819), a kind of modern EDDA.

Oenghus See MAPONOS

Oerter \'ȯr-tər\, **Al(fred)** (born 1936) U.S. discus thrower. Born in Astoria, N.Y., he won gold medals at four consecutive Olympic Games (1956, 1960, 1964, 1968) and set world records four times between 1962 and 1964. He was the first to throw the discus over 200 ft.; he recorded his best throw (212 ft 6 in., or 64.78 m) at the 1968 Olympics.

O P Q R

O'Faolain \ō-ˈfā-lən, ō-ˈfa-lən\, **Sean** *orig.* **John Francis Whelan** (1900–1991) Irish writer. He became involved in anti-British activities during the Irish insurrection (1918–21) and taught 1926–33. After achieving success with his first story collection, *Midsummer Night Madness* (1932), and the novel *A Nest of Simple Folk* (1933), he wrote full-time. He is known for carefully crafted, lyrical short stories about Ireland's lower and middle classes, often examining the decline of the nationalist struggle or the oppressive provincialism of Irish Catholicism. His other works include *Bird Alone* (1936), *A Life of Daniel O'Connell* (1938), and *Vive moi!* (1964), his autobiography.

Off-Broadway Small-scale theatrical productions in New York. The term was first used to refer to experimental plays produced on low budgets in small theaters, which provided an alternative to the commercially oriented BROADWAY theaters. Off-Broadway theaters grew after 1952 with the success of JOSE QUINTERO's productions. Plays by EDWARD ALBEE, SAM SHEPARD, and LANFORD WILSON were first produced off-Broadway, as were avant-garde works by EUGENE IONESCO, SAMUEL BECKETT, and HAROLD PINTER. Many new plays are now staged in well-equipped off-Broadway houses, and off-Broadway theater has its own set of awards, the Obies. As production costs increased, smaller and more experimental theaters emerged, which were quickly labeled off-off-Broadway.

Offa \ˈȯ-fə\ (died 796) One of the most powerful kings in Anglo-Saxon England. He became king of Mercia (757–96) after seizing power during a civil war. He extended his rule over most of southern England and married his daughters to the rulers of Wessex and Northumbria. Eager to form European diplomatic ties, Offa signed a commercial treaty with CHARLEMAGNE (796) and allowed the pope to increase his control over the English church. He built OFFA'S DYKE to divide Mercia from Welsh lands.

Offa's Dyke Earthwork in western England. It stretches 169 mi (270 km) from the SEVERN RIVER near Chepstow to the seaward end of the Dee River estuary. It was built by OFFA of Mercia to fortify the boundary between his kingdom and the lands of the Welsh; for centuries it marked the England–Wales boundary. It consisted of a plain bank (in places some 60 ft, or 18 m, high) and a ditch (12 ft, or 3.7 m, deep). Many sections remain, and a walking path now runs its length.

Offenbach \ˈȯ-fən-ˌbäk\, **Jacques** *orig.* **Jacob** (1819–1880) German-French composer. Son of a cantor, he studied at the Paris Conservatoire but had to leave for lack of funds. He first wrote theater music as conductor of the Théâtre-Français (from 1850); he later opened his own Bouffes Parisiens, for which he wrote 22 one-act works (1855–58). He began writing longer operettas and had a string of hits, including *Orpheus in the Underworld* (1858), *La belle Hélène* (1864), *Bluebeard* (1866), *La vie Parisienne* (1866), and *The Grand Duchess of Gérolstein* (1868). Dismissed by serious musicians but loved by the public, he suffered setbacks after the Franco-Prussian War and spent his last three years on his masterpiece, *The Tales of Hoffmann* (1881).

Office of Management and Budget (OMB) U.S. agency of the federal executive branch. It assists the president in preparing the federal budget and in supervising its administration in executive agencies. It is involved in the development and resolution of all budget, policy, legislative, regulatory, procurement, and management issues on behalf of the president. It evaluates the effectiveness of, and sets funding priorities for, agency programs, policies, and procedures.

Office of Strategic Services (OSS) (1942–45) U.S. agency formed for the purpose of obtaining information about and sabotaging the military efforts of enemy nations during World War II. It was headed by William J. ("Wild Bill") Donovan (1883–1959). Many of its functions were later assumed by the CENTRAL INTELLIGENCE AGENCY.

offset printing *or* **offset lithography** *or* **litho-offset** In commercial PRINTING, a widely used technique in which the inked image on a printing plate is imprinted on a rubber cylinder and then transferred (offset) to PAPER or other material. The rubber cylinder gives great flexibility, permitting printing on wood, cloth, metal, leather, and rough paper. In offset printing the matter to be printed is neither raised above the surface of the printing plate (as in LETTERPRESS PRINTING) nor sunk below it (as in intaglio, or gravure, printing). Offset printing, a development of LITHOGRAPHY, is based on the principle that water and grease do not mix, so that a greasy ink can be deposited on grease-treated printing areas of the plate, while nonprinting areas, which hold water, reject the ink. The offset plate is usually of zinc or aluminum or a combination of metals, with the surface treated to render it porous and then coated with a photosensitive material. Exposure to an image hardens the coating on printing areas; the coating on nonprinting areas is washed away, leaving wetted metal that will reject ink. See also XEROGRAPHY.

offshore bar See SANDBAR

O'Flaherty, Liam (1896–1984) Irish novelist and short-story writer. He abandoned his training for the priesthood and became a soldier in World War I, a migrant laborer in North and South America and the Middle East, and a revolutionary in Ireland. A leading writer of the IRISH LITERARY RENAISSANCE, he combined brutal naturalism, psychological analysis, poetry, and biting satire with an abiding respect for the Irish people. His novels include *Thy Neighbour's Wife* (1923), *The Informer* (1925; film, 1935), *Skerrett* (1932), *Famine* (1937), and *Insurrection* (1950).

Ogaden \ˌō-gə-ˈden\ Region, eastern Ethiopia. In the triangular wedge that juts into Somalia, it is a dry, barren, plain sparsely populated by Somali-speaking nomadic pastoralists. Conquered in the late 19th century by the Ethiopian emperor MENILEK II, it was invaded by Italy in 1935 and made part of Italian East Africa. Liberated in 1941, it remained under British administration until 1948. It was invaded by Somalia in 1977 and retaken by Ethiopia in 1978, with help from Cuba and the Soviet Union.

ogam writing *or* **ogham writing** *or* **ogum writing** \ˈä-gəm\ Alphabetic script used for writing the IRISH and Pictish (see PICTS) languages on stone monuments, mostly c. AD 400–600. In its simplest form, it consists of four sets of strokes, or notches, each set containing five letters composed of from one to five strokes, thus creating 20 letters. A fifth set of five symbols, called *forfeda* ("extra letters"), was probably a later development. Most inscriptions are short and consist only of names. Of the more than 400 inscriptions known, about 330 are from Ireland.

Ogata Kenzan \ō-ˈgä-tä-ˈken-ˌzän\ *orig.* **Ogata Shinsei** (1663–1743) Japanese potter, calligrapher, and painter. Many of his designs reflect his classical Chinese and Japanese education. The *iro-e* ("color painting") of his pottery is particularly fine, and his calligraphy, seen in his wares and paintings, was distinctive. His best-known works include a plate with a picture of a cedar grove and the *Hana-kago* ("Flower Baskets"), a watercolor hanging scroll.

Ogbomosho \ˌōg-bō-ˈmō-shō\ City (pop., 1996 est.: 730,000), southwestern Nigeria. Founded in the mid-17th century, it was an outpost of the OYO EMPIRE until the Muslim FULANI conquests in the early 19th century. As a center of resistance, the walled town attracted many Oyo refugees. Located northeast of IBADAN, it is one of Nigeria's largest urban centers. It is also a trading center and rail junction.

Ogilvy \ˈō-gəl-vē\, **David M(ackenzie)** (1911–1999) British advertising executive. After an Oxford education, he worked as an apprentice chef and stove salesman before taking a job in an advertising agency. He spent a year in the U.S. learning U.S. advertising techniques. In 1948, with Anderson Hewitt, he formed Hewitt, Ogilvy, Benson & Mather, which became one of the world's largest advertising firms. He is noted for reminding his colleagues that "the consumer is not a moron," and his ads for brands such as Schweppes and Rolls-Royce were admired for their creativity.

Oglethorpe, James (Edward) (1696–1785) English colonist. He served in the British army 1712–22, then entered Parliament, where he became interested in prison reform. In 1732 he secured a charter for a colony in what became Georgia, where debtors could start a new life and persecuted Protestants could practice freely. He accompanied the first settlers to found Savannah (1733) and led the defense of his territory against attacks by Spain (1739, 1742), returning to England in 1743.

Ögödei \ˈō-gə-ˌdā\ (1185–1241) Son of GENGHIS KHAN who succeeded his father in 1229 and greatly expanded the MONGOL empire. He established his headquarters in central Mongolia and built the capital city of KARAKORUM. Like his father, he carried out simultaneous campaigns by relying on generals who acted independently but were subject to his orders. Allying himself with China's Southern SONG DYNASTY, Ögödei attacked the JUCHEN DYNASTY in northern China, taking its capital in 1234. Meanwhile, his nephew BATU defeated Russia while other generals were attacking Iran and Iraq. Only Ögödei's death (during a drinking bout) prevented the invasion of Western Europe. See also GOLDEN HORDE, KUBLAI KHAN, MÖNGKE.

Ogooué River *or* **Ogowe River** \ˌō-gō-ˈwā\ River, western central Africa, mainly in GABON. It rises in Gabon and flows northwest, then west, emptying into the Atlantic Ocean south of Port-Gentil after a course of 750 mi (1,200 km). It is navigable for about 250 mi (400 km) and is heavily used for shipping goods, including lumber, to the coast.

O'Hara, John (Henry) (1905–1970) U.S. novelist and short-story writer. A native of Pottsville, Pa., O'Hara developed the objective, straightforward style he used in his fiction while working as a critic and reporter in New York City. His works stand as a social history of upwardly mobile Americans of the 1920s through the 1940s. Among them are the popular novels *Appointment in Samarra* (1934); *Butterfield 8* (1935; film, 1960); *Pal Joey* (1940), adapted as a successful musical; *Ten North Frederick* (1955; film, 1958); and *From the Terrace* (1958; film, 1960).

O'Higgins, Bernardo (1776?–1842) South American revolutionary leader and first Chilean head of state (1817–23). The illegitimate son of a Spanish officer of Irish origin, he was educated in Peru, Spain, and England, where his Chilean nationalism was awakened. When NAPOLEON invaded Spain (1808) and Spanish control of Chile relaxed, he became a member of Chile's new congress. He led the defensive forces when Chile was invaded by royalists from Peru in 1814; defeated, he fled to Argentina. He returned in 1817 with JOSÉ DE SAN MARTÍN and defeated the Spanish. Elected supreme director of Chile, he established a working governmental organization, but his reforms antagonized conservatives and he resigned.

Ohio State (pop., 1997 est.: 11,186,000), U.S., northern central region. It covers 41,222 sq mi (106,765 sq km); its capital is COLUMBUS. Lake ERIE is on its northern boundary; the OHIO RIVER forms part of its southeastern and southern boundary. Ohio was originally inhabited by prehistoric HOPEWELL mound builders, who disappeared c. AD 400. The earliest European explorers found the area occupied by MIAMI, SHAWNEE, and other Indian tribes. The region was ceded to Britain by France after the FRENCH AND INDIAN WAR. In 1803 it became the 17th state, and the first state carved out of the Northwest Territory (see NORTHWEST ORDINANCES). During the 19th century, it became one of the first great industrial states because of its location, transport facilities, and natural resources, including coal, petroleum, and natural gas. Although manufacturing is its most important economic activity, nearly two-thirds of the state is still farmland. It was the birthplace or residence of eight U.S. presidents—WILLIAM H. HARRISON, ULYSSES S. GRANT, RUTHERFORD B. HAYES, JAMES GARFIELD, BENJAMIN HARRISON, WILLIAM MCKINLEY, WILLIAM H. TAFT, and WARREN G. HARDING. Its major cities include COLUMBUS, CLEVELAND, CINCINNATI, TOLEDO, AKRON, and DAYTON.

Ohio Co. Organization of Englishmen and Virginia colonists, established in 1748 to promote trade with American Indians and secure British control of the Ohio River valley for settlement. Activity in the area claimed by France led to the last FRENCH AND INDIAN WAR (1754). A separate organization, the Ohio Co. of Associates (1786), founded Marietta, Ohio, the first permanent settlement north of the Ohio River.

Ohio Idea Proposal to redeem AMERICAN CIVIL WAR bonds in paper money instead of gold. The plan, part of the debate between hard-money advocates and soft-money or GREENBACK MOVEMENT supporters after the Civil War, was sponsored by GEORGE PENDLETON and was especially popular in the Midwest. Endorsed by the Democratic Party in 1868, it died with the election of ULYSSES S. GRANT and passage of the Public Credit Act (1869), which provided for payment of government obligations in gold.

Ohio River Major river, eastern central U.S. Formed by the confluence of the ALLEGHENY and MONONGAHELA rivers, it flows northwest out of Pennsylvania, and west and southwest to form the state boundaries of Ohio–West Virginia, Ohio–Kentucky, Indiana–Kentucky, and Illinois–Kentucky. After a course of 975 mi (1,569 km), it empties into the MISSISSIPPI RIVER at Cairo, Ill. It is navigable and has supported commerce since the earliest settlements. The river's strategic importance was recognized by the 1750s. After the FRENCH AND INDIAN WAR, the English controlled the territory around the river.

Ohio State University, The State university system consisting of a main campus in Columbus and branches in five other locations. It was established in 1870 as a land-grant institution. The main campus is a comprehensive research institution, with colleges of agriculture, dentistry, law, medicine, and veterinary medicine. Research facilities include a transportation research center, a freshwater laboratory, a supercomputer center, and a polar research center. The Columbus campus has the highest enrollment in the U.S., approx. 48,000.

Ohio University Public university in Athens, Ohio, with branches in Chillicothe, Ironton, Lancaster, St. Clairsville, and Zanesville. It offers a range of undergraduate and graduate degrees and a doctorate in osteopathic medicine. Research facilities include Edwards Accelerator Laboratory, a Center for Geotechnical and Environmental Research, and an Institute for Local Government and Rural Development. When founded in 1804, it was the first institution of higher education in the Northwest Territory. Total enrollment is about 20,000.

Ohm, Georg Simon (1789–1854) German physicist. While teaching mathematics at the Jesuits' College in Cologne (1817–27), he discovered that the flow of electric current through a conductor is directly proportional to the potential difference, or voltage, and inversely proportional to the resistance. He resigned when his theory (OHM'S LAW) was coldly received. His theory soon came to be widely recognized, and he subsequently taught in Nuremberg (1833–49) and Munich (1849–54). The physical unit measuring electrical resistance was named for him.

Ohm, detail of a lithograph.
HISTORIA-PHOTO

Ohm's law Relationship between the potential difference (voltage), ELECTRIC CURRENT, and RESISTANCE in an electric CIRCUIT. In 1827 GEORG SIMON OHM discovered that at constant temperature, the current I in a circuit is directly proportional to the potential difference V, and inversely proportional to the resistance R, or $I = V/R$. Resistance is generally measured in ohms (Ω). Ohm's law may also be expressed in terms of the ELECTROMOTIVE FORCE E of an electric energy source, such as a battery, or $E = IR$. In an ALTERNATING-CURRENT circuit, when the combination of resistance and reactance, called impedance Z, is constant, Ohm's law is applicable and $V/I = Z$.

oil Any greasy substance liquid at room temperature and insoluble in water. It may be a fixed (nonvolatile) oil, an ESSENTIAL OIL, or a mineral oil (see PETROLEUM). Fixed oils and (animal) FATS are both ESTERS of GLYCEROL and FATTY ACIDS. These oils have a variety of industrial and food uses. Linseed, tung, and other drying oils are highly unsaturated (see SATURATION); these and large quantities of soybean, sunflower, and safflower oils (also used in foods) are used in paints and varnishes. When exposed to air they absorb oxygen and polymerize (see POLYMERIZATION), forming a tough coating. Some specialty oils and oil derivatives are also used in leather dressing and textile manufacture.

oil-drop experiment See MILLIKAN OIL-DROP EXPERIMENT

oil painting Painting in oil colors, a medium consisting of pigments suspended in drying oils. Oil paint enables both fusion of tones and crisp effects, and is unsurpassed for textural variation. The standard consistency of oil paint is a smooth, buttery paste. It is applied with brushes or a thin palette knife, usually onto a stretched linen canvas. Finished oil paintings are often coated with varnish. Oil as a painting medium is recorded as early as the 11th century, though the practice of easel painting with oil colors stems directly from 15th-century techniques of painting with tempera, in which the medium is egg yolk rather than oil. In the 16th century, oil color emerged as the basic painting material in Venice; it has been the most widespread medium for easel paintings ever since.

oil seal *or* **shaft seal** In MACHINES, a device that prevents the passage of fluids along a rotating shaft. Seals are necessary when a shaft extends from a housing (enclosure) containing oil, such as a pump or a gearbox. Leather, synthetic rubber, and silicones are among the materials used for the sealing ring. See also BEARING.

oil shale Any fine-grained SEDIMENTARY ROCK that contains solid organic matter (KEROGEN) and yields significant quantities of oil when heated. This SHALE OIL is a potentially valuable FOSSIL FUEL, but the present methods of mining and refining it are expensive, damage the land, pollute the water, and produce carcinogenic wastes. Thus, oil shale will probably not be exploited on a wide scale until other petroleum resources have been nearly depleted. Estonia, China, and Brazil have facilities for producing relatively limited quantities, and the U.S. government operates an experimental plant in Colorado.

Oise River \'wäz\ River, northern France. It is formed by the confluence of two streams, one rising near Chimay in Belgium and the other near Rocroi in France. It flows southwest into the SEINE, and is 188 mi (302 km) long. It is a link in the canal system between the Seine and the canals of northern France. Several battles of World War I were fought along its banks.

Oisín \'ōsh-yin\ *or* **Ossian** \'äs-ē-ən, 'äsh-ən\ Irish warrior-poet of the FENIAN CYCLE of hero tales. The name Ossian became known throughout Europe in 1762–63 when the Scottish poet James Macpherson (1736–1796) published the epics *Fingal* and *Temora,* which he represented as translations of works by the 3rd-century Gaelic poet. The poems were widely acclaimed and influential in the Romantic movement, but their authorship was later doubted, notably by SAMUEL JOHNSON (1775), and they were eventually determined to have been written largely by Macpherson.

Oistrakh \'ȯi-ˌsträk\, **David (Fyodorovich)** (1908–1974) Russian violinist. After his debut in 1928, he entered and won a number of prestigious competitions. He performed for Soviet troops at the front during World War II and made debuts in the West in the 1950s. D. SHOSTAKOVICH dedicated both his violin concertos to Oistrakh. He taught at the Moscow Conservatory from 1934, where one of his most distinguished students was his son Igor (born 1931), who himself joined the conservatory's faculty (from 1958).

Ojibwa \ō-'jib-wā\ *or* **Chippewa** \'chi-pə-ˌwȯ\ ALGONQUIAN-SPEAKING Indian people who formerly inhabited a region north of the Great Lakes but who during the 17th–18th century moved west to what is now northern Minnesota. Each Ojibwa tribe was divided into migratory bands. In the autumn, bands separated into family units for hunting; in summer, families gathered at fishing sites. They grew corn and collected wild rice. The Midewiwin, or Grand Medicine Society, was the major Ojibwa religious organization. The Ojibwa are one of the largest Native American groups in North America today, numbering about 50,000 in the U.S. and over 100,000 in Canada.

Ojukwu \ō-'jük-wü\, **Odumegwu** (born 1933) Governor of the Eastern Region of Nigeria (1966–67) and head of the secessionist state of BIAFRA (1967–70). A member of the IGBO, Ojukwu was educated at Oxford University. He was appointed head of the traditional Igbo homelands in the east following the overthrow of Nigeria's civilian government by Igbo military leaders. He stayed on in that capacity even after members of the opposition HAUSA and YORUBA staged a successful countercoup. Mounting secessionist pressures compelled him to declare the Eastern Region an independent state in 1967. Following the Biafra conflict he fled to the Ivory Coast; he returned to Nigeria in 1982.

Oka River \ō-'kä\ River, central Russia. The largest right-bank tributary of the VOLGA RIVER, it flows 932 mi (1,500 km) north to Kaluga, then east to join the Volga at NIZHNIY NOVGOROD. Navigable for most of its length, except during winter, it is an important trade artery for lumber and grain.

okapi \ō-'kä-pē\ RUMINANT species *(Okapia johnstoni)* in the GIRAFFE family that lives alone in Congo rain forests, eating leaves and fruit. Its neck and legs are proportionately shorter than the giraffe's, and females, which are larger than males, stand about 5 ft (1.5 m) at the shoulder. The sleek coat is deep brown on the front of the body; the upper legs are black-and-white-striped, and the lower legs are white, with black rings above the hooves. The male's short horns are covered with skin except at the tips.

Okapi (*Okapia johnstoni*).
KENNETH W. FINK—ROOT RESOURCES

Okavango River \ˌō-kä-'väŋ-gō\ *in Angola* **Cubango River** River, southwestern central Africa. It is the fourth-longest river system in the region. Rising in central Angola, it forms a section of the boundary between Angola and Namibia. It empties into the Okavango Swamp, a large marsh north of Lake NGAMI in northern Botswana, after a course of about 1,000 mi (1,600 km). It is unnavigable except for small craft, and its banks are sparsely settled; a major problem for inhabitants is control of the TSETSE FLY. The Moremi Wildlife Reserve in the northeastern corner of the swamp teems with wildlife.

Okeechobee \ˌō-kə-'chō-bē\, **Lake** Lake, southern central Florida. It is the largest lake in the southern U.S., and the third-largest freshwater lake wholly within the country. It drains to the sea through the EVERGLADES. A remnant of the prehistoric Pamlico Sea, its name means "Big Water" in the language of the SEMINOLE Indians, who still live on the lake's northwestern shore.

O'Keeffe, Georgia (1887–1986) U.S. painter. Born in Sun Prairie, Wis., she studied art in Chicago and New York, where she met and married the photographer ALFRED STIEGLITZ. By the early 1920s, her highly individualistic painting style had emerged, as typified by such works as *Black Iris* (1926). Her subjects were often enlarged views of the skulls and other bones of animals, flowers and plant organs, shells, rocks, mountains, and other natural forms. Her mysteriously suggestive images of bones and flowers set against a perspectiveless space have inspired a variety of erotic, psychological, and symbolic interpretations. Her later works celebrate the clear skies and desert landscapes of New Mexico, where she moved after her husband's death in 1946. She is regarded by critics as one of the most original and important American artists, and her works are highly popular among the general public.

"Near Abiquiu, New Mexico," oil on canvas by Georgia O'Keeffe, 1930; in the Metropolitan Museum of Art, New York City.

Okefenokee Swamp \ˌō-kə-fə-'nō-kē\ Swamp and wildlife refuge, southeastern Georgia and northeastern Florida. It has an area of more than 600 sq mi (1,550 sq km). Located about 50 mi (80 km) inland from the Atlantic coast, it is bounded by the low, sandy Trail Ridge, which prevents direct drainage into the Atlantic. It has diverse and abundant wildlife. Exotic flowers, such as rare orchids, abound. In 1937 a large area of the swamp, almost all in Georgia, was made the Okefenokee National Wildlife Refuge.

Okhotsk \ə-'kȯtsk\, **Sea of** Arm of the northwestern Pacific Ocean. Bounded by the Siberian coast, the KAMCHATKA Peninsula and the KURIL ISLANDS, HOKKAIDO, and SAKHALIN, it covers 611,000 sq mi (1.58 million sq km). It connects the ports of the Russian Far East. In winter, ice floes impede navigation, and dense fog is a hindrance during the summer.

Okinawa \ˌō-kē-'nä-wä\ Island of Japan, located in the RYUKYU archipelago, in CHINA SEA. The largest island in the Ryukyu chain, it is about 70 mi (112 km) long and 7 mi (11 km) wide, with an area of 463 sq mi (1,199 sq km). It was the site of severe fighting between the U.S. and Japan in WORLD WAR II. In April 1945 U.S. troops made an amphibious landing on Okinawa, which was heavily defended by the Japanese. In a three-month-long campaign both sides sustained heavy casualties before U.S. forces gained control of the island. In 1972 the United States returned Okinawa to Japan, though U.S. military installations remained.

Oklahoma State (pop., 1997 est.: 3,317,000), U.S., southwestern central region. It covers 69,956 sq mi (181,186 sq km); its capital is OKLAHOMA CITY. The RED RIVER forms its southern boundary; the ARKANSAS RIVER flows across northeastern Oklahoma. Its highest point is Black Mesa (4,973 ft, or 1,516 m), located in the Panhandle. Evidence of inhabitation by the CLOVIS and FOLSOM cultures, 15,000–10,000 years ago, has been found. In more modern times, until the expedition of FRANCISCO VAZQUEZ DE CORONADO in 1541, the area was home to representatives of at least three major Indian language groups. Spanish control of the area lasted until 1800, when it passed to the French. In 1803 the area became part of the U.S. with the LOUISIANA PURCHASE. In 1828 the U.S. Congress reserved Oklahoma for settlement by Indians, and it became known as INDIAN TERRITORY. In 1890 the western part was organized as Oklahoma Territory. The two were merged and admitted to the union as the 46th state in 1907. Cattle raising and farming are the mainstays of the economy. Mineral products include natural gas, petroleum, coal, and stone. The state's heritage is reflected in Indian and cowboy museums. A barge system links the state's second major city, TULSA, to the Gulf of Mexico.

Oklahoma, University of Public university in Norman, founded in 1890. The main campus comprises 19 colleges, including those of architecture, business administration, education, engineering, law, and arts and sciences. Research facilities include a meteorological center and a political communication center. Total enrollment is about 20,000. A campus in Oklahoma City houses the medical school and health-sciences center.

Oklahoma City City (pop., 1996 est.: 470,000), capital of Oklahoma. Settled during the Oklahoma land rush in 1889, it was incorporated as a city in 1890 and became the state capital in 1910. It expanded rapidly after the discovery of petroleum in the area in 1928. The largest city in the state and its main commercial, financial, industrial, and transportation center, it is the chief marketing and processing point for the livestock industry. It is home to the National Cowboy Hall of Fame, Myriad Gardens, and an annual rodeo competition. In 1995 it was the site of a deadly act of domestic terrorism, when the Murrah Federal Building was bombed, killing 168 people and injuring 500.

okra Herbaceous, hairy, annual plant *(Hibiscus,* or *Abelmoschus, esculentus)* of the MALLOW FAMILY, grown for its edible, gummy fruit. Okra leaves are heart-shaped; flowers are yellow with a crimson center. The fruit or pod is a tapering, 10-angled CAPSULE, 4–10 in. (10–25 cm) long and hairy at the base. Only the tender, unripe fruit is eaten; it is prepared in a number of ways and is a defining ingredient of the gumbos of the southern U.S. Because of its large amount of mucilage (a gelatinous substance), okra is used as a broth and soup thickener. In some countries the seeds are used as a substitute for coffee.

Okra (*Hibiscus esculentus*, or *Abelmoschus esculentus*).

DEREK FELL

Oktoberfest Annual festival in MUNICH, Germany, lasting two weeks and ending on the first Sunday of October. It began in 1810 as a horse race celebrating the wedding of the crown prince of Bavaria, later King Louis I (1786–1868). The race was soon combined with the state agricultural fair, and food and drink were offered. In the late 20th century the Munich breweries celebrated Oktoberfest by setting up large temporary beer halls, each seating 3,000–5,000 people, and hiring bands to entertain the crowds as they ate and drank. Total beer consumption during the festival exceeds a million gallons.

Okubo Toshimichi \'ō-kü-bō-ˌtō-shē-'mē-chē\ (1830–1878) Japanese SAMURAI leader from the domain of SATSUMA who, with SAIGO TAKAMORI, arranged an alliance with the domain of CHOSHU to work for the overthrow of the TOKUGAWA SHOGUNATE and the restoration of the emperor. After the MEIJI RESTORATION of 1868, Okubo became a dominant figure in the new government. He traveled to the West and returned convinced that Japan needed rapid economic development and modernization to survive. He supported the establishment of technical schools, loans to private businesses, and government-sponsored factory development. In 1873 he argued against those who favored invading Korea and prevailed. He was assassinated in 1878 by discontented samurai. See also KIDO TAKAYOSHI, MEIJI PERIOD.

Okuma Shigenobu \'ō-kü-mä-ˌshē-ge-'nō-bü\ (1838–1922) Japanese politician of the MEIJI PERIOD who twice served as prime minister. His initial contribution to the new government was to oversee the reorganization of Japan's fiscal system. Later, his radical proposals for a new Japanese constitution and exposing of corruption in proposed sales of government property led to his being forced out of government. In 1882 he formed the Rikken Kaishinto ("Progressive Party"), which favored English parliamentary government. With ITAGAKI TAISUKE he created a new party in 1898, the Kenseito ("Constitutional Party"). They formed a short-lived government with Okuma as prime minister. Okuma's second tenure as prime minister (1914–16) was more successful. He is also remembered as the founder of Waseda University (1882). See also MEIJI CONSTITUTION.

Okumura Masanobu \ˌō-kü-'mür-ä-ˌmä-sä-'nō-bü\ *or* **Genpachi** \gen-'pä-chē\ *orig.* **Okumura Shinmyo** (1686–1764) Japanese painter and publisher of illustrated books. His style is noted for its vividness and graceful, restrained lines. He was one of the first Japanese artists to adopt Western perspective, to which he was introduced by Chinese prints. He produced large-scale prints depicting scenes such as the insides of theaters and stores. Such prints were called *uki-e* ("looming picture") for their foreshortened perspective. He is also said to have founded the format of *habahiro hashira-e,* or wide, vertical prints.

Okuninushi \'ō-kü-nē-'nü-shē\ Central hero in the mythology of the Izumo branch of SHINTO in Japan. Okuninushi built the world with the help of the dwarf deity Sukunahikona, and he ruled Izumo until the appearance of the divine grandchild, Ninigi. In modern Japanese folk belief, Okuninushi is a god who heals and who makes marriages happy.

Olaf I Tryggvason \'ō-läf...'trüg-və-sȯn\ (964?–c. 1000) Viking king of Norway (995–c. 1000). The son of a Norwegian chieftain, he joined Viking attacks on England in 991 and 994. He returned to Norway and was accepted as king on the death of Haakon the Great in 995. Olaf imposed Christianity on the Norwegian coast but had little influence in the interior. His missionaries, including LEIF ERIKSSON, introduced Christianity to the Shetland, Faeroe, and Orkney islands and to Iceland and Greenland. He was killed in the Battle of Svolder, celebrated in medieval Scandinavian poetry.

Olaf II Haraldsson \hä-räl-sȯn\ *or* **St. Olaf** (c. 995–1030) King of Norway (1016–28). A Viking warrior, he fought against the English in 1009–11 but assisted ETHELRED II against the Danes in 1013. He returned to Norway after his conversion to Christianity and gained control over the country by 1016. Olaf sent out missionaries throughout his realm, and his religious code (1024) established the Church of Norway. He was driven out of Norway by CANUTE THE GREAT (1028) and was killed trying to reconquer the country two years later. He became a national hero and the patron saint of Norway.

Olaf V *Norwegian* **Olav Alexander Edward Christian Frederik** (1903–1991) King of Norway (1957–91). Son of King HAAKON VII, Olaf became a celebrated sportsman, winning the gold medal in yachting at the 1928 Olympics. In World War II he lived in exile with his family in England and was named head of the Norwegian armed forces in 1944. From 1955 he served as regent for his father, whom he succeeded as king in 1957. Like other constitutional monarchs, Olaf's duties were largely ceremonial.

Olaf V, 1973.

KNUDSENS FOTOSENTER

Olajuwon \ə-'lä-zhü-ˌwän\, **Hakeem (Abdul)** (born 1963) Nigerian-U.S. basketball player. Born in Lagos, he did not play basketball until he was 15. Two years later he went to the University of Houston, and in 1984 he led its team to the NCAA semifinals. In 1994 the 7-ft, 255-lb Olajuwan led the Rockets to the NBA championship. Nicknamed "the Dream," he holds the all-time record for blocked shots (3,582 to the end of the 1998–99 season) and has continued to record high marks for steals, rebounds, points, and assists.

Olbers' paradox Paradox of why the sky is dark at night. If the universe is endless and uniformly populated with luminous stars, every line of sight must end at the surface of a star and the night sky should be bright with no dark spaces between stars. This paradox is widely attributed to Heinrich Wilhelm Olbers (1758–1840), who discussed it in 1823, though JOHANNES KEPLER first advanced the problem in 1610 as an argument against the notion of a limitless universe with infinite stars. The paradox has since been resolved: we can see no farther than the light-travel distance within the lifetime of the universe, and light becomes red-shifted (see RED SHIFT).

Olbia \'ōl-byä\ *formerly* **Terranova Pausania** Town (pop., 1991: 41,000), northeastern SARDINIA, Italy. Originally a Greek colony, it passed to the Romans and was the site of a Roman victory over the Carthaginian general Hanno in 259 BC. It was rebuilt by Pisan colonists in 1198 and named Terranova Pausania. Renamed Olbia in 1939, it is the main passenger port for connections with the Italian mainland. It has Phoenician and Roman ruins.

old age *or* **senescence** Final stage of the normal life span, often defined as beginning at age 60 or 65 for retirement or certain benefits (e.g., MEDICARE AND MEDICAID, SOCIAL SECURITY). With an increasing proportion of the population over 65, age-related medical problems (including certain cancers and heart disease) have also increased (see GERONTOLOGY AND GERIATRICS). Many problems once thought to result from aging have been found to be due to disease (including Alzheimer's disease). Exercising the mind and the muscles minimizes loss or deterioration of function. Sexual activity may decrease, but in healthy persons no age limit exists for it. See also AGING.

Old Believers Russian dissenters who refused to accept liturgical reforms imposed on the Russian Orthodox Church by NIKON in 1652–58. Numbering in the millions in the 17th century, the Old Believers endured persecution for years, and several of their leaders were executed. They split into a variety of sects, of which the two main groups were the Popovtsy (priestly sects) and Bezpopovtsy (priestless sects). In 1971 the council of the Russian Orthodox Church rescinded all the anathemas of the 17th century and recognized the full validity of the old rites.

Old Catholic church Any of a group of Western Catholic churches that separated from Rome after the First Vatican Council promulgated the doctrine of PAPAL INFALLIBILITY (1869–70). Old Catholic churches in the Netherlands, Germany, Switzerland, Austria, Poland, and elsewhere joined together in 1889 to form the Union of Utrecht. The Old Catholics accept the Bible, the Apostles' and NICENE creeds, and the seven SACRAMENTS. Their chief authority in church government is the conference of bishops. They have long used the vernacular in public worship; confession to a priest is not obligatory, and in some Old Catholic churches the celibacy of the clergy is optional.

Old Church Slavic language Oldest attested SLAVIC LANGUAGE, known from a small corpus of 10th- or 11th-century manuscripts, most written in the Glagolitic alphabet (see CYRILLIC ALPHABET). The Old Church Slavic (or Old Church Slavonic) documents, all translations from Christian ecclesiastical texts, resulted from the mission to the Moravian Slavs of Sts. CYRIL AND METHODIUS, though all but one of the surviving manuscripts were actually copied in South Slavic-speaking areas. Beginning already in the 11th century, the influence of the vernacular languages in cultural focal areas (Serbia, Bulgaria-Macedonia, Ukraine, and Russia) led to regional variations in Church Slavic. Church Slavic remained the literary language of EASTERN ORTHODOXY in South Slavic and East Slavic lands into modern times and is still the liturgical language of Slavic orthodoxy and the Slavic EASTERN RITE CHURCH. Old Church Slavic and Church Slavic are more archaic than any living Slavic language in completely retaining both the original Slavic verbal system and the full set of seven nominal cases and three numbers.

Old English *or* **Anglo-Saxon** Language spoken and written in England before AD 1100. It belongs to the Anglo-Frisian group of GERMANIC LANGUAGES. Four dialects are known: Northumbrian (in northern England and southeastern Scotland), Mercian (central England), Kentish (southeastern England), and West Saxon (southern and southwestern England). Mercian and Northumbrian are often called the Anglian dialects. Most extant Old English writings are in the West Saxon dialect. The great epic poem of Old English is *BEOWULF*; the first period of extensive literary activity occurred in the 9th century. Old English had three genders (masculine, feminine, neuter) for nouns and adjectives; nouns, pronouns, and adjectives were also inflected for case. Old English had a greater proportion of strong (irregular) verbs than does Modern English, and its vocabulary was more heavily Germanic. See also ENGLISH LANGUAGE.

Old English script See BLACK LETTER SCRIPT

Old English sheepdog Shaggy WORKING DOG developed in early-18th-century England and used primarily to drive sheep and cattle to market. It has a shuffling, bearlike gait and a dense solid-colored or white-marked grayish coat. It stands 21–26 in. (53–66 cm) and weighs over 55 lbs (25 kg). Its long, dense, weather-resistant coat covers the eyes but does not obscure vision. The coat may be gray or blue-gray, with or without white markings. The tail is usually removed soon after birth.

Old Farmer's Almanac See FARMER'S ALMANAC

Old Ironsides See USS CONSTITUTION

Old Norse language Classical GERMANIC LANGUAGES used c. 1150–1350, the literary language of the Icelandic SAGAS, SKALDIC POETRY, and EDDAS. The terms Old Norse and Old Icelandic are sometimes used interchangeably because Icelandic records of this period are more plentiful and of greater literary value than those in the other Scandinavian languages, but Old Norse also embraces the ancestors of modern NORWEGIAN, DANISH, SWEDISH, and Faeroese.

Old Point Comfort Historic point and part of the city of HAMPTON, southeastern Virginia. It is located at the entrance to HAMPTON ROADS, opposite NORFOLK. Named by the colonists of JAMESTOWN in 1607, it has been the site of fortifications, including Fort George and Fort Monroe, since 1609. The latter was a Union base during the AMERICAN CIVIL WAR. It was a popular seaside resort in the 19th and early 20th century.

Old Testament Sacred scriptures of JUDAISM and, with the NEW TESTAMENT, of CHRISTIANITY. Written almost entirely in the HEBREW LANGUAGE between 1200 and 100 BC, the Old Testament (also called the Hebrew Bible or Tanakh) is an account of God's dealings with the Hebrews as his chosen people. In the Hebrew Bible, the first six books tell how the Israelites became a people and settled in the Promised Land, the following seven books describe the development of Israel's monarchy and the messages of the prophets, and the last 11 books contain poetry, theology, and some additional historical works. Christians divided some of the original Hebrew books into two or more parts, specifically, Samuel, Kings, and Chronicles (two parts each), Ezra-Nehemiah (two separate books), and the Minor Prophets (12 separate books). The content of the Old Testament varies according to religious tradition, the Jewish, Roman Catholic, and Protestant canons all differing from each other as to which books they include. See also APOCRYPHA, BIBLE.

Old Vic London theater company. The company's theater opened in 1818 as the Royal Coburg; renamed the Royal Victoria in 1833, it became popularly known as the Old Vic. The company, managed by LILIAN M. BAYLIS, began a regular Shakespeare season in 1914. From the 1930s it was noted for its memorable productions of Shakespeare's plays and other classics with such actors as JOHN GIELGUD, LAURENCE OLIVIER, and RALPH RICHARDSON. The company was dissolved in 1963 and formed the nucleus of the new National Theatre, which performed at the Old Vic theater until moving to a new building in 1976.

Old World monkey Any of certain anthropoid PRIMATES of Africa and Asia, also called catarrhines, as distinguished from the NEW WORLD MONKEYS (platyrrhines). Catarrhines are generally distinguished from platyrrhines in having a narrow nose, narrow septum, close-set nostrils directed forward or down, bony ear passages, two premolars in each half of each jaw, a nonprehensile tail (if any), and hard patches of naked skin (ischial callosities) on the buttocks. The terms Old World monkey and catarrhine usually apply only to members of the families Cercopithecidae (monkeys with cheek pouches: guenons, BABOONS, and others) and Colobidae (leaf monkeys) but may also include the families Hylobatidae

(GIBBONS), Pongidae (APES), and Hominidae (human beings). See also COLOBUS MONKEY, PROBOSCIS MONKEY, VERVET MONKEY.

Oldenbarnevelt \ˌōl-dən-ˈbär-nə-vəlt\, **Johan van** (1547–1619) Dutch statesman and a founding father of Dutch independence. A lawyer in the province of Holland, in 1579 he helped WILLIAM I negotiate the Union of Utrecht. Appointed "great pensionary" of Holland, he mobilized Dutch resources for the military goals of MAURICE OF NASSAU. As foreign secretary of the Union's seven provinces, he negotiated a triple alliance with France and England against Spain (1596). He later concluded the Twelve Years' Truce with Spain (1609), which reaffirmed Holland's dominant role in the republic. In 1617 he sided with the moderate Arminians in religious strife against the stricter Calvinists (known as Counter-Remonstrants) and Prince Maurice; he was arrested in 1618, convicted of religious subversion, and beheaded.

Oldenburg Former German state, since 1946 part of Lower SAXONY, Germany. It was held by the counts of Oldenburg from c. 1100 until 1667, when it passed to Denmark. In the late 18th century it was ruled by the bishop of Lübeck, who was made duke of Oldenburg by the Holy Roman emperor JOSEPH II. It became a grand duchy in the early 19th century and took Prussia's side in the Austro–Prussian War of 1866. It joined the German empire in 1871. Its last grand duke abdicated in 1918. The 17th-century grand-ducal palace in the city of Oldenburg (pop., 1992 est.: 145,000), is now a state museum of art and culture.

Oldenburg, Claes (Thure) (born 1929) Swedish-U.S. POP ART sculptor. The son of a consular official, he spent part of his early life in the U.S. He graduated from Yale University and attended the Art Institute of Chicago before doing freelance illustrating for magazines. He turned to sculpture after moving to New York in 1956. Like other practitioners of Pop art, he chose banal subjects from consumer culture, but for "soft sculptures" such as *Giant Clothespin* (1976) and *Giant Soft Shuttlecock* (1995) he chose subjects with close human associations, and his frequent use of soft, yielding vinyl gave the objects human, often sexual overtones.

Oldowan industry \ˈäl-də-wən\ STONE-TOOL INDUSTRY of the early PALEOLITHIC (beginning c. 2.5 million years ago) characterized by crudely worked pebble tools made of quartz, quartzite, or basalt and chipped in two directions to form simple, rough implements for chopping, scraping, or cutting. The industry is associated with early hominids such as *HOMO HABILIS* and possibly also *AUSTRALOPITHECUS robustus*, and has been found at OLDUVAI GORGE (from which its name derives), Lake Turkana (see LAKE TURKANA REMAINS), and the Afar region of Ethiopia. Oldowan tools were made for nearly 1.5 million years before the emergence of the ACHEULIAN INDUSTRY.

Olduvai Gorge \ˈōl-də-ˌwā, ˈōl-də-ˌvī\ Archaeological site in the eastern Serengeti Plains, northern Tanzania. It is a steep-sided ravine about 30 mi (48 km) long and 295 ft (90 m) deep. Deposits exposed in the sides of the gorge cover a time span from c. 2.1 million to 15,000 years ago and have yielded the remains of more than 50 HOMINIDS as well as the most complete sequence of STONE-TOOL INDUSTRIES. The site first came to public notice when L. S. LEAKEY FAMILY, after nearly 30 years of work, uncovered the remains of the first australopithecine found outside southern Africa. Remains of *HOMO HABILIS* and *HOMO ERECTUS* have since been found. See also OLDOWAN INDUSTRY.

oleander \ˈō-lē-ˌan-dər\ Any of the ornamental evergreen shrubs of the genus *Nerium* (DOGBANE FAMILY), which have poisonous milky juice. Numerous varieties of flower color in the common oleander, or rosebay *(N. oleander)*, have been introduced from greenhouse culture and are grown outdoors in warmer climates. All parts of the plant are very toxic if eaten, and contact with them may cause skin irritation.

oleaster family \ˈō-lē-ˌas-tər\ Family Elaeagnaceae, composed of three genera of hardy shrubs and small trees, found in the Northern Hemisphere, especially in steppe and coastal regions. The plants' tiny, distinctive scales give them a silvery or rust-colored sheen. Many members of the family perform NITROGEN FIXATION. The berries of several species are edible. Ornamental shrubs in this family include buffalo berry or silverberry *(Shepherdia argentea)*, oleaster or Russian olive *(Elaeagnus angustifolia)*, and sea buckthorn *(Hippophae rhamnoides)*.

olefin \ˈō-lə-fən\ *or* **alkene** Any unsaturated HYDROCARBON containing one or more pairs of carbon atoms linked by a double bond (see COVALENT BOND, SATURATION). Olefins may be classified by whether the double bond is in a ring (cyclic) or a chain (acyclic, or aliphatic) or by the number of double bonds (monoolefin, diolefin, etc.). Rare in nature, olefins are obtained by the cracking of PETROLEUM fractions at high temperatures. The simplest ones (ETHYLENE, propylene, butylene, butadiene, and isoprene) are the basis of the PETROCHEMICALS industry. They react by adding other chemical agents at the double bond to form derivatives or POLYMERS.

Olga, St. *or* **St. Helga** (c. 890–969) Princess of Kiev. The first recorded female ruler in Russia, she served as regent of Kiev (945–64) after the assassination of her husband Igor I (877?–945); she avenged his death by having his murderers scalded to death. Probably baptized (c. 957) at Constantinople, she became the first member of the ruling family of Kiev to adopt Christianity. She was canonized as the first Russian saint of the Orthodox Church.

oligarchy \ˈä-li-ˌgär-kē, ˈō-li-ˌgär-kē\ Rule by the few, often seen as having self-serving ends. Aristotle used the term pejoratively for unjust rule by bad men, contrasting oligarchy with rule by an ARISTOCRACY. Most classic oligarchies have resulted when governing elites were recruited exclusively from a ruling class, which tends to exercise power in its own interest. The term is considered outmoded today because "few" conveys no information about the nature of the ruling group.

Oligocene epoch \ˈä-li-gō-ˌsēn\ Major division of the TERTIARY PERIOD, from c. 33.7 to 23.8 million years ago. It follows the EOCENE EPOCH and precedes the MIOCENE EPOCH. The term (from the Greek for "few recent forms") refers to the small number of modern animals that originated during this epoch. Oligocene climates appear to have been temperate, and many regions were nearly tropical. Grasslands expanded, and forested regions dwindled. The vertebrates of the northern continents had an essentially modern aspect that is a result less of the appearance of new forms than of the extinction of archaic vertebrates at the close of the Eocene.

oligopoly \ˌäl-ə-ˈgä-pə-lē\ Market situation in which producers are so few that the actions of each of them have an impact on price and on competitors. Each producer must consider the effect of a price change on the others. A cut in price by one may lead to an equal reduction by the others, with the result that each firm will retain about the same share of the market as before but with a lower profit margin. Competition in oligopolistic industries thus tends to manifest itself in nonprice forms such as advertising and product differentiation. Oligopolies in the U.S. include the steel, aluminum, and automobile industries. See also CARTEL, MONOPOLY.

oligosaccharide \ˌä-li-gō-ˈsa-kə-ˌrīd\ Any CARBOHYDRATE with three to six units of simple SUGARS (MONOSACCHARIDES). A wide variety of oligosaccharides are made by partially breaking down POLYSACCHARIDES. Few oligosaccharides occur naturally, mostly in plants; those in animals tend to be combined in glycoproteins.

olive Subtropical, broad-leaved, evergreen tree *(Olea europaea)* and its edible fruit. The edible olive was being grown on the island of Crete c. 3500 BC, the Semitic peoples apparently were cultivating it as early as 3000 BC, and it was used by the ancient Greeks and Romans, after which olive growing spread to all the countries bordering the Mediterranean. Today olives are grown primarily for olive oil, which has in recent decades become highly popular in North America, valued both for its distinctive taste and fragrance and for healthful properties that have become widely known. Fresh olives must be treated to neutralize their extreme bitterness before they can be eaten. The olive family (Oleaceae) comprises about 900 species in 24 genera of woody plants. Native to forested regions, members of the olive family grow worldwide except in the Arctic, as evergreens in tropical and warm temperate climes and as deciduous trees in colder zones. ASH trees yield HARDWOOD timber; horticultural favorites include LILACS, JASMINES, PRIVETS, and FORSYTHIA. Many members of the family are cultivated for their beautiful and fragrant flowers.

Oliver, King *orig.* **Joseph** (1885–1938) U.S. cornetist and bandleader, one of the important early figures in jazz. Oliver grew up in New Orleans and established himself as the city's preeminent cornetist, coleading a band with trombonist Kid Ory before moving to Chicago in 1918. In 1922, Oliver hired his New Orleans protégé LOUIS ARMSTRONG to join him in Chicago in his Creole Jazz Band. Their recordings together, including "Dipper Mouth Blues," are jazz classics.

Olives, Mount of Limestone ridge, east of JERUSALEM. Frequently mentioned in the BIBLE, it is holy both in Judaism and in Christianity. Politically it is part of the municipality of Greater Jerusalem under Israeli administration. Its slopes have been the most sacred burial ground in Judaism for centuries. The peak generally regarded as the Mount of Olives is 2,652 ft (808 m) high. Nearby is the traditional site of the Garden of GETHSEMANE.

Olivetti & C. SpA \ˌä-lə-ˈve-tē\ Italian electronics and telecommunications company. Founded by Camillo Olivetti (1868–1943), the firm began making typewriters in 1908. Camillo's son Adriano studied manufacturing and plant management in the U.S. in the 1920s, and as company president from 1938 made Olivetti into Europe's principal maker of business machines. The company later produced calculators, microcomputers, and copiers. In 1982 its U.S. subsidiary was purchased by Docutel Corp. and became Docutel/Olivetti Corp. In the late 1990s Olivetti sold off its money-losing computer business and remade itself as a telecommunications company with holdings in mobile and fixed-line telephones.

Olivier \ə-ˈli-vē-ˌā\, **Laurence (Kerr)** *later* **Baron Olivier (of Brighton)** (1907–1989) British actor, director, and producer. He began his professional career in 1926 and joined the OLD VIC company in 1937, playing many major Shakespearean roles. With RALPH RICHARDSON he co-directed the Old Vic (1944–50), and he acted in some of its greatest productions, including *Richard III, Henry IV,* and *Oedipus Rex.* He was knighted in 1947. From 1950 he directed and acted under his own management; his notable productions included *Antony and Cleopatra* and *The Entertainer* (1957). He was the founding director of the National Theatre (1962–73), one of whose theaters is now named for him. In 1970 he was created a life peer, the first actor ever to be so honored. His many films included *Wuthering Heights* (1939), *Rebecca* (1940), *Henry V* (1944), *Hamlet* (1948, Academy Award), *Richard III* (1955), *The Entertainer* (1960), *Othello* (1965), *Sleuth* (1972), and *The Boys from Brazil* (1978). He was married to the actresses VIVIEN LEIGH and (from 1961) Joan Plowright (born 1929).

olivine \ˈä-lə-ˌvēn\ Any member of a group of common magnesium, iron silicate minerals. Olivines occur in many IGNEOUS ROCKS and are a major constituent of the earth's upper MANTLE. They also have been found in some lunar rocks and in many meteorites. Olivine forms yellow to greenish yellow crystals and is sometimes used in making bricks. Transparent green olivine (precious olivine) is called PERIDOT.

Olmec \ˈäl-ˌmek\ First elaborate pre-Columbian culture of Mesoamerica. The Olmec lived in the lowlands of southern Mexico's Gulf Coast. Developing a wide trading network, their cultural influence spread north to the Valley of Mexico and south to Central America; later native religions and iconography throughout Mesoamerica have Olmec roots. Their oldest known building site, San Lorenzo, which dates to c. 1150 BC, is remarkable for its colossal stone sculptures of human heads. The dominant motif in Olmec art is the figure of a god that is a hybrid of a jaguar and a human infant. Olmec buildings, monuments, and art style all indicate a complex and nonegalitarian society.

Olmsted, Frederick Law (1822–1903) U.S. landscape architect. Born in Hartford, Conn., he traveled in the South in the 1850s and won fame for several books describing its slaveholding culture. During an extended vacation in Europe, he became profoundly impressed with English landscaping, which he described in *Walks and Talks of an American Farmer in England* (1852). In 1857 he was hired as superintendent of New York's newly planned CENTRAL PARK. With the architect Calvert Vaux (1824–1895), he won a competition to design the park and became its chief architect in 1858. The result was a nature-lover's paradise incorporating lawns, woods, ponds, and meandering paths. Other Olmsted parks include Prospect Park in Brooklyn, Niagara Falls, an extensive system of parks and parkways in Boston, and the World's Columbian Exposition (later Jackson Park) in Chicago. He founded the magazine *The NATION.* As chairman of the first Yosemite commission, he helped secure the area as a permanent public park.

Olmütz \ˈōl-ˌmu̇ets\, **Humiliation of** (1850) Agreement signed at Olmütz (now Olomouc, Czech Republic) between Prussia and Austria. In response to an appeal from the elector of Hesse for help against rebellious subjects, Prussia and Austria sent troops. They threatened to clash, and when Russia sided with Austria, Prussia withdrew. In the Olmütz agreement, Prussia gave up its plans to create a union of German states without Austria and accepted Austria's reconstitution of the GERMAN CONFEDERATION. Prussia resented the diplomatic reverse and considered itself humiliated.

Olney, Richard (1835–1917) U.S. statesman. Born in Oxford, Mass., he served as U.S. attorney general (1893–95) under Pres. GROVER CLEVELAND and set a precedent by using an injunction to break the PULLMAN STRIKE (1894). As U.S. secretary of state (1895–97), he dealt with Venezuela's request for support in its border dispute with British Guiana by demanding that Britain arbitrate the dispute to avoid war. His note to Britain, called the Olney Corollary, reasserted U.S. sovereignty in the western Hemisphere and reinforced the MONROE DOCTRINE.

Olt River \ˈōlt\ River, southern Romania. It rises close to the headwaters of the MURES RIVER in eastern Transylvania at an elevation of 5,900 ft (1,800 m). It is 308 mi (496 km) long and flows south through the southern CARPATHIAN MTNS. to enter the DANUBE RIVER opposite Nikopol. There are several resorts and spas along its course through the mountains.

Olympia Ancient sanctuary and site of the OLYMPIC GAMES, northwestern Peloponnese, southern Greece. Located 10 mi (16 km) inland from the Ionian Sea, it was on the northern bank of the ALPHEUS RIVER. A center of Greek religious worship, it held the primarily athletic contests in honor of ZEUS every four years, beginning in 776 BC. In the temple of Zeus, built c. 460 BC, was the statue of Zeus by PHIDIAS, one of the SEVEN WONDERS OF THE WORLD. Excavations have uncovered many ruins, including temples and the stadium.

Olympia City (pop., 1995 est.: 39,000), capital of Washington state. It is at the southern end of PUGET SOUND, southwest of TACOMA. Originally called Smithfield, it was renamed for the nearby OLYMPIC MTNS. and incorporated as a city in 1859. It developed port facilities and a lumber-based economy, supplemented by oyster farming and other industries. Its harbor is the site of a large merchant reserve fleet. Located at the base of the Olympic Peninsula, it is the gateway to OLYMPIC NATIONAL PARK.

Olympic Games In ancient Greece, a Panhellenic festival held every fourth year and made up of contests of sports, music, and literature. Since 1896, the name has been used for a modified revival of the ancient games consisting of international athletic contests held at four-year intervals. The original Greek games included footraces, the discus and javelin throws, the long jump, boxing, wrestling, the pentathlon, and chariot races. After the subjugation of Greece by Rome, the games declined; they were finally abolished in AD 393. They were revived in the late 19th cent through the efforts of the baron de COUBERTIN, the first modern games being held in Athens. The first Winter Games were held in 1924. The direction of the modern Olympic movement and the regulation of the games is vested in the International Olympic Committee,

Sites of the Modern Olympic Games

Year	Summer	Winter	Year	Summer	Winter
1896	Athens	*	1960	Rome	Squaw Valley
1900	Paris	*	1964	Tokyo	Innsbruck
1904	St. Louis	*	1968	Mexico City	Grenoble
1908	London	*	1972	Munich	Sapporo
1912	Stockholm	*	1976	Montreal	Innsbruck
1916	†	*	1980	Moscow	Lake Placid
1920	Antwerp	*	1984	Los Angeles	Sarajevo
1924	Paris	Chamonix	1988	Seoul	Calgary
1928	Amsterdam	St. Moritz	1992	Barcelona	Albertville
1932	Los Angeles	Lake Placid	1994	‡	Lillehammer
1936	Berlin	Garmisch-Partenkirchen	1996	Atlanta	‡
			1998	‡	Nagano
1940	†	†	2000	Sydney	‡
1944	†	†	2002	‡	Salt Lake City
1948	London	St. Moritz	2004	Athens	‡
1952	Helsinki	Oslo	2006	‡	Turin
1956	Melbourne	Cortina	2008	Beijing	‡

*The Winter Games were not held until 1924.
†Games were not held during World Wars I and II.
‡After 1992 the Summer and Winter Games were held on a staggered two-year schedule.

headquartered at Lausanne, Switzerland. Until the 1970s the games adhered to a strict code of amateurism, but since that time professional players have also been allowed to participate. Programs for the Summer Games include competition in ARCHERY, BASKETBALL, BOXING, CANOEING, CYCLING, DIVING, equestrian sports, FENCING, FIELD HOCKEY, football (SOCCER), GYMNASTICS, HANDBALL, JUDO, modern PENTATHLON, ROWING, SAILING, SHOOTING, SWIMMING, TABLE TENNIS, TENNIS, TRACK AND FIELD (athletics), VOLLEYBALL, WATER POLO, WEIGHT LIFTING, and WRESTLING. The program for the Winter Games includes the BIATHLON, BOBSLEDDING, ICE HOCKEY, LUGEING, and numerous ice-SKATING and SKIING events. The programs may also include demonstration sports and exhibitions.

Olympic Mountains Segment of the Pacific Coast Ranges, northwestern Washington. The mountains extend across the Olympic Peninsula south of the Strait of JUAN DE FUCA and west of PUGET SOUND within OLYMPIC NATIONAL PARK. The chief peaks are Mount Olympus, at 7,965 ft (2,428 m), and Mount Constance, at 7,743 ft (2,360 m). There is heavy rainfall creating rain forests dominated by Douglas fir and Sitka spruce. Some trees are nearly 300 ft (90 m) high and 8 ft (2.5 m) in diameter.

Olympic National Park National park, northwestern Washington. Established in 1938 to preserve the OLYMPIC MTNS. and their forests and wildlife, it covers 1,442 sq mi (3,735 sq km); it includes a strip of Pacific Northwest shoreline geographically separated from the rest of the park. There are more than 60 glaciers in the park. The western part includes rain forests; the eastern slopes feature lakes; and the ocean shore section contains scenic beaches and three Indian reservations.

Olympus, Mt. Mountain peak, northeastern Greece. At 9,570 ft (2,917 m), it is the highest mountain in Greece. It is part of the Olympus range, lying on the border between Macedonia and THESSALY, near the Gulf of Salonika. The summit is snowcapped and often has cloud cover. In ancient Greece, it was regarded as the abode of the gods and the site of the throne of ZEUS.

Olympus Mons Large VOLCANO on MARS, the largest known volcano in the solar system. It consists of a central structure about 17 mi (27 km) high and 335 mi (540 km) wide at the base, surrounded by an outward-facing cliff up to about 6 mi (10 km) high. At the summit is a crater 53 mi (85 km) in diameter. For comparison, earth's largest volcano, MAUNA LOA, is 74 mi (120 km) wide at the base and rises 5.5 mi (9 km) above the ocean floor.

Olynthus \ō-'lin-thəs\ Ancient Greek city, MACEDONIA, on the Chalcidice Peninsula, northeastern Greece. From the late 5th century BC it was the head of a strong confederacy of Greek towns known as the Chalcidian League. It was destroyed by PHILIP II in 348 BC. Excavations have revealed the grid plan of the ancient town and provided material for studying the relationship between Classical and Hellenistic Greek art.

om \'ōm\ In HINDUISM and other Indian religions, a sacred syllable considered the greatest of all MANTRAS. The syllable om is composed of the three sounds *a-u-m* (in the SANSKRIT LANGUAGE, the vowels *a* and *u* join to become *o*), which represent three important triads: earth, atmosphere, and heaven; the major Hindu gods, BRAHMA, VISHNU, and SHIVA; and the sacred Vedic scriptures, Rig, Yajur, and Sama (see VEDIC RELIGION). Thus om mystically embodies the essence of the universe. It is uttered at the beginning and end of Hindu prayers, chants, and meditation and is also freely used in Buddhist and Jain rituals.

Omagh \'ō-mä\ District (population 1995 est.: 47,000) and town (pop., 1991: 18,000), Northern Ireland. Formerly in County Tyrone, the district was established in 1973. The area was ruled by the ancient O'Neill family (5th–16th century), passing to English rule after the flight of Hugh O'Neill in 1607. Most of the land is grazed by dairy cattle or sheep, and the rivers contain salmon and trout. Omagh town, the district seat, is a market and light-manufacturing center.

Omaha \'ō-mə-ˌhò, 'ō-mə-ˌhä\ City (pop., 1996 est.: 364,000), eastern Nebraska, on the Missouri River, north of its junction with the Platte River. The city's name, meaning "upstream people," referred to the Omaha Indians. Omaha was founded in 1854 and incorporated as a city in 1857. In 1863 it became the starting point for the UNION PACIFIC RAILROAD Co.'s first transcontinental railroad, and soon grew into a center of trade and industry. The largest city in the state, it is a major livestock and grain market, as well as a railroad, meat-packing, and insurance center. It is home to the University of NEBRASKA and the Joslyn Art Museum.

O'Mahony, John (1816–1877) Irish-American political leader. An Irish resistance leader, he fled to New York in 1853. There he founded and led (1858–66) the U.S. branch of the Fenian Brotherhood, an Irish secret revolutionary society. By 1865 the American Fenian group had become large and prosperous and was sending money and arms to Ireland. O'Mahony reluctantly backed the Irish Fenians' decision to send military raids into Canada against the British, part of a scheme to hold Canada hostage for the cause of Irish freedom. The raids failed and he resigned, but was later called out of retirement (1872–77). See also JOHN O'NEILL

Oman \ō-'män\ *officially* **Sultanate of Oman** *formerly* **Muscat and Oman** Nation, southeastern coast of the ARABIAN PENINSULA. Area: 119,500 sq mi (309,500 sq km). Population (1997 est.): 2,265,000. Capital: MASQAT, or Muscat. The Omanis are predominantly Arab and tribal in organization. There are also many people from S.East Asia and East Africa working there. Language: Arabic (official), Baluchi. Religions: Islam (official), Hinduism. Currency: rial Omani. Oman is a hot, arid country with high humidity along the coasts. The Al-Hajar Mountains parallel the Gulf of Oman coast, reaching a height of more than 10,000 ft (3,000 m). A broad expanse of gravel desert extends southwestward to cover three-fourths of the country. It has a developing mixed economy, with the production and export of petroleum as its largest sector. It is a monarchy, with an advisory council; its head of state and government is the sultan. The land has been inhabited for at least 10,000 years. The Arab migration to Oman began in the 9th century BC. Tribal warfare continued until the conversion to Islam in the 7th century AD. It was ruled by Ibadi IMAMS until 1154, when a royal dynasty was established. The Portuguese controlled the coastal areas c. 1507–1650, when they were expelled. The Al Bu Said dynasty, founded in the mid-18th century, still rules Oman. The kingdom expanded into eastern Africa in the 18th–19th century, and the capital was in ZANZIBAR. Oil was discovered in 1964. In 1970 the sultan was deposed by his son, who began a policy of modernization and joined the ARAB LEAGUE and the UNITED NATIONS. In the PERSIAN GULF WAR, Oman cooperated with the allied forces against Iraq. In the 1990s it continued to expand its foreign relations.

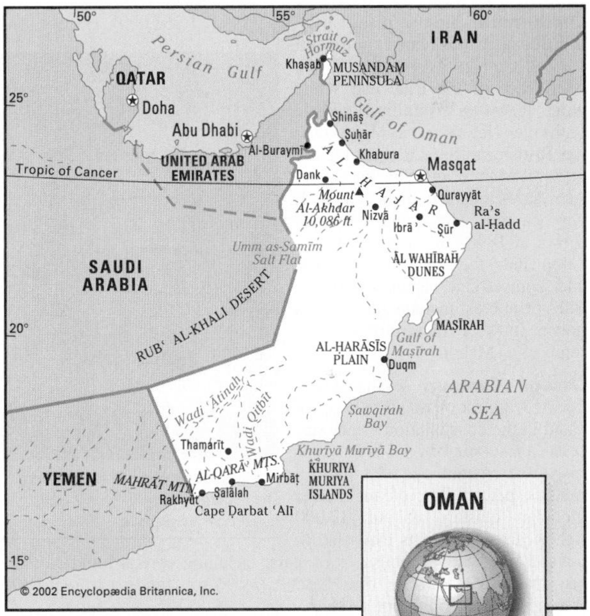

Oman, Gulf of Northwest arm of the Arabian Sea, between the eastern part of the ARABIAN PENINSULA and Iran. It is about 230 mi (370 km) wide, about 340 mi (545 km) long, and connects with the PERSIAN GULF through the Strait of HORMUZ. It is the only entrance to the Persian Gulf

O P Q R

from the Arabian Sea and Indian Ocean, and is important as a shipping route for the oil-producing area around the Persian Gulf.

Omar, Mosque of See DOME OF THE ROCK

Omar Khayyam \ˌō-ˌmär-ˌkī-ˈyäm\ *Persian* **Abu ol-Fath Omar ebn Ebrahim ol-Khayyami** (1048–1131) Persian poet, mathematician, and astronomer. Educated in the sciences and philosophy, he was renowned in his country and time for his scientific achievements, but few of his prose writings survive. His verses attracted little attention until his *robaiyat* ("quatrains") were loosely translated into English by EDWARD FITZGERALD and published in 1859. Many of the quatrains (each of which was intended as an independent poem) are of doubtful attribution; most scholars agree on the authenticity of about 50, with controversy over some 200 others.

ombudsman \ˈäm-ˌbu̇dz-mən\ (Swedish: "representative") Representative assigned by a large organization or a government to investigate citizen complaints and suggest solutions. An ombudsman's office was established by the Swedish constitution of 1809. The idea soon spread to other Scandinavian countries, and later to New Zealand, Britain, Germany, Israel, and some states or provinces in the U.S., Australia, and Canada. An ombudsman's responsibility is to receive and investigate complaints and to serve as an independent and impartial arbiter in recommending what may be done to satisfy the complainant or in explaining why no action is necessary. Its use has spread to universities, corporations, municipalities, and institutions such as hospitals.

Omdurman \ˌäm-dər-ˈman\ City (pop., 1993: 1,267,000), eastern central Sudan. It is situated on the left bank of the NILE RIVER just below the confluence of the Blue and White Niles. It was an insignificant village until the victory of al-MAHDI over the British in 1885. It grew rapidly after al-Mahdi and his successor, ABD ALLAH, made it their capital. It was captured by Anglo-Egyptian forces in 1898 but continued to develop into the cultural, religious, and commercial center of Sudan. Sites of interest include Abd Allah's house (now a museum) and the tomb of al-Mahdi.

The tomb of al-Mahdi in Omdurman, The Sudan.
CHARLES BEERY—SHOSTAL/EB INC.

Omega Centauri \ō-ˈmā-gə-sen-ˈtȯr-ī\ Brightest GLOBULAR CLUSTER, located in the constellation Centaurus. It has a MAGNITUDE of 3.7 and is visible to the unaided eye as a faint luminous patch. One of the nearer globular clusters (about 17,000 light-years away), it is estimated to contain hundreds of thousands of stars, including several hundred VARIABLE STARS. John Herschel (see HERSCHEL FAMILY) was the first to recognize it as a star cluster and not a NEBULA.

omen Observed phenomenon that is interpreted as signifying good or bad fortune. The many and varied omens that the ancients noted included lightning, cloud movements, the flights of birds, and the paths of sacred animals. Each type of omen was gauged according to specific meaningful characteristics, such as the kinds of bird in flight or the direction of flight in relation to the observer.

Ometecuhtli \ˌō-mā-ˈtā-ˌku̇t-lē\ AZTEC deity, the Lord of Duality or Lord of Life. With his female counterpart, Omecíhuatl (Lady of Duality), he lived in Omeyocan, the 13th and highest Aztec heaven. He was represented by symbols of fertility, and his image was adorned with ears of corn. He was the only Aztec god to have neither a temple nor a formal cult. Seeing him as remote in the heavens, the Aztecs assumed he would never interact with them directly, but they felt his presence in rituals and in the rhythms of nature.

omnivore \ˈäm-nə-ˌvōr\ Animal that eats both plant and animal matter. Most omnivorous species do not have highly specialized food-processing structures or food-gathering behavior. Many animals generally considered CARNIVORES are actually omnivorous; for example, the red fox eats fruits and berries as well as mammals and birds. See also HERBIVORE.

Omsk \ˈȯmsk\ City (pop., 1996 est.: 1,200,000), southwestern Russia, at the confluence of the IRTYSH and Om rivers. Founded in 1716 as a military stronghold, Omsk became a city in 1804. It remained the headquarters of the Siberian COSSACKS until the late 19th century. In 1918–19 it was the seat of the anti-Bolshevik government of Adm. ALEKSANDR KOLCHAK. Its growth was spurred by the building of the TRANS-SIBERIAN RAILROAD in the 1890s and the onset of World War II. Pipelines from the Volga-Urals and western Siberian oil fields supply the refinery and the petrochemical industry.

On See HELIOPOLIS

Onassis, Aristotle (Socrates) (1906–1975) Greek shipping magnate and international businessman. Born in Smyrna, Greece (now Turkey), the son of a tobacco dealer, he started a tobacco-importing business in Buenos Aires. He was made consul general after negotiating a trade agreement for the Greek government. A millionaire by age 25, he bought his first freight ships in 1932. In the 1940s and '50s his fleet grew until it was larger than the navies of many countries. He acquired business interests in Monte Carlo, and from 1957 to 1974 owned and operated Olympic Airways, the Greek national airline. He conducted a long affair with M. CALLAS, and in 1968 married Jacqueline Kennedy (see JACQUELINE KENNEDY ONASSIS).

Onassis, Jacqueline Kennedy *orig.* **Jacqueline Bouvier** (1929–1994) U.S. public figure. Born in East Hampton, N.Y., in 1953 she married Sen. JOHN F. KENNEDY, who became president in 1961. As first lady, she restored the WHITE HOUSE to its original Federal style and conducted a televised tour of the residence. Her graciousness, elegance, and beauty endeared her to the American public; her broad culture and ease in speaking Spanish and French won over foreign leaders. After her husband's assassination, she moved to New York with their children, Caroline (born 1957) and John, Jr. (1960–1999). In 1968 she married ARISTOTLE ONASSIS. After his death in 1975, she returned to New York, where she became noted as a book editor.

Oñate \ōn-ˈyä-tā\, **Juan de** (1550?–1630) Spanish CONQUISTADOR. Born in New Spain (Mexico), he received permission to govern the colony of New Mexico, which he founded in 1598. He sent exploring parties throughout the American Southwest to search for gold and led an expedition into present-day Kansas in 1601. Still searching for gold, he explored the region west to the Colorado River and south to the Gulf of California (1604). He resigned in 1607. Tried for his brutal treatment of the Indians and settlers while governor, he was found guilty and exiled from the colony in 1614.

onchocerciasis See RIVER BLINDNESS

oncogene \ˈäŋ-kə-ˌjēn\ GENE that can cause CANCER. It is a sequence of DNA that has been altered or mutated from its original form, the proto-oncogene (see MUTATION). Proto-oncogenes promote the specialization and division of normal cells. A change in their genetic sequence can result in uncontrolled cell growth, ultimately causing the formation of a cancerous tumor. In humans, proto-oncogenes can be transformed into oncogenes in three ways: point mutation (alteration of a single nucleotide base pair), translocation (in which a segment of the chromosome breaks off and attaches to another chromosome), or amplification (increase in the number of copies of the proto-oncogene). Oncogenes were first discovered in certain RETROVIRUSES and were later identified as cancer-causing agents in many animals. About 60 human oncogenes have been identified, including some that cause breast and lung cancer. See also J. MICHAEL BISHOP, HAROLD VARMUS.

Ondaatje \än-ˈdä-chā\, **(Philip) Michael** (born 1943) Sri Lankan-Canadian novelist and poet. He emigrated to Montreal at 19 and attended the University of Toronto and Queen's University. His fascination with the American West led to one of his most celebrated works, the pastiche *The Collected Works of Billy the Kid* (1970). His novel *The English Patient* (1992, Booker Prize; film, 1996) won him international recognition; it was followed by *Anil's Ghost* (2000). His musical poetry and prose are a blend of myth, history, jazz, memoirs, and other forms. He also has directed several films.

Onega \ə-ˈnye-gə\, **Lake** Lake, northwestern Russia. Located between Lake LADOGA and the WHITE SEA, it is the second-largest lake in Europe. It has an area of 3,753 sq mi (9,720 sq km) and is 154 mi (248 km) long. It empties into the Svir River and is frozen for about half of each year. It is connected with the BALTIC and White seas by canal and with the VOLGA RIVER basin by a waterway, enabling it to play an important part in international trade and transport.

Oneida \ō-ˈnī-də\ IROQUOIAN-speaking North American Indian people of what is now central New York, one of the original five nations of the IROQUOIS CONFEDERACY. The Oneida were semisendentary and practiced corn agriculture. LONGHOUSES sheltered families related through maternal descent. Each community had a local council that guided the chief or chiefs. The Oneida supported the colonist cause in the American Revolution and were attacked by the pro-British Iroquois under JOSEPH BRANT. By the mid-19th century, most Oneida had dispersed. They number about 5,000 today, with concentrations in Canada, Wisconsin, and central New York.

Oneida Community Utopian religious community founded by JOHN H. NOYES in Oneida, N.Y., in 1847. Noyes and his disciples formed their first religious society in Putney, Vt., in 1841, but their practice of communal marriage aroused the hostility of the townspeople, and they were obliged to move to Oneida. The Oneida group flourished for 30 years, supporting itself by manufacturing steel traps, silverware, and other items. After it broke up in 1879, remaining members reorganized it as a commercial enterprise, which is noted for the manufacture of silver plate.

O'Neill, Eugene (Gladstone) (1888–1953) U.S. playwright. Born in New York City, the son of a touring actor, he spent an itinerant youth as a seaman, heavy drinker, and derelict, then began writing plays while recovering from tuberculosis (1912). His one-act *Bound East for Cardiff* (1916) was produced by the experimental PROVINCETOWN PLAYERS, which also staged his other early plays (1916–20). *Beyond the Horizon* was produced on Broadway in 1920, earning him his first Pulitzer Prize. Enormously prolific, he often wrote about tortured family relationships and the conflict between idealism and materialism. Soon recognized as a major dramatist, he became widely translated and produced. His many plays of the 1920s include *The Emperor Jones* (1921), *The Hairy Ape* (1922), *Anna Christie* (1922, Pulitzer Prize), *Desire Under the Elms* (1925), *The Great God Brown* (1926), and *Strange Interlude* (1928, Pulitzer Prize). Among his later plays are *Mourning Becomes Electra* (1931), *Ah! Wilderness* (1933; his only comedy), *The Iceman Cometh* (1946), and the autobiographical *Long Day's Journey into Night* (produced 1956; Pulitzer Prize), considered his masterpiece. O'Neill was awarded the Nobel Prize in 1936, the first U.S. playwright so honored.

O'Neill, John (1834–1878) U.S. (Irish-born) political leader. He arrived in the U.S. in 1848 and settled in Tennessee, where he joined the U.S. branch of the secret Irish nationalist Fenian Brotherhood. A supporter of its scheme to invade Canada to win Irish freedom from Britain, in 1866 he led a group of 600 men across the Niagara River to capture Fort Erie, but was forced to flee back to the U.S. In 1870 he led a raid from Vermont that Canadians repulsed, and he led another on Manitoba in 1871. See also JOHN O'MAHONY.

Onin War \ˈō-nin\ (1467–77) Civil war in central Japan that destroyed the remnants of central governmental authority and led to 100 years of warfare. The war sprang from a shogunal succession dispute, with one powerful clan supporting the brother of the ruling SHOGUN and another supporting the shogun's infant son. It ended in stalemate, but clans across Japan became involved in hopes of increasing their territory through victory. The nation was at last reunified under ODA NOBUNAGA, TOYOTOMI HIDEYOSHI, and TOKUGAWA IEYASU. See also ASHIKAGA SHOGUNATE, WARRING STATES PERIOD.

onion Herbaceous biennial plant *(Allium cepa)* of the LILY FAMILY, probably native to South Asia but now grown worldwide, and its edible bulb. Among the hardiest and oldest garden-vegetable plants, onions bear a cluster of small, greenish-white flowers on one or more leafless stalks. The leaf base swells to form the underground mature, edible onion. Onions are pungent and cause eye tearing when peeled or sliced because they contain a sulfur-rich volatile oil. They vary in size, shape, color, and pungency.

Onion (*Allium cepa*).
WALTER CHANDOHA

Though low in standard nutrients, they are valued for their flavor. Onions have been claimed to cure colds, earaches, and laryngitis and have been used to treat animal bites, powder burns, and warts; like their close relative GARLIC, they are being studied for other suspected beneficial qualities. See also ALLIUM.

Onnes, Heike Kamerlingh See Heike KAMERLINGH ONNES

Onsager \ˈȯn-ˌsä-gər\, **Lars** (1903–1976) Norwegian-U.S. chemist. He emigrated to the U.S. and taught principally at Yale University. His development of a general theory of irreversible chemical processes, described as the "fourth law of THERMODYNAMICS," gained him a 1968 Nobel Prize. He also applied the laws of thermodynamics to systems not in EQUILIBRIUM. His explanation of the movement of IONS in SOLUTION as related to TURBULENCES and fluid DENSITIES had a major effect on the development of PHYSICAL CHEMISTRY.

Ontario Province (pop., 2001: 11,874,400), the second largest in Canada. It is situated between HUDSON and JAMES bays and the ST. LAWRENCE RIVER–Great Lakes chain; its capital is TORONTO. Before European settlement, the area was inhabited by IROQUOIS and Algonquian Indian tribes. In the 17th century it was visited by French explorers and missionaries. It passed to the British in 1763 after the FRENCH AND INDIAN WAR. It was the scene of many battles in the WAR OF 1812. In 1867 it became one of four provinces of the new Dominion of Canada. northern Ontario has a rocky and rugged terrain with thick forests, bogs, lakes, and extensive mineral reserves. southern Ontario is an important farming and industrial region and is the center of Canada's population and urban development. OTTAWA, the national capital, is also in Ontario.

Ontario, Lake Smallest and easternmost of the GREAT LAKES of North America. Bounded by New York and Ontario, and with the U.S.–Canada border passing through it, the lake is roughly elliptical; its major axis, 193 mi (311 km) long, lies nearly east to west, and its greatest width is 53 mi (85 km). The NIAGARA RIVER is the lake's main feeder. There are five islands at its eastern end, where the lake discharges into the ST. LAWRENCE RIVER near Kingston, Ont. The Welland Canal and the Niagara River connect it to Lake ERIE to the southwest. It was visited by SAMUEL DE CHAMPLAIN in 1615; its early French name was Lac Frontenac. Ports on the lake include TORONTO and HAMILTON, Ont., and ROCHESTER and Oswego, N.Y.

ontological argument Argument that proceeds from the idea of God to the reality of God. It was first clearly formulated by St. ANSELM in his *Proslogion* (1077–78); a later famous version is given by DESCARTES. Anselm began with the concept of God as that than which nothing greater can be conceived. To think of such a being as existing only in thought and not also in reality involves a contradiction, since a being that lacks real existence is not a being than which none greater can be conceived. A yet greater being would be one with the further attribute of existence. Thus the unsurpassably perfect being must exist; otherwise it would not be unsurpassably perfect. This is among the most discussed and contested arguments in the history of thought.

ontology Theory of being as such. Ontology is synonymous with METAPHYSICS as defined by ARISTOTLE, but because metaphysics came to include other studies (including philosophical COSMOLOGY and RATIONAL PSYCHOLOGY), ontology has become the preferred term for the study of being. In the 18th century CHRISTIAN WOLFF understood ontology as a deductive discipline leading to necessary truths about the essences of beings. Wolff's successor, IMMANUEL KANT, presented influential refutations of ontology as a purported system of knowledge. Ontology again became important in the 20th century, notably among students of PHENOMENOLOGY and EXISTENTIALISM, particularly MARTIN HEIDEGGER.

onychophoran \ˌä-ni-ˈkä-fə-rən\ Any of about 90 species of free-living terrestrial INVERTEBRATES in the class Onychophora (sometimes considered a phylum). They are sometimes called velvet worms for their velvety skin. The common genus *Peripatus* occurs in the West Indies, Central America, and northern South America. Onychophorans are slender and segmented; each segment has a pair of short legs. Species range from 0.6 to 6 in. (14–150 mm) long. They live in humid, hidden spots: in forest litter, wood crevices, termite nests, or the soil, sometimes to a depth of more than 3 ft (1 m). They use their jaws to open captured prey (often small insects) and suck out the juices.

onyx \ˈä-niks\ Striped, semiprecious variety of the silica mineral AGATE with white and black alternating bands. Other varieties include carnelian

O P Q R

onyx, with white and red bands, and sardonyx, with white and brown bands. Its properties are the same as those of QUARTZ. Onyx is used in carved cameos and intaglios because its layers can be cut to show a color contrast between the design and the background. It is found worldwide, but chiefly in India and South America.

Oort cloud Vast spherical cloud of small, icy bodies orbiting the sun at distances ranging from about 0.3 light-year to one light-year or more, that is probably the source of most long-period COMETS. In 1950 the Dutch astronomer Jan Hendrik Oort (1900–1992) noted that no comets have orbits that would indicate an interstellar origin. He proposed that the sun is surrounded by billions of these objects, which are only occasionally detectable when they enter the inner solar system. The Oort cloud is believed to be composed of primordial bodies dating from the formation of the solar system (see SOLAR NEBULA). Whether it merges into the disk-shaped KUIPER BELT in its inner region is not known.

Op art *or* **Optical art** Branch of mid-20th-century geometric abstract art that deals with optical illusion. Op art painters devised complex optical spaces by manipulating repetitive forms such as parallel lines, checkerboard patterns, and concentric circles or by creating chromatic tension from the juxtaposition of complementary colors, creating the illusion of movement. Principal artists of the Op movement in the late 1950s and 1960s include VICTOR VASARELY, Bridget Riley (born 1931), and Larry Poons (born 1937).

opal A hydrated, noncrystalline SILICA MINERAL used extensively as a gemstone. Its chemical composition is similar to that of QUARTZ but generally with a variable water content. Pure opal is colorless, but impurities generally give it various dull colors ranging from yellow and red to black. Black opal is especially rare and valuable. White opal and fire opal, characterized by yellow, orange, or red color, are much more common. Various forms of common opal are widely used as abrasives, insulation material, and ceramic ingredients. Opal is most abundant in volcanic rocks, especially in areas of hot-spring activity. The finest gem opals have been found in Australia; other areas that yield gem material include Japan, Mexico, Honduras, India, New Zealand, and the U.S.

Black opal from Australia; in the collection of the Department of Earth Sciences, Washington University, St. Louis, Mo.

JOHN H. GERARD

OPEC See ORGANIZATION OF PETROLEUM EXPORTING COUNTRIES

open cluster *or* **galactic cluster** Any group of Population I (see POPULATIONS I AND II) stars with a common origin, held together by mutual gravitation (not to be confused with a CLUSTER OF GALAXIES). Stars in open clusters are much more scattered than those in GLOBULAR CLUSTERS. All known open clusters contain from about 10 to 1,000 or more stars (about half contain fewer than 100) and have diameters of 5–75 light-years. More than 1,000 have been discovered in the Milky Way galaxy; well-known examples include the PLEIADES and the HYADES.

Open Door policy Statement of U.S. foreign policy toward China. Initiated by U.S. secretary of state JOHN HAY (1899), the policy reaffirmed the principle that all nations should have equal access to Chinese ports open to trade. The U.S. sent notes to Britain, Germany, France, Italy, Japan, and Russia explaining the policy to prevent them from establishing separate spheres of influence in China. Their replies were evasive, but the U.S. considered them acceptances of the policy. Japan's violation of the policy in 1937 led the U.S. to cut off supplies to Japan. The policy ended with the communist takeover of China (1949).

open-heart surgery Any surgical procedure opening the HEART and exposing one or more of its chambers, most often to repair valve disease or correct congenital HEART MALFORMATIONS. Invention of the heart-lung machine (see ARTIFICIAL HEART), which allows the heart to be stopped during surgery, made it possible. The first successful open-heart surgery was performed in the U.S. in 1953 by John H. Gibbon, Jr., to close an atrial septal defect.

open-hearth process *or* **Siemens-Martin process** Steelmaking technique that for most of the 20th century accounted for most STEEL made in the world. WILLIAM SIEMENS made steel from pig iron in a reverberatory furnace of his design in 1867. The same year the French manufacturer Pierre-Émile Martin (1824–1915) used the idea to produce steel by melting wrought iron with steel scrap. Siemens used the waste heat given off by the furnace: he directed the fumes from the furnace through a brick checkerwork, heating it to a high temperature, and then used the same path to introduce air into the furnace; the preheated air significantly increased the flame temperature. The open-hearth process furnace (which replaced the BESSEMER PROCESS) has itself been replaced in most industrialized countries by the BASIC OXYGEN PROCESS and the ELECTRIC FURNACE. See also REVERBERATORY FURNACE.

open-market operation Any of the purchases and sales of government SECURITIES and commercial paper by a CENTRAL BANK in an effort to regulate the MONEY SUPPLY and credit conditions. Open-market operations can also be used to stabilize the prices of government securities. When the central bank buys securities on the open market, it increases the reserves of commercial banks, making it possible for them to expand their loans and investments. It also increases the price of government securities, equivalent to reducing their interest rates, and decreases interest rates generally, thus encouraging investment. If the central bank sells securities, the effects are reversed. Open-market operations are usually performed with short-term government securities such as TREASURY BILLS.

opera Musical drama made up of vocal pieces with orchestral accompaniment, overtures, and interludes. Opera was invented at the end of the 16th century in an attempt by the Camerata, an academy of Florentine poets, musicians, and scholars, to imitate ancient Greek drama, which was known to have been largely sung or chanted. Since no actual Greek music was known, composers had considerable freedom in reconceiving it. Imitations of Greek pastoral poetry became the basis for early opera libretti. The first operas, by Jacopo Peri (*Dafne,* 1598; lost) and G. CACCINI (*Euridice*, 1600), consisted throughout of lightly accompanied melody closely imitating inflected speech. C. MONTEVERDI, the greatest early operatic figure, composed the first masterpiece, *Orfeo,* in 1607; unlike its predecessors, *Orfeo* is scored for a small orchestra, and RECITATIVE here begins to be clearly distinguished from ARIA, an achievement that would prove decisive for opera's future success. In France, J.-B. LULLY produced a prototype for courtly opera whose influence would dominate French opera through the mid-18th century. J.-P. RAMEAU, G.F. HANDEL, and C.W. GLUCK were the most significant opera composers of the first two-thirds of the 18th century; their works were surpassed by the brilliant operas of W.A. MOZART. In the early 19th century, G. ROSSINI and G. DONIZETTI dominated Italian opera. The later 19th century saw the great works of G. VERDI and RICHARD WAGNER; the latter, with his bold innovations, became the most influential operatic figure since Monteverdi. R. STRAUSS and G. PUCCINI wrote the most popular 20th-century operas. See also BALLAD OPERA, BEIJING OPERA, OPERETTA.

operating system (OS) SOFTWARE that controls the operation of a COMPUTER, directs the input and output of data, keeps track of files, and controls the processing of computer PROGRAM. Its roles include managing the functioning of the computer hardware, running the applications programs, serving as an interface between the computer and the user, and allocating computer resources to various functions. When several jobs reside in the computer simultaneously and share resources (MULTITASKING), the OS allocates fixed amounts of CPU time and MEMORY in turn, or allows one job to read data while another writes to a printer and still another performs computations. Through a process called time-sharing, a large computer can handle interaction with hundreds of users simultaneously, giving each the perception of being the sole user. Modern computer operating systems are becoming increasingly machine-independent, capable of running on any HARDWARE platform; a widely used platform-independent operating system in use today is UNIX. Most personal computers run on Microsoft's WINDOWS operating system, which grew out of and eventually replaced MS-DOS. See also LINUX.

operationalism In the philosophy of SCIENCE, the view that theoretical propositions are meaningful only insofar as scientific practice includes specific operations—either manual measuring operations, or computational pencil-and-paper operations—in terms of which those propositions are given meaning. Thus, nothing is to be read into scientific knowledge beyond its operational meaning. The idea of nature as a thing-in-itself is eliminated, as an intellectual superstition and an obstacle to better scientific understanding, a survival from an earlier metaphysical era. Operationalism is closely associated with the work of the U.S. physicist Percy W. Bridgman (1882–1961).

operations management See PRODUCTION MANAGEMENT

operations research Application of scientific methods to management and administration of military, government, commercial, and industrial systems. It began during World War II in Britain when teams of scientists worked with the Royal Air Force to improve radar detection of enemy aircraft, leading to coordinated efforts to improve the entire system of early warning, defense, and supply. It is characterized by a systems orientation, or systems engineering, in which interdisciplinary research teams adapt scientific methods to large-scale problems that must be modeled, since laboratory testing is impossible. Examples include resource allocation and replacement, inventory control, and scheduling of large-scale construction projects.

operator, differential See DIFFERENTIAL OPERATOR

operetta Musical drama similar to OPERA, usually with a romantically sentimental plot, employing songs, dances, and orchestral interludes interspersed with spoken dialogue. The modern tradition begins with J. OFFENBACH, who wrote some 90 operettas and inspired a Viennese tradition that began with the works of Franz von Suppé (1819–1895) and JOHANN STRAUSS, JR. In Britain, most of the 14 comic operettas (1871–96) of W.S. GILBERT and A. SULLIVAN have been enduringly popular. In the U.S., the works of such European immigrant composers as V. HERBERT and R. FRIML were widely popular in the early 20th century. See also MUSICAL.

operon \'ä-pər-ˌän\ Genetic regulatory system of single-celled organisms (PROKARYOTES) and their viruses, in which GENES coding for functionally related proteins are clustered along the DNA, enabling their expression to be coordinated in response to the cell's needs. By providing a means to produce proteins only when and where they are required, the operon allows the cell to conserve energy. A typical operon consists of a group of structural genes that code for enzymes involved in a metabolic pathway, such as the biosynthesis of an amino acid. A single unit of messenger RNA is transcribed from the operon and is then translated into separate proteins. Operons are controlled by various regulatory elements that respond to environmental cues. The operon system was first proposed by FRANÇOIS JACOB and JACQUES MONOD in the early 1960s.

Opet \'ō-ˌpet\ Ancient Egyptian festival of the New Year. In the celebration of Opet, statues of AMON and MUT and their son KHONS were carried down the Nile on barges in a ritual journey from their shrines at KARNAK to the temple of LUXOR. There the statues remained about 24 days, a festival time for Luxor. The images were returned to Karnak by the same route in a second public appearance that closed the festival.

Ophite \'ä-ˌfīt, 'ō-ˌfīt\ Member of any of several Gnostic sects that flourished in the Roman empire in the 2nd century AD and for several centuries thereafter. The sects shared a dualistic theology, opposing a beneficent and entirely spiritual Supreme Being to a chaotic and evil material world. To the Ophites, the human dilemma resulted from the mixture of these conflicting spiritual and material elements in human nature. Only gnosis, the esoteric knowledge of good and evil, could redeem one from the bonds of matter. See also DUALISM, GNOSTICISM.

ophthalmology \ˌäf-thəl-'mä-lə-jē\ Medical specialty dealing with the EYES, dating to 1805. FRANS C. DONDERS's 1864 advances in OPTICS allowed EYEGLASSES to be fitted to vision problems. The ophthalmoscope made it possible to look inside the eye and relate eye defects to internal conditions. More recent advances include eye exams, early treatment of congenital defects, and eye banks to store corneas for transplants. Ophthalmologists test visual function and examine the eye for faulty development, disease, injury, degeneration, aging, or refractive errors. They prescribe treatment for eye disease and lenses for refraction and perform surgery when needed. See also OPTOMETRY, VISUAL-FIELD DEFECT.

Ophüls \'ō-fūels\, **Max** *orig.* **Max Oppenheimer** (1902–1957) German film director. An actor, stage director, and producer in Germany and Austria (1921–30), he gained renown as a film director with *Liebelei* (1933). He left Germany for France, where he made *The Tender Enemy* (1936), then moved to Hollywood, where he directed *The Exile* (1947), *Letter from an Unknown Woman* (1948), and *The Reckless Moment* (1949). He returned to France to make *La ronde* (1950), *Le plaisir* (1952), and *Lola Montez* (1955), considered his masterpiece. His son, Marcel (born 1927), has worked in France principally as a documentary filmmaker; his controversial *The Sorrow and the Pity* (1971), examining French conduct under German occupation, earned him international acclaim, as did *Hotel Terminus* (1988, Academy Award).

Opie, Eugene Lindsay (1873–1971) U.S. pathologist. Born in Staunton, Va., he received his MD from Johns Hopkins University. Early in his career, he correctly deduced that degenerative changes in the islets of Langerhans caused DIABETES MELLITUS and theorized that blockage of the junction of the bile and pancreatic ducts caused acute PANCREATITIS. He later showed that TUBERCULOSIS (TB) was spread by contact, including from one family member to another. His work led to use of X-ray films to detect asymptomatic TB, the sputum test to predict the chance of its spread, and injection of heat-killed tubercle bacilli to prevent infection.

opium Organic compound, a NARCOTIC drug known since ancient Greek times, obtained from exuded juice of immature fruit capsules of the OPIUM POPPY. Opium has legitimate medical uses, as the source of the ALKALOIDS CODEINE and MORPHINE and their derivatives. It is also used illicitly, either raw or purified as alkaloids and their derivatives (including HEROIN). Opium alkaloids of one type (e.g., morphine, codeine) act on the NERVOUS SYSTEM, mimicking the effects of ENDORPHINS; they are ANALGESIC, narcotic, and potentially addicting (see DRUG ADDICTION). Those of a second type, including papaverine and noscapine, relieve smooth muscle spasms and are not analgesic, narcotic, or addicting. Habitual opium use produces physical and mental deterioration and shortens life. Overdose can cause death by depressing RESPIRATION.

opium poppy Flowering plant *(Papaver somniferum)* of the family Papaveraceae, native to Turkey. OPIUM, MORPHINE, CODEINE, and HEROIN are all derived from the milky fluid in the unripe seed capsule. A common garden annual in the U.S., the opium poppy bears wide (5 in., or 13 cm) blue-purple or white flowers on plants about 3–16 ft (1–5 m) tall, with lobed or toothed silver-green foliage. It is also grown for its tiny nonnarcotic ripe seeds, kidney-shaped and grayish-blue to dark blue, which are used for in bakery goods and for seasoning, oil, and birdseed.

Opium Wars Two trading wars (1839–42, 1856–60), the first between China and Britain and the second (also called the Arrow War or Anglo-French War) between China and a British-French alliance. Historically, China believed that the West had nothing of interest to offer in trade; if Western nations desired Chinese goods, they had to pay for them in hard currency. To offset this negative currency flow, the British took to the illegal importation of opium, which the Chinese population was eager to buy. When China tried to stop the practice, hostilities broke out. Britain triumphed, and the resultant Treaty of NANJING was a blow to China. The second opium war resulted in the Treaty of Tianjin (Tientsin), which required further Chinese concessions. When China refused to sign the treaties, Beijing was captured and the emperor's summer palace burned. A deeper reason for the Opium Wars was mutual arrogance: China saw itself as the center of the world to which peripheral nations came humbly to trade; Britain and the West saw China as backward and therefore coercible. See also CANTON system, British EAST INDIA CO., LIN ZEXU.

Oporto See PORTO

opossum Any of about 66 species (family Didelphidae) of New World, mostly arboreal, nocturnal MARSUPIALS. Highly adaptable and reproductively fertile, opossums have changed little in millions of years. The North American species, the stout-bodied common, or Virginia, opossum *(Didelphis marsupialis)*, grows to 40 in. (100 cm) long. It is largely white, and has an opposable clawless toe on each hind foot; with

Common opossum (*Didelphis marsupialis*).

ROBERT J. ELLISON—THE NATIONAL AUDUBON SOCIETY COLLECTION/PHOTO RESEARCHERS its long, naked, prehensile tail, it resembles a large rat. Up to 25 grublike, 0.07-oz (2-g) newborns compete for the 13 nipples in the pouch, where the survivors spend four or five weeks; they spend the following eight to nine weeks clinging to the mother's back. The common opossum may feign death ("play possum") if surprised. It eats small animals, insects, and fruit, and sometimes domestic poultry and cultivated grain.

Oppenheimer, J(ulius) Robert (1904–1967) U.S. theoretical physicist. Born in New York City, he graduated from Harvard Univ., did research at Cambridge Univ., and earned a doctorate from Göttingen University. He returned to the U.S. to teach at Caltech (1929–47). His research focused on energy processes of subatomic particles, and he trained a generation of American physicists. In World War II he was named director of the Army's atomic-bomb project, later known as the MANHATTAN PROJECT, and set up the laboratory in Los Alamos, N.M., that remains a principal weapons-research laboratory. He directed the Institute for Advanced Study in Princeton 1947–66. He strongly opposed the development of the hydrogen bomb, and in 1953 he was suspended from secret nuclear research as an alleged communist and a security risk; the case, which pitted him against EDWARD TELLER, became a worldwide cause célèbre. In 1963 he was reinstated and awarded the Enrico Fermi Award.

opportunity cost In economic terms, the opportunities forgone in the choice of one expenditure over others. For a consumer with a fixed income, the opportunity cost of buying a new dishwasher might be the value of a vacation trip never taken or several suits of clothes unbought. The concept of opportunity cost allows economists to examine the relative monetary values of various goods and services.

opposition, square of Geometrical representation of the traditional logical relations of opposition (contradictories, contraries, subalterns) among the four types of propositions (universal affirmative or A-proposition, universal negative or E, particular affirmative or I, particular negative or O) in the Aristotelian doctrine of the SYLLOGISM. At the top left is the A; at the top right is the E; below the A is the I; and below the E is the O. The A and the O, like the E and I, are contradictories (diagonal relations); the A and the E are contraries; and the I is subaltern to (hence implied by) the A, the O subaltern to the E. Whereas contradictories have opposite truth-values (one true, the other false), contraries cannot both be true but can both be false.

optical activity Ability of a substance to rotate the plane of POLARIZATION of a beam of light passed through it, either as CRYSTALS or in SOLUTION. Clockwise rotation as one faces the light source is "positive," counterclockwise rotation "negative." LOUIS PASTEUR was the first to recognize that molecules with optical activity are stereoisomers (see ISOMERISM). Optical ISOMERS occur in mirror-image pairs whose physical and chemical properties are the same except that they rotate the plane of polarized light in opposite directions and interact differently with other stereoisomers (see ASYMMETRIC SYNTHESIS).

optical character recognition See OCR

optical scanner See optical SCANNER

optics Science concerned with the production and propagation of light, the changes it undergoes and produces, and closely related phenomena. Physical optics deals with the nature and properties of light; geometric optics deals with the formation of images by mirrors, lenses, and other devices that use light. Optical data processing involves manipulation of the information content of an image formed by coherent (one-wavelength) optical systems. The study of optics has led to the development of devices such as EYEGLASSES and CONTACT LENSES, TELESCOPES, MICROSCOPES, CAMERAS, BINOCULARS, LASERS, and optical fibers (see FIBER OPTICS).

Optimates and Populares \ˌäp-ti-ˈmā-tēz...ˌpäp-yə-ˈlar-ēz\ Ideological positions in ancient Rome that became defined in the early 1st century BC. Both groups came from the wealthier classes. The Optimates (Latin: "Best Ones," "Aristocrats") promoted the dominance of the Senate and the proper balance of the constitution; the Populares ("Demagogues," "Populists") used and defended the powers of the popular assemblies and the office of tribune and advocated such measures as land distribution, debt cancellation, and subsidized grain allowances. Their polarization led to civil wars—notably between Julius CAESAR and POMPEY and between Octavian (AUGUSTUS) and Mark ANTONY—and the fall of the republic with Augustus' accession.

optimization Field of applied mathematics whose principles and methods are used to solve quantitative problems in disciplines including physics, biology, engineering, and economics. Questions of maximizing or minimizing FUNCTIONS arising in the various disciplines can be solved using the same mathematical tools (see MAXIMUM, MINIMUM). In a typical optimization problem, the goal is to find the values of controllable factors determining the behavior of a system (e.g., a physical production process, an investment scheme) that maximize productivity or minimize waste. The simplest problems involve functions (systems) of a single variable (input factor) and may be solved with DIFFERENTIAL CALCULUS. LINEAR PROGRAMMING was developed to solve optimization problems involving two or more input variables. See also SIMPLEX METHOD.

optometry \äp-ˈtä-mə-trē\ Profession concerned with examining the eyes for defects or faults of refraction. Optometrists prescribe optical aids (e.g., EYEGLASSES, CONTACT LENSES), supervise eye exercise programs to treat vision problems, and examine the eyes for disorders such as GLAUCOMA and CATARACTS. They are generally not licensed to prescribe drugs or trained to perform surgery. See also OPHTHALMOLOGY.

opuntia \ō-ˈpən-shə\ Any plant of the largest genus of the CACTUS family, *Opuntia,* native to the New World and featuring characteristic small bristles with backward-facing barbs. Subgroups are based on the form of the stem segments: CHOLLAS have cylindrical joints; PRICKLY PEARS have flat joints. Sizes range from tiny, cold-hardy forms to treelike varieties. In the Northern Hemisphere, opuntia is the most northern-ranging cactus.

Opus Dei (Latin: "work of God") Roman Catholic lay and clerical organization whose actions and beliefs have been both criticized and praised. Its members seek personal Christian perfection, strive to implement Christian ideals in their chosen occupations, and promote Christian values to society as a whole. Opus Dei, in full Prelature of the Holy Cross and Opus Dei, was founded in 1928 in Spain by Josemaría Escrivá de Balaguer y Albá (beatified in 1992). It is theologically conservative and accepts the teaching authority of the church without question. It was granted special status as the first and only personal prelature in the church by Pope JOHN PAUL II in 1982 and has established numerous vocational schools and universities. It is also highly controversial, accused of secrecy, using cult-like recruiting practices, and having grand political ambitions. There are separate organizations for men and women, which, since 1982, have been headed by a prelate elected by its members. At the end of the 20th century priests constituted only a tiny percentage of the organization, numbering roughly 1,600 of the nearly 84,000 members living in 80 countries.

oracle Source of a divine communication delivered in response to a petitioner's request. Ancient Greece and Rome had many oracles. The most famous was that of APOLLO at DELPHI, where the medium was a woman over 50 called the Pythia. After bathing in the Castalian spring, she apparently would descend into a basement cell, mount a sacred tripod, and chew the leaves of the laurel, sacred to Apollo. Her utterances, which were often highly ambiguous, were interpreted by priests. Other oracles, including those at Claros (Apollo), Amphicleia (DIONYSUS), OLYMPIA (Zeus), and EPIDAURUS (ASCLEPIUS), were consulted through various other methods; for example, the oldest of the oracles, that of ZEUS at Dodona, spoke through the whispering of the leaves of a sacred oak. At some shrines, the inquirer would sleep in the holy precinct and receive an answer in a dream.

oral tradition Cultural information passed on from one generation to the next by storytellers. The forms of oral tradition include POETRY (often chanted or sung), folktales, and PROVERBS as well as magical spells, religious instruction, and recollections of the past. Music and rhyme commonly serve as both entertainment and aids to memory. Epic poems concerning the destiny of a society or summarizing its myths often begin as oral tradition and are later written down. In oral cultures, oral tradition is the only means of communicating knowledge. The prevalence of radio, television, and newspapers in Western culture has led to the decline of oral tradition, though it survives among old people and some minority groups as well as among children, whose games, counting rhymes, and songs are transmitted orally from generation to generation.

Oran \ō-ˈrän\ City (pop., 1987: 619,000), northwestern Algeria. Situated on the Mediterranean Sea, it is about midway between TANGIER, Morocco, and ALGIERS. With the adjacent Mers el-Kebir, it is the country's second-largest port. Founded in the 10th century by Andalusians as a base for trade with the northern African hinterland, it was held by the

Spanish until 1708, when it fell to the Turks. It was devastated by a 1790 earthquake. In 1792 the Turks settled a Jewish community there. In 1831 it was occupied by the French and became a modern port and naval base. In World War II it came under Allied forces. Most of its European inhabitants left after Algerian independence in 1962. It is divided into a waterfront and the old and new city sections built on terraces above it.

orange Any of several species of small trees or shrubs in the genus *Citrus* of the RUE (OR CITRUS) FAMILY, grown in tropical and subtropical regions, and their nearly round fruits, with leathery, oily rinds and edible, juicy inner flesh rich in vitamin C. Key commercial species include the China (or sweet, or common) orange; the mandarin orange (including TANGERINES); and seedless navel oranges. The tree has broad, glossy, medium-sized evergreen leaves, leafstalks with narrow wings, and very fragrant flowers. It bears fruit abundantly for 50–80 years. Oranges do not improve in quality off the tree, so they are picked when fully ripe. A sizeable portion of the U.S. crop is processed for frozen concentrated juice. By-products include essential oils, pectin, candied peel, orange marmalade, and stock feed.

Orange Free State Former province, central Republic of South Africa. Before the arrival of the Europeans, the area was the home of BANTU-speaking peoples. AFRIKANERS came in large part during the GREAT TREK of the 1830s. Britain administered the territory 1848–54; then the independent Orange Free State was established. British rule was reimposed following the SOUTH AFRICAN WAR in 1902, though self-government was later restored. In 1910 it became the Orange Free State province of the Union of South Africa (from 1961 the Republic of South Africa). After the South African elections of 1994, it became the province of Free State. Blacks make up about 80% of the population; most of the whites speak AFRIKAANS. The province's capital is BLOEMFONTEIN.

Orange-Nassau, House of Princely dynasty and royal family of the Netherlands. The title began with WILLIAM I THE SILENT, prince of Orange-Nassau, who was stadtholder (viceroy) of the Netherlands, as were his descendants until 1795. In 1815 William VI became WILLIAM I, king of the Netherlands. Through his descendants, the male line of the royal dynasty continued until 1890, when WILHELMINA, daughter of WILLIAM III, became queen. In 1908 she decreed that her descendants should be styled princes and princesses of Orange-Nassau.

Orange River River, southern Africa. It rises in the Lesotho Highlands as the Sinqu River and flows west as the Orange across the Republic of South Africa. It passes the southern edge of the KALAHARI DESERT, and winds through the NAMIB DESERT before draining into the Atlantic Ocean in South Africa. It forms the border between South Africa and Namibia. It is about 1,300 mi (2,100 km) long. There are some irrigated sections along the river and many dams but no large towns.

orangutan \ə-ˈraŋ-ə-ˌtaŋ\ *or* **orang** Species (*Pongo pygmaeus*, family Pongidae) of diurnal, mostly arboreal great APE, found only in the lowland swamp forests of Borneo but originally in the jungles of South Asia as well. The orangutan (Malaysian for "man of the forest") has a short thick body, long arms, short legs, and shaggy reddish hair. Males are about 4.5 ft (137 cm) tall and weigh about 185 lbs (85 kg); females are smaller. Orangutans are placid, deliberate, ingenious, and persistent. Males have fatty cheek flaps and a baglike, pendulous swelling at the throat. Orangutans use all four limbs to walk and climb. They eat mostly figs and other fruits and some leaves, bark, and insects. They sleep in trees on a platform built of interwoven branches. Adults are solitary, coming together only for a brief courtship, and live far apart. The mother carries and nurses the single young for almost three years. Though generally remarkably silent, the adult male has a loud, roaring "long call." The orangutan is an endangered species protected by law.

Orangutan (*Pongo pygmaeus*).
RUSS KINNE—PHOTO RESEARCHERS

Oranjestad \ō-ˈrän-yə-ˌstät\ Seaport and chief administrative town (pop., 1998: 28,000), ARUBA, Netherlands Antilles. It is located on the western coast of this Caribbean island. It is a free port and a petroleum processing and shipping center.

oratorio Large-scale musical composition on a sacred subject for solo voices, chorus, and orchestra. The term derives from the oratories, community prayer halls set up by ST. PHILIP NERI in the mid-16th century in a COUNTER-REFORMATION attempt to provide locales for religious edification outside the church itself, and the oratorio remained a nonliturgical (and non-Latin) form for moral musical entertainment. The first oratorio, really a religious OPERA, was written in 1600 by Emilio de' Cavalieri (c. 1550–1602), and the oratorio's development closely followed that of opera. G. CARISSIMI produced an important body of Italian oratorios, and M.-A. CHARPENTIER transferred the oratorio to France in the later 17th century. In Germany the works of H. SCHUTZ anticipate the oratorio-like PASSIONS of J.S. BACH. The most celebrated oratorio composer was G.F. HANDEL; his great English works include the incomparable *Messiah* (1742). Handel inspired F.J. HAYDN's great *Creation* (1798) and exerted great influence on the 19th-century oratorio, whose composers include H. BERLIOZ, F. MENDELSSOHN, and F. LISZT. Though the oratorio thereafter declined, 20th-century oratorio composers included E. ELGAR, I. STRAVINSKY, A. HONEGGER, and K. PENDERECKI.

Orbison, Roy (1936–1988) U.S. singer and songwriter. Born in Vernon, Texas, he began playing guitar on the radio at 8. His first single, "Ooby Dooby" (1956), was followed by a string of hits, including "Only the Lonely," "I Can't Stop Loving You," "Crying," "In Dreams," and "Oh, Pretty Woman." His career waned after the death of his wife in a motorcycle accident (1966) and the death of two sons in a fire (1968). He enjoyed a comeback in the 1980s; with B. DYLAN, George Harrison, and Tom Petty he formed the band the Traveling Wilburys.

orbital Mathematical expression, called a WAVE FUNCTION, that describes properties characteristic of no more than two ELECTRONS near an atomic nucleus or molecule. An orbital can be considered a three-dimensional region in which there is a 95% probability of finding an electron. Atomic orbitals are designated by a combination of numerals and letters (e.g., $1s$, $2p$, $3d$, $4f$). The numerals are the principal quantum number and are related to the atomic energy level and distance from the nucleus; the letters indicate the orbital's angular momentum and hence its shape. An s orbital with zero net orbital angular momentum is spherical. A p orbital with one fundamental unit of angular momentum, $\hbar$, is shaped somewhat like a dumbbell ($\hbar$ is Planck's constant, h, divided by 2π). The shapes of the other orbitals are more complicated. Molecular orbitals have geometries determined by the overlap of two or more atomic orbitals, and are designated by Greek symbols, e.g., σ and π.

orca See KILLER WHALE

Orcagna \ȯr-ˈkän-yä\, **Andrea** *orig.* **Andrea di Cione** (c. 1315/20–1368) Florentine painter, sculptor, and architect. A goldsmith's son, he was the leading member of a family of painters and the most prominent Florentine artist of the mid-14th century. His altarpiece for the Strozzi Chapel in Florence's Santa Maria Novella (1354–57) shows his ability to unify the multiple panels of a polyptych. As a sculptor he is known for a single work, the tabernacle in the guild oratory of Or San Michele (1352–60), a decorative structure of great complexity that is among the finest examples of the expressive art that sprang up in Tuscany after the BLACK DEATH. He was employed as architect on Florence's Duomo (cathedral) in 1357 and 1364–67.

orchestra Instrumental ensemble of varying size and composition. Today the term orchestra usually refers to the traditional large Western ensemble of bowed STRINGED INSTRUMENTS with BRASS, WOODWIND, and PERCUSSION instruments, with several players to each string part. The development of the orchestra coincides with the early history of OPERA. The form of the modern orchestra owes most to that of the mid-17th-century French court, especially as employed by J.-B. LULLY, which was dominated by 24 bowed strings but also often included woodwind instruments. Trumpets, horns, and timpani were often added in the early 18th century and were standard by the time of F.J. HAYDN. The 19th century saw a considerable expansion, particularly in the number and variety of wind and percussion instruments; some works called for well over 100 musicians. The symphony orchestra changed little in the 20th century. See illustration on following page. See also ORCHESTRATION.

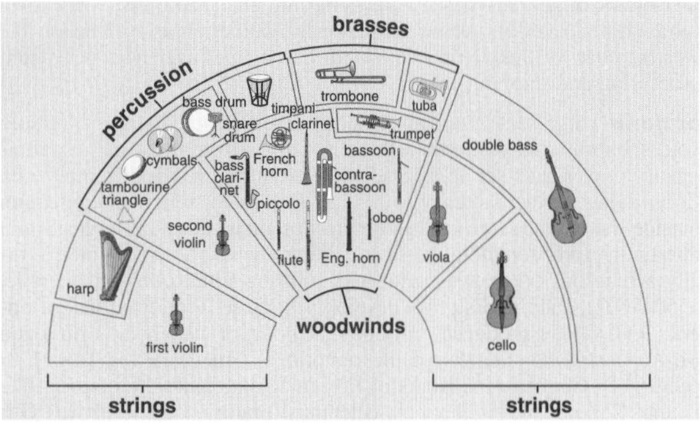

Standard layout of a modern symphony orchestra.

orchestration Art and science of choosing which instruments to use for a given piece of music. Once entirely dependent on what was available or customary, composers began to explore the musical potential of instrumental combinations with the advent of the modern orchestra in the mid- to late 18th century. The sections of the orchestra historically were separate ensembles: the stringed instruments for indoors, the woodwind instruments for outdoors, the horns for hunting, and trumpets and drums for battle or royal ceremony. Enterprising composers had availed themselves of different combinations earlier, but standardization put exact knowledge at the service of imagination. The first great orchestration text was written by H. BERLIOZ (1843).

orchid Any of the 15,000–35,000 species in 400–800 genera of nonwoody perennial plants that make up the family Orchidaceae. Bearing attractive flowers, orchids grow in most of the nonpolar world, especially in tropical regions, in soil or on other plants. Hybrids with showy flowers for the commercial trade come from the genera *Cattleya, Cymbidium, Vanda,* and *Laelia.* Flowers vary widely in size, color, and shape, but all are bilaterally symmetrical and have three sepals. Most orchids photosynthesize, but some live on dead organic material or absorb food from a fungus living in their roots. VANILLA is extracted from the seedpod of the genus *Vanilla.* Many folk medicines, local beverages, and foods are prepared from parts of orchid plants.

Orchid (*Polystachya bella*).

orchitis \òr-ˈkī-təs\ INFLAMMATION and swelling of the TESTES, caused by infection (most often MUMPS) or chemical or physical injury. The testicles' rich blood and lymphatic supply block most infections in the absence of severe injury. Usual symptoms are high fever, sudden pain in the testicle, nausea and vomiting, and swelling, tightness, and tenderness of the gland. Fluids with pus or blood may accumulate in the scrotum, which is generally red and thickened. Treatment may include antibiotics, bed rest, support of the testes, compresses, and surgery or drainage.

Orchomenus \òr-ˈkä-mə-nəs\ Ancient city, northwestern BOEOTIA, Greece. It was the northernmost fortified town in MYCENAEAN times and controlled a large part of Boeotia. In c. 550 BC it became one of the first cities to coin money, thereby gaining fame for its wealth. It was frequently attacked and finally destroyed by THEBES in the 4th century BC. Excavations have revealed that it was an important NEOLITHIC and BRONZE AGE site, with a beehive temple and palace.

Orczy \ˈōrt-sē\, **Emmuska (Magdalena Rosalia Marie Josepha Barbara), Baroness** (1865–1947) Hungarian-British novelist. The daughter of a noted musician, she was educated in Brussels and Paris and studied art in London. She became famous as the author of *The Scarlet Pimpernel* (1905), a swashbuckling adventure set in the era of the French Revolution. Her sequels did not match its great popular success. She also wrote detective stories.

Ord River River, northeastern Western Australia. It rises in the Albert Edward Range and flows east and north to Cambridge Gulf; it is about 200 mi (320 km) long. Discovered in 1879 by Alexander Forrest, it was named for Harry Ord, governor of Western Australia. The Ord River Project is designed to prevent flooding and collect irrigation water.

ordeal In customary law, a test of guilt or innocence in which the accused undergoes dangerous or painful tests believed to be under supernatural control. Ordeals by fire or water are the most common. Burns suffered while passing through fire (as in Hindu custom) or rejection (i.e., being buoyed up) by a body of water (as in witch trials) would be regarded as proof of guilt. In ordeal by combat, as in the medieval duel, the victor is said to win not by his own strength but because supernatural powers have intervened on the side of the right.

order In CLASSICAL ARCHITECTURE, any of several styles defined by the particular type of COLUMN, base, CAPITAL, and ENTABLATURE they use. There are five major orders: Doric, Ionic, and Corinthian (all developed in Greece), and Tuscan and Composite (developed in Rome). The form of the capital is an order's most distinguishing characteristic. Both the Doric and Ionic orders originated in wooden temples. The Doric is squat and simple. The Ionic, distinguished by the scrolls, or volutes, on its capital, resembles a capital I. The Corinthian capital is more ornate, with carved acanthus leaves and scrolls. The Romans modified the Greek orders to produce the Tuscan (a simplified form of the Doric) and Composite (a combination of the Ionic and Corinthian) orders. See also COLOSSAL ORDER.

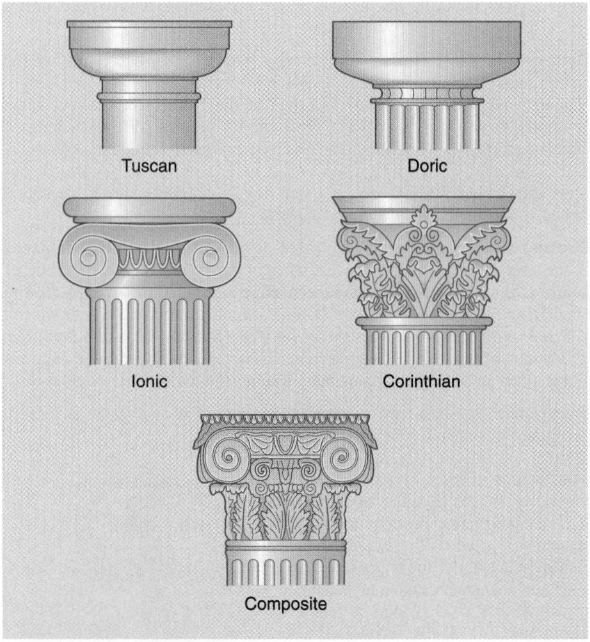

Capital styles for the five major orders of Classical architecture.

order in council In Britain, a regulation traditionally issued by the sovereign on the advice of the PRIVY COUNCIL. In modern practice, an order is issued only on the advice of ministers, and the minister in charge of the department concerned with the order's subject matter is responsible to Parliament for its contents. Most orders in council today are issued to implement legislation passed by Parliament.

Order of the Garter See Order of the GARTER

ordinary differential equation Equation containing DERIVATIVES of a FUNCTION of a single VARIABLE. Its order is the order of the highest derivative it contains (e.g., a first-order DIFFERENTIAL EQUATION involves only the first derivative of the function). Because the derivative is a rate of change, such an equation states how a function changes but does not specify the function itself. Given sufficient initial conditions, however, such as a specific function value, the function can be found by various methods, most based on INTEGRATION.

Ordovician period \ˌȯr-də-ˈvi-shən\ Interval of geologic time, 490–443 million years ago, the second oldest period of the PALEOZOIC ERA. It follows the CAMBRIAN and precedes the SILURIAN. During the Ordovician, many of the landmasses were aligned in the tropics. Life was dominated by marine invertebrates, but some forms of land plants may have appeared during the middle of the period. Spores suggesting a tropical terrestrial environment have been found in rocks of that age.

Ordzhonikidze \ər-jən-yik-ˈyēd-zə\, **Grigory (Konstantinovich)** (1886–1937) Russian communist leader. After the RUSSIAN REVOLUTION OF 1917, he became chairman of the Caucasian bureau (1921) and helped the Red Army conquer Georgia, forcing its merger with Armenia and Azerbaijan into the Transcaucasian Federal Republic and then into the Soviet Union. He became a member of the Politburo (1930) and commissar for heavy industry (1932), but in the mid-1930s he opposed JOSEPH STALIN's industrial policy. His sudden death was ascribed to natural causes, but NIKITA KHRUSHCHEV later charged (1956) that Stalin had driven him to suicide.

ore Aggregate of economically important MINERALS that is sufficiently rich to separate for a profit. Although more than 3,500 mineral species are known, only about 100 are considered ore minerals. The term originally applied only to metallic minerals (see NATIVE ELEMENT) but now includes such nonmetallic substances as SULFUR, calcium fluoride (FLUORITE), and barium sulfate (BARITE). Ore is always mixed with unwanted rocks and minerals, known collectively as gangue. The ore and the gangue are mined together and then separated. The desired element is then extracted from the ore. The metal may be still further refined (purified) or alloyed with other metals.

ore dressing *or* **mineral processing** Mechanical treatment of crude ORES to separate the valuable MINERALS. Ore dressing was at first applied only to ores of precious metals, but later came to be used to recover other metals and nonmetallic minerals. It is also used during coal preparation to enrich the value of raw coal. The primary operations are comminution and concentration. Comminution is carried out by large jaw crushers and by smaller cylindrical grinding mills. Common methods of concentration are gravity separation and FLOTATION separation. Gravity methods include jigging (ground ore is fed into a pulsating body of water so that the heavier mineral fractions settle out, leaving lighter wastes at the top) or washing the ore down inclined planes, spirals, or shaking tables so that mineral and waste fractions settle in different areas. See also BENEFICIATION, MINING.

oregano Flavorful dried leaves and flowering tops of any of various perennial herbs of the MINT family, particularly *Origanum vulgare*. Oregano is an essential ingredient of Mediterranean cuisines; in the U.S., use of oregano rose sharply in the later 20th century, largely because of the popularity of pizza. Native to the Mediterranean and western Asia, the herbs are now naturalized in parts of Mexico and the U.S.

Oregon State (pop., 1997 est.: 3,243,000), U.S., northwestern region. It covers 97,073 sq mi (251,419 sq km); its capital is SALEM. The COLUMBIA RIVER forms its northern boundary; the SNAKE RIVER is its upper eastern boundary. The CASCADES RANGE, with Mount HOOD, is in western central Oregon. First sighted by Spanish explorers, it was visited by FRANCIS DRAKE in 1579 and by JAMES COOK in 1778. The area was inhabited by many American Indian peoples when in 1792 Capt. Robert Gray explored the COLUMBIA RIVER, giving the U.S. a claim to the region. The river's mouth was reached by the LEWIS AND CLARK EXPEDITION in 1805. The first white settlement was founded at Astoria in 1811 by the fur trader JOHN J. ASTOR. Settlement of the area accelerated from c. 1843 with mass migration over the OREGON TRAIL. It was part of the Oregon Territory and was admitted to the Union as the 33rd state in 1859. The state's economy is dependent on its forests, farms, and livestock. Salmon and shellfish are the bases of the fishing industry. Centers of population, arts, and education are PORTLAND, EUGENE, and Medford.

Oregon, University of Public university in Eugene, founded in 1876. It comprises colleges of arts and sciences, business administration, and education, and schools of architecture, law, music, and journalism and communication. University facilities include a solar research center, a marine biology institute, and an observatory. The campus itself is a registered arboretum. Total enrollment is 17,000.

Oregon Caves National Monument National monument, southwestern Oregon. It is a single cave comprising a series of chambers joined by subterranean corridors on four levels. Located in the Siskiyou Mountains near the California border, the monument was established in 1909. It has an area of 488 acres (197 hectares). It contains many stalagmites, STALACTITES, and other formations.

Oregon Question Dispute over ownership of the Pacific Northwest region of North America. Spain, Russia, the U.S., and Britain all had claims to the region based on exploration or settlement. Spain vacated its claims after the NOOTKA SOUND CONTROVERSY and in an 1819 treaty with the U.S. The U.S. and Britain established a joint claim over the Oregon Country in 1818. Russia abandoned its claims in separate treaties (1824–25). A compromise Oregon Treaty between the U.S. and Britain (1846) drew the U.S.–Canada land boundary at 49°N.

Oregon Trail Major U.S. route to the Northwest in the 19th century. It stretched about 2,000 mi (3,200 km), from Independence, Mo., to the Columbia River region of Oregon. First used by fur traders and missionaries, it was heavily used in the 1840s by travelers to Oregon, including settlers of the "great migration," led by MARCUS WHITMAN. Of all western trails, it was in use for the longest period, surviving competition from the railroad by serving as a trail for eastward cattle and sheep drives.

Orestes \ȯ-ˈres-tēz\ In GREEK MYTHOLOGY, the son of AGAMEMNON and Clytemnestra. According to HOMER, Orestes was away when his father returned from TROY to meet his death at the hands of Aegisthus, his wife's lover. On reaching manhood, Orestes avenged his father by killing Aegisthus and Clytemnestra. AESCHYLUS' dramatic trilogy the *Oresteia* recounts the murder and the pursuit of Orestes by the FURIES for the crime of matricide. In EURIPIDES' *Iphigeneia in Tauris,* Orestes is reunited with his sister IPHIGENEIA and regains his father's kingdom.

Øresund \ˈœ-rə-ˌsən\ *English* **The Sound** Almost tideless strait between SJÆLLAND island, Denmark, and Sweden, connecting the Kattegat Strait with the BALTIC SEA. It is one of the busiest sea lanes in the world, though ice sometimes impedes navigation in severe winters. Three large islands within it divide the waters into channels. COPENHAGEN and Helsingør are the principal ports on the Danish side, MALMÖ and Hälsingborg, on the Swedish side.

Orff, Carl (1895–1982) German composer and music educator. He trained at the Munich Academy and held several musical posts thereafter. In the 1920s he grew interested in early Baroque music and the association of music with movement; from 1930 he rewrote his earlier pieces to conform to these interests. In 1924 he cofounded a school for which he devised a comprehensive music-education program (Orff Schulwerk) involving improvisation on specially designed gamelan-like percussion instruments; the program has since come into wide international use. After writing his best-known work, *Carmina Burana* (1937), he withdrew all his earlier compositions. His later propulsively rhythmic theater works include the operas *Der Mond* (1939) and *Die Kluge* (1943).

organ Keyboard instrument in which pressurized air produces notes by means of a series of tuned pipes. Organs include the largest and most complex of all instruments, with the widest range of pitch and timbre and the greatest variety of designs, as well as the oldest repertoire and the most involved history. The simplest organs consist of a single rank of pipes, each corresponding to a single key. They are arranged over a wind chest connected to the keys by a set of valves and fed with a supply of air by electrically or mechanically activated bellows. By pulling out knobs, called stops, the player engages new ranks of pipes. Two dis-

The Bruckner Organ, 18th century; in the church of the Abbey of Sankt Florian, Austria.

TONI SCHNEIDERS

O P Q R

tinct types of pipes are used: flue pipes (both open and stopped) produce sound by directing air against the edge of an opening in the pipe, whereas reed pipes sound by means of a thin metal tongue inside the pipe that vibrates against a fixed projection next to it. Different shapes and materials produce a variety of tone colors. A large organ may have five or more banked keyboards, or manuals, each of which controls a distinctive group of pipes. Most organs also have pedalboards played with the feet. A large organ's pipes may vary in length from about 1 in to 32 ft (2.5 cm–10 m), resulting in a huge nine-octave range. The earliest organ (c. 250 BC) was the Greek *hydraulis,* in which the wind was regulated by water pressure. The bellows-fed organ appeared around the 7th century AD. The organ became firmly associated with the church by the 10th century. As organs became widespread, different regions pursued different modes of construction and sought different tonal ideals. The baroque German organ is ideally suited to polyphony, while the French taste for variety of timbres eventuated in A. CAVAILLE-COLL's vast "orchestral" organs. See also HARMONIUM.

Organ Pipe Cactus National Monument National monument, southwestern Arizona, at the Mexican border. Established in 1937, and with an area of 330,689 acres (133,929 hectares), it preserves segments of the mountainous SONORAN DESERT and is named for the organ-pipe cactus. Wildlife includes GILA MONSTERS, antelope, coyotes, and a variety of birds.

organic compound Substance whose MOLECULES contain one or more (often many more) CARBON ATOMS (excluding carbonates, cyanides, carbides, and a few others; see INORGANIC COMPOUND). Until 1828 (see UREA), scientists believed that organic compounds could be formed only by life processes (hence the name). Since carbon has a far greater tendency to form chains and rings than other elements, its COMPOUNDS are vastly more numerous (many millions have been described) than all others known. Living organisms consist mostly of water and organic compounds: PROTEINS, CARBOHYDRATES, FATS, NUCLEIC ACIDS, HORMONES, VITAMINS, and a host of others. Natural and synthetic fibers and most fuels, drugs, and plastics are organic. HYDROCARBONS contain only carbon and hydrogen; organic compounds with other FUNCTIONAL GROUPS include CARBOXYLIC ACIDS, ALCOHOLS, ALDEHYDES, KETONES, PHENOLS, ETHERS, and other, more complex, molecules, including HETEROCYCLIC COMPOUNDS, ISOPRENOIDS, and AMINO ACIDS.

organic farming *or* **organic gardening** System of CROP cultivation that uses biological methods of fertilization and pest control as substitutes for chemical FERTILIZERS and PESTICIDES, which are regarded by supporters of organic methods as harmful to health and the environment and unnecessary for successful cultivation. It was initiated as a conscious rejection of modern agri-chemical techniques in the 1930s by the British agronomist Sir Albert Howard. Miscellaneous organic materials, including animal MANURE, COMPOST, grass turf, STRAW, and other crop residues, are applied to fields to improve both soil structure and moisture-holding capacity and to nourish soil life, which in turn nourishes plants. (Chemical fertilizers, by contrast, feed plants directly.) Biological pest control is achieved through preventive methods, including diversified farming, CROP ROTATION, the planting of pest-deterrent species, and the use of INTEGRATED PEST MANAGEMENT techniques. Bioengineered strains are avoided. Since organic farming is time-consuming, organically grown produce tends to be expensive. Organic produce formerly accounted for a minuscule portion of total American farm output, but it has seen a huge proportional increase in sales in recent years.

O
P
Q
R

Organization for Economic Cooperation and Development See Organization for ECONOMIC COOPERATION AND DEVELOPMENT

Organization of African Unity (OAU) Intergovernmental organization established in 1963 to promote unity and solidarity of African states and eliminate vestiges of colonialism. Membership has varied somewhat over the years because of political disputes. The OAU, whose chief policy unit was the annual assembly of heads of state and government, successfully mediated the Algeria-Morocco dispute of 1964–65 and the Somalia-Ethiopia and Kenya-Somalia border disputes of 1965–67, but it was less successful with the Biafra conflict (1968–70). From the 1970s the OAU concentrated on economic cooperation and human rights. In 2002 the organization's name was changed to the African Union. Its headquarters remained in ADDIS ABABA, Ethiopia.

Organization of American States (OAS) International organization formed in 1948 to replace the PAN-AMERICAN UNION. Its goals include the strengthening of hemispheric peace and security through a pro-U.S., anticommunist policy, the settling of disputes among its members, provision for collective security, and the encouraging of socioeconomic cooperation. In the post–Cold War era it has promoted democracy among its members (e.g., by monitoring elections and safeguarding human rights), which include most countries in the Western Hemisphere. See also ALLIANCE FOR PROGRESS, INTER-AMERICAN DEVELOPMENT BANK.

Organization of Petroleum Exporting Countries (OPEC) Multinational organization established in 1960 to coordinate the petroleum policies of its members. Iran, Iraq, Kuwait, Saudi Arabia, and Venezuela were the original members; they were joined by Qatar (1961), Indonesia and Libya (1962), Abu Dhabi (1967; membership transferred to the United Arab Emirates, 1974), Algeria (1967), and Nigeria (1971). Ecuador (1973) and Gabon (1975) are no longer OPEC members. Policy decisions are taken by consensus at its Vienna headquarters. The dominant Middle Eastern members used oil price increases as a political weapon in retaliation against Western support of Israel in the 1973 ARAB-ISRAELI WAR, and OPEC members' income greatly increased as a result. Internal dissent, the development of alternative energy sources, and the exploitation of non-OPEC oil sources subsequently combined to reduce OPEC's influence.

organizational psychology See INDUSTRIAL PSYCHOLOGY

organizational relations See INDUSTRIAL RELATIONS

organized crime Crime committed on a national or international scale by a criminal association; also, the associations themselves. Characteristics include a hierarchy of ranks with assigned responsibilities; a conspiracy among groups to coordinate activities, divide territory geographically, and allocate resources from the community to the international level; a commitment to secrecy; and corruption of law-enforcement authorities. One source of income is the provision of illegal goods and services, including narcotics, gambling, and prostitution; other sources include extortion, fraud, theft, and robbery. Organized crime arose in the U.S. during PROHIBITION to provide bootlegged liquor. In recent years organized crime has become immensely powerful in Russia, taking advantage of a weak and impoverished government and widespread official corruption. See also MAFIA, YAKUZA.

organum \'ȯr-gə-nəm\ Early polyphonic setting of plainchant (see GREGORIAN CHANT), the earliest form of COUNTERPOINT. The oldest written organum (c. 900), which evidently reflects a prevailing improvisational practice, consists of two lines moving simultaneously, note against note, the added line often paralleling the chant line a 4th or a 5th below. Later the added line acquired greater melodic individuality and independence. Organum consisting of more than one note against each chant note (florid or melismatic organum) appears by the early 12th century. Three- and four-voice organum were first composed by the NOTRE-DAME SCHOOL. Organum died out with the advent of the 13th-century MOTET.

Orhon River *or* **Orkhon River** \'ȯr-ˌkȯn\ River, northern Mongolia. It is 698 mi (1,123 km) long and rises from the slopes of the Hangayn Mountains. It flows east, then north past KARAKORUM. The 8th-century funerary stelae discovered in the river's valley in 1889 contain some of the oldest known Turkic writing and are called the Orhon inscriptions. The river is navigable for shallow-draft vessels only in July and August.

oriel Bay window in an upper story, supported from below by projecting CORBELS. Usually semihexagonal or rectangular in plan, oriels first became prevalent early in the 15th century. They were often placed over gateways or entrances to manor houses and public buildings of the late Gothic and Tudor periods. In cities of North Africa and the Middle East, the *moucharaby* is an oriel that uses grills or lattices in place of glass and shutters. See also BRISE-SOLEIL.

Orient Express Luxury train that ran from Paris to Constantinople (Istanbul) for over 80 years (1883–1977). Developed by the Belgian businessman Georges Nagelmackers, its luxuriously furnished cars became the symbol of glamour for European society. Europe's first transcontinental express train, it covered over 1,700 mi (2,740 km); after 1919 the route extended from Calais and Paris to Lausanne and via the Simplon Pass to Milan, Venice, Zagreb, and beyond. Service was suspended during both world wars. Discontinued in 1977, it was revived in 1982 to run between London and Venice as the "Venice Simplon Orient Express."

orientation In architecture, the position of a building on its site. In Mesopotamia and Egypt, as well as in pre-Columbian Central America, a building's important features, such as entrances and passages, faced the rising sun. Mosques are oriented so that the MIHRAB faces Mecca. Christian churches have usually been oriented with the apse or altar at the eastern end. Orientation is frequently planned to take maximum advantage of daily and seasonal variations of sunlight. A structure's optimal orientation is usually a compromise between its function, location, and the prevailing environmental factors of solar radiation, light, humidity, and wind that make up the site's microclimate.

orienteering Cross-country footrace in which each participant uses a map and compass to navigate between checkpoints along an unfamiliar course. Introduced in Sweden in 1918, it later spread throughout Europe. World championships have been held since 1966. Runners set out at intervals; the winner is the runner who completes the course in the fastest time. Orienteering is also practiced by cyclists, canoeists, horseback riders, and skiers.

origami See PAPER FOLDING

Origen \'ȯr-i-jən\ *orig.* **Oregenes Adamantius** (c. AD 185–254?) Greek theologian, one of the Fathers of the Church. Probably the son of a Christian martyr, Origen studied philosophy in Alexandria and served as head of its catechetical school for 20 years. He later settled in Palestine and founded a school of philosophy and theology. He traveled widely as a preacher. His greatest work, the *Hexapla,* is a synopsis of six versions of the Old Testament. His writings, influenced by Neoplatonism and Stoicism, stress that providence seeks to restore all souls to their original blessedness and emphasize the centrality of the Word (LOGOS) in the cosmos. He held that even Satan was not beyond repentance and salvation, a view for which he was condemned.

original sin In Christian doctrine, the condition or state of SIN into which each human being is born, or its origin in ADAM's disobedience to God when he ate the fruit of the tree of knowledge of good and evil. His guilt was transmitted to his descendants. Though GENESIS describes Adam's sufferings as the consequence of his disobedience, it does not make Adam's sin hereditary. The main scriptural basis of the doctrine is found in the writings of St. PAUL; St. AUGUSTINE helped make humanity's sinful nature a central element in orthodox Christian theology.

Orinoco River \ˌōr-ē-'nō-kō\ Major river, South America. It rises on the western slopes of the Sierra Parima Mountains along the Venezuela–Brazil border. It flows in a giant arc through Venezuela for 1,700 mi (2,740 km) and enters the Atlantic Ocean near the island of Trinidad. It forms part of the border between Colombia and Venezuela. With its tributaries, it is the northernmost of South America's four major river systems. The water fauna include the PIRANHA and the Orinoco CROCODILE. The river basin is largely inhabited by indigenous Indian groups.

oriole Any songbird of 24 species in the Old World genus *Oriolus* (family Oriolidae) or 30 species in the New World genus *Icterus* (family Icteridae). Males typically are black and yellow or black and orange, with some white. Females are less colorful. Orioles are not easily seen but may be detected by their loud whistling and jarring notes. All are insect eaters (several species also eat fruit) in woodlands and gardens, chiefly in warm regions. The only European species is the 9.5-in. (24-cm) golden oriole *(O. oriolus).* Other *Oriolus* species are found in Africa, Asia, and Australia. The Baltimore oriole *(I. galbula)* breeds in North America east of the Rockies.

Golden oriole (*Oriolus oriolus*).
H. SCHREMPP—BRUCE COLEMAN INC.

Orion \ə-'rī-ən\ In GREEK MYTHOLOGY, a powerful hunter. He was sometimes said to be the son of POSEIDON. He drove the wild beasts out of the island of Chios and fell in love with Merope, daughter of the king. Disapproving of Orion, the king had him blinded, but his vision was restored by the rays of the rising sun. He later went to Crete to live and hunt with ARTEMIS. Some legends hold that he was killed by Artemis or APOLLO out of jealousy; another tells that he was fatally bitten by a scorpion. After his death the gods placed him in the sky as a constellation.

Orion Nebula \ə-'rī-ən\ Bright NEBULA, faintly visible to the unaided eye in the sword of the hunter's figure in the constellation Orion. About 1,500 light-years from earth, it contains hundreds of very hot young stars clustered about a group of four massive stars known as the Trapezium. Radiation primarily from these four stars excites the nebula to glow. Discovered in the early 17th century, it was the first nebula to be photographed (1880).

Orissa State (pop., 1994 est: 33,795,000), eastern India. It occupies an area of 60,178 sq mi (155,861 sq km); its capital is BHUBANESWAR, and Cuttack is the largest city. Part of the ancient and medieval kingdom of KALINGA, it was a stronghold of HINDUISM before its conquest by the Afghan rulers of Bengal in 1568, when it became part of the Mughal empire. It was ruled by Britain from 1803 until India's independence in 1947, and received statehood in 1950. Situated in a tropical savanna that is subject to cyclones, it has a largely rural population, which is engaged mainly in agriculture. Crops include rice, oilseed, jute, and sugarcane. It has a rich artistic heritage and contains some of the best examples of Indian art and architecture.

Orizaba See CITLALTÉPETL

Orkhon River See ORHON RIVER

Orkney Islands Group of more than 70 islands and islets (pop., 1995 est.: 20,000), Scotland. Lying north of the Scottish mainland, they make up the Orkney administration region. The Orkneys, only 20 of which are inhabited, were the Orcades of ancient classical literature. There is much evidence of prehistoric inhabitants. Norse raiders arrived in the late 8th century AD and colonized the islands in the 9th century. Thereafter they were ruled by Norway and Denmark until Scotland annexed them in 1472. It is a prosperous agricultural area. KIRKWALL is the administrative seat.

Orlando City (pop., 1996 est.: 174,000), central Florida. Settlement began c. 1844 around an army post. It was renamed in 1857 to honor Orlando Reeves, an army sentry killed during the SEMINOLE WARS. After 1950 the development of the aerospace complex at Cape CANAVERAL and, after 1971, of nearby DISNEY WORLD boosted the city's population and economy. It is also the center of a citrus farming region.

Orlando, Vittorio Emanuele (1860–1952) Italian politician and prime minister (1917–19). He was elected to Italy's Chamber of Deputies in 1897 and served in cabinet positions from 1903. As prime minister, he led Italy's delegation to the PARIS PEACE CONFERENCE but was unable to obtain concessions from the Allies for Italian-claimed territory and resigned. President of the Chamber of Deputies 1919–25, he resigned in protest against Fascist electoral fraud. He was president of the postwar Constituent Assembly 1946–47.

Orléans \ȯr-lā-'ä^{n}\, *ancient* **Aurelianum** City (pop., 1990: 108,000), northern central France. It was conquered by Julius CAESAR in 52 BC and became an intellectual center under CHARLEMAGNE. It was a major cultural center in the Middle Ages and became a royal duchy under PHILIP VI in 1344. During the HUNDRED YEARS' WAR, the English siege in 1429 was relieved by JOAN OF ARC, known as the Maid of Orléans, and her troops. Located on the LOIRE RIVER in a fertile valley, it is important for market gardening, horticulture, and textile production.

Orléans, House of Name of the cadet or junior branch of the Valois and BOURBON houses of France. Of the four dynasties of princes, Philippe I (1336–1375) died without heirs. Descendants of the second dynasty, headed by Louis I (1372–1407), held the title until 1545. The third dynasty was headed by Gaston (1608–1660), whose title from 1626 passed to the fourth dynasty under Philippe I (1640–1701), younger brother of LOUIS XIV. Philippe's descendants included Louis-Philippe-Joseph, duc d'ORLÉANS, and LOUIS-PHILIPPE, king of the French from 1830.

Orléans, Louis-Philippe-Joseph, duc (Duke) d' *known as* **Philippe Égalité** (1747–1793) French Bourbon prince who supported popular democracy in the FRENCH REVOLUTION. A cousin of LOUIS XVI, he disapproved of MARIE-ANTOINETTE and lived away from the royal court at Versailles. In 1787 he was exiled to his estates for challenging the king's authority. In 1789 he was elected to the Estates General and soon joined the Third Estate. After joining the Jacobins (1791), he renounced his title of nobility (1792) and accepted the name Philippe Égalité from the

Paris Commune. In the National Convention, he supported the radicals, but after his son Louis-Philippe defected to the Austrians, he was accused of conspiracy, arrested, and guillotined.

Orlov \ər-'lȯf\, **Aleksey (Grigoryevich), Count** (1737–1808) Russian military officer. He became an officer in the Russian guards and adviser to his brother Count Grigory G. Orlov, with whom he planned the overthrow of Peter III (1762) and the installation of Catherine II as empress. Promoted to major general, he was given command of the Russian fleet in the Russo–Turkish War.

Orlov, Grigory (Grigoryevich), Count (1734–1783) Russian military officer and lover of Catherine II. An artillery officer, he fought in the Seven Years' War. While stationed in St. Petersburg, he met the grand duke Peter (later Peter III) and his wife, Catherine, whose lover Orlov became c. 1760. After Peter ascended the throne (1762), Orlov and his brother, Count Aleksey G. Orlov, planned the coup d'état that overthrew Peter and made Catherine empress of Russia. As Catherine's close adviser, he proposed agrarian reforms to help the serfs, but little was accomplished. He lost favor at court c. 1772.

Ormandy, Eugene *orig.* **Jenö Blau** (1899–1985) Hungarian-U.S. conductor. A violin prodigy, he became professor of violin at the Budapest Royal Academy at 17. He came to New York in 1921, playing in and conducting a theater orchestra, then served as conductor of the Minneapolis Symphony (1931–36). He shared the Philadelphia Orchestra with L. Stokowski for two years before becoming sole conductor in 1938, and he led the orchestra until he was made laureate in 1980. His background as a string player had much to do with maintaining the rich "Philadelphia sound" created by his predecessor, and the orchestra made scores of recordings under him.

ormolu \'ȯr-mə-ˌlü\ (from French, *dorure d'or moulu:* "gilding with gold paste") Gold-colored alloy made up of copper, zinc, and sometimes tin in various proportions, but usually at least 50% copper. It is used in mounts (ornaments on borders, edges, and as angle guards) for furniture and for other decorative purposes. After the molten alloy has been poured into a mold and allowed to cool, it is gilded with powdered gold mixed with mercury. It is then fired at a temperature that evaporates the mercury, leaving a gold surface. Ormolu was first produced in France in the mid-17th century, and France remained its main center of production.

Secretary decorated with ormolu mounts, marquetry, and intarsia, French, c. 1770; in the Wallace Collection, London.

BY COURTESY OF TRUSTEES OF THE WALLACE COLLECTION, LONDON

Ormonde, Duke of *orig.* **James Butler** (1610–1688) Anglo-Irish statesman. Born into the prominent Butler family of Ireland, he succeeded to the earldom of Ormonde in 1632. In service to the English crown in Ireland from 1633, he fought against the Catholic rebellion from 1641. He concluded a peace with the Catholic confederacy in 1649, then rallied support for Charles II, but was forced to flee when Oliver Cromwell landed at Dublin. He was Charles's adviser in exile (1650–60). After the Restoration he was appointed lord lieutenant of Ireland (1662–69, 1677–84), where he encouraged Irish commerce and industry. He was created a duke in 1682.

Ormuz See Hormuz

ornamentation In music, the addition of notes for expressive and aesthetic purposes. For example, a long note may be ornamented by repetition or by alternation with a neighboring note ("trill"); a skip to a nonadjacent note can be filled in with the intervening notes; or the resolution of a dissonance (see consonance and dissonance), because of its inevitability, can be delayed.

ornamentation, architectural Applied embellishment in various styles that is a distinguishing characteristic of buildings, furniture, and household items. Ornamentation often occurs on entablatures, columns, and the tops of buildings and around entryways and windows, especially in the form of moldings. Throughout antiquity and into the Renaissance, and later for religious buildings, applied ornament was very important, often having symbolic meaning. The anthemion petal motif was especially popular on the moldings of ancient Greek cornices. Other motifs from antiquity include the Egyptian cartouche (oval), fretwork (banding) of capitals, fluting and reeding of columns, bas-relief egg-and-dart moldings (with alternating oval and pointed forms), and scrollwork such as that found on Ionic capitals and in the running-dog pattern (or wave scroll). Brattishing refers to the continuous embellishment around the top of a wall common in the Gothic period. The diaper motif, an allover pattern of small repeated shapes, was also often used in this period. Characteristic of Mannerist architecture and furniture is the use of strapwork (interlaced scrollwork), which originated with Islamic metalwork.

Orne River \'ȯrn\ River, northwestern France. It is 94 mi (152 km) long, and flows through the Orne and Calvados departments past Caen into the English Channel. Its bridges were seized by the Allied forces during the World War II Normandy Campaign in June 1944.

ornithischian \ˌȯr-nə-'this-kē-ən\ Any "bird-hipped" dinosaur species (order Ornithischia), herbivores with hip bones arranged like those of modern birds, with the pubis bone pointed backward. Many species had a toothless, horny beak and powerful cheek teeth. Ornithischians flourished from the Late Triassic to the Late Cretaceous periods (227–65 million years ago). Many species (in the suborder Cerapoda) were bipedal, and defensive armor, if present, was only on the massive head and culminated in a great bony frill. Other species (in the suborder Thyreophora) were heavily plated and armored along the back, and some species also had armor on the flanks and head. See also protoceratops, saurischian, stegosaur, triceratops.

ornithology Branch of zoology dealing with the study of birds. Early writings on birds were largely anecdotal (including folklore) or practical (e.g., treatises on falconry and game-bird management). From the mid-18th century on, ornithology progressed from the description and classification of new species discovered in scientific expeditions to examination of internal anatomy to the study of the bird ecology and ethology. Ornithology is one of the few scientific fields in which nonprofessionals make substantial contributions; the field observations of birders provide valuable information on behavior, ecology, distribution, and migration. Other information is gained by means of radar, radio transmitters, portable audio equipment, and bird banding, which provides information on longevity and movements.

orogeny \ȯ-'rä-jə-nē\ Mountain-building event, generally one that occurs in a geosyncline. Orogeny tends to occur during a relatively short geologic time frame. It is usually accompanied by folding and faulting of strata and by the deposition of sediments in areas adjacent to the orogenic belt. Orogenies may result from continental collisions, the underthrusting of continents by oceanic plates, the overriding of oceanic ridges by continents, and other causes. See also Acadian orogeny, Alleghenian orogeny, Alpine orogeny, Laramide orogeny, Taconic orogeny.

Oromo \ō-'rō-mō\ *or* **Galla** Major ethnic group of Ethiopia, numbering 20 million, or nearly half the population, and occupying much of its central and southern central regions. They speak a Cushitic language of the Afroasiatic family. They are a diverse group, having assimilated and intermarried with other peoples since the 16th century. Traditionally the Oromo were nomadic herders, but today most are settled agriculturalists. Politically they are largely subjugated to the dominant Amhara. In religion they are divided among Islam, the Ethiopian Orthodox faith, and traditional beliefs.

Orontes River \ō-'rän-tēz\ River, southwestern Asia. Rising in the Bekaa Valley of Lebanon and flowing north between the Lebanon and Anti-Lebanon Mtns., it passes the cities of Homs and Hamah in Syria, where it has been dammed to form Hims Lake. Northwest of Hamah it enters Turkey, where it flows west past Antakya, the ancient Greek city of Antioch, and empties into the Mediterranean Sea. It is unnavigable for most of its 355 mi (571 km) length but is an important source for irrigation.

Orozco \ō-'rōs-kō\, **José Clemente** (1883–1949) Mexican mural painter. When he lost his left hand at 17, he abandoned architectural studies for painting, pursuing Mexican themes. As a caricaturist for a revolutionary paper, he explored Mexico City's slums and painted a series of watercolors, *House of Tears,* on the lives of prostitutes. The reaction of moralists forced him to flee to the U.S. in 1917, but in 1919 the new government of Alvaro Obregon welcomed him back, and he joined Diego Rivera and David A. Siqueiros in creating large-scale murals for public buildings, in which he continued his radical social commentary. Again forced to abandon Mexico in 1927, he worked until 1934 in the U.S., where his style evolved and matured in murals from coast to coast. In 1934, his international reputation firmly established, he returned to Mexico and embarked on his most technically impressive and emotionally expressive murals, including *Catharsis* (1934), in the Palacio de Bellas Artes. He was a leader among those who raised Mexican art to a position of international eminence.

Orpheus Greek legendary hero who sang and played the lyre so beautifully that animals, trees, and rocks danced around him. When his wife, Eurydice, was killed by a snake, he went to the underworld in search of her, and his music and grief so moved Hades that he agreed to let Orpheus take Eurydice to the land of the living on condition that neither of them was to look back as they left. On seeing the sun, Orpheus turned to share his delight with Eurydice, and she disappeared. Orpheus was later torn to pieces by maenads, and his head, still singing, floated to Lesbos, where an oracle of Orpheus was established. By the 5th century BC, a Hellenistic mystery religion (the Orphic mysteries) had arisen based on his songs and teachings. His story became the subject of some of the earliest operas.

Orphic mysteries See mystery religions

Orphism Trend in Cubism that gave priority to color. Its name, bestowed in 1912 by Guillaume Apollinaire, recalls not only the legendary Orpheus but the Symbolist painters' description of Paul Gauguin's orchestration of color as "Orphic art." Among the painters who worked in this style were Robert Delaunay, Fernand Leger, Francis Picabia, and Marcel Duchamp. The best-known example is Delaunay's abstract *Simultaneous Composition: Sun Disks* (1912–13), in which superimposed circles of color have their own rhythm and movement.

Orr, Bobby *orig.* **Robert Gordon** (born 1948) Canadian-U.S. ice-hockey player. Born in Parry Sound, Ontario, he was signed to a junior amateur contract by Boston Bruins scouts when he was 12. He joined the Bruins in 1966 and played with them for 10 seasons, helping them to the play-offs in eight consecutive seasons and to two Stanley Cup victories. The first defenseman to lead the National Hockey League in scoring (1970, 1975), he is the only player ever recognized as the most valuable defenseman eight years in a row (1967–68 to 1974–75).

Orr (number 4), 1968.
CANADA WIDE–PICTORIAL PARADE/EB INC.

Ørsted \'œr-stəd\, **Hans Christian** (1777–1851) Danish physicist and chemist. In 1820 he discovered that electric current in a wire can deflect a magnetized compass needle, a phenomenon that inspired the development of electromagnetic theory. His 1820 discovery of piperine, one of the pungent components of pepper, was an important contribution to chemistry, as was his preparation of metallic aluminum in 1825. In 1824 he founded a society devoted to the spread of scientific knowledge among the general public. In 1932 the name oersted was adopted for the physical unit of magnetic field strength.

Ortega (Saavedra) \ȯr-'tā-gə\, **Daniel** (born 1945) President of Nicaragua (1984–90). In 1963 he became a member of the Sandinista National Liberation Front and organized urban resistance to the corrupt dictatorship of the Somoza family. Jailed and later exiled, he returned secretly to Nicaragua and helped unite opposition to Somoza. After the Sandinistas prevailed in 1979, he coordinated the ruling junta; in 1984 he was elected Nicaragua's president. U.S. efforts to destabilize his government led to economic hardship and a protracted war, and Ortega lost his bid for reelection in 1990. See also Violeta Chamorro, contras.

Ortega y Gasset \ȯr-'tā-gä-ē-gä-'set\, **José** (1883–1955) Spanish philosopher. He taught at the University of Madrid from 1911, and lived abroad 1931–46. Though influenced by Neo-Kantianism, he diverged from it in such works as *Adam in Paradise* (1910), *Quixote's Meditations* (1914), and *Modern Theme* (1923). He saw individual life as the fundamental reality; for absolute truth he substituted the perspective of each individual. Sharing his generation's preoccupation with Spain's problems, he founded the periodicals *España* (1915), *El sol* (1917), and *Revista de Occidente* (1923). Of his other works, the best known are *Invertebrate Spain* (1922) and *The Revolt of the Masses* (1929), which foreshadowed the Spanish Civil War. He greatly influenced Spain's 20th-century cultural and literary renaissance.

orthoclase \'ȯr-thə-ˌklās\ Common alkali feldspar mineral, potassium aluminosilicate ($KAlSi_3O_8$), that usually occurs as variously colored grains in granite. Orthoclase is used in the manufacture of glass and ceramics; occasionally, transparent crystals are cut as gems. It is primarily important as a rock-forming mineral, however, and is abundant in igneous rocks, pegmatites, and gneisses. The feldspar minerals consist of sodium, potassium, and calcium aluminosilicates, and any feldspar may be chemically classed by the percentage of each of these three pure compounds, called end-members. Orthoclase is the potassium-bearing end-member of the system. Microcline is a lower temperature structural form of the same chemical composition as orthoclase.

Orthoclase from Serra de Peneda, Portugal.
EMIL JAVORSKY

Orthodox Catholic Church See Eastern Orthodoxy

Orthodox Judaism Religion of Jews who adhere strictly to traditional beliefs and practices; the official form of Judaism in Israel. Orthodox Jews hold that both the written law (Torah) and the oral law (codified in the Mishna and interpreted in the Talmud) are immutably fixed and remain the sole norm of religious observance. Orthodox Judaism has held fast to such practices as daily worship, dietary laws, intensive study of the Torah, and separation of men and women in the synagogue. It also enjoins strict observance of the Sabbath and does not permit instrumental music during communal services. A leading center of Orthodoxy in the U.S. is New York's Yeshiva Univ.

orthogonal polynomial Any of an infinite set of special polynomials useful in solving differential equations arising in physics and engineering. If two polynomials are orthogonal, the integral of their product (inner product; see inner product space) calculated over an appropriate interval is zero. An infinite set of mutually orthogonal polynomials can serve as a basis for the set of all continuous functions, meaning that any continuous function can be represented as a linear combination (see linear transformation) of such polynomials. The simplest example is the set of Legendre polynomials, which satisfy a second-order differential equation called the Legendre equation and are orthogonal on the interval from to 1. Other examples are the sets of Hermite and Chebyshev polynomials.

orthogonality \ȯr-ˌthä-gə-'na-lə-tē\ In mathematics, a property synonymous with perpendicularity when applied to vectors but applicable more generally to functions. Two elements of an inner product space are orthogonal when their inner product—for vectors, the dot product (see vector operations); for functions, the definite integral of their product—is zero. A set of orthogonal vectors or functions can serve as the basis of an inner product space, meaning that any element of the space can be formed from a linear combination (see linear transformation) of the elements of such a set.

orthopedics \ˌȯr-thə-'pē-diks\ *or* **orthopedic surgery** Medical specialty concerned with the skeleton and its associated structures. It treats fractures, strained muscles, torn ligaments and tendons, and other injuries, and deals with acquired and congenital skeletal deformities and the effects of degenerative diseases such as osteoarthritis. Originally dependent on heavy braces and splints, it now uses bone grafts, hip and other joint replacements, prostheses (see prosthesis), special footwear, and braces to enhance mobility. Orthopedics uses the techniques of physical medicine and rehabilitation and occupational therapy in addition to those of traditional medicine and surgery.

Orton, Joe *orig.* **John Kingsley** (1933–1967) British dramatist. Originally an unsuccessful actor, he turned to writing, finding success in 1964 when his radio play *The Ruffian on the Stair* was broadcast by the BBC. His three full-length black comedies, *Entertaining Mr. Sloane* (1964), *Loot* (1965), and *What the Butler Saw* (produced posthumously, 1969), scandalized audiences with their examination of moral corruption, violence, and sexual rapacity. Orton's career was cut short when he was murdered by K. L. Halliwell, his lifelong companion, who afterward committed suicide.

Orumiyeh, Daryacheh-ye See Lake URMIA

Orwell, George *orig.* **Eric Arthur Blair** (1903–1950) British novelist, essayist, and critic. Instead of accepting a scholarship to a university, Orwell went to Burma to serve in the Indian Imperial Police 1922–27, an experience that changed him into a literary and political rebel. On returning to Europe, he lived in self-imposed poverty, gaining material for *Down and Out in Paris and London* (1933), and became a socialist. He went to Spain to report on the Spanish Civil War and stayed to join the Republican militia. His war experiences, which gave him a lifelong dread of communism (he would later provide British intelligence services with lists of his fellow British communists), are recounted in *Homage to Catalonia* (1938). His novels typically portray a sensitive, conscientious, emotionally isolated individual at odds with an oppressive or dishonest social environment. His most famous works are the anti-Soviet satirical fable *Animal Farm* (1945), and *Nineteen Eighty-four* (1949), a dystopic vision of totalitarianism whose influence was widely felt in the postwar decades. His literary essays are also admired. He died of tuberculosis.

Orwell.

BBC COPYRIGHT

oryx Any of four species (genus *Oryx*) of large stocky ANTELOPES living in herds on African and Arabian deserts and plains. Oryxes are 40–47 in. (102–120 cm) high. They have a mane and a tufted tail. The coat is grayish brown, whitish, or white, depending on the species, with dark patches on the face and forehead, a dark streak on either side of the eye, and various dark markings on the body and legs. Both sexes have long, sharp-tipped, straight or curved horns.

Arabian oryx (*Oryx leucoryx*).

ROD MOON—THE NATIONAL AUDUBON SOCIETY COLLECTION/PHOTO RESEARCHERS

Osage \ō-'sāj\ North American Indian people of SIOUAN LANGUAGE stock who lived variously in the Piedmont and Ozark plateaus and the western Missouri and southeastern Kansas prairies. Osage culture was of the prairie type, marked by the combination of village agriculture and buffalo hunting. Their villages consisted of LONGHOUSES; TEPEES were used during the hunting season. Their religious ceremonies divided clans into symbolic sky and earth groups. In the late 19th century the Osage were removed to a reservation in Oklahoma. The discovery of oil there made them a uniquely prosperous tribe. Today they number about 8,000.

Osage River \ō-'sāj, 'ō-ˌsāj\ River, western Missouri. Formed by the junction of the Marais des Cygnes and Little Osage rivers, it is about 500 mi (800 km) long and is the largest tributary of the MISSOURI RIVER. It flows east and northeast through Lake of the OZARKS and enters the Missouri just east of Jefferson City, Mo.

Osaka \ō-'sä-kä, *Jap* 'ō-sä-kä\ *ancient* **Naniwa** City (pop., 1995 est.: 2,602,000) and seaport, southern central HONSHU, Japan, on the northeastern shore of Osaka Bay. A long-established city and port, Naniwa was made a castle town by TOYOTOMI HIDEYOSHI in the 16th century. It was the leading commercial city of Japan during the feudal era and the leading industrial city from the late 19th century. It was badly damaged by U.S. bombing during World War II. Once noted for its large textile industry, it is now a leading financial center with heavy industries including machinery, iron and steel, and chemicals. With KOBE and KYOTO, it is part of Japan's second-largest urban and industrial center. It is also a cultural and educational center, with several universities and theaters.

Osborne, John (James) (1929–1994) British playwright. Initially an actor, he cowrote his first play *The Devil Inside Him* (1950) with Stella Linden. His *Look Back in Anger* (1956; film, 1959) ushered in a spate of vigorously realistic plays about contemporary British working-class life, and Osborne became the first of the postwar ANGRY YOUNG MEN. *The Entertainer* (1957; film, 1960) starred LAURENCE OLIVIER as a failing music-hall comedian. He produced film adaptations of both plays and wrote the screenplay for *Tom Jones* (1963, Academy Award). His later plays include *Luther* (1961) and *Inadmissible Evidence* (1964).

John Osborne.

UPI/BETTMANN NEWSPHOTOS

Oscan language \'äs-kən\ ITALIC LANGUAGE formerly spoken in southern and central Italy, related closely to UMBRIAN and more distantly to LATIN. It was probably the native tongue of the SAMNITE people of Italy's central mountainous region. Oscan was gradually displaced by Latin and apparently became extinct by the end of the 1st century AD. Modern knowledge of it comes from some 250 inscriptions written in a colonial LATIN ALPHABET, the GREEK ALPHABET, and an alphabet derived from the one used for ETRUSCAN.

Osceola \ˌä-sē-'ō-lə\ (1804?–1838) SEMINOLE Indian leader during the Second SEMINOLE WAR. The war began in 1835 when the U.S. government attempted to force the Seminole off their traditional lands in Florida and into the Indian territory west of the Mississippi River. Osceola and his followers employed guerrilla tactics and forced a truce. During negotiations he was arrested and removed to a military fort at Charleston, S.C., where he died.

Osceola, detail of a lithograph by George Catlin, 1838.

BY COURTESY OF THE LIBRARY OF CONGRESS, WASHINGTON, D.C.

oscillator Mechanical or electronic device that produces a back-and-forth PERIODIC MOTION. A PENDULUM is a simple mechanical oscillator that swings with a constant amplitude, requiring the addition of energy at each swing only to compensate for the energy lost because of air resistance or friction. In electronic oscillators, ELECTRONS oscillate with a constant period and also require the addition of energy to replace energy loss. Electronic oscillators are used to generate ALTERNATING CURRENT and high-frequency currents for carrier waves in radio broadcasting. They are incorporated in a wide variety of electronic equipment.

oscilloscope \ə-'si-lə-ˌskōp\ *or* **cathode-ray oscilloscope** Electronic display device used to produce patterns on a screen that are the graphical representations of electrical signals. Time is normally on the horizontal axis, and a function of the voltage generated by the input signal to the oscilloscope on the vertical axis; four or more plots can be simultaneously shown. Because almost any physical phenomenon can be converted into a corresponding electric voltage, oscilloscopes find commercial, engineering, and scientific applications in acoustic research, television-production engineering, and electronics design.

OSHA *in full* **Occupational Safety and Health Administration** Agency of the U.S. Department of LABOR. Formed in 1970, it is charged with ensuring that employers furnish their employees with a working environment free from recognized health and safety hazards. It enforces occupational safety and health standards, develops regulations, conducts investigations and workplace inspections, and issues citations and penalties for noncompliance.

Oshogbo \ō-'shōg-bō\ City (pop., 1996 est.: 477,000), Nigeria. Located northeast of IBADAN, it lies along the Oshun River. Originally settled by the Ilesha from Ibokun, it remained a small town until the early 19th century when an influx of YORUBAS fleeing from FULANI conquerors arrived. In 1840 it was the scene of a battle won by Ibadan that proved to be the turning point in the Fulani-Yoruba wars. It was made part of Oyo state in 1976 and the capital of the newly created state of Osun in 1991. It is a trade center for cocoa and palm oil; weaving and dyeing cotton cloth and growing tobacco are other local occupations.

Osiris \ō-'sī-rəs\ Ancient Egyptian god of the underworld. According to myth, Osiris was slain by the god SETH, who tore apart the corpse and flung the pieces all over Egypt. The goddess ISIS, consort of Osiris, and her sister Nephthys found the pieces and gave new life to Osiris, who became the ruler of the underworld. Isis and Osiris then conceived HORUS. In the Egyptian concept of divine kingship, the king at death became Osiris and the new king was identified with Horus. Osiris also represented the power that brought life out of the earth. Festivals reenacting his fate were celebrated annually in towns throughout Egypt.

Osler \'ōs-lər\, **William** *later* **Sir William** (1849–1919) Canadian physician and professor. Born in Bond Head, Ontario, he became the first to identify blood PLATELETS (1873), and later taught at the medical school at McGill University (1875–84) and later at Johns Hopkins Univ.'s new medical school (1889–1905). There he helped transform clinical teaching; students studied patients in the wards and took their problems to the lab, and experts pooled their knowledge to benefit both patient and student in public teaching sessions. Osler's *Principles and Practice of Medicine* (1892) became the most popular medical textbook of its day. He was involved in the formation of two physicians' associations and the *Quarterly Journal of Medicine*. Osler's nodes on the hand are seen in some cardiac infections, and two blood disorders also bear his name.

Osler at the bedside of a patient while professor of medicine at Johns Hopkins, 1888–1904.

BY COURTESY OF THE OSLER LIBRARY, MCGILL UNIVERSITY, MONTREAL

Oslo \'äz-lō, *Norwegian* 'üs-lü\ *formerly (1624–1925)* **Christiania** *or* **Kristiania** City (metro. area pop., 1997 est.: 494,000), capital of Norway. It lies at the northern end of Oslo Fjord and constitutes a separate county. It was founded by King HARALD III SIGURDSSON c. 1050. Haakon V built the Akershus fortress c. 1300. After it was destroyed by fire in 1624, King CHRISTIAN II of Denmark-Norway built a new town farther west and called it Christiania. It grew in the 19th century, partly by absorbing neighboring towns, and replaced BERGEN as Norway's largest and most influential city. It was renamed Oslo in 1925 and developed rapidly after World War II. It is the country's principal commercial, industrial, and transportation center, and its harbor is the largest and busiest in Norway.

osmosis \äz-'mō-səs\ Spontaneous passage or DIFFUSION of water or other SOLVENT through a semipermeable membrane. If a solution is separated from a pure solvent by a membrane that is permeable to the solvent but not to the solute, the solution will tend to become more dilute by absorbing solvent through the membrane. The pressure caused by the migration of solvent through the membrane is called osmotic pressure.

osprey \'äs-prē, 'äs-prā\ *or* **fish hawk** Species *(Pandion haliaetus)* of long-winged HAWK found along seacoasts and large interior waterways. Ospreys are about 26 in. (65 cm) long and brown above and white below, with some white on the head. An osprey flies over the water, hovers above its prey, and then plunges feet first, seizing the fish in its long, curved talons. Ospreys breed on all continents except South America, where they live only in winter. They usually nest, singly or in colonies, high in trees or on cliffs. Bioaccumulation of pesticides caused populations to dwindle in the 20th century, but they are now recovering.

Osroene *or* **Osrhoene** \ˌäz-rə-'wē-nē\ Ancient kingdom, northwestern MESOPOTAMIA. Located between the TIGRIS and EUPHRATES rivers, it was situated across the modern frontier of Turkey and Syria, with its capital at EDESSA. Founded c. 136 BC, it commanded strategic trade and military routes 1st century BC–2nd century AD. At different times it was allied with either PARTHIA or ROME. The kingdom was abolished by Roman emperor CARACALLA in AD 216. In the 4th–7th century AD it was dominated by the wars between Byzantium and Persia. Under its Arab dynasties, it became a center of reaction against Hellenism, and the headquarters of Chaldean Syriac literature and learning. It fell to the Muslims in 638.

OSS See OFFICE OF STRATEGIC SERVICES

Osservatore romano \ò-ˌser-vä-'tò-rā-rō-'mä-nō\, **L'** (Italian: "The Roman Observer") Daily newspaper published in Vatican City, one of the most influential papers in Italy and the de facto voice of the Holy See. Founded in 1861, it was subsidized by the Vatican from its start and was bought outright in 1890 by Pope LEO XIII. It regularly details the pope's activities and prints the text of papal speeches as the Vatican newspaper of record; it also reports and comments on political developments, stressing editorials and comment over news and noting the religious and moral implications of events, institutions, and trends.

Ossian See OISÍN

Ossianic ballads \ˌä-sē-'a-nik, ˌä-shē-'a-nik\ Irish Gaelic and Scottish lyric and narrative poems dealing with the legendary Finn MacCumhaill and his war band. They are named for Oisín (Ossian), the chief bard of the FENIAN CYCLE. Part of a common Scots-Irish Gaelic tradition, the ballads consist of more than 80,000 lines dating from the 11th to the 18th century. Unlike earlier Fenian literature, which reflected mutual respect between pagan and Christian tradition, they are stubbornly pagan and anticlerical, full of lament for past glories and contempt for the Christian present. Most of the poetry claimed for Oisín was in fact written by Scottish poet James Macpherson (1736–1796).

Ossianic cycle See FENIAN CYCLE

Ossory \'ä-sə-rē\ Ancient kingdom, Ireland. It became a semi-independent state within the kingdom of Leinster, c. 1st century AD. In the 9th century its king, Cerball, allied himself with the Norse invaders. His Irish descendants became known as the Fitzpatricks. The modern diocese of Ossory, with its see at Kilkenny, approximates the size of the ancient state.

Ostade \òs-'tä-də\, **Adriaen van** (1610–1685) Dutch painter and printmaker. Known for his genre paintings of peasant life, he also did religious subjects, portraits, and landscapes. The most important influence on his style was ADRIAEN BROUWER. Like Brouwer, he delighted in scenes such as tavern brawls, usually in dimly lit interiors, as in *Carousing Peasants in an Interior* (c. 1638). He employed a broad, vigorous technique in a subdued range of colors. After he adopted a brighter palette in the 1640s, his subjects became less ribald, and from the 1650s he painted many of them in outdoor settings (e.g., *The Itinerant Fiddler*, 1672).

osteitis deformans See PAGET'S DISEASE OF BONE

Ostend Manifesto \ä-'stend\ (1854) Secret document written by U.S. diplomats at Ostend, Belgium, describing a plan to acquire Cuba from Spain. On orders from U.S. secretary of state WILLIAM MARCY, three U.S. diplomats—minister to Britain JAMES BUCHANAN, minister to France John Y. Mason, and minister to Spain Pierre Soulé—devised a plan to purchase or, if necessary, seize Cuba during the U.S. expansionist drive in the Caribbean. Publication of the aggressively worded document, and Soulé's advocacy of slavery, caused Marcy to denounce it.

osteoarthritis \ˌäs-tē-ō-är-'thrī-təs\ *or* **osteoarthrosis** *or* **degenerative joint disease** Most common JOINT disorder, afflicting over 80% of those who reach age 70. It does not involve excessive inflammation, and may have no symptoms, especially at first. CARTILAGE softens and wears away, and bone grows in its place, distorting the joint's surface and causing pain, stiffness, and limited movement, usually in weight-bearing joints (vertebrae, knees, hips). Treatment may include ANALGESICS, rest, weight loss, corticosteroids, and/or PHYSICAL MEDICINE AND REHABILITATION or an exercise program. Hip or knee replacement or surgical removal of unhealthy tissue may be needed.

osteogenesis imperfecta \ˌäs-tē-ō-ˈje-nə-səs-ˌim-pər-ˈfek-tə\ Hereditary connective-tissue disease in which the BONES are very fragile. Several forms probably reflect different degrees of expression of the same disorder. Babies with osteogenesis imperfecta congenita, if not stillborn, are born with FRACTURES, which continue to occur, causing severe crippling. Survival to adulthood is rare. Those with osteogenesis imperfecta tarda are normal at birth, but fractures occur easily. In van der Hoeve syndrome, the sclerae are also bluish and bone deformities in the skull cause deafness, with double-jointedness and abnormally thin skin.

osteopathy \ˌäs-tē-ˈä-pə-thē\ Health-care profession founded by the U.S. physician Andrew Taylor Still (1828–1917) as a reform movement against the rather primitive 19th-century drugs and surgical techniques. It emphasizes the relationship between musculoskeletal structure and organ function. Osteopathic physicians learn to recognize and correct structural problems through manipulative and other therapies and earn a doctor of osteopathy (DO) degree. They are licensed to practice in all U.S. states and have the same professional rights and responsibilities as MDs in most states. Osteopathic hospitals provide general or specialized health care, including maternity and emergency care.

osteoporosis \ˌäs-tē-ō-pə-ˈrō-səs\ Generalized loss of bone density, causing skeletal weakness. Around age 40, the rate of bone resorption in humans starts to exceed the rate of bone formation. Women experience accelerated bone loss after menopause. When the amount of bone falls below a certain threshold, fractures occur with little or no trauma. Prevention begins with adequate calcium intake in youth, when bone mass is built, and then throughout life. Weight-bearing exercise and VITAMIN D are important at all ages. In women, hormone-replacement therapy helps arrest osteoporosis, as ESTROGEN deficiency is a major cause of accelerated bone loss. Bisphosphonates inhibit bone resorption or prevent bone loss in patients not yet suffering from osteoporosis. Growth factors are under investigation as stimulants of new bone growth.

Ostia \ˈä-stē-ə\ Ancient Roman town. Originally at the mouth of the TIBER RIVER, it would now be about 4 mi (6 km) upstream. The modern seaside resort of Ostia is near the ancient city. It was probably founded in the 4th century BC, and developed as a naval station, major port, and center of the grain trade. It reached the height of its prosperity in the 2nd century AD with a population of about 50,000. It suffered from the decline of the Roman economy in the 3rd century and from barbarian raids in 5th century. Its Roman ruins were quarried for building materials in the Middle Ages and for sculptors' marble during the Renaissance. Excavations began in the 19th century, and about two-thirds of the Roman town can now be seen.

ostomy \ˈäs-tə-mē\ Surgical opening in the body, or the operation creating it, usually to allow discharge of wastes through the abdominal wall. It may be temporary, to relieve strain on damaged organs, or permanent, to replace normal channels congenitally missing or surgically removed (usually to treat cancer). A loop of bowel (the COLON in COLOSTOMY and the ILEUM in ileostomy) is cut and the end brought through to the abdominal surface. Waste usually exits into a self-adhering bag worn over the opening, or an internal pouch may be made from body tissue.

Ostpolitik \ˈȯst-pȯ-li-ˌtēk\ (German: "Eastern Policy") West German foreign policy begun in the late 1960s. Initiated by WILLY BRANDT as foreign minister and then chancellor, the policy was one of détente with Soviet-bloc countries, recognizing the East German government and expanding commercial relations with other Soviet-bloc countries. Treaties were concluded in 1970 with the Soviet Union, renouncing the use of force in their relations, and with Poland, recognizing Germany's 1945 losses east of the ODER-NEISSE LINE. The policy was continued by Chancellor HELMUT SCHMIDT.

Ostrasia See AUSTRASIA

Ostrava \ˈō-strə-və\ City (pop., 1996 est.: 325,000), northeastern Czech Republic, at the confluence of the Opava and ODER rivers near the Moravian Gap. It was founded c. 1267 as a fortified town by Bruno, bishop of Olomouc, to protect the entry to MORAVIA from the north. Its castle was demolished in 1495. Historic buildings include a 13th-century church. The major industry is coal mining.

ostrich Two-toed, long-necked, RATITE (*Struthio camelus,* family Struthionidae) found in Africa, the largest living bird. An adult male ostrich may be 8 ft (2.5 m) tall and weigh up to 350 lbs (155 kg). Males are black, with white wing and tail plumes; females are brown. Ostriches live in flocks of 5–50, usually among grazing animals, eating plants and an occasional animal. Roaring, hissing males fight for three to five hens, which lay 15–60 eggs in a communal nest scraped in the ground. The male sits at night; the females take turns by day. One-month-old chicks can run with adults, at 40 mph (65 kph). To escape detection, ostriches may lie on the ground with neck outstretched, a habit that may have given rise to the notion that they bury their head in the sand.

Ostrogoths \ˈäs-trə-ˌgäths\ Division of GOTHS (Ostrogoth means "Eastern Goth") who built an empire north of the Black Sea in the 3rd century and established a kingdom in Italy in the late 5th century. At its zenith in the 4th century, the Ostrogoth empire stretched from the Don to the Dniester (in present-day Ukraine) and from the Black Sea to southern Belarus. After their subjugation by the HUNS (c. 370), some Ostrogoths settled along the Danube River (c. 450). When the Hun empire collapsed (455), THEODORIC led the Ostrogothic invasion of Italy and declared himself king (493). JUSTINIAN I fought the Ostrogoths in Italy for almost 20 years (c. 535–54) and ended their national existence.

Ostrovsky \ə-ˈstrȯf-skē\, **Aleksandr (Nikolayevich)** (1823–1886) Russian playwright. His second play, *The Bankrupt* (1850), exposed bogus bankruptcy cases and led to his dismissal from the civil service. His later plays, most of which treat characters from the Russian merchant class, include the comedies *Poverty Is No Disgrace* (1853), *The Thunderstorm* (1859), and *The Snow Maiden* (1873), adapted as an opera by N. RIMSKY-KORSAKOV. With his 47 plays Ostrovsky created a Russian national repertoire, and he is considered the greatest representative of the Russian realistic period.

Ostwald \ˈȯst-ˌvält\, **(Friedrich) Wilhelm** (1853–1932) Russian-German physical chemist. Born in Riga, Latvia, he moved to Germany in 1887. He wrote the influential *Textbook of General Chemistry* (2 vols., 1885–87). With JACOBUS H. VAN'T HOFF in 1887 he founded the *Zeitschrift für physikalische Chemie,* which became for many years the most important journal in the field. His work at the University of Leipzig (1887–1906) established it as a great school of PHYSICAL CHEMISTRY. In 1888 he discovered Ostwald's law of dilution of an electrolyte. He gave the first modern definition of a catalyst in 1894, and was awarded the Nobel Prize in 1909 for his work on CATALYSIS. His process for the conversion of ammonia to nitric acid proved of great industrial importance. He is regarded as one of the founders of the field of physical chemistry.

O'Sullivan, Timothy H. (1840–1882) U.S. photographer. Raised in New York (but possibly born in Ireland), he learned photography in MATHEW B. BRADY's studio there, and during the Civil War he photographed on many fronts as one of Brady's team. Perhaps his best-known picture is *Harvest of Death* (1863), showing Confederate dead at Gettysburg. He took part in surveys in Panama as well as in the western and southwestern U.S., and was appointed chief photographer for the Treasury Department in 1880.

Oswald, Lee Harvey (1939–1963) U.S. assassin of Pres. JOHN F. KENNEDY. Born in New Orleans, he served in the U.S. Marines 1956–59. Expressing pro-Soviet views, he moved to the Soviet Union and unsuccessfully tried to become a Soviet citizen. He returned to the U.S. in 1962 with his Russian wife and daughter, but retained his radical political beliefs. In April 1963 he allegedly shot at but missed Edwin Walker, an ultrarightist retired general. In October he took a job at the Texas School Book Depository in Dallas. On November 22, from a window on its sixth floor, he allegedly fired three shots that killed Kennedy and wounded Gov. John B. Connally. Soon afterward he killed a patrolman who had detained him, and he was soon captured and arraigned. On November 24, while being transferred to an interrogation office, he was fatally shot by Jack Ruby, a nightclub owner.

other minds, problem of In EPISTEMOLOGY, the problem of explaining how it is possible for one person to know anything about the quality of another person's inner experience, or even that other people have inner experiences at all. For example, because each person's pain sensation is private, one cannot really know that what another person describes as pain is really qualitatively the same as what one describes as pain oneself. Though the physical manifestations the other person exhibits can be perceived, it seems that only the other person can know the contents of his or her mind.

Otis, Harrison Gray (1765–1848) U.S. politician. Born in Boston, a nephew of JAMES OTIS, he practiced law and served in the Massachusetts legislature (1796–97, 1802–5), U.S. House of Representatives (1797–1801), state senate (1805–13, 1814–17), and U.S. Senate (1817–22), and was mayor of Boston (1829–32). A Federalist, he opposed the War of 1812 and was a leader of the HARTFORD CONVENTION.

Otis, James (1725–1783) American Revolutionary statesman. Born in West Barnstable, Mass., he argued before the colonial court against the British-imposed Writs of ASSISTANCE (1761), reportedly stating "Taxation without representation is tyranny." He served in the provincial legislature (1761–69) and was a leader with SAMUEL ADAMS in opposing the STAMP ACT. He wrote political pamphlets upholding the colonists' cause, including *The Rights of the British Colonies Asserted and Proved* (1764). Struck on the head in a scuffle with a British official in 1769, he later became mentally unbalanced.

otitis \ō-'tī-təs\ INFLAMMATION of the EAR. Otitis externa is DERMATITIS, usually bacterial, of the auditory canal and sometimes the external ear. It can cause a foul discharge, pain, fever, and sporadic DEAFNESS. Otitis media is due to allergy or viral or bacterial infection of the middle ear. The bacterial form may be acute (causing earache, fever, and pus and requiring antibiotics) or chronic. It can invade the bone (MASTOIDITIS), requiring surgery. Otitis in the INNER EAR (labyrinthitis) often arises from respiratory infection, SYPHILIS, or otitis media. Symptoms include vertigo, vomiting, and hearing loss. Recovery is usually quick unless there is pus formation, which can destroy the inner-ear structures, causing permanent deafness in that ear.

otolaryngology \ˌō-tō-ˌlar-ən-'gä-lə-jē\ *or* **otorhinolaryngology** \ˌō-tō-ˌrī-nō-ˌlar-ən-'gä-lə-jē\ Medical specialty dealing with the EAR, NOSE, and throat (see LARYNX, PHARYNX). The connection of these structures became known in the late 19th century. Otolaryngologists use an otoscope to examine the eardrum and a laryngoscope (developed in 1855) to inspect the larynx. They also test hearing and prescribe hearing aids. The operating microscope (developed in 1921) and flexible ENDOSCOPY now permit them to operate on delicate internal structures.

Otomanguean languages \ˌō-tə-'mäŋ-gā-ən\ Diverse family of more than 20 American Indian languages and language clusters concentrated in central and southern Mexico, with over a million speakers. Several of the language clusters, such as Otomí (dispersed through eastern central Mexico), Chinantecan, Mixtecan, and Zapotecan (all spoken in the state of Oaxaca), are highly differentiated and may be considered language families in themselves. The profile of a typical Otomanguean language stands out among American Indian languages: TONE plays a significant role, verbal MORPHOLOGY is simple, syllables may be closed only by a glottal stop, and initial consonant clusters have several distinctive features.

Otomi \ˌō-tə-'mē\ Mesoamerican Indian population living in the central plateau region of Mexico. Traditionally, they practice slash-and-burn agriculture and raise livestock. Their crafts include spinning, weaving, pottery, and basketry, and their dress varies from traditional to modern. *Compadrazgo,* fictive kinship based on the godparent/godchild relationship, is central to their society. Ritual obligations bind a child's parents and godparents in a close relationship. They profess Roman Catholicism but identify the major saints with pre-Christian divinities.

O'Toole, Peter (born 1932) British actor. The son of a bookie, he studied drama at the Royal Academy of Dramatic Art and served in the navy. He made his London debut in 1956, and played Hamlet in the National Theatre's inaugural production in 1963. He made his film debut in *Kidnapped* (1960) and won international acclaim for *Lawrence of Arabia* (1962). Noted for his wit and intensity, he often played eccentrics and heavy drinkers, starring in such films as *Becket* (1964), *The Lion in Winter* (1968), *The Ruling Class* (1972), *The Stunt Man* (1980), and *My Favorite Year* (1982).

ottava rima \ō-'tä-və-'rē-mə\ Italian stanza form composed of eight 11-syllable lines, rhyming *abababcc*. It originated in the late 13th and early 14th century and was established by GIOVANNI BOCCACCIO as the standard form for Italian epic and narrative verse. When the form appeared in English, the lines were shortened to 10 syllables. In the 17th–18th century, English ottava rima was written in iambic pentameter and used for heroic poetry. Notably effective in Lord BYRON's *Beppo* (1818) and *Don Juan* (1819–24), it was also used by EDMUND SPENSER, JOHN MILTON, JOHN KEATS, PERCY B. SHELLEY, ROBERT BROWNING, and WILLIAM BUTLER YEATS.

Ottawa \'ä-tə-wə\ City (pop., 1991: 314,000), capital of CANADA. It is located in southeastern Ontario, on the OTTAWA, Gatineau, and Rideau rivers. The area was inhabited by American Indians when it was visited by SAMUEL DE CHAMPLAIN in 1613, and the nearby rivers served traders and explorers over the next two centuries. Its settlement developed after the construction of the Rideau Canal in 1826. Originally named Bytown, it was incorporated as the city of Ottawa in 1855. To resolve political disputes between TORONTO and QUEBEC CITY, and MONTREAL and Kingston, it was selected as Canada's capital by Queen VICTORIA in 1857. The federal government is the major employer; many commercial and financial associations are located there. It is the site of several educational and cultural institutions, including the National Arts Centre and the National Gallery of Canada.

Ottawa River River, eastern central Canada, the chief tributary of the ST. LAWRENCE RIVER. It rises in the Laurentian plateau of western QUEBEC and flows west to form the Quebec–Ontario border before joining the St. Lawrence west of MONTREAL. It is 790 mi (1,271 km) long and forms innumerable lakes. Explored by SAMUEL DE CHAMPLAIN in 1613, it became a major route for explorers, fur traders, and missionaries to the GREAT LAKES. In the 19th century the Rideau Canal was completed, linking OTTAWA to Lake ONTARIO, and lumbering became important. It is now a source of hydroelectric power.

otter Any of several carnivore species in four genera of semiaquatic, web-footed members of the WEASEL family (Mustelidae), found throughout Africa, North and South America, Europe, and Asia. Otters have the same general proportions as weasels. Size varies among species; total length is typically 3–7 ft (1–2 m) and weight is 6.5–60 lbs (3–27 kg); the large SEA OTTER is an exception. Otter fur, especially that of northern animals, is highly valued. Most species live near rivers; some live near lakes or streams; the sea otter is completely marine. Otters eat small aquatic animals. They are inquisitive and playful; a favorite sport is sliding down a mudbank and plunging into water.

River otter (*Lutra canadensis*).
KENNETH W. FINK—ROOT RESOURCES

Otter, William Dillon *later* **Sir William** (1843–1929) Canadian army officer. Born in Clinton, Ontario, he joined the army and helped suppress the North-West Rebellion (1885). He became the first commanding officer of the Royal Canadian regiment of infantry (1893) and led a Canadian force in the SOUTH AFRICAN WAR. Appointed chief of the general staff (1908) and inspector general of the Canadian militia (1910–12), he directed internment operations in World War I.

Otto, Nikolaus August (1832–1891) German engineer who developed the four-stroke INTERNAL-COMBUSTION ENGINE. He built his first gasoline-powered engine in 1861, and in 1876 he built an internal-combustion engine using the four-stroke cycle (four strokes of the piston for each explosion), which offered the first practical alternative to the STEAM ENGINE as a POWER source. Though the four-stroke cycle was patented in 1862 by Alphonse Beau de Rochas (1815–1893), it is commonly known as the Otto cycle since Otto was the first to build such an engine.

Otto, Rudolf (1869–1937) German theologian, philosopher, and historian of religion. He taught at the Univs. of Göttingen and Breslau, then settled in Marburg in 1917. His theories on religion were influenced by his journeys to Africa and Asia to study non-Christian faiths and by the writings of IMMANUEL KANT and FRIEDRICH SCHLEIERMACHER. In *The Idea of the Holy* (1917), Otto coined the term "numinous" to designate the non-

O
P
Q
R

rational element of religious experience—the awe, fascination, and blissful exultation inspired by the perception of the divine. He believed that religion provided an understanding of the world that was distinct from and beyond that of science. His other books include *Mysticism East and West* (1926), *India's Religion of Grace and Christianity* (1930), and *The Kingdom of God and Son of Man* (1938).

Rudolf Otto, 1925.
FOTO—JANNASCH, MARBURG/L.

Otto I *known as* **Otto the Great** (912–973) Duke of Saxony (936–61), German king (936–73), and Holy Roman Emperor (962–73). He extended the frontiers of the German kingdom, winning territory from the Slavs in the east, forcing the Bohemians to pay tribute (950), and gaining influence in Denmark and Burgundy. In 951 Otto became king of the Lombards and married the queen of Italy. He quelled a rebellion by his son in 955 and defeated the MAGYARS in the Battle of LECHFELD. Crowned emperor by Pope John XII in 962, he deposed John in 963 and replaced him with Leo VIII. He returned to Italy (966–72) to subdue Rome, and he betrothed his son, Otto II, to a Byzantine princess (972).

Otto III (980–1002) German king (983–1002) and Holy Roman Emperor (996–1002). He was elected German king at age 3, and his mother and grandmother served as regents until he came of age in 994. He went to Rome to put down a rebellion (996) and installed his cousin as Gregory V, the first German pope. After returning in 997 to quell another revolt, he made Rome the center of his empire. He saw himself as leader of world Christianity and hoped to revive the glory of ancient Rome in a universal Christian state. When Rome rebelled against him (1001), he requested help from Bavaria but died before it arrived.

Otto IV *or* **Otto of Brunswick** (c. 1175–1218) German king and Holy Roman Emperor. He was elected German king (1198) by the Guelph faction (see GUELPHS AND GHIBELLINES) but was opposed by the HOHENSTAUFENS, who elected PHILIP of Swabia. The two factions were at war for several years, but after Philip's murder in 1208 a new election gave the throne to Otto. He was crowned emperor (1209) by INNOCENT III after agreeing not to claim Sicily. When he violated this pact and conquered southern Italy (1210), the German princes invited FREDERICK II to replace him. With his uncle, JOHN of England, Otto invaded France, Frederick's ally; defeated at the Battle of BOUVINES, he was deposed in 1215.

Ottoman empire Former Turkish empire centered in ASIA MINOR. It was named for Osman I (1259–1326), a Muslim prince in BITHYNIA who conquered neighboring regions once held by the SELJUQ DYNASTY and founded his own dynasty c. 1300. Ottoman troops first invaded Europe in 1345, sweeping through the Balkans. Though defeated by TIMUR in 1402, by 1453 the Ottomans, under Muhammad II the Conquerer (1429–1481), had destroyed the BYZANTINE EMPIRE and captured its capital, Constantinople (ISTANBUL), which henceforth served as the Ottoman capital. Under Selim I (1467–1520) and his son SÜLEYMAN I the Magnificent, the Ottoman empire became the largest in the world, Süleyman taking control of Persia, Arabia, Hungary, and the Balkans. By the early 16th century the Ottomans had also defeated the MAMLUKS in Syria and Egypt; and their navy under BARBAROSSA soon seized control of much of the BARBARY COAST. Beginning with Selim, the Ottoman sultans also held the title of CALIPH, the spiritual head of Islam. Ottoman power began to decline in the late 16th century with the destruction of the imperial fleet in 1571 at the Battle of LEPANTO. Ottoman forces besieged Vienna in 1683; their defeat and subsequent losses led to their relinquishing Hungary in 1699. Continuing corruption and decadence gradually undermined the government. In the 18th century the RUSSO-TURKISH WARS and wars with Austria and Poland further weakened the empire, which in the 19th century came to be called the "sick man of Europe." Most of its remaining European territory was lost in the BALKAN WARS (1912–13). It sided with Germany in World War I; postwar treaties dissolved the empire, and in 1922 the sultanate was abolished by MUSTAFA KEMAL ATATURK, who proclaimed the Republic of Turkey. See also JANISSARY, TURKS, YOUNG TURKS.

Ottonian art \ä-'tō-nē-ən\ Painting, sculpture, and other visual arts produced during the reigns of the German Ottonian emperors and their first successors from the Salic house (950–1050). Though it drew on the heritage of CAROLINGIAN ART, it developed a style of its own, particularly in painting and sculpture. Manuscript illuminators of the period were less concerned with naturalism than with expression through sober, dramatic gesture and heightened coloration. Ottonian large-scale wooden crucifixes and wooden reliquaries covered with gold leaf marked a return to sculpture in the round. Bronze casting, an antique art practiced by the Carolingians, flourished as well. Ottonian architecture was more regulated than Carolingian, with simple interior spaces and a more systematic layout. Ottonian architects provided impetus for the monumentality of ROMANESQUE ARCHITECTURE.

Otway, Thomas (1652–1685) English dramatist and poet. A failed actor, he turned to writing and had immense success with *Don Carlos* (produced 1676), considered the best of his rhymed heroic plays. His other plays include *The Orphan* (1680), a blank-verse domestic tragedy; *The Souldier's Fortune* (1680), a comedy; and his masterpiece, *Venice Preserv'd* (1682), one of the greatest theatrical successes of the period. A forerunner of sentimental drama, he is outstanding for his convincing presentations of human emotions in an age of heroic but artificial tragedies. *The Poet's Complaint of His Muse* (1680) is a powerful, gloomy autobiographical poem.

Ouachita River \'wä-shə-,tȯ\ *formerly* **Washita River** River, southwestern Arkansas and eastern Louisiana. Rising in the Ouachita Mtns., it flows southeast to join the RED RIVER after a course of 605 mi (973 km). Its lower reaches are known as the Black River. It has been a navigation route since the late 18th century; six locks and dams were built on it by 1924.

Ouagadougou \,wä-gä-'dü-gü\ City (pop., 1993 est.: 690,000), capital of Burkina Faso, western Africa. It was the capital of the historic MOSSI kingdom of Wagadugu, which was founded in the 15th century. The Mossi king still lives in the city, though his powers have been eclipsed by the French colonial and post-independence administrations. A manufacturing center, it is the nation's largest city and is connected by rail to ABIDJAN, Ivory Coast.

Oudh \'au̇d\ Former province of British India. Now the northeastern portion of UTTAR PRADESH state, it received its name from AJODHYA, the capital of the ancient kingdom of KOSALA, which was nearly coextensive with modern Oudh. It was taken by Muslim invaders in the 12th century, became part of the Mughal empire in the 16th century, and was annexed by the British in 1856. In 1877 it was joined with AGRA to form the United Provinces of Agra and Oudh. After India's independence in 1947 it became part of Uttar Pradesh.

Oudry \ü-'drē\, **Jean-Baptiste** (1686–1755) French Rococo painter, tapestry designer, and illustrator. Like his paintings, Oudry's tapestries were highly regarded for their tonal subtlety and lively study of nature. His services were sought by PETER I THE GREAT of Russia, the queen of Sweden, and LOUIS XV, who commissioned him to paint portraits of his dogs and appointed him official painter of the royal hunts.

Ouida \'wē-də\ *orig.* **Maria Louise Ramé** *or* **Maria Louise de la Ramée** (1839–1908) English novelist. Among her novels, most of them extravagant, melodramatic romances of fashionable life, are *Held in Bondage* (1863), *Strathmore* (1865), *Chandos* (1866), *Under Two Flags* (1867), and *Moths* (1880). She also wrote animal stories, including the popular *A Dog of Flanders* (1872). She settled in Florence in 1874, where reckless extravagance reduced her to acute poverty in later life.

Ouija board \'wē-jə\ Device for obtaining messages from the spirit world, sometimes used by a medium during a séance. The name derives from the French and German words for "yes" (oui/ja). The Ouija board is an oblong piece of wood or cardboard with letters of the alphabet inscribed in a half-moon along the edge. A small heart-shaped board is placed on top of it. Participants each lightly place a finger on the small board, which spirits supposedly move around on the larger board. As it touches the letters it may spell out words or sentences.

ounce Unit of weight in the avoirdupois system, the traditional European system of weight, which was incorporated into the British Imperial

O P Q R

system and the U.S. system of weights and measures (see MEASUREMENT). The ounce is equal to 1/16 lb (437.5 grains). In the troy and apothecaries' systems (two other traditional systems of weight), it is equal to 1/12 troy or apothecaries' lb (480 grains). The avoirdupois ounce is equal to 28.35 g, the troy ounce to 31.1 g. As a unit of volume, the fluid ounce is equal to 1/16 of a pint (29.57 ml) in the U.S. system, and to 1/20 of a pint (28.41 ml) in the British Imperial system. See also GRAM, INTERNATIONAL SYSTEM OF UNITS, METRIC SYSTEM, POUND.

ounce See SNOW LEOPARD

Ouranus See URANUS

Ouse River *or* **Great Ouse River** \'üz\ River, central and eastern England. It rises in NORTHAMPTONSHIRE, and flows 156 mi (251 km) past Buckingham, BEDFORD, Huntington, and St. Ives to Earith, then to the NORTH SEA. Locks make the river navigable upstream to Bedford.

Ouse River River, northeastern England. It is formed in North Yorkshire and flows through YORK and Selby to join the Aire River. It merges with the TRENT RIVER to form the Humber River (see HUMBER ESTUARY). The lower Ouse is a major transport route for industrial products and raw materials, including steel, coal, and textiles.

Outer Banks Chain of barrier islands, North Carolina coast. Extending southward 175 mi (282 km) along the coast, it stretches from the Virginia border to Cape Lookout. Generally covered with sand dunes, the islands range from a few feet to more than 100 ft (160 m) in height. Most are linked by roads and causeways; there are numerous beaches, making the Outer Banks a popular resort area. Once a hideout for pirates and a place of shipwrecks, the islands have several historical sites, including ROANOKE ISLAND and Kitty Hawk, site of the WRIGHT BROTHERS' first powered flight.

Outer Mongolia See MONGOLIA

outwash Deposit of sand and gravel carried by running water from the melting ice of a GLACIER and laid down in stratified deposits. An outwash may be as much as 330 ft (100 m) thick at the edge of a glacier, and it may extend for many miles. Outwashes are the largest glacial deposits and provide a considerable source of windblown material.

Ouyang Xiu *or* **Ou-yang Hsiu** \'ō-'yäŋ-'shyü\ (1007–1072) Chinese poet, historian, and statesman. He served in various official positions, but was repeatedly demoted for outspokenness and personal scandals. After one scandal he took to drink and built a pavilion that he named Zuiweng ting ("Old Drunkard Pavilion") and made the subject of an essay that became one of the most celebrated works in Chinese literature. Later put in charge of civil-service examinations, he favored those who wrote in the simple, ancient style known as *guwen* and failed those who used literary embellishments, thus setting a new course in Chinese literature. His own writings in the *guwen* style, including *Xin Tang shu* (1060; "New History of the Tang Dynasty"), became a model that was long emulated.

ouzel *or* **ousel** \'ü-zəl\ Species *(Turdus torquatus)* of songbird in the THRUSH family, characterized by a white crescent on the breast. A blackish bird, about 10 in. (25 cm) long, it breeds locally in uplands from Britain and Norway to the Middle East. The name was formerly applied to a closely related European BLACKBIRD *(T. merula).* The DIPPER is often called water ouzel.

Ring-ouzel (*Turdus torquatus*).
DRAWING BY JOHN P. O'NEILL

ovarian cancer Malignant TUMOR of the OVARIES. Risk factors include early age of first menstruation (before age 12), late onset of menopause (after age 52), absence of pregnancy, presence of specific genetic mutations, use of fertility drugs, and personal history of breast cancer. Symptoms such as abdominal swelling, pelvic pressure or pain, and unusual vaginal bleeding often do not appear until ovarian cancer is advanced. Surgery, sometimes followed by chemotherapy or radiation therapy, is an effective treatment for most ovarian cancers.

ovary \'ō-və-rē\ In zoology, the female reproductive organ (see REPRODUCTIVE SYSTEM) that produces EGGS and SEX HORMONES (ESTROGEN and PROGESTERONE). Humans have two ovaries, almond-shaped organs about 1.5 in. (4 cm) long. They contain hollow balls of cells (follicles) that hold immature eggs. About 150,000–500,000 follicles usually are present at birth; by young adulthood, only about 34,000 remain. The number continues to decrease until MENOPAUSE, when the few remaining follicles decay and the ovaries shrink and produce far less estrogen. Only 300–400 follicles mature and release an egg, which develops into an EMBRYO if fertilized or, if not, passes from the body with MENSTRUATION. In botany, an ovary is the enlarged base of a flower's female organ (pistil). It contains ovules, which develop into seeds when fertilized, and matures into a fruit.

over-the-counter market Trading in STOCKS and BONDS that does not take place on STOCK EXCHANGES. Such trading occurs most often in the U.S., where requirements for listing stocks on the exchanges are strict. Schedules of fees for buying and selling SECURITIES are not fixed in the over-the-counter market, and dealers derive their profits from the markup of their selling price over the price they paid. Many bond issues and preferred-stock issues, including U.S. government bonds, are listed on the NEW YORK STOCK EXCHANGE but have their chief market over-the-counter. Other U.S. government securities, as well as state and municipal bonds, are traded over-the-counter exclusively. Institutional investors such as MUTUAL FUNDS often trade over-the-counter because they are given volume discounts not offered on the exchanges. The regulation of the over-the-counter market is carried out largely by the National Association of Securities Dealers, created by Congress in 1939 to establish rules of conduct and protect members and investors from abuses. See also NASDAQ.

overpopulation Situation in which the number of individuals of a given species exceeds the number that its environment can sustain. Possible consequences are environmental deterioration, impaired quality of life, and a population crash (sudden reduction in numbers caused by high mortality and failure to produce viable offspring).

overtone *or* **harmonic** In acoustics, a series of higher tones contained within almost any musical tone. HERMANN VON HELMHOLTZ first demonstrated the long-suspected physical fact that a body producing a musical pitch—such as a taut string, or a column of air within the tubular body of a wind instrument—vibrates not only as a unit but simultaneously also as integral fractions (half, third, etc.), resulting in the presence of a series of overtones within the fundamental tone (i.e., the one identified as the actual pitch). These higher tones contribute greatly to the TIMBRE of a given sound source, even though few listeners are aware of hearing any pitch except the fundamental, or first (lowest) harmonic. The second harmonic sounds an octave higher than the fundamental; the third sounds a 5th above the second harmonic; the fourth sounds a 4th above the third (two octaves above the fundamental); the 5th sounds a major 3rd above the fourth; and so on. It is widely believed that the special consonance of the octave and the 5th, and even the major 3rd, derive from their strength in the overtone series (see CONSONANCE AND DISSONANCE).

overture Musical introduction to a larger, often dramatic, work. Originating with C. MONTEVERDI's *Orfeo* (1607), overtures served as openings for operas. The large-scale two- or three-part "French overture" invented by J.-B. LULLY (1658) for his operas and ballets was widely imitated for a century. The sinfonia, a development of the latter that became the standard Italian overture form, was a principal precursor of SONATA FORM, which itself became the standard form for later operatic overtures. In the 19th century, overtures independent of any larger work usually illustrated a literary or historical theme (see SYMPHONIC POEM). Overtures to OPERETTAS and MUSICALS have traditionally been medleys of their themes.

overweight Body weight greater than the optimum. If moderate, it is not necessarily OBESITY, particularly in muscular or large-boned persons, but even small reductions in excess weight can improve health. An increasing proportion (more than one-third by some estimates) of the U.S. population is currently overweight, and health problems associated with it are increasing. The long-term effectiveness of diet programs and products in combating overweight is doubtful. Better approaches include educational and preventive efforts starting in childhood, and reduction of food intake (especially fat) combined with exercise.

Ovett \ō-'vet\, **Steve** *orig.* **Stephen Michael** (born 1955) British runner. Born in Brighton, he was the winner of gold (in the 800-m race) and bronze medals at the 1980 Olympic Games. In the course of his career Ovett set six world records.

Ovid \'ä-vid\ *Latin* **Publius Ovidius Naso** (43 BC–AD 17) Roman poet. A member of Rome's knightly class, Ovid dutifully started an official career but soon abandoned it for poetry. His first work, *The Loves,* was an immediate success. It was followed by *Epistles of the Heroines; The Art of Beauty; The Art of Love,* one of his best-known works; and *Remedies for Love*, all reflecting the sophisticated, pleasure-seeking society in which he lived through themes of love and amorous intrigue. He was a well-established poet when he undertook perhaps his greatest work, *Metamorphoses,* on legends of transformations of human beings into nonhuman forms by gods; and *Fasti* ("Calendar"), an account of the Roman year and its religious festivals. His verse had immense influence because of its imaginative interpretations of classical myth and its supreme technical accomplishment. For unclear reasons, in AD 8 AUGUSTUS banished him to Tomis on the Black Sea; despite Ovid's many pleas, he was never allowed to return. He described his life in an autobiographical poem in *Sorrows.* Extensively read and imitated in the Renaissance, he is the classical poet who most influenced WILLIAM SHAKESPEARE.

Oviedo \ō-'vyā-t͟hō\ *ancient* **Asturias** City (pop., 1995 est.: 202,000), capital of ASTURIAS, northwestern Spain. It lies on a hill surrounded by mountains and a fertile plain. Founded as a monastery in AD 757, it became the capital of the kingdom of Asturias in 810. It was one of the few Spanish towns never conquered by the MOORS in the Middle Ages and contains many medieval landmarks, including the 14th-century cathedral. It was badly damaged during the SPANISH CIVIL WAR. It is the center of a mining region that produces coal and iron.

Ovimbundu \ˌō-vim-'bün-dü\ Bantu-speaking people of central Angola. Numbering about 4 million, the Ovimbundu provided the major popular support for JONAS M. SAVIMBI and the National Union for the Total Independence of Angola (UNITA). They were formerly traders; today they farm, hunt, and raise livestock. About half the 22 Ovimbundu chiefdoms were tributary to a larger chiefdom before Portuguese intervention in the 20th century.

ovum See EGG

Owen, Robert (1771–1858) Welsh manufacturer and philanthropist. At his New Lanark cotton mills (Lanarkshire, Scotland), in partnership with JEREMY BENTHAM, he set up innovative social and industrial welfare programs, including improved housing and schools for young children. In *A New View of Society* (1813) he contended that character is wholly formed by one's environment. By 1817 his work had evolved into ideas presaging socialism and the cooperative movement, ideas he would spend much of his life preaching. He sponsored several experimental utopian communities of "Owenites" in Britain and the U.S., including one at New Harmony, Ind. (1825–28), all of which proved short-lived. He strongly supported early labor unions, but opposition and repression swiftly dissolved them, and it was two generations before socialism again influenced unionism. He was the father of ROBERT DALE OWEN.

Owen, Robert Dale (1801–1877) Scottish-American social reformer. In 1825 he emigrated with his father, ROBERT OWEN, to establish a community at New Harmony, Ind. He moved to New York with FANNY WRIGHT and edited the *Free Enquirer,* an advocate for radical free thought; they were active in the WORKINGMEN'S PARTY. Owen returned to New Harmony in 1832. In the U.S. House of Representatives (1843–47) he introduced a bill establishing the SMITHSONIAN INSTITUTION. He served as U.S. minister to Italy 1855–58. A strong advocate of emancipation, he urged an end to slavery in a letter to ABRAHAM LINCOLN and wrote *The Wrong of Slavery* (1864).

Owen, Wilfred (1893–1918) British poet. Owen was already writing verse before he enlisted in the army in 1915, but the experience of trench warfare brought him to rapid maturity; the poignant poems he wrote after January 1917 are full of anger at the cruelty and waste of war and pity for its victims. A week before the armistice, he died in action at 25. His single volume of poems, published posthumously, is noted for its experiments in assonance. BENJAMIN BRITTEN's celebrated *War Requiem* (1962) is a setting of Owen's poems.

Owens, Jesse *orig.* **James Cleveland** (1913–1980) U.S. track-and-field athlete. Born in Oakville, Ala., he starred in high school in Cleveland, Ohio. At Ohio State University in 1935, he broke or equaled four world track records in one day, setting a new long-jump record that would stand for 25 years. In the 1936 Olympics in Berlin he won four gold medals, tying the Olympic record in the 100-m run, breaking the Olympic record in the 200-m run, running the final segment for the world-record-breaking U.S. 400-m relay team, and breaking the listed world record for the long jump. As a black man, he thereby dramatically foiled ADOLF HITLER's intention to use the games to show Aryan racial superiority. For a time he held alone or shared the world records for all sprint distances recognized by the International Amateur Athletic Federation.

Owens, 1936.
AP/WIDE WORLD PHOTOS

owl Any of the mostly nocturnal BIRDS OF PREY in the order Strigiformes: typical owls (family Strigidae), BARN and grass owls (Tytonidae), and bay owls (Phodilidae). Their virtually noiseless flight and protective (usually brown) coloration aid in capturing insects, birds, and small mammals. Owls have round, forward-looking eyes, a sharply hooked beak, and acute hearing and vision. They are 5–28 in. (13–70 cm) long. Some species have a disk framing the face or ear tufts that help locate prey by reflecting sound to the ears. Owls can turn their head 180° (some species can turn as much as 270°). They nest in buildings, trees, or on the ground. Typical owls occur worldwide except in Antarctica. See also HORNED OWL, SCREECH OWL, SNOWY OWL.

owlet moth See MILLER

ox Domesticated form of large BOVID (species *Bos taurus*) that once moved in herds across North America and Europe (where they have disappeared) and Asia and Africa (where some still exist in the wild). The docile castrated male is used as a draft animal in many countries. Oxen are used for food in some areas. The term is also applied to a castrated male of any CATTLE breed. See also AUROCHS, YAK.

oxalic acid \äk-'sa-lik\ Colorless, crystalline, toxic CARBOXYLIC ACID found in many plants, especially rhubarb, wood sorrel, and spinach. Because it forms soluble CHELATES with iron, some of the iron in these plants is not available nutritionally. However, this property makes it useful for removing blood and rust stains, cleaning metals other than iron, and flushing car radiators. Oxalic acid and its SALTS (oxalates) are used in many chemical processes.

oxalis \äk-'sa-ləs\ Any of about 850 species of small herbaceous plants that make up the genus *Oxalis,* native mostly to southern Africa and tropical and South America. Most members are familiar garden ornamentals. The name (Greek for "acid") reflects the plant's sharp acidic taste. The common wood sorrel *(O. acetosella)* of eastern North America and Britain is a small, stemless plant with cloverlike three-part leaves, whose leaflets fold back and droop at night. The flowers have five white, purple-veined petals. After the fruit splits open, the fleshy coat of the seed curls back elastically, ejecting the true seed.

oxbow lake Small lake located in a former MEANDER loop of a river or stream channel. It is generally formed as a river cuts through a meander neck to shorten its course, blocks off the old channel, and then migrates away from the lake. If only one loop is cut off, the lake is crescent-shaped; if more than one loop is cut off, the lake is serpentine (winding). Eventually, oxbow lakes silt up to form marshes and finally meander scars.

Oxenstierna (af Södermöre) \'ük-sen-ˌsher-nå\, **Axel (Gustafsson), Count** (1583–1654) Swedish statesman. Born into a noble family, he became a member of the council of state and in 1612 was appointed chancellor by GUSTAV II ADOLF. He worked with the king to stabilize administrative reforms. As a diplomat, he negotiated peace treaties with Denmark (1613) and Poland (1622). In the THIRTY YEARS' WAR, he was appointed governor-general of Prussia (1626) and military commander in Germany (1631). He directed Swedish policy in Germany

O P Q R

until 1636, when he returned to Sweden. As a regent during Queen Christina's minority (1636–44), he effectively ruled the country.

oxeye daisy Garden perennial plant *(Chrysanthemum leucanthemum)* in the composite family. The compound flower has 15–30 white ray flowers surrounding a bright yellow disk flower, about 1–2 in. (2.5–5 cm) across. It grows about 2 ft (60 cm) high and has oblong, notched leaves and long petioles (leafstalks). Native to Europe and Asia, it has become a common wild plant in the U.S. See also daisy.

Oxford *ancient* **Oxonia** City (pop., 1994 est.: 133,000), county seat of Oxfordshire, England. Situated on the Thames River, it is best known for the University of Oxford. First occupied in Saxon times as a fording point, it became a burg, built to defend the northern frontier of Wessex from Danish attack; it was first mentioned in the Anglo-Saxon Chronicle of AD 912. Little remains of the town's Norman period of occupation. It is generally known as the "City of Spires" because of its skyline of 15th–17th century. Gothic towers and steeples, most of which belong to the university. The city was the Royalist headquarters in the English Civil Wars. Its modern economy is varied and includes, in addition to educational services, printing and publishing industries and automobile manufacturing.

Oxford, Earl of *orig.* **Edward de Vere** (1550–1604) English lyric poet. A brilliantly gifted linguist and one of the most dashing figures of his time, Oxford was also reckless, hot-tempered, and disastrously spendthrift. He was the patron of an acting company, Oxford's Men, and possibly later of the Lord Chamberlain's Men (as hereditary Lord Great Chamberlain of England), as well as of such writers as John Lyly and Edmund Spenser. He wrote highly praised poems and plays in his earlier years, though none of the plays are known to have survived. A 1920 book by J. Thomas Looney made Oxford the leading candidate, next to William Shakespeare himself, for the authorship of Shakespeare's plays, a theory supported by the coincidence that Oxford's literary output apparently ceased just before Shakespeare's work began to appear.

Oxford, Earl of See Robert Harley

Oxford, Provisions of (1258) Plan of reform accepted by Henry III of England. On the verge of bankruptcy, Henry asked Parliament for a grant of revenue and agreed in return to a program of reform drafted by a royal commission. Regarded as England's first written constitution, the Provisions placed the government under the direction of the king and a 15-member baronial council, provided for Parliament to meet three times a year, and reformed local administration. They were annulled by the Dictum of Kenilworth (1266).

Oxford, University of Autonomous university at Oxford, England. It was founded in the 12th century and modeled on the University of Paris, with initial faculties of theology, law, medicine, and the liberal arts. Of the earliest colleges, University College was founded in 1249, Balliol c. 1263, and Merton in 1264. Early scholars of note include Roger Bacon, John Duns Scotus, William of Ockham, and John Wycliffe. In the Renaissance, Desiderius Erasmus and St. Thomas More helped enhance its already considerable reputation. By then faculties of physical science, political science, and other fields had been added. The first women's college, Lady Margaret Hall, was established in 1878. There are 32 other colleges and collegial institutions. Oxford houses the Bodleian Library and the Ashmolean Museum of Art and Archaeology. Oxford University Press (1478) is the world's oldest, largest, and most famous university publisher. Oxford has been associated with many of the greatest names in British history. Current enrollment is about 16,000.

Oxford English Dictionary, The (OED) Definitive historical dictionary of the English language. It was conceived by London's Philological Society in 1857, and sustained editorial work began in 1879 under James Murray. Published in 10 volumes between 1884 and 1928, it first appeared under its current name in 1933. Its definitions are arranged mostly in order of historical occurrence and illustrated with dated quotations from English-language literature and records. Its second edition was published in 20 volumes in 1989.

Oxford movement *or* **Tractarian movement** (1833–45) Movement within the Church of England that aimed to emphasize the church's Catholic inheritance as a source of legitimacy and deeper spirituality. Its main intent was to defend the Church of England as a divine institution against the threats of liberal theology, rationalism, and government interference. Though some in the movement (notably John Henry Newman and Henry E. Manning) ended up converting to Catholicism, most did not. Their concern for a higher standard of worship influenced not only the Church of England but also other British Protestant sects. The movement was also instrumental in the establishment of Anglican monasteries and convents.

Oxfordshire \'äks-fərd-ˌshir\ County (pop., 1995 est.: 598,000), southern central England. It consists of two upland areas divided by a broad vale. Evidence of inhabitation dates from the Paleolithic, Mesolithic, and Neolithic eras. Dorchester was an important Roman settlement; subsequent Saxon settlement was concentrated along the Thames River valley. The county saw action during the English Civil Wars. The economy is basically agricultural, with sheep farming and wool production. Cowley, a suburb of the county seat of Oxford, is the major industrial center.

oxidation-reduction *or* **redox** Any chemical reaction in which electrons are transferred. Addition of hydrogen or electrons is reduction, and removal of hydrogen or electrons is oxidation (originally applied to combination with oxygen but now including transfer of hydrogen or electrons). The processes always occur simultaneously: one substance is oxidized by the other, which it reduces. The conditions of the substances before and after are called oxidation states, to which numbers are given and with which calculations can be made. (Valence is a similar but not identical concept.) The chemical equation that describes the electron transfer can be written as two separate half reactions that can in theory be carried out in separate compartments of an electrolytic cell (see electrolysis), with electrons flowing through a wire connecting the two. Strong oxidizing agents include fluorine, ozone, and oxygen itself; strong reducing agents include alkali metals such as sodium and lithium.

oxide Any chemical compound in which oxygen is combined with another element. Metal oxides contain the metal cation and the oxide anion (O_2^-); they typically react with water to form bases or with acids to form salts. Oxides of nonmetallic elements are volatile compounds in which a covalent bond joins the oxygen and the nonmetal; they react with water to form acids or with bases to form salts. A few substances (e.g., aluminum, zinc) form amphoteric oxides, which form salts with both acids and bases. Certain organic compounds form oxides in which the oxygen is covalently bonded to a nitrogen (amine oxides), phosphorus (phosphine oxides), or sulfur (sulfoxides) atom in the organic molecule.

oxide mineral Any naturally occurring inorganic compound with a structure based on close-packed oxygen atoms in which smaller, positively charged metal or other ions occur. Oxide minerals are common in all rock types, whether igneous, sedimentary, or metamorphic.

Oxus River See Amu Darya

oxygen Gaseous chemical element, chemical symbol O, atomic number 8. It constitutes 21% (by volume) of air and over 46% (by weight) of the earth's crust, where it is the most plentiful element. It is a colorless, odorless, tasteless gas, occurring as the diatomic molecule O_2. In respiration, it is taken up by animals and some bacteria (and by plants in the dark), which give off carbon dioxide (CO_2). In photosynthesis, green plants assimilate carbon dioxide in the presence of sunlight and give off oxygen. The small amount of oxygen that dissolves in water is essential for the respiration of fish and other aquatic life. Oxygen takes part in combustion and in corrosion but does not itself burn. It has valence 2 in compounds; the most important is water. It forms oxides and is part of many other molecules and functional groups, including nitrate, sulfate, phosphate, and carbonate; alcohols, aldehydes, carboxylic acids, and ketones; and peroxides. Obtained for industrial use by distillation of liquefied air, oxygen is used in steelmaking and other metallurgical processes and in the chemical industry. Medical uses include respiratory therapy, incubators, and inhaled anesthetics. Oxygen is part of all gas mixtures for spacecraft, scuba divers, workers in closed environments, or hyperbaric chambers. It is also the oxidizer in rocket engines and in water and waste treatment processes.

oxygen process, basic See basic oxygen process

Oxyrhynchus \ˌäk-si-ˈriŋ-kəs\ Archaeological site, Egypt, on the west-ern bank of the Nile River. Many ancient papyri dating from 250 BC to AD 700 were discovered here in the late 19th and early 20th century. The papyri, written mainly in Greek and Latin, contain both religious texts and masterpieces of Greek classical literature. Some of these texts, once considered lost, were by Pindar and Callimachus. The modern village of Al-Bahnasa is located on the site.

Oyo empire Yoruba state in present-day southwestern Nigeria that dominated the land between the Volta and Niger rivers 1650–1750. Two waves of immigrants probably entered the area c. AD 700–1000, the second wave forming a state at Oyo. Oyo became preeminent among Yoruba states because of its good trading position, natural resources, and industrious inhabitants. Though at first less powerful than its neighbors, by the end of the 16th century its ruler, Orompoto, had used trade-derived wealth to maintain a trained army. In the 18th century Oyo subjugated the Dahomey kingdom and had begun trading with European merchants at Dahomey's ports. Though its wealth increased, neglect of the army and of possibilities for territorial expansion by Abiodun (r.c. 1770–90) led to weakened central authority for his successor, and soon after 1800 Oyo was captured by Fulani Muslims from Hausaland. See also Hausa.

oyster Any bivalve of two families, Ostreidae (true oysters) or Aviculidae (pearl oysters), found in temperate and warm coastal waters worldwide. Both valves (halves) have a rough, often dirty-gray outer surface and a smooth white lining (nacre). The lower valve, which affixes to a surface, is flattish. The smaller upper valve is convex and has rougher edges. The oyster filters its food, minute organic particles, from the water. Oysters are cultivated as a food, which is regarded as a delicacy. Pearls are the accumulation of nacre around a piece of foreign matter.

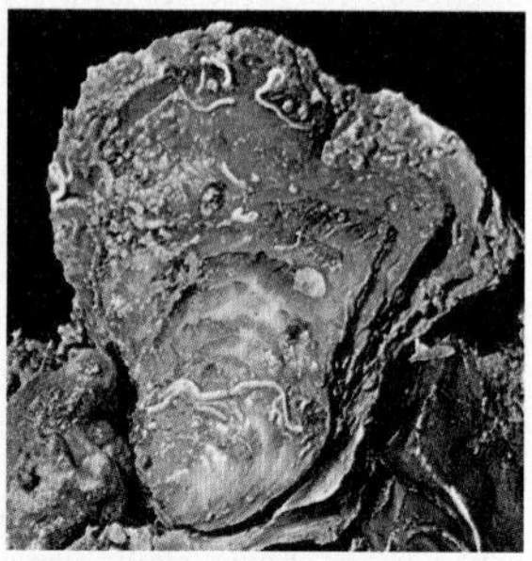

European flat oyster (*Ostrea edulis*).
G. TOMSICH—PHOTO RESEARCHERS

oyster plant See salsify

oystercatcher Any of about seven species (genus *Haematopus,* family Haematopodidae) of stout-bodied shorebirds inhabiting temperate and tropical seacoasts and inland waters in Europe, Asia, Africa, the Western Hemisphere, and Australia. Oystercatchers are 16–20 in. (40–50 cm) long, with thick pinkish legs; long pointed wings; and a long, flattened, wedge-shaped, orange-red bill. Their plumage varies from black-and-white, including a bold white wing patch, to entirely black. They attack mollusks as the tide ebbs, when the shells are exposed and still partially open.

Oz, Amos *orig.* **Amos Klausner** (born 1939) Israeli novelist, short-story writer, and essayist. A second-generation Israeli, Oz lived primarily on a kibbutz from the 1950s to the 1980s. He served in the Israeli Army (1957–60, 1967, and 1973) but later became a leading advocate of peace. His symbolic works—including *Where the Jackals Howl, and Other Stories* (1965); *My Michael* (1968), perhaps his best-known novel; and *Black Box* (1987)—reflect the conflicts in Israeli life.

Özal \ō-'zäl\, **Turgut** (1927–1993) Turkish prime minister (1983–89) and president (1989–93). After studying electrical engineering, he oversaw Turkey's electrification program in the 1950s and '60s. After working as a World Bank economist for most of the 1970s, he was elected prime minister as head of his own Motherland Party in 1983, and reelected in 1987. In 1989 he persuaded the parliament to make him president, a traditionally nonpolitical position, and used the office to claim for Turkey an important role in the Persian Gulf War.

Ozark Mountains *or* **Ozark Plateau** Heavily forested highlands, southern central U.S. Extending southwest from St. Louis to the Arkansas River, they occupy an area of about 50,000 sq mi (130,000 sq km) in Missouri, Arkansas, Illinois, and Kansas. Many of the highest peaks exceed 2,000 ft (600 m). Tourism is one of the region's chief industries. Lake of the Ozarks provides power and recreational facilities. The name Ozark probably derives from the French trading post, Aux Arc, established in the area in the 1700s.

Ozarks, Lake of the Lake, southern central Missouri. One of the largest man-made lakes in the U.S., it is located in the scenic Ozark Mtns. It is about 125 mi (200 km) long, with an area of 93 sq mi (242 sq km). It is formed by the Bagnell Dam in the Osage River. The area of Lake of the Ozarks State Park has recreational fishing and water sport facilities and is a popular resort destination. Nearby are several limestone caverns.

Ozawa \ō-'zä-wə\, **Seiji** (born 1935) Japanese-U.S. (Manchurian-born) conductor. After initial conducting experience in Japan, and study at Tanglewood, he went to Europe to study with H. v. Karajan. He became assistant to Leonard Bernstein at the New York Philharmonic (1961–65), then held posts in Toronto (1965–69) and San Francisco (1970–76) before becoming music director of the Boston Symphony Orchestra in 1973. He has also had a distinguished opera-conducting career in Europe.

Ozick \'ō-zik\, **Cynthia** (born 1928) U.S. novelist and short-story writer. Born in New York City, she graduated from NYU and received an MA from Ohio State University Jewish themes, and the notion that artistic creation can be a hubristic attempt to rival the Creator, are strong in Ozick's works, which include *Trust* (1966), *Leviathan* (1982), *The Messiah of Stockholm* (1987), *The Shawl* (1990), and *The Puttermesser Papers* (1997). Collections of her essays include *Metaphor and Memory* (1989) and *Fame and Folly* (1996).

Ozma, Project Attempt in 1960 to detect radio signals generated by hypothetical intelligent beings from planets of other stars. Frank D. Drake (born 1930), director of the search, named the project for the princess of L. Frank Baum's imaginary Oz. The search used a special receiver attached to a radio telescope at the U.S. National Radio Astronomy Observatory at Green Bank, W.V. Some 150 hours of occasional observation over four months detected no recognizable signals. See also Drake equation, SETI.

ozone Pale blue gas (O_3) that is irritating, explosive, and toxic. Like ordinary oxygen gas (O_2), it contains oxygen atoms, but the bonding of three atoms per molecule gives it distinctive properties. It is formed in electrical discharges, and accounts for the odor of the air after thunderstorms or near electrical equipment. Usually manufactured on the spot by passing an electric discharge through oxygen or air, it is used in water purification, deodorization, bleaching, and various chemical reactions that require a strong oxidizing agent (see oxidation-reduction). Small amounts that occur naturally in the ozone layer absorb ultraviolet (UV) radiation, which otherwise could severely damage living organisms. Ozone contributes to air pollution, ozone produced by auto emissions in the presence of sunlight being a deletrious component of smog, and also accelerates the deterioration of rubber.

ozone layer *or* **ozonosphere** Region in the upper atmosphere, about 6–30 mi (10–50 km) high, with significant concentrations of ozone, formed by the effect of solar ultraviolet (UV) radiation on oxygen and also present in trace quantities elsewhere in earth's atmosphere. Ozone strongly absorbs solar UV radiation, causing atmospheric temperature to climb to about 30°F (0°C) at the top of the layer, and preventing much of this radiation from reaching earth's surface, where it would injure many living things. Chlorofluorocarbons, or CFCs, and some other air pollutants that diffuse into the ozone layer destroy ozone. In the mid-1980s, scientists discovered that a "hole"—an area where the ozone is up to 50% thinner than normal—develops periodically in the ozone layer above Antarctica. This severe regional depletion, explained as a natural seasonal depletion, appears to have been exacerbated by the effects of CFCs, and may have led to an increase in skin cancer caused by UV exposure. Restrictions on the manufacture and use of CFCs and other ozone-destroying pollutants were imposed in 1978.

Ozu \'ō-zü\, **Yasujiro** (1903–1963) Japanese film director. He joined the Shochiku movie studio as a cameraman in 1923 and directed his first film three years later. He originated the genre known as *shomin-geki* ("common-people's drama"), which treated lower-middle-class Japanese family life, with such films as the silent comedies *I Graduated, But . . .* (1929) and *I Was Born, But . . .* (1932) and *The Toda Brother and His Sisters* (1941). His later films, noted for their detailed character portrayals, pictorial beauty, and quiet, contemplative mood, include *Late Spring* (1949), *Tokyo Story* (1953), *Early Spring* (1956), *Late Autumn* (1960), *The End of Summer* (1961), and *An Autumn Afternoon* (1962).

P-47 *or* **Thunderbolt** FIGHTER and fighter-bomber aircraft used by Allied air forces in World War II. A single-seat, single-engine monoplane, it was developed in the U.S. to meet the need for a high-speed long-range fighter. First flown in 1941, it carried eight .50-caliber machine guns, had a maximum bomb load of 2,500 lbs (1,100 kg), and could carry ten 5-in. (127-mm) rockets beneath its wings. It had a maximum speed of 440 mph (700 kph) and a ceiling of 40,000 ft (12,000 m). More P-47s (15,683) were built for the Allied air services than any other fighter.

P-51 *or* **Mustang** FIGHTER AIRCRAFT of World War II. A single seat, single-engine monoplane produced for Britain's RAF, it went into service in 1941 and later was adopted by the U.S. Army Air Force. The original P-51 had four .50-caliber and four .30-caliber machine guns and a camera for photoreconnaissance; its maximum speed was 390 mph (630 kph). The P-51D, a later model, had six .50-caliber machine guns and a maximum speed of 440 mph (700 kph). A superb long-range fighter, it played a significant part in defeating the German Luftwaffe.

***p-n* junction** Electric contact in TRANSISTORS and related devices between two different types of material called *p*-type and *n*-type SEMICONDUCTORS. These materials are pure semiconductor materials, such as SILICON, to which impurities have been added. Materials of *p*-type contain "holes" (vacancies formerly occupied by ELECTRONS) that behave like positively charged particles, whereas *n*-type materials contain free electrons. ELECTRIC CURRENT flows more easily across a *p-n* junction in one direction than in the other. If the positive pole of a battery is connected to the *p*-side of the junction, and the negative pole to the *n*-side, charge flows across the junction. If the battery is connected in the opposite direction, very little charge can flow. The *p-n* junction forms the basis for COMPUTER CHIPS, SOLAR CELLS, and other electronic devices.

Paar, Jack (born 1918) U.S. television talk-show host. Born in Canton, Ohio, he worked in radio in the late 1940s before hosting his first television show, *Up to Paar,* in 1952. As host of the late-night talk show *Tonight,* renamed *The Jack Paar Show* (1957–62), he established the now-standard format of celebrity interviews, monologues, and variety skits, and was noted for his witty conversation, high-strung mannerisms, and mercurial temper. He later hosted the weekly *Jack Paar Program* (1962–65).

Paasikivi \'pä-si-ki-vē\, **Juho Kusti** (1870–1956) Finnish statesman. He served in the Finnish parliament 1907–13, as minister of finance 1908–9, and as independent Finland's first prime minister in 1918. After World War I, he was prominent as a banker and businessman. As minister to Sweden (1936–39), he negotiated a treaty to end the RUSSO-FINNISH WAR (1940). After World War II, he served as Finland's prime minister (1944–46) and later president (1946–56). While accepting the necessity of friendly relations with the Soviet Union, he was uncompromising in his defense of Finnish independence and resisted the growth of communist influence in Finland.

Pabst \'päpst\, **G(eorg) W(ilhelm)** (1885–1967) Austrian film director. The son of a railroad official, he toured Europe as an actor from age 20 and was directing plays by 1912. He later directed films in Berlin, beginning with *The Treasure* (1923) and continuing with *The Joyless Street* (1925), *Secrets of a Soul* (1926), and *The Love of Jeanne Ney* (1927). His masterpieces, *Pandora's Box* (1929) and *Diary of a Lost Girl* (1929), both starred LOUISE BROOKS. Later films include *Kameradschaft* (1931) and *The Threepenny Opera* (1931). He moved to France in 1933, and to Austria after the war.

PAC See POLITICAL ACTION COMMITTEE

pacemaker Source of rhythmic electrical impulses that trigger HEART contractions. In the heart's electrical system, impulses generated at a natural pacemaker are conducted to the atria and ventricles. Heart surgery or certain diseases can interrupt conduction (heart block), requiring use of a temporary or permanent artificial pacemaker. A small electrode attached to an electric generator outside the body is threaded through a vein into the heart. The generator, inserted beneath the skin, produces regular pulses of electric charge to maintain the heartbeat. Permanent pacemakers can also be implanted on the heart's surface.

Pachacamac \pä-'chä-kä-ˌmäk\ Site of a pre-Incan city, southeast of LIMA, Peru. It has remains of a temple to the god Pachacamac, a later Incan Temple of the Sun, and the ruins of the surrounding city. The earlier temple and terraced adobe pyramid date from c. 200 BC to AD 600. The city was sacked by Spanish soldiers under FRANCISCO PIZARRO c. 1523 and is now occupied by the village of La Mamacoma.

Pachelbel \päk-'el-ˌbel, *Engl* 'pä-kəl-ˌbel\, **Johann** (1653–1706) German composer and organist. Conservative musically, he was friendly with DIETRICH BUXTEHUDE and was the teacher of Johann Christoph Bach (1671–1721), who later gave lessons to his younger brother J.S. BACH. Though he wrote a huge amount of music, of which his organ chorale variations and Magnificat settings are especially remarkable, he is principally known today for a single piece, the extremely popular *Canon in D Major*, which he may not have written.

Pacher \'päk-ər\, **Michael** (1435–1498) Austrian painter and sculptor. His colossal altarpiece for the Pilgrimage Church of St. Wolfgang in Upper Austria (1479–81) is a masterpiece of late Gothic painting, sculpture, and architecture. The painted panels, with their deep architectural perspective and dramatic foreshortening, indicate knowledge of MANTEGNA. The sculptural portions, with their intricate detail, bright polychrome, and sweeping draperies, show his attachment to northern traditions; and the architectural elements show an extravagant version of the late Gothic style. Pacher was one of the earliest artists to introduce the principles of Renaissance painting into German-speaking regions.

Pachuca (de Soto) City (pop., 1990: 179,000), capital of HIDALGO state, central Mexico. Founded in 1534, it was one of the first settlements in NEW SPAIN. It lies in a rich mining area in the Sierra Madre Oriental, 8,150 ft (2,484 m) above sea level. Its silver mines date from the 16th century, when the Mexican process of separating silver from the ore by amalgamation with mercury was perfected there. Industries include smelting works and metallic-ore reduction plants.

Pacific, War of the (1879–83) Conflict involving Chile, Bolivia, and Peru over disputed territory on the Pacific coast rich in mineral resources. National boundaries in the region were not definitively established, and in the 1870s Chile controlled nitrate fields located in Peru and Bolivia. As demand for nitrates rose, war broke out over the territory. Chile defeated both countries and took control of valuable mining areas in each. Bolivia lost its entire Pacific coast. A 1904 treaty gave Bolivian commerce freedom of transit through Chilean territory, but it continued to try to escape its landlocked status (see CHACO WAR). Peru foundered economically for decades after the war. A final accord between Peru and Chile was only reached in 1929 through U.S. mediation.

Pacific Coast Ranges See COAST RANGES

Pacific Islands, Trust Territory of the Former UNITED NATIONS trusteeship, administered by the U.S. 1947–86. It consisted of more than 2,000 islands scattered over about 3,000,000 sq mi (7,770,000 sq km) of the tropical western Pacific Ocean, north of the equator. It covered the region known as MICRONESIA and comprised three major island groups: the MARIANAS, the CAROLINES, and the MARSHALLS. The seat of government was SAIPAN in the NORTHERN MARIANA ISLANDS. In 1986 the U.S. declared the trust territory agreements no longer in effect. The Federated States of Micronesia and the Republic of the Marshall Islands thus became sovereign states and the Northern Mariana Islands became a commonwealth of the U.S. The Republic of PALAU became a sovereign state in 1994.

Pacific Ocean Body of salt water extending from the Antarctic region in the south to the Arctic circle in the north and lying between the continents of Asia and Australia on the west and North and South America on the east. It occupies about one-third of the surface of the earth and is by far the largest of the world's OCEANS. Its area, excluding adjacent seas, is approximately 63,800,000 sq mi (165,250,000 sq km), twice that of the ATLANTIC OCEAN and more than the whole land area of the globe. Its mean depth is 14,040 ft (4,280 m). The western Pacific is noted for its many peripheral seas.

Pacific Railway Acts (1862, 1864) Measures providing federal aid for construction of a U.S. transcontinental railroad. The first act granted rights of way to the UNION PACIFIC RAILROAD to build westward from Omaha, Neb., and to the Central Pacific Railroad to build eastward from Sacramento, Cal. The second act doubled the size of the land grants adjacent to the rights of way and allowed the railroads to sell bonds to raise more money. Congressional investigations later showed that some railroad owners had illegally profited from the railway acts (see CRÉDIT MOBILIER SCANDAL).

Pacific Security Treaty See ANZUS PACT

Pacification of Ghent See Pacification of GHENT

pacifism \'pa-sə-ˌfi-zəm\ Opposition to war and violence as a means of settling disputes. The tenets of BUDDHISM made it the first genuinely pacifist movement: the Buddhist king ASHOKA renounced war, though in other times and places Buddhist doctrines did not prevent rulers from waging war. The Greek conception of peace was an individual one, while the Pax Romana of the Roman empire did not apply to so-called barbarians. Aspects of Christianity supported pacifism, but by the Middle Ages the Christian peace, like the Pax Romana, was only for those within the fold. In the 17th–18th century, pacifist thought focused on the idea that transferring power from sovereigns to the people would result in peace, because, it was claimed, wars were a product of sovereigns' ambitions and pride. In the 19th–20th century, the pacifist theme led to interest in general disarmament and the founding of international organizations such as the LEAGUE OF NATIONS and the UNITED NATIONS. Pacifism on a national level has yet to satisfactorily address the problem of an aggressor that does not possess the same moral scruples. Personal pacifism may lead one to become a CONSCIENTIOUS OBJECTOR. LEO TOLSTOY, MOHANDAS K. GANDHI, and MARTIN LUTHER KING became well known for their pacifism.

Pacino \pə-'chē-nō\, **Al(fredo James)** (born 1940) U.S. actor. Born in New York City, he began his career as a stage actor, winning Tony awards for *Does a Tiger Wear a Necktie?* (1969) and later for *The Basic Training of Pavlo Hummel* (1977). He won the important film role of Michael Corleone in *The Godfather* (1972) and its sequels (1974, 1990), and also starred in such films as *Serpico* (1973), *Dog Day Afternoon* (1975), *And Justice for All* (1979), *Scarface* (1983), *Sea of Love* (1989), *Glengarry Glen Ross* (1992), *Scent of a Woman* (1992, Academy Award), *Devil's Advocate* (1997), and *The Insider* (1999), earning a reputation as one of the finest of all American actors.

pack ice Floating mass of ice formed from seawater in polar regions. Pack ice expands during winter to cover about 5% of the northern oceans and 8% of the southern oceans. When melting occurs in spring and summer, the margins of the pack ice retreat. The pack ice of the Northern Hemisphere covers an average area of about 4 million sq mi (10 million sq km), filling the Arctic Ocean basin and adjacent North Atlantic Ocean. About twice as much pack ice forms in the oceans surrounding Antarctica as in the Arctic. The maximum area of Antarctic pack ice is about 7.5 million sq mi (20 million sq km).

pack rat See WOOD RAT

Pact of Paris See KELLOGG-BRIAND PACT

Pact of Steel Alliance between Germany and Italy. Signed by ADOLF HITLER and BENITO MUSSOLINI on May 22, 1939, it formalized the 1936 ROME–BERLIN AXIS agreement, linking the two countries politically and militarily.

Packard, Alpheus Spring (1839–1905) U.S. entomologist. Born in Brunswick, Me., in 1867 he founded *American Naturalist*, and he served as its editor until 1887. He taught at Brown University 1878–1905. He described some 50 genera of insects and marine invertebrates; his books include *The Cave Fauna of North America* (1888), *The Labrador Coast* (1891), and *Textbook of Entomology* (1898).

paddle tennis Game like tennis that is played with a rectangular paddle and a slow-bouncing rubber ball on a small court. Frank P. Beal introduced it on New York playgrounds in the early 1920s. National championship tournaments are still held in the U.S. See also PLATFORM TENNIS.

paddlefish Either of two species (family Polyodontidae) of archaic freshwater fishes with a paddlelike snout, wide mouth, smooth skin, and cartilaginous skeleton. It feeds with mouth gaping open, gill rakers straining plankton from the water. The American paddlefish, or spoonbill *(Polyodon spathula)*, is greenish or gray and averages 40 lbs (18 kg); it lives in the open waters of the Mississippi basin. The other known species *(Psephurus gladius)*, a larger fish with a more slender snout, inhabits the Chang (Yangtze) River basin. The flesh of both species resembles CATFISH; the roe can be made into CAVIAR.

Paderewski \ˌpa-də-'ref-skē\, **Ignacy Jan** (1860–1941) Polish pianist, composer, and statesman. After teaching at the Warsaw Conservatory (1878–83), a period when he wrote most of the pieces he is remembered for (including the famous Minuet in G), he studied with T. LESCHETIZKY in Vienna from 1884. His U.S. debut at Carnegie Hall (1891) was followed by a 117-concert North American tour, during which his pianism and dashingly Romantic image brought him a wild popularity. During World War I he worked for Polish independence; in 1919 he served briefly as the first premier of the new state, representing it at the Paris Peace Conference.

Padre Island \'pä-drē, 'pä-drā\ Barrier island, southern Texas. It is 113 mi (182 km) long and up to 3 mi (5 km) wide, lying along the Gulf Coast of Texas. It extends south from CORPUS CHRISTI to Port Isabel and is separated from the mainland by Laguna Madre. It contains a recreational preserve with a large variety of birdlife, excellent fishing, and a broad beach.

Padua \'pa-dyü-wə\ *Italian* **Padova** \'pä-dō-vä\ *ancient* **Patavium** City (pop., 1991: 215,000), northern Italy. Legend holds that it was founded by the Trojan hero ANTENOR. First mentioned in 302 BC, it prospered as a Roman city and was under Lombard rule in the 7th–8th century. A leading Italian commune in the 11th–13th century, it passed to VENICE, which held it from 1405 to 1797. Under Austrian rule 1815–66, it was active in the RISORGIMENTO. It was heavily bombed in World War II, but was rebuilt. Its historic buildings contain works by many artists, including GIOTTO, TITIAN, DONATELLO, and MANTEGNA. The University of Padua (1222), the second-oldest in Italy, had GALILEO among its teachers and DANTE, PETRARCH, and TASSO among its students. Padua's botanical garden (1545) is the oldest in Europe. The city is now a commercial and industrial center.

Paekche \'pak-ˌchə\ One of three kingdoms into which Korea was divided before 660. It is traditionally said to have been founded in 18 BC by the legendary leader Onjo. In the 3rd century AD Paekche emerged as a fully developed kingdom, and by the 4th century it had extended its territory from the southwestern tip of the Korean peninsula to the whole Han River basin in central Korea. By then it was a centralized aristocratic state. Confucianism and Buddhism flourished, and Paekche's visual arts revealed technical maturity and warm human qualities. In the 5th century it was pushed back south by the northern Korean kingdom of KOGURYO, and in 660 it fell to an alliance of the southern Korean state of SILLA and the TANG-DYNASTY China.

Paeonia \pē-'ō-nē-ə\ Ancient land, in what is now northern Greece, Macedonia, and western Bulgaria. It originally included the whole Vardar River valley. The Paeonians were weakened by the Persian invasion of 490 BC, and the tribes living along the Strymon River fell under Thracian control. The growth of Macedonia forced the remaining tribes north, and they were defeated by PHILIP II in 358 BC. It became part of the Roman province of Macedonia, and by AD 400 the Paeonians had lost their identity.

Paestum \'pes-təm, 'pēs-təm\ Ancient city, southern Italy, on the Gulf of Salerno (the ancient Bay of Paestum). It was founded in the 6th century BC by Greek colonists from SYBARIS, who called it Poseidonia. It was taken by the Lucanians, an indigenous Italic people, in the 4th century BC. They ruled until 273 BC, when the city was captured by the Romans. Deserted after its sack by Muslim raiders in AD 871, the abandoned site's remains were discovered in the 18th century. It is known for its three Doric temples and its city walls of travertine blocks.

The Temple of Athena at Paestum.

ALINARI—ART RESOURCE

Pagan \pə-ˈgän\ Village, central Myanmar. Extending along the left bank of the Irrawaddy River, southwest of Mandalay, it was founded c. AD 849 and was the capital of a powerful dynasty from the 11th to the 13th century. It was conquered by the Mongols in 1287. As a center of Buddhist learning, it is a pilgrimage center and contains Buddhist shrines that have been restored and redecorated and are in current use. Ruins of other shrines and pagodas cover a wide area. An earthquake in 1975 severely damaged more than half of the important structures and irreparably destroyed many of them. The village also has a school for lacquerware, for which the region is noted.

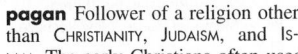

The Ananda temple, Pagan; its top portion, a restoration, was broken off in an earthquake in 1975.

VAN BUCHER—PHOTO RESEARCHERS

pagan Follower of a religion other than Christianity, Judaism, and Islam. The early Christians often used the term to refer to non-Christians who worshiped multiple deities. Christian missionaries frequently sought to stamp out pagan practices by building churches on the sites of pagan shrines or by associating Christian holidays with pagan rituals (e.g., linking Christmas with the celebration of the winter solstice). The term pagan was also used to refer to non-Christian philosophers.

Paganini \ˌpa-gə-ˈnē-nē\, **Niccolò** (1782–1840) Italian violinist and composer. A prodigy, he joined an orchestra by age 9. He toured Italy 1810–28, renowned as its greatest violin virtuoso in the world though dismissed by serious musicians as a showman. In the 1820s he underwent mercury treatment for syphilis, which left him looking romantically haggard. His long-deferred international tour (1830–34), by which time his expressiveness was equal to his technique, created frenzy, and some believed he had made a pact with the devil for his amazing talent. Paganini greatly extended violin technique; his numerous compositions include 24 *Caprices* for solo violin and six violin concertos.

Paganini, etching by Luigi Calamatta after a drawing by J.-A.-D. Ingres, 1818.

THE GRANGER COLLECTION, NEW YORK CITY

Page, Alan (Cedric) (born 1945) U.S. football player. Born in Canton, Ohio, he was an All-America defensive end for Notre Dame. Playing tackle for the Minnesota Vikings (1967–78), he became part of its legendary "Purple People Eaters" front line. In 1971 he became the first defensive player to win the NFL's Most Valuable Player award. He earned a law degree in 1978, and continued playing with the Chicago Bears (to 1981) while engaging in private practice. He earned a record for highest number of safeties and blocked kicks, and never missed a game in his 15-year career. In 1993 he was named to the Minnesota Supreme Court.

Page, Geraldine (1924–1987) U.S. actress. Born in Kirksville, Mo., she studied drama in Chicago and New York, and won fame on Broadway as Alma Winemiller in *Summer and Smoke* (1952; film, 1961). Noted for her portrayals of fragile and troubled women, she starred in such other plays as *The Rainmaker* (1954–55), *Separate Tables* (1957–58), *Strange Interlude* (1963), and *Agnes of God* (1982). Her films include *Hondo* (1953), *Sweet Bird of Youth* (1962), and *The Trip to Bountiful* (1985, Academy Award). She won Emmy awards for *A Christmas Memory* (1966) and *The Thanksgiving Visitor* (1968).

pageant \ˈpa-jənt\ Large-scale, spectacular theatrical production or procession. In the Middle Ages, a pageant was the wagon on which religious plays such as mystery plays were performed. Because the plays were associated with ceremony and spectacle, the term came to refer to any extravagant dramatic event or colorful celebration. Pageants often serve to express the shared identity of a community or religious group. Secular pageants include coronations and royal weddings; other modern examples are seen in Mardi Gras and other carnival processions.

Paget \ˈpa-jət\, **James** *later* **Sir James** (1814–1899) British surgeon and physiologist. In 1834 he discovered the parasite that causes trichinosis. He gave excellent descriptions of breast cancer, Paget's disease (an inflammatory cancerous condition around the nipple in elderly women), and Paget's disease of bone (1877). He was one of the first to recommend surgical removal of bone-marrow tumors instead of amputation of the limb.

Paget's disease of bone *or* **osteitis deformans** \ˌäs-tē-ˈī-təs\ Chronic disease of middle age named for James Paget, with locally disorganized bone destruction (in which bones soften, pooling of blood may lead to heart or circulatory trouble, and high blood calcium can lead to kidney stones or systemic calcium poisoning) alternating with disordered bone construction (with dense, brittle bones and deformity that can compress internal structures). The long bones, vertebrae, pelvis, and skull are most often affected, more often in men. The risk of cancer, usually osteosarcoma, is high. Calcitonin (which regulates bone growth) and bisphosphonates (which block excessive bone breakdown) are drugs of treatment.

Pago Pago \ˈpäŋ-ō-ˈpäŋ-ō, ˈpä-gō-ˈpä-gō\ Town (pop., 1990: 4,000), capital of American Samoa. Located on the southern shore of Tutuila Island, in the South Pacific Ocean, it was selected in 1872 as the site of a U.S. Navy coaling station. An active naval base until 1951, it is now a regular port of call. Its airport, opened in 1964, has stimulated tourist traffic and modernization.

pagoda Towerlike, multistoried structure of stone, brick, or wood, usually associated with a Buddhist temple complex and enshrining sacred relics. The pagoda evolved from the Indian stupa. The pagoda's crowning ornament is bottle-shaped in Tibet and pyramidal or conical in Myanmar, Thailand, Cambodia, and Laos. In China, Korea, and Japan, a pagoda is a tall tower repeating a basic story unit in diminishing proportions. The stories may be circular, square, or polygonal. The pagoda form is intended mainly as a monument and has very little usable interior space.

Pahang River \pä-ˈhaŋ\ River, Malaysia, the longest on the Malay Peninsula. Forming in the northwestern part of the state, it flows south and east to the China Sea. It is 285 mi (459 km) long and navigable by boats for most of its length. Deforestation in the river's basin has led to heavy flooding during the monsoon season.

Pahari painting \pə-ˈhä-rē\ *or* **Hill painting** Style of miniature painting and book illustration that developed in the independent states of the Himalayan foothills in India c. 1690–1790. Combining the bold intensity of the Basohli school with the delicacy and lyricism of the Kangra school, Pahari painting is closely related to Rajasthani painting. It shares with the Rajput art of the northern Indian plains a preference for depicting legends of the cowherd god Krishna.

Pahlavi \ˈpa-lə-ˌvē\, **Mohammad Reza Shah** (1919–1980) Shah of Iran (1941–79), noted for his pro-Western orientation and autocratic rule. After an education in Switzerland, he replaced his father, Reza Shah Pahlavi, as ruler when the latter was forced into exile. His rule was marked by a power struggle with his premier, Muhammad Mosaddeq, who almost succeeded in deposing him in 1953; intervention by British and U.S. intelligence returned him to the throne the next year. His program of rapid modernization and oil-field development initially brought him popular support, but his autocratic style and suppression of dissent, along with corruption and the unequal distribution of Iran's new oil wealth, led to increasing opposition, led by the exiled Ruhollah Khomeini. In 1979 he was forced into exile, where he died of cancer.

Pahlavi, Reza Shah (1878–1944) Shah of Iran (1926–41). Born to a family of chiefs of the Pahlevan clan, he rose through the army ranks and in 1921 led a coup that overthrew the Qajar dynasty in order to end Iran's political chaos and its domination by Britain and the Soviet Union following World War I. He constructed roads, schools, and hospitals, opened a university, and built the Trans-Iranian Railway. He emancipated women and banned the veil, nationalized several economic sectors, and reduced the clergy's power by repressive methods that eventually cost him his popularity. During World War II the U.S. and Britain occupied Iran to prevent an alliance with Germany, forcing him to abdicate in favor of his son, MOHAMMAD REZA SHAH PAHLAVI.

Pai River See BAI RIVER

Paige, Satchel *orig.* **Leroy Robert** (1906?–1982) U.S. baseball pitcher. Born in Mobile, Ala., he earned legendary fame during his many years in the NEGRO LEAGUES. He was 42 when he was finally allowed to enter the major leagues in 1948, shortly after JACKIE ROBINSON broke baseball's race barrier. Joining the Cleveland Indians, he helped that team win the World Series that year. He retired after six seasons. A right-handed, loose-jointed "beanpole" standing 6 ft 4 in. (1 m 93 cm), Paige had considerable pitching speed and a comprehensive mastery of slow-breaking deliveries. He is reputed to have won 2,000 of a total of 2,500 games pitched during his nearly 30-year career. Among his well-known rules for staying young is the admonition "Don't look back, something might be gaining on you."

Satchel Paige, 1942.

UPI

Paijanne \'pā-ˌya-ne\, **Lake** Lake, southern Finland. It is 75 mi (121 km) long and 14 mi (23 km) wide. The lake system is drained southward to the Gulf of Finland by the Kymi River. The irregular shoreline is heavily forested and supports important timber operations that use the lake for transport. It contains thousands of islands, numerous villages along the lakeshore, and many private villas off its southern end.

Paik \'pāk, 'pīk\, **Nam June** (born 1932) Korean-U.S. sculptor and video and performance artist. He studied music at the Univs. of Tokyo and Munich, and came to the U.S. in 1964. Inspired by JOSEPH BEUYS and J. CAGE, he joined the FLUXUS group. He is considered the father of video art. His sophisticated video displays, such as *TV Buddha* (1974), an installation with a Buddha contemplating himself on television, were seen as uniquely appropriate to the Information Age, in which fascination with electronic media has replaced spirituality as the focus of life.

pain Physical suffering associated with a bodily disorder (such as a disease or injury) and accompanied by mental or emotional distress. Pain, in its simplest form, is a warning mechanism that helps protect an organism by influencing it to withdraw from harmful stimuli (such as a pinprick). In its more complex form, such as in the case of a chronic condition accompanied by depression or anxiety, it can be difficult to isolate and treat. Pain receptors, found in the skin and other tissues, are nerve fibers that react to mechanical, thermal, and chemical stimuli. Pain impulses enter the spinal cord and are transmitted to the brain stem and thalamus. The perception of pain is highly variable among individuals; it is influenced by previous experiences, cultural attitudes (including gender stereotypes), and genetic makeup. Medication, rest, and emotional support are the standard treatments. The most potent pain-relieving drugs are OPIUM and MORPHINE, followed by less-addictive substances and non-narcotic ANALGESICS such as ASPIRIN and IBUPROFEN.

Paine, Robert Treat (1731–1814) American jurist. He practiced law in his native Boston from 1757 and gained recognition as a prosecuting attorney in the murder trial of the British soldiers involved in the BOSTON MASSACRE. He was a member of the Continental Congress and a signer of the DECLARATION OF INDEPENDENCE. He served as Massachusetts' first attorney general (1777–90) and as a judge in the state supreme court (1790–1804).

Paine, Thomas (1737–1809) British-American political philosopher. After an early life of failed prospects in England, he met BENJAMIN FRANKLIN, who advised him to emigrate to America. He arrived in Philadelphia in 1774 and helped edit the *Pennsylvania Magazine.* In January 1776 he wrote *Common Sense,* a 50-page pamphlet eloquently advocating independence; more than 500,000 copies were quickly sold, and it greatly strengthened the colonists' resolve. In the AMERICAN REVOLUTION he served as a volunteer aide to Gen. NATHANAEL GREENE and wrote the 16 *Crisis* papers (1776–83), each signed "Common Sense"; the first, beginning "These are the times that try men's souls," was read to the troops at Valley Forge on GEORGE WASHINGTON's order. Paine traveled to England in 1787 and became involved in debate over the French Revolution; his *The Rights of Man* (1791–92) defended the revolution and espoused republicanism; seen as an attack on the monarchy, it was banned and Paine was declared an outlaw in England. He went to France, where he was elected to the National Convention (1792–93). He criticized the REIGN of Terror and was soon imprisoned by MAXIMILIEN ROBESPIERRE (1793–94). After his release, he remained in Paris and wrote *The Age of Reason* (1794, 1796), a work on DEISM and an attack on organized religion. He returned to the U.S. in 1802; criticized for his Deist writings and little remembered for his service to the Revolution, he died in poverty.

Thomas Paine, detail of a portrait by John Wesley Jarvis; in the Thomas Paine Memorial House, New Rochelle, N.Y.

BY COURTESY OF THE THOMAS PAINE NATIONAL HISTORICAL ASSOCIATION

paint Decorative and protective coating commonly applied to rigid surfaces as a liquid consisting of a PIGMENT suspended in a vehicle, or binder. The vehicle, usually a RESIN dissolved in a SOLVENT, dries to a tough film, binding the pigment to the surface. Paint was used for pictorial and decorative purposes in the caves of France and Spain as early as 15,000 BC.

paintbrush See INDIAN PAINTBRUSH

Painted Desert Region, northern central Arizona. It stretches about 150 mi (240 km) from the GRAND CANYON to PETRIFIED FOREST NATIONAL PARK and has an area of about 7,500 sq mi (19,425 sq km). The name was first used in 1858 by a government explorer to describe the area's brilliantly colored rock surfaces, exposed by erosion. A large part of the desert lies within NAVAJO and HOPI Indian reservations. The Navajo tribes use the variegated sands for their ceremonial sand paintings.

painted lady Either of two species of BUTTERFLIES in the genus *Vanessa* (family Nymphalidae): *V. cardui* of Africa and Europe or *V. virginiensis* of North and Central America. They have broad, elaborately patterned wings of reddish orange, brown, white, and blue. In spring, vast numbers of *V. cardui* travel thousands of miles across the Mediterranean from Africa to Europe. A few members of the subsequent generation travel south in late summer, but most perish in the northern winter. North American painted ladies travel in spring from northwestern Mexico to the Mojave Desert and sometimes as far as Canada. Their larvae eat plants in the aster family; *V. cardui* larvae eat thistles and stinging nettles.

American painted lady (*Vanessa virginiensis*).

E.S. ROSS

painted turtle Species (*Chrysemys picta,* family Emydidae) of brightly marked North American TURTLE found from southern Canada to northern Mexico. It has a smooth shell, 4–7 in. (10–18 cm) long, with red and yellow markings on its relatively flat, black or greenish brown upper shell. It usually lives in quiet, shallow bodies of fresh water, especially those with thickly planted

Painted turtle (*Chrysemys picta*).

LEONARD LEE RUE III—THE NATIONAL AUDUBON SOCIETY COLLECTION/PHOTO RESEARCHERS mud bottoms, feeding on plants, small animals, and some carrion. It often basks in large groups on logs and other objects. In many areas it hibernates.

Painter, Theophilus Shickel (1889–1969) U.S. zoologist and cell biologist. Born in Salem, Va., he received his PhD from Yale in 1913. He was the first to identify individual genes in the chromosomes of drosophila. Painter realized that the unusually large cells of the salivary glands of drosophila were particularly well suited for studies of genes and chromosomes. In 1933 he published a drawing of a section of a drosophila chromosome showing more than 150 bands, which for the first time allowed the precise positions of genes to be determined.

painting Art consisting of representational, imaginative, or abstract designs produced by application of colored paints to a two-dimensional, prepared, flat surface. The elements of design (i.e., line, color, tone, texture) are used in various ways to produce sensations of volume, space, movement, and light. The range of media (e.g., tempera, FRESCO, oil, WATERCOLOR, ink, GOUACHE, encaustic, casein) and the choice of a particular form (e.g., MURAL, easel, panel, MINIATURE, ILLUMINATED MANUSCRIPT, SCROLL, screen, FAN) combine to realize a unique visual image. The early cultural traditions of tribes, religions, guilds, royal courts, and states controlled the craft, form, imagery, and subject matter of painting and determined its function (e.g., ritualistic, devotional, decorative). Painters were considered skilled artisans rather than creative artists until eventually, in the Far East and Renaissance Europe, the fine artist emerged with the social status of a scholar and courtier.

pair production Formation of an ELECTRON and a POSITRON from high-energy ELECTROMAGNETIC RADIATION traveling through matter, usually in the vicinity of an atomic NUCLEUS. It is a direct conversion of radiant energy into matter in accordance with the equation $E = mc^2$, where E is the amount of energy, m is the mass, and c is the speed of light. It is one of the principal ways in which high-energy GAMMA RAYS are absorbed in matter. The positrons quickly disappear by being reconverted into PHOTONS in the process of ANNIHILATION with other electrons. Pair production may sometimes refer to the formation of other particle/antiparticle pairs as well.

Paisiello \ˌpä-ē-zē-ˈye-lō\, **Giovanni** (1740–1816) Italian composer. Trained in Naples, he served CATHERINE II THE GREAT as chapel master in St. Petersburg (1776–84), writing many short operas. He enjoyed his first operatic success in Vienna in 1784, while returning to Naples to become dramatic composer to Ferdinand IV, and remained there despite changes in regime until 1815. He composed over 80 operas, including a very popular *Barber of Seville* (1782).

Paisley, Ian (Richard Kyle) (born 1926) Protestant leader in Northern Ireland. After being ordained in the Reformed Presbyterian church (1946), he cofounded a new sect, the Free Presbyterian Church of Ulster (1951), which soon grew to over 30 churches. In the 1960s he became the voice of extreme Protestant opinion in the sectarian strife of Northern Ireland, opposed to any concessions to the Catholics. He led demonstrations throughout Northern Ireland and was repeatedly imprisoned for unlawful assembly. Elected to the House of Commons in 1970, he cofounded the Democratic Unionist Party in 1971, and also organized a paramilitary group of Protestant fighters called the Third Force.

Paiute \ˈpī-ˌyüt\ Either of two distinct American Indian groups that speak languages of the Numic branch of the UTO-AZTECAN family. The Southern Paiute occupied southern Utah, northwestern Arizona, southern Nevada, and southwestern California. The Northern Paiute occupied eastern central California, western Nevada, and eastern Oregon. Both groups were primarily food collectors who subsisted on wild plant foods, supplemented by small game. They occupied temporary brush shelters, used rabbit-skin clothing, and made baskets for food gathering. They were organized in loosely knit BANDS. Most Paiute were directed onto reservations in the 19th century; today they number about 7,500. See also UTE.

Pakistan *officially* **Islamic Republic of Pakistan** Nation, southern Asia. Area: 307,374 sq mi (796,095 sq km). Population (1997 est.): 136,183,000. Capital: ISLAMABAD. The population is a complex mix of indigenous peoples that have been affected by successive waves of Aryans, Persians, Greeks, Pashtuns, Mughals, and Arabs. Languages: Urdu (official), Punjabi, Pashto, Sindhi, Balochi. Religions: Islam (official), Hinduism, Christianity. Currency: Pakistan rupee. Pakistan may be divided into four regions: the great highlands, the Baluchistan Plateau, the Indus Plain, and the desert areas. The Himalayan and Trans-Himalayan ranges form the great highlands, in the northernmost part of the country; some of the highest peaks are K2 and NANGA PARBAT. It has a developing mixed economy based largely on agriculture, light industries, and services. Unemployment is widespread and emigration has depleted the workforce; remittances from Pakistanis working abroad are a major source of foreign exchange. It is an Islamic republic with two legislative houses; its chief of state is the president, and the head of government is the prime minister. The area has been inhabited since c. 3500 BC. From the 3rd century BC to the 2nd century AD, it was part of the Mauryan and Kushan kingdoms. The first Muslim conquests were in the 8th century AD. The British EAST INDIA CO. subdued the reigning MUGHAL DYNASTY in 1757. During the period of British colonial rule, what is now (Muslim) Pakistan was part of (Hindu) India. The new state of Pakistan came into existence in 1947 by act of the British Parliament. Kashmir remained a disputed territory between Pakistan and India, resulting in military clashes and full-scale war in 1965. Civil war between East and West Pakistan in 1971 resulted in independence for Bangladesh (formerly East Pakistan) in 1972. Many Afghan refugees migrated to Pakistan during the Soviet–Afghan War in the 1980s. Pakistan elected BENAZIR BHUTTO, the first woman to head a modern Islamic state, in 1988. She was ousted in 1990 when her party was defeated by a conservative coalition. During the 1990s conditions were volatile. Border flare-ups with India continued and Pakistan conducted nuclear tests. Political conditions worsened and the army carried out a coup in 1999.

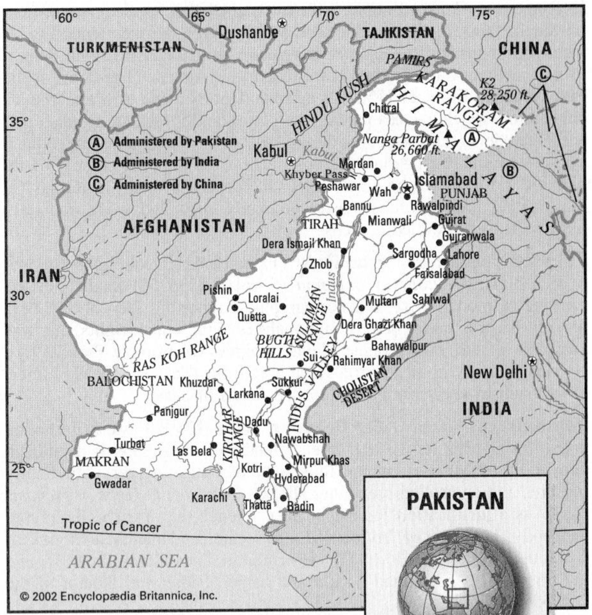

Pakula \pə-ˈkü-lə\, **Alan J.** (1928–1998) U.S. film producer and director. Born in New York City, he worked in Hollywood from 1949. He formed a production company with the director Robert Mulligan (born 1925) to produce *To Kill a Mockingbird* (1962) and other movies. His directorial debut, *The Sterile Cuckoo* (1969), was followed by such films as *Klute* (1971), *All the President's Men* (1976), *Sophie's Choice* (1982), *Presumed Innocent* (1990), and *The Pelican Brief* (1993).

Pala bronze See EASTERN INDIAN BRONZE

palace Royal residence, and sometimes a seat of government or religious center. The word derives from Rome's Palatine Hill, where the emperors built their residences. The earliest known palaces are those of the Egyptian kings at Thebes, with an outer wall enclosing a labyrinth of rooms and courtyards. Other ancient cultures also built vast palaces (e.g., the Assyrian palaces at Nimrud, Khorsabad, and Nineveh; the Minoan palace at Knossos; and the Persian palaces at Persepolis and Susa).

In Rome and Constantinople, palaces reached their peak as centers of power. In Western Europe after the Middle Ages, palaces tended to be single buildings. In Renaissance Italy every prince had his royal palace, usually with an internal court surrounded by an arcade. The court of the Pitti Palace in Florence (1560) is an important example of Mannerist architecture. French palaces include the LOUVRE and VERSAILLES; Spanish palaces include EL ESCORIAL and the ALHAMBRA. In contrast to the typical Western format, East Asia's palaces, such as the imperial palaces of Japan and those in Beijing's FORBIDDEN CITY, consist of many buildings (in these cases, low pavilions mostly of highly decorated wood construction) within vast, walled gardens.

Palacký \'pä-lats-kē\, **František** (1798–1876) Czech historian and politician. His *History of Bohemia* (5 vols., 1836–67) made him the founder of modern Czech historiography. Supporting the concept of a federal Austria composed of nationalities with equal rights, he was chairman of the 1848 Prague Slavic congress to promote PAN-SLAVISM. He was a deputy in the Austrian assembly from 1861. His ideas of liberal nationalism later strongly influenced TOMAS MASARYK.

Palamas \,pä-lä-'mäs\, **St. Gregory** (1296–1359) Eastern Orthodox priest. From 1332 he was the chief defender of the school of mysticism known as Hesychasm, which integrated repetitive prayer with bodily postures and controlled breathing. His *Apology for the Holy Hesychasts* (1338) is a justification for mystical experience that involves both soul and body; his *Book of Holiness* (1344) is the fundamental textbook of Byzantine mysticism. He was made bishop of Thessaloniki in 1347, and in 1368 he was acclaimed a saint and named Father and Doctor of the Orthodox Church.

palate \'pa-lət\ Roof of the MOUTH, separating the oral and nasal cavities. The front two-thirds, the hard palate, is a plate of bone covered by mucous membrane. It gives the tongue a surface against which to make speech sounds and shape food during chewing and keeps pressures in the mouth from closing off the nasal passage. The flexible soft palate behind it is made of muscle and connective tissue and ends in the uvula, a fleshy projection. It rises to block the nasal cavity (see NOSE) and upper PHARYNX off from the mouth and lower pharynx for swallowing or to create a vacuum for drinking. Cleft palate, a CONGENITAL DISORDER involving a gap in the palate, can be corrected surgically.

Palatinate \pə-'la-tᵊn-ət\ *German* **Pfalz** \'pfälts\ Historical region, now part of Germany. It was once under the jurisdiction of the counts palatine, who in the 14th century became ELECTORS of the HOLY ROMAN EMPIRE. In the 16th and 17th century it was a stronghold of Protestantism. It was divided into two parts: the Lower, or Rhenish, Palatinate, on both sides of the RHINE RIVER in the area south of the MAIN RIVER; and the Upper Palatinate, in northern Bavaria around Amberg and Regensburg. The capital of the Lower Palatinate was HEIDELBERG until the 18th century.

Palau \pə-'lau̇\ *or* **Belau** \bə-'lau̇\ *officially* **Republic of Palau** *formerly* **Pelew** Independent island republic, western Pacific Ocean. Area: 188 sq mi (487 sq km). Population (1997 est.): 17,000. Capital: KOROR. The population is of mixed Malay, Melanesian, Filipino, and Polynesian ancestry. Languages: Palauan, Sonsorolese-Tobian, English (all official). Religions: Roman Catholicism, Protestantism, Modekne. Currency: U.S. dollar. The islands of the Palau group are fertile, with mangrove swamps along the coasts, backed by savanna and palms rising to rain forests in the hills. The major source of employment is government service. Subsistence farming and fishing are the main occupations in the rural areas. It is a republic with two legislative houses; its head of state and government is the president. The islands were under nominal Spanish ownership for more than three centuries when they were sold to Germany in 1899. They were seized by Japan in 1914 and taken by Allied forces in 1944 during World War II. Palau became part of the U.S. Trust Territory of the PACIFIC ISLANDS in 1947 and became a sovereign state in 1994; the U.S. provides economic assistance and maintains a military presence in the islands.

Palawan \pä-'lä-wän\ Island, southwestern Philippines. It is long and narrow and extends northeast–southwest between the CHINA SEA and Sulu seas. It has a mountainous backbone that runs its entire length, with the highest peak at Mount Mantalingajan (6,839 ft, or 2,085 m). The capital is Puerto Princesa. Remnants of a PLEISTOCENE EPOCH land bridge that connected it to BORNEO explain the similarity of the two islands' vegetation. A coastal plain supports most of Palawan's population and is the main agricultural area. Scattered settlement and shifting agriculture predominate, with rice as the main food crop. Oil drilling off the northern coast began in 1992.

pale District separated from the surrounding country by defined boundaries or set apart by a distinctive administrative and legal system. In imperial Russia from the late 18th century, the Pale of Settlement was the area in which Jews were permitted to live. By the 19th century it included all of Russian Poland, Lithuania, Belarus, Crimea, Bessarabia, and most of Ukraine. It ceased to exist during World War I, when Jews in great numbers fled to the interior, and it was abolished in 1917. The English maintained a pale in Ireland until the entire island was subjugated under ELIZABETH I in the 16th century.

Palembang \,pä-lem-'bäŋ\ City (pop., 1995 est.: 1,352,000) and river port, Indonesia. It is located on both banks of the Musi River. It was the capital of a Buddhist kingdom 7th–14th century AD; then it was overthrown by the Hindu MAJAPAHIT EMPIRE. The Dutch EAST INDIA CO. established a trading post there and in 1659 built a fort. Occupied by the Japanese during World War II, it was the capital of the state of South Sumatra until it was included in the Republic of Indonesia in 1950. The port is accessible to ocean traffic and has considerable trade with ports on the MALAY PENINSULA and in Thailand and China.

Palenque \pä-'leŋ-kā\ Ruined ancient Mayan city of the Late Classic period (c. AD 600–900) in what is now Chiapas state, Mexico, considered the most beautiful of Mayan sites. The Palenque builders designed temple pyramids and palaces with mansard-style roofs and walls embellished with delicate stucco reliefs of rulers, gods, and ceremonies. The principal structure is the Palace, a labyrinth of galleries with interior courts and a four-story square tower. The great Temple of the Inscriptions is noted for its hieroglyphics and a vast funerary crypt, filled with jade, discovered in 1952.

Paleo-Siberian languages *or* **Paleo-Asiatic languages** \,pā-lē-ō\ Group of four unrelated language families spoken in northeastern Asia. Believed to have covered much larger areas of Siberia and perhaps Manchuria in the past, they have lost ground to URALIC and ALTAIC languages, and more recently to RUSSIAN (see SIBERIAN PEOPLES). Of the Yeniseian languages, the only survivors are Ket, spoken by fewer than 500 people, and the virtually extinct Yug (Yugh). The two extant Yukaghir languages, North or Tundra Yukaghir and South or Kolyma Yukaghir, together have fewer than 100 speakers. The Chukotko-Kamchatkan (Luoravetlan, Chukotian) family includes Chukchi, with about 10,000 speakers in extreme northeastern Siberia; Koryak, with fewer than 5,000 speakers south of Chukchi; and Itelmen, spoken on the Kamchatka Peninsula by fewer than 100 people. The two Nivkh (Gilyak) varieties, Amur Nivkh and Sakhalin Nivkh, together have fewer than 1,000 speakers.

Paleocene epoch *or* **Palaeocene epoch** \'pā-lē-ə-,sēn\ Earliest division of the TERTIARY PERIOD, from 65 to 54.8 million years ago. It precedes the EOCENE EPOCH and follows the CRETACEOUS PERIOD. The Paleocene was characterized by a generally warming climate, with little or no frost; seasonal variation probably consisted of alternating dry and wet seasons. By the Paleocene the dinosaurs and other reptilian groups that were dominant during the Cretaceous had disappeared, and the epoch saw the rapid proliferation and evolution of mammals.

paleoclimatology *or* **palaeoclimatology** Scientific study of the extended climatic conditions of past geologic ages. Paleoclimatologists seek to explain climate variations for all parts of the earth during any given geologic period, beginning with the time of the earth's formation. The basic research data are drawn mainly from geology and paleobotany; speculative attempts at explanation have come largely from astronomy, atmospheric physics, meteorology, and geophysics.

paleogeography *or* **palaeogeography** Geography of selected portions of the earth's surface at specific times in the geologic past. The simplest kind of paleogeography is a map showing the locations of ancient lands and seas, but paleogeographic maps may also show the occurrence and distribution of fossil, plant, and animal communities; environments of sedimentation (e.g., deltas, reefs, deserts, or deep-sea basins); areas undergoing uplift and erosion or subsidence and deposition; and major climatic zones.

paleogeology *or* **palaeogeology** Geology of a region at any given time in the distant past. Paleogeologic reconstructions in map form show not only the ancient topography of a region but also the distribution of rocks beneath the surface and such structural features as FAULTS

O P Q R

and FOLDS. Maps of this kind help investigators determine deformation events in a region, stream-drainage patterns now buried under layers of sediment, and the extent of ancient oceans and seas. They also provide a useful tool for petroleum geologists, enabling them to identify geologic structures where oil or natural gas may be trapped.

paleohydrology *or* **palaeohydrology** Scientific discipline concerned with hydrologic systems as they existed during previous periods of earth history. Changing hydrologic conditions are inferred from the evidence of the alteration, deposition, and erosion in rocks. Paleohydrology also deals with the changes in animals and plants through geologic time that have been greatly influenced by hydrologic change.

Paleolithic period \ˌpā-lē-ə-ˈli-thik\ ("Old Stone Age") Ancient technological or cultural stage characterized by the use of rudimentary chipped stone tools. During the Lower Paleolithic (c. 2.5 million–200,000 years ago), simple pebble tools and crude stone choppers were made by the earliest human ancestors. About 700,000 years ago, the first rough hand ax appeared, later refined and used with other tools in the ACHEULIAN INDUSTRY. A flake-tool tradition emerged in the Middle Paleolithic, as exemplified by implements of the MOUSTERIAN INDUSTRY. The Upper Paleolithic (40,000–10,000 BC) saw the emergence of more complex, specialized, and diverse regional stone-tool industries, such as the AURIGNACIAN, SOLUTREAN, and MAGDALENIAN. The two principal forms of Paleolithic art are small sculptures, such as the so-called Venus figurines and various carved or shaped animal and other figures, and monumental paintings, incised designs, and reliefs on the walls of caves such as ALTAMIRA and LASCAUX. The end of the Paleolithic is marked by the emergence of the settled agricultural villages of the NEOLITHIC PERIOD.

paleomagnetism *or* **palaeomagnetism** *or* **remanent magnetism** Permanent magnetism in rocks, resulting from the orientation of the earth's magnetic field at the time of rock formation in a past geologic age. It is a source of information for the paleomagnetic studies of POLAR WANDERING and PLATE TECTONICS.

paleontology *or* **palaeontology** Scientific study of life of the geologic past, involving analysis of plant and animal fossils preserved in rocks. It is concerned with all aspects of the biology of ancient life forms: their shape and structure, evolutionary patterns, taxonomic relationships with each other and with modern species, geographic distribution, and interrelationships with the environment. Paleontology has played a key role in reconstructing the earth's history and has provided evidence to support the theory of evolution. Data from paleontologic studies have also aided petroleum geologists in locating deposits of oil and natural gas, which are frequently associated with the remains of certain ancient life forms.

Paleozoic era *or* **Palaeozoic era** \ˌpā-lē-ə-ˈzō-ik\ Major interval of geologic time, c. 543–248 million years ago. From the Greek for "ancient life," it is the first era of the PHANEROZOIC EON and is followed by the MESOZOIC ERA. It is divided into six periods: (from oldest to youngest) the CAMBRIAN, ORDOVICIAN, SILURIAN, DEVONIAN, CARBONIFEROUS, and PERMIAN. During the early Paleozoic, much of North America was covered by a warm, shallow sea with many coral reefs. Fossils from this time include marine invertebrates and primitive fish; the plants were predominantly algae, with some mosses and ferns. During the late Paleozoic, huge, swampy forest regions covered much of the northern continents. Plant and animal life flourished. Amphibians left the oceans to live on land, reptiles evolved as fully terrestrial life forms, and insect life began. Ferns grew to tree size, and precursors of the conifers appeared.

Palermo *ancient* **Panormus** City (metro. area pop., 2000 est.: 683,794), seaport, and capital of SICILY, on the Bay of Palermo. Founded by Phoenician traders in the 8th century BC, it was later a Carthaginian settlement. It was taken by the Romans in 254 BC. Conquered by the Arabs in 831, it flourished as a center of trade with North Africa. The period of Norman rule was its golden age, when it became the capital of the Norman kingdom of Sicily founded by King ROGER II in 1130. In 1194 Germany's Hohenstaufen ruler, FREDERICK II took over. In 1282 a popular uprising known as the SICILIAN VESPERS ended the subsequent French rule. It was taken by Italian patriot GIUSEPPE DE GARIBALDI in 1860 and made part of the kingdom of Italy. Heavily bombed during World War II, it was captured by Allied forces in 1943. Notable buildings from the Norman and later periods include the cathedral that contains the tombs of Roger II and Frederick II. It is Sicily's chief port, and ship repair is an important industry.

Palestine *biblical* **Canaan** Region, at the eastern end of the MEDITERRANEAN SEA. It extends east to the JORDAN RIVER, north to the border between Israel and Lebanon, west to the Mediterranean, and south to the NEGEV desert, reaching the Gulf of AQABA. The political status and geographical area designated by the term have changed considerably over the course of some three millennia. The eastern boundary has been particularly fluid, often understood as lying east of the Jordan and extending at times to the edge of the ARABIAN DESERT. A land of sharp contrasts, it includes the DEAD SEA and mountain peaks more than 2,000 ft (610 m) above sea level. In the 20th century it has been the object of conflicting claims by Jewish and Arab national movements. The region is sacred to Judaism, Christianity, and Islam. Settled since early prehistoric times, mainly by Semitic groups, it was occupied in biblical times by the kingdoms of Israel, JUDAH, and JUDAEA. It was subsequently held by virtually every power of the Middle East, including the Assyrians, Persians, Romans, Byzantines, Crusaders, and Ottoman Turks. It was governed by Britain under a U.N. mandate from the end of World War I until 1948, when the State of Israel was proclaimed. Armies from Egypt, Transjordan, Syria, and Iraq attacked the next day. They were defeated by the Israeli army. See ISRAEL, JORDAN, WEST BANK, and GAZA STRIP for the later history of the region.

Palestine Liberation Organization (PLO) *Arabic* **Munazzamat al-Tahrir al-Filastiniyyah** Umbrella political organization representing the Palestinian people in their drive for a Palestinian state. It was formed in 1964 to centralize the leadership of various groups. After the SIX-DAY WAR of 1967, the PLO promoted a distinctively Palestinian agenda. In 1969 YASIR ARAFAT, leader of FATAH, the PLO's largest faction, became its chairman. From the late 1960s the PLO engaged in GUERRILLA attacks on ISRAEL from bases in Jordan; in 1971 King HUSSEIN expelled them, and PLO headquarters moved to Lebanon. In 1974 Arafat advocated limiting PLO activity to direct attacks against Israel, and the Arab community recognized the PLO as the sole legitimate representative of all Palestinians. It was admitted to the ARAB LEAGUE in 1976. In 1982 Israel invaded Lebanon and expelled PLO forces based there. In 1988 the PLO leadership, then based in Tunis, declared a Palestinian state and the following year elected Arafat its president. It also recognized Israel's right to exist, though several militant factions dissented. In 1993 Israel recognized the PLO by signing an agreement with it granting Palestinian self rule in parts of the WEST BANK and GAZA STRIP. The PLO became an integral part of the Palestinian National Authority. See also PALESTINE, LEBANESE CIVIL WAR, HAMAS, and INTIFADA.

Palestinian Talmud See TALMUD

Palestrina See PRAENESTE

Palestrina \ˌpa-lə-ˈstrē-nə\, **Giovanni Pierluigi da** (1526?–1594) Italian composer. He sang in Rome as a choirboy, then worked as an organist in his nearby hometown of Palestrina. He was appointed director of the Vatican's Cappella Giulia by Pope Julius II in 1551, and later worked at the other great Roman churches. When the Council of TRENT dictated a musical style that permitted the words to be readily understood, a legend grew up that Palestrina's *Pope Marcellus Mass*, written in the simpler style, had actually saved church polyphony from being banned altogether by the council. He later worked for the d'Este family in Tivoli, but returned to the Cappella Giulia in 1571 and remained there the rest of his life. He wrote 104 masses, almost 400 motets, and at least 140 madrigals. After his death, his superbly balanced and serene music was proclaimed as a model for composers in the Roman Catholic church. The modern study of counterpoint dates from the codification of his practice in the 18th century.

Paley, Grace *orig.* **Grace Goodside** (born 1922) U.S. short-story writer and poet. Born in New York City in the Jewish Bronx, whose accents are vividly reproduced in her fiction, Paley was active in the opposition to the Vietnam War in the 1960s and continued her political activism after the war ended. Her stories, compassionate and often comic explorations of family and neighborhood life and of individuals struggling against loneliness, are collected in *The Little Disturbances of Man* (1959), *Enormous Changes at the Last Minute* (1974), and *Later the Same Day* (1985). Her poetry appears in *Leaning Forward* (1985) and *Begin Again* (1992).

Paley, William S(amuel) (1901–1990) U.S. broadcaster. Born in Chicago, he worked in his family's cigar business from 1922. His success at increasing sales through radio advertisements sparked his interest in the medium. He invested in a small radio network, Columbia Phonographic Broadcasting System, becoming its president in 1928 and rapidly adding member stations. He built CBS into one of the world's leading radio and television networks, serving as president 1928–46 and chairman of the board 1946–90. He launched CBS News in 1933 and built its outstanding staff, and he hired top entertainment stars for its other radio and television shows.

Palgrave, Francis Turner (1824–1897) English critic and poet. He spent many years in the civil service's education department and taught poetry at Oxford. His *Golden Treasury of English Songs and Lyrics* (1861), a comprehensive, well-chosen, and carefully arranged lyric anthology, influenced the poetic taste of several generations and was important in popularizing the works of WILLIAM WORDSWORTH.

Pali canon See TRIPITAKA

Pali language \'pä-lē\ Middle INDO-ARYAN LANGUAGE of the 5th century BC in which the most essential documents of THERAVADA Buddhism are written. Linguistically, Pali is a homogenization of the northern Middle Indo-Aryan dialects in which the BUDDHA's teachings were orally recorded and transmitted. According to the tradition of Sri Lankan chronicles, the Theravada canon was first written down in the 1st century BC, though its oral transmission continued long afterward. No single script was ever developed for Pali; scribes used scripts of their own languages to copy canonical texts and commentaries (see INDIC WRITING SYSTEMS), and most extant palm-leaf manuscripts of Pali are of relatively recent date.

Palikir \ˌpä-lē-'kir\ Capital of the Federated States of MICRONESIA. It is located on the island of Pohnpei (formerly Ponape, pop., 1994: 32,000). Nearby is Kolonia (pop., 1994: 7,000), one of the Micronesian states' larger towns.

Palissy \på-lē-'sē\, **Bernard** (1510–1590) French potter and writer. Known for his decorated rustic ware, a type of EARTHENWARE covered with colored lead glazes, he was appointed "inventor of rustic pottery to the king and the queen mother" in 1565. His public lectures on natural history, published in 1580, revealed him to be a writer and scientist, and a pioneer of the scientific method. A Huguenot, he was imprisoned in 1588 in the Bastille, where he died.

Palladio \pä-'läd-yō\, **Andrea** *orig.* **Andrea di Pietro della Gondola** (1508–1580) Italian architect. While a young mason, he was noticed by an Italian scholar and soon found himself studying mathematics, music, philosophy, and classical authors. From 1541 he made several trips to Rome to study ancient ruins. His first palace design, the Palazzo Civena (1540–46), was innovative for its use of an arcaded area behind the main elevation, in imitation of a Roman forum. In his villas, Palladio tried to recreate the Roman villa based on ancient descriptions. His first, Villa Godi at Lonedo (c. 1540–42), contained elements for which he is famous, including symmetrical wings and a walled court. His most widely copied villa was the Villa Rotonda (1550–51), near Vicenza. His reconstruction of the Basilica (town hall) in Vicenza (begun 1549) employs a two-story arcade with a motif that came to be known as Palladian: rounded arches flanked by rectangular openings. His facades for San Francesco della Vigna (c. 1565), San Giorgio Maggiore (begun 1566), and Il Redentore (begun 1576), all in Venice, became prototypes for attaching classical temple fronts to basilican churches. Palladio was the first to systematize the plan of a house and to use the ancient Greco-Roman temple front as a portico. His *Four Books of Architecture* was possibly the most influential architectural pattern book ever printed. His influence climaxed during the 18th-century Classical Revival; the resulting Palladianism spread through Europe and the U.S.

palm Any of about 2,800 species of flowering, subtropical trees, shrubs, and vines that make up the family Arecaceae (or Palmae). Many are economically important. Palms furnish food, shelter, clothing, timber, fuel, building materials, fibers, starch, oils, waxes, and wines for local populations in the tropics. Many species have very limited ranges; some grow only on single islands. Their fast growth and many by-products make exploitation of the rain forest appealing to agribusiness. The usually tall, unbranched, columnar trunk is crowned by a tuft of large, pleated, fan- or feather-shaped leaves, with often prickly petioles (leafstalks), the bases of which remain after leaves drop, often clothing the trunk. Trunk height and diameter, leaf length, and seed size vary greatly. Small flowers are produced in large clusters. Among the most important palms are the sugar palm *(Arenga pinnata,* or *saccharifera),* COCONUT PALM, DATE PALM, and cabbage PALMETTO.

palm PC Computer small enough to fit in a person's palm. Palm PCs (also called palmtops, handheld computers, or personal data assistants) typically use pens instead of keyboards for data input. They have limited memory and lack built-in peripheral devices (e.g., disk drives and modems), though such devices can be plugged in through peripheral slots. They run a limited set of application programs, such as calendars, address books, and memo pads.

Palm Springs Resort city (population 1995 est.: 43,000), southern California. It is located in the COACHELLA VALLEY. Originally known as Agua Caliente for its hot springs, it was a stagecoach stop by 1872. In 1884 John G. McCallum established the Palm Valley Colony there. Incorporated as a city in 1938, it developed into a glamorous desert resort and residential area, frequented by celebrities, including Hollywood stars. Nearby is JOSHUA TREE NATIONAL MONUMENT.

Palm Sunday *or* **Passion Sunday** In Christianity, the first day of Holy Week and the Sunday before EASTER, commemorating JESUS' triumphal entry into Jerusalem. It usually includes a procession of members of the congregation carrying palms, representing the palm branches the crowd scattered in front of Jesus as he rode into the city. The liturgy also includes readings recounting the suffering and death of Jesus. Palm Sunday was celebrated in Jerusalem as early as the 4th century and in the West by the 8th century.

Palma (de Mallorca) City (pop., 1995 est.: 318,000), capital of the BALEARIC ISLANDS and of MAJORCA island, Spain, in the western Mediterranean Sea. It lies on the southwestern coast of Majorca on Palma Bay. Romans conquered Majorca in 123 BC, and it was later ruled by Byzantines and Arabs before being taken by JAMES I of Aragon in 1229. The city's old sections have many notable homes built in the 16th and 18th century. Historic buildings include the Gothic cathedral and Bellver Castle. The economy is varied, and includes tourism and light manufacturing.

Palma, Arturo Alessandri See Arturo ALESSANDRI PALMA

Palmas, Las See LAS PALMAS

Palme \'päl-mə\, **(Sven) Olof (Joachim)** (1927–1986) Swedish prime minister (1969–76, 1982–86). After studying in Sweden and the U.S., he was elected to the Swedish parliament (1958) and became a leader of the Swedish Social Democratic Workers' Party. He served in ministerial posts from 1963 and became prime minister in 1969. A strong pacifist, he attacked U.S. policy in the Vietnam War and later acted as a U.N. special envoy to mediate in the Iran–Iraq War. After his reelection in 1982, he tried to reinstate socialist economic policies in Sweden. He was shot to death by an assassin in 1986; his murder remains unsolved.

Palmer, A(lexander) Mitchell (1872–1936) U.S. politician. Born in Moosehead, Pa., he served in the U.S. House of Representatives (1909–15) and helped secure the Democratic nomination for WOODROW WILSON in 1912. Appointed U.S. attorney general (1919–21), Palmer used the espionage and sedition acts (1917, 1918) to attack political radicals, dissidents, and aliens in the "Red Scare" period after World War I. The government-led roundup of suspected communists became known as the "Palmer raids."

Arnold Palmer, 1984.
ARNOLD PALMER ENTERPRISES

Palmer, Arnold (Daniel) (born 1929) U.S. golfer. Born in Youngstown, Ohio, the son of a greenskeeper, he turned professional in 1954 after winning the U.S. Amateur championship. He was the first player to win the MASTER'S TOURNA-

O P Q R

MENT four times (1958, 1960, 1962, 1964); his other major titles include the U.S. Open (1960) and the British Open (1961–62). From 1954 (when he turned professional) through 1975, he won 61 tournaments. He won the PGA Senior Open in 1980 and 1981. He was the first golfer to earn $1 million in tournament prize money. His exciting play and amiable personality won him wide popularity among fans who became known as "Arnie's Army."

Palmer, Samuel (1805–1881) British painter and etcher. He began exhibiting conventional landscapes at the Royal Academy by 14. After converting to a personal form of High Anglicanism and discovering medieval art, he developed a visionary style, displaying a mystical but precise depiction of nature and an overflowing religious intensity, united by a vivid re-creation of the pastoral conventions. In these works he was encouraged and influenced by WILLIAM BLAKE. As his religious fervor faded after 1830, the precarious balance between realism and vision was lost.

Palmerston (of Palmerston), Viscount *orig.* **Henry John Temple** *known as* **Lord Palmerston** (1784–1865) English politician and prime minister (1855–58, 1859–65). He entered Parliament in 1807 as a Tory and served as secretary for war (1809–28). Associated with the Whig Party from 1830, he served many years as foreign secretary (1830–34, 1835–41, 1846–51) and supported British interests and liberal causes abroad. He played a key role in establishing the independence of Belgium (1830–31) and Greece (1832) and secured Turkey's integrity against France (1840). Appointed prime minister in 1855, he brought an end to the Crimean War, approved the creation of the independent kingdom of Italy, and supported a policy of neutrality in the American Civil War. Nicknamed "Pam," he was a symbol of British nationalism and one of Britain's most popular leaders.

palmetto \pal-'me-tō\ *or* **cabbage palmetto** Tree *(Sabal palmetto)* of the PALM family, occurring in the southeastern U.S. and the West Indies. Commonly grown for shade and as ornamentals along avenues, palmettos grow to about 80 ft (24 m) tall and have fan-shaped leaves. The water-resistant trunk is used as wharf piling. Mats and baskets are sometimes made from the leaves, and stiff brushes are made from the stems. The buds are edible. *S. texana,* a similar species, occurs in the southwestern U.S. and in Mexico.

palmistry Reading of an individual's character and DIVINATION of the future by interpreting lines on the palm of the hand. Palmistry may have originated in ancient India, and it was probably from their original Indian home that the traditional fortune-telling of the GYPSIES was derived. It was also practiced in China, Tibet, Persia, Mesopotamia, Egypt, and ancient Greece. In medieval Europe it was used to discover witches, who were thought to have pigmentation spots as signs of a pact with the devil. Though palmistry is still practiced, there is no known scientific basis for it.

Palmyra \pal-'mī-rə\ *biblical* **Tadmor** Ancient city, Syria, northeast of DAMASCUS, at the modern city of Tadmur. Said to have been built by King SOLOMON, it became prominent in the 3rd century BC, when the SELEUCIDS made the road through Palmyra one of the routes of east–west trade. Under Roman control by the reign of TIBERIUS, it briefly regained autonomy in the 3rd century AD under the Arab queen ZENOBIA. The main military station on the road that linked Damascus to the EUPHRATES RIVER, it was conquered by the Muslims in 634. Inscriptions in the ARAMAIC LANGUAGE supply knowledge of the city's trade with India via the Persian Gulf and with Egypt, Rome, and Syria. Ancient ruins reveal the city's plan.

Temple of Bel, Palmyra, Syria.
H. ROGER-VIOLLET

Palomar Observatory Astronomical OBSERVATORY on Mount Palomar, near San Diego, Cal., site of the famous Hale TELESCOPE, a reflecting telescope with a 200-in. (5-m) aperture that has proved instrumental in cosmological research. Built in 1948 and named in honor of George Ellery Hale (1868–1938), it was the largest instrument of its kind until 1976, when a Soviet telescope became the largest (now also superseded). Founded in 1948 by Caltech, the observatory was operated jointly with the MOUNT WILSON OBSERVATORY as the Hale Observatories until 1980.

palomino \ˌpa-lə-'mē-nō\ Color type of HORSE, cream, yellow, or gold with a white or silver mane. It is popular in pleasure and parade classes. Palominos may conform to the breed types of several light breeds, including the ARABIAN HORSE and the American QUARTER HORSE.

palsy See CEREBRAL PALSY, PARALYSIS

Pamirs \pə-'mirz\ High altitude region, central Asia, mostly in Tajikistan. It is partly on the borders of XINJIANG UYGUR, China; JAMMU AND KASHMIR, India; and Afghanistan. The range contains many peaks that are more than 20,000 ft (6,100 m) high and many glaciers. COMMUNISM PEAK rises in the northwest. It is sparsely populated, and almost all the inhabitants are Tajiks. It is a central mountain knot from which extend several great ranges, including the KARAKORAMS and HINDU KUSH.

Pamlico Sound \'pam-li-ˌkō\ Shallow body of water, eastern shore of North Carolina. It is separated from the Atlantic Ocean by the OUTER BANKS. It extends 80 mi (130 km) south from ROANOKE ISLAND and is 8–30 mi (13–48 km) wide. Numerous waterfowl nest along the coastal waters; there is some commercial fishing, especially for oysters.

Pampas Vast, grass-covered plain extending west from the Atlantic coast to the Andean foothills, primarily in Argentina. The Argentine pampas covers 295,000 sq mi (760,00 sq km) and slopes gradually downward from northwest to southeast. The western portion is dry and largely barren; the humid eastern portion is the nation's economic heart. Herds of wild cattle and horses, introduced by the Spaniards and rounded up by Argentina's famed GAUCHOS, roamed the pampas until the later 19th century, when the land was fenced into huge *estancias* (ranches). The region is prominent in Argentina's gaucho literature and musical folklore.

pamphlet Unbound printed publication with a paper cover or no cover. Among the first printed materials, pamphlets were widely used in England, France, and Germany from the early 16th century, often for religious or political propaganda; they sometimes rose to the level of literature or philosophical discourse. In North America, pre-Revolutionary War agitation stimulated extensive pamphleteering; foremost among the writers of political pamphlets was THOMAS PAINE. By the 20th century, the pamphlet was more often used for information than for controversy.

Pamplona *ancient* **Pompaelo** City (pop., 1991 est.: 182,000), capital of NAVARRA, northern Spain. According to tradition, it was founded in 75 BC by POMPEY THE GREAT as a military settlement. It was almost derelict after Moorish and Frankish invasions in the 5th century AD. It was captured from the Moors by CHARLEMAGNE in 778 and became the capital of the kingdom of NAVARRE under SANCHO III. The citadel built by King PHILIP II of Spain in 1571 made it the most strongly fortified town of the north. In 1841 it became the capital of the new Navarra province. The chief tourist attraction is the Fiesta de San Fermín, honoring its first bishop, which is celebrated with bullfights and the running of the bulls through the city streets. The fiesta is described in ERNEST HEMINGWAY'S *The Sun Also Rises.*

Pan Greek fertility deity with a half-human, half-animal form. The Romans associated him with FAUNUS. Pan was usually said to be the son of HERMES. He was often represented as a vigorous and lustful figure with the horns, legs, and ears of a goat; in later art his human parts were more emphasized. Some Christian depictions of the devil bear a striking resemblance to Pan. Pan haunted the high hills, where he was chiefly concerned with flocks and herds. Like a shepherd, Pan was a piper, and he rested at noon. He could inspire irrational terror in humans, and the word *panic* comes from his name.

pan See PLAYA

Pan-African movement Movement dedicated to establishing independence for African nations and cultivating unity among black people throughout the world. It originated in conferences held in London (1900, 1919, 1921, 1923) and other cities. W. E. B. DU BOIS was a principal early leader. The important sixth Pan-African conference (Manchester, 1945) included JOMO KENYATTA and KWAME NKRUMAH. The first truly intergovernmental conference was held in Accra, Ghana, in 1958, where PATRICE LUMUMBA was a key speaker. The Pan-Africanist Congress (PAC) was founded by ROBERT M. SOBUKWE and others in South Africa in 1959 as a political alternative to the AFRICAN NATIONAL CON-

GRESS, which was seen as contaminated by non-African influences. The founding of the ORGANIZATION OF AFRICAN UNITY (OAU) by JULIUS NYERERE and others in 1963 was a milestone, and the OAU soon became the most important Pan-Africanist organization.

Pan American (Sports) Games Quadrennial sports event for the nations of the Western Hemisphere, patterned after the Olympic Games and sanctioned by the International Olympic Committee. The games, conceived in 1940 but first held in 1951, are conducted by the Pan American Sports Organization (PASO), or Organización Deportiva Panamericana (ODEPA), headquartered in Mexico City. All major international sports and several more specialized events are included in the regular program. They are held the year preceding the Olympics, in various host cities.

Pan-American Highway International highway system connecting North and South America. Conceived in 1923 as a single route, the road grew to include a number of designated highways in participating countries, including the Inter-American Highway from Nuevo Laredo, Mexico, to Panama City. The whole system, extending from Alaska and Canada to Chile, Argentina, and Brazil, totals nearly 30,000 mi (48,000 km). Only some 240 miles (400 km) in the Panama–Colombia border area remains uncompleted.

Pan-American Union Organization to promote cooperation among the countries of Latin America and the U.S. It was established (as the International Union of American Republics) in 1890 at the first Pan-American conference, initiated by U.S. secretary of state JAMES BLAINE, with the aim of promoting economic, social, and cultural agreement among the nations of the Americas. In 1948 it was reconstituted as the ORGANIZATION OF AMERICAN STATES.

Pan American World Airways, Inc. *known as* **Pan Am** Former U.S. airline. It was founded in 1927 by former World War I pilot JUAN TRIPPE, who secured a contract to fly mail between Key West, Fla., and Havana. In 1929 Pan Am established passenger service to the Caribbean and Central America. It inaugurated the first transpacific flights (San Francisco–Manila) in 1936, the first transatlantic flights (New York City–Lisbon) in 1939, and the first round-the-world flights in 1947, and it pioneered commercial jet travel in the 1950s. Its business declined in the 1960s and '70s, and its acquisition of National Airlines in 1980 failed to improve its position. Despite selling its Asian and South Pacific routes to UNITED AIRLINES and its transatlantic, European, and Middle Eastern routes to Delta Air Lines, it was forced to declare bankruptcy in 1991.

Pan-Arabism Nationalist concept of cultural and religious unity among Arab countries that developed after their liberation from Ottoman and European dominance. An important event was the founding in 1943 of the BAATH PARTY, which now has branches in several countries and is the ruling party in Syria and Iraq. Another was the founding of the ARAB LEAGUE in 1945. Pan-Arabism's most charismatic and effective proponent was Egypt's GAMAL ABDEL NASSER. Since Nasser's death, Syria's HAFIZ AL-ASSAD, Iraq's SADDAM HUSSEIN, and Libya's MUAMMAR AL-QADDAFI have all tried to assume his mantle.

Pan-Germanism Movement to politically unify all German-speaking people. The desire for German unification began in the early 19th century and was advanced by ERNST ARNDT and other early nationalists. The Pan-German League was organized in 1894 by Ernst Hasse (1846–1908) to heighten German nationalist awareness, especially among German-speaking people outside Germany. The movement, which pressed for German expansion in Europe, gained support after World War I under the WEIMAR REPUBLIC and was actively promoted by ADOLF HITLER and the NAZI PARTY. After Germany's defeat in 1945 and the expulsion of Germans from formerly German areas of Eastern Europe, the movement declined.

Pan Gu *or* **P'an Ku** \'pän-'gü\ In Chinese Taoist legend, the first man. He came forth from CHAOS (an egg) with two horns, two tusks, and a hairy body. He used his knowledge of YIN-YANG to separate heaven and earth, set the sun, moon, stars, and planets in place, and divide the four seas. He also shaped the earth by chiseling out valleys and stacking up mountains. Another legend says that the universe derived from Pan Gu's gigantic corpse. His eyes became the sun and moon, his blood formed rivers, his hair grew into trees and plants, and the human race sprang from parasites that infested his body. In art, he is often shown as a dwarf clothed with leaves.

Pan-p'o See BANPO

Pan-Slavism Movement to unite Slav peoples of Eastern and central Europe. It began in the early 19th century when Slav intellectuals studied their common cultures. Political goals for Slavic unity increased in 1848, when a Slav congress organized by FRANTISEK PALACKY met in Prague to press for equal rights under Austrian rule. In the 1860s the movement became popular in Russia, to which Pan-Slavs looked for protection from Turkish and Austro-Hungarian rule; this led Russia and Serbia into wars against the Ottoman empire in 1876–77. In the 20th century, nationalist rivalries among the Slav peoples prevented their effective collaboration.

Pan-Turkism Political movement of the late 19th and early 20th century, which had as its goal the political union of all Turkic-speaking peoples in the OTTOMAN EMPIRE, Russia, China, Iran, and Afghanistan. The movement, which began among the Turks in the Crimea and on the Volga, initially sought to unite the Turks of the Ottoman and Russian empires against growing Russian domination. MUSTAFA KEMAL ATATURK later de-emphasized Pan-Turkism, encouraging Turkish nationalism only within Turkey.

Panaji \pä-'nä-jē\ *or* **New Goa** Town (pop., 1991: 43,000), seaport, and capital of GOA, western India. It is on the Arabian Sea at the mouth of the Mandavi River. It replaced Old Goa as the residence of the Portuguese viceroy in 1759 and as the capital of Portuguese India in 1843. It contains colonial houses and plazas and has a tourist industry.

Panama *officially* **Republic of Panama** Nation, CENTRAL AMERICA. It is bounded by the Caribbean Sea, Colombia, the Pacific Ocean, and Costa Rica. Area: 29,157 sq mi (75,517 sq km). Population (1997 est.): 2,719,000. Capital: PANAMA CITY. The people are mostly mestizo (mixed Spanish-Indian) and Indian groups, including the Guaymí, Kuna, and

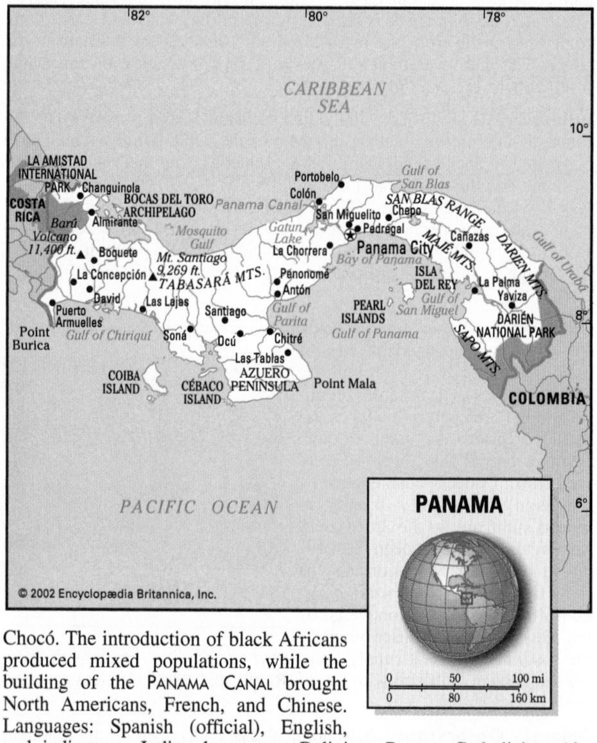

Chocó. The introduction of black Africans produced mixed populations, while the building of the PANAMA CANAL brought North Americans, French, and Chinese. Languages: Spanish (official), English, and indigenous Indian languages. Religion: Roman Catholicism (the majority). Currency: balboa. Panama consists of three distinct areas: the lowlands, or hot lands (more than 85% of the country); the temperate lands; and the highlands, or cold lands. It has a market economy based on services. Most of this is transportation, communications, and storage connected with the Panama Canal, as well as international banking and tourism. It is a republic with one legislative house; its head of state and government is the president, assisted by vice presidents. The land was inhabited by American Indians when the Spanish arrived in 1501. The first successful Spanish settlement was founded by VASCO NUNEZ DE BALBOA in 1510. Panama was part of the viceroyalty of NEW GRANADA until it declared its independence from Spain in 1821 to join Colombia. In 1903 it revolted against Colombia and was recognized by the U.S., to whom it ceded the CANAL ZONE. The completed canal was opened in 1914; its jurisdiction reverted from the U.S. to Panama in 1999. An invasion by U.S. troops in 1989 overthrew the de facto ruler, Gen. MANUEL NORIEGA. In 1999 the country elected its first female president, Mireya Moscoso.

Panama Canal Ship canal, Panama. Extending across the Isthmus of Panama, it connects the Atlantic and Pacific oceans. It is about 51 mi (82 km) long from deepwater to deepwater, with a minimum width of 300 ft (91 m) and a minimum depth of 41 ft (12 m). In 1879 a French company began constructing the canal, but the enterprise collapsed in 1889. Under a 1903 treaty Panama granted the U.S. the Panama CANAL ZONE and the rights to build and operate a canal. Work began in 1904; facing enormous obstacles, GEORGE GOETHALS directed the construction from 1907 and the canal opened on August 15, 1914. After disputes over sovereignty, a 1977 treaty provided for Panama to take control of the canal in 2000; it did so in 1999. Except for small craft, no vessel can pass through the canal under its own power. Ships are towed by electric locomotives, and it takes 15–20 hours to complete the passage. Duplicate locks enable ships to pass in opposite directions simultaneously. It allows ships sailing between the eastern and western coasts of the U.S. to shorten their voyage by about 8,000 nautical miles.

Panama Canal Zone See CANAL ZONE

Panama City City (pop., 2000: 415,964), capital of Panama. Near the Pacific entrance of the PANAMA CANAL, on the Bay of Panama, the site was originally an Indian fishing village. The old city was founded in 1519 and completely destroyed by British buccaneer HENRY MORGAN in 1671. It was rebuilt in 1674 just west of the old site by a Spanish CONQUISTADOR. In 1751 the area became part of NEW GRANADA and later part of Colombia. It was the center of the Panamanian revolt against Colombia in 1903, when it became the capital of Panama. After the opening of the canal in 1914, it developed rapidly, becoming the commercial and transportation center of the country. The economy depends largely on canal traffic and canal personnel.

Panathenaea \ˌpan-ˌa-thə-ˈnē-ə\ In GREEK RELIGION, an Athenian festival of great antiquity. Originally an annual event, it was eventually celebrated every fourth year, probably in deliberate rivalry to the OLYMPIC GAMES. It consisted of the sacrifices and rites proper to the season (mid-August) in the cult of ATHENA, the city's protectress. Representatives of all the dependencies of ATHENS came to the Panathenaea. The great procession, made up of the heroes of the Battle of MARATHON, is the subject of the frieze of the PARTHENON. The participants offered Athena an embroidered robe and sacrificed animals; there were also poetry recitations (later replaced by a musical contest) and athletic competitions.

Panay \pə-ˈnī\ Island (pop., 1990: 3,136,425), westernmost of the Visayan group, central Philippines. It is surrounded by the Sibuyan, Visayan, and Sulu seas, and the Guimaras Strait separates it from NEGROS island. Roughly triangular in shape, it has an area of 4,446 sq mi (11,515 sq km). A rugged, almost unpopulated mountain range parallels its western coastline. Between the range and a hilly eastern portion, a densely populated, intensely farmed fertile plain extends north–south. Its chief city is ILOILO.

Pañca-tantra *or* **Panchatantra** \ˌpən-chə-ˈtən-trə\ ("Five Chapters") Collection of Indian beast fables originally written in Sanskrit that has had extensive circulation throughout the world. The original work, now lost, may have originated between 100 BC and AD 500. A textbook for instructing three sons of a king, it contained aphorisms that tend to glorify shrewdness and cleverness more than the helping of others. As early as the 11th century one version reached Europe, where it was known as *The Fables of Bidpai* (after the narrator, an Indian sage).

panchayat raj \pən-ˈchä-yət\ In India, government by the village council, or panchayat. When India gained its independence, it was stated that the government "should take steps to organize village panchayats." The first village panchayat was inaugurated in 1959 in Rajasthan, and in 1993 panchayats were incorporated into the Indian Constitution. Their members are elected, and one-third of them are required to be women. Scheduled castes and tribes are also guaranteed representation in proportion to their population. Today the role and success of the panchayats are still the topic of heated discussion. See also INDIAN NATIONAL CONGRESS.

Panchen Lama \ˈpän-chən-ˈlä-mə\ Any of the line of reincarnated LAMAS who head the Tashilhunpo Monastery in TIBET, second only to the DALAI LAMA in spiritual authority in the dominant sect of TIBETAN BUDDHISM. A Panchen Lama installed by the Chinese government remained in Tibet after the 13th Dalai Lama fled into exile in 1959. He refused to brand the Dalai Lama a traitor and was imprisoned by the Chinese in 1964, he was released in the late 1970s and died in 1989. The six-year-old boy chosen as the new Panchen Lama in 1995 was seized by the government and a different boy was substituted, in an effort to undermine the Dalai Lama's authority.

pancreas \ˈpaŋ-krē-əs\ Compound GLAND functioning as both an exocrine (secreting through a duct) and an endocrine (ductless) gland. It continuously secretes pancreatic juice (containing water, bicarbonate, and enzymes needed to digest carbohydrates, fat, and protein) through the pancreatic duct to the DUODENUM. Scattered among the enzyme-producing cells are the islets of LANGERHANS, which secrete INSULIN and glucagon directly into the bloodstream. Disorders include inflammation (PANCREATITIS), INFECTIONS, TUMORS, and CYSTS. If more than 80–90% of the pancreas must be removed, the patient will need to take insulin and pancreatic extracts. See also DIABETES MELLITUS, HYPOGLYCEMIA.

pancreatic cancer Malignant TUMOR of the PANCREAS. Risk factors include smoking, a diet high in fat, exposure to certain industrial products, and diseases such as diabetes and chronic pancreatitis. Pancreatic cancer is more common in men. Symptoms often do not appear until pancreatic cancer is advanced; they include abdominal pain, unexplained weight loss, and difficulty digesting fatty foods. Surgery, radiation therapy, chemotherapy, or some combination of these may be used to treat the disease.

pancreatitis \ˌpaŋ-krē-ə-ˈtī-təs\ INFLAMMATION of the PANCREAS, associated with alcohol, trauma, or pancreatic-duct obstruction. Activated enzymes escaping into pancreatic tissues cause irritation and inflammation. If it does not subside, bleeding, tissue death and scarring, pus formation, and infection may occur. Symptoms include severe pain (worst when lying on the back), low fever, nausea, and HYPERTENSION. Acute cases are treated by controlling pain, preventing or relieving shock, inhibiting pancreatic-juice secretion (including eliminating oral intake of food), avoiding infection, and replacing lost fluids and salts. Chronic pancreatitis can destroy enough of the pancreas to cause pancreatic-juice deficiency and DIABETES MELLITUS. Treatment may include a low-fat diet, avoiding overeating and alcohol, pancreatic extracts, and INSULIN.

panda *or* **giant panda** Species (*Ailuropoda melanoleuca,* family Ursidae) of white-and-black forest-dwelling carnivore, found in western central China, that subsists mainly on bamboo. Because they cannot digest cellulose, wild pandas (of which there are fewer than 1,000) spend 10–12 or more hours a day eating up to 66 lbs (30 kg) of bamboo leaves, stems, and shoots to obtain needed nutrients. Pandas in captivity (currently about 100 individuals, mostly in China) will eat cereals, milk, fruits, and garden vegetables. Giant pandas grow to 5 ft (1.5 m) long and weigh over 200 lbs (100 kg). They live alone except when breeding. They are difficult to breed in captivity.

Giant panda (*Ailuropoda melanoleuca*).
TOM MCHUGH—PHOTO RESEARCHERS

panda, lesser *or* **cat bear** *or* **bear cat** Long-tailed nocturnal raccoonlike carnivore (*Ailurus fulgens,* family Procyonidae) that inhabits high mountain forests in the Himalayas and adjacent eastern Asia. It is 20–26 in. (50–65 cm) long, excluding the 12–20-in. (30–50-cm) bushy, faintly ringed tail. It weighs 6–10 lbs (3–4.5 kg) and has soft, thick, reddish brown fur. The face is white, with a red-brown stripe from the eyes

O
P
Q
R

to the mouth. It eats plants, especially bamboo, and fruits and insects. Though an agile climber, it mostly feeds while on the ground.

Pandora In GREEK MYTHOLOGY, the first woman. After PROMETHEUS stole fire from heaven and bestowed it on mortals, ZEUS decided to counteract this blessing and commissioned HEPHAESTUS to fashion a woman out of earth, upon whom the gods bestowed their choicest gifts. After marrying Prometheus' brother, Pandora opened a jar containing all kinds of misery and evil, which escaped and flew out over the earth. In one version, Hope alone remained inside, the lid having been shut before she could escape.

panegyric \ˌpa-nə-ˈjir-ik\ Eulogistic oration or laudatory discourse that originally was a speech delivered at an ancient Greek general assembly *(panegyris),* such as the Olympic and Panathenaic festivals. Speakers frequently advocated Hellenic unity by expounding on the former glories of Greek cities; hence the elaborate and flowery connotations of the term. Later Roman speakers praised and flattered eminent persons, especially emperors, in panegyrics. The form was also used in the European Middle Ages, Renaissance, and Baroque era.

Pangaea \pan-ˈjē-ə\ Hypothetical protocontinent proposed by ALFRED WEGENER in 1912 as part of his theory of CONTINENTAL DRIFT. Pangaea (from Greek: *pangaia,* "all earth") supposedly covered about half the earth and was completely surrounded by a world ocean called Panthalassa. Late in the TRIASSIC PERIOD (248–206 million years ago), Pangaea began to break apart. Its segments, LAURASIA (composed of all the present-day northern continents) and GONDWANA (all of the present southern continents) gradually receded, resulting in the formation of the Atlantic Ocean.

Pangkor Engagement \ˈpäŋ-ˌkȯr\ (1874) Treaty between the British government and Malay chiefs, named for the island where it was signed. In return for British backing in a complicated Perak succession dispute, Raja Abdullah accepted a British resident (adviser) with broad powers at his court, the first step in the establishment of British dominion over the Malay states.

pangolin \ˈpaŋ-gə-lən\ *or* **scaly anteater** Any of about eight species of armored placental MAMMALS (genus *Manis,* order Pholidota) of tropical Asia and Africa. Scales formed of cemented hairs cover the upper body, legs, and tail. Pangolins are 2–6 ft (60–180 cm) long and weigh 10–60 lbs (5–27 kg). They have a conical head, no teeth, a long tongue, short legs, and a long prehensile tail. Some are arboreal; terrestrial species live in burrows. Nocturnal animals, pangolins locate prey, mainly termites, by smell, ripping open nests with their front claws. When threatened, the pangolin (Malayan for "rolling over") curls up or emits an odoriferous secretion. See also ANTEATER, ECHIDNA.

panic In economics, a severe financial disturbance, such as widespread bank failures, feverish stock speculation followed by a market crash, or a climate of fear caused by economic crisis or anticipation of such a crisis. The term is applied only to the initial, violent stage of financial upheaval rather than the whole decline in the BUSINESS CYCLE (see DEPRESSION and RECESSION). Until the 19th century, economic fluctuations were largely connected with shortages of goods, market expansion, and speculation (as in the SOUTH SEA BUBBLE). Panics in the industrialized societies of the 19th–20th century have reflected the increasing complexity of advanced economies. The Panic of 1857 in the U.S. had its seeds in the railroads' defaulting on their BONDS and in the decline in the value of railroad SECURITIES; its effects were complex, including not only the closing of many banks but also severe unemployment in the U.S. and a money-market panic in Europe. The Panic of 1873, which began with financial crises in Vienna and New York, marked the start of a long-term contraction in the world economy. The greatest panic began with the U.S. stock-market crash of 1929 (see GREAT DEPRESSION).

Panjabi language See PUNJABI LANGUAGE

Pankhurst, Emmeline *orig.* **Emmeline Goulden** (1858–1928) British feminist. In 1879 she married Richard Pankhurst (1834–1898), author of Britain's first women's-suffrage bill and the Married Women's Property acts (1870, 1882). In 1889 she founded the Women's Franchise League, which in 1894 secured for married women the right to vote in local elections. After holding municipal offices in Manchester, in 1903 she founded the Women's Social and Political Union. From 1912 she advocated extreme militancy, mainly in the form of arson, and was arrested 12 times in one year. Weeks before her death in 1928, Britain passed a bill to give voting rights to all women. Her daughter Christabel H. Pankhurst (1880–1958)—later Dame Christabel—organized the militant tactics of the WSPU and directed actions that included hunger strikes and huge outdoor rallies. She later became a religious evangelist and moved to the U.S.

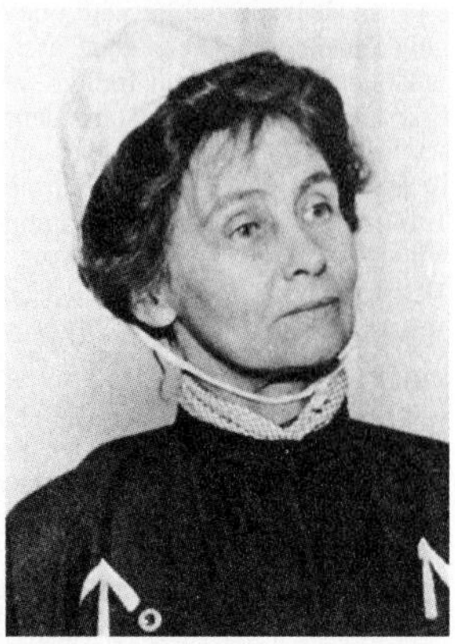

Emmeline Pankhurst in prison clothes, 1908.

BBC HULTON PICTURE LIBRARY

Pannini \pän-ˈnē-nē\, **Giovanni Paolo** *or* **Giovanni Paolo Panini** (1691–1765) Italian painter. After gaining fame for his fresco painting, he specialized in Roman topography and became the foremost artist in that field in the 18th century. His real and imaginary views of ancient Roman ruins embody precise observation and tender nostalgia, and combine elements of late classical art of the baroque period with incipient Romanticism. His work was popular both with tourists and his peers: he was admitted to the French Academy in 1732 and became its professor of perspective.

Pannonia Province, Roman empire, corresponding to modern western Hungary and parts of eastern Austria, Slovenia, and northern Yugoslavia. The original inhabitants were mainly Illyrians, with some Celts in the western part. Conquered by Rome beginning in 35 BC, it revolted in AD 6, posing the greatest threat to Italy since HANNIBAL's invasion. It was split in AD 106, and Pannonia Superior became a center of the Roman wars under MARCUS AURELIUS. The Romans withdrew after 395.

Panofsky \pə-ˈnȯf-skē\, **Erwin** (1892–1968) German-U.S. art historian. A professor at the University of Hamburg (1926–33), he fled Nazi Germany for the U.S. and in 1935 began teaching at Princeton's Institute for Advanced Study. He gained prominence for his studies in iconography, the study of symbols and themes in works of art. His writings are distinguished by their variety of subjects, critical penetration, erudition, and rich allusions to literature, philosophy, and history. Among his major works are the groundbreaking *Studies in Iconology* (1939), *Albrecht Dürer* (1943), and *Early Netherlandish Painting* (1953).

panorama Narrative scene or landscape painted to conform to a curved or flat background, which surrounds or is unrolled before the viewer. Popular in the late 18th and 19th century, it was an antecedent of the stereopticon and motion pictures. The true panorama is exhibited on the walls of a large cylinder, and the viewer stands on a platform in the cylinder's center and turns around to see all points of the horizon. The first panorama, a view of Edinburgh, was executed in 1788 by the Scottish painter Robert Barker (1739–1806). In the mid-19th century the rolled panorama became popular: a painting on canvas was wound between two poles and slowly unrolled behind a frame or revealed in sections.

panpipe *or* **syrinx** Wind instrument consisting of pipes of different lengths made of cane (less often wood, clay, or metal) arranged in a row. It is blown across the top, each pipe producing a different note. The panpipe dates from c. 2000 BC and is found worldwide, especially in eastern Africa, South America, and Melanesia.

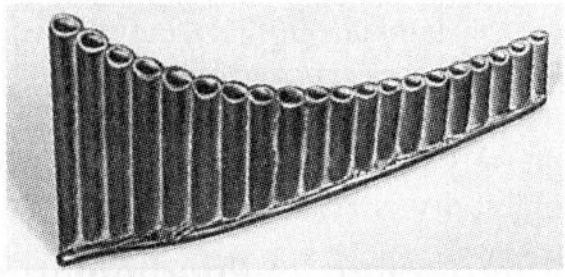

Romanian panpipe; in the Horniman Museum, London.

BY COURTESY OF THE HORNIMAN MUSEUM, LONDON

p'ansori Korean "story singing," a form of sung folk narrative. Once a narrative performance that incorporated shamanistic chants, *p'ansori* became a vehicle for treating popular customs and everyday life.

pansy Any of several popular cultivated VIOLETS (genus *Viola*). Pansies have been grown for so long under such diverse conditions with such striking variations in color and form that their origin is uncertain. Probably the garden pansy *(V. wittrockiana)* is a cultivated form of *V. tricolor,* a weed of European grainfields. Annuals or short-lived perennials, pansies grow 6–12 in. (15–30 cm) tall and have heart-shaped leaves at the base and oblong leaves growing from the stems. Velvety flowers occur in combinations of blue, yellow, and white. The smaller, usually purple, wild pansy is also known as Johnny-jump-up, heartsease, and love-in-idleness.

Pansy (*Viola tricolor*).
KITTY KOHOUT–ROOT RESOURCES

pantheism Doctrine that the universe is God and, conversely, that there is no god apart from the substance, forces, and laws manifested in the universe. Pantheism characterizes many Buddhist and Hindu doctrines and can be seen in such Hindu works as the VEDAS and the BHAGAVADGITA. Numerous Greek philosophers contributed to the foundations of Western pantheism. In the Middle Ages and the Renaissance, the tradition was continued in NEOPLATONISM and Judeo-Christian MYSTICISM. In the 17th century BENEDICT DE SPINOZA formulated the most thoroughly pantheistic philosophical system, arguing that God and Nature are merely two names for one reality.

Pantheon Building in Rome begun 27 BC probably as an ordinary rectangular Classical temple and completely rebuilt by HADRIAN (AD 118–28). It is remarkable for its size and design; the exact method of construction has never been determined. A circular building of concrete faced with brick, it has a great concrete dome, 142 ft (43 m) in diameter, and a front porch of Corinthian columns with a triangular pediment. The vast space is lit solely by the 27-ft (8-m) oculus at the dome's center. The interior is lined with colored marble; the walls are marked by seven deep recesses screened by pairs of columns.

Pantheon, Rome, begun by Agrippa in 27 BC, completely rebuilt by Hadrian c. AD 118–c. 128.
FREDERICO ARBORIO MELLA

panther See COUGAR, LEOPARD

pantomime See MIME AND PANTOMIME

pantothenic acid \ˌpan-tə-ˈthe-nik, ˌpan-tə-ˈthē-nik\ Organic compound, part of the VITAMIN B COMPLEX, essential in animal METABOLISM. Found in all living cells and tissues, in animals it occurs in the combined form called COENZYME A, which promotes many reactions necessary for growth and well-being. Since it is synthesized by bacteria normally in the human intestine, deficiency leading to disease does not occur.

Pánuco River \ˈpä-nü-ˌkō\ River, central Mexico. Rising in HIDALGO state and flowing northeast into the Gulf of Mexico below TAMPICO, it is about 100 mi (160 km) long and has considerable economic importance. It has served to drain TEXCOCO and other interior lakes via a system of tunnels and channels. Its waters are used to irrigate the fertile La Huasteca lowlands, and its lower course is navigable.

panzer division \ˈpan-zər, ˈpänt-sər\ (German: "armored division") Self-contained MILITARY UNIT of the German army, built around the capabilities of ARMORED VEHICLES. In World War II, it consisted of a tank brigade with four battalions; a motorized infantry brigade with four rifle battalions; an artillery regiment; and reconnaissance, antitank, and military-engineering battalions and service units. Germany had six panzer divisions in 1939 and 20 by 1941. It remains the principal offensive element of the German army.

pao-chia See BAOJIA

Paoli \ˈpau̇-lē\, **Pasquale** (1725–1807) Corsican patriot. Son of Giacinto Paoli, who led the Corsicans against Genoa in 1735, he lived with his father in exile in Naples 1739–55. On his return, he overcame the Genoese faction and was elected to rule Corsica. He suppressed the vendetta system, substituted order and justice, and instituted national schools. He continued the fight for independence, but after France invaded Corsica in 1769 he fled to England, where he lived until 1790. Recalled to Corsica as military commandant, he expelled the French with British naval support (1794) and offered the island's sovereignty to England. He retired to England in 1795.

Paolo, Giovanni di See GIOVANNI DI PAOLO

Pap smear *or* **Papanicolaous smear** \ˌpäp-ə-ˈnē-kə-ˌlau̇z\ Sample of cells from the VAGINA and cervix of the UTERUS for laboratory staining and examination to detect genital herpes and early-stage CANCER, especially of the cervix. Developed by the Greek-U.S. physician George Nicolas Papanicolaou (1883–1962), this technique also can be applied to cells obtained from other surfaces.

papacy \ˈpā-pə-sē\ System of central government of the Roman Catholic church. BISHOPS led the early Church, with the bishop of Rome being accorded special respect by the end of the 1st century AD. St. CYPRIAN challenged that position of honor in the 3rd century, and in the 4th–5th century the power of the see of Constantinople rose to challenge that of Rome; the rivalry would culminate in the SCHISM OF 1054 between the Eastern and Western Churches. After the collapse of the Roman empire, the papacy found protection under the wing of CHARLEMAGNE and his successors; in the 9th–10th century the German emperors controlled it. In 1059 Pope LEO IX responded by vesting the right to name a new pope exclusively with the College of CARDINALS. To establish the papacy's supremacy over the state, GREGORY VII decreed in 1075 that civil rulers could not invest churchmen with temporal power (see INVESTITURE CONTROVERSY) and excommunicated HENRY IV of Germany. In the next centuries, the worldliness and corruption of the papal court and the "Babylonian Captivity" of the papacy at Avignon (see AVIGNON PAPACY) led to the Western SCHISM and eventually to the REFORMATION. The Council of TRENT inaugurated the COUNTER-REFORMATION. In the 19th century the papacy lost its remaining temporal powers when the PAPAL STATES were incorporated into the new Kingdom of Italy. It maintained a conservative religious position, proclaiming infallibility in doctrinal matters and espousing the idea that the pope is the absolute ruler of the church. The Second VATICAN COUNCIL gave the bishops, clergy, and laity more voice. See also ROMAN CATHOLICISM.

Papago \ˈpä-pə-ˌgō\ North American Indian people of UTO-AZTECAN LANGUAGE stock who traditionally inhabited the desert regions of Arizona and northern Sonora, Mexico. Closely related to the PIMA, they probably descend from ancient HOHOKAM peoples. The Papago practiced food gathering and flash-flood farming in the dry region they inhabited. Because of the wide dispersal of their fields, their largest viable political unit was a group of temporarily related villages. The Papago had less contact with whites than other Indian groups and have retained elements of their traditional culture. Today they number about 7,500 and live primarily on reservations in southern Arizona.

Papal Curia See ROMAN CURIA

papal infallibility In ROMAN CATHOLICISM, the doctrine that the pope, acting as supreme teacher and under certain conditions, as when he speaks *ex cathedra* ("from the chair"), cannot err when he teaches in matters of faith or morals. It is based on the belief that the church, entrusted with the teaching mission of Jesus, will be guided by the Holy Spirit in remaining faithful to that teaching. The First Vatican Council (1869–70) stated the conditions under which a pope may be said to have spoken infallibly: he must intend to demand irrevocable assent from the entire church in some aspect of faith or morals. The doctrine remains a major obstacle to ecumenical endeavors and is the subject of controversy even among Roman Catholic theologians.

Papal Inquisition See INQUISITION

Papal States *Italian* **Stati Pontifici** \ˈstä-tē-pōn-ˈtē-fē-chē\ Territories of central Italy over which the POPE had sovereignty 756–1870. The extent of the territory and the degree of papal control varied over the centuries. The temporal power of the medieval papacy was based on the DONATION OF PEPIN in AD 754. The papacy acquired the duchy of Benevento in 1077, and Popes INNOCENT III and JULIUS II expanded the papal domain. The rise of communes and rule by local families weakened papal authority in the towns, and by the 16th century the papal territory was one of a number of petty Italian states. They were an obstacle to

Italian unity until 1870, when ROME was taken by Italian forces and became the capital of Italy. In 1929 the LATERAN TREATY settled the pope's relation to the Italian state and set up an independent city-state (see VATICAN CITY).

Papandreou \ˌpä-pän-ˈdrā-ü\, **Andreas (Georgios)** (1919–1996) Greek educator and prime minister (1981–89, 1993–96). Son of GEORGIOS PAPANDREOU, he taught at UC–Berkeley 1955–63, then returned to Greece when his father became premier (1963) and was elected to the Greek parliament. After the military coup in 1967 he went into exile. He returned in 1974 to form the left-wing Panhellenic Socialist Movement (Pasok). The party gained a majority in 1981, and Papandreou became premier. He promoted generous social-welfare programs, but his government was weakened by financial scandals and mounting budget deficits, and he resigned in 1989 but remained the leader of Pasok. He again became prime minister in 1993, but ill health forced him to retire in 1996.

Papandreou, Georgios (1888–1968) Greek prime minister (1944, 1963, 1964–65). He began his political career as a liberal in 1915 and served as minister of education 1929–33. In 1935 he founded the Democratic Socialist Party, then went into exile. He briefly headed a coalition government in 1944, then held ministerial posts 1946–52. He merged his party with the Liberal Party and formed the Center Union in 1961. As prime minister in 1964 he introduced far-reaching social reforms, but he was dismissed by the king in 1965. After the military coup in 1967, he was jailed briefly with his son, ANDREAS PAPANDREOU.

papaw *or* **pawpaw** \ˈpä-ˌpȯ\ Deciduous tree or shrub *(Asimina triloba)* of the CUSTARD APPLE family, native to the eastern and midwestern U.S. It can grow to 40 ft (12 m) tall and has pointed, broadly oblong, drooping leaves up to 12 in. (30 cm) long. The purple flowers bloom with a foul odor before the leaves emerge in spring. The edible fruit looks like a stubby banana; its skin turns black as it ripens. Handling pawpaw fruits produces a skin reaction in allergic individuals. The name is also sometimes applied to the PAPAYA.

papaya \pə-ˈpī-ə\ Large palmlike plant (*Carica papaya;* family Caricaceae), cultivated throughout the tropics and warm subtropics, and its succulent juicy fruit. A popular breakfast fruit in many countries, it is also used in salads, pies, sherbets, juices, and confections. The juice of the unripe fruit contain an enzyme that is useful in various remedies for indigestion and in meat tenderizers.

Papeete \ˌpä-pā-ˈā-tā\ Seaport (pop., 1988: 24,000), capital of French Polynesia, northwestern coast of Tahiti. A tropical city with tall palms and exotic flowers, it is one of the largest urban and commercial centers in the South Pacific. By 1829 its excellent harbor made it a place of trade and a port of call for whalers. In 1880 it was annexed by the French, and it became a commune in 1890. It is a major tourist base and a center for Pacific Rim trade.

Papen \ˈpä-pən\, **Franz von** (1879–1969) German politician. He served as military attaché in Washington, D.C. (1913–15), but was recalled on espionage charges. A monarchist member of the German Reichstag (1921–32), he was chosen chancellor in 1932, but was soon ousted by KURT VON SCHLEICHER. In revenge, Papen persuaded PAUL VON HINDENBURG to appoint ADOLF HITLER as chancellor and himself as vice chancellor. Papen resigned in 1934 when he was unable to restrain the Nazis' push for power. As ambassador to Austria (1934–38), he worked for Austria's annexation to Germany. He was ambassador to Turkey 1939–44. Arrested in 1945, he was tried and acquitted at the NUREMBERG TRIALS; sentenced to prison by a German court as a Nazi, he was released on appeal in 1949.

Papen.
CAMERA PRESS

paper Matted or felted sheet, usually made of CELLULOSE fibers, formed on a wire screen from water suspension. Source materials include wood pulp, rags, and recycled paper. The fibers are separated (by processes that may be mechanical, chemical, or both) and wetted to produce paper pulp, or stock. The pulp is filtered on a woven screen to form a sheet of fiber, which is pressed and compacted to squeeze out most of the water. The remaining water is removed by evaporation, and the dry sheet is further compressed and often (depending on the intended use) coated or infused with other substances. Types of paper in common use include bond paper, book paper, bristol (or bristol board), groundwood and newsprint, kraft paper, paperboard, and sanitary paper (for towels, napkins, etc.). See also CALENDERING, FOURDRINIER MACHINE, KRAFT PROCESS.

paper birch Ornamental, shade, and timber tree *(Betula papyrifera)* of the BIRCH family, native to northern and central North America. Also called canoe birch, silver birch, or white birch, it is one of the best-known birches. The smooth, varicolored or white bark of young trees peels horizontally in thin sheets, which once were used as writing surfaces as well as for roofing, canoes, and shoes. The water-impervious bark, which burns even when wet, is a boon to campers and hikers.

paper chromatography (PC) Type of CHROMATOGRAPHY using filter or other special papers as the stationary phase. Spots of and reference materials are applied near one edge (or corner, for two-dimensional PC) of the paper. The edge of the paper is dipped in a solvent, which travels along it by CAPILLARITY, moving the components of the sample at rates depending on their relative solubilities in the solvent. In two-dimensional PC, the paper is turned 90° and dipped it in a different solvent. The components of the sample mixture, visible as separated spots, are identified by comparing the distances they have traveled with those of the known reference materials. PC is especially useful for complex mixtures of AMINO ACIDS, PEPTIDES, CARBOHYDRATES, STEROIDS, and many other organic compounds and inorganic IONS.

paper folding *Japanese* **origami** Art of folding objects out of paper without cutting, pasting, or decorating. Its early history is unknown, but it seems to have developed from the older art of folding cloth. Origami has reached its greatest development in Japan, with hundreds of traditional folds and an extensive literature dealing with the art. There are two types of Japanese folds: figures used in ceremonial etiquette, and objects such as animals, flowers, furniture, and human figures. Some objects have amusing action features; best known is the bird that flaps its wings when its tail is pulled. Paper folding has also flourished in Spain, South America, and Germany.

Paphlagonia Ancient district, northern ASIA MINOR, on the BLACK SEA. A mountainous country, one of the oldest in Asia Minor, it submitted to ALEXANDER THE GREAT in 333 BC. In the 3rd–2nd century BC it was gradually absorbed by the Pontic kingdom on its eastern border. In 65 BC the coastal districts, including the capital, Sinope, were attached to Roman BITHYNIA. The area was incorporated into the Roman province of GALATIA c. 6 BC; the interior regions were left under native rulers. It was part of the Byzantine empire, and all but its coastal regions were lost after the Battle of MANZIKERT (1071).

papillomavirus \ˌpa-pə-ˈlō-mə-ˌvī-rəs\ Any of a group of VIRUSES that cause WARTS and other harmless tumors in humans. These small viruses contain circular DNA. More than 50 distinct types are known. Different types are responsible for warts of the hands, plantar warts (of the feet), flat warts, and throat warts. Genital warts are caused by other types, which are spread by sexual intercourse. Some papillomaviruses have been linked with various cancerous tumors, especially cervical cancers; their presence can be detected through an ordinary PAP SMEAR.

papillon \ˌpä-pē-ˈyō^{n}\ Breed of TOY DOG known from the 16th century, when it was called a dwarf SPANIEL. A favorite of MARIE-ANTOINETTE, it appeared in paintings by Old Masters. It acquired its name (French for "butterfly") in the late 19th century, when a variety with large, flaring ears became fashionable. Another variety has drooping ears. A slender, graceful dog with a plumed tail, it stands 11 in. (28 cm) or less and weighs up to 11 lbs (5 kg). The soft, full coat is usually white, with darker patches.

Papineau \pȧ-pē-ˈnō\, **Louis Joseph** (1786–1871) Canadian politician. Born in Montreal, he was elected to the legislative assembly of Lower Canada (now Quebec) in 1808 and became speaker in 1815. A leader of the French-Canadian Party, he opposed the British-dominated government of Lower Canada and opposed union with Upper Canada. In 1834 he helped draft the 92 Resolutions, demanding control of revenues and an elective provincial council. When the British governor rejected the demands, hostilities broke out. Papineau escaped to the U.S., then to France, where he lived 1839–44. He returned to Canada under an amnesty and served in the Canadian House of Commons (1848–54).

Papp, Joseph *orig.* **Joseph Papirofsky** (1921–1991) U.S. theatrical producer and director. Born in Brooklyn, N.Y., he studied acting and directing and worked as a stage manager for CBS television. In 1954 he founded the New York Shakespeare Festival, which gave free performances of Shakespeare's plays in city parks. He produced and directed most of the plays, and by 1962 he had persuaded city officials and arts organizations to sponsor the building of the Delacorte Theater in Central Park. In 1967 he founded the Public Theater to produce new and classic dramas, creating a seven-theater complex in the old Astor Library. Several productions traveled to Broadway, including *Hair* (1967) and *A Chorus Line* (1975). Papp remained one of OFF-BROADWAY's most active producers into the 1980s, championing many young playwrights and actors. He served as artistic director of the Shakespeare Festival and the Public Theater until his death.

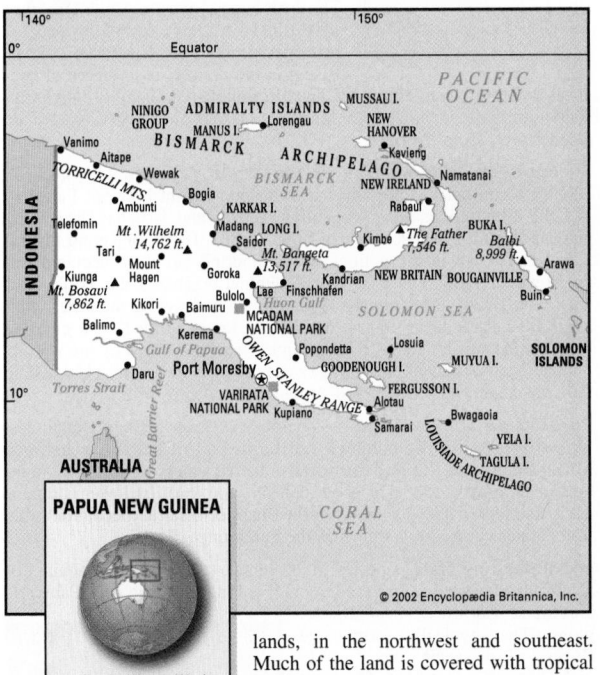

Papua New Guinea \'pa-pyü-wə...'gi-nē\ *officially* **Independent State of Papua New Guinea** Island nation, South Pacific Ocean. Area: 178,704 sq mi (462,840 sq km). Population (1997 est.): 4,496,000. Capital: PORT MORESBY. Most of the people are Papuan (four-fifths) and Melanesian; minorities are Polynesian, Chinese, and European. Languages: English (official), Tok Pisin, Motu, indigenous languages. Religions: Anglicanism and other Protestant sects, Roman Catholicism. Currency: kina. About 85% of the total land area is on the island of NEW GUINEA; the nation also includes BOUGAINVILLE island and the BISMARCK ARCHIPELAGO. The New Guinea terrain ranges from swampy lowland plains in the south and north to high central mountains, the Highlands, in the northwest and southeast. Much of the land is covered with tropical rain forest. Some of the outlying islands are volcanic. It has a developing mixed economy based largely on the export of mineral and agricultural products. It is a constitutional monarchy with one legislative house; its chief of state is the British monarch represented by the governor-general, and the head of government is the prime minister. The area has been inhabited since prehistoric times, with hunters as the earliest settlers. The Portuguese sighted the coast in 1512, and in 1545 the Spanish claimed the island. The first colony was founded in 1793 by the British. In 1828 the Dutch claimed the western half as part of the Dutch East Indies. In 1884 Britain annexed the southeastern part and Germany took over the northeastern sector. The British part became the Territory of Papua in 1906 and passed to Australia, which also governed the German sector after World War I. After World War II, Australia governed both sectors as the Territory of Papua and New Guinea. Dutch New Guinea was annexed to Indonesia in 1969 as the province of Irian Jaya. Papua New Guinea achieved independence in 1975 and joined the British COMMONWEALTH. It moved to resolve its war with Bougainville independence fighters in 1997.

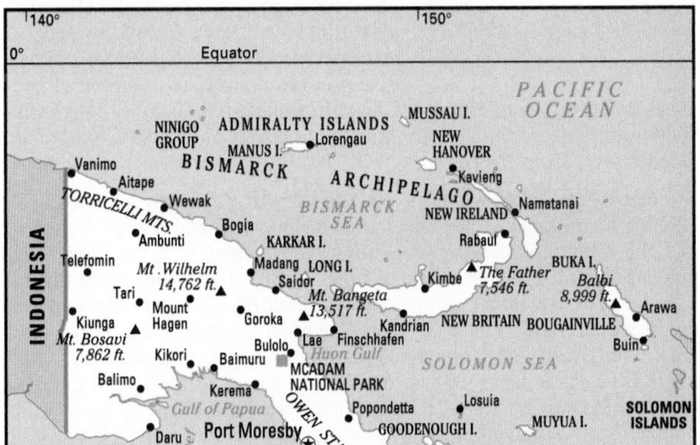

Papuan languages \'pa-pyə-wən\ Group of about 750 languages spoken by indigenous peoples of New Guinea and parts of some neighboring islands, including Alor, Bougainville, Halmahera, New Britain, New Ireland, and Timor. Spoken by perhaps 5 million people, Papuan languages belong to about 60 families, the higher genetic relationships of which are still uncertain. This diversity, conjoined with the numerous AUSTRONESIAN LANGUAGES spoken on smaller parts of New Guinea and on adjacent islands, makes the region the most linguistically heterogeneous area of the world. The vast majority of Papuan languages have fewer than 100,000 speakers; among those with more are Chimbu and Enga, spoken in the highlands of Papua New Guinea. Linguistically, Papuan languages show great variation, though PHONEME inventories tend to be small, verbs follow subjects and objects in nearly all Papuan languages, and verbal MORPHOLOGY is typically complex.

papyrus \pə-'pī-rəs\ Writing material of ancient times and the plant from which it comes, *Cyperus papyrus* (SEDGE FAMILY), also called paper plant. This grasslike aquatic plant has woody, bluntly triangular stems and grows to about 15 ft (4.6 m) high in quietly flowing water up to 3 ft (90 cm) deep. The ancient Egyptians used the stem of the plant to make sails, cloth, mats, cords, and principally paper. Paper made from papyrus was the chief writing material in ancient Egypt, Greece, and Rome. In the 8th–9th century AD, other plant fibers replaced papyrus in the manufacture of paper. The plant is now often used as a pool ornamental in warm areas or in conservatories.

Pará River \pá-'rä\ Channel of the AMAZON RIVER that passes to the south and east of Marajó Island, in northeastern Pará state, northern Brazil. It is about 200 mi (320 km) long and 40 mi (64 km) wide at its mouth. It carries a small part of the discharge of the Amazon east and north to the Atlantic Ocean, and its entire length is navigable.

parabola \pə-'ra-bə-lə\ Open curve, one of the CONIC SECTIONS. It results when a right circular cone intersects a plane that is parallel to an edge of the cone. It is also the path of a point moving so that its distance from a fixed line (directrix) is always equal to its distance from a fixed point (focus). In ANALYTIC GEOMETRY its equation is $y = ax^2 + bx + c$ (a second-degree, or quadratic, POLYNOMIAL FUNCTION). Such a curve has the useful property that any line parallel to its axis of SYMMETRY reflects through its focus, and vice versa. Rotating a parabola about its axis produces a surface (paraboloid) with the same reflection property, making it an ideal shape for satellite dishes and reflectors in headlights. Parabolas occur naturally as the paths of projectiles. The shape is also seen in the design of bridges and arches.

Paracel Islands \,par-ə-'sel\ *Chinese* **Xisha Qundao** \'shē-,shä-'chün-'daù\ *Vietnamese* **Quan Dao Hoang Sa** \'kwän-'daù-'hwäŋ-'sä\ Group of about 130 small coral islands and reefs, CHINA SEA, east of central Vietnam and southeast of HAINAN island, China. The low, barren islands, none of which exceeds 1 sq mi (2.5 sq km) in area, lack fresh water, and there are no permanent human residents. In 1932 they were claimed by FRENCH INDOCHINA, and Japan occupied some of the islands during World War II. China, Taiwan, and Vietnam all claim them. In 1974 China assumed control, and they remain a matter of contention.

Paracelsus \,par-ə-'sel-səs\ *orig.* **Philippus Aureolus Theophrastus Bombastus von Hohenheim** (1493–1541) German-Swiss physician and alchemist. He claimed to have received his doctoral degree at the University of Ferrara. He adopted the name "para-Celsus"—meaning "beyond Celsus" (the Roman authority on medicine)—and wandered throughout Europe and the Middle East, studying with alchemists. He valued the common sense of common people more than the dry teachings of ARISTOTLE, GALEN, and AVICENNA, and stressed nature's healing power. All were welcome at his lectures (which he gave in German, not Latin) at the University of Basel, but such broadmindedness scandalized the authorities, and eventually he was forced to flee the city. His written works include *Der grossen Wundartzney* (1536; "Great Surgery Book"). He anticipated by centuries the treatment of syphilis by mercury com-

O P Q R

pounds, the realization that inhaled dust causes miners' SILICOSIS, and HOMEOPATHY, and was the first to connect GOITER with minerals in drinking water.

parachute Umbrella-like device for slowing the descent of a body falling through the atmosphere. Separate panels sewn together form a canopy attached by suspension lines to a harness worn by the user. Originally designed to provide a safe escape from a disabled aircraft, parachutes are also used for dropping supplies and for slowing returning space capsules. The parachute was conceived by the 14th century, but practical demonstrations began only in the 1780s in France, leading in 1797 to a 3,200-ft (1,000-m) exhibition jump from a balloon by André-Jacques Garnerin (1769–1823); in 1802 he made a jump of 8,000 ft (2,400 m). Early parachute material was canvas, which was later replaced by silk and then nylon. See also SKYDIVING.

Paraclete See HOLY SPIRIT

paradox Apparently self-contradictory statement whose underlying meaning is revealed only by careful scrutiny. Its purpose is to arrest attention and provoke fresh thought, as in the statement "Less is more." In poetry, paradox functions as a device encompassing the tensions of error and truth simultaneously, not necessarily by startling juxtapositions but by subtle and continuous qualifications of the ordinary meanings of words. When a paradox is compressed into two words, as in "living death," it is called an oxymoron.

paradoxes of Zeno \'zē-ˌnō\ Arguments by which ZENO OF ELEA upheld the doctrine of PARMENIDES that real Being is unique and immobile. Zeno's arguments were aimed at discrediting the beliefs in plurality and motion that were inconsistent with Parmenides' doctrine. His best-known arguments are those against the reality of motion. One argument begins from the fact that a body in motion can reach a given point only after having traversed half the distance. But before traversing half, it must traverse half of this half, and so on ad infinitum; consequently, the goal can never be reached.

paraffin Paraffin WAX, an organic compound derived from PETROLEUM. It usually consists of a mixture of alkane hydrocarbons (also called paraffins) and is used for coating and sealing, for candles, and in cosmetics. See also ALKANE.

Paragua See PALAWAN

Paraguaná Peninsula \ˌpä-rä-gwä-'nä\ Peninsula, northwestern Venezuela, between the CARIBBEAN SEA and the Gulf of Venezuela. It has a low elevation, infertile soil, and sparse population. It became important in the 1950s and 1960s with the development of the petroleum industry. Pipelines lead from the oil fields to the large refineries on the western side of the peninsula, which is accessible to deep-draft tankers.

Paraguay \ˌpä-rä-'gwī, *Engl* 'par-ə-ˌgwā\ *officially* **Republic of Paraguay** Nation, southern central South America. Area: 157,043 sq mi (406,741 sq km). Population (1997 est.): 5,089,000. Capital: ASUNCIÓN. Most of the people are mestizo (mixed Spanish and GUARANÍ Indian); there are much smaller groups of Indians, blacks, Caucasians, and Asians. Languages: Spanish and Guaraní (both official). Religion: Roman Catholicism (88% of the population). Currency: Guaraní. Paraguay is a landlocked country of plains and swampland. The PARAGUAY RIVER, flowing from north to south, divides the country into two geographic regions: the Eastern Region, which is an extension of the Brazilian Plateau; and the Western Region, which forms the northern part of the GRAN CHACO plains. It has a developing market economy that is based largely on agriculture, trade, and light industries. It is a republic with two legislative houses; its chief of state and government is the president. Seminomadic tribes speaking Guaraní were in the area long before it was settled by Spain in the 16th–17th century. Paraguay was part of the viceroyalty of RIO DE LA PLATA until it became independent in 1811. It suffered from dictatorial governments in the 19th century and from the 1865 war with Brazil, Argentina, and Uruguay. The CHACO WAR with Bolivia over disputed territory was settled primarily in Paraguay's favor by the peace treaty of 1938. Military governments, including that of ALFREDO STROESSNER, predominated in the mid-20th century until the election of a civilian president, Juan Carlos Wasmosy, in 1993. It suffered from a financial crisis in the late 1990s, and democratic government was in jeopardy. See map above.

Paraguay River River, South America. The fifth-largest river in South America, it is 1,584 mi (2,550 km) long and the principal tributary of the PARANÁ RIVER. Rising in the Mato Grosso region of Brazil at 980 ft (300 m) above sea level, it crosses Paraguay to its confluence with the Paraná near the Argentine border. The GRAN CHACO plain extends west from the river.

Paraguayan War *or* **War of the Triple Alliance** (1864/65–70) Bloodiest conflict in Latin American history, fought between Paraguay and the allied countries of Argentina, Brazil, and Uruguay. The Paraguayan dictator Francisco Solano López (1827–1870), objecting to Brazil's interference in the politics of neighboring Uruguay, declared war on Brazil in 1864. The next year Argentina organized the Triple Alliance with Brazil and Uruguay. After three bloody years the allies annihilated the Paraguayan forces, but Solano López carried on a guerrilla war until he was killed in 1870. Paraguay was devastated by the war; its population was halved and territory covering 55,000 sq mi (140,000 sq km) was annexed by Brazil and Argentina.

Paraíba do Sul River \ˌpä-rà-'ē-bə-dü-'sül\ River, eastern Brazil, east of SÃO PAULO. It flows northeast and forms part of the border between Minas Gerais and Rio de Janeiro states before emptying into the Atlantic Ocean, after a course of about 600 mi (965 km). Its lower course is navigable, and it plays a vital role in Brazil's social and economic life. In its upper course, it is known as the Parahitinga.

parakeet Any of 115 species in 30 genera (subfamily Psittacinae) of small, slender seed-eating PARROTS with a long, tapering tail. Parakeets are found worldwide in warm regions. They typically form large flocks. Most species lay four to eight eggs in a tree hole. The most popular caged parakeet is the budgerigar *(Melopsittacus undulatus)*, mistakenly called LOVEBIRD; about 8 in. (19 cm) long, it may be any color but usually has cheek spots and close barring on the upper parts.

Budgerigar (*Melopsittacus undulatus*).
BRUCE COLEMAN LTD.

parallax \'par-ə-laks\ Difference in the direction of a celestial object as seen by an observer from two widely separated points, a measurement used to find a body's distance. The two positions of the observer and that of the object form a triangle; its apex angle (at the object) is twice the parallax, which becomes smaller when the distance is larger. Observations for calculating solar parallax can be made simultaneously from two different places on the earth's surface, reaching a maximum of 8,794 seconds of arc for observers at points diametrically opposed. The difference in a star's position as seen from earth at points six months apart in its orbit (stellar, or annual, parallax) allows measurements of distances too large to be made from two places on earth's surface. The nearest star system, ALPHA CENTAURI, has a stellar parallax of 0.76 seconds of arc. The parallax of stars over 30 PARSECS from earth has been determined from the EUROPEAN SPACE AGENCY's Hipparcos satellite.

parallel bars Event in men's gymnastics in which a pair of wooden bars supported horizontally above the floor at the same height is used to perform acrobatic feats. Competitors combine swings and vaults with stationary positions requiring strength and balance, though swings and vaults must predominate. It has been included as an Olympic gymnastics event since the modern games began in 1896. See also UNEVEN PARALLEL BARS.

Parallel bars.
STEWART FRASER—COLORSPORT

parallel evolution EVOLUTION of geographically separated groups in such a way that they show physical resemblances. A notable example is the similarity between the marsupial mammals of Australia and placental mammals elsewhere, which have arrived at remarkably similar forms through the separate courses of their evolution.

parallel postulate One of the five postulates of EUCLID underpinning EUCLIDEAN GEOMETRY. It states that through any given point not on a line there passes only one line parallel to that line in the same plane. Unlike Euclid's other four postulates, it is not self-evident, nor can it be derived from the AXIOMS of geometry. Nor, it turns out, is the parallel postulate necessary. In the 19th century, CARL FRIEDRICH GAUSS, NIKOLAY LOBACHEVSKY, BERNHARD RIEMANN, and others discovered NON-EUCLIDEAN GEOMETRIES that result when the parallel postulate is altered.

paralysis *or* **palsy** Loss or impairment of voluntary use of one or more MUSCLES. It may be flaccid (with loss of muscle tone) or spastic (stiff). Hemiplegia (one-sided paralysis) is usually caused by STROKE or brain TUMOR on the opposite side. Diplegia (two-sided paralysis, as in CEREBRAL PALSY) results from generalized brain disease. SPINAL-CORD DAMAGE (from bone or joint disease, FRACTURE, or tumor affecting the vertebrae; inflammatory and degenerative diseases; or PERNICIOUS ANEMIA) paralyzes the body at and below the level of the damage (paraplegia if the legs and lower body only; quadriplegia if arms and legs). POLIOMYELITIS and polyneuritis (NEURITIS of multiple nerves) result in paralysis with muscle wasting. Bell's palsy (a type of neuritis) paralyzes the muscles of one side of the face. MUSCULAR DYSTROPHY causes paralysis by attacking muscle. Metabolic causes include MYASTHENIA GRAVIS. Paralysis may also have psychiatric causes (see HYSTERIA).

paramagnetism Kind of MAGNETISM that occurs in materials weakly attracted by a strong magnet. Compounds containing iron, palladium, platinum, and the rare-earth elements exhibit strong paramagnetism because they have atoms with some incomplete inner ELECTRON shells. Their unpaired electrons make the atoms behave like tiny permanent magnets that align with and strengthen an applied MAGNETIC FIELD. As the temperature rises, strong paramagnetism decreases because of the greater random motion of the atoms. Weak paramagnetism, found in many solid metallic elements, is independent of temperature.

Paramaribo \ˌpä-rä-ˈmä-rē-bō\ City (pop., 1993 est.: 201,000), seaport, and capital of Suriname, on the SURINAME RIVER near the Atlantic Ocean. Originally an Indian village, it became a French settlement c. 1640. In 1651 it became a British colony. It was ceded to the Dutch in 1667. It is built on a shingle reef that stands 16 ft (5 m) above the river at low tide. Much of the distinctive Dutch colonial architecture and a canal system remain. Since 1945 the city has grown considerably because of tourism and industries.

paramecium \ˌpar-ə-ˈmē-sē-əm\ Any of the free-living single-celled PROTOZOANS that make up the genus *Paramecium,* all easily cultivated in the laboratory. Most are about the size of the period at the end of this sentence. They vary in shape and are surrounded by a rigid protein layer (pellicle) covered with hundreds of cilia that beat rhythmically to propel them and to direct bacteria and other food particles into their oral groove. Food particles are collected into food VACUOLES, where digestion takes place. Two (occasionally three) contractile vacuoles close to the surface near the ends of the cell expand and contract as they discharge metabolic wastes and excess fluid. Paramecia have two kinds of nuclei: a large macronucleus (the center of all metabolic activities) and at least one small micronucleus (which stores the genetic material necessary for sexual reproduction).

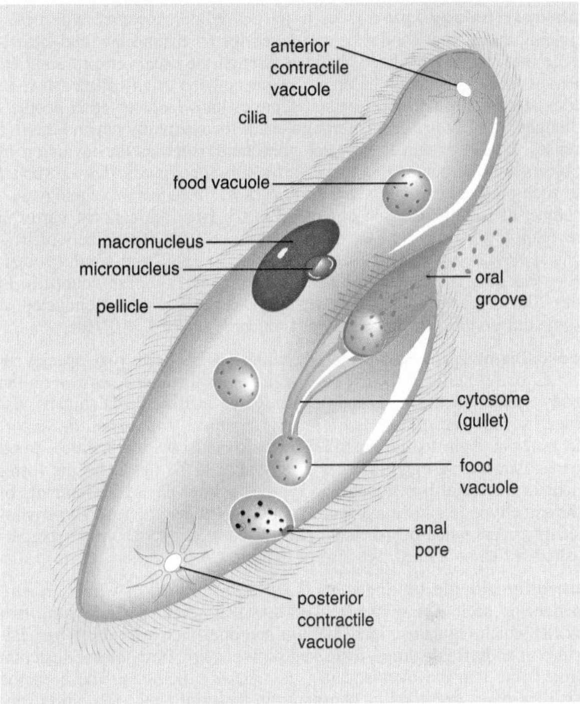

General features of a paramecium.

Paramount Communications Media and communications corporation. It was founded (as Paramount Pictures Corp.) by W. W. Hodkinson in 1914 as a film distributor. It became a motion-picture company two years later and won attention with stars such as MARY PICKFORD, GLORIA SWANSON, and RUDOLPH VALENTINO. In the late 1920s and 1930s the studio added CLAUDETTE COLBERT, Gary COOPER, and MARLENE DIETRICH to its roster. Forced to declare bankruptcy after its chain of theaters suffered losses during the transition to sound, the company was reorganized two years later as Paramount Pictures, Inc. Among its successes of the 1940s and '50s were the films of PRESTON STURGES and BILLY WILDER. In 1966 Gulf & Western Industries took control of Paramount, and the new company later changed its name to Paramount Communications. In 1994 it was acquired by Viacom Inc., which in 2000 merged with CBS.

Paraná River \ˌpä-rä-ˈnä\ River, South America, the second-longest after the AMAZON RIVER. It rises on the plateau of southeastern central Brazil and flows generally south 3,032 mi (4,880 km) to join the URUGUAY RIVER and form the Río de la PLATA estuary on the Atlantic Ocean. Its drainage basin includes most of southeastern Brazil, Paraguay, eastern Bolivia, and northern Argentina. From its origin at the confluence of the Rio Grande and PARANAÍBA RIVER to its junction with the PARAGUAY RIVER, it is known as the Alto (Upper) Paraná. Completion of the Itaipú Dam between Paraguay and Brazil in the 1980s submerged the massive Guaíra Falls and created a large reservoir.

Paranaíba River \ˌpä-rä-nä-ˈē-bə\ River, southern central Brazil. Rising on the western slopes of the Serra da Mata da Corda, it flows southwest for about 600 mi (1,000 km). It collects eight large tributaries along its course to join the Rio Grande and form the PARANÁ RIVER. In the 1970s Brazil began irrigation projects for cattle raising and agriculture in the river valley.

paranoia Mental disorder characterized by delusions of persecution or grandeur, usually without HALLUCINATIONS. Paranoia was formerly classified as a distinct PSYCHOSIS but is now generally treated as one of several varieties of SCHIZOPHRENIA or, in milder cases, of PERSONALITY DISORDER. The paranoid person generally suffers from exaggerated self-reference, a tendency to construe independent events and acts as pertaining to him- or herself.

parapsychology \ˌpar-ə-ˌsī-ˈkä-lə-jē\ Discipline concerned with investigating events that cannot be accounted for by natural law and knowledge that cannot have been obtained through the usual sensory abilities. Parapsychology studies the cognitive phenomena often called EXTRASENSORY PERCEPTION, in which a person acquires knowledge of other people's thoughts or of future events through channels apparently beyond the five senses. It also examines physical phenomena such as the levitation of objects and the bending of metal through psychokinesis. Though belief in such phenomena may be traced to earliest times, parapsychology as a subject of serious research originated in the late 19th century, partly in reaction to the growth of the spiritualist movement. The Society of Psychical Research was established in London in 1882, and similar societies were later founded in the U.S. and in many European countries. In the 20th century research into parapsychology was also conducted at some universities, notably at Duke University under J. B. Rhine.

parasitism \ˈpar-ə-sə-ˌti-zəm\ Relationship between two species in which one benefits at the expense of the other. Ectoparasites live on the body surface of the host; endoparasites live in their hosts' organs, tissues, or cells and often rely on a third organism (the carrier, or vector) to transmit them to the host. The CUCKOO and COWBIRD practice brood parasitism, laying eggs in other birds' nests to be raised by the foster parents. In social parasitism, one type of animal parasitizes animals of the same type (e.g., one ant species on different ant species). Hyperparasitism occurs when parasites are parasitized (e.g., PROTOZOANS hyperparasitize a flea on a dog). See also PREDATION.

parathyroid gland Endocrine GLAND, two to eight of which are embedded in each side of the THYROID GLAND. It secretes parathyroid HORMONE, which regulates blood calcium and phosphorus levels. When calcium in body fluids drops, increased hormone secretion releases calcium from BONE into the bloodstream (see CALCIUM DEFICIENCY). The hormone also increases excretion of phosphate in the urine, lowering blood concentrations, and may play a role in magnesium metabolism. When thyroid removal is required, the parathyroid glands must be separated out and left in place. See also ENDOCRINE SYSTEM.

parchment Processed skins of certain animals (chiefly sheep, goats, and calves) that have been prepared for the purpose of writing on them. Parchment was probably invented in Greece in the 2nd century BC. Skins had been used for writing material even earlier (c. 2400 BC), but the new, more thorough method of cleaning, stretching, and scraping made possible the use of both sides of a manuscript leaf, leading to the replacement of the rolled manuscript by the bound book (CODEX). Especially fine parchment is known as vellum. In modern usage, the terms "parchment" and "vellum" are sometimes used for a type of high-quality paper.

pardo (Spanish: "brown") In Venezuela, a person of mixed African, European, and Indian ancestry. In the colonial period, pardos, like all nonwhites, were kept in a state of servitude, with no hope of gaining wealth or political power. Nevertheless, most pardos remained royalists during much of the war for independence because they relied on Spain for protection in their conflicts with the Venezuelan-born whites, toward whom the European Spaniards took a superior attitude. In Brazil, a pardo is a person of mixed European and African descent.

pardon In law, release from guilt or remission of punishment. The power to pardon is generally exercised by the state's chief executive officer. A pardon may be full or conditional. A conditional pardon imposes a lesser punishment or some other obligation. Some states still bar pardoned offenders from holding public office or obtaining professional licenses.

Paré \pà-ˈrā\, **Ambroise** (1510–1590) French physician and surgeon. Employed as an army surgeon in 1537, Paré preferred less drastic measures than those then in use (including castration in hernia surgery, and searing of large arteries with hot irons during amputation) and operated only when necessary. He introduced the implantation of gold and silver teeth, artificial limbs, and artificial eyes (see PROSTHESIS) and invented many instruments, popularized the truss for hernias, and first suggested that syphilis caused aneurysms. He published books on a wide variety of medical matters; his surgical works were especially influential.

Pareto \pä-ˈre-tō\, **Vilfredo** (1848–1923) Italian economist and sociologist. Educated at the University of Turin, he worked as an engineer and later served as a director of a large Italian railway. He taught at the University of Lausanne from 1893. His law of income distribution used a complex mathematical formula to trace historical patterns in the distribution of wealth. In 1906 he laid the foundation of modern WELFARE ECONOMICS with his concept of the Pareto optimum, which stated that a society's resources are not optimally allocated as long as it is possible to make at least one person better off while keeping others as well off as before.

Parhae \ˈpò-ˈhī\ *Chinese* **Bohai** \ˈbò-ˈhī\ State established in the 8th century in northern Manchuria and northern Korea. Founded by a former Korean general, Tae Cho-yang, it was considered a successor state to KOGURYO, which had occupied much of the same territory before its conquest by SILLA in 668. Like Silla, Parhae was a tributary state of TANG-DYNASTY China. It traded with the nomadic tribes of the north and with China and Japan. Parhae was conquered in 926 by the Khitan tribes almost 20 years after their creation of the LIAO DYNASTY on China's northern borders.

pari-mutuel \ˌpar-i-ˈmyü-chə-wəl\ Betting pool in which those who bet on competitors finishing in the first three places share the total amount bet minus a percentage for the management. First introduced in France c. 1870, it soon became one of the most popular methods of betting on horse races internationally. Today computers calculate betting pools and current odds on each horse and flash the figures to the public at regular intervals. The system is used largely for off-track betting. Pari-mutuel betting is also practiced in dog racing and JAI ALAI.

Paria \pə-ˈrē-ə\, **Gulf of** Inlet of the Caribbean Sea, between the Venezuela coast and Trinidad. Extending about 100 mi (160 km) east–west and 40 mi (65 km) north–south, it is linked with the Caribbean to the north and the Atlantic Ocean to the south. Its ports, including PORT-OF-SPAIN, Trinidad, handle shipments of petroleum, iron ore, and agricultural products. In 1498, on his third voyage to the western Hemisphere, CHRISTOPHER COLUMBUS probably first sighted South America when he sailed into the gulf.

Paricutin \pä-ˈrē-kü-ˌtēn\ Volcano, western Michoacán state, western central Mexico, on the site of the former village of Parícutin. It is about 9,100 ft (2,775 m) high and is one of the youngest volcanoes on earth. It began to erupt in an open field in 1943 and buried the village. Eruptions ceased in 1952.

Parilia \pə-ˈri-lē-ə\ Ancient Roman festival celebrated annually on April 21 in honor of the goddess Pales, protector of flocks and herds. It was celebrated first by the early kings of Rome and later by the PONTIFEX maximus. The VESTAL VIRGINS opened the festival by distributing straw and the ashes and blood of sacrificed animals. Ritual cleaning, anointing, and adornment of herds and stalls followed. The celebrants jumped over a bonfire three times to complete the rite of purification.

Paris In GREEK MYTHOLOGY, a son of King PRIAM of TROY and his wife, HECUBA. An evil portent prompted his parents to abandon him as an infant. Unknown to them, he was raised as a shepherd, and as a young man he was received home again after winning a boxing contest against Priam's other sons. ZEUS chose him to determine which of three goddesses was most beautiful—HERA, ATHENA, or APHRODITE. In the famous "judgment of Paris," he chose Aphrodite because she offered to help him win the most beautiful woman alive. His seduction of HELEN was the cause of the TROJAN WAR. Near the end of the war, Paris shot the arrow that killed ACHILLES and soon afterward was himself killed.

O P Q R

Paris City (pop., 1999: 2,125,246; metro. area pop., 9,644,507), river port, and capital of France, on both banks of the SEINE RIVER. Lutetia, the original settlement, on an island in the Seine, was in existence by the late 3rd century BC. It was captured and fortified by the Romans in 52 BC. During the 1st century AD the city spread to the left bank of the Seine. By the early 4th century it was known as Paris. It withstood several Viking sieges 885–87 and became the capital of France in 987, when HUGH CAPET, the count of Paris, became king. The city was improved during the reign of PHILIP II, who formally recognized the University of PARIS c. 1200. In the 14th–15th century its development was hindered by the BLACK DEATH and the HUNDRED YEARS' WAR. In the 17th–18th century it was improved and beautified. Leading events of the FRENCH REVOLUTION took place there 1789–99. NAPOLEON III commissioned GEORGES HAUSSMANN to modernize the city's infrastructure and add several new bridges over the Seine. It was the site of the PARIS PEACE CONFERENCE, ending WORLD WAR I. During World War II it was occupied by German troops. It is now the financial, commercial, transportation, artistic, and intellectual center of France. The city's many attractions include the EIFFEL TOWER, NOTRE-DAME DE PARIS, the LOUVRE, Pantheon, POMPIDOU CENTER, and PARIS OPERA, as well as boulevards, public parks, and gardens.

Paris, Congress of (1856) Conference in Paris to produce the treaty that ended the CRIMEAN WAR. The treaty was signed between Russia on one side and France, Britain, Sardinia-Piedmont, and Turkey on the other. It guaranteed the independence and territorial integrity of Turkey. Russia was forced to surrender Bessarabia to Moldavia, warships of all nations were barred from the Black Sea, and the Danube River was opened to shipping of all countries. The congress also adopted the first codified law of the sea, which banned privateering and defined a legal naval blockade.

Paris, Treaty of (1229) Treaty by which RAYMOND VII of Toulouse conceded defeat to LOUIS IX of France after the ALBIGENSIAN CRUSADE. It arranged the marriage of Raymond's daughter and Louis's brother and provided for the eventual return of LANGUEDOC to the crown, thus destroying the independence of the princes of the south.

Paris, Treaty of (1259) Peace treaty signed by HENRY III of England and LOUIS IX of France. It allowed the English to keep Aquitaine and nearby territories but obliged Henry to acknowledge himself the vassal of the French king. The agreement kept peace between England and France until the outbreak of the HUNDRED YEARS' WAR in 1337.

Paris, Treaty of (1763) Treaty concluding the SEVEN YEARS' WAR (including the FRENCH AND INDIAN WAR). It was signed by Britain and Hanover on one side and France and Spain on the other. France renounced to Britain the mainland of North America east of the Mississippi, its conquests in India since 1749, and four West Indian islands. Britain restored to France four other West Indian islands and the West African colony of Gorée (Senegal). In return for recovering Havana and Manila, Spain ceded Florida to Britain and received Louisiana from the French.

Paris, Treaty of (1814) Treaty signed in Paris that ended the NAPOLEONIC WARS between France and the Allies (Austria, Britain, Prussia, Russia, Spain, Sweden, and Portugal). The terms were generous to France, since NAPOLEON had abdicated and the Bourbon dynasty was restored. France was allowed to retain its boundaries of 1792 and ceded only several islands to Britain. Other terms were left to be discussed later.

Paris, Treaty of (1815) Second treaty between France and the Allies, following NAPOLEON'S HUNDRED DAYS and final defeat. It was harsher than the first Treaty of PARIS (1814). France was required to return to its borders of 1790 and was stripped of the Saar and Savoy regions; it was also obliged to pay an indemnity of 700 million francs and to support a 150,000-man army of occupation for three to five years.

Paris, University of Second-oldest European university (after the University of BOLOGNA), founded c. 1170. It grew out of the cathedral schools of Notre-Dame, and, with papal support, soon became a great center of Christian orthodox teaching. In the medieval period its professors included St. BONAVENTURE, ALBERTUS MAGNUS, and THOMAS AQUINAS. Its most celebrated early college was the Sorbonne, founded c. 1257. The university declined somewhat under the impact of the Reformation and Counter-Reformation. With the French Revolution and Napoleon's reforms, teaching became more independent of religion and politics. By the mid-20th century the university had again become a preeminent scientific and intellectual center. In May 1968 a Sorbonne student protest grew into a serious national crisis. This led to decentralizing reforms, the old university being replaced in 1970 by a system in Paris and its suburbs called the Universities of Paris I–XIII. Enrollment systemwide is about 310,000.

Paris Commune *or* **Commune of Paris** (March 18–May 28, 1871) Insurrection of Paris against the French government. After France's defeat in the FRANCO-PRUSSIAN WAR and the collapse of the SECOND EMPIRE, the republican Parisians feared that the conservative majority in the National Assembly would restore the monarchy. On March 18 the National Guard in Paris resisted orders to disarm, and after municipal elections were won by the revolutionaries, they formed the Commune government. Factions included the so-called Jacobins, who wanted the Paris Commune to control the revolution (as its namesake had in the French Revolution); the Proudhonists, socialist followers of PIERRE JOSEPH PROUDHON who supported a federation of communes; and the Blanquistes, socialist followers of LOUIS AUGUSTE BLANQUI who demanded violent action. Government forces quickly suppressed communes elsewhere in France, then entered Paris on May 21. In a week of fierce fighting, they crushed the Communards, who had set up barricades in the streets and burned public buildings, including the Tuileries Palace. About 20,000 insurrectionists and 750 government troops were killed. In the aftermath, the government took harsh repressive action; 38,000 suspects were arrested and over 7,000 were deported.

Paris-Match \på-rē-'mȧch\ Weekly pictorial magazine published in France since 1949 as the successor to *L'Illustration* (1843–1944). A popular news and current-events magazine aimed at the middle class, it features picture-stories on such subjects as public affairs, entertainment, fashion, and consumer products. Its format resembles that of *Life*, and it is similarly noted for topicality and outstanding photography. Under the ownership of Jean Prouvost (died 1978), it achieved prestige and financial success. It is now published by Hachette Filipacchi Medias, one of the world's largest magazine publishers.

Paris Opera *or* **Opéra Garnier** \ō-per-'ä-gårn-'yā\ Opera house in Paris, designed by Charles Garnier (1825–1898). The extraordinarily lavish building, considered one of the masterpieces of the Second Empire (BEAUX-ARTS STYLE), was begun in 1861 and opened in 1875. The floor plan is as elaborate as the exterior. The interior, with its generous circulation space, including a grand staircase and numerous richly decorated galleries, foyers, and corridors, provided a place to be seen as well as a splendid performance space.

Paris Peace Conference (1919–20) Meeting that inaugurated the international settlement after WORLD WAR I. It opened on January 12, 1919, with representatives from over 30 countries. The principal delegates were France's GEORGES CLEMENCEAU, Britain's DAVID LLOYD GEORGE, the U.S.'s WOODROW WILSON, and Italy's VITTORIO EMANUELE ORLANDO, who with their foreign ministers formed a Supreme Council. Commissions were appointed to study specific financial and territorial questions, including REPARATIONS. The major products of the conference were the LEAGUE OF NATIONS; the Treaty of VERSAILLES, presented to Germany; the Treaty of SAINT-GERMAIN, presented to Austria; and the Treaty of NEUILLY, presented to Bulgaria. The inauguration of the League of Nations on January 16, 1920, brought the conference to a close. Treaties were subsequently concluded with Hungary (Treaty of TRIANON, 1920) and Turkey (Treaties of SÈVRES, 1920, and LAUSANNE, 1923).

parity In economics, equality in price, rate of exchange, purchasing power, or wages. In international exchange, parity exists when the EXCHANGE RATE between two CURRENCIES makes the purchasing power of both currencies equal. Adjustments to maintain parity can occur in the marketplace as prices change in response to SUPPLY AND DEMAND, or through the intervention of national governments or international agencies such as the INTERNATIONAL MONETARY FUND. In U.S. agricultural economics, the term parity is used for a system of regulating the prices of farm commodities, usually by government price supports and production quotas, to guarantee farmers the purchasing power they had in a past base period. Parity is also used in personnel administration to establish equitable wage rates for various classes of employees.

parity In physics, a property related to the symmetry of the WAVE FUNCTION representing a system of fundamental particles. It plays an important role in QUANTUM MECHANICS in the description of a physical system.

Parity transformation replaces a system with a type of mirror image in which the spatial coordinates describing the system are inverted, so that the coordinates x, y, and z are replaced with $-x$, $-y$, and $-z$. If a system is identical to the original system after parity transformation, its parity is even. If the image is the negative of the original, its parity is odd. In either case, the physical observables of the system remain unchanged. In 1957 Chien-Shiung Wu (1912–1997) and coworkers made the surprising discovery that BETA DECAY reactions do not conserve parity; in other words, the inverted image of the process does not exist in nature. This is a general property of the WEAK FORCE.

park Large outdoor area set aside for recreation. The earliest parks were hunting grounds of the Persian kings; such reserves became shaped by riding paths and shelters. A second type of park derived from the open-air meeting places of Greece, where the functions of an area for exercise, social concourse, and athletes' training ground were combined with elements of a sculpture gallery and religious center. Parks of post-Renaissance times featured extensive woods, raised galleries, and often elaborate aviaries and cages for wild animals. What often differentiates present-day parks is their accommodation for active recreation; facilities may include outdoor theaters, zoos, concert shells, concessions for dining and dancing, amusement areas, boating areas, and areas for sports. See also NATIONAL PARK.

Park, Mungo (1771–1806) Scottish explorer of the Niger. A trained surgeon, Park had traveled to the East Indies before being chosen by the African Association to head an expedition to find the source of the NIGER RIVER (1795–97). He lost most of his crew and supplies, was imprisoned and tortured for four months by hostile Arabs, and suffered severe illness, reaching Ségou (now in Mali) but not the river's source. His *Travels in the Interior Districts of Africa* (1797) became a great popular success. On a second expedition (1805–6) he reached BAMAKO, but was killed on the return trip.

Park, Robert E(zra) (1864–1944) U.S. sociologist. Born in Harveyville, Pa., he worked for BOOKER T. WASHINGTON and later taught principally at the University of Chicago—where he was a leading figure in the "Chicago school" of sociology, characterized by empirical research and the use of human ecology models—and at Fisk University. He is noted for his work on ethnic groups, particularly American blacks, and on human ecology, a term he has been credited with coining. Park wrote *Introduction to the Science of Sociology* (1921) and *The City* (1925) with Ernest W. Burgess; *Race and Culture* (1950) and *Human Communities* (1952) were published posthumously.

Parker, Alan (born 1944) British-U.S. film director. After working as an advertising copywriter and director of TV commercials, he formed a production company with Alan Marshall and produced several short television films. He wrote and directed *Bugsy Malone* (1976), and won acclaim for *Midnight Express* (1978). His later work includes such varied films as *Fame* (1980), *Mississippi Burning* (1988), *The Commitments* (1991), and *Evita* (1996).

Parker, Alton B(rooks) (1852–1926) U.S. jurist. Born in Cortland, N.Y., he served in county and state judicial posts. As chief justice of the New York court of appeals (1898–1904), he was noted for upholding the rights of labor. He was the Democratic presidential candidate in 1904; soundly defeated by Pres. THEODORE ROOSEVELT, he resumed his law practice.

Charlie Parker, 1949.
AP/WIDE WORLD PHOTOS

Parker, Charlie *orig.* **Charles Christopher** (1920–1955) U.S. saxophonist and composer, one of the originators of BEBOP and among the greatest improvisers in jazz. Born in Kansas City, Parker played with Jay McShann's big band (1940–42) and those of EARL HINES (1942–44) and BILLY ECKSTINE (1944) before leading his own small groups in New York. (A nickname acquired in the early 1940s, Yardbird, was shortened to Bird and used throughout his career.) Parker frequently worked with DIZZY GILLESPIE in the mid-1940s, making a series of small-group recordings that heralded the arrival of bebop as a mature outgrowth of the improvisation of the late swing era. His direct, cutting tone and unprecedented dexterity on the alto saxophone made rapid tempos and fast flurries of notes trademarks of bebop, and his complex, subtle harmonic understanding brought an altogether new sound to the music. Easily the most influential jazz musician of his generation, his chronic drug addiction and early death contributed to making him a tragic legend.

Parker, Dorothy *orig.* **Dorothy Rothschild** (1893–1967) U.S. short-story writer and poet. Born in West End, N.J., she grew up in affluence in New York City. She was a drama critic for *Vanity Fair* and wrote book reviews for the *New Yorker* (1927–33). Her poetry volumes include *Enough Rope* (1926) and *Death and Taxes* (1931). Her short stories were collected in *Laments for the Living* (1930) and *After Such Pleasures* (1933). She also worked as a film writer, reported on the Spanish Civil War, and collaborated on several plays. A member of the Algonquin Round Table, she is chiefly remembered for her wit.

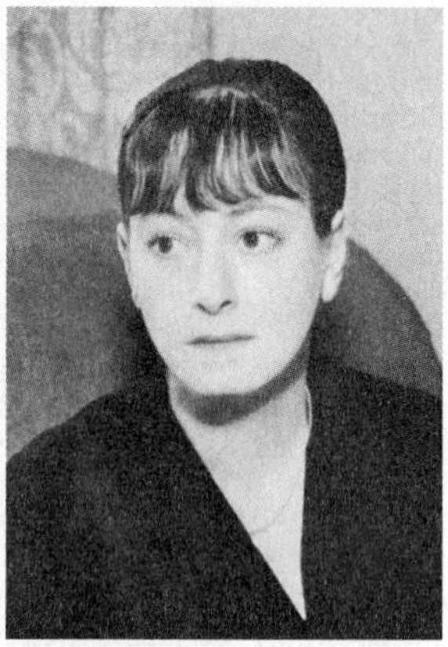
Dorothy Parker, 1939.
CULVER PICTURES

Parkinson, C(yril) Northcote (1909–1993) British historian and writer. He received a PhD from Kings College, London, and later taught at various schools in England and Malaya. He is most famous for his 1955 formulation of the satiric "Parkinson's Law," which stated that "Work expands to fill the time available for its completion." In *The Law and the Profits* (1960) he discussed a second law, "Expenditure rises to meet income."

parkinsonism Neurological disorder causing progressive loss of control of movement. It was first described in 1817 by the British physician James Parkinson (1755–1824). The cause of primary parkinsonism, or Parkinson's disease, is unknown. The mean age of onset is about 57, but juvenile parkinsonism is also known. Neurons in the brain that normally produce DOPAMINE deteriorate. When 60–80% are destroyed, signals suppressing unintended movement are disrupted and symptoms appear, including tremor at rest, muscle rigidity, trouble in starting movements, and loss of balance. Known causes include SLEEPING SICKNESS; certain poisons; repeated blows to the head, as in boxing; and the "designer drug" MPTP. Environmental toxins or genetic susceptibility may account for some cases. Drug therapy requires careful scheduling and combinations to delay development of tolerance and side effects. Surgical pallidotomy (destruction of the globus pallidus, a brain structure involved in motor control) and transplantation of fetal dopamine-producing tissue remain experimental.

Parkman, Francis (1823–1893) U.S. historian. A native of Boston, Parkman graduated from Harvard University before embarking in 1846 on a journey to the West that resulted in *The California and Oregon Trail* (1849). He is noted for his seven-part history *France and England in North America*, covering the colonial period from the beginnings to 1763; its volumes include *Pioneers of France in the New World* (1865); *Montcalm and Wolfe* (1884), which demonstrates how biography can penetrate the spirit of an age; and *A Half-Century of Conflict* (1892), which exemplifies his literary artistry.

Parks, Gordon (born 1912) U.S. writer, photographer, and film director. Born in Fort Scott, Kan., Parks worked as a staff photographer for *Life* (1948–72), becoming known for his portrayals of ghetto life, black nationalists, and the civil-rights movement. His first work of fiction was *The Learning Tree* (1963), a novel about a black adolescent in Kansas in the 1920s. He has combined poetry and photography in collections such as *A Poet and His Camera* (1968) and *Glimpses Toward Infinity* (1996). He has also directed several motion pictures, including *Shaft* (1971).

O P Q R

Parks, Rosa *orig.* **Rosa McCauley** (born 1913) U.S. black civil-rights activist. Born in Tuskegee, Ala., she worked as a seamstress in Montgomery, where she was active in the NAACP (1943–56). In 1955 she was arrested after refusing to give her seat on a public bus to a white man. The resultant boycott of the bus system organized by MARTIN LUTHER KING and others brought the CIVIL RIGHTS MOVEMENT to new prominence. In 1957 Parks moved to Detroit, where she was a staff assistant (1965–88) to U.S. Rep. John Conyers. She was awarded the Congressional Gold Medal in 1999.

Parlement \'pär-lə-mənt\ Supreme court under the ancien régime in France. It developed out of the *curia regis* ("king's court") in which the CAPETIAN kings convened their chief vassals and prelates to consider feudal and political issues. By the mid-13th century this judicial institution was known as Parlement and served as a court of appeals against the judgments of royal officials. Later Parlements also reviewed the king's edicts to determine whether they were just and lawful. The chief Parlement was located in Paris, and others were established in the provinces. The Parlements were abolished in the FRENCH REVOLUTION.

Parliament Legislative assembly of Britain and of other governments modeled after it. The British Parliament consists of the monarch, the House of LORDS, and the House of COMMONS, and traces its roots to the union (c. 1300) of the Great Council and the King's Court, two bodies that treated with and advised the king. In the 14th century, Parliament was split into two houses, with the lords spiritual and temporal (i.e., not only the nobility but also high officials of the church) debating in one and the knights and burgesses in the other. In the 14th century Parliament also began to present petitions ("bills") to the king, which with his assent would become law. ROBERT WALPOLE was the first party leader to head the government as PRIME MINISTER (1721–42). See also PARLIAMENTARY DEMOCRACY.

Parliament, Canadian Legislature of Canada, created by the BRITISH NORTH AMERICA ACT. The 301 members of its House of Commons are elected for maximum terms of five years from the provinces on the principle of representation by population. The 105 members of its Senate are appointed by Canada's governor-general from the regions of Canada and serve until age 75. The parliament has authority over the armed forces, regulates trade and commerce, levies taxes, and is in charge of banking, credit, currency and bankruptcy, criminal law, postal services, fisheries, patents and copyrights, the census, navigation and shipping, railways, canals, and telegraphs. It also retains powers not specifically assigned to provincial legislatures. The leader of the party winning the most seats in a general election becomes prime minister and is called on by the governor-general to form a government. He generally chooses elected party colleagues to form the CABINET. The party winning the second-largest number of seats in the House becomes the official opposition party.

Parliament Act of 1911 Act passed in the British Parliament that deprived the House of LORDS of its absolute power of veto on legislation. Proposed by a Liberal majority in the House of COMMONS, the act stated that any bill passed unchanged by the Commons in three separate sessions over two years could be presented for the royal assent (necessary for a bill to become law) without the Lords' consent. By subordinating the Lords to the Commons, the act was seen as another step in making the British Constitution more democratic.

parliamentary democracy Democratic form of government in which the party with the greatest representation in the parliament forms the government, its leader becoming PRIME MINISTER or chancellor. Executive functions are exercised by members of the parliament appointed by the prime minister to the CABINET. The parties in the minority serve in opposition to the majority and have the duty to regularly challenge it. The prime minister may be removed from power whenever he or she loses the confidence of a majority of the ruling party or of the parliament. Parliamentary democracy originated in Britain (see PARLIAMENT) and was adopted in several of its former colonies.

parliamentary procedure *or* **rules of order** Generally accepted rules, precedents, and practices used in the governance of deliberative assemblies. They are intended to maintain decorum, ascertain the will of the majority, preserve the rights of the minority, and facilitate the orderly transaction of business. Rules of parliamentary procedure originated in Britain in the 16th–17th century, and were subsequently adopted by legislatures around the world. *Robert's Rules of Order*, codified in 1876 by U.S. Gen. Henry M. Robert (1837–1923), has been regularly refined and enlarged in the decades since and remains the standard in the U.S.

Parma City (pop, 1996 est.: 166,000), EMILIA-ROMAGNA region, northern Italy, on the Parma River. Founded by the Romans in 183 BC, it became an episcopal see in the 4th century AD. It was destroyed by the Ostrogoths under THEODORIC I, but was rebuilt in the Middle Ages. Made part of the duchy of Parma and Piacenza in 1545, it was held by the FARNESE FAMILY and later passed to the Austrians. In 1815 Napoleon gave the city to his second consort, MARIE-LOUISE. In 1861 it became part of united Italy. It was badly damaged during World War II, but was rebuilt. It is the commercial center of an agricultural region and is famous for its parmesan cheese. Sites of interest include the 12th-century Romanesque cathedral, the 13th-century baptistery, and the university (founded in the 11th century).

Parmenides \pär-'men-ə-ˌdēz\ (born c. 515 BC) Greek philosopher, leader of the ELEATICS. His general teaching has been reconstructed from the few surviving fragments of his lengthy verse composition *On Nature*. He held that the multiplicity of existing things, their changing forms and motion, are but an appearance of a single eternal reality ("Being"), thus giving rise to the Parmenidean principle that "all is one." He went on to say that all claims of change or of non-Being are illogical. Because he introduced the method of basing claims about appearances on a logical concept of Being, he is considered a founder of METAPHYSICS. PLATO's dialogue *Parmenides* deals with his thought.

Parmigianino \ˌpär-mi-jä-'nē-nō\ *orig.* **Girolamo Francesco Maria Mazzola** (1503–1540) Italian painter and etcher. Born in Parma (the source of his nickname), he painted some of his early frescoes for San Giovanni Evangelista; they were influenced by CORREGGIO, who had recently worked in the same church. His originality is seen in his *Self-Portrait in a Convex Mirror* (1524). His *Madonna of the Long Neck* (1534) is typical of his later work, which is characterized by ambiguity of spatial composition, elongation of the human figure, and the pursuit of a rhythmical, sensuous beauty beyond nature. Among the most remarkable portrait painters of his age, he was one of the first artists to develop the elegant and sophisticated version of MANNERISM that influenced the next generation of painters, and one of the first Italian artists to practice etching.

Parnaíba River \ˌpär-nȧ-'ē-bə\ River, northeastern Brazil. It rises in the Serra da Tabatinga and flows northeast for 1,056 mi (1,700 km) to empty into the Atlantic Ocean, forming a delta at its mouth. The river has great economic importance. It is navigable by shallow-draft vessels from its mouth at least as far south as the junction of the Rio Canindé. The port of Parnaíba (pop., 1991: 128,000), located near the river's mouth, is a commercial center.

Parnassian poets \pär-'na-sē-ən\ Members of a French school of poetry of the second half of the 19th century that was headed by C.-M.-R. Leconte de Lisle (1818–1894) and THEOPHILE GAUTIER. The Parnassians stressed restraint, objectivity, technical perfection, and precise description as a reaction against the emotionalism and verbal excess of ROMANTICISM. Their name came from the anthology to which they contributed, *Le Parnasse contemporain* (1866, 1871, 1876). Their influence was evident in movements such as MODERNISMO and led to experimentation in meters and verse forms and the revival of the SONNET.

Parnassus \pär-'na-səs\, **Mt.** Mountain in central Greece. Located in the Pindus range, it rises to a height of 8,061 ft (2,457 m). In the ancient world it was sacred to APOLLO and the Corycian nymphs, probably because of its proximity to DELPHI and its oracle. For Roman poets the Castalian spring on Parnassus was a source of inspiration, and the mountain was regarded as the home of the MUSES.

Parnell \pär-'nel\, **Charles Stewart** (1846–1891) Irish nationalist leader. After an education at Cambridge Univ., he returned to Ireland and served in the British Parliament (1875–91), introducing obstructionist legislative tactics to call attention to Ireland's needs. In 1877 he became president of the Home Rule Confederation. He was jailed for making violent speeches against the new land act (1881–82), then released to curb an increase in terrorist acts. Reaction against the PHOENIX PARK MURDERS enabled him to unite factions in Ireland to win support for parliamentary measures, such as WILLIAM E. GLADSTONE's HOME RULE proposals. He remained popular in Ireland until he was named in the divorce suit of his mistress, Katherine O'Shea (1890).

parochial education Education offered institutionally by a religious group. In the U.S. and Canada, parochial education refers to elementary and secondary schools maintained by Roman Catholic parishes, Protestant churches, or Jewish organizations and are separate from the public school system. The curriculum usually includes both religious and general studies.

parody In literature, a work in which the style of an author is closely imitated for comic effect or in ridicule. Differing both from BURLESQUE (by the depth of its technical penetration) and from travesty (which treats dignified subjects in a trivial manner), parody mercilessly exposes the tricks of manner and thought of its victim, and therefore cannot be written without a thorough appreciation of the work it ridicules. Examples date from as early as ancient Greece and occur in nearly all literatures and all periods.

parole Supervised conditional liberty from prison granted prior to the expiration of a prisoner's sentence. Modern use of parole stems from a change in penal philosophy to emphasize rehabilitation rather than retribution. In some jurisdictions, those convicted of certain crimes (e.g., rape or murder) are not eligible for parole. Conditions of parole vary, but in all cases their violation may constitute grounds for reincarceration. Parole supervision ranges from little more than a periodic police check to intensive supervision by trained personnel. See also PROBATION.

Parr, Catherine (1512–1548) Sixth and last wife of HENRY VIII of England. The daughter of an official in the royal household, she had been widowed twice by the time she married Henry in 1543. She exerted a beneficial influence on the increasingly paranoid king and developed close friendships with his children by previous marriages. After Henry's death in 1547, she married Baron Thomas Seymour but died shortly after giving birth to a daughter.

Parra, Nicanor (born 1914) Chilean poet. A student of mathematics and physics, Parra began teaching theoretical physics at the University of Chile in 1952. One of the most important Latin-American poets of his time, he is known for originating so-called antipoetry (poetry that opposes traditional poetic techniques or styles). In *Poems and Antipoems* (1954), he sought to make poetry accessible to the masses by treating everyday problems of a grotesque world in clear language with black humor and ironic vision. In later works he experimented with language and continued his antipoetic techniques.

Parrhasius *or* **Parrhasios** \pə-'rā-zhəs\ (5th century BC) Greek painter. A native of Ephesus (now in Turkey) who settled in Athens, he was praised by ancient critics as a master of outline drawing. He apparently succeeded in portraying various psychological states in his depictions of the face. Many of his drawings on wood and parchment were preserved and highly valued by later painters for purposes of study. His picture of Theseus adorned the Capitol in Rome; other works were chiefly mythological groups. No works or copies survive.

Parrish \'par-ish\, **(Frederick) Maxfield** (1870–1966) U.S. illustrator and painter. Born in Philadelphia and trained at the Pennsylvania Academy of Fine Arts and Drexel Institute of Art, he was the highest-paid commercial artist and muralist in the U.S. by the 1920s. He is best known for his depictions of fantasy landscapes populated by attractive young women. He used meticulously defined outlines and intricately detailed natural backgrounds; his unusual colors, especially the luminous "Parrish blue," give his pictures a dreamlike quality. Though his popularity declined in the late 1930s, appreciation of his work revived in the 1960s and '70s.

parrot Any of the approximately 300 species of birds in the family Psittacidae. About 220 species of true parrots (subfamily Psittacinae) are found worldwide in warm regions (see PARAKEET). Many are brilliantly colored. They have a blunt tongue and eat seeds, buds, and some fruit and insects. Their vocal apparatus permits many species to mimic human speech with great accuracy. The African gray parrot *(Psittacus erithacus)*, almost unsurpassed as a talker, is about 13 in. (33 cm) long and is gray except for a red tail and white face; it lives up to 80 years. The 26 species of Amazon parrots (genus *Amazona*), also good mimics, are 10–16 in. (25–40 cm) long and predominantly green. Five other subfamilies are found chiefly around New Zealand and Australia. See also COCKATIEL, COCKATOO, KEA, LOVEBIRD, MACAW.

Rainbow lorikeet (*Trichoglossus haematodus*).
BRUCE COLEMAN LTD.

parrot fish Any of about 80 species (family Scaridae) of slender, blunt-headed, deep-bodied fishes found on tropical reefs. They are often brightly colored and have large scales. The fused teeth form a "beak" used to scrape algae and the soft part of coral from reefs. Platelike teeth in the throat grind the ingested food and bits of coral. Some species grow to 4 ft (1.2 m) long and weigh 45 lbs (20 kg). The Indo-Pacific surf, or rivulated, parrot fish *(Callyodon fasciatus)* grows to 18 in. (46 cm) or more. The queen parrot fish *(Scarus vetula)* is an Atlantic species.

Parrot fish (*Calotomus*).
DOUGLAS FAULKNER

parsec Unit of measure used by astronomers to express distances to stars and galaxies. It is the distance at which the radius of earth's orbit would subtend an angle of 1 second of arc, so an object 1 parsec away would have a PARALLAX of 1 second. An object's distance in parsecs is the reciprocal of its parallax in seconds of arc. For example, ALPHA CENTAURI, with a parallax of 0.76 second, is 1.33 parsecs from the sun and earth. One parsec equals 3.26 light-years, or 1.92×1013 mi (3.09×1013 km).

Parsi *or* **Parsee** Zoroastrian of India. The Parsis, whose name means "Persians," are descended from Persian Zoroastrians who emigrated to India to escape persecution by Muslims. The migration occurred sometime between the 8th and 10th century. The Parsis settled in Gujarat and became a farming community. When the British EAST INDIA CO. took control of the region around Bombay (now Mumbai) in the late 17th century and established religious freedom, many Parsis moved there, and by the 19th century they had become a wealthy merchant class. The Parsis still live chiefly in the Mumbai area, though other Parsi communities exist in Bangalore, India, and Karachi, Pakistan. See also ZOROASTRIANISM AND PARSIISM.

Parsiism See ZOROASTRIANISM AND PARSIISM

parsley Hardy biennial herb *(Petroselinum crispum)* of the family Apiaceae, or Umbelliferae, native to Mediterranean lands. The compound leaves are used in cooking. The family Apiaceae, sometimes called the parsley family, contains 300–400 genera of plants found in a wide variety of habitats, mostly in northern temperate regions. Most are aromatic herbs with feathery leaves. The flowers are often arranged in a conspicuous umbel (a flat-topped cluster). Many species are poisonous, including POISON HEMLOCK. Popular members of the family include CARROT, CELERY, PARSNIP, and FENNEL. Species used as herbs and spices include ANISE, DILL, CORIANDER, CARAWAY, and cumin *(Cuminum cyminum)*.

parsnip Plant *(Pastinaca sativa)* of the PARSLEY family, cultivated for its large, tapering, fleshy, edible white root, which has a distinctive, sweet flavor and is usually served as a cooked vegetable. At the end of summer the solids of the root consist largely of starch, but a period of low temperature changes much of the starch to sugar. The root is hardy and not damaged by hard freezing of the soil. Native to Britain, Europe, and temperate Asia, the parsnip has become extensively naturalized in North America.

Parsnip (*Pastinaca sativa*).
G.R. ROBERTS

Parsons, Charles Algernon *later* **Sir Charles** (1854–1931) British mechanical engineer. He began

O P Q R

work at the Armstrong engineering works in Newcastle upon Tyne in 1877, and formed his own company to manufacture turbines and other heavy machinery in 1889. He developed the multiple-stage turbine in 1884, and had introduced it in power plants to generate electricity by 1891. Modern steam and nuclear power plants still use turbines of this type to turn their generators. He demonstrated his marine turbine in "Turbinia," a vessel that attained a speed of over 34 knots in 1897; Parsons turbines made high-speed ocean liners possible.

Parsons, Elsie *orig.* **Elsie Worthington Clews** (1875–1941) U.S. sociologist, anthropologist, and folklorist. Born in New York City, she was trained in sociology. Her early works, advocating women's rights, included *The Family* (1906) and *The Old-Fashioned Woman* (1913). She later turned to anthropology under the influence of FRANZ BOAS and ALFRED L. KROEBER. Her *Pueblo Indian Religion* (1936) and *Mitla* (1936) remain standard studies of Pueblo and Zapotec Indian cultures. She also produced notable collections of West Indian and African-American folklore.

Parsons, Talcott (1902–1979) U.S. sociologist. Born in Colorado Springs, he taught at Harvard University from 1927 to 1973. He advocated a structural-functional analysis, a study of the ways that interrelated and interacting units forming the structures of a social system contribute to the system's development and maintenance. He was largely responsible for introducing the work of É. DURKHEIM and MAX WEBER to American sociologists. His major work is *The Structure of Social Action* (1937). See also FUNCTIONALISM.

Parson's Cause Dispute involving English clergy in colonial Virginia over payment of salaries. When the British vetoed colonial laws that substituted currency for tobacco as payment for clerical salaries (1759), the clergy sued for back pay. In the most publicized case (1763), PATRICK HENRY defended a colonial parish against a suit by a clergyman, citing interference by the British and convincing a jury to return only one penny in damages. The clergy soon gave up their protest.

Parsvanatha \'pärsh-və-'nä-tə\ (fl. 8th century BC) In JAINISM, the 23rd TIRTHANKARA, or saint, of the present age. He founded a religious order and formulated four vows binding on its members (not to kill, steal, lie, or own property; a vow of celibacy was added later by MAHAVIRA). According to legend, Parsvanatha once saved a family of serpents trapped in a log in an ascetic's fire. One of the snakes, later reborn as Dharana, the lord of the underworld kingdom of NAGAS (snakes), sheltered Parsvanatha from a storm sent by an enemy demon. In sculpture and painting Parsvanatha is identified by a canopy of snake hoods over his head.

Pärt, Arvo (born 1935) Estonian-German composer. A devoutly Orthodox Christian, he developed a style based on the slow change of sounds like bells and pure voice tones, reminiscent of the medieval Notre-Dame school and the sacred music of Eastern Orthodoxy. His major works include the violin concerto *Tabula Rasa* (1977), *Cantus in Memory of Benjamin Britten* (1977), *Magnificat-Antiphones* (1988), *The Beatitudes* (1991), *Summa* (1991), and *Litany, Psalom, and Trisagion.*

Partch, Harry (1901–1974) U.S. composer and instrument maker. Born in Oakland, Cal., he grew up in Arizona and was largely self-taught musically. He traveled as a hobo, conceiving many of his musical ideas while doing so. Around 1930 he began building a remarkable instrumentarium of original percussion and string instruments, tunable to 43 divisions of the octave. His works often involve theatrical elements, reflecting his interest in African, Japanese, and Native American ritual. They include *Lyrics by Li Po* (1931), *Barstow—8 Hitchhiker Inscriptions from a Highway Railing at Barstow, California* (1941), *US Highball* (1943), and *On the 7th Day Petals Fell on Petaluma* (1966).

parterre \pär-'ter\ Division of garden beds in an ornamental pattern. The parterre grew out of the knot garden, a medieval form of bed in which various plant types were separated from each other by hedges. In the 16th century, the hedges were replaced by wooden or leaden shapes or by lines of shells or coal, and the areas between were filled with colored sand or stone chips. The naturalistic English garden of the 18th century displaced the elaborate parterre.

Parthenon \'pär-thə-,nän\ Chief temple of ATHENA on the ACROPOLIS at Athens. Built 447–432 BC by Ictinus and Callicrates under Pericles, it is considered the culmination of the Doric ORDER. Though the white marble temple has suffered damage over the centuries, including the loss of most of its sculpture, its basic structure remains intact. The colonnade supports an entablature consisting of a plain architrave, a frieze of alternating triglyphs (grooved blocks) and metopes (plain blocks with relief sculpture) and, at the two ends, a triangular pediment. The colonnade consists of eight columns on the ends and 17 on the sides, enclosing a cella; the interior originally held a great gold-and-ivory statue by PHIDIAS. Such architectural devices as entasis of the columns and an upward curvature of the base are used to correct optical illusions. Its sculpture rivaled its architecture. The pediment sculptures represent the birth of Athena and her battle with Poseidon; a continuous frieze shows the annual Panathenaic procession of citizens honoring Athena. The entire work is a marvel of harmony and clarity. See also ELGIN MARBLES.

Parthenon, on the Acropolis, Athens, by Ictinus and Callicrates, 447–432 BC.
ALISON FRANTZ

Parthia Ancient land, western Asia. Corresponding roughly to modern northeastern Iran, it formed a province of the PERSIAN empire and later of the empire of ALEXANDER THE GREAT. After the dissolution of the SELEUCID empire c. 250 BC, a new Parthian kingdom was founded by Arsaces. His was the first of the ARSACID DYNASTY that ruled until it was overthrown by Persia c. AD 226. At its height in the early 1st century BC, it was known as the Parthian empire and included the area between the EUPHRATES and INDUS rivers and between AMU DARYA and the Arabian Sea. It was weakened by internal disorder and Roman advances in the 1st century BC. One of its later capitals was HECATOMPYLOS. The ruins of CTESIPHON, another major Parthian city, are in modern Iraq. The Parthians were famous as horsemen and archers.

Parti Québécois \pär-tē-kā-be-'kwä\ Minor Canadian political party founded in 1968 by RENE LEVESQUE and other French-Canadian separatists in the province of Quebec. In the 1976 provincial election it won a majority in the assembly, which then decreed French as the province's only official language of government and business. After a separatist referendum on independence failed (1980), the party lost membership. It revived in the 1990s and won the 1994 provincial election. In 1995 the party held another referendum on secession, but it was narrowly defeated.

partial derivative In DIFFERENTIAL CALCULUS, the DERIVATIVE of a function of several VARIABLES with respect to change in just one of its variables. Partial derivatives are useful in analyzing surfaces for MAXIMUM and MINIMUM points and give rise to PARTIAL DIFFERENTIAL EQUATIONS. As with ordinary derivatives, a first partial derivative represents a rate of change or a SLOPE of a TANGENT LINE. For a three-dimensional surface, two first partial derivatives represent the slope in each of two perpendicular directions. Second, third, and higher partial derivatives give more information about how the function changes at any point.

partial differential equation In mathematics, an equation that contains PARTIAL DERIVATIVES, expressing a process of change that depends on more than one independent variable. It can be read as a statement about how a process evolves without specifying the formula defining the process. Given the initial state of the process (such as its size at time zero) and a description of how it is changing (i.e., the partial differential equation), its defining formula can be found by various methods, most based on INTEGRATION. Important partial differential equations include the heat equation, the wave equation, and LAPLACE'S EQUATION, which are central to MATHEMATICAL PHYSICS.

particle accelerator Device that accelerates a beam of fast-moving, electrically charged atoms (IONS) or SUBATOMIC PARTICLES. Accelerators are used to study the structure of atomic nuclei (see ATOM) and the nature of subatomic particles and their FUNDAMENTAL INTERACTIONS. At speeds close to that of light, particles collide with and disrupt atomic nuclei and subatomic particles, allowing physicists to study nuclear components and to make new kinds of subatomic particles. The CYCLOTRON accelerates positively charged particles, while the betatron accelerates negatively charged ELECTRONS. SYNCHROTRONS and LINEAR ACCELERATORS are used either with positively charged particles or electrons. Accelerators are also used for radioisotope production, cancer therapy, biological sterilization, and one form of radiocarbon dating.

particle physics *or* **high-energy physics** Study of the fundamental SUBATOMIC PARTICLES, including both MATTER (and ANTIMATTER) and the carrier particles of the FUNDAMENTAL INTERACTIONS as described by QUANTUM FIELD THEORY. Particle physics is concerned with structure and forces at this level of existence and below. Fundamental particles possess properties such as ELECTRIC CHARGE, SPIN, MASS, MAGNETISM, and other complex characteristics, but are regarded as pointlike. All theories in particle physics involve QUANTUM MECHANICS, in which symmetry is of primary importance. See also ELECTROWEAK THEORY, LEPTON, MESON, QUANTUM CHROMODYNAMICS, QUARK.

parting In METALLURGY, the separation of GOLD and SILVER by chemical or electrochemical means. Gold and silver are often extracted together from the same ores or recovered as by-products from the extraction of other metals. A solid mixture of the two, known as bullion or doré, can be parted by boiling in nitric acid. The silver is dissolved as SILVER NITRATE, leaving a gold residue that is filtered off and washed; silver is precipitated out of solution by adding ferrous sulfate. This is the traditional method used in ASSAYING the content of gold and silver samples.

partnership Association of two or more persons or entities that conduct a business for profit as co-owners. Except in the case of the LIMITED liability partnership, which shares with the corporation the characteristic of being treated as a single entity whose members have limited personal liability, a partnership is traditionally viewed as an association of individuals rather than an entity with a separate and independent existence. A partnership cannot exist beyond the lives of the partners. The partners are taxed as individuals and are personally liable for TORTS and contractual obligations. Each is viewed as the agent of the others, and traditionally all are jointly and severally liable for the tortious acts of any partner.

partridge Any of certain species of Old World game bird in the family Phasianidae. The European gray partridge *(Perdix perdix),* introduced into North America, has a reddish face and tail, gray breast, barred sides, and a dark U shape on the belly. Males may be 12 in. (30 cm) long. The hen lays about 15 eggs in a grassy cup in grainfields or hedges. Family groups (coveys) forage for seeds and insects. The five Asian and 35 African species of francolins (genus *Francolinus*) have leg spurs and are 10–16 in. (25–40 cm) long. The snow partridge *(Lerwa lerwa)* inhabits high Asian mountains. Partridges are larger than QUAIL and have a stronger bill and feet. GROUSE and BOBWHITES are often erroneously called partridge.

parturition *or* **birth** *or* **childbirth** *or* **labor** *or* **delivery** Process of bringing forth a child from the UTERUS, ending PREGNANCY. It has three stages. In dilation, uterine contractions lasting about 40 seconds begin 20–30 minutes apart, and progress to severe labor pains about every three minutes. The opening of the cervix widens as contractions push the FETUS. Dilation averages 13–14 hours in first-time mothers, less if a woman has had previous babies. When the cervix dilates fully, expulsion begins. The "water" (amniotic sac) breaks (if it has not already), and the woman may actively push. Expulsion lasts 1–2 hours or less. Normally, the baby's head emerges first; other positions make birth more difficult and risky. In the third stage, the PLACENTA is expelled, usually within 15 minutes. Within six to eight weeks, the mother's REPRODUCTIVE SYSTEM returns to nearly the prepregnancy state. See also CESAREAN SECTION, LACTATION, MIDWIFERY, MISCARRIAGE, NATURAL CHILDBIRTH, OBSTETRICS AND GYNECOLOGY, PREMATURE BIRTH.

party system Political system in which individuals who share a common set of political beliefs organize themselves into parties to compete in elections for the right to govern. Single-party systems are found in countries that do not allow genuine political conflict. Multiparty and two-party systems represent means of organizing political conflict within pluralistic societies and are thus indicative of democracy. Multiparty systems allow for greater representation of minority viewpoints; since the coalitions that minority parties must often form with other minority parties to achieve a governing majority are often fragile, such systems may be marked by instability. See also ELECTORAL SYSTEM.

Parvati \'pär-və-ˌtē\ Wife of the Hindu god SHIVA. Parvati is the benevolent aspect of Shakti, the Hindu supreme goddess (see SHAKTISM). According to the traditional account of her marriage, she won Shiva's notice only after severe ascetic discipline. The couple had two children, the elephant-headed GANESHA and the six-headed Skanda. In sculpture Parvati is always depicted as a mature and beautiful woman. The sacred TANTRAS are framed as a discussion between Parvati and Shiva.

Parvati, bronze image, early Cola period, 10th century AD; in the Freer Gallery of Art, Washington, D.C.

BY COURTESY OF THE SMITHSONIAN INSTITUTION, FREER GALLERY OF ART, WASHINGTON, D.C.

Pas de Calais See Strait of DOVER

pas de deux \pä-də-'dœ̄\ (French: "step for two") Dance for two performers. A characteristic part of classical BALLET, it includes an adagio, or slow dance, by the ballerina and her partner; solo variations by the male dancer and then the ballerina; and a coda, or conclusion, with both partners dancing together to display their virtuosity. Celebrated pas de deux occur in *Sleeping Beauty, Swan Lake,* and *Giselle.*

Pasadena City (pop., 1996 est.: 134,000), southwestern California, at the base of the SAN GABRIEL MTNS. Founded in 1874, it was incorporated as a city in 1886. It grew as a winter resort and citrus center after the construction of the Santa Fe Railway, and the freeway system that links it to LOS ANGELES to the southwest. It is a center of scientific research, based on the CALIFORNIA INSTITUTE OF TECHNOLOGY and its Jet Propulsion Laboratory. It is the site of the annual college football ROSE BOWL and the New Year's Day Tournament of Roses, a flower festival begun in 1890.

Pasadena City (pop., 1996 est.: 132,000), southeastern Texas, east of HOUSTON. Founded in 1895, it was incorporated in 1929. After World War II the city grew rapidly, stimulated by nearby industrial development, especially in petrochemicals and aerospace. Northeast of the city is the site of the 1836 capture of Mexican Gen. ANTONIO SANTA ANNA after the Battle of San Jacinto.

Pasargadae \pə-'sär-gə-ˌdē\ Ruined city, ancient Persia, northeast of PERSEPOLIS and of modern SHIRAZ, Iran. It was the capital of CYRUS THE GREAT, founder of the ACHAEMENIAN DYNASTY. He was said to have founded the city on the site of his victory over the last king of the Medes, c. 550 BC. The city was surrendered to ALEXANDER THE GREAT in 330 BC. It was known for the majestic simplicity of its architecture; its ruins include the bases of several large buildings and the nearly intact tomb of Cyrus.

pascal Unit of PRESSURE, abbreviated Pa, in the INTERNATIONAL SYSTEM of Units. Named for BLAISE PASCAL, the unit is a pressure of one NEWTON per square meter (1 N/m^2). It is inconveniently small for many purposes, and the kilopascal (kPa), 1,000 N/m^2, is more commonly used in engineering work (1 lb per sq in. equals 6.895 kPa).

Pascal \pas-'kal\ Computer PROGRAMMING LANGUAGE named for BLAISE PASCAL and based partly on ALGOL. It was developed by Niklaus Wirth of Zurich's Federal Institute of Technology in the late 1960s as an educational tool for systematic teaching of programming, with fast, reliable

O
P
Q
R

COMPILERS. It was made available to the public in 1974 and was used by many universities for the next 15 years. Pascal strongly influenced languages developed later, such as ADA. Complex DATA STRUCTURES and ALGORITHMS can be described concisely by Pascal, and its programs are easy to read and debug.

Pascal \pas-'kal\, **Blaise** (1623–1662) French mathematician, physicist, and religious philosopher. The son of a mathematician, he was a child prodigy, earning the envy of RENE DESCARTES with an essay he wrote on conic sections in 1640. In the 1640s and '50s he made contributions to physics (formulating PASCAL'S LAW) and mathematics (working on the arithmetic triangle, inventing a calculating machine, and contributing to the advance of differential calculus). For work done in his early years, he is regarded as the founder of the modern theory of probability. At the same time he became increasingly involved with JANSENISM. *Les provinciales* were a series of letters defending Jansenism and attacking the JESUITS. His great work of Christian apologetics, *Apologie de la religion chrétienne,* was never finished, but he put together most of his notes and fragments between 1657 and 1658; these were published posthumously as *Pensées* (1670). He returned to scientific work, contributing to the *Élements de géométrie* and publishing his findings on cycloid curves, but he soon returned to devotional life and spent his last years helping the poor. The PASCAL was named in his honor. See also PASCAL'S WAGER.

Pascal's law *or* **Pascal's principle** In FLUID MECHANICS, the statement that in a fluid at rest in a closed container, a PRESSURE change in one part is transmitted without loss to every portion of the fluid and to the walls of the container. The principle was first stated by BLAISE PASCAL, who also discovered that the pressure at a point in a fluid at rest is the same in all directions, and that the pressure would be the same on all planes passing through a specific point.

Pascal's wager Practical argument for belief in God formulated by BLAISE PASCAL. In his *Pensées* (1657–58), Pascal posed the following argument to show that religious belief is reasonable: If God does not exist, the agnostic loses little by believing in him and gains correspondingly little by not believing. If God does exist, the agnostic gains eternal life by believing in him and loses an infinite good by not believing.

Paschal II \pas-'kal\ *orig.* **Raniero** (died 1118) Pope (1099–1118). He fostered the First CRUSADE and favored Gregorian reforms, but his pontificate was dominated by the INVESTITURE CONTROVERSY. Paschal came to terms on the issue of lay investiture with HENRY I of England and Philip I of France (1107). His negotiations with Emperors HENRY IV and Henry V were unsuccessful, and he was imprisoned by Henry V (1111). While a prisoner, he agreed to royal investiture of bishops and crowned Henry emperor, but a church council declared his concessions invalid and excommunicated the emperor.

Pascin \pȧs-'ka^n\, **Jules** *orig.* **Julius Pincas** (1885–1930) Bulgarian painter. He traveled widely and lived in Austria and Germany, producing drawings for satirical journals, before moving to Paris in 1905. He moved to New York during World War I and became a U.S. citizen, but returned to Paris in 1920 and became associated with other Jewish artists, including MARC CHAGALL, AMEDEO MODIGLIANI, and CHAIM SOUTINE. He painted portraits and a series of large-scale biblical and mythological scenes, but his most notable works are thinly painted ironic studies of women. Though financially successful, he was emotionally unstable; he hanged himself at 45.

Pashtuns \,pȧsh-'tünz\ Pashto-speaking people of southeastern Afghanistan and northwestern Pakistan. The Pashtuns, who number about 7.5 million in Afghanistan and 14 million in Pakistan, constitute the majority of the population of Afghanistan. Their origins are unclear: Pashtun tradition asserts that they are descended from Afghana, grandson of King Saul of Israel, but most scholars believe that they arose from an intermingling of ancient ARYANS from the north or west with subsequent invaders. Each Pashtun tribe is divided into clans, subclans, and patriarchal families. Disputes among the Pashtun over property, women, and personal injury often result in blood feuds between families and whole clans. Most tribesmen are sedentary farmers; some are migratory herdsmen and caravaners. Large numbers of the Pashtun have always been attracted to military service.

Pašić \'pä-shēt^y, *Engl* 'pä-shich\, **Nikola** (1845–1926) Serbian and Yugoslav statesman. The editor of a socialist newspaper in Serbia, he was elected in 1878 to the legislature, where he opposed the authoritarian monarchy and advocated a parliamentary democracy. In 1881 he helped found the Radical Party, but he was forced to flee to Bulgaria in 1883. Returning to Serbia in 1889 under a new king, he served as premier (1891–92) and as ambassador to Russia (1893–94). Forced into exile again because of his political radicalism (1899–1903), he returned to support the KARAGEORGEVIC DYNASTY and King PETER I. As leader of the Radical Party, he served as premier of Serbia during most of the period 1904–18, then helped create the new Kingdom of SERBS, CROATS, AND SLOVENES (later Yugoslavia). Despite opposition from the historically separate regions, as premier (1921–26) he pushed for a unitary constitution that confirmed Serbia's dominance.

Pašić.
H. ROGER-VIOLLET

Pasionaria, La See Dolores IBÁRRURI

Pasolini \,pä-sō-'lē-nē\, **Pier Paolo** (1922–1975) Italian film director, poet, and novelist. He wrote novels about Rome's slum life as well as a significant body of poetry, and became a screenwriter in the mid-1950s, collaborating most notably on FEDERICO FELLINI'S *Nights of Cabiria* (1956). His directorial debut, *Accattone* (1961), was based on his novel *A Violent Life* (1959). His best-known film, stylistically unorthodox and implicitly radical, is perhaps *The Gospel According to Saint Matthew* (1964). Later films include *Oedipus Rex* (1967), *Teorema* (1968), *Medea* (1969), *The Canterbury Tales* (1972), and *The Arabian Nights* (1974). His use of eroticism, violence, and depravity were criticized by Italian religious authorities. He died after a brutal beating apparently suffered during a homosexual encounter.

pasqueflower See ANEMONE

passage, rite of Any of numerous ceremonial events, existing in all societies, that mark the passage of an individual from one social or religious status to another. The term was coined by the French anthropologist Arnold van Gennep (1873–1957) in 1909. Many of the most important rites are connected with the biological stages of life—birth, maturity, reproduction, and death. Other rites celebrate changes that are wholly cultural, such as initiation into special societies. In modern societies, graduation from school is a rite of passage. Scholars often interpret rites of passage as mechanisms by which society confronts and incorporates change without disrupting the equilibrium necessary to social order. See also SECRET SOCIETY.

Passamaquoddy Bay Inlet of the Bay of FUNDY, between southwestern New Brunswick, Canada, and southeastern Maine, at the mouth of the St. Croix River. Deer Island and Campobello Island are in its southern part. It has an immense tidal flow, with about 70 billion cu ft (2 billion cu m) entering and leaving twice daily on the turn of the tide.

passenger pigeon Extinct species *(Ectopistes migratorius)* of PIGEON (subfamily Columbinae, family Columbidae). Passenger pigeons were about 13 in. (32 cm) long and had a long pointed tail; the male was pinkish, with a blue-gray head. Billions inhabited eastern North America in the early 19th century; migrating flocks darkened the skies for days at a time. Gunners began to slaughter them in huge numbers for shipping by railway carloads for sale in city meat markets. Martha, the last known passenger pigeon, died in 1914 in the Cincinnati Zoo. The bird's extinction was largely responsible for ending the marketing of game birds and gave major impetus to the conservation movement.

Passenger pigeon, mounted (*Ectopistes migratorius*).
BILL REASONS—THE NATIONAL AUDUBON SOCIETY COLLECTION/PHOTO RESEARCHERS

passerine Any perching bird. All passerines belong to the largest order of birds, Passeriformes, and have feet specialized for holding onto a horizontal branch (perching). The passerine foot has three forward-directed toes and one backward-directed toe. Most passerines have moderately curved, sharp claws. Some ground-dwelling species (e.g., LARKS, PIPITS) have flatter, longer feet. Species that spend much time airborne (e.g., SWALLOWS) have small, weak feet. Species that cling and climb (e.g., NUTHATCHES) have strong, sharp, curved claws. Passerines include about 4,000 species of oscines (SONGBIRDS; suborder Passere, or Oscines) and 1,100 species of suboscines (suborders Eurylaimi, called broadbills; Tyranni, including FLYCATCHERS; and Menurae, including LYREBIRDS). Suboscines lack the syrinx of the songbirds or have only a poorly developed one, but some can utter complex vocalizations. All passerines are land birds, abundant worldwide except in Antarctica. Most are insectivorous, solitary nesters that build a cup-shaped open nest.

Passion Musical setting of the suffering and crucifixion of Christ. The early Passion consisted entirely of plainchant. Liturgical enactments of Christ's Passion date from the early Middle Ages, the characters' parts being sung by individual celebrants and the crowd's role by the congregation. Polyphonic Passions began appearing in the 15th century. In the German tradition exemplified by H. SCHUTZ, the Passion closely resembles the dramatic ORATORIO, with solo arias and other ensembles contrasting with choral sections; the alternative motet-style Passion lacked solo sections and avoided dramatic oppositions. After the 18th century, Passions ceased to be widely composed.

Passion play Religious drama of medieval origin dealing with the suffering, death, and resurrection of JESUS. Early Passion plays were written in Latin and consisted of Gospel readings alternating with poetic descriptions of the events of Christ's Passion (i.e., his sufferings between the Last Supper and his death). Use of the vernacular for these poetic passages led to the development of independent vernacular plays. By the 16th century many of the plays had been overtaken by secular influences and had become mere popular entertainments. Some survived into the 20th century, most notably the one performed by local villagers every 10 years at Oberammergau, Germany. See also LITURGICAL DRAMA, MIRACLE PLAY, MYSTERY PLAY.

passionflower family Family Passifloraceae, composed of about 600 species of herbaceous or woody vines, shrubs, and trees in 20 genera. Members of this family grow mostly in warm regions. Many species produce edible fruits. Members of the largest genus, *Passiflora,* are highly prized for their showy, unusual flowers. A pedestal-like structure in the center of the flower carries the reproductive parts of both sexes. The passionflower blossom is often used to symbolize events in the last hours (Passion) of JESUS, which accounts for the name of the group.

passive resistance See CIVIL DISOBEDIENCE, SATYAGRAHA

Passover In JUDAISM, the holiday commemorating the liberation of the Hebrews from slavery in Egypt. Before sending a plague to destroy the firstborn of the Egyptians, God instructed MOSES to tell the Israelites to place a special mark above their doors as a signal for the angel of death to pass over (i.e., spare the residents). The festival of Passover begins on the 15th and ends on the 22nd (in Israel, the 21st) day of the month of Nisan (March or April). During Passover only unleavened bread may be eaten, symbolizing the Hebrews' suffering in bondage and the haste with which they left Egypt. On the first night of Passover, a SEDER is held, and the HAGGADAH is read aloud.

passport Document issued by a national government identifying a traveler as a citizen with a right to protection while abroad and a right to return to the country of citizenship. It is normally a small booklet containing a description and photograph of the bearer. Most nations require entering travelers to obtain a visa, an endorsement on the passport showing that the proper authorities have examined it and permitting the bearer to enter the country and remain for a specified period.

pasta Any of several starchy food pastes *(pasta alimentaria)* made from semolina, the purified middlings (endosperm) of a hard WHEAT called durum. Pasta is traditionally associated with Italian cuisine, though it may have entered Europe from Asia during the Mongol invasions of the 13th century. In making pasta, semolina dough is compacted and forced through perforated plates, or dies, that form it into the desired shape. It is produced in the form of ribbons, cords, tubes, and other shapes, each with its own name (e.g., spaghetti, macaroni). The formed dough is then dried under controlled conditions. Pasta is boiled and combined with other foods before serving.

pastel Drawing medium consisting of fragile, finger-size crayons called pastels, made of powdered pigments combined with a minimum of nongreasy binder (usually gum tragacanth or, from the mid-20th century, methyl cellulose). Because pigment applied with pastel does not change in color value, the final effect can be seen immediately. Pastel remains on the surface of the paper and thus can be easily obliterated unless protected by glass or a fixative spray of glue size or gum solution. When pastel is applied in short strokes or linearly, it is usually classed as drawing; when it is rubbed, smeared, and blended to achieve painterly effects, it is often regarded as a painting medium.

Pasternak, Boris (Leonidovich) (1890–1960) Russian poet and prose writer. He studied music and philosophy and after the Russian Revolution of 1917 worked in the library of the Soviet commissariat of education. His early poetry, though avant-garde, was successful, but in the 1930s a gap widened between his work and officially approved literary modes, and he supported himself by doing translations. The novel *Doctor Zhivago* (1957; film, 1965), an epic of wandering, spiritual isolation, and love amid the harshness of the revolution and its aftermath, was a best-seller in the West but until 1987 circulated only in secrecy in the Soviet Union. He was awarded the Nobel Prize in 1958, but was forced to decline it because of Soviet opposition to his work.

Pasteur \pas-'tər\, **Louis** (1822–1895) French chemist and microbiologist. Early in his career, after studies at the École Normale Supérieure, he researched the effects of polarized light on chemical compounds. In 1857 he became director of scientific studies at the École. His studies of FERMENTATION of alcohol and milk (souring) showed that yeast could reproduce without free oxygen (the Pasteur effect); he deduced that fermentation and food spoilage were due to the activity of microorganisms and could be prevented by excluding or destroying them. His work overturned the concept of spontaneous generation (life arising from nonliving matter) and led to heat PASTEURIZATION, allowing vinegar, wine, and beer to be produced and transported without spoiling. He saved the French silk industry by his work on silkworm diseases. In 1881 he perfected a way to isolate and weaken germs, and went on to develop VACCINES against anthrax in sheep and cholera in chickens following EDWARD JENNER's example. He turned his attention to researching rabies, and in 1885 saved the life of a boy bitten by a rabid dog by inoculating the boy with a weakened virus. In 1888 he founded the Pasteur Institute for rabies research, prevention, and treatment.

Pasteurella \ˌpas-chə-'rel-ə\ Genus (named after LOUIS PASTEUR) of rod-shaped BACTERIA that cause several serious diseases in domestic animals and milder infections in humans. Members are gram-negative (see GRAM STAIN), do not move, and do not require oxygen. The widespread infections they cause, referred to by the general term pasteurelloses, are transmitted by direct contact and, in some cases, by ticks and fleas. Control by vaccine is variable, as is treatment with penicillin and other antibiotics.

pasteurization Partial STERILIZATION of a substance, especially MILK or other beverages, by using heat to destroy microorganisms while leaving its chemical makeup unaltered. The process is named for LOUIS PASTEUR, its originator. Pasteurization of milk requires temperatures of about 145°F (63°C) for about 30 minutes, or higher temperatures for shorter periods. The treatment destroys any disease-causing organisms (principally *Mycobacterium tuberculosis*) as well as organisms that cause spoilage. See also FOOD PRESERVATION.

Tony Pastor.
CULVER PICTURES

Pastor, Tony *orig.* **Antonio** (1837–1908) U.S. impresario and comic singer, considered the father of VAUDEVILLE in the U.S. Born in New York City, he appeared at P. T. BARNUM's American Museum as a child prodigy and first performed in a variety show in 1861. After managing a series of New York theaters, he opened the Fourteenth Street Theater in 1881. Though variety shows of the time featured coarse humor and were considered unsuitable for ladies, he advertised his theater as "the first specialty and vaudeville theater of America, catering to polite tastes." His unexpected success spurred other theater managers to follow suit and led to the creation of vaudeville. See also MUSIC HALL AND VARIETY THEATER.

pastoral \ˌpas-tə-ˈräl\ Literary work dealing in a usually artificial manner with shepherds or rural life, typically contrasting the innocence and serenity of the simple life with the misery and corruption of city or court life. The characters are often the vehicles for the author's moral, social, or literary views. The poet and his friends are often presented as shepherds and shepherdesses; two or more shepherds sometimes contend in "singing matches." The conventions of pastoral poetry were largely established by THEOCRITUS, whose bucolics are its earliest examples. VIRGIL's *Eclogues* were influential as well, as was EDMUND SPENSER's *Shepheardes Calender* in the Renaissance. The idea of pastoral as meaning a simpler world that somehow mirrors a more complex one also appears in novelists as different as FYODOR DOSTOYEVSKY, LEWIS CARROLL, and WILLIAM FAULKNER. See also ECLOGUE.

Pastoureaux \ˌpas-tủr-ˈō\ (French: "shepherds") Participants in two outbreaks of mob violence in medieval France. The first Pastoureaux were peasants in northeastern France aroused by news in 1251 of the reverses suffered by LOUIS IX on the Seventh CRUSADE. Accusing the nobles, clergy, and bourgeoisie of indifference to the king's fate, they began pillaging churches and towns. The second Pastoureaux converged on Paris in 1320 to punish Philip V for failing to undertake a crusade. They sacked the city, opened the prisons, and marched into the countryside, where they carried out pogroms against Jews and lepers.

Pasupata \ˈpä-shủ-ˌpə-tə, ˌpä-shủ-ˈpə-tə\ Early Hindu sect that worshiped SHIVA as the supreme deity. Numerous subsects flourished in northern and northwestern India until at least the 12th century and spread to Java and Cambodia. Pasupata teachings were believed to have originated with Shiva himself, reincarnated as the teacher Lakulin. The sect's rise is dated roughly between the 2nd century BC and the 2nd century AD. The ascetic practices adopted by the Pasupatas included smearing their bodies thrice-daily with ashes. Out of Pasupata doctrine developed two extreme schools, KAPALIKA AND KALAMUKHA, as well as one moderate sect, SHAIVISM.

Patagonia Semi-arid scrub plateau, southern Argentina. It is the largest desert region in the Americas, with an area of about 260,000 sq mi (673,000 sq km). Its approximate boundaries are the Río Colorado in the north, the Atlantic Ocean in the east, the Río Coig in the south, and the ANDES in the west. A region of vast and virtually treeless plains, it has a variety of wildlife, including llamas, pumas, and eagles. Natural resources include petroleum, iron ore, copper, uranium, and manganese.

Patarine *or* **Patarene** \ˈpa-tə-rən\ Member of a group of craftsmen, tradesmen, and peasants organized in Milan c. 1058 to call for reform of the imperial church. Named for the Pataria, the quarter of Milan where they assembled, the Patarines attacked clerical concubinage and marriage and opposed the papacy's moral corruption and temporal powers. They drew support from Pope GREGORY VII and subsequent reform popes. They anticipated the movements for religious reform that were to develop in the 12th century.

patch test Controlled application of biological or chemical substances to the skin to test for ALLERGY. Small amounts of diluted test substances applied under a patch of cloth or soft paper and an impermeable membrane are left in place for 48 hours, and the skin reaction is then examined and scored from 0 (none) to 4+ (severe blistering and redness).

Patel \pə-ˈtäl\, **Vallabhbhai (Jhaverbhai)** *known as* **Sardar Patel** (1875–1950) Indian statesman. Educated in India, he set up his own law office in 1900, and later studied law in Britain; he did not become involved in politics until 1917. Like MOHANDAS K. GANDHI and unlike JAWAHARLAL NEHRU, he advocated dominion status within the British Commonwealth rather than independence for India. He opposed armed struggle on practical rather than moral grounds, and he was not interested in Hindu-Muslim unity. Patel was repeatedly a candidate for the presidency of the Indian National Congress, but his uncompromising attitude toward the Indian Muslims cost him Gandhi's support and, ultimately, the presidency. After Indian independence (1947), he held several cabinet positions. He is remembered for achieving the peaceful integration of the princely Indian states into the Indian Union and the political unification of India.

patent Government grant to an inventor of the exclusive right to make, use, or sell an invention, usually for a specified term. It may be granted for a process or method that is new, useful, and not obvious, or for a new use of a known process, machine, or composition of matter or material, including asexually reproduced plants and genetically engineered organisms. It may also be granted for any new, original, and ornamental design for an article of manufacture. In the U.S., design patents are issued for 14 years, other patents for 20 years. Patents are considered personal property and may be sold, assigned, or otherwise transferred.

Pater \ˈpā-tər\, **Walter (Horatio)** (1839–1894) English critic, essayist, and humanist. Elected a fellow at Oxford in 1864, Pater made his reputation as a scholar and aesthete with essays collected in *Studies in the History of the Renaissance* (1873). Written in a delicate, fastidious style, the essays introduced his influential advocacy of "art for art's sake," which contrasted with the prevailing emphasis on art's moral or educational values and became a cardinal doctrine of AESTHETICISM. *Marius the Epicurean* (1885), a philosophical romance on the ideal life, is his most substantial work.

Paterson City (pop., 2000: 149,222), northeastern New Jersey. It is located on the Passaic River, north of NEWARK, N.J. It was founded in 1791 as an industrial settlement by advocates of U.S. industrial independence from Europe. The successful enterprise, begun by ALEXANDER HAMILTON, was known as the Society for Establishing Useful Manufactures. In the 19th century it was a center of cotton textile production, the silk industry, and locomotive manufacturing. It received a city charter in 1851 and was the scene of many labor disputes. By the 20th century its industries were widely diversified.

Paterson, William (1745–1806) U.S. (Irish-born) jurist. He emigrated as a child to New Jersey. He was the state's attorney general 1776–83. At the Constitutional Convention, he played a leading role in the debate over representation and, in opposition to the Virginia (or large-state) Plan, submitted the New Jersey (or small-state) Plan, which called for an equal vote for all states. He secured ratification of the U.S. Constitution in New Jersey and was elected one of the state's first U.S. senators (1789–90). He was governor of New Jersey 1790–93, then served as a justice of the U.S. Supreme Court (1793–1806).

Pathan See PASHTUN

Pathé \pȧ-ˈtā, *Engl* pa-ˈthā\, **Charles** (1863–1957) French film executive. In 1896 he and his brother Émile founded Pathé Frères, which distributed THOMAS ALVA EDISON's Kinetoscope viewing device to French theaters. The firm entered film production using the camera developed by the LUMIÈRE brothers. In 1909 Pathé produced his first "long film," *Les misérables,* and launched the *Pathé Gazette,* an internationally popular newsreel that ran until 1956. In 1914 Pathé Frères released the first episodes of *The Perils of Pauline,* one of the earliest screen SERIALS. With facilities throughout the world, Pathé Frères dominated the film market in the early 20th century, and it remained a film distributor after Charles's retirement in 1929.

pathology Medical specialty dealing with causes of disease and structural and functional changes in abnormal conditions. As AUTOPSIES, initially prohibited for religious reasons, became more accepted in the late Middle Ages, people learned more about the causes of death. In 1761 Giovanni Battista Morgagni (1682–1771) published the first book to locate disease in individual organs. In the mid-19th century, the humoral theories of infection were replaced first by cell-based theories (see RUDOLF VIRCHOW) and then by the bacteriologic theories of ROBERT KOCH and LOUIS PASTEUR. Today, pathologists work mostly in the laboratory and consult with a patient's physician after examining specimens including surgically removed body parts, blood and other fluids, urine, feces, and discharges. Culturing of infectious organisms, staining, fiber optic endoscopy, and electron microscopy have greatly expanded the information available to the pathologist.

patina See DESERT VARNISH

Patinir \ˌpȧ-tə-ˈnir\, **Joachim (de)** *or* **Joachim de Patinier** *or* **Joachim de Patenier** \ˌpȧ-tə-ˈnēr\ (c. 1480–1524) Netherlandish

O
P
Q
R

painter. Nothing is known of his early life, but his work reflects knowledge of the paintings of GERARD DAVID. He is the first Western artist known to have specialized in landscape painting, though his work has a nominal religious subject and he never painted pure landscapes. His novelty lay in the fact that the religious motif in such works as *Flight into Egypt* (1515–20) was overshadowed by the phenomena of the natural world. He apparently made a practice of supplying landscape settings for figure compositions painted by other Flemish masters. His landscapes combine realistic detail with a sense of fantasy that suggests his familiarity with the works of HIERONYMUS BOSCH.

patio In Spanish and Latin-American architecture, a courtyard open to the sky within a building. A Spanish development of the Roman ATRIUM, it is comparable to the Italian *cortile* but provides more seclusion, possibly due to Moorish custom. The patio of the contemporary U.S. house is a paved outdoor area adjoining or partially enclosed by the building and often used for outdoor dining.

patio process *or* **Mexican process** Method of isolating SILVER from its ORE, apparently dating from pre-Columbian times. The ore was crushed and ground by mule power in ARRASTRAS, reducing it to a fine mud. This was then spread over a courtyard or patio, sprinkled with MERCURY, salt, and copper sulfate, and mixed by driving mules over it. Chemical reactions caused the silver to dissolve in the mercury. When the amalgamation was complete, the material was agitated with water in large tubs and the mud run off. The AMALGAM at the bottom was collected and heated to drive off the mercury. Used for much of the world's silver production for 350 years, the process was replaced by the CYANIDE PROCESS early in the 20th century.

Patna \'pət-nə\ City (pop., 1991: 1,100,000) and capital of BIHAR state, northeastern India. On the GANGES RIVER, it was founded in the 5th century BC as Pataliputra; it was the capital of MAGADHA until the 1st century BC. It was ruled later by the MAURYAN EMPIRE. A center of learning, it became the GUPTA DYNASTY's capital in the 4th century AD but declined and was deserted by the 7th century. Revived as Patna in 1541 by an Afghan ruler, it became prosperous under the MUGHAL DYNASTY and passed to the British in 1765. Extensive archaeological excavations have been made in its vicinity.

Paton, Alan (Stewart) (1903–1988) South African writer and political activist. While principal of a reformatory housing black youths, Paton introduced controversial progressive reforms and wrote his best-known work, the novel *Cry, the Beloved Country* (1948), focusing international attention on the issue of APARTHEID. To offer a nonracial alternative to apartheid, he helped found the Liberal Party of South Africa in 1953, and led the organization until it was banned in 1968. His other works include the novel *Too Late the Phalarope* (1953) and the biographies *Hofmeyr* (1964) and *Apartheid and the Archbishop* (1973).

Paton, 1961.
UPI

patria potestas \'pä-trē-ə-pō-'tes-ˌtäs\ ("power of the father") In Roman family law, the power that the male head of a family exercised over his children and descendants in the male line, natural or adopted. Originally this power was absolute, and included the right to inflict capital punishment. He could free his male descendants or turn over his daughter to the power of her husband, and all property belonged to him. By the end of the republic (from about the 1st century BC), the father could inflict only light punishment and sons could keep what they earned.

patriarch Title applied to OLD TESTAMENT leaders such as METHUSELAH, ABRAHAM, Isaac, and JACOB. It was once given also to some Roman Catholic BISHOPS who wielded great authority. It is still used in EASTERN ORTHODOXY, which now has nine patriarchates: Constantinople, Alexandria, Antioch, Jerusalem, Moscow, Georgia, Serbia, Romania, and Bulgaria.

patrician In ancient Rome, any member of a group of citizen families who, in contrast to the PLEBEIANS, formed a privileged nobility. They attempted to hold on to magistracies, priesthoods, and legal and religious knowledge, and the great civil struggle of the ROMAN REPUBLIC was the plebeians' effort to achieve equality and break their monopoly. The patricians gradually lost their monopoly except in a few areas, such as selected priesthoods and the office of interrex, and in the late republic (1st century BC) the distinction lost political importance. After 27 BC, patrician rank was necessary for ascent to the imperial throne. After Constantine's reign (AD 337), the term became an honorary title with no peculiar power.

Patrick, St. (fl. 5th century) Patron saint of Ireland. Born in Britain of a Romanized family, he was captured at 16 by Irish raiders and carried into slavery in Ireland. He spent six years as a herdsman before escaping from his master and being reunited with his family in Britain. Called in a dream to bring Christianity to the Irish, he returned to Ireland and journeyed far and wide, baptizing chiefs and kings and converting whole clans. One popular legend says that he explained the notion of the Holy Trinity using the shamrock, now the national flower of Ireland. He is also said to have rid Ireland of snakes.

patristic literature Body of literature that comprises those works (excluding the New Testament) written by Christians before the 8th century AD. It refers to the works of the Church Fathers. Most patristic literature is in Greek or Latin, but much survives in Syriac and other Near Eastern languages. The works of the Apostolic Fathers contain the earliest patristic literature. By the mid-2nd century AD, Christians wrote to justify their faith to the Roman government and to refute GNOSTICISM. Significant patristic authors include JUSTIN MARTYR, ORIGEN, TERTULLIAN, EUSEBIUS OF CAESAREA, ATHANASIUS, BASIL THE GREAT, St. GREGORY OF NYSSA, GREGORY OF NAZIANZUS, John CHRYSOSTOM, AMBROSE, AUGUSTINE of Hippo, Ephraem Syrus (306?–373), St. JEROME, THEODORE OF MOPSUESTIA, St. CYRIL OF ALEXANDRIA (c. 375–444), St. Maximus the Confessor (c. 580–662), and Pope GREGORY I.

patron saint Saint to whose protection and intercession a person, society, church, place, profession, or activity is dedicated. The choice is usually made on the basis of some real or presumed relationship (e.g., St. PATRICK is the patron saint of Ireland because he is credited with introducing Christianity there).

patronage system See SPOILS SYSTEM

pattern recognition In computer science, the imposition of identity on input data, such as speech, images, or a stream of text, by the recognition and delineation of patterns it contains and their relationships. Stages in pattern recognition may involve measurement of the object to identify distinguishing attributes, extraction of features for the defining attributes, and comparison with known patterns to determine a match or mismatch. Pattern recognition has extensive application in astronomy, medicine, robotics, and remote sensing by satellites. See also SPEECH RECOGNITION.

patternmaking In materials processing, the first step in CASTING and molding processes, the making of an accurate model of the part, somewhat oversize to allow for shrinkage of the cast material as it cools. Foundry workers then make a MOLD from the pattern, introduce the liquid into the mold, and remove the hardened part from the mold. The processing of materials in liquid form is commonly known as casting when it involves metals, glass, and ceramics; it is called molding when it involves plastics and some other nonmetallic materials. Patternmaking is a highly skilled trade learned by apprenticeship.

Patterson, Floyd (born 1935) U.S. boxer. Born in Waco, N.C., he was reared in Brooklyn, N.Y. He won an Olympic gold medal as a middleweight in 1952. As a professional he moved up to heavyweight, and in 1956 succeeded ROCKY MARCIANO as world heavyweight champion by knocking out ARCHIE MOORE. He lost the title to Ingemar Johansson in 1959, regained it in 1960 (becoming the first to hold the heavyweight championship twice), and lost it again in 1962 to Sonny Liston.

Patton, George S(mith) (1885–1945) U.S. Army officer. Born in San Gabriel, Cal., he graduated from West Point and fought in World War I with the newly formed tank corps. He later became a major general in command of the 2nd Armored Division (1940). In World War II, he led military operations in Morocco (1942) and Sicily (1943), then commanded the 3rd Army in its sweep across northern France (1944) into

O P Q R

Germany (1945). His bold use of mobile tank warfare strategies, coupled with his strict, highly disciplined leadership, earned him his troops' respect and the nickname "Old Blood-and-Guts." He was criticized for striking a hospitalized soldier he suspected of malingering, and later publicly apologized. He died in a car crash in Germany.

Paul, Les *orig.* **Lester Polfus** (born 1916) U.S. guitarist and inventor. Born in Waukesha, Wis., he played many styles of popular music, initially country but later jazz, and in the 1940s was a sideman for NAT KING COLE and BING CROSBY. He invented the first solid-body electric guitar, and was instrumental in developing modern-day multitrack recording. His overdubbed, sped-up records from the late 1940s and early 1950s—including "Brazil" (1948), "Nola" (1950), and "How High the Moon" (1951), often with his wife, Mary Ford (1924–1977) singing harmony with herself—demonstrated the potential of tape. He continued to perform occasionally into his eighties.

Paul, Lewis (died 1759) British inventor. Working with JOHN WYATT from c. 1730, he developed the first power spinning machine (see DRAWING FRAME), which they patented in 1738. It operated by drawing cotton or wool through pairs of successively faster rollers. It was eventually replaced by R. ARKWRIGHT's water frame. Paul also patented a CARDING MACHINE in 1748.

Paul, St. *orig.* **Saul** (c. AD 10–67?) Early Christian missionary and theologian, known as the Apostle to the gentiles. Born a Jew in TARSUS, Asia Minor, he was trained as a rabbi but earned his living as a tentmaker. A zealous PHARISEE, he persecuted the first Christians until a vision of Jesus, experienced while on the road to Damascus, converted him to Christianity. Three years later he met St. PETER and Jesus' brother James, and was henceforth recognized as the 13th Apostle. From his base in Antioch, he traveled widely preaching to the gentiles. By asserting that non-Jewish disciples of Christ did not have to observe Jewish law, he helped to establish Christianity as a separate religion rather than a Jewish sect. On a journey to Jerusalem, he aroused such hostility among the Jews that a mob gathered, and he was arrested and imprisoned for two years. The circumstances of his death are unknown. Paul's ministry and religious views are known largely from his letters, or epistles, collected in the NEW TESTAMENT, which are the first Christian theological writing and the source of much Christian doctrine. It was due to Paul more than anyone else that Christianity became a world religion.

Paul I *Russian* **Pavel Petrovich** (1754–1801) Czar of Russia (1796–1801). He was the son of PETER III and CATHERINE II the Great, whom he succeeded as emperor in 1796. He reversed many of Catherine's policies, strengthened the autocracy, and established the law of succession within the male line of the ROMANOV DYNASTY. He provoked the hostility of the nobles and the army with his tyrannical rule and capricious foreign policy, which drew Russia into war with France. In a plot by the nobles to depose him and place his son Alexander (later ALEXANDER I) on the throne, Paul was assassinated.

Paul III *orig.* **Alessandro Farnese** (1468–1549) Pope (1534–49). The son of a noble Tuscan family, he was made a cardinal-deacon in 1493 and served as bishop in Parma and Ostia before being named dean of the College of Cardinals by LEO X. Ordained a priest in 1519, he was unanimously elected pope in 1534. Though loose in morals in earlier years (he had three sons and a daughter), he became an efficient promoter of reform, convening the Council of TRENT in 1545 and initiating the COUNTER-REFORMATION. He also supported the newly founded JESUITS and was a patron of the arts, the last in the tradition of the Renaissance popes.

Paul VI *orig.* **Giovanni Battista Montini** (1897–1978) Pope (1963–78). Educated at Brescia and ordained in 1920, he continued his studies in Rome, earning degrees in civil and canon law. He was a church diplomat for much of his career, until he was named archbishop of Milan in 1954. He became a cardinal in 1958, and in 1963 he was elected pope. Paul VI presided over the final sessions of the Second VATICAN COUNCIL and appointed commissions to carry out its reforms, including revisions in the MASS. He also relaxed rules on fasting and removed a number of questionable saints from the church's calendar. He promoted ECUMENISM and was the first pope to travel widely, visiting Israel, India, Asia, and Latin America.

Pauli, Wolfgang (1900–1958) Austrian–U.S. physicist. At the age of 20, he wrote a 200-page encyclopedia article on the theory of relativity. He taught physics in Zurich (1928–40) and later at the Institute for Advanced Study in Princeton. In 1924 he proposed that a spin quantum number, +½ or –½, is necessary to specify electron energy states; and in 1930 he proposed that the energy and momentum apparently lost when an electron is emitted from an atomic nucleus in beta decay is carried away by an almost massless, uncharged, and difficult-to-detect particle (the neutrino). He was awarded a 1945 Nobel Prize for his 1925 discovery of the PAULI EXCLUSION PRINCIPLE.

Pauli exclusion principle Assertion proposed by WOLFGANG PAULI that no two ELECTRONS in an ATOM can be in the same state or configuration at the same time. It accounts for the observed patterns of light emission from atoms. The principle has since been generalized to include the whole class of particles called FERMIONS. The SPIN of such particles is always an odd whole-number multiple of ½. For example, electrons have spin ½, and can occupy two distinct states with opposite spin directions. The Pauli exclusion principle indicates, therefore, that only two electrons are allowed in each atomic energy state, leading to the successive buildup of ORBITALS around the NUCLEUS. This prevents matter from collapsing to an extremely dense state.

Pauling, Linus (Carl) (1901–1994) U.S. chemist. Born in Portland, Ore., he received his doctorate from the California Institute of Technology and became a professor there in 1931. He was one of the first researchers to apply quantum mechanics to the study of molecular structures; to calculate interatomic distances and the angles between chemical bonds (see BONDING), he effectively used X-RAY DIFFRACTION, electron diffraction, magnetic effects, and the heat of REACTION. His book *The Nature of the Chemical Bond, and the Sturcture of Molecules and Crystals* (1939) became one of the century's most influential chemistry texts. He was the first recipient of the American Chemical Society's Langmuir Prize (1931), and later the first recipient of its Lewis medal (1951), and in 1954 he received the Nobel Prize for Chemistry. In 1962 his efforts on behalf of control of NUCLEAR WEAPONS and against nuclear testing brought him the Nobel Peace Prize, making him the first recipient of two unshared Nobel Prizes. In later years he devoted himself to the study of the prevention and treatment of illness by taking high doses of vitamins and minerals, particularly VITAMIN C.

Linus Pauling, photograph by Yousuf Karsh.

paulistas \pau̇-'lēs-täs\ Residents of the Brazilian state of SÃO PAULO, Latin America's foremost industrial center. Paulistas are credited with exploring much of Brazil's interior during the colonial years, helping the country extend its borders in the process. In the 16th–17th century BANDEIRAS, expeditions in search of mineral wealth and Indians to enslave, were central to the economy and culture of São Paulo. The early paulistas were known for their skills in the wilderness, their distrust of authority, and their prowess as Indian fighters. Today's paulistas are known for their aggressiveness and acumen in business and their fast-paced lives.

Paulus \'pau̇-ləs\, **Friedrich** (1890–1957) German general in World War II. He became deputy chief of the German general staff in World War II, and commanded the German 6th Army in the Soviet Union. He was defeated in the Battle of STALINGRAD in 1943, and the surrender of his army of 300,000 men ended Germany's offensive in Russia. While a prisoner, Paulus agitated against ADOLF HITLER among the other German prisoners of war and later testified at the NUREMBERG TRIALS. After his release from prison (1953), he settled in East Germany.

Pausanias \pȯ-'sā-nē-əs\ (fl. AD 143–176) Greek traveler and geographer. His *Description of Greece* is an invaluable guide to ancient ruins. He describes the religious art and architecture of OLYMPIA and DELPHI, the pictures and inscriptions at ATHENS, the statue of Athena on the ACROPOLIS, and (outside the city) the monuments of famous men and of Athenians fallen in battle. According to JAMES GEORGE FRAZER, without Pausa-

O P Q R

nias the ruins of Greece would be "a labyrinth without a clue, a riddle without an answer."

pavane \pə-'vän\ Stately court dance introduced from southern Europe into England in the 16th century. The dance, consisting of forward and backward steps to music in duple time, was originally used to open ceremonial balls; later its steps became livelier and it came to be paired with the quick galliard in triple time.

Pavane, "The Dance in the Garden" illumination from the *Roman de la rose*, Toulouse, early 16th century; in the British Library (Harley MS 4425, fol. 14v).

Pavarotti, Luciano (born 1935) Italian tenor. He started out as a schoolteacher, beginning his vocal training only in his twenties. He made his professional debut in 1961, and two years later was singing throughout Europe. He debuted at La Scala in 1965, and at the Metropolitan Opera in 1968. He retained the beautiful tone and thrilling high notes that his audiences loved into his sixties, nurturing his broad appeal by recording many light pieces in addition to the traditional Italian repertoire in which he specializes. The most famous male classical singer of the late 20th century, he came to personify the Italian tenor worldwide.

pavement Durable surfacing of a road, path, court, patio, plaza, airstrip, or other such area. The Romans, the greatest road builders of the ancient world, built their roads of stone and concrete. By AD 75 several methods of road construction were known in India, including brick and stone slab pavements, and street paving was common in towns. Smaller cobblestones began to be used for European paving in the late Middle Ages. The 18th–19th century saw the development of pavement systems (e.g., MACADAM) that used light road surfaces of broken or crushed stone. Modern flexible pavements contain sand and gravel or crushed stone compacted with a bituminous binder (e.g., asphalt or tar); such a pavement has enough plasticity to absorb shock. Rigid pavements are made of concrete, composed of coarse and fine aggregate and portland cement, and usually reinforced with steel rod or mesh.

Pavese \pä-'vā-sā\, **Cesare** (1908–1950) Italian poet, critic, novelist, and translator. Pavese founded, and was long an editor with, the publishing house of Einaudi. Denied a creative outlet by fascist control of literature, he did translations in the 1930s and '40s that introduced many modern U.S. and English writers to Italy. Much of his own work appeared between the end of World War II and his death by suicide at 41; some was published posthumously. His best works include *Dialogues with Leucò* (1947), poetic conversations on the human condition; the novel *The Moon and the Bonfire* (1950); and the journal *This Business of Living* (1952). The Pavese Prize for literature was established in 1957.

Pavia \pä-'vē-ə\ *ancient* **Ticinum** City (pop., 1991: 76,000), LOMBARDY, northern Italy, on the TICINO RIVER. Originally a settlement of the Papiria tribe, it was conquered by Rome c. 220 BC. Pillaged by ATTILA and ODOACER in the 5th century AD, it became a center of Gothic resistance against the Byzantine empire. Ruled by the Visconti family (see GIAN GALEAZZO VISCONTI) from c. 1359, it became a leading Italian city-state. In 1525 it was the scene of a decisive victory by the Holy Roman emperor CHARLES V over the French under FRANCIS I, who was captured. It was active in the RISORGIMENTO and joined the kingdom of Italy in 1859. It still retains the ancient plan of the Roman fortified town, and medieval structures remain. The University of Pavia (founded 1361) is linked with the ancient law school, which dates to 825. It is a center of communications, agriculture, and industry.

Pavlov \'päv-ˌlȯf\, **Ivan (Petrovich)** (1849–1936) Russian physiologist. He is known chiefly for the concept of the conditioned reflex. In his classic experiment, he found that a hungry dog trained to associate the sound of a bell with food salivated at the sound even in the absence of food. He expanded on CHARLES SHERRINGTON's explanation of the spinal reflex. He also tried to apply his laws to human psychoses and language function. His ability to reduce a complex situation to a simple experiment and his pioneering studies relating human behavior to the nervous system laid the basis for the scientific analysis of behavior. After the Russian Revolution, he became an outspoken opponent of the Communist government. He won a 1904 Nobel Prize for his work on digestive secretions.

Pavlova \'pav-lə-və\, **Anna (Pavlovna)** (1881–1931) Russian ballerina, considered the greatest ballerina of the early 20th century. She studied at the Imperial Ballet school from 1891 and joined the MARIINSKY THEATER company in 1899, becoming prima ballerina in 1906. From 1908 she toured in Europe as a guest artist with many companies. In 1913 she left Russia to tour with her own company, which showcased her outstanding classical performances in such ballets as MICHEL FOKINE's *Dying Swan, Pavillon d'Armide,* and *Chopiniana,* as well as various short solos. Her many tours brought ballet to audiences in many countries for the first time and did much to popularize ballet worldwide.

Anna Pavlova.

pawnbroking Business of advancing loans to customers who have pledged household goods or personal belongings as security. The pawnbroker's trade is one of the oldest known, having existed 2,000–3,000 years ago in China, as well as in ancient Greece and Rome. Pawnbroking was common in medieval Europe despite laws against USURY. Private pawnbrokers were usually those exempt from the laws, notably the Jews. In 1462 the FRANCISCANS set up the *montes pietatis,* which granted interest-free loans to the poor, though they were later forced to charge interest to prevent premature exhaustion of their funds. Public pawnshops existed briefly in the Middle Ages but were reestablished in the 18th century to free debtors from the high interest rates of private pawnshops. Most European countries now maintain public pawnshops; in the U.S. only private pawnshops exist. Social-welfare programs and increased access to easy CREDIT has led to a decline in pawnbroking's importance. See also INTEREST, CONSUMER CREDIT, CREDIT CARD.

Pawnee \pȯ-'nē\ PLAINS INDIAN people of Caddoan language stock who traditionally lived along the Platte River in what is now Nebraska. The Pawnee tribe comprised relatively independent BANDS, each divided into villages. They lived in large, dome-shaped, earth-covered lodges but used TEPEES on buffalo hunts. Women raised corn, squash, and beans. Chiefs, priests, and shamans constituted the dominant class. Pawnee religion focused on a variety of deities, including the supreme being Tirawa, the sun god, and morning and evening stars. The Pawnee had military societies, and many Pawnee served as scouts for the U.S. armies of the frontier. Pawnee lands were ceded to the U.S. in the mid-19th century and most Pawnee were relocated to a reservation in Oklahoma. Today they number about 2,300.

pawpaw See PAPAW

Pax Romana \'paks-rō-'ma-nə, 'päks-rō-'mä-nə\ (Latin: "Roman Peace") State of comparative tranquility throughout the Mediterranean world from the reign of AUGUSTUS (27 BC–AD 14) to that of MARCUS AURELIUS (AD 161–80). The concord also included northern Africa and Persia. The empire protected and governed provinces, each of which legislated and administered its own laws while accepting Roman taxation and military control. It was the Pax Romana that ensured the survival and eventual transmission of the classical Greek and Roman heritage.

Paxton Boys uprising (1763) Attack by Pennsylvania frontiersmen on an Indian settlement. In the Pontiac Indian uprising, about 57 drunken men from Paxton, Pa., killed 20 peaceful Indians. The colonial governor ordered the arrest of the "Paxton Boys," but sympathetic colonists refused to prosecute. Instead, angered by appropriations insufficient to defend the western frontier, over 600 armed frontiersmen marched on Philadelphia in 1764. They were met by leading Philadelphians, including BENJAMIN FRANKLIN, who promised the men a hearing.

payments, balance of See BALANCE OF PAYMENTS

Payton, Walter (Jerry) (1954–1999) U.S. football player. Born in Columbia, Miss., he played in college for Jackson State University. From 1975 to 1987 he played for the Chicago Bears. He holds the all-time career record for yardage (16,726), combined yardage (rushing and pass receiving; 21,803 yds), seasons with 1,000 or more yards rushing (10), and yards gained in a single game (275). In 1999 it was revealed that he was suffering from a rare liver disease. He is considered by some the greatest running back in football history.

Paz \ˈpäs\, **Octavio** (1914–1998) Mexican poet, writer, and diplomat. Educated at the University of Mexico, Paz published his first book of poetry, *Luna Silvestre* ("Savage Moon"), in 1933. He later founded and edited several important literary reviews. Influenced in turn by Marxism, surrealism, existentialism, Buddhism, and Hinduism, his poetry uses rich imagery in dealing with metaphysical questions, and his most prominent theme is the human ability to overcome existential solitude through erotic love and artistic creativity. His prose works include *The Labyrinth of Solitude* (1950), an influential essay on Mexican history and culture. He was Mexico's ambassador to India 1962–68. He was awarded the Nobel Prize in 1990.

Paz Estenssoro \ˈpäs-ˌes-ten-ˈsȯr-ō\, **Víctor** (1907–2001) President of Bolivia (1952–56, 1960–64, 1985–89). Originally an economics professor, he was elected to the Chamber of Deputies and became president when the National Revolutionary Movement (MNR), a left-wing organization that he helped found, seized power in 1952. He extended the vote to Indians, implemented agrarian reform, and expropriated three major tin companies. He was elected again in 1964 but was overthrown by a military coup the same year. He regained the presidency in 1985 and instituted a program of economic austerity that reduced the hyperinflation that had imperiled the Bolivian economy.

Pazzi conspiracy \ˈpät-sē\ (April 16, 1478) Unsuccessful plot to overthrow the MEDICI rulers of Florence. It was led by the rival Pazzi family, with the backing of Pope SIXTUS IV, who wanted to consolidate papal rule over northern central Italy. The conspirators tried to assassinate two Medici brothers during mass at the Cathedral of Florence; they killed Giuliano de' Medici, but Lorenzo de' MEDICI escaped. The people of Florence rallied to the Medici and killed many of the conspirators, leaving Lorenzo more powerful than before and setting off a two-year war with the papacy.

PBS *in full* **Public Broadcasting Service** Private, nonprofit U.S. corporation of public television stations. PBS provides its member stations, which are supported by public funds and private contributions rather than by commercials, with educational, cultural, news, and children's programs that are produced by its members and by independent producers worldwide. Its popular programs have included *Sesame Street, Masterpiece Theatre, Great Performances, NewsHour with Jim Lehrer,* and *Nova.* PBS was founded in 1969 to coordinate and provide services to its member stations, which now number about 350. Funding is provided mainly by viewers' contributions, state governments, and grants from businesses and private foundations; the U.S. government, through the Corporation for Public Broadcasting, supplies about 15%.

PC See PERSONAL COMPUTER

PCB *in full* **polychlorinated biphenyl** \bī-ˈfe-nᵊl, bī-ˈfē-nᵊl\ Any of a class of highly stable organic compounds prepared by the reaction of CHLORINE with biphenyl, a two-ring compound. The commercial product, a mix of several PCB ISOMERS, is a colorless, viscous liquid that hardly dissolves in water, does not degrade under high temperatures, and is a good DIELECTRIC. PCBs became widely used as lubricants, heat-transfer fluids, and fire-resistant dielectric fluids in transformers and capacitors in the 1930s and '40s. In the mid-1970s they were found to cause liver dysfunction in humans and came under suspicion as CARCINOGENS; their manufacture and use were consequently restricted in the U.S. and many other countries, though illegal dumping by manufacturers continued. They persist in the environment and have entered the FOOD CHAIN, causing great harm especially to invertebrates and fish.

pea Any of several species, comprising hundreds of varieties, of herbaceous annual plants belonging to the family Leguminosae (or Fabaceae), also known as the pea family (see LEGUME), grown virtually worldwide for their edible seeds. *Pisum sativum* is the common garden pea of the Western world, which GREGOR MENDEL used for his pioneering studies of HEREDITY. While their origins have not been definitely determined, it is known that peas are one of the oldest cultivated crops. Some varieties, called sugar peas, snow peas, or mange-touts, have edible pods, and are popular in East Asian cuisines. See also SWEET PEA.

Pea (*Pisum sativum*).
WALTER CHANDOHA

Peabody \ˈpē-bə-dē\, **Elizabeth (Palmer)** (1804–1894) U.S. educator. Born in Billerica, Mass., she served as secretary to WILLIAM ELLERY CHANNING (1825–34) and worked with BRONSON ALCOTT in his Temple School. She opened a Boston bookshop in 1839, which became a center for Transcendentalist activities. She published works by MARGARET FULLER and NATHANIEL HAWTHORNE and also published and wrote articles for *The Dial.* Inspired by the work of FRIEDRICH FROEBEL, she opened the first kindergarten in the U.S. in 1860 and thereafter devoted herself to organizing public and private kindergartens. Her sisters married HORACE MANN and NATHANIEL HAWTHORNE.

Peabody \ˈpē-ˌbä-dē\, **George** (1795–1869) U.S. merchant and financier. Born in South Danvers, Mass. (renamed Peabody in his honor), he earned an early fortune as a partner in a wholesale dry-goods business and as president of the Eastern Railroad (from 1836). On a trip to England he negotiated an $8 million loan for the near-bankrupt state of Maryland. In 1837 he moved to London permanently and founded a merchant banking house specializing in FOREIGN EXCHANGE; his banking operations helped establish U.S. CREDIT abroad. He spent most of his fortune on philanthropy to promote education and the arts; his gifts include a natural-history museum at Yale University, an archaeology museum at Harvard, and an Asian export art museum in Salem, Mass.

Peace Corps U.S. government agency of volunteers, formed in 1961 by Pres. JOHN F. KENNEDY. Its purpose is to assist other countries in their development efforts by providing skilled workers in the fields of education, agriculture, health, trade, technology, and community development. Volunteers are expected to serve for two years as good neighbors in the host country, to speak its language, and to live on a level comparable to that of the local residents. By 2002, over 165,000 volunteers had served in the corps.

Peace of God Movement within the medieval Roman Catholic Church to end private warfare. First heard of in 990 at synods in southern and central France, the peace decrees forbade, under pain of excommunication, private warfare or violence against churches, clerics, pilgrims, merchants, women, peasants, and cattle. All those who lived in an area under the Peace of God had to swear to observe and enforce it. The peace was also decreed at the councils of Limoges (994), Poitiers (999), and Bourges (1038).

peace pipe See CALUMET

Peace River River, western Canada. Formed by the confluence of the Finlay and Parsnip rivers in the Canadian Rockies of British Columbia, it flows east across the border of Alberta to join the Slave River just north of its outlet from Lake ATHABASCA. It is 1,195 mi (1,923 km) long. It was explored by ALEXANDER MACKENZIE in 1792–93 and became a major fur trading route. It is an important source of hydroelectric power.

Peace River River, western central Florida. It rises in Polk Co. and flows south and southwest into Charlotte Harbor on the southwestern coast. It is about 85 mi (135 km) long.

peach Small to medium-sized fruit tree *(Prunus persica)* of the ROSE family, grown throughout the warmer temperate regions of both hemispheres, and the fruit it produces. It probably originated in China and spread westward. Peach trees are intolerant of severe cold but require winter chilling to induce spring growth. The long, pointed leaves are glossy green and lance-shaped. Pink or white flowers grow singly or

O
P
Q
R

clustered. The fleshy, juicy exterior of the fruit is edible; the hard interior is called the stone or pit. In freestone types, stones separate easily from ripe flesh; in clingstone types, the flesh adheres firmly to the stone. Thousands of varieties have been developed. Peach skin is downy or fuzzy; smooth-skinned peaches are NECTARINES. Peaches are widely eaten fresh and are baked in desserts. Canned peaches are a staple commodity in many regions. Related plants include ALMOND, PLUM, and CHERRY.

Peach (*Prunus persica*).
GRANT HEILMAN

peacock Any of three species (family Phasianidae) of resplendent birds of open lowland forests. Blue, or Indian *(Pavo cristatus),* and green, or Javanese *(P. muticus),* peacock males are 35–50 in. (90–130 cm) long and have a 60-in. (150-cm) train of metallic green tail feathers tipped with an iridescent eyespot ringed with blue and bronze. The train is erected, fanned out, and vibrated during courtship. Females (peahens) are duller and have no train. The male forms a harem of two to five hens, which lay their eggs in a depression in the ground. The blue and green male Congo peacock *(Afropavo congensis)* has a short rounded tail; the reddish and brown hen has a topknot.

Peacock, Thomas Love (1785–1866) English novelist and poet. For most of his life Peacock worked for the East India Co. He was a close friend of PERCY B. SHELLEY, who greatly inspired his writing. His best verse is interspersed in his novels, which are dominated by the conversations of their characters and satirize the intellectual currents of the day. His best-known work, *Nightmare Abbey* (1818), satirizes romantic melancholy and includes characters based on Shelley, SAMUEL TAYLOR COLERIDGE, and Lord BYRON.

Peale, Charles Willson (1741–1827) U.S. painter, inventor, and naturalist. Born in Maryland, he began his career by exchanging a saddle for painting lessons. He later went to London to study with BENJAMIN WEST. On his return he became the preeminent portrait painter of the middle colonies. He damaged his professional career by entering enthusiastically into the revolutionary movement. In 1786 he founded an institution in Philadelphia for the study of natural law and display of natural history and technological objects; the Peale Museum, the first major U.S. museum, was widely imitated by other museums of the period and later by P. T. BARNUM. He is best remembered for his portraits of the leading figures of the American Revolution.

Peale, Norman Vincent (1898–1993) U.S. Protestant clergyman. Born in Bowersville, Ohio, son of a Methodist preacher, he attended Ohio Wesleyan University and was ordained a pastor in the Methodist Episcopal Church. After leading congregations in Brooklyn and Syracuse, N.Y., in 1933 he became pastor of Marble Collegiate Church in New York City, where he remained for the rest of his career. In 1937 he cofounded the Religio-Psychiatric Clinic, which combined religion and psychiatry in the interests of mental health. He gained fame through radio and television sermons and through his books, including the best-selling *Power of Positive Thinking* (1952). In 1969 he was elected president of the Reformed Church in America.

Peale, Rembrandt (1778–1860) U.S. painter and writer. A son of CHARLES WILLSON PEALE, he studied with his father and at the Royal Academy in London. In Paris in 1808–10 he was offered the post of court painter to Napoleon I. His early portrait of THOMAS JEFFERSON (1805) was his masterpiece. Following his father's example, he opened a museum and portrait gallery in Baltimore, where he established the first illuminating gasworks. When he resumed painting, he turned to formal subject pieces (e.g., *The Court of Death,* 1820) before returning to portraiture with the first of a series of portraits of GEORGE WASHINGTON.

peanut *or* **groundnut** Annual LEGUME *(Arachis hypogaea)* and its edible seeds, which have the peculiar habit of ripening underground in pods. Native to tropical South America, peanuts were introduced early into the Old World tropics. Each pod contains one to three oblong seeds with whitish to dark-purple seed coats. Peanuts are a concentrated food; pound for pound they have more protein, minerals, and vitamins than beef liver, more fat than heavy cream, and more calories than sugar. They are pressed for edible oil, ground into peanut butter, eaten as snacks, and used in cooking. The plant is fed to livestock.

pear Any of several species of trees of the genus *Pyrus,* especially *P. communis,* of the ROSE family, which is one of the most important fruit trees in the world and is cultivated in all temperate-zone countries of both hemispheres. The thousands of varieties include Bartlett (by far the most widely grown), Beurre Bosc, and Beurre d'Anjou. In the U.S., much of the crop is canned; in Europe, pears are more commonly eaten fresh or used for perry (fermented pear juice). The tree is taller and more upright than the APPLE tree; pear fruits are sweeter and softer than apples. Hard cells (grit, or stone cells) dot the flesh.

Pear (*Pyrus communis*).
GRANT HEILMAN

pearl Concretion formed by a MOLLUSK consisting of the same material (called nacre, or mother-of-pearl) as the mollusk's shell. Long treasured as gemstones, pearls are valued for their translucence and luster and for the delicate play of surface color. The more perfect a pearl's shape and the deeper its luster, the greater its value. The color varies with the mollusk and its environment. Jewelers of the 16th–17th century often used irregularly shaped "baroque" pearls, formed from muscular tissue, to form the bodies of animals and other figures. In Europe and China, mother-of-pearl has been used as an inlay material for decorating furniture. The discovery that a pearl could be cultivated by insertion of a foreign object inside the mollusk's shell is said to have been made in 13th-century China.

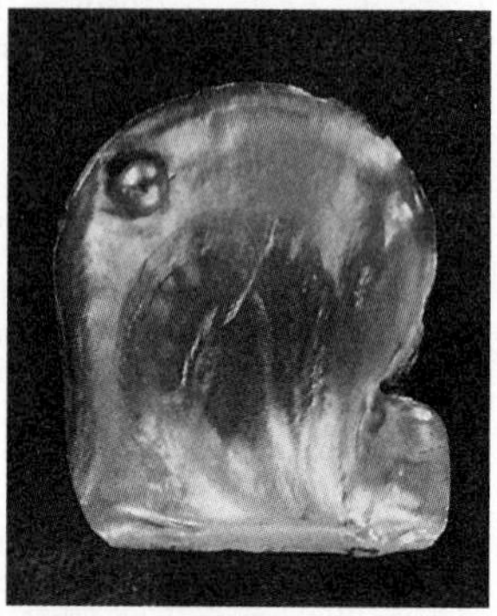
Blister pearl attached to the shell of an Oriental pearl oyster (*Pinctada martensii Dunker*).
BY COURTESY OF THE AMERICAN MUSEUM OF NATURAL HISTORY, NEW YORK

Pearl Harbor Inlet, southern coast of OAHU island, Hawaii, 6 mi (10 km) west of HONOLULU, forming a landlocked harbor connected with the Pacific Ocean. In 1887 Hawaii granted the U.S. the exclusive use of the harbor as a coaling and repair station, and in 1908 a naval station was established. In 1941 the harbor was attacked without warning by the Japanese air force, causing great loss of life and precipitating U.S. entry into WORLD WAR II. It is now the headquarters of the U.S. Pacific Fleet.

Pearl River River, central Mississippi. It flows southwest through JACKSON, then into Louisiana and the Gulf of Mexico. About 410 mi (660 km) long, it forms the boundary between Mississippi and Louisiana. Honey Island Swamp, lying in the mid-delta area southwest of Picayune, Miss., is noted for its wildlife and fishing.

pearlstone See PERLITE

Pearson, Drew *orig.* **Andrew Russell** (1897–1969) U.S. newspaper columnist. Born in Evanston, Ill., Pearson taught industrial geography at the University of Pennsylvania before turning to journalism. He was fired from the *Baltimore Sun* for writing *Washington Merry-Go-Round* (1931, with Robert S. Allen), a gossipy book about the scene in the U.S. capital. From 1932 he wrote an influential syndicated column of the same name (with Allen until 1942; from 1965 with Jack Anderson, who inherited it on Pearson's death), which specialized in muckraking. Among the many world leaders he interviewed was NIKITA KHRUSHCHEV.

Pearson, Lester B(owles) (1897–1972) Prime minister of Canada (1963–68). Born in Toronto, he taught at the University of Toronto (1924–28), then joined the Canadian foreign service in 1928. He was posted to Britain (1935–41) and the U.S. (1942–45), serving as ambassador to the U.S. 1945–46. He served in the Canadian House of Commons 1948–68, and was minister of external affairs 1948–56. He led the

Canadian delegation to the U.N. 1948–56, and served as president of its General Assembly 1952–53. In 1957 he received the Nobel Peace Price for his help in resolving the SUEZ CRISIS. Head of the Liberal Party from 1958, he rebuilt it to win the 1963 election. As prime minister he was involved with the growing Quebec separatist movement and rebuked visiting CHARLES DE GAULLE for his expressed support. He retired in 1968.

Peary, Harold *orig.* **Harrold Jese Pereira de Faria** (1909–1985) U.S. actor. Born to Portuguese immigrants in San Leandro, Cal., he created the character Throckmorton F. Gildersleeve on the hit comedy series *Fibber McGee and Molly* in 1937. He starred in his own popular radio serial, *The Great Gildersleeve* (1941–50), considered the first spin-off created from another series. He later acted in such television series as *Blondie* (1957) and *Fibber McGee and Molly* (1959), and he continued to perform on radio into the 1970s.

Peary, Robert E(dwin) (1856–1920) U.S. explorer. Born in Cresson, Pa., he joined the U.S. Navy in 1881 but was granted leaves of absence to pursue his Arctic expeditions. He explored Greenland by dog sledge (1886, 1891), finding evidence that it was an island, and returned there (1893–94, 1895, 1896) to transport large meteorites to the U.S. After announcing his intention to reach the North Pole, he made several attempts between 1898 and 1905, sailing on a specially built ship and sledging to within 175 mi (280 km) of the pole. On April 6, 1909, accompanied by Matthew Henson (1866–1955) and four Eskimo, he reached what he saw as his goal, and he became widely acknowledged as the first explorer to reach the pole. (The claim of his former colleague Frederick A. Cook (1865–1940) to have reached the pole in 1908 was later discredited.) Examination of Peary's expedition diary and new documents in the 1980s suggested he may only have reached a point 30–60 mi (50–100 km) short of the pole.

peasant Any member of a class that tills the soil as small landowners or agricultural laborers. The peasant economy generally has a simple technology and a DIVISION OF LABOR by age and sex. The basic unit of production is the family or household. Peasant families traditionally consume what they produce, though a portion of their output may be sold in the market or paid to a landlord. Productivity per worker and yields per unit of land are usually low. Peasants as a class tend to disappear as a society industrializes, though peasantlike social structures may persist under new economic regimens. See also EJIDO, FEUDALISM, HACIENDA, SERFDOM.

Peasants' Revolt *or* **Wat Tyler's Rebellion** (1381) First great popular rebellion in English history. It was triggered by the poll tax of 1381, which angered laborers and artisans already resentful of the limits on wages fixed by the Statute of Laborers (1351). Centered in southeastern England and East Anglia, the revolt was led by Wat Tyler (died 1381), who marched into London with a band of Kentish rebels. They captured the Tower of London and beheaded officials responsible for the poll tax. RICHARD II promised reforms, but Tyler was killed in his presence by the mayor of London. The last of the rebels were subdued in East Anglia two weeks later.

Peasants' War (1524–25) Peasant uprising in Germany. Inspired by reforms brought by the REFORMATION, peasants in western and southern Germany invoked divine law to demand agrarian rights and freedom from oppression by nobles and landlords. As the uprising spread, some peasant groups organized armies. Though supported by HULDRYCH ZWINGLI and THOMAS MUNTZER, the revolt was condemned by MARTIN LUTHER, which contributed to its defeat, principally by the army of the Swabian League. Some 100,000 peasants were killed. Reprisals and increased restrictions discouraged further attempts to improve the peasants' plight.

peat Organic fuel consisting of a light, spongy material formed in temperate humid environments by the accumulation and partial decomposition of vegetable remains under conditions of poor drainage. Vast beds occur in Europe, North America, and northern Asia but are worked only where there is little coal. Peat deposition is the first step in the formation of COAL. Dried peat burns readily, with a smoky flame and a characteristic odor. It is used for domestic heating and to fire boilers. In Ireland, millions of tons are consumed annually; Russia, Sweden, Germany, and Denmark also use considerable quantities.

peat moss *or* **sphagnum moss** \'sfag-nəm\ Any of more than 160 species of plants that make up the bryophyte genus *Sphagnum,* which grow in dense clumps around ponds, in swamps and bogs, on moist, acid cliffs, and on lakeshores from tropical to subpolar regions. These pale-green to deep-red plants can hold 20 times their weight in water. As they die and are compressed, they form organic peat, which is harvested and dried as fuel, as seedbed cover, and as shipping packaging for plants and live aquatic animals. Gardeners stir peat into soil to increase soil moisture, porosity, and acidity and to reduce erosion.

pecan NUT and tree (*Carya illinoinensis*) of the WALNUT family, native to temperate North America. Occasionally reaching a height of about 160 ft (50 m), the tree has deeply furrowed bark and feathery leaves. Pecan nut meat, rich and distinctive in flavor and texture, has one of the highest fat contents of any vegetable product and a caloric value close to that of butter. Pecan production is a considerable industry of the southeastern U.S., where pecan pie and pecan praline candy are traditional sweets.

Pecan (*Carya illinoinensis*).
GRANT HEILMAN

peccary \'pe-kə-rē\ *or* **javelin** \'ja-və-lən\ Any of three species (family Tayassuidae) of New World even-toed UNGULATES resembling pigs. Found in deserts and wet tropical forests from Texas to Patagonia, peccaries are gray with white markings and have small, erect ears and almost no tail. They grow to 30–35 in. (75–90 cm) long and weigh 30–65 lbs (15–30 kg). A scent gland that opens on the back and emits a strong, musky odor inspired the belief that peccaries have two navels. Peccaries have spearlike upper canines and eat plants, small animals, and carrion. They live in groups of five to 25 or 50–100, depending on the species.

Collared peccary (*Tayassu tajacu*).
JEN AND DES BARTLETT—BRUCE COLEMAN INC.

Pechora River \pi-'chȯ-rə\ River, northeastern Russia. It rises in the northern URAL MTNS. and flows south, then west and north to enter the BARENTS SEA by a delta, after a course of 1,124 mi (1,809 km). It is frozen from early November to early May. Its basin contains large deposits of coal, petroleum, and natural gas.

Pechora Sea *Russian* **Pechorskoye More** \pi-'chȯr-skə-yə-'mȯr-yə\ Sea, southeastern extension of the BARENTS SEA, north of European Russia. It is located between Kolguyev Island and the Yugorsky Peninsula. Although it is blocked by floating ice from November to June, its cod, seals, and other marine life are exploited. The main port is Naryan-Mar on the PECHORA RIVER.

Peck, (Eldred) Gregory (born 1916) U.S. film actor. Born in La Jolla, Cal., he appeared on Broadway in *The Morning Star* (1942) and played several other stage roles before making his film debut in *Days of Glory* (1944). Known for playing likeable, honest men of high moral quality, he starred in such movies as *The Keys of the Kingdom* (1944), *Spellbound* (1945), *The Yearling* (1946), *Gentleman's Agreement* (1947), *Twelve O'Clock High* (1949), *The Gunfighter* (1950), *Roman Holiday* (1953), *Moby Dick* (1956), and *To Kill a Mockingbird* (1962, Academy Award). His later films included *MacArthur* (1977), *The Old Gringo* (1989), and *Cape Fear* (1991).

pecking order Basic pattern of social organization within a flock of poultry in which each bird pecks another lower in the scale without fear of retaliation and submits to pecking by one of higher rank. For groups of mammals (e.g., BABOON, WOLF) or other birds, the term "dominance hierarchy" is usually used, and the ranking often involves feeding or mating.

Peckinpah \'pe-kin-ˌpä\, **(David) Sam(uel)** (1925–1984) U.S. film director. Born to ranchers in Fresno, Cal., he served in the Marines, studied drama at USC, and began working in television in the mid-1950s, writing for and directing such programs as *Gunsmoke* and *The*

O P Q R

Rifleman. He made his debut as a film director with *The Deadly Companions* (1961), which was followed by *Ride the High Country* (1962) and *Major Dundee* (1965). Among his later films were *The Wild Bunch* (1969), considered his finest, *Straw Dogs* (1971), *Pat Garrett and Billy the Kid* (1973), and *Cross of Iron* (1977). Peckinpah was known as a heavy drinker, perpetually at odds with the Hollywood establishment, and his films were noted for their magnificent landscapes, embittered characters, and brutal violence.

Pecos River \ˈpā-kəs\ River, eastern New Mexico and western Texas. It rises in the Sangre de Cristo Mtns. of New Mexico and flows southeast about 500 mi (800 km) across the Texas border. It empties into the Rio Grande at the Amistad National Recreation Area. There are many dams along the river, including the Alamogordo, Avalon, and Red Bluff dams.

pectin Any of a class of carbohydrates found in certain plant cell walls and tissues. They are principally composed of a galactose derivative, galacturonic acid. In fruits, pectin keeps the walls of adjacent cells joined together, helping them remain firm and hold their shape. As fruits become overripe, the pectin breaks down to simple sugars that dissolve more readily, so the fruits become soft and lose their shape. Because it forms a thick, gel-like solution when added in small amounts to fruit acids, sugar, and water, pectin is used to make jellies, jams, and marmalades. Its thickening properties also make it useful in the confectionery, pharmaceutical, and textile industries.

Pedersen \ˈpit͟h-ər-sən\, **Holger** (1867–1953) Danish linguist. He specialized in comparative Celtic grammar but made influential contributions to many other areas of linguistics. In addition to his *Comparative Grammar of the Celtic Languages* (2 vols., 1909–13), he published works on Albanian, Armenian, Russian, and Indo-European dialects; on Lithuanian, Hittite, Tocharian, Czech, and Turkish phonology; on the relationship of Indo-European languages to the Semitic and Finno-Ugric languages; and on the origin of runes.

pedestal In classical architecture, a support or base for a column, statue, vase, or obelisk. It may be square, octagonal, or circular. A single pedestal may also support a group of columns, or colonnade (see podium). The pedestal, which was first employed by Roman architects, consists (from bottom to top) of three parts: the plinth, the dado (or die), and the cornice (or cap).

pediatrics \ˌpē-dē-ˈa-triks\ Medical specialty dealing with the development, health, and diseases of children. It did not become a specialized area of study until the 18th century, when the first children's hospitals were founded. Early pediatricians studied childhood diseases (see Thomas Sydenham) but could do little to cure them. By the mid-20th century, when antibiotics and vaccines had controlled most of these diseases in the developed world and infant and child mortality had fallen, pediatrics changed its focus to normal growth and child development. Recently, behavioral and social aspects of children's health have been incorporated.

pedigree Record of ancestry or purity of breed. Pedigrees of domesticated animals are maintained by governmental or private record associations or breed organizations in many countries. In human genetics, pedigree diagrams are used to trace the inheritance of a specific trait, abnormality, or disease. Standard symbols are used to represent males, females, mating (marriage), and offspring. The offspring symbols appear from left to right in the order of birth and are connected to the marriage line by a vertical line. Possession of the character under study is shown by a solid or blackened symbol, and absence is shown by an open or clear symbol.

pediment In classical architecture, a triangular gable crowning a portico or facade. The pediment was the crowning feature of the Greek temple front. The pediment's triangular wall surface, or tympanum, was often decorated with sculpture. The Romans adapted the pediment as a purely decorative form to finish doors, windows, and niches, sometimes using a series of alternating triangular and segmentally curved pediments, a motif revived in the Italian High Renaissance. Baroque-era designers developed many varieties of broken, scrolled, and reverse-curved pediments.

pediment In geology, any relatively flat surface of bedrock (exposed or lightly covered with soil or gravel) that occurs at the base of a mountain or as a plain having no associated mountain. Pediments are most conspicuous in basin-and-range-type desert areas throughout the world, but they also occur in humid areas. In the tropics, the surfaces tend to be covered with soil and obscured by vegetation. Many tropical river towns are situated on pediments, which offer easier building sites than the steep hillsides above or the river marshes below.

pedology \pi-ˈdä-lə-jē\ Scientific discipline concerned with all aspects of soils, including their physical and chemical properties, the role of organisms in soil production and in relation to soil character, description and mapping of soil units, and origin and formation of soils. Pedology embraces such subdisciplines as soil chemistry, soil physics, and soil microbiology. Usually, a soil auger is used to obtain core samples in places where no subsurface exposure can be found, and the soil units are defined, delineated, and mapped in a manner somewhat similar to procedures used in the mapping of surficial geologic deposits or landforms.

Pedra Furada \ˈpā-drə-fü-ˈrä-də\ Controversial archaeological site, northeastern Brazil. It was thought to contain hearths and stone artifacts as old as 48,000 years, about 35,000 years earlier than the commonly accepted dates for the first human settlement of the Americas. Experts have concluded that the early "occupation deposits" and associated stone "artifacts" were probably formed by natural geologic phenomena.

Pedrell \pā-ˈt͟hrel\, **Felipe** (1841–1922) Spanish musicologist and composer. He was largely self-taught as a musician. A scholarship for study in Rome exposed him to the great past of Spanish music preserved in archives there, and he determined to revive the tradition by bringing to light both folk and older art music and by promoting a national style of composition. His own works include operas and orchestral and choral works. He is regarded as the father of Spanish musical nationalism.

Pedro I \ˈpā-drō, ˈpā-drü\ *known as* **Dom Pedro** (1798–1834) First emperor of Brazil (1822–31) and, briefly, king of Portugal. The son of John VI of Portugal, he became regent of Brazil in 1821, but in 1822 he broke with Lisbon and declared Brazil's independence. The former colony became a constitutional monarchy with Pedro its emperor. Strong opposition to his autocratic manner and impatience with parliamentary procedure induced him to abdicate in favor of his 5-year-old son, Pedro II. When John VI died, Pedro I became Portugal's King Pedro IV, but quickly abdicated in favor of his daughter, the future Queen Maria II. See also Jose Bonifacio de Andrada e Silva.

Pedro II *orig.* **Dom Pedro de Alcântara.** (1825–1891) Second and last emperor of Brazil (1831–89). He became emperor at age 5 when his father, Pedro I, abdicated. After a period of regency, he was crowned in 1841. His concern for his subjects, skill at arbitrating political disputes, and leadership in economic matters brought stability to the country. He led Brazil into the Paraguayan War, which brought Brazil prestige and territory. His support eroded primarily over the issue of the imperial prerogatives. Emancipation was proclaimed in 1888; in 1889 Pedro II was removed in a military coup and a republic was established. See also Jose Bonifacio de Andrada e Silva.

Pee Dee River River, North and South Carolina. Rising as the Yadkin River in the Blue Ridge Mtns. in northwestern North Carolina, it flows southeast into Winyah Bay near Georgetown, S.C. It is 233 mi (375 km) long. The lower Pee Dee is navigable for 90 mi (145 km).

Peel, detail of an oil painting by John Linnell, 1838; in the National Portrait Gallery, London.

Peel, Sir Robert (1788–1850) British prime minister (1834–35, 1841–46) and principal founder of the Conservative Party. A member of Parliament from 1809, Peel served as chief secretary for Ireland (1812–18) and resisted efforts to admit Catholics to Parliament. As home secretary (1822–27, 1828–30) he reorganized England's criminal code. He established London's first disciplined police force, whose members were nicknamed after him "bobbies" or "peelers." After a brief first term as prime minister, Peel led the newly formed Conservative Party to a strong victory in the 1841 elections and became prime minister again. He imposed an income tax, reorganized the Bank of ENGLAND, and initiated reforms in Ireland. Favoring reduced tariffs on imports, he repealed the CORN LAWS, which caused his government to fall, but he continued to support free-trade principles in Parliament. He was the chief architect of the mid-Victorian age of stability and prosperity that he did not live to see.

Peel River River, northwestern Canada. It rises in western Yukon Territory and flows east and then north into the MACKENZIE RIVER in the Northwest Territories, near Fort McPherson, a fur-trading post. It is 425 mi (684 km) long. Its upper course through Peel Plateau is characterized by canyons as deep as 1,000 ft (300 m). Its lower valley consists primarily of nature preserves and game sanctuaries.

peerage Body of peers or titled nobility in Britain. The five ranks, in descending order, are DUKE, MARQUESS, earl (see COUNT), VISCOUNT, and BARON. Until 1999, peers were entitled to sit in the House of LORDS and exempted from jury duty. Titles may be hereditary or granted for life.

Pegasus \'pe-gə-səs\ In GREEK MYTHOLOGY, a winged horse. It sprang from the blood of MEDUSA as she was beheaded by PERSEUS. BELLEROPHON captured Pegasus and rode him in several of his exploits, including his fight with the CHIMERA, but when he tried to ride the winged horse to heaven he was unseated and killed, and Pegasus was placed in the sky as a constellation. The flight of Pegasus is often regarded as a symbol of poetic inspiration.

pegmatite \'peg-mə-ˌtīt\ Almost any wholly crystalline IGNEOUS ROCK that is at least in part very coarse-grained, the major constituents of which include minerals typically found in ordinary igneous rocks (such as granites) and in which extreme textural variations, especially in grain size, are characteristic. Usually found as irregular dikes, lenses, or veins, pegmatite deposits occur in all parts of the world and are the chief source of commercial FELDSPAR, sheet MICA, and beryllium, tantalum-niobium, and lithium minerals.

Pei \'pā\, **I(eoh) M(ing)** (born 1917) Chinese-U.S. architect. He emigrated to the U.S. in 1935 and studied at MIT and Harvard University. After working for Webb & Knapp, he formed his own partnership in 1955. His National Center for Atmospheric Research, Boulder, Col., mimics the broken silhouettes of the surrounding peaks. His innovative East Building of the National Gallery of Art (1978) was hailed as one of his finest achievements. Other works include Boston's John Hancock Tower (1973), Beijing's Fragrant Hill Hotel (1982), and a controversial glass pyramid for a courtyard at the LOUVRE MUSEUM (1989). The Miho Museum of Art, Shiga, Japan (1997), much of it underground, was acclaimed for the harmony between the building and its mountain environment. Pei received the 1983 Pritzker Architecture Prize.

peine forte et dure \'pen-'fȯrt-ā-'du̇r\ (French: "strong and hard punishment") Formerly in English law, punishment inflicted on those accused of a felony who refused to enter a plea. By a statute of 1275, the *peine* was usually to imprison and starve the prisoner until he submitted; in 1406 pressing by heavy weights was added to this. The practice was abolished in 1772.

Peipus \'pī-pəs\, **Lake** *Estonian* **Lake Peipsi** \'pāp-sē\ Lake, northern central Europe, forming the boundary between Estonia and Russia. It is 60 mi (97 km) long and 31 mi (50 km) wide, and it is frozen for half the year. In 1242 the Russians under ALEXANDER NEVSKY defeated the Teutonic knights (see TEUTONIC ORDER) on the frozen lake in the "Battle on the Ice," forcing them to relinquish claims to Russian lands.

Peirce \'pərs, 'pirs\, **Charles Sanders** (1839–1914) U.S. scientist, logician, and philosopher. Born in Cambridge, Mass., son of the mathematician and astronomer Benjamin Peirce (1809–1880), he attended Harvard University and later spent 30 years as a scientist with the U.S. Coast Guard Survey (1861–91). As a scientist, he is noted for his contributions to the theory of probability, his studies of gravity, and the logic of scientific methodology. He eventually abandoned the physical sciences to study logic, which in its widest sense he identified with SEMIOTICS. He lectured on logic at Johns Hopkins University 1879–94, then spent the rest of his life writing in seclusion. He is regarded as the founder of PRAGMATISM. Though he made eminent contributions to deductive logic, he was a student primarily of "the logic of science"—of INDUCTION and of "retroduction," or "abduction," the forming and accepting on probation of a hypothesis to explain surprising facts. His lifelong ambition was to establish abduction and induction permanently in the very conception of logic.

Peisistratus \pi-'sis-trə-təs\ (early 6th century–527 BC) TYRANT of Athens (c. 560–559, 556–555, 546–527 BC). Born an aristocrat, he gained military honors early. He first became tyrant in 560 after claiming an attempt had been made on his life and appealing to the people to grant him a bodyguard, which he used to help seize the Acropolis. His reign was short-lived, but he gained power again briefly in 556, before being ousted by LYCURGUS and Megacles. After several years in exile, he returned with an army in 546, took control, and remained in power until his death. A patron of the arts, he executed many public works and tried to help small farmers. His unification of Attica and improvement of Athens's prosperity helped make the city preeminent in Greece.

Peking See BEIJING

Peking man See ZHOUKOUDIAN

Pekingese \ˌpē-kə-'nēz\ Breed of long-haired TOY DOG developed in ancient China, where it was held sacred and was kept in Peking's Imperial Palace. Looting English forces introduced the breed to the West in 1860. Known as the "lion dog" for its full mane but perhaps also for its courage, it stands 6–9 in. (15–23 cm) and weighs up to 14 lbs (6.5 kg). It has hanging ears, a short, wrinkled muzzle, and a black mask across the face. The coat may be solid or variegated. Chinese royalty carried very small Pekingese, called "sleeve dogs," in their sleeves.

Pekingese.
SALLY ANNE THOMPSON—EB INC.

Peko \'pā-kȯ\ In Estonian religion, an agricultural deity who aided the growth of grain, especially barley. Peko was represented by a wax image that was kept buried in the grain in the granary and brought out in early spring for a ritual of agricultural fertility. At the end of a ceremonial feast, leftovers were distributed among the poor, and the men competed in wrestling or fence jumping to determine who had the right to keep Peko in his granary until the following year.

Pelagianism \pə-'lā-jē-ə-ˌni-zəm\ Christian HERESY of the 5th century that emphasized free will and the goodness of human nature. Pelagius (354?–after 418), a British monk who settled in Africa in 410, was eager to raise moral standards among Christians. Rejecting the arguments of those who attributed their sins to human weakness, he argued that God made humans free to choose between good and evil and that sin is an entirely voluntary act. His disciple Celestius denied the church's doctrine of ORIGINAL SIN and the necessity of infant BAPTISM. Pelagius and Celestius were excommunicated in 418, but their views continued to find defenders until the Council of Ephesus condemned Pelagianism in 431.

Pelé \'pā-ˌlā\ *orig.* **Edson Arantes do Nascimento** (born 1940) Brazilian soccer player, in his time perhaps the most famous and best-paid athlete in the world. Born in Três Corações, he joined the Santos Football Club in 1956 and helped lead that team to a world club championship in 1962. He led the Brazilian national team to three World Cup victories (1958, 1962, 1970). In 1969, during his 909th match, he scored his 1,000th goal. Of average stature, he combined kicking power and accuracy with a remarkable ability to anticipate other players' moves. In 1975 he joined the New York Cosmos of the North American Soccer League (NASL); he retired after leading the team to the league championship in 1977. He was the 1978 recipient of the International Peace Award, and in 1980 he was named Athlete of the Century.

Pelé.
A.F.P.—PICTORIAL PARADE/EB INC.

Pelée \pə-'lā\, **Mt.** Active volcanic mountain, northern MARTINIQUE, West Indies. It is northwest of FORT-DE-FRANCE and is 4,583 ft (1,397 m) high. A gently sloping cone, it supports luxuriant forests. A violent eruption in 1902 destroyed the port of Saint-Pierre, killing about 30,000 people. A minor eruption occurred in 1929.

Pelew See PALAU

Pelham, Henry (1696–1754) British prime minister (1743–54). He was elected to Parliament in 1717 and, as a supporter of ROBERT WALPOLE, became secretary for war (1724) and paymaster of the forces (1730). He succeeded Walpole as prime minister and chancellor of the exchequer in 1743 and led a stable Whig ministry with parliamentary assistance from his brother, the duke of NEWCASTLE. Pelham resisted attempts to prolong the War of the AUSTRIAN SUCCESSION and signed the Treaty of AIX-LA-CHAPELLE (1748). After the war, he introduced financial reforms, including lower military expenditures, a reduced land tax, and a consolidation of the national debt.

Pelham-Holles, Thomas See Duke of NEWCASTLE

pelican Any of about eight species constituting the genus *Pelecanus* (family Pelecanidae), white or brown birds distinguished by a large, elastic throat pouch. Some species are 70 in. (180 cm) long, have a wingspan of 10 ft (3 m), and weigh up to 30 lbs (13 kg). Most species drive fish into shallow water and, using the pouch as a dip net, scoop them up and immediately swallow them. Pelicans inhabit freshwaters and seacoasts in many parts of the world; they breed in colonies on islands, laying one to four eggs in a stick nest. Chicks thrust their bills down the parent's gullet to obtain regurgitated food.

Brown pelican (*Pelecanus occidentalis*).
NORMAN TOMALIN—BRUCE COLEMAN INC.

Pella Ancient capital, MACEDONIA. Located in northern Greece northwest of THESSALONIKI, it flourished at the end of the 5th century BC. Originally known as Bounomos, it developed rapidly under PHILIP II, but after the Romans defeated the last Macedonian king, it became a small provincial town. Archaeological excavations began in 1957 and revealed large, well-built houses with rooms with mosaic floors dating from the late 4th century. It was the birthplace of ALEXANDER THE GREAT.

pellagra \pə-ˈla-grə\ Nutritional disorder caused largely by a deficiency of NIACIN, marked by skin lesions and digestive and neurological disturbances. DERMATITIS usually appears first, with abnormal sensitivity to sunlight. It may look like a severe sunburn, later becoming reddish brown, rough, and scaly. Diarrhea usually alternates with constipation, along with mouth and tongue inflammation and cracking and dry scaling of the lips. Later, mental abnormalities may include nervousness, depression, and delirium. Mild cases of niacin deficiency respond to a well-balanced diet alone. Pellagra still occurs where diets consist mostly of corn, which is low in both niacin and TRYPTOPHAN (converted to niacin in the body), with little or no protein-rich food. It can also be a side effect of chronic alcoholism.

Peloponnese \ˈpe-lə-pə-ˌnēz\ Peninsula, forming southern part of mainland Greece. A large, mountainous body of land jutting south into the Mediterranean Sea, it has an area of 8,278 sq mi (21,439 sq km) and is joined to the rest of mainland Greece by the Isthmus of Corinth. The Mycenaean civilization flourished there in the 2nd millennium BC at MYCENAE and Pylos. Its chief cities during the classical period were CORINTH and SPARTA. Under the Romans it was part of the province of Achaea from 146 BC to c. 4th century AD. It was part of the Byzantine empire until it was taken by the FRANKS; they held it in the 13th–15th century, when it was often known as Morea. The modern city of Patras (pop., 1991: 155,000), in the northern part, is a commercial center.

Peloponnesian League *or* **Spartan Alliance** Military coalition of Greek city-states led by SPARTA, formed in the 6th century BC. League decisions about war, peace, or alliance were determined by congresses summoned by the Spartans. The league was a major force in Greek affairs, forming the core of resistance to the Persian invasions in 490 and 480 and fighting Athens in the PELOPONNESIAN WAR. Its power declined after its defeat at Leuctra in 371, and the league disbanded in 366/365.

Peloponnesian War (431–404 BC) War fought between ATHENS and SPARTA, the leading city-states of ancient Greece, along with their allies, which included nearly every other Greek city-state. Its principal cause was a fear of Athenian imperialism. The Athenian alliance relied on its strong navy, the Spartan alliance on its strong army. The war fell into two periods, separated by a six-year truce. Fighting broke out in 431, with PERICLES commanding the Athenians. In the first 10 years, Archidamus led the Spartans to defeats. Plague struck Athens in 429, killing Pericles and much of the army. In 428 CLEON almost convinced Athens to massacre the rebellious citizens of Mytilene on Lesbos, but Athens rescinded the order. In 421 both states agreed to accept the Peace of NICIAS. This lasted six years, until Athens launched its disastrous Sicilian expedition. By 413 Athens's forces were demolished. In 411 an oligarchy briefly took power. When democratic leaders were restored by the navy later that year, they refused Spartan peace offers, and the war continued until 405, when the Athenian navy was destroyed at the Battle of AEGOSPOTAMI with Persian help. Under blockade, Athens surrendered in 404. Its empire was dismantled, and the Spartans installed the THIRTY TYRANTS.

Pelops \ˈpē-ˌläps, ˈpe-ˌläps\ In GREEK MYTHOLOGY, founder of the Pelopid dynasty at MYCENAE. Pelops was a grandson of ZEUS. His father, TANTALUS, cooked and served Pelops to the gods at a banquet, and only DEMETER, mourning the loss of her daughter, PERSEPHONE, was distracted enough to eat from the dish. The gods ordered the body restored, but the shoulder, Demeter's portion, was missing, and the boy was given a replacement of ivory. In another story, POSEIDON, helped Pelops gain the hand of Hippodamia, daughter of King Oenomaus of Pisa.

pelota \pə-ˈlō-tə\ (Spanish: "little ball") Any of several games in which players take turns, using a glove or implement, hitting a rubber ball either directly at one another or off a wall. The latter version is related to HANDBALL and JAI ALAI, which are played by two or four players on one-, two-, or three-walled courts using gloves, rackets, or bats. In Spain and elsewhere, pelota is a professional sport on which spectators wager.

Pelusium \pə-ˈlü-shē-əm\ Ancient Egyptian city. Located on the easternmost mouth (long silted up) of the NILE RIVER, it is southeast of modern PORT SAID. It was the main frontier fortress against Palestine in the 26th Egyptian dynasty and later, and was a customs post for Asian goods. In 522 BC the Persians, under Cambyses II, defeated the pharaoh Psamtik III there. In Roman times it was a station on the route to the RED SEA; its ruins date from the Roman period.

pelvic girdle *or* **bony pelvis** Basin-shaped complex of BONES that connects the trunk and legs, supports and balances the trunk, and contains and supports the intestines, bladder, and internal sex organs. It is formed by the hipbones, each consisting of three bones—the ilium above and to the side, the ischium behind and below, and the pubis in front—which join in front at the pubic symphysis and behind at the sacrum (see VERTEBRAL COLUMN). It also contains the socket of the hip joint. It transmits body weight from the spine to the leg. Women's wider, rounder pelvic girdle allows the birth canal to accommodate the fetal head.

pelvic inflammatory disease (PID) Acute INFLAMMATION of the pelvic cavity in women, caused by bacterial infection (usually GONORRHEA or CHLAMYDIA) of REPRODUCTIVE SYSTEM structures. Usually a SEXUALLY TRANSMITTED DISEASE, it occurs mainly in sexually active women under 25, more often in those using intrauterine devices (IUDs). PID can resemble gonorrhea, with abdominal and lower pelvic pain, chills, nausea, fever, and thick, smelly vaginal discharge. Fallopian-tube scarring can cause infertility and ECTOPIC PREGNANCY. Treatment requires antibiotics, bed rest, pain medication, and sexual abstinence until the infection disappears. Sexual partners must also be treated to prevent reinfection.

Pemex *officially* **Petróleos Mexicanos.** Mexico's state-owned oil company. In 1938 Pres. LAZARO CARDENAS nationalized 17 foreign oil companies to create Pemex, the largest Latin American petroleum company and a major world exporter of fossil fuel. Pemex engages in exploration, production, refining, transportation, storage, distribution, and sales of oil and natural gas. In the 1970s promising oil discoveries gave rise to a national spending spree, led by the flamboyant Pres. JOSE LOPEZ PORTILLO and financed by massive borrowing. Crude-oil production tripled. When the price of oil dropped in 1981, 87% of Pemex's assets were owed to foreign banks; by 1982 the country was virtually bankrupt. By the end of the 1990s Pemex had been reorganized and partially privatized.

pen drawing Artwork executed wholly or in part with pen and ink, usually on paper. It is fundamentally a linear method of making images. Artists who wish to suggest three-dimensional forms use hatching and cross-hatching, or washes of color laid onto the drawing with a brush. The three most common types of ink are black carbon ink, the finest type being Chinese ink or the modern India ink; brown ink, which was popular with the old masters; and iron gall, a chemical ink. The three pen types are quill, reed, and metal. Quill pens were most popular for their flexibility and ability to be sharpened to extreme fineness. Steel became the predominant pen type by the 20th century.

penal colony Distant or overseas settlement established to punish criminals with forced labor and isolation from society. Such colonies were developed mostly by the English, French, and Russians. Britain sent criminals to its American colonies until the Revolutionary War; Australia was principally a penal colony from its colonization until the mid-19th century. FRENCH GUIANA, site of a French penal colony, was infamous for its inhumanity; DEVIL'S ISLAND was still operating during World War II. Russian penal colonies were established in Siberia under the czars but were most widely used during the Stalin era. Notorious for their harsh punishments and underfeeding, most penal colonies have now been abolished.

Penang \pə-ˈnaŋ\ Island (pop., 1991: 1,100,000), Malaysia, off the northwestern coast of the MALAY PENINSULA, part of the state of Penang. The capital and chief port is George Town (pop., 1991: 220,000), in the northeast. British colonization began in 1786. In 1826 Penang (known until 1867 as Prince of Wales Island) combined with MALACCA and SINGAPORE to form the STRAITS SETTLEMENTS. From the mid-19th century it was a market for tin and rubber. In 1948 it became part of the Federation of Malaya, later Malaysia. In the late 20th century it became Malaysia's prime tourist center, with resort hotels mainly on the northern coast at Batu Feringgi.

Penates \pə-ˈnā-tēz, pə-ˈnä-tēz\ Roman household gods. They were worshiped privately as protectors of the household and also publicly as protectors of the Roman state. They were sometimes associated with other deities of the house, such as VESTA, and their name was often used interchangeably with that of the LARES. Each house had a shrine with their images, which were worshiped at the family meal and on special occasions. Offerings were portions of the regular meal or of special cakes, wine, honey, and incense. The number and precise identities of the Penates were a puzzle even to the ancients.

pencil drawing Drawing executed with a pencil, an instrument made of GRAPHITE enclosed in a wood casing. Though graphite was mined in the 16th century, its use by artists is not known before the 17th century. In the 17th–18th century, graphite was used primarily to make preliminary sketches for more elaborate work in another medium, seldom for finished works. By the late 18th century, an ancestor of the modern pencil was constructed by inserting a rod of natural graphite into a hollow cylinder of wood. Pencil rods produced from mixtures of graphite and clays, true prototypes of the modern graphite pencil, were introduced in 1795. This improvement allowed for better control and encouraged wider use. The great masters of pencil drawing kept the elements of a simple linearism with limited shading, but many artists in the 18th–19th century created elaborate effects of light and shade by rubbing the soft graphite particles with a tightly rolled paper or chamois.

pendant *or* **pendent** In architecture, a sculpted ornament suspended from a VAULT or ceiling, especially an elongated boss (carved keystone) at the junction of the intersecting ribs of the fan vaulting associated with the English PERPENDICULAR STYLE. In stone ceilings, the use of pendant vaulting was a solution to the difficulty of adapting fan vaulting to very wide church NAVES. Strong transverse arches were made to span the area, and these in turn supported the elongated keystones. Intermediate rib and panel vaults sprang from these pendants.

pendant Ornament suspended from a bracelet, earring, or necklace, and derived from the primitive practice of wearing amulets or talismans around the neck. The practice dates from the Stone Age, when pendants consisted of objects such as teeth, stones, and shells. Commemorative and decorative pendants were common in ancient Egypt, Greece, and Rome. In the Middle Ages, reliquaries, or devotional pendants, and crosses were created with jewels. By the beginning of the 16th century, Renaissance artists were creating pendants for decorative rather than religious use. The late-19th-century Art Nouveau movement often featured women's figures, butterflies, or flowers on pendants.

Art Nouveau pendant by L. Gautrait, c. 1900; in the Schmuckmuseum, Pforzheim, Ger.

BY COURTESY OF THE SCHMUCKMUSEUM, PFORZHEIM, GER

pendentive In architecture, a triangular segment of a spherical surface forming the transition between the circular plan of a DOME and the polygonal plan of its supporting structure. The problem of placing a round dome on a square base assumed growing importance to Roman builders, but it remained for Byzantine architects to recognize the possibilities of the pendentive and fully develop it (see HAGIA SOPHIA). One of the great architectural inventions of all time, the pendentive became very important in the Renaissance and baroque periods. As a result of Byzantine influence, pendentives are also frequent in ISLAMIC ARCHITECTURE. A vaulting form in which the curve of the pendentive and dome is continuous is known as a pendentive dome.

Penderecki \ˌpen-də-ˈret-skē\, **Krzysztof** (born 1933) Polish composer and conductor. He studied composition at the Kraków Conservatory, and would later served as its director (1972–87). His early music (1960–74) involved blocks of sound and ritual, and he developed graphic notation to convey the desired effects, resulting in vivid works that attracted international attention, including *Threnody for the Victims of Hiroshima* (1960), *Stabat mater* (1962), the *St. Luke Passion* (1965), and the opera *The Devils of Loudun* (1969). After 1975 his music became more traditional, in such works as the opera *Paradise Lost* (1978), concertos for violin (1977), cello (1982), and viola (1983), and *Lux aeterna* (1983).

Pendergast, Thomas J(oseph) (1872–1945) U.S. politician. Born in St. Joseph, Mo., he was active in municipal politics in Kansas City, Mo., and became the political boss of the city's Democrats by 1916. His political machine dominated city and state politics for almost 25 years and influenced national Democratic conventions. He helped HARRY TRUMAN in his early political career. Attacked by opponents for allowing corrupt practices in Kansas City, Pendergast was convicted of income-tax evasion in 1939 and served one year in prison.

Pendleton, George (Hunt) (1825–1889) U.S. politician. Born in Cincinnati, he served in the U.S. House of Representatives 1857–65, and was the Democratic candidate for vice president (with GEORGE B. MCCLELLAN) in 1864. A member of the GREENBACK MOVEMENT, he advocated the OHIO IDEA for redeeming Civil War bonds. He served in the U.S. Senate 1879–85, where he sponsored the PENDLETON CIVIL SERVICE ACT. He served as minister to Germany 1885–89.

Pendleton Civil Service Act (1883) U.S. legislation establishing the modern civil-service system of permanent federal employment based on merit. Public demand for civil-service reform to replace the system based on political party affiliation (the SPOILS system) resulted in the bill sponsored by Sen. GEORGE PENDLETON, which provided for selection of government employees by competitive examination administered by a civil-service commission. Only 10% of government jobs were initially covered by the law, but successive Congresses expanded its scope to include over 90% of federal employees.

pendulum Body suspended from a fixed point so that it can swing back and forth under the influence of gravity. A simple pendulum consists of a bob (weight) suspended at the end of a string. The PERIODIC MOTION of a pendulum is constant, but can be made longer or shorter by increasing or decreasing the length of the string. A change in the mass of the bob alone does not affect the period. Because of their constancy, pendulums were long used to regulate the movement of clocks. Other, special kinds of pendulums are used to measure the value of g, the acceleration due to gravity, and to show that the earth rotates on its axis (see FOUCAULT PENDULUM).

peneplain \'pē-nə-ˌplān\ Gently undulating, almost featureless plain near sea level. This would form, theoretically, by various erosional processes that reduce areas of initially high relief produced by active uplift to areas of virtually no relief. The lack of present-day peneplains tends to discredit the theory, but some geomorphologists propose that large areas of low relief at high altitude in some mountains are evidence of uplifted peneplains. Others question whether the dynamic relationship between erosion and rock type would ever allow the development of a peneplain, even over very long timespans.

Peneus River See PINIÓS RIVER

penguin Any of 18 species (order Sphenisciformes) of flightless seabirds that breed mainly on islands in subantarctic waters and on cool coasts of Africa, Australia, New Zealand, and South America. A few species inhabit temperate regions, and the Galápagos penguin *(Spheniscus mendiculus)* lives in the equatorial tropics off South America. Species differ mainly in size and head pattern; all have a dark back and a white belly. The smallest species, the little blue penguin *(Eudyptula minor),* is about 16 in. (40 cm) tall; the largest, the emperor penguin *(Aptenodytes forsteri),* is almost 4 ft (120 cm) tall. At sea for weeks at a time, flocks feed on fish, squid, and crustaceans.

penicillin ANTIBIOTIC derived from the PENICILLIUM mold. It was discovered in 1928 by ALEXANDER FLEMING; by 1940, HOWARD WALTER FLOREY, ERNST BORIS CHAIN, and others had produced commercial quantities that proved vital to the treatment of war casualties, making penicillin the first successful antibiotic for human bacterial infections. Many natural and semisynthetic (ampicillin, amoxicillin) variants have since been produced. All work by inhibiting the enzymes responsible for bacterial cell wall synthesis (and therefore do not work against microorganisms without cell walls or with certain variant cell walls; e.g., the tuberculosis bacillus). Among the bacteria susceptible to penicillin are those causing strep throat, spinal MENINGITIS, gas GANGRENE, SYPHILIS, and GONORRHEA. Overuse has led to DRUG RESISTANCE in some strains. Penicillin's chief side effect is ALLERGY, which can be life-threatening.

penicillium \ˌpe-nə-'si-lē-əm\ Any blue or green MOLD in the genus *Penicillium* (division Mycota; see FUNGUS). Common on foodstuffs, leather, and fabrics, they are economically important in producing ANTIBIOTICS (see PENICILLIN), organic acids, and cheeses such as English Stilton, Italian Gorgonzola, and French Roquefort.

Peninsular War (1808–14) Part of the NAPOLEONIC WARS, fought on the Iberian Peninsula. After French forces occupied Portugal (1807) and NAPOLEON installed his brother JOSEPH BONAPARTE as king of Spain (1808), a rebellion in Madrid began what was called in Spain "the War of Independence," and insurrections soon erupted in other cities. By 1810 the French overcame the Spanish rebels in Madrid and elsewhere in Spain. Meanwhile, the British under the future duke of WELLINGTON landed in Portugal (1808), where they fought the French in inconclusive campaigns until 1812. After Napoleon withdrew French forces to bolster his invasion of Russia, Wellington began his gradual advance into Spain. The British victory at the Battle of Vitoria (1813) and their march into southwestern France forced the French to withdraw from Spain and to reinstall FERDINAND VII as king (1814).

penis Male sex organ, which also provides the channel for urine to leave the body. Three long columns of tissue extend through its length, covered by elastic tissue and a thin layer of skin. One expands at the tip into a mushroom-shaped structure (glans penis) and contains the urethra (see URINARY SYSTEM), which ends in a slitlike opening. In sexual arousal, blood fills spaces in the tissue, and blood vessels constrict to hold it there, enlarging and hardening the penis in an erection. The foreskin, a circular fold of skin covering the glans, is often removed (see CIRCUMCISION). See also REPRODUCTIVE SYSTEM.

Penn, Irving (born 1917) U.S. photographer. Born in Plainfield, N.J., he aspired to be a painter but at 26 took a job designing photographic covers for *Vogue* and soon was established as a fashion photographer. He branched out into portraiture after World War II and became much admired as a portraitist of celebrities. His austere images conveyed elegance and sophistication through clarity of line and composition rather than from props or backdrops.

Penn, William (1644–1718) English Quaker leader and founder of Pennsylvania. Expelled from Oxford for his Puritan beliefs, he was sent to manage the family estates in Ireland, where he joined the Society of FRIENDS in 1667. He was imprisoned four times for publishing books and pamphlets and speaking in support of Quaker doctrines; one of his trials resulted in the precedent-setting Bushell's Case, which established the independence of juries. In *The Great Case of Liberty of Conscience* (1670) Penn advocated religious toleration and envisioned a colony based on religious and political freedom. On his father's death, he inherited his estates and influence with CHARLES II, who granted him a vast province on the Delaware River in payment for debts owed his father. He arrived in Pennsylvania in 1682. He drafted a Frame of Government that established freedom of worship, laid out the city of Philadelphia, and established peaceful relations with the Indians. In 1684 he returned to England to defend his interests against claims by neighboring Maryland. With the accession of his friend the duke of York as JAMES II, he effected the release of imprisoned Quakers and the Declaration of Indulgence (1687), which permitted religious toleration. He returned to Pennsylvania (1699–1701) and wrote the Charter of Privileges, which allowed the assembly greater autonomy. He returned to England, where he later faced financial problems.

Penney, J(ames) C(ash) (1875–1971) U.S. merchant. Born in Hamilton, Mo., he became a partner in a dry-goods store in Wyoming in 1902 and five years later bought out his partners' shares to launch what became the J. C. Penney Co. His stores offered a wide variety of inexpensive merchandise, and he offered profit-sharing plans, first to managers and later to all employees. By 1929 the company had 1,392 stores across the U.S., and at the time of Penney's death it was the second-largest merchandiser in the country, behind SEARS, ROEBUCK AND CO.

Pennines \'pe-ˌnīnz\ *or* **Pennine Chain** Mountain range, northern England, extending south from the Scottish border to DERBYSHIRE. The highest peak is Cross Fell, at 2,930 ft (893 m) high. Water action has developed underground caverns in the range's limestone, which is extensively quarried. Sheep farming is also important. Archaeological remains in the area include the ancient Roman HADRIAN'S WALL.

Pennsylvania State (pop., 1997 est.: 12,020,000), U.S., middle Atlantic region. It covers 45,333 sq mi (117,412 sq km); its capital is HARRISBURG. The DELAWARE RIVER forms part of its eastern boundary. The MONONGAHELA RIVER unites with the ALLEGHENY RIVER at PITTSBURGH to form the OHIO RIVER. The area was inhabited by Indian peoples, including the SHAWNEE and DELAWARE, when Europeans arrived in the 17th century. In 1664 the English seized control of the region, and in 1681 the English king granted a charter to WILLIAM PENN, who established a Quaker colony based on religious tolerance in 1682. Much of the fighting of the FRENCH AND INDIAN WAR took place there. The first and second CONTINENTAL CONGRESSES met in PHILADELPHIA, and the DECLARATION OF INDEPENDENCE was signed there in 1776. One of the original states of the Union, it was the second state to ratify the U.S. Constitution in 1787. During the AMERICAN CIVIL WAR it was a center of military activity (see Battle of GETTYSBURG). The postwar period brought great economic, industrial, and population growth, consolidating the state's position as a major commercial power. It is one of the most prosperous states, with an economy based on farming, mining, manufacturing, and high technology. The state continues to produce much of the nation's specialty steel and an abundance of coal. Philadelphia and Pittsburgh are major ports with fine educational, cultural, and musical institutions.

Pennsylvania, University of Private university in Philadelphia, a traditional member of the IVY LEAGUE. Founded in 1740 as a charity school, it became an academy in 1753, with BENJAMIN FRANKLIN as president of the first board of trustees. With the founding of the first medical school in North America (1765), it became a university. Today, in addition to its college of arts and sciences and its medical school, it includes a college of general studies and schools of business (the Wharton School), communication (the Annenberg School), education, engineering, fine arts, law, nursing, dentistry, veterinary medicine, and social work. Its institutes include the Wistar Institute of Anatomy and Biology and the Phipps Institute of Genetics and Community Diseases. The University Museum (of archaeology and ethnology) is a teaching and research organization. Total enrollment is about 21,000.

Pennsylvania Railroad Co. Major U.S. railroad. It was chartered in 1846 by the Pennsylvania legislature to build a line between Harrisburg and Pittsburgh, and its passenger service began two years later. By purchasing the Pittsburgh, Fort Wayne and Chicago Railway in 1856, the company extended its service to Chicago. After the Civil War it expanded to St. Louis and Cincinnati in the west and Norfolk, Va., in the south, with 10,000 mi (16,000 km) of track at its greatest extent. It began to lose money in the mid-20th century, and in 1968 it merged with its competitor, the NEW YORK CENTRAL, to form the Penn Central Transportation Co. Penn Central declared bankruptcy in 1970; its passenger service was taken over by AMTRAK in 1971 and its assets by CONRAIL in 1976. See also J. EDGAR THOMSON.

Pennsylvania State University Public state system of higher education with a main campus in University Park and numerous other campuses and locations, including the Milton S. Hershey Medical Center in Hershey and the Dickinson School of Law in Carlisle. The university originated with the charter of the Farmers' High School in 1855 and was designated the commonwealth's land-grant college in 1862. It took its current name only in 1953. Research facilities include the Biotechnology Institute, the Center for Applied Behavioral Science, and the Center for Particle Science and Engineering. Total enrollment for the system is almost 80,000.

Pennsylvanian period In North America, the interval of geologic time roughly equivalent to what is internationally designated the Late CARBONIFEROUS epoch (323–290 million years ago). Because the rocks that originated during this span of time are widespread in the state of Pennsylvania, some U.S. geologists favor the term over Late Carboniferous period, which was first adopted in Europe.

Penobscot River \pə-'näb-skət\ River, central Maine, flowing south into Penobscot Bay. The state's longest river, about 350 mi (560 km) long, it is navigable for 60 mi (97 km) to Bangor. Once an important source of salmon, it has become economically important to the lumber, pulp, and paper industries because of its hydropower facilities. Navigated by French and English voyagers in the early 17th century, it was named for the Penobscot Indians.

penology \pē-'nä-lə-jē\ Branch of CRIMINOLOGY dealing with prison management and the treatment of offenders. Penological studies have sought to clarify the ethical bases of punishment, along with the motives and purposes of society in inflicting it; differences throughout history and between nations in penal laws and procedures; and the social consequences of the policies in force at a given time. Influential historical works have included Cesare Beccaria's *On Crimes and Punishments* (1764), JEREMY BENTHAM's "Panopticon" scheme (c. 1800), Cesare Lombroso's *Crime* (1876), and MICHEL FOUCAULT's *Discipline and Punish* (1975).

pension Series of periodic money payments made to a person who retires from employment because of age, disability, or the completion of an agreed span of service. The payments generally continue for the rest of the recipient's natural life, and they are sometimes extended to a widow or other survivor. Military pensions have existed for many centuries; private pension plans originated in Europe in the 19th century. There are two basic types of pension plans: defined contribution and defined benefit. A defined contribution plan invests a defined amount each pay period. The individual may have some discretion as to how the money is invested. The benefit, the amount of the pension, depends on the success of those investments. A defined benefit plan pays a known amount according to some formula, but the amount invested in the fund may vary. Pensions may be funded by making payments into a pension TRUST FUND or by the purchase of ANNUITIES from insurance companies. In plans known as multiemployer plans, various employers contribute to one central trust fund administered by a joint board of trustees.

Pentagon Huge five-sided building (1941–43) in Arlington, Va., that is the headquarters of the U.S. Department of Defense. Designed by George Edwin Bergstrom, it was, on its completion, the world's largest office building, covering 34 acres (14 hectares) and offering 3.7 million sq ft (about 344,000 sq m) of usable floor space for as many as 25,000 workers. Built of structural steel and reinforced concrete with some limestone facing at a cost of $83 million, the five-story structure actually consists of five concentric pentagons, with 10 spokelike corridors connecting the whole. In 2001 more than 180 people were killed and many more were injured when part of the Pentagon's southwest side was destroyed in the SEPTEMBER 11 ATTACKS.

Pentagon Papers Secret documents detailing the U.S. role in Indochina from World War II to 1968. The U.S. Defense Department commissioned the study; a project associate, Daniel Ellsberg (born 1931), opposed to U.S. participation in the VIETNAM WAR, leaked details of the documents to the press. In June 1971 the *New York Times* began publishing articles based on the study. The U.S. Justice Department, citing national security, obtained a temporary court order halting publication. The U.S. Supreme Court ruled that the government had failed to justify restraint of publication, and the documents were published widely, fueling dissent over the U.S.'s Vietnam policy.

Pentateuch See TORAH

pentathlon Athletic contest entailing five distinct types of competition. In the ancient Olympic Games, the pentathlon included a sprint, or short-distance footrace, and the LONG JUMP, DISCUS THROW, JAVELIN THROW, and a WRESTLING match. A modified version (with a medium-distance race substituted for the wrestling match) was included in the revived Olympic Games 1912–24. The modern, or military, pentathlon, included in the Olympics from 1912 and made a team event in 1952, includes an equestrian STEEPLECHASE, FENCING, pistol SHOOTING, a freestyle swim, and a CROSS-COUNTRY RUN. Women's pentathlon competition (SHOT PUT, HIGH JUMP, HURDLING race, sprint, and long jump) was replaced in 1981 by the HEPTATHLON.

Pentecost (Greek, *pentecoste:* "fiftieth day") Christian festival commemorating the descent of the HOLY SPIRIT on the disciples of Jesus, occurring on the Jewish Pentecost, after Jesus' death, resurrection, and ascension. The disciples began to speak in the many languages of the people assembled there, a sign that the disciples should spread the Christian message throughout the world. Jewish Pentecost was a thanksgiving feast for the first fruits of the wheat harvest and was associated with remembrance of God's gift of the Law to Moses on Mount Sinai. Christian Pentecost is celebrated on the Sunday concluding the 50-day period following Easter.

Pentecostalism Protestant religious movement that originated in the U.S. in the 19th–20th century. It is characterized by a belief that all Christians should seek a postconversion religious experience called BAPTISM with the HOLY SPIRIT. The experience corresponds to the descent of the Holy Spirit on the twelve APOSTLES (PENTECOST) and is evidenced by speaking in tongues, prophesying, and healing. Pentecostalism grew out of the 19th-century HOLINESS MOVEMENT and shares its emphasis on biblical literalism, conversion, and moral rigor. The charismatic movement in Roman Catholic and mainstream Protestant denominations represents the same spirit. Today there are many Pentecostalist denominations in the U.S. and around the world, including the ASSEMBLIES OF GOD. Penetcostalism has been especially successful in the Caribbean, Latin America, and Africa.

penthouse Enclosed area on top of a building. A penthouse can be an apartment on the roof or top floor of a building or a structure on the roof housing the top of an elevator shaft, air-conditioning equipment, or stairs leading to the roof. A penthouse is usually set back from the vertical face of a building, but as a real-estate term, penthouse may refer to any top floor, regardless of setbacks. Though the word now often suggests a luxurious apartment with a panoramic view, historically a penthouse was a lean-to, shed, or other small structure attached to a comparatively large building.

Pentium Family of MICROPROCESSORS developed by INTEL CORP. Introduced in 1993 as the successor to Intel's 80486 microprocessor, the Pentium contained two processors on a single chip and about 3.3 million TRANSISTORS. Using a CISC (complex instruction set computer) architecture, its main features were a 32-BIT address BUS, a 64-bit data bus, built-in floating-point and memory-management units, and two 8KB caches. It was available with processor speeds ranging from 60 megahertz (MHz) to 200 MHz. The Pentium quickly became the processor of choice for personal computers. It was superseded by ever faster and more powerful processors, the Pentium Pro (1995), the Pentium II (1997), the Pentium III (1999), and the Pentium 4 (2000).

Penutian languages \pə-'nü-tē-ən\ Hypothetical superfamily of North American Indian languages that unites a number of languages and language families mainly of the far western U.S. and Canada. The Penutian hypothesis was proposed by Roland B. Dixon and ALFRED L. KROEBER in 1913 and refined by EDWARD SAPIR in 1921. Like the Hokan hypothesis (see HOKAN LANGUAGES), it attempted to reduce the number of unrelated language families in one of the world's most linguistically diverse areas.

At its core was a group of languages spoken along California's central coast and in the CENTRAL VALLEY, including Ohlone (Costanoan), Miwok, Wintuan, Maidu, and Yokuts. Sapir added Oregon Penutian (languages once spoken in eastern Oregon), Chinookan (spoken along the lower Columbia River), Plateau Penutian (languages of PLATEAU INDIAN peoples), Tsimshian (spoken in western British Columbia), and Mexican Penutian (spoken in southern Mexico). Aside from the Mexican group, all the languages are today either extinct or spoken almost exclusively by older adults. Though the hypothesis remains unproven, at least some languages of the group are probably related to each other.

Penzias \'pent-sē-əs\, **Arno (Allan)** (born 1933) U.S. (German-born) astrophysicist. His family fled Nazi Germany, and he received his PhD from Columbia Univ., after which he joined Bell Telephone Laboratories, where he worked with ROBERT W. WILSON monitoring radio emissions from a ring of gas around the Milky Way galaxy. The two detected an unexpected uniform background static that suggested a thermal energy throughout the universe at a temperature of about −454°F (−269°C), which most scientists now agree is residual COSMIC BACKGROUND RADIATION stemming from the explosion billions of years ago from which the universe was created. They shared a 1978 Nobel Prize with Pyotr Kapitsa (1894–1984) for their work. In 1981 Penzias became vice president of Bell Laboratories.

peonage \'pē-ə-nij\ Form of involuntary servitude, the origins of which date back to the Spanish conquest of Mexico, when the conquerors forced the poor, especially Indians, to work for Spanish planters and mine operators. In the U.S., the word peon referred to workers compelled by contract to pay their creditors in labor. Though prohibited under U.S. federal law, peonage persisted in some southern states through state laws that made labor compulsory. Another form of peonage exists when prisoners sentenced to hard labor are farmed out to labor camps.

peony \'pē-ə-nē\ Any of about 33 species of flowering plants in the genus *Paeonia,* sole genus of the family Paenoiaceae, found in Europe, Asia, and western North America and known for their large, showy blossoms. Herbaceous peonies are perennials that grow to about 3 ft (1 m). Their annual stems bear large, glossy, much-divided leaves and produce large single and double flowers of white, pink, rose, and deep crimson. Tree peonies are shrubs about 4–6 ft (1.2–1.8 m) high with permanent rootstocks and woody stems that bear flowers varying in color from white to lilac, violet, and red.

People's Liberation Army Unified organization of China's land, sea, and air forces. Its 3 million troops make it one of the largest forces in the world. The PLA traces its roots to the 1927 Nanchang Uprising of the Communists against the Nationalists. Initially called the Red Army, it grew under ZHU DE from 5,000 troops in 1929 to 200,000 in 1933. This force survived the LONG MARCH in retreat from the Nationalists. A large portion of it, the Eighth Route Army, fought with the Nationalists against the Japanese in northern China. After World War II, the Communist forces, renamed the People's Liberation Army, defeated the Nationalists, making possible the formation of the People's Republic of China in 1949. See also LIN BIAO, MAO ZEDONG.

Peoria City (pop, 1996 est.: 112,000), central Illinois, on the Illinois River where it widens to form Peoria Lake. The first settlement on the site was a French fort established in 1680 by R.-R. LA SALLE. Later settlements were by the French, Indians, and other colonists. It was incorporated as a city in 1845. It is a major port, trade, and shipping center for a large agricultural area. It is highly industrialized, and its products include earth-moving equipment and chemicals.

Pepin, Donation of See DONATION OF PEPIN

Pepin III \'pe-pən\ *known as* **Pepin the Short** (714?–768) King of the Franks (751–68), the first king of the CAROLINGIAN DYNASTY and the father of CHARLEMAGNE. A son of CHARLES MARTEL, he became mayor of Neustria, Burgundy, and Provence in 741 and de facto ruler of the Franks when his brother entered a monastery in 747. With the backing of the pope, he deposed the last MEROVINGIAN ruler, Childeric III, in 751 and was crowned king. Pepin helped STEPHEN II combat the Lombards (754, 756) in Italy. He also put down revolts in Saxony and Bavaria and struggled to subdue rebellious Aquitaine.

pepper *or* **garden pepper** Any of many plants in the genus *Capsicum* of the NIGHTSHADE FAMILY, notably *C. annuum, C. frutescens,* and *C. boccatum,* native to Central and South America and cultivated extensively throughout tropical Asia and the equatorial New World for their edible, pungent fruits. Red, green, and yellow mild bell or sweet peppers, rich in vitamins A and C, are used in seasoning and as a vegetable food. The pungency of hot peppers, including tabasco, chili, and cayenne peppers, comes from the compound capsaicin in the internal partitions of the fruit. The spice BLACK PEPPER comes from an unrelated plant.

Red peppers (*Capsicum annuum*) from which paprika is made.

G.R. ROBERTS

pepper, black See BLACK PEPPER

Pepper, Claude (Denson) (1900–1989) U.S. politician. Born in Dudleyville, Ala., he practiced law in Florida before being elected to the U.S. Senate (1936–50), where he supported legislation that created Social Security, minimum wages, and medical assistance for the elderly. He returned to his law practice 1950–62. In the U.S. House of Representatives (1962–89), he chaired the committee on aging and sponsored legislation that abolished mandatory retirement in federal agencies and raised the retirement age to 70 in the private sector (1968). In 1989 he was awarded the Medal of Freedom.

peppermint Strongly aromatic perennial herb (*Mentha piperita,* MINT family), source of a widely used flavoring. Native to Europe and Asia, it has been naturalized in North America. The stalked, smooth, dark-green leaves and blunt, oblong clusters of pinkish-lavender flowers are dried for use as a flavoring agent. Oil of peppermint is widely used to flavor confectionery, chewing gum, toothpastes, and medicines. The oil also contains MENTHOL, long used medicinally as a soothing balm.

PepsiCo, Inc. U.S. conglomerate. The SOFT DRINK Pepsi-Cola was created by a pharmacist, Caleb D. Bradham, who gave his tonic its name (from Greek *pepsis,* "digestion") in 1898 and incorporated the Pepsi-Cola Co. in 1902. After two bankruptcies and several reincorporations, the Pepsi-Cola trademark and assets were bought in 1931 by Charles G. Guth, who improved the formula and marketed a 12-ounce bottle for five cents with huge success. Pepsi-Cola merged with the soda-fountain chain Loft, Inc., in 1941, and in 1965 it merged with Frito-Lay, Inc., adopting its current name, PepsiCo, Inc. In the 1970s and '80s PepsiCo bought restaurant chains such as Pizza Hut, Taco Bell, and Kentucky Fried Chicken, but in 1997 it spun off its restaurant business into a separate company, Tricon Global Restaurants. PepsiCo's headquarters are in Purchase, N.Y.

pepsin Powerful ENZYME in gastric juice (see STOMACH) that partially digests PROTEINS in food. Glands in the stomach lining make pepsinogen, a ZYMOGEN converted to pepsin by the HYDROCHLORIC ACID in gastric juice. Pepsin is active only in the acid environment of the stomach (PH 1.5–2.5 or less); it is ineffective in the intestine (pH 7). It is used commercially in some cheesemaking, in the leather industry to remove hair and residual tissue from hides, and in the recovery of silver from discarded photographic films by digesting the gelatin layer that holds the silver.

peptic ulcer Sore that develops in the mucous membrane of the STOMACH (more frequent in women) or DUODENUM (accounting for 80% of ulcers, and more frequent in men) when its ability to resist acid in gastric juice is reduced. It causes burning ache and hungerlike pain. Ulcers can bleed, perforate the abdominal wall, or block the gastrointestinal tract. Stress and diet were blamed until *Helicobacter pylori* bacteria and long-term use of ASPIRIN and similar drugs were shown to be the two major causes. The former is treated with combination drug therapy, the latter by stopping the causative drugs if possible or with drugs that reduce acid production. A rare cause is Zollinger-Ellison syndrome, in which a tumor causes increased acid secretion. Cigarette smoking slows healing and promotes recurrence.

peptide Organic compound composed of a series of AMINO ACIDS linked by peptide bonds (see COVALENT BOND) between the carbon of one and the nitrogen of the next. Peptide chains longer than a few dozen amino acids are PROTEINS. Biosynthesis of peptides from a succession of amino acids carried by transfer RNA molecules takes place on RIBOSOMES and is catalyzed and controlled by ENZYMES. Many HORMONES, ANTIBIOTICS, and other compounds that participate in life processes are peptides.

Pepys \'pēps\, **Samuel** (1633–1703) English diarist and public official. Born into a humble family, Pepys was appointed about 1659 as a clerk in the office of the Exchequer, where on January 1, 1660, he began the diary for which he is chiefly known. He steadily improved his position, in time becoming secretary of the Admiralty, a member of Parliament, president of the Royal Society, trusted confidant of CHARLES II and JAMES II, and friend of the great scholars of his age. His diary (published 1825), which he kept through 1669, presents a fascinating picture of the official and upper-class life in Restoration London, with vivid, honest accounts of ordinary as well as great events, including the Plague and the GREAT FIRE OF LONDON.

Pepys, oil painting by John Hayls, 1666; in the National Portrait Gallery, London.

BY COURTESY OF THE NATIONAL PORTRAIT GALLERY, LONDON

Pequot \'pē-ˌkwät\ Any of a group of ALGONQUIAN-speaking Indian peoples who lived in the Thames valley in what is now eastern Connecticut. Their subsistence was based on corn cultivation, hunting, and fishing. For a brief period they lived amicably with the American colonists, but relations became strained as land pressures grew. Puritan clergymen encouraged violence against the Pequot as infidels, and in 1636 war broke out, resulting in large losses. Further destruction was caused by a revolt of the MOHEGAN, who had earlier been ruled by a Pequot chief. In 1655 the few remaining Pequot were resettled on the Mystic River. Today they number about 500.

Perahia \pə-'rī-ə\, **Murray** (born 1947) U.S.-British pianist. Born in New York City, he was trained at the Mannes College of Music. He won the Leeds International Piano Competition by unanimous vote in 1972, and in 1975 shared the first Avery Fisher Prize. From 1982 he was music director of the Aldeburgh Festival and made his home in England. He has recorded music from G.F. HANDEL to BELA BARTOK, and is best known for his sensitive recordings of W.A. MOZART's concertos, conducted from the keyboard.

Peranakans \ˌper-ə-'nä-kənz\ In Indonesia, native-born people of mixed Indonesian and foreign ancestry. The term often refers to the Peranakan Chinese, the largest and most important Peranakan group, who formed a stable community by the mid-19th century, partly adopting the indigenous way of life and generally speaking the native tongue. By contrast, in the early 20th century a large wave of Chinese immigration created a Totok (foreign-born) Chinese community. Unlike the Peranakans, the Totoks retained their own Chinese dialects and remained China-oriented.

perception Process of registering sensory stimuli as meaningful experience. The dividing line between SENSATION and perception has varied according to how the terms are defined. A common distinction is that sensations are simple sensory experiences, while percepts are complex constructions of simple elements joined through association. Another is that perception is more subject to the influence of learning. Though hearing, smell, touch, and taste perceptions have all been explored, vision has received the most attention. Structuralist researchers such as EDWARD BRADFORD TITCHENER focused on the constituent elements of visual perceptions, whereas GESTALT PSYCHOLOGY has stressed the need to examine organized wholes, believing humans are disposed to identifying patterns. Visual objects tend to appear stable despite continually changing stimulus features (such as ambient light, perspective, ground vs. figure arrangement), which enables an observer to match a perceived object with the object as it is understood to exist. Perceptions may be influenced by expectancies, needs, unconscious ideas, values, and conflicts.

Perceval Hero of ARTHURIAN LEGEND. His childlike innocence protected him from worldly temptation. In CHRÉTIEN DE TROYES's *Le conte du graal,* Perceval visits the castle of the wounded Fisher King and sees the GRAIL, but fails to ask about it and therefore fails to heal the Fisher King. He later sets out in search of the grail and grows spiritually. He was displaced by GALAHAD as the hero of the grail quest but continued to play an important role. His story was told in WOLFRAM VON ESCHENBACH's *Parzifal*, which provided the basis for RICHARD WAGNER's opera *Parsifal* (1882).

Perceval \'pər-sə-vəl\, **Spencer** (1762–1812) British prime minister (1809–12). He entered Parliament in 1796 and supported WILLIAM PITT's policy of war with France. He served as attorney general 1802–6, and as chancellor of the exchequer 1807–9. As premier from 1809, he was noted as an efficient administrator but also for his opposition to religious tolerance. He was assassinated by a deranged man who had applied to him for redress of a complaint against the government.

perch Either of two species (family Percidae, order Perciformes) of popular food and sport fishes: the Eurasian common perch *(Perca fluviatilis)* or the North American yellow perch *(P. flavescens)*. Some consider the two a single species. Both have one spiny and one soft-rayed dorsal fin. Perches are carnivores of quiet ponds, lakes, streams, and rivers. The common perch is greenish, with dark vertical bars on the sides and reddish in the lower fins. It grows to 6 lbs (3 kg), rarely more. The yellow perch, similar but yellower, grows to about 15 in. (40 cm) and weighs up to 2 lbs (1 kg); it is a popular game fish. See also SAUGER, SEA BASS, WALLEYE.

Percheron \'pər-chə-ˌrän\ Heavy breed of draft HORSE that originated in France's Perche region. The breed probably stems from the medieval Flemish "great horse," modified by Oriental and draft-type blood to produce animals for heavy farm work. Percherons became popular in the U.S. in the 1850s and influenced U.S. agriculture more than any other draft breed. They average 16–17 hands (64–68 in., 163–173 cm) high and weigh 1,900–2,100 lbs (860–950 kg). Common colors are black and gray. Agile and energetic for their size, they have a mild disposition.

percussion instruments Musical instruments that are struck (or sometimes shaken or scraped) to produce sound. They include instruments whose own hard substance is made to vibrate (idiophones) and instruments that include a tight membrane that vibrates (membranophones). They may produce tones of definite or indefinite pitch. Their primary function is often rhythmic, but many are used as melody instruments. They include the BELL, CARILLON, CYMBAL, DRUM, DULCIMER, GAMELAN, GLOCKENSPIEL, MARIMBA, PIANO, STEEL DRUM, TABLA, TAMBOURINE, TIMPANI, VIBRAPHONE, and XYLOPHONE.

Percy, John (1817–1889) British metallurgist. He turned to metallurgy after obtaining a medical degree, and in 1848 devised a process for extracting silver from its ores, which soon came into widespread use. He improved the BESSEMER PROCESS for making steel, and he was the first to survey British iron ores. At London's Metropolitan School of Sciences, he trained a generation of metallurgists. His multivolume *Treatise on Metallurgy* (1861–80), though unfinished, quickly attained classic status.

Percy, Walker (1916–1990) U.S. novelist. Born in Birmingham, Ala., he was orphaned in late childhood and was raised by a cousin in Mississippi. While working as a pathologist he contracted tuberculosis; during his recuperation he decided on a writing career and converted to Roman Catholicism. His first and best-known novel, *The Moviegoer* (1961), introduced his concept of malaise, a sense of spiritual emptiness characteristic of the rootless modern world. His other works, often about the search for faith and love in a New South transformed by industry and technology, include *Love in the Ruins* (1971), *The Second Coming* (1980), and *The Thanatos Syndrome* (1987).

peregrine falcon \'per-ə-grən\ *or* **duck hawk** FALCON species *(Falco peregrinus)* found worldwide but rare today because of bioaccumulation of pesticides. Peregrines are 13–19 in. (33–48 cm) long and gray above, with black-barred whitish underparts. They fly high and dive at tremendous speed (up to 175 mph, or 280 kph—the greatest speeds attained by any bird), striking with clenched talons and killing by impact. They usually nest in a scrape on a high cliff ledge near water, where bird prey is plentiful. Breeding programs have reintroduced the species into the wild and introduced it into urban areas, where it finds a clifflike habitat

O P Q R

among skyscrapers and preys chiefly on the rock dove (see PIGEON). Despite the programs' success, the species remains vulnerable.

Peregrine falcon (*Falco peregrinus*).
KENNETH W. FINK—ROOT RESOURCES

Pereira \pə-'rā-rä\ City (pop., 1997 est.: 434,000), western central Colombia. It is in the western foothills of the Cordillera Central above the Cauca River valley. Founded in 1863 on the former site of Cartago, it is a center for coffee and cattle and has some light manufacturing.

Perelman \'per-əl-mən\, **S(idney) J(oseph)** (1904–1979) U.S. humorist. Born in Brooklyn, N.Y., Perelman attended Brown University and soon began writing screenplays for such early Marx Brothers films as *Monkey Business* (1931) and *Horse Feathers* (1932). A master of wordplay, he regularly contributed essays to the *New Yorker*; many were collected in such books as *Westward Ha!* (1948) and *The Road to Miltown* (1957). He collaborated with K. WEILL on the musical *One Touch of Venus* (1943). His later screenplays include *Around the World in 80 Days* (1956, Academy Award).

perennial Any plant that persists for several years, usually with new herbaceous growth from a part that survives from season to season. Trees and shrubs are perennial, as are some herbaceous flowers and vegetative ground covers. Perennials have only a limited flowering period, but with maintenance throughout the growing season, they provide a leafy presence and shape to the garden landscape. Popular flowering perennials include BELLFLOWERS, CHRYSANTHEMUMS, COLUMBINES, LOCKSPURS, HOLLYHOCKS, PHLOX, PINKS, POPPIES, and PRIMROSES. See also ANNUAL, BIENNIAL.

Peres, Shimon \'per-es\ *orig.* **Shimon Perski** (born 1923) Israeli (Polish-born) statesman. He emigrated to Palestine with his family in 1934 and joined the HAGANA in 1947. After Israel achieved independence, he held a number of defense positions (1948–65). In 1967 he helped establish the ISRAEL LABOUR PARTY. The indecisive 1984 election led to a power-sharing arrangement with the Likud candidate, YITZHAK SHAMIR, the two men alternating as prime minister. Peres's tenure (1984–86) saw Israel's withdrawal from Lebanon (see LEBANESE CIVIL WAR). He was foreign minister under YITZHAK RABIN (1992–95), with whom, along with YASIR ARAFAT, he shared the Nobel Peace Prize in 1994. He became prime minister on Rabin's assassination, and was narrowly defeated by Benjamin Netanyahu in 1996.

perestroika \,per-ə-'strói-kə\ (Russian: "restructuring") Program instituted in the Soviet Union by MIKHAIL GORBACHEV in the mid-1980s to restructure Soviet political and economic policy. Gorbachev proposed reducing the direct involvement of the Communist Party leadership in the country's governance and increasing the local governments' authority. Seeking to bring the Soviet Union up to economic par with such capitalist countries as Germany, Japan, and the U.S., he decentralized economic controls and encouraged enterprises to become self-financing. The economic bureaucracy, fearing loss of its power and privileges, obstructed much of his program.

Peretz \'per-ets\, **Isaac Leib** *(or* **Loeb** *or* **Löb)** *or* **Yitskhok Leybush Perets** (1852?–1915) Polish writer. Peretz wrote prolifically, mostly in Yiddish, bringing to it new expressive force and modernizing influences from Western European art and literature. His tales of Hasidic lore (e.g., the *Silent Souls* series) are elegiac meditations on traditional values that draw material from the lives of impoverished Eastern European Jews. Among his works are story collections, including *Folktales* (1908), the drama *The Golden Chain* (1909), and articles on many subjects to encourage Jews toward wider secular knowledge.

Pérez (Rodríguez), Carlos (Andrés) (born 1922) President of Venezuela (1974–79, 1989–93). He began his political career at 18. A founder of Democratic Action (AD), he was elected president in 1973 with the support of the liberal ROMULO BETANCOURT. He nationalized the oil industry while retaining experienced foreign personnel to ensure efficiency, slowed production to conserve resources, stimulated small business and agriculture, and channeled petroleum income into hydroelectric projects, education programs, and steel mills. Reelected in 1989, Pérez promoted free-market economic reforms. After surviving two attempted coups, he was imprisoned in 1993 on charges of embezzlement and misuse of public funds.

Pérez de Cuéllar \'per-es-thā-'kwā-yär\, **Javier** (born 1920) Fifth secretary-general of the UNITED NATIONS (1982–91). Born in Peru, he joined the foreign ministry (1940) and later the foreign service (1944), serving in France, Britain, Bolivia, and Brazil. After serving as ambassador to Switzerland and as Peru's first ambassador to the Soviet Union, he was appointed ambassador to the U.N., a post he held until he was appointed secretary-general. As secretary-general he advocated the use of the UNITED NATIONS SECURITY COUNCIL for keeping the peace and serving as a forum for negotiations. In his second term, he negotiated the cease-fire that ended the IRAN–IRAQ WAR (1988).

Pérez Galdós \'pā-rāth-gäl-'dōs\, **Benito** (1843–1920) Spanish novelist. In the 1870s he began a cycle of 46 short historical novels, *Episodios nacionales* (1873–1912), that earned him comparison with HONORE DE BALZAC and CHARLES DICKENS. Some of his finest works chronicle contemporary Spain, including *The Disinherited Lady* (1881) and his masterpiece, *Fortunata y Jacinta* (1886–87), a study of two unhappily married women. His earlier works show a reforming zeal and anticlericalism, but after the 1880s he displayed greater sympathy for Spain and its idiosyncrasies, as in *Nazarín* (1895), *Compassion* (1897), and a series featuring the character Torquemada. He also wrote plays, some very popular but of less artistic value. He was regarded as Spain's greatest novelist since MIGUEL DE CERVANTES.

Pérez Jiménez \'per-ez-hē-'men-ez\, **Marcos** (1914–2001) Soldier and president of Venezuela (1953–58). He graduated from the Venezuelan Military Academy and in 1945 and 1948 participated in coups d'état. Appointed to the presidency by the military and elected in 1953 by the constituent assembly, which he controlled, he embarked on a program of vast public works. He and his associates received commissions on every project. His regime was marked by extravagance, corruption, police oppression, unemployment, and high inflation. He was forced out of office in 1958 and later jailed for embezzling government funds. His attempts to reenter political life were thwarted repeatedly.

perfect gas *or* **ideal gas** Gas whose physical behavior conforms to the general GAS LAW, which states that for a given quantity of gas, the product of the volume V and pressure P is proportional to the absolute temperature, or $PV = kT$, where k is a constant. A perfect gas is assumed to consist of a large number of MOLECULES in random motion, which obey NEWTON'S LAWS OF MOTION. Their volume is assumed to be negligibly small, and no forces are presumed to act on the molecules except during momentary collisions. Though no gas has these properties, real gases at sufficiently high temperatures and low pressures can be described this way.

performance art Art form that arose in Europe and the U.S. in the 1960s. Early examples, often called "happenings," represented a challenge to orthodox art forms and cultural norms by creating a type of art experience that could not be captured or purchased. Performance art typically employs live performers with props, and may draw on such arts as poetry, music, dance, and painting. It may be staged in unconventional venues such as coffeehouses or bars or on the street. Today many performance artists are principally monologuists. Prominent performance artists have included J. CAGE, Dennis Oppenheim, Yoko Ono, NAM JUNE PAIK, Meredith Monk, and LAURIE ANDERSON.

perfume Fluid preparation used for scenting, composed of natural essences or synthetics and a fixative. Perfumes are concocted by the artful blending of certain fragrant substances in appropriate proportions. The art of perfumery was apparently known to the ancient Chinese, Hindus, Egyptians, Israelites, Carthaginians, Arabs, Greeks, and Romans; references to perfumes are found in the Bible. Raw materials used in perfumery include natural products, of plant or animal origin, and synthetic materials. Fine perfumes may be blends of more than 100 ingredients.

perfume bottle Vessel made to hold scent. The earliest example is Egyptian and dates to c. 1000 BC. The fashion for PERFUME later spread to Greece, where terra-cotta and glass containers were made in a variety of shapes such as animals and human heads. Romans made perfume bottles out of molded and blown glass. The spread of Christianity marked a decline in perfume production, as well as of glassmaking. The revival of perfume making in France in the 12th century and the popularity of VENETIAN GLASS in the 13th century revived the production of perfume bottles.

Pergamum \'pər-gə-məm\ *or* **Pergamus** \'pər-gə-məs\ Ancient Greek city, western ASIA MINOR, near the modern town of Bergama, Turkey. It existed from at least the 5th century BC but became important in the HELLENISTIC period, when it was the residence of the Attalid dynasty and reached its height 263–133 BC. Then it was bequeathed to Rome. After the fall of Rome, it was ruled by the Byzantines until it passed into Ottoman hands in the early 14th century AD. It is one of the most outstanding examples of city planning in antiquity, and its library was excelled only by that in ALEXANDRIA, Egypt. Excavations begun in 1878 by the Berlin Museum unearthed many artistic treasures.

pergola \'pər-gə-lə\ Garden walk or terrace typically formed by two rows of columns or posts roofed with an open framework of beams and cross rafters over which plants are trained. Its purpose is to provide a foundation on which climbing plants can be viewed and to give shade. Known in ancient Egypt, pergolas were a common feature of early Renaissance gardens in Italy and subsequently throughout Europe. They had a marked revival during the ARTS AND CRAFTS MOVEMENT in Britain. See also ARBOR.

Pergolesi \,pər-gə-'lā-zē\, **Giovanni Battista** (1710–1736) Italian composer. His first successes came in 1732 with his appointment as chapel master to a Neapolitan prince. His comic opera *Lo frate 'nnamorato* (1732) was followed in 1733 by an opera seria, which had a comic intermezzo that became his best-known work, *La serva padrona*. His health failing, he moved into a Franciscan monastery (1736), where he wrote his famous *Stabat mater* and *Salve Regina* before dying at 26. Traveling opera troupes took up *La serva padrona*, and in 1752 the success of a Paris production set off the controversy known as the *querelle des bouffons*. Because of his posthumous popularity, many works by others were attributed to him.

Periander, marble bust in the Vatican Museum, Rome.
THE MANSELL COLLECTION

Periander \,per-ē-'an-dər\ (died 588? BC) Second tyrant of CORINTH (628?–588? BC). He was the son of CYPSELUS, founder of the Cypselid dynasty. One of the most violent of the early Greek tyrants, he killed his wife and avenged the death of his son in Corcyra by sending 300 Corcyran boys to be castrated (they managed to escape). He treated the nobility harshly, but built a strong, prosperous Corinthian economy. His extensive building program included construction of the Diolkos, a portage used to transport ships across the Isthmus of Corinth.

Pericles, detail of a marble herm; in the Vatican Museum.
ANDERSON–ALINARI FROM ART RESOURCE/EB INC.

Pericles \'per-ə-,klēz\ (c. 495–429 BC) Athenian general and statesman largely responsible for the full development of Athenian democracy and the Athenian empire. Related to the influential ALCMAEONIDS, he was elected to power sometime after 461, and he quickly helped adopt essential democratic reforms. He asserted Athenian control over the DELIAN LEAGUE and used the league's treasury to rebuild the Acropolis, sacked by the Persians. His influential consort ASPASIA bore him a son, who was legitimated when his legitimate sons died. In 447–446 Athens lost Megara, giving Sparta direct access to Attica. Though Athens and Sparta agreed on a Thirty Years' Peace (446–445), Pericles had the Long Walls from Athens to the port at Piraeus strengthened for protection. When war broke out in 431, he relied on the navy to keep the city supplied. Attica's population was brought inside the Long Walls, leaving the countryside open to Spartan pillaging. When plague broke out, killing one-fourth of the population, he was deposed and fined. Though reelected, he too died of the plague. His great funeral oration (c. 430) remains one of the greatest defenses of democracy, and his era is remembered as the Golden Age of Athens.

peridot \'per-ə-,dät, 'per-ə-,dō\ *or* **precious olivine** \'ä-lə-,vēn\ Gem-quality, transparent green OLIVINE. Very large crystals are found in Myanmar; peridots from the U.S. are seldom larger than two carats. Yellow-green peridot has been called chrysolite (Greek for "golden stone"); this term, used for various unrelated minerals, is now less common for the gemstone.

peridotite \pə-'ri-də-,tīt\ Coarse-grained, heavy, igneous rock that contains at least 10% OLIVINE, other iron- and magnesium-rich minerals (generally PYROXENES), and not more than 10% FELDSPAR. Peridotite is the ultimate source of all CHROMIUM ore and naturally occurring DIAMONDS, and of nearly all chrysotile asbestos. Nearly all peridotite is more or less altered to SERPENTINE; in warm, humid climates peridotite and serpentine have weathered to soils and related deposits that, though now worked on a relatively small scale, are potential sources of iron, nickel, cobalt, and chromium.

Périer \pār-'yā\, **Casimir (-Pierre)** (1777–1832) French statesman. Son of a financier, he cofounded a bank in 1801 and by 1814 was a leading banker in Paris. He was elected to the French Chamber of Deputies (1817), where he opposed CHARLES X. After the JULY REVOLUTION of 1830 made LOUIS-PHILIPPE king, Périer became premier (1831) and quickly restored civic order in France. Active in foreign affairs, he sent an army to defend Belgium against the Dutch (1831) and ordered the occupation of Ancona to check Austrian predominance in the Papal States (1832). His authoritarian approach brought attacks from both left and right and sometimes alienated the king.

Périgord \,pā-rē-'gȯr\ Historic and cultural region, southern France. The counts of Périgord played a part in the troubled affairs of AQUITAINE, and control of Périgord was disputed by the French and the English from 1259. The area was transferred to the house of Albret in 1470. After it was inherited by the crown of NAVARRE, HENRY IV united it with the French crown (1607).

period In geology, the basic unit of the geologic time scale. During these spans of time, specific systems of rocks were formed. Originally, the method for defining the sequence of periods was relative; it was based on STRATIGRAPHY and PALEONTOLOGY. CARBON-14 DATING and similar methods are now used to determine absolute ages for various periods.

periodic motion Motion that is repeated in equal intervals of time. The time of each interval is the period. Examples of periodic motion include a rocking chair, a bouncing ball, a vibrating guitar string, a swinging PENDULUM, and a water wave. See also SIMPLE HARMONIC MOTION.

periodic table Organized array of all the chemical elements in approximately increasing order of their ATOMIC WEIGHT. They show a periodic recurrence of certain properties, first discovered in 1869 by DMITRY I. MENDELEYEV. Those in the same column of the table as usually arranged have similar properties. In the 20th century, when the structure of ATOMS was understood, the table was seen to precisely reflect increasing order of ATOMIC NUMBER. Members of the same group in the table have the same number of ELECTRONS in the outermost shells of their atoms and form bonds of the same type, usually with the same VALENCE; the NOBLE GASES, with full outer shells, generally do not form bonds. The periodic table has thus greatly deepened understanding of BONDING and chemical behavior.

periodical Publication whose issues appear at fixed or regular intervals. Periodicals generally are considered to include NEWSPAPERS, which usually have large, unfastened pages and contents with considerable immediacy; and MAGAZINES, or journals, which have smaller pages, are usually fastened or bound, and often have more specialized, less time-dependent contents.

periodontitis \ˌper-ē-ə-ˌdän-ˈtī-təs\ INFLAMMATION of soft tissues around the teeth (see TOOTH). Poor dental hygiene leads to deposition of bacterial plaque on the teeth below the gum line, irritating and eroding nearby tissues. If it is not treated, the gum margin recedes, exposing the roots of the teeth. The process eventually involves the bone anchoring the teeth, which loosen and may fall out. Removal of all plaque deposits and affected soft tissues can arrest but not reverse bone deterioration.

periosteum \ˌper-ē-ˈäs-tē-əm\ Dense membrane over BONES. The fibrous outer layer contains nerve fibers and many blood vessels, which supply cells in the bone. The bone-producing cells of the inner layer are most prominent in fetal life and early childhood, when bone formation is at its peak. In adulthood they are less active but vital to continuous bone remodeling. When bone is injured, they multiply profusely to produce new bone.

periscope Optical instrument (see OPTICS) used in land and sea warfare, submarine NAVIGATION, and elsewhere to enable an observer to see the surroundings while remaining under cover, behind armor, or submerged. A periscope includes two mirrors or reflecting PRISMS to change the direction of the light coming from the scene observed: the first deflects it down through a vertical tube, the second diverts it horizontally so that the scene can be viewed conveniently.

peristalsis \ˌper-ə-ˈstȯl-səs\ Progressive wavelike MUSCLE contractions in the ESOPHAGUS, STOMACH, and intestines, and sometimes in the ureters and other hollow tubes. The waves can be short, local REFLEXES or long, continuous contractions along the length of the organ. In the esophagus, peristaltic waves push food into the stomach. In the stomach, they help mix stomach contents and propel food to the SMALL INTESTINE, where they expose food to the intestinal wall for absorption and move it forward. Peristalsis in the LARGE INTESTINE pushes waste toward the ANAL CANAL and is important in removing gas and dislodging potential bacterial colonies.

peritoneoscopy See LAPAROSCOPY

peritonitis \ˌper-ə-tᵊn-ˈī-təs\ INFLAMMATION of the peritoneum (see ABDOMINAL CAVITY), with pus accumulating between the parietal and the visceral peritoneum, abdominal pain and distension, vomiting, and fever. It may be acute or chronic, local or generalized. Acute peritonitis usually results from inflammation elsewhere (e.g., by spread of bacterial infection). Primary peritonitis often comes from a perforated gastrointestinal tract, as with rupture in appendicitis. Control of the source problem may be followed by remission, adhesions, or ABSCESSES (much rarer since the development of antibiotics).

periwinkle In botany, any of various plants of the genus *Vinca* of the DOGBANE FAMILY. The lesser periwinkle *(V. minor),* which has small lilac-blue flowers, is a dependable, trailing, evergreen perennial that is native to Europe and has become widespread over much of eastern North America. The greater periwinkle *(V. major),* with larger leaves and larger purplish-blue flowers, is native to continental Europe and has become naturalized in England. ALKALOIDS derived from the periwinkle plant have had some success in inhibiting cancer growth.

periwinkle In zoology, any of some 80 species (family Littorinidae) of widely distributed, chiefly herbivorous, shore SNAILS. Periwinkles are usually found on rocks, stones, or pilings between high- and low-tide marks. The common periwinkle *(Littorina littorea),* the largest northern species, may grow to 1.5 in. (4 cm) long. It is usually dark gray and has a solid spiral shell. Introduced into North America c. 1857, it is now common on Atlantic coasts. All periwinkle species are a favorite food of many shorebirds.

Periwinkles (*Littorina*).
JANE BURTON—BRUCE COLEMAN LTD.

Periyar River \ˌper-i-ˈyär\ River, central KERALA state, southwestern India. It is 140 mi (225 km) long and rises in the western GHATS range near the border with TAMIL NADU state. It flows north to Periyar Lake, an artificial reservoir created by damming the river. A tunnel carries water from the lake eastward through the mountains to the Vaigai River, where it is used for irrigation. From the lake it flows northwest and empties into the Arabian Sea.

perjury In law, act or crime of knowingly making a false statement while under oath. The statement must be material to the issue of inquiry. Perjuries that have the effect of obstructing the adjudication of a case may be given increased punishment for that reason. A person who makes a false statement and later corrects it is usually not considered to have committed perjury.

Perkins, Anthony (1932–1992) U.S. film actor. Born in New York City, the son of the actor Osgood Perkins, he studied at Columbia University. After making his screen debut in *The Actress* (1953), he appeared in such films as *Friendly Persuasion* (1956) and *Fear Strikes Out* (1957), but became best known as the murderous motel owner Norman Bates in ALFRED HITCHCOCK's *Psycho* (1960). He later appeared in several films in Europe, including *The Trial* (1963), *The Champagne Murders* (1967), and *Ten Days' Wonder* (1972), and in such U.S. films as *Pretty Poison* (1968), *Catch-22* (1970), and *WUSA* (1970). He died of complications from AIDS.

Perkins, Frances *orig.* **Fannie Coralie** (1882–1965) U.S. public official. Born in Boston, she became a social worker in New York City, and a leader in organizations to improve women's working conditions. She served as state industrial commissioner 1929–33 under Gov. FRANKLIN ROOSEVELT. As president, Roosevelt appointed her U.S. secretary of labor, the first woman to hold a cabinet post. In her long term (1933–45), she advocated such reforms as a minimum wage, maximum workweek, and unemployment compensation, helped draft the Social Security Act, and supervised the Fair Labor Standards Act (1938). She was later a U.S. Civil Service commissioner (1945–53).

Perkins, Jacob (1766–1849) U.S. inventor. Born in Newburyport, Mass., he built a machine to cut and head NAILS in one operation c. 1790. He developed a method of engraving paper money that made counterfeiting difficult; lack of interest in the U.S. led him to set up a bank-note factory in England (1819). He experimented with high-pressure steam BOILERS, built a horizontal STEAM ENGINE (1827), designed an improved paddle wheel (1829), and invented a means for the free circulation of water in boilers (1831) that led to the design of modern water-tube boilers.

Perkins, Maxwell (Evarts) (1884–1947) U.S. editor. Born in New York City, he worked as a reporter for the *New York Times* before joining the publishing firm of Charles Scribner's Sons, of which he would later became editorial director and vice president. He is best known for the intensive editorial work that shaped THOMAS WOLFE's sprawling manuscripts into publishable form, but he also assisted the early careers of F. SCOTT FITZGERALD, ERNEST HEMINGWAY, RING LARDNER, ERSKINE CALDWELL, EDMUND WILSON, and ALAN PATON.

Perl *in full* **Practical Extraction and Reporting Language** High-level computer PROGRAMMING LANGUAGE, the most popular language for writing CGI scripts and the premier scripting (or interpreted) language of the WORLD WIDE WEB. Since it has roots in UNIX, its syntax is similar to C and it includes several UNIX utilities. Because of its excellent text-processing capability, it is widely used by system administrators (for writing administrative tasks) and is especially suited for developing prototype versions of programs. Because it is an interpreted language, its programs are highly portable across different operating systems. Originally developed by Larry Wall at NASA's Jet Propulsion Laboratory in 1986, it has since been improved by hundreds of volunteer developers. Like LINUX, it can be obtained free of charge.

perlite *or* **pearlstone** Natural glass with concentric cracks such that the rock breaks into small, pearl-like bodies. It is formed by the rapid cooling of viscous LAVA or MAGMA. Perlite is porous and has a waxy to pearly luster and is commonly gray or greenish but may be brown, blue, or red. Since c. 1950, large deposits have been worked in New Mexico, Nevada, California, and other western states. Heat-treated perlite is a substitute for sand in lightweight wall plaster and concrete aggregate. Perlite is used for heat and sound insulation, lightweight ceramic products, and filters.

Perlman, Itzhak (born 1945) Israeli-U.S. violinist. Despite a bout with polio as a child of 4 that left him crippled, he was a prodigy, and he made his U.S. television debut at 13. He studied with Ivan Galamian (1903–1981) and Dorothy DeLay (born c. 1915) at Juilliard. Recognition of his gifts led to a highly successful career as orchestral soloist and chamber-music player, with scores of recordings. Blessed with a popular touch, he has appeared on television, played jazz and klezmer music, and involved himself in educating young musicians.

permafrost Perennially frozen earth, with a temperature below 32°F (0°C) continuously for two years or more. Permafrost is estimated to underlie 20% of the earth's land surface and reaches depths of 5,000 ft (1,500 m) in northern Siberia. It occurs in 85% of Alaska, more than half of Russia and Canada, and probably all of Antarctica. Permafrost has a significant effect on plant and animal life, and it presents special problems in engineering projects. All land use in permafrost environments must take into account the terrain's special sensitivity; if the delicate natural balance is not maintained, extensive degradation and ecological damage may result.

permeability, magnetic See MAGNETIC PERMEABILITY

Permian period Interval of geologic time, 290–248 million years ago. The last of the six periods of the PALEOZOIC ERA, it follows the CARBONIFEROUS PERIOD. During the Permian, the continents joined to form a single supercontinent, PANGAEA. Hot, dry conditions prevailed almost everywhere, and deserts were widespread. Life evolved as a continuation of established lines. Marine invertebrates evolved into several lineages. Marine and freshwater fish and amphibians thrived. Reptiles evolved into three distinct groups: the cotylosaurs, the pelycosaurs, and the therapsids. Land plants evolved from ferns and seed ferns to conifers and adapted to drier and well-drained land conditions. Toward the close of the Permian, many forms of life suffered mass extinction, whose causes are unknown.

permittivity \ˌpər-ˌmi-ˈti-və-tē\ Universal electric constant that appears in the mathematical formulation of the ELECTROSTATIC FORCE. The permittivity of an insulating, or DIELECTRIC, material is commonly symbolized by the Greek letter epsilon (ε). The permittivity of a VACUUM is symbolized ε_0. The ratio $\varepsilon/\varepsilon_0$ is the dielectric constant of the material. The SI units of permittivity are square coulombs per newton-square meter (C_2/N-m^2).

permutations and combinations Number of ways a subset of objects can be selected from a given set of objects. In a permutation, order is important; in a combination, it is not. Thus, there are six permutations of the letters A, B, C selected two at a time (AB, AC, BC, BA, CA, CB) yet only three combinations (AB, AC, BC). The number of permutations of r objects chosen from a set of n objects, expressed in FACTORIAL notation, is $n! \div (n - r)!$ The number of combinations is $n! \div [r!(n - r)!]$. The $(r + 1)$st coefficient in the binomial expansion of $(x + y)^n$ coincides with the combination of n objects chosen r at a time (see BINOMIAL THEOREM). PROBABILITY THEORY evolved from the study of gambling, including figuring out combinations of playing cards or permutations of win-place-show possibilities in a horse race, and such counting methods played an important role in its development in the 17th century.

Pernambuco See RECIFE

pernicious anemia Slow-developing disease in which vitamin B_{12} (see VITAMIN B COMPLEX) deficiency impairs red-blood-cell production. It can result from a diet lacking in vitamin B_{12} or when intrinsic factor, a substance needed for intestinal absorption of B_{12}, either is not produced by stomach cells or cannot bind to the vitamin. It causes weakness, waxy pallor, shiny tongue, and stomach, intestinal, and neurological problems. Its slow development can allow ANEMIA to become very severe by the time of diagnosis. Monthly B_{12} injections into muscle soon reverses the anemia, but the injections must be continued for life.

Perón \pā-ˈrōn\, **Eva (Duarte de)** *known as* **Evita** *orig.* **María Eva Duarte** (1919–1952) Second wife of Argentine president JUAN PERON and a powerful though unofficial political leader. Born into poverty, she was an actress when she married Perón. She was instrumental in the success of his first presidential campaign and won the adulation of the masses. Evita acted as de facto minister of health and labor, awarding generous wage increases to workers. With "voluntary" contributions from businesses, labor unions, and the elite, she established thousands of hospitals, schools, and orphanages. After her death of cancer at 33, her grief-stricken working-class followers sought to have her canonized.

Perón, Isabel (Martínez de) *orig.* **María Estela Martínez Cartas** (born 1931) Third wife of JUAN PERON and president of Argentina (1974–76). Born into a lower-middle-class family, she was a dancer when she met Perón in 1955 or 1956. They married during his exile in 1961, and she became his running mate in the 1973 presidential election. She succeeded him when he died in 1974, inheriting problems of inflation and political violence, which she tried ineffectively to solve by printing money and imposing a state of siege. She was deposed in 1976; after five years of house arrest, she was convicted of corruption but permitted to go into exile in Spain.

Perón, Juan (Domingo) (1895–1974) President of Argentina (1946–55, 1973–74). After attending military school, he served in the 1930s in Italy, where he observed the successes of the Fascists. In 1943 he helped overthrow Argentina's ineffective civilian government. As secretary of labor and social welfare he built a loyal following among industrial workers, who helped elect him president in 1946. Perón's political views drew on both the far left and the far right: while he showered workers with much-needed benefits, he restricted civil liberties severely. The charisma of his wife, EVA PERON, greatly increased the regime's standing with the populace. He was reelected in 1951, but a disastrous economic decline and increasing disaffection among many elements of Argentine society led to his overthrow in 1955 by democratically inspired military officers. He lived in exile in Spain for two decades, but continued to influence Argentine affairs. When the PERONIST party was made legal, he was reelected president in absentia; he died less than a year after returning to Argentina and assuming the presidency. See also ISABEL PERON.

Peronist \pə-ˈrō-nist\ Member of Argentina's Justicialist Nationalist Movement, supporter of JUAN PERON, or adherent of his populist and nationalist policies. Perón's poorly defined political philosophy embraced elements of both left- and right-wing ideology, combining a commitment to the redistribution of wealth with authoritarian nationalism and disregard for civil rights. After his death in 1974, the Justicialist movement was weakened by factionalism, but it has continued to play an important role in Argentine politics and has adherents elsewhere. See also CARLOS MENEM.

Perot \pə-ˈrō\, **H(enry) Ross** (born 1930) U.S. businessman. Born in Texarkana, Texas, he graduated from Annapolis and served in the U.S. Navy 1953–57. After working for IBM (1957–62), he formed his own company, the data-processing contract company Electronic Data Systems, and successfully directed it until he sold it in 1984 to General Motors for $2.5 billion. He became nationally known in 1992 as an independent candidate for U.S. president; appealing to voters dissatisfied with traditional party politics, he won 19% of the popular vote. His Reform Party gradually established its autonomy from Perot himself.

Pérouse Strait, La See SOYA STRAIT

peroxide Any of a class of chemical compounds in which two OXYGEN atoms are linked by a single COVALENT BOND. Several organic (see ORGANIC COMPOUND) and inorganic (see INORGANIC COMPOUND) peroxides are useful as bleaching and oxidizing agents (see OXIDATION-REDUCTION), as initiators of POLYMERIZATION reactions, and in the preparation of hydrogen peroxide (a mild bleach and antiseptic) and other oxygen compounds. The peroxide ANION (chemical formula O_2^{2-}) is present in peroxides of inorganic compounds.

Perpendicular style Phase of late GOTHIC ARCHITECTURE in England roughly parallel in time to the French FLAMBOYANT STYLE. The style, concerned with creating rich visual effects through decoration, was characterized by a predominance of vertical lines in stone window TRACERY, enlargement of windows to great proportions, and conversion of the interior stories into a single unified vertical expanse. Fan VAULTS, springing from slender columns or PENDANTS, became popular. The oldest surviving example of the style is probably the choir of Gloucester Cathedral (begun c. 1335). Other major monuments include King's College Chapel, Cambridge (1446–1515), and the chapel of Henry VII in WESTMINSTER ABBEY. In the 16th century, the grafting of Renaissance elements onto the Perpendicular style resulted in the TUDOR STYLE.

Perpignan \ˌper-pē-ˈnyäⁿ\ City (pop., 1990: 108,000), southern France. Located just north of the Spanish border, it was founded c. 10th century. It was the capital of ROUSSILLON in the 12th century, and of the kingdom of MAJORCA 1276–1344. It was heavily fortified during the struggle between France and Spain for the area; it became French in 1659. It is now a market center for the surrounding agricultural area; its many medieval buildings have made tourism economically important.

Perrault \pe-'rō\, **Charles** (1628–1703) French poet, prose writer, and storyteller. Perrault began to win a literary reputation c. 1660 with light verse and love poetry. He is best remembered for his collection of charming fairy stories written to amuse his children, *Contes de ma mère l'oye,* or *Tales of* MOTHER GOOSE (1697). He spent the rest of his life promoting the study of literature and the arts. A leading member of the ACADÉMIE FRANÇAISE, he was involved in a famous controversy with NICHOLAS BOILEAU on the relative merits of ancient and modern literature; his support for the modern was of landmark significance in the revolt against the confines of prevailing tradition.

Perrot \pe-'rō\, **Jules (Joseph)** (1810–1892) French dancer and choreographer, known for his Romantic ballets. He studied with S. VIGANO and other exponents of the expressive tradition. He debuted at the Paris Opera in 1830 and partnered MARIE TAGLIONI until 1835, when he left the company to tour in Europe. He choreographed several ballets for Carlotta Grisi (1819–1899), probably including the famous solos in *Giselle.* He worked as dancer and ballet master in London (1842–48) and St. Petersburg (1848–58), where he continued to choreograph in the expressive, dramatic style.

Jules Perrot, engraving after a drawing.

BY COURTESY OF THE BIBLIOTHEQUE DE L'OPERA, PARIS; PHOTOGRAPH, PIC

Perry, Matthew C(albraith) (1794–1858) U.S. naval officer. Born in South Kingston, R.I., he followed his brother OLIVER PERRY into the navy and commanded the first U.S. navy steamship, the *Fulton* (1837–40). He led naval forces in the MEXICAN WAR and assisted WINFIELD SCOTT at Veracruz. In 1852 Pres. MILLARD FILLMORE sent Perry to head a naval expedition to induce Japan to establish diplomatic relations with the U.S. Concluding that Japan's centuries-old policy of isolation would be ended only by a show of force, Perry led four ships into the fortified harbor of Uraga (1853) and convinced the Japanese to accept his message. In 1854 he entered Edo (now Tokyo) Bay with nine ships and concluded the first treaty between Japan and the U.S., allowing U.S. trading privileges and opening the Far East to U.S. influence.

Perry, Oliver Hazard (1785–1819) U.S. naval officer. Born in South Kingston, R.I., the older brother of MATTHEW PERRY, he entered the navy in 1799 and served in the West Indies and the Mediterranean. In 1813 he was ordered to Erie, Pa., to assemble a naval squadron to challenge British control of the Great Lakes in the WAR OF 1812. With 10 small ships, he engaged six British warships in Lake Erie (September 10, 1813). After his flagship was disabled, he was rowed to the *Niagara,* from which he won the battle by sailing directly into the British line, firing broadside. In reporting the British surrender he wrote "We have met the enemy and they are ours."

Perse, Saint-John See SAINT-JOHN PERSE

Persephone \pər-'se-fə-nē\ *Latin* **Proserpina** In GREEK MYTHOLOGY, daughter of ZEUS and DEMETER. She was gathering flowers when she was seized by HADES, who carried her off to the underworld to make her his wife. On learning of the abduction, Demeter was so distraught that she allowed barrenness and famine to spread over the earth. Zeus commanded Hades to allow Persephone to return to her mother, but because she had eaten some (or, in some versions, just one) pomegranate seeds in the underworld, she had to remain one-third of the year with Hades, spending the other two-thirds with Demeter. This myth accounts for the change of the seasons and the annual cycle of growth and decay. See photograph above.

Persephone abducted by Hades, marble sculpture by Gian Lorenzo Bernini, 1621–22; in the Borghese Gallery, Rome.

ANDERSON—ALINARI FROM ART RESOURCE/EB INC.

Persepolis \pər-'se-pə-ləs\ Ancient city and capital of PERSIA, northeast of SHIRAZ, in modern southwestern central Iran. It was built in a remote and mountainous area under DARIUS I, who made it the capital of Persia, replacing PASARGADAE. In 330 BC ALEXANDER THE GREAT plundered the city and burned the palace of XERXES. The city's ruins cover an extensive area and comprise a number of colossal buildings, including palaces of early Persian kings, a great staircase, an audience hall, and a treasury.

Perseus (212?–c. 165 BC) Last king of Macedonia (179–168). Son of PHILIP V, he fought against Rome (199) and Aetolia (189). He persuaded the king to execute his brother Demetrius. As king, he extended his influence in neighboring states and tried to gain the trust of the Greek world, but alarmed Greece by visiting Delphi with an army. EUMENES II of Pergamum informed Rome of Perseus' allegedly aggressive designs, provoking the Third MACEDONIAN WAR (171–168). The struggle ended in a final defeat of the Macedonians by the Romans, ending the monarchy, and Perseus spent the rest of his life in captivity.

Perseus In GREEK MYTHOLOGY, the slayer of the GORGON MEDUSA. He was the son of ZEUS and DANAË. His grandfather had him thrown into the sea in a chest with his mother as an infant because of a prophecy that Perseus would kill him. Perseus and his mother survived, and as a young man Perseus set out to gain the head of Medusa. On his way home he rescued the Ethiopian princess ANDROMEDA from a sea monster, and she became his wife. When he took his mother back to her native Argos, he threw a discus that accidentally killed his grandfather, thus fulfilling the prophecy.

Pershing \'pər-zhiŋ, 'pər-shiŋ\, **John J(oseph)** (1860–1948) U.S. Army officer. Born in Laclede, Mo., he graduated from West Point and served on the western frontier (1886–98), in the Spanish-American War, in the Philippines (1899–1903, 1906–13), and as commander of a punitive raid against PANCHO VILLA (1916). In World War I he was appointed commander in chief of the American Expeditionary Force (AEF). He maintained the AEF as an independent army of 2 million men and resisted Allied efforts to use U.S. forces as replacement units for French and British troops. He led the successful assault of the St. Mihiel salient in September 1918 and helped defeat German forces in the Meuse-Argonne offensive. He was promoted to general of the armies in 1919 and was army chief of staff 1921–24. His nickname, "Black Jack," derived from his service with a black regiment early in his career. His memoirs won a Pulitzer Prize (1931).

John J. Pershing, 1917.

BY COURTESY OF THE LIBRARY OF CONGRESS, WASHINGTON, D.C.

Persia Historical name for the kingdom of Iran, South Asia. It was used for centuries, chiefly in the West, and originated from a region of southern Iran formerly known as Persis or Parsa. Parsa was the name of an Indo-European nomadic people who migrated into the area c. 1000 BC; the use of the name was gradually extended by the ancient Greeks and other Western peoples to apply to the whole Iranian plateau. The people of Iran have always called their country Iran, and in 1935 the government requested that the name Iran be used instead of Persia.

Persian cat Breed of stocky, round-headed DOMESTIC CAT that has a long, silky coat (many colors possible), large round eyes, snub nose, and thick ruff. The breed is often referred to as the LONGHAIR.

Persian Gulf Arm of the Arabian Sea. It is 550 mi (885 km) long, and has an average depth of 328 ft (100 m). It is connected with the Gulf of OMAN and the Arabian Sea through the Strait of HORMUZ. It contains the island state of Bahrain and is bordered by Iran, the United Arab Emirates, Oman, Saudi Arabia, Qatar, Kuwait, and Iraq. Its economy is dominated by petroleum production. It was the scene of the PERSIAN GULF WAR in 1991.

Persian Gulf War *or* **Gulf War** (1990–91) International conflict triggered by Iraq's invasion of Kuwait in August 1990. Though justified by S. Hussein, the Iraqi leader, on grounds that Kuwait was illegally taking oil from an Iraqi field, the invasion was presumed to be principally motivated by desire to acquire Kuwait's own rich oil fields. The U.S. and its NATO allies, supported by a coalition of Arab nations, began massing troops in Saudi Arabia that month; when a U.N. Security Council deadline for Iraq's withdrawal was ignored, a massive U.S.-led air offensive against Iraq began (January 16/17, 1991). SADDAM HUSSEIN, the Iraqi leader, responded by pumping millions of gallons of Kuwaiti oil into the gulf. A powerful ground offensive (February 24–28) achieved victory almost immediately, though not before Hussein had had scores of oil wells set alight; the last were not extinguished for some eight months. Estimates for Iraqi military deaths range from 8,000 to 100,000; the Allies lost about 300 troops. Hussein subsequently faced widespread popular uprisings, which he managed to quell. A U.N.-sanctioned trade embargo remained in effect, pending destruction of Iraq's chemical- and nuclear-weapons research facilities, through the decade.

Persian language *or* **Farsi language** IRANIAN LANGUAGE spoken by more than 25 million people in Iran as a first language, and by millions more as a second. Modern Persian is a KOINE developed from southwestern dialects in the 7th–9th century, after the introduction of Islam brought a massive infusion of loanwords from ARABIC. Its standardization and literary cultivation took place in northeastern Persia and Central Asia in the 11th–12th century. Polities outside Persia itself (e.g., Mughal India, Ottoman Turkey) have at times been major literary centers. Its status in those countries led to a very strong Persian influence on URDU and Ottoman TURKISH. Other TURKIC and INDO-ARYAN languages, CAUCASIAN LANGUAGES, and Iranian languages have also borrowed heavily from Persian. Like other Modern Iranian languages, Persian shows marked changes in sound structure from Old Iranian, as well as a drastic reduction in the repertoire of verbal forms and complete loss of case inflections for nouns and adjectives. It is written in a slightly modified form of the ARABIC ALPHABET.

Persian Wars *or* **Greco-Persian Wars** (492–449 BC) Series of wars between Greek states and Persia, particularly two invasions of Greece by Persia (490, 480–479). When DARIUS I came to power in Persia in 522, the Ionian Greek city-states in Anatolia were under Persian control. They rose up unsuccessfully in the IONIAN REVOLT (499–494). The support lent by Athens provoked Darius to invade Greece (492). His fleet was destroyed in a storm. In 490 he assembled a huge army on a plain near Athens; his devastating defeat at the Battle of MARATHON sent him back to Persia. In 480 the Persians under XERXES I invaded Greece again, seeking to avenge the defeat. This time all Greece fought together, with Sparta in charge of the army and Athens of the navy. A band of Spartans under LEONIDAS was overcome at the Battle of THERMOPYLAE, allowing the Persian army to reach Athens, which they sacked (480). When the Persian navy was soundly defeated at the Battle of SALAMIS, Xerxes withdrew it to Persia. His army was defeated at the Battle of PLATAEA in 479 and driven from Greece, and the navy met a similar fate at Mycale on the Anatolian coast. Sporadic fighting went on for 30 more years, during which Athens formed the DELIAN LEAGUE to free the Ionians. The Peace of Callias (449) ended the hostilities.

persimmon Either of two trees of the genus *Diospyros* in the EBONY family, and their globular, edible fruits. The native American persimmon *(D. virginiana),* a small tree with dark-red to maroon fruits that contain several large, flattened seeds, grows from the Gulf states north to central Pennsylvania and central Illinois. The Oriental persimmon *(D. kaki),* grown extensively in China and Japan, has larger, more astringent, yellow to red fruit. Good sources of vitamins A and C, persimmons are eaten fresh or stewed or cooked as jam.

American persimmon (*Diospyros virginiana*).
H.R. HUNGERFORD

personal computer (PC) MICROCOMPUTER designed for use by one person at a time. A typical PC assemblage comprises a CPU; internal MEMORY consisting of RAM and ROM; data storage devices (including a HARD DISK, a FLOPPY DISK, or CD-ROM); and input/output devices (including a display screen, keyboard, MOUSE, and PRINTER). The PC industry began in 1977 when Apple Computer introduced the Apple II. Radio Shack and Commodore Business Machines also introduced PCs that year. IBM entered the PC market in 1981. The IBM PC, with increased memory capacity and backed by IBM's large sales organization, quickly became the industry standard. Apple's Macintosh (1984) was particularly useful for DESKTOP PUBLISHING. MICROSOFT CORP. introduced MS WINDOWS (1985), a GRAPHICAL USER INTERFACE that gave PCs many of the capabilities of the Macintosh, initially as an overlay of MS-DOS. Windows went on to replace MS-DOS as the dominant operating environment for personal computers. Uses of PCs multiplied as the machines became more powerful and application SOFTWARE proliferated. Today, PCs are used for word processing, Internet access, and many other daily tasks.

personal-liberty laws Laws passed by U.S. states in the North to counter the FUGITIVE SLAVE ACTS. Such states as Indiana (1824) and Connecticut (1828) enacted laws giving escaped slaves the right to jury trials on appeal. Vermont and New York (1840) assured fugitives the right of jury trial and provided them with attorneys. Other states forbade state authorities to capture and return fugitives. After the COMPROMISE OF 1850, most Northern states enacted further guarantees of jury trials and punishment for illegal seizure. These laws were cited by proslavery interests as assaults on states' rights and as justification for SECESSION.

personal property See REAL AND PERSONAL PROPERTY

personalismo (Spanish: "personalism") In Latin America, the practice of glorifying a leader. It often involves sacrificing the interests of political parties, ideologies, and constitutional government out of loyalty to a leader. Political parties throughout Latin America have often consisted of the personal following of a leader, a fact reflected in the popular terms for the partisans. Members of Argentina's Justicialist National Movement, for example, are called *peronistas* (PERONISTS), after its charismatic founder, and the followers of FIDEL CASTRO are *fidelistas.* See also CAUDILLO.

personality Totality of an individual's behavioral and emotional characteristics. Personality embraces a person's moods, attitudes, opinions, motivations, and style of thinking, perceiving, speaking, and acting. It is part of what makes each individual distinct. Theories of personality have existed in most cultures and throughout most of recorded history. The ancient Greeks used their ideas about physiology to account for differences and similarities in TEMPERAMENT. In the 18th century, IMMANUEL KANT, C.-L. MONTESQUIEU, and GIAMBATTISTA VICO proposed ways of understanding individual and group differences; in the early 20th century ERNST KRETSCHMER and the psychoanalysts SIGMUND FREUD, ALFRED ADLER, and CARL GUSTAV JUNG offered competing personality theories. Freud's model rested on the power of psychosexual drives as mediated by the structural components of the ID, EGO, and SUPEREGO and the interplay of conscious and unconscious motives. Particularly important was the array of DEFENSE MECHANISMS an individual employed. Jung, like Freud, emphasized unconscious motives but de-emphasized sexuality and advanced a typal theory that classified people as INTROVERTS AND EXTROVERTS, and claimed that an individual personality was a persona (social facade) drawn from the "collective unconscious," a pool of inherited racial memories. Later theories by ERIK ERIKSON, GORDON W. ALLPORT, and CARL R. ROGERS were also influential. Contemporary personality studies tend to be empirical (based on the administration of projective tests or personality inventories) and less theoretically sweeping, and to emphasize personal identity and development. Personality traits are usually seen as the product of both genetic predisposition and experience. See also PERSONALITY DISORDER, PSYCHOLOGICAL TESTING.

personality disorder General behavioral pattern or manner of being that is integral to an individual's PERSONALITY and yet is considered maladaptive or abnormal. Rather than being illnesses, personality disorders are enduring and pervasive features of the personality that deviate markedly from the cultural norm. They include the dependent, histrionic, narcissistic, obsessive-compulsive, antisocial, avoidant, borderline (unstable), paranoid, and schizoid types. The causes appear to be both hereditary and environmental. The most effective treatment combines behavioral and psychotherapeutic therapies (see BEHAVIOR THERAPY, PSYCHOTHERAPY).

personnel administration See INDUSTRIAL RELATIONS

perspective Depiction of three-dimensional objects and spatial relationships on a two-dimensional plane. In Western art, illusions of volume and space are generally created by use of the linear perspective system, based on the observation that objects appear to shrink and parallel lines to converge at an infinitely distant vanishing point as they recede in space from the viewer. The vanishing point may have been known to the Greeks and Romans but had been lost until FILIPPO BRUNELLESCHI rediscovered the principles of linear or "mathematical" perspective early in the 15th century. Linear perspective dominated Western painting until the late 19th century, when PAUL CEZANNE flattened the conventional picture plane. The Cubists and other 20th-century painters abandoned depiction of three-dimensional space altogether. See also AERIAL PERSPECTIVE.

Perspex See LUCITE

perspiration Fluid given off by the SKIN as vapor by simple evaporation or as sweat actively secreted from SWEAT GLANDS to evaporate and cool the body. When the body temperature rises, the sympathetic nervous system stimulates eccrine sweat glands to secrete water to the skin surface, where it cools the body by evaporation. Human eccrine sweat is essentially a dilute sodium-chloride solution with trace amounts of other plasma electrolytes. In extreme conditions, human beings may excrete several liters of such sweat in an hour.

Perth City (pop., 1996 est.: 1,097,000), capital of WESTERN AUSTRALIA state, Australia. Located on the SWAN RIVER, 10 mi (16 km) from its mouth, it was settled in 1829. It developed rapidly after the discovery of gold fields at Coolgardie in 1890, and the opening of Fremantle Harbor in 1897. It is now a major industrial center, with a rapidly expanding economy. The site of the 1987 AMERICA'S CUP, it is the seat of the University of Western Australia and Murdoch Univ.

Perth Town (pop., 1995 est.: 42,000), central Scotland, on the TAY RIVER, northwest of EDINBURGH. A Roman settlement, it became a royal burgh in 1210. It was the capital of Scotland until 1437, when King JAMES I of Scotland was murdered there. At the Church of St. John the Baptist in 1559 JOHN KNOX denounced idolatry; the result was the plunder of the town's monasteries and altars. It was a JACOBITE city during the Scottish uprisings of 1715 and 1745. The economy is based on whisky blending and distilling, and manufacturing. It is also an agricultural market center.

pertussis See WHOOPING COUGH

Peru *officially* **Republic of Peru** Country, western South America. Area: 496,225 sq mi (1,285,216 sq km). Population (2002 est.): 26,724,000. Capital: LIMA. Almost half of the people are QUECHUA Indians, and nearly one-third are MESTIZOS of combined Indian and Spanish ancestry; smaller groups include whites and Aymara Indians. Languages: Spanish, Quechua, and Aymara (all official). Religions: Roman Catholicism (official), Protestantism. Currency: new sol. Peru is the third largest nation in South America and may be divided into three geographic regions from west to east: the coast, a long, narrow belt of desert lowlands; the highlands, the Peruvian portion of the ANDES; and the vast, forested eastern foothills and plains, consisting mainly of the tropical rainforests of the AMAZON RIVER basin. Peru has a developing mixed economy based largely on services, manufacturing, agriculture, and mining. Most industries, including the petroleum industry, were nationalized in the late 1960s and early 1970s, but many were privatized again in the 1990s. It is a republic with one legislative house; its head of state and government is the president. Peru was the center of the INCA empire, which was established c. 1230 with its capital at CUZCO. In 1533

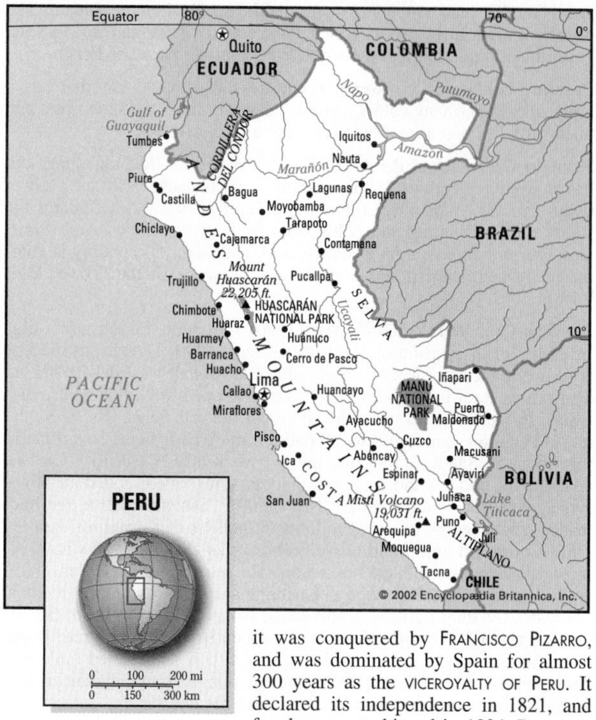

it was conquered by FRANCISCO PIZARRO, and was dominated by Spain for almost 300 years as the VICEROYALTY OF PERU. It declared its independence in 1821, and freedom was achieved in 1824. Peru was defeated in the WAR OF THE PACIFIC with Chile (1879–84). A boundary dispute with Ecuador erupted into war in 1941, which gave Peru control over a larger part of the Amazon basin; further disputes ensued until the border was demarcated again in 1998. The government was overthrown by a military junta in 1968, and civilian rule was restored in 1980. The government of ALBERTO FUJIMORI dissolved the legislature in 1992 and promulgated a new constitution the following year. It later successfully combated the SHINING PATH and TUPAC AMARÚ rebel movements. Fujimori won a second term in 1995, but charges of fraud accompanied his election to a third term in 2000; his government crumbled later that year. In 2001 Alejandro Toledo became Peru's first democratically elected president of Quechua ethnicity.

Peru, viceroyalty of Second of the four viceroyalties that Spain created to govern its domains in the Americas. Established in 1543, it initially included most of South America, but it lost jurisdiction over much of its territory to other viceroyalties over time. Peru, with its wealth of silver, was considered Spain's most valuable possession in the Americas. By the late 18th century, Indian rebellions had destabilized the region, and the viceroyalty was unable to defend itself when the revolutionary forces of JOSE DE SAN MARTIN entered Lima in 1821. It became part of Peru and Chile in 1824. See also NEW GRANADA, NEW SPAIN, viceroyalty of RÍO DE LA PLATA.

Perugia \pā-ˈrü-jä\ City (pop., 1996 est.: 151,000), capital of UMBRIA region, central Italy. It lies north of Rome between the TIBER RIVER and Lake TRASIMENO. Founded by the Umbrians, it became one of the 12 major cities of the ETRUSCANS; it later was ruled by Rome from 310 BC. It became a Lombard duchy in AD 592. It was the center of the great Umbrian school of painting, which flourished in the 15th century (see PERUGINO, PINTURICCHIO). It played an active role in the Italian RISORGIMENTO and became part of Italy in 1860. It is an agricultural trade center noted for its chocolate. There are notable remains of buildings and fortifications from Etruscan and medieval times.

Perugino \ˌper-ə-ˈjē-nō\ *orig.* **Pietro di Cristoforo Vannucci** (c. 1450–1523) Italian painter. Born near Perugia (the source of his nickname), he was probably a pupil of PIERO DELLA FRANCESCA and VERROCCHIO. One of his most famous frescoes, *Giving of the Keys to St. Peter* (1481–82), in the Sistine Chapel, anticipated High Renaissance ideals in its compositional clarity and sense of spaciousness. He was at the height of his powers c. 1490–1500, when he painted the *Crucifixion* fresco for the convent of Santa Maria Maddalena dei Pazzi in Florence. Perugino's art declined in his later years, and c. 1505 he left the highly critical Florentine art scene to work in Umbria. In 1508 he made a brief comeback by painting roundels on the ceiling of the Stanza dell'Incendio in the Vatican. The commission for the wall frescoes went to his pupil RAPHAEL, who had already proved himself the greater artist.

"Vision of St. Bernard," wood panel by Perugino, c. 1491–94; in the Alte Pinakothek, Munich.
BY COURTESY OF THE ALTE PINAKOTHEK, MUNICH

Perun \p^{y}i-'rün\ In ancient SLAVIC RELIGION, the thunder god. He purified the earth and made it fertile, and he was the overseer of right and order. His powers were believed to be evident in the thunderbolt, the rattle of stones, the bellow of a bull, the bleat of a goat, and the touch of an ax blade. In the Christian period the worship of Perun was gradually transferred to St. Elijah, but folk belief in his powers continued. Sacrifices and communal feasts on July 20 in his honor were celebrated in Russia until modern times.

Perutz \pə-'rüts\, **Max Ferdinand** (1914–2002) Austrian-British biochemist. With JOHN COWDERY KENDREW he founded the Medical Research Council Unit for Molecular Biology at Cambridge. His discovery that HEMOGLOBIN's structure changes when it picks up or releases oxygen led to the full understanding of the molecular mechanism of respiratory oxygen transport by hemoglobin. For his X-ray diffraction analysis of hemoglobin's structure, he and Kendrew shared a 1962 Nobel Prize. Perutz also used CRYSTALLOGRAPHY to study the flow of GLACIERS.

Pesaro \'pā-zä-ˌrō\ *ancient* **Pisorum** City (pop., 2001 est.: 90,311), MARCHE region, northern central Italy. A seaport on the Adriatic Sea, it was destroyed by the OSTROGOTHS in AD 536. Rebuilt and fortified by the Byzantine general Belisarius as one of the cities of the Pentapolis, it was sold to the SFORZA FAMILY in 1445. It became part of the PAPAL STATES in 1631. It was the birthplace of composer GIOACCHINO ROSSINI in 1792. In World War II, Pesaro suffered heavily in the Allied advance of 1944, but many of its old buildings escaped with minor damage. It is a seaside resort surrounded by an agricultural area. Its museum of MAJOLICA is the richest in Italy.

Peshawar \pə-'shä-wər\ City (pop., 1998 est.: 988,055), capital of North-West Frontier province, Pakistan. It is located west of the Bara River near the KHYBER PASS. Once the capital of the ancient Buddhist kingdom of Gandhara, it was a center of the caravan trade with Afghanistan and central Asia. It became the capital of the Indo-Scythian Kushan empire c. 1st century AD. It was captured by the Muslims in 988. By the 16th century Peshawar was ruled by the Afghans. It was under British control 1849–1947 and served as an important military base. The city is still militarily important; its ancient bazaar remains a meeting place for foreign merchants and traders.

Pessoa \pes-'sō-ə\, **Fernando António Nogueira** (1888–1935) Portuguese poet. While living in South Africa, where his stepfather was Portugal's consul, Pessoa became fluent in English. On returning to Lisbon he worked as a translator while contributing to avant-garde reviews, especially *Orpheu* (1915), the organ of Brazilian-Portuguese Modernismo, of which he became a leading aesthetician. Only after his death did the rich dream world of his poetry, peopled with fictional alter egos called "heteronyms," become well known. His important volumes include *Poesias de Fernando Pessoa* (1942), *Poesias de Álvaro de Campos* (1944), *Poemas de Alberto Caeiro* (1946), and *Odes de Ricardo Reis* (1946).

pest Any organism, usually an animal, judged as a threat to humans. Most pests either compete with humans for natural resources or transmit disease to humans, their crops, or their livestock. Invertebrate pests include some protozoans, flatworms, nematodes, mollusks, arachnids, and especially insects. Mammals and birds can also be pests. Human activities, such as monocultural farming practices, use of broad-spectrum pesticides, and introduction of exotic species, often result in the proliferation of pest species. Certain fungi, bacteria, and viruses are also considered pests. Plant pests are usually called WEEDS.

Pestalozzi \ˌpes-tə-'lōt-sē\, **Johann Heinrich** (1746–1827) Swiss educational reformer. Between 1805 and 1825 he directed the Yverdon Institute (near Neuchâtel), which drew pupils and educators (including FRIEDRICH FROEBEL) from all over Europe. His teaching method emphasized group rather than individual recitation and focused on such participatory activities as drawing, writing, singing, physical exercise, model making, collecting, mapmaking, and field trips. Among his ideas, considered radically innovative at the time, were making allowances for individual differences, grouping students by ability rather than age, and encouraging formal teacher training.

pesticide Any toxic substance used to kill animals or plants that damage crops or ornamental plants or are hazardous to the health of domestic animals or humans. All pesticides act by interfering with the target species' normal METABOLISM. They are often classified by the type of organisms they are intended to control (e.g., INSECTICIDE, HERBICIDE, FUNGICIDE). Many also inadvertently harm other organisms in the environment, either directly or via consumption of the target organism.

pet Any animal kept by humans for companionship or pleasure rather than for utility. The main distinction between pets and domesticated livestock is the degree of contact between owner and animal. Another distinction is the owner's affection for the animal, which is often returned. Dogs are known to have been kept as pets since prehistoric times; cats, since the 16th century BC; and horses, since at least 2000 BC. Other common pets include birds, rabbits, rodents, raccoons, reptiles, amphibians, and even insects. The trend toward making pets of exotic animals (e.g., monkeys and ocelots) is worrisome because owners can rarely provide for their needs, and the animals' already precarious populations are further depleted when members are sold for pets.

PET See POSITRON EMISSION TOMOGRAPHY

Pétain \pā-'ta^{n}\, **(Henri-) Philippe** (1856–1951) French general. He served in the French army from 1876 and later taught at the war college. His successful defense in the Battle of VERDUN (1916) made him a national hero, and in 1918 he became commander in chief and a marshal of France. After the war he was appointed vice president of the Supreme War Council (1920–30) and minister of war (1934). After the German invasion of France (1940), Pétain was appointed premier at age 84. He concluded an armistice with Germany, and as head of VICHY FRANCE he attempted to obtain concessions by cooperating with the Germans. In 1942 the Germans forced him to accept PIERRE LAVAL as premier and he withdrew to a nominal role as head of state. After the Allied invasion of France, he fled to Germany. In 1945 he was tried and condemned to death; the sentence was commuted to life in prison, where he died at 95.

Petén Itzá \pe-ˌten-ēt-'sä\, **Lago** Lake, northern Guatemala. It is about 27 mi (48 km) long and covers an area of 38 sq mi (98 sq km). The region was a stronghold of the Maya Itzá Indians, who were not conquered by the Spanish until 1697. The lakeshore is now dotted with modern towns, including Flores and San Benito. Much of the surrounding land is covered with dense rain forest, but there is some cultivation of cacao, sugarcane, and tropical fruits around Flores.

Peter I (died 969) Czar of Bulgaria (927–69). The second son of SIMEON I, he inherited the throne on his father's death in 927 but could not maintain the power of the Bulgarian empire, which was undermined by internal divisions and by the invasions of the MAGYARS, Byzantines, and others. Peter was forced to make concessions to the Byzantine emperor, ROMANUS I LECAPENUS, whose granddaughter he married.

Peter I *Russian* **Pyotr Alekseyevich** *known as* **Peter the Great** (1672–1725) Czar of Russia (1682–1725). Son of Czar ALEXIS, he reigned jointly with his half brother IVAN V 1682–96, and alone from 1696. Interested in progressive influences from Western Europe, he visited several countries there (1697–98). After returning to Russia, he introduced Western technology, modernized the government and military system, and transferred the capital to the new city of St. Petersburg (1703). He further increased the power of the monarchy at the expense of the nobles and the Orthodox church. Some of his reforms were implemented brutally, with considerable loss of life. Suspecting that his son Alexis was conspiring against him, he had Alexis tortured to death in 1718. He pursued foreign policies to give Russia access to the Baltic and Black seas, engaging in war with the Ottoman empire (1695–96) and with Sweden in the Second NORTHERN WAR (1700–21). His campaign against Persia (1722–23) secured for Russia the southern and western shores of the Caspian Sea. In 1721 he was proclaimed emperor; his wife succeeded him as the empress CATHERINE I. For raising Russia to a recognized place among the great European powers, Peter is widely considered one of the outstanding rulers and reformers in Russian history, but he has also been decried by nationalists for discarding much of what was unique in Russian culture, and his legacy has been seen as a model for JOSEPH STALIN's brutal transformation of Russian life.

Peter I (1844–1921) King of Serbia (1903–18) and of the Kingdom of Serbs, Croats, and Slovenes (later Yugoslavia) from 1918. The son of Prince Alexander Karageorgeviæ, who was forced to abdicate in 1858, he lived with his family in exile. He fought with the French army in the FRANCO-PRUSSIAN WAR and with the Serb revolt against the Turks (1875). After the assassination of Alexander Obrenovich (1903), Peter was elected king of Serbia. He advocated a constitutional government and won recognition for his liberal policies. In World War I, he allied Serbia with France and Russia but was defeated by the Central Powers. In 1918 he returned to Belgrade and was proclaimed king of the Serbs, Croats, and Slovenes.

Peter II *Russian* **Pyotr Alekseyevich** (1715–1730) Czar of Russia (1727–30). The grandson of PETER I, he was named heir to the throne by CATHERINE I and on her death was crowned at age 11. Peter's regency was directed by ALEKSANDR MENSHIKOV. He fell under the influence of the aristocratic Dolgoruky family, which ousted Menshikov as regent, moved the capital to Moscow (1728), and arranged Peter's betrothal to one of its princesses. On the day set for the wedding, Peter died of smallpox at 14.

Peter II (1923–1970) Last king of Yugoslavia. The son of ALEXANDER I, he became titular king on his father's assassination (1934), but ruled under the regency of his uncle Prince Paul (1893–1976). After a coup deposed Paul (1941), Peter ruled for several weeks until the German invasion forced him to flee to London. He led a government-in-exile until the Yugoslav monarchy was abolished in 1945. He moved to the U.S., where he worked in public relations.

Peter III *Spanish* **Pedro** *known as* **Peter the Great** (1239–1285) King of Aragon (1276–85) and of Sicily (as Pedro I, 1282–85). He married the Hohenstaufen heiress of Sicily (1262) and ended the Sicilian revolt (1282), becoming king despite Guelph and papal opposition (see SICILIAN VESPERS). Unhappy with his Sicilian venture, nobles and municipalities in Aragon forced Peter to confirm their legal rights and diminish crown rights. In 1285 he defeated Philip III of France, who had invaded Aragon in an effort to dethrone him.

Peter III *Russian* **Pyotr Fyodorovich** *orig.* **Karl Peter Ulrich, Herzog (Duke) von Holstein-Gottorp** (1728–1762) Czar of Russia (1762). Grandson of PETER I, the young duke was brought to Russia by his aunt ELIZABETH when she became empress (1741). Proclaimed the heir to the Russian throne, he was unpopular at court for his pro-Prussian attitude. After he succeeded Elizabeth (1762), he reversed her foreign policy, making peace with Prussia and withdrawing from the SEVEN YEARS' WAR. He offended the Orthodox church by trying to force it to adopt Lutheran practices. After six months he was forced to abdicate by a group of nobles, in collusion with his own wife, Catherine (later CATHERINE II), and COUNT GRIGORY G. ORLOV, and was murdered while in the conspirators' custody.

Peter IV *Spanish* **Pedro** *known as* **Peter the Cruel** (1319?–1387) King of Aragon (1336–87). He took the Balearic Islands and Roussillon from Majorca (1343–44), defeated the Aragonese nobles (1348), and became duke of Athens and Neopatras (1380). He waged war against Castile (1356–66) but failed to gain any territory; after 1369 France favored Castile over Aragon. Peter tried to maintain neutrality in the HUNDRED YEARS' WAR, and he quarreled with his heir, the future John I, who became the tool of French intrigues.

Peter Damian \'dā-mē-ən\, **St.** (1007–1072) Italian cardinal and doctor of the church. He was prior of Fonte Avellana in the Apennines before being named a cardinal in 1057. A leader of the 11th-century monastic reform movement, he played a leading role in the papal reforms of clerical celibacy and SIMONY and in the promotion of voluntary poverty. He defended Pope Alexander II against the ANTIPOPE Honorius II and reconciled Alexander with the city of Ravenna.

Peter Lombard (c. 1100–1160) French bishop and theologian. He studied in Bologna and taught theology in the school of Notre-Dame, Paris. He was consecrated bishop of Paris in 1159. His *Four Books of Sentences* (1148–51), a systematic collection of teachings of the Church Fathers and opinions of medieval theologians, served as the standard theological text of the Middle Ages. In it Peter touched on every doctrinal issue, from God and the Trinity to the "four last things" (death, judgment, hell, and heaven). He asserted that sacraments are the cause and not merely the signal of grace and that human actions may be judged good or bad according to their cause and intention.

Peter the Apostle, St. *orig.* **Simon** (died c. AD 64) Disciple of JESUS, recognized as the leader of the twelve APOSTLES. Jesus called him Cephas (Aramaic for "rock"; rendered in Greek as "Petros") and said "Upon this rock I will build my church." When Jesus was arrested, Peter denied him three times, as Jesus had foretold. Accounts of Peter's life and ministry rely on the four GOSPELS, the Acts of the Apostles, the epistles of Peter, and the epistles of St. PAUL. Peter worked with Paul in Antioch and later carried on missionary work in Asia Minor. He eventually suffered martyrdom. ST. PETER'S BASILICA is said to have been built on the site of his grave in Rome. In Roman Catholicism he is regarded as the first in the unbroken succession of POPES. Jesus' promise to give him the "keys of the kingdom" led to the popular perception of Peter as the gatekeeper of heaven.

Peter the Great See PETER I (RUSSIA), PETER III (Aragon)

Peter the Great Bay Inlet, Sea of JAPAN, northwestern Pacific Ocean, in southeastern Russia. It extends for 115 mi (185 km) from the mouth of the TUMEN RIVER northeast across to Cape Povorotny. The bay reaches inland for 55 mi (88 km) and contains the port of VLADIVOSTOK. The bay freezes from early December to mid-April.

Peter the Hermit (c. 1050–1115) French religious leader. A charismatic ascetic, he preached widely in Europe in support of the First CRUSADE and led his enthusiastic followers to Constantinople in 1096. They advanced to Nicomedia (modern Izmir, Turkey), but Peter was unable to maintain discipline; he returned to Constantinople to ask for help from ALEXIUS I, and in his absence his army was annihilated by the Turks. Peter reached Jerusalem in 1099 and afterwards returned to France, where he became prior of an Augustinian monastery.

Peter the Venerable (1092?–1156) French abbot of Cluny (from 1122). He joined BERNARD DE CLAIRVAUX in supporting Pope Innocent II and weakened the position of the antipope ANACLETUS II. He befriended PETER ABELARD and reconciled him to Bernard and the pope. Peter's reforms restored Cluny to its prominence among the religious establishments of Europe.

Peterhof See PETRODVORETS

Peterloo Massacre (August 16, 1819) Brutal dispersal of a meeting held on St. Peter's Fields in Manchester, England. Called to protest unemployment and high food prices and demand parliamentary reform, the meeting drew about 60,000 people, including many women and children. Alarmed by its size, city officials ordered the city's volunteer cavalry to arrest the speakers. The untrained cavalry also attacked the peaceable crowd with sabers, and professional soldiers were sent to join the attack. After a 10-minute rout, about 500 people lay injured and 11 were dead. The incident (likened to Waterloo) came to symbolize Tory tyranny.

Peters, Carl (1856–1918) German explorer and colonizer in East Africa. After studying British principles of colonization, he founded the Society for German Colonization (1884) and made treaties with chiefs in East Africa to cede their territories to him. He helped establish the German East African protectorate of Tanganyika and formed the German East Africa Co. in 1885. He served as imperial high commissioner for Kilimanjaro (1891–97) and explored the Zambezi River (1899–1901), where he discovered relics of ancient cities and gold mines.

Peter's Pence In medieval England, an annual tax of a penny paid by landowners to the papal treasury in Rome. Peter's Pence was instituted during the 7th or 8th century and continued until the 16th century. It also existed in several northern European kingdoms.

Petersburg Campaign (1864–65) Series of military operations in southern Virginia at the end of the AMERICAN CIVIL WAR. The rail center of Petersburg, Va., was a strategic defense point near the Confederate capital of Richmond. In June 1864 the Union army began a siege of both cities, and each side built fortifications 35 mi (56 km) long. Confederate troops under ROBERT E. LEE held the cities, but supplies were scarce and Lee's 50,000 troops were immobilized by lack of horses. In April 1865 the 120,000 Union troops under ULYSSES S. GRANT drove the Confederates behind the city's inner defenses. This forced the evacuation of both cities, and was soon followed by the surrender at Appomattox.

Peterson, Oscar (Emmanuel) (born 1925) Canadian pianist and composer, the greatest virtuoso of modern jazz piano. Peterson grew up in Montreal and studied classical piano. His jazz playing, influenced by ART TATUM and NAT KING COLE, is characterized by cascades of notes and an effervescent swing. After a Carnegie Hall debut in 1949 he became one of the busiest pianists in jazz, in demand as an accompanist, solo pianist, and leader of his own trio. An outstanding, extroverted improviser and sensitive accompanist, Peterson's playing demonstrates his roots in SWING as well as BEBOP.

Peterson, Roger Tory (1908–1996) U.S. ornithologist. Born in Jamestown, N.Y., he started drawing birds in high school. His *Field Guide to the Birds* (1934), illustrated with paintings that stressed the features that best identified a species in the field, greatly stimulated public interest in bird study in the U.S. and Europe. Many other guides followed. More responsible than any other person for fostering a widespread awareness of birds by the American public, he received such awards as the American Ornithologists' Union's Brewster Medal (1944) and the World Wildlife Fund's Gold Medal (1972).

Petipa \pā-tē-'pä\, **Marius** (1819–1910) French-Russian dancer and choreographer who greatly influenced modern classical Russian ballet. Born in Marseilles, he received his early training from his ballet-master father and was a principal dancer in France, Belgium, and Spain before joining the Imperial Theater in St. Petersburg in 1847. There he also created several ballets, including *The Pharaoh's Daughter,* which led to his appointment as chief choreographer in 1869. By his retirement in 1903, he had produced over 60 ballets for the imperial theaters in St. Petersburg and Moscow—including *Don Quixote* (1869), *La Camargo* (1872), *Sleeping Beauty* (1890), *Swan Lake* (1895), and *The Seasons* (1900)—which formed the core of the classical Russian repertoire.

Petit \pə-'tē\, **Roland** (born 1924) French dancer and choreographer. He danced with the Paris Opera Ballet in 1940–44. He then formed several companies, with which he toured Europe and the U.S. His dramatic ballets combined fantasy with elements of contemporary realism and included *Les forains* (1945), *Le jeune homme et la mort* (1946), and *Carmen* (1949). He choreographed dances in films in the 1950s, and later staged revues featuring his wife, Zizi Jeanmaire. In 1973 he became director of the Ballet de Marseille.

petit jury \'pe-tē\ *or* **trial jury** Jury of usually 12 persons that is impaneled to examine and decide the facts at issue in a trial. It is the standard jury for civil and criminal trials. It has less discretion than is often imagined. The trial judge supervises it, rules on what EVIDENCE it may view and which laws are applicable, and sometimes directs or, at the end of the trial, sets aside its verdict. See also GRAND JURY.

petition Written instrument directed to an individual, government official, legislative body, or court in order to seek redress of grievances or request a favor. When brought by a sufficient number of people (represented by their signatures), a petition can enable a candidate to get on a ballot, cause an issue to be submitted to the electorate (see REFERENDUM AND INITIATIVE), and exert pressure on legislators to vote in a certain way. In the U.S., the right to petition is guaranteed by the 1st Amendment to the Constitution.

Petition of Right (1628) Petition sent by Parliament to King CHARLES I complaining of a series of breaches of law. The petition sought recognition of four principles: no taxation without the consent of Parliament, no imprisonment without cause, no quartering of soldiers on subjects, and no martial law in peacetime. To continue receiving subsidies for his policies, Charles was compelled to accept the petition, but he later ignored its principles.

Petőfi \'pet-œ-fē\, **Sándor** (1823–1856?) Hungarian poet and revolutionary. He became famous with his first poetry volume, *Versek* (1844). Before the revolution of 1848 he wrote poems that glowed with political passion; one of them, "Talpra magyar" ("Rise, Hungarian"), became an anthem. He disappeared and was assumed dead in battle in 1849, but archives found in the 1980s revealed that he was marched to Siberia and died there. His works are characterized by realism, humor, descriptive power, and a peculiar vigor and have a direct style adapted from national folk songs. *János vitéz* (1845), an entrancing fairy tale, is his most popular epic.

Petra \'pē-trə\ Ruined city, southwestern Jordan. It was the capital of the Nabataean kingdom from c. 312 BC until its defeat by the Romans in AD 106, when it became part of the province of Arabia. After several centuries as a flourishing trade center, it declined with the shifting of trade routes to the EUPHRATES RIVER and the PERSIAN GULF. It was captured by the Muslims in the 7th century. Its ruins were discovered in 1812 by the Swiss traveler, Johann L. Burckhardt. Excavations have revealed many rock-cut monuments, including tombs with elaborate facades carved in the rose, crimson, and purple sandstone of the surrounding hills.

The Nabataean rock-cut monument of Ad-Dayr, Petra, Jordan.
BRIAN BRAKE FROM RAPHO/PHOTO RESEARCHERS—EB INC.

Petrarch \'pē-ˌträrk, 'pe-ˌträrk\ *Italian* **Francesco Petrarca** (1304–1374) Italian scholar, poet, and humanist. Born in Arezzo, after 1326 he abandoned the study of law for his true interests, literature and the religious life. He took minor ecclesiastical orders and moved to Avignon, where in 1327 he first saw Laura, the idealized subject of his chaste love and of his celebrated Italian love lyrics; mainly sonnets and odes written over about 20 years, most were included in his *Canzoniere* or *Rime* (1360). The greatest scholar of his age, especially of classical Latin, he traveled widely, visiting learned men, searching out manuscripts, and undertaking diplomatic missions. He strongly advocated the continuity between classical culture and the Christian message; in combining the two ideals he is considered the founder and a great representative of HUMANISM. His Latin works, reflecting his religious and philosophical interests, include *On Illustrious Men* (begun c. 1337), the epic poem *Africa* (begun c. 1338), the autobiographical treatise *Petrarch's Secret* (written 1342–58), *De vita solitaria* (1345–47; "The Life of Solitude"), and *Epistolae metricae* (begun c. 1345; "Metrical Letters"). After 1367 he lived in and near Padua. His influence on European literature was enormous and lasting, and his deep consciousness of the classical past as a source of literary and philosophical meaning for the present was of great importance in paving the way for the RENAISSANCE.

petrel Any of numerous seabirds (order Procellariiformes, particularly family Procellariidae), including 24 species (genera *Pterodroma* and *Bulweria*) called gadfly petrels because of their fluttering flight. Most are dark above and light below, with long wings and a short, wedge-shaped tail. They nest in colonies on tropical and subtropical islands. Both parents tend the single chick until it is almost fully fledged. During the nonbreeding season, petrels roam the open ocean, eating squid and small fishes. Species in the family Pelecanoididae are called diving petrels. See also FULMAR, SHEARWATER, STORM PETREL.

Petrie \'pē-trē\, **(William Matthew) Flinders** *later* **Sir Flinders** (1853–1942) British archaeologist who made valuable contributions to the techniques of EXCAVATION and DATING. During excavations in Egypt in the mid-1880s Petrie developed a sequence dating method, based on a comparison of potsherds at various levels, that made possible the reconstruction of ancient history from material remains. His excavations, together with those of HEINRICH SCHLIEMANN at Troy, marked the beginning of the examination of successive levels of a site, rather than the previously haphazard digging. He made many important discoveries in Egypt and Palestine. His *Methods and Aims in Archaeology* (1904) was the definitive work of its time. He taught at the University of London (1892–1933).

Petrified Forest National Park National park, eastern Arizona. Established as a national monument in 1906 and as a national park in 1962, it has an area of 146 sq mi (378 sq km). It features extensive exhibits of petrified wood in several "forest" areas, fossilized leaves, plants, and broken logs, and the PAINTED DESERT. Other features include petroglyphs and ancient PUEBLO INDIAN ruins.

petrified wood Fossil formed by the infiltration of minerals into cavities between and within cells of natural wood, usually by SILICA (silicon dioxide, SiO_2) or CALCITE (calcium carbonate, $CaCO_3$). Often this replacement of organic tissue by mineral deposits is so precise that the internal structure as well as the external shape is faithfully represented; sometimes even the cell structure may be determined.

Petrobrás \'pe-trō-ˌbräs\ *officially* **Petróleo Brasileiro SA** Brazilian oil and natural-gas company, the largest corporation in South America. It was founded in 1953 as a government-owned monopoly to prospect, extract, and refine domestic petroleum and to transport that oil and its derivatives. A government agency sets its policies and oversees its development. Although mainly devoted to developing petroleum sources in Brazil, Petrobrás also has interests in the Middle East, North Africa, and Colombia. In 1995, as part of a campaign to privatize state-owned industries, the Brazilian government ended the company's monopoly and allowed foreign competition. Petrobrás subsequently developed joint ventures with foreign businesses.

petrochemical Strictly, any of a large class of chemicals (as distinct from fuels) derived from PETROLEUM and NATURAL GAS. The category has been broadened to include a much larger range of organic compounds and a few inorganic compounds (including carbon black, SULFUR, and AMMONIA). Some materials are hard to classify because they have alternative sources (BENZENE from coal, ETHANOL from fermentation). Like crude oil and natural gas, most petrochemicals consist mainly of carbon and hydrogen and are called HYDROCARBONS. Petrochemicals used as raw materials ("feedstocks") include ETHYLENE (highest volume), propylene, butadiene, benzene, TOLUENE, xylene, and NAPHTHALENE. Petrochemical products include PLASTICS (POLYETHYLENE, polypropylene, polystyrene), SOAPS and DETERGENTS, SOLVENTS, DRUGS, FERTILIZERS, PESTICIDES, EXPLOSIVES, synthetic fibers, RUBBERS, paints, EPOXIES, flooring and insulating materials, luggage, and recording disks and tapes.

Petrodvorets \ˌpyi-trə-dvȧ-'ryets\ *formerly (until 1944)* **Peterhof** City (pop., 1995 est.: 82,000), northwestern Russia. Located near St. Petersburg, it was founded by PETER I THE GREAT as a country estate in 1709. After visiting France in 1717, he decided to create a residence that would rival the Palace of VERSAILLES. The Baroque Grand Palace (1714–28) was designed by Domenico Trezzini, and its gardens by Alexandre Le Blond (1679–1719). It became the most lavish and popular of the Russian royal summer residences. Today the Grand Palace (now a museum) and the vast park, with 39 mi (63 km) of canals that connect the intricate system of fountains, are part of the 2,500-acre (1,000-hectare) preserved area in the city of Petrodvorets.

Petrograd See SAINT PETERSBURG

petrol See GASOLINE

Petróleos de Venezuela, SA \ˌpe-trō-'lā-ōs-thā-ˌve-nəz-'wā-lə\ State-owned Venezuelan oil and natural-gas company. It was created in 1976 through the nationalization of Venezuela's petroleum industry, which had been controlled by foreign companies since the end of World War I. Petróleos de Venezuela engages in the exploration, refining, and marketing of oil, petrochemicals, and natural gas, including the export of petroleum and petroleum products. It earns the largest share of Venezuela's foreign currency. A member of the ORGANIZATION OF PETROLEUM EXPORTING COUNTRIES (OPEC), it tends to be a voice of moderation within the group. Its headquarters are in Caracas.

petroleum *or* **crude oil** Complex mixture of HYDROCARBONS derived from the geological transformation and decomposition of plants and animals that lived hundreds of millions of years ago. It occurs in the earth in liquid (crude oil), gaseous (NATURAL GAS), or solid (BITUMINOUS COAL, ASPHALT) forms. Petroleum and natural gas are the most important primary FOSSIL FUELS. Asphalt has been used since ancient times to caulk ships and pave roads. In the mid-1800s, oil began to replace whale oil in lamps, and the first well specifically for oil was drilled in 1859. The development of the automobile gave petroleum a new role as the source of GASOLINE. Petroleum and its products have since been used as fuels for heating, for land, air, and sea transport, and for electrical power generation, and as PETROCHEMICAL sources and lubricants. Crude oil and natural gas, produced mostly in Saudi Arabia, the U.S., and Russia, now account for about 60% of world energy consumption; the U.S. is by far the largest consumer. At present rates of consumption, the known supply will be exhausted by the mid-21st century. Petroleum is recovered from drilled wells, transported by pipeline or tanker ship to refineries, and there converted to fuels and petrochemicals.

petroleum trap Subsurface reservoir of petroleum. The oil is always accompanied by water and often by NATURAL GAS; all are confined in porous rock. The natural gas, being lightest, occupies the top of the trap and is underlain by the oil and then the water. A layer of impervious rock, called the roof rock, prevents the escape of the petroleum. The part of the trap that is actually occupied by the oil and gas is called the petroleum reservoir.

petrology Scientific study of rocks, including their composition, texture, and structure; occurrence and distribution; and conditions of origin. Petrology is concerned with all three major types of rocks: igneous, metamorphic, and sedimentary. The subdiscipline of experimental petrology involves synthesizing rocks in the laboratory to ascertain the physical and chemical conditions under which they form. The subdiscipline of petrography is concerned primarily with the systematic study and description of rocks using a petrographic microscope.

Petronas Towers \pe-'trō-nəs\ Twin stainless-steel-clad skyscrapers, linked by a skybridge, in Kuala Lumpur, Malaysia. With 88 stories and a height of 1,483 ft (452 m), a figure that includes the pinnacle atop each tower, the towers are considered the world's tallest buildings (though, when measured by the roof line, the SEARS TOWER is higher). Designed by Cesar Pelli (born 1926), the circular, step-tapered towers, completed in 1998, house the headquarters of Malaysia's national petroleum company. Their structural frames consist of high-strength, steel-reinforced concrete.

Petronius Arbiter, Gaius *orig.* **Titus Petronius Niger** (died AD 66) Roman writer. Of a noble family, Petronius belonged to a class of idle pleasure-seekers, but served ably as governor of the Asian province of Bithynia and as consul in Rome. After being appointed NERO's authority on taste (hence "Arbiter"), he was accused of plotting to kill the emperor and, though innocent, committed suicide. He is the reputed author of the *Satyricon*, a comic picaresque novel vividly portraying contemporary Roman society through the escapades of a disreputable trio of adventurers, with unrelated stories and the author's commentaries on Roman life interspersed.

Petty, Richard (born 1937) U.S. stock-car racer. Born in Level Cross, N.C., he entered professional stock-car racing in 1958. In his long professional career he would win 200 races. In 1975 he set the NASCAR record of 13 victories in one season. "King Richard" also won seven Daytona 500 races and seven NASCAR grand national championships. His father, son, and grandson were all former or current NASCAR racers.

Petty, William *later* **Sir William** (1623–1687) British political economist and statistician. He gave up a life at sea to study medicine, and taught anatomy at Oxford. He founded mines, ironworks, and fisheries in Ireland, was responsible for several inventions, and was a founder of the Royal Society. He was an originator of political arithmetic, which he defined as the art of reasoning by figures upon things relating to government. In his best-known work, *Treatise of Taxes and Contributions* (1662), he favored giving free rein to the forces of individual self-interest but declared the maintenance of a high level of employment to be a duty of the state. He also argued that the labor necessary for production was the main determinant of exchange value.

petunia Any of many species of flowering plants in the genus *Petunia,* in the nightshade family, which originated in South America. The innumerable varieties of showy, trumpet-shaped flowers are immensely popular. There are two types: the compact, erect sort seen in summer garden beds, and the sprawling, long-stemmed sort seen in hanging baskets and window boxes. From early summer until frost, petunias bloom profusely with single or double blossoms; crisped, fringed, or ruffled flowers; and spectacular hues from pure white to deep crimson or purple, speckled or veined in contrasting colors. Leaves are soft, flabby, and covered with fine, sticky hairs. Technically perennials, petunias are most often grown as annuals.

Pevsner \'pevz-nər\, **Antoine** *orig.* **Natan Borisovich Pevzner** (1886–1962) Russian-French sculptor and painter. After travels to Paris and Oslo, he returned to become a professor at Moscow's school of fine arts. He helped form the Suprematist group (see Suprematism), and in 1920 he and his brother, Naum Gabo, issued the *Realist Manifesto* of Constructivism. He settled in Paris in 1923. He used zinc, brass, copper, and celluloid for his early sculptures; later he relied mainly on parallel arrays of bronze wire soldered together to form plates, which he joined to form intricate shapes.

Pevsner \'pefs-nər\, **Nikolaus** *later* **Sir Nikolaus** (1902–1983) German-British art historian. He studied at various German universities and taught at Göttingen University (1929–33) before moving to England to escape Nazism. There he taught at the Univs. of London, Oxford, and Cambridge. He is best known for his writings on architecture, especially his 46-volume series of county-by-county guides, *The Buildings of England* (1951–74), one of the great achievements of 20th-century scholarship. He conceived and edited the *Pelican History of Art* series (1953–), many of whose individual volumes have become classics.

pewter Tin-based alloy used to make domestic utensils. Pewter dates back at least 2,000 years, to Roman times. Ancient pewter contained about 70% tin and 30% lead. Such pewter, also called black metal, darkened greatly with age, and the lead readily leached out in contact with acidic foods. Pewter with little or no lead is of finer quality, and alloys that include antimony and bismuth are more durable and shinier. Modern pewter is about 91% tin, 7.5% antimony, and 1.5% copper; the absence of lead makes it safe to use for foods and beverages. The surface of modern pewter is bluish white with either a bright finish or a soft, satin sheen. It resists tarnish, retaining its color and finish indefinitely.

peyote \pā-'ō-tē\ Either of two species of the genus *Lophophora* in the cactus family, native to North America, almost exclusively to Mexico. The body of the peyote cactus is spineless, soft, usually blue-green, and only 3 in. (8 cm) wide and 2 in. (5 cm) tall. The more common species, mescal *(L. williamsii),* has pink to white flowers. *L. diffusa,* more primitive, has white to yellow flowers and a yellow-green body. Well known for its hallucinogenic effects (primarily due to the alkaloid mescaline), peyote figures prominently in old and recent religious rituals of certain American Indian peoples. The sale, use, or possession of dried mescal buttons (flowering heads) or live plants is prohibited by law in many places.

Peyote (*Lophophora williamsii*).
DENNIS E. ANDERSON

peyotism See Native American Church

Pfeiffer \'fī-fər\, **Michelle** (born 1957) U.S. film actress. Born in Santa Ana, Cal., she made her movie debut in 1980. After winning acclaim in *The Witches of Eastwick* (1987) she became a major star, noted for her beauty and air of vulnerability. Her many films include *Dangerous Liaisons* (1988), *The Fabulous Baker Boys* (1989), *Frankie and Johnny* (1991), *Batman Returns* (1992), *The Age of Innocence* (1993), and *Dangerous Minds* (1995).

pH Quantitative measure of the strength of the acid (and base) in a solution, defined as the negative common logarithm of the concentration of hydrogen ions (H^+) in moles/liter (written in square brackets): $pH = -\log_{10}[H^+]$. Its name comes from the fact that pH is the absolute value of the power (p) of the hydrogen ion concentration (H). The product of the concentrations in water of H^+ and OH^- (the hydroxide ion) is always about 10^{-14}. The strongest acid solution has about 1 mole/liter of H^+ (and about 10^{-14} of OH^-), for a pH of 1. The strongest basic solution has about 10^{-14} moles/liter of H^+ (and about 1 of OH^-), for a pH of 14. A neutral solution has about 10^{-7} moles/liter of both H^+ and OH^-, for a pH of 7. The pH value, measured by a pH meter, titration, or indicator (e.g., litmus) strips, helps inform chemists of the nature, composition, or extent of reaction of substances, biologists of the composition and environment of organisms or their parts or fluids, physicians of the functioning of bodily systems, and agronomists of the suitability of soils for crops and any treatments needed. The pH is now defined in electrochemical terms (see electrochemistry).

Phaedra \'fē-drə\ In Greek legend, the daughter of King Minos. She became the second wife of Theseus after he abandoned her sister Ariadne. She later fell in love with her stepson Hippolytus; rejected, she accused him of rape. He was killed, and she hanged herself.

Phaedrus \'fē-drəs\ (c. 15 BC–c. AD 50) Roman fabulist. A slave by birth, Phaedrus became a freedman in Augustus' household. He was the first writer to Latinize whole books of fables, producing free versions in iambic meter of Greek prose fables then circulating under the name of Aesop. Phaedrus' renderings, noted for their charm, brevity, and didacticism, became very popular in medieval Europe; they include such favorites as "The Fox and the Sour Grapes" and "The Wolf and the Lamb."

Phaethon \'fā-ə-thən\ In Greek mythology, the son of Helios, the sun god, and a nymph. Taunted as illegitimate, Phaethon asked for permission to drive the chariot of the sun through the heavens for a single day in order to prove that Helios was his father. He proved unable to control the horses, and, after making a gash in the heavens that became the Milky Way, he rode too close to earth and began to scorch it. To prevent further damage, Zeus hurled a thunderbolt, killing him.

Phag-mo-gru family \'fäg-mō-grü\ Tibetan family that in the 14th century liberated Tibet from Mongol control. At that time Tibet was governed by lamas from the Sa-skya monastery who resided at the Mongol (Yuan) court in China. Under Byang-chub rgyal-mtshan (1302–1364), the Phag-mo-gru liberated central Tibet. For the next 100 years, a semblance of central authority was reestablished in the country.

phage See bacteriophage

phalanger See possum

phalanx \'fā-,laŋks\ Tactical formation consisting of a block of heavily armed infantry standing shoulder to shoulder in files several ranks deep. First used by the Sumerians and fully developed by the ancient Greeks, it is viewed today as the beginning of European military development. The Greek city-states adopted a phalanx eight men deep during the 7th century BC. The spectacle of Greek hoplites marching forward in solid ranks was frightening to the enemy, but the phalanx was difficult to maneuver and easily thrown into confusion if its ranks were broken.

phalarope \'fa-lə-ˌrōp\ Any of three species (genus *Phalaropus,* family Scolopacidae) of slim-necked shorebirds, 6–10 in. (25–25 cm) long, with lobed toes and a straight, slender bill. In summer, their gray-and-white plumage has red markings. Females fight for nesting territory and court the males; males, smaller and duller, do all the nesting duties and lead the young south in autumn. Two species breed around the Arctic Circle and winter on tropical oceans, where they are known as sea snipe. Wilson's phalarope *(P. tricolor)* breeds in western North America and migrates to the Argentine pampas.

Phan Boi Chau \'pän-'bȯi-'chau̇\ *or* **Phan Giai San** \'pän-'gyī-'sän\ *orig.* **Phan Van San** (1867–1940) Vietnamese resistance figure. Son of a poor scholar, he received a doctorate in 1900, by which time he was already a firm nationalist. Opposed to French rule in Vietnam, he organized efforts to place the nationalist Prince Cuong De (1882–1951) on the throne. In 1905 he moved his resistance movement to Japan, where he met SUN YAT-SEN and PHAN CHAU TRINH. His monarchist scheme failed, as did a plan to assassinate the French governor-general of Indochina, and Chau was imprisoned 1914–17. Hundreds of Vietnamese protested when he was arrested again in 1925; subsequently released, he spent his remaining years in quiet retirement.

Phan Chau Trinh \'pän-'chü-'trin\ (1872–1926) Vietnamese nationalist leader and reformer. Trinh, who fought in the resistance movement even as a boy, came to believe that modernization was a prerequisite for development of an autonomous state, and thus made modernization his primary goal. He urged replacing the civil-service system with vocational schools and commercial firms, but his attempts to persuade the French to undertake major reforms failed and he was twice imprisoned. He was mourned as a national hero after his death. See also PHAN BOI CHAU.

Phanerozoic eon \ˌfa-nə-rə-'zō-ik\ Span of geologic time from c. 543 million years ago, the end of the PROTEROZOIC EON, to the present. The Phanerozoic, the eon of visible life, is divided into three major eras: the PALEOZOIC, MESOZOIC, and CENOZOIC. Although life originated in PRECAMBRIAN TIME, it was in the Phanerozoic that many forms arose and evolved. The earth gradually assumed its present configuration and physical features through such processes as PLATE TECTONICS, mountain building, and glaciation.

pharaoh \'fer-ō\ Title applied to Egyptian kings from c. 1500 BC on. Pharaohs were regarded as gods, retaining their divine status even after death. A pharaoh's will was supreme, and he governed by royal decree, with the assistance of VIZIERS. The common people nevertheless judged a pharaoh by his deeds; many were criticized, plotted against, and even deposed and killed. See also AKHENATON, AMENEMHET I, AMENHOTEP II, AMENHOTEP III, RAMSES II, THUTMOSE III, TUTANKHAMEN.

Pharisee \'far-ə-ˌsē\ Member of a Jewish religious party in Palestine that emerged c. 160 BC in opposition to the SADDUCEES. The Pharisees held that the Jewish oral tradition was as valid as the TORAH. They struggled to democratize the Jewish religion, arguing that the worship of God was not confined to the Temple of JERUSALEM and fostering the SYNAGOGUE as an institution of worship. Their belief that reason must be applied in the interpretation of the Torah and its application to contemporary problems is now basic to Jewish theology.

pharmaceutical industry Producers of pharmaceuticals, substances used in the diagnosis, treatment, and prevention of disease and the modification of organic functions. The earliest records of medicinal plants and minerals are those of the ancient Chinese, Hindu, and Mediterranean civilizations. Medicines were prepared first by physicians and later by apothecary shops. The modern pharmaceutical industry began in the 19th century with the discovery of highly active medicinal compounds that could be manufactured most efficiently on a large scale. As these drugs replaced the herbal medicines of earlier times, the occurrence and severity of such diseases as rheumatic fever, typhoid fever, pneumonia, poliomyelitis, syphilis, and tuberculosis were greatly reduced. Many drugs are extracted from plant substances; alkaloids such as quinine, cocaine, and morphine are among the best-known examples. Others are made from animal substances, such as the glandular extracts that are used to produce insulin. Pharmaceutical industry research has greatly aided medical progress, and many new drugs have been discovered and produced in industrial laboratories. Increasing health-care costs, government regulation, and research ethics are all issues of concern to the industry.

pharmacology \ˌfär-mə-'käl-ə-jē\ Branch of MEDICINE dealing with the actions of DRUGS in the body—both therapeutic and toxic effects—and development and testing of new drugs and new uses of existing ones. Though the first Western pharmacological treatise (a listing of herbal plants) was compiled in the 1st century AD, scientific pharmacology was only possible from the 18th century on, when drugs could be purified and standardized. In the U.S., the FOOD AND DRUG ADMINISTRATION regulates drug development. Pharmacologists develop drugs from plant and animal sources and create synthetic versions of these, along with new drugs based on them or their chemical structure. They also test drugs, first in vitro (in the laboratory) for biochemical activity and then in vivo (on animals, human volunteers, and patients) for safety, effectiveness, side effects, and interactions with other drugs and to find the best dose, timing, and route (mouth, injection, etc.). Drug products are constantly tested for potency and purity. See also MEDICINAL POISONING, PHARMACY.

pharmacy Science dealing with collection, preparation, and standardization of DRUGS. Pharmacists, who must earn a qualifying degree, prepare and dispense prescribed medications. They formerly mixed and measured drug products from raw materials according to doctors' prescriptions, and are still responsible for formulating, storing, and providing correct dosages of medicines, now usually produced by pharmaceutical companies as premeasured tablets or capsules. They also advise patients on the use of both prescription and over-the-counter drugs. Laws regulating the pharmaceutical industry are based on the national pharmacopoeia (in the U.S., the U.S. Pharmacopoeia or USP), which outlines the purity and dosages of numerous medicinal products.

Pharsalus \fär-'sā-ləs\, **Battle of** (48 BC) Decisive engagement in the Roman civil war between Julius CAESAR and POMPEY. Caesar had recently been defeated by Pompey when the two met again in Greece. Though Pompey had twice as many men, Caesar used unorthodox tactics to overwhelm him. Pompey fled and about half his men surrendered; the rest were killed or took flight.

pharyngeal tonsils See ADENOIDS

pharyngitis \ˌfar-ən-'jī-təs\ INFLAMMATION and INFECTION (usually bacterial or viral) of the PHARYNX. Symptoms include pain (sore throat, worse on swallowing), redness, swollen lymph nodes, and fever. Throat culture may be the only way to distinguish infection with STREPTOCOCCUS bacteria (strep throat), which can cause RHEUMATIC FEVER if not treated in time with ANTIBIOTICS, from viral infections, which do not respond to antibiotics and require only symptom relief.

pharynx \'far-iŋks\ Inside of the throat, from the oral and nasal cavities (see MOUTH, NOSE) to the TRACHEA and ESOPHAGUS. It has three connected sections: the nasopharynx, at the back of the nasal cavity; the oropharynx, in the back of the oral cavity down to the epiglottis (a flap of tissue that closes off the LARYNX during swallowing); and the laryngopharynx, from the epiglottis to the esophagus. The oropharynx contains the palatine TONSILS. The eustachian tubes connect the middle EARS to the pharynx, allowing air pressure on the eardrum to be equalized. Disorders include PHARYNGITIS, TONSILLITIS, and cancer.

phase In THERMODYNAMICS, a chemically and physically uniform quantity of matter that can be separated mechanically from a nonhomogeneous mixture. It may consist of a single substance or of a mixture of substances. The three basic phases of matter are SOLID, LIQUID, and GAS; other phases that are considered to exist include crystalline (see CRYSTAL), colloidal (see COLLOID), GLASS, amorphous, and PLASMA. The different phases of a pure substance are related to each other in terms of TEMPERATURE and PRESSURE. For example, if the temperature of a solid is raised enough, or the pressure is reduced enough, it will become a liquid.

phase In wave motion, the fraction of the time required to complete a full cycle that a point completes after last passing through the reference position. Two PERIODIC MOTIONS are said to be in phase when corresponding points of each reach maximum or minimum displacements at the same time. If the crests of two waves pass the same point at the same time, they are in phase for that position. If the crest of one and the trough of the other pass the same point at the same time, the phase angles differ by 180° and the waves are said to be of opposite phase. Phase differences are important in alternating electric current technology (see ALTERNATING CURRENT).

pheasant Any of about 50 species of mostly long-tailed birds in the family Phasianidae (order Galliformes), chiefly Asian but naturalized elsewhere. Most species inhabit open woodlands and brushy fields. All have a hoarse call. The feet and lower legs are unfeathered. Females are inconspicuous. Most males are strikingly colored and have one or more leg spurs; some have a fleshy facial ornament. Males sometimes fight to the death for a harem of hens. Male ring-necked or common pheasants *(Phasianus colchicus),* 35 in. (90 cm) long, have a streaming tail, coppery breast, purplish green neck, and ear tufts; they are widespread in the northern U.S. Japanese green pheasants *(P. versicolor)* call in concert when an earthquake is imminent.

Common pheasant (*Phasianus colchicus*).

H. REINHARD—BRUCE COLEMAN INC./EB INC.

Pheidias See PHIDIAS

phenol \'fē-ˌnōl, 'fē-ˌnȯl\ Any of a class of organic compounds with a hydroxyl group (–OH; see FUNCTIONAL GROUP) attached to a carbon atom in a ring of an AROMATIC COMPOUND. The simplest one, CARBOLIC ACID (C_6H_5OH), is also called phenol. Phenols are similar to ALCOHOLS but form stronger hydrogen bonds with water (see BONDING), so they dissolve more readily in water and boil at higher temperatures. They may be colorless liquids or white solids; many have a sharp, spicy odor. Some are found in ESSENTIAL OILS. Phenols with higher MOLECULAR WEIGHTS and phenol derivatives have supplanted phenol itself as industrial ANTISEPTICS.

phenol See CARBOLIC ACID

phenomenalism View that facts about material objects are reducible to facts about actual and possible SENSE-DATA. According to phenomenalists, a material object is not a mysterious something "behind" the appearances presented in sensation. If it were, the material world would be unknowable; indeed, the term matter itself would be unintelligible unless it somehow could be defined by reference to sensations. In speaking about a material object, then, reference must be made to a system of possible and actual sense-data. In this way, an "empirical cash value" can be given to the concept of matter by analyzing it in terms of sensations. See also GEORGE BERKELEY.

phenomenology Philosophical discipline originated by EDMUND HUSSERL. Husserl developed the phenomenological method to make possible "a descriptive account of the essential structures of the directly given." Phenomenology emphasizes the immediacy of experience, the attempt to isolate it and set it off from all assumptions of existence or causal influence and lay bare its essential structure. Phenomenology restricts the philosopher's attention to the pure data of consciousness, uncontaminated by metaphysical theories or scientific assumptions. Husserl's concept of the life-world—as the individual's personal world as directly experienced—expressed this same idea of immediacy. With the appearance of the *Annual for Philosophical and Phenomenological Research* (1913–30), under Husserl's editorship, his personal philosophizing flowered into an international movement. Its most notable adherents were MAX SCHELER and MARTIN HEIDEGGER.

phenotype \'fē-nə-ˌtīp\ All the observable characteristics of an organism, such as shape, size, color, and behavior, that result from the interaction of its GENOTYPE (total genetic makeup) with the environment. The common type of a group of physically similar organisms is sometimes also known as the phenotype. The phenotype may change throughout the life of an individual because of environmental changes and the changes associated with aging. Different environments can influence the development of inherited traits (e.g., size is affected by available food supply) and can alter expression by similar genotypes (e.g., twins brought up in dissimilar families may mature differently). Furthermore, not all inherited possibilities in the genotype are expressed in the phenotype, because some are the result of inactive, recessive, or inhibited genes. See also VARIATION.

phenylalanine \ˌfe-nᵊl-'a-lə-ˌnēn, ˌfē-nᵊl-'a-lə-ˌnēn\ One of the essential AMINO ACIDS, present in many common PROTEINS, especially HEMOGLOBIN. It is used in medicine and nutrition and as one of the two amino acids making up ASPARTAME. Persons with PHENYLKETONURIA do not metabolize phenylalanine properly and must adhere to a diet free of it.

phenylketonuria \ˌfe-nᵊl-ˌkē-tᵊn-'u̇r-ē-ə\ **(PKU)** *or* **phenylpyruvic oligophrenia** \ˌfe-nᵊl-pī-ˌrü-vik-ˌäl-i-gō-'frē-nē-ə\ Inability to normally metabolize PHENYLALANINE, whose accumulation interferes with normal childhood development. Central NERVOUS-SYSTEM effects include mental retardation and seizures (see EPILEPSY), with behavioral signs seen at four to six months of age. Abnormal metabolism also leads to low MELANIN levels, with light hair, eye, and skin color. Tests detect this recessive genetic disorder (see CONGENITAL DISORDER, RECESSIVENESS) in two-thirds of the one in 10,000 newborns born with high levels of phenylalanine. Keeping phenylalanine out of the diet (by total avoidance of meat, dairy, and high-protein foods, and ASPARTAME) until adolescence permits normal development. Protein is supplied in a phenylalanine-free drink. Pregnant women with PKU must resume the diet to prevent severe damage to the unborn child.

pheromone \'fer-ə-ˌmōn\ Any chemical compound secreted by an organism in minute amounts to elicit a particular reaction from other organisms of the same species. Pheromones are widespread among insects and vertebrates (except birds) and are present in some fungi, slime molds, and algae. The chemicals may be secreted by special GLANDS or incorporated into other substances (e.g., urine), shed freely or deposited in selected locations. Pheromones are used to bring creatures together (e.g., in termite, bee, and ant colonies), lead them to food (e.g., in scent trails laid by ants), signal danger (e.g., when released by wounded fish to alert others), attract a mate and elicit sexual behavior (numerous examples, possibly including humans), and influence sexual development (in many mammals and certain insects). Alarm pheromones often last a shorter time and travel a shorter distance than other types. In vertebrates, chemical stimuli often influence parent–young responses. Sex-attractant pheromones are used in certain products to lure and trap unwanted or harmful insects.

Phi Beta Kappa Leading honor society in the U.S., which draws its membership from college and university students. The oldest Greek-letter society in the U.S., it was founded in 1776 as a secret literary and philosophical society at College of WILLIAM AND MARY. It became an honor society in the 19th century. Membership is now based on general scholarship, and new members are usually elected by Phi Beta Kappa faculty.

Phibunsongkhram \'pē-bu̇n-sȯŋ-ˌkräm\, **Luang** *orig.* **Plaek Khittasangkha** (1897–1964) Field marshal and premier of Thailand (1938–44, 1948–57). After military training in France, he helped organize the PROMOTERS REVOLUTION of 1932 that ended absolute monarchy in Siam. In 1939 he changed the country's name to Thailand. As premier during World War II he allied himself with Japan; as the war turned against Japan, his government collapsed. The army seized power in 1947 and he was reinstalled as premier in 1948. Opposed to communism, he further allied Thailand to the West during the Cold War by helping establish the S.EAST ASIA TREATY ORGANIZATION. He was ousted by his military colleagues in 1957 and fled to Japan.

Phidias \'fid-ē-əs\ *or* **Pheidias** \'fī-dē-əs\ (c. 490–430 BC) Greek sculptor. Placed in charge of the great building program initiated by PERICLES in Athens, he supervised and probably designed the overall sculptural decoration of the PARTHENON. He also created its most important religious images, including the colossal statue of the Athena Parthenos (438–436). Many of the Parthenon's sculptures (the ELGIN MARBLES) are now in the British Museum. Ancient writers considered his masterpiece to be the statue of Zeus (c. 430) for the Temple of Zeus at Olympia. He initiated the idealistic classical style that distinguishes Greek art in the later 5th and 4th century BC.

"Heracles," marble statue produced in the workshop of Phidias, from the eastern pediment of the Parthenon, the Acropolis, Athens, c. 5th century BC; in the British Museum.

BY COURTESY OF THE TRUSTEES OF THE BRITISH MUSEUM; PHOTOGRAPH, J.R. FREEMAN & CO. LTD.

Philadelphia City (pop., 1996 est.: 1,478,000) and port, southeastern Pennsylvania, at the confluence of the Delaware and Schuylkill rivers. The site was occupied by the Delaware Indians before William Penn founded the city in 1682. It was the capital of Pennsylvania 1683–1799 and the capital of the U.S. 1790–1800. It played a prominent role in opposing British policies and was the site of the first and second Continental Congresses, the signing of the Declaration of Independence, and the Constitutional Convention. The population grew in the 18th century, with many immigrants from Scotland, Ireland, and Germany. It was the largest and most important city of the U.S. in the 19th century and a center of the antislavery movement. In 1876 it was the site of the U.S. Centennial Exposition. It is also the site of the U.S.'s oldest art museum (1805) and the first U.S. hospital (1751). It is the largest city in the state and a center of commerce, finance, industry, and culture. Its numerous educational institutions include the University of Pennsylvania.

Philadelphia Inquirer Morning newspaper, long one of the most influential dailies in the eastern U.S. Founded in 1847 as the *Pennsylvania Inquirer,* it took its present name c. 1860. It was a strong supporter of the North in the American Civil War. In the 19th and early 20th century it survived circulation wars by providing broad news coverage and by constantly modernizing its plant and equipment. Bought by Moses Annenberg in 1936, it stayed in his family's hands until 1969, when it was acquired by John S. Knight. In 1974 it became part of the merged Knight-Ridder Newspapers group.

Philae \'fī-lē\ Former island in the Nile River in Upper Egypt. It was sacred to Isis and contained many temples, the earliest dating from the 7th century BC. After the completion of the Aswan High Dam in 1970, the temples were moved to the nearby island of Agilkia before Philae was submerged by the waters behind the dam.

philanthropy In Christian theology, love of humanity; more broadly, love of, or beneficent service on behalf of, humanity. Philanthropy is rooted in Christian anthropology, which sees Christ in everyone. In the fellow human, Christians see the image of the present Lord, who became human, suffered, died, and was resurrected in order to lead all humanity back into the Kingdom of God. From the beginning of church history, the doctrine of election (see Calvinism, predestination) has been opposed by the idea that God's love of humanity is greater than the righteousness that craves the eternal damnation of the guilty. Since the time of Origen, this second attitude is found among mystics, both in the Eastern Church and in Western Christendom.

Philaretus See Arnold Geulincx

philately \fə-'la-tᵊl-ē\ Collection and study of postage stamps. The first postage stamps were issued in England in 1840, and in the U.S. in 1842. Stamp collectors usually specialize, collecting stamps of one country, one period of time, or one subject (e.g., birds, flowers, art). Value depends on rarity and condition. An issue of stamps that includes a printer's error may have increased value.

Inverted airplane airmail stamp, U.S., 1918.
LEE BOLTON

Philby, Kim *orig.* **Harold Adrian Russell** (1912–1988) British intelligence officer and Soviet spy. He became a communist at Cambridge University in the 1930s, and in 1933 a Soviet agent. Recruited into the MI-6 section of British intelligence by Guy Burgess (1940), he became head of counterespionage operations. In 1949 he was sent to Washington, D.C., as top liaison officer between British and U.S. intelligence services. He revealed top-secret information to the Soviets and in 1951 warned Burgess and Donald Maclean (1913–1983) that they were under suspicion, enabling them to escape. Philby himself came under suspicion and was dismissed from MI-6 in 1955. He worked as a journalist in Beirut, then fled to the Soviet Union in 1963. There he worked for the KGB and rose to the rank of colonel. The most successful Soviet double agent of the Cold War period, he was responsible for the deaths of many Western agents.

Philemon and Baucis \fi-'lē-mən...'bȯ-sis\ In Greek mythology, a pious old couple in Phrygia. When Zeus and Hermes, disguised as wayfarers, had been turned away by the couple's richer neighbors, Philemon and Baucis extended them hospitality. As a reward they were spared when a flood swept the countryside. Their cottage was turned into a temple, and they became priest and priestess of it. Years later they were granted their wish to die at the same moment, and they were turned into trees.

Philip (of Swabia) *German* **Philipp** (1178–1208) German Hohenstaufen king (1198–1208). The youngest son of Frederick I Barbarossa, he was elected German king on the death of Emperor Henry VI. The rival Welf dynasty elected Otto IV king, and a civil war broke out. A truce was finally called in 1207; Innocent III recognized Philip and promised to crown him emperor (1208), but Philip was murdered first.

Philip, Duke of Edinburgh *known as* **Prince Philip** (born 1921) Husband of Queen Elizabeth II of Britain. Son of Prince Andrew of Greece and Denmark (1882–1944) and Princess Alice (1885–1969), a great-granddaughter of Queen Victoria, he was reared in Britain. In World War II he served in combat with the Royal Navy. In 1947 he became a British subject, taking his mother's surname, Mountbatten, and renouncing his right to the Greek and Danish thrones. He married Princess Elizabeth in 1947 and continued on active service in the navy until her accession to the throne in 1952. Charles, Prince of Wales, is their son.

Philip, King See Metacom

Philip II *French* **Philippe** *known as* **Philip the Bold** (1342–1404) Duke of Burgundy (1363–1404). He was granted the duchy of Burgundy by his father, John II, and by marriage and purchase he acquired additional lands in northern and central France, Flanders, and the Netherlands. He shared the government with his brothers during the minority of his nephew Charles VI, ensuring friendly relations with England and Germany. When Charles went insane (1392), Philip became virtual ruler of France. He formed an alliance with England (1396) and withdrew his support of the Avignon papacy (1398).

Philip II *French* **Philippe** *known as* **Philip Augustus** (1165–1223) French king (1179–1223). The first of the great Capetian kings, he gradually reconquered the French territories held by the kings of England. He joined with Richard I on the Third Crusade, but the two kings soon quarreled. Philip returned to France (1191) and attacked English possessions; imprisoned in Austria on his journey home, Richard was freed in 1194 and promptly went to war with the French. When Richard was killed (1199), his brother John signed a treaty with Philip (1200), but within two years France and England were again at war. Philip conquered Normandy (1204) and subdued Maine, Touraine, Anjou, and most of Poitou (1204–5). John later organized a coalition against France, but he was defeated by Philip at the Battle of Bouvines (1214). Philip also expanded his territory into Flanders and Languedoc.

Philip II *or* **Philip of Macedonia** (382–336 BC) 18th king of Macedonia (359–336 BC), father of Alexander the Great. Appointed regent for his nephew, he seized the throne. He initially promoted peace with his neighbors, using the time gained to build his forces, introducing innovations in arms, tactics, and training and stabilizing his western frontier. His movements on the eastern frontier provoked the Greeks into forming a coalition against him. He intervened in the Sacred War to free Delphi from the Phocians, becoming the ally of Thebes and the Thessalian League, whose president he became. Demosthenes turned Athens against him with his *Philippics* (346–342), and Thebes also came to view Philip as a threat. He defeated both at the Battle of Chaeronea, becoming leader of all Greece. He formed the Greek states into the League of Corinth to attack Persia, but was undone by family politics. As he had taken a second wife, his first wife, Olympias, left him, taking Alexander. Philip was assassinated by a Macedonian nobleman, possibly in collusion with Olympias and Alexander.

Philip II *Spanish* **Felipe** \fā-'lē-pā\ (1527–1598) King of Spain (1556–98) and of Portugal (as Philip I, 1580–98). The son of Emperor Charles V, Philip received from his father the duchy of Milan (1540), the kingdoms of Naples and Sicily (1554), the Netherlands (1555), and Spain and its overseas empire (1556). He ruled from the Netherlands from 1555 and waged a successful war against France in 1557. From 1559 he ruled from Spain, where he built the palace of El Escorial and encouraged Spain's literary golden age. He was a champion of the COUNTER-REFORMATION but failed to put down rebellions in the Netherlands (from 1568) and to conquer England, suffering the defeat of the Spanish ARMADA (1588). He gained a victory in the Mediterranean with the defeat of the Ottoman offensive at the Battle of LEPANTO (1571) and unified the Iberian Peninsula as king of Portugal from 1580. During his reign the Spanish empire attained its greatest power, extent, and influence.

Philip II, detail of an oil painting by Titian; in the Corsini Gallery, Rome.
ALINARI–ART RESOURCE

Philip III *French* **Philippe** *known as* **Philip the Good** (1396–1467) Duke of BURGUNDY (1419–67). The most important of the VALOIS dukes of Burgundy, he founded the Burgundian state that rivaled France in the 15th century. He confirmed his right to Burgundy by signing the Treaty of Troyes with HENRY V of England (1420), and he maintained an alliance with England, breaking it only during his unsuccessful attempt to capture Calais (1435–39). Philip avoided conflict with France and instead attacked his smaller neighbors, conquering Hainaut, Brabant, Holland and Zeeland, and Luxembourg by 1443. A renowned patron of the arts, he presided over one of Europe's most extravagant courts.

Philip III *Spanish* **Felipe** (1578–1621) King of Spain and of Portugal (1598–1621). The son of PHILIP II, he was an indifferent ruler and allowed royal favorites to govern in his place. From 1609 his government continued the policy of expelling the Moriscos (Christians of Moorish ancestry), which caused serious economic problems. The huge sums he spent on court entertainments exacerbated Spain's growing economic problems.

Philip IV *French* **Philippe** *known as* **Philip the Fair** (1268–1314) King of France (1285–1314). On inheriting the French throne he modeled himself on his grandfather, LOUIS IX. He was also king of Navarre (as Philip I, 1284–1305), ruling jointly with his wife, Joan I of Navarre. War with England (1294–1303) ended with a peace treaty and the betrothal of his daughter to the future EDWARD II. Philip forced a harsh treaty on Flanders in 1305. He conducted a long struggle with Boniface VIII (1297–1303) but was pacified by succeeding popes, including CLEMENT V, who began the AVIGNON PAPACY. Philip expelled the Jews from France (1306) and persecuted the Knights TEMPLAR (1307).

Philip IV *Spanish* **Felipe** (1605–1665) King of Spain (1621–65) and of Portugal (as Philip II, 1621–40). He succeeded his father, PHILIP III, and left the administration of his rule to his chief ministers, the duke de Olivares (1621–43) and the duke's nephew Luis Méndez de Haro (1643–61). Spain's industry and commerce declined, and wars against Holland, France, and Germany further drained Spain's economy. Portugal regained its independence (1640), and Holland was lost by the Peace of WESTPHALIA (1648). A poet and patron of the arts, Philip was the friend and frequent subject of DIEGO VELAZQUEZ.

Philip V (238–179 BC) King of Macedonia (221–179). Son of Demetrius II, he succeeded Antigonus Doson. Supporting the Hellenic League against Sparta, Aetolia, and Elis (220–217), he allied with HANNIBAL in 215 and attacked Roman client states in Illyria. Rome responded in the First MACEDONIAN WAR. Intrigue against Egypt and his unsuccessful sea battle with Rhodes and Pergamum led Rome to initiate the Second Macedonian War, in which it prevailed at Cynoscephalae (197). Rome's harsh terms eased after Philip made common cause against its Greek foes. Fearing that Rome would turn on him again, he attempted to expand by attacking the Balkans (184, 183, 181); he died on a fourth attempt in 179.

Philip V *Spanish* **Felipe** *orig.* **Philippe, duc (Duke) d'Anjou** (1683–1746) King of Spain (1700–46). Grandson of LOUIS XIV of France and great-grandson of PHILIP IV of Spain, Philip was named to succeed the childless CHARLES II as king in 1700. Louis's refusal to exclude Philip from the line of succession to the French throne led to the War of the SPANISH SUCCESSION. The resultant Peace of UTRECHT (1713) deprived Philip of the SPANISH NETHERLANDS and parts of Italy, but left him Spain and Spanish America. Initially influenced by his French advisers through his wife, Maria Luise of Savoy, after her death (1714) he was influenced by his second wife, ELIZABETH FARNESE, and her Italian advisers. Attempts to secure territories in Italy caused the formation of the QUADRUPLE ALLIANCE (1718) against Spain. Philip later brought Spain into the War of the AUSTRIAN SUCCESSION. His reign marked the beginning of the Bourbon dynasty in Spain (see BOURBON, HOUSE OF).

Philip VI *or* **Philip of Valois** \väl-ˈwä\ *French* **Philippe de Valois** (1293–1350) First French king of the Valois dynasty (1328–50). He continued CAPETIAN efforts to centralize the state but made concessions to the nobility, clergy, and bourgeoisie. His knights killed thousands of rebellious Flemings at the Battle of Cassel (1328). His disputes with EDWARD III of England led to the outbreak of the HUNDRED YEARS' WAR (1337). French defeats at the battles of Sluys (1340) and CRÉCY (1346) caused crises in France until the spread of the BLACK DEATH (from 1348) overshadowed other considerations.

Philip Augustus See PHILIP II (France)

Philip Morris Cos. Inc. U.S. HOLDING COMPANY. The company began with the incorporation of Philip Morris & Co. in New York in 1919; it became a principal maker of cigarettes in the 1930s and '40s, and the popularity of its Marlboro cigarettes grew with its use of cowboy imagery to advertise them in the mid-1950s. Its other cigarette brands include Benson and Hedges, Virginia Slims, and Merit, and it is now the world's largest tobacco company. In 1969 Philip Morris acquired the Miller Brewing Co. It further reduced its dependence on tobacco by acquiring General Foods (1985), KRAFT FOODS (1988), and NABISCO (2000), among others. In 1998, as part of the settlement of a suit brought against it and other cigarette manufacturers by almost all the U.S. states, it agreed to participate in paying $206 billion to the states for smoking-related health-care costs. Miller Brewing was sold to South African Breweries in 2002.

Philip of Hesse (1504–1567) German nobleman, landgrave of Hesse and champion of the Reformation. His skillful management made HESSE a sovereign state. Won to the cause of MARTIN LUTHER, Philip became a Reformation leader in Germany. In 1529 he founded the first Protestant university at Marburg (1529), and in 1531 he united several princes and towns to form the SCHMALKALDIC LEAGUE. However, his folly in contracting a bigamous second marriage damaged his reputation. After the emperor crushed the league, Philip was imprisoned (1547–52). Long imprisonment undermined his influence and his health, though he finally saw Lutheranism gain a position of legal equality with Catholicism in the Peace of AUGSBURG (1555). In the year of his death, he divided Hesse among his four sons.

Philip of Macedonia See PHILIP II

Philip the Bold See PHILIP II (Burgundy)

Philip the Good See PHILIP III (Burgundy)

Philipon \fē-lē-ˈpōⁿ\, **Charles** (1802–1862) French caricaturist, lithographer, and journalist. An excellent draftsman with a fertile sense of satire and vigorous political opinions, he published a series of journals of political satire. *La Caricature*, which he introduced in 1830, was suppressed in 1835; *Le Charivari*, introduced in 1832, became the inspiration for *Punch*, subtitled *The London Charivari*. His drawing showing the transformation of LOUIS-PHILIPPE into the shape of a pear established the pear as the common symbol for the king. He attracted and inspired the best caricaturists in France, including HONORÉ DAUMIER and GUSTAVE DORÉ.

Philippe Égalité See duc d'ORLÉANS

Philippi \ˈfi-lə-ˌpī\ Ruined hill town, northern central Macedonia, Greece. In c. 357 BC it was fortified by King PHILIP II to control nearby gold mines. In 42 BC it was the scene of the decisive Roman battle in which MARK ANTONY and Octavian (later AUGUSTUS) defeated BRUTUS and CASSIUS, the leading assassins of Julius CAESAR. Many Christian ruins, especially of the 5th–6th century AD, are spread over the site. St. PAUL preached the gospel to Christian converts there.

Philippine–American War *or* **Philippine Insurrection** (1899–1902) War between the U.S. and Filipino revolutionaries, which may be seen as a continuation of the PHILIPPINE REVOLUTION against Spanish rule.

The Treaty of Paris (1898) transferred Philippine sovereignty from Spain to the U.S. but was not recognized by Filipino leaders, whose troops controlled the entire archipelago except the capital city of Manila. By 1902 U.S. troops had defeated the insurgency, though sporadic fighting continued until 1906. The U.S. retained possession of the islands until 1946.

Philippine Revolution (1896–98) Filipino independence struggle that failed to end Spanish colonial rule in the Philippines. There had been numerous quasi-religious uprisings during the more than 300 years of colonial rule, but the late-19th-century writings of JOSE RIZAL and others helped stimulate a more broad-based movement for Philippine independence. Spain was unwilling to reform its colonial government, and armed rebellion broke out in 1896. Rizal, who had advocated reform but not revolution, was shot for sedition; his martyrdom fueled the revolution. The rebel forces of EMILIO AGUINALDO were unable to defeat the Spanish, but in the wake of Spain's defeat in the SPANISH-AMERICAN WAR (1898) the Filipinos proclaimed their independence. The Treaty of Paris ceded the Philippines to the U.S., however, and Agui-naldo was obliged to continue the revolutionary struggle, now against the U.S. See also PHILIPPINE–AMERICAN WAR.

Philippine Sea \'fil-ə-ˌpēn\, **Battle of the** (June 19–20, 1944) Naval battle of WORLD WAR II between the U.S. and Japan. On June 19, after the U.S. invaded SAIPAN, Japan sent 430 planes to destroy U.S. ships but suffered heavy losses from U.S. carrier aircraft before retiring the next day. Called the greatest carrier battle of the war, it ended with the loss of over 300 Japanese planes and two carriers, while U.S. aircraft losses totaled 130, with minor damage to ships.

Philippines *officially* **Republic of the Philippines** Nation, an archipelago off the southeastern coast of Asia. Area: 115,651 sq mi (299,536 sq km). Population (1997 est.): 71,539,000. Capital: MANILA; QUEZON CITY is the designated center of national government. Filipinos are predominantly of Malay descent, frequently admixed with Chinese and

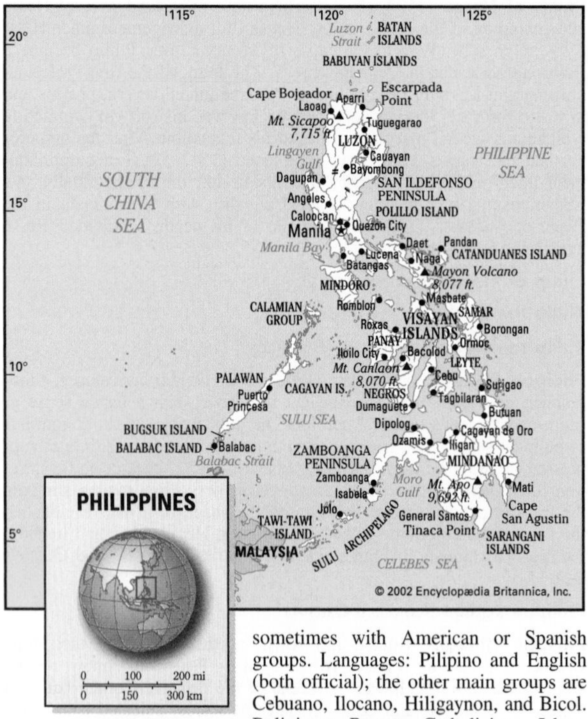

sometimes with American or Spanish groups. Languages: Pilipino and English (both official); the other main groups are Cebuano, Ilocano, Hiligaynon, and Bicol. Religions: Roman Catholicism, Islam, Protestantism. Currency: Philippine peso. The Philippines consist of about 7,100 islands and islets. The two principal islands are LUZON in the north and MINDANAO in the south. The VISAYAN group is in the central Philippines, MINDORO is directly south of Luzon, and PALAWAN is isolated in the west. The topography of the archipelago is varied, with inactive volcanoes and mountain ranges the main features of most of the larger islands. The country has a predominantly market economy based largely on agriculture, light industries, and services. It is a republic with two legislative houses; its chief of state and head of government is the president. Discovered by FERDINAND MAGELLAN in 1521, the islands were colonized by the Spanish, who retained control until the Philippines were ceded to the U.S. in 1898 following the SPANISH-AMERICAN WAR. The Commonwealth of the Philippines was established in 1935 to prepare the country for political and economic independence, which was delayed by World War II and the Japanese invasion. The islands were liberated by U.S. forces 1944–45, and the Republic of the Philippines was proclaimed in 1946, with a government patterned on that of the U.S. In 1965 FERDINAND MARCOS was elected president. He declared martial law in 1972, and it lasted until 1981. After 20 years of dictatorial rule, he was driven from power in 1986. CORAZON AQUINO became president and instituted a period of democratic rule that continued with the 1992 election of Fidel Ramos. Through the 1990s the government tried to come to terms with independence fighters in the southern islands.

Philips Electronics NV *Dutch* **Philips' Gloeilampenfabrieken, NV** Major Dutch manufacturer of consumer electronics, household appliances, lighting equipment, and computer equipment. It was founded by the Dutch engineer Gerard Philips in 1891 to make incandescent lamps, and incorporated under its present name in 1912. Its strong research efforts were consolidated in 1914 in a separate organization that became the Philips Research Laboratories. It began manufacturing radios in the 1920s, and after World War II it marketed stereo equipment, televisions, and other products under such brand names as Philips, Magnavox, and Norelco. Philips helped create the compact disc, the cassette tape, and the videocassette recorder. It has manufacturing and marketing subsidiaries throughout the world.

Philistines People of Aegean origin who settled on the southern coast of PALESTINE around the 12th century BC, about the time of the Israelites' arrival. They lived in five cities that together made up Philistia, from which the Greeks derived the name Palestine. They first fought the Israelites in the 11th century BC. In the 10th century they were defeated by the Israelite king DAVID; the Bible recounts his slaying of their champion, the giant Goliath. They were later ruled by Assyria, Egypt, Babylonia, Persia, Greece, and Rome. They left no written records.

Phillips, Irna (1901–1973) U.S. radio producer and director. Born in Chicago, she worked as a teacher before turning to writing for radio and creating the first SOAP OPERA, *Painted Dreams* (1930). Later known as "Queen of the Soaps," she introduced such techniques as the organ bridge to give a smooth flow between scenes and the cliff-hanger ending to each episode. Her daytime radio serials included *Today's Children* (1933–38, 1943–50); *The Guiding Light* (1937–56; television, 1952–); *Road of Life* (1937–59); and *Women in White* (1938–42, 1944–48), the first hospital soap opera. She also created the television serials *As the World Turns* (1956) and *Another World* (1964).

Phillips, Wendell (1811–1884) U.S. reformer and abolitionist. A lawyer in his native Boston, he joined the antislavery movement. His reputation as an inspirational orator began with his address at an abolitionist meeting to protest the murder of ELIJAH LOVEJOY (1837). He became an associate of WILLIAM LLOYD GARRISON and lectured widely at meetings of the AMERICAN ANTI-SLAVERY SOCIETY, serving as its president 1865–70. He also advocated prohibition, women's suffrage, prison reform, regulation of corporations, and labor reform.

Wendell Phillips.

BY COURTESY OF THE LIBRARY OF CONGRESS, WASHINGTON, D.C.

Phillips curve Graphic representation of the inverse relationship between the rate of UNEMPLOYMENT and the rate of change in money wages. In 1958 A. W. Phillips plotted British unemployment rates and rates of change in money wages and found that when unemployment rates were low, employers were more likely to bid wages up to lure good employees away from their competitors. He claimed that this was a stable relationship. In the 1960s macroeconomists substituted the rate of price INFLATION for the rate of change in money wages and promulgated the curve as a tool of economic policy, arguing that the simultaneous achievement of low unemployment and low inflation was problematic. Monetarists, including MILTON FRIEDMAN, claimed the relationship was not stable.

Philo Judaeus \'fī-lō-jü-'dē-əs\ *or* **Philo of Alexandria** (15/10 BC–AD 45/50) Greek-speaking Jewish philosopher. A leader of the Jewish community of Alexandria, Egypt, he led a delegation to the emperor CALIGULA c. AD 40 to ask that Jews not be forced to worship him. His writings provide the clearest view of this development of Judaism in the Diaspora. His philosophy was influenced by PLATO, ARISTOTLE, the Neo-Pythagoreans, the CYNICS, and STOICISM. In his view of God, Philo was original in insisting on an individual Providence able to suspend the laws of nature, in contrast to the prevailing Greek view of a universal Providence who is himself subject to the laws of nature. As the first to attempt to synthesize revealed faith and philosophic reason, he occupies a unique position in the history of philosophy. He is regarded as the most important representative of Hellenistic Judaism and a forerunner of Christian theology.

philodendron \,fi-lə-'den-drən\ Any of about 200 species of climbing herbaceous plants that make up the genus *Philodendron* in the ARUM FAMILY, native to the New World tropics. Some are popular indoor foliage plants in colder areas and landscape plants in warmer climates. The leaves are often large and smooth-edged to variously lobed and cut. The inflorescence is seldom produced indoors. Many forms are available in cultivation, foremost among them the common heart-leaf *(Philodendron scandens oxycardium).* Large varieties include the spade-leaf philodendron *(P. domesticum* or *P. hastatum),* with triangular leaves up to 2 ft (60 cm) long, and the selloum philodendron *(P. selloum),* with deeply cut leaves up to 3 ft (1 m) long.

Philopoemen \,fi-lə-'pē-mən\ (252?–182 BC) General of the ACHAEAN LEAGUE. Elected federal cavalry commander (c. 210) and general of the league (208–207, 206–205, 201–200), he won victories against the Aetolians and the Spartans, using Macedonian armor and tactics. In his fourth generalship (193–192) he failed against the Spartans by sea but crushed their army on land. The Roman FLAMININUS stopped his capture of Sparta, but when its leader was assassinated he added that state to the confederation. He was captured when Messene rebelled, and given poison.

philosophe \,fē-lə-'zȯf\ Any of the literary men, scientists, and thinkers of 18th-century France who were united, in spite of divergent personal views, in their conviction of the supremacy and efficacy of human reason. Inspired by the philosophy of RENE DESCARTES, the SKEPTICISM of the libertines (or freethinkers), and the popularization of science by Bernard de Fontenelle (1657–1757), they were dedicated to the advancement of science and secular thought and to the open-mindedness of the ENLIGHTENMENT. They included VOLTAIRE, MONTESQUIEU, DENIS DIDEROT, JEAN LE ROND D'ALEMBERT, and JEAN-JACQUES ROUSSEAU. The philosophes compiled the *ENCYCLOPÉDIE,* one of the great intellectual achievements of the century.

philosophical anthropology Study of human nature conducted by the methods of philosophy. It is concerned with such questions as the status of mankind in the universe, the purpose or meaning of human life, and whether mankind can be made an object of systematic study. Among the most important works in philosophical anthropology are MAX SCHELER'S *Man's Place in the Universe* (1928), Helmuth Plessner's *The Levels of the Organic and Man* (1928), Arnold Gehlen's *Der Mensch* (1940), and ERNST CASSIRER'S *An Essay on Man* (1944)

philosophy Critical examination of the grounds for fundamental beliefs and analysis of the basic concepts employed in the expression of such beliefs. Philosophy may also be defined as reflection on the varieties of human experience, or as the rational, methodical, and systematic consideration of the topics that are of greatest concern to mankind. Philosophical inquiry is a central element in the intellectual history of many historical civilizations. Difficulty in achieving a consensus about the definition of the discipline partly reflects the fact that philosophers have frequently come to it from different fields and have preferred to reflect on different areas of experience. The world's great religions have all produced significant allied philosophical schools. Such Western philosophers as THOMAS AQUINAS, GEORGE BERKELEY, and SOREN KIERKEGAARD saw philosophy as a means to defend religion and dispel the antireligious errors of MATERIALISM and RATIONALISM. PYTHAGORAS, RENE DESCARTES, and BERTRAND RUSSELL, among others, were primarily mathematicians whose views of reality and knowledge were influenced by mathematics. Such figures as PLATO, THOMAS HOBBES, and JOHN STUART MILL were primarily concerned with POLITICAL PHILOSOPHY. The PRE-SOCRATICS, FRANCIS BACON, and ALFRED NORTH WHITEHEAD, among many others, started from an interest in the physical composition of the natural world. Other philosophical fields include AESTHETICS, EPISTEMOLOGY, ETHICS, LOGIC, METAPHYSICS, philosophy of MIND, and PHILOSOPHICAL ANTHROPOLOGY. See also ANALYTIC PHILOSOPHY, CONTINENTAL PHILOSOPHY, FEMINIST PHILOSOPHY, POLITICAL PHILOSOPHY, philosophy of SCIENCE.

phlebitis \fli-'bī-təs\ INFLAMMATION of the wall of a VEIN. Causes include nearby infection, trauma, surgery, and childbirth. The area over the vein is painful, swollen, red, and hot. A tender, cordlike mass may be felt under the skin. It usually occurs in surface veins in the lower leg and can be treated with pain relievers and bed rest, with mild exercise after inflammation subsides. Phlebitis can last for years; in such cases, irritation of the vein's inner lining leads to blood-clot formation, a condition known as thrombophlebitis (see THROMBOSIS). In deeper veins, this requires anticoagulants to prevent EMBOLISMS.

phloem \'flō-,em\ *or* **bast** Plant tissues that conduct foods made in the leaves to all other parts of the plant. Phloem is composed of several types of specialized cells, including sieve-tube cells and phloem fibers. Sieve tubes (columns of sieve-tube cells), which have perforated areas in their walls, provide the main channels in which food substances travel. Phloem fibers are long, flexible cells that make up the soft fibers used commercially (e.g., FLAX and HEMP).

phlox Any of about 65 species of plants (genus *Phlox*), belonging to the family Polemoniaceae, admired both in gardens and in the wilds for their clustered heads of flowers. All species but one are native to North America. Phlox is herbaceous, usually with oval or linear leaves; it has heads of massed tubular flowers with five flaring lobes. A few species are woody, but most are herbaceous annuals or perennials. Sizes range from the 5-ft-high (1.5-m) summer phlox *(P. paniculata)* to the 18-in.-high (45-cm) woodland PERENNIAL blue phlox *(P. divaricata)* to the low-creeping, freely branching, evergreen moss pink, or creeping phlox *(P. subulata).*

Moss pink (*Phlox subulata*).
RUSS KINNE—PHOTO RESEARCHERS/EB INC.

Phnom Penh \pə-'nȯm-'pen\ City (pop., 1994 est.: 920,000), capital of Cambodia, at the junction of the TONLE SAP River with the MEKONG RIVER. Founded in 1434 as the capital of the KHMER nation, it was abandoned several times before being reestablished in 1865. It was a cultural center, with many institutions of higher learning. When the KHMER ROUGE came to power in Cambodia in 1975, they forced the city's population into the countryside to work in the fields. It was repopulated beginning in 1979, and the city's educational institutions began a difficult period of recovery from the virtual extermination of the country's educated class. Although it is 180 mi (290 km) from the sea, it is a major port of the Mekong River valley; it is linked to the CHINA SEA via Vietnam by a channel of the Mekong delta.

phobia Extreme and irrational fear of a particular object, class of objects, or situation. Phobias are classified as forms of ANXIETY disorder (a NEUROSIS), since anxiety is its chief symptom. They are generally believed to result when fear produced by an original threatening situation (such as a near-drowning in childhood) is transferred to other similar situations (such as encounters with bodies of water), the original fear often being repressed or forgotten. BEHAVIOR THERAPY is often successful in overcoming phobias, the phobic person being gradually exposed to the anxiety-provoking object or situation in a way that demonstrates that no threat really exists.

Phocaea \fō-'sē-ə\ Ancient city, on the Aegean Sea, northernmost of the IONIAN cities on the western coast of ASIA MINOR. An important mar-

O P Q R

itime state c. 1000–550 BC, it founded a number of colonies, including Massilia (MARSEILLE) in the western Mediterranean. It declined after the Persian conquest c. 545 BC. The modern town of Foça is located in an olive- and tobacco-growing region and attracts tourists to the ancient city's ruins.

Phocis \'fō-sis\ Ancient territory, central Greece. It extended north from the Gulf of Corinth over the range of Mount PARNASSUS to the Locrian Mtns., which formed the northern frontier. Its chief towns were Elateia, DELPHI, and Daulis. Mainly a pastoral region, its early history is obscure. Traditionally, the Phocians controlled the sanctuary and oracle at Delphi, but they lost control after a war with neighboring Greek states c. 590 BC. It was allied with SPARTA in the PELOPONNESIAN WAR and was conquered by PHILIP II OF MACEDON in 346 BC.

phoebe \'fē-bē\ Any of three species (family Tyrannidae, suborder Tyranni) of suboscine PASSERINES with a habit of twitching their tail when perching. The eastern phoebe *(Sayornis phoebe)* of North America is 7.5 in. (18 cm) long, plain brownish gray above, and paler below. Its call is a brisk "fee-bee" uttered over and over. It makes a mossy nest, strengthened with mud, on a ledge, often under a bridge. Say's phoebe *(S. saya),* a slightly larger bird with buff-hued underparts, occurs in open country in western North America. The black phoebe *(S. nigricans),* occurring from the southwestern U.S. to Argentina, is dark above with a white belly.

Phoenicia \fi-'nē-shə\ Ancient country, corresponding to modern Lebanon, with adjoining parts of modern Syria and Israel. Its chief cities were Sidon, TYRE, and Berot (modern BEIRUT). The PHOENICIANS were notable merchants, traders, and colonizers of the Mediterranean in the 1st millennium BC. The country was conquered successively by the Assyrians, Babylonians, Persians, and ALEXANDER THE GREAT. In 64 BC it was incorporated into the Roman province of Syria.

Phoenicians \fi-'nē-shənz\ People of ancient PHOENICIA. They were merchants, traders, and colonizers who probably arrived from the Persian Gulf c. 3000 BC. By the 2nd millennium BC they had colonies in the Levant, North Africa, Anatolia, and Cyprus. They traded wood, cloth, dyes, embroideries, wine, and decorative objects; ivory and wood carving became their specialties, and their goldsmiths' and metalsmiths' work was well known. Their alphabet became the basis of the Greek alphabet.

Phoenix \'fē-niks\ City (pop., 1996 est.: 1,159,000), capital of Arizona. It is located on the SALT RIVER. The river valley was occupied as early as AD 1300 by prehistoric Indians, now known as the HOHOKAM CULTURE, who disappeared in the early 15th century. Modern Phoenix was founded in 1870 and incorporated as a city in 1881. It became the territorial capital in 1889 and state capital in 1912. There was widespread expansion after World War II, with the population quadrupling between 1950 and 1960. It occupies a semi-arid valley surrounded by mountains and irrigated fields; its economy is based on farming, manufacturing, mining, and tourism.

phoenix In ancient Egypt and in classical antiquity, a fabulous bird associated with the worship of the sun. The Egyptian phoenix was said to be as large as an eagle, with brilliant scarlet and gold plumage and a melodious cry. Only one phoenix existed at a time, and it lived no less than 500 years. As its end approached, it built a nest of aromatic boughs and spices, set it on fire, and was consumed in the flames. From the pyre was born a new phoenix, which sealed its predecessor's ashes in an egg of myrrh and flew to HELIOPOLIS to deposit them on the altar of the sun god. The phoenix thus symbolized immortality. See also FENGHUANG.

Phoenix Islands Group of eight small coral atolls, part of Kiribati, in the western central Pacific Ocean, 1,650 mi (2,650 km) southwest of Hawaii. The low, sandy atolls have a total land area of about 11 sq mi (28 sq km) and were discovered in the 19th century by U.S. whaling ships. Annexed by Britain in 1889, they were joined to the GILBERT AND ELLICE ISLANDS in 1937. They became part of independent Kiribati in 1979. Kanton is the only inhabited atoll.

Phoenix Park murders (May 6, 1882) Assassination in Dublin of British officials. The newly arrived chief secretary of Ireland, Lord Frederick Cavendish, and his undersecretary, Thomas Burke, were walking in Dublin's Phoenix Park when they were stabbed to death by members of the Invincibles, a radical Irish nationalist secret society. The murders caused a revulsion against terrorism and enabled CHARLES STEWART PARNELL to subordinate the Irish National League to the more moderate Home Rule Party in Parliament.

phoneme Smallest unit of speech distinguishing one word (or word element) from another (e.g., the sound *p* in *tap,* which differentiates that word from *tab* and *tag*). The term is usually restricted to VOWELS and CONSONANTS, but some linguists include differences of pitch, STRESS, and rhythm. A phoneme may have variants, called allophones, that differ phonetically without affecting meaning. Phonemes may be recorded with special symbols, such as those of the INTERNATIONAL PHONETIC ALPHABET. In transcription, linguists conventionally place symbols for phonemes between slash marks: /p/.

phonetics Study of SPEECH sounds. It deals with their ARTICULATION (articulatory phonetics), their acoustic properties (acoustic phonetics), and how they combine to make syllables, words, and sentences (linguistic phonetics). The first phoneticians were Indian scholars (c. 300 BC) who tried to preserve the pronunciation of Sanskrit holy texts. The classical Greeks are credited as the first to base a WRITING system on a phonetic alphabet. Modern phonetics began with Alexander Melville Bell (1819–1905), whose *Visible Speech* (1867) introduced a system of precise notation for writing down speech sounds. In the 20th century, linguists have focused on developing a classification system that can permit comparison of all human speech sounds. Another concern of modern phonetics is the mental processes of speech perception.

phonics \'fä-niks\ Method of reading instruction that breaks language down into its simplest components. Children learn the sounds of individual letters first, then the sounds of letters in combination and in simple words. Simple reading exercises with a controlled vocabulary reinforce the process. Phonics-based instruction has declined in recent years in the face of competition from "whole-language" instruction, in which children are introduced to whole words at a time, are given real literature rather than reading exercises, and are encouraged to keep journals in which they were permitted to spell creatively. A strong backlash against whole-language teaching has made reading instruction a battlefield, and most teachers today favor a combination of the two techniques.

phonograph *or* **record player** Instrument for reproducing SOUNDS. A phonograph record stores a copy of sound waves as a series of undulations in a wavy groove inscribed on its rotating surface by the recording stylus. When the record is played back, another stylus (needle) responds to the undulations, and its motions are then reconverted into sound. Its invention is generally credited to THOMAS ALVA EDISON (1877). Stereophonic systems, with two separate channels of information in a single groove, became a commercial reality in 1958. All modern phonograph systems had certain components in common: a turntable that rotated the record; a stylus that tracked a groove in the record; a pickup that converted the mechanical movements of the stylus into electrical impulses; an amplifier that intensified these electrical impulses; and a LOUDSPEAKER that converted the amplified signals back into sound. Phonographs and records were the chief means of reproducing recorded sound at home until the 1980s, when they were largely replaced by recorded cassettes (see TAPE RECORDER) and COMPACT DISCS.

phonology \fə-'nä-lə-jē\ Study of sound patterns within languages. Diachronic (historical) phonology traces and analyzes changes in speech sounds and sound systems over time (e.g., the process by which *sea* and *see,* once pronounced with different vowel sounds, have come to be pronounced alike). Synchronic (descriptive) phonology investigates sound patterns at a single stage in a language's development, to identify which ones can occur (in English, for example, *nt* and *rk* appear within or at the end of words but not at the beginning).

phonon \'fō-ˌnän\ In SOLID-STATE PHYSICS, a quantum of lattice vibrational energy. In analogy to a PHOTON (a quantum of light), a phonon is viewed as a wave packet with particlelike properties (see WAVE-PARTICLE DUALITY). The way phonons behave determines or affects various properties of SOLIDS. Thermal conductivity, for instance, is explained by phonon interactions. Phonons also provide the basis for understanding SUPERCONDUCTIVITY in certain metals.

Phony War (1939–40) Early months of WORLD WAR II, marked by no major hostilities. The term was coined by journalists to derisively describe the six-month period (October 1939–March 1940) during which no land operations were undertaken by the Allies or the Germans after the German conquest of Poland in September 1939.

phosgene \'fäz-,jēn\ *or* **carbonyl chloride** \'kär-bə-,nil\ Colorless, highly toxic gas used in CHEMICAL WARFARE as well as in industrial processes including the making of dyestuffs and polyurethane resins. Either alone or in combination with CHLORINE, it was used against troops in World War I. It smells like musty hay. Inhalation causes severe lung injury several hours after exposure. First prepared in 1811, it is manufactured by the reaction of CARBON MONOXIDE and chlorine in the presence of a catalyst. Gaseous phosgene is usually stored and transported as a liquid under pressure in steel cylinders or as a solution in TOLUENE. Mixed with water, it forms CARBON DIOXIDE and HYDROCHLORIC ACID.

phosphate Any of numerous chemical compounds related to phosphoric acid (H_3PO_4). Phosphate SALTS are inorganic compounds containing the phosphate ION (PO_4^{3-}), the hydrogen phosphate ion (HPO_4^{2-}), or the dihydrogen phosphate ion ($H_2PO_4^-$), along with any CATION. Phosphate ESTERS are organic compounds in which the hydrogens of phosphoric acid are replaced by organic groups (e.g., methyl, ethyl, phenyl), with one of their carbon atoms bonding to an oxygen atom in the phosphate group. NUCLEIC ACIDS and ATP both contain phosphate; bones and teeth contain calcium phosphate. Phosphate rock (mainly calcium phosphate) is one of the four most important basic chemical commodities. Phosphates were formerly used in DETERGENTS, which washed into rivers and lakes, causing WATER BLOOMS of algae and bacteria (see EUTROPHICATION); such use is now generally outlawed or regulated. Phosphates are still used in fertilizers, baking powder, and toothpaste.

phospholipid \,fäs-fō-'li-pəd\ *or* **phosphatide** Any member of a large class of fat-like organic compounds with PHOSPHATE in their structure, as well as carbon, hydrogen, oxygen, and perhaps nitrogen. One end of each molecule is soluble in water and water solutions (including CYTOPLASM), the other end in FATS. They naturally combine to form a two-layer structure (LIPID bilayer) with the fat-soluble ends sandwiched in the middle and the water-soluble ends sticking out. Such lipid bilayers are the structural basis of cell MEMBRANES. Phospholipids are the principal components of the myelin sheaths of NEURONS. Examples of phospholipids include LECITHIN, cephalins, phosphoinositides (in brain), and cardiolipin (in heart).

phosphorescence Emission of light from a substance exposed to RADIATION and persisting as an afterglow after the exciting radiation has been removed. Unlike FLUORESCENCE, in which the absorbed light is emitted about 10^{-8} second after excitation, in phosphorescence the extra energy absorbed is stored in METASTABLE STATES and reemitted later. Phosphorescence may last from about 10^{-3} second to days or even years. The term phosphorescence is often applied to LUMINESCENCE of living organisms, as well.

phosphorite \'fäs-fər-,īt\ *or* **phosphate rock** Rock with a high concentration of phosphates in nodular or compact masses. The phosphates may be derived from a variety of sources, including marine invertebrates that secrete shells of calcium phosphate and the bones and excrement of vertebrates. Typical phosphorite beds contain about 30% phosphorus pentoxide (P_2O_5) and constitute the primary source of raw materials for phosphate fertilizers. Significant deposits in the U.S. include the Phosphoria Formation in Idaho and the Monterey Formation in California. Major deposits also occur in the Sechura Desert in Peru.

phosphorus Nonmetallic chemical ELEMENT, chemical symbol P, atomic number 15. The ordinary ALLOTROPE, "white phosphorus," is a poisonous, colorless, semitransparent, soft, waxy solid that glows in the dark (PHOSPHORESCENCE) and combusts spontaneously in air, producing dense white fumes of the OXIDE; it is used as a rodenticide and a military smokescreen. Heat or sunlight converts it to "red phosphorus," a violet-red powder that does not phosphoresce or combust. Much less reactive and soluble than white phosphorus, it is used in manufacturing other phosphorus compounds and in semiconductors, fertilizers, and safety matches. "Black phosphorus," made by heating the white form under pressure, is flaky like GRAPHITE. Phosphorus seldom occurs uncombined in nature. As the PHOSPHATE ion, it is abundant and widely distributed, in APATITE, PHOSPHORITE, and many other minerals. Phosphorus has VALENCE 3 or 5 in compounds, which have many uses in industry. Phosphine (PH_3) is a chemical raw material and a doping agent (deliberately added impurity) for solid-state electronics components. Organic phosphorus compounds are used as plasticizers, gasoline additives, insecticides (e.g., parathion), and nerve gases.

Photian Schism See Photian SCHISM

Photius \'fō-shē-əs\, **St.** (c. 820–891?) Patriarch of Constantinople (858–67, 877–86). A high-ranking civil servant, he was promoted swiftly through the ecclesiastical orders to become patriarch after the deposition of Ignatius, an action that offended Pope Nicholas I. Photius added to the conflict by refusing to restore dioceses earlier transferred from the Roman to the Byzantine church. Angry that Nicholas would not recognize him, Photius excommunicated the pope (867), thus beginning the Photian SCHISM. Photius was deposed the same year but restored in 877 after his successor died. He and Pope John VIII agreed to return Bulgaria to the Roman church but to allow Greek bishops to remain.

Photo-Secession Group of U.S. photographers influenced by the ART NOUVEAU movement. Founded in 1902 by ALFRED STIEGLITZ, the Photo-Secession sought recognition of photography as an art to be judged on its own terms. It was akin to such groups as the Linked Ring in London, and its name reflected that of the SEZESSION movement (though it was also known by the number 291, the address of Stieglitz's gallery). Stieglitz did not believe in retouching or manipulating negatives or prints, but others of the group, such as EDWARD STEICHEN, were adherents of the impressionistic soft-focus school and the new techniques. The record of the Photo-Secession is contained in the quarterly *Camera Work* (1903–17).

photocell *or* **photoelectric cell** *or* **electric eye** SOLID-STATE DEVICE with a photosensitive CATHODE that emits ELECTRONS when illuminated and an ANODE for collecting the emitted electrons. Illumination excites electrons, which are attracted to the anode, producing current proportional to the intensity of the illumination. In a photovoltaic cell, light is used to produce voltage. In a photoconductive cell, light is used to regulate the flow of current. Photocells are used in control systems, where interrupting a beam of light opens a circuit, actuating a relay that supplies power to a mechanism to bring about a desired operation, such as opening a door or setting off a burglar alarm. Photocells are also used in PHOTOMETRY and SPECTROSCOPY.

photochemical reaction CHEMICAL REACTION initiated by absorption of ENERGY in the form of visible (LIGHT), ULTRAVIOLET, or INFRARED radiation. Primary photochemical processes occur as an immediate result, and secondary processes may follow. The most important example is PHOTOSYNTHESIS. Vision depends on photochemical reactions that occur in the eye (see RETINA, RHODOPSIN). In photography, light activates the silver nitrate to a state that is easy to reduce to metallic silver grains during development. Bleaching of laundry, tanning of skin, storage of energy in solar batteries, and many industrial reactions are also photochemical. Certain air pollutants become more reactive and form noxious compounds in photochemical reactions.

photocopier Device for producing copies of text or graphic material by the use of light, heat, chemicals, or electrostatic charge. Most modern copiers use a method called XEROGRAPHY. Fast and efficient photocopiers have benefited businesses tremendously, but have created copyright problems and have led to voluminous consumption of paper with its attendant environmental consequences.

photoelectric effect Phenomenon in which charged particles are released from a material when it absorbs radiant energy (see RADIATION). It is often thought of as the ejection of ELECTRONS from the surface of a metal plate when visible light falls on it. It can also occur if the radiation is in the wavelength range of ULTRAVIOLET RADIATION, X RAYS, or GAMMA RAYS. The emitting surface may be a solid, liquid, or gas, and the emitted particles may be electrons or ions. The effect was discovered in 1887 by HEINRICH HERTZ and explained by ALBERT EINSTEIN in work for which he received the Nobel Prize.

photoengraving Any of several processes for producing PRINTING plates by photographic means (see PHOTOGRAPHY). In general, a plate coated with a photosensitive substance is exposed to an image, usually on film; the plate is then treated in various ways, depending on the printing process to be used. Photoengraving is particularly useful for reproducing photographs via the HALFTONE PROCESS. See also OFFSET PRINTING.

photography Method of recording permanent images by the action of light projected by a lens in a camera onto a film or other light-sensitive material. It was developed in the 19th century through the artistic aspirations of two Frenchmen, NICEPHORE NIEPCE and L.-J.-M. DAGUERRE, who invented the first commercially successful process, the DAGUERREOTYPE

(1837), and two Englishmen, Thomas Wedgwood and (W.H.) FOX TALBOT, who patented the negative-positive calotype process that became the forerunner of modern photographic technique. Photography has had a profound impact on society. It was initially used for portraiture and landscapes. In the 1850s and '60s, MATHEW B. BRADY and ROGER FENTON pioneered war photography and photojournalism. Related processes include radiography (the recording of images by X rays, electron beams, and nuclear radiation), and television and videotape (recording the transmission of light images with electromagnetic signals). See also DIGITAL CAMERA.

photolysis \fō-'tä-lə-səs\ Breakdown of MOLECULES into smaller units via absorption of LIGHT. Flash photolysis, an experimental technique developed by MANFRED EIGEN, R. G. W. Norrish, and G. Porter, studies short-lived chemical intermediates formed in many PHOTOCHEMICAL REACTIONS An intense, brief flash of light splits molecules into short-lived fragments, which are analyzed by SPECTROPHOTOMETRY in a second, less intense flash.

photometry \fō-'tä-mə-trē\ Precision measurement of the brightness, color, and spectrum of stars and other celestial objects to obtain data on their structure, temperature, and composition. About 130 BC, HIPPARCHUS used a system that divided the stars into six MAGNITUDES, from brightest to faintest. Beginning in the 17th century, use of the TELESCOPE led to the discovery of many fainter stars, and the scale was extended downward. Since the 1940s, use of photographic and then photoelectric equipment has vastly extended the sensitivity and wavelength range of astronomical photometry. The main (UBVRI) classification system uses wave bands in the ultraviolet, blue, visual, red, and infrared ranges. More elaborate systems can distinguish giant and dwarf stars, detect metals in stars, and determine surface gravity.

photon *or* **light quantum** Minute energy packet of ELECTROMAGNETIC RADIATION. In 1900 MAX PLANCK found that heat radiation is emitted and absorbed in distinct units, which he called quanta. In 1905 ALBERT EINSTEIN explained the PHOTOELECTRIC EFFECT, proposing the existence of discrete energy packets in light. The term photon came into use for these packets in 1926. The energies of photons range from high-energy gamma rays and X rays to low-energy infrared and radio waves, though all travel at the same speed, the speed of light. Photons have no ELECTRIC CHARGE or rest mass and are the carriers of the ELECTROMAGNETIC FIELD.

photoperiodism Response by an animal or plant to changes in daily, seasonal, or yearly cycles of light and darkness. Among animals, sleep, migration, reproduction, and the changing of coats or plumage are regulated to some extent by day length. In the poultry industry, photoperiodism is commonly induced by artificial lighing to maximize egg laying and body weight. Plant growth, seed setting, germination, flowering, and fruiting are also affected by day length. Other environmental factors that modify an organism's responses include temperature and nutrition.

Photorealism Late-20th-century painting style based on photography, in which realistic scenes are rendered in meticulous detail. An offshoot of POP ART, it became a trend in U.S. painting in the 1970s among artists fascinated by camera images. Though photographs had been used by 19th-century painters such as EUGENE DELACROIX as substitutes for reality, the Photorealists relied on the photograph itself, replicating it in large-scale detail as the reality on which to base an ACRYLIC PAINTING. Its subjects often included reflecting surfaces (chrome-plated diners, motorcycles, glass-fronted buildings, etc.). Its awesome technical precision, brilliant color schemes, and visual complexity earned the style wide popularity. Its most notable practitioners were Don Eddy (*New Shoes for H*, 1974), Richard Estes (*Food Shop*, 1967), and Audrey Flack (*Queen*, 1976).

photoreception Biological responses to stimulation by light, most often referring to the mechanism of vision. In one-celled organisms such as the amoeba, the whole cell may be sensitive to light. Earthworms have photoreceptive cells scattered over their bodies to help them orient themselves by comparison of light intensities in different directions. Most animals have localized photoreceptors of varying complexity. In humans, photoreception relies on the chemical response of a light-sensitive pigment, RHODOPSIN, in photoreceptor cells in the RETINA of the EYE. Stimulation of those cells results in a stimulus being conducted toward the NERVOUS SYSTEM. Humans, like other vertebrates, have two types of photosensitive cells, rod cells and cone cells. Rod cells are responsible for vision when there is little light; cone cells mediate daylight vision and color. Photoreception also refers to PHOTOSYNTHESIS in plants. See also SENSE.

photosphere Visible surface of the SUN, about 250 mi (400 km) thick. It emits most of the sun's light that reaches earth directly. Temperatures range from about 18,000°F (10,000°C) at the bottom to 8,000°F (4,000°C) at the top; its density is about 1/1,000 that of air at the surface of earth. SUNSPOTS are photospheric phenomena. The photosphere has a granular structure. Each grain (cell), a mass of hot gas several hundred miles in diameter, rises from inside the sun, radiates energy, and sinks back within minutes to be replaced by others in a constantly changing pattern.

photosynthesis Process by which green plants and certain other organisms transform light into chemical energy. In green plants, light energy is captured by CHLOROPHYLL in the CHLOROPLASTS of the leaves and used to convert water, carbon dioxide, and minerals into oxygen and energy-rich organic compounds (simple and complex sugars) that are the basis of both plant and animal life. Photosynthesis consists of a number of photochemical and enzymatic reactions. It occurs in two stages. During the light-dependent stage (light reaction), chlorophyll absorbs light energy, which excites some electrons in the pigment molecules to higher energy levels; these leave the chlorophyll and pass along a series of molecules, generating formation of NADPH (an enzyme) and high-energy ATP molecules. Oxygen, released as a by-product, passes into the atmosphere through pores in the leaves. NADPH and ATP drive the second stage, the dark reaction (or Calvin cycle, discovered by MELVIN CALVIN), which does not require light. During this stage glucose is generated using atmospheric carbon dioxide. Photosynthesis is crucial for maintaining life on earth; if it ceased, there would soon be little food or other organic matter on the planet, and most organisms would disappear. See illustration on following page.

phototube See PHOTOCELL

photovoltaic effect Process in which two dissimilar materials in close contact act as an electric cell when struck by light or other radiant energy. In CRYSTALS of certain elements, such as SILICON and GERMANIUM, the ELECTRONS are usually not free to move from atom to atom. Light striking the crystal provides the energy needed to free electrons from their bound condition. These electrons can cross the junction between two dissimilar crystals more easily in one direction than another, so one side of the junction acquires a negative voltage with respect to the other. As long as light falls on the two materials, the photovoltaic BATTERY can continue to provide voltage and current. The current can be used to measure the brightness of the light or as a source of power, as in a SOLAR CELL.

Phrachomklao See MONGKUT

Phrachunlachomklao See CHULALONGKORN

Phramongkutklao See VAJIRAVUDH

phratry \'frā-trē\ In ancient Greece, tribal subdivisions of households or families claiming a common kin relation. At the apex of each phratry were aristocratic clans that had certain hereditary rights, such as the right to hold priestly offices. Both phratries and clans were patrilineal. The Athenian phratry is well known. Every native Athenian male belonged to a phratry; they were concerned with such matters as legitimacy of descent and inheritance.

Phraya Taksin See TAKSIN

phrenology \fri-'nä-lə-jē\ Study of the shape of the SKULL as an indication of mental abilities and character traits. FRANZ JOSEPH GALL stated the principle that each of the innate mental faculties is based in a specific brain region ("organ"), whose size reflects the faculty's prominence in a person and is reflected by the skull's surface. He examined the skulls of persons with particular traits (including "criminal" traits) for a feature he could identify with it. His followers Johann Kaspar Spurzheim (1776–1832) and George Combe (1788–1858) divided the scalp into areas they labeled with traits such as combativeness, cautiousness, and form perception. Though popular well into the 20th century, phrenology has been wholly discredited.

Phrygia \'fri-jē-ə\ Ancient country, western central ASIA MINOR. It was named after a people whom the Greeks called Phryges and who dominated Asia Minor between the HITTITE collapse (12th century BC) and ascent of LYDIA (7th century BC). The Phrygians were possibly of Thracian

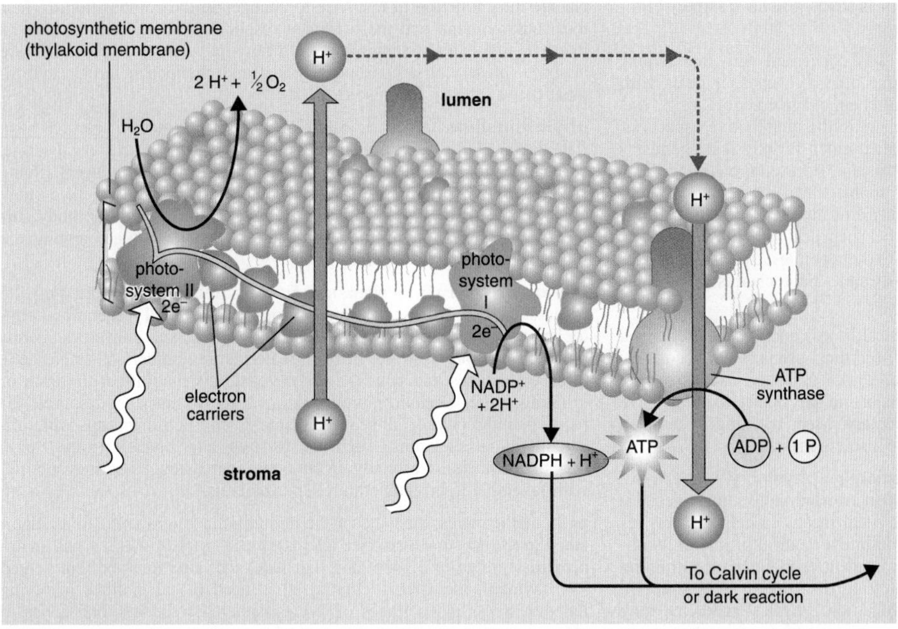

The light reaction of photosynthesis. The light reaction occurs in two photosystems (units of chlorophyll molecules). Light energy (indicated by wavy arrows) absorbed by photosystem II causes the formation of high-energy electrons, which are transferred along a series of acceptor molecules in an electron transport chain to photosystem I. Photosystem II obtains replacement electrons from water molecules, resulting in their split into hydrogen ions (H+) and oxygen atoms. The oxygen atoms combine to form molecular oxygen (O_2), which is released into the atmosphere. The hydrogen ions are released into the lumen. Additional hydrogen ions are pumped into the lumen by electron acceptor molecules. This creates a high concentration of ions inside the lumen. The flow of hydrogen ions back across the photosynthetic membrane provides the energy needed to drive the synthesis of the energy-rich moleculeATP. High-energy electrons released as photosystem I absorbs light energy are used to drive the synthesis of NADPH. Photosystem I obtains replacement electrons from the electron transport chain. ATP provides the energy and NADPH provides the hydrogen atoms needed to drive the subsequent photosynthetic dark reaction, or Calvin cycle.

origin (see THRACE) and had their capital at Gordium. The kingdom of their legendary king, MIDAS, ended c. 700 BC with the invasion of the Cimmerians, who burned the capital. The Phrygians excelled in metalwork, wood carving, carpet making, and embroidery. Their religious cult of the GREAT MOTHER OF THE GODS was passed on to the Greeks. After 1945, U.S. archaeologists discovered carved stone tombs and shrines there.

Phumiphon Adunlayadet See BHUMIBOL ADULYADEJ

Phyfe \'fīf\, **Duncan** *orig.* **Duncan Fife** (1768–1854) Scottish-U.S. furniture designer. His family settled in Albany, N.Y., c. 1784; there he became an apprentice cabinetmaker and eventually opened his own shop. In 1792 he moved to New York City, where he changed the spelling of his name and became so successful that he employed 100 carvers and cabinetmakers. He was one of the first Americans to use the factory method of manufacturing furniture successfully. Though he did not originate a new furniture style, he interpreted fashionable European styles—SHERATON, REGENCY, DIRECTOIRE, EMPIRE—with such grace that he became a major exponent of Neoclassicism. His furniture, decorated with typical period ornaments such as harps and acanthus leaves, was generally of high-quality mahogany.

Mahogany side chair designed by Phyfe, 1807; in The Henry Francis du Pont Winterthur Museum, Delaware.

BY COURTESY OF THE HENRY FRANCIS DU PONT WINTERTHUR MUSEUM, DELAWARE

phyle \'fī-lē\ Any of several TRIBES that formed the largest political subgroups in all Dorian and most Ionian Greek city-states. Phylae were simultaneously kinship groups, corporations with their own officials and priests, and local units for administrative and military purposes. Athens's original four phylae were replaced by 10 under CLEISTHENES' reorganization (508/7 BC); Sparta's original three were supplanted by five in the 8th century BC.

phyllite \'fi-ˌlīt\ Fine-grained METAMORPHIC ROCK formed by the recrystallization of fine-grained, parent SEDIMENTARY ROCKS, such as mudstones or shales. Phyllite has a marked tendency to split into sheets or slabs; it may have a sheen on its surfaces due to tiny plates of micas. Its grain size is larger than that of SLATE but smaller than that of SCHIST.

phylloxera \ˌfi-ˌläk-'sir-ə, fə-'läk-sə-rə\ Any of numerous, chiefly North American, INSECT species (genus *Phylloxera,* order Homoptera), many of which are serious pests of plants. Phylloxera form galls on and can defoliate trees, especially HICKORY and PECAN. See also GRAPE PHYLLOXERA.

phylogenetic tree \ˌfī-lō-jə-'ne-tik\ Diagram showing the evolutionary interrelations of a group of organisms that usually originated from a shared ancestral form. The ancestor is in the tree trunk; organisms that have arisen from it are placed at the ends of tree branches. The distance of one group from the other groups indicates the degree of relationship; that is, closely related groups are located on branches close to one another. Though phylogenetic trees are speculative, they provide a convenient method for studying phylogenetic relationships and EVOLUTION. See also PHYLOGENY.

phylogeny \fī-'lä-jə-nē\ History of the EVOLUTION of a species or group, especially lines of descent and relationships among broad groups. The fundamental proposition is that plants or animals of different species descended from common ancestors. Because the evidence for such relationships is almost always incomplete, most judgments of phylogenicity are based on indirect evidence and cautious speculation. Modern TAXONOMY, the science of classifying organisms, is based on phylogeny. Early taxonomic systems had no theoretical basis; organisms were grouped according to apparent similarity. Biologists who propose a phylogeny obtain evidence from the fields of paleontology, comparative anatomy, comparative embryology, biochemistry, and molecular biology. The data and conclusions of phylogeny indicate that today's living creatures are the product of a historical process of evolution and that degrees of resemblance within and between groups correspond to degrees of relationship by descent from common ancestors. See also PHYLOGENETIC TREE.

physical anthropology Branch of ANTHROPOLOGY concerned with the study of HUMAN EVOLUTION and human biological variation. Research on human evolution involves the discovery, analysis, and description of fossilized human remains. Two key goals are the identification of differences between humans and their human and nonhuman ancestors, and the clarification of the biological emergence of humankind. A variety of quantitative methods are used, including the comparative analysis of genetic codes. Research on biological variation among contemporary humans once relied heavily on the concept of RACE, but today principles of

GENETICS and the analysis of such factors as BLOOD TYPE have largely eliminated race as a scientific category.

physical chemistry Branch of CHEMISTRY concerned with interactions and transformations of materials. Unlike other branches, it deals with the principles of physics underlying all chemical interactions (e.g., GAS LAWS), measuring, correlating, and explaining the quantitative aspects of reactions. QUANTUM MECHANICS has clarified much for physical chemistry by modeling the smallest particles, ATOMS and MOLECULES, enabling theoretical chemists to use computers and sophisticated mathematical techniques to understand the chemical behavior of matter. Chemical thermodynamics deals with the relationship between heat and other forms of chemical energy, kinetics with CHEMICAL REACTION rates. Subdisciplines of physical chemistry include ELECTROCHEMISTRY, photochemistry, surface chemistry, and CATALYSIS.

physical education Training in physical fitness and in skills requiring or promoting it. In the U.S. it is required in most primary and secondary schools. It generally includes CALISTHENICS, GYMNASTICS, various sports, and some study of health. College majors in physical education have been available since the early 20th century. Most teaching is done in gymnasiums, though outdoor sports are also emphasized.

physical medicine and rehabilitation *or* **physiatry** \ˌfiz-ē-ˈa-trē\ *or* **physical therapy** *or* **rehabilitation medicine** Medical specialty treating chronic disabilities through physical means to help patients return to a comfortable, productive life, despite a medical problem. Its objectives are pain relief, functional improvement or maintenance, training in essential activities, and functional testing of areas such as strength, mobility, breathing capacity, and coordination. Physical medicine may use DIATHERMY, HYDROTHERAPY, MASSAGE, exercise, and functional training. The last can mean learning to work with a guide dog or a PROSTHESIS or learning new ways to carry out everyday activities with a limb missing, sometimes by using assistive devices. Physician specialists head rehabilitation teams including a physical therapist, rehabilitation engineer, rehabilitation nurse, and psychological counselor, and sometimes a respiratory or speech therapist. See also OCCUPATIONAL THERAPY, ORTHOPEDIC surgery.

physics Science that deals with the structure of MATTER and the interactions between the fundamental constituents of the observable universe. Long called natural philosophy (from the Greek *physikos*), physics is concerned with all aspects of nature, covering the behavior of objects under the action of given forces and the nature and origin of gravitational, electromagnetic, and nuclear force fields. The goal of physics is to formulate comprehensive principles that bring together and explain all discernible phenomena. See also AERODYNAMICS, ASTROPHYSICS, ATOMIC PHYSICS, BIOPHYSICS, MECHANICS, NUCLEAR PHYSICS, PARTICLE PHYSICS, QUANTUM MECHANICS, SOLID-STATE PHYSICS, STATISTICAL MECHANICS.

physics, mathematical See MATHEMATICAL PHYSICS

physiocrat Member of a school of economics, founded in 18th-century France, that held that government should not interfere with the operation of natural economic laws and that land is the source of all wealth. It is generally regarded as the first scientific school of economics. The physiocratic school (the name refers to the "rule of nature") was founded by FRANCOIS QUESNAY, who demonstrated the economic relation between a workshop and a farm and asserted that the farm alone added to a nation's wealth. The physiocrats envisaged a society in which written law would be in harmony with NATURAL LAW. They pictured a predominantly agricultural society, attacking MERCANTILISM for its emphasis on manufacturing and foreign trade and its mass of economic regulations. Quesnay's disciples included Victor Riqueti, the comte de MIRABEAU, and Pierre Samuel du Pont de Nemours (1739–1817). The school was in decline by 1768, and after the dismissal of a sympathetic comptroller general in 1776 the leading physiocrats were exiled. Though many of their theories, notably their theory of wealth, were later demolished, their introduction of SCIENTIFIC METHOD to economics had a permanent effect on the discipline.

physiology \ˌfi-zē-ˈä-lə-jē\ Study of the functioning of living organisms or their constituent tissues or cells. Physiology was usually considered separately from ANATOMY until the development of high-powered microscopes made it clear that structure and function were inseparable at the cellular and molecular level. An understanding of BIOCHEMISTRY is fundamental to physiology. Physiological processes are dynamic; cells change their function in response to changes in the composition of their local environment, and the organism responds to alterations in both its internal and external environment. Many physiological reactions are aimed at preserving a constant physical and chemical internal environment (HOMEOSTASIS). See also CYTOLOGY.

phytoflagellate \ˌfī-tō-ˈfla-jə-lət\ Any of several PROTOZOANS that have flagella in addition to sharing many characteristics with typical ALGAE, especially the pigment CHLOROPHYLL and various other pigments. Some species, though similar in form, lack chlorophyll. Phytoflagellates may obtain nutrients by photosynthesis, by absorption through the body surface, or by ingestion of food particles. CRYPTOMONADS are among the more important phytoflagellates.

phytoplankton \ˌfī-tō-ˈplaŋk-tən\ FLORA of freely floating, often minute organisms that drift with water currents. Like land vegetation, phytoplankton uses carbon dioxide, releases oxygen, and converts minerals to a form animals can use. In fresh water, large numbers of green ALGAE often color lakes and ponds, and CYANOBACTERIA may affect the taste of drinking water. Oceanic phytoplankton is the primary food source, directly or indirectly, of all sea organisms. Composed of groups with silica-containing skeletons, such as DIATOMS and DINOFLAGELLATES, phytoplankton varies seasonally in amount, increasing in spring and fall with favorable light, temperature, and minerals.

pi In mathematics, the RATIO of the circumference of a CIRCLE to its diameter. An IRRATIONAL NUMBER (see also TRANSCENDENTAL NUMBER), it has an approximate value of 3.14159265, but its exact value must be represented by a symbol, the Greek letter π. Pi is used in calculations involving lengths, areas, and volumes of circles, spheres, cylinders, and cones. It also arises frequently in problems dealing with certain periodic phenomena (e.g., motion of pendulums, alternating electric currents). To make such calculations precise, modern computers have carried pi to more than 200 billion decimal places.

Piaf, Edith \ˈpyȧf *Engl* ˈpē-ˌaf\ *orig.* **Edith Giovanna Gassion** (1915–1963) French popular singer. Her mother, a café singer, abandoned her at birth; Piaf became blind at 3 as a result of meningitis, but recovered her sight four years later. Her father, a circus acrobat, took her along on tours and encouraged her to sing. She sang for years in the streets of Paris, living a raffish life, until discovered by a cabaret owner who suggested she change her name to Piaf, Parisian slang for "sparrow." She was soon singing her chansons in the large music halls of Paris. During World War II she entertained French prisoners of war and aided several in their escapes. She spent the postwar years touring, gaining worldwide fame with her intense performances of such songs as "La vie en rose" and "Non, je ne regrette rien." In the 1950s she became the most highly paid performer in the world. Despite her success, her life was marred by illness, accidents, and unhappiness; she died at 47.

Piaget \pyä-ˈzhā\, **Jean** (1896–1980) Swiss psychologist. Trained in zoology and philosophy, Piaget later studied psychology in Zurich (from 1918) with CARL GUSTAV JUNG and EUGEN BLEULER, and was subsequently affiliated with the University of Geneva from 1929 until his death. He developed a theory of "genetic epistemology," a natural timetable for the development of the child's ability to think in which he traced four stages—the sensorimotor (ages 0–2), preoperational or symbolic (2–7), concrete operational (7–12), and formal operational (through adulthood)—each marked by increased cognitive sophistication and ability to use symbols. In 1955 Piaget founded and became director (to 1980) of an international center for genetic epistemology in Geneva. His numerous books include *The Language and Thought of the Child* (1923), *Judgment and Reasoning in the Child* (1924), *The Origin of Intelligence in Children* (1948), and *The Early Growth of Logic in the Child* (1964). He is regarded as the foremost developmental psychologist of the 20th century.

piano *or* **pianoforte** Keyboard instrument with wire strings that sound when struck by hammers activated by the keys. It was invented in Florence by B. CRISTOFORI before 1720, with the particular aim of permitting note-to-note dynamic variation (lacking in the HARPSICHORD). It differs from the older CLAVICHORD in that its hammers (rather than tangents) are thrown at the strings and bounce back, permitting the struck string to vibrate loudly, and its dynamic range is far wider. A cast-iron frame is needed to withstand the strings' tremendous tension. Pianos have taken various shapes. The original harpsichord (or wing) shape has survived in the modern grand piano; the less-expensive square (actually rectangular)

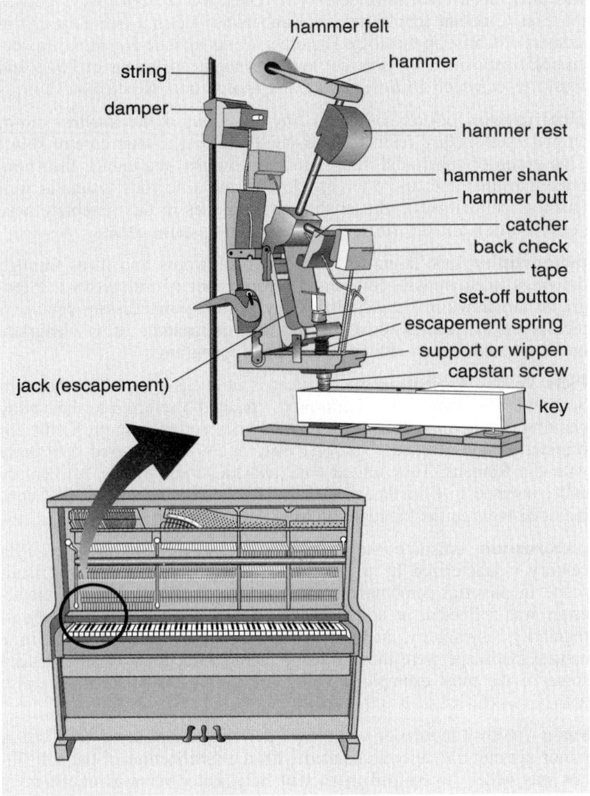

Each key of a piano actuates a complex mechanical system to strike a taut string and produce a musical tone. Depending on how the keys and pedals are operated, the mechanism may produce a variety of effects on the same note, from muffled to brilliant and from quick to sustained.

piano, standard in the early 19th century, was replaced by the upright piano, in which the strings are vertical. For at least 150 years the piano was the most important instrument in Western music.

piano nobile \ˌpyä-nō-ˈnȯ-bi-lā\ (Italian: "noble floor") In a Renaissance building, the first floor above ground level. In the typical palace erected by an Italian prince, the large, high-ceilinged reception rooms were in this upper, main story. Often a grand exterior staircase or pair of staircases led from ground level up to the piano nobile.

Piave River \ˈpyä-vā\ River, northeastern Italy. Rising in the Carnic Alps south of Lienz near the Austrian frontier, it flows south and southeast into the Adriatic Sea, east of VENICE. It is 137 mi (220 km) long. During World War I, its valley was the scene of several battles against the Austrians (see Battle of CAPORETTO). In 1966 the river burst its dikes in a major flood.

piazza \pē-ˈät-sə, pē-ˈa-zə\ Open square or marketplace, surrounded by buildings, in an Italian town or city. It was equivalent to the plaza of Spanish-speaking countries. The term became more widely used in the 16th–18th century, denoting any large open space with buildings around it. In 17th–18th-century Britain, long covered walks or galleries with roofs supported by columns were called piazzas; in the U.S. in the 19th century, piazza was another name for a veranda formed by projecting eaves.

Piazzetta \pyät-ˈtsāt-tä\, **Giovanni Battista** *or* **Giambattista Piazzetta** (1682–1754) Italian painter, illustrator, and designer. Trained as a wood carver by his father, he turned to painting and became one of the outstanding Venetian artists of the 18th century. His art evolved from Italian baroque traditions of the 17th century to the Rococo style. He had a strong influence on the young GIOVANNI BATTISTA TIEPOLO at the time he painted the finest of his early religious works, *St. James Led to Martyrdom* (1722). His most popular work is the celebrated *Fortune Teller* (1740). On the founding of the Venetian Academy in 1750, he was made its first director.

Piazzolla \pyät-ˈsō-lə\, **Astor** (1921–1992) Argentine composer. Born in Buenos Aires, he lived in the Bronx, N.Y., until he was 15, then returned to Argentina to play bandoneon (a type of accordion) in a tango band led by Anibal Troilo (1917–1975). From 1944 he led his own groups. His interest in classical music led to study with N. BOULANGER (1954–55) and the development of his own compositional style, infusing elements of jazz and modern music into tango. Not always initially popular with tango fans, his music is now recognized as having revived the genre and greatly expanded its artistic potential.

Picabia \pē-kȧb-ˈyȧ\, **Francis** (1879–1953) French painter, illustrator, designer, writer, and editor. The son of a Cuban diplomat and a Frenchwoman, he was successively involved in Impressionism, Neo-Impressionism, Fauvism, Cubism, and Surrealism. In New York in 1915, he joined MARCEL DUCHAMP and MAN RAY in founding the U.S. DADA movement. Back in Europe in the 1920s, he plunged into the Surrealist style, then produced abstract and figurative paintings. Notable for his inventiveness and absurdist humor as well as his disconcerting changes of style, he founded an avant-garde magazine (1917–24), contributed to others, and published a variety of pamphlets.

Picardy \ˈpi-kər-dē\ *French* **Picardie** \ˌpē-kȧr-ˈdē\ Historical region, northern France. Before 1790 it was bounded by the Strait of Dover, Artois, and Flanders, and by Champagne, Normandy, and the ENGLISH CHANNEL. In the 13th century the area included the countships of Amiénois and Vermandois, which were united to the French crown by PHILIP II from 1185. It was joined to BURGUNDY in 1435 and became a province of France in 1482. The region was the scene of heavy fighting in both World Wars, especially in the Battle of the SOMME (1916).

picaresque novel Early form of the NOVEL, usually a first-person narrative, relating the episodic adventures of a rogue or lowborn adventurer (Spanish, *pícaro*) who drifts from place to place and from one social milieu to another in an effort to survive. The genre originated in Spain and had its prototype in MATEO ALEMAN's *Guzmán de Alfarache* (1599). It appeared in various European literatures until the mid-18th century, when the growth of the realistic novel led to its decline. Because of the opportunities for satire they present, picaresque elements enriched many later novels, such as NIKOLAY GOGOL's *Dead Souls* (1842), MARK TWAIN's *Huckleberry Finn* (1884), and THOMAS MANN's *Confessions of Felix Krull* (1954).

Picasso, Pablo (Ruiz y) (1881–1973) Spanish-French painter, sculptor, printmaker, ceramicist, and stage designer. Trained by his father, a professor of drawing, he exhibited his first works at 13. After moving permanently to Paris in 1904, he replaced the predominantly blue tones of his so-called Blue Period (1901–4) with those of pottery and flesh in his Rose Period (1904–6). His first masterpiece, *Les demoiselles d'Avignon* (1907), was controversial for its violent treatment of the female body and the masklike faces derived from his study of African art. The next year, he and his friend GEORGES BRAQUE found inspiration in PAUL CEZANNE before beginning to experimenting with CUBISM, depicting multiple views of an object on the same canvas. By 1912 they had taken Cubism further by gluing paper and other materials onto their canvases. Between 1917 and 1924 Picasso designed stage sets for five ballets for SERGEY DIAGHILEV's BALLETS RUSSES. In the 1920s and '30s, the Surrealists spurred him to explore new subject matter, particularly the image of the Minotaur. The SPANISH CIVIL WAR inspired perhaps his greatest work, the enormous *Guernica* (1937), whose violent imagery condemned the useless destruction of life. After World War II he joined the Communist Party and devoted his time to sculpture, ceramics, and lithography as well as painting. In his late years he created variations on the works of earlier artists, the most famous being a series of 58 pictures based on *Las Meninas* of DIEGO VELAZQUEZ. An innovator throughout his 80-year career, Picasso seemed to move beyond criticism and made his influence felt by virtually every 20th-century artist.

Piccard \pē-ˈkär\, **Auguste** (1884–1962) Swiss-Belgian physicist and BALLOON and undersea explorer. He studied and taught physics in Zurich, and later at the University of Brussels (1922–54). In 1930 he designed a balloon with an airtight, pressurized cabin to ascend into the stratosphere to study cosmic rays. In 1932 he ascended over 55,500 ft (16,650 m). The undersea BATHYSCAPHE he designed with his son, Jacques, descended in 1953 more than 10,000 ft (3,000 m). His grandson Bernard Piccard made the first round-the-world balloon flight in 1999.

Piccolomini (-Pieri) \ˌpēk-kō-ˈlō-mē-nē\, **Ottavio** (1599–1656) Italian general. He entered the service of the Habsburgs in 1616 and became a trusted lieutenant to ALBRECHT W. E. VON WALLENSTEIN. Overlooked for advancement, he turned against his superior and conspired in his assassination (1634). He served Spain against the French in the Netherlands and won the Battle of Thionville (1639), for which he was created duke of Amalfi. In 1648 Emperor FERDINAND III named him commander in chief and he conducted the last campaign of the THIRTY YEARS' WAR. He represented Austria at the Congress of Nuremberg (1649), which negotiated issues left unsettled by the Peace of WESTPHALIA.

picker Machine for harvesting a crop (e.g., corn, cotton) and preparing it for storage. The mechanical picker removes mainly the desired portion of the plant (e.g., grain and cobs of corn, bolls of cotton) rather than harvesting the entire plant.

pickerel Any of several North American PIKES (family Esocidae), distinguished from the northern pike and MUSKELLUNGE by their smaller size, completely scaled cheeks and gill covers, and banded or chainlike markings. The chain pickerel *(Esox niger)* grows to about 2 ft (0.6 m) and a weight of about 3 lbs (1.4 kg). The barred *(E. americanus)* and grass *(E. vermiculatus)* pickerels reach a maximum weight of about 1 lb (0.5 kg).

Pickering, Timothy (1745–1829) American politician. Born in Salem, Mass., he joined the militia in 1766 and served in the American Revolution under GEORGE WASHINGTON, becoming adjutant general (1777–78) and quartermaster general (1780–85). He later served as U.S. postmaster general (1791–95), secretary of war (1795), and secretary of state (1795–1800). A leader of the FEDERALIST PARTY, he served in the U.S. Senate (1803–11) and House of Representatives (1813–17). He opposed the War of 1812 and was a member of the ESSEX JUNTO. After retiring from politics, he turned to experimental farming and education.

picketing Act by workers of standing in front of or near a workplace to call attention to their grievances, discourage patronage, and, during STRIKES, to discourage strikebreakers. Picketing is also used in non-work-related protests. The U.S. Norris-LaGuardia Act (1932) made it easier for workers to picket by restricting the use of court injunctions against strikes, but the TAFT-HARTLEY ACT (1947) outlawed mass picketing.

Pickett, George Edward (1825–1875) U.S. and Confederate army officer. Born in Richmond, Va., he graduated from West Point and served in the Mexican War. He resigned his commission in 1861 to enter the Confederate army. He rose to major general and commanded a division at the Battle of Fredericksburg. At the Battle of GETTYSBURG, he led the climactic attack known as Pickett's Charge, in which 4,300 men of his division constituted almost half the attacking force under JAMES LONGSTREET. The attempt to breach the Union lines on Cemetery Ridge was repulsed with the loss of about 60% of his men. Though criticized for his leadership, he retained his command.

Pickford, Mary *orig.* **Gladys Mary Smith** (1893–1979) U.S. film actress. Born in Toronto, she acted with a stock company from age 5, went on tour at 8, and was performing on Broadway by 18. She starred in D. W. GRIFFITH'S *The Lonely Villa* (1909) and by 1913 was acting in movies exclusively. One of the first movie stars, she became a symbol of innocence and was known as "America's sweetheart." Her silent films included *Tess of the Storm Country* (1914), *Rebecca of Sunnybrook Farm* (1917), *Poor Little Rich Girl* (1917), and *Pollyanna* (1920). A shrewd businesswoman, she formed UNITED ARTISTS CORP. (1919) with her second husband, DOUGLAS FAIRBANKS, and others. She received an Academy Award for her first sound film, *Coquette* (1929). She retired from acting in 1933 and received a special Academy Award in 1975.

Pico Bolívar See Pico BOLÍVAR

Pico della Mirandola \ˈpē-kō-ˌdāl-lä-mē-ˈrän-dō-ˌlä\, **Giovanni, conte (count) di Concordia** (1463–1494) Italian scholar, philosopher, and humanist. He settled in Florence in 1484 as a protégé of LORENZO DE'MEDICI and MARSILIO FICINO. In 1486 he posted in Rome a list of 900 theses on logic, mathematics, physics, and other subjects that he proposed to defend against any opponent. His *Oration on the Dignity of Man* (1486), which accompanied the posting, epitomizes Renaissance HUMANISM. Accused of heresy by the pope, he was later cleared, and he was later reconverted to orthodoxy by GIROLAMO SAVONAROLA. Pico was the first Christian scholar to use Kabbalistic doctrine (see KABBALA) in support of Christian theology. His other works include *Heptaplus* (a seven-point exposition of Genesis) and a synoptic treatment of PLATO and ARISTOTLE, of which *Of Being and Unity* is a portion. He died at 31.

picornavirus \pē-ˌkȯr-nə-ˈvī-rəs\ Any of a group of the smallest known animal VIRUSES. (*Pico* refers to their small size, *rna* to their core of RNA.) This group of spheroidal viruses includes viruses that attack the vertebrate intestinal tract and often invade the central nervous system as well (such as polioviruses), viruses that infect tissues in the vertebrate nose (RHINOVIRUSES), and the virus agent of FOOT-AND-MOUTH DISEASE.

pictography \pik-ˈtä-grə-fē\ Expression of words and ideas through drawings (pictographs), considered a forerunner of true WRITING. Pictographs are drawn in a standardized way, omitting unnecessary details. A pictograph that stands for a specific idea or meaning is an ideogram; one that stands for an individual word is a logogram.

Picts \ˈpikts\ Ancient people of what is now eastern and northeastern Scotland. The name (from Latin *picti,* "painted") referred to their body painting or tattooing. They were probably descended from pre-Celtic aborigines. They attacked HADRIAN'S WALL in 297 and warred constantly with the Romans. They united their two kingdoms by the 7th century and converted to Christianity, and in 843 KENNETH I, king of the Scots, included them in the kingdom of Alba, later Scotland.

picturesque Artistic concept and style of the late 18th and early 19th century characterized by a preoccupation with architecture and landscape in pictorial combination with each other. In Britain, the picturesque was defined as an aesthetic quality marked by pleasing variety, irregularity, asymmetry, and interesting textures; medieval ruins in a natural landscape were thought to be picturesque. JOHN NASH produced some of the most exemplary works embodying the concept. See also FOLLY.

Picus \ˈpī-kəs\ In ROMAN MYTHOLOGY, a woodpecker sacred to MARS. A minor agricultural deity associated with the fertilization of the soil, Picus was widely worshiped in ancient Italy. Later versions of the myth made him an early king of Italy, whose bride, CIRCE, changed him into a woodpecker. In art he was shown as a woodpecker mounted on a pillar, and later as a youth with a woodpecker on his head. The woodpecker was also an important bird in augury.

pidgin \ˈpi-jən\ Language with a very limited vocabulary and a simplified grammar. Pidgins usually arise to permit communication between groups with no language in common; if a pidgin becomes established as the native language of a group, it is known as a CREOLE. Pidgins such as Chinese Pidgin English and Melanesian Pidgin English arose through contact between English-speaking traders and inhabitants of the Far East and the Pacific islands. Other pidgins appeared with the slave trade in Africa and with the importation of West African slaves to Caribbean plantations. Most of the small vocabulary of a pidgin language (Melanesian Pidgin has only 2,000 words, Chinese Pidgin English only 700) is usually drawn from a single language (Melanesian Pidgin, for example, has an English word stock of more than 90%).

Piedmont \ˈpēd-ˌmänt\ *Italian* **Piemonte** \pyā-ˈmȯn-tā\ Autonomous region (pop., 1996 est.: 4,289,000), northwestern Italy. With its capital at TURIN, it borders on France and Switzerland. In Roman times its passes connected Italy with the transalpine provinces of GAUL. In the Middle Ages, the House of SAVOY was the region's most important power. It was a center during the 19th-century RISORGIMENTO to unite Italy. VICTOR EMMANUEL II, originally king of Piedmont and Sardinia, became modern Italy's first king in 1861. Surrounded by mountains, it is centered on the PO RIVER valley, which contains some of Italy's best farmland, producing wheat, rice, and wines. Its hydroelectric plants supply energy for much of northern Italy.

Piedmont Geographic region, eastern U.S. Lying between the APPALACHIAN MTNS. and the Atlantic coastal plain, it is about 600 mi (950 km) long, and stretches between the Hudson River and central Alabama. A relatively low, rolling plateau crossed by many rivers, it is a fertile agricultural region.

Pielinen \ˈpē-ə-ˌlē-nən\, **Lake** Lake, southeastern Finland, near the border with Russia. It is 56 mi (90 km) long and has an area of 422 sq mi (1,093 sq km). It has many islands and is drained southward into Lake

O
P
Q
R

SAIMAA by the Pielis River. It is surrounded by dense forests, especially on its western shore. The shore is capped by Koli Hill, the center of a winter sports area.

Pieman River \'pī-mən\ River, northwestern TASMANIA, Australia. It is formed near Tullah by the confluence of the Macintosh and MURCHISON rivers. Rising on the western edge of the central highlands, it is about 70 mi (115 km) long and flows west to the Indian Ocean. There was some gold and tin mining in the area during the 1870s and 1890s. It was named for an infamous convict, Alexander Pierce (Jimmy the Pieman), who was recaptured at its mouth after escaping from the MACQUARIE HARBOUR penal colony.

pier In building construction, a vertical load-bearing member such as an intermediate support for adjacent ends of two BAYS or spans. Bulkier than a column but smaller than a wall, a pier can support an arch or beam. The lower portion of a pier may be widened to better distribute the downward pressure of a massive overlying structure. In Romanesque and Gothic architecture, a feature of the NAVE arcade is the compound pier, which is cross-shaped in cross section, with shafts placed in the recesses.

Pierce, Franklin (1804–1869) 14th president of the U.S. (1853–57). Born in Hillsboro, N.H., he practiced law and served in the U.S. House of Representatives (1833–37) and Senate (1837–42). He returned to his law practice, serving briefly in the Mexican War. At the deadlocked Democratic convention of 1852, he was nominated as the compromise candidate; though largely unknown nationally, he unexpectedly trounced WINFIELD SCOTT in the general election. For the sake of harmony and business prosperity, he was inclined to oppose antislavery agitation so as to placate Southern opinion. He promoted U.S. territorial expansion, resulting in the diplomatic controversy of the OSTEND MANIFESTO. He reorganized the diplomatic and consular service and created the U.S. Court of Claims. He encouraged plans for a transcontinental railroad and approved the GADSDEN PURCHASE. To promote northwestern migration and conciliate sectional demands, he approved the KANSAS-NEBRASKA ACT but was unable to settle the resultant problems. Defeated for renomination by JAMES BUCHANAN in 1856, he retired from politics.

Franklin Pierce.

BY COURTESY OF THE LIBRARY OF CONGRESS, WASHINGTON, D.C.

Piero della Francesca \fran-'ches-kə\ (c. 1420–1492) Italian painter. Son of a prosperous tanner and wool merchant in the Republic of Florence, he became known for his serene, disciplined exploration of perspective. His fresco cycle for San Francesco at Arezzo, *The Legend of the True Cross* (1450s), exemplifies his simplicity and clarity of structure, controlled use of perspective, and aura of serenity. His famous diptych portrait of his patrons, Count Federico da Montefeltro and his wife (c. 1470), is known for its unidealized depiction of their features and the use of landscape in the background. Though he had little influence on his contemporaries, Piero's important scientific and poetic contributions to Renaissance painting are now well recognized. Also a writer, he produced theoretical treatises on geometry and perspective.

"The Baptism of Christ," panel painting by Piero della Francesca, c. 1440–45; in the National Gallery, London.

BY COURTESY OF THE TRUSTEES OF THE NATIONAL GALLERY, LONDON; PHOTOGRAPH, A.C. COOPER LTD.

Piero di Cosimo \kò-'sē-mō\ *orig.* **Piero di Lorenzo** (1461/62–1521) Italian painter. His name derives from that of his master, Cosimo Rosselli, whom he assisted on frescoes for the Sistine Chapel. His later mythological paintings exhibit a bizarre romantic style. Many are filled with fantastic hybrid human-animal forms engaging in revels (*The Discovery of Honey,* c. 1500) or fights (*Battle of the Centaurs and the Lapiths,* c. 1500). His art reflects his eccentric personality. He belonged to no school of painting but borrowed from many artists, including SANDRO BOTTICELLI and LEONARDO DA VINCI.

Pierre \'pir\ City (pop., 1993 est.: 13,000), capital of South Dakota. It is located on the MISSOURI RIVER, in the geographic center of the state. The area was originally inhabited by Arikara Indians. The city was founded in 1880 as the western terminus of the Chicago and North Western Railway, which spurred its growth as a mining and trade center. It became the state capital in 1889. It is the hub of a large, diversified agricultural area with a significant tourist industry based on nearby lakes.

Pietà \pyā-'tä\ (Italian: "Pity") Depiction of the Virgin Mary supporting the body of the dead Christ. The theme grew out of that of the Lamentation, the moment between the Descent from the Cross and the Entombment. It first appeared in Germany in the early 14th century. It enjoyed greater popularity in northern Europe than in Italy through the 15th century, yet the supreme representation is MICHELANGELO's (1499), in ST. PETER'S BASILICA. The Pietà was widely represented in both painting and sculpture. Michelangelo's conception of Mary bearing Jesus' body on her knees was standard until the 16th century, when artists began to place Jesus at Mary's feet. Though most religious art declined after the 17th century, the Pietà retained its popularity through the 19th century.

"Pietà," marble sculpture by Michelangelo, 1499; in St. Peter's Basilica, Rome.

SCALA/ART RESOURCE, NEW YORK CITY

Pietism \'pī-ə-ˌti-zəm\ Reform movement in German LUTHERANISM that arose in the 17th century. Philipp Jakob Spener (1635–1705), a Lutheran pastor, originated the movement when he organized an "assembly of piety," a regular meeting of Christians for devotional reading and spiritual exchange. Spener advocated greater involvement of the laity in worship, more extensive study of Scripture, and ministerial training that emphasized piety and learning rather than disputation. Under Spener's successor, August Hermann Francke (1663–1727), the University of Halle became a center of the movement. Pietism influenced the MORAVIAN and Methodist churches (see METHODISM).

Pietro da Cortona *orig.* **Pietro Berrettini** (1596–1669) Italian painter, architect, and decorator. The son of a stonemason of Cortona, Tuscany, he was apprenticed to a painter in Florence. His first major work, a series of frescoes in the small church of Santa Bibiana in Rome (1624–26), was commissioned by Pope Urban VIII, and the patronage of the pope's family, the Barberinis, advanced Pietro's career. The rich exuberance of those frescoes was a prelude to his best-known work, the large ceiling fresco *Allegory of Divine Providence and Barberini Power* (1632–39) in the Barberini Palace. Here he demonstrated his mastery of illusion, for the center of the vault appears open to the sky and the figures seem to hover in space. He provided a series of frescoes for the Pitti Palace in Florence. Also a master architect, his greatest architectural accomplishment is the church of Sts. Martina e Luca in Rome (1634), the first baroque church built as a unitary whole.

piezoelectricity \pē-ˌā-zō-ə-ˌlek-'tri-sə-tē\ Appearance of an ELECTRIC FIELD in certain nonconducting CRYSTALS as a result of the application of mechanical PRESSURE. Pressure polarizes some crystals, such as quartz, by slightly separating the centers of positive and negative charge. The resultant electric field is detectable as a voltage. The converse effect also occurs: an applied electric field produces mechanical deformation in the crystal. Using this effect, a high-frequency alternating electric current (see ALTERNATING CURRENT) can be converted to an ultrasonic wave of the same frequency, while a mechanical vibration, such as sound, can be converted into a corresponding electrical signal. Piezoelectricity is utilized in microphones, phonograph pickups, and telephone communications systems.

pig Any wild or domestic even-toed UNGULATE (family Suidae) that is a stout-bodied, short-legged omnivore, with thick, sparsely bristled skin, a long mobile snout, small tail, and hooves with two functional and two nonfunctional digits. Pigs are native to European, Asian, and North African forests. Wild pigs use their tusklike teeth to forage and for defense; the teeth of domestic pigs, which were developed from wild pigs in Europe c. 1500 BC, are less developed. Pigs are regarded as highly intelligent. Domestic pigs are classified as lard (thick fat, carcass weighing at least 220 lbs, or 100 kg), bacon (carcass about 150 lbs, or 70 kg), and PORK (carcass about 100 lbs, or 45 kg) pigs, depending on the principal product derived from them; they are also a source of leather. Today they are usually bred in almost complete confinement. See also BOAR, HOG.

pig iron Crude IRON obtained directly from the BLAST FURNACE and cast in molds (see CAST IRON). The crude ingots, called pigs, are then remelted along with scrap and alloying elements and recast into molds to produce various iron and STEEL products (see BESSEMER PROCESS, FINERY PROCESS, PUDDLING PROCESS).

Pigalle \pē-ˈgȧl\, **Jean-Baptiste** (1714–1785) French sculptor. Born into a family of master carpenters, he began training as a sculptor in Paris at 18 and then studied in Rome (1736–40). Returning to France, he modeled the first version of his famous *Mercury Fastening His Sandals,* which in a later version won him admission to the Royal Academy (1744). The statue became so popular that in 1748 LOUIS XV commissioned a life-size marble version to present to FREDERICK II of Prussia. He was also noted for his portrait sculptures. His *Nude Voltaire* (1776), an anatomically realistic rendering of the aged philosopher, caused a furor when it was first shown.

pigeon Any species (family Columbidae) of plump, small-billed, monogamous birds, found almost worldwide and recognizable by their head-bobbing strut. Unlike other birds, pigeons suck liquids and provide the young with regurgitated "pigeon's milk." The 175 species of true pigeons include the Old and New World *Columba* species and the Old World *Streptopelia* species; all eat seeds and fruit. Common street pigeons, or rock doves, are descendants of the Eurasian rock *(Columba livia).* From antiquity pigeons were trained to carry messages over long distances. About 115 species of fruit pigeons occur in Africa, southern Asia, Australia, and Pacific islands. The three species of crowned pigeons (genus *Goura*), of New Guinea, are nearly the size of a turkey. See also DOVE, MOURNING DOVE, PASSENGER PIGEON, TURTLEDOVE.

pigeon hawk See MERLIN

pigment Any intensely colored compound used to color other materials. Unlike DYES, pigments do not dissolve; they are applied as fine solid particles mixed with a liquid. In general, the same ones are used in oil- and water-based PAINTS, printing INKS, and plastics. They may be inorganic compounds (usually brighter and longer-lasting) or organic compounds. Natural organic pigments have been used for centuries, but today most are synthetic or inorganic. The primary white pigment is titanium dioxide. Carbon black is the most usual black pigment. Iron oxides give browns, ranging from yellowish through orange to dark brown. Chromium compounds yield chrome yellows, oranges, and greens, cadmium compounds brilliant yellows, oranges, and reds. The most common blues, Prussian blue and ultramarine, are also inorganic. Organic pigments, usually synthesized from aromatic HYDROCARBONS, include the nitrogen-containing azo pigments (red, orange, and yellow; see AZO DYES) and the copper phthalocyanines (brilliant, strong blues and greens). CHLOROPHYLL, CAROTENE, RHODOPSIN, and MELANIN are pigments produced by plants and animals for specialized purposes.

pika \ˈpē-kə, ˈpī-kə\ Any of numerous round-eared, tailless members (genus *Ochotona,* family Ochotonidae) of the RABBIT order (Lagomorpha), found in Asia, eastern Europe, and parts of western North America. Though not HARES, they are sometimes called mouse hare and little chief hare. The hind legs are less developed than a rabbit's; pikas scamper rather than bound. Their brownish or reddish fur is soft, long, and thick. Pikas are 6–12 in. (15–30 cm) long and weigh 4–14 oz (125–440 g). Most species live in rocky, mountainous areas, but some Asian species inhabit burrows. Pikas do not seem to hibernate, but in summer and autumn they "harvest" vegetation, dry it in the sun, then store the hay in protected places (e.g., under rocks) to be eaten in winter.

American pika (*Ochotona princeps*).
KENNETH W. FINK—ROOT RESOURCES

pike Ancient and medieval INFANTRY weapon consisting of a long, metal-pointed spear with a heavy wooden shaft 10–20 ft (3–6 m) in length. Its use by Swiss foot soldiers in the 14th century contributed to the decline of the feudal knights. A variation is used by the picador in BULLFIGHTING.

pike Any of several voracious freshwater fishes (family Esocidae, order Salmoniformes) with a slender body, small scales, long head, shovel-like snout, large mouth, and strong teeth, and with dorsal and anal fins far back on the tail. The northern pike *(Esox lucius)* of North America, Europe, and northern Asia may grow to 4.5 ft (1.4 m) long and weigh 45 lbs (20 kg). A solitary hunter, it lies motionless or lurks among weeds, then suddenly lunges, seizing an approaching fish or invertebrate. Large species also take waterfowl and small mammals. See also MUSKELLUNGE, PICKEREL.

Northern pike (*Esox lucius*).
RUSS KINNE—PHOTO RESEARCHERS

Pike, Kenneth L(ee) (born 1912) U.S. linguist and anthropologist. Born in Woodstock, Conn., Pike has been associated throughout his career with the Summer Institute of Linguistics (now SIL International), an organization dedicated to linguistic study of little-known, unwritten languages, as an ancillary to Bible translation. He originated the linguistic theory known as tagmemics. The tagmeme, a unit comprising a function (e.g., a subject) and a class of items fulfilling that function (e.g., nouns), is identified by semantic as well as syntactic function.

Pike, Zebulon Montgomery (1779–1813) U.S. explorer. Born in Lamberton, N.J., he joined the army at 15. In 1805 he led an expedition to find the headwaters of the Mississippi River; he traveled 2,000 mi (3,200 km) from St. Louis to northern Minnesota, where he erroneously identified Leech Lake as the river's source. In 1806 he was sent to the Southwest to explore the Arkansas and Red rivers. Passing through Colorado, he tried unsuccessfully to climb the 14,110-ft (4,301-m) mountain later named PIKES PEAK. His party continued into northern New Mexico (1807); his report on the Santa Fe region encouraged later expansion into the Southwest. In the WAR OF 1812 he was killed in the attack on York (Toronto).

Pikes Peak Mountain peak, eastern Colorado. It is located in the Front Range of the ROCKY MTNS., near COLORADO SPRINGS. At 14,110 ft (4,301 m) in height, it is known for the panoramic view from its summit. It was discovered in 1806 by U.S. explorer ZEBULON PIKE. The view from it is said to have inspired Katharine Lee Bates to write "America the Beautiful" in 1893.

pilaster \pi-ˈlas-tər\ In CLASSICAL ARCHITECTURE, a shallow rectangular column built into a wall and projecting slightly beyond it. It has a capital and base and conforms to one of the ORDERS. In Roman architecture the pilaster gradually became more and more decorative rather than structural, and served to break up otherwise empty expanses of wall.

Pilate \ˈpī-lət\, **Pontius** (died after AD 36) Roman prefect of JUDAEA (AD 26–36) who presided at the trial of JESUS and gave the order for his

CRUCIFIXION. The NEW TESTAMENT represents Pilate as a weak and vacillating man, who found no fault with Jesus but ordered his execution to please the mob calling for his death. Known for his severity toward the Jews, he was eventually ordered back to Rome to stand trial for cruelty and oppression. A tradition of uncertain accuracy holds that he killed himself on orders from CALIGULA in AD 39; another legend relates that both Pilate and his wife became converts to Christianity.

pilchard \'pil-chərd\ Local name in Britain and elsewhere for the European SARDINE *(Sardina,* or *Clupea, pilchardus).* It is found in the Mediterranean and off the Atlantic coasts of Spain, Portugal, France, and Britain.

Pilcomayo River \ˌpēl-kō-'mä-yō\ River, southern central South America, the chief western tributary of the PARAGUAY RIVER. It rises in the eastern ANDES in western central Bolivia and flows southeast through the GRAN CHACO of Paraguay to join the Paraguay River opposite ASUNCIÓN, after a course of 1,550 mi (2,500 km). It forms part of the boundary between Argentina and Paraguay.

pile In building construction, a postlike foundation member used from prehistoric times. Piles transfer building loads down to a suitable bearing stratum when the soil mass immediately below a construction is unsuitable for the direct bearing of footings (see FOUNDATION). Piles support loads either by bearing directly on rock or suitable soil or by developing friction along their very ample length. In modern civil engineering, piles of timber, steel, or concrete are driven into the ground to support a structure; bridge piers and building foundations may be supported on groups of piles.

pile See HEMORRHOID

pileworm See SHIPWORM

pilgrimage Journey to a shrine or other sacred place undertaken to gain divine aid, as an act of thanksgiving or penance, or to demonstrate devotion. Medieval Christian pilgrims stayed at hospices set up specifically for pilgrims, and on their return trip they wore on their hats the badge of the shrine visited. The chief attractions for pilgrims in the Middle Ages were the Holy Land, SANTIAGO DE COMPOSTELA in Spain, and Rome, but there were hundreds of local pilgrimage sites, including the tomb of St. FRANCIS OF ASSISI and that of ST. THOMAS BECKET in CANTERBURY. More recent pilgrimage sites include the shrine of Our Lady of Guadalupe in Mexico (1531), LOURDES in France (1858), and FÁTIMA in Portugal (1917). The tradition of pilgrimage is also important in Buddhism, with sites including Bodh Gaya, where the BUDDHA received enlightenment, and VARANASI, where he delivered his first sermon. In Islam all members of the faith are enjoined to perform the HAJJ, the pilgrimage to MECCA, at least once in their lifetime.

Pilgrimage of Grace (1536) Uprising in the northern counties of England against the REFORMATION legislation of HENRY VIII. Royal mandates to dissolve the monasteries in the north triggered riots in Lincolnshire and Yorkshire, where 30,000 armed rebels under Robert Aske occupied York, demanding a return to papal obedience and a parliament free from royal influence. Playing for time to assemble enough royal forces to oust the rebels, the 3rd duke of NORFOLK made vague promises, and the rebels dispersed, believing they had won, only to be arrested later; about 220 were executed, including Aske.

Pilgrims First settlers of Plymouth (Massachusetts), the first permanent colony in New England (1620). The members of the English Separatist Church, a radical faction of PURITANISM, composed a third of the 102 colonists who sailed aboard the *Mayflower* to North America, and became the dominant group. The settlers were later collectively referred to as the Forefathers; the term "Pilgrim Fathers" was applied to them by DANIEL WEBSTER at the bicentennial celebration (1820). See also MAYFLOWER COMPACT, PLYMOUTH CO.

pill bug Any species of terrestrial CRUSTACEAN in the genera *Armadillidium* and *Armadillo* (both in the order Isopoda), native to Europe and introduced worldwide. Pill bugs (sometimes called wood lice) resemble tiny armadillos in appearance and behavior; they have a gray, oval body covered with platelike armor, and, when disturbed, roll into a ball. They are about 0.75 in. (19 mm) long. Pill bugs live in dry, sunny places, in dry leaf litter, and on forest edges. See also SOW BUG. See photograph above.

Pill bugs (*Armadillidium vulgare*).
E.S. ROSS

pillar Relatively slender isolated vertical structural member such as a PIER or (usually squat) column. It may be constructed of a single piece of stone or wood or built up of units, such as bricks. A pillar commonly has a load-bearing or stabilizing function, but it may also stand alone, as do commemorative pillars.

Pillars of Hercules Two promontories at the eastern end of Strait of GIBRALTAR. They include the Rock of Gibraltar (at GIBRALTAR) in Europe and Jebel Musa in CEUTA, northern Africa. They are fabled to have been set there by HERACLES as a memorial in his travels to seize the cattle of the three-bodied giant Geryon.

Pillars of Islam See Pillars of ISLAM

Pillsbury Co. U.S. food-products company. It was established in Minneapolis in 1871 as C. A. Pillsbury & Co. Its founder, Charles Alfred Pillsbury (1842–1899), built the company into one of the world's largest milling concerns in the 1880s, expanding the business by obtaining favorable freight rates and building his own grain elevators throughout the Northwest. He sold it to an English syndicate but remained its managing director until his death. Pillsbury later became a successful manufacturer of food products, with subsidiaries including Burger King, Häagen-Dazs, and Green Giant. It was acquired by Grand Metropolitan PLC (now Diageo PLC) in a hostile takeover in 1989.

Pilon \pē-'lō^{n}\, **Germain** (c. 1525–1590) French sculptor. His decoration of the tomb of FRANCIS I (1558), a relatively early work, shows an Italian influence, but he later developed a distinctively French expression by fusing elements of classical and Gothic art with the Fontainebleau adaptation of MANNERISM. His best-known works are funerary sculptures for HENRY II and Catherine de Médicis at St.-Denis (1561–70). His work represents a transitional link between the Gothic tradition and baroque sculpture.

pilot fish Widely distributed species (*Naucrates ductor,* family Carangidae) of carnivorous fish that inhabits warm and tropical open seas. It is slender and has a forked tail, a lengthwise keel on each side of the tail base, and a few small spines in front of the dorsal and anal fins. It may grow to 2 ft (60 cm) but is usually about 14 in. (35 cm) long. Five to seven distinctive vertical dark bands mark the bluish body. Pilot fishes follow sharks and ships, apparently to feed on parasites and leftover scraps. It was formerly thought that they were leading, or "piloting," the larger fishes to food.

pilot whale Any of one to three species (genus *Globicephala,* family Delphinidae) of TOOTHED WHALE found in all oceans except the Arctic and Antarctic, also called caa'ing whale for a roaring sound it makes when stranded. It is black, usually with a lighter splash on the throat and chest, and has a round, bulging forehead, a short beaklike snout, and slender, pointed flippers, and grows to 13–20 ft (4–6 m) long. Pilot whales live in large schools, sometimes hundreds or thousands, feeding mainly on squid. They have been kept in oceanariums and trained to perform.

Pilsudski \pil-'süt-skē, pil-'züt-skē\, **Józef (Klemens)** (1867–1935) Polish revolutionary leader. Born in Poland under the Russian Empire, he was reared with a hatred for Russian oppression. Banished to Siberia for socialist activism (1887–92), he became a leader of the Polish Socialist Party on his return. In 1908 he organized the secret Union of Military Action, which fought in World War I under Austro-Hungarian command against the Russians. In 1916 he demanded recognition of Poland's independence, which was granted in 1918. He served as Poland's first head of state until the constitution was established in 1922. After staging a coup in 1926, he served as premier (1926–28) and minister of defense (1926–35) under handpicked premiers, which allowed him to rule as the dictator of Poland.

Piltdown hoax Forgery of human fossil remains that impeded early-20th-century progress in the study of human evolution. The apparently fossilized skull found at Piltdown Common near Lewes, England, was first proposed as a new species of prehistoric man ("Piltdown man") in 1912. Only in 1954 was the skull shown to consist of a human cranium skillfully joined to the jaw of an orangutan. The hoax may have been perpetrated by the skull's discoverer, Charles Dawson, or British Museum staff member, Martin A.C. Hinton.

Pima \'pē-mə\ North American Indian people of UTO-AZTECAN LANGUAGE stock who traditionally lived in southern Arizona in what was the core area of the prehistoric HOHOKAM CULTURE, from which they probably descend. The Pima originally were sedentary corn farmers who lived in one-room houses and used the Gila and Salt rivers for irrigation. Some hunting and gathering were also done. Their villages were larger than those of the related PAPAGO Indians, and they possessed a stronger tribal unity. The Pima were long friendly with whites but enemies of the APACHE. Today 10,000 Pima live mainly on reservations in Arizona.

pimiento *or* **pimento** Any of various mild PEPPERS of the genus *Capsicum* that have distinctive flavor but lack pungency, including the European paprikas. A common flavoring in Hungarian dishes, paprika is made by grinding dried peppers. The term "pimento" sometimes refers to ALLSPICE because early Spanish explorers of the West Indies and Central America mistook the highly aromatic berries of the tropical allspice tree for a type of pepper and called it *pimenta.*

pin (fastener) In mechanical and civil engineering, a peg or bar designed to fasten machine and structural components together or to keep them aligned. Dowel pins are used to keep machine components aligned, sometimes without making a rigid joint (as in a pin-connected truss). Taper pins are used to fix the hub of a gear or a pulley to a shaft. Split cotter pins prevent nuts from turning on bolts and keep loosely fitting pins in place. The clevis pin has a ridge at one end and is kept in place by a cotter pin inserted through a hole in the other end. Many other types of pins are used in various machines.

Pinatubo \ˌpē-nä-'tü-bō\, **Mt.** Mountain, western LUZON, Philippines. Located about 55 mi (90 km) northwest of MANILA, it rose to a height of about 4,800 ft (1,460 m) before its eruption in 1991 (for the first time in 600 years). Its explosions produced a column of smoke and ash more than 19 mi (30 km) high, and left about 100,000 people homeless. The ashfalls forced the evacuation and eventual closing of a nearby U.S. Air Force base. Its eruption may have been the largest in the 20th century.

Pinchback, Pinckney (Benton Stewart) (1837–1921) U.S. politician. Born in Macon, Ga., to a former slave and a white planter, he became a riverboat steward. In the Civil War, he reached Union-held New Orleans, where he raised and led a company of black Union volunteers, called the Corps d'Afrique (1862–63). After the war he was elected to the Louisiana senate (1868), and served as lieutenant governor (1871). Elected to the U.S. House of Representatives (1872) and Senate (1873), he was denied his seat in each body on unproved charges of election fraud. He subsequently became a lawyer and moved to Washington, D.C.

Pinchot \'pin-shō\, **Gifford** (1865–1946) U.S. forestry and conservation pioneer. Born in Simsbury, Conn., he graduated from Yale University and studied forestry in Europe. In 1892 he became the first professional U.S. forester. In 1896 he joined the national forest commission of the National Academy of Sciences and helped plan the U.S. system of forest reserves (later NATIONAL FORESTS). As chief of the U.S. Forest Service (1898–1910), he established the nation's forest-service system. He founded the Yale School of Forestry and taught there 1903–36. He served as governor of Pennsylvania 1923–27 and 1931–35.

Pinckney, Charles (1757–1824) U.S. diplomat. Born in Charleston, S.C., a cousin of CHARLES C. PINCKNEY and THOMAS PINCKNEY, he fought in the American Revolution. He served in the Continental Congress (1784–87) and was instrumental in calling for the CONSTITUTIONAL CONVENTION. As a delegate from South Carolina, he proposed numerous provisions that were incorporated in the final draft of the Constitution. He helped write the South Carolina constitution and served as governor 1789–92, 1796–98, and 1806–8. He served in the U.S. Senate 1798–1801, and as U.S. minister to Spain 1801–5.

Pinckney, Charles Cotesworth (1746–1825) American diplomat. Born in Charleston, S.C., a cousin of CHARLES PINCKNEY and brother of THOMAS PINCKNEY, he was an aide to GEORGE WASHINGTON in the American Revolution, commanded at Savannah, and was promoted to brigadier general in 1783. He was a delegate to the Constitutional Convention. Appointed minister to France (1796), he was involved in negotiations that ended in the XYZ AFFAIR. He was the unsuccessful Federalist candidate for vice president in 1800 and for president in 1804 and 1808.

Pinckney, Eliza *orig.* **Elizabeth Lucas** (1722–1793) British-American planter. Born in Antigua, West Indies, the daughter of a British landowner in South Carolina, she managed his plantations from 1739. She experimented with various crops and succeeded in marketing the first American crop of indigo. After her marriage to the lawyer Charles Pinckney (1744), she revived the cultivation of silkworms and manufacture of silk on his plantation. She continued to manage their extensive landholdings after his death (1758). CHARLES C. PINCKNEY and THOMAS PINCKNEY were her sons.

Pinckney, Thomas (1750–1828) American diplomat. Born in Charleston, S.C., the brother of CHARLES C. PINCKNEY and cousin of CHARLES PINCKNEY, he served as governor of South Carolina 1787–89 and as minister to Britain 1792–96. As special envoy to Spain (1795), he negotiated the Treaty of San Lorenzo, also called Pinckney's Treaty, which fixed the southern border of the U.S. and granted the U.S. navigation rights on the Mississippi River and the right of deposit (storage of goods) at New Orleans. He was a major general in the War of 1812.

Pindar (518/522 BC–438? BC) Greek poet. A Boeotian of aristocratic birth, Pindar was educated in neighboring Athens and lived much of his life in Thebes. Almost all his early poems have been lost, but his reputation was probably established by his later hymns in honor of the gods. He developed into the greatest lyric poet of ancient Greece, respected throughout the Greek world. Of his 17 volumes, comprising almost every genre of choral lyric, only four have survived complete, and those lack his musical settings. The extant poems, probably representing his masterpieces, are odes (see PINDARIC ODE) in the epinicion form, commissioned to celebrate triumphs in various Hellenic athletic games. Lofty and religious in tone, they are noted for their complexity, rich metaphors, and intensely emotive language.

Pindaric ode Ceremonious poem in the manner of PINDAR, who employed a triadic, or three-part, structure consisting of a strophe (two or more lines repeated as a unit) followed by a metrically harmonious antistrophe and an epode (summary line) in a different meter. The three parts correspond to movements onstage by the CHORUS in Greek drama. After the 16th-century publication of Pindar's choral ODES in the epinicion form, poets writing in various vernaculars created irregular rhymed odes that suggest his style. Such odes in English are among the greatest poems in the language, including JOHN DRYDEN's "Alexander's Feast," WILLIAM WORDSWORTH's "Ode: Intimations of Immortality," and JOHN KEATS's "Ode on a Grecian Urn."

pine Any of 10 genera of coniferous trees (rarely shrubs) of the family Pinaceae (see CONIFER), native to northern temperate regions, especially about 90 species of ornamental and timber evergreen conifers of the genus *Pinus.* Needlelike leaves and cones are solitary or in bunches. Shallow root systems make pines susceptible to wind and surface disturbance. The family includes FIR, DOUGLAS FIR, HEMLOCK, SPRUCE, LARCH, and CEDAR. Many species are sources of softwood timber, paper pulp, oils, and resins. Some are cultivated as ornamentals.

Cluster of pollen-bearing male cones of Austrian (black) pine (*Pinus nigra*).
GRANT HEILMAN–EB INC.

pineal gland \'pī-nē-əl, pī-'nē-əl\ *or* **pineal body** *or* **epiphysis cerebri** \i-'pif-ə-səs-'ser-ə-brē\ Endocrine GLAND in the BRAIN that regulates MELATONIN production. It is large in children and begins to shrink at puberty, weighing little more than 0.0035 oz (0.1 g) in adults. The gland may play a significant role in sexual maturation, CIRCADIAN RHYTHM and SLEEP induction, and SEASONAL AFFECTIVE DISORDER and DEPRESSION. In animals it is known to play a major role in sexual development, HIBERNATION, METABOLISM, and seasonal breeding.

pineapple Fruit-bearing plant *(Ananas comosus)* of the family Bromeliaceae, native to the New World tropics and subtropics but introduced elsewhere. Pineapple is served fresh where available and in canned form worldwide. It is a key ingredient in Polynesian cuisine. Like AGAVE and some YUCCAS, the plant has a rosette of 30–40 stiff, succulent leaves on a thick, fleshy stem. A determinate inflorescence forms 15–20 months after planting. After fertilization, the many lavender flowers fuse and become fleshy to form the 2–4 lb (1–2 kg) fruit. Ripening takes 5–6 months.

Pineapple (*Ananas comosus*).
BY COURTESY OF DOLE COMPANY

Pinero \pi-ˈnir-ō\, **Arthur Wing** *later* **Sir Arthur** (1855–1934) British playwright. He entered the theatrical world as an actor with HENRY IRVING's theater company. His first play, *£200 a Year,* was produced in 1877. He wrote a series of farces such as *The Magistrate* (1885) before turning to dramas of social issues. *The Second Mrs. Tanqueray* (1893), the first of his plays depicting women confronting their situation in society, established his reputation, and he followed it with such works as *The Notorious Mrs. Ebbsmith* (1895) and *Trelawny of the "Wells"* (1898).

Ping Pong See TABLE TENNIS

Pinilla, Gustavo Rojas See Gustavo ROJAS PINILLA

pinion See GEAR, RACK AND PINION

Piniós River \ˌpē-nē-ˈȯs\ *or* **Peneus River** \pi-ˈnē-əs\ River, THESSALY, northern central Greece. It rises in the Pindus Mountains and flows about 125 mi (200 km) southeast and northeast through the plain of Thessaly and the Vale of TEMPE into the Gulf of Salonika. In prehistoric times it formed a great lake before it broke through the Vale of Tempe. It is navigable in its lower course.

pink family Family Caryophyllaceae, composed of 2,070 species of flowering plants in 89 genera found mainly in northern temperate regions. The approximately 300 species of true pinks belong to the genus *Dianthus;* relatively easy to grow, these are popular in rock gardens for their fragrant, showy flowers. Though members of the pink family are diverse in appearance and habitat, most have swollen leaf and stem joints. The family includes CARNATIONS, BABY'S BREATH, SWEET WILLIAM, CAMPION, and CHICKWEED.

pink salmon Food fish (*Oncorhynchus gorbuscha,* family Salmonidae) of the North Pacific that constitutes half of the commercial fishery of Pacific SALMON. It weighs about 4.5 lbs (2 kg) and is marked with large, irregular spots. Pink salmon often spawn on tidal flats. The young enter the sea immediately after hatching.

Pinkerton National Detective Agency U.S. independent police force. The agency was founded in 1850 by Allan Pinkerton (1819–1884), former deputy sheriff of Cook Co., Ill. It initially specialized in railway theft cases. It solved the $700,000 Adams Express Co. theft in 1856 and thwarted a 1861 assassination plot against president-elect ABRAHAM LINCOLN. It later participated in anti-labor union activities (see HOMESTEAD STRIKE) and was instrumental in breaking up the MOLLY MAGUIRES.

Pinkham \ˈpiŋk-əm\, **Lydia E(stes)** (1819–1883) U.S. patent-medicine proprietor. Born in Lynn, Mass., Pinkham began making her Vegetable Compound as a home remedy, which she shared with her neighbors. The compound, a blend of ground herbs, was 18% alcohol. In 1875 the Pinkham family decided to sell the medicine, which Pinkham claimed could cure any "female complaint" from nervous prostration to a prolapsed uterus. The business was soon grossing almost $300,000 a year. Not until the 1920s, when federal regulation of drugs and advertising increased, did the Lydia E. Pinkham Medicine Co. reduce both the alcoholic content of the medicine and the claims for its efficacy.

pinniped \ˈpi-nə-ˌped\ Any member of the three existing families of aquatic, fin-footed mammals that constitute the suborder Pinnipedia (order Carnivora; see CARNIVORE). They include the Odobenidae (see WALRUS) and the Phocidae and Otariidae (see SEAL).

Pinochet (Ugarte) \ˌpē-nə-ˈshā, *Span* ˌpē-nō-ˈche\, **Augusto** (born 1915) Head of Chile's military government (1974–90). A career military officer, he planned and led the coup d'état in which Pres. SALVADOR ALLENDE died. He moved to crush liberal opposition and in the next three years arrested about 130,000 Chileans and foreigners, many of whom were tortured and some of whom were killed. He led a rapid transition to a free-market economy, which led to acute hardship for the lower classes. A new constitution in 1981 granted him eight more years as president. Rejected in a plebiscite in 1989, he stepped down after free elections installed Patricio Aylwin in 1990. In 1998 he was arrested in England at the request of Spain and held for trial for crimes against Spanish citizens in Chile during his tenure; he was released 16 months later.

pinochle \ˈpē-ˌnə-kəl\ Card game played with a 48-card pack containing two sets of each suit from ace through nine. Bidding is based on certain combinations of cards within the player's hand and an estimation of the number of tricks, or hands, he or she can win.

Pinsky, Robert (born 1940) American poet and critic. Pinsky was poetry editor of *The New Republic* from 1979 to 1986. His own poems, many of which are to be found in *The Figured Wheel: New and Collected Poems* (1996), often explore the meaning of ordinary acts. He also did a notable verse translation of Dante's *Inferno* (1994). Pinsky was poet laureate consultant from 1997 to 2000.

pintail Any of four species (genus *Anas,* family Anatidae) of sleek, long-tailed, long-necked DABBLING DUCKS that are swift fliers and popular game birds. The common, or northern, pintail *(A. acuta),* widespread in the Northern Hemisphere, is a long-distance flier; some Alaskan birds winter in Hawaii. It is 26–30 in. (66–75 cm) long. The male has a white breast, gray back, and black tail; the female is mottled brown. The preferred diet is seeds. The brown, or yellow-billed, and the Bahama, or white-cheeked, pintails are primarily found in South America. The red-billed pintail is a grayish African species.

Pinter, Harold (born 1930) British playwright. Born into a working-class family, he acted with touring companies until 1959. His early one-act plays *The Room* (1957) and *The Dumbwaiter* (1957) were followed by the full-length *The Birthday Party* (1958). *The Caretaker* (1960) and *The Homecoming* (1965)—which, like his earlier works, use disjointed small talk and lengthy pauses in dialogue to convey a character's thought, which often contradicts his speech—established his reputation as an innovative and complex dramatist. His later plays include *Betrayal* (1978; film, 1983), *Mountain Language* (1988), and *Moonlight* (1993). He has also written radio and television plays and such screenplays as *The Servant* (1963), *The Go-Between* (1971), and *The French Lieutenant's Woman* (1981).

pinto Spotted HORSE, also called paint, piebald, and other terms to describe variations in color and markings. The American Indian ponies of the western U.S. were often pintos. Most pure-breed associations refuse to register pintos. Their color patterns are called overo (white spreading irregularly up from the belly, mixed with a darker color) and tobiano (white spreading down from the back in smooth, clean-cut patterns).

Pinturicchio \ˌpēn-tü-ˈrēk-kyō\ *or* **Pintoricchio** \ˌpēn-tȯ-ˈrēk-kyō\ *orig.* **Bernardino di Betto di Biago** (1452?–1513) Italian painter. Born in Perugia, he assisted PERUGINO on the frescoes in the Vatican's SISTINE CHAPEL (1481–82). His most important work, the fresco decoration of six rooms in the Borgia Apartments for Pope ALEXANDER VI (1492–94), features brilliant colors, gilding, and ancient Roman ornamental motifs. His last major works were 10 scenes from the life of PIUS II in the Piccolomini Library of Siena Cathedral. He was also a prolific panel painter.

pinworm Common species *(Enterobius,* or *Oxyuris, vermicularis)* of NEMATODE parasitic to humans, especially children. Female pinworms may be 0.5 in. (13 mm) long; males are much smaller. Pinworms have a very long tail that gives them a pin-like appearance. They mate in the upper gastrointestinal tract, usually in the large intestine; the females

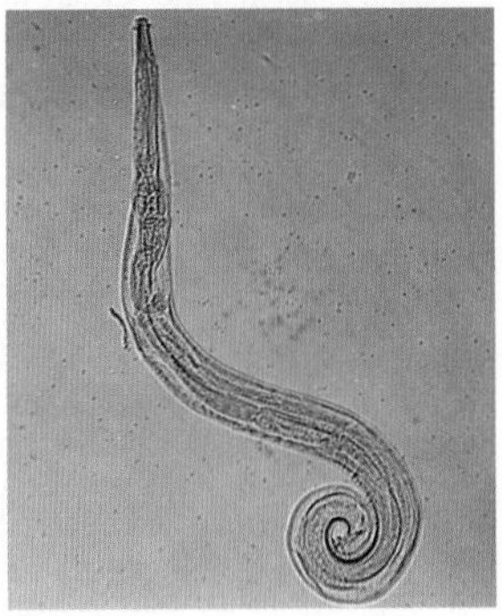

Pinworm (*Enterobius vermicularis*).
WALTER DAWN

travel to the anus, deposit their fertilized eggs on the skin near the anal opening, and die. The worms' movements cause itching; eggs transferred to the fingernails when the victim scratches may be passed to the mouth. Eggs can also be inhaled with air dust. The eggs or larvae make their way to the intestine, and the cycle begins again.

Pio, Padre *orig.* **Francesco Forgione** (1887–1968) Italian priest. Born into a devout Catholic family, he consecrated himself to Jesus at 5. At 15 he joined the Capuchins and took the name Pio; in 1910 he became a priest. That same year he received the stigmata for the first time. They were healed, but he received them again in 1918; this time they remained with him until his death. This and other signs of his holiness (perfume and, reportedly, the ability to be in two places at once), drew growing numbers of pilgrims to him. He was canonized in 2002.

Piombo, Sebastiano del See SEBASTIANO DEL PIOMBO

Pioneer First series of unmanned U.S. deep-space probes. Pioneer 1 was the first spacecraft launched by NASA (1958). Pioneers 1–4 were intended to be lunar missions, but only Pioneer 4 succeeded in escaping earth's gravity (1964). Pioneers 6–9 were successfully launched into solar orbits (1965–68) to study the solar wind, solar magnetic field, and cosmic rays. Pioneer 10, launched in 1972, was the first space probe to traverse the asteroid belt and to fly by JUPITER (1973), where it discovered Jupiter's huge magnetic tail. It then became the first manmade object to exit the solar system. Pioneer 11's data and photographs (1979) enabled scientists to identify two previously undiscovered moons and an additional ring around SATURN and radiation belts in its magnetosphere. Pioneer Venus 1 and 2 began orbiting VENUS in 1978, sending back observations of its clouds and lower atmosphere and radar maps of its surface; Pioneer Venus 2 also released four probes into its atmosphere.

pipe, sacred See CALUMET

Pipestone National Monument National monument, southwestern Minnesota. Established in 1937, it has an area of 282 acres (114 hectares) and contains quarries of a reddish-colored stone that was used by the PLAINS INDIANS to make ceremonial peace pipes. The stone is reserved for use by the Indians, who quarry it under special permits from the National Park Service. HENRY W. LONGFELLOW popularized the quarries in "The Song of Hiawatha."

pipit *or* **fieldlark** Any of about 50 species (family Motacillidae) of small, slender-bodied, ground-dwelling songbirds (especially in the genus *Anthus*) found worldwide except in polar regions and on some islands. They are brownish-streaked and 5–9 in. (12–23 cm) long. They have a thin, pointed bill, pointed wings, and elongated hind toes and claws. Named for their twittering sounds, they walk and run rapidly, searching the ground for insects. Their flight is strongly undulating. Their white outer tail feathers show best in flight. See also WAGTAIL.

Pippin, Horace (1888–1946) U.S. folk painter. Pippin served in the infantry in World War I, but he was wounded in 1918 and discharged with a partially paralyzed right arm. His first large canvas was an eloquent protest against war, *End of the War: Starting Home* (1931–34). His primary theme became the African American experience, as seen in his series entitled *Cabin in the Cotton* (mid-1930s) and his paintings of episodes in the lives of the antislavery leader John Brown and President Abraham Lincoln. After the art world discovered Pippin in 1937, he received wide acclaim as the greatest black painter of his time.

piracy Illegal act of violence, detention, or plunder committed for private ends by the crew of, usually, a private ship against another ship on the HIGH SEAS. Air piracy (i.e., the HIJACKING of an aircraft) is a more recent phenomenon. Piracy has occurred in all stages of history: the Phoenicians, Greeks, and Romans engaged in it, as did the Vikings, Moors, and other Europeans. It also occurred among Asian peoples. During the Elizabethan wars with Spain in the late 16th century, treasure-laden Spanish galleons leaving Mexico were a natural target for pirates. In the 16th–18th centuries, pirates from North Africa's BARBARY COAST threatened commerce in the Mediterranean. The increased size of merchant vessels, improved naval patrolling, and recognition by governments of piracy as an international offense led to its decline in the late 19th century. In the late 20th century, incidents of piracy occurred with increasing frequency in the seas of East and Southeast Asia. See also BLACKBEARD, FRANCIS DRAKE, JEAN LAFFITE, HENRY MORGAN.

Piraeus \pī-ˈrē-əs\ City (pop., 1991: 170,000), port of ATHENS, Greece. The port and its "long walls," fortified barriers connecting it with Athens, were completed in the mid-5th century BC. The walls were destroyed by SPARTA at the end of the PELOPONNESIAN WAR. Rebuilt under the Athenian leader Conon in 393 BC, it was burned in 86 BC by the Roman commander LUCIUS CORNELIUS SULLA. It regained importance after 1834, when Athens became capital of the newly independent Greece. The largest port in Greece, it is the center for all sea communication with the Greek islands.

Pirandello, Luigi (1867–1936) Italian playwright and novelist. He earned a doctorate in philology at the University of Bonn but turned to writing poetry, short stories, and several novels, including the successful *The Late Mattia Pascal* (1904). His first major play, *Right You Are (If You Think You Are)* (1917), explored the relativity of truth, a lifelong subject for Pirandello. *Six Characters in Search of an Author* (1921) contrasted art and life; it was followed by the tragedy *Henry IV* (1922). His other plays include *Each in His Own Way* (1924) and *Tonight We Improvise* (1930). He established the Teatro d'Arte in Rome and toured the world with his company (1925–27). Recognized as a major figure in 20th-century theater, he was awarded the Nobel Prize in 1934.

Pirandello.
BY COURTESY OF THE ITALIAN INSTITUTE, LONDON

Piranesi \ˌpē-rä-ˈnā-sē\, **Giovanni Battista** *or* **Giambattista Piranesi** (1720–1778) Italian draftsman, printmaker, architect, and art theorist. Born near Venice, he went to Rome at 20 as a draftsman for the Venetian ambassador. After settling there in 1747, he developed a highly original etching technique that produced rich textures and bold contrasts of light and shadow. His many prints of classical and postclassical Roman structures contributed to the growth of classical archaeology and the Neoclassical art movement. He is best known today for his extraordinary series of imaginary prisons (*Carceri d'invenzione,* 1745). His prints are among the most impressive architectural representations in Western art.

piranha \pə-ˈrä-nə, pə-ˈrän-yə\ *or* **caribe** \kə-ˈrē-bē\ Any of several species in the genus *Serrasalmus* (family Characidae), deep-bodied, carnivorous fishes abundant in rivers of eastern and central South America and noted for voracity and ferocity. One of the most dangerous species, *S. nattereri,* grows to 2 ft (60 cm) long, but most species are smaller. Some species are silvery, with an orange belly and throat; others are almost completely black. All have saw-edged teeth that close in a scissorlike bite. Piranhas travel in groups, usually preying on other fishes. They are attracted to the scent of blood and can quickly reduce even a large animal to a skeleton.

Pirquet \pir-ˈkā\, **Clemens, Freiherr (Baron) von** (1874–1929) Austrian physician. In 1906 he noticed that patients who received two injections of horse serum or smallpox vaccine usually had quicker, more severe reactions (which he called "allergies") to the second injection. While studying cowpox vaccination symptoms, he also developed a new theory about infectious diseases' incubation times and about antibody formation. In Pirquet's test, a drop of tuberculin is scratched into the skin; a red, raised area developing at the site (Pirquet's reaction) indicates tuberculosis.

Pisa \ˈpē-zə, *Italian* ˈpē-sä\ *ancient* **Pisae** City (pop., 2001 prelim.: 85,379), central Italy. Located on the ARNO RIVER, it probably began as an Etruscan town. It became a Roman colony c. 180 BC. A Christian bishopric by AD 313, it flourished during the Middle Ages as the urban center of TUSCANY. Pisa's participation in the CRUSADES made it a rival of GENOA and VENICE. It became part of the kingdom of Italy in 1860. The city was the scene of heavy fighting during World War II. It is now an important railway junction. Its cathedral, the LEANING TOWER OF PISA, and other attractions make it a tourist destination. It is the site of the University of Pisa (founded 1343) and the birthplace of GALILEO.

Pisano \pi-ˈsä-nō, pi-ˈzä-nō\, **Andrea** *or* **Andrea da Pontedera** (c. 1295–c. 1348) Italian sculptor and architect. He created the earliest of three bronze doors for the Baptistery of the cathedral of Florence (1330–36). On GIOTTO's death in 1337, Andrea succeeded him as chief architect of the cathedral's bell tower, to which he added two stories adorned with panel reliefs. In 1347 he was appointed superintending architect of the cathedral of Orvieto. One of the most important Italian sculptors of the 14th century, he is known for his restrained style and skillful arrangement of figures.

Pisano, Giovanni (c. 1250–1319) Italian sculptor and architect. His early work is similar to that of NICOLA PISANO, his father and teacher. Around 1285 he began work on the facade of Siena's cathedral, whose lavish and ordered design and ornamentation became the model for future Gothic facade decoration in central Italy. His other great achievement, the Pistoia pulpit (c. 1298–1301), is characterized by extreme agitation, its figures, animals, drapery, and landscape being wrenched into physically impossible configurations. His pulpit for the Pisa cathedral (1302–10) is much more classical, perhaps to accord with GIOTTO's monumental style, then in the ascendancy. Though regarded as Italy's only true Gothic sculptor, he never lost sight of the heritage of classical Rome.

Pisano, Nicola (c. 1220–1278?) Italian sculptor. His work, along with that of his son, GIOVANNI PISANO, created a new sculptural style for the late 13th and 14th century in Italy. His greatest work, the pulpit in the Baptistery of Pisa Cathedral (1260), is extraordinary in its assertion of a new style, distinct from all its predecessors though indebted to them. The work draws on many motifs, including Roman reliefs, early Christian frescoes and mosaics, and French Gothic architecture and sculpture, but assimilates them, creating a unified whole that gave a new sense of direction to Tuscan art.

"Adoration of the Magi," detail of the marble pulpit in the Baptistery at Pisa, by Nicola Pisano, c. 1259–60.

ALINARI—ART RESOURCE/EB INC.

Pisces \'pī-ˌsēz\ (Latin: "Fishes") In astronomy, the constellation lying between Aries and Aquarius; in ASTROLOGY, the twelfth sign of the ZODIAC, governing approximately the period February 19–March 20. Its symbol is two fish tied together. These are a reference to the Greek myth of APHRODITE and EROS, who jumped into a river to escape the monster TYPHON and were changed into fish. In another version of the myth, two fish carried them to safety.

Pishpek See BISHKEK

Pisidia \pi-'si-dē-ə\ Ancient region, southern ASIA MINOR. Most of it was composed of the TAURUS MTNS., which provided refuge for a lawless population that resisted successive conquerors. It was incorporated into the Roman province of GALATIA in the early 1st century AD and became part of LYCIA and Pamphylia under Emperor VESPASIAN in AD 74. DIOCLETIAN included Pisidia in the diocese of Asia c. AD 297. During Byzantine times it continued to be a region of revolt. By 1204 the Byzantines had ceded control of the region to the Turks.

Pissarro \pə-'sär-ō\, **(Jacob-Abraham-) Camille** (1830–1903) West Indian-French Impressionist painter. The son of a prosperous Jewish merchant in the Danish West Indies, he moved in Paris in 1855. His earliest canvases are broadly painted figure paintings and landscapes that show the careful observation of nature that was to remain a characteristic of his art. In 1871 he took a house in Pontoise, in the countryside outside Paris. These surroundings formed the theme of his art for some 30 years. Despite acute eye trouble, his later years were his most prolific. The Parisian and provincial scenes of this period include *Place du Théâtre Française* (1898) and *Bridge at Bruges* (1903). Pissarro was the only Impressionist painter who participated in all eight of the group's exhibitions.

Self-Portrait by Camille Pissarro, oil on canvas, 1903; in the Tate Gallery, London.

BY COURTESY OF THE TRUSTEES OF THE TATE GALLERY, LONDON

pistachio \pə-'sta-shē-ˌō\ Any of nine species of aromatic trees and shrubs, some ornamental, that make up the genus *Pistacia* of the SUMAC (or cashew) family, native to Eurasia, with one species in southwestern North America and another in the Canary Islands. Commercial pistachio nuts are seeds from the fruit of *P. vera.* They have a pleasing, mild, resinous flavor and are used extensively as food and for yellowish-green coloring in confections. The tree bears leaves with thick, wide, leathery, featherlike leaflets and small fruit in clusters.

pistil Female reproductive part of a FLOWER. Centrally located, the pistil typically has a swollen base called the ovary, which contains the potential SEEDS (ovules). The stalk (style) arises from the ovary and has a pollen-receptive tip, the stigma, which is variously shaped and often sticky. There may be a single pistil, as in the LILY, or several to many pistils, as in the BUTTERCUP. Each pistil is constructed of one to many rolled leaflike structures, or CARPELS. Differences in the composition and form of the pistil are useful in classifying flowering plants. See also STAMEN.

pistol Small firearm designed to be operated with one hand. The name may derive from the city of Pistoia, Italy, where handguns were made as early as the 15th century. It was originally a cavalry weapon. The two classes of pistol are REVOLVERS and automatics. Automatics have a mechanism, actuated by the energy of recoil, that feeds cartridges from a magazine in the butt.

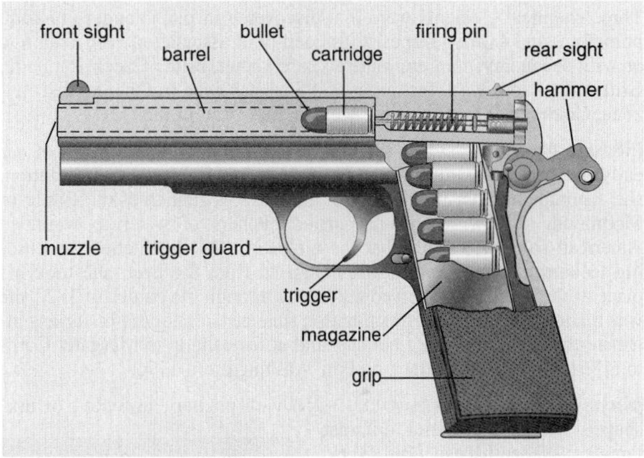

Parts of a semiautomatic pistol.

piston and cylinder In mechanical engineering, a sliding cylinder with a closed head (the piston) that moves up and down (or back and forth) in a slightly larger cylindrical chamber (the cylinder) by or against pressure of a fluid, as in an engine or pump. The cylinder of a STEAM ENGINE is closed by plates at both ends, with provision for the piston rod, which is rigidly attached to the piston, to pass through one of the end cover plates. The cylinder of an INTERNAL-COMBUSTION ENGINE is closed at one end by a plate called the head and open at the other end to permit free oscillation of the connecting rod, which joins the piston to the crankshaft.

pit bull terrier *or* **Staffordshire terrier** Dog breed developed in 19th-century Britain for fighting other dogs in pits. It was created by crossing the BULLDOG (which at the time was longer-legged and more agile) with a terrier, possibly the FOX TERRIER. Once known by such names as bull-and-terrier and half-and-half, the pit bull is a stocky, muscular, unusually strong dog with powerful jaws, standing 17–19 in. (43–48 cm) and weighing 30–50 lbs (14–23 kg). Its stiff, short coat may be any color, solid or variegated. See also BULL TERRIER.

pit viper Any species of VIPER (subfamily Crotalinae) that has, in addition to two movable fangs, a heat-sensitive pit organ between each eye and nostril which together help it accurately aim its strike at its warm-blooded prey. Pit vipers are found from deserts to rain forests, primarily in the New World. They may be terrestrial, arboreal, or aquatic. Some species lay eggs; others produce live young. See also Bushmaster, Copperhead, Fer-de-lance, Moccasin, Rattlesnake.

Pitcairn Island Island (pop., 1992 est.: 52), southern central Pacific Ocean. It is the only inhabited island of the Pitcairn Island group, which also includes Henderson, Ducie, and Oeno. It has an area of about 2 sq mi (5 sq km). Discovered in 1767 by the British, it was uninhabited until 1790, when it was settled by mutineers from HMS *Bounty,* led by Fletcher Christian. It was annexed by Britain in 1839. The inhabitants were removed to Norfolk Island in 1856 because of overpopulation. Some returned to Pitcairn, and their descendants make up the present population, who subsist on fishing and farming. In 1970 the British High Commissioner in New Zealand was appointed the colony's governor.

pitch Quality of a musical tone that varies with the number of vibrations per second (hertz, Hz) of the sounding body and is perceived as highness or lowness. A higher pitch has a higher number of vibrations. The sounds of bodies vibrating in ratios of multiples of two seem to be related to each other; such pitches are said to demonstrate "octave equivalence," so they share a letter designation (like "C" or "F sharp"). Pitch today is generally standardized; the A above middle C is widely standardized as 440 Hz, which implies the pitches of all other notes in the equal-tempered scale. See also Interval, Tuning and Temperament.

pitchblende Amorphous, dense, black, pitchy form of the crystalline uranium oxide mineral uraninite; it is one of the primary mineral ores of uranium. Pitchblende is found in granular masses and has a greasy luster. Three chemical elements were first discovered in pitchblende: uranium, polonium, and radium. Deposits, frequently in association with uraninite or with secondary uranium minerals, are known in the Czech Republic, Britain, the Northwest Territories and Saskatchewan in Canada, and Arizona, Colorado, Montana, New Mexico, and Utah in the U.S.

Pitcher, Molly (1753?–1832) American patriot. Little is known of her early life; she is thought to have been Irish. In the American Revolution, she accompanied her husband, William Hays, a gunner, at the Battle of Monmouth (1778), where she carried pitchers of water to wounded American soldiers, earning her the nickname "Molly Pitcher." According to legend, after her husband collapsed from the heat, she took his place at the cannon and served heroically through the battle. In 1822 she was recognized for her heroism with a state pension. Some historians attribute the act of replacing her husband at the cannon to Margaret Corbin (1751–1800) in the attack on Fort Washington in 1776.

pitcher plant Any carnivorous plant with pitcher-, trumpet-, or urn-shaped leaves, in several different families: Nepenthaceae (Old World pitcher plants), Cephalotaceae, Asclepiadaceae (milkweed family), and especially Sarraceniaceae (New World pitcher plants, particularly those in the eastern North American genus *Sarracenia*). Pitcher plants inhabit bogs, swamps, wet or sandy meadows, or savannas where the soils are water-saturated, acidic, and deficient in nitrates or phosphates. Their unusual tubular leaves have a series of nectar-secreting glands that extend from the lip down into the interior and attract insects. Once in the plant, the prey tumbles down into a liquid pool and drowns, after which an enzyme secreted within the leaf digests it, releasing nitrates and other nutrients, which supplement the meager nutrient supply of bogs. Most pitcher plants produce a crop of pitchered, insect-catching leaves in the spring, and a second crop of tubeless leaves in the fall. Pitcher-plant flowers are showy and have an agreeable scent.

Yellow pitcher plant (*Sarracenia flava*).

© JEFF LEPORE/PHOTO RESEARCHERS

pitot tube \'pē-,tō\ Instrument for measuring the velocity (speed) of a flowing fluid. Invented by Henri Pitot (1695–1771), it consists of a tube with a short, right-angled bend, which is placed vertically in a moving fluid with the mouth of the bent part directed upstream; the pressure, measured with an attached device, depends on the fluid flow and can be used to calculate the velocity. Pitot tubes are used to measure airspeed in wind tunnels and aboard aircraft in flight; they are also used to measure the flow of liquids (see flow meter).

Pitt, William *later* **Earl of Chatham** *known as* **the Elder Pitt** (1708–1778) British statesman and orator, twice virtual prime minister (1756–61, 1766–68). He entered Parliament in 1735 and provoked controversy with his maiden speech, which criticized the ministry of Robert Walpole. With the outbreak of the Seven Years' War, he was named secretary of state and became virtual prime minister. His leadership brought many British victories that greatly extended the British empire. His wide popular appeal led to the nickname "the Great Commoner," though he was disliked by many in government for his high-handedness. He resigned in 1761 when the cabinet refused to declare war on Spain. Though ill with gout, he became a champion of liberty and spoke in favor of American colonial resistance to the Stamp Act. He formed another government in 1766, in which he served as lord privy seal, but resigned in 1768 because of ill health. Widely mourned on his death in 1778, he was buried in Westminster Abbey.

Pitt, William *known as* **the Younger Pitt** (1759–1806) British statesman and prime minister (1783–1801, 1804–6). The son of William Pitt, he entered Parliament in 1781 and served as chancellor of the exchequer (1782–83). He was appointed prime minister in 1783 and undertook reforms that reduced the large national debt incurred by the American Revolution, reduced tariffs, placed the East India Co. under government control, and restructured the government in India. Forced into conflict with France by the French Revolutionary Wars, he formed a series of coalitions with European states against France (1793, 1798, 1805). Pitt responded to demands by radicals for parliamentary reform with repressive measures. In 1800 he secured the Act of Union with Ireland but resigned in 1801 when his proposal for Catholic emancipation was denied. His second term as premier (1804–6) was marked by the collapse of the Third Coalition after the Battles of Ulm and Austerlitz, the news of which weakened his already fragile health.

William Pitt, the Younger, detail of an oil painting by John Hoppner; in the National Portrait Gallery, London.

BY COURTESY OF THE NATIONAL PORTRAIT GALLERY, LONDON

pittosporum \pə-'täs-pə-rəm\ Any of various evergreen shrubs or trees, mainly from Australia and New Zealand, that make up the genus *Pittosporum* (family Pittosporaceae), commonly known as Australian laurel. They are planted especially as ornamentals in warm regions. The most popular and hardiest species, called tobira, or house-blooming mock orange *(P. tobira),* is native to China and Japan; it is a popular fragrant hedge plant in warm climates and a handsome indoor plant elsewhere.

Pittsburgh City (pop., 1996 est.: 350,000), southwestern Pennsylvania. It is situated at the confluence of the Allegheny and Monongahela rivers where they form the Ohio River. In 1758 the French Fort Duquesne was captured there by the British, and the site was renamed Pitt. It was incorporated as a borough in 1794 and as a city in 1816. In the 19th century it developed rapidly as a steel-manufacturing center. The American Federation of Labor began there in 1881 (see AFL-CIO). The second-largest city in the state, it is the center of an urban industrial complex that includes several neighboring cities. There are more than 150 industrial research laboratories in the area. It is home to the University of Pittsburgh, Carnegie-Mellon Univ., and other educational institutions.

Pittsburgh, University of State university system comprising a main campus in Pittsburgh and branches at four other locations. It was founded as Pittsburgh Academy in 1787. The main campus is a comprehensive research institution and includes schools of medicine, dentistry, law, engineering, and social work, among others. Campus facilities include centers for the study of ecology and of learning and development. Enrollment at the main campus is about 26,000.

Pittsburgh Platform Manifesto of Reform Judaism drawn up in 1885 by a conference of rabbis in Pittsburgh, Pa. It declared that Judaism was in the process of evolution, and asserted that the Talmud was to be considered as religious literature rather than as immutable law. It remained the official philosophy of the U.S. Reform movement until 1937, when the Columbus Platform moved Reform Judaism back to a more traditional position.

pituitary gland \pə-'tü-ə-,ter-ē\ *or* **hypophysis** \hī-'päf-ə-səs\ Endocrine gland lying on the underside of the brain. It plays a major part in regulating the endocrine system. Its anterior lobe secretes most of the pituitary hormones, which stimulate growth (see growth hormone); egg and sperm development; milk secretion; release of other hormones by the thyroid gland, adrenal glands, and reproductive system; and pigment production. The posterior lobe stores and releases hormones from the hypothalamus that control pituitary function, uterine contraction and milk release, and blood pressure and fluid balance.

Pius, Sextus Pompeius Magnus See Sextus Pompeius Magnus Pius

Pius II \'pī-əs\ *orig.* **Enea Silvio Piccolomini** (1405–1464) Pope (1458–64). An Italian diplomat who became bishop of Trieste (1447) and Siena (1449), he mediated between the German princes and the papacy, arranged the coronation of Frederick III as Holy Roman Emperor (1452), and made peace with Aragon and Naples. As pope he tried to unite Europe in a crusade against the Turks, but he was unable to win the support of the Christian princes. Pius was also a noted humanist and a prolific writer on the events of his day.

Pius V, St. *orig.* **Antonio or Michele Ghislieri** (1504–1572) Pope (1566–72). Born in Alessandria, he joined the Dominican order at 14 and was ordained in 1528. A relentless pursuer of heretics, he was named Commissary General of the Inquisition in 1551. By 1556 he was a cardinal, and in 1566 he was elected pope. He zealously carried out church reforms and succeeded in keeping Protestantism out of Italy. In 1570 he excommunicated Elizabeth I, thus worsening the position of Catholics in England. He organized the campaign that led to the victory of the Spanish, Venetian, and papal fleets over the Turks in the Battle of Lepanto in 1571.

Pius IX *orig.* **Giovanni Maria Mastai-Ferretti** (1792–1878) Pope (1846–78). Born in the Papal States, he became an archbishop in 1827, a cardinal in 1840, and pope on the death of Gregory XVI. He set out to make liberal reforms, but the revolutionary fervor of 1848 frightened him into extreme conservatism. He proclaimed the dogma of the Immaculate Conception (1854) and convened the First Vatican Council (1869–70), which promulgated the doctrine of papal infallibility. After losing temporal power to Victor Emmanuel II upon Italian unification, he regarded himself as a prisoner in the Vatican and refused any contact with the Italian government. Pius's pontificate was the longest in history.

Pius IX.
FELICI

Pius X, St. *orig.* **Giuseppe Melchiorre Sarto** (1835–1914) Pope (1903–14). Born in the Italian region of Venetia, he became bishop of Mantua in 1884 and patriarch of Venice in 1893. He was elected pope in 1903 and soon became known both for his piety and for his staunch religious and political conservatism. Pius suppressed the Catholic intellectual movement known as Modernism and opposed the political movement for social reform known as Christian Democracy. He worked to organize the laity for collaboration in the church's apostolic work, and he reformed the Catholic liturgy and systematized canon law. He was canonized in 1954.

Pius XII *orig.* **Eugenio Maria Giuseppe Giovanni Pacelli** (1876–1958) Pope (1939–58). Born in Rome, he served in the papal diplomatic service and as secretary of state to the Holy See before succeeding Pius XI in 1939. He was active in humanitarian work with prisoners and refugees during World War II, but has been criticized for his failure to speak out against the Holocaust. In the postwar era he was a defender of persecuted Catholics in communist countries. Known for his austere conservatism, he defined the dogma of the bodily assumption of the Virgin in 1950.

Pius XII, photograph by Yousuf Karsh.

pixel *in full* **picture element** Smallest resolved unit of a video image that has specific luminescence and color. Its proportions are determined by the number of lines making up the scanning raster (the pattern of dots that form the image) and the resolution along each line. In the most common form of computer graphics, the thousands of tiny pixels that make up an individual image are projected onto a display screen as illuminated dots that from a distance appear as a continuous image. An electron beam creates the grid of pixels by tracing each horizontal line from left to right, one pixel at a time, from the top line to the bottom line. A pixel may also be the smallest element of a light-sensitive device, such as cameras that use charged-coupled devices (see CCD).

Pizarro, Francisco (c. 1475–1541) Conquistador who seized the Inca empire for Spain. In 1510 he enrolled in an expedition of exploration in the New World, and three years later he joined Vasco Nunez de Balboa on the expedition that discovered the Pacific. He made two voyages of discovery down the Colombian coast (1524–25, 1526–28) and continued his explorations southward, naming the new territory Peru. In 1531 he set sail for Peru with his four brothers, 180 men, and 37 horses. He soon encountered emissaries of the Inca emperor, Atahuallpa, and arranged a meeting. There his men slaughtered the emperor's unarmed retainers and took him hostage. After accepting a rich ransom for Atahuallpa's release, Pizarro had him garroted. He spent the rest of his life consolidating Spain's hold on Peru. He founded Lima (1535), where he was killed by fellow Spaniards he had betrayed.

Pizarro, Gonzalo (1502?–1548) Spanish explorer and conqueror. With his half brother Francisco Pizarro, he took part in the conquest of Peru (1531–33), for which he received extensive land grants and was made governor of Quito (1539). In 1541–42 he led a disastrous expedition into the unexplored region east of Quito that cost the lives of almost 200 Spaniards and 4,000 Indians. He returned to find that Spain had restricted the conquerors' privileges; the conquistadores revolted against the viceroy, and Pizarro led the antiroyalist forces to victory at the Battle of Anaquito (1546), but they were defeated in 1548 and he was executed.

Pizarro, Hernando (1475?–1578) Spanish conqueror. With his half brother Francisco Pizarro, he took part in the conquest of Peru (1531–33), then returned to Spain. Back in Peru (1536), he was seized at Cuzco by Diego de Almagro. After his release, Pizarro commanded his brother's army and captured and executed Almagro (1538). He returned to Spain to argue in favor of the Pizarros' claims in Peru, but was imprisoned for 20 years (1540–60).

pizza Food of Neapolitan origin consisting of a flattened disk of bread dough topped with olive oil, tomatoes, and mozzarella cheese, baked quickly and served hot. Pizza is now eaten throughout Italy, with regional variations in toppings. Pizza came to the U.S. with Italian immigrants; the first U.S. pizzeria opened in 1905, and pizza became one of the nation's favorite foods after World War II. Toppings include such unusual items as oysters and pineapple.

PKK See Kurdistan Workers Party

PKU See phenylketonuria

PL Kyodan \'pē-'el-'kyō-dän\ *in full* **Perfect Liberty Kyodan** Religious group founded in Japan by Miki Tokuchika in 1946 as a revival of his father's group, Hito-no-michi. Unaffiliated with any of the major religious traditions of Japan, it teaches that the goal of human life is joyful self-expression. Misfortune and suffering come from forgetting God, but the believer may pray that his troubles be transferred to the patriarch, who is strengthened for vicarious suffering by the group's collective prayers. Today PL Kyodan claims more than 2.5 million adherents worldwide. The sect's headquarters are at Habikino, near Osaka.

placenta \plə-'sen-tə\ Organ in most mammals that develops in the uterus along with a fetus to mediate metabolic exchange. The umbilical cord attaches it to the fetus at the navel. Nutrients and oxygen in the mother's blood pass across the placenta to the fetus, and metabolic wastes and carbon dioxide from the fetus cross in the other direction; the two blood supplies do not mix. Other substances (e.g., alcohol or drugs) in the mother's blood can also cross the placenta, with effects including congenital disorders and drug addiction in the newborn (see fetal alcohol syndrome); some microorganisms can cross it to infect the fetus, but so do the mother's antibodies. The placenta, weighing a pound or more at the end of pregnancy, is expelled at parturition. Some animals eat it as a source of nutrients; in some species this stimulates lactation.

placer deposit Natural concentration of heavy minerals caused by the effect of gravity on moving particles. When heavy, stable minerals are freed from their matrix by weathering processes, they are slowly washed downslope into streams that quickly winnow the lighter matrix. Thus the heavy minerals become concentrated in stream, beach, and lag (residual) gravels and constitute workable ore deposits. Minerals that form placer deposits include gold, platinum, cassiterite, magnetite, chromite, ilmenite, rutile, native copper, zircon, monazite, and various gemstones.

placer mining Oldest method of recovering gold from alluvial deposits. It takes advantage of gold's high density, which causes it to sink more rapidly from moving water than the lighter siliceous materials with which it is found. Panning, used by 19th-century miners, employed a pan in which a few handfuls of the gold-bearing soil or gravel and a large amount of water were placed; by swirling the pan's contents, the miner washed the siliceous material over the side, leaving the gold and heavy materials behind. Dredging is the most important placer-mining method today. Used worldwide is the bucket-ladder dredge, with its continuous chain of buckets rotating around a rigid adjustable frame called the ladder. In sluicing, a slightly sloping wooden trough called a box sluice, or a ditch cut in hard gravel or rock called a ground sluice, is used as a channel along which gold-bearing gravel is carried by a stream of water. Riffles placed transversely along the bottom of the sluice cause the water to eddy into small basins, retarding the current so that gold may settle.

Placid, Lake See Lake Placid

plagioclase \'plā-jē-ə-ˌklās\ Any member of the series of abundant feldspar minerals that usually occur as light- to medium-grey-colored, transparent to translucent grains or crystals. Plagioclase ranges in composition from albite to anorthite. It is used in the manufacture of glass and ceramics; iridescent varieties are valued as gemstones. The primary importance of plagioclase, however, derives from its role as a rock-forming mineral.

plague \'plāg\ Infectious fever caused by the bacterium *Yersinia pestis,* carried by the rat flea. It usually spreads to humans only when the flea runs out of rodent hosts. It takes three forms. Bubonic, the mildest, has characteristic swollen lymph nodes (buboes) and is spread only by the flea. It accounts for three-fourths of plague cases. Pneumonic plague has extensive lung involvement and is spread in droplets from the lungs; it is often fatal in three or four days without treatment. In septicemic plague, bacteria overwhelm the bloodstream and often cause death within 24 hours, before other symptoms have a chance to develop. In the 14th century, plague ravaged Europe and Asia and was called the Black Death. Plague does not respond to penicillin, but other antibiotics are effective. Sanitary measures against fleas and rodents, quarantine, and extreme caution in handling infectious materials help to suppress epidemics. A vaccine can prevent plague.

plaice Commercially valuable European flatfish *(Pleuronectes platessa).* At most 36 in. (90 cm) long, the plaice normally has both eyes on the right side of the head and four to seven bony bumps near its eyes. It is brown with red or orange spots. The American plaice *(Hippoglossoides platessoides)* is found in both Europe (where it is called the rough dab) and the U.S. It is reddish or brownish and grows to about 24 in. (60 cm) long.

Plaice (*Pleuronectes platessa*).
JACQUES SIX

plain Any relatively level area of the earth's surface that exhibits gentle slopes and small local relief (differences in elevation). Occupying slightly more than one-third of the terrestrial surface, plains are found on all continents except Antarctica. Some are tree-covered and others are grassy. Still others support scrub brush and bunch grass, and a few are nearly waterless deserts. With certain exceptions, plains have become the sites of major centers of population, industry, commerce, and transportation.

Plain, the *French* **la Plaine** In the French Revolution, the centrist deputies in the National Convention. They formed the majority of the assembly's members and were essential to the passage of any measures. Their name derived from their place on the floor of the assembly; above them sat the members of the Mountain, or Montagnards. Led by Emmanuel Joseph Sieyès, the Plain initially voted with the moderate Girondins but later joined the Montagnards in voting for the execution of Louis XVI. In 1794 they helped overthrow Maximilien Robespierre and other extreme Jacobins (see Jacobin Club).

Plain of Esdraelon See Plain of Esdraelon

Plain of Reeds See Plain of Reeds

Plain of Sharon See Plain of Sharon

Plains Indians Any of various Native American tribes that formerly inhabited the Great Plains of the U.S. and southern Canada. They included the Arapaho, Assiniboin, Blackfoot, Cheyenne, Comanche, Plains Cree, Crow, Hidatsa, Kiowa, Mandan, Osage, Pawnee, and Sioux.

Plains of Abraham See Plains of Abraham

planarian \plə-'nar-ē-ən\ Any of about 3,000 species of widely distributed, mostly free-living flatworms of the family Planariidae and related families (class Turbellaria), usually found in freshwater but also in marine and terrestrial environments. The soft, ciliated body is leaf-shaped when elongated. The spade-shaped head has two eyes and sometimes tentacles. The tail is pointed. The mouth is on the lower side, often more than halfway toward the tail. Most species are 0.1–0.6 in. (3–15 mm) long; some grow to about 1 ft (30 cm). Planarians swim with an undulating motion or creep like slugs. Most feed at night on protozoans, snails, and other worms.

Planck \'plänk\, **Max (Karl Ernst Ludwig)** (1858–1947) German physicist. He studied at the Univs. of Munich and Kiel, then became professor of theoretical physics at the University of Berlin (1889–1928). His work on the second law of thermodynamics and blackbody radiation led him to formulate the revolutionary quantum theory of radiation, for which he received a Nobel Prize in 1918. He also discovered the quantum of action, now known as Planck's constant, h. He championed Albert Einstein's special theory of relativity, but he opposed the indeterministic, statistical worldview introduced by Niels Bohr, Max Born, and Werner Heisenberg after the advent of quantum mechanics. As the influential president of the Kaiser Wilhelm Society (later the Max Planck Society) until his resignation in 1937, he appealed to Adolf Hitler to reverse his devastating racial policies. His son was later implicated in the July Plot against Hitler, and was executed.

plane tree Any of ten species of large trees that make up the genus *Platanus,* sole genus of the family Platanaceae, native to North America, eastern Europe, and Asia. Plane trees are planted widely in cities for their resistance to diseases and to air pollution and because they grow rapidly and furnish quick shade. They are characterized by scaling bark; large, deciduous, usually lobed leaves; and globular heads of flower and seed. Ball-shaped smooth or bristly seed clusters, which dangle singly and often persist after leaf fall, are key identifiers. Winter bark is patchy and picturesque; as the outer bark flakes off, inner bark shows shades of white, gray, green, and yellow.

planer Metal-cutting machine tool in which the workpiece is firmly attached to a horizontal table that moves back and forth under a single-point cutting tool. The tool-holding device is mounted on a crossrail so that the tool can be moved across the table in small sideward movements. Since the cutting tool can be moved at almost any angle, a wide variety of grooves and surfaces can be generated. Mechanical planers, or surfacers, are also used to smooth wood to an even thickness. Planers perform the same operations as SHAPERS but can machine workpieces up to 50 ft (15 m) long.

planet Any large body orbiting the SUN or another STAR (see PLANETS OF OTHER STARS), except COMETS, meteoroids (see METEOR), or SATELLITES of a larger body. The word comes from the Greek for "wanderer," because their positions change relative to those of the stars. The nine major planets known to revolve around the sun, in order of distance from it, are MERCURY, VENUS, EARTH, MARS, JUPITER, SATURN, URANUS, NEPTUNE, and PLUTO. The first four are called terrestrial planets and the next four Jovian planets. Pluto, distinct from either group, resembles the icy satellites of the Jovian planets. The terrestrial planets are less than 8,000 mi (13,000 km) in diameter and rocky, with comparatively thin or negligible atmospheres. The sun's heat is thought to have prevented the abundant gases in the original SOLAR NEBULA from condensing in them. The Jovian planets formed farther out, where the gases were cool enough to condense, so the planets grew very massive and retained huge atmospheres of light gases, mainly hydrogen and helium. Called gas giants, the Jovian planets appear to be similar in structure; none has an accessible surface. Pluto is by far the smallest major planet. There may be planets beyond it (e.g., PLANET X). The inner and outer planets are separated by tens of thousands of minor planets, making up the ASTEROID belt. In ASTROLOGY, great importance is placed on the planets' positions in the 12 constellations of the ZODIAC. See also PLANETESIMAL, SOLAR SYSTEM.

Planet X Supposed distant PLANET of the solar system, hypothesized on the basis of calculations of effects on the orbits of Uranus and Neptune. The term was first used by PERCIVAL LOWELL c. 1905, and though his prediction eventually resulted in the discovery of Pluto, Pluto's mass was insufficient to explain the apparent perturbations of Uranus and Neptune. However, modern measurements suggest that there may be no significant discrepancies in the outer planets' orbits.

planetarium Institution devoted to popular education in ASTRONOMY and related fields, especially space science, whose main teaching tool is a hemispheric screen onto which images of celestial objects as seen from the earth are projected from an instrument also known as a planetarium, or planetarium projector. Major planetariums have extensive exhibit space, museum collections, sizable staffs, projection domes 80 ft (25 m) or more across, and seating capacities of over 600.

planetary nebula Any of a class of bright nebulae (see NEBULA) that may somewhat resemble planets when viewed through a small telescope but are in fact expanding shells of luminous gas around dying stars. A planetary nebula is the outer envelope shed by a red GIANT STAR not massive enough to become a SUPERNOVA. Instead, the star's intensely hot core becomes exposed (see WHITE DWARF) and ionizes the surrounding shell of gas, which is expanding at tens of miles per second.

planetesimal \ˌpla-nə-ˈte-sə-məl\ One of a class of hypothetical bodies that joined to form the PLANETS after condensing from dust and gas early in the history of the solar system. According to the nebular hypothesis, a cloud of interstellar dust and gas underwent gravitational contraction, eventually forming a SOLAR NEBULA. Clumps of dust left behind in its midplane as it contracted coalesced into planetesimals the size of pebbles, of boulders, and then a few to several hundred miles across. These then combined under the force of gravity to form protoplanets, precursors of the current planets.

planets of other stars *or* **extrasolar planets** Planets that orbit stars other than the sun. The existence of extrasolar planets, many light-years from earth, has been confirmed in recent years. Current detection methods, based on the planets' gravitational effects on the stars they orbit, can discover only very massive planets. At present, planets ranging from half to 60 times the mass of JUPITER have been detected around more than 30 stars. About one-third have highly elliptical orbits, and most of the rest are closer to their stars than MERCURY is to the sun. This raises questions about whether our own solar system is typical, but the current methods are sensitive only to massive planets near to the stars. One such planet, discovered in 1995, orbits a sunlike star, 51 Pegasi.

plankton Marine and freshwater organisms that, because they are unable to move or are too small or too weak to swim against water currents, exist in a drifting, floating state. Plankton is the productive base of both marine and freshwater ecosystems, providing food for larger animals and indirectly for humans, whose fisheries depend on plankton. As a human resource, plankton has only begun to be developed and used. The plantlike community of plankton is called PHYTOPLANKTON, and the animal-like community is called ZOOPLANKTON, but many planktonic organisms are better described as PROTISTS. Most phytoplankton serves as food for zooplankton, but some of it is carried below the light zone. Zooplankton is used directly as food by fish (including herring) or mammals (including whales), but several links on the food chain usually have been passed before plankton is available for human consumption.

plant Any organism in the kingdom Plantae, consisting of multicellular, eukaryotic life forms (see EUKARYOTE) with six fundamental characteristics: PHOTOSYNTHESIS as the almost exclusive mode of nutrition, essentially unlimited growth at MERISTEMS, cells that contain CELLULOSE in their walls and are therefore somewhat rigid, the absence of organs of movement, the absence of sensory and nervous systems, and life histories that show ALTERNATION OF GENERATIONS. No definition of the kingdom completely excludes all nonplant organisms or even includes all plants. Many plants, for example, are not green and thus do not produce their own food by photosynthesis, being instead parasitic on other living plants (see PARASITISM). Others obtain their food from dead organic matter. Many animals possess plantlike characteristics, such as a lack of mobility (e.g., SPONGES) or the presence of a plantlike growth form (e.g., some CORALS and BRYOZOANS), but in general such animals lack other plant characteristics. Some past classification systems (see TAXONOMY) placed difficult groups such as PROTOZOANS, BACTERIA, ALGAE, SLIME MOLDS, and fungi (see FUNGUS) in the plant kingdom, but structural and functional differences between these organisms and plants have convinced most scientists to classify them elsewhere.

plant virus Any of various VIRUSES that can cause plant disease (e.g., the tobacco mosaic virus). Plant viruses are economically important because many of them infect crop and ornamental plants. Numerous plant viruses are rodlike and can be extracted readily from plant tissue and crystallized. Most lack the fatty membrane found in many animal viruses, and all contain RNA. Plant viruses are transmitted in various ways, most importantly through insect bites, mainly by aphids and plant hoppers. Symptoms of virus infection include color changes, dwarfing, and tissue distortion. The appearance of streaks of color in certain tulips is caused by a virus. See also REOVIRUS.

Plantagenet \plan-ˈta-jə-nət\, **House of** *or* **House of Anjou** \ˈan-jü\ Royal house of England (1154–1485) that provided 14 kings, including six from the cadet houses of LANCASTER and YORK. The line descended from Geoffrey, count of Anjou (died 1151), and the empress MATILDA, daughter of the English king HENRY I. Some historians apply the name House of Anjou, or ANGEVIN DYNASTY, to only HENRY II, RICHARD I, and JOHN, and label their successors, including EDWARD I, EDWARD II, and EDWARD III, as Plantagenets. The name may have originated as a nickname (Plante-geneste) for Count Geoffrey, who planted broom shrubs (Latin *genista*) to improve his hunting covers. The Wars of the ROSES saw the defeat of the last Plantagenet king, RICHARD III, in 1485. The legitimate line ended with Edward of Warwick (died 1499).

plantain \ˈplan-tᵊn\ Any of about 265 species of familiar garden, lawn, and roadside WEEDS in the genus *Plantago* of the family Plantaginaceae. Distinctively, the leaves lack a proper blade. What appears to be a blade is an expanded petiole (leafstalk), with several parallel main veins, emerging at the base of the stalk. Small flowers are borne in spikes or heads atop long leafless stalks. The greater plantain *(P. major)* provides seed spikes for bird food. Ribwort, or English, plantain *(P. lanceolata)* and hoary plantain *(P. media)* are troublesome weeds. Some species have been useful in medicine (e.g., as an ingredient in laxatives).

plantain Tall plant *(Musa paradisiaca)* of the BANANA family that is closely related to the common banana *(M. sapientum)*. Believed to have originated in S.East Asia, the plantain grows 10–33 ft (3–10 m) tall and has a conical false "trunk" formed by the leaf sheaths of its spirally arranged, long, thin leaves. The green-colored fruit is larger than that of the banana and contains more starch. Because the starch is maximal before the fruit ripens, the fruit is not eaten raw but is boiled or fried, often with coconut juice or sugar as flavoring. It may also be dried for later use in cooking or ground for use as meal, which can be further refined to a flour. The plantain is a staple food and beer-making crop for East African peoples, and is also eaten in the Caribbean and Latin America.

plantation walking horse See TENNESSEE WALKING HORSE

Plante, (Joseph) Jacques (Omer) (1929–1986) Canadian hockey player. Born in Shawinigin Falls, Quebec, he recorded a shutout in his first NHL game. He was an integral member of the powerful Montreal Canadiens, which won a record five successive STANLEY CUPS (1956–60). He was the first goalie to wear a protective face mask (1959). Honored throughout his 18-year NHL career, he was one of the most successful of all NHL goaltenders.

Planudes \plā-'nü-dēz\, **Maximus** *orig.* **Manuel** (1260–1310?) Greek Orthodox scholar, anthologist, and polemicist. He established a school in Constantinople that gained a strong reputation for its humanities curriculum. His Greek translations of Latin philosophy and literature and of Arabic mathematics publicized these areas of learning throughout the Greek Byzantine cultural world. Though chiefly known for his theological writings, he made a distinctive contribution to the history of Greek literature with his revision of the *Greek Anthology,* a collection of Greek prose and poetry c. 700 BC–AD 1000.

plasma \'plaz-mə\ Liquid part of blood (including dissolved chemicals but not the cells and PLATELETS). This straw-colored fluid serves as the blood's transport medium, helps maintain BLOOD PRESSURE, distributes body heat, and maintains the PH balance in the bloodstream and body. More than 90% consists of water, about 7% proteins, and the rest other substances, including waste products of METABOLISM. Important plasma proteins include ALBUMIN, COAGULATION factors, and GLOBULINS, including GAMMA GLOBULIN and a hormone that stimulates ERYTHROCYTE formation. Serum is the liquid part of the blood that remains after clotting.

plasma Electrically conducting medium in which there are roughly equal numbers of positively and negatively charged particles, produced when the atoms in a gas become ionized (see IONIZATION). Plasma is sometimes called the fourth state of MATTER (the first three being solid, liquid, and gas). A plasma is unique in the way it interacts with itself, with ELECTRIC and MAGNETIC fields, and with its environment. It can be thought of as a collection of ions, electrons, neutral atoms and molecules, and photons in which some atoms are being ionized at the same time as electrons are recombining with other ions to form neutral particles, while photons are continuously being produced and absorbed. It is estimated that more than 99% of the matter in the universe exists in the plasma state.

plasmid \'plaz-məd\ Genetic element not contained within a CHROMOSOME. It occurs in many bacterial strains. Plasmids are circular DNA molecules that replicate independently of the bacterial chromosome. They are not essential for the bacterium but may give it a selective advantage. Some plasmids determine the production of proteins that can kill other bacteria; others make bacteria resistant to antibiotics. Plasmids are extremely valuable tools in the fields of molecular biology and genetics, specifically in the area of GENETIC ENGINEERING.

plasmodium \plaz-'mō-dē-əm\ Any of the parasitic PROTOZOANS that make up the genus *Plasmodium,* the cause of MALARIA. Infecting red blood cells in mammals, birds, and reptiles, plasmodia occur worldwide, especially in tropical and temperate zones. They are transmitted to humans by the bite of the *Anopheles* mosquito. From the bloodstream, young plasmodia enter liver cells, where they divide and form an adult stage that is then released back into the bloodstream and infects red blood cells. Rapid division of the parasites results in the destruction of the red blood cells, which release toxins that cause the periodic chill and fever cycles typical of malaria.

plaster of paris Quick-setting GYPSUM plaster consisting of a fine white powder, calcium sulfate hemihydrate, which hardens when moistened and allowed to dry. It is made by heating gypsum to 250–360°F (120–180°C). Used since ancient times, plaster of paris is so called because of its preparation from the abundant gypsum found in Paris. It is used to make molds and casts for ceramics and sculptures, to precast and hold ornamental plasterwork on ceilings and cornices, and for orthopedic bandages (casts). In medieval and Renaissance times, gesso (plaster of paris mixed with glue) was applied to wood panels, plaster, stone, or canvas to provide the ground for tempera and oil painting.

plasticity Ability of certain SOLIDS to flow or to change shape permanently when subjected to STRESSES between those that produce temporary deformation, or elastic behavior, and those that cause failure of the material, or rupture (see FRACTURE). Plasticity allows a solid under the action of outside forces to become permanently deformed without rupturing; ELASTICITY enables a solid to return to its original shape after the load is removed. Plastic deformation occurs in many metal-forming processes (ROLLING, pressing, FORGING, WIRE DRAWING) and in geologic processes (rock folding and rock flow within earth under extremely high pressures and at elevated temperatures).

plastics POLYMERS that can be molded or shaped, usually by heat and pressure. Most are lightweight, transparent, tough organic compounds that do not conduct electricity well. They fall into two classes: Thermoplastics (e.g., POLYETHYLENE, polystyrene) can be melted and formed again and again; thermosetting plastics, or thermosets (e.g., POLYURETHANE, EPOXY), once formed, are destroyed rather than melted by heating. Few plastics contain only RESIN; many also contain plasticizers (to change the melting point and make them softer), colorants, reinforcements, and fillers (to improve mechanical properties such as stiffness), and stabilizers and antioxidants (to protect against aging, light, or biological agents). Plastics are not biodegradable (see BIODEGRADABILITY), but RECYCLING of plastics, especially thermoplastics, has become an important industry. Major industrial uses of plastics include cars, buildings, packaging, textiles, paints, adhesives, pipes, electrical and electronic components, prostheses, toys, brushes, and furniture. Common plastics include polyethylene terephthalate, or PET (used, e.g., in beverage bottles), PVC (hoses), foamed polystyrene, or Styrofoam (insulated food containers), and LUCITE (shatterproof windows). See also LEO BAEKELAND.

plastic surgery SURGERY to correct disfigurement, restore function, or improve appearance. It may involve reshaping or moving tissues to fill a depression, cover a wound, or improve appearance. Cosmetic surgery solely to improve appearance is not the main focus of plastic surgery. It is utilized after disfigurement by burns or tumor removal, or for reconstructive work, and may involve hiding incisions in skin folds or using buried sutures to hold wounds closed. Reconstructive plastic surgery corrects severe functional impairments, fixes physical abnormalities, and compensates for tissue lost to trauma or surgery. MICROSURGERY and computerized DIAGNOSTIC IMAGING techniques have revolutionized the field.

Plata, Río de la Estuary, PARANA and URUGUAY rivers, between Uruguay and Argentina. It is about 170 mi (275 km) long, with a maximum width at its mouth of about 140 mi (220 km); at MONTEVIDEO it is about 60 mi (97 km) wide, and opposite BUENOS AIRES and above, 25–28 mi (40–45 km) wide. Discovered by the Spanish in 1516, it was explored by FERDINAND MAGELLAN in 1520 and by SEBASTIAN CABOT, 1527–29. The first permanent settlement in the area was at Asunción in 1537.

Plata, viceroyalty of Río de la See viceroyalty of RÍO DE LA PLATA

Plataea \plə-'tē-ə\ Ancient city, BOEOTIA, eastern central Greece, south of THEBES. It was settled by Boeotians, who expelled the earlier Bronze Age inhabitants. The Plataeans fought along with the Athenians against the Persians at the Battle of MARATHON (490 BC). It was the scene of the Greek victory over the invading Persians in the Battle of PLATAEA (479 BC). It was destroyed by the Spartans in 427 BC but was rebuilt under the Macedonian kings PHILIP II and ALEXANDER THE GREAT as a symbol of Greek courage in resisting Persia.

Plataea, Battle of (479 BC) Battle between Greek and Persian forces near Plataea (modern Plataiaí) in Boeotia on the slopes of Mount Cithaeron. A largely Spartan force, including HELOTS, defeated the Persian army of XERXES I, led by Mardonius; the victory marked the end of Persian attempts to invade mainland Greece.

plate tectonics Theory that the earth's LITHOSPHERE (the crust and upper portion of the mantle) is divided into about 12 large plates and several small ones that float on and travel independently over the ASTHENOSPHERE. The theory revolutionized the geological sciences in the 1960s by combining the earlier idea of CONTINENTAL DRIFT and the new concept of SEAFLOOR SPREADING into a coherent whole. Each plate consists of rigid rock created by upwelling magma at OCEANIC RIDGES, where plates diverge. Where two plates converge, a SUBDUCTION ZONE forms, in which one plate is forced under another and into the earth's mantle. The majority of the earthquakes and volcanoes on the earth's surface occur along the margins of tectonic plates. The interior of a plate moves as a rigid body, with only minor flexing, few earthquakes, and relatively little volcanic activity. See illustration on following page.

plateau Extensive area of flat upland, usually bounded by an escarpment on all sides but sometimes enclosed by mountains. Plateaus are extensive, and together with enclosed basins they cover about 45% of the

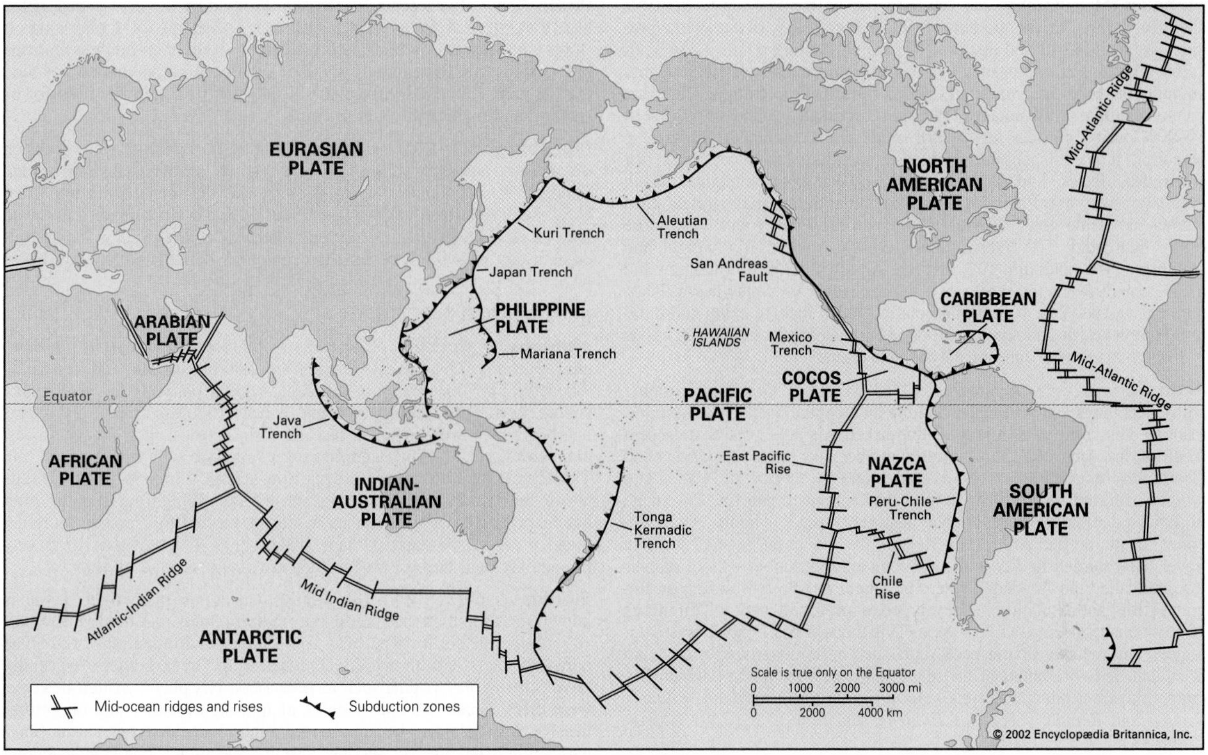

Major tectonic plates of the earth's lithosphere. New lithosphere is created by upwelling magma at certain plate boundaries, called spreading centers or oceanic ridges, where the plates diverge. At other boundaries, called subduction zones, plates converge until one is forced under the other (subducted) into the earth. The continents are rigidly connected to their respective plates and move as the plates move, a few inches a year.

earth's land surface. The essential criteria for a plateau are low relative relief and some altitude. Low relief distinguishes plateaus from MOUNTAINS, although their origin may be similar. Plateaus, being high, often create their own local climate; the topography of plateaus and their surroundings often produce arid and semiarid conditions.

Plateau Indians Any of various Native American tribes that inhabited the high plateau between the Rocky Mountains on the east and the Cascade Range on the west. Among this group were the Coeur d'Alene, FLATHEAD, KLAMATH, Kutenai, MODOC, NEZ PERCÉ, Spokan, Thompson, and Salish.

platelet *or* **thrombocyte** Small, colorless, irregular blood cell crucial in COAGULATION. Produced in BONE MARROW and stored in the SPLEEN, platelets accumulate to block a cut in a blood vessel and provide a surface for fibrin strands to adhere to, contract to pull the strands together, and take part in the conversion sequence of coagulation factors. They also store and transport several chemicals and absorb foreign bodies, including viruses. Antibodies to platelets may develop after repeated platelet or whole-blood transfusions.

Plateresque \ˌpla-tə-ˈresk\ Main architectural style in Spain and its New World colonies in the late 15th and 16th century. The name (which comes from a comparison to the intricate work of silversmiths) came to be generally applied to late Gothic and early Renaissance Spanish architecture, which was characterized by minutely detailed relief ornament derived from Moorish, Gothic, and Italian Renaissance sources and applied without regard for structure. Favorite motifs include twisted columns, heraldic escutcheons, and sinuous scrolls. Clusters of ornament contrast with broad expanses of flat wall surface. Outstanding examples of the style include the College of San Gregorio, Valladolid (1488), the town hall of Seville (begun 1527), and Granada Cathedral (1528–43). Philip II's reaction to Plateresque excess was to build EL ESCORIAL.

platform tennis Variation of PADDLE TENNIS played on a platform enclosed by a wire fence. It was devised in 1928 in Scarsdale, N.Y. The short-handled oval paddles are made of perforated plywood; the balls are made of sponge rubber. The rules are the same as for TENNIS, except that balls may be taken off back or side walls after first striking inside the court.

Plath, Sylvia (1932–1963) U.S. poet. Born in Boston, the daughter of an entomologist, Plath was driven to excel as a writer from an early age and published her first poem at 8. At Smith College she made an early suicide attempt and submitted to electroshock treatment. While attending Cambridge University on a Fulbright grant, she married TED HUGHES. After their separation, she committed suicide at 30. Though she was not widely recognized in her lifetime, her reputation grew rapidly afterward; by the 1970s she was considered a major contemporary poet. Her works, often confessional and preoccupied with alienation, death, and self-destruction, include the volumes *The Colossus* (1960), *Ariel* (1965), and *The Collected Poems* (1981, Pulitzer Prize) and a semiautobiographical novel, *The Bell Jar* (1963).

plating Coating a METAL or other material, such as plastic or china, with a hard, nonporous metallic surface to improve durability and beauty. Early plated goods ("old SHEFFIELD PLATE") are made by the process invented by THOMAS BOULSOVER, and consist of a sandwich of copper between two layers of silver. Today surfaces such as gold, silver, stainless steel, palladium, copper, and nickel are applied by dipping an object into a solution containing the desired surface material, which is deposited by chemical or electrochemical action (see ELECTROPLATING). Much plating is done for decorative purposes, but still more is done to increase the durability and CORROSION resistance of softer materials. Most automotive parts, appliances, housewares and flatware, hardware, plumbing and electronic equipment, wire goods, aircraft and aerospace products, and machine tools are plated for durability. See also GALVANIZING, TERNEPLATE, TINPLATING.

platinum Metallic chemical ELEMENT, one of the TRANSITION ELEMENTS, chemical symbol Pt, atomic number 78. A very heavy, silvery-white precious METAL, it is soft and ductile, with a high melting point (3,216°F, or 1,769°C) and good resistance to corrosion and chemical attack. Small amounts of IRIDIUM are commonly added for a harder, stronger ALLOY that retains platinum's advantages. Platinum is usually found as alloys of 80–90% purity in PLACER DEPOSITS, or more rarely combined with arsenic or sulfur. It is indispensable in high-temperature laboratory work, for electrodes, dishes, and electrical contacts that resist chemical attack even when very hot. Platinum is used in dental alloys, and surgical pins. Known as "white gold," it is used in expensive jewelry and is far more costly than gold. The international primary standards for weight and length are 90% platinum, 10% iridium. An alloy of 76.7% platinum and 23.3% cobalt forms the most powerful permanent MAGNETS known. Platinum has VALENCE 2 or 4 in its compounds, which include many coordination complexes. It and some compounds are useful CATALYSTS, particularly for HYDROGENATION and in catalytic converters.

Plato \'plā-tō\ *orig.* **Aristocles** (428?–347? BC) Greek philosopher whose teachings and writings constitute an essential part of Western philosophy. His family was highly distinguished; his father claimed descent from the last king of Athens, and his mother was related to Critias and Charmides, extremist leaders of the oligarchic terror of 404. Plato (whose acquired name refers to his broad forehead, and thus his range of knowledge) must have known SOCRATES from boyhood. After Socrates' death, he fled Athens for Megara, then spent the next 12 years in travel. He returned in 387 and soon founded the famous school of philosophy called the Academy, where he taught ARISTOTLE. Building on Socrates' life and thought, he developed a profound and wide-ranging philosophical system (see PLATONISM). His thought has logical, epistemological, and metaphysical aspects, but much of its underlying motivation is ethical. It is presented in his many dialogues, in most of which Socrates plays a leading role (e.g., *Apology, Protagoras, Meno, Phaedo, Symposium, Republic, Sophist, Timaeus,* and *Laws*). See also NEOPLATONISM.

Platonism \'plā-tə-,ni-zəm\ Any philosophy that embodies some major idea of Plato's, especially in taking abstract forms as metaphysically more basic than material things. Though there was in antiquity a tradition about Plato's "unwritten doctrines," Platonism then and later was based primarily on a reading of the dialogues. It is characterized by an intense concern for the quality of human life—always ethical, often religious, and sometimes political, based on a belief in unchanging and eternal realities (the Platonic Forms), independent of the changing things of the physical world perceived by the senses. This belief in absolute values rooted in an eternal world distinguishes Platonism from the philosophies of Plato's immediate predecessors and successors and from later philosophies inspired by them. See also NEOPLATONISM.

platoon Principal subdivision of a military company, battery, or troop. Usually commanded by a lieutenant, it consists of 25–50 soldiers organized into two or more squads led by noncommissioned officers. The term was first used in the 17th century to refer to a small body of musketeers who fired together in a volley alternately with another platoon. It has been used in U.S. military manuals since 1779, and throughout the 19th century it meant half a company. It was reintroduced into the British army in 1913. See also MILITARY UNIT.

Platt, Orville Hitchcock (1827–1905) U.S. politician. Born in Washington, Conn., he served in the state legislature (1861–62, 1864, 1869) and later the U.S. Senate (1879–1905), where he sponsored legislation relating to patents and copyrights, including the international copyright act of 1891. He was chairman of the committee on territories (1887–93), which recommended admission of six new western states. He is remembered for sponsoring the PLATT AMENDMENT (1901).

Platt Amendment (1901) Rider appended to a U.S. Army appropriations bill, stipulating conditions for withdrawal of U.S. troops remaining in Cuba since the SPANISH-AMERICAN WAR. The amendment, which was added to the Cuban constitution of 1901, affected Cuba's rights to negotiate treaties and permitted the U.S. to maintain its naval base at Guantánamo Bay and to intervene in Cuban affairs "for the preservation of Cuban independence." In 1934 Pres. FRANKLIN ROOSEVELT supported abrogation of the amendment's provisions except for U.S. rights to the naval base. See also GOOD NEIGHBOR POLICY.

Platte River River, central Nebraska. Formed by the confluence of the NORTH PLATTE and SOUTH PLATTE rivers, it is 310 mi (500 km) long. It flows southeast into a big bend at Kearney, Neb., then empties into the MISSOURI RIVER at Plattsmouth, south of OMAHA. It is too shallow for navigation and is almost dry for much of the year. Its waters are used for irrigation and municipal water systems.

Plattsburgh City (pop., 1995 est.: 19,000), northeastern New York, on the western shore of Lake CHAMPLAIN, south of the Canadian border. Founded by Zephaniah Platt in 1784, it was the scene of an important U.S. victory during the WAR OF 1812 on Lake Champlain that saved New York from British invasion via the HUDSON RIVER valley. Incorporated as a city in 1902, it became the center of the Lake Champlain resort area.

platyhelminth See FLATWORM

platypus *or* **duckbill** MONOTREME amphibious MAMMAL *(Ornithorhynchus anatinus)* of lakes and streams in eastern Australia and Tasmania. About 23 in. (60 cm) long, the squat-bodied platypus has a ducklike snout, short legs, webbed feet, and a beaverlike tail. Each day it eats nearly its own weight in crustaceans, fishes, frogs, mollusks, tadpoles, and earthworms; lacking teeth, it crushes its food with ridges in the bill. The female lays one to three eggs in a nest in a long twisting passage above the waterline. The young are weaned about four months after hatching. The male's heel bears a spur connected to a poison-secreting gland. Large fishes and perhaps snakes prey on platypuses. Formerly trapped for their dense, soft fur, they are now protected by law.

Plautus \'plȯ-təs\ (254?–184 BC) Roman comic playwright. Little is known for certain about his life, but tradition holds that he was associated with the theater from an early age. Like other Roman playwrights, he borrowed plots and dramatic techniques from Greek authors, especially NEW COMEDY playwrights such as MENANDER. His plays, written in verse, were often farces marked by cases of mistaken identity and opportunities for slapstick, and he popularized such character types as the braggart soldier and the sly servant. Twenty-one of his comedies—among the earliest surviving works in Latin—are extant, including *The Pot of Gold, The Captives, The Two Menaechmuses, The Braggart Warrior,* and *Pseudolus*. His work influenced European comedy from the Renaissance onward, notably WILLIAM SHAKESPEARE's *Comedy of Errors* and MOLIÈRE's *The Miser*.

play In zoology, actions that have all the elements of purposeful behavior but are performed for no apparent reason. Play has been documented only among mammals and birds. It is most common among immature animals, but adult animals also play. Horses, cattle, and other ungulates run and kick up their heels even when not fleeing from predators or defending themselves. Dogs adopt an aggressive posture to entice others to join in mock combat. Otters are well known for their mudsliding. Male birds may spontaneously perform their territorial songs when there is no intruding rival.

play See THEATER

playa \'plī-ə\ *or* **pan** *or* **flat** *or* **dry lake** Flat-bottomed depression that is periodically covered by water. Playas occur in interior desert basins and adjacent to coasts in arid and semiarid regions. The water that periodically covers the playa slowly filters into the groundwater system or evaporates into the atmosphere, causing the deposition of salt, sand, and mud along the bottom and around the edges of the depression.

Player, Gary (Jim) (born 1935) South African golfer. Born in Johannesburg, he entered the U.S. PGA circuit in 1955. He won the British Open three times (1959, 1968, 1974), the Master's three times (1961, 1974, 1978), the U.S. PGA twice (1962, 1972), and the U.S. Open once (1965). The span of his major championship victories covered three decades, longer than that of any previous golfer.

player piano Piano that mechanically plays music encoded as perforations on a paper roll. An early version, invented in 1897 by the American E. S. Votey, was a cabinet placed in front of an ordinary piano, with wooden "fingers" projecting over the keyboard. A paper roll with perforations corresponding to the notes passed over a tracker bar to activate the release of air by pneumatic devices that set the fingers in motion; the user could control tempo and loudness by levers and pedals. Soon this mechanism was built into the piano itself. The later reproducing player piano could reproduce the nuances of tempo and dynamics in great performances, the roll being produced by the performance itself. After the 1920s the phonograph led to the instrument's quick decline. Modern versions, such as the Yamaha Disklavier, are operated by digital memory on a computer disk.

Steinway-Welte player piano, 1910; in the British Piano and Musical Museum, Brentford, Middlesex, Eng.

playing cards Small rectangular cards used for playing games, and sometimes for divination and conjuring. Modern cards are divided into four suits: spades, hearts, diamonds, and clubs. A complete pack, or deck, of cards includes 13 cards in each suit (10 numbered cards and three court cards—king, queen, and knave); two extra cards, called jokers (portraying a medieval jester), are often included as well. The origin of playing cards is obscure—China and India being the two most likely sources—as is the meaning of their symbols. The earliest reference to cards in Europe occurs in Italy in 1299. The 52-card French deck is now standard throughout the world, but decks with fewer cards evolved in Germany and Spain. Other suit emblems were also used (e.g., bells in Germany, cups in Spain and Italy). See also TAROT.

plea bargaining Negotiation of an agreement between the prosecution and the defense whereby the defendant pleads guilty to a lesser offense or (in the case of multiple offenses) to one or more of the offenses charged, in exchange for more lenient sentencing, recommendations, a specific sentence, or a dismissal of other charges. Supporters claim plea bargaining speeds court proceedings and guarantees a conviction; opponents believe it prevents justice from being served.

plebeian \ple-'bē-ən\ (Latin, *plebs*) Member of the general citizenry, as opposed to the PATRICIAN class, in the ancient ROMAN REPUBLIC. Plebeians were originally excluded from the SENATE and from all public offices except military TRIBUNE, and they were forbidden to marry patricians. Seeking to acquire equal rights, they carried on a campaign called Conflict of the Orders, developing a separate political organization and seceding in protest from the state at least five times. The campaign ceased when a plebeian dictator (appointed 287 BC) made measures passed in the plebeian assembly binding on the whole community.

plebiscite \'ple-bə-ˌsīt\ Vote by the people of an entire country or district to decide an issue. Voters are asked to accept or reject a given proposal rather than choose between alternative proposals. By means of plebiscites, intermediaries such as political parties can be bypassed. Because plebiscites offer a way to claim a popular mandate without permitting an opposition party, totalitarian regimes have used them to legitimize their power. See also REFERENDUM AND INITIATIVE.

Plehve \'plā-vyi\, **Vyacheslav (Konstantinovich)** (1846–1904) Russian government administrator. In 1881 he was appointed director of the secret police in the ministry of the interior. He became head of the imperial chancellery (1894), state secretary for Finland (1899), and minister of the interior (1902). Concerned with upholding autocratic principles, he suppressed revolutionary and liberal movements, harshly pursued Russification policies against minority nationality groups, and backed police-controlled labor unions. He was assassinated by a member of the Socialist Revolutionary Party.

Pleiades \'plē-ə-ˌdēz\ OPEN CLUSTER of stars in the constellation Taurus, about 400 light-years from earth. It contains a large amount of bright nebulous material and several hundred stars, of which six or seven can be seen by the unaided eye and have figured prominently in the myths and literature of many cultures. In the Northern Hemisphere, the rising of the Pleiades near dawn in spring has from ancient times marked the opening, and their morning setting in autumn the end, of seafaring and farming seasons.

Pleistocene epoch \'plīs-tə-ˌsēn\ Earlier and longer of the two epochs that constitute the QUATERNARY PERIOD. The Pleistocene began c. 1.8 million years ago and ended c. 10,000 years ago. It was preceded by the PLIOCENE EPOCH of the TERTIARY PERIOD and followed by the HOLOCENE EPOCH. At the height of the Pleistocene glacial ages, more than 30% of the land area of the earth was covered by glacial ice; during the interglacial stages, probably only about 10% was. The animals and plants of the Pleistocene began to resemble those of today. Flowering plants proliferated, and new groups of land mammals, including humans, appeared. At the end of the epoch, mass extinctions occurred: in North America more than 30 genera of large mammals became extinct within a span of roughly 2,000 years. Of the many causes that have been proposed for these extinctions, the two most likely are changing environment with changing climate and disruption of the ecological pattern by early humans.

Plekhanov \pli-'k̲ä-nȯf\, **Georgy (Valentinovich)** (1856–1918) Russian Marxist theorist. From 1874 he was active in the Populist movement and became a leader of the Land and Freedom group (1877–80). To avoid arrest, he went into a long exile in Geneva (1880–1917). In 1883 he founded the first Russian Marxian revolutionary organization, Liberation of Labor, which became the RUSSIAN SOCIAL-DEMOCRATIC WORKERS' PARTY (1898). In *Socialism and Political Struggle* (1883) and *Our Differences* (1885), he described a two-phase revolutionary scheme that influenced Russian Marxist thought. Followers in the 1890s included VLADIMIR ILICH LENIN. After the party split (1903), Plekhanov joined the MENSHEVIKS but spent years trying to reunite the party. He supported the Allies in World War I and opposed the Bolshevik seizure of power. After returning briefly to Russia in 1917, he died in exile in Finland.

Plessy v. Ferguson U.S. Supreme Court decision (1896) that established the legality of racial SEGREGATION so long as facilities were "separate but equal." The case involved a challenge to Louisiana laws requiring separate rail cars for blacks and whites. Though the laws were upheld, a famous dissent by JOHN MARSHALL HARLAN advanced the idea that the U.S. Constitution is "color-blind." The *Plessy* decision was overturned in 1954 by *BROWN V. BOARD OF EDUCATION*.

Pleurococcus See PROTOCOCCUS

Pleven \plā-'ven\, **René** (1901–1993) French politician and premier (1950–51, 1951–52). A lawyer and industrial executive, he served in CHARLES DE GAULLE's wartime government (1940–45). Elected to the National Assembly in 1945, he cofounded with FRANCOIS MITTERRAND the Democratic and Socialist Union of the Resistance, serving as its president 1946–53. He held several postwar cabinet posts, including minister of defense (1949–50, 1952–54). He sponsored the Pleven Plan for a unified European army, but the EUROPEAN DEFENSE COMMUNITY, based on his plan, collapsed in 1954. He served as minister of justice 1969–73.

Plexiglas See LUCITE

Pleyel \ple-'yel, *Engl* 'plī-əl\, **Ignace Joseph** *orig.* **Ignaz Josef** (1757–1831) Austrian-French music publisher, piano maker, and composer. He studied with F.J. HAYDN c. 1772–77, then held posts in Vienna and Strasbourg and traveled in Italy before settling in Paris. His publishing house, Maison Pleyel, published Haydn's complete string quartets (1801), and in 1802 published the first miniature scores for study, but it survived its founder by only three years. His piano firm lasted until the 1960s. Pleyel's music, including 45 symphonies and over 70 string quartets, was once very popular.

Plimsoll \'plim-səl\, **Samuel** (1824–1898) British reformer. A London coal merchant, he served in Parliament 1868–80. With his book *Our Seamen* (1873), he helped overcome resistance to the Merchant Shipping Act, which instituted such reforms as the loading limit for cargo ships. A load line (the Plimsoll mark or line) was marked on the hull of every cargo ship, indicating the maximum depth to which the ship could be safely loaded.

plinth Lowest part, or foot, of a PEDESTAL, PODIUM, or architrave (molding around a door). It can also refer to the bottom support of a piece of furniture or the usually projecting stone coursing that forms a platform for a building. Tall stone plinths are often used to add monumentality to temple settings and MAUSOLEUMS (see TAJ MAHAL).

Pliny the Elder \'plin-ē\ *Latin* **Gaius Plinius Secundus** (AD 23–79) Roman scholar. Descended from a prosperous family, Pliny pursued a military career, held official positions (including procurator of Spain), and later spent years in semiretirement, studying and writing. His fame rests on his *Naturalis historia,* or *Natural History* (AD 77), an encyclopedic work of uneven accuracy that was the European authority on scientific matters up to the Middle Ages. Six other works ascribed to him were probably lost in antiquity. He died while observing the great eruption of VESUVIUS.

Pliny the Younger *Latin* **Gaius Plinius Caecilius Secundus** (AD 61/62–113?) Roman author and administrator. The nephew of PLINY THE ELDER, he practiced law and held official posts, including consul and head of the military and senatorial treasuries. He is known for the nine books of private letters he published in AD 100–109. The carefully composed letter, at that time a fashion among the wealthy, was transformed by Pliny into an art. His are charming and meticulous occasional pieces on diverse literary, social, and domestic themes that intimately illustrate public and private life in the heyday of the Roman empire.

Pliocene epoch \'plī-ə-ˌsēn\ Last and shortest epoch of the TERTIARY PERIOD, from c. 5.3 to c. 1.8 million years ago. It follows the MIOCENE EPOCH and precedes the PLEISTOCENE EPOCH of the QUATERNARY PERIOD. Pliocene environments were generally cooler and drier than those of preceding Tertiary epochs. In general, Pliocene mammals grew larger than those of earlier epochs. The more advanced primates continued to evolve, and it is possible that the australopithecines (see AUSTRALOPITHECUS), the first creatures that can be termed human, developed late in the Pliocene.

Plisetskaya \pli-'set-skə-yə\, **Maya (Mikhaylovna)** (born 1925) Russian prima ballerina, noted for her technical virtuosity and ability to integrate acting with dancing. She studied at the BOLSHOI's school in Moscow, joining the company as a soloist in 1943. She toured worldwide with the Bolshoi Ballet and appeared as a guest artist with several companies, including the Paris Opera. She also danced in several films, including *Swan Lake* (1957). In the 1980s she was a guest ballet director in Rome and later in Madrid.

Maya Plisetskaya in *Swan Lake*, 1961.
PARIS MATCH—PICTORIAL PARADE

PLO See PALESTINE LIBERATION ORGANIZATION

ploidy \'plȯi-dē\ Number of sets of CHROMOSOMES in the nucleus of a cell. In normal human body cells, chromosomes exist in pairs, a condition called diploidy. During MEIOSIS the cell produces sex cells (gametes), each containing half the normal number of chromosomes, a condition called haploidy. When an egg and a sperm unite in fertilization, the diploid condition is restored. Polyploid cells have three or more times the number of chromosomes found in haploid cells; polyploid organisms usually cannot reproduce. Aneuploid cells have an abnormal number of chromosomes that is not a multiple of the haploid number. Aneuploidy is most often caused by an error leading to an unequal distribution of chromosomes during division.

Plotinus \plō-'tī-nəs\ (AD 205–270) Egyptian-Roman philosopher. Probably born in Egypt, he studied in Persia and moved to Rome in AD 244, where he became the center of an influential circle of intellectuals. His attempt to form a Platonic republic in Campania c. 265 was halted by GALLIENUS. He was the founder of NEOPLATONISM; his collected works, the *Enneads* (from Greek, *enneas:* "set of nine") consisting of six sets of nine treatises each, arranged by his disciple Porphyry (232?–c. 305), are the first and greatest collection of Neoplatonic writings. For Plotinus, philosophy was not only a matter of abstract speculation but also a way of life and a religion. His works strongly influenced early Christian theology, and his philosophy was widely studied and emulated for many centuries.

Plovdiv \'plȯv-ˌdif\ City (pop., 1996 est.: 344,000), southern central Bulgaria. It is situated on the MARITSA RIVER, north of the RHODOPE MTNS. In 341 BC it fell to PHILIP II and was renamed Philippopolis. From AD 46 it was called Trimontium and was the capital of the Roman province of THRACE. It changed hands repeatedly during the Middle Ages until 1364, when it was captured by the Turks. It was united with Bulgaria in 1885 and assumed its present name after 1919. It is a major railroad junction and a food-processing center with diversified industries.

plover \'plə-vər, 'plō-vər\ Any of about 36 species (family Charadriidae, order Charadriiformes) of plump-breasted shorebirds found almost worldwide. Plovers are 6–12 in. (15–30 cm) long and have long wings, longish legs, a short neck, and a straight, short bill. Many species are plain brown, gray, or sandy above and whitish below. Others, including the golden and black-bellied plovers, are finely patterned above and black below in breeding season. Many species run along the shoreline, snapping up small aquatic invertebrates. They have a melodious whistled call. Both parents incubate the two to five eggs and care for the young. See also KILLDEER.

Golden plover (*Pluvialis apricaria*).
KENNETH W. FINK—ROOT RESOURCES

plow *or* **plough** Most important agricultural implement since the beginning of history, used to turn and break up SOIL, to bury CROP residues, and to help control WEEDS. The forerunner of the plow is the prehistoric digging stick. The earliest plows were undoubtedly digging sticks with handles for pulling or pushing. By Roman times, plows were pulled by oxen or horses, and today they are drawn by TRACTORS.

plum Any of various trees in the genus *Prunus* of the ROSE family, and their edible fruits. In the U.S. and Europe, plums are the most extensively distributed of the stone (drupe) fruits, most varied in native and cultivated kinds, and most adapted to a wide range of soils and climatic conditions. The fruits show a wide range of size, flavor, color, and texture. They are widely eaten fresh, cooked, or baked in pastries. In full bloom, plum trees are covered with densely packed, showy flower clusters. The smooth-skinned fruit has a fleshy, juicy exterior and a hard interior stone or pit. Plum varieties that can be or have been dried without resulting in fermentation are called prunes.

plumbago See GRAPHITE

plumbing System of pipes and fixtures installed in a building for the distribution of potable water and the removal of waterborne wastes. Plumbing is usually distinguished from water and sewage systems, which serve a group of buildings or a city. Improvement in plumbing systems was very slow, with virtually no progress made from the time of the Roman system of AQUEDUCTS and lead pipes until the 19th century. Eventually the development of separate, underground water and sewage systems eliminated open sewage ditches. Present-day water pipes are usually made of steel, copper, brass, plastic, or other nontoxic material. A building's waste-disposal system has two parts: the drainage system and the venting system. The drainage portion comprises pipes leading from various fixture drains to the central main, which is connected to the sewage system. The venting system consists of pipes leading from an air inlet (usually on the roof) to various points within the drainage system; by providing the circulation of air within the system, it protects the trap seals of fixtures from siphonage and back pressure. See also SEWAGE SYSTEM, WATER POLLUTION, WATER-SUPPLY SYSTEM. See illustration opposite on following page.

Plunket, St. Oliver (1629–1681) Irish prelate, the last man to suffer martyrdom for the Catholic faith in England. He was ordained in Rome, where he taught theology and represented the Irish bishops at the Holy See. In 1669 he was appointed archbishop of Armagh and primate of

Ireland, and worked to restore the disorganized church in Ireland. Renewed persecution forced him into hiding in 1673. In the anti-Catholic hysteria caused by the TITUS OATES plot (1678), he was betrayed and imprisoned in Dublin in 1679. After a farcical trial in London, he was convicted of treason and was hanged, drawn, and quartered. He was canonized in 1975.

pluralism In social and political thought, the autonomy enjoyed by disparate groups within a society, or the doctrine that the existence of such groups is beneficial. In a pluralistic society, no single interest group or class predominates. Pluralism was strongly championed in the early 20th century by such writers as FREDERIC W. MAITLAND and HAROLD J. LASKI, and in the later 20th century by ROALD DAHL and David B. Truman.

pluralism In METAPHYSICS, the doctrine opposed to MONISM. Whereas monists such as PARMENIDES, BENEDICT DE SPINOZA, and G. W. F. HEGEL maintain that reality consists of only one ultimate substance, pluralists assert that reality consists of manifold entities of many different types, and that the diversity of things is more striking and important than their unity. WILLIAM JAMES, especially in *A Pluralistic Universe* (1909), held that it is characteristic of empirically minded thinkers to note the changeability of things, their multiplicity of their being and their relations with one another, and the unfinished character of the world.

plurality system Electoral process in which the candidate who polls more votes than any other candidate is elected. It is distinguished from the majority system, in which, to win, a candidate must receive more votes than all other candidates combined. It is the most common method of selecting candidates for public office. Its chief advantage is that it avoids the need for runoffs to produce a winner. Its chief disadvantage is that it may result in a winner who has received a minority of the votes cast. It operates best in a two-party system, where the small vote for any third party will rarely result in an outcome seriously at odds with the voters' will.

Plutarch \'plü-ˌtärk\ *Greek* **Plutarchos** ***Latin*** **Plutarchus** (AD 46?–after 119) Greek biographer and author. The son of a biographer and philosopher, Plutarch studied in Athens, taught in Rome, traveled widely, and made many important friends before returning to his native town in Boeotia. His literary output was immense, but his popularity rests primarily on his *Parallel Lives,* a series of pairs of biographies of famous Greeks and Romans. Displaying impressive learning and research, the *Lives* exhibit noble deeds and characters and provide model patterns of behavior. The *Moralia*, or *Ethica,* contains his surviving writings on ethical, religious, physical, political, and literary topics. His works profoundly influenced the evolution of the essay, biography, and historical writing in 16th–19th-century Europe, especially through translations such as Sir Thomas North's *Lives of the Noble Grecians and Romanes* (1579), WILLIAM SHAKESPEARE's source for his Roman history plays.

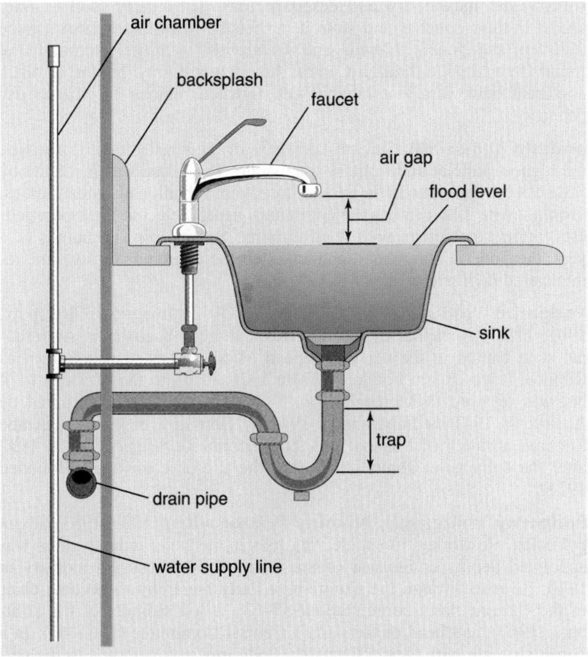

The basic components of a plumbing fixture include the water-supply pipes, a valve or faucet for controlling the flow of water, and a drainpipe to carry wastewater away. An air chamber may be added to the supply line to cushion the effects of water hammer. A trap in the drain line leaves a plug of water in the pipe to prevent unwanted sewer gases from entering the room via the drain.

Pluto Ninth planet from the sun. It was discovered in 1930 by Clyde W. Tombaugh (1906–1997) and named after the Greek god of the underworld. It is usually the outermost of the known planets, averaging about 3.7 billion mi (5.9 billion km) from the sun, but its eccentric orbit brings it closer to the sun than NEPTUNE for 22 years during its 248-year orbit. Because of its distance and size, Pluto always appears relatively faint, even through a telescope. Its axis is tipped 122°, so it rotates nearly on its side and "backwards," once every 6.387 days, locked synchronously with the orbit of its single moon, Charon, discovered in 1978. Pluto has a diameter of about 1,500 mi (2,400 km), roughly two-thirds that of the moon, and has less than 1% of earth's mass and only about 6% of its surface gravity. Infrared observations (see INFRARED ASTRONOMY) suggest that Pluto has methane ice polar caps, which sometimes appear to extend halfway to its equator. Its estimated average surface temperature is −380°F (−205°C). Its thin atmosphere contains methane and probably some heavier gases, possibly nitrogen.

plutonium Radioactive (see RADIOACTIVITY) metallic chemical ELEMENT, chemical symbol Pu, atomic number 94. A member of the ACTINIDE series of TRANSITION ELEMENTS, it is the most important TRANSURANIUM ELEMENT because of its use in certain types of nuclear reactors (see NUCLEAR POWER) and in NUCLEAR WEAPONS. It is found in nature only in traces produced by natural NEUTRON irradiation in URANIUM ores. It is produced by neutron irradiation of uranium-238. Plutonium is a silvery METAL that tarnishes in air; it is warm because of energy released in ALPHA DECAY. Its ISOTOPES, all radioactive, are highly toxic radiological poisons (see RADIATION INJURY) because they give off alpha particles and are specifically absorbed by bone marrow. Though potentially lethal, its toxicity has frequently been exaggerated.

Plymouth City (metro. area pop., 1995 est.: 258,000), in DEVON, southwestern England, on Plymouth Sound southwest of London. It was named Sudstone in the DOMESDAY BOOK of 1086; its harbor is still called Sutton Harbor. It was the port from which the English fleet sailed against the Spanish ARMADA in 1588. It was the last port touched by the *Mayflower* before its voyage to America in 1620. In 1690 its dockyard was built on the western bank of the Tamar River. During World War II it suffered bomb damage from air raids. The rebuilt city has some of the finest commercial, shopping, and civic centers in Britain and new bridges over the Plym and Tamar rivers.

Plymouth City (pop., 1995 est.: 48,000), southeastern Massachusetts, on Plymouth Bay. It was the site of the first permanent European settlement in New England, the Colony of New Plymouth, founded by the PILGRIMS in 1620 and governed under the MAYFLOWER COMPACT until 1691, when it became part of MASSACHUSETTS BAY COLONY. Its seaside location and historic associations make Plymouth an outstanding summer resort. A tourist-based economy is supplemented by light industry, fishing, and cranberry growing. Historical attractions include Plimoth Plantation (a recreation of the original Pilgrim village) and many restored early colonial houses.

Plymouth Co. (1606–9) Commercial trading company chartered by the English crown to colonize the eastern coast of North America in present-day New England. Also called the Virginia Colony of Plymouth, its shareholders were merchants of Plymouth, Bristol, and Exeter. Its twin company was the more successful LONDON CO. The Plymouth Co. established a colony on the coast of Maine in 1607, but soon abandoned it. Inactive after 1609, it was reorganized under a new charter in 1620 as the Council for New England.

plywood Manufactured panel made up of three or more thin plies (layers) of wood. Each ply is laid down with its grain running perpendicular to the one before it. Like other glued-wood products, plywood provides a strong, inexpensive alternative to solid wood. It is widely used both in cabinetmaking (for chests, dressers, wardrobes, and tables) and in house construction (for walls, ceilings, subfloors, doors, and in forms for casting concrete). See also GLUE-LAMINATED TIMBER.

PMS See PREMENSTRUAL SYNDROME

pneumatic device \nü-'ma-tik\ Any of various TOOLS and instruments that generate and use COMPRESSED AIR. Examples include rock drills, pavement breakers, riveters, forging presses, paint sprayers, blast cleaners, and atomizers. Compressed-air power is flexible, economical, and safe. In general, pneumatic systems have relatively few moving parts, contributing to high reliability and low maintenance costs.

pneumatic structure MEMBRANE STRUCTURE that is stabilized by the pressure of compressed air. Air-supported structures are supported by internal air pressure. A network of cables stiffens the fabric, and the assembly is supported by a rigid ring at the edge. The air pressure within this bubble is increased slightly above normal atmospheric pressure and maintained by compressors or fans. Air locks are required at entrances to prevent loss of internal air pressure. Air-supported membranes were first devised by Walter Bird in the late 1940s and were soon put to use as covers for swimming pools, temporary warehouses, and exhibition buildings. Air-inflated structures are supported by pressurized air within inflated building elements that are shaped to carry loads in a traditional manner. Pneumatic structures are perhaps the most cost-effective type of building for very long spans.

pneumococcus \,nü-mə-'kä-kəs\ Spheroidal bacterium *(Streptococcus pneumoniae)* that causes human diseases including pneumonia, sinusitis, ear infection, and meningitis. Usually occurring in the upper respiratory tract, this gram-positive (see GRAM STAIN) COCCUS is often found in a chain configuration and surrounded by a POLYSACCHARIDE capsule. Pneumococci are separated into types depending on the specific capsular polysaccharide formed. Their disease-causing ability resides in the capsule, which delays or prevents their destruction by cells in the bloodstream that normally engulf foreign material.

pneumoconiosis \,nü-mə-,kō-nē-'ō-səs\ Any LUNG disease caused by inhalation of organic or inorganic dusts or chemical irritants, usually over time. Some dusts (e.g., SILICA MINERALS, ASBESTOS) produce grave reactions in small quantities. Dust collects in the PULMONARY ALVEOLI, causing inflammation that scars lung tissue, reducing its elasticity. Chest tightness and shortness of breath may progress to chronic BRONCHITIS and EMPHYSEMA. Cigarette smoking worsens many types. The most common cause of severe disease is silica (see SILICOSIS). Asbestos (see ASBESTOSIS), beryllium, and aluminum dusts can cause worse disease, often on brief exposure. Organic causes include mold spores (see ALLERGY) and textile fibers. Chemical irritants such as ammonia, acid, and sulfur dioxide are soon absorbed by the lung lining; their irritant effect can cause pulmonary EDEMA, and they can lead to chronic bronchitis.

pneumonia \nü-'mōn-yə\ INFLAMMATION and solidification of LUNG tissue caused by infection, foreign particle inhalation, or irradiation, but usually by BACTERIA. *Mycoplasma pneumoniae* is the most common cause in healthy individuals. The bronchi and alveoli may be inflamed. Coughing becomes severe and may bring up flecks of blood. It can be serious but is rarely fatal. *Streptococcus pneumoniae* is more common and generally more severe but usually affects only those with low resistance, especially in hospitals. A highly lethal form caused by *Klebsiella pneumoniae* is almost always confined to hospitalized patients with low immunity. Other bacterial pneumonias include *Pneumocystis carinii* pneumonia (rare except in AIDS) and LEGIONNAIRES' DISEASE. Most respond to ANTIBIOTIC treatment. VIRUSES set the stage for bacterial pneumonia by weakening the individual's immune system more often than they cause pneumonia directly. Fungal pneumonia usually occurs in hospitalized persons with low resistance, but contaminated dusts can cause it in healthy individuals. It can develop rapidly and may be fatal. X-RAY treatment (see RADIATION THERAPY) of structures in the chest may cause temporary lung inflammation.

Po Chü-i See BO JUYI

Po Hai See BO HAI

Po River *ancient* **Padus** River, northern Italy. The country's longest river, it is about 405 mi (652 km) long. It rises in the Cottian Alps on the western frontier and flows northeast to TURIN, then east across PIEDMONT and LOMBARDY into the ADRIATIC SEA. Its delta is one of the most complex of any European river, with at least 14 mouths. It is navigable from its mouth to PAVIA. Industrial cities in its valley include MILAN, PADUA, and VERONA. It has suffered devastating autumn floods, including those in 589, 1438, 1951, and 1966.

Pobedonostsev \pə-byi-də-'nòst-syif\, **Konstantin (Petrovich)** (1827–1907) Russian government administrator. He wrote and lectured on civil law at Moscow University (1859–65), tutored the sons of Czar ALEXANDER II, and later became a close adviser to ALEXANDER III, influencing him to adopt reactionary policies. As director general of the Holy Synod of the Russian Orthodox Church (1880–1905), he assumed great power over domestic policy in education, religion, and censorship. Nicknamed "the Grand Inquisitor," he became the symbol of Russian monarchical absolutism.

Pocahontas \,pō-kə-'hän-təs\ (1595?–1617) POWHATAN Indian woman who helped maintain peace between English colonists and Native Americans by befriending the settlers at JAMESTOWN, Va. Daughter of the powerful chief POWHATAN, Pocahontas intervened to spare the life the colony's captive leader, JOHN SMITH. She subsequently converted to Christianity and wedded the colonist JOHN ROLFE, which furthered efforts toward peace. She traveled to England, where she was received at court, but died of smallpox there.

Pocahontas, detail of a portrait by an unknown artist, 1616.

BY COURTESY OF THE LIBRARY OF CONGRESS, WASHINGTON, D.C.

pocket billiards See POOL

pocket gopher See GOPHER

pocket mouse Any of about 30 species of nocturnal North American RODENTS constituting the genus *Perognathus* (family Heteromyidae), having fur-lined, external cheek pouches that open alongside the mouth. Pocket mice are yellowish brown to dark gray and are 2.5–5 in. (6–13 cm) long, excluding a tail of about the same length. They are usually solitary and inhabit dry and desert regions. They carry food (mainly seeds) in their pouches and store it in their burrows. Spiny pocket mice (most in the genera *Liomys* and *Heteromys;* family Heteromyidae), found from Mexico through Central America, are gray, brown, or black nocturnal burrowers that inhabit wet, forested regions as well as dry country.

podesta \,pō-də-'stä\ (Italian: "power") In medieval Italian COMMUNES, the highest judicial and military magistrate. The office was instituted by FREDERICK I BARBAROSSA in an attempt to govern rebellious Lombard cities. From the late 12th century the communes usually elected their own podesta, often a nobleman with legal training. Serving for six months or a year, the podesta summoned councils, led the communal army, and administered civil and criminal jurisdiction.

Podgorica \'pòd-,gòr-ēt-sä\ *formerly (1946–92)* **Titograd** City (pop., 1991: 118,000), capital of MONTENEGRO, southern Yugoslavia. As a feudal state capital in the early European Middle Ages, it was known as Ribnica; it was called Podgorica from 1326. It fell to the Turks in 1474 but was restored to Montenegro in 1878. In 1916 it was occupied by Austria, in 1941 by Italy, and in 1943 by Germany. In 1946 it became Titograd in honor of Marshal TITO, but restored its former name in 1992 after the collapse of communism. It is the site of a university (founded 1974).

Podgorny \pòd-'gòr-nē\, **Nikolay (Viktorovich)** (1903–1983) Soviet politician. He worked in engineering jobs in the sugar industry, then was appointed deputy commissar of the Soviet food-processing industry in 1940. He rose through the Communist Party hierarchy to become chair of the Ukraine party committee (1957–63), a full member of the Politburo (1960), and head of the party's Central Committee (1963–65). In a power struggle with LEONID BREZHNEV, Podgorny was demoted to the ceremonial post of chairman of the Presidium of the Supreme Soviet (1965–77).

podiatry \pə-'dī-ə-trē\ *or* **chiropody** \,kə-'räp-əd-ē\ Medical specialty dealing with the FOOT. Podiatrists diagnose and treat foot diseases, disabilities, and deformities by means of PHYSICAL MEDICINE AND REHABILITA-

TION, special shoes and other mechanical devices, drugs, and minor surgery.

podium In architecture, a PEDESTAL on a large scale. It may be any of various elements that form the base of a structure, such as the platform forming the floor and substructure of a Classical temple, a low wall supporting columns, or the structurally or decoratively emphasized lowest portion of a wall. The term is also applied to other types of raised platform, such as an orchestra conductor's dais.

Poe, Edgar Allan (1809–1849) U.S. poet, critic, and short-story writer. Born in Boston, Poe was raised by foster parents in Richmond, Va., following his mother's death in 1811. He briefly attended the University of Virginia and then returned to Boston, where in 1827 he published a pamphlet of youthful Byronic poems. By 1835 he was in Richmond as editor of the *Southern Literary Messenger,* the first of several periodicals he was to edit or write for. There he married a 13-year-old cousin, who would die in 1847. At various times he lived in Baltimore, New York, and Philadelphia. Alcohol, the bane of his irregular and eccentric life, caused his death at 40. His works are famous for his cultivation of mystery and the macabre. Among his tales are "The Fall of the House of Usher," "The Masque of the Red Death," "The Black Cat," "The Tell-Tale Heart," and "The Pit and the Pendulum." "The Murders in the Rue Morgue" and "The Purloined Letter" initiated the modern DETECTIVE STORY. His poems (less highly regarded now than formerly) are musical and sensuous, as in "The Bells," a showcase of sound effects; they include touching lyrics inspired by women (e.g., "Annabel Lee") and the uncanny (e.g., "The Raven").

poet laureate Title first granted in England for poetic excellence. Begun in 1616, the office was formally established in 1668 and has been continuous since then. Its holder, a salaried member of the British royal household, was formerly expected to compose poems for court or national occasions, but since the appointment of WILLIAM WORDSWORTH in 1843 the office has been a reward for eminence in poetry and has carried no specific duties. In 1985 the U.S. government created the title of poet laureate, to be held by the consultant in poetry to the Library of CONGRESS.

poetry Writing that formulates a concentrated imaginative awareness of experience in language chosen and arranged to create a specific emotional response through its meaning, sound, and rhythm. It may be distinguished from PROSE by its compression, frequent use of conventions of METER and RHYME, use of the line as a formal unit, heightened vocabulary, and freedom of syntax. Its emotional content is expressed through a variety of techniques, from direct description to symbolism, including the use of METAPHOR and SIMILE. See also PROSE POEM, PROSODY.

Poetry U.S. poetry magazine founded in Chicago in 1912 by HARRIET MONROE, who became its longtime editor. It became the principal organ for modern poetry of the English-speaking world and survived through World War II. Because its inception coincided with the CHICAGO LITERARY RENAISSANCE, it is often associated with the raw, local-color poetry of CARL SANDBURG, EDGAR LEE MASTERS, VACHEL LINDSAY, and SHERWOOD ANDERSON, but it also championed new formalistic movements, including IMAGISM. EZRA POUND was its European correspondent; among the authors it published were T. S. ELIOT, WALLACE STEVENS, MARIANNE MOORE, D. H. LAWRENCE, and WILLIAM CARLOS WILLIAMS.

Poggio Bracciolini \'pòd-jō-ˌbrät-chō-'lē-nē\, **Gian Francesco** (1380–1459) Italian humanist and calligrapher. While working as a copyist of manuscripts, Poggio invented the humanist script, which later became the prototype for Roman fonts in printing. He traveled to various monasteries in Europe, uncovering lost, forgotten, or neglected classical Latin manuscripts, including works by CICERO and LUCRETIUS. He also translated works by LUCIAN, XENOPHON, and others into Latin. His own writings include moral dialogues and *Facetiae* (1438–52), a collection of humorous tales containing satires of his contemporaries.

pogrom \pə-'gräm\ (Russian: "devastation, riot") Mob attack, condoned by authorities, against persons and property of a religious, racial, or national minority. The term is usually applied to attacks on Jews in Russia in the late 19th and early 20th century. After the assassination of Czar ALEXANDER II (1881), false rumors associating Jews with the murder aroused Russian mobs in over 200 cities and towns to attack Jews and destroy their property. Mob attacks diminished in the 1890s but again became common in 1903–6. Though the government did not organize pogroms, its anti-Semitic policy (1881–1917) and reluctance to stop the attacks led many anti-Semites to believe that their violence was legitimate. Pogroms also occurred in Poland and in Germany during ADOLF HITLER's regime.

pogy See MENHADEN

Poincaré \pwaⁿ-kä-'rā\, **(Jules-) Henri** (1854–1912) French mathematician, theoretical astronomer, and philosopher of science. Born into a distinguished family of civil servants (see RAYMOND POINCARÉ), he excelled at mental calculation and possessed an unusually retentive memory. He wrote a doctoral dissertation on DIFFERENTIAL EQUATIONS (1879), then joined the University of Paris (1881), where he remained the rest of his life. Working in celestial mechanics and mathematical analysis, he independently obtained many of ALBERT EINSTEIN's results relating to the special theory of relativity, and published them in a paper on the dynamics of the electron (1906). He later wrote books for the general public on the meaning and importance of science and mathematics.

Henri Poincaré, 1909.
H. ROGER-VIOLLET

Poincaré \pwaⁿ-kä-'rā\, **Raymond** (1860–1934) French politician. A lawyer, he served in the Chamber of Deputies (1887–1903) and the Senate (1903–12) and as minister of education (1893, 1895) and finance minister (1894, 1906). As prime minister and foreign minister (1912–13), he strengthened France's ties with Russia and Britain. As president of the THIRD REPUBLIC (1913–20), he vigorously supported national unity. As prime minister again in 1922–24 and 1926–29, he was credited with solving France's financial crisis by stabilizing the franc, enabling a period of new prosperity.

poinsettia \pòin-'se-tē-ə\ Popular flowering plant *(Euphorbia pulcherrima),* best-known member of the diverse SPURGE family. Native to Mexico and Central America, it grows in moist, wet, wooded ravines and on rocky hillsides. What appear to be flower petals are actually colored leaflike BRACTS that surround a central cluster of tiny yellow flowers. Cultivated varieties are available with white, pink, mottled, and striped bracts, but the solid-red varieties are in greatest demand during the Christmas season. Milky latex in the stems and leaves can be irritating to sensitized persons or animals, but the claim that poinsettias are deadly poisonous is greatly exaggerated.

Poinsettia (*Euphorbia pulcherrima*).
GRANT HEILMAN—EB INC.

Point Four Program U.S. policy of technical assistance and economic aid to underdeveloped countries. Pres. HARRY TRUMAN proposed the plan as the fourth point of his 1949 inaugural address. It was approved by Congress and administered by a special State Department agency until it was merged with other foreign-aid programs in 1953. Technical assistance, mainly in agriculture, public health, and education, was provided through contracts with U.S. business and educational organizations. Such organizations as the INTER-AMERICAN DEVELOPMENT BANK were created to help develop the program.

Pointe-Noire \ˌpwaⁿt-'nwär\ City (pop., 1992 est.: 576,000) and port, southwestern Republic of the Congo. It was the capital (1950–58) of the Middle Congo region of FRENCH EQUATORIAL AFRICA. With independence in 1958, it was replaced by BRAZZAVILLE as the national capital, but it remained important for trade. Its port facilities were completed in 1939 and expanded during World War II. The Congo's second-largest city, it is a principal port and commercial center, especially for the oil industry.

pointer Dog breed of HOUND, SPANIEL, and SETTER ancestry, first recorded c. 1650 in Britain and named for the dog's rigid posture in the direction of quarry. Pointers were originally used to point hares and were later trained as bird dogs. The pointer stands 23–28 in. (58–71 cm) and weighs 50–75 lbs (23–34 kg); it has a long muzzle, hanging ears, tapered tail, and a short, smooth coat, usually white with dark markings. The German short-haired pointer tracks, points, and retrieves; it is about the size of a pointer and has a short coat of solid liver color or liver and gray-white.

German short-haired pointer.
SALLY ANNE THOMPSON

pointillism \'pwa^{n}-tē-ˌyi-zəm, 'pȯin-t^{ə}l-ˌi-zəm\ In painting, the practice of applying small strokes or dots of contrasting color to a surface so that from a distance they blend together. The term (and its synonym, divisionism) was first used to describe the paintings of GEORGES SEURAT. See also CAMILLE PISSARRO, PAUL SIGNAC.

Poiret \pwȧ-'re\, **Paul** (1879–1944) French fashion designer. After working in the Parisian fashion house of CHARLES FREDERICK WORTH, he opened his own shop in 1902. In 1908 he revived the Empire style, popular in France during the reign of Napoleon I. He invented the brassiere c. 1911. Seeking to restore naturalness to female garb, he was principally responsible for the decline of the corset. He is best known for the hobble skirt, to which he later added draped and belted knee-length tunics. Fringed and tasseled capes, multicolored feathers, and fox stoles imparted a theatrical look to his designs. His flowing Greek costumes were extremely popular in the prewar era, but his popularity faded in the 1920s and he died in poverty. He is often regarded as the most influential fashion designer of all time.

poison Any substance (natural or synthetic) that damages living tissues and injures or kills. Poisons spontaneously produced by living organisms are often called TOXINS, or VENOMS if produced by animals. Poisons may be ingested, inhaled, injected, or absorbed through the skin. They do not always have an all-or-none effect; some are far more toxic than others (e.g., 0.25 g of potassium CYANIDE may kill, whereas a massive single dose of table salt can kill). Poisoning may be acute (a single dose does significant damage) or chronic (repeated or continuous doses produce an eventual effect, as with chemical CARCINOGENS). The effects produced by poisons may be local (hives, blisters, inflammation) or systemic (hemorrhage, convulsions, vomiting, diarrhea, clouding of the senses, paralysis, respiratory or cardiac arrest). Agricultural PESTICIDES are often poisonous to humans. Some industrial chemicals can be very toxic or carcinogenic. Most drugs and health-care products can be poisons if taken inappropriately or in excess. Most forms of RADIATION can be toxic (see RADIATION INJURY). See also ANTIDOTE, ARSENIC POISONING, FISH POISONING, FOOD POISONING, LEAD POISONING, MEDICINAL POISONING, MERCURY POISONING, MUSHROOM POISONING.

poison hemlock Any of several poisonous herbaceous plants of the PARSLEY family, especially *Conium maculatum,* believed to be the plant that killed SOCRATES. It is now common in the U.S. as well as in Europe. A tall biennial, this plant has green stems spotted with red or purple, large compound leaves, and white flowers. Though the poison is concentrated in the seeds, the entire plant is dangerous to livestock when fresh. Despite their common name, poison hemlocks are not CONIFERS (see HEMLOCK). Water hemlocks (*Cicuta* species) are similar and also dangerous.

poison ivy Either of two species of white-fruited woody vines or shrubs of the SUMAC, or cashew, family, native to North America. The species found in eastern North America *(Toxicodendron radicans)* is abundant; a western species known as POISON OAK is less common. Classification specialists place both species in either of two genera, *Toxicodendron* or *Rhus.* Poisonous to the touch, the plant causes severe inflammation and blistering of the skin. Key identifiers are leaves with three mitten-shaped leaflets. The principal toxin (urushiol) may be carried from the plant on clothing, shoes, tools, or soil; by animals; or by smoke from burning plants. Because the toxin is nonvolatile, poisoning may result from wearing clothing a year after its contact with the plant.

Poison ivy (*Toxicodendron radicans*).
WALTER CHANDOHA

poison oak Species of POISON IVY *(Toxicodendron diversilobum),* in the SUMAC (or cashew) family, native to western North America. Like many other lobe-leafed plants commonly called oak, poison oak is not an OAK tree of species *Quercus.*

poison sumac Attractive, narrow shrub or small tree *(Rhus,* or *Toxicodendron, vernix)* of the SUMAC, or cashew, family, also called poison elder, native to swampy acidic soils of eastern North America. Unlike the upright reddish, fuzzy fruit clusters of other SUMACS, whitish waxy berries droop loosely from its stalks. The clear sap, which blackens on exposure to air, is extremely toxic and irritating to the skin for many people.

Poitier \'pwä-tē-ˌā\, **Sidney** (born 1924) U.S. actor. Born in Miami, he was raised in the Bahamas, then studied and acted with the American Negro Theatre in New York. He made his film debut in *No Way Out* (1950) and played notable roles in *Blackboard Jungle* (1955), *The Defiant Ones* (1958), *Lilies of the Field* (1963, Academy Award), *In the Heat of the Night* (1967), *To Sir with Love* (1967), and *Guess Who's Coming to Dinner* (1967). He won acclaim on Broadway for his role in *A Raisin in the Sun* (1959). As one of the first black actors to play dignified film roles, he was a central figure in the breaking of the color barrier in the U.S. film industry. He also directed several films, including *Buck and the Preacher* (1972), *Let's Do It Again* (1975), and *Stir Crazy* (1980).

Poitiers, Battle of (732) See Battle of TOURS/POITIERS

Poitiers \pwä-'tyā\, **Battle of** (September 19, 1356) Catastrophic defeat of the French king JOHN II in the HUNDRED YEARS' WAR between France and England. English troops under EDWARD THE BLACK PRINCE were under pursuit from the probably superior French forces. South of Poitiers the English secured themselves in thickets and marshes, where the French knights became bogged down and made easy targets for the English archers. John II was taken prisoner and for his freedom had to consent to the disadvantageous Treaties of BRETIGNY and Calais.

Poitou \pwä-'tü\ Historical region, western central France. It was bounded by BRITTANY, ANJOU, TOURAINE, Marche, and the Atlantic Ocean. It was inhabited by the ancient Gallic tribe of Pictones and became part of Roman Aquitania. A meeting place of northern and southern cultures, its golden age (11th–12th century) was characterized by great ROMANESQUE ART and architecture. The counts of Poitiers were succeeded by the Angevin kings of England, but by 1375 the French had won the region back. It was a province of France until the FRENCH REVOLUTION, when it was divided into three departments. It is predominantly a rural area; regional specialties include seafood and white wine.

poker Any of several card games in which a player bets that the value of his or her hand is greater than that of the hands held by others. Each subsequent player must either equal or raise the bet or drop out, and the player holding the highest hand at the end of the betting wins the pot.

Two principal forms have developed: straight poker, in which all cards of the standard five-card hand are dealt facedown; and stud poker, in which one or two cards are dealt facedown and the rest faceup (five-card) or the last card down (seven-card). In draw poker, cards may be discarded and additional cards drawn. The traditional ranking of hands is (1) straight flush (five cards of the same suit in sequence, the highest sequence—ace-king-queen-jack-ten—being called a royal flush), (2) four of a kind, (3) full house (three of a kind, plus a pair), (4) flush (five of a single suit), (5) straight (five in sequence), (6) three of a kind, (7) two pair, (8) one pair. Similar five-card games were played in Europe from the 16th century; the French game Poque was brought to Louisiana by French settlers in the 18th century and moved north and west in the early 19th century.

pokeweed *or* **pokeberry** *or* **poke** Strong-smelling shrublike plant *(Phytolacca americana)* with a poisonous root resembling the shape of horseradish, native to wet or sandy areas of eastern North America. It has white flowers, reddish-black berries, and dark-green leaves that often are red-veined or borne on red leafstalks. The berries contain a red dye used to color wine, candies, cloth, and paper. Like the roots, the red or purplish mature stalks are poisonous. Very young green shoots (up to about 6 in., or 15 cm), however, are edible.

Pokrovsky Cathedral See SAINT BASIL THE BLESSED

Pol Pot *orig.* **Saloth Sar** (c. 1925–1998) Prime minister of Cambodia (1975–79). Born in a small village, Pol Pot joined the anti-French resistance under HO CHI MINH in the 1940s and became a member of the Cambodian Communist party in 1946. After studying radio technology in Paris, he returned to Cambodia in 1953 and taught French until he fell under police suspicion in 1963. For the next 12 years he built up the Communist Party. U.S. anticommunist activity in Cambodia, including the toppling of NORODOM SIHANOUK and a bombing campaign in the countryside, drove many to join him. In 1975 his KHMER ROUGE forces captured Phnom Penh, which he ordered entirely evacuated. Even the sick were wheeled out in hospital beds, and in the first weeks it is estimated that tens of thousands died. The ruthlessness with which he pursued his intention to return to "year zero" and create an ethnically pure, agrarian, communist state resulted in as many as 2 million deaths. Overthrown by the Vietnamese in 1979, he led an anti-Vietnamese guerrilla war until he was repudiated by the Khmer Rouge and sentenced to life imprisonment (1997); he died the next year.

Poland *officially* **Republic of Poland** Nation, central Europe. Area: 120,728 sq mi (312,685 sq km). Population (2002 est.): 38,644,000. Capital: WARSAW. Most of the people are Polish; there are minorities of Ukrainians, Germans, and Belarusans. Language: Polish (official). Religions: Roman Catholicism, Orthodoxy. Currency: zloty. Poland consists almost entirely of lowlands in the northern and central regions. The southern border is largely formed by the Sudeten and CARPATHIAN MTNS. The VISTULA and ODER, the principal river systems, both drain into the BALTIC SEA. Industries include mining, manufacturing, and public utilities. Poland is a republic with two legislative houses; its chief of state is the president, and its head of government is the prime minister. Established as a kingdom in 922 under MIESZKO I, Poland was united with Lithuania in 1386 under the JAGIELLON DYNASTY (1386–1572) to become the dominant power in eastern central Europe, and enjoyed a prosperous golden age. In 1466 it wrested western and eastern Prussia from the TEUTONIC ORDER, and its lands eventually stretched to the Black Sea. Wars with Sweden (see First and Second NORTHERN WAR) and Russia in the later 17th century led to the loss of considerable territory. In 1697 the electors of Saxony became kings of Poland, virtually ending Polish independence. In the late 18th century Poland was divided between Prussia, Russia, and Austria (see Partition of POLAND) and ceased to exist. After 1815 the former Polish lands came under Russian domination, and from 1863 Poland was a Russian province, subjected to intensive Russification. After World War I an independent Poland was established by the Allies. The invasion of Poland in 1939 by the U.S.S.R. and Germany precipitated World War II, during which the Nazis sought to purge its culture and its large Jewish population. Reoccupied by Soviet forces in 1945, Poland was controlled by a Soviet-dominated government from 1947. In the 1980s the SOLIDARITY labor movement, led by LECH WALESA, achieved major political reforms, and free elections were held in 1989. An economic austerity program instituted in 1990 sped the transition to a market economy. Poland became a member of NATO in 1999. See map above.

Poland, Partitions of (1772, 1793, 1795) Territorial divisions of Poland by Russia, Prussia, and Austria that progressively reduced its territory until it ceased to exist as a state. In the First Partition (1772), a Poland weakened by civil war and Russian intervention agreed to a treaty signed by Russia, Prussia, and Austria that deprived it of half its population and almost one-third of its land area. In the Second Partition (1793), Poland was forced to cede additional lands to Prussia and Russia. To quell a nationalist uprising led by TADEUSZ KOSCIUSZKO, Russia and Prussia invaded Poland and divided the remnants of the state among themselves and Austria in the Third Partition (1795). Only with the establishment of the Polish Republic in 1918 were the results of the partitions reversed.

Polanski \pə-'lan-skē\, **Roman** (born 1933) Polish-French film director. Born to Polish-Jewish parents in Paris, he grew up in Poland and survived a traumatic wartime childhood under the Nazis. His first feature film, *Knife in the Water* (1962), brought him international fame. He left Poland that year for Britain, where he made *Repulsion* (1965), and later the U.S., where his *Rosemary's Baby* (1968) had a huge success. In 1969 his new wife, the actress Sharon Tate, was murdered by followers of CHARLES MANSON. He directed a graphic adaptation of *Macbeth* in 1971, and the acclaimed thriller *Chinatown* in 1974. Arrested for statutory rape in 1977, he fled to France while out on bail, and there directed *Tess* (1979), *Frantic* (1988), *Bitter Moon* (1992), and *Death and the Maiden* (1994).

polar bear White semiaquatic BEAR *(Ursus maritimus)* found throughout Arctic regions, generally on drifting oceanic ice floes. A swift, wide-ranging traveler and a good swimmer, it stalks and captures its prey. It primarily eats seal but also fish, seaweed, grass, birds, and caribou. The male weighs 900–1,600 lbs (410–720 kg) and is about 5.3 ft (1.6 m) tall at the shoulder and 7–8 ft (2.2–2.5 m) long. It has a short tail. The hairy soles of its broad feet protect it from the cold and help it move across the ice. Though shy, it is dangerous when confronted.

Polar bear (*Ursus maritimus*).
FRANCOIS GOHIER/ARDEA LONDON

polar wandering Migration of the magnetic poles of the earth through geologic time. Scientific evidence indicates that the magnetic poles have slowly and erratically wandered across the surface of the earth. Pole locations calculated from measurements on rocks younger than about 20 million years do not depart from the present pole locations by very much, but successively greater "virtual pole" distances are revealed for rocks older than 30 million years, indicating that substantial deviations occurred. Calculations of polar wandering formed one of the first important pieces of evidence for CONTINENTAL DRIFT.

Polaris \pə-'lar-əs\ *or* **North Star** Earth's present northern polestar (the star visible from the Northern Hemisphere toward which the axis of earth points), at the end of the "handle" of the Little Dipper in the constellation Ursa Minor. Polaris is actually a triple star, composed of a BINARY STAR and a CEPHEID VARIABLE. PRECESSION of earth's axis made the star Thuban, in the constellation Draco, the North Star in ancient Egyptian times and will cause the North Pole to point toward Vega, in the constellation Lyra, 12,000 years from now.

polarization Property of certain types of ELECTROMAGNETIC RADIATION in which the direction and magnitude of the vibrating ELECTRIC FIELD are related in a specified way. The electric VECTOR representing the magnitude and direction of the electric field in a wave of light is perpendicular to the direction in which the wave is moving. Unpolarized light consists of waves moving in the same direction with their electric vectors pointing in random orientations about the axis of propagation. Plane-polarized light consists only of waves that vibrate in one direction. In circular polarization the electric vector rotates about the propagation direction. Light may be polarized by reflection or by passing it through polarizing filters, such as certain crystals, that transmit vibrations in one plane but not in others. Polarized light has useful applications in crystallography, liquid-crystal displays, optical filters, and the identification of optically active chemical compounds.

Polaroid Corp. Major U.S. manufacturer of photographic equipment and supplies. The company was established as Land-Wheelwright Laboratories in 1932 by EDWIN LAND and George Wheelwright to produce Land's first invention, an inexpensive plastic-sheet light polarizer (see POLARIZATION). By 1936 Land was using polarized material in sunglasses and other optical devices, and in 1937 the company was incorporated under the Polaroid name. After World War II Land invented the first instant camera, marketed in 1947 as the Polaroid Land camera, which delivered a finished sepia-toned print 60 seconds after exposure. The company introduced color film for its Polaroid cameras in the 1960s and instant motion pictures in 1977. Its headquarters are in Cambridge, Mass. See also EASTMAN KODAK CO.

Pole, Reginald (1500–1558) English Catholic prelate. A cousin of HENRY VII, Pole was sent by HENRY VIII to study in Italy (1521–27) and given minor offices in the church. Critical of Henry's antipapal policies, he wrote *In Defense of Ecclesiastical Unity* (1536) to defend the pope's spiritual authority. As cardinal, he was sent by Pope PAUL III on missions to persuade Catholic monarchs to depose Henry. These efforts angered Henry, who executed Pole's brother, Lord Montague (1538), and his mother, Margaret, countess of Salisbury (1541). Pole was named papal governor of the Patrimony of St. Peter and later was presiding legate at the Council of TRENT. When the Catholic Mary Tudor became queen as MARY I in 1553, he was appointed legate for England, where he instituted church reforms and was a strong influence on the queen. He was appointed archbishop of Canterbury (1556), but a conflict between the papacy and England's ally Spain caused the pope to cancel Pole's authority and declare him a heretic. Demoralized, he died 12 hours after the death of Queen Mary.

pole construction Method of building that dates back to the Stone Age. Excavations in Europe show rings of stones that may have braced huts made of wooden poles or weighted down the walls of tents made of animal skins supported by central poles. Two types of American Indian pole structures were the WIGWAM and LONGHOUSE. Pole-and-thatch dwellings are common in the Caribbean, Mesoamerica, and the Pacific Islands; bamboo-pole dwellings constructed on piles are found in many wet areas of Asia. A southern African method utilizes a ring of poles inserted into the ground and brought together in a crest and expertly thatched. Today, pole construction employs a vertical structure of pressure-treated wood poles firmly embedded in the ground as a pier foundation. See also TENT STRUCTURE.

pole vault TRACK-AND-FIELD event consisting of a vault for height over a crossbar with the aid of a long pole. It became a competitive sport in the mid-19th century and was included in the first modern Olympic Games. It is generally for men only. In competition, each vaulter is given three chances to clear a specific height. The bar is raised progressively until a winner emerges.

polecat Any of several principally terrestrial mammals of the CARNIVORE family Mustelidae, found in Eurasia and Africa. The polecat hunts at night, feeding on small mammals, birds, reptiles, frogs, fishes, and eggs. Species differ in size and color. The European, or common, polecat *(Mustela putorius),* also called foul marten for its odor, weighs 1–3 lbs (0.5–1.4 kg) and is 14–21 in. (35–53 cm) long, excluding the 5–8-in. (13–20-cm) bushy tail. Its long, coarse fur is brown above, black below. In the U.S., SKUNKS are often called polecats. See also FERRET.

European polecat (*Mustela putorius*).
RUSS KINNE—PHOTO RESEARCHERS

Polesye \pȯ-'lye-sye\ *or* **Pripet Marshes** \'pri-ˌpet\ *or* **Pripyat Marshes** \'pri-pyət\ Vast marsh region, southern Belarus and northwestern Ukraine. The largest swamp of the European continent, the marshes lie in the thickly forested basin of the PRIPYAT RIVER. They cover an area of about 104,000 sq mi (270,000 sq km). Densely wooded and largely uninhabited, the region has supported a diversified lumber industry. A vast amount of land reclamation has taken place during the 20th century, including the regulation of water drainage, permitting the development of agricultural areas.

Polhem \'pä-ləm\, **Christopher** (1661–1751) Swedish mechanical and mining engineer. From 1693 to 1709 he devised water-powered machinery that mechanized operations at the great Falun copper mine. In 1704 he built a factory in Stjaernsund that used division of labor, hoists, and conveyor belts to minimize manual labor, anticipating mass-production techniques later adopted in America and England. His alphabet of machines demonstrated the basic elements of mechanism used by later machine builders. His rolling mill was later adapted by HENRY CORT to the production of wrought iron in England.

police Body of agents organized to maintain civil order and public safety, enforce the law, and investigate crime. Characteristics common to most police forces include a quasi-military organization, a uniformed patrol and traffic-control force, plainclothes divisions for criminal investigations, and a set of enforcement priorities that reflects the community's way of life. Administration may be centralized at the national level downward, or decentralized, with local police forces largely autonomous. Recruits usually receive specialized training and take an exam. The modern metropolitan police force began with SIR ROBERT PEEL in Britain c. 1829. SECRET POLICE are often separate, clandestine organizations established by national governments to maintain political and social orthodoxy, which typically operate with little or no restraint.

police power Power of a government to exercise reasonable control over people and property within its jurisdiction in the interest of general security, health, safety, morals, and welfare. It is generally regarded as one of the powers reserved to the states under the U.S. Constitution. In considering cases involving the exercise of police power, the courts have applied a doctrine called "balance of interests" to determine when the public's right to health and well-being outweighs private or individual concerns. Of equal concern is that DUE PROCESS of law be observed.

O P Q R

poliomyelitis \ˌpō-lē-ō-ˌmī-ə-ˈlī-təs\ *or* **polio** *or* **infantile paralysis** Acute infectious viral disease that can cause flaccid PARALYSIS of voluntary MUSCLES. Severe epidemics killed or paralyzed many people, mostly children and young adults, until the 1960s, when JONAS SALK's injectable killed VACCINE and ALBERT B. SABIN's oral attenuated live vaccine controlled polio in the developed world. Flulike symptoms with diarrhea may progress to back and limb pain, muscle tenderness, and stiff neck. Destruction of SPINAL-CORD motor cells causes paralysis, ranging from transient weakness to complete permanent paralysis, in fewer than 20% of patients. Patients may lose the ability to use the limbs, to breathe, or to swallow and speak. They may need PHYSICAL MEDICINE AND REHABILITATION, mechanical breathing assistance, or tracheal suction to remove secretions. A "postpolio syndrome" occurs decades later in some cases, with weakness of muscles that had recovered.

polis \ˈpä-ləs\ In ancient Greece, an independent city and its surrounding region under a unified government. A polis might originate from the natural divisions of mountains and sea and from local tribal and cult divisions. Usually the town was walled and contained a citadel on raised ground (ACROPOLIS) and a marketplace (AGORA). Government was centered in the town; usually there was an assembly of citizens, a council, and magistrates. Ideally, all citizens participated in the government and in the cults, defense, and economy. Noncitizens included women, minors, METICS, and slaves. Hellenism spread many of the institutions into the Middle East. See also ATHENS, CITY-STATE, SPARTA, THEBES.

Polisario \ˌpō-li-ˈsä-rē-ō\ *officially* **Popular Front for the Liberation of Saguia el Hamra and Rio de Oro** North African politico-military group. Initially an insurgency against Spanish control of the western Sahara region, it turned to agitation against Morocco and Mauritania when the Spanish withdrew in 1976 and left the territory to those two nations. Mauritania made peace in 1979, whereupon Morocco annexed the whole territory. Polisario continued its resistance. In 1991 it agreed to a ceasefire and a referendum, which has been repeatedly postponed by Morocco. See also HASSAN II, SAHARAN ARAB DEMOCRATIC REPUBLIC.

Polish Corridor Strip of land that gave Poland access to the Baltic Sea. Transferred to the newly constituted state of Poland as part of the Treaty of VERSAILLES (1919), the corridor, 20–70 mi (30–110 km) wide, separated eastern Prussia from the main part of Germany. The Germans resented the transfer, though the region had been historically Polish before the Partitions of POLAND and was inhabited by a Polish majority. When Poland refused to accede to ADOLF HITLER's demands for extraterritorial highways across the corridor and cession of the free port city of Danzig (Gdańsk), Germany seized the pretext to invade Poland (1939), beginning World War II.

Polish language West SLAVIC LANGUAGE of Poland, spoken by over 41 million people, including 2–3 million in North America and perhaps 1.5 million in the former Soviet Union. The earliest continuous text in Polish dates from the 14th century. The standard language, formulated in the 16th century, combines features of western and southeastern dialects. Polish is written in the LATIN ALPHABET, and utilizes both digraphs (combinations of letters) and diacritics to distinguish its fairly elaborate repertory of consonants. Stress is fixed on the next-to-last syllable.

Polish Succession, War of the (1733–38) European conflict waged ostensibly to determine the successor to AUGUSTUS II the Strong of Poland. Austria and Russia supported his son AUGUSTUS III, while most Poles, France, and Spain supported STANISLAW I, a former Polish king (1704–9) and father-in-law of France's LOUIS XV. Stanislaw was elected king in 1733, but a Russian threat forced him to flee and Augustus was elected in his place. France, with Sardinia and Spain, declared war on Austria (1733), seeking to reclaim territory in Italy held by Austria. An inconclusive campaign ended in the preliminary Peace of Vienna (1735), which redistributed the disputed Italian territory and recognized Augustus as king. A final treaty was signed in 1738.

Politburo \ˈpä-lət-ˌbyu̇r-ō\ Supreme policy-making body of the COMMUNIST PARTY OF THE SOVIET UNION, the model for the politburos in other countries. The first Politburo, created in 1917 to provide leadership during the BOLSHEVIK uprising, was dissolved when the coup was accomplished. The party congress of 1919 instructed the Central Committee to elect a new Politburo, which soon overshadowed the Central Committee in power. In 1952 it was replaced by a larger Presidium of the Central Committee; after JOSEPH STALIN's death, stress was placed on "collective leadership" to correct for his abuses. The name Politburo was revived in 1966. Its members included the general secretary of the Communist Party, the minister of defense, the head of the KGB, and the heads of the most important republics or urban party branches. It was dissolved with the breakup of the Soviet Union in 1991.

Politian \pō-ˈli-shən\ *orig.* **Angelo Poliziano** *or* **Angelo Ambrogini** (1454–1494) Italian poet and humanist. He demonstrated his poetic abilities early and became a friend and protégé of LORENZO DE'MEDICI. One of the foremost classical scholars of the Renaissance, he produced between 1473 and 1478 Latin and Greek verses that are among the best examples of humanist poetry. He was also, with Lorenzo, a leader in the revaluation of literature in Italian. His vernacular works include *Stanzas Begun for the Tournament of the Magnificent Giuliano de' Medici* (1475–78), a masterpiece in OTTAVA RIMA; and the drama *Orfeo* (1480).

political action committee (PAC) In U.S. politics, an organization whose purpose is to raise and distribute campaign funds to candidates seeking political office. PACs rose to prominence after the Federal Election Campaign Act (1971) limited the amount of money any corporation, union, or private individual could give to a candidate. By soliciting smaller contributions from a much larger number of individuals, PACs can circumvent these limits. By the end of the century, the vast amounts of money raised by PACs had greatly increased the cost of running for office and inspired debate about campaign finance reform.

political convention In U.S. politics, an election-year meeting of POLITICAL-PARTY activists at the local, state, or national level to select candidates for office and decide on party policy. Conventions also serve as morale-boosting rallies for the campaigns that follow. Conventions were instituted in the 1830s to replace the often exclusive and secretive caucus system; it was hoped that the conventions' openness would make them less amenable to control by party bosses. Today, candidates at the state and local level are nominated by PRIMARY ELECTIONS and the convention merely endorses the nominee. At the national level as well, the growth of presidential primaries has meant that conventions are largely limited to ratifying the candidate already selected by the voters.

political economy Academic discipline that explores the relationship between individuals and society and between markets and the state using methods drawn from economics, political science, and sociology. The term is derived from the Greek terms *polis* (city or state) and *oikonomos* (one who manages a household). Political economy is thus concerned with how countries are managed, taking into account both political and economic factors. The field today encompasses several areas of study, including the politics of economic relations, domestic political and economic issues, the comparative study of political and economic systems, and the study of international political economy.

political machine In U.S. politics, a political-party organization that controls enough votes to maintain political and administrative control of its community. The rapid growth of cities in the 19th century created huge problems for city governments, which were often poorly structured and unable to provide services. Enterprising politicians were able to create support by doing favors for newcomers in exchange for votes, including giving out patronage jobs and housing. Though machines often helped restructure city governments to the benefit of their constituents, they just as often resulted in poorer service (when jobs were doled out as political rewards), corruption (when contracts or concessions were awarded in return for kickbacks), and aggravation of racial or ethnic hostilities (when the machine did not reflect the city's diversity). Reforms, suburban flight, and a more mobile population with fewer ties to city neighborhoods have all contributed to weakening machine politics. Famous machines have included those of WILLIAM MARCY TWEED (New York), JAMES MICHAEL CURLEY (Boston), THOMAS PENDERGAST (Kansas City, Mo.), and RICHARD DALEY (Chicago). See also CIVIL SERVICE.

political party Organized group seeking political power, whether by election or revolution. Parties may be mass-based, appealing for support to the whole electorate, or cadres, with membership confined to an active elite; most parties have features of both types. All parties have an ideology designed to attract supporters. Most countries now have single-party, two-party, or multiparty systems (see PARTY SYSTEM). Formal parties arose in Britain and the U.S. in the early 19th century; parties are not mentioned in either country's constitution. In the U.S., PRIMARY ELECTIONS at the state level are generally employed to select party candidates.

political philosophy Branch of philosophy that analyzes the state and related concepts such as political obligation, law, social justice, and constitution. The first major work of political philosophy in the Western tradition was Plato's *Republic.* Aristotle's *Politics* is a detailed empirical study of political institutions. The Roman tradition is best exemplified by Cicero and Polybius. St. Augustine's *City of God* began the tradition of Christian political thinking, which was developed by Thomas Aquinas. Niccolo Machiavelli studied the nature and limits of political power. Thomas Hobbes's *Leviathan* (1651) raised the problem of political obligation in its modern form. Hobbes was followed by Benedict de Spinoza, John Locke, and J.-J. Rousseau in the exposition of a social-contract theory. This was rejected by David Hume and also by G. W. F. Hegel, whose *Philosophy of Right* (1821) was fundamental for 19th-century political thought. Hegel's defense of private property stimulated Karl Marx's critique of it. John Stuart Mill developed Jeremy Bentham's utilitarian theory of law and political institutions, so as to reconcile them with a demand for individual liberty. Recent work has been characterized by a division between Marxists and traditional liberal thinkers, but there is much diversity within each of those traditions.

political science Academic discipline concerned with the study of government and politics. It studies such subjects as the nature of states, the functions performed by governments, voter behavior, political parties, political culture, political economy, and public opinion. Though it has roots in the writings of Plato and Aristotle, its development in the modern era arose with the creation of the social sciences. Its scientific character was developed by Henri de Saint-Simon and Auguste Comte in the 19th century; the first institution dedicated to its study, the Free School of Political Science, was founded in Paris in 1871.

Polk, James K(nox) (1795–1849) 11th president of the U.S. (1845–49). Born in Mecklenburg Co., N.C., he became a lawyer in Tennessee and a friend and supporter of Andrew Jackson, who helped Polk win election to the U.S. House of Representatives (1825–39). He left the House to become governor of Tennessee (1839–41). At the deadlocked 1844 Democratic convention Polk was nominated as the compromise candidate; he is considered the first dark-horse presidential candidate. A proponent of western expansion, he campaigned with the slogan "Fifty-four Forty or Fight," to bring a solution to the Oregon Question. Elected at 49, the youngest president to that time, he successfully concluded the Oregon border dispute with Britain (1846) and secured passage of the Walker Tariff Act (1846), which lowered import duties and helped foreign trade. He led the prosecution of the Mexican War, which resulted in large territorial gains but reopened the debate over the extension of slavery. His administration also established the Department of the Interior, the U.S. Naval Academy, and the Smithsonian Institution, oversaw revision of the treasury system, and proclaimed the validity of the Monroe Doctrine. Though an efficient and competent president, deft in his handling of Congress, he was exhausted by his efforts and did not seek reelection; he died three months after leaving office.

James K. Polk, daguerreotype by Mathew Brady, 1849.

BY COURTESY OF THE LIBRARY OF CONGRESS, WASHINGTON, D.C.

polka Lively couple dance of Bohemian folk origin (*polka* is Czech for "Polish woman") in duple time, characterized by three quick steps and a hop. Originating in the early 19th century, it became popular in ballrooms across Europe and in North and South America. It has remained popular in the 20th century as both a folk dance and a ballroom dance.

poll tax Tax of a uniform amount levied on each individual. The most famous British poll tax was the one levied in 1380, a main cause of the 1381 Peasants' Revolt. In the U.S., poll taxes were used as a voting prerequisite in the southern states; when payment was made a prerequisite to voting, impoverished blacks (and often poor whites) were effectively denied the vote. In 1966 the U.S. Supreme Court ruled that states could not levy a poll tax as a prerequisite for voting in state and local elections.

pollack *or* **pollock** \'pä-lək\ Either of two commercially important North Atlantic species of food fish in the cod family (Gadidae). *Pollachius* (or *Gadus*) *virens,* called saithe or coalfish in Europe, is deep green with a pale belly. It has a small chin barbel (fleshy protuberance) and three dorsal and two anal fins. A carnivorous, lively, usually schooling fish, it grows to about 3.5 ft (1.1 m) long and weighs up to 35 lbs (16 kg). The other species, *Theragra chalcogramma,* or walleye pollack, closely resembles *P. virens.*

Pollack \'pä-lək\, **Sydney** (born 1934) U.S. film director, producer, and actor. Born in Lafayette, Ind., he acted in and directed television plays in the early 1960s before directing his first feature film, *The Slender Thread,* in 1965. He earned acclaim for the drama *They Shoot Horses, Don't They?* (1969) and followed it with a series of hits, including *The Way We Were* (1973), *The Electric Horseman* (1979), *Tootsie* (1982), *Out of Africa* (1985, Academy Award), and *The Firm* (1993). He also acted in such films as *Husbands and Wives* (1992) and *Eyes Wide Shut* (1999).

Pollaiuolo \ˌpōl-lī-'wȯ-lō\, **Antonio del and Piero del** *orig.* **Antonio and Piero di Jacopo d'Antonio Benci** (c. 1432–1498, c. 1441–1496) Italian sculptors, painters, engravers, and goldsmiths. Antonio probably trained in goldsmithing and metalworking with Lorenzo Ghiberti, while Piero may have studied painting with Andrea del Castagno. The brothers collaborated consistently after 1460, producing their works under a combined signature, and their individual contributions are hard to determine. Antonio is recognized as a superb draftsman and was among the first to practice anatomical dissection in the study of the human form; Piero's individual work is less artistically significant. In Florence they created an altarpiece in San Miniato al Monte and *The Martyrdom of St. Sebastian* (1475) in the Pucci Chapel of the Church of the Santissima Annunziata. In Rome their works included the tombs of Popes Sixtus IV and Innocent VIII. Antonio's famous *Battle of Nudes* is one of the largest and most important Italian engravings of the 15th century.

pollen Mass of microscopic spores in a seed plant that appears usually as a fine dust. Each pollen grain is tiny, varies in shape and structure, is formed in the stamens in seed plants, and is transported by various means (see pollination) to the pistil, where fertilization occurs. The outer layer of a pollen grain is very resistant to disintegration; treatment with intense heat, strong acids, or strong bases has little effect on it. Because the grains often are very distinctive, some plant species may be identified by their pollen grains alone. Common components of both recent and ancient geologic sediments, pollen grains have provided much information on the origin and geologic history of plant life on land. Pollen is produced in such quantities that it is a significant part of the airborne components of earth's atmosphere. The protein-containing substance in many pollen grains (e.g., ragweed and many grasses) causes the allergic reaction commonly known as hay fever.

pollination Transfer of pollen grains in seed plants from the stamens, where they form, to the pistil. Pollination is required for fertilization and the production of seeds. On the surface of the pistil the pollen grains germinate (see germination) and form pollen tubes that grow downward toward the ovules. During fertilization, a sperm cell in a pollen tube fuses with the egg cell of an ovule, giving rise to the plant embryo. The ovule then grows into a seed. Since the pollen-bearing parts of the stamens are rarely in direct contact with the pistil, plants commonly rely on external agents for pollen transport. Insects (especially bees) and wind are the most important pollinators; other agents include birds and a few mammals (notably certain bats). Water transport of pollen is rare. An egg may be fertilized by self-pollination (when the sperm comes from pollen produced by the same flower or by another flower on the same plant) or by cross-pollination (when the sperm comes from the pollen of a different plant).

Pollini, Maurizio (born 1942) Italian pianist. He made his debut at 9, winning the Warsaw Chopin Competition in 1960 at 18, as the youngest of the contestants. He first played in the U.S. in 1968. His recordings and performances range from works by J.S. Bach to K. Stockhausen, with a particular specialty in Ludwig van Beethoven, playing all with equal dedication. His combination of intellectual grasp and seriousness and extraordinary technical brilliance have given him a unique standing in the concert world.

polliwog See TADPOLE

Pollock, Frederick *later* **Sir Frederick** (1845–1937) British legal scholar. He taught at Oxford University 1883–1903, and was made a king's counsel in 1920. He was noted for his *History of English Law Before the Time of Edward I* (with FREDERIC W. MAITLAND, 1895) and several standard textbooks. He kept up a 60-year correspondence with OLIVER WENDELL, JR. HOLMES; the *Holmes-Pollock Letters* were published in 1941.

Pollock \'pä-lək\, **(Paul) Jackson** (1912–1956) U.S. painter. Born in Cody, Wyo., he grew up in California and Arizona. In the early 1930s he studied in New York under THOMAS HART BENTON, and later he was employed on the WPA FEDERAL ART PROJECT. In 1947, after several years of semiabstract work stimulated by psychotherapy, Pollock began to lay his canvas on the floor and pour or drip paint onto it in stages, a style exemplified by *Number Ten, 1949,* the black-and-white *Number Thirty-two, 1950,* and the mural-size *Lavender Mist* (1950). Though the novelty of his "drip" technique tended to overshadow the personal expression that the technique permitted him, he was recognized in his lifetime as a leading practitioner of ABSTRACT EXPRESSIONISM, particularly the form known as ACTION PAINTING. Championed by CLEMENT GREENBERG and others, he became a celebrity. Separated from his wife, the artist Lee Krasner (1908–1984), he died in a car crash at 44.

Pollock painting in his studio on Long Island, New York, 1950.
HANS NAMUTH

Pollock v. Farmers' Loan and Trust Co. U.S. Supreme Court ruling (1895) that voided portions of an 1894 act that imposed a direct tax on the incomes of U.S. citizens and corporations, thus declaring the federal INCOME TAX unconstitutional. The decision was mooted in 1913 when ratification of the 16th Amendment to the U.S. Constitution gave Congress the power "to lay and collect taxes on incomes."

pollution See AIR POLLUTION, WATER POLLUTION

Pollux, Castor and See DIOSCURI

polo Game played by teams of players on horseback using mallets with long flexible handles to drive a wooden ball through goalposts. It was first played in Persia in the 6th century BC; from there it spread to Arabia, Tibet (*polo* is Balti for "ball"), South Asia, and the Far East. The first British polo clubs were formed in India in the mid-19th century; the game came to the U.S. a few decades later. Polo has long been primarily played by the wealthy, because of the expense of acquiring and maintaining a stable of polo "ponies" (actually full-sized adult horses, bred for docility, speed, endurance, and intelligence). The standard team is made up of four players whose positions are numbered 1–4. A game consists of six 7½-minute periods called chukkers or chukkas. The field is 300 yards (274.3 m) long by 160 yards (146.3 m) wide; an indoor version of the game is played on a smaller field.

Polo, Marco (1254?–1324) Venetian merchant and traveler who journeyed from Europe to Asia (1271–95). Born into a Venetian merchant family, he joined his father and uncle on a journey to China, traveling along the SILK ROAD and reaching the court of KUBLAI KHAN c. 1274. The Polos remained in China for about 17 years, and the Mongol emperor sent Marco on several fact-finding missions to distant lands. Marco may also have governed the city of Yangzhou (1282–87). The Polos returned to Venice in 1295, after sailing from eastern China to Persia and then journeying overland through Turkey. Captured by the Genoese soon after his return, Marco was imprisoned along with a writer, Rustichello, who helped him to write the tale of his travels. The book, *Il Milione*, was an instant success, though most medieval readers considered it an extravagant romance rather than a true story. See photograph opposite.

polonaise \,pä-lə-'nāz\ Dignified ceremonial dance in 3/4 time, frequently employing dotted rhythms, that often opened court balls in the 17th–19th century. It likely began as a warrior's triumphal dance, and was adopted by the Polish court as a formal march c. 1573. The dancers promenaded with gliding steps accented by bending the knee slightly on every third step. It often appeared in ballets, and polonaises were composed by G.F. HANDEL, LUDWIG VAN BEETHOVEN, and especially F. CHOPIN, whose piano polonaises were martial and heroic.

Poltava \pəl-'tä-və\, **Battle of** (June 1709) Decisive victory of Russia over Sweden in the Second NORTHERN WAR. The battle was fought near Poltava, Ukraine, between 80,000 Russian troops under PETER I THE GREAT and ALEKSANDR MENSHIKOV and 17,000 Swedish troops under CHARLES XII. Despite the lack of reinforcements for his depleted forces, Charles besieged Poltava in May 1709. The Russians set up a countersiege line and forced the Swedes to attack. Charles planned a daring charge through the Russian line, but he had been injured and his commanders failed to execute the attack. The Russian counterattack killed or captured the entire Swedish army except for Charles and 1,500 followers. Sweden's defeat ended its status as a major power and marked the beginning of Russian supremacy in Eastern Europe.

Polybius \pə-'lib-ē-əs\ (c. 200–118? BC) Greek statesman and historian. Son of an Achaean statesman, Polybius was one of 1,000 eminent Achaeans deported to Rome in 168 BC for supposed disloyalty to the Romans. There he became mentor to SCIPIO AFRICANUS THE YOUNGER, with whom he witnessed the destruction of Carthage soon after his political detention had ended. When hostilities broke out between Achaea and Rome, he negotiated for his countrymen and sought to reestablish order. His reputation rests on his history of the rise of Rome; of its 40 volumes, only five survive in their entirety.

polychaete \'pä-lē-,kēt\ Any of about 5,400 species of marine WORMS of the ANNELID class Polychaeta, having a segmented body with many setae (bristles) on each segment. Species, often brightly colored, range from less than an inch (2.5 cm) to about 10 ft (3 m) long. Most body segments bear two bristly parapodia (lobelike outgrowths). The head has short sensory projections and tentacles. Adults may be free-swimming or sedentary; larvae are free-swimming. Found worldwide, polychaetes are important for turning over sediment on the ocean bottom. One species, the bloodworm, is a popular saltwater fish bait. See also TUBE WORM.

Polyclitus *or* **Polycleitus** *or* **Polykleitos** \,pä-li-'klī-təs\ (5th century BC) Greek sculptor. His *Doryphorus* (*Spear Bearer,* c. 440 BC) was known as "the Canon" because it illustrated his book of that name, which set forth his theory of the ideal mathematical proportions of the human body and proposed that the sculptor strive for a dramatic counterbalance between the relaxed and tense body parts and the directions in which they move. His balanced and rhythmical bronze statues of young athletes, such as the *Diadumenus* (*Man Tying on a Fillet,* c. 420 BC), demonstrated his principles and freed Greek sculpture from its tradition of rigid frontal poses. With PHIDIAS, Polyclitus was the most important Greek sculptor of his age.

Marco Polo, title page of the first printed edition of *The Travels of Marco Polo,* 1477.
BY COURTESY OF THE COLUMBIA UNIVERSITY LIBRARIES, NEW YORK

Polycrates \pə-'lik-rə-,tēz\ (6th century BC) Tyrant of the Aegean island of SAMOS c. 535–522 BC. He took control during a festival of Hera, eliminating his two brothers, who shared his power. He quickly became notorious for piracy, as he sought to dominate nearby islands and Ionia. Initially a supporter of Egypt, he joined the Persians against Egypt in 525 BC. Attempts to remove him by his opponents, with Spartan help, were unsuccessful until the Persian governor of Sardis lured him to the mainland

and had him crucified. Polycrates brought wealth and prominence to Samos and was a patron of writers, including ANACREON.

polycystic ovary syndrome *or* **Stein-Leventhal syndrome** Endocrine disorder in women in which high ANDROGEN levels block ovulation (see REPRODUCTIVE SYSTEM). It causes a high proportion of female INFERTILITY cases. Symptoms vary but often include hirsutism, acne, and obesity. MENSTRUATION may be irregular, absent, or excessive. The OVARIES are usually enlarged and contain CYSTS. The disease may not be diagnosed until a woman tries to conceive. The underlying cause is not fully understood. Treatment attempts to reduce androgen production. Infertility may be treated with clomiphene citrate to induce ovulation or with LAPAROSCOPY.

polyester Organic compound, any of a class of POLYMERS formed by ESTER linkages between MONOMERS. They are usually prepared from equivalent amounts of GLYCOLS and dibasic CARBOXYLIC ACIDS, which undergo condensation POLYMERIZATION to produce the polyester and water. Polyesters are strong, colorfast, and resistant to corrosion and chemical attack but tend to build up a static charge. Besides the familiar fibers and films (e.g., Dacron, Mylar), polyesters are used to make reinforced plastics, automotive parts, boat hulls, foams, laminates, tapes, piping, bottles, disposable filters, encapsulations, and coatings.

polyethylene (PE) Any of the POLYMERS of ETHYLENE, the largest class of PLASTICS. Its simple basic structure, of ETHYLENE MONOMERS, can be linear (e.g., high-density or HDPE, and ultrahigh molecular weight polyethylene UHMWPE) or branched (low-density or LDPE, and linear low-density polyethylene LLDPE). LDPE and LLDPE have similar structures (low crystalline content), properties (high flexibility), and uses (packaging film, plastic bags, mulch, insulation, squeeze bottles, toys, and housewares). HDPE has a dense, highly crystalline structure of high strength and moderate stiffness; blow-molded HDPE bottles are accepted by most recycling programs, unlike injection-molded HDPE pails, appliance housings, and toys. UHMWPE is made with molecular weights 6–12 times that of HDPE; it can be spun and stretched into stiff, highly crystalline fibers with tensile strength many times that of steel; uses include bulletproof vests.

polygamy \pə-'li-gə-mē\ Marriage to more than one spouse at a time. The term is often used as a synonym for polygyny (marriage to more than one woman), which appears to have formerly been common in most of the world and is still found widely in non-Western cultures. Polygyny seems to offer the husband increased prestige, economic stability, and sexual companionship while offering cowives a shared labor burden and an institutionalized role where a surplus of unmarried women might otherwise exist. The polygynous family is often fraught with bickering and sexual jealousy; to preserve harmony, one wife may be accorded seniority, and each wife and her children may have separate living quarters. Polyandry (marriage to more than one man) is relatively rare; in Tibet and Nepal, where brothers may marry a single woman, the practice serves to limit the number of descendants and keep limited land within the household.

Polygnotus *or* **Polygnotos** \ˌpä-lig-'nō-təs\ (c. 475 BC–c. 450 BC) Greek painter. None of his works are extant, but accounts exist of monumental wall paintings in a severely classical style at the hall of the Cnidians at Delphi: the *Iliupersis* (*Sack of Troy*) and the *Nekyia* (*Ulysses Visiting Hades*). His compositions were noted for the expression of emotion on faces and for the distribution of figures throughout the composition rather than on a single base line, as was the convention of the day.

polygon In geometry, any closed CURVE consisting of a set of line segments (sides) connected such that no two segments cross. The simplest polygons are triangles (three sides), quadrilaterals (four sides), and pentagons (five sides). If none of the sides, when extended, intersects the polygon, it is a convex polygon; otherwise it is concave. A polygon with all sides equal is equilateral. One with all interior angles equal is equiangular. Any polygon that is both equilateral and equiangular is a regular polygon (e.g., equilateral triangle, square).

polygraph See LIE DETECTOR

polyhedron \ˌpä-lē-'hē-drən\ In EUCLIDEAN GEOMETRY, a three-dimensional object composed of a finite number of polygonal surfaces (faces). Technically, a polyhedron is the boundary between the interior and exterior of a solid. In general, polyhedrons are named according to number of faces. A tetrahedron has four faces, a pentahedron five, and so on; a cube is a six-sided REGULAR POLYHEDRON (hexahedron) whose faces are squares. The faces meet at line segments called edges, which meet at points called vertices. See also EULER'S FORMULA.

polymer \'pä-lə-mər\ Any of a class of natural or synthetic substances composed of MACROMOLECULES that are multiples of MONOMERS. The monomers need not all be the same or have the same structure. Polymers may consist of long chains of unbranched or branched monomers or may be cross-linked networks of monomers in two or three dimensions. Their backbones may be flexible or rigid. Inorganic polymers can be elements or compounds, including DIAMOND, GRAPHITE, FELDSPAR, and GLASS. Many important natural materials are organic polymers, including CELLULOSE (from sugar monomers), LIGNIN, RUBBER, PROTEINS (from amino acids), and NUCLEIC ACIDS (from NUCLEOTIDES). Synthetic organic polymers include many PLASTICS, including POLYETHYLENE, the NYLONS, POLYURETHANES, POLYESTERS, vinyls (e.g., PVC), and synthetic RUBBERS. The SILICONES, with an inorganic backbone of silicon and oxygen atoms and organic side groups, are the most important mixed organic–inorganic compounds.

polymerase chain reaction \pä-'lə-mə-ˌrās\ **(PCR)** Laboratory technique used to make numerous copies of a specific DNA segment quickly and accurately. These are needed for various experiments and procedures in MOLECULAR BIOLOGY, forensic analysis (DNA FINGERPRINTING), evolutionary biology (to amplify DNA fragments found in ancient specimens), and medicine (to diagnose genetic disease or detect low viral counts). Invented by KARY MULLIS, PCR requires a DNA template (as little as one molecule) to copy, NUCLEOTIDES to go into the copies, and the ENZYME DNA polymerase to catalyze the formation of bonds between the nucleotide monomers. A three-step cycle (separating DNA strands, marking the ends of the segment to be copied, and catalyzing the formation of bonds) lasting a few minutes doubles the number of DNA strands. Repetition of this cycle many times results in an exponential increase in the amount of DNA.

polymerization \pə-ˌli-mə-rə-'zā-shən\ Any process in which MONOMERS combine chemically to produce a POLYMER. The monomer molecules—usually from at least 100 to many thousands—may or may not all be the same. In nature, ENZYMES carry out polymerization under ordinary conditions to form PROTEINS, NUCLEIC ACIDS, and CARBOHYDRATE polymers; in industry, the reaction is usually done with a CATALYST, often under high pressure or heat. In addition polymerization, FREE RADICALS at the ends of the growing chains usually attach the monomer to the chain and put a free radical at the new end. In condensation polymerization, the reaction with each new monomer splits off a molecule of a side product, often water.

polymorphism Discontinuous genetic VARIATION that results in the occurrence of several different forms or types of individuals among the members of a single species. The most obvious example of polymorphism is the separation of most higher organisms into male and female sexes. Another example is the different blood types in humans. A polymorphism that persists over many generations is usually maintained because no one form has an overall advantage or disadvantage over the others in terms of NATURAL SELECTION. Some polymorphisms have no visible manifestations. The CASTES that occur in social insects are a special form of polymorphism that results from differences in nutrition rather than from genetic variation.

Polynesia \ˌpä-lə-'nē-zhə\ Group of islands scattered across a huge triangular area of the eastern central Pacific. A subdivision of OCEANIA, Polynesia includes New Zealand, Hawaii, SAMOA, the LINE ISLANDS, FRENCH POLYNESIA, the COOK ISLANDS, the PHOENIX ISLANDS, TUVALU, TONGA, and EASTER ISLAND. FIJI is sometimes included in the group because of its Polynesian population. The islands are mostly small coral atolls, and some are of volcanic origin. Most of the inhabitants are Polynesians, some of whom might be related to the Malay. Their languages belong to a subfamily of the AUSTRONESIAN LANGUAGES. Contact with European culture began in the late 1700s with the arrival of Spanish explorers and radically altered life in Polynesia. Colonizers, imposing western belief systems and cultural ways, effectively wiped out local traditions and customs. Samoa and Tonga retain more of the traditional culture than the other islands.

polynomial In algebra, an expression consisting of numbers and variables grouped according to certain patterns. Specifically, polynomials are sums of monomials of the form ax^n, where a (the coefficient) can be any real number and n (the degree) must be a whole number. A polynomial's degree is that of its monomial of highest degree. Like whole numbers, polynomials may be prime or factorable into products of primes. They may contain any number of VARIABLES, provided that the power of each variable is a nonnegative integer. They are the basis of algebraic equation solving. Setting a polynomial equal to zero results in a polynomial EQUATION; equating it to a variable results in a polynomial FUNCTION, a particularly useful tool in modeling physical situations. Polynomial equations and functions can be analyzed completely by methods of ALGEBRA and CALCULUS. See also ORTHOGANAL POLYNOMIAL.

polynomial, orthogonal See ORTHOGANAL POLYNOMIAL

polyoma virus \ˌpä-lē-ˈō-mə\ Minute infectious agent normally present in extremely small amounts in wild mice without causing obvious ill effects. It may induce cancerous tumors if grown in tissue culture and injected in large quantities into newborn mice or young hamsters, guinea pigs, and rabbits. It belongs to the papova group of VIRUSES.

polyp \ˈpä-ləp\ Growth projecting from the wall of a cavity lined with a mucous membrane. Shape varies widely; it may have a stalk or many lobes. Polyps most often occur in the nose, urinary bladder, and digestive tract, especially in the rectum and colon. Symptoms, if any, depend on location and size; they may result from pressure or from blockage of a passage. Polyps occasionally bleed. Because a small percentage are precursors to cancers or actually contain cancers, it is advisable to have them removed and examined microscopically and to undergo routine colonoscopy after age 50.

polyp In zoology, one of two principal CNIDARIAN body forms and, sometimes, an individual in a BRYOZOAN colony. The cnidarian polyp body is a hollow cylindrical structure. The lower end attaches to another body or surface. The upper, or free, end is directed upward and has a mouth surrounded by extensible tentacles that bear stinging structures called nematocysts. The tentacles capture prey, which is then drawn into the mouth. The polyp may be solitary (see SEA ANEMONE) or colonial (see CORAL). The body wall consists of three dermal layers. The other cnidarian body form is the MEDUSA.

Polyphemus \ˌpä-lə-ˈfē-məs\ In GREEK MYTHOLOGY, a CYCLOPS. He was the son of POSEIDON and the nymph Thoösa. When ODYSSEUS and his companions were cast ashore on the coast of Sicily, Polyphemus imprisoned them in his cave with the intention of eating them. Odysseus got the giant drunk and then blinded him by plunging a burning stake into his single eye. When Polyphemus opened his cave in the morning, Odysseus and the six men the giant had not yet devoured made their escape by clinging to the bellies of sheep let out to pasture.

polyphony See COUNTERPOINT

polyploidy See PLOIDY

polysaccharide \ˌpä-lē-ˈsa-kə-ˌrīd\ Any of a large class of long-chain SUGARS composed of MONOSACCHARIDES. Because the chains may be unbranched or branched and the monosaccharides may be of one, two, or occasionally more kinds, polysaccharides can be categorized in various ways. CELLULOSE, STARCH, GLYCOGEN, and dextran are all polysaccharides of GLUCOSE, with different CONFIGURATIONS. PECTINS are composed of a GALACTOSE derivative, CHITIN of a glucose derivative. Connective tissues, joint fluid, and cartilage contain two-component polysaccharides, including HEPARIN.

polysiloxane See SILICONE

polytheism Belief in many gods. Though Judaism, Christianity, and Islam are monotheistic (see MONOTHEISM), most other religions throughout history have been polytheistic. The numerous gods may be dominated by a supreme god or by a small group of powerful gods. The gods originated as abstractions of the forces of nature such as the sky or the sea and of human and social functions such as love, war, marriage, or the arts. In many religions the sky god is powerful and all-knowing (e.g., DIEVS), and the earth goddess is maternal and associated with fertility. Gods of death and the underworld (e.g., OSIRIS and HEL) are also important. In addition to many gods, polytheistic religions generally also include malevolent or benevolent spiritual forces or powers. See also GOD AND GODDESS.

polyurethane Any of a class of very versatile POLYMERS that are made into flexible and rigid foams, fibers, elastomers (elastic polymers), and surface coatings. They are produced by reacting an isocyanate (with the functional group —NCO) with an alcohol (with the —OH group). Foamed polyurethanes are made with organic compounds containing carboxyl groups, causing a reaction that liberates carbon dioxide bubbles throughout the product. Spandex fibers are highly elastic and have replaced natural and synthetic rubber fibers for many textile purposes. Polyurethane elastomers are made into auto parts, rollers, flexible molds, medical equipment, and shoe soles. Polyurethane surface coatings are applied as sealants to wood, concrete, and machine parts.

polyvinyl chloride See PVC

Pombal \pə-ˈbäl\, **marquês (Marquess) de** *orig.* **Sebastião (José) de Carvalho (e Mello)** (1699–1782) Portuguese reformer. After serving as ambassador to England and Vienna, he became chief minister to King Joseph and came to dominate Portuguese politics (1750–77). He encouraged industry and commerce and stimulated trade with Brazil. After the 1755 earthquake that devastated Lisbon, he organized aid and reconstruction efforts. He restricted the power of the nobility, had the Jesuits imprisoned or deported to Rome (1759), reorganized Portugal's army, and reformed the university educational system. After Joseph's death (1777), Pombal's power disappeared; under Queen Maria I, he was accused of abuse of power and banished from Lisbon to his estates.

pomegranate \ˈpä-mə-ˌgra-nət\ Fruit of *Punica granatum,* a bush or small tree of Asia, which with a little-known species from the island of Socotra constitutes the family Punicaceae. Native to Iran and long cultivated around the Mediterranean and in India, it also grows in the warmer parts of the New World. The orange-sized and obscurely six-sided fruit has smooth, leathery, brownish-yellow to red skin. Several chambers contain many thin, transparent vesicles of reddish, juicy pulp, each containing an angular, elongated seed. The fruit is eaten fresh, and the juice is the source of the grenadine syrup used in flavorings and liqueurs. The plant grows 16–23 ft (5–7 m) tall and has elliptical, bright-green leaves and handsome orange-red flowers. Throughout the Orient, the pomegranate has since earliest times occupied a position of importance alongside the grape and the fig. It is mentioned in the Bible, by the Prophet Muhammad, and in Greek mythology.

Pomerania \ˌpä-mə-ˈrā-nē-ə\ Historical region, northwestern central Europe, on the BALTIC SEA between the ODER and VISTULA rivers. Occupied by Slavs and other peoples, it was ruled by Polish princes in the 10th century. German immigration into western and central Pomerania began in the late 12th century eastern Pomerania was held by the Knights of the TEUTONIC ORDER from 1308, until it was reconquered by Poland in 1466. Polish dukes ruled those regions under the HOLY ROMAN EMPIRE until the 17th century. The elector of BRANDENBURG acquired the duchies in 1637. Prussia united western and central Pomerania in 1815 as the province of Pommern. Most of the area is now in Poland; its westernmost section is in eastern Germany.

Pomeranian \ˌpä-mə-ˈrā-nē-ən\ Breed of TOY DOG developed from the same SLED-DOG ancestors as the Keeshond, SAMOYED, and Norwegian elkhound. It is said to have been bred down in size from a 30-lb (14-kg) dog in the duchy of Pomerania in the early 19th century. Spirited but docile, it has a foxlike head and small, erect ears. Its long coat, especially full on the neck and chest, is white, black, brown, or reddish brown. It stands about 6–7 in. (14–18 cm) and weighs about 3–7 lbs (1.5–3 kg).

pommel horse See SIDE HORSE

Pomo Hokan-speaking North American Indian people whose territory was centered in California's Russian River valley. Fish, waterfowl, deer, and wild plant foods were plentiful in this region. Coastal Pomo constructed dwellings of heavy timber and bark; inland Pomo used poles, brush, and grass. Pomo religion involved SECRET SOCIETIES, dances, rituals, and impersonations of spirits. Pomo basketry is often considered the finest in California. Today about 3,000 Pomo live in some 20 communities in their original territory.

Pomona \pə-ˈmō-nə\ Ancient Roman goddess of fruit. Vertumnus, god of the seasons, fell in love with her, but she rejected him and all other suitors, preferring to cultivate her orchards. Refusing to give up, Vertumnus came to her in the form of an old woman and pleaded his case so effectively that Pomona changed her mind and agreed to be his.

Pompadour \'päm-pə-ˌdōr\, **marquise (Marchioness) de** *orig.* **Jeanne-Antoinette Poisson** *known as* **Madame de Pompadour** (1721–1764) French mistress of Louis XV. Educated in art and literature, she married Charles-Guillaume Le Normant d'Étoiles in 1741 and became admired by Parisian society and by the king, who installed her at Versailles as his mistress in 1745. She obtained a separation from her husband and was created marquise de Pompadour. She, the king, and her brother, appointed director of the king's buildings, planned and built the École Militaire and the Place de la Concorde in Paris, the Petit Trianon palace at Versailles, and many other buildings. She and Louis also encouraged painters, sculptors, and craftsmen, making her 20 years in power the height of artistic taste. Her political influence was less astute; the alliance with Austria against the German Protestant princes that she urged led to the disastrous Seven Years' War.

Madame de Pompadour, detail of a portrait by François Boucher; in the National Gallery of Scotland, Edinburgh.

BY COURTESY OF THE NATIONAL GALLERIES OF SCOTLAND, EDINBURGH

pompano \'päm-pə-ˌnō\ Any of several species of deep-bodied, toothless, silvery fishes in the order Perciformes (especially in the genus *Trachinotus,* family Carangidae) inhabiting warm coastal waters worldwide. Some are highly prized as food. Pompanos have small scales, a narrow tail base, and a forked tail. The Florida, or common, pompano *(T. carolinus),* of the U.S. Atlantic and Gulf coasts, is about 18 in. (45 cm) long and weighs about 2 lbs (1 kg). The African pompano, or threadfish *(Alectis crinitis),* of the Atlantic and eastern Pacific, is 35 in. (90 cm) long and has long, threadlike rays extending from the dorsal and anal fins. The Pacific pompano *(Peprilus simillimus)* is in the family Stromateidae.

Florida pompano (*Trachinotus carolinus*).

ROBERT REDDEN—ANIMALS ANIMALS

Pompeii \päm-'pā\ Ancient city, southern Italy, southeast of Naples. Founded in the 6th century BC or earlier by the Oscans, who were descendants of the Neolithic inhabitants of Campania, it came under Greek and Etruscan influence and was occupied by the Samnites, an Italic tribe, in the late 5th century BC. It was allied with Rome and colonized by 80 BC. It was damaged by an earthquake in AD 63 and completely destroyed by the eruption of Mount Vesuvius in 79. Volcanic debris buried the town and protected the ruins for years. Archaeological excavations, begun in 1748, have uncovered much of the city, including forums, temples, baths, theaters, and hundreds of private homes. See also Herculaneum.

Temple of Apollo, Pompeii, Italy, with Mount Vesuvius in the background.

EDWIN SMITH

Pompeius Magnus Pius \päm-'pē-əs-'mag-nəs-'pī-əs\, **Sextus** *or* **Pompey the Younger** (67?–35 BC) Son of Pompey the Great and an opponent of Pompey's rivals. After his father was killed fighting Julius Caesar in 48, he fled to Spain to continue the struggle. Mark Antony gave him a naval command after Caesar's assassination (44), but he was outlawed in 43 under a law targeting those complicit in Caesar's death. He ravaged the coast of Italy, helped Antony against Octavian (later Augustus), and tried in vain to force both to make him governor of Sicily (39). Finally defeated by Octavian's forces, he fled to Asia Minor but was caught and executed.

Pompey the Great \'päm-pē\ *Latin in full* **Gnaeus Pompeius Magnus** (106–48 BC) Statesman and general of the Roman republic. His early military career was illustrious. He fought effectively for Sulla against Marius in the Social War, reconquered Spain (76–71), destroyed the last of Spartacus' army (71), destroyed the pirates of the eastern Mediterranean (from 67), defeated Mithradates (63), and consolidated and extended the eastern provinces and frontier kingdoms. In 61 he formed the First Triumvirate with Julius Caesar and Marcus Licinius Crassus. After Crassus' death (53), Pompey and Caesar fell out. By 52, with Rome in a state of anarchy, he was named sole consul. In 49 Caesar defied the Senate and provoked the civil war by crossing the Rubicon in pursuit of Pompey, who fled east with his navy. Defeated at the Battle of Pharsalus (48), Pompey fled with his fleet to Egypt, not realizing the Egyptians would take Caesar's side, and was killed as he prepared to step on land from the boat they had sent to bring him ashore.

Pompidou \'päm-pi-ˌdü\, **Georges (-Jean-Raymond)** (1911–1974) French premier (1962–68) and president (1969–74). He taught school before serving in World War II, and was an aide to Charles de Gaulle 1944–46. After joining the Rothschild bank in Paris, he rose rapidly to become director general (1959). As de Gaulle's chief aide (1958–59), he helped draft the constitution of the Fifth Republic. He secretly negotiated a cease-fire in the Algerian War in 1961, and was appointed premier in 1962. In 1968 he skillfully negotiated an end to the French student-worker strikes. Elected president of France in 1969, he continued de Gaulle's policies. The Pompidou Center is named for him.

Pompidou.

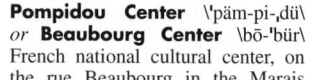

DENNIS BRACK—BLACK STAR

Pompidou Center \'päm-pi-ˌdü\ *or* **Beaubourg Center** \bō-'bür\ French national cultural center, on the rue Beaubourg in the Marais section of Paris. Its full name, the Georges Pompidou National Art and Cultural Center, recognizes the president of the Republic under whose administration it was commissioned. When formally opened in 1977, the building attracted notoriety for its brightly colored exterior pipes, ducts, and other exposed architectural elements, and it soon became one of the most visited cultural sites in the world. Though primarily a museum for 20th-century visual arts, it also houses temporary exhibitions, a library, a center for industrial design, a film museum, and a Center for Musical and Acoustical Research.

Ponce de León \ˌpän-sə-ˌdā-lē-'ōn\, **Juan** (1460–1521) Spanish explorer. He may have accompanied Christopher Columbus's expedition in 1493 and later fought in the West Indies (1502), becoming governor of eastern Hispaniola. He colonized Puerto Rico (1508–9) and founded a settlement near modern San Juan. Rumors of a fountain of youth in the Bahamas inspired him to lead an expedition in 1513, but he landed instead on the northern coast of Florida near modern St. Augustine. He sailed along Florida's southern and western coasts, then returned to Spain to secure the title of military governor (1514). He sailed again to colonize Florida in 1521, but was wounded in an Indian attack and died in Cuba.

Pondicherry Union territory (pop., 1994 est.: 894,000), India. It was formed in 1962 from the four former French colonies of Pondicherry, Karikal, and Yanam, on the eastern seaboard, and Mahe, on the western seaboard. One of the smallest of the union territories, it is united by little other than Hinduism. The city of Pondicherry is the administrative capital.

Pondicherry City (pop., 1991: 203,000), seaport, and capital of Pondicherry union territory, southeastern India. Lying on the Coromandel Coast, it originated as a French trade center in 1674, when it was purchased from a local ruler. Held by the Dutch 1693–97, it was taken by the British several times between 1761 and 1803. It was a French possession 1816–1954. A seaside tourist resort, it contains an international study center at a Hindu religious retreat, or ashram.

Pondoland Region, Eastern Cape province, southern Republic of South Africa, on the coast of the Indian Ocean. It was settled at the end of the 16th century by the Pondos or Mpondos, a Bantu-speaking people. It was annexed to Cape Colony in 1894. It occupies a narrow strip from the coast to the interior plateaus in the west. The interior is rich cattle country with fertile farmlands.

Pont-Aven school \ˌpō^{n}-tə-ˈven\ Group of young painters who espoused a style known as Synthetism and united under the tutelage of Paul Gauguin at Pont-Aven, Brittany, in the late 1880s and early 1890s. The artists included Émile Bernard, Charles Laval, Maxime Maufra, Paul Sérusier, Charles Filiger, Jacob Meyer de Haan, Armand Séguin, and Henri de Chamaillard. Their paintings showed an overall simplification, a highly expressive use of color, and an intensely spiritual subject matter. When Gauguin left for Tahiti, members of the school became increasingly involved in developing the theories and techniques of Symbolism.

Pontchartrain \ˈpän-chər-ˌtrān\, **Lake** Lake, southeastern Louisiana. It is 40 mi (64 km) long and 25 mi (40 km) wide, with an area of 625 sq mi (1,619 sq km). More a tidal lagoon than a lake, it is brackish and teems with game fish. It is connected through Lake Borgne with the Gulf of Mexico and by canal with the Mississippi River. It is spanned by Pontchartrain Causeway, at 23.8 mi (38.4 km) long, the world's longest concrete bridge, which crosses the lake north from New Orleans.

Pontecorvo \ˌpän-tə-ˈkȯr-vō\, **Guido** (1907–1999) Italian-British geneticist. In 1938, influenced by Hermann Joseph Muller, he designed a method for studying genetic differences among species that usually produce sterile hybrids when interbred. His technique permitted him to study evolutionary divergence in the fruit fly. His conviction that research in microbial genetics could lead to increased production of penicillin, much needed in World War II, led him to the genetics of fungi, and in 1950 he found that recombination of genes can occur in the fungus *Aspergillus nidulans* without sexual reproduction. Nonsexual gene recombination became a useful technique in exploring the nature of gene action.

Pontiac (1720?–1769) Ottawa Indian chief who organized the combined resistance to British power in the Great Lakes area known as Pontiac's War (1763–64). At first friendly with whites, Pontiac realized that his people would lose their ancestral lands if white encroachment were not stopped. He coordinated the attack on 12 fortified British posts by a confederacy of individual tribes, winning a great victory. He himself led the attack on the fort at Detroit. Continuing British action took its toll, and in 1766 Pontiac finally agreed to a peace treaty. His murder in 1769 by an Illinois Indian provoked the vengeance of several northern Algonquian tribes, resulting in the virtual destruction of the Illinois.

Pontifex See Quintus Mucius Scaevola

pontifex Member of a council of priests in ancient Rome. The pontifices were responsible for administration of the *jus divinum* (laws concerning religious practices). There were three pontifices under the monarchy, but by the time of Julius Caesar the number had grown to 16, of which one was designated chief priest, or pontifex maximus. Also included in the *collegium* (college) of pontifices were the Vestal Virgins. Among the duties of the pontifices were regulation of the calendar and of expiatory rituals, consecration of temples and sacred objects, superintendence of marriage and the family, and administration of the laws of adoption and succession.

Pontoppidan \pȯn-ˈtȯp-ē-dan\, **Henrik** (1857–1943) Danish realist writer of novels and short stories. He studied engineering and worked as a teacher before taking up writing. His works, typically written in a cold, aloof, epic style, present a comprehensive picture of his country and his epoch. His earlier works are informed with a desire for social progress; his later ones despair of its realization. His major novels include the semiautobiographical *Lucky Peter* (1898–1904) and the five-volume cycle *The Realm of the Dead* (1912–16). He shared the 1917 Nobel Prize with Karl Gjellerup.

Pontormo \pōn-ˈtȯr-mō\, **Jacopo da** *orig.* **Jacopo Carrucci** (1494–1556) Florentine painter. The son of a painter, he was apprenticed to Leonardo da Vinci and later to Piero di Cosimo and Andrea del Sarto, who exerted the greatest influence on him. The agitated, almost neurotic emotionalism of his work reflects a departure from the balance and tranquillity of the High Renaissance. His expressive style is sometimes considered an early manifestation of Mannerism. Primarily a religious painter, he also did sensitive portraits and was employed by the Medici family to decorate their villa at Poggio a Caiano with mythological subjects.

Pontus Ancient district, northeastern Asia Minor adjoining the Black Sea. An independent kingdom, with its capital at Amasia, it was established in the 4th century BC. It continued expanding its borders until 66 BC, when its last king, Mithradates VI Eupator, was defeated by Pompey the Great. It was incorporated into the Roman empire in 63 BC.

pony Any of several breeds of small horses standing less than 14.2 hands (57 in., 144 cm) high and noted for gentleness and endurance. Among the common pony breeds are the Shetland; the stylish and hardy Welsh; the high-stepping Welsh Cob; the Exmoor and Dartmoor, natives of the English moors that are used to breed polo ponies; and the Highland, a thick, gray saddle animal.

Pony Express (1860–61) U.S. system of mail delivery by horse and rider relays. The 1,800-mi (2,900-km) route between St. Joseph, Mo., and Sacramento, Cal., included 157 stations. Riders changed horses every 10–15 miles, and it took about 10 days to complete the route. The sponsoring company of Russell, Majors & Wadell employed such riders as William F. Cody and Pony Bob Haslam. The system provided an important mail link with the West, but it was a financial failure and became obsolete after 18 months with the completion of the transcontinental telegraph system.

poodle German water retriever. Poodles have a long muzzle, hanging ears, and docked tail. The dense, solid-colored, wiry topcoat covers a woolly undercoat. Poodles' hair was traditionally clipped to permit them to swim efficiently when retrieving; today they are usually clipped in ornamental patterns. A dog with unclipped hair, which forms ropelike cords, is called a corded poodle. The standard poodle is more than 15 in. (38 cm) tall and weighs up to 70 lbs (32 kg); the miniature stands 10–15 in. (25.5–38 cm); the toy is under 10 in. (25.5 cm) and weighs about 7 lbs (3 kg). The poodle is the national dog of France, where it was once trained to scent and dig up truffles. Poodles are regarded as the most intelligent of all domestic dog breeds.

Standard poodle.

SALLY ANNE THOMPSON

pool *or* **pocket billiards** Billiards game played on an oblong table having six pockets with 15 object balls and a white cue ball. At the beginning of play, the balls are arranged (racked) in a pyramid formation with its apex on a spot near the foot of the table. The first player breaks the formation by driving the cue ball into it; to continue play, he or she must pocket a ball. In the popular "8-ball" game, the first player (or team) to sink either the seven solid-colored balls (numbered 1–7) or the seven banded (striped) balls (9–15), finishing with the black 8-ball, wins. In "9-ball," only the balls numbered 1–9 are used, and they must be sunk sequentially; the player who sinks the 9-ball wins. Pool probably reached its present form in England and France by c. 1800; today it is most popular in North America.

Poona See Pune

Poor Laws In British history, a body of laws undertaking to provide relief for the poor, developed in 16th-century England and maintained, with various changes, until after World War II. The original laws provided relief, including care for the aged, sick, and infant poor as well as work for the able-bodied through local parishes. Their scope was curtailed in the early 19th century, when poverty among the able-bodied was considered a moral failing. In the 1930s and '40s the Poor Laws were replaced by a comprehensive system of public WELFARE services.

Pop art Art in which commonplace objects from the world of popular culture—comic strips, soup cans, road signs, hamburgers, etc.—are used as subject matter. Pop art was, among other things, an attempt to achieve an objective, impersonal, and nonelitist art after the highly subjective, personal, and often intimidating ABSTRACT EXPRESSIONISM. It has its origins in DADA and the work of MARCEL DUCHAMP; its immediate predecessors were JASPER JOHNS, LARRY RIVERS, and ROBERT RAUSCHENBERG. Though commonly regarded as largely an American phenomenon of the late 1950s and 1960s, exemplified by the work of ROY LICHTENSTEIN, ANDY WARHOL, CLAES OLDENBURG, ROBERT INDIANA, and GEORGE SEGAL, its effects—including its decisive destruction of the boundary between "high" and "low" art—have continued to be powerfully felt throughout the visual arts up to the present.

Popé \pō-'pā\ (died 1692) Tewa PUEBLO medicine man who led an Indian revolt in 1680 against the Spanish invaders in what is now the southwestern U.S., driving them out of Santa Fe and temporarily restoring the old Pueblo way of life. Popé believed that he was guided in his actions by tribal ancestral spirits (KACHINAS). After leading what came to be known as the Pueblo Revolt, Popé was accorded great honors; but success made him despotic, and he was eventually deposed.

pope Ecclesiastical title of the BISHOP of Rome, head of the Roman Catholic church. In the early church, especially in the 3rd–5th century, it was a title of affectionate respect for any bishop. It is still used for the Eastern Orthodox PATRIARCH of Alexandria and for Orthodox priests, but around the 9th century it came to be reserved in the West exclusively for the bishop of Rome. Catholic doctrine regards the pope as the successor of St. PETER THE APOSTLE and accords him supreme jurisdiction over the church in matters of faith and morals, as well as in church discipline and government. Papal infallibility in matters of doctrine was asserted by the First Vatican Council in 1870. See also PAPACY, ROMAN CATHOLICISM. See table on the following pages.

Pope, Albert Augustus (1843–1909) U.S. manufacturer. Born in Boston, he served in the Civil War and subsequently made a fortune in a Boston shoe supply business. In 1877 he founded a successful bicycle factory in Hartford, Conn. In the 1890s he began producing gasoline and electric AUTOMOBILES in Hartford, Indianapolis, and Toledo.

Pope, Alexander (1688–1744) English poet and satirist. A precocious boy precluded from formal education by his Roman Catholicism, Pope was mainly self-educated. A deformity of the spine and other health problems limited his growth and physical activities, leading him to devote himself to reading and writing. His first major work was *An Essay on Criticism* (1711), a poem on the art of writing containing brilliant epigrams (e.g., "To err is human, to forgive, divine") that have become proverbs. His witty mock-epic *The Rape of the Lock* (1712, 1714) ridicules fashionable society. The great labor of his life was his verse translations of HOMER's *Iliad* (1720) and *Odyssey* (1726), whose success made him financially secure. He became involved in many literary battles, prompting him to write such poems as the scathing mock-epic *The Dunciad* (1728) and *An Epistle to Dr. Arbuthnot* (1735). The philosophical *An Essay on Man* (1733–34) was intended as part of a larger work that he never completed.

Alexander Pope, portrait by Thomas Hudson; in the National Portrait Gallery, London.

BY COURTESY OF THE NATIONAL PORTRAIT GALLERY, LONDON

Pope, John (1822–1892) U.S. Army officer. Born in Louisville, Ky., he graduated from West Point and served in the Mexican War. At the outbreak of the AMERICAN CIVIL WAR, he was appointed brigadier general of volunteers, and he commanded operations that secured Union navigation of the Mississippi River almost to Memphis. In 1862 he was given command of the Army of Virginia. At the second Battle of BULL RUN, his forces were defeated. He tried to blame the rout on his subordinates, including F.-J. PORTER, but was relieved of command and sent to Minnesota to quell a Sioux uprising. After the war he commanded the Department of the Missouri (1870–83).

John Pope.

BY COURTESY OF THE LIBRARY OF CONGRESS, WASHINGTON, D.C.

Popish Plot (1678) In English history, a fictitious but widely believed rumor that Jesuits planned to assassinate CHARLES II and replace him with his brother, the Catholic duke of York (later JAMES II). The rumor was fabricated by TITUS OATES, who gave a sworn deposition of his "evidence" to a London justice of the peace. When the latter was found murdered, a panic among the people was followed by accusations and trials, leading to the execution of about 35 innocent people. When Oates was finally discredited, the panic subsided.

poplar Any of at least 35 species and many natural hybrids of trees that make up the genus *Populus* (WILLOW family). Poplars grow throughout northern temperate regions, some even beyond the Arctic Circle. They are rapid-growing but relatively short-lived. Their leaves flutter in the slightest breeze because of their laterally compressed petioles (leafstalks). The relatively soft wood is used to make cardboard boxes, crates, paper, and veneer. North America has three groups of native poplars: COTTONWOODS, ASPENS, and BALSAM POPLARS.

poplar, yellow See TULIP TREE

Popocatépetl \ˌpō-pə-'ka-tə-ˌpe-tᵊl\ Volcano, PUEBLA state, southeastern central Mexico, west of the city of PUEBLA. The perpetually snowcapped, symmetrical cone rises to 17,930 ft (5,465 m). The first Spanish ascent is thought to have been made in 1519. After being inactive for more than 50 years, it erupted in 1994, with recurrences in 1996.

Popol Vuh \'pō-pȯl-'vü\ Mayan document that provides valuable information on ancient MAYA mythology and culture. It was written between 1554 and 1558 in the QUICHE language using Spanish letters. It tells of the creation of man, the acts of the gods, and the origin and history of the Quiche people and also gives a chronology of their kings. The book was discovered early in the 18th century by Francisco Jiménez, a parish priest in the Guatemalan highlands, who copied out the original, now lost, and translated it into Spanish.

popolo \'pō-pō-lō\ (Italian: "people") In the COMMUNES (city-states) of 13th-century Italy, a pressure group instituted to protect the interests of the commoners against the nobility. Until then noblemen had exclusively controlled the commune governments, and the popolo was the means by which wealthy merchants sought to extend their power. The popolo in Florence controlled the government 1250–60 and again after 1282. By the beginning of the 14th century, its elders formed the supreme executive of the commune.

Popper, Karl (Raimund) *later* **Sir Karl** (1902–1994) Austrian-British philosopher of natural and social science. In *The Logic of Scientific Discovery* (1934), he rejected the traditional conception of INDUCTION, which held that a scientific hypothesis may be verified through the accumulation of confirming observations, arguing instead that scientific hypotheses can at best only be falsified. His later works include *The Open Society and Its Enemies* (1945), *The Poverty of Historicism* (1957), and *Postscript to the Logic of Scientific Discovery* (3 vols., 1981–82).

poppy family Family Papaveraceae, containing about 200 species of mostly herbaceous plants and some woody small trees and shrubs. Most species of this family, which is outstanding for its many garden ornamentals (largely of the genus *Papaver*) and for pharmaceutically important plants, are found in the Northern Hemisphere. All have cup-shaped flowers, a CAPSULE fruit, leaves that are usually deeply cut or divided into leaflets, and colored sap. Members include the OPIUM POPPY and the corn, or Flanders, poppy *(P. rhoeas),* the seeds of which may lie dormant for

Popes and Antipopes[1] (antipopes in italics)

Peter	?–c.64
Linus	c.67–76/79
Anacletus	76–88 or 79–91
Clement I	88–97 or 92–101
Evaristus	c.97–c.107
Alexander I	105–115 or 109–119
Sixtus I	c.115–c.125
Telesphorus	c.125–c.136
Hyginus	c.136–c.140
Pius I	c.140–55
Anicetus	c.155–c.166
Soter	c.166–c.175
Eleutherius	c.175–89
Victor I	c.189–99
Zephyrinus	c.199–217
Calixtus I (Callistus)	217?–22
Hippolytus	*217, 18–235*
Urban I	222–30
Pontian	230–35
Anterus	235–36
Fabian	236–50
Cornelius	251–53
Novatian	*251*
Lucius I	253–54
Stephen I	254–57
Sixtus II	257–58
Dionysius	259–68
Felix I	269–74
Eutychian	275–83
Gaius	283–96
Marcellinus	291/96–304
Marcellus I	308–9
Eusebius	309/10
Miltiades (Melchiades)	311–14
Sylvester I	314–35
Mark	336
Julius I	337–52
Liberius	352–66
Felix (II)	*355–58*
Damasus I	366–84
Ursinus	*366–67*
Siricius	384–99
Anastasius I	399–401
Innocent I	401–17
Zosimus	417–18
Boniface I	418–22
Eulalius	*418–19*
Celestine I	422–32
Sixtus III	432–40
Leo I	440–61
Hilary	461–68
Simplicius	468–83
Felix III (or II)[2]	483–92
Gelasius I	492–96
Anastasius II	496–98
Symmachus	498–514
Laurentius	*498, 501–c. 505/507*
Hormisdas	514–23
John I	523–26
Felix IV (or III)[2]	526–30
Dioscorus	*530*
Boniface II	530–32
John II	533–35
Agapetus I	535–36
Silverius	536–37
Vigilius	537–55
Pelagius I	556–61
John III	561–74
Benedict I	575–79
Pelagius II	579–90
Gregory I	590–604

Sabinian	604–6
Boniface III	607
Boniface IV	608–15
Deusdedit (also called Adeodatus I)	615–18
Boniface V	619–25
Honorius I	625–38
Severinus	640
John IV	640–42
Theodore I	642–49
Martin I	649–55
Eugenius I	654–57
Vitalian	657–72
Adeodatus II	672–76
Donus	676–78
Agatho	678–81
Leo II	682–83
Benedict II	684–85
John V	685–86
Conon	686–87
Sergius I	687–701
Theodore	*687*
Paschal	*687*
John VI	701–5
John VII	705–7
Sisinnius	708
Constantine	708–15
Gregory II	715–31
Gregory III	731–41
Zacharias (Zachary)	741–52
Stephen (II)[3]	752
Stephen II (or III)[3]	752–57
Paul I	757–67
Constantine (II)	*767–68*
Philip	*768*
Stephen III (or IV)[3]	768–72
Adrian I	772–95
Leo III	795–816
Stephen IV (or V)[3]	816–17
Paschal I	817–24
Eugenius II	824–27
Valentine	827
Gregory IV	827–44
John	*844*
Sergius II	844–47
Leo IV	847–55
Benedict III	855–58
Anastasius (the Librarian)	*855*
Nicholas I	858–67
Adrian II	867–72
John VIII	872–82
Marinus I	882–84
Adrian III	884–85
Stephen V (or VI)[3]	885–91
Formosus	891–96
Boniface VI	896
Stephen VI (or VII)[3]	896
Romanus	897
Theodore II	897
John IX	898–900
Benedict IV	900–903
Leo V	903
Christopher	*903–4*
Sergius III	904–11
Anastasius III	911–13
Lando	913–14
John X	914–28
Leo VI	928
Stephen VII (or VIII)[3]	929–31
John XI	931–35
Leo VII	936–39
Stephen VIII (or IX)[3]	939–42
Marinus II	942–46
Agapetus II	946–55
John XII	955–64

Leo VIII[4]	963–65
Benedict V[4]	964–66?
John XIII	965–72
Benedict VI	973–74
Boniface VII (1st time)	*974*
Benedict VII	974–83
John XIV	983–84
Boniface VII (2nd time)	*984–85*
John XV (or XVI)[5]	985–96
Gregory V	996–99
John XVI (or XVII)[5]	*997–98*
Sylvester II	999–1003
John XVII (or XVIII)[5]	1003
John XVIII (or XIX)[5]	1004–9
Sergius IV	1009–12
Gregory (VI)	*1012*
Benedict VIII	1012–24
John XIX (or XX)[5]	1024–32
Benedict IX *(1st time)*	1032–44
Sylvester III	1045
Benedict IX *(2nd time)*	1045
Gregory VI	1045–46
Clement II	1046–47
Benedict IX *(3rd time)*	1047–48
Damasus II	1048
Leo IX	1049–54
Victor II	1055–57
Stephen IX (or X)[3]	1057–58
Benedict X	*1058–59*
Nicholas II	1059–61
Alexander II	1061–73
Honorius (II)	*1061–72*
Gregory VII	1073–85
Clement (III)	*1080–1100*
Victor III	1086–87
Urban II	1088–99
Paschal II	1099–1118
Theodoric	*1100–2*
Albert (Aleric)	*1102*
Sylvester (IV)	*1105–11*
Gelasius II	1118–19
Gregory (VIII)	*1118–21*
Calixtus II (Callistus)	1119–24
Honorius II	1124–30
Celestine (II)	*1124*
Innocent II	1130–43
Anacletus (II)	*1130–38*
Victor (IV)	*1138*
Celestine II	1143–44
Lucius II	1144–45
Eugenius III	1145–53
Anastasius IV	1153–54
Adrian IV	1154–59
Alexander III	1159–81
Victor (IV)	*1159–64*
Paschal (III)	*1164–68*
Calixtus (III)	*1168–78*
Innocent (III)	*1179–80*
Lucius III	1181–85
Urban III	1185–87
Gregory VIII	1187
Clement III	1187–91
Celestine III	1191–98
Innocent III	1198–1216
Honorius III	1216–27
Gregory IX	1227–41
Celestine IV	1241
Innocent IV	1243–54
Alexander IV	1254–61
Urban IV	1261–64
Clement IV	1265–68
Gregory X	1271–76
Innocent V	1276
Adrian V	1276
John XXI[5]	1276–77

Nicholas III	1277–80
Martin IV[6]	1281–85
Honorius IV	1285–87
Nicholas IV	1288–92
Celestine V	1294
Boniface VIII	1294–1303
Benedict XI	1303–4
Clement V (at Avignon, from 1309)	1305–14
John XXII 5 (at Avignon)	1316–34
Nicholas (V) (at Rome)	*1328–30*
Benedict XII (at Avignon)	1334–42
Clement VI (at Avignon)	1342–52
Innocent VI (at Avignon)	1352–62
Urban V (at Avignon)	1362–70
Gregory XI (at Avignon, then Rome from 1377)	1370–78
Urban VI	1378–89
Clement (VII) (at Avignon)	*1378–94*
Boniface IX	1389–1404
Benedict (XIII) (at Avignon)	*1394–1423*
Innocent VII	1404–6
Gregory XII	1406–15
Alexander (V) (at Bologna)	*1409–10*
John (XXIII) (at Bologna)	*1410–15*
Martin V[6]	1417–31
Clement (VIII)	*1423–29*
Eugenius IV	1431–47
Felix (V) (also called Amadeus VIII of Savoy)	*1439–49*
Nicholas V	1447–55
Calixtus III (Callistus)	1455–58
Pius II	1458–64
Paul II	1464–71
Sixtus IV	1471–84
Innocent VIII	1484–92
Alexander VI	1492–1503
Pius III	1503
Julius II	1503–13
Leo X	1513–21
Adrian VI	1522–23
Clement VII	1523–34
Paul III	1534–49
Julius III	1550–55
Marcellus II	1555
Paul IV	1555–59
Pius IV	1559–65
Pius V	1566–72
Gregory XIII	1572–85
Sixtus V	1585–90
Urban VII	1590
Gregory XIV	1590–91
Innocent IX	1591
Clement VIII	1592–1605
Leo XI	1605
Paul V	1605–21
Gregory XV	1621–23
Urban VIII	1623–44
Innocent X	1644–55
Alexander VII	1655–67
Clement IX	1667–69
Clement X	1670–76
Innocent XI	1676–89
Alexander VIII	1689–91
Innocent XII	1691–1700
Clement XI	1700–21
Innocent XIII	1721–24
Benedict XIII	1724–30
Clement XII	1730–40
Benedict XIV	1740–58
Clement XIII	1758–69
Clement XIV	1769–74
Pius VI	1775–99
Pius VII	1800–23
Leo XII	1823–29

Popes and Antipopes[1] (antipopes in italics) (continued)

Pius VIII	1829–30	Pius XI	1922–39
Gregory XVI	1831–46	Pius XII	1939–58
Pius IX	1846–78	John XXIII	1958–63
Leo XIII	1878–1903	Paul VI	1963–78
Pius X	1903–14	John Paul I	1978
Benedict XV	1914–22	John Paul II	1978–

[1]Until the 4th cent., the popes were usually known only as bishops of Rome.
[2]The higher number is used if Felix (II), who reigned 355–58 and is ordinarily classed as an antipope, is counted as a pope.
[3]Though elected on March 23, 752, Stephen (II) died two days later before he could be consecrated and thus is ordinarily not counted. The issue has made the numbering of subsequent Stephens somewhat irregular.
[4]Either Leo VIII or Benedict V may be considered an antipope.
[5]A confusion in the numbering of popes named John after John XIV (r.983–84) resulted because some 11th-cent. historians mistakenly believed that there had been a pope named John between antipope Boniface VII and the true John XV (r.985–86). Therefore they mistakenly numbered the real popes John XV to XIX as John XVI to XX. These popes have since customarily been renumbered XV to XIX, but John XXI and John XXII continue to bear numbers that they themselves formally adopted on the assumption that there had indeed been 20 Johns before them. In current numbering, there thus exists no pope by the name of John XX. In the 13th cent. the papal chancery misread the names of the two popes Marinus as Martin, and as a result of this error Simon de Brie in 1281 assumed the name of Pope Martin IV instead of Martin II. The enumeration has not been corrected, and thus there exist no Martin II and Martin III.

years. The latter became a symbol of World War I because it bloomed in fields that had been disturbed by battle. See also California poppy.

popular art Any dance, literature, music, theater, or other art form intended to be received and appreciated by ordinary people in a literate, technologically advanced society dominated by urban culture. It tends to be narrative, to reinforce uncontroversial beliefs and sentiments, to support institutions, and to create identity in a social group. In the 20th century it is usually dependent on such technologies of reproduction or distribution as television, photography, digital compact disc and tape recording, motion pictures, radio, and videocassettes.

popular front Coalition of working-class and middle-class political parties that united to defend democracy from an expected fascist assault in the 1930s. The policy of a "united front" against fascism was announced at the communist Third International (1935), to include not only communists and socialists but also liberals, moderates, and even conservatives. Popular-front governments were formed in France and Spain in 1936, but the financial consequences of the reforms undertaken by the France government, under Leon Blum, proved its undoing, and the Spanish government was brought down by Francisco Franco in the Spanish Civil War.

Popular Front for the Liberation of Oman (PFLO) *orig.* Dhofar Liberation Front. Resistance group founded in 1963 by Arab nationalists and religious conservatives to depose Sultan Said ibn Taimur (r.1932–70). In 1968 its leadership was taken over by Marxists. In 1970 the sultan was deposed by his son, Qabus ibn Said, who softened the resistance with a combination of military pressure and economic rewards.

popular music Historically, any non-folk-music form that acquired mass popularity—from the songs of the medieval minstrels to those elements of fine art music originally intended for a small, elite audience but that became widely popular. After the Industrial Revolution, true folk music began to disappear, and the popular music of the Victorian era and the early 20th century was that of the music hall and vaudeville, with its upper reaches dominated by waltz music and the operettas of J. Offenbach, V. Herbert, and others. In the U.S., minstrel shows performed the compositions of such songwriters as S. Foster. In the 1890s Tin Pan Alley emerged, and later the musical, which achieved great sophistication. Beginning with ragtime in the 1890s, black Americans had begun combining complex African rhythms with European harmonic structures, a synthesis that would eventually create jazz. The music audience greatly expanded, partly because of technology. By 1930, phonograph records had replaced sheet music as the chief source of music in the home, enabling those without musical training to hear popular songs. The microphone relieved singers of the need for trained voices that could fill large halls. The ability of radio broadcasting to reach rural communities aided the dissemination of new styles, notably country music, and to a lesser extent blues. U.S. popular music achieved international dominance in the decades after World War II. By the 1950s, the migration of American blacks to cities in the North had resulted in the cross-fertilization of elements of blues with the uptempo rhythms of jazz to create rhythm and blues. Rock and roll, with such figures as E. Presley and Little Richard, soon developed as an amalgam of rhythm and blues with country music and other influences (see rock music). In the 1960s, British rock groups, including the Beatles and the Rolling Stones, became internationally influential. Rock quickly attracted the allegiance of Western teenagers, who, with new disposable incomes, replaced young adults as the chief audience for popular music. From the late 1960s black pop gained a huge white audience. The history of pop through the 1990s was basically that of rock and its variants, including disco, heavy metal, punk rock, and rap, which have spread throughout the world and become the standard musical idiom for young people in many countries.

Popular Party (Italy) See Italian Popular Party

Popular Republican Movement (MRP) French social-reform party. Founded in 1944, the MRP was a strong center party of the Fourth Republic and the French expression of Christian Democracy. After winning about 25% of the vote, it declined in the 1950s, losing strength to both right and left factions. In 1966 it was merged with other right-center parties to become the Centre Démocrate, which won only 13% of the vote. By 1968 it had become little more than a political club.

popular sovereignty Political doctrine that allowed the settlers of U.S. federal territories to decide whether to enter the Union as free or slave states. It was applied by Sen. Stephen A. Douglas as a means to reach a compromise through passage of the Kansas-Nebraska Act. Critics of the doctrine called it "squatter sovereignty." The resulting violence between pro- and antislavery factions (see Bleeding Kansas) showed its failure as a workable compromise. See also Dred Scott decision.

Populares See Optimates and Populares

Populations I and II Two broad classes of stars and stellar groupings, whose members differ primarily in age, chemical composition, and location in galaxies. They were distinguished and named by Walter Baade (1893–1960). Population I consists of younger stars, clusters, and associations. These occur in and near the arms of the Milky Way system and other spiral galaxies and have been detected in irregular galaxies (e.g., the Magellanic Clouds). Population I objects are thought to have originated from interstellar gas that has undergone various processes, including supernova explosions, which enriched their constituent matter with heavier elements. Population II consists of older (generally 1 billion–15 billion years old) stars and clusters, presumably formed from interstellar gas clouds that emerged very early in a galaxy's history. Consisting almost entirely of hydrogen and helium, they are found in the galactic halos of spiral galaxies, in globular clusters, and, in large numbers, in elliptical galaxies. Astronomers sometimes refer to a Population III as the very first generation of stars to emerge after the big bang.

populism Political philosophy that champions the common person, usually by favorable contrast with an elite. Populism usually combines elements of the left and right, opposing large corporate and financial interests but also frequently targeting ethnic and racial minorities and immigrants for discrimination. The term arose from the U.S. Populist Movement of the 1890s.

Populist *or* **Narodnik** \nä-ˈrȯd-ˌnik\ Member of a 19th-century socialist movement in Russia. In the 1860s and '70s, the movement attracted intellectuals who believed that political propaganda among the peasants (*narod:* "people") would lead to their revolt and the liberalization of the czarist regime. Attempts to arouse the peasants produced police persecution and arrests, which drove the socialists to more radical methods, including terrorism. The revolutionary group Land and Freedom, led by Georgy Plekhanov, was formed in the mid-1870s and continued to work among the peasantry until it split in 1879. The movement's populist ideology was revived in the 20th century by the Socialist Revolutionary Party.

Populist Movement Coalition of U.S. agrarian reformers in the Midwest and South in the 1890s. The movement developed from farmers' alliances formed in the 1880s in reaction to falling crop prices and poor credit facilities. The leaders organized the Populist, or People's, Party (1892), which advocated a variety of measures to help farmers. The party's presidential candidate, James B. Weaver (1833–1912), won over 1 million votes. Many state and local Populist candidates were elected in the Midwest. In the 1896 election the party joined with the Democratic Party to support the Free Silver Movement and the unsuccessful candidacy of William Jennings Bryan. The movement declined thereafter.

Populonium *ancient* **Pupluna** Ancient Roman city, western coast of central Italy. It was originally Etruscan. Silver and iron ores from the nearby island of Elba supplied its metal-manufacturing industry. During the 5th century BC it became wealthy as the first city in Etruria to coin silver. It was conquered by Romans and suffered during the wars between Sulla and Marius in the 1st century BC. It has remains of Etruscan walls and tombs, and ruins of a medieval castle.

porcelain Vitrified pottery with a white, fine-grained body that is usually translucent. It was first made in China during the Tang dynasty (618–907) and in its advanced form during the Yuan dynasty (1279–1368). The three main types are true (or hard-paste) porcelain, artificial (or soft-paste) porcelain, and bone china. Attempts by medieval European potters to imitate true porcelain led to the discovery of soft-paste porcelain, which can be cut with a file. The secret of true porcelain was discovered c. 1707 in Saxony. Standard English bone china was produced c. 1800 when Josiah Spode II (1754–1827) added calcined bones to the hard-paste porcelain formula. Hard-paste porcelain, though strong, chips more readily than bone china. See also Bow porcelain, Chantilly porcelain, Chelsea porcelain, Meissen porcelain, Nymphenburg porcelain, Saint-Cloud porcelain, Sèvres porcelain, stoneware.

porch Roofed structure, usually open at front and sides, projecting from the face of a building and used to protect an entrance. If colonnaded, it may be called a portico. A veranda is typically a long porch surrounded by a railing, often extending along more than one side of a building. Simple porches were exceedingly common in the domestic architecture of Britain and the U.S. from the late 18th century. In Gothic cathedrals the porch was often a small gabled structure projecting from the northern or southern walls of the nave. See also loggia, narthex.

porcupine Heavy-bodied, solitary, slow-moving, nocturnal rodent with quills (modified hairs) along the back, tail, and, on certain crested species, the neck and shoulders. The quills are easily detached when touched. The New World species (four genera in family Erethizontidae) are arboreal and have barbed quills; the Old World species (four genera in family Hystricidae) are terrestrial and have unbarbed quills. The North American porcupine *(Erethizon dorsatum),* about 30 in. (75 cm) long, with a tail about 8 in. (20 cm) long and quills about 3 in. (8 cm) long, drives its powerful tail against an assailant. For food, it favors the tender tissue beneath tree bark. Crested porcupines, the typical Old World porcupines, run backward, quills erect, into the enemy. They eat roots, fruit, and other vegetation. The African crested porcupine, the largest terrestrial rodent in Europe and Africa, may weigh 60 lbs (27 kg) and have quills 14 in. (35 cm) long.

porgy \'pȯr-jē\ Any of about 100 species (family Sparidae) of generally shallow-water fishes found throughout tropical and temperate seas. Porgies, sometimes called sea breams, are typically high-backed, with a single dorsal fin, a small mouth, and teeth strong enough to handle fishes and hard-shelled invertebrates. Most species do not exceed 1 ft (30 cm) long, but some may grow to 4 ft (120 cm). The South African musselcrackers, popular sport fishes, grow to 100 lbs (45 kg). In Australia and Japan, several species of *Chrysophrys* are important food fish (called snappers in Australia). The red sea bream inhabits deep European waters. See also sheepshead.

Northern porgy (*Stenotomus chrysops*).
RUNK/SCHOENBERGER FROM GRANT HEILMAN

pork Flesh of hogs, usually slaughtered between the ages of six months and one year. It is consumed as cooked fresh meat in various cuts or preparations, including chops and sausage, or cured or smoked for ham, bacon, dry sausage, or other products. Because pigs may be infected by the parasitic disease trichinosis, fresh pork must be cooked to an internal temperature of 160°F (71°C) to destroy the parasite. Pork is proscribed by the dietary laws of Islam and Judaism.

pornography Depiction of erotic behavior intended to cause sexual excitement. The word originally signified any work of art or literature depicting the life of prostitutes. Though pornography is clearly ancient in origin, its early history is obscure because it was customarily not thought worthy of transmission or preservation. The invention of printing led to the production of ambitious pornographic written works intended to entertain as well as to arouse. The first modern works designed solely to arouse appeared in 18th-century Europe. The development of photography and motion pictures contributed greatly to the proliferation of pornography. Since World War II, written pornography has been largely superseded by explicit visual representations.

porphyrin \'pȯr-fə-rən\ Any of a class of heterocyclic compounds, biological pigments of a characteristic chemical constitution and structure having four fused rings and nitrogen atoms. When their derivatives are combined with proteins and metal ions, the resulting compounds include the hemoproteins (e.g., hemoglobin, cytochromes, and catalase, an enzyme that accelerates hydrogen peroxide breakdown).

porphyry copper deposit \'pȯr-fə-rē\ A large body of igneous rock, having distinct crystals in a relatively fine-grained base, that contains chalcopyrite and other sulfide minerals. These deposits contain vast amounts of ore that averages a fraction of 1% copper by weight; although low-grade, the deposits are important because they can be worked on a large scale at low cost. Large porphyry copper deposits are worked in the southwestern U.S. (where molybdenum may be produced as a by-product), the Solomon Islands, Canada, Peru, Chile, Mexico, and elsewhere.

porpoise Any toothed whale in the family Phocoenidae (or, by some authorities, part of the dolphin family Delphinidae). The four species (genus *Phocoena*) of the common, or harbor, porpoise are primarily fish eaters that travel in pairs or large groups. They are gray or black above and white below. The shy *P. phocoena,* found throughout the Northern Hemisphere, rarely leaps. The other species of *Phocoena* are found along Californian and South American coasts. The active, gregarious Dall porpoise *(Phocoenoides dalli)* of the North Pacific and the True porpoise *(P. truei)* of Japan often swim with ships, usually in groups of two to 20. Both eat cephalopods and fishes and are black with a large white patch on each side. The black finless porpoise *(Neomeris phocoenoides),* a small, slow animal, inhabits the Pacific and Indian oceans. At most 7 ft (2 m) long, porpoises are shorter and chubbier than dolphins and have a blunt snout. Like the dolphins, they are known for their high intelligence.

port Input/output conduit for personal computers. The serial port was created as an interface between data terminal equipment and data-communications equipment. It processes data sequentially, as a series of bits, and is used to connect equipment (e.g., a modem or mouse) to the computer. The parallel port processes several data bits in parallel and is used to connect peripherals such as computer printers and optical scanners to the computer. The parallel port is faster, but the serial port is cheaper and requires less power. See also USB.

port Sweet, fortified red wine of rich taste and aroma made in Portugal. The name derives from Porto, the town where it is traditionally aged and bottled. Peculiar to the manufacture of port is a large dose of brandy given to the still-fermenting liquid (called must). Much time, often decades, is needed for the maturing of fine ports.

Port Arthur See Lüshun

Port-au-Prince \,pōr-tō-'prins\ City (metro. area pop., 1995 est.: 1,4216,000), seaport, and capital of Haiti, West Indies, on the southeastern shore of the Golfe de la Gonâve. Founded by the French in 1749, it was destroyed by earthquakes in 1751 and 1770 and has frequently suffered from fires and civil strife. In 1807 the port was opened to foreign commerce. It is the country's principal port and commercial center, producing sugar, flour, cottonseed oil, and textiles.

Port Blair City (pop., 1991: 75,000), capital of Andaman and Nicobar Islands union territory, India, in the Bay of Bengal. It was occupied by the British in 1789 but soon abandoned. The town was made a penal colony in 1858. It was occupied by the Japanese 1942–45. The penal colony was abolished in 1945. It is a market town with several local museums and an airport.

Port-de-France See Nouméa

Port Jackson Inlet of the South Pacific, New South Wales, southeastern Australia, one of the world's finest natural harbors. It was sighted in 1770 by Capt. James Cook. Its entrance is between North and South Heads, where naval and military stations are located. Sydney is on its southern shore, and the northern suburbs of Sydney are on its northern shore; they are joined by the Sydney Harbour Bridge, which was built in 1932.

Port Louis City (pop., 2000: 148,506), capital, and main port of Mauritius. It was founded c. 1736 by the French as a port for ships rounding the Cape of Good Hope to and from Asia and Europe. With the completion of the Suez Canal in 1869, the city's importance declined. It is the principal commercial center of the island; its primary export is sugar.

Port Moresby City (pop., 1997: 271,813), capital of Papua New Guinea, on the southeastern coast of the Gulf of Papua. Its large, sheltered harbor was explored by British Capt. John Moresby in 1873. The British annexed the area 1883–84. The town became a main Allied base in World War II. The National Capital District, established in 1974, includes all of Port Moresby; it became the capital when Papua New Guinea became independent in 1975. A commercial center, it is also the site of a university.

Port of Spain City (pop., 1995 est.: 52,000), seaport, and capital of Trinidad and Tobago. Formerly the capital of the West Indies Federation, it is located in the northwestern part of the island of Trinidad on the Gulf of Paria. It is an air transport center for the Caribbean and has a diversified economy, producing rum, beer, and lumber. It is also a principal port and shipping center; exports include oil, sugar, citrus, and asphalt.

Port Said \sä-'ēd, 'sīd\ Seaport city (pop., 1996 est.: 470,000), northeastern Egypt, on the Mediterranean Sea at the northern end of the Suez Canal. Founded in 1859 on a narrow, sandy strip separating the Mediterranean from Lake Manzala, it became the world's most important coaling station. It was the landing point of French and British troops during the Suez Crisis (1956) that followed Egypt's nationalization of the Suez Canal. In the Six-Day War of 1967, Israeli forces occupied the eastern bank of the canal, which was closed until 1975. The city was revitalized after 1975 and its industries include textiles, clothing, cosmetics, and glass.

Port-Vila \ˌpȯr-vē-'lä\ *or* **Vila** Seaport, capital, and largest town (pop., 1999: 30,139) of Vanuatu, South Pacific. Although French in appearance, the town has a multinational population, including British, French, and Vietnamese. It served as a base for the U.S. in World War II and is the commercial center of Vanuatu.

porte cochere \ˌpōrt-kō-'sher\ (French: "coach door") Passageway through a building, or gateway in an outer wall, designed to let vehicles pass from the street to an interior courtyard. Such gateways are common features of homes and palaces built in the grand style of Louis XIV and Louis XV. The term also applies to a roofed structure extending from the entrance of a building over an adjacent driveway.

Porter, Cole (Albert) (1891–1964) U.S. composer and lyricist. Born to an affluent family in Peru, Ind., Porter studied violin and piano as a child and composed an operetta at 10. At Yale University he composed about 300 songs, including "Bulldog." He studied law and later music at Harvard. He made his Broadway debut with *See America First* (1916). He later went to France and became an itinerant playboy; though rather openly homosexual, he married a wealthy divorcée. Songs written for the Broadway success *Paris* (1928) led to a series of hit musicals, incl. *Gay Divorcée* (1932), *Anything Goes* (1934), *Red, Hot and Blue* (1934), the superb *Kiss Me, Kate* (1948), *Can-Can* (1953), and *Silk Stockings* (1955). He also worked on a number of films, including *High Society* (1956). Porter's witty, sophisticated songs, for which he wrote both words and music, include "Night and Day," "I Get a Kick Out of You," "Begin the Beguine," "I Love Paris," and "You're the Top." A riding accident in 1937 left him a semi-invalid; he underwent 30 operations and eventually the amputation of a leg.

Porter, David (1780–1843) U.S. naval officer. Born in Boston, he joined the navy (1798) and served in the Tripolitan War. In the War of 1812 he commanded the *Essex,* the first U.S. warship active in the Pacific Ocean; he captured several British whaling vessels and took possession of Nuku Hiva, the largest of the Marquesas Islands (1813). He was blockaded by British frigates in Valparaíso, Chile, where he surrendered (1814). He served on the board of naval commissioners (1815–23) and commanded a squadron to suppress piracy in the West Indies (1823–25). For unauthorized action against Spanish authorities in Puerto Rico, he was court-martialed and suspended from duty. He resigned in 1826 and became commander of the Mexican navy (1826–29).

Porter, David Dixon (1813–1891) U.S. naval officer. Born in Chester, Pa., he served under his father, David Porter, in the West Indies and in the Mexican navy before joining the U.S. Navy (1829). Promoted to commander in the Civil War, he served under his foster brother, David Farragut, to help win the Battle of New Orleans. In 1863 he succeeded in running his fleet past the Confederate fort at Vicksburg to meet Ulysses S. Grant's troops and complete the effort to open the Mississippi River to Union forces. After the war he served as superintendent of the U.S. Naval Academy (1865–69) and was promoted to admiral (1870).

David Dixon Porter, photograph; in the Mathew Brady collection.
BY COURTESY OF THE LIBRARY OF CONGRESS, WASHINGTON, D.C.

Porter, Fitz-John (1822–1901) U.S. Army officer. Born in Portsmouth, N.H., he graduated from West Point and later taught there (1849–55). In the Civil War he was made a brigadier general of volunteers. In the Second Battle of Bull Run he served under Gen. John Pope, who blamed Porter for the Union defeat. At his court-martial Porter claimed that Pope's orders were confusing and impossible to execute, but he was found guilty and cashiered. In 1879 he won a review of his case, which supported his claim of innocence.

Porter, Katherine Anne (1890–1980) U.S. writer. Born in Indian Creek, Texas, she worked as a journalist in Chicago and Denver before leaving in 1920 for Mexico, the scene of several of her stories. Her collections include *Flowering Judas* (1930), her first and most popular; *Pale Horse, Pale Rider* (1939), a set of three novellas; and *Collected Short Stories* (1965, Pulitzer Prize, National Book Award). Her stories have a richness of texture and complexity of character delineation usually achieved only in the novel. *Ship of Fools* (1962) is her only novel.

portico Colonnaded porch or entrance to a structure, or a covered walkway supported by regularly spaced columns. The portico is a principal feature of Greek temple architecture and thus a prominent element in Roman and all subsequent Classically inspired structures.

Portillo, José López See José López Portillo

Portland Seaport city (pop., 2000: 64,249), southwestern Maine. First settled in 1632, it was destroyed by Indians in 1676 and 1690. It was incorporated as a town in 1786 and was the state capital 1820–32. A fire destroyed much of the city center in 1866, but Portland was again rebuilt. The state's largest city, it is the hub of a metropolitan area that includes the cities of South Portland and Westbrook and many towns. It is built largely on two hilly peninsulas overlooking Casco Bay. Industries include pulp and paper, shipbuilding, publishing, commercial fishing, and lumber. It was the birthplace of Henry W. Longfellow.

Portland City (pop., 2000: 529,121) and port, northwestern Oregon, on the Willamette River, southeast of its confluence with the Columbia River. Settled in 1829 on the site of an early Indian campground, it was laid out in 1844 and incorporated in 1851. Early growth was stimulated by gold rushes and the flow of immigrants along the Oregon Trail. It is the state's largest city and principal port. Exports include lumber, aluminum, and wheat. Shipbuilding and meat-packing are important industries. It is the site of many educational institutions, including Lewis and Clark College (1867) and Reed College.

portland cement Binding agent of present-day CONCRETE. It is a finely ground powder made by burning and grinding a limestone mixed with clay or shale. Its inventor, Joseph Aspdin (1799–1855), patented the process in 1824, naming the material for its resemblance to the limestone of the Isle of Portland, England. The cement combines chemically with the water it is mixed with, then hardens and strengthens.

Portland Vase Roman vase (1st century AD) of dark-blue glass decorated with white figures, the finest surviving Roman example of CAMEO GLASS. It came into the possession of the duke of Portland in the 18th century. The vase has been extensively copied, particularly in the Victorian period. The most accurate copies were made in jasperware with white figures in relief (by JOSIAH WEDGWOOD, 1790) and in glass (1876). In 1845, while in the British Museum (where it still resides), the original vase was smashed, necessitating painstaking restoration.

Portland Vase, Roman cameo glass, 1st century AD; in the British Museum.

Porto \'pōr-tü\ *Portuguese* **Oporto** Seaport city (pop., 1991: 311,000), northwestern Portugal, on the right bank of the DOURO RIVER. It was called Portus Cale in Roman times and was earlier a flourishing settlement on the Douro's south bank. Held successively by the Alani, Visigoths, Moors, and Christians, it became an important port in the 14th century. HENRY THE NAVIGATOR was born there in 1394. It was the site of a British victory over the French in the 1809 PENINSULAR WAR. World famous for its PORT wine, Porto is Portugal's second-largest city and the region's commercial and industrial center.

Pôrto Alegre \'pōr-tü-ä-'lā-grē\ Seaport city (metro. area pop., 2000: 3,507,624), southern Brazil, near the Atlantic coast. Founded c. 1742 by immigrants from the AZORES, it was first known as Pôrto dos Casais. It received many German and Italian settlers in the 19th century. Located on the Guaíba River, it is a center of inland navigation. It is the most important Brazilian commercial center south of SÃO PAULO; exports include rice, tobacco, and hides. Industries include shipbuilding and the manufacture of textiles, pharmaceuticals, and chemicals. It is also an educational center.

Porto-Novo \ˌpōr-tō-'nō-vō\ City (pop., 1994 est.: 200,000), seaport, and capital of Benin, on the Gulf of GUINEA, western Africa. Situated on a coastal lagoon in the southeastern part of the country, it was probably founded in the late 16th century as the center of the indigenous kingdom of Porto-Novo. The Portuguese established a trading post in the 17th century, and it became a center of the SLAVE TRADE. It became a French protectorate in 1863. In 1904 it became the capital of the French West African colony of Dahomey. The ruins of old African palaces remain, and there are many colonial style buildings, including the old Portuguese cathedral.

Portsmouth \'pōrt-smәth\ City (pop., 1999 est.: 190,400) and seaport, HAMPSHIRE, southern England, on the island of Portsea in the ENGLISH CHANNEL. It was founded and received its first charter in 1194. A naval dockyard was established in 1496 and greatly expanded after 1698. Covering more than 300 acres (120 hectares), the dockyard is the city's main source of employment. Portsmouth suffered extensive damage from German bombing in World War II. Important industries are shipbuilding and aircraft engineering. The city was the birthplace of CHARLES DICKENS.

Portsmouth City (pop., 2000: 100,565) and seaport, southeastern Virginia, on the Elizabeth River opposite NORFOLK. With Norfolk and NEWPORT NEWS, it comprises the Port of HAMPTON ROADS. Founded in 1752, and named after PORTSMOUTH, England, it was occupied by both British and American troops during the AMERICAN REVOLUTION. It was incorporated as a city in 1858. During the AMERICAN CIVIL WAR the U.S. Navy Yard was evacuated by Union troops, allowing Southern troops access to stores of equipment; it was recaptured in 1862. It is part of the U.S. military complex at Hampton Roads. Shipbuilding and ship repair are the main economic activities, augmented by various manufactures.

Portsmouth, Treaty of (1905) Peace settlement that ended the RUSSO-JAPANESE WAR. It was mediated by Pres. THEODORE ROOSEVELT and signed at the U.S. naval base near Portsmouth, N.H. By its terms, Russia recognized Japan as the dominant power in Korea and ceded its leases to Port Arthur (now Lüshun) and the Liaodong Peninsula, as well as the southern half of Sakhalin, to Japan. Both powers agreed to restore Manchuria to China.

Portugal *officially* **Portuguese Republic** *ancient* **Lusitania** Country, western coast of the IBERIAN PENINSULA, southwestern Europe. Area: 35,662 sq mi (92,365 sq km). Population (2000 est.): 10,005,000. Capital: LISBON. Most of the people are Portuguese. Language: Portuguese (official). Religion: Roman Catholicism. Monetary unit: euro. Administratively, the Atlantic islands of the AZORES and MADEIRA are part of Portugal. Portugal is divided roughly in half by the TAGUS RIVER; the highlands rise mostly north of the Tagus and stretch northeast into Spain. It has an industrialized economy in which both the public and private sectors participate. Major industries were nationalized after a military coup in 1974, but many were returned to the private sector in the late 1980s. Light industries predominate, and products include textiles and clothing, paper and wood products, and chemicals. It is a republic with one legislative house; the chief of state is the president, and the head of government is the prime minister. In the 1st millennium BC, Celtic peoples settled the Iberian peninsula. They were conquered c. 140 BC by the Romans, who ruled until the 5th century AD, when the area was invaded by Germanic tribes. A Muslim invasion in 711 left only the northern part of Portugal in Christian hands. In 1179 it became the kingdom of Portugal and expanded as it reconquered the Muslim-held sectors. The boundaries of modern continental Portugal were completed in 1270 under King AFONSO III. In the 15th and 16th centuries the monarchy encouraged exploration that took Portuguese navigators to Africa, India,

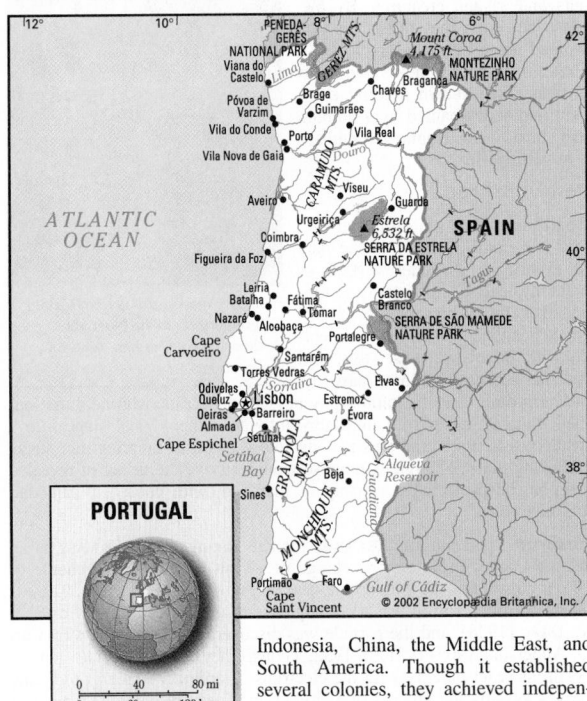

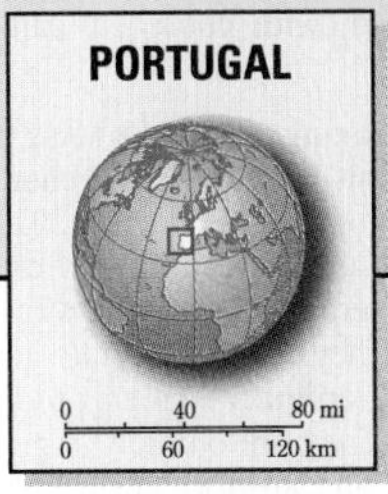

Indonesia, China, the Middle East, and South America. Though it established several colonies, they achieved independence over the years (see BRAZIL, GOA, CAPE VERDE Islands, EAST TIMOR, ANGOLA, GUINEA-BISSAU, MOZAMBIQUE, MACAO). ANTÓNIO DE OLIVEIRA SALAZAR ruled Portugal as a dictator in the mid-20th century; he was removed from office in 1968. A new constitution was adopted in 1976 (revised 1982), and civilian rule resumed. It was a charter member of NATO and is a member of the EUROPEAN UNION.

Portuguese East Africa See MOZAMBIQUE

Portuguese Guinea See GUINEA-BISSAU

Portuguese language ROMANCE LANGUAGE spoken by about 170 million people in Portugal, Brazil, and other former Portuguese colonies. The first literary works in Portuguese date from the 13th–14th century. Standard Portuguese is based on the dialect of Lisbon. Dialectal variation in Portugal is limited, but the differences between Brazilian and European Portuguese are more extensive, including changes in PHONOLOGY, verb conjugation, and SYNTAX. The four major dialect groups are Northern (Galician, spoken in northwestern Spain), Central, Southern (including the Lisbon dialect), and Insular (including Brazilian and Madeiran) Portuguese.

Portuguese man-of-war Any of various floating, warm-water marine CNIDARIANS (genus *Physalia,* class Hydrozoa) found worldwide but mostly in the Gulf Stream and the Indian and Pacific oceans. The MEDUSA-form body consists of a translucent, jellylike, gas-filled float, which may be 3–12 in. (9–30 cm) long. POLYPS beneath the float bear hanging tentacles up to 165 ft (50 m) long. Nematocysts on some polyps paralyze fish and other prey. Other polyps then attach to, spread over, and digest the victim. A third type of polyp is involved in reproduction. The painful sting of *Physalia* can cause fever, shock, or disruption of heart and lung function.

Portuguese West Africa See ANGOLA

Poseidon \pə-ˈsī-dən\ Greek god of water and the sea, son of CRONUS and RHEA. His brothers were ZEUS and HADES. When the three brothers deposed their father, the kingdom of the sea fell by lot to Poseidon. Unpredictable and sometimes violent, he was also god of earthquakes, and he was closely associated with horses. Most of his offspring were giants and savage creatures. By MEDUSA he was the father of the winged horse PEGASUS. The ISTHMIAN GAMES were held in his honor. In art he was often shown holding a trident and accompanied by a dolphin and tuna. The Romans identified him with NEPTUNE.

Poseidon, marble statue from Melos, 2nd century BC; in the National Archaeological Museum, Athens.
ALINARI—ART RESOURCE

Posen See POZNAN

positivism Any philosophical system that confines itself to the data of experience, excludes A PRIORI or metaphysical speculations, and emphasizes the achievements of science. Positivism is closely connected with EMPIRICISM, PRAGMATISM, and LOGICAL POSITIVISM. More narrowly, the term designates the philosophy of AUGUSTE COMTE, who held that human thought had passed inevitably through a theological stage into a metaphysical stage and was passing into a positive, or scientific, stage. Believing that the religious impulse would survive the decay of revealed religion, he projected a worship of mankind, with churches, calendar, and hierarchy.

positron \ˈpä-zə-ˌträn\ SUBATOMIC PARTICLE having the same MASS as an ELECTRON but with an electric charge of +1 (an electron has a charge of −1). It constitutes the antiparticle (see ANTIMATTER) of an electron. The existence of the positron was a consequence of the electron theory of P. A. M. DIRAC (1928), and the particle was discovered in COSMIC RAYS by Carl D. Anderson (1905–1991) in 1932. Though they are stable in a vacuum, positrons react quickly with the electrons of ordinary matter, producing GAMMA RAYS by the process of ANNIHILATION. They are emitted in positive BETA DECAY of proton-rich radioactive nuclei and are formed in PAIR PRODUCTION.

positron emission tomography (PET) Imaging technique used in diagnosis and biomedical research. A chemical that emits POSITRONS is injected into the body, and detectors measure their activity as they combine with ELECTRONS and are annihilated. Computers analyze, integrate, and reconstruct to produce images of the organs scanned. PET is particularly useful for studying BRAIN and HEART functions.

possession, adverse See ADVERSE POSSESSION

possible world Conception of a total way things might have happened. It is often contrasted with the way things have actually happened. In his *Theodicy* (1710), G. W. LEIBNIZ used the concept of a possible world in attempting to solve the theological problem of moral and physical evil, arguing that an all-perfect God would actualize the best of all possible worlds, an idea later satirized by VOLTAIRE in *Candide* (1759). Philosophers have since constructed several different formalizations of the concept of a possible world.

possum *or* **phalanger** \fə-ˈlan-jər, ˈfā-ˌlan-jər\ Any of several species (family Phalangeridae) of nocturnal, arboreal MARSUPIALS of Australia and New Guinea. They are 22–50 in. (55–125 cm) long, including the long prehensile tail, and have woolly fur. All species eat fruits, leaves, and blossoms; some also eat insects and small vertebrates. Possums grasp branches with their hind feet. Most species bear their young in tree hollows and unused birds' nests; a few build leafy nests. Several species are endangered because of predation, fur trapping, or habitat loss, but the common brush-tailed possum is considered a pest. See also OPOSSUM.

Post, C(harles) W(illiam) (1854–1914) U.S. manufacturer of breakfast CEREALS. Post grew up in Springfield, Ill., and worked as a traveling salesman. In the 1880s he became a patient of JOHN H. KELLOGG at a health sanitarium in Battle Creek, Mich., where he became interested in producing healthful foods like those Kellogg served. In 1895 he founded Postum Cereal Co., the precursor to GENERAL FOODS CORP. His first product, the cereal beverage Postum, was followed by Grape Nuts and Post Toasties.

Post, Emily *orig.* **Emily Price** (1872–1960) U.S. authority on social behavior. Born in Baltimore to wealth and social position, she was left in straitened circumstances after a divorce and began writing light fiction and magazine articles. At her publisher's suggestion, she undertook her major work, *Etiquette: The Blue Book of Social Usage* (originally *Etiquette in Society, in Business, in Politics and at Home*), in which, unlike earlier writers on the subject, she directed her commonsense views to the ordinary person of moderate means. First published in 1922, it appeared in 10 editions in her lifetime. The outpouring of letters it provoked inspired her newspaper column, which became widely syndicated.

Emily Post.
BROWN BROTHERS

post-and-beam system In building construction, a system in which two upright members, the posts, hold up a third member, the beam, laid horizontally across their top surfaces. In Britain it is called post-and-lintel system, but in the U.S. "lintel" is usually reserved for a short beam that spans a window or door opening. The post and beam formed the basis of architecture from prehistoric to Roman times, and is illustrated by such ancient structures as STONEHENGE. All structural openings evolved from this system, which is seen in pure form only in COLONNADES and in FRAMED STRUCTURES, the posts of doors, windows, ceilings, and roofs usually being hidden in walls. The beam must bear loads that rest on it as well as its own load without deforming or breaking. Post-and-beam construction has largely been supplanted by the modern steel frame.

post-traumatic stress disorder Psychological reaction occurring after a highly stressing event, characterized by DEPRESSION, ANXIETY, flashbacks, recurrent nightmares, and avoidance of reminders of the event. The traumatic events can include automobile accidents, rape or assault, military combat, torture, incarceration in a concentration camp, and such natural disasters as floods, fires, or earthquakes. Long-term effects include marital and family problems, difficulties at work, and abuse of alcohol and other drugs. PSYCHOTHERAPY, including GROUP THERAPY, is used in treating the disorder.

postal system System of delivering written or packaged communications to any addressee anywhere in the world. Such systems are usually government-run and are paid for by a combination of user charges and government subsidy. The earliest references to postal services are in Egypt c. 2000 BC and in Zhou-dynasty China c. 1000 BC. The Roman empire developed various centralized methods of relaying messages. In the Middle Ages there were no centralized postal services. Private postal systems developed with the development of nation-states in the Renaissance, and later became government monopolies. Charging on the basis of weight rather than distance and using prepaid stamps were first proposed in 1837. The General Postal Union (1875; later Universal Postal Union) improved international mail delivery by establishing that member countries would retain the postage they collected on outgoing international mail and would treat incoming international mail as they treated domestic mail. Airmail and automated mail handling were 20th-century developments.

poster Eye-catching printed paper announcement or advertisement that is exhibited to promote a product, event, or idea. Posters were popularized by the mid-19th-century invention of LITHOGRAPHY, which allowed colored posters to be produced cheaply and easily. HENRI DE TOULOUSE-LAUTREC was noted for his poster art, which often advertised Parisian cabaret performers. Poster art flourished with the rise of the ART NOUVEAU style, as seen in the work of ALPHONSE MUCHA. During World War I, posters were used for recruiting and propaganda, and the industrial boom of the early 20th century gave rise to advertising posters for every conceivable product and event. The later rise of film and television advertising led to an eclipse in poster art.

Postimpressionism Movement in Western painting that represented both an extension of IMPRESSIONISM and a rejection of its limitations. The term was coined by ROGER FRY for the works of PAUL CEZANNE, GEORGES SEURAT, PAUL GAUGUIN, HENRI DE TOULOUSE-LAUTREC, and others. Most of these painters began as Impressionists, yet each abandoned that style to form his own highly personal art. The work of these painters formed a basis for several contemporary trends and for modern art in general. The Postimpressionists often exhibited together but, unlike the Impressionists, a close-knit, convivial group, they painted mainly alone. See also NEO-IMPRESSIONISM.

postmodernism Any of several artistic movements that have challenged the philosophy and practices of modern arts or literature since about the 1960s. In literature this has amounted to a reaction against an ordered view of the world and therefore against fixed ideas about the form and meaning of texts. In its reaction against modernist ideals (see MODERNISM) such as autotelic art and the original masterpiece, postmodern writing and art emphasize devices such as pastiche and parody and the stylized technique of the antinovel and magic realism. Postmodernism has also led to a proliferation of critical theories, most notably DECONSTRUCTION and its offshoots, and the breaking down of the distinction between "high" and pop culture.

postmortem See AUTOPSY

poststructuralism Movement in LITERARY CRITICISM begun in France in the late 1960s. Based on the linguistic theories of FERDINAND DE SAUSSURE, the anthropology of CLAUDE LEVI-STRAUSS (see STRUCTURALISM), and the deconstructionist theories of JACQUES DERRIDA (see DECONSTRUCTION), it centers on the idea that language is not a transparency through which we see "truth" or "reality" but rather a structure or code that cannot possess absolute meaning in itself. Poststructuralists believe that all meaning resides in "intertextuality," the relationship of the text to past and nonliterary text and codes, and reject the traditional Western insistence on a single correct reading of a text. Writers associated with the movement include ROLAND BARTHES, JACQUES LACAN, JULIA KRISTEVA, and MICHEL FOUCAULT.

Potala Palace \'pō-tə-lə\ Religious and administrative complex, near LHASA, Tibet, China. It covers 5 sq mi (13 sq km) atop a hill 425 ft (130 m) above the Lhasa River valley. Potrang Karpo (the White Palace, completed 1648) once served as the seat of the Tibetan government and the main residence of the DALAI LAMA; from the mid-18th century it was used as a winter palace. Potrang Marpo (the Red Palace, 1694) houses several chapels, sacred statues, and the tombs of eight Dalai Lamas; it remains a major pilgrimage site for Tibetan Buddhists. The complex, which has a total of 1,000 rooms, was declared a WORLD HERITAGE SITE in 1994.

potash \'pät-ˌash\ Name used for various inorganic compounds of POTASSIUM, chiefly the CARBONATE (K_2CO_3), a white crystalline material formerly obtained from wood ashes. They are used to make special types of glass, potassium silicate (a dehydrating agent), pigments, printing inks, and soft soaps; for washing raw wool; and as a lab reagent and general-purpose food additive. Potassium hydroxide is frequently called caustic potash, and in the fertilizer industry, potassium oxide is called potash.

potash mica See MUSCOVITE

potassium Chemical ELEMENT, one of the ALKALI METALS, chemical symbol K, atomic number 19. It is a soft, silvery-white METAL, not found free in nature and hardly ever used as the metal (except as a chemical reagent) because of its extreme reactivity. Potassium is essential for life and is present in all soils. Potassium IONS (K^+) and SODIUM ions act at cell membranes in electrochemical impulse transmission and in TRANSPORT. Potassium in compounds has VALENCE 1. The chloride is used as a fertilizer and a raw material for producing other compounds and the HYDROXIDE for making liquid soaps and detergents and in preparing various SALTS. The iodide is added to table salt to protect against IODINE DEFICIENCY. The NITRATE is also called SALTPETER, and the CARBONATE is called POTASH.

potassium-argon dating Method for determining the age of igneous rocks based on the amount of argon-40 in the rock. Radioactive potassium-40 decays to argon-40 with a half-life of about 1.3 billion years, making this method useful for dating rocks that are billions of years old. A more sophisticated method, called argon-argon dating, provides a more accurate estimate of the original potassium-40 content by means of the ratio of argon-40 to argon-39 in the rock, thus yielding a more accurate age determination.

potato Herbaceous annual *(Solanum tuberosum)* in the NIGHTSHADE FAMILY. One of the world's main food crops, the potato differs from other food crops in that the edible portion is a TUBER. Highly digestible, potatoes are prepared for eating in many ways and are a major source of starch as well as amino acids, protein, vitamin C, and B vitamins. The stem grows 20–40 in. (50–100 cm) tall, sprouting spirally arranged compound leaves. Underground, stems extend as STOLONS, the ends of which enlarge into 1–20 tubers of variable shape and size. The tubers have spirally arranged buds (eyes) that may remain dormant after the tuber is fully grown for up to 10 weeks or more; they grow into plants identical to the parent plant. A native of the Andes, the potato (also known as the common potato, white potato, or Irish potato) was carried by Spaniards into Europe during the 16th century. A century later, it had become the major food crop in Ireland; disastrous damage to the crop by a fungal blight caused the IRISH POTATO FAMINE in the mid-1800s. See also SWEET POTATO.

Potato (*Solanum tuberosum*).
GRANT HEILMAN

potato beetle Destructive species *(Lema trilineata)* of leaf BEETLE (family Chrysomelidae). Less than 0.25 in. (6 mm) long, it is yellow and has three black stripes on its wing covers. Eggs are laid on the underside of a potato leaf, on which both larvae and adults feed. The larvae are camouflaged by excrement the beetles pile on their back. Two generations are produced each year; the second overwinters in the ground in the pupal stage. See also COLORADO POTATO BEETLE.

potato bug See COLORADO POTATO BEETLE

Potemkin \pə-'tyem-kin\, **Grigory (Aleksandrovich)** (1739–1791) Russian army officer. He entered the horse guards (1755) and helped bring CATHERINE II to power (1762). He fought with distinction in the RUSSO-TURKISH WAR (1768–74), then became Catherine's lover (1774–76) and was made governor-general of "New Russia" (S Ukraine). In 1783 she made him prince of Tauris. As a field marshal from 1784, he introduced reforms in the army, built the harbor of Sevastopol, and constructed a fleet in the Black Sea. He attempted unsuccessfully to colonize the Ukrainian steppes, but underestimated the costs, leaving many projects half-complete; his successful disguising of the weak points of his administration led to the claim that he erected mere facades—"Potemkin villages"—to show Catherine on her tour of the region. He commanded the Russian army in the second Russo-Turkish war.

Potemkin, engraving by James Walker, 1789, after a portrait by Johann Baptist Lampi.

potential, electric See ELECTRIC POTENTIAL

potential energy Energy stored by an object by virtue of its position. For example, an object raised above the ground acquires potential energy equal to the WORK done against the force of gravity; the energy is released as KINETIC ENERGY when it falls back to the ground. Similarly, a stretched spring has stored potential energy that is released when the spring is returned to its unstretched state. Other forms of potential energy include electrical potential energy, CHEMICAL ENERGY, and NUCLEAR ENERGY.

Potenza \pō-'tent-sä\ *ancient* **Potentia** City (pop., 2001 est.: 69,295), capital of BASILICATA region, southern Italy. Located at 2,684 ft (819 m) above sea level in the APENNINES, the Roman city Potentia was founded in the 2nd century BC and became an important road junction and flourishing community. In medieval times it had a succession of feudal overlords. In 1860 it was the first town in southern Italy to expel the Bourbon rulers of the kingdom of the Two SICILIES. The town has been rebuilt several times after earthquake damage. It is an agricultural center and ships fruit and vegetables.

potestas patria See PATRIA POTESTAS

potlatch Ceremonial distribution of property and gifts practiced among the American Indians of the northwestern Pacific coast, particularly the KWAKIUTL. A potlatch was given by an heir or successor to assert and validate his newly assumed social position. Ceremonial formalities were observed in inviting guests, in speechmaking, and distributing goods according to the social rank of the recipients. Great feasts and generous hospitality accompanied the potlatch. The ceremony has been much studied by anthropologists for the light it sheds on the nature of property, wealth, prestige, and SOCIAL STATUS. See also GIFT EXCHANGE.

Potok \'pō-täk\, **Chaim** *orig.* **Herman Harold Potok** (1929–2002) U.S. rabbi and novelist. The son of Polish immigrants, he was reared in an Orthodox Jewish home and was ordained a Conservative rabbi. He taught until he began a career as an editor and writer of scholarly and popular articles and reviews in the 1960s. His novels, which have introduced to U.S. fiction the spiritual and cultural life of Orthodox Jews, include *The Chosen* (1967; film, 1981), *The Promise* (1969), *My Name Is Asher Lev* (1972), *Davita's Harp* (1985), and *The Gift of Asher Lev* (1990).

Potomac River \pə-'tō-mək\ River, eastern central U.S. Rising in the APPALACHIAN MTNS. of West Virginia, it is about 287 mi (462 km) long. It flows southeast through the DISTRICT OF COLUMBIA into CHESAPEAKE BAY. It is navigable by large vessels to WASHINGTON, D.C., above which it descends in a series of rapids and falls, including Great Falls. Noted for its beauty, the Potomac is also rich in history. MOUNT VERNON, home of GEORGE WASHINGTON, is on its banks below Washington, D.C. The CHESAPEAKE AND OHIO CANAL NATIONAL HISTORICAL PARK parallels the river.

Potosí \ˌpō-tō-'sē\ City (pop., 2001: 132,966), southwestern Bolivia. Founded in 1545 after the discovery of silver in a neighboring mountain, it grew to be the most populous city in Latin America. Its population declined (after peaking at 160,000 c. 1650) drastically with the slackening of silver production but expanded in the 19th–20th century with the introduction of industries, including tin mining. One of the highest cities in the world, at an altitude of 13,700 ft (4,176 m), it is a major Bolivian industrial center.

Potsdam City (pop., 1998 est.: 136,077) and capital of BRANDENBURG state, Germany. It is located on the HAVEL RIVER, southwest of BERLIN. First mentioned in 993 as a Slav settlement, it was chartered in 1317. It became the electoral residence of the margrave of Brandenburg in 1640 under FREDERICK WILLIAM, the Great Elector. It was the Prussian royal residence under FREDERICK II, during whose reign it was a military and intellectual center. It was severely damaged during World War II, but many monuments survived and others have been restored. In 1945 it was the site of the POTSDAM CONFERENCE. Industries include locomotives, engineering, and textiles. It is the site of several scientific and technical institutions.

Potsdam Conference (July 17–August 2, 1945) Allied conference held in the Berlin suburb of Potsdam after Germany's surrender in WORLD WAR II. HARRY TRUMAN, JOSEPH STALIN, and WINSTON CHURCHILL (later replaced by CLEMENT R. ATTLEE) met to discuss European peace settlements, occupation of Germany and Austria, reparations, political and territorial plans for Eastern Europe, and the continuing war against Japan. France was allowed to share in the occupation, the Polish-German borders were redrawn, and Stalin refused to let the Western powers interfere with his control of Eastern Europe.

Potter, (Helen) Beatrix (1866–1943) English author and illustrator of children's books. In her childhood Potter spent holidays in Scotland and the English Lake District, which inspired her love of animals and stimulated her imaginative and technically superb watercolor drawings. The illustrated animal stories she sent to a sick child when she was 27 were published as *The Tale of Peter Rabbit* (1902), which became one of the best-selling children's book of all time. More than 20 sequels followed, featuring such original characters as Jeremy Fisher, Jemima Puddle-Duck, and Mrs. Tiggy-Winkle.

Beatrix Potter, 1913.

Potter, Dennis (Christopher George) (1935–1994) British dramatist. Educated at Oxford, he thereafter devoted himself to writing, especially of television plays. His innovative serial *Pennies from Heaven* (1978) combined fantasy sequences and musical interludes in which actors lip-synched to old recordings of period songs. His best-known teleplay, the eight-part *The Singing Detective* (1986), an autobiographical account of his crippling bouts of psoriatic arthropathy, combined humor, pathos, and fantastic musical numbers. His other teleplays included the allegedly sacrilegious *Brimstone and Treacle* (1976, televised 1987) and *Lipstick on Your Collar* (1993). His movie screenplays include *Gorky Park* (1983) and *Dreamchild* (1985).

pottery One of the oldest and most widespread of the decorative arts, consisting of objects (mostly useful ones, such as vessels, plates, and bowls) made of clay and hardened with heat. EARTHENWARE is the oldest and simplest form; STONEWARE is fired at a high temperature to cause it to vitrify and harden; and PORCELAIN is a fine, generally translucent form of pottery. The Chinese began their sophisticated production of pottery in the Neolithic Period and produced porcelain as early as the 7th century AD. Chinese porcelain, or "china," was widely exported to Europe and had a profound influence on European manufacturers and on taste. Classical Greece and Islamic cultures are also known for their artistic and technical innovations in pottery.

Poujade \pü-'zhäd\, **Pierre (-Marie)** (born 1920) French political leader. The owner of a bookstore in St-Céré, in 1953 he organized a local shopkeepers' strike to protest high taxation. Expanding his activities to other towns, he enrolled 800,000 members in his Union for the Defense of Tradesmen and Artisans. His right-wing movement, known as Poujadism, attracted discontented farmers and merchants; in 1956 it won 52 seats in the national assembly. Poujade's influence soon waned, but in the 1970s he founded an organization for nonunion workers.

Poulenc \'pü-ˌlaŋk\, **Francis (Jean Marcel)** (1899–1963) French composer. In his teens, he studied piano with Ricardo Viñes (1875–1943) and met ERIK SATIE and the composers of Les SIX. He wrote piano and orchestral music, including concertos for harpsichord, two pianos, and organ, and chamber music, but is best known for his vocal music, including the operas *Les mamelles de Tirésias* (1944), *Dialogues of the Carmelites* (1956), and *La voix humaine* (1958), such sacred choral works as the Mass in G (1937), the *Stabat mater* (1950), and the *Gloria* (1959), reflecting his devout Catholicism, and many admired songs.

poultry farming Raising birds commercially or domestically for meat, eggs, and feathers. Chickens, ducks, turkeys, and geese are the birds of primary commercial importance. GUINEA FOWL and squabs are chiefly of local interest. Though chickens have been domesticated for at least 4,000 years, their meat and eggs have been mass-production commodities only since c. 1800.

pound Unit of weight in the avoirdupois system, the traditional European system of weight (incorporated into the British Imperial system and the U.S. system of weights and measures), equal to 16 oz, 7,000 grains, or 0.4536 kg. It is also a unit of weight in the troy and apothecaries' systems (two other traditional systems of weight), equal to 12 troy or apothecaries' oz, 5,760 grains, or 0.37 kg. Its Roman ancestor, the *libra*, is the source of the abbreviation *lb*. The troy pound is used for precious metals, the apothecaries' pound for drugs. The British monetary pound is linked historically with the minting of silver coins (sterlings). Large payments were reckoned in "pounds of sterlings," later shortened to "pounds sterling." See also GRAM, INTERNATIONAL SYSTEM OF UNITS, MEASUREMENT, METRIC SYSTEM, OUNCE.

Pound, Ezra (Loomis) (1885–1972) U.S. poet and critic. Born in Hailey, Idaho, Pound attended Hamilton College and the University of Pennsylvania, where he studied various languages. In 1908 he sailed for Europe, where he would spend most of his life. He soon became a leader of IMAGISM and a dominant influence in Anglo-American verse, helping promote such writers as WILLIAM BUTLER YEATS, JAMES JOYCE, ERNEST HEMINGWAY, ROBERT FROST, D. H. LAWRENCE, and T. S. ELIOT, whose *Waste Land* he brilliantly edited. After World War I he published two of his most important poems, "Homage to Sextus Propertius" (1919) and *Hugh Selwyn Mauberley* (1920). He also began publishing *The Cantos,* an attempt at an epic sequence of poems, which would remain his major poetic occupation throughout his life. With the onset of the Great Depression, he increasingly pursued his interest in history and economics, became obsessed with monetary reform, and declared his admiration for BENITO MUSSOLINI. In World War II he made pro-Fascist radio broadcasts; detained by U.S. forces for treason in 1945, he was initially held at Pisa; *The Pisan Cantos* (1948, Bollingen Prize), written there, are notably moving. He was subsequently held in an American mental hospital until 1958, when he returned to Italy. *The Cantos* (1970) collects his 117 completed cantos.

Pound, Roscoe (1870–1964) U.S. legal educator and botanist. Born in Lincoln, Neb., he became a lawyer after studying at Harvard, and later obtained a PhD in botany (1897). At the University of Nebraska he directed the state botanical survey (1892–1903) and discovered a rare fungus (*Roscopoundia*). He later taught at several law schools, most notably Harvard (1910–37), where he also served as dean (1916–36), instituting many reforms. He was perhaps the chief U.S. advocate of sociological jurisprudence, which holds that statutes and court decisions are affected by social conditions; his ideas apparently influenced FRANKLIN ROOSEVELT'S NEW DEAL programs. After World War II he helped reorganize the Nationalist Chinese judicial system.

Roscoe Pound.
BY COURTESY OF THE LIBRARY OF CONGRESS, WASHINGTON, D.C.

Poussin \pü-'sa^n\, **Nicolas** (1594–1665) French painter. Except for two years as court painter to Louis XIII, he spent his entire career in Rome, where he became an admirer of ancient Roman civilization. In early works, he depicted themes from classical mythology in a painterly style reminiscent of such Venetian masters as TITIAN. Turning to RAPHAEL for inspiration, he began in the mid-1630s to develop a style marked by classical clarity and monumentality (e.g., *The Rape of the Sabine Women*, c. 1637, and the *Seven Sacraments* series, 1634–42). His late masterworks, such as *Holy Family on the Steps* (1648), employ a style calculated to express virtue and rectitude, featuring only a few figures painted in harsh colors against a severe background. In his landscapes, such as *Landscape with Polyphemus* (1649), the disorder of nature is reduced to the order of geometry. His austere and highly ordered compositions influenced generations of French painters, including J.-L. DAVID, J.-A.-D. INGRES, and PAUL CEZANNE.

powder metallurgy Fabrication of METAL objects from a powder rather than CASTING from molten metal or FORGING at softening temperatures. In some cases the powder method is more economical, as in making metal parts such as gears for small machines, in which casting would involve considerable scrap loss. In other cases, melting is impractical (e.g., because the melting point of the metal is too high). Powder metallurgy is also used to produce a porous product that will allow a liquid or gas to pass through it. See also METALLURGY, SINTERING.

Powder River River, northern Wyoming and southeastern Montana. It rises in the foothills of the BIGHORN MTNS. in Wyoming and flows north 486 mi (782 km) to join the YELLOWSTONE RIVER near Terry, Mont. Tributaries include the Little Powder River and Crazy Woman Creek.

Powderly, Terence V(incent) (1849–1924) U.S. labor leader. Born in Carbondale, Pa., the son of Irish immigrants, he became a railroad worker at age 13 and a machinist's apprentice at 17. He joined the Machinists' and Blacksmiths' Union in 1871. Three years later he joined the secret order of the KNIGHTS OF LABOR, and in 1879 he was chosen for its highest post, grand master workman. He presided over the union in its period of greatest membership, but attacks by opponents such as JAY GOULD caused membership to decline. Powderly became absorbed in internal disputes and finally resigned in 1893. See also LABOR UNION, URIAH SMITH STEPHENS.

Powell, Adam Clayton, Jr. (1908–1972) U.S. politician. Born in New Haven, Conn., he succeeded his father as pastor of the Abyssinian Baptist Church in New York's Harlem (1937) and built its membership to 13,000. He was elected to the New York City Council (1941), the first black to serve on that body. In the U.S. House of Representatives (1945–67, 1969–71), he sponsored much social legislation and effected passage of antipoverty acts and federal aid to education. Known for his flamboyance and unconcern for House decorum, he was the target of a libel suit and was investigated for financial misconduct. In 1967 the House voted to exclude him, but the U.S. Supreme Court later overturned its decision.

Powell \'pō-əl, 'pau̇(-ə)l\, **Anthony (Dymoke)** (1905–2000) British novelist. He published his first novel, *Afternoon Men* (1931), while working in a London publishing house. He worked in journalism and served in World War II before publishing the first of 12 novels in the autobiographical and satiric series *A Dance to the Music of Time* (1951–75). His best-known work, it reflects his outlook and experiences of English society in the decades before and after the war. His later novels include *The Fisher King* (1986).

Anthony Powell, 1974.
FAY GODWIN

Powell, Bud *orig.* **Earl Rudolph** (1924–1966) U.S. pianist and composer, one of the most influential piano soloists in modern jazz. Born in New York City, Powell played in Cootie Williams's big band (1942–44) before becoming part of the burgeoning activity of BEBOP in late-1940s. His style became the predominant approach for post–swing-era pianists: he did away with most accepted functions of the left hand, playing brief, syncopated chords supporting long melody lines by the right hand. He moved to Paris in 1959 and returned to the U.S. in 1964. His career was interrupted several times due to nervous breakdowns thought to derive from head injuries sustained in a racially motivated attack in 1945.

Powell, Colin (Luther) (born 1937) U.S. Army officer. Born in New York City, he entered the army after college and served in the Vietnam War. He held posts in the U.S. Department of Defense and in 1983 became senior military assistant to the secretary of defense. A staff member on the National Security Council (1987), he was appointed assistant for national security affairs to RONALD REAGAN (1988). Promoted to four-star general (1989), he was appointed by GEORGE BUSH as chairman of the Joint Chiefs of Staff, the first black officer to hold that post. He helped plan the invasion of Panama (1989) and the operations of the PERSIAN GULF WAR. Immensely popular, he declined to run for president in 1996. He became U.S. secretary of state under GEORGE W. BUSH in 2001.

Powell, John Wesley (1834–1902) U.S. geologist and ethnologist. Born in Mount Morris, N.Y., Powell became director of the U.S. Geological Survey in 1881, where he worked extensively on mapping water sources and advancing irrigation projects. He developed the first comprehensive classification of American Indian languages (1877) and was the first director of the SMITHSONIAN INSTITUTION's Bureau of American Ethnology (1879–1902). He described some of his many expeditions down the Colorado River (1871–79) in *Exploration of the Colorado River of the West and Its Tributaries* (1875).

Powell, Lewis F(ranklin), Jr. (1907–1998) U.S. jurist. Born in Suffolk, Va., he studied law at Washington and Lee University and Harvard Univ., then returned to practice law in Virginia. As chairman of the Richmond school board, he oversaw peaceful school integration in 1959; he later chaired the state board of education and served as president of the American Bar Association. He reluctantly acquiesced when Pres. RICHARD NIXON nominated him for the U.S. Supreme Court in 1971; he took his seat in 1972 and served until 1987. He took moderate-to-liberal stances on civil rights, affirmative action, and separation of church and state, and was conservative on law enforcement.

Powell, Michael (Latham) (1905–1990) British film director. He directed his first movie, *Two Crowded Hours,* in 1931 and made over 20 low-budget films before ALEXANDER KORDA teamed him with screenwriter Emeric Pressburger (1902–1988) to make the successful *U-Boat 29* (1939). Forming their own production company, they made such movies as *The Thief of Bagdad* (1940), *The Life and Death of Colonel Blimp* (1943), *Stairway to Heaven* (1946), *Black Narcissus* (1947), *The Red Shoes* (1948; often called their greatest film), *The Tales of Hoffmann* (1951), and the controversial *Peeping Tom* (1960). Powell's films were notable for their use of brilliant color, fantasy, and experimental cinematography.

Powell, Robert Baden- See Robert S. BADEN-POWELL

Powell, William (1892–1984) U.S. film actor. Born in Pittsburgh, he acted on Broadway from 1912 and made his screen debut in *Sherlock Holmes* (1922). He played villains in the silent movies, and with the coming of sound he moved into light mysteries, playing his first detective in *The Canary Murder Case* (1929). He became a leading star as the sophisticated, bemused detective Nick Charles, opposite MYRNA LOY, in the hit *The Thin Man* (1934) and its successful sequels. His later notable films included *The Great Ziegfeld* (1936), *My Man Godfrey* (1936), and *Life with Father* (1947).

power In science and engineering, the time rate of doing WORK or delivering ENERGY. Power (P) can be expressed as the amount of work done (W), or energy transferred, divided by the time interval (t): $P = W/t$. A given amount of work can be done by a low-powered motor in a long time or by a high-powered motor in a short time. Units of power are those of work (or energy) per unit time, such as foot-pounds per minute, joules per second (called watts), or ergs per second. Power can also be expressed as the product of the FORCE (f) applied to move an object and the speed (v) of the object in the direction of the force: $P = fv$. See also HORSEPOWER.

Power, Charles Gavan (1888–1968) Canadian politician. Born in Sillery, Quebec, he was seriously wounded in World War I. He served in the Canadian House of Commons 1917–55. In W.L. MACKENZIE KING's government he served as minister for pensions and national health (1935–39) and postmaster general (1939–40). As minister for national defense for air (1940–44), he promoted the interests of Canadian air forces serving under British command and created Canadian squadrons in Europe.

Power, Tyrone (Edmund) (1914–1958) U.S. actor. Born in Cincinnati, the descendant of a long line of actors, he toured with a Shakespearean repertory company before making his Broadway debut in *Romeo and Juliet* (1935). His first film hit was *Lloyds of London* (1936). He became noted for his action-adventure roles in such movies as *The Rains Came* (1939), *The Mark of Zorro* (1940), *Blood and Sand* (1941), *Nightmare Alley* (1947), and *The Mississippi Gambler* (1953), while continuing to act on stage in such plays as *Saint Joan* (1936), *Mister Roberts* (1950), and *Back to Methuselah* (1958).

power of attorney See power of ATTORNEY

Powers, Hiram (1805–1873) U.S.-Italian sculptor. Born in Woodstock, Vt., he worked as an artist-assistant in a waxworks museum in Cincinnati, then moved to Washington, D.C., where he modeled busts of such figures as ANDREW JACKSON (1834). In 1837 he settled permanently in Florence. He attracted international notoriety with his marble *Greek Slave* (1843), an image of a nude young woman in chains, which caused a sensation at London's Crystal Palace Exposition in 1851. An artist of outstanding technical ability, he was one of the most popular sculptors of his time.

"Greek Slave," marble statue by Hiram Powers, 1843; in the Corcoran Gallery of Art, Washington, D.C.

BY COURTESY OF THE CORCORAN GALLERY OF ART, WASHINGTON, D.C.

Powhatan \ˌpau̇-ə-ˈtan, pau̇-ˈha-tᵊn\ (died 1618) North American Indian chief, father of POCAHONTAS. At the peak of his power he allegedly controlled 128 villages (about 9,000 inhabitants) of the POWHATAN confederacy. He did not oppose the English settlement at JAMESTOWN, but some of his tribesmen persistently attacked isolated groups of settlers. In 1614 Pocahontas married a settler, and shortly thereafter Powhatan negotiated a peace agreement.

Powhatan Confederacy of at least 30 ALGONQUIAN-speaking North American Indian tribes that once occupied most of tidewater Virginia and the eastern shore of Chesapeake Bay. It was named for its powerful chief, POWHATAN, to whom the tribes provided military support and paid taxes in the form of goods. Many of the villages, consisting of long dwellings covered with bark or reed mats, were palisaded. Powhatan women cultivated corn, beans, and squash; the men hunted and waged war, chiefly against the IROQUOIS. The intermittent hostilities with the English settlers often called the Powhatan War (1622–44) ended with the breaking of the confederacy. Today about 3,000 Powhatan live along the Virginia coast.

powwow American Indian ceremony or gathering of any of various kinds. The term was originally used for healing ceremonies, but it could also refer to exuberant celebrations, with dancing and singing, of success in hunting or victory in battle. Meetings of tribal councils were also often termed powwows. Today the word is used for large-scale Indian social gatherings, often representing more than one tribe, with traditional drumming, singing, and dancing. Modern powwows draw tourists as well as participants, and craft items and souvenirs are offered for sale.

Powys \ˈpō-əs\ Area, eastern central Wales. Now a Welsh county, with its seat at LLANDRIDOD WELLS, it is named after the Welsh princedom of Powys, located in the border country between Wales and England. At its most powerful in the 12th century, the princedom was unable to gain ascendancy in Wales because it was so close to the border area where the cultures of Wales and England intermingled. Main elements in the landscape are the valley lowlands leading to SHREWSBURY and HEREFORD. There are remains of Iron Age and Roman settlements.

poxvirus Any of a group of VIRUSES responsible for a wide range of pox diseases in humans and other animals. Poxvirus was the cause of SMALLPOX. (Human CHICKEN POX is caused by herpes varicella–zoster.) The virus particle is somewhat brick-shaped, and its surface is studded with hollow spikes. It contains DNA. Unlike other DNA viruses, poxviruses appear to develop entirely within the CYTOPLASM of affected cells. The virus of rabbit pox has been used with mixed success in Australia to control the wild rabbit population.

Poynings \'pȯi-ˌniŋz\, **Edward** *later* **Sir Edward** (1459–1521) English soldier and administrator. A supporter of Henry Tudor (later HENRY VII), he served as the king's lord deputy of Ireland (1494–95), where he enacted legislative measures ("Poynings' Laws") that applied all English public laws to Ireland and required every act of the Irish parliament to be approved by the king and privy council.

Poznań \'pȯz-ˌnän\ *German* **Posen** \'pōz-ᵊn\ City (pop., 1996 est.: 582,000), western central Poland, on the WARTA RIVER. One of the oldest cities in Poland, dating from the 9th century AD, it reached the height of prosperity as a trade center from the 15th to the 17th century, but declined after the Second NORTHERN WAR. In 1793 it was annexed to PRUSSIA, intensifying a Germanization that had begun in the 13th century. In 1918 it reverted to Poland. During World War II it was occupied by the Germans and suffered extensive damage. Rebuilt after the war, it has become the administrative, industrial, and cultural center of western Poland. It is also an academic center with scientific and literary institutes. Its varied industries include textile mills, metallurgical works, and chemical plants.

Practical Learning School *or* **Silhak** School of thought that arose in 18th-century Korea, dedicated to a practical approach to statecraft. It attacked NEO-CONFUCIANISM, particularly its formalism and concern with ritual. Members of the school originated many ideas for social reform and the development of farming. Notable contributors include Yi Ik (1681–1763), who wrote on land reform and the abolition of class barriers, and Pak Chi-won (1737–1805), who advocated the development of commerce and technology. The school contributed to the wave of modernization that occurred after the introduction of Western culture into Korea in the late 19th century.

practical reason Rational capacity by which (rational) agents guide their conduct. In IMMANUEL KANT's moral philosophy, it is defined as the capacity of a rational being to act according to principles (i.e., according to the conception of laws). Unlike the ethical intuitionists (see INTUITIONISM), Kant never held that practical reason intuits the rightness of particular actions or moral principles. For him, practical reason was basically formal rather than material, a framework of formative principles rather than a source of specific rules. This is why he put such stress on his first formulation of the CATEGORICAL IMPERATIVE. Lacking any insight into the moral realm, humans can only ask themselves if what they are proposing to do has the formal character of law, namely, the character of being the same for all persons similarly circumstanced.

Prado Museum \'prä-dō\ Spain's national art museum, housing the world's greatest collection of Spanish painting as well as other European works. Founded in Madrid in 1818 by FERDINAND VII, it was opened to the public in 1819 as the Royal Museum of Painting. Its holdings were formed over three centuries from the various royal collections of the Habsburg and Bourbon monarchs in Spain. In 1868 it became the National Museum of the Prado after the exile of ISABELLA II. In 1872 it acquired many notable paintings formerly owned by Spanish convents and monasteries. It owns the outstanding collections of the works of El GRECO, DIEGO VELAZQUEZ, and FRANCISCO GOYA, and numerous works by such other Spanish masters as JOSE DE RIBERA and FRANCISCO ZURBARAN. Among its other holdings are collections of Greco-Roman statuary and many Flemish and Italian masterpieces.

Praeneste \prē-'nes-tē\ *modern* **Palestrina** Ancient city, LATIUM, in central Italy, on a spur of the APENNINES. Founded before the 8th century BC, it saw many battles with Rome before becoming part of the ROMAN EMPIRE. It was a major center for the cult of the goddess Fortuna, whose sanctuary and temple oracle were surrounded by an immense complex of buildings. It became a favorite summer resort of wealthy Romans, including AUGUSTUS, HADRIAN, and PLINY THE YOUNGER. The modern town was the birthplace of G.P. DA PALESTRINA.

praetor \'prē-tər\ In ancient Rome, an officer with authority to judge cases of equity and, in the absence of CONSULS, in the government. He also produced the public games. After a one-year term, a praetor typically went on to govern a province. Originally open only to PATRICIAN magistrates, the post could be held by PLEBEIANS from c. 337 BC. The number of praetors increased to eight by the 1st century BC, two for civil matters and six for specific courts. It continued to vary under different government leaders and emperors; by the late empire, only the city praetor for public games remained.

Praetorian Guard \prē-'tōr-ē-ən\ (Latin, *cohors praetoria*) Household troops of the Roman emperors. In the 2nd century BC they were bodyguards for Roman generals, their name taken from the general's tent (*praetorium).* During the civil wars, military leaders had personal bodyguards, but in 27 BC AUGUSTUS created a permanent corps to guard the emperor and stationed its members around Rome. In AD 23, with SEJANUS as commander, they gained political influence; from then on, they usually had an important voice in appointing emperors. They were responsible for the accession of CLAUDIUS (41), the disorders of 68–69, the lynching of DOMITIAN's murderers (97), and the murder of ELAGABALUS (222). CONSTANTINE I disbanded the body in 312.

Pragmatic Sanction (1713) Decree by Emperor CHARLES VI requiring the undivided descent of his Habsburg domains. It stipulated that his heritage go to his eldest son or, in the absence of a son, to his eldest daughter. It became law in 1720 within the Habsburg states, and much of Charles's later reign was directed toward securing acceptance of the sanction from the other European powers. Since his son died soon after birth (1716), his daughter MARIA THERESA became his heir. On Charles's death (1740), the sanction was contested by Prussia and Bavaria, which led to the War of the AUSTRIAN SUCCESSION.

Pragmatic Sanction of Bourges \'bürzh\ (July 7, 1438) Decree issued by King Charles VII of France after the Council of BASEL, confirming the supremacy of a council over the pope. The decree also confirmed the Council's assertion of the "liberties" of the Gallican Church, restricting the rights of the pope and in many cases making his jurisdiction subject to the king's. Revoked by LOUIS XI in 1461, the Pragmatic Sanction was reasserted periodically until the 16th century.

pragmatics Branch of LINGUISTICS and philosophy of language that studies the relationship between linguistic expressions and their users. It is usually defined in contrast to SYNTAX and SEMANTICS as the study of the rules and conventions governing the use of meaningful expressions to perform communicative acts (see SPEECH ACT THEORY). A distinction between semantics and pragmatics is reflected in the distinction between the strict and literal meaning of the words uttered by a speaker (studied in semantics) and their meaning when uttered on a particular occasion (studied in pragmatics). Irony and metaphor provide examples of the divergence between a sentence's literal meaning and the meaning of a particular utterance of the sentence.

pragmatism Philosophical movement first given systematic expression by CHARLES SANDERS PEIRCE and WILLIAM JAMES and later taken up and transformed by JOHN DEWEY. Pragmatists emphasize the practical function of knowledge as an instrument for adapting to reality and controlling it. Pragmatism agrees with EMPIRICISM in emphasizing the priority of experience over A PRIORI reasoning. While truth had traditionally been explained either in terms of coherence (see COHERENTISM) or in terms of correspondence with reality, pragmatism held that truth is to be found in the process of verification. Pragmatists interpret ideas as instruments and plans of action. In contrast to the conception of ideas as images of reality, pragmatism emphasizes the functional character of ideas: ideas are suggestions and anticipations of possible conduct, hypotheses or forecasts of what will result from a given action, or ways of organizing behavior in the world rather than replicas of the world. See also W. V. O. QUINE, RICHARD RORTY.

Prague \'präg\ City (pop., 1996 est.: 1,210,000), capital of the Czech Republic, situated on both sides of the VLTAVA RIVER. The site was settled as early as the 9th century AD. By the 14th century it was one of Europe's leading cultural and trade centers. It was the center of opposition to the HABSBURGS in the early 17th century (see Defenestration of PRA-

O P Q R

GUE). The treaty ending the Austro–Prussian War was signed there in 1866. It became the capital of an independent Czechoslovakia in 1918. It was occupied by Germany during World War II and by the U.S.S.R. and other WARSAW PACT military forces in 1968 (see PRAGUE SPRING). In 1989 it was the center of a movement that led to the peaceful overthrow of the Communist government. Prague is the country's major economic and cultural center, famous for its music, literature, and architecture.

Prague, Defenestration of (May 23, 1618) Incident of Bohemian resistance to Habsburg authority. In 1617 Catholic officials in Bohemia closed Protestant chapels in violation of the religious-liberty guarantee of 1609. At an assembly called by the Protestants, the imperial regents were found guilty of violating the guarantee and were thrown from the windows of the council room of Prague Castle. Though the victims were not seriously hurt, the incident sparked the Bohemian revolt against Emperor FERDINAND II and led to the THIRTY YEARS' WAR.

Prague Spring (1968) Brief period of liberalization in Czechoslovakia under ALEXANDER DUBCEK. In April 1968 he instituted agricultural and industrial reforms, a revised constitution to guarantee civil rights, autonomy for Slovakia, and democratization of the government and the Communist Party. By June, many Czechs were calling for more rapid progress toward real democracy. Though Dubček believed he could control the situation, the Soviet Union and the WARSAW PACT countries, alarmed by the threat of a social-democratic Czechoslovakia, invaded the country in August, deposed Dubček, and gradually restored control by reinstalling hard-line communists as leaders.

Praia \'prī-ə\ City (pop., 1995 est.: 68,000), port, and capital of Cape Verde. It is located on the southern shore of São Tiago (Santiago) Island, in the Atlantic Ocean, about 400 mi (640 km) off the western African bulge. It ships agricultural products, including bananas, coffee, and sugarcane, and is a submarine cable station.

prairie Level or rolling grassland, especially that found in central North America. Decreasing amounts of rainfall, from 40 in. (100 cm) at the forested eastern edge to less than 12 in. (30 cm) at the desertlike western edge, affect the species composition of the prairie grassland. The vegetation is composed primarily of perennial grasses, with many species of flowering plants of the pea and composite families. The three main types of prairie are the tallgrass prairie; midgrass, or mixed-grass, prairie; and shortgrass prairie, or shortgrass plains. Coastal prairie, Pacific or California prairie, Palouse prairie, and desert plains grassland are covered primarily with combinations of mixed-grass and shortgrass species.

prairie chicken Either of two species of North American GROUSE (genus *Tympanuchus*) noted for lek displays (group courtship displays). The greater prairie chicken is about 18 in. (45 cm) long and may weigh almost 2 lbs (1 kg). Its brown plumage is strongly barred below, and it has a short, rounded, dark tail. It occurs locally from Saskatchewan to coastal Texas and Louisiana; northernmost birds are somewhat migratory. The eastern subspecies, the heath hen, is extinct. The lesser prairie chicken, smaller and paler, inhabits the arid western central Great Plains. The sharp-tailed grouse *(Pedioecetes)* is locally called prairie chicken.

prairie dog Any of five species (genus *Cynomys*) of stout, short-legged, terrestrial SQUIRRELS, named for their barklike call. Once abundant throughout the western U.S. and northern Mexican plains, they are now found mostly in protected areas of Wyoming, Texas, Oklahoma, and South Dakota. They are 12–17 in. (30–43 cm) long, including a 1–5-in. (3–12-cm) tail. Their main diet is grass. Colonies consist of well-defined territories defended by a male, several females, and young. The burrows of the black-tailed prairie dog have carefully tended funnel-shaped entry mounds that prevent flooding and serve as lookout posts. The white-tailed prairie dog inhabits higher altitudes, hibernates, and is less colonial.

Prairie school Style of architecture produced in the American Midwest by FRANK LLOYD WRIGHT, George Grant Elmslie (1871–1952), Barry Byrne (1883–1967), and others c. 1900–17. Prairie houses were generally built of brick, wood, and plaster, with stucco walls and bands of casement windows. The Prairie architects emphasized horizontal lines, using low roofs with wide, projecting eaves. They discarded elaborate floor plans and detailing for flowing internal spaces organized around a central fireplace or hearth. The resulting low, spreading structures are characterized by light, crossing volumes and spaces; they reach out to nature, not other buildings.

Prajapati \prə-'jä-pə-tē\ Creator figure in the Vedic period of India. In early Vedic literature (see VEDA), the name was applied to various primal figures. Later it signified one deity, the "lord of all creatures," who was said to have produced the universe and all its beings after preparing himself through ascetic practices. Other stories allude to his own creation from the primal waters. His female emanation was Vac, the personification of the sacred word; Usas, the dawn, was identified as his female partner or his daughter. In the post-Vedic age, Prajapati came to be identified with BRAHMA.

Prajnaparamita \'prəg-ˌnyä-'pär-ə-mē-ˌtä\ Body of SUTRAS and their commentaries in MAHAYANA Buddhism. The main texts, written 100 BC–AD 150, represent *prajna* (wisdom) as the supreme perfection and the primary avenue to NIRVANA. The content of this wisdom is the realization that all phenomena are illusory. The name Prajnaparamita also refers to the personification of the literature or of wisdom, often depicted as a woman with hands in the teaching gesture or holding a lotus and sacred book.

Prajnaparamita, 13th-century stone sculpture from Singosari, East Java; in the Museum Pusat, Jakarta, Indonesia.

BY COURTESY OF THE RIJKSMUSEUM VOOR VOLKENKUNDE, LEIDEN, NETH.

prakriti and purusha \'prə-kri-tē...'pu̇-ru̇-shə\ In the SAMKHYA school of Indian philosophy, material nature and the soul. Prakriti is material nature in its germinal state, eternal and beyond perception. When it comes into contact with the soul or self (purusha), it starts a process of evolution that leads through several stages to the creation of the existing material world. In the Samkhya view, only prakriti is active; the self, trapped in materiality, does nothing but observe and experience. The self escapes from prakriti by recognizing its total difference from and noninvolvement in the material world.

Pramudya Ananta Tur *or* **Pramoedya Ananta Toer** \prä-'müd-yä-ä-'nän-tä-'tür\ (born 1925) Javanese novelist and short-story writer. While imprisoned by the Dutch (1947–49) for his role in the Indonesian revolt against renewed colonial rule, Pramudya wrote his first published novel, *The Fugitive* (1950). After Indonesia gained independence in 1949, he began to produce works written in a rich style that incorporates everyday speech and images from classical Javanese culture. Imprisoned 1965–79 for his role in a communist coup attempt, he wrote a series of four novels—*This Earth of Mankind* (1980), *Child of All Nations* (1980), *Footsteps* (1985), and *House of Glass* (1988)—that depict Javanese society under Dutch rule. He is the preeminent prose writer of postindependence Indonesia.

Prandtl \'prän-tᵊl\, **Ludwig** (1875–1953) German physicist, considered the father of AERODYNAMICS. He taught at the University of Göttingen 1904–53. His 1904 discovery of the BOUNDARY LAYER at the surface of a body moving in air or water led to an understanding of skin friction DRAG and of the way streamlining (see STREAMLINE) reduces the drag of airplane wings and other moving bodies. His work on wing theory explained the process of airflow over airplane wings.

prasada \prə-'sä-də\ In HINDUISM, consecrated food offered to the deity and then distributed to worshipers, who consume it as a sign of the god's favor. Prasada is used both in temple ceremonies, where it may be offered to a god such as KRISHNA and then distributed by the priests, and at household shrines, where it is offered to the god and then handed out to household members. See also PUJA.

pratitya-samutpada \prə-'tēt-yə-ˌsə-mu̇t-'pä-də\ In BUDDHISM, the chain of causation that leads from rebirth to death. Existence is seen as an interrelated flux of transient events that occur in a series, one producing another, usually described as a chain of 12 links: (1) ignorance, which leads to (2) faulty perceptions of reality, which provide the structure of (3) knowledge, which addresses (4) name and form, or the principle of individual identity and the sensory perception of an object, experienced through (5) the six domains (the five senses and their object, along with the mind), whose presence leads to (6) contact (between objects and the senses), followed by (7) sensation, which, being pleasant, leads to (8) thirst and then (9) grasping (as of sex partners), which leads to (10) the process of becoming, culminating in (11) birth, and at last (12) old age and death.

Pratt, E(dwin) J(ohn) (1883–1964) Canadian poet. Born in Western Bay, Newfoundland, he trained for the ministry and later taught many years at the University of Toronto. The early collection *The Titans* (1926) contains his widely read "The Cachalot." *Brébeuf and His Brethren* (1940), perhaps his best work, chronicles the martyrdom of Jesuit missionaries. Later collections include *Dunkirk* (1941), *They Are Returning* (1945), *Behind the Log* (1947), and *Towards the Last Spike* (1952).

Pratt, Francis Ashbury (1827–1902) U.S. inventor. With Amos Whitney he founded the Pratt & Whitney Co. in Hartford, Conn., to manufacture machine tools. He was instrumental in bringing about adoption of a standard system of gauges. He also invented a metal-planing machine (1869), a gear cutter (1884), and a milling machine (1885).

Pratt Institute Private institution of higher learning in Brooklyn, N.Y. It was founded as a trade school in 1887 by the industrialist Charles Pratt (1830–1891). It comprises schools of architecture, art and design (for which it is especially renowned), liberal arts and sciences, professional studies, and information and library science. It has both bachelor's and master's degree programs. Enrollment is about 3,400.

pratyaya \prət-ˈyä-yə\ In Buddhism, an auxiliary, indirect cause, as distinguished from a direct cause *(hetu)*. A seed, for example, is the direct cause of a plant, whereas sunlight, water, and earth are the auxiliary causes. Sometimes pratyaya is used to refer to cause in general. The idea of causation is important in the Buddhist concept of the cycle of death and rebirth (see pratitya-samutpada).

pratyeka-buddha \prət-ˈyā-kə\ In Buddhism, one who attains enlightenment through his own efforts rather than by listening to the teachings of a buddha. The way of the self-enlightened buddha was retained only in the Theravada tradition. Mahayana Buddhism rejects the path of self-enlightenment as too limiting and embraces the ideal of the bodhisattva, who postpones final enlightenment to work for the salvation of others.

Pravda \ˈpräv-də\ (Russian: "Truth") Former daily newspaper published in Moscow and distributed nationwide, the official organ of the Communist Party of the Soviet Union 1918–91. It was founded in St. Petersburg as an underground paper by Vladimir Ilich Lenin and two colleagues in 1912. As a Soviet state newspaper and organ of information and education, it offered well-written articles and analyses on science, economics, cultural topics, and literature as well as materials to indoctrinate and inform readers on Communist theory and programs. International relations was largely left to the government paper *Izvestiya*. After Communist power ended in 1991, most of its readership evaporated; it became the voice of the conservative-nationalist opposition and ceased publication in 1996.

Praxiteles \prak-ˈsi-tᵊl-ˌēz\ (fl. c. 370–330 BC) Greek sculptor. His only known surviving work, the marble *Hermes Carrying the Infant Dionysus*, displays delicate modeling and exquisite surface finish. A few other works survive in Roman copies. His most celebrated work was the *Aphrodite of Cnidus,* which Pliny the Elder considered the best statue in the world. Through Praxiteles' influence, figures were increasingly shown standing in graceful, sinuous poses, leaning lightly on some support, a pose further developed by sculptors of the Hellenistic Age. Greatest and most original of the 4th-century Attic sculptors, he profoundly influenced the later course of Greek sculpture.

prayer Silent or spoken petition made to God or a god. Prayer has been practiced in all religions throughout history. Its characteristic postures (bowing the head, kneeling, prostration) and position of the hands (raised, outstretched, clasped) signify an attitude of submission and devotion. Prayer may involve confessions of sin, requests, thanks, praise, offerings of sacrifice, or promises of future acts of devotion. In addition to spontaneous private prayer, most religions have fixed formulas of prayer (e.g., the Lord's Prayer), often recited in group worship. The four prophetic religions (Judaism, Christianity, Islam, and Zoroastrianism) prescribe a daily set form of individual prayer, such as the *shema,* to be recited twice a day by every male Jew, and the Islamic *salat,* performed five times a day.

prayer wheel In Tibetan Buddhism, a mechanical device used as an equivalent to the recitation of a mantra. The prayer wheel consists of a hollow metal cylinder, often beautifully embossed, mounted on a rod and containing a consecrated paper bearing a mantra. Each turn of the wheel by hand is considered equivalent to orally reciting the prayer. Variants to the hand-held prayer wheel are large cylinders that can be set in motion by hand or attached to windmills or waterwheels and thus kept in continuous motion.

Tibetan prayer wheel, gilt silver, 18th–19th century; in the Seattle (Washington) Art Museum.

BY COURTESY OF THE SEATTLE ART MUSEUM, WASHINGTON, EUGENE FULLER MEMORIAL COLLECTION

Praygraj *formerly* **Allahabad** \ˈä-lä-hä-ˌbäd\ City (metro. area pop., 2001 prelim.: 1,049,579), northern India, on the Ganges and Yamuna rivers. An ancient holy city sacred to Hindu pilgrims, it is the site of the Pillar of Ashoka (erected 240 BC). Under Muslim rule 1194–1801, it was then ceded to the British. The Mughal emperor Akbar built a fort there in the late 16th century. It was the scene of a serious outbreak in the 1857 Indian Mutiny. As the home of the Nehru family, it was later a center of the Indian independence movement. It is the site of the Jama Masjid (Great Mosque) and Allahabad University.

praying mantis See mantis

Pre-Raphaelites \ˌprē-ˈrä-fē-ə-ˌlīts\ Group of young British painters, led by Dante Gabriel Rossetti, William Holman Hunt, and John Everett Millais, who banded together in 1848 in reaction against what they considered the unimaginative and artificial historical painting of the 18th and early 19th century, seeking to express a new moral seriousness and sincerity in their works. Their name, the Pre-Raphaelite Brotherhood, honored the simplicity in depicting nature in Italian art before Raphael, and the symbolism, imagery, and mannered style of their paintings often suggest a faux-medieval world. Later members included Edward Burne-Jones and George Frederic Watts (1817–1904). The group also functioned as a school of writers who often used medieval settings, sometimes with shocking effect, as in William Morris's *The Defence of Guenevere* (1858), which deals with issues of love and sex. Though active less than 10 years, the group had a profound influence on the arts.

pre-Socratics Earliest Greek philosophers (those who preceded Socrates) whose attention to questions about the origin and nature of the physical world has led to their being called cosmologists or naturalists. Among the most significant were the Milesians Thales, Anaximander, and Anaximenes, Xenophanes of Colophon, Parmenides, Heracleitus of Ephesus, Empedocles, Anaxagoras, Democritus, Zeno of Elea, and Pythagoras.

Preakness Stakes One of the three classic U.S. horse races making up the Triple Crown. It is held annually in mid-May at Baltimore's Pimlico Race Course. The course distance is 1 3/16 mi. (1.9 km). The field is limited to 3-year-old Thoroughbreds.

Prebisch \ˈprā-bish\, **Raúl** (1901–1986) Argentine economist and statesman. Serving in various positions in Argentine government and academia, he advised developing countries to stimulate domestic manufacturing to reduce their reliance on imports and thus their dependence on the industrialized nations. He also advocated economic integration of Latin America to achieve economies of scale and land reform to reduce the income inequalities that impeded growth of the domestic market. As the influential head of the U.N.'s Economic Commission for Latin

America, he addressed inequities in the trade relationships between wealthy and poor nations.

Precambrian time Interval of geologic time from c. 4 billion years ago, the age of the oldest known rocks, to 543 million years ago, the beginning of the CAMBRIAN PERIOD. This interval represents more than 80% of the geologic record and thus provides important evidence of how the continents evolved. The Precambrian is divided into the ARCHEAN and PROTEROZOIC eons, with the boundary between them at 2.5 billion years ago. It was originally defined as the era that predated the emergence of life in the CAMBRIAN PERIOD. It is now known, however, that life on the earth had begun by the early Archean. Soft-bodied organisms without skeletons began to appear toward the end of the Precambrian.

precast concrete Concrete cast into structural members under factory conditions and then brought to the building site. A 20th-century development, precasting increases the strength and finish durability of the member and decreases time and construction costs. Concrete cures slowly; the design strength is usually reached 28 days after initial setting. Using precast concrete eliminates the lag between the time on-site concrete is placed and the time it can carry loads. Precast concrete components include slabs, beams, columns, walls, stairways, modular boxes, and even kitchens and bathrooms with precast fixtures. See also PREFABRICATION.

precession Phenomenon associated with the action of a GYROSCOPE or a spinning top and consisting of a comparatively slow rotation of the axis of rotation of a spinning body about a line intersecting the spin axis. It arises as a result of external TORQUE acting on the body. One example of precession is the smooth, slow circling of a spinning top (the uneven wobbling is called nutation). Precession of the earth's axis of rotation is the reason that the positions of celestial bodies appear to drift systematically with the passage of time. See also precession of the EQUINOXES.

precipitation All liquid and solid water particles that fall from clouds and reach the ground, including drizzle, RAIN, SNOW, ice crystals, and HAIL. The essential difference between a precipitation particle and a cloud particle is size; an average raindrop has a mass equivalent to that of about 1 million cloud droplets. Precipitation elements (ice crystals or droplets that form around soluble particles such as salt) form directly from the vapor state and get larger through collision and coalescence. Eventually they become large enough to respond to gravity, and they fall to the ground.

Precisionism Smooth, precise technique used primarily in the 1920s by several U.S. painters in representational canvases depicting sharply defined forms, such as urban skylines; the industrial landscape of factories and smokestacks, buildings, and machinery; and country landscapes with grain elevators and barns or empty desert and sky. The scenes are always devoid of people or signs of human activity. Precisionism is a "cool" art, which keeps the viewer at a distance. It had its origins in Cubism, Futurism, and Orphism; in turn it influenced Pop art. Though it was not a school or movement with a formal program, the Precisionist artists, including CHARLES DEMUTH and GEORGIA O'KEEFFE, often exhibited together.

predation Form of food getting in which one animal, the predator, eats an animal of another species, the prey, immediately after killing it or, in some cases, while it is still alive. Most predators are generalists; they eat a variety of prey species. Specialist predators, such as ANTEATERS, eat only one or a few prey species. Cannibalism is a type of predation in which an animal eats another of its own species. Seed consumption is also considered predation because the entire living embryo of a plant is destroyed.

predestination In CHRISTIANITY, the doctrine that God has long ago determined who will be saved and who will be damned. Three types of predestination doctrine have developed. One doctrine holds that God singled out the saved because he foresaw their future merits. A second doctrine (often identified with JOHN CALVIN) states that from eternity God has determined the saved and the damned, regardless of their merit or lack thereof. A third doctrine, set forth by THOMAS AQUINAS and MARTIN LUTHER, ascribes salvation to the unmerited GRACE of God but links the lack of grace to SIN. In ISLAM, issues of predestination and free will were argued extensively. The MUTAZILA held that God would be unjust if he predestined all human actions; the ASHARIYA advocated a strict predestination that became the mainstream Islamic view.

predicate calculus Part of modern symbolic logic which systematically exhibits the logical relations between propositions involving quantifiers such as "all" and "some." The predicate calculus usually builds on some form of the PROPOSITIONAL CALCULUS and introduces quantifiers, individual variables, and predicate letters. A sentence of the form "All F's are either G's or H's" is symbolically rendered as $(\forall x)[Fx \supset (Gx \vee Hx)]$, and "Some F's are both G's and H's" is symbolically rendered as $(\exists x)[Fx \wedge (Gx \wedge Hx)]$. Once conditions of truth and falsity for the basic types of propositions have been determined, the propositions formulable within the calculus are grouped into three mutually exclusive classes: (1) those that are true on every possible specification of the meaning of their predicate signs, such as "Everything is F or is not F"; (2) those false on every such specification, such as "Something is F and not F"; and (3) those true on some specifications and false on others, such as "Something is F and is G." These are called, respectively, the valid, inconsistent, and contingent propositions. Certain valid proposition types may be selected as axioms or as the basis for rules of inference. There exist multiple complete axiomatizations of first-order (or lower) predicate calculus ("first-order" meaning that quantifiers bind individual variables but not variables ranging over predicates of individuals). See also LOGIC.

preeclampsia and eclampsia \ˌprē-i-ˈklamp-sē-ə\ Hypertensive conditions induced by PREGNANCY. In preeclampsia, HYPERTENSION, PROTEIN in the urine, and hand and face EDEMA develop late in pregnancy or soon after. Persistent hypertension compromises the fetus's blood supply and damages the mother's kidneys. Monitoring of blood pressure and weight gain may detect it before symptoms (headaches, visual disturbances, stomach pain) begin. Eclampsia follows in about 5% of cases, with convulsions that pose a serious threat to mother and child. It can usually be prevented by special diets, drugs, and limited activity or early delivery.

preemption \prē-ˈemp-shən\ U.S. policy that allowed the first settlers, or squatters, on public land to buy the land they had improved. Since improved land, coveted by speculators, was often priced too high for squatters to buy at auction, temporary preemptive laws allowed them to acquire it without bidding. The Pre-Emption Act (1841) gave squatters the right to buy 160 acres at $1.25 per acre before the land was auctioned. The Homestead Act (1862) made preemption an accepted part of U.S. land policy. See also HOMESTEAD MOVEMENT.

prefabrication Assembly of standardized building components at a location other than the building site. Units may include doors, stairs, window walls, wall panels, floor panels, roof trusses, room-sized components, and even entire buildings. Prefabrication requires the cooperation of architects, suppliers, and builders regarding the size of basic modular units. In the U.S. building industry, the 4-by-8-ft (1.2-by-2.4-m) panel is a standard unit; the architect's drafted building plans and the supplier's prefabricated wall units are based on multiples of that MODULE. Advantages of prefabrication include the cost savings of mass production, the opportunity to use specialized equipment to produce components, and standardization of parts for quick assembly and erection. The major drawback is in assigning responsibility for quality control. See also PRECAST CONCRETE.

prefect In ancient Rome, any of various high officials primarily with judicial and administrative responsibilities. In the early republic, a prefect of the city *(praefectus urbi)* took over the CONSULS' duties during their absence from Rome. They lost some importance after the introduction of PRAETORS (mid-4th century BC). AUGUSTUS revitalized the office when he appointed five prefects to supervise the city government, the fire brigade, the grain supply, and the PRAETORIAN GUARD. The praetorian prefects acquired great power and often became virtual prime ministers.

pregnancy Process of human gestation that takes place in the female's body as a FETUS develops, from FERTILIZATION to birth (see PARTURITION). It begins when a viable SPERM from the male and EGG from the OVARY merge in the fallopian tube (see FERTILITY, FERTILIZATION). The fertilized egg (zygote) grows by cell division as it moves toward the UTERUS, where it implants in the lining and grows into an EMBRYO and then a fetus. A PLACENTA and umbilical cord develop for nutrient and waste exchange between the circulations of mother and fetus. A protective fluid-filled amniotic sac encloses and cushions the fetus. Early in pregnancy, higher ESTROGEN and PROGESTERONE levels halt MENSTRUATION, cause nausea, often with vomiting (morning sickness), and enlarge the breasts and prepare them for LACTATION. As the fetus grows, so does the uterus, displacing

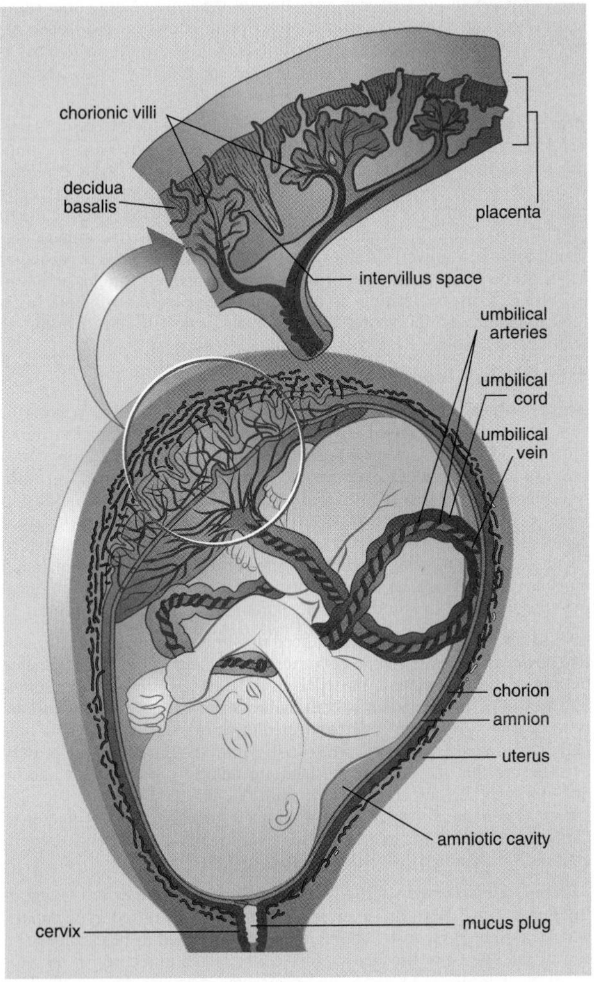

Full-term fetus in the uterus. The amnion, formed from the inner embryonic membrane, encloses the fetus. The space between the amnion and fetus (amniotic cavity) is filled with the watery amniotic fluid. The outermost embryonic membrane, the chorion, has developed fingerlike projections (villi) on its outer surface, which have enlarged and penetrated the decidua basalis layer of the uterus. The chorionic villi and the decidua basalis form the placenta. Maternal blood fills the spaces around the villi (intervillous spaces); oxygen and nutrients diffuse into the villi and pass on to the fetus via the umbilical vein. Waste materials that leave the fetus via the umbilical arteries diffuse out of the villi into the mother's blood.

other organs. Normal weight gain in pregnancy is 20–25 lbs (9–11.5 kg). The fetus's nutritional needs require the mother to take in more calories and especially protein, water, calcium, and iron. FOLIC-ACID supplements are recommended during early pregnancy to prevent NEURAL TUBE DEFECTS. Smoking, alcohol, and many legal and illegal drugs can cause CONGENITAL DISORDERS and should be avoided during pregnancy. ULTRASOUND imaging is often used to monitor structural and functional progress of the growing fetus. The due date is estimated as 280 days from the time of last menstruation; 90% of babies are born within two weeks of the estimated date. See also AMNIOCENTESIS, PREECLAMPSIA AND ECLAMPSIA, PREMATURE BIRTH.

prehistoric religion Religious practices and beliefs of prehistoric peoples, as inferred from archaeological findings. The oldest burials that attest to a belief in life after death date from 50,000–30,000 BC. Corpses were buried with goods such as stone tools and parts of animals, suggesting an attempt to placate the dead or equip them for the next world. The Middle PALEOLITHIC PERIOD provides the first evidence of animal SACRIFICES, which may have been offerings to the dead, to a higher power, or to the fertility of the animal species. Prehistoric human sacrifices have also been found, usually of women and children. From the BRONZE AGE on, weapons and jewelry were often thrown into springs, wells, and other bodies of water as sacrifices (probably of war booty). Animals such as bears were important in prehistoric religion from the Upper Paleolithic period on, probably seen as guardian spirits and associated with magical powers. Fertility rites were also practiced, as evidenced by small corpulent female figures known as Venus statuettes, with highly emphasized breasts and buttocks.

prelude Musical composition, usually brief, generally played as an introduction to another piece. The prelude originated as an organ genre, short pieces being traditionally improvised by the organist to establish the key of a following piece or to fill brief interludes in a church service. Their improvisatory origins were often reflected in rhythmic freedom and virtuosic runs. A section in this style would often lead to a closing fugal section; in time this turned into a separate movement, and preludes came to be paired with FUGUES. In the 17th century, preludes began to be frequently written for lute or harpsichord. In later years the term came to be used for short piano pieces, often in sets, by such composers as F. CHOPIN, A. SCRIABIN, and C. DEBUSSY. See also CHORALE PRELUDE.

premature birth Birth less than 37 weeks after conception. Infants born as early as 23–24 weeks may survive but many face lifelong disabilities (e.g., cerebral palsy, blindness, deafness). Premature infants account for 8–9% of live births but two-thirds of infant deaths. 40–50% of cases have no explanation; other cases can be attributed to such causes as maternal hypertension or diabetes, multiple pregnancy, or placental separation. With good care, about 85% of live-born premature infants should survive. Infants born very early (before 32–34 weeks) lack fully developed lungs and often develop RESPIRATORY DISTRESS SYNDROME. They also have problems maintaining body temperature and fighting infection. Most deaths result from breathing problems, infections, and brain or lung hemorrhages. Premature infants are characterized by low birth weight, small size, irregular breathing, absence of subcutaneous fat, and thin skin.

premenstrual syndrome (PMS) Variable group of symptoms occurring before MENSTRUATION in 40% of women, severe in about 10% of those. Physical symptoms may include headache, cramps, bloating, and constipation or diarrhea. Emotional symptoms range from irritability, lethargy, and mood swings to hostility, confusion, and depression. Theories as to the cause center on hormones, nutrition, and stress (known to affect severity). Depending on the symptoms, treatment may involve exercise, stress management, nutritional therapy, or drugs. Dietary measures include low sodium and high protein and complex carbohydrate intake and avoidance of xanthines (including caffeine). Increasing calcium intake has recently been shown to prevent or reduce cramps, which are best treated with ibuprofen.

premier See PRIME MINISTER

Preminger \'pre-min-jər\, **Otto** (1906–1986) Austrian-U.S. film director. While studying law in his native Vienna, he worked with MAX REINHARDT's theater and soon became its director. In 1935 he went to the U.S. to direct *Libel* on Broadway. Invited to Hollywood, he made the successful thriller *Laura* (1944), which helped establish FILM NOIR. Forming his own production company, he made such landmark films as *The Moon Is Blue* (1953), which challenged Hollywood censorship; the all-black *Carmen Jones* (1954); and *The Man with the Golden Arm* (1955), a tale of drug addiction. His later films included *Anatomy of a Murder* (1959), *Exodus* (1960), *The Cardinal* (1963), and *Hurry Sundown* (1967).

Prendergast, Maurice (Brazil) (1858–1924) U.S. (Canadian-born) painter. Born in Saint John's, Newfoundland, he moved with his family to Boston in 1868. After study in Paris (1891–94), he spent much of his career traveling and painting abroad. He was the first U.S. artist to fully absorb French Impressionism and Postimpressionism. His lively street scenes feature floating geometric areas of brilliant decorative color with a mosaiclike effect (e.g., *Central Park in 1903*). He produced his most outstanding works in watercolor (*Picnic: Boston Garden*, c. 1895; *Venice*, 1899). In his later years he lived in New York and exhibited with The EIGHT and in the 1913 ARMORY SHOW.

O P Q R

Prensa \'pren-sä\, **La** (Spanish: "The Press") Argentine daily newspaper, widely regarded as the finest Spanish-language newspaper in the world. Founded in Buenos Aires in 1869, it soon broke with the traditional emphasis on propaganda to stress professional, accurate news reporting and independence in editorial opinion. It displayed a concern for human welfare that persisted in the face of government harassment, notably in the 1940s under the regime of JUAN PERON. In 1951 it was seized and became a Peronist propaganda organ; after Perón's overthrow, it reappeared as an independent daily in 1956.

Preobrajenska, Olga *orig.* **Olga Yosifovna Preobrazhenskaya** (1871–1962) Russian ballerina and teacher. She joined the Mariinsky Ballet in 1889, earning the title of prima ballerina in 1900. Her lyrical creativity and love of improvisation were praised by audiences and critics. She also taught at the Imperial Theatre School (1901–02 and 1914–21, during which time the school was renamed the Petrograd State Ballet School). As an instructor, she helped to form the next generation of Russian dancers. In 1922 she emigrated from Russia and taught at her own ballet school in Paris (1923–60).

preparatory school School that prepares students for entrance to a higher school. In Europe, where SECONDARY EDUCATION has been selective, preparatory schools have been those that catered to pupils wishing to enter the academic secondary schools. In North America, where access to secondary education has been less competitive, the term usually refers to private secondary schools that prepare students for college.

Preparedness Movement Pre–World War I campaign to increase U.S. military capabilities and convince the public of the need for U.S. involvement in a European conflict. Such leaders as THEODORE ROOSEVELT and Gen. LEONARD WOOD sought to persuade Pres. WOODROW WILSON to strengthen U.S. national defenses, and various organizations sponsored preparedness parades to build public awareness and support. It resulted in passage of the National Defense Act (1916); the U.S. entered the war the next year.

prerogative court \pri-'rä-gə-tiv\ In English law, a court through which the powers, privileges, and immunities reserved to the sovereign were exercised. Such courts were originally formed during the period when the sovereign's power was greater than the Parliament's. The STAR CHAMBER, the High Commission, and the Court of CHANCERY all achieved importance in the 16th century. By the 17th century they were being challenged by the COMMON LAW courts and competing political interests, and they were soon put out of business. See also PRIVY COUNCIL.

Presbyterianism Form of church government based on rule by elders, or presbyters. The presbyters who govern the church are grouped in a hierarchy of courts, the highest of which is the general assembly. They are elected by the members of the congregation for fixed terms, in a system intended to affirm the equality of all Christians. The term Presbyterianism also refers to a denomination, the Presbyterian Church. The modern Presbyterian churches trace their origins to the Calvinist churches of the British Isles; in continental Europe such congregations were known as REFORMED CHURCHES. The Presbyterian Church is strongest in Scotland, where it was founded by JOHN KNOX in 1557, but it is also well established in England, Wales, and the U.S. See also CALVINISM.

preschool education Childhood education during the period from infancy to the age of 5 or 6. Institutions for preschool education vary widely around the world, as do their names (e.g., infant school, day care, maternal school, nursery school, crèche, kindergarten). The first systematic theory of early childhood pedagogy was propounded by FRIEDRICH FROEBEL, the founder of the KINDERGARTEN. Other influential theorists include MARIA MONTESSORI and JEAN PIAGET. Of major concern in preschool education is language development; teachers often conduct listening and language games. See also ELEMENTARY EDUCATION.

Prescott, William H(ickling) (1796–1859) U.S. historian. Born in Salem, Mass., to a prosperous family, Prescott graduated from Harvard University in 1814 but was prevented by poor health and eyesight from taking up a career in law or business. His friends, including WASHINGTON IRVING, led him to his life's work: recounting the history of 16th-century Spain and its colonies. He is best known for his *History of the Conquest of Mexico* (1843) and *History of the Conquest of Peru* (1847), for which he made rigorous use of original sources, and which earned him a reputation as the first scientific U.S. historian.

prescription In property law, the effect of the lapse of time in creating and destroying rights. Acquisitive prescription allows an individual, after unequivocal possession for a specific period, to acquire an interest in REAL PROPERTY, such as an easement, but not the property itself. See also ADVERSE POSSESSION.

prescriptivism In metaethics, the view that moral judgments are prescriptions and therefore have the logical form of imperatives. Prescriptivism was first advocated by Richard M. Hare (born 1919) in *The Language of Morals* (1952). Hare argued that it is impossible to derive any prescription from a set of descriptive sentences, but tried nevertheless to provide a foothold for moral reasoning in the constraint that moral judgments must be "universalizable": that is, that if one judges a particular action to be wrong, one must also judge any relevantly similar action to be wrong. Universalizability is not a substantive moral principle but a logical feature of the moral terms: anyone who uses such terms as "right" and "ought" is logically committed to universalizability.

preservation, food See FOOD PRESERVATION

preservative Any of numerous chemical additives used to prevent or slow food spoilage caused by chemical changes (e.g., oxidation, mold growth) and maintain a fresh appearance and consistency. Antimycotics (e.g., sodium and calcium propionate, sorbic acid) inhibit mold growth; ANTIOXIDANTS (e.g., butylated hydroxytoluene or BHT) delay rancidity in foods containing fats and oils; ANTIBIOTICS (e.g., tetracyclines) prevent bacterial growth; humectants retain moisture in products like shredded coconut; and antistaling agents (e.g., glyceryl monostearate) maintain moisture and softness in baked goods. Some preservatives also improve the appearance of the product (e.g., sodium nitrate and NITRITE in meats).

president In government, the officer in whom a nation's chief executive power is vested. In some countries, the president is the chief of state but not of the government, in which case the role is primarily ceremonial. Elsewhere, the president is both the leader of the government and the head of state. Presidents may be elected directly or indirectly, for a limited or unlimited number of terms. In the U.S., the president's chief duty is to ensure that the laws of the land are faithfully executed, which he does through various agencies and with the aid of his CABINET. He also serves as commander in chief of the armed forces, nominates judges to the SUPREME COURT, and makes treaties with foreign governments (contingent on Senate approval). See also PRIME MINISTER.

Presley, Elvis (Aaron) (1935–1977) U.S. popular singer, the "King of Rock and Roll." Born in Tupelo, Miss., Presley was raised in Memphis, where he sang Pentecostal church music and listened to black bluesmen and Grand Ole Opry broadcasts. In 1954 he began to record for the producer Sam Phillips. In 1956, under his new manager, "Colonel" Tom Parker, he released "Heartbreak Hotel," the first of numerous million-selling hits, including "Hound Dog" and "All Shook Up." In the same year, he appeared in *Love Me Tender,* the first of 33 mediocre films, and on several TV shows, notably the "Ed Sullivan Show." Presley's intensely charismatic style—including his sexy hip shaking, ducktail haircut, and characteristic sneer—excited young fans, especially females, to wild adulation. After a stint in the army (1958–60) he resumed recording and acting, but his earlier raucous style was moderated. In 1968 he introduced a Las Vegas-based touring act with orchestra and gospel-type choir. Battling public pressures, weight gain, and drug dependence, he underwent a personal decline. His death at 42, attributed to natural causes, was mourned by hundreds of thousands of fans at Graceland, his Memphis estate, which remains a place of pilgrimage. Over 500 million of his records are claimed to have been sold during his lifetime, making him the most successful solo recording artist in history.

Pressburg See BRATISLAVA

Pressburg, Treaty of (December 26, 1805) Agreement signed by Austria and France at Pressburg (now Bratislava, Slovakia) after NAPOLEON's victories at the Battles of ULM and AUSTERLITZ. Austria gave up Venetia to Napoleon's kingdom of Italy, and the Tirol and Vorarlberg to Bavaria. Austria agreed to admit the electors of Bavaria and Württemberg, allied with Napoleon, to the rank of kings, which further reduced Austrian influence in Germany. Austria's influence was also excluded from Italy. The treaty enabled Napoleon to create a ring of French client states beyond France.

pressure Perpendicular force per unit area, or STRESS at a point within a confined fluid. A solid object exerts pressure on a floor equal to its WEIGHT divided by the area of contact. The weight of the earth's atmosphere on the earth constitutes ATMOSPHERIC PRESSURE, which varies from place to place but always decreases with altitude. The pressure exerted by a confined gas results from the average effect of the forces produced on the walls of the container by the continual, numerous collisions by gas molecules. Hydrostatic pressure is the stress, or pressure, exerted equally in all directions at points within a confined fluid. Lithostatic pressure is the stress exerted on a body of rock in the earth's crust by surrounding rock, which increases with depth below the earth's surface. The SI unit of pressure is the pascal (Pa), which is equal to one newton of force per square meter.

pressure gauge Instrument for measuring the condition of a fluid (liquid or gas) that is specified by the FORCE the fluid would apply, when at rest, to a unit area, such as pounds per square inch (psi) or PASCALS (Pa). The reading on the gauge, called the gauge pressure, is always the difference between two PRESSURES. When the lower of the pressures is that of the atmosphere, the total (or absolute) pressure is the sum of the gauge and atmospheric pressures.

Prester John Legendary Christian ruler of the East. He was believed to be a NESTORIAN and a king-priest (Prester being short for Presbyter, "elder" or "priest") reigning in an unspecified part of the Far East. The legend arose during the CRUSADES in the 12th century, among European Christians who hoped that Prester John would prove an ally in the effort to regain the Holy Land from the SARACENS. In the 13th–14th century various missionaries and travelers, including Marco POLO, searched for his kingdom in Asia. After the mid-14th century, Ethiopia was the center of the quest, as Prester John became identified with the emperor of that African Christian nation.

Prestes \'prā-tās\, **Luís Carlos** (1898–1990) Brazilian revolutionary. In 1924 he led a rebel force on a three-year trek through Brazil's interior in an effort to spark a rebellion in the countryside. Though the effort failed, he became a romantic hero. He went on to lead the Brazilian Communist Party, which advocated ending payments on the national debt, nationalization of foreign-owned companies, and LAND REFORM. Imprisoned after a violent uprising in 1935, he was released after World War II, and later served briefly as a senator.

Preston City (pop., 1994 est.: 133,000), county seat of LANCASHIRE, England, on the RIBBLE RIVER. It grew near the site of a Roman fort and received its first charter in 1179. As a market center, it became known for its woolen and linen weaving and its cotton mills. It was the site of the Lancashire Royalist headquarters during the ENGLISH CIVIL WARS. The Royalists were defeated there by OLIVER CROMWELL in 1648. Despite the decline of the cotton textile industry, the economy has remained strong through diversification, and it produces aircraft and motor vehicles.

prestressed concrete Concrete reinforced by either pretensioning or posttensioning, allowing it to carry a greater load or span a greater distance than ordinary REINFORCED CONCRETE. In pretensioning, lengths of steel wire or cables are laid in the empty mold and stretched. The concrete is placed and allowed to set, and the cables are released, placing the concrete into compression as the steel shrinks back to its original length. In posttensioning, the steel in the concrete is stretched after the curing process. Prestressing places a concrete member in compression; these compressive stresses counteract the tensile bending stresses of an applied load. The process was developed by the French engineer Eugène Fressinet in the early 20th century.

Pretoria \pri-'tōr-ē-ə\ City (metro. area pop., 1991: 1,080,000), administrative capital of the Republic of South Africa. Founded in 1855, it became the capital of the TRANSVAAL in 1860, the administrative capital of South Africa in 1910, and a city in 1931. During the SOUTH AFRICAN WAR in 1899, WINSTON CHURCHILL was imprisoned there until his escape. Pretoria is primarily a seat of government, and most people are employed in the service sector. It is also an important rail center, with an industrial economy based on iron and steel. Its educational institutions include the University of South Africa and the University of Pretoria. See also BLOEMFONTEIN, CAPE TOWN.

Pretorius \prə-'tü-rē-ūs\, **Andries** (1798–1853) Boer leader in the GREAT TREK from British-dominated Cape Colony who became the dominant military and political figure in Natal and the TRANSVAAL. Pretorius's forces defeated the ZULU at Blood River in 1838 and at Magono in 1840. In 1842 he led an unsuccessful fight with the British over the annexation of Natal. Following British annexation of Transvaal in 1848, his forces again attacked and were again defeated. In 1852 he participated in the Sand River Convention, where Transvaal independence was recognized. He led negotiations for independence of the Orange River Sovereignty, finally guaranteed by the Bloemfontein Convention of 1854. His son Marthinus Wessel Pretorius (1819–1901) was the first president of the South African Republic (1857, 1864, 1869) and president of the Orange Free State (1859–63). After British annexation of the Transvaal, Marthinus joined insurgent Boer leaders and helped win recognition of its independence. He was a member of the ruling triumvirate until the election of PAUL KRUGER as president in 1883.

preventive medicine Efforts toward disease prevention in the community and the individual. It covers patient interviews and testing to detect risk factors; sanitary measures in homes, communities, and medical facilities; patient education; and diet and exercise programs as well as preventive drugs and surgery. It has three levels: primary (e.g., prevention of coronary heart disease in a healthy person), secondary (e.g., prevention of heart attack in a person with heart disease), and tertiary (e.g., prevention of disability and death after a heart attack). The first is by far the most economical. Important advances in preventive medicine include vaccination (see VACCINE), ANTIBIOTICS, DIAGNOSTIC IMAGING, and recognition of psychological factors. See also EPIDEMIOLOGY, IMMUNOLOGY, INDUSTRIAL MEDICINE, QUARANTINE.

Prévert \prā-'ver\, **Jacques (-Henri-Marie)** (1900–1977) French poet and screenwriter. A shop worker, he began writing after his military service. Influenced by the Symbolist movement, he renewed the ancient tradition of oral poetry, creating "song poems" about Paris street life, collected in the anthology *Words* (1945). Many were put to music and became extremely popular. His excellent screenplays for MARCEL CARNE include *The Children of Paradise* (1945), *Spectacle* (1951), and *Things and Other Things* (1972). He also worked for French television and on animated films for children.

Previn \'pre-vin\, **André (George)** *orig.* **Andreas** (Ludwig) Priwin (born 1929) U.S. (German-born) pianist, composer, and conductor. Born in Berlin, he fled Nazi persecution with his family and moved to Los Angeles in 1939. He orchestrated and arranged music for MGM in the 1940s and '50s, and thereafter scored films for several studios. Meanwhile he had become a noted classical and jazz pianist and started conducting. He has served as principal conductor of the Houston Symphony, London Symphony, Pittsburgh Symphony, Los Angeles Philharmonic, and Royal Philharmonic orchestras. He has also composed a symphony, concertos, and the opera *A Streetcar Named Desire* (1998), as well as popular songs. He was awarded a British knighthood (KBE) in 1996 and a Kennedy Center Honor in 1998.

Prévost d'Exiles \prā-,vō-dāg-'zēl\, **Antoine-François** *known as* **Abbé Prévost** (1697–1763) French novelist. From an early age Prévost alternated between enlistments in the army and entries into the religious life, which he eventually fled in 1728. Subsequent years were marked by numerous love affairs and debt. His fame rests entirely on one work—*Manon Lescaut* (1731), a sentimental novel about a young man of good family who ruins his life for a courtesan, which became the basis of two famous operas, J. MASSENET's *Manon* and G. PUCCINI's *Manon Lescaut*.

PRI See INSTITUTIONAL REVOLUTIONARY PARTY

Priam \'prī-əm\ In GREEK MYTHOLOGY, the last king of TROY. He succeeded his father Laomedon as king and gradually expanded Troy's control over the Hellespont. By his wife, HECUBA, he had many children, including HECTOR and PARIS. He reigned during the TROJAN WAR; in its final year he lost 13 sons, three of whom were killed by ACHILLES in a single day. Hector's death broke his spirit, and he went humbly to Achilles to ask for the corpse. When Troy fell, Achilles' son Neoptolemus killed the elderly Priam on an altar.

Priapus \prī-'ā-pəs\ Greek god of animal and vegetable fertility. He was represented in a caricature of the human form, grotesquely misshapen, with an enormous phallus. The ass was sacrificed in his honor, probably because it symbolized lecherousness and was associated with the god's sexual potency. His father was DIONYSUS and his mother was either a local nymph or APHRODITE. In Hellenistic times the worship of Priapus spread throughout the ancient world, and he was adopted as the god of gardens.

Pribilof Islands \'pri-bə-ˌlȯf\ Group of islands, southeastern BERING SEA, Alaska. It includes St. Paul, St. George, and two islets, and is about 300 mi (500 km) west of the mainland. Control of the islands was transferred from Russia to the U.S. with the ALASKA PURCHASE (1867). The islands are hilly with no harbors and are breeding grounds from April to November for most of the world's fur seals. Commercial seal killing is governed by a convention signed by the U.S., U.S.S.R., Japan, and Canada in 1957. The islands are also home to enormous numbers of birds and blue and white foxes. The indigenous population is made up of ALEUTS.

price Amount of MONEY that has to be paid to acquire a given good, service, or resource. Operating as a measure of value, prices perform a significant economic function, distributing the scarce supply of goods, services, and resources to those who most want them through the adjustments of SUPPLY AND DEMAND. Prices of resources are called wages, interest, and rent. This system, known as the price mechanism, is based on the principle that only by allowing prices to move freely will the supply of any given commodity match demand. If supply is excessive, prices will be low and production will be reduced; this will cause prices to rise until there is a balance of demand and supply. If supply is inadequate, prices will be high, prompting an increase in production that in turn will lead to a reduction in prices until supply and demand are in equilibrium. A totally free price mechanism does not exist in practice; even in free-market economies, MONOPOLIES or government regulation may limit the efficiency of price as a determinant of supply and demand. In centrally planned economies, the price mechanism may be supplanted by centralized government control. Attempts to operate an economy without a price mechanism usually result in surpluses of unwanted goods, shortages of desired products, BLACK MARKETS, and stunted economic growth.

Price, (Mary Violet) Leontyne (born 1927) U.S. soprano. Born in Laurel, Miss., she was trained at the Juilliard School. Picked by V. THOMSON for a revival of *Four Saints in Three Acts*, she made her name in the international tour of *Porgy and Bess* (1953–55). She sang Aïda at La Scala in 1960, and made her Metropolitan Opera debut in 1961. She was one of the Met's most popular stars for more than two decades, creating the role of Cleopatra in S. BARBER's *Antony and Cleopatra* (1966), which opened the new Met at Lincoln Center, and singing her last Aïda in 1985.

Price, Vincent (1911–1993) U.S. actor. Born in St. Louis, he made his London stage debut as Prince Albert in *Victoria Regina* (1935), then reprised the role on Broadway. In 1938 he went to Hollywood, where he became known for his cultivated manner and silken voice. He played historical roles in *The Private Lives of Elizabeth and Essex* (1939), *Hudson's Bay* (1941), and *The Three Musketeers* (1948). He was the menacing villain in horror movies such as *House of Wax* (1953) and *Diary of a Madman* (1963) as well as a series of ROGER CORMAN movies adapted from EDGAR ALLAN POE stories, including *The Masque of the Red Death* (1964).

price discrimination Practice of selling a commodity at different prices to different buyers, even though sales costs are the same for all the transactions. Buyers may be discriminated against on the basis of income, race, age, or geographic location. For price discrimination to succeed, other entrepreneurs must be unable to purchase goods at the lower price and resell them at a higher one.

price index Measure of change in a set of PRICES, consisting of a series of numbers arranged so that a comparison of the values for any two periods or places will show the change in prices between periods or the difference in prices between places. Price indexes were first developed to measure changes in the cost of living in order to determine the wage increases necessary to maintain a constant STANDARD OF LIVING. There are two basic types. Laspeyres-type indexes define a market basket of goods in a base period, then use the prices for those goods to examine change over space and time. In its simplest form, this is simply the ratio of what those goods cost today to what they cost in the base period. The two most familiar indexes of this type are the CONSUMER PRICE INDEX (CPI) and the producer price index (PPI). The CPI measures changes in retail prices in such component parts as food, clothing, and shelter. The PPI (formerly called the wholesale price index) measures changes in the prices charged by manufacturers and wholesalers. Paasche-type indexes define a market basket of goods in the current period, then use the prices of those goods from past periods. The most familiar index of this type is the GDP deflator, used in the U.S. in the NATIONAL INCOME ACCOUNTING to differentiate amounts in constant dollars from those in current dollars.

prickly pear Any of a group of flat-stemmed, spiny OPUNTIA cacti (see CACTUS), native to the Western Hemisphere, or the edible fruit of certain species. Engelmann prickly pear *(Opuntia engelmannii)* and beaver tail cactus *(O. basilaris)* commonly occur in the southwestern U.S. The Indian fig *(O. ficus-indica)* is an important food in tropical and subtropical countries. Because their stems have a high water content, prickly pears can be used as forage crops and emergency stock feed during drought. Some species are cultivated as ornamentals and valued for their large flowers.

Engelmann prickly pear (*Opuntia engelmannii*).
GRANT HEILMAN

Pride, Thomas *later* **Sir Thomas** (died 1658) English soldier. Joining the Parliamentary army in the ENGLISH CIVIL WARS, he commanded a regiment in the Battle of Naseby (1645), then served with OLIVER CROMWELL and helped rout the invading Scots at Preston (1648). When the army, dominated by the Independents, occupied London later that year, Pride arrested or expelled about 140 Presbyterian members from the House of Commons ("Pride's Purge"). He was a member of the commission that tried CHARLES I.

Pridi Phanomyong \'prē-dē-'pä-nȯm-ˌyȯŋ\ *or* **Luang Pradist Manudharm** \lü-'äŋ-prä-'dist-ˌmä-nü-'därm\ (1900–1983) Thai political leader and prime minister. He earned a doctorate in law in France, where he was influenced by socialism and where, with LUANG PHIBUNSONGKHRAM and others, he plotted the overthrow of Siam's absolute monarchy. Pridi participated in the PROMOTERS REVOLUTION and helped write the constitution of December 1932. He engineered the downfall of Phibunsongkhram's pro-Japanese government (1944) and in 1946 became Thailand's first popularly elected prime minister. Unjustly held responsible for the assassination of King Ananda that year, he was forced to resign and flee the country in 1947. He lived in China until 1970, when he moved to France.

Priene \prī-'ē-nē\ Ancient city of IONIA, north of the MENDERES RIVER, southwestern Turkey. According to STRABO it was founded by Ionians and Thebans. It was sacked in the 7th century BC but regained its position in the 6th century BC. It prospered under the Romans and Byzantines but gradually declined. After passing into Turkish hands in the 13th century AD, it was abandoned. Archaeological excavations revealed a Greek town built on terraces; atop a nearby hill is the temple of Athena Polias, dedicated by ALEXANDER THE GREAT in 334 BC.

priesthood Office of a spiritual leader expert in the ceremonies of worship and the performance of religious rituals. Though chieftains, kings, and heads of households have sometimes performed priestly functions, in most civilizations the priesthood is a specialized office. The priest's duties are concerned less with magic than with the right performance of ritual acts required by the divine powers. Many African societies, for example, differentiated between SHAMANS and the priests responsible for the worship of tribal ancestors. SACRIFICE is often one of the most important duties of the priesthood. Not every highly developed religion possesses a priesthood, the most notable exception being ISLAM. The idea of the "priesthood of all believers" was also a cardinal doctrine of the REFORMATION, and the Protestant belief that priests are not needed as intermediaries between church members and the HOLY SPIRIT is seen most clearly in sects such as the Society of FRIENDS.

Priestley, Joseph (1733–1804) English theologian, political theorist, and physical scientist. He worked as a teacher and lecturer in various subjects before joining the ministry in 1767. His early scientific studies resulted in his *History and Present State of Electricity* (1767), which became a fundamental text in the field. His *Essay on Government* (1768) influenced later UTILITARIANISM. He did important work in the field of chemical reactions and change. He is considered the discoverer of nitro-

O P Q R

gen, carbon monoxide, ammonia, and several other gases, and in 1774 he became the first to identify oxygen; his report led ANTOINE LAVOISIER to repeat the experiment, deduce oxygen's nature and role, and name it. His theological works include *History of the Corruptions of the Christian Church* (1782), burned as sacrilegious in 1785, and *A General History of the Christian Church* (6 vols., 1790–1802). His nonconformist religious views and his political activities, particularly in support of the French Revolution, made him increasingly controversial in England, and he emigrated to the U.S. in 1794.

primary education See ELEMENTARY EDUCATION

primary election Electoral device for choosing a party's candidates for public office. The formal primary system is peculiar to the U.S., where it came into widespread use in the early 20th century. Most U.S. states use the primary system for statewide offices, and most states hold primary elections for the national president, in which delegates supporting a presidential candidate are selected to attend a national convention, where they vote for the candidate. A closed-vote primary is restricted to party members; an open-vote primary is open to all voters in the district. Names can be placed on the ballot by an eligible citizen's declaration of candidacy, nomination at a pre-primary convention, or by a petition signed by a required number of voters. See also ELECTORAL SYSTEMS, PARTY SYSTEM.

primate Placental MAMMAL (order Primates) that originated as a forest-dweller perhaps 97.5 million years ago. Primates are distinguished from other mammals by one or more of the following: unspecialized structure, specialized behavior, short muzzle, poor smell, prehensile five-digit hands and feet, flat nails, no claws, depth perception with acute vision that is binocular to some degree, forward-facing eyes, large brain, and prolonged pre- and postnatal development. Most species bear a single young and live in troops headed by a male. The prosimians include eight families: LEMURS (Lemuridae, Indriidae, Cheirogaleidae, Megaladapidae), the aye-aye (Daubentoniidae), GALAGOS (Galagonidae), and LORISES (Loridae), TARSIERS (Tarsiidae). The anthropoids (a a group called the Catarrhini) include nine families: NEW WORLD monkeys (families Callitrichidae, Cebidae, Aotidae, Atelidae, and Pitheciidae), OLD WORLD monkeys (Cercopithecidae), the lesser APES (Hylobatidae), the great apes (Pongidae), and humans (Hominidae). The great apes are sometimes classified with humans in Hominidae.

Primaticcio \ˌprē-mə-ˈtēt-chō\, **Francesco** (1504/5–1570) Italian-French painter, sculptor, and architect. In 1532 FRANCIS I invited him to help redecorate the FONTAINEBLEAU Palace, and Primaticcio became one of the principal artists in France; he remained there the rest of his life, making only brief trips to Italy. His decorative style in painting and stucco sculpture stressed the human figure; the exaggerated musculature and active, elongated forms of his figures greatly influenced 16th-century French art. One of the first artists in France to replace religious themes with those of classical mythology, he brought a quiet French elegance to Italian Mannerism.

prime minister *or* **premier** \pri-ˈmir, pri-ˈmyir\ Head of the executive branch of government in states with a parliamentary system (see PARLIAMENTARY DEMOCRACY). The prime minister is the leader of the POLITICAL PARTY or coalition with a governing majority, and is formally appointed by the head of state. The office was developed in Britain by ROBERT WALPOLE; its powers were consolidated by WILLIAM PITT the Younger. The British prime ministry has served as a model for the heads of government in many Commonwealth countries, Europe, and Japan. The prime minister has appointive powers and is responsible for the government's legislative program, budget, and other policies. His term of office lasts until the next scheduled election or until he loses legislative support. In France, which has both a PRESIDENT and a prime minister, the president wields greater power but the prime minister controls the domestic legislative agenda. See also CHANCELLOR.

prime number Any positive INTEGER greater than 1 and divisible without remainder only by 1 and itself. Their sequence begins 2, 3, 5, 7, 11, 13, 17, 19, 23, 29 . . . but follows no discernible pattern. The issues of the regularities and irregularities in the distribution of primes are among the most important questions in NUMBER THEORY and the most interesting open questions in mathematics. Primes have been recognized since at least 300 BC, when they were studied by ERATOSTHENES and by EUCLID, who devised an elegant PROOF that there are infinitely many primes. The prime-number FACTORS of an integer are the prime numbers whose product is that integer (see fundamental theorem of ARITHMETIC).

primitive culture Term sometimes used of societies characterized by lack of a written language, relative isolation, small population, simple technology, and a slow rate of sociocultural change. The term has developed negative connotations as a result of its association with COLONIALISM and outdated notions of SOCIOCULTURAL EVOLUTION, whereby "simpler" signifies "lower" or morally or intellectually inferior, and anthropologists today generally prefer such terms as "nonliterate" or "small-scale."

Primo de Rivera \ˈprē-mō-t͟hā-ri-ˈver-ə\, **José Antonio** (1903–1936) Spanish politician. Son of the dictator MIGUEL PRIMO DE RIVERA, he began a legal career in 1925. In 1933 he founded the Spanish fascist party, the FALANGE, and was elected to the Cortes (parliament). He expounded his views in his periodicals *F.E.* (1934) and *Arriba* (1935) and made speeches across Spain. After the leftist Popular Front came to power (1936), he was arrested, given a summary trial, and executed at 33. He was treated as a martyr by FRANCISCO FRANCO's Nationalist movement.

Primo de Rivera, Miguel (1870–1930) Spanish general and dictator of Spain (1923–30). A military officer from 1888, he served as military governor of Cádiz (1915–19), Valencia (1919–22), and Barcelona (1922–23), where he firmly suppressed disorder. Believing the parliamentary system to be corrupt, he took power in a coup in 1923, dissolved the Cortes, and suspended constitutional guarantees. He successfully ended the Moroccan war (1927), settled labor disputes, and undertook public works, but failed to implement agrarian reforms. Increasing discontent with his repressive government and lack of support from the army forced him to resign in 1930. JOSE ANTONIO PRIMO DE RIVERA was his son.

primogeniture \ˌprī-mō-ˈje-nə-ˌchu̇r\ Preference in INHERITANCE that is given by law or custom to the eldest son and his issue. The motivation for such a practice has usually been to keep the estate of the deceased, or some part of it, whole and intact, and to acknowledge the importance of age-seniority within the social hierarchy. It is no longer a recognized principle of inheritance in most jurisdictions.

primrose Any flowering plant of the genus *Primula,* one of 28 genera of the family Primulaceae. *Primula* includes more than 500 species, which occur chiefly in the Northern Hemisphere in cool or mountainous regions. The plants are low-growing, usually perennial herbs; a few are biennials. Most species grow 25–50 cm (10–20 inches) tall, but some are as short as 5 cm and others as tall as 120 cm. Many species are cultivated for their attractive, five-petaled flowers, which may be red, pink, purple, blue, white, or yellow. Other plants in the primrose family include CYCLAMENS and pimpernels. The EVENING PRIMROSE (family Onagraceae) is not a true primrose.

Primus \ˈprī-məs\, **Pearl** (1919–1994) U.S. (Trinidad-born) dancer, choreographer, and anthropologist. She lived in New York City from age 2. She made her dance debut as the first black member of the New Dance Group in 1943 and formed her own company the next year. Her performances drew on the African-American experience and on her own anthropological research in Africa and the Caribbean. Such works as *African Ceremonial* (1944) and *The Wedding* (1961) reflect the interests that also led her to obtain a PhD from Columbia Univ.

Prince *orig.* **Prince** (Rogers) Nelson (born 1958) U.S. singer and songwriter. Born in Minneapolis, the son of a jazz pianist, he taught himself several instruments and formed his own bands as a teenager. At 19 he released his first album, on which he played all the instruments. His second album, *Prince* (1979), was followed by many others, including the bestselling *1999* (1982), the soundtrack to the film *Purple Rain* (1983), in which he also starred, and *Diamonds and Pearls* (1991). His sexually suggestive lyrics and stage behavior kept him at the center of controversy. In 1993 he changed his name to an unpronounceable symbol and became known as "The artist formerly known as Prince," but in 2000 he resumed his previous name.

prince European title of rank, usually denoting a person exercising complete or almost complete sovereignty or a member of a royal family. The wife of a prince is a princess. In Britain, the title was not used until 1301, when EDWARD I invested his son, the future EDWARD II, as Prince of Wales. From EDWARD III's time, the king's (or queen's) eldest son and heir has usually been so invested.

Prince, Hal *orig.* **Harold Smith** (born 1928) U.S. theatrical producer and director. Born in New York City, he worked for the producer GEORGE ABBOTT, before coproducing the successful musical *The Pajama Game* (1954). He went on to produce or coproduce over 30 hit musicals, including *Damn Yankees* (1955), *West Side Story* (1957), *A Funny Thing Happened on the Way to the Forum* (1962), and *Fiddler on the Roof* (1964). Frequently working with S. SONDHEIM, he won Tony awards for his direction of the musicals *Cabaret* (1966), *Company* (1970), *Follies* (1971), *Candide* (1974) *Sweeney Todd* (1979), *Evita* (1979), *The Phantom of the Opera* (1986), and *Show Boat* (1995).

Prince Albert National Park Park, central Saskatchewan. Its main entrance is northwest of the city of Prince Albert. Established in 1927, it has an area of 1,496 sq mi (3,875 sq km) and is mostly woodland and lakes, interlaced with streams and nature trails. It is a sanctuary for birds, moose, elk, caribou, and bears.

Prince Edward Island Province (pop., 2000 est.: 138,900), Canada. One of the MARITIME PROVINCES and Canada's smallest province, it is an island in the southern GULF OF ST. LAWRENCE, separated from Nova Scotia and New Brunswick by the Northumberland Strait. Its capital is CHARLOTTETOWN. Discovered by JACQUES CARTIER in 1534, it was used by MICMAC Indians for fishing and hunting. It was colonized by the French in 1720, then ceded to the British in 1763. Known as the "Cradle of Confederation," it was the site of the CHARLOTTETOWN CONFERENCE of 1864, which led to the federation of Canada. It became a province in 1873. It has good natural harbors on its eastern and southern sides. There has been little industrial development, and more than half of the island is used for agriculture. Fishing and tourism are also of economic importance. In 1997 a road bridge opened between Prince Edward Island and the mainland.

Prince of Wales Strait Narrow channel between BANKS ISLAND and northwestern VICTORIA ISLAND, in the southwestern ARCTIC ARCHIPELAGO, Northwest Territories, Canada. It is about 170 mi (274 km) long and forms part of the NORTHWEST PASSAGE between the Atlantic and Pacific oceans. It was discovered in 1850 by the Irish explorer Robert McClure.

Prince Rupert's Land See RUPERT'S LAND

Prince William Sound Inlet of the Gulf of ALASKA, southern Alaska. It lies east of the Kenai Peninsula and spans 90–100 mi (145–160 km). It was named by the British captain GEORGE VANCOUVER in 1778 to honor a son of GEORGE III. In 1989 the largest oil spill in history occurred when the tanker *Exxon Valdez* ran aground on Bligh Reef and lost 10.9 million gallons of crude oil into the sound, with disastrous effects on its ecology.

princeps (Latin: "first one," "leader") Unofficial title used by Roman emperors from AUGUSTUS (r.27 BC–AD 14) to DIOCLETIAN (r.284–305), a period called the principate. The title originated during the ROMAN REPUBLIC, when it was held by the leading member of the Senate. Augustus' use of it strengthened his claim to be the restorer of republican institutions and virtues, though he and his successors were in fact autocrats. See also PRINCE.

Princeton, Battles of Trenton and See Battles of TRENTON AND PRINCETON

Princeton University Private university in Princeton, N.J., a traditional member of the IVY LEAGUE. Founded as the College of New Jersey in 1746, it is the fourth-oldest university in the U.S. and one of the most prestigious. WOODROW WILSON served as university president 1902–10. In addition to an undergraduate college and a graduate school, Princeton has a school of engineering and applied science and a school of architecture and urban planning. Its Woodrow Wilson School of Public and International Affairs continues a long Princeton tradition of training government officials. The university has admitted women since 1969. Total enrollment is about 6,500.

Princip \'prēnt-sēp\, **Gavrilo** (1894–1918) Serbian nationalist and assassin of Archduke FRANCIS FERDINAND. A Bosnian Serb, he sought to unite the South Slav peoples and destroy Austro-Hungarian rule in the Balkans, and was trained in terrorism by the BLACK HAND society. When the Austro-Hungarian archduke made an official visit to Sarajevo in June 1914, Princip shot him and his wife, Sophie. The assassinations precipitated WORLD WAR I. Princip was sentenced to 20 years in prison, where he died after the amputation of his arm.

Príncipe See SÃO TOMÉ AND PRÍNCIPE

Pringle, John *later* **Sir John** (1707–1782) British physician. As physician general to the British armed forces (1740–48), he applied his knowledge to hospitals and army camps. In *Observations on the Diseases of the Army* (1752), he outlined procedures for hospital ventilation and camp sanitation. He recognized the various forms of DYSENTERY as one, equated hospital and jail fevers, and coined the term INFLUENZA. His suggestion that military hospitals be respected as sanctuaries by both sides in a conflict led to the establishment of the Red Cross.

printed circuit Electrical device in which the wiring and certain components consist of a thin coat of electrically conductive material applied in a pattern on an insulating substrate. Printed circuits replaced conventional wiring after World War II in much electronic equipment, greatly reducing size and weight while improving reliability and uniformity over the hand-soldered circuits formerly used. They are commonly used to mount INTEGRATED CIRCUITS on boards for use as plug-in units in computers, televisions, and other electronic devices. Mass-produced printed circuit boards allow automated assembly of electronic components, considerably reducing their cost.

printer, computer Electronic device that accepts text files or images from a computer and transfers them to a medium such as paper or film. It can be connected directly to the computer or indirectly via a network. Printers are classified as impact printers (in which the print medium is physically struck) and non-impact printers. Most impact printers are dot-matrix printers, which have a number of pins on the print head that emerge to form a character. Non-impact printers fall into three main categories: laser printers use a laser beam to attract toner to an area of the paper, ink-jet printers spray a jet of liquid ink, and thermal printers use heated pins to imprint an image on specially treated paper. Important printer characteristics include resolution (in dots per inch), speed (in sheets of paper printed per minute), color (full-color or black-and-white), and cache memory (which affects the speed at which a file can be printed).

printing Process for reproducing text and illustrations, traditionally by applying INK to PAPER under pressure, but today including various other methods. In modern commercial printing, three basic techniques are used. LETTERPRESS PRINTING relies on mechanical pressure to transfer a raised inked image to the surface to be printed. Gravure printing transfers ink from recessed cells of varying depths. In OFFSET PRINTING the printing and nonprinting areas of the plate differ not in height but in wettability.

printmaking Art form consisting of the production of images, usually on paper but occasionally on fabric, parchment, plastic, or other support, by various techniques of multiplication, under the direct supervision of or by the hand of the artist. Such fine prints are considered original works of art, even though they can exist in multiple copies. Major techniques include relief, intaglio, and surface printing (e.g., LITHOGRAPHY and stenciling). Early printmaking was influenced by a desire for multiple prints, but artists discovered that when a drawing is translated into a print, it takes on entirely new characteristics, and the metamorphosis became the strongest attraction for artists. See also ENGRAVING, ETCHING, MEZZOTINT, WOODCUT.

prion \'prē-,än\ Disease-causing agent, discovered by STANLEY PRUSINER, responsible for various fatal neurodegenerative diseases called transmissible spongiform encephalopathies. An abnormal form of a normally harmless protein found in mammals and birds, the disease-causing prion can enter the brain through infection, or it can arise from a MUTATION in the gene that encodes the protein. Once present in the brain it causes normal proteins to refold into the abnormal shape. As prion proteins multiply, they accumulate within nerve cells, destroying them and eventually causing brain tissue to become riddled with holes. Diseases caused by prions include CREUTZFELDT-JAKOB DISEASE, MAD COW DISEASE, and scrapie. Prions are unlike all other known disease-causing organisms in that they appear to lack NUCLEIC ACID (DNA or RNA).

Pripyat Marshes See POLESYE

Pripyat River \'pri-pyət\ *or* **Pripet River** \'pri-,pet\ River, northwestern Ukraine and southern Belarus. Rising in northwestern Ukraine near the Polish border, it flows east through the Pripet Marshes (POLESYE) to Mazyr, then joins the DNIEPER RIVER in the Kiev Reservoir after a course of 480 mi (775 km). It is navigable for 300 mi (483 km) and is connected by canals with the BUG and NEMAN rivers.

Priscian \'pri-shən\ *Latin* **Priscianus Caesariensis** (fl. c. AD 500) Latin grammarian. He used the writings of APOLLONIUS DYSCOLUS on Greek GRAMMAR as a guide in producing his own classic works on Latin grammar. His *Institutiones grammaticae* ("Grammatical Foundations"), with citations from Latin authors, became the standard work for teaching grammar in the Middle Ages. His other writings include treatises on weights and measures and on the meters of TERENCE.

prism Piece of glass or other transparent material cut with precise angles and plane faces. Prisms are useful for analyzing and refracting light (see REFRACTION). A triangular prism can separate white light into its constituent colors by refracting each different WAVELENGTH of light by a different amount. The longer wavelengths (those at the red end of the SPECTRUM) are bent the least, the shorter ones (those at the violet end) the most. The result is the spectrum of visible light, or the rainbow. Prisms are used in certain kinds of SPECTROSCOPY and in various optical systems.

prison Institution for the confinement of people convicted of major crimes. Prisons are distinguished from jails by the level of government responsible for them and the term of confinement. Jails are usually under local jurisdiction and house inmates sentenced to less than a year, whereas prisons are overseen by higher levels of government and house inmates for longer terms. Suspects were originally imprisoned while awaiting trial, but imprisonment came to be viewed as a possible punishment for crime. In early U.S. prisons, prisoners were kept in isolation; in the 19th century, prisoners were permitted to work together, but in silence. At the end of the 19th century, prison reformers successfully advocated segregation of criminals by type of crime, age, and sex, rewards for good behavior, indeterminate sentencing, vocational training, and parole.

prisoner's dilemma Imaginary situation employed in GAME THEORY. In one version, it is as follows. Two prisoners are accused of a crime. If one confesses and the other does not, the one who confesses will be released immediately and the other will spend 20 years in prison. If neither confesses, each will be held only a few months. If both confess, they will each be jailed 15 years. They cannot communicate with one another. If each does a purely self-interested calculation, he will decide to confess. Paradoxically, when each pursues his own interest, both end up worse than if they were not egoists (see EGOISM).

Pristina \'prēsh-tē-ˌnä\ City (pop., 2000 est.: 186,611), southern Yugoslavia. It is the capital of the KOSOVO autonomous region of the republic of Serbia. It was the capital of the Serbian state before the Turks defeated the Balkan Christian armies in 1389 at the Battle of KOSOVO. A cultural center for Kosovar Albanians, it lost many of its ethnic Albanian inhabitants in 1999, when they were driven out by the Serbian campaign of "ethnic cleansing" (see KOSOVO CONFLICT).

Pritchett, V(ictor) S(awdon) *later* **Sir Victor** (1900–1997) British novelist, short-story writer, and critic. A full-time journalist from 1922 and a literary critic for the *New Statesman* 1928–65, Pritchett became known for his perceptive essays and reviews and for his penetrating and finely crafted short stories. His collections, which offer lively, ironic portraits of middle-class life, include *You Make Your Own Life* (1938), *Blind Love* (1969), and *A Careless Widow* (1989). He also wrote novels, travel books, and the admired memoirs *A Cab at the Door* (1968) and *Midnight Oil* (1971).

Prithvi Narayan Shah \'prit-vē-'nä-rä-yän\ (1723?–1775) Member of the ruling Shah family of Gurkha (Gorkha) principality, Nepal, who conquered the three Malla kingdoms (MALLA ERA) and consolidated them to found the modern state of Nepal. After unifying Nepal he went on to annex territory in northern India, as well as large portions of the Tibet plateau and of the valleys of the Inner Himalayas. He sealed Nepal's border and refused to trade with the British.

Pritzker Architecture Prize World's most prestigious honor in the field of architecture. Established through the philanthropic efforts of the Pritzker family, a prominent Chicago business family, the prize, first awarded in 1979, bestows an annual award of $100,000 on an architect whose built contributions to the field and to society are judged worthiest. The international jury has included architects, artists, historians, academicians, critics, and business executives.

privacy, right of Right of a person to be free from intrusion into matters of a personal nature. Although not explicitly mentioned in the U.S. Constitution, a right to privacy has been held to be implicit in the BILL OF RIGHTS, providing protection from unwarranted government intrusion into areas such as marriage and contraception. A person's right to privacy may be overcome by a compelling state interest. In TORT law, privacy is a right not to have one's intimate life and affairs exposed to public view or otherwise invaded. Less broad protections of privacy are afforded public officials and others defined by law as "public figures" (e.g., movie stars).

privateer Privately owned vessel commissioned by a state at war to attack enemy ships, usually merchant vessels. All nations engaged in privateering from the earliest times until the 19th century. Crews were not paid by the government but were entitled to receive portions of the value of any cargo they seized. Limiting privateers to the activities laid down in their commissions was difficult, and the line between privateering and PIRACY was often blurred. In 1856, by the Declaration of Paris, Britain and other major European countries (except Spain) declared privateering illegal; the U.S. finally repudiated it at the end of the 19th century, and Spain agreed to the ban in 1908. See also BUCCANEER, FRANCIS DRAKE, WILLIAM KIDD, JEAN LAFFITE.

privatization Transfer of government services or assets to the private sector. State-owned assets may be sold to private owners, or statutory restrictions on competition between privately and publicly owned enterprises may be lifted. Services formerly provided by government may be contracted out. The objective is often to increase government efficiency; implementation may affect government revenue either positively or negatively. Privatization is the opposite of nationalization, a policy resorted to by governments that want to keep the revenues from major industries, especially those that might otherwise be controlled by foreign interests.

privet \'pri-vət\ Any of about 40–50 species of shrubs and small trees in the genus *Ligustrum* of the OLIVE family that are widely used for hedges, screens, and ornamental plantings. Native to Europe, Asia, Australia, and the Mediterranean, these evergreen or deciduous plants have usually oval, smooth-edged leaves; creamy-white, often odorous clusters of flowers; and black berries. The hardy common privet *(L. vulgare)*, native to northeastern Europe and Britain and naturalized in northeastern North America, is used widely as a hedge plant. Mock privets belong to the genus *Phillyrea* (same family) and bear small, bright-red fruits that turn purple-black as they mature.

privileged communication *or* **confidential communication** In law, communication between parties to a confidential relation such that the communication's recipient is exempted from disclosing it as a witness. Communications between attorney and client, husband and wife, doctor (especially psychiatrist) and patient, and, often, clergy and parishioner as well as journalist and source are generally recognized by the courts as privileged.

Privy Council \'pri-vē\ Historically, the British sovereign's private council. Once powerful, it is today chiefly concerned with issuing royal charters, conducting government research, and serving as an appeals body for ecclesiastical and other lesser courts. It grew out of the medieval CURIA *(curia regis)* but lost most of its judicial and political functions in the mid-17th century. See also PREROGATIVE COURT.

Prix de Rome \'prē-də-'rōm\ *in full* **Grand Prix de Rome** Art scholarships awarded by the French government. First established in 1666 by LOUIS XIV and CHARLES LE BRUN, these prizes enable young French painters, sculptors, architects, engravers, and musicians to study in Rome. Grand-prize winners in each artistic category study at the Académie de France in Rome for four years. Many of the greatest French artists and musicians of past centuries have been prizewinners, including J.-H. FRAGONARD, J.-L. DAVID, H. BERLIOZ, and C. DEBUSSY. The prizes are still being awarded, though their prestige has diminished.

prize cases (1863) Legal dispute in which the U.S. Supreme Court upheld Pres. ABRAHAM LINCOLN's seizure of ships (prizes). In April 1861, three months before Congress declared a state of war, Lincoln authorized a blockade of Confederate ports. In that three-month period, several merchant ships ran the blockade and were captured by the Union navy. The legality of the seizures was challenged in court; on appeal, the Supreme Court ruled that the president had acted legally to resist insurrection, sanctioning presidential use of emergency powers.

probability theory Branch of mathematics that deals with analysis of random events. Probability is the numerical assessment of LIKELIHOOD on a scale from 0 (impossibility) to 1 (absolute certainty). Probability is usually expressed as the RATIO between the number of ways an event can happen and the total number of things that can happen (e.g., there are 13 ways of picking a diamond from a deck of 52 cards, so the probability of picking a diamond is $\frac{13}{52}$, or $\frac{1}{4}$). Probability theory grew out of attempts to understand card games and GAMBLING. As science became more rigorous, analogies between certain biological, physical, and social phenomena and games of chance became more evident (e.g., the sexes of newborn infants follow sequences similar to those of coin tosses). As a result, probability became a fundamental tool of modern genetics and many other disciplines. Probability theory is also the basis of the insurance industry, in the form of actuarial statistics.

probate In law, the process of proving in a court (probate court) that an instrument is the valid last WILL and testament of a deceased person. The term also refers broadly to the process of administering an estate. Unless it is contested or shown to contain obvious anomalies, a document purporting to be a will requires little authenticating proof for certification (admission to probate). Probate courts also often supervise the administration of estates by executors and oversee the guardianship of minors and others lacking capacity under the law.

probation Conditional suspension of an offender's sentence upon the promise of good behavior and agreement to accept supervision and abide by specified requirements. It differs from PAROLE in that the offender is not required to serve any of the sentence. Those convicted of serious offenses and those previously convicted of other offenses are usually not considered for probation. Studies in several countries show that 70–80% of probationers successfully complete their probation; additional limited evidence suggests that recidivism may be less than 30%.

problem play *or* **thesis play** Type of drama that developed in the 19th century to deal with controversial social issues in a realistic manner, expose social ills, and stimulate thought and discussion. It is exemplified by the works of HENRIK IBSEN, who exposed hypocrisy, greed, and hidden corruption of society in a number of masterly plays. His influence encouraged others to use the form. GEORGE BERNARD SHAW brought it to an intellectual peak with his plays and their long, witty prefaces. More recent examples include works of SEAN O'CASEY, ATHOL FUGARD, ARTHUR MILLER, and AUGUST WILSON.

problem solving Process involved in finding a solution to a problem. Many animals routinely solve problems of locomotion, food finding, and shelter through trial and error. Some higher animals, such as apes and cetaceans, have demonstrated more complex problem-solving abilities, including discrimination of abstract stimuli, rule learning, and application of language or languagelike operations. Humans use not only trial and error but also insight based on an understanding of principles, inductive and deductive reasoning (see DEDUCTION, LOGIC), and divergent or creative thinking (see CREATIVITY), and problem-solving abilities and styles may vary considerably by individual.

proboscis monkey \prə-ˈbä-səs, prə-ˈbäs-kəs\ Species (*Nasalis larvatus,* family Cercopithecidae) of long-tailed arboreal OLD WORLD MONKEY of swampy mangrove forests on Borneo. Diurnal vegetarians, they live in groups of about 20. They are red-brown with pale underparts; the young monkey has a blue face. The male's nose is long and pendulous, the female's is smaller, and the young's is upturned. Males are 22–28 in. (56–72 cm) long, have a 26–29-in. (66–75-cm) tail, and weigh 26–53 lbs (12–24 kg); females are smaller and much lighter.

procedural law Law that prescribes the procedures and methods for enforcing rights and duties and for obtaining redress (e.g., in a suit). It is distinguished from substantive law (i.e., law that creates, defines, or regulates rights and duties). Procedural law is a set of established forms for conducting a trial and regulating the events that precede and follow it. It prescribes rules relative to jurisdiction, pleading and practice, jury selection, evidence, appeal, execution of judgments, representation of counsel, costs, registration (e.g., of a stock offer), prosecution of crime, and conveyancing (transference of deeds, leases, etc.), among other matters.

process philosophy 20th-century school of philosophy that emphasizes the elements of becoming, change, and novelty in experienced reality and opposes the traditional Western philosophical stress on being, permanence, and uniformity. Reality, including both the natural world and the human sphere, is essentially historical in this view, emerging from (and bearing) a past and advancing into a novel future. Hence, it cannot be grasped by old static spatial concepts that ignore the temporal and novel aspects of the universe given in human experience. The foremost contributors to process philosophy have been HENRI BERGSON and ALFRED NORTH WHITEHEAD.

Proclamation of 1763 Proclamation by Britain at the end of the FRENCH AND INDIAN WAR that prohibited settlement by whites on Indian territory. It established a British-administered reservation from west of the Appalachians and south of Hudson Bay to the Floridas and ordered white settlers to withdraw. It formalized Indian land titles and forbade land patents without a purchase from, or treaty agreement with, the title-holding tribe. After American colonists and pioneers objected, the proclamation was replaced by the Treaties of FORT STANWIX.

proconsul In the ancient ROMAN REPUBLIC, a CONSUL whose powers had been extended for a definite period beyond his regular one-year term. Such extensions were necessitated by events such as long periods of war. Extensions were originally voted by the people, but the power was soon taken by the Senate. Provincial governors were usually magistrates whose terms had been extended. Under the empire (after 27 BC), governors of senatorial provinces were called proconsuls.

Procopius \prə-ˈkō-pē-əs\ (born 490–507) Byzantine historian. He advised BELISARIUS on his first Persian campaign (527–31) and fought the Vandals in Africa until 536. He was in Sicily with Belisarius and fought the Goths in Italy until 540, and he described the plague in Constantinople in 542. His books *Polemon* ("Wars"), *Peri Krismaton* ("Buildings"), and *Anecdota* ("Secret History") are valuable sources.

Procter & Gamble Co. Major U.S. manufacturer of soaps, cleansers, and other household products. It was formed in 1837 when William C. Procter, a British candlemaker, and James Gamble, an Irish soapmaker, merged their businesses in Cincinnati. The company supplied soap and candles to the Union Army in the Civil War and continued to prosper when the war was over. Among its products were Ivory soap (1879), Crisco shortening (1911), Tide, the first synthetic laundry detergent (1946), and Joy, the first liquid synthetic detergent (1949). In 1932 Procter & Gamble also sponsored the first radio soap opera. The company later began to make personal-care items such as toothpaste, shampoo, and deodorant; food products such as cake mixes and coffee; and miscellaneous products such as cellulose pulp and chemicals.

proctoscope \ˈpräk-tə-ˌskōp\ Lighted tube used to inspect the RECTUM and lower COLON. It is 10 in. (25 cm) long, allowing the entire rectal lining to be examined for disease. It is inserted into the ANAL CANAL and advanced as far as is comfortable for the patient. Modern fiber-optic proctoscopes allow more extensive observation with less discomfort. Proctoscopy or proctosigmoidoscopy (which includes the lower colon) is standard in physical examinations of older persons. See also ENDOSCOPY.

Prodi, Romano (born 1939) Italian prime minister (1996–98) and from 1999 president of the European Commission, one of the governing bodies of the EUROPEAN UNION. Prodi graduated from Catholic University in Milan in 1961 and did postdoctoral work at the London School of Economics. After serving as a professor of economics at the University of Bologna, he entered government in 1978. In 1996, after two productive stints as chairman of the Institute for Industrial Reconstruction (1982–89 and 1993–94), he was narrowly elected prime minister as head of the center-left Olive Tree coalition. During his 28 months in office, Prodi privatized telecommunications and reformed the government's employment and pension policies. Budget disputes with members of his own party led to his resignation in October 1998. His nomination as president of the European Commission was approved by the EUROPEAN PARLIAMENT in May 1999, and his term began in September.

producer goods *or* **capital goods** *or* **intermediate goods** Goods manufactured and used in further manufacturing, processing, or resale. Intermediate goods either become part of the final product or lose their distinct identity in the manufacturing stream, while capital goods are the plant, equipment, and inventories used to produce final products. The contribution of intermediate goods to a country's GROSS DOMESTIC PRODUCT may be determined through the value-added method, which calculates the amount of value added to the final CONSUMER GOOD at each stage of production. This series of values is summed to estimate the total value of the final product.

product rule Rule for finding the DERIVATIVE of a product of two functions. If both f and g are differentiable, then so is fg. That is, $(fg)' = fg' + gf'$ or $(fg)' = f'g + g'f$.

production function Equation that expresses the relationship between the quantities of productive factors (such as LABOR and CAPITAL) used and the amount of product obtained. It states the amount of product that can be obtained from every combination of factors, assuming that the most efficient available methods of production are used. The production function can thus measure the MARGINAL PRODUCTIVITY of a particular factor of production and determine the cheapest combination of productive factors that can be used to produce a given output.

production management *or* **operations management** Planning and control of industrial production processes to ensure smooth and efficient operation. Production-management techniques are used in SERVICE industries as well as manufacturing. Production-management responsibilities include the traditional "five M's": men (and women), machines, methods, materials, and money. Managers are expected to maintain a flexible production process with a workforce that can readily adapt to new equipment and schedules. They may use industrial-engineering methods, such as time-study measurements, to design efficient work methods. They are responsible for managing both physical (raw) materials and information materials (paperwork). Of their duties involving money, inventory control is the most important. They must track component parts, work in process, finished goods, packaging materials, and general supplies. The production cycle requires that sales, financial, engineering, and planning departments exchange information—such as sales forecasts, inventory levels, and budgets—until detailed production orders are dispatched by a production-control division. Managers must also monitor operations to ensure that they produce at planned output levels while meeting cost and quality objectives.

productivity In economics, a measure of productive efficiency calculated as the ratio of what is produced to what is required to produce it. Any of the traditional factors of production—LAND, LABOR, or CAPITAL—can be used as the denominator of the ratio, though productivity calculations are actually seldom made for land or capital since their capacity is difficult to measure. Labor is in most cases easily quantified—for example, by counting workers engaged on a particular product. In industrial nations, the effects of increasing productivity are shown most clearly in the use of labor. Productivity can be seen not only as a measure of efficiency but also as an indicator of economic development. Productivity increases as a primitive extractive economy develops into a technologically sophisticated one. The pattern of increase typically exhibits long-term stability interrupted by sudden leaps that represent major technological advances. Productivity in Europe and the U.S. made great strides following the development of such technologies as the steam power, the railroad, and the gasoline motor. Increases in productivity tend to lead to long-term increases in real wages.

proenzyme See ZYMOGEN

profiler Machine tool for cutting complex, irregular shapes, invented by FREDERICK W. HOWE. A rapidly rotating cutter is guided by a finger that traces around the outline of a pattern. The profiler was an important component of the AMERICAN SYSTEM OF MANUFACTURE that made mass production possible.

profit In business usage, the excess of total revenue over total COST during a specific period of time. In economics, profit is the excess over the returns to CAPITAL, LAND, and LABOR. Since these resources are measured by their OPPORTUNITY COSTS, economic profit can be negative. There are various sources of profit: an innovator who introduces a new production technique can earn entrepreneurial profits; changes in consumer tastes may bring some firms windfall profits; or a firm may restrict output to prevent prices from falling to the level of costs (monopoly profit).

profit sharing System by which employees are paid a share of the PROFITS of the business enterprise in which they are employed, in keeping with a plan outlined in advance. These payments, which may vary according to salary or wage, are in addition to regular earnings. Profit-sharing plans were probably first developed in France in the early 19th century as worker incentives. Today such plans are used by businesses in Western Europe, the U.S., and parts of Latin America. Profit shares may be distributed on a current or deferred basis or through some combination of the two. Under current distribution, profits are paid out to employees immediately in the form of cash or company stock. In deferred-payment plans, profit shares may be paid into a TRUST FUND from which employees can draw ANNUITIES in later years.

progeria \prō-ˈjir-ē-ə\ Disorder with characteristics of premature aging. Affected persons have thin skin, go bald or gray early, and develop diseases of aging decades earlier than normal individuals. Not all systems are affected; there is no senility and no aging in the central nervous system. There are two major types. In the extremely rare Hutchinson-Gilford syndrome, children look 60 years old by age 10 and die at an average age of 13. The unrelated Werner's syndrome is a recessive hereditary disease that begins in young adulthood and makes patients look 30 years older than they are; their average lifespan is 47 years.

progesterone \prō-ˈjes-tə-ˌrōn\ STEROID HORMONE secreted by the female REPRODUCTIVE SYSTEM that functions mainly to regulate the condition of the endometrium (see UTERUS), preparing it to accept a fertilized egg. If the egg is not fertilized, the level of progesterone drops, the uterine lining breaks down, and MENSTRUATION ensues. If the egg is fertilized (see PREGNANCY), the placenta produces progesterone, whose effects include preparing the MAMMARY GLANDS for LACTATION. Many forms of oral CONTRACEPTION use a synthetic progesterone.

program, computer Set of ordered instructions that enable a computer to carry out a specific task. A program is prepared by first formulating the task and then expressing it in an appropriate PROGRAMMING LANGUAGE. Programmers may work in MACHINE LANGUAGE or in ASSEMBLY LANGUAGES. But most applications programmers use one of the high-level languages (such as BASIC or C++) or FOURTH-GENERATION LANGUAGES that more closely resemble human communication. Other programs then translate the instructions into machine language for the computer to use. Programs are stored on permanent media (such as a HARD DISK), and loaded into RAM to be executed by the computer's processor, which executes each instruction in the program, one at a time. Programs are often divided into applications and system programs. Applications perform tasks such as WORD PROCESSING, DATABASE functions, or accessing the INTERNET. System programs control the functioning of the computer itself; an OPERATING SYSTEM is a very large program that controls the operations of the computer, the transfer of files, and the processing of other programs.

programmed cell death See APOPTOSIS

programming language Language in which a computer programmer writes instructions for a computer to execute. Some languages, such as COBOL, FORTRAN, PASCAL, and C, are known as procedural languages because they use a sequence of commands to specify how the machine is to solve a problem. Others, such as LISP, are functional, in that programming is done by invoking procedures (sections of CODE executed within a program). Languages that support OBJECT-ORIENTED PROGRAMMING take the data to be manipulated as their point of departure. Programming languages can also be classified as high-level or low-level. Low-level languages address the computer in a way that it can understand directly, but they are very far from human language. High-level languages deal in concepts that humans devise and can understand, but they must be translated by means of a COMPILER into language the computer understands.

Progressive Conservative Party of Canada *known as* **Conservative Party** Major political party in Canada. It originated with the informal coalition of conservatives and moderate liberals to form the Liberal-Conservative Party led by JOHN MACDONALD (1854). It held power until 1873 and regained dominance as the renamed Conservative Party (1878–96). After Macdonald's death (1891), it was led by ROBERT BORDEN (1901–20), and it regained power in coalition with the Quebec nationalists (1911–20). The party was out of power except briefly in 1926 and in 1930–35. When John Bracken, a Progressive, became leader in 1942, its name was changed to its current name, though it is often called by the shorter name Conservative. It regained power under JOHN G. DIEFENBAKER (1958–63), Joe Clark (1979–80), and BRIAN MULRONEY (1984–93).

progressive education Movement that took form in Europe and North America during the late 19th century as a reaction to the alleged narrowness and formalism of traditional education. A main objective was to educate the "whole child"—that is, to attend to physical and emotional as well as intellectual growth. Creative and manual arts gained importance in the curriculum, and children were encouraged toward experimentation and independent thinking. Progressive educational ideas and practices were most powerfully advanced in the U.S. by JOHN DEWEY. See also SUMMERHILL SCHOOL.

progressive locomotor ataxia See TABES DORSALIS

Progressive Party U.S. independent political party, short-lived at three periods. The first Progressive Party, known as the BULL MOOSE PARTY, was organized in 1911. The second was assembled in 1924, selecting ROBERT LA FOLLETTE as its presidential candidate; it dissolved when La Follette died in 1925. The third Progressive Party was founded in 1947 by HENRY WALLACE. It differed from the previous groups by focusing on changes in foreign policy, favoring a conciliatory policy toward the Soviet Union. Wallace won over 1 million votes in the 1948 election, but the party was never again influential.

progressive systemic sclerosis See SCLERODERMA

progressive tax Tax levied at a rate that increases as the quantity subject to taxation increases. Designed to collect a greater proportion of tax revenue from wealthy people, progressive taxes reflect the view that those who are able to pay more should carry a heavier share of the tax burden. Progressive INCOME TAXES may provide for exemption from tax liability for incomes under a specified amount, or may establish progressively greater rates for larger and larger incomes. The presence of deductions can also make a tax progressive. Progressive taxes are a stabilizing force in periods of INFLATION or RECESSION because the amount of tax revenue changes more than proportionately with an increase or decrease in income. For example, in an inflationary economy, as prices and incomes rise, a greater percentage of taxpayers' income goes toward taxes. Government revenues increase, and the government has more leverage over the economy. A side effect of this system is that lower-income taxpayers have an especially difficult time making ends meet when inflation is high. To compensate, many economists advocate INDEXATION; several countries adjust their tax rates annually in times of inflation, usually in line with the CONSUMER PRICE INDEX. See also REGRESSIVE TAX.

Prohibition Legal prevention of the manufacture, sale, or transportation of alcoholic beverages. In the U.S., the Prohibition movement arose out of the religious revivalism of the 1820s. Maine passed the first state Prohibition law in 1846, ushering in a wave of such state legislation. The drive toward national Prohibition was fueled by the Anti-Saloon League, founded in 1893. With Prohibition already adopted in 33 states, the 18th Amendment to the U.S. Constitution went into effect in 1920. Prohibition was embraced with varying degrees of enthusiasm in different parts of the country, and enforced accordingly. In urban areas, BOOTLEGGING gave rise to ORGANIZED CRIME, with such gangsters as AL CAPONE. In part because of the rise in crime, its supporters gradually became disenchanted with it. The 21st Amendment repealed the 18th in 1933, and by 1966 all states had also abandoned Prohibition.

Prohibition Party Oldest minor U.S. political party still in existence. It was founded in 1869 to campaign for legislation to prohibit the manufacture and sale of liquor. The party was strong in rural regions and among small-town voters affiliated with Protestant evangelical churches. It nominated candidates for state and local offices and attained national strength in the 1888 and 1892 presidential elections, when its candidates polled 2.2% of the vote. Since 1900 it has been active mainly on local levels.

projective geometry Branch of mathematics that deals with the relationships between geometric figures and the images (mappings) of them that result from projection. Examples of projections include motion pictures, maps of the earth's surface, and shadows cast by objects. One stimulus for the subject's development was the need to understand PERSPECTIVE in drawing and painting. Every point of the projected object and the corresponding point of its image must lie on the projection ray, a line that passes through the center of projection. Modern projective geometry emphasizes the mathematical properties (such as straightness of lines and points of intersection) preserved in projections despite the distortion of lengths, angles, and shapes.

prokaryote \prō-ˈkar-ē-ˌōt\ Any cellular organism that lacks a distinct NUCLEUS. BACTERIA (including blue-green algae, or CYANOBACTERIA) are prokaryotes; all other organisms are EUKARYOTES. Prokaryotic cells lack a nuclear membrane and most of the components of eukaryotic cells. A nuclear region usually consists of circular, double-stranded DNA. Many prokaryotes also contain accessory, self-replicating genetic structures called plasmids. The flagella are distinct from those of eukaryotes in design and movement. The organelles (small, self-contained cellular parts that perform specific functions) that are present, such as storage vesicles, are surrounded by a membrane consisting mainly of proteins.

Prokofiev \prə-ˈkȯ-fyif\, **Sergei (Sergeievich)** (1891–1953) Russian composer and pianist. Son of a pianist, he began writing piano pieces at age 5 and wrote an opera at 9. He studied at the St. Petersburg Conservatory (1904–14) with N. RIMSKY-KORSAKOV and others. Prolific and arrogant, from 1910 he made a living by performing as a virtuoso. He played his own first concerto at his graduation recital. During World War I he wrote his *Scythian Suite* (1915) and First ("Classical") Symphony (1917). His opera *The Love for Three Oranges* premiered in 1921 in Chicago. Paris was his base from 1922, and the 1920s saw three new symphonies and the completed operas *The Fiery Angel* (1927) and *The Gambler* (1928). In the 1930s, he was drawn back to Russia; there he wrote scores for the ballet *Romeo and Juliet* (1936), *Peter and the Wolf* (1936), and SERGEI EISENSTEIN's film *Alexander Nevsky* (1938). World War II inspired the score to Eisenstein's *Ivan the Terrible* (1942–45) and the opera *War and Peace* (1943). The government's denunciation of his work in 1948 was a harsh blow; his health failed, and he died on the same day as JOSEPH STALIN.

prolapse Protrusion of an internal organ out of its normal place, usually of the RECTUM or UTERUS outside the body when supporting muscles weaken. The membrane lining the rectum can push out through the anus, most often in old people with constipation who strain during defecation. Chronic rectal prolapse requires surgical repair. The uterus may prolapse into the vagina after gravity adds to weakness from childbirth injuries. Temporary supports and pelvic exercises can relieve mild uterine prolapse, but severe prolapse may require HYSTERECTOMY.

proletariat \ˌprō-lə-ˈter-ē-ət\ Lowest-ranking socioeconomic classes. In ancient Rome, they were the poor landless freemen who, crowded out of the labor market by the extension of slavery, became parasites on the economy. KARL MARX used the term to refer to the class of wage earners engaged in industrial production only (the broader term "working class" included all those obliged to work for their living). Another of Marx's category, the *lumpenproletariat* (*lumpen:* "rags"), were marginal and unemployable workers, paupers, beggars, and criminals.

proline \ˈprō-ˌlēn\ One of the nonessential AMINO ACIDS, found in many PROTEINS, especially COLLAGEN. Because its amino nitrogen is part of a ring structure (making it a HETEROCYCLIC COMPOUND), its chemical properties differ from those of the other amino acids in proteins. It is used in biochemical, nutritional, and microbiological research and as a dietary supplement.

promenade \ˌprä-mə-ˈnād, ˌprä-mə-ˈnäd\ Public place where people walk (or, in the past, rode) at leisure for pleasure, exercise, or display. Promenades are pedestrian avenues pleasingly landscaped or commanding a view, often located along waterfronts and in parks. Vehicular traffic may or may not be restricted.

Prometheus \prə-ˈmē-thē-əs\ In GREEK RELIGION, one of the TITANS and a god of fire. He was a master craftsman and a supreme trickster, and he was sometimes associated with the creation of humans. According to legend, Prometheus stole fire from the gods and gave it to humans. In vengeance, ZEUS created PANDORA, who married Prometheus's brother and set loose all the evils of the world. Another tale held that ZEUS had Prometheus chained to a mountain and sent an eagle to devour his liver, which regenerated every night so that he could suffer the same torment the next day.

promissory note Short-term credit instrument consisting of a written promise by one person to pay a specified amount of money to another on demand or at a given future date. They are often negotiable and may be secured by the pledge of collateral. Promissory notes were in use in Europe as early as the Renaissance. The instrument has changed substantially during the 20th cent, both in form and in use. Various clauses have been added regarding payment and other provisions—for example, authorizing the sale of collateral, permitting extensions of time, and allowing acceleration of payment in the event of default. See also ACCEPTANCE, BILL OF EXCHANGE.

Promoters Revolution (1932) Bloodless coup that put an end to absolute monarchy in Siam (Thailand) and initiated the Constitutional Era. The coup was headed by the "promoters," a group that included members of the Thai elite, noted intellectuals, and disaffected army officers. Their first constitution, the Temporary Constitution, stripped the king of power and put it in the hands of the promoters themselves. The Permanent, or December, Constitution restored some of the royal prestige and dignity and introduced some liberal, Western-style reforms. None of Thailand's subsequent constitutions effectively limited political power or provided a means by which political contests could be decided. See also Luang Phibunsongkhram, Pridi Phanomyong.

pronghorn Ruminant *(Antilocapra americana)* of North American plains and semideserts, the only living member of the family Antilocapridae. The pronghorn stands 30–40 in. (80–100 cm) tall. It is reddish brown with a short, dark-brown mane, white underparts, two white bands on the throat, and a circular white patch on the rump. Both sexes bear erect, two-pronged horns; the longer prong curves backward, the shorter prong forward. Pronghorns live alone or in small bands in summer, and in large herds in winter. The fastest mammal of North America, the pronghorn can run 45 mph (70 kph) and can bound up to 20 ft (6 m). Though tens of millions once roamed the West, they were nearly exterminated by hunters in the early 20th century; conservation efforts have since allowed their populations to increase.

Pronghorn (*Antilocapra americana*).
LEONARD LEE RUE III

Prony \prō-ˈnē\, **(Gaspard-Clair-François-Marie) Riche, Baron de** (1755–1839) French mathematician and engineer. He invented the Prony brake (1821), a device for measuring the power developed by an engine. Friction developed on the edge of a rotating pulley by means of brake blocks that are squeezed against the wheel by tightening bolts applies torque to a lever; a scale measures the force needed to hold the lever in place.

proof In logic and mathematics, an argument that establishes a proposition's validity. Formally, it is a finite sequence of formulas generated according to accepted rules. Each formula either is an axiom or is derived from a previously established theorem, and the last formula is the statement that is to be proven. The essence of deductive reasoning (see deduction), this is the basis of Euclidean geometry and all scientific methods inspired by it. An alternative form of proof, called mathematical induction, applies to propositions defined through processes based on the counting numbers. If the proposition holds for $n = 1$ and can be shown to hold for $n = k + 1$ whenever $n = k$ (a constant) is also true, then it holds for all values of n. An example is the assertion that the sum of the first n counting numbers is $n(n + 1)/2$.

propaganda Manipulation of information to influence public opinion. The term comes from *Congregatio de propaganda fide* ("Congregation for Propagation of the Faith"), a missionary organization established by the pope in 1622. Propagandists emphasize the elements of information that support their position and deemphasize or exclude those that do not. Misleading statements and even lies may be used to create the desired effect in the public audience. Lobbying, advertising, and missionary activity are all forms of propaganda, but the term is most commonly used in the political arena. Until the 20th century, pictures and the written media were the principal instruments of propaganda; radio, television, and motion pictures later joined their ranks. Authoritarian and totalitarian regimes use propaganda to win and keep the support of the populace; in wartime, propaganda boosts civilian and soldier morale, while propaganda aimed at the enemy is an element of psychological warfare.

propane Colorless, easily liquefied, hydrocarbon gas (C_3H_8, or more fully, $CH_3CH_2CH_3$). Separated in large quantities from natural gas, light crude oil, and oil-refinery gases, it is available as liquefied propane or as a major constituent of liquefied petroleum gas (LPG). It is an important raw material for the manufacture of ethylene and for the petrochemical industry. It is also used as a refrigerant, extractant, solvent, and aerosol propellant and in the mixture in bubble chambers.

propeller Device with a central hub and radiating blades placed so that each forms part of a helical (spiral) surface, used to propel a vehicle such as a ship or airplane. By its rotation in water or air, the propeller produces thrust on the blades, which gives forward motion to the vehicle.

proper motion Apparent motion of a star across the celestial sphere at right angles to the observer's line of sight, generally measured in seconds of arc per year. Any radial motion (toward or away from the sun) is not included. Edmond Halley was the first to detect proper motions; the largest known is that of Barnard's star, about 10 seconds yearly.

Propertius \prō-ˈpər-shəs, prō-ˈpər-shē-əs\, **Sextus** (55/43 BC–after 16 BC) Roman poet. Very few details of his life are known. The first and best known of his four books of elegies, *Cynthia,* was published in 29 BC, the year he met its heroine (his mistress, whose real name was Hostia). She emerges from his poems as beautiful, uninhibited, jealous, and irresistible. In Book II his main theme is still love, but he also contemplates writing an epic, is preoccupied with thoughts of death, and attacks the materialism of his time. Books III and IV demonstrate a bold command of language and various literary forms; among the subjects are Roman mythology and history.

property In law, something that is owned or possessed. Concepts of property vary widely among cultures. In Western society, it is generally regarded as either tangible (e.g., land or goods) or intangible (e.g., stocks and bonds or a patent). Individual ownership of property is emphasized in the West, whereas in many non-Western societies property ownership is de-emphasized or conceived on a more strictly communal basis. The use of property is extensively regulated throughout the West. Landowners injured by adjoining land uses may sue in nuisance in the Anglo-American countries; similar actions exist in civil-law countries. Throughout the West, property may be acquired in various ways. "Occupancy" allows one to become the owner of property formerly not owned by anyone. A far more common means of acquiring property is by transfer from the previous owner or owners. Such transfers include sales, donations, and inheritance. See also adverse possession, community property, easement, intellectual property, prescription, real and personal property.

property tax Levy imposed on real estate (land and buildings) and on personal property such as automobiles, jewelry, and furniture. In some countries it may also extend to farm equipment, business equipment, and inventories as well as intangibles such as stocks and bonds. Property taxes are usually levied by local or state governments rather than national governments, and they are a major source of tax revenue. Property taxes existed in the ancient world first as land taxes and later as taxes on farmhouses, livestock, and so on. The administration of a property tax involves identifying the property to be taxed, assessing its value, determining the appropriate tax rate, and collecting the requisite sum of money. Though sometimes burdensome to the poor, property taxes generally tend to redistribute the benefits of wealth from higher to lower income groups, since they often pay for schools and other services used by low-income groups. See also capital-gains tax, consumption tax, income tax, progressive tax, regressive tax.

prophet Person who speaks by divine inspiration, revealing or interpreting the will of a god. Prophets have appeared in many religions throughout history. The most familiar in the West are such Old Testament leaders as Moses, Isaiah, and Daniel, along with the Prophet Muhammad. In contrast to the diviner or interpreter of omens (see divination), who may answer private questions, prophets often address the destiny and moral life of a whole people. Some prophets seek to create a new society that will realize their message and thus found new religions. Others may look only to reform or purify an existing society and religion. The tone of prophecy ranges widely, from ecstasy, inspired utterance, and ethical fervor to passionate social criticism, prediction of the future, and expectation of apocalypse.

Prophet, The *orig.* **Tenskwatawa** (1768–1834) North American Indian leader. Born in Old Chillicothe, Ohio, the brother of Tecumseh, he became a religious revivalist and maintained a strong following among the Shawnee based on his 1805 declaration that he had received a message from the "Master of Life" and had contact with the supernatural. Advocating a return to traditional ways of life, he rejected the white man's introduction of alcohol, textile clothing, and individual ownership of property, and he worked with Tecumseh for an Indian confederacy to resist U.S. encroachment. In Tecumseh's absence he allowed the Shawnee to be drawn into and defeated at the Battle of Tippecanoe (1811).

Prophet's Mosque House of worship built on the site of MUHAMMAD's house in MEDINA, considered one of the three holiest places in ISLAM. It was originally a simple brick structure surrounding an enclosed courtyard where people gathered to hear Muhammad. He later built roofed galleries to shelter his visitors, and in 628 a pulpit was added to raise him above the crowd. In 706 Caliph al-Walid I pulled down the original building and built a MOSQUE on the site, which contains Muhammad's tomb. The mosque served as the model for later Islamic architecture.

proportional representation Electoral system in which the share of seats held by a POLITICAL PARTY in the LEGISLATURE closely matches the share of popular votes received. It was devised in Europe in the mid-19th century to guarantee minority groups more representation than was possible under the majority or PLURALITY SYSTEMS. Its supporters claim that it creates a more accurate reflection of public opinion; its opponents claim that more parties in a legislature result in a weaker and less stable government. Two methods for apportioning seats are the single-transferable-vote method, under which voters rank candidates by preference, and the list system, under which voters vote for a party's list of candidates rather than individuals. See also LEGISLATIVE APPORTIONMENT.

proportion/proportionality In algebra, equality between two RATIOS. In the expression $a/b = c/d$, a and b are in the same proportion as c and d. For example, if one triangle is twice the size of a second, then each side of the first triangle is in the same proportion to the corresponding side of the second as 2 is to 1. A proportion is typically set up to solve a word problem in which one of its four quantities is unknown. It is solved by multiplying one numerator by the opposite denominator and equating the product to that of the other numerator and denominator. The term *proportionality* describes any relationship that is always in the same ratio. The number of apples in a crop, for example, is proportional to the number of trees in the orchard, the ratio of proportionality being the average number of apples per tree.

propositional attitude Psychological state expressed by a verb that may take a subordinate clause beginning with "that" as its complement. Such verbs as "believe," "hope," "fear," "desire," "intend" and "know" all express propositional attitudes. The linguistic contexts created by their use are typically referentially opaque (see INTENTIONALITY) in the sense that co-referential expressions are not freely intersubstitutable within those contexts. Thus, to use BERTRAND RUSSELL's example, Peter may believe that WALTER SCOTT was a Scotsman but not believe that the author of *Waverley* (which Scott wrote) was a Scotsman. Peter may, for instance, believe that an American wrote it.

propositional calculus FORMAL SYSTEM of propositions and their logical relationships. As opposed to the PREDICATE CALCULUS, the propositional calculus employs simple, unanalyzed propositions rather than predicates as its atomic units. Simple (atomic) propositions are denoted by lowercase Roman letters (e.g., p, q), and compound (molecular) propositions are formed using the standard symbols $\wedge$ for "and," $\vee$ for "or," $\supset$ for "if . . . then," and $\neg$ for "not." As a formal system, the propositional calculus is concerned with determining which formulas (compound proposition forms) are provable from the axioms. Valid inferences among propositions are reflected by the provable formulas, because (for any formulas A and B) $A \supset B$ is provable if and only if B is a logical consequence of A. The propositional calculus is consistent in that there exists no formula A in it such that both A and $\neg$ A are provable. It is also complete in the sense that the addition of any unprovable formula as a new axiom would introduce a contradiction. Further, there exists an effective procedure for deciding whether a given formula is provable in the system. See also LOGIC, PREDICATE CALCULUS, laws of THOUGHT.

propositional function Sentencelike expression that may be thought of as obtained from a sentence by substituting variables for constants occurring in the sentence. For example, "x was a parent of y" may be thought of as obtained from "Adam was a parent of Abel." A propositional function therefore has no truth-value, becoming true or false only when its free variables are replaced by constants of appropriate syntactic categories (e.g., "Abraham was a parent of Isaac").

proprietary colony Type of settlement in British North America (1660–90). To repay political and financial debts, the British crown, beginning with CHARLES II, awarded supporters vast tracts of land in colonial New York, New Jersey, Pennsylvania, Maryland, and the Carolinas. The proprietors were to supervise and develop the colonies, which became successful enterprises. By 1690 concern about the colonies' growing independence from control by British officials led to the end of proprietary grants.

proprioception \ˌprō-prē-ō-ˈsep-shən\ Perception of stimuli relating to position, posture, equilibrium, or internal condition. Receptors (nerve endings) in skeletal MUSCLES and on TENDONS provide constant information on limb position and muscle action for coordination of limb movements. Awareness of equilibrium changes usually involves perception of gravity. In humans, gravity, position, and orientation are registered by tiny grains called otoliths moving within two fluid-filled sacs in the INNER EAR in response to any change in position or orientation. Their motion is detected by sense hairs. Rotation is detected by the inertial lag of fluid in the semicircular canals acting on the sense hairs. The central NERVOUS SYSTEM integrates signals from the canals to perceive rotation in three dimensions. See also SENSE.

propylaeum \ˌprä-pə-ˈlē-əm, ˌprō-pə-ˈlē-əm\ In ancient Greek architecture, a structure forming an entrance or gateway to a sacred enclosure, usually consisting, at the least, of a porch supported by columns both outside and within the actual gate. The term is often used in the plural (propylaea). The most famous example is the great Propylaea designed by Mnesicles for the Athenian ACROPOLIS. The name propylaea was also applied to various 18th–19th-century Neoclassical and Romantic monumental gateways.

proscenium \prō-ˈsē-nē-əm\ In a THEATER, the frame or arch separating the stage from the AUDITORIUM, through which the action of a play is viewed. In ancient Greek theaters, the *proskenion* was an area in front of the SKENE that eventually functioned as the stage. The first permanent proscenium in the modern sense was built in 1618 at the Farnese Theater in Parma. Though the arch contained a stage curtain, its main purpose was to provide a sense of spectacle and illusion; scene changes were carried out in view of the audience. Not until the 18th century was the curtain commonly used to hide scene changes. The proscenium opening was of particular importance to 19th-century realistic playwrights, for whom it served as a picture frame through which the audience experienced the illusion of spying on the characters.

prose Literary medium distinguished from POETRY especially by its greater irregularity and variety of rhythm and its closer correspondence to the patterns of everyday speech. Though it is readily distinguishable from poetry in that it does not treat a line as a formal unit, the significant differences between prose and poetry are of tone, pace, and sometimes subject matter.

prose poem Work in prose that has some of the technical or literary qualities of POETRY (such as regular rhythm, definitely patterned structure, or emotional or imaginative heightening) but that is set on a page as PROSE. The form took its name from CHARLES BAUDELAIRE's *Petits poèmes en prose* (1869; "Little Poems in Prose"). Other writers of prose poems include, in the 19th century, STEPHANE MALLARME, ARTHUR RIMBAUD, FRIEDRICH HOLDERLIN, NOVALIS, and RAINER MARIA RILKE, and in the 20th, AMY LOWELL (in her "polyphonic prose") and such contemporary poets as JOHN ASHBERY.

prosecutor Government attorney who presents the state's case against the defendant in a criminal prosecution. In some countries (France, Japan), public prosecution is carried out by a single office. In the U.S., states and counties have their own prosecutors. Only at the federal level is the system unitary; the U.S. attorney general's office appoints a U.S. attorney for each federal district. In most state and local jurisdictions, prosecutors are elected to office. Whether elected or appointed, prosecutors are often subject to political pressures. A prosecutor takes charge of the investigation once a crime has been committed, presents evidence at a hearing before a grand jury, and questions witnesses during the trial. See also INDEPENDENT COUNSEL.

Proserpina See PERSEPHONE

prosody \ˈprä-sə-dē, ˈprä-zə-dē\ Study of the elements of language, especially METER, that contribute to rhythmic and acoustic effects in poetry. The basis of "traditional" prosody in English is the classification of verse according to the syllable stress of its lines. Effects such as RHYME scheme, alliteration, and assonance further influence a poem's "sound meaning." Nonmetrical prosodic study is sometimes applied to modern poetry, and visual prosody is used when verse is "shaped" by its typographical arrangement. Prosody also involves examining the subtleties of a poem's rhythm, its "flow," the historical period to which it belongs, the poetic genre, and the poet's individual style.

Prosser, Gabriel See GABRIEL

prostaglandin \ˌpräs-tə-ˈglan-dən\ Any of a class of organic compounds that occur in many animal tissues and have diverse hormonelike effects in animals (see HORMONE). Their common chemical structure is derived from a FATTY ACID with 20 carbon atoms. They have important effects on BLOOD PRESSURE, blood clotting, pain sensation, and reproduction mechanisms, but one prostaglandin may have different and even opposite effects in different tissues. They hold promise for treating HEART DISEASE and VIRAL DISEASES and may be useful in CONTRACEPTION. Some substances that inhibit prostaglandin synthesis (see ASPIRIN) are useful in controlling pain, asthma attacks, or anaphylactic shock or as ANTICOAGULANTS.

prostate cancer Malignant TUMOR of the PROSTATE GLAND. Prostate cancer commonly occurs in men over age 50, and in North America the disease is twice as common in black men as it is in whites. Symptoms include frequent or painful urination, blood in the urine, sexual dysfunction, swollen lymph nodes in the groin, and pain in the pelvis, hips, back, or ribs. The likelihood of developing prostate cancer doubles if there is a family history. Treatment may include surgery, radiation therapy, hormone therapy, chemotherapy, or a combination of two or more of these approaches.

prostate gland \ˈpräs-ˌtāt\ Chestnut-shaped male reproductive organ, located under the bladder, which adds secretions to the SPERM during ejaculation of SEMEN. It surrounds the urethra (see URINARY SYSTEM) and is rounded at the top, narrowing to a blunt point. The prostate consists of 30–50 GLANDS, supported by CONNECTIVE TISSUE, that discharge fluids into the urethra and two ejaculatory ducts. Those ducts, which also carry sperm and fluid discharged by the seminal vesicles, join the urethra inside the prostate. The prostate contributes 15–30% of the seminal fluid. It reaches its mature size at PUBERTY. Around age 50, it commonly shrinks and decreases its secretions; an increase in size after midlife may be due to INFLAMMATION or malignancy. See also PROSTATIC DISORDER.

prostatic disorder \prä-ˈsta-tik\ Abnormality or disease of the PROSTATE GLAND. About half of all men over 60 have some nonmalignant enlargement, or benign prostatic hyperplasia (BPH). The gland may eventually compress the urethra, causing problems urinating. Severe cases can lead to infection, bladder stones, obstruction, and kidney failure. Prostate cancer, also found mainly in older men, can be deadly but usually grows so slowly that most patients die of something else before the cancer spreads. Since surgery and radiation therapy often lead to incontinence and impotence, many cases are monitored (through prostate-specific antigen, or PSA, tests) and treated only if necessary. Gonorrhea and other bacterial infections involving the prostate are treated with antibiotics.

prosthesis \präs-ˈthē-səs\ Artificial substitute for a missing part of the body, usually an arm or leg. Prostheses have evolved from wooden legs and hooks that replaced hands, to sophisticated plastic, fiberglass, and metal devices, designed to fit limbs amputated at different points. They may have working joints and allow motion either by amplification of electric current generated by muscle contractions or by actual attachment to the patient's muscles. Arm prostheses usually allow some degree of grasping and manipulation. External or implanted breast prostheses are used after mastectomy.

prostitution Practice of engaging in sexual activity, usually with individuals other than a spouse or friend, in exchange for immediate payment in money or other valuables. Prostitutes may be of either sex and may engage in either heterosexual or homosexual activity, but most prostitution has been by females with males as clients. Prostitution is a very old and universal phenomenon; also universal is the condemnation of the prostitute but relative indifference toward the client. Prostitutes are often set apart in some way. In ancient Rome they were required to wear distinctive dress; under Hebrew law only foreign women could be prostitutes; in prewar Japan they were required to live in special sections of the city. In the European Middle Ages prostitution was licensed and regulated by law; an epidemic of venereal disease in the 16th century and post-Reformation morality led to the closure of brothels. In the U.S. prostitution was first curtailed by the Mann Act (1910), and by 1915 most states had banned brothels (Nevada being a notable exception). Prostitution is nevertheless tolerated in most U.S. and European cities, where police activity focuses instead on associated crimes. Prostitutes are very often poor and lack skills to support themselves; in many traditional societies, there are few other available money-earning occupations for women without family support. In developing African and Asian nations, prostitution has been largely responsible for the spread of AIDS and the orphaning of hundreds of thousands of children.

Protagoras \prō-ˈtag-ə-rəs\ (c. 485–410 BC) Greek philosopher, first and most famous of the SOPHISTS. He spent most of his life at Athens, where he considerably influenced contemporary thought on moral and political questions. He claimed to teach men "virtue" in the conduct of their daily lives. He is best known for his dictum "Man is the measure of all things," an expression of RELATIVISM. He expressed his agnosticism in *Concerning the Gods*. He was accused of impiety, his books were publicly burned, and he was exiled from Athens c. 415 BC.

protectionism Policy of protecting domestic industries against foreign competition by means of TARIFFS, SUBSIDIES, import QUOTAS, or other handicaps placed on imports. The chief protectionist measures, government-levied tariffs, raise the price of imported articles, making them less attractive to consumers than cheaper domestic products. Import quotas, which limit the quantities of goods that can be imported, are another protectionist device. Wars and economic depressions historically have resulted in increases in protectionism, while peace and prosperity have tended to encourage FREE TRADE. Protectionist policies were common in Europe in the 17th–18th century under MERCANTILISM. Britain abandoned many of its protectionist laws in the 19th century, and by World War I tariffs were low throughout the Western world. Economic and political dislocation led to rising customs barriers in Europe in the 1920s, and the GREAT DEPRESSION spawned an epidemic of protectionist measures; world trade shrank drastically as a result. The U.S. had a long history of protectionism, with tariffs reaching high points in the 1820s and the Great Depression, but in 1947 it became one of 23 nations to sign the GENERAL AGREEMENT ON TARIFFS AND TRADE (GATT), which substantially reduced customs tariffs. Despite trade agreements such as GATT, calls for protectionism are still heard in many countries when industries suffer severely from foreign competition. See also TRADE AGREEMENT, WORLD TRADE ORGANIZATION.

protectorate Relationship in which one country exercises some decisive control over another country or region. The degree of control may vary from one in which the protecting state guarantees the safety of the other to one that is a disguised form of annexation. Though the relationship is an ancient one, the use of the term dates only from the 19th century. In modern times most protectorates have been established by treaties requiring the weaker state to surrender management of its international relations, thus losing part of its SOVEREIGNTY.

protein Any of numerous organic compounds, complex POLYMERS of AMINO ACIDS needed for biochemical processes. Twenty different amino acids can occur in proteins, in chains of hundreds to thousands of units. An active protein has three important levels of structure: primary (the amino acid sequence), determined by the GENES; secondary (the geometric shape, often a helix), determined by the angles of the COVALENT BONDS between (peptide bonds) and within amino acids; and tertiary (the looped and folded overall shape), determined by the hydrogen bonds (see HYDROGEN BONDING) between amino-acid side chains. The tertiary structure, globular or sheetlike with ridges, crevices, or pockets, holds the key to an ENZYME's activity. Some proteins are simple (amino acids only), some conjugated (see CONJUGATION) to other groups, often VITAMINS or METALS needed in tiny amounts in the diet. HEMOGLOBIN is a conjugated protein. Proteins may be covalently linked to sugars (glyco-proteins), phosphorus (phospho-proteins), or sulfur (sulfo-proteins). Structural proteins include COLLAGEN and KERATIN. Almost all enzymes are proteins. Other biologically active proteins include HORMONES (e.g., INSULIN, ACTH, GROWTH HORMONE); transport proteins, which carry substances across membranes or to different parts of the body; and ANTIBODIES. Proteins have industrial uses in adhesives, plastics, and fibers, but most uses are in foods.

proteolysis \ˌprō-tē-ˈä-lə-səs\ Process in which a PROTEIN is broken down partially, into PEPTIDES, or completely, into AMINO ACIDS, by proteolytic ENZYMES, present in bacteria and in plants but most abundant in animals. Proteins in food are attacked in the stomach by PEPSIN and in the SMALL INTESTINE mainly by trypsin and chymotrypsin from the PANCREAS. Proteolytic enzymes are secreted as ZYMOGENS, which are themselves converted by proteolysis to their active forms. Many other zymogens or precursors undergo proteolysis to form active enzymes or proteins (e.g., fibrinogen to fibrin). In cells, proteolytic degradation of old proteins is part of cellular maintenance.

Proterozoic eon \ˌprä-tə-rə-ˈzō-ik, ˌprō-tə-rə-ˈzō-ik\ Younger of the two divisions of PRECAMBRIAN time, from 2.5 billion to 543 million years ago. Proterozoic rocks have been identified on all the continents and often constitute important sources of metallic ores, notably of iron, gold, copper, uranium, and nickel. The many small protocontinents that had formed during early Precambrian time had coalesced into one or several large landmasses by the beginning of the Proterozoic. Rocks of the Proterozoic contain many traces of primitive life forms, such as the fossil remains of BACTERIA and blue-green algae (see CYANOBACTERIA).

Protestant ethic Value attached to hard work, thrift, and self-discipline under certain Protestant doctrines, particularly those of CALVINISM. MAX WEBER, in *The Protestant Ethic and the Spirit of Capitalism* (1904–5), held that the Protestant ethic was an important factor in the economic success of Protestant groups in the early stages of European CAPITALISM, in that worldly success came to be interpreted as a sign of the individual's election to eternal salvation. Weber's thesis was variously criticized and expanded throughout the 20th century. See also PROTESTANTISM, RICHARD H. TAWNEY.

Protestantism One of the three major branches of CHRISTIANITY, originating in the 16th-century REFORMATION. The term applies to the beliefs of Christians who do not adhere to ROMAN CATHOLICISM or EASTERN ORTHODOXY. A variety of Protestant denominations grew out of the Reformation. The followers of MARTIN LUTHER established the evangelical churches of Germany and Scandinavia; those of JOHN CALVIN and more radical reformers such as HULDRYCH ZWINGLI founded REFORMED churches in other countries such as Switzerland and Scotland (PRESBYTERIANISM). Another important branch of Protestantism, represented by the Church of ENGLAND and EPISCOPAL CHURCH, had its origins in 16th-century England and is now the Protestant denomination closest to Roman Catholicism in theology and worship. The doctrines of the various Protestant denominations vary considerably, but all emphasize the supremacy of the BIBLE in matters of faith and order, JUSTIFICATION by GRACE through faith and not through works, and the PRIESTHOOD of all believers. See also ADVENTIST, BAPTIST, Society of FRIENDS, MENNONITE, METHODISM.

Proteus \ˈprō-tē-əs\ In GREEK MYTHOLOGY, the prophetic old man of the sea and the shepherd of sea animals such as seals. He was subject to POSEIDON. He knew all things—past, present, and future—but disliked telling what he knew. Those who wanted information from him had to catch him sleeping and bind him. He would try to escape by changing his form, but if a captor held him fast he gave the wished-for answer and plunged into the sea.

prothrombin \prō-ˈthräm-bin\ Carbohydrate-protein compound in PLASMA essential to COAGULATION. In response to bleeding, a complex series of clotting-factor interactions leads to its conversion by thromboplastin to thrombin, which transforms fibrinogen in plasma into fibrin. Fibrin and PLATELETS combine to form a clot. HEMOPHILIA is caused by a hereditary lack of one of the clotting factors. VITAMIN K is needed to synthesize prothrombin, so conditions that impair the vitamin's absorption result in prothrombin deficiency and a tendency to prolonged bleeding.

protist \ˈprō-təst\ Any member of a kingdom (Protista) of diverse EUKARYOTES, including ALGAE, PROTOZOANS, and lower fungi (see FUNGUS). Most are single-celled organisms, though the algae tend to be multicellular. Many can move, mainly by using flagella (see FLAGELLUM), cilia (see CILIUM), or footlike extensions (pseudopodia). The kingdom was developed to accommodate intermediate organisms that, even though they possessed some plant or animal characteristics, did not exhibit the specialized features indicative of those groups. Some protists are considered the ancestors of multicellular plants, animals, and fungi. The term was first suggested in 1866 by ERNST HAECKEL. With the development of advanced biochemical, genetic, and imaging techniques, previously established relationships have come under scrutiny, and it is now thought that some groups are less closely related to one another than once believed. As a result, the classification of protists, while convenient, is no longer entirely satisfactory.

Proto-Geometric style Visual art style of ancient Greece that signaled the reawakening of technical proficiency and conscious creative spirit after the collapse of the MINOAN and MYCENAEAN civilizations, around the 12th century BC. The vocabulary of the style was limited to circles, arcs, triangles, and wavy lines, all derived from Minoan-Mycenaean representations of aquatic and plant life. On pottery, these design elements were carefully placed in horizontal bands, mainly at a vase's shoulder or belly. Its lower portion was usually either left plain or painted in a solid glossy black pigment inherited from BRONZE AGE artists.

Proto-Geometric amphora from Athens, early 10th century BC; in the Kerameikos Museum, Athens.
HIRMER FOTOARCHIV, MUNICH

protoceratops \ˌprō-tə-ˈser-ə-ˌtäps\ Any member of a genus of quadrupedal DINOSAURS found as fossils in Gobi deposits of the CRETACEOUS PERIOD (144–65 million years ago). The hind limbs were more strongly developed than the forelimbs; the back was arched. Adults were about 7 ft (2 m) long and probably weighed about 400 lbs (180 kg). The skull was about one-fifth the body length. Bones in the skull grew backward into a perforated frill. The jaws were beaklike and toothed. There may have been a hornlike structure on top of the snout. Long spines on the well-developed tail suggest that protoceratops was semiaquatic.

Protococcus \ˌprō-tə-ˈkä-kəs\ *or* **Pleurococcus** Genus of green ALGAE. Popularly called MOSS though not actually classified as such, it is found as a thin, green covering on the moist, shaded side of trees, rocks, and soil. The spherical cells, either solitary or clumped together forming short false filaments, have heavy cell walls that protect them against excessive water loss. Each cell contains a large dense CHLOROPLAST. The position of *Protococcus* in classification systems is uncertain.

protocol In computer science, a set of rules or procedures for transmitting data between electronic devices, such as computers. In order for computers to exchange information, there must be a preexisting agreement as to how the information will be structured and how each side will send and receive it. Without a protocol, a transmitting computer, for example, could be sending its data in 8-BIT packets while the receiving computer might expect the data in 16-bit packets. Protocols are established by international or industrywide organizations. Perhaps the most important computer protocol is OSI (Open Systems Interconnection), a set of guidelines for implementing networking communications between computers. The most important sets of Internet protocols are TCP/IP, HTTP, and FTP.

proton Stable SUBATOMIC PARTICLE (one of the BARYONS) with a unit of positive ELECTRIC CHARGE and a mass 1,836 times that of the ELECTRON. Protons are found in the atomic nucleus along with NEUTRONS. For each ELEMENT, the number of protons in the nucleus is always the same and is its ATOMIC NUMBER. Protons have ANTIMATTER counterparts (antiprotons), with the same mass but a negative charge. Protons are used as projectiles in PARTICLE ACCELERATORS to produce and study nuclear reactions. They are the chief constituent of primary COSMIC RAYS and are among the products of radioactive decay (see RADIOACTIVITY) and nuclear reactions.

protoplasm CYTOPLASM and NUCLEUS of a CELL. In 1835, when the term was first defined, it referred to the ground substance of living material responsible for all living processes. Cells were seen as either fragments or containers of protoplasm, but the origin of formed structures within the cell, especially the nucleus, was unaccounted for. Today the term is used to mean simply the cytoplasm and nucleus.

protozoal diseases \ˌprō-tə-ˈzō-əl\ Diseases caused by PROTOZOANS. These organisms may remain in the human host for their entire life cycle, but many carry out part of their reproductive cycle in insects or other hosts. For example, mosquitoes are vectors of PLASMODIUM, the cause of MALARIA. See also ENTAMOEBA, *GIARDIA LAMBLIA*, *SLEEPING SICKNESS*.

protozoan \ˌprō-tə-ˈzō-ən\ Any of a group of small (usually microscopic) single-celled PROTISTS. They are found worldwide in most soils, fresh water, and oceans. While most are solitary individuals, various colonial forms exist. The taxonomic relationships of protozoans to one another and to other protists continue to be revised. The smallest known protozoans are tiny blood parasites less than 2 microns long; the largest may be 16 mm long and visible to the naked eye. Protozoan shapes vary, but all share such eukaryotic features as lipid-protein membranes and membrane-enclosed vacuoles and organelles (see EUKARYOTE). They show wide variation in modes of movement, nutrition, and reproduction. Various classification systems exist to group the protozoans. The major phyla include Sarcomastigophora (flagellated forms and forms possessing cytoplasmic extensions called pseudopodia), Ciliophora (ciliated forms), and Apicomplexa, Microspora, and Myxozoa (spore-producing forms). Apicomplexa and Microspora are sometimes included in the single phylum Sporozoa. Commonly known protozoans include DINOFLAGELLATES, AMOEBAS, and paramecia (see PARAMECIUM).

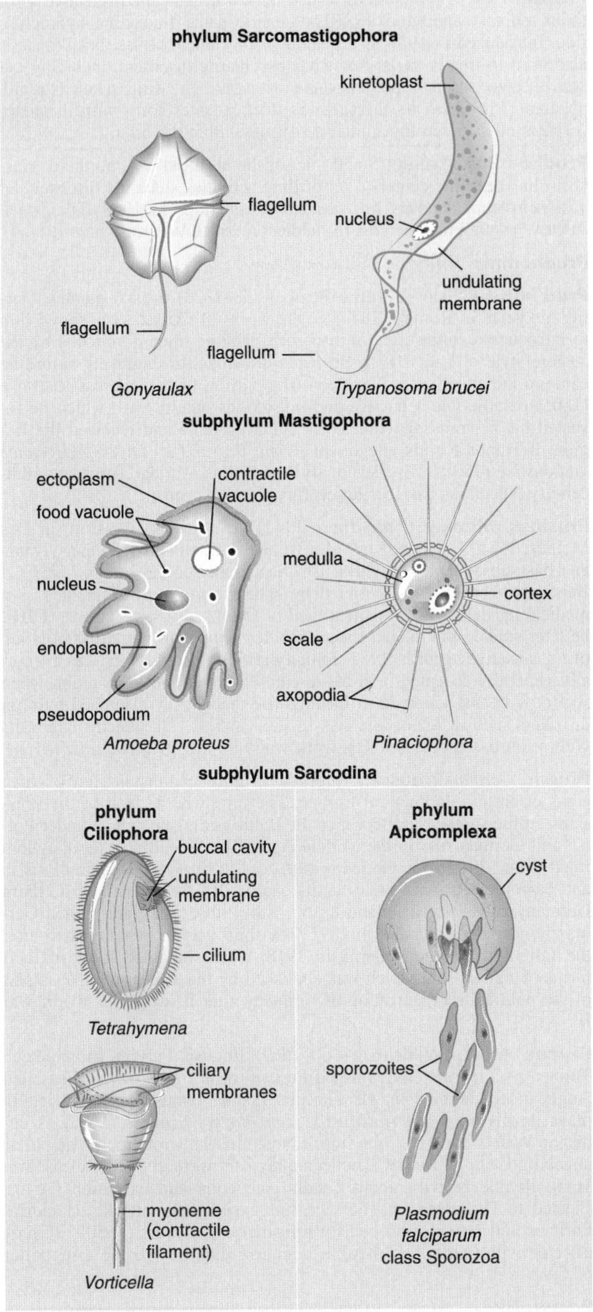

Representative protozoans. The zooflagellate *Trypanosoma brucei* is the causative agent of African sleeping sickness. The phytoflagellate *Gonyaulax* is one of the dinoflagellates responsible for the occurrence of red tides. The amoeba is one of the most common sarcodines. Other members of the subphylum Sarcodina, such as the radiolarians, heliozoans, and foraminiferans, usually possess protective coverings. The heliozoan *Pinaciophora* is shown covered with scales. The subphylum Ciliophora, which includes the ciliated *Tetrahymena* and *Vorticella,* contains the greatest number of protozoan species but is the most homogeneous group. The malaria-causing *Plasmodium* is spread by the bite of a mosquito that injects infective spores (sporozoites) into the bloodstream.

protractor Instrument for constructing and measuring plane ANGLES. The simplest protractor is a semicircular disk marked in degrees from 0° to 180°. A more complex protractor, for plotting position on NAVIGATION charts, is called a three-arm protractor, or station pointer, and consists of a circular scale connected to three arms. The center arm is fixed, while the outer two can be rotated to any desired angle relative to the center one. A related instrument is the course protractor, which allows navigators to measure the angular distance between north and the course plotted on a navigation chart.

Proudhon \prü-ˈdōⁿ\, **Pierre-Joseph** (1809–1865) French journalist and socialist. After working as a printer, he moved to Paris in 1838 and joined the socialist movement. His *What Is Property?* (1840) created a sensation with such phrases as "property is theft." While working in Lyon (1843–48) he encountered the Mutualists, a weavers' anarchist society whose name he later adopted for his form of ANARCHISM. His *System of Economic Contradictions* (1846) was attacked by KARL MARX and initiated the split between anarchists and Marxists. In Paris in 1848, Proudhon published radical newspapers; imprisoned 1849–52, he was harassed by the police after his release and fled to Belgium in 1858. On his return in 1862 he gained influence among the workers, including some of the founders of the FIRST INTERNATIONAL.

Proulx \ˈprü\, **(Edna) Annie** (born 1935) U.S. writer. Born in Norwich, Conn., she studied at the University of Vermont. She began professional writing with commissioned nonfiction books on cooking, gardening, and country living. She founded and edited (1984–86) *Behind the Times,* a rural Vermont newspaper, and published stories in men's outdoor magazines. Her first novel, *Postcards* (1992), depicting the decline of the small farm, received the PEN/Faulkner Award. It was followed by *The Shipping News* (1993, Pulitzer Prize, National Book Award), and *Accordion Crimes* (1996). Her story collections *Heart Songs* (1988) and *Close Range* (1999) also won high praise.

Proust \ˈprüst\, **Marcel** (1871–1922) French novelist. Born to a wealthy family, he studied law and literature. His social connections allowed him to become an observant habitué of the most exclusive drawing rooms of the nobility, and he wrote social pieces for Parisian journals. He published essays and stories, including the story collection *Pleasures and Days* (1896). He had suffered from asthma since childhood, and c. 1897 he began to disengage from social life as his health declined. Half-Jewish himself, he became a major supporter of ALFRED DREYFUS in the affair that made French anti-Semitism into a hugely controversial national issue. Deeply affected by his mother's death in 1905, he withdrew further from society. An incident of involuntary revival of childhood memory through the taste of a rusk biscuit in 1909 led him to retire almost totally into an eccentric seclusion in his cork-lined bedroom to write *À la recherche du temps perdu* (1913–27; *In Search of Lost Time,* or *Remembrance of Things Past*). The vast seven-part novel is at once a kind of autobiography, a vast social panorama of France in the years just before and during World War I, and an im-

Marcel Proust, oil painting by Jacques-Émile Blanche; in a private collection.

O P Q R

mense meditation on love and jealousy and on art and its relation to reality. One of the supreme achievements in fiction of all time, it brought him worldwide fame and affected the entire climate of the 20th-century novel.

Provençal language See OCCITAN LANGUAGE

Provence \prō-'vä^{n}s\ Historical and cultural region, southeastern coastal France. It was part of Roman Gallia NARBONENSIS. With the breakdown of the Roman empire in the late 5th century, it was invaded successively by the Visigoths, Burgundians, and Ostrogoths. It came under the rule of the Franks c. 536. During the 13th century it was involved in the ALBIGENSIAN CRUSADE. It was united with the French crown in 1481. Its language, Provençal, was important in medieval literature, and its ROMANESQUE ARCHITECTURE was an outstanding cultural achievement of the Middle Ages. It suffered in the 16th-century Wars of RELIGION. In 1790, during the FRENCH REVOLUTION, it lost its political institutions and was divided into several departments.

proverb Succinct and pithy saying that is in general use and expresses commonly held ideas and beliefs. Proverbs are part of every spoken language and folk literature, originating in oral tradition. Often the same proverb is found in many variants in different parts of the world. Literate societies from the ancient Egyptians on have collected their proverbs. One of the earliest English proverb collections, *The Proverbs of Alfred,* dates from c. 1150–80. In North America the best-known collection is probably that of *Poor Richard's,* an almanac published 1732–57 by BENJAMIN FRANKLIN.

Providence City (pop., 2000: 173,618), capital of Rhode Island. It is located at the head of NARRAGANSETT BAY on the Providence River. Founded in 1636 by ROGER WILLIAMS as a refuge for religious dissenters, it was partly destroyed in KING PHILIP'S WAR in 1676. It played an important role in the AMERICAN REVOLUTION and was a major port in trade with the WEST INDIES in the 18th century. Incorporated as a city in 1831, it became the sole capital of the state in 1900, an honor it had shared with NEWPORT since 1854. A seaport and an industrial and commercial center, it is the focus of a metropolitan area that includes Pawtucket and East Providence. Educational institutions include BROWN UNIV. and the RHODE ISLAND SCHOOL OF DESIGN.

Provincetown Town (pop., 2000: 3,431), eastern Massachusetts, northern tip of CAPE COD. It was the first landing place of the PILGRIMS in 1620, and the MAYFLOWER COMPACT was drawn up in its harbor. Incorporated as a town in 1727, it was a whaling and fishing port in the 19th century. Bounded by the Cape Cod National Seashore, it is a popular summer resort and noted artists' colony. The PROVINCETOWN PLAYERS theater group originated there.

Provincetown Players U.S. theatrical company (1915–29), founded by a group of writers and artists in Provincetown, Mass., to encourage new and experimental works. One of their first productions, which were often staged in members' homes, was of the first play of EUGENE O'NEILL, a founding member whose career was launched by the Players. In 1916 the players moved to New York's Greenwich Village. There they introduced several more of O'Neill's plays as well as works by EDNA ST. VINCENT MILLAY, Susan Glaspell, Paul Green, and dozens of other playwrights. The company disbanded after the stock-market crash of 1929, though the Provincetown Playhouse has continued to serve intermittently as a theater into the 21st century.

Provisions of Oxford See Provisions of OXFORD

Provisors, Statute of (1351) Law passed by the English Parliament during the reign of EDWARD III. It set up procedures to increase royal control over the papal practice of making appointments to church benefices in England, and damaged English relations with the church.

Provo City (pop., 2000: 105,166), northern central Utah. Situated on the Provo River between Utah Lake and the WASATCH MTNS., it was founded in 1849 by MORMON colonists. Construction of railroads in the 1870s spurred the city's development as a center for the mining of silver, lead, copper, and gold. The founding in 1875 of Brigham Young Academy (now BRIGHAM YOUNG UNIV.) also contributed to Provo's growth. The city's industries include steel, canning, electronics, and textiles. Nearby is TIMPANOGOS CAVE NATIONAL MONUMENT.

Proxima Centauri See ALPHA CENTAURI

Prozac First of the class of ANTIDEPRESSANT drugs called selective serotonin reuptake inhibitors (SSRIs), generic name fluoxetine hydrochloride. Introduced in 1986 as a treatment for clinical DEPRESSION, Prozac is also used to treat a variety of other psychiatric disorders, including OBSESSIVE-COMPULSIVE DISORDER and BULIMIA NERVOSA. The drug, taken as a pill, apparently achieves its therapeutic effect by interfering with the reabsorption of the neurotransmitter SEROTONIN within the brain.

Prudhoe Bay \'prü-dō\ Small inlet of the BEAUFORT SEA, northern Alaska. It has been the center of oil-drilling activities since the discovery of vast petroleum deposits on Alaska's North Slope in 1968. The TRANS-ALASKA PIPELINE links the area to Valdez on PRINCE WILLIAM SOUND.

Prudhomme, Sully See SULLY PRUDHOMME

Prud'hon \prūē-'dō^{n}\, **Pierre-Paul** (1758–1823) French painter. During his years in Rome (1784–88), the works of CORREGGIO inspired him to introduce a softer effect into French painting, then dominated by the austere style of J.-L. DAVID. He made drawings for engravers before he came to the attention of Napoleon. His portrait of the empress JOSEPHINE (1805) exhibits the seductive and mysterious quality with which he invested his portraits of women. He achieved fame and received the Legion of Honor for his allegorical *Crime Pursued by Divine Vengeance and Justice* (1808). His elegant style served as a bridge from late-18th-century Neoclassicism to 19th-century Romanticism.

Prusiner, Stanley (Ben) (born 1942) U.S. neurologist. Born in Des Moines, Iowa, he earned his MD from the University of Pennsylvania and has subsequently taught at UC–San Francisco (1974–84) and UC–Berkeley (from 1984). Intrigued by spongiform encephalopathies as a medical resident when a patient died of CREUTZFELDT-JAKOB DISEASE (CJD), he later studied the related sheep disorder scrapie and reported isolation of its causative agent in 1982. Initially criticized, his theory was eventually generally accepted, and his research received world attention when MAD COW DISEASE emerged in Britain. The theory may also shed light on disorders such as ALZHEIMER'S DISEASE and PARKINSONISM, which share traits with prion-based diseases. His work won him a 1997 Nobel Prize.

Prussia *German* **Preussen** \'prȯs-^{ə}n\ In European history, any of three areas of eastern and central Europe. The first was the land of the Prussians on the southeastern coast of the Baltic Sea, which came under Polish and German rule in the Middle Ages. The second was the kingdom ruled from 1701 by the German HOHENZOLLERN DYNASTY, including Prussia and BRANDENBURG, with BERLIN as its capital. It seized much of northern Germany and western Poland in the 18th–19th century and united Germany under its leadership in 1871. The third was the state created after the fall of the Hohenzollerns in 1918, which included most of their former kingdom and which was abolished by the Allies in 1947 as part of the political reorganization of Germany after its defeat in World War II.

Prynne \'prin\, **William** (1600–1669) English Puritan pamphleteer. Trained as a lawyer, he published Puritan tracts from 1627 and assailed Anglican ceremonialism. He attacked popular amusements, especially plays, in his book *Histrio Mastix: The Players Scourge* (1633). Archbishop WILLIAM LAUD had him imprisoned; after he wrote more pamphlets attacking Laud and other Anglicans, his ears were cut off. Released in 1640, Prynne brought about Laud's conviction and execution (1645). Elected to Parliament in 1648, he was expelled for attacks on radical Puritans and later imprisoned for refusing to pay taxes (1650–53). Disaffected with OLIVER CROMWELL's Commonwealth, he became a supporter of CHARLES II.

Przewalski's horse \pshə-'väl-skēz, ˌpər-zhə-'väl-skēz\ Last wild EQUINE subspecies *(Equus caballus przewalskii)* surviving into the 20th century. It is yellowish or light red (dun) and stands 12–14 hands (48–56 in., 122–142 cm) high. It has a dark mane and tail and usually a stripe on the back. The mane is short and erect with no forelock. It was discovered in western Mongolia in the 1870s. The horse disappeared in the wild in the 1960s, but the descendants of specimens that

Przewalski's horse (*Equus caballus przewalskii*).

KENNETH W. FINK FROM ROOT RESOURCES

had earlier been taken to European zoos began to be reintroduced into the Mongolian steppe in the 1990s.

psalm \'säm\ Sacred song or poem. The term is most widely known from the Book of Psalms in the OLD TESTAMENT. The 150 psalms, ranging in subject from songs of joyous faith and thanksgiving to songs of bitter protest and lamentation, rank among the immortal poetry of all time. They have had a profound influence on the liturgies of Judaism and Christianity. Their dating and authorship are highly problematic, and the tradition of assigning them to King DAVID is no longer accepted. In the original Hebrew text the book had no name. When the Hebrew Bible was translated into Greek (the SEPTUAGINT), it was titled *Psalterion,* referring to a stringed instrument to accompany such songs.

Pseudo-Demetrius See False DMITRY

Pseudo-Dionysius the Areopagite (fl. c. 500) Probably a Syrian monk. Under the pseudonym DIONYSIUS THE AREOPAGITE, he wrote a series of treatises that united Neoplatonic philosophy (see NEOPLATONISM), Christian theology, and mystical experience. Their doctrinal content covers the Trinity, the angelic world, the incarnation and redemption, and provides an explanation of all that is. His treatise "On Divine Names" discussed the nature and effects of contemplative prayer. The Dionysian corpus was absorbed into Greek and Eastern Christian theologies and also influenced mystics in the Western church. THOMAS AQUINAS was among those who wrote commentaries on the works.

pseudomonad \ˌsü-də-'mō-ˌnad\ Any of a large and varied group of rod-shaped, often curved BACTERIA. Many can move, propelled by one or more flagella. Some aquatic species are attached to surfaces by long strands or stalks. Most are found in soil or water; some cause diseases in plants, and a few cause serious diseases in humans and other mammals. One very common and widespread species, *Pseudomonas aeruginosa,* is a serious cause of disease in humans, causing antibiotic-resistant infections in individuals with weakened resistance. Pseudomonads have been implicated in hospital-acquired infections of surgical wounds and severely burned tissue and in fatal infections of cancer patients treated with immunosuppressive drugs.

psilomelane \ˌsī-lō-'me-ˌlān\ Barium and manganese hydrous oxide, $BaMnMn_8O_{16}(OH)_4$, an important ore mineral of MANGANESE. What was formerly called psilomelane is now known to be a mixture of several manganese oxides of which romanechite is a major constituent. Such manganese oxide mixtures may form large deposits and may occur in lake or swamp bedded deposits and clays; it has been found in Germany, France, Belgium, Scotland, Sweden, India, and the U.S. The name *psilomelane* (from the Greek words for "smooth" and "black") refers to its typical black, smooth-surfaced, grape-bunch-shaped or stalactitic masses.

psoriasis \sə-'rī-ə-səs\ Chronic, recurrent skin disorder with reddish, slightly elevated patches or bumps covered with silvery-white scales. Spots may coalesce into large patches around a normal area. If the nails are involved, they may become pitted, thick, and separated from the nail bed. Skin injury, infection, stress, and certain drugs may trigger psoriasis. Skin cells move at an accelerated rate from the dermis into the epidermis, where they slough off, causing inflammation. In some cases, patients also have arthritis. Psoriasis often becomes less severe in the summer and during pregnancy. There is no cure, but treatment with drugs and ultraviolet light may help.

Psyche, depicted with wings, classical sculpture; in the Louvre, Paris.
ALINARI—ART RESOURCE/EB INC.

Psyche \'sī-kē\ In Greek and Roman mythology, a beautiful princess who won CUPID's love. Her beauty was such that worshipers began to turn away from VENUS, and the envious goddess commanded her son Cupid to make Psyche fall in love with the most despicable of men. But Cupid himself fell in love, and hid Psyche in a remote place where he visited her secretly under cover of darkness. One night she lit a lamp and discovered her lover's identity. He left angrily, and Psyche wandered the earth searching for him. Venus captured her, but after Cupid rescued her, JUPITER made her immortal and gave her in marriage to Cupid.

psychiatry Branch of medicine concerned with mental disorders. Until the 18th century, mental-health problems were considered forms of demonic possession; gradually they came to be seen as illnesses requiring treatment. In the 19th century, research into and classification and treatment of mental illnesses advanced. SIGMUND FREUD's psychoanalytic theory dominated the field for many years before it was challenged by behavioral and cognitive therapy and humanistic PSYCHOLOGY in the mid-20th century. Psychiatrists hold MD degrees and can prescribe drugs and other medical treatments in addition to conducting psychotherapy. The psychiatrist often works as a member of a mental-health team that includes clinical psychologists and social workers.

psychoanalysis Method of treating MENTAL DISORDERS that emphasizes the probing of unconscious mental processes. It is based on the psychoanalytic theory devised by SIGMUND FREUD in Vienna in the late 19th and early 20th century. It calls for patients to engage in free ASSOCIATION of ideas, speaking to therapists about anything that comes to mind. DREAMS and slips of the tongue are examined as a key to the workings of the unconscious mind, and the "work" of therapy is to uncover the tensions existing between the instinctual drive of the ID, the perceptions and actions of the EGO, and the censorship imposed by the morality of the SUPEREGO. Careful attention is paid to early childhood experiences (especially those with a sexual dimension), the memory of which may have been repressed because of guilt or trauma; recalling and analyzing these experiences is thought to help free patients from the ANXIETY and neuroses caused by REPRESSION as well as from more serious illnesses known as psychoses (see NEUROSIS, PSYCHOSIS). Some of Freud's early associates, notably CARL GUSTAV JUNG and ALFRED ADLER, rejected his theories on many points and devised alternative methods of analysis. Other important figures in psychoanalysis, including ERIK ERIKSON, KAREN HORNEY, and ERICH FROMM, accepted the basic Freudian framework but contributed their own additions or modifications.

psycholinguistics Study of the mental processes involved in the perception, production, and acquisition of LANGUAGE. Much psycholinguistic work has been devoted to the learning of language by children and on speech processing and comprehension by both children and adults. In the 1960s and '70s, the theories of NOAM CHOMSKY stimulated much research; in recent years psycholinguists have employed other models as well. See also LINGUISTICS.

psychological development Development of cognitive, emotional, intellectual, and social capabilities and functioning over the course of one's life. It is the subject matter of the discipline of DEVELOPMENTAL PSYCHOLOGY. In INFANCY, language is acquired, PERCEPTION, EMOTION, and MEMORY take shape, and learning and motor skills develop. In childhood, SPEECH emerges, cognitive abilities advance from concrete to abstract operations, emotional responses become more sophisticated, and EMPATHY and moral reasoning begin to be employed. ADOLESCENCE is a time of rapid emotional and intellectual growth, while ADULTHOOD is characterized by the maturing of all developmental processes.

psychological testing Use of tests to measure the skill, knowledge, intelligence, capacities, or aptitudes of an individual or group. Best known is the IQ test; other tests include achievement tests, designed to evaluate a student's grade or performance level, and PERSONALITY tests. The latter include both inventory-type (question-and-response) tests and projective tests such as the Rorschach (inkblot) and thematic apperception (picture-theme) tests, which are used by clinical psychologists and psychiatrists to help diagnose mental disorders and by psychotherapists and counselors to help assess their clients. Experimental psychologists routinely devise tests to obtain data on PERCEPTION, LEARNING, and MOTIVATION. See also EXPERIMENTAL PSYCHOLOGY, PSYCHOMETRICS.

psychological warfare Use of propaganda against an enemy, supported by whatever military, economic, or political measures are required, and usually intended to demoralize an enemy or to win it over to a different point of view. It has been carried on since ancient times. The conquests of GENGHIS KHAN were aided by expertly planted rumors about large numbers of ferocious MONGOL horsemen in his army. Specialized units were a major part of the German and Allied forces in World War II and the U.S. armed forces in the Korean and Vietnam wars. Strategic psychological warfare is mass communications directed to a very large audience or over a considerable expanse of territory; tactical psychological warfare implies a direct connection with combat operations (e.g., the surrender demand). Consolidation psychological warfare consists of messages distributed to the rear of one's own advancing forces for the sake of protecting the line of communications, establishing military government, and carrying out administrative tasks within such a government.

psychology Scientific discipline that studies mental processes and behavior in humans and other animals. Literally meaning "the study of the mind," psychology focuses on both individual and group behavior. Clinical psychology is concerned with the diagnosis and treatment of MENTAL DISORDERS. Other specialized fields of psychology include CHILD PSYCHOLOGY, EDUCATIONAL PSYCHOLOGY, sports psychology, SOCIAL PSYCHOLOGY, and COMPARATIVE PSYCHOLOGY. The issues studied by psychologists cover a wide spectrum, including LEARNING, COGNITION, INTELLIGENCE, motivation, EMOTION, PERCEPTION, PERSONALITY, and the extent to which individual differences are shaped by genetics or environment. The methods used in psychological research include observation, interviews, psychological testing, laboratory experimentation, and statistical analysis.

psychometrics Science of psychological measurement. Psychometricians design and administer psychological tests (see PSYCHOLOGICAL TESTING), both to generate empirical data on mental processes and to refine their understanding of measurement techniques and the statistical analysis of results. Major concerns include test reliability and validity and the norming or standardization of results.

psychomotor seizure \,sī-kə-'mōt-ər\ Type of EPILEPSY involving subjective sensations (aura) followed by clouded consciousness and automatic behavior. It may include hallucinations of various senses, a sense of unreality of objects or people, déjà vu, intense fear, abdominal sensations, or awareness of increased respiration or heartbeat. Afterwards, the individual is unresponsive or shows depressed awareness for a few minutes, remembering only the aura. Rarely, frequent mild seizures merge into a period of confusion lasting hours or days, with fluctuating levels of awareness and inappropriate behavior. Different types of attacks originate in different brain regions.

psychoneurosis See NEUROSIS

psychopathology See ABNORMAL PSYCHOLOGY

psychopharmacology Study of the effect of drugs on the mind and behavior, particularly in the context of developing treatments for mental disorders. Major psychopharmacological advances in the 20th century include the development of TRANQUILIZERS, ANTIDEPRESSANTS, lithium carbonate (for BIPOLAR DISORDER), certain stimulants (including AMPHETAMINES), and antipsychotic agents such as chlorpromazine (Thorazine), fluphenazine (Prolixin), and haloperidol (Haldol).

psychophysics Branch of psychology concerned with the effect of physical stimuli (such as sound waves) on mental processes. Psychophysics was established by GUSTAV THEODOR FECHNER in the mid-19th century, and since then its central inquiry has remained the quantitative relation between stimulus and SENSATION. A key tenet has been WEBER'S LAW. Psychophysical methods are used today in vision research and audiology, PSYCHOLOGICAL TESTING, and commercial product comparisons (e.g., tobacco, perfume, and liquor).

psychosis \sī-'kō-səs\ Serious mental derangement characterized by defective or lost contact with reality. The primary psychoses are SCHIZOPHRENIA and the delusional disorders (e.g., megalomania), but extreme cases of DEPRESSION and BIPOLAR DISORDER, substance-induced DELIRIUM, and certain varieties of DEMENTIA are also understood to share important features with the psychoses. The major symptoms, aside from delusions and HALLUCINATIONS, are disorganized speech and behavior and often mood disturbances. Treatment usually consists of medication and counseling in an institutional setting.

psychosomatic disorder Bodily ailment or symptom, caused by mental or emotional disturbance, in which psychological stresses adversely affect physiological (somatic) functioning to the point of distress. Psychosomatic disorders may include HYPERTENSION, respiratory ailments, gastrointestinal disturbances, migraine and tension HEADACHES, SEXUAL DYSFUNCTIONS, DERMATITIS, and ULCERS. Many patients suffering from psychosomatic conditions respond to a combination of drug therapy and PSYCHOTHERAPY. See also HYPOCHONDRIASIS.

psychosurgery Treatment of PSYCHOSIS or other MENTAL DISORDERS by means of brain surgery. The first such technique was the prefrontal LOBOTOMY. Fairly common from the 1930s through the 1950s, lobotomy reduced neurotic symptoms such as agitation and aggressiveness, but also left patients apathetic and with a limited range of emotions; it has since been largely replaced by the use of tranquilizing and antipsychotic drugs (see PSYCHOPHARMACOLOGY). A form of psychosurgery developed more recently involves the placement of tiny lesions in specific areas of the brain and has little effect on intellectual function or quality of life; it has been used to treat OBSESSIVE-COMPULSIVE DISORDER and occasionally cases of severe ANXIETY.

psychotherapy Treatment of mental or emotional disturbance through interpersonal communications between the sufferer and a trained counselor or therapist. The goal of many modern individual and GROUP THERAPIES is to establish a central relationship of trust in which the client or patient can feel free to express personal thoughts and emotions and thus gain insight into his or her condition and generally share in the healing power of words. Such therapies include PSYCHOANALYSIS and its variants (see ALFRED ADLER, CARL GUSTAV JUNG), client-centered or NONDIRECTIVE PSYCHOTHERAPY, Gestalt therapy (see GESTALT PSYCHOLOGY), play and art therapy, and general COUNSELING. In contrast, BEHAVIOR THERAPY focuses on modifying behavior by reinforcement techniques without concerning itself with internal states.

Ptah \'ptä\ In EGYPTIAN RELIGION, the creator god. The patron of craftsmen, especially sculptors, Ptah was identified by the Greeks with HEPHAESTUS, the divine blacksmith. He was represented as a man in mummy form, wearing a skullcap and a short, straight false beard. He was originally the local deity of MEMPHIS, capital of Egypt from the 1st dynasty onward; the political importance of Memphis caused Ptah's cult to spread across Egypt. With Sekhmet and Nefertem, he was one of the Memphite Triad of deities.

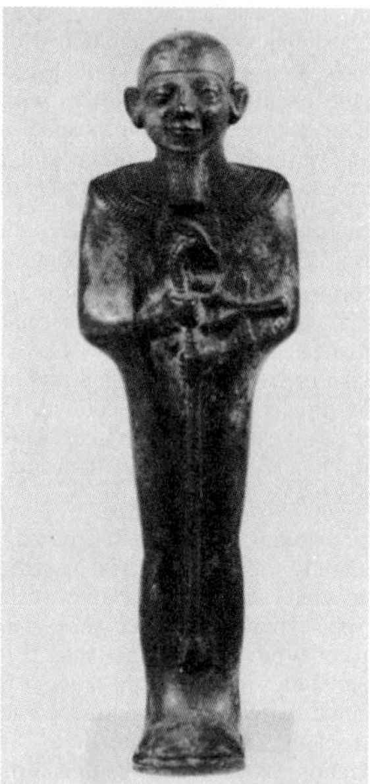

Ptah, holding the emblems of life and power, bronze statuette, Memphis, c. 600–100 BC; in the British Museum.
BY COURTESY OF THE TRUSTEES OF THE BRITISH MUSEUM

ptarmigan \'tär-mi-gən\ Any of three or four species of GROUSE (genus *Lagopus*) of cold regions. Ptarmigan plumage changes from white in winter to gray or brown, with barring, in spring and summer. The toes are covered with stiff feathers above and below. The common ptarmigan *(L. mutus)* occurs throughout the British Isles, Europe, and North America, where it is called rock ptarmigan. Ptarmigans survive winter in the Arctic and on mountaintops by browsing shrubs and scratching up lichens and leaves; they burrow in snow to sleep. Males begin group displays in early spring and then separate and display singly in adjoining territories.

Pteranodon \tə-'ra-nə-,dän\ Genus of extinct flying REPTILES, descendants of the PTERODACTYL. Fossils are known from Late Cretaceous (99–65 million years ago) deposits of Europe, Asia, and North America. *Pteranodon* had a wingspan of 23 ft (7 m) or more. The largest specimen had a wingspan of 50 ft (15.5 m). The body was about the size of a modern turkey. *Pteranodon* had a crest at the back of the skull and long, pelican-like, toothless jaws. They probably made nests and spent much time gliding over the ocean searching for fish. They probably depended on air currents for liftoff rather than on flapping their wings.

pterodactyl \,ter-ə-'dak-t^{ə}l\ Any member of the PTEROSAUR suborder Pterodactyloidea, known from Late Jurassic and Cretaceous fossils

(159–65 million years ago) in eastern Africa and Europe. Members of the typical genus, *Pterodactylus,* ranged from the size of a sparrow to that of an albatross. Pterodactyls had slender, delicate teeth that were angled forward (possibly for use as straining devices), long metacarpal bones, and a short tail. They were probably able gliders but not efficient as active fliers, and they apparently lacked feathers. Unlike the ARCHAEOPTERYX, the pterodactyl was not an ancestor of the birds.

pterosaur \'ter-ə-ˌsȯr\ Any of several extinct flying REPTILES (order Pterosauria) that flourished during the Jurassic and Cretaceous periods (206–65 million years ago). Pterosaurs hung by their long, slender hind limbs when at rest. They soared and glided on fragile, membranous wings that were attached to the long fourth finger of each forelimb and extended along the flank. The first three fingers were slender, clawed, clutching structures. Pterosaurs had a long, slender beak and a large brain. *Ramphorhynchus* had strong, sharply pointed teeth, a long tail, and a wingspread of about 3 ft (1 m). It probably obtained food by diving for fish. See also PTERODACTYL.

Ptolemaïs \ˌtä-lə-'mā-əs\ Ancient coastal city, CYRENAICA, on the left bank of the NILE RIVER, south of MEMPHIS. It received its name in the 3rd century BC from PTOLEMY III, who united Cyrenaica with Egypt. Its economy was based on trade with the interior, and it flourished in Hellenistic times, in the early period of the Roman empire, and again from the late 3rd century AD, when DIOCLETIAN made it the metropolis of the Roman province of Upper Libya.

Ptolemy \'tä-lə-mē\ *Latin* **Claudius Ptolemaeus** (fl. AD 127–145) Greek astronomer and mathematician. He worked principally in Alexandria. It is often difficult to determine which findings in his great astronomical book, the *ALMAGEST*, are Ptolemy's and which HIPPARCHUS's. The sun, moon, planets, and stars, he believed, were attached to crystalline spheres, centered on the earth, which turned to create the cycles of day and night, the lunar month, and so on. In order to explain retrograde motion of the planets, he refined a complex geometrical model of cycles within cycles that was highly successful at predicting the planets' positions in the sky. The earth-centered Ptolemaic system became dogmatically asserted in Western Christendom until the sun-centered COPERNICAN SYSTEM replaced it. His *Geography* contained an estimate of the size of the earth, a description of its surface, and a list of places located by latitude and longitude. Ptolemy also dabbled in mechanics, optics, and music theory.

Ptolemy I Soter \'tä-lə-mē...'sō-tər\ (c. 365–283/282 BC) Ruler of Egypt (323–285) and founder of the Ptolemaic dynasty. A Macedonian general of ALEXANDER THE GREAT, he and the other generals divided the empire after Alexander's death, Ptolemy becoming SATRAP of Egypt. Alexander's successors were soon at war. Ptolemy was defeated in 306 by ANTIGONUS I MONOPHTHALMUS, though he and the others rebuffed Antigonus' attack on Egypt. He earned the name Soter ("Savior") after defeating Antigonus on Rhodes (304), but Antigonus was not finally crushed until 301 at the Battle of IPSUS. Ptolemy secured and expanded his empire through alliances and marriages. He and his fellow kings won a final war (288–286) against DEMETRIUS of Macedonia, freeing Athens from Macedonian occupation. He obtained control of the League of Islanders (including most of the Aegean islands), which formed the basis of Egypt's maritime supremacy. As king he respected Egyptian culture, blended Greek and Egyptian peoples and religions, and founded the Library and Museum of ALEXANDRIA. After his death the Egyptians raised him to the level of a god. He was succeeded by his son, PTOLEMY II PHILADELPHUS.

Ptolemy II Philadelphus (308–264 BC) King of Egypt (285–246 BC), second king of the Ptolemaic dynasty. He reigned as co-ruler (285–282) with his father, PTOLEMY I SOTER, then purged his family of rivals, including his first wife, and married his sister, ARSINOE II. Wars with the rulers of the SELEUCID and ANTIGONID dynasties weakened his influence in the Aegean and brought near-disaster to his allies Athens and Sparta. He concluded these wars by diplomacy and marriage alliances and managed to regain his influence in the Aegean. He devised a buffer zone of possessions to protect Egypt from attack, and he dealt with reverses through diplomacy. A prudent and enlightened ruler, he promoted economic development and made Alexandria into a center for poets and scholars.

Ptolemy III–XV (r.246–30 BC) Macedonian kings of the Ptolemaic dynasty in Egypt. Ptolemy III Euergetes ("Benefactor") (fl. 246–221) defeated the ruler of the SELEUCID DYNASTY in the Third Syrian War (245–241). Ptolemy IV Philopator ("Father-loving") allowed Egypt to decline under his debauched rule (r.221–205). Ptolemy IX Soter II ruled with his mother (116–110, 109–107), until she expelled him and installed his brother Ptolemy X Alexander (r.107–88). Alexander's unpopularity resulted in his expulsion, and he died at sea in 88. Soter II assumed sole rule (88–81), installing his brother's widow, his own daughter, with him. Ptolemy XI Alexander II (r.80 BC) was the last fully legitimate Ptolemaic king of Egypt. He took Ptolemy IX Soter II's widow as wife and co-ruler, on SULLA's command, then murdered her and took sole power, for which the people of Alexandria killed him; his rule lasted 19 days. Ptolemy XIV Theos Philopator II shared power (47–44 BC) with his sister CLEOPATRA; it was probably she who had him assassinated, to make way for her son by Julius CAESAR. Ptolemy XV Caesar, or Caesarion, shared power with his mother from 44 BC; he was killed by Octavian (later AUGUSTUS) after Cleopatra's suicide in 30 BC. His death marked the Roman conquest of Egypt and the dynasty's end.

puberty In human physiology, the period of first becoming capable of reproducing sexually. Occurring at about age 12 in girls and age 14 in boys, puberty is characterized by the maturing of the genital organs, development of secondary sex characteristics, and, in girls, onset of MENSTRUATION. Both sexes experience a swift increase in body size and changes in body shape and composition. Puberty marks the beginning of ADOLESCENCE.

pubic louse See human LOUSE

Public Broadcasting Service See PBS

public debt See NATIONAL DEBT

public health Science and art of preventing disease, prolonging life, and promoting health through organized community efforts. These include sanitation, control of contagious infections, hygiene education, early diagnosis and preventive treatment, and adequate living standards. It requires understanding not only of epidemiology, nutrition, and antiseptic practices but also of social science. Historical public-health measures included quarantine of leprosy victims in the Middle Ages and efforts to improve sanitation following the 14th-century plague epidemics. Population increases in Europe in the 1750s brought with them increased awareness of infant deaths and a proliferation of hospitals. Britain's Public Health Act of 1848 established a special public-health ministry. In the U.S. today, public health is studied and coordinated on a national level by the CENTERS FOR DISEASE CONTROL AND PREVENTION; internationally, the WORLD HEALTH ORGANIZATION plays an equivalent role.

public house *or* **pub** Establishment that serves alcoholic beverages for consumption on the premises, especially in Britain. Under English common law, inns and taverns were declared public houses responsible for the well-being of travelers. They were expected to receive all travelers in reasonable condition who were willing to pay for food, drink, and lodging. In Tudor England, certain innkeepers were obliged by royal act to maintain stables; others served as unofficial postmasters. The early public houses were identified by simple signs that featured creatures such as lions, dolphins, or swans. In the 18th century, the word Arms was added to many pub names to indicate that the establishment was under the protection of a noble family. Though British public houses were traditionally owned and operated by independent licensed proprietors, by the early 20th century many were owned or associated with brewery companies.

public relations (PR) Aspect of communications that involves promoting a desirable image for a person or group seeking public attention. It originated in the U.S. in the early 20th century with pioneers such as EDWARD L. BERNAYS, who first developed the idea of the professional publicist, and IVY LEDBETTER LEE. Government agencies in Britain and the U.S. soon began hiring publicists to engineer support for their policies and programs, and the public-relations business boomed after World War II. Clients may include individuals such as politicians, performers, and authors, and groups such as business corporations, government agencies, charities, and religious bodies. The audience addressed may be as narrow as male alternative-music fans between the ages of 21 and 30 or as broad as the world at large. A publicist's functions include generating favorable publicity and knowing what kind of story is likely to be printed or broadcast. The task is complicated by the variety of existing media: besides newspapers, magazines, radio, and television, there are publications of professional associations, direct-mail lists, on-site promotional events, and so on. It consists largely of optimizing good news and forestalling bad news; if disaster strikes, the publicist must assess the situation, organize the client's response so as to minimize damage, and marshal and present information to the media.

Public Safety, Committee of See COMMITTEE OF PUBLIC SAFETY

public school *or* **independent school** In Britain, any of a small group of tuition-charging secondary schools that specialize in preparing students for university and for public service. The name public school dates from the 18th century, when the schools began attracting students from beyond their immediate environs, and thus became "public" as opposed to local. Such schools are thus in fact private schools independent of the state system. Important boys' schools include Winchester (1394), ETON, Westminster (1560), and Harrow (1571); well-known girls' schools include Cheltenham, Roedean, and Wycomb Abbey. Public schools cultivated a class-conscious code of behavior, speech, and appearance that set the standard for British officialdom from the early 19th century. See also COLLEGE, SECONDARY EDUCATION.

public television See PBS

public transportation See MASS TRANSIT

public utility Enterprise that provides certain classes of services to the public, including common-carrier transportation (buses, airlines, railroads); telephone and telegraph services; power, heat and light; and community facilities for water and sanitation. In most countries such enterprises are state-owned and state-operated; in the U.S. they are mainly privately owned, but operate under close regulation. Given the technology of production and distribution, they are considered natural MONOPOLIES, since the capital costs for such enterprises are large and the existence of competing or parallel systems would be inordinately expensive and wasteful. Government regulation, particularly at the state level, aims to ensure safe operation, reasonable rates, and service on equal terms to all customers. In recent years some states have experimented with deregulation of electricity and natural-gas operations to stimulate price reductions and improved service through competition.

Public Works Administration U.S. government agency (1933–39). Part of the NEW DEAL, the agency was established to reduce unemployment through the construction of highways and public buildings. Authorized by the National Industrial Recovery Act (1933), it was administered by HAROLD ICKES. It spent about $4 billion to build schools, courthouses, city halls, public-health facilities, and roads, bridges, dams, and subways. It was gradually dismantled as the nation moved to a military-industrial economy in World War II.

Public Works of Art Project (PWAP) First of the U.S. federal art programs conceived as part of the NEW DEAL during the Great Depression. Organized in 1933, it provided work to thousands of unemployed artists. PWAP projects (many of which were left unfinished) included some 7,000 easel paintings and watercolors, 1,400 murals and sculptures, 2,500 works of graphic art, and numerous other works designated to embellish nonfederal public buildings and parks. Prominent works include the murals in San Francisco's Coit Memorial Tower, GRANT WOOD's mural at Iowa State College, and BEN SHAHN's mural designs on the theme of PROHIBITION. Many projects left incomplete when the PWAP ended in 1934 were finished under the WPA FEDERAL ART PROJECT.

publishing Traditionally, the selection, preparation, and distribution of printed matter—including books, newspapers, magazines, and pamphlets. Contemporary publishing includes the production of materials in digital formats such as CD-ROMs, as well as materials created or adapted for online, electronic distribution. Publishing has evolved from small, ancient, and law- or religion-bound origins into a vast industry that disseminates every kind of information imaginable. In the modern sense of a copying industry supplying a lay readership, publishing began in Hellenistic Greece, in Rome, and in China. After paper reached the West from China in the 11th century, the central innovation in Western publishing was JOHANNES GUTENBERG's invention of movable type. In the 19th and 20th centuries, technological advances, the rise of literacy and leisure, and ever-increasing information needs contributed to an unprecedented expansion of publishing. Issues that modern publishing must contend with include attempts at censorship, copyright laws, royalties for authors and commissions for literary agents, new marketing techniques, pressures from advertisers affecting editorial independence, acquisition of independent publishing concerns by conglomerates, and the growth of competing media such as television and the Internet.

Pucci \'pü-chē\, **Emilio, marchese (Marquess) di Barsento** (1914–1992) Italian fashion designer and politician. He became a designer when a fashion photographer for *Vogue* noticed his original ski outfit and asked him to design women's ski clothes. He is best known for his tight shantung "Pucci pants" and vividly printed silk dresses and blouses. His colorful, less formal uniforms for Braniff flight attendants were the first of their kind. Later he branched into men's fashions, perfume, and ceramics. He was a member of the Italian Parliament 1963–72.

Puccini \pü-'chē-nē\, **Giacomo (Antonio Domenico Michele Secondo Maria)** (1858–1924) Italian composer. Born into a family of organists and choirmasters, he decided to write operas after hearing G. VERDI's *Aïda*. At the Milan Conservatory he worked with Amilcare Ponchielli (1834–1886). His first opera, *Le villi* (1883), was performed after the publisher Giulio Ricordi and A. BOITO heard him sing through it. His second, *Edgar* (1889), was a failure, but *Manon Lescaut* (1893) brought him international recognition. *La bohème* (1896) was not initially a success, but *Tosca* (1900) was. A paid claque disrupted the La Scala premiere of *Madam Butterfly* (1904), but the next year's revival was a hit. A domestic scandal distracted him, and it was 1910 before *The Girl of the Golden West* premiered at the Metropolitan Opera. The trilogy *Il trittico* (including *Gianni Schicchi*) followed in 1918. He was the most popular opera composer in the world at the time of his death; his unfinished *Turandot* was completed by Franco Alfano (1875–1954).

Pucelle \pǖ-'sel\, **Jean** (fl. c. 1319–1334) French manuscript illuminator. Little is known of his background, but his large workshop dominated Parisian painting in the early 14th century, when he enjoyed court patronage and his work commanded high prices. His most celebrated work, the *Hours of Jeanne d'Evreux* (c. 1325–28), a tiny private prayer book commissioned by the queen, featured numerous drolleries (marginal designs), a style he popularized, and reveals his genius for using sources from Italian and French art to give a playful tone to an essentially religious work.

puddling process Method of converting PIG IRON into WROUGHT iron by subjecting it to heat and frequent stirring in a furnace in the presence of oxidizing substances (see OXIDATION-REDUCTION). Invented by HENRY CORT in 1784 (superseding the FINERY PROCESS), it was the first method that allowed wrought iron to be produced on a large scale.

Puebla State (pop., 1995 est.: 4,624,000), southeastern central Mexico. It has an area of 13,090 sq mi (33,902 sq km); the capital is PUEBLA city. It occupies part of the Anáhuac Plateau and varies in elevation from 5,000 ft to 8,000 ft (1,500 to 2,400 m), with fertile valleys formed by the SIERRA MADRE Oriental. The region has long been densely populated. Pre-Columbian peoples had a highly developed civilization in the area, and there are many archaeological sites. The Spanish made Puebla an economic and religious center, and since the 19th century it has been an important agricultural and industrial center.

Puebla (de Zaragoza) City (pop., 1990: 1,100,000), capital of PUEBLA state, southeastern Mexico. Founded in 1532, it lies on a plain 7,093 ft (2,162 m) above sea level in the SIERRA MADRE Oriental foothills. Located between MEXICO CITY and VERACRUZ, it was occupied by U.S. forces during the MEXICAN WAR. Its Spanish colonial architecture is similar to that of the city of TOLEDO, Spain. The center of an important agricultural and industrial region, it is also known for its glazed ceramic tiles, glass, and pottery. In 1973 it was badly damaged by an earthquake that rocked central Mexico.

pueblo (Spanish: "town") Community of the PUEBLO INDIANS of the southwestern U.S., consisting of multistoried apartment houses constructed of large ADOBE blocks beginning c. AD 1000. Freestanding structures up to five stories tall were built around a central court. Each floor is set back from the floor under it; the whole structure resembles a zigzag pyramid, with terraces formed by the rooftops of the level below. Though rooms often have connecting doorways, movement between levels is by means of ladders through holes in the ceilings. Ground-floor rooms, used for storage, have no outside doors. Each pueblo has at least two KIVAS. Many of the pueblos are still occupied; ACOMA pueblo is believed to be the oldest continuously inhabited place in the U.S. Some of the largest pueblos are at Taos, Isleta, Laguna, and Zuni. See also CLIFF DWELLING.

O
P
Q
R

Pueblo Incident (1968) Capture of the USS *Pueblo* by North Korea off its coast. Maintaining that the ship, a navy intelligence vessel, had been in international waters, the U.S. negotiated with North Korea to secure release of its 83 crewmen. The agreement allowed the U.S. to publicly disavow the confession the crew had signed while admitting the ship's intrusion, apologizing, and formally acknowledging the confessions obtained in captivity. An inquiry into the confessions and the conduct of the ship's commander produced no apparent disciplinary action.

Pueblo Indians Historic descendants of the prehistoric ANASAZI peoples who have for centuries lived in settled PUEBLOS in what is now northeastern Arizona and northwestern New Mexico. The contemporary pueblos are divided into eastern and western. The eastern group includes settlements along the Rio Grande in New Mexico (most notably TAOS Pueblo), while the western group includes the HOPI villages of northeastern Arizona and the ZUNI, ACOMA, and Laguna villages of northwestern New Mexico.

Pueblo pottery One of the most highly developed of the Native American arts. Pueblo pots, made only by women of the tribe, are constructed of long "sausages" of clay that are coiled upward and then smoothed out. Designs include geometric, floral, and animal patterns. The method was developed during the Classical Pueblo period (c. 1050–1300) and is still being used today.

Pottery made by the Pueblo Indians (Left) Acoma waterjar, 1890, (center) Santa Clara vase, c. 1880, (right) San Ildefonso waterjar, 1906; in the Denver Art Museum, Colo.

BY COURTESY OF THE DENVER ART MUSEUM, DENVER, COLO.

Puente \'pwen-tā\, **Tito** *orig.* **Ernesto Antonio Puente, Jr.** (1923–2000) U.S. bandleader, percussionist, and composer, a leading figure in SALSA music. Born in New York to Puerto Rican parents, Puente served in the Navy during World War II, and later studied at Juilliard. In the late 1940s, he formed his own band and rose to prominence with the mambo and cha-cha-cha fads of the 1950s. Always experimenting, he became a pioneer of Latin-jazz fusion. His compositions include "Pare Cochero" and "Oye Como Va." He performed with many artists, especially C. CRUZ, and recorded well over 100 albums.

puerperal fever \pyü-'ər-pə-rəl\ *or* **childbed fever** Infection of the female REPRODUCTIVE SYSTEM after childbirth or abortion, with fever over 100°F (38°C) in the first 10 days. The inner surface of the uterus is most often infected, but lacerations of any part of the genital tract can give BACTERIA (often *Streptococcus pyogenes*) access to the bloodstream and lymphatic system to cause SEPTICEMIA, cellulitis (cellular inflammation), and pelvic or generalized PERITONITIS. Severity varies. Puerperal fever has become very rare in developed countries but is still seen after abortions performed in unhygienic surroundings.

Puerto Rico *officially* **Commonwealth of Puerto Rico** Self-governing island commonwealth of the WEST INDIES, in union with the U.S. Area: 3,515 sq mi (9,104 sq km). Population (1998 est.): 3,786,000. Capital: SAN JUAN. The population is a mixture of diverse ethnic groups, mainly of Spanish and African descent. Languages: Spanish and English (both official). Religion: Roman Catholicism. Currency: U.S. dollar. Puerto Rico is a mountainous island and may be divided into three geographic regions: the mountainous interior, the northern plateau, and the coastal plains. It has a developing free-market economy, and manufacturing, financial services, and trade (mostly with the U.S.) are its main components. Tourism is also an important source of income. Its chief of state is the U.S. president, and its head of government is the commonwealth governor. The island was inhabited by Arawak Indians when it was settled by the Spanish in the early 16th century. It remained largely undeveloped economically until the late 18th century. After 1830 it gradually developed a plantation economy based on the export crops of sugarcane, coffee, and tobacco. The independence movement began in the late 19th century, and Spain ceded the island to the U.S. in 1898, after the SPANISH-AMERICAN WAR. In 1917 Puerto Ricans were granted U.S. citizenship, and in 1952 the island became a commonwealth with autonomy in internal affairs. The question of Puerto Rican statehood has been a political issue, with commonwealth status approved by voters in 1967 and again, in 1993.

Puerto Vallarta \'pwer-tō-bä-'yär-tä\ City (pop., 1990: 111,000), western central Mexico. It is situated on Banderas Bay, in the Pacific coastal lowland, south of the mouth of the Ameca River. The major port of JALISCO state, it exports bananas, coconut oil, hides, and fine woods. It is also an international tourist resort, known for aquatic sports, fishing (especially for sharks), and hunting.

Pufendorf \'pü-fən-ˌdȯrf\, **Samuel** *later* **Freiherr (Baron) von Pufendorf** (1632–1694) German jurist and historian. The son of a pastor, he left the study of theology for jurisprudence, philosophy, and history. Influenced by HUGO GROTIUS and THOMAS HOBBES, his most notable works are *Elementorum jurisprudentiae universalis* (1660; "Elements of Universal Jurisprudence") and *De jure naturae et gentium* (1672; "Of the Law and Nature of Nations"), in which he defended the idea of NATURAL LAW and argued that there is no such creature as a natural slave—that all men have a right to equality and freedom. He taught at the Univs. of Heidelberg (1661–68) and Lund (1670–77) before becoming official historiographer to CHARLES XI of Sweden (1677–88) and to the elector of Brandenburg (1688–94).

puffball Any of various fungi (see FUNGUS) in the order Lycoperdales of the class Basidiomycetes, found in soil or on decaying wood in grassy areas and woods. Puffballs are named for the fact that puffs of spores are released when the dry and powdery tissues of the mature spherical fruiting body (basidiocarp) are disturbed. Many are edible before maturity.

puffer *or* **blowfish** Any of about 90 species (family Tetraodontidae) of fishes that, when disturbed, inflate themselves into a globular shape with air or water. Most species occur in warm and temperate seas worldwide; some occur in brackish or fresh water. Puffers have tough, usually prickly, skin; their fused teeth form a beaklike structure, split in the center of each jaw. The largest grow to 3 ft (90 cm) long, but most are considerably smaller. Though they contain a lethal toxin, they are sometimes eaten, especially in Japan, where puffers (called fugu) are prepared by a specially trained chef.

Puffer (*Arothron stellatus*).

DOUGLAS FAULKNER

puffin *or* **sea parrot** Any of three species (family Alcidae) of diving birds with a large, brightly colored, triangular beak. Puffins nest in large colonies on seaside and island cliffs. Both parents carry up to 10 fish crosswise in the bill to the nest (a deep burrow), feeding the single chick for about six weeks. They then leave, and the chick waits alone for its flight feathers to grow, living on stored fat, then flies out to sea by itself. The common, or Atlantic, puffin *(Fratercula arctica)* is about 12 in. (30 cm) long. The Pacific species are the horned puffin *(F. corniculata)* and the tufted puffin *(Lunda cirrhata)*.

Common puffin (*Fratercula arctica*).

BEN GOLDSTEIN—ROOT RESOURCES

pug Breed of TOY DOG that probably originated in China. Dutch traders brought it to England in the late 17th century. Squarely built and muscular, the pug has a short muzzle, tightly curled tail, large head, prominent eyes, and small, drooping ears. It stands 10–11 in. (26–28 cm) and weighs about 13–18 lbs (6–8 kg). Its short, glossy coat can be black, silver, or apricot fawn; there is a black mask on the face. Loyal and alert, pugs are valued as companions.

Pug.

SALLY ANNE THOMPSON—EB INC.

Pugachov \ˌpü-gə-ˈchȯf\, **Yemelyan (Ivanovich)** (1742?–1775) Russian COSSACK leader. He fought in the Russian army (1763–70) then wandered among settlements of the dissident OLD BELIEVERS. Learning of Cossack discontent after their unsuccessful rebellion in 1772, he claimed to be Czar Peter III and decreed the abolition of serfdom. Vowing to depose CATHERINE II, he gathered a large following of Cossacks and peasants in the Ural region. After initial victories against the Russian army, he was defeated, captured, and executed.

Puget \pǖ-ˈzhe\, **Pierre** (1620–1694) French sculptor, painter, and architect. As a young man he was employed by PIETRO DA CORTONA to work on the ceiling decorations of the Pitti Palace in Florence. Thereafter he worked chiefly in France as painter and sculptor. While his work is in the tradition of Roman baroque, such sculptures as *Milo of Crotona* (c. 1671–82), in which the athlete is attacked by a lion while his hand is caught in a tree stump, show a strain and anguish that suggest the works of MICHELANGELO.

Puget Sound \ˈpyü-jət\ Arm of the Pacific Ocean. Extending south in western Washington state from the eastern end of the Strait of JUAN DE FUCA, it was explored by the British navigator GEORGE VANCOUVER in 1792. It has many deepwater harbors, including SEATTLE, TACOMA, Everett, and Port Townsend, which are shipping ports for the rich farmlands along the river estuaries. It provides a sheltered area for recreational boating and salmon fishing.

Puglia \ˈpü-lyä\ *or* **Apulia** \ä-ˈpü-lyä\ Autonomous region (pop., 2000 est.: 4,085,239), southeastern Italy. It is located between the Adriatic Sea, the APENNINES and the Gulf of Taranto. It was ruled in the early Middle Ages by Goths, Lombards, and Byzantines and achieved its greatest glory under the HOHENSTAUFEN emperors, especially the 13th-century Holy Roman emperor FREDERICK II. In 1861 it became part of the Italian kingdom. The wines of the region are the strongest in Italy and are used to fortify other, lighter varieties. There are chemical and petrochemical industries in BARI, the regional capital, and iron and steel plants in TARANTO.

Pugwash Conferences Series of international meetings of eminent scientists to discuss problems of nuclear weapons and world security. The first meeting was held in 1957 at the estate of CYRUS EATON in Pugwash, Nova Scotia. The Pugwash organization was established to convene subsequent conferences to discuss arms control and disarmament; these were held in the Soviet Union, Britain, India, and the U.S., among other countries. The organization and its president and founding member, Joseph Rotblat (born 1908), received the 1995 Nobel Prize for Peace.

puja \ˈpü-jä\ In HINDUISM, a form of ceremonial worship. It may range from brief daily rites in the home to an elaborate temple ritual. A typical puja offers the image of a deity the honors accorded to a royal guest. The god is gently roused from sleep, ritually bathed and dressed, served three meals during the day, and ceremonially put to bed. Rituals may also include a sacrifice and oblation to the sacred fire. Some pujas are performed by the worshiper alone; others require a ritually pure person. A puja may be performed for a specific purpose or simply as an act of devotion.

Pukaskwa National Park \pü-ˈkas-kwə\ National park, central Ontario, on the northeastern shore of Lake SUPERIOR. Established in 1971, it is Ontario's largest national park, covering 725 sq mi (1,878 sq km). It includes areas of rugged CANADIAN SHIELD wilderness as well as 50 mi (80 km) of the shoreline of Lake Superior, with rocky islets and coves and spectacular cliffs. Excavations of prehistoric Indian remains have been made. Wildlife includes timber wolf, black bear, mink, lynx, white-tailed deer, moose, and woodland caribou. The park has vast forests of white and black spruce, jack pine, poplar, and birch.

Pulcher, Publius Clodius See Publius CLODIUS PULCHER

Pulitzer \ˈpu̇-lət-sər\, **Joseph** (1847–1911) U.S. (Hungarian-born) newspaper editor and publisher. He emigrated to the U.S. in 1864 to serve in the American Civil War. After the war he became a reporter and then proprietor at German-language newspapers in St. Louis and entered Missouri politics. In 1878 he merged the *St. Louis Dispatch* (founded 1864) and the *Post* (founded 1875) into the *Post-Dispatch*, which soon became the city's dominant evening newspaper. Shifting his interests to New York, he purchased the *World* (1883) and founded the *Evening World* (1887). He helped establish the pattern of the modern newspaper by combining exposés of political corruption and crusading investigative reporting with publicity stunts, self-advertising, and sensationalism. In his will he endowed the Columbia University School of Journalism and established the PULITZER PRIZES.

Pulitzer Prize \ˈpu̇-lət-sər, ˈpyü-lət-sər\ Any of a series of annual prizes awarded by Columbia University for outstanding public service and achievement in American journalism, letters, and music. Fellowships are also awarded. The prizes, originally endowed with a gift of $500,000 from JOSEPH PULITZER, are highly esteemed and have been awarded each May since 1917 on the recommendation of the Pulitzer Prize Board, composed of judges appointed by the university. The numbers and categories of prizes have varied over the years. Today they include 14 awards in journalism, six in letters, one in music, and four fellowships.

pulley In mechanics, a WHEEL that carries a flexible ROPE, cord, cable, chain, or belt on its rim. Pulleys are used singly or in combination to transmit ENERGY and MOTION. In BELT DRIVES, pulleys are attached to shafts at their axes, and power is transmitted between the shafts by means of endless belts running over the pulleys. One or more independently rotating pulleys can be used to gain MECHANICAL ADVANTAGE, especially for lifting weights. The shafts around which the pulleys turn may attach them to frames or blocks, and a combination of pulleys, blocks, and rope is called a BLOCK AND TACKLE. The pulley is considered one of the five simple MACHINES.

Pullman, George M(ortimer) (1831–1897) U.S. industrialist. Born in Brocton, N.Y., he moved to Chicago as a young man and worked as a cabinetmaker for his brother. In 1858 he remodeled two day coaches for a local railroad company into sleeping coaches; eventually he set up his own firm, and the first true Pullman sleeping car appeared in 1865. Becoming wealthy from his invention, in 1867 he founded the Pullman Palace Car Co.; the next year he created the first dining car. In 1880 he built the town of Pullman (now incorporated into Chicago) for its workers; a much-discussed social experiment, the town was also the scene of the famous PULLMAN STRIKE of 1894.

Pullman Strike Widespread railroad strike, May 11–July 20, 1894. After financial reverses caused the Pullman Palace Car Co. to cut wages by 25%, local union members called a strike. The company's president, GEORGE PULLMAN, refused arbitration, and union president EUGENE V. DEBS called for a nationwide boycott of Pullman cars. Sympathy strikes followed in 27 states. Violence broke out in Chicago, and Gov. JOHN PETER ALTGELD refused to intervene. The U.S. attorney general, RICHARD OLNEY, obtained an injunction against the strikers for impeding mail service, and federal troops were called in. Debs's conviction for conspiring against interstate commerce established the use of antitrust laws against labor-union activities.

pulmonary alveolus \ˈpu̇l-mə-ˌner-ē-al-ˈvē-ə-ləs\ Any of the 300 million or so small air spaces in the LUNGS where carbon dioxide leaves the blood and oxygen enters it. Alveoli form clusters (alveolar sacs) connected by alveolar ducts to the bronchioles. Their thin walls contain numerous capillaries, supported by a mesh of elastic and collagenous fibers; gas exchange between them occurs by DIFFUSION. A film of fatty substances (surfactant) over the walls reduces surface tension, keeping the alveoli from collapsing and making it easier to expand the lungs. Alveolar macrophages (see LEUKOCYTE, LYMPHOID TISSUE) act as mobile scavengers, engulfing foreign particles in the lungs.

pulmonary circulation System of blood vessels forming a closed circuit between the HEART and the LUNGS. Unlike the SYSTEMIC CIRCULATION, it carries oxygenated blood in VEINS and deoxygenated blood in ARTERIES. The right ventricle pumps blood into the pulmonary artery, which branches to the right and left lungs. In the CAPILLARIES, blood releases carbon dioxide into the air in the PULMONARY ALVEOLI and takes up oxygen, which it brings back to the left atrium of the heart through the pulmonary veins. From the left atrium it is pumped into the left ventricle and from there into the AORTA and systemic circulation. See also CARDIOVASCULAR SYSTEM, CIRCULATION.

pulmonary heart disease *or* **cor pulmonale** \ˌkȯr-pu̇l-mə-ˈnäl-ē\ Enlargement and eventual failure of the right ventricle of the heart due to disorders of the lungs or their blood vessels or chest-wall abnormalities. Chronic disease is most often caused by chronic BRONCHITIS or EMPHYSEMA. Symptoms include chronic cough, trouble in breathing after exertion, wheezing, weakness, leg EDEMA, right upper abdominal pain, and neck vein distension. The lungs' CAPILLARY network is slowly destroyed; pressure in the pulmonary artery rises and the right ventricle enlarges in response, leading, if uncorrected, to heart failure. Treatment includes a respirator, low-sodium diet, DIURETICS, DIGITALIS, and ANTIBIOTICS for respiratory infection. Acute disease, due to pulmonary EMBOLISM, is often treated by removal of the blockage.

pulsar *in full* **pulsating radio star** Any of a class of cosmic objects that appear to emit extremely regular pulses of radio waves. A few give off short rhythmic bursts of visible light, X rays, and gamma radiation as well. Thought to be rapidly spinning NEUTRON STARS, they were discovered by ANTONY HEWISH and JOCELYN BELL BURNELL in 1967 with a specially designed radio telescope. More than 500 have been detected since. All behave similarly, but the intervals between pulses range from one-thousandth of a second to four seconds long. Charged particles from the surface enter the star's magnetic field, which accelerates them so that they give off radiation, released as intense beams from the magnetic poles. These do not coincide with the pulsar's own axis of rotation, so as it spins the radiation beams swing around like a lighthouse and they are seen as pulses. Radio pulsars have been shown to be slowing down, typically by a millionth of a second per year. It has been calculated that pulsars "switch off" after about 10 million years, when their magnetic fields weaken enough.

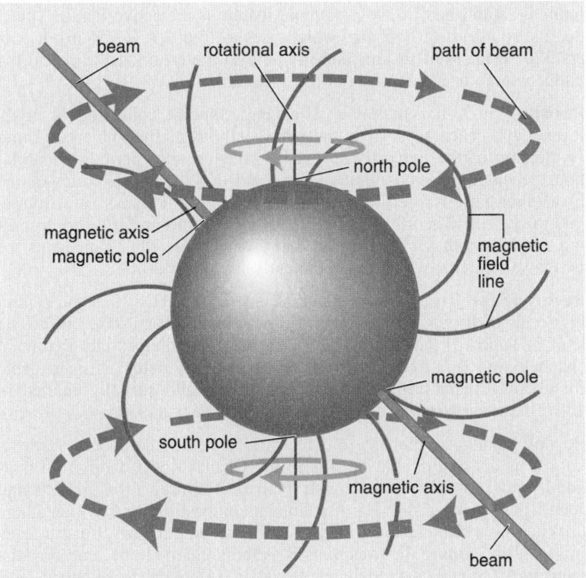

A pulsar emits two beams (of radio waves, for instance) along its magnetic axis. If the magnetic axis is offset from the rotational axis, the beams will sweep out circular paths as the star rotates, instead of remaining in one constant position. An observer in the path of such a beam will thus see a periodic pulse of radio waves as the beam sweeps by.

pulse Pressure wave in the ARTERIES from contraction of the HEART. It can be felt where arteries are near the skin's surface; it is usually read at the carotid artery in the neck or at the wrist. Its rate, strength, and rhythm and the contour of the wave provide valuable information but must be viewed in context (e.g., rapid pulse occurs with serious heart disease, simple fever, or vigorous exercise). The average adult pulse rate is 70–80 beats per minute; the rate decreases with age and is generally faster in women.

puma See COUGAR

pumice \ˈpə-məs\ Very porous, frothlike volcanic glass that has long been used as an abrasive in cleaning, polishing, and scouring compounds. It is also used in precast masonry units, poured concrete, insulation and acoustic tile, and plaster. Pumice is IGNEOUS ROCK that cooled so rapidly there was no time for it to crystallize. When it solidified, the vapors dissolved in it were suddenly released, and the whole mass swelled up into a froth that immediately consolidated. Any type of LAVA may become pumiceous under favorable conditions.

pump Machine that uses ENERGY to raise, transport, or compress fluids. Pumps are classified by how they transfer energy to the fluid. The basic methods are volume displacement, addition of KINETIC ENERGY, and use of ELECTROMAGNETIC FORCE. Pumps in which displacement is accomplished mechanically are called positive displacement pumps. Kinetic pumps pass kinetic energy to the fluid by means of a rapidly rotating impeller (blade). To use electromagnetic force, the fluid being pumped must be a good electrical conductor. Pumps used to transport or pressurize gases are called COMPRESSORS, blowers, or fans.

pumpkin Fruit of certain varieties of *Cucurbita pepo* or *C. moschata*, of the GOURD family. In the U.S., the thick-growing, small-fruited bush, or nontrailing, varieties of *C. pepo* are called SQUASH, and the long-season, long-trailing, large-fruited varieties are called pumpkin. Pumpkins produce very long vines and large (9–18 lb, or 4–8 kg), globe-shaped, orange fruits. Giant and miniature species are available. The usually lightly furrowed or ribbed rind is smooth, and the fruit stem is hard and woody. Pumpkins mature in early autumn and can be stored for a few months in a dry, warm place. They are commonly grown in North America, Britain, and Europe for human food and livestock feed. In Europe pumpkin is served mainly as a vegetable; in the U.S. and Canada pumpkin pie is a traditional Thanksgiving and Christmas dessert. Pumpkins are used in the U.S. for HALLOWEEN decorations.

Punch Hooknosed, humpbacked character in MARIONETTE and puppet shows (see PUPPETRY). Adapted from a stock character of the COMMEDIA DELL'ARTE, the puppet character was brought to France and England by Italian puppeteers in the 1660s. By 1700 every English puppet show featured Punch (from Punchinello) and his wife, Judy. As marionettes became less popular in the 1790s, smaller glove puppets were used in the popular Punch-and-Judy play. The outrageous behavior of the deceitful Punch, established by the 19th century, continues to delight puppet-show audiences today.

Punch English illustrated periodical published 1841–1992 and revived in 1996 with a revised format. Initially a weekly radical paper, it became famous for its satiric humor, caricatures, and cartoons. Among its famous early staff members were WILLIAM THACKERAY and JOHN TENNIEL. A cover drawing by Richard Doyle was used continuously from 1849 to 1956, when each issue's cover was made different, though the traditional figures of Punch and his dog Toby usually appeared somewhere.

punch press MACHINE TOOL that changes the size or shape of a piece of material, usually sheet metal, by applying PRESSURE to a DIE in which the workpiece is held. The form and construction of the die determine the shape produced on the workpiece. A punch press has two components: the punch, which is attached to the reciprocating (back and forth, or up and down) ram (plunger) of the machine; and the die, which is clamped onto a bed or anvil whose flat surface is perpendicular to the path of the ram. The punch pushes against the workpiece, which is held in the die. Punch presses are usually driven by electric motors. See also HYDRAULIC PRESS.

punctuation Standard set of marks used in written and printed texts to clarify meaning and to separate sentences, words, and parts of words. It often marks discourse features such as intonational contours and pauses. It may also convey information about a word (e.g., hyphens in compound words) unrelated to speech patterns. In English, the period (.) marks the end of a sentence or abbreviation. The comma (,) usually separates clauses, phrases, or items in a series. The colon (:) often introduces an explanation or series of examples. The semicolon (;) usually separates independent clauses. The dash (—) marks an abrupt transition. The exclamation point (!) signals surprise. The question mark (?) signals a question. The apostrophe (') marks the possessive case or the omission of letters. Quotation marks (" ") set off either quoted words or words used with special significance. Interpolations in a sentence are marked by brackets ([ ]) or parentheses ().

Pune \'pü-nə\ *formerly* **Poona** City (metro. area pop., 1995: 2,940,000), western India. Called "Queen of the DECCAN," it is the cultural capital of the Maratha peoples (see MARATHA CONFEDERACY). It first gained importance as the capital of the Bhonsle Marathas in the 17th century. Temporarily captured by the Mughals, it again became the Maratha capital from 1714 until 1817, when it fell to the British. It served as the seasonal capital of the Bombay presidency, and its mild weather has made it a popular tourist resort. It is a major educational center, and headquarters of the Indian army's southern command; it is ringed by a sprawling complex of industrial suburbs.

Punic Wars \'pyü-nik\ *or* **Carthaginian Wars** Three wars (264–241 BC, 218–201, 149–146) between Rome and CARTHAGE. The first concerned control of Sicily and of the sea lanes in the western Mediterranean; it ended with Rome victorious but with great loss of ships and men on both sides. In 218 HANNIBAL attacked Roman territory, starting from Spain and marching overland into Italy with troops and elephants. After an initial Carthaginian victory, FABIUS MAXIMUS CUNCTATOR harassed him wherever he went without offering battle. Abandoning this tactic resulted in a major Roman loss at the Battle of CANNAE (216); that defeat drew the Romans together and, though worn down, they managed to rally, eventually defeating Hannibal and driving him out of Italy (203). The Third Punic War was essentially the siege of Carthage; it led to the destruction of Carthage, the enslavement of its people, and Roman hegemony in the western Mediterranean. The Carthaginian territory became the Roman province of Africa.

Punjab \,pən-'jäb\ State (pop., 1994 est.: 21,695,000), northwestern India. Bounded by Pakistan, it occupies an area of 19,448 sq mi (50,370 sq km). The city of CHANDIGARH is the joint administrative capital of Punjab and HARYANA. In the 18th century the Sikhs (see SIKHISM) built a powerful kingdom in the Punjab, which came under British rule in 1849. In 1947 the area was split between the new nations of India and Pakistan, the smaller eastern portion going to India. It is the only Indian state with a majority of Sikhs. Hindus make up about one-third of the population, and there are smaller minorities of Christians, Jains, and Muslims. The economy is based on agriculture and small- and medium-scale industry.

Punjabi language *or* **Panjabi language** \,pən-jä-bē\ Indo-Aryan language of the Punjab in India and Pakistan. Punjabi has about 26 million speakers in India and perhaps more than 60 million in Pakistan—nearly half the population of the latter—but linguists have sometimes considered the dialects of southwestern, western, and northern Punjab province in Pakistan a different language. Inhabitants of southern Punjab province have agitated for consideration of their speech as a distinct language, Siraiki (with over 12 million speakers), though Siraiki and Punjabi are mutually intelligible. A linguistically significant feature of Punjabi is its development of phonemically distinctive TONE in syllables that have (or originally had) breathy-voiced consonants.

punk rock Term originally applied to 1960s U.S. garage bands that came to denote a genre that represented a reaction against both the hippy ideals and the soft rock prevalent on radio in the 1970s. Originating in the countercultural rock of such artists as the Velvet Underground and Iggy (Pop) and the Stooges, punk rock evolved in New York in the mid-1970s with artists such as Patti Smith and the Ramones. It soon took root in London—where distinctly "punk" fashions, including spiked hair and ripped clothing, were popularized—with such bands as the Sex Pistols and the Clash, and later in California, with X, Black Flag, and the Dead Kennedys. It is often marked by a fast, aggressive beat, loud guitar with abrupt chord changes, and nihilistic lyrics. Variants include new wave (more pop-oriented and accessible) and hardcore (characterized by brief, harsh songs played at breakneck speed); the latter continued to thrive through the 1990s.

Punnett \'pən-ət\, **Reginald Crundall** (1875–1967) British geneticist. Through contact with WILLIAM BATESON he came to support the theories of GREGOR MENDEL, and in 1905 he published the first textbook on Mendelian genetics. Using poultry and sweet peas, Punnett and Bateson discovered some of the fundamental processes of Mendelian genetics, including linkage, sex determination, sex linkage, and the first example of nonsexual chromosome linkage. Punnett demonstrated the value of using sex-linked plumage-color factors to distinguish male from female chickens, making possible early identification of the less valuable males, a process now known as autosexing.

Punt \'pùnt\ In ancient Egyptian and Greek geography, the southern coast of the RED SEA and adjacent coasts of the Gulf of ADEN, corresponding to modern coastal Ethiopia and Djibouti. Visited by Egyptian expeditions as early as 2200 BC, it was a place of ancient legend and fable and Egypt's source for incense, ivory, and ostrich feathers. Queen HATSHEPSUT made a voyage to Punt and had the details of the journey recorded on the walls of the Deir el-Bahri temple near THEBES. Only in the late 4th century BC were the trade routes to Punt opened to the Greeks.

pupa \'pyü-pə\ Inactive, nonfeeding stage in the life of insects that undergo complete METAMORPHOSIS. In a protective covering (cocoon or chrysalis), the LARVA is transformed into an adult. During pupation, a process controlled by hormones, larval structures break down and adult structures form; wings appear for the first time. The adult emerges either by splitting the pupal skin and chewing its way out or by secreting a fluid that softens the cocoon.

puppetry Art of creating and manipulating puppets in a theatrical show. Puppets are figures that are moved by human rather than mechanical aid. They may be controlled by one or several puppeteers, who are screened from the spectators. Varieties include glove (or hand) puppets, rod puppets, shadow puppets, and MARIONETTES (or string puppets). Puppetry had its beginnings in tribal society and has been part of every civilization. By the 18th century it was so popular in Europe that permanent theaters were built for the usually itinerant puppeteers. Companies presented favorite stories of the French Guignol, the Italian Arlecchino, the German Kasperle, and the English PUNCH and Judy. By the mid-20th century puppetry had reached television with JIM HENSON's Muppets. See also BUNRAKU, SERGEY OBRAZTSOV.

Puracé National Park \,pü-rä-'sā\ National park, southwestern Colombia. Established in 1961, its main feature is the active Puracé Volcano, just southeast of Popayán, which rises to 15,603 ft (4,756 m). It covers 320 sq mi (830 sq km) and is home to the SPECTACLED BEAR and the pudu, a small deer that is about one foot tall.

Purana \pù-'rä-nə\ In HINDUISM, an encyclopedic collection of myth, legend, and genealogy. A Purana traditionally treats five subjects: primary creation of the universe, secondary creation after periodic annihilation, genealogy of gods and saints, grand epochs, and histories of the royal dynasties. Written in narrative couplets, the Puranas date from c. 400 to c. 1000. The 18 principal surviving Puranas are grouped according to whether they exalt VISHNU, SHIVA, or BRAHMA. Most popular is the Bhagavata Purana, which treats the early life of KRISHNA.

Purari River River, eastern central NEW GUINEA. Rising in the central highlands of Papua New Guinea, it flows about 290 mi (470 km) to the Gulf of Papua of the CORAL SEA. Its lower course divides into five main channels that lace through a well-settled swampy delta. It is navigable for about 120 mi (190 km). Although found and partially charted in 1887, the river system was not fully traced until the 1930s.

Purcell \'pər-səl\, **Henry** (c. 1659–1695) British composer. Little is known of his origins, but he was in the Chapel Royal choir from boyhood, and probably studied with Pelham Humfrey (1647–1674) and John Blow (1649–1708). His first known composition was written at age 8. When his voice changed, he assisted in keeping the royal instruments in repair and tuning the Westminster Abbey organ. He became organist there in 1679 and at the Chapel Royal in 1682. He wrote music in a number of genres. His highly important opera *Dido and Aeneas* (1689) was followed by the "semi-operas" *King Arthur* (1691), *The Faery Queen* (1692), and *The Indian Queen* (1695). He also wrote much incidental music, some 250 songs, 12 fantasias for viol consort, and many anthems and services. He is regarded as the greatest English composer after W. BYRD and before the 20th century.

purdah Seclusion of women from public observation by means of concealing clothing (including the veil) and walled enclosures as well as screens and curtains within the home. The custom seems to have originated in Persia and was adopted by Muslims during the Arab conquest of what is now Iraq in the 7th century. The Muslim domination of northern India led to its adoption by the Hindu upper classes, but it was discarded by Hindus after the end of British rule in India. The custom of purdah still continues in many Islamic countries.

Purdue University State university system with a main campus in West Lafayette, Ind., and branches in two other locations. Founded in 1869 as a land-grant university under the Morrill Act, it was named for John Purdue, a founding donor. Two campuses operated jointly with Indiana Univ. and nine technology sites throughout the state are also part of the system. The main campus is a comprehensive research university; it includes schools of management, pharmacy, veterinary medicine, and eight other fields. Research facilities include an engineering experiment station and a rare-isotope measuring laboratory. Enrollment at the main campus is about 35,000.

pure culture In microbiology, laboratory culture containing a single species of organism. A pure culture is usually derived from a mixed culture (containing many species) by methods that separate the individual cells so that, when they multiply, each will form an individually distinct colony, which may then be used to establish new cultures with the assurance that only one type of organism will be present. Pure cultures may be more easily isolated if the growth medium of the original mixed culture favors the growth of one organism to the exclusion of others.

Pure Land Buddhism Devotional cult of the buddha Amitabha. It is one of the most popular forms of Mahayana Buddhism in East Asia today. Pure Land schools believe that rebirth in the Western Paradise (the Pure Land) is given to all those who invoke Amitabha's name with sincere devotion. In China the Pure Land cult can be traced back to the 4th century, when the scholar Huiyuan (333–416) formed a society of monks and laymen who meditated on the name of Amitabha. His successors systematized and spread the doctrine in the 6th–7th century. The Pure Land teaching was transmitted to Japan by monks of the Tiantai school.

purgatory In Roman Catholic doctrine, the condition of those who have died in a state of grace but have not been purged of sin. These remaining sins include unforgiven venial sins or forgiven mortal sins. Souls burdened by such sins must be purified before entering heaven. The church also teaches that souls in purgatory may be aided by efforts of the living faithful through prayers, almsgiving, indulgences, and other works. The existence of purgatory has been denied as unbiblical by Protestant churches and most Eastern Orthodox churches.

Purge Trials Soviet trials of critics of Joseph Stalin. After the assassination of Sergey Kirov, prominent Bolsheviks were accused of conspiracy to remove Stalin from power. In three widely publicized show trials (1936–38), which presented confessions obtained under torture or fabricated by the secret police, the accused were found guilty and executed or sent to prison. Numerous closed, unpublicized trials of Soviet military leaders were also held and resulted in a massive purge throughout the armed forces. The trials eliminated such potential rivals and critics of Stalin as Nikolay I. Bukharin, Lev Kamenev, Aleksey Rykov, Mikhayl Tukhachevsky, Genrikh Yagoda, and Grigory Y. Zinovyev, but earned worldwide condemnation.

Purim \'pu̇r-im, pu̇-'rēm\ Jewish festival celebrating the survival of the Jews marked for death in Persia in the 5th cent BC. According to the Book of Esther, Haman, chief minister of King Ahasuerus, planned a general massacre of the Jews and set the date by casting lots. Ahasuerus' wife Esther interceded for the Jews, and they were allowed to attack their enemies. The ritual observance begins with a day of fasting on the 13th of Adar (in February or March), the day before the actual holiday. The Book of Esther is read in the synagogue, and Jews are enjoined to exchange gifts and make donations to the poor. Purim is a day of merrymaking and feasting.

purine \'pyu̇r-ˌēn\ Any of a class of heterocyclic compounds with a two-ring structure composed of carbon and nitrogen atoms. The simplest member, purine itself ($C_5H_4N_4$), is not common, but its derivatives with the structure are. Examples are uric acid, caffeine, and two of the nucleotides in nucleic acids, guanine and adenine.

Puritan Revolution See English Civil Wars

Puritanism Movement in the late 16th and 17th century that sought to "purify" the Church of England, leading to civil war in England and to the founding of colonies in North America. Many Puritans joined the Parliamentary party during the English Civil War and gained considerable power, but after the Restoration they were once again a dissenting minority. Believing themselves chosen by God to revolutionize history, some Puritans founded settlements in America (see Pilgrims), notably the Massachusetts Bay Colony. The Puritans of Massachusetts emphasized the conversion experience, by which the elect experienced the descent of grace. In their theocracy only the elect were allowed to vote and rule, though the privileges of church membership were extended to all baptized and orthodox persons.

Purkinje \pər-'kin-jē\, **Jan Evangelista** (1787–1869) Czech experimental physiologist. He discovered the Purkinje effect (as light decreases, red objects appear to fade faster than blue ones), Purkinje cells (large branching neurons in the cerebellum), and Purkinje fibers (which conduct impulses from the natural pacemaker throughout the heart). At Breslau he created the world's first independent physiology department and first official physiology laboratory. He introduced the term protoplasm, devised new methods for preparing microscope samples, discovered the skin's sweat glands and the nucleus of the unripe ovum, recognized the uniqueness of fingerprints, and noted that pancreatic extracts digest protein.

Purkinje.
CTK–CZECHOSLOVAK NEWS AGENCY

purpura \'pər-pə-rə\ Presence of hemorrhages in the skin, due to failure of hemostasis (arrest of bleeding). The major causes are damage to small artery walls, platelet deficiency, clotting-factor deficiency, development in the body of circulating anticoagulants, and fibrinolysis, in which a usually dormant system destroys clots. Each of these occurs in a variety of conditions. Depending on the type, treatment may consist of administration of steroids, administration of deficient blood components, or removal of the spleen.

Purus River \pü-'rüs\ River, northwestern central South America. One of the most crooked rivers in the world, it rises in Peru and flows generally northeast through the rain forests of Peru and Brazil. In Brazil, it meanders to join the stretch of the Amazon River upstream from Manaus known as the Solimões River. At its mouth it divides into numerous branches. Most of its 1,995-mi (3,211-km) course is navigable, as are the many lakes formed near its shores. Rubber is gathered from forests along its course.

purusha See prakriti and purusha

Pusan \'pü-ˌsän\ City (pop., 1995: 3,814,000) and port, South Korea, at the southeastern tip of the Korean Peninsula. Pusan was opened to Japanese trade in 1876 and to general foreign trade in 1883. It developed into a major port (called Fusan) under Japanese rule 1910–45. It served as the country's temporary capital during the Korean War. It is the nation's largest port and second-largest city. Administratively it has the status of a special city equal to that of a province. Industries include shipbuilding and manufacturing. Hot springs are located in the northeastern suburbs.

Pushkin, Aleksandr (Sergeyevich) (1799–1837) Russian writer. Born into an aristocratic family, Pushkin began his literary career while still a student at the Imperial Lyceum at Tsarskoye Selo (later renamed Pushkin). His first major work was the romantic poem *Ruslan and Ludmila* (1820). With his political verses and epigrams, he became associated with a revolutionary movement that culminated in the unsuccessful Decembrist revolt of 1825. Banished to several provincial locations, he produced a cycle of romantic narrative poems that confirmed him as the leading Russian poet of the day and the leader of the Romantic generation of the 1820s. He also worked on his important historical tragedy, *Boris Godunov* (1831), and his central masterpiece, the novel in verse *Eugene Onegin* (1833). After Nicholas I allowed him to return to Moscow in 1826, Pushkin abandoned his revolutionary sentiments, turning to the figure of Peter the Great in poems such as *The Bronze Horseman* (1837). Other works from this period include the classic short story

"The Queen of Spades" (1834) and the drama *The Stone Guest* (1839). In his late works the motif of peasant rebellion is prominent. The object of suspicion in court circles, he died at 37 after being forced into a duel. He is often considered his country's greatest poet and the founder of modern Russian literature.

Putin \'pü-tyin\, **Vladimir (Vladimirovich)** (born 1952) Russian president (from 2000). His long career with the KGB, based in Dresden, ended with his transfer to Leningrad. He was soon being referred to as deputy mayor, and by 1993 he was essentially exercising mayoral control. He moved to Moscow in 1996, apparently in a continuation of a KGB operation, and was responsible for determining the fate of assets in countries where Russia's missions had closed. In 1997 BORIS YELTSIN promoted him to deputy head of his administration; in 1999 he named Putin prime minister, and at the end of 1999 Yeltsin stepped down as president in Putin's favor. Three months later he won a resounding electoral victory, partly the result of his success in the battle to keep Chechnya from seceding.

Putnam, Hilary (born 1926) U.S. philosopher of science. Born in Chicago, he taught at Princeton, MIT, and Harvard (from 1965). He has made significant contributions to epistemology, logic, philosophy of language, and philosophy of mind, and is best known for his advocacy of scientific REALISM. In *Reason, Truth, and History* (1981), he defends "internal realism," which maintains that scientific truth is to be defined as the ideal limit of the process of improving our scientific theory.

Putnam, Israel (1718–1790) American Revolutionary army officer. Born in Salem Village, Mass., he worked as a farmer in Connecticut from 1740. He served in the French and Indian War, winning fame as an Indian fighter. Appointed a major general in the Continental Army (1775), he fought with distinction at Bunker Hill, but his troops were defeated at the Battle of Long Island. He was charged with defense of the Hudson highlands but abandoned Fort Montgomery and Fort Clinton to the British. He served in lesser commands until he suffered a stroke in 1779.

Putnam, Rufus (1738–1824) American Revolutionary army officer. Born in Sutton, Mass., a cousin of ISRAEL PUTNAM, he fought in the French and Indian War. Entering the Continental Army (1775), he organized fortifications in Boston and New York (1776–77) and at West Point (1778) and fought at the Battle of Saratoga. In 1783 he was promoted to brigadier general. After the war he helped found the Ohio Co. of Associates to obtain a land grant for settlement by war veterans; he led the group that founded Marietta, Ohio (1788). He served as U.S. surveyor general 1796–1803.

putting-out system See DOMESTIC SYSTEM

Putumayo River \,pü-tü-'mä-yō\ River, northwestern South America. Rising in southwestern Colombia, it is about 980 mi (1,575 km) long and flows southeast through tropical rain forests, forming a large section of the Peru–Colombia boundary. It crosses the border into Brazil, where it is known as the Içá, and empties into the AMAZON RIVER. It is navigable for almost its entire length and is a major transport route, especially for the rubber produced in the region.

Puvis de Chavannes \pᵫe-'vē-də-shȧ-'vän\, **Pierre (-Cécile)** (1824–1898) French painter. He studied briefly with EUGENE DELACROIX in Paris and exhibited regularly at the Paris Salons. He is best known for his large canvas paintings for the walls of public buildings in Paris, including the Pantheon (1874–78, 1893–98), the Sorbonne (1889–91), and the Hôtel de Ville (1891–94), as well as the museum in Amiens (1880–82). He also decorated the staircase of the Boston Public Library (1895–96). His works are usually idealized depictions of antiquity or allegorical representations of abstract themes, in simplified forms and pale, flat, frescolike colors. The leading French mural painter of the later 19th century, he exerted a strong influence on the Postimpressionists.

Puzo, Mario (1920–1999) U.S. novelist. Born in New York City to Italian immigrant parents, he studied at the New School for Social Research and Columbia University. His novel *The Godfather* (1969), the saga of a Mafia family, remained a huge bestseller for more than five years and was the basis for acclaimed films by FRANCIS FORD COPPOLA. His later novels included *The Sicilian* (1984), *The Last Don* (1996), and *Omerta* (2000). Often questioned about the Mafia, Puzo confessed that he had never met a gangster before publishing *The Godfather.*

PVC *in full* **polyvinyl chloride** Synthetic RESIN, an organic POLYMER made by treating VINYL CHLORIDE MONOMERS with a PEROXIDE. It may be blended with more rubbery polymers or copolymerized with other vinyls to obtain products with desired properties. PVC resin mixed with plasticizers (see WALDO SEMON), stabilizers, and pigments is made into flexible articles (e.g., raincoats, toys, containers). Nonplasticized resin has been used for rigid products (e.g., water pipes, plumbing fittings, phonograph records). Concern over leaching of vinyl chloride into foods has resulted in restrictions on its use in food containers; its decomposition into hydrogen chloride when burned has also raised concerns. Today it is produced in larger quantities than any other plastic except polyethylene.

Pydna \'pid-nə\, **Battle of** (168 BC) Decisive confrontation in the Roman victory over PERSEUS and Macedonia in the Third MACEDONIAN WAR. It took place on a plain near Pydna (present-day Kítros, Greece). The Roman general Lucius Paullus (229?–160 BC) adroitly outmaneuvered the Macedonians; their PHALANX was penetrated by the Roman LEGIONS, whose short swords were more effective than the Macedonian PIKES. When defeat was imminent, Perseus fled. The Romans ended the Macedonian monarchy and divided the country into four republics.

pyelonephritis \,pī-ə-lō-ni-'frī-təs\ INFECTION (usually bacterial) and INFLAMMATION of KIDNEY tissue and the renal pelvis. Acute pyelonephritis is usually localized and may have no apparent cause. Symptoms include fever, chills, lower-back pain, and bacteria and white blood cells in the urine. Treatment with ANTIBIOTICS requires one to three weeks. Scar tissue forms, but kidney function is usually not impaired. Chronic pyelonephritis results from repeated bacterial infections, which may have no symptoms but destroy more and more tissue over years. If it is diagnosed before too much function is lost, surgery may help, but UREMIA, severe infections, and heart and blood-vessel disorders can lead to death. DIALYSIS or KIDNEY TRANSPLANT sometimes prolongs life.

Pygmalion In GREEK MYTHOLOGY, a king of Cyprus who fell in love with a statue of APHRODITE. The goddess took pity on him and brought the statue to life, and he married her. In some versions of the myth Pygmalion was a sculptor who carved the statue himself because he was disgusted with the faults of ordinary women, and when it was brought to life he gave it the name Galatea.

Pygmy Any of a class of people of equatorial Africa ranging under 5 ft (1.5 m) in height. The name is also sometimes loosely applied to the SAN of southern Africa and the so-called Negrito peoples of Asia (such as the Philippine Ilongot). Besides their short stature, Pygmies are notable in having the highest basal-metabolism rate in the world and a high incidence of SICKLE-CELL ANEMIA. The MBUTI of the Ituri Forest are a well-studied example. See also RACE.

Pyle \'pīl\, **Ernie** *orig.* **Ernest Taylor** (1900–1945) U.S. journalist. Born near Dana, Ind., Pyle left Indiana University to become a reporter for a small-town newspaper. Later he acquired a roving assignment for the Scripps-Howard newspaper chain; his experiences provided material for a column that appeared in as many as 200 newspapers before World War II. His reporting of the campaigns in North Africa, Sicily, Italy, and France won a Pulitzer Prize in 1944. He was killed at 44 by Japanese machine-gun fire during the Okinawa campaign. Compilations of his columns include *Ernie Pyle in England* (1941), *Brave Men* (1944), and *Last Chapter* (1946).

pylon \'pī-,län\ (Greek: "gateway") In modern construction, a tower that gives support, such as the steel towers between which electrical wires are strung or the piers of a bridge. Originally, pylons were monumental gateways to ancient Egyptian temples, either a pair of tall truncated pyramids with a doorway between them or a masonry mass pierced by a doorway.

Pym \'pim\, **John** (1584–1643) English politician. As a member of Parliament (1621–43), he soon became an expert on finances and colonial affairs. He was an architect of Parliament's victory over CHARLES I in the first phase of the ENGLISH CIVIL WARS. He helped form the system of taxation that survived in England until the 19th century. His skill as a parliamentary tactician preserved the unity of Parliament and led to close relations between the government and the city of London.

Pynchon \'pin-chən\, **Thomas** (born 1937) U.S. writer. Born in Glen Cove, N.Y., he studied physics at Cornell and worked briefly as a technical writer before devoting himself to fiction. Beginning with his first novel, *V* (1963), a complex, cynically absurd tale that juxtaposes scenes of 1950s hipster life with symbolic images of the entire century, his works have combined black humor and fantasy to depict human alienation in the chaos of modern society. The idea of conspiracy is central to *The Crying of Lot 49* (1966) and to his masterpiece, *Gravity's Rainbow* (1973), an extraordinary novel about the end of World War II, full of paranoid fantasy, grotesque imagery, and esoteric scientific and anthropological material. Later works include the novels *Vineland* (1990) and *Mason & Dixon* (1997) and the story collection *Slow Learner* (1984). He has lived in hiding or incognito for decades, refusing to grant interviews or be photographed.

Pyongyang \ˌpyəŋ-ˈyaŋ\ City (pop., 1996 est.: 2,500,000), capital of North Korea, on the Taedong River. Founded in 1122 BC according to legend, it is said to be the oldest city in Korea. In 108 BC the Chinese established a trading colony there. It was the capital of the Koguryo kingdom AD 427–668, then was captured by Chinese invaders. It fell to the Japanese in 1592 and was devastated by the Manchus in the early 17th century. Much of it was destroyed during the Sino-Japanese War. During the Japanese occupation of Korea 1910–45, it was built up as an industrial city. Captured by U.N. forces during the Korean War in 1950, it was retaken by Chinese Communist troops. After 1953 it was rebuilt with Soviet and Chinese aid. It is a heavy industry and transportation center.

pyramid Ancient monumental structure constructed of or faced with stone or brick and having a rectangular base and four sloping triangular sides meeting at an apex. Pyramids have been built at various times and places; the best-known are those of Egypt and of Central and South America. The pyramids of ancient Egypt were royal tombs. Each contained an inner sepulchral chamber that housed the deceased (usually mummified) ruler, members of his entourage, and artifacts. The rest of the pyramid complex consisted of a large enclosure, an adjacent mortuary temple, and a causeway leading down to a pavilion. About 80 royal pyramids survive in Egypt, the greatest being those at Giza. American pyramids include the Pyramids of the Sun and Moon at Teotihuacán, the Castillo at Chichén Itzá, and various Inca and Chimu structures in Andean settlements. These pyramids were generally built of earth and faced with stone; they are typically of stepped form and topped by a platform or temple structure used for rituals, including human sacrifice.

Pyramus and Thisbe \ˈpir-ə-məs...ˈthiz-bē\ Hero and heroine of a Babylonian love story related in Ovid's *Metamorphoses.* Their parents forbade them to meet, so they communicated through a hole in the wall between their two houses before at last deciding to run away together. They agreed to meet at a mulberry tree. Arriving first, Thisbe was scared away by a lion, which shredded the veil she dropped when she fled. Pyramus, finding the veil, believed her dead and stabbed himself; she returned and, finding Pyramus dying, killed herself. The fruit of the mulberry tree, white until then, was stained dark purple by the lovers' blood.

Pyrenees \ˈpir-ə-ˌnēz\ Mountain range, southwestern Europe. It extends 270 mi (430 km) from the Mediterranean Sea to the Bay of Biscay of the Atlantic Ocean. It forms a high wall between France and Spain. Generally, the crest of the range marks the boundary between the two countries. The tiny, autonomous principality of Andorra lies among its peaks. The highest point is Aneto Peak, at 11,169 ft (3,404 m) tall. There are few passes through the mountains. The pass at Roncesvalles was made famous in the 12th-century *Chanson de Roland,* based on the Battle of Roncesvalles (778).

Pyrenees, Treaty of the (November 7, 1659) Peace treaty between France and Spain. From the end of the Thirty Years' War (1648) until 1659, Spain and France fought almost continuously. When Philip IV of Spain did not receive the expected Habsburg support against France, he concluded a peace settlement that ceded border regions to France. The treaty also involved a marriage compact between Louis XIV and the Spanish infanta Maria Teresa, which established Louis as the most powerful monarch in Europe.

pyrethrum \pī-ˈrē-thrəm\ Any of certain plant species of the genus *Chrysanthemum* (see chrysanthemum) native to South Asia, whose aromatic flower heads, when powdered, constitute the active ingredient in the insecticide pyrethrin (or pyrethrum). The concentrations of pyrethrum powder used in insecticides are nontoxic to plants and higher animals; these insecticides therefore find wide use in household and livestock sprays as well as in dusts for edible plants. The typical species, the perennial *C. coccineum,* also is the florists' pyrethrum, or painted lady. Large deep-rose-colored petals surrounding the yellow center, or disk, are borne on long simple stems above the crown of finely cut leaves.

pyridine \ˈpir-ə-ˌdēn\ Any of a class of aromatic compounds with a six-member aromatic ring composed of five carbon atoms and one nitrogen atom, making it a heterocyclic compound. The simplest one is pyridine itself (C_5H_5N). Natural compounds with pyridine rings include niacin and pyridoxine (see vitamin B complex), the tuberculosis drug isoniazid, and other plant products (e.g., nicotine). Pyridine is used as a raw material for various drugs, vitamins, and fungicides and as a solvent. It has a nauseating odor and a burning taste, so it may be added to ethanol and antifreezes to make them undrinkable (see denaturation).

pyrimidine \pə-ˈrim-ə-ˌdēn\ Any of a class of heterocyclic compounds with a ring structure of four carbon and two nitrogen atoms. The simplest member, pyrimidine itself ($C_4H_4N_2$), is not common, but derivatives with the structure are. Examples include thiamine (vitamin B_1), several sulfa drugs, barbiturates, and three of the bases in nucleic acids (cytosine, thymine, and uracil).

pyrite *or* **iron pyrite** \ˈpī-ˌrīt\ *or* **fool's gold** Naturally occurring gold-colored iron disulfide mineral. Pyrite has frequently fooled prospectors into thinking they had discovered gold. Pure pyrite (FeS_2) contains 47% iron and 53% sulfur, by weight. Pyrite is used commercially as a source of sulfur, particularly for the production of sulfuric acid. Because there are much better sources of iron, it is not generally used as an iron ore. For many years Spain was the largest producer; other countries include Japan, the U.S., Canada, Italy, Norway, Portugal, and Slovakia.

pyrometer \pī-ˈrä-mə-tər\ Instrument for measuring relatively high temperatures, as in furnaces. Most pyrometers work by measuring radiation from the body whose temperature is to be measured (radiation devices have the advantage of not having to touch the material being measured). Optical pyrometers measure the temperature of glowing bodies by comparing them visually with an incandescent filament of known temperature whose temperature can be adjusted. In resistance pyrometers, a fine wire is put in contact with the object; the instrument converts the change in electrical resistance caused by heat to a reading of the temperature of the object.

pyroxene \pī-ˈräk-ˌsēn\ A group of important rock-forming silicate minerals of variable composition, among which calcium-, magnesium-, and iron-rich varieties predominate. Common pyroxenes belong to either the low-calcium enstatite-(ortho)ferrosilite series, $(Mg,Fe)SiO_3$, or the high-calcium diopside-hedenbergite series, $Ca(Mg,Fe)Si_2O_6$. Rare pyroxenes include jadeite, aegirine, and johannsenite. See also enstatite.

pyroxenite \pī-ˈräk-sə-ˌnīt\ Dark medium- to coarse-grained igneous rock that consists chiefly of pyroxene. Accessory minerals include hornblende, biotite, or olivine. Pyroxenites are not abundant.

pyrrhotite \ˈpir-ə-ˌtīt\ Iron sulfide mineral in which the ratio of iron to sulfur atoms is somewhat variable but is always slightly less than 1. It commonly is found in association with other sulfides. The variety troilite, with a composition near that of iron sulfide (FeS), is an important constituent of some meteorites.

Pyrrhus \ˈpir-əs\ (319–272 BC) King of Hellenistic Epirus. After being allied to Demetrius and taken hostage, he was befriended by Ptolemy I Soter and restored to his kingdom. In 281 he was asked for help against Rome by the Greek enclave of Tarentum (Taranto), and won costly victories at Heraclea and Ausculum. Crossing to Sicily, he conquered most of the Punic territory, but the Greek Sicilians revolted against his despotism. He suffered serious losses on his return to Italy (275) but defeated Antigonus II Gonatas in Macedonia (274) and became king there. He died in a skirmish in Argos trying to help Sparta. His costly victories gave rise to the term "Pyrrhic victory."

Pythagoras \pə-ˈtha-gə-rəs\ (c. 580–c. 500 BC) Greek philosopher and mathematician. Probably born in Samos, he settled in Croton (S Italy), where he established a community of followers who adhered to a way of life he prescribed. His school of philosophy reduced all meaning to numerical relationships and proposed that all existing objects are fundamentally composed of form and not material substance. The principles of PYTHAGOREANISM, including belief in the immortality and reincarnation of the soul and in the liberating power of abstinence and asceticism, influenced the thought of PLATO and ARISTOTLE and contributed to the development of mathematics and Western rational philosophy. The proportions of musical intervals and SCALES were first studied by Pythagoras, and he was the first influential Western practitioner of VEGETARIANISM. None of his writings survive, and it is difficult to distinguish the ideas he originated from those of his disciples. His memory is kept alive partly by the PYTHAGOREAN THEOREM, probably developed by his school after he died.

Pythagorean theorem \pə-ˌtha-gə-ˈrē-ən\ Rule relating the lengths of the sides of a right triangle. It says that the sum of the squares of the lengths of the legs is equal to the square of the length of the hypotenuse (the side opposite the right angle). That is, $a^2 + b^2 = c^2$, where c is the length of the hypotenuse. Triads of whole numbers that satisfy it (e.g., 3, 4, and 5) are called Pythagorean triples. See also law of COSINES, law of SINES.

Pythagoreanism \pə-ˌtha-gə-ˈrē-ə-ˌni-zəm\ Philosophical school, probably founded by PYTHAGORAS c. 525 BC. It originated as a religious brotherhood or an association for the moral reformation of society; brothers were sworn to strict loyalty and secrecy. The brotherhood had much in common with the Orphic communities (see ORPHISM), which sought by rites and abstinence to purify the believer's soul and enable it to escape from the "wheel of birth." Pythagoreanism held that reality, at its deepest level, is mathematical, that philosophy can be used for spiritual purification, that the soul can rise to union with the divine, and that certain symbols have mystical significance. It was the first important Western system of thought to advocate vegetarianism. The school became extinct in the mid-4th century.

Pythian Games \ˈpi-thē-ən\ In ancient Greece, various athletic and musical competitions held in honor of APOLLO, chiefly at DELPHI, from before the 5th century BC to the 4th century AD. They took place in August of the third year of each Olympiad (the four-year period between OLYMPIC GAMES). Events were similar to those of the ancient Olympics.

python \ˈpī-ˌthän\ Any of 20–25 species (subfamily Pythoninae, family Boidae) of sluggish, docile, nonvenomous SNAKES found in tropical and temperate regions from western Africa to China, Australia, and the Pacific islands. (The dwarf python of Central America is sometimes placed in this subfamily.) Pythons feed on birds and mammals, killing them by constriction. Most species are found near water; some are arboreal. All lay 15–100 eggs, depending on body size. The Asian reticulated python may be the world's longest snake (the ANACONDA is heavier); specimens over 30 ft (9 m) long have been recorded.

Qadariya \ˌkä-də-ˈrē-ə\ In Islam, adherents of the doctrine of free will. The name was also applied to the Mutazila. The issue of free will was a major point of controversy in Islamic theology, and the Qadariya took the most extreme stand in its defense. They based their argument on the necessity of divine justice, maintaining that without responsibility and freedom one cannot fairly be held accountable for one's actions. See free will problem.

Qaddafi \kə-ˈdä-fē\, **Muammar al-** *or* **Muammar al-Khadafy** (born 1942) Ruler of Libya (from 1969). Son of a Bedouin farmer, he was born in a tent in the desert. He graduated from the University of Libya and Libya's military academy as a devout Muslim and ardent nationalist. As a captain in the army, he led the 1969 coup that deposed King Idris I. He has espoused his own form of Islamic socialism, and his foreign policy has been anti-Western and anti-Israel. In 1970 he closed U.S. and British military bases and expelled Italians and Jews. He banned alcohol and gambling, and in 1973 he nationalized the oil industry. He has made unsuccessful attempts to unify Libya with other countries. His government has repeatedly been linked with terrorist incidents in Europe and elsewhere, and he has supported groups trying to overthrow neighboring governments. He narrowly escaped death in 1986 when U.S. planes bombed sites in Libya.

qadi \ˈkä-ˌdē\ Muslim judge who renders decisions according to the Sharia, the canon law of Islam. The qadi hears only religious cases, such as those involving inheritance, pious bequests, marriage, and divorce, though theoretically his jurisdiction extends to civil and criminal matters. The second caliph, Umar ibn al-Khattab, was the first to appoint a qadi to eliminate the necessity of his personally judging every dispute that arose in the community.

Qadisiyya \ˌkä-di-ˈsē-ə\, **Battle of** (636?) Battle fought between Sasanian forces (see Sasanian dynasty) and Arab invaders on one of the Euphrates canals, near Hirah in present-day Iraq. The Arab victory over Yazdegerd (r. 632–51) marked the end of the last native Persian dynasty.

Qajar dynasty \kä-ˈjär\ (1794–1925) Ruling dynasty of Iran. It was founded by Agha Mohammad Khan, who reunified Iran and reasserted Iran's rule over territories in Georgia and the Caucasus by defeating his rivals, including the last ruler of the Zand dynasty. His successor (r.1797–1834) lost land to Russia and increased contacts with the West. Nasir al-Din Shah's successful manipulation of Russia and Britain preserved Persia's independence, but his successors could not cope with European meddling and the aftermath of World War I, and the dynasty was abolished in 1925. See also Reza Shah Pahlavi.

Qantas Airways Limited Australian airline, the oldest in the English-speaking world, founded in 1920 as Queensland and Northern Territory Aerial Services Ltd. (later abbreviated to Qantas). By 2002 it had more than 140 destinations in over 30 countries.

Qara Qoyunlu See Kara Koyunlu

Qaraghandy See Karaganda

Qaraism See Karaism

Qarqar See Karkar

Qasimi \kä-ˈsē-mē\, **Sheikh Sultan bin Muhammad al-** (born 1942) Ruler of the Persian Gulf emirate of Sharjah since 1972. He succeeded his brother, who was assassinated. A political moderate, he has favored strengthening the federal government of the United Arab Emirates. In the wake of a failed coup attempt by another brother, he agreed to implement financial and administrative reforms and also agreed to make his brother crown prince, with the right to succeed him, but changed his mind and exiled his brother in 1990.

Qatar \ˈkä-tər\ *officially* **State of Qatar** Independent emirate on the eastern coast of the Arabian Peninsula. Area: 4,412 sq mi (11,427 sq km). Population (2001 est.): 606,000. Capital: Doha. Most of the population is Arab, with South Asian and Iranian minorities who are often migrant workers. Languages: Arabic (official), English. Religion: Islam (official). Currency: Qatar riyal. Qatar is mostly stony, sandy, and barren, and consists of salt flats, dune desert, and arid plains. Largely because of oil and natural gas exports, Qatar's gross national product per capita is one of the highest in the world. The government owns all of the agricultural land and generates most of the economic activity. The private sector participates in trade and contracting on a limited scale. It is a monarchy, and its basis of legislation is Islamic law. The head of state and government is the emir assisted by the prime minister. It was partly controlled by Bahrain in the 18th–19th century and was nominally part of the Ottoman empire until World War I. In 1916 it became a British protectorate. Oil was discovered in 1940, and the country rapidly modernized. Qatar declared independence in 1971, when the British protectorate ended. In 1991 it served as a base for air strikes against Iraq in the Persian Gulf War. See map below.

Qazvin *or* **Kazvin** \kaz-ˈvēn\ City (pop., 1996: 291,117), northwestern Iran. Founded as Shad Shahpur in AD 250, it flourished under Muslim rule in the 7th century. Genghis Khan laid waste to the city, but it later revived and was made the capital of Persia (1548–98). In the late 18th century it became a base for foreign trade with areas of the Caspian Sea, Persian Gulf, and Asia Minor. A coup d'état was launched from Qazvin in 1921 that led to Iran's consolidation under Reza Shah Pahlavi. It is a regional communications center, with some manufacturing.

qedesha \ˈkä-de-shȧ\ One of a class of sacred prostitutes found throughout the ancient Middle East and associated especially with the worship of the fertility goddess Astarte. Prostitutes, who often played an important part in official temple worship, could be either male or female. The early Israelites adopted Canaanite rites of sacred prostitution, and despite the denunciations of Israelite prophets, the practice continued until the reforms of Josiah in the 7th century BC.

Qi *or* **Ch'i** One of the largest and most powerful of the many states into which early China was divided (771?–221 BC). During the Eastern Zhou dynasty, Qi was the first state to fully institute a uniform tax system, a central army, and a centralized bureaucracy based on talent rather than hereditary rank. It formed a league of states in 651 BC to stave off invasions from the north and south, but its hegemony was short-lived. In 221 BC it was absorbed into the Qin dynasty.

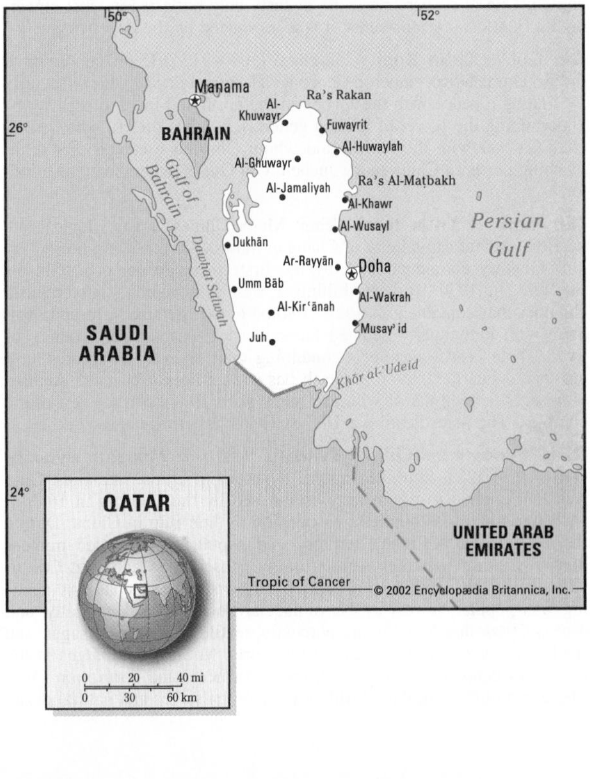

qi *or* **ch'i** \'chē\ In Chinese philosophy, the ethereal substance of which everything is composed. Early Taoist philosophers and alchemists regarded it as a vital force associated with breath and bodily fluids and sought to control its movement within the body in order to achieve longevity and spiritual power. Manipulation of qi is central to Chinese meditation, medicine, and MARTIAL ARTS. In the 10th–13th century NEO-CONFUCIANISM regarded qi as emanating from the Great Ultimate by way of *li,* the ordering principle of the universe, transformed into the elements through yin and yang (see YIN-YANG).

Qianlong emperor *or* **Ch'ien-lung emperor** \chē-'en-'lůŋ\ *orig.* **Hongli** (1711–1799) Fourth emperor of the QING DYNASTY in China. His reign (1735–96) was one of the longest in Chinese history. China's boundaries reached their greatest extent, encompassing Mongolia, Tibet, Nepal, Taiwan, and portions of Central Asia. Qianlong sponsored a compilation of the Confucian Classics (see FIVE CLASSICS); the compilation's descriptive catalog is still used today. At the same time, he was ordering the expurgation or destruction of all books containing anti-Manchu sentiments; some 2,600 titles were ordered destroyed. He enjoyed excellent personal relationships with JESUIT missionaries in Beijing, though Roman Catholic preaching remained officially forbidden. In the first half of his reign, agriculture made great strides and was superior to that in much of Europe. Taxes were light and education was widespread, even among the peasantry. Subsequently, military expeditions and increasing governmental corruption permanently harmed the dynasty, sowing the seeds for its decline in the 19th century. See also HESHEN, KANGXI EMPEROR, MANCHU.

qilin *or* **ch'i-lin** \chē-'lin\ In Chinese mythology, a kind of UNICORN whose rare appearance often coincides with the imminent birth or death of a sage or illustrious ruler. Appearances could also indicate the benevolence of living emperors. It has a single horn on its forehead, a yellow belly, a multicolored back, a horse's hooves, a deer's body, and an ox's tail. Legend has it that a qilin appeared to the pregnant mother of CONFUCIUS.

Qin dynasty *or* **Ch'in dynasty** \'chin\ (221–206 BC) Dynasty that established the first great Chinese empire. The Qin (from which the name China is derived), established the approximate boundaries and basic administrative system that all subsequent dynasties were to follow. Qin accomplishments include standardization of the CHINESE WRITING SYSTEM and the building of the GREAT WALL; the dynasty is also notorious for the "Qin bibliocaust," in which all nonutilitarian books were ordered burned. Due to its harshness, the dynasty only outlasted its first emperor, SHI HUANGDI, by four years; it was succeeded by the HAN DYNASTY.

Qin Gui *or* **Ch'in Kuei** \'chin-kü-'ā\ (1090–1155) Chief counselor to the Southern SONG emperor Gaozong. He maintained external security by signing a peace with the Juchen in the north and internal security by undermining the power of leading generals, notably YUE FEI, who had argued for war with the Juchen and whom Qin Gui executed. For relinquishing northern China to the Juchen, Qin Gui is remembered as a traitor.

Qin tomb *or* **Ch'in tomb** \'chin\ Major Chinese archaeological site near the ancient capital city of Changan (now Xi'an), a 20-sq-mi (50-sq-km) funerary compound built by the first sovereign emperor, Qin SHI HUANGDI. In 1974 workers drilling a well discovered a subterranean chamber that contained an army of some 6,000 life-size terra-cotta soldiers with individually detailed faces, horses, weapons, and other objects. Three nearby chambers containing more than 1,400 figures have also been unearthed; the tomb itself has not yet been excavated. Archaeologists anticipate that it will take many years to unearth the rest of the complex. The mausoleum is a UNESCO world heritage site.

Qing dynasty *or* **Ch'ing dynasty** \'chiŋ\ *or* **Manchu dynasty** (1644–1911/12) Last of the imperial dynasties in China. The name Qing was first applied to the dynasty established by the MANCHU in 1636 in Manchuria and then applied by extension to their rule in China. During the Qing dynasty, China's territory and population expanded tremendously. Cultural attitudes were strongly conservative and NEO-CONFUCIANISM was the dominant philosophy. The arts flourished: LITERATI painting was popular, novels in the vernacular developed substantially, and BEIJING OPERA developed. Qing porcelain, textiles, tea, paper, sugar, and steel were exported to all parts of the world. Military campaigns in the later 18th century depleted government finances, and corruption grew. These conditions, combined with population pressures and natural disasters, led to the TAIPING and NIAN Rebellions, which in turn so weakened the dynasty that it was unable to rebuff the demands of foreign powers in the later 19th century. The dynasty ended with the Republican Revolution of 1911 and the abdication of the last emperor in 1912.

Qinghai *or* **Ch'ing-hai** \'chiŋ-'hī\ *formerly* **Koko Nor** Lake, QINGHAI province, China. The largest drainless mountain lake of central Asia, it is 65 mi (105 km) long and 40 mi (64 km) wide; its surface area fluctuates seasonally between 1,600 and 2,300 sq mi (4,200–6,000 sq km). Formed by melting glaciers during the late Pleistocene, it is located in the Nan Mountains at an elevation of 10,515 ft (3,205 m). Twenty-three rivers and streams empty into it.

Qinghai *or* **Tsinghai** *or* **Ch'ing-hai** Province (pop., 2000 est.: 5,180,000), western central China. The capital is XINING. Located in a remote region of China, to the west of the historic provinces of China proper, it forms the northeastern part of the plateau of Tibet, with its greater part above 10,000 ft (3,048 m) high. In one of its mountain ranges, the HUANG HE (Yellow River) has its source. Parts of it came under Chinese control in the 3rd century BC. For centuries it was sparsely occupied by nomadic herdsmen, chiefly Tibetans and Mongols, and a few Chinese farmers. The Chinese population increased over the years; it was made a Chinese province in 1928. Economic activities include farming, herding, mining, timbering, and manufacturing. It possesses some of China's best pasturelands and is noted for its horse breeding.

Qishon River *or* **Kishon River** \'kī-ˌshän\ River, northern Israel. It rises near Mount Gilboa and flows northwest through the Plain of Esdraelon to the Mediterranean Sea just north of HAIFA. It is about 25 mi (40 km) long. It was the scene of biblical events, including the Israelite victory of DEBORAH over the Canaanite Gen. Sisera, and of ELIJAH's slaying of the prophets of BAAL. In modern times, the river's mouth has been developed as part of Haifa's port complex. It is the main base of Israel's fishing fleet.

Qiu Chuji *or* **Ch'iu Ch'u-chi** \'jyü-'jü-'jē\ *orig.* **Changchun** \'chäŋ-'chůn\ (1148–1227) Taoist monk and alchemist. His disciple Li Zhichang chronicled Qiu's journey to meet GENGHIS KHAN (who wished to learn from Qiu) in *The Travels of an Alchemist,* which describes the land and people between the Great Wall and Kabul and between the Yellow and Aral Seas. Qiu Chuji was a member of a sect known for its extreme asceticism and the doctrine of *xingming,* which held that man's lost natural state could be recovered through prescribed practices.

Qu Yuan *or* **Ch'ü Yüan** \'chü-'ywen\ (343?–289? BC) Chinese poet. Born into the ruling house of Chu, in youth Qu Yuan was a favorite of the region's ruler. Later he was banished and wandered in despair, writing and observing folk customs, which would influence his works. He eventually drowned himself. His most famous poem is the melancholy *Li sao* ("Encountering Sorrow"). One of the greatest poets of ancient China, he exerted enormous influence on later poets with his highly original verse.

quack grass See COUCH GRASS

quadrangle Rectangular open space completely or partially enclosed by buildings of an academic or civic character. The grounds of a quadrangle are often grassy or landscaped. Such an area, intended as an environment for contemplation, study, or relaxation, was a feature of monastic establishments and the colleges that evolved from them. The quadrangular layout at New College in Oxford University (completed 1386), with its partially connected buildings, was enormously influential in subsequent collegiate building.

quadratic equation Algebraic equation of particular importance in OPTIMIZATION. A more descriptive name is second-degree POLYNOMIAL equation. Its standard form is $ax^2 + bx + c = 0$, and its solution is given by the quadratic formula

$$x = \frac{-b \pm \sqrt{b^2 - 4ac}}{(2a)}$$

which guarantees two REAL-NUMBER solutions, one real-number solution, or two COMPLEX-NUMBER solutions, depending on whether $b^2 - 4ac$ is greater than, equal to, or less than 0.

quadrille \kwä-'dril\ Dance for four couples in square formation, fashionable in the late 18th and 19th century. Imported to England from Parisian ballrooms in 1815, it consisted of four or five contredanses (see COUNTRY DANCE), each danced with prescribed combinations of intertwining figures rather than depending on intricate individual steps. It was often danced to opera melodies. See also American SQUARE DANCE.

Quadros, Jânio da Silva (1917–1992) President of Brazil (1961). A colorful and eccentric populist, he campaigned with a broom to dramatize his pledge to "sweep out corruption." In his seven months as president, he banned bikini swimsuits and cockfights, reestablished relations with the Soviet Union, decorated CHE GUEVARA, and refused to support the U.S. in the BAY OF PIGS INVASION of Cuba. He attributed his sudden resignation to "terrible forces" conspiring against him. Stripped of political rights and exiled in 1968, he was granted amnesty in 1980 and returned to serve two terms as mayor of São Paulo.

Quadruple Alliance (1718) Alliance between Austria, Britain, the Dutch Republic, and France, formed to prevent Spain from altering the terms of the Peace of UTRECHT (1713). When PHILIP V of Spain seized Sardinia and Sicily, the British fleet brought Austrian troops to Sicily and the French occupied northern Spain, and Philip was forced to renounce his claims in Italy.

Quadruple Alliance (1815) Alliance between Britain, Russia, Austria, and Prussia first formed in1813 to oppose France in the final phase of the NAPOLEONIC WARS. It was officially renewed in 1815 to enforce the peace settlement concluded at the Congress of VIENNA. The allies agreed to meet occasionally to keep European political development within terms of the 1815 settlement. This program was partially carried out by the Congresses of AIX-LA-CHAPELLE (1818), TROPPAU (1820), LAIBACH (1821), and VERONA (1822).

quaestor \'kwe-stər, 'kwē-stər\ (Latin: "investigator") In ancient Rome, an officer appointed by a CONSUL as his deputy. Around 450 BC they became magistrates, a class of high-level government administrators that included the consuls, PRAETORS, and PREFECTS. Quaestors, the lowest level of this class, were elected by the people. After 421 there were four quaestors, two public treasurers and two who assisted the consuls, accompanying them to war and taking charge of supplies and payment of troops. From AUGUSTUS' time there were 20 quaestors, many of whom acted as finance officers and assistants to provincial governors.

quahog \'kō-,hȯg, 'kwȯ-,hȯg\ Thick-shelled edible CLAM of the U.S. The northern quahog *(Mercenaria mercenaria),* also known as the cherrystone, littleneck, or hard-shell clam, is 3–5 in. (8–13 cm) long. The dingy white shell is thick and rounded and has prominent concentric lines. It is found in the intertidal zone from the Gulf of St. Lawrence to the Gulf of Mexico. It is the most important food clam of the Atlantic coast. The southern quahog *(M. campechiensis),* found in the intertidal zone from Chesapeake Bay to the West Indies, is about 3–6 in. (8–15 cm) long and has a heavy, white, plump shell.

quail Any of several species of short-tailed game birds (family Phasianidae), some with a head plume that is straight or curled forward. Species range from 5 to 13 in. (13–33 cm) long. Some of the 95 Old World species have leg spurs, but the 36 New World species never do. Quails prefer open country and brushy borders. The male may help incubate the 12 eggs. Quails mainly eat seeds and berries but also leaves, roots, and insects. The common quail *(Coturnix coturnix)* of Eurasia and Africa is the only migratory bird in the order Galliformes. Quails are generally smaller than PARTRIDGES. See also BOBWHITE.

California quail (*Callipepla californica*).

Quaker Oats Co. International manufacturer of grocery products. It was formed in 1901 by the merging of three milling companies from Ohio and Iowa, including the country's largest cereal mill. The company initially produced oat and wheat cereals, cornmeal, and baby food. By the late 20th century, hundreds of food products had been added. In the 1960s and '70s, the company diversified into chemical products, restaurants, and toys, but most nonfood assets were sold in the 1990s. Headquartered in Chicago, the company has several foreign subsidiaries.

Quakers See Society of FRIENDS

quality In philosophy, a property that applies to things taken singly, in contrast to a RELATION, which applies to things taken in pairs, triples, etc. The distinction drawn by GALILEO and JOHN LOCKE between primary and secondary qualities is motivated by the fact that modern science seems to reveal that unaided sensory perception gives false or incomplete information about the intrinsic qualities of physical objects. Mathematical formulations of physical phenomena seem to indicate that most sensory information may contribute nothing to knowledge of objects. In this view, primary qualities, such as shape, quantity, and motion, are genuine properties of things that are describable by mathematics, whereas secondary qualities, such as odor, taste, sound, color, or warmth, exist only in human consciousness and do not belong to the objects.

Quant, Mary (born 1934) English designer of youth-oriented fashions, responsible in the 1960s for the "Chelsea look" of England and the widespread popularity of the miniskirt and "hot pants." After opening a successful boutique called Bazaar in 1957, she went on to mass-produce her designs on a multimillion-dollar annual scale.

Quantrill \'kwän-trəl\, **William C(larke)** (1837–1865) U.S. outlaw and Confederate guerrilla. Born in Canal Dover, Ohio, he worked as an itinerant schoolteacher, then moved to Kansas, where he failed at farming. By 1860 he was a horse thief and murderer. In the Civil War he joined the Confederate army, but later gathered a gang of guerrillas to raid and rob Union towns and farms. Quantrill's Raiders were given official status by the Confederates in 1862. In 1863 his group of about 450 men sacked the free-state town of Lawrence, Kan., killing 150 people. They later defeated a Union detachment and killed 90 soldiers. Quantrill was mortally wounded in a raid into Kentucky.

quantum In physics, a discrete natural unit, or packet, of energy, charge, angular momentum, or other physical property. Light, for example, which appears in some respects as a continuous electromagnetic wave, on the submicroscopic level is emitted and absorbed in discrete amounts, or quanta; for light of a given wavelength, the magnitude of all the quanta emitted or absorbed is the same in both energy and momentum. These particlelike packets of light are called PHOTONS, a term also applicable to quanta of other forms of electromagnetic energy such as X RAYS and GAMMA RAYS. Submicroscopic mechanical vibrations in the layers of atoms comprising CRYSTALS also give up or take on energy and momentum in quanta called PHONONS. See also QUANTUM MECHANICS.

quantum chromodynamics (QCD) Theory that describes the action of the STRONG FORCE. The strong force acts only on certain particles, principally QUARKS that are bound together in the PROTONS and NEUTRONS of the atomic NUCLEUS, as well as in less stable, more exotic forms of matter. Quantum chromodynamics has been built on the concept that QUARKS interact via the strong force because they carry a form of "strong charge," which has been given the name "color." The three types of charge are called red, green, and blue, in analogy to the primary colors of light, though there is no connection with the usual sense of color.

quantum computing Experimental method of computing that makes use of quantum-mechanical phenomena. It incorporates quantum theory and the UNCERTAINTY PRINCIPLE. Quantum computers would allow a BIT to store a value of 0 and 1 simultaneously. They could pursue multiple lines of inquiry simultaneously, with the final output dependent on the interference pattern generated by the various calculations. See also DNA COMPUTING, QUANTUM MECHANICS.

quantum electrodynamics (QED) Quantum theory of the interactions of charged particles with the ELECTROMAGNETIC FIELD. It describes the interactions of light with matter as well as those of charged particles with each other. Its foundations were laid by P. A. M. DIRAC when he discovered an equation describing the motion and spin of electrons that incorporated both QUANTUM MECHANICS and the theory of special RELATIVITY. The theory, as refined and developed in the late 1940s, rests on the idea that charged particles interact by emitting and absorbing PHOTONS. It has become a model for other QUANTUM FIELD THEORIES.

quantum field theory Theory that brings QUANTUM MECHANICS and special RELATIVITY together to account for subatomic phenomena. In particular, the interactions of SUBATOMIC PARTICLES are described in terms of their interactions with fields, such as the ELECTROMAGNETIC FIELD. However, the fields are quantized and represented by particles, such as PHOTONS for the electromagnetic field. QUANTUM ELECTRODYNAMICS is the quantum field theory that describes the interaction of electrically charged particles via electromagnetic fields. QUANTUM CHROMODYNAMICS describes the action of the STRONG FORCE. The ELECTROWEAK THEORY, a unified theory of electromagnetic and WEAK FORCES, has considerable experimental support, and can likely be extended to include the strong force. Theories that include the gravitational force (see GRAVITATION) are more speculative. See also GRAND UNIFIED THEORY, UNIFIED FIELD THEORY.

quantum mechanics Branch of mathematical physics that deals with atomic and subatomic systems. It is concerned with phenomena that are so small-scale that they cannot be described in classical terms, and is formulated entirely in terms of statistical probabilities. Considered one of the great ideas of the 20th century, quantum mechanics was developed mainly by NIELS BOHR, ERWIN SCHRODINGER, WERNER HEISENBERG, and MAX BORN and led to a drastic reappraisal of the concept of objective reality. It explained the structure of ATOMS, atomic nuclei (see NUCLEUS), and MOLECULES; the behavior of SUBATOMIC PARTICLES; the nature of chemical bonds (see BONDING); the properties of crystalline solids (see CRYSTAL); NUCLEAR ENERGY; and the forces that stabilize collapsed STARS. It also led directly to the development of the LASER, the ELECTRON MICROSCOPE, and the TRANSISTOR.

Qu'Appelle River \kwä-'pel\ River, southern Saskatchewan. It is about 270 mi (435 km) long and flows east through several lakes and Indian reservations and across the Manitoba border into the ASSINIBOINE RIVER. Its French name, meaning "who calls," was derived from its CREE Indian name, which referred to the cries of a legendary spirit that haunted its waters. Once a fur-trapping region, its basin is now farmed for wheat.

quarantine Detention of humans or animals suspected to have communicable disease until they are proved free of infection. The term is often used interchangeably with isolation (separation of a known infected individual from healthy ones until the danger of transmission passes). It derives from the 40-day (quarantina) isolation period instituted in an attempt to prevent spread of plague in the Middle Ages. Though appropriate in some cases (e.g., DIPHTHERIA), it is ineffective for diseases that are spread by other means (e.g., PLAGUE) or are contagious before symptoms appear. In some cases, contacts (e.g., the family of a hepatitis patient) are notified, educated on precautions, and monitored for development of illness. Quarantine is more often applied to animals (e.g., for RABIES).

quark Any of a group of SUBATOMIC PARTICLES thought to be among the fundamental constituents of matter, more specifically, of PROTONS and NEUTRONS. The concept of the quark was first proposed by MURRAY GELL-MANN and George Zweig (born 1937); its name was taken from JAMES JOYCE's novel *Finnegans Wake*. Quarks include all particles that interact by means of the STRONG FORCE. They have MASS and SPIN, and they obey the PAULI EXCLUSION PRINCIPLE. They have never been resolved into smaller components, and they never occur alone. Their behavior is explained by the theory of QUANTUM CHROMODYNAMICS, which provides a means of calculating their basic properties. There are six types of quark, called up, down, strange, charmed, bottom, and top. Only the up and down quarks are needed to make protons and neutrons; the others occur in heavier, unstable particles.

Quarles, Francis (1592–1644) English religious poet. Quarles is remembered for his *Emblemes* (1635), the most notable of English-language emblem books (collections of symbolic pictures, usually with verse and prose). Its success led him to produce another, *Hieroglyphikes of the Life of Man* (1638). Printed together in 1639, they formed perhaps the most popular volume of verse of the 17th century. He also wrote *Enchiridion* (1640), a highly popular book of aphorisms.

quarter horse Breed of light HORSE developed in the U.S. from THOROUGHBRED, MORGAN, AMERICAN SADDLEBRED, and other stock as a quarter-mile racer. Though overshadowed by the Thoroughbred, it found a place in the western and southwestern U.S. as a stock horse (see CUTTING HORSE). Modern quarter horses are short and stocky, with a muscular build and a deep, broad chest. They are noted for fast starting, turning, and stopping ability, short-distance speed, and intelligence. They stand 14.3–16 hands (57–64 in., 145–163 cm) high, weigh 950–1,200 lbs (431–544 kg), and have a calm, cooperative temperament.

quarter-horse racing Racing of QUARTER HORSES. It originated among British settlers in Virginia shortly after Jamestown was established in 1607. The course was traditionally a quarter-mile (400 m); today there are 11 officially sanctioned races, ranging from 220 to 870 yards (201–796 m). Timing is to the nearest 1⁄100 second.

quartermaster Officer who oversees arrangements for the quartering and movement of troops. The office dates at least to the 15th century in Europe. The French minister of war under LOUIS XIV created a quartermaster general's department that dotted the countryside with strategically located stockpiles of food, forage, ammunition, and equipment. By the 18th century his duties in some European countries included coordinating marches and deployments and drafting operational orders; in the U.S. he remained a specialized administrative and logistical functionary until 1962, when the Quartermaster Corps was absorbed by other agencies.

quartz Second most abundant mineral (after FELDSPAR) in the earth's crust, present in many rocks. Quartz, which consists of silica, or silicon dioxide (SiO_2), has great economic importance. Many varieties are gemstones, including AMETHYST, CITRINE, SMOKY QUARTZ, and rose quartz. SANDSTONE, composed mainly of quartz, is an important building stone. Large amounts of quartz sand (or silica sand) are used in the manufacture of glass and ceramics and for molds in metal casting. Crushed quartz is used as an abrasive in sandpaper; silica sand is employed in sandblasting; and sandstone is used whole to make whetstones, millstones, and grindstones. Silica glass (or fused quartz) is used in optics to transmit ultraviolet light. Tubing and various vessels of fused quartz have important laboratory applications, and quartz fibers are employed in extremely sensitive weighing devices.

quartzite SANDSTONE that has been converted into a solid QUARTZ rock. Quartzites are usually white; they fracture smoothly and break up into rubble under frost action. Sandstone may be converted to quartzite by precipitation of silica from waters below the earth's surface; such rocks are called orthoquartzites, whereas those produced by recrystallization (METAMORPHISM) are metaquartzites. Because they weather slowly, they tend to project as hills or mountain masses. Many prominent ridges in the Appalachian Mountains are composed of quartzite. Pure quartzites are a source of silica for metallurgical purposes and for the manufacture of silica brick. Quartzite is also quarried for paving and roofing materials.

quasar \'kwā-ˌzär\ *in full* **quasi-stellar radio source** Any of a class of rare cosmic objects of high luminosity and strong radio emission observed at extremely great distances. The term is also often applied to closely related objects that have the same optical appearance but do not emit radio waves, the so-called QSOs (quasi-stellar objects). Most quasars exhibit very large RED SHIFTS, suggesting that they are moving away from earth at tremendous speeds (approaching the speed of light) and are some of the most distant known objects in the universe. Quasars are no more than a light-year or two across but up to 1,000 times more luminous than a giant galaxy with a diameter of 100,000 light-years, allowing them to be observed at distances of more than 10 billion light-years. Many investigators attribute such energy generation to gas spiraling at high velocity into a supermassive BLACK HOLE at the center of an otherwise normal GALAXY. See also ACTIVE galactic nuclei.

Quasimodo \ˌkwä-zē-'mō-dō\, **Salvatore** (1901–1968) Italian poet, critic, and translator. He spent 10 years as an engineer for the Italian government while writing poetry in his spare time. He gradually became a leader of HERMETICISM after the publication of his first poetry collection, *Acque e terre* (1930; "Waters and Land"). After World War II his social convictions shaped his work, beginning with *Giorno dopo giorno* (1947; "Day After Day"). He published an astonishing range of translations, edited anthologies, and wrote essays, including those in *The Poet and the Politician* (1960). He received the Nobel Prize in 1959.

Quaternary period \'kwä-tər-ˌner-ē, kwə-'tər-nə-rē\ Interval of geologic time, 1.8 million years ago to the present. The Quaternary follows the TERTIARY PERIOD and is the more recent of the two periods of the CENOZOIC ERA. The Quaternary is subdivided into the PLEISTOCENE EPOCH and the HOLOCENE EPOCH, and is characterized by major cyclical changes of climate on a global scale. Because these led to repeated invasions of vast areas by ice sheets, the period is frequently referred to as the Great Ice Age. Its major biologic feature was the evolution and dispersion of humans. The dramatic changes of climate and environment in the Quaternary led to high rates of evolution and extinction, particularly among the mammals. The extinction of many large mammals toward the end of the last ice age may also be related to the rapid territorial expansion of humans.

Quayle, (James) Dan(forth) (born 1947) U.S. politician. Born in Indianapolis, he served as associate publisher of his family's *Huntington Herald-Press* (1974–76). He was elected to the U.S. House of Representatives (1976–80) and Senate (1980–88). Chosen as the Republican candidate for vice president, he was elected with GEORGE BUSH in 1988. During his term, Quayle traveled widely on goodwill missions but was criticized for various gaffes. In 1992 he and Bush were defeated for reelection.

Quebec Province (pop., 2001: 7,410,500), eastern Canada. It is bounded by the Hudson Strait, UNGAVA BAY, Newfoundland, the Gulf of ST. LAWRENCE, New Brunswick, the U.S., Ontario, and HUDSON BAY. Its capital is QUEBEC city. The original inhabitants were Inuits (see ESKIMO) and members of the Algonquian, Cree, and other Indian tribes. Settled by the French in the early 17th century, it was lost to the British in the FRENCH AND INDIAN WAR, but the struggle for authority between the French and British groups led to a rebellion by French Canadians in 1837. The rebellion was quelled, and in 1867 Quebec united with New Brunswick and Nova Scotia to form the Dominion of Canada. Most of the population is of French descent. Various movements for independence have continued during the 20th century; the PARTI QUÉBÉCOIS won provincial elections in 1976, but its independence referendum was defeated in 1980. A second independence referendum was defeated in 1995 by a close margin. Principal industries include mining, hydroelectric power, and forestry.

Quebec *or* **Quebec City** City (metro. area pop., 2001: 682,757), port, and capital of QUEBEC province. It lies at the confluence of the ST. LAWRENCE and St. Charles rivers, about 150 mi (240 km) northeast of MONTREAL, on a rocky promontory above the rivers. Canada's oldest city, it was settled by the French in 1608 as a trading post. It was the capital of NEW FRANCE from 1663 to 1763, when it was lost to the British. It was the capital of Lower Canada 1791–1841 and CANADA EAST 1841–67. It became the provincial capital in 1867. Most of the population is French speaking and Roman Catholic. It is the site of LAVAL UNIV. and other colleges and cultural institutions. Manufactures include newsprint, milled grain, cigarettes, and clothing. Shipbuilding and tourism are important industries.

Quebec, Battle of (September 13, 1759) Decisive battle of the FRENCH AND INDIAN WAR. In June, JAMES WOLFE led a British force of 250 ships with 8,500 soldiers to take up positions in the St. Lawrence River around Quebec. French forces under the Marquis de MONTCALM withstood a two-month siege of the city. In September the British secretly landed 4,000 men near the city and forced a confrontation with French troops on the Plains of ABRAHAM. The defending French were routed in the battle, in which both Wolfe and Montcalm were mortally wounded.

Quebec Act (1774) British statute establishing Quebec's government and extending its borders. It provided for a governor and appointed council, religious freedom for Roman Catholics, and use of the French civil code. The act attempted to resolve the problem of making the colony a province of British North America and tried to build French-Canadian loyalty to the British. It also extended the borders of Quebec to include the land between the Ohio and Mississippi rivers, a region claimed by American colonists. It was considered one of the INTOLERABLE ACTS, which led to the AMERICAN REVOLUTION.

Québécois, Parti See PARTI QUÉBÉCOIS

Quechua \'ke-chə-wə\ South American Indian population of the Andes from Ecuador to Bolivia. In the early 15th century the Quechuas were conquered by the Chancas, who in turn were subdued by the INCAS. Much of the traditional Quechua way of life endured under the Incas, but it was drastically altered by the 16th-century Spanish conquest. Traditional Quechuas now lead isolated lives as marginal farmers in the high Andes. Their religion combines Roman Catholicism with folk beliefs. See also QUECHUAN LANGUAGES.

Quechuan languages \'ke-chə-wən\ Family of closely related South American Indian languages still spoken by some 12 million people in southern Columbia and Ecuador, Bolivia, and northern Argentina. Southern Peruvian Quechua, one language of the family, was a KOINE and administrative language within the INCA empire and was spread by Inca colonization. Quechua was formerly placed in a single family with Aymara, another important Andean language spoken chiefly in Bolivia, which is typologically and phonetically similar to Southern Peruvian Quechua; however, this hypothesis has been disputed.

Queen, Ellery *pseudonym of* **Frederic Dannay** *orig.* **Daniel Nathan** *and* **Manfred Bennington Lee** *orig.* **Manford Lepofsky** (1905–1982; 1905–1971) U.S. writers. The two cousins, born respectively in Brooklyn and White Plains, N.Y., collaborated on more than 35 best-selling detective novels featuring the detective Ellery Queen. They took turns writing stories about Queen after winning a detective-story contest with *The Roman Hat Mystery* (1929). The pair used the pseudonym Barnaby Ross to write about a second detective, Drury Lane. They also cofounded *Ellery Queen's Mystery Magazine* (1941), edited numerous anthologies, and cofounded Mystery Writers of America.

Queen Anne style Style of English decorative arts that reached its apex during the reign (1702–14) of Queen ANNE. The most distinctive feature of Queen Anne furniture is the cabriole leg, shaped in a double curve (the upper part convex, the lower concave) and ending in either a claw-and-ball or paw foot. The Queen Anne chair is identifiable by a splat back curved to fit the hollow of the spine. The wood used was almost exclusively walnut, often embellished with marquetry, inlay, veneering, and lacquerwork. Ornamentation motifs include scallop shells, scrolls, Oriental figures, and animals.

Queen Anne's lace *or* **wild carrot** Bristly biennial *(Daucus carota)* of the PARSLEY family, native to Eurasia but now found almost worldwide. An ancestor of the cultivated CARROT, it grows 5 ft (1.5 m) tall and has divided, long, feathery leaves. Flat-topped clusters (umbels) of white or pink flowers have a single dark-purple flower in the center and resemble lace. The enlarged root is edible but very bitter, and the ribbed fruits have sharp spines.

Queen Anne's War (1702–13) Second in a series of wars between Britain and France for control of North America. It was the American phase of the War of the SPANISH SUCCESSION. American colonial settlements along the New York and New England borders with Canada were raided by French forces and their Indian allies. The British capture of Port Royal (1710) resulted in French-held Acadia's becoming the British province of Nova Scotia. Under the Treaty of Utrecht (1713), Britain also acquired Newfoundland and the Hudson Bay region from France.

Queen Charlotte Islands Group of about 150 islands (pop., 1991: 5,000) off western British Columbia. They have an area of 3,705 sq mi (9,596 sq km). The two largest islands, Graham and Moresby, are irregular in shape and rise to nearly 4,000 ft (1,200 m). The inhabitants, including HAIDA Indians, engage in fishing and ranching.

Queen Charlotte Sound Broad, deep inlet of the Pacific Ocean indenting western British Columbia. Bounded on the north by the QUEEN CHARLOTTE ISLANDS and on the south by VANCOUVER ISLAND, the sound feeds into a series of straits that once were avenues followed by the continental GLACIERS as they pushed out to sea. Its eastern border is a complex of islands, inlets, and fjords.

Queen Elizabeth Islands Island group, northern Canada. Part of the Canadian Arctic archipelago, it comprises all the islands north of latitude 74°30′ N, including the Parry and Sverdrup island groups. The islands, the largest of which are ELLESMERE, MELVILLE, Devon, and Axel Heiberg, have a total land area of over 150,000 sq mi (390,000 sq km). Probably first visited by the Vikings c. AD 1000, they were partially explored (1615–16) by English navigators William Baffin and Robert Bylot. The islands, which are administratively split between the NORTHWEST TERRITORIES and NUNAVUT, were named in 1953 to honor Queen ELIZABETH II.

Queen Elizabeth National Park *or* **Ruwenzori National Park** National park, southwestern Uganda. Established in 1952, it has an area of 764 sq mi (1,978 sq km) and lies east of Lake EDWARD. One of the largest parks in Uganda, it has areas of rain forest and savanna grassland. It is within the western branch of the GREAT RIFT VALLEY and is dotted with PLEISTOCENE volcanic craters. Wildlife includes chimpanzees, leopards, lions, and elephants.

Queens Borough (pop., 1990: 1,950,000) of NEW YORK CITY, coextensive with Queens county, southeastern New York. The largest of the five boroughs, it lies on western LONG ISLAND and extends across the width of the island from the junction of the EAST RIVER and LONG ISLAND SOUND to the Atlantic Ocean. The first settlements, made by the Dutch 1636–56, came under English control in 1664. It became a county in 1683 and a borough in 1898. Queens was primarily rural during the 19th century, but some of its shore communities began attracting summer vacationers. Development was spurred by the construction of the Queensboro Bridge and the Long Island Railroad tunnel. It is mostly residential, though it has extensive manufacturing around Long Island City, and storage and shipping facilities lining the East River. It is the site of New York City's major airports, Kennedy and La Guardia.

Queen's University at Kingston Privately endowed university in Kingston, Ontario. It was founded in 1841 and modeled after the University of EDINBURGH. It is a comprehensive research institution, offering undergraduate, graduate, and professional degrees in most major fields. Research facilities include centers for the study of international relations, industrial relations, and natural resources. Total enrollment is about 17,000.

Queensberry rules Code of BOXING rules written by John Graham Chambers (1843–1883) and published in 1867 under the sponsorship of John Sholto Douglas, Marquess of Queensberry (1844–1900), known also for precipitating the downfall of OSCAR WILDE. Besides calling for the wearing of gloves, the rules forbade wrestling holds, required a fallen man to be given a free count of 10 to recover, established the three-minute round with a one-minute rest period, and disallowed seconds from entering the ring during the round.

Queensland State (pop., 1996: 3,369,000), northeastern Australia. Bounded on the north by the Pacific Ocean and the GREAT BARRIER REEF, it has an area of 667,000 sq mi (1,727,530 sq km); the capital is BRISBANE. Its coastal region, the most tropical part of Australia, attracts many tourists. Inland from the GREAT DIVIDING RANGE, which runs the entire length of the state, mining and cattle ranching are important. Capt. JAMES COOK charted the coast in 1770. In the 19th century the state housed several penal colonies, and drew settlers to mine its gold. It became a constituent state in 1901 when the Commonwealth of Australia was proclaimed.

quenching Rapid cooling, as by immersion in oil or water, of a METAL object from the high temperature at which it is shaped. Quenching is usually done to maintain mechanical properties that would be lost with slow cooling. It is commonly applied to STEEL objects, to which it gives HARDNESS. The quenching media and the type of agitation during quenching are selected to obtain specified physical properties with minimum internal stresses and distortions. Oil is the mildest medium, and salt brine has the strongest quenching effect. In special cases, steel is cooled and held for some time in a molten salt bath, which is kept at a temperature either just above or just below the temperature where martensite begins to form. These two heat treatments, called martempering and austempering, both result in even less distortion of the metal. Copper objects hardened by hammering or other deformation at ordinary temperatures can be restored to malleability by heating and quenching. See also TEMPERING.

Queneau \kə-'nō\, **Raymond** (1903–1976) French author. After working as a reporter, he became a reader for the prestigious *Encyclopédie de la Pléiade*, a scholarly edition of past and present classical authors; by 1955 he was its director. Verbal play, black humor, pessimism, and a derisive posture toward authority appear often in his more than 30 works of prose and poetry, which include the novels *Zazie* (1959), perhaps his best-known work, and *The Blue Flowers* (1965).

Quercia, Jacopo della See JACOPO DELLA QUERCIA

Quercy \ker-'sē\ Historical and cultural region, southwestern France. The district was organized in Gallo-Roman times and was occupied by the FRANKS in the 6th century. It was contested by England and France throughout the Middle Ages. United with the French crown in 1472, it suffered severely during the Wars of RELIGION of the 16th century. It is well forested with oaks of the genus *Quercus* that give the region its name. There are vineyards around Cahors that produce rich red wines.

Querétaro \kā-'rā-tä-ˌrō\ State (pop., 1995 est.: 1,250,000), central Mexico. It has an area of 4,420 sq mi (11,449 sq km), and its capital is QUERÉTARO city. Situated on the central plateau, it is almost evenly divided between mountainous areas in the north and plains and valleys in the south that form part of Mexico's Bajío region. In 1531 the area was conquered by Spain, which began colonization in the 1550s. It was administered with Guanajuato before it became a state in 1824. Chief mineral products are opals and mercury. Medicinal plants, sweet potatoes, fruits, and grains are among the many crops cultivated.

Querétaro City (pop., 1990: 386,000), capital of QUERÉTARO state, Mexico. Situated on the Mexican Plateau, 6,119 ft (1,865 m) above sea level, it is considered an excellent example of a Spanish colonial city. Founded by the OTOMI Indians, it was incorporated into the AZTEC empire in 1446. Brought under Spanish control in 1531, it became an important supply center for the rich mining districts of GUANAJUATO and ZACATECAS. Emperor MAXIMILIAN was executed here in 1867 after his defeat by the forces of BENITO JUAREZ. The Mexican Constitution of 1917 was written in Querétaro. It is the site of one of Mexico's oldest and largest cotton factories; textiles and pottery are also produced there.

Quesada, Gonzalo Jiménez de See Gonzalo JIMÉNEZ DE QUESADA

Quesnay \kā-'nā\, **François** (1694–1774) French physician and economist. He served as consulting physician to LOUIS XV at Versailles, where he developed an interest in economics. In his *Tableau économique* (1758), he described the relationship between the different economic classes of society and the flow of payments among them, and he developed the concept of economic equilibrium used by many later economic analysts. An advocate of LAISSEZ-FAIRE economic policy, he became the intellectual leader of the PHYSIOCRATS, the first systematic school of political economy.

Quételet \ket-'le\, **(Lambert) Adolphe (Jacques)** (1796–1874) Belgian statistician, sociologist, and astronomer. He is known for his application of STATISTICS and the theory of probability to social phenomena. He collected and analyzed government statistics on crime, mortality, and other subjects, and devised improvements in census taking. In *Sur l'homme* (1835) and *L'Anthropométrie* (1871) he developed the notion of the *homme moyen,* the statistically "average man." A founder of quantitative social science, he was nonetheless widely criticized for the crudeness of his methodology.

quetzal \ket-'säl\ Any of several tropical arboreal, short-billed, fruit-eating birds (genus *Pharomachrus*) in the trogon family (Trogonidae), whose weak feet have, uniquely, the second toe directed backward. It was the sacred bird of the ancient MAYAS and AZTECS. Today the quetzal, found in remote parts of cloud forests from southern Mexico to Bolivia, is the national emblem of Guatemala (whose monetary unit is the quetzal). The resplendent, or Guatemalan, quetzal is about 50 in. (125 cm) long. Long blue-green plumes cover the tail; the breast and head, with a rounded hairlike crest, are gold-green; the blue back has a curly gold-tinged mantle; and the belly is red. The quetzal is now listed as endangered.

Quetzalcóatl \ˌkāt-säl-'kō-ä-təl, ˌkāt-säl-kō-'ä-təl\ Feathered Serpent, a major deity of ancient Mexico. Quetzalcóatl began as a god of vegetation in the TEOTIHUACÁN civilization. For the TOLTECS he was the god of the morning and evening star. The AZTECS revered him as the patron of priests, the inventor of the calendar and of books, and the protector of goldsmiths and other craftsmen. He was also identified with the planet Venus and was a symbol of death and resurrection. One myth held that he was a white priest-king who sailed away on a raft made of snakes. The belief that

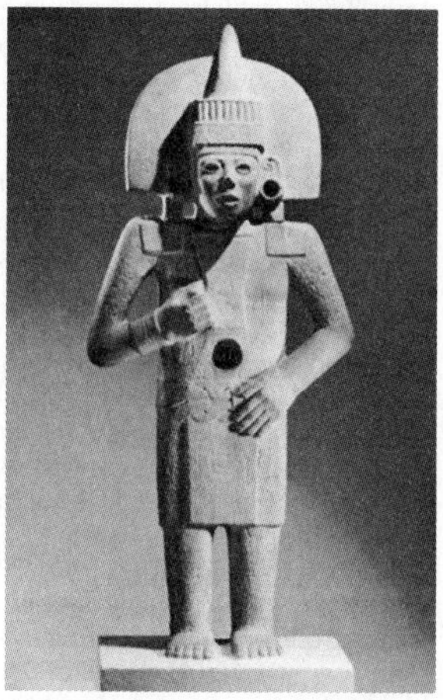

Quetzalcóatl, limestone figure of the Huastec culture, Mexico, AD 900–1250; in The Brooklyn Museum, New York.

BY COURTESY OF THE BROOKLYN MUSEUM, NEW YORK, HENRY L. BATTERMAN AND FRANK S. BENSON FUNDS

he would someday return from the east led Montezuma II to regard Hernan Cortes as the fulfillment of the prophecy.

queuing theory \'kyü-iŋ\ Study of the behavior of queues (waiting lines) and their elements. Queuing theory is a tool for studying several performance parameters of computer systems and is particularly useful in locating the reasons for "bottlenecks," compromised computer performance caused by too much data waiting to be acted on at a particular phase. Queue size and waiting time can be looked at, or items within queues can be studied and manipulated according to factors such as priority, size, or time of arrival.

Quevedo, Leonardo Torres See Leonardo Torres Quevedo

Quezon (y Molina) \'kā-sȯn\, **Manuel (Luis)** (1878–1944) Filipino statesman. Quezon fought in the Philippine–American War, but became convinced after the Philippines' defeat that the only way to independence was through cooperation with the U.S. He served in the Philippine Assembly (1907–9). As the Philippines' representative in the U.S. House of Representatives (1909–16), he played a major role in obtaining Congress's pledge of independence for the Philippines (1916) and fought for passage of the Tydings-McDuffie Act (1934), which laid out a timetable for independence. He became president of the Commonwealth (a precursor to the independent republic) in 1935 and was reelected in 1941; when Japan occupied the Philippines in 1942, he formed a government-in-exile in the U.S. He did not live to see full independence for the Philippines. Quezon City is named in his honor.

Quezon City \'kā-ˌsōn\ City (pop., 1994 est.: 1,677,000), Luzon Island, Philippines, northeast of Manila. Named for Pres. Manuel Quezon, who selected the site in 1939, it replaced Manila as the capital in 1948. Considered part of metropolitan Manila, it began to grow after World War II with the construction of many government buildings. The seat of government moved back to Manila in 1976. The city is home to two universities.

Quiche *or* **K'iche** *or* **Kiche** \kē-'chā\ Indian population of the Guatemalan highlands, largest of all ethnic groups speaking a Mayan language. The Quiche Mayas had an advanced civilization in pre-Columbian times. Records of their history and mythology are preserved in the *Popol Vuh*. Traditional Quiche are agricultural. Their homes are thatched huts, and they practice weaving and pottery. Nominally Roman Catholic, they conduct pagan rituals as well. Many were killed or displaced during the Guatemalan military's counterinsurgency campaign of the early 1980s. At present they number between 700,000 and 800,000.

quicklime See lime

quicksand State in which water-saturated sand loses its supporting capacity and acquires the characteristics of a liquid. Quicksand is usually found in a hollow at the mouth of a large river or along a flat stretch of stream or beach where pools of water become partly filled with sand and an underlying layer of stiff clay or other dense material prevents drainage. Mixtures of sand, mud, and vegetation in bogs often act like true quicksands. Any sand may become "quick" if its effective weight is being carried by water between the grains. In that case, even a footstep may collapse the loose structure. The sand-water suspension is denser than an animal or human body, so the body cannot sink below the surface, but struggling may lead to loss of balance and drowning.

quicksilver See mercury

Quiller-Couch, Arthur (Thomas) *later* **Sir Arthur** (1863–1944) English poet, novelist, and anthologist. Educated at Oxford, he worked as a journalist and editor in London before settling in his native Cornwall. He taught at Cambridge from 1912. He is noted for compiling *The Oxford Book of English Verse 1250–1900* (1900; revised 1939) and *The Oxford Book of Ballads* (1910). His works, written in a clear and apparently effortless style, include many novels and short stories, verse, and criticism, including *On the Art of Writing* (1916) and *On the Art of Reading* (1920).

quilombo \kē-'lȯm-bō\ *or* **mocambo** In colonial Brazil, a community organized by fugitive slaves. Quilombos were located in inaccessible areas and usually consisted of fewer than 100 people, who survived by farming and raiding. The largest and most famous was Palmares, which grew into an autonomous republic and by the 1690s had 20,000 inhabitants. It owed its prosperity to abundant irrigated land and the abduction of slaves from Portuguese plantations. The abducted slaves were kept in bondage to the runaways. Several Portuguese and Dutch expeditions attempted to destroy Palmares; a bandeira finally succeeded in 1694.

quilting Process of stitching together two layers of fabric, usually with a soft, thick substance placed between them. The layer of wool, cotton, or other stuffing provides insulation; the stitching keeps the stuffing evenly distributed and also provides opportunity for artistic expression. Quilting has long been used for clothing in many parts of the world, especially in the Far and Middle East, and the Muslim regions of Africa. It reached its fullest development in the U.S., where it was popularly used for petticoats and comforters. By the end of the 18th century, the U.S. quilt had distinctive features, such as colored fabric sewn on the outer layers (appliqué) and stitching that echoed the appliqué pattern.

quince Any of the fruit shrubs and small trees that make up the genus *Cydonia*, in the rose family. Common quince *(C. oblonga)* is native to Iran, Turkey, and perhaps Greece and the Crimea. The raw golden-yellow fruit has a strong fragrant aroma and astringent taste; it takes on a pink color when cooked and makes an excellent preserve. The Japanese quince (*Chaenomeles* species) is an ornamental shrub widely used for its flowers, which appear on the tightly branched stems before the leaves open fully in late winter and early spring.

Quince (*Cydonia oblonga*).
WALTER CHANDOHA

Quincey, Thomas De See Thomas De Quincey

Quine, W(illard) V(an) O(rman) (1908–2000) U.S. logician and philosopher. Born in Akron, Ohio, he was trained in mathematics and later studied under Rudolf Carnap, then taught at Harvard University 1936–78. He advocated systematic constructivist analysis of philosophy. Though his early career emphasized technical aspects of logic as a basis for philosophy, his later work investigated more general philosophical issues within a systematic linguistic framework. He is widely known for his attacks on the analytic–synthetic distinction and the atomistic view of confirmation. He is also known as a proponent of philosophical naturalism. His works include *A System of Logistic* (1934), *Word and Object* (1960), *Philosophy of Logic* (1970), and *Theories and Things* (1981).

quinine \'kwī-ˌnīn\ Alkaloid found in the bark of cinchona trees and shrubs. The chemical structure of this heterocyclic compound is large and complex, with several rings. For the 300 years preceding the 1940s, when newer antimalarials were developed, quinine was the only drug known to Western medicine for the prevention and treatment of malaria. The first chemical compound ever used successfully against an infectious disease, it has benefited more people than any other such drug in history. Quinine is also occasionally used to treat pain and fever and is a flavoring agent in some carbonated beverages, including tonic water.

Quinn, Anthony (1915–2001) U.S. (Mexican-born) film actor. Of mixed Irish-Mexican parentage, he began appearing in movies in 1936, initially playing bit parts as Indians or foreign characters. After appearing on Broadway in *A Streetcar Named Desire,* he returned to Hollywood, where he won Academy Awards for his supporting roles in *Viva Zapata!* (1952) and *Lust for Life* (1956). Noted for his earthy masculinity, he acted in over 100 other films, notably Federico Fellini's *La Strada* (1954), *Requiem for a Heavyweight* (1962), and *Zorba the Greek* (1964).

quinone \kwi-'nōn\ Any member of a class of aromatic compounds with two oxygen atoms bonded to the ring as carbonyl groups (—C=O; see functional group). This structure plays an important role in theories of chemical structure and color, since quinones occur as pigments in bacteria, fungi, and certain higher plants; animals containing quinones obtain them from plants they eat. The K vitamins (see vitamin K) are naphthoquinones. Quinone often denotes *para*-benzoquinone ($C_6H_4O_2$), a bright yellow solid with a sharp odor used in manufacturing dyes and fungicides and in photography.

Quintana Roo \kē-'tä-nä-'rō\ State (pop., 1995 est.: 704,000), eastern YUCATÁN PENINSULA, southeastern Mexico. Bounded by the Caribbean Sea and Belize, its northern shore is on the Yucatán Channel between the Gulf of Mexico and the Caribbean Sea. It has an area of 19,397 sq mi (50,212 sq km). The capital is CHETUMAL. The region was used as a place of exile for political prisoners for many years. Originally created as a territory from parts of YUCATÁN and CAMPECHE states, it became a state in 1974. It is the site of many MAYAN ruins. Its main products are chicle and a small amount of copra, produced on the coast near Cozumel island, where HERNAN CORTES landed in 1519.

Quinte \'kwin-tē\, **Bay of** Arm of Lake ONTARIO, southeastern Ontario. It extends for 75 mi (121 km) from its entrance near Amherst Island to Murray Canal at the western end. A resort area, it is a scenic, narrow bay with many small inlets. Among the major settlements around the bay are Trenton, Belleville, Deseronto, and Picton. The bay's name was derived from Kenté, an Indian village on the bay's western shore.

Quintero \kēn-'ter-ō\, **José (Benjamín)** (1924–1999) U.S. (Panamanian-born) theatrical director. After studying theater at USC, he directed his first play in 1949. He was a founder of the off-Broadway theater Circle in the Square, where he directed regularly from 1950, establishing the house as a major center for serious theater. His direction of TENNESSEE WILLIAMS's *Summer and Smoke* (1952) confirmed his reputation and made a star of GERALDINE PAGE. He was best known for his productions of 20th-century plays, especially those of Williams and EUGENE O'NEILL, including *The Iceman Cometh* (1956), *Long Day's Journey Into Night* (1956), and *A Moon for the Misbegotten* (1973, Tony award).

Quintilian *Latin* **Marcus Fabius Quintilianus** (AD 35?–after 96) Latin teacher and writer. Born in Spain, Quintilian was probably educated and trained in oratory in Rome. From about 68 to 88 he taught rhetoric, becoming Rome's leading teacher, and was an eminent advocate in the law courts. His *Institutio oratoria* is a practical survey of rhetoric in 12 books and a major contribution to educational theory and literary criticism. His dual emphasis on intellectual and moral training appealed to humanists of the 15th–16th century and through them influenced the modern view of education as all-around character training to equip a student for life.

Quirino \kē-'rē-nō\, **Elpidio** (1890–1956) Second president of the independent Republic of the Philippines. Quirino served in numerous elected and appointed posts in the Philippines prior to independence. In 1934 he accompanied MANUEL QUEZON to the U.S. to secure passage of the Tydings-McDuffie Act, which set a date for Philippine independence. He became vice president to MANUEL ROXAS after independence, succeeding to the presidency on Roxas's death in 1948. Quirino's presidency saw notable postwar reconstruction and economic gains, but social problems remained unsolved (leading to the HUKBALAHAP REBELLION) and government corruption was widespread.

Quirinus \kwə-'rī-nəs\ Major Roman deity ranking close to JUPITER and MARS. The *flamines* (see FLAMEN) of these three gods were the three major priests of Rome. Despite his importance, little is known about Quirinus, who was originally a god of the SABINES. He may have been another form of Mars. By the late republic he was identified with ROMULUS. His festival, the Quirinalia, was celebrated on February 17, and his temple was one of the oldest in Rome.

Quisling, Vidkun (Abraham Lauritz Jonsson) (1887–1945) Norwegian politician and German collaborator in World War II. After serving as military attaché in Petrograd and Helsinki, he became Norway's minister of defense in 1931. He resigned in 1933 to form the fascist National Union party. He actively collaborated in the German conquest of Norway (1940) and served in the occupation government. His attempts to convert Norwegians to NATIONAL SOCIALISM aroused strong opposition. After Norway's liberation, he was found guilty of treason and executed. His name became a synonym for "traitor."

Quito \'kē-tō\ City (pop., 1997 est.: 1,488,00), capital of Ecuador. Situated on the lower slopes of the Pichincha, a volcano that last erupted in 1666, it lies in a narrow Andean valley at an altitude of 9,350 ft (2,850 m). A pre-Columbian town, it was captured by the INCAS in 1487 and taken by the Spanish in 1534. It is the oldest of all South American capitals and preserves much of its colonial atmosphere. In 1535 the Franciscans established an art school there, the first of its kind in South America. One of Ecuador's two major industrial centers, it produces textiles and light consumer goods. It is the site of several institutions of higher learning.

quiz show See GAME SHOW

Qumran \kùm-'rän\ Site on the northwestern shore of the DEAD SEA, where the DEAD SEA SCROLLS were discovered in 1947. Excavations have revealed the ruins of buildings less than a mile from the sea, believed by some scholars to have been occupied by ESSENES, the probable authors of the scrolls. The buildings include a scriptorium, a potter's workshop, and a flour mill; water was supplied through an aqueduct. The Essenes are thought to have founded a monastic community at Qumran in the mid-2nd century BC. They temporarily abandoned the settlement after an earthquake and fire in 31 BC, but later returned and lived there until Roman legions destroyed the community in AD 68.

quoin \'kȯin, 'kwȯin\ In architecture, both the external corner of a building and, more often, one of the stones used to form that corner. These stones are both structural and decorative in that they often differ in jointing, color, texture, or size from the masonry of the adjoining walls. Usually quoins are toothed (i.e., set in short courses in a regular pattern of alternating lengths). Such construction dates back to ancient Rome.

quoits \'kȯits, 'kwȯits\ Game in which flattened rings of iron or circles of rope (both called quoits) are thrown at an upright pin (hob) in an attempt to ring it or come as near to it as possible. Quoits may have been played in Roman-occupied Britain (1st–5th century AD), and it may have given rise to HORSESHOE PITCHING.

quota In international trade, a government-imposed limit on the quantity of goods and services that may be exported or imported over a specified period of time. Quotas are more effective than TARIFFS in restricting trade, since they limit the availability of goods rather than simply increasing their price. By limiting foreign goods, a quota aims to allow domestic goods to compete more successfully, though the price of the goods may also rise. Quotas restricting trade were first imposed on a large scale during World War I. In the 1920s, quotas were progressively abolished and replaced by tariffs, but their use was revived in the wave of PROTECTIONISM set off by the GREAT DEPRESSION. After World War II, the Western European countries began a gradual dismantling of quantitative import restrictions, but the U.S. was slower to discard them. See also FREE TRADE.

quotient rule Rule for finding the DERIVATIVE of a quotient of two functions. If both f and g are differentiable, then so is the quotient $F(x) = f(x)/g(x)$. In abbreviated notation, it says $(f/g)' = (gf' - fg')/g^2$.

Quqon \kə-'kȯn\ *or* **Kokand** \kə-'känt\ Region, eastern Uzbekistan. A powerful khanate by the 18th century, it recognized Chinese sovereignty c. 1760. It was conquered by Russia in 1876, and was made a province of Turkistan under its ancient name, Fergana. It became part of the new Uzbek S.S.R. in 1924, and of independent Uzbekistan in 1991. Its chief city, also called Quqon (pop., 1993 est.: 184,000), was founded in 1732, though its settlement dates back to the 10th century.

Quran \kù-'rän\ *or* **Koran** \kə-'ran, kə'rän\ Sacred SCRIPTURE of ISLAM, regarded by Muslims as the infallible word of God, revealed to the Prophet MUHAMMAD. The book, first compiled in its authoritative form in the 7th century, consists of 114 chapters (SURAS) of varying length, written in Arabic. The earliest suras call for moral and religious obedience in light of the coming Day of Judgment; the ones written later provide directives for the creation of a social structure that will support the moral life called for by God. The Quran also provides detailed accounts of the joys of paradise and the terrors of hell. Muslims believe the God who spoke to Muhammad is the God worshiped by Jews and Christians, but that the revelations received by those religions are incomplete. Emphasis on the stern justice of God is tempered by frequent references to his mercy and compassion. The Quran demands absolute submission *(islam)* to God and his word, and it serves as the primary source of Islamic law. It is regarded as immutable in both form and content; traditionally translation was forbidden. The translations available today are regarded as paraphrases to facilitate understanding of the actual scripture.

qurra \kù-'rä\ Professional class of reciters of the QURAN. MUHAMMAD's early disciples often memorized his divine revelations, and even after the Quran was assembled in written form, it was common for pious Muslims to memorize it in its entirety. Such reciters were often called on by scholars to elucidate points of pronunciation and meaning, and by the 9th century they formed an established class. Religious men employed in mosques still memorize the Quran to aid them in interpreting its revelations to the faithful. In some Arab countries the professional duties of reciting the Quran are usually reserved for blind men.

Qutb \'kü-tüb\, **Sayyid** (1906–1966) Egyptian religious leader and writer executed by Pres. GAMAL ABDEL NASSER. He was from a family of rural notables who had fallen on hard times. His most important book, *Signposts,* harshly criticized Nasser's rule. When the MUSLIM BROTHERHOOD tried to assassinate Nasser in 1954, he was among those arrested and imprisoned (1954–64). Rearrested in 1966, he was accused of conspiracy, convicted of treason, and executed.

Qwa Qwa \'kwä-ˌkwä\ Former black enclave, South Africa. It bordered Lesotho and the province of NATAL. With an area of 253 sq mi (655 sq km), it was the smallest of South Africa's black states. Established in 1974, it had industries that included brickworks, gravel quarries, and furniture making. It was incorporated into ORANGE FREE STATE province in 1994, which was called Free State province after 1995.

O
P
Q
R

Ra See RE

Rabanus Maurus *or* **Hrabanus Maurus** \rä-'bä-nůs-'maů-růs\ (c. 780–856) German theologian. A Benedictine monk, he became director of the school at the Fulda monastery near Frankfurt am Main in 803, and he built Fulda into a leading European center of learning. He was elected abbot in 822 and used the monastery as a base for Christian missions throughout Europe. He was named archbishop of Mainz in 847. His many writings include *On the Nature of Things* (842–47), an encyclopedia drawing on all past knowledge. He also wrote treatises on education and grammar and commentaries on the Bible. His work contributed so much to the development of German literature that he received the title Praeceptor Germaniae ("Teacher of Germany").

Rabat \rə-'bät\ *Arabic* **Ribat** \ri-'bät\ City (metro. area pop., with SALÉ, 1994: 1,386,000), capital of Morocco. It is situated on the Atlantic coast at the mouth of the Bou Regreg River, opposite Salé. One of Morocco's four imperial cities, it was founded in the 12th century by ALMOHAD ruler ABD AL-MUMIN as a ribat (camp) quartering troops for his holy war against Spain. After 1609 the unified community of Rabat-Salé became the home of large numbers of Andalusian MOORS who had been driven from Spain and, later, of the Sallee Corsairs, the most dreaded of BARBARY COAST pirates. Under the French, it was made the administrative capital of a French protectorate after 1912. Now a center of the textile industry, it is noted for its carpets, blankets, and leather handicrafts.

Rabban Gamaliel See GAMALIEL I

rabbi \'ra-ˌbī\ *or* **rebbe** \'re-bə\ In Judaism, a person qualified by study of the Hebrew scriptures and the TALMUD to serve as spiritual leader of a Jewish community or congregation. Ordination can be conferred by any rabbi, but it usually depends on a written statement issued by the candidate's teacher. Though rabbis are considered teachers rather than priests, they conduct religious services, assist at BAR MITZVAHS, perform marriages, and are present at funerals. In questions of divorce, a rabbi's role depends on an appointment to a special court of Jewish law. The rabbi also counsels and consoles members of his congregation and oversees the religious education of the young.

rabbinic Judaism \rə-'bi-nik\ Principal form of JUDAISM that developed after the fall of the Second Temple of JERUSALEM (AD 70). It originated in the teachings of the PHARISEES, who emphasized the need for critical interpretation of the TORAH. Rabbinic Judaism is centered on study of the TALMUD and debate about the legal and theological issues it raises. Its mode of worship and life discipline continue to be practiced by Jews worldwide.

rabbit Any small, bounding, gnawing mammal of the family Leporidae. Rabbits have long ears, a short tail, long hind legs, and two pairs of upper incisors—one pair behind a larger, functional pair. Most species are gray or brown. They grow to 10–18 in. (25–45 cm) long and weigh 1–4 lbs (0.5–2 kg). They feed primarily on grasses. Their reproductive rate is very high; unlike HARES, rabbits are born naked, blind, and helpless. Most species are nocturnal and live alone in burrows, but the European, or Old World, rabbit *(Oryctolagus cuniculus)* of Europe and Asia, ancestor to all domestic breeds, lives in warrens consisting of many burrows. The 13 species of North American cottontail rabbits (genus *Sylvilagus*) have white on the underside of the tail.

Eastern cottontail rabbit (*Sylvilagus floridanus*).
STEVE AND DAVE MASLOWSKI

Rabéarivelo \rá-bā-á-rē-'vā-lō\, **Jean-Joseph** (1901–1937) Malagasy writer. Largely self-educated, he earned his living as a proofreader for a publishing concern. He wrote seven volumes of poetry in French, of which *Presque-songes* (1934; "Near-Dreams") and *Traduit de la nuit* (1935; "Translation of the Night") are considered the most important. The mythical and surrealistic world created in his poems is intensely personal and dominated by visions of death, catastrophe, and alienation. Harassed by French authorities and addicted to drugs, he committed suicide. He is regarded as the father of modern literature in his native land.

Rabelais \rá-'ble, *Engl* 'ra-bə-ˌlā\, **François** (1494?–1553) French writer and priest. After apparently studying law, he took holy orders as a Franciscan, but later, because of a dispute, removed to a Benedictine house. In 1530 he left the Benedictines to study medicine, a profession he would follow the rest of his life. He became a significant humanist scholar, publishing translations of HIPPOCRATES and GALEN. His fame rests on the five comic novels (one of doubtful authenticity) known collectively as *Gargantua and Pantagruel,* including the masterpieces *Pantagruel* (1532) and *Gargantua* (1534) as well as *Le tiers livre* (1546; "The Third Book"), his most profound work. These works display a delight in words, a mastery of storytelling, and deep humanist learning in a mosaic of scholarly, literary, and scientific parody that is unlike any previous work in French. They were banned by civil and church authorities for their satirical content and earthy humor, but were nevertheless read throughout Europe. Throughout his career, Rabelais owed his freedom to the protection of powerful patrons.

Rabi \'rä-bē\, **I(sidor) I(saac)** (1898–1988) U.S. (Polish-born) physicist. He earned his PhD at Columbia Univ., where he later taught physics (from 1929). In 1940–45 at MIT he led a group of scientists who helped develop radar, and succeeded J. ROBERT OPPENHEIMER as chairman of the Atomic Energy Commission's General Advisory Committee (1952–56). He was the first to propose the joint European laboratory CERN, and he helped found New York's Brookhaven National Laboratory. His method for measuring the magnetic properties of atoms atomic nuclei, and molecules (1937) led to the atomic clock, the maser, the laser, magnetic resonance imaging, and the central technique for molecular and atomic beam experimentation, and won him a 1944 Nobel Prize.

rabies \'rā-ˌbēz\ Acute, usually fatal infectious disease of warm-blooded animals that attacks the central NERVOUS SYSTEM. It is spread by contact with an infected animal's saliva, usually from a bite. The RHABDOVIRUS that causes it spreads along nerve tissue from the wound to the brain. Symptoms usually appear four to six weeks later, often beginning with irritability and aggressiveness. Wild animals lose their fear of humans but are easily provoked to bite, as are pets. Depression and paralysis soon follow. Death usually comes three to five days after symptoms begin. In humans, death can result from a seizure in the early phase even before symptoms of central-nervous-system depression develop. One name for rabies, hydrophobia ("fear of water"), comes from painful throat contraction on trying to swallow. If not treated in time (within a day or two) with a serum containing antibodies and then a series of vaccinations, rabies in humans is almost always fatal. Immediate cleansing of animal bites with soap and water can remove much of the virus.

Rabin \rə-'bēn\, **Yitzhak** (1922–1995) First native-born prime minister of Israel. He fought in the Israeli war of independence and became chief of staff in 1964. His strategies helped win the SIX-DAY WAR in 1967. After retiring from the army (1968), he served as ambassador to the U.S. (1968–73). As head of the ISRAEL LABOUR PARTY, he twice served as prime minister (1974–77, 1992–95). During his first tenure, he secured a cease-fire with Syria in the Golan Heights and ordered the raid on Entebbe (see ENTEBBE INCIDENT). As defense minister (1984–90), he responded forcefully to the Palestinian INTIFADA. In 1993 secret negotiations with the Palestinians at last yielded a political settlement calling for limited Palestinian self-rule in the GAZA STRIP and the WEST BANK, for which he shared the 1994 Nobel Peace Prize with SHIMON PERES and YASIR ARAFAT. He was assassinated by a right-wing Jewish extremist.

raccoon *or* **ringtail** Any member of from two to seven species of omnivorous, nocturnal CARNIVORES (genus *Procyon,* family Procyonidae) characterized by a bushy, ringed tail and a black mask on the face. The North American raccoon *(P. lotor)* has a stout body, short legs, pointed muzzle, and small erect ears. It is 30–36 in. (75–90 cm) long, including the 10-in. (25-cm) tail, and weighs over 20 lbs (10 kg). The shaggy, coarse fur is iron-gray to blackish. The feet resemble slender human hands. Raccoons eat arthropods, rodents, frogs, berries, fruit, and plants;

in towns and cities they thrive on garbage. They prefer woods near water and usually live in hollow trees. The crab-eating raccoon *(P. cancrivorus)* of South America is similar but has coarser fur.

North American raccoon (*Procyon lotor*).

LEONARD LEE RUE III

race Term once commonly used in PHYSICAL ANTHROPOLOGY to denote a division of humankind possessing traits that are transmissible by descent and sufficient to characterize it as a distinct human type (e.g., Caucasoid, Mongoloid, Negroid). Today the term has little scientific standing, as older methods of differentiation, including hair form and body measurement, have given way to the comparative analysis of DNA and gene frequencies relating to such factors as BLOOD TYPING, the excretion of AMINO ACIDS, and inherited ENZYME deficiencies. Because all human populations today are extremely similar genetically, most researchers have abandoned the concept of race for the concept of the cline, a graded series of differences occurring along a line of environmental or geographical transition. This reflects the recognition that human populations have always been in a state of flux, with genes constantly flowing from one gene pool to another, impeded only by physical or ecological boundaries. While relative isolation does preserve genetic differences and allow populations to maximally adapt to climatic and disease factors over long periods of time, all groups currently existing are thoroughly "mixed" genetically, and such differences as still exist do not lend themselves to simple typologizing. "Race" is today primarily a sociological designation, identifying a class sharing some outward physical characteristics and some commonalities of culture and history. See also CLIMATIC ADAPTATION, ETHNIC GROUP, RACISM.

racemate \rā-ˈsē-ˌmāt\ Mixture of equal quantities of two enantiomers, substances whose molecular structures are mirror images of one another (see ISOMER). The two enantiomers rotate polarized light through opposite angles, canceling each other out so that the racemic mixture has no OPTICAL ACTIVITY. Racemization is the conversion of an optically active form of a compound into a racemic mixture; reversing this process is called resolution.

racer Any of several slender, swift SNAKES (subspecies of *Coluber constrictor,* family Colubridae) of North and Central America and Asia. Racers have a long tail, big eyes, and smooth scales. Color and pattern vary among subspecies, some of which grow to 6 ft (1.8 m) long. Among the fastest of snakes, racers can move at 3.5 mph (5.6 kpm). They hold down their prey, usually a small warm-blooded animal, by the weight of their coils and then swallow it. If cornered, they vibrate the tail and strike repeatedly with a sideways motion that tears a victim's skin. See also BLACK SNAKE.

Racer (*Coluber constrictor*).

Rachel In the Book of GENESIS, one of JACOB's two wives. Jacob was forced to serve her father Laban for seven years to win her, but at the end of that time he was tricked into marrying her sister Leah. He was then allow to marry Rachel as well, in return for seven more years of labor. At first childless, she eventually gave birth to JOSEPH, and she died giving birth to Benjamin.

Rachmaninoff \räk-ˈmä-nə-ˌnȯf\, **Sergei (Vassilievich)** (1873–1943) Russian-U.S. composer and pianist. He studied at the St. Petersburg and Moscow conservatories. After playing his first concerto for his graduation as a piano student (1891), he stayed on to earn a composition degree, writing his first opera, *Aleko* (1892), in 17 days. His first symphony (1897) was such a disaster that he could not compose for three years. Known for his titanic virtuosity as a pianist, he toured widely while returning to composing prolifically. He moved to the U.S. after the 1917 revolution. His works, most of them in a lush late-Romantic style, include three symphonies, four piano concertos, the opera *Francesca da Rimini* (1906), the tone poem *From the Isle of the Dead* (1909), a *Liturgy of St. John Chrysostom* (1910), and *Symphonic Dances* (1940).

Racine \rà-ˈsēn\, **Jean (-Baptiste)** (1639–1699) French playwright and master of French classical tragedy. Orphaned at an early age, he was educated in a Jansenist convent, and he chose drama in defiance of his upbringing. His first play was produced by MOLIÈRE in 1664. Their friendship ended when Racine took his next play, *Alexandre le grand* (1665), to a competing theater and seduced Molière's mistress and leading actress. She starred in Racine's successful *Andromaque* (1667), which explored his theme of the tragic folly of passionate love. His only comedy, *The Litigants* (1668), was followed by his great tragedies *Britannicus* (1669) and *Bérénice* (1670)—which together led to a breach with PIERRE CORNEILLE, the declining idol of older playgoers—and *Bajazet* (1672). After writing his masterpiece, *Phèdre* (1677), a tragedy drawn from Greek mythology, he retired to become official historian to LOUIS XIV. His final plays, *Esther* (1689) and *Athalie* (1691), were commissioned by the king's wife, Mme. de MAINTENON.

racism Any action, practice, or belief that reflects the racial worldview—the ideology that humans are divided into separate and exclusive biological entities called "races," that there is a causal link between inherited physical traits and traits of personality, intellect, morality, and other cultural behavioral features, and that some races are innately superior to others. Racism was at the heart of North American SLAVERY and the colonization and empire-building activities of some Western Europeans overseas, especially in the 18th century. The idea of RACE was invented to magnify the differences between people of European origin in the United States and those of African descent whose ancestors had been brought against their will to function as slaves in the American South. By projecting Africans and their descendants as lesser human beings, the proponents of slavery attempted to justify and maintain this system of exploitation while at the same time portraying the United States as a bastion and champion of human freedom, with human rights, democratic institutions, unlimited opportunities, and equality. The contradiction between slavery and the ideology of human equality, accompanying a philosophy of human freedom and dignity, seemed to demand the dehumanization of those enslaved. By the 19th century, racism had matured and the idea spread around the world. Racism differs from ethnocentrism in that it is linked to physical and therefore immutable differences among people. Ethnic identity is acquired, and ethnic features are learned forms of behavior. Race, on the other hand, is a form of identity that is perceived as innate and unalterable. In the last half of the 20th century many conflicts around the world were interpreted in racial terms even though their origins were in the ethnic hostilities that have long characterized many human societies (e.g., Arabs and Jews, English and Irish). Racism reflects an acceptance of the deepest forms and degrees of divisiveness and carries the implication that differences among groups are so great that they cannot be transcended. See also ETHNIC GROUP, SOCIOCULTURAL EVOLUTION.

rack and pinion Mechanical device consisting of a bar of rectangular cross section (the rack), having teeth on one side that mesh with teeth on a small GEAR (the pinion). If the pinion rotates about a fixed axis, the rack will move in a straight path. Some AUTOMOBILE steering mechanisms have rack-and-pinion drives that use this principle. If the rack is fixed and the pinion is carried in bearings on a table guided on tracks parallel to the rack, rotation of the pinion shaft will move the table parallel to the rack. On MACHINE TOOLS, this principle is used to obtain rapid movements of worktables.

racketeering See ORGANIZED CRIME

rackets Game for two or four players with ball and racket on a four-walled court. Rackets is played with a hard ball in a relatively large court (approx. 9×18 m), unlike the related games of SQUASH and RACQUETBALL. As in these other games, the object of rackets is to bounce, or rebound, the ball off the front and other walls in such a way as to defeat an opponent's attempt to reach and return it. It appears to have developed in England in the early 19th century.

Rackham, Arthur (1867–1939) British artist and illustrator. While a staff artist for a London newspaper, he also began illustrating books. He became skillful using the new halftone process, and his highly detailed drawings revealed a unique imagination. He achieved renown with a

1900 edition of *Grimm's Fairy Tales*, and his illustrations for *Rip Van Winkle* (1905) brought him recognition in America as well. Altogether he illustrated more than 60 books, including classics of children's literature as well as works of WILLIAM SHAKESPEARE, CHARLES DICKENS, JOHN MILTON, RICHARD WAGNER, and EDGAR ALLAN POE.

racquetball Game similar to HANDBALL, played on a four-walled court with a short-handled racquet and a ball larger than that used in handball. The game was invented in 1950 by Joseph G. Sobek (1918–1998), who was unhappy with the indoor racquet sports then available. By the late 1990s there were 8.5 million racquetball players in 91 countries.

radar System that uses electromagnetic echoes to detect and locate objects in space. It can also measure precisely the distance (range) to an object and the speed at which the object is moving toward or away from the observing unit. Radar (the name is derived from *ra*dio *d*etecting *a*nd *r*anging) originated in the experimental work of HEINRICH HERTZ in the late 1880s. During World War II, British and U.S. researchers developed a high-powered MICROWAVE radar system for military use. Radar is used today in identification and monitoring of artificial satellites in earth orbit, as a navigational aid for airplanes and marine vessels, and for air-traffic control around major airports.

radar astronomy See RADIO AND RADAR ASTRONOMY

Radcliffe, Ann *orig.* **Ann Ward** (1764–1823) English gothic novelist. Brought up in a well-to-do family, in 1787 she married a journalist who encouraged her literary pursuits. She achieved fame with her third novel, *The Romance of the Forest* (1791). With her fourth, *The Mysteries of Udolpho* (1794), she became the most popular novelist in England. *The Italian* (1797), which displays rare psychological insight, reveals her full powers. In her tales, scenes of terror and suspense are infused with an aura of romantic sensibility.

Radcliffe, William (1760–1841) British inventor. The son of a weaver, in 1789 he set up his own spinning and weaving business in Stockton. His name is principally linked to the dressing (i.e., starching) machine, actually invented by one of his machinists. He patented essential improvements to EDMUND CARTWRIGHT'S power loom, enabling the explosive success of the technology. His house and mill were destroyed by LUDDITES in 1812; his wife's subsequent death was blamed on the attack.

Radcliffe-Brown, A(lfred) R(eginald) (1881–1955) British social anthropologist. He taught at the Univs. of Cape Town, Sydney, Chicago, and Oxford. In his version of FUNCTIONALISM, he viewed the component parts of society (e.g., the kinship system, the legal system) as having an indispensable function for one another, the continued existence of one component being dependent on that of the other, and he developed a systematic framework of concepts relating to the social structures of small-scale societies. He had a profound impact on British and American social anthropology. Among his major works are *The Andaman Islanders* (1922) and *Structure and Function in Primitive Society* (1952).

Radek \'rä-dyik\, **Karl (Bernhardovich)** *orig.* **Karl Sobelsohn** (1885–1939?) Russian communist politician. He took part in the RUSSIAN REVOLUTION OF 1905, then wrote for leftist newspapers in Poland and Germany (1906–14). After meeting VLADIMIR ILICH LENIN in 1915, he helped reorganize the German Communist Party in 1918. He returned to Russia in 1919 and rose to leadership in the COMINTERN but was ousted in 1924 for his support of LEON TROTSKY. After recanting in 1929, he became a fervent Stalinist and editorial-board member of *IZVESTIYA* (1931–36). Despite his conversion, he was arrested and tried in the PURGE TRIALS and sentenced to 10 years in prison, where he died.

Radetzky \rä-'det-skē\, **Joseph, Graf (Count)** (1766–1858) Austrian army officer. He fought with distinction against the French in the Napoleonic Wars. As army chief of staff, he attempted to modernize the Austrian army. As commander in chief of the Austrian army in northern Italy (1831–57), he suppressed the revolt in the Austrian-ruled provinces of Lombardy and Venetia in 1848. He served as governor-general of these provinces 1849–57. His status among conservatives as a national hero inspired Johann Strauss the Elder to compose the *Radetzky March*.

Radha \'rä-dä\ In Hindu mythology, mistress of the god KRISHNA when he lived among the cowherds of Vrndavana. Though Radha was the wife of another cowherd, she was the most beloved of Krishna's consorts and his constant companion. In the BHAKTI movement of VAISHNAVISM, Radha symbolizes the human soul and Krishna the divine. The allegorical love of Radha and Krishna has been celebrated in the poetry of many Indian languages, and Radha is often worshiped along with Krishna, especially in northern and eastern India.

radial engine Type of INTERNAL-COMBUSTION ENGINE used mainly in small airplanes, in which the cylinders (ranging from five to as many as 28, depending on engine size) are mounted in a circle around the crankshaft, sometimes in banks of two or more. Once the dominant piston-engine type, radials are now in only limited production; most new requirements are met by remanufacturing existing stock.

radiant heating HEATING system in which heat is transmitted by radiation from a heated surface. Radiant heating systems usually employ either electric-resistance wiring or hot-water heating pipes, which may embedded in the floor, ceiling, or walls. Panel heating is a form of radiant heating characterized by very large surfaces (typically an entire ceiling or floor) containing electrical conductors, hot-water pipes, or hot-air ducts. With many such systems there is no visible heating equipment in the room.

radiation Process by which energy is emitted from a source and propagated through the surrounding medium, or the energy involved in this process. Radiation consists of a flow of atomic or subatomic particles or of waves. Familiar examples are light (a form of ELECTROMAGNETIC RADIATION) and sound (a form of acoustic radiation). Both electromagnetic and acoustic radiation can be described as waves with a range of frequencies and intensities. Electromagnetic radiation is also often treated as discrete packets of energy, called PHOTONS. All matter is constantly bombarded by radiation from cosmic and terrestrial sources, and radioactive elements emit several types of radiation (see RADIOACTIVITY). See also CHERENKOV RATIATION, HAWKING RADIATION, INFRARED RADIATION, SYNCHROTRON RADIATION, THERMAL RADIATION, ULTRAVIOLET RADIATION.

radiation injury Tissue damage caused by exposure to ionizing RADIATION. Structures with rapid cell turnover (e.g., skin, stomach or intestinal lining, and bone marrow) are most susceptible. High-dose irradiation of the last two causes radiation sickness. Nausea and vomiting subside in a few hours. They are followed in intestinal cases by abdominal pain, fever, and diarrhea leading to dehydration and a fatal shocklike state, and in bone-marrow cases (two to three weeks later) by fever, weakness, hair loss, infection, and hemorrhage. In severe cases, death occurs from infection and uncontrollable bleeding. Lower radiation doses can cause cancer (notably LEUKEMIA and BREAST CANCER), sometimes years later. Radiation exposure in early pregnancy can produce abnormalities in the embryo, whose cells are multiplying rapidly.

radiation pressure PRESSURE on a surface resulting from ELECTROMAGNETIC RADIATION that impinges on it. The pressure is a result of the MOMENTUM carried by the radiation. When radiation is reflected rather than absorbed, the radiation pressure is doubled. Radiation pressure can sometimes be great enough to produce a force that is useful.

radiation therapy *or* **radiotherapy** *or* **therapeutic radiology** Use of RADIATION sources to treat or relieve diseases, usually CANCER (including LEUKEMIA). The ionizing radiation primarily used to destroy diseased cells works best on fast-growing cancers. However, radiation can also cause cancer (see RADIATION INJURY) and is no longer used for benign conditions. Other complications include nausea, hair loss, weight loss, and weakness. Radioactive substances may be implanted in tumors (see NUCLEAR MEDICINE). External radiation involves 10–20 sessions over several months, either after surgical removal of the growth or when surgery is impossible; it can deliver higher doses to deep tumors than implantation. INFRARED and ULTRAVIOLET radiation is applied with lamps to relieve INFLAMMATION.

radical Term used in chemistry with one predominant and two subsidiary, looser meanings. It most often refers to a FREE RADICAL. It can also mean an ION or a FUNCTIONAL GROUP.

radical In politics, one who desires extreme change of part or all of the social order. The term (which derives from the Latin word for "root," and thus implies change beginning at a system's roots) was given this sense by CHARLES JAMES FOX in 1797 when he demanded "radical reform" consisting of universal manhood suffrage. In France before 1848, republicans and advocates of universal male suffrage were called radicals. The term was later applied to Marxists (see MARXISM) who called for fundamental social change to eradicate divisions among social classes.

In popular usage, it is applied to political extremism, not necessarily violent, of both the left and the right.

Radical Republican Member of the REPUBLICAN PARTY in the 1860s committed to emancipation of the slaves and racial justice. Zealous antislavery advocates in the Congress pressed Pres. ABRAHAM LINCOLN to include emancipation as a war aim. They later opposed his process of lenient RECONSTRUCTION of the South under presidential control and countered with the harsh WADE-DAVIS BILL. After Lincoln's death the Radicals supported Pres. ANDREW JOHNSON, but soon demanded congressional control of Reconstruction. Johnson's attempt to break the Radicals' power led them to pass the TENURE OF OFFICE ACT; his challenge of the act led to impeachment proceedings. Radical Republican leaders included Henry Winter Davis (1817–1865), THADDEUS STEVENS, CHARLES SUMNER, and BENJAMIN BUTLER. Their influence waned as white control over Southern governments gradually returned in the 1870s.

Radical-Socialist Party French political party. The oldest of France's political parties, it was founded in 1901 but had its origins in the 19th century. In the 1870s the reformist wing of the French Republican party, led by GEORGES CLEMENCEAU, became known as the Radicals, and was important in administrations into the early 20th century. Traditionally a centrist party, it was most prominent in the THIRD and FOURTH Republics. In the 1920s and '30s it joined coalition governments with the FRENCH SOCIALIST PARTY. After 1945 it led other centrist groups to form politically important coalitions.

radio ELECTROMAGNETIC RADIATION of lower frequency (hence longer wavelength) than visible light or INFRARED RADIATION, and consisting of the range of frequencies used for navigation signals, AM and FM broadcasting, TELEVISION transmissions, CELL-PHONE communications, and various forms of RADAR. For radio transmission, information is imparted to a carrier wave by varying (modulating) its amplitude, frequency, or duration. The technology of radio arose from the work of MICHAEL FARADAY, JAMES CLERK MAXWELL, HEINRICH HERTZ, GUGLIELMO MARCONI, and others, and improvement followed the development of the VACUUM TUBE, the electronic-tube OSCILLATOR, the TUNED CIRCUIT, and other components. Later innovations have included the replacement of tubes by TRANSISTORS and of wires by PRINTED CIRCUITS. See also RADIO AND RADAR ASTRONOMY.

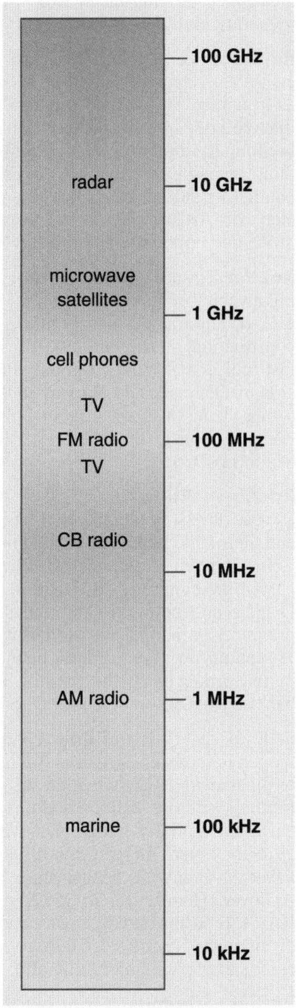

Radio waves lie at the low-frequency end of the electromagnetic spectrum. They are primarily used in various types of communications signals. Also of importance is the detection of natural radio sources in radio and radar astronomy. A few applications are shown at their approximate positions in the spectrum (on a logarithmic scale). Microwaves are a subset of the radio spectrum, ranging from about 1 to 1000 mm in wavelength, or a frequency between about 1 and 100 GHz. The microwave region is used especially in various forms of radar, in communications with spacecraft and satellites (as in the Global Positioning System), and in microwave ovens. Amateur communications, such as CB (citizens' band) and short-wave radio, occur around 10 MHz. Marine navigation and communications systems operate especially below 1 MHz. Other devices or systems using radio waves include metal detectors, loran, and magnetic resonance imaging.

radio and radar astronomy Study of celestial bodies by measuring the energy they emit or reflect at radio wavelengths. It began in 1931 with KARL JANSKY's discovery of radio waves from an extraterrestrial source. After 1945, huge radar-dish antennas, improved receivers and data-processing methods, and radio interferometers let astronomers study fainter sources and obtain greater detail. Radio waves penetrate much of the gas and dust in space, giving a much clearer picture of the center and structure of the Milky Way than optical observation can. This has allowed detailed studies of the INTERSTELLAR MEDIUM in our galaxy and the discovery of previously unknown cosmic objects (e.g., PULSARS, QUASARS). In radar astronomy, radio signals are sent to near-earth bodies or phenomena (e.g., meteor trails, the moon, asteroids, nearby planets) and the reflections measured, providing precise measurement of the objects' distances and surface structure. Because radar waves can penetrate even dense clouds, they have provided our only maps of the surface of VENUS. Radio and radar studies of the moon revealed its sandlike surface before landings were made. Radio observations have also contributed greatly to knowledge about the sun. See also RADIO TELESCOPE.

radio broadcasting See BROADCASTING

radio telescope Combination of RADIO receiver and ANTENNA, used for observation in radio astronomy (see RADIO AND RADAR ASTRONOMY). Radio telescopes vary widely but all have two basic components, a large radio antenna and a radiometer or radio receiver. Because some astronomical radio sources are extremely faint on earth, radio telescopes are usually very large, and only the most sensitive radio receivers are used. The first large fully steerable radio telescope was completed in 1957 at Jodrell Bank, England. The world's largest fully steerable radio telescope is the 100-m (328-ft) antenna operated by the Max Planck Institute for Radio Astronomy in Germany. The largest single radio telescope in the world is the 1,000-ft (305-m) fixed spherical reflector at the ARECIBO OBSERVATORY in Puerto Rico. Radio telescopes enabled investigators to discover intense radio emissions from Jupiter and have been used to measure the temperatures of all the planets.

Lovell Telescope, a fully steerable radio telescope at Jodrell Bank, Macclesfield, Cheshire, Eng.

JODRELL BANK SCIENCE CENTRE

radio wave WAVE from the portion of the ELECTROMAGNETIC SPECTRUM at lower frequencies than INFRARED RADIATION. The wavelengths of radio waves vary from around 1 millimeter to thousands of meters. Radio waves are used in the transmission and detection of communications signals that travel through the air in a straight line or by reflection from the ionosphere, or to and from a communications satellite in space. They are used in television, navigation, air-traffic control, telecommunications, radar, and remote-controlled toys, and for many other purposes. See illustration opposite.

radioactive series Any of four sets of unstable heavy atomic nuclei that undergo a series of ALPHA DECAY and BETA DECAY until a stable nucleus is achieved. The natural series are the thorium series, the URANIUM series, and the actinium series. These are headed by naturally occurring species of unstable nuclei that have HALF-LIVES comparable to the age of the earth. The fourth set, the neptunium series, is headed by neptunium-237, which has a half-life of 2 million years. Its members do not occur naturally but are artificially produced by nuclear reactions and have short half-lives.

radioactivity Property exhibited by certain types of matter of emitting radiation spontaneously. The phenomenon was first reported in 1896 by Henri Becquerel for a uranium salt, and it was soon found that all uranium compounds are radioactive due to the uranium's radioactivity. In 1898 Marie Curie and her husband discovered two other naturally occurring, strongly radioactive elements, radium and polonium. The radiation is emitted by unstable atomic nuclei (see nucleus) as they attempt to become more stable. The main processes of radioactivity are alpha decay, beta decay, and gamma decay. In 1934 it was discovered that radioactivity could be induced in ordinary matter by artificial transmutation.

radiocarbon dating See carbon-14 dating

radiology Branch of medicine that uses radiation for diagnosis (diagnostic imaging) and treatment (radiation therapy) of disease. Originally, it involved X rays for diagnosis and X rays, gamma rays, and other ionizing radiation for treatment. Diagnostic methods now include isotope scanning (see nuclear medicine), use of nonionizing radiation, as in ultrasound and magnetic resonance imaging, and radioimmunoassay (in which radioactive isotopes in antibodies against hormones detect minute amounts of hormones for diagnosis of endocrine disorders). Radiotherapy now includes, in cancer treatment, radioactive hormones and chemotherapeutic drugs.

radiotherapy See radiation therapy

radish Annual or biennial plant *(Raphanus sativus)* of the mustard family, probably of Oriental origin, grown for its large, succulent root. Low in calories and high in bulk, radishes have a sharp taste and are usually eaten raw. The shape of the edible portion of the root varies greatly, as does the color (from white through pink to red, purple, and black). Radishes may weigh only a few ounces (U.S. and European varieties) or, in the case of the Japanese daikon, more than 2 lbs (1 kg).

Radish (*Raphanus sativus* variety *radicula*).

INGMAR HOLMASEN

Radishchev \rə-'dyēsh-chif\, **Aleksandr (Nikolayevich)** (1749–1802) Russian political writer. Though a nobleman, he pursued a career as a civil servant, in which he met people from all social classes. Influenced by such writers as J.-J. Rousseau, he wrote *A Journey from St. Petersburg to Moscow* (1790), in which he described examples of social injustice, hoping that his criticism of serfdom, autocracy, and censorship would enlighten Catherine II. Instead, he was arrested and exiled to Siberia. He was pardoned by Alexander I in 1801 but committed suicide a year later. He inspired later revolutionaries, including those who instigated the Decembrist revolt.

radium Chemical element, heaviest alkaline earth metal, chemical symbol Ra, atomic number 88. It was discovered by Marie Curie in 1898 and isolated by 1910. All its isotopes are radioactive (see radioactivity). Radium does not occur free in nature but occurs in natural ores such as pitchblende as a disintegration product of radioactive decay of heavier elements, including uranium. Its use in medicine (see radiation therapy, radiology, nuclear medicine) has declined because of its cost, and its use in consumer goods (to illuminate watch and clock hands and numbers, as well as instrument dials) was halted because it can cause radiation injury. It is still used for some radiography and as a source of neutrons.

radon \'rā-ˌdän\ Chemical element, chemical symbol Rn, atomic number 86. The heaviest noble gas, it is colorless, odorless, tasteless, radioactive (see radioactivity), and relatively unreactive (forming compounds only with fluorine). It is rare in nature because all its isotopes are short-lived and because radium, its source, is scarce. It seeps from certain soils and rocks (such as granite) into the atmosphere and can accumulate in poorly ventilated spaces near ground level, including house basements; using such spaces is now known to increase the risk of lung cancer more than any other common factor except smoking. Radon is used in radiotherapy, radiography, and in research.

Raeburn, Henry *later* **Sir Henry** (1756–1823) Scottish portrait painter. Though apprenticed early to a goldsmith, he lacked formal training as a painter. He worked principally as a miniaturist and evolved a distinctive style of oil portraiture, painting directly on the canvas without preliminary drawings. His portraits are characterized by a vigorous handling of paint and vivid and experimental lighting effects, usually from behind the sitters' heads. He was elected president of the Edinburgh Society of Artists (1812) and Royal Academician (1815), knighted in 1822, and appointed His Majesty's Limner for Scotland (1822).

Raeder \'rā-dər\, **Erich** (1876–1960) German naval officer. After serving as chief of staff to an admiral in World War I, he himself rose to the rank of admiral. As naval commander in chief from 1928, he urged the construction of submarines (forbidden by the Treaty of Versailles) and fast cruisers. Appointed grand admiral in 1939, he supervised the invasion of Denmark and Norway in 1940. Differences with Adolf Hitler led to his dismissal from supreme command in 1943. He was sentenced to life in prison at the Nuremberg Trials, but was released because of ill health in 1955.

Raetia *or* **Rhaetia** \'rē-shē-ə\ Ancient Roman province south of the Danube River. It comprised parts of present-day Austria, Switzerland, and Germany. Its native inhabitants were probably of mixed Illyrian and Celtic descent. Conquered by Rome in 15 BC, it became an important part of the empire for its position on the highways between Italy and the Danube and between Gaul and the Balkans. Because it was a frontier province, its boundaries shifted when German tribes encroached; in the 1st century AD, the northern boundary extended to the Neckar River, but in the 3rd century the western and northern boundaries were pulled back. By 450, Rome controlled only the alpine regions.

RAF \'är-'ā-'ef\ *in full* **Royal Air Force** Armed service charged with the air defense of Britain and other international defense obligations. It originated in 1911, when an air battalion of the Royal Engineers was formed, with one balloon and one airplane company. In World War I the naval and military wings of the British air forces were separate, but in 1918 they were merged into the RAF. An RAF cadet college was established at Cranwell, Lincolnshire, in 1920, and an RAF staff college at Andover, Hampshire, in 1922. At the outbreak of World War II, the RAF's first-line strength was about 2,000 aircraft. RAF fighter pilots distinguished themselves during the Battle of Britain against the numerically superior German Luftwaffe.

Raffles, (Thomas) Stamford *later* **Sir Stamford** (1781–1826) Administrator in the British East India Co. and founder of Singapore. He joined the British East India Co. at 14, and his hard work won him an appointment as assistant secretary to the government of Penang (in present-day Malaysia). There he undertook an intensive study of the Malayan peoples, and his knowledge allowed him to play a key role in the British defeat of Dutch-French forces in Java, where he became lieutenant governor in 1811. He inaugurated a mass of reforms aimed at transforming the Dutch colonial system and improving the condition of the native population. He was recalled by the company, which deemed his reforms too costly; though he was popular in London (he was knighted in 1816), his authority when he resumed his Eastern service was severely restricted. Undeterred, he went on to found the port city of Singapore in 1819 to ensure British access to the China seas; in 1824 the Dutch relinquished all claims to Singapore. Raffles is credited with the creation of Britain's Far Eastern empire.

raga In classical Indian music, a principle akin to mode. A raga can be regarded as a vocabulary of melodic figures that tend, as a group, to emphasize certain tones of a scale, giving the raga a specific emotional character and implying the kind of music to be improvised. The emphasis on certain pitches effectively divides the scale into primary and secondary tones; the secondary tones serve to ornament the primary tones, thus reinforcing the emphasis. Each scale can have several different ragas, depending on which tones of the scale are made primary. Two additional factors contribute to the artistic potential of the raga: the division of tones between primary and secondary is not always hard and fast; moreover, a tertiary level (ornaments of the ornaments) is often made available to the performer. The concept of raga, introduced sometime before the 9th century, became influential throughout South and East Asia.

Ragae See RHAGAE

Raglan (of Raglan), Baron *orig.* **FitzRoy James Henry Somerset** (1788–1855) English army officer. He served as aide and, later, military secretary to the duke of WELLINGTON. Appointed commander in chief of British forces in the CRIMEAN WAR (1854), he gave an ambiguous order in the Battle of BALAKLAVA that led to the disastrous charge of the Light Cavalry Brigade under the Earl of CARDIGAN. Raglan became the scapegoat for the campaign's lack of progress and the inadequate supplies to the troops in the winter of 1854–55. His name was applied to the raglan sleeve, probably designed to adapt his coat to the arm he had amputated after the Battle of WATERLOO.

Ragnarok \'räg-nə-ˌrœk, 'räg-nə-ˌräk\ In Scandinavian mythology, the end of the divine and human worlds. As described in the 10th-century Icelandic poem *Völuspá* and other sources, Ragnarok will be preceded by cruel winters and moral chaos. Giants and demons will attack the gods, who will face death like heroes. The sun will be darkened, the stars will vanish, and the earth will sink into the sea. Afterward the earth will rise again, the innocent will return from the dead, and the hosts of the just will live in a hall roofed with gold. The title of RICHARD WAGNER's opera *Götterdämmerung* ("Twilight of the Gods") is a German equivalent of Ragnarok.

ragtime U.S. popular music of the late 19th and early 20th century distinguished by its heavily syncopated rhythm. Ragtime found its characteristic expression in formally structured piano compositions, the accented left-hand beat opposed in the right hand by a fast, bouncing melody that gave the music its powerful forward impetus. (The term probably derives from "ragged time,"a description of syncopation.) Ragtime compositions typically featured three or four discrete 16-bar strains performed at a moderate tempo. The most celebrated ragtime composer was SCOTT JOPLIN. The rhythm and structure of ragtime were important influences on the development of JAZZ.

ragweed Any of about 15 species of weedy plants (see WEED) that make up the genus *Ambrosia* in the COMPOSITE FAMILY, most of which are native to North America. They have rough hairy stems, mostly lobed or divided leaves, and inconspicuous greenish flowers borne in small heads. Common ragweed *(A. artemisiifolia)* is found across North America. POLLEN shed by ragweeds in great abundance in late summer is the principal cause of HAY FEVER in eastern and middle North America. Since ragweeds are annuals, mowing before pollination season eradicates them.

rail Any of about 100 species (family Rallidae) of slender marsh birds found almost worldwide. Rails have short rounded wings, a short tail, large feet, and long toes. Their loud call, especially at night, reveals their presence in dense vegetation. They are mostly dull grays and browns, often with barred patterns. Species vary from 4 to 18 in. (11–45 cm) long. Short-billed species are often called crakes. The king *(Rallus elegans)*, clapper *(R. longirostris)*, and Virginia *(R. limicola)* rails and the sora, or Carolina rail *(Porzana carolina)*, have been hunted in the U.S.; several of the rails are now endangered, and some species have been exterminated.

Virginia rail (*Rallus limicola*).

JOHN H. GERARD FROM THE NATIONAL AUDUBON SOCIETY COLLECTION/PHOTO RESEARCHERS

railroad Mode of land transportation in which flange-wheeled vehicles move over two parallel steel rails or tracks, drawn by a LOCOMOTIVE or propelled by self-contained motors. The earliest railroads were built in European mines in the 16th century, using cars pulled on tracks by men or horses. With the advent of the steam locomotive and construction of the first railway in 1825, the modern railroad developed quickly. The first U.S. railroad, the Baltimore and Ohio, began operation in 1827. Specialized railroad cars were built to transport freight and passengers, including the sleeping cars developed by George Pullman in 1859. In the 19th century the railroad had an important influence on every country's economic and social development. In the U.S. the transcontinental railroad, completed in 1869, began an era of railroad expansion and consolidation that involved such financial empire builders as CORNELIUS VANDERBILT, JAY GOULD, EDWARD H. HARRIMAN, JAMES J. HILL, and LELAND STANFORD. The railroad's importance in the U.S. began to diminish from the early 20th century, but in Europe, Asia, and Africa it continues to provide vital transportation links within and between countries. See also ORIENT EXPRESS, TRANS-SIBERIAN RAILROAD.

Railway Express Agency U.S. company that once operated the nation's largest ground and air express services. It was founded by the U.S. government as the American Railway Express Co. in 1918, when the nation's major express carriers—Adams & Co., AMERICAN EXPRESS CO., WELLS, FARGO & CO., and Southern Express Co.—were merged into a public corporation. An association of railroads bought out the business in 1929 and began to operate it as the Railway Express Agency. Its name was changed to REA Express in 1970. Poor management, strikes, and competition led to heavy losses, and REA filed for bankruptcy in 1975.

railways, national Rail transportation services owned and operated by national governments. U.S. railways are privately owned and operated, though the CONRAIL corporation was established by the federal government and AMTRAK uses public funds to subsidize privately owned intercity passenger trains. Canada has several small, privately owned railways, but its major passenger railway, Canadian National, was government-funded until 1995. In many countries, the central government owns and operates a national rail system, though some nations have privatized their national rail services in hopes of increasing efficiency and lowering cost through competition. These systems were usually formed from the union of various private railroads purchased or nationalized by the government. France's private railroads were gradually acquired by the government in the early 20th century; in 1938 the last remaining private lines were nationalized and incorporated into the SNCF, or French National Railways. All British railroads were nationalized as British Railways in 1948, but were privatized in 1994. Japan privatized its national railway in 1987. A major concern when national railways are privatized is that service to unprofitable areas will be cut, adversely affecting local populations; privatization plans attempt to address this issue with varying success.

Raimondi \rī-'män-dē, rī-'mōn-dē\, **Marcantonio** (c. 1480–1534) Italian engraver. He trained in Bologna under FRANCIA, but his energetic lines and use of cross-hatching in modeling were influenced by ALBRECHT DURER. After he moved to Rome c. 1510, he specialized in reproducing works by other artists, particularly RAPHAEL. He retained Raphael's idealized figures but provided his own background and landscapes. His engravings sold in large numbers and did much to spread High Renaissance style throughout Europe during the master's lifetime.

rain PRECIPITATION of liquid water drops with diameters greater than 0.02 in. (0.5 mm). When the drops are smaller, the precipitation is usually called drizzle. Raindrops may form by the coalescence of colliding small water droplets or from the melting of snowflakes and other ice particles as they fall into warm air near the ground. Hawaii's Mount Waialeale, with a 20-year annual average of 460 in. (11,700 mm), is the earth's wettest known point; the driest areas are in parts of deserts where no appreciable rain has ever been observed. Less than 10 in. (250 mm) and more than 60 in. (1,500 mm) per year represent approximate extremes of rainfall for all the continents.

rain dance Ceremonial dance performed to bring rain needed to water crops. Rain dances have been customary in many cultures, from the ancient Egyptians to the civilization of the MAYAS and the people of the 20th-century Balkans. Rain dances often include dancing in a circle, the participation of young girls, decoration with green vegetation, nudity, the pouring of water, and whirling, meant to act as a wind charm. They may also include phallic and fertility rites.

rain forest Lush FOREST, generally composed of tall, broad-leaved trees and usually found in wet tropical regions around the equator, mainly in South and Central America, West and Central Africa, Indonesia, parts of Southeast Asia, and tropical Australia, where the climate is relatively humid, with no marked seasonal variation. Depending on the amount of annual rainfall, the trees may be evergreens or mainly deciduous. The former require more water. Temperatures remain high, usually about 86°F (30°C) during the day and 68°F (20°C) at night. Soil conditions vary with location and climate, though most rain-forest soils tend to be permanently moist and not very fertile, because the hot, humid weather causes organic matter to decompose rapidly and to be absorbed quickly by tree roots and fungi. Rain forests have many vertical layers of plant and animal development. The highest plant layer, the tree canopy, extends to heights of 100–165 ft (30–50 m). Animals there mostly feed and escape from predators among leaves and branches. The next-highest layer is filled with small trees, LIANAS, and EPIPHYTES. Above the ground surface the space is occupied by tree branches, twigs, and foliage. Many species of animals live in the undergrowth. Contrary to popular belief, the rain forest floor is not impassable, being bare except for a thin layer of HUMUS and fallen leaves. Animals inhabiting this layer (e.g., rhinoceroses, gorillas, elephants, leopards, and bears) are adapted to walking and climbing short distances. Burrowing animals, such as armadillos and caecilians, are found below the soil surface, as are microorganisms that help decompose and free much of the organic litter accumulated by other plants and animals from all layers. The climate of the ground layer is unusually stable because the upper stories of tree canopies and the lower branches filter sunlight and heat radiation and reduce wind speeds, keeping the temperatures fairly even.

rainbow Series of concentric colored arcs that may be seen when light from a distant source—usually the sun—falls on a collection of water drops such as in rain, spray, or fog. The colored rays of the rainbow are caused by the REFRACTION and internal REFLECTION of light rays that enter the drop, each color being bent through a slightly different angle. Hence, the combined colors are separated upon emerging from the drop. The most brilliant and most common rainbow is the so-called primary bow, which results from light that emerges from the drop after one internal reflection. The colors of the arc (from outside to inside) are red, orange, yellow, green, blue, indigo, and violet. Occasionally a less-intense secondary bow may be observed; it has its color sequence reversed.

Rainbow Bridge National Monument National monument, southern Utah on the Navajo Indian Reservation near the Utah–Arizona border. Established in 1910, the site occupies 160 acres (65 hectares). It centers on a rainbow-shaped bridge of pink sandstone 290 ft (88 m) above a creek that winds toward the COLORADO RIVER. The bridge is 278 ft (85 m) long and is probably the world's largest natural bridge. Embedded among canyons, it is accessible only on foot, by horseback, or by boat on Lake Powell.

rainbow trout Species *(Oncorhynchus mykiss)* of fish in the SALMON family (Salmonidae) noted for spectacular leaps and hard fighting when hooked. It has been introduced from western North America to many other countries. A brightly colored fish of lakes and swift streams, it is covered with small black spots and has a reddish band along either side. The steelhead, a large, bluish, oceangoing form, is also a prized game fish. Rainbow trout may weigh 6 lbs (2.8 kg); steelheads (and rainbows in large lakes) may weigh 10–20 lbs (4.5–9 kg) or more. Another form of rainbow, the Kamloops, or Kootenay, trout of Idaho, may exceed 30 lbs (14 kg).

Rainer \'rī-nər\, **Luise** (born 1909) Austrian (German-born) film actress. She grew up in Munich, Switzerland, and Vienna, and was a distinguished stage actress with MAX REINHARDT's company (from 1927) before making films in Europe. Moving to Hollywood, she starred in *The Great Ziegfeld* (1936) and *The Good Earth* (1936), winning Academy Awards for both pictures. After a brief career and a stormy marriage to CLIFFORD ODETS, she retired to Europe, only returning to the screen many years later in *The Gambler* (1997).

Rainey, Ma *orig.* **Gertrude Malissa Nix Pridgett** (1886–1939) U.S. singer. Born in Columbus, Ga., Rainey began touring southern tent shows, levee camps, and cabarets at 17 in a song-and-dance team with her husband, the minstrel comic William ("Pa") Rainey. She performed through the 1920s, leading her own troupes, including at times BESSIE SMITH and THOMAS DORSEY. An earthy stage presence, known for her flamboyant dress, Rainey recorded more than 90 songs (including "See See Rider" and "Ma Rainey's Black Bottom") from 1923 to 1928 with country blues musicians and black jazz players. She retired in 1933. The first great professional blues vocalist, she earned the sobriquet "Mother of the Blues."

Rainier \rə-'nir\, **Mt.** Mountain, western central Washington state, southeast of TACOMA. At 14,410 ft (4,392 m), it is the highest point in the CASCADE RANGE and in the state. It covers 100 sq mi (260 sq km) and is surrounded by the largest single-mountain glacier system in the U.S. outside Alaska, with 41 glaciers radiating from the broad summit. A dormant volcano that last erupted 2,000 years ago, it is the major part of Mount Rainier National Park, established in 1899 and comprising 235,612 acres (95,423 hectares). It is a popular tourist and recreation area.

Rainier III \ren-'yā, *Engl* rā-'nir\ *orig.* **Rainier-Louis-Henri-Maxence-Bertrand de Grimaldi** (born 1923) Prince of Monaco (from 1949), 31st in a line of hereditary rulers. He intensified, expanded, and diversified Monaco's enterprises, including its industry. Through land retrieval from the seas, he expanded the national territory by one-fifth. His most significant political reform was the promulgation of a new constitution, based on modern principles without repudiating tradition. His wedding to GRACE KELLY in 1956 attracted worldwide attention.

Rainy Lake Narrow lake astride the Canadian–U.S. border, between Minnesota and southwestern Ontario. It is about 50 mi (80 km) long and has an area of 360 sq mi (932 sq km). Its shores are irregular and deeply indented, and it contains more than 500 islands. The region is the site of several Indian reservations and is popular for hunting, fishing, and canoeing.

Rajang River \'rä-ˌjäŋ\ *or* **Rejang River** \'rā-ˌjäŋ\ Chief river, central Sarawak, on the island of BORNEO, Malaysia. It flows southwest and west into the CHINA SEA and is about 350 mi (565 km) long. It is navigable for about 80 mi (130 km) to Sibu by oceangoing vessels and has a wide, swampy delta. Several market towns are along its banks.

Rajasthan \'rä-jə-ˌstän\ State (pop., 1994 est.: 48,040,000), northwestern India. Bounded by Pakistan, it covers an area of 132,149 sq mi (342,266 sq km); its capital is JAIPUR. Archaeological evidence shows continuous human habitation for about 100,000 years. In the 7th–11th cent AD, several RAJPUT dynasties arose, reaching their height in the 16th century. The emperor AKBAR brought the Rajput states into the MUGHAL empire. In the 19th century, the British came into control of the region. After Indian independence (1947), the area was organized as the Union of Rajasthan, and then reorganized in 1956. It is dominated by the Aravalli Range and the THAR DESERT. Predominantly an agricultural and pastoral state, it is the largest producer of wool in India.

Rajneesh \'rəj-ˌnēsh, räj-'nēsh\, **Bhagwan Shree** *orig.* **Chandra Mohan Jain** (1931–1990) Indian spiritual leader. A teacher of philosophy, he lectured throughout India and established an ASHRAM in Pune (Poona). He preached an eclectic doctrine of Eastern mysticism, individual devotion, and a notorious sexual freedom while amassing vast personal wealth. By the early 1970s he had attracted 200,000 devotees, many from Europe and the U.S. He lived with a community of followers in Oregon from 1981 to 1985, when he was deported from the U.S. for immigration fraud. He spent his last years in Pune, where he reestablished his ashram.

Rajputana \ˌräj-pə-'tä-nə\ Region of northwestern India that now comprises RAJASTHAN state and small sections of MADHYA PRADESH and GUJARAT. The Aravalli Range crosses the southern part of the region from northeast to southwest. The northwestern part is largely the THAR DESERT, but to the southeast the country is very fertile. The Rajput states came under British protection by treaties in 1818; most of the area was formed into Rajasthan state in 1948.

Rajputs \'räj-ˌpu̇ts\ Caste of landowners organized in patrilineal clans and located mainly in central and northern India, numbering about 12 million. The Rajputs regard themselves as descendants or members of the Kshattriya (warrior ruling) class, though in fact they vary greatly in status. After the fall of the GUPTA DYNASTY, invaders and indigenous peoples in northwestern India were probably integrated, the leaders in both groups becoming Kshattriyas. In the 9th–10th century the Rajputs became important politically, and for centuries they prevented complete Muslim domination of Hindu India. They eventually accepted Mughal overlordship and, later, British suzerainty (1818).

Rakaia River \rə-'kī-ə\ River, eastern central SOUTH ISLAND, New Zealand. Rising in the glaciers of the SOUTHERN ALPS, it flows east and southeast for 90 mi (145 km) before entering Canterbury Bight of the Pacific Ocean through a delta west of BANKS PENINSULA.

Rákóczi family \'rä-kōt-sē\ Noble MAGYAR family prominent in 17th-century Hungary. Its members included György I (1593–1648), who as prince of Transylvania (1630–48) allied himself with Sweden against the Habsburgs and won religious freedom for Protestants in Hungary. His son György II (1621–1660), prince of Transylvania (1648–60), joined

Sweden in attacking Poland (1656) but was forced to retreat; he was killed in battle by the invading Turks, who restored Turkish control over Transylvania. György's son Ferenc I (1645–1676) became a Catholic and joined Croatia in an unsuccessful revolt against Habsburg rule in Hungary. His son Ferenc II (1676–1735), prince of Transylvania (1704–11), led a Hungarian uprising for independence from the Habsburg empire (1703) that was initially successful, but his forces were defeated by the Austrians in 1711.

Raleigh \'rò-lē, 'rä-lē\ City (pop., 1996 est.: 244,000), capital of North Carolina. It was selected as the state capital in 1788 and laid out in 1792. It is a major retail shipping point for eastern North Carolina and a wholesale distributing point for food stores. Manufactures include textiles, electronic equipment and computers, and processed foods. An educational center, it is part of North Carolina's Research Triangle, along with Durham and Chapel Hill, an area of cultural, scientific, and educational institutions, including DUKE UNIV. and the University of NORTH CAROLINA.

Raleigh, Walter *later* **Sir Walter** (1554?–1618) English adventurer and favorite of ELIZABETH I. He joined his half brother HUMPHREY GILBERT on a piratical expedition against the Spanish (1578), then fought against the Irish rebels in Munster (1580). His outspoken views on English policy in Ireland caught the attention of ELIZABETH I, who made him her favorite at court. In 1584 he sent an expedition to explore the coast north of Florida, which he named Virginia, and to establish an unsuccessful colony at ROANOKE ISLAND. He was knighted by Elizabeth in 1585. Out of favor at court from c. 1592, he led an unsuccessful expedition up the Orinoco River in search of gold, which he described in *The Discoverie of Guiana* (1596). When Elizabeth died (1603), he was accused of plotting to depose JAMES I and imprisoned in the Tower of London. Released in 1616, he led another unsuccessful expedition to search for gold in Guyana. When his men burned a Spanish settlement, he was rearrested by James and executed, at the demand of the Spanish ambassador, under Raleigh's original sentence for treason.

rally driving Automobile competition using public roads and ordinary traffic rules. The object is to maintain a specified average speed between checkpoints; the route is unknown to the driver and navigator until the start of the event. Rally racing began in 1907 with a Peking-to-Paris race (7,500 mi, or 12,000 km). The Monte-Carlo rally began in 1911. The longest rally held regularly is the 3,874-mi (6,234-km) East African Safari.

Rally for the Republic *or* **Gaullists** (RPR) French political party. It was founded by JACQUES CHIRAC in 1976 as the successor to the various Gaullist coalitions that dominated the political life of the FIFTH REPUBLIC under CHARLES DE GAULLE and GEORGES POMPIDOU. The party had its antecedents in the group Rally of the French People, organized by de Gaulle in 1947. It evolved into the Union for the New Republic (1958–62) and then the Union of Democrats for the New Republic (1968–76) before assuming its present name.

ram Projection fixed to the front end of a fighting vessel and designed to damage enemy ships struck by it. It may have been developed by the Egyptians as early as 1200 BC, but it was most commonly used on Phoenician, Greek, and Roman GALLEYS. It was briefly revived in the mid-19th century, notably in the American Civil War, when rams mounted on armored, steam-driven warships were used effectively against wooden sailing ships. Improvements in naval weaponry and the spread of metal-hulled ships soon made it obsolete again. See also BATTERING RAM.

RAM \'ram\ *in full* **random-access memory** Computer main MEMORY in which specific contents can be accessed (read or written) directly by the CPU in a very short time regardless of the sequence (and hence location) in which they were recorded. Two types of memory are possible with random-access circuits, static RAM (SRAM) and dynamic RAM (DRAM). A single memory chip is made up of several million memory cells. In a SRAM chip, each memory cell stores a binary digit (1 or 0) for as long as power is supplied. In a DRAM chip, the charge on individual memory cells must be refreshed periodically in order to retain data. Because it has fewer components, DRAM requires less chip area than SRAM; hence a DRAM chip can hold more memory, though its access time is slower.

Rama Major Hindu deity. The name became associated with Ramacandra, the seventh incarnation of VISHNU, whose story is told in the *RAMAYANA*. Conceived as a model of reason, virtue, and right action, Rama was one of the chief objects of the BHAKTI cults. He is often depicted as a standing figure, holding an arrow in his right hand and a bow in his left. In temples his image is attended by the figures of his wife, SITA, his half-brother, Laksmana; and the monkey general, HANUMAN.

Rama IV See MONGKUT

Rama V See CHULALONGKORN

Rama VI See VAJIRAVUDH

Rama IX See BHUMIBOL ADULYADEJ

Ramadan \rà-mä-'dän\ In ISLAM, a holy month of fasting, the ninth month of the Muslim year, commemorating the revelation of the QURAN to MUHAMMAD. As an act of atonement, Muslims are required to fast and abstain from sexual activity during the daylight hours of Ramadan. Determined according to the lunar calendar, Ramadan can fall in any season of the year. The Ramadan fast is considered one of the Five Pillars of ISLAM, and the end of the fast is celebrated as one of the important religious holidays of Islam.

Ramakrishna (Paramahamsa) *orig.* **Gadadhar Chattopadhyaya** (1836–1886) Indian mystic. Born into a poor Brahman family, he worked as a priest in a temple of Kali in Calcutta (now Kolkata), where he had a vision and commenced spiritual practices in a number of different religious traditions. He denounced sexual desire and money as the twin evils that put spiritual enlightenment beyond reach, rejected the caste system, and held that all religions are in essence the same and that all are true. His teachings were spread by his disciples, notably VIVEKANANDA. A religious order bearing his name, with headquarters in Kolkata, sends missionaries throughout the world.

Raman \'rä-mən\, **Chandrasekhara Venkata** *later* **Sir Chandrasekhara** (1888–1970) Indian physicist influential in the growth of science in India. He received a Nobel Prize in 1930 for discovering that when LIGHT passes through a transparent material, some of the light that emerges at a right angle to the original beam is of other FREQUENCIES (Raman frequencies) characteristic of the material. He contributed to the building up of nearly every Indian research institution in his time, founded a scholarly physics journal and an academy of sciences, and trained hundreds of students.

Ramana Maharshi \'rə-mə-nə-mə-'hər-shē\ *orig.* **Venkataraman Aiyer** (1879–1950) Hindu spiritual leader. Born into a Brahman family in southern India, he left his village at 17 to become a hermit on Mount Arunachala, where SHIVA was said to have entered the world at creation. One of India's youngest GURUS, he held that evil and death were an illusion, which could be dissipated through his technique of *vicara* (self-pondering inquiry), and that to achieve liberation from rebirth it was necessary to practice BHAKTI (devotional surrender) either to Shiva or to Ramana Maharshi himself.

Ramananda \,rä-mə-'nən-də\ (c. 1400–c. 1470) Indian spiritual leader. He lived as an ascetic before settling in Varanasi (Benares) to study Vedic texts and the philosophy of RAMANUJA. He was fifth in succession in the lineage of Ramanuja, but his determination to ignore caste distinctions led to a break with the philosopher's other followers. With 12 disciples he founded his own sect, the Ramanandis, who practiced devotion to RAMA. His teachings were similar to Ramanuja's, but he dropped the ban on intercaste dining and the strict rule that all teaching and all texts must be in Sanskrit, himself teaching in the vernacular Hindi in order to reach the masses who did not know Sanskrit.

Ramanuja, bronze sculpture, 12th century; from a Visnu temple in Tanjore district, India.

BY COURTESY OF THE INSTITUT FRANCAIS D'INDOLOGIE, PONDICHERRY

Ramanuja \rä-'mä-nù-jə\ (1017?–1137) Indian theologian and philosopher, the most influential thinker of devotional HINDUISM. After a long pilgrimage through India, he found-

O P Q R

ed centers to spread devotion to VISHNU and LAKSHMI. He provided an intellectual basis for the practice of BHAKTI in major commentaries on the Vedas, the Brahma-sutras, and the Bhagavadgita. He was a major figure in the school of VISISTADVAITA, which emphasized the need for the soul to be united with a personal god. His chief philosophical contributions follow from his conviction that the phenomenal world is real and provides real knowledge, and that the exigencies of daily life are not contrary to the life of the spirit.

Ramanujan \rä-ˈmän-u̇-jə^n\, **Srinivasa (Aaiyangar)** (1887–1920) Indian mathematician. Extremely poor, he was largely self-taught from age 15. In 1913 he began a correspondence with Godfrey H. Hardy (1877–1947) that took him to England, where he made advances especially in the theory of numbers, the partition of numbers, and the theory of continued fractions. He published papers in English and European journals, and in 1918 became the first Indian elected to the Royal Society of London. He died of tuberculosis at 32, generally unknown but recognized by mathematicians as a phenomenal genius.

Ramatirtha \ˌrä-mə-ˈtir-tə\ *orig.* **Tirath Ram** (1873–1906) Hindu religious leader. He was a professor of mathematics before a meeting with VIVEKANANDA strengthened his desire to pursue a religious life. In 1901 he left his wife and children and went into seclusion in the Himalayas, and he later traveled to Japan and the U.S. He became known for his poetic manner of interpreting VEDANTA and for his joyful approach to religious learning as a means to the liberation of the individual. He died by drowning in the Ganges.

Ramayana \rä-ˈmä-yə-nə\ Indian epic poem, composed in Sanskrit c. 300 BC. With the *MAHABHARATA,* it is one of the two great epic poems of India. Consisting of 24,000 couplets in seven books, it describes the royal birth of RAMA and the loss of his throne. Banished to the forest with his wife, SITA, and his half-brother, Laksmana, he spends 14 years in exile. When a demon king carries off Sita, Rama enters into an alliance with Sugriva, king of the monkeys, and HANUMAN, the monkey general, who help him rescue her. Rama regains his kingdom, but Sita is banished when her chastity is questioned, and she is swallowed by the earth after proving her innocence.

Rambert \räm-ˈber\, **Marie** *later* **Dame Marie** *orig.* **Cyvia Rambam** (1888–1982) Polish-English ballet producer and director. She studied with E. JAQUES-DALCROZE, and taught eurythmics to the BALLETS RUSSES, where it influenced VASLAV NIJINSKY's avant-garde choreography. She continued to study ballet with Enrico Cecchetti (1850–1928) and used his methods when she founded a ballet school in 1920. She helped found the Camargo Society in 1930 and established the Ballet Club (later Ballet Rambert) in 1935. She encouraged new choreographers such as FREDERICK ASHTON and gave support to new dancers and stage designers, helping to establish the importance of English ballet. Her troupe, renamed the Rambert Dance Co. in 1987, has continued to perform.

Rameau \rà-ˈmō\, **Jean-Philippe** (1683–1764) French composer and music theorist. Son of an organist, he held organist posts until he was 49. From 1733 he wrote a series of highly successful operas, incl. *Hippolyte et Aricie* (1733) and *Les Indes galantes* (1735), assuring his place as the most important French opera composer since J.-B. LULLY. The *querelles des bouffons* (1752–53), a famous artistic controversy about the relative merits of French and Italian opera, was settled in favor of the French style by Rameau's music. He also won renown for his many keyboard pieces, mostly for harpsichord. His *Treatise on Harmony* (1722) established him as a major music theorist. In it he asserted that harmony is the basis of music, and that chords, which had been understood principally as collections of intervals above a bass, should instead be seen as representing inversions of more fundamental harmonic entities—both a valuable insight and an oversimplification which itself proved productive.

ramjet Air-breathing JET ENGINE that operates with no major moving parts. It relies on the craft's forward motion to draw in air and on a specially shaped intake passage to compress the air for combustion. After fuel sprayed into the engine has been ignited, combustion is self-sustaining. As in other jet engines, forward thrust is obtained as a reaction to the rearward rush of hot exhaust gases. Ramjets work best at speeds of Mach 2 (twice the speed of sound) and higher. See also TURBOJET.

Ramkhamhaeng \ˌräm-k̲äm-ˈhaŋ\ (1239?–1298) Third king of Sukhothai (N-central Thailand) who created and ruled the first major TAI state in 13th-century S.East Asia. He united a region that shared a common religion (THERAVADA Buddhism). Under him, the arts developed distinctively Tai expressions and accomplished bronze sculptures were created. He is also credited with inventing the Thai alphabet, a modification of Mon Khmer script. He was remembered only in legend until King MONGKUT of Siam, then a Buddhist monk, rediscovered his 1292 inscription in 1834. As a result, he came to be regarded as a national hero, a just and liberal ruler who imparted a sense of cultural unity to the region. The inscription's authenticity has since been questioned.

rammed earth *or* **pisé de terre** \ˌpē-ˌzā-də-ˈter\ Building material made by compacting and drying a stiff mixture of clay, sand or other aggregate, and water. It has been used by many civilizations. The most durable of the earth-building forms, it is formed into building blocks (see ADOBE) or rammed within removable wooden forms in layers or lifts to construct walls. China's Erligang (c. 1600 BC) is an example of a rammed-earth fortification; it covers an area of 1.2 sq mi (3.2 sq km) and may have taken 10,000 people more than 12 years to build.

Rampal \räm-ˈpäl\, **Jean-Pierre (Louis)** (1922–2000) French flutist. From 1947 he appeared widely in chamber music and solo recitals. In the 1950s he founded his own chamber groups, while also playing in the pit at the Paris Opéra 1956–62. Works were written for him by F. POULENC and others. His sweetness of tone and virtuosity in a largely baroque repertoire, as evidenced on a great many admired recordings, made him the first flutist to attain major international stardom.

Ramses II \ˈram-ˌsēz\ *known as* **Ramses the Great** (died 1213 BC) King of ancient Egypt, 1279–1213 BC. His family came to power some decades after the reign of AKHENATON. He set about restoring Egypt's power, subduing rebellion in southern Syria and fighting the HITTITES inconclusively at the famous battle of KADESH. He captured towns in Galilee and Amor, but, unable to defeat the Hittites, he assented to a peace treaty in 1258 BC. He married one and perhaps two of the Hittite king's daughters, and the later part of his reign was free from war. Its prosperity may be measured by the amount of construction he undertook. Early on he built himself a residence city in the Nile delta as a base for military campaigns and resumed construction of the temple of Osiris begun by his father. He added to the temple at KARNAK and completed a funerary temple for his father at LUXOR. In Nubia he built six temples, most famously those at ABU SIMBEL.

Ramses II, upper portion of a granite figure from Thebes, 1250 BC; in the British Museum.

Ramses III (died 1156 BC) King of ancient Egypt, 1187–1156 BC. Son of Setnakht, the founder of Egypt's 20th dynasty, he fought off Libyan invaders in the fifth year of his reign and the Sea Peoples (a conglomeration of migrating peoples from Asia Minor and the Mediterranean) two years later. After another conflict with the Libyans, he achieved a lasting peace. He then reorganized society into classes grouped by occupation and resumed temple building. He encouraged trade and industry, and the nation prospered. A delay in sending monthly rations to temple builders in Thebes c. 1158 BC resulted in the first recorded labor dispute.

Ramses III, detail of the lid of a granite sarcophagus, about 1187–56 BC; in the Fitzwilliam Museum, Cambridge.

Ramu River \'rä-mü\ River, Papua New Guinea. One of the country's longest rivers, it is about 400 mi (645 km) long. It rises in the southeast and flows northwest through the great Central Depression, where it receives numerous streams draining the mountainous region. During World War II its valley was taken from the Japanese by Allied forces (1943). It was the scene of an earthquake in 1993.

Rana era (1846–1951) In Nepal, the period during which control of the government lay in the hands of the Rana family. Jung Bahadur (1817–1877) seized power in 1846 and made himself permanent prime minister. He was given the hereditary title of Rana. Under the Ranas, Nepal maintained relations with the British, who provided it with support. When the British withdrew from India in 1947, the Rana family was exposed to new dangers. They faced a revolution in 1950, and in 1951, under pressure from India, Nepal's King Tribhuvan took the throne with restored sovereignty.

ranch Large farm for breeding and raising cattle, sheep, or horses. Ranching originated in South America and Mexico in early colonial times, when Spanish settlers introduced cattle and horses and tended them on the pampas. It was an itinerant form of LIVESTOCK farming: herds were tended on open range, and biannual roundups were held for branding calves and driving mature animals to market. Itinerant ranching reached its peak in the 1880s. By the early 20th century, overstocking, quarantine laws, railroad competition, and barbed-wire fences had put an end to cattle drives and open-range farming. Ranching today is nearly all sedentary, but huge ranches still exist.

Rand, Ayn *orig.* **Alice Rosenbaum** *or* **Alissa Rosenbaum** (1905–1982) Russian-U.S. writer. She emigrated to the U.S. in 1926 after graduating from the University of Petrograd, and worked as a screenwriter in Hollywood. She won a cult following with two best-selling novels presenting her belief that all real achievement comes from individual ability and effort, that laissez-faire capitalism is most congenial to the exercise of talent, and that selfishness is a virtue, altruism a vice. In *The Fountainhead* (1943), a superior individual transcends traditionalism and conformism. The allegorical *Atlas Shrugged* (1957) combines science fiction and a political message. She expounded her philosophy, which she called objectivism, in nonfiction works and as editor of two journals, and became an icon of radical libertarianism.

RAND Corp. Nonpartisan think tank whose original focus was national security. It grew out of a research-and-development project (its name is a contraction of "research and development") by Douglas Aircraft Co. for the Army Air Force in 1945. In 1948 it became a private nonprofit corporation. In the 1960s it expanded its focus to address domestic public-policy issues. Its mission today is to improve policy and decision making through research and analysis. It employs several hundred scholars in many disciplines. Its funding comes from government contracts, charitable foundations, private corporations, and earnings on its endowment. Its headquarters are in Santa Monica, Cal., and it has offices in Washington, D.C., New York, and overseas.

Randolph, A(sa) Philip (1889–1979) U.S. civil-rights leader. Born in Crescent City, Fla., he moved to New York in 1911. In 1917 he cofounded the journal *The Messenger* (later *Black Worker*) and called for more positions for blacks in the war industry and the armed forces. In 1925 he founded the Brotherhood of Sleeping Car Porters, the first successful black trade union, and remained its president until 1968. In 1941 he lobbied Pres. FRANKLIN ROOSEVELT to ban discrimination in defense industries and federal bureaus. In 1948 he influenced Pres. HARRY TRUMAN to bar segregation in the armed forces. In 1955 he was made a vice president of the newly combined AFL-CIO, and in 1960 he formed the Negro American Labor Council to fight discrimination within the AFL-CIO.

Randolph, Edmund Jennings (1753–1813) U.S. politician. Born in Williamsburg, Va., he helped draft the state's constitution (1776), and served in the Continental Congress 1779–82. He was a delegate to the Annapolis Convention and the CONSTITUTIONAL CONVENTION, where he presented the Virginia Plan that influenced the final draft of the U.S. Constitution. As governor of Virginia (1786–88), he effected the state's ratification of the Constitution. He served as U.S. attorney general (1789–94) and secretary of state (1794–95), resigning after he was falsely accused of accepting a bribe from the French to influence the U.S. government against Britain. He returned to his law practice and served as chief counsel for AARON BURR in his 1807 trial.

Randolph, John (1773–1833) American politician. Born in Prince George Co., Va., he was elected in 1799 to the U.S. House of Representatives, where he served almost continuously until 1829. A noted orator, he was a staunch advocate of states' rights and opposed a national bank and federal protective tariffs. He supported slavery and led the resistance to the MISSOURI COMPROMISE. His denunciation of HENRY CLAY's support of JOHN QUINCY ADAMS for president led to a harmless duel with Clay (1826).

random-access memory See RAM

Random House U.S. publishing company. It was founded by BENNETT CERF and Donald S. Klopfer in 1925. As it grew it published many successful and prestigious writers and gathered under its corporate roof many other firms, including Alfred A. Knopf, Inc. (acquired 1960), Pantheon Books (1961), Ballantine Books (1973), Fawcett Books (1982), and the Crown Publishing Group (1988). It was itself bought several times before becoming in 1998 a part of one of the world's largest media companies, Bertelsmann AG.

random variable In statistics, a FUNCTION that can take on either a finite number of values, each with an associated probability, or an infinite number of values, whose probabilities are summarized by a DENSITY FUNCTION. Used in studying chance events, it is defined so as to account for all possible outcomes of the event. When these are finite (e.g., the number of heads in a three-coin toss), the random variable is called discrete and the probabilities of the outcomes sum to 1. If the possible outcomes are infinite (e.g., the life expectancy of a light bulb), the random variable is called continuous and corresponds to a density function whose INTEGRAL over the entire range of outcomes equals 1. Probabilities for specific outcomes are determined by summing probabilities (in the discrete case) or by integrating the density function over an interval corresponding to that outcome (in the continuous case).

range finder Instrument used to measure the distance from the instrument to a selected point or object. The optical range finder, used chiefly in CAMERAS, consists of an arrangement of LENSES and PRISMS set at each end of a tube. The object's range is determined by measuring the ANGLES formed by a line of sight at each end of the tube; the smaller the angles, the greater the distance, and vice versa. Since the mid-1940s, radar has replaced optical range finders for most military targeting, and the laser range finder, developed in 1965, has largely replaced optical range finders for SURVEYING and radar in certain military applications.

Rangeley Lakes \'rānj-lē\ Chain of lakes, western Maine. It includes Rangeley, Mooselookmeguntic, Richardson, and Umbagog lakes. They extend more than 50 mi (80 km) in length, cover an area of 80 sq mi (207 sq km), and have elevations between 1,200 and 1,500 ft (365 and 460 m).

Ranger Any of a series of nine unmanned probes launched 1961–65 by NASA. The project was NASA's earliest attempt to explore the MOON's surface. Ranger 4 (1962) became the first U.S. spacecraft to hit the moon, crash-landing on its surface as planned. The last three probes in the series (1964–65) sent more than 17,000 high-resolution photographs of the moon before crashing. See also LUNA, PIONEER, SURVEYOR.

Rangoon See YANGON

Ranjit Singh \'rən-jit-'siⁿ-hə\ (1780–1839) Founder and maharaja (1801–39) of the Sikh kingdom of the Punjab. He became chief of the Shukerchakias (a Sikh group located in what is now Pakistan) on the death of his father in 1792. In 1799 he seized Lahore, the capital of the Punjab, and in 1801 he proclaimed himself maharaja of the Punjab. In 1802 he captured Amritsar, a city sacred to the Sikhs, and by 1820 he had consolidated his rule over the whole Punjab between the Sutlej and the Indus rivers. The Sikh state he created, which had included Sikhs, Muslims, and Hindus in both the army and the cabinet, collapsed soon after his death.

Rank, J(oseph) Arthur *later* **Baron Rank (of Sutton Scotney)** (1888–1972) British motion-picture distributor and producer. His British National Film Co. made its first commercial picture in 1935. That year he and Charles Woolf established General Film Distributors to distribute UNIVERSAL PICTURES films in Britain. By 1941 Rank controlled two of the three largest movie-theater chains in Britain. The J. Arthur Rank Organisation (incorporated 1946) dominated British film production in the late 1940s and '50s. Rank served as chairman (1946–62) and president

(1962–72) of the Rank Organisation, which shifted from filmmaking to hotel ownership and other more profitable enterprises in the late 1960s.

Rank \'räŋk\, **Otto** *orig.* **Otto Rosenfeld** (1884–1939) Austrian psychologist. Born in Vienna, he became a protégé of SIGMUND FREUD. In his early books, including *The Artist* (1907) and *The Myth of the Birth of the Hero* (1909), he extended psychoanalytic theory to explain the significance of myths. He edited the *International Journal of Psychoanalysis* 1912–24. The publication of *The Trauma of Birth* (1924), which was seen to undermine the principles of psychoanalysis by arguing that the basis of anxiety neurosis is psychological trauma occurring during birth, led to his expulsion from the Vienna Psychoanalytic Society. Rank settled in New York in 1936, and his later work focused on the will as the guiding force in personality development.

Ranke \'räŋ-kə\, **Leopold von** *orig.* **Leopold Ranke** (1795–1886) German historian. Ranke taught at the University of Berlin 1825–71. Inspired by the scientific method of historical study used by BARTHOLD GEORG NIEBUHR, he championed objective writing based on philological and textual criticism of source materials. His scholarly technique and way of teaching (he was the first to establish a historical seminar) had great influence on Western historiography. His many works covering a wide variety of topics typically are subtle accounts of particular limited periods in European state and political history that, like his source materials, take comparatively little notice of social and economic forces.

Rankin, Jeannette (1880–1973) U.S. reformer, first woman member of the U.S. Congress (1917–19, 1941–43). Born in Missoula, Mont., she was a social worker from 1909 and became active in women's-suffrage work. Elected to the U.S. House of Representatives in 1916, she introduced the first bill to give women the vote. A pacifist, she voted against declaring war on Germany (1917). She lost her bid for a U.S. Senate seat (1918) and returned to social work. In 1940 she won reelection to the House, where she became the only legislator to vote against declaration of war on Japan. Declining to seek reelection, she continued to lecture on social reform. In 1968, at 87, she led 5,000 women, the "Jeannette Rankin Brigade," to protest the Vietnam War.

Jeannette Rankin, 1918.

BY COURTESY OF THE LIBRARY OF CONGRESS, WASHINGTON, D.C.

Rankine \'raŋ-kən\, **William J(ohn) M(acquorn)** (1820–1872) Scottish engineer and physicist, one of the founders of THERMODYNAMICS. His classic *Manual of the Steam Engine and Other Prime Movers* (1859) was the first attempt at a systematic treatment of the theory of STEAM ENGINES. He worked out a thermodynamic cycle of events (the RANKINE CYCLE) that was used as a standard for the performance of steam-power installations in which a condensable vapor provides the working fluid. He also did notable work on earth pressures and the stability of retaining walls.

Rankine cycle Ideal cyclical sequence of changes of PRESSURE and TEMPERATURE of a fluid, such as water, used in an engine, such as a STEAM ENGINE. Described in 1859 by WILLIAM RANKINE, it is used as a standard for rating the performance of steam power plants. In the Rankine cycle, the working substance of the engine undergoes four successive changes: (1) heating at constant volume (as in a boiler), (2) evaporation and superheating (if any) at constant pressure, (3) isentropic expansion in the engine, and (4) condensation at constant pressure with return of the fluid to the boiler. See also CARNOT CYCLE.

Ransom, John Crowe (1888–1974) U.S. poet and critic. Born in Pulaski, Tenn., Ransom attended and later taught at Vanderbilt Univ., where he became the leader of the Fugitives, a group of poets who shared a belief in the South and its regional traditions and published the influential journal *The Fugitive* (1922–25). At Kenyon College, he founded and edited (1939–59) the *Kenyon Review*. His literary studies include *The New Criticism* (1941), which gave its name to an important critical movement (see NEW CRITICISM), and he became recognized as a leading theorist of the post–World War I Southern literary renaissance. His *Selected Poems* (1945; rev. ed., 1969) won the National Book Award.

rap Musical style in which rhythmic and/or rhyming speech is chanted ("rapped") to musical accompaniment that can include digital sampling (music and sounds extracted from other recordings). This backing music is also called hip-hop, the name used to refer to a broader cultural movement that includes rap, deejaying (turntable manipulation), graffiti painting, and breakdancing. Rap, which originated in African American communities in New York City, came to national prominence with the Sugar Hill Gang's "Rapper's Delight" (1979). Rap's early stars included Grandmaster Flash and the Furious Five, Run-D.M.C., LL Cool J, Public Enemy (who espoused a radical political message), and the Beastie Boys. The late 1980s saw the advent of "gangsta rap," with lyrics that were often misogynistic or which glamorized violence. More recent stars have included Sean "Puffy" Combs, Jay-Z, OutKast, and Eminem.

Rapa Nui See EASTER ISLAND

Rapallo \rä-'pä-lō\, **Treaty of** (April 16, 1922) Treaty between Germany and the Soviet Union, signed at Rapallo, Italy. Negotiated by Germany's WALTHER RATHENAU and the Soviet Union's GEORGY V. CHICHERIN, it reestablished normal relations between the two nations. The nations agreed to cancel all financial claims against each other, and the treaty strengthened their economic and military ties. As the first agreement concluded by Germany as an independent agent since World War I, it angered the Western Allies.

rape Annual plant *(Brassica napus)* of the MUSTARD FAMILY, native to Europe. This 1-ft-tall (30-cm) plant has a long, thin taproot; smooth, bluish-green, deeply scalloped leaves; and clusters of yellow flowers. Each round, elongated seedpod has a short beak and contains many seeds. The seeds yield an oil (rapeseed oil, or canola) that is the lowest in saturated fat of any edible oil, making it popular for use in cooking. It is also used as an ingredient in soap and margarine and as a lamp fuel.

Rape (*Brassica napus*).

INGMAR HOLMASEN

rape Unlawful sexual activity, usually sexual intercourse, carried out forcibly or under threat of injury and against the will of the victim. Though traditionally limited to attacks on women by men, in recent years the definition of rape has been broadened to cover same-sex attacks and attacks against those who, because of mental illness, intoxication, or other reasons, are incapable of valid consent. Statutory rape, or intercourse with a person younger than a certain age (from 14 to 18 years), has long been a serious crime in most jurisdictions. Rape is generally considered an expression of anger or aggression and a pathological assertion of power by the rapist. Victims' psychological responses vary but usually include feelings of shame, humiliation, confusion, fear, and rage. Many rape victims fail to report the crime, deterred by the prospect of a distressing cross-examination in court and the difficulty in proving a crime for which there usually are no witnesses. See also ASSAULT AND BATTERY.

Raphael In the BIBLE and the QURAN, one of the archangels. In the apocryphal *Book of Tobit* he appears in human disguise and conquers the demon Asmodeus. His name in Hebrew means "God has healed," and in Tobit his business is to heal the earth. Raphael is reckoned among the saints in both Eastern and Western churches.

Raphael \'ra-fē-əl, 'rā-fē-əl\ *orig.* **Raffaello Sanzio** (1483–1520) Italian painter and architect. As a member of PERUGINO's workshop, he established his mastery by 17 and began receiving important commissions. In 1504 he moved to Florence, where he executed many of his famous Madonnas; his unity of composition and suppression of inessentials is evident in *The Madonna* of the Goldfinch (c. 1506). Though influenced by LEONARDO DA VINCI's chiaroscuro and sfumato, his figure types were his own creation, with round, gentle faces that reveal human sentiments raised to a sublime serenity. In 1508 he was summoned to Rome to decorate a suite of papal chambers in the Vatican. The frescoes in the Stanza della Segnatura are probably his greatest work; the most famous, *The School of Athens* (1510–11), is a complex and magnificently ordered allegory of secular knowledge showing Greek philosophers in an architectural setting. The Madonnas he painted in Rome show him turning away from his earlier work's serenity to emphasize movement and grandeur, partly under MICHELANGELO's influence. The *Sistine Madonna* (1513) shows the richness of color and new boldness of compositional invention typical of his Roman period. He became the most important portraitist in Rome, designed 10 large tapestries to hang in the SISTINE CHAPEL, designed a church and a chapel, assumed the direction of work on ST. PETER'S BASILICA at the death of DONATO BRAMANTE, and took charge of virtually all the papacy's projects in architecture, painting, and the preservation of antiquities. When he died on his 37th birthday, his last masterpiece, the *Transfiguration* altarpiece, was placed at the head of his bier.

Rapier \'rāp-yər\, **James T(homas)** (1837–1883) U.S. politician. Born in Florence, Ala., son of a slave and a wealthy planter, he was educated in Canada and Scotland. After the Civil War he returned to Alabama, where he became a successful cotton planter and a delegate to the state's first Republican convention. Elected to the U.S. House of Representatives in 1873, he worked for passage of the Civil Rights Act of 1875 but was defeated for reelection. He returned to Alabama, where he was active as a labor organizer and publisher of the *Montgomery Sentinel.*

raptor \'rap-tər\ In general, any BIRD OF PREY, including OWLS. The raptors are sometimes restricted to EAGLES, FALCONS, HAWKS, and VULTURES (birds of the order Falconiformes), all diurnal predators that "seize and carry off" (Latin *raptare*) their prey.

raptures of the deep See NITROGEN NARCOSIS

rare earth metal Any of a large class of chemical ELEMENTS including scandium (atomic number 21), yttrium (39), and the 15 elements from 57 (lanthanum) to 71 (see LANTHANIDES). The rare earths themselves are pure or mixed OXIDES of these METALS, originally thought to be quite scarce; however CERIUM, the most plentiful, is three times as abundant as lead in the earth's crust. The metals never occur free, and the pure oxides never occur in minerals. These metals are similar chemically because their atomic structures are generally similar; all form compounds in which they have VALENCE 3, including stable oxides, CARBIDES, and borides.

Ras Nasrani \'räs-ˌnäs-'rä-nē\ *formerly* **Sharm al-Sheikh** \'shärm-äl-'shēk\ Inlet and cape, southeastern coast of the SINAI Peninsula, Egypt. The site of an Egyptian military base, it was captured by Israeli forces in the Sinai campaign of 1956 (see ARAB–ISRAELI WARS). After the SIX-DAY WAR in 1967, Israel again occupied the site until its withdrawal from the Sinai Peninsula in the early 1980s. In 1972 a new town, Ophira, was built there. The region has been developed as a recreational and tourist area.

Rashi \'rä-shē\ *in full* **Rabbi Shlomo Yitzhaqi** (1040–1105) Medieval French commentator on the Bible and the Talmud. He studied in the schools of Worms and Mainz, and became a local Jewish leader in the valley of the Seine c. 1065. His influential writings on the Bible examined the literal meaning of the text and used allegory, parable, and symbolism to analyze its nonliteral meaning. His landmark commentary on the Talmud is a classic introduction to biblical and postbiblical Judaism.

Rashid Rida \rä-'shēd-rē-'dä\, **Muhammad** (1865–1935) Syrian Islamic scholar. As founder (1898) and publisher of the newspaper *al-Manar,* he helped Muslims formulate an intellectual response to the problem of reconciling their religious heritage with the modern world. He was concerned with the backwardness of the Muslim countries, which he proposed to remedy by reviving the original principles of Islam. He advocated that rulers consult with religious leaders in formulating government policies. He also urged Arabs to emulate the scientific and technological progress of the West.

Rashidun \ˌrä-shi-'dün\ First four CALIPHS of the Islamic community: ABU BAKR, UMAR IBN AL-KHATTAB, UTHMAN IBN AFFAN, and ALI. As ISLAM's first rulers after MUHAMMAD, they assumed all his duties except prophecy. They led the congregation in prayer, delivered the Friday sermons, and commanded the army. The caliphate of the Rashidun expanded the Islamic state beyond Arabia into Iraq, Syria, Palestine, Egypt, Iran, and Armenia. They were also responsible for the adoption of the Islamic calendar and the establishment of an authoritative reading of the QURAN.

Rashnu \'räsh-nü\ In ZOROASTRIANISM, the god of justice, who determines the fates of the dead. Assisted by MITHRA and SRAOSHA, Rashnu stands at the Bridge of the Requiter and weighs on his golden scales the deeds of the souls that wish to pass. The divine triad sometimes attempts to intercede for souls and obtain forgiveness for their sins. The 18th day of the month is sacred to Rashnu.

Rasht City (pop., 1994 est.: 374,000), northern central Iran, south of the Caspian Sea on a branch of the Safid River. Its importance as the main city of the Gilan region dates from Russia's expansion southward in the 17th century. It was severely damaged by Russian occupation during both World Wars. Surrounded by rice fields and areas of half-cleared jungle, it is a market and processing center for rice, tea, peanuts, and silk.

Rask \'räsk\, **Rasmus (Kristian)** (1787–1832) Danish linguist. A scholar of INDO-EUROPEAN LANGUAGES, he was a principal founder of the science of comparative LINGUISTICS. His observation that sound shifts between corresponding words in GERMANIC and other Indo-European languages followed predictable patterns was the basis of a fundamental law of linguistics later enunciated by JACOB GRIMM (Grimm's law). Rask also carried out extensive research on OLD NORSE, publishing his *Investigation of the Origin of the Old Norse or Icelandic Language* in 1818. By the end of his life he had mastered 25 languages and dialects.

Raskob \'ras-kəb\, **John Jakob** (1879–1950) U.S. financier. Born in Lockport, N.Y., he went to work for E.I. du Pont de Nemours & Co. in 1902 and played a major role in DU PONT's expansion in the early 20th century. He joined the board of GENERAL MOTORS in 1915; as chairman of its finance committee from 1918, he greatly increased sales and earnings, establishing the General Motors Acceptance Corp. (GMAC) to allow dealers to finance their inventory and offer credit and long-term financing to their customers. He left in 1928 to head the Democratic National Committee and run ALFRED E. SMITH's unsuccessful presidential campaign; later he and Smith helped direct the construction of the EMPIRE STATE BUILDING.

raspberry Any of many species of fruit-bearing bushes of the genus *Rubus* in the ROSE family. When picked, the juicy red, purple, or black berry separates from its core; in the related BLACKBERRY, the core is part of the fruit. Red raspberries are propagated by suckers (see SUCKERING) from the roots of the parent plant or from root CUTTINGS. Black and purple varieties have arched canes and are propagated by LAYERING of the shoot tips. Raspberries contain iron and vitamin C. They are eaten fresh and are also very popular in jams, as a pastry filling, and as a flavoring for liqueurs.

Black raspberry (*Rubus occidentalis*).
GRANT HEILMAN

Rasputin \ra-'spyü-t^{ə}n\, **Grigory (Yefimovich)** *orig.* **Grigory (Yefimovich) Novykh** (1872?–1916) Russian mystic influential at the court of the Czar NICHOLAS II and ALEXANDRA. An illiterate peasant, he earned the name *rasputin* ("debauched one") for his early licentious behavior. After undergoing a religious experience, he gained a reputation among the peasants as a holy man, able to heal the sick. He became known to Nicholas and the susceptible Alexandra, and proved capable of stopping the bleeding of their hemophiliac son, probably by means of hypnotism. He became a favorite at court, despite reports of his continuing and flagrant debauchery. When Nicholas left Alexandra in charge of Russia's internal affairs in 1915, Rasputin influenced her appointment of church officials and incompetent cabinet ministers. After several attempts to remove his harmful influence, a group of noblemen including Prince Felix Yusupov assassinated him by successively poisoning him, shooting him, and finally throwing him into the ice-filled Neva River. The RUSSIAN REVOLUTION OF 1917 followed weeks later.

Rastafarian \ˌras-tə-ˈfer-ē-ən\ Member of a political and religious movement among blacks in Jamaica and several other countries. Rastafarians worship Haile Selassie, considering him the messiah. They believe that blacks are the Israelites reincarnated, who have been subjected to the evil and inferior white race in divine punishment for their sins; they will eventually be redeemed by repatriation to Africa and will compel the whites to serve them. These beliefs, first enunciated in 1953, can be traced to several independent prophets, particularly Marcus Garvey. As the movement grew, ideas of repatriation tended to give way to either black militancy or mysticism. The Rastafarian life usually includes vegetarianism, the wearing of dreadlocks, and the smoking of marijuana.

Rastatt and Baden \ˈrä-ˌshtät...ˈbäd-ᵊn\, **Treaties of** (March 6 and September 7, 1714) Two peace treaties between Emperor Charles VI and France that ended Charles's attempt to continue the War of the Spanish Succession. In these treaties, Charles renounced his claims to the Spanish throne but did not actually make peace with Spain.

Rastenburg Assassination Plot See July Plot

rat Any of more than 500 forms of Asian rodent (genus *Rattus,* family Muridae) that have been introduced worldwide. The black rat *(Rattus rattus)* and the Norway rat *(R. norvegicus)* are the aggressive, omnivorous animals commonly associated with the name. They prefer areas of human habitation, where they can easily find food. They have keen senses and can climb, jump, burrow, or gnaw their way into seemingly inaccessible places. They reproduce extremely rapidly (up to 150 offspring a year) and have few natural predators. Rats transmit numerous human diseases and have often destroyed grain supplies. The black rat is about 8 in. (20 cm) long, excluding the slightly longer tail. The Norway rat (also called the brown, barn, sewer, or wharf rat) has proportionately smaller ears and a shorter tail. Laboratory rats are strains of the Norway rat. The name rat is applied, without scientific basis, to other rodents (e.g., kangaroo rat, wood rat).

Norway rat (*Rattus norvegicus*).
JOHN H. GERARD

rat snake Any of 40–55 snake species in the genus *Elaphe* (family Colubridae) and similar forms, found in woodlands and barnyards in North America, Europe, and Asia. Nonvenomous, they kill rats and mice by constriction, and also eat eggs and poultry. Some hunt birds in trees. These egg-laying snakes are normally slow and docile, but in self-defense they vibrate the tail, discharge a foul liquid, and strike from an upreared position. The black rat, or pilot black, snake *(E. obsoleta obsoleta)* of the eastern U.S. may exceed 8 ft (2.5 m).

Aesculapian snake (*Elaphe longissima*).
ANTON THAU–BAVARIA VERLAG

ratchet Mechanical device that transmits intermittent motion or permits a shaft to rotate in one direction but not in the opposite one. Reversible ratchets are used on socket wrench handles and are convenient for tightening or loosening bolts in positions where a complete revolution of a wrench handle is impossible. They are used in mechanical jacks to lock the jack rod after each successive lift.

Rathbone, Basil (1892–1967) British actor. He made his stage debut in 1911 and later played classical roles in London and New York. From 1924 he appeared in Hollywood movies, often in romantic roles. With his distinctive voice and gaunt appearance, he was cast as a villain in several swashbuckling movies starring Tyrone Power and Errol Flynn. He won praise for his roles in *Romeo and Juliet* (1936) and *If I Were King* (1938), but became best known for portraying Sherlock Holmes in a series of films that began with *The Hound of the Baskervilles* (1939).

Rathenau \ˈrä-tᵊn-ˌau̇, *Engl* ˈra-thən-ˌau̇\, **Walther** (1867–1922) German industrialist and statesman. From 1915 he headed the AEG conglomerate developed by his father, Emil Rathenau (1838–1915). In World War I he organized the conservation and distribution of raw materials for the War Ministry. In 1918 he cofounded the liberal German Democratic Party and supported cooperation with the Social Democratic Party. After serving as minister of reconstruction (1921–22), he was appointed foreign minister and negotiated the Treaty of Rapallo with the Soviet Union. Reviled by extreme nationalists as a Jew and a promoter of "creeping Communism," he was assassinated.

Rathke \ˈrät-kə\, **Martin H(einrich)** (1793–1860) German anatomist and embryologist. He was the first to describe gill slits and gill arches in mammal and bird embryos. He thought they were vestigial gills but recognized their significance in development of the associated blood vessels. He first described Rathke's pouch (1839), an embryonic structure that develops into the pituitary gland's anterior lobe. He also did pioneering marine zoology research.

ratio Quotient of two values. The ratio of *a* to *b* can be written *a*:*b* or as the fraction *a*/*b*. In either case, *a* is the antecedent and *b* the consequent. Ratios arise whenever comparisons are made. They are usually reduced to lowest terms for simplicity. Thus, a school with 1,000 students and 50 teachers has a student/teacher ratio of 20 to 1. The ratio of the width to the height of a rectangle is called an aspect ratio, an example of which is the golden ratio of classical architecture. When two ratios are set equal to each other, the resulting equation is called a proportion.

rational number Any number that can be represented as the quotient of two integers (i.e., the denominator cannot equal zero). The set of rational numbers includes all integers as well as all fractions. In decimal form, rational numbers are either terminating or repeating decimals.

rational psychology Metaphysical discipline that attempted to determine the nature of the human soul by a priori reasoning. In Christian Wolff's division of metaphysics, rational psychology was one of three disciplines included under the heading of "special metaphysics" (the others being rational cosmology and rational theology). Immanuel Kant, in his *Critique of Pure Reason*, criticized the pretensions of rational psychology.

rationalism Philosophical view that regards reason as the chief source and test of knowledge. Rationalism has long been the rival of empiricism, the doctrine that all knowledge ultimately comes from, and must be tested by, sense experience. As against this doctrine, rationalism holds reason to be a faculty that can lay hold of truths beyond the reach of sense perception, both in certainty and in generality. In stressing the existence of a "natural light," rationalism has also been the rival of systems claiming esoteric knowledge, whether from mystical experience, revelation, or intuition, and has been opposed to various irrationalisms that tend to stress the biological, the emotional or volitional, the unconscious, or the existential at the expense of the rational.

rationing Government allocation of scarce resources and consumer goods, usually adopted during wars, famines, or other national emergencies. Rationing according to use prohibits the less important uses of a commodity (e.g., the use of gasoline for pleasure trips as opposed to work-related travel). Rationing by quantity limits the amounts of a commodity available to each claimant (e.g., a pound of butter per month). Rationing by value limits the amount of money consumers can spend on commodities that are difficult to standardize (e.g., clothing). Point rationing assigns a point value to each commodity and allocates a certain number of points to each consumer. These can be tracked through coupons, which are issued to consumers and must be exchanged for the approved amounts of rationed goods. Consumers in a rationed economy are usually encouraged to save their money or invest in government bonds so that unspent money will not be used for unrationed items or purchases on the black market.

ratite \ˈra-ˌtīt\ Any bird species that cannot fly because its smooth, or raftlike, sternum (breastbone) lacks a keel to which flight muscles can be anchored. The group includes some of the largest birds of all time. Two extinct types, the slow-moving, heavy-bodied elephant bird of Madagascar and the moas of New Zealand, grew to 10 ft (3 m) tall. Extant ratites include the cassowary, emu, kiwi, ostrich, and rhea.

Rattigan, Terence (Mervyn) *later* **Sir Terence** (1911–1977) British playwright. After writing two comedies, he won acclaim for the drama *The Winslow Boy* (1946; film, 1948). His best-known work, *Separate*

Tables (1955; film, 1958), explored the isolation created by rigidly imposed social conventions. His other plays included *The Browning Version* (1948), *Ross* (1960), and *A Bequest to the Nation* (1970). He wrote screenplays for the film adaptations of his plays and for *The Yellow Rolls-Royce* (1965) and *Goodbye Mr. Chips* (1969).

rattlesnake Any of about 30 species in two genera of New World PIT VIPERS having a tail rattle that produces a buzzing sound when vibrated. The rattle is composed of horny, loosely connected segments added one at a time with each molt. *Sistrurus* species have large scales on the top of the head. *Crotalus* species have mostly small scales on the head. Species range from 1 to 8 ft (30–250 cm) long. Most eat small animals, primarily rodents, birds, and lizards. All bear live young. In hot areas rattlesnakes become nocturnal; in cold areas they hibernate in groups. Heat-sensitive organs on the sides of the head help them locate and strike their prey. A rattlesnake bite, though painful, is not fatal if treated. See also SIDEWINDER.

Timber rattlesnake (*Crotalus horridus*).
JACK DERMID

Ratzenhofer, Gustav (1842–1904) Austrian general, philosopher, and sociologist. After a successful military career in which he attained the rank of field marshal, he developed an interest in the social sciences, particularly SOCIAL DARWINISM. He believed human interaction was characterized by "absolute hostility" between ethnic groups, but that the species could evolve higher forms of association through sociology. His works included *The Essence and Objective of Politics* (3 vols., 1893) and *Sociological Perception* (1898).

Rauschenberg \'raú-shən-,bərg\, **Robert** (*orig.* Milton) (born 1925) U.S. painter and graphic artist. Born in Port Arthur, Tex., he studied under JOSEF ALBERS. His "combine" paintings of the 1950s, incorporating such objects as soda bottles, traffic barricades, and stuffed birds, anticipated the Pop art movement. In later work, he used silkscreen and other techniques to transfer images from the commercial print media and his own photographs to canvas, reinforcing the images and unifying them compositionally with bold strokes of paint. His work has roots in Dada and the ready-mades of MARCEL DUCHAMP.

Ravana \'rä-və-nə\ In Hinduism, king of the demons. Ravana is depicted with 10 heads and 20 hands and flying a magic chariot. He ruled in the kingdom of Lanka, from which he had expelled his brother Kubera. His abduction of SITA and defeat by her husband, RAMA, are the central events of the epic *RAMAYANA*. The demon king is also remembered for shaking Mount Kailasa until SHIVA intervened and imprisoned him beneath it for 1,000 years. The popular annual Ram Lila festival climaxes with the defeat of Ravana and the burning of huge effigies of demons.

Ravana, the 10-headed demon-king, detail from a Guler painting of the *Ramayana*, c. 1720; in the Cleveland Museum of Art.
BY COURTESY OF THE CLEVELAND MUSEUM OF ART, OHIO, GIFT OF GEORGE P. BICKFORD

Ravel \rà-'vel\, **(Joseph) Maurice** (1875–1937) French composer. At 14 he was admitted to the Paris Conservatoire. Completing his piano studies, he returned to study composition with G. FAURE, writing the important piano piece *Jeux d'eau* and a string quartet. In the next decade he produced some of his best-known music, including *Gaspard de la nuit* for piano (1908) and *Rapsodie espagnole* (1908). His great ballet *Daphnis et Chloé* (1912) was commissioned by SERGEY DIAGHILEV. Other works include the operas *L'heure espagnole* (1911) and *L'enfant et les sortileges* (1925), the suites *Valses nobles et sentimentales* (1911) and *Le tombeau de Couperin* (1917), the orchestral works *La valse* (1920) and *Bolero* (1928), two piano concertos, and many beautiful songs. A careful, precise worker, Ravel possessed great gifts as an orchestrator, and his works are universally admired for their superb craftsmanship; he has remained the most widely popular of all French composers.

raven Any of several species (genus *Corvus*, CROW family Corvidae) of heavy-billed, usually solitary, songbirds, once abundant throughout the Northern Hemisphere but now restricted to undisturbed areas. The common raven *(C. corax),* the biggest PASSERINE, grows to 26 in. (66 cm) long and has a wingspan of more than 4 ft (1.3 m). The dark, iridescent plumage is shaggy, especially around the throat. Ravens eat rodents, insects, grain, birds' eggs, and, in winter, carrion and refuse. Captive nestlings may learn to mimic a few words. The large nest, a crude structure of sticks, is built high on a cliff or treetop.

Ravenna \rə-'ve-nə\ City (metro. area pop., 1996 est.: 137,000), northeastern Italy. It is located inland from the Adriatic Sea, with which it is connected by a canal. It was the capital of the western Roman empire in the 5th century AD and of the Ostrogothic kingdom and Byzantine Italy in the 6th–8th century. Its art and architecture reflect a fusion of Roman forms with Byzantine mosaics and other decoration; sites include the 6th-century basilica of Sant'Apollinare Nuovo and the octagonal church of San Vitale. It became part of the kingdom of Italy in 1861 and today is an agricultural and industrial city, with enterprises that include petroleum and natural-gas refining.

Ravi River \'rä-vē\ River, northwestern India and northeastern Pakistan, one of the five rivers of the PUNJAB. It rises in the HIMALAYAS in HIMACHAL PRADESH state, India, and flows past Chamba, turning southwest at the boundary of JAMMU AND KASHMIR. It then flows to the Pakistani border and along it before entering Pakistani Punjab. It flows past LAHORE, Pakistan, and turns west near Kamalia, emptying into the CHENAB RIVER after a course of about 450 mi (725 km).

Rawalpindi \,rä-wəl-'pin-dē\ City (pop., 1998: 1,406,214), PUNJAB province, northern Pakistan, southwest of ISLAMABAD. In ancient times, the locality was included in the Achaemenid Persian empire. The ancient city of TAXILA has been identified with nearby ruins. Strategically located, it controls the routes to Kashmir and was the site of an important British military station. The capital of Pakistan 1959–69, it is the headquarters of the Pakistan army and an administrative, commercial, and industrial center. Wheat, barley, corn, and millet are the chief crops grown in the area. Mankial, south of the city, is a 3rd-century-BC Buddhist STUPA site.

Rawlings, Jerry J(ohn) (born 1947) Ghanaian military and political leader who twice (1979, 1981) overthrew the government and seized power. After the first coup Rawlings, a junior air-force officer, yielded power to a freely elected civilian president, Hilla Limann, but ousted Limann two years later. As Ghana's ruler, he created workers' councils and established production and price controls, but later abandoned these measures. His policies afforded GHANA relative political and economic stability. He was returned to office by election in 1996 and stepped down from the presidency in 2001.

Rawlings, Marjorie Kinnan (1896–1953) U.S. short-story writer and novelist. Born in Washington, D.C., Rawlings worked as a journalist before moving to backwoods Florida and devoting herself to fiction. Taking her material from the people and land around her, she wrote richly atmospheric works that resemble vivid factual reporting and are noted for their magical descriptions of landscape. Her best-known novel is *The Yearling* (1938, Pulitzer Prize), about a boy from a hardscrabble family and the fawn he adopts. Her later works include *Cross Creek* (1942) and *The Sojourner* (1953).

Rawls, John (born 1921) U.S. philosopher. Born in Baltimore, he taught at Cornell (1962–79) and later Harvard (from 1979). He has written primarily on ethics and political philosophy. In his *Theory of Justice* (1971), he offered an alternative to UTILITARIANISM that led to very different conclusions about justice. He asserted that if people had to choose principles of justice from behind a "veil of ignorance" that restricted what they could know of their own position in society, they would not seek to maximize overall utility but would instead both protect their liberty and safeguard themselves against the worst possible outcome. They would thus sanction only the kinds of inequalities (e.g., in wealth) that are to the benefit of the worst off (e.g., because the inequalities are necessary for incentives that benefit all).

ray Any of 300–350 mostly marine species of cartilaginous fish (order Batoidei) found worldwide and classified as ELECTRIC RAYS, SAWFISHES,

SKATES, and STINGRAYS. Many species are slow-moving bottom-dwellers. The gill openings and mouth are on the underside of the flattened body. Winglike pectoral fins extend along the sides of the head. All but electric rays have a long, slender tail, often with saw-edged, venomous spines, and rough, often spiny, skin. See also MANTA RAY.

Cow-nosed ray (*Rhinoptera bonasus*), a stingray.
PAINTING BY RICHARD ELLIS

Ray, James Earl (1928–1998) U.S. assassin. Ray was born in Alton, Illinois; he became a small-time criminal and was sentenced several times to prison, and he escaped from the Missouri state prison in 1967. In Memphis, Tennessee, on April 4, 1968, he shot MARTIN LUTHER KING from the window of a rooming house as King emerged from his motel room across the street. Ray fled to Toronto, London, Lisbon, and back to London, where he was arrested on June 8. Back in Memphis, he pleaded guilty and was sentenced to 99 years in prison. He later recanted his confession. He tried many times, even with the support of the King family, to have his case reopened, but to no avail.

Ray, John (1627–1705) British naturalist and botanist. Son of a blacksmith, he was enabled to attend Cambridge University by a special fund, and spent many years there as a fellow. With Francis Willughby (1635–1672) he undertook a complete catalog of living things, of which he published numerous volumes. His enduring legacy to botany was the establishment of species as the ultimate unit of taxonomy. He attempted to base his systems of classification on all the structural characteristics of organisms, including internal anatomy, rather than on a single feature. By insisting on the importance of lungs and heart structure, he effectively established the class of mammals, and he divided insects according to the presence or absence of multiple metamorphoses. Coming closer to a truly natural system of taxonomy than had any of his contemporaries, Ray helped make possible CAROLUS LINNAEUS's later contributions.

Ray, Man *orig.* **Emmanuel Radnitsky** (1890–1976) U.S. photographer, painter, and filmmaker. Born in Philadelphia, he grew up in New York, where he studied architecture, engineering, and art. With MARCEL DUCHAMP he formed the New York DADA group in 1917 and produced READY-MADES. In 1921 he moved to Paris and became associated with the Surrealists. He rediscovered the technique for making "cameraless" pictures or photograms, which he called "rayographs," by placing objects on light-sensitive paper, and the technique of solarization, which makes part of the image negative and part positive. He turned to portrait photography and made a virtually complete record of the celebrities of Parisian cultural life of the 1920s and '30s. He also made important contributions as an avant-garde filmmaker in the 1920s.

Ray, Nicholas *orig.* **Raymond Nicholas Kienzle** (1911–1979) U.S. film director. Born in Galesville, Wis., he studied architecture and drama and began directing plays in the mid-1930s. After working in New York with JOHN HOUSEMAN and ELIA KAZAN, he followed them to Hollywood, where he directed *They Live By Night* (1948). Much admired by believers in the AUTEUR THEORY, Ray was praised for demonstrating a personal style in such movies as *In a Lonely Place* (1950), *The Lusty Men* (1952), *Johnny Guitar* (1954), the landmark film of youthful rebellion *Rebel Without a Cause* (1955), *Bigger Than Life* (1956), *Bitter Victory* (1958), and *55 Days at Peking* (1963).

Satyajit Ray.
CAMERA PRESS

Ray, Satyajit (1921–1992) Indian film director. After studying with RABINDRANATH TAGORE, he became art director of an ad agency and a book illustrator. He sold all his possessions to make his first film, *Pather Panchali* (1955), a story of village life that was extremely successful at the Cannes Film Festival. With *Aparajito* (1956) and *The World of Apu* (1959), he completed the brilliant Apu Trilogy and brought Indian cinema to world attention. He later won acclaim for *Devi* (1960), *Two Daughters* (1961), *The Big City* (1964), *The Lonely Wife* (1964), *The Chess Players* (1977), *The Home and the World* (1984), and *The Visitor* (1990). He wrote all his own screenplays, noted for their humanism and poetry, and often composed the music for his films, though his short stories and novellas became his main source of income. In 1992 he received an honorary Academy Award.

ray flower See COMPOSITE FAMILY

Rayburn, Sam(uel) (Taliaferro) (1882–1961) U.S. politician. Born in Roane Co., Tenn., he taught school before becoming a lawyer in Texas, where he served in the legislature 1907–13. He was elected as a Democrat to the U.S. House of Representatives in 1912, where he served for 48 years, including 17 years as speaker (1940–46, 1949–53, 1955–61). A skillful tactician, he influenced the passage of much NEW DEAL legislation and cowrote the bill enacting rural electrification. He was the long-time political mentor to LYNDON B. JOHNSON and a trusted adviser to presidents from FRANKLIN ROOSEVELT to JOHN F. KENNEDY.

Rayleigh (of Terling Place) \'rā-lē\, **Baron** *orig.* **John William Strutt** (1842–1919) English physicist. In 1873 he succeeded to his father's title and built a research laboratory on his estate. He taught physics at Cambridge University 1879–84 and was secretary of the Royal Society 1884–95. His research included work on electromagnetism, color, acoustics, and diffraction gratings, and his theory explaining the blue color of the sky evolved into the RAYLEIGH SCATTERING law. In 1904 he was awarded the Nobel Prize for Physics for his isolation of argon. In 1908 he became chancellor of Cambridge University. His influential *Theory of Sound* (1877, 1878) examines questions of vibrations and resonance of media.

Rayleigh scattering Dispersion of ELECTROMAGNETIC RADIATION by particles with radii less than 1/10 the WAVELENGTH of the radiation. It is named for Baron RAYLEIGH, who described it in 1871. Since blue light is at the short wavelength end of the visible SPECTRUM, it is scattered in the atmosphere much more than the longer-wavelength red light. This causes the blue color of the sky, since the observer sees only the scattered light. The Rayleigh laws predict the variation of the intensity and the POLARIZATION of scattered light.

Raymond, Antonin (1888–1976) Czech-U.S. architect. He emigrated to the U.S. in 1910. He assisted FRANK LLOYD WRIGHT in building the Imperial Hotel, Tokyo (1916). Remaining in Japan, he and his partner, Ladislav Rado, built numerous structures, mostly for Americans. As one of the few modernist architects working in Japan at the time, he influenced such architects as Junzo Yoshimura and KUNIO MAEKAWA. Among his works were the Reader's Digest Building, Tokyo (1951; since destroyed) and the Nagoya International School (opened 1967), a circular structure serving a flexible, progressive educational program.

Raymond IV *French* **Raimond** *known as* **Raymond of St. Gilles** \sa^n-'zhēl\ (1041?–1105) Count of Toulouse (1093–1105) and marquis of Provence (1066–1105). The first Western European ruler to join the First CRUSADE, he helped to capture Antioch (1098) and Jerusalem (1099) but refused the crusaders' crown of Jerusalem. He also conquered and ruled Tripoli (1102–5).

Raymond VI *French* **Raimond** (1156–1222) Count of TOULOUSE (1194–1222). He at first tolerated the heretical CATHARI but later joined the ALBIGENSIAN CRUSADE against them. Raymond fought the crusaders to save his own dominions, and though he lost his title by decree of the fourth LATERAN COUNCIL (1215), despite the effort of Pope INNOCENT III to arrange a compromise, he regained most of his lands by conquest. Twice excommunicated, he was refused Christian burial.

Raymond VII *French* **Raimond** (1197–1249) Count of Toulouse (1222–49). He helped recover lands taken from his father, RAYMOND VI, and negotiated a truce (1223) with land-hungry crusaders from northern France. For failing to suppress the heretical CATHARI he was excommunicated (1226) and subjected to a French invasion. He ceded territory to France by treaty and agreed to permit the ALBIGENSIAN CRUSADE to continue in Languedoc (1229). Allied with HENRY III of England, he rebelled unsuccessfully against Louis VIII of France (1242) and was forced to accept greater French authority over Toulouse.

Raymond of Peñafort \ˌpān-yə-ˈfȯrt\, **St.** *Spanish* **Raimundo** (c. 1185–1275) Catalan Dominican friar influential in defining church law. He studied and taught CANON LAW at Bologna, then returned to Barcelona, where he joined the Dominicans and wrote a manual for confessors widely used in the late Middle Ages. Appointed papal chaplain by Pope GREGORY IX (1230), he was commissioned to codify the papal statues and rulings on canon law; these *Decretals* (1234) remained part of church law until 1917. He later organized schools of Arabic and Hebrew studies in Tunis and Murcia.

Rayonism \ˈrā-ə-ˌni-zəm\ (Russian, *Luchizm:* "ray-ism") Russian art movement founded 1912–13 by Mikhail Larionov (1881–1964) and his wife, Natalia Goncharova (1881–1962), which represented one of the first steps toward the development of abstract art in Russia. A synthesis of Cubism, Futurism, and Orphism, Rayonism was described by Larionov as "concerned with spatial forms that are obtained through the crossing of reflected rays from various objects." It apparently ended after 1914, when its founders departed for Paris.

Rayonnant style \re-yən-ˈäⁿ\ French style (13th century) that represents the height of GOTHIC ARCHITECTURE. During this period architects became less interested in achieving great size than in decoration, which took such forms as pinnacles, moldings, and especially window TRACERY. The style's name reflects the radiating character of the ROSE WINDOW. Other features include the thinning of vertical supporting members, the enlargement of windows, and the combination of the triforium gallery and CLERESTORY into one large glazed area, until walls became largely undifferentiated screens of tracery, mullions, and glass. Amiens Cathedral (1220–70) is cited as its earliest manifestation. Especially fine achievements include NOTRE-DAME DE PARIS, the church of Saint-Urbain in Troyes (founded 1262), and the extraordinary Sainte-Chapelle, Paris (consecrated 1248), Louis IX's palace chapel. See also CATHEDRAL.

Razi \ˈrä-zē\, **ar-** *in full* **Abu Bakr Muhammad ibn Zakariya' ar-Razi** *Latin* **Rhazes** (865?–925?) Persian alchemist and philosopher. He saw himself as the Islamic version of SOCRATES in philosophy and of HIPPOCRATES in medicine. In *Kitab al-hawi* ("The Comprehensive Book") he surveyed Greek, Syrian, early Arabic, and some Indian medical knowledge, adding his own comments. His philosophical writings include *The Spiritual Physick of Rhazes,* a popular ethical treatise and major alchemical study. He called himself a follower of PLATO but disagreed with Arabic interpreters of Plato. His theory of the composition of matter is similar to that of DEMOCRITUS. He was considered the greatest physician of the Islamic world.

Razin \ˈrå-zyin\, **Stenka** *orig.* **Stepan Timofeyevich** (c. 1630–1671) Russian COSSACK rebel. Born in the prosperous Don Cossack area, he supported the runaway serfs from Poland and Russia who escaped into the region to find land. In 1667 he led a band of newcomers to establish an outpost on the upper Don River. They raided Russian and Persian settlements on the Caspian Sea (1667–70), acquiring great fame and wealth. He then led his Cossack anarchists on a campaign into the Volga River region, where he was joined by disaffected peasants. After seizing Tsaritsyn (now Volgograd), Astrakhan, and Saratov, his force of 20,000 undisciplined rebels was defeated by the Russian army at Simbirsk. Razin was captured, tortured, and executed. He became a popular Russian folk hero and was immortalized in songs and legends.

razor clam Any of several species of marine CLAMS (family Solenidae) common in intertidal sands and muds, particularly of temperate seas. Razor clams have narrow and elongated shells (shaped like straight razors) up to 8 in. (20 cm) long. A large active foot enables them to move rapidly up and down within their burrow and retreat quickly when disturbed. With their short siphons (tubes) they feed on particulate material in seawater. Some species can swim short distances by jetting water through their siphons.

razorback whale See FIN WHALE

RCA Corp. Major U.S. electronics and broadcasting conglomerate. It is a unit of GENERAL ELECTRIC CO., with headquarters in New York City; its subsidiaries include NBC. RCA was founded as the Radio Corp. of America by General Electric in 1919 to acquire Marconi Wireless Telegraph Co. of America, at that time the only company capable of handling commercial transatlantic radio communications. RCA founded NBC in 1926 to carry on the company's radio broadcasting. In 1939 RCA developed the first experimental television set, and its black-and-white sets went on the market seven years later. General Electric acquired RCA in 1986, and in 1987 it sold RCA's consumer-electronics division to the French corporation Thomson-Brandt, SA. RCA is also active in military and space electronics and satellite communications.

Re \ˈrā\ *or* **Ra** \ˈrä\ In ancient EGYPTIAN RELIGION, the creator god and god of the sun. He was believed to sail across the sky in his solar bark and at night to travel in another bark through the underworld, where he had to vanquish a serpent before he could be born again. As the creator, he rose from the ocean of chaos, creating himself and then engendering eight other gods. From the 4th dynasty, kings held the title Son of Re, and Re later became part of the throne name they adopted at accession and was appended to the names of such gods as AMON and SEBEK.

reactance Measure of the opposition that an electrical CIRCUIT or a part of a circuit presents to ELECTRIC CURRENT (see ELECTRICAL IMPEDANCE) insofar as the current is varying or alternating. Steady electric currents flowing along conductors in one direction undergo opposition called electrical RESISTANCE, but no reactance. Reactance is present in addition to resistance when conductors carry ALTERNATING CURRENT. Reactance also occurs for short intervals when DIRECT CURRENT is changing as it approaches or departs from steady flow (e.g., when switches are closed or opened). Reactance is of two types, inductive and capacitive. Inductive reactance is associated with the varying magnetic field that surrounds a wire or a coil carrying a current. Capacitive reactance is associated with the changing electric field between two conducting surfaces (plates) separated from each other by an insulating medium. The ohm is the unit of reactance.

reaction, heat of Amount of HEAT that must be added or removed during a CHEMICAL REACTION to keep all substances involved at the same temperature. If it is positive (heat must be added), the reaction is endothermic; if it is negative (heat is given off), the reaction is exothermic. Accurate heat of reaction values are needed for proper design of equipment used in chemical processes; they are usually estimated from compiled tables of THERMODYNAMICS data (heats of formation and heats of combustion of many known materials). The ACTIVATION ENERGY is unrelated to the heat of reaction.

reaction rate Speed at which a CHEMICAL REACTION proceeds, in terms of amount of product formed or amount of reactant consumed per unit of time. The reaction rate depends on the nature of the reacting substances and the type of chemical change, as well as temperature and pressure, especially if GASES are involved. In general, the reactions of IONS occur very rapidly, but those in which COVALENT BONDS are formed or broken are slower. CATALYSTS usually accelerate reaction rates. The prediction, measurement, and interpretation of reaction rates are subjects of the branch of chemistry known as chemical kinetics. See also law of MASS ACTION.

Read, Nathan (1750–1849) U.S. engineer and inventor. Born in Warren, Mass., he attended and taught at Harvard Univ., and soon thereafter invented technology to adapt JAMES WATT'S STEAM ENGINE to boats and road vehicles. He devised a chain-wheel method of using paddle wheels to propel a STEAMBOAT, and in 1791 was one of four recipients (with John Fitch, James Rumsey, and JOHN STEVENS) of the original U.S. steamboat patents. He was also an innovator in windmill, waterpower, and threshing technology.

read-only memory See ROM

Reade, Charles (1814–1884) English novelist and dramatist. Though trained in law and an officer at Oxford Univ., he put much of his time and resources into writing and staging his melodramatic plays. His novels expose, with passionate indignation, the social injustices of his times. He is best remembered for the historical romance *The Cloister and the Hearth* (1861); his other novels include *It Is Never Too Late to Mend* (1856), attacking prison conditions; *Hard Cash* (1863), on the abuse of mental patients; and *Put Yourself in His Place* (1870), about terrorism by trade unionists.

Reader's Digest U.S.-based monthly magazine. Founded by DEWITT AND LILA WALLACE, it was first published in 1922 as a digest of condensed articles of topical interest and entertainment value taken from other periodicals. From 1934 it published condensed versions of current books; later it began publishing books containing original material. Though initially conceived as an impartial journal, the *Digest* has tended to reflect its publishers' generally conservative outlook. It probably has the largest circulation of any periodical in the world, appearing in 48 editions and 19 languages worldwide.

Reading \'re-diŋ\ City (pop., 1994 est.: 139,000), county seat of BERKSHIRE, England, west of LONDON. It was a Danish encampment as early as AD 871 and was given a town charter by King HENRY III in 1253. It suffered severely in the ENGLISH CIVIL WARS of the mid-17th century. By that time the town's trade, notably in clothing, had begun to decline. OSCAR WILDE was imprisoned in Reading Gaol in 1897. It is now an agricultural center noted for the bulbs produced in its nurseries. It is the site of a university, and its industries include computer production, and malting and brewing.

ready-made Everyday object selected and designated as art. The name was coined by MARCEL DUCHAMP, whose first ready-mades included a snow shovel that he picked up on a snowy day in New York, and a wheel mounted on a stool (1913). They represented a protest against the excessive importance attached to works of art. Duchamp's anti-aesthetic gestures made him one of the leading Dadaists of his day, and his ready-made concept, though widely regarded for decades as an insult to art, was adapted by such later artists as ROBERT RAUSCHENBERG, ANDY WARHOL, and JASPER JOHNS.

Reagan \'rā-gən\, **Ronald W(ilson)** (born 1911) 40th president of the U.S. (1981–89). Born in Tampico, Ill., he attended Eureka College and worked as a radio sports announcer before going to Hollywood in 1937. In his career as a movie actor, he had roles in 50 films and was twice president of the Screen Actors Guild (1947–52, 1959–60). He became a spokesman for the General Electric Co. and hosted its television theater program 1954–62. Having gradually changed his political affiliation from liberal Democrat to conservative Republican, he was elected governor of California and served 1967–74. In 1980 he defeated incumbent Pres. JIMMY CARTER to become president. Shortly after taking office, he was wounded in an assassination attempt. He adopted SUPPLY-SIDE ECONOMICS to promote rapid economic growth and reduce the federal deficit. Congress approved most of his proposals (1981), which succeeded in lowering inflation but doubled the national debt by 1986. He began the largest peacetime military buildup in U.S. history and in 1983 proposed construction of the STRATEGIC DEFENSE INITIATIVE. His foreign policy included the INF Treaty to restrict INTERMEDIATE-RANGE NUCLEAR WEAPONS and the invasion of GRENADA. In 1984 he defeated WALTER MONDALE in a landslide for reelection. Details of his administration's involvement in the IRAN-CONTRA AFFAIR emerged in 1986 and significantly weakened his popularity and authority. Though his intellectual capacity for governing was often disparaged, his artful communication skills enabled him to pursue numerous conservative policies with conspicuous success. In 1994 he revealed that he had Alzheimer's disease.

real and personal property Basic types of property in English COMMON LAW, roughly corresponding to the division between immovables and movables in CIVIL LAW. Real property consists of land, buildings, crops, and other resources, improvements, or fixtures still attached to the land. Personal property is essentially all property other than real property, including goods, animals, money, and vehicles.

real number In mathematics, a quantity that can be expressed as a finite or infinite decimal expansion. The counting NUMBERS, INTEGERS, RATIONAL NUMBERS, and IRRATIONAL NUMBERS are all real numbers. Real numbers are used in measuring continuously varying quantities (e.g., size, time), in contrast to measurements that result from counting. The word *real* distinguishes them from the IMAGINARY NUMBERS.

realism In the visual arts, an aesthetic that promotes accurate, detailed, unembellished depiction of nature or of contemporary life. Realism rejects imaginative idealization in favor of close observation of outward appearances. It was a dominant current in French art between 1850 and 1880. In the early 1830s, the painters of the BARBIZON school espoused realism in their faithful reproduction of the landscape near their village. GUSTAVE COURBET was the first artist to proclaim and practice the realist aesthetic; his *Burial at Ornans* and *The Stone* Breakers (1849) shocked the public and critics with their frank depiction of peasants and laborers. In his satirical caricatures, HONORE DAUMIER used an energetic linear style and bold detail to criticize the immorality he saw in French society. Realism emerged in the U.S. in the work of WINSLOW HOMER and THOMAS EAKINS. In the 20th century, German artists associated with the NEUE SACHLICHKEIT worked in a realist style to express their disillusionment after World War I. The Depression-era movement known as SOCIAL REALISM adopted a similarly harsh realism to depict the injustices of U.S. society. See also NATURALISM.

realism In literature, the theory or practice of fidelity to nature or to real life and to accurate representation without idealization of everyday life. The 18th-century works of DANIEL DEFOE, HENRY FIELDING, and TOBIAS SMOLLETT are among the earliest examples of realism in English literature. It was consciously adopted as an aesthetic program in the mid-19th century in France, when interest arose in recording previously ignored aspects of contemporary life and society; GUSTAVE FLAUBERT's *Madame Bovary* (1857) established the movement in European literature. The realist emphasis on detachment and objectivity, along with lucid but restrained social criticism, became integral to the novel in the late 19th century. The word has also been used critically to denote excessive minuteness of detail or preoccupation with trivial, sordid, or squalid subjects. See also NATURALISM.

realism In philosophy, any viewpoint that accords to the objects of human's knowledge an existence that is independent of whether they are perceiving or thinking about them. Against nominalism, which denies that UNIVERSALS have any reality at all (except as words), and conceptualism, which grants universals reality only as concepts within the mind, realism asserts that universals exist independently of their being expressed in language and conceived by human minds. Against IDEALISM and PHENOMENALISM, it asserts that the existence of material objects and their QUALITIES is independent of their being perceived. Similarly, moral realism asserts that moral qualities of actions (such as being morally good, bad, or indifferent, or being ethically right, wrong, or obligatory) belong to the actions themselves and are not to be explained as mere products of a mind that perceives and feels attracted to or repelled by the actions. In opposition to conventionalism, realism holds that scientific theories are objectively true (or false) based on their correspondence (or lack of it) to an independently existing reality.

realpolitik Politics based on practical objectives rather than on ideals. The word does not mean "real" in the English sense but rather connotes "things"—hence a politics of adaptation to things as they are. Realpolitik thus suggests a pragmatic, no-nonsense view and a disregard for ethical considerations. In diplomacy it is often associated with relentless, though realistic, pursuit of the national interest.

reamer Rotary cutting TOOL of cylindrical or conical shape, used for enlarging and finishing to accurate dimensions holes that have been drilled, bored, or cored. A reamer cannot be used to start a hole. All reamers have lengthwise flutes or grooves; either the sides of the tool or the tip may be used for cutting. Reamers are made from high-carbon STEEL, HIGH-SPEED STEEL, or cemented CARBIDES.

reaper Any farm machine that cuts grain (CEREAL). Early reapers simply cut the crop and dropped it unbound. Modern machines include harvesters, combines (see COMBINE HARVESTER), and binders, which also perform other harvesting operations. See also CYRUS H. MCCORMICK.

reason, practical See PRACTICAL REASON

Réaumur \rā-ō-'mu̅e̅r, *Engl* ˌrā-ō-'myu̇r\, **René-Antoine Ferchault de** (1683–1757) French physicist and entomologist. He invented the thermometric scale that bears his name (see THERMOMETRY); on the Réaumur scale, 0° marks the freezing point of water and 80° marks the boiling point. He invented the opaque white glass known as Réaumur porcelain, improved techniques for making iron and steel, discovered that crayfish can regenerate lost appendages, and isolated gastric juice. His *Memoirs Serving as a Natural History of Insects* (1734–42), though unfinished, was a milestone in entomological history.

rebate Retroactive refund or credit given to a buyer who has paid the full list price for a product or service. Fair and equitable rebates are used simply as incentives available to all customers. So-called deferred (or exclusive-patronage) rebates are used by large vendors of perishables and consumer durable goods. To receive such a rebate, the purchaser must agree to buy certain goods or services exclusively from a particular vendor for a fixed period of time. Rebating was a common pricing tactic in the 19th century, often used by large industrialists to undercut competition. The U.S. railroad industry practiced PRICE discrimination by granting secret rebates to important customers; the rebates granted to STANDARD OIL CO. helped it acquire a monopoly over the oil industry.

rebbe See RABBI

Récamier \rā-kȧm-ˈyā\, **Jeanne-Françoise-Julie-Adélaïde, dame (lady) de** *orig.* **Jeanne-Françoise-Julie-Adélaïde Bernard** *known as* **Madame de Récamier** (1777–1849) French hostess. Daughter of a prosperous banker, she married a wealthy banker and began to entertain widely. Her great charm and wit attracted to her salon most of the important political and literary figures of early 19th-century Paris, including many opponents of NAPOLEON, who exiled her in 1805. After Napoleon's defeat in 1815 she returned to Paris, where in her later years F.-A.-R. CHATEAUBRIAND became her companion and the central figure in her salon. Her friend GERMAINE DE STAEL created her literary portrait in the novel *Corinne*.

receivership In law, state of being in the hands of a receiver, a person appointed by the court to administer, conserve, rehabilitate, or liquidate the assets of an insolvent corporation for the protection or relief of creditors. It is a legal solution to a financial difficulty; it does not necessarily entail the termination of the corporate charter. See also BANKRUPTCY, INSOLVENCY.

Recent epoch See HOLOCENE EPOCH

recession Downward trend in the BUSINESS CYCLE characterized by a decline in production and employment, which in turn causes the incomes and spending of households to decline. Even though not all households and businesses experience actual declines in income, their expectations about the future become less certain and cause them to delay making large purchases or investments. Consumers buy fewer durable household goods, and businesses are less likely to purchase machinery and equipment and more likely to use up existing inventory instead of adding goods to their stock. This drop in demand leads to a corresponding fall in output and thus worsens the economic situation. Whether a recession develops into a severe and prolonged DEPRESSION depends on a number of circumstances. Among them are the extent and quality of CREDIT extended during the previous period of prosperity, the amount of speculation permitted, the ability of government MONETARY and FISCAL policies to reverse the downward trend, and the amount of excess productive capacity in existence. See also PANIC.

recessiveness Failure of one of a pair of genes (ALLELES) present in an individual to express itself in an observable manner because of the greater influence, or DOMINANCE, of its opposite-acting partner. Both alleles affect the same inherited characteristic, but the presence of the recessive gene cannot be determined by observation of the organism; that is, though present in the organism's GENOTYPE (gene makeup), the recessive trait is not evident in its PHENOTYPE (observable characteristics). The term recessive is applied both to the trait in the organism having the alleles of a gene pair in the recessive condition and to the allele whose effect can be masked by another allele of the same gene.

Recife \ri-ˈsē-fē\ *formerly* **Pernambuco** \ˌper-nəm-ˈbü-kü\ Seaport (pop., 1991 est.: 1,297,000), northeastern Brazil. Founded by the Portuguese in the first half of the 16th century, it was raided and sacked by British privateers in 1595. It was occupied by the Dutch 1630–54. It has been called the Venice of Brazil because it is crossed by waterways and its component parts are linked by numerous bridges. Situated at the confluence of the Capibaribe and Beberibe rivers, near Point Plata, the easternmost point of South America, it is one of the leading ports of Brazil, with extensive modern facilities. It is an educational and cultural center, with several universities and theaters.

reciprocity \ˌre-sə-ˈprä-sə-tē\ In international trade, the granting of mutual concessions on TARIFFS, QUOTAS, or other commercial restrictions. Reciprocity implies that these concessions are neither intended nor expected to be generalized to other countries with which the contracting parties have commercial treaties. Reciprocity agreements may be made between individual countries or groups of countries. Membership in the WORLD TRADE ORGANIZATION to some extent precludes the signing of reciprocity treaties because WTO nations are obliged to grant MOST-FAVORED-NATION TREATMENT to all other members.

recitative \ˌre-sə-tə-ˈtēv\ Style of accompanied solo singing that imitates the rhythms and tones of speech. Representing an attempt at an ideally expressive musical text setting, which the ancient Greeks were thought to have mastered, it came into existence in tandem with OPERA c. 1600, the first operas being largely written in recitative. Recitative style gradually began to separate from lyrical ARIA style. Regular alternation of recitative with aria became the rule for both opera and CANTATA, and recitative became essential to the dramatic ORATORIO as well. It remains basic to operatic composition; the presence of recitative (as opposed to spoken dialogue) most clearly distinguishes opera from the MUSICAL and related genres.

recognizance \ri-ˈkäg-nə-zənts\ In law, obligation entered into before a court or magistrate requiring the performance of an act (e.g., appearance in court), usually under penalty of a money forfeiture. The most common use of recognizance is in connection with BAIL in criminal cases. The accused may also be released on his or her "own recognizance" when no bail is required.

recombination In genetics, regrouping of the maternal and paternal GENES during the formation of sex cells (gametes). Recombination occurs randomly in nature as a normal event of MEIOSIS. It is enhanced by crossing-over (see LINKAGE GROUP). Recombination acts to ensure that no two daughter cells are identical, nor are any identical in genetic content to the parent cell. Laboratory study of recombination has contributed significantly to the understanding of genetic mechanisms, allowing scientists to map CHROMOSOMES, identify linkage groups, isolate the causes of certain genetic mistakes, and manipulate recombination itself by transplanting genes from one chromosome to another. See also GENETIC ENGINEERING, MOLECULAR BIOLOGY.

recompression chamber See HYPERBARIC CHAMBER

Reconstruction (1865–77) Period after the AMERICAN CIVIL WAR affecting former Confederate states. Problems associated with readmitting the 11 Southern states were confronted first by Pres. ABRAHAM LINCOLN, who planned to readmit states in which at least 10% of the voters had pledged loyalty to the Union. This lenient approach was opposed by the RADICAL REPUBLICANS, who passed the WADE-DAVIS BILL. Pres. ANDREW JOHNSON continued Lincoln's moderate policies, but enactment in the South of the BLACK CODES and demand in the North for stricter legislation resulted in the Reconstruction Acts of 1867. These established military districts in the South and required the Southern states' acceptance of the 14th and 15th Amendments to the Constitution to ensure the freedmen's civil rights. Southern resentment of the imposed government, which included Republicans, CARPETBAGGERS, and SCALAWAGS, and of the activities of the FREEDMEN'S BUREAU led to the formation of such terrorist groups as the KU KLUX KLAN and the Knights of the White Camelia. By the 1870s conservative Democrats again controlled most state governments in the South. While Reconstruction was often seen as a period of corruption, many constructive legal and educational reforms were introduced.

Reconstruction Finance Corporation (RFC) U.S. government agency established (1932) to provide loans to railroads, banks, and businesses. The RFC was an attempt by Pres. HERBERT HOOVER to counter the early effects of the GREAT DEPRESSION by rescuing institutions from default. It was widely used by Pres. FRANKLIN ROOSEVELT in the NEW DEAL and to finance defense plants in World War II. After the war, the RFC's powers and functions were gradually transferred to other agencies.

Reconstructionism Movement that originated in U.S. Judaism in the 1920s. It regards Judaism only as a specific human culture, rejects the tradition of a transcendent deity who made a COVENANT with his chosen people, and does not accept the BIBLE as the inspired word of God. Its principles, as enunciated by MORDECAI MENAHEM KAPLAN, are based on the belief that Jews can live a distinctively Jewish cultural life without being religiously observant. Reconstructionists today number about 60,000.

record player See PHONOGRAPH

recorder Cylindrical, usually wooden, wind instrument with finger-holes. As a fipple (duct) flute, its rather soft tones are produced by air blown against the sharp edge of an opening in the tube. The large recorder family includes instruments ranging from the sopranino to the contrabass. The recorder emerged in the 14th century and was widely used in ensembles and orchestras in the late Renaissance and throughout the Baroque era. Displaced by the transverse FLUTE, it was revived in the 20th century.

rectum End segment of the LARGE INTESTINE (see DIGESTION) in which FECES accumulate just prior to discharge. It is 5–6 in. (13–15 cm) long and lined with mucous membrane. One set of muscles separates it from the ANAL CANAL; another shortens it to expel feces. The rectal walls distend as feces enter, which stimulates the urge for DEFECATION.

recycling *or* **materials salvage** Recovery and reuse of materials from consumed products. The main motives for recycling have been the increasing scarcity and cost of natural resources (including oil, gas, coal, mineral ores, and trees) and the pollution of air (see AIR POLLUTION), water (see WATER POLLUTION), and land by waste materials. There are two types of recycling, internal and external. Internal recycling is the reuse in a manufacturing process of materials that are a waste product of that process, and is common in the metals industry (see SCRAP METAL). External recycling is the reclaiming of materials from a product that is worn out or no longer useful; an example is the collection of old newspapers and magazines for the manufacture of newsprint or other paper products.

Red Army Army of the Soviet Union. Formed in the aftermath of the RUSSIAN REVOLUTION OF 1917, its first civilian leader was LEON TROTSKY, who proved a brilliant strategist and administrator. Formed of workers and peasants, it initially lacked an officers' corps, and Trotsky was forced to mobilize officers of the former imperial army until a new, politically reliable corps could be trained. The COMMUNIST PARTY placed commissars in all army units to ensure political orthodoxy. JOSEPH STALIN purged the military leadership in 1937, leaving the army demoralized and unprepared for the German surprise attack in 1941. It had recovered enough by 1945 to be surpassed in strength only by the U.S. Army, with forces numbering over 11 million. In 1946 the word Red was dropped; in 1960 the commissars' duties were transferred to its officers.

Red Army Faction See BAADER-MEINHOF GANG

red blood cell See ERYTHROCYTE

Red Brigades *Italian* **Brigate Rosse** Extreme left-wing terrorist organization in Italy. Its self-proclaimed aim was to undermine the Italian state and pave the way for a Marxist upheaval led by a "revolutionary proletariat." Reputedly founded by Renato Curcio (born 1945), it began carrying out violent acts with firebombings (1970), escalating to kidnappings (1971) and murders (1974), most notably that of ALDO MORO (1978). At its height, it probably had 400–500 full-time members, perhaps 1,000 sporadic members, and a few thousand supporters. Arrest and imprisonment of many leaders and ordinary members greatly weakened the organization in the 1980s.

Red Cloud *orig.* **Mahpiua Luta** (1822–1909) American Indian leader. Born in present-day Nebraska, Red Cloud, as principal chief of the Oglala Teton Dakota (SIOUX), led the opposition of both Sioux and Cheyenne to the U.S. government's development of the Bozeman Trail to goldfields in Montana Territory (1865–67). Relentlessly attacking workers along the route from Fort Laramie (in modern Wyoming) to Montana, he refused offers to negotiate until the U.S. agreed to halt the project, whereupon he laid down his arms and allowed himself to be settled on the Red Cloud Agency in Nebraska.

Red Cross *officially* **International Movement of the Red Cross and Red Crescent** *formerly* **International Red Cross** Humanitarian agency with national affiliates worldwide. It was established for the care of victims of battle, but it now aids in the prevention and relief of human suffering generally. It arose out of the work of J.-H. DUNANT, who proposed the formation of voluntary relief societies in all countries, the first of which came into being in 1864. The name Red Crescent, adopted in 1906 at the insistence of the Ottoman empire, is used in Muslim countries. In peacetime, the Red Cross aids victims of natural disasters, maintains blood banks, and provides supplementary health-care services. In wartime, it serves as an intermediary between belligerents and visits prisoner-of-war camps to provide relief supplies, mail, and information for and from their relatives. Its operating principles are humanity, impartiality, and neutrality. Its headquarters are in Geneva. Individual national organizations run community programs and coordinate natural-disaster relief efforts. The American Red Cross was founded by CLARA BARTON in 1881 and first chartered by Congress in 1900; it runs the world's largest donor blood service. In 1901 Dunant received the first Nobel Peace Prize, and the Red Cross itself received the prize in 1917, 1944, and 1963.

red deer Species of DEER *(Cervus elaphus),* sometimes called ELK, native to Europe, Asia, and North Africa. It is found in woodlands and hunted for sport and food. Red deer live in sexually segregated herds except in the breeding season, when males (harts) fight for harems of females (hinds). Red deer stand about 4 ft (1.2 m) high at the shoulder. The coat is reddish brown, with lighter underparts and a light rump. The hart has long, regularly branched antlers bearing 10 or more tines. There are several endangered subspecies. See also WAPITI.

red elm See SLIPPERY ELM

Red Eyebrows Chinese peasant band that formed in response to the unrest and civil war following the floods and famines that accompanied disastrous changes in the course of the Huang (Yellow) River between AD 2 and 11. They painted their faces to look like demons, and their leader spoke through mediums. In AD 23 their forces overthrew WANG MANG, the usurper whose reign interrupted the HAN DYNASTY.

red-figure pottery Type of Greek POTTERY that flourished from the late 6th to the late 4th century BC. Developed in Athens c. 530 BC, the red-figure pottery quickly overtook the older BLACK-FIGURE POTTERY as the preferred style of vase painting. In red-figure technique, the background was painted black, and the outline details on the figures were also painted (rather than incised) in black, but the rest of each figure was unpainted and so retained the orange-red color of the natural vase. By comparison with incising, the painting of the details allowed more flexibility in rendering human form, movements, expressions, and perspective. Since most of the ornamentation was narrative, such technical advantages were of utmost importance.

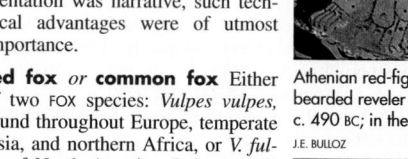

Athenian red-figure cup, detail of a bearded reveler by the Brygos Painter, c. 490 BC; in the Louvre, Paris.

J.E. BULLOZ

red fox *or* **common fox** Either of two FOX species: *Vulpes vulpes,* found throughout Europe, temperate Asia, and northern Africa, or *V. fulva* of North America. It has a reddish brown coat. The tail is white-tipped; the ears and legs are black. Red foxes are 36–42 in. (90–105 cm) long, including the 15-in. (38-cm) tail; stand about 16 in. (40 cm) tall; and weigh about 15 lbs (7 kg). They eat small mammals, eggs, fruit, and birds. They are hunted for sport and fur and are raised commercially for pelts. North American red foxes exhibit black and silver color phases.

Red Guards Radical university and high-school students formed into paramilitary units of the Chinese CULTURAL REVOLUTION. They responded in 1966 to MAO ZEDONG's call to revitalize the revolutionary spirit of the Chinese Communist Party and went so far as to attempt purging the country of its pre-Communist culture. With a membership in the millions, they attacked and persecuted local party leaders, schoolteachers, and other intellectuals. By early 1967 they had overthrown party authorities in many localities. Internal strife ensued as units argued over which best represented MAOIST thought. Their disruptions of industrial production and urban life led the government to redirect them to the countryside in 1968, where the movement gradually subsided.

Red River *Chinese* **Yuan Chiang** \'ywän-'jyäŋ\ *Vietnamese* **Song Hong** \'sòŋ-'hòŋ\ River, Southeast Asia. It rises in central YUNNAN province, southern China, and flows southeast across northern Vietnam, past HANOI, into the Gulf of TONKIN. The principal river of northern Vietnam, it is about 500 mi (805 km) long and has a wide, fertile delta east of Hanoi.

Red River River, southern central U.S. It rises in the high plains of eastern New Mexico and flows southeast across Texas and Louisiana to a point northwest of Baton Rouge, where it enters the ATCHAFALAYA RIVER. It is 1,290 mi (2,080 km) long and forms part of the Texas–Oklahoma and Texas–Arkansas borders. In Texas it was the site of the RED RIVER INDIAN WAR (1874).

Red River Indian War (1874–75) Uprising of Indian warriors from reservation tribes (ARAPAHO, CHEYENNE, COMANCHE, KIOWA, and Kataka). After settlement of southwestern tribes on reservations in Oklahoma and Texas (1867), discontented braves broke out repeatedly to raid white travelers and settlers. An attack in 1874 killed 60 Texans. Federal troops under WILLIAM T. SHERMAN converged on Indians concentrated in the Red

O P Q R

River valley of Texas. Indian resistance forced 14 pitched battles with U.S. troops before the Indians' eventual surrender and return to the reservations.

Red River of the North River, northern U.S. and southern Manitoba. It flows north, forming the Minnesota–North Dakota boundary, before entering Manitoba and emptying into Lake Winnipeg after a course of 545 mi (877 km). After it was explored 1732–33, the river, named after the reddish-brown silt it carries, was a transportation link between Lake Winnipeg and the Mississippi River system. The Red River Settlement, an agricultural colony, was founded in 1811 near Winnipeg. Its fertile valley produces cereals, potatoes, and sugar beets, and supports cattle raising.

red salmon See sockeye salmon

Red Sea Narrow inland sea between the Arabian Peninsula and North Africa. It extends southeast from Suez, Egypt, for about 1,200 mi (1,930 km) to the Bab el-Mandeb Strait, which connects with the Gulf of Aden and then with the Arabian Sea. It separates the coasts of Egypt, the Sudan, and Eritrea from those of Saudi Arabia and Yemen. It contains some of the world's warmest and saltiest seawater. With its connection to the Mediterranean Sea via the Suez Canal, it is one of the most heavily traveled waterways in the world, carrying traffic between Europe and Asia. Its name is derived from the color changes observed in its waters.

red shift Displacement of the spectrum of an astronomical object toward longer wavelengths (visible light shifts toward the red end of the spectrum). In 1929 Edwin Hubble reported that distant galaxies had red shifts proportionate to their distances (see Hubble's constant). Since red shifts can be caused by motion of an object away from the observer (the Doppler effect), Hubble concluded that galaxies are receding from the Milky Way. This became the cornerstone of theories of an expanding universe. In modern cosmological theories, the red shift is understood to arise from stretching of the photon's wavelength as it travels through expanding space.

red soil Any of a group of soils that develop in a warm, temperate, moist climate under deciduous or mixed forests and that have thin organic and organic-mineral layers overlying a yellowish-brown leached layer resting on an illuvial (see illuviation) red layer. Red soils generally form from iron-rich sedimentary rock. They are usually poor growing soils, low in nutrients and humus and difficult to cultivate.

red spider See spider mite

Red Square Open square, central Moscow. It lies north of the Moskva River and covers almost 800,000 sq ft (73,000 sq mi). Dating from the late 15th century, it has long been a busy market area as well as a focal point in Russian history, the scene of executions, demonstrations, riots, and parades. Located around it are the State Historical Museum (1875–81), the eight-towered St. Basil's Cathedral (1555–60), the former state department store GUM, and Lenin's tomb.

red tide Discoloration of seawater caused by dinoflagellates during periodic blooms (population increases). Toxic substances released by these organisms into the water may be lethal to fish and other marine life, and they irritate the human respiratory system. Coastal resorts sometimes close when breaking waves release the toxic substances into the air. The causes of red tide are uncertain; it may require the confluence of several natural phenomena, in which human influence may or may not play a part.

Red Turbans Peasant rebel movement that flourished in northern China at the end of the Yuan dynasty (1206–1368). The Red Turbans, whose leader was regarded as an incarnation of the bodhisattva Maitreya, were opposed to alien Mongol rule; their movement gained momentum from the famine that resulted from crop failures and floods in the 1330s. Their marauding, which began in the 1350s, took them as far as Korea, where their incursions contributed to the downfall of the Koryo dynasty. Though their rebellion was put down, rival rebel forces under Zhu Yuanzhang (1328–1398) toppled the Yuan dynasty and founded the Ming. See also Hongwu emperor.

redbird See cardinal

redbud Any of the shrubs or small trees that make up the genus *Cercis* (family Leguminosae), native to North America, southern Europe, and Asia, and widely planted for their showy early-spring flowers and interesting branch patterns. Clusters of small, purplish-pink flowers appear on old stems and branches before the leaves unfurl. The heart-shaped to roundish leaves quickly turn from bronzy to bright green, then to yellow in fall. The eastern redbud *(C. canadensis)* is the hardiest species.

Eastern redbud (*Cercis canadensis*).
KENNETH & BRENDA FORMANEK-EB INC.

redfish *or* **rosefish** *or* **ocean perch** Commercially important food fish *(Sebastes marinus)* of the scorpion fish family (Scorpaenidae), found in the Atlantic along European and North American coasts. It has a large mouth, large eyes, and spines on its head and cheeks. It grows to about 40 in. (1 m) long. Related species include *S. owstoni,* a food fish of the Orient, and the Norway haddock *(S. viviparus)* of Europe. Both are red and grow to about 10 in. (25 cm) long.

Redford, (Charles) Robert (born 1937) U.S. film actor and director. Born in Santa Monica, Cal., he made his Broadway debut in 1959 and won acclaim in *Barefoot in the Park* (1963; film, 1967). The blond, appealing Redford began acting in films in the mid-1960s, appearing with Paul Newman in the hits *Butch Cassidy and the Sundance Kid* (1969) and *The Sting* (1973), and also starring in *The Candidate* (1972), *Jeremiah Johnson* (1972), *The Natural* (1984), *All the President's Men* (1976), *Out of Africa* (1985), and *Indecent Proposal* (1993). His directorial debut, *Ordinary People* (1980, Academy Award), was followed by *The Milagro Beanfield War* (1988), *A River Runs Through It* (1992), *Quiz Show* (1994), and *The Horse Whisperer* (1998). In 1980 he founded the Sundance Institute to sponsor young filmmakers' works, and by the 1990s its film festival was the major showcase for U.S. independent films.

Redgrave, Michael (Scudamore) *later* **Sir Michael** (1908–1985) British actor. He made his stage debut in 1934 and acted with the Old Vic and the National Theatre in classic roles from Shakespeare, Ibsen, and Chekhov and in such modern works as *Family Reunion* (1939) and *Tiger at the Gate* (1955). Noted for his refined good looks and expressive voice, he began his film career in *The Lady Vanishes* (1938) and continued with roles in *Dead of Night* (1945), *Mourning Becomes Electra* (1947), and *The Browning Version* (1951).

Redgrave, Vanessa (born 1937) British actress. The daughter of Michael Redgrave, she made her London stage debut in 1958 and won praise as Rosalind in *As You Like It* (1961). Her performances in such movies as *Morgan!* (1966), *Blow-Up* (1966), *Camelot* (1967), *Isadora* (1968), *Mary, Queen of Scots* (1971), and *Julia* (1977, Academy Award) won her critical adulation, and she was acclaimed as one of the world's greatest actresses. Though criticized for her left-wing political activism, especially on behalf of Palestinians, she continued to win acclaim for her work on stage and screen. Her later films included *The Bostonians* (1984), *Howards End* (1992), and *Mrs. Dalloway* (1998). Her sister Lynn (born 1943) has had a distinguished stage career in London and New York, much of it in the classical repertory. Highlights of her film career include her performances in *Georgy Girl* (1966), *Shine* (1996), and *Gods and Monsters* (1998).

Redi \'re-dē\, **Francesco** (1626–1697) Italian physician and poet. While working as physician to the dukes of Tuscany, he demonstrated in 1668, in one of the first biological experiments with proper controls, that the presence of maggots in rotting meat does not result from spontaneous generation. Redi set up a series of flasks containing different meats; half were sealed, half open. He repeated the experiment, replacing the sealed flasks with gauze-covered flasks. Though the meat in all the flasks rotted, Redi found that only in the uncovered flasks, which flies had entered freely, did the meat contain maggots. As a poet, he is known chiefly for his *Bacco in Toscana* (1685).

Redon \rə-'dō^{n}\, **Odilon** (1840–1916) French painter, lithographer, and etcher. He studied under J.-L. Gérome and learned lithography under Henri Fantin-Latour. He came to be associated with the Symbolist painters (see Symbolism). His oils and pastels, chiefly still lifes with flowers, won him admiration as a colorist from HENRI MATISSE and other painters. His prints (nearly 200 in all), which explore fantastic, often macabre themes, foreshadowed Surrealism and Dada.

Redon, self-portrait, 1904; in a private collection.
ARCHIVES PHOTOGRAPHIQUES, PARIS

Redouté \rə-dü-'tā\, **Pierre Joseph** (1759–1840) French botanical painter. Born in Belgium, he became a favored artist at the court of France, patronized by kings from LOUIS XVI to LOUIS-PHILIPPE. His delicate botanical prints were not only framed as pictures but also used for china. His *Les Liliacées* (1802–15) contained 500 plates of lilies. However, roses became his specialty; *Les Roses* (1817–21) is considered his finest series, and its classic images are still widely reproduced.

redox See OXIDATION-REDUCTION

redstart Any of about 11 species of Old World chat-thrush (see CHAT) in the genus *Phoenicurus* (family Turdidae) or about 12 New World species of WOOD WARBLER (family Parulidae) of similar appearance and behavior. Old World redstarts have a red tail, which they constantly flit or shiver. They are about 6 in. (14 cm) long. The male common redstart *(P. phoenicurus)* is gray, with a black face and throat and reddish breast. New World redstarts (genera *Setophaga* and *Myioborus*) are usually strikingly marked with black, white, and red.

Common, or American, redstart (*Setophaga ruticilla*).
HAL H. HARRISON FROM GRANT HEILMAN

reduction Any of a class of CHEMICAL REACTIONS in which the number of ELECTRONS associated with an ATOM or group of atoms is increased. The electrons taken up by the substance reduced are supplied by another substance, often hydrogen (H_2) which is thereby oxidized. See also OXIDATION-REDUCTION.

reduction division See MEIOSIS

redwood *or* **sequoia** Coniferous evergreen timber tree *(Sequoia sempervirens)* of the family Taxodiaceae, found in the fog belt of the coastal range from southwestern Oregon to central California at elevations up to 3,300 ft (1,000 m). The genus name commemorates the Cherokee Indian SEQUOYAH. The redwood is sometimes called coast redwood to distinguish it from the Sierra redwood (or BIG TREE) and the Japanese redwood (or Japanese cedar). Redwoods are the tallest living trees, often exceeding 300 ft (90 m) in height; one has reached 368 ft (112 m). Typical trunk diameters are 10–20 ft (3–6 m) or more. The redwood tree takes 400–500 years to reach maturity; some are known to be more than 1,500 years old. As the tree ages, the lower limbs fall away, leaving a clear, columnar trunk. Redwood timber has been used in carpentry, for furniture, shingles, fence posts, and paneling, and for fine wood objects. Today many of the remaining redwood stands are protected (see REDWOOD NATIONAL PARK, SEQUOIA NATIONAL PARK). See also DAWN REDWOOD.

Redwood National Park National park, northwestern corner of California. Established in 1968, and with a boundary change in 1978, it preserves virgin groves of ancient redwood trees, including the world's tallest at 367.8 ft (112.1 m) high. It also includes 40 mi (65 km) of scenic Pacific coastline. It covers an area of 172 sq mi (445 sq km), including land in three state parks.

reed In botany, any of several species of large aquatic GRASSES, especially the four species in the genus *Phragmites* (family Poaceae, or Gramineae). The common, or water, reed *(P. australis)* occurs along the margins of lakes, fens, marshes, and streams from the Arctic to the tropics. It is a broad-leaved grass, about 5–15 ft (1.5–5 m) tall, with feathery flower clusters and stiff, smooth stems. Bur reed (genus *Sparganium*) and reed mace (genus *Typha*) are plants of other families. Dried reed stems have been used for millennia as thatching and construction material, in basketry, for arrows and pens, and in musical instruments (see REED INSTRUMENTS).

Reed, Carol *later* **Sir Carol** (1906–1976) British film director. He made his stage debut as an actor in 1924 and as a director in 1927, staging EDGAR WALLACE's detective thrillers. He began directing films in 1935, winning praise for *The Stars Look Down* (1939), *Night Train* (1940), and the wartime semidocumentary *The True Glory* (1945). His greatest successes included the thrillers *Odd Man Out* (1947), *The Fallen Idol* (1948), and the classic *The Third Man* (1949). His later films include *The Key* (1958), *Our Man in Havana* (1959), and *Oliver!* (1968, Academy Award).

Reed, John (1887–1920) U.S. journalist. Born to a wealthy family in Portland, Ore., he attended Harvard University and began writing for the radical socialist journal *The Masses* in 1913. He covered the revolutionary fighting in Mexico (1914) and was frequently arrested for leading labor strikes. A war correspondent during World War I, he became a close friend of VLADIMIR ILICH LENIN and witnessed the RUSSIAN REVOLUTION OF 1917, described in his book *Ten Days That Shook the World* (1919). He became head of the U.S. Communist Labor Party; indicted for sedition, he escaped to the Soviet Union, where he died of typhus and was buried beside the Kremlin wall.

Reed, Thomas B(rackett) (1839–1902) U.S. politician. Born in Portland, Me., he served in the U.S. House of Representatives 1877–99. As speaker of the House (1889–91, 1895–99) he introduced procedural changes that strengthened legislative control by the majority party and increased the power of the speaker and the rules committee. The Reed Rules were attacked by opponents, who called Reed "Czar Reed" for his vigorous promotion of their passage. Ten years later the speaker's powers were reduced.

Reed, Walter (1851–1902) U.S. pathologist and bacteriologist. Born in Belroi, Va., he received a medical degree at 18 from the University of Virginia and entered the Army Medical Corps in 1875. He investigated the spread of TYPHOID fever in military camps during the Spanish-American War and was later curator of the Army Medical Museum in Washington, D.C. Yellow fever was believed to be spread by bedding and other articles, but CARLOS FINLAY had theorized in 1886 that it was carried by insects, and Reed's team ruled out a bacterium suspected as the cause and found patterns of spread that supported the insect theory. Controlled experiments proved transmission by mosquito bite, and in 1901 efforts to combat an outbreak in Havana succeeded within 90 days.

Walter Reed.
THE BETTMANN ARCHIVE

Reed, Willis (born 1942) U.S. basketball player. Born in Hico, La., he averaged 19.5 points in his rookie year and was named Rookie of the Year. Playing for the New York Knicks (1964–74), in 1970 he became the only player ever to win the Most Valuable Player award for the regular season, the championships, and the All-Star game. After retiring he coached the Knicks (1977–79) and other teams.

Reed College Private liberal-arts college in Portland, Ore. Founded in 1909, it is named after Simeon Reed, a prosperous Portland businessman. It offers undergraduate programs in the physical and biological sciences, the humanities, and the social sciences. Its curriculum emphasizes both traditional academic courses and independent learning. Enrollment is about 1,300.

reed instruments Any wind instrument whose sound results from air that causes a thin blade, or reed, of cane or metal to vibrate, thereby setting up a sound wave in an enclosed air column or in the open air. Reed pipes have single or double reeds. A single reed may hit against a frame (beating reeds), as in the CLARINET or SAXOPHONE, or may vibrate freely through a closely fitting frame (free reeds), as in a HARMONICA or ACCORDION. Beating reeds in WOODWIND INSTRUMENTS depend on the pipe's sounding length (as determined by the fingering) to determine the pitch. Free reeds have their own single pitch, determined by their thickness and length. A double reed, as in the OBOE or BASSOON, consists of two cane blades tied together that beat against each other. See also ENGLISH HORN, SHAWM.

reed organ See HARMONIUM

Reeds, Plain of *Vietnamese* **Dong Thap Muoi** \'dȯŋ-'täp-'mwȯi\ Low, swampy region, a northwestern extension of the MEKONG RIVER delta, southern Vietnam and eastern Cambodia. It has been partially reclaimed by a levee and drainage system.

reef, coral See CORAL REEF

Refah Party \re-'fä\ *or* **Welfare Party** Turkish religious political party founded by NECMETTIN ERBAKAN in 1983. After doing well in local elections in the early 1990s, it won the most seats (29%) in the 1995 national legislative elections, becoming the first religious party in Turkey to win a general election. It took office in 1996 at the head of a new coalition after a center-right coalition formed to oppose it collapsed after a few months. The liberal foreign policies it favored were tempered by warnings from the conservative military.

reference frame *or* **frame of reference** Coordinate system that allows description of time and position of points relative to a body. The axes, or lines, emanate from a position called the origin. As a point moves, its VELOCITY can be described in terms of changes in displacement and direction. Reference frames are chosen arbitrarily. For example, if a person is sitting in a moving train, the description of the person's motion depends on the chosen frame of reference. If the frame of reference is the train, the person is considered to be not moving relative to the train; if the frame of reference is the earth, the person is moving relative to the earth.

referendum and initiative Electoral devices by which voters may express their wishes regarding government policy or proposed legislation. Optional referenda are put on the ballot when a sufficient number of voters sign a PETITION demanding that a law passed by the legislature be ratified by the people. Obligatory referenda are those required by law; voluntary referenda are submitted by the legislature to voters to decide an issue or test public opinion. Initiatives are used to invoke a popular vote on a proposed law or constitutional amendment. Direct initiatives are submitted by a required number of voters directly to the public for a vote; indirect initiatives are submitted to the legislature for a vote. Referenda and initiatives are most commonly used in the U.S. and Switzerland. See also PLEBISCITE.

referential opacity See INTENTIONALITY

reflection Change in the direction of propagation of a WAVE that strikes a boundary between different media through which it cannot pass. When a wave strikes such a boundary it bounces back, or is reflected, just as a ball bounces off the floor. The angle of incidence is the angle between the path of the wave and a line perpendicular to the boundary. The angle of reflection is the angle between the same line and the path of the reflected wave. All reflected waves obey the law of reflection, which states that the angle of reflection is equal to the angle of incidence. The reflectivity of a material is the fraction of energy of the oncoming wave that is reflected by it.

reflex In biology, an automatic and inborn response to a stimulus that involves a nerve impulse passing from a sensory nerve cell to a muscle or gland without reaching the level of consciousness. Simple reflexes include sucking, swallowing, blinking, scratching, and the knee jerk. Most reflexes consist of complex patterns of many unconsciously coordinated muscular actions that form the basis of much instinctive behavior in animals. Examples include walking, standing, the cat's righting reflex, and basic sexual acts.

Reform Bill of 1832 British parliamentary act that expanded the electorate. It transferred voting privileges from the small rural boroughs controlled by the nobility and gentry to the heavily populated but underrepresented industrial towns. Conceived by Prime Minister EARL GREY and introduced by EARL RUSSELL, it passed in the House of Commons three times but was opposed by the House of Lords until Grey's threat to create 50 new liberal peers (enough to carry the bill) finally brought their agreement. The act redistributed seats in the Commons and lowered the electoral qualifications to allow voting by small property owners (much of the middle class).

Reform Bill of 1867 British parliamentary act that extended the vote to many workingmen in the towns and cities, creating a major working-class constituency for the first time. It was largely conceived by BENJAMIN DISRAELI, who hoped to expand his base of potential supporters.

Reform Bill of 1884–85 British parliamentary act that gave the vote to agricultural workers. In 1885 the Redistribution Act equalized representation on the basis of 50,000 voters for each member of parliament. Together the two acts tripled the electorate and prepared the way for universal male suffrage.

Reform Judaism Religious movement that has modified or abandoned many traditional Jewish beliefs and practices in an effort to adapt Judaism to the modern world. It originated in Germany in 1809 and spread to the U.S. in the 1840s under the leadership of Rabbi ISAAC MAYER WISE. Reform Judaism permits men and women to sit together in the synagogue, incorporates choir and organ music in the service, holds a confirmation ceremony for girls parallel to the boys' BAR MITZVAH, and does not observe daily public worship, strict dietary laws, or the restriction of normal activities on the SABBATH. Its principles, initially enunciated in the PITTSBURGH PLATFORM (1885), were revised in the COLUMBUS PLATFORM (1937) to support traditional customs and ceremonies and the liturgical use of Hebrew. The Reform movement continues to move toward ORTHODOX JUDAISM without embracing all its strictures.

Reform Party Political movement in Canada in the 1830s and '40s. Reformers in Upper Canada (later Ontario) led by ROBERT BALDWIN urged that provincial governments be made accountable to elected legislative assemblies ("responsible government"). An extremist group led by WILLIAM L. MACKENZIE opposed the government in the rebellion of 1837. Reformers in Lower Canada (later Quebec) joined LOUIS PAPINEAU and his Patriote Party. Reform Party candidates were elected premier (1842–43, 1848–54) in the province of Canada (union of Upper and Lower Canada). In the 1850s the party split between a moderate group, which allied with JOHN MACDONALD'S PROGRESSIVE-CONSERVATIVE PARTY, and a radical faction, the CLEAR GRITS, from which the LIBERAL PARTY emerged.

Reforma, La Liberal political and social revolution in Mexico (1854–76) under the principal leadership of BENITO JUAREZ. It began with the removal of the dictator ANTONIO SANTA ANNA and went on to abolish special privileges of the church and the military, confiscate church lands, suppress monasteries, institute civil marriage, establish a liberal federalist constitution, and place the army under civilian control. Confiscated church property was to be allocated to the landless, but this policy proved to be La Reforma's outstanding failure, as the number and wealth of large landholders instead increased. La Reforma came to a close when PORFIRIO DIAZ seized power in 1876.

Reformation *or* **Protestant Reformation** Break with ROMAN CATHOLICISM and the establishment of Protestant churches in the 16th century. Though reformers such as JAN HUS and JOHN WYCLIFFE attacked abuses in the Roman Catholic church in the late medieval period, the Reformation is usually dated from 1517, when MARTIN LUTHER posted his NINETY-FIVE THESES on the church door in Wittenberg. Various Protestant denominations were soon founded by more radical reformers, such as HULDRYCH ZWINGLI and the ANABAPTISTS. JOHN CALVIN established a theocracy in Geneva after his conversion to the Protestant cause. The Reformation spread to other European countries and soon dominated northern Europe. Spain and Italy remained resistant to Protestantism and became centers of the COUNTER-REFORMATION. In England, where HENRY VIII founded the Church of ENGLAND in 1534, the Reformation's roots were primarily political rather than religious, motivated by the pope's refusal to grant Henry a divorce. In Scotland, the Calvinist JOHN KNOX led in the establishment of the Presbyterian church (see PRESBYTERIANISM).

Reformed church Any of several Protestant groups strongly influenced by CALVINISM. They are often called by national names (Swiss Reformed, Dutch Reformed, etc.). The name was originally used by all the Protestant churches that arose out of the 16th-century REFORMATION, but was later confined to the Calvinistic churches of continental Europe, most of which use a Presbyterian form of church government. The Calvinistic churches of the British Isles became known as Presbyterian churches (see PRESBYTERIANISM).

refraction Change in direction of a WAVE as it leaves one medium and enters another. Waves, such as sound and light waves, travel at different speeds in different media. When a wave enters a new medium at an angle of less than 90°, the change in speed occurs sooner on one side of the wave than on the other, causing the wave to bend, or refract. When water waves approach shallower water at an angle, they bend and become parallel to the shore. Refraction explains the apparent bending of a pencil when it is partly immersed in water and viewed from above the surface. It also causes the optical illusion of the MIRAGE.

refractory Material that is not deformed or damaged by high temperatures, used to make CRUCIBLES, incinerators, insulation, and furnaces, particularly metallurgical furnaces. Refractories are produced in several forms: molded bricks of various shapes, bulk granular materials, plastic mixtures consisting of moistened aggregates that are rammed into place, castables composed of dry aggregates and a binder that can be mixed with water and poured like concrete, and mortars and cements for laying brickwork.

refrigeration Process of removing HEAT from an enclosed space or from a substance in order to lower the temperature. In industrialized nations and prosperous regions in the developing world, refrigeration is used chiefly to store foodstuffs at low temperatures, thus inhibiting the destructive action of bacteria, yeasts, and molds. Many perishable products can be frozen, permitting them to be kept for months and even years with little loss in nutrition or flavor or change in appearance. See also AIR-CONDITIONING, COOLING SYSTEM, HEAT EXCHANGER.

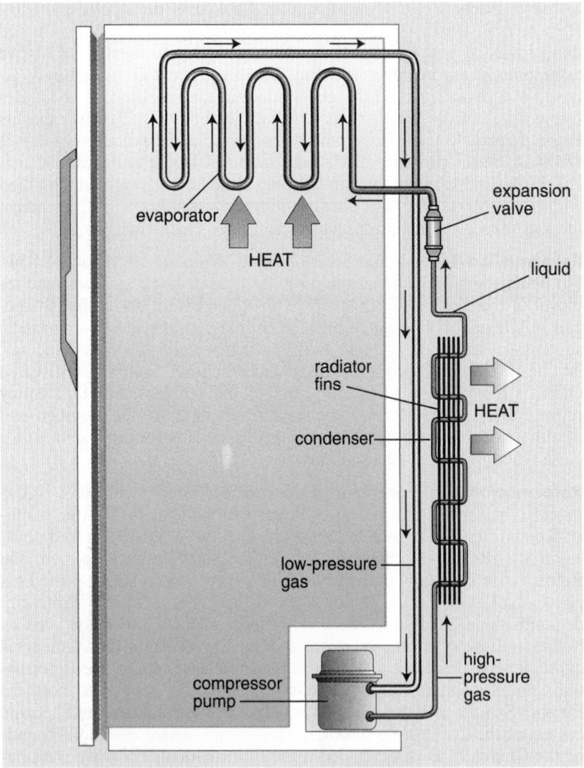

Components of a refrigerator. A compressor pressurizes the refrigerant gas, heating it and forcing it through the system. The gas cools and liquefies in the condenser, giving up its heat to the outside air. The liquid's temperature and pressure are lowered when it passes through an expansion valve. The cold liquid passes into the evaporator coils, where heat drawn from the warmer refrigerator compartment causes it to vaporize. The gas is then returned to the compressor to repeat the cycle.

refugee Person involuntarily displaced from his or her homeland. Until the late 19th century and the emergence of fixed and closed national boundaries, waves of refugees were always absorbed by neighboring countries. Immigration restrictions and increasing numbers of refugees necessitated special action to aid them. In 1921 FRIDTJOF NANSEN created a League of Nations Passport to allow refugees to move freely across national boundaries. Refugee status at that time was accorded to migrants only if their departure was involuntary and asylum was sought in another country. In 1938 its definition was expanded to include a fear of persecution because of ethnicity, religion, nationality, group membership, or political opinion. Later the criteria were expanded again to include flight from home within one's own country. Refugee status ends when the migrant is either resettled or returns home. Today most of the world's refugees (over 5 million) are in Africa, though conflict in the former Yugoslavia and elsewhere in post–Cold War Europe have also significantly increased the number of refugees. See also INTERNATIONAL REFUGEE ORGANIZATION, Office of the UNITED NATIONS HIGH COMMISSIONER FOR REFUGEES, UNITED NATIONS RELIEF AND REHABILITATION ADMINISTRATION.

Refusés, Salon des See SALON DES REFUSÉS

Régence style \rā-ˈzhäⁿs\ French style in the decorative arts that developed c. 1710–1730, when Philippe II, duc d'Orléans, was regent of France. It marks the transition from the massive rectilinear forms of furniture in the LOUIS XIV STYLE to the ROCOCO forms of LOUIS XV STYLE. In reaction against the pomposity of Louis XIV's court, smaller, more intimate rooms replaced formal state apartments and called for a more graceful style. The delicately styled Régence furniture replaced heavy, carved ornamentation with flat, curving motifs, often foliage and bouquets framed by flowing ribbons and bows. Walnut, rosewood, and mahogany supplied rich but tasteful contrasts in veneering. Intricate tracery in brass and tortoiseshell marquetry on ebony was adapted to the new taste. The commode and writing table were introduced during this period.

Regency style Style in the decorative arts and architecture produced in England during the regency (1811–20) and reign (1820–30) of GEORGE IV. Designers borrowed both structural and ornamental elements from Greek and Roman antiquity. Egyptian motifs, inspired by Napoleon's Egyptian campaign of 1798, became part of the Regency fashion. A resurgence of a taste for chinoiserie is seen in imitation bamboo and in "japanned" lacquerwork. The prince's taste for French furniture popularized pieces ornamented with brass marquetry in the French style. Ornamentation relied on rich contrasts of exotic wood veneers and application of metal or painting rather than extensive carving.

Regents of the University of California v. Bakke \ˈba-kē\ U.S. Supreme Court decision (1978) that ruled unconstitutional the use of fixed quotas for minority applicants at professional schools. At issue was a state medical school's AFFIRMATIVE-ACTION program that, because it required a certain number of minority admissions, twice denied entrance to a qualified white candidate (Allan Bakke). The Court concluded that schools "may take race into account" in making admissions decisions, but that fixed quotas violate the EQUAL-PROTECTION clause of the U.S. Constitution.

Reger \ˈrā-gər\, **(Johann Baptist Joseph) Max(imilian)** (1873–1916) German composer and organist. The local organist secretly sent some of his compositions to Hugo Riemann (1849–1919), who took Reger on as his student and assistant. He became a prolific composer of songs, piano pieces, and especially organ music. His music, combining progressive and conservative elements and often highly chromatic, has always been more popular in Germany than elsewhere.

reggae \ˈre-gā\ Jamaican popular music and dance style. It originated in the mid-1960s as a music of the Jamaican poor, reflecting social discontent and the RASTAFARIAN movement. Its instrumentation features an electric bass played at high volume as a lead instrument, around which an ensemble of organ, piano, drums, and lead and rhythm electric guitars plays short ostinato phrases with regular accents on the offbeats. Reggae was popularized in the U.S. by the film *The Harder They Come* (1973), starring the singer Jimmy Cliff, and through tours by B. MARLEY and the Wailers and by Toots (Hibbert) and the Maytals, whose influence was felt among white rock musicians.

Reggio di Calabria \ˈred-jō-dē-kä-ˈlä-brē-ə\ *ancient* **Rhegium.** City (metro. area pop., 1996 est.: 180,000), former capital of the CALABRIA region, southern Italy, on the Strait of MESSINA. Founded as a Greek colony at the end of the 8th century BC, it was allied with Athens in the 5th century BC and with Rome c. 280 BC. From the 5th century AD it was ruled successively by the Visigoths, Ostrogoths, Byzantines, and Arabs. It was conquered by the Normans under ROBERT GUISCARD c. 1060 and became part of the kingdom of the Two SICILIES. Destroyed many times by Saracen invaders and by earthquakes, it has been repeatedly rebuilt. It is a tourist resort and seaport that exports dried herbs and essential oils for the perfume and pharmaceutical industries.

regiment In most armies, a body of troops headed by a colonel and divided into companies, BATTALIONS, or squadrons. French CAVALRY units were called regiments as early as 1558. In early U.S. service, as in European armies up to that time, the usual number of companies in a regiment was 10. Early in the 19th century, NAPOLEON divided the regiments of the French army into three battalions each, and in 1901 the U.S. Army adopted the three-battalion INFANTRY regimental system.

Regina \ri-ˈjī-nə\ City (pop., 1991: 179,000), capital of Saskatchewan. It is located on Wascana Creek, in the southern central part of the province. It originated as a hunters' camp and was known as Pile O'Bones for the heaps of bones left there after skinning and cutting buffalo. It was the administrative headquarters of the Northwest Territories 1882–1905, then became the provincial capital. It was the headquarters of the ROYAL CANADIAN MOUNTED POLICE until 1920. After World War II it expanded rapidly to become an important transportation, manufacturing, and distributing center for a vast agricultural area. Local mineral resources and fertile prairies support an economy based largely on oil, natural gas, potash refining, and food processing.

regional development program Any government program designed to encourage the industrial and economic development of regions depressed or plagued by high unemployment. Most industrialized countries have adopted some type of regional development program since World War II. The most common method of encouraging development is to offer grants, loans, and loan guarantees to companies relocating or expanding in the region. France, for example, has offered SUBSIDIES related to the amount of investment and the number of new jobs created, as well as loans, interest subsidies, and free land sites. Area development plans in Britain, Germany, Japan, The Netherlands, and the U.S. have also extended loan assistance. Tax incentives are also used to encourage companies to invest in depressed areas. The government may also offer low-cost housing for workers and assistance in developing power, light, transportation, and sanitation facilities. See also DEVELOPMENT BANK.

regression In statistics, a process for determining a line or curve that best represents the general trend of a data set. Linear regression results in a line of best fit, for which the sum of the squares of the vertical distances between the proposed line and the points of the data set are minimized (see LEAST SQUARES METHOD). Other types of regression may be based on higher-degree POLYNOMIAL functions or EXPONENTIAL FUNCTIONS. A quadratic regression, for example, uses a quadratic function (second-degree polynomial function) to produce a PARABOLA of best fit.

regressive tax Tax levied at a rate that decreases as its base increases. Regressivity is considered undesirable because poorer people pay a greater percentage of their income in tax than wealthier people. CONSUMPTION TAXES and SALES TAXES are usually considered regressive because of their set rate structures. Tobacco, gasoline, and liquor sales taxes, all major sources of tax revenue, are the most regressive taxes. In an effort to limit regressivity, a number of U.S. states have exempted medicine and grocery items from sales tax. PROPERTY TAX is often judged regressive because poorer people spend a larger percentage of their income on housing than wealthier people. See also PROGRESSIVE TAX.

regular polyhedron Geometric solid all of whose faces are identical regular POLYGONS and all of whose angles are equal. There are only five such POLYHEDRONS. The cube is constructed from the square, the dodecahedron from the regular pentagon, and the tetrahedron, octahedron, and icosahedron (with 20 faces) from the equilateral triangle. Though described by EUCLID, they are often called the Platonic solids because of PLATO's attempt to relate each to one of the five elements of which the world was then believed to be made.

Regulators of North Carolina (1764–71) Vigilance group formed in the western frontier counties of North Carolina. Opposed to the high taxes and corruption imposed by the colonial government, the group sought vainly to obtain reforms, then refused to pay taxes, agitated against public officials, and committed acts of violence. Gov. William Tryon sent troops to crush the insurrection at the Battle of Alamance (1771). The leaders were hanged for treason and many followers fled to Tennessee, where they sided with the Loyalists in the American Revolution.

regulatory agency Independent government commission charged by the legislature with setting and enforcing standards for specific industries in the private sector. The concept was invented by the U.S. government in 1887, and regulatory agencies exist almost exclusively in the U.S. The theory is that a commission of experts on the industry being regulated is better equipped to regulate it than the legislature or executive departments. Designed to operate with a minimum of executive or legislative supervision, agencies have executive, legislative, and judicial functions, and their regulations have the force of law. Important regulatory agencies include the FOOD AND DRUG ADMINISTRATION, OSHA, the FEDERAL COMMUNICATIONS COMMISSION, and the SECURITIES AND EXCHANGE COMMISSION.

Rehnquist \ˈren-ˌkwist\, **William H(ubbs)** (born 1924) U.S. jurist. Born in Milwaukee, he received his law degree from Stanford University and served as clerk to ROBERT JACKSON. He later practiced law in Phoenix (1953–69), where he became active in the conservative wing of the Republican Party. At the U.S. Justice Department (1969–71), he opposed civil-rights legislation and advocated greatly enlarged police powers. He was nominated for the Supreme Court by Pres. RICHARD NIXON in 1972; his highly conservative views and polished opinions prompted Pres. RONALD REAGAN to name him chief justice (1986). He has led the Court along a conservative path, while administratively working to reduce its caseload. He presided over the U.S. Senate during the impeachment trial of Pres. WILLIAM JEFFERSON CLINTON (1999).

Reich \ˈrīk\, **Steve** *orig.* **Stephen Michael** (born 1936) U.S. composer. Born in New York City, he majored in philosophy at Cornell University. After study with D. MILHAUD and L. BERIO, he pursued interests in Balinese and African music, learning drumming in Ghana. His early music explored the process of simultaneous repeated patterns gradually slipping out of phase ("process music"). With Terry Riley (born 1935) and P. GLASS, he was among the most prominent of the early "minimalists" of the 1970s. His early works include *Drumming* (1971) and *Music for 18 Musicians* (1976); later works such as *The Desert Music* (1983) and *Different Trains* (1988) show a considerably expanded compositional vocabulary.

Reich \ˈrīk\, **Wilhelm** (1897–1957) Austrian-U.S. psychologist. Trained at the Berlin Psychoanalytic Institute, he joined the faculty of the Vienna Psychoanalytic Institute in 1924. In *The Function of the Orgasm* (1927), he argued that the failure to achieve orgasm could produce neurosis. An advocate of sexual education and freedom as well as of radical left-wing politics, he left Germany in 1933 and settled in the U.S. in 1939. After breaking with the psychoanalytic movement in 1934, he developed a pseudoscientific system called orgonomy. He conceived of mental illness and some physical illnesses as deficiency of cosmic energy (measured in units called "orgones"), which he treated by placing the patient in a cabinet with reflective inner surfaces known as the orgone box. Reich's views brought him into conflict with U.S. authorities in the early 1950s; he was convicted of contempt of court and died in prison.

Reichstadt, Duke of See NAPOLEON II

Reichstag fire \ˈrīks-ˌtäk\ (February 27, 1933) Burning of the German parliament building (Reichstag) in Berlin. Allegedly set by a Dutch communist, the fire was used by ADOLF HITLER to turn public opinion against his opponents, especially the communists. He enacted a decree suspending constitutional protection of personal rights, which effectively began the NAZI PARTY dictatorship. The fire was widely believed to have been set by the Nazis themselves, while others have argued there was no proof of Nazi complicity; it remains the subject of debate and research.

Reid, Thomas (1710–1796) Scottish philosopher. Originally a pastor, he became a philosophy professor, and succeeded ADAM SMITH in the chair of moral philosophy at the University of Glasgow (1764–80). He rejected the skeptical empiricism of DAVID HUME in favor of a "philosophy of common sense," holding that Hume's SKEPTICISM was incompatible with common sense, since both human behavior and ordinary language provide overwhelming evidence to support the existence of a material world and personal identity amidst continuous change. His important works include *An Inquiry into the Human Mind* (1764), *Essays on the Intellectual Powers of Man* (1785), and *Essays on the Active Power of Man* (1788).

Reign of Terror *French* **la Terreur** (1793–94) Period in the FRENCH REVOLUTION. It was established by the government on September 5, 1793, to take harsh measures against those suspected of being enemies of the Revolution (including nobles, priests, and hoarders). Controlled by the radical COMMITTEE OF PUBLIC SAFETY and MAXIMILIEN ROBESPIERRE, the Terror eliminated enemies on the left (JACQUES R. HÉBERT and his followers) and the right (GEORGES J. DANTON and the Indulgents). A law passed in June 1794 that suspended a suspect's right to public trial or legal defense caused the THERMIDORIAN REACTION, and the Terror ended on July 27, 1794, with Robespierre's overthrow. About 300,000 suspects were arrested during the period; about 17,000 were executed and many others died in prison.

Reims *or* **Rheims** \'rēmz, *French* 're^{n}s\ City (pop., 1990: 185,000), northeastern France. The ancient capital of the Gallic tribe of the Remi, it was conquered by the Romans. In the 5th century the Frankish king CLOVIS was baptized there; in honor of this occasion most later French kings were crowned there. It was badly damaged in World Wars I and II and was the scene of Germany's unconditional surrender in May 1945. It is a major wine-producing center, noted especially for champagne. Other industries include aircraft and automobile equipment manufacturing. The 13th-century cathedral of Notre-Dame is one of the most notable Gothic cathedrals in France.

The cathedral of Notre-Dame, Reims, Fr.
PAUL ALMASY

reincarnation *or* **transmigration of souls** *or* **metempsychosis** Doctrine of the rebirth of the SOUL in one or more successive existences, which may be human, animal, or vegetable. Belief in reincarnation is characteristic of Asian religions, especially HINDUISM, JAINISM, BUDDHISM, and SIKHISM. All hold to the doctrine of KARMA, the belief that actions in this life will have their effect in the next. In Hinduism, a person may be freed from the cycle of birth and rebirth only by reaching a state of enlightenment. Likewise in Buddhism, discipline and MEDITATION may enable a seeker to reach NIRVANA and escape the wheel of birth and rebirth. MANICHAEISM and GNOSTICISM accepted the concept of reincarnation, as do such modern spiritual movements as THEOSOPHY.

reindeer Any species of Arctic DEER in the genus *Rangifer* (family Cervidae), especially Old World species, some of which are domesticated. New World species are usually called CARIBOU. The reindeer herded by the SAMI (Lapps) are used as draft and pack animals and as a source of meat and milk; their skins are used for tents, boots, and other clothing. In Siberia they are used as pack animals and as mounts.

Reiner, Carl (born 1922) U.S. actor, writer, director, and producer. Born in the Bronx, N.Y., he acted on the stage before appearing with SID CAESAR in the television comedy series *Your Show of Shows* (1950–54). He created and produced *The Dick Van Dyke Show* (1961–66), for which he won several Emmy awards. His novel *Enter Laughing* (1958) was adapted as a play (1963) and a movie (1967). He directed such film comedies as *Where's Poppa* (1970), *Oh, God!* (1977), and *Fatal Instinct* (1993). His son Rob Reiner (born 1945) acted in various television series, becoming famous as "Meathead" in *All in the Family* (1971–78). Rob began his film-directing career with *This Is Spinal Tap* (1984), which was followed by such successes as *Stand By Me* (1986), *The Princess Bride* (1987), *When Harry Met Sally . . .* (1989), *Misery* (1990), and *A Few Good Men* (1992).

Reiner \'rī-nər\, **Fritz** (1888–1963) Austro-Hungarian-U.S. conductor. After piano studies with BELA BARTOK, he conducted opera in Budapest (1911–14) and Dresden (1914–22). He emigrated to the U.S. in 1922, where he conducted orchestras in Cincinnati (1922–31) and Pittsburgh (1938–48). From 1953 to 1962 he led the Chicago Symphony Orchestra, which under Reiner first won international acclaim. He also taught conducting at the Curtis Institute (LEONARD BERNSTEIN was among his students). A stern taskmaster, he inspired devotion on the part of many players.

reinforced concrete Concrete in which steel is embedded in such a manner that the two materials act together in resisting forces. The reinforcing steel—rods, bars, or mesh—absorbs the tensile, shear, and sometimes the compressive stresses in a concrete structure. Plain concrete does not easily withstand tensile and shear stresses caused by wind, earthquakes, vibrations, and other forces and is therefore unsuitable in most structural applications. In reinforced concrete, the tensile strength of steel and the compressive strength of concrete work together to allow the member to sustain these stresses over considerable spans. The invention of reinforced concrete in the 19th century revolutionized the construction industry, and concrete became one of the world's most common building materials.

Reinhardt, Ad(olf Frederick) (1913–1967) U.S. painter. Born in Buffalo, N.Y., he studied art after graduating from Columbia University. He employed several abstract styles in the 1930s and '40s, but by the early 1950s he had restricted his works to monochrome paintings incorporating symmetrically placed squares and oblong shapes against backgrounds of similar color, in which drawing, line, brushwork, texture, light, and most other visual elements were suppressed. He explained his style as a conscious search for an art that would be entirely separate from life. He influenced the MINIMALISM of the 1960s, more as a polemicist than as a painter.

Reinhardt, Django *orig.* **Jean-Baptiste** (1910–1953) French guitarist, the first great European jazz soloist. Of Gypsy parentage, Reinhardt learned guitar at an early age, adapting his technique to accommodate the loss of the use of two fingers burned in a caravan fire in 1928. With jazz violinist Stéphane Grappelli (1908–1997), he formed the Quintette du Hot Club de France in 1934. Reinhardt toured the U.S. with DUKE ELLINGTON in 1946. One of the first important guitar soloists in jazz, his blend of SWING and the Gypsy tradition as well as his unconventional technique made him a unique and legendary figure.

Django Reinhardt, 1947.
BY COURTESY OF DOWN BEAT MAGAZINE

Reinhardt, Max *orig.* **Max Goldmann** (1873–1943) German theatrical director. After studying drama in Vienna and acting in Salzburg, he joined Otto Brahm's company in Berlin in 1894. He directed his first play in 1902 and managed a small theater from 1903. He had directed over 40 plays by 1905, when he became famous for his creative staging of *A Midsummer Night's Dream*. He bought Berlin's Deutsches Theater and remodeled it with the latest innovations in scenic design and lighting. Known for the extravagant theatricality and stunning visual effects of his productions, he won much praise for his staging of the religious spectacle *The Miracle* (1911). He cofounded the Salzburg Festival in 1920, where he staged *Jedermann* (an adaptation of *Everyman*) in the cathedral square. He left Germany in 1933 and eventually settled in the U.S. A major influence on 20th-century drama, he helped increase the creative authority of the director.

Reinsurance Treaty (June 18, 1887) Secret agreement between Germany and Russia. Arranged by OTTO VON BISMARCK after the collapse of the THREE EMPERORS' LEAGUE, it provided that each party would remain neutral if either became involved in a war with a third nation, and that this would not apply if Germany attacked France or if Russia attacked Austria. Germany acknowledged the Russian sphere of influence in Bulgaria. After the treaty was not renewed in 1890, a Franco-Russian alliance began to take shape.

Rejang River See RAJANG RIVER

relapsing fever Infectious disease with recurring fever, caused by several SPIROCHETES of the genus *Borrelia,* transmitted by lice, ticks, and bedbugs. Onset is sudden, with high fever, which breaks within a week with profuse sweating. Symptoms return about a week later. There may be two to 10 relapses, usually decreasing in severity. Mortality usually ranges from 0 to 6%, up to 30% in rare epidemics. Central-nervous-system involvement causes various, usually mild, neurological symptoms. The first microscopic organisms clearly associated with serious human disease (1867–68), the spirochetes mutate repeatedly, changing their antigens so that the host's immunity no longer is effective, which produces the relapses. Antibiotics can be effective, but inadequate therapy may leave spirochetes alive in the brain, and they may reinvade the bloodstream.

relation In LOGIC, a relation R is defined as a set of ordered pairs, triples, quadruples, and so on. A set of ordered pairs is called a two-place (or dyadic) relation; a set of ordered triples is a three-place (or triadic) relation; and so on. In general, a relation is any set of ordered n-tuples of objects. Important properties of relations include symmetry, transitivity, and reflexivity. Consider a two-place (or dyadic) relation R. R can be said to be symmetrical if, whenever R holds between x and y, it also holds between y and x (symbolically, $(\forall x)\ (\forall y)\ [Rxy \supset Ryx]$); an example of a symmetrical relation is "x is parallel to y." R is transitive if, whenever it holds between one object and a second and also between that second object and a third, it holds between the first and the third (symbolically, $(\forall x)\ (\forall y)\ (\forall z)\ [(Rxy \wedge Ryz) \supset Rxz]$); an example is "x is greater than y." R is reflexive if it always holds between any object and itself (symbolically, $(\forall x)\ Rxx$); an example is "x is at least as tall as y" since x is always also "at least as tall" as itself.

relational database DATABASE in which all data are represented in tabular form. The description of a particular entity is provided by the set of its attribute values, stored as one row or record of the table, called a tuple. Similar items from different records can appear in a table column. The relational approach supports queries that involve several tables by providing automatic links across tables. Payroll data, for example, can be stored in one table and personnel benefits data in another; complete information on an employee can be obtained by joining the tables on employee identification number. In more powerful relational data models, entries can be programs, text, unstructured data in the form of binary large objects (BLOBs), or any other format the user requires. The relational approach is currently the most popular model for DATABASE MANAGEMENT SYSTEM. See also OBJECT-ORIENTED PROGRAMMING.

relative density See SPECIFIC GRAVITY

relativism Any view which maintains that the truth of statements about a specified subject matter is not determinable by a universally valid method but varies depending on the person or society considering the statements or the circumstances in which the statements are made. See also ETHICAL RELATIVISM.

relativity Concept in physics that measurements change when considered by observers in various states of motion. In classical physics, it was assumed that all observers anywhere in the universe would obtain identical measurements of space and time intervals. According to relativity theory, this is not so; all measurements depend on the relative motions of the observer and the observed. There are two distinct theories of relativity, both proposed by ALBERT EINSTEIN. The special theory of relativity (1905) developed from Einstein's acceptance that the speed of LIGHT is the same in all REFERENCE FRAMES, irrespective of their relative motion. It deals with non-accelerating reference frames, and is concerned primarily with electric and magnetic phenomena and their propagation in space and time. The general theory (1916) was developed primarily to deal with GRAVITATION and involves accelerating reference frames. Both theories are major milestones in the history of modern physics. See also EQUIVALENCE PRINCIPLE, SPACE-TIME.

relay race Race between teams in which each team member successively covers a specified portion of the course. In track events, such as the 400-m (4×100-m) and 1,600-m (4×400-m) relays, the runner finishing one leg passes a baton to the next runner while both are running within a marked exchange zone. In swimming competitions, such as the 4×100-m and 4×200-m freestyle races and the 4×100-m medley, the swimmer completing one leg touches the edge of the pool to signal the start of the next teammate's leg.

relief *or* **rilievo** \ril-'ye-vō\ (from Italian, *rilievare:* "to raise") In sculpture, any work in which the figures project from a supporting background, usually a plane surface. Bas-reliefs ("low reliefs"), in which the design projects only slightly, were common on the walls of stone buildings in ancient Egypt, Assyria, and elsewhere in the Middle East. High reliefs, in which the forms project at least half or more of their natural circumference, were first employed by the ancient Greeks. Italian Renaissance sculptors combined high and low relief in strikingly illusionistic compositions, as in LORENZO GHIBERTI's bronze doors in Florence. Baroque sculptors continued these experiments, often on a larger scale (e.g., ALESSANDRO ALGARDI's *Meeting of Attila and Pope Leo,* 1646–53). The dramatic possibilities of the Renaissance concept of relief were later notably employed by FRANCOIS RUDE (*The Marseillaise,* 1833–36) and AUGUSTE RODIN (*The Gates of Hell).*

Athena mourning, mezzo-relievo from the Acropolis, 5th century BC, in the Acropolis Museum, Athens.
ALINAR—ART RESOURCE

relief Public or private aid to people in economic need because of natural disasters, wars, economic upheaval, chronic unemployment, or other conditions that prevent self-sufficiency. A distinction may be drawn between relief targeting upheavals and natural disasters and relief of chronic social conditions, now usually referred to as WELFARE. In 17th-century China the government maintained EVER-NORMAL GRANARIES for use in the event of famine. Through the 19th century, disaster relief in Europe consisted largely of emergency grants of food, clothing, and medical care through hastily organized local committees. In the 20th century, disaster relief became one of the chief activities of the International RED CROSS and other international agencies. Assistance to the needy from public funds has traditionally been strictly limited; in England, the Poor Law Reform Act of 1834 required people able to work to enter a workhouse in order to receive public assistance. The U.S. government responded to the Great Depression with the NEW DEAL, which emphasized work relief programs such as the WORKS PROGRESS ADMINISTRATION. In the later 20th century, the work requirement was abandoned in most countries, and the needy received direct cash payments, though in the U.S. the movement for welfare reform resulted in the passage in 1996 of "workfare" laws cutting off relief for most able-bodied welfare recipients who fail to take government-sponsored jobs.

relief printing See LETTERPRESS PRINTING

religion Relation of human beings to God or the gods or to whatever they consider sacred or, in some cases, merely supernatural. Archaeological evidence suggests that religious beliefs have existed since the first human communities. They are generally shared by a community, and they express the communal culture and values through myth, doctrine, and ritual. Worship is probably the most basic element of religion, but moral conduct, right belief, and participation in religious institutions also constitute elements of the religious life. Religions attempt to answer basic questions intrinsic to the human condition (Why do we suffer? Why is there evil in the world? What happens to us when we die?) through the relationship to the sacred or supernatural or (e.g., in the case of BUDDHISM) through perception of the true nature of reality. Broadly speaking, some religions (e.g., JUDAISM, CHRISTIANITY, and ISLAM) are outwardly focused, and others (e.g., JAINISM, Buddhism) are inwardly focused.

religion, philosophy of Branch of philosophy that studies key metaphysical and epistemological concepts, principles, and problems of religion. Topics considered include the existence and nature of God, the possibility of knowledge of God, human freedom (the FREE WILL PROBLEM), personal identity, immortality, and the problems of moral and natural evil and suffering. Natural THEOLOGY is the attempt to establish knowledge of God without dependence on revelation. Traditional arguments for the existence of God include the ONTOLOGICAL ARGUMENT, the COSMOLOGICAL ARGUMENT, and the ARGUMENT FROM DESIGN.

Religion, Wars of (1562–98) Conflicts in France between Protestants and Catholics. The spread of French CALVINISM persuaded the French ruler CATHERINE DE MÉDICIS to show more tolerance for the HUGUENOTS, which angered the powerful Catholic de GUISE family. Its partisans massacred a Huguenot congregation at Vassy (1562), causing an uprising in the provinces. Many inconclusive skirmishes followed, and compromises were reached in 1563, 1568, and 1570. After the murder of the Huguenot leader GASPARD II DE COLIGNY in the SAINT BARTHOLOMEW'S DAY MASSACRE (1572), the civil war resumed. A peace compromise in 1576 allowed the Huguenots freedom of worship. An uneasy peace existed until 1584, when the Huguenot leader Henry of Navarre (later HENRY IV) became heir to the French throne. This led to the War of the THREE HENRYS and later brought Spain to aid the Catholics. The wars ended with Henry's embrace of Catholicism and the religious toleration of the Huguenots guaranteed by the Edict of NANTES (1598).

Religious Science Movement founded in the U.S. by Ernest Holmes (1887–1960). After publishing his major work, *The Science of the Mind* (1926), he established the Institute of Religious Science and Philosophy (1927). In 1949 Religious Science was established as a denomination; it soon split into two groups. It teaches that the individual mind and the Universal Mind are one, and that the universe is the material manifestation of the Universal Mind. Like NEW THOUGHT, it teaches that evil stems from ignorance of humanity's true higher identity, and that prayer can bring about healing not only of spiritual but of physical ailments.

Remagen \'rā-ˌmäg-ᵊn\ Town (pop., 1992 est.: 15,000), western Germany. Located on the left bank of the RHINE RIVER, southeast of BONN, it originated as a Roman fortress and still has Roman remains. In World War II its railroad bridge was the site where Allied troops forced a crossing of the Rhine (1945) for the first time in the war.

Remak \'rā-ˌmäk\, **Robert** (1815–1865) German embryologist and neurologist. He discovered and named the three germ layers of cells that develop in the early embryo: the ectoderm, mesoderm, and endoderm. He also discovered Remak's fibers (nerve fibers with no myelin sheath) and Remak's ganglia (neurons in the heart) and was a pioneer in electrotherapy for nervous diseases. He achieved enough eminence to obtain a lectureship at the University of Berlin despite Prussian laws barring Jews from teaching.

remanent magnetism See PALEOMAGNETISM

Remarque \rə-'märk\, **Erich Maria** *orig.* **Erich Paul Remark** (1898–1970) German-U.S.-Swiss novelist. Drafted into the German army at 18, he served in World War I and was wounded several times. He is chiefly remembered for *All Quiet on the Western Front* (1929), a brutally realistic account of the daily routine of ordinary soldiers and perhaps the best-known and most representative novel about that war. He came to the U.S. in 1939, but settled in Switzerland after World War II. His other works include *The Road Back* (1931), *Arc de Triomphe* (1946; film, 1948), and *The Black Obelisk* (1956).

Rembrandt (Harmenszoon) van Rijn \rīn\ (1606–1669) Dutch painter and etcher. The son of a prosperous miller in Leiden, he was apprenticed to masters there and in Amsterdam. His early works show the spotlight effects of light and shadow that were to dominate his later works. After moving to Amsterdam in 1631, he quickly became the city's most fashionable portrait painter, and in 1632 he was commissioned to paint the celebrated *Anatomy Lesson of Dr. Nicolaes Tulp*. Yearning for recognition as a biblical and mythological painter, in 1635 he produced his *Sacrifice of Isaac* and in 1636 the unconventional masterpiece *Danaë*. In 1634 he had married Saskia van Uylenburgh, a woman of property, and until 1642 he painted many tender pictures of her. That year, when Saskia died and he completed his largest painting, the extraordinary but controversial *The Militia* Company of Captain Frans Banning Cocq (known as *The Night Watch*), was a watershed in his life and art. His portrait commissions thereafter declined and he turned increasingly to etchings and biblical subjects. His *Christ at Emmaus* (1648) exemplifies the quiet dignity and vulnerability of his later spirituality. In 1656, after transferring most of his property to his son, he applied for bankruptcy. In his last decade he treated biblical subjects like portraits, and also did a wealth of self-portraits; many of these paintings evoke a timeless world of quiet, deep emotion. His paintings are characterized by luxuriant brushwork, rich color, and a mastery of chiaroscuro. The silent human figure, Rembrandt's central subject, contributes to the sense of a shared dialogue between viewer and picture, the foundation of Rembrandt's greatness and of his popularity today.

Remington, Eliphalet (1793–1861) U.S. firearms manufacturer and inventor. Son of a blacksmith in Suffield, Conn., he grew up on his father's farm near Utica, N.Y., where he made his first FLINTLOCK rifle (1816). In 1828 he built a large arms factory at present-day Ilion, N.Y. He and his son Philo improved arms manufacture with the reflection method of straightening gun barrels and the first successful cast-steel, drilled rifle barrel made in the U.S. In 1847 he supplied the U.S. Navy with its first breech-loading rifle. His Remington Arms Co. made small arms for the U.S. government during the American Civil War and World Wars I and II.

Remington, Frederic (1861–1909) U.S. painter, illustrator, sculptor, and war correspondent. Born in Canton, N.Y., he studied at Yale University and New York's Art Students League. He traveled widely and specialized in depicting Indians, cowboys, soldiers, horses, and other aspects of life on the Plains. His work is notable for its rendering of swift action and its accuracy of detail. He covered the Spanish-American War (1898) as a correspondent. The countless reproductions of his works as newspaper engravings brought him wealth and fame.

remora \'re-mə-rə\ *or* **sharksucker** *or* **suckerfish** Any of 8–10 species of marine fishes (family Echeneidae) noted for attaching themselves to, and riding about on, SHARKS, other marine animals, and oceangoing ships. Remoras adhere by means of a flat, oval sucking disk on top of the head. They are thin and dark, 1–3 ft (30–90 cm) long. They live in warm waters worldwide, feeding on the leavings or the external parasites of their hosts.

A remora (*Echeneis naucrates*) and its host, a leopard shark.
DOUGLAS FAULKNER

ren *or* **jen** \'rən\ In CONFUCIANISM, the most basic of all virtues, variously translated as "humaneness" or "benevolence." It originally denoted the kindness of rulers to subjects. CONFUCIUS identified ren as perfect virtue, and MENCIUS made it the distinguishing characteristic of humanity. In NEO-CONFUCIANISM it was a moral quality imparted by Heaven.

Renaissance \'re-nə-ˌsäns\ (French: "rebirth") Late-medieval cultural movement in European civilization that brought renewed interest in classical learning and values. The Renaissance began in Italy during the late 13th century and spread throughout Europe in the 15th century, ending finally in the 16th and early 17th century. Inspired by the works of ancient Greece and Rome, Renaissance artists produced painting and sculpture based on the observation of the visible world and practiced according to mathematical principles of balance, harmony, and perspective. The new aesthetic tenets found expression in the works of such Italian artists as LEONARDO DA VINCI, SANDRO BOTTICELLI, RAPHAEL, TITIAN, and MICHELANGELO, and the city of Florence became the center of Renaissance art. In the world of letters, HUMANISTS such as DESIDERIUS ERASMUS rejected religious orthodoxy in favor of the study of human nature, and such writers as PETRARCH and GIOVANNI BOCCACCIO in Italy, FRANCOIS RABELAIS in France, and WILLIAM SHAKESPEARE in England produced works that emphasized the intricacies of human character. See also RENAISSANCE ARCHITECTURE.

Renaissance architecture Style of architecture, reflecting the rebirth of Classical culture, that originated in Florence in the early 15th century and spread throughout Europe, replacing the medieval Gothic style. There was a revival of ancient Roman forms, including the column and round arch, the tunnel VAULT, and the dome. The basic design element was the ORDER. Knowledge of CLASSICAL ARCHITECTURE came from the ruins of ancient buildings and the writings of VITRUVIUS. As in the Classical period, proportion was the most important factor of beauty; Renaissance architects found a harmony between human proportions and buildings. This concern for proportion resulted in clear, easily comprehended space and mass, which distinguishes the Renaissance style from the more complex Gothic. FILIPPO BRUNELLESCHI is considered the first Renaissance architect. LEON BATTISTA ALBERTI's *Ten Books on Architecture*, inspired by

Vitruvius, became a bible of Renaissance architecture. From Florence the early Renaissance style spread through Italy. DONATO BRAMANTE's move to Rome ushered in the High Renaissance (c. 1500–20). Mannerism, the style of the Late Renaissance (1520–1600), was characterized by sophistication, complexity, and novelty rather than the harmony, clarity, and repose of the High Renaissance. The Late Renaissance also saw much architectural theorizing, with Sebastiano Serlio (1475–1554), Giacomo da Vignola (1507–1573), and ANDREA PALLADIO publishing influential books.

renal calculus See KIDNEY STONE

renal carcinoma \'rē-n^{ə}l-ˌkär-sə-'nō-mə\ *or* **clear-cell carcinoma** *or* **hypernephroma** Malignant TUMOR of the cells that cover and line the KIDNEY. It usually affects persons over 40 with vascular disorders of the kidneys, seldom causing pain until advanced. It often metastasizes to other organs (e.g., lungs, liver, brain, bone) and may go unrecognized until these secondary tumors cause symptoms. Blood can appear in the urine early on but is painless and usually disregarded. Even in early stages, X-ray films can show deformity in kidney structures. Renal carcinoma may spontaneously regress. After surgical removal, the cancer may recur as much as 20 years later, or not at all.

renal cyst Any of several types of CYSTS in the KIDNEYS. Some are present at birth; others are caused by tubular obstruction. Large cysts can cause backaches and a dragging sensation. Multiple cysts occur as a result of various disorders, including kidney vascular diseases, lymphatic vessel blockage, congenital diseases, and tapeworm infestation. The most serious is medullary cystic disease, which has no warning symptoms but causes ANEMIA, low blood sodium levels, and UREMIA. The kidneys become shrunken, grainy, and scarred. Cysts should usually be checked surgically to rule out cancer. See also UROGENITAL MALFORMATION.

renal failure See KIDNEY FAILURE

renal system See URINARY SYSTEM

renal transplant See KIDNEY TRANSPLANT

Renan \rə-'nä^{n}\, **(Joseph-) Ernest** (1823–1892) French philosopher, historian, and scholar of religion. He trained for the priesthood but left the Catholic church in 1845, feeling that its teachings were incompatible with the findings of historical criticism, though he retained a quasi-Christian faith in God. His five-volume *History of the Origins of Christianity* (1863–1880) included his *Life of Jesus* (1863); an attempt to reconstruct the mind of Jesus as a wholly human person, it was virulently denounced by the church but widely read by the general public. His later works include the series *History of the People of Israel* (1888–96).

Renan, detail of an oil painting by Léon Bonnat, 1892; in the Musée Renan, Tréguier, Fr.
ARCHIVES PHOTOGRAPHIQUES

renga \'reŋ-ˌgä\ Genre of Japanese linked-verse poetry in which two or more poets supply alternating sections of a poem. The form began with the composition of a traditional five-line poem by two people. A popular pastime from ancient times, even in remote rural areas, it developed fully in the 15th century. Composition spread to court poets, who drew up "codes" to establish renga as an art. An example of renga is the melancholy *Minase sangin hyakuin* (1488), composed by SOGI, Shohaku, and Socho. Later the initial verse *(hokku)* of a renga developed into the HAIKU form.

Reni \'rā-nē\, **Guido** (1575–1642) Italian painter. Apprenticed to the Flemish painter Denis Calvaert at 10, he was later influenced by the novel naturalism of the CARRACCI FAMILY of his native Bologna, the frescoes of RAPHAEL, and ancient Greco-Roman sculpture. He executed many important commissions in Rome, including the celebrated ceiling fresco *Aurora* (1613–14). In his religious and mythological works, he tempered baroque exuberance and complexity with classical restraint, tender emotion, and delicate coloring. Until JOHN RUSKIN scorned him in the 19th century, he was highly regarded; his status as one of the great painters of the 17th century has since been reestablished.

Renner, Karl (1870–1950) Austrian chancellor (1918–20, 1945) and president (1945–50). A lawyer, he served in the Reichsrat (lower house) from 1907. He became the first chancellor of the new Austrian republic in 1918 but was unable to prevent territorial losses at the end of World War I. In the 1920s he led the right wing of the Social Democratic Party and in 1938 favored the ANSCHLUSS with Germany. In 1945 he worked to reestablish Austrian home rule and was elected president of the republic. He wrote numerous works on government and law.

Rennes \'ren\ City (pop., 1990: 204,000), western France, at the confluence of the Ille and Vilaine rivers. Once under Roman occupation, it was the capital of BRITTANY in the Middle Ages, and a rival of NANTES. It was the seat of the Brittany parliament 1561–1675. It was almost completely destroyed by fire in 1720 and was rebuilt. It was bombed and partly destroyed in World War II. It is a commercial and industrial city, producing railway equipment, automobiles, and chemicals. It is also the cultural center of Brittany.

Rennie, John (1761–1821) Scottish civil engineer. He built three bridges across the Thames at London: Waterloo Bridge (since replaced), the old Southwark Bridge (1814–19), and the New London Bridge (completed 1831 and since replaced). He worked on extensive drainage projects in the Lincolnshire fens; built the London and East India docks on the Thames; improved naval dockyards at Plymouth, Portsmouth, Chatham, and Sheerness; and began the great breakwater that shelters Plymouth Sound.

Reno \'rē-nō\ City (pop., 1996 est.: 155,000), western Nevada. It is located on the Truckee River, near the California border, Lake TAHOE, and the SIERRA NEVADA foothills. Until 1900 it was primarily a distribution point, but after several well-known people were granted divorces or were quickly married there under liberal state laws, it became famous as a busy divorce and marriage center. It is also a year-round vacation center. When gambling was legalized in Nevada in 1931, Reno began to attract tourists to its many casinos.

Renoir \rən-'wär\, **(Pierre-) Auguste** (1841–1919) French painter. His father, a tailor in Limoges, moved with his large family to Paris in 1844. Renoir began working as a decorator of porcelain at 13 and studied painting at night. He formed a close friendship with his fellow student CLAUDE MONET and became a leading member of the Paris Impressionists. His early works were typically Impressionist snapshots of real life, full of sparkling color and light. Among his early masterpieces are *Le Moulin de la Galette* (1876) and *The Luncheon of the Boating Party* (1881). A visit to Italy (1881–82) introduced him to RAPHAEL and the expressive force of clear line and smooth painting, and by the mid-1880s he had broken with IMPRESSIONISM to employ a more disciplined, formal technique. In works such as *Bathers* (1884–87), he emphasized volume, form, contours, and line. In his later works, he departed from the strict rules of Classicism to paint colorful still lifes, portraits, nudes, and landscapes of southern France, where he settled in 1907. Rheumatism confined him to a wheelchair by 1912, but he never ceased to paint, often with his brush attached to his hand. JEAN RENOIR was his son.

Renoir, Jean (1894–1979) French film director. The son of AUGUSTE RENOIR, he discovered a passion for the cinema while recovering from wounds suffered in World War I. He directed his first film, *La fille de l'eau*, in 1924. His films were marked by a keen pictorial sense and a deep appreciation for the unpredictability of human character. He cowrote the screenplays for many of his films, including *Boudu Saved from Drowning* (1932), *Madame Bovary* (1934), *The Crime of Monsieur Lange* (1936), and *La bête humaine* (1938) as well as his two masterpieces, *Grand Illusion* (1937) and *The Rules of the Game* (1939), among the greatest films

Jean Renoir.
GLOBE PHOTOS

ever made. He lived in the U.S. 1940–51, where he directed *The Southerner* (1945), *The Diary of a Chambermaid* (1946), and *The River* (1951). He received an honorary Academy Award in 1975.

Rensselaer Polytechnic Institute \ˌren-sə-ˈlēr\ Private institution of higher learning in Troy, N.Y. Founded in 1824 by Stephen Van Rensselaer, it was one of the first U.S. colleges dedicated to the study of science and civil engineering. It comprises schools of architecture, engineering, humanities and social sciences, management, and science, and offers both undergraduate and advanced degrees. Research facilities include a technology park, a communications center, and a center for industrial innovation. Total enrollment is about 6,500.

rent In common usage, payment made in return for the right to use property belonging to another. In CLASSICAL ECONOMICS, rent was the income gained from cultivated or improved land after the deduction of all production costs. In modern economic usage, rent is the difference between the total return to a factor of production (LAND, LABOR, CAPITAL) and its supply PRICE, the minimum amount necessary to attain its services. Rent plus OPPORTUNITY COST make up the total income paid to a productive resource. Efforts made by a resource owner to obtain MONOPOLY profit is considered rent-seeking behavior.

Renta, Oscar de la See Oscar DE LA RENTA

Reorganized Church of Jesus Christ of Latter-day Saints Faction of the sect founded by JOSEPH SMITH in 1830, whose main body became the Church of Jesus Christ of Latter-day Saints, or MORMON church. The Reorganized Church broke away in 1852, rejecting the leadership of BRIGHAM YOUNG in favor of Smith's son; it also rejected the practice of polygamy and the label Mormon. Its teachings are based on the BIBLE, the Book of MORMON, and the *Doctrine and Covenants,* a book of revelations received by its prophets. Today it has about 200,000 members and is headquartered in Independence, Mo.

reovirus \ˌrē-ō-ˈvī-rəs\ Any of a small group of animal and plant VIRUSES that appear spheroidal and contain a core of RNA. Among the best-known genera are *Orthoreovirus, Orbivirus, Rotavirus,* and *Phytoreovirus.* The first three infect animals; the last can destroy rice, corn, and other crops.

reparations Payment in money or materials by a nation defeated in war. After WORLD WAR I, reparations to the ALLIED POWERS were required of Germany by the Treaty of VERSAILLES. The original amount of $33 billion was later reduced by the DAWES PLAN and the YOUNG PLAN and was canceled after 1933. In the 1920s German resentment over reparations was used by ultranationalists to foment political unrest.

repertory theater Production of several different plays in a single season by a resident acting company. The plays chosen may be classic works by famous dramatists or new works by emerging playwrights, and the companies that perform them often serve as a training ground for young actors. In Britain the practice, intended to make high-quality theater available throughout the country, began in the early 20th century. Repertory companies, or stock companies, originally presented a different play each night of the week while preparing and rehearsing new plays. The system evolved to the current practice of presenting a series of short, continuous runs of each play.

Repin \ˈryā-pyin, *Engl* ˈrā-pin\, **Ilya (Yefimovich)** (1844–1930) Russian painter. After training with a provincial icon painter and at the St. Petersburg Academy of Fine Arts, he visited France and Italy on an academy scholarship. On his return he began painting subjects from Russian history. In 1873 he achieved international fame with *Volga Boatmen*, a grim, powerful image that became the model for Soviet Socialist Realism. Among his best-known works is *Ivan the Terrible and His Son Ivan* (1895), depicting Ivan's murder of his son. He also painted vigorous portraits (including LEO TOLSTOY and M. MUSSORGSKY). In 1894 he became professor of historical painting at the St. Petersburg Academy.

replacement deposit In geology, a mineral deposit formed by chemical processes that dissolve the original rock and deposit a new assemblage of minerals in its place. See also METASOMATIC REPLACEMENT.

representation In politics, a method or process of enabling a constituency to participate in shaping legislation and government policy through deputies chosen by it. Representation is necessary in modern politics because the populations governed are too large to allow for direct assembly. See also PROPORTIONAL REPRESENTATION.

Representation of the People Acts (1918, 1928) Parliamentary acts that expanded suffrage in Britain. The act of 1918 gave the vote to all men over 21 and all women over 30, which tripled the electorate. The act of 1928 extended the franchise to women aged 21–30. The acts continued the voting reforms begun by the Reform Bills (see REFORM BILL OF 1832, REFORM BILL OF 1867, REFORM BILL OF 1884–85).

representationalism Theory of knowledge based on the assertion that the mind perceives only mental representations of material objects outside the mind, not the objects themselves. The validity of human knowledge is thus called into question because of the need to show that such images accurately correspond to the external objects. The doctrine, still current in certain philosophical circles, has roots in CARTESIANISM, the EMPIRICISM of JOHN LOCKE and DAVID HUME, and the IDEALISM of IMMANUEL KANT.

repression In metabolism, a control mechanism by which a protein molecule, called a repressor, prevents the synthesis of an ENZYME by binding to (and thus hindering the action of) the DNA that controls the enzyme's synthesis. Though the process has been studied mainly in microorganisms, it is believed to occur in a similar way in higher organisms. See also INHIBITION.

repression In psychoanalytic theory, the exclusion of distressing memories, thoughts, or feelings from the conscious mind. Often involving sexual or aggressive urges or painful childhood memories, these unwanted mental contents are pushed into the unconscious mind. Repression is thought to give rise to ANXIETY and to neurotic symptoms, which begin when a forbidden drive or impulse threatens to enter the conscious mind. PSYCHOANALYSIS seeks to uncover repressed memories and feelings through free ASSOCIATION as well as to examine the repressed wishes released in DREAMS.

reproduction Process by which organisms replicate themselves, assuring continuation of their species. The two basic forms are asexual and sexual. Asexual reproduction (e.g., fission, spore formation, regeneration, and vegetative reproduction) produces an offspring genetically identical to its single parent. Sexual reproduction produces a new individual through the union of special sex cells (gametes), usually from different parents. Gametes result from MEIOSIS. Gamete union results in a zygote, the first cell of a new organism. Sexual reproduction ensures that each offspring is genetically unique (except in cases of multiple offspring derived from divisions of one zygote). Most animals, including all vertebrates, reproduce sexually.

reproductive behavior In animals, any activity directed toward perpetuation of a species. Sexual reproduction, the most common mode, occurs when a female's egg is fertilized by a male's sperm. The resulting unique combination of genes produces genetic variety that contributes to a species' adaptability. The stages of approach, identification, and copulation are well developed to avoid predators and the wastage of eggs and sperm. Most one-celled and some more-complex organisms reproduce asexually. See also COURTSHIP BEHAVIOR.

reproductive system, human Organ system by which humans reproduce. In females, the OVARIES sit near the openings of the fallopian (uterine) tubes, which carry EGGS from the ovaries to the UTERUS. The cervix extends from the lower end of the uterus into the VAGINA, whose opening, as well as that of the urethra (see URINARY SYSTEM), is covered by four folds of skin (the labia); the clitoris, a small erectile organ, is located where the labia join in front. The activity of the ovaries and uterus goes through a monthly cycle of changes (see MENSTRUATION) throughout the reproductive years except during PREGNANCY and nursing. In males, the TESTES lie in a sac of skin (the scrotum). A long duct (the vas deferens) leads from each testis and carries SPERM to the ejaculatory ducts in the PROSTATE GLAND; these join the urethra, which continues through the PENIS. In the urethra, sperm mixes with secretions from the seminal vesicles, prostate gland, and Cowper's gland to form SEMEN. In early embryos, the reproductive systems are undetermined. By birth the organs appropriate to each sex have typically developed but are not functioning. They continue to grow, and at puberty their activity increases and maturation occurs, enabling sexual reproduction. See illustration opposite on following page.

reptile Any of the approximately 6,000 species of the class Reptilia, air-breathing VERTEBRATES that have internal fertilization and a scaly body and are cold-blooded. Most species have short legs (or none) and have long tails, and most lay eggs. Living reptiles include the scaly reptiles (SNAKES and LIZARDS; order Squamata), the CROCODILES (Crocodilia), the TURTLES (Chelonia), and the unique TUATARA (Rhynchocephalia). Being cold-blooded, reptiles are not found in very cold regions, and in regions with cold winters they usually hibernate. They range in size from GECKOS that measure about 1 in. (3 cm) long to the PYTHON, which grows to 30 ft (9 m); the largest turtle, the marine leatherback, weighs about 1,500 lbs (680 kg). Extinct reptiles include the DINOSAURS, the PTEROSAURS, and the dolphinlike ichthyosaurs.

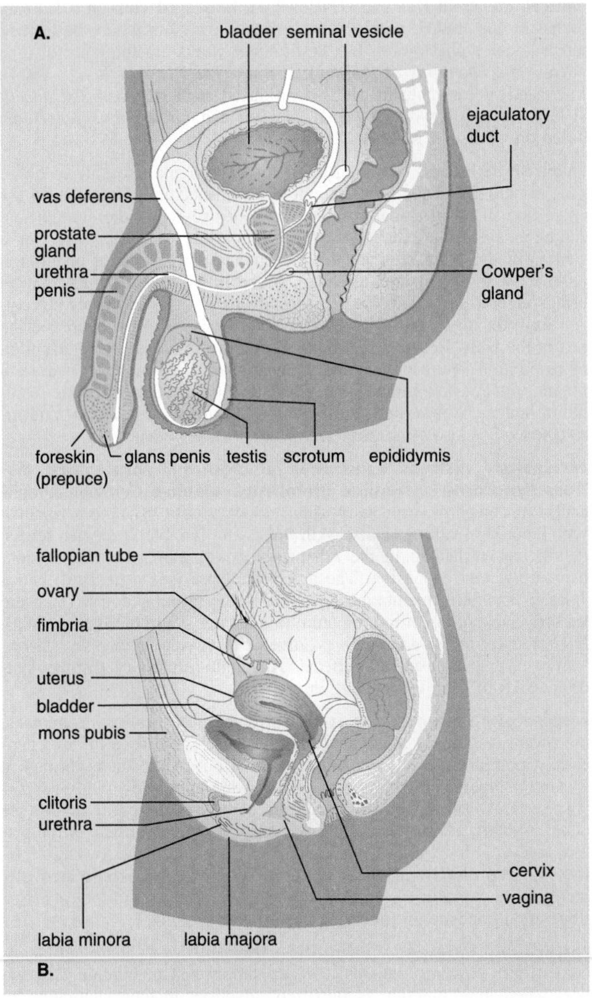

A. Male reproductive system. The scrotum, a pouch of skin, is divided into two sacs, each containing a testis and its associated epididymis. Tubules within the testes contain sperm cells at different stages of development. As sperm leaves the testes, it passes into the epididymis, a highly coiled tube that serves as a reservoir for sperm. The vas deferens, a duct leading out from the epididymis, joins with the duct of the seminal vesicles as it passes through the prostate gland to form a single tube (ejaculatory duct) which opens into the urethra, the tube that conveys both sperm and urine out through the penis. B. Female reproductive system. In a menstruating woman, a follicle containing an egg matures each month in either of two ovaries. Ovulation occurs as the mature follicle ruptures and releases an egg, which is drawn into the ovary's associated fallopian (uterine) tube, which contains a fringe of fingerlike projections (fimbriae). Fertilization usually occurs in the fallopian tube as the egg travels to the uterus. Successful implantation of a fertilized egg in the uterus results in development of an embryo. The vagina, a muscular tube that leads to the uterus, allows sperm to pass into the uterus and serves as a passageway for the fetus during childbirth.

republic Form of government in which the leader is periodically appointed under a constitution. It was originally contrasted with governments in which leadership was hereditary, but is now understood to mean a state ruled by representatives elected by its populace, all of which is enfranchised. Republics may also be distinguished from direct DEMOCRACIES, but representative democracies are by and large republics.

Republican, Radical See RADICAL REPUBLICAN

Republican Party *or* **GOP (Grand Old Party)** One of two major U.S. political parties. It was formed in 1854 by former members of the WHIG, DEMOCRATIC, and FREE SOIL parties who chose the party's name to recall the Jeffersonian Republicans' concern with the national interest above sectional interests and states' rights. The new party opposed slavery and its extension into the territories, as provided by the KANSAS-NEBRASKA ACT. Its first presidential candidate, JOHN C. FREMONT, won 11 states in 1856; its second, ABRAHAM LINCOLN, won the 1860 election by carrying 18 states. Its association with the Union victory in the AMERICAN CIVIL WAR allowed it a long period of dominance. Republican candidates won 14 of 18 presidential elections between 1860 and 1932, through support from an alliance of northern and midwestern farmers and big-business interests. The presidency of THEODORE ROOSEVELT produced a progressive wing of the party, which divided it and gave control to the Democrats 1913–21. The party's inability to counter the impact of the GREAT DEPRESSION led to its ouster from power (1933–53) until DWIGHT D. EISENHOWER's presidency brought a moderate wing to prominence. But the party's platform remained conservative, calling for a strong anti-Communist stance, a reduction of government regulation of the economy, lower taxes, and resistance to civil-rights legislation. The GOP gained new support from middle-class suburbanites and white Southerners disturbed by the integrationist stance of 1960s Democrats. RICHARD NIXON lost the 1960 presidential race; conservatives regained control in 1964, but their candidate, BARRY GOLDWATER, lost. Nixon won narrowly in 1968 and by a landslide in 1972 but resigned in 1974 as a result of the WATERGATE SCANDAL. Conservatives regained control of the party with the election of RONALD REAGAN (1980, 1984) and his vice president, GEORGE BUSH (1988). The 1992 election of Democrat WILLIAM JEFFERSON CLINTON as president was offset by the Republicans' regaining control of Congress (1994) for the first time in 40 years.

Republican Party, National See NATIONAL REPUBLICAN PARTY

Republican River River, central U.S. Rising in eastern Colorado, it is 422 mi (679 km) long. It flows northeast and east through southern Nebraska, then southeast through northeastern central Kansas to unite with the Smoky Hill River at Junction City and form the KANSAS RIVER. It is part of the Missouri River Basin flood-control and land-reclamation project.

Requiem Musical setting of the MASS for the dead. (*Requiem*, Latin for "rest," is the first word of the mass.) The Requiem's text differs from the standard mass Ordinary in omitting its joyous sections and keeping only the Kyrie, Sanctus, and Agnus Dei, which are combined with other sections including the Dies Irae ("Day of Wrath"). The first surviving polyphonic setting is by J. OCKEGHEM; celebrated later Requiems include those of W.A. MOZART, H. BERLIOZ, G. VERDI, G. FAURE, J. BRAHMS, and BENJAMIN BRITTEN.

resale price maintenance Measures taken by manufacturers or distributors to control the resale prices of their products (i.e., the prices charged by businesses that resell them). Such measures have been applied to a limited array of goods, including pharmaceuticals, books, photographic supplies, and liquor. Resale price maintenance first began to be employed in the 1880s, reflecting the success of brand promotion and the resulting increase in competition among retailers. It became especially common in the U.S., but declined after World War II. It is prohibited in some countries, including Canada and Sweden. The complexity of marketing channels in industrialized countries makes it increasingly difficult for manufacturers to establish and enforce a single price or even a minimum price for their goods. See also FAIR-TRADE LAW.

research and development (R&D) In industry, two closely related processes by which new products and new forms of old products are created through technological innovation. The work generally focuses on two types of research, basic and applied. Basic research is directed toward a generalized goal (e.g., genetic research in a pharmaceutical laboratory). Applied research directs the results of basic research toward the needs of a specific industry and results in the development of new or modified products or processes. In addition to carrying out basic and applied research and developing models, R&D staff may evaluate the efficiency and cost of the product.

resin \'re-zᵊn\ Any natural or synthetic organic compound consisting of a noncrystalline (amorphous) solid or viscous liquid substance or mixture. Natural resins are usually transparent or translucent yellow to brown and can melt and burn. Most are exuded from trees, especially pines and firs (see CONIFER), when the bark is injured. The fluid secretion usually dries out and hardens (and is thus a "drying oil"). Natural resins may be spirit-soluble (e.g., BALSAMS, used in healing; TURPENTINE; and mastics and shellac, used in varnishes) or oil-soluble (e.g., amber, Oriental lacquer). Synthetic resins are not clearly differentiated from PLASTICS; the term resin is often used for the raw plastic product or the POLYMER fluid to be processed into it. Certain synthetic resins are useful as ion-exchange media (see ION-EXCHANGE RESIN).

resistance Opposition that a material or electrical CIRCUIT offers to the flow of ELECTRIC CURRENT. It is the property of a circuit that transforms electrical energy into heat energy as it opposes the flow of current. The resistance R, the ELECTROMOTIVE FORCE or voltage V, and the current I are related by OHM'S LAW. The resistance of an electrical CONDUCTOR generally increases with increasing temperature and is utilized in devices such as lamps and heaters. The ohm (Ω) is the common unit of electrical resistance; one ohm is equal to one volt (see ELECTROMOTIVE FORCE) per ampere.

Resistance *or* **Underground** Clandestine groups opposed to Nazi rule in German-occupied Europe in World War II. The groups included civilians who worked secretly against the occupation and armed bands of partisans or guerrilla fighters. Resistance activities ranged from assisting the escape of Jews and Allied airmen shot down over enemy territory to committing sabotage, ambushing German patrols, and sending intelligence information to the Allies. Resistance groups were not always unified; in some countries, rival groups divided along communist and noncommunist lines. However, in France the clandestine National Council of the Resistance coordinated all French groups, which gave support to the NORMANDY CAMPAIGN and participated in the August 1944 uprising that helped liberate Paris. Resistance groups in other northern European countries also undertook military actions to help the Allied forces in 1944–45.

resistivity Electrical RESISTANCE of a CONDUCTOR of unit cross-sectional area and unit length. The resistivity of a conductor depends on its composition and its temperature. As a characteristic property of each material, resistivity is useful in comparing various materials on the basis of their ability to conduct ELECTRIC CURRENT. As temperature increases, the resistivity of a metallic conductor usually increases and that of a SEMICONDUCTOR usually decreases.

Resnais \rə-'nā\, **Alain** (born 1922) French film director. After studying at the French cinema school IDHEC, he made short films on the visual arts (*Van Gogh*, 1948) and documentaries (*Night and Fog*, 1956). His first feature film, *Hiroshima mon amour* (1959), created a sensation with its alternation between past and present and is considered one of the earliest and best films of the NEW WAVE. He continued his exploration of the complex themes of time and memory in *Last Year at Marienbad* (1961). His later films include *Muriel* (1963), *Stavisky* (1974), *My American Uncle* (1980), *Love Unto Death* (1984), and *I Want to Go Home* (1989).

Resnais.
BY COURTESY OF THE FRENCH FILM OFFICE, NEW YORK

resonance In physics, the relatively large selective response of an object or a system that vibrates in step with an externally applied VIBRATION. Acoustical resonance is the vibration induced in a string of a given pitch when a note of the same pitch is produced nearby, in the sound box of an instrument such as a guitar, or in the mouth or nasal cavity when speaking. Mechanical resonance, such as that produced in a bridge by wind or by marching soldiers, can eventually produce wide swings great enough to cause the bridge's destruction. Resonance in frequency-sensitive electrical CIRCUITS makes it possible for certain communication devices to accept signals of some frequencies while rejecting others. MAGNETIC RESONANCE occurs when electrons or atomic nuclei respond to the application of MAGNETIC FIELDS by emitting or absorbing ELECTROMAGNETIC RADIATION. See also NUCLEAR MAGNETIC RESONANCE.

Respighi \re-'spē-gē\, **Ottorino** (1879–1936) Italian composer. After musical studies in Bologna (1891–1901), he played viola in a Russian orchestra and studied with N. RIMSKY-KORSAKOV, from whom he learned much about orchestration. His best-known works are the colorful tone poems *The Fountains of Rome* (1916) and *The Pines of Rome* (1924). Interested in early music, he also produced such works as *Gli uccelli* (1927), based on works by J.-P. RAMEAU, and *La boutique fantasque*, based on works by G. ROSSINI.

respiration Process of taking in air for oxygen and releasing it to dispose of carbon dioxide. The amount of air inhaled and exhaled in an average human breath (tidal volume) is about one-eighth the amount that can be inhaled after exhaling as much as possible (vital capacity). Nerve centers in the brain regulate the movements of muscles of respiration (DIAPHRAGM and chest-wall muscles). Blood in the PULMONARY CIRCULATION brings carbon dioxide from the tissues to be exhaled and takes up oxygen from the air in the PULMONARY ALVEOLI to carry it to the heart and the rest of the body. Because the body stores almost no oxygen, interruption of respiration—by asphyxiation, drowning, or chest-muscle PARALYSIS—for more than a few minutes can cause death. Disorders affecting respiration include ALLERGY, ASTHMA, BRONCHITIS, EMPHYSEMA, PNEUMONIA, and TUBERCULOSIS. See also RESPIRATORY SYSTEM, RESPIRATORY THERAPY.

respiratory distress syndrome *or* **idiopathic respiratory distress syndrome** *or* **hyaline membrane disease** Common complication in newborns, especially after PREMATURE BIRTH. Symptoms include very labored breathing, bluish skin tinge, and low blood oxygen levels. Insufficient surfactant in the PULMONARY ALVEOLI raises surface tension, hampering lung expansion. The alveoli collapse (see ATELECTASIS) and a "glassy" (hyaline) membrane develops in the alveolar ducts. Once the leading cause of death in premature infants, the syndrome is now usually treated for a few days with positive-pressure ventilation (see RESPIRATORY THERAPY), with no aftereffects. An adult respiratory distress syndrome (ARDS) can follow lung injury.

respiratory system Organ system involved in RESPIRATION. In humans, the DIAPHRAGM and, to a lesser extent, the muscles between the ribs generate a pumping action, moving air in and out of the lungs through a system of pipes (conducting airways), divided into upper and lower airway systems. The upper airway system comprises the nasal cavity (see NOSE), SINUSES, and PHARYNX; the lower airway system consists of the LARYNX, TRACHEA, bronchi, bronchioles, and alveolar ducts (see PULMONARY ALVEOLUS). The blood and CARDIOVASCULAR system can be considered elements of a working respiratory system. See also THORACIC CAVITY. See illustration opposite on following page.

respiratory therapy *or* **inhalation therapy** Medical specialty concerned with ensuring patients' oxygen supply and maintaining RESPIRATION when lung function is impaired. Practices include suctioning to clear secretions from the airway, use of oxygen tents and aerosol mists (sometimes medicated) to ease breathing, and tilting the body to promote drainage. More complex mechanical techniques include positive-pressure ventilation, which delivers a gas mixture with various programmed pressure patterns. The gases may be given through a mask over the nose and mouth, a tube inserted into the TRACHEA through the nose or mouth (intubation), or a skin incision (tracheotomy) when swelling or bleeding blocks the airway.

restaurant Establishment where refreshments or meals are served to paying guests. Though inns and taverns served simple fare to travelers for centuries, the first modern restaurant where guests could order from a varied menu is thought to have belonged to A. Boulanger, a soup vendor who opened his business in Paris in 1765. The sign above his door advertised restoratives, or *restaurants*, referring to his soups and broths. By 1804 Paris had more than 500 restaurants, and France soon became internationally famous for its cuisine. Other European restaurants include the Italian *trattorie*, taverns featuring local specialties; the German

O P Q R

Weinstuben, informal restaurants with a large wine selection; the Spanish tapas bars, which serve a wide variety of appetizers; and the PUBLIC HOUSES of England. Asian restaurants include the Japanese sushi bars and teahouses serving formal Kaiseki cuisine as well as the noodle shops of China. Most U.S. restaurant innovations have revolved around speed. The cafeteria originated in San Francisco during the 1849 gold rush; cafeterias feature self-service and offer a variety of foods displayed on counters. The U.S. also pioneered fast-food restaurants such as White Castle (founded 1921) and McDonald's (see RAY KROC), usually operated as chains and offering limited menus.

Reston, James (Barrett) (1909–1995) U.S. (Scottish-born) columnist and editor. His family moved to the U.S. when he was 10. He was a sportswriter before joining the *New York Times* in 1939, where he worked as a reporter, a nationally syndicated columnist, Washington bureau chief (1953–64), executive editor (1968–69), and vice president (1969–74) before retiring in 1989. One of the most influential U.S. journalists, he had unrivaled personal access to U.S. presidents and world leaders and was often the first to break major stories. He won two Pulitzer Prizes (1945, 1957), helped create the first Op-Ed page (1970), and recruited and trained many talented young journalists.

Restoration Restoration of the monarchy in England in 1660. It marked the return of CHARLES II as king (1660–85) following the period of OLIVER CROMWELL's Commonwealth. The bishops were restored to Parliament, which established a strict Anglican orthodoxy. The period, which also included the reign of JAMES II (1685–88), was marked by an expansion in colonial trade, the ANGLO-DUTCH WARS, and a revival of drama and literature (see RESTORATION LITERATURE).

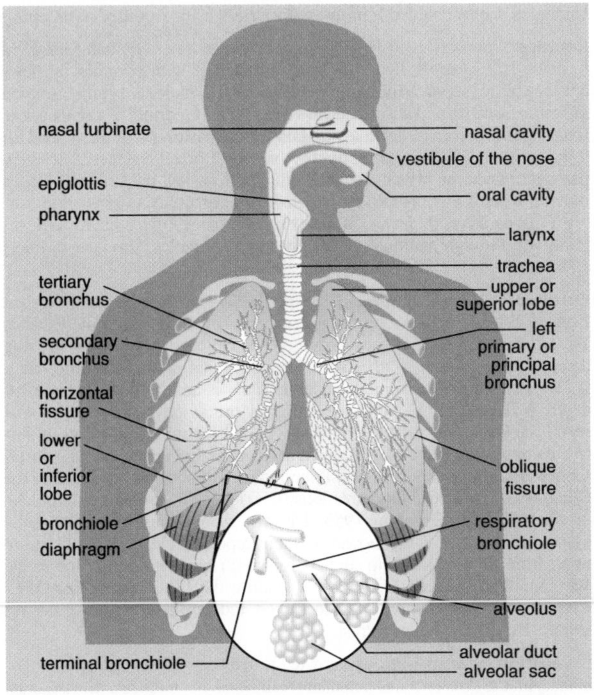

As air enters the nasal cavity through the nostrils, it is warmed and moistened by mucous membranes of the nasal turbinates before entering the pharynx. Stiff hairs lining the vestibule inside the nostrils help filter the entering air. The air-filled sinuses adjacent to the nasal cavity produce mucus. The larynx connects the pharynx with the trachea or windpipe. The cartilaginous epiglottis prevents food from entering the larynx during swallowing. A left and right primary bronchus supply each lung with air from the trachea. They divide into smaller secondary and tertiary bronchi; the smallest divisions, bronchioles, lead to the cup-shaped, thin-walled alveoli, which occur in clusters (alveolar sacs). Oxygen and carbon dioxide are exchanged between the alveoli and surrounding capillaries. Oblique fissures or grooves of each lung separate the upper lobe from the lower lobe. The horizontal, or transverse, fissure of the right lung forms a middle lobe. Movement of the diaphragm along with the ribs and rib muscles causes expansion and contraction of the lungs during breathing.

Restoration literature English literature written after the RESTORATION of the monarchy in 1660 following the period of the Commonwealth. Some literary historians equate its era with the reign of CHARLES II (1660–85), while others add the reign of JAMES II (1685–88). Many typical modern literary forms (e.g., the novel, biography, history, travel writing, and journalism) began to develop with sureness during the Restoration period. Pamphlets and poetry (notably that of JOHN DRYDEN) flourished, but the age is chiefly remembered for its glittering, critical, and often bawdy comedies of manners by such playwrights as GEORGE ETHEREGE, THOMAS SHADWELL, WILLIAM WYCHERLY, JOHN VANBRUGH, WILLIAM CONGREVE, and GEORGE FARQUHAR.

restraint of trade Preventing of free competition in business by some action or condition such as price-fixing or the creation of a MONOPOLY. The U.S. has a long-standing policy of maintaining competition among business enterprises through ANTITRUST LAWS, the best known of which, the SHERMAN ANTITRUST ACT of 1890, declared illegal "every contract, combination . . . or conspiracy in restraint of trade or commerce."

restriction enzyme PROTEIN (endonuclease) produced by BACTERIA that cleaves DNA at specific sites along its length. Thousands have been found, from many different bacteria; each recognizes a specific nucleotide sequence. The bacteria's own DNA is disguised with methyl (—CH_3) groups at the recognition sites to protect it. In the bacterial cell, these ENZYMES destroy (i.e., "restrict") the DNA of invading VIRUSES (BACTERIOPHAGES), eliminating the infection. In the laboratory they are used to manipulate DNA fragments, such as those that contain GENES, and have become a very powerful tool of recombinant DNA BIOTECHNOLOGY (see DNA RECOMBINATION).

restrictive covenant In property law, an agreement acknowledged in a deed or lease that restricts the free use or occupancy of property, such as by forbidding commercial use or certain types of structures. The restrictive covenant is as old as the law of property, being well-established in Roman law. The term is also used in business law to refer to an agreement whereby one party promises not to engage in the same business or a similar business in a particular area for a period of time.

retailing Selling of merchandise directly to the consumer. Retailing began several thousand years ago with peddlers hawking their wares at the earliest marketplaces. It is extremely competitive, and the failure rate of retail establishments is relatively high. Price is the most important arena of competition, but other factors include convenience of location, selection and display of merchandise, attractiveness of the establishment, and reputation. The diversity of retailing is evident in the many forms it now takes, including VENDING MACHINES, door-to-door and telephone sales, DIRECT-MAIL MARKETING, discount houses, specialty stores, DEPARTMENT STORES, supermarkets, and consumer COOPERATIVES.

retaining wall *or* **revetment** Wall constructed to hold in place a mass of earth or prevent the erosion of an embankment. It may also be battered, with the face inclined toward the load it is bearing. The most basic type of reinforced retaining wall is the massive concrete gravity wall, which is prevented from falling over by the sheer weight and volume of its mass. A CANTILEVER (L-shaped) retaining wall resists overturning by means of cantilever footings, spread footings (see FOUNDATION) shaped to resist overturning and sliding.

reticuloendothelial system \re-ˌtik-yə-lō-ˌen-də-ˈthē-lē-əl\ *or* **macrophage system** \ˈmak-rə-ˌfāj\ *or* **mononuclear phagocyte system** Part of the body's defenses consisting of a class of cells widely distributed in the body. Reticuloendothelial cells filter out and destroy BACTERIA, VIRUSES, and foreign substances, and destroy worn-out or abnormal cells and tissues. Precursor cells in bone marrow develop into monocytes (see LEUKOCYTE), which are released into the bloodstream. Most enter body tissues, developing into much larger cells called macrophages, with different appearances in various locations. Some roam through the circulation and between cells and can coalesce into a single cell around a foreign object to engulf it. Reticuloendothelial cells also interact with LYMPHOCYTES in immune reactions. Cells in the SPLEEN destroy old red blood cells and recycle their HEMOGLOBIN; uncontrolled, this process causes ANEMIA. TUMORS of the reticuloendothelial system can be localized or widespread throughout the body. See also LYMPHATIC SYSTEM.

retina \'re-tᵊn-ə\ Layer of nerve tissue covering the back two-thirds of the eyeball. Light focused onto the retina by the lens of the EYE stimulates two types of light-sensitive cells: rods, which are sensitive to low light levels, and cones, which provide detailed vision and color perception. Chemical changes in these cells trigger nerve impulses, which are assembled by complex connections among retinal nerves into a pattern to be carried through the optic nerve to the visual centers of the brain. Disorders affecting the retina or the macula in its center decrease vision and can cause BLINDNESS. See also DETACHED RETINA, MACULAR DEGENERATION.

retraining program Occupational training program designed to aid workers in obtaining new employment. Formal retraining programs were first developed in Europe at the end of World War II to help military personnel return to civilian life and to reduce UNEMPLOYMENT. Retraining programs are also used to respond to labor shortages in specific occupations. They have been put forward as at least a partial solution to the problem of structural unemployment in declining industries or industries severely affected by competition from imports. Such programs, which are most common in Western Europe, may include monetary allowances during training, relocation expenses, and family allowances. In several countries, refusal to participate in a retraining program disqualifies a worker from eligibility for unemployment compensation benefits.

retriever Any of several dog breeds, bred to retrieve game, that have a thick, water-resistant coat, keen sense of smell, and "soft" mouth that does not damage game. Retrievers are 22–24 in. (55–62 cm) tall and weigh 55–75 lbs (25–34 kg). The golden retriever has a golden-brown coat that is long on the neck, legs, and tail. The Labrador retriever has a short black or brown coat. Both are often used as guide dogs, and both are highly popular as pets. Other retriever breeds include the Chesapeake Bay, curly-coated, and flat-coated retrievers.

Golden retriever.
SALLY ANNE THOMPSON

retrograde motion In astronomy, the actual or apparent motion of a body in a direction opposite to that of the predominant ("direct") motions of similar bodies. Observationally and historically, retrograde motion refers to the apparent reversal of the planets' motion through the stars for several months in each SYNODIC PERIOD. This required a complex explanation in earth-centered models of the universe (see PTOLEMY), but was naturally explained in heliocentric models (see COPERNICAN SYSTEM) by the apparent motion as the earth passed by a planet in its orbit. It is now known that nearly all bodies in the SOLAR SYSTEM revolve and rotate in the same counterclockwise direction as viewed from a position in space above earth's North Pole. This common direction probably arose during the formation of the SOLAR NEBULA. The few objects with clockwise motions (e.g., the rotation of Venus, Uranus, and Pluto) are also described as retrograde.

retrovirus \,re-trō-'vī-rəs\ Any of a group of VIRUSES that, unlike most other viruses and all cellular organisms, carry their genetic blueprint in the form of RNA. Retroviruses are responsible for some cancers and viral infections of animals, and they cause at least one type of human cancer. The retrovirus HIV is the cause of AIDS in humans. The name signifies that they use RNA to synthesize DNA, the reverse of the usual cell process. This process makes it possible for genetic material from a retrovirus to enter and become a permanent part of the GENES of an infected cell.

Retton, Mary Lou (born 1968) U.S. gymnast. Born in Fairmont, W.V., she began studying dance and acrobatics at age 4. At the 1984 Olympic Games she received perfect scores in her final two events to win a dramatic victory in the combined exercises, becoming the first American woman gymnast to win an individual Olympic gold medal. Her style, exhibiting speed, accuracy, and power, served to transform women's gymnastics. She was the first gymnast inducted into the U.S. Olympics Hall of Fame (1985).

Reuchlin \'ròik-lin\, **Johannes** (1455–1522) German humanist. After obtaining his law degree in 1481, he held court and judicial posts in Württemberg and its capital, Stuttgart, from the 1480s until 1512. Second only to DESIDERIUS ERASMUS among the German humanists, Reuchlin was a pioneer in the scientific study of classical Greek and translated many classical texts. His grammar and lexicon, *On the Fundamentals of Hebrew* (1506), revolutionized Hebrew studies and advanced Old Testament research. He opposed the Dominicans' plan to destroy all Hebrew literature, and in 1516 he was acquitted of heresy by a papal commission. PHILIPP MELANCHTHON was his nephew.

Réunion \rē-'yün-yən\ Island (pop., 1997: 681,000) and French overseas department, Mascarene Islands, western Indian Ocean. Located 425 mi (684 km) east of Madagascar, it is about 39 mi (63 km) long and 28 mi (45 km) wide, with an area of 970 sq mi (2,512 sq km). Its capital is ST.-DENIS. It consists mainly of rugged mountains dissected by torrential rivers. Most of the population is of mixed descent (Creole), with African descent predominant. It was settled in the 17th century by the French, who brought slaves from eastern Africa to work on coffee and sugar plantations. It was a French colony until 1946, then became an overseas department of France. Its economy is based almost entirely on sugar for export. Other products include rum, molasses, tobacco, geraniums, and vanilla.

Reuter \'ròi-tər\, **Paul Julius** *later* **Freiherr (baron) von Reuter** *orig.* **Israel Beer Josaphat** (1816–1899) German founder of the news agency REUTERS. He was a bank clerk and partner in a small publishing concern before initiating a prototype news service in Paris in 1849, using electric telegraphy and carrier pigeons in his network. He moved to England in 1851 and opened a telegraph office serving banks, brokerage houses, and leading business firms. He steadily extended his commercial news service, acquiring his first subscribing newspaper client in 1858. Undersea cables enabled him to expand the service to other continents.

Reuters \'ròi-tərz\ British cooperative NEWS AGENCY. Founded in 1851 by PAUL JULIUS REUTER, it was initially concerned with commercial news but began to serve a growing newspaper clientele after the London *Morning Advertiser* subscribed in 1858. After a period of competition, Reuters and two rival agencies agreed on a division of territory and for many years held a virtual monopoly on world press services. The company remained in private hands until 1925, when its structure began moving toward a cooperative of British and Australasian press interests. As a cooperative, it draws on an extensive range of resources and, directly or through national news agencies, provides services in most countries.

Reuther \'rü-thər\, **Walter (Philip)** (1907–1970) U.S. labor leader. Born in Wheeling, W.V., he became an apprentice tool- and diemaker at 16. He traveled around the world in the 1930s, developing a lifelong distaste for communism after spending two years in a Soviet auto factory. He became a local union leader in Detroit and helped organize sit-down strikes—during which he suffered brutal physical attacks—that made the UNITED AUTOMOBILE WORKERS (UAW) a power in the auto industry. As president of the UAW from 1946 until his death, he was an effective negotiator of wages-and-hours gains. He became president of the Congress of Industrial Organizations (CIO) in 1952 and was an architect of the AFL-CIO merger in 1955. He was second in power to GEORGE MEANY at the AFL-CIO; however, their repeated clashes, partly stemming from Reuther's strong support for civil rights and opposition to the Vietnam War, resulted in Reuther's leading the UAW out of the AFL-CIO in 1968 and forming a short-lived federation with the TEAMSTERS UNION. He died in a plane crash.

revelation Transmission of knowledge from a god or the gods to humans. In the Western monotheistic religions of Judaism, Christianity, and Islam, revelation is the basis of religious knowledge. Humans know God and his will because God has chosen to reveal himself to them. He may communicate with his chosen servants through dreams, visions, or physical manifestations and may inspire PROPHETS who relay his message to the people. His will may also be translated directly into writing through the handing down of divine law (e.g., the TEN COMMANDMENTS) or SCRIPTURE (e.g., the BIBLE and the QURAN). Other religions emphasize "cosmic" revelation, in which any and all aspects of the world may reveal the nature of a single underlying divine power (e.g., BRAHMAN in the VEDAS).

Revelation, Book of *or* **Revelations** *or* **Apocalypse of John** Last book of the NEW TESTAMENT. It consists of two main parts, the first containing moral admonitions to several Christian churches in Asia Minor, and the second composed of extraordinary visions, allegories, and symbols that have been the subject of varying interpretations throughout history. A popular interpretation is that Revelation deals with a contemporary crisis of faith, possibly the result of Roman persecutions. It exhorts Christians to remain steadfast in their faith and hold firm to the hope that God will ultimately vanquish their enemies. References to "a thousand years" have led some to expect that the final victory over evil will come after the completion of a millennium (see MILLENNIALISM). Modern scholarship accepts that the book was written not by St. JOHN THE APOSTLE but by various unknown authors in the late 1st century AD. See also APOCALYPSE.

Revels, Hiram R(hoades) (1822–1901) U.S. clergyman and politician. Born to free blacks in Fayetteville, N.C., he was educated in the North. Ordained a minister, he became a pastor and principal of a Baltimore school for blacks. In the Civil War he helped organize black volunteer regiments for the Union army. After the war he moved to Natchez, Miss., and was elected state senator in 1869. In 1870 he was elected to the U.S. Senate to fill the unexpired term of JEFFERSON DAVIS, becoming the first black elected to the Senate. He later served as president of Alcorn A&M College for blacks (1871–74, 1876–83).

revenue bond *or* **limited obligation bond** BOND issued by a municipality, state, or public agency authorized to build, acquire, or improve a revenue-producing property such as a waterworks, electric generating plant, or railroad. Unlike general-obligation bonds, which are repaid through a variety of tax sources, revenue bonds are payable from specified revenues only, usually the revenues from the facility for which the bond was originally issued. Revenue bonds typically pay interest rates higher than those of general-obligation bonds. The separation of the revenue bond obligation from a municipality's other bond obligations allows the municipality to circumvent legislated debt limits.

revenue sharing Funding arrangement in which one government unit grants a portion of its tax income to another government unit. For example, provinces or states may share revenue with local governments, or national governments may share revenue with provinces or states. Laws determine the formulas by which revenue is shared, limiting the controls that the unit supplying the money can exercise over the receiver and specifying whether matching funds must be supplied by the receiver. Forms of revenue sharing have been used in several countries, including Canada, India, and Switzerland. From 1972 to 1986 the U.S. pursued a revenue-sharing program in which state and local governments received federal funds to spend as they saw fit.

reverberatory furnace Furnace used for SMELTING, refining, or melting in which the fuel is not in direct contact with the contents but heats it by a flame blown over it from another chamber. Such furnaces are used in COPPER, TIN, and NICKEL production, in the production of certain CONCRETES and CEMENTS, and in ALUMINUM recycling. In steelmaking, this process (now largely obsolete) is called the OPEN-HEARTH PROCESS. The heat passes over the hearth and then radiates back (reverberates) onto the contents. The roof is arched, with the highest point over the firebox. It slopes downward toward a bridge of flues that deflects the flame so that it reverberates.

Revere, Paul (1735–1818) American patriot and silversmith. Born in Boston, he entered his father's trade as a silversmith and engraver. An ardent supporter of the colonists' cause, he took part in the BOSTON TEA PARTY. As the principal rider for Boston's Committee of Safety, he arranged to signal the British approach by having lanterns placed in Boston's Old North Church steeple: "One if by land and two if by sea." On April 18, 1775, he set off to ride to Lexington to alert colonists that British troops were on the march and to warn SAMUEL ADAMS and JOHN HANCOCK to flee. Though stopped by a British patrol, he was able to alert the patriot leaders; because of his warning, the MINUTEMEN were prepared for the Battle of LEXINGTON and the start of the AMERICAN REVOLUTION. His ride was celebrated in a famous poem by HENRY W. LONGFELLOW (1863). In the Revolution, Revere constructed a powder mill to supply colonial arms. After the war he discovered a process for rolling sheet copper and opened a rolling mill that produced sheathing for such ships as the USS *CONSTITUTION*. He continued to design handsome silver bowls, flatware, and utensils that are museum pieces today.

revetment See RETAINING WALL

Revillagigedo \rə-ˌvi-lə-gə-ˈgē-dō\ Group of islands, Mexico, in the Pacific Ocean, about 300 mi (500 km) south of the BAJA CALIFORNIA peninsula and 370 mi (595 km) west of Mexico. Covering a total land area of 320 sq mi (830 sq km), it consists of numerous volcanic islands. The largest, Socorro, rises to an elevation of 3,707 ft (1,130 m). The islands are rich in sulfur, fish, and guano, and are administered by COLIMA state, Mexico.

revivalism Reawakening of Christian values and commitment. The spiritual fervor of revival-style preaching, typically performed by itinerant, charismatic preachers before large gatherings, is thought to have a restorative effect on those who have been led away from the right path. Various Protestant sects have experienced periods of revivalism at different times since the 17th century, and many came into being during revivalist periods, notably METHODISM. Common themes are stricter interpretation of the BIBLE, rejection of literary or historical study of the Bible, emphasis on the conversion experience, and a call to live devoutly. Revivalism can be interpreted as a precursor of 20th-century Christian FUNDAMENTALISM. See also GREAT AWAKENING, DWIGHT MOODY.

revolution Fundamental, rapid, and often irreversible change in the established order. In the political sense, revolution is a radical change in government, usually accomplished through violence, that may also result in changes to the economic system, social structure, and cultural values. The Greeks saw revolution as possible only after societal breakdown; a strong value system, firmly adhered to, was thought to protect against it. With the advent of Renaissance humanism and the belief that changes in government might sometimes be necessary and good, revolution took on more positive connotations. JOHN MILTON saw revolution as the means of achieving freedom, IMMANUEL KANT believed it was a force for the advancement of mankind, and G. W. F. HEGEL held revolution to be the fulfillment of human destiny. Hegel's philosophy in turn influenced KARL MARX. See also COUP D'ÉTAT.

Revolution of 1688 See GLORIOUS REVOLUTION

Revolutionary War See AMERICAN REVOLUTION

Revolutions of 1848 Series of republican revolts against European monarchies. They began in Sicily and spread to France, the German and Italian states, and the Austrian empire. In France the revolution established the SECOND REPUBLIC, and in Central Europe liberal political reform and national unification appeared likely. However, the armies loyal to the monarchies soon reestablished their power and rescinded most of the promised reforms. The revolts eventually ended in failure and repression, and were followed by widespread disillusionment among liberals.

revolver PISTOL with a revolving cylinder that provides multishot action. Some early versions, known as pepperboxes, had several barrels, but as early as the 17th century pistols were being made with a revolving chamber to load cartridges into a single barrel. The first practical revolver was not designed until 1835, when SAMUEL COLT patented his version. He established the standard of a cylinder with multiple chambers, each of which successively locked in position behind the barrel and was discharged by pressure on the trigger. In Colt's early single-action revolvers, the cylinder revolved as the hammer was cocked manually. Double-action revolvers, in which the hammer is cocked and the cylinder revolves as the trigger is pulled, were developed soon afterward, along with metal cartridges.

revue Theatrical production of brief, loosely connected, often satirical skits, songs, and dances. Originally derived from the medieval French street fair, the modern revue dates from the early 19th century with the Parisian *Folies Marigny* and later at the FOLIES BERGÈRE. The English revue developed in two forms: one as the costume display and spectacle of the Court Theatre productions in the 1890s, and another as the *André Charlot Revues* of the 1920s and the London Hippodrome shows, which emphasized clever repartee and topicality. In the U.S., the *Ziegfeld Follies* began in 1907 and usually featured a star personality. Revues appeared periodically on Broadway and West End stages until competition from movies and television moved the form to small nightclubs and improvisational theaters.

Rexroth, Kenneth (1905–1982) U.S. painter, essayist, poet, and translator. Born in South Bend, Ind., the largely self-educated Rexroth spent much of his youth traveling in the West, organizing and speaking for unions. His early poems were experimental, influenced by Surrealism; his later work was praised for its tight form and its wit and humanistic passion. He was an early champion of the BEAT MOVEMENT. His works include essays in *Assays* (1962) and *With Eye and Ear* (1970); and many translations of Japanese, Chinese, Greek, Latin, and Spanish poetry.

Rey See RHAGAE

Reye's syndrome \'rīz, 'rāz\ Acute neurological illness in children following INFLUENZA, CHICKEN POX, or other viral infections. Vomiting, lethargy, and confusion begin as the child appears to be recovering, followed hours or days later by drowsiness, disorientation, seizures, respiratory arrest, and coma. At worst, it causes fatty liver degeneration and potentially fatal brain swelling. There is no specific cure, but treatment of imbalances helps over 70% of patients survive (some with brain damage). Its incidence has decreased since the recognition that it often follows use of ASPIRIN or other SALICYLIC-ACID derivatives in children during a viral illness; parents are now warned. It can also result from AFLATOXIN or WARFARIN poisoning.

Reykjavík \'rā-kyä-ˌvēk\ City (pop., 1996 est.: 105,000), capital of Iceland, at the southeastern corner of FAXA BAY. According to tradition, it was founded in 874 by the Norseman Ingólfur Arnarson. Until the 20th century it was a small fishing village, ruled and largely inhabited by Danes. It became the capital of a self-governing Iceland under the Danish king in 1918 and of the independent Republic of Iceland in 1944. In World War II it was a U.S. naval and air base. In 1986 arms-control talks between the U.S. and U.S.S.R. were held there. It is the commercial, industrial, and cultural center of the island, its major fishing port, and the site of nearly half of the nation's industries.

Reymont \'rā-ˌmȯnt\, **Wladyslaw (Stanislaw)** *orig.* **Wladyslaw Stanislaw Rejment** (1867–1925) Polish novelist. He never finished his schooling and worked in his youth as a shop apprentice, a lay brother in a monastery, a railway official, and an actor. His short stories and novels are written in a naturalistic, factual style with short sentences. His best work, *The Peasants* (1904–9), is a four-volume chronicle of peasant life over the course of a year, written in peasant dialect. Translated into many languages, it won Reymont the 1924 Nobel Prize.

Reynaud \rā-'nō\, **Paul** (1878–1966) French politician and premier (1940). After serving in World War I, he served in the Chamber of Deputies (1919–24, 1928–40) and in cabinet positions (1930–32). As minister of finance (1938–40) and premier (1940), he called on France to resist Nazi Germany. After the German invasion, Reynaud resigned rather than conclude an armistice; he was arrested and kept in captivity 1940–45. Returning to the Chamber of Deputies (1946–62), he helped draft the constitution of the FIFTH REPUBLIC.

Reynolds, Joshua *later* **Sir Joshua** (1723–1792) British portrait painter. Son of a clergyman-schoolmaster, he was apprenticed to a London portraitist in 1740. His large group portrait *The Eliot Family* (c. 1746) reveals the influence of ANTHONY VAN DYCK. The impressions gained during two years in Italy (1750–52), particularly in Venice, inspired his painting for the rest of his life. He established a portrait studio in London in 1753 and was immediately successful. His early London portraits introduced new vigor into English portraiture. After 1760, with the increasing vogue for Greco-Roman antiquity, his style became increasingly classical and self-conscious. He was elected the first president of the Royal Academy in 1768. Through his art and teaching, Reynolds led British painting away from the anecdotal pictures of the early 18th century toward the formal rhetoric of continental academic painting. His *Discourses Delivered at the Royal Academy* (1769–90), advocating rigorous academic training and study of the old masters, ranks among the most important art criticism of the time.

Reynolds, Osborne (1842–1912) British engineer and physicist. Educated at Cambridge Univ., he became the first professor of engineering at the University of Manchester (1868). Best known for his work in HYDRAULICS and hydrodynamics, he formulated the law of resistance in parallel channels (1883), the theory of LUBRICATION (1886), and the standard mathematical framework used in TURBULENCE work (1889). He studied wave engineering and tidal motions in rivers and made pioneering contributions to the concept of group velocity. The Reynolds stress in fluids with turbulent motion and the REYNOLDS NUMBER are named for him.

Reynolds number In FLUID MECHANICS, a number that indicates whether the flow of a fluid (liquid or gas) is absolutely steady (in streamlined, or LAMINAR FLOWd) or on the average steady with small, unsteady changes (in turbulent flow; see TURBULENCE). The Reynolds number, abbreviated N_{Re} or Re, has no dimensions (see DIMENSIONAL ANALYSIS), and is defined as the size of the flow—as, for example, the diameter of a tube (D) times the average speed of flow (v) times the mass density of the fluid (ρ)—divided by its absolute VISCOSITY (μ). OSBORNE REYNOLDS demonstrated in 1883 that the change from laminar to turbulent flow in a pipe occurs when the value of the Reynolds number exceeds 2,100.

Rg Veda See RIG VEDA

Rh blood-group system System for classifying BLOOD according to presence or absence of the Rh ANTIGEN (factor) in ERYTHROCYTES. Rh-negative persons who receive Rh-positive BLOOD TRANSFUSIONS produce ANTIBODIES to Rh factor, which attack red blood cells with the factor if they are ever received again, causing serious illness and sometimes death. The antibodies also attack the red cells of an Rh-positive fetus carried by an Rh-negative woman if she has had a previous Rh-positive transfusion or pregnancy (see ERYTHROBLASTOSIS FETALIS). The Rh-negative trait is rare worldwide but more common in some ethnic groups. See also BLOOD TYPING.

rhabdovirus \ˌrab-dō-'vī-rəs\ Any of a group of VIRUSES responsible for RABIES and vesicular stomatitis (an acute disease of cattle and horses, characterized by blisters in and about the mouth, that resembles foot-and-mouth disease). The bullet-shaped virus particle is encased in a fatty membrane and contains RNA.

Rhaetia See RAETIA

Rhaetian Alps \'rē-tēən\ Segment of the central ALPS extending along the Italian–Swiss and Austrian–Swiss borders but mainly in eastern Switzerland. Bernina Peak, on the Italian border, is the highest point at 13,284 ft (4,049 m) tall. In the eastern part is the Swiss National Park, founded in 1914, with an area of 65 sq mi (169 sq km); it is known for its rugged alpine scenery and its wildlife.

Rhagae *or* **Ragae** \'rā-jē\ *Persian* **Rey** Ancient city, MEDIA. It was formerly one of the great cities of Iran; its ruins are at modern Rey, near TEHRAN. A settlement there dates from the 3rd millennium BC. Under the SASANIANS (3rd–7th century AD), it was a center of ZOROASTRIANISM. It was captured by the Muslims in AD 641. It grew in importance until the 12th century, when it was weakened by religious conflicts. In 1220 it was destroyed by the MONGOLS, and its inhabitants were massacred. It was famous for its decorated silks and for ceramics. HARUN AL-RASHID, memorialized in *The THOUSAND AND ONE NIGHTS*, was born here c. 765. Only two architectural towers survive.

Rhazes See ar-RAZI

Rhea \'rē-ə\ Greek goddess, one of the TITANS. Daughter of URANUS and GAEA, she married her brother CRONUS, who swallowed all their children except ZEUS, whom Rhea concealed. Zeus then overcame Cronus and restored his siblings.

rhea \'rē-ə\ Either of two ostrich-like species of South American three-toed RATITE birds (family Rheidae). The common rhea *(Rhea americana)* is about 4 ft (120 cm) tall and weighs about 50 lbs (20 kg). It has luxuriant plumage, brown or gray above and whitish below. Darwin's rhea *(Pterocnemia pennata)* is smaller and has white-tipped brownish plumage. Rheas live in open country, often among grazing animals, and run from predators. They eat a wide variety of plants and animals. Both species are listed as endangered.

Rhee, Syngman (1875–1965) First president of the Republic of Korea (South Korea). The first Korean to earn a PhD at a U.S. university (Princeton), he returned to Korea in 1910, the year Japan annexed Korea. Unable to hide his hostility toward Japanese rule, he left again for the U.S. in 1912. For the next 30 years he spoke out for Korean independence; in 1919 he was elected president of a provisional government in exile. As the only Korean leader well known to the U.S., Rhee was returned to Korea ahead of his rivals at the end of World War II; he was elected president of the Republic of Korea in 1948. He held that post until 1960, when opposition to his authoritarian policies (which included outlawing the opposition Progressive Party) forced his resignation. He died in exile in Hawaii.

Rheims See REIMS

rhesus monkey \'rē-səs\ Sand-colored MACAQUE *(Macaca mulatta)*, widespread in southern and South Asian forests. Rhesus monkeys are 17–25 in. (47–64 cm) long, excluding the furry 8–12-in. (20–30-cm) tail, and weigh 10–24 lbs (4.5–11 kg). They eat fruits, seeds, roots, herbs, and insects. They are held sacred in some parts of India. Hardy in captivity, highly intelligent, and lively, they make good pets when young but may become bad-tempered as adults. They have been used frequently in medical research. The determination of the Rh (from rhesus) factor in human blood involves reaction with the blood of this species. See also RH BLOOD-GROUP SYSTEM.

Rhesus monkeys (*Macaca mulatta*).
YLLA FROM RAPHO/PHOTO RESEARCHERS—EB INC.

rhetoric Art of speaking or writing effectively. It may entail the study of principles and rules of composition formulated by critics of ancient times, and can also involve the study of writing or speaking as a means of communication or persuasion. Classical rhetoric probably developed along with democracy in Syracuse in the 5th century BC, when dispossessed landowners argued claims before their fellow citizens. Shrewd speakers sought help from teachers of oratory, called rhetors. This use of language was of interest to philosophers such as PLATO and ARISTOTLE because the oratorical arguments called into question the relationships among language, truth, and morality. The Romans recognized separate aspects of the process of composing speeches, a compartmentalization that grew more pronounced with time. Renaissance scholars and poets studied rhetoric closely, but by the 19th century the term had come to mean empty political discourse or elaborate style without substance.

rheumatic fever \rü-'ma-tik\ Generalized disease caused by certain types of STREPTOCOCCUS bacteria. It occurs mostly in children and young adults. Symptoms may be mild, or sudden fever, joint pain, and inflammation may begin days to weeks after a streptococcal infection, usually of the throat (see PHARYNGITIS), with skin nodules and rashes, CHOREA, abdominal pain, nosebleeds, and weight loss. HEART inflammation, with accompanying rapid heartbeat, murmurs, and enlargement, can lead to valve scarring, markedly shortening life. After recovery, survivors are prone to future attacks. PENICILLIN given when the initial infection is diagnosed can prevent it. Otherwise, SALICYLIC-ACID derivatives or STEROIDS help the symptoms.

rheumatoid arthritis \'rü-mə-ˌtȯid\ Chronic, progressive AUTOIMMUNE DISEASE causing CONNECTIVE-TISSUE INFLAMMATION, mostly in synovial JOINTS. It can occur at any age, is more common in women, and has an unpredictable course. It usually starts gradually, with pain and stiffness in one or more joints, then swelling and heat. Muscle pain may persist, worsen, or subside. Membrane inflammation and thickening scars joint structures and destroys CARTILAGE. In severe cases, adhesions immobilize and deform the joints, and adjacent skin, bones, and muscles atrophy. If high-dose aspirin, ibuprofen, and other NSAIDs do not relieve pain and disability, low-dose steroids may be tried. Physical medicine and rehabilitation reduce pain and swelling with heat and then range-of-motion exercises. Orthopedic appliances correct or prevent gross deformity and malfunction. Surgery can replace destroyed hip, knee, or finger joints with prostheses. There is also a juvenile form.

Rhiannon \hrē-'ä-nōn\ Welsh manifestation of the Gaulish horse goddess EPONA and the Irish goddess Macha. She is best known from the *MABINOGION*, in which she makes her appearance on a pale, mysterious steed and meets King Pwyll, whom she marries. Unjustly accused of killing her infant son, she was forced to carry people on her back like a horse until she was vindicated by her son's return.

Rhine, Confederation of the See CONFEDERATION OF THE RHINE

Rhine River *German* **Rhein** River, western Europe. Rising in the Swiss ALPS, it flows north and west through western Germany to drain through the delta region of the Netherlands into the North Sea. It is 820 mi (1,319 km) long and navigable for 540 mi (870 km). Its many canals connect it with the RHÔNE, MARNE, and DANUBE river systems. It has been an international waterway since 1815 (see Congress of VIENNA). It has played a prominent part in German history and legend. In World War II its course was a major line of defense. Major cities along its banks include BASEL, MANNHEIM, KOBLENZ, COLOGNE, DUISBURG, and ROTTERDAM.

Rhineland *German* **Rheinland** Region of Germany, west of the RHINE RIVER, with an area of about 9,000 sq mi (23,300 sq km). The chief city is COLOGNE. In the 19th century it became the most prosperous area of Germany. After World War I, Allied troops occupied portions of the area on the border with France, and it was the scene of recurrent crises and controversies during the 1920s. In 1936 ADOLF HITLER ordered German troops to enter the demilitarized zone of the Rhineland; weak objections by the Allies foreshadowed Hitler's later annexation of the SUDETENLAND.

rhinoceros Any of five extant African and Asian species (family Rhinocerotidae) of three-toed UNGULATES. One of the largest of all land animals (the white rhinoceros is second only to the elephant), the rhinoceros is particularly distinguished by one or two horns—growths of keratin, a fibrous hair protein—on its upper snout. All have thick, virtually hairless skin that forms platelike folds at the shoulders and thighs. Rhinos grow to 8–14 ft (2.5–4.3 m) long and 3–6.5 ft (1.5–2 m) tall; adults weigh 3–5 tons. Most are solitary inhabitants of open grassland, scrub forest, or marsh, but the Sumatran rhino lives in deep forest. The African black rhino browses on succulent plants, the white and great Indian rhinos graze on short grasses, and the Sumatran and Java rhinos browse on bushes and bamboo. In the second half of the 20th century, the rhinoceros was brought to the brink of extinction by hunters, mostly seeking the horn, which is valued in Asia as an aphrodisiac. Only a few thousand survive, almost all on reserves.

African black rhino (*Diceros bicornis*).
CAMERA PRESS—PICTORIAL PARADE/EB INC.

rhinovirus \ˌrī-nō-'vī-rəs\ Any of a group of PICORNAVIRUSES capable of causing common COLDS in humans. The virus is thought to be transmitted to the upper respiratory tract by airborne droplets. Because of the great number of cold viruses, VACCINES against them are virtually impossible to develop. See also ADENOVIRUS.

rhizome Horizontal underground plant stem capable of producing the upward shoot and downward root systems of a new plant. This capability allows vegetative (asexual) propagation and enables plants to survive an annual unfavorable season underground. In some plants (e.g., WATER LILIES, many FERNS, and forest herbs), the rhizome is the only stem of the plant. In such cases, only the leaves and flowers are readily visible.

Rhode Island *officially* **Rhode Island and Providence Plantations** State (pop., 1997 est.: 987,000), northeastern U.S. One of the NEW ENGLAND states and the smallest U.S. state, it covers 1,212 sq mi (3,139 sq km); its capital is PROVIDENCE. It borders the Atlantic Ocean. The original inhabitants were Narragansett Indians. The first European settlement was in 1636 by ROGER WILLIAMS and his followers, who were banished from Massachusetts; in 1663 King CHARLES II granted a charter to Williams. Though it never officially joined the New England colonies in KING PHILIP'S WAR, it suffered greatly when many settlements were burned. It was in the forefront fighting British customs laws leading up to the AMERICAN REVOLUTION. An original state of the Union, it was the 13th to ratify the Constitution, in 1790, only after the BILL OF RIGHTS was included. The cotton-textile mill built by SAMUEL SLATER in Pawtucket in 1790 initiated the INDUSTRIAL REVOLUTION in the U.S. Its original charter remained in effect until Dorr's Rebellion (see THOMAS W. DORR) in 1842 led to extension of suffrage. Manufacturing is important to the economy, and products include jewelry and silverware, textiles and clothing, and electrical machinery and electronics.

Rhode Island, University of Public university in Kingston, R.I., with branch campuses at Narragansett Bay, in Providence, and at the largely forested 2,400-acre West Alton Jones Campus in West Greenwich. It is a land- and sea-grant institution; first chartered in 1888, it attained university standing in 1951. It offers a range of master's and doctoral degree programs and has a Graduate School of Oceanography. Total enrollment is about 16,000.

Rhode Island School of Design (RISD) One of the most eminent fine-arts colleges in the U.S., located in Providence, R.I. It was founded in 1877 but did not offer college-level instruction until 1932. It combines professional arts training with a broad liberal-arts curriculum, offering bachelor's and master's degrees in the fine arts, design, and other fields. Its art museum has extensive collections of American painting and decorative arts. Enrollment is about 2,000.

Rhodes *Greek* **Ródhos** \'rò-ˌthòs\ Island of Greece, the largest of the Dodecanese group and the most easterly in the Aegean Sea. The main city of Rhodes (pop., 1995 est.: 45,000) lies at the northern tip of the island. The earliest known settlers were the Dorians c. 1000 BC. In the classical period, it vacillated between Athens, Sparta, and Persia. A devastating earthquake c. 225 BC destroyed the Colossus of RHODES, located there. In the medieval period it was occupied by the Byzantines, Saracens, and the Knights of St. John (see KNIGHTS OF MALTA). The knights converted the island into a fortress and held it for two centuries until 1523, when the Turks took control. In 1912 it was taken from Turkey by Italy, and in 1947 it was awarded by treaty to Greece. A year-round tourist industry has brought prosperity to the island.

Rhodes, Alexandre de (1591–1660) French missionary, the first Frenchman to visit Vietnam. He established a Jesuit mission in Indochina in 1619, and he later estimated that he had converted some 6,700 Vietnamese to Catholicism. Expelled in 1630, he spent 10 years teaching philosophy in Macao before returning, only to be exiled again in 1646. The Vatican sponsored a Vietnamese missionary program in 1658 based on de Rhodes's ideas, but he himself was sent to Persia, where he died. He wrote a Vietnamese-Latin-Portuguese dictionary and perfected the romanized script Quoc-ngu (developed by earlier missionaries), which facilitated communication of Christian doctrines to the Vietnamese and increased the literacy rate among the population.

Rhodes, Cecil (John) (1853–1902) Financier, statesman, and empire builder of British South Africa. Rhodes grew up in the English countryside, and in 1871 was sent to assist his brother in business in South Africa, where he became interested in diamond mining. He founded DE BEERS CONSOLIDATED MINES (1888), and by 1891 his company was mining 90% of the world's diamonds. Seeking expansion to the north and dreaming of building a Cape-to-Cairo railway, he persuaded Britain to establish a protectorate over Bechuanaland (1884), clashing with Boer president PAUL KRUGER. He obtained digging concessions from LOBENGULA (1889), but later overran him militarily (1893). At his instigation Britain chartered the British South Africa Co. (1889) and put Rhodes in charge. He extended the company's control to two northern provinces, which were eventually named after him as Southern Rhodesia (now Zimbabwe) and Northern Rhodesia (now Zambia). His interest in the mineral-rich TRANSVAAL led to his plotting to overthrow Kruger (1895), but the attempt was botched by LEANDER STARR JAMESON and Rhodes was forced to resign as prime minister of Cape Colony and head of the British South Africa Co. His last years were marked by disappointment and scandal brought about by the scheming of Princess Radziwill. His will bequeathed most of his fortune to establishing the RHODES SCHOLARSHIPS.

Rhodes, Colossus of Enormous bronze statue of the sun god Helios that towered more than 100 ft (30 m) over the harbor at the city of Rhodes in Greece. The work of Chares of Lindos, the statue commemorated the raising of Demetrios Poliorcetes' long siege of Rhodes (305–304 BC). One of the SEVEN WONDERS OF THE WORLD, it was toppled by an earthquake c. 225 BC. The fallen Colossus was left in place until AD 653, when raiding Arabs broke up its remains and sold the bronze for scrap.

Colossus of Rhodes, constructed c. 292–280 BC, wood engraving reconstruction by Sidney Barclay, c. 1875.

HISTORICAL PICTURES SERVICE, CHICAGO

Rhodes scholarship Grant to attend the University of OXFORD The program was established in 1902 by the will of CECIL RHODES. Until 1976, candidates had to be unmarried males resident in a Commonwealth country, the U.S., or South Africa. In 1976 women were accepted. Two candidates each year are also chosen from Germany. The scholarships, which are highly competitive, are usually for two years.

Rhodesia Region, southern central Africa, now divided into Zimbabwe in the south and Zambia in the north. Named after British colonial administrator CECIL RHODES, it was administered by the British South Africa Co. in the 19th century and exploited mostly for its gold, copper, and coal deposits. In 1911 it was divided into Northern and Southern Rhodesia; Southern Rhodesia became a self-governing British colony (1923), and Northern Rhodesia, a British protectorate (1924). They joined with Nyasaland to become the Federation of Rhodesia and Nyasaland 1953–63. See also MALAWI.

Rhodesia See ZIMBABWE

Rhodesian ridgeback *or* **African lion dog** South African hound breed characterized by a narrow band of hair growing forward along its back, against the direction of the rest of the coat. The ridge is inherited from a half-wild local hunting dog that was crossbred with European dogs. Strong, active, and of great endurance, it is trim and short-haired, with hanging ears and a glossy brown coat. It stands 24–27 in. (61–69 cm) and weighs 65–75 lbs (30–34 kg). It is an able guard and hunter (especially of lions) and a good companion.

Rhodesian ridgeback.

WALTER CHANDOHA

Rhodian Sea Law \'rō-dē-ən\ Regulations governing trade and navigation in the Byzantine Empire. Based on a statute in the Code of JUSTINIAN and on ancient maritime law in Rhodes, the Rhodian Sea Law focused on liability for lost or damaged cargo. It divided the cost of the losses among the shipowner, the owners of the cargo, and the passengers, thus serving as a form of insurance against storms and piracy. It was effective from the 7th through the 12th century.

rhodochrosite \ˌrō-də-'krō-ˌsīt\ CARBONATE MINERAL composed of manganese carbonate ($MnCO_3$), a source of MANGANESE for the ferromanganese alloys used in steel production. It is commonly found in ore veins formed at moderate temperatures, in high-temperature metamorphic deposits, and in sedimentary deposits.

rhododendron \ˌrō-də-'den-drən\ Any of about 800 diverse species of woody plants that make up the genus *Rhododendron* in the HEATH FAMILY, notable for their attractive flowers and handsome foliage. They are native chiefly in the northern temperate zone, especially in South Asia and Malaysia. Some are evergreens, others deciduous. Some are low-growing ground covers; others are tall trees. Flowers are usually tubular to funnel-shaped and occur in a wide range of colors: white, yellow, pink, scarlet, purple, and blue. See also AZALEA.

rhodonite \'rō-də-ˌnīt\ SILICATE MINERAL that occurs in various MANGANESE ores, often with RHODOCHROSITE. A manganese silicate, $MnSiO_3$, with small amounts of iron and calcium, it is found in the Ural Mtns., Sweden, Australia, California, New Jersey, and elsewhere. Rhodonite is the primary source of some important manganese oxide deposits, such as the manganese ores of India. Fine-grained rhodonite of clean, pink color is a desirable gem and ornamental stone.

Rhodonite from Pajsberg, Swed.

BY COURTESY OF THE FIELD MUSEUM OF NATURAL HISTORY, CHICAGO; PHOTOGRAPH, JOHN H. GERARD

Rhodope Mountains \'rä-də-pē\ Mountain range, BALKAN PENINSULA, southeastern Europe. Extending southeast along the border between Bulgaria and Macedonia, Greece, the range is drained by tributaries of the MARITSA RIVER. It forms an important climatic barrier, protecting the Aegean lowlands from cold northerly winds. The mountains were a refuge for Slavic peoples during the period of Turkish rule (15th–19th century), and ancient customs survive. The lakes, river valleys, and extensive forests form the basis of a tourist industry.

rhodopsin \rō-'däp-sən\ *or* **visual purple** Organic compound contained in the light-sensitive rod cells in the RETINA that helps the eye adapt to dim light. It is composed of opsin, a PROTEIN, linked to retinal, a pigment-carrying substance formed from VITAMIN A. In bright light rhodopsin breaks down into retinal and opsin, both of which are colorless; in dim light or darkness the process is reversed and the purple-red rhodopsin is reformed.

Rhone River River, Switzerland and France. An historic southern gateway, and the only major river of the continent that flows directly to the Mediterranean Sea, it is 505 mi (813 km) long and is navigable for about 300 mi (485 km). It is alpine in character, and its course has been shaped by neighboring mountain systems. Rising in the Swiss ALPS, it flows into Lake GENEVA, then crosses into France through the JURA MTNS. It continues south through LYON, AVIGNON, and Tarascon to ARLES and enters the Mediterranean west of MARSEILLE.

rhubarb Any of several species of the genus *Rheum* (family Polygonaceae), especially *R. rhaponticum* (or *R. rhabarbarum*), a hardy perennial grown for its large, succulent, edible leafstalks. Rhubarb is best adapted to the cooler parts of the temperate zones. The fleshy, tart, and highly acid leafstalks are used in pies, compotes and preserves, and sometimes as the base of a wine or an aperitif. The roots withstand cold well. The huge leaves that unfold in early spring are toxic to cattle and humans; later in the season a large central flower stalk may bear numerous small, greenish-white flowers and angular, winged fruits. Rhubarb root has long been considered to have cathartic and purgative properties.

Rhubarb (*Rheum rhaponticum*).
DEREK FELL

rhyme Type of echoing produced by the close placement of two or more words with similarly sounding final syllables. Rhyme is used in poetry (and occasionally in prose) to produce sounds that appeal to the ear and to unify and establish a poem's stanzaic form. End rhyme (i.e., rhyme used at the end of a line to echo the end of another line) is most common, but internal rhyme (occurring before the end of a line) is frequently used as an embellishment. Types of "true rhyme" include masculine rhyme, in which the two words end with the same vowel-consonant combination (stand/land); feminine rhyme (or double rhyme), in which two syllables rhyme (profession/discretion); and trisyllabic rhyme, in which three syllables rhyme (patinate/latinate).

rhyolite \'rī-ə-,līt\ IGNEOUS ROCK that is the volcanic equivalent of GRANITE, whose chemical composition is similar. Rhyolites are known from all parts of the earth and from all geologic ages; they are found mostly on the continents or their immediate margins, but small quantities have been described from remote islands.

Rhys \'rēs\, **Jean** *orig.* **Ella Gwendolen Rees William** (1890–1979) Dominican-British novelist. Rhys left the West Indies for London to study acting at 16. She later moved to Paris, where she was encouraged to write by FORD MADOX FORD. She earned acclaim for short stories and novels set in the bohemian world of Europe in the 1920s and '30s, including *Good Morning Midnight* (1939). After settling in Cornwall, she published nothing for nearly three decades before producing *Wide Sargasso Sea* (1966), a memorable novel about Mr. Rochester's West Indian first wife in BRONTE FAMILY's *Jane Eyre;* and two story collections.

rhythm and blues (R&B) Any of several closely related musical styles developed in the U.S. by black artists. The various styles were based on a mingling of European influences with JAZZ rhythms and tonal inflections, particularly syncopation and the flatted blues chords. They grew out of the BLUES of the rural South, which blended work chants with songs of deep emotion, and were greatly influenced by GOSPEL MUSIC. Three major forms were distinguishable. The earliest, called "race," was the style of the "jump" band, which emphasized strong rhythm, solo work (especially by saxophones), and vocals in a shout-blues manner. A second form, often called "Chicago blues," was exemplified by such performers as M. WATERS and typically played by a small group with amplified instruments. The third major form was primarily vocal, featuring close, gospel-influenced harmonies often backed by an orchestra. In the mid-1950s the term rhythm and blues was adopted by the music industry for music intended for the black audience; with the gradual disappearance of racial barriers, the Chicago blues style began to seem less a vital form than a folk tradition, while the gospel style was transformed into the SOUL MUSIC of vast appeal. Rhythm and blues was the chief antecedent of ROCK MUSIC.

rhythm and meter Two aspects of the organization of time in Western music. Rhythm consists of the pattern of longer and shorter notes, measured from the beginning of one note to that of the next, and is frequently irregular. Meter, like poetical METER, is usually a regular pattern of accented and unaccented beats, and provides the context in which rhythm is understood. In notated music, meter is indicated by means of a time signature—in which the lower number specifies the basic unit or subunit of the beat (e.g., 8 usually indicates that eighth-notes are the basic subunit) and the upper number specifies the number of beats in a measure—at the beginning of a piece or movement, and by the vertical barlines that divide the piece into measures.

rhythmic sportive gymnastics Athletic competition related to GYMNASTICS and dance in which participants, individually or in groups, perform exercise routines with the aid of hand apparatuses such as ropes, hoops, balls, clubs, and ribbons. In scoring points, artistry counts more than acrobatics. The sport dates from the 18th century. Though some gymnasts participated at the Olympic Games from 1948 to 1956, not until 1984 did it become an official Olympic competitive event.

Ribalta \rē-'bäl-tä\, **Francisco** (1565–1628) Spanish painter. His early works are Mannerist. After settling in Valencia in 1598, he developed a darker and more naturalistic style (e.g., his *Santiago* altarpiece, 1603), under the influence of CARAVAGGIO. After 1612 he achieved originality and grandeur in such paintings as *Christ Embracing St. Bernard.* His later paintings, marked by powerfully modeled forms, simplicity of composition, and naturalistic lighting, anticipate the work of DIEGO VELAZQUEZ, FRANCISCO ZURBARAN, and JOSE DE RIBERA.

Ribaut \rē-'bō\, **Jean** (1520?–1565) French colonizer. He served in the French navy under GASPARD II DE COLIGNY, who in 1562 sent him to found a French Huguenot colony in Florida. He landed at the mouth of the St. Johns River (Florida) then sailed north to establish Charlesfort (now in South Carolina). He returned to France, then was sent back to Florida (1565) to reinforce the French colony of Fort Caroline on the St. Johns River. Spanish claims to the region led to the attack and destruction of the colony by PEDRO MENENDEZ DE AVILES, who massacred the French, including Ribaut.

Ribbentrop \'ri-bən-,träp\, **Joachim von** (1893–1946) German diplomat and foreign minister under the Nazi regime. After serving in World War I, he became a wine merchant. He met ADOLF HITLER in 1932 and became his chief adviser on foreign affairs. He negotiated the ANGLO-GERMAN NAVAL AGREEMENT and served as ambassador to Britain (1936–38), advising Hitler that Britain could not aid Poland effectively. As foreign minister (1938–45), he negotiated the PACT OF STEEL with Italy, the GERMAN-SOVIET NONAGGRESSION PACT, and the Tripartite Pact with Japan and Italy. His influence waned in World War II, after which he was found guilty at the NUREMBERG TRIALS and hanged.

Ribble River River, northwestern England. It is 75 mi (120 km) long. It rises in North Yorkshire and flows south and west through Lancashire into the Irish Sea through an estuary extending from PRESTON. The channel to the Irish Sea coast has been straightened to provide a shipping lane to Preston.

Ribera \rē-'ber-ə\, **José de** *or* **Jusepe de Ribera** (1591–1652) Spanish painter and printmaker. Though born in Spain, where he is said to have trained under FRANCISCO RIBALTA, he spent most of his life in Naples (then a Spanish possession). Most of his works are of religious subjects. Dramatic light and shadow and sometimes horrific detail emphasize the mental and physical suffering of penitent or martyred saints, as in *The Martyrdom of St. Bartholomew* (c. 1630). In later works his modeling is softer, his colors are richer, and he demonstrates strong human sympathy, as in *The Clubfooted Boy* (1642). His etchings are among the finest produced in Italy and Spain in the baroque period.

riboflavin \ˌrī-bə-ˈflā-vən\ *or* **vitamin B$_2$** Yellow, water-soluble organic compound, abundant in whey, egg white, and other foods. It has a complex structure incorporating three rings. Green plants and most microorganisms can synthesize it; animals need to acquire it in their diet. It exists in combined forms as COENZYMES and functions in the METABOLISM of CARBOHYDRATES and AMINO ACIDS. A syndrome resembling PELLAGRA is thought to result from riboflavin deficiency. See also FLAVIN.

ribose \ˈrī-ˌbōs\ Five-carbon SUGAR found in RNA. (In DNA the corresponding sugar is the closely related deoxyribose.) A ribose molecule combined with ADENINE, GUANINE, CYTOSINE, or URACIL forms a NUCLEOSIDE; adding a PHOSPHATE group forms a NUCLEOTIDE. The ribose of one nucleotide joins with the phosphate of the next to form the RNA backbone. Ribose phosphates are components of various COENZYMES and are used by microorganisms in synthesizing HISTIDINE.

ribosome \ˈrī-bə-ˌsōm\ Tiny particle, the site of PROTEIN synthesis, that is present in large numbers in living cells. These tiny granules occur both as free particles within cells and as particles attached to the membranes of the ENDOPLASMIC RETICULUM. They are 40% protein and 60% RNA. Ribosomes account for a large proportion of the total RNA of a cell. Proteins newly formed on ribosomes detach and migrate to other parts of the cell to be used.

Ricardo, David (1772–1823) British economist. The son of a Dutch Jew, he followed his father into the London stock exchange, where he made a fortune before turning to the study of political economy, in which he was influenced by the writings of ADAM SMITH. His writings in support of a metal currency standard were influential. In his major work, *The Principles of Political Economy and Taxation* (1817), he examined the movement of wages and the determination of value, asserting that the domestic values of commodities were largely determined by the labor required for their production. His Iron Law of Wages stated that attempts to improve the real income of workers were futile and that wages tended to stabilize at subsistence level. Though many of his ideas are obsolete, he was a major figure in the development of CLASSICAL ECONOMICS, and is credited as the first person to systematize economics.

Ricci \ˈrēt-chē\, **Matteo** (1552–1610) Italian Jesuit missionary who introduced Christianity to China. From a noble family, he was educated by the Jesuits, whose order he joined after studying law in Rome. He volunteered for missionary work overseas, arrived in Goa in 1578, and proceeded to China in 1582. China's interior was closed to foreigners when he arrived, but his willingness to adopt the Chinese language and culture gave him entry. In 1597 he was appointed director of Jesuit activities in China. In 1599 he settled in Nanjing, where he studied astronomy and geography. In 1601 he was finally admitted to Beijing, where he preached the Gospel, taught science to scholars, and translated Christian works into Chinese.

Riccio \ˈrēt-chō, *Engl* ˈrich-ē-ˌō\, **David** *orig.* **Davide Rizzio** (1533?–1566) Italian musician and favorite of MARY, QUEEN OF SCOTS. He accompanied the duke of Savoy's ambassador to Scotland and entered Mary's service as a musician (1561). He became her close adviser and helped arrange her marriage to Lord DARNLEY (1565). Disliked because of his arrogance, Riccio was an impediment to the Scottish nobles' plan to remove Mary. While at dinner in Mary's palace, he was seized by an armed band of nobles, including Lord RUTHVEN, and stabbed to death.

Rice (*Oryza sativa*).
GRANT HEILMAN

rice Edible starchy CEREAL grain and the annual GRASS (*Oryza sativa*, family Poaceae, or Gramineae) that produces it. Roughly one-half the world's population, including almost all of East and Southeast Asia, depends on rice as its principal staple food. First cultivated in India more than 4,000 years ago, rice gradually spread westward and is now cultivated widely in flooded fields (paddies) and river deltas of tropical, semitropical, and temperate regions. Growing to about 4 ft (1.2 m) in height, rice has long, flattened leaves and an inflorescence made up of spikelets bearing flowers that produce the fruit, or grain. Removal of just the husk produces brown rice, containing 8% protein and a source of iron, calcium, and B vitamins. Removal of the bran layer leaves white rice, greatly diminished in nutrients. Enriched white rice has added B vitamins and minerals. So-called wild rice *(Zizania aquatica)* is a coarse annual grass of the same family whose cereal grain, now often considered a delicacy, has long been an important food of North American Indians.

Rice, Jerry (Lee) (born 1962) U.S. football player. Born in Starkville, Miss., he won All-America honors at Mississippi Valley State University. A member of the San Francisco 49ers since 1985, he holds several all-time career records, incl. those for receptions (1,139+), yardage (17,612+), and touchdowns (164+), as well as various single-season and Super Bowl records. He is considered by many the greatest wide receiver of all time.

Rice University Private university in Houston. It was founded in 1891 and endowed by William Marsh Rice. It has schools of humanities, social sciences, architecture, music, natural sciences, and engineering and a graduate school of administration. It offers both undergraduate and graduate degrees in numerous fields. Total enrollment is about 4,500.

Rich, Adrienne (Cecile) (born 1929) U.S. poet, scholar, and critic. Born in Baltimore, she was a student at Radcliffe College when her poems were chosen for publication in the Yale Younger Poets series; the resulting volume, *A Change of World* (1951), reflected her formal mastery. Her subsequent work traces a transformation from well-crafted but imitative poetry to a highly personal and powerful style. Her increasing commitment to the women's movement and a lesbian/feminist aesthetic came to politicize much of her work. Among her collections are *Diving into the Wreck* (1973, National Book Award) and *The Dream of a Common Language* (1978). Her nonfiction *Of Woman Born* (1976; National Book Award) was widely read.

Rich, Buddy *orig.* **Bernard** (1917–1987) U.S. bandleader and one of the most energetic and dazzling drummers in jazz. Born in New York City, Rich was a child-prodigy vaudeville performer known as "Baby Traps, the Drum Wonder." He played with several of the great SWING bands, notably ARTIE SHAW (1939) and TOMMY DORSEY (1939–42, 1944–46), before forming his own big band. In small ensembles, he worked with many of the greatest musicians in jazz in concerts and recordings during the 1950s. The clarity and speed of his drumming made him legendary.

Richard, (Joseph Henri) Maurice (1921–2000) Canadian ice-hockey player. Born in Montreal, he played right wing for the Montreal Canadiens (1942–60). He was the first National Hockey League player to score 50 goals in a regular (50-game) season (1943–44). His nickname, "Rocket," acknowledged his speed and aggressive play, and he was particularly noted for his clutch scoring.

Richard I *known as* **Richard the Lionheart(ed)** *French* **Richard Coeur de Lion** (1157–1199) Duke of Aquitaine (1168–99) and Poitiers (1172–99) and king of England, duke of Normandy, and count of Anjou (1189–99). He inherited Aquitaine from his mother, ELEANOR OF AQUITAINE. Denied real authority there, he rebelled against his father, HENRY II (1173–74), and later enlisted PHILIP II of France in a successful campaign against Henry (1189). Crowned king of England on Henry's death that year, Richard embarked on the Third CRUSADE (1190), stopping in Sicily to name TANCRED king and conquering Cyprus. He won victories in the Holy Land, but after failing to gain Jerusalem he signed a truce (1192) with SALADIN. On his way home Richard was captured by Leopold of Austria and turned over to HENRY VI of Germany, who imprisoned him until a ransom was paid (1194). Richard returned to England and reclaimed the throne from his brother JOHN, then spent the rest of his life in Normandy fighting against PHILIP II.

Richard II (1367–1400) King of England (1377–99). The grandson of EDWARD III, he inherited the throne during his boyhood, and his uncle JOHN OF GAUNT and other nobles dominated the government. The BLACK DEATH brought on economic problems, leading to the PEASANTS' REVOLT

(1381), which Richard quelled with false promises. His enemies among the nobility placed limits on his royal power (1386–89), but he later took revenge on them. He banished John of Gaunt's son, Henry, and confiscated his vast Lancastrian estates. While Richard was absent in Ireland, Henry invaded England (1399) and seized power as HENRY IV. Richard abdicated the throne and died in prison.

Richard III (1452–1485) Last Yorkist king of England. He was made duke of Gloucester in 1461 after his brother Edward of York had deposed the weak Lancastrian king HENRY VI and assumed power as EDWARD IV. Richard and Edward were driven into exile in 1470 but returned and defeated the Lancastrians in 1471. On Edward's death (1483), Richard became protector for Edward's son, the 12-year-old King Edward V, but he usurped the throne and confined Edward and his little brother to the Tower of London, where they were murdered. Henry Tudor (later HENRY VII) raised an army against Richard, who was defeated and killed at the Battle of BOSWORTH FIELD. Later Tudor histories painting Richard as a monster may have been exaggerated.

Richards, I(vor) A(rmstrong) (1893–1979) English critic and poet. While a lecturer at Cambridge, Richards wrote influential works, including *Principles of Literary Criticism* (1924), in which he introduced a new way of reading poetry that led to the NEW CRITICISM. A student of psychology, he concluded that poetry performs a therapeutic function by coordinating various human impulses into an aesthetic whole. In the 1930s he spent much of his time developing Basic English, a language system of 850 basic words that he believed would promote international understanding. He taught at Harvard University from 1944.

Richards, (Isaac) Vivian (Alexander) (b. 1952) West Indian professional CRICKET player, widely regarded as one of the greatest batsmen in the game. Born into a sporting family, Richard's appeared in his first Test match for the West Indies against India in 1974, but he came to prominence with a score of 192 while batting against India in his second Test in that same year. In 1976 Richard's scored a record 1,710 runs. His 56-ball century (scoring 100 points on 56 balls bowled) in 1985 is a record in Test cricket. Richards played a vital role in the West Indies' two World Cup triumphs. He captained the West Indies in 50 Tests with 27 victories and holds the record for never having lost a series as captain. He was selected Wisden Cricketer of the Year in 1977 and was also one of the five cricketers of the century selected by Wisden in 2000. He began coaching the West Indies team upon his retirement as a player in 1991. Richards was knighted in 1999 by the government of Antigua.

Richardson, Dorothy M(iller) (1873–1957) English novelist. From age 17 she engaged in teaching, clerical work, and journalism. For much of her life she worked on her sequence novel *Pilgrimage,* comprising 13 volumes beginning with *Pointed Roofs* (1915). The final volume, *March Moonlight*, was published a decade after her death. A sensitive autobiographical account of a woman's developing consciousness, it was a pioneering work in STREAM-OF-CONSCIOUSNESS fiction. Though well received and much discussed among her peers in her lifetime, it remains little read.

Richardson, Henry Handel *orig.* **Ethel Florence Lindesay Richardson** (1870–1946) Australian-English novelist. In 1888 she left Australia to study music in Germany, and she spent the rest of her life abroad, settling in England in 1904 with her husband, J. G. Robertson. *Maurice Guest* (1908), her antiromantic first novel, concerns a music student's disastrous love affair. Her masterpiece, *The Fortunes of Richard Mahony* (3 vols., 1917–29), combining description of an Australian immigrant's life and work in the goldfields with a powerful character study, is considered the crowning achievement of modern Australian fiction to that time.

Richardson, Henry Hobson (1838–1886) U.S. architect. Born in Priestley Plantation, La., he studied at Harvard University and the École des Beaux-Arts in Paris. His designs for Boston's Brattle Square (1870–72) and Trinity (1872–77) churches won him a national reputation. He designed houses, libraries, suburban railroad stations, educational buildings, and commercial and civic structures. Instead of the narrow vertical proportions and Gothic features used by his contemporaries, he favored horizontal lines, simple silhouettes, and large-scale Romanesque or Byzantine-inspired details. The Crane Memorial Library in Quincy, Mass. (1880–82), with its granite base, clerestory windows, tiled gable roof, and cavernous entrance arch, stands with his finest mature works. His Romanesque style had an integrity seldom achieved by his many imitators, and the functionalism of his designs presaged the work of LOUIS SULLIVAN.

Richardson, John (1796–1852) Canadian writer. His experience in the British army in the War of 1812 and later abroad provided material for some of his writings. The first Canadian novelist to write in English, he won acclaim with his third novel and only enduring work, *Wacousta* (1832), a gothic story about the Indian uprising led by PONTIAC. His nonfiction includes *Personal Memoirs of Major Richardson* (1838) and *War of 1812* (1842).

Richardson, Ralph (David) *later* **Sir Ralph** (1902–1983) British actor. He began his acting career at 18, and gained prominence in the 1930s and '40s at the OLD VIC in such roles as Peer Gynt, Petruchio, Falstaff, and Volpone, gaining a reputation as one of the greatest actors of his time. He made his screen debut in 1933 and became known for playing urbane, witty characters and later for eccentric old men. His many films included *The Fugitive* (1939), *The Fallen Idol* (1948), *The Heiress* (1949), *Long Day's Journey into Night* (1962), *Doctor Zhivago* (1965), *David Copperfield* (1970), and *Greystoke* (1984).

Richardson, Samuel (1689–1761) English novelist. After moving with his family to London at 10, Richardson was apprenticed to a printer before setting up in business for himself in 1721. He soon became quite prosperous. In the 1730s he began to edit and write pamphlets, and eventually hit on the idea of writing a book using a series of letters on the same subject. His major novels were the EPISTOLARY NOVEL *Pamela* (1740), about a servant who avoids seduction and is rewarded by marriage; and his huge masterpiece *Clarissa* (7 vols., 1747–48), a tragedy with multiple narrators that develops a profoundly suggestive interplay of opposed voices. *The History of Sir Charles Grandison* (1753–54), which blends moral discussion and a comic ending, influenced later writers, especially JANE AUSTEN.

Richardson, Tony *orig.* **Cecil Antonio** (1928–1991) British director. With the English Stage Co. he won acclaim with JOHN OSBORNE's *Look Back in Anger* (1956), and led the company in reinterpreting classic plays and in productions of EUGENE IONESCO and SAMUEL BECKETT. He directed *The Entertainer* (1958) and *A Taste of Honey* (1960) on Broadway. He and Osborne formed a film company (1958), which produced screen versions of Osborne's plays as well as *The Loneliness of the Long Distance Runner* (1962) and *Tom Jones* (1963, Academy Award). His later films include *The Charge of the Light Brigade* (1968), *Ned Kelly* (1970), and *Blue Sky* (1993). He was married to VANESSA REDGRAVE; their daughters Miranda and Joely Richardson are both film actresses. His death resulted from AIDS.

Richelieu \ˈri-shə-ˌlü, *French* rē-shə-ˈlyœ̄\, **cardinal et duc (Duke) de** *orig.* **Armand-Jean du Plessis** (1585–1642) French statesman and chief minister to LOUIS XIII. Born to a minor noble family, he was ordained a priest in 1607 and became bishop of Luçon. As the first bishop in France to implement reforms decreed by the Council of TRENT, he brought order to a diocese ruined by the Wars of RELIGION. In 1614 he was elected a deputy of the clergy in the ESTATES GENERAL, where he was noted as a conciliatory force. He became an adviser to MARIE DE MÉDICIS in 1616, and later councillor to her son, Louis XIII. Named a cardinal in 1622, he served as chief minister from 1624 and became the controlling influence in France's policies. He established royal absolutism in France by suppressing the political power of the HUGUENOTS and reducing the influence of the nobles. In foreign policy, he sought to weaken Habsburg control of Europe and entered the THIRTY YEARS' WAR. Devious and brilliant, he increased the power of the BOURBON dynasty and established orderly government in France. He also founded the ACADÉMIE FRANÇAISE and rebuilt the Sorbonne.

Cardinal de Richelieu, detail of a portrait by Philippe de Champaigne; in the Louvre, Paris.

GIRAUDON—ART RESOURCE/EB INC.

Richelieu River \'ri-shə-,lü\ River, southern Quebec. It is 210 mi (338 km) long and flows north from Lake Champlain to join the St. Lawrence River at Sorel. Explored in 1609 by Samuel de Champlain, it was used by the warring French and English colonists and later by commercial loggers and fishermen. A canal enables shallow-draft vessels to navigate between Montreal and New York City via the St. Lawrence and Richelieu rivers, Lake Champlain, and the Hudson River.

Richler, Mordecai (1931–2001) Canadian novelist. Born in Montreal, he grew up in a Jewish working-class neighborhood in which many of his novels are set. In 1951–52 he lived in Paris; he later lived in England. *The Apprenticeship of Duddy Kravitz* (1959) is a bawdy account of a Jewish boy in Montreal and his transformation into a ruthless businessman. *Cocksure* (1968) and *St. Urbain's Horseman* (1971) examine North Americans in England. His later novels include *Joshua Then and Now* (1980) and *Solomon Gursky Was Here* (1989).

Richmond City (pop., 2000: 197,790), capital of Virginia. It is located in the eastern central part of the state, on the James River. Established as a trading post in 1637 and incorporated as a town in 1742, it became the state capital in 1779 and played an important role in the American Revolution. During the American Civil War it was the capital of the Confederate States of America. It was taken by Gen. Ulysses S. Grant in 1865, and much of the business district was burned. It is now a major tobacco market and commercial and government center; its universities include the University of Richmond (founded 1830) and Virginia Commonwealth University (1838).

Richter \'rik-tər\, **Conrad (Michael)** (1890–1968) U.S. short-story writer and novelist. Born in Pine Grove, Pa., he became fascinated with U.S. history and spent years researching frontier life. He is best known for *The Sea of Grass* (1936), an epic on the settling of the Southwest, and for his trilogy of pioneer life, *The Trees* (1940), *The Fields* (1946), and *The Town* (1950, Pulitzer Prize). *The Waters of Kronos* (1960, National Book Award) is an autobiographical novel.

Richter \'rik-tər\, **Curt Paul** (1894–1988) U.S. biologist. Born in Denver, he received a PhD from Johns Hopkins University. He introduced the concept of the biological clock in a 1927 paper on animals' internal cycles (see biological rhythm). He theorized that ancient peoples' discovery of fire changed their habits, resulting in brain-structure changes that increased their ability to learn and communicate. He helped discover relationships between behavior and biochemistry governing sleep, stress, and disease onset.

Richter, Gerhard (born 1932) German painter. Beginning in the early 1960s, Richter created paintings that were faithful enlargements of black-and-white photographs, often family snapshots and landscapes; he would continue this pursuit throughout his career. In the 1970s he also created monochromatic paintings, which explored the act of painting at its purest, while by the 1980s he experimented with an expressionistic, gestural style. Notably, Richter never allied himself to one movement—he has been alternatively described as a Pop artist, Minimalist, and postmodernist. Instead, he has consistently carried out a rigorous, personal exploration of the process of painting.

Richter, Sviatoslav (Teofilovich) (1915–1997) Russian pianist. He became accompanist to the Odessa Opera at 15 and began conducting there at 18. In 1949, two years after graduating from the Moscow Conservatory, his gifts won him the Stalin Prize. He toured Europe, East Asia, and the U.S., becoming legendary for the powerful technique and fiery energy in his solo performances. Highly regarded as an accompanist and chamber player as well, he made celebrated trio recordings with M. Rostropovich and David Oistrakh.

Richter scale \'rik-tər\ Widely used measure of the magnitude of an earthquake, introduced in 1935 by U.S. seismologists Beno Gutenberg (1889–1960) and Charles F. Richter (1900–1985). The scale is logarithmic, so that each increase of one unit represents a 10-fold increase in magnitude (amplitude of seismic waves). The magnitude is then translated into energy released. Earthquakes that are fainter than the ones originally chosen to define magnitude zero are accommodated by using negative numbers. Though the scale has no theoretical upper limit, the most severe earthquakes have not exceeded a scale value of 9. The moment magnitude scale, in use since 1993, is more accurate for large earthquakes; it takes into account the amount of fault slippage, the size of the area ruptured, and the nature of the materials that faulted.

Richthofen \'rikt-,hō-fən\, **Manfred, Freiherr (Baron) von** *known as* **The Red Baron** (1892–1918) German World War I ace. Born to a famous and wealthy family, he began his military career in 1912 as a cavalry officer. In 1915 he transferred to the air force and in 1916 took command of a fighter group that came to be known as "Richthofen's Flying Circus" for its decorated scarlet planes. He had been acclaimed Germany's greatest aviation ace, credited with shooting down 80 enemy airplanes, before he himself was shot down at the age of 25.

Manfred, Freiherr von Richthofen.
PICTORIAL PARADE

Ricimer \'ri-sə-mər\ *orig.* **Flavius Ricimer** (died 472) Roman general. He rose high in the Roman army, but he was barred from the imperial throne as a barbarian and instead became a kingmaker in the empire. He defeated the Vandals in Sicily and deposed the emperor Avitus for Majorian (457), who elevated him to consul. In 461 Ricimer deposed and executed Majorian and appointed Libius Severus as Western emperor. The Eastern emperor later made Anthemius ruler in the West, but Ricimer elevated Olybrius (472) and killed Anthemius.

Rickenbacker, Eddie *orig.* **Edward Vernon** (1890–1973) U.S. World War I ace and industrialist. Born in Columbus, Ohio, he was a top racing driver by 1917, when he entered the army as a driver for an air-corps colonel, who helped him become a fighter pilot. For shooting down 26 enemy airplanes in World War I, he was awarded the Medal of Honor. He later founded and directed his own automobile company, and from 1932 he was an executive with several airlines. As president of Eastern Air Lines (1938–59), he oversaw its growth into a major corporation.

rickets *or* **vitamin D deficiency** Disease of infancy and childhood characterized by defective bone growth due to lack of vitamin D. Calcium phosphate is not properly deposited in the bones, which become soft, curved, and stunted. Early symptoms include restlessness, profuse sweating, lack of limb and abdominal-muscle tone, soft skull bones, and developmental delays. Muscles may cramp and twitch. Without early treatment, effects may include bowlegs, knock-knees, and beadiness where the ribs meet the breastbone. A narrow chest and pelvis can increase susceptibility to lung diseases and impede childbirth. Treatment is with high-dose vitamin D supplementation, sunlight, and a balanced diet.

Ricketts, Howard T(aylor) (1871–1910) U.S. pathologist. Born in Findlay, Ohio, he received his medical degree from Northwestern University. He discovered the bacteria (named rickettsia) that cause Rocky Mountain spotted fever and epidemic typhus. He demonstrated in 1906 that the former could be transmitted by the bite of a certain tick, and identified a bacterium in the blood of infected animals, in the ticks, and in their eggs. He found that epidemic typhus in Mexico was transmitted by a louse and found a related bacterium in the victim's blood and in the lice. He transmitted the disease to monkeys, which developed immunity. He died of typhus later that year.

rickettsia \ri-'ket-sē-ə\ Any of the rod-shaped bacteria that make up the family Rickettsiaceae (named for Howard Ricketts). They are rod-shaped or variably spherical, and most are gram-negative (see gram stain). Natural parasites of certain arthropods, they can cause serious diseases in humans and other animals, to which they are usually transmitted by a bite from an arthropod carrier. Rickettsias can also be transmitted when arthropod feces are inhaled or enter the skin through abrasion. Typhus, trench fever, and Rocky Mountain spotted fever are rickettsial infections. The most effective treatment includes prolonged administration of broad-spectrum antibiotics.

Rickey, Branch (Wesley) (1881–1965) U.S. baseball executive. Born in Stockdale, Ohio, he began playing professional baseball while a student at Ohio Wesleyan University. In 1917 he began a long association with the St. Louis Cardinals (president, 1917–19; field manager, 1919–25; general manager, 1925–42). In 1919 he devised the farm system of training ballplayers. He later became president and general manager of the Brooklyn Dodgers (1943–50). In 1945 he broke a long-standing race barrier by hiring the first two black players in non-Negro League baseball (1945), including Jackie Robinson, defying strong resistance. He was later associated with the Pittsburgh Pirates (1950–59).

Rickover, Hyman G(eorge) (1900–1986) U.S. (Russian-born) naval nuclear engineer. His family emigrated to the U.S. in 1906 and he grew up in Chicago. After graduating from Annapolis, he served on submarines and other ships, then headed the electrical section of the Navy's Bureau of Ships in World War II. From 1947 he led the Navy's nuclear-propulsion program; his team developed the first atomic-powered submarine, the USS *Nautilus*, launched in 1954. He headed research on reactor development for the Atomic Energy Commission, and helped develop the nation's first full-scale, civilian-use nuclear power plant, at Shippingport, Pa. (1956–57). Promoted to admiral in 1973, he was noted for his outspoken views and singleminded advocacy of nuclear power development.

Rida, Muhammad Rashid See Muhammad Rashid Rida

riddle Deliberately enigmatic or ambiguous question requiring a thoughtful and often witty answer. The riddle is a form of guessing game that has been a part of the folklore of most cultures from ancient times. Western scholars generally recognize two main kinds of riddle: the descriptive riddle, usually describing an animal, person, plant, or object in an intentionally enigmatic manner (thus an egg is "a little white house without door or window"); and the shrewd or witty question. A classical Greek example of the latter type is "What is the strongest of all things?"—"Love: iron is strong, but the blacksmith is stronger, and love can subdue the blacksmith."

Ride, Sally (Kristen) (born 1951) U.S. astronaut. Born in Los Angeles, she received a PhD in physics from Stanford University in 1977 and joined NASA the same year. In 1983 she participated in the seventh space-shuttle mission, aboard the *Challenger*, as flight engineer, becoming the first American woman and the third woman internationally (after the Russians Valentina Tereshkova, in 1963, and Svetlana Savitskaya, in 1982) to fly into outer space. She went on to become director of the California Space Institute at UC–San Diego.

Ridgway, Matthew B(unker) (1895–1993) U.S. Army officer. Born in Fort Monroe, Va., he graduated from West Point and served in staff positions until World War II. In 1942 he commanded an airborne division in the invasion of Sicily (1943), the first airborne assault in U.S. military history. He led his paratroopers in the Normandy Campaign and commanded airborne operations across Europe. In the Korean War he led the U.S. 8th Army, rallying U.N. forces and forcing the Chinese out of South Korea. Promoted to general, he succeeded Douglas MacArthur as Allied commander in the Far East (1951). He later served as supreme commander of NATO forces (1952) and army chief of staff (1953–55).

Riefenstahl \'rē-fən-ˌshtäl\, **Leni** *orig.* **Berta Helene Amalie** (born 1902) German film director and photographer. In the 1920s she was a dancer and actress in German nature films. After forming a production company, she made and starred in the mystical *The Blue Light* (1932). For Adolf Hitler she directed the propaganda film *Triumph of the Will* (1935), a documentary glorifying the Nuremberg Rallies. She was praised for the technical brilliance of *Olympia* (1938), her documentary on the 1936 Berlin Olympics. Imprisoned after World War II, she was eventually cleared of complicity in Nazi war crimes, but her film career never recovered, and she worked principally as a photographer thereafter.

Riel \rē-'el\, **Louis** (1844–1885) Canadian leader of the Métis people in western Canada. Riel was born in St. Boniface, Manitoba. In 1869 he headed a revolt against Canadian expansion in the west that resulted in the establishment of the province of Manitoba (1870). Intermittent hostilities continued for several years thereafter, and Riel was officially outlawed. In 1885 he led a Métis uprising in Saskatchewan that was crushed by the Canadians. Riel was found guilty of treason and hanged. His death led to ethnic conflicts in Quebec and Ontario and marked the beginning of the nationalist movement.

Riemann \'rē-ˌmän\, **(Georg Friedrich) Bernhard** (1826–1866) German mathematician. He studied at the Univs. of Berlin and Göttingen, and later taught principally at Göttingen. His dissertation (1851) was on function theory. He became convinced that mathematical theory could link magnetism, light, gravitation, and electricity and suggested field theories, in which the space surrounding electrical charges may be mathematically described. While continuing to develop unifying mathematical themes in the laws of physics, he created Riemannian geometry (or elliptic geometry), which proved essential to Albert Einstein's model of space-time in relativity theory. Riemann surfaces, Riemann integrals, and Riemann curvature, among other concepts, contributed to the understanding of curves and surfaces, as well as of calculus. With Carl Friedrich Gauss, Riemann helped establish Göttingen's reputation as a world leader in mathematical research. His work widely influenced geometry and analysis.

Riemannian geometry See elliptic geometry

Riemenschneider \'rē-mən-ˌshnī-dər\, **Tilman** (c. 1460–1531) German sculptor. Son of a mint master, he settled in Würzburg in 1483 and opened a highly successful workshop. He was a city councillor (1504–20) and burgomeister (1520–25), but his sympathies with the revolutionaries in the Peasants' Revolt led to a brief imprisonment. His wood and stone sculpture, characterized by sharply folded, flowing drapery, included monumental tombs and altarpieces as well as independent statues and reliefs, and made him one of the major masters of late Gothic art in Germany.

Rienzo, Cola di See Cola di Rienzo

Riesener \rēz-'ner\, **Jean-Henri** (1734–1806) French cabinetmaker. Son of an usher in the law courts of the elector of Cologne, he joined a workshop in Paris and became its head when his master died. In 1774 he was made royal cabinetmaker and from then on was the regular supplier of furniture to Marie-Antoinette. His preferred wood was mahogany; occasionally he used lacquer and mother-of-pearl to enrich his surfaces. His furniture exemplified Louis XVI style.

Jewel casket on a stand, veneered with mahogany, sycamore, and purplewood, by Riesener, c. 1780; in the Victoria and Albert Museum, London.

BY COURTESY OF THE VICTORIA AND ALBERT MUSEUM, LONDON

Riesman, David (1909–2002) U.S. sociologist. Born in Philadelphia and educated at Harvard University and Harvard Law School, he clerked for Louis Brandeis and taught at the Univs. of Buffalo and Chicago before returning to Harvard to teach (1958–80). He studied primarily the social character of the urban middle class and is noted for *The Lonely Crowd* (1950), whose title became a catchphrase for the alienation of the individual in modern urban society.

Rietveld \'rēt-ˌvelt\, **Gerrit (Thomas)** (1888–1964) Dutch architect and furniture designer. He was an apprentice in his father's cabinetmaking business (1899–1906) and later studied architecture in Utrecht. In 1918 he created his famous red-and-blue armchair, which, with its emphasis on geometry and use of primary colors, became a symbol of De Stijl. His masterpiece is the Schroeder House in Utrecht (1924), remarkable for its interplay of right-angle forms, planes, and lines.

Rif Muslim Berber people who live in Er Rif of northern Morocco. Their culture is based on cultivation, herding, and fish processing. They speak a dialect of Berber, but Arabic and Spanish are also widely used. They have traditionally flouted central-government control and have often instigated uprisings and attempted coups. Led by Abd al-Krim, they declared a short-lived independent republic, the Rif Republic (1919–26), which was quashed by a French-Spanish alliance. See also Kabyle.

Rif See Er Rif

rifle Firearm whose barrel is rifled (i.e., has spiral grooves cut inside it to give a spin to the projectile). Though usually applied to a weapon fired from the shoulder, the name can also refer to a rifled cannon. Rifled firearms date to at least the 15th century, when it was discovered that imparting a spin to the bullet improved its range and accuracy. The earliest muzzle-loading rifles were more difficult to load than smoothbore MUSKETS, but the invention of metallic cartridges made possible the development of breech-loading mechanisms. Bolt-action rifles, which use a manually operated cylinder to drive the cartridge into the rifle's chamber, are the most common type for hunting. See also ASSAULT RIFLE.

Rift Valley See GREAT RIFT VALLEY

rift valley Elongated trough formed by the subsidence of a segment of the earth's crust between dip-slip, or normal, FAULTS. Rift valleys are usually narrow and long and have a relatively flat floor. The sides drop away steeply in steps and terraces. Rift valleys are found on the continents and along the crests of OCEANIC RIDGES. They occur where two plates that make up the earth's surface are separating (see PLATE TECTONICS). Submarine rift valleys are usually centers of SEAFLOOR SPREADING, where magma wells up from the MANTLE. The most extensive continental rift valleys are those of the East African Rift System; other notable examples include Russia's Baikal Rift Valley and Germany's Rhine Rift Valley.

Rig Veda *or* **Rg Veda** \rig-ˈvā-də\ Oldest religious SCRIPTURE in the world and most revered of the VEDAS, dating from the second millennium BC or earlier. Consisting of more than 1,000 hymns addressed to DEVAS (gods), it reflects a POLYTHEISM that is mainly concerned with the propitiation of divinities associated with the sky and atmosphere. It makes reference to such rituals as marriage and funeral rites, which differ little from those practiced today in Hinduism. It is the source of much Indian thought, and many consider its study essential to understanding India.

Riga \ˈrē-gə\ City (pop., 2000 est.: 788,283), capital of Latvia. It is situated on both banks of the Western DVINA RIVER, above its mouth on the Gulf of RIGA. It was founded as a trading post in 1201 on the site of an ancient Liv settlement and joined the HANSEATIC LEAGUE in 1282. In the Middle Ages it was dominated by the TEUTONIC ORDER, and it was fought over by Poles and Russians in the 16th century. It was captured by Sweden in 1621 and granted self-government but was ceded to Russia in 1721. It was the capital of an independent Latvia 1918–40, then was incorporated into the U.S.S.R. It again became the capital of an independent Latvia in 1991. It is a principal Baltic port and a major administrative, cultural, and industrial center. Its medieval remains include a 13th-century church and a 14th-century castle.

Riga, Gulf of Large gulf of the BALTIC SEA. Bounded by Latvia and Estonia, it covers about 7,000 sq mi (18,000 sq km). The gulf, icebound from December to April, has a maximum depth of 177 ft (54 m). The coasts are mostly low and sandy, and several important rivers, including the Western DVINA, reach the sea there. Several ports and resorts, including RIGA, line its shores.

Riga, Treaty of (1921) Treaty between Poland and Russia signed in Riga, Latvia that ended the Russo-Polish War of 1919–20 and set their mutual border. It gave Poland parts of Byelorussia (Belarus) and Ukraine and lasted until World War II, after which a new treaty established a new border.

right Portion of the political spectrum associated with conservative political thought. The term derives from the seating arrangement of the French revolutionary parliament (c. 1790s) in which the conservative representatives sat to the presiding officer's right. In the 19th century, the term applied to conservatives who supported authority, tradition, and property. In the 20th century a divergent, radical form developed that was associated with FASCISM. See also LEFT.

right-to-work law In the U.S., any state law prohibiting labor agreements that require all employees to be union members. Supporters of such laws maintain that they are more equitable because they allow a person to choose whether or not to join a LABOR UNION. Opponents maintain that they reduce workers' job security by weakening the bargaining power of unions.

right whale Any of five species (genera *Balaena, Eubalaena,* and *Caperea*) of BALEEN WHALES (family Balaenidae) with a stout body and an enormous head. (The name refers to two species considered the "right" whales to hunt because of their value, slowness, and buoyancy after death.) The upper jaw is strongly arched, and the lower lip curves upward along the side, giving the lower jaw a scooplike form. There is no dorsal fin except in the pygmy right whale, a small, seldom-seen whale of the Southern Hemisphere. The bowhead whale *(Balaena mysticetus),* inhabiting Arctic and northern temperate waters, is black, with a white chin, throat, and sometimes underparts. It grows to about 65 ft (20 m). The northern right whale *(E. glacialis)* grows to 60 ft (18 m). Similar to the bowhead but with a smaller, less strongly arched head, it may also have a "bonnet," a horny growth infested with parasites, on its snout. Both species have been protected since 1946.

Southern right whale (*Eubalaena australis*).
ILLUSTRATION BY LARRY FOSTER

rights of the accused See rights of the ACCUSED

Riis \ˈrēs\, **Jacob A(ugust)** (1849–1914) Danish-U.S. reporter and social reformer. He emigrated to the U.S. at 21 and became a police reporter for the *New York Tribune* (1877–88) and the *New York Evening Sun* (1888–99). He publicized the deplorable living conditions in the slums of New York's Lower East Side, photographing the rooms and hallways of tenements. He compiled his findings in *How the Other Half Lives* (1890), a book that stirred the nation's social conscience and spurred the state's first significant legislation to improve tenements.

Rijn, Rembrandt van See REMBRANDT VAN RIJN

Rikken Seiyukai \ˈrik-ˌen-ˈsā-yu̇-ˌkī\ Dominant Japanese political party from its inception in 1900 until 1940. Founded by ITO HIROBUMI, it initially stood for increased parliamentary participation in government. It was supported by the landlord class and ZAIBATSU business interests, and was generally more conservative than its chief rival, the Minseito.

Riley, James Whitcomb (1849–1916) U.S. poet. Born in Greenfield, Ind., he came into touch with the populace of rural Indiana through his early work experiences. His verse contributions to the *Indianapolis Daily Journal*, written in Hoosier dialect ostensibly by a farmer, established his reputation as "the poet of the common people." His best-known poems include "When the Frost Is on the Punkin" and "The Raggedy Man." Among his many collections are *The Old Swimmin' Hole* (1883), *Pipes o' Pan at Zekesbury* (1888), and *Home Folks* (1900).

rilievo See RELIEF

Rilke \ˈril-kə\, **Rainer Maria** *orig.* **René Maria Rilke** (1875–1926) Austrian-German poet. After an unhappy childhood and an ill-planned preparatory education, Rilke began a life of wandering that took him across Europe. His visits to Russia inspired his first serious work, the long poem cycle *The Book of Hours* (1905). For 12 years beginning in 1902 his geographic center was Paris, where he developed a new style of lyrical poetry that attempted to capture the plastic essence of a physical object; the results were *New Poems* (1907–8) and its prose counterpart, the novel *The Notebook of Malte Laurids Brigge* (1910). After 13 years of writing very little because of writer's block and depression, in 1922 he finally completed the 10 poems of the *Duino Elegies* (1923), a profound meditation on the paradoxes of human existence and one of the century's poetic masterpieces. Unexpectedly and with astonishing speed, he then composed *Sonnets to Orpheus* (1923), a superb 55-poem cycle inspired by the death of a young girl, which continues the *Elegies*' meditations on death, transcendence, and poetry. The two works brought him international fame.

Rimbaud \raⁿ-'bō\, **(Jean-Nicolas-) Arthur** (1854–1891) French poet and adventurer. The provincial son of an army captain, he had begun by age 16 to write violent, blasphemous poems, and he formulated an aesthetic doctrine stating that a poet must become a seer, break down the restraints and controls on personality, and thus become the instrument for the voice of the eternal. He was invited to Paris by PAUL VERLAINE, with whom he entered a homosexual relationship and engaged in a wild and dissipated life. *The Drunken Boat* (written 1871), perhaps his finest poem, displays his astonishing verbal virtuosity and a daring choice of images and metaphors. In *Les illuminations* (written 1872–74), a collection of mainly PROSE POEMS, he tried to abolish the distinction between reality and hallucination. *A Season in Hell* (1873), which alternates prose passages with dazzling lyrics, became his farewell to poetry at age 19. After a falling-out, Verlaine shot and wounded Rimbaud; later their final meeting ended in a violent quarrel. Rimbaud abandoned literature and from 1875 led an international vagabond life as a merchant and trader, mainly in Ethiopia; he died after his leg was amputated at 37. The Dionysian power of his verse and his liberation of language from the constraints of form greatly influenced the SYMBOLIST MOVEMENT and 20th-century poetry.

Rimbaud, detail from "Un Coin de table," oil painting by Henri Fantin-Latour, 1872; in the Louvre, Paris.
GIRAUDON—ART RESOURCE

Rimsky-Korsakov, Nikolai (Andreyevich) (1844–1908) Russian composer. While at St. Petersburg's College of Naval Cadets, he met other composers; M. BALAKIREV took a special interest in him, and from 1867 he was included among the MIGHTY FIVE. Returning from his first cruise as a midshipman in 1865, he finished a symphony, which Balakirev conducted. In 1873 he managed to have the post of Inspector of Naval Bands created for himself. He helped A. BORODIN orchestrate *Prince Igor* and revised several of M. MUSSORGSKY's works. He wrote many colorful operas, much loved in Russia, including *Sadko* (1896), *Mozart and Salieri* (1897), *The Tale of Tsar Saltan* (1903), *The Legend of the Invisible City of Kitezh* (1905), and *The Golden Cockerel* (1908); other works include three symphonies, the suite *Scheherazade* (1888), and the *Russian Easter Festival* overture. All his works are distinguished by brilliant orchestration. His many students included A. GLAZUNOV, S. PROKOFIEV, O. RESPIGHI, and I. STRAVINSKY.

rinderpest Acute, highly contagious viral disease of RUMINANTS (including wild cloven-hoofed ones), common in Africa, the Indian subcontinent, and the Middle East. The virus spreads by close direct or indirect contact. It is the most severe infectious disease of cattle, with sudden onset and high mortality; fever and appetite loss are followed by symptoms including eye and nasal discharge, labored breathing, and diarrhea; prostration, coma, and death follow within 6–12 days. Local eradication depends on controlling it in wild animals and eliminating infected domestic animals; vaccination combined with quarantine is effective.

ring Circular band of gold, silver, or other precious or decorative material usually worn on the finger, but sometimes on the toes, the ears, or the nose. The earliest examples were found in the tombs of ancient Egypt. In addition to being worn as adornment, rings have functioned as symbols of authority, fidelity, or social status. In the early Roman republic, most were made of iron, gold being reserved for persons of high status; but by the 3rd century BC anyone except a slave could wear a gold ring. The Romans are thought to have originated engagement rings, symbolizing a promise of marriage. In the Middle Ages, signet rings were important in religious, legal, and commercial transactions; memorial, posy, and keepsake rings served sentimental purposes; occult rings supposedly had magical powers; and poison rings had hollow bezels that could be filled with poison for the purpose of suicide or homicide.

ring In modern ALGEBRA, a set of elements and two operations, addition and multiplication, that conform to certain conditions. These specify that the set be closed under addition and multiplication, form a commutative group with respect to addition (see GROUP THEORY) but be merely associative with respect to multiplication, and that it obey the distributive law of multiplication over addition. If the set also contains a multiplicative inverse for each nonzero element, it is called a division ring. The set of INTEGERS is a ring, while the sets of RATIONAL, REAL, and COMPLEX numbers each form a field.

Ring of Fire Belt of seismic and volcanic activity roughly surrounding the Pacific Ocean. It includes the ANDES, the coastal regions of Central and North America, the ALEUTIAN and KURIL islands, KAMCHATKA peninsula, Taiwan, eastern Indonesia, New Zealand, the Japanese and Philippine islands, and the island arcs of the western Pacific. About 70% of all historically recorded active volcanoes have occurred in this belt. See also PLATE TECTONICS.

Ringgold, Faith (born 1930) U.S. artist, author, and political activist. Born in New York City, she began teaching art in New York's public schools in the 1950s. In 1963 she began her "American People" series of paintings, which dealt with the civil-rights movement from a female perspective. In the 1970s she became active in promoting feminist art and the racial integration of the New York art world. Her famous "story quilts," inspired by Tibetan tankas, depict stories set in the context of African-American history. She adapted one of her quilts, *Tar Beach,* as a children's book, and went on to publish other books for children.

Ringling Brothers Family of U.S. circus owners. After five of the seven brothers formed a song-and-dance troupe (1882), they began to add circus acts to their show. In 1884 they organized their first small circus in their hometown, Baraboo, Wis., and began to tour the Midwest in circus wagons. In 1890 they began moving their wagons by railway. They acquired smaller circuses from 1900, and in 1907 bought the Barnum & Bailey Circus to form the leading U.S. circus. The guiding managers were Charles Ringling (1863–1926) and later John Ringling (1866–1936), whose acquisition of American Circus Corp. in 1929 brought 11 major circuses under Ringling control. The Ringling Brothers and Barnum & Bailey Circus continues to perform, though it passed out of Ringling family hands in 1967.

John Ringling.
KEYSTONE—EB INC.

rings Event in men's GYMNASTICS in which a pair of rubber-coated metal rings suspended from a ceiling or crossbar are used to perform hanging, swinging, and balancing feats. The rings themselves must remain essentially stationary. There must be at least two handstands in an exercise, one attained by strength and the other utilizing body swing. Strength movements on the rings include the iron cross (holding the body vertical with the arms fully stretched sideways) and the lever (hanging with straight arms with the body stretched out horizontally).

ringworm Superficial skin changes caused by certain fungi (see FUNGUS) that live on the skin, feeding on KERATIN. Skin responses vary from slight scaling to blistering and marked disruption of the keratin layer (depending on body area and type of fungus), usually in a ring shape. It includes ATHLETE'S FOOT, jock itch, and fungal infections of the body, hands, nails, beard, and scalp. While the last is very contagious, spread of other types depends on susceptibility and predisposing factors (e.g., excessive perspiration). Ringworm is treated with medications applied to the skin or taken orally. Limited ultraviolet-light exposure may also help.

Rio de Janeiro City (pop., 1995 est.: 5,474,000) and port, southeastern Brazil. The site was discovered by the Portuguese in the early 16th century and became important in the 18th century as an outlet for mineral exports from gold and diamond mines. Located on one of the largest harbors in the world and known for its scenic views, it was the capital of Brazil from 1822 to 1960, when the national capital was moved to BRASILIA. It is the country's second-largest manufacturing center after SÃO PAULO. Major industries include metallurgy and food processing. Noted for its wide streets, public buildings, beaches (see COPACABANA), and public parks and gardens, it is a leading tourist and resort center.

Río de la Plata See Río de la PLATA

Río de la Plata, viceroyalty of Last of the four viceroyalties that Spain created to govern its New World colonies. Established in 1776 as part of a decentralization of rule in the Spanish empire, it controlled an area previously administered by the viceroyalty of PERU and included what is now Argentina, Uruguay, Paraguay, and Bolivia. Successive viceroys defended the territory against encroachment by Portugal and Britain and helped Buenos Aires become a flourishing outpost of the Spanish empire. Salted meat from the cattle ranches of the interior, exported to meet the demand for cheap food for slaves, brought unprecedented wealth to the colony. In 1810 the Creoles created a provisional junta and sent the viceroy into exile. See also NEW GRANADA, NEW SPAIN.

Río de Oro Southern region, WESTERN SAHARA. Its principal town, Dakhla (formerly Villa Cisneros), has a small port and must rely on imported drinking water. The narrow inlet of the Atlantic Ocean at Dakhla was called Río de Oro (River of Gold) by the Portuguese because of the trade in gold dust from western Africa. From the 1880s until 1976 it was ruled by Spain. In 1979 it was occupied by Morocco. The indigenous inhabitants are Muslim and largely nomadic BERBERS.

Rio Grande \'rē-ō-'grand\ *in Mexico* **Río Bravo** River, North America. One of the longest rivers of North America, it flows 1,900 mi (3,000 km) from its sources in the southern ROCKY MTNS. of southwestern Colorado to the Gulf of MEXICO. It rises high in the SAN JUAN MTNS. and flows generally south, passing southeast between Texas and Mexico, marking the entire border. The earliest European settlements were along the lower course of the river in the 16th century, but many of the PUEBLO INDIAN settlements of New Mexico date from before the Spanish conquest. During the Spanish period, the middle and upper portions were called the Río del Norte and the lower course was called the Río Bravo. It is a major source of irrigation. It flows through BIG BEND NATIONAL PARK.

Rio Treaty *officially* **Convention on Biological Diversity** International environmental agreement approved at the 1992 EARTH SUMMIT. Negotiations began in 1988 under the auspices of the U.N. Environment Program. Its goals are the conservation of the planet's biodiversity and the fair use of its resources. The agreement had gained the signatures of 168 governments within a year after the summit.

Riopelle \rē-ō-'pel\, **Jean-Paul** (born 1923) Canadian painter, sculptor, and graphic artist. Born in Montreal, he moved to Paris in 1947 and, with P.-E. BORDUAS, became associated with the group of Canadian painters known as Les Automatistes, who practiced AUTOMATISM. His early lyrical, abstract paintings evolved into a denser, more powerful impasto style; he is renowned for his use of various media (including watercolor, ink, oils, crayon, and chalk) and he also produced large collage murals. He achieved international acclaim with the huge triptych *Pavane* (1954). He is the leading Canadian abstract painter of his generation.

rip current *or* **riptide** Narrow jetlike stream of water that flows sporadically seaward for several minutes, in a direction perpendicular to a beach. The term *riptide* is a misnomer because the currents are in no way related to tides. Rip currents form at long coasts that are approached by wave trains that are nearly parallel to the shoreline. In shallow water, normal wave motion displaces the water small distances shoreward with each passing wave. During periods of large waves, water builds up at the beach and cannot escape as longshore currents, which require oblique wave approach. The buildup continues until water can escape by surging for several minutes through a low point in a breaker, creating an undertow that can be dangerous for swimmers.

riparian right \ri-'par-ē-ən\ In law, the right of one who owns riparian land (land abutting or including a stream or river) to have access to and use of the shore and water. These rights are a form of real property (see REAL AND PERSONAL PROPERTY) and are inherited with the land. A landowner whose property abuts an ocean, sea, lake, or pond is said to possess littoral rights. Specific water-use laws vary from state to state.

Ripken, Cal(vin Edwin), Jr. (born 1960) U.S. baseball player. He was born into a baseball family in Havre de Grace, Md.; his father and brother both played professionally. He played for the Baltimore Orioles from 1981. In 1990 he set single-season records for highest fielding percentage by a shortstop (.996) and fewest errors by a shortstop (3), and in 1993 he broke the home-run record for a shortstop. In 1995 he broke LOU GEHRIG's long-standing record of consecutive games played (2,130), eventually running his streak to 2,632 games before taking a day off in 1998.

Ripley, George (1802–1880) U.S. journalist and reformer. Born in Greenfield, Mass., he became a Unitarian minister after graduating from Harvard Divinity School. A member of the Transcendental Club and an editor of *The Dial,* its literary magazine, he founded the utopian community BROOK FARM in 1841 and served as its director and leading promoter. When it closed in 1847, he took a job with the *New York Tribune* to pay off its debts. His own financial position did not become secure until he published *The Cyclopedia* (1862), a popular reference book.

ripple mark One of a series of small marine, lake, or riverine features, consisting of repeating wavelike forms with symmetric slopes, sharp peaks, and rounded troughs. Ripple marks are formed in sandy bottoms by oscillation waves, in which only the wave form advances rapidly, the actual water-particle motion consisting of almost closed vertical orbits. The presence of the bottom restricts the lowermost orbits into nearly flat ellipses, and the bottom water moves back and forth rhythmically. If the maximum horizontal velocity of this motion is capable of moving the grains composing the bed, ripple marks develop. See also WAVE.

RISC \'risk\ *in full* **Reduced Instruction Set Computer** COMPUTER ARCHITECTURE that uses a limited number of instructions. RISC became popular in microprocessors in the 1980s. The traditional CISC (Complex Instruction Set Computer) architecture uses many instructions that do long, complex operations. Each RISC instruction is executed much more quickly than a CISC instruction, and most computational tasks can be processed faster. Many instruction sets combine attributes of CISC and RISC.

risk In economics and finance, an allowance for the hazard (risk) in an investment or loan. Default risk refers to the chance that a borrower will not repay a loan. If a banker believes that a borrower may not repay a loan, the banker will charge the true INTEREST plus a premium for the default risk, the premium depending on the degree of presumed risk. All stock investment carried an implicit risk since there is no guarantee of return on investment. Trading or variability risk is the amount that the return may vary, up or down, from the expected return on investment.

Risorgimento \rē-,zȯr-ji-'men-tō\ (Italian: "Resurgence") 19th-century movement for Italian unification. Reforms introduced by France into its Italian states in the Napoleonic period remained after the states were restored to their former rulers in 1815 and provided an impetus for the movement. Secret groups such as YOUNG ITALY advocated Italian unity, and such leaders as CAMILLO CAVOUR, who founded the journal *Il Risorgimento* (1847), GIUSEPPE DE GARIBALDI, and GIUSEPPE MAZZINI called for liberal reforms and a united Italy. After the failure of the REVOLUTIONS OF 1848, leadership passed to Cavour and Piedmont, which formed an alliance with France against Austria (1859). The unification of most of Italy in 1861, followed by the annexation of Venetia (1866) and papal Rome (1870), marked the end of the Risorgimento.

Ritalin A mild form of AMPHETAMINE used in the treatment of ATTENTION-DEFICIT HYPERACTIVITY DISORDER (ADHD), generic name methylphenidate. Ritalin, taken as a pill, also has been effective for the treatment of other conditions such as NARCOLEPSY. Although the drug acts as a stimulant in most people, Ritalin calms and focuses those with ADHD. Ritalin's mode of action is unknown, but it is thought that the drug reduces symptoms by increasing the amount and activity of a neurotransmitter in the brain.

rite of passage See rite of PASSAGE

Ritsos \'rēt-sȯs\, **Yannis** (1909–1990) Greek poet. He joined the Greek Communist Party in 1934, the year his first collection of poems, *Tractors,* appeared. It and a second collection mixed socialist philosophy with images of his personal suffering. His third collection, *Funeral Procession* (1936), provided the words for the anthem of the Greek Left. He fought as a Communist during the Nazi occupation and Greek civil war, and spent four years in prison camps. Arrested and exiled in 1967, he was prohibited from publishing until 1972. Despite those obstacles, he wrote a total of 117 books, including plays and essays.

Ritt, Martin (1914–1990) U.S. film director. Born in New York City, he joined his friend ELIA KAZAN at the GROUP THEATRE and worked as an actor, then began directing plays on Broadway (1946–47) and on television (1948–51). Blacklisted as a former Communist in 1951, he returned to directing with his first film, *Edge of the City* (1957), and became noted for addressing social themes. His films include *Hud* (1963), *The Spy Who Came in from the Cold* (1965), *Sounder* (1972), and *Norma Rae* (1979).

Rittenhouse, David (1732–1796) U.S. astronomer and inventor. Born in Germantown, Pa., he was a clockmaker by trade but also built mathematical instruments and, it is believed, the first TELESCOPE in the U.S. In 1769 he observed VENUS moving across the face of the sun and noted that Venus has an atmosphere. Rittenhouse served as treasurer of Pennsylvania (1777–89), first director of the U.S. Mint in Philadelphia (1792–95), and president of the American Philosophical Society (1791–96).

Rivadavia \ˌrē-vä-t͟hä-vē-ə\, **Bernardino** (1780–1845) First president of the Argentine republic (1826–27). Active in the 1810 movement for independence from Spain, he came to dominate the ruling revolutionary triumvirate in 1811. He disbanded the Spanish courts, abolished censorship, and ended the slave trade. Elected president of the United Provinces in 1826, he continued to advance reforms but was unable to extricate his country from a fruitless war with Brazil and was constantly embroiled with provincial CAUDILLOS. Unable to win acceptance for a centralist constitution, he resigned. His cultural initiatives, including the founding of the University of Buenos Aires, were among his greatest achievements. Most of his later years were spent in exile.

river Natural stream of water that flows in a channel with more or less defined banks. Rivers are a fundamental link in the HYDROLOGIC CYCLE, and they play a major role in shaping the surface features of the earth. Even apparently arid desert regions are greatly influenced by river action when periodic floodwaters surge down usually dry watercourses. River flow is sustained by the difference between water input and output. Rivers are fed by overland runoff, groundwater seepage, and meltwater released along the edges of snowfields and glaciers. Direct precipitation contributes only very small amounts of water. Losses of river water result from percolation into porous and permeable rock, gravel, or sand; evaporation; and ultimately outflow into the ocean.

river blindness *or* **onchocerciasis** \ˌäŋ-kō-ˌsər-ˈkī-ə-səs\ Human disease caused by a filarial worm native to Africa but also found in parts of tropical America and transmitted by several BLACKFLIES. It is so called because the flies that transmit the disease breed on rivers and mostly affect riverine populations. Blindness is caused by dead microfilariae—the larvae that can be produced for some 15–18 years by adult worms—inside the eye. River blindness is common in savannah areas of Africa and in Guatemala and Mexico. In 1987 the World Health Organization began to distribute the drug ivermectin (originally developed for use against livestock parasites), which eliminates the microfilariae, though it does not kill the adult parasite.

Rivera, Diego (1886–1957) Mexican muralist. After study in Mexico City and Spain, he settled in Paris from 1909 to 1919. He briefly espoused CUBISM but abandoned it c. 1917 for a visual language of simplified forms and bold areas of color. Returning to Mexico in 1921, he sought to create a new national art on revolutionary themes in the wake of the MEXICAN REVOLUTION. He painted many public murals, the most ambitious of which is in the National Palace (1929–57). From 1930 to 1934 he worked in the U.S. His mural for New York's Rockefeller Center aroused a storm of controversy and was ultimately destroyed because it contained the figure of VLADIMIR ILICH LENIN; he later reproduced it at the Palace of Fine Arts in Mexico City. With JOSÉ CLEMENTE OROZCO and DAVID A. SIQUEIROS, he created a revival of FRESCO PAINTING that became Mexico's most significant contribution to 20th-century art. His large-scale, didactic murals contain scenes of Mexican history, culture, and industry, with Indians, peasants, conquistadores, and factory workers drawn as simplified figures in crowded, shallow spaces. Rivera was married to FRIDA KAHLO almost uninterruptedly from 1929 to 1954.

Rivera, José Antonio Primo de See José Antonio PRIMO DE RIVERA

Rivera, Luis Muñoz See Luis MUÑOZ RIVERA

Rivers, Joan (born 1937) U.S. entertainer. Born in Brooklyn, N.Y., she graduated from Barnard College. She appeared with the Chicago comedy troupe Second City and performed in nightclubs and on television. She created the television series *Husbands and Wives* (1976–77). Known for her grating voice and gossipy humor, she backed up JOHNNY CARSON as permanent guest host on *The Tonight Show* (1983–86), hosted the short-lived *The Late Show Starring Joan Rivers* (1986–87) and a daytime talk show, and continued to make television appearances.

Rivers, Larry *orig.* **Yitzroch Loiza Grossberg** (1923–2002) U.S. painter associated with ABSTRACT EXPRESSIONISM and POP ART. Born in New York, he studied at the Juilliard School and was a professional jazz saxophonist before turning to painting and studying with HANS HOFMANN. His early works are characterized by frequent use of complex, fragmentary, and multiple views; perhaps the best known is the harshly realistic *Double Portrait of Berdie* (1955). From the 1960s he introduced commercial images into his work, as well as elements of collage, construction, and sculpture; an elaborate example of his mixed-media works is *The History of the Russian Revolution* (1965).

Riverside City (pop., 2000: 255,166), southern California, on the Santa Ana River. With SAN BERNARDINO and Ontario, it forms a metropolitan complex east of LOS ANGELES. Settled in the 1870s, it was incorporated as a city in 1883 and became a citrus-growing area. Its economy now includes manufacturing and educational activities.

Riviera \ˌri-vē-ˈer-ə\ Coastal region bordering on the Mediterranean Sea in southeastern France and northwestern Italy. It extends from CANNES, France, to La Spezia, Italy. The Italian Riviera is divided into the Riviera di Ponente west of GENOA and the Riviera di Levante east of Genoa. The French Riviera is also called the CÔTE D'AZUR. Noted for its scenery and pleasant climate, it is one of the major tourist centers of Europe. Because of its mild winters, many delicate plants flourish there, and flowers are grown out of season for export to northern markets. See also CANNES, NICE, MONTE CARLO.

Riyadh \rē-ˈyäd\ City (metro. area pop., 1997 est.: 2,800,000), capital of Saudi Arabia, in the eastern central part of the country. Chosen as the capital of the SAUD DYNASTY in 1824, it remained the center of Saud rule until 1881, when the Rashid family gained control of the region. In 1902 IBN SAUD regained control, and it became the center for his conquest of the ARABIAN PENINSULA. When the kingdom of Saudi Arabia was proclaimed in 1932, Riyadh became the capital. Discovery of immense petroleum deposits in the kingdom in the 1930s transformed the old provincial town into a showplace of modern technology. The old city walls were demolished in the 1950s to make room for rapid expansion. In addition to its administrative role, it is the kingdom's commercial, educational, and transportation center.

Rizal (y Alonso) \rē-ˈsäl\, **José** *in full* **José Protasio Rizal Mercado y Alonso Realonda** (1861–1896) Filipino patriot, physician, and man of letters. From his youth Rizal committed himself to the reform of Spanish rule in his home country. He lived in Europe 1882–92, where he published novels exposing the evils of Spanish rule and became the leader of the Propaganda Movement, which produced reform-oriented articles, magazines, and poetry. He returned to the Philippines to found a nonviolent-reform society; he was deported to Mindanao, where he spent four years. When the Katipunan nationalist secret society revolted in 1896, the Spanish arrested and executed Rizal, though he had no connection with the group and had taken no part in the insurrection. His martyrdom convinced Filipinos that there was no alternative to independence from Spain.

R.J. Reynolds Tobacco Holdings, Inc. U.S.-based tobacco company. Its origins date to the establishment of Richard Joshua Reynolds's tobacco-plug factory in Winston, N.C., in 1875. The Reynolds Tobacco Co. became a major manufacturer of tobacco products, notably Camel, Winston, and Salem cigarettes. Reynolds began to diversify in the 1960s, and in 1970 adopted the name R. J. Reynolds Industries, Inc. In 1985 R.J. Reynolds Industries acquired NABISCO Brands. The new company, named RJR Nabisco in 1986, was acquired by Kohlberg Kravis Roberts & Co. (KKR) in 1989. It was the largest corporate transaction ($25 billion) of its time. KKR divested its ownership in 1995. In 1999 R.J. Reynolds Tobacco Company became a subsidiary of R.J. Reynolds Tobacco Holdings, Inc. Nabisco was acquired by PHILIP MORRIS COS. Inc. in 2000.

RKO Radio Pictures, Inc. U.S. film studio. It was created in 1928 as Radio-Keith-Orpheum when the Radio Corp. of America (RCA CORP.) acquired the Keith-Albee-Orpheum theater chain and a production firm. In the 1930s RKO was noted for producing a series of FRED ASTAIRE–G. ROGERS musicals and KATHARINE HEPBURN's early movies, as well as such films as *Cimarron* (1931), *The Informer* (1935), and *Citizen Kane* (1941). It was bought by Howard R. Hughes in 1948; his inattention doomed the company, and it ceased production in 1953 and was sold to Desilu Productions (1957). After numerous reorganizations, it continued as RKO General, operating radio and television stations and theaters.

RNA *in full* **ribonucleic acid** \ˌrī-bō-nu̇-ˈklē-ik, ˌrī-bō-nu̇-ˈklā-ik\ One of the two main types of nucleic acid (the other being DNA), which functions in cellular protein synthesis in all living cells and replaces DNA as the carrier of genetic information in some viruses. Like DNA, it consists of strands of nucleotides joined along their length, but the strands are single and it has uracil (U) where DNA has thymine. Messenger RNA (mRNA), a single strand copied from a DNA strand that acts as its template, carries the message of the genetic code from DNA (in chromosomes) to the site of protein synthesis (on ribosomes). Ribosomal RNA (rRNA), part of the building material of ribosomes, participates in protein synthesis. Transfer RNA (tRNA), the smallest type, has fewer than 100 nucleotide units (mRNA and rRNA contain thousands). Each nucleotide triplet on mRNA specifies which amino acid comes next on the protein being synthesized, and a tRNA molecule with that triplet's complement on its protruding end brings the specified amino acid to the site to be linked into the protein. Various minor types of RNA also exist; at least some act as catalysts (ribozymes), a function long ascribed only to proteins.

roach Common European sport fish *(Rutilus rutilus)* of the carp family (Cyprinidae), found in lakes and slow rivers. A high-backed, yellowish green fish with red eyes and reddish fins, the roach is 6–16 in. (15–40 cm) long and weighs up to 4.5 lbs (2 kg). It lives in small schools and eats plants, insects, and small animals. It is sometimes eaten or used as bait. In North America, other fishes are called roach, including the rudd, the golden shiner (both cyprinids), and several members of the sunfish family (Centrarchidae).

roach See cockroach

Roach, Hal *orig.* **Harold Eugene** (1892–1992) U.S. film producer. Born in Elmira, N.Y., he tried gold prospecting before becoming a bit player in Hollywood (1912). He befriended Harold Lloyd and directed and produced his *Just Nuts* (1915), then formed the Hal Roach Studio (1919) and went on to produce such other Lloyd comedies as *Safety Last* (1923). In the 1920s and '30s he produced thousands of comedy shorts, winning Academy Awards for *The Music Box* (1932) and *Bored of Education* (1936). In addition to producing the Will Rogers films and the "Our Gang" shorts, he teamed Laurel and Hardy in their first film together in 1927 and produced a series of their films, including *Leave 'em Laughing* (1928) and *Way Out West* (1937), as well as such other successes as *Topper* (1937) and *Of Mice and Men* (1939). In 1984 he received an Academy Award for lifetime achievement.

Roach, Max(well) (born 1924) U.S. bandleader and composer, and one of the most important drummers in modern jazz. Born in New Land, N.C., Roach performed with many of the key bebop players of the mid-1940s, including Dizzy Gillespie and Charlie Parker. He developed a light, flexible manner of keeping time with the ride cymbal rather than the bass drum, updating the role of the drumset for the new music and exploring the melodic possibilities of the drums in his solos. He formed a quintet with trumpeter Clifford Brown in 1954, and continued as leader of his own group following Brown's death in 1956.

road Traveled way on which people, animals, or wheeled vehicles move. The earliest roads developed from paths and trails and appeared with the invention of wheeled vehicles, around 3000 BC. Road systems developed to facilitate trade in early civilizations; the first major road extended 1,775 mi (2,857 km) from the Persian Gulf to the Aegean Sea and was used c. 3500–300 BC. The Romans used roads to maintain control of their empire, with over 53,000 mi (85,000 km) of roadways extending across its lands; Roman construction techniques and design remained the most advanced until the late 1700s. In the early 19th century invention of macadam road construction provided a quick and durable method for building roads, and asphalt and concrete also began to be used. Motorized traffic in the 20th century led to the limited-access highway, the first of which was a parkway in New York City (1925). Superhighways also appeared in Italy and Germany in the 1930s. In the 1950s the U.S. interstate highway system was inaugurated to link the country's major cities. See illustration opposite.

roadrunner *or* **chaparral cock** \ˌsha-pə-ˈral\ Either of two species of terrestrial cuckoo, especially *Geococcyx californianus* (family Cuculidae), of Mexican and southwestern U.S. deserts. About 22 in. (56 cm) long, they have streaked brown-and-white plumage, a short shaggy crest, bare blue and red skin behind the eyes, stout bluish legs, and a long tail carried at an angle. Clumsy, weak fliers, they prefer to run. Using their stout bill, they pound insects, lizards, and snakes to death, then swallow the victim head first. The lesser roadrunner *(G. velox),* of Mexico and Central America, is smaller, buffier, and less streaked.

Roadrunner (*Geococcyx californianus*).

RUSS KINNE—PHOTO RESEARCHERS/EB INC.

Roanoke \ˈrō-ə-ˌnōk\ City (pop., 1990: 96,000), western Virginia. It is located on the Roanoke River at the southern end of the Shenandoah Valley. Settled in 1740, it developed after 1882, when it became a rail junction and outlet for Virginia and West Virginia coal. Chartered in 1874 as the town of Big Lick, it was renamed Roanoke (1882) after the Indian term for shell money. Manufactures now include railroad cars, metal and steel products, clothing, chemicals, and furniture.

Roanoke Island Island, off North Carolina coast. Situated near the southern entrance to Albemarle Sound, it is about 12 mi (19 km) long and 3 mi (5 km) wide. It was the site of the first English settlement in North America; its original colonists, led by Walter Raleigh, remained for only 10 months in 1585. The second group arrived in 1587 and shortly after, Virginia Dare was born there. When a supply ship arrived in 1590 all the colonists had vanished; their fate was never known. During the American Civil War the island was captured in 1862 by Union forces under Gen. Ambrose E. Burnside. It is now a resort and residential area.

Roanoke River River, southern Virginia and northeastern North Carolina. Formed by the confluence of forks in West Virginia, it flows southeast for 380 mi (612 km) into Albemarle Sound, on the Atlantic coast of North Carolina. Just north of the Virginia–North Carolina boundary, it joins the Dan River, its principal tributary. It is navigable by small craft from its mouth to Weldon, N.C.

roasting In metallurgy, usually the first step in smelting ore to extract metal. The ore is heated in the presence of an abundant flow of air to drive off moisture and, if the metal-bearing mineral is a sulfide, convert it to an oxide. Sulfur fumes from ore roasting have been a major source of environmental pollution in the past.

Rob Roy *orig.* **Robert MacGregor** (1671–1734) Scottish Highland outlaw. Nephew of the chief of the MacGregor clan, he became a freebooter and apparently engaged in the time-honored Border practices of cattle stealing and blackmail. After the penal laws against the MacGregors were reintroduced (1693), he took the surname Campbell and frequently signed himself Rob Roy ("Red Rob"), in reference to his red hair. He became a brigand after his financial ruin in 1712 and exacted

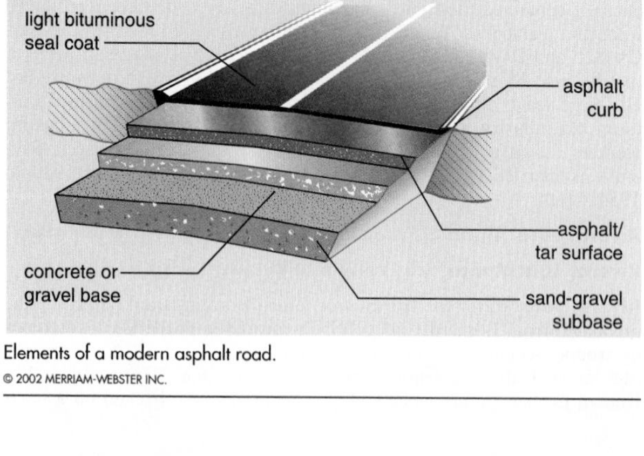

Elements of a modern asphalt road.

tribute for protection against thieves. Arrested in 1722, he was pardoned in 1727. He was glamorously portrayed as a Scottish Robin Hood in WALTER SCOTT's novel *Rob Roy*.

Robbe-Grillet \rōb-grē-'yā\, **Alain** (born 1922) French writer. Trained as a statistician and agronomist, he became a writer and leading theoretician of the *nouveau roman* ("new novel"), the French ANTINOVEL that emerged in the 1950s. His narratives lack conventional elements such as chronological plot and are composed largely of recurring images and repeated fragments of dialogue. Among his works are fiction, including *The Erasers* (1953), *Jealousy* (1957), and *Djinn* (1981); the essay *Towards a New Novel* (1963); and the memoir *Ghosts in the Mirror* (1984). He is also a screenwriter and film director; his best-known work in the medium is his screenplay for *Last Year at Marienbad* (1961).

robber fly *or* **assassin fly** Any of about 4,000 species of predatory DIPTERANS in the family Asilidae, found worldwide. Robber flies are the largest of all dipterans; some species are 3 in. (8 cm) long. Most have a dull-colored, stout body resembling that of a bumblebee and a moustache of bristles between the large-faceted eyes. They use their long legs to capture insects in flight and hold them while eating; a fluid injected into the victim breaks down muscle tissue. A few species are serious pests of apiaries.

Robber fly (Asilidae).
WILLIAM E. FERGUSON

robbery See THEFT

Robbia family, Della See DELLA ROBBIA FAMILY

Robbins, Jerome (1918–1998) U.S. dancer, choreographer, and director. He was born in New York City. He joined the Ballet Theatre (later AMERICAN BALLET THEATRE) in 1940, creating roles in such ballets as *Bluebeard* and *Romeo and Juliet.* His first choreographic success was LEONARD BERNSTEIN's *Fancy Free,* which became the musical *On the Town* (1944); this was followed by many successful Broadway musicals and films, including *West Side Story* (1957), *Gypsy* (1959), and *Fiddler on the Roof* (1964). He joined the NEW YORK CITY BALLET in 1949, and was associate director (1950–59), resident choreographer and ballet master (1969–83), and codirector with PETER MARTINS until retiring in 1990. His choreography is marked by a blend of modern, academic, and popular dance styles in a variety of American idioms.

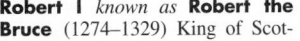

Jerome Robbins in *Fancy Free*, 1944.
FRED FEHL

Robert I *known as* **Robert the Bruce** (1274–1329) King of Scotland (1306–29). Though Robert was of Anglo-Norman ancestry and held lands in both England and Scotland, he sided with the Scots against England and fought under WILLIAM WALLACE. He gained the Scottish throne in 1306 after stabbing a rival to death in a quarrel. Twice defeated by EDWARD I (1306), he became a fugitive, hiding on a remote island off the Irish coast. Within a year, Robert returned to Scotland and began gathering supporters, and in 1314 he defeated EDWARD II at the Battle of BANNOCKBURN. EDWARD III finally recognized him and confirmed Scottish independence in 1328.

Robert II *known as* **Robert Curthose** \'kůr-tōz\ (1054?–1134) Duke of Normandy (1087–1106). The eldest son of WILLIAM I, he was named heir to Normandy but rebelled twice (c. 1077, c. 1082). Robert was exiled to Italy but returned as duke on his father's death. He pawned Normandy to his brother WILLIAM II, and joined the First CRUSADE, in which he fought bravely and helped to capture Jerusalem (1099). He led an unsuccessful invasion of England after HENRY I became king (1100); Henry then invaded Normandy (1105–6) and captured Robert, who spent the rest of his life as a prisoner.

Robert II (1316–1390) King of Scotland (1371–90). Grandson of ROBERT I the Bruce, he served as regent during the periods of exile and of imprisonment by the English of his uncle, DAVID II, and took the throne on David's death in 1371 as the first Stuart king and thus the founder of the House of STUART. His reign proved anticlimactic; he had little effect on political and military affairs, taking no active part in the renewed war with England (1378–88). Succession after his death was disputed by his numerous children (legitimate and illegitimate) and their descendants.

Robert III (1337?–1406) King of Scotland (1390–1406). After having ruled in the name of his father, ROBERT II, 1384–88, he assumed the throne in his own right on his father's death. Physically disabled by a kick from a horse in 1388, he was never the real ruler of Scotland. His brother Robert, earl of Fife, later duke of Albany, governed during Robert II's last years and continued to govern throughout Robert III's reign, except for three years when Robert III's eldest son, David, duke of Rothesay, took his place. Robert III's other son became JAMES I.

Robert Guiscard \gēs-'kär\ (c. 1015–1085) Norman adventurer and duke of Apulia (1059–85). Born into a family of Norman knights, he joined his brothers and half brothers in southern Italy, defeating the Byzantines, Lombards, and papacy (1053) and taking over Apulia. He allied with the papacy (1059), agreeing to oppose the Byzantines and expel the Arabs from Sicily. His brother Roger (later ROGER I) helped him to conquer Sicily and Calabria, and he gained control of Salerno in 1076, making it the capital of his duchy. Robert made an abortive attempt to gain the Byzantine throne (1083) but returned to Italy to defend Pope GREGORY VII from his enemies.

Robert-Houdin \rō-ber-ü-'da^{n}\, **Jean-Eugène** *orig.* **Jean-Eugène Robert** (1805–1871) French magician, considered the father of modern CONJURING. Trained as a watchmaker, he became a magician at the Palais-Royal (1845–55), performing on a bare stage in evening dress rather than the usual wizardlike costume. He used familiar objects to create his illusions, then gave a plausible explanation of the technical procedures involved. He was the first magician to use electricity, and he exposed magicians who relied on supernatural explanations for their feats. In 1856 he was sent to Algeria by the French government to counter the influence of the dervishes by duplicating their feats.

Roberts, Charles G(eorge) D(ouglas) *later* **Sir Charles** (1860–1943) Canadian poet. At first a teacher and editor, he became a journalist in New York City and lived in London before settling in Toronto. His best-known poems are simple descriptive lyrics about the scenery and rural life of his native New Brunswick and Nova Scotia. He published some 12 verse volumes, including *In Divers Tones* (1887) and *The Vagrant of Time* (1927). His prose includes short stories that display his intimate knowledge of the Canadian woods, including *Earth's Enigmas* (1896) and *Red Fox* (1905). He is remembered as the first writer to express national feeling after the confederation of 1867.

Roberts, Oral (born 1918) U.S. evangelist. Born near Ada, Okla., the son of a Pentecostal preacher, he underwent a conversion experience in 1935. He spent 12 years as a pastor in several towns in the South and built up his own organization, the Pentecostal Holiness Church. He studied at Oklahoma Baptist College (1943–45), emerging as a Methodist. Claiming direct communications from God, he began an itinerant ministry of faith healing in the late 1940s. The Oral Roberts Evangelistic Assn., based in Tulsa, became the parent organization for other endeavors, including a publishing firm, and Roberts became known for his luxurious way of life. From the 1950s he reached wide audiences through radio and television. In 1963 he founded Oral Roberts University in Tulsa, from which he retired as president in the early 1990s.

Roberts, Richard (1789–1864) British inventor. He was an uneducated Welsh quarryman before he took a position with HENRY MAUDSLAY and then established his own machine-tool factory. He was one of the inventors of the metal PLANER, and he made important improvements to the LATHE. His automatic SPINNING MULE marked an important advance in spinning technology. He developed a screw-cutting lathe and built gear-cutting and slotting machines, railway locomotives with INTERCHANGEABLE PARTS, automatic machinery for punching holes in plate, and the first successful gas meter. Though he was said to have improved everything he touched, he was not a shrewd businessman, and he died in poverty.

Robertson, Oscar (Palmer) (born 1938) U.S. basketball player. Born in Charlotte, Tenn., he became the first African-American to play for the University of Cincinnati. As a member of the Cincinnati Royals (1960–69), "the Big O" twice led the league in combined average for points, rebounds, and assists (1961–62, 1963–64). He played for the Milwaukee Bucks 1970–74. He ended his career with 26,710 points, 7,804 rebounds, and 9,887 assists.

Robertson, Pat *orig.* **Marion Gordon Robertson** (born 1930) U.S. evangelist. Born in Lexington, Va., he attended Washington and Lee Univ., served in the Marine Corps, and earned a law degree from Yale University. After undergoing a religious conversion, he studied at New York Theological Seminary and was ordained a Southern Baptist minister in 1959. In 1960 he started the nation's first Christian television station, at Portsmouth, Va., and he built it into the Christian Broadcasting Network. Its mainstay was his talk show, "The 700 Club." In 1988 he campaigned for the Republican presidential nomination. In 1989 he founded the Christian Coalition, a conservative political organization that went on to exercise wide influence.

Roberval \rō-ber-ˈväl\, **Jean-François de la Rocque, sieur (Lord) de** (c. 1500–1560/61) French colonizer in Canada. A member of the court of FRANCIS I, he was appointed lieutenant general of the North American territory discovered earlier by JACQUES CARTIER and sent to colonize the region. In 1542 he reached Cartier's former headquarters at Cap Rouge, near present-day Quebec. Cartier was to have served as his guide, but he had left in 1541. After a harsh winter, the settlement failed to establish a colony and Roberval returned to France.

Robeson \ˈrōb-sən\, **Paul (Bustill)** (1898–1976) U.S. singer, actor, and activist. Born in Princeton, N.J., to a former slave turned preacher and a Quaker mother, Robeson attended Rutgers Univ., where he was an All-America football player. Graduating at the head of his class, he went on to earn a law degree at Columbia University. Because of a lack of opportunity for blacks in law, he turned to theater, joining a group that included EUGENE O'NEILL and appearing in his *All God's Chillun Got Wings* (1924) and *The Emperor Jones* (1924; film, 1933), a huge success in New York and London. Robeson's superb bass-baritone brought him worldwide renown with his performance of "Ol' Man River" in *Show Boat* (1928). His lead role in *Othello* won high praise in London (1930) and on Broadway (1943). He visited the Soviet Union in 1934, and became identified with strong left-wing commitments, while continuing his artistic success. In 1950 his passport was withdrawn because he refused to disclaim membership in the Communist Party. Viciously harassed and ostracized, Robeson left the U.S. to live in Europe and travel in Soviet-bloc countries, but returned in 1963 because of ill health.

Robeson Channel \ˈrōb-sən\ Northernmost part of the sea passage connecting BAFFIN BAY with the Arctic Ocean. Located between ELLESMERE ISLAND and northwestern Greenland, it extends north for 50 mi (80 km) from the Hall Basin to the Lincoln Sea. For brief periods during the summer, the channel is open to navigation.

Robespierre \ˌrō-bes-ˈpyer\, **Maximilien (François-Marie-Isidore) de** (1758–1794) French revolutionary. A successful lawyer in Arras (1781–89), he was elected to the National Assembly (1789), where he became notorious as an outspoken radical in favor of individual rights. He became a leading member of the MONTAGNARDS in the National Convention. After calling for the death of LOUIS XVI, he led the Jacobins (see JACOBIN CLUB) and the COMMITTEE OF PUBLIC SAFETY (1793) in establishing the REIGN OF TERROR, during which, as virtual dictator of France, he had former friends such as GEORGES J. DANTON executed. Despite earlier support from the people of Paris, who called him "the Incorruptible," he lost his dominating authority and was overthrown and guillotined in the THERMIDORIAN REACTION. Often regarded as a bloodthirsty dictator, he was later valued for his social ideals of reducing inequality and ensuring work for all.

robin Either of two THRUSH species (family Turdidae). The American robin *(Turdus migratorius),* 10 in. (25 cm) long, with gray-brown upper parts and a rusty breast, lives in deciduous forests and sometimes towns. It eats earthworms, insects, and berries. The European robin, or robin redbreast *(Erithacus rubecula),* breeds throughout Europe, western Asia, and part of North Africa. It is 5.5 in. (14 cm) long, with olive-brown upper parts, white belly, and rusty-orange face and breast.

Robin Hood Legendary English outlaw. The hero of ballads dating from as early as the 14th century, Robin Hood was a rebel who robbed and killed landowners and government officials and gave his gains to the poor. He treated women and common people with courtesy, and he ignored the laws of the forest that restricted hunting rights. His greatest enemy was the sheriff of Nottingham. The ballads emerged during a time of agrarian unrest that culminated in the PEASANTS' REVOLT of 1381. There is no evidence of Robin Hood's historical existence, though later tradition places him in the reign of King JOHN. In postmedieval ballads and stories he was a nobleman who took refuge in Sherwood Forest after losing his lands. His men included Little John and Friar Tuck; his beloved was Maid Marion.

Robinson, Bill *orig.* **Luther** *known as* **Bojangles** (1878–1949) U.S. tap dancer. Born in Richmond, Va., he developed extraordinary tap-dancing skills. He became the first black to appear in white vaudeville shows, and later the first black in FLORENZ ZIEGFELD's Follies. He danced in most of the leading U.S. theaters and nightclubs and also appeared in films, notably in four with SHIRLEY TEMPLE and in the all-black *Stormy Weather* (1943). On the anniversary of his 60th year in show business, New York's mayor proclaimed "Bill Robinson Day," and on his death he received tributes from royalty and the White House. See also TAP DANCE.

Robinson, Edward G. *orig.* **Emmanuel Goldenberg** (1893–1973) U.S. (Romanian-born) film actor. He was brought up on New York's Lower East Side and won a scholarship to the American Academy of Dramatic Art. He was largely a stage actor until the advent of sound movies. After winning fame as a gangster boss in *Little Caesar* (1931), he often played tough guys and criminals. His later films include *Barbary Coast* (1935), *Double Indemnity* (1944), *The Woman in the Window* (1944), *Scarlet Street* (1945), *All My Sons* (1948), *Key Largo* (1948), and *The Cincinnati Kid* (1965). In 1973 he was posthumously awarded an honorary Academy Award.

Robinson, Edwin Arlington (1869–1935) U.S. poet. Raised in Head Tide, Me., he attended Harvard briefly, then endured years of poverty and obscurity before his poetry began to attract attention. He is best known for short dramatic lyrics about the people in a small New England village, especially their tragedies and defeats, including "Richard Cory" and "Miniver Cheevy." His collections include *The Children of the Night* (1897), *The Man Against the Sky* (1916), and *Collected Poems* (1921, Pulitzer Prize). He also wrote long narrative poems, including *Merlin* (1917), *Lancelot* (1920), *The Man Who Died Twice* (1924, Pulitzer Prize), *Tristram* (1927, Pulitzer Prize), and *Amaranth* (1934).

Robinson, Frank (born 1935) U.S. baseball player and the first black manager in major-league baseball. Born in Beaumont, Texas, he played principally for the Cincinnati Reds (1956–65) and Baltimore Orioles (1966–71). In 1966 he won the triple crown, leading the league in home runs (49), runs batted in (122), and batting average (.316). He later managed the Cleveland Indians (1975–77), San Francisco Giants (1981–84), and Baltimore Orioles (1988–91).

Robinson, Henry Peach (1830–1901) British photographer. Tiring of doing portraits, he turned to "high art" photographs, which imitated the anecdotal genre paintings popular at the time, creating them by pasting together parts of several negatives ("combination printing"). *Fading Away* (1858), depicting the peaceful death of a young girl surrounded by her grieving family, skillfully combines five different negatives. He used costumed models to shoot even bucolic scenes in his studio. His *Pictorial Effect in Photography* (1869) was for decades the most influential book in English on photographic practice.

Robinson, Jackie *orig.* **Jack Roosevelt** (1919–1972) U.S. baseball player, the first black player in the major leagues. Born in Cairo, Ga., Robinson became an outstanding performer in several sports at Pasadena Junior College and UCLA before leaving college to help his mother care for the family. He served in the army in World War II as a second lieutenant. He played baseball with the Kansas City Monarchs of the NEGRO LEAGUES before being signed by BRANCH RICKEY to a Brooklyn Dodgers farm team (1945–46). On being advanced to the majors in 1947, he endured with notable dignity the early opposition to his presence, opposition quickly silenced by Robinson's immediate success as he led the league in stolen bases and was chosen rookie of the year. In 1949 he won the batting championship with a .342 average and was voted the league's most valuable player. He retired from the Dodgers team in 1956 with a career batting average of .311. In his later years he strongly supported the cause of civil rights for black Americans.

Jackie Robinson, 1946.
UPI

Robinson, James Harvey (1863–1936) U.S. historian. Born in Bloomington, Ill., Robinson received his doctorate from the University of Freiburg and returned to the U.S. to teach European history, principally at Columbia University (1895–1919). In *The New History* (1912), he called for the use of the social sciences in historical scholarship and put forth his controversial contention that the study of the past should serve primarily to improve the present. Among his other works are *The Mind in the Making* (1921) and several influential textbooks, including *The Development of Modern Europe* (1907–8; with CHARLES BEARD).

Robinson, Joan (Violet) *orig.* **Joan (Violet) Maurice** (1903–1983) British economist. A professor at Cambridge University (1931–71), she helped develop Keynesian theory, establishing her reputation in 1933 with *The Economics of Imperfect Competition*, in which she analyzed distribution and allocation, dealing particularly with the concept of exploitation (see MONOPOLISTIC COMPETITION). In the 1940s she began to incorporate aspects of MARXISM into her work. Her unorthodox views and sympathy with noncapitalist systems—including China's, on which she wrote three books—involved her in controversy throughout her career.

Robinson, Mary *orig.* **Mary Bourke** (born 1944) Irish politician, first woman president of Ireland (1990–97). She earned a law degree at the University of Dublin, where she became a professor of law (1969–75). She served in the Irish senate 1969–89 as a Labour Party member. In 1990 she was a coalition candidate for president, and narrowly defeated the expected winner from the Fianna Fáil Party. In 1997 she was appointed U.N. high commissioner for human rights.

Robinson, Smokey *orig.* **William** (born 1940) U.S. singer and songwriter, a leading figure in the history of MOTOWN. Born in Detroit, Robinson formed a group while still in high school. As the Miracles, they released their first single, produced by Berry Gordy, Jr., who shortly thereafter founded the Motown label. Their first Motown hit, "Shop Around" (1961), was followed by "You Really Got a Hold on Me," "I Second That Emotion," and "The Tracks of My Tears"; Robinson also wrote such other Motown hits as the Temptations' "My Girl" and Mary Wells's "My Guy." He became president of Motown in 1972, by which time he was performing as a solo artist. He was inducted into the Rock and Roll Hall of Fame in 1987.

Robinson, Sugar Ray *orig.* **Walker Smith, Jr.** (1921–1989) U.S. boxer. Born in Detroit, he began boxing in high school in New York City and won all of his 89 amateur fights. He was six times a world champion, once (1946–51) as a welterweight (147 lbs) and five times (1951–60) as a middleweight (160 lbs). In 201 professional bouts, he made 109 knockouts. He suffered only 19 defeats, most when he was past 40. His outstanding ability and flamboyant personality made him a hero of boxing fans throughout the world, and he is sometimes considered the best fighter in history.

robot Any automatically operated machine that replaces human effort, though it may not look much like a human being or function in a humanlike manner. The term comes from the play *R.U.R.* by KAREL CAPEK (1920). Major developments in microelectronics and computer technology since the 1960s have led to significant advances in robotics. Advanced, high-performance robots are used today in automobile manufacturing and aircraft assembly, and electronics firms use robotic devices together with other computerized instruments to sort or test finished products.

robotics Design, construction, and use of machines (robots) to perform tasks done traditionally by human beings. Robots are widely used in such industries as automobile manufacture to perform simple repetitive tasks, and in industries where work must be performed in environments hazardous to humans. Many aspects of robotics involve ARTIFICIAL INTELLIGENCE; robots may be equipped with the equivalent of human senses such as vision, touch, and the ability to sense temperature. Some are even capable of simple decision making, and current robotics research is geared toward devising robots with a degree of self-sufficiency that will permit mobility and decision-making in an unstructured environment. Today's industrial robots do not resemble human beings; a robot in human form is called an android.

Roca \'rō-kə\, **Cape** Promontory in Portugal and the westernmost point of continental Europe. It lies on the Atlantic coast northwest of LISBON. Known to the Romans as Promontorium Magnum, the cape is a narrow granite cliff, 472 ft (144 m) high, forming the western end of the Sintra Mtns.

rocaille \rō-'kī\ (French: "rock work") In Western architecture and decorative arts, an 18th-century style featuring elaborately stylized shell-like, rocklike, flower, fern, and scroll motifs. Originally designating the fanciful shellwork of artificial grottoes, rocaille came to be synonymous with LOUIS XV STYLE. It is most often found in small pieces of furniture and such personal articles as snuffboxes. The term "Rococo" combines "rocaille" and "barocco" (baroque).

Rochambeau \ˌrō-ˌsham-'bō\, **comte (Count) de** *orig.* **Jean-Baptiste-Donatien de Vimeur** (1725–1807) French army officer. He served in the War of Austrian Succession and became a brigadier general in 1761. He was put in command of a French army of 6,000 to join the Continental Army in the American Revolution (1780). After waiting in vain for French naval support, he joined forces with GEORGE WASHINGTON at White Plains, N.Y., in 1781. They marched to YORKTOWN, where they besieged British forces and forced their surrender. He returned to France in 1783, where he commanded the Army of the North in the French Revolution and was made a marshal of France.

Roche \'rōsh\, **(Eamonn) Kevin** (born 1922) Irish-U.S. architect. After studying under MIES VAN DER ROHE, he became EERO SAARINEN's principal design associate (1954–61), working with John Dinkeloo (1918–81) on such projects as the Dulles International Airport Terminal Building (1962) and St. Louis's Gateway Arch (1965). The two launched their own firm in 1966. Roche's approach, though similar to Saarinen's, resulted in simpler geometric forms. Well-known works include the Ford Foundation headquarters in New York City (1968), General Foods headquarters in Rye, N.Y. (1977), and the Bouygues world headquarters outside Paris (1983). Roche received the Pritzker Architecture Prize in 1982.

Roche, Mazo de la See Mazo DE LA ROCHE

Roche limit \'rȯsh\ Minimum distance at which a large SATELLITE can orbit its primary body without being torn apart by tidal forces. If satellite and primary are of similar composition, the theoretical limit is about 2.5 times the radius of the larger body. The rings of SATURN lie inside Saturn's Roche limit and may be the debris of a demolished moon. The limit was first calculated by Édouard Roche in 1850.

Rochefoucauld, duc de La See duc de LA ROCHEFOUCAULD

Rochester City (pop., 1996 est.: 222,000) and port, northwestern New York. Founded in 1811 and incorporated as a city in 1834, it became a boom town with construction of the ERIE CANAL and rail connections. It was the home of Margaret and Kate Fox, spiritualists who attracted world attention in the 1840s with their seances known as the "Rochester rappings." FREDERICK DOUGLASS published his anti-slavery newspaper there in 1847, and the city was a terminus of the UNDERGROUND RAILROAD. SUSAN B. ANTHONY lived there 1866–1906. In the 1890s GEORGE EASTMAN developed photographic equipment there; the city's manufacturing still includes cameras and photographic equipment. It is a cultural and educational center and the home of the University of ROCHESTER, EASTMAN SCHOOL OF MUSIC, and Rochester Institute of Technology.

Rochester, Earl of *orig.* **John Wilmot** (1647–1680) English poet and wit. The most notorious debauchee of the RESTORATION court, Rochester was also its best poet and one of the most original and powerful English satirists. *A Satyr Against Mankind* (1675) is a scathing denunciation of rationalism and optimism that contrasts human perfidy with animal wisdom, and "History of Insipids" (1676) is a devastating attack on the government of CHARLES II. In 1680 he became ill, experienced a religious conversion, and recanted his past, ordering "all his profane and lewd writings" burned. His single dramatic work is *Valentinian* (1685).

Rochester, University of Private university in Rochester, N.Y., founded in 1850. It consists of a college of arts and sciences, a college of engineering and applied science, and schools of music (the EASTMAN SCHOOL), business administration, and education and human development. A medical center includes schools of medicine, dentistry, and nursing. Research facilities include the Frederick Douglass Institute for African and African-American Studies. Total enrollment is about 8,400.

rock In geology, a naturally occurring and coherent aggregate of MINERALS. The three major classes of rock—IGNEOUS, SEDIMENTARY, and METAMORPHIC—are based on the processes that formed them. These three classes are further subdivided on the basis of various factors, especially chemical, mineralogical, and textural attributes (see e.g., acid and basic rocks, CRYSTALLINE ROCK, EXTRUSIVE ROCK). See also FELSIC ROCK, INTRUSIVE ROCK, MAFIC ROCK.

rock art Ancient or prehistoric drawing, painting, or similar work on or of stone. Rock art includes pictographs (drawings or paintings), petroglyphs (carvings or inscriptions), engravings (incised motifs), petroforms (rocks laid out in patterns), and geoglyphs (ground drawings). The ancient animals, tools, and human activities depicted often help shed light on daily life in the distant past, though the images are frequently symbolic. Sometimes the art at a single site may extend over several centuries. Rock art may have played a role in prehistoric religion, possibly in connection with ancient MYTHS or the activities of SHAMANS. Important sites occur in southern Africa, Europe, North America, and Australia.

rock crystal Transparent variety of the SILICA MINERAL QUARTZ that is valued for its clarity and total lack of color or flaws. Rock crystal formerly was used extensively as a gemstone, but it has been replaced by glass and plastic; rhinestones originally were quartz pebbles found in the Rhine River. The optical properties of rock crystal led to its use in lenses and prisms; its piezoelectric properties (see PIEZOELECTRICITY) are used to control the oscillation of electrical circuits.

rock glacier Tonguelike body of coarse rock fragments, found above the timberline on mountains, that moves slowly down a valley. The rock material usually has fallen from the valley walls and may contain large boulders; it resembles the material left at the end (terminus) of a true GLACIER. A rock glacier may be 100 ft (30 m) deep and nearly a mile (1.5 km) long.

rock music *or* **rock and roll** Musical style that arose in the U.S. in the mid-1950s and became the dominant form of popular music in the world. Though rock has used a wide variety of instruments, its basic elements were one or several vocalists, heavily amplified electric guitars (including bass, rhythm, and lead), and drums. It began as a simple style, relying on heavy, dance-oriented rhythms, uncomplicated melodies and harmonies, and lyrics sympathetic to its teenage audience's concerns—young love, the stresses of adolescence, and automobiles. Its roots lay principally in RHYTHM AND BLUES and COUNTRY MUSIC. Both R&B and country lay outside the mainstream of popular music in the early 1950s, when the Cleveland disc jockey Alan Freed (1921–1965) and others began programming R&B, which until then had been played only to black audiences. Freed's success gave currency to the term rock and roll. The highly rhythmic, sensual music of CHUCK BERRY, BILL HALEY and the Comets, and particularly ELVIS PRESLEY in 1955–56 struck a responsive chord in newly affluent postwar teenagers. In the 1960s, several influences combined to lift rock out of what had already declined into a bland and mechanical format. In England, where rock's development had been slow, the BEATLES and the ROLLING STONES were found to have retained the freshness of its very early years and achieved enormous success in the U.S., where a new generation had grown up unaware of the musical influences of the new stars. At the same time BOB DYLAN, JONI MITCHELL, the Byrds, and others were blending the traditional ballads and verse forms of FOLK MUSIC with rock, and musicians began to explore social and political themes. Such performers as the GRATEFUL DEAD, JIM MORRISON of the Doors, and FRANK ZAPPA combined imaginative lyrics with instrumental virtuosity, typically featuring lengthy solo improvisation, and JANIS JOPLIN and JIMI HENDRIX won large followings with their exotic elaborations on R&B. The 1970s saw the rise of singer-songwriters such as PAUL SIMON, NEIL YOUNG, ELTON JOHN, DAVID BOWIE, and BRUCE SPRINGSTEEN, and rock assimilated other forms to produce JAZZ-rock, HEAVY METAL, and PUNK ROCK. In the 1980s the DISCO-influenced rock of MADONNA, MICHAEL JACKSON, and PRINCE was balanced by the post-punk "new wave" music of such performers as LAURIE ANDERSON, Talking Heads (led by DAVID BYRNE), and the Eurythmics—all of whom illustrated their songs with music videos. By the 1990s rock music had incorporated grunge, RAP, TECHNO, and other forms.

Rock River River, northern central U.S. It rises in southeastern Wisconsin and flows across the northwestern corner of Illinois, emptying into the Mississippi River at Rock Island, Ill.; it is 300 mi (480 km) long. The bottomlands along the lower course are subject to spring floods and require levee protection.

Rockefeller, David (born 1915) U.S. banker and philanthropist. Born in New York City, a grandson of JOHN D. ROCKEFELLER and brother of NELSON ROCKEFELLER, he joined the staff of the Chase National Bank of New York in 1946 after earning a PhD and serving in World War II. He became senior vice president in 1952 and effected the merger with the Bank of Manhattan Co. that resulted in the CHASE MANHATTAN BANK (1955), for which he served as chairman of the board 1969–81.

Rockefeller, John D(avison) (1839–1937) U.S. industrialist and philanthropist. Born in Richford, N.Y., he moved with his family to Cleveland in 1853. In 1859 he established a commission business dealing in hay, grain, meats, and other goods. In 1863 he built an oil refinery that soon was the largest in the area. With a few associates he incorporated STANDARD OIL CO. (Ohio) in 1870. He bought out competitors to control the oil-refinery business in Cleveland (1872) and in the U.S. (1882). He placed the stock of the company and its affiliates in other states under control of a board of trustees, establishing the first major U.S. business trust company. As a result of antitrust proceedings, he later converted the trust into a holding company. In the 1890s he turned his attention to philanthropy. He founded the University of CHICAGO in 1892, the Rockefeller Institute for Medical Research (later ROCKEFELLER UNIV.) in 1901, and the ROCKEFELLER FOUNDATION in 1913. He donated over $500 million in his lifetime, and his philanthropy continued through donations by his son John D. Rockefeller, Jr. (1874–1960), and other descendants.

Rockefeller, Nelson (Aldrich) (1908–1979) U.S. politician. Born in Bar Harbor, Me., a grandson of JOHN D. ROCKEFELLER, he worked for several family enterprises, including Creole Petroleum in Venezuela (1935–40). He became coordinator of inter-American affairs at the U.S. State Department (1940–44), assistant secretary of state (1944–45), and undersecretary of health, education, and welfare (1953–55). As governor of New York (1959–73), he oversaw expansion of the state's fiscal, cultural, and educational systems. He sought the Republican presidential nomination in 1964 and 1968, but conservatives opposed his liberal views. He served as U.S. vice president (1974–77) under GERALD FORD. A major art patron, he founded the Museum of Primitive Art (later incorporated into the METROPOLITAN MUSEUM OF ART).

Rockefeller Center Complex of 14 limestone skyscrapers broadly spaced on a 12-acre (5-hectare) site, built between 1929 and 1940 in midtown Manhattan. It was designed by a team of architects headed by Henry Hofmeister, H. W. Corbett, RAYMOND HOOD, and Wallace K. Harrison. Wood veneering, mural painting, mosaics, sculpture, metalwork, and other allied arts were integrated with the architecture. Radio City Music Hall (1932) is noted for its ART DECO interior.

Rockefeller Foundation U.S. philanthropic organization. It was endowed by JOHN D. ROCKEFELLER and chartered in 1913. Rockefeller was assisted in its management by his son John D. Rockefeller, Jr. The foundation supports medical research and education and provides grant and fellowship programs in the social sciences, agricultural sciences, and global environmental studies, and in building democracy.

Rockefeller University Private university in New York City devoted to research and graduate education in the biomedical sciences. Founded by JOHN D. ROCKEFELLER in 1901, it became affiliated with the State University of NEW YORK in 1954. It offers tuition-free advanced instruction and research opportunities to a small number (approx. 125) of gifted students. Rockefeller graduates and faculty have included more than 15 Nobel Prize laureates.

rocket Type of jet-propulsion device that uses either solid or liquid propellants to provide the fuel and oxidizer needed for combustion. The term is also commonly applied to any of various vehicles, including fireworks, skyrockets, GUIDED MISSILES, and SPACECRAFT LAUNCH VEHICLES, that are driven by such a propulsive device. Typically, thrust (forward motion) is produced by reaction to a rearward expulsion of hot gases at extremely high speed (see NEWTON'S LAWS OF MOTION). The most common types of rockets burn chemical propellants, either solid or liquid. Combustion provides the hot gases that are ejected in a jet through a nozzle at the rear of the rocket.

rocket See ARUGULA

rockfish *or* **stonefish** Name applied to species in the SCORPION-FISH family (Scorpaenidae), including the LIONFISH, REDFISH, and ZEBRA FISH. In North America the name is also applied to the eastern mudminnow (*Umbra pygmaea,* family Umbridae), one of several hardy fishes of cool, mud-bottomed ponds, lakes, and streams. Eastern mudminnows frequently bury themselves, tail first, in the mud. They are often used as bait.

Rockford City (pop., 2000: 150,111), northern Illinois, on the ROCK RIVER. The state's second-largest city, it was founded by New Englanders in 1834. Originally called Midway, it was renamed for the ford across the river and incorporated as a city in 1852. Waterpower supplied by a dam built in 1844 led to its development as a manufacturing center in the middle of an agricultural area. Principal products include machine tools and hardware, farm implements, furniture, and seeds.

Rockingham, Marquess of *orig.* **Charles Watson-Wentworth** (1730–1782) British politician. From 1751 to 1762 he served as gentleman of the bedchamber for GEORGE II and then GEORGE III, who appointed him prime minister in 1765. He obtained repeal of the unpopular STAMP ACT but agreed to passage of the DECLARATORY ACT. His ministry collapsed through internal dissension in 1766. He and EDMUND BURKE led the parliamentary opposition to the ministries in power and spoke in favor of independence for the American colonies. In his brief second ministry (1782), he began peace negotiations with the U.S. and obtained legislative independence for the Irish parliament.

Rockne \'räk-nē\, **Knute (Kenneth)** (1888–1931) U.S. (Norwegian-born) football coach who built the University of NOTRE DAME into a major football power. He emigrated with his family to Chicago in 1893. He ran track and played end on the Notre Dame football team, becoming part of a passing combination that established the forward pass as a major weapon. He later played end for numerous professional teams. After his playing career, he became an assistant coach (1914–18) and then head coach (1919–32) at Notre Dame. In Rockne's 13 seasons, his "Fighting Irish" won 105 games, lost 12, and tied five. He trained such famous players as George "The Gipper" Gipp and the members of the FOUR HORSEMEN, and his colorful personality captured the public's imagination.

Rockwell, Norman (1894–1978) U.S. illustrator. Born in New York City, he studied at the Art Students League and received his first freelance assignment at 17. From 1916 to 1963 he produced 317 covers for *The Saturday Evening Post.* Most of his works are humorous treatments of idealized small-town and family life. During World War II, posters of his *Four Freedoms* were distributed by the Office of War Information. Though loved by the public, Rockwell's work was often dismissed by critics. Late in his career, he turned to more serious subjects (e.g., a series on racism for *Look* magazine) and began to receive more serious attention, and in the 1990s his critical reputation enjoyed a positive reassessment.

Rocky Mountain goat See MOUNTAIN GOAT

Rocky Mountain National Park National park, northern central Colorado, established in 1915. Enclosing part of the Front Range of the ROCKY MTNS., it has an area of 262,191 acres (106,109 hectares). It contains many peaks exceeding 10,000 ft (3,000 m), including Longs Peak (14,255 ft or 4,345 m), as well as broad valleys and alpine lakes. The tundra in the park's high country is an island of arctic vegetation surrounded by plants of lower latitudes. Animal life includes bighorn sheep, deer, mountain lions, and a variety of birds.

Rocky Mountain spotted fever TYPHUS-like disease first seen in the Rocky Mountain region, caused by the bacterium *Rickettsia rickettsii* (see RICKETTSIA) and transmitted by various TICKS. In severe cases the rash bleeds more and is especially prominent on the wrists and ankles. Central-nervous-system involvement causes restlessness, insomnia, and delirium. Prostration may progress to coma, with death possible in a week or more. Mortality increases with age. Recovery is slow but usually complete as visual disturbances, deafness, and mental confusion pass. Prompt antibiotic treatment hastens it and reduces mortality. Prevention depends on avoiding tick bites by wearing long, light-colored clothing and insect repellent and inspecting for ticks. A vaccine reduces the risk of infection somewhat and of death greatly.

Rocky Mountains *or* **Rockies** Mountain system, western North America. It extends some 3,000 mi (4,800 km) from the Mexican frontier to the Arctic Ocean, through the western U.S. and Canada. The highest peak in the U.S. Rockies is Mount Elbert in Colorado, at 14,433 ft (4,399 m) tall; in the Canadian Rockies, it is Mount Robson in British Columbia, at 12,972 ft (3,954 m) tall. The CONTINENTAL DIVIDE, located in the mountains, separates rivers flowing to the east and to the west. Wildlife includes grizzly bear, brown bear, elk, bighorn sheep, and cougar. The area is rich in deposits of copper, iron ore, silver, gold, lead, zinc, phosphate, potash, and gypsum. ROCKY MTN., YELLOWSTONE, and GRAND TETON national parks in the U.S. are major recreational facilities.

Rococo style \rə-'kō-,kō, rō-kə-'kō\ *or* **Late Baroque** Style in interior design, the decorative arts, painting, architecture, and sculpture that originated in Paris in the early 18th century. The word Rococo is derived from French *rocaille,* denoting the shell-covered rockwork used to decorate artificial grottoes. Reacting against the ponderous baroque that had become the official style of LOUIS XIV'S reign, Rococo was light, elegant, and elaborately ornamented. Walls, ceilings, and moldings feature interlacings of curves and countercurves based on S and C shapes as well as on shell forms and other natural shapes. Chinese motifs were also employed (see CHINOISERIE). Painting was characterized by easygoing treatments of mythological and courtship themes, delicate brushwork, and sensuous coloring; notable practitioners include ANTOINE WATTEAU, FRANCOIS BOUCHER, and J.-H. FRAGONARD. Rococo style spread throughout France and other countries, principally Germany and Austria. Among the finest German examples is the church at Vierzehnheiligen, designed by BALTHASAR NEUMANN.

Rodchenko \räd-'cheŋ-kō\, **Aleksandr (Mikhailovich)** (1891–1956) Russian painter, sculptor, designer, and photographer. He initially embraced a completely abstract, highly geometric style, using a ruler and compass. His series of black-on-black geometric paintings (1918) was a direct response to KAZIMIR MALEVICH's *White on White.* In 1919, influenced by VLADIMIR TATLIN, he began to make hanging three-dimensional constructions that were, in effect, MOBILES. As leader of a wing of CONSTRUCTIVISM that sought to produce works appropriate to workers' daily lives, he renounced easel painting and took up photography and book, furniture, and set design. His innovations in lighting in his photography influenced SERGEI EISENSTEIN. He returned to easel painting in the 1930s.

Roddenberry, Gene (1921–1991) U.S. television and film producer. Born in El Paso, Tex., he worked as a pilot (1945–49) and police officer (1949–53) before becoming a writer for such television series as *Dragnet* and *Dr. Kildare.* He created the idea for the *Star Trek* series and produced the show from 1966 until it ended in 1969; later rerun in syndication, it developed a durable cult following among fans known as "Trekkies." He produced six *Star Trek* movies, and from 1987 produced the TV series *Star Trek: The Next Generation.*

rodent Any member of the order Rodentia, which contains 50% of all living MAMMAL species. Rodents are gnawing, mostly herbivorous, placental mammals. They have one pair of upper and one pair of lower, continuously growing, incisors. When the lower jaw is pulled back, the cheek teeth connect for grinding; when it is pulled forward and down, the incisors meet at the tips for gnawing. Rodent families include SQUIRRELS (Sciuridae); Old World mice (see MOUSE) and RATS (Muridae); deer mice (see DEER MOUSE), GERBILS, HAMSTERS, LEMMINGS, MUSKRATS, WOOD RATS, and VOLES (Cricetidae); BEAVER (Castoridae); GOPHERS (Geomyidae); GUINEA PIGS (Caviidae); pocket mice (see POCKET MOUSE) and KANGAROO RATS and mice (Heteromyidae); New and Old World PORCUPINES (Erethizontidae and Hystricidae); and hutia (Capromyidae).

rodeo Public performance featuring competitive or exhibition bronco riding, calf roping, steer wrestling, and Brahma bull riding. Rodeo developed from informal competitions among COWBOYS held from the mid-

19th century. Denver is traditionally accepted as the birthplace of paid spectator rodeo, in 1887. The oldest surviving annual show is the one at Cheyenne, Wy. (established 1897). In calf roping and steer wrestling, the contestant seeks to bring down the animal in the shortest possible time. In riding events, contestants seek to stay on their mounts as long as possible and are awarded points for style, control, and other factors.

Rodgers, Jimmie *orig.* **James Charles** (1897–1933) U.S. COUNTRY-MUSIC singer and guitarist. Born in Meridian, Miss., he left school at the age of 14 to work on the trains, and would be known throughout his career as the "Singing Brakeman." While working on the railroad he learned guitar and banjo, absorbed BLUES techniques from black railroad workers, and eventually created his characteristic sound—a blend of traditional work, blues, hobo, and cowboy songs, and his trademark "blue yodel." By c. 1924 his tuberculosis had made continued railroad work impossible; he began instead to perform, and soon became a best-selling recording artist, the first solo star of country music. His more than 110 recordings include "Blue Yodel No. 1" and "Mississippi River Blues." He died at 35. He was one of the first three inductees into the Country Music Hall of Fame.

Rodgers, Richard (1902–1979) U.S. composer, one of the greatest figures in musical theater. A New York City native, Rodgers studied at Columbia Univ., where he met L. HART, and later studied composition at the Institute of Musical Art. His first success with Hart was a revue, *The Garrick Gaieties* (1925). Their comedy *On Your Toes* (1936), with the jazz ballet *Slaughter on Tenth Avenue,* established serious dance as a permanent part of musical comedy. Among their other collaborations were *Babes in Arms* (1937), *The Boys from Syracuse* (1938), and *Pal Joey* (1940), which was revived in 1952 with enormous success. After Hart's death, Rodgers worked with O. HAMMERSTEIN. Their *Oklahoma!* (1943, Pulitzer Prize) enjoyed a then-unprecedented Broadway run of 2,248 performances; their 17-year partnership produced such successes as *South Pacific* (1949*), The King and I* (1951), and *The Sound of Music* (1959) and made them the foremost team in the history of the American musical.

Rodin \rō-'dan\, **(François-) Auguste (-René)** (1840–1917) French sculptor. Insolvent and repeatedly rejected by the École des Beaux-Arts, he earned his living by doing decorative stonework. Not until his late thirties, after a trip to Italy, did he develop a personal style free of academic restraints and establish his reputation as a sculptor with *The Age of Bronze* (exhibited 1878), whose realism was so great that he was accused of forming its mold on a living person. His *Gates of Hell*, a bronze door commissioned in 1880 for a proposed Musée des Arts Décoratifs, remained unfinished at his death, but two of its many figures were the bases of his most famous images, *The Thinker* (1880) and *The Kiss* (1886). His portraits include monumental figures of VICTOR HUGO and HONORE DE BALZAC. Though these and many other works caused controversy for their unconventionality, he was successful enough that he could establish a workshop where he executed only molds, leaving the casting of bronze and the carving of marble to assistants. To his sculpture he added book illustrations, etchings, and numerous drawings, mostly of female nudes. He revitalized sculpture as an art of personal expression and has been considered one of its greatest portraitists.

Rodney, Caesar (1728–1784) American Revolutionary leader. Born in Dover, Del., he was a delegate to the Stamp Act Congress (1765) and the Continental Congress (1774–76, 1777–78). He cast the tie-breaking vote in the Delaware delegation that decided the Congress's resolution for independence. A signer of the DECLARATION OF INDEPENDENCE, he became commander of the Delaware militia (1777) and served as "president" of Delaware (1778–81).

Rodrigo \\, **Joaquín** (1901–1999) Spanish composer. Rodrigo, who was blind from age three, studied music from an early age. Best known for his highly successful *Concierto de Aranjuez* for guitar and orchestra (1939), Rodrigo wrote a great variety of music, including concertos for piano and orchestra and harp and orchestra, solo guitar and piano, a ballet, an opera and some 60 songs.

roe deer Almost tailless Eurasian DEER *(Capreolus capreolus),* found in small family groups in lightly forested regions. It stands 26–34 in. (66–86 cm) at the shoulder. Its coat is reddish brown in summer and grayish brown, with a conspicuous white rump patch, in winter. The male has short, usually three-tined antlers roughened at the base. When alarmed, the deer barks like a dog.

Roe v. Wade U.S. Supreme Court decision (1973) that established a woman's right to have an ABORTION without undue restrictive interference from the government. A Texas law prohibiting abortions was challenged by an unmarried pregnant woman (Roe), and the Court ruled in her favor, finding that the state had violated her right to privacy. HARRY BLACKMUN wrote for the seven-member majority that the state's legitimate concern for the protection of prenatal life increased as a pregnancy advanced. While allowing that the state might forbid abortions during the third trimester, he held that a woman was entitled to obtain an abortion freely, after medical consultation, during the first trimester and in an authorized clinic during the second. The *Roe* decision, perhaps the most controversial in the Court's history, remains at the center of the issue of abortion rights.

Roebling \'rœb-liŋ, *Engl* 'rō-bliŋ\, **John Augustus** (1806–1869) German-U.S. civil engineer, a pioneer in the design of suspension bridges. He emigrated to the U.S. in 1831. His best-known work is New York's BROOKLYN BRIDGE. In the 1850s and '60s Roebling and his son Washington (1837–1926) built four suspension bridges: two at Pittsburgh, one at Niagara Falls (1855), and one at Cincinnati (1866). When his design for a bridge connecting Brooklyn and Manhattan was accepted, he was appointed chief engineer. He died from an injury he received as construction began. Washington completed the project in 1883; himself incapacitated from 1872 by decompression sickness, his completion of the work depended heavily on his wife, Emily Warren Roebling.

Roentgen \'rœnt-gən\, **Abraham** (1711–1793) German furniture designer and cabinetmaker. In 1750 he established a shop in Neuwied, near Cologne. The Rococo-style furniture he produced there was of outstanding quality and was often decorated with inlay work of ivory and other semiprecious materials. Much of his work was created for various German courts. His son David Roentgen (1743–1807), who succeeded him as head of the firm in 1772, was appointed cabinetmaker to MARIE-ANTOINETTE of France. Under his direction, the family workshop became famous for music boxes, clocks, and mechanical toys as well as for its fine furniture. The Roentgens' shop was perhaps the most successful firm of furniture production in the 18th century.

Roentgen, Wilhelm Conrad See Wilhelm Conrad RÖNTGEN

Roethke \'ret-kē\, **Theodore** (1908–1963) U.S. poet. Born in Saginaw, Mich., he was educated at the University of Michigan and Harvard University. He later taught at several colleges and universities, notably the University. of Washington (1947–63). His verse, characterized by introspection and intense lyricism, is collected is such volumes as *Open House* (1941), *The Waking* (1953, Pulitzer Prize), *Words for the Wind* (1957, Bollingen Prize, National Book Award), and *The Far Field* (1964, National Book Award). His later career was interrupted by hospitalizations for manic depression.

Roger I *known as* **Roger Guiscard** \gēs-'kär\ (1031–1101) Count of Sicily (1072–1101). A Norman knight, he went to Italy (1057) to help his brother ROBERT GUISCARD take Calabria from the Byzantines (1060). They launched a campaign to conquer Sicily from the Muslims (1061), and when they captured Palermo (1072), Roger was granted a limited right to govern Sicily and Calabria. After Robert's death he gained full right to govern and created an efficient centralized government.

Roger II (1095–1154) Grand count of Sicily (1105–30) and king of Sicily (1130–54). The son of ROGER I, he was a capable and energetic ruler who incorporated the mainland territories of Calabria (1122) and Apulia (1127). He was crowned king by the antipope ANACLETUS II, and he forced Innocent II to confirm him in 1139. He built a powerful navy but refused to join the Second CRUSADE, preferring as the ruler of a largely Arab population to show tolerance toward Muslims. He promulgated a law code (1140), and his court was an intellectual center for both Arab and Western scholars.

Rogers, Carl R(ansom) (1902–1987) U.S. psychologist. He trained at Columbia Univ.'s Teachers College (PhD, 1931) and directed a children's agency in New York before taking teaching positions in various universities. In 1963 he helped found an institute for the study of the person in La Jolla, Cal. He is known as the originator of client-centered, or NONDIRECTIVE, PSYCHOTHERAPY and helped establish HUMANISTIC PSYCHOLOGY. His writings include *Counseling and Psychotherapy* (1942), *Client-Centered Therapy* (1951), *Psychotherapy and Personality Change* (1954), and *On Becoming a Person* (1961).

Rogers, Fred (born 1928) U.S. television host and producer. Born in Latrobe, Pa., he produced the local public-television show *The Children's Corner* (1954–61) and later created a similar program, *Mister Rogers,* for Canadian television (1963–64). In 1968 he developed it into *Mister Rogers' Neighborhood.* Known for his gentleness and his desire to educate, Rogers, who was ordained a Presbyterian minister in 1962, uses puppets, music, and guests to teach his viewers about various subjects and emotions. His show, the longest-running U.S. children's television program of all time, has garnered many honors.

Rogers, Ginger *orig.* **Virginia Katherine McMath** (1911–1995) U.S. film actress. Born in Independence, Mo., she began her career as a dancer in vaudeville and made her Broadway debut in 1929. After starring in *Girl Crazy* (1930–31), she moved to Hollywood. Her first performance with FRED ASTAIRE, in *Flying Down to Rio* (1933), was so popular that they continued the partnership in nine more movies, including *The Gay Divorcee* (1934), *Top Hat* (1935), and *Swing Time* (1936). She also acted in the drama *Kitty Foyle* (1940, Academy Award) and in light comedies such as *Tom, Dick, and Harry* (1941) and *The Major and the Minor* (1942).

Rogers, Robert (1731–1795) American frontier soldier. Born in Methuen, Mass., he raised and commanded a militia called Rogers's Rangers, which earned fame in the French and Indian War and in Pontiac's War. He led the first English exploration of the upper Mississippi River and Great Lakes region (1766) but failed to reach the Pacific Ocean, his intended goal. In the American Revolution he was regarded as a Loyalist spy; imprisoned by GEORGE WASHINGTON, he escaped to organize the Queen's Rangers, which he led in operations around New York. Defeated in 1780, he fled to England.

Rogers, Roy *orig.* **Leonard Franklin Slye** (1911–1998) U.S. actor and singer. Born in Cincinnati, he moved to California with his family to pick fruit in 1929. There he formed the singing group Sons of the Pioneers, which performed on radio and later in movies. He acted in westerns with GENE AUTRY, whom he replaced as "King of the Cowboys" when Autry went to war. His films include *Tumbling Tumbleweeds* (1935), *Red River Valley* (1941), and *Yellow Rose of Texas* (1944). He acted in several with his wife, Dale Evans, usually riding his famous horse, Trigger. He also starred in the radio show *The Roy Rogers Show* (1944–55) as well as the television series of the same name (1951–57).

Rogers, Will(iam Penn Adair) (1879–1935) U.S. humorist and actor. Raised in Indian Territory (now Oklahoma), he demonstrated his rope-twirling skills in Wild West shows and vaudeville and gradually wove bits of homespun wit into his act. He was popular in New York from 1905 and starred in FLORENZ ZIEGFELD's *Midnight Frolic* (1915). Noted for his good-natured but sharp criticism of current affairs, he wrote a newspaper column in the *New York Times* (from 1922) as well as several books. He performed on radio and in movies such as *State Fair* (1933) and *Steamboat Round the Bend* (1935). His death in a plane crash in Alaska with the aviator Wiley Post (1899–1935) was widely mourned.

Will Rogers.
CULVER PICTURES

Roget \rō-'zhā\, **Peter Mark** (1779–1869) English physician and philologist. In 1814 he invented a slide rule for calculating the roots and powers of numbers. He was instrumental in founding the University of London (1828). He is best known for his *Thesaurus of English Words and Phrases* (1852), a comprehensive classification of synonyms or verbal equivalents which he assembled during his retirement. He was a fellow (from 1815) and secretary (from 1827) of the Royal Society.

Rohan \rò-'ä^{n}\, **Henri, duc (Duke) de** (1579–1638) French HUGUENOT leader. At 16 he entered the army of HENRY IV, who made him a peer of France in 1603. After Henry's death (1610), Rohan led the Huguenots in revolt against the government of MARIE DE MÉDICIS (1615–16) and became the Huguenots' foremost general in the civil wars of the 1620s. He recounted the events of the War of La Rochelle (1627–29) in his celebrated *Mémoires.* He then went to Venice. After his return to France (1635), he successfully commanded a French expedition against the Habsburgs in Lombardy. In 1637 he went to Switzerland, where he died in the THIRTY YEARS' WAR battle at Rheinfelden.

Rohan, Louis-René-Édouard, prince de (1734–1803) French clergyman. A cardinal and bishop of Strasbourg (1779–1801), he spent much of his time at the French court. He was involved in the Affair of the DIAMOND NECKLACE (1785) when he was duped into purchasing a necklace for MARIE-ANTOINETTE without her authority. Tried for fraud, he was acquitted but was exiled from the court in disgrace, and became a martyr to the queen's enemies and the critics of royal absolutism.

Rohe, Ludwig Mies van der See Ludwig MIES VAN DER ROHE

Röhm \'rœm\, **Ernst** (1887–1934) German leader of the SA. He rose to the rank of major in World War I. Soon thereafter, he helped found the NAZI PARTY. A supporter of ADOLF HITLER, he offered Hitler the use of his private strong-arm force (later the SA). After brief imprisonment for his part in the BEER HALL PUTSCH (1923), Röhm went to Bolivia as a military instructor (1925–30), then was recalled by Hitler to reorganize and command the SA. Röhm's ambition that the SA supplant or absorb the regular army came to be opposed by Hitler and his advisers. On the pretext that he and the SA were preparing to overthrow Hitler, Röhm was murdered during the NIGHT OF THE LONG KNIVES.

Röhm, 1933.
HEINRICH HOFFMANN, MUNICH

Rohmer \'rō-mər\, **Eric** *orig.* **Jean-Marie-Maurice Scherer** (born 1920) French film director. After working as a schoolteacher, he became a founding editor of *La Gazette du Cinéma* in 1950 and later editor of the influential NEW WAVE periodical *Cahiers du Cinéma* (1957–63). After directing several short films, he made a series of *contes moraux* ("moral tales") that included the successful films *My Night at Maud's* (1968), *Claire's Knee* (1970), and *Chloe in the Afternoon* (1972), sensitively observed studies of romantic love. His later films include *The Marquise of O* (1976), *Full Moon in Paris* (1984), and *Autumn Tale* (1999).

Rojas Pinilla \'rō-häs-pē-'nē-yä\, **Gustavo** (1900–1975) Soldier and dictator of Colombia (1953–57). He rose through the ranks of the army to seize power from the brutal regime of Laureano Gómez (1889–1965). Though he promised peace, justice, and liberty, he instead ruled by decree, silencing the opposition press, stirring up violence against Protestants, and embezzling government money. He was exiled and impeached, but returned to form an opposition party and run for president. In 1970 he was narrowly defeated in elections he claimed were fraudulent; his supporters rioted and martial law was declared. His daughter sought the presidency in 1974 but was soundly defeated.

Rokitansky \,rō-kē-'tän-skē\, **Karl, Freiherr (Baron) von** (1804–1878) Austrian pathologist. He inspired IGNAZ SEMMELWEIS to study medicine and supported his efforts to eliminate puerperal fever by antiseptic procedures. He was the first to detect bacteria in malignant endocarditis and to describe spondylolisthesis (forward displacement of one vertebra over another). He differentiated pneumonias originating in lobes of the lung and in bronchioles, made a fundamental study of acute yellow atrophy of the liver, and established the micropathology of emphysema. His *Treatise of Pathological Anatomy* (3 vols., 1842–46) elevated pathology to an established science. During his career he performed more than 30,000 autopsies.

Rokossovsky \rə-kə-'sȯf-skē\, **Konstantin (Konstantinovich)** (1896–1968) Russian army officer. He joined the Red Army in 1917 and rose through the ranks. Imprisoned in 1938 during the Stalinist purges, he was released when Germany invaded the Soviet Union in 1941. He became a noted commander in World War II, especially at the Battle of STALINGRAD. After the war he was minister of defense in Soviet-dominated Poland (1949–56) and deputy minister of defense in the Soviet Union (1956–62).

Roland, Chanson de See CHANSON DE ROLAND

Rolfe \'rälf\, **John** (1585–1622?) English colonial official. He arrived in Virginia in 1610, where his experiments with tobacco cultivation produced the first export crop and built the colony's economy. In 1614 he married POCAHONTAS, which helped assure peaceful relations with local tribes. In 1617 the couple and their infant son traveled to England; they were enthusiastically received, but Pocahontas became ill and died. Rolfe returned to Virginia and was appointed to the colony's council. He was apparently killed in a massacre.

Rolland \rȯ-'läⁿ\, **Romain** (1866–1944) French novelist, dramatist, and essayist. At 14 he went to Paris to study and found a society in spiritual disarray, and his life and writings came to reflect his concern with major social, political, and spiritual events. From 1910 he taught music history at the Sorbonne. His best-known novel is *Jean-Christophe* (1904–12), a 10-volume epic whose protagonist is modeled half on LUDWIG VAN BEETHOVEN and half on himself. His pamphlet *Above the Battle* (1915) calls on France and Germany to respect truth and humanity during World War I. In the 1920s he turned to interpreting the mystical philosophy of Asia, especially India, in such works as *Mahatma Gandhi* (1924). He wrote several other major biographies, including *Beethoven* (1910). He was awarded the Nobel Prize in 1915.

Rolle \'rōl\, **Richard (de Hampole)** (c. 1300–1394) English mystic. He left Oxford University without a degree, dissatisfied with the subjects of study, and became a hermit. Writing in the vernacular for the sake of women readers, he exalted the contemplative life and emphasized a rapturous mystical union with God. He may have been spiritual adviser to the nuns of Hampole in his late years.

roller bearing One of the two types of rolling, or antifriction, BEARINGS, the other being the BALL BEARING. Like a ball bearing, a roller bearing has two grooved tracks, but the balls are replaced by rollers. The rollers may be cylinders or shortened cones. If the rollers are cylindrical, only radial loads (perpendicular to the axis of rotation) can be carried, but with conical rollers both radial and thrust, or axial, loads (parallel to the axis of rotation) can be carried. In a given space, a roller bearing can carry a greater radial load than a ball bearing can.

roller-skating Sport in which the participants use roller skates (shoes with sets of wheels attached) to move about on special rinks or paved surfaces. The invention of roller skates is traditionally credited to the Belgian Joseph Merlin in the 1760s, but the first practical four-wheel skate was designed in 1863 by James Plimpton of Medford, Mass. Roller-skating speed events became popular in the early 20th century. Later, team competitions in "roller derbies" on banked tracks became a spectator sport. In the late 20th century, roller skates gave way to in-line (Rollerblade) skates, in which a single row of wheels is used in place of the standard rectangular configuration.

Rolle's theorem \'rȯlz\ Special case of the MEAN-VALUE THEOREM of differential calculus. It states that if a continuous curve passes through the *x*-axis twice within a given interval and has a unique TANGENT LINE at every point of that interval, then somewhere between the two points of interception it has a tangent parallel to the *x*-axis.

rolling In technology, the main method of forming molten METALS, GLASS, or other substances into shapes that are small in cross-section in comparison with their length, such as bars, sheets, rods, rails, and girders. Rolling is the most widely used method of shaping metals and is particularly important in the manufacture of STEEL. The process consists of passing the metal between pairs of rollers revolving at the same speed but in opposite directions and spaced so that the distance between them is slightly less than the thickness of the metal.

Rolling Stones British musical group. Its original members were Mick Jagger (born 1943), Keith Richards (born 1943), Brian Jones (1944–1969), Bill Wyman (born 1936), and Charlie Watts (born 1941). Jones was succeeded by Mick Taylor (born 1948) in 1969, who was replaced in turn by Ron Wood (born 1947) in 1976. The band was formed in 1962 when Jagger, Richards, and Jones, who had been performing sporadically in a blues band, recruited Wyman and formed their own group. Watts joined the band in 1963. Jagger was the lead vocalist, while Jones and Richards played guitars, Wyman played bass, and Watts played drums. The band's name was adopted from a M. WATERS song. By 1966 a series of outstanding songs had made the band second in popularity only to the BEATLES. Jagger and Richards wrote most of its songs; their songs are marked by a driving backbeat, biting and satirical lyrics, and simple but expressive instrumental accompaniments. The group reached the height of its popularity with such albums as *Beggar's Banquet* (1968) and *Exile on Main Street* (1972). They have continued to perform long after the other classic rock bands of the 1960s disbanded.

Rollins, Sonny *orig.* **Theodore Walter** (born 1930) U.S. saxophonist and composer, a dominant influence on the tenor saxophone and one of the greatest improvisers in jazz. Born in New York City, Rollins was inspired by COLEMAN HAWKINS and CHARLIE PARKER and performed with many musicians in the late 1940s, including MILES DAVIS. A member of the CLIFFORD BROWN–M. ROACH quintet in 1955–57, he has since worked as leader of his own groups. Rollins's robust tone and technical dexterity are matched with athletic endurance in the service of the logical evolution of ideas in his solos.

Rollo (c. 860–932?) Scandinavian rover who founded the duchy of NORMANDY. After raiding Scotland, England, Flanders, and France on pirating expeditions, he took lands along the Seine River as his base (c. 911). He battled CHARLES III of France, who gave him the part of Neustria that came to be called Normandy in return for Rollo's promise to end his pillaging.

Rolls-Royce PLC British manufacturer of aircraft engines and propulsion and power systems and, for much of the 20th century, a maker of luxury automobiles. Charles S. Rolls, a pioneer motorist and aviator, and Henry Royce, an engineer and carmaker, incorporated Rolls-Royce Ltd. in 1906. The firm's handsome, immaculately engineered cars included the Silver Ghost (introduced 1906 as "40/50 hp" model), a series of Phantoms (1925), the Silver Dawn (1949), Silver Cloud (1955), Silver Shadow (1965), and Silver Seraph (1998). In 1931 Rolls-Royce acquired Bentley Motors Ltd., another maker of fine cars. Rolls-Royce also developed a series of notable piston and jet aircraft engines, beginning with the Eagle (1914); eventually its turbine-engine operations accounted for the largest part of its sales. A fixed-price contract with Lockheed Aircraft (see LOCKHEED MARTIN CORP.) to produce an engine for its L-1011 TriStar jetliner drove Rolls-Royce into bankruptcy in 1971. It was split into two companies: its jet-engine division was taken over by the British government and later privatized as Rolls-Royce PLC, while its automobile operations were restructured into Rolls-Royce Motor Holdings Ltd. and privatized. The latter was acquired in 1980 by Vickers Ltd., which sold it to VOLKSWAGEN AG in 1998 as part of a novel agreement in which BMW AG would take over the manufacture of cars with the Rolls-Royce name in 2003, while Volkswagen retained the Bentley line.

Rølvaag \'rōl-ˌväg\, **Ole (Edvart)** (1876–1931) Norwegian-U.S. novelist and educator. He emigrated to the U.S. in 1896 and spent most of his life at St. Olaf College (Northfield, Minn.), teaching Norwegian language and literature and the history of Norwegian immigration. His works, written in Norwegian, are noted for their realistic portrayals of Norwegian settlers on the Dakota prairies and of the clash between transplanted and native cultures in the U.S. His best-known work is *Giants in the Earth* (1927), a translation of two of his novels.

Rom See GYPSIES

ROM \'räm\ *in full* **read-only memory** Form of computer MEMORY that does not lose its contents when the power supply is cut off and that is not rewritable once it is manufactured or written. It is generally employed for programs designed for repeated use without modification, such as the start-up procedures of a PERSONAL COMPUTER; the ROM is used for storing the program used in the control unit of the computer. See also CD-ROM, COMPACT DISC.

Romains \rō-'ma^n\, **Jules** *orig.* **Louis-Henri-Jean Farigoule** (1885–1972) French novelist, dramatist, and poet. A teacher of philosophy, Romains first became known as a poet and as founder (c. 1908–11), with Georges Chennevière, of the literary movement Unanimisme, which combined belief in universal brotherhood with the psychological concept of group consciousness. His most popular work was the comedy *Knock* (1923), a satire on doctors. His masterpiece, *Men of Good Will* (27 vols., 1932–46), is a vast novel cycle attempting to recreate the spirit of French society from 1908 to 1933 and exemplifying the Unanimiste interest in collective life.

roman Typeface used most widely in Western TYPOGRAPHY, the general term for the type of this book's text. Characterized by simple, unembellished shapes, roman was developed by 15th-century printers as an alternative to the heavy-bodied, spiky BLACK LETTER SCRIPT. Models for a new type that was easier to cut and read were found in the scriptoria, where scribes, probably at the urging of humanist scholars, were experimenting with a letter face they believed had been used in ancient Rome. Historians now trace its ancestry instead to the letter forms developed for Charlemagne's decrees by ALCUIN in the 9th century. Within a century, roman had superseded all other typefaces throughout Europe; the sole exception was Germany, where black letter continued to hold sway into the 20th century.

roman à clef \rō-män-ȧ-'klā\ ("novel with a key") Novel that has the extraliterary interest of portraying identifiable people more or less thinly disguised as fictional characters. The tradition dates to 17th-century France, when members of aristocratic literary coteries included in their historical romances representations of well-known figures in the court of LOUIS XIV. A more recent example is W. SOMERSET MAUGHAM's *Cakes and Ale* (1930), widely held to portray THOMAS HARDY and HUGH WALPOLE. A more common type of roman à clef is one in which the disguised characters are easily recognized only by a few insiders, as in SIMONE DE BEAUVOIR's *The Mandarins* (1954).

Roman Africa See Roman AFRICA

Roman alphabet See LATIN ALPHABET

Roman Catholicism Largest single Christian denomination in the world, with some one billion members, or about 18% of the world's population. The Roman Catholic church has had a profound effect on the development of Western civilization and has been responsible for introducing Christianity in many parts of the world. It regards itself as the only legitimate inheritor of the ministry of JESUS, by virtue of an unbroken succession of leaders beginning with St. PETER THE APOSTLE and continuing to the present day. It holds that the POPE is the infallible interpreter of divine revelation. Church organization is strictly hierarchical. The pope appoints and presides over about 150 CARDINALS. Each of the church's 500 ARCHBISHOPS is the head of an archdiocese. These in turn are divided into about 1,800 dioceses, each headed by a BISHOP. Within dioceses are parishes, each served by a church and a priest. Only men can enter the priesthood, but women who wish to enter holy orders can become nuns, who are organized into orders and convents. The basic form of worship is the MASS, which celebrates the SACRAMENT of the EUCHARIST. Theologically, Roman Catholicism differs from PROTESTANTISM with regard to its understanding of the sources of REVELATION and the channels of GRACE. With EASTERN ORTHODOXY it asserts that both SCRIPTURE and church tradition are revelatory of the basis of Christian belief and church polity. It sets the number of sacraments at seven (BAPTISM, penance, Eucharist, matrimony, ordination, CONFIRMATION, and anointing of the sick); its rich sacramental life is supplemented by other devotions, chiefly Eucharistic services and devotions to the SAINTS. The Second VATICAN COUNCIL (1962–65) liberalized many aspects of the church; the role of women in the church, clerical celibacy, church opposition to divorce, contraception by artificial means, homosexuality, and abortion remain contentious issues.

Roman Curia Group of Vatican bureaus that assist the pope in exercising his jurisdiction over the Roman Catholic Church. The work of the Curia is traditionally associated with the College of CARDINALS. A cardinal named as secretary of state coordinates the activities of the Curia, and various sacred congregations handle administrative matters—for example, the Sacred Congregation for the Causes of Saints is concerned with beatification and canonization and with the preservation of relics. The judicial branch of the Curia consists of three tribunals, of which the highest is the Apostolic Signatura.

Roman de la Rose \rō-'mä^n-də-lä-'rōs\ ("Romance of the Rose") One of the most popular French poems of the late medieval period. Modeled on OVID's *Art of Love*, it survives in more than 300 manuscripts. Its first 4,058 lines were written c. 1230 by Guillaume de Lorris; they form a charming dream allegory drawing on COURTLY-LOVE traditions. About 1280 Jean de Meun wrote the rest of the more than 21,000 lines, incorporating a vast mass of encyclopedic information and opinions on many contemporary topics, which secured the poem's fame. The *Roman* was translated by GEOFFREY CHAUCER and was one of the most important literary influences on his writings.

Roman law Law of the ROMAN REPUBLIC AND EMPIRE. Roman law has influenced the development of law in most of Western civilization. It dealt with matters of succession (or inheritance), obligations (including contracts), property (including slaves), and persons. Most laws were passed by assemblies dominated by the patrician families, though the rulings of magistrates were also important. Later emperors bypassed these forms and issued their own decrees. The interpretations of jurists also came to have the weight of law. Though various attempts were made to gather and simplify existing laws (beginning with the TWELVE TABLES), by far the most successful effort was that of JUSTINIAN I, whose code superseded all previous laws and formed the Roman Empire's legal legacy. Roman legal procedure is the basis for modern procedure in CIVIL-LAW countries. In the early Republic, the plaintiff was required to call the defendant to court or bring him by force. A magistrate then decided whether the case should go before a *judex,* or prominent layman. The judex heard advocates give arguments and question witnesses; he made a decision but had no power to execute it. In the later Republic, much greater power was placed in the hands of the magistrates and courts: the summons was issued by the court, the trial was held only before a magistrate, and the court became responsible for the execution of the sentence.

Roman mythology Oral and literary traditions of the ancient Romans concerning their gods and heroes and the nature and history of the cosmos. Much of what became Roman mythology was borrowed from GREEK MYTHOLOGY at a later date, as Greek gods were associated with their Roman counterparts. As in Greek mythology, legendary Roman heroes (such as ROMULUS AND REMUS and AENEAS) were given semidivine status. See also ROMAN RELIGION.

Roman numerals System of representing numbers devised by the ancient Romans. The numbers are formed by combinations of the symbols I, V, X, L, C, D, and M, standing, respectively, for 1, 5, 10, 50, 100, 500, and 1,000 in the HINDU-ARABIC NUMERAL system. A symbol placed after another of equal or greater value adds its value; for example, II = 2 and LX = 60. A symbol placed before one of greater value subtracts its value; for example, IV = 4 and XL = 40. A bar over a symbol indicates that its value should be multiplied by 1,000.

1	I	8	VIII	40	XL	900	CM
2	II	9	IX	50	L	1,000	M
3	III	10	X	60	LX	5,000	$\overline{V}$
4	IV	11	XI	90	XC	10,000	$\overline{X}$
5	V	19	XIX	100	C	50,000	$\overline{L}$
6	VI	20	XX	200	CC	100,000	$\overline{C}$
7	VII	30	XXX	500	D	500,000	$\overline{D}$

Roman question Dispute between church and state in Italy. With the completed unification of Italy in 1870, the papacy objected to the Italian seizure of Rome and the PAPAL STATES. The conflict was ended in 1929 by the LATERAN TREATY, which created VATICAN CITY and resolved the dispute.

Roman religion Religious beliefs of the Romans from ancient times until official acceptance of Christianity in the 4th century AD. The Romans believed that everything was subordinate to the rule of the gods, and the object of their religion was to secure divine cooperation and benevolence. Prayer and sacrifice were used to propitiate the gods and were often carried out at temples dedicated to particular divinities and presided over by priests (see FLAMEN). The chief Roman priest, head of the state religion, was known as the PONTIFEX maximus; notable among the other groups of priests were the *augures,* who practiced DIVINATION to determine whether the gods approved of an action. The earliest Roman gods were the sky god JUPITER, the war god MARS, and QUIRINUS; other important early gods were JANUS and VESTA. Many other deities were borrowed from GREEK RELIGION or associated with Greek gods, and the stories woven into ROMAN MYTHOLOGY were often taken directly from GREEK MYTHOLOGY. Domestic shrines were devoted to divine ancestors or protectors, the LARES and PENATES. During the Roman empire, dead emperors were also raised to the status of divinities and were venerated.

Roman Gods and Goddesses

Apollo	god of sunlight, music, poetry, and, prophecy	Mars	god of war
Aurora	goddess of the dawn	Mercury	messenger god and god of commerce
Bacchus	god of wine	Minerva	goddess of wisdom, the arts, and trades
Bellona	goddess of war	Mithra	god of light
Ceres	goddess of agriculture	Neptune	god of the sea
Cupid	god of love	Ops	goddess of abundance
Diana	goddess of fertility, hunting, and the moon	Pales	goddess of flocks and shepherds
Dis or Orcus	god of the underworld	Pomona	goddess of fruit trees and fruit
Faunus	god of pastures, forests, and herds	Proserpine	goddess of the underworld
Flora	goddess of flowers	Saturn	god of seed time and harvest
Janus	god of gates and doors	Venus	goddess of beauty and love
Juno	goddess of marriage and women	Vertumnus	god of the seasons
Jupiter	supreme god and god of the sky and weather	Vesta	goddess of the hearth
Libitina	goddess of funerals	Vulcan	god of fire
Maia	goddess of growth and increase		

Roman republic and empire Ancient state that once ruled the Western world. It centered on the city of Rome from the founding of the republic (509 BC) through the establishment of the empire (27 BC) to the final eclipse of the empire in the west (5th century AD). The republic's government consisted of two CONSULS, the SENATE, and magistrates, originally all PATRICIANS, and two popular PLEBEIAN assemblies: the military centuriate assembly and the civilian tribal assembly. A written code, the Law of the TWELVE TABLES (451 BC), became the basis of Roman private law. By the end of the 3rd century BC, Roman territory included all of Italy; by the late republican period it encompassed most of western Europe, northern Africa, and the Near East, organized into provinces. After a period of civil war, Julius CAESAR took power as DICTATOR. Following his assassination (44 BC), conflict among Mark ANTONY, LEPIDUS, and Octavian resulted in Octavian's victory (31) and his accession as emperor AUGUSTUS (r.27 BC–AD 14). The imperial government, a principate, combined aspects of the republic and a monarchy. In AD 395 the empire split into eastern and western halves, with the west under severe pressure from the barbarians. Rome was sacked in 410 by the Visigoths, and the western empire fell to German invaders in 476; the east continued as the Byzantine Empire until 1453. See table opposite.

romance Literary form that developed in the aristocratic courts of mid-12th-century France and had its heyday in France and Germany between the mid-12th and mid-13th century in the works of such masters as CHRÉTIEN DE TROYES and GOTTFRIED VON STRASSBURG. The staple subject matter is chivalric adventure (see CHIVALRY), though love stories and religious allegories are sometimes interwoven. Most romances draw their plots from classical history and legend, ARTHURIAN LEGEND, and the adventures of CHARLEMAGNE and his knights. Written in the vernacular, they share a taste for the exotic, the remote, and the miraculous. Lingering echoes of the form can be found in later centuries, as in the ROMANTICISM of the 18th–19th century.

Romance languages Group of related languages derived from LATIN, with nearly 920 million native speakers. The major Romance languages—FRENCH, SPANISH, PORTUGUESE, ITALIAN, and ROMANIAN—are national languages. French is probably the most internationally important, but Spanish, the official language of 19 American countries and Spain and Equatorial Guinea, has the most speakers. Languages spoken in smaller areas include CATALAN, OCCITAN, SARDINIAN, and Rhaeto-Romance. The Romance languages began as DIALECTS of Vulgar Latin, which spread during the Roman occupation of Italy, the Iberian Peninsula, Gaul, and the Balkans and developed into separate languages in the 5th–9th century. Later, European colonial and commercial contacts spread them to the Americas, Africa, and Asia.

Romanesque architecture Architecture current in Europe from about the mid-11th century to the advent of GOTHIC ARCHITECTURE. A fusion of Roman, Carolingian and Ottonian, Byzantine, and local Germanic traditions, it was a product of the great expansion of MONASTICISM in the 10th–11th century. Larger churches were needed to accommodate the numerous monks and priests, as well as the pilgrims who came to view saints' relics. For the sake of fire resistance, masonry vaulting began to replace timber construction. Romanesque churches characteristically incorporated semicircular arches for windows, doors, and arcades; barrel or groin VAULTS to support the roof of the NAVE; massive piers and walls, with few windows, to contain the outward thrust of the vaults; side aisles with galleries above them; a large tower over the crossing of nave and transept; and smaller towers at the church's western end. French churches commonly expanded on the early Christian BASILICA plan, incorporating radiating chapels to accommodate more priests, ambulatories around the sanctuary APSE for visiting pilgrims, and large TRANSEPTS between the sanctuary and nave.

Romanesque art Sculpture and painting that reached its height in Western Europe c. 1075–1125, a fusion of Roman, CAROLINGIAN and OTTONIAN, and BYZANTINE art with local Germanic traditions. The expansion of monasticism in the 10th–11th century revived the art of monumental sculpture after almost 600 years of dormancy. RELIEF sculpture depicted

Roman Emperors*

Augustus	27 BC–AD 14	Carus	282–83
Tiberius	14–37	Carinus	283–85
Caligula	37–41	Numerian	283–84
Claudius	41–54	Constantine I	312–37
Nero	54–68	Constantine II	337–40
Galba	68–69	Constans I	337–50
Otho	69	Constantius II	337–61
Vitellius	69	Magnentius	350–53
Vespasian	69–79	Julian	361–63
Titus	79–81	Jovian	363–64
Domitian	81–96	Theodosius I	379–95
Nerva	96–98	**East only**	
Trajan	98–117	Diocletian	284–305
Hadrian	117–38	Galerius	305–11
Antoninus Pius	138–61	Licinius	308–24
Marcus Aurelius	161–80	Valens	364–78
Lucius Verus	161–69	Procopius	365–66
Commodus	177–92	Arcadius	395–408
Pertinax	193	Theodosius II	408–50
Didius Julianus	193	Marcian	450–57
Septimius Severus	193–211	Leo I	457–74
Caracalla	198–217	Leo II	474
Geta	209–12	Zeno	474–91
Macrinus	217–18	**West only**	
Elagabalus	218–22	Maximian	286–305
Severus Alexander	222–35	??	306–8
Maximin	235–38	Constantius I Chlorus	305–6
Gordian I	238	Severus	306–7
Gordian II	238	Maxentius	306–12
Maximus	238	Valentinian I	364–75
Balbinus	238	Gratian	375–83
Gordian III	238–44	Valentinian II	375–92
Philip	244–49	Honorius	395–423
Decius	249–51	Constantius III	421
Hostilian	251	Valentinian III	425–55
Gallus	251–53	Petronius Maximus	455
Aemilian	253	Avitus	455–56
Valerian	253–60	Majorian	457–61
Gallienus	253–68	Libius Severus	461–67
Claudius II Gothicus	268–70	Anthemius	467–72
Quintillus	269–70	Olybrius	472
Aurelian	270–75	Glycerius	473–74
Tacitus	275–76	Julius Nepos	474–75
Florian	276	Romulus Augustulus	475–76
Probus	276–82		

*For Eastern emperors after the fall of Rome, see BYZANTINE EMPIRE.

biblical history and church doctrine on column capitals and around the massive doors of churches. Natural objects were freely transformed into visionary images that derive their power from abstract linear design and expressive distortion. Linear stylization is seen also in the capital letters and marginal decoration of ILLUMINATED MANUSCRIPTS. Romanesque art was concerned with transcendental values, in sharp contrast to the naturalism and humanism of the earlier classical and later GOTHIC ART traditions. Monumental painting that imitated the sculptural style covered the interior walls of churches. Both sculpture and painting incorporated a broad range of subject matter, including theological works, reflecting the revival of learning. See also ROMANESQUE ARCHITECTURE.

Romania *or* **Rumania** Nation, southeastern Europe. Area: 91,699 sq mi (237,500 sq km). Population (1997 est.): 22,572,000. Capital: BUCHAREST. Most of the people are Romanian, with Hungarians a minority. Language: Romanian (official). Religion: Romanian Orthodoxy. Currency: leu. The land is dominated by the great arc of the CARPATHIAN MTNS., whose highest peak, Moldoveanu, is 8,346 ft (2,544 m) tall. The DANUBE RIVER forms the southern boundary with Bulgaria. Under communist rule 1948–89, Romania had a centrally planned economy that was transformed from an agricultural into an industrial economy. From 1991, the post-communist government began returning industrial and commercial

enterprises to the private sector. Romania is a republic with two legislative houses; its chief of state is the president, and the head of government is the prime minister. Romania was formed in 1862 by the unification of Moldavia and WALACHIA (for the earlier history, see DACIA). During World War I, it sided with the Allies and doubled its territory in 1918 with the addition of TRANSYLVANIA, BUKOVINA, and BESSARABIA. Allied with Germany in World War II, it was occupied by Soviet troops in 1944 and became a satellite country of the U.S.S.R. in 1948. During the 1960s Romania's foreign policy was frequently independent of the Soviet Union's. The communist regime of NICOLAE CEAUSESCU was overthrown in 1989, and free elections were held in 1990. Throughout the 1990s Romania struggled with rampant corruption and organized crime as it tried to stabilize its economy.

Romanian language \rů-ˈmā-nē-ən, rō-ˈmā-nē-ən\ ROMANCE LANGUAGE spoken mainly in ROMANIA and MOLDOVA. The name Romanian is usually identified with Daco-Romanian, one of the four major dialects of Balkan Romance. Other dialects are Aromanian (Macedo-Romanian), spoken in scattered communities in Greece, Macedonia, Albania, and Bulgaria; the nearly extinct Megleno-Romanian, spoken in northern Greece; and Istro-Romanian, spoken on Croatia's Istrian Peninsula. The earliest known continuous text in Romanian dates from 1521. Romanian's phonology, grammar, and vocabulary reflect its relative isolation from other Romance languages and its close contact with the SLAVIC LANGUAGES. Written in the CYRILLIC ALPHABET until the 19th century, Romanian now uses the LATIN ALPHABET.

Romano, Giulio See GIULIO ROMANO

Romanov, Michael See MICHAEL

Romanov dynasty \rō-ˈmä-nȯf, ˈrō-mə-ˌnȯf\ Rulers of Russia from 1613 to 1917. The name derived from Roman Yurev (died 1543), whose daughter Anastasiya Romanovna was the first wife of IVAN IV the Terrible. Her nephews assumed the surname Romanov, and the dynasty began with the election of MICHAEL ROMANOV as czar in 1613. He was succeeded by his son ALEXIS (r.1645–76), followed by Alexis's sons FYODOR III and joint rulers IVAN V and PETER I. When Peter was sole ruler, he decreed in 1722 that the monarch could choose his successor, but he was unable to effect the law, so the crown passed to his wife CATHERINE I, his grandson PETER II, and Ivan V's daughter ANNA. The line of descent returned to Peter's daughter ELIZABETH (r.1741–62), her nephew PETER III and his wife CATHERINE II the Great, and their son PAUL I. Paul established a definite order of succession and was followed by his sons ALEXANDER I (r.1801–25) and NICHOLAS I (r.1825–55). Nicholas was succeeded by his son ALEXANDER II, grandson ALEXANDER III, and great-grandson NICHOLAS II (r.1894–1917), the last ruler of the Russian monarchy.

Romanticism Literary, artistic, and philosophical movement that began in Europe in the 18th century and lasted roughly until the mid-19th century. In its intense focus on the individual consciousness, it was both a continuation of and a reaction against the ENLIGHTENMENT. Romanticism emphasized the individual, the subjective, the irrational, the imaginative, the personal, the spontaneous, the emotional, the visionary, and the transcendental. Among its attitudes were a deepened appreciation of the beauties of nature; a general exaltation of emotion over reason and of the senses over intellect; a turning in upon the self and a heightened examination of human personality; a preoccupation with the genius, the hero, and the exceptional figure; a new view of the artist as a supremely individual creator; an emphasis on imagination as a gateway to transcendent experience and spiritual truth; a consuming interest in folk culture, national and ethnic cultural origins, and the medieval era; and a predilection for the exotic, the remote, the mysterious, the weird, the occult, the monstrous, the diseased, and even the satanic. See also CLASSICISM and TRANSCENDENTALISM.

Romanus I Lecapenus \rō-ˈmā-nəs...ˌle-kə-ˈpē-nəs\ (872?–948) Byzantine emperor (920–44). He was admiral of the Byzantine fleet on the Danube before being chosen to share the throne with his son-in-law CONSTANTINE VII. He exercised all real power of the imperial throne until 944. His reign was ended by his own sons, who compelled him to become a monk.

Romanus III Argyrus \ˈär-jə-rəs\ (968?–1034) Byzantine emperor (1028–34). An undistinguished Byzantine patrician, he was compelled by the dying emperor Constantine VIII to marry his daughter Zoe and become his successor. Romanus proved inept in military and financial matters, and his effort to repel Muslim invaders was unsuccessful (1030). He is believed to have been poisoned by his wife.

Romanus IV Diogenes \dī-ˈä-jə-ˌnēz\ (died 1072) Byzantine emperor (1067–71). A member of the military aristocracy, he married the widow of the emperor Constantine X Ducas in 1067. He led military expeditions against the SELJUQ Turks, who defeated and captured him at the Battle of MANZIKERT (1071). During his imprisonment Constantine's son was crowned as Michael VII Ducas. On his release the new emperor blinded Romanus and exiled him to an island in the Sea of Marmara.

Romany language \ˈrō-mə-nē\ Indo-Aryan language of the Roma (see GYPSIES), spoken in many countries of the world, with its greatest concentration of speakers in eastern Europe. Romany is believed to have separated from the northern Indian languages c. AD 1000. Its DIALECTS, which include many loanwords from languages where the Roma have lived, are classified according to the languages that influenced them: Greek, Romanian, Hungarian, Czecho-Slovak, German, Polish, Russian, Finnish, Scandinavian, Italian, Serbo-Croatian, Welsh, and Spanish. Romany has no tradition of writing but a rich oral tradition. In the 20th century some collections of Romany poems and folktales have been published in eastern Europe.

Romberg, Sigmund (1887–1951) Hungarian-U.S. composer. Romberg studied engineering and composition in Vienna, becoming a skilled violinist and organist. In 1909 he went to New York, where he conducted a restaurant orchestra and played piano in cafés. As staff composer for the impresario Jacob Shubert, Romberg prepared scores for about 40 musical shows. His first notable operetta, *Maytime* (1917), was followed in the 1920s by *Blossom Time* (1921), *The Student Prince* (1924), *The Desert Song* (1926), and *The New Moon* (1928). His last success was *Up in Central Park* (1945). In all he wrote almost 80 stage shows.

Rome *Italian* **Roma** City (metro. area pop., 2000 est.: 2,643,581), capital of Italy. It is situated in the central part of the country, on the TIBER RIVER. The historical site of Rome on its seven hills was occupied as early as the Bronze Age (c. 1500 BC), and the city was politically unified by the early 6th century BC. It became the capital of the Roman empire (see ROMAN REPUBLIC AND EMPIRE). The Romans gradually conquered the Italian peninsula (see ETRUSCANS), extended their dominion over the entire Mediterranean basin (see PUNIC WARS), and expanded their empire into continental Europe. Under POMPEY THE GREAT and Julius CAESAR, Rome's influence was extended over Syria, Jerusalem, Cyprus, and Gaul. After the battle of ACTIUM, all Roman lands were controlled by Octavian (AUGUSTUS), the first Roman emperor. As the imperial capital, Rome became the site of magnificent public buildings, including palaces, temples, public baths, theaters, and stadiums. It reached the peak of its grandeur and ancient population during the late 1st and early 2nd century AD. It remained the capital of the Roman empire until Emperor CONSTANTINE THE GREAT dedicated Constantinople (now ISTANBUL) in AD 330. By the end of the 6th century, the protection of the city was in the hands of the Roman Catholic church (see HOLY ROMAN EMPIRE), which achieved absolute rule only in the 15th century. The city flourished during the RENAISSANCE and was the seat of the PAPACY and the PAPAL STATES. In 1870 it became the capital of a united Italy. It was transformed into a modern capital in the 1920s and '30s, and is Italy's administrative, cultural, and transportation center. See also VATICAN CITY.

Rome, March on (October 1922) Insurrection that brought BENITO MUSSOLINI to power in Italy. Social discontent gave Fascist Party leaders the opportunity to take control of the Italian government. Assisted by the armed squads known as BLACKSHIRTS, they planned to march on Rome and force King VICTOR EMMANUEL III to call on Mussolini to form a government. Since the king was unwilling to use the Italian army to defend Rome, the government capitulated to the Fascists' demands. The March on Rome turned into a parade to show the Fascist Party's support for Mussolini as the new prime minister.

Rome, Treaties of Two international agreements signed in Rome in 1957 by Belgium, France, West Germany, Italy, Luxembourg, and the Netherlands. One established the EUROPEAN ECONOMIC COMMUNITY; the other created the EUROPEAN ATOMIC ENERGY COMMUNITY.

Rome–Berlin Axis Coalition formed in 1936 between Italy and Germany. An agreement formulated by Italy's foreign minister GALEAZZO CIANO informally linking the two fascist countries was reached on October 25, 1936. It was formalized by the PACT OF STEEL in 1939. The term AXIS POWERS came to include Japan as well.

Rommel \'rò-məl\, **Erwin (Johannes Eugen)** (1891–1944) German army commander in WORLD WAR II. A teacher at military academies, he wrote the acclaimed textbook *Infantry Attacks* (1937). He commanded a PANZER DIVISION in the invasion of France (1940), then led his Afrika Korps troops in early successes against the Allies in the NORTH AFRICA CAMPAIGN. He became known as the "Desert Fox" for his audacious surprise attacks, and was promoted to field marshal. In 1942 he was ordered to attack Cairo and the Suez Canal, despite his request to withdraw his exhausted troops. After his defeat in the Battles of EL ALAMEIN and retreat into Tunisia, he returned to Germany and in 1944 was given command of the defense of the northwestern French coast. His tactical suggestions were ignored, and after the Allied NORMANDY CAMPAIGN began, he became convinced that the war could not be won. Implicated in the JULY PLOT to kill ADOLF HITLER, he was ordered to take poison so that Hitler could avoid a trial of the esteemed "people's marshal."

Rommel, 1941.

ULLSTEIN BILDERDIENST, BERLIN

Romney, George (1734–1802) British portrait painter. Son of a Lancashire cabinetmaker, he began his career by touring the northern counties, painting portraits for a few guineas each. In 1762 he established himself as a portraitist in London and quickly won favor among society patrons. His success depended on the flattery of his likenesses; he avoided any suggestion of the sitter's character or sensibilities. Infatuated with Emma Hart (later Lady HAMILTON) c. 1781–82, he went on to paint more than 50 images of her. Line rather than color dominates his work, and the flowing rhythms and easy poses of Roman classical sculpture underlie the smooth patterns of his compositions.

George Romney, "Self Portrait," oil painting, 1782; in the National Portrait Gallery, London.

BY COURTESY OF THE NATIONAL PORTRAIT GALLERY, LONDON

Romulus and Remus Twins of Roman legend who were the legendary founders of ROME. They were the offspring of MARS and Rhea Silvia, a VESTAL VIRGIN and princess in Alba Longa. As infants they were thrown into the TIBER RIVER by their great-uncle Amulius, who feared they would lay claim to his title. Suckled by a she-wolf and raised by a shepherd, the twins later deposed Amulius, restored their grandfather Numitor to the throne, and founded a city on the site where they had been saved from the river. When Romulus built a city wall, Remus jumped over it and was killed by his brother. The city was named for Romulus, who ruled until his disappearance in a storm. Believing that he had become a deity, the Romans worshiped him as QUIRINUS.

Romulus and Remus with their wolf foster-mother, bronze sculpture; in the Museo Nuovo in the Palazzo dei Conservatori, Rome.

ALINARI—ART RESOURCE

Roncesvalles \ˌròn-thās-'bäl-ˌyās\, **Battle of** *or* **Battle of Roncevaux** \rōü-sə-'vō\ (August 15, 778) Basque attack on CHARLEMAGNE's army at a pass in the Pyrenees in northern Spain. It occurred when Charlemagne was returning to Aquitaine after a campaign against the Muslims in Spain, and his rear guard was ambushed and massacred by Basque soldiers. The battle is treated in the 11th-century *Chanson de Roland*, in which the attackers are Moors and the rear guard is led by Charlemagne's nephew Roland.

O P Q R

Rondane National Park \ˈrȯn-dä-nə\ Park, southern central Norway. Established as a national park in 1970, it covers an area of 221 sq mi (572 sq km) of mountainous terrain. The highest peak is Rondeslottet at 7,146 ft (2,178 m) tall. Vegetation is sparse, and the few trees are mostly dwarf birch and conifers.

rondeau \ˈrän-dō, *French* rōⁿ-ˈdō\ One of several FORMES FIXES (fixed forms) in French lyric poetry and song of the 14th–15th century, later popular with many English poets. The rondeau has only two rhymes (allowing no repetition of rhyme words) and consists of 13 or 15 lines of 8 or 10 syllables divided into three stanzas. The beginning of the first line of the first stanza serves as the refrain of the second and third stanzas.

rondo Musical form characterized by the initial statement and periodic restatement of a melody alternately with contrasting material. It originated in the French baroque harpsichord rondeau, which was later influenced by vocal rondo forms in Italian opera buffa. Most rondos fall into either a five part *(abaca)* or a seven-part *(abacaba)* form. The rondo was very popular in the late 18th and 19th century, providing the form particularly for romping final movements of sonatas, quartets, symphonies, and concertos.

Rondon \rōn-ˈdōn\, **Cândido (Mariano da Silva)** (1865–1958) Brazilian explorer and protector of Indians. As a young soldier he was assigned to extend telegraph lines into the Brazilian backlands. In 1913–14 he and U.S. Pres. THEODORE ROOSEVELT headed an expedition that explored a tributary of the Madeira River, coming into close contact with the Indian tribes of the interior. Appalled by their mistreatment by outsiders, he helped create a government agency for their protection. The state of Rondônia, created in 1982 from the former Guaporé territory, was named for him.

ronin \ˈrō-nin\ Japanese masterless SAMURAI. Because samurai received their livelihood from their lord in return for service, a masterless samurai was essentially a vagabond unless he could enter the service of another lord. Ronin could be disruptive to society; in the early 17th century ronin led unsuccessful revolts against the TOKUGAWA SHOGUNATE. The most famous ronin were the 47 whose actions were celebrated in CHIKAMATSU MONZAEMON's play *Chushingura.* By avenging their lord's death in defiance of a shogunal order forbidding the vendetta, the 47 ronin, who were subsequently forced to commit suicide, came to be seen as embodiments of the ideals of BUSHIDO, the warrior's code.

Ronsard \rōn-ˈsår\, **Pierre de** (1524–1585) French poet. Of a noble family, Ronsard turned to scholarship and literature after an illness left him partially deaf. He was the foremost poet of La Pléiade, a literary group that used classical and Italian models to elevate the French language as a medium for literary expression. He was recognized in his lifetime as a prince of poets; among his diverse works were *Odes* (1550), inspired by HORACE; *Les amours* (1552); the unfinished *La Franciade* (1572), in imitation of VIRGIL's *Aeneid,* meant to be the national epic; and *Sonnets pour Hélène,* now perhaps his most famous collection. He perfected and established the ALEXANDRINE as the classic form in French for scathing satire, elegiac tenderness, and tragic passion.

Röntgen \ˈrent-gən, ˈrənt-jən\, **Wilhelm Conrad** *or* **Wilhelm Conrad Roentgen** (1845–1923) German physicist. He taught at the Univs. of Giessen (1879–88), Würzburg (1888–1900), and Berlin (1900–20). In 1895 he discovered rays that did not exhibit properties such as reflection or refraction, and mistakenly thought they were unrelated to light. Because of their mysterious nature, he called them X RAYS. He later produced the first X-ray photographs, showing the interiors of metal objects and the bones in his wife's hand. He also did important research in a wide variety of other fields. In 1901 he was awarded the first Nobel Prize for Physics.

Röntgen.
HISTORIA-PHOTO

roof Covering of the top of a building. Roofs have been constructed in a wide variety of forms—flat, pitched, vaulted, domed, or in combinations—as dictated by regional, technical, and aesthetic considerations. Thatched roofs, usually sloping, were the earliest type and are still used in rural Africa and elsewhere. Flat roofs have historically been used in arid climates where drainage of water off the roof is not important, as in the Middle East and the southwestern U.S. They came into more widespread use in the 19th century, when new waterproof roofing materials and the use of structural steel and concrete made them more practical. Sloping roofs come in many different varieties. The simplest is the lean-to (or shed) roof, which has only one slope. A roof with two slopes that form a triangle at each end is called a gable roof. A hipped (or hip) roof has sloping sides and ends meeting at inclined projecting angles called hips. The gambrel roof has two slopes on each of its two sides, the upper being less steep than the lower. The mansard roof has two slopes on all four sides, a shallower upper part and a steeper lower part. See also HAMMER-BEAM ROOF, LAMELLA ROOF.

roof pendant Downward extension of the surrounding rock that protrudes into the upper surface of intrusive rocks. Most intrusions that contain roof pendants are relatively shallow; the roof pendants occur as isolated pieces of the surrounding rock within the intrusive mass. Because roof pendants are exposed by erosion of the overlying rock, their presence indicates that the igneous body is being observed near its upper surface. Roof pendants can be studied to determine some of the conditions that existed at the time of intrusion, such as the temperature and composition of the MAGMA.

rook Most abundant Eurasian bird *(Corvus frugilegus)* of the CROW family (Corvidae). Rooks, 18 in. (45 cm) long, are black and have shaggy thigh feathers and bare white skin at the base of the sharp bill. They are migratory and range discontinuously from Britain to Iran and Manchuria. They dig for larvae and worms in meadows and plowed fields. They nest in large colonies (rookeries) in tall trees, sometimes within towns; the nest, solidly constructed of twigs and soil, is used year after year.

Roon \ˈrōn\, **Albrecht Theodor Emil, Graf (Count) von** (1803–1879) Prussian army officer. He aided Prince William (later Emperor WILLIAM I) in suppressing the insurrection in Baden (1848). As minister of war (1859–73), he improved the Prussian army by requiring universal military service and a permanent reserve. His reforms contributed to the army's decisive victories in the SEVEN WEEKS' WAR (1866) and the FRANCO-PRUSSIAN WAR (1870–71), which helped make Germany the leading power on the European continent.

Rooney, Mickey *orig.* **Joe Yule, Jr.** (born 1920) U.S. film actor. Born in Brooklyn, N.Y., he joined his family in their vaudeville act from age 2 and made his film debut playing a midget in 1926. He starred in 50 RKO short comedies as Mickey McGuire (1927–33) and won praise for his roles in *A Midsummer Night's Dream* (1935) and *Boys Town* (1938). From 1937 he played the cocky, energetic Andy Hardy in a series of popular films, often teamed with JUDY GARLAND. His later film successes include *The Human Comedy* (1943), *National Velvet* (1944), *Baby Face Nelson* (1957), and *The Black Stallion* (1979). He made a successful Broadway debut in *Sugar Babies* in 1979, and received an honorary Academy Award in 1983.

Roosevelt \ˈrō-zə-ˌvelt, ˈrō-zə-vəlt\, **(Anna) Eleanor** (1884–1962) U.S. first lady and diplomat. Born in New York City, the niece of THEODORE ROOSEVELT, she married her distant cousin, FRANKLIN ROOSEVELT, in 1905. She raised their five children and became active in politics after her husband's polio attack (1921). As first lady (1933–45), she traveled around the U.S. to report on living conditions and public opinion for her husband, and supported such humanitarian causes as child welfare, equal rights, and social reforms. During World War II, she traveled in Britain and the South Pacific as well as to U.S. military bases to help raise morale. She

Eleanor Roosevelt, 1950.
BROWN BROTHERS

wrote the syndicated column "My Day" and several books. After her husband's death, she was appointed a delegate to the U.N. (1945, 1949–52, 1961), whose founding she had strongly advocated. As chair of its Commission on Human Rights (1946–51), she helped draft the UNIVERSAL DECLARATION OF HUMAN RIGHTS (1948). In the 1950s she traveled around the world for the U.N. and remained active in the Democratic Party.

Roosevelt, Franklin D(elano) (1882–1945) 32nd president of the U.S. (1933–45). Born in Hyde Park, N.Y., he was attracted to politics as an admirer of his cousin THEODORE ROOSEVELT, and became active in the Democratic Party. In 1905 he married ELEANOR ROOSEVELT, who would become a valued adviser in future years. He served in the state senate (1910–13) and as U.S. assistant secretary of the navy (1913–20). In 1920 he was nominated for vice president. The next year he was stricken with polio; though unable to walk, he remained active in politics. As governor of New York (1929–33), he set up the first state relief agency in the U.S. In 1932 he won the Democratic presidential nomination with the help of JAMES FARLEY and easily defeated Pres. HERBERT HOOVER. In his inaugural address to a nation of more than 13 million unemployed, he pronounced that "the only thing we have to fear is fear itself." Congress passed most of the changes he sought in his NEW DEAL program in the first hundred days of his term. He was overwhelmingly reelected in 1936 over ALF LANDON. To solve legal challenges to the New Deal, he proposed enlarging the U.S. Supreme Court, but his "court-packing" plan aroused strong opposition and had to be abandoned. By the late 1930s economic recovery had slowed, but Roosevelt was more concerned with the growing threat of war. In 1940 he was reelected to an unprecedented third term, defeating WENDELL WILLKIE. He maintained U.S. neutrality toward the war in Europe, but approved the principle of LEND-LEASE and in 1941 met with WINSTON CHURCHILL to draft the ATLANTIC CHARTER. With U.S. entry into WORLD WAR II, he mobilized industry for military production and formed an alliance with Britain and the Soviet Union; he met with Churchill and JOSEPH STALIN to form war policy at TEHRAN (1943) and YALTA (1945). Despite declining health, he won reelection for a fourth term against THOMAS DEWEY (1944) but served only briefly before his death. His presidency is widely regarded as one of the greatest in U.S. history.

Roosevelt, Theodore *known as* **Teddy Roosevelt** (1858–1919) 26th president of the U.S. (1901–9). Born in New York City, he was elected to the New York legislature in 1882, where he became a Republican leader opposed to the Democratic political machine. After political defeats and the death of his wife, he went to the Dakota Territory to ranch. He returned to New York to serve on the U.S. Civil Service Commission (1889–95) and as head of the city's board of police commissioners (1895–97). A supporter of WILLIAM MCKINLEY, he served as assistant secretary of the navy (1897–98). When the SPANISH–AMERICAN WAR was declared, he resigned to organize a cavalry unit, the ROUGH RIDERS. He returned to New York a hero and was elected governor in 1899. As the Republican vice-presidential nominee, he took office when McKinley was reelected, and he became president on McKinley's assassination in 1901. One of his early initiatives was to urge enforcement of the SHERMAN ANTITRUST ACT against business monopolies. He won election in his own right in 1904, defeating ALTON PARKER. At his urging, Congress regulated railroad rates and passed the Pure Food and Drug Act and Meat Inspection Act (1906) to provide new consumer protections. He set aside national forests, parks, and mineral, oil, and coal lands for conservation. He and secretary of state ELIHU ROOT announced the Roosevelt corollary to the MONROE DOCTRINE, which reinforced the U.S. position as defender of the Western Hemisphere. For mediating an end to the RUSSO–JAPANESE WAR, he received the 1906 Nobel Peace Prize. He secured a treaty with Panama for construction of a trans-isthmus canal. Declining to seek reelection, he secured the nomination for WILLIAM H. TAFT. After traveling in Africa and Europe, he tried to win the Republican presidential nomination in 1912; when he was rejected, he organized the BULL MOOSE PARTY and ran on a policy of NEW NATIONALISM, but failed to win the election. Throughout his life he continued to write, publishing extensively on history, politics, travel, and nature. See also BIG STICK POLICY, T. ROOSEVELT NATIONAL PARK.

Roosevelt Island *formerly (until 1921)* **Blackwell's Island** *or (1921–73)* **Welfare Island** Island in the EAST RIVER, between the boroughs of MANHATTAN and QUEENS, NEW YORK CITY. Administratively part of Manhattan, it has an area of 139 acres (56 hectares). In 1637 the Dutch bought the island from the Indians. In 1828 the city acquired it and built a penitentiary there. It was renamed in 1973 to honor Pres. FRANKLIN ROOSEVELT. Now the site of moderate-income housing and shopping complexes, it is connected to Manhattan by aerial tramway and to Queens by bridge.

root In botany, the underground anchoring part of a plant. It grows downward in response to gravity, absorbs water and dissolved minerals, and stores reserve food. Primary root systems have a deep sturdy taproot (in GYMNOSPERMS and dicots; see COTYLEDON) plus secondary or lateral smaller roots, and root hairs. Grasses and other monocots produce a shallow diffuse mass of fibrous secondary roots. Additional support (e.g., in CORN and ORCHIDS) comes from stem offshoots called adventitious, or prop, roots. Fleshy roots that store food may be modified taproots (e.g., CARROTS, TURNIPS, and BEETS) or modified adventitious roots (e.g. CASSAVA). TUBERS such as the POTATO are modified, fleshy, underground stems, or RHIZOMES. Aerial roots arise from the stem and either pass for some distance through the air before reaching the soil or remain hanging in the air.

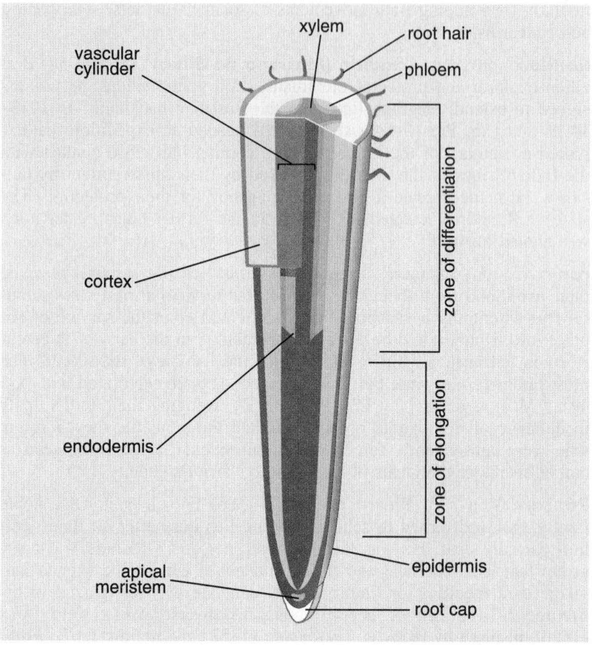

Structure of a root. The apical meristem is an area of actively dividing cells that forms all the root's cells. The root cap provides a protective covering that facilitates passage of the root through soil. Cells become specialized for specific functions in the zone of differentiation, or maturation zone. The epidermal layer allows passage of water and dissolved materials into the interior. Cells of the cortex store food and transport water and substances to the endodermis, which regulates their entry into the vascular cylinder, containing the xylem and phloem.

Root, Elihu (1845–1937) U.S. lawyer and diplomat. Born in Clinton, N.Y., he became a U.S. attorney in 1883. He served as secretary of war 1899–1904, and after the Spanish–American War he set up a civil government in Puerto Rico and organized U.S. control of the Philippines. As secretary of state (1905–9) under THEODORE ROOSEVELT, he concluded treaties with Japan and South American countries to improve relations with the U.S. He was awarded the Nobel Peace Prize in 1912. He served in the U.S. Senate 1909–15. A supporter of the League of Nations, he helped frame the statute establishing the World Court.

Root, Elisha King (1808–1865) U.S. inventor, engineer, and manufacturer. Born in Ludlow, Mass., he worked in a cotton mill from age 10 and later as a machinist. He became superintendent of SAMUEL COLT's firearms company in 1849, and he succeeded Colt as president on the latter's death. In 1853 he designed a drop hammer, which was soon being used in every forge (see FORGING) in the world. His numerous inven-

O P Q R

tions and innovations were principally responsible for Colt's preeminence in small arms.

rope Assemblage of fibers, filaments, or wires compacted by twisting or braiding into a long, flexible line. Wire rope is often referred to as cable. The basic requirement for service is that the rope remain firmly compacted and structurally stable, even while being bent, twisted, and pulled. The most important property of a rope is its TENSILE STRENGTH. Because even short fibers can be spun into long flexible YARNS, practically any fiber can be made into a rope. Braided ropes deteriorate more slowly than twisted ropes.

Roper River River, NORTHERN TERRITORY, Australia. It flows east to Limmen Bight on the Gulf of CARPENTARIA; it is about 325 mi (525 km) long and is navigable for about 90 mi (145 km). It marks the southern limit of the region known as ARNHEM LAND. North of the river's mouth is the "Ruined City of Arnhem Land," a region of sandstone whose weathered shapes suggest ruined buildings.

Rorik See RURIK

rorqual \'rór-kwəl\ Any of five species of BALEEN WHALES in the genus *Balaenoptera* (family Balaenopteridae), namely, the BLUE, FIN, SEI, Bryde's, and minke whales. The term often includes the HUMPBACK WHALE, the only other member of the family.

Rorschach \'rōr-ˌshäk\, **Hermann** (1884–1922) Swiss psychiatrist. The son of an art teacher, he was given the nickname Kleck, meaning "inkblot," as a schoolboy because of his interest in sketching. After receiving an M.D. from the University of Zurich in 1912, he became a practitioner of psychoanalysis and became vice president of the Swiss Psychoanalytic Society in 1919. He devised the Rorschach test to gauge the perceptions, intelligence, and emotional traits of his patients and used it to gather the data summarized in *Psychodiagnostics* (1921).

Rorty, Richard (McKay) (born 1931) U.S. philosopher. Born in New York City, he has taught at Princeton University (1961–82) and the University of Virginia (from 1982). He is noted for promoting a rapprochement between ANALYTIC PHILOSOPHY and CONTINENTAL PHILOSOPHY. His *Philosophy and the Mirror of Nature* (1979) is a critique of REPRESENTATIONALISM, which he claims has operated as an unquestioned assumption in philosophy from RENÉ DESCARTES on. In place of representationalism, he advocates a position inspired by PRAGMATISM. His rejection of representationalism means that there is no longer any point to the traditional epistemological project of establishing a criterion of correspondence between our ideas and reality. His later books include *Contingency, Irony and Solidarity* (1988).

Rosa, Salvator (1615–1673) Italian painter and etcher. He studied in Naples, where he came under the influence of José de RIBERA, but most of his career was spent in Rome, with an interlude in Florence under the patronage of a Medici cardinal. His landscapes, marine paintings, and battle scenes are known for their picturesquely wild, romantic qualities. A flamboyant personality, he was also an accomplished poet, satirist, actor, and musician.

Rosario City (metro. area pop., 1999 est.: 1,000,000) and river port, eastern central Argentina, on the PARANÁ RIVER. Founded in 1725, it began to develop into a major city in the late 19th century. It is the third-largest city in Argentina. In 1819 the city was burned by revolutionaries. In 1860 it welcomed domestic and foreign oceangoing ships to its natural harbor, which became a major port. The city exports grain, meat, and lumber. It is also an industrial city, producing steel, automobiles, and agricultural machinery, and an educational center.

rosary Religious exercise in which prayers are recited and counted on a string of beads or knotted cord, which is also called a rosary. Many of these devices are highly ornamental and incorporate jewels. The practice of using a rosary or "counting beads" occurs widely in world religions, including Christianity, Hinduism, Buddhism, and Islam. In Christianity, the most common rosary is that of the Virgin MARY. Its origin is uncertain, but it is associated with St. DOMINIC and reached its definitive form in the 15th century.

rosary pea *or* **Indian licorice** Tropical plant (*Abrus precatorius;* family Leguminosae). Its hard, red and black seeds, though highly poisonous, are strung into necklaces and rosaries in India and other tropical areas. In India the seeds are also used as a unit of weight *(ratti).*

Rosas \'rō-säs\, **Juan Manuel de** (1793–1877) Argentinian military and political leader. Born to a wealthy family, Rosas emerged a Federalist hero from the country's long civil war and was made governor of Buenos Aires in 1829. He left office in 1833 to pursue a war against the Indians, and in 1835 he again became governor of Buenos Aires, this time with dictatorial powers. He was the quintessential CAUDILLO, a tyrant who cultivated a fiercely loyal personal following and ruled by intimidation and patronage. Despite his professed allegiance to federalism, he established central control over all of Argentina until he was finally overthrown in 1852 and forced to flee to England.

rose Any of about 100 species in the genus *Rosa* (family Rosaceae) characterized by their beautiful, fragrant flowers. *Rosa* species are probably the most widely recognized and universally favored of ornamental flowering plants. Hundreds of varieties are cultivated in all types of settings, and there are many hybrids. Roses are susceptible to numerous diseases, most caused by fungi. The rose family contains about 3,000 species and accounts for 45% of the species in the rose order (Rosales). Other popular garden plants and ornamentals in the rose family include SPIREA, CINQUEFOIL, HAWTHORN, MOUNTAIN ASH, and flowering CHERRY. The family also contains many important fruits, including the APPLE, PEACH, STRAWBERRY, PEAR, PLUM, APRICOT, ALMOND, QUINCE, BLACKBERRY, and RASPBERRY. Plants of some species contain dangerous CYANIDE compounds. Many members have thorns or prickles.

Prairie rose (*Rosa setigera*).
JOHN H. GERARD

Rose, Fred (1897–1954) U.S. singer and songwriter, a pioneer of COUNTRY MUSIC. Born in Indiana, he grew up in St. Louis, and he performed at Chicago nightclubs as a teenager. He wrote and recorded popular music in the 1920s, including "Honest and Truly." As country music emerged, Rose became one of its foremost songwriters. He had his own Nashville radio show, and later wrote songs for GENE AUTRY's films. Many of his songs have become classics, including "Tears on My Pillow" (1941) and "A Mansion on the Hill" (1948), cowritten with HANK WILLIAMS, whose career he helped foster. In 1942 he and ROY ACUFF cofounded the Acuff-Rose Publishing Co. Rose was one of the first three musicians elected to the Country Music Hall of Fame.

Rose, Pete(r Edward) (born 1942) U.S. baseball player. He began playing organized baseball at 8. He played for the Cincinnati Reds (1963–79, 1984–86), the Philadelphia Phillies (1980–83), and the Montreal Expos (1984). His 4,256 career hits and 3,562 games played both remain all-time records, and his career mark for runs (2,165) is exceeded only by TY COBB, BABE RUTH, and HANK AARON. In 1989, after being investigated for allegedly betting on baseball games, including those of his own Reds, Rose was banned from the sport for life.

Rose Bowl *formally* **Pasadena Tournament of Roses** Oldest U.S. postseason college football contest, held annually in Pasadena, Cal., usually on New Year's Day. Each Rose Bowl game is preceded by the Tournament of Roses Parade featuring floats of elaborate floral design. The first festival was held in 1890, and the first football game in 1902. The Rose Bowl stadium opened in 1922. From 1947 to 2001 participation was limited to teams from the Big Ten and Pacific Ten conferences. Starting in 2002, this arrangement would be suspended every fourth year in order to allow the Rose Bowl to host a national championship game.

Rose of Lima, St. *orig.* **Isabel de Flores** (1586–1617) Patron saint of Peru and of all South America, the first person born in the Western Hemisphere to be canonized by the Roman Catholic church (1671). Born to a wealthy family in Lima, in 1606 she overcame her mother's objections and joined a Dominican order. She went into seclusion in a hut in the family garden, where she lived with great austerity, fasting, wearing a crown of thorns, and sleeping on a bed of broken glass, and experienced many visions, particularly of the devil. Only in her last three years did she leave her seclusion. Many miracles were reported after her death.

rose of Sharon Shrub or small tree *(Hibiscus syriacus,* or *Althaea syriaca)* in the MALLOW FAMILY, native to eastern Asia but widely planted as an ornamental for its showy flowers. It can grow to 10 ft (3 m) and generally assumes a low-branching pyramid shape. The mallowlike flowers range from white and pinkish-lavender to purple, generally with a crimson base; some varieties have double flowers. The name also sometimes refers to the unrelated Aaron's-beard *(Hypericum calycinum),* a shrubby relative of ST.-JOHN'S-WORT.

rose quartz Translucent, coarse-grained variety of the SILICA MINERAL QUARTZ found in PEGMATITES. Rose quartz is valued for its pale to rich pink color, which is due to very small amounts of TITANIUM. It has been carved since early times and has been faceted to provide gems of good brilliance. Its milky aspect is attributed to tiny needlelike inclusions of RUTILE, which, when oriented, give the polished stone an asterism (optical phenomenon of a star-shaped figure) like that found in sapphire, but not as sharp or intense. Rose quartz occurs in Brazil, Madagascar, Sweden, Namibia, California, and Maine, among other sites.

rose window In GOTHIC ARCHITECTURE, a decorated circular window, often glazed with stained glass, that first appeared in mid-12th-century cathedrals. It was used mainly at the western end of the NAVE and the ends of the TRANSEPT. The bar TRACERY of a High Gothic rose window consisted of a series of radiating forms, each tipped by a pointed arch at the outside of the circle. The rose windows of NOTRE-DAME DE PARIS are particularly noteworthy. In later FLAMBOYANT-STYLE tracery, the radiating elements consisted of an intricate network of wavy, double-curved bars.

Roseau \rō-'zō\ Town (pop., 1991: 16,000), capital of Dominica, WEST INDIES. It lies on the island's southwestern coast, at the mouth of the Roseau River. Its port exports limes, tropical vegetables, and spices. There are botanical gardens and nearby waterfalls and thermal springs. The town was burned by the French in 1805 and again suffered nearly total destruction by a hurricane in 1979.

Rosebery \'rōz-bə-rē\, **Earl of** *orig.* **Archibald Philip Primrose** (1847–1929) British politician. He served in WILLIAM E. GLADSTONE'S governments as undersecretary for Scottish affairs (1881–83) and foreign secretary (1886, 1892–94). He succeeded Gladstone as prime minister (1894–95) but was ineffective in resolving conflicts within the Liberal Party and in passing legislation through the Conservative-dominated House of Lords. He broke with the Liberal Party by opposing Irish HOME RULE (1905) and retired from public life.

Rosecrans \'rō-zə-ˌkranz\, **William S(tarke)** (1819–1898) U.S. general. Born in Kingston Township, Ohio, he served in the army before resigning to become an architect and civil engineer. In the AMERICAN CIVIL WAR he led Union forces to victory at Iuka and Corinth, Miss., and at Murfreesboro, Tenn. In 1863 he advanced on Confederate troops under BRAXTON BRAGG at Chattanooga, forcing them out of the city. An ill-planned move precipitated the Battle of CHICKAMAUGA and forced his troops to retreat into Chattanooga, where they were besieged; Rosecrans's error led to his being removed from command. He later served as minister to Mexico and as a U.S. Representative (1881–85).

rosefish See REDFISH

rosemary Small perennial evergreen shrub *(Rosmarinus officinalis)* of the MINT family whose leaves are used to flavor a wide variety of food. The bush grows 3–7.5 ft (1–2.3 m) tall and has short linear leaves that resemble curved pine needles, dark green and shiny above, white beneath. Bluish flowers grow in small clusters. Bees are particularly fond of rosemary. In ancient times rosemary was believed to strengthen memory; in literature and folklore it is an emblem of remembrance and fidelity. Native to the Mediterranean, it has been naturalized throughout Europe and temperate America.

Rosenberg, Alfred (1893–1946) German Nazi ideologue. As editor of the Nazi Party newspaper from 1921, he drew on the ideas of the English racist HOUSTON STEWART CHAMBERLAIN for his books espousing German racial purity and anti-Semitism, which reinforced ADOLF HITLER'S own extreme prejudices. In World War II he oversaw the transport of stolen art into Germany and was a government official in the occupied eastern territories. After the war he was tried at the Nuremberg Trials and hanged as a war criminal.

Rosenberg, Julius and Ethel *orig.* **Ethel Greenglass** (1918–1953, 1915–1953) U.S. spies. They were both born in New York City and both joined the Communist Party. In 1940 Julius became an engineer with the U.S. Army Signal Corps. He and his wife Ethel apparently gave military secrets to the Soviet military in a conspiracy with Ethel's brother, Sgt. David Greenglass, a machinist on the atomic-bomb project at Los Alamos, and Harry Gold, a courier for the U.S. espionage ring. They were all arrested in mid-1950. Greenglass and Gold received prison terms, but the Rosenbergs were sentenced to death. Despite several appeals and a worldwide campaign for mercy, they were executed at Sing Sing Prison in 1953, the only U.S. civilians ever executed for espionage.

Rosenquist, James (born 1933) U.S. painter associated with the POP ART movement. Born in Grand Forks, N.D., he began his career as an abstract painter but was later drawn to Pop art. Such features of his large canvases as pop-culture iconography, advertising logos, and superimposed images may be traceable in part to his youthful employment as a billboard painter. He has also created large works combining lithography, screenprinting, etching, and collage.

Rosenzweig \'rō-zən-ˌtsvīk\, **Franz** (1886–1929) German-Jewish existentialist and religious philosopher. As a student at Berlin and Freiburg, he rejected the idealism of G. W. F. HEGEL. He briefly thought of converting to Christianity, but turned instead to an intensive reading of the Hebrew classics. While serving in World War I he began to formulate the existentialist understanding of faith and belief that would eventuate in his major work, *The Star of Redemption* (1921). He collaborated on a translation of the Old Testament with MARTIN BUBER in which he tried to restore what he thought was the existentialist tone of the original.

Roses, Wars of the (1455–85) Series of dynastic civil wars between the Houses of LANCASTER and YORK for the English throne. The wars were named for the emblems of the two houses, the white rose of York and the red of Lancaster. Both claimed the throne through descent from EDWARD III. Lancastrians held the throne from 1399, but the country fell into a state of near anarchy during the reign of HENRY VI, and during one of Henry's bouts with madness in 1453 the duke of York was declared protector of the realm. Henry reestablished his authority in 1455, and the battle was joined. The Yorkists succeeded in putting EDWARD IV on the throne in 1461, but the wars continued, and in 1471 they murdered HENRY VI in the Tower of London. In 1483 RICHARD III overrode the claims of his nephew Edward V to seize the throne, alienating many Yorkists. The Lancastrian Henry Tudor (HENRY VII) defeated and killed Richard at the Battle of BOSWORTH FIELD, ending the wars. He united the houses by marriage and defeated a Yorkist rising in 1487.

Rosetta Stone \rō-'ze-tə\ Inscribed stone slab, now in the British Museum, that provided an important key to the decipherment of Egyptian HIEROGLYPHS. An irregularly shaped block of black basalt with inscriptions in hieroglyphs, Demotic EGYPTIAN, and Greek, it was discovered by Napoleon's troops near the town of Rosetta (Rashid), northeast of Alexandria, in 1799. The text concerns the deeds of Ptolemy V Epiphanes (205–180 BC), and dates from the ninth year of his reign. Its decipherment was begun by THOMAS YOUNG, who isolated the proper names in the Demotic version, and decisively completed by J.-F. CHAMPOLLION, who grasped that some hieroglyphs were phonetic.

The Rosetta Stone, with Egyptian hieroglyphics in the top section, demotic characters in the middle, and Greek at the bottom; in the British Museum.

BY COURTESY OF THE TRUSTEES OF THE BRITISH MUSEUM

Rosewall, Ken(neth Ronald) (born 1934) Australian tennis player. Born in Sydney, he won his first major titles, the Wimbledon men's doubles and the French singles, in 1956. He remained a major competitor for 25 years, winning 18 Grand Slam titles. His last major victory came in 1973 as part of the Australian Davis Cup team.

Rosh Hashanah \ˌräsh-hə-'shä-nə\ Jewish New Year. Sometimes called the Day of Judgment, Rosh Hashanah falls on Tishri 1 (in September or October) and ushers in a 10-day period of self-examination and penitence that ends with YOM KIPPUR. The liturgy includes the blowing of the ram's horn, or shofar, a call for spiritual awakening associated with the giving of the Law to Moses on Mount Sinai. It is also called the Day of Remembrance, since it celebrates the creation of the world and the responsibilities of the Jews as God's chosen people. It is a solemn but hopeful holiday; bread and fruit dipped in honey are eaten as omens of sweetness for the year ahead.

Rosicrucian \ˌrō-zə-ˈkrü-shən\ Member of a secret worldwide brotherhood claiming to possess esoteric wisdom handed down from ancient times. The name derives from the order's symbol, a combination of a rose and a cross. Its origins are obscure. Its earliest known document, *Account of the Brotherhood* (1614), tells the story of the supposed founder, Christian Rosenkreuz ("Rose Cross"), allegedly born in 1378, who is said to have acquired his wisdom on trips to the Middle East and imparted it to his followers on his return to Germany. He is now generally considered a symbolic rather than a real character. Some regard Paracelsus as the true founder; others say Rosicrucianism is only the accumulated wisdom passed down from Plato, Jesus, Philo Judaeus, Plotinus, and others. No reliable evidence dates the order's history earlier than the 17th century. The international "Ancient Mystical Order Rosae Crucis" was founded in 1915; it and other Rosicrucian groups continue to operate today.

Ross, Betsy *orig.* **Elizabeth Griscom** (1752–1836) American patriot. Born in Philadelphia, she worked as a seamstress and upholsterer, carrying on her husband's upholstery business after he was killed in the American Revolution. According to legend, in 1776 she was visited by George Washington, Robert Morris, and her husband's uncle George Ross, who asked her to make a flag for the new nation based on a sketch by Washington. Though Ross made flags for the navy, no firm evidence supports this legend of the national flag. In 1777 the Continental Congress adopted the Stars and Stripes as the U.S. flag.

Ross, Diana See Supremes

Ross, Harold W(allace) (1892–1951) U.S. editor. Born in Aspen, Col., he worked as a reporter and editor before launching *The New Yorker* in 1925 with the financial backing of a wealthy friend. The new magazine soon attracted established writers and artists as well as young talent drawn by its innovative style and Ross's encouragement. His famously unvarnished speech and bluster, which seemed at odds with his magazine's sophistication, masked extraordinary editorial instincts and capacities. Ross remained the guiding force behind *The New Yorker* until his death, though he relinquished many of his duties in his later years.

Ross, John *Indian name* **Tsan-Usdi ("Little John")** (1790–1866) American Indian chief. Born near Lookout Mtn., N.C., the son of a Scottish father and part-Cherokee mother, he grew up as a Cherokee. He fought in the Creek war under Andrew Jackson (1813–14). He later became president of the National Council of Cherokees (1819–26). As principal chief of the Cherokee Nation (1828–39), he resisted government attempts to seize Cherokee farms and lands in Georgia and unsuccessfully petitioned Jackson to defend the Indians' rights. In 1838 he was forced to lead his people on the infamous Trail of Tears to the Oklahoma Territory. There he became chief of the new United Cherokee Nation (1839–66).

Ross, Martin See Edith Somerville

Ross, Ronald *later* **Sir Ronald** (1857–1932) British bacteriologist. After earning a medical degree, he entered the Indian Medical Service and served in the third Anglo-Burmese War (1885). He studied bacteriology in London, then returned to India, where he discovered the plasmodium parasite (cause of malaria) in the gastrointestinal tract of the *Anopheles* mosquito in 1897. He used infected and healthy birds to learn its entire life cycle, including its presence in the mosquito's salivary glands, showing how it is transmitted by a bite. He received a 1902 Nobel Prize.

Ross, William David *later* **Sir William** (1877–1971) Scottish moral philosopher. He served many years as provost at Oriel College, Oxford (1902–47) and later as Oxford's vice chancellor. A critic of utilitarianism, he proposed a form of ethical intuitionism. He maintained that "good" (which pertains to motives) and "right" (which pertains to acts) are indefinable and irreducible terms (see naturalistic fallacy) and that certain commonsensical moral principles (e.g., those requiring promise-keeping, truth-telling, and justice) are knowable by mature reflection. His writings include *Aristotle* (1923), *The Right and the Good* (1930), *Foundations of Ethics* (1939), *Plato's Theory of Ideas* (1951), and *Kant's Ethical Theory* (1954).

Ross Ice Shelf World's largest body of floating ice, lying at the head of Ross Sea, an enormous indentation in Antarctica. Its area is estimated to be about the size of France. The great white barrier wall of the shelf's front, first seen in 1841 by British explorer Capt. James C. Ross, rises in places to 200 ft (60 m). The ice shelf has been an important gateway for explorations of the Antarctic interior, including expeditions by Roald Amundsen and Robert Falcon Scott in 1911–12 to the South Pole, and for R. E. Byrd's expeditions (1928–41). It is the site of several permanent research stations.

Rosse, Earl of *orig.* **William Parsons** (1800–1867) Irish astronomer. His "Leviathan," 54 ft (16.2 m) long, was the largest reflecting telescope of the 19th century, and its mirror had a diameter of 72 in. (183 cm). With it Rosse discovered the spiral shape of many objects then classed as nebulae, now recognized as galaxies, and he studied and named the Crab Nebula. He was also the first to discover binary and triple stars. As Lord Oxmantown, he served in the House of Commons 1821–34; on inheriting his father's earldom in 1841, he joined the House of Lords.

Rossellini \ˌrōs-säl-ˈlē-nē\, **Roberto** (1906–1977) Italian film director. He directed his first feature film, *White Ship,* in 1941. During World War II he made Fascist propaganda films but also secretly filmed anti-Fascist activities. He used the documentary footage in *Open City* (1945), acclaimed as one of the first examples of Italian Neorealism. The screenplay was written with Federico Fellini, who also collaborated with him on *Paisan* (1946). He made several films starring Ingrid Bergman, beginning with *Stromboli* (1949), but the scandal of their adulterous affair and marriage damaged their careers. He later directed *General della Rovere* (1959) and works for the stage and television, including a series of didactic historical works. His daughter Isabella Rossellini (born 1952) has appeared in such films as *Blue Velvet* (1986) and *Big Night* (1996).

Rossellino \ˌrōs-säl-ˈlē-nō\, **Bernardo** (1409–1464) Italian architect and sculptor. Influenced by Donatello, Filippo Brunelleschi, and Luca Della Robbia, he developed a moderately classical style. His tomb for Leonardo Bruni (1444–50) in Santa Croce, Florence, was one of the greatest achievements of early Renaissance sculpture and inaugurated a new type of sepulchral monument. Its fine balance between sculpture and architecture, figure and decoration, made it the prototypical niche tomb of its time. He also designed the apse of St. Peter's Basilica and the cathedral and Piccolomini Palace in Pienza (1460–64). He presumably trained his brother Antonio (1427–1479), who regularly assisted him. A master of portraiture in sculpture, Antonio achieved extremely detailed and realistic likenesses. His greatest work is the Chapel of the Cardinal of Portugal, an elaborate combination of architecture and figurative sculpture in San Miniato al Monte, outside Florence.

Rossetti \rō-ˈze-tē\, **Christina (Georgina)** (1830–1894) English poet. The youngest child of Gabriele Rossetti and the sister of Dante Gabriel Rossetti, she found her highest inspiration in her deep religious faith. The collections *Goblin Market* (1862) and *The Prince's Progress* (1866) contain most of her finest work. Her best poetry is strong, personal, and unforced; her success arises from her ability to unite the devotional and the passionate sides of her nature. Her *Sing-Song* (1872; enlarged 1893), a collection of nursery rhymes, is among the most outstanding children's books of the 19th century. After the onset of a thyroid disorder in 1871, she wrote mainly devotional verse.

Christina Rossetti, chalk drawing by Dante Gabriel Rossetti, 1866; in a private collection.

Rossetti \rō-ˈzet-ē, rō-ˈset-ē\, **Dante Gabriel** *orig.* **Gabriel Charles Dante** (1828–1882) British painter and poet. Son of Gabriele Rossetti and brother of Christina Rossetti, he trained at the Royal Academy, but vacillated between painting and poetry. As an informal pupil of

FORD MADOX BROWN, he absorbed Brown's admiration for the German NAZARENES, and in 1848, with several friends, he formed the PRE-RAPHAELITES. Rossetti expanded the Brotherhood's aims by linking poetry, painting, and social idealism and by treating "Pre-Raphaelite" as synonymous with a romanticized medieval past. When his oil paintings were severely criticized, he turned to watercolors based on literary works, which he could more easily sell to acquaintances, and became very successful. The group broke up in 1852, but Rossetti revived it in 1856 with EDWARD BURNE-JONES and WILLIAM MORRIS. After the death of his long-ailing wife in 1862, possibly by suicide, literary themes gave way to pictures of women, particularly Morris's wife, Jane. His poetry, including the sonnet sequence "The House of Life," was widely admired. He broke with Morris in 1875 over his love for Jane, and spent his later years as an alcoholic recluse.

Dante Gabriel Rossetti, photograph by Lewis Carroll, 1863.

THE BETTMANN ARCHIVE

Rossetti, Gabriele (Pasquale Giuseppe) (1783–1854) Italian poet, revolutionary, and scholar. A librettist and later curator of a museum in Naples, he was condemned for his spirited verse on contemporary politics and for membership in a revolutionary group. In 1824 he fled to England, where in 1831 he published an eccentric interpretation of DANTE, claiming a chiefly political and antipapal meaning in the *Divine Comedy*. The work led to a post as professor of Italian at King's College, London, from 1831 to 1847. He is best known as the father of four talented children, including CHRISTINA ROSSETTI and DANTE GABRIEL ROSSETTI.

Rossini, Gioacchino (Antonio) (1792–1868) Italian composer. He sang in church and in minor opera roles as a child, began composing at 12, and at 14 entered Bologna's conservatory, where he wrote mostly sacred music. From 1812 he produced theater works at a terrific rate, and for 15 years he was the dominant voice of Italian opera; his major successes included *L'Italiana in Algeri* (1813), *Otello* (1816), *The Barber of Seville* (1816), *La Cenerentola* (1817), *Mosè in Egitto* (1818), *The Siege of Corinth* (1826), and *Semiramide* (1823). His speed and nonchalant attitude made him seem more careless than he was; the musical formulas he devised would shape Italian opera until GIUSEPPE VERDI, but his wit and invention using them was unparalleled. From 1824 he spent much time in Paris, where he wrote his masterpiece, *William Tell* (1829). After 1832 his health was poor, and he composed little until the series of wonderful piano pieces and songs collected as *Sins of My Old Age* (1868).

Rosso \'rōs-sō\, **Giovanni Battista (di Jacopo)** *known as* **Rosso Fiorentino** *or* **Il Rosso** (1494–1540) Italian painter and decorator. He trained under ANDREA DEL SARTO, alongside JACOPO DA PONTORMO, with whom he became a leading figure in the development of MANNERISM. In his later work, the highly charged emotionalism of his early works (e.g., the *Assumption* fresco, 1513–14, in Florence's Santissima Annunziata) is more subdued; his new style is seen in his *Dead Christ with Angels* (1525–26). In 1530 he went to France at the invitation of FRANCIS I; there he became a founder of the FONTAINEBLEAU SCHOOL, and the ornamental style he developed influenced decorative arts across northern Europe. He remained in the royal service until his death.

Rostand \rȯs-'tän\, **Edmond (-Eugène)** (1868–1918) French playwright. He wrote poetry, essays, and plays for puppet theater before his first stage play, *The Red Glove,* was performed in 1888. His most popular work is the heroic comedy *Cyrano de Bergerac* (1898), the story of an ugly, long-nosed soldier who despairs of winning the lady he loves and helps a friend woo her instead. The final example of French Romantic drama, it was enormously successful internationally. He also wrote *L'aiglon* (1900) for SARAH BERNHARDT.

Rostock \'rȯ-,stȯk\ City (pop., 1996 est.: 228,000) and seaport, northeastern Germany, on the Warnow River, 8 mi (13 km) from the BALTIC SEA. Founded in 1218, it was a powerful member of the HANSEATIC LEAGUE in the 14th century. Wooden ships were built in its shipyards from the medieval period until 1851, when the first German steam-propelled vessel was built there. It was heavily damaged in World War II by Allied bombing. After the war the town center was rebuilt, and it was developed as East Germany's principal ocean port. It is an important fishing and shipbuilding center and manufactures diesel engines and chemical products.

Rostov \rə-'stȯf\ City (pop., 1991 est.: 36,000), western central Russia. First mentioned in chronicles in AD 862, Rostov was an outstanding center of early medieval Russia. It was the capital of the Rostov-Suzdal principality, which came under the control of MOSCOW in 1474. In the late 16th century it became an important trade center on the route between Moscow and the WHITE SEA. It still produces traditional handmade enamelware.

Rostov-na-Donu \rə-'stȯf-nä-'dȯ-nü\ *English* **Rostov-on-Don** City (pop., 1996 est.: 1,000,000), southern Russia in Europe. Located on the DON RIVER about 28 mi (45 km) from the Sea of AZOV, it was founded as a customs post in 1749. It was fortified soon after, and because of its key position as a transport center and port, it grew steadily with the 19th-century Russian colonization. Occupied by the Germans in World War II, it suffered extensive damage, but was rebuilt. It is a transportation and industrial center; the nearby DONETS BASIN led to major industrialization in recent decades.

Rostropovich \,rȯs-trə-'pō-vich\, **Mstislav (Leopoldovich)** (born 1927) Russian-U.S. cellist and conductor. Born in Azerbaijan, he studied composition (with D. SHOSTAKOVICH), piano, and cello at the Moscow Conservatory from 1943. He had pieces written for him by such composers as Shostakovich, S. PROKOFIEV, and BENJAMIN BRITTEN. A political dissident, he left the Soviet Union in 1974 and made his career in the West. Settling in the U.S., he served as music director of the National Symphony Orchestra (1977–96), while continuing to make many solo appearances, becoming perhaps the world's most famous cellist. As a pianist, he has accompanied his wife, the soprano Galina Vishnevskaya (born 1926).

Roswitha See HROSVITHA

Rota, Nino (1911–1979) Italian composer of film scores. Born in Milan, Rota had composed an oratorio and an opera by age 13. After studies at Philadelphia's Curtis Institute he began writing film scores. From 1950 to 1978 he served as director of Bari's Liceo Musicale. In 1950 he also began his long association with FEDERICO FELLINI, for whom he would score such films as *La Strada* (1955), *La Dolce Vita* (1960), *8½* (1963), and *Amarcord* (1973; U.S. release, 1974). His many other film scores included FRANCIS FORD COPPOLA's *The Godfather* (1972) and *The Godfather: Part II* (1974).

rotary engine INTERNAL-COMBUSTION ENGINE in which the combustion chambers and cylinders rotate with the driven shaft around a fixed control shaft to which pistons are attached. The gas pressures of combustion are used to rotate the shaft. In the Wankel engine, the most fully developed and widely used rotary engine, a triangular rotor rotates with an orbital motion in a specially shaped casing, and forms rotating crescent-shaped combustion chambers between its sides and the curved wall of the casing.

rotary press PRINTING press that prints on PAPER passing between a supporting cylinder and a cylinder containing the printing plates. In contrast, the flatbed press has a flat printing surface. The rotary press is used mainly in high-speed, web-fed operations in which the press takes paper from a roll, as in newspaper printing. Many of these large presses not only print as many as four colors but also cut and fold and bind in a cover, all in one continuous automatic process. Paper passes through some presses at nearly 20 mph (30 kph); large presses can print up to 60,000 copies of 128 standard-size pages in an hour. See also R. HOE.

Roth, Philip (Milton) (born 1933) U.S. writer. A native of Newark, N.J., Roth attended the University of Chicago, and first achieved fame with *Goodbye Columbus* (1959), whose title story candidly depicts the boorish materialism of a suburban family. His works are characterized by an acute ear for dialogue, a concern with Jewish middle-class life, and the painful entanglements of sexual and familial love. Among his subsequent novels are the comic and scandalous *Portnoy's Complaint* (1969) and an admired series centering on a writer named Nathan Zuck-

O P Q R

erman, including *The Ghost Writer* (1979), *Zuckerman Unbound* (1981), *The Anatomy Lesson* (1983), and *The Counterlife* (1986). Later works include the scabrously hilarious and poignant *Sabbath's Theater* (1995, National Book Award) and *American Pastoral* (1997, Pulitzer Prize).

Rothko, Mark *orig.* **Marcus Rothkowitz** (1903–1970) U.S. (Russian-born) painter. His family settled in Portland, Ore., in 1913, and he took up painting (largely self-taught) after moving to New York in 1925. His early realistic style culminated in the *Subway* series (late 1930s). The semiabstract forms of *Baptismal Scene* (1945) developed into a highly personal contemplative form of ABSTRACT EXPRESSIONISM by 1948. He spent the rest of his career refining a basic style featuring two or three soft-edged rectangles that nearly filled his wall-sized canvases, eschewing the violent brush strokes and paint splattering of his fellow Abstract Expressionists. In 1965–66 he completed 14 immense canvases, whose somber intensity reveals his deepening mysticism; they are now housed in a chapel in Houston, which was named the Rothko Chapel after his suicide.

Rothschild family European banking dynasty. It was founded by Mayer Amschel Rothschild (1744–1812), who started out in a Frankfurt banking house. The family name derived from the red shield *(rote Schild)* on the house in the Jewish ghetto where Mayer's ancestors lived. The financial transactions of the Napoleonic Wars of 1792–1815 were the foundation of the Rothschild fortune. Mayer and his oldest son, Amschel (1773–1855), supervised the growing business from Frankfurt, while Nathan (1777–1836) established a branch in London in 1804. James (or Jakob, 1792–1868) settled in Paris in 1811, and Salomon (1774–1855) and Karl (1788–1855) opened offices in Vienna and Naples, respectively, in the 1820s. The Rothschild business later focused on government securities and industrial companies, including railway, coal, ironworking, oil, and metallurgical investments. Their powerful position was eventually threatened by the new commercial banks, and by the late 19th century the Rothschild group was no longer the first banking consortium. The Rothschilds received many honors: Mayer's five sons were made barons of the Austrian empire, a Rothschild was the first Jew to enter the British Parliament, and another was the first to be elevated to the British peerage. Members of the British and French families—the only ones still engaged in banking after the seizure of the Austrian house by the Nazis—distinguished themselves as scientists and philanthropists. Baron Philippe de Rothschild (1902–1988) became a premier winemaker, of the vineyard Mouton-Rothschild.

rotifer \'rō-tə-fər\ Any of about 2,000 species of microscopic, multicellular, water-dwelling INVERTEBRATES constituting the class Rotifera, or Rotaria (phylum Aschelminthes; see WORM). Currents created by the rotifer's corona (moving cilia arranged in a circle at the head) sweep bacteria, protozoans, and detritus into the mouth. Rotifers also eat larger items (other rotifers, crustaceans, algae). The muscular pharynx contains hard jaws. Body shape varies greatly among species. Rotifers are common in freshwater on all continents, but some live in saltwater. The species vary widely in mode of living: they may be free-living or parasitic, solitary or colonial, and free-swimming, crawling, or sedentary.

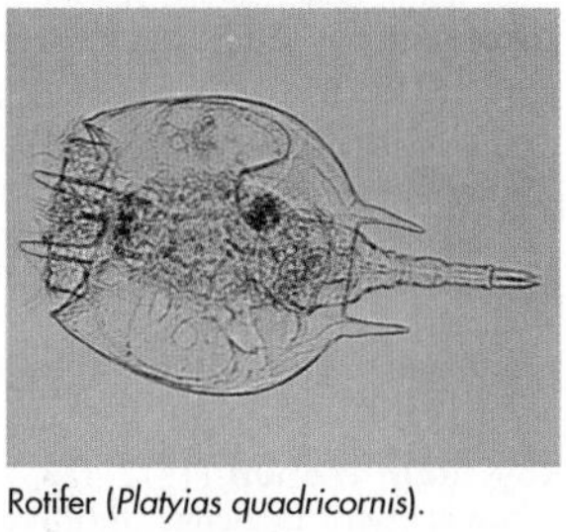
Rotifer (*Platyias quadricornis*).
RUNK/SCHOENBERGER FROM GRANT HEILMAN

Rotterdam City (pop., 1996 est.: 593,000) and seaport, western Netherlands. It is situated on both sides of the Nieuwe Maas River, near the NORTH SEA. Founded in the 13th century, it developed into a major port and commercial city. From 1795 to 1813 it was occupied by the French. Heavily damaged by the Germans during World War II, it was extensively rebuilt on a new plan. One of the world's busiest cargo-handling ports, it is a major transshipment port for inland Europe, with tens of thousands of RHINE RIVER barges using its facilities. The second-largest city in the Netherlands, it has several large oil refineries and produces chemicals, paper, and clothing. It is also a cultural and educational center.

Rottluff, Karl Schmidt- See Karl SCHMIDT-ROTTLUFF

Rottweiler \'rät-,wī-lər, 'rōt-,vī-lər\ Breed of dog descended from a breed of cattle dog left by the Roman legions in Rottweil, Germany. From the Middle Ages to c. 1900, it accompanied butchers on buying expeditions, carrying money in a neck pouch. It has also served as a guard dog, drover's dog, draft dog, and police dog. Stocky and muscular, it stands 22–27 in. (56–69 cm) and weighs 90–110 lbs (41–50 kg). It has a short, black coat, with tan markings on the head, chest, and legs.

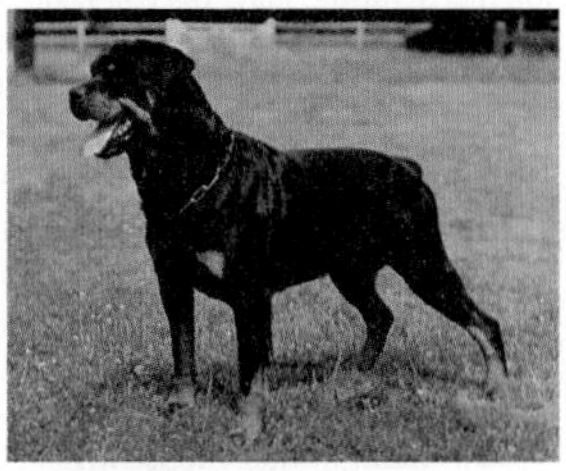
Rottweiler.
SALLY ANNE THOMPSON

rotunda In Classical and Neoclassical architecture, a building or room that is circular in plan and covered with a dome. The PANTHEON is a Classical Roman rotunda. The Villa Rotonda at Vicenza, designed by ANDREA PALLADIO, is an Italian Renaissance example. The central hall of the U.S. CAPITOL is an example of the rotunda in its familiar role as part of a monumental public building.

Rouault \rü-'ō\, **Georges (-Henri)** (1871–1958) French painter. His apprenticeship in a glazier's shop restoring medieval stained glass (1885–90) influenced his mature style as a painter. After an early academic period, his style evolved toward FAUVISM before he established a highly personal form of EXPRESSIONISM. An ardent Roman Catholic, he painted subjects apparently fallen from grace—prostitutes, tragic clowns, and pitiless judges. After 1914 his subject matter became more specifically religious, with greater emphasis on redemption, and he shifted from watercolor to oil. His layers of paint became thick and rich, his forms simplified, and his colors and black lines reminiscent of stained glass. In the 1930s he produced a splendid series on Christ's Passion, while reworking many earlier paintings. His series of clowns in the 1940s are virtual self-portraits. He also produced many engravings as well as ceramics, tapestry designs, and stained glass.

Rouen \rü-'ä^{n}\ City (pop., 1990: 105,000), northwestern France, on the SEINE RIVER. It became important in the 3rd century AD, with the arrival of Christianity with St. Mellon. Sacked by the Normans in 876, it became the medieval capital of NORMANDY. It came under English rule in 1066 and again in 1419. JOAN OF ARC was imprisoned and executed there in 1431. It was recaptured by the French in 1449. Historic buildings include the 14th-century abbey of St. Ouen and the great Gothic cathedral, whose oldest parts date to the 11th century. It was the birthplace of PIERRE CORNEILLE and GUSTAVE FLAUBERT.

Rough Riders 1st Volunteer Cavalry regiment in the SPANISH–AMERICAN WAR. The group, organized and led by THEODORE ROOSEVELT and LEONARD WOOD, included cowboys, miners, policemen, and college athletes. The most famous of its exploits in the fighting in Cuba was an uphill charge in the Battle of Santiago (July 1, 1898) in which the group helped capture Kettle Hill and then charged across a valley to assist in the seizure of San Juan Ridge and its high point, San Juan Hill. The regiment received wide coverage in the U.S. press that helped establish Roosevelt's reputation.

roulette \rü-'let\ Gambling game in which players bet on which red or black numbered compartment of a revolving wheel a small ball will come to rest in. Roulette (French for "small wheel") emerged in the late 18th century in the casinos of Europe. All bets are placed against the "house," or casino bank. Bets may be made until the ball slows down and is about to drop from its track into a compartment. Bets may be on a single number or various combinations of numbers that pay off at lesser odds if the winner is among them. Betting that a red or black or odd or even number will come up are other options.

roundworm See NEMATODE

Rousseau \rü-'sō\, **Henri** *known as* **Le Douanier Rousseau** (1844–1910) French painter. After service in the army, he began working as a toll collector (not as a *douanier,* or customs officer, the epithet his friends later used), but found time to paint and draw. Completely self-taught, he exhibited some early paintings, including *Carnival Evening,* at the SALON DES INDÉPENDANTS in 1886. Like his later works, it is typical of NAIVE ART; everything is drawn literally, the clouds look solid, and the costumes receive more attention than the figures themselves—but it achieves a striking mood and mystery. In 1893 he retired to devote himself to painting, and in 1894 his *War* won him his first recognition by the avant-garde. His best-known works are richly colored images of lush jungles, wild beasts, and exotic figures (e.g., *The Sleeping Gypsy,* 1897). He exhibited *The Hungry Lion* with the Fauves (see FAUVISM) in 1905. He died a pauper; only after his death was his greatness recognized.

Rousseau, Jean-Jacques (1712–1778) Swiss-French philosopher. He ran away from Geneva to Italy in 1728, traveled for years, and settled in Paris in 1741. He wrote on music and economics for DENIS DIDEROT's ENCYCLOPÉDIE. His *Discourse on the Arts and Sciences* (1750) asserted that humans had been corrupted and enslaved by society and civilization, which, though not inherently bad, had become increasingly harmful with their growing sophistication—an idea to which he returned throughout his life and which set him apart from both conservatives and radicals. His light opera *Le devin du village* (1752) had a long-running success, despite its naive music, and made him famous. His *Discourse on the Origin and Foundations of Inequality Among Men* (1754) attacked private property. His *Social Contract* (1762) argued that if a civil society, or state, could be based on a genuine SOCIAL CONTRACT, people would receive in exchange for their natural independence a better kind of freedom. The work became the basic text of the French Revolution, though it has long been seen to support totalitarian regimes as well as radical democracy. His novel *Émile* expressed his ideas on education, and became widely influential over the following century, but the controversy its publication aroused forced him to flee to Switzerland. He began showing signs of mental instability c. 1767, and he died insane. His *Confessions* (published 1781–88) is a famous autobiography.

Rousseau \rü-'sō\, **(Pierre-Etienne-) Théodore** (1812–1867) French painter. A tailor's son, he began to paint at 14 and soon was painting outdoors directly from nature, a novel practice at the time. Because he strayed from the academic path, his work was consistently rejected by the Salon. From the 1830s he painted regularly in the village of Barbizon, where he became a leader of the BARBIZON SCHOOL of landscape painters. His paintings, which show nature as a wild, undisciplined force, counter the calmly idealized landscapes of Neoclassicism, and his small, highly textured brush strokes presage those of the Impressionists.

Roussel \rü-'sel\, **Albert (Charles Paul Marie)** (1869–1937) French composer. He served as a midshipman before deciding to make music his career, and studied for the next 10 years at Paris's Schola Cantorum. His early music was much influenced by his teacher V. D'INDY. His opera-ballet *Padmâvatî* (1918), with its Indian scales, won enthusiasm from younger composers; his other works include the ballets *The Spider's Feast* (1913) and *Bacchus et Ariane* (1930) and the third and fourth symphonies (1930, 1934).

Roussillon \ˌrü-sē-yōⁿ\ Historical and cultural region, southern France. Originally inhabited by Iberians, the region was conquered by Rome in the 2nd century BC. It was held by the VISIGOTHS in the 5th century AD, and successively by Arabs and Carolingian Franks. It was acquired by the counts of BARCELONA in the 9th century. Monasticism flourished from the 10th century on, and the area is rich in ROMANESQUE ARCHITECTURAL remains. It became part of the kingdom of ARAGON in the 12th century. It was acquired from Spain by treaty in 1659. The chief city is PERPIGNAN. CATALAN is widely spoken.

Rowe \'rō\, **Nicholas** (1674–1718) English writer. His plays, which did much to assist the rise of domestic tragedy (in which the protagonists are middle-class rather than aristocratic), include *The Ambitious Step-Mother* (1700), *Tamerlane* (1702), *The Fair Penitent* (1703), *The Tragedy of Jane Shore* (1714), and *The Tragedy of the Lady Jane Grey* (1715). He is also remembered as the first to attempt a critical edition of WILLIAM SHAKESPEARE (*The Works of Mr. William Shakespear,* 1709, 1714). He became poet laureate in 1715. Rowe is regarded as the foremost 18th-century English tragic dramatist.

rowing Propulsion of a boat by means of oars. As a sport, it involves one of two kinds of boat: (1) the shell, a narrow, light racing boat propelled by eight rowers pulling single oars under the direction of a coxswain; and (2) the scull, a racing shell propelled by one or two rowers using sculls (pairs of oars). Organized racing began at the Univs. of Oxford and Cambridge in the 1820s, culminating in 1839 in the Henley Regatta (from 1851 the Henley Royal Regatta). In the U.S., Harvard and Yale universities first raced in 1851. Rowing events in the Olympic Games have been held for men since 1900 and for women since 1976.

Rowlandson \'rō-lənd-sən\, **Mary** *orig.* **Mary White** (1637–1710/11) American (British-born) colonial author. She was the daughter of the original proprietor of Lancaster, Mass., where she lived with her minister husband and their four children. When Indians razed the settlement in 1676, she was captured and held hostage for 11 weeks. Ransomed, she moved to Connecticut with her husband and two surviving children. Her narrative of captivity, published in 1682, became popular in the colonies and in London.

Rowlandson, Thomas (1756–1827) British caricaturist. The son of a merchant, he studied at the Royal Academy and in Paris. After establishing a portrait studio, he began to draw caricatures to supplement his income, and found such success with them that caricature became his major occupation. The comic images he created lampooned familiar social types of his day—the antiquarian, the blowzy barmaid, the hack writer. He also illustrated editions of the novels of TOBIAS SMOLLETT, OLIVER GOLDSMITH, and LAURENCE STERNE.

Rowling, J(oanne) K(athleen) (born 1965) British author, creator of the popular and critically acclaimed Harry Potter series. The first book in the proposed seven-volume series, *Harry Potter and the Philosopher's Stone* (U.S. title *Harry Potter and the Sorcerer's Stone*), was published in 1997. Featuring vivid descriptions and an imaginative story line, it followed the unlikely hero Harry Potter, a lonely orphan who discovers that he is actually a wizard and enrolls in the Hogwarts School of Witchcraft and Wizardry. The book was an immediate success, appealing to both children (its intended audience) and adults. Succeeding volumes—*Harry Potter and the Chamber of Secrets* (1998), *Harry Potter and the Prisoner of Azkaban* (1999), and *Harry Potter and the Goblet of Fire* (2000)—were also best-sellers, and a film based on the first book was released in 2001. Rowling was credited with renewing children's interest in reading, and in 2001 she was appointed OBE (Officer of the British Empire).

Roxas (y Acuna) \'rō-ḵäs\, **Manuel** (1892–1948) First president (1946–48) of the Republic of the Philippines. A lawyer, he began his political career in 1917. An advocate for Philippine independence from the U.S., he was a member of the convention that drew up a constitution under the revised Philippine Independence and Commonwealth Act (Tydings-McDuffie Act; 1934). He collaborated with the pro-Japanese administration during World War II but was defended in postwar trials by Gen. DOUGLAS MACARTHUR. He became president of the Philippines when independence was achieved (1946). Roxas obtained rehabilitation funds from the U.S., but was forced to permit U.S. military bases and make other major concessions. His government was marred by corruption and police brutality, setting the stage for the HUKBALAHAP REBELLION.

Roy, Jamini (1889–1972) Indian artist. In the late 1920s and early '30s he rejected his academic training and instead developed a linear, decorative, colorful style based on Bengali folk traditions. During the 1930s and '40s, the popularity of his paintings represented the passage of modern Indian art from its earlier academic leanings to new nativist predilections. Roy's subject matter ranged from the *Ramayana* to Christ to portraits of contemporary figures such as Mahatma Gandhi. He is one of the best-known Indian artists of the 20th century.

Roy, Ram Mohun (1772–1833) Indian religious, social, and political reformer. Born in Bengal to a prosperous Brahman family, he traveled widely in his youth, exposing himself to various cultures and developing unorthodox views of Hinduism. In 1803 he composed a tract denouncing India's religious divisions and superstitions and advocating a monotheistic Hinduism that would worship one supreme god. He provided modern translations of the VEDAS and UPANISHADS to provide a philosophical basis for his beliefs, advocated freedom of speech and of religion, and denounced the caste system and suttee. In 1826 he founded the Vedanta College, and in 1828 he formed the BRAHMO SAMAJ.

Royal Academy of Arts Britain's national academy of art. It was founded in 1768 by GEORGE III. Its first president (1768–92) was JOSHUA REYNOLDS. The number of its members, who are selected by members and associates, is fixed at 40; members' names are frequently followed by the initials R.A. ("Royal Academician"). Its galleries contain works by such former members as THOMAS GAINSBOROUGH and J.M.W. TURNER. The academy opened a new wing, the Sackler Galleries, in 1991.

Royal Air Force See RAF

O
P
Q
R

Royal Ballet English ballet company and school. In 1931 NINETTE DE VALOIS and Lilian Baylis organized the Vic-Wells Ballet, naming it for the two theaters (Old Vic and Sadler's Wells) where it performed. In the 1940s the group was called the Sadler's Wells Ballet, after its theater; it moved to Covent Garden in 1946. ALICIA MARKOVA, M. FONTEYN, and ROBERT HELPMANN were among the company's early members. By the 1950s the Sadler's Wells Ballet had expanded to include its own school and a separate touring company; it was reorganized and in 1956 received a royal charter to become the Royal Ballet. Such dancers as RUDOLF NUREYEV and such choreographers as FREDERICK ASHTON, KENNETH MACMILLAN, and BRONISLAVA NIJINSKA have been associated with the company.

Royal Botanic Gardens, Kew See KEW GARDENS

Royal Canadian Mounted Police *or* **Mounties** Federal police force of Canada. It is also the criminal and provincial force in all provinces except Ontario and Quebec and the only force in the Yukon, Northwest, and Nunavut territories. It was founded as the North West Mounted Police (1873) with a force of 300 men to bring order to western Canada, where U.S. traders were creating havoc by trading whiskey to the Indians for furs. That success was followed by peacekeeping in the KLONDIKE GOLD RUSH (1898) and later settlement of the west. The group assumed its current name when it became a federal force in 1920 and its headquarters moved to Ottawa.

Royal Dutch/Shell Group Multinational corporate group owned by Royal Dutch Petroleum Co. Ltd. of The Hague and Shell Transport and Trading Co., PLC, of London. The two parent companies began as rivals. In London in 1878, Marcus Samuel took over his father's import-export business (which included oriental shells) and started handling kerosene; he later entered the oil business in the Far East, and in 1897 he founded Shell Transport and Trading Co., Ltd. Meanwhile, in 1890 a group of Dutch businessmen founded the Royal Dutch Co. for the Exploitation of Oil Wells in the Dutch Indies, which built its first refinery in Sumatra in 1892. In 1907 the two companies merged into the Royal Dutch/Shell Group, which acquired producing concerns in Egypt, Iraq, Romania, Russia, Mexico, Venezuela, California, and Oklahoma. The group's principal U.S. subsidiary is Shell Oil Co. (founded 1922). Today Royal Dutch/Shell is one of the 10 largest corporate groups in the world.

Royal Greenwich Observatory \'gre-nich\ Astronomical OBSERVATORY, oldest scientific institution in Britain, founded for navigational purposes in 1675 by Charles II at GREENWICH, England. Its main contributions have been in navigation, timekeeping, determination of star positions, and almanac publication. In 1767 it began publishing *The Nautical Almanac,* based on the time at the longitude of Greenwich; its popularity among navigators led in part to the Greenwich meridian's being made earth's prime meridian and the starting point for international time zones in 1884 (see GREENWICH MEAN TIME).

Royal National Theatre British theater company. It was formed in 1962 as the National Theatre with LAURENCE OLIVIER as director (1963–73) and included many actors from the OLD VIC company. In 1976 the company moved from London's Old Vic Theatre to a newly constructed three-theater complex on the southern bank of the Thames. In 1988 Queen Elizabeth II gave the company permission to add "Royal" to its name. Partly subsidized by the state, the theater presents a mixed classic and modern repertoire. Its directors have included PETER HALL (1973–88) and Richard Eyre (from 1988).

Royal Navy Naval military organization of Britain. Organized SEA POWER was first used in England by ALFRED the Great, who launched ships to repel a Viking invasion. In the 16th century, HENRY VIII built a fleet of fighting ships armed with large guns and created a naval administration. Under ELIZABETH I the navy developed into Britain's major defense and became the means for extending the British Empire around the globe. The maritime forces were given the name Royal Navy by CHARLES II. In the 18th century, it engaged in a long struggle with the French for maritime supremacy, and it later played a key role in Britain's stand against NAPOLEON. For the rest of the 19th century, it helped enforce what became known as the Pax Britannica, the long period of relative peace in Europe that depended on British maritime supremacy. It remained the world's most powerful navy until the mid-20th century, and it was active in protecting shipping from submarine attack in World Wars I and II. Today it maintains a fleet of nuclear-armed submarines and various surface vessels.

Royal Shakespeare Co. (RSC) Major British theatrical company. It was originally attached to the Shakespeare Memorial Theatre in Stratford-upon-Avon, which opened in 1879 as the site of an annual festival of WILLIAM SHAKESPEARE'S plays. The resident company was called the Shakespeare Memorial Co. until 1961, when it was renamed and reorganized into two units, one to play at Stratford and the other in London. The Stratford unit performs plays by Shakespeare and other Elizabethan and Jacobean playwrights, while the London unit, based at the Barbican arts complex, also performs modern plays and classics of other eras.

Royal Society (of London for the Promotion of Natural Knowledge) Oldest scientific society in Britain. Founded in 1660, its early members included ROBERT HOOKE, CHRISTOPHER WREN, ISAAC NEWTON, and EDMOND HALLEY. It provided an impetus to scientific thought and developments in England, and its achievements became internationally famous. *Philosophical Transactions,* one of the earliest periodicals in the West (1665), publishes scientific papers; abstracts of papers appear in the *Proceedings*. The society awards several prestigious medals. Today it has more than 1,000 fellows and 90 foreign members.

Royall \'ròi-əl\, **Anne Newport** *orig.* **Anne Newport** (1769–1854) U.S. writer, generally considered the nation's first newspaperwoman. Born in Maryland, she was widowed in her 50s. Royall journeyed across the country and during 1826–31 published 10 accounts of her travels, which remain valuable sources of social history. An eccentric and acerbic woman, she was convicted in Washington, D.C., in 1829 of being a "common scold," the result of her antagonism to a local Presbyterian church. In 1831 she began to publish her outspoken and controversial views on various subjects in her muckraking Washington newspaper, *Paul Pry* (1831–36), which was succeeded by *The Huntress* (1836–54).

Royce, Josiah (1855–1916) U.S. philosopher. Born in Grass Valley, Cal., he studied engineering before turning to philosophy. He taught at Harvard University from 1882 to his death. An absolute idealist in the Hegelian tradition, he taught a monistic IDEALISM (see MONISM) and helped raise the intellectual standards for philosophy. A diverse thinker, he also made contributions to psychology, social ethics, literary criticism, history, and metaphysics. His many books include *The Religious Aspect of Philosophy* (1885), *The Spirit of Modern Philosophy* (1892), *Studies of Good and Evil* (1898), *The World and the Individual* (1900–1), and *The Philosophy of Loyalty* (1908). His emphasis on individuality and will over intellect strongly influenced later U.S. philosophy.

Royko, Mike *orig.* **Michael** (1932–1997) U.S. columnist. A native of Chicago, Royko cut short his college education to serve in the Air Force during the Korean War. In 1959 he joined the *Chicago Daily News*, becoming a full-time columnist in 1964. His irreverent, acerbic, and insightful political and social essays reflected his working-class ethnic origins, often exposing injustices visited on ordinary people. He later moved to the *Chicago Sun-Times* and then to the *Chicago Tribune*. His widely syndicated column earned him a Pulitzer Prize in 1972. He published collections of his columns and the best-selling *Boss* (1971), on RICHARD DALEY.

Rozelle, Pete *orig.* **Alvin Ray** (1926–1996) U.S. sports executive and commissioner of the NATIONAL FOOTBALL LEAGUE. Born in South Gate, Cal., he graduated from the University of San Francisco and initially worked in public relations. Named commissioner in 1960, he doubled the league's size, helped create the SUPER BOWL, and negotiated lucrative television deals with the networks. In 1966 Rozelle secured an agreement to merge the NFL with the rival American Football League. In 1970 he persuaded ABC to broadcast "Monday Night Football," which proved a huge success. NFL attendance more than tripled during his tenure, which lasted until 1989.

RU-486 Common name for mifepristone, a drug used in the first several weeks of pregnancy for inducing abortion. RU-486 blocks the receptors for progesterone, a hormone necessary for the maintenance of pregnancy. The drug causes the breakdown of the uterine lining, which, along with the embryo, is shed through the vagina. It has been available in France for the termination of early pregnancy since 1988 and was approved for use in the United States in 2000. The name RU-486 is derived from the manufacturer Roussel-Uclaf and a serial number.

Ruanda-Urundi \rü-'än-dä-ü-'rün-dē\ Former territory, central eastern Africa. It was administered by Belgium 1922–62, during which time, as a U.N. trust territory from 1946. It was part of the Belgian Congo 1925–

60. In 1962 it was divided into the independent states of Rwanda and Burundi.

Rub al-Khali \'rüb-ȧl-'k̲ȧ-lē\ Vast desert, southern ARABIAN PENINSULA. It covers about 250,000 sq mi (650,000 sq km), mainly in southeastern Saudi Arabia, and has lesser portions in Yemen, Oman, and the United Arab Emirates. It is the largest area of continuous sand in the world and occupies more than one-quarter of Saudi Arabia. It is virtually uninhabited and largely unexplored. In 1948 Al-Ghawar, the world's largest oilfield, was discovered there.

rubber *or* **natural rubber** Organic compound, an elastic POLYMER made from the LATEX of various RUBBER TREES and RUBBER PLANTS, especially *Hevea brasiliensis.* Natural rubber, still important industrially, now competes with synthetic alternatives (see NEOPRENE). Rubber's usefulness is based on its unique elasticity, which allows it to be deformed (stretched) and to recover its shape; it is made possible by vulcanization with SULFUR or another cross-linking agent (essentially changing the polymer from thermoplastic to thermosetting; see PLASTICS), along with accelerators and activators. Fillers and other additives allow tailoring of properties to the desired use (e.g., by foaming, shaping, and curing). More than half of all rubber goes into making tires; the rest is used principally in belts, hoses, gaskets, shoes, clothing, furniture, and toys.

rubber plant *or* **India rubber plant** Tropical tree *(Ficus elastica)* of the MULBERRY FAMILY. The rubber plant is large in its native S.East Asia and other warm areas; elsewhere it is a common indoor potted plant. It has large, thick, oblong leaves and figlike fruits in pairs along its branches. The milky sap, or LATEX, was once an important source of an inferior natural RUBBER. Young plants available in the florist's trade are durable and grow well under less-than-ideal indoor conditions. Some cultivated varieties have broader, darker-green leaves; others are variegated. See also RUBBER TREE.

rubber tree South American tropical tree *(Hevea brasiliensis)* of the SPURGE family. Cultivated on plantations in the tropics and subtropics, especially in S.East Asia and western Africa, it replaced the RUBBER PLANT in the early 20th cent as the chief source of natural RUBBER. It has soft wood, high, branching limbs, and a large area of bark. The milky liquid (LATEX) that oozes from any wound to the tree bark is concentrated to 60% RUBBER content for making dipped goods (surgical gloves, prophylactics, toys, bottles, shoes, and balls).

rubella \rü-'be-lə\ *or* **German measles** Viral disease with a usually mild course, except in women in the first 20 weeks of pregnancy, in whom it can cause fetal birth defects (of eyes, heart, brain, and large arteries) or death. Sore throat and fever are followed by swollen glands and a rash. Up to 30% of infections may have no symptoms. Lifelong immunity follows infection. ENCEPHALITIS is a rare complication. Rubella was not distinguished from MEASLES (rubeola) until the early 19th century and was not known to be dangerous until 1941. The virus was isolated in 1962, and a vaccine became available in 1969.

Rubens, Peter Paul (1577–1640) Flemish painter and diplomat. After apprenticeships in Antwerp, he was admitted to its painters' guild in 1598. He went to Italy in 1600 and until 1608 worked for the duke of Mantua, who in 1603 sent him to Spain to present paintings and other gifts to PHILIP III, the first of many diplomatic missions he would perform for various courts over three decades. The enormous fame he would achieve made him welcome at royal courts, and sovereigns often discussed affairs of state while they sat for portraits. Returning to the Spanish Netherlands (now Belgium) in 1608, he was appointed court painter to the Spanish Habsburg regents, and over the next decade produced numerous altarpieces. A devout Catholic, he became the Counter-Reformation's chief artistic proponent in northern Europe. In 1620 he contracted to design 39 ceiling paintings for the Jesuit church, to be completed by assistants, including the young ANTHONY VAN DYCK. In France he did 21 large canvases for MARIE DE MÉDICIS and a tapestry cycle for LOUIS XIII; for Britain his *Allegory of Peace and War* (1629–30) commemorated the success of his own diplomatic efforts to end hostilities between Britain and Spain, and he decorated the royal Banqueting House for CHARLES I; in Spain he did more than 60 oil sketches for PHILIP IV's hunting lodge. Both Charles and Philip knighted him. His output was prodigious. His style was a fusion of Flemish realism, Italian Renaissance classicism, and his own astounding invention. The opulent figures in his paintings generate a pervasive sense of movement in vivid, dynamic compositions. His profound stylistic influence extended over three centuries.

rubeola See MEASLES

Rubicon \'rü-bi-ˌkän\ Small stream that separated Cisalpine GAUL from Italy in the era of the Roman republic. The movement of Julius CAESAR's forces over the Rubicon into Italy in 49 BC violated the law that forbade a general to lead an army out of the province to which he was assigned. Caesar's act thus amounted to a declaration of war against the Roman Senate and resulted in the three-year civil war that left Caesar ruler of the Roman world. "Crossing the Rubicon" became a popular phrase describing a step that irrevocably commits a person to a given course of action.

rubidium-strontium dating \rü-'bi-dē-əm-'strän-shē-əm\ Method of estimating the age of rocks, minerals, and meteorites from measurements of the amount of the stable isotope strontium-87 formed by the decay of the unstable isotope rubidium-87 that was present in the rock at the time of its formation. The method is applicable to very old rocks because the transformation is extremely slow: the half-life, or time required for half the initial quantity of rubidium-87 to disappear, is approximately 48.8 billion years.

Rubinstein, Anton (Grigor'yevich) (1829–1894) Russian composer and pianist. Touring as a piano virtuoso, he met F. CHOPIN and F. LISZT in Paris and G. MEYERBEER in Berlin. After several years' study, he settled in St. Petersburg in 1848, where in 1862 he founded the St. Petersburg Conservatory, and thereafter devoted much energy to improving the quality of Russian musical education. His once popular compositions, including six symphonies, five piano concertos, and many chamber works and piano pieces (including "Melody in F") have largely disappeared from the repertoire. His brother Nicolai (1835–1881), also a famous pianist and teacher, founded the Moscow Conservatory in the 1860s.

Anton Rubinstein.
BY COURTESY OF THE ROYAL COLLEGE OF MUSIC, LONDON

Rubinstein, Arthur (1887–1982) Polish-U.S. pianist. His studies with J. JOACHIM led to a debut in Berlin in 1900. He later studied with I. PADEREWSKI as well and performed with moderate success. After some years accompanying the violinist Eugène Ysaye (1858–1931), he stopped performing for five years (1932–37) to improve his technique, and reemerged as a giant of 20th-century music. Moving to the U.S., he became equally noted as soloist and chamber musician, with such partners as J. HEIFETZ and Gregor Piatigorsky (1903–1976). Active through his eighties, his repertoire ranged from J.S. BACH to 20th-century Spanish composers; his playing of F. CHOPIN and J. BRAHMS was particularly admired.

Rubinstein, Helena (1870–1965) Polish-U.S. cosmetician, business executive, and philanthropist. She went to Australia in 1902, where she opened a beauty salon in which she offered free consultation along with a special cream brought from Poland. An immediate success, she returned to Europe and opened a salon in London in 1908 and another in Paris in 1912. In 1914 she emigrated to the U.S. to open salons in New York and other cities. She began wholesale distribution of her products in 1917. After World War II she built factories on five continents. In 1953 she established the Helena Rubinstein Foundation to coordinate her gifts to museums, colleges, and institutions for the needy.

Rublev \rəb-'lyȯf\, **Andrei** *or* **Andrei Rublyov** (c. 1360–1430) Russian painter. He was trained wholly in the stylized tradition of Byzantine art, but to the more humanistic approach it had adopted by the 14th century he added a truly Russian element, a complete unworldliness that distinguishes his work from that of his predecessors and successors. He assisted Theophanes the Greek in decorating the Cathedral of the Annunciation in Moscow. The greatest of medieval Russian ICON painters, he is best known for *The Old Testament Trinity* (c. 1410). He became a monk fairly late in life.

rubrication \ˌrü-bri-'kā-shən\ In calligraphy and typography, the use of handwriting or type of a different color on a page, derived from the practice of setting off liturgical directions, headings of statutes, and the like in red. Specifically, it applied to the rules prescribed for the conduct of religious services as set forth in breviaries, prayer books, and missals. Though red is the traditional color for rubrication (from Latin, *rubricare:* "to color red"), the term is now extended to include inks of other colors either applied by hand or printed.

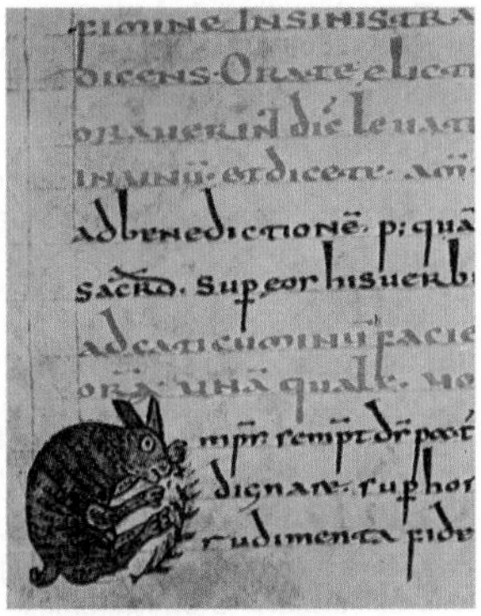

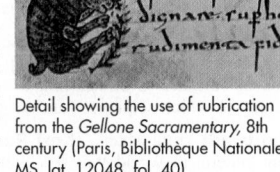

Detail showing the use of rubrication from the *Gellone Sacramentary,* 8th century (Paris, Bibliothèque Nationale, MS. lat. 12048, fol. 40).
BY COURTESY OF THE BIBLIOTHEQUE NATIONALE, PARIS

ruby Gemstone composed of transparent red CORUNDUM. Its color varies from deep to pale red, in some cases with a tinge of purple, depending on chromium and iron content; the most valued is a pigeon-blood red. When it is cut and polished, ruby is a brilliant (light-deflecting) stone, but it lacks fire (flashes of color). Ruby is a mineral of very limited distribution. Its best-known source is in Myanmar, and rubies have also been found in Thailand, Sri Lanka, and elsewhere. Rubies have been produced synthetically with much success; those containing 2.5% chromic oxide have the prized pigeon-blood red color.

Rude \'rūed\, **François** (1784–1855) French sculptor. He won the Prix de Rome in 1812 but was prevented from going to Rome by the Napoleonic Wars. His early work was in the Neoclassical tradition, but he was uncomfortable within its restrictions and soon adopted a dynamic, emotional style. An ardent Bonapartist, he is best known for *Departure of the Volunteers of 1792* (1833–36), on the ARC DE TRIOMPHE; also called *La Marseillaise,* it catches the martial spirit of the Napoleonic era.

Rudolf (1858–1889) Archduke and crown prince of AUSTRIA. The son of Emperor FRANCIS JOSEPH, he received a broad education and traveled widely. As heir to the throne of Austria-Hungary, he hoped to bring reform to the empire, but his liberal views alienated his father and he was excluded from the business of government. From 1881 he considered having himself crowned king of Hungary and reviving a kingdom of Poland. He then became despondent and allegedly formed a suicide pact with his mistress, Maria Vetsera; the two were found shot dead in the hunting lodge at Mayerling. Efforts to disguise the facts provoked many rumors, while romantic writers found inspiration in the story.

Rudolf, Lake See Lake TURKANA

Rudolf I *or* **Rudolf of Habsburg** (1218–1291) First German king (1273–91) of the HABSBURG DYNASTY. He inherited lands in Alsace, the Aargau, and Breisgau and extended his territory by marriage and through negotiation. Crowned German king (1273), he was recognized by GREGORY X only after promising to lead a new Crusade and to renounce imperial rights in Rome, the papal territories, and Italy. Rudolf defeated his rival Otakar II (1276, 1278) and gained lands in Austria, which he granted to his sons. He fought the expansionist policies of France, but French influence at the papal court kept him from being crowned Holy Roman Emperor.

Wilma Rudolph, 1961.
AP/WIDE WORLD PHOTOS

Rudolph, Wilma (Glodean) (1940–1994) U.S. sprinter. Born in St. Bethlehem, Tenn., she was a sickly child who wore an orthopedic shoe until she was 11. After setting a world record in the 200-m dash (22.9 sec), she won the 100-m and 200-m dashes and was a member of the winning 4×100-m relay team at the 1960 Olympic Games, becoming the first American woman to win three track-and-field gold medals in a single Olympics.

Rudolphi's rorqual See SEI WHALE

rue family *or* **citrus family** Family Rutaceae, made up of about 1,700 species of woody shrubs and trees (and a few herbaceous perennials) in 160 genera. Valuable for timber, edible fruits, and as ornamentals, members are found worldwide in warm temperate and tropical regions. The flowers are conspicuous for their color, fragrance, and nectar. Economically important fruits in the family include the LEMON, LIME, ORANGE, GRAPEFRUIT, CITRON, and KUMQUAT. Among the ornamentals are common rue *(Ruta graveolens)* and the unusual burning bush, or gas plant *(Dictamnus albus),* whose aromatic leaves contain oil glands that, when squeezed, release a gas ignitable by a match.

ruffed grouse North American species *(Bonasa umbellus)* of GROUSE, sometimes incorrectly called a PARTRIDGE. Ruffed grouse live mainly on berries, fruits, seeds, and buds but also eat insects and small animals. They are 16–20 in. (40–50 cm) long and have feathered lower legs and a black band on the fan-shaped tail. The male's ruff consists of erectile black feathers on the sides of the neck. Males beat their wings rapidly against the air (called drumming) to proclaim their territory.

Ruffin, Edmund (1794–1865) U.S. agriculturist and secessionist. Born in Prince George Co., Va., he managed his father's tobacco plantation from 1813. He found that overuse and poor farming methods produced an acid soil unable to retain fertilizers; in 1832 he published an influential book advocating the use of marl to reduce soil acidity, which helped restore Southern plantations to productivity. He also published the *Farmer's Register* (1833–42) and lectured widely on agriculture. In the 1850s he defended slavery and advocated secession. He fired one of the first shots at FORT SUMTER (1861). Unable to accept the South's defeat, he killed himself.

rug and carpet Any decorative textile normally made of a thick material and intended as a floor covering. Floor coverings made of plaited rushes date from the 5th or 4th millennium BC. Carpets were first made in central and western Asia as coverings for earthen floors; they were also used as blankets, saddle covers, storage bags, tent doorways, and tomb covers. The prayer rug was designed to be carried everywhere. Oriental carpets imported into Europe in the 16th–17th century were considered too valuable to be put on the floor and were often used as wall decoration. They are still popular wall decorations in Russia. Carpet weaving reached its peak of artistry in 16th-century Persia. In the West, outstanding carpets were produced at factories in 17th-century France and 18th-century England. Most handmade carpets are made from sheep's wool, which was colored with natural dyes until the 19th century, when chemical dyes were introduced. See also AUBUSSON CARPET, AXMINSTER CARPET, BAKU RUG.

rugby Football sport comprised of two variant codes—rugby union and rugby league. The sport was first developed in the 1820s at the Rugby School in England. In 1895 a dispute over professionalism between the Rugby Football Union and several clubs in northern England led to the creation of rugby league (always a professional sport). Rugby union became fully professional in 1995. The game is played by teams of 15 (union) or 13 (league) members each, using an inflated oval ball. The ball may be kicked, carried, or passed laterally or backward (but not forward). The object is to score goals (worth three points) by kicking the ball between the uprights of the opponent's goal, or tries (worth five points in union play, four in league), by grounding the ball behind the opponent's goal line. A conversion kick (worth two points) is attempted after scoring a try. Both rugby union and rugby league have international play and world cup tournaments. Rugby is most popular in the United Kingdom, South Africa, Australia, and New Zealand.

Ruhr occupation (1923–25) Occupation of the industrial RUHR RIVER valley region in Germany by French and Belgian troops. The action was provoked by German deficiencies in the coal and coke deliveries to France required by the reparations agreement after World War I. French occupation of Düsseldorf, Duisburg, and Ruhrort in 1921 was followed by French-Belgian occupation of the entire region in 1923. Passive resistance by German workers paralyzed the Ruhr's economy and precipitated the collapse of the German currency. The dispute was settled by the DAWES PLAN, and the occupation ended in 1925.

Ruhr River \'rür\ River, western Germany. An important tributary of the lower RHINE RIVER, it rises on the northern side of Winterberg and flows 146 mi (235 km) west. The Ruhr valley is a major industrial and mining region; it includes the industrial cities of ESSEN, DÜSSELDORF, and DORTMUND. The Ruhr coalfield is one of the world's largest and produces the bulk of Germany's bituminous coal. Industries begun by the Krupp and Thyssen families flourished in the 19th–20th century (see THYSSEN-KRUPP STAHL). The river was militarily important in World War I, and the river valley was occupied 1923–25 by France and Belgium (see RUHR OCCUPATION). As the industrial heart of Nazi Germany, it was severely bombed in World War II and occupied by Allied troops in 1945; full control was returned to West Germany in 1954. It is now a center of steel production and diversified chemical manufacturing.

Ruisdael \'röis-ˌdäl\, **Jacob (Isaakszoon) van** (1628/29–1682) Dutch landscape painter. He was probably trained by his father, a frame-maker and artist. He was enrolled in the Haarlem painters' guild in 1648 and settled in Amsterdam c. 1656. He was a remarkably versatile artist, and some 700 paintings have been attributed to him. Whereas earlier Dutch artists used trees merely as decorative devices, Ruisdael (whose name was also spelled Ruysdael) made them the subject of his paintings and imbued them with forceful personalities through vigorous brush-work and strong colors. The emotional force of his work is evident in the famous *Jewish Cemetery* (c. 1660), where three tombstones crumble to ruin amid an ever-renewing nature. His late works include numerous panoramas of the flat Dutch countryside, in which a low, distant horizon is dominated by a vast, clouded sky.

Ruisdael, Salomon van See Salomon van RUYSDAEL

Ruiz \rü-'ēth\, **Juan** (1283?–1350?) Spanish poet and cleric. Educated at Toledo, Ruiz was serving as a village archpriest when he finished his masterpiece, *Libro de buen amor* (1330, expanded 1343; *The Book of Good Love*). Perhaps the most important long poem in medieval Spanish literature, it contains 12 narrative poems, each describing a different love affair. Its title refers to the distinction the author makes between the (good) love of God and carnal love. Drawing on material from an impressive range of literary and other sources, it presents a vigorous, high-spirited, satirical glimpse of medieval life.

Rukwa \'rü-kwä\, **Lake** Shallow lake, southwestern Tanzania, eastern Africa. It covers an area of about 1,000 sq mi (2,600 sq km) and lies midway between Lake TANGANYIKA and Lake MALAWI at an elevation of about 2,600 ft (800 m). It has no outlet, and at times it is completely dry. Its water is brackish, and there are salt pans near its southwestern end. Crocodile and hippopotamus inhabit the lake, and fish abound.

Rule of the Community See MANUAL OF DISCIPLINE

rules of order See PARLIAMENTARY PROCEDURE

rum DISTILLED LIQUOR made from SUGARCANE products, primarily molasses. It is first mentioned in records from Barbados c. 1650. Rum figured in the slave trade: slaves from Africa were traded in the West Indies for molasses, the molasses was made into rum in New England, and the rum was then traded to Africa for more slaves. British sailors received regular rum rations from the 18th century until the 1970s. Two major types are marketed. The light-bodied rums, traditionally of Puerto Rico and Cuba, employ cultivated yeast and are distilled in continuous-operation stills before being blended and aged 1–4 years. The heavier dark rums, traditionally of Jamaica, employ yeast spores from the air and are distilled in simple pot stills before being blended and aged 5–7 years. Rum is drunk straight or mixed, and is used in dessert sauces and other dishes.

Rumania See ROMANIA

Rumi \'rü-ˌmē\, **Jalal ad-Din ar-** *or* **Mawlana** (1207?–1273) Anatolian-Persian mystic and poet. He was a theologian and teacher in Anatolia when he met Shams ad-Din, a holy man who revealed to him the mysteries of divine majesty and beauty; their intimate relationship scandalized Rumi's followers, who had Shams murdered. *The Collected Poetry of Shams* contains Rumi's verses on his love for Shams. His main work, the didactic epic *Masnavi-ye Manavi* ("Spiritual Couplets"), widely influenced Muslim mystical thought and literature. He is believed to have composed poetry while in a state of ecstasy and often accompanied his verses by a whirling dance. After his death, his disciples were organized as the Mawlawiyah order, called in the West the whirling DERVISHES. Rumi is regarded as the greatest Sufi mystic and poet in the Persian language. In English translation, his work has become widely popular in recent years.

ruminant \'rü-mə-nənt\ Any UNGULATE of the suborder Ruminantia (order Artiodactyla), including ANTELOPE, CAMELS, CATTLE, DEER, GIRAFFES, GOATS, OKAPIS, PRONGHORN, and SHEEP. Most ruminants have a four-chambered stomach, two-toed feet, and small or absent upper incisors. Camels and CHEVROTAINS have three-chambered stomachs. Ruminants eat quickly, storing masses of grass (grazers) or foliage (browsers) in the first stomach chamber, the rumen, where it softens. They later regurgitate the material, called cud, and chew it again to further break down the undigestible cellulose. The chewed cud goes directly to the other chambers, where various microorganisms help in its digestion.

rummy Any of several card games for two or more players in which each player tries to assemble groups of three or more cards of the same rank or suit and to be the first to meld them all. CANASTA is a type of rummy in which sequences are not permitted. See also GIN RUMMY.

Rundstedt \'rünt-ˌshtet\, **(Karl Rudolf) Gerd von** (1875–1953) German general in World War II. Chief of staff of an army corps in World War I, he was active after the war in Germany's secret rearmament. In World War II he was promoted to field marshal (1940) and commanded armies in the invasions of Poland, France, and the Soviet Union. As commander in chief on the Western Front (1942–45), he fortified France against the expected Allied invasion. Removed briefly from command (1944), he returned to direct the Battle of the BULGE. He was captured in 1945 but released because of ill health.

Runeberg \'rü-nə-ˌberʸ\, **Johan Ludvig** (1804–1877) Finnish poet who wrote in Swedish. During an interruption in his academic career, he became a tutor at a country estate, where he encountered Finland's landscape and tales of the heroic past. His works, combining classicism with Romantic feeling and an understanding of peasant life and character, include the epic poems *The Moose Hunters* (1832) and *Hanna* (1836), which won him a place in Swedish letters; and *Kung Fjalar*, a cycle of romances derived from old legends. His patriotic poem "Our Country," from *Tales of Ensign Stål* (1848, 1860), became the Finnish national anthem. Runeberg is considered Finland's national poet.

runic writing *or* **futhark** \'fü-ˌthärk\ Writing system used by Germanic peoples of northern Europe, Britain, Scandinavia, and Iceland from roughly the 3rd to the 16th or 17th century AD. Of uncertain origins, it is clearly derived from one of the alphabets of the Mediterranean area. Three main varieties were used in different regions and time periods: Early, or Common Germanic (Teutonic); Anglo-Saxon, or Anglian; and Nordic, or Scandinavian. More than 4,000 runic inscriptions and several runic manuscripts are extant, of which about 2,500 come from Sweden.

runner See STOLON

Runyon, (Alfred) Damon (1884–1946) U.S. journalist and short-story writer. Born in Manhattan, Kan., he served in the Spanish-American War as a teenager. After returning to the U.S. he wrote for newspapers in the West. In 1911 he moved to New York, where he developed a style focusing on the underside of city life and began to write stories. He is best known for *Guys and Dolls* (1931), stories about a racy section of Broadway written in the uniquely rendered slang that became his trademark, which became a highly successful musical by F. LOESSER (1950).

rupa-loka \'rü-pə-'lō-kə\ In BUDDHISM, any of the 16 planes of existence into which those beings who have renounced sense desires are reborn. It is intermediate between the kama-loka, where material beings are born, and the ARUPA-LOKA, where only the mind exists. Its upper levels are called the Pure Abodes, the birthplace of those beings who do not return to lower planes in subsequent births. The rupa-loka, free from sensuous desire but still conditioned by form, is inhabited by gods. See also KARMA.

Rupert, Prince (1619–1682) Royalist commander in the ENGLISH CIVIL WARS. Son of the Palatine elector FREDERICK V and Elizabeth, daughter of JAMES I of England, Rupert became a favorite of his uncle, CHARLES I, whom he joined in England in 1642. In the ENGLISH CIVIL WARS, he was given command of the cavalry and became known for his daring tactics in winning victories at Bristol (1643) and in Lancashire (1644). He met defeat at the Battle of MARSTON MOOR but was appointed commander of the king's army. When he surrendered Bristol (1645), he was dismissed and then banished from England. He commanded a small Royalist fleet that preyed on English shipping (1648–50), then retired to Germany (1653–60). With the Restoration (1660), he was given naval commands in the Anglo–Dutch Wars. He was a founder and first governor of the Hudson's Bay Co.

Rupert's Land *or* **Prince Rupert's Land** Historical region, northern and western Canada, comprising the drainage basin of Hudson Bay. In 1670 it was granted by King Charles II to the Hudson's Bay Co. It was named after Prince Rupert, the king's cousin and the company's first governor. In 1869 the land became part of the Dominion of Canada.

Rupnarayan River \'rüp-nä-ˌrä-yən\ River, West Bengal state, northeastern India. It rises as the Dhaleshwari in the Chota Nagpur plateau foothills northeast of Purulia and follows a tortuous southeasterly course past the town of Bankura, where it is known as the Dwarkeswar. It flows 150 mi (240 km) to join the Hugli River. It originally formed a western exit of the Ganges River and is important for its irrigation potential.

rural electrification Project of the U.S. government in the 1930s. As part of the New Deal, the Rural Electrification Administration (REA) was established (1935) to bring electric power to farms, thereby raising the standard of rural living and slowing the migration of farm workers to cities. Providing low-interest loans to construct power plants and power lines to rural areas, the project eventually equipped over 98% of U.S. farms with electricity.

Rurik *or* **Rorik** (died 879?) Semilegendary founder of the Rurik dynasty of Kievan Rus. He was a Viking (Varangian) prince, and according to one 12th-century Russian chronicle, the people of Novgorod invited him to take over their strife-ridden government (c. 862). Other historians think that he conquered Novgorod or that he and his army were rebellious mercenaries. Igor, probably his son, is held to be the real founder of the Russian princely house.

Rus See Kievan Rus

rusalka \rü-'säl-kə\ In Slavic folklore and mythology, a water nymph who embodies the soul of either a drowned virgin or a child that died unbaptized. Details of their appearance and behavior vary widely, but a common feature is that they attempt to entice men. In some areas, they are the subject of an early-summer festival, when they are thought to emerge from the water and dance by night. In A. Dvorak's opera *Rusalka,* a rusalka attempts to marry a human prince but is reclaimed by her element.

rush Any of several flowering plants distinguished by cylindrical stalks or hollow, stemlike leaves. They are found in temperate regions, particularly in moist or shady locations. The rush family (Juncaceae) includes the genera *Juncus,* the common rushes, and *Luzula,* the wood rushes. In many parts of the world, common rushes are woven into chair bottoms, mats, and basketwork, while rush pith serves as wicks in open oil lamps and tallow candles (rushlights). Other rushes include the bulrush (family Typhaceae), the horsetail (or scouring rush), the flowering rush (*Butomus umbellatus,* family Butomaceae), and the sweet rush, or sweet flag (*Acorus calamus*, arum family).

Rush, Benjamin (1746–1813) U.S. physician and political leader. Born near Philadelphia, he attended the College of New Jersey at Princeton. As a doctor, he was a dogmatic theorist who proposed that all diseases are fevers caused by overstimulation of blood vessels, with a simple remedy—bloodletting and purges. He advocated humane treatment for insane patients; his idea that insanity often had physical causes marked a significant advance. He wrote the first chemistry textbook and the first psychiatry treatise in the U.S. An early and active American Patriot and a member of the Continental Congress, Rush drafted a resolution urging independence and signed the Declaration of Independence.

Rush, Richard (1780–1859) U.S. diplomat. Born in Philadelphia, the son of Benjamin Rush, he served as U.S. attorney general 1814–17 and secretary of the treasury 1825–29. As acting secretary of state (1817), he negotiated the Rush-Bagot Agreement with Britain, which limited naval forces on the Great Lakes after the War of 1812. As U.S. minister to Britain (1817–25), he negotiated an agreement fixing the border between Canada and the U.S. at the 49th parallel. In conferences on Latin America, he helped formulate the Monroe Doctrine.

Rushdie \'ru̇sh-dē, *commonly* 'rəsh-dē\, **(Ahmed) Salman** (born 1947) Indian-British novelist. Educated at Cambridge Univ., he worked as an advertising copywriter in London in the 1970s before winning unexpected success with *Midnight's Children* (1981, Booker Prize), an allegorical novel about modern India. His second novel, *Shame* (1983), is a scathing portrait of politics and sexual morality in Pakistan. *The Satanic Verses* (1988), which includes among its bizarre happenings some episodes based on the life of Muhammad, was denounced as blasphemous by outraged Muslim leaders, and in 1989 Rushdie was condemned to death by Iran's Ruhollah Khomeini. He became the focus of enormous international attention and was compelled to remain in hiding for years. His later novels include *The Moor's Last Sigh* (1995) and *The Ground Beneath Her Feet* (1999).

Rushing, Jimmy *orig.* **James Andrew** (1903–1972) U.S. singer, one of the great voices of the blues during the swing era. Born in Oklahoma City, Rushing joined Count Basie's first group in 1935, gaining exposure through many recordings and remaining until 1950. He thereafter worked leading his own small groups or with the bands of Benny Goodman, Buck Clayton, and occasionally Basie. Rushing's full tenor voice, although associated with the blues-based repertoire of the Basie period, was also well suited to popular songs and ballads.

Rushmore, Mt. Peak and national memorial, Black Hills, southwestern South Dakota. Sculptures of the heads of presidents George Washington, Thomas Jefferson, Abraham Lincoln, and Theodore Roosevelt are carved on the granite face of the mountain, which is 6,000 ft (1,829 m) high. The four heads, each about 60 ft (18 m) high, represent, respectively, the nation's founding, political philosophy, preservation, and expansion and conservation. The memorial was dedicated in 1925. Work on it was carried out during 1927–41 under the direction of Gutzon Borglum.

Rusk, (David) Dean (1909–1994) U.S. public official and educator. Born in Cherokee Co., Ga., he taught at Mills College 1934–40, then served in World War II on Gen. Joseph Stilwell's staff. He later held positions in the state and war departments, helping prosecute the Korean War as an assistant secretary of state (1950). After serving as president of the Rockefeller Foundation (1952–60), he became U.S. secretary of state under John F. Kennedy and Lyndon B. Johnson (1961–69). A consistent defender of U.S. participation in the Vietnam War, he became a target of antiwar protests. He also opposed diplomatic recognition of Communist China. After retiring from public life, he taught at the University of Georgia until 1984.

Ruskin, John (1819–1900) English art critic. Born into a wealthy family, Ruskin was largely educated at home. He was a gifted painter but the best of his talent went into his writing. His multivolume *Modern Painters* (1843–60), planned as a defense of J.M.W. Turner, expanded to become a general survey of art. In Turner he saw "truth to nature" in landscape painting, and he went on to find the same truthfulness in Gothic architecture. His other writings include *The Seven Lamps of Architecture* (1849) and *The Stones of Venice* (1851–53). He was a defender of the Pre-Raphaelites. In 1869 he was elected Oxford's first Slade professor of fine art; he resigned in 1879 after James M. Whistler won a libel suit against him. Ruskin's personal life was troubled. His marriage was never consummated, and his wife obtained an annulment to marry John Everett Millais. In later years he used his inherited wealth to promote idealistic social causes, but his powerful rhetoric, which still contained striking insights, became marred by bigotry and occasional incoherence. Ruskin remains the preeminent art critic of 19th-century Britain.

Ruskin, detail of an oil painting by Sir John Everett Millais, 1853–54; in a private collection.
BY COURTESY OF THE ROYAL ACADEMY OF ARTS, LONDON

Russell, Bertrand (Arthur William), 3rd Earl Russell (1872–1970) British logician and philosopher, best known for his work in mathematical logic and for his advocacy on behalf of a variety of social and political causes, especially pacifism and nuclear disarmament. Russell was born into the British nobility as the grandson of Earl Russell, who was twice prime minister of Britain in the mid-19th century. He studied mathematics and philosophy at Cambridge University, where he came under the influence of the idealist philosopher J.M.E. McTaggart, though he soon rejected idealism in favor of an extreme Platonic realism. In an early paper, "On Denoting" (1905), he solved a notorious puzzle in the philosophy of language by showing how phrases such as "The present king of France," which have no referents, function logically as general statements rather than as proper names. Russell later regarded this discovery, which came to be known as the "theory of descriptions," as one of his most important contributions to philosophy. In *The Principles of Mathematics* (1903) and the epochal *Principia Mathematica* (3 vols., 1910–13), which he wrote with Alfred North Whitehead, he sought to demonstrate that the whole of mathematics derives from logic. For his pacifism in World War I he lost his lectureship at Cambridge and was later imprisoned. (He would abandon pacifism in 1939 in the face of Nazi aggression.) Russell's best-developed metaphysical doctrine, logical atomism, strongly influenced the school of logical positivism. His later philosophical works include *The Analysis of Mind* (1921), *The Analysis of Matter* (1927), and *Human Knowledge: Its Scope and Limits* (1948). His *A History of Western Philosophy* (1945), which he wrote for a popular audience, became a best-seller and was for many years the main source of his income. Among his many works on social and political topics are *Roads to Freedom* (1918); *The Practice and Theory of Bolshevism* (1920), a scathing critique of Soviet communism; *On Education* (1926); and *Marriage and Morals* (1929). In part because of the controversial views he espoused in the latter work, he was prevented from accepting a teaching position at the City College of New York in 1940. After World War II he became a leader in the worldwide campaign for nuclear disarmament, serving as first president of the international Pugwash Conferences on nuclear weapons and world security and of the Campaign for Nuclear Disarmament. In 1961, at the age of 89, he was imprisoned for a second time for inciting civil disobedience. He received the Nobel Prize for Literature in 1950.

Bertrand Russell, 1960.

BY COURTESY OF THE BRITISH BROADCASTING CORPORATION, LONDON

Russell, Bill *orig.* **William Felton** (born 1934) U.S. basketball player. Born in Monroe, La., the 6-ft. 10-in. center led the University of San Francisco to two NCAA championships (1955–56). Playing for the Boston Celtics (1956–69), Russell led his team to 11 NBA championships in 13 seasons—the last two as coach, having become in 1967 the first black coach of a major professional sports team. Russell's career mark for rebounds (21,620) is second only to that of his great rival Wilt Chamberlain, and he is regarded as one of the finest defensive centers of all time. He was voted most valuable player in the NBA five times, and the Associated Press selected him as the outstanding professional basketball player of the 1960s. He later coached the Seattle SuperSonics (1973–77).

Russell, Charles Taze (1852–1916) U.S. religious leader. Born in Pittsburgh, he was raised in the Congregational church but rejected its teachings, unable to reconcile God's mercy with the idea of hell. Influenced by the Adventists, he adopted a doctrine of millennialism. He founded the International Bible Students Association in 1872 (renamed Jehovah's Witnesses in 1931) and taught that the final days would come in 1914, and that Christ's kingdom on earth would begin after a war between capitalism and socialism. In 1884 he founded the Watch Tower Bible and Tract Society, today one of the world's largest publishers. His books, pamphlets, and periodicals were widely circulated, and he won many converts despite the apparent failure of his apocalyptic prediction.

Russell (of Kingston Russell), Earl *orig.* **John Russell** (1792–1878) British politician and prime minister (1846–52, 1865–66). A member of the prominent Russell family, he entered Parliament in 1813. He was a strong advocate of reform and made it a cause of the Whig Party, leading the effort to pass the Reform Bill of 1832. He served in Viscount Melbourne's government as home secretary (1835), reducing the number of crimes liable to capital punishment and beginning state support of public education. In the 1840s he advocated free trade and forced Sir Robert Peel out of office. Russell became prime minister in 1846 and established the 10-hour day in factories (1847) and a board of public health (1848), but party disunity defeated his attempts at wider social and economic reform.

Russell, (Henry) Ken(neth Alfred) (born 1927) British film director. As a documentary film director for the BBC, he became known for his fictionalized "biopics" of famous composers and artists. His first feature film was *French Dressing* (1963), and he later won a wide audience with his lush adaptation of *Women in Love* (1969). He was criticized for using shock and sensationalism in many of his later films, which include *The Music Lovers* (1971), *The Devils* (1971), *Savage Messiah* (1972), *Tommy* (1975), *Altered States* (1980), and *The Lair of the White Worm* (1988).

Russell, Lillian *orig.* **Helen Louise Leonard** (1861–1922) U.S. singer and actress. Born in Iowa, she made her stage debut while still in her teens. She achieved stardom in *Grand Mogul* (1881), and later won acclaim in *La Grande-Duchesse de Gérolstein* (1890). From 1899 to 1904 she appeared in England and the U.S. with a burlesque company. Representing the feminine ideal of her generation, she was as famous for her flamboyant personal life as for her hourglass figure, her beauty, and her voice. After her fourth marriage in 1912, she wrote a syndicated column on health, beauty, and love and lectured on these topics before vaudeville audiences.

Russell, William, Lord (1639–1683) English Whig politician. A member of the House of Commons, he joined the opposition to the pro-French policies of Charles II. In 1678 he was convinced by Titus Oates's fabricated Popish Plot, and by 1680 led the fight in the Commons to exclude Charles's brother James (later James II) from the succession. After Charles dissolved Parliament (1681), Russell continued to associate with Whig dissidents. In 1683 he was accused of participating in the Rye House Plot to murder Charles. The charges were never proved, but Russell was found guilty of treason and beheaded.

Russell Cave National Monument National Monument, northeastern Alabama, south of the Alabama–Tennessee border. It constitutes part of a cavern that was discovered c. 1953. The cave is about 210 ft (64 m) long, 107 ft (33 m) wide, and 26 ft (8 m) high. It contains an almost continuous record of human habitation dating to at least 7000 BC. The national monument was established in 1961.

Russell family English Whig family. It first became prominent under the Tudors, when John Russell (died 1555) was created earl of Bedford (1549) for helping suppress a rebellion against the Protestant reforms of Edward VI. The family was connected with the Parliamentary party in the English Civil Wars. Its first notable Whig member was William, Lord Russell. Later members included John, Earl Russell, and his grandson, the philosopher Bertrand Russell.

Russia *officially* **Russian Federation** Nation, eastern Europe and northern Asia, former republic of the U.S.S.R.. Area: 6,592,812 sq mi (17,075,383 sq km). Population (2001 est.): 144,536,000. Capital: Moscow. Most of the people are Russian; minorities include Tatars and Ukrainians. Languages: Russian (official), various Turkic and Uralic languages. Religion: Russian Orthodox Christianity, Islam, but most of the people are nonreligious. Currency: ruble. The land and its environments are varied, including the Ural Mtns. and ranges in eastern Siberia, with the highest peaks in Kamchatka. The Russian plain contains the great Volga and Northern Dvina rivers, and in the Siberian plain are the valleys of the Ob, Yenisey, Lena, and Amur rivers. Tundra covers extensive portions in the north, and in the south there are forests, steppes, and fertile areas. The economy was industrialized from 1917 to 1945 but was in serious decline by the 1980s. In 1992 the government decreed radical reforms to convert the centrally planned economy into a market economy based on private enterprise. Russia is a republic with a bicameral legislative body; its head of state is the president, and the head of government is the prime minister. The region between the Dniester and the Volga rivers was inhabited from ancient times by various peoples, including the Slavs. The area was overrun in the 8th century BC–6th century AD by successive nomadic peoples, including the Sythians, Sarma-

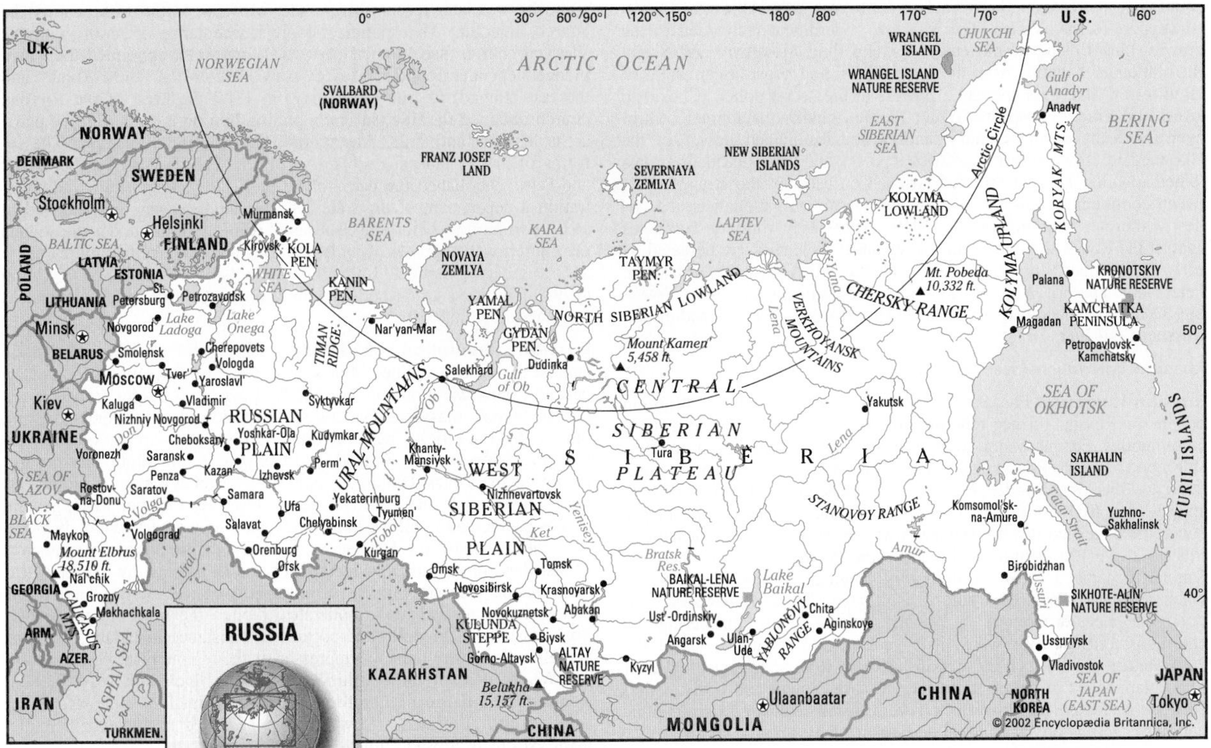

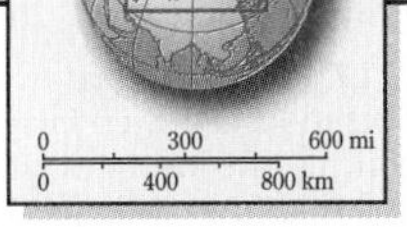

tians, Goths, Huns, and Avars. KIEVAN RUS, a confederation of principalities ruling from KIEV, emerged c. 10th century. It lost supremacy in the 11th–12th century to independent principalities, including NOVGOROD and Vladimir. Novgorod ascended in the north and was the only Russian principality to escape the domination of the Mongol GOLDEN HORDE in the 13th century. In the 14th–15th century the princes of MOSCOW gradually overthrew the Mongols. Under IVAN IV, Russia began to expand. The ROMANOV DYNASTY arose in 1613. Expansion continued under PETER I (the Great) and CATHERINE II (the Great). The area was invaded by NAPOLEON in 1812; after his defeat, Russia received most of the grand duchy of WARSAW (1815). Russia annexed Georgia, Armenia, and Caucasus territories in the 19th century. The Russian southward advance against the OTTOMAN EMPIRE was of key importance to Europe (see CRIMEA). Russia was defeated in the CRIMEAN WAR. Chinese cession of the AMUR RIVER's left bank in 1858 marked Russia's expansion in the Far East. It sold Alaska to the U.S. in 1867 (see ALASKA PURCHASE). Its defeat in the RUSSO–JAPANESE WAR led to an unsuccessful uprising in 1905 (see RUSSIAN REVOLUTION OF 1905). In World War I it fought against the CENTRAL POWERS. The popular overthrow of the Czarist regime in 1917 marked the beginning of a government of soviets (see RUSSIAN REVOLUTION OF 1917). The BOLSHEVIKS brought the main part of the former empire under Communist control and organized it as the Russian Soviet Federated Socialist Republic (coextensive with present-day Russia). The Russian S.F.S.R. joined other soviet republics in 1922 to form the U.S.S.R. (See UNION OF SOVIET SOCIALIST REPUBLICS for history 1922–91.) Upon the dissolution of the U.S.S.R. in 1991, the Russian S.F.S.R. was renamed and became the leading member of the COMMONWEALTH OF INDEPENDENT STATES. It adopted a new constitution in 1993. During the 1990s, it struggled on several fronts, beset with economic difficulties, political corruption, and independence movements (see CHECHNYA).

Russian Civil War (1918–20) Conflict between the newly formed BOLSHEVIK government and its RED ARMY against the anti-Bolshevik forces in Russia. The unfavorable Treaty of BREST-LITOVSK concluded with Germany caused the anti-Lenin socialists to break with the Bolsheviks and join the right-wing Whites and their volunteer army under ANTON DENIKIN. In

Leaders of Muscovy, Russia, and the Russian Empire

Princes of Muscovy:		**Interregnum**	1610–12
Danilovich dynasty*		**Czars and Empresses of Russia: Romanov dynasty****	
Daniel (son of Alexander Nevsky)	c.1276–1303		
Yury	1303–25	Michael III	1613–45
Ivan I	1325–40	Alexis	1645–76
Semyon (Simeon)	1340–53	Fyodor III	1676–82
Ivan II	1353–59	Peter I (Ivan V coruler 1682–96)	1682–1725
Dmitry Donskoy	1359–89	Catherine I	1725–27
Vasily I	1389–1425	Peter II	1727–30
Vasily II	1425–62	Anna	1730–40
Ivan III	1462–1505	Ivan VI	1740–41
Vasily III	1505–33	Elizabeth	1741–61 (O.S.)
Ivan IV	1533–47		
Czars of Russia:			
Danilovich dynasty		Peter III***	1761–62 (O.S.)
Ivan IV	1547–84		
Fyodor I	1584–98	Catherine II	1762–96
Czars of Russia:		Paul	1796–1801
Time of Troubles		Alexander I	1801–25
Boris Godunov	1598–1605	Nicholas I	1825–55
Fyodor II	1605	Alexander II	1855–81
False Dmitry	1605–6	Alexander III	1881–94
Vasily (IV)	1606–10	Nicholas II	1894–1917

*The Danilovich dynasty is a late branch of the Rurik dynasty, named after its progenitor, Daniel.
**In 1721 Peter I the Great took the title of "emperor" (Russian: *imperator*), considering it a larger, more European title than the Russian "czar." However, every male sovereign continued usually to be called czar (and his consort czarina, or czaritsa), though every female sovereign was conventionally called empress (*imperatritsa*).
***The direct line of the Romanov dynasty came to an end in 1761 with the death of Elizabeth, daughter of Peter I, but subsequent rulers of the "Holstein–Gottorp dynasty" (the first, Peter III, was son of Charles Frederick, duke of Holstein–Gottorp, and Anna, daughter of Peter I) took the family name of Romanov.

an attempt to create another front in World War I, the Allies gave limited support to the Whites. The Moscow government responded to the growing anti-Bolshevik movement by expelling Menshevik and Social Revolutionary deputies from the government, and began a campaign of "Red terror" that gave increased powers to the secret police (Cheka) to arrest and execute suspects. While the Bolsheviks maintained control over the heart of the country, anti-Bolsheviks gained power in the Ukraine and Omsk, where Aleksandr Kolchak and other dissident groups joined together to fight the Red Army. Confused by the struggles between communists, Russian Whites, and Ukrainian nationalists, the Allies withdrew their support by 1919. After early military successes against the Red Army, the White forces under Kolchak were defeated by early 1920. Other White troops under Nikolay Yudenich failed to take St. Petersburg. The last White stronghold in the Crimea under Pyotr Wrangel, Denikin's successor, was defeated in November 1920, ending the Russian Civil War.

Russian Formalism See Formalism

Russian language East Slavic language spoken by about 170 million people in Russia, former republics of the Soviet Union, and emigré communities. For many non-Russian ethnic groups both within and outside contemporary Russia it is a common second language and lingua franca. Since the Middle Ages, Russian has gradually expanded its speech area from its historical locus in the upper Volga and Dnieper River drainages northward and eastward. Russian-speakers penetrated Siberia in the 16th century and reached the Pacific in the 17th century. Russian became a full-fledged literary language in the 18th century, when it finally displaced Church Slavic (see Old Church Slavic language). Dialect differences in Russian are not great, considering the enormous territory over which it is spoken, and the upheavals of the 20th century eroded such distinctions as exist. Russian is typical of most Slavic languages in having an elaborate case system and a distinction between perfective and imperfective verb forms, expressed by a combination of prefixation and suffixal derivation.

Letters	English Sound	Letters	English Sound	Letters	English Sound
А а	a	К к	k	Х х	kh
Б б	b	Л л	l	Ц ц	ts
В в	v	М м	m	Ч ч	ch
Г г	g	Н н	n	Ш ш	sh
Д д	d	О о	o	Щ щ	shch
Е е	e *or* ye	П п	p	Ъ ъ	(the hard sign)
Ё ё	o *or* yo	Р р	r	Ы ы	y
Ж ж	zh	С с	s	Ь ь	(the soft sign)
З з	z	Т т	t	Э э	e
И и	i	У у	u	Ю ю	yu
Й й	y	Ф ф	f	Я я	ya

The Russian Cyrillic alphabet, with English sound equivalents. Originally used for writing Old Church Slavonic, the alphabet in its various modern forms is used in writing several Slavic languages as well as some non-Slavic languages of the former Soviet Union.

Russian Orthodox Church Eastern Orthodox church of Russia, its de facto national church. In 988 Prince Vladimir of Kiev (later St. Vladimir) embraced Byzantine Orthodoxy and ordered the baptism of his population. By the 14th century, the metropolitan of Kiev and all Russia (head of the Russian church) was residing in Moscow; dissatisfied western Russian principalities obtained temporary separate metropolitans, but authority was later recentralized under Moscow. In the 15th century the church, rejecting Metropolitan Isidore's acceptance of union with the Western church (see Council of Ferrara-Florence), appointed their own independent metropolitan. Moscow saw itself as the "third Rome" and the last bulwark of true Orthodoxy; in 1589 the head of the Russian church obtained the title patriarch, putting him on a level with the patriarchs of Constantinople, Alexandria, Antioch, and Jerusalem. The reforms of Nikon caused a schism within the church (see Old Believers), and Peter I abolished the patriarchate in 1721, making church administration a department of the state. The patriarchate was reestablished in 1917, two months before the Bolshevik revolution, but under the soviets the church was deprived of its legal rights and practically suppressed. It saw a great resurgence following the collapse of the Soviet Union (1991). The Russian Orthodox Church in the U.S. became independent from Moscow in 1970.

Russian Revolution of 1905 Unsuccessful uprising in Russia against the czarist regime. After several years of mounting discontent, a peaceful demonstration was crushed by Czar Nicholas II's troops in the Bloody Sunday massacre. General strikes followed in St. Petersburg and other industrial cities. The revolt spread to non-Russian parts of the empire, including Poland, Finland, and Georgia. Antirevolutionary groups, including the Black Hundreds, opposed the rebellion with violent attacks on socialists and pogroms against Jews. By October 1905, general strikes had spread to all the large cities, and the workers' councils or soviets, often led by the Mensheviks, became revolutionary governments. The strikes' magnitude convinced Nicholas II, advised by Sergey Witte, to issue the October Manifesto, promising an elected legislature. The concessions satisfied most moderates, though the more ardent revolutionaries refused to yield, and pockets of resistance in Poland, Georgia, and elsewhere were harshly suppressed as the regime restored its authority. While most of the revolutionary leaders, including Leon Trotsky, were arrested, the revolution forced the czar to institute such reforms as a new constitution and a Duma, though he failed to adequately implement various promised reforms.

Russian Revolution of 1917 Revolution that overthrew the imperial government and placed the Bolsheviks in power. Increasing governmental corruption, the reactionary policies of Nicholas II, and catastrophic Russian losses in World War I contributed to widespread dissatisfaction and economic hardship. In February 1917, riots over food scarcity broke out in Petrograd (St. Petersburg). When the army joined the rebels, Nicholas was forced to abdicate. A provisional government, headed by Georgy Y. Lvov, was appointed in March and tried to continue Russia's participation in World War I, but it was opposed by the powerful Petrograd workers' soviet, which favored Russian withdrawal from the war. Other soviets were formed in major cities and towns, choosing members from factories and military units. The soviet movement was dominated by the Socialist Revolutionary Party, followed by the Mensheviks and the Bolsheviks. Between March and October, the Provisional Government was reorganized four times; Aleksandr Kerensky became its head in July, and put down a coup attempted by Lavr Kornilov but was unable to halt Russia's slide into political and military chaos. By September the Bolsheviks, led by Vladimir Ilich Lenin, had achieved majorities in the Petrograd and Moscow soviets and won increasing support among the hungry urban workers and soldiers. In October they staged a nearly bloodless coup (the "October Revolution"), occupying government buildings and strategic points. Kerensky tried unsuccessfully to organize resistance, then fled the country. The congress of soviets approved the formation of a new government composed mainly of Bolsheviks. See also April Theses, Aleksandr Guchkov, July Days, Russian Civil War.

Russian Social-Democratic Workers' Party Marxist revolutionary party that preceded the Communist Party of the Soviet Union. Founded in Minsk in 1898, it held that Russia could achieve socialism only after developing a bourgeois society with an urban proletariat. The party split in 1903 because of the argument between the Bolshevik wing, led by Vladimir Ilich Lenin, and the Menshevik wing, led by L. Martov, over Lenin's proposals for a party composed of professional revolutionaries. Party members were active in the Russian Revolution of 1905. In the turmoil of the Russian Revolution of 1917, the Bolsheviks broke completely with the Mensheviks and changed their name to "Russian Communist Party (Bolshevik)."

Russo-Finnish War *or* **Winter War** (1939–40) War waged by the Soviet Union against Finland at the start of World War II, following the signing of the GERMAN–SOVIET NONAGGRESSION PACT. When Finland refused to grant the Soviets a naval base and other concessions, Soviet troops attacked on several fronts in November 1939. The heavily outnumbered Finns under CARL GUSTAV EMIL MANNERHEIM put up a skillful defense until February 1940, when heavy Russian bombardments breached the Finns' southern defenses. A peace treaty in March 1940 ceded western Karelia to Russia and allowed construction of a Soviet naval base on the Hanko peninsula.

Russo–Japanese War (1904–5) Conflict between Russia and Japan over territorial expansion in East Asia. After Russia leased the strategically important Port Arthur (now Lüshun, China) and expanded into Manchuria, it faced the increasing power of Japan. When Russia reneged on its agreement with Japan to withdraw troops from Manchuria, the Japanese fleet attacked the Russia naval squadron at Port Arthur and began a siege of the city in February 1904. Japanese land forces cut the Russian army off from coming to aid Port Arthur and pushed it back to Mukden (now Shenyang). The reinforced Russian army took the offensive in October, but poor military leadership blunted its effectiveness. After the long Japanese siege of Port Arthur, in January 1905 the corrupt Russian commander surrendered the garrison without consulting his officers, despite adequate stores and ammunition for its continued defense. Heavy fighting around Mukden ended in March 1905 with the withdrawal of Russian troops under ALEKSEY KUROPATKIN. The decisive naval Battle of TSUSHIMA gave the Japanese the upper hand and brought Russia to the peace table. With the signing of the Treaty of PORTSMOUTH, Russia abandoned its expansionist policy in eastern Asia and Japan gained effective control of Korea and much of Manchuria.

Russo–Turkish Wars Series of 12 wars (1676–1878) fought between Russia and the Ottoman empire. Russia waged the early wars in an attempt to establish a warm-water port on the Black Sea. In the war of 1695–96, PETER I captured the fortress of Azov, but early-18th-century attempts to seize the Balkans failed. In CATHERINE II's reign, the first major Russo–Turkish war (1768–74) pushed Russian borders south and gave Russia a vague right of protection over the Ottoman sultan's Christian subjects. Catherine annexed the Crimean Peninsula (1783) and in 1792 Russia gained the entire western Ukrainian Black Sea coast. In the 19th century wars were fought over the Dardanelles and Bosporus straits, the Caucasus, and Crimea (see CRIMEAN WAR). The 1877–78 Russo–Turkish War pitted Russia and Serbia against Turkey over Bosnia and Herzegovina. Russia was victorious, but its gains were restricted by the Congress of BERLIN (1878), imposed by an anxious Britain and Austria-Hungary.

rust, blister See BLISTER RUST

rustication In architecture, decorative masonry achieved by cutting back the edges of stones to a plane surface while leaving the central portion of the face either rough or projecting markedly. Rustication provides a rich, bold surface for exterior walls. It was used as early as the 6th century BC in the tomb of Cyrus the Great. Italian Early Renaissance architects used rustication to decorate palaces. In the Mannerist (Late Renaissance) and baroque periods, rustication assumed great importance in garden and villa design. Fantastic surfaces were achieved, as in vermiculated work, in which the surface is covered with wavy, serpentine patterns or vertical, dribbled forms.

Rustin, Bayard (1910–1987) U.S. civil-rights leader. Born in West Chester, Pa., he organized the New York branch of the Congress on Racial Equality in 1941 and worked for the Fellowship of Reconciliation (1941–53). In the 1950s he was an adviser to MARTIN LUTHER KING and helped organize the SOUTHERN CHRISTIAN LEADERSHIP CONFERENCE. He was the chief organizer of the 1963 March on Washington to rally support for pending civil-rights legislation. He later served as president (1966–79) of the A. Philip Randolph Institute, a civil-rights organization.

rutabaga \ˌrü-tə-ˈbā-gə\ Swedish TURNIP *(Brassica napus)* in the MUSTARD FAMILY. A hardy biennial, the rutabaga is a cool-season plant cultivated for its fleshy roots and tender leaves. Related to the turnip, it requires a longer growing season but is more tolerant of cold; in addition, its flesh is firmer and more nutritious and its roots keep much better during winter. White-fleshed varieties have a rough, green skin and bright canary-colored flowers. Yellow-fleshed varieties have a smooth green, purple, or bronze skin and buff-yellow or pale-orange flowers. Rutabagas are extensively cultivated as a vegetable and as a cattle fodder crop in Canada, Britain, and northern Europe, and to a lesser extent in the U.S.

Rutgers, The State University of New Jersey State university system with its main campus at New Brunswick and smaller campuses at Newark and Camden. It was founded as Queens College in 1766 and renamed in 1825 for the philanthropist Henry Rutgers. At the New Brunswick campus are the original college and three other residential colleges, one of them (Douglass) enrolling only women and another (Cook) devoted to agricultural and environmental science; a graduate school for the liberal arts; colleges of engineering and pharmacy; and schools or graduate schools of education, psychology, social work, communications, business, and the arts. The Newark and Camden campuses each have a college of arts and sciences, a graduate school, and schools of law, business management, and other professional subjects. Total enrollment is about 48,000.

Ruth, Babe *orig.* **George Herman** (1895–1948) U.S. baseball player, one of the greatest hitters and most popular figures in the sport's history. He was born in Baltimore and raised in poverty. He began his career in 1914 as a member of Baltimore's minor-league team, and joined the Boston Red Sox later that season. He started as a pitcher, compiling an outstanding record (94 wins, 46 losses), but switched to the outfield because of his powerful hitting. Sold to the New York Yankees in 1920, he remained with the team until 1934; he played his last year with the Boston Braves (1935). He coached the Brooklyn Dodgers in 1938, but his reputation for irresponsibility prevented his obtaining a permanent coaching or manager's job. His prodigious slugging earned him the nickname "Sultan of Swat." In 1927 he set the most famous of all baseball records when he hit 60 home runs in a single season, a mark that stood until 1961. He hit at least 50 home runs in four separate seasons and at least 40 in each of 11 seasons. His career slugging percentage (.690) remains an all-time record; he ranks second in career home runs (714, behind HANK AARON), runs (2,174, behind TY COBB), and runs batted in (2,213, again behind Aaron), and third in extra-base hits (1,356, behind Aaron and STAN MUSIAL).

Babe Ruth.
UPI

Ruthenian language See UKRAINIAN LANGUAGE

Rutherford, Ernest *later* **Baron Rutherford** (of Nelson) (1871–1937) New Zealand–British physicist. After studies at Canterbury College, he moved to Britain to attend Cambridge Univ., where he worked with J. J. THOMSON at the Cavendish Laboratory. He would later teach at McGill University in Montreal (1898–1907) and Victoria University in Manchester (1907–19), before becoming chair of the Cavendish Laboratory (from 1919). At the laboratory in the years 1895–97 he discovered and named two types of radioactivity, ALPHA DECAY and BETA DECAY. He later identified the alpha particle as a helium nucleus, and used it in his discovery of the atomic nucleus. With FREDERICK SODDY he formulated the transformation theory of radioactivity (1902). In 1919 he became the first person to artificially disintegrate an element, and in 1920 he hypothesized the existence of the neutron. His work contributed greatly to understanding the disintegration and transmutation of radioactive elements and became fundamental to much of 20th-century physics. In 1908 he was awarded the Nobel Prize. He was knighted in 1914 and ennobled in 1931. Element 104, rutherfordium, is named in his honor.

Ruthven family \ˈri-vən, ˈrüth-vən\ Noble Scottish family prominent in the 16th century. Its members included Lord Patrick Ruthven (c. 1520–1566), provost of Perth (1553–66) and Protestant privy councillor to MARY, QUEEN OF SCOTS. He helped arrange her marriage to Lord DARNLEY (1565) and led the plot to murder her secretary, DAVID RICCIO, after which he fled to England. His son William Ruthven (1541?–1584) also took part in the plot against Riccio and became lord high treasurer (1571). He was the chief conspirator in the "raid of Ruthven" that in 1582 captured the boy king James VI (later JAMES I of England), after which Ruthven was pardoned but later beheaded for treason. His son

John Ruthven, earl of Gowrie (1577?–1600), continued the family tradition of intrigue by offering to serve Queen ELIZABETH I, then leading the opposition to James VI. In the so-called Gowrie conspiracy, Ruthven was killed in his house in Perth, possibly in an abortive attempt to take James VI prisoner.

rutile \'rü-ˌtīl\ Commercially important TITANIUM mineral (titanium dioxide, TiO_2). It forms red to reddish brown, hard, brilliant metallic, slender crystals. Rutile has minor uses in porcelain and glass manufacture as a coloring agent and in making some steels and copper alloys. It is also used as a gem, but synthetic rutile is actually superior to natural crystals for gem use; it has fire (flashes of color) and brilliance (light deflection) like those of diamond. Rutile is mined in Norway and is widespread in the Alps, the southern U.S., Mexico, and elsewhere.

Rutile on pyrophyllite from Mono County, Calif.

B.M. SHAUB

Ruwenzori National Park See QUEEN ELIZABETH NATIONAL PARK

Ruysdael, Jacob van See Jacob van RUISDAEL

Ruysdael \'rȯis-ˌdäl\, **Salomon van** *orig.* **Salomon de Goyer** (c. 1600–1670) Dutch landscape painter. Uncle of JACOB VAN RUISDAEL, he entered the Haarlem painters' guild in 1623 and became its head in 1648. Unlike other landscape painters of the period, including his nephew, Ruysdael generally painted actual landscapes, sometimes combining motifs from several places in one picture. His powerful later work exhibits a command of landscape elements and an increasing use of color for effect.

Rwanda \rə-'wän-də\ *officially* **Republic of Rwanda** Nation, eastern central Africa. Area: 9,757 sq mi (25,271 sq km). Population (1997 est.): 7,738,000. Capital: KIGALI. The population is mostly HUTU, with a TUTSI minority. Languages: Rwanda, French, English (all official). Religions: Roman Catholicism, Islam, indigenous beliefs. Currency: Rwanda franc. Rwanda is a mountainous, landlocked country. Most of it is at an elevation of more than 5,000 ft (1,500 m). There are bamboo forests, wooded regions, and grassy savannas with rich and varied wildlife. It is a developing country with a mainly free-enterprise economy based on agriculture. It is ruled by a transitional regime with one legislative body; its head of state and government is the president, in conjunction with the prime minister and vice president. Originally inhabited by the Twa, a PYGMY people, it then became home to the Hutu, who were well established there when the Tutsi appeared in the 14th century. The Tutsi conquered the Hutu and in the 15th century founded a kingdom near Kigali. The kingdom expanded steadily, and by the early 20th century Rwanda was a unified state with a military structure. The Belgians occupied Rwanda in 1916, and the LEAGUE OF NATIONS created RUANDA-URUNDI as a Belgian mandate in 1923. The Tutsi retained their dominance until shortly before Rwanda reached independence in 1962, when the Hutu took control of the government and stripped the Tutsi of much of their land. Many Tutsis fled Rwanda, and the Hutu dominated the country's political system, waging sporadic civil wars until mid-1994, when the death of the country's leader in a plane crash led to massive violence. The Tutsi-led Rwandan Patriotic Front (RPF) took over the country by force after the massacre of almost 500,000 Tutsis by Hutus. Two million refugees, mostly Hutu, fled to neighboring Congo (Zaire) after the RPF's victory.

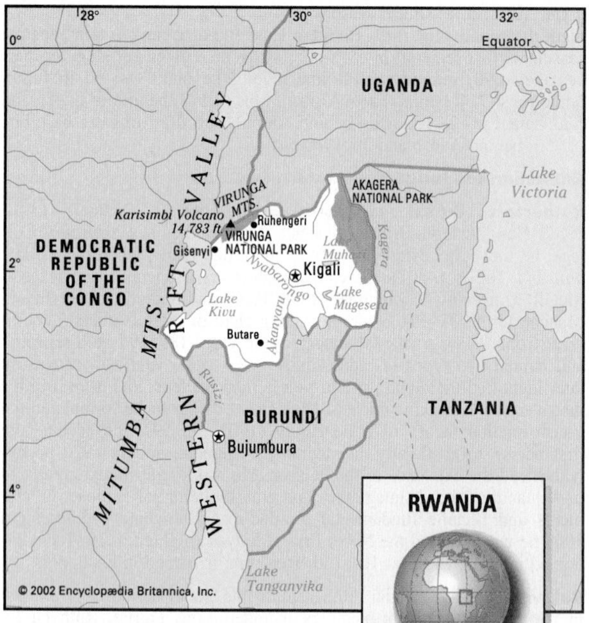

Ryan, (Lynn) Nolan, Jr. (born 1947) U.S. baseball player. Born in Refugio, Texas, he was signed to a New York Mets minor-league team in 1965. He played for the Mets (1968–71), California Angels (1972–79), Houston Astros (1980–88), and Texas Rangers (1989–93). In 1983 he became the first pitcher to surpass WALTER JOHNSON's 1927 record of 3,508 career strikeouts, and he retired in 1993 at the advanced age of 46 with an astonishing 5,714. He also set records for most strikeouts in a season (383 in 1973) and most no-hit games (7).

Ryan, Robert (1909–1973) U.S. film actor. Born in Chicago, he trained for the stage at MAX REINHARDT's workshop in Hollywood, and after World War II he became a successful character actor. Often playing tough guys and bullies, he earned acclaim for his roles in *The Woman on the Beach* (1947), *Crossfire* (1947), *The Set-Up* (1949), and *Act of Violence* (1949). His later films included *Bad Day at Black Rock* (1955), *Men in War* (1957), *Odds Against Tomorrow* (1959), *Billy Budd* (1962), and *The Wild Bunch* (1969).

Rybinsk Reservoir \'ri-bənsk\ Lake, on the upper VOLGA RIVER, northwestern Russia. It was created by two dams on the Volga and its tributary, the Sheksna. When the project was completed in 1947, a lake of 1,768 sq mi (4,580 sq km) in area was formed; it was the world's largest artificial body of water. It regulates the flow of the Volga, provides power for MOSCOW and other cities, and is part of the Volga-Baltic Waterway.

Ryder, Albert Pinkham (1847–1917) U.S. painter. Born in New Bedford, Mass., a fishing port, he never lost his obsession with the sea. He settled in New York c. 1870 and briefly studied painting. His highly personal seascapes, including *Toilers of the Sea,* reflect his feeling of human helplessness against the forces of nature. Thick yellow light (usually moonlight) heightens the mood of mystery in such paintings as *The Race Track* and *Death on a Pale Horse.* He was a strikingly imaginative painter, and though he was a solitary one, his works became well known in his lifetime.

"Toilers of the Sea," oil on wood panel by Ryder, before 1884; in the Metropolitan Museum of Art, New York City.

BY COURTESY OF THE METROPOLITAN MUSEUM OF ART, NEW YORK, GEORGE A. HEARN FUND, 1915

Ryder Cup Biennial team golf event first held in 1927. It was originally played between teams of golfers from the U.S. and Britain; since 1979 players opposing the U.S. have been chosen from all of Europe. The trophy was donated by the British seed merchant Samuel Ryder.

rye CEREAL GRASS (Secale cereale) and its edible grain, used to make rye bread and rye whiskey, as livestock feed, and as a pasture plant. Native to South Asia, today it is grown extensively in Europe, Asia, and North America, mainly where climate and soil are relatively unfavorable for other cereals and as a winter crop where temperatures are too cool for winter WHEAT. Rye thrives at high altitudes and is the most winter-hardy of all small grains. It is high in carbohydrates and provides small quantities of protein, potassium, and B vitamins. Only rye and wheat have the necessary qualities to make a loaf of bread, but rye lacks the elasticity of wheat and thus is frequently blended with wheat flour. The tough fibrous STRAW of rye is used for animal bedding, thatching, mattresses, hats, and paper. Rye may be grown as a GREEN MANURE crop.

Rye House Plot (1683) In English history, an alleged Whig conspiracy to assassinate CHARLES II because of his pro-Catholic policies. The plot drew its name from Rye House at Hoddeston, Hertfordshire, near the road where Charles was supposed to be killed as he traveled from a horse meet. The king's unexpected early departure supposedly foiled the plot, which was later revealed by an informer. The facts remained cloudy, but the main plotters included the duke of MONMOUTH, WILLIAM, LORD RUSSELL, Algernon Sidney (1622–1683), and Sir Thomas Armstrong. The last three were tried, convicted of treason, and beheaded.

Ryerson Polytechnic University Privately endowed institution of higher learning in Toronto. It was founded in 1948 and named after the educator Egerton Ryerson (1803–1882). It has faculties of engineering and applied science, arts (including the humanities and social sciences), applied arts, business, community services, and continuing education. It is primarily a four-year baccalaureate institution. Enrollment is about 14,000.

Rykov \'rik-əf\, **Aleksey (Ivanovich)** (1881–1938) Soviet official. Active in Bolshevik revolutionary activities from age 18, he became a party leader and, after VLADIMIR ILICH LENIN's death, chairman of the Council of People's Commissars (1924–29). A strong supporter of the NEW ECONOMIC POLICY, he was joined by JOSEPH STALIN to defeat the economic radicals (and Stalin's rivals) LEON TROTSKY, GRIGORY Y. ZINOVYEV, and LEV KAMENEV. When Stalin then adopted his rivals' radical ideas, Rykov was stripped of his posts and forced to recant his "Right Opposition" views (1929). In 1936 he was implicated in fabricated conspiracies, tried in Stalin's PURGE TRIALS, and executed for treason.

Ryle, Gilbert (1900–1976) British philosopher. He taught at Oxford University (1945–68), where he became a leading figure in the "Oxford philosophy," or "ordinary language," movement, which attempted to dissipate confusion arising from the misapplication of language. His classic *The Concept of Mind* (1949) challenged RENE DESCARTES's traditional distinction between body and mind. What Ryle deems the logically incoherent dogma of Cartesian DUALISM he labels as the doctrine of the ghost-in-the-machine. In *Dilemmas* (1954) he analyzes propositions that appear irreconcilable. His other noteworthy books include *Philosophical Arguments* (1945), *A Rational Animal* (1962), *Plato's Progress* (1966), and *The Thinking of Thoughts* (1968).

Ryle, Martin *later* **Sir Martin** (1918–1984) British radio astronomer. After receiving a PhD in physics from Oxford Univ., he helped design radar equipment during World War II. He was an early investigator of extraterrestrial radio signals. Ryle guided the Cambridge radio astronomy group in the production of radio source catalogs. The *Third Cambridge Catalogue* (1959) helped lead to the discovery of the first QUASAR. To map distant radio sources, he developed a technique called aperture synthesis, which provided tremendously increased resolving power for radio telescopes and was used to locate the first PULSAR. In 1974 he and ANTONY HEWISH shared a Nobel Prize.

Rymer \'rī-mər\, **Thomas** (1643?–1713) English critic. Though called to the bar in 1673, Rymer almost immediately turned to literary criticism. He is known for introducing into England the principles of French formalist Neoclassical criticism. Among his works are *The Tragedies of the Last Age* (1678) and *A Short View of Tragedy* (1693), both highly critical of modern drama and favoring classical tragedy. His views were very influential until the 19th century. Appointed historiographer royal in 1692, he compiled most of the *Foedera,* a collection of treaties entered into by England that is of considerable value to the medievalist.

Ryoan-ji \ˌrē-ō-'än-ˌjē\ Japanese Buddhist temple in Kyoto, famous for its abstract garden (c. 1500). An area approximately 30 by 70 ft (10 by 20 m) is covered with raked sand and set with 15 stones divided into five unequal groups. If anything is represented, it may be rocky islets in a sea, but the garden's appeal lies essentially in the charm of its relationships and the arrangement of rocks such that all 15 are not visible from any single vantage point.

Ryukyu Islands \rē-'yü-ˌkyü\ Island chain (pop., 1990: 1,222,000), Japan. It extends in an arc 600 mi (970 km) long from southern Japan to the northern tip of Taiwan. The 55 islands and islets have a total land area of 870 sq mi (2,254 sq km). In ancient times it was an independent kingdom, but Chinese and Japanese sovereignty were successively imposed on the archipelago from the 14th to the 19th century. In 1879 the Ryukyus became an integral part of Japan. After Japan's defeat in World War II, the U.S. took control of the islands; it returned them all by 1972. The U.S. maintains military bases on OKINAWA. The islands are primarily rural, and agriculture is the dominant occupation.

SA *in full* **Sturmabteilung (German: "Assault Division")** *known as* **Storm Troopers** *or* **Brownshirts** Nazi paramilitary organization that played a key role in Adolf Hitler's rise to power. The SA was founded by Hitler in Munich in 1921 and drew its early membership from the Freikorps. Outfitted in brown uniforms after the fashion of the Italian Fascist Blackshirts, the SA protected Nazi Party meetings and assaulted political opponents. From 1931 it was headed by Ernst Rohm, and by 1932 it had grown to a force of over 400,000. Röhm wanted to merge the regular army with the SA under his leadership, but Hitler had become wary of the organization's growing power. In 1934 he ordered a "blood purge" of the SA, which became known as the Night of the Long Knives. Thereafter the SA was reduced to a minor political role.

Sa-skya pa \'sás-kyə-'pá\ Tibetan Buddhist sect granted sovereignty over Tibet by Kublai Khan and noted also for contributions to philosophy and linguistics. The Sa-skya pandita Kun-dga'-rgyal-mtshan (1182–1251) wrote a major treatise developing Buddhist logic.

Saadia ben Joseph \'sá-dē-á-ben-'jō-zəf\ *Arabic* **Said ibn Yusuf al-Fayyumi** (882–942) Egyptian-Babylonian Jewish philosopher and polemicist. He left Egypt c. 905 and eventually settled in Babylonia, where he headed the rabbinic Academy of Sura. He wrote a Hebrew-Arabic dictionary and translated much of the Old Testament into Arabic. He produced his greatest work, *The Book of Beliefs and Opinions,* in 935. His theology hinges on the unity of God and the principle of justice. The latter takes issue with the view (widespread in Islam) that the definition of what is just depends solely on God's will, to which none of the moral criteria found among humans is applicable. Against this principle, Saadia and the Mutazilites (see Mutazila) believed that just and unjust are intrinsic characteristics of human actions and cannot be changed by divine decree.

Saale River \'zä-lə, *Engl* 'sä-lə\ River, eastern central Germany. A left tributary of the Elbe River, it rises in the Bavarian highlands and flows north to join the Elbe just above Barby. As it crosses Thuringia, it enters a deep valley dominated by castles. It is 265 mi (426 km) long.

Saar, Betye (born 1926) U.S. artist and educator. Born in Los Angeles, California, Saar studied design, education, and printmaking. By 1968 she developed an interest in three-dimensional objects and began working in assemblage. Her works incorporate found objects of all sorts—from those suggesting ritual folk art to traditional Christianity. Many also challenge racist myths and stereotypes. Saar's *The Liberation of Aunt Jemima* (1972), for example, is a "mammy" doll placed in front of the eponymous pancake syrup labels; she carries a broom in one hand and a shotgun in the other. Saar's works expanded in size and scope from the late 1970s. Her room-size installations often featured mystical themes and sometimes included shrines.

Saar River \'sär, 'zär\ *French* **Sarre** \'sär\ River, France and Germany. A right-bank tributary of the Moselle River, it flows 153 mi (246 km) across northeastern France into Germany and enters the Moselle above Trier, Germany. The northern part of the valley is a wine-growing district. The middle stretch between Saarbrücken and Dillingen is a center of heavy industry.

Saarbrücken \zär-'brü̅-kən\ City (pop., 1996 est.: 187,000), capital of Saarland state, southwestern Germany, on the Saar River. Chartered in 1321, it belonged to the counts of Nassau-Saarbrücken until it was occupied by the French in 1793. It passed to Prussia in 1815 and became the capital of the Saar region in 1919. The present city was formed in 1909 by the union of the former Saarbrücken with Burbach-Malstatt, Sankt Johann, and Sankt Arnual. In 1959 it was made capital of Saarland. Historic buildings include the 18th-century baroque Ludwigskirche, the Gothic abbey church of St. Arnual (c. 1270–1330), and the Old Bridge over the Saar (1546).

Saaremaa *or* **Sarema** \'sär-ə-ˌmä\ Largest of the islands in the Muhu archipelago that divides the Baltic Sea from the Gulf of Riga. A part of Estonia, it has an area of 1,031 sq mi (2,671 sq km). It was occupied in the 13th century by the Livonian Knights and was ruled successively by Denmark, Sweden, and Russia before becoming part of Estonia in 1918. It was occupied by German troops in World War II. Economic activities include agriculture, livestock raising, and fishing.

Saarinen \'sär-ə-nən\, **Eero** (1910–1961) U.S. (Finnish-born) architect. His father, Eliel Saarinen (1873–1950), was the foremost Finnish architect of his time; his major works include the Helsinki railway station (1904–14) and—after emigrating to the U.S. in 1923—the buildings of the Cranbrook Foundation, Bloomfield Hills, Mich. (1925–41). Eero joined his father's practice after studying at Yale. His vast General Motors Technical Center in Warren, Mich. (1948–56), was followed in 1948 by his design for St. Louis's Gateway Arch (completed 1965). In the Kresge Auditorium and chapel at MIT (1955), he used a "handkerchief" dome resting on three points for the auditorium and a stark red-brick cylinder for the chapel. His TWA terminal at Kennedy International Airport (1956–62) employs two cantilevered concrete shells that extend dramatically outward, suggesting wings.

Saarland \'zär-ˌlänt, *Engl* 'sär-ˌland\ *or* **Saargebiet** \'zär-gə-ˌbēt\ State, southwestern Germany. It has an area of 992 sq mi (2,569 sq km). The capital, Saarbrücken, lies along the Saar River. The region was contested by France and Germany from the 17th century until 1815, when France ceded most of it to Prussia by the Treaty of Paris. When Alsace-Lorraine was added to the German empire in 1871, the Saar ceased to be a boundary state and developed rapidly as a coal-mining and industrial area, producing iron and steel. French military forces occupied it after World War II, but it was restored to Germany and became a state in 1957.

Saba Island (pop., 1990: 1,100) of the Netherlands Antilles in the Caribbean Sea. It lies 16 mi (26 km) northwest of St. Eustatius, with which it forms the Lesser Antilles. It has an area of 5 sq mi (13 sq km) and is the peak of an extinct volcano, Mount Scenery. It was settled by the Dutch in 1632, but its inaccessibility and ruggedness prevented it from achieving economic importance and it was often a buccaneers' stronghold. The economy depends heavily on tourism.

Sabah dynasty Ruling family of Kuwait since 1756. In that year the Banu Utub, a group of families of the Anizah tribe living in what is now Kuwait, appointed a member of the Sabah family, Sabah bin Jaber (r.c. 1752–64), to be their ruler. There have been 13 emirs to the present day. The present emir rules with the assistance of a prime minister, a council of ministers, and a national assembly, but the Sabah family reserves the right to choose succeeding emirs from within the family.

Sabbath Day of the week set aside for worship and observance of religious duties in Judaism and Christianity. The Jewish Sabbath begins at sunset on Friday and lasts until sunset the next day, during which time no ordinary work or act of labor is performed. For most Christian denominations, the Sabbath is on Sunday; prescribed conduct varies considerably, but attendance at worship services is a feature common to all. In Islam, Friday is the day of worship.

saber-toothed tiger *or* **saber-toothed cat** Any of the extinct cat species forming the subfamily Machairodontinae. They had two long, bladelike canine teeth in the upper jaw. They lived from 36.6 million years ago to about 10,000 years ago, arising in North America and Europe and spreading to Asia, Africa, and South America. The best-known, the short-limbed *Smilodon* of the Americas, was bigger than the modern lion. Its "sabers," which grew to 8 in. (20 cm) long, were used to stab and slash prey, including the mastodon, whose pattern of extinction paralleled their own.

Sabi River See Save River

Sabin \'sā-bin\, **Albert Bruce** (1906–1993) U.S. (Polish-born) physician and microbiologist. He emigrated to the U.S. with his parents in 1921 and received an MD from New York University. He grew polio virus in human nerve tissue outside the body, showed that it does not enter the body through the respiratory system, and proved that poliomyelitis is primarily an infection of the digestive tract. He postulated that an oral vaccine would work longer than Jonas Salk's injections of killed virus, and isolated weakened strains of each of the three types of polio virus that would stimulate antibody production but not produce disease. The Sabin oral polio vaccine, approved for use in the U.S. in 1960, became the main defense against polio throughout the world.

Sabine \'sab-in\, **Edward** *later* **Sir Edward** (1788–1883) British (Irish) astronomer and geodesist. He accompanied the expeditions of

John Ross (1818) and William Parry (1819) in search of the Northwest Passage. In 1821 he began experiments to determine the earth's shape more precisely by observing the motion of a pendulum. He thereafter devoted most of his efforts to researches on terrestrial magnetism, overseeing the establishment of magnetic observatories throughout the world. In 1852 he discovered that the periodic variation of sunspots is correlated with certain changes in magnetic disturbances. He was president of London's Royal Society 1861–71. Knighted in 1869, he was promoted to the rank of general in 1870.

Sabine River \sə-'bēn\ River, eastern Texas and western Louisiana. Rising in northeastern Texas, it flows southeast and south, broadens near its mouth to form Sabine Lake, and continues from Port Arthur through Sabine Pass to enter the Gulf of Mexico after a course of 578 mi (930 km). The river forms the southern section of the Texas–Louisiana boundary and is a link in the GULF INTRACOASTAL WATERWAY.

Sabines \'sā-,bīnz\ Ancient Italic tribe located east of the Tiber River. According to legend, ROMULUS invited them to a festival and then carried off ("raped") their women to provide wives for his men. The second king of Rome, Numa Pompilius, probably a Sabine, supposedly created virtually all the Romans' religious institutions and practices. Later groups displaced the Sabines from Rome. The Romans conquered them and granted them partial citizenship in 290; they became full citizens in 268.

sable CARNIVORE (*Martes zibellina,* family Mustelidae) that inhabits forests of northern Asia and is highly valued for its fur. The name is sometimes applied to related European and Asian species and to the American MARTEN. The sable is 13–20 in. (32–51 cm) long, excluding the 5–7-in. (13–18-cm) tail, and weighs 2–4 lbs (0.9–1.8 kg). The coat varies from brown to almost black. The solitary, arboreal sable eats small animals and eggs.

Sabra and Shatila massacres \'säb-rə...shá-'tē-lə\ (1982) Massacre of Palestinian civilians by Christian militiamen in two Beirut refugee camps during the Israeli invasion of Lebanon. The goal of Israel's invasion was to expel Palestinian guerrillas from Lebanon. To achieve this objective, Israel allied itself with several Lebanese Christian groups, including the Phalange party, who fought the Palestinians during the brutal LEBANESE CIVIL WAR (1975–90). Following the U.S.-brokered evacuation of PALESTINE LIBERATION ORGANIZATION (PLO) fighters from Beirut, Israeli forces under Defense Minister ARIEL SHARON allowed Phalange militiamen to enter the two camps, ostensibly to root out further PLO fighters. Estimates of the number of women, children, and elderly who were killed over the next several days ranged from 800 to several thousand. Although no militiamen were ever prosecuted for those atrocities, Sharon—who an Israeli commission of inquiry later found indirectly responsible through negligence—was condemned in Arab popular opinion as the culprit of the massacre.

Sabrata *or* **Sabratha** \'sa-brə-tə\ Ancient city in Roman Africa, the westernmost of the three cities of TRIPOLIS. Founded by the Carthaginians as a trading post, it was first permanently settled in the 4th century BC. Archaeological excavations have uncovered more than half the area of the city, including Roman and Byzantine fortifications, temples, fountains, the forum, theater, basilica, and several churches.

Sabre \'sā-bər\ *or* **F-86** U.S. single-seat, single-engine jet FIGHTER manufactured by North American Aviation, Inc. Built with wings swept back to limit transonic drag as flight speed approached the sound barrier, it could exceed the speed of sound in a dive. The first squadron became operational in 1949, and the fighter saw combat in the Korean War; production ended in 1956. It was 37.5 ft (11.5 m) long and had a wingspan of over 37 ft (11 m). Powered by a series of turbojet engines, its top speed was almost 700 mph (1,100 kph) in level flight. It carried guided missiles, machine guns or cannon in the fuselage, and rockets or bombs under the wings.

Sabzavari \'sab-zə-,vä-rē\, **Hajji Hadi** (1797/98–1878) Iranian philosopher and religious scholar. In his native city of Sabzavar he founded a school that attracted students of philosophy from all over the Muslim world. His two main philosophical works, *The Secrets of Wisdom* and *A Treatise on Logic in Verse,* in which he advanced the *hikma* (wisdom) school of thought, are still studied in Iran. He lived a devoutly religious and ascetic life and is said to have performed miracles.

Sac See SAUK

Sacagawea \,sa-kə-jə-'wē-ə\ (1786?–1812) SHOSHONE Indian woman who, carrying her infant son on her back, traveled thousands of wilderness miles with the LEWIS AND CLARK EXPEDITION (1804–6). Though she had been separated from her people for nearly 10 years when the expedition began, Sacagawea was instrumental in obtaining horses and guides from a band of Shoshone (led by her brother Cameahwait) at a point when the expedition might well have ended. Her fortitude in the face of hazards and deprivations became legendary.

saccharin \'sa-kə-rən\ Synthetic organic compound, $C_7H_5NSO_3$, that is 200–700 times as sweet as cane sugar. The sodium or calcium salt of saccharin is widely used as a diet sweetener. Though approved by the Food and Drug Administration, its safety is controversial because it appears to be a weak CARCINOGEN. See also ASPARTAME.

Sacchi \'säk-kē\, **Andrea** (1599–1661) Italian painter. He studied with FRANCESCO ALBANI in Bologna and in Rome, where he would work all his life. He was employed, with PIETRO da Cortona, to decorate the Sacchetti family villa (1628) and the Barberini Palace, for which he produced the ceiling fresco *Allegory of Divine Wisdom* (1629–31). His two altarpieces in the church of Santa Maria della Concezione (1631–38) are distinguished by their Classicism. Other notable works include eight canvases in the cupola of the Baptistery of St. John in Rome (1639–45). He was a skilled draftsman and the leading exponent of the Classical tradition in 17th-century Roman painting.

Sacco-Vanzetti case Murder trial in Massachusetts (1920–27). After the robbery and murder of a paymaster and a guard at a shoe factory (1920), police arrested the Italian immigrant anarchists Nicola Sacco (1891–1927), a shoemaker, and Bartolomeo Vanzetti (1888–1927), a fish peddler. They were tried and found guilty. Radicals and socialists protested the men's innocence, and many others felt they had been convicted for their beliefs. In 1925 a convicted murderer confessed to participating in the crime, but attempts to obtain a retrial failed and the two were sentenced to death in 1927. Protest meetings were held throughout the U.S. Gov. Alvin Fuller appointed an advisory panel, which agreed with his refusal to grant clemency, and the men were executed. They became martyrs to radicals' belief that the legal system was biased. Though opinion remained divided on the men's guilt, most agreed that defects in the trial warranted a retrial.

Sachs \'zäks, *Engl* 'saks\, **Curt** (1881–1959) German-U.S. musicologist. He studied clarinet and composition as a teenager, but earned a doctorate in art history. After working as an art critic, he returned to musicology, becoming one of the most significant scholars of that field, especially in the systematic study of musical instruments (with E. v. HORNBOSTEL). After emigrating to the U.S. in 1937, he wrote important textbooks and surveys and supervised the growth of the discipline, lecturing at such institutions as Columbia and NYU.

Sachs, Nelly (Leonie) (1891–1970) German poet and dramatist. Born to a prosperous family, Sachs wrote poems mainly for her own entertainment until the advent of Nazism darkened her work and forced her to flee to Sweden. Her lyrics from those years combine lean simplicity with imagery variously tender, searing, or mystical. In the famous title poem of her collection *O the Chimneys* (1967), Israel's body drifts upward as smoke from the Nazi death camps. Her best-known play is *Eli* (1951). She shared the 1966 Nobel Prize with S. Y. AGNON.

Nelly Sachs, 1966.
UPI

Sachsen See SAXONY

Sachsenhausen \'zäk-sən-,haù-zən\ German Nazi CONCENTRATION CAMP. Located near the village of Sachsenhausen in northern Germany, it was established in 1936 as part of a system of camps that included BUCHENWALD (for central Germany) and DACHAU (for southern Germany). The camp's early prisoners included 10,000 Jews rounded

S T U V

up from Berlin and Hamburg after the KRISTALLNACHT raids. Of the 200,000 prisoners who went through Sachsenhausen during World War II, 100,000 died there from disease, execution, and overwork in the local armaments factories; many of the rest were transferred to other camps. See also HOLOCAUST.

Sackler, Arthur M(itchell) (1913–1987) U.S. physician, medical publisher, and art collector. Born in New York City, he earned an MD from New York University. In 1949 he founded the Creedmore Institute of Psychobiological Studies in New York, and did pioneering research in the field of psychobiology. He edited the *Journal of Clinical and Experimental Psychopathology* and founded the biweekly *Medical Tribune* newspaper. He funded research at several universities, and endowed art galleries at universities and museums, donating art from his own vast collection, including the world's largest collection of ancient Chinese art, to the Metropolitan Museum of Art.

Sacks, Oliver (Wolf) (born 1933) British-U.S. neurologist and writer. He emigrated to the U.S. in 1960 to study neurology at the University of California, and in 1965 he joined the faculty at New York's Albert Einstein College of Medicine. Many of his books relate case histories of neurologically damaged people. His empathy with those afflicted with strange conditions, including Tourette's syndrome, amnesia, and autism, has been the hallmark of his writings. *Awakenings,* about the long-term effects of SLEEPING SICKNESS, was filmed in 1990; other books include *The Man Who Mistook His Wife for a Hat* (1986) and *An Anthropologist on Mars* (1995).

Sackville, Thomas *later* **Earl of Dorset** (1536–1608) English politician and poet. A London barrister, he entered Parliament in 1558. He was a member of the Privy Council (1585) and conveyed the death sentence to MARY, QUEEN OF SCOTS, in 1586. He later served on diplomatic missions to The Hague and served as lord high treasurer 1599–1608. He was also noted as the coauthor of *The Tragedie of Gorboduc* (1561), the earliest English drama in blank verse, and for his "Induction," the most famous part of the verse collection *A Myrrour for Magistrates* (1563).

Sackville-West, Vita *orig.* **Victoria Mary** (1892–1962) British novelist and poet. The daughter of a baron, she married the diplomat and author Harold Nicolson (1886–1968) in 1913; her journal was the basis of *Portrait of a Marriage* (1973) by their son Nigel, which described a happy marriage in which both partners were principally homosexual. Her gift for evoking the beauty of the Kentish countryside was evident in her long poem *The Land* (1926). Her best-known novels are *The Edwardians* (1930) and *All Passion Spent* (1931). She also wrote biographies and gardening books. She was the inspiration for the title character in her friend VIRGINIA WOOLF's novel *Orlando*.

sacrament Religious action or symbol in which spiritual power is believed to be transmitted through material elements or the performance of ritual. The concept is ancient; prehistoric people believed that they could advantageously influence events in the natural world, such as weather patterns, through the performance of ritual. In modern religions, the sacrament is primarily associated with CHRISTIANITY and is said to derive from such practices instituted by JESUS as BAPTISM, the washing of the feet, and the casting out of DEMONS. As codified by St. THOMAS AQUINAS and promulgated by the Council of TRENT, the sacraments of ROMAN CATHOLICISM are seven in number: baptism, CONFIRMATION, the EUCHARIST, penance, anointing of the sick, ordination, and matrimony. See also SAMSKARA.

Sacramento City (pop., 1996 est.: 376,000), capital of California. It is located in the CENTRAL VALLEY, where the SACRAMENTO and American rivers meet. First settled in 1839 as New Helvetia by JOHN SUTTER, it became an important trading center during the GOLD RUSH. The present city was laid out in 1848 and named for the river. It became the state capital in 1854 and prospered as a transportation and agricultural center. It was the terminus of the first California railroad in 1856 and the western terminus of the PONY EXPRESS in 1860. A ship canal completed in 1963 made the city a deepwater port. The city's main industries in addition to government services, include food processing, printing, and aerospace products. It is the site of several institutions of higher learning.

Sacramento River River, northern California. Rising near Mount SHASTA, it flows 382 mi (615 km) southwest between the Cascade and Sierra Nevada ranges, through the northern CENTRAL VALLEY. It forms a common delta with the SAN JOAQUIN RIVER before entering the northern arm of SAN FRANCISCO BAY. California's largest river, it is navigable for 180 mi (290 km) and accommodates oceangoing vessels as far as SACRAMENTO. Scene of the GOLD RUSH of 1849, the river flows through one of the world's richest agricultural regions.

sacrifice Act of offering objects to a divinity, thereby making them holy. The motivation for sacrifice is to perpetuate, intensify, or reestablish a connection between the human and the divine. It is often intended to gain the favor of the god or to placate divine wrath. The term has come to be applied specifically to blood sacrifice, which entails the death or destruction of the thing sacrificed (see HUMAN SACRIFICE). The sacrifice of fruits, flowers, or crops (bloodless sacrifice) is more often referred to as an offering.

sacrifice, human See HUMAN SACRIFICE

Sadat \sə-ˈdat\, **(Muhammad) Anwar al-** (1918–1981) President of Egypt (1970–81). A graduate of the Cairo Military Academy, he joined GAMAL ABDEL NASSER's conspiracy to depose the monarchy in 1950, and later served as vice president (1964–66, 1969–70). He became president when Nasser died in 1970. In 1973 he joined with Syria in a surprise attack on Israel, losing militarily but gaining politically. In 1977 he went to Jerusalem to offer peace to Israel, and in 1979 he concluded a peace treaty with MENACHEM BEGIN. The two men shared the 1978 Nobel Peace Prize. At home, faced with a worsening economy, Sadat suppressed public dissent. His assassination by KHALID AL-ISLAMBULI, a Muslim extremist, elicited shock and grief worldwide. See also ARAB–ISRAELI WARS, CAMP DAVID ACCORDS, HOSNI MUBARAK.

saddle Seat for a rider on the back of an animal, usually a horse. The leather saddle was developed between the 3rd century BC and the 1st century AD, probably by peoples of the Asian steppes, where the stirrup and the horse collar also originated. The saddle greatly improved a rider's ability to control a moving horse, especially in combat. Improvements made in medieval Europe were related to feudal battles among knights. Modern saddles are mainly divided into two types: the light, flat English or Hungarian style used for sport and recreation, and the sturdy Western style used originally for cattle roping and now also for recreation.

Sadducee \ˈsa-jə-ˌsē\ Member of a Jewish priestly sect that flourished for about two centuries, until the destruction (AD 70) of the Second Temple of JERUSALEM. Sadducees were generally wealthier, more conservative, and better connected politically than their rivals, the PHARISEES. They believed in strict interpretation of the TORAH and thus rejected such ideas as immortality of the soul, bodily resurrection after death, and the existence of angels. They viewed JESUS' ministry with mistrust and are believed to have played some part in his death. Their wealth and complicity with Roman rulers made them unpopular with the common people.

Sade \ˈsäd\, **Marquis de** *orig.* **Donatien-Alphonse-François, comte** (count) de Sade (1740–1814) French novelist and philosopher. After abandoning a military career at the end of the Seven Years' War, he married and became involved in a life of debauchery and outrageous scandal with prostitutes and with local young people he abducted, for which he was repeatedly imprisoned, once narrowly escaping execution. Despite his noble birth, he supported the French Revolution, which he saw as representing political liberation on a level parallel to the sexual liberation he himself represented. He was twice sent to the insane asylum at Charenton (1789–90, 1801–14), where he would eventually die. He overcame boredom and anger in prison and the asylum by writing sexually graphic novels and plays. *The 120 Days of Sodom* (written 1785) was a tale of four libertines who kidnap victims for a nonstop orgy of perversion. In his most famous novel, *Justine* (1791), the heroine suffers because she fails to perceive that there is no moral God and that desire is the only reality. His other works include *Philosophy in the Bedroom* (1793) and *Crimes of Passion* (1800).

sadhu and swami In India, a religious ascetic or holy person. Sadhus are typically wandering ascetics who subsist on alms. They may follow the tenets of a particular belief system, such as HINDUISM or JAINISM, but are more typically regarded as saintly in their own right. The term swami refers to a sadhu ordained in a specific order and is associated particularly with VEDANTA. Sadhus and swamis may live either in communities or in solitude; they typically possess little, eschew conventional and modern dress, and have shaven heads or matted, unkempt hair.

sadism \'sā-ˌdi-zəm, 'sa-ˌdi-zəm\ Psychosexual disorder in which sexual urges are gratified by inflicting pain on another person. The term is derived from the name of the Marquis de SADE, who chronicled his own such practices. The level and extent of sadistic violence may vary from mild pain to extreme brutality, sometimes leading to serious injury or death. Sadism is often linked to MASOCHISM, and many individuals who have one tendency also have the other. The sadist, however, often seeks a victim who is not a masochist, since some of the sexual excitement derives from the victim's unwillingness.

Sadowa, Battle of See Battle of KÖNIGGRÄTZ

Saenredam \'sän-re-ˌdäm\, **Pieter Jansz(oon)** (1597–1665) Dutch painter. Son of an engraver, he became a friend of the architect Jacob van Campen (1595–1657), which may have influenced him to specialize in architectural painting. A pioneer of the "church portrait," he was the first Dutch artist to abandon the Mannerist tradition of fanciful invention in architectural painting in favor of a new realism in rendering specific buildings. His paintings of church interiors show a scrupulous precision and convey a majestic spaciousness and serenity.

Safaqis See SFAX

Safavid dynasty \sä-'fä-vəd\ (1502–1736) Persian dynasty. It was founded by ISMAIL I, who, by converting his people from Sunni Islam to Shiite Islam, helped create a sense of nationhood. He captured Tabriz from the Ak Koyunlu and became shah of Azerbaijan (1501) and Persia (1502). ABBAS I (r.1588–1629) brought the dynasty to its peak; his capital, ESFAHAN, was the center of Safavid architectural achievement. The dynasty declined in the century following his reign, pressed by the Ottomans and the Mughals, and fell when a weak shah, Tahmasp II, was deposed by his lieutenant, NADIR SHAH.

Safdie \'säf-dē\, **Moshe** (born 1938) Israeli-Canadian architect. Educated at McGill University School of Architecture, he began his career in the offices of LOUIS KAHN. His Habitat '67, a prefabricated concrete housing complex of individual apartment units stacked irregularly along a zigzagged framework evocative of an Italian hill town or a PUEBLO, was a bold experiment in prefabricated housing using modular units; it aroused intense international interest but failed to catch on as a low-cost housing construction method. Later works include Yeshivat Porat Joseph Rabbinical College in Jerusalem (1971–79) and Coldspring New Town near Baltimore (1971). He served as director of urban design at Harvard University 1978–84.

safe sex Practices that reduce the risk of contracting SEXUALLY TRANSMITTED DISEASES, especially AIDS, during SEXUAL INTERCOURSE and similar activities. The term usually refers to use of condoms, which greatly reduce the chance of infection but are not 100% effective. Abstinence and staying monogamous with an uninfected and monogamous partner are completely safe.

safety Activities that seek to minimize or to eliminate hazardous conditions that can cause bodily injury. Occupational safety is concerned with risks in areas where people work: offices, manufacturing plants, farms, construction sites, and commercial and retail facilities. Public safety is concerned with hazards in the home, in travel and recreation, and in other situations that do not fall within the scope of occupational safety. See also LIFE-SAFETY SYSTEMS, OSHA (Occupational Safety and Health Administration).

safflower Flowering annual plant *(Carthamus tinctorius)* of the COMPOSITE FAMILY. Native to parts of Asia and Africa, it is now widely grown as an oil crop in the U.S., Canada, Australia, Israel, and Turkey. Oil obtained from the seeds, an ingredient of soft margarines, salad oil, and cooking oil, is valued for its high proportion of polyunsaturated fats. Since the oil does not yellow with age, it is also a useful base for varnish and paint. The plant, which grows 1–4 ft (0.3–1.2 m) high, has flowers in red, orange, yellow, or white, which were formerly a source of textile dyes.

Safflower (*Carthamus tinctorius*).
J.C. ALLEN AND SON

saffron Golden-colored, pungent seasoning and dye obtained from the dried stigmas of flowers of the saffron crocus *(Crocus sativus)*, a bulbous perennial of the IRIS FAMILY. Because 1 lb (0.45 kg) of saffron represents 75,000 blossoms, it is the world's most expensive spice. The color and flavor are essential ingredients for certain Mediterranean and Asian dishes, as well as for special English, Scandinavian, and Balkan baked goods. Since ancient times, saffron has been the official color for the robes of Buddhist priests and for royal garments in several cultures. Greeks and Romans scattered saffron as a perfume in halls, courts, theaters, and baths.

Saffron (*Crocus sativus*).
EMIL MUENCH—OSTMAN AGENCY

Safi al-Din \sä-'fē-äl-'dēn\ (1253–1334) Iranian SHEIKH who founded the Safavid order of mystics, which in time developed into the SAFAVID DYNASTY. He was influenced by mystics of the Sufi order and by Sheikh Zahid, a religious leader whose daughter he eventually married. On Sheikh Zahid's death, Safi al-Din assumed his leadership and gradually attracted many more adherents, largely through his policy of hospitality to all who sought refuge. He is commemorated by a shrine in Ardabil, northwestern Iran, the city of his birth.

Safire \'sa-ˌfīr\, **William** (born 1929) U.S. journalist. Born in New York City and educated at Syracuse Univ., he worked as a newspaper reporter and at radio and television stations before entering the public-relations field, eventually founding his own successful firm. He was a speechwriter for SPIRO AGNEW and then for RICHARD NIXON. In 1973 he began his conservative and vigorously written "Essay" column for the *New York Times*, which earned him a Pulitzer Prize in 1978. He also writes on linguistic issues in the *New York Times Magazine*. Among his books are the novels *Full Disclosure* (1977) and *Sleeper Spy* (1995) and works of lexicographical interest.

saga Genre of prose narrative typically dealing with prominent figures and events of the heroic age in Norway and Iceland, especially as recorded in Icelandic manuscripts of the late 12th and 13th century. Once thought to be orally transmitted history that had finally been written down, sagas are now usually regarded as reconstructions of the past, imaginative in varying degrees and created according to aesthetic principles. Important ideals in sagas are heroism and loyalty; revenge often plays a part. Action is preferred to reflection, and description of the inner motives and point of view of protagonists is minimized. Subdivisions of the genre include kings' sagas, recounting the lives of Scandinavian rulers; legendary sagas, treating themes from myth and legend; and ICELANDERS' SAGAS. See also GRETTIS SAGA, NJÁLS SAGA.

Sagan \'sā-gən\, **Carl (Edward)** (1934–1996) U.S. astronomer and science writer. Born in Brooklyn, N.Y., he received his PhD from the University of Chicago. At the Smithsonian Astrophysical Observatory (1962–68), he worked on planetary astronomy and on the SETI project. He gained prominence as a popular science writer and commentator noted for his clear writing and enthusiasm; his *Dragons of Eden* (1977) won a Pulitzer Prize. He coproduced and narrated the television series *Cosmos* (1980); its companion book became the best-selling English-language science book of all time. In the 1980s he studied the environmental effects of nuclear war and helped popularize the term "nuclear winter."

Sagan \sä-'gäⁿ\, **Françoise** *orig.* **Françoise Quoirez** (born 1935) French novelist and dramatist. While attending the Sorbonne, she published her best known novel, the poignant *Bonjour tristesse* (1954; "Hello Sadness"), when she was 19. It became an international best-seller, and was followed by *A Certain Smile* (1956). Her later novels often feature aimless people in tangled relationships. Her plays, including *Opposite Extremes* (1987), resemble her novels in their subject matter.

sage Aromatic perennial herb *(Salvia officinalis)* of the MINT family, native to the Mediterranean. Its leaves are used fresh or dried as a flavoring in many foods. The stems, 2 ft (60 cm) tall, have rough or wrinkled, downy, gray-green or whitish-green oval leaves. The flowers may be purple, pink, white, or red. Since the Middle Ages, sage tea has been brewed as a spring tonic and a stimulant believed to strengthen the memory and promote wisdom. See also Salvia.

Sage (*Salvia officinalis*).
INGMAR HOLMASEN

Sage, Russell (1816–1906) U.S. financier. Born in Shenandoah, N.Y., in 1839 he started a wholesale grocery business, which earned him enough money to start a Hudson River shipping trade. He served in Congress 1853–57. He invested successfully in the La Crosse Railroad in Wisconsin, and eventually acquired an interest in more than 40 railroads, serving as director or president of 20. He helped organize the Atlantic & Pacific Telegraph Co. In 1872 he originated stock-market puts and calls (options to buy or sell a set amount of stock at a set price and within a given time limit), but stopped dealing in them after losing $7 million in the panic of 1884.

sagebrush Any of various shrubby species of Artemisia of the Composite family. Native to semiarid plains and mountain slopes in western North America, these shrubs are adapted both to dry, hot summers and to moist, mild winters with intermittent polar Pacific winds. Common sagebrush *(Artemisia tridentata)* is a many-branched shrub, usually about 3–6.5 ft (1–2 m) high, with silvery gray, bitter-aromatic foliage.

Sager \'sā-jər\, **Ruth** (1918–1997) U.S. geneticist. Born in Chicago, she received her PhD from Columbia and later taught at Hunter College and Harvard University Questioning the traditional belief that chromosomal genes are the only apparatus for transmitting genetic information to a cell, she discovered (1953) in the alga *Chlamydomonas* the existence of a second genetic-transmitting system, a gene not located on the alga's chromosomes that controls the cell's sensitivity to the antibiotic streptomycin, and observed that both male and female *Chlamydomonas* can transmit the nonchromosomal gene.

Sagittarius \ˌsa-jə-'ter-ē-əs\ (Latin: "Archer") In astronomy, the constellation lying between Capricorn and Scorpio; in astrology, the ninth sign of the zodiac, governing approximately the period November 22–December 21. Its symbol is a centaur shooting a bow and arrow, or an arrow drawn across a bow. The association of this constellation with a mounted archer originated in Babylonia as early as the 11th century BC.

Sagittarius A Strongest source of cosmic radio waves, lying in the direction of the constellation Sagittarius. Discovered by Karl Jansky in 1932, it has been identified as the nucleus of the Milky Way galaxy. The region is relatively small and constitutes an intense source of infrared radiation thought to be emitted partly by stars and partly by dust around them. Observations indicate that the galactic nucleus contains collapsed matter in the form of a black hole with a mass 10,000–1 million times that of the sun. These properties resemble those of other active galactic nuclei but on a much smaller scale.

sago \'sā-gō\ Food starch prepared from carbohydrate material stored in the trunks of several palms, chiefly *Metroxylon rumphii* and *M. sagu*, sago palms native to Indonesia. Composed of 88% carbohydrate, sago is a basic food of the South Pacific, where it is used in meal form to prepare soups, cakes, and puddings. Elsewhere its use in cookery is mainly as a pudding and sauce thickener. In industry it is used as a textile stiffener. The thick trunk grows to 30 ft (9 m) tall in low marshy areas. At 15 years the core of the mature trunk is engorged with starchy material. If allowed to form and ripen, the fruit absorbs the starch, leaving the stem hollow and dying. Cultivated plants thus are cut down when the flower spike appears, and the starchy pith is extracted from the stems.

saguaro \sə-'wär-ə, sə-'gwär-ō\ Large, candelabra-shaped, branched cactus *(Cereus giganteus,* or *Carnegiea gigantea)* native to Mexico, Arizona, and California. Slow-growing at first, mature saguaros may eventually reach 50 ft (15 m) in height. They bloom for the first time when 50–75 years old. They may die at 150–200 years (at a weight of up to 10 tons, or 9,000 kg), most commonly by being uprooted by wind or washouts. Shallow, wide-ranging roots gather moisture from a large area of desert to support the weighty top growth. The white, night-blooming flowers, which remain open into the next day, are the Arizona state flower. The red fruits have been an important food of Native Americans.

Saguaro National Monument Mountain and desert region, southeastern Arizona. Established in 1933, it comprises an area of 124 sq mi (321 sq km), east of Tucson, Ariz., and contains forests of saguaro. Plant life also includes paloverde, mesquite trees, and ocotillo.

Saguenay River \ˌsa-gə-'nā\ River, southern central Quebec. It drains Lac St.-Jean into the St. Lawrence River at Tadoussac, northeast of Quebec city. Flowing east, it descends about 300 ft (90 m) in a turbulent stream in the first third of its 105-mi (169-km) course. Its fall is a source of hydroelectric power; its shores are in many places high cliffs 1,000–1,800 ft (300–550 m) high. It is a recreational area.

Sahara Largest tropical desert in the world, encompassing almost all of northern Africa. Covering an area of about 3,500,000 sq mi (9,065,000 sq km), it is bounded by the Atlantic Ocean, the Atlas Mtns., the Mediterranean Sea, the Red Sea, and the Sahel. It includes parts of several countries, including Morocco, Algeria, Tunisia, Libya, Egypt, Mauritania, Mali, Niger, Chad, and Sudan. Principal topographic features include large oasis depressions, extensive stony plains, rock-strewn plateaus, abrupt mountains, and sand sheets, dunes, and seas. Huge areas of it are empty, but scattered clusters of inhabitants survive in fragile ecological balance wherever vegetation or water sources occur. Sedentary living is restricted to oasis areas. See also Libyan Desert.

Saharan Arab Democratic Republic Disputed territory of Western Sahara occupied by Morocco. It was a Spanish colony from c. 1884 to 1976. After Spain left, native Saharawi guerrillas (see Polisario) based in Algeria declared a government-in-exile, and fought Morocco and Mauritania for control. Mauritania made peace in 1979, whereupon Morocco claimed the whole territory. A promised referendum on whether the territory will remain part of Morocco or to become independent continues to be postponed. See also Hassan II.

Sahel \sä-'hel\ Semiarid region, western and northern central Africa. Extending from Senegal eastward to the Sudan, it forms a transitional zone between the arid Sahara to the north and the humid savannas to the south. In the late 20th century it was afflicted by desertification and soil erosion due to overgrazing and overfarming. It suffered a devastating drought and famine in the early 1970s, and by 1973 sections of the Sahara had advanced southward as much as 60 mi (100 km). Severe drought and famine again struck in 1983–85. Despite government reforestation programs in recent decades, it continued to expand southward.

Sahibdin (fl. 17th century) Indian miniature painter. His work dominated the Mewar school of Rajasthani painting. Though he was a Muslim, Sahibdin was fully at ease with Hindu themes. He produced abstract compositions that are full of brilliant color and endowed with religious fervor. Among the important surviving examples of his paintings are a *ragamala* (musical modes) series (1628); a series on the *Bhagavata-Purana,* a scriptural text (1648); and the sixth book (*Yuddhakanda*) of the Hindu epic the *Ramayana* (1652).

Saicho \'sī-ˌchō\ *or* **Dengyo Daishi** (767–822) Monk who established the Tendai (Tiantai) sect of Buddhism in Japan. Ordained at 13, he studied in China and returned with the teachings of Tendai Buddhism, which embraced the Lotus Sutra. Unlike other Buddhist sects in Japan, it asserted that the material world could hold meaning and value and that the teachings of the Buddha are accessible to all, not just a select few. Saicho enjoyed favor with the government but often incurred the enmity of the leaders of other Japanese Buddhist sects. The monastery he built on Mount Hiei became one of the great centers of Buddhist learning.

Said \sä-'ēd\, **Edward W(illiam)** (born 1935) Palestinian-U.S. literary critic. Said was educated in Western schools in Jerusalem and Cairo before moving to the United States to attend Princeton and Harvard universities. He has taught at Columbia University since 1963. In *Orientalism* (1978), perhaps his best-known work, he examines Western stereotypes of the Islamic world and argues that Orientalist scholarship is based on Western imperialism. An outspoken proponent of Palestinian issues, he has written on the Middle East in such works as *The Question of Palestine* (1979) and *The Politics of Dispossession* (1994). His general concern is the interaction of literature and politics, which he treats in *Beginnings* (1975), *The World, the Text, and the Critic* (1983), and *Culture and Imperialism* (1993).

Said ibn Sultan \sä-'ēd-ˌib-ən-sůl-'tän\ *or* **Said Sayyid** \sä-'ēd-'sī-əd\ (1791–1856) Ruler of Muscat and Oman and of Zanzibar (1806–56), who made Zanzibar the principal power in eastern Africa and the commercial capital of the western Indian Ocean. Under Said, Zanzibar caravans were sent into central Africa to extract ivory, slaves, and other products. In 1822 he forbade his subjects to sell slaves to European traders. From 1828 he developed the islands of Zanzibar and Pemba into the world's largest clove producers, and he built up a large navy that helped expand his commercial interests.

Saigo Takamori \'sī-gō-ˌtä-kä-'mō-rē\ (1827–1877) Japanese military and political leader. A SAMURAI from the domain of SATSUMA, Saigo joined OKUBO TOSHIMICHI and KIDO TAKAYOSHI in working for the overthrow of the TOKUGAWA SHOGUNATE and the return of the emperor. He commanded the troops that seized control of the imperial palace from the shogunate, and went on to lead a campaign against the shogunate's supporters. After the Restoration, he was given command of the new Imperial Guard. In 1873 he supported a war with Korea; when this plan was cancelled, he resigned from government. He opened a military school in Kagoshima that drew to it disaffected former samurai (class distinctions had been abolished in 1871). In 1877 some of his disciples attacked a government arsenal and he found himself the unwilling head of a rebellion. It lasted for six months and resulted in some 12,000 dead on both sides, including Saigo himself. He is regarded as a tragic hero by the Japanese.

Saigon See HO CHI MINH CITY

Saikaku See IHARA SAIKAKU

sailfish Valued food and game fish in the genus *Istiophorus* (family Istiophoridae) of warm and temperate waters worldwide. It has a long, rounded spear extending from its snout but is distinguished from MARLINS and related species by its slimmer form, long pelvic fins, and especially its large, sail-like dorsal fin, which is bright blue and spotted. Deep blue above and silvery below, they grow to about 11 ft (3.4 m) long and 200 lbs (90 kg) or more. They feed mainly on other fishes. Its classification is uncertain, and one *(I. platypterus)* to several species may be recognized.

Sailfish (*Istiophorus platypterus*).

D. CORSON—SHOSTAL

sailing *or* **yachting** Sport or pastime of racing or cruising a sailboat or yacht. A modern yacht (from a Dutch word meaning "ship for chasing") is a sailboat used for racing. In the 17th century Dutch royalty sailed early yachts for pleasure; CHARLES II brought the sport to England. Organized yacht racing on the Thames began in the mid-18th century; in North America yachting began with the Dutch in New York in the 17th century and continued under the British. The first U.S. yacht clubs were founded in the mid-19th century. Sailboat races are held over two kinds of courses, point-to-point and closed. Yacht racing has been part of the OLYMPIC GAMES since 1900. The AMERICA'S CUP is the preeminent prize in yachting. See illustration opposite.

sailplane See GLIDER

Saimaa \'sī-ˌmä\, **Lake** Lake, southeastern Finland, northeast of HELSINKI. It has an area of 443 sq mi (1,147 sq km) and is the primary lake in the Great Saimaa lake system, the largest in Finland. About 120 lakes and numerous rivers and streams in the system drain most of southeastern Finland through Lake Saimaa, the Vuoksi River, and the Saimaa Canal to the Gulf of Finland. The lake system provides essential transportation links and hydroelectric power among the major towns of the region, and its scenic forests attract many tourists.

saint Holy person. In the New Testament, St. PAUL used the term to mean a member of the Christian community, but the term more commonly refers to those noted for their holiness and venerated during their lifetimes or after death. In Roman Catholicism and Eastern Orthodoxy, saints are publicly recognized by the church and are considered intercessors with God for the living. They are honored on special feast days, and their remains and personal effects are venerated as relics. Often Christian saints perform miracles in their lifetime, or miracles occur in their names after their death. In Islam, *wali* ("friend of God") is often translated as saint; in Buddhism, ARHATS and BODHISATTVAS are roughly equivalent to saints. Hindu SADHUS are somewhat similar. See also CANONIZATION.

Saint Albans Raid (October 19, 1864) Raid by Confederates in the AMERICAN CIVIL WAR. About 25 Confederate soldiers based in Canada raided the Union town of St. Albans, Vt., where they killed one man and robbed three banks. They retreated to Canada, where a pursuing U.S. posse captured several of them but was forced to surrender them to Canadian authorities. The Canadians returned the stolen money but later released the soldiers, causing strained relations between the two countries.

Saint Andrews City (pop., 1995 est.: 15,000) and seaport, FIFE region, eastern Scotland. It was formerly the ecclesiastical capital of Scotland; its religious traditions began in the 6th century AD, when St. Kenneth is believed to have formed a Celtic religious community there. It received a charter in 1160 and was one of the principal towns in Scotland in the Middle Ages. In 1472 its archbishop was recognized as the primate of Scotland, and it took part in the important events of the Scottish Reformation. A popular seaside and golfing resort, it is noted for its golf courses and for University of ST. ANDREWS.

Saint Andrews, University of Oldest university in Scotland, founded in 1411 on the outskirts of St. Andrews. The university buildings include St. Salvator's College (1450), St. Leonard's College (1512;

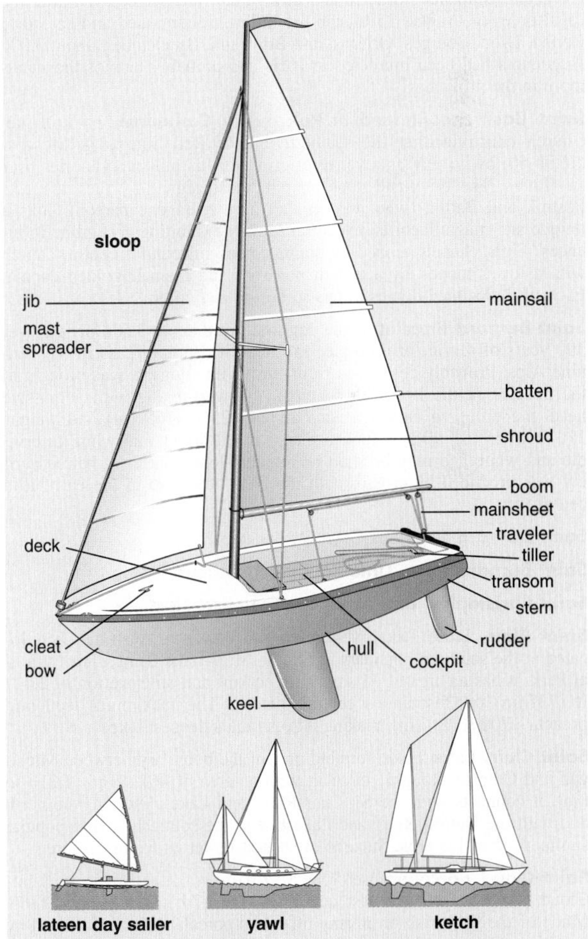

Principal parts of a simple sailboat. The weight of the keel helps the boat remain upright; the rudder provides steering control. The principal sail is called the mainsail; the jib is a smaller headsail. The shrouds are ropes that provide lateral support to the mast.

S T U V

merged with St. Salvator's in 1747), and the University Library (1612). A third college, St. Mary's (1537), has always taught theology exclusively. Total enrollment is about 5,000. The medical and dental school became independent as the University of Dundee in 1967.

Saint Augustine \'ȯ-gə-ˌstēn\ City (pop., 1992 est.: 12,000), northeastern Florida. It is the oldest continuously settled U.S. city. In 1513 JUAN PONCE DE LEON landed there, in search of the Fountain of Youth, and claimed the territory for Spain. It became part of the U.S. in 1821. The CASTILLO DE SAN MARCOS, now a national monument, is a symbol of the era of Spanish control. During the AMERICAN REVOLUTION the city was a refuge for LOYALISTS, and during the Indian Wars it was the place of imprisonment for OSCEOLA and other Seminoles. It is a winter and summer resort and a port on the ATLANTIC INTRACOASTAL WATERWAY. The economy is based on tourism and fishing.

Saint Bartholomew's Day, Massacre of (August 24–25, 1572) Murder of French HUGUENOTS in Paris by Catholics. As part of the ongoing Wars of RELIGION, CATHERINE DE MÉDICIS agreed to a plot by the Guise family (see House of GUISE) family to assassinate the Huguenot GASPARD II DE COLIGNY. When he was only wounded, Catherine feared discovery of her complicity and secretly urged faithful nobles to murder all the Huguenot leaders, who were in Paris for the wedding of the future HENRY IV. The massacre began on August 24 and spread rapidly; after the leaders had been murdered, Huguenot homes and shops were pillaged and their occupants murdered and thrown into the Seine. Even after the royal order on August 25 to stop the killing, it continued and spread to Rouen, Lyon, Bourges, Orléans, and Bordeaux. By October, about 3,000 Huguenots had been murdered in Paris and probably tens of thousands more in the provinces.

Saint Basil the Blessed *or* **Pokrovsky Cathedral** \pə-'krȯf-skē\ Church constructed at the southern end of Red Square in Moscow (1554–60) by IVAN IV as a votive offering for his military victories over the Tatars. The brick-and-stone church was designed by the architects Postnik and Barma (who may in fact have been one person). It is a unique and magnificent architectural fantasy exhibiting Byzantine influences. Eight chapels topped by onion domes surround a central church with a tower topped by a tent-shaped roof and a small golden cupola. Each of the painted domes differs in design and color.

Saint Bernard Breed of rescue dog that saved about 2,500 people over 300 years of service at a hospice in Great St. Bernard pass in the Pennine Alps. Probably descended from MASTIFF-like dogs, it was brought to the hospice in the late 17th century. A powerful dog with a massive head and drooping ears, it stands at least 25 in. (65 cm) and weighs 110–200 lbs (50–90 kg). Its dense coat is red-brown and white or brindle and white and may be short or medium-long. The long-haired variety was produced by crosses with the NEWFOUNDLAND in the early 19th century.

Saint Bernard Pass See GREAT ST. BERNARD PASS

Saint Bernard Pass, Little See LITTLE ST. BERNARD PASS

Saint Christopher and Nevis See SAINT KITTS-NEVIS

Saint Clair, Lake Lake, western central TASMANIA, Australia. It is located at the southern boundary of Cradle Mtn.–Lake Saint Clair National Park. It has an area of 11 sq mi (28 sq km) and an elevation of 2,417 ft (737 m) on Tasmania's central plateau. The maximum depth approaches 700 ft (215 m), making it Australia's deepest lake.

Saint Clair, Lake Lake, forming part of the boundary between Michigan and Ontario. Roughly circular, with an area of 467 sq mi (1,210 sq km), it connects with the St. Clair River and Lake HURON to the north and with the Detroit River and Lake ERIE to the south. It is in a popular summer recreation area. Suburbs of DETROIT lie on its western shore.

Saint-Cloud porcelain \seⁿ-'klü\ Soft-paste PORCELAIN made in Saint-Cloud, France, from the last quarter of the 17th century until 1766. Much of the yellowish or creamy off-white porcelain was influenced by late Ming Chinese white porcelain—hence the plum-blossom decoration molded in low relief and figures in the Chinese manner.

Saint Croix \'krȯi\ Largest island (pop., 1990: 50,000) of the U.S. VIRGIN ISLANDS. Located south of ST. THOMAS, it has an area of 84 sq mi (218 sq km). Its capital is Christiansted; the town of Frederiksted is the commercial center. In 1493 it was visited by CHRISTOPHER COLUMBUS, who named it Santa Cruz. In the mid-17th century it was colonized in turn by the Dutch, English, Spanish, and French. It was purchased by Denmark in 1733 and sold to the U.S. in 1917. In 1989 it was devastated by a hurricane, but recovered with U.S. aid. Tourism is the main industry; rum is distilled and exported.

Saint-Denis \ˌseⁿ-də-'nē\ City (pop., 1990: 91,000), northern France. Now a suburb of PARIS, until the mid-19th century it was only a small township centered on its famous abbey church, which had been the burial place of French kings. King DAGOBERT I founded the abbey in the 7th century and built it over the tomb of St. DENIS, patron saint of France. Abbot SUGER built there a new basilica which later transformed Western architecture from the ROMANESQUE to the GOTHIC: most late-12th-century French cathedrals, including CHARTRES, are based on that of St.-Denis. Remarkable tombs found there include those of LOUIS XII, ANNE OF BRITTANY, HENRY II, and CATHERINE DE MÉDICIS. The city is now an industrial center.

Saint-Denis \ˌsaⁿ-də-'nē\ City (pop., 1990: 101,000), capital of the French overseas department of RÉUNION, in the western Indian Ocean. It lies in a basin at the mouth of the St.-Denis River on the northern coast of the island, wedged between the ocean and a mountain rising abruptly behind it. It was originally the main port of Réunion, but an artificial harbor at Le Port, on the northwestern coast, replaced it in the 1880s. It is primarily an administrative town.

Saint Denis \ˌsānt-'den-əs\, **Ruth** *orig.* **Ruth Dennis** (1877–1968) U.S. modern-dance innovator and teacher. She was born in Newark, N.J. She was a vaudeville performer before developing her dramatic dance act based on Asian dance forms. She toured in Europe (1906–9) to wide acclaim, returning to tour in the U.S. In 1915 she and her husband, TED SHAWN, established the Denishawn dance company and school to present a new choreographic style of abstract "music visualization." She toured with the company until it disbanded in 1931 when she and Shawn separated. She founded a society of spiritual arts to study the use of dance in religion. She continued to perform, teach, and lecture into the 1960s.

Saint Elias Mountains \ˌə-'lī-əs\ Segment of the Pacific COAST RANGES, southwestern Yukon Territory and eastern Alaska. The mountains extend southeast about 250 mi (400 km) from the WRANGELL MTNS. to Cross Sound along the Canada–U.S. border. Many peaks exceed 17,000 ft (5,200 km), including Mount St. Elias (18,008 ft, or 5,489 km) high on the Canada–U.S. border, and Mount LOGAN. In 1741 VITUS BERING sighted Mount St. Elias from his ship and became the first official European discoverer of North America. The mountains contain the world's most extensive ice fields outside the polar ice caps. The southern end of the range forms part of GLACIER BAY NATIONAL PARK.

Saint Elmo's fire Glow accompanying the brushlike discharges of atmospheric electricity that usually appears as a tip of light on the extremities of such pointed objects as church towers or the masts of ships during stormy weather. It is commonly accompanied by a crackling or fizzing noise. It is commonly observed on the periphery of propellers and along the wing tips, windshield, and nose of aircraft flying in dry snow, in ice crystals, or near thunderstorms. St. Elmo is an Italian corruption of St. Erasmus, patron saint of Mediterranean sailors, who traditionally regarded St. Elmo's fire as a sign of his guardianship over them.

Saint-Exupéry \saⁿ-tāg-zǖ-pā-'rē\, **Antoine (-Marie-Roger) de** (1900–1944) French aviator and writer. He flew as a commercial, test, and military reconnaissance pilot and was a publicity attaché for Air France and a reporter. He died when he was shot down on a wartime Air Force mission over the Mediterranean. His writings exalt perilous adventure and aviation, as in the novels *Southern Mail* (1929) and *Night Flight* (1931). *Wind, Sand, and Stars* (1939) is a lyrical memoir with philosophical musings and meditations. *The Little Prince* (1943) is a child's fable for adults.

Saint Francis River River, southeastern Missouri and eastern Arkansas. Rising in southeastern Missouri and flowing south, it enters the MISSISSIPPI RIVER just above Helena, Ark., after a course of 425 mi (684 km). For part of its course it forms a portion of the Missouri–Arkansas boundary. It is navigable for 125 mi (201 km).

Saint-Gaudens \sānt-'gȯ-dᵊnz\, **Augustus** (1848–1907) U.S. (Irish-born) sculptor. Son of an Irish mother and a French father, he was brought to the U.S. in infancy and at 13 was apprenticed to a cameo cutter. He studied sculpture in New York and at the École des Beaux-Arts in Paris (1867–70), then settled in New York in 1872. Between 1880 and 1897 he executed most of the works that earned him his reputation as the foremost American sculptor of the late 19th century. His first important commission was the monument to DAVID FARRAGUT (1878–81) in New York's Madison Square Park. For Boston he produced his great relief monument to Col. Robert G. Shaw and his black Civil War regiment (1884–97). The memorial to the wife of HENRY ADAMS (1886–91) in Washington, D.C., a mysterious draped figure with a shadowed face, is often considered his greatest work.

Saint George's Town (pop., 1991 est.: 5,000), capital of Grenada, in the WEST INDIES. It lies on the island's southwestern coast, on a small peninsula. Founded by the French in 1650, it became the capital of the WINDWARD ISLANDS (1885–1958). Now a port, it exports cacao, nutmeg, mace, and bananas. It was the scene of fighting in 1983 during the military intervention in Grenada by U.S. and Caribbean forces.

Saint George's Channel Wide passage between the Irish Sea and the northern Atlantic Ocean. It extends for 100 mi (160 km) and has a minimum width of 47 mi (76 km) between Carnsore Point, Ireland, and St. David's Head, Wales. The name derives from the legend of St. GEORGE, in which he traveled to England by sea.

Saint-Germain \ˌsaⁿ-zher-ˈmaⁿ\, **Treaty of** (1919) Treaty ending WORLD WAR I between Austria and the ALLIED POWERS. Signed at Saint-Germain-en-Laye, near Paris, on September 10, 1919, it came into force on July 16, 1920. It registered the breakup of the Habsburg empire and recognized the independence of Czechoslovakia, Poland, Hungary, and the Kingdom of the SERBS, CROATS, AND SLOVENES (YUGOSLAVIA). Such areas as eastern Galicia, southern Tirol, and Trieste were also ceded by Austria. The treaty limited Austria's army to 30,000 men, dismantled the Austro-Hungarian navy, and barred the union of Austria with Germany.

Saint Gotthard Pass \ˈgä-tərd\ Mountain pass, LEPONTINE ALPS, southern Switzerland. An auto and railway route between central Europe and Italy, it lies at an elevation of 6,916 ft (2,108 m) and is 16 mi (26 km) long. Though the pass was known to the Romans, it was not generally used until the early 13th century. A long, winding auto route leads across the pass, and the St. Gotthard Tunnel extends for more than 9 mi (14 km) beneath it. The railway through the tunnel connects LUCERNE with MILAN.

Saint Helena \ˈhe-lə-nə, hə-ˈlē-nə\ Island (pop., 1991 est.: 6,000), southern Atlantic Ocean. Located 1,200 mi (1,950 km) west of Africa, it has an area of 47 sq mi (122 sq km). The capital and port is Jamestown. With Ascension Island and Tristan da Cunha Islands, it constitutes a British crown colony (119 sq mi or 308 sq km; pop., 1993 est.: 7,400). Discovered in 1502, it became a port of call for ships sailing between Europe and the East Indies. It was owned by the British EAST INDIA CO. in the 17th century; because of its remoteness, it was used as the final place of exile for NAPOLEON (1815–21). It declined in importance after the SUEZ CANAL was opened in 1869.

Saint Helens, Mt. Volcanic peak in the CASCADE RANGE, southwestern Washington. Dormant since 1857, it erupted in 1980 in one of the greatest volcanic explosions ever recorded in North America. The earthquake, eruption, and avalanche killed 60 people and thousands of animals, and 10 million trees were blown down by the lateral air blast. It was over 9,600 ft (2,925 m) tall before the eruption which reduced it to 8,366 ft (2,550 m). Further eruptions have occurred since 1980, and a dome of lava has grown in the crater. Mount St. Helens National Volcanic Monument was established in 1982.

Saint-Jean \saⁿ-ˈzhäⁿ\, **Lac** Lake, southern central Quebec. A shallow lake, it has an area of 387 sq mi (1,003 sq km) and discharges into the SAGUENAY RIVER. In the 20th century, logging operations on its feeder streams led to the establishment of large paper mills on the lake. Since 1926 the lake's seasonal fluctuations have been controlled by two hydroelectric dams. It is a tourist resort center famous for its salmon fishing.

Saint John City (pop., 1991: 75,000), southern New Brunswick. It is situated on the Bay of FUNDY, at the mouth of the ST. JOHN RIVER. The site, visited by SAMUEL DE CHAMPLAIN in 1604 and fortified in the 1630s, was occupied by the British in 1758. It was chartered as the first city in Canada in 1785. The city recovered from a disastrous fire in 1877. Its year-round ice-free harbor fostered shipping, shipbuilding, and fishing. It is the province's largest city and principal port. Industries include lumbering and pulp and paper products.

Saint John, Henry See Viscount BOLINGBROKE

Saint-John Perse \saⁿ-dzhȯn-ˈpers\ *orig.* **Marie-René-Auguste-Aléxis Saint-Léger Léger** (1887–1975) French poet and diplomat. He served in various diplomatic posts from 1914 until his dismissal by the collaborationist Vichy government in 1940. He spent the years 1940–57 in exile in the U.S. The language of his poetry, admired especially by poets for its precision and purity, is difficult, and he made little appeal to the general public. His works include *Anabasis* (1924; translated by T. S. ELIOT), *Exile* (1942), *Winds* (1946), *Seamarks* (1957), and *Birds* (1962). He was awarded the Nobel Prize in 1960.

Saint John River River, northeastern U.S. and southeastern Canada. Rising in northwestern Maine, it flows northeast to the Canadian border, then southeast to form the international boundary; in Canada, it flows through New Brunswick into the Bay of FUNDY at ST. JOHN. It is 418 mi (673 km) long. At its mouth in St. John Harbor are the "reversing falls" rapids, caused by the strong tides of the bay, which at high tide force the river to reverse its flow for several miles upstream.

Saint John's City (pop., 1991 est.: 22,000), capital of Antigua and Barbuda, West Indies. It lies on Antigua's northwestern coast. It is a resort and the island's main port, handling sugar, cotton, machinery, and lumber. Nearby Fort St. John's was damaged over the centuries (1690–1847) by earthquakes, fire and a hurricane.

Saint John's City (pop., 1996: 174,000), port, and capital of Newfoundland, on the southeastern Atlantic coast. A small fishing base from the early 16th century, it was colonized by the British in 1583. Attacked several times by the French, it was securely British from 1762 and prospered as a fishing port, despite several disastrous fires in the 19th century. It is a commercial and industrial center, a major ocean port, and the base for the province's fishing fleet. Industries include shipbuilding and fish processing. The annual regatta is one of the oldest sports events in North America. Signal Hill Historic Park memorializes several events, including GUGLIELMO MARCONI's reception of the first transatlantic wireless message from Europe (1901).

Saint Johns River River, northeastern Florida. It rises in the eastern central part of the state and flows north parallel to the coast until it turns at JACKSONVILLE to empty into the Atlantic Ocean, after a course of 285 mi (459 km). It is important for both shipping and recreation.

Saint-John's-wort Common name for plants in the family Hypericaceae, which contains 350 species of herbs or low shrubs in eight genera. The family is sometimes considered part of the family Guttiferae. The majority of species (about 300) belong to the genus *Hypericum.* Their leaves are opposite or whorled, dotted with glands, and usually have smooth margins. Several species are cultivated in temperate regions for their handsome flowers. *H. perforatum*, a showy golden flower grown in both the Old and New Worlds whose buds contain a red oil, has long been credited with magical and medicinal powers; today it is being widely used and studied for its possible efficacy against depression.

Saint-Just \saⁿ-ˈzhūest\, **Louis (-Antoine-Léon) de** (1767–1794) French Revolutionary leader. In support of the French Revolution, he wrote the radical *Esprit de la révolution et de la constitution de France* (1791) and was elected to the National Convention in 1792. A close associate of MAXIMILIEN ROBESPIERRE and a member of the COMMITTEE OF PUBLIC SAFETY, he was elected president of the Convention in 1793 and sponsored the Ventôse (March) Decrees, which confiscated property

Louis de Saint-Just, portrait after a red chalk drawing by Christophe Guérin, 1793.

BY COURTESY OF THE BIBLIOTHEQUE NATIONALE, PARIS

S T U V

of the Revolution's enemies and redistributed it to the poor. He led the victorious attack against the Austrians at Fleurus (in modern Belgium). A fanatical leader of the Reign of Terror, he was arrested in the Thermidorian Reaction and guillotined at 26.

Saint Kitts-Nevis *officially* **Federation of Saint Kitts and Nevis** *or* **Saint Christopher and Nevis** Independent nation of the Leeward Islands in the eastern Caribbean. Area: 104 sq mi (269 sq km). Population (1997 est.): 42,000. Capital: Basseterre (on St. Kitts). Most of the population is of African descent. Language: English (official). Religion: Protestantism. Currency: Eastern Caribbean dollar. The islands—Saint Kitts, Nevis, and Sombrero—are of volcanic origin, with mountain ranges rising to 3,793 ft (1,156 m). The climate is tropical, and heavy vege-

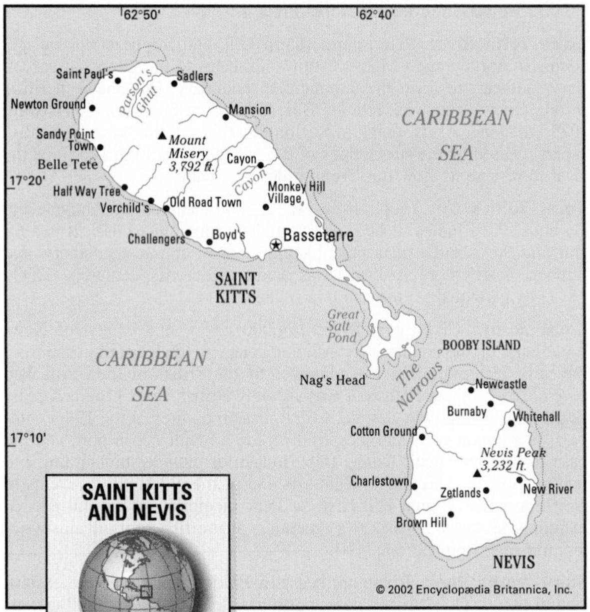

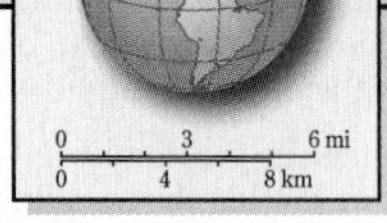

tation covers most of the mountainous interior. The economy is based on agriculture. Sugar has long been the mainstay, and tourism is also important. It is a constitutional monarchy with one legislative house; its chief of state is the British monarch represented by the governor-general, and the head of government is the prime minister. St. Kitts became the first British colony in the West Indies in 1623. Anglo–French rivalry grew in the 17th century and lasted more than a century. In 1783, by the Treaty of Versailles, the islands became wholly British possessions. They were united with Anguilla 1882–1980 but became an independent federation within the British Commonwealth in 1983. In 1997 Nevis considered becoming independent.

Saint Laurent \'sa^n-lȯ-'rä^n\, **Louis (Stephen)** (1882–1973) Prime minister of Canada (1948–57). Born in Compton, Quebec, he served in the Canadian House of Commons 1942–58 and in W.L. Mackenzie King's cabinet as minister of justice and attorney general (1942–46) and minister of external affairs (1945–48). As leader of the Liberal Party (1948), he succeeded King as prime minister. He promoted Canadian unity by equalizing provincial revenues and expanded social security and university education. He supported Canadian membership in NATO and helped establish the St. Lawrence Seaway.

Saint Laurent \sa^n-lȯ-'rä^n\, **Yves (-Henri-Donat-Mathieu)** (born 1936) Algerian-French fashion designer. He left for Paris after secondary school to pursue a fashion career and at 17 was hired as Christian Dior's assistant. When Dior died four years later, he was named head of the House of Dior. In 1962 he opened his own fashion house and quickly emerged as one of the world's most influential designers, noted especially for his popularization of women's trousers for all occasions and his extensive ready-to-wear line.

Saint Lawrence, Gulf of Deep gulf of the Atlantic Ocean, off eastern Canada. It has an area of about 60,000 sq mi (155,000 sq km). It touches the shores of half the provinces of Canada, providing a gateway to the interior of the entire North American continent. Its boundaries are the maritime estuary at the mouth of the St. Lawrence River, the Strait of Belle Isle between Newfoundland and the mainland, and Cabot Strait. It has many islands, including Prince Edward Island and the Magdalen Islands.

Saint Lawrence River River, southern Quebec and southeastern Ontario. It flows northeast out of Lake Ontario into the Gulf of St. Lawrence and is about 760 mi (1,225 km) long. It passes through the Thousand Islands and for about 120 mi (195 km) forms the boundary between New York and Ontario. Entering Quebec, it widens into Lake St. Francis, then flows past Montreal island. Below Quebec city it widens to 90 mi (145 km) at its mouth in the Gulf of St. Lawrence. Major tributaries include the Ottawa, Saguenay, Richelieu, and Manicouagan rivers, all in Canada. It links the Atlantic Ocean with the Great Lakes through the St. Lawrence Seaway.

Saint Lawrence Seaway U.S.–Canadian waterway and lock system. Located along the upper St. Lawrence River, it links the Atlantic Ocean with the Great Lakes. Its construction, carried out in 1954–59, involved clearing a 186-mi (299-km) stretch of the St. Lawrence River between Montreal and Lake Ontario. It included lakes, rivers, locks, and canals that extended for 2,340 mi (3,766 km) to connect Duluth, Minn., with the head of the Gulf of St. Lawrence. With the Great Lakes, it provides 9,500 mi (15,285 km) of navigable waterways. It allows deep-draft ocean vessels access to the Great Lakes' rich industrial and agricultural regions. It is navigable from April to mid-December.

Saint-Léon \sa^n-lā-'ō^n\, **(Charles-Victor-) Arthur (Michel)** (1821–1870) French dancer, choreographer, and violinist. He trained with his ballet-master father and toured extensively throughout Europe (1838–59), often playing the violin as he danced. He was ballet master at the Imperial Theater in St. Petersburg (1859–69); his *The Humpbacked Horse* was the first ballet based on Russian folk themes. In 1870 he became ballet master at the Paris Opera, where he choreographed his most famous ballet, *Coppélia.* He developed an early system of dance notation, which he published in 1852.

Saint Louis City (pop., 2000: 348,189), eastern central Missouri. Located on the Mississippi River, below its confluence with the Missouri River, it was founded in 1764 by the French as a trading post and was named for King Louis IX of France. It became the crossroads of westward expansion for exploring parties, fur-trading expeditions, and pioneers traveling the Santa Fe and Oregon trails. Since the 19th-century steamboat era and the arrival of the railroads in the 1850s, it has been a major transportation hub. Its diversified industries include brewing, food processing, and the manufacture of aircraft. The largest city in the state, it is home to many educational institutions, including Washington University and St. Louis University. It also features the Gateway Arch designed by Eero Saarinen.

Saint Lucia \'lü-shə\ Island nation, Windward Islands, eastern Caribbean Sea. Area: 238 sq mi (616 sq km). Population (1997 est.): 148,000. Capital: Castries. Most of the population is of African descent. Languages: English (official), French patois. Religions: Roman Catholicism, Protestantism. Currency: Eastern Caribbean dollar. St. Lucia is of volcanic origin, and its Qualibou volcano, which continues to emit steam and gases, is a prime tourist sight. Wooded mountains run north–south, culminating in Mount Gimie (3,117 ft, or 950 m). It is a constitutional monarchy with a parliament of two legislative houses; its chief of state is the British monarch represented by the governor-general, and the head of government is the prime minister. Caribs replaced early Arawak inhabitants c. AD 800–1300. Settled by the French in 1650, it was ceded to Great Britain in 1814 and became one of the Windward Islands in 1871. It became fully independent in 1979. The economy is based on agriculture and tourism. See map on following page.

Saint-Malo \sa^n-mä-'lō\, **Gulf of** Gulf of the English Channel indenting the northern coast of Brittany, France. It extends from the island of Bréhat to the peninsula of Cotentin, Normandy. It includes the rocky islet of Mont-St.-Michel. At low tide, a huge tract of land is uncovered in spring and fall at the gulf's main port, St.-Malo. The shore is lined with numerous small resorts.

S
T
U
V

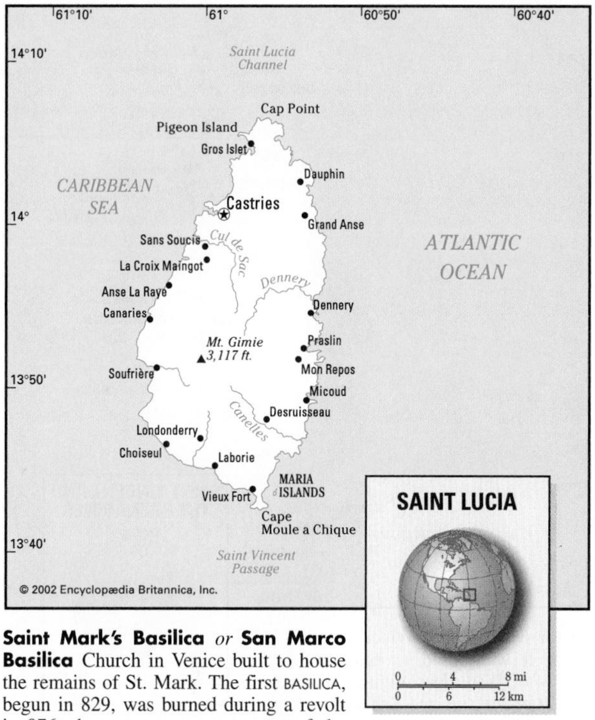

Saint Mark's Basilica *or* **San Marco Basilica** Church in Venice built to house the remains of St. Mark. The first BASILICA, begun in 829, was burned during a revolt in 976; the present structure, one of the most beautiful buildings in Europe, was completed in 1071. The plan is an Eastern symmetrical Greek cross (see CHURCH) surmounted by five domes. The design is distinctly Byzantine, and both Byzantine and Italian architects and craftsmen probably worked on it. The interior is decorated with mosaics on gold background; the floor is of inlaid marble and glass. In the restricted light their colors glow fantastically. Over the centuries, the church has benefited richly from the addition of sculpture, mosaics, and ceremonial objects.

Saint Martin *or Dutch* **Sint Maarten** Island, LEEWARD ISLANDS, eastern West Indies. Located northwest of ST. KITTS–NEVIS, it covers an area of 33 sq mi (85 sq km). Discovered by CHRISTOPHER COLUMBUS, it was divided in 1648 between the French and the Dutch. The northern section of the island (20 sq mi or 52 sq km) is a dependency of the French overseas department of GUADELOUPE; its chief town is Marigot (pop., 1990: 26,000). The island's southern section (13 sq mi or 34 sq km) is administratively part of the NETHERLANDS ANTILLES; its main town is the island's capital, Philipsburg (pop., 1990: 32,000). The island's economy is based on tourism.

Saint-Maurice River \sa^n-mō-'rēs\ River, southern Quebec. It is 325 mi (523 km) long and a major tributary of the ST. LAWRENCE RIVER, flowing south from Gouin Reservoir into the St. Lawrence at Trois Rivières. It is a major logging river, serving large pulp and paper factories at La Tuque, Grand-Mère, Shawinigan, and Trois Rivières. Since 1900 it has also been a major source of hydroelectric power.

Saint Paul City (pop., 1996 est.: 260,000), capital of Minnesota. It is in the eastern part of the state, on the MISSISSIPPI RIVER just east of MINNEAPOLIS, with which it forms the Twin Cities. In 1805 ZEBULON PIKE made an unofficial treaty there with the Dakota (Sioux) for possession of the region. First settled in 1838, it was known as Pig's Eye until 1841, when a log chapel dedicated to St. Paul was built there. It became the capital of the Minnesota Territory in 1849 and of the state in 1858. It was important in the development of the upper Midwest because of its location on the Mississippi and its rail links, which promoted its livestock market. It is a major transportation, commercial, and industrial center with diversified manufactures, including automobiles, electronic equipment, and food products. Educational institutions include Macalaster and Concordia colleges, among others.

Saint Paul River River, western Africa. Rising in southeastern Guinea, its upper reach forms part of the border between Guinea and Liberia. It enters Liberia north of Gbarnga and discharges into the Atlantic Ocean after a southwesterly course of about 280 mi (450 km). Navigable for 18 mi (29 km) upstream, the river and its major tributaries drain much of Liberia and Guinea. Two arms of the river enclose Bushrod Island, site of the port of MONROVIA.

Saint Paul's Cathedral Cathedral of the Church of England in London. The present building is a domed church of great openness designed in a restrained, classical baroque style by CHRISTOPHER WREN and constructed (1675–1710) of Portland stone. It replaced Old St. Paul's, destroyed in the Great Fire of 1666. The interior is characterized by ironwork and woodcarving by master craftsworkers. The majestic dome, set on a colonnaded drum, rises 365 ft (111 m). The superbly detailed cathedral that Wren built bears only a slight resemblance to the Classical-Gothic design that had been accepted; why this is so remains a mystery.

Saint Peter's Basilica Present church of St. Peter's in Rome, begun by Pope JULIUS II in 1506 and completed in 1615. It is the church of the popes and one of the world's largest churches. It was built to replace Old St. Peter's, erected by Constantine over Peter's traditional burial place. According to the original plan of DONATO BRAMANTE, it was to take the form of a Greek cross around a central dome. Successive architects, including RAPHAEL, drew fresh plans after Bramante's death, modifying the original Greek-cross plan to a Latin cross. ANTONIO DA SANGALLO THE YOUNGER returned to Bramante's symmetrical plan. MICHELANGELO, who followed da Sangallo, nearly completed the drum for the massive dome before his death. Pope Paul V (r.1605–21) then insisted on a longitudinal plan for liturgical reasons, and adopted the plan of Carlo Maderno (1556–1629), which extended the nave to the east. GIAN LORENZO BERNINI added the elliptical piazza, lined by colonnades, that serves as the approach to the basilica. The interior is filled with Renaissance and baroque masterpieces, including Michelangelo's Pietà and Bernini's BALDACHIN, statue of St. Longinus, tomb of Urban VIII, and bronze Throne of St. Peter.

Saint Petersburg *Russian* **Sankt-Peterburg** \'sȧnkt-,p^{y}ə-t^{y}ər-'bu̇rk\ *formerly (1914–24)* **Petrograd** *or (1924–91)* **Leningrad** City (pop., 1996 est.: 4,200,000) and port, northwestern Russia. Located on the delta of the NEVA RIVER where it enters the Gulf of Finland, it is Russia's second-largest city after MOSCOW. Founded by PETER I (Peter the Great) in 1703, it was the capital of the Russian empire from 1712 to 1917. It was the scene of the DECEMBRIST REVOLT in 1825, and the BLOODY SUNDAY attack on workers in the RUSSIAN REVOLUTION OF 1905. The original center of the BOLSHEVIK revolution (see RUSSIAN REVOLUTION OF 1917), it lost its capital status to MOSCOW in 1918. In World War II it underwent a seige by German forces (September 1941–January 1944), during which as many as one million people died (see Siege of LENINGRAD). From 1990 a reformist city council and mayor helped swing the country from Communist control. It is a cultural, educational, and industrial center and Russia's largest seaport. Industries include engineering, printing, manufacturing, and shipbuilding. One of Europe's most beautiful cities, it is intersected by many canals and crossed by more than 600 bridges; it is the site of many palaces, cathedrals, museums (see HERMITAGE), and historical monuments.

Saint Petersburg City (pop., 1996 est.: 236,000), western central Florida. It is near the tip of Pinellas Peninsula, adjacent to TAMPA BAY. Settled in 1876, it became in the late 1940s one of the first Florida cities to encourage tourists to spend their retirement years there. It is a winter resort and a center for yachting and sport fishing. It is connected by bridges to the city of TAMPA and the mainland and with a string of sand-reef island resorts known as the Holiday Isles.

Saint-Pierre and Miquelon \'sānt-'pir...'mi-kə-,län *French* se^n-'pyer-ā-mē-'klō^n\ French overseas territorial collectivity (pop., 1993 est.: 6,000). It consists of two islands in the Atlantic Ocean off the southern coast of Newfoundland. Miquelon has an area of 83 sq mi (215 sq km). St.-Pierre, with an area of 10 sq mi (26 sq km), is the administrative and commercial center; almost 90% of the population live there. First settled by seafarers from western France early in the 17th century, the islands changed hands several times between France and Britain until an 1814 treaty made French possession final. They were classified as a French territory in 1946, a department in 1976, and a territorial collectivity in 1985. The economy is based on cod fishing.

Saint-Saëns \sa^n-'sä^{n}s\, **(Charles) Camille** (1835–1921) French composer. Astonishingly gifted from childhood, with a phenomenal memory (at his debut piano recital at 11, he offered to play any Beethoven sonata without music), he became a darling of the salons and a celebrated improviser. To promote new music by French composers, he founded the Société Nationale de Musique in 1871. His compositions are often brilliant in their effects but not always profound. Of his 13 operas, *Samson et Dalila* (1877) had the greatest success. He wrote five piano concertos, three symphonies (including the "Organ" Symphony), two cello concertos, and three violin concertos; his tone poem *Danse macabre* (1874) and the suite *Carnival of the Animals* (1886) are widely known.

Saint-Simon \sa^n-sē-'mō^n\, **(Claude-) Henri (de Rouvroy, comte) de** (1760–1825) French social theorist. He joined the French army at 17 and was sent to aid the colonists in the American Revolution. After his return to France (1783), he made a fortune in land speculation but gradually dissipated it. He turned to the study of science and technology as the solution to society's problems, and wrote *On the Reorganization of European Society* (1814) and (with AUGUSTE COMTE) *Industry* (1816–18), in which he envisioned an industrialized state directed by modern science. In *The New Christianity* (1825), he stated that religion should guide society toward improving life for the poor. His disciples helped influence the rise of CHRISTIAN SOCIALISM.

Henri de Saint-Simon, lithograph by L. Deymaru, 19th century.

BBC HULTON PICTURE LIBRARY

Saint Thomas Chief island (pop., 1990: 48,000), U.S. VIRGIN ISLANDS. Located east of Puerto Rico, it covers an area of 32 sq mi (83 sq km). The capital, CHARLOTTE AMALIE, has a well-sheltered harbor. Sighted in 1493 by CHRISTOPHER COLUMBUS, St. Thomas was colonized first by the Dutch (1657) and then by the Danish (1666). After 1673, when slavery was introduced, the island became one of the chief Caribbean sugar producers and a major slaving center. Falling sugar prices after 1820, and the abolition of slavery in 1848, led to a decrease in profits. The U.S. bought St. Thomas for use as a naval base in 1917. The chief industry is tourism.

Saint Vincent, Cape Cape, southwesternmost point of Portugal. To the Greeks and Romans it was known as Promontorium Sacrum (Sacred Point) because of a shrine there. Pastoralism and fishing are the economic mainstays of the region. Near Sagres, the main settlement, was the town of Vila do Infante, where c. 1420 Prince HENRY THE NAVIGATOR established a naval observatory and school for navigators. Many naval battles have taken place off the cape.

Saint Vincent, Gulf Triangular inlet of the Indian Ocean. It is located on the southeastern coast of South Australia, between Yorke Peninsula and the mainland. About 90 mi (145 km) long and 45 mi (73 km) wide, it is linked to the ocean by Investigator Strait and Backstairs Passage. KANGAROO ISLAND lies across its entrance, and Port Adelaide (pop., 1991: 38,000), South Australia's leading port, is on its eastern side.

Saint Vincent and the Grenadines \'gre-nə-ˌdēnz\ Island nation, WINDWARD ISLANDS in the eastern Caribbean. It is comprised of St. Vincent island and the northern GRENADINES. Area: 150 sq mi (388 sq km). Pop. (1997 est.): 112,000. Capital: KINGSTOWN. Most of the population is of African descent. Languages: English (official), French patois. Religion: Protestantism. Currency: Eastern Caribbean dollar. The islands are composed of volcanic rock. Thickly wooded volcanic mountains run north–south and are cut by many swift streams. Mount Soufrière (4,048 ft, or 1,234 m), the highest of the mountains, has had devastating volcanic eruptions. Agriculture is the mainstay of the economy, and export crops include bananas and arrowroot. Tourism is also important. It is a constitutional monarchy with one legislative house; its chief of state is the British monarch represented by the governor-general, and the head of government is the prime minister. The French and the British contested for control of St. Vincent until 1763, when it was ceded to England by the Treaty of PARIS. The original inhabitants, the CARIBS, recognized British sovereignty but revolted in 1795. Most of the Caribs were deported; many who remained were killed in volcanic eruptions in 1812 and 1902. In 1969 St. Vincent became a self-governing state in association with the United Kingdom, and in 1979 it achieved full independence.

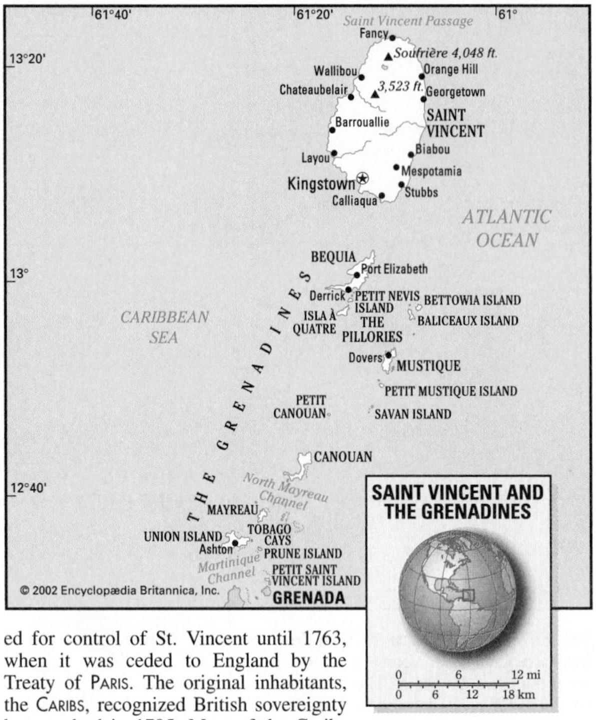

Sainte-Beuve \sa^{n}t-'bœ̄v\, **Charles-Augustin** (1804–1869) French literary historian and critic. In 1825 he began contributing critical articles to periodicals. In essays collected in *Critiques et portraits littéraires* (1832–39) and *Portraits contemporains* (1846), he developed a new approach to critiquing living writers that involved extensive biographical research to understand their mental attitudes. His famous *Causeries du lundi* ("Monday Chats"), published in newspapers 1849–69, were detailed, well-rounded literary studies in which he applied historical frames of reference to contemporary writing.. His methods revolutionized French criticism by freeing it from personal prejudice and partisan passions. His *Port-Royal* (1840–48) is a scholarly history of an abbey and of 17th-century France.

Saintsbury, George (Edward Bateman) (1845–1933) English literary historian and critic. When the school at which he was teaching failed in 1876, he decided to write for a living. He produced several successful volumes of criticism of French literature and extensive writings on English literature. Though he formulated no philosophy of criticism, his works were influential because they combined authoritative scholarship with the popular appeal of entertaining prose. They include *A History of Criticism and Literary Taste in Europe from the Earliest Texts to the Present Day* (1900–4), one of the first surveys of critical literary theory and practice.

Saipan \sī-'pan, sī-'pän\ Island (pop., 1990: 39,000), NORTHERN MARIANA ISLANDS, in the western Pacific Ocean. It has an area of 47 sq mi (122 sq km). Its chief settlement, Chalan Kanoa, is the Northern Marianas' commonwealth center. Ruled by Spain 1565–1899, it then passed to Germany 1899–1914. It was a Japanese mandate 1920–44, then was captured after fierce fighting by U.S. forces in World War II. It was the headquarters of the U.S.-administered U.N. Trust Territory of the PACIFIC ISLANDS (terminated 1990). Copra is the island's chief product.

Saïs \'sā-is\ Ancient Egyptian city. Located in the Nile Delta on the Canopic, or Rosetta, branch of the NILE RIVER, it was from prehistoric times, the site of the chief shrine of NEITH, goddess of war and the loom. It became the capital of Egypt under Psamtik I (r.664–609 BC). His successors of the 26th dynasty also had their capital there. Enriched by Mediterranean and African trade, the Saite kings built fine temples, palaces, and tombs. Inscribed stones found on the site and in nearby villages are all that remain of the once-great city.

Saivism See SHAIVISM

saivo \'sī-ˌvü\ One of the SAMI regions of the dead, where the deceased lead happy lives with their families and ancestors, acting in every way as they did on earth. In Norway the saivo world was thought to exist in the mountains, whereas in Finland it was usually believed to be under special double-bottomed lakes. These localities were regarded as sacred and as sources of power that could be used by the SHAMAN, or NOAIDE. When the noaide wished to go into a trance, he would ask his guardian spirits from the saivo to aid him.

Sakakura \ˌsä-kä-'kü-rä\, **Junzo** (1904–1969) Japanese architect. He was one of the first to combine 20th-century European architecture with traditional Japanese elements. His first outstanding East-West blend was the Japanese pavilion at the 1937 World Exposition in Paris. He worked in the Paris office of LE CORBUSIER (1931–36), and was known as Le Corbusier's leading advocate in Japan. His major works include the Museum of Modern Art in Kamakura (1951) and Shinjuku Station Square and Odakyu Department Store in Tokyo (1964–67).

sake \'sä-kē\ Japanese ALCOHOLIC BEVERAGE made from fermented RICE. It dates to at least the 3rd century AD. Sake is light in color and non-carbonated, with a sweet flavor; its alcohol content is about 18% by volume. Often mistakenly called a wine, sake is closer in its method of manufacture to BEER. Steamed rice is combined with a mold that converts the rice STARCH to fermentable sugars; the mix is kneaded into a paste, twice fermented (with fresh rice and water added), filtered, and bottled. In Japan, where it is the national beverage and the traditional drink of the SHINTO gods, sake is warmed in a small earthenware or porcelain vessel before being blessed and served in small porcelain cups.

Sakha See YAKUT

Sakhalin \ˌsä-kä-'lēn\ Island, extreme eastern Russia. Together with the KURIL ISLANDS, it forms an administrative region (pop., 1995: 648,000) of Russia. It is 589 mi (948 km) long, 16–100 mi (26–161 km) wide, and covers an area of 28,597 sq mi (74,066 sq km). Sakhalin was first settled by Russians in 1853, and it came under Russian control in 1875 when Japan ceded it in exchange for the Kuril Islands. Japan held the southern part 1905–1945, then ceded it and the Kurils to the U.S.S.R. The economy is dominated by fishing, lumbering, coal mining, and the extraction of oil and natural gas in the north.

Sakharov \'sä-k̲ə-ˌrȯf\, **Andrey (Dmitriyevich)** (1921–1989) Russian nuclear physicist and human-rights advocate. He worked with I. Y. Tamm (1895–1971) to develop the Soviet Union's first hydrogen bomb, but in 1961 he opposed NIKITA KHRUSHCHEV's plan to test a 100-megaton hydrogen bomb in the atmosphere. In 1968 he published in the West "Progress, Coexistence, and Intellectual Freedom," which called for nuclear-arms reduction and criticized Soviet repression of dissidents. He and his wife, Yelena G. Bonner, continued to advocate civil liberties and reform in the Soviet Union. In 1975 Sakharov received the Nobel Peace Price but was forbidden to travel to Oslo to receive it. In 1980 he was exiled to the closed city Gorky (now Nizhniy Novgorod); his wife was exiled there in 1984. They were released in 1986 and returned to Moscow. Sakharov's honors were restored in 1989, and many of his causes became official policy under MIKHAIL GORBACHEV.

Saki \'sä-kē\ *orig.* **H(ector) H(ugh) Munro** (1870–1916) Scottish writer. A journalist early in his career, he wrote political satires and worked as a foreign correspondent before settling in London in 1908. His comic short stories and sketches, which satirize the Edwardian social scene, were published in *Reginald* (1904), *Reginald in Russia* (1910), *The Chronicles of Clovis* (1911), and *Beasts and Super-Beasts* (1914); the best-known include "Tobermory" and "The Open Window." Studded with epigrams and with well-contrived plots, his stories reveal a vein of cruelty and a self-identification with the enfant terrible. He was killed in action in World War I.

Sakkara See SAQQARA

sakti See SHAKTI

Saktism See SHAKTISM

Sakyamuni \'säk-yə-ˌmu̇-nē\ Epithet of the BUDDHA Gautama meaning "sage of the Sakyas." The Sakyas were a clan into which the Buddha was born a prince; their kingdom covered an area that is today in southern Nepal and part of what is now northern UTTAR PRADESH, India.

Saladin \'sa-lə-dᵊn\ *in full* **Salah al-Din Yusuf ibn Ayyub** (1137/8–1193) Kurdish sultan of Egypt, Syria, Yemen, and Palestine and founder of the AYYUBID DYNASTY. Though as a youth he preferred religious to military studies, he began his military career under his uncle. On his uncle's death Saladin ordered Shawar, the powerful vizier of the Egyptian FATIMID DYNASTY, assassinated, and became vizier of Egypt. In 1171 he abolished the Shiite Fatimid caliphate and announced a return to Sunni Islam. From 1174, as sultan of Egypt and Syria, he succeeded in uniting Egypt, Syria, northern Mesopotamia, and Palestine. His reputation as a generous and virtuous but firm ruler rekindled Muslim resistance to the crusaders. In 1187, turning his full strength against the Latin crusader kingdoms, he retook Jerusalem from the crusaders after 88 years. Whereas the Christian conquest had been marked by slaughter, Saladin's troops demonstrated courteous and civilized behavior. His victory deeply shocked the West and led to the call for the Third CRUSADE (1189–92), which matched him against RICHARD I; their stalemate resulted in a peace that gave the crusaders only a small strip of land from Tyre to Yafo (Jaffa). Saladin is considered one of the greatest of Muslim heroes.

Salado River \sä-'lä-t͟hō\ River, eastern Argentina. It flows through the PAMPAS, generally southeast for about 400 mi (640 km) to the Atlantic Ocean, where it empties, southeast of BUENOS AIRES. Before 1800 it marked the frontier between Spanish colonization to the northeast and indigenous Indians to the southwest.

Salamanca *ancient* **Salmantica** *or* **Helmantica.** City (pop., 1994 est.: 167,000), western Spain. An important Iberian settlement, it was sacked by HANNIBAL in 217 BC. It later became a Roman station. Captured by Moors in the 8th century, it was reconquered by Christians 1087–1102. It was occupied by the French in the PENINSULAR WAR. It is a cultural center as well as the commercial center of an agricultural district. Its many landmarks include the 12th-century Romanesque cathedral, the Gothic-style cathedral (begun 1513), and the University of Salamanca (founded 1218).

salamander Any member of about 400 species in 10 AMPHIBIAN families (order Caudata), commonly found in freshwater and damp woodlands, principally in temperate regions of the Northern Hemisphere. Salamanders are generally nocturnal, short-bodied, 4–6 in. (10–15 cm) long, and brightly colored. They have a tail; two pairs of limbs of roughly the same size; moist, smooth skin; teeth on the jaws and roof of the mouth; and, usually, internal fertilization. The largest species, the Chinese giant salamander *(Andrias davidianus),* is 5 ft (1.5 m) long. Salamanders eat insects, worms, snails, and other small animals, including members of their own species. See also HELLBENDER, NEWT.

Salamander (*Salamandra terrestris*).
JACQUES SIX

Salamis \'sa-lə-məs\ Ancient city, Cyprus. Located on Cyprus' eastern coast, it had an active trade with PHOENICIA, EGYPT, and CILICIA. According to tradition, it was founded by Teucer, a hero of the TROJAN WAR. A major Hellenic center during the struggles between Greece and Persia, it was the scene of a Greek naval victory in 449 BC, and again in 306 BC when DEMETRIUS I POLIORCETES defeated PTOLEMY I SOTER of Egypt. It was visited later by Sts. PAUL and Barnabas. Under the Byzantine empire it was known as Constantia after Constantius II rebuilt it AD 337–61. It was abandoned after its destruction by the Arabs in 647–48.

Salamis, Battle of (480 BC) Battle in the PERSIAN WARS, the first great naval battle ever recorded. The Greeks, with about 370 TRIREMES led by THEMISTOCLES, lured the Persian fleet of about 800 GALLEYS into the narrow strait between the island of Salamis and the Athenian port of Piraeus, where they sank about 300 vessels while losing only about 40 of their own. XERXES had to postpone his planned land offensive, giving the Greek city-states time to unite against him.

Salan \sá-'lä^{n}\, **Raoul (-Albin-Louis)** (1899–1984) French military officer who sought to prevent Algerian independence. During a military career in which he became the French army's most decorated soldier, he served in France and French West Africa (1941–44), Indochina (1945–53), and Algeria (1956–62). Rebelling against Charles de Gaulle's decision to free Algeria, in 1961 he formed a right-wing extremist group, which terrorized France and Algeria before his eventual capture (1962) and trial for treason.

Salazar \ˌsa-lə-'zär\, **António de Oliveira** (1889–1970) Portuguese prime minister (1932–68). A professor of economics, he was appointed by Antonio Carmona as finance minister (1928) and later prime minister (1932). His new constitution established the authoritarian New State, curtailing political freedom and concentrating on economic recovery, and he thenceforth ruled as a virtual dictator. Sympathetic to Francisco Franco and the Axis Powers, he maintained Portugal's neutrality in World War II. He greatly improved the country's transportation, utilities, and education systems. He fought to preserve Portugal's African colonies after the general decolonization. Incapacitated by a stroke in 1968 after 36 years in power, he was not told when he was replaced as prime minister.

Salé \sa-'lā\ *Arabic* **Sla** \'slä\ City (metro. area population with Rabat, 1994: 1,386,000), northwestern Morocco. Located at the mouth of the Bou Regreg River, opposite Rabat, it was founded in the 10th century, and reached its peak as a medieval merchant port. After 1627 Salé, with Rabat as its vassal, became the corsair republic of Bou Regreg and the base for the Sallee Corsairs, the most dreaded of the Barbary Coast pirates. The two cities grew together until the Bou Regreg silted up and Salé port was closed. It has many mosques and mausoleums; its greatest shrine is the tomb of Sidi Abd Allah ibn Hasan, the city's patron saint.

Salem City (pop., 1996 est.: 123,000), capital of Oregon. It lies along the Willamette River, southwest of Portland. Founded in 1840, the town prospered as migration increased over the Oregon Trail. It became the state capital in 1859. It was an early river port whose growth was stimulated by rail connections in the 1870s. It is a food-processing center for a dairy and fruit-growing area, and has wood and light manufacturing industries.

Salem witch trials (May–October 1692) American colonial persecutions for witchcraft. In the town of Salem, Massachusetts Bay Colony, several young girls, stimulated by supernatural tales told by a West Indian slave, claimed to be possessed by the devil and accused three women of witchcraft. Under pressure, the accused women named others in false confessions. Encouraged by the clergy, a special civil court was convened with three judges, including Samuel Sewall, to conduct the trials. They resulted in the conviction and hanging of 19 "witches" and the imprisonment of nearly 150 others. As public zeal abated, the trials were stopped and then condemned. The colonial legislature later annulled the convictions.

Salerno City (pop., 1994 est.: 144,000), southern Italy. Located on the Gulf of Salerno, it was founded by the Romans in 197 BC on the site of an earlier town. Part of a Lombard duchy from AD 646, it was the capital of an independent Lombard principality 839–c. 1076. Then it was conquered by the Norman Robert Guiscard and became his capital. It later became part of the kingdom of Naples. In World War II, its coast was the scene of a major battle (September 1943) between Allied landing forces and the Germans. It is an active seaport in an industrial area; its landmarks include a medical school (the earliest in Europe, probably founded in the 9th century) and the cathedral (845, rebuilt 1076–85), which contains the tombs of St. Matthew and Pope Gregory VII.

sales tax Levy imposed on the sale of goods and services. A sales tax on the manufacture, purchase, sale, or consumption of a specific commodity is known as an excise tax. Though excise taxes have been used since ancient times, the general sales tax is a comparatively recent innovation. Sales taxes are ad valorem taxes, imposed "according to the value" (i.e., monetary value) of the taxable commodity. They are classified according to the levels of business activity at which they are imposed—production, wholesale, or retail. They account for significant portions of the revenue of most U.S. states and Canadian provinces. In Western Europe a variation of the sales tax, the value-added tax, is widely used. Most sales taxes are borne by the consumer, since even where they are levied on production or wholesale goods, part or all of the cost is shifted to the consumer in the form of higher prices. Because sales taxes at the retail level are regressive taxes, essential goods such as food, clothing, or drugs are sometimes exempted. See also progressive tax, income tax.

Salesbury \'sālz-ˌber-ē\, **William** (c. 1520–1584?) Welsh lexicographer and translator. He spent most of his life at Llanrwst, Wales, following antiquarian, botanical, and literary pursuits. His collection of Welsh proverbs, *The Whole Sense of a Welshman's Head* (1546), may be the first book printed in Welsh. Salesbury compiled the first Welsh-English dictionary (1547) and, with Richard Davies, translated the New Testament into Welsh (1567).

Salgado, Sebastião (born 1944) Brazilian photojournalist. Born in Aimorés, Brazil, Salgado briefly pursued a career as an economist before switching his focus to photography in 1971. Over the next decade Salgado photographed stories such as the famine in Niger and the civil war in Mozambique. In 1979 he joined the prestigious Magnum Photos cooperative for photojournalists, and two years later he gained prominence as a result of his photograph of John Hinckley's attempt to assassinate President Ronald Reagan. By the mid-1980s Salgado devoted himself almost entirely to long-term projects that told a story through a series of images, often focusing on the homeless and downtrodden. Among his critically acclaimed books of photographs are *Other Americas* (1986), *Workers* (1993), and *Migrations: Humanity in Transition* (2000).

salicylic acid \ˌsa-lə-'si-lik\ White, crystalline solid organic compound used chiefly to make aspirin and other pharmaceutical products, including methyl salicylate (oil of wintergreen, for medicines and flavorings), phenyl salicylate (for sunburn creams and pill coatings), and salicylate (a cutaneous fungicide). It and certain derivatives occur naturally in some plants, particularly species of *Spiraea* and *Salix* (willow). Large amounts are used in producing certain dyes.

Salieri \säl-'yer-ē\, **Antonio** (1750–1825) Italian composer. He moved to Vienna in 1766 with Florian Gassmann (1729–1774), and remained there most of his career. On Gassmann's death, he became composer and conductor of the Italian opera at the imperial court, and later court kapellmeister (1788). Vienna's most popular opera composer for much of the last quarter of the 18th century, he had many important students, including Ludwig van Beethoven, F. Schubert, and F. Liszt. In addition to his more than 40 operas, he wrote much other secular and sacred music. Though he and W.A. Mozart were rivals, there is no basis to the story that he poisoned Mozart, and it is unlikely that he claimed to have done so on his deathbed or earlier.

Salinas \sə-'lē-nəs\ City (pop., 1996 est.: 112,000), western California. Located in the Salinas valley east of Monterey, it was a crossroads on El Camino Real, the old Spanish trail between San Diego and San Francisco. It was settled in 1856 and became a cattle center. The arrival of the Southern Pacific Railroad in 1868 stimulated agricultural development. It was the birthplace of John Steinbeck, who often referred to it in his books, especially in *East of Eden*.

Salinas (de Gortari) \sä-'lē-näs\, **Carlos** (born 1948) President of Mexico (1988–94). Son of a Mexican senator, Salinas earned a PhD in economics at Harvard University and held various governmental posts until he was elected president in 1988 by a slim margin; vote fraud was widely charged. He pursued a program of economic retrenchment and privatization, selling off hundreds of inefficient state-owned corporations and spending part of the proceeds on infrastructure and social services. In 1991–92 his government conegotiated the North American Free Trade Agreement. The economic collapse immediately following his term made him the target of bitter criticism. The assassination of his party's nominee as his successor was linked to Salinas's associates, and Salinas fled to the U.S. and eventually Ireland. His brother Raúl, widely suspected of extensive corruption, was convicted in 1999 of complicity in another assassination.

Salinger \'sa-lin-jər\, **J(erome) D(avid)** (born 1919) U.S. writer. Born in New York City, he began to publish short stories in periodicals in 1940. After World War II his stories, some based on his army experiences, appeared increasingly in the *New Yorker*. His entire literary output comprises 13 stories and novellas—collected in *Nine Stories* (1953), *Franny and Zooey* (1961), and *Raise High the Roof Beam, Carpenters, and Seymour: An Introduction* (1963)—and *The Catcher in the Rye* (1951), a novel of adolescent anguish that won great critical and popular admiration, especially among college students. He retreated into a mysterious seclusion in New Hampshire and ceased to publish. A 1998 memoir by a woman who had pursued a relationship with him as a 19-year-old brought unwelcome notoriety.

Salisbury See HARARE

Salisbury, Earl of See Robert CECIL

Salisbury \'sȯlz-bə-rē\, **Harrison E(vans)** (1908–1993) U.S. author and journalist. Born in Minneapolis, he was a reporter with United Press (1930–48) before joining the *New York Times,* where he won a 1955 Pulitzer Prize. He later held editorial positions with the *Times,* rising to associate editor (1972–74). The first Western journalist to visit Hanoi during the Vietnam War, he wrote eyewitness accounts that contributed to skepticism in the U.S. about the war's purpose. His 29 books include 10 on Russia and six on China.

Salisbury, Marquess of *orig.* **Robert Arthur Talbot Gascoyne-Cecil** (1830–1903) British prime minister (1885–86, 1886–92, 1895–1902). He served in BENJAMIN DISRAELI's government as secretary for India (1874–78) and foreign secretary (1878–80), helping to convene the Congress of BERLIN. He led the Conservative Party opposition in the House of Lords, then became prime minister on three occasions beginning in 1885, usually serving concurrently as foreign secretary. He opposed alliances, maintained strong national interests, and presided over an expansion of Britain's colonial empire, especially in Africa. He retired in 1902 in favor of his nephew, ARTHUR JAMES BALFOUR.

Salishan languages \'sā-li-shən\ Family of about 23 North American Indian languages, spoken or formerly spoken in the Pacific Northwest and adjoining areas of Idaho, Montana, and southern British Columbia. Today Salishan languages are spoken almost exclusively by older adults. They are remarkable for their elaborate consonant inventories and small number of vowels. Grammatically, all words except for particles tend to assume predicative function, so there is no clear demarcation between nouns and verbs.

saliva Thick, colorless fluid constantly present in the mouth, composed of water, mucus, proteins, mineral salts, and amylase, an enzyme that breaks down starches. One to two liters are produced daily by the SALIVARY GLANDS. Small amounts are continually discharged into the mouth, but the presence, smell, or even thought of food increases flow. Saliva's main function is to keep the inside of the mouth moist, making speech more fluid, dissolving food molecules for taste, and easing swallowing. It also helps control the body's water balance, since lack of it stimulates thirst when water intake has been low. Saliva reduces dental CARIES and infection by removing food debris, dead cells, bacteria, and white blood cells.

salivary gland \'sal-ə-ˌver-ē\ Any of the organs that secrete SALIVA. Three pairs of major glands secrete saliva into the mouth through distinct ducts: the parotid glands (the largest), between the ear and the back of the lower JAW; the submaxillary glands, along the side of the lower jaw; and the sublingual glands, in the floor of the mouth near the chin. There are also numerous small glands in the tongue, palate, lips, and cheeks. The presence, smell, or thought of food normally increases secretion.

Saljuq dynasty See SELJUQ DYNASTY

Salk \'sȯk\, **Jonas (Edward)** (1914–1995) U.S. physician and researcher. Born in New York City, he received his MD from New York University Working with other scientists to classify polio virus, he confirmed earlier studies that identified three strains. He showed that killed virus of each strain could induce antibody formation without producing disease. Salk's vaccine was released for use in the U.S. in 1955. From 1963 he directed the Salk Institute in La Jolla, Cal. He was awarded the Presidential Medal of Freedom in 1977.

Sallé \sȧ-'lā\, **Marie** (1707–1756) French dancer and choreographer. She made her debut at the Paris Opera in 1721. In London and Paris, she performed in a new expressive, dramatic style that later was championed as the *ballet d'action* by J.-G. NOVERRE. With *Pygmalion* (1734), she became the first woman to choreograph a ballet in which she danced, and also the first to discard the traditional restrictive costume for a muslin dress. Her rivalry with MARIE CAMARGO led her to appear more frequently in London, where she danced in several of G.F. HANDEL's opera ballets. She retired from the Paris Opera in 1740.

Sallust \'sa-ləst\ *Latin* **Gaius Sallustius Crispus** (86?–35/34 BC) Roman historian. Sallust probably had military experience before taking political office during the strife of the 50s. He began to write after his political career ended c. 45 BC, becoming one of the great Latin literary stylists, noted for his narrative writings about political personalities, corruption, and party rivalry. His works, whose influence pervades later Roman historiography, are *Catiline's War* (43–42 BC), dealing with corruption in Roman politics; *The Jugurthine War* (41–40), exploring party struggles in Rome in the late 2nd century BC; and *Histories*, of which only fragments remain.

salmon Name that originally referred to the ATLANTIC SALMON *(Salmo salar)* and now also refers to six species of Pacific salmon (genus *Oncorhynchus,* family Salmonidae): CHUM, CHINOOK, PINK, and SOCKEYE salmon; COHO; and the cherry salmon *(O. masu)* of Japan. Adult salmon live at sea, then migrate, fighting rapids and leaping high falls, to the stream where they hatched to spawn. Pacific salmon die soon after spawning; many Atlantic salmon live to spawn again. See also TROUT.

Salmon River River, central Idaho. It flows northeast past the town of Salmon, where it is joined by the Lemhi River, and then northwest to join the SNAKE RIVER south of the Idaho–Oregon–Washington border. It is about 420 mi (676 km) long. It is the largest tributary of the Snake and flows through an extensive wildlife area of national forests.

salmon trout See LAKE TROUT

salmonella \ˌsal-mə-'ne-lə\ Any of the rod-shaped, gram-negative, non-oxygen-requiring BACTERIA that make up the genus *Salmonella.* Their main habitat is the intestinal tract of humans and other animals. Some of the 2,200 species exist in animals without causing disease; others are serious pathogens. Any of a wide range of mild to serious infections caused by salmonellae are called salmonellosis, including TYPHOID and paratyphoid fever in humans. Refrigeration prevents their reproduction but does not kill them; as a result, many salmonellae can develop in foods, which, when eaten, can cause GASTROENTERITIS. Chickens are major reservoirs of salmonella, and chicken and eggs are the principal source of human poisoning, whose symptoms include diarrhea, vomiting, chills, and painful headaches. Other food sources include unpasteurized milk, ground meat, and fish.

salmonellosis \ˌsal-mə-ˌne-'lō-səs\ Any of several bacterial infections caused by SALMONELLA, including TYPHOID and similar fevers and GASTROENTERITIS (see FOOD POISONING). Meat from diseased animals carries the BACTERIA, and any food can pick it up from infected feces in the field or during storage, or from contaminated food or utensils during food preparation. The source is often hard to trace. Eggs from infected hens can carry it within, not just on the shells. Onset is sudden and sometimes severe, with nausea, vomiting, diarrhea, prostration, and low fever. Most patients recover within days, with some degree of immunity. Prevention requires care in food handling, especially thorough cooking.

Salome \sə-'lō-mē, 'sa-lə-(ˌ)mā\ Stepdaughter of HEROD ANTIPAS, who caused the death of JOHN THE BAPTIST. The event is recounted in the gospels of Matthew and Mark, though her name is given only by the historian JOSEPHUS. John had been imprisoned for denouncing Herod's adulterous marriage to Herodias, but Herod was afraid to kill him. When Salome, daughter of Herodias, danced before the king, he promised to give her anything she asked as a reward, and she requested John's head on a platter. The scene was a popular subject in Christian art.

Salomon \'zä-lō-mȯn\, **Erich** (1886–1944) German photographer. He studied law at the University of Munich but soon abandoned his practice to pioneer in photojournalism. He specialized in photographing heads of state in unguarded moments at international conferences and social gatherings. His purpose was to show the human qualities of world leaders, who up to that time had been stereotyped in stiff formal portraits. Of Jewish extraction, he went into hiding in Holland during World War II but was caught and died at the AUSCHWITZ death camp.

Salomon \'sa-lə-mən\, **Haym** (1740–1785) Polish-American patriot and financier. Forced to flee Poland for his revolutionary activities, he arrived in New York in 1772 and soon became a successful merchant and financier. A supporter of the colonists in the American Revolution, he was arrested and imprisoned by the British. In 1778 he escaped to Philadelphia, where he opened a brokerage office. He made loans totaling over $600,000 to help finance the new government, gave interest-free private loans to JAMES MADISON, THOMAS JEFFERSON, JAMES MONROE, and others, and obtained French loans to the American government.

Salon \sȧ-ˈlōü\ Official exhibition of art sponsored by the French government. It originated in 1667 when LOUIS XIV sponsored an exhibit of the works of the members of the Royal Academy of Painting and Sculpture. The Salon derives its name from the exhibition's location in the Salon d'Apollon of the Louvre Palace. After 1737 it became an annual event, and in 1748 the jury system of selection was introduced. During the French Revolution, the Salon was opened to all French artists, though academicians continued to maintain near-total control over the teaching and exhibition of art through most of the 19th century. In 1881 the new Société des Artistes Français began to oversee the Salon, and with the growing importance of independent exhibitions of the works of avant-garde artists, it gradually lost its influence and prestige.

Salon des Indépendants \sȧ-ˈlō^{n}-dā-za^{n}-dā-pä^{n}-ˈdä^{n}\ Annual unjuried exhibition of the Société des Artistes Indépendants, held in Paris since 1884. Organized as a second SALON DES REFUSÉS, it was established in response to the rigid traditionalism of the official government-sponsored SALON. Its first show exhibited works by PAUL CEZANNE, PAUL GAUGUIN, HENRI DE TOULOUSE-LAUTREC, VINCENT VAN GOGH, and GEORGES SEURAT. By 1905 HENRI ROUSSEAU, PIERRE BONNARD, HENRI MATISSE, and the Fauves had all exhibited there.

Salon des Refusés \sȧ-ˈlō^{n}-dā-rə-fue̅-ˈzā\ Art exhibition held in 1863 in Paris by command of NAPOLEON III for those artists whose works had been refused by the jury of the official SALON. Among the exhibitors were CAMILLE PISSARRO, HENRI FANTIN-LATOUR, JAMES M. WHISTLER, and EDOUARD MANET, whose scandalous *Le déjeuner sur l'herbe* was officially regarded as an affront to taste.

Salonika See THESSALONÍKI

salsa (Spanish: "sauce") Contemporary Latin-American dance music. Salsa developed in Cuba in the 1940s, drawing on local musical styles such as *charanga* (featuring primarily strings and flute) and the dance music of the *conjuntos* (bands), which included vocals, trumpet, and African percussion instruments, and blending in elements of jazz. In the 1950s salsa began to flourish in New York, where it incorporated traditional Puerto Rican rhythms, and later elements from Venezuelan and Colombian music and RHYTHM AND BLUES as well. Its stars have included C. CRUZ, T. PUENTE, and Willie Colon.

salsify \ˈsal-sə-fē, ˈsal-sə-ˌfī\ *or* **oyster plant** *or* **vegetable oyster** Biennial herbaceous plant *(Tragopogon porrifolius)* of the COMPOSITE FAMILY, native to the Mediterranean. The thick white taproot is cooked as a vegetable and tastes somewhat like oysters. The plant has purple flowers and narrow leaves whose bases usually clasp the stem. Goatsbeard, or meadow salsify *(T. pratensis),* is a weedy European species, naturalized in North America, that has a large yellow flower head. It is occasionally cultivated as an ornamental, and its leaves, flowers, and roots are sometimes eaten in salads.

Flower of goatsbeard (*Tragopogon pratensis*).
LOUISE K. BROMAN FROM ROOT RESOURCES

salt Chemical COMPOUND formed when the hydrogen of an ACID is replaced by a METAL or its equivalent, such as ammonium (NH_4). Typically, an acid and a BASE react to form a salt and water. Most inorganic salts ionize (see ION) in water solution. SODIUM CHLORIDE—common table salt—is the most familiar salt; sodium bicarbonate (BICARBONATE OF SODA), SILVER NITRATE, and calcium carbonate are others.

SALT *in full* **Strategic Arms Limitation Talks** Negotiations between the U.S. and the Soviet Union aimed at curtailing the manufacture of strategic nuclear missiles. The first round of negotiations began in 1969 and resulted in a treaty regulating ANTIBALLISTIC MISSILES and freezing the number of intercontinental ballistic missiles and submarine-launched ballistic missiles. It was signed by LEONID BREZHNEV and RICHARD NIXON in 1972. A second round of talks (SALT II, 1972–79) addressed the asymmetry between the two sides' strategic forces and ended with an agreement to limit strategic launchers (see MIRV). It was signed by Brezhnev and JIMMY CARTER; though never formally ratified by the U.S. Senate, its terms were observed by both sides. Subsequent negotiations took the name Strategic Arms Reduction Talks (START). See also INTERMEDIATE-RANGE NUCLEAR WEAPONS, NUCLEAR TEST-BAN TREATY.

Salt, Titus *later* **Sir Titus** (1803–1876) British manufacturer. He took over the family textile factories in 1834, and soon developed machinery for using coarse Russian wool and discovered a method of manufacturing fabrics from ALPACA wool (1836). In 1853 he created one of the first planned industrial communities, the model manufacturing town of Saltaire (near Bradford, West Yorkshire).

salt dome Largely subsurface geologic structure that consists of a vertical cylinder of SALT embedded in horizontal or inclined strata. In the broadest sense, the term includes both the core of salt and the strata that surround and are "domed" by the core. Major accumulations of oil and NATURAL GAS are associated with salt domes in the U.S., Mexico, the North Sea, Germany, and Romania; domes along the Gulf Coast contain large quantities of SULFUR. Salt domes are also major sources of salt and potash on the Gulf Coast and in Germany, and they have been used for underground storage of liquefied propane gas. Storage "bottles," made by drilling into the salt and then forming a cavity by subsequent solution, have been considered as sites for disposal of radioactive wastes.

Salt Lake City City (pop., 2000: 181,743), capital of Utah. Located on the Jordan River, near the southeastern end of GREAT SALT LAKE, it was founded in 1847 by BRIGHAM YOUNG and a group of 148 MORMONS as a refuge from religious persecution. It was known as Great Salt Lake City until 1868. It prospered from rail connections to become a hub of western commerce, and became the state capital in 1896. The largest city in the state, it lies at an altitude of 4,390 ft (1,338 m). It is a commercial center for nearby mining operations and has diversified manufacturing industries. As the headquarters of the Mormon Church of Jesus Christ of Latter-day Saints, it influences the social, economic, political, and cultural life of the state and region. It is the site of the Mormon Temple and Tabernacle. It was the host city of the 2002 Winter Olympic Games.

Salt River River, eastern central Arizona. A tributary of the GILA RIVER, it is formed at the confluence of the Black and White rivers. It flows west 200 mi (320 km) and empties into the Gila River southwest of PHOENIX. It is part of the COLORADO RIVER drainage basin. A system of dams forms a chain of lakes that provide hydroelectric power. In pre-Columbian times, the river valley was cultivated by HOHOKAM Indians, who constructed systems of irrigation canals.

Salta City (metro. area pop., 1991: 371,000), northwestern Argentina. It lies in the irrigated Andean valley of Lerma, on a headstream of the SALADO RIVER. Founded in 1582 as San Felipe de Lerma, it was the scene of the defeat of the Spanish royal forces in 1813 during the Argentine war of independence. The economy is based on farming, lumbering, stock raising, and mining. It is a tourist center with nearby thermal springs, and has grown in importance as a center of archaeological investigations of pre-Columbian Indian cultures, including the INCA.

saltbox CLAPBOARD house of the original New England settlers having two stories in front, a single story in the rear, and a double-sloped roof that is longer over the rear section. It arose from the tradition of locating the kitchen in a lean-to behind the house; the roof was simply extended over the lean-to, creating the characteristic long-in-back silhouette.

Saltillo \säl-ˈtē-yō\ City (pop., 1990: 441,000), capital of COAHUILA state, northeastern Mexico. Founded in 1575, it was the first Spanish settlement in the area. In 1824–36 it was the capital of a vast province that included what is now Texas and other areas of the American Southwest. It is now a commercial, communications, and manufacturing center; its products include woolen fabrics, knitted goods, and flour. Gold, silver, lead, and coal are mined in the nearby mountains. At an elevation of 5,246 ft (1,599 m), it has a cool, dry climate that has made it a summer resort.

Salton Sea Saline lake, southeastern California. The area that is now the lake was a salt-covered sink or depression about 280 ft (85 m) below sea level until 1905–6, when diversion controls on the COLORADO RIVER broke below the California–Mexico border and floodwaters rushed north, filling the depression. In 1907 a line of protective levees was built to prevent further deepening of the depression. The lake has an area of 344 sq mi (890 sq km). Its surface is now about 235 ft (72 m) below sea level, and its salinity is similar to that of seawater. Part of a state recreation area, it has swimming, boating, and camping facilities.

saltpeter *or* **niter** Transparent, colorless, or white powder or crystals of POTASSIUM NITRATE, found native in deposits. It is a strong oxidizing agent (see OXIDATION-REDUCTION), used in fireworks, EXPLOSIVES, matches, fertilizers, glassmaking, steel TEMPERING, and food curing; as a reagent; and as an oxidizer in solid rocket propellants. The term is also used for sodium nitrate (Chile saltpeter) and calcium nitrate (lime saltpeter), both of which are used in the NITRIC-ACID industry and as fertilizers, and for ammonium nitrate (Norway saltpeter), a high explosive and fertilizer.

Saluda River \sə-'lü-də\ River, western central South Carolina. Rising in the BLUE RIDGE MTNS., in northern and southern forks that join northwest of Greenville, the main stream flows southeast past Pelzer. After a course of about 145 mi (232 km), it joins the Broad River at COLUMBIA, S.C., to form the Congaree River. The name Saluda is of Indian origin, probably meaning "river of corn."

saluki \sə-'lü-kē\ Breed of HOUND whose ancestors may date to 7000 BC. It was sacred to the Egyptians, who called it the "royal dog of Egypt" and used it to hunt gazelle. Keen-sighted and hardy, it resembles a GREYHOUND, with long ears and silky coat. Colors can be solid white, tan, or reddish brown or a combination of black, tan, and white. It stands 18–28 in. (46–71 cm) and weighs 45–60 lbs (20–27 kg).

Salvador *or* **Bahia** City (pop., 1991: 2,070,000), port, and capital of BAHIA state, northeastern Brazil. Located at the southern tip of a peninsula that separates All Saints Bay from the Atlantic Ocean, it is one of Brazil's oldest cities, and was founded in 1549 as the Portuguese colonial capital. At the center of the sugar trade along the bay, it became a prize for pirates, and the Dutch captured it briefly in 1624. Retaken by the Portuguese, it became a major center for the African slave trade. It has grown continuously since 1940, and its port is one of the nation's finest. Important industries include food and tobacco processing, ceramics, and shipbuilding.

salvation In religion, deliverance from fundamentally negative conditions, such as suffering, evil, death, or SAMSARA, or the restoration or elevation of the natural world to a higher, better state. Eastern religions tend to stress self-help through individual discipline and practice, sometimes over the course of many lifetimes, though in MAHAYANA Buddhism BODHISATTVAS and certain buddhas may act as intervening divine agents. In Christianity, JESUS is the source of salvation and faith in his saving power is stressed. Islam emphasizes submission to God. Judaism posits collective salvation for the people of Israel.

Salvation Army International Christian charitable movement. It was founded in 1865 by WILLIAM BOOTH, with the aim of feeding and housing the poor of London. He adopted the name Salvation Army in 1878 and established the organization on a military pattern. Members are called soldiers, and officers earn ranks that range from lieutenant to brigadier. Converts are required to sign Articles of War and to volunteer their services. Doctrines are similar to those of other evangelical Protestant denominations, though Booth saw no need for SACRAMENTS. The meetings are characterized by singing and hand clapping, instrumental music, personal testimony, free prayer, and an open invitation to repentance. Headquartered in London, the Salvation Army now provides a wide variety of social services in more than 100 countries.

salvia \'sal-vē-ə\ Any of about 700 species of herbaceous and woody plants that make up the genus *Salvia,* in the MINT family. Some members (e.g., SAGE) are important as sources of flavoring. Easy to propagate, transplant, and grow in poor soil and drought conditions, salvias are a garden staple. Best known is the 1–3-ft (30–90-cm) annual scarlet sage *(S. splendens)* from Brazil, whose blazing spikes contrast with dark-green, oval leaves from midsummer to frost. Blue sage *(S. farinacea),* of southwestern North America, is a favorite in dried winter bouquets.

Salween River \'sal-ˌwēn\ *Chinese* **Nu** River, S.East Asia. Rising in eastern Tibet, it flows generally south for about 1,500 mi (2,400 km) through YUNNAN province, China, and eastern Myanmar, emptying into the Gulf of Martaban of the ANDAMAN SEA at Moulmein. In its lower course, it forms the frontier between Myanmar and Thailand for about 80 mi (130 km). The longest river in Myanmar, it is navigable by small craft in certain sections, but dangerous rapids hinder its use as a major waterway.

Salyut \sȧl-'yüt\ Any of a series of seven Russian SPACE STATIONS (of two designs) that served as scientific laboratories and living quarters in earth orbit for the crews aboard several SOYUZ spacecraft. Soyuz craft and Progress cargo ferries routinely rendezvoused and docked with Salyut to transfer cosmonauts and supplies to the space station. Salyut 1, launched in 1971, was the world's first space station but orbited too low and reentered earth's atmosphere within six months. Salyut 7, launched in 1982, was succeeded by MIR.

Salzburg *ancient* **Juvavum** City (pop., 1991: 144,000), northern central Austria. Located on the Salzach River, it began as a Celtic settlement and later became the site of a Roman town. It was made a bishopric by St. BONIFACE in 739 and was raised to an archbishopric in 798. Its archbishops became princes of the HOLY ROMAN EMPIRE in 1278; it became the seat of their powerful ecclesiastical principality. A music center for centuries, it was the birthplace of W.A. MOZART; the annual Salzburg Festival is held there. Notable buildings include Renaissance and baroque houses, archepiscopal palaces, and a 17th-century cathedral.

sama \sȧ-'ma\ In SUFISM, the practice of listening to music, chanting, and dancing as a means of producing a state of religious ecstasy and mystical trance. Practitioners hold that music prepares the soul for a deeper comprehension of divine realities and a better appreciation of divine music. God, as the source of beauty, is taken to be approachable through these activities because they contain or exemplify beauty. It is stressed that music is only a means to approach the spiritual realm, and strong ascetic training is required to ensure that music so employed does not arouse base instincts.

samadhi \sə-'mä-dē\ State of intense concentration or absorption of consciousness, the product of meditation. In Hinduism, it is achieved through YOGA, in which the consciousness is absorbed in the object of meditation. In Buddhism, samadhi is the result of mind-development as distinct from insight-development (see VIPASSANA), and is attainable by non-Buddhists as well as Buddhists. In ZEN Buddhism, samadhi allows the meditator to overcome dualistic subject–object awareness through unity with the object of meditation.

Samar \'sä-ˌmär\ Island (pop., 1990: 1,247,000), eastern central part of the Philippines. The third-largest after LUZON and MINDANAO, it is one of the VISAYAN ISLANDS and has an area of 5,050 sq mi (13,080 sq km). Occupied by the Japanese in 1942, it was retaken by the U.S. in 1944. The rugged interior is sparsely settled; permanent settlements are generally coastal. Coconuts and abaca are the main cash crops. The island is well forested, and there are logging and sawmill operations on the eastern coast.

Samara \sə-'mä-rə\ *formerly (1935–91)* **Kuybyshev** \'kü-ē-bə-shəf\ City (pop., 1996 est.: 1,200,000) and river port, eastern Russia. Located on the left bank of the VOLGA RIVER where the Samara River joins the Volga, it was founded in 1586 as a fortress protecting the Volga trade route. It was the scene of the rebellion of YEMELYAN PUGACHOV against CATHERINE II in 1773–74. It later became a major trade center. Its growth was stimulated during World War II by the relocation there of numerous government functions when MOSCOW was threatened by German attack. It is one of Russia's industrial cities, and the center of a network of pipelines. Oil and petrochemicals are the major industries.

Samaria \sə-'mar-ē-ə\ Central region, ancient Palestine. Extending for about 40 mi (65 km) north–south and 35 mi (56 km) east–west, it was bounded by GALILEE, JUDAEA, the Mediterranean Sea, and the JORDAN RIVER. Ancient Shechem (near modern Nablus) was the region's crossroads and political center until the Assyrian conquest of Israel in the 8th century BC. The town of Samaria, its capital, was built by King Omri c. 880 BC. It was taken by SARGON II c. 724–721 BC and its inhabitants were transported into captivity. It was rebuilt by King HEROD THE GREAT, who renamed it Sebaste in honor of the Roman emperor AUGUSTUS (Greek, *Sebastos*). In AD 6 the region became part of the Roman province of Judaea.

Samaritans Inhabitants of SAMARIA in ancient Palestine. Samaria was home to Jews who were not deported in 722 BC when the Assyrians conquered Israel, and Jews who returned to the homeland refused the help of these people, later identified as Samaritans, in rebuilding the

Temple of JERUSALEM. In the 4th century BC, the Samaritans built their own temple in Nablus (now in Jordan), where a small remnant of the community lives today. They speak Arabic but pray in Hebrew. The dislike of Jews for Samaritans was the background of the parable of the Good Samaritan (Luke 10:25–37).

Samarqand *or* **Samarkand** \ˌsä-mər-ˈkänd\ City (pop., 1998 est.: 388,000), eastern central Uzbekistan. One of the oldest cities in central Asia, it was known as Maracanda in the 4th century BC. It was captured by ALEXANDER THE GREAT in 329 BC. From the 6th century AD it was ruled successively by the Turks, Arabs, and Samanids of Iran and was an important point on the SILK ROAD from China to Europe until its destruction by GENGHIS KHAN in 1220. It became the capital of the empire of TIMUR (Tamerlane) c. 1370; he made it the most important economic and cultural center in the region. The old city contains several medieval buildings. It became a provincial capital of the Russian empire in 1887. It expanded considerably during the Soviet period.

samba Ballroom dance of Brazilian origin, popular in the U.S. and Europe in the 1940s. Danced to music in 4/4 time with a syncopated rhythm, the dance is characterized by simple forward and backward steps and tilting, rocking body movements. In Brazil, an older African type of samba is also danced in circles or double lines as a type of group dance. For decades the samba has dominated Brazilian popular music.

Sambhar Lake \ˈsäm-bər\ Salt lake, eastern central RAJASTHAN state, India. Located west of JAIPUR, it is about 90 sq mi (230 sq km) in area and is India's largest lake. The soluble sodium compounds stored in the lake's underlying silt have accumulated by the evaporation of water brought down by annual river flooding. Salt sheets, which from a distance resemble snow, cover the lake's bed; it is usually dry in the hot months.

Samhain See HALLOWEEN

Sami \ˈsȧ-mē\ *or* **Lapp** Descendants of ancient nomadic peoples who inhabited northern Scandinavia. They may be Paleo-Siberian or alpine peoples from central Europe. Reindeer hunting was the basis of their life from earliest times; herding was the basis of their economy until recently. They became nomadic a few centuries ago. The three Sami languages, mutually unintelligible, are sometimes considered dialects of one language of the FINNO-UGRIC branch of the Uralic family. Today they number about 30,000.

samizdat \ˈsä-mēz-ˌdät\ System whereby literature suppressed by the Soviet government was clandestinely written, printed, and distributed; also, the literature itself. Samizdat began appearing in the 1950s, first in Moscow and Leningrad, then throughout the Soviet Union. It typically took the form of carbon copies of typewritten sheets that were passed from reader to reader. The subjects included dissident activities, protests addressed to the regime, transcripts of political trials, analyses of socioeconomic and cultural themes, and even pornography. Samizdat disappeared when media outlets independent of the government emerged in the early 1990s.

Samkara See SANKARA

Samkhya \ˈsəŋ-kyä, ˈsəm-kyä\ One of the six orthodox systems (DARSHANS) of Indian philosophy. It adopts a consistent DUALISM between matter and soul (see PRAKRITI AND PURUSHA), which are sufficient to account for the existence of the universe; it does not hypothesize the existence of a god. Samkhya also makes a thoroughgoing distinction between psychological and physical functions on the one hand and pure "personhood" on the other.

Samnites Ancient warlike tribes of the mountainous center of southern Italy. They were probably related to the SABINES. Originally allies of Rome against the Gauls (354 BC), they later fought three wars against the Romans (343–341, 316–304, 298–290). Though defeated, the Samnites later helped PYRRHUS and HANNIBAL in their wars against Rome. They also fought in the SOCIAL WAR and unsuccessfully took part in the civil war against SULLA (82 BC).

Samoa *officially* **Independent State of Samoa** *formerly* **Western Samoa** Independent state, southern central Pacific Ocean, northeast of New Zealand. Area: 1,093 sq mi (2,831 sq km). Population (2001 est.): 179,000. Capital: APIA (on Upolu Island). The people are mainly Polynesian, closely akin to Tongans and to New Zealand's MAORIS. Languages: Samoan and English (both official). Religion: Christianity. Currency: tala. Samoa is part of the Samoan archipelago and consists of two major islands, Upolu and Savai'i, both of which are volcanic. There are also seven small islands, two of which, Apolima and Manono, are inhabited. It has a developing economy based mainly on agriculture, with some light manufacturing, fishing, lumbering, and tourism. It is a constitutional monarchy with one legislative house; the chief of state is the head of state, and the head of government is the prime minister. Polynesians inhabited the islands for thousands of years before they were visited by Europeans in the 18th century. The islands were contested by the U.S., Britain, and Germany until 1899, when they were divided between the U.S. and Germany. In 1914, Western Samoa was occupied by New Zealand, which received it as a League of Nations mandate in 1920. After World War II, it became a U.N. trust territory administered by New Zealand and achieved independence in 1962. In 1997, the word Western was dropped from the country's name.

Samoa, American See AMERICAN SAMOA

Samori Ture *or* **Samory Touré** \sä-ˈmȯr-ē-tü-ˈrā\ (c. 1830–1900) Muslim reformer and military adventurer. A member of the MALINKE people, Samori in 1868 proclaimed himself a religious chief and led a band of warriors in establishing a chiefdom in the Kankan region of Guinea. He fought the French in 1883, 1886, and 1891, managing to expand into the Sudan, but was ultimately forced to transfer his kingdom to the upper Ivory Coast. Captured in 1898, he died two years later.

Sámos \ˈsä-ˌmōs\ Island (pop., 1991: 42,000) in the Aegean Sea, Greece. It is located off the western coast of Turkey, from which it is separated by Samos Strait. Wooded and mountainous, it has an area of 184 sq mi (476 sq km). Settled by the IONIANS in the 11th century BC, it was a leading commercial center of Greece by the 7th century BC. It was noted for its cultural achievements, especially in sculpture, during the 6th-century-BC reign of POLYCRATES. Ruled successively by Persia, Athens, Sparta, Rome, Byzantium, and Turkey, it was annexed to Greece in 1912. The island is fertile and produces wine, olives, fruit, cotton, and tobacco.

Samoyed *or* **Samoyede** \ˈsa-mə-ˌyed\ Breed of sturdily built, husky-like dog developed in Siberia, where SIBERIAN PEOPLES kept it as a sled dog, companion, and herd dog for their reindeer. It has erect ears, dark almond-shaped eyes, and a characteristic "smile." Its long, heavy coat is white, cream-colored, grayish yellow (biscuit), or white-and-biscuit. It stands 19–24 in. (48–60 cm) and weighs 50–65 lbs (23–30 kg). Gentle, loyal, and intelligent, it makes a capable guard and a good companion.

Samoyed.
SALLY ANNE THOMPSON—EB INC.

sampo \ˈsäm-pȯ\ In Finnish mythology, a mysterious object that has been variously identified but is typically believed to be a cosmological pillar that supports the vault of heaven. Because it is the axis around which the heavens revolve, all life is dependent on it as the source of all good. In one legend, the creator-smith Ilmarinen forged the sampo for Louhi, the hag-goddess of the underworld, and then stole it back, resulting in its near-destruction. In the *KALEVALA*, sampo is a magic mill that grinds out an endless supply of salt, gold, and meal for its possessor.

Sampras, Pete (born 1971) U.S. tennis player. Born in Washington, D.C., he learned tennis after moving to southern California. He is a five-time U.S. Open champion (1990, 1993, 1995–96, 2002), seven-time Wimbledon champion (1993–95, 1997–2000), and two-time Australian Open champion (1994, 1997). In 2002 he won his fifth U.S. Open men's singles trophy, setting a world record of 14 Grand Slam victories. He is known for his high-powered serves, accurate volleys, and unassuming demeanor.

Sampson, William T(homas) (1840–1902) U.S. naval officer. Born in Palmyra, N.Y., he graduated from Annapolis and served in the Civil War. He was superintendent of the U.S. Naval Academy 1886–90, and chief of the ordnance bureau 1893–97. In the Spanish–American War he commanded the Atlantic squadron in its blockade of the Spanish fleet at Santiago de Cuba (1898). When the Spanish tried to escape from the harbor, his squadron destroyed the fleet. Though he had outlined the battle plans, he was absent on shore during the battle. Credited with the victory, he was promoted to rear admiral.

samsara \səm-'sär-ə, səŋ-'sär-ə\ In BUDDHISM and HINDUISM, the endless round of birth, death, and rebirth to which all conditioned beings are subject. Samsara is conceived as having no perceptible beginning or end. The particulars of an individual's wanderings in samsara are determined by KARMA. In Hinduism, MOKSHA is release from samsara. In Buddhism, samsara is transcended by the attainment of NIRVANA. The range of samsara stretches from the lowliest insect (sometimes the vegetable and mineral kingdoms are included) to BRAHMA, the highest of the gods.

samskara \səm-'skär-ə, səŋ-'skär-ə\ In HINDUISM, any of the personal sacraments traditionally observed at every stage of life, from the moment of conception to the scattering of one's funeral ashes. The observance of the samskaras is based on custom and on such texts as the PURANAS, and differs considerably according to region, CASTE, or family. The most generally accepted list of 16 traditional samskaras includes ceremonies for conception, a male birth, name-giving, the UPANAYANA, and marriage. There is also a body of noncanonical samskaras performed by and for the benefit of women.

Samson Israelite warrior hero of the OLD TESTAMENT Book of Judges. His mother had been told by an angel that she would bear a son whose life would be dedicated to God and whose hair must never be cut. Samson performed many powerful acts, including slaying a lion and moving the gates of GAZA. When he revealed to a Philistine woman, Delilah, that his hair was the source of his strength, she shaved his head while he was sleeping, leaving him powerless. He was blinded and enslaved by the PHILISTINES, but later his strength was restored and he pulled down the pillars of a temple where 3,000 Philistines had gathered, killing them and himself.

Samuel (c. 11th century BC) OLD TESTAMENT prophet, the first after MOSES and the last of the judges of ancient Israel. His story is told in two biblical books (1 and 2 Samuel) that relate the history of Israel in the 11th–10th century BC. During this period, the first monarchy of Israel was established and the tribes of Israel united under a single kingdom with its capital at Jerusalem. Samuel received a revelation that led to the installation of SAUL as king, but later announced an oracle rejecting Saul and secretly anointed DAVID as king. Scholars dispute whether the historical Samuel was the author of the two books that bear his name.

Samuel (died 1014) Czar of Western Bulgaria (980–1014). Ruling originally in Macedonia, he conquered Serbia, northern Bulgaria, Albania, and northern Greece. He revived the Bulgarian patriarchate and in the 980s defeated BASIL II. However, his struggle with the Byzantines continued until 1014, when Basil defeated Samuel's army at the Battle of Belasitsa. At Basil's order, the 15,000 Bulgarian prisoners were blinded and then returned to Samuel, who is said to have died of shock.

Samuel, Herbert Louis *later* **Viscount Samuel (of Mount Carmel and of Toxteth)** (1870–1963) British politician. A social worker in the London slums, he entered the House of Commons in 1902, where he effected legislation that established juvenile courts and the Borstal system for youthful offenders. As postmaster general (1910–14, 1915–16), he nationalized the telephone system. Appointed the first British high commissioner for Palestine (1920–25), he improved the region's economy and promoted harmony among its religious communities. He led the Liberal Party 1931–35; after being made viscount (1937), he led the Liberals in the House of Lords 1944–55. As president of the British (later Royal) Institute of Philosophy (1931–59), he wrote such popular works as *Practical Ethics* (1935) and *Belief and Action* (1937).

Samuelson, Paul (Anthony) (born 1915) U.S. economist. Born in Gary, Ind., he received his PhD from Harvard. He taught at MIT from 1940, becoming an emeritus professor in 1986. His *Foundations of Economic Analysis* (1947) outlines a basic theme of his work, the universal nature of consumer behavior as the key to economic theory. His studies included the dynamics of economic systems, analyses of public goods, welfare economics, and public expenditure. His most influential work was perhaps his mathematical formulation of multiplier and accelerator effects and, in consumption analysis, his development of the theory of revealed preference. His classic *Economics* (1948) is the best-selling U.S. economics textbook of all time. For his fundamental contributions to nearly all branches of economics, he became in 1970 the third person to be awarded the Nobel Prize in Economics.

samurai Member of the Japanese warrior class. In early Japanese history, culture was associated with the imperial court and warriors were looked down on. The samurai became important with the rise in private estates (SHOEN), which needed samurai protection. Their power increased, and when MINAMOTO YORITOMO established the KAMAKURA SHOGUNATE (1192–1333), they became the ruling class. They were characterized by an ethic of discipline, stoicism, and service (see BUSHIDO). Samurai culture developed further during the ASHIKAGA SHOGUNATE (1338–1573). During two centuries of peace under the TOKUGAWA SHOGUNATE (1603–1867), they were largely transformed into civil bureaucrats. As government employees, they received a fixed stipend that was worth less and less in the flourishing merchant economy of the 18th–19th century in Edo (Tokyo) and Osaka. By the mid-19th century, lower-ranking samurai, eager for societal change and anxious to create a strong Japan in the face of Western encroachment, overthrew the shogunal government in the MEIJI RESTORATION of 1868. Feudal distinctions were abolished in 1871. Some samurai rebelled (see SAIGO TAKAMORI) but most threw themselves into the modernization of Japan. See also DAIMYO, HAN.

San *formerly* **Bushmen** Group of peoples now living mainly in and around the KALAHARI DESERT region of southern Africa. San languages belong to the KHOISAN family. Two well-known San groups are the *!*Kung (Ju/'Hoansi) and the G/wi. Traditional San society centers on the nomadic BAND of related families. San shelters are semicircular structures of branches, twigs, and grass; their equipment is portable, their possessions few and light. They have traditionally hunted using bows and snares, and gathered wild vegetables, fruits, and nuts. Numbering about 50,000, most have been restricted, because of historical and political factors, to harsh, semiarid areas, and work for wages on European farms or serve other Africans, notably the TSWANA.

San \'sán\, **Saya** *orig.* **Ya Gyaw** (1876–1931) Burmese political leader. A Buddhist monk, physician, and astrologer in Siam and Burma, he joined an extreme nationalist group dedicated to organizing peasant discontent. Claiming the throne of Burma, he had himself crowned in 1930 and initiated an anti-British revolt in the Tharrawaddy district. The rebels, armed only with spears and swords and charms to make them invulnerable to bullets, were defeated by British troops with machine guns by 1932, and Saya San was hanged. The revolt exposed the precarious and unpopular position of the British in Burma.

San Andreas Fault \ˌsan-an-'drā-əs\ Zone of transform faults at the boundary between two tectonic plates, running along the coast of northern California for 650 mi (1,050 km) and passing seaward in the vicinity of SAN FRANCISCO. Movement along the FAULT is characterized by frequent EARTHQUAKES, including the major San Francisco quake of 1906, when parts of the fault line moved as much as 21 ft (6.4 m), and the less serious earthquake of 1989.

San Antonio City (pop., 1996 est.: 1,068,000), southern central Texas. It is situated at the headwaters of the San Antonio River. Founded in 1718 by the Spanish as a mission on the site of an Indian village, it was laid out as a town in 1731. The mission, called the ALAMO, became a military post in 1794; it was the site of the historic siege in 1836. In the late 19th century, it became a major cattle center as the starting point of the CHISHOLM TRAIL. Military installations, especially for aviation and aerospace, spurred the city's rapid growth after 1940. The economy is now balanced among government, business, manufacturing, education, and tourism.

San Bernardino City (pop., 1996 est.: 183,000), southern California. It is located about 62 mi (100 km) east of LOS ANGELES. It was laid out as a town by MORMONS in 1852 and developed as a trade center chiefly for the surrounding citrus groves and vineyards. Other industries, including aerospace, electronics, and steel, are now the economic mainstays. It is part of the San Bernardino-Riverside-Ontario metropolitan complex.

San Bernardino Pass Mountain pass, LEPONTINE ALPS, southeastern Switzerland. Its altitude is 6,775 ft (2,065 m). The village of San Bernardino, just south of the pass, is a popular year-round resort. A tunnel beneath the pass was opened in 1967, improving travel through the region. The pass was named for St. BERNARDINE OF SIENA, who preached in the area in the early 15th century.

San Cristóbal Island \ˌsän-krēs-'tō-bäl\ One of the GALÁPAGOS ISLANDS, eastern Pacific Ocean. It is the most populated and fertile island of the archipelago, producing sugar, coffee, cassava, and lime. Volcanic in origin, and about 24 mi (39 km) long and 8 mi (13 km) wide, it is the only island of the group that has a regular water supply. CHARLES DARWIN landed there at the settlement of San Cristóbal in 1835 and compiled data that he later used in his *Origin of Species.*

San Diego City (pop., 1996 est.: 1,171,000) and port, southwestern California. It is located on San Diego Bay, the site of major naval and military bases. Sighted by the Spanish in 1542 and named San Miguel, the area was renamed San Diego in 1602. In 1769 the Spanish established a military post on the site and JUNIPERO SERRA dedicated the first California mission there. It was captured from Mexico in 1846, and a new city was laid out in 1867. The arrival of the Santa Fe railroad in 1884 stimulated the city's growth. Industrial development is dominated by aerospace, electronics, and shipbuilding, and the city is the main commercial outlet for the farm produce of southern California. Balboa Park and its SAN DIEGO ZOO are renowned, as are the area universities.

San Diego Zoo World's largest collection of mammals, birds, and reptiles, located in San Diego, Cal., and administered by the Zoological Society of San Diego. The 100-acre (40.5-hectare) zoo, founded in 1916, has some 800 animal species and some 6,500 plant species. The 1,800-acre (729-hectare) San Diego Wild Animal Park opened in 1972 some 32 mi (52 km) northeast, in the San Pasqual Valley; there over 250 species of animals roam through Asian, African, and Australian habitats. A research department, the Center for Reproduction of Endangered Species (1975) has contributed to the zoo's success in managing and breeding endangered species.

San Fernando Valley Valley, southern California, northwest of central LOS ANGELES. It is bounded by the SAN GABRIEL, Santa Susana, and Santa Monica mountains and the Simi Hills. Originally an agricultural area, it occupies 260 sq mi (670 sq km) and now contains several residential suburbs of Los Angeles, including Encino, North Hollywood, Studio City, and Van Nuys.

San Francisco City (pop., 1996 est.: 735,000) and port, northern California. It is on the northern end of a peninsula between the Pacific Ocean and SAN FRANCISCO BAY. Founded in the 18th century by the Spanish, it came under Mexican control after Mexican independence in 1821. Occupied by U.S. forces in 1846, it grew rapidly after the discovery of gold in nearby areas (see GOLD RUSH). In 1869 it became the terminus of the first transcontinental railroad. It suffered extensive damage from the earthquake and fire of 1906. It was prominent in the American cultural revolution of the 1960s. It suffered heavy earthquake damage in 1989. It is a commercial, cultural, and financial center and one of the country's most cosmopolitan cities. A noted educational center, it is also the site of the GOLDEN GATE BRIDGE.

San Francisco Bay Large, nearly landlocked bay indenting western central California. A drowned river valley paralleling the coastline, it is connected with the Pacific Ocean by the Golden Gate Strait, which is spanned by the GOLDEN GATE BRIDGE. The bay is one of the world's finest natural harbors. Treasure, Yerba Buena, Angel, and ALCATRAZ islands are there; the cities of SAN FRANCISCO, OAKLAND, and BERKELEY are nearby.

San Gabriel Mountains Segment of the Pacific COAST RANGES, southern California. Many peaks exceed 9,000 ft (2,700 m); the highest is San Antonio Peak, or "Old Baldy," at 10,080 ft (3,072 m) tall. The range also includes MOUNT WILSON OBSERVATORY, northeast of PASADENA. The mountains are largely within the Angeles National Forest.

San Jacinto Mountains \ˌsan-jə-'sin-tō\ Segment of the Pacific COAST RANGES, southwestern California. San Jacinto Peak is the highest point, at 10,804 ft (3,293 m) tall. The city of PALM SPRINGS lies at its eastern base. The range is largely within conservation areas, including the Mount San Jacinto State Park and a division of the San Bernardino National Forest. The mountains attract tourists, provide outdoor recreation, and are an important watershed for the surrounding area.

San Joaquin River \ˌsan-wä-'kēn\ River, central California. Formed by forks rising in the SIERRA NEVADA, it flows past STOCKTON, Cal., to join the SACRAMENTO RIVER above Suisun Bay. It is 350 mi (560 km) long and is dammed for hydroelectric power. Its valley is the southern part of the CENTRAL VALLEY, one of the most productive agricultural regions in the U.S.

San José \ˌsäŋ-hō-'sā\ City (metro. area pop., 1996 est.: 968,000), capital of Costa Rica. Founded c. 1738 as Villa Nueva, in a broad, fertile valley 3,800 ft (1,160 m) above sea level, it developed slowly as a tobacco center in the Spanish colonial era. In 1823 it became the capital and in the 1840s the center of coffee production, which remained the chief source of the country's income through the 19th century. The political, social, and economic center of Costa Rica, it grew rapidly in the 20th century in both population and area.

San Jose \ˌsan-hō-'zā\ City (pop., 1996 est.: 839,000), western central California. It is located southeast of SAN FRANCISCO. The first civil settlement in California, it was founded in 1777 as a Spanish military supply base and became the state's first capital (1849–51). In 1850 it became the first chartered city in California. It was a trade depot for the California gold fields. The railroad from San Francisco improved trade connections for the produce of nearby farms. It is a processing and distribution center for a rich agricultural area producing fruit and wine. It is part of SILICON VALLEY, and its industries include the manufacture of electronic, computer, and aerospace components, auto parts, and consumer goods.

San Jose scale Species *(Aspidiotus perniciosus)* of SCALE INSECT first discovered in North America at San Jose, Cal., in 1880 but probably a native of China. A waxy gray secretion (the scale) covers the yellow females, which are about 0.06 in. (1.5 mm) in diameter. The scale is elevated in the center and is surrounded by a yellow ring. The female produces several generations of living young each year. San Jose scales can completely cover tree branches and may eventually kill the tree.

San Juan \sän-'hwän\ City (metro. area pop., 1996 est.: 434,000), seaport, and capital of Puerto Rico. It was visited in 1508 by JUAN PONCE DE LEON and founded in the early 16th century by the Spanish. It became heavily fortified and was a starting point for expeditions to unknown parts of the New World. Several times it was attacked by the British, including FRANCIS DRAKE in 1595. During the SPANISH–AMERICAN WAR, it fell to the U.S in 1898. It expanded rapidly in the 20th century and is one of the major ports and tourist resorts of the West Indies. Industries include petroleum and sugar refining, brewing, and distilling. San Juan is the commonwealth's financial capital, and many U.S. banks and corporations maintain offices there. El Morro and San Cristóbal fortifications are among the city's historic remnants.

San Juan Island National Historical Park Historical park, San Juan Islands, northwestern Washington. Established in 1966, it covers 1,752 acres (710 hectares). The San Juan Islands archipelago consists of 172 islands, and make up a Washington state county.

San Juan Mountains Segment of the southern ROCKY MTNS., southwestern Colorado. It extends from southwestern Colorado, along the course of the RIO GRANDE to the Chama River, in northern New Mexico. Many peaks in the northern section exceed 14,000 ft (4,300 m), including Mts. Eolus, Sneffels, and Redcloud. Uncompahgre Peak is the highest, at 14,309 ft (4,361 m). Composed mainly of volcanic rocks, the mountains have a rugged, well-forested terrain.

San Juan River River and outlet of Lake NICARAGUA, southern Nicaragua. It flows from the lake's southeastern end, forms the Nicaragua–Costa Rica border, and empties into the Caribbean Sea; it is 124 mi (199 km) long. Near its mouth it forms three arms: the Juanillo Menor, the Río Colorado, and the San Juan proper.

San Juan River River, southwestern U.S. It rises in the SAN JUAN MTNS. of southern Colorado, on the western side of the CONTINENTAL DIVIDE. It flows southwest into New Mexico, northeast into Utah, and west to the COLORADO RIVER. It is 360 mi (580 km) long and not navigable. The section of the river where the boundaries of New Mexico, Utah, Arizona, and Colorado meet, into which it has carved numerous S-shaped canyons more than 1,000 ft (300 m) deep, is known as the Goosenecks.

San Luis Potosí \sän-'lwēs-pō-tō-'sē\ State (pop., 1995 est.: 2,201,000), northeastern Mexico. It has an area of 24,351 sq mi (63,068 sq km). The capital is SAN LUIS POTOSÍ. It is a fertile area, and crops are cultivated in the uplands and in the lower tropical valleys. Livestock-raising is important, and hides, tallow, and wool are exported. Some of the richest silver mines in Mexico are located in the state.

San Luis Potosí City (pop., 1990: 526,000), capital of SAN LUIS POTOSÍ state, Mexico. Situated on the central plateau, it is 6,158 ft (1,877 m) above sea level. Founded as a Franciscan mission in 1583 and made a city in 1658, it was the center of the region's colonial administration. It was the site of Benito Juarez's government in 1863. In 1910 Francisco Madero drew up the basic social and political program of the Mexican Revolution in the city. It is the hub of a rich silver mining and agricultural region and is a leading manufacturing and metal smelting and refining center.

San Marco Basilica See Saint Mark's Basilica

San Marino *officially* **Republic of San Marino** Nation, central Italian Peninsula, southern Europe. It is located near the Adriatic Sea and is surrounded by Italy. Area: 24 sq mi (62 sq km). Population (1997 est.): 26,000. Capital: San Marino. Most of the people are Italian. Language: Italian (official). Religion: Roman Catholicism. Currency: Italian lira. The territory has an irregular rectangular form with a maximum length of 8 mi (13 km). It is crossed by streams that flow into the Adriatic Sea. It is dominated by Mount Titano, 2,424 ft (739 m) high, on which the capital, the town of San Marino (pop., 1992 est.: 2,300), is located, sur-

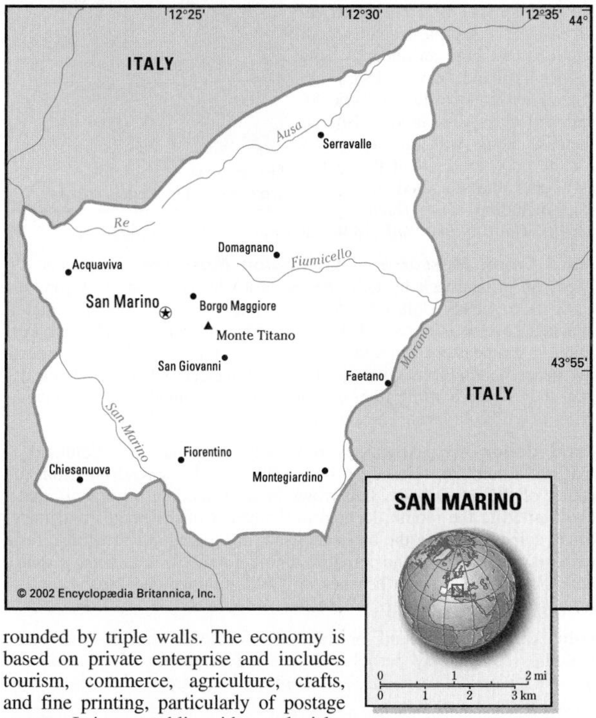

rounded by triple walls. The economy is based on private enterprise and includes tourism, commerce, agriculture, crafts, and fine printing, particularly of postage stamps. It is a republic with one legislative house; its heads of state and government are two captains-regent. According to tradition, it was founded in the early 4th century AD by St. Marinus. By the 12th century it had developed into a commune and remained independent despite challenges from neighboring rulers, including the Malatesta family in nearby Rimini, Italy. San Marino survived the Renaissance as a relic of the self-governing Italian city-state and remained an independent republic after the unification of Italy in 1861. It is one of the smallest republics in the world, and may be the oldest one in Europe.

San Marino City (pop., 1995 est.: 13,000), southwestern California. It is east of Los Angeles and south of Pasadena. In 1903 railroad magnate Henry E. Huntington (1850–1927) purchased the San Marino Ranch and founded the community, which was incorporated in 1913. His estate, deeded to the public, includes the Huntington Library (with rare English and American books and manuscripts), Art Gallery (where Thomas Gainsborough's *Blue Boy* is displayed), and Botanical Gardens.

San Martín \,sän-mär-'tēn\, **José de** (1778–1850) National hero of Argentina who helped lead the revolutions against Spanish rule in Argentina (1812), Chile (1818), and Peru (1821). Son of a professional soldier and colonial administrator, he was educated in Spain. Initially he fought loyally for Spain against the Moors (1791), the British (1798), and the Portuguese (1801), but in 1812 he returned to the New World to help the revolutionaries. His greatest campaign was the liberation of Lima, without which the independence of the Argentine provinces could not have been secured. His bold strategy was to lead an army over the Andes, a daunting undertaking. In 1817 he liberated Chile, which he turned over to Bernardo O'Higgins, and proceeded to Peru by ship, where he blockaded the chief port until the royalists withdrew. He then entered Lima and declared the independence of Peru, though he lacked adequate forces to subdue the royalists in the interior. The following year he met with Simon Bolivar; what passed between them is unknown, but San Martín soon afterward went into exile in France, leaving Bolívar to complete the liberation of Peru.

San Pedro Sula \sän-'pā-thrō-'sü-lä\ City (metro. area pop., 1995 est.: 384,000), northwestern Honduras. It is located about 100 mi (160 km) northwest of Tegucigalpa. Founded by the Spanish in 1536, the city has been almost completely rebuilt. It is the country's chief industrial center and second-largest city; it produces a wide variety of items, including textiles, foodstuffs, clothing, beverages, and furniture.

San Salvador See Bahamas

San Salvador City (metro. area pop., 1992 est.: 1,522,000), capital of El Salvador. Founded near Suchitoto by the Spanish in 1525, it was moved to its present site in 1528 and declared a city in 1546. It became the capital of the country in 1839. During the late 1970s it became the focus of violence between the government and left-wing political groups. It is the country's financial, commercial, and industrial center, producing textiles and clothing, leather goods, and wood products. It is also the site of the University of El Salvador. Ruined by earthquakes in 1854, 1873, and 1917 and by heavy floods in 1934, it often has been reconstructed. Another earthquake in 1986 killed more than 900 people.

San Sebastián \,sän-sā-,bäs-'tyän\ *Basque* **Donostia** \,thō-nō-'stē-ä\ Seaport (pop., 1991: 190,000), northern Spain. It is situated at the mouth of the Urumea River on the Bay of Biscay, near the French border. First mentioned in 1014, it was chartered by Sancho the Wise of Navarre c. 1175. The town was burned in 1813 after Anglo-Portuguese troops took it from the French during the Peninsular War. Formerly the summer residence of the Spanish royal court, it is now a fashionable seaside resort. Nearby is Mount Urgull, with the 16th-century Mota Castle at its summit.

San Simeon Former estate of William Randolph Hearst, southern California. It was built on a vast private estate of 245,000 acres (99,000 hectares), developed in the 1860s by Hearst's father. In 1919–20, with the architect Julia Morgan, Hearst began construction of a complex of luxurious buildings and gardens to serve as a country house. The main residence, later called Hearst Castle, is a Spanish Renaissance building with 150 rooms, a cathedral-like façade, and two bell towers. Lavish interior decorations were obtained from European churches and palaces. The site's embellishment continued (1919–48) with numerous subsidiary buildings, Mediterranean gardens, statuary, pools, fountains, a pergola, and priceless art treasures collected worldwide. The complex is now a state historical monument.

San Stefano \sän-'ste-fä-,nō\, **Treaty of** (1878) Peace settlement imposed on the Ottoman government by Russia at the end of the Russo-Turkish War. It established an independent Bulgarian principality that included most of Macedonia, realigned other European provinces of the Ottoman empire, and ceded parts of Asian Turkey to Russia. Opposed by Austria-Hungary and Britain, it was modified at the Congress of Berlin.

Sanaa \sä-'nä\ City (pop., 1995 est.: 972,000), capital of Yemen. Located in the western part of the country, it was built on the site of the ancient pre-Islamic stronghold of Ghumdan, traditionally dated to the 1st century AD. It was converted to Islam in 632. Nominally under Ottoman sovereignty from 1516, it was effectively controlled by the Zaydi imams from the early 17th century to 1872. It became the capital of an independent Yemen after the Ottoman defeat in World War I. In 1990, after Yemen's merger with the People's Democratic Republic of Yemen, it became the capital of the unified nation. For many centuries it has been the chief economic, political, and religious center of the Yemen highlands.

Sanaga River \,sä-nä-'gä\ River, central Cameroon. It flows southwest into the Bight of Biafra opposite the island of Bioko. It is about 325 mi

(525 km) long. Falls and rapids are found along much of its upper course. Dams and reservoirs regulate water flow and harness the river's hydroelectric power.

Sánchez Cotán \'sän-chāth-kō-'tän\, **Juan** (1560–1627) Spanish painter. Profoundly religious, he was early influenced by the spirit of Catholic mysticism that dominated the intellectual life of Toledo, where he was a still-life painter. He entered a monastery in 1603 and remained a Carthusian lay brother till his death. Though his religious paintings are not exceptional, his still lifes are considered among the best produced in Europe, their detailed realism, visual harmony, and illusion of depth conveying humility and mystic spirituality.

"Quince, Cabbage, Melon, and Cucumber," oil on canvas by Juan Sánchez Cotán, c. 1602; in the San Diego Museum of Art, Calif.

SAN DIEGO MUSEUM OF ART, GIFT OF ANNE R. AND AMY PUTNAM

Sanchi sculpture \'sän-chē\ Early Indian sculpture that embellished the gateways of the Buddhist relic mound called the Great Stupa at Sanchi, in Madhya Pradesh, a magnificent monument of the 1st century BC. The two square posts of each gateway are topped by capitals of sculptured animals or dwarfs, surmounted by three crossbars that end in spirals and are covered with crowded relief sculptures depicting events of the Buddha's life. In the angle between the lowest crossbar and the pillar are sensuous figures of female earthly spirits.

Architraves of the north gateway (toran) to the Great Stupa (stupa No. 1) at Sanchi, Madhya Pradesh, India.

ART RESOURCE—EB INC.

Sancho I *known as* **Sancho the Founder** (1154–1211) Second king of Portugal (1185–1211). The son of AFONSO I, he resettled depopulated areas of Portugal, established new towns, and rebuilt frontier strongholds and castles. He encouraged foreign settlers and granted large tracts to military orders. When Portugal was invaded by the Almohad Moors, he sent a crusader fleet against them (1189), but he lost control of Portuguese lands south of the Tagus River (1191).

Sancho II *known as* **Sancho the Cowled** (1207–1248) Fourth king of Portugal (1223–45). His reign was marked by a series of vain attempts to bring political stability to his strife-ridden realm. He renewed the war against the MOORS and gained control over most of the Algarve (1238–39). He was deposed (1245) in favor of his brother AFONSO III.

Sancho III Garcés \'sän-chō...gär-'thās\ *known as* **Sancho the Great** (992?–1035) King of Navarre (1000–1035). Son of García III, he proved a skilled politician and succeeded in extending control over all the Christian states of Spain. In 1010 he married Munia, daughter of the count of Castile, and he elevated Castile to a kingdom in 1029. By dividing his kingdom among his four sons, he made fratricidal wars inevitable after his death.

Sancho IV *known as* **Sancho the Brave** (1257–1295) King of Castile and Leon (1284–95). The second son of Afonso X, he won the backing of nobles and military orders in his effort to gain recognition as heir, and he usurped the throne on his father's death. Sancho defeated an invasion of Andalusia by the king of Fès (1290) and won the support of Aragon by marrying his daughter to JAMES II (1291). He depended greatly on his warrior-queen, María de Molina (died 1321).

sand Mineral, rock, or soil particles that are 0.0008–0.08 in. (0.02–2 mm) in diameter. Most rock-forming minerals are found in sand, but QUARTZ is by far the most common. Most sands also contain a small quantity of FELDSPAR, as well as white MICA. All sands contain small quantities of heavy rock-forming minerals, including garnet, tourmaline, zircon, rutile, topaz, pyroxenes, and amphiboles. In the pottery and glass-making industries very pure quartz sands are used as a source of silica. Similar sands are used for lining the hearths of steel furnaces. Molds used in foundries for casting metal are made of sand with a clay binder. Quartz and garnet sands are used extensively as abrasives. Among ordinary sand's many uses, it is a basic ingredient of mortar, cement, and concrete. See also TAR SAND.

Sand, George \'sä^{n}d, *Engl* 'sand\ *orig.* **Amandine-Aurore-Lucile Lucie Dupin** (1804–1876) French writer. During childhood she gained a love of the countryside that would inform most of her works. Married in 1822, she soon tired of her husband, Casimir Dudevant, and began a series of liaisons; her lovers included PROSPER MERIMEE, ALFRED MUSSET, and, most importantly, F. CHOPIN. She became famous (under her pseudonym) with her novel *Indiana* (1832), a protest against conventions that bind an unhappy wife to her husband. *Lélia* (1833) extended her iconoclastic views on social and class associations. Similar themes, along with her sympathy for the poor, are evident in her finest works, the so-called rustic novels, including *The Devil's Pool* (1846), *The Country Waif* (1848), and *Little Fadette* (1849).

George Sand.

BY COURTESY OF THE MUSEE CARNAVALET, PARIS

Sand Creek Massacre *or* **Chivington Massacre** (November 29, 1864) Surprise attack by U.S. troops on a Cheyenne camp. A force of 1,200 men, mostly Colorado volunteers, under Col. John M. Chivington attacked several hundred Cheyenne camped on Sand Creek near Fort Lyon in southeastern Colorado Territory. The Indians had been conducting peace negotiations with the fort's commander; when the attack began, they raised a white flag, but the troops continued to attack, massacring over 200 Indians. The slayings led to the PLAINS INDIAN wars.

sand dollar Any ECHINODERM (order Clypeastroida, class Echinoidea) that has a coinlike, thin-edged body. Five "petals" spread out from the center of the upper body. It burrows in sand, feeding on organic particles wafted to the mouth, located in the center of the body's underside. Small spines covering the body are used for digging and crawling. Tests (external skeletons) of the common sand dollar *(Echinarachnius parma),* which often wash up on beaches in North America and Japan, are 2–4 in. (5–10 cm) in diameter.

sand dune Hill, mound, or ridge of windblown sand or other loose material such as clay particles. Dunes are commonly associated with desert regions and seacoasts, and there are large areas of dunes in nonglacial parts of Antarctica.

sand flea *or* **beach flea** Hopping terrestrial CRUSTACEAN (family Talitridae). The European sand flea *(Talitrus saltator)* is about 0.6 in. (1.5 cm) long. The long-horned sand flea *(T. longicornis),* found on the North American Atlantic coast, has antennae the same length as the waxy white body, up to 1 in. (2.5 cm) long. During the day, sand fleas lie buried near the high-tide mark; at night, they forage for organic debris. The common sand flea *(Orchestia agilis,* or *platensis)* lives along Atlantic coasts of Europe and the Americas.

sand fly Any of several species in the DIPTERAN family Phlebotomidae (sometimes considered part of the family Psychodidae) with aquatic larvae that live in the intertidal zone of coastal beaches, in mud, or in wet organic debris. The genus *Phlebotomus* transmits the pappataci fever virus, and in parts of South America, Africa, and Asia it carries the protozoan parasites that cause kala azar, Oriental sore, espundia, and bartonellosis. The name is also used for species of the BLACKFLY and biting MIDGE families.

sand shark Any of about six species of shallow-water, bottom-dwelling SHARKS in the genus *Odontaspis* (family Odontaspididae), found along tropical and temperate coastlines of all oceans. They are 10–20 ft (3–6 m) long and are brown or gray above, paler below. Voracious but generally sluggish, they have long, slim, pointed teeth and prey on fishes and INVERTEBRATES. Two species, the sand tiger *(O. taurus)* of the At-

Sand shark (*Odontaspis*).
GRANT HEILMAN—EB INC.

lantic and the gray nurse *(O. arenarius)* of Australia, are potentially dangerous.

sandalwood Any semiparasitic plant of the genus *Santalum* (family Santalaceae; the sandalwood family), or its wood, especially the wood of the true, or white, sandalwood, *Santalum album,* which is used in making furniture and from which oil used in making perfumes, soaps, candles, and incense is derived. The approximately 10 species of *Santalum* are distributed throughout South Asia and the islands of the South Pacific. The sandalwood family contains more than 400 species of semiparasitic shrubs, herbs, and trees in about 36 genera, found in tropical and temperate regions. In some genera the leaves are reduced to scalelike structures. The green leaves contain some chlorophyll, which allows the plants to make food, but all sandalwoods are parasites to a certain extent, obtaining water and nutrients from their hosts. Most, including *S. album,* are root parasites, but some are stem parasites.

Sandalwood Island See SUMBA

sandbar *or* **offshore bar** Submerged or partly exposed ridge of sand or coarse sediment that is built by waves offshore from a beach. The swirling turbulence of waves breaking off a beach excavates a trough in the sandy bottom. Some of this sand is carried forward onto the beach and the rest is deposited on the offshore flank of the trough. Sand suspended in the backwash and in rip currents adds to the bar, as does some sand moving shoreward from deeper water. The bar's top is kept below still-water level by the plunge of the waves breaking over it.

Sandburg, Carl (1878–1967) U.S. poet, historian, novelist, and folklorist. Born in Galesburg, Ill., Sandburg tried many occupations and fought in the Spanish-American War before moving to Chicago in 1913, where he worked in journalism. He won recognition in 1914 with poems, including perhaps his best known, "Chicago," in POETRY magazine. His Whitmanesque free verse eulogizing American workers appeared in such volumes as *Smoke and Steel* (1920) and *The People, Yes* (1936). *The American Songbag* (1927) and *New American Songbag* (1950) collect folksongs he performed. His other works include *Abraham Lincoln: The Prairie Years* (1926); *Abraham Lincoln: The War Years* (1939, Pulitzer Prize); *Remembrance Rock* (1948); and four children's books, including *Rootabaga Stories* (1922).

Sandburg, 1949.
BY COURTESY OF THE ILLINOIS STATE HISTORICAL LIBRARY, SPRINGFIELD

Sanders, Barry (born 1968) U.S. football player. Born in Wichita, Kan., he attended Oklahoma State Univ., where he won the HEISMAN TROPHY (1988) and set 34 college rushing records. As a running back for the Detroit Lions from 1989, in his first 10 seasons he rushed for 15,269 yards, placing him second behind WALTER PAYTON in all-time career yardage. He holds records for the most games with 150 yards or more rushing (25), the most 100-yard games in a season (14), and the most touchdown runs of 50 or more yards (15). He stunned the football world by announcing his retirement before the start of the 1999 season.

Sanders, Otto Liman von See Otto LIMAN VON SANDERS

sandhill crane CRANE species (*Grus canadensis,* family Gruidae), 35–43 in. (90–110 cm) long, with a red crown, a bluish or brownish gray body tinged with sandy yellow, and a long, harsh, penetrating call. It is one of the oldest of all bird species. It breeds from Alaska to Hudson Bay; it formerly bred in southern central Canada and the Great Lakes region of the U.S. but is now rare in those regions. A smaller, nonmigratory subspecies breeds in Florida and southern Georgia; others are classified as rare or critically endangered. Sandhill cranes have been used as surrogate parents in efforts to save the WHOOPING CRANE from extinction.

Sandinistas Members of Nicaragua's Sandinista National Liberation Front (FSLN). The group was founded in 1962 to oppose the SOMOZA FAMILY's dictatorship and organized support among students, workers, and peasants. From bases in Honduras and Costa Rica, they attacked the Nicaraguan National Guard. They split into factions in the mid-1970s but reunited during the revolution of 1978–79 that finally succeeded in overthrowing Pres. Anastasio Somoza. A junta headed by DANIEL ORTEGA led the Sandinista government (1979–90), which implemented literacy and community health programs. In an effort to topple the government, the U.S. imposed a trade embargo, pressured international lending institutions to withhold aid, and trained and supported the CONTRAS. The FSLN lost support over time and was voted out of power in 1990. See also VIOLETA CHAMORRO.

sandpainting Type of art practiced among the NAVAJO and PUEBLO INDIANS and among Tibetan Buddhists. Sandpaintings are stylized, symbolic pictures (in Tibet, MANDALAS) prepared by trickling small quantities of crushed, colored sandstone, charcoal, or pollen on a background of clean smoothed sand. The pictures may include representations of deities, cosmic worlds, animals, lightning, rainbows, plants, and other SYMBOLS described in chants that accompany various religious and healing rites.

sandpiper Any of numerous shorebirds (family Scolopacidae) found breeding or wintering nearly worldwide. Sandpipers, 6–12 in. (15–30 cm) long, have a moderately long bill and legs, long, narrow wings, and a fairly short tail. Their plumage has a complicated "dead-grass" pattern of browns, buffs, and blacks above, white or cream below. They run along ocean and inland beaches and mudflats, picking up insects, crustaceans, and worms and uttering utter thin, piping cries. Many species migrate in great flocks, from the Arctic to South America and New Zealand.

White-rumped sandpiper (*Calidris fuscicollis*).
HELEN CRUICKSHANK FROM THE NATIONAL AUDUBON SOCIETY COLLECTION/PHOTO RESEARCHERS

sandstone Sedimentary rock formed from sand-sized grains (0.0025–0.08 in., or 0.06–2 mm, in diameter). The spaces between grains may be empty or filled with either a chemical cement of SILICA or CALCIUM carbonate or a fine-grained matrix of silt and clay particles. The principal mineral constituents of the grain framework are QUARTZ, FELDSPAR, and rock fragments. Sandstones are quarried for use as building stone. Because of their abundance, diversity, and mineralogy, sandstones are also important to geologists as indicators of erosional and depositional processes. See also GRAYWACKE.

Sandwich, Earl of *orig.* **John Montagu** (1718–1792) British first lord of the admiralty (1748–51, 1771–82). He served as secretary of state for the north (1763–65, 1770–71) and led the prosecution of JOHN WILKES. Appointed first lord of the admiralty during the American Revolution, he was criticized for keeping much of the British fleet in European waters to avoid French attack. His promotion of exploration led Capt. JAMES COOK to name the Sandwich Islands (later Hawaii) after him in 1778. The sandwich was named after him in 1762 when he spent 24 hours at a gaming table without other food.

Sangallo the Younger, Antonio da See Antonio DA SANGALLO THE YOUNGER

Sanger, Frederick (born 1918) British biochemist. Educated at Cambridge Univ., he thereafter worked principally at the Medical Research Council in Cambridge (1951–83). He spent 10 years elucidating the structure of the insulin molecule, determining the exact order of all its amino acids by 1955. His techniques for determining the order in which amino acids are linked in proteins made it possible to discover the structure of many other complex proteins. In 1958 he won the Nobel Prize for Chemistry for his work. In 1980 Sanger became the fourth person ever to be awarded a second Nobel Prize (also for Chemistry), which he shared with PAUL BERG and Walter Gilbert (born 1932), for determining the sequences of nucleotides in the DNA molecule of a small virus.

Sanger, Margaret *orig.* **Margaret Higgins** (1879–1966) U.S. birth-control pioneer. Born in Corning, N.Y., she practiced obstetrical nursing in New York's Lower East Side, where she noticed a relationship between poverty, uncontrolled fertility, and high rates of infant and maternal deaths. In 1914 she published *The Woman Rebel* (later *Birth Control Reviews*), which was banned as obscene. She was arrested in 1916 for mailing birth-control literature, and again when she opened the nation's first birth-control clinic. Her legal appeals brought publicity and support to her cause, and the federal courts soon granted physicians the right to prescribe contraceptives. In 1921 she founded the American Birth Control League. She soon took her campaign worldwide, organizing the first World Population Conference (1927) and becoming the founding president of the International Planned Parenthood Federation (1953).

Margaret Sanger.

BY COURTESY OF PLANNED PARENTHOOD-FEDERATION OF AMERICA, INC.

sangha \'seŋ-gə\ Buddhist monastic order, traditionally composed of four groups: monks, nuns, laymen, and laywomen. Established by the BUDDHA, it is the world's oldest body of celibate clerics. Together with the Buddha and the DHARMA, it makes up the Threefold Refuge, a basic creed of Buddhism. Buddha established the BHIKSU sangha for men and later the bhiksuni sangha for women. Members depend on alms from the community, since they are discouraged from engaging in commerce or agriculture. They live according to the VINAYA PITAKA.

Sangre de Cristo Mountains \'saŋ-grē-də-'kris-tō\ Segment of the southern ROCKY MTNS. It extends southeast for about 250 mi (400 km) from southern central Colorado to northern central New Mexico. Many of the peaks exceed 14,000 ft (4,300 m); Blanca Peak, at 14,345 ft (4,372 m) tall, is the highest. Tourism and mining are the main economic activities.

Sanhedrin \san-'hē-drən, san-'he-drən\ Jewish council that operated in Roman Palestine from the time of the MACCABEES (c. 165 BC) to the end of the patriarchate (AD 425). While the term refers to the supreme Jewish court, the Sanhedrin's exact composition and powers—religious, judicial, and legislative—are reported variously in different sources. It is mentioned in various books of the Bible (Mark, Luke, Acts) as having taken part in or adjudicated the trials of JESUS, St. PETER THE APOSTLE, and St. JOHN THE BAPTIST. According to Talmudic sources, the Great Sanhedrin was a court of 71 sages that met on fixed occasions in the Temple of JERUSALEM, acting as a religious legislative body, trial court, and administrator of rituals.

Sankara \'shən-kə-rə\ *or* **Samkara** \'shəm-kə-rə\ (c. 700–750) Indian philosopher and theologian. Born into a pious Brahman family in Kerala, he became a SANNYASI after his father's death. He is said to have traveled all over India, holding discussions with philosophers of different creeds. He is the reputed author of more than 300 Sanskrit works, most of them commentaries on and expositions of Vedic literature. The most renowned exponent of the ADVAITA school of VEDANTA philosophy, he is credited with laying the foundation for Hindu orthodoxy in India after centuries of challenge from Jainism and Buddhism.

sankin kotai \'san-ˌkin-kō-'tī\ Under Japan's TOKUGAWA SHOGUNATE, a system of alternate attendance, whereby DAIMYO were required to reside alternately in their HAN (feudal domains) and in the capital city of Edo. This system was inaugurated in 1635 and lasted until 1862. It kept the daimyo from building up a potentially threatening power base in their domains, and, because of the expense of maintaining two residences, kept them from becoming too rich. It also contributed to the flowering of an urban culture and a commercial economy, and led to improved roads and communications.

sannyasi \ˌsən-'yä-sē\ In HINDUISM, one who renounces all ties with family and society and pursues spiritual liberation. Sannyasis are a class of SADHU that do not live in communities, instead leading a mendicant, itinerant life. Those recognized as having achieved full self-knowledge are considered free of all worldly rules and duties, including those pertaining to CASTE, and are not required to carry out image worship or offerings. After death, their bodies, rather than being cremated, are buried in a seated, meditative posture.

sansculotte \ˌsäⁿ-kü̅-'lȯt, *Engl* ˌsanz-kü-'lät\ (French, *sans-culotte:* "without breeches") In the FRENCH REVOLUTION, one of the ill-clad and ill-equipped volunteers of the Revolutionary army; also a Parisian ultrademocrat of the Revolution. The working-class sansculottes wore long trousers to distinguish themselves from the upper classes, who wore knee-breeches *(culotte).* Allied with the Jacobins (see JACOBIN CLUB) in the REIGN OF TERROR, sansculottes included ultrademocrats of all classes. Their influence waned after the fall of MAXIMILIEN ROBESPIERRE in 1794.

Sanskrit language Old INDO-ARYAN LANGUAGE, the classical literary language of HINDUISM. The most ancient form is Vedic, attested in its earliest form in parts of the RIG VEDA, dating from the late 2nd millennium BC. Late Vedic Sanskrit was described and codified in a grammar by Panini, dating from about the 5th century BC. Literary activity in so-called Classical Sanskrit, in many respects close to the language described by Panini, flourished c. 500 BC–c. AD 1000. Today Sanskrit (now usually written in the Devanagari script) serves as a learned language and LINGUA FRANCA for Brahman scholars. It is an archaic INDO-EUROPEAN LANGUAGE with an elaborate system of nominal and verbal inflection.

Sansovino \ˌsän-sō-'vē-nō\, **Andrea** *orig.* **Andrea Contucci** (c. 1467–1529) Italian sculptor. The fine detail and high emotional pitch of his marble Altar of the Sacrament in Florence's Santo Spirito (1485–90) typify his early work; his marble *Baptism of Christ* (1502), above one of the Baptistery doors in Florence, marks a shift to High Renaissance style with its dignified poses and strong but controlled emotion. His tombs for two cardinals in Rome's Santa Maria del Popolo (completed 1509) were his most influential innovation, with their triumphal-arch form and the novel sleeping attitude of the deceased cardinals. His works display the transition from early to High Renaissance, and his graceful style acted as a counterbalance to MICHELANGELO'S titanic, muscular sculpture throughout the 16th century.

Sansovino \ˌsän-sō-'vē-nō\, **Jacopo** *orig.* **Jacopo Tatti** (1486–1570) Italian sculptor and architect. He trained in Florence under ANDREA SANSOVINO, whose name he adopted. In 1505–6 he moved to Rome to study architecture and work on the restoration of ancient sculpture. After the sack of Rome in 1527 he fled to Venice, where he was appointed state architect (1529). His Library of St. Mark's (begun 1537) is one of the major architectural works of the 16th century. His vivid sculptures were often important decorative elements of his buildings. His best-known statues are the colossal figures of Mars and Neptune on the staircase of the Doges' Palace (1554–66). He was more successful than any other Renaissance architect in fusing architecture and sculpture.

Santa Ana \ˌsän-tä-'ä-nä\ City (metro. area pop., 1992 est.: 202,000), northwestern El Salvador. It is one of the country's largest cities and a major coffee-producing center with one of the world's largest coffee mills. Other industries include the manufacture of cotton textiles, furniture, and leather goods. There are summer resorts at nearby Lake Coatepeque, and the ruined Indian city of Chalchuapa is 9 mi (14 km) west. The Santa Ana Volcano, 7,755 ft (2,365 m) high, is also nearby.

Santa Ana City (pop., 1996 est.: 302,000), southwestern California. Located east of LONG BEACH, the site was laid out in 1869. The community developed as a center for the farm produce of the Santa Ana valley after the Southern Pacific Railroad connected it to LOS ANGELES in 1878.

Nearby military installations and freeway construction spurred residential and industrial growth after World War II.

Santa Anna, Antonio (López de) (1794–1876) Soldier and several times president of Mexico (1833–36, 1844–45, 1847, 1853–55). He fought on both sides of nearly every issue of the day. He is famous for his glorious victories, including his thwarting of Spain's attempt to reconquer Mexico (1829), and for his ignominious failures, including his defeat and capture by SAM HOUSTON at San Jacinto in the Texas revolt (1836). When the MEXICAN WAR broke out, he contacted Pres. JAMES POLK to broker a peace, but on arriving in Mexico he led Mexican forces against the U.S. (1846–47) and was driven into exile. When MAXIMILIAN was made emperor of Mexico, Santa Anna offered his services both to Maximilian and to his opponents; neither side accepted. He lived abroad 1855–74, finally returning to Mexico to die in poverty. See also ALAMO, CAUDILLO, La REFORMA.

Santa Anna, daguerreotype by F.W. Seiders.

Santa Barbara City (pop., 1996 est.: 86,000), southern California, on the Pacific coast. Named for the patron saint of mariners in 1602, it became the site of a Spanish military post in 1782. The mission of Santa Barbara was built in 1786; it is the western headquarters of the FRANCISCAN Order and has been in continuous use since its founding. The city developed into a busy port and was incorporated as a city in 1850. After the arrival (1887) of the Southern Pacific Railroad, it became a popular seaside resort. Its economy is bolstered by livestock farms and petroleum production. Its educational institutions include the University of California at Santa Barbara (1891).

Santa Barbara Islands See CHANNEL ISLANDS (California)

Santa Claus See St. NICHOLAS

Santa Cruz \ˌsän-tä-ˈkrüs\ City (pop., 1993 est.: 767,000), eastern central Bolivia. Founded by Spaniards from Paraguay in 1561 at what is now San José de Chiquitos, it was attacked repeatedly by Indians until 1595. Then it was moved to its present location and renamed Santa Cruz de la Sierra. In 1811 its inhabitants declared their independence from Spain. Bolivia's second-largest city, it is a trade center for crops, including sugarcane and rice, grown in the surrounding area. It has an oil refinery and is the seat of a university.

Santa Cruz de Tenerife \ˌsän-tä-ˈkrüth-thā-ˌtā-nē-ˈrē-fā\ Port city (metro. area pop., 1995 est.: 205,000), capital of the island of Tenerife in the CANARY ISLANDS, Spain. Founded in 1494, it occupies a small plain between two usually waterless ravines. It was attacked by the British in 1657 and 1797; the latter assault was led by HORATIO NELSON. After 1877 growth was spurred by the banana and tomato trade and, later, by harbor improvements and tourism. FRANCISCO FRANCO, then captain general of the Canary Islands, organized in Santa Cruz the national uprising that led to the SPANISH CIVIL WAR in 1936. Industries include oil refining.

Santa Fe City (pop., 1996 est.: 66,000), capital of New Mexico. It lies at the foot of the SANGRE DE CRISTO MTNS. Founded by the Spanish in 1610, it was the administrative, military, and missionary headquarters of a vast, sparsely populated Spanish colonial province during the 18th century. In the MEXICAN WAR in 1846, the city was occupied by U.S. forces under Gen. STEPHEN KEARNY. After New Mexico was ceded to the U.S., Santa Fe became the capital of the territory in 1851. In 1912 it became the state capital. It was the western terminus of the SANTA FE TRAIL. It is a major tourist center noted for Indian and Mexican handicrafts, and its large Spanish–American population has made it the cultural capital of the southwest. A popular summer resort, it also attracts winter skiers.

Santa Fe Railway See ATCHISON, TOPEKA AND SANTA FE RAILROAD CO.

Santa Fe Trail Historic wagon trail from INDEPENDENCE, Mo., to SANTA FE, N.M. An important commercial route from 1821 to 1880, it was opened by WILLIAM BECKNELL and used by merchant wagon caravans. From the MISSOURI RIVER, it followed the divide between the tributaries of the Arkansas and Kansas rivers to the site of modern Great Bend, Kan., then proceeded along the Arkansas River. At the western end, three routes turned south to Santa Fe, the shortest being the Cimarron Cutoff through the valley of the CIMARRON RIVER. When the Santa Fe railroad was completed in 1880, use of the trail ceased.

Santa Gertrudis Heaviest breed of beef CATTLE, developed in the 20th century by the King Ranch in Texas by crossing BRAHMAN bulls with SHORTHORN cows. It is usually solid red with occasional small white markings on the forehead or the flanks. It has a long, deep body and much loose skin about the neck, brisket, and navel.

Santa Isabel See MALABO

Santa Isabel *or* **Santa Ysabel** Island (pop., 1986: 14,000) central SOLOMON ISLANDS, South Pacific Ocean. Located 50 mi (80 km) northwest of GUADALCANAL, it is about 130 mi (209 km) long and 20 mi (32 km) wide at its widest point. Mount Marescot, at 4,000 ft (1,219 m) tall, is the highest peak. The island was under German control 1886–99; Rekata Bay on the northwestern coast was a Japanese base during World War II. Coconut plantations and timber development are important to the economy.

Santa River River, western central Peru. Rising in the Andean Cordillera Blanca, it flows northwest, descending to form the Callejón de Huaylas, a densely populated agricultural region. Below Huallanca, it veers west and plunges through a spectacular gorge, the Cañon del Pato, to enter the Pacific Ocean after a course of 200 mi (300 km). It powers hydroelectric stations.

Santa Rosa City (pop., 1996 est.: 122,000), western California. It is at the foot of the Sonoma Mtns., northwest of SAN FRANCISCO. Founded in 1833 and incorporated in 1868, it developed as a processing and shipping center for the agricultural produce of the Sonoma valley. The economy relies on retail services catering to an increasing residential population. The city was the site of the home and gardens of plant breeder LUTHER BURBANK. Nearby is the JACK LONDON Memorial.

Santander \ˌsän-ˌtän-ˈder\ Port city (metro. area pop., 1995 est.: 195,000), capital of the autonomous community of CANTABRIA, northern Spain. A major seaport and summer resort, it is situated on the southern shore of Cape Mayor, a rocky peninsula extending east and sheltering the Santander Bay, an inlet of the Bay of BISCAY. The city was rebuilt after a disastrous fire in 1941. In addition to tourism, the economy is based on fishing, iron refining, and shipbuilding. The caves of ALTAMIRA and Castillo are nearby.

Santayana \ˌsän-tä-ˈyä-nä\, **George** *orig.* **Jorge Augustín Nicolás Ruiz de Santillana** (1863–1952) Spanish-U.S. philosopher, poet, and humanist. Born in Madrid, Santayana moved to the U.S. as a boy in 1872. After graduating from Harvard, he taught philosophy there (with WILLIAM JAMES and JOSIAH ROYCE) 1889–1912, and began producing important contributions to aesthetics, speculative philosophy, and literary criticism, including *The Sense of Beauty* (1896), *Interpretations of Poetry and Religion* (1900), and *The Life of Reason* (1905–6). He returned to Europe in 1912. *Scepticism and Animal Faith* (1923) best conveys his theory of immediately apprehended essences and describes the role played by "animal faith" in various forms of knowledge. He also wrote a novel, *The Last Puritan* (1935), and an autobiography, *Persons and Places* (3 vols., 1944–53).

Santee River \san-ˈtē\ River, southeastern central South Carolina. It flows southeast into the Atlantic Ocean after a course of 143 mi (230 km). It has been dammed to form the reservoir Lake Marion, which is connected by a navigable waterway, Lake Moultrie, and the Cooper River to CHARLESTON, S.C. The entire river system is the most important waterway and source of hydroelectric power in South Carolina.

Santería \ˌsän-te-ˈrē-ə\ Religious movement that originated in Cuba. It combines West African YORUBA beliefs and practices with elements of ROMAN CATHOLICISM. It includes belief in one supreme being, but worship and rituals center on *orishas,* deities or patron saints (with parallels among the Roman Catholic saints) that combine a force of nature and humanlike characteristics. Practices may include trance dancing, rhythmic drumming, spirit possession, and animal sacrifice. Santería has a considerable following in the U.S., particularly in Florida and in other areas with large African and Hispanic populations. See also CANDOMBLÉ, MACUMBA, VODUN.

Santiago (de Chile) \ˌsan-tē-'ä-gō\ City (metro. area pop., 1995: 5,077,000), capital of Chile. It is located in central Chile, on the Mapocho River, at an altitude of 1,706 ft (520 m). Founded in 1541 by the Spanish, the city has suffered repeatedly from earthquakes, floods, and civil disorders; it was occupied in 1817 during the war for independence. It became the capital of an independent Chile in 1818. It is the country's economic and cultural center and principal industrial city; it produces textiles, footwear, and foodstuffs. The city boasts a cosmopolitan cultural life, and is the home of the University of Chile.

Santiago (de los Caballeros) City (metro. area pop., 1993: 365,000), northern central Dominican Republic. Founded c. 1500, it was destroyed by an earthquake in 1562 and rebuilt a few miles away. Ruins of the old city are still visible in the district of San Francisco de Jacagua. It is the country's second-largest city; its economy depends mainly on the production of pharmaceuticals, cigarettes, rum, and coffee.

Santiago (de Compostela) City (pop., 1991: 88,000), capital of GALICIA autonomous community, northwestern Spain. It contains a Romanesque cathedral completed in 1211 that was built on the tomb of the apostle St. JAMES. The tomb, discovered in the 9th century, became the most important Christian pilgrimage site in Europe after that of Rome. The town that grew up around the tomb was destroyed in 997 by the Moors and was rebuilt in the Middle Ages. Chief economic activities include agriculture, silverwork, wood engraving, and the manufacture of linen and paper. The city is home to several colleges and a university.

Santiago de Cuba Seaport city (pop., 1994 est.: 440,000), eastern Cuba. The second-largest city in Cuba, it was founded in 1514 and moved to its present site in 1522. It commanded a strategic location on the northern Caribbean Sea in the early colonial period and was the capital of Cuba until 1589. It was a focal point of the SPANISH–AMERICAN WAR, and in 1898 the entire Spanish fleet was destroyed near its coast. In 1953 it was the scene of FIDEL CASTRO's attack against the Moncada army barracks. It is the center of an agricultural and mining region and exports copper, iron, manganese, sugar, and fruit.

Santo Domingo City (metro. area pop., 1993: 1,556,000), capital of the Dominican Republic. It is situated on the southeastern coast of the island of HISPANIOLA, at the mouth of the Ozama River. Founded in 1496 by CHRISTOPHER COLUMBUS brother Bartolomeo as the capital of the first Spanish colony in the New World, it became the oldest permanent city established by Europeans in the western hemisphere. It was under French control 1795–1809, and it was annexed to Spain 1861–65. It became the capital of the Dominican Republic when the country gained independence from Spain in 1865. The city was renamed Ciudad Trujillo in 1936 for Pres. RAFAEL TRUJILLO but reverted to its original name after his assassination in 1961. It is the commercial and cultural center of the republic and its principal seaport. Important industries include metallurgy and petrochemicals. It is the reputed site of the tomb of C. Columbus.

Santo Tomé de Guayana See CIUDAD GUAYANA

Santorini See THÍRA

Santorio, Santorio *Latin* **Sanctorius** (1561–1636) Italian physician. He adapted several of GALILEO's inventions to develop a medical thermometer and a pulse clock. To test GALEN's assertion that respiration also occurs through the skin as "insensible perspiration," Santorio built a large scale on which he frequently ate, worked, and slept, so he could study his body-weight changes in relation to his solid and liquid intake and output. After 30 years, he found the total of visible excreta was less than the amount ingested; his study marked the introduction of quantitative procedure into medical research. His *De statica medicina* (1614; "On Medical Measurement") was the first systematic study of basal METABOLISM.

Sanusi \sä-'nü-sē\, **al-** *in full* **Sidi Muhammad ibn Ali al-Sanusi al-Mujahiri al-Hasani al-Idrisi** (1787?–1859) North African Muslim theologian. He received his religious training in Fès, Morocco, which was under strong French influence at the time. He became convinced that the Islamic community needed to revitalize itself in order to shake off foreign domination. Using tactics he had developed among Bedouins in the Hejaz, he organized tribes in Cyrenaica to resist Italian domination, founding a militant mystical movement, the Sanusiya (1837), that helped Libya win its independence in the 20th century. IDRIS I was his grandson.

São Francisco River \ˌsau̇ⁿm-fräⁿ-'sēs-kü\ River, eastern Brazil. The largest river wholly within Brazil, it flows north and east across the great central plateau for about 1,811 mi (2,914 km) to its mouth on the Atlantic Ocean. The upper river valley is an area of thorny forest vegetation; the climate of the river basin is dry and hot. The fish of the river are an important food source. Hydroelectric dams provide power throughout northeastern Brazil.

São Paulo \sau̇ⁿm-'pau̇-lü\ City (metro. area pop., 1995: 16,417,000), southeastern Brazil. It is located 30 mi (48 km) from its Atlantic port of Santos. Founded by Portuguese Jesuits in 1554, it became a base for exploration in the 17th century and a city in 1711. In 1822 it was the scene of the declaration of Brazilian independence by Emperor PEDRO I. It developed rapidly from the late 19th century. It is the foremost industrial center in LATIN AMERICA, producing steel, motor vehicles, machine tools, and a wide range of consumer goods, including textiles and appliances. It is also Brazil's largest city, an important cultural and publishing center, and one of the most populous cities in the western hemisphere.

São Tomé \sau̇ⁿ-tü-'mā\ City (pop., 1991 est.: 43,000), capital of São Tomé and Príncipe. It is on the northeastern coast of the island of São Tomé, located on the equator in the Gulf of GUINEA. It is the country's largest city and its major port.

São Tomé and Príncipe \sau̇ⁿ-tü-'mā...'prēn-sē-pē\ *officially* **Democratic Republic of São Tomé and Príncipe** Nation, central Africa. It is situated on the equator in the Gulf of GUINEA, west of the African mainland. Area: 386 sq mi (1,001 sq km). Population (1997): 137,000. Capital: SÃO TOMÉ. Most of the people are African. Languages: Portu-

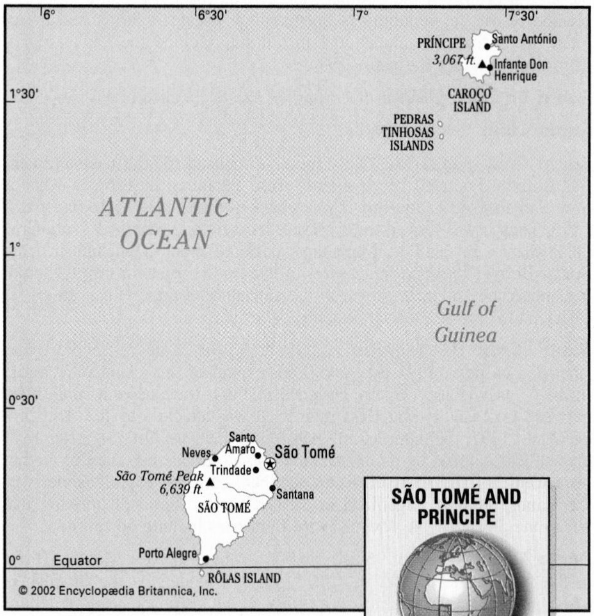

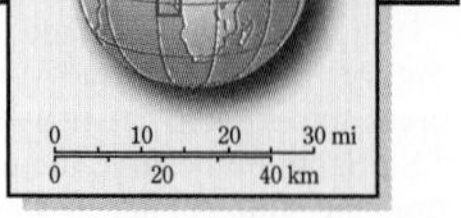

guese (official), Creole dialects. Religion: Christianity. Currency: dobra. The country consists of the two main islands, São Tomé and Príncipe, which are separated by about 90 mi (145 km), and a number of islets. The two main islands each have northeastern lowlands, central volcanic highlands, and swift-flowing streams. The economy is partly government controlled and partly private and is based on agriculture and fishing. It is a republic with one legislative house; its chief of state is the president, and the head of government is the prime minister.

First visited by European navigators in the 1470s, the islands were colonized by the Portuguese in the 16th century and were used in the trade and transshipment of slaves. Sugar and cocoa were the main cash crops. The islands became an overseas province of Portugal in 1951 and achieved independence in 1975. During recent decades its economy was heavily dependent on international assistance.

Saône River \'sōn\ *ancient* **Arar** River, eastern France. It flows generally south to join the RHONE RIVER at LYON. It is navigable upstream from Lyon for 233 mi (373 km) and has 30 locks along its course, which is almost completely canalized. Barge traffic is heavy along its lower course, and it is connected by canal to both the RHINE and SEINE rivers.

Saoshyant \saủsh-'yänt\ In ZOROASTRIANISM AND PARSIISM, the final savior of the world. He is the foremost of the three saviors who are posthumous sons of ZOROASTER. He is expected to appear at the end of the last millennium of the world, miraculously conceived by a virgin who has swum in a lake where Zoroaster's seed is preserved. He will vanquish demonic power and resurrect the bodies of the dead, bestowing eternal perfection on them after all souls have been cleansed.

Sapir \sə-'pir\, **Edward** (1884–1939) U.S. (Polish-born) linguist and anthropologist. He was a founder of ethnolinguistics, which considers the relationship of culture to language, and a principal developer of the American (descriptive) school of structural LINGUISTICS. He became widely known for his contributions to the study of AMERICAN INDIAN LANGUAGES. His best-known work is *Language* (1921).

sapodilla \,sa-pə-'di-lə\ Tropical evergreen tree *(Manilkara,* or *Achras, zapota)* of the family Sapotaceae, native to southern Mexico and northern Central America, and its distinctive fruit. The rusty-brown fruit is eaten fresh in many tropical and subtropical areas. Its sweet flavor has been compared to a combination of pears and brown sugar. When the fruit is ripe, its shiny black seeds are surrounded by clear, yellowish-brown, juicy flesh; when immature, its flesh contains both tannin and milky latex and is distasteful. The latex is the chief source of gum chicle, once important in the CHEWING-GUM industry.

Sapodilla (*Manilkara,* or *Achras, zapota*).
WALTER DAWN

sapper Military engineer. The name is derived from the French word *sappe* ("trench"), which became connected with MILITARY ENGINEERING in the 17th century, when attackers dug covered trenches to approach the walls of a besieged fort and also undermined the walls by tunneling beneath them. In modern armies, sappers provide tactical support by carrying out construction, including earthworks, portable bridges, and tank traps; build major facilities such as airports, supply roads, fuel depots, and barracks; and handle additional tasks, including disarming and disposing of LAND MINES and unexploded bombs and preparing and distributing maps.

sapphire Transparent to translucent natural or synthetic variety of CORUNDUM that is highly prized as a gemstone. Its color is due mainly to the presence of small amounts of iron and titanium and normally ranges from very pale blue to deep indigo. Colorless, gray, yellow, pale pink, orange, green, violet, and brown varieties also are known as sapphire; red varieties are called RUBY. Synthetic sapphire has been produced commercially since 1902. Much is used in jewelry, but most is used in the manufacture of jewel bearings, gauges, dies, and other specialized components; some also is used as a high-grade abrasive. It is found in Sri Lanka, Myanmar, and India and occurs in Montana in the U.S.

Sappho \'sa-fō\ (fl. c. 610–c. 580 BC) Greek lyric poet. Little is known of her life beyond the facts that she was born on the island of Lesbos and became the leading spirit of an informal women's society, of a type common among women of good family in her era, formed to pursue graceful pleasures, among them composing and reciting verse. Her principal themes are the loves, jealousies, and hates that flourished in that atmosphere. Her writing, mostly vernacular and not formally literary, is concise, direct, and picturesque and expresses a range of feelings, including her love for other women, which produced the word "lesbian" (from the island's name). Though much admired in antiquity, most of her work was lost by the early Middle Ages; only quotations by other authors of two poems and a number of fragments survive.

Sapporo \sä-'pō-rō\ City (pop., 1995 est.: 1,757,000), HOKKAIDO, Japan. Located on the ISHIKARI RIVER, the city was laid out in 1871 with wide, tree-lined streets; it became the capital in 1886. It is a major commercial center, with Otaru, on the Sea of JAPAN, as its port. Chief industries are lumbering, printing, and publishing. A popular center for skiing and winter sports, it was the site of the Winter OLYMPIC GAMES in 1972. The annual Snow Festival features giant sculptures carved from packed snow. It is the site of two universities.

sapsucker Either of two species of North American WOODPECKERS that drill holes in neat, close rows to obtain sap and insects. The yellow-bellied sapsucker *(Sphyrapicus varius),* about 8 in. (20 cm) long, is one of the few migratory species of woodpecker, breeding in northern regions and southern mountains and migrating as far as the West Indies and Central America. Both sexes have bold head markings. Williamson's sapsucker *(S. thyroideus),* which lives in high pine forests of the western U.S., is uncommon throughout its range.

Yellow-bellied sapsucker (*Sphyrapicus varius*).
KENNETH W. FINK FROM ROOT RESOURCES

Saqqara *or* **Sakkara** \sə-'kär-ə\ Site of ancient ruins, Lower Egypt. Part of the necropolis of the ancient city of MEMPHIS, it is located southwest of CAIRO and west of the modern village of Saqqara. The earliest remains are those in the Archaic period cemetery at the northernmost end of the site, where large mud-brick tombs, or MASTABAS, have been found that date to the beginning of Egyptian history. South of the Archaic cemetery lies the Step Pyramid, the oldest PYRAMID in Egypt. It was built by Djoser, second king of the 3rd dynasty, who ruled c. 2650–c. 2575 BC.

sarabande \'sar-ə-,band\ Stately processional dance in triple meter popular in the French court and throughout Europe in the 17th–18th century. Of Spanish or Mexican origin, it began as a vigorous dance, set to lively music and castanets, for a double line of couples. At first considered improper, it was forbidden in Spain in 1583. In the early 17th century, it was modified to its slow, dignified court version in France and Italy. The slow sarabande, usually with an accented dotted note on the second beat, became a standard movement of the baroque SUITE.

Saracens \'sar-ə-səns\ In the Middle Ages, any person—Arab, Turk, or other—who professed the religion of Islam. The name spread into Western Europe through the Byzantines and the crusaders. It was also applied to nomadic people of the deserts between Syria and Arabia.

Saragossa \,sar-ə-'gä-sə\ *Spanish* **Zaragoza** \,zä-rä-'gō-sä\ City (metro. area pop., 1995 est.: 608,000), capital of ARAGON autonomous community, northeastern Spain. It is located on the southern bank of the EBRO RIVER. The Celtiberian town of Salduba at the site was taken by the Romans at the end of the 1st century BC and made a colony named Caesaraugusta, from which its present name derives. It became an episcopal see in the 3rd century AD, and was taken by the Moors c. 714. It was the capital of Aragon 12th–15th century. It underwent two sieges (1808–9) by the French, which were commemorated in Lord BYRON's *Childe Harold*. It is an industrial center and the site of the annual National Trade Fair. Notable buildings include Romanesque and Gothic churches and palaces. Its university was founded in 1474.

Sarah (fl. early 2nd millennium BC) In the Old Testament, the wife of ABRAHAM and mother of Isaac. She was childless until age 90. In GENESIS, God promised Abraham that she would be "a mother of nations," but

Sarah refused to believe, and had already given her maidservant Hagar to Abraham, with whom he fathered Ishmael. Nevertheless, Sarah did conceive in her old age and give birth to Abraham's son Isaac.

Sarah Lawrence College Private liberal-arts college in Bronxville, N.Y. It was founded as a women's college in 1926 and named for the wife of its founding donor, William V. Lawrence. It became coeducational in 1968. Enrollment is about 1,300.

Sarajevo \'sä-rä-ye-ˌvȯ, *Engl* ˌsar-ə-'yā-vō\ City (pop., 1997 est.: 360,000), capital of Bosnia and Herzegovina. After the Turks invaded in the late 15th century, it developed as a trading center and stronghold of Muslim culture. From 1878 it was part of the Austro-Hungarian empire (see AUSTRIA-HUNGARY). In 1914 Archduke FRANCIS FERDINAND was assassinated by a Serbian nationalist, which action precipitated World War I. After Bosnia and Herzegovina declared independence in 1992, it became a focal point of fierce civil war as Serb militias drove thousands of Bosnian Muslims from the countryside to take refuge in the city (see BOSNIAN CONFLICT). Its pre–civil war industries included a brewery, furniture factory, tobacco factory, and an automobile plant. It was the host of the 1984 Winter OLYMPIC GAMES, and is the center of a road network with a rail connection to the Adriatic Sea. It retains a strong Muslim character, with many mosques and an ancient marketplace.

Saramago \ˌsä-rä-'mä-gü\, **José** (born 1922) Portuguese novelist. From a poor family, Saramago was unable to finish university but continued his studies part-time while working in a welder's shop. Later he moved into journalism and translation work. He published his first novel, *Country of Sin,* in 1947 but had to wait until 1982 for his breakthrough work, *Baltasar and Blimunda* (1982). His later novels, in which magic realism is mixed with outspoken political commentary, include *The Stone Raft* (1986), perhaps his best-known work, and *Blindness* (1995). He received the Nobel Prize in 1998.

Saranac Lakes \'sar-ə-ˌnak\ Three lakes, northeastern New York. Located in the ADIRONDACK MTNS. region, they are Upper, Middle, and Lower Saranac Lakes. They range in size from about 2.5 mi (4 km) wide to about 8 mi (13 km) long. Their elevation is 1,540 ft (469 m) above sea level. The village of Saranac Lake (pop., 1990: 5,000) is a summer and winter sports resort. Tourism and wood-based industries are the chief sources of income.

Sarandon \sə-'ran-dən\, **Susan** *orig.* **Susan Abigail Tomalin** (born 1946) U.S. film actress. Born in New York City, she married the actor Chris Sarandon and made her screen debut in 1970. After winning fans in the campy *Rocky Horror Picture Show* (1975), she proved her talent in films such as *Pretty Baby* (1978), *Atlantic City* (1981), and *The Witches of Eastwick* (1987). While working on *Bull Durham* (1988), she began a long relationship with the actor Tim Robbins (born 1958), who shared her commitment to progressive political activism. Her later films include *Thelma and Louise* (1991), *Lorenzo's Oil* (1992), and *Dead Man Walking* (1996, Academy Award).

Sarapeum \ˌser-ə-'pē-əm\ Either of two temples of ancient Egypt that were dedicated to the worship of the Greco-Egyptian god Sarapis. The original temple was built on the western bank of the Nile, near SAQQARA, during the reign of RAMSES II on a site originally dedicated to the worship of OSIRIS. The other Sarapeum was at ALEXANDRIA and was built during the reign of PTOLEMY I SOTER. In Roman times, other Sarapeums were constructed throughout the empire.

Sarasate (y Navascuéz) \ˌsä-rä-'sä-tā\, **Pablo (Martín Melitón) de** (1844–1908) Spanish violinist. After his debut at 8, he was sent to study in Madrid, where the queen gave him the Stradivarius that he would play his whole life. After finishing his studies in Paris, he toured the world. He had many pieces written for him (by M. BRUCH, C. SAINT-SAENS, etc.) and wrote scores of brilliant virtuoso works himself, including *Zigeunerweisen* (1878) and the *Carmen Fantasy* (1883).

Saratoga, Battles of (1777) Engagements in the AMERICAN REVOLUTION. British troops under JOHN BURGOYNE marched from Canada to join with other British troops, and, after camping at Saratoga, N.Y., engaged the Continental Army under HORATIO GATES at the Battle of Freeman's Farm, or First Battle of Saratoga (September 19). Failing to break the American lines, the British met a counterattack led by BENEDICT ARNOLD at the Battle of Bemis Heights, or Second Battle of Saratoga (October 7). With his forces reduced to 5,000 men, Burgoyne began to retreat, but Gates, with 20,000 men, surrounded the British at Saratoga and forced their surrender (October 17). The American victory induced the French to offer open recognition and military aid.

Saratov \sə-'rä-təf\ City (pop., 1995: 902,000), western Russia. Located on the VOLGA RIVER, it was founded in 1590 as a fortress to protect the trade route along the Volga. It was moved to a new site in 1616 and again in 1674 after the fortress was destroyed in a revolt. Linked to MOSCOW by railroad in the 1870s, Saratov became a major commercial center. Its road bridge across the Volga (opened 1965) is the largest in Europe. Now a major industrial center, it produces electric and petrochemical equipment and machine tools. Its educational institutions include a university (founded 1919) and a music conservatory.

Sarazen \'sar-ə-zən\, **Gene** *orig.* **Eugene Saraceni** (1902–1999) U.S. golfer, prominent in the 1920s and '30s. Born in Harrison, N.Y., to a poor Italian immigrant family, he won the U.S. Open (1922, 1932), the British Open (1932), the Masters (1935), and the PGA championship (1922–23, 1933). His Masters victory was highlighted by his famous double eagle 2 (three under par) on the par-5 15th hole.

sardine Any of certain species of small (6–12 in., or 15–30 cm, long) food fishes of the HERRING family (Clupeidae), especially in the genera *Sardina, Sardinops,* and *Sardinella.* The common herring *(Clupea harengus)* is found throughout the North Atlantic. The five species of *Sardinops* live in the Pacific and Indian oceans. Sardines are small, silvery, slender fishes with a single short dorsal fin and no scales on the head. They live in dense schools, migrating along the coast. They are usually fished with an encircling net, particularly the purse seine, and mainly at night, when they surface to feed on plankton. See also PILCHARD, SPRAT.

Sardinia *Italian* **Sardegna** \sär-'dān-yä\ Island and Italian autonomous region (pop., 1996 est.: 1,661,000), off southern Italian coast. The second-largest island in the western Mediterranean Sea, it measures 9,194 sq mi (23,813 sq km); its capital is CAGLIARI. Thousands of structures made of basalt blocks, called nuraghi, are a dominating feature of the island. Some date to c. 1500–400 BC. Phoenicians were its first recorded settlers c. 800 BC. Greeks and Carthaginians followed; Roman rule began in 238 BC. In the early Middle Ages, PISA and GENOA struggled over its domination. The kingdom of Sardinia, centered on the lands of Piedmont in northwestern Italy and the island of Sardinia, was ruled by the House of SAVOY from 1720 until the unification of Italy in 1861. Agriculture, fishing, and mining are economic mainstays.

Sardinian language ROMANCE LANGUAGE spoken in SARDINIA, the most similar to Vulgar LATIN of the modern Romance languages. Its only standard form is the *sardo illustre,* a literary language used mostly for folk verse. Italian is the island's official language, and few literary works exist in Sardinian. The earliest written materials date from c. 1080.

Sardis \'sär-dəs\ *or* **Sardes** \'sär-dēz\ Ancient city, ASIA MINOR, east of Smyrna. It was the chief city and capital of the kingdom of LYDIA from the 7th century BC and the first city where gold and silver coins were minted. It fell to the Persians c. 546 BC and passed to the Romans in 133 BC. Destroyed by an earthquake in AD 17, it was rebuilt and remained one of the great cities of ASIA MINOR until the later Byzantine period. It was obliterated by TIMUR in 1402. Its ruins include the ancient Lydian citadel, but excavations have uncovered more remains of the Hellenistic and Byzantine city than of the ancient Lydian town.

Sardou \sȧr-'dü\, **Victorien** (1831–1908) French playwright. He owed his initial success to the actress Pauline Déjazet, for whom he wrote several of his 70 works, including *A Scrap of Paper* (1860). Several later works, including *Fédora* (1882), were written for SARAH BERNHARDT. His *La Tosca* (1887) was adapted by G. PUCCINI as an opera. His last success was *Madame Sans-Gêne* (1893). In 1877 he was elected to the Académie Française. His plays rely heavily on theatrical devices and plot contrivances, and he is remembered as a craftsman of the bourgeois drama that GEORGE BERNARD SHAW belittled as "Sardoodledom."

Sarekat Islam \'sȧr-ə-kȧt\ First nationalist political party in Indonesia to gain wide popular support. Founded in 1912 to promote the interests of Muslim merchants, it soon began working for the self-government of the Dutch East Indies. Its religious appeal helped it grow rapidly, and by 1916 it claimed 350,000 members. As it became more and more involved in revolutionary activities, communist elements entered the organization, and a struggle for power between religious leaders and communists culminated in its division in 1921. With the departure of its left wing, Sarekat Islam declined.

Sarema See SAAREMAA

Sargasso Sea Body of still water in the North Atlantic Ocean. Elliptical in shape and strewn with a brown floating seaweed of the genus *Sargassum*, it lies between the parallels 20° N and 35° N and the meridians 30° W and 70° W and encompasses the BERMUDA islands. It was first mentioned by CHRISTOPHER COLUMBUS, who crossed it in 1492. The presence of the seaweed suggested the proximity of land and encouraged him to continue, but many early navigators feared becoming entangled in the floating vegetation and turned back.

sargassum \sär-'ga-süm\ Any of the brown ALGAE that make up the genus *Sargassum.* They are adapted for a free-floating tropical environment, even though many species grow attached to rocks along the coast. The SARGASSO SEA, a free-floating mass of seaweed (mostly *S. natans*), occurs in the Atlantic Ocean. Sargassums are also known as sea holly because of their highly branched stems with hollow, berrylike floats and many leaflike, sawtooth-edged blades. They are used as fertilizer in New Zealand and as a component of soups and soy sauce in Japan.

Sargent, John Singer (1856–1925) U.S.-British painter. Son of wealthy American parents, he was born in Italy and grew up in Europe, not seeing the U.S. until 1876. Having studied painting in Paris, in 1879 he traveled to Madrid and Haarlem to study the works of DIEGO VELAZQUEZ and FRANS HALS; his finest works were painted soon afterward. Best known is his *Madame X*, which created a scandal at the 1884 Salon; critics found it eccentric and erotic, and the sitter's mother claimed it made her daughter a laughingstock. Discouraged, he moved permanently to London, though he often visited the U.S. The *Pall Mall Gazette* voted his *Miss Vickers* (1884) the worst painting of the year, and not until 1886 did he achieve the acclaim he was to enjoy in the U.S. and England the rest of his life. His elegant portraits created an enduring image of high society of the Edwardian age; the best, painted with his slashing brush strokes, capture his subjects in revealing, off-guard moments. He largely gave up portraiture in 1907 and devoted the rest of his life to murals and landscapes.

Sargon \'sär-gän\ (r.2334–2279? BC) Ancient Mesopotamian ruler. What is known of him comes from legends and tales; his capital city, Agade, has never been located. Perhaps originally a royal cupbearer, he came to prominence by defeating a Sumerian king, thereby attaining an empire in southern Mesopotamia and becoming the first emperor whose native tongue was Akkadian rather than Sumerian. He enlarged the empire from Iraq to Anatolia, and trade flourished with the Indus valley, Oman, the Persian Gulf coast, Cappadocia, and the Mediterranean.

Sargon II (died 705 BC) Assyrian king (721–705 BC). He continued the empire-building work of his father, TIGLATH-PILESER III. One of his aims was to prove the might of the Assyrian god Ashur by enlarging the empire he had inherited. His conquests ranged from southern Babylonia to Armenia to the Mediterranean. He probably died in battle in northwestern Persia. His son, SENNACHERIB, succeeded him.

Sargon II, detail of a relief from the palace at Khorsabad; in the Louvre, Paris.

BY COURTESY OF THE MUSEE DU LOUVRE, PARIS; PHOTOGRAPH, MAURICE CHUZEVILLE

Sarmatians \sär-'mā-shənz\ People originally of Iranian stock who migrated from Central Asia to the Ural Mountains in the 6th–4th century BC and settled in southern European Russia and the eastern Balkans. Closely related to the SCYTHIANS, they were expert horsemen and warriors and gained wide influence through administrative and political astuteness. Women fought alongside men and may have inspired Greek tales of AMAZONS. By the 5th century BC they controlled the land between the Urals and the Don, and by the 2nd century they had conquered the Scythians to rule almost all southern Russia. Allied with Germanic tribes, they continued to pose a threat to the West until the 1st century AD. After invading Dacia and the lower Danube, they were overrun by the GOTHS. Many joined the Gothic invasion of western Europe. Sarmatia was destroyed by HUNS after AD 370. Their descendants cannot be traced after the 5th century.

Sarmiento \särm-'yān-tō\, **Domingo Faustino** (1811–1888) Educator, statesman, writer, and president of Argentina (1868–74). A rural schoolteacher, he entered provincial politics and was exiled to Chile by JUAN MANUEL DE ROSAS for his outspokenness. There he became an important figure in journalism and education. In his important book *Facundo* (1845), he denounced the Rosas dictatorship and the culture of the GAUCHOS. He returned to Argentina to help overthrow Rosas in 1852. Elected president in 1868, he ended the PARAGUAYAN WAR, developed the public school system, established technical and professional schools, and upheld civil liberties.

Sarnoff, David (1891–1971) U.S. (Russian-born) communications executive. After emigrating with his family to New York in 1900, he left school to become a telegraph messenger boy and later a radio operator for the Marconi telegraph company. In 1912 he heard the distress signal from the sinking *Titanic* and remained at his instrument for 72 hours relaying news. Rapidly promoted, he became general manager of the newly formed Radio Corp. of America (RCA CORP.) in 1921. He had proposed the first commercially marketed radio receiver in 1916, and by 1924 it had earned $80 million in sales. He formed the radio network NBC in 1926. Perceiving television's potential, he set up an experimental television station (1928) and demonstrated the new medium at the New York World's Fair (1939). During World War II he was a communications consultant to Gen. DWIGHT D. EISENHOWER and was made a brigadier general. President of RCA 1930–47, he served as chairman of the board until 1970.

Sarnoff, 1971.

AP/WIDE WORLD PHOTOS

Saro-Wiwa \,sä-rō-'wē-wə\, **Ken** *orig.* **Kenule Benson Tsaro-Wiwa** (1941–1995) Nigerian writer and activist. He taught at the University of Lagos and held government office before turning to writing. His first novels were *Songs in a Time of War* and *Sozaboy* (both 1985); his television series *Basi and Company* satirized the Nigerian desire to get rich with little effort. He also wrote poetry, children's stories, and a newspaper column. His support of the Ogoni people against the oil industry put him at odds with the government; he was spuriously charged with four murders and executed despite worldwide protest.

Saronic Gulf \sə-'rä-nik\ Gulf of the AEGEAN SEA, southeastern coast of Greece. Some 50 mi (80 km) long and 30 mi (50 km) wide, it separates ATTICA and the PELOPONNESE and is linked to the Gulf of Corinth by the Corinth Canal. It was the site of a major Athenian victory over the Persians in 480 BC (see Battle of SALAMIS). Its ports include PIRAEUS and MEGARA.

Saroyan \sə-'rói-ən\, **William** (1908–1981) U.S. writer. Born in Fresno, Cal., Saroyan was the largely self-educated son of an Armenian immigrant. He made his initial impact during the Depression with brash, original, and irreverent stories celebrating the joy of living in spite of poverty, hunger, and insecurity. Much of his fiction is based on his childhood and family. His story collections include *The Daring Young Man on the Flying Trapeze* (1934), *Inhale and Exhale* (1936), and *My Name is Aram* (1940). His other works include the play *The Time of Your Life* (1939, Pulitzer Prize) and *The Human Comedy* (1943), a sentimental novel of life in a small California town.

Sarpi \'sär-pē\, **Paolo** (1552–1623) Italian patriot, scholar, and state theologian. A native of Venice, Sarpi at age 20 became court theologian to the duke of Mantua, a post that gave him leisure to study Greek, Hebrew, mathematics, anatomy, and botany. Later, as consultor to the government, he incurred the wrath of Pope Paul V by supporting Venice's right to restrict church construction in the city and to try priests accused of crimes unrelated to religion (e.g., murder) in the state's courts. His *History of the Council of Trent* (1619), an important work decrying papal absolutism, was published under a pseudonym; though placed on the INDEX LIBRORUM PROHIBITORUM, it enjoyed a success.

Sarraute \sä-ˈrōt\, **Nathalie** *orig.* **Nathalie Ilyanova Tcherniak** (1900–1999) French novelist and essayist. She practiced law until c. 1940, when she became a full-time writer. *Tropismes* (1939), a collection of sketches, introduced her idea of tropisms, the "things that are not said and the movements that cross our consciousness very rapidly." An early practitioner and leading theorist of the *nouveau roman* ("new novel"), the French ANTINOVEL, she discarded conventions of plot, chronology, characterization, and point of view. Her novels—including *Portrait of a Man Unknown* (1948), *Martereau* (1953), *Le planétarium* (1959), and *Here* (1997)—and her plays focus on the unspoken "subconversations" in human interactions.

sarsaparilla \ˌsas-pə-ˈri-lə\ Aromatic flavoring agent originally made from the dried roots of several tropical SMILAX vines. Native to the southern and western coasts of Mexico to Peru, the plants are large, perennial, climbing or trailing vines with short, thick, underground stems that produce many prickly, angular, aboveground stems supported by tendrils. Once a popular tonic, sarsaparilla now is blended with WINTERGREEN and other flavors and used in root beer and other carbonated beverages, or to flavor and mask the taste of medicines. In North America, the strongly aromatic roots of the wild sarsaparilla *(Aralia nudicaulis)* and false, or bristly, sarsaparilla *(A. hispida),* of the GINSENG family, are sometimes substituted for true sarsaparilla.

Sarto, Andrea del See ANDREA DEL SARTO

Sartre \ˈsärtrᵊ\, **Jean-Paul** (1905–1980) French philosopher, novelist, and playwright, the foremost exponent of EXISTENTIALISM. He studied at the Sorbonne, where he met SIMONE DE BEAUVOIR, his lifelong companion and intellectual collaborator. His first novel, *Nausea* (1938), narrates the feeling of revulsion that a young man undergoes when confronted with the contingency of existence. *Huis-clos* (1944, *No Exit*) became the most widely celebrated of his several plays. In *Being and Nothingness* (1943) he places human consciousness, or nothingness *(néant),* in opposition to being, or thingness *(être);* consciousness is nonmatter and thus escapes all determinism. With his treatise *Existentialism and Humanism* (1946), these works formed the foundations of postwar existentialism. He learned the PHENOMENOLOGY of EDMUND HUSSERL and used it in *Imagination* (1936), *Sketch for a Theory of the Emotions* (1939), and *The Psychology of Imagination* (1940), and he later examined Marxism in *Critique of Dialectical Reason* (1960). His final works included an autobiography, *The Words* (1963), and the huge study *Flaubert* (4 vols., 1971–72). A central figure of the French left, he opposed the Vietnam War and supported the 1968 revolutionaries. He declined the 1964 Nobel Prize for Literature.

Sartre, photograph by Gisèle Freund, 1968.
GISELE FREUND

Sarvastivada \sər-ˌväs-ti-ˈvä-də\ One of the 18 schools of HINAYANA Buddhism to develop during the first four or five centuries after the Buddha's death. The name literally means the teaching that everything exists, which related to the notion that the past, present, and future all exist. The Sarvastivada school was particularly influential in northwestern India and portions of S.East Asia.

Sasanian dynasty *or* **Sassanian dynasty** \sa-ˈsā-nē-ən\ Persian dynasty (AD 224–651). Founded by Ardashir I (r.AD 224–41) and named for his ancestor Sasan (c. 1st century AD), it replaced the Parthian empire (see PARTHIA). Its capital was CTESIPHON. The dynasty battled Rome and Byzantium in the west and the Kushans and Hephthalites in the east throughout much of its existence. In the 3rd century its empire stretched from Sogdiana and Georgia to northern Arabia, and from the Indus River to the Tigris and Euphrates. Traditions of the ACHAEMENIAN DYNASTY were revived, Zoroastrianism was reestablished as the state religion, and art and architecture experienced a renaissance. Its important rulers included Shapur I (died 272), Shapur II (309–379), KHOSROW I, and KHOSROW II. The Sasanians were the last native Persian dynasty before the Arab conquest of the region.

Saskatchewan \sas-ˈka-chə-ˌwän\ Province (pop., 1996: 1,024,000), western Canada. It is bounded by Alberta, Manitoba, the Northwest Territories, and the U.S. The capital is REGINA. A plains region, with prairie to the south and wooded country to the north, it supports rich and varied wildlife. The Cree Indians inhabited the region for some 5,000 years before it was claimed by the HUDSON'S BAY CO., which controlled the area from 1670 until it surrendered the land to the British in 1868. It was part of the Northwest Territory until 1869, and in 1870 became part of the Dominion of Canada. From 1882 the extension of the railroad brought large numbers of European settlers. The province was created in 1905. Its economy is based on oil, gas, and potash production, grains, and livestock. The largest city is SASKATOON.

Saskatchewan, University of Public university in Saskatoon, Saskatchewan, founded in 1907. It has colleges of arts and sciences, graduate studies, agriculture, veterinary medicine, engineering, law, medicine, dentistry, nursing, pharmacy, commerce, education, and physical education. Total enrollment is about 18,000.

Saskatchewan River River, southwestern and southern central Canada. The largest river system of Alberta and Saskatchewan, it rises in the Canadian Rockies as the North and South Saskatchewan rivers, which are 800 mi (1,287 km) and 865 mi (1,392 km) long, respectively. The combined streams continue east 340 mi (550 km) to enter Lake WINNIPEG. Once important as a fur-trading route, it now provides hydroelectric power and irrigation.

Saskatoon \ˌsas-kə-ˈtün\ City (pop., 1991: 186,000), southern central Saskatchewan. It was founded on the SASKATCHEWAN RIVER in 1883 as the proposed capital of a temperance colony. It grew rapidly following the arrival of the railroad in 1890 and the town's amalgamation with two adjoining settlements in 1906. Saskatchewan's largest city, it is a cultural and educational center and a major transportation hub and distribution center. Its educational institutions include the University of Saskatchewan (founded 1907).

Sasquatch See BIGFOOT

sassafras \ˈsa-sə-ˌfras\ North American tree *(Sassafras albidum)* of the LAUREL FAMILY. The aromatic leaf, bark, and root are used as a flavoring, as a traditional home medicine, and as a tea. The aromatic roots yield about 2% oil of sassafras, once the characteristic ingredient of root beer. The tree is native to sandy soils from Maine to Ontario and Iowa and south to Florida and Texas. It is usually small but may attain a height of 65 ft (20 m) or more. It has furrowed bark, bright-green twigs, small clusters of yellow flowers followed by dark-blue berries, and three distinctive forms of leaves, often on the same twig: three-lobed, two-lobed (mitten-shaped), and entire.

Sassandra River \sə-ˈsan-drə\ River, western Ivory Coast. It rises as the Tienba in the northwestern highlands and becomes the Sassandra at its confluence with the Férédougouba. It courses southeast 400 mi (650 km) to empty into the Gulf of GUINEA at the seaport of Sassandra. Its upper reaches have been panned for diamonds; its lower course marks the eastern boundary of the Taï Reserve, known for its pygmy hippopotamus.

Sassetta *orig.* **Stefano di Giovanni** (died c. 1450) Italian painter. His interest in Florentine art is evident in his monumental *Madonna of the Snow* altarpiece for Siena Cathedral (1430–32) and in his most ambitious work, an altarpiece for San Francesco at Sansepolcro (1437–44). His fusion of traditional and contemporary elements transformed Sienese painting from the Gothic to the Renaissance style, and he is considered one of the greatest Sienese painters of the 15th century.

SAT *in full* **Scholastic Aptitude Test** Standardized test taken by U.S. high-school students applying to colleges. It is divided into two principal sections, verbal and mathematical. Promulgated largely through the efforts of JAMES B. CONANT as a means of promoting merit-based (rather than class-based) college admissions, it was administered to few students before the end of World War II but today is taken by millions each year. Scores declined as the test came to be more widely administered, and in 1995 the score of 500 for each section (midway between the extremes of 200 and 800) was reestablished as the actual mean score of those tested. The test, which most colleges use as one measure of a student's ability, has been insistently criticized for a claimed bias in favor of the white middle class, and for its multiple-choice format, which critics claim is inadequate to test various important capacities.

satanism Worship of Satan, or the DEVIL, the personality or principle regarded in the Judeo-Christian tradition as embodying absolute evil, in complete antithesis to God. Cults associated with satanism have been documented, however sketchily, back to the 17th century. Their central feature is the black MASS, a corrupted and inverted rendition of the Christian EUCHARIST. Practices are said to include animal SACRIFICE and deviant sexual activity. Worship is motivated by the belief that Satan is more powerful than the forces of good, and so is more capable of bringing about the results sought by his adherents.

satellite Natural or artificial object orbiting a larger astronomical object, usually a planet. The MOON is the most obvious example and the only one known until the discovery of the GALILEAN SATELLITES. All the sun's planets except Mercury and Venus have natural satellites, which vary greatly in size and composition, from almost entirely rocky (e.g., the moon) to volcanic or mostly ice. The first artificial satellite was SPUTNIK 1 (1957). Since then, many hundreds have been sent into orbit around earth and around Venus, Mars, and Jupiter, as well as the sun and moon. Artificial satellites are used for scientific research and other purposes, such as communication (see COMMUNICATIONS SATELLITE), weather forecasting, earth resources management, and military intelligence. See also LANDSAT.

satellite, communications See COMMUNICATIONS SATELLITE

sati See SUTTEE

Satie \sȧ-'tē\, **Erik** *orig.* **Eric Alfred Leslie** (1866–1925) French composer. His Scottish mother died when he was 7; sent back to his grandparents in Normandy, he was given music lessons by the local organist. Returning to Paris, he attended the Conservatoire 1879–82. From 1888 he played piano at Le Chat Noir, a bohemian hangout, and he became "official composer of the Rosicrucians." Living in austere poverty in a working-class district, he gained prominence in 1911 when M. RAVEL played his *Three Sarabandes* (1887), and was acknowledged as a forerunner of modern music. Though lionized, he retained his eccentric way of life and always ended up at odds with his admirers, including C. DEBUSSY, JEAN COCTEAU, and Les SIX. His mostly short piano works are as odd, witty, and charming as he was, and often sport such bizarre titles as *Three Pieces in the Form of a Pear.*

satin Fabric constructed by the satin WEAVING method, one of the three basic TEXTILE weaves. Satin weave superficially resembles TWILL, but does not have the regular step in each successive weft that characterizes twills. Thus, there is no strong diagonal line, and the fabric is smooth-faced, with an unbroken surface made up of long floating warp yarns. Because satins are susceptible to the wear caused by rubbing and snagging, they are considered luxury fabrics. Satin is made in different weights for various uses, including dresses (particularly evening wear), linings, bedspreads, and upholstery. Though originally of silk, it may be made of yarns of other fibers.

satire Artistic form in which human or individual vices, folly, abuses, or shortcomings are held up to censure by means of ridicule, derision, burlesque, irony, or other methods, sometimes with an intent to bring about improvement. Literature and drama are its chief vehicles, but it is also found in such mediums as film, the visual arts (e.g., caricatures), and political cartoons. Though present in Greek literature, notably in the works of ARISTOPHANES, satire generally follows the example of either of two Romans, HORACE or JUVENAL. To Horace the satirist is an urbane man of the world who sees folly everywhere but is moved to gentle laughter rather than to rage. Juvenal's satirist is an upright man who is horrified and angered by corruption. Their different perspectives produced the subgenres of satire identified by JOHN DRYDEN as comic satire and tragic satire.

Satnami sect \ˌsət-'nä-mē\ Religious community in India that challenges political and religious authority by worshiping the supreme god Satnam. Combining practices from ISLAM and HINDUISM, Satnamis typically reject both the worship of images and the CASTE system, while retaining an underlying orthodox VEDANTA philosophy. Modern Satnamis are confined almost entirely to the low-status Camar caste, and they advocate social equality as well as ethical and dietary self-restraint.

Sato \'sä-tō\, **Eisaku** (1901–1975) Prime minister of Japan (1964–1972) who presided over Japan's post-World War II reemergence as a major world power. For his policies on nuclear weapons, which led to Japan's signing the nuclear nonproliferation treaty, he shared the 1974 Nobel Peace Prize. As prime minister Sato improved relations with other Asian countries and oversaw the return of the Ryukyu Islands from the U.S. to Japan.

satrap Provincial governor in the ACHAEMENIAN empire. DARIUS I (r.522–486 BC) established 20 satrapies with an annual tribute. Appointed by the king, satraps were usually of the royal family or Persian nobility and held office indefinitely. They collected taxes, were the highest judicial authority, and were responsible for internal security and raising and maintaining an army. Controls guarded against abuse of power, but after the mid-5th century BC, with central authority weakened, satrapies became virtually independent. ALEXANDER THE GREAT and his successors retained the satraps.

Satsuma \'sät-sü-ˌmä\ Japanese feudal domain (HAN) in southern Kyushu; modern-day Kagoshima Prefecture. Satsuma was ruled by the Shimazu family from the end of the 12th century until the MEIJI RESTORATION in 1868. In 1609 the family had conquered the RYUKYU ISLANDS, and trade with the Ryukyus continued during the TOKUGAWA SHOGUNATE, when the rest of the country was forbidden contact with the outside world. This trade both enriched Satsuma and provided experience with foreign affairs that would prove useful in the 19th century when Western powers started pressuring Japan to end its isolation. The domain also had expertise in Western learning: Shimazu Shigehide (1745–1833) founded schools of medicine, mathematics, and astronomy, while Shimazu Nariakira (1809–1858) adopted Western-style military techniques and armaments. These advantages, along with a traditional enmity toward the Tokugawa family, put the men of Satsuma in a prime position to become leaders in the movement to overthrow the shogunal government. See also OKUBO TOSHIMICHI, SAIGO TAKAMORI.

Satsuma Rebellion See SAIGO TAKAMORI

saturation State of an ORGANIC COMPOUND in which all its CARBON atoms are linked by single bonds. Saturation also means the state of a SOLUTION or vapor (see VAPORIZATION) in which it has the highest possible concentration of the dissolved or vaporized material at a given pressure and temperature. Though it is sometimes possible to bring about supersaturation (a concentration exceeding the equilibrium value), such solutions or vapors are unstable and spontaneously revert to the saturated state. See also FATTY ACID, HYDROGENATION.

Saturn Roman god of agriculture, equated with the Greek deity CRONUS. His wife was Ops, the goddess of plenty, and his children included JUNO, NEPTUNE, and CERES. His festival, Saturnalia (beginning December 17), became the most popular Roman festival; its influence is still felt in the celebration of CHRISTMAS and the Western New Year. During Saturnalia, all business transactions were suspended, presents were exchanged, and slaves were given token freedom. The remains of Saturn's temple are located in the Forum in Rome. Saturday is named for Saturn.

Saturn Sixth PLANET from the sun, named after the Roman god of sowing and seed. The second-largest nonstellar object in the SOLAR SYSTEM after Jupiter, it is about 95 times as massive as earth and has more than 700 times its volume. Its outer layers are gaseous, mainly hydrogen. Models of its interior suggest a rocky core surrounded by a shallow layer of liquid metallic hydrogen encased by an envelope of molecular hydrogen. Saturn has at least 18 icy satellites (including TITAN, the biggest) and an extensive ring system, with seven main sections visible from earth with a telescope. Saturn's rings, first observed in 1610 by GALILEO, are made up of countless separate particles of all sizes, estimated to range from grains of fine dust to a small number of bodies possibly tens of miles across. Water ice observed on the surfaces of the particles probably constitutes most of the ring material. Saturn's day is about 10.5 hours; its year is 29.5 earth years. Its rapid rotation, acting on electric currents in the core, generates a strong magnetic field and large magnetosphere. Its gravity at the top of its atmosphere is 16% greater than earth's. Its average distance from the sun is 887 million mi (1,427 billion km).

Saturn Any of a series of large two- and three-stage vehicles for launching spacecraft, developed by the U.S. beginning in 1958, and first fired in 1961. Saturn I, the first U.S. rocket specifically developed for spaceflight, was a two-stage vehicle that placed test versions of APOLLO spacecraft into orbit and launched unmanned spacecraft. Saturn V was the largest rocket booster ever built by the U.S. and was used for the lunar missions of Apollo and to launch SKYLAB.

saturniid moth \sə-ˈtər-nē-əd\ *or* **giant silkworm moth** Any of some 800 MOTH species of the principally tropical family Saturniidae. Adults have a stout, hairy body and broad wings, often vividly colored and patterned. Most species have a central eyespot on each wing. Among the saturniids are the io moth *(Automeris io);* the giant cecropia moth *(Hyalophora cecropia),* the largest moth native to North America, with a wingspan of 6 in. (15 cm); several species of *Antheraea* that are used as a source of commercial silk; the emperor moth *(Saturnia pavonia);* and the LUNA MOTH.

Polyphemus moth (*Antheraea polyphemus*).
WILLIAM E. FERGUSON

Saturninus \ˌsa-tər-ˈnī-nəs\, **Lucius Appuleius** (died 100 BC) Roman politician. From 104 he opposed the Senate, which objected to his extremist liberal positions. As TRIBUNE (103) he supported Rome's proletariat by reducing the price of grain, assigning land grants to veterans, and setting up a court to try cases of treason. The consul, MARIUS, initially supported him, but later withdrew his backing. When Saturninus and his followers seized the Capitoline Hill, Marius restored order, locking the leaders of the action in the Senate house. Their enemies tore off the roof and stoned them to death. The Senate then rescinded most of Saturninus' legislation.

satyagraha \ˌsət-ˈyä-grə-hə\ Philosophy of nonviolent protest, or passive resistance. MOHANDAS K. GANDHI introduced it in South Africa (1906) and, from 1917, developed it in India in the period leading up to independence from Britain. Satyagraha seeks to conquer through submission. It involves refusing to submit to or cooperate with anything perceived as wrong, while adhering to the principle of nonviolence in order to maintain the tranquillity of mind required for insight and understanding. The principle played a significant role in the U.S. CIVIL RIGHTS MOVEMENT led by MARTIN LUTHER KING. See also CIVIL DISOBRDIENCE.

satyr and silenus \ˈsā-tər...sī-ˈlē-nəs\ In GREEK MYTHOLOGY, wild woodland creatures that are part man and part beast, the bestial part being represented as the legs of a goat or horse. From the 5th century BC, the name Silenus was applied to the foster father and tutor of DIONYSUS. Satyrs and sileni are depicted in art and literature in the company of NYMPHS, whom they constantly pursue. PRAXITELES' sculptures represented a new artistic type in which the satyr was young and handsome.

Saud \sà-ˈüd\ *in full* **Saud ibn Abdul Aziz al-Faisal al-Saud** (1902–1969) King of Saudi Arabia (1953–64). Son and successor of IBN SAUD, he continued his father's program of modernization, emphasizing the construction of medical and educational facilities. His financial mismanagement led to increasing opposition. He was deposed in favor of his brother, Faisal ibn Abd al-Aziz (1905–1975), who proved far more financially competent.

Saud dynasty \sà-ˈüd\ Rulers of present-day Saudi Arabia. In the 18th century Muhammad ibn Saud (died 1765), chief of an Arabian village that had never fallen under Ottoman control, rose to power together with the WAHHABI religious movement. He and his son Abd al-Aziz I (r.1764–1803) conquered much of Arabia; Saud I (r.1803–14) conquered Medina in 1804 and Mecca in 1806. The Ottoman sultan induced the viceroy of Egypt to crush the Saudis and Wahhabis, which was accomplished by 1818. A second Saudi state was formed in 1824 by Muhammad ibn Saud's grandson Turki (r.1823–34), who made Riyadh his capital. When Turki's son Faisal (r.1843–65) died, succession disputes led to civil war. Power did not return to Saudi hands until 1902, when IBN SAUD recaptured Riyadh. He established the kingdom of Saudi Arabia by royal decree in 1932. One of his sons, Fahd (born 1923), is the country's current ruler.

Saudi Arabia \ˈsau̇-dē, ˈsȯ-dē\ *officially* **Kingdom of Saudi Arabia** Country, South Asia. It occupies four-fifths of the ARABIAN PENINSULA and is bounded by the Red Sea and the Persian Gulf. Area: 865,000 sq mi (2.24 million sq km). Population (2001): 22,757,000. Capital: RIYADH. The people are predominantly Arab. Language: Arabic (official). Religion: Islam (official) (Sunnite). Currency: Saudi riyal. The country is a plateau region, with bands of imposing highlands rising from the narrow Red Sea coast. More than 95% is desert, including the world's largest continuous sand area, the RUB AL-KHALI (Empty Quarter). The largest petroleum producer of the ORGANIZATION OF PETROLEUM EXPORTING COUNTRIES (OPEC) and the third-largest producer in the world, its reserves represent one-fourth of the world total. Other products include natural gas, gypsum, dates, wheat, and desalinated water. It is a monarchy; its head of state and government is the king. Saudi Arabia is the historical home of ISLAM, founded by MUHAMMAD in MEDINA in 622. During medieval times, local and foreign rulers fought for control of the peninsula; in 1517 the Ottomans prevailed. In the 18th–19th century Islamic leaders supporting religious reform struggled to regain Saudi territory, all of which was restored by 1904. The British held Saudi lands as a protectorate 1915–27; then they acknowledged the sovereignty of the Kingdom of the Hejaz and Najd. The two kingdoms were unified as the Kingdom of Saudi Arabia in 1932. Since World War II, it has supported the Palestinian cause in the Middle East and maintained close ties with the U.S. In 2000 Saudi Arabia and Yemen settled their longstanding border dispute.

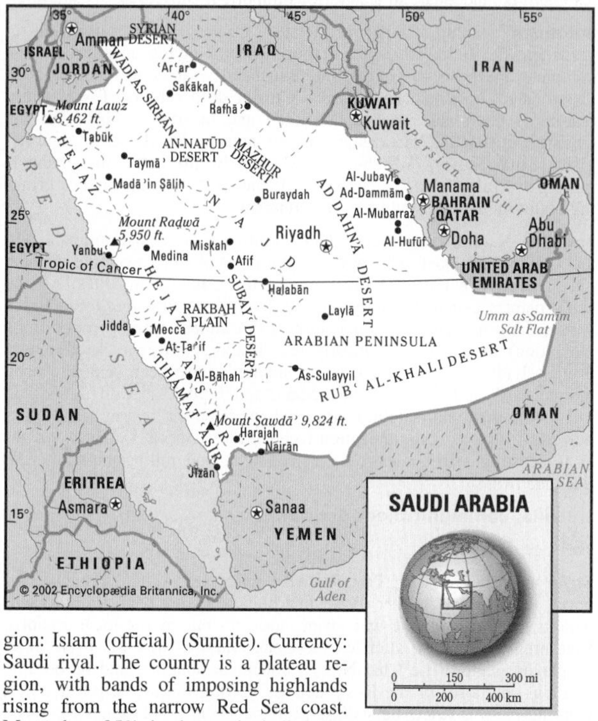

sauger \ˈsȯ-gər\ Species *(Stizostedion canadense)* of pikeperch (family Percidae), carnivorous food and game fishes found in lakes and silty rivers of eastern North America. Saugers are slender and darkly mottled. They have two dorsal fins and rarely exceed a length of 12 in. (30 cm) or a weight of about 2 lbs (1 kg).

Saugus Iron Works First successful ironworks in colonial America. It was established in 1646 in Saugus, Mass., just north of Boston, by Robert Bridges and JOSEPH JENKS, after large quantities of bog iron were discovered there. It principally cast utensils and rolled and slit nail rods for the settlers. It closed c. 1688. Parts have been restored as a national historic site.

Sauk \ˈsȯk\ *or* **Sac** ALGONQUIAN-speaking North American Indian people closely related to the FOX and KICKAPOO who traditionally inhabited the region of what is now Green Bay, Wisc. In summer the Sauk lived in bark-house villages near fields where women raised corn and other crops. In winter the village separated into patrilineal family groups that erected pole-and-thatch houses. In spring the groups gathered on the Iowa prairie to hunt bison. By c. 1800 the Sauk had settled along the Mississippi River in central Illinois, but they were forced to cede these lands to the U.S. In 1832 a group of Sauk and Fox led by BLACK HAWK made a tragically unsuccessful attempt to return to their Illinois lands. Today about 1,000 Sauk live in Oklahoma.

Saul *Hebrew* **Shaul** First king of Israel (r. 1021–1000 BC). All that is known of Saul comes from the biblical books of Samuel I and II. He was anointed king by the prophet SAMUEL after delivering the town of Jabesh-Gilead from Ammonite oppression. Samuel's rejection of Saul and Saul's jealousy of DAVID led to Saul's decline. He died battling the Philistines at Mount Gilboa; David delivered the Israelites and paid tribute to the fallen Saul.

Saule \'saù-le\ In Baltic mythology, the sun goddess who determines the well-being and regeneration of all life on earth. She is said to ride each day through the sky on a chariot with copper wheels, drawn by horses that never tire or sweat. Toward evening, she washes the horses in the sea before retreating into her castle at the end of the sea. The major event in her honor was the midsummer Ligo feast, during which great fires were lit on hills to ward off evil spirits.

Sault Sainte Marie \ˌsü-ˌsānt-mə-'rē\ City (pop., 2000: 16,542), eastern Upper Peninsula, Michigan. Located on the rapids of the St. Marys River between Lakes SUPERIOR and HURON, it is linked to its Canadian twin city, Sault Sainte Marie, Ontario (pop., 2001: 74,566), by road and rail bridges. The U.S. and Canada each operate a part of the Sault Sainte Marie Canals, or Soo Canals, a hub of the ST. LAWRENCE SEAWAY. The first U.S. canal went into operation in 1855; it has since been replaced and is now divided into the northern canal (completed 1919) and the southern canal (completed 1896). The Canadian canal, which has one lock, was completed in 1895.

sauna Bath in steam from water thrown on heated stones. Known in ancient times in various places, saunas are most closely identified with the Finnish people, who made saunas a national tradition. Typically, a wooden hut is built near the edge of a lake, with rows of flat stones inside. These are heated by burning wood in a space under the floor. Cold water is then thrown on them to create steam. The unclothed users sit on wooden benches in the steam-filled hut, then beat themselves with branches until their skin is red and tingling and dive into the cold water, or in winter roll in the snow. These extreme temperature changes are thought to have a beneficial effect on the circulation. In an adapted form, saunas are popular today in gymnasiums and health clubs.

Saura (Atarés) \'saù-rä\, **Carlos** (born 1932) Spanish film director. He won notice as a director with *The Hunt* (1965), the first of his allegorical films criticizing Spanish society under FRANCISCO FRANCO. Writing or cowriting all his screenplays, he directed *The Garden of Delights* (1970), *Anna and the Wolves* (1972), and *Cousin Angelica* (1973). He collaborated with the choreographer-dancer Antonio Gades on the flamenco dramas *Blood Wedding* (1981), *Carmen* (1983), and *Love the Magician* (1986). His later films include *Flamenco* (1995), *Tango* (1998), and *Goya in Bordeaux* (1999).

saurischian \sò-'ris-kē-ən\ Any "lizard-hipped" DINOSAUR species (order Saurischia), with hip bones arranged like those of modern REPTILES, the pubis bone pointed forward and down. The order includes all carnivorous and some giant herbivorous dinosaurs. Saurischians evolved from small bipedal dinosaurs called thecodonts; they first appeared in the Late TRIASSIC epoch (227–206 million years ago). The order consists of three suborders: THEROPODS, SAUROPODS, and staurikosaurs (suborder Staurikosauria). Staurikosaurs, known only from the incomplete remains of a few species, seem to have been medium-sized flesh-eaters similar to the theropods. See also ORNITHISCHIAN.

sauropod \'sòr-ə-ˌpäd\ Any species of four-legged, herbivorous, SAURISCHIAN dinosaur in the suborder Sauropoda. The sauropods include the largest of all dinosaurs and the largest land animals that ever lived. They existed from the Late Triassic into the Cretaceous period (227–65 million years ago). All species had a small head, extremely long neck, massive body, thick pillarlike legs, and a very long, tapering, whiplike tail. With their weak, sparse teeth, they cropped vegetation from even the tallest trees, apparently depending on swallowed stones or bacteria in the gut to digest plant matter. Species ranged from 50 ft (15 m) long to the 98-ft (30-m) *Brachiosaurus,* which weighed 80 metric tons. See also BRONTOSAURUS, DIPLODOCUS, THEROPOD.

sausage Highly seasoned minced meat, usually PORK or BEEF, traditionally stuffed in casings of prepared animal intestine. Sausage has been known since ancient times. Some varieties came to be known by their city of origin: the frankfurter from Frankfurt am Main, bologna from Bologna, the wiener from Vienna (Wien). Sausage meat may be eaten fresh, smoked, dried, or pickled. It may be mixed with other meats and additives such as cereals, vegetable starch, soy flour, preservatives, artificial colorings, and various spices. Casings may be intestine, paraffin-treated fabric bags, or synthetic sleeves of plastic or reconstituted COLLAGEN. All but dry (cured) sausages require refrigerated storage. Cooked and dry sausages are ready to eat; fresh (and fresh-frozen) sausages must be cooked.

Saussure \sō-'sɶ̄r\, **Ferdinand de** (1857–1913) Swiss linguist. Though his only written work appeared while he was still a university student, Saussure became very influential as a teacher, principally at the University of Geneva (1901–13). Two of his students reconstructed lecture notes and other materials as *Course in General Linguistics* (1916), often considered the starting point of 20th-century LINGUISTICS. He saw language as a structured system that may be approached both as it exists at a particular time and as it changes over time, and he formalized principles and methods of study for each approach. His concepts may be regarded as the beginning of STRUCTURALISM.

Sauveur \sō-'vœr\, **Albert** (1863–1939) Belgian-U.S. metallurgist. He emigrated to the U.S. in 1887, and taught at Harvard University 1899–1939. His microscopic and photomicroscopic studies of metal structures make him one of the founders of physical METALLURGY. His work in HEAT TREATING of metals is regarded as a scientific landmark. He wrote the influential treatise *Metallography and Heat Treatment of Iron and Steel* (1912).

Sava River \'sä-vä\ River, western Balkans, southern Europe. It flows for 584 mi (940 km), and its basin covers much of Slovenia, Croatia, Bosnia, and northern Serbia. It rises in the JULIAN ALPS as two rivers, which join at Radovlijica. It then flows through Slovenia and Croatia, forming the border between Croatia and Bosnia before entering Serbia and joining the DANUBE RIVER at BELGRADE.

Savannah City (pop., 2000: 131,510), southeastern Georgia, U.S. Located at the mouth of the SAVANNAH RIVER, it is the oldest city in Georgia and its principal seaport. It was established in 1733 by JAMES OGLETHORPE and was the birthplace of the Georgia colony, the colonial government seat, and capital of the state until 1786. A major Confederate supply port during the AMERICAN CIVIL WAR, the city was the objective of Union Gen. WILLIAM T. SHERMAN's march to the sea in 1864. Noted for its beautiful historic buildings built around a system of small parks, it is a leading tourist center. It is the site of several institutions of higher learning.

Savannah River River, eastern Georgia, U.S. Formed by the confluence of the Tugaloo and Seneca rivers at Hartwell Dam, it flows southeast to form the boundary between Georgia and South Carolina. It empties into the Atlantic Ocean at SAVANNAH after a course of 314 mi (505 km). It is navigable for ocean vessels to 5 mi (8 km) above Savannah and for barge traffic to AUGUSTA.

Save River \'sä-vē\ *or* **Sabi River** \'sä-bē\ River, Mozambique. It rises in Zimbabwe and flows east-southeast across the border into Mozambique, continuing east into the MOZAMBIQUE CHANNEL. It is about 400 mi (645 km) long and is navigable by light craft for 100 mi (160 km) above its mouth.

Savigny \'zä-vin-yē\, **Friedrich Karl von** (1779–1861) German jurist and legal historian. He was nobly born, and his privileged position enabled him to devote his life to scholarship. Teaching at the University of Berlin (1810–42), he helped found the influential "historical school" of jurisprudence. His *History of Roman Law in the Middle Ages* (6 vols., 1815–31) laid the foundation for the modern study of medieval law. He founded a system for establishing a modern German CIVIL LAW with his *System of Modern Roman Law* (8 vols., 1840–49). A product of Romanticism, he regarded law as a reflection of a people's customs and spirit that could not be imposed artificially by means of rational, formal legislation.

Savimbi \sə-'vim-bē\, **Jonas (Malheiro)** (1934–2002) Angolan guerrilla leader and politician. After obtaining a doctorate abroad, Savimbi returned to found the National Union for the Total Independence of Angola (UNITA) in 1966. With aid from China, South Africa, and the U.S., UNITA developed a large guerrilla army and embarked on an extended war against the Soviet-backed Angolan government. In 1991 Savimbi agreed to participate in free multiparty elections, but after losing he resumed his military campaign. A peace accord (1994) and later agreements (1996) permitted UNITA to join a coalition government, but Savimbi declined to become vice president and violence continued until his death. UNITA signed a peace agreement in April 2002.

saving Process of setting aside a portion of current income for future use, or the resources accumulated in this way over a given period of time. Savings may take the form of bank deposits and cash holdings or securities. How much individuals save is affected by their preferences for future over present consumption and their expectations of future income. If individuals consume more than the value of their income, then their saving is negative and they are said to be dissaving. Individual saving may be measured by estimating disposable income and subtracting current CONSUMPTION expenditures. A measure of business saving is the increase in net worth shown on a BALANCE SHEET. Total national saving is measured as the excess of national income over consumption and taxes. Saving is important to economic progress because of its relation to INVESTMENT: an increase in productive wealth requires that some individuals abstain from consuming their entire income and make their savings available for investment.

savings and loan association Financial institution that accepts savings from depositors and uses those funds primarily to make loans to home buyers. Savings and loan associations (S&Ls) originated with 18th-century British building societies, in which workmen banded together to finance the building of their homes. The first U.S. savings and loan was established in Philadelphia in 1831. S&Ls were initially cooperative institutions in which savers were shareholders in the association and received dividends in proportion to profits, but today are mutual organizations that offer a variety of savings plans. They are not obliged to rely on individual deposits for funds but are permitted to borrow from other financial institutions and to market mortgage-backed SECURITIES, money-market certificates, and STOCK. Because high INFLATION and rising interest rates in the 1970s made fixed-rate mortgages unprofitable, regulations were altered to permit S&Ls to renegotiate mortgages. In the late 1980s, a growing number of S&Ls failed because inadequate regulation had allowed risky investments and fraud to flourish. The government was obliged to cover vast losses in excess of $200 billion, and the Federal Savings and Loan Insurance Corp. (FSLIC) became insolvent in 1989. Its insurance functions were taken over by a new organization supervised by the FEDERAL DEPOSIT INSURANCE CORP., and the Resolution Trust Corp. was established to handle the bailout of the failed S&Ls.

savings bank Financial institution that gathers savings and pays INTEREST or DIVIDENDS to savers. It channels the savings of individuals who wish to consume less than their incomes to borrowers who wish to spend more. This function is performed by mutual savings banks, SAVINGS AND LOAN ASSOCIATIONS, CREDIT UNIONS, postal savings systems, and municipal savings banks. Unlike a COMMERCIAL BANK, a savings bank does not accept demand deposits. Many savings banks originated as part of a philanthropic effort to encourage saving among people of modest means. The earliest municipal savings banks developed from the municipal pawnshops of Italy (see PAWNBROKING). Other early savings banks were founded in Germany in 1778 and The Netherlands in 1817. The first U.S. savings banks were nonprofit institutions established in the early 1800s for charitable purposes.

Savonarola, painting by Fra Bartolomeo; in the Museo di S. Marco, Florence.

ALINARI–ART RESOURCE/EB INC.

Savonarola \ˌsa-və-nə-'rō-lə, *Italian* ˌsä-vō-nä-'rȯ-lä\, **Girolamo** (1452–1498) Italian preacher, religious reformer, and martyr. He joined the DOMINICAN order in 1475 and was sent to Florence to lecture at the convent of San Marco, where he became known for his learning and asceticism. He preached that the church needed reforming, that it would be scourged and then renewed. After the overthrow of the MEDICI FAMILY (1494), Savonarola became leader of Florence, setting up a democratic but severely puritanical government and seeking to establish a Christian republic as a base for reforming Italy and the church. He was opposed by the Arrabiati, supporters of the Medici, and by Pope ALEXANDER VI, who attempted to restrain his unusual interpretations of scripture and his claim of prophecy. Savonarola was tried, convicted of heresy (1498), and hanged and burned. Despite popular veneration, attempts to bring about his canonization have been unsuccessful.

savory Aromatic annual herb *(Satureja hortensis)* of the MINT family, native to southern Europe. The dried leaves and flowering tops are used as a flavoring and in herb bouquets. Winter, or dwarf, savory *(S. montana)* is smaller and flowers in winter. It is used for culinary purposes almost interchangeably with the summer species.

Savoy *French* **Savoie** \sȧ-'vwȧ\ *Italian* **Savoia** \sä-'vȯ-yä\ Historical region, southeastern France and northwestern Italy. From the 11th century the counts of Savoy ruled it as part of the kingdom of ARLES under the suzerainty of the HOLY ROMAN EMPIRE. It became virtually independent and expanded across the ALPS to include the plain of PIEDMONT in Italy. In the 18th century Piedmont and Savoy were incorporated into the kingdom of SARDINIA, and the dukes of Savoy became kings of Sardinia. Savoy and Piedmont were ceded to France in 1792, but Savoy was restored to its traditional rulers in 1815, with the addition of GENOA. In 1860 Sardinia, Genoa, and Piedmont joined other Italian states to form the kingdom of Italy. The House of SAVOY was the ruling house of Italy until 1946, when the Italian Republic was established.

Savoy, House of Historic dynasty of Europe and the ruling house of Italy 1861–1946. Its founder was Umberto I the Whitehanded (died 1048?), who held the county of Savoy and areas east of the Rhône River and south of Lake Geneva. His medieval successors, including AMADEUS VI, added territory in the western Alps where France, Italy, and Switzerland converge. In 1416 the house was raised to ducal status in the Holy Roman Empire, after which it declined until the late 16th century. Though under French domination in the 17th century, the house under VICTOR AMADEUS II acquired territory in northeastern Italy and attained the royal title, first of the kingdom of Sicily (1713), which he exchanged for Sardinia (1720). The house was powerful in the RISORGIMENTO, and under the kings VICTOR EMMANUEL I and II and CHARLES ALBERT it contributed to the 19th-century unification of Italy. It then lost its prominence, and the monarchs UMBERTO I and VICTOR EMMANUEL III served mainly as figureheads until the vote for a republic in 1946 ended Savoy rule.

saw TOOL for cutting solid materials to prescribed lengths or shapes. Most saws take the form of a thin metal strip with teeth on one edge or a thin metal disk with teeth on the edge. The teeth are usually set to alternate sides so that the kerf (groove) cut by the saw is wider than the thickness of the saw; the saw blade can thus move freely in the groove without binding. Thin-strip saws are used in various ways in both hand and machine operations; circular, or disk, saws are always machine powered (see SAWING MACHINE, MACHINE TOOL).

saw palmetto Any of several shrubby PALMS chiefly of the southern U.S. and West Indies that have spiny-toothed petioles (leafstalks), especially a common palm *(Serenoa repens)* of the southeastern U.S., with a usually creeping stem. Saw palmettos make up part of the vegetation found in the Florida EVERGLADES. When undisturbed, they grow into great masses of foliage. The saw palmetto has recently drawn attention as the source of a possible treatment for prostate cancer.

Sawatch Range \sə-'wäch\ Range of the ROCKY MTNS., central Colorado. It is 100 mi (160 km) long and is bounded by the ARKANSAS RIVER and the Elk Mountains. Its middle portion, with Mts. Yale, Harvard, and Princeton, is usually called the Collegiate Range. Many summits exceed 14,000 ft (4,300 m), including Mount Elbert (14,433 ft, or 4,399 m), the highest point in the Rockies. The discovery of gold in 1860 attracted settlers to the region. Ranching, dairying, and tourism are the main industries today.

Sawchuk \'sȯw-chək\, **Terry** *orig.* **Terrence Gordon** (1929–1970) Canadian-U.S. hockey goalie. Born in Winnipeg, Manitoba, he played two seasons in other leagues before coming to the National Hockey

League (1949), in which he played for the Detroit Red Wings (1949–54, 1957–64), Boston Bruins (1955–56), Toronto Maple Leafs (1964–67), and other teams. His career record of 103 shutouts still stands, as do his records of most wins (435) and most games (971).

sawfish Any of about six species (genus *Pristis,* family Pristidae) of sharklike RAY. Sawfishes have a long head, long body, and a long, toothed, bladelike snout. The largest attain lengths of 23 ft (7 m) or more. These bottom-dwellers inhabit shallow waters of subtropical and tropical bays and estuaries and sometimes swim up rivers. Some live in the freshwaters of Lake Nicaragua. They are not generally dangerous. Their saws are used either to dig out bottom animals or, when lashed about, to kill or maim schooling fishes. Sawfishes are good to eat when small; they are fished in some areas for food, oil, skins, and other products.

Sawfish (*Pristis*).
KARL H. MASLOWSKI

sawfly Any of numerous, widely distributed insect species in five families (superfamily Tenthredinoidea, order Hymenoptera). Typical sawflies (family Tenthredinidae) are often brightly colored and are commonly found on flowers; the North American pear slug eats pear, cherry, and plum leaves. The larvae of many species in the other four families also damage trees. Argid sawflies (family Argidae) feed on rose bushes and willow, oak, and birch trees. The North American elm sawfly (family Cimbicidae) feeds on elm and willow. The North American conifer sawflies (family Diprionidae) are common, sometimes serious, pests of coniferous trees. The pergid sawflies (family Pergidae) consist of a single genus in South America and Australia.

Sawfly (*Cimbex*).
WILLIAM E. FERGUSON

sawing machine MACHINE TOOL for cutting up bars of material or for cutting out shapes in plates of raw material. The cutting tools (SAWS) may be thin metallic disks with teeth on their edges, thin metal blades or flexible bands with teeth on one edge, or thin grinding wheels. The tools may use any of three actions: true cutting, grinding, or friction-created melting.

sawmill Machine or plant with power-driven machines for sawing logs into rough-squared sections or into planks and boards. A sawmill may be equipped with planing, molding, tenoning, and other machines for finishing processes. Cutting is performed on various large machines; reciprocating saws, band saws, or circular saws cut the log into various thicknesses as it moves past the saw on a feeder table. The biggest mills are usually located where timber can be brought by river or rail, and mill design is affected by the mode of transportation.

Sax, Adolphe *orig.* **Antoine Joseph** (1814–1894) Belgian instrument maker. Son of an accomplished instrument maker, he worked for his father until 1842, making improvements on the clarinet and bass clarinet. He then set up shop in Paris, supported by such musicians as H. BERLIOZ and Fromental Halévy (1799–1862) but opposed by French instrument makers, and invented several new families of instruments, including the saxhorns, the saxtrombas, and most successfully, the SAXOPHONES. A fine woodwind player, he taught saxophone at the Paris Conservatory 1857–71.

Saxe, (Hermann-) Maurice, comte (Count) de (1696–1750) German-French general. The illegitimate son of Frederick Augustus I of Saxony, he served under EUGENE OF SAVOY in Flanders and was made Count of Saxony (Saxe) in 1711. He commanded a German regiment in the French service (1719) and made innovations in military training, especially in musketry. He served with distinction in the French army against his half brother AUGUSTUS III in the War of the POLISH SUCCESSION and was made a general (1734). He successfully led French forces in the War of the AUSTRIAN SUCCESSION, capturing Prague (1741) and invading the Austrian Netherlands. There he won the Battle of Fontenoy (1745) and captured Brussels and Antwerp (1746). Appointed marshal general of France by LOUIS XV, Saxe led the successful invasion of Holland in 1747.

Saxe-Coburg-Gotha, House of See House of WINDSOR

saxifrage \'sak-sə-frij\ Any of about 300 species of the genus *Saxifraga,* of the family Saxifragaceae, which is composed of 36 genera of mostly perennial herbaceous plants. Members of the saxifrage family are known for their ability to grow and thrive on exposed rocky crags and in fissures of rocks. They are adapted to the full range of moisture conditions, but most grow in moist, shaded woodlands in northern cold and temperate regions. Leaves characteristically alternate along the stem and sometimes are deeply lobed or form rosettes. Flowers generally are borne in branched clusters and range in color from greenish to white or yellow and from pink or red to purple. The fruit is a CAPSULE. *Saxifraga* species are planted in rock gardens or as border ornamentals, prized for their small, bright flowers, fine-textured foliage, and early spring flowering. Other well-known genera in the saxifrage family are *Astilbe, Heuchera,* and *Mitella.*

Saxo Grammaticus \'sak-sō-grə-'ma-ti-kəs\ (fl. mid-12th century–early 13th century) Danish historian. Little is known of Saxo's life except that he was a Zealander from a family of warriors and probably served as clerk to the archbishop of Lund. His 16-volume *Gesta Danorum* ("Story of the Danes") is the first important work on the history of Denmark and the first Danish contribution to world literature. A panorama of his country's antiquity and traditions, it inspired many 19th-century Danish Romantic poets and was the original source of the story of WILLIAM SHAKESPEARE's *Hamlet.* Saxo's brilliant, ornate Latin earned him the name "Grammaticus" in the 14th century.

Saxons Germanic people who lived along the Baltic coast in ancient times and later migrated west as far as the British Isles. The Saxons became pirates in the North Sea during the decline of the Roman empire, and in the early 5th century they spread through northern Germany and along the coasts of Gaul and Britain. They fought CHARLEMAGNE (772–804) before being incorporated into the Frankish kingdom, and they settled Britain along with other Germanic invaders, including the ANGLES and the Jutes.

Saxony *German* **Sachsen** \'zäk-sən\ Historical region, former state, and recreated state, Germany. Before 1180 the name was applied to the territory conquered c. AD 200–700 by the Germanic Saxon tribe. They were conquered and Christianized by CHARLEMAGNE in the late 8th century. In the mid-9th century it became part of the German kingdom of the FRANKS. The territory was broken up in 1180 and divided into two smaller and widely separated areas, Saxe-Lauenburg on the lower ELBE RIVER and Saxe-Wittenberg on the middle Elbe. From 1422 the name was applied to a large region, including the country from THURINGIA to Lusatia, bordering Bohemia. It was part of the German empire 1871–1918, and a free state in the WEIMAR REPUBLIC 1919–33. The state was abolished in 1952 and divided among East German districts. Upon German reunification in 1990, a new state of Saxony was recreated.

saxophone Single-reed wind instrument with a conical metal tube and finger keys. Though made of brass, it is classified as a WOODWIND INSTRUMENT. Its mouthpiece resembles the CLARINET's. The saxophone family includes instruments with at least eight different ranges, the tenor and alto instruments being the most common. The smallest (highest-range) saxophones are straight; the rest have curved necks and their bells are bent up and out. Transposing instruments in B-flat and E-flat, all have the same written 3½-octave range. The saxophone was patented in 1846 by A. SAX, who created two separate instrument families, for military and orchestral use respectively. Though few composers included saxophones in their orchestral scores, they became centrally important in military, dance, and jazz bands.

Say \'se, *Engl* 'sā\, **J(ean-)B(aptiste)** (1767–1832) French economist. He edited a magazine and started a spinning mill before joining the faculty of the Conservatory of Arts and Crafts (1817–30) and the Collège de France (1830–32). In his major work, *A Treatise on Political Economy* (1803), he advanced his law of markets, which claims that supply creates its own demand. He attributed economic DEPRESSION not to a general deficiency in demand but rather to temporary overproduction for some markets and underproduction for others, an imbalance that must automatically adjust itself as overproducers redirect their production to conform with consumers' preferences. Say's law remained a central tenet of orthodox economics until the GREAT DEPRESSION.

Sayan Mountains \sə-'yän\ Large upland region on the frontiers of eastern central Russia and Mongolia. The mountains form a rough arc stretching from the ALTAY SHAN to Lake BAIKAL and connecting with the Khamar-Daban mountain system of the Transbaikalia. The western and eastern ranges, each with a different geologic history, meet in a central knot where elevations exceed 10,000 ft (3,000 m).

Sayers, Dorothy L(eigh) (1893–1957) English scholar and writer. In 1915 Sayers became one of the first women to graduate from Oxford University. Her first major work was *Whose Body?* (1923), in which she created the detective Lord Peter Wimsey, a witty, dashing young gentleman-scholar who would be featured in such later short-story collections and novels as *Strong Poison* (1930), *The Nine Tailors* (1934), and *Busman's Honeymoon* (1937). After the 1930s she concentrated on theological dramas and books, radio plays, and scholarly translations, notably of DANTE's *Divine Comedy.*

Sayers, Gale (Eugene) (born 1943) U.S. football player. Born in Wichita, Kan., he attended the University of Kansas, where he twice made All-American. He became an explosive running back for the Chicago Bears (1965–71), a leading touchdown scorer and yardage gainer; in 1965 he scored a record-tying six touchdowns in a single game. He was forced to retire early by knee injuries.

Sayles, John (born 1950) U.S. film director. Born in Schenectady, N.Y., he graduated from Williams College and wrote short stories and novels, including *Union Dues* (1977), before becoming a screenwriter for ROGER CORMAN. He made his directorial debut with the acclaimed *Return of the Secaucus Seven* (1980). Usually writing his own screenplays, he has explored social and political issues in other thoughtful films such as *Lianna* (1982), *Matewan* (1987), *Eight Men Out* (1988), *City of Hope* (1991), and *Lone Star* (1996). He also directed the children's movie *The Secret of Roan Inish* (1994).

Sazonov \sə-'zȯ-nəf\, **Sergey (Dmitriyevich)** (1860–1927) Russian diplomat. After became minister of foreign affairs in 1910. He promoted close relations with Britain and France and supporting the BALKAN LEAGUE against Turkey. He contributed to the precipitating events of World War I by affirming Russia's support for Serbia against Austria and insisting that NICHOLAS II order the mobilization of the Russian army (July 30, 1914); two days later, Germany declared war on Russia. He set Russia's war aim as the annexation of Constantinople and the Turkish straits, but was dismissed when he urged the czar to grant Poland autonomy. After the Russian Revolution of 1917, he moved to France.

scabious \'skā-bē-əs\ Any of about 100 species of annual and perennial herbaceous plants that make up the genus *Scabiosa* (family Dipsaceae), native to temperate Eurasia, the Mediterranean, and mountains of eastern Africa. Some are important garden plants, including the southern European annual pincushion flower *(S. atropurpurea),* also called sweet scabious, mourning bride, or garden scabious. All species have leaf rosettes at the base of the plant, and leafy stems. Flower heads have an outer ring of female flowers and a circle of leaflike bracts below. Devil's bit scabious belongs to the genus *Succisa* (see BLUEBONNET).

Perennial scabious (*Scabiosa caucasica*).

VALERIE FINNIS

Scaevola \'sē-və-lə\, **Quintus Mucius** *or* **Pontifex** (died 82 BC) Roman lawgiver. He served successively as consul, as governor of the province of Asia, and from c. 89 BC as pontifex maximus. Around 95 he obtained the passage of the Lex Licinia Mucia, removing certain groups from the citizen rolls, which led to the SOCIAL WAR of 90–88. His major work was an 80-volume systematic treatise on civil law, which was frequently quoted and followed by subsequent writers. His handbook *Horoi* ("Definitions") was the oldest work excerpted in JUSTINIAN I's Digest.

scaffold Temporary platform used to elevate and support workers and materials during work on a structure or machine. It consists of one or more wooden planks and is supported by either a timber or a tubular steel or aluminum frame; bamboo is used in parts of Asia. Scaffolding may be raised and lowered by means of cables controlled by a ratchet or electric motor.

scalawag U.S. Southerner who supported RECONSTRUCTION. Opponents also applied the pejorative term to those who joined with CARPETBAGGERS and freedmen to support REPUBLICAN PARTY policies. The term, of unknown origin, was used from the 1840s to denote a worthless farm animal and later a worthless person. Scalawags included former Whigs and hill-country farmers with Unionist sympathies and comprised almost 20% of the white electorate after the AMERICAN CIVIL WAR. Many held government positions in the South and advocated moderate reforms.

scale Primary pitches of a KEY or MODE arranged within an octave. Scales are distinguished by the pattern of the INTERVALS between adjacent notes. A scale can be seen as an abstraction from MELODY—that is, the pitches of a melody arranged in stepwise order.

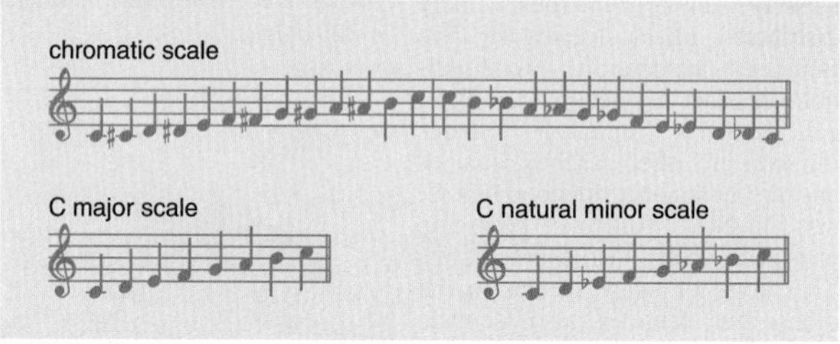

Examples of the chromatic, major, and minor scales.

scale insect Any member of several families of sap-sucking INSECTS (order Homoptera) whose bodies are covered by a waxy shell (the scale). The eggs are protected by the female's body or scale or a waxy filamentous mass. Scale insects may attack any part of a plant, but each species is host-specific. Many species are serious plant pests; others have commercial value. The lac insect is used in a red dye and in shellac. Cochineal, a red dyestuff, consists of the dried, pulverized bodies of females of the species *Dactylopius coccus.* See also COTTONY-CUSHION SCALE, SAN JOSE SCALE.

Scalia \skə-'lē-ə\, **Antonin** (born 1936) U.S. jurist. Born in Trenton, N.J., he studied at Georgetown University and Harvard Law School, where he edited its law review. He worked for a Cleveland law firm (1961–67), taught at the University of Virginia (1967–74), served as an assistant U.S. attorney general (1974–77), and taught at the University of Chicago (1977–82). A staunch conservative, he was appointed by Pres. RONALD REAGAN to the U.S. Court of Appeals (1982) and then to the U.S. Supreme Court (1986). There Scalia has opposed judicial activism and applied narrow interpretations to acts of Congress while granting some leniency to state and local laws, provided they do not conflict with federal law or with conservative constitutional principles.

Scaliger \'ska-lə-jər\, **Julius Caesar and Joseph Justus** (1484–1558, 1540–1609) Classical scholars. Julius was born in Italy but settled in France. He worked in botany, zoology, and grammar but was chiefly interested in developing an understanding and critical evaluation of the ancients. His most widely read book was his *Poetics* (1561), in which Greco-Roman rhetoric and poetics are used as a foundation for literary criticism. His son Joseph, a precocious student of language, studied in France, Germany, and Italy and taught in France before he was called to the University of Leiden, where he became known as the most erudite scholar of his time. His major works are the *Opus de emendatione tempore* (1583; "Study on the Improvement of Time") and *Thesaurus temporum* (1609; "Thesaurus of Time"), which brought order to ancient chronology.

scallop Any of more than 400 species (family Pectinidae) of marine BIVALVES found worldwide, from the intertidal zone to deep waters. The two halves of the shell (valves) are usually fan-shaped, except for a winglike projection at either side of the straight hinge. The shells are 1–6 in. (2.5–15 cm) long. They may be smooth or ribbed and red, purple, orange, yellow, or white. Cilia filter microscopic plants and animals from the water and move them toward the mouth. Scallops swim by clapping the valves, propelling themselves forward. The muscle that closes the valves is a popular food item.

scalping Removal of all or part of the scalp, with hair attached, from an enemy's head. It is best known as a practice of North American Indian warfare. At first confined to eastern tribes, it spread as a result of bounties offered by the French, English, Dutch, and Spanish for the scalps of enemy Indians and sometimes of enemy whites. Many American frontiersmen and soldiers adopted the custom. Among PLAINS INDIANS, scalps were taken for war honors, usually from dead enemies, although some warriors preferred a live victim. The operation was not necessarily fatal, and some victims were released alive.

scaly anteater See PANGOLIN

Scamander River See MENDERES RIVER

scampi *or* **Dublin Bay prawn** *or* **Norway lobster** Edible LOBSTER *(Nephrops norvegicus),* widespread in the Mediterranean and northeastern Atlantic. It is sold as a delicacy over much of its range. Scampi live in burrows on soft sea bottoms at depths of 33 to 820 ft (10–250 m). They grow to about 8 in. (200 mm) long and weigh about 7 oz (200 g). The slender claws may be almost as long as the body. Most scampi are trawled, but some are caught in baited lobster pots.

Scandinavia Region of northern Europe, usually defined as comprising Norway, Sweden, and Denmark. It is sometimes used more broadly to include Finland and Iceland. Norway and Sweden occupy the SCANDINAVIAN PENINSULA, though Denmark is part of the North European Plain. The Scandinavian peoples are linked by cultural similarities, and they speak a closely related group of GERMANIC LANGUAGES.

Scandinavian Peninsula Large promontory, northern Europe. Occupied by Norway and Sweden, it is about 1,150 mi (1,850 km) long, with an area of 290,000 sq mi (750,000 sq km), and extends south from the BARENTS SEA. It is largely mountainous; its eastern side slopes gently to the Baltic Sea, while the western side has mountains reaching the coast and is deeply dissected by fjords.

scanner, optical Computer input device that uses a light beam to scan codes, text, or graphic images directly into a computer or computer system. BAR-CODE scanners are used widely at point-of-sale terminals in retail stores. A handheld scanner or bar-code pen is moved across the code, or the code itself is moved by hand across a scanner built into a checkout counter or other surface, and the computer stores or immediately processes the data in the bar code. After identifying the product through its bar code, the computer determines its price and feeds that information into the cash register. Optical scanners are also used in FAX machines and to input graphic material directly into PERSONAL COMPUTERS. See also OCR.

Scapa Flow Sea basin, ORKNEY ISLANDS. Located off the northern tip of Scotland, it is about 15 mi (24 km) long and 8 mi (13 km) wide. Its extensive sheltered waters served as a major British naval base during World Wars I and II. The Germans scuttled their fleet there after World War I. The base was fortified in World War II following German attacks and the sinking of the battleship *Royal Oak* in 1939. The base closed in 1956.

scapegoat In the Old Testament, a goat that was symbolically burdened with the SINS of the people and then killed on YOM KIPPUR to rid Jerusalem of its iniquities. Similar rituals were held elsewhere in the ancient world to transfer guilt or blame. In ancient Greece, human scapegoats were beaten and driven out of cities to mitigate calamities. In early Roman law, an innocent person was allowed to assume the penalty of another; CHRISTIANITY reflects this notion in its belief that JESUS died to atone for the sins of mankind.

scar Mark left on the skin after a wound heals. Cells called fibroblasts produce COLLAGEN fibers, which form bundles that make up the bulk of scar tissue. Scars have a blood supply but no oil glands or elastic tissue, so they can be slightly painful or itchy. Hypertrophic scars grow overly thick and fibrous but remain within the original wound site. Scars can also develop into tumorlike growths called keloids, which extend beyond the wound's limits. Both can inhibit movement when they result from serious burns over large areas, especially around a joint. All scars, especially those from unaided healing of third-degree burns, can become malignant. Treatment of serious scars is one of the most important problems in PLASTIC SURGERY.

scarab \'skar-əb\ In EGYPTIAN RELIGION, a symbol of immortality much used in funerary art. It was inspired by the life cycle of the SCARAB BEETLE; the dung balls that the beetles consume, lay their eggs in, and use to feed their young represented a cycle of rebirth and were associated with immortality and with the passage of the sun across the heavens. Many scarabs were made of precious metals and were worn as amulets or used as seals. First appearing c. 2575–c. 2130 BC, they were fashioned in great numbers during the Middle Kingdom and New Kingdom.

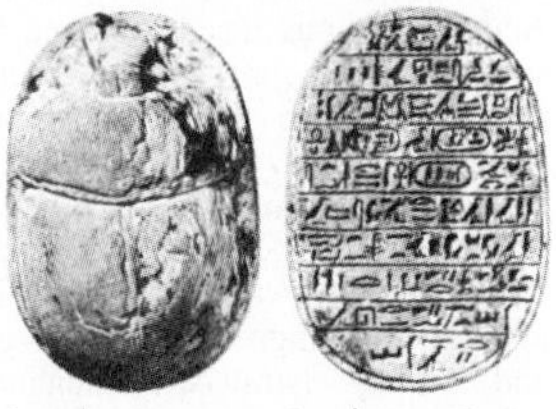

Scarab commemorating the marriage of Amenhotep III and Queen Tiy, 18th dynasty; in the Oriental Institute, Chicago.

BY COURTESY OF THE ORIENTAL INSTITUTE, THE UNIVERSITY OF CHICAGO

scarab beetle Any of about 30,000 BEETLE species (family Scarabaeidae), found worldwide, that are compact, heavy-bodied, and oval. Each antenna terminates in three flattened plates that fit together to form a club. The outer edges of the front legs may be toothed or scalloped. Species range from about 0.2 to 5 in. (5–120 mm) long and include one of the heaviest known insects. One species of DUNG BEETLE, *Scarabaeus sacer,* was sacred to the ancient Egyptians. Many species are agricultural pests (e.g., CHAFER, JAPANESE BEETLE, JUNE BEETLE); many are popular with insect collectors because they are large and have beautifully colored, hard, highly polished forewings.

Scarborough City (pop., 1991: 525,000), southeastern Ontario. With the cities of EAST YORK, ETOBICOKE, YORK, NORTH YORK, and TORONTO, it constitutes the municipality of Metropolitan Toronto. First called Glasgow, it was renamed in 1793 because its coastal bluffs reminded settlers of SCARBOROUGH, England. Originally a farming community, it later became an industrial and residential urban compound.

Scarborough City (pop., 1994 est.: 109,000), NORTH YORKSHIRE, England. Located on the North Sea coast, it originated as a 10th-century Viking fishing settlement at the site of a 4th-century Roman signal station. In the 12th century a Norman castle was built on the headland. After 1626, spa development made it a fashionable resort. It remains the most popular seaside resort in northeastern England.

Scarborough Town (pop., 1990: 4,000) and deepwater harbor of Tobago island, Trinidad and Tobago. First named Port Louis, it is steeply laid out on the slopes of a hill overlooking the harbor. It succeeded Georgetown as the island of Tobago's capital in 1796. It is located in a coconut growing area.

Scarlatti, (Pietro) Alessandro (Gaspare) (1660–1725) Italian composer. He may have studied with G. CARISSIMI in Rome. His first known opera was a success (1679), and by 1680 he was chapel master in Rome for Queen CHRISTINA of Sweden. He left this secure position to become chapel master of the viceroy of Naples (1684–1702). Most of the operas produced in the city during this period were his own, and they were increasingly heard in other cities as well, including Leipzig and London. Most of his instrumental music comes from his late period, as do his comic operas. He wrote at least 70 and perhaps over 100 operas, as well as some 600 secular cantatas; his opera overtures *(sinfonie)* were important forerunners of the symphony. D. SCARLATTI was his son.

Scarlatti \skär-'lät-ē\, **(Giuseppe) Domenico** (1685–1757) Italian composer and keyboard player. Son of A. SCARLATTI, he worked as his father's assistant in Naples. By 1705 he was living in Rome. His father subsequently sent him to Venice, where he stayed until c. 1708. There he probably met G.F. HANDEL and A. VIVALDI; he is said to have had a contest with Handel in which the German won at organ playing but Scarlatti won at the harpsichord. By 1723 he was tutor to the Spanish infanta (later crown princess) Maria Barbara, in whose service he remained for much of his life. Though he wrote operas, oratorios, cantatas, and other works, his reputation rests on the 555 brilliant one-movement keyboard sonatas he wrote for her, one of the greatest bodies of work by any baroque composer.

Domenico Scarlatti, engraving.

BY COURTESY OF THE BIBLIOTHEQUE NATIONALE, PARIS; PHOTOGRAPH, J.P. ZIOLO

scarlet fever *or* **scarlatina** Acute infectious disease caused by some types of STREPTOCOCCUS bacteria. Fever, sore throat, headache, and, in children, vomiting are followed in two to three days by a rash. The skin peels in about one-third of cases. After a coating disappears, the tongue is swollen, red, and bumpy (strawberry tongue). Glands are usually swollen. Complications frequently involve the sinuses, ears (sometimes with MASTOIDITIS), and neck. ABSCESSES are common. NEPHRITIS, ARTHRITIS, or RHEUMATIC FEVER may occur later. Treatment involves PENICILLIN or GAMMA GLOBULIN, bed rest, and adequate fluid intake. Scarlet fever has become uncommon and much milder since the mid-20th century, independent of the use of antibiotics.

Scarron \skä-'rō^{n}\, **Paul** (1610–1660) French writer. With his first works, Scarron helped make the BURLESQUE a characteristic literary form of his time. *Virgile travesty* (7 vols., 1648–53) was a very successful parody of VIRGIL's *Aeneid*. Scarron's plays, often based on Spanish originals, were important in the theatrical life of Paris. He is now remembered for a single novel, *Le roman comique* (3 vols., 1651–57; "The Comic Novel"), which recounts the comical adventures of a company of strolling players; its realism makes it an invaluable source of information about conditions in the French provinces in the 17th century. His widow, Madame de Maintenon, was later married to Louis XIV.

scattering In physics, the change in direction of MOTION of a particle because of a collision with another particle. The collision can occur between two charged particles; it need not involve direct physical contact. Experiments show that the trajectory of the scattered particle is a hyperbola and that as the bombarding particle is aimed more closely toward the scattering center, the angle of deflection decreases. The term scattering is also used for the diffusion of electromagnetic waves by the atmosphere, resulting, for example, in long-range radio reception on the ground. See also RAYLEIGH SCATTERING.

scaup Any of three species (genus *Aythya,* family Anatidae) of DIVING DUCKS. The greater scaup, or big bluebill *(A. marila),* breeds across Eurasia and most of the Nearctic region. The lesser scaup, or little bluebill *(A. affinis),* breeds in northwestern North America. Both are popular game birds, 15–20 in. (38–51 cm) long, that winter along the U.S. coasts. Males have a dark breast and grayish back but differ in head color and wing markings; females are brown with white patches around the blue bill. Scaups eat mainly clams. The third species is the New Zealand scaup *(A. novaeseelandiae).*

Schacht \'shäkt\, **(Horace Greeley) Hjalmar** (1877–1970) German financier. He served as vice director of the Dresdner Bank and director of the German National Bank before becoming a commissioner in the finance ministry (1923), where he developed a rigorous monetary program that halted German inflation and stabilized the mark. He became president of the Reichsbank (1923–30, 1933–39) and minister of economics (1934–37), but was dismissed when he opposed ADOLF HITLER's rearmament expenditure. Imprisoned after the JULY PLOT against Hitler's life (1944), he was later captured by the Allies and acquitted at the NUREMBERG TRIALS. He later founded a bank in Düsseldorf and served as an international financial consultant.

Schally \'sha-lē\, **Andrew V(ictor)** (born 1926) Polish-U.S. endocrinologist. His family fled Poland in 1939, and he received his PhD in biochemistry from McGill University in 1957. He shared a 1977 Nobel Prize for his work with ROGER C.L. GUILLEMIN and ROSALYN YALOW in isolating and synthesizing HORMONES produced by the HYPOTHALAMUS.

Scharnhorst \'shärn-ˌhȯrst\, **Gerhard Johann David von** (1755–1813) Prussian general. He joined the Hanoverian army in 1778 and served with distinction in Belgium against the French in the 1790s. An officer in the Prussian army from 1801, he taught at the war academy and became chief of staff in the war against Napoleon (1806). As head of the army reform commission (from 1807), he developed the modern general staff system and reorganized the Prussian army; with AUGUST, COUNT GNEISENAU he devised the system of rapid military training and use of army reserves. After a forced retirement, he became chief of staff to GEBHARD VON BLUCHER (1813) and died of a wound received in the Battle of Lützen.

Schaumburg-Lippe \'shau̇m-ˌbu̇rk-'li-pə\ Former German state. Schaumburg was the ancestral seat of a line of counts recorded from the early 12th century. The line died out in 1640 and the lands were partitioned. It joined the GERMAN CONFEDERATION in 1815 and the German empire in 1871. It joined the WEIMAR REPUBLIC in 1918 as a free state; in 1946 it was merged into the state of Lower Saxony.

Schechter Poultry Corp. v. United States \'shek-tər\ U.S. Supreme Court decision (1935) that abolished the National Industrial Recovery Act (NIRA; see NATIONAL RECOVERY ADMINISTRATION), a cornerstone of the NEW DEAL. By unanimous vote, the Court held that Congress had exceeded its authority by delegating too much legislative power to the president and industrial groups. It also found that NIRA's "codes of fair practice" went beyond the regulation of interstate commerce in attempting to control intrastate activity. With NIRA's successor, the National Labor Relations Act (1935), FRANKLIN ROOSEVELT's administration produced a workable solution to the economic emergency created by the GREAT DEPRESSION that proved acceptable to the Court.

Scheherazade *or* **Sheherazade** \shə-ˌher-ə-'zäd\ Fictional sultan's wife who narrates *The THOUSAND AND ONE NIGHTS*. According to the story that serves as the collection's framework, the Sultan Shahrya found his first wife unfaithful, and after deciding that he hated all women, he married and killed a new wife each day. Scheherazade, daughter of his vizier, in an effort to avoid his previous wives' fate, related to him a fascinating story every night, promising to finish it on the following night. The sultan enjoyed the stories so much that he put off her execution indefinitely and finally abandoned the idea altogether.

Scheidt \'shīt\, **Samuel** (1587–1654) German composer. After study in Amsterdam with J.P. SWEELINCK, he returned to his native Halle and spent his entire life there in various musical offices, including court organist and later kapellmeister to the Margrave of Brandenburg, working with H. SCHUTZ. The Thirty Years' War hurt music in Halle, but through professional trials and personal tragedies Scheidt continued to write prolifically. He wrote much sacred vocal music in both German and Latin, including *Geistliche Concerte* (1631–40). His chief work for keyboard (mostly organ) was *Tabulatura nova* (1624), written in open score rather than traditional organ tablature.

Schein \'shīn\, **Johann Hermann** (1586–1630) German composer. After singing as a boy in the chapel of the elector of Saxony, he studied music at the University of Leipzig. In 1616 he became cantor of St. Thomas' Church in Leipzig, the post later held by J.S. BACH. In this capacity, he was an important teacher, became friends with S. SCHEIDT and H. SCHUTZ and wrote sacred works that combined the vocal lyricism of Italian music with the Northern contrapuntal style. His *Banchetto musicale* (1617) is a collection of dances, perhaps the first in which dances are gathered into unified suites, with common thematic motifs. His sacred vocal works include *Opella nova* (1618–26) and the hymn collection *Cantional* (1627).

Schelde River \'skel-də\ *or* **Scheldt River** \'skelt\ *French* **Escaut** \es-'kō\ River, western Europe. It rises in northern France, flows through western Belgium to the city of ANTWERP, turns northwest, and empties into the NORTH SEA in Dutch territory, after a course of 270 mi (435 km). Along with the Lower RHINE and the MEUSE rivers, it drains one of the world's most densely populated areas. A channel in the western Schelde allows oceangoing vessels to reach Antwerp at full tide.

Scheler \'shā-lər\, **Max** (1874–1928) German philosopher. He is remembered primarily for his contributions to PHENOMENOLOGY. His *Formalism in Ethics and Non-Formal Ethics of Values* (1913–16) contains a detailed critique of IMMANUEL KANT's ethics. In *Man's Place in the Universe* (1928), he asserts that humanity, God, and world are one cosmic process with two poles, spirit and life-urge. By itself, spirit is powerless, unless its ideas can "functionalize" with life-factors allowing their realization, a concept similar to those of PRAGMATISM.

Schelling \'shel-iŋ\, **Friedrich Wilhelm Joseph von** (1775–1854) German philosopher and educator. Inspired by IMMANUEL KANT, JOHANN GOTTLIEB FICHTE, and BENEDICT DE SPINOZA, he tried in his *System of Transcendental Idealism* (1800) to unite his concept of nature with Fichte's philosophy. He held that art mediates between the natural and physical spheres when the natural (or unconscious) and spiritual (or conscious) productions are united in artistic creation. His view that the Absolute expresses itself in all beings as the unity of the subjective and the objective was criticized by G. W. F. HEGEL. In *Of Human Freedom* (1809), he declared that mankind's freedom is real only if it is freedom for both good and evil, a position that forms the basis of his later philosophy. A major figure of post-Kantian IDEALISM, Schelling had an important influence on Romanticism.

Schenker \'sheŋ-kər\, **Heinrich** (1868–1935) Austro-Hungarian music theorist. Born in Poland, he studied piano with Karol Mikuli (1819–1897). He studied law and composition in Vienna before settling there as a private teacher and occasional performer. He proposed that J.-P. RAMEAU's harmonic theory had erred in making harmony fundamental at the expense of counterpoint. His own study of C.P.E. BACH led him to posit counterpoint as equally fundamental and to recognize the subtle integration of the two. His most influential perception was that tonal music consists effectively of layers of ornamentation of simpler musical statements, providing the best explanation of how an entire piece can be grasped by the ear. His controversial theories and graphic notation—presented in such texts as *Harmony* (1906), *Counterpoint* (1910–22), and *Free Composition* (1935)—were widely disseminated in the 1970s and by the end of the century had become the basis of the most widely employed analytical techniques for tonal music.

scherzo \'skert-ˌsō\ (Italian: "joke") Musical movement in rapid triple time, which replaced the MINUET in such genres as the SYMPHONY, SONATA, and STRING QUARTET in the 19th century. The name was first used for light vocal and instrumental pieces of the baroque era. It formally often resembles the minuet, being in rounded binary form and having a contrasting trio section between two statements of the scherzo proper, but its tempo is often much faster and its style may range from playful to vehement or grotesque.

Schiaparelli \ˌskyä-pä-'rel-lē\, **Elsa** (1890–1973) Italian-French fashion designer. After working in the U.S. as a film scriptwriter and translator, she settled in Paris and opened her first shop in the 1920s. By 1935 she was a leader in haute couture and was expanding into perfume, cosmetics, lingerie, jewelry, and swimsuits. Her designs combined eccentricity with simplicity and a trim neatness with flamboyant color. Her "shocking pink," the sensation of the 1947 season, is still regularly revived. With CHRISTIAN DIOR, she was instrumental in the worldwide commercialization of Parisian fashion.

Schickard \'shi-ˌkärd\, **Wilhelm** (1592–1635) German astronomer, mathematician, and cartographer. In 1623 he invented one of the first calculating machines. He proposed to JOHANNES KEPLER the development of a mechanical means of calculating ephemerides (predicted positions of celestial bodies at regular intervals of time), and he contributed to the improvement of accuracy in mapmaking.

Schiele \'shē-lə\, **Egon** (1890–1918) Austrian painter, draftsman, and printmaker. He was strongly influenced by the JUGENDSTIL movement, and the linearity and subtlety of his work owe much to GUSTAV KLIMT's decorative elegance; yet he always emphasized expression over decoration, heightening the emotive power of line with a feverish intensity. His candid, agitated, erotic images caused a sensation, and in 1912 he was briefly imprisoned for indecency. His landscapes exhibit the same febrile quality of color and line. A special room was reserved for his work at a Viennese exhibition in 1918, just before he died in the influenza epidemic of that year. He has since been recognized as one of the great artists of EXPRESSIONISM.

Schiff \'shif\, **Dorothy** (1903–1989) U.S. newspaper publisher. Born in New York City, Schiff was a wealthy socialite who in 1939 used family money to buy majority control of the *New York Post.* In 1943 she took the title of owner and president, and in 1962 became editor in chief. Under her direction the *Post* became a crusading liberal paper, staunchly supporting unions and social-welfare legislation. She converted it to a tabloid format and included popular features and columnists, with the result that in the 1960s it became the city's only surviving afternoon daily. In 1976 she sold the *Post* to RUPERT MURDOCH.

Schiff, Jacob H(enry) (1847–1920) German-U.S. financier and philanthropist. He emigrated to the U.S. in 1865, and in 1875 joined the investment-banking firm of Kuhn, Loeb & Co. He succeeded his father-in-law as head of the firm in 1885, and became one of the leading railroad bankers in the U.S. He played a pivotal role in the reorganization of several transcontinental lines, notably the UNION PACIFIC RAILROAD and the NORTHERN PACIFIC RAILWAY. During the Russo-Japanese War he sold Japanese bonds in the U.S., for which he was decorated by the emperor of Japan. His extensive philanthropies included large contributions to Barnard College and the Jewish Theological Seminary.

Schiller \'shil-ər\, **(Johann Christoph) Friedrich (von)** (1759–1805) German dramatist, poet, and literary theorist, one of greatest figures in his nation's literature. Schiller was educated at the direction of a domineering duke, whose tyranny he eventually fled to write. With his successful first play, *The Robbers* (1781), he took up the exploration of freedom, a central theme throughout his works. *Don Carlos* (1787), his first major poetic drama, helped establish BLANK VERSE as the recognized medium of German poetic drama. His jubilant "Ode to Joy" was later used in LUDWIG VAN BEETHOVEN's Symphony No. 9. Appointed professor of history at the University of Jena in 1789, he developed his epic masterpiece, the historical drama *Wallenstein* (1800). During a period spent formulating his views on aesthetic activity, he produced philosophical essays, exquisite reflective poems, and some of his most popular ballads. He spent his last years in ill health in Weimar, near his friend JOHANN W. VON GOETHE. His mature plays, including *Maria Stuart* (performed 1800) and *Wilhelm Tell* (1804), examine the inward freedom of the soul that enables the individual to rise above physical frailties and the pressure of material conditions.

Schinkel \'shiŋ-kəl\, **Karl Friedrich** (1781–1841) German architect and painter. As state architect of Prussia (from 1815), he executed many commissions for FREDERICK WILLIAM III and other royal family members. He based his work on the revival of various historical styles. His mausoleum for Queen Louise (1810) and the brick and terra-cotta Werdersche Kirche, Berlin (1821–30), are among the earliest GOTHIC REVIVAL designs in Europe. Other works included the GREEK REVIVAL Schauspielhaus (1818) and Altes Museum (1822–30), both in Berlin. In 1830 Schinkel became director of the Prussian Office of Public Works; his work as a city planner resulted in new boulevards and squares in Berlin. He is also remembered for his stage sets and ironwork designs.

schipperke \'ski-pər-kē, 'shi-pər-kē\ Dog breed that originated in Flanders and was used as a guard on barges. The schipperke ("little captain") is descended from the Leauvenaar, which also gave rise to the Belgian SHEEPDOG. A short, thickset, tailless dog with a dense black coat and a foxlike head, it stands 12–13 in. (31–33 cm) and weighs up to 18 lbs (8 kg). It has a lively, inquisitive expression and is generally hardy and energetic, an able vermin hunter, and a good watchdog.

Schism \'si-zəm\, **Photian** Controversy between Eastern and Western Christianity in the 9th century, triggered by the opposition of the Roman pope to the appointment of PHOTIUS as patriarch of Constantinople. Ecclesiastical rights of jurisdiction in the Bulgarian church and a doctrinal dispute over the insertion of the *Filioque* ("and from the Son") clause in the NICENE CREED were also at issue. Photius withdrew from communion with Rome in 867; he himself was finally exiled in 886.

Schism, Western *or* **Great Schism** (1378–1417) In Roman Catholic history, a period when there were two, and later three, rival popes, each with his own College of CARDINALS. The schism began soon after the papal residence was returned to Rome from Avignon (see AVIGNON PAPACY). URBAN VI was elected amid local demands for an Italian pope, but a group of cardinals with French sympathies elected an antipope, Clement VII, who took up residence at Avignon. Cardinals from both sides met at Pisa in 1409 and elected a third pope in an effort to end the schism. The rift was not healed until the Council of Constance vacated all three seats and elected MARTIN V as pope in 1417.

Schism of 1054 *or* **East-West Schism** Event that separated the Byzantine and Roman churches. The Eastern and Western churches had long been estranged over doctrinal issues such as the relationship of the

Holy Spirit to the Father and the Son. The Eastern Church resented the Roman enforcement of clerical celibacy and the limitation of the right of confirmation to the bishop. There were also jurisdictional disputes between Rome and Constantinople. In 1054 Pope LEO IX and the patriarch of Constantinople, MICHAEL CERULARIUS, excommunicated each other, an event that marked the final break between the two churches. The rift widened in subsequent centuries, and the churches have remained separate, though the excommunications were lifted by the papacy and the patriarch in the 20th century. See also EASTERN ORTHODOXY, ROMAN CATHOLICISM.

schist \'shist\ Crystalline METAMORPHIC ROCK that has a highly developed tendency to split into layers. Most schists are composed largely of platy minerals such as MUSCOVITE, CHLORITE, TALC, BIOTITE, and GRAPHITE. The green color of many schists and their formation under a certain range of temperature and pressure conditions have led to distinction of the GREENSCHIST FACIES in the mineral facies classification of metamorphic rocks. Schists are usually classified on the basis of their mineralogy, with varietal names that indicate the characteristic mineral present.

schistosomiasis \ˌshis-tə-sə-'mī-ə-səs\ *or* **bilharziasis** \ˌbil-ˌhär-'zī-ə-səs\ Group of chronic disorders caused by parasitic FLATWORMS of the genus *Schistosoma* (blood FLUKES). Depending on the infecting species, thousands of eggs released by the females reach either the intestine or the bladder, are excreted in feces or urine, and hatch on contact with freshwater. The larvae invade snails, develop to the next stage, emerge into the water, and invade mammals to feed and breed in the bloodstream. An initial allergic reaction (inflammation, cough, late-afternoon fever, hives, liver tenderness) and blood in the stools and urine give way to a chronic stage, in which eggs impacted in the walls of organs cause fibrous thickening (fibrosis). This condition can lead to serious liver damage in the intestinal types and to bladder stones, fibrosis of other pelvic organs, and urinary-tract bacterial infection. In most cases, early diagnosis and persistent treatment to kill the adult worms ensure recovery.

schizophrenia \ˌskit-sə-'frē-nē-ə\ Any of a group of severe mental disorders that have in common such symptoms as HALLUCINATIONS, delusions, blunted emotions, disorganized thinking, and withdrawal from reality. Four main types are recognized: the paranoid, characterized by delusions of persecution or grandeur combined with unrealistic, illogical thinking and frequent auditory hallucinations; the disorganized (hebephrenic), characterized by disordered speech and behavior and shallow or inappropriate emotional responses; the catatonic, characterized by motor inflexibility, stupor, or stereotyped movements along with mutism, echolalia, or other speech abnormalities; and the undifferentiated, a nonspecific type. Schizophrenia seems to occur in 0.5–1% of the general population. There is strong evidence that genetic inheritance plays a role, but no single cause has been identified. Stressful life experiences may help trigger its onset. Treatment consists of drug therapy and counseling. About one-third of all patients make a full recovery, one-third have recurring episodes, and one-third deteriorate into a chronic condition.

Schlegel \'shlā-gəl\, **August Wilhelm von** (1767–1845) German scholar and critic. He worked as a tutor and wrote for FRIEDRICH SCHILLER's short-lived periodical *Die Horen* before cofounding with his brother FRIEDRICH VON SCHLEGEL the periodical *Athenäum* (1798–1800), which became the organ of German ROMANTICISM. While a professor at the University of Jena, he undertook translations of the works of WILLIAM SHAKESPEARE (1797–1810) that became standard editions and are among the finest of all German literary translations. His *Lectures on Dramatic Art and Literature* (1809–11) was widely translated and helped spread fundamental Romantic ideas throughout Europe. From 1818 until his death he taught at the University of Bonn.

Schlegel, Friedrich von (1772–1829) German writer and critic. He contributed many of his projects and theories to journals such as *Athenäum* (1798–1800), the quarterly he and his brother AUGUST W. VON SCHLEGEL founded at Jena. His study of Sanskrit led him to publish *Concerning the Language and Wisdom of India* (1808), a pioneering attempt at comparative Indo-European linguistics and the starting point of the study of Indo-Aryan languages and comparative philology. His conception of a universal, historical, and comparative literary scholarship has been profoundly influential, and he is regarded as the originator of many of the philosophical ideas that inspired early German ROMANTICISM.

Schleicher \'shlī-k̲ər\, **August** (1821–1868) German linguist. He began his career studying classical and Slavic languages. Influenced by G. W. F. HEGEL and CHARLES DARWIN, he formed the theory that a language is an organism, with periods of development, maturity, and decline. He invented a system of language classification that resembled a botanical taxonomy, tracing groups of related languages and arranging them in a genealogical tree. His model, the *Stammbaumtheorie* ("family-tree theory"), was a major development in the study of INDO-EUROPEAN LANGUAGES. His great work was *A Compendium of the Comparative Grammar of the Indo-European, Sanskrit, Greek and Latin Languages* (1874–77), in which he attempted to reconstruct Proto-Indo-European.

Schleicher, Kurt von (1882–1934) German army officer and last chancellor in the WEIMAR REPUBLIC. A career army officer, he rose to major general by 1929, and became a key figure in the Weimar Republic. His political intrigues helped secure for him the posts of defense minister (1932) and chancellor (1932–33). Seeking to keep the Nazis under the army's control, he offered to participate in a government with ADOLF HITLER, but Hitler refused him and thereafter regarded Schleicher as his chief enemy. Dismissed by PAUL VON HINDENBURG in favor of Hitler, Schleicher was murdered during the NIGHT OF THE LONG KNIVES.

Kurt von Schleicher, 1932.
ARCHIV FUR KUNST UND GESCHICHTE, BERLIN

Schleiden \'shlī-dən\, **Matthias Jakob** (1804–1881) German botanist. Trained as a lawyer, he soon left the profession to study natural science. He and THEODOR SCHWANN developed the cell theory, which states that organisms are composed of cells or substances made by cells; they were thus the first to formulate what was then an informal belief as a principle of biology equal in importance to the atomic theory of chemistry. He also recognized the importance of the cell nucleus and sensed its connection with cell division. He was one of the first German biologists to accept CHARLES DARWIN's theory of evolution.

Schleiden.
BY COURTESY BILDARCHIV PREUSSISCHER KULTURBESITZ BPK, WEST BERLIN

Schleiermacher \'shlī-ər-ˌmäk̲-ər\, **Friedrich (Ernst Daniel)** (1768–1834) German theologian, preacher, and classical philologist. He joined the clergy in 1796, and in *On Religion* (1799) he addressed the Romantics, declaring that they were not as far from religion as they thought. From 1810 to his death, he taught at the University of Berlin. He helped unite Prussia's Lutheran and Reformed churches in 1817. His major work, *The Christian Faith* (1821–22), is a systematic interpretation of Christian dogmatics. His thought influenced theology through the 19th and early 20th century, and he is generally recognized as the founder of modern Protestant theology.

Schlesinger \'shlā-ziŋ-ər, 'shle-sin-jər\, **Arthur M(eier) and Arthur M(eier), Jr.** (1888–1965, born 1917) U.S. historians. Born in Xenia, Ohio, the elder Schlesinger taught at Harvard University for three decades beginning in 1924. He helped to broaden the study of U.S. history by emphasizing social and urban developments. His books include *The Colonial Merchants and the American Revolution, 1763–1776* (1917) and *Rise of the City, 1878–1898* (1933), and he coedited (with Dixon Ryan Fox) the series *A History of American Life* (1928–43). His son, born in Columbus, Ohio, has taught at Harvard (1946–61) and the City University of New York (1966–95). Long active in liberal politics, he was an adviser to ADLAI STEVENSON and JOHN F. KENNEDY during their presidential campaigns and served as Kennedy's special assistant. His books include *The Age of Jackson* (1946, Pulitzer Prize), *The Age of Roosevelt* (3 vols., 1957–60), *A Thousand Days* (1965, National Book Award, Pulitzer Prize), *The Imperial Presidency* (1973), and *The Cycles of American History* (1986).

Schlesinger, John (Richard) (born 1926) British film and theater director. He worked as an actor before becoming a documentary director for BBC television, where he won praise for his *Terminus* (1960). His feature films *A Kind of Loving* (1962) and *Billy Liar* (1963) were caustic depictions of English urban life. The successful *Darling* (1965) mocked the shallowness of the jet set, and he followed it with *Far From the Madding Crowd* (1967). His first U.S. film, *Midnight Cowboy* (1969), won him an Academy Award. His later films include *Sunday Bloody Sunday* (1971), *Marathon Man* (1976), *Yanks* (1979), *Madame Sousatzka* (1988), and *Cold Comfort Farm* (1995).

Schleswig-Holstein \'shlās-ˌvik-'hōl-ˌshtīn\ Historical area and state (pop., 1996 est.: 2,726,000), northwestern Germany. It occupies the southern half of the JUTLAND Peninsula and includes Fehmarn Island in the Baltic and various islands in the FRISIAN ISLANDS group. Its capital is KIEL. From the 15th century the former duchies of Schleswig and Holstein were subject to the claims and counterclaims of Denmark, Sweden, the Holy Roman Empire, Prussia, and Austria. The Danes ceded them to Prussia and Austria in 1864, and in 1866 both areas became part of Prussia (see SCHLESWIG-HOLSTEIN QUESTION). The northern part of Schleswig was awarded to Denmark in 1920. The German part of Schleswig-Holstein was organized as a state of West Germany after World War II. Industries include shipbuilding, electrical engineering, paper, textiles, clothing, and tourism.

Schleswig-Holstein Question \'shles-ˌwig-'hōl-ˌstīn\ Conflict between Denmark and Prussia over SCHLESWIG-HOLSTEIN. In the 1840s the Danish-speaking population of northern Schleswig, supported by the Danish government, wanted to detach Schleswig from Holstein and incorporate it with Denmark, whereas the German-speaking majority of the two duchies wanted to combine them as a state within the GERMAN CONFEDERATION. An 1848 uprising by Germans in the region was aided by the Prussian army in a war that ousted Denmark's troops (1848–51). The agreements of 1851–52 restored the region's status quo. In 1863 a renewed attempt by Denmark to annex Schleswig caused Prussia and Austria to declare war in 1864. After the Danish defeat at Dybbøl and the occupation of Jutland, Denmark was forced to surrender all of Schleswig-Holstein to Prussia and Austria.

Schlieffen Plan \'shlē-fən\ Plan of attack used by the German armies at the outbreak of WORLD WAR I. It was named after its developer, Count Alfred von Schlieffen (1833–1913), former chief of the German general staff. To meet the possibility of Germany's facing a war against France in the west and Russia in the east, Schlieffen proposed that, instead of aiming the first strike against Russia, Germany should aim a rapid, decisive blow with a large force at France's flank through Belgium, then sweep around and crush the French armies against a smaller German force in the south. The plan used at the beginning of World War I had been modified by HELMUTH VON MOLTKE, who reduced the size of the attacking army and was blamed for Germany's failure to win a quick victory.

Schliemann \'shlē-män\, **Heinrich** (1822–1890) German archaeologist and excavator of TROY, MYCENAE, and TIRYNS. As a boy he loved the Homeric poems, and he eventually learned ancient and modern Greek and many other languages. As a military contractor in the Crimean War he made a sufficient fortune to retire (at 36) and devote himself to archaeology. In 1873, at Hissarlik, Turkey, he discovered the remains of ancient Troy (verifying the historical event of the TROJAN WAR) and a treasure of gold jewelry ("Priam's Treasure"), which he smuggled out of the country. Because the Ottoman government prevented his return, he began excavating Mycenae in Greece, where he found more invaluable remains and treasures. He and Wilhelm Dörpfeld (1853–1940) resumed work at Hissarlik in 1878, exposing the stratigraphy more clearly and advancing archaeological technique. In 1884 they excavated the great fortified site at Tiryns. Schliemann's excavations helped lengthen considerably the perspective of history and popularize archaeology. His contributions were genuine, though his written accounts contain many self-serving fabrications.

Schliemann, detail of an engraving by A. Weger, after a photograph.

BY COURTESY OF THE DEUTSCHE STAATSBIBLIOTHEK, EAST BERLIN

Schlöndorff \'shlœn-ˌdȯrf\, **Volker** (born 1939) German-U.S. film director. He studied filmmaking in Paris and worked for LOUIS MALLE and ALAIN RESNAIS. He returned to Germany to make his first feature film, *Young Torless* (1968). He displayed a cool directorial style that distinguished him from others in the New German cinema movement. Forming his own production company, he made such movies as *The Last Honor of Katharina Blum* (1975) and *Coup de Grace* (1976); with *The Tin Drum* (1979, Academy Award), he won international fame. His later films include *Circle of Deceit* (1981), *Swann in Love* (1984), *Voyager* (1991), and *The Ogre* (1998).

Schmalkaldic Articles \shmäl-'käl-dik\ One of the confessions of faith of LUTHERANISM, written by MARTIN LUTHER in 1536 and considered by heads of state of the SCHMALKALDIC LEAGUE in 1537. A response to a bull issued by Pope PAUL III calling for a general council of the Roman Catholic church to deal with the REFORMATION, the articles were prepared in order to determine which issues could be negotiated with ROMAN CATHOLICISM and which could not be compromised. The first section discusses the unity of God, the Holy TRINITY, the INCARNATION, and JESUS; on these subjects there was no disagreement with the Catholics. The second discusses JUSTIFICATION by faith, the chief point of contention. The third deals with such matters as SIN, repentance, the SACRAMENTS, and CONFESSION.

Schmalkaldic League \'shmäl-ˌkäl-dik\ Defensive alliance by Protestant states of the HOLY ROMAN EMPIRE. It was established in 1531 at Schmalkalden, Germany, to defend the newly formed Lutheran churches from attack by the Catholic emperor CHARLES V. Fearing that the league would ally itself with his enemy, FRANCIS I of France, Charles gave it de facto recognition until 1544, when he made peace with Francis. Charles then moved against the league militarily and by 1547 had effectively destroyed it. See also SCHMALKALDIC ARTICLES.

Schmidt \'shmit\, **Helmut** (born 1918) German politician, chancellor of West Germany (1974–82). A member of the Social Democratic Party, he served in the Bundestag 1953–61 and 1965–87. He was minister of defense (1969–72) and minister of finance (1972–74) before succeeding WILLY BRANDT as chancellor in 1974. A popular and capable chancellor, he continued the policy of OSTPOLITIK while maintaining West Germany's key position in NATO and the European Community. He resigned in 1982 after a split in the government coalition over social-welfare policy. He has written numerous books on German politics and international relations.

Schmidt-Rottluff \'shmit-'rȯt-lu̇f\, **Karl** *orig.* **Karl Schmidt** (1884–1976) German painter and printmaker. As an architecture student in Dresden, he helped form Die BRÜCKE in 1905. He soon realized the expressive potential of flat, patterned design; his mature style, seen in *Self-Portrait with Monocle* (1910), is characterized by boldly dissonant colors and jagged forms. After 1911, when he moved to Berlin, his paintings and woodcuts show an interest in Cubism and African sculpture. Though his works had become more conventional by the 1930s, the Nazis officially declared them "degenerate." After World War II he taught art and resumed painting, but his work never regained its former power.

"Self-Portrait with Monocle," oil on canvas by Schmidt-Rottluff, 1910; in the Nationalgalerie, Berlin.

BY COURTESY OF THE NATIONALGALERIE, STAATLICHE MUSEEN PREUSSISCHER KULTURBESITZ, BERLIN

S T U V

Schnabel \'shnä-bəl\, **Artur** (1882–1951) Austrian pianist and composer. When he was 7, his family moved to Vienna. There he studied with T. LESCHETIZKY, who told him his musical gifts transcended his instrument, and also met J. BRAHMS and others. He made his debut in 1890. Based in Berlin 1900–33, he composed, taught, and gave legendary performances of the complete sonatas of LUDWIG VAN BEETHOVEN and F. SCHUBERT for centenary celebrations. In the 1930s he became the first to record the complete Beethoven cycle. During the Nazi period, he moved to London, then to the U.S. Though he mostly played the works of the past, his own music was ultramodern. Today he is uniquely revered by serious pianists.

Schnabel \'shnä-bəl\, **Julian** (born 1951) U.S. painter. Born in New York City, he studied at the University of Houston and the Whitney Museum of American Art. In the 1980s he was a leading exponent of NEO-EXPRESSIONISM. His works exhibit an ambivalent emotional tone, jarring color harmonies, and a primitive style; his best-known works incorporate shards of broken plates. Though he has enjoyed considerable success, there has been controversy regarding both the quality of his art and his aggressive self-promotion. Starting in the 1990s, Schnabel began to pursue film. He received widespread critical acclaim for his direction of *Before Night Falls* (2000), a film about Cuban poet Reinaldo Arenas.

schnauzer \'shnaůt-sər, 'shnaů-zər\ Any of three German dog breeds having a wiry black, salt-and-pepper, or black-and-tan coat. The standard, 17–20 in. (43–51 cm) high and weighing 26–37 lbs (12–17 kg), dates to the 15th century; it has a blunt, heavily whiskered muzzle and a squared body. The miniature, 12–14 in. (30–36 cm) high and weighing 13–15 lbs (6–7 kg), was developed in the 19th century from standard schnauzers and AFFENPINSCHERS. The giant schnauzer, a cross between the standard and various working dogs, stands 21–26 in. (53–66 cm) and weighs 66–77 lbs (30–35 kg).

Schnittke \'shnit-kə\, **Alfred (Garrievich)** (1934–1998) Russian composer. He began musical training in Vienna and continued in Moscow, then taught at the Moscow Conservatory 1962–72. He scored more than 60 films, and was one of the first Soviet composers to experiment with serialism. After the death of D. SHOSTAKOVICH, he became the Soviet Union's leading composer, and gained a major international reputation as he evolved a highly eclectic style ("polystylistics"). He suffered the first of several serious strokes in 1985, but continued to compose. He wrote nine symphonies, six concerti grossi, many concertos, four string quartets, and the operas *Life with an Idiot* (1992), *Gesualdo* (1995), and *Historia von D. Johann Fausten* (1995).

Schnitzler \'shnits-lər\, **Arthur** (1862–1931) Austrian playwright and novelist. He practiced medicine in Vienna most of his life, and also studied psychiatry. He became known for his psychological dramas and for his fearlessness in depicting the erotic lives of his characters, beginning with the early play *Anatol* (1893). His best-known play, *Reigen* (*Merry-Go-Round,* 1897), was a cycle of 10 dramatic dialogues that traced the links connecting the partners in a series of sexual encounters; considered scandalous when first performed in 1920, it was filmed as *La Ronde* by MAX OPHULS in 1950. His drama *Playing with Love* (1896) and his most successful novel, *None but the Brave* (1901), revealed the hollowness of the Austrian military code of honor.

Schoenberg.
PICTORIAL PARADE

Schoenberg \'shœn-ˌberk, *Engl* 'shərn-ˌbərg\, **Arnold (Franz Walter)** (1874–1951) Austrian-U.S. composer. Raised Catholic by his Jewish-born parents, he began studying violin at 8 and later taught himself cello. Alexander Zemlinsky (1871–1942) became his only composition teacher, and later his brother-in-law. His first string quartet (1898) was acclaimed, and with R. STRAUSS's help he obtained a teaching post in Berlin, but soon returned to Vienna, having composed his huge *Gurrelieder* (1901, orchestrated 1913). In 1904 A. BERG and A. WEBERN began their studies with him, which would profoundly shape their later artistic careers. Around 1906 Schoenberg came to believe that tonality had to be abandoned. His period of "free ATONALITY" (1907–16) saw such remarkable works as the monodrama *Erwartung*, the *Five Orchestral Pieces* (both 1909), and the notorious *Pierrot lunaire* (1912). From 1916 to 1923 he issued almost nothing, being occupied with teaching and conducting but also seeking a way to organize atonality; his thought eventuated in his epochal development of the twelve-tone method (see SERIALISM). In 1930 he began work on a three-act opera based on a single tone row; *Moses und Aron* remained unfinished at his death. The rise of Nazism moved him to reassert his Jewishness and forced him to flee to the U.S., where he remained, teaching at UCLA 1936–44. Though never embraced by a broad public, he may have exercised a greater influence on 20th-century music than any other composer.

Scholasticism Theological and philosophical movement, beginning in the 11th century, that sought to integrate the secular understanding of the ancient world, as exemplified by ARISTOTLE, with the dogma implicit in the revelations of Christianity. Its aim was a synthesis of learning in which theology surmounted the hierarchy of knowledge. Principal figures in early Scholasticism were PETER ABELARD, St. ANSELM OF CANTERBURY, St. ALBERTUS MAGNUS, and ROGER BACON. The movement flourished in the 13th century, drawing on the writings and doctrines of St. THOMAS AQUINAS. By the 14th century Scholasticism was in decline, but it had laid the foundations for many revivals and revisitations in later centuries, particularly under Pope LEO XIII (1879), who sought to modernize the insights of the medieval scholastics. Modern philosophers influenced by Scholasticism include JACQUES MARITAIN and Étienne Gilson (1884–1978).

Schönerer \'shœ-nə-rər\, **Georg, Ritter (Knight) von** (1842–1921) Austrian political extremist. In 1873 he was elected to the federal parliament as a left-wing liberal. He became an ardent German nationalist and outspoken anti-Semite and in 1885 founded the Pan-German Party. Reelected to the parliament in 1897, he opposed the pro-Czech language ordinances and was credited with driving the prime minister from office. He helped 21 Pan-German candidates win election to the parliament in 1901. His violent temperament so disrupted the party that by 1907 it had virtually disappeared from Austrian politics, but his ideological influence continued undiminished.

Schongauer \'shōn-ˌgaů-ər\, **Martin** (c. 1435/50–1491) German painter and printmaker. Though a prolific painter whose panels were sought in many countries, it is as an engraver that he was unrivaled in northern Europe. His engravings, consisting of about 115 plates, represent a highly refined manifestation of the late Gothic spirit. He brought engraving to maturity by expanding its range of contrasts and textures, bringing an artist's sensibility to an art hitherto the domain of goldsmiths. The grace of his work became proverbial in his lifetime, giving rise to such nicknames as Hübsch ("Charming") Martin and Schön ("Beautiful") Martin.

school psychology Branch of APPLIED PSYCHOLOGY that deals largely with educational assessment, PSYCHOLOGICAL TESTING, and student consultation in elementary and secondary schools. School psychologists train in EDUCATIONAL and DEVELOPMENTAL psychology as well as in general psychology, COUNSELING, and other fields. The school psychologist usually must be certified to practice in a particular school district.

Schoolcraft, Henry Rowe (1793–1864) U.S. explorer and ethnologist. Born in Albany, N.Y., he explored mineral deposits in southern Missouri and Arkansas (1817–18) and served as topographer on an expedition to the Lake Superior region (1820), then took an OJIBWA wife and became an Indian agent. In 1832 he discovered the source of the MISSISSIPPI RIVER at Lake Itaska, Minn. In 1836 he concluded a treaty in which the Ojibwa ceded much of northern Michigan to the U.S. His six-volume *Indian Tribes of the United States* (1851–57) was a pioneering, though flawed, work.

schooling behavior Behavior characteristic of clupeiform fish (HERRINGS, ANCHOVIES, and allies) in which many fish swim together, appearing to act as a single organism. A school of herring may contain many millions of individuals of roughly similar size. Fishes above or below the size limit break away and form schools among themselves. The primary advantage to the fish seems to be safety for the individual. When threatened, a school of thousands of anchovies, spread over several hundred meters, will contract to a writhing sphere only a few meters across, thereby thwarting the attempt of a natural predator to catch a single individual.

schooner \'skü-nər\ Sailing ship rigged with fore-and-aft sails on its two or more masts. Though apparently developed from a 17th-century Dutch design, the first genuine schooner was built in the American colonies, probably at Gloucester, Mass., in 1713, by Andrew Robinson. Compared to square-rigged ships, they were ideal for coastal sailing; they handled better in the varying coastal winds, had shallower drafts for shallow waters, and required a smaller crew in proportion to their size. By the end of the century, they were the most important North American ship, used for the coastal trade and for fishing. After 1800 they became popular in Europe and around the world. Clipper ships married the schooner design to that of the old three-masted merchantman.

Schopenhauer \'shō-pən-,hau̇-ər\, **Arthur** (1788–1860) German philosopher. Son of a banker and a novelist, he studied in several fields before earning his doctorate in philosophy. He regarded the Upanishads, together with the works of Plato and Immanuel Kant, as the foundation of his philosophical system, and was primarily important as the exponent of a metaphysical doctrine of the will in immediate reaction against the idealism of G. W. F. Hegel. His magnum opus, *The World as Will and Representation* (1819), consists of two comprehensive series of reflections that include successively the theory of knowledge and the philosophy of nature, aesthetics, and ethics. His turning from spirit and reason to the powers of intuition, creativity, and the irrational, affected (partly via Friedrich Nietzsche) the ideas and methods of vitalism, life philosophy, existentialism, and anthropology. His other works include *On the Will in Nature* (1836), *The Two Main Problems of Ethics* (1841), and *Parerga und Paralipomena* (1851). An unhappy and solitary man, his works earned him the sobriquet "the philosopher of pessimism."

Schopenhauer, 1855.
ARCHIV FUR KUNST UND GESCHICHTE, WEST BERLIN

Schouten Islands \'skau̇-tᵊn\ Archipelago, Pacific Ocean across the entrance to Cenderawasih Bay, northern coast of Irian Jaya, Indonesia. The islands cover an area of 1,231 sq mi (3,188 sq km). The chief islands are Biak, Supiori, and Numfoor and are among the most densely populated areas of Irian Jaya. Another island group of the same name is located off the northeastern coast of New Guinea island; it is part of Papua New Guinea.

Schreiner \'shrī-nər\, **Olive (Emilie Albertina)** (1855–1920) South African writer. She had no formal education but read widely, developing a powerful intellect and militantly feminist and liberal views. After working as a governess she published (as Ralph Iron) the semiautobiographical *The Story of an African Farm* (1883). The first great South African novel, it concerns a girl living on an isolated farm in the veld who struggles to attain independence in the face of rigid Boer social conventions. Her later works include *Trooper Peter Halkett of Mashonaland* (1897), attacking Cecil Rhodes, and *Woman and Labour* (1911), an acclaimed bible of the women's movement.

Schröder \'shrœ-dər\, **Gerhard** (born 1944) Chancellor of Germany. In his youth he joined the Social Democratic Party and the Young Socialists, and as a law student at Göttingen he participated in the student protests of 1968. He served in the Bundestag 1980–86, and succeeded to the premiership of the state of Lower Saxony in 1990. His election as federal chancellor in 1998 ended 16 years of conservative rule under Helmut Kohl.

Schröder-Devrient \'shrœ-dər-dəv-rē-'äⁿ, -dev-'rēnt\, **Wilhelmine** (1804–1860) German soprano. Daughter of a baritone, she achieved international renown with her 1822 performance as Ludwig van Beethoven's Leonora. Though her voice showed signs of wear by her thirties, she was known for her dramatic prowess—she genuinely cried onstage and was called the "Queen of Tears"—and she created three early Wagnerian roles: Adriano (*Rienzi*, 1842), Senta (*The Flying Dutchman*, 1843), and Venus (*Tannhäuser*, 1845).

Schrödinger \'shrœ-diŋ-ər\, **Erwin** (1887–1961) Austrian physicist. He taught physics in Zurich (1921–27) and Berlin (1927–33), then left Germany, objecting to the persecution of Jews. He settled in Ireland, where he joined the Dublin Institute for Advanced Studies (1940–56). He made fundamental contributions to quantum mechanics, and shared a 1933 Nobel Prize with P. A. M. Dirac for his development in 1926 of the wave equation now called the Schrödinger equation. In addition to his scientific research, he made contributions to philosophy and the history of science; his books include *What Is Life?* (1944), *Nature and the Greeks* (1954), and *My View of the World* (1961).

Schrödinger equation \'shrœ-diŋ-ər\ Fundamental equation developed in 1926 by Erwin Schrodinger that established the mathematics of quantum mechanics. The equation determines the behavior of the wave function that describes the wavelike properties of a subatomic system. It relates kinetic energy and potential energy to the total energy, and is solved to find the different energy levels of the system. Schrödinger applied the equation to the hydrogen atom and predicted many of its properties with remarkable accuracy. The equation is used extensively in atomic, nuclear, and solid-state physics. See also wave-particle duality.

Schubert \'shü-,bert\, **Franz Peter** (1797–1828) Austrian composer. He learned violin from his schoolteacher father and piano from his brother. He joined the precursor of the Vienna Boys Choir (1808), making such quick progress that A. Salieri undertook to guide his training (1810–16). At his family's insistence, he was trained as a schoolteacher. That same year, his first mass was performed, and he composed his first important songs. In 1815 he wrote two symphonies, more than 100 songs, and four stage works. In 1818, seeking independence, he quit teaching at his father's school to tutor Johann Esterházy's daughters. In 1819–20 he wrote the great "Trout" Quintet and a mass. In 1821, 20 of his most popular songs were published with great success, and he wrote the opera *Alfonso und Estrella*. His amazing production continued in 1822, despite his first awareness of the disease (possibly syphilis) that would kill him, with the Unfinished Symphony and the "Wanderer" Fantasy. He was often ill during his last five years, but continued his production of music, including the song cycles *Die schöne Müllerin* and *Winterreise*, the last three piano sonatas, and the "Great C Major" Symphony. His last years were made miserable by illness, not poverty; in fact, his greatness was widely recognized. He died at 31, having produced more masterpieces by that age than almost any other composer in history. His 600 songs made the lied a serious genre and sparked its great development in subsequent decades.

Schuller \'shu̇l-ər\, **Gunther (Alexander)** (born 1925) U.S. composer, conductor, and educator. Born in New York City, son of a violinist, he trained at the Manhattan School of Music. He played French horn with the Cincinnati Orchestra from age 18, and in the Metropolitan Opera orchestra 1945–59, as well as with such jazz musicians as Miles Davis and the Modern Jazz Quartet. His "third stream" music (combining classical and jazz styles) has included such compositions as *Seven Studies on Themes of Paul Klee* (1959). He was president of the New England Conservatory of Music 1967–77, and directed the Berkshire Music Center 1974–84. A preeminent authority on jazz, he is the author of the acclaimed *Early Jazz* (1968) and *The Swing Era* (1988).

Schultz \'shu̇lts\, **Dutch** *orig.* **Arthur Flegenheimer** (1902–1935) U.S. gangster. Born in the Bronx, N.Y., Schultz (who borrowed his pseudonym from an old-time gangster) advanced from burglaries to bootlegging, ownership of breweries and speakeasies, and policy rackets in the Bronx and Manhattan. When the murderous "Dutchman" made plans to assassinate Thomas Dewey, who had made him the target of an investigation, he himself was murdered at 33 by N.Y. crime bosses, who feared his plan would result in a crackdown on organized crime.

Schulz \'shu̇lts\, **Charles** (1922–2000) U.S. cartoonist. Son of a Minneapolis barber, he took a correspondence course in cartooning and worked as a freelance cartoonist before creating *Peanuts* (originally *Li'l Folks,* 1950), which would become the most widely syndicated comic strip of all time. The strip, whose characters are boys and girls ranging in age from 3 to 5 and a beagle with a grandiose imagination, deals with the frustrations of everyday life and the cruelty that exists among children, often with philosophical and psychological overtones. Just before his death, after 50 years of continuous production, Schulz announced the end of his strip.

Schumacher \'shü-,mäk-ər, *Engl* 'shü-,māk-ər\, **E(rnst) F(riedrich)** (1911–1977) German-British economist. After studying in England and the U.S., he settled in England in 1937. During World War II he worked on theories for full-employment policies and, under WILLIAM H. BEVERIDGE, plans for Britain's postwar welfare state. In 1950–70 he was an adviser to Britain's nationalized coal industry. After a visit to Burma in 1955, he came to believe that poor countries needed an "intermediate technology" adapted to the unique needs of each in order to develop. In the influential *Small Is Beautiful* (1973) he argued that capitalism brought higher living standards at the cost of deteriorating culture and that bigness—especially large industries and large cities—was unaffordable.

Schuman \'shü-,män\, **Robert** (1886–1963) French statesman. He was a member of the French National Assembly from 1919. After working in the French Resistance in World War II, he helped found the POPULAR REPUBLICAN MOVEMENT. He served as finance minister (1946), premier (1947–48), foreign minister (1948–52), and minister of justice (1955–56). In 1950 he proposed the Schuman Plan to promote European economic and military unity, which led to the EUROPEAN COAL AND STEEL COMMUNITY and the EUROPEAN ECONOMIC COMMUNITY (EEC). He served as president of the EEC's consultative assembly (1958–60).

Schuman \'shü-mən\, **William (Howard)** (1910–1992) U.S. composer and administrator. Born in New York City, he wrote songs in high school with his friend F. LOESSER. In 1930 he began studying composition with R. HARRIS. He enjoyed success with his *American Festival Overture* (1939), and his *Secular Cantata No. 2: A Free Song* won the first Pulitzer Prize for music (1943). Other works include ballets for MARTHA GRAHAM, the popular *New England Triptych* (1956), and 10 symphonies. As president of the Juilliard School (1945–62), he modernized its curriculum. As the first president of Lincoln Center (1962–68), he brought together several music organizations and established its Chamber Music Society and Mostly Mozart program.

Schumann \'shü-,män\, **Clara (Josephine)** *orig.* **Clara Josephine Wieck** (1819–1896) German pianist. Trained by her father, the noted piano teacher Friedrich Wieck (1785–1873), she debuted as a prodigy with Leipzig's Gewandhaus Orchestra in 1830, then toured for two years. By 1835 she had fallen in love with R. SCHUMANN, the Wiecks' boarder since 1830. When Clara turned 21, they eloped against her father's wishes. Her artistic stature had already been established by her tours, but the birth of eight children limited her career, and she stopped writing music in 1853 after showing considerable promise as a composer. Robert's mental deterioration led to her resuming touring full-time; she retired from performing and teaching in the 1890s only because of ill health. From 1853 she had a close lifelong relationship with J. BRAHMS.

Robert and Clara Schumann, lithograph by J. Hofelich.
THE BETTMANN ARCHIVE

Schumann, Robert (Alexander) (1810–1856) German composer. Son of a bookseller, he considered becoming a novelist. After taking up law studies to please his mother, he began studying piano with Friedrich Wieck instead of attending classes. In 1830 he took a term off to become a virtuoso and moved in with Wieck. In 1831 he began composing. The poor reception of an early symphony, a mysterious hand injury, and a long illness led to a suicide attempt in 1833. He emerged from it by starting a music journal, *Neue Zeitschrift für Musik*, in 1834. He was attracted by the 16-year-old Clara Wieck, who returned his feelings, to her father's alarm; the latter's efforts failed to prevent their marriage in 1840. The first phase of Schumann's compositional life ended with the publication (1837–39) of much piano music, including *Davidsbündlertänze*, *Carnaval*, *Kinderszenen*, and *Kreisleriana*, and he thereafter concentrated on a single genre at a time. The "year of song," 1840, resulted in the song cycles *Dichterliebe* and *Frauenliebe und -leben* and over 100 other songs. His next year was spent with orchestral music, producing two of his four symphonies (nos. 1 and 4) and his piano concerto; in 1842 he concentrated on chamber music. In his last productive years, he turned to dramatic or semidramatic works. His mental deterioration (probably associated with both syphilis and a family history of mental illness) accelerated; he was placed in a sanatorium and died there two years later.

Schumpeter \'shu̇m-,pā-tər\, **Joseph A(lois)** (1883–1950) Moravian-U.S. economist and sociologist. Educated in Austria, he taught at several European universities before joining the faculty of Harvard University (1932–50). He became known for his theories of capitalist development and the BUSINESS CYCLE. His popular book *Capitalism, Socialism, and Democracy* (1942) argued that capitalism would eventually perish of its own success. His posthumous *History of Economic Analysis* (1954) is an exhaustive study of the development of analytic methods in economics.

Schurz \'shu̇rts, 'shərts\, **Carl** (1829–1906) German-U.S. politician and journalist. After being involved in a failed revolutionary movement, he fled to the U.S. in 1852. He settled in Wisconsin, where he became active in the antislavery movement and the Republican Party. In the Civil War he was appointed brigadier general of volunteers and saw action in several battles. After the war he became a newspaper editor in St. Louis (1867–69), where he won election to the U.S. Senate in 1869. As U.S. secretary of the interior (1877–81), he promoted civil-service reform and an improved Indian policy. He later edited the *New York Evening Post* and the *Nation* (1881–83) and wrote editorials for *Harper's Weekly* (1892–98). Pursuing his reform interests, he joined the mugwumps (1884) and headed the National Civil Service Reform League (1892–1901).

Schurz.
BY COURTESY OF THE LIBRARY OF CONGRESS, WASHINGTON, D.C.

Schuschnigg \'shu̇sh-nik\, **Kurt von** (1897–1977) Austrian politician and chancellor (1934–38). Elected to the Austrian parliament in 1927, he served in the government of ENGELBERT DOLLFUSS as minister of justice (1932) and education (1933–34). After Dollfuss was assassinated, Schuschnigg was named chancellor. He disbanded the paramilitary Heimwehr in 1936 and tried to prevent the German takeover of Austria. After making concessions to ADOLF HITLER in February 1938, he sought to reassert national independence through a plebiscite to be held on March 13. However, on March 11 Germany invaded Austria and carried out the ANSCHLUSS, and Schuschnigg was imprisoned until the war ended. He later lived and taught in the U.S. (1948–67).

Schutz \'shu̇ts\, **Alfred** (1899–1959) Austrian-U.S. sociologist and philosopher who developed a social science based on PHENOMENOLOGY. Originally a banker, he emigrated to the U.S. in 1939. He drew attention to the social presuppositions underlying everyday life and to the creation of social reality through SYMBOLS and human action. His work laid the basis for the field of ethnomethodology, the study of people's commonsense understandings of the structure of social interaction. His principal work is *The Phenomenology of the Social World* (1932). See also INTERACTIONISM.

Schütz \'shu̅e̅ts\, **Heinrich** (1585–1672) German composer. An innkeeper's son, he was heard singing by a nobleman staying at the inn, who underwrote his education, and he went on to the University of Marburg. In 1609 he began study with G. GABRIELI in Venice. The elector of Saxony in Dresden "borrowed" Schütz for a "few months" in 1614, then refused to let him return. As kapellmeister in Dresden from 1619, he published his first collection of sacred music, *Psalms of David*. He traveled to Italy in 1628, where C. MONTEVERDI acquainted him with new musical developments, and he adopted aspects of the Italian style in his great *Symphoniae sacrae* (1629) for chorus and instruments; he later published a second and third collection of *Symphoniae sacrae* (1647, 1650). He spent much time in Denmark and elsewhere over the next 15 years. Economic conditions deteriorated, and in the early 1650s he was no longer even being paid; he was released by the elector's death in 1656.

Schuyler \'skī-lər\, **Philip John** (1733–1804) American Revolutionary officer. Born in Albany, N.Y., he served in the French and Indian War and helped settle colonial war claims with Britain (1761–63). He served in the New York legislature 1768–75 and in the Continental Congress 1775–77 and 1778–80. In the American Revolution he was commissioned one of four major generals in the Continental Army. As commander of the northern department, he planned to invade Canada; illness prevented his leading that debacle, and his later defeat at the Battle of Ticonderoga led to his replacement by Horatio Gates. He subsequently served as one of New York's first U.S. senators (1789–91, 1797–98).

Schwab, Charles M(ichael) (1862–1939) U.S. entrepreneur and steel-industry pioneer. Born in Williamsburg, Pa., he joined Andrew Carnegie's steelworks at Braddock, Pa., as a laborer and rose swiftly in the Carnegie empire. In 1892 Carnegie delegated to him the task of returning the plant in Homestead to normal production after the bloody Homestead Strike. His success in improving labor relations and increasing production led to his appointment as president of Carnegie Steel Co. in 1897 at the age of 35. Schwab proposed the merger of the competing steel companies that would create the U.S. Steel Corp., and became its first president in 1901. He resigned in 1903 to devote himself to the Bethlehem Steel Corp., which he built into one of the nation's largest steel producers.

Schwann \'shvän\, **Theodor** (1810–1882) German physiologist. He founded modern histology by recognizing the cell as the basic unit of animal structure. A year after Matthias Jakob Schleiden, a colleague Schwann knew well, advanced the cell theory for plants, Schwann extended it to animals. While investigating digestive processes, he isolated a substance responsible for digestion in the stomach, the first enzyme prepared from animal tissue, and named it pepsin. He studied muscle contraction and nerve structure, discovering the striated muscle in the upper esophagus and the myelin sheath covering nerve cells. He coined the term metabolism, identified the role played by microorganisms in the decomposition of organic matter, and formulated the basic principles of embryology by observing that the egg is a single cell that eventually develops into a complete organism.

Schwartz, Arthur See Howard Dietz

Schwartz \'shwȯrts\, **Delmore** (1913–1966) U.S. poet, short-story writer, and critic. Born in Brooklyn, N.Y., he taught at Harvard and other schools and edited and was an editor of *Partisan Review* (1943–55). His works include *In Dreams Begin Responsibilities* (1939), consisting of a short story and poetry; *Shenandoah* (1941), a verse play; and *The World Is a Wedding* (1948) and *Successful Love* (1961), collections of short stories dealing primarily with middle-class Jewish family life. His work is noted for its lyrical descriptions of cultural alienation and the search for identity. Brilliant but unstable, he became alcoholic and declined into insanity.

Schwarz inequality \'shwȯrts\ Fundamental rule of functional analysis. It states that in a vector space, function space, or other inner product space, the inner product of two elements is less than or equal to the product of their norms. In symbols, $|(x, y)| \leq |x| \cdot |y|$.

Schwarzenberg \'shvärt-sən-ˌberk\, **Felix, Fürst (Prince) zu** (1800–1852) Austrian statesman who restored the Habsburg empire as a European power. Entering the diplomatic service, he became a protégé of Klemens, Furst von Metternich and served in several Austrian embassies. In the Revolutions of 1848, he helped Joseph Radetzky defeat rebel forces in Italy. As prime minister and foreign minister of Austria (1848–52), he secured the replacement of Emperor Ferdinand by Francis Joseph. He reestablished order in Austria with a new constitution that transformed the Habsburg empire into a unitary, centralized state. He also imposed the Humiliation of Olmütz on Prussia.

Schwarzenegger \'swȯrts-ə-ˌneg-ər\, **Arnold** (born 1947) Austrian-U.S. film actor. A bodybuilder in Austria, he moved to the U.S. in 1968 and won the title of Mr. Universe five times and Mr. Olympia seven times before retiring undefeated in 1980. After appearing in the documentary *Pumping Iron* (1977), he starred in the hit *Conan the Barbarian* (1982) and its sequel (1984). Noted for his extraordinary physique and heavy accent, he became a huge international star with *The Terminator* (1984). His other films include *Twins* (1988), *Kindergarten Cop* (1990), *Total Recall* (1990), *True Lies* (1994) and *Eraser* (1996).

Schwarzkopf \'shwȯrts-ˌkȯf\, **(Olga Maria) Elisabeth (Fredericke)** *later* **Dame Elisabeth** (born 1915) German-British soprano. After studies at the Berlin Hochschule, she debuted as a flower maiden in *Parsifal* in 1938. A 1942 recital in Berlin caused Karl Bohm to invite her to the Vienna State Opera. She made her Covent Garden debut in 1947 with that company, and remained there for five years. Her voice bloomed, and she began her long associations with the Salzburg Festival (1949–64) and La Scala (1949–63). Her annual lieder recitals were legendary. Her opera farewell (1972) was in her famous role as the Marschallin in *Der Rosenkavalier*, and she retired in 1975.

Schwarzkopf, H. Norman (born 1934) U.S. Army commander. Born in Trenton, N.J., he graduated from West Point and fought in the Vietnam War (1965–66, 1969–70). After various other assignments, he was promoted to major general (1983) and commanded forces in the invasion of Grenada. In 1988 he became a four-star general and commander of the U.S. Central Command, which included operations in the Middle East. To confront Iraq's invasion of Kuwait in 1990, he directed the buildup of 700,000 U.S. and allied troops in Saudi Arabia, and he commanded the successful Desert Storm operations in the Persian Gulf War (1991), after which he retired from active service. His autobiography is *It Doesn't Take a Hero* (1992).

Schwarzschild \'shwȯrt-ˌshilt\, **Karl** (1873–1916) German astronomer. He published his first paper (on celestial orbits) at 16. In 1901 he became professor and director of the observatory at the University of Göttingen. He gave the first exact solution of Albert Einstein's general equations of gravitation, which led to a description of how mass curves space. He also laid the foundation of the theory of black holes, using the gravitational equations to show that bodies of sufficient mass would have an escape velocity greater than the speed of light and therefore would not be directly observable. See also Schwarzschild radius.

Schwarzschild radius *or* **gravitational radius** Radius below which the gravitational attraction between a body's particles must cause its irreversible gravitational collapse, named for Karl Schwarzschild. This is thought to be the final fate of the most massive stars (see black hole). The gravitational radius (R_g) of an object of mass M is given by $R_g = 2GM/c^2$, where G is the universal gravitational constant and c the speed of light. For a star like the sun, the Schwarzschild radius would be about 1.8 mi (3.0 km).

Schweitzer \'shwīt-sər\, **Albert** (1875–1965) Alsatian-German theologian, philosopher, organist, and mission doctor. In his early years he took a degree in philosophy (1899) and became an accomplished organist. In his huge biography of J.S. Bach (2 vols., 1905), he viewed Bach as a religious mystic. He also wrote on organ construction and produced an edition of Bach's organ works. His books on religion include several on St. Paul; his *Quest of the Historical Jesus* (1910) became widely influential. In 1905 he announced he would become a mission doctor and devote himself to philanthropic work. He and his wife moved in 1913 to Lambaréné in French Equatorial Africa (now Gabon), and with local helpers built a hospital on the banks of the Ogooué River, to which they later added a leper colony. In 1952 he received the Nobel Peace Prize for his efforts on behalf of "the Brotherhood of Nations." Two years before his death, his hospital and leper colony was serving 500 patients. His philosophical books discuss his famous principle of "reverence for life."

Schweitzer, photograph by Yousuf Karsh.

Schwitters \'shvit-ərz\, **Kurt** (1887–1948) German Dada artist and poet. Associated with the Berlin Dadaists from 1918, he moved to Hanover in 1924. He assembled collages and other constructions from everyday objects (train tickets, wooden spools, newspapers, postage stamps); his poems were composites of newspaper headlines, advertising slogans, and other printed ephemera. He referred to all his artistic activities—and later to all his daily activities and even to himself—as *Merz,* the syllable left when he snipped letters from *Kommerzbank* ("Commercial Bank"). When the Nazis declared his art "degenerate" in 1937, he moved to Norway and later to England.

"Picture with Light Centre," collage of paper with oil on cardboard by Kurt Schwitters, 1919; in the Museum of Modern Art, New York City.

BY COURTESY OF THE MUSEUM OF MODERN ART, NEW YORK CITY

sciatica \sī-'a-ti-kə\ Pain along the course of the sciatic nerve, from the lower back down each leg. It often begins after lower-back strain and is associated with spinal-disk herniation. Pain is increased by coughing, sneezing, or bending the neck forward. Muscle relaxants, painkillers, and nerve stimulation are among the treatments, but surgery to relieve pressure on the nerve is needed if pain is disabling or nerve function is progressively disturbed (with leg weakness and loss of feeling). Rarely, sciatica arises from other causes of nerve compression (e.g., tumor) or disorders involving the peripheral nervous system.

science, philosophy of Branch of philosophy that attempts to elucidate the nature of scientific inquiry—observational procedures, patterns of argument, methods of representation and calculation, metaphysical presuppositions—and evaluate the grounds of their validity from the points of view of EPISTEMOLOGY, formal LOGIC, SCIENTIFIC METHOD, and METAPHYSICS. Historically, it has had two main preoccupations, ontological and epistemological. The ontological preoccupations (which frequently overlap with the sciences themselves) ask what kinds of entities can properly figure in scientific theories and what sort of existence such entities possess. Epistemologically, philosophers of science have analyzed and evaluated the concepts and methods employed in studying natural phenomena, both the general concepts and methods common to all scientific inquiries and the specific ones that distinguish special sciences.

science fiction Fiction dealing principally with the impact of actual or imagined science on society or individuals, or more generally, literary fantasy including a scientific factor as an essential orienting component. From beginnings in the works of JULES VERNE and H.G. WELLS, it emerged as a genre in the pulp magazine *Amazing Stories,* founded in 1926. It came into its own as serious fiction in the magazine *Astounding Science Fiction* in the late 1930s and in works by such writers as ISAAC ASIMOV, ARTHUR C. CLARKE, and ROBERT HEINLEIN. A great boom in popularity followed World War II, when numerous writers' approaches included predictions of future societies on earth, analyses of the consequences of interstellar travel, and imaginative explorations of intelligent life in other worlds. Much recent fiction has been written in the "cyberpunk" genre, which deals with the effects of computers and artificial intelligence on anarchic future societies.

Scientific American U.S. monthly magazine interpreting scientific developments to lay readers. It was founded in 1845 as a newspaper describing new inventions. By 1853 its circulation had reached 30,000 and it was reporting on various sciences, such as astronomy and medicine, apart from inventions. In 1921 it became a monthly. From its founding it used woodcut illustrations, and it was one of the first papers to use halftone illustrations. Its articles—solidly based on scholarly research, well written, carefully edited, and accompanied by definitions of scientific terms and by illustrations—have made it the most highly regarded magazine of its genre.

scientific method Mathematical and experimental techniques employed in the natural sciences. Many empirical sciences, especially the social sciences, use mathematical tools borrowed from PROBABILITY THEORY and STATISTICS, together with such outgrowths of these as DECISION THEORY, GAME THEORY, utility theory, and OPERATIONS RESEARCH. Philosophers of science have addressed general methodological problems, such as the nature of scientific EXPLANATION and the justification of INDUCTION. See also MILL'S METHODS.

scientific visualization Process of interpreting mental conceptions in the sciences in visual terms. It is a vital procedure in the creative realization of scientific ideas, particularly in COMPUTER SCIENCE. Basic visualization techniques include surface rendering, volume rendering, and animation. High-performance workstations or SUPERCOMPUTERS are used to show SIMULATIONS, and high-level PROGRAMMING LANGUAGES are being developed to support visualization programming. Scientific visualization has applications in medicine, biology, chemistry, education, business, engineering, and computer science.

Scientology, Church of Religious and pseudoscientific movement established in the U.S. by L. RON HUBBARD in 1954. It uses a system of psychotherapy, known as Dianetics, that seeks to free subjects from the destructive imprints of past experiences, called engrams. Scientology also includes a highly structured system of belief dealing with the origins of life and the universe and involving the human soul, or thetan (actually each person's spiritual self). The organization has often been the subject of controversy, facing claims of exerting unreasonable control over its followers, as well as charges of fraud, tax evasion, and financial mismanagement.

Scilly \'si-lē\, **Isles of** *or* **Scilly Isles** Group of about 50 small islands and many more islets, off LAND'S END, southwestern England. Totaling about 6 sq mi (16 sq km), the islands are a continuation of the granite masses of the Cornish mainland. During the ENGLISH CIVIL WARS, Prince Charles sheltered there until his escape to JERSEY in 1646. The islands were a haunt of pirates and notorious for smuggling activities. They are administratively part of the county of CORNWALL.

Scipio Africanus the Elder \'si-pē-ō, 'ski-pē-ō\ *in full* **Publius Cornelius Scipio Africanus** (236–184/183 BC) Roman general in the Second PUNIC WAR. He was born into a patrician family that had produced several consuls. As a military TRIBUNE, he fought at the Battle of CANNAE (216), managing to escape from the defeat. While still young, he secured Spain for Rome by 206, driving the Carthaginians out and avenging his father's death. As CONSUL in 205 he won the right to attack the Carthaginians in Africa. In 202 he won a major victory over HANNIBAL at the Battle of ZAMA, ending the Second Punic War and winning the name Africanus. His political opponents, led by CATO, accused Scipio and his brother Lucius of offering too lenient terms to Macedonia after their engagement there and of not being able to account for money supposedly received in those terms. Though there was no evidence of his guilt, Scipio withdrew from public life and died a virtual exile.

Scipio Africanus the Younger *or* **Scipio Aemilianus** \i-ˌmil-ē-'ā-nəs\ *in full* **Publius Cornelius Scipio Aemilianus Africanus Numantinus** (185/184–129 BC) Roman general credited with the final subjugation of CARTHAGE. He was the natural son of Paullus and the adoptive son of Publius Scipio, son of SCIPIO AFRICANUS THE ELDER. POLYBIUS instilled in him the ideals of honor, glory, and military success. He first distinguished himself in the Third MACEDONIAN WAR (168). He then campaigned in Spain and went on to Africa (150), where he displayed great military skill against Carthage while serving as military TRIBUNE, and demand arose that he take the command against Carthage. Though under age, he was elected CONSUL in 147 and returned to Africa. He besieged and destroyed Carthage (146), ending the Third PUNIC WAR and establishing the province of Africa. Again made consul (134), he was given command of the Celtiberian War (see CELTIBERIA), and he secured Spain by besieging and destroying Numantia (133). Back in Rome, he took an unpopular position on a bill supported by his friend Tiberius GRACCHUS; he was due to speak on the question when he died unexpectedly.

scirocco See SIROCCO

scissors Cutting instrument or tool consisting of a pair of opposed metal blades that meet and cut when the handles at their ends are brought together. Modern scissors are of two types: the more usual pivoted blades have a rivet or screw connection between the cutting ends and the handle ends; spring shears have a C-shaped spring connection at the handle ends.

SCLC See SOUTHERN CHRISTIAN LEADERSHIP CONFERENCE

scleroderma \ˌskler-ə-ˈdər-mə\ *or* **progressive systemic sclerosis** \sis-ˈtem-ik-sklə-ˈrō-səs\ Chronic disease that hardens the SKIN and fixes it to underlying structures. Swelling and COLLAGEN buildup lead to loss of elasticity. The cause is unknown. It usually begins at age 25–55, more often in women, with severe inflammation of underlying tissue and stiffness, pain, and skin tautness and thickening. Systemic problems that may arise years later include fever, trouble in breathing, fibrous tissue in the lungs, inflammation of heart muscle or membranes, gastrointestinal disorders, and kidney malfunction. Calcium deposits build up under the skin. The disease may finally stabilize or gradually regress. STEROIDS may help, and physical medicine and rehabilitation with heat, massage, and passive exercise (movement of the limbs by the therapist) help prevent limb fixation and deformity.

Scofield, (David) Paul (born 1922) British actor. After entertaining the troops in World War II, he joined the theater company at Stratford-upon-Avon (later the ROYAL SHAKESPEARE CO.) in 1946, winning acclaim as Henry V and Hamlet. He had his greatest success in *A Man for All Seasons* in London (1960) and New York (1961–62) and reprised the role on film (1966, Academy Award). He continued to excel onstage, notably in *Uncle Vanya* (1970) and *Amadeus* (1979). He appeared in the film versions of *King Lear* (1971), *A Delicate Balance* (1973), and *Henry V* (1989) and later in *Quiz Show* (1994) and *The Crucible* (1996).

Scone \ˈskün\, **Stone of** Rectangular block of yellow sandstone decorated with a Celtic cross, which has been associated with the crowning of Scottish kings since medieval times. Legend says it was Jacob's pillow in the Holy Land, and it was taken to Ireland and then carried off by invading Scots. KENNETH I MACALPIN brought it to the Scottish village of Scone c. 840. EDWARD I took it to England (1296), where it was later placed under the Coronation Chair in Westminster Abbey as a symbol of the authority of English kings over Scotland. It was finally returned to Scotland in 1996.

Scopas *or* **Skopas** \ˈskō-pəs\ (fl. 4th century BC) Greek sculptor and architect. Ancient writers ranked him with PRAXITELES and LYSIPPUS as one of the major sculptors of the late Classical period. He helped establish the expression of powerful emotions as an artistic theme. He apparently worked on three monuments: the temple of Athena Alea at Tegea, the temple of Artemis at Ephesus, and the Mausoleum at Halicarnassus. Of many freestanding sculptures attributed to him, the *Maenad* in Dresden and the *Pothos* in Rome are the most noteworthy.

Scopes trial (July 10–21, 1925) Widely publicized trial in Dayton, Tenn. John T. Scopes (1900–1970), a high-school teacher, was charged with teaching CHARLES DARWIN's theory of EVOLUTION, which violated a state law prohibiting the teaching of any doctrine that denied the divine creation of humans. The trial, often called the Monkey Trial, was broadcast live on radio and attracted worldwide interest. The prosecutor was WILLIAM JENNINGS BRYAN; the defense attorney was CLARENCE DARROW. The judge limited arguments to the basic charge to avoid a test of the law's constitutionality and a discussion of Darwin's theory. Scopes was found guilty and fined $100; he was later acquitted on a technicality.

score In music, the parts of all the instruments or singers of an ensemble notated with simultaneous sounds aligned vertically, on a system of parallel staffs arranged one above another. Polyphonic music was being composed for some 600 years before the score came into regular use in the 16th–17th century. Early examples of scores exist for works of the NOTRE-DAME SCHOOL, and early composers may have used temporary scores during composition, perhaps on chalkboards, from which the parts for individual singers were then copied.

Scorel \ˈskȯr-əl\, **Jan van** (1495–1562) Dutch humanist, architect, engineer, and painter. He studied briefly with JAN GOSSART, who encouraged him to travel. Five years of work and study in Europe took him eventually to Rome. Returning to Holland in 1524, he introduced such Italian Renaissance elements as nudes, classical draperies and architecture, and spacious imaginary landscapes. His greatest works are his portraits, which show his gift for characterization. He successfully combined the idealism of Renaissance Italy with the naturalism of northern European art in his paintings, and bequeathed the style to successive generations of Dutch artists.

Scoresby Sound \ˈskōrz-bē\ Deep inlet, Norwegian Sea, eastern central coast of Greenland. It runs inland for 70 mi (110 km) and has numerous fjords (the longest is 280 mi, or 451 km) and two large islands. It was charted by William Scoresby in 1822.

scoria \ˈskōr-ē-ə\ Heavy, dark, glassy IGNEOUS ROCK that contains many bubblelike cavities. Foamlike scoria, in which the bubbles are very thin shells of solidified basaltic magma, occurs as a product of explosive eruptions (as on Hawaii) and as frothy crusts on some lavas. Other scoria, sometimes called volcanic cinder, resembles clinkers, or cinders from a coal furnace.

Scorpio *or* **Scorpius** (Latin: "Scorpion") In astronomy, the constellation lying between Libra and Sagittarius; in ASTROLOGY, the eighth sign of the ZODIAC, governing approximately the period October 24–November 21. Its symbol, a scorpion, refers to the Greek myth of the scorpion that stung ORION. The story explains why the constellation of Orion sets as Scorpius rises in the sky. Another Greek myth says that a scorpion caused the horses of the sun to bolt when they were being driven by the inexperienced PHAETHON.

scorpion Any of some 1,300 nocturnal ARACHNID species (order Scorpionida, subphylum Chelicerata) having a slender body, a segmented tail tipped with a venomous stinger, and six pairs of appendages. The small first pair tear apart insect and spider prey. Strong, clawlike pincers on the large second pair, held horizontally in front, are used as feelers and for grasping prey while sucking the tissue fluids. The last four pairs, each with a pincer, are walking legs. The venom is either a hemotoxin that, in humans, causes swelling, redness, and pain or a neurotoxin that may cause convulsions, paralysis, cardiac irregularities, and death. Most scorpions will sting a human only if provoked. Nocturnal hunters, most species are tropical or subtropical.

scorpion fish Any of the numerous species of carnivorous marine fish of the family Scorpaenidae, especially those in the genus *Scorpaena,* widely distributed in temperate and tropical waters. They have large, spiny heads and strong, sometimes venomous, fin spines. Many species blend with their surroundings by virtue of their dull color, but some are brightly colored, often red. The largest species grow to about 40 in. (1 m) long. Scorpion fish lie quietly on the bottom, often among rocks. See also LIONFISH, REDFISH, ROCKFISH, ZEBRA FISH.

California scorpion fish (*Scorpaena guttata*).

BUD MEESE FROM ROOT RESOURCES—EB INC.

Scorsese \skȯr-ˈsā-zē\, **Martin** (born 1942) U.S. film director. Born into a Sicilian family in New York's Little Italy, he earned a graduate degree in filmmaking at NYU. After directing several short films, he won critical attention for his feature film *Mean Streets* (1973) and was widely praised for *Taxi Driver* (1976), which starred his frequent lead actor ROBERT DE NIRO. Noted for his realistic, violent portrayals of New York street life, innovative camera work, classic film knowledge, and a spirited cynicism, he rose to the top rank of American directors with such films as *New York, New York* (1977), the acclaimed *Raging Bull* (1980), *The King of Comedy* (1983), *The Color of Money* (1986), the controversial *Last Temptation of Christ* (1988), *GoodFellas* (1990), *Cape Fear* (1991), *The Age of Innocence* (1993), *Casino* (1995), and *Gangs of New York* (2002).

scotch See WHISKEY

scoter *or* **sea coot** Any of three species (genus *Melanitta*) of DIVING DUCK that are mainly marine except during the breeding season. The males are shiny black. The surf scoter *(Melanitta perspicillata)* breeds in the forests and tundra of Canada and Alaska and winters on seacoasts as far south as Florida and southern California. The white-winged, or velvet, scoter *(M. deglandi,* or *fusca)* and the black, or common, scoter *(M.* or sometimes *Oidemia, nigra)* occur north of the equator nearly worldwide. All three feed mainly on marine animals such as clams.

Scotland Northernmost country of the United Kingdom. Area: 30,421 sq mi (78,789 sq km). Population (2001 est.): 5,109,000. Capital: EDINBURGH. The population is a blend of Celtic, Angle, and Norman ancestry. Languages: English (official), Scottish Gaelic, and Scots. Religion: Church of Scotland (Presbyterian) (official). Currency: pound sterling. Scotland has three major geographic regions. The Highlands, in the north, are occupied by a series of lakes and the GRAMPIAN MOUNTAINS;

the Lowlands include some of Scotland's best farmland; and the Southern Uplands feature narrow, flat valleys separating table mountains. It has a temperate oceanic climate. Important industries are coal and oil production, electronics, forestry, and marine fishing. PICTS inhabited the region when it was invaded by the Romans c. AD 80. In the 5th century it split into four kingdoms under the Picts, Scots, Britons, and Angles. Scottish unification began in the 9th century. It came under a heavy anglicizing influence from the 11th century, and its ruler was forced to pay homage to the English crown in 1174, leading to numerous future disputes. The Scottish and English kingdoms were united in 1603 when James VI, son of MARY, QUEEN OF SCOTS, ascended the English throne as JAMES I. Scotland became part of the United Kingdom of Great Britain in 1707, when the parliaments of both governments passed the Act of Union. The English prevailed in two Scottish rebellions in the 18th century, and after 1745, the history of Scotland became part of the history of Great Britain. It has no sovereign executive but retains vestiges of ancient sovereignty in its own legal and educational systems. In 1997, the Scots passed a referendum that allowed them to establish their own parliament in Edinburgh to vote on wide-ranging political issues while remaining part of the United Kingdom. The Scottish Parliament first convened in 1999.

Scotland Yard *officially* **New Scotland Yard** Headquarters of the London Metropolitan Police, and, by extension, the force itself. The London police force was created in 1829 by SIR ROBERT PEEL and housed at 4 Whitehall Place, which had an entrance in Great Scotland Yard. In 1890 it moved to a new building; that location became New Scotland Yard, a name that was kept when it moved again in 1967. In addition to duties common to all metropolitan police forces (including crime detection and prevention and traffic management), it is entrusted with civil defense in times of emergency, and it maintains a special branch for guarding visiting dignitaries, royalty, and political dignitaries. It keeps records on all known criminals in Britain, and other British police forces often seek its assistance. It also helps train the police of Commonwealth nations.

Scott, George C(ampbell) (1927–1999) U.S. actor. Born in Wise, Va., he served in the Marines before beginning to act on stage and television. He won praise for his early film roles in *Anatomy of a Murder* (1959), *The Hustler* (1961), and *Petulia* (1968). A strong screen personality, he was noted for his bull neck and barking voice. He won an Academy Award for *Patton* (1970) but refused to accept it, calling the competition a "meat parade." Among his later films were *The Hospital* (1972), *Hardcore* (1979), *Taps* (1981), and *Malice* (1993). His television work included *The Price* (1970, Emmy award, also refused), and the role of Scrooge in *A Christmas Carol* (1984).

Scott, Paul (Mark) (1920–1978) British novelist. Scott entered military service in India in the 1940s and later was a director of a London literary agency; he resigned in 1960 to write full-time. He is known for works chronicling the decline of the British occupation of India, notably *The Raj Quartet*—consisting of *The Jewel in the Crown* (1966), *The Day of the Scorpion* (1968), *The Towers of Silence* (1971), and *A Division of the Spoils* (1975)—and *Staying On* (1977, Booker Prize). All his works, including those set outside India, employ Indian themes or characters.

Scott, Peter Markham *later* **Sir Peter** (1909–1989) British conservationist and artist. Son of ROBERT FALCON SCOTT, he graduated from Cambridge University and soon gained renown as a wildlife painter. In 1946 he founded the Severn Wildfowl Trust (later renamed the Wildfowl and Wetlands Trust). Through a captive breeding program at his sanctuary, he saved the NENE from extinction in the 1950s. In 1961 he founded the World Wildlife Fund (World Wide Fund for Nature). As a member of the Species Survival Commission of the International Union for Conservation of Nature and Natural Resources (1962–81), he created the *Red Data Book* (see ENDANGERED SPECIES). He was knighted in 1973.

Scott, Ridley (born 1937) British film director. He studied art and worked as a set designer and director in British television, then formed his own production company in 1967 to make television commercials. His first feature film was *The Duellists* (1977). It was followed by the science-fiction thrillers *Alien* (1979) and *Blade Runner* (1982), a box-office hit that became a cult classic for its vividly dark images. His later films include *Legend* (1985), *Black Rain* (1989), the widely acclaimed *Thelma and Louise* (1991), *G.I. Jane* (1997), and *Gladiator* (2000).

Scott, Robert Falcon (1868–1912) British explorer. He joined the Royal Navy in 1880, proved his competence leading an Antarctic expedition (1901–4), and was promoted to captain. In 1910 he embarked on a second expedition, and in October 1911 he and 11 others started overland for the South Pole. After their motor sledges broke down and seven men returned to base camp, Scott and four others trekked for 81 days to reach the pole in January 1912, only to find that ROALD AMUNDSEN had preceded them by about a month. Exhausted and beset by bad weather and insufficient supplies, the men died on the return trip, Scott and the last two survivors only 11 miles from their base camp. In England Scott was celebrated as a national hero for his courage, though his judgment has been questioned.

Scott, Walter *later* **Sir Walter** (1771–1832) Scottish writer, often considered both the inventor and the greatest practitioner of the historical novel. From childhood Scott was familiar with stories of the Border region of Scotland. Apprenticed to his father, a lawyer, in 1786, he later became sheriff depute of Selkirk and clerk to the Court of Session in Edinburgh. His interest in border ballads led to the collection *Minstrelsy of the Scottish Border* (1802–3). His first original poetic romance, *The Lay of the Last Minstrel* (1805), established his reputation; *The Lady of the Lake* (1810) was his most successful contribution to the genre. He produced editions of the works of JOHN DRYDEN (18 vols., 1808) and JONATHAN SWIFT (19 vols., 1814). Troubled with debt, from 1813 he wrote in part to make money. He tired of narrative poetry and turned to prose romances. The extremely popular series now known as the Waverley novels consists of more than two dozen works dealing with Scottish history, including the masterpieces *Old Mortality* (1816), *Rob Roy* (1817), and *The Heart of Midlothian* (1818). He drew on English history and other themes for *Ivanhoe* (1819), *Kenilworth* (1821), and *Quentin Durward* (1823). All his novels were published anonymously until 1827.

Sir Walter Scott, detail of an oil painting by Sir Edwin Henry Landseer, 1824; in the National Portrait Gallery, London.

BY COURTESY OF THE NATIONAL PORTRAIT GALLERY, LONDON

Scott, Winfield (1786–1866) U.S. Army officer. Born in Petersburg, Va., he fought in the War of 1812 at the battles of Chippewa and Lundy's Lane (1814). Promoted to major general, he traveled to Europe to study military tactics. He advocated a well-trained and disciplined army and earned the nickname "Old Fuss and Feathers" for his emphasis on military formalities. In 1841 he became commanding general of the U.S. Army. He directed operations during the MEXICAN WAR and led the U.S. invasion at Veracruz and the victory at the Battle of CERRO GORDO. He was the Whig Party's nominee in the 1852 presidential election, but lost to FRANKLIN PIERCE.

Scott v. Stanford See DRED SCOTT DECISION

Scottish fold cat Breed of DOMESTIC CAT with ears that fold forward and down. A Scottish shepherd discovered the foundation cat—Susie, a white barn cat—in 1961. Scottish folds may be longhaired or shorthaired and of any color or pattern. Susie's fold was caused by a genetic mutation that does not appear in every kitten. The folded ear and a pedigree that leads back to Susie are required for show. Scottish folds are gentle and quiet.

Scottish Gaelic language CELTIC LANGUAGE of northern Scotland, a descendant of the Irish speech introduced into northern Britain by invaders in the 4th–5th century. Gaelic gradually supplanted Pictish (see PICTS) as well as the British Celtic Lowlands dialects, and by the Middle Ages was the language of all of the Scottish Highlands and part of the Lowlands. Until the 17th century, Classical Modern Irish (see IRISH LANGUAGE) was the literary medium of Gaeldom, and only after its collapse did writers regularly begin to use features that distinguish Scottish Gaelic dialects from Irish dialects. Increasing Anglicization, suppression of tra-

S T U V

ditional culture after the Battle of CULLODEN, and the 19th-century land clearances precipitated a marked decline; today it is probably a true community language for fewer than 80,000 people, most on the northwestern coast and the Hebrides.

Scottish law Legal practices and institutions of Scotland. When the English and Scottish parliaments were joined in 1707, the legal systems of the two countries were very dissimilar. Scotland had supplemented its customary law with civil-law principles adapted from the systems of France and Holland. Its assimilation of English law following the union was significant, particularly in the area of mercantile law. The supreme Scottish civil court is the Court of Sessions, composed of 18 judges and divided into Outer and Inner houses. The supreme criminal court is the High Court of Justiciary. Below these two bodies are six sheriffdoms, each with its own sheriff court, an institution of great antiquity. Lesser cases are heard by district courts.

Scottish terrier *or* **Scottie** Short-legged TERRIER breed, perhaps the oldest of the Highland terriers. A strong and plucky dog, the Scottie is squat and bewhiskered, with alert-looking eyes and a distinctive rolling gait, and about 10 in. (25.5 cm) high and weigh 18–22 lbs (8–10 kg). Its hard, wiry coat may be of various colors.

Scotts Bluff National Monument National monument, western Nebraska. Established in 1919, it has an area of 5 sq mi (13 sq km). Its focus is a large bluff that rises 800 ft (244 m) above the NORTH PLATTE RIVER and was a prominent landmark on the OREGON TRAIL. A museum at the base of the bluff highlights the history of the pioneer travelers.

Scottsboro case U.S. civil-rights controversy. In April 1931, in Scottsboro, Ala., nine black youths were charged with the rape of two white women. Despite testimony by doctors that no rape had occurred, the all-white jury convicted them and sentenced all but the youngest to death. In 1932, following public outcry, the U.S. Supreme Court overturned the convictions on the grounds that the defendants had not received adequate legal counsel. Alabama retried and convicted one of the youths; this conviction too was overturned by the Supreme Court since blacks had systematically been excluded from the state's juries. Alabama retried and reconvicted the defendants individually, but yielded to public pressure and freed or paroled all but one, who later escaped.

Scotus, John Duns See John DUNS SCOTUS

scouting Activities of various national and worldwide organizations for youth aimed at developing character, citizenship, and individual skills. Scouting began when ROBERT S. BADEN-POWELL published *Scouting for Boys* (1908), in which he described the games and contests he used to train cavalry troops in scouting, envisioning small groups of boys who would learn tracking, reconnaissance, mapping, and other outdoor skills under a peer leader. The Boy Scouts, as established by Baden-Powell, was for boys 11–15 years old. The concept became so popular that separate organizations for girls (Girl Guides or Girl Scouts, 1910) and for younger boys (Wolf Cubs or Cub Scouts, 1916) and older boys (Explorers) were also formed.

Scrabble Game in which two to four players compete in forming words with lettered wooden tiles on a 225-square board. Words spelled out by letters on the tiles interlock like words in a crossword puzzle. Words are scored by adding up the point values of their letters. The game (originally called Lexico) was developed by Alfred Butts, an unemployed architect, in 1931. It was redesigned and renamed Scrabble by Butts and James Brunot in 1948. Tens of millions of sets have been sold in many languages worldwide.

scrap metal Used METALS that are an important source of industrial metals and ALLOYS, particularly in the production of steel, copper, lead, aluminum, and zinc. Smaller amounts of tin, nickel, magnesium, and precious metals are also recovered from scrap. Impurities consisting of such organic materials as wood, plastic, paint, and fabric can be burned off. Scrap is usually blended and remelted to produce alloys similar to or more complex than those from which the scrap was derived. See also RECYCLING.

screech owl Any of numerous OWLS of the genus *Otus* (family Strigidae). Both New World species and Old World species (called scops owls) have a facial disk and ear tufts. In spite of their name, they do not in fact screech. Their coloring resembles tree bark, and they are 8–12 in. (20–30 cm) long. They eat mostly small mammals, birds, and insects. Notable species are the common screech owl *(O. asio)* of North America, the flammulated owl *(O. flammeolus)* of western North America, and the common scops owl *(O. scops)* of southern Europe, Asia, and Africa.

screenplay Written text that provides the basis for a film production. Screenplays usually include not only the dialogue spoken by the characters but also a shot-by-shot outline of the film's action. Screenplays may be adapted from novels or stage plays or developed from original ideas suggested by the screenwriters or their collaborators. They generally pass through multiple revisions, and screenwriters are called on to incorporate suggestions from directors, producers, and others involved in the filmmaking process. Early drafts often include only brief suggestions for planned shots, but by the date of production a screenplay may evolve into a detailed shooting script, in which action and gestures are explicitly stated.

screw In machine construction, a usually circular cylindrical member with a continuous spiral rib or thread, used either as a FASTENER or as a FORCE and MOTION modifier. Various types of screws are used to clamp machine parts together. Wood screws are made in a wide variety of diameters and lengths; when using wood screws, small starting holes called pilot holes are often drilled first to avoid splitting the wood. Screws that modify force and motion are known as power screws. The screw is considered one of the five simple MACHINES. See also WEDGE.

screwworm Any of several North and South American BLOWFLY species named for the screwlike appearance of the LARVA's body, which is ringed with small spines. Screwworms attack livestock and other animals, including humans. The true screwworm *(Cochliomyia hominivorax)* and the secondary screwworm *(Callitroga macellaria)* develop in decaying flesh; they may also attack healthy tissue. Each female deposits 200–400 eggs near an open wound. The larvae burrow into the tissue and, when mature, drop to the ground to pupate. Severe infestations (myiasis) may kill the affected animal.

Scriabin \'skryä-bin\, **Alexander (Nikolaevich)** (1872–1915) Russian composer and pianist. He studied piano at the Moscow Conservatory and then launched a successful concert career. His early music was mostly for piano (including études, preludes, and sonatas) but also included two symphonies and a piano concerto. Obsessed with RICHARD WAGNER and FRIEDRICH NIETZSCHE, he began composing in an entirely new nontonal style based on his "mystic chord," producing a third symphony and the *Divine Poem* (1904). He became involved in theosophy, writing the tone poem *Poem of Ecstasy* (1908), and experimenting with "light shows" coordinated with the harmonies in his *Prometheus* (1910) in preparation for a huge operatic ritual, *Mysterium,* which was never composed. A lip tumor led to his death at 43.

Alexander Scriabin.
NOVOSTI PRESS AGENCY

Scribe \'skrēb\, **(Augustin) Eugène** (1791–1861) French playwright and librettist. He wrote some 350 dramas, most of which proved extremely successful, and became the most popular opera librettist of his time. His librettos include G. ROSSINI's *Le comte Ory* (1828), V. BELLINI's *La sonnambula* (1831), G. DONIZETTI's *L'elisir d'amore* (1832), G. MEYERBEER's *Les Huguenots* (1836), and G. VERDI's *Les vêpres siciliennes* (1855).

Scribner, Charles *orig.* **Charles Scrivener** (1821–1871) U.S. publisher. In 1846, in partnership with Isaac D. Baker (died 1850), Scribner established the publishing firm of Baker & Scribner in his native New York City. In 1878 the firm was renamed Charles Scribner's Sons. Its list initially consisted of philosophical and theological (mainly Presbyterian) books, but later included reprints and translations of British and continental European literature. Among the firm's periodicals was *Scribner's Monthly* (1870–81). After his death other members of the SCRIBNER FAMILY continued the business.

Scribner family Family of U.S. publishers whose firm, named Charles Scribner's Sons from 1878, issued books and periodicals. After the death of its founder, Charles Scribner, the company was headed successively by his sons John Blair (1850–1879), Charles (1854–1930), and Arthur Hawley (1859–1932). During the long presidency (1879–1928) of the second Charles Scribner, the firm published such authors as Henry James, Theodore Roosevelt, Edith Wharton, Ernest Hemingway, George Meredith, and Rudyard Kipling. Later presidents were Charles Scribner (1890–1952), son of the second Charles; and his son Charles, Jr. (1921–1995), who also served as president of Princeton University Press, founded in 1905 by his grandfather. Charles Scribner's Sons was purchased in 1984 by Macmillan Inc.

scrimshaw Decoration of bone or ivory objects, such as whale's teeth and walrus tusks, with fanciful designs, traditionally carved by Anglo-American and Native American whale fishermen with a jackknife or sail needle and emphasized with black pigments (e.g., lampblack). Among the traditional subjects are whaling scenes, ships, naval battles, flower bouquets, Masonic emblems, coats of arms, and the Irish harp. The earliest surviving examples date from the late 17th century, but the craft reached its peak in 1830–50. It is still practiced by whalers in Siberia and Alaska.

Scripps, Edward Wyllis (1854–1926) U.S. newspaper publisher. Born near Rushville, Ill., he was first employed by his half brother, James Edmund Scripps (1835–1906), on newspapers in Detroit. He began publishing his own papers in 1878 and eventually owned 34 in 15 states. He was a partner in forming the first major U.S. newspaper chain, the Scripps-McRae League of Newspapers (1894). In 1907 he consolidated regional Scripps news services as United Press (after 1958, United Press International). In 1922 he transferred his interests to his son, Robert Paine Scripps (1895–1938), who with Roy W. Howard formed the Scripps-Howard chain. Today's the E.W. Scripps Co. includes varied media holdings in addition to newspapers.

scripture Sacred writings of religions, comprising a large portion of the literature of the world. Scriptures vary in form, volume, age, and degree of sacredness. Nearly all scriptures were originally oral and were passed down as memorized texts through several generations before being put in writing. In some religions, notably Islam, Hinduism, and Buddhism, there is still strong emphasis on the value of reciting or chanting the scriptures aloud. The Hebrew Bible (Old Testament) is the scripture of Judaism; the Bible (Old and New Testaments together) is the scripture of Christianity; and the Quran is the scripture of Islam. Scriptures of Hinduism include the Vedas and Upanishads. See also Adi Granth, Avesta, Book of Mormon, sutra, Tripitaka.

scrod Young fish (as a cod or haddock), especially one split and boned for cooking. The origin of the term is not known for certain, but it is thought to come from an Old Dutch word meaning "to shred." It seems to have first been used around 1841.

scroll painting Art form practiced primarily in the Far East. The two dominant types are the Chinese landscape scroll and the Japanese narrative scroll. China's greatest contribution to the history of painting, the landscape hand scroll, reached its greatest period in the 10th–11th century with such masters as Xu Daoning and Fan Kuan. The Japanese scroll paintings of the 12th–13th century developed the storytelling potential of painting to its greatest extent. In the earliest, Murasaki Shikibu's literary masterpiece *The Tale of Genji,* the narrative is told in pictures alternating with text. Eventually the illustration stood nearly alone. Typical subjects were the stories and biographies popular during Japan's Middle Ages.

Scruggs, Earl See Lester Flatt

SCSI \'skə-zē\ *in full* **Small Computer System Interface** Type of standard interface used to connect peripheral devices (disks, modems, printers, etc.) to small and medium-sized computers. Because all SCSI hardware devices and software drivers must meet the SCSI standard, this means that all SCSI-compliant equipment (both computers and devices) can work together, sometimes daisy-chained together.

scuba diving Swimming done under water with a self-contained underwater-breathing apparatus (SCUBA), as opposed to skin diving, which requires only a snorkel, goggles, and flippers. Scuba gear was invented by J.-Y. Cousteau and Émile Gagnan in 1943. Diving clubs formed quickly as the new technology became widely available. Scuba diving is used in oceanography, in underwater exploration and salvage work, in the study of water pollution, and for recreation.

sculpin *or* **bullhead** *or* **sea scorpion** Any of about 300 species (family Cottidae) of inactive, bottom-dwelling fishes found principally in northern regions. Sculpins are slender and tapered and have one or more spines on the gill covers, large fanlike pectoral fins, and naked or spiny skin. The head is usually wide and heavy. Most species live in shallow seawaters, some live in deeper waters, and others inhabit freshwater. The largest species grow to 2 ft (60 cm) long; the miller's-thumb *(Cottus gobio),* common in European lakes and rivers, is only about 4 in. (10 cm) long. Other species of *Cottus* are found in Asia and North America.

sculpture Three-dimensional art produced especially by forming hard or plastic materials into three-dimensional objects, usually by carving or modeling. The designs may be produced in freestanding objects (i.e., in the round), in relief, or in environments, and a variety of media may be used, including clay, wax, stone, metal, fabric, wood, plaster, rubber, and found objects. Materials may be carved, modeled, molded, cast, wrought, welded, sewn, or assembled and combined. Until the 20th century, sculpture was considered a representational art, but since the early 1900s nonrepresentational works have been produced. See also environmental sculpture, kinetic sculpture.

scurvy *or* **vitamin C deficiency** Nutritional disorder caused by deficiency of vitamin C. Deficiency interferes with tissue synthesis, causing swollen, bleeding gums, loose teeth, sore, stiff joints and legs, bleeding under the skin and in deep tissues, slow wound healing, and anemia. The scourge of sailors on long sea voyages, scurvy was recognized as diet-related in 1753, when James Lind showed that drinking citrus juice could cure and prevent it, leading to the concept of deficiency diseases. Full-blown scurvy is now rare, and adequate vitamin C usually cures even severe cases in days.

Scutari \'skü-tä-rē\, **Lake** Largest lake in the Balkan Peninsula. Located on the frontier between Montenegro and Albania, it has an area of 150 sq mi (390 sq km). It was formerly an arm of the Adriatic Sea. Steep mountains, plains, and marshland border the lake, as do many small villages that are noted for their old monasteries and fortresses.

Scylla and Charybdis \'si-lə...kə-'rib-dis\ In Greek mythology, two monsters that guarded the narrow passage through which Odysseus had to sail in his wanderings. These waters are now identified with the Strait of Messina. On one shore was Scylla, a monster with six snaky heads, who reached out of her cave to seize and devour six of Odysseus' companions. On the opposite shore was Charybdis, the personification of a whirlpool, who drank down and belched forth the waters three times a day. The shipwrecked Odysseus saved himself by clinging to a tree on the shore until his raft floated to the surface.

Scythian art \'si-thē-ən\ Decorative objects, mainly jewelry and trappings for horses, tents, and wagons, produced by nomadic Scythian tribes that roamed Central Asia and eastern Europe between the 7th century BC and the 2nd century AD. Also known as Steppes art, it largely features representations of real or mythical beasts worked in a wide variety of materials, including wood, leather, bone, appliqué felt, bronze, iron, silver, gold, and electrum. Outstanding are gold stags about 12 in. (30 cm) long, their legs tucked under them, probably used as central ornaments on round shields.

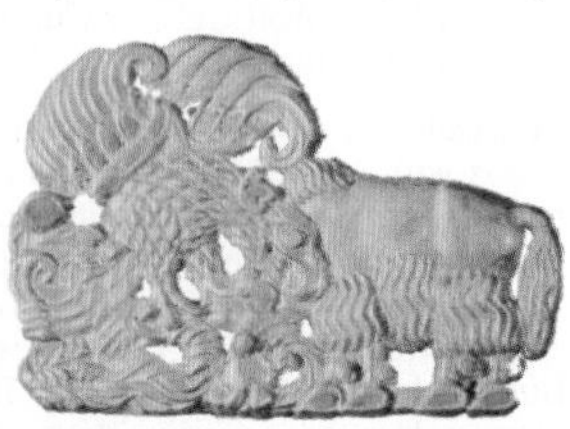

Scythian gold belt buckle with turquoise inlay, from Siberia; in the Hermitage, St. Petersburg.
NOVOSTI PRESS AGENCY

Scythians \'si-thē-ənz\ Nomadic people of Iranian stock who migrated from Central Asia to southern Russia in the 8th–7th century BC. Fierce warriors, they were among the first expert horsemen, which enabled them to establish an empire from western Persia through Syria and Judaea to Egypt and to expel the Cimmerians from their territory in the Caucasus and north of the Black Sea. Though driven out of Anatolia by the Medes (see Media), they held territory from the Persian border into southern Russia; they repelled an invasion by the Persian Darius I c. 513

BC. Their civilization produced wealthy aristocrats ("Royal Scyths"), whose graves held richly worked articles of gold and other precious materials. The army consisted of freemen; on presentation of an enemy's head, a soldier could share in the booty. They fought with double-curved bows, trefoil-shaped arrows, and Persian swords. Burial called for the sacrifice of the dead man's wife and servants. In the 5th century BC, the royal family intermarried with Greeks. The community fell to the SARMATIANS in the 2nd century BC. See also SCYTHIAN ART.

SDI See STRATEGIC DEFENSE INITIATIVE

SDS See STUDENTS FOR A DEMOCRATIC SOCIETY

Sea, Law of the International law codified in a treaty signed in 1982 by 117 nations and covering the status and use of TERRITORIAL WATERS, sea lanes, and ocean resources. It was not initially signed by the U.S., England, West Germany, Israel, Italy, and several other industrialized nations, but by 1998 the U.S. had accepted most of its provisions. The code defines territorial waters as those extending 12 nautical mi (22 km) beyond a nation's coast and gives to each nation exclusive fishing and mining rights in waters extending to 200 nautical mi (370 km) from its coast. Some nations not signing the treaty objected to these provisions and to the setting of production ceilings on seabed mining in international waters (areas outside the 200-mi limit). See also HIGH SEAS.

sea anemone \ə-ˌne-mə-ˌnē\ Any of more than 1,000 CNIDARIAN species in the order Actiniaria, found from the tidal zone of all oceans to depths of more than 30,000 ft (10,000 m) and occasionally in brackish water. Species vary from less than 1 in. (3 cm) to about 5 ft (1.5 m) in diameter. The mouth, at the upper end of the cylindrical body, is surrounded by petal-like, usually colorful, tentacles that bear stinging nematocysts for paralyzing prey such as fishes. Some species eat only microorganisms. Most species remain permanently attached to a hard surface such as a rock or the back of a crab.

Sea anemone, *Tealia*.
M. WOODBRIDGE WILLIAMS

sea bass Any of about 400 species (family Serranidae) of carnivorous fishes, most of which inhabit shallow regions of warm and tropical seas. Sea bass have a slender body, small scales, large mouth, and straight-edged or rounded tail. The spiny frontal section and the soft-rayed rear section of the dorsal fin are usually joined but may be separated by a notch. Species range from about 1 in. (3 cm) to 6 ft (1.8 m) long and may weigh 500 lbs (225 kg). About 12 species in the family Moronidae (sometimes considered a subfamily of Serranidae) inhabit temperate waters. See also BASS.

sea coot See SCOTER

sea cow *or* **Steller's sea cow** Extinct aquatic mammal *(Hydrodamalis gigas)* that lived around islands in the Bering Sea. It was discovered in 1741 and described by a member of VITUS BERING's expedition. At least 24 ft (7.5 m) long, it had no teeth, a small head, and a broad, horizontal, forked tail fluke; its dark brown skin was sometimes streaked or spotted with white. It browsed on seaweed. Russian sealers hunted it for food and fur; by 1768 the entire population, estimated at about 5,000, had been exterminated. The term also refers to DUGONGS and MANATEES.

sea cucumber Any of 1,100 species of ECHINODERMS constituting the class Holothurioidea, found in all oceans, mostly in shallow water. The soft, cylindrical body is 0.75 in. (2 cm) to 6.5 ft (2 m) long and 0.4–8 in. (1–20 cm) thick. It is usually dull, dark, and often warty. The internal skeleton consists merely of numerous tiny bits in the skin. Most species have five rows of tube feet extending from mouth to anus. The 10 or more retractile tentacles surrounding the mouth are used for taking food (mud containing nutrients or small aquatic animals) or burrowing. Locomotion is sluglike. See also SHELLFISH.

sea eagle Any of various large fish-eating EAGLES (especially in the genus *Haliaeetus*), of which the best known is the BALD EAGLE. Sea eagles live along rivers, big lakes, and tidewater worldwide except in South America. Some reach over 3 ft (1 m) long. All have an exceptionally large, high-arched beak and bare lower legs. The toes' undersurfaces are roughened for grasping slippery prey. They eat mostly carrion but sometimes kill, snatching fish from the water surface and often robbing their chief competitor, the OSPREY. Asian species include the gray-headed, or greater, fishing eagle and the lesser fishing eagle.

sea fan Any of about 500 CORAL species (genus *Gorgonia*) especially abundant in shallow waters along the Atlantic coasts of Florida, Bermuda, and the West Indies. POLYPS grow colonially in a flat, fanlike pattern. Each polyp has some multiple of six tentacles, which it spreads out to form a plankton-catching net. An internal skeleton supports all branches of the colony. The living tissues (often red, yellow, or orange) entirely cover the skeleton. The fan-shaped colonies usually grow across the current, increasing their ability to ensnare prey. All species grow to about 2 ft (60 cm) high.

Sea fan.
DOUGLAS FAULKNER

sea horse Any of about 24 species (family Syngnathidae) of fishes that usually live along warm seashores, clinging to plants with their forward-curled, prehensile tail. Species range from 1.5 to 12 in. (4–30 cm) long. Sea horses have bony rings instead of scales, and their eyes can move independently. They swim upright, propelling themselves horizontally with their fins and vertically with their swim bladder. They catch small organisms by sucking them quickly into their small mouths. The female deposits her eggs into a brood pouch beneath the male's tail, and the male expels the newly hatched young.

Sea horse (*Hippocampus erectus*).
DES BARTLETT—BRUCE COLEMAN LTD.

sea lavender Any of about 300 species of chiefly perennial herbaceous plants that make up the genus *Limonium* of the family Plumbaginaceae, especially *L. vulgare*. Bearing small flowers in dense spikes, *L. vulgare* grows in large tracts that sometimes turn acres lilac-colored in late summer. The flower spikes of this and other sea lavenders are often used in dry-flower arrangements for their lasting qualities and permanent colors.

sea leopard See LEOPARD SEAL

sea level Position of the air-sea boundary, to which all terrestrial elevations and submarine depths are referred. The sea level at any location changes constantly with changes in tides, atmospheric pressure, and wind conditions. Longer-term changes are influenced by changes in the earth's climates. Consequently, the level is better defined as mean sea level, the height of the sea surface averaged over all stages of the tide over a long period of time.

sea lion Any of five species (family Otariidae) of eared SEALS found along coasts on both sides of the Pacific, from Alaska to Australia. Sea lions have short, coarse hair that lacks a distinct undercoat. The males of all but the California sea lion have a mane. Sea lions feed principally on fish, squid, and octopus. They breed in large herds; males establish a harem of 3–20 females. The California sea lion *(Zalophus californianus)* is the trained seal of circuses and zoos. Males of the various species range from 8 to 11 ft (2.5–3.3 m) long and weigh 600–2,200 lbs (270–1,000 kg).

sea otter *or* **great sea otter** Rare, completely marine OTTER *(Enhydra lutris)* of the northern Pacific, usually found in kelp beds. Floating on its back, it opens mollusks by smashing them on a stone balanced on its chest. The large hind feet are broad and flipperlike. It is 40–65 in. (100–160 cm) long and weighs 35–90 lbs (16–40 kg). The thick lustrous coat is reddish to dark brown. By 1910 it had been hunted almost to extinction for its fur; now fully protected, it is gradually increasing in numbers.

sea parrot See PUFFIN

Sea Peoples Any of the groups of aggressive seafarers who invaded eastern Anatolia, Syria, Palestine, Cyprus, and Egypt toward the end of the BRONZE AGE. They were especially active in the 13th century BC. Though the extent and origin of the upheavals remain uncertain, Sea Peoples are believed responsible for the destruction of old powers such as the HITTITE empire. The Egyptians waged two wars against them (1236–1223 BC and c. 1198–1166). The only major tribe to settle permanently in Palestine were the Peleset (i.e., PHILISTINES).

sea power Means by which a nation extends its military power onto the seas. Measured in terms of a nation's capacity to use the seas in defiance of rivals, it consists of combat vessels and weapons, auxiliary craft, commercial shipping, bases, and trained personnel. It includes aircraft based on carriers or used in support of shipping. Its main purpose is to protect friendly shipping from enemy attack and to destroy or hinder the enemy's shipping. It may also be used to enforce a BLOCKADE. Finally, naval forces have been used to bombard land targets from the sea. The AIRCRAFT CARRIER added a new dimension to this capability, as did the missile-firing nuclear SUBMARINE. The classic exposition of the role of sea power as the basis of national greatness is ALFRED THAYER MAHAN's *The Influence of Sea Power upon History* (1890).

sea scorpion See SCULPIN

sea slug See NUDIBRANCH

sea snake Any of some 50 species (family Hydrophiidae) of venomous, marine SNAKES with an oarlike tail and flattened body. Most are found along coasts and in estuaries of Australia and Asia, sometimes basking on the surface in a large group, though the yellow-bellied, or pelagic, sea snake ranges throughout the Pacific. The nostrils, usually on top of the snout, have valvelike closings. The body of several species is much thicker than the head and neck. Most species are 3–4 ft (1–1.2 m) long; *Laticauda semifasciata,* a Japanese delicacy, may be twice as long. Though generally slow to strike, their venom may be lethal.

sea squirt Any TUNICATE in the class Ascidiacea; found in seas worldwide. Resembling potatoes more than animals, they are permanently fixed to a surface. A forceful contraction of the adult's vaselike body shoots a jet of seawater when it is disturbed. They filter-feed near the shore on debris from dead plants and animals and, in deeper water, on plankton. Adults, from less than 1 in. to 1 ft (2–30 cm) long, have functional male and female reproductive organs. The free-swimming, tadpolelike larvae hatch from eggs shed by one individual and fertilized by another. Some species live individually, others in colonies.

sea star See STARFISH

sea trout See WEAKFISH

sea urchin Any of about 700 species (class Echinoidea) of ECHINODERMS found worldwide. Sea urchins have a globular body covered with movable, sometimes poisonous, spines up to 12 in. (30 cm) long. Pores along the internal skeleton accommodate slender, extensible, often sucker-tipped tube feet. Sea urchins live on the seafloor and use their tube feet or spines to move about. The mouth is on the body's underside; teeth are extruded to scrape algae and other food from rocks. Some species excavate hiding places in coral, rock, or even steel. Roe of some species is eaten in certain countries.

Slate-pencil urchin (*Heterocentrotus mammillatus*).
DOUGLAS FAULKNER

Seaborg \'sē-ˌbȯrg\, **Glenn (Theodore)** (1912–1999) U.S. nuclear chemist. Born to Swedish parents in Ishpeming, Mich., he pursued graduate study at UC–Berkeley. Working with John Livingood, Emilio Segré, and others, he discovered some 100 isotopes, including many that would prove to be of major importance, such as iodine-131 and technetium-99. However, his best-known work would involve the isolation and identification of TRANSURANIUM ELEMENTS. In 1941 he and his colleagues discovered PLUTONIUM. He went on to discover and isolate the elements americum, curium, berkelium, californium, einsteinium, fermium, mendelevium, and nobelium (atomic numbers 95–102). He joined the MANHATTAN PROJECT in 1942 and was instrumental in the development of the ATOMIC BOMB, which he pleaded unsuccessfully with Pres. Truman not to use on civilian targets. He shared a 1951 Nobel Prize with Edwin Mattison McMillan (1907–1991). Prediction of new elements' chemical properties and placement in the PERIODIC TABLE was helped greatly by an important organizing principle enunciated by Seaborg, the actinide concept. He served as head of the Atomic Energy Commission 1961–71. A strong advocate of nuclear disarmament, he led the negotiations that eventuated in the Limited Nuclear Test-Ban Treaty (1963) and later played a leading role in the passage of the NUCLEAR NONPROLIFERATION TREATY. In 1997 his name was given to the new element seaborgium, the first time a living person had been so honored.

seafloor spreading Theory that oceanic crust forms along submarine mountain zones, known collectively as the OCEANIC RIDGE system, and spreads out laterally away from them. This idea, proposed by U.S. geophysicist Harry H. Hess (1906–1969) in 1960, was pivotal in the development of the theory of PLATE TECTONICS.

seafood Edible aquatic animals, excluding mammals, but including both freshwater and ocean creatures. Seafood includes bony and cartilaginous FISHES, CRUSTACEANS, MOLLUSKS, edible JELLYFISH, sea TURTLES, FROGS, SEA URCHINS, and SEA CUCUMBERS. The roe, or eggs, of some species are eaten as CAVIAR. After cereals, seafood may be humanity's most important food, furnishing about 15% of the world's protein intake. Lean fish is equivalent to beef or poultry in its protein yield (18–25% by weight), but much lower in calories. Much seafood is eaten uncooked, either raw, dried, smoked, salted, pickled, or fermented. Otherwise it is cooked whole or cut into steaks, fillets, or chunks. It is often used in stews or soups.

Seagram Building High-rise office building in New York City (1958). Designed by LUDWIG MIES VAN DER ROHE and PHILIP JOHNSON, this sleek Park Avenue skyscraper is a pure example of a rectilinear prism sheathed in glass and bronze; it took the INTERNATIONAL STYLE to its zenith. Despite its austere and forthright use of the most modern materials, it demonstrates Mies's exceptional sense of proportion and concern for detail.

Seagram Co. Ltd. Formerly the world's largest producer and marketer of distilled spirits. The company began when Distillers Corp., Ltd., a Montreal distillery owned by Samuel Bronfman, acquired Joseph E. Seagram & Sons in 1928. The new company, Distillers Corp.–Seagrams Ltd., grew rapidly. Originally a maker of blended whiskies, the firm diversified in the 1950s and '60s into scotch, bourbon, rum, vodka, gin, and wines, which were sold around the world. In the 1990s it entered the field of music and entertainment, purchasing Universal Studios, media firm MCA, and Dutch music giant Polygram NV. The company was acquired by French media conglomerate Vivendi in 2000 to form Vivendi Universal. The beverage businesses were later sold to Diageo and Pernod Ricard. See also SEAGRAM BUILDING.

seal Aquatic carnivore with webbed flippers and streamlined body. Earless (true, or hair) seals (of the family Phocidae, with 18 species) lack external ears. In water, they propel themselves by side-to-side strokes of the hind limbs and maneuver with their forelimbs. On land, they wriggle on their belly or pull themselves with their forelimbs. Earless species include the ELEPHANT SEAL, HARBOR SEAL, HARP SEAL, and LEOPARD SEAL. The eared seals (family Otariidae, with five species of SEA LION and nine of fur seal) have external ears and longer flippers. In water, they propel themselves by a rowing motion of their forelimbs; on land, they use all four limbs to move about.

Sealyham terrier Breed of TERRIER developed in the late 19th century by Capt. John Edwardes for hunting foxes, otters, and badgers on his Welsh estate, Sealyham. A small, short-legged, sturdy dog, it was bred for courage, stamina, and hunting ability. It has a double coat, soft underneath and wiry on top, and may be solid white or white with darker markings on its head and drooping ears. It stands about 10 in. (25.5 cm) and weighs about 20 lbs (9 kg).

Seami See ZEAMI

S T U V

seamount Large submarine volcanic mountain rising at least 3,000 ft (1,000 m) above the surrounding seafloor; smaller submarine volcanoes are called sea knolls, and flat-topped seamounts are called guyots. Seamounts are abundant and occur in all major ocean basins. By the late 1970s more than 10,000 seamounts had been reported in the Pacific Ocean basin alone. Virtually every oceanographic expedition discovers new seamounts, and it is estimated that about 20,000 exist worldwide.

seaplane Aircraft that can land, float, and take off on water. The first practical seaplanes were built and flown in 1911–12 by GLENN H. CURTISS, who developed both the float seaplane, essentially a land plane with pontoons instead of landing wheels, and the flying boat, a boatlike plane that combined a main float and fuselage in a single body. A retractable landing wheel was later added to create an amphibian aircraft. By the late 1920s seaplanes held the speed and range records for aircraft. During the 1940s their utility diminished with the building of long-range land-based airplanes, new airports, and aircraft carriers.

search and seizure In law enforcement, an exploratory investigation of a premises or a person and the taking into custody of property or an individual in the interest of gaining evidence of unlawful activity or guilt. The latitude allowed police in carrying out searches and seizures varies greatly from country to country. In the U.S., the 4th Amendment to the Constitution prohibits unreasonable searches and seizures and requires that a warrant be issued following a finding of probable cause. The warrant must specify the place to be searched and the persons and things to be seized.

search engine Tool for finding information, especially on the INTERNET or WORLD WIDE WEB. Search engines are essentially massive DATABASES that cover wide swaths of the Internet. Most consist of three parts: at least one program, called a spider, crawler, or bot, which "crawls" through the Internet gathering information; a database, which stores the gathered information; and a search tool, with which users search through the database by typing in keywords describing the information desired (usually at a Web site dedicated to the search engine). Increasingly, metasearch engines, which search a subset (usually 10 or so) of the huge number of search engines and then compile and index the results, are being used.

Searle, Ronald (William Fordham) (born 1920) British cartoonist, painter, and author. He published his first cartoons in the late 1930s. Taken prisoner during World War II, he later published a book of grim sketches based on his years in a Japanese prison camp. In 1941 Searle created the bizarre schoolgirls who became the subject of four films, beginning with *The Belles of St. Trinian's* (1954). He joined the staff of *Punch* in 1956 before moving to Paris in 1961. He has published more than 50 books.

Sears, Isaac (1730–1786) American patriot. Born in West Brewster, Mass., he became a merchant in New York City. He supported the patriots' cause in the Stamp Act riots. As a member of the radical Sons of Liberty, he led a boycott of British goods to protest the Townshend Acts. He led the ouster of Loyalist officials from New York City, and seized control of the municipal government until GEORGE WASHINGTON's troops arrived (1775). From Boston he organized privateers to prey on British ships.

Sears, Roebuck and Co. U.S. merchandising company, one of the world's largest retailers. It was founded in 1893 by Richard W. Sears (1863–1914) and Alvah C. Roebuck (1864–1948) The company grew rapidly, selling mail-order merchandise at low prices to rural residents who lacked access to competitive retail outlets. Under Robert E. Wood (president 1928–54), Sears built retail stores across the U.S., and by 1931 its retail sales had topped its mail-order sales. It diversified into financial services in the 1980s and introduced the Discover credit card (now owned by Morgan Stanley) in 1985, but in 1992 it began shedding its financial-services subsidiaries. It discontinued its famous catalog in 1993 and spun off insurance subsidiary Allstate (founded by Sears in 1931) in 1995. In 2002 Sears acquired catalog retailer Land's End, Inc.

Sears Tower Skyscraper office building in Chicago. With 110 floors and a height of 1,450 ft (442 m), it became the world's tallest building at its completion in 1974. Its architect, Fazlur Khan (1928–1982), designed it as a bundled-tube (see SKYSCRAPER) structure to resist lateral forces. It is modular in plan, with nine 75-ft- (23-m-) square, column-free units. The exterior is sheathed in black aluminum and bronze-tinted glass. Louvers clad the four floors devoted to the building's mechanical operations. It was the world's tallest building until 1996, when it was surpassed by the PETRONAS TOWERS (1,483 ft [452 m]) in Kuala Lumpur, Malaysia.

season Any of four divisions of the year according to consistent annual changes in the weather. In the Northern Hemisphere, winter formally begins on the winter SOLSTICE, December 21 or 22; spring on the vernal

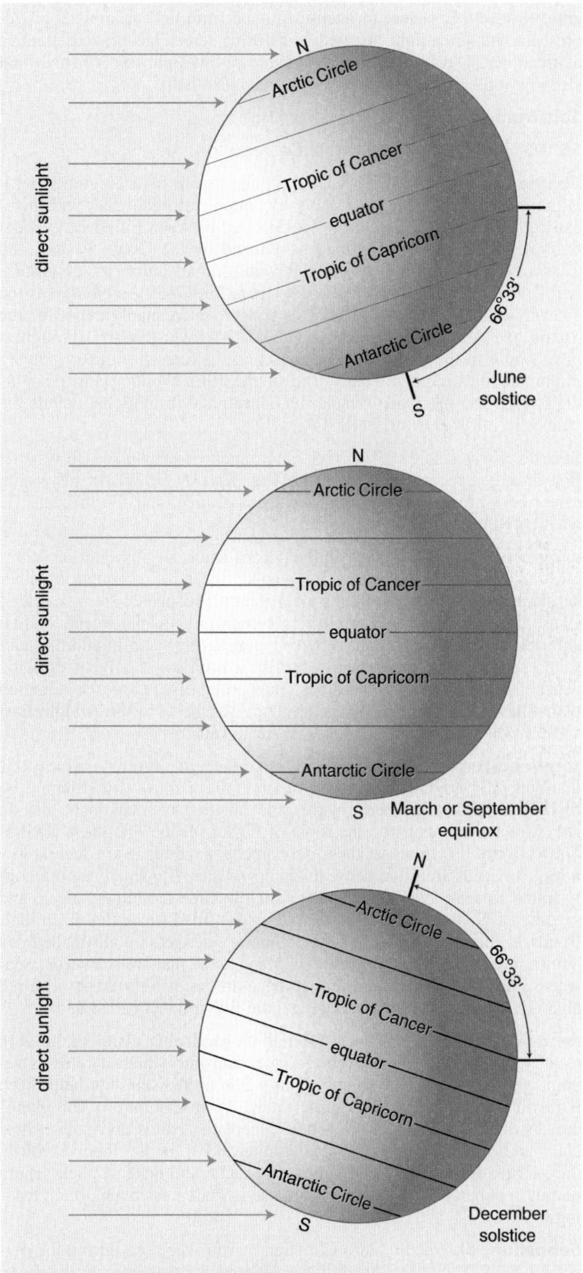

Because the earth is tilted on its axis with respect to the plane of its orbit around the sun, different parts of its surface are in direct (overhead) sunlight at different times of the year. The change in the amount of sunlight reaching the surface at various latitudes is the primary cause of the seasons.

S T U V

EQUINOX, March 20 or 21; summer on the summer solstice, June 21 or 22; and fall or autumn on the autumnal equinox, September 22 or 23. In the Southern Hemisphere, the dates of onset of summer and winter are reversed, as are those of spring and fall.

seasonal affective disorder (SAD) Cyclical DEPRESSION occurring in winter, apparently caused by insufficient sunlight. It is most common in places at high latitudes and therefore with long winters and very short daylight hours. Symptoms can include all those of major depression, and there is a risk of suicide. The cause may be related to regulation of the body's temperature and hormones and may involve the PINEAL GLAND and MELATONIN. Exposure to intense full-spectrum light from a set of fluorescent bulbs in a light box with a diffusing screen has proved effective as treatment. Dawn simulation (exposure to low light levels in the final sleep period) and negative-ion therapy can also help.

Seastrom, Victor See Victor SJÖSTRÖM

SEATO See SOUTHEAST ASIA TREATY ORGANIZATION

Seattle City (pop., 1996 est.: 525,000) and seaport, Washington state. It is the largest city in the state and the commercial, industrial, and financial center of the Pacific Northwest. Situated between Elliott Bay (PUGET SOUND) and Lake Washington, it is flanked by the OLYMPIC MTNS. and CASCADE RANGE. Laid out in 1853, it withstood an Indian attack (1856), anti-Chinese riots (1880s), and a disastrous fire (1889) to emerge as the gateway to the Orient and Alaska. It was the main supply depot for the Yukon and Alaskan gold rushes in the 1890s. World War II brought a great boom to the city, with shipyards and the aircraft industry playing important roles. Seattle Center, site of the 1962 World's Fair, contains the 607-ft (185-m) Space Needle. Its educational institutions include the University of WASHINGTON (1861).

Seattle Slew (foaled 1974) U.S. Thoroughbred racehorse. He was the first unbeaten racer ever to win the TRIPLE CROWN (1977). In his racing career of 17 races, he won 14, was second twice, and fourth once. He was retired to stud in 1978.

seawater Water that makes up the oceans and seas. Seawater is a complex mixture of 96.5% water, 2.5% salts, and small amounts of other substances. Much of the world's magnesium is recovered from seawater, as are large quantities of bromine. In certain parts of the world, sodium chloride (table salt) is obtained by evaporating seawater. In addition, desalted seawater can theoretically furnish a limitless supply of drinking water, but the high processing costs are prohibitive. Large desalination plants have been built in dry areas along seacoasts in the Middle East and elsewhere to relieve shortages of fresh water.

seaweed Any of certain species of red, green, and brown marine ALGAE that generally are anchored to the sea bottom or to a solid structure by rootlike holdfasts that perform the sole function of attachment and do not extract nutrients as do the roots of higher plants. The most obvious seaweeds are brown algae; mosslike carpets of red algae are seen at low tides. Seaweeds are often dense in shallow water. Brown algae commonly found as seaweeds include KELP, which include the largest algae, and SARGASSUM. Some seaweeds have hollow, gas-filled floats that keep their fronds at the surface of the water. *Ulva* species, commonly called sea lettuce, are among the relatively few green algae that are seaweeds. Seaweeds are used as food, and brown algae are used in FERTILIZERS. The red alga *Gelidium* is used to make the gelatin-like product called agar.

sebaceous gland \si-'bā-shəs\ Small OIL-producing gland in the SKIN, usually connected to a HAIR follicle by a duct into which it releases sebum, a component of the slightly greasy film on the skin that helps keep it flexible and prevents too much water loss or absorption. The glands are distributed over the entire body except the palms and soles, most abundantly on the scalp and face. Large and well developed at birth, they shrink during childhood but enlarge again and increase their sebum output at puberty (apparently in response to male hormones), often leading to ACNE.

Sebastian, St. (died c. 288) Christian martyr who died during the persecutions of DIOCLETIAN. According to legend, he was born in Gaul and went to Rome to serve in the army. When officials learned that he was a Christian seeking converts, they ordered his execution by archers. Left for dead, he was nursed back to health by a Christian widow. He presented himself before the emperor, who condemned him to death by beating. His body was thrown into a sewer but was afterwards found and buried. In Renaissance art he was often depicted as a handsome youth pierced by arrows.

Sebastiano del Piombo \se-bäs-'tyä-nō-del-'pyȯm-bō\ *orig.* **Sebastiano Luciani** (1485/86–1547) Italian painter. While in Venice, he was highly influenced by his teacher, GIORGIONE. In 1511 he moved to Rome and became a member of MICHELANGELO's circle. Michelangelo thought so highly of him that he provided sketches for him to execute. In Sebastiano's *Pietà* (1513), *Flagellation* (1516–24), and *Raising of Lazarus* (1516–18), all based on Michelangelo's sketches, he combined the warm coloring of the Venetian school with Michelangelo's anatomical clarity and firm sculptural drawing. After Raphael's death, Sebastiano's reputation as a portraitist was unparalleled. In 1531 Pope Clement VII, the subject of one of his finest portraits (1526), appointed him keeper of the papal seal; his nickname derives from the fact that the seal was of lead (Italian, *piombo*). The lucrative post gave him financial security, and his output declined.

Sebastopol See SEVASTOPOL

Sebek \'se-ˌbek\ In ancient Egyptian religion, a crocodile god. His chief sanctuary in Fayyum province included a sacred crocodile, which was believed to be an incarnation of the god. Sebek may have been associated with fertility or death and burial before becoming a major deity and patron of kings in the Middle Kingdom (c. 1938–c. 1600? BC). He was merged with RE, the sun god, to constitute a crocodile form of that deity known as Sebek-Re. The worship of Sebek continued in Ptolemaic and Roman times.

Sebou River \sə-'bü\ River, northern Morocco. From its source as the Wadi Guigou, it flows north to FÈS and then east to the Atlantic Ocean at Mehdiya, a distance of 280 mi (450 km). Its basin is a major olive, rice, wheat, sugar beet, and vineyard region. Kenitra (pop., 1982: 188,000), 10 mi (16 km) from its mouth, is a busy port at the head of navigation for oceangoing vessels.

Sebek, wearing horns, solar disk with uraeus, and plumes, bronze figurine, c. 600–300 BC; in the British Museum.

BY COURTESY OF THE TRUSTEES OF THE BRITISH MUSEUM

secession (1860–61) Withdrawal of 11 Southern states from the U.S. The precipitating event was the election of ABRAHAM LINCOLN as president (1860). Most slaveholding states had vowed to secede if the Republican candidate won, since the party strongly opposed slavery and its extension into the new territories. Secession had been proclaimed by states'-rights advocates as a corollary to the compact that united the states, permitting them to withdraw as easily as they had joined. Earlier threats of secession were made at the HARTFORD CONVENTION (1814), in the NULLIFICATION crisis (1832), and in the 1850s before the MISSOURI COMPROMISE. Secession was first approved by South Carolina (1860); six other states followed in the period before Lincoln was inaugurated in March 1861. After Lincoln resisted the South's attack on FORT SUMTER, four other slaveholding states voted to secede, joining the newly formed CONFEDERATE STATES OF AMERICA.

Second Empire (1852–70) Period in France under the rule of Emperor NAPOLEON III (the original empire having been that of NAPOLEON). In its early years (1852–59), the empire was authoritarian but enjoyed economic growth and pursued a favorable foreign policy. Liberal reforms were gradually introduced after 1859, but such measures as a low-tariff treaty with Britain alienated French businessmen and political liberalization led to increased opposition to the government. In 1870 a new constitution establishing a quasi-parliamentary regime was widely approved, but France's defeat at the Battle of SEDAN in the FRANCO–PRUSSIAN WAR was followed by an uprising in Paris on September 4, 1870. This resulted in the overthrow of the government, the abdication of Napoleon III, and the end of the Second Empire.

Second Empire style See BEAUX-ARTS STYLE

Second International *or* **Socialist International** (1889–1914) Federation of socialist political parties and trade unions that greatly influenced the European labor movement while supporting parliamentary democracy and opposing anarchism. Unlike the centralized FIRST INTERNATIONAL, it was a loose federation that met in a number of cities at various intervals. By 1912 it represented the socialist parties of all European countries, the U.S., Canada, and Japan, with a membership of about 9 million. It reaffirmed Marxist doctrine, but its main concern became the prevention of a general European war. When that failed, the International ended in 1914.

Second Republic (1848–52) French republic established after the REVOLUTION of 1848 (following the original republic during the FRENCH REVOLUTION). The liberal republicans' hopes of establishing an enduring democratic regime were soon frustrated. In 1848 Louis-Napoléon (later NAPOLEON III) was elected president and a monarchist majority was elected to the legislative assembly, which passed conservative measures restricting voting rights and freedom of the press and giving the church increased control over education. Soon realizing that his power and future reelection were limited by the assembly's actions, Louis-Napoléon organized a coup d'état in 1851. A new constitution reduced the assembly's power, and a plebiscite to approve the change was accompanied by officially inspired petitions for the empire's restoration. In 1852 Louis-Napoléon was proclaimed emperor and the SECOND EMPIRE was born.

secondary education Traditional second stage in formal education, beginning at age 11–13 and ending usually at age 15–18. The distinction between ELEMENTARY EDUCATION and secondary education has gradually become less marked, owing to the proliferation of middle schools, junior high schools, and other divisions. In the U.S., over 80% of students of secondary-school age attend a HIGH SCHOOL. In the British system, most students (90% in Britain) attend comprehensive schools similar to American high schools; the rest attend either grammar schools (i.e., publicly funded PREPARATORY SCHOOLS), technical schools, or PUBLIC SCHOOLS, which are actually private. In France, students 15–18 years of age who have completed the first part of their secondary education (the so-called "guidance cycle") attend a lycée, either a general (academic) or a vocational lycée. In Germany, students who have completed grade 9 may enter a *Hauptschule,* a school for further general education that leads to apprenticeship training; a *Realschule,* a school for both general and specialized education that leads to either vocational school or apprenticeship training; or an academically oriented GYMNASIUM.

Secord \'sē-ˌkȯrd\, **Laura** *orig.* **Laura Ingersoll** (1775–1868) Canadian loyalist in the War of 1812. Born in Great Barrington, Mass., she moved to Canada with her family in the 1780s. On learning of an impending U.S. attack on the British outpost of Beaver Dams (1813), she walked through the U.S. lines to warn the British commander; with the advance information, the British were able to defeat the U.S. force.

secret police Police established by national governments to maintain political and social control. Generally clandestine, secret police have operated independently of the civil police. Notorious 20th-century examples were the Nazi GESTAPO and the Russian KGB. Secret-police tactics include arrest, imprisonment, torture, and execution of political enemies and intimidation of potential opposition members.

secret society Any of various oath-bound societies devoted to brotherhood (or sisterhood), moral discipline, and mutual assistance. Such societies usually conduct rituals of initiation to instruct new members in the rules of the group (see rite of PASSAGE). Greek and Roman MYSTERY RELIGIONS had their secular counterparts in clandestine social clubs, some of which served as platforms for political dissent. In western Africa, secret societies such as Poro (for men) and Sande (for women) served to translate slight advantages of wealth and prestige into political authority. In parts of New Guinea, secret men's societies serve as repositories of tribal knowledge. Fraternal orders such as the Freemasons (see FREEMASONRY) may be considered secret societies, as may criminal groups such as the MAFIA and the Chinese TRIADS and hate groups such as the KU KLUX KLAN.

Secretariat (foaled 1971) U.S. Thoroughbred racehorse. In 1973 he became the first TRIPLE CROWN winner since CITATION in 1948. At the BELMONT STAKES he won by an unprecedented 31 lengths. In his two-year career, he came in first 16 times, second three times, and third once. He is often regarded as the greatest Thoroughbred in history.

secretary bird African RAPTOR (*Sagittarius serpentarius,* family Sagittaridae), the only living BIRD OF PREY that hunts on foot. It has long scaly legs, a light-gray body that is 4 ft (1.2 m) long, and a 7-ft (2.1-m) wingspread. It weighs about 8 lbs (3.5 kg). Twenty black crest feathers make it appear to be carrying quill pens behind its ears. Secretary birds kill snakes (their main prey) by stamping on them, flailing them against the ground, or dropping them from aloft. They make their large stick-built nests in thorn trees. Both parents feed the offspring by regurgitation. Secretary birds are protected in most African nations.

Secretary bird (*Sagittarius serpentarius*).

Secular Games *Latin* **Ludi saeculares.** Celebrations held in ancient Rome at the beginning of a new *saeculum,* or generation. Similar games were originally held by the ETRUSCANS as offerings to the underworld gods. The Romans at first also worshiped the underworld gods, but later introduced APOLLO, DIANA, and LETO in a festival that lasted three days and nights. More days were added later. The first known Roman games were held in 249 BC, the second in 146, and the third in 17 under Caesar AUGUSTUS. Later games were held in AD 47, 88, 147, 204, 248, and 262 and included sports, music, theater, and circuses. The games ceased in the 4th century AD under CONSTANTINE I, who converted to Christianity.

Securities and Exchange Commission (SEC) U.S. regulatory commission established by Congress in 1934. Its purpose was to restore investor confidence by ending the misleading sales practices and stock manipulations that had led to the stock market's 1929 collapse. It prohibited the buying of stock without adequate funds to pay for it, initiated registration and supervision of securities markets and stockbrokers, established rules regarding proxies, and prohibited unfair use of nonpublic information in stock trading (see INSIDER TRADING). It also required that companies offering securities make full public disclosure of all relevant information.

security In finance, written evidence of ownership conferring the right to receive property not currently in the holder's possession. The most common securities are STOCKS and BONDS. Governments, companies, and financial institutions use securities to raise money. Stocks are securities issued in the form of equity ownership. Bonds are securities that take the form of DEBT. They constitute promises to pay a specified amount at a specified date and to pay interest at a specified rate in the interim. Most government securities are bonds that pay a fixed amount of interest per year; unlike commercial securities, their repayment is guaranteed. Both stocks and bonds are traded publicly on organized exchanges. The world's principal exchanges are the NEW YORK STOCK EXCHANGE, the LONDON STOCK EXCHANGE, and the TOKYO STOCK EXCHANGE. External forces such as international troubles, changes in government policies, and trends in foreign stock markets all have an effect on security prices. For individual stocks, the company's current and prospective financial performance play an important role, as do overall trends within its business sector. See also INVESTMENT, SAVING.

Security Council, U.N. See UNITED NATIONS SECURITY COUNCIL

Sedan \sə-ˈdä^{n}, *Engl* sə-ˈdan\, **Battle of** (September 1, 1870) Defeat of the French army in the FRANCO–PRUSSIAN WAR that led to the fall of the SECOND EMPIRE. At the French border fortress of Sedan on the Meuse River, 120,000 French troops under MARIE EDME PATRICE DE MAC-MAHON were attacked by over 200,000 German troops under HELMUTH VON MOLTKE. After Mac-Mahon was wounded, the confused French command tried unsuccessfully to break through the encircling German lines with massive cavalry charges. Emperor NAPOLEON III, who had accompanied Mac-Mahon, realized the French position was hopeless and surrendered with 83,000 troops.

Seder \ˈsā-dər\ Ritual meal served on the first night of PASSOVER, commemorating the flight of the Jews from Egypt. Presided over by the head of the family, the Seder follows a liturgy, the HAGGADAH, that reminds participants of the story of the EXODUS. The ritual includes blessings, the pouring of wine, and ritual questions about the meaning of the event ("Why does this night differ from all other nights?") asked by the youngest child present. The meal includes unleavened bread and bitter herbs, the bread symbolizing the haste with which the Israelites left Egypt and the herbs symbolizing the bitterness of slavery. A cup of wine is poured for ELIJAH, the precursor of the MESSIAH.

sedge family Family Cyperaceae, one of the 10 largest families of flowering plants, composed of about 5,000 species of grasslike herbs that inhabit wet regions worldwide. Sedges are monocots (see COTYLEDON) of extraordinary ecological importance; forming the base of food webs, they provide food and shelter for aquatic and wetland animals. They are also important as ornamentals and weeds, and are used in woven products such as mats, baskets, screens, and sandals. Key identifying characteristics that distinguish sedges from GRASSES are solid stems that are often triangular in cross section; leaves, when present, that clasp the stem with a sheath; and small spikes of minute flowers that are not enclosed in bracts. They range in height from about 1 in. to 13 ft (2 cm–4 m). The genus *Carex* represents the true sedges. PAPYRUS and BULRUSHES are also included in this family.

Sedgwick, Adam (1785–1873) English geologist. A pioneer in the establishment of geology as a university discipline (at Trinity College, Oxford Univ.), he named the CAMBRIAN PERIOD and (with Roderick Murchison) the DEVONIAN PERIOD. His grandnephew, the zoologist Adam Sedgwick (1854–1913), first established the evolutionary link between the annelids and the arthropods.

sedimentary facies \ˈfā-shēz\ Different, but contemporaneous and juxtaposed, SEDIMENTARY ROCKS. Terrigenous facies are accumulations of particles eroded from older rocks and transported to the depositional site. Biogenic facies are accumulations of whole or fragmented shells and other hard parts of animals. Chemical facies result from precipitation of inorganic material from solution. The shapes and characteristics of facies may change as conditions change over time.

sedimentary rock Rock formed at or near the earth's surface by the accumulation and LITHIFICATION of fragments of preexisting rocks or by precipitation from solution at normal surface temperatures. Sedimentary rocks can be formed only where sediments are deposited long enough to become compacted and cemented into hard beds or strata. They are the most common rocks exposed on the earth's surface but are only a minor constituent of the entire crust. Their defining characteristic is that they are formed in layers. Each layer has features that reflect the conditions during deposition, the nature of the source material (and, often, the organisms present), and the means of transport. See also SEDIMENTARY FACIES.

sedimentation In geology, the process of deposition of a solid material from a state of suspension or solution in a fluid (usually air or water). Broadly defined it also includes deposits from glacial ice and materials collected under the effect of gravity alone, as in talus deposits, or accumulations of rock debris at the base of cliffs.

sedimentology Scientific discipline concerned with the physical and chemical properties of SEDIMENTARY ROCKS and the processes involved in their formation, including transportation, deposition, and LITHIFICATION of sediments. The aim of much sedimentological research is to interpret ancient environmental conditions by studying the constituents, textures, structures, and fossil content of the deposits.

sedition Crime of creating a revolt, disturbance, or violence against lawful civil authority with the intent to cause its overthrow or destruction. Because it is limited to organizing and encouraging opposition to government rather than directly participating in its overthrow, sedition is regarded as falling one step short of the more serious crime of TREASON. In the U.S., the display of a certain flag or the advocacy of a particular movement, such as SYNDICALISM, ANARCHISM, or COMMUNISM, has periodically been declared seditious. In recent decades the courts have applied a more stringent test to ensure that constitutional guarantees regarding FREEDOM OF SPEECH are not abridged. See also ALIEN AND SEDITION ACTS.

sedum \ˈsē-dəm\ Any of about 600 species of succulent plants that make up the genus *Sedum,* in the stonecrop, or orpine, family (Crassulaceae), native to temperate zones and to mountains in the tropics. Some species are grown in greenhouses for their unusual foliage and sometimes showy flowers of white, yellow, pink, or red. Low-growing varieties are popular in rock gardens and rock walls, and as edging in garden borders. Some species form mosslike mats on rocks and walls.

Seeckt \ˈzākt\, **Hans von** (1866–1936) German general. A career army officer, in World War I he was chief of staff of the 11th army and then chief of staff of the Turkish army. After the war he became head of the German Reichswehr (1919–26) and secretly built a small but efficient army, circumventing the Treaty of VERSAILLES prohibition. He supported cooperation with Russia and encouraged the Treaty of RAPALLO. He later served as an adviser to the Chinese Nationalist Army (1934–35).

seed Reproductive structure in plants that consists of a plant embryo, usually accompanied by a supply of food (endosperm, which is produced during fertilization) and enclosed in a protective coat. Seed embryos contain one or more COTYLEDONS. In typical FLOWERING PLANTS, seed production follows POLLINATION and fertilization. As seeds mature, the ovary that enclosed the ovules develops into a fruit containing the seeds. Most seeds are small, weighing less than a gram; the smallest contain no food reserve. At the opposite extreme, the seed of the double coconut palm may weigh up to about 60 lb (27 kg). Seeds are highly adapted to transportation by animals, wind, and water. When circumstances are favorable, water and oxygen penetrate the seed coat, and the new plant begins to grow (see GERMINATION). The longevity of seeds varies widely: some remain viable for only about a week; others have been known to germinate after hundreds or even thousands of years.

seed plant *or* **spermatophyte** \spər-ˈma-tə-ˌfīt\ Any of the FLOWERING PLANTS (angiosperms) and the CONIFERS and related plants (GYMNOSPERMS). Seed plants share many features with FERNS, including the presence of vascular tissue (see XYLEM and PHLOEM), but unlike ferns, they have stems that branch sideways and vascular tissue that is arranged in strands (bundles) around the core. Seed plants have generally more complex plant bodies and reproduce via SEEDS. As the main dispersal unit of seed plants, the seed represents a significant improvement over the SPORE, with its limited capacity for survival. Seed plants also differ from ferns in having GAMETOPHYTES that are reduced in size and are embedded in the SPOROPHYTES (and thus are less vulnerable to environmental stress). Another land-based adaptation of seed plants is POLLEN dispersed by wind or animals. The dispersal of pollen, in addition to dispersal of seeds, promotes genetic RECOMBINATION and distribution of the species over a wide geographic area.

Seeger, 1971.
DAVID GAHR

Seeger, Pete(r) (born 1919) U.S. folk singer and songwriter. Born in New York City, son of the pioneering ethnomusicologist Charles Seeger (1886–1979) and stepson of the composer RUTH CRAWFORD SEEGER, he studied at Harvard but left to travel the country by hopping freight trains, gathering tunes, and learning to play the banjo. In 1940 he organized the Almanac Singers with W. GUTHRIE, and performed widely at union halls and farm meetings. In 1948, with Lee Hays, Ronnie Gilbert, and Fred Hellerman, he formed the Weavers. Shortly after the group became successful, it was blacklisted because of Seeger's previous left-wing activities. They broke up in 1952, but reunited three years later for a triumphant Carnegie Hall concert. Seeger continued to suffer from blacklisting even after the overturning of a 1961 conviction for noncooperation with the House Committee on Un-American Activities. He fostered the growth of the hootenanny (a gathering of performers playing and singing for each other, with audience participation), and he wrote such folk standards as "Where Have All the Flowers Gone" and "If I Had a Hammer." He is also known as a prominent supporter of antiwar, civil-rights, and environmental causes.

Seeger, Ruth Crawford See Ruth CRAWFORD SEEGER

Seeing Eye dog See GUIDE DOG

Sefarim, Mendele Moykher See MENDELE MOYKHER SFORIM

Sefer ha-bahir \'se-fer-ˌhä-bä-'hir\ (Hebrew: "Book of Brightness") Hebrew commentary on the OLD TESTAMENT that had a major influence on the development of the KABBALA. It also influenced the symbology of JUDAISM in general by calling attention to the mystical significance of the shapes and sounds of the HEBREW ALPHABET. The *Bahir* first appeared in France in the 12th century, though Kabbalists consider it much older. It introduced the concept of the transmigration of souls and the notion of a cosmic or spiritual tree that symbolizes the flow of divine creative power. Though Kabbalists view it as authoritative, mainstream Judaism rejects it as heretical.

Sefer ha-zohar \'se-fer-hä-'zō-ˌhär\ (Hebrew: "Book of Splendor") Classical text central to KABBALA that has influenced all mystical movements within JUDAISM. Many Kabbalists invest it with a sanctity normally accorded only to the TORAH and the TALMUD. Written mostly in Aramaic, it is believed to be mainly the work of MOSES DE LEÓN. The main part of the *Zohar* provides a mystical and symbolic interpretation of biblical texts, especially those of the TORAH, Ruth, and the Song of SOLOMON. Other sections deal with the mystery of creation, the problem of evil, and the cosmic significance of prayer and good deeds.

Sefer Torah \'se-fer-tō-'rä\ (Hebrew: "Book of the Law") In JUDAISM, the Pentateuch (see TORAH), when written in Hebrew by a qualified calligrapher on vellum or parchment and enshrined in the Ark of the Law in a synagogue. It is used for public readings during services on the Sabbath, Mondays, Thursdays, and religious festivals. Sephardic Jews often enclose it in a wooden or metal case; Ashkenazi Jews cover it with an ornate mantle of cloth with ritual ornaments. Its scrolls are handled according to prescribed ritual that reflects the esteem in which they are held.

Seferis \se-'fer-ēs\, **George** *orig.* **Giorgios Stylianou Seferiades** *or* **Yeoryios Stilianou Sepheriades** (1900–1971) Greek poet, essayist, and diplomat. He studied law in Paris and held various diplomatic posts 1926–62. His poetry appeared in a number of collections beginning with *I strofí* (1931; "The Turning Point"). He is considered the leading Greek poet of "the generation of the '30s," which introduced Symbolism to modern Greek literature. He was awarded the Nobel Prize in 1963.

Segal \'sē-gəl\, **George** (1924–2000) U.S. sculptor. Born in New York City, he attended several universities. He began his career as a figurative painter. In the early 1960s he was associated with the POP ART movement, but his distinctive sculptures, consisting of monochromatic life-size plaster figures cast from live models, alone or in groups, situated in mundane environments, are distinguished by their ability to capture a mood of anonymity and alienation. Notable works include *The Gas Station* (1963), *The Truck* (1966), and *The Hot Dog Stand* (1978).

Segesta \sē-'jes-tə\ Ancient city, northwestern Sicily, located near modern Calatafimi. It was the chief city of the Elymi, a people of supposedly Trojan origin (see TROY). Culturally, it was Greek, but it generally took the Carthaginian side against its Greek neighbors, and boundary disputes with SELINUS were frequent. Early in the First PUNIC WAR, it was allied with Rome. Its ruins include a well-preserved 3rd-century-BC theater and a 5th-century-BC temple to Artemis.

segoni-kun \se-'gō-nē-'kün\ Highly sculptural mask of the Tyiwara society of the western African BAMBARA tribe. Derived from the antelope's form and emphasizing its head, neck, and horns, the masks were worn by dancers imitating the antelope's graceful movements at cultivation ceremonies. It was believed that the spirit of the *tyi-wara* (work animal), which held great power over agricultural fertility, was embodied in the masks.

Segovia, Andrés (1893–1987) Spanish guitarist. Almost entirely self-taught, he made his debut in Grenada in 1909 and by the 1920s was touring internationally; he would continue to perform into his nineties. He was by far the most important force in making the guitar a concert instrument. He commissioned works by M. DE FALLA, A. ROUSSEL, and H. VILLA-LOBOS, and himself arranged music ranging from the Renaissance to the 19th century for solo guitar.

Segovia.
AP/WIDE WORLD PHOTOS

Segrè \sə-'grā\, **Emilio (Gino)** (1905–1989) Italian-U.S. physicist. He worked under ENRICO FERMI before becoming director of the physics laboratory at the University of Palermo in 1936. In 1937 he discovered TECHNETIUM, the first man-made element not found in nature. While visiting California in 1938, he was dismissed from the university by the Fascist government. He continued his research at UC–Berkeley, where he and his associates discovered the element astatine and the isotope plutonium-239, which he found to be fissionable. In 1955, using the new bevatron particle accelerator, Segrè and Owen Chamberlain (born 1920) produced and identified antiprotons, antiparticles having the same mass as protons but opposite electrical charge, setting the stage for the discovery of many additional antiparticles. The two men shared a 1959 Nobel Prize.

segregation Separation of individuals or groups. Racial segregation provides a means of maintaining the economic advantages and higher social status of the politically dominant group. In recent times it has been used primarily by white populations to maintain their ascendancy over other groups through legal and social color bars. In the Southern states of the U.S., public facilities were segregated from the late 19th century into the 1950s (see JIM CROW LAWS). The CIVIL-RIGHTS MOVEMENT and the CIVIL RIGHTS ACT of 1964 helped end segregation in education and the use of public facilities, but socially sanctioned racial discrimination continues. See also APARTHEID.

sei whale \'sā\ *or* **Rudolphi's rorqual** \'ròr-kwəl\ Swift species *(Balaenoptera borealis)* of BALEEN WHALE in the RORQUAL family. It is 40–50 ft (13–15 m) long and is bluish gray or blackish above and paler below. It has small flippers, about 50 short lengthwise grooves on its chest, and dark baleen with pale, silky, inner fringes. It inhabits oceans from the Arctic to the Antarctic, migrating between cold and temperate summer waters and winter breeding grounds in warmer regions.

Seifert \'sā-fert\, **Jaroslav** (1901–1986) Czech poet. He made a living as a journalist until 1950. Though his early works reflect youthful expectations for the future of communism in the Soviet Union, he broke with the Communist Party in 1929. More lyrical elements were evident in his later poems, and the history and current events of Czechoslovakia were the most common subjects in his approximately 30 volumes. In the 1980s and '90s many of his works were translated, including *Honeymoon Ride* (1938), *Bozena Nemcova's Fan* (1940), and *Halley's Comet* (1967). He also contributed to journals and wrote children's literature and memoirs. In 1984 he became the first Czech to win the Nobel Prize.

seigniorage \'sān-yə-rij\ Charge over and above the expenses of coinage that is deducted from the bullion brought to a mint to be coined. From early times, coinage was the prerogative of kings, who prescribed the amount they were to receive as seigniorage. This was sometimes compensated for by replacing part of the gold or silver with base metal, resulting in debased coinage. In England all such charges were abolished in 1666. Because coins are now issued only as token money, they no longer need to possess a high intrinsic value, and low-standard silver or base-metal alloys are sufficient. The margin between the cost of producing a coin and its currency value is known as seignoriage.

seignorialism See MANORIALISM

Seine River \'sen\ *ancient* **Sequana** Second-longest river in France. It rises on the Langres plateau, 18 mi (30 km) northwest of DIJON, and flows through PARIS before emptying into the ENGLISH CHANNEL at LE HAVRE after a course of 485 mi (780 km). Its tributaries include the MARNE and OISE rivers. It drains an area of about 36,400 sq mi (78,700 sq km) in northern France; its network carries most of France's inland waterway traffic.

Seinfeld, Jerry (born 1954) U.S. comedian and television actor. Born in Brooklyn, N.Y., he initially worked as a stand-up comic in nightclubs and on television. He cocreated and starred in the hit television series *Seinfeld* (1990–98), which was inspired by his stand-up routines about life in New York City. One of the most successful situation comedies in history, it featured a collection of selfish and neurotic characters obsessed with the fear of commitment and the minutiae of everyday life.

seismic sea wave See TSUNAMI

seismic wave \'sīz-mik\ Vibration generated by an EARTHQUAKE, explosion, or similar phenomenon and propagated within the earth or along its surface. Earthquakes generate two principal types of waves: body waves, which travel within the earth, and surface waves, which travel along the surface. Seismograms (recorded traces of the amplitude and frequency of seismic waves) yield information about the earth and its subsurface structure; artificially generated seismic waves are used in oil and gas prospecting.

seismology \sīz-'mä-lə-jē\ Scientific discipline concerned with the study of EARTHQUAKES and of the propagation of SEISMIC WAVES. A branch of GEOPHYSICS, it has provided much information about the composition and state of the planet's interior. Recent work has focused on predicting earthquakes in hopes of minimizing the risk to humans. Seismologists have also studied quakes induced by human activities—such as impounding water behind high dams, injecting fluids into deep wells, and detonating underground nuclear explosions—in an effort to find ways of controlling natural earthquakes.

Seistan See SISTAN

Seiyukai See RIKKEN SEIYUKAI

Sejanus \si-'jā-nəs\, **Lucius Aelius** (died AD 31) Administrator of the Roman empire for TIBERIUS. In AD 14 he became PREFECT of the PRAETORIAN GUARD and gained the emperor's confidence. After the suspicious death of Tiberius' son DRUSUS (23), he sought to discredit Agrippina the Elder, mother of Tiberius' probable heirs. Forbidden to marry Drusus' widow, Sejanus moved the emperor to Capri (27) and had Agrippina and her son NERO exiled (29). The emperor suspected Sejanus of plotting a coup and had him executed, to widespread relief.

Sejong \'se-'jȯŋ\ (1397–1450) Monarch of the CHOSON dynasty in Korea during whose reign (1419–50) Korean cultural achievements reached a high point. Sejong created hangul, the Korean alphabet (see KOREAN LANGUAGE), and banned Buddhist monks from Seoul, thereby reducing the power and wealth of the Buddhist hierarchy.

Seku, Ahmadu See AHMADU SEKU

Selassie, Haile See HAILE SELASSIE

Seldes \'sel-dəs\, **George** (1890–1995) U.S. journalist. Born in Alliance, N.J., he became a reporter in 1909. He worked for the *Chicago Tribune* 1918–1928, then quit to pursue independent journalism. In *You Can't Print That* (1928) he criticized censorship and strictures on journalists, a continuing theme in his career. He reported on the rise of fascism in Italy and Spain in the 1930s, and he and his wife published *In Fact,* a journal devoted to press criticism, in the years 1940–50. His other targets included the tobacco industry and J. EDGAR HOOVER. He published his memoirs, *Witness to a Century,* in 1987. His brother, the critic Gilbert Seldes (1893–1970), was managing editor of *The Dial* during the 1920s. His best-known book was *The Seven Lively Arts* (1924). He was a columnist for the *New York Evening Journal* and the *Saturday Evening Post,* film critic for *The New Republic,* first director of television for CBS News, and first dean of the University of Pennsylvania's Annenberg School for Communication.

selection In biology, the preferential survival and reproduction or preferential elimination of individuals with certain GENOTYPES, by means of natural or artificial controlling factors. The theory of evolution by NATURAL SELECTION was proposed by CHARLES DARWIN and ALFRED RUSSEL WALLACE in 1858. Artificial selection differs from natural selection in that inherited variations in a species are manipulated by humans through controlled BREEDING in order to create qualities economically or aesthetically desirable to humans, rather than useful to the organism in its natural environment.

Selene \sə-'lē-nē\ *Latin* **Luna** In GREEK and ROMAN religion, the goddess that personified the moon. Her parents were the TITANS Hyperion and Theia; her siblings were HELIOS and Eos, the goddess of dawn. Selene fell in love with Endymion, a handsome young shepherd; her husband ZEUS cast Endymion into eternal sleep, but she visited him in the cave where he slept, and he fathered her 50 daughters. In art Selene is often represented as a woman with the crescent moon on her head. As Luna she had temples in Rome on the Aventine and Palatine hills.

Selenga River \ˌsi-liŋ-'gä\ River, Mongolia and eastern central Russia. It rises in Mongolia south of Lake Hövsgöl and joins the ORHON RIVER at Sühbaatar to become the Selenga. It continues north into Russia, eventually flowing into Lake BAIKAL after a course of 920 mi (1,480 km). It is navigable from its mouth to beyond Sühbaatar in May–October, when it is ice-free.

selenium \sə-'lē-nē-əm\ Semimetallic chemical ELEMENT, chemical symbol Se, atomic number 34. It is widely distributed, usually in small amounts, occasionally uncombined but more often as selenides of iron, lead, silver, or copper. Selenium has several ALLOTROPES; the gray metallic crystalline form is the most stable at room temperature. Its electrical conductivity increases when light strikes it and it can convert LIGHT directly into ELECTRICITY, so selenium is used in PHOTOCELL, SOLAR CELLS, and light meters. It is also used in rectifiers to convert alternating to direct ELECTRIC CURRENT. It serves as a red colorant for glass and glazes. Selenium has VALENCE 2, 4, and 6 in its compounds, many of which are toxic though the element is not. Selenium dioxide is an important reagent in organic chemistry. Vital to living cells, it works as an ANTIOXIDANT in the body and is being studied for a variety of possible beneficial effects; it is used in nutritional supplements and animal feeds.

Seles \'se-ləs\, **Monica** (born 1973) Yugoslav-U.S. tennis player. Born in Novi Sad, she came to the U.S. to train in 1985. She developed quickly and became one of the dominant women stars of the 1990s, achieving multiple wins in all Grand Slam tournaments (French Open, 1990–92; Australian Open, 1991–93, 1996; U.S. Open, 1991–92) except Wimbledon, which she lost in 1991 and 1992 to her rival STEFFI GRAF. In 1993 she stopped competing temporarily after being stabbed by a Graf fan on a court in Hamburg.

Seleucia (on the Tigris) \sə-'lü-shə\ Ancient city, on the TIGRIS RIVER, central Iraq. Founded by SELEUCUS I NICATOR in the late 4th century BC as his eastern capital, it replaced BABYLON as MESOPOTAMIA's leading city. The population, which PLINY THE ELDER estimated at 600,000, was composed largely of Macedonians and Greeks and also included Jews and Syrians. During the Parthian domination of the Tigris-Euphrates valley that began in the 2nd century BC, it maintained its position and trade despite its Greek sympathies. In 165 AD the Romans burned the city, marking the end of Hellenism in Mesopotamia. See also SELEUCID DYNASTY.

Seleucid dynasty \sə-'lü-səd\ Macedonian Greek dynasty (312–64 BC) founded by SELEUCUS I NICATOR. Carved from ALEXANDER THE GREAT's empire, the Seleucid domain stretched from Thrace to the border of India and included Babylonia, Syria, and Anatolia. Seleucus was succeeded in 281 by ANTIOCHUS I SOTER, who reigned until 261. He was followed by Antiochus II (r.261–246), SELEUCUS II CALLINICUS (r.246–225), Seleucus III (r.225–223), and ANTIOCHUS III the Great (r.223–187). Under the last, the empire was at its height. Resistance to the power and spread of Hellenistic culture soon began to manifest itself in the Asian lands. Antiochus III's encounter with the Romans signaled decline, especially after the defeat of 190. The decline accelerated after the death of Antiochus IV (r.175–164), who lost JUDAEA to the MACCABEES. The efforts of Demetrius I and Antiochus VII could not forestall the dynasty's inevitable end at the hands of the Roman POMPEY THE GREAT in 64 BC.

Seleucus I Nicator \sə-ˈlü-kəs...ni-ˈkā-tər\ (359/354–281 BC) Macedonian army officer, founder of the SELEUCID DYNASTY. Following the death of ALEXANDER THE GREAT, under whom he served, Seleucus won an empire centered on Syria and Iran. In 312, after being ousted by ANTIGONUS I MONOPHTHALMUS and serving PTOLEMY, he reconquered Babylon. He declared himself king in 305. By 303 he had extended his empire to India. In 301 he helped defeat Antigonus at the Battle of IPSUS and received Syria, later taking southern Syria from Ptolemy. A marriage alliance with DEMETRIUS I POLIORCETES' daughter soured, and in 294, when his son became sick with love for Seleucus' wife (the son's stepmother), he gave her to him and made the son coregent. Hoping to reestablish Alexander's empire, Seleucus captured Demetrius (285) and defeated Lysimachus (281), another of Alexander's former generals who had become a satrap in Asia Minor. Later he entered Macedonia, where he was murdered.

Seleucus II Callinicus \ˌka-lə-ˈnī-kəs\ (died 225 BC) Fourth king (r.246–225) of the SELEUCID DYNASTY. He became ruler when his mother poisoned his father, Antiochus II, and proclaimed him king. Her supporters made away with his Egyptian stepmother, Bernice, daughter of PTOLEMY II, whom Antiochus had briefly married. Her brother Ptolemy III responded by invading Seleucus' kingdom and taking the eastern provinces. Seleucus managed to regain northern Syria and part of Iran, but was defeated by his brother (c. 235), now supported by their mother, and ceded territory beyond the Taurus River. He died in a fall from his horse.

self-defense In CRIMINAL LAW, an affirmative defense (e.g., to a murder charge) alleging that the defendant used serious force necessarily for self-protection. The claim of self-defense must normally rely on a reasonable belief that the other party intended to inflict great bodily harm or death and that avoidance by retreating was impossible. See also HOMICIDE.

Self-Defense Force Japan's military after World War II. In Article 9 of Japan's postwar constitution, the Japanese renounced war and pledged never to maintain land, sea, or air forces. The rearming of Japan in the 1950s was therefore cast in terms of self-defense. In 1950 a small military force called the National Police Reserve was created; this became the National Safety Force in 1952 and the Self-Defense Force in 1954. Ostensibly it was never to be used outside Japan or its waters; consequently, Self-Defense Force participation in U.N. peacekeeping missions or relief work has sparked vigorous debate in Japan and abroad, especially among nations that were victims of Japanese aggression in World War II.

self-determination Process by which a group of people, usually possessing a degree of political consciousness, form their own state and government. The idea evolved as a byproduct of NATIONALISM. According to the U.N. charter, a people has the right to form itself into a state or to otherwise determine the form of its association with another state, and every state has the right to choose its own political, economic, social, and cultural systems. Moreover, the administering authorities of dependent territories are enjoined to ensure political advancement and the development of self-government in those territories.

self-esteem Sense of personal worth and ability that is fundamental to an individual's identity. Family relationships during childhood are believed to play a crucial role in its development. Parents may foster self-esteem by expressing affection and support for the child as well as by helping the child set realistic goals for achievement instead of imposing unreachably high standards. KAREN HORNEY asserted that low self-esteem leads to the development of a personality that excessively craves approval and affection and exhibits an extreme desire for personal achievement. According to ALFRED ADLER's theory of personality, low self-esteem leads people to strive to overcome their perceived inferiorities and to develop strengths or talents in compensation.

self-fertilization Fusion of male and female sex cells (gametes) produced by the same individual. This type of FERTILIZATION occurs in bisexual organisms, including most flowering plants, numerous protozoans, and many invertebrates. Many organisms capable of self-fertilization can also reproduce by means of CROSS-FERTILIZATION. As an evolutionary mechanism, self-fertilization allows an isolated individual to create a local population and stabilizes desirable genetic strains, but it fails to provide a significant degree of variability within a population and thereby limits the possibilities for adaptation to environmental change.

self-heal Perennial weed *(Prunella vulgaris)* in the MINT family, native to North America and widespread throughout the continent. Growing 6–14 in. (14–36 cm) tall, self-heal is often a low weed in lawns. The often-prostrate branches root readily wherever they touch soil. Tiny, two-lipped, lilac-colored or white flowers are clustered into noticeable dense, spikes. Leaves have sparsely toothed or smooth margins. Regarded in medieval times as a cure-all, the dried leaves and flowers are still brewed for soothing sore throats.

self-incrimination In CRIMINAL LAW, incrimination of and by oneself, particularly through testimony. The 5th Amendment to the U.S. Constitution contains a provision that protects a person from being compelled to make self-incriminating statements, one intention being to prevent coercion of testimony. Though people may be required to testify, they are permitted to refuse to answer questions if an answer would be potentially self-incriminating. See also rights of the ACCUSED, EXCLUSIONARY RULE.

Selim III \se-ˈlēm\ (1761–1808) Ottoman sultan (1789–1807). He inherited the throne during a losing war with Austria and Russia (1787–92), with whom he signed treaties. NAPOLEON's invasion of Egypt in 1798 drove him into an alliance with Britain and Russia, but, impressed with Napoleon's successes, he switched sides in 1806. At home he attempted tax and land reform and established a European-style military corps, but, unable to enforce his reforms in the face of mutinies, he rescinded them. He was strangled on orders from his successor, Mustafa IV.

Selim III, detail of a portrait by H. Berteaux, early 19th century; in the Topkapi Palace Museum, Istanbul.
SONIA HALLIDAY

Selinus \si-ˈlī-nəs\ Ancient Greek city, southern coast of Sicily. Founded by Greek colonists in the 7th century BC, it achieved great prosperity in the 5th century BC, when its Doric temples were built. In 409 BC it was destroyed by a Carthaginian army aiding the inhabitants of the rival city of SEGESTA. It never truly recovered, and in 250 BC the Carthaginians finally demolished it. Its extensive ruins include the remains of eight temples.

Seljuq dynasty \ˈsel-jük\ *or* **Saljuq dynasty** \ˈsal-jük\ (c. 11th–13th century) Muslim TURKMEN dynasty that ruled Persia, Iraq, Syria, and Anatolia. Seljuq was the chief of a nomadic Turkish tribe. His grandsons Chaghri Beg and TOGHRÏL BEG conquered realms in Iran. Under ALP-ARSLAN and Malik-shah, the empire came to include all of Iran, Mesopotamia, Syria, and Palestine; Alp-Arslan's victory over the Byzantine emperor led to several CRUSADES. Adherents of Sunni Islam, the Seljuqs adopted Persian culture, and the Persian language displaced Arabic in Iran. By 1200 Seljuq power remained only in their sultanate of Rum in Anatolia, which collapsed in a war against the KHWAREZM-SHAH in 1230 and was overrun by MONGOLS in 1243. See also NIZAM AL-MULK.

Selkirk Mountains \ˈsel-ˌkərk\ Mountain range, southeastern British Columbia, northern Idaho, and Montana. It extends some 200 mi (320 km) and in many places rises abruptly more than 8,000 ft (2,400 m). The highest summit is Mount Sir Sanford at 11,555 ft (3,522 m) tall. Crossed by the Canadian Pacific Railway, the range contains parts of GLACIER and Mount Revelstoke national parks.

Sellars, Peter (born 1957) U.S. stage director. Born in Pittsburgh, he attended Harvard Univ., where he began developing his innovative and often controversial style of directing. He is best known for staging plays and operas for numerous international theaters in settings far different than those suggested by the text. His controversial production of *Ajax* (1986) took the form of a post-Vietnam military trial, and among his many striking opera productions, W.A. MOZART's *Don Giovanni* was staged in an urban ghetto, his *Cosí fan tutte* in a diner, and his *Marriage of Figaro* in a corporate high-rise.

Sellers, Peter *orig.* **Richard Henry** (1925–1980) British film actor. The son of vaudeville performers, he acted from childhood in his parents' comedy act. In the early 1950s he performed on radio in the popular comedy series *The Goon Show.* He began appearing in the movies in the mid-1950s; his performances in *The Mouse That Roared* (1959), *I'm All Right, Jack* (1959), *Lolita* (1962) and *Dr. Strangelove* (1964), in which he played three characters, were especially well received. He was enormously popular as the bumbling Inspector Clouseau in the comedy *The Pink Panther* (1964) and its sequels, and later won praise for his role as a simpleminded gardener in *Being There* (1979).

Sellers, William (1824–1905) U.S. engineer and manufacturer. He was born in Delaware Co., Pa., to a distinguished scientific family. The first of his firms manufactured machinists' tools and mill gearing. His formulas for matching screw threads and nuts (1864) became the U.S. standards. In 1868 he founded Edge Moor Iron Co., which became the largest plant in the world for supplying and building iron bridges (it provided all the structural work for the BROOKLYN BRIDGE) and other large structures. He was president from 1873 of Midvale Steel Co. (Nicetown, Pa.), which became the major metal supplier for U.S. government ordnance and small arms.

Selye \'zel-yə\, **Hans (Hugo Bruno)** (1907–1982) Austro-Hungarian-Canadian endocrinologist. In early work on the effects of STRESS, he injected ovarian hormones into rats; this stimulated the adrenal glands, causing deterioration of the thymus gland, ulcers, and finally death. He later showed that physical injury, environmental stress, and toxins could have similar effects. Extending his theory to humans, he proved that a stress-induced hormonal-system breakdown could lead to so-called "diseases of adaptation," including heart disease and hypertension. He was president of the International Institute of Stress and wrote 33 books, including *Stress Without Distress* (1974).

Selznick, David O(liver) (1902–1965) U.S. film producer. Born in Pittsburgh, he trained with his father, a movie executive, before moving to Hollywood in 1926. Working for MGM, RKO, and other studios, he produced such films as *Dinner at Eight* (1933), *King Kong* (1933), *David Copperfield* (1935), and *A Tale of Two Cities* (1935). He formed his own company, Selznick International, in 1936 and produced such hits as *A Star Is Born* (1937). He was essential to the enormous success of *Gone with the Wind* (1939), overseeing its entire production with detailed memos about every aspect of the movie. He brought ALFRED HITCHCOCK to the U.S. and produced *Rebecca* (1940) and *Spellbound* (1945). He also produced *Duel in the Sun* (1946), *The Third Man* (1949), and *A Farewell to Arms* (1957), which starred his second wife, JENNIFER JONES.

semantics Study of meaning, one of the major areas of linguistic study (see LINGUISTICS). Linguists have approached it in a variety of ways. Members of the school of interpretive semantics study the structures of language independent of their conditions of use. In contrast, the advocates of generative semantics insist that the meaning of sentences is a function of their use. Still another group maintains that semantics will not advance until theorists take into account the psychological questions of how people form concepts and how these relate to word meanings.

semaphore \'se-mə-ˌfȯr\ Method of visual signaling, usually with flags or lights. Before radio, a semaphore system was widely used to send messages between ships. A person would stand with arms extended, moving two flags to specific angles to indicate letters or numbers. Before the invention of the telegraph, semaphore signaling with lights on high towers was used to transmit messages between distant points; messages were read by telescope. Modern semaphores have included movable arms or rows of light simulating arms, displayed from towers and used to signal railroad trains.

Semarang \sə-'mär-ˌäŋ\ City (pop., 1995 est.: 1,367,000), JAVA, Indonesia. Located on Java's northern coast, it lies on the banks of the Semarang River which is canalized for traffic to and from the sea. Despite being one of the largest ports in Java, its harbor is unprotected against monsoons, which can cause suspension of port operations. It is the seat of a university.

Sembène \sem-'ben\, **Ousmane** (born 1923) Senegalese writer and film director. He fought with the Free French in World War II. After the war he worked as a docker and taught himself French. His writings, often on historical-political themes, include *The Black Docker* (1956), *God's Bits of Wood* (1960), and *Niiwam and Taaw* (1987). Around 1960 he became interested in film; since studying in Moscow, he has made films reflecting a strong social commitment, including *Black Girl* (1966), the first feature produced in sub-Saharan Africa. With *Mandabi* (1968), he began to film in the Wolof language; his later films have included *Xala* (1974), *Ceddo* (1977), *Camp de Thiaroye* (1987), and *Guelwaar* (1994).

Semele \'se-mə-ˌlē\ In GREEK MYTHOLOGY, a daughter of CADMUS and Harmonia, and the mother of DIONYSUS. When Semele became the lover of ZEUS, HERA was enraged, and she coaxed Semele into asking to see the god in all his splendor. Having promised to grant Semele's every wish, Zeus was forced to comply. The firebolts emanating from him destroyed Semele, but Zeus rescued the unborn Dionysus from the ashes. Some stories hold that Dionysus later descended into HADES and brought Semele back to take her place among the immortals.

semen \'sē-mən\ *or* **seminal fluid** Whitish viscous fluid emitted from the male reproductive tract that contains SPERM and liquids (seminal plasma) that help keep them viable. Sperm cells, produced by the TESTES in humans, represent 2–5% of semen volume; fluids from tubules, glands, and storage areas of the REPRODUCTIVE SYSTEM bathe them as they travel down, nourishing them, keeping them motile, or participating in certain chemical reactions. During ejaculation, liquids from the PROSTATE GLAND and seminal vesicles dilute the sperm and provide a suitable, slightly alkaline environment. An average ejaculation of a human male expels 0.1–0.3 cu inches (2–5 ml), containing 200–300 million sperm.

Semey \ˌse-mā'\ *formerly (until 1991)* **Semipalatinsk** \ˌse-mē-pə-'lä-tinsk\ Port city (pop., 1995 est.: 320,000) on the IRTYSH RIVER, eastern Kazakhstan. Founded as a Russian fort in 1718 and moved to its present site in 1778, it lay at the junction of caravan trails, and before 1917 more than 11,000 camels passed through annually. In the early 20th century, it was connected by rail to Siberia and central Asia. It has one of the largest meat-packing plants in Kazakhstan. Its name was changed after Kazakhstani independence in 1991.

semi-Pelagianism \ˌse-mē-pə-'lā-jē-ə-ˌni-zəm\ Religious movement that flourished AD 429–529 in southern France, considered a HERESY by the Roman Catholic church. Unlike their near-contemporaries, the Pelagians (see PELAGIANISM), the semi-Pelagians believed in the universality of ORIGINAL SIN as a corruptive force in mankind and held that it could not be overcome without the GRACE of God. They endorsed BAPTISM, but contrary to AUGUSTINE, they taught that the innate corruption of mankind was not so great that it was beyond the will of mankind to subdue through asceticism. Its principal exponents were Sts. John Cassian (360–435), Vincent of Lérins (died c. 450), and Faustus of Riez (c. 400–c. 490).

semiconductor Class of crystalline solids with electrical conductivity between that of a CONDUCTOR and an INSULATOR. Such materials can be treated chemically to allow transmission and control of an ELECTRIC CURRENT. Semiconductors are used in the manufacture of electronic devices such as DIODES, TRANSISTORS, and INTEGRATED CIRCUITS. Intrinsic semiconductors have a high degree of chemical purity, but their conductivity is poor. Extrinsic semiconductors contain impurities that produce much greater conductivity. Some common intrinsic semiconductors are single crystals of SILICON, GERMANIUM, and gallium arsenide; such materials can be converted into the technologically more important extrinsic semiconductors by addition of small amounts of impurities, a process called doping (see DOPANT). Advances in semiconductor technology in recent years have gone hand in hand with increased operational speed in COMPUTERS.

seminary Educational institution, usually for training in theology. In the U.S. the term was formerly also used to refer to institutions of higher learning for women, often teachers' colleges. Since at least the 4th century there have been seminaries for the training of clergy. The first known group of seminarians was gathered by St. Basil of Ancyra. The term dropped out of general use in the Middle Ages, when most theological training was in monasteries, and later, in the universities. After the REFORMATION and the emergence of new denominations, seminaries again came into use, especially in the U.S. The 16th-century Council of TRENT ordered seminaries to be opened in every diocese.

Seminole \'se-mə-ˌnōl\ North American Indian people of MUSKOGEAN LANGUAGE stock who split off from the CREEK in the later 18th century and settled in northern Florida, where they were joined by runaway slaves, Indian and black, from Georgia. The Seminoles lived more by hunting and fishing than by agriculture, constructed shelters of thatched roofs supported by poles, and wore tailored hide clothing decorated in bright-colored strips. In an effort to stem white encroachment, they fought a succession of wars (the SEMINOLE WARS). Today about 2,000 Seminole live in Florida and 5,000 in Oklahoma.

Seminole Wars (1817–18, 1835–42, 1855–58) Three conflicts between the U.S. and the SEMINOLE Indians of Florida. The first began when U.S. authorities tried to recapture runaway black slaves living among Seminole bands. After U.S. forces seized Spanish-held Pensacola and St. Marks, Spain ceded its Florida territory under the Transcontinental Treaty (1819). The second conflict followed the refusal of most Seminoles to relocate under the INDIAN REMOVAL ACT. Led by OSCEOLA, the Seminole warriors hid in the Everglades and used guerrilla tactics to defend their land; about 2,000 U.S. soldiers were killed in the prolonged fighting. After Osceola was captured, resistance declined and most Seminoles agreed to emigrate west. The third conflict arose from efforts to oust the remaining Seminoles from Florida.

semiotics \ˌsē-mē-ˈä-tiks, ˌse-mē-ˈä-tiks\ *or* **semiology** Study of signs and sign-using behavior, especially in language. In the late 19th and early 20th century, the work of FERDINAND DE SAUSSURE and CHARLES SANDERS PEIRCE led to semiotics' emergence as a mode for examining phenomena in different fields, today including aesthetics, anthropology, communications, psychology, and semantics. Interest in the structure behind the use of particular signs links semiotics with the methods of STRUCTURALISM. Saussure's theories are also fundamental to POSTSTRUCTURALISM.

Semite Person speaking one of a group of related languages, presumably derived from a common language, Semitic (see SEMITIC LANGUAGES). The term came to include ARABS, Akkadians, Canaanites, some Ethiopians, and ARAMAEAN tribes including Hebrews. Semitic tribes migrated from the ARABIAN PENINSULA, beginning c. 2500 BC, to the Mediterranean coast, MESOPOTAMIA, and the Nile delta. In PHOENICIA, they became seafarers. In Mesopotamia, they blended with the civilization of SUMER. The Hebrews settled at last with other Semites in PALESTINE, founding a new religion and nation. See also JUDAISM.

Semitic languages \sə-ˈmi-tik\ Family of AFROASIATIC LANGUAGES spoken in northern Africa and South Asia. No other language family has been attested in writing over a greater time span—from the late 3rd millennium BC to the present. Both traditional and some recent classifications divide the family into an eastern and western group. Until recently the sole known East Semitic language was AKKADIAN; now some scholars add Eblaite, the language of a CUNEIFORM archive found at the ancient city of EBLA, with documents dating from c. 2300–2250 BC. West Semitic contains as one major subgroup Northwest Semitic, which includes Ugaritic, known from alphabetic cuneiform texts of c. 1400–1190 BC; the closely related Canaanite languages (including Moabite, Phoenician, and Ancient HEBREW); and ARAMAIC. Further subgrouping is controversial; traditionally, ARABIC was placed in a distinct South Semitic subgroup of West Semitic, though a more recent classification puts it together with Northwest Semitic. The South Semitic languages include Epigraphic South Arabian; Modern South Arabian (or Modern South Arabic), a group of six languages spoken in eastern Yemen, southwestern Oman, and the island of Socotra; and ETHIOPIC.

Semliki River \ˈsem-lē-kē\ River, eastern central Africa. It connects Lake EDWARD and Lake ALBERT and is 143 mi (230 km) long. The latter part of its course forms part of the border between Congo (Zaire) and Uganda. Wildlife, including elephants, hippopotamuses, crocodiles, and antelope, is abundant. The river's delta, choked with ambatch (a fast-growing thorny tree) and papyrus, is steadily encroaching on Lake Albert.

Semmelweis \ˈze-məl-ˌvīs\, **Ignaz (Philipp)** *Hungarian* **Ignác Fülöp Semmelweis** (1818–1865) Hungarian-Austrian physician. As an assistant at Vienna's obstetric clinic, at a time when European maternity hospitals saw death rates from puerperal fever of up to 30%, Semmelweis noticed that far fewer women died in the midwives' division of the clinic than in the division where students were taught, often after coming from the dissecting room. Concluding that students carried the infection, he had them wash their hands in chlorinated lime before each exam, and mortality dropped from 18% to 1%. Though his ideas were accepted in Hungary, his *Etiology, Understanding, and Preventing of Childbed Fever* (1861) was widely rejected abroad, including by RUDOLF VIRCHOW.

Semmes \ˈsemz\, **Raphael** (1809–1877) U.S. naval officer. Born in Charles Co., Md., he joined the U.S. Navy in 1826. In the Mexican War he commanded the naval landing at Veracruz. A resident of Alabama, he resigned his commission in 1861 and was appointed a commander in the Confederate navy. He captured 17 Union merchant ships before assuming command of the man-of-war *Alabama* in 1862. On numerous raids, he captured, sank, or burned 82 Union ships, disrupting Union commerce. In 1864 he was defeated in a battle with the *Kearsarge* in the English Channel, but escaped capture. See also ALABAMA CLAIMS.

Semon \ˈsē-mən\, **Waldo** (1898–1999) U.S. chemist. Born in Boise, Idaho, he obtained his doctorate from Harvard University and subsequently worked at various research labs and universities. He is known principally for his discovery of plasticized PVC, which, in combinations of up to 50% with plasticizer, is now familiar as floor tile, garden hose, imitation leather, shower curtains, and coatings. He also made pioneering contributions in polymer science, including new rubber antioxidants, and his technical leadership led to discovery of three major new polymer families: thermoplastic polyurethane, synthetic "natural" rubber, and oil-resistant synthetic rubbers.

Semyonov \sə-ˈmyo-nəf\, **Nikolay (Nikolayevich)** (1896–1986) Russian physical chemist. His specialty was the mechanisms of chain and branched-chain CHEMICAL REACTIONS, which he showed were the norm in chemical transformations. He shared a 1956 Nobel Prize with Cyril Hinshelwood (1897–1967).

Sen, Amartya (b.1933) Indian economist who was awarded the 1998 NOBEL PRIZE in Economic Sciences for his work in WELFARE ECONOMICS and social choice. Sen is best known for his work on the causes of FAMINE, and his research led to the development of solutions for limiting the effects of food shortages. After attending Presidency College in Calcutta (now Kolkata), Sen studied at Trinity College, University of Cambridge (B.A., 1955; M.A. and Ph.D., 1959). He taught economics at the Universities of Jadavpur (1956–58) and Delhi (1963–71), the London School of Economics, the University of London (1971–77), the University of Oxford (1977–88), and Harvard University (1988–98). In 1998 he was appointed master of Trinity College. His *Poverty and Famines: An Essay on Entitlement and Deprivation* (1981) showed that declining wages, unemployment, rising food prices, and inefficient food distribution could lead to starvation. His views encouraged policy makers to maintain stable prices for food.

Senate In ancient Rome, the governing and advisory council that was the most permanent element in the Roman constitution. Under the monarchy, it served as an advisory council, with undefined powers. During the republic, it advised the CONSULS and supposedly stood second to them in power. Senators were appointed by the consuls, but since they served for life, by the late republic the Senate became independent of the consuls, with extensive powers. About 312 BC the selection of senators was transferred from the consuls to the CENSORS. In 81 BC SULLA made selection automatic, routinely admitting all former QUAESTORS. It became the chief governing body, and controlled the republic's finances. Julius CAESAR increased the number of senators to 900. AUGUSTUS dropped the number to 300 and reduced the Senate's power, while giving it new judicial and legislative functions. The number later increased to about 2,000; many were provincials, the most important being the great landowners. The Senate's power faded until it disappeared in the 6th century AD.

Sendak, Maurice (Bernard) (born 1928) U.S. artist and writer. Born to Polish immigrant parents in New York City, he studied at the Art Students League. He illustrated more than 80 children's books by other writers before writing one himself. His *Kenny's Window* (1956) was followed by the innovative trilogy *Where the Wild Things Are* (1963), *In the Night Kitchen* (1970), and *Outside Over There* (1981). He collaborated with Carole King on the musical *Really Rosie* (1978) and designed stage productions of *The Magic Flute* (1980) and *The Nutcracker*(1983).

Sendero Luminoso See SHINING PATH

Seneca \ˈse-ni-kə\ North American Indian people of the IROQUOIAN linguistic group, the largest nation of the IROQUOIS CONFEDERACY, who lived in what is now western New York and eastern Ohio. Families linked by maternal kinship lived together in LONGHOUSES. Each community had a council of adult males, which guided the village chief. In the autumn small parties would leave the villages for the annual hunt, returning about midwinter; spring was the fishing season. Seneca women cultivated corn and other vegetables. Warfare with other Indian nations was frequent. In the American Revolution the Seneca were British allies, resulting in the destruction of their villages by Gen. John Sullivan in 1779. In 1797 they secured land for 12 reservations in western New York, four of which still exist. Today the Seneca number about 4,500. See also CORNPLANTER, HANDSOME LAKE.

Seneca \'se-ni-kə\, **Lucius Annaeus** (4 BC?–AD 65). Roman philosopher, statesman, and playwright. Born in Spain, he was trained as an orator and began a career in politics and law in Rome c. AD 31. While banished to Corsica for adultery (41–49), he wrote the philosophical treatises *Consolationes.* He later became tutor to the future emperor NERO, and from 54 to 62 was a leading intellectual figure in Rome. An adherent of STOICISM, he wrote other philosophical works including the *Epistilae morales,* a collection of essays on moral problems. He also left a series of verse tragedies marked by violence and bloodshed, including *Thyestes*, *Hercules*, and *Medea.* His plays influenced the development of Elizabethan drama during the Renaissance, notably WILLIAM SHAKESPEARE's *Titus Andronicus* and JOHN WEBSTER's *Duchess of Malfi.*

Seneca, marble bust, 3rd century, after an original bust of the 1st century; in the Staatliche Museen zu Berlin, Germany.

BY COURTESY OF THE STAATLICHE MUSEEN ZU BERLIN, GERMANY

Seneca Falls Convention (July 19–20, 1848) Assembly held at Seneca Falls, N.Y., that launched the U.S. WOMEN'S SUFFRAGE MOVEMENT. The meeting was initiated by ELIZABETH CADY STANTON and LUCRETIA MOTT. Over 200 people attended the meeting. The group passed the Declaration of Sentiments, a list of grievances and demands modeled on the Declaration of Independence that called on women to organize and petition for their rights. A demand for the right to vote passed by a narrow margin.

Senegal \,se-ni-'gȯl\ *officially* **Republic of Senegal** Nation, western Africa. Area: 75,951 sq mi (196,712 sq km). Population (2002 est.): 9,905,000. Capital: DAKAR. There are seven major ethnic groups in Senegal, including the WOLOF, Serer, FULANI, and MALINKE, each speaking a separate language, and a number of smaller groups. Language: French (official). Religion: Islam (more than 90% of the population). Currency: CFA franc. The climate varies from dry desert to moist tropics. Forests cover about 31% of the total area, about 27% is arable, and approximately 30% is pasture or rangeland. Agriculture is the main industry; peanuts are the most important cash and export crop. Other important industries are fishing, mining, manufacturing, and tourism. Senegal has large reserves of phosphates and iron ore. It is a republic with one legislative house; its chief of state is the president, and the head of government is the prime minister. Links between the peoples of Senegal and North Africa were established in the 10th century AD. Islam was introduced in the 11th century, although ANIMISM retained a hold on the country into the 19th century. The Portuguese explored the coast in 1445, and in 1638 the French established a trading post at the mouth of the SENEGAL RIVER. Throughout the 17th–18th century, Europeans exported slaves, ivory, and gold from Senegal. The French gained control over the coast in the early 19th century, and moved inland, checking the expansion of the TUKULOR empire; in 1895 Senegal became part of FRENCH WEST AFRICA. Its inhabitants were made French citizens in 1946, and it became an overseas territory of France. It became an autonomous republic in 1958 and was federated with Mali 1959–60. It became an independent state in 1960. In 1982 it entered a confederation with Gambia, called SENEGAMBIA, which was dissolved in 1989. More recently uprisings in part of the country caused political disorder.

Senegal River River, western Africa. It rises in Guinea and flows northwest across Mali, then west to the Atlantic Ocean, forming the border between Mauritania and Senegal. It is 1,020 mi (1,641 km) long. Its two major headstreams, the Bafing and Bakoye, meet in Mali to form the Senegal proper. Dams control floodwaters and prevent the encroachment of saltwater during the dry season.

Senegambia Confederation of Senegal and Gambia, 1982–89. The two countries agreed to integrate their military and security forces; form an economic and monetary union; coordinate their foreign policies and communications; and establish confederal institutions controlled by Senegal. Each country maintained its independence. It was dissolved in 1989. The term also refers to the region around the SENEGAL and GAMBIA rivers.

senescence See OLD AGE

Senghor \seŋ-'gȯr\, **Léopold (Sédar)** (1906–2001) Poet, president of Senegal (1960–80), and cofounder of the NEGRITUDE movement in African art and literature. He completed his studies in Paris and became a teacher there. Drafted in 1939, he was captured and spent two years in Nazi concentration camps, where he wrote some of his finest poems. He was elected to the French National Assembly in 1945. In 1948 he edited *Hosties noires,* an anthology of French-language African poetry that became a seminal Negritude text. That same year he founded the Senegalese Progressive Union (from 1976 the Socialist Party). When Senegal gained independence in 1960, he was unanimously elected president. He became an internationally respected spokesman for Africa and the Third World. In 1984 he became the first black inducted into the Académie Française.

senile dementia \'sē-,nīl-di-'men-chə\ DEMENTIA of OLD AGE (mostly after age 75), with loss of NEURONS and BRAIN-tissue shrinkage. Onset is usually gradual. Memory loss may progress until the patient cannot remember basic social and survival skills or function independently. Language skills, spatial or temporal orientation (see SPATIAL DISORIENTATION), judgment, and other cognitive capacities may also decline, and there may be personality changes. ALZHEIMER'S DISEASE accounts for about 50% of cases. Next most common is multi-infarct dementia, in which a series of small STROKES destroy more and more of the brain; treatment of the underlying vascular disorder can sometimes prevent or delay it.

senna Any of several plants, especially of the genus *Cassia,* in the pea family (see LEGUME), mostly of subtropical and tropical regions. Many are used medicinally; some yield tanbark used in preparing leather. In the eastern U.S., wild sennas *(C. hebecarpa* and *C. marilandica)* grow up to 4 ft (1.25 m) high and have showy spikes of yellow flowers. Some species are Old World shrubs or small trees.

Sennacherib \sə-'na-kə-rəb\ (died 681 BC) King of Assyria (r. 705/4–681 BC), son and successor of SARGON II. Between 703 and 689 he undertook six campaigns against ELAM (SW Iran); the last campaign saw the sack of BABYLON. He dealt firmly with an Egyptian-backed rebellion in Palestine in 701, sparing Jerusalem after receiving payment of a heavy indemnity. He rebuilt the city of NINEVEH, around which he planted fruit trees and exotic plants, including cotton, building extensive canals to bring water to the plantations. He devised less laborious methods of bronze casting and improved methods of raising water from wells. He was assassinated by a son during a rebellion.

Sennett, Mack *orig.* **Michael Sinnott** (1880–1960) U.S. (Canadian-born) film director. Born in Quebec, he performed in burlesque and vaudeville before joining the Biograph studio in 1908, and soon was directing comedies under D. W. GRIFFITH. He formed Keystone Co. in 1912. He produced the first U.S. feature-length comedy, *Tillie's Punctured Romance* (1914), but became most famous for over 1,000 comedy shorts, often featuring the slapstick comedy and wild antics of the Keystone Kops. He hired such stars as Mabel Normand, Fatty Arbuckle, and CHARLIE CHAPLIN. He excelled in comic timing, improvisation, and effective editing, and used trick camera work and high-speed and slow-motion photography to produce his famous comic chase scenes. In 1937 he received a special Academy Award.

Sennett.

BY COURTESY OF THE MUSEUM OF MODERN ART FILM STILLS ARCHIVE, NEW YORK

sensation Mental process (such as seeing, hearing, or smelling) due to immediate bodily stimulation, usually as distinguished from PERCEPTION. When a stimulus impinges on a SENSE organ and the organism responds, the stimulus has been sensed. See also PSYCHOPHYSICS, SENSE-DATA.

sense *or* **sensory reception** *or* **sense perception** Mechanism by which information is received about one's external or internal environment. Stimuli received by nerves, in some cases through specialized organs with receptor cells sensitive to one type of stimulus, are converted into impulses that travel to specialized areas of the brain, where they are analyzed. In addition to the "five senses"—sight, hearing, smell, taste, and touch—humans have senses of motion (kinesthetic sense), heat, cold, pressure, pain, and balance. Temperature, pressure, and pain are cutaneous (skin) senses; different points on the skin are particularly sensitive to each. See also CHEMORECEPTION, EAR, EYE, INNER EAR, MECHANORECEPTION, NOSE, PHOTORECEPTION, PROPRIOCEPTION, TASTE, THERMORECEPTION, TONGUE.

sense-data Entities that are the direct objects of sensation. The image one sees with one's eyes closed after staring at a bright light is a sense-datum. When Macbeth hallucinates a dagger floating before him, he is aware of sense-data, even though there is no actual dagger. In both cases there is something of which one is directly aware that is the same in both veridical and nonveridical instances of perception. Even in cases of normal vision, one may be said to be seeing sense-data; when one looks at a penny from a certain angle and sees it as elliptical, for example, there is an elliptical sense-datum in one's visual field.

sensitive plant Either of two plants in the pea family (see LEGUME) that close up their leaves and droop when touched. This unusually quick response is due to rapid water release from specialized cells at the bases of leaftsalks. The more common plant is *Mimosa pudica* (see MIMOSA). Spiny and shrubby, with fernlike leaves and small, globular, mauve flower puffs, it grows about 1 ft (30 cm) high as a widespread tropical weed and a greenhouse curiosity. Wild sensitive plant *(Cassia nictitans)* is less sensitive to touch; a larger plant, 20 in. (50 cm) high, it is native to the eastern U.S. and the West Indies.

sensitivity training Instruction in a group setting designed to cultivate awareness of the needs and emotions of all members of the group. Derived from GROUP THERAPY, sensitivity training is intended to build trust and communication among individuals and groups, and has been used in a wide variety of contexts, including business and industry.

sentence In CRIMINAL LAW, a judgment formally pronouncing the punishment to be inflicted on a person convicted of a crime. Among the major types are the concurrent sentence, which runs at the same time as another; the consecutive sentence, which runs before or after another; the mandatory sentence, which is specifically required by statute as punishment for an offense; and the suspended sentence, the imposition of which is suspended by the court. See also CAPITAL PUNISHMENT, PAROLE.

Seoul \ˈsōl\ City (pop., 2000 prelim.: 9,891,000), capital of the Republic of Korea (South Korea) since 1946, with the administrative status of a province. Located on the HAN RIVER near the center of the Korean peninsula, Seoul was the capital of the Korean CHOSON DYNASTY 1394–1910, and the center of Japanese rule of Korea 1910–45. During the KOREAN WAR it was the capital of the U.S. military government and suffered extensive damage; it has been largely rebuilt since 1953. In 1988 it was the site of the Summer OLYMPIC GAMES. The commercial, cultural, and industrial center of South Korea, it is a center of higher education, with several universities, including Seoul National University (1946).

separation of powers Division of governmental powers among separate and independent bodies; typically the executive, legislative, and judicial branches of government. Such division prevents the concentration of power in any one branch, since the cooperation of all three is necessary for the development, execution, and administration of public policy. The concept received its first modern formulation from MONTESQUIEU, who declared it the best way to safeguard liberty; he influenced the framers of the CONSTITUTION OF THE U.S., who in turn influenced the writers of later constitutions. See also CHECKS AND BALANCES.

Sephardi \sə-ˈfär-dē\ Member of the Jews, or their descendants, who lived in Spain and Portugal from the Middle Ages until their expulsion in the late 15th century. They fled first to North Africa and other parts of the Ottoman empire and eventually settled in such countries as France, Holland, England, Italy, and the Balkan states. They differ from the ASHKENAZI Jews in their traditional language, LADINO, and in their preservation of Babylonian rather than Palestinian Jewish ritual traditions. Of today's estimated 700,000 Sephardic Jews, many live in Israel.

Sepik River \ˈsā-pik\ River, northeastern New Guinea. It enters the Bismarck Sea through a delta about 700 mi (1,100 km) from its source in the central highlands. Because of the amount of sediment it carries, it discolors the waters for 20 mi (32 km) beyond its mouth, which is more than 1 mi (1.6 km) wide. It is navigable by shallow-draft vessels for more than 300 mi (483 km). The river's small tribal groups have extensive artistic traditions, known as the Sepik River style.

Sepoy Mutiny See INDIAN MUTINY

seppuku \ˈse-pə-ˌkü\ *or* **hara-kiri** Japanese ritual suicide by disembowelment, practiced by members of the SAMURAI class. Suicide by disembowelment was favored because it was slow and painful, and therefore demonstrated courage, self-control, and strong resolve. Voluntary seppuku was performed to avoid the dishonor of capture, show loyalty to one's lord by following him into death, protest against some policy of a superior, or atone for failure. Obligatory seppuku was a method of capital punishment for a samurai, who would be beheaded by a second once he had made an initial stab wound himself. Obligatory seppuku was abolished in 1873, but voluntary seppuku continued to occur. A notable 20th-century example is that of YUKIO MISHIMA. See also BUSHIDO.

September 11 attacks Series of airline hijackings and suicide bombings against U.S. targets perpetrated by 19 militants associated with the Islamic extremist group AL-QAEDA. The attacks were planned well in advance; the militants—most of whom were from Saudi Arabia—traveled to the U.S. beforehand, where a number received commercial flight training. Working in small groups, the hijackers boarded 4 domestic airliners in groups of 5 (a 20th alleged militant had been detained by U.S. authorities) on Sept. 11, 2001, and took control of the planes soon after takeoff. At 8:46 AM (local time), the terrorists piloted the first plane into the north tower of the WORLD TRADE CENTER in NEW YORK CITY. A second plane struck the south tower some 15 minutes later. Both structures erupted in flames and, badly damaged, soon collapsed. A third plane struck the southwest side of the PENTAGON near WASHINGTON, D.C., at 9:40, and within the next hour the fourth crashed in Pennsylvania after its passengers—aware of events via cellular telephone—attempted to overpower their assailants. Some 2,800 victims were killed in New York, 184 at the Pentagon, and 40 in Pennsylvania. All 19 terrorists died.

septic arthritis Acute INFLAMMATION of one or more JOINTS caused by INFECTION. Suppurative arthritis may follow certain bacterial infections; joints become swollen, hot, sore, and filled with pus, which erodes their CARTILAGE, causing permanent damage if not promptly treated by giving ANTIBIOTICS, draining the pus, and resting the joint. Nonsuppurative arthritis can accompany several diseases caused by bacteria, viruses, or fungi; joints become stiff, swollen, and painful to move. Treatment includes rest, drugs, and, in the case of TUBERCULOSIS, orthopedic care to prevent skeletal deformity.

septicemia \ˌsep-ti-ˈsē-mē-ə\ *or* **blood poisoning** Invasion of the bloodstream after surgery or infectious disease by microorganisms—typically gram-negative (see GRAM STAIN) BACTERIA—and the TOXINS they release. The latter trigger immune responses and widespread COAGULATION in blood vessels. High fever, chills, weakness, and sweating are followed by a drop in blood pressure. Multiple INFECTIONS are often present, requiring broad-spectrum ANTIBIOTICS as well as drainage of foci of infection. Without immediate treatment, septic shock follows, with a mortality rate over 50%. Microorganisms may lodge in mucous membranes, causing ABSCESSES and pus formation. Invasive technology and antibiotic-resistant bacteria in hospitals have made septicemia more severe and more common. See also BACTEREMIA.

Septimania \ˌsep-tə-ˈmā-nē-ə\ Ancient territory, southwestern France. Located between the GARONNE and RHÔNE rivers and the PYRENEES and Cevennes mountains, it was settled during the reign of the Roman emperor AUGUSTUS by veterans of the Seventh Legion (Septimani). It was the last Gallic holding of the Visigoths of Spain. The region was occupied by the FRANKS 732–768, was part of the kingdom of AQUITAINE under the CAROLINGIANS, and became a separate duchy in 817. In the 9th century it was subsumed under the counts of TOULOUSE.

Septuagint \sep-ˈtü-ə-jənt\ Earliest extant Greek translation of the OLD TESTAMENT from the original Hebrew, presumably made for the use of the Jewish community in Egypt when Greek was the lingua franca. The Pentateuch was translated near the middle of the 3rd century BC; the rest of the Old Testament was translated in the 2nd century BC. The name Septuagint was derived from a legend that 72 translators worked on the project. Its influence was far-reaching. The Septuagint rather than the original Hebrew Bible was the main basis for the Old Latin, Coptic, Ethiopic, Armenian, Georgian, Slavonic, and some Arabic translations of the BIBLE.

sequencing Determining of the order of AMINO acids in a PROTEIN or of NUCLEOTIDES in a NUCLEIC ACID. The results have increased understanding of the mechanisms of life processes and have numerous applications. Whereas FREDERICK SANGER required 10 years to determine the structure and sequence of INSULIN and about as long to determine the sequence of nucleotides in the DNA of a small VIRUS, automated laboratory instruments and techniques can now do either task in days or hours. See also GENETIC CODE, POLYMERASE CHAIN REACTION.

sequestration In law, a WRIT authorizing a law-enforcement official to take into custody the property of a defendant in order to enforce a judgment or to preserve the property until a judgment is rendered. In some CIVIL-LAW jurisdictions, contested property may be deposited with a third party until it is determined to whom it properly belongs.

sequoia See REDWOOD

sequoia, giant See BIG TREE

Sequoia National Park National park, SIERRA NEVADA range, California. The 629-sq-mi (1,629-sq-km) area was set aside in 1890 to protect groves of big trees (*Sequoiadendron giganteum*) which are among the world's largest and oldest living things. The largest tree in the park is thought to be 3,000–4,000 years old. KINGS CANYON NATIONAL PARK adjoins it to the north; Mount WHITNEY is on the eastern boundary.

Sequoyah *or* **Sequoya** *or* **Sequoia** \si-ˈkwȯi-ə\ (c. 1760–1843) Creator of the CHEROKEE writing system. Convinced that the secret of the white people's power was written language, Sequoyah set about developing a Cherokee system. Adapting letters from English, Greek, and Hebrew, he created a system of 86 symbols representing all the syllables of the Cherokee language. Most Cherokee became literate as a result.

Seram See CERAM

seraph \ˈser-əf\ In Jewish, Christian, and Islamic literature, a celestial being with two or three pairs of wings who guards the throne of God. In Christian angelology, seraphim are the highest-ranking in the hierarchy of ANGELS. In art they are often painted red, symbolizing fire. They appear in the Old Testament in a vision of ISAIAH as six-winged creatures praising God. See also CHERUB.

Serbia *Serbo-Croatian* **Srbija** \ˈsər-bē-ˌyä\ Constituent republic of the Federal Republic of YUGOSLAVIA, comprising 80% of its area. The formerly autonomous provinces of VOJVODINA and KOSOVO are within its borders. Area: 34,116 sq mi (88,361 sq km). Population (2001 est.): 10,003,000. Capital: BELGRADE. Ethnic Serbs, Croats, Bosnians, and Albanians live in the republic. Language: Serbo-Croatian (official). Religions: Serbian Orthodox, Roman Catholic, Islam. Currency: Yugoslav new dinar. Serbia is mountainous, with forests in the central area and low-lying plains in the north. The fertile plains of Vojvodina supply much of the nation's grain, tobacco, and sugar beets, while the hilly central areas specialize in dairy, fruit, and livestock. Before the 1990s civil war, mining and manufacturing were the economic mainstays, with industries noted for textiles and with deposits of lead, zinc, coal, copper, and oil. Serbs settled the region in the 6th–7th century AD. In the 9th century, nominally under Byzantine suzerainty, the Serbs converted to Eastern Orthodox Christianity. The Ottoman Turks triumphed at the BATTLE OF KOSOVO in 1389; after a period of resistance, it became part of the Ottoman Empire in 1459. After the Russo-Turkish War of 1828–29, it became an autonomous principality under Turkish suzerainty and Russian protection. It became completely independent of Turkey in 1878. After World War I, it became part of the Kingdom of Serbs, Croats, and Slovenes, which was renamed Yugoslavia in 1929. In 1946 Serbia was made one of six federated republics of Yugoslavia. As the Yugoslav economy faltered in the 1980s, the country began to break apart. After an unsuccessful attempt to prevent Slovenia's secession in 1991, Serb elements of the Yugoslav armed forces began assisting Bosnian Serbs in sweeping Muslims and Croats from eastern and northern Bosnia and Herzegovina. After Yugoslavia's breakup, Serbia joined with Montenegro to form a new Yugoslav federation. The area remained in turmoil (see BOSNIAN CONFLICT). The 1995 signing of the Dayton peace accords ultimately brought little relief. SLOBODAN MILOSEVIC retained power through the end of the century, and the push for more autonomy by Albanian Kosovars provoked another round of fighting in 1998–99 (see KOSOVO CONFLICT). NATO retaliated with a bombing campaign as the violence escalated, which led to a peace accord in June 1999. A change in the Yugoslav government late in 2000 brought reinstatement in the United Nations, and in 2002 the governments of the two component states agreed to remain united under the name Serbia and Montenegro.

Serbian and Croatian language *or* **Serbo-Croatian language** \krō-ˈā-shən\ South SLAVIC LANGUAGE spoken by some 21 million people in Croatia, Bosnia-Herzegovina, Serbia, Montenegro, and Kosovo. As the dominant language of pre-1991 Yugoslavia, it was used or understood by most ethnic groups of the federation. The Central Neo-štokavian dialect forms the basis for both Standard Serbian and Standard Croatian. Historically, Serbia's literary language was the Serbian recension of Church Slavic (see OLD CHURCH SLAVIC LANGUAGE). In the 19th century a new literary language based on colloquial Serbian was successfully promulgated by VUK STEFANOVIC KARADZIC. Croatian written in the LATIN ALPHABET first appears in the mid-14th century. In the 19th century, the Zagreb-based Illyrian political movement, which aimed at a union of all South Slavs, turned to the Central Neo-štokavian dialect as the basis for a literary language that would unite Croatians and bring them closer to their Slavic brethren. The move toward a unified "Serbo-Croatian" was supported by the politically unified Yugoslav kingdom (1918–41) and communist Yugoslavia (1945–91). Since Yugoslavia's political disintegration, movement has been away from linguistic unity, leading to declarations of distinct Serbian, Croatian, and Bosnian languages.

Serbs, Croats, and Slovenes \ˈkrō-ˌäts\, **Kingdom of** Balkan state formed in 1918 after World War I. It included the previously independent kingdoms of Serbia and Montenegro and the southern Slav territories formerly subject to the Austro-Hungarian empire, including Dalmatia, Croatia-Slavonia, Slovenia, and Bosnia and Herzegovina. The kingdom was ruled by the Serbian KARAGEORGEVIC DYNASTY. In 1929 King ALEXANDER I sought to combat local nationalisms by proclaiming a royal dictatorship and renaming the state Yugoslavia.

Serengeti National Park \ˌser-ən-ˈge-tē\ Wildlife refuge, northern central Tanzania. Established in 1951, the park covers 5,700 sq mi (14,763 sq km). An international tourist attraction, it is the only place in Africa where vast land animal migrations still take place. More than 35 species of plains animals, 200 species of birds, and lions, leopards, elephants, rhinoceroses, hippopotamuses, giraffes, and baboons inhabit the park. Poaching is a major problem.

serfdom Condition in medieval Europe in which a tenant farmer was bound to a hereditary plot of land and to the will of his landlord. Serfs differed from slaves in that slaves could be bought and sold without reference to land, whereas serfs changed lords only when the land they worked changed hands. From about the 2nd century AD, large privately owned estates in the Roman empire that had been worked by slaves were broken up and given to peasant farmers. These farmers came to depend on larger landowners for protection in turbulent times, and swearing fealty to a proprietor became common practice. In 332 CONSTANTINE I established serfdom legally by requiring tenant farmers to pay labor services to their lords. As serfs, they could not marry, change occupations, or move without their lord's permission, and they had to give a major portion of their harvest to their lord. The development of centralized political power, the labor shortage caused by the BLACK DEATH, and endemic peasant uprisings in the 14th–15th century led to the gradual emancipation of serfs in Western Europe. In Eastern Europe serfdom became more entrenched during that period; the peasants of the Austro-Hungarian empire were not freed until the late 18th century, and Russia's serfs were not freed until 1861. See also FEUDALISM.

serial Film presented in a series of episodes over several months. The serials, usually adventure melodramas, probably developed from the adventure stories published in monthly installments in magazines. The first internationally popular serial, *The Perils of Pauline* (1914), starring Pearl White, was followed by such other serials as *The Hazards of Helen,* which ran for 119 episodes (1914–17). Serials focused on action sequences, with cliff-hanging endings for each episode. They remained popular with movie audiences, especially children, into the 1940s.

serial murder Unlawful homicide of at least two people, carried out in a series over a period of time. Serial murder is distinguished from mass murder, in which several victims are murdered at the same time and place. Criminologists have distinguished between two types of serial murder: classic serial murder, which usually involves stalking and is often sexually motivated, and spree serial murder, which is usually motivated by thrill-seeking. Cases of serial murder have been documented since ancient times. The known incidence of serial murder increased dramatically in the early 19th century, particularly in Europe, though this development has been attributed to advances in law-enforcement techniques and increased news coverage rather than to an actual rise in the number of occurrences. From the late 19th century serial murderers received considerable attention in the press, and their cases inspired numerous books and films. These accounts, however, tended to mislead the public by suggesting that serial murder is a common phenomenon, when in fact it represented less than 2 percent of all murders in the late 20th century.

serialism Use of an ordered set of pitches as the basis of a musical composition. The terms twelve-tone music and serialism, though not entirely synonymous, are often used interchangeably. The serial method was worked out by A. SCHOENBERG in the years 1916–23, though another serial method was being devised simultaneously by Josef Matthias Hauer (1883–1959). To Schoenberg, it represented the culmination of the growth of CHROMATICISM in the late 19th and early 20th century. Concerned to erase the system of TONALITY, which he regarded as outworn but which he realized would frequently assert itself even in the music of composers who desired to transcend it, Schoenberg's original method stipulated (among several other requirements) that no note could be repeated before all 11 other notes of the chromatic scale had been used. Serialism, a broader term than twelve-tone music, can apply to use of fewer than 12 tones. "Total serialism," a concept that arose in the late 1940s, attempts to organize not only the 12 pitches but such other elements as rhythm, dynamics, register, and instrumentation into ordered sets as well.

serigraphy See SILKSCREEN

serine \'ser-ˌēn\ One of the nonessential AMINO acids, found in substantial concentrations (sometimes 5–10%) in many common PROTEINS. It is also an important component of PHOSPHOLIPIDS. It is used in biochemical and microbiological research and as a dietary supplement and feed additive.

Serkin, Rudolf (1903–1991) Austro-Hungarian-U.S. pianist. He made his debut at 12, in Vienna, and from 1920 was a close associate of ADOLF BUSCH, whose daughter he married in 1935. He emigrated to the U.S. in 1939 and began teaching at the Curtis Institute, which he served as director 1968–75. In 1950 he and Busch cofounded the Marlboro Music Festival in Vermont, which under Serkin's direction would become the preeminent locus for chamber music in the U.S. He was known for his highly intelligent and expressive but self-effacing playing of the German-Austrian classics. His son, Peter (born 1947), is a well-known pianist, with a wide repertoire.

Serling, (Edward) Rod(man) (1924–1975) U.S. television writer and producer. Born in Syracuse, N.Y., he began his career in radio but soon shifted to television, becoming a freelance screenwriter in 1953. He wrote teleplays for such series as *Kraft Television Theater, Studio One,* and *Playhouse 90,* including *Requiem for a Heavyweight* (1956, Emmy award). He created, narrated, and was the main writer of the famous supernatural series *The Twilight Zone* (1959–65), and narrated the similar series *Night Gallery* (1970–73).

Sermon on the Mount Biblical collection of religious teachings and ethical sayings attributed to JESUS, as reported in the Gospel of St. MATTHEW. The sermon was addressed to disciples and a large crowd of listeners to guide them in a life of discipline based on a new law of love, even of enemies, as opposed to the old law of retribution. It is the source of many familiar Christian homilies and oft-quoted passages from the BIBLE, including the Beatitudes and the LORD'S PRAYER. The sermon is often regarded as a blueprint for Christian life.

serotonin \ˌser-ə-'tō-nən\ Chemical (5-hydroxytryptamine, or 5-HT) derived from the amino acid TRYPTOPHAN. It occurs in brain and intestinal tissue, platelets, and certain connective-tissue cells and is a component of many animal VENOMS (e.g., wasp, toad). A strong stimulator of blood-vessel constriction and a NEUROTRANSMITTER, serotonin concentrates in certain brain areas, especially the midbrain and HYPOTHALAMUS. Some cases of DEPRESSION are apparently caused by reduced amounts or activity of serotonin in the brain; many ANTIDEPRESSANTS counteract that condition. Excessive brain serotonin activity may cause MIGRAINE HEADACHES and NAUSEA. LSD may act by inhibiting the action of serotonin.

serpentine \'sər-pən-ˌtēn\ Any of a group of magnesium-rich silicate minerals whose composition resembles $Mg_3Si_2O_5(OH)_4$. Serpentine generally occurs in three forms: as CHRYSOTILE, the most common variety of ASBESTOS; and as antigorite or lizardite, both of which are commonly massive and fine-grained. Named in allusion to its resemblance to a snake's skin, serpentine is usually grayish, white, or green but may be yellow or green-blue. It takes a high polish and is sometimes used as an ornamental stone.

Serra \'ser-ə\, **Junípero** (1713–1784) Spanish missionary. He was ordained a Franciscan priest in 1730 and worked as a missionary in Mexico 1750–67. When Spain began its occupation of Alta California (now California), he joined the expedition and in 1769 founded Mission San Diego. From 1770 to 1782 he founded eight more Californian missions, thereby strengthening Spain's control of the area. His work earned him the title of Apostle of California, and he was beatified in 1988.

Serra, Richard (born 1939) U.S. sculptor. Born in San Francisco, he paid for his education at the University of California by working in steel factories. From 1961 he studied with JOSEF ALBERS at Yale University. He settled in New York c. 1966 and began to experiment with new materials; in 1968 he exhibited rubber and neon sculptures. In 1969–70 gravity became a major element of his work; the *Prop* series consisted of huge plates of lead or steel leaning against each other, supported only by their opposing weights. He is best known for his enormous, sometimes controversial outdoor pieces that interact with the environment, particularly *Tilted Arc,* installed in New York's Federal Plaza in 1981 but removed in 1989.

Sertorius \sər-'tōr-ē-əs\, **Quintus** (123?–72 BC) Roman statesman and military commander who ruled most of Spain 80–72 BC. He commanded an army in the SOCIAL WAR, and he helped MARIUS take Rome (87–86) in his struggle against SULLA. As PRAETOR in 83 he was sent to Spain; he fled to Mauretania when Sulla pursued him, but later overthrew Sulla's governor in Farther Spain and by 77 was ruler of most of Spain. When POMPEY THE GREAT and Metellus Pius arrived to put down the rebellion, he skillfully kept them at bay until the tide turned in his favor. When troop morale sank, he was murdered by a conspiracy of officers.

serval \'sər-vəl\ Long-limbed CAT *(Felis serval)* of sub-Saharan Africa found in grass- and bush-covered country near water. It has a long neck and large, cupped ears. It is 32–40 in. (80–100 cm) long, has an 8–12-in. (20–30-cm) tail, stands about 20 in. (50 cm), and may weigh over 30 lbs (15 kg). Its long coat is yellowish to reddish brown above and whitish below, with black spots or stripes; there are some all-black servals in Kenya.

Serval (*Felis serval*).
CHRISTINA LOKE–PHOTO RESEARCHERS

server Network computer, computer program, or device that processes requests from a client (see CLIENT-SERVER ARCHITECTURE). On the WORLD WIDE WEB, for example, a Web server is a computer that uses the HTTP protocol to send Web pages to a client's computer when the client requests them. On a LOCAL AREA NETWORK, a print server manages one or more printers, and prints files sent to it by client computers. Network servers (which manage network traffic) and file servers (which store and retrieve files for clients) are two more examples of servers.

Servetus \sər-'vē-təs\, **Michael** (1511?–1553) Spanish physician and theologian. His views alienated both Roman Catholics and Protestants, beginning with the publication of his first book, *De Trinitatis erroribus* (1531), in which he denied the Holy Trinity. His most important work, *Biblia sacra ex Santis Pagnini translatione* (1542), was notable for its theory of prophecy. Elsewhere he questioned the usefulness of baptism and criticized the promulgation of the NICENE CREED. Persecuted by JOHN CALVIN, he was convicted of heresy in Geneva and burned at the stake. His notable contribution to medicine was the first accurate description of cardiopulmonary circulation of the blood (1553).

Service, Robert (William) (1874–1958) English-Canadian popular verse writer. He emigrated to Canada in 1894 and lived eight years in the Yukon. His *Songs of a Sourdough* (1907) and *Ballads of a Cheechako* (1909), about life in the "frozen North," were enormously popular. He became known as "the Canadian Kipling" with such rollicking ballads as "The Shooting of Dan McGrew" and "The Cremation of Sam McGee." His other works include the novel *The Trail of '98* (1910) and *Rhymes of a Red Cross Man* (1916).

service academies, U.S. See UNITED STATES SERVICE ACADEMIES

service industry Industry that provides services rather than goods. Economists divide the products of all economic activity into two broad categories, goods and services. Industries that produce goods (tangible objects) include agriculture, mining, manufacturing, and construction. Service industries include everything else: banking, communications, wholesale and retail trade, all professional services such as engineering and medicine, all consumer services, and all government services. The proportion of the world economy devoted to services rose rapidly in the 20th century. In the U.S., the service sector accounted for more than half the gross domestic product in 1929, two-thirds in 1978, and more than three-quarters in 1993. As increases in AUTOMATION facilitate productivity, a smaller workforce is able to produce more goods, and the service functions of distribution, management, FINANCE, and sales become relatively more important.

servitude In property law, a right by which property owned by one person is subject to a specified use or enjoyment by another. As used in CIVIL-LAW jurisdictions, servitude most often refers to the obligation of one item of immovable property (e.g., a tract of land) in favor of another. Such servitude is transferred along with the ownership of the dominant estate. The servient estate cannot be transferred separately from the dominant estate. See also EASEMENT.

servomechanism Device used to correct the performance of a mechanism automatically, by means of error-sensing feedback. The term properly applies only to systems in which the feedback and error-correction signals control mechanical position or velocity. Servomechanisms were first used in military and marine navigation equipment. Today they are used in automatic machine tools, satellite-tracking antennas, celestial-tracking systems on telescopes, automatic navigation systems, and antiaircraft-gun control systems. The design of servomechanisms is considered to be a branch of both ROBOTICS and CYBERNETICS.

sesame Erect, annual plant *(Sesamum indicum)* of numerous types and varieties in the family Pedaliaceae. It has been cultivated since antiquity for its seeds, which are used as food and flavoring and yield a prized oil. The hulled seeds, creamy or pearly white and tiny, have a mild, nutlike aroma and taste. The whole seed is used extensively in the cuisines of the Middle East and Asia. Sesame oil, noted for its stability and its resistance to becoming rancid, is used as a salad or cooking oil, in shortening and margarine, in the manufacture of soaps, pharmaceuticals, and lubricants, and as an ingredient in cosmetics.

Sessions, Roger (Huntington) (1896–1985) U.S. composer. Born in Brooklyn, N.Y., he attended Harvard and Yale, lived in Italy and Germany (1925–33), and later taught principally at Princeton University (1935–45, 1953–65). His early neoclassicism preceded his adoption of serialism c. 1953. His works include the operas *The Trial of Lucullus* (1947) and *Montezuma* (1963), incidental music to *The Black Maskers* (1923), eight symphonies, a *Concerto for Orchestra* (1982, Pulitzer Prize), and the cantata *When Lilacs Last in the Door-yard Bloom'd* (1970), as well as several widely read books on music. His seriousness has kept his works from a wide audience.

set In mathematics and logic, any collection of objects (elements), which may be mathematical (e.g., numbers, FUNCTIONS) or not. The intuitive idea of a set is probably even older than that of NUMBER. Members of a herd of animals, for example, could be matched with stones in a sack without members of either set actually being counted. The notion extends into the infinite. For example, the set of integers from 1 to 100 is finite, whereas the set of all integers is infinite. A set is commonly represented as a list of all its members enclosed in braces. A set with no members is called an empty, or null, set, and is denoted ∅. Because an infinite set cannot be listed, it is usually represented by a formula that generates its elements when applied to the elements of the set of counting numbers. Thus, {2x‡ = 1,2,3,...} represents the set of positive even numbers (the vertical bar means "such that").

set theory Branch of mathematics that deals with the properties of SETS. It is most valuable as applied to other areas of mathematics, which borrow from and adapt its terminology and concepts. These include the operations of union (∪), and intersection (∩). The union of two sets is a set containing all the elements of both sets, each listed once. The intersection is the set of all elements common to both original sets. Set theory is useful in analyzing difficult concepts in mathematics and LOGIC. It was placed on a firm theoretical footing by GEORG CANTOR, who discovered the value of clearly formulated sets in the analysis of problems in symbolic logic and NUMBER THEORY.

setback In architecture, a steplike recession in the profile of a high-rise building. Usually dictated by BUILDING CODES to allow sunlight to reach streets and lower floors, the building must take another step back from the street for every specified added height interval. Without building setbacks, many of New York City's streets would be in constant shadow. In the 1920s, architects drew attention to their setbacks with decorative devices—mosaics; Chinese, Mayan, or Greek motifs; or Cubistic blocks; later architects deemphasized them. The INTERNATIONAL STYLE glass-wall skyscraper was typically built without intermittent setbacks, zoning requirements being met by one huge setback at ground level that created a plaza. The late 20th century saw a return to decorative setbacks.

Seth *or* **Set** Ancient Egyptian god and patron of the 11th nome, or province, of Upper Egypt. A trickster, he was a sky god, lord of the desert, and master of storms, disorder, and warfare. He was the brother of OSIRIS, whom he killed, and he was antagonistic to HORUS, the child of Osiris' sister, ISIS. Seth's cult largely died out in the 1st millennium BC, and he was gradually ousted from the Egyptian pantheon. He was later regarded as entirely evil and identified as a god of the Persians and other invaders of Egypt.

SETI *in full* **Search for Extraterrestrial Intelligence** Ongoing project designed to search for extraterrestrial life. Based in the U.S., SETI focuses on receiving and analyzing signals, mostly in the RADIO region of the ELECTROMAGNETIC SPECTRUM, from space, looking for nonrandom patterns likely to have been sent by intelligent beings. Approaches include targeted searches examining sunlike stars and systematic sweeps covering all directions. The search remains controversial; NASA funded a SETI project beginning in 1988, but Congress ended its funding in 1992; it has been funded privately since then. See also DRAKE EQUATION, Project OZMA.

Seti I (died 2379 BC) Egyptian king of the 19th dynasty (r.2390–2379 BC). His father, Ramses I, had reigned only two years. It was Seti who was the real founder of the greatness of the Ramessids, though his son

RAMSES II is more famous. Seti did much to promote Egypt's prosperity. He fortified the frontier, opened mines and quarries, dug wells, and rebuilt temples and shrines; he continued work on the great hall at KARNAK and built a temple at ABYDOS decorated with reliefs of great delicacy.

Seton \'sē-tᵊn\, **Ernest Thompson** *orig.* **Ernest Evan Thompson** (1860–1946) Canadian-U.S. naturalist and animal fiction writer. Seton's family emigrated to Canada from England in 1866. He earned a living for a time as a wild-animal artist, and in 1898 published his most popular book, the story collection *Wild Animals I Have Known.* Deeply concerned for the future of the North American prairie, he fought to establish reservations for American Indians and parks for endangered animals. In 1902 he founded the Woodcraft Indians to give children opportunities for nature study. He chaired the committee that established the Boy Scouts of America.

Seton \sē-tᵊn\, **St. Elizabeth Ann** *orig.* **Elizabeth Ann Bayley** *known as* **Mother Seton** (1774–1821) U.S. religious leader and educator, the first native-born U.S. citizen canonized by the Roman Catholic church. Born into an upper-class family in New York City, in 1794 she married William Magee Seton. In 1797 she founded the Society for the Relief of Poor Widows with Small Children, and in 1803 she was herself left a widow with five children. After converting from Episcopalianism to Roman Catholicism in 1805, she opened a free Catholic elementary school in Baltimore in 1809. In 1813 she founded the Sisters of Charity, the first U.S. religious order, and she served as its superior until her death. She is often considered the mother of the parochial-school system in the U.S. She was canonized in 1975.

setter Any of three breeds derived from a medieval hunting dog that would set (lie down) when it found birds so that it and the birds could be covered with a net. Setters have long hair on the ears, chest, legs, and tail. They weigh 44–70 lbs (20–32 kg) and stand 23–27 in. (58–69 cm). The English setter, developed in the 15th century, may be all white, black and white-and-tan, or white with dark flecks. The Gordon setter originated in 17th-century Scotland; its soft, wavy coat is black with tan markings. The Irish setter, bred in Ireland in the 18th-cent, has a straight red coat.

Irish setter.
SALLY ANNE THOMPSON

Settignano, Desiderio da See DESIDERIO DA SETTIGNANO

settlement In law, a compromise or agreement between litigants to settle the matters in dispute between them in order to dispose of and conclude their litigation. Generally, as a result of the settlement, prosecution of the action is withdrawn or dismissed without any judgment being entered. The parties may, however, incorporate the terms of the settlement into a consent decree, recorded by the court. Most suits brought today are either withdrawn or settled.

Settlement, Act of (June 12, 1701) Act of Parliament that thereafter regulated the succession to the English throne. It decreed that if King WILLIAM III or Princess (later Queen) ANNE died without issue, the crown was to pass to JAMES I's granddaughter Sophie of Hanover (1630–1714) and her Protestant heirs. The act resulted in the accession of the House of HANOVER in 1714. It also decreed that future monarchs must belong to the Church of England, that judges were to hold office on the basis of good behavior rather than at the sovereign's pleasure, and that impeachment by the House of Commons was not subject to pardon by the sovereign.

settlement house *or* **social settlement** *or* **community center** Neighborhood social-welfare agency. The staff of a settlement house may sponsor clubs, classes, athletic teams, and interest groups; they may employ such specialists as vocational counselors and caseworkers. The settlement movement began with the founding of Toynbee Hall in London in 1884 by Samuel Augustus Barnett (1844–1913). It spread to the U.S. in the late 19th century with the establishment of such institutions as Hull House in Chicago (founded by JANE ADDAMS). Most countries now have similar institutions. In the late 19th and early 20th cent, U.S. settlement houses were active among the masses of new immigrants and worked for reform legislation such as workers' compensation and child-labor laws.

settling In building construction, the gradual subsiding of a structure as the soil beneath its foundation consolidates under loading. This may continue for several years after the structure's completion. Primary consolidation occurs as water is squeezed out from the voids within the soil mass. Secondary consolidation results from adjustments in the internal structure of the soil mass under a sustained load. Whenever the possibility of settlement exists, care must be taken to choose a structural system and FOUNDATION capable of adapting. Fixed-end beams present a problem as they are incapable of rotating under uneven settlement loads and bend in response to the stress; simply supported beams, the ends of which act as hinges, will rotate slightly and remain straight. Special columns with jacking devices may then be used to level the beams. Floating foundations and PILES are often used to overcome the problems of building on yielding soils. See also SOIL MECHANICS.

Seurat \sœ̄-'rä\, **Georges (-Pierre)** (1859–1891) French painter. He entered the École des Beaux-Arts in 1878 and exhibited at the 1883 Salon, though he had already lost sympathy with its conservative policies. He studied scientific works in an effort to achieve scientifically the color effects that the Impressionists had pursued, and developed POINTILLISM, the technique of juxtaposing tiny brush strokes of contrasting colors to portray the play of light. Employing this method, he created huge compositions, including *Une Baignade, Asnières* (1883–84) and his masterpiece, *Sunday Afternoon on the Island of La Grande Jatte* (1884–86). As an aesthetic theorist, he explored the effects that could be achieved with the three primary colors and their complements.

Seuss, Dr. See Theodor GEISEL

Sevan \sə-'vän\ Lake, northern Armenia. It has an area of 525 sq mi (1,360 sq km). Lying at 6,250 ft (1,905 m) above sea level in a mountain-enclosed basin, it is Armenia's largest lake, and is in two connected parts: the smaller Maly Sevan and the Bolshoy Sevan. It is rich in fish. Several ancient Armenian churches lie along the shores.

Sevastopol *formerly* **Sebastopol** \sə-'vas-tə-ˌpōl\ Seaport city (pop., 1996 est.: 365,000) in the CRIMEA, southern Ukraine. In 1783 the Russians annexed the Crimea, and, near the ancient Greek colony of Chersonesus, they began construction of a naval base on Sevastopol Bay, an inlet of the BLACK SEA. It became a commercial port in the early 19th century. It was besieged by Anglo-French forces for 11 months (1854–55) during the CRIMEAN WAR, an ordeal chronicled by LEO TOLSTOY in his *Sevastopol Sketches.* The devastated town was later rebuilt, and it was the anti-Bolshevik White Army headquarters in the RUSSIAN CIVIL WAR (1918–20). In World War II it was destroyed after a months-long siege by the Germans, but it was again reconstructed. The chief base of the Russian Black Sea fleet since the early 19th century, it has extensive dockyard facilities and arsenals.

Seven, Group of Toronto-centered group of Canadian painters devoted to landscape painting (especially of northern Ontario subjects) and the creation of a national style. A number of future members met in 1913 while working as commercial artists in Toronto. The group adopted its name on the occasion of a group exhibition held in 1920. The original members included J.E.H. MacDonald (1873–1932), Lawren S. Harris, Arthur Lismer, F.H. Varley, Franklin Carmichael, Frank H. Johnston, and ALEXANDER YOUNG JACKSON. The group was particularly influential in the 1920s and '30s. In 1933 the name was changed to the Canadian Group of Painters.

Seven Cities of Cíbola See Seven Cities of CÍBOLA

Seven Days' Battles (June 25–July 1, 1862) AMERICAN CIVIL WAR battles that prevented Union capture of Richmond, Va. In a series of attacks and counterattacks by both sides, the Confederate army under ROBERT E. LEE forced Union troops under GEORGE B. MCCLELLAN to retreat from a position 4 mi (6 km) east of the Confederate capital to a new base on the James River. The Union failure to take Richmond and the withdrawal of the Army of the Potomac ended the Peninsular Campaign. Casualties were estimated at 16,000 for the Union and 20,000 for the Confederates.

Seven Oaks Massacre (1816) Destruction of a Canadian fur-trading settlement. Sixty MÉTIS directed by an agent of the NORTH WEST CO. set out to run provisions past the rival HUDSON'S BAY CO. settlement on the Red River. They were intercepted by the colony's governor and 25 sol-

S
T
U
V

diers at Seven Oaks, near the settlement. An argument grew into a fight in which the Métis killed 20 men, including the governor. They then threatened the remaining settlers with massacre, forcing them to abandon the colony. The settlement was restored the next year.

Seven Weeks' War *or* **Austro-Prussian War** (June–August 1866) Conflict between Prussia on one side and Austria, Bavaria, Saxony, Hanover, and minor German states on the other. A contrived dispute by Prussia's Otto von Bismarck over the Schleswig-Holstein Question resulted in the June 1866 Prussian attack on Austrian forces in Bohemia. The Prussian army, modernized and reorganized by Graf von Albrecht T. E. Roon and Helmuth von Moltke, decisively defeated Austria at the Battle of Königgrätz and elsewhere. By August the war was formally concluded by the Treaty of Prague, which assigned Schleswig-Holstein and other territories to Prussia. The effect of the war was to exclude Austria from Germany.

Seven Wonders of the World Preeminent architectural and sculptural achievements of antiquity, as listed by various Greco-Roman observers. Included on the best known list were the Pyramids of Giza (the oldest of the wonders and the only one substantially in existence today), the Hanging Gardens of Babylon (a series of landscaped rooftop terraces on a ziggurat, ascribed to either Nebuchadnezzar II or the semilegendary Queen Sammu-ramat), the Statue of Zeus at Olympia (a large gold-and-ivory figure of the god on his throne by Phidias), the Temple of Artemis at Ephesus (a temple, built in 356 BC, famous for its imposing size and the works of art that adorned it), the Mausoleum of Halicarnassus, the Colossus of Rhodes, and the Pharos of Alexandria (a lighthouse built c. 280 BC on the island of Pharos off Alexandria, said to have been more than 350 ft, or 110 m, high). These wonders inspired the compilation of many other lists of seven attractions, or "wonders," by later generations.

Seven Years' War (1756–63) Major European conflict between Austria and its allies France, Saxony, Sweden, and Russia on one side against Prussia and its allies Hanover and Britain on the other. The war arose out of Austria's attempt to win back the rich province of Silesia, taken by Prussia in the War of the Austrian Succession. Early victories by Frederick II the Great in Saxony and Bohemia (1756–58) were offset by a decisive Prussian defeat by Austria and Russia near Frankfurt (1759). After inconclusive fighting in 1760–61, Frederick concluded a peace with Russia (1762) and drove the Austrians from Silesia. The war also involved the overseas colonial struggles between Britain and France in North America (see French and Indian War) and in India. The European conflict was settled with the Treaty of Hubertusburg, by which Frederick confirmed Prussia's stature as a major European power.

Seventh-day Adventist See Adventist

Severn River \'se-vərn\ *Welsh* **Hafren** \'hä-vren\ *ancient* **Sabrina** River, eastern Wales and western England. Britain's longest river, it is 180 mi (290 km) long from its source to tidal waters. It rises in eastern central Wales and crosses the English border near Shrewsbury, continuing south to the Bristol Channel and the Atlantic Ocean.

Severus \sə-'vir-əs\, **Septimius** *in full* **Lucius Septimius Severus Pertinax** (AD 146–211) Roman emperor (193–211). He was in Europe in command of Rome's largest army when the emperor Publius Helvius Pertinax was murdered. Named emperor by his troops, he marched on Rome and took the throne. He effectively made Rome a military monarchy, giving the army a dominant role in government, ignoring the Senate, choosing officials from among the equites (see eques), and granting control of the courts to the Praetorian prefect. He annexed Mesopotamia, and he died attempting to subdue non-Roman Britain, having named his son Caracalla his successor, thereby founding a personal dynasty.

Severus Alexander *in full* **Marcus Aurelius Severus Alexander** ***orig.*** **Gessius Bassianus Alexianus** (AD 208–235) Roman emperor (222–35). At 14 he succeeded Elagabalus, who had been murdered at the prompting of Severus' mother and grandmother, both of whom held real power during his reign. A council of senators gave nominal ruling power to the Senate. Civil lawlessness reigned, and Severus' military incompetence led to defeat by the Persians. When he bought peace from the Alemanni tribes, his indignant soldiers murdered him and his mother.

Sevier \sə-'vir\, **John** (1745–1815) American frontiersman and politician. Born in New Market, Va., he moved to what is now eastern Tennessee in 1773, where he fought in Lord Dunmore's War. In the American Revolution he helped win the Battle of King's Mountain (1780). He participated in a settlers' revolt against North Carolina that formed the temporary state of Franklin (1784) and was elected its governor (1785–88). He served in the U.S. House of Representatives from North Carolina 1789–91. When Tennessee joined the Union, he served as governor 1796–1801 and 1803–9.

Sévigné \sā-vēn-'yā\, **Marquise de** *orig.* **Marie de Rabutin-Chantal** (1626–1696) French writer. Of old Burgundian nobility, she was well educated and moved in court society in Paris after her marriage in 1644. She was devoted to her children, and after her daughter married and moved to Provence she began writing letters to her, without literary intention, that recounted events, described people and details of daily life, and commented on many topics. The stories and gossip in the 1,700 letters of this correspondence, related in a natural, spontaneous tone, provide a vivid picture of the 17th-century French aristocracy.

Seville \sə-'vil\ *Spanish* **Sevilla** \sā-'bē-yä\ *ancient* **Hispalis** City (metro. area pop., 1995 est.: 720,000), capital of Andalusia autonomous community, Spain. Located on the Guadalquivir River, it is Spain's leading inland port and fourth-largest city. Originally an Iberian town, it prospered under the Romans in the 2nd century BC. In the 5th–8th century AD, it was the chief city in southern Spain under the Vandals and the Visigoths. In 711 it came under the Moors and was a cultural and commercial center until the 13th century, when Spanish Christians under Ferdinand III captured it. After 1492 it became the center of the Spanish colonial trade with the Americas. The French occupied the city 1808–12, and during the Spanish Civil War (1936–39) it was held by the Nationalists. It is one of Spain's main tourist centers, with historic mosques, cathedrals, and the 12th-century Alcázar Palace. It was the site of the Spanish-American Exposition in 1929 and the World Exposition in 1992. The University of Seville was founded in 1502.

Sèvres \'sevr^{ə}\, **Treaty of** (August 10, 1920) Pact at the end of World War I between the Allied Powers and the government of Ottoman Turkey, signed at Sèvres, France. It abolished the Ottoman empire, obliged Turkey to renounce rights over Arab Asia and North Africa, and provided for an independent Armenia, an autonomous Kurdistan, and Greek control over the Aegean islands commanding the Dardanelles. These provisions were rejected by the new Republic of Turkey, and the treaty was replaced in 1923 by the Treaty of Lausanne.

Sèvres porcelain \'sev-rə\ French hard-paste, or true, porcelain as well as soft-paste porcelain, made at the royal (now national) factory of Sèvres from 1756 until the present. On the decline of Meissen porcelain after 1756, Sèvres became the leading porcelain factory in Europe, thanks in large part to the patronage of Louis XV's mistress, Madame de Pompadour, who involved the foremost artists of the day (e.g., François Boucher and E.-M. Falconet) in the enterprise. Sèvres porcelain is famous for many styles and techniques, including white figures representing cupids, shepherdesses, or nymphs and the embellishment of grounds with minute patterns in gold.

Sèvres soft-paste porcelain jardiniere decorated with flowers and cupids painted in reserves on *rose Pompadour* ground, 1761; in the Victoria and Albert Museum, London.

BY COURTESY OF THE VICTORIA AND ALBERT MUSEUM, LONDON; PHOTOGRAPH, WILFRID WALTER—EB INC.

Sewa River \'sē-wə\ River, Sierra Leone. Formed by the junction of the Bagbe and Bafi rivers, it flows 150 mi (240 km) to join the Waanje River and form the Kittam, which empties into the Atlantic. The country's most important commercial river, it is extensively panned for diamonds.

sewage system Collection of pipes and mains, treatment works, and discharge lines (sewers) for the wastewater of a community. Early civilizations often built drainage systems in urban areas to handle storm runoff. The Romans constructed elaborate systems that also drained wastewater from the public baths. In the Middle Ages these systems fell into disrepair. As the populations of cities grew, disastrous epidemics of cholera and typhoid fever broke out, the result of ineffective separation of sewage and drinking water. In the mid-19th century the first steps were taken to treat wastewater. The concentration of population and the addition to sewage of manufacturing waste that occurred during the INDUSTRIAL REVOLUTION increased the need for effective sewage treatment. Sewer pipe is laid following street patterns, and access holes with metal covers allow periodic inspection and cleaning. Catch basins at street corners and along street gutters collect surface runoff of storm water and direct it to the storm sewers. Civil engineers determine the volume of sewage likely, the route of the system, and the slope of the pipe to ensure an even flow by gravity that will not leave solids behind. In flat regions, pumping stations are sometimes needed. Modern sewage systems include domestic and industrial sewers and storm sewers. Sewage treatment plants remove organic matter from waste water through a series of steps. As sewage enters the plant, large objects (such as wood and gravel) are screened out; grit and sand are then removed by settling or screening with finer mesh. The remaining sewage passes into primary sedimentation tanks where suspended solids (sludge) settle out. The remaining sewage is aerated and mixed with microorganisms to decompose organic matter. A secondary sedimentation tank allows any remaining solids to settle out; the remaining liquid effluent is discharged into a body of water. Sludge from the sedimentation tanks may be disposed of in landfills, dumped at sea, used as fertilizer, or decomposed further in heated tanks (digestion tanks) to produce methane gas to power the treatment plant.

Sewall \'sü-əl\, **Samuel** (1652–1730) American (British-born) colonial merchant and jurist. He emigrated to America as a boy and became manager of the New England colonial printing press (1681–84) and a member of the governor's council (1684–1725). In 1692 he was appointed to preside at the SALEM WITCH TRIALS. He later admitted the error of the court's decision to execute the 19 people convicted and stood alone to hear his confession read aloud. His three-volume *Diary* (published 1878–82) provides a view of New England Puritan life.

Sewanee See University of the SOUTH

Seward \'sü-ərd\, **William H(enry)** (1801–1872) U.S. politician. Born in Florida, N.Y., he served in the New York state senate 1830–34, and as governor 1839–43. In the U.S. Senate (1849–61), he was an antislavery leader in the Whig and Republican parties. A close adviser to Pres. ABRAHAM LINCOLN, he served as U.S. secretary of state 1861–69. He helped prevent foreign recognition of the Confederacy and obtained settlement in the TRENT AFFAIR. In 1865 he was stabbed by a co-conspirator of JOHN WILKES BOOTH, but recovered. He is best remembered for successfully negotiating the ALASKA PURCHASE (1867), which critics called Seward's Folly.

Seward Peninsula \'sü-ərd\ Peninsula, western Alaska. Its tip, Cape Prince of Wales, on the Bering Strait, is the most westerly point of North America. It is about 180 mi (290 km) long and 130 mi (208 km) wide; its highest peak is 4,720 ft (1,439 m) tall, in the Kigluaik Mountains. The city of NOME is on its southern coast.

Sewell \'sü-əl\, **Anna** (1820–1878) British writer. She was introduced to writing by her mother, the author of juvenile best-sellers, and her concern for the humane treatment of horses began early in life. Confined to her house as an invalid, she spent her last years writing the children's classic *Black Beauty* (1877), a fictional autobiography of a gentle, highbred horse. It had a strong moral purpose and is said to have been instrumental in abolishing the cruel practice of using the checkrein.

sewing machine Machine for stitching material (such as cloth or leather), usually having a NEEDLE and SHUTTLE to carry THREAD and powered by treadle or electricity. Invented by ELIAS HOWE in 1846 and successfully manufactured by Howe and ISAAC MERRITT SINGER, it became the first widely distributed mechanical home appliance and has also been an important industrial machine. Modern sewing machines are usually powered by an electric motor, but the foot-treadle machine is still in wide use in much of the world.

sex Sum of features by which a member of a plant or animal species can be placed into one of two complementary reproductive groups, male or female. Males and females may or may not have apparent structural differences, but they always have functional, hormonal, and chromosomal differences. Patterns of behavior, sometimes elaborate, may also distinguish the sexes in some species. See also REPRODUCTIVE BEHAVIOR.

sex chromosome Either of a pair of CHROMOSOMES that determine whether an individual is male or female. The sex chromosomes of mammals are designated X and Y; in humans, they constitute one pair of the total 23 pairs of chromosomes. Individuals possessing two X chromosomes (XX) are female; those having one X and one Y chromosome (XY) are male. The X chromosome is larger and carries more genetic information than the Y. Traits controlled only by genes found on the X chromosome (e.g., hemophilia, red-green color blindness) are said to be sex-linked. Sex-linked traits occur far more frequently in males than in females, since a male inheriting an allele for a recessive (see RECESSIVENESS) trait on the X chromosome lacks a corresponding allele on the Y chromosome that might counteract its effects. Several disorders are associated with an abnormal number of sex chromosomes, including TURNER'S SYNDROME and KLINEFELTER'S SYNDROME.

sex hormone Organic compound produced by the sex glands (OVARIES and TESTES) or other organ that has an effect on the sexual features of an organism. Like many other kinds of HORMONES, sex hormones may be artificially synthesized. See also ANDROGEN, ESTROGEN, PROGESTERONE.

sex linkage See LINKAGE GROUP

sextant Instrument for determining the ANGLE between the horizon and a celestial body such as the sun, the moon, or a star, used in celestial NAVIGATION to determine LATITUDE AND LONGITUDE. It consists of a metal arc, marked in degrees, and a movable radial arm pivoted at the center of the arc's circle. A TELESCOPE, mounted rigidly to the framework, is lined up with the horizon. The radial arm, on which a mirror is mounted, is moved until the star is reflected into a half-silvered mirror in line with the telescope and appears, through the telescope, to coincide with the horizon. The angular distance of the star above the horizon is then read from the graduated arc of the sextant. From this angle and the exact time of day (e.g., noon) as registered by a CHRONOMETER, the latitude can be determined (within a few hundred meters) by means of published tables. Invented in 1731, the sextant replaced the octant and became an essential tool of navigation.

Sexton, Anne *orig.* **Anne Gray Harvey** (1928–1974) U.S. poet. Born in Newton, Mass., she worked as a model, librarian, and teacher. Her first book of poetry, *To Bedlam and Part Way Back* (1960), examines her mental breakdowns and subsequent recoveries with confessional intensity. She continued probing her personal life in *All My Pretty Ones* (1962) and *Live or Die* (1966, Pulitzer Prize). Her other works include the nonfiction collection *No Evil Star* (1985). She died a suicide. Several volumes of poetry were published posthumously.

sexual dysfunction Inability to experience arousal or achieve sexual satisfaction under ordinary circumstances, as a result of psychological or physiological problems. The most common sexual dysfunctions have traditionally been referred to as impotence (applied to males) and frigidity (females), but these terms have gradually been replaced by more specific terms. Most sexual dysfunctions can be overcome through use of COUNSELING, PSYCHOTHERAPY, or drug therapy.

sexual harassment Unsolicited verbal or physical behavior of a sexual nature. Sexual harassment today may embrace any sexually motivated behavior considered offensive by the recipient. Legal recourse is available in cases that occur in the workplace, though it is very difficult to obtain convictions. In 1994 the U.S. Supreme Court ruled that behavior can be considered sexual harassment and an abridgment of an individual's civil rights if it creates a hostile and abusive environment.

sexual intercourse *or* **coitus** *or* **copulation** Act in which the male reproductive organ enters the female reproductive tract (see REPRODUCTIVE SYSTEM). Various sexual activities (foreplay) lead to physiological changes that progress to orgasm (climax) and resolution (see SEXUAL RESPONSE). If it is completed, SEMEN passes from the male's into the female's body. If conditions favor FERTILIZATION, a SPERM joins with an EGG and PREGNANCY begins (see FERTILITY, REPRODUCTION); CONTRACEPTION can prevent this. Intercourse with an unwilling female is RAPE. See also REPRODUCTIVE BEHAVIOR, SAFE SEX, human SEXUALITY, SEXUALLY TRANSMITTED DISEASE.

sexual response Four-stage series of physiological reactions to sexual stimulation. Persons do not necessarily progress through all four stages, nor need two persons pass through them simultaneously. Self-stimulation is called MASTURBATION; if two persons stimulate each other, it is mutual masturbation; if the two are of opposite sex, sexual response may lead to SEXUAL INTERCOURSE. In excitement, muscles tense and heart rate increases; in males, the PENIS becomes erect; in females, the inner VAGINA widens, its walls become moist, and the clitoris enlarges. In the plateau stage, breathing accelerates and muscles continue tensing; the TESTES and glans of the penis enlarge; the outer vagina contracts and the clitoris retracts. At orgasm the muscle tension is quickly released; the penis contracts repeatedly, ejaculating SEMEN; the vagina contracts regularly. In resolution, the genitals of both return to their pre-arousal condition; men cannot become aroused for some minutes or hours; women can quickly become aroused again.

sexuality, human Tendencies and behavior of human beings with regard to any activity that causes or is otherwise associated with sexual arousal. It is strongly influenced by the genetically inherited SEXUAL RESPONSE patterns that ensure reproduction (see REPRODUCTIVE BEHAVIOR), societal attitudes toward sex, and each individual's upbringing. Physiology sets only very broad limits on human sexuality; most of the enormous variation found among humans results from learning and conditioning. What is deviant in one society may be normal in another. Sexuality covers gender identity, sexual orientation, and actual practices, as well as one's acceptance of these aspects of one's personality, which may be more important than their specifics. See also HOMOSEXUALITY, TRANSSEXUALISM.

sexually transmitted disease (STD) Disease transmitted primarily by direct sexual contact. STDs usually affect the genitals and REPRODUCTIVE and URINARY systems but can be spread to the mouth or rectum by oral or anal sex. In later stages they may attack other organs and systems. The best known are SYPHILIS, GONORRHEA, AIDS, and HERPES SIMPLEX type II. Yeast infections (see CANDIDA) produce a thick, whitish vaginal discharge and genital irritation and itch in women and sometimes irritation of the penis in men. Crab-louse infestation (see human LOUSE) can also be considered an STD. The incidence of STDs has been affected by such factors as ANTIBIOTICS, BIRTH-CONTROL methods, and sexual behavior. See also CHLAMYDIA, HEPATITIS, PELVIC INFLAMMATORY DISEASE, TRICHOMONAD, WART.

Seybouse River \sā-'büz\ River, northeastern Algeria. It rises at the eastern edge of the Sétif plains, rushes through a narrow gorge in Mount Nador, and flows through a tree-lined valley to the Mediterranean Sea south of ANNABA. Unnavigable except for its estuary, it is 145 mi (232 km) long.

Seychelles \sā-'shel, sā-'shelz\ *officially* **Republic of Seychelles** Island republic, western Indian Ocean. Area: 175 sq mi (453 sq km). Population (1997 est.): 77,000. Capital: VICTORIA. The mixed population is of French, black, and Asian ancestry. Languages: Creole, English, French. Religion: Roman Catholicism. Currency: Seychelles rupee. Located east of northeastern Tanzania, the Seychelles are composed of two main island groups: the Mahé group of 40 central mountainous islands, and a second group of over 70 outlying, flat, coralline islands. The country's developing economy is heavily dependent on tourism. Exports include fish, copra, and cinnamon. It is a republic with one legislative house; its head of state and government is the president. The first recorded landing on the uninhabited Seychelles was made in 1609 by an expedition of the British EAST INDIA CO. The archipelago was claimed by the French in 1756 and surrendered to the British in 1810. In 1903 the Seychelles became a British crown colony, and a republic within the COMMONWEALTH in 1976. A one-party socialist state since 1979, the Seychelles began moving toward democracy in the 1990s; it adopted a new constitution in 1993. See map opposite.

Seymour, Jane (1509?–1537) Third wife of HENRY VIII of England. A lady-in-waiting to Henry's wives CATHERINE OF ARAGON and ANNE BOLEYN, she first attracted Henry's attention c. 1535 but refused to be his mistress. This probably hastened Boleyn's downfall and execution (1536), after which Seymour and Henry were married privately. She restored Henry's daughter Mary (later MARY I) to his favor, and gave birth to his only male heir, the future EDWARD VI, but died 12 days later, to Henry's genuine sorrow.

Seyss-Inquart \'zīs-'iŋk-ˌvärt\, **Arthur** (1892–1946) Austrian Nazi leader. A leader of the moderate faction of the Austrian Nazis, he served on the federal council of state (1937–38). In response to German pressure, he was named minister of interior and security and then replaced KURT VON SCHUSCHNIGG as chancellor (1938). He welcomed the ANSCHLUSS by Germany and became governor of the Austrian administration (1938–39). In World War II he was German high commissioner of the Netherlands (1940–45) and carried out the Nazi policy against Dutch Jews. He was tried at the NUREMBERG TRIALS and executed as a war criminal.

Sezession \zā-tses-'yōn\ Name for several groups of progressive artists that broke away from established and conservative artists' organizations in Austria and Germany. The first secession group was formed in Munich in 1892. It was followed by the Berlin Sezession movement, formed by Max Liebermann (1847–1935) in 1892, which included such artists as LOVIS CORINTH. The most famous of the groups, formed in Vienna in 1897 by GUSTAV KLIMT, favored a highly ornamental ART NOUVEAU style over the prevailing academicism. Shortly thereafter, murals created by Klimt for the ceiling of the University of Vienna auditorium were rejected as scandalous because of their erotic symbolism. The Sezession movement influenced such artists and architects as EGON SCHIELE and JOSEF HOFFMANN. See also PHOTO-SECESSION.

Sfax \'sfaks\ *or* **Safaqis** \sə-'fä-kis\ Port city (pop., 1994: 231,000), eastern central Tunisia. Built on the site of two ancient settlements, the city grew as an Islamic trading center. It was occupied by the Normans in the 12th century and the Spanish in the 16th century, and later served as a stronghold of the BARBARY COAST pirates. The town was bombarded by the French in 1881 prior to their occupation of Tunisia and again in World War II, when it was a base for German forces until taken by the British in 1943. Tunisia's second-largest city, it is a transportation hub and a major fishing port.

Sforim, Mendele Moykher See MENDELE MOYKHER SFORIM

Sforza \'sfȯrt-sä\, **Carlo, Conte (Count)** (1873–1952) Italian diplomat. He entered the diplomatic service in 1896 and served in embassies worldwide. He was minister for foreign affairs 1920–21, and ambassador to France in 1922, then resigned after refusing to serve under BENITO MUSSOLINI. A strong anti-Fascist, he lived in voluntary exile in Belgium until 1939 and in the U.S. (1940–43). He returned to Italy to serve in various government posts, including minister of foreign affairs (1947–51).

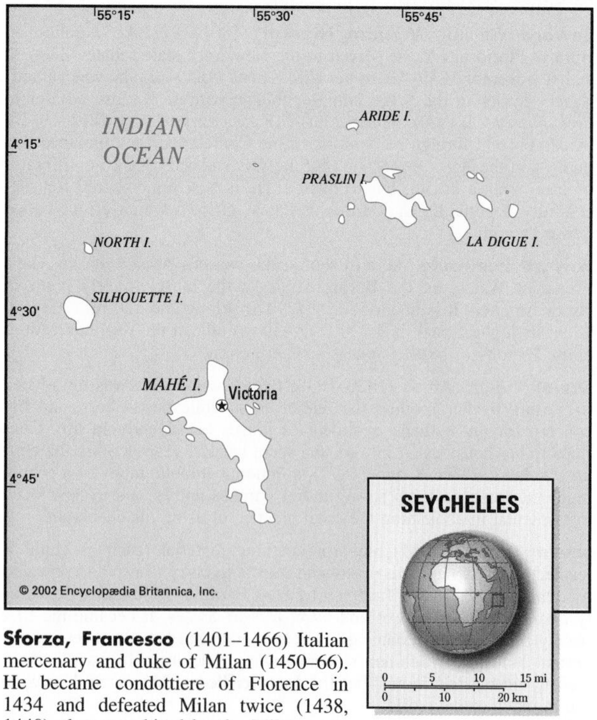

Sforza, Francesco (1401–1466) Italian mercenary and duke of Milan (1450–66). He became condottiere of Florence in 1434 and defeated Milan twice (1438, 1440), then was hired by the Milanese to serve as captain general in their struggle to found a republic (1447). He later blockaded the city and seized control, becoming duke of Milan in 1450, and he allied with Florence to secure the Peace of LODI (1454). See also SFORZA FAMILY.

Sforza, Ludovico (1452–1508) Regent (1480–94) and duke of Milan (1494–98). The second son of FRANCESCO SFORZA, he was known as "the Moor" because of his dark complexion and black hair. He plotted to take over as regent for his young nephew. He made Milan supreme among the Italian states, and his patronage of scholars and artists such as LEONARDO DA VINCI made his court renowned in Europe. He bribed MAXIMILIAN I to declare him duke of Milan and fought to expel the French from Italy. After LOUIS XII conquered Milan (1498), Ludovico tried unsuccessfully to retake it (1500); he was captured and died in prison.

Sforza family Italian family that ruled Milan 1450–1535. The family began with the prosperous farmer and later condottiere leader Muzio Attendolo (1369–1424), who was given the nickname Sforza ("Force"). His illegitimate son Francesco SFORZA became duke of Milan in 1450. Galeazzo Maria Sforza (1444–1476) succeeded his father in 1466 and, though a despotic ruler, he introduced the cultivation of rice, built canals and encouraged commerce, and was a patron of the arts; he was assassinated by conspirators who vainly hoped to provoke a popular uprising. Gian Galeazzo Sforza (1469–1494) succeeded his father in 1476 under the regency of his mother and uncle, Ludovico SFORZA, who usurped the government in 1481 and established Milan's supremacy. After Ludovico was driven from power by LOUIS XII of France in 1499, his son Massimiliano Sforza (1493–1530) returned to rule briefly (1513–16) before yielding the duchy to France. Another son, Francesco Maria Sforza (1495–1535), returned after the French defeat to rule from 1522, until his death without heirs ended the ducal line in 1535. The duchy then passed to CHARLES V and the Habsburgs. Descendants of Sforza Secondo (an illegitimate son of Francesco Sforza) became the counts Sforza and included the diplomat CARLO, CONTE SFORZA.

SGML *in full* **Standard Generalized Markup Language** MARKUP LANGUAGE for organizing and tagging elements of a document, including headings, paragraphs, tables, and graphics. The elements are marked according to their meaning and relationship to other elements rather than to the format of their presentation. The tagged elements can then be formatted in different ways according to the unique rules for different applications. Readable by both humans and computer programs, SGML is usable in a wide range of applications, including print publishing, CD-ROMs, and database systems. Generic coding of electronic manuscripts was first proposed in the late 1960s; in 1969 an IBM team developed GML, which was adopted by the U.S. Internal Revenue Service and Department of Defense. In the late 1970s the American National Standards Institute (ANSI) established a committee to create SGML from GML; it was accepted by the International Organization for Standards in 1986. See also HTML, XML.

Shaanxi \'shän-'shē\ *or* **Shensi** \'shen-'sē\ Province (pop., 2000 est.: 36,050,000), eastern central China. Its capital is XI'AN. It has three distinct natural regions: the mountainous southern region, the central WEI RIVER valley, and the northern upland plateau. The valley is especially vulnerable to earthquakes. Its northern parts were some of the earliest settled in China, and the remains of ancient construction projects found there include part of the GREAT WALL. From 221 BC until the Tang dynasty, it was wealthy, and the center of much political activity. As its irrigation system deteriorated the area declined. In the 13th century, under the MONGOLS, it assumed its present form as a province. MAO ZEDONG's LONG MARCH ended here in 1935; it came under Communist control in 1937. Its ancient irrigation system has been rehabilitated in modern times, and the region is again a rich agricultural region. Crops include corn, winter wheat, fruits, tobacco, and cotton.

Shabbetai Tzevi \'shä-bə-ˌtī-tsə-'vē\ (1626–1676) False Jewish MESSIAH. Born in Smyrna, he studied the mystical learning of the Kabbala and proclaimed himself the messiah at 22. He traveled around the Levant, gaining both followers and enemies. With the support of powerful religious and political figures, his movement spread to parts of Europe and North Africa. In 1666, the year he was prophesied to bring about the restoration of Israel, he was imprisoned by the Ottoman sultan and, under threat of torture, converted to Islam. His following largely fell away, though some remained faithful to him and strove to reconcile his claims with his seeming betrayal of Judaism.

Shabeelle River \sha-'be-lē\ *in Ethiopia* **Shebele River** \she-'be-lē\ River, eastern Africa. It rises in the Ethiopian Highlands and flows southeast through the arid OGADEN Plateau. After crossing into Somalia, it approaches the coast near MOGADISHU, then turns southwest to flow for some 200 mi (322 km) parallel with the coast. Its total length is 1,250 mi (2,011 km). During rainy periods in Ethiopia, it joins the JUBBA RIVER and the combined waters then flow to the Indian Ocean. In drier years it disappears in a series of marshes and sand flats northeast of the Jubba confluence.

Shackleton, Ernest Henry *later* **Sir Ernest** (1874–1922) British explorer. In 1901 he joined ROBERT FALCON SCOTT's expedition to the Antarctic. He returned to Antarctica in 1908 and led a sledging party to within 97 mi (156 km) of the pole. In 1914 he led the British Trans-Antarctic Expedition, which planned to cross Antarctica via the South Pole. His expedition ship *Endurance* was caught in pack ice and drifted for 10 months before being crushed. Shackleton and his crew drifted on ice floes for another five months until they reached Elephant Island. He and five others sailed 800 mi (1,300 km) to South Georgia Island to get help, then he led four relief expeditions to rescue his men. He died on South Georgia at the outset of another Antarctic expedition.

shad Any of several saltwater food fishes of the HERRING family (Clupeidae) that swim up rivers to spawn. Shad eggs (roe) are a delicacy in the U.S. Adult shad are toothless. The lower jaw of shad in the genus *Alosa* fits into a notch at the tip of the upper jaw. The American shad *(A. sapidissima),* an Atlantic fish introduced into the Pacific, is a migratory plankton eater and a good game fish. The Allis (or Allice) shad *(A. alosa)* of Europe is about 30 in. (75 cm) long and weighs about 8 lbs (3.6 kg). See also WHITEFISH.

Shadwell, Thomas (1642?–1692) English dramatist. One of the court wits after the Restoration (1660), he wrote 18 plays, of which his broad comedies of manners are the best remembered. *Epsom-Wells* (1672), his greatest success, played for nearly half a century. After his friendship with JOHN DRYDEN ended over differences in politics and dramatic techniques, both men produced satires attacking the other, Dryden's (including the devastating *MacFlecknoe*), being the more memorable. In 1688 Shadwell succeeded Dryden as poet laureate and historiographer royal.

Shaffer, Peter (Levin) (born 1926) British playwright. He first won notice for his comedy *Five Finger Exercise* (1958) and his epic tragedy *The Royal Hunt of the Sun* (1964). His *Equus* (1973, Tony award; film, 1977) was a hit in London and New York. He was also acclaimed for *Amadeus* (1979), which treated A. SALIERI's one-sided rivalry with W.A. MOZART, and adapted the play for film (1984, Academy Award). His later plays include *Yonadab* (1985), *Lettice and Lovage* (1988), and *The Gift of the Gorgon* (1992).

Shafii \'sha-fi-ˌē\, **Abu Abd Allah (Muhammad ibn Idris) al-** (767–820) Muslim legal scholar and founder of the Shafiiya school of law. A distant relative of MUHAMMAD, he was brought up in poverty in Mecca and studied with Islamic scholars across Arabia and the Levant. His great contribution was the creation of a synthesis of Islamic legal thought that put into coherent form many familiar but unsystematized ideas. He dealt primarily with the identification of the sources of Islamic law and their application to contemporary events. His book the *Risala* (c. 817) earned him the title "father of Muslim jurisprudence."

shaft seal See OIL SEAL

Shaftesbury, 1st Earl of *orig.* **Anthony Ashley Cooper** (1621–1683) English politician. He served in the English Civil War, fighting first for the king (1643), then for Parliament (1644). He was appointed by OLIVER CROMWELL to the council of state (1653–54, 1659) and also served in Parliament (1654–60). One of 12 commissioners sent to invite CHARLES II to return to England, he was appointed to Charles's privy council (1660) and served as chancellor of the exchequer (1661–72) and lord chancellor (1672–73). As head of the Council of Trade and Foreign Plantations (1672–74) he drew up a constitution for the North American province of Carolina, aided by his protégé JOHN LOCKE. Dismissed by Charles for supporting the anti-Catholic TEST ACT and opposing the marriage of Charles's brother James (later JAMES II) to another Catholic, Shaftesbury became a leader of the WHIG opposition. He exploited the political chaos caused by TITUS OATES to consolidate his parliamentary power and tried unsuccessfully to pass the Exclusion Bill, to keep James from the throne. In 1681 Charles dissolved the Parliament; Shaftesbury was arrested and tried for treason but acquitted. In 1682 he fled to Holland, where he died.

Shaftesbury, 3rd Earl of *orig.* **Anthony Ashley Cooper** (1671–1713) English politician and philosopher. Grandson of the 1st earl of SHAFTESBURY, he received his early education from JOHN LOCKE. He entered Parliament in 1695; succeeding to his title in 1699, he served three years in the House of Lords. His numerous philosophical essays were influenced by NEOPLATONISM; published as *Characteristicks of Men, Manners, Opinions, Times* (1711), they became the chief source of English DEISM and influenced such writers as ALEXANDER POPE, SAMUEL TAYLOR COLERIDGE, and IMMANUEL KANT.

Shaftesbury, 7th Earl of *orig.* **Anthony Ashley Cooper** (1801–1885) English politician and social reformer. When his father succeeded to the earldom in 1811, Cooper became Lord Ashley. As a member of Parliament (1826–51), he opposed the REFORM BILL OF 1832 but supported Catholic emancipation and repeal of the CORN LAWS. From 1833 he led the factory reform movement in Parliament and effected passage of the Mines Act (1842) and the Ten Hours Act (1847), known as Lord Ashley's Act, which shortened the working day in textile mills. As president of the Ragged Schools Union (1843–83), he promoted the free education of destitute children. Succeeding to his father's title in 1851, he continued his work as one of the most effective social reformers of 19th-century England. He also led the evangelical movement within the Church of England and financially supported several missionary societies.

Shah Jahan \'shä-jə-'hän\ (1592–1666) Mughal emperor of India (1628–58). During his father JAHANGIR's reign, he was part of the clique that dominated MUGHAL-DYNASTY politics. After Jahangir's death, he garnered enough support to proclaim himself emperor. His reign was notable for its successes against the Deccan states. Though attempts to reconquer lost territory almost bankrupted the empire, his reign marked the zenith of Mughal court splendor. Of his great architectural undertakings (including a fortress-palace built when he transferred the capital from Agra to Delhi), the most famous is the TAJ MAHAL. Though a more orthodox Muslim than his father, he was less orthodox than his son and successor, AURANGZEB, and he was relatively tolerant of his Hindu subjects.

Shah of Iran See M. R. Shah PAHLAVI, R. Shah PAHLAVI

Shahn, Ben(jamin) (1898–1969) U.S. (Lithuanian-born) painter and graphic artist. His family emigrated to New York in 1906. As a youth he worked as a lithographer's apprentice; he later attended New York University and the National Academy of Design. In 1931–33 he achieved fame with a series of gouache paintings inspired by the Sacco-Vanzetti case, combining realism and abstraction in the service of sharp sociopolitical comment. In 1933 he assisted DIEGO RIVERA with his Rockefeller Center mural and worked for the PUBLIC WORKS OF ART PROJECT. In 1935–38 he depicted rural poverty as an artist and photographer for the Farm Security Administration. After World War II he concentrated on easel painting, poster design, and book illustration.

Ben Shahn, 1966.

Shaivism *or* **Saivism** \'shī-ˌvi-zəm\ One of three main forms of modern HINDUISM, centered on the worship of SHIVA. The earliest of the cults devoted to Shiva date from the 4th century BC. Texts written by devotees of Shiva in the 3rd century AD are the basis of TANTRA in Hinduism and other Indian religions. Today Shaivism includes diverse movements, both religious and secular, all of which take Shiva as the supreme and all-powerful deity and teacher, and view gaining the nature of Shiva as the ultimate goal of existence. This is believed to be brought about by the performance of complex ritual. See also SHAKTISM, VAISHNAVISM.

Shaka \'shä-kə\ (1787?–1828) ZULU chief (1816–28), founder of southern Africa's Zulu Empire. Raised as an outcast because his parents' marriage violated Zulu custom, Shaka proved himself a brilliant warrior and by 1816 had established himself as head of the Zulu. He worked to improve weapons systems, institute a regimental system, and develop standard tactics, ruling his warriors with an iron hand. He attacked and subjugated tribes of coastal ZULULAND, contributing to the MFECANE disturbances of the 1820s. After his mother's death in 1827, he became psychotic and began terrifying and killing his own people; he was murdered by his two half brothers.

Shaka, lithograph by W. Bagg, 1836.

Shaker Member of the United Society of Believers in Christ's Second Appearing, a celibate millenarian sect that established communal settlements in the U.S. in the 18th century. Derived from a branch of radical English Quakers (see Society of FRIENDS), the movement was brought to the U.S. in 1774 by ANN LEE, an illiterate textile worker whose followers accepted her as the second incarnation of Christ. The movement spread throughout New England from its base near Albany, N.Y., and later into Kentucky, Ohio, and Indiana, eventually establishing 19 communities. Communities held property in common, observed celibacy, and pursued a life of productive labor. Though sometimes persecuted for their pacifism and for bizarre beliefs falsely attributed to them, Shakers won admiration for their model farms and orderly, prosperous communities. Their talent for simple, functional design led to numerous inventions and innovations (see SHAKER FURNITURE). The movement reached its height in the 1840s and thereafter gradually declined; today the lone remaining community is at Canterbury, N.H.

Shaker furniture Furniture designed for the religious colonies of SHAKERS founded in the U.S. in the last quarter of the 18th century. The Shakers' designs reflected their beliefs that good craftsmanship was in itself an act of prayer and that form should follow function, an attitude that anticipated the concept of FUNCTIONALISM a century later. Constructed of pine or other inexpensive wood, each item was fashioned solely to serve its intended use and was devoid of decoration. Interest in Shaker furniture and other Shaker crafts revived in the 20th century, after most Shaker colonies had dissolved, and imitations are now widely produced.

Shakespeare, William (1564–1616) British poet and playwright, often considered the greatest writer in world literature. He spent his early life in Stratford-upon-Avon, receiving at most a grammar-school education, and at 18 he married a local woman, Anne Hathaway. By 1594 he was apparently a rising playwright in London and an actor in a leading theater company, the Lord CHAMBERLAIN'S (LATER KING'S) MEN; the company performed at the GLOBE THEATRE from 1599. The order in which his plays were written and performed is highly uncertain. His earliest plays seem to date from1590 to the mid-1590s and include the comedies *Love's Labour's Lost*, *The Comedy of Errors*, *The Taming of the Shrew*, and *A Midsummer Night's Dream*; history plays based on the lives of the English kings, including *Henry VI*, *Richard III*, and *Richard II*; and the tragedy *Romeo and Juliet*. The plays apparently written between 1596 and 1600 are mostly comedies, including *The Merchant of Venice*, *The Merry Wives of Windsor*, *Much Ado About Nothing*, and *As You Like It*, and histories, including *Henry IV*, *Henry V*, and *Julius Caesar*. Between 1600 and 1607 he may have written the comedies *Twelfth Night*, *All's Well That Ends Well*, and *Measure for Measure*, as well as the great tragedies *Hamlet* (probably begun in 1599), *Othello*, *Macbeth*, and *King Lear*, which mark the summit of his art. Among his later works (about 1607 to 1614) are the tragedies *Antony and Cleopatra*, *Coriolanus*, and *Timon of Athens*, as well as the fantastical romances *The Winter's Tale* and *The Tempest*. Shakespeare's plays, all of them written largely in iambic pentameter verse, are marked by extraordinary poetry, vivid, subtle, and complex characterizations, and a highly inventive use of English. His 154 sonnets, published in 1609 but apparently written mostly in the 1590s, often express strong feeling within an exquisitely controlled form. Shakespeare retired to Stratford before 1610 and lived as a country gentleman until his death. The first collected edition of his plays, or First Folio, was published in 1623. As with most writers of the time, little is known about his life and work, and other writers, particularly the 17th Earl of OXFORD, have frequently been proposed as the actual authors of his plays and poems.

shakti *or* **sakti** \'shək-tē\ In HINDUISM, the "creative energy" inherent in and proceeding from God. It is exemplified by the female principle, the female reproductive organs, or the female goddess Shakti, wife of SHIVA. As energy, shakti is viewed as the merging of powers emanating from male gods, and is possessed by each person. In tantric Hinduism, shakti is associated with the lowest of the CHAKRAS, lying dormant within the body as a coiled serpent (KUNDALINI) that must be aroused to reach spiritual liberation by uniting with Shiva at the top of the head. See also SHAKTISM.

Shaktism *or* **Saktism** \'shək-ˌti-zəm\ Worship of the supreme Hindu goddess Shakti (see SHAKTI). Together with VAISHNAVISM and SHAIVISM, it is one of the major forms of HINDUISM practiced today. Particularly prominent in the Bengal and Assam, Shaktism takes various forms depending on conceptions of Shakti. In popular worship she has many names, and some scholars consider most female deities in Hinduism to be various manifestations of her. Shakti is worshiped and cultivated as a power that can lead to spiritual liberation. Shaktism is inseparably related to the system of practices for the purification of mind and body that are grouped under tantric Hinduism.

shakuhachi \ˌshä-kü-'hä-chē\ Japanese bamboo flute. Its notes are produced by blowing across the open upper end, resulting in a distinctively breathy tone. It has five fingerholes. The shakuhachi is of great antiquity; it has been widely played as a solo instrument and in small ensembles, especially with the KOTO and samisen.

shale Any of a group of fine-grained, laminated SEDIMENTARY ROCKS consisting of silt- and clay-sized particles. Shale constitutes roughly 60% of the sedimentary rock in the earth's crust. Shales are commercially important, particularly in the ceramics industry. They are a valuable raw material for tile, brick, and pottery and constitute a major source of alumina for portland cement. In addition, advances in recovery methods may one day make OIL SHALE a practical source for liquid petroleum.

shale oil Synthetic crude oil that is extracted from OIL SHALE by pyrolysis, or destructive distillation. The oil obtained from oil shale cannot be refined by the methods that have been developed for crude oil, however, because shale oil is low in hydrogen and contains large amounts of nitrogen and sulfur compounds. To be made usable, shale oil must be hydrogenated and then chemically treated to remove the nitrogen and sulfur, a process too expensive to make shale oil commercially competitive with crude oil. See also KEROGEN, PETROLEUM.

shallot Mildly aromatic herbaceous plant *(Allium ascalonicum)* of the LILY FAMILY, probably of Asiatic origin, used to flavor foods. Closely related to the ONION and GARLIC, the shallot is a hardy perennial with short, small, cylindrical, and hollow leaves; lavender to red flowers in a compact umbel; and small, elongated, angular BULBS. Much like garlic, the bulbs develop in clusters on a common base. The leaves are sometimes eaten when green. The so-called shallot marketed extensively as green spring onions is in fact a form of onion.

shaman \'shä-mən\ Person who uses MAGIC to cure the sick, divine the unknown, or control events. Shamanism is classically associated with certain Arctic and Central Asian peoples, but today the term is applied to analogous religious and quasi-religious systems throughout the world. As MEDICINE MAN and priest, the shaman cures illnesses, directs communal sacrifices, and escorts the SOULS of the dead to the other world. He operates by using techniques of ecstasy, the power to leave his body at will during a trancelike state. In cultures where shamanism occurs, sickness is usually thought of as soul loss; it is thus the shaman's task to enter the spirit world, capture the soul, and reintegrate it in the body. A person becomes a shaman either by inheritance or by self-election. See also ANIMISM.

Shamash \'shä-ˌmäsh\ In MESOPOTAMIAN RELIGION, the god of the sun, who, with his father, SIN, and the goddess ISHTAR, was part of an astral triad of divinities. As the solar god, Shamash was the heroic conqueror of night and death, and he became known as the god of justice and equity. He was said to have presented the Code of HAMMURABI to the Babylonian king. At night he served as judge of the underworld. The chief centers of his cult were at LARSA and SIPPAR.

Shamil *or* **Shamyl** \'shä-ˌmēl\ (1797?–1871) Leader of Muslim Dagestan and Chechen mountaineers. In 1830 he joined a Sufi sect that had become involved in a holy war against the Russians for Dagestan, formerly part of northern Iran but occupied by the Russians from 1813. He eventually became IMAM of Dagestan and established an independent republic (1834), then led successive raids against the Russians in the Caucasus for 25 years. Determined to suppress him, the Russians attacked from all sides, compelling his surrender in 1859 and effectively ending Caucasian resistance to Russian subjugation.

Shamir \shə-'mēr\, **Yitzhak** *orig.* **Yitzhak Jazernicki** (born 1915) Polish-Israeli statesman. He emigrated in 1935 to Palestine, where he helped found the Israel Freedom Fighters, later known as the Stern Gang. Twice arrested by British authorities (1941, 1946), he twice escaped and eventually found asylum in France. After Israel achieved independence, he served as a Mossad secret-service operative until 1965. He was speaker of the Knesset (1977–80) and later foreign minister under MENACHEM BEGIN (1980–83). He became prime minister in 1983; in 1984 an indecisive election led to his sharing power with the Labour Party leader SHIMON PERES, and Shamir acted as prime minister for the six years beginning in 1986, which included another indecisive election in 1988 and the formation of a coalition government in 1990, but lost power in 1992.

Shamun, Camille See Camille CHAMOUN

Shan *Shan* **Tai** Southeast Asian people who live primarily in eastern and northwestern Myanmar and also in Yunnan province, China. The Shan are the largest minority group in Myanmar, numbering more than 4 million. They live mainly in the valleys and plains on the Shan Plateau, where they grow rice or practice slash-and-burn agriculture. They are THERAVADA Buddhists and have their own written language and literature. They dominated much of Myanmar in the 13th–16th century; in recent decades they have been at odds with the national government over the issue of local autonomy. See also TAI.

Shandong *or* **Shantung** *or* **Shan-tung** \'shän-'dùŋ\ Coastal province (pop., 2000 est.: 90,790,000), northeastern China. It contains the SHANDONG PENINSULA and an inland zone that includes a fertile, intensely cultivated area that forms part of the HUANG HE (Yellow River) basin. The peninsula has been occupied since the 3rd millennium BC, and by the 8th century BC it had become a center of political and military activity. It became northern China's leading maritime center in the 3rd century AD and retained that position for centuries. In the 19th century devastating floods resulted in substantial emigration. It came under German, British, and Japanese influence in the late 19th century. The Japanese occupied it 1937–45; it came under communist control in 1948. Its products include wheat, corn, iron ore, gold, fish, and silk. CONFUCIUS and MENCIUS were born in Shandong.

Shandong Peninsula *or* **Shantung Peninsula** *or* **Shan-tung Peninsula** Peninsula, eastern China. Occupying the eastern section of SHANDONG province, it extends northeastward between BO HAI and the YELLOW SEA. The terrain is hilly, with elevations around 600 ft (180 m), but rising to 3,707 ft (1,130 m) in the Lao Mountains. Fishing is important along the coast, while fruit is grown in the hills. Iron ore, magnesite, and gold are abundant. Some of China's best ports are located along the peninsula's rocky, indented coast.

Shang dynasty *or* **Yin dynasty** Traditionally, the second of China's dynasties, following the XIA DYNASTY. Until recent excavations provided archaeological evidence for the Xia, the Shang was the first verifiable Chinese dynasty. Dates for its founding vary; traditionally its rule was said to have spanned 1766–1122 BC. Shang society was stratified: it included a king, local governors, nobles, and the masses, who engaged in agriculture. The Shang developed a 12-month, 360-day calendar with intercalary months added as necessary. The CHINESE WRITING SYSTEM began to develop; numerous records and ceremonial inscriptions survive. Surviving artifacts include musical instruments, superb bronze vessels, pottery for ceremonial and daily use, and jade and ivory ornaments. Cowrie shells were used as currency. See also ERLITOU CULTURE, ZHOU DYNASTY.

Shanghai \'shaŋ-'hī\ Municipality with provincial status (pop., 1999 est.: city, 8,937,175; municipality, 14,740,000), eastern central China. It is located on the Huangpu River, which gives oceangoing vessels access to the city. It was settled c. AD 1000, and later under the MING DYNASTY it was an area of intense cotton production. This changed when Shanghai became the first Chinese port opened to trade with the West after China's defeat by Britain in the OPIUM WARS (1842); it came to dominate the nation's commerce. The site of the CHINESE COMMUNIST PARTY's founding in 1921, it saw severe fighting in the SINO-JAPANESE WAR and was occupied by Japan during World War II. Since the communist victory in 1949, it has become China's chief industrial and commercial center, and one of its leading centers of higher education and scientific research.

Shankar \'shäŋ-ˌkär\, **Ravi** (born 1920) Indian sitar player. Born in Benares (now Varanasi), he studied music and dance, toured as a member of his brother Uday's dance troupe, and spent years learning the sitar. After serving as music director of All-India Radio (1948–56), he began a series of European and U.S. tours. He scored SATYAJIT RAY's *Apu* film trilogy (1955–59). He was a founder of the National Orchestra of India, and in 1962 he founded the Kinnara School of Music in Bombay (now Mumbai) and later in Los Angeles. His performances with Y. MENUHIN and his association with the BEATLES' George Harrison were primarily responsible for bringing Indian music to a broad Western audience.

Shannon, Claude (Elwood) (1916–2001) U.S. electrical engineer. Born in Petoskey, Mich., he received his PhD from MIT. He had a long career as a research mathematician at Bell Laboratories (1941–72) and professor at MIT (1957–78). On the basis of his 1948 paper "The Mathematical Theory of Communication," he is considered the founder of COMMUNICATION THEORY. He was awarded the National Medal of Science in 1966 and the Kyoto Prize in 1985.

Shannon River River, Ireland. The country's longest river, it rises in northwestern Co. Cavan and flows for about 230 mi (370 km) to enter the Atlantic Ocean below Limerick. It is surrounded by marshes and bogs for much of its course and widens at various points into lakes, many with islands. In the early 19th century, it was a vital link in the waterways of Ireland; today it is used by pleasure craft.

Shanxi \'shän-'shē\ *or* **Shansi** \'shän-'sē\ Province (pop., 2000 est.: 32,970,000), northern China. The capital is TAIYUAN. Largely a vast plateau covered by great loess deposits, it was the home of early Chinese agriculture. Most of the people are Han Chinese; other ethnic groups include Chinese Muslims, Mongols, and Manchus. Since ancient times it has been an integral part of the various northern kingdoms of China, serving as a buffer against invaders from the north and as a key trade route. It was one of the major avenues by which BUDDHISM came to China from India. After the overthrow of the QING DYNASTY in 1911–12, the warlord Yen Hsi-shan ruled as absolute dictator until the end of World War II. Japan occupied part of the province during the SINO-JAPANESE WAR. Communist forces assumed control of Shanxi in 1949. It has vast reserves of coal and iron, the largest titanium and vanadium deposits in China, and is China's largest provincial producer of cotton.

Shao Yong *or* **Shao Yung** \'shau̇-'yu̇ŋ\ (1011–1077) Chinese philosopher who greatly influenced the development of the idealist school of NEO-CONFUCIANISM. Originally a Taoist, he refused all offers of government office and lived in a hermitage outside Henan. He became interested in Confucianism by studying the *YI JING*, from which he developed his theory that numbers are the basis of all existence. He believed that the key to the world hinged on the number four; thus the universe is divided into four sections (sun, moon, stars, and zodiac), the body into four sense organs (eye, ear, nose, and mouth), and the earth into four substances (fire, water, earth, and stone). He also introduced to Confucianism the Buddhist concept of the universe's repeating cycles.

shape-note singing Congregational singing using hymnals that employ specially shaped noteheads to facilitate reading for untrained singers. The seven-note scale is sung not to the syllables do-re-mi-fa-sol-la-ti but to a four-syllable system brought to America by early English colonists: fa-sol-la-fa-sol-la-mi. The system reflects the fact that a series of three intervals repeats itself in the major scale. A differently shaped notehead is used for each of the four syllables. The singer reads the music by following the shapes; singers unfamiliar with the system can ignore them. The tradition largely died out around the 1880s but has enjoyed a revival in recent years. The traditional shape-note hymnal, *The Sacred Harp,* first published in 1844, remains in use today.

shaper Metal-cutting MACHINE TOOL in which the workpiece is usually held in a VISE or similar device that is clamped to a table and can be manually operated or power-driven at right angles to the path of a chisel-like cutting tool with only one cutting edge. A moving table feeds the workpiece in small, individual steps at the end of each stroke of the tool. The adjustable mounting of the tool permits the cutting of grooves and generating of surfaces at almost any angle to one another. The largest shapers have a 36-in. (0.9-m) cutting stroke and can machine parts up to 36 in. (0.9 m) long. See also PLANER.

Shapley, Harlow (1885–1972) U.S. astronomer. Born in Nashville, Mo., in 1911 he began finding the dimensions of the components of numerous binary stars from measurements of their light variation when they eclipse one another, and proposed that Cepheid variables are pulsating variable stars. In 1914 he joined the staff of the Mount Wilson Observatory. His study of the distribution of globular clusters in the galaxy led him to deduce that the sun, previously thought to lie near the center of the galaxy, was 50,000 light-years from the center (now estimated at about 28,000), leading to the first realistic estimate of the galaxy's size. Shapley also studied neighboring galaxies, especially the Magellanic Clouds, and found that galaxies tend to occur in clusters.

shar-pei \'shär-'pā\ Ancient breed of dog that originated in China. Shar-peis are notable for their loose, wrinkled skin, especially when young. They have a short bristly coat, wide blunt muzzle, blue-black tongue, and unusual black gums.

Sharani \ˌsha-rä-'nē\, **al-** *orig.* **Abd al-Wahhab ibn Ahmad** (1492–1565) Egyptian scholar and mystic, founder of the Sufi order known as the Sharawiya. Throughout his career he sought to avoid the extremism he saw in the various theological sects of Islam, as well as in other Sufi orders; his aim was to take the best from each, ignoring conflicts between them. Since his thoughts and writings were unsystematic and confused, the appeal of his teachings depended largely on his personal presence. The order gradually declined after his death, though it remained fairly popular until the 19th century.

Sharansky, Natan See Anatoly SHCHARANSKY

sharecropping See TENANT FARMING

Shari River See CHARI RIVER

Sharia \'shȧ-'rē-ȧ\ Legal and moral code of ISLAM, systematized in the early centuries of the Muslim era (8th–9th century AD). It rests on four bases: the QURAN; the SUNNA, as recorded in the HADITH; *ijma,* or agreement among scholars; and *qiyas,* or analogical reasoning. Sharia differs fundamentally from Western law in that it purports to be grounded in divine revelation. Among modern Muslim countries, Saudi Arabia and Iran retain Sharia as the law of the land, in both civil and criminal proceedings, but the legal codes of most other Muslim countries combine elements of Islamic and Western law where necessary. Most Islamic fundamentalist groups insist that Muslim countries should be governed by Sharia.

shark Any of more than 300 species of predatory cartilaginous fish (order Selachii). An ancient animal, it has changed little in 100 million years. The skin typically is dull gray and tough and has toothlike scales. Most sharks have a muscular, asymmetrical, upturned tail; pointed fins; a pointed snout; and sharp triangular teeth. Sharks have no swim bladder and must swim perpetually to keep from sinking. Most species bear living young. Several species can be dangerous to humans (e.g., GREAT WHITE SHARK, HAMMERHEAD SHARK, SAND SHARK, TIGER SHARK); smaller ones, called topes, hounds, and DOGFISHES, are fished commercially. See also BASKING SHARK, MACKEREL SHARK, MAKO SHARK, THRESHER SHARK, WHALE SHARK.

sharksucker See REMORA

Sharm al-Sheikh See RAS NASRANI

Sharon \shə-'rōn\, **Ariel** (born 1928) Israeli soldier and politician. Born in Palestine, he received military training and did intelligence and reconnaissance work after Israel achieved independence. During the SUEZ CRISIS, and again during the SIX-DAY WAR, a unit under his command captured the strategic Mitla Pass. In the 1973 Yom Kippur War, he led the Israeli counterattack. Appointed minister of agriculture in charge of settlements (1977), he actively promoted Jewish settlement of occupied Arab territory. As minister of defense (1981–83), he oversaw Israel's invasion of Lebanon (see LEBANESE CIVIL WAR). An Israeli court of inquiry held Sharon indirectly responsible for the SABRA AND SHATILA MASSACRES, and he was forced to resign in 1983. He held several further cabinet positions throughout the 1980s and '90s and in 1999 became head of the LIKUD party. In 2001 he was elected prime minister.

Sharon, Plain of Mediterranean coastal plain, western Israel. Extending 55 mi (89 km) from Mount Carmel to TEL AVIV-JAFFA, and roughly triangular in shape, it has been inhabited since remote antiquity. Its name occurs in the Bible and is mentioned in Egyptian pharaonic inscriptions. Modern settlement was undertaken as part of the ZIONIST movement to resettle the agricultural lands of Palestine in the late 19th century, and by the early 1930s it had become the most densely settled area of Jewish Palestine. It produces citrus fruits, vegetables, and cotton, and is a popular tourist destination.

Shasta, Mt. Peak, CASCADE RANGE, northern California. A double-peaked extinct volcano, 14,162 ft (4,317 m) high, it dominates the landscape for a hundred miles. The several glaciers on its slopes are popular with skiers and climbers. The first ascent was made in 1854.

shath \'shath\ In SUFISM, a divinely inspired statement that a practitioner utters in a mystical state. The Sufis claim that there are moments of ecstatic fervor when they are overwhelmed by the divine presence to such a degree that they lose touch with worldly realities. In such moments they utter statements that may seem incoherent or blasphemous if taken literally, and so must be interpreted allegorically. Since the state of mystical trance is normally brief, the statements rarely exceed six or seven words, but Sufis regard all their writings, particularly their poetry, as possessing an element of shath.

Shatila See SABRA AND SHATILA MASSACRES

Shatt al Arab \'shät-ál-'ár-əb\ River, southeastern Iraq, formed by the confluence of the TIGRIS and EUPHRATES rivers. It flows southeastward for 120 mi (193 km) and passes the Iraqi port of BASRA and the Iranian port of Abadan before emptying into the Persian Gulf. For about the last half of its course the river forms the border between Iraq and Iran. In the 1980s it was the scene of prolonged fighting in the IRAN–IRAQ WAR.

Shatuo Turks *or* **Sha-t'o Turks** \'shä-'tō\ Nomadic people who came to the aid of the TANG DYNASTY (618–907) after the rebel Huang Zhao captured the capitals of Luoyang and Changan in 880 and 881. Their leader, Li Keyong (856–908), became one of the aspirants to imperial power during the collapse of the Tang dynasty.

Shaughnessy \'shȯ-nə-sē\, **Thomas George** *later* **Baron Shaughnessy (of Montreal and Ashford)** (1853–1923) U.S.-Canadian railway executive. Born in Milwaukee, he initially worked as a clerk for the Chicago, Milwaukee & St. Paul Railway. In 1882 he joined the CANADIAN PACIFIC RAILWAY as general purchasing agent, becoming vice president (1891–99), president (1899–1918), and chairman of the board (from 1918). He oversaw the greatest expansion in the railroad's history and added shipping and mining industries to its holdings.

Shaw, Anna Howard (1847–1919) U.S. (British-born) suffragist. She arrived in the U.S. with her family in 1851. By age 15 she was a frontier school teacher, and in 1880 she became the first woman minister of the Methodist Protestant Church. She took up the causes of temperance and women's suffrage in 1885 and became an important spokesperson for both. She earned a medical degree the next year. She served as president of the National American Woman Suffrage Association 1904–15, and died shortly before women gained the right to vote.

Shaw, Artie *orig.* **Arthur Arshawsky** (born 1910) U.S. clarinetist and leader of one of the most popular big bands of the SWING era. Born in New York City, Shaw was a technically brilliant clarinetist and worked freelance before leading his own groups. In 1936 he performed with a string quartet, later expanding the group into a more conventional dance band. He led a Navy band during World War II, and afterward led various ensembles until his retirement in 1954. His best-known recordings are "Begin the Beguine" and "Frenesi."

Shaw, George Bernard (1856–1950) Irish playwright and critic. After moving to London in 1876, he worked for years as a music and art critic, wrote book and theater reviews, and was an active member of the socialist FABIAN SOCIETY. In his first play, *Widowers' Houses* (1892), he emphasized social and economic issues instead of romance, adopting the ironic comedic tone that would characterize all his work. He described his first plays as "unpleasant" because they forced the spectator to face unpleasant facts; these included *Mrs. Warren's Profession* (1893), which concerned prostitution and was barred from performance until 1902. He then wrote four "pleasant" plays, including the comedies *Arms and the Man* (1894) and *Candida* (1895). His next plays included *Caesar and Cleopatra* (1899) and *Man and Superman* (1905). He used high comedy to explore society's foibles in *Major Barbara* (1905), *The Doctor's Dilemma* (1911), and *Pygmalion* (1913), his comedic masterpiece. Other notable plays include *Androcles and the Lion* (1912), *Heartbreak House* (1919), and *Saint Joan* (1923). His other writings and speeches made him a controversial public figure for much of his life. He received the Nobel Prize in 1925.

George Bernard Shaw, photograph by Yousuf Karsh.
KARSH—WOODFIN CAMP AND ASSOCIATES

Shaw, Lemuel (1781–1861) U.S. jurist. Born in Barnstable, Mass., he drafted Boston's first charter in 1822; it remained in effect until 1913. In 1830 he was appointed chief justice of the Supreme Judicial Court of Massachusetts, where he served for 30 years. His rulings were formative in the development of both Massachusetts and national jurisprudence. His daughter married HERMAN MELVILLE.

shawm Double-reed Renaissance WOODWIND INSTRUMENT, ancestor of the OBOE. Its conical bore and bell are wider than the oboe's. A disk called a pirouette usually supports the player's lips. Shawms were constructed in many sizes, from treble to great bass. They were in use in the Middle East perhaps 2,000 years ago, and were introduced into Europe during the Crusades. With their powerful tone, shawms were classed with the "loud" or "outdoor" instruments and used in dance and ceremonial music.

Shawn, Ted (originally Edwin Myers) (1891–1972) U.S. modern dancer, teacher, and choreographer. Born in Kansas City, Mo., he married RUTH SAINT DENIS in 1914, soon after beginning his dance career. They cofounded their Denishawn school and company in 1915; their tours brought modern dance to many parts of the U.S. for the first time. After they separated in 1931, Shawn established a company of male dancers and choreographed works that embodied a vigorous, masculine style. In 1933 he founded the Jacob's Pillow Dance Festival in Becket, Mass., as a summer residence and theater for his dancers. He continued to dance and choreograph into the 1960s.

Shawn in *Frohsinn*.
PICTORIAL PARADE

Shawnee \shȯ-'nē\ ALGONQUIAN-speaking North American Indian people from the central Ohio River Valley. Closely related in language and culture to the FOX, KICKAPOO, and SAUK, the Shawnee were also influenced by the SENECA and DELAWARE. In the summer the Shawnee lived in bark-covered houses grouped into large villages near fields in which women cultivated corn. The primary male occupation was hunting. In winter the village broke into small patrilineal family groups, which moved to hunting camps. In the 17th century the Shawnee were driven from their home by the IROQUOIS, scattering into widely separated areas. After 1725 the tribe reunited in Ohio. Following their defeat by Gen. ANTHONY WAYNE (1794), they broke into three independent branches that eventually settled in Oklahoma. Today they number about 4,000.

shaykh See SHEIKH

Shays' Rebellion Uprising in western Massachusetts, 1786–87. In a period of economic depression and land seizures for debt collection, several hundred farmers led by Daniel Shays (1747?–1825) marched on the state supreme court in Springfield, which they prevented from carrying out foreclosures and debt collection. Shays then led a force of about 1,200 men in attacking the nearby federal arsenal, but they were repulsed by troops under BENJAMIN LINCOLN. As a result of the uprising, the state enacted laws easing the economic condition of debtors.

Shcharansky \shə-'ran-skē\, **Anatoly (Borisovich)** *later* **Natan Sharansky** (born 1948) Soviet dissident. Born in Ukraine, he worked as a computer specialist and became an interpreter for ANDREY SAKHAROV. A Jew, he applied for permission to emigrate to Israel in 1973 but was refused and discharged from his job. He became an advocate for dissidents, contacting Western journalists to publicize their cause. In 1977 he was arrested by the KGB for treason and espionage, sentenced to 13 years in prison, and sent to the Siberian Gulag. His wife, Avital, who had emigrated to Israel in 1974, championed his cause. Released in 1986, he settled in Israel, where he founded a party stressing immigrants' concerns and won a cabinet seat in 1996.

She-Ji *or* **She-Chi** \'shə-'jē\ Ancient Chinese compound deity of the soil and harvests. China's earliest legendary emperors worshiped She (earth), for they alone had responsibility for the entire earth and country. Since ordinary people had no part in this courtly worship, they came to focus their worship on the god of grain (Ji). Local shrines held two images, one of She and one of Ji, and eventually the two images were considered man and wife.

shear legs Device, often temporary, for lifting heavy weights. It consisted of three poles lashed together at the top with a block and tackle attached. Shear legs were often used for placing masts in sailing ships.

shear wall In building construction, a rigid vertical diaphragm capable of transferring lateral forces from exterior walls, floors and roofs to the ground foundation in a direction parallel to their planes. Examples are the reinforced concrete wall or vertical TRUSS. Lateral forces caused by wind, earthquake, and uneven settlement loads, in addition to the weight of structure and occupants, create powerful twisting (torsional) forces. These forces can literally tear (shear) a building apart. Reinforcing a frame by attaching or placing a rigid wall inside it maintains the shape of the frame and prevents rotation at the joints. Shear walls are especially important in high-rise buildings subject to lateral wind and seismic forces.

shearing In TEXTILE manufacturing, the cutting of the raised nap of a pile fabric to a uniform height to enhance appearance. Shearing machines operate much like rotary lawn mowers, and the amount of shearing depends on the desired height of the nap or pile. Shearing may also be applied to create stripes and other patterns by varying surface height. In animal husbandry, shearing is the cutting off of the fleece of SHEEP and other wool-bearing animals, using special shears.

shearwater Any of numerous species (family Procellariidae) of long-winged seabirds named for their habit of gliding on stiff wings along wave troughs. Typical shearwaters are the 12–17 drab, slender-billed species of *Puffinus,* 14–26 in. (35–65 cm) long. Shearwaters nest in a burrow on offshore islands and coastal hills in the Atlantic and Mediterranean and throughout most of the Pacific. A colony may consist of hundreds of thousands of pairs; at night, when the calling adults move in and out of the burrows, the din is deafening. See also FULMAR, PETREL.

sheathed bacteria Group of BACTERIA found widely in nature in slow-running water. Many species are attached to underwater surfaces. They are characterized by a threadlike, branching arrangement of cells enclosed in a sheath. The sheaths of some are variously encrusted with iron or manganese oxides, depending on the water. One of the best known is a common species, *Sphaerotilus natans,* which in polluted water has thin, colorless sheaths, and in unpolluted water containing iron has yellow-brown iron-encrusted sheaths that often grow into long slimy tassels.

Sheba, Queen of (fl. 10th century BC) In Jewish and Islamic traditions, ruler of the Kingdom of Saba (Sheba) in southwestern Arabia. In an Old Testament story, she visited King SOLOMON to test his wisdom. In Islamic tradition she is known as Bilqis and is converted from worship of the sun to worship of God, marrying either Solomon himself or a Hamdani tribesman. In Persian folklore she is considered the daughter of a Chinese king and a peri. Ethiopian tradition names her Makeda; her son by Solomon is seen as the founder of the Ethiopian royal dynasty.

Shebele River See SHABEELLE RIVER

Sheeler, Charles (1883–1965) U.S. painter and photographer. Born in Philadelphia and educated at the Pennsylvania Academy of Fine Arts, he initially earned a living as a photographer. His acclaimed series of photographs of the Ford automobile plant at River Rouge, Mich. (1927) was followed by a series on Chartres Cathedral (1929). In his paintings, early Cubist influence led to the PRECISIONISM of his maturity. He treated industrial and architectural subjects in an abstract-realist style, emphasizing their formal qualities, as in his painting *Rolling Power* (1939), which revealed the abstract power of a locomotive's driving wheels.

Sheen, Fulton J(ohn) (1895–1979) U.S. religious leader. Born in El Paso, Ill., he attended parochial school and St. Viator College before being ordained to the priesthood in 1919. He pursued further studies in the U.S. and Belgium. He taught at Catholic University (Washington, D.C.) from 1926 to 1950. In 1930 he began his 22-year radio career on the program *The Catholic Hour,* with which he reached an estimated 4 million listeners. In 1951 he became a bishop. In the 1950s he began a weekly television series, *Life Is Worth Living;* it was followed by two more series. At his death he was one of the best-known clerics in the U.S.

sheep RUMINANTS (BOVID genus *Ovis*) that have scent glands in the face and hind feet and horns that, if present, are more divergent than those of the GOAT. Species range from 80 to 400 lbs (35–180 kg). The coat of wild species consists of outer hair underlain by WOOL. Sheep graze in flocks, preferably on short, fine grasses and legumes. They have been domesticated from at least 5000 BC in the Middle East, Europe, and central Asia. Most domesticated breeds produce fine wool; the few that produce only hair or coarse or long wool are generally raised for meat. The flesh of mature sheep is called mutton; that of immature sheep is called LAMB.

sheep laurel *or* **lambkill** Open upright woody shrub *(Kalmia angustifolia)* of the HEATH FAMILY. Growing 1–4 ft (0.3–1.2 m) high, it has glossy, leathery, evergreen leaves and showy pink to rose flowers. Like other *Kalmia* species (including MOUNTAIN LAUREL) and other members of the heath family, it contains a poison (andromedotoxin). In northwestern North America, where these plants occur, livestock (especially sheep) that graze on nonfertile soils of abandoned pastures and meadows may ingest enough of the plant to become poisoned, potentially fatally.

sheepdog In general, any dog breed developed to herd sheep; specifically, the BORDER COLLIE. Most sheepdog breeds stand about 2 ft (60 cm) and weigh over 50 lbs (23 kg). The French briard has bushy brows and a long, waterproof coat. The Belgian sheepdog has long black hair and erect ears. The Hungarian puli has a coat of long ropelike cords. It stands 16–19 in. (41–48 cm) and weighs about 30 lbs (14 kg). See also OLD ENGLISH SHEEPDOG, SHETLAND SHEEPDOG.

sheepshead Species *(Archosargus probatocephalus)* of popular edible sport fish in the PORGY family, common along southern North American Atlantic and Gulf of Mexico coasts. The species has inexplicably become very rare from New England to the Chesapeake Bay area, where it was once prevalent. Sheepsheads have a high forehead and a compressed silver body with wide, dark, vertical bands, most distinct in juveniles. The large flat teeth crush and grind crustaceans and hard-shelled mollusks. Adults are typically 2–2.5 ft (60–75 cm) long and weigh about 20 lbs (9 kg).

sheet See SILL

sheet erosion Detachment of soil particles by raindrop impact and their removal downslope by water flowing overland as a sheet instead of in definite channels or rills. A more or less uniform layer of fine particles is removed from the entire surface of an area, sometimes resulting in an extensive loss of rich topsoil. Sheet erosion commonly occurs on recently plowed fields or on other sites having poorly consolidated soil material with scant vegetative cover.

Sheffield City (pop., 1995: 529,000), SOUTH YORKSHIRE, England. It is situated at the foot of the PENNINES. An Anglo-Saxon village that became the site of a castle and parish church early in the 12th century, it has been known for its cutlery since medieval times. By 1700 it had a monopoly of the English cutlery trade, and it remains the center of the industry today. It developed a steel industry from the mid-19th century, and several metallurgical innovations, including the process for making STAINLESS STEEL, originated there. In 1568 MARY, QUEEN OF SCOTS, was imprisoned in its Norman castle (now in ruins).

Sheffield plate Articles made of copper coated with silver by fusion. The technique was discovered c. 1742 by the Sheffield (Yorkshire) cutler THOMAS BOULSOVER, who noted that the combination of fused silver and copper retained the ductility of both metals and acted as one when manipulated. Other workshops in Britain, continental Europe, and North America also produced cooking and eating utensils of Sheffield plate. After the introduction of ELECTROPLATING in 1840, production of Sheffield plate declined; by the 1870s it had all but disappeared. Admired for its soft, glowing gray luster, Sheffield-plate ware soon came to be prized and collected.

Sheffield plate chamber candlestick by Matthew Boulton, c. 1820; in the Sheffield City Museum, Sheffield, South Yorkshire.

BY COURTESY OF SHEFFIELD CITY MUSEUM; MOTTERSHAW PHOTOGRAPHY

Sheherazade See SCHEHERAZADE

sheikh \'shēk, 'shāk\ Among Arabic-speaking tribes, especially BEDOUIN, the male head of the family, as well as of each successively larger social unit making up the tribal structure. The sheikh is assisted by an informal tribal council of male elders. The word may also be used as a title or form of respectful address or to designate a religious authority.

Shekhina \shə-kē-'nä, shə-'kē-nə\ In JUDAISM, the worldly presence of God, sometimes conceived of as a divine light. It is said that the Shekhina descended on the TABERNACLE and on SOLOMON's Temple, though it was one of the five things lacking in the Second Temple of JERUSALEM. There is an affinity between the Shekhina and the HOLY SPIRIT; though the two are not identical, both signify divine immanence, are associated with prophecy, can be lost due to sin, and are connected with the study of the TORAH.

shelduck *or* **sheldrake** Any of several short-billed, somewhat gooselike, Old World DUCKS with long legs and an upright stance. They are smaller members of the duck tribe Tadornini (family Anatidae). The common shelduck *(Tadorna tadorna),* of Europe and Asia, is black and white with a reddish chest band; the drake has a knob on his red bill. The ruddy shelduck *(Casarca ferruginea),* ranging from northern Africa and Spain to Mongolia, is orangish, with a pale head and white wing patches. Drakes usually have melodious whistling calls and are aggressive. In North America, MERGANSERS are sometimes called sheldrakes.

shelf fungus See BRACKET FUNGUS

Shelikhov \'she-li-ˌkəf\, **Gulf of** *Russian* **Zaliv Shelikhova** \zə-'lʸif-'she-li-kə-və\ Gulf, eastern Russia. Lying between the Siberian mainland and the KAMCHATKA Peninsula, it is an extension of the Sea of OKHOTSK. It extends northward 420 mi (670 km) and has a maximum width of 185 mi (300 km). The tidal ranges in its northern bays are among the greatest in the world. It is closed by ice from December to May.

shell ARTILLERY projectile, cartridge case, or shotgun cartridge. It originated in the 15th century as a container for metal or stone shot, dispersed when the container burst after leaving the GUN. Explosive shells, in use by the 16th century, were hollow cast-iron balls filled with GUNPOWDER and lit by a fuse. Until the 18th century, such shells were used only in high-angle fire (including MORTARS). In the 19th century, shells were adopted for direct-fire artillery, notably in the form of SHRAPNEL. Modern artillery shells consist of a casing (usually steel), a propelling charge, and a bursting charge; the propelling charge is ignited by a primer at the base of the shell and the bursting charge by a fuse in the nose. In RIFLE, PISTOL, and MACHINE-GUN ammunition, the word usually signifies the brass casing that contains the propulsive charge. In shotgun ammunition, the shell is the entire cartridge, including shot, powder, primer, and case.

Shell See ROYAL DUTCH/SHELL GROUP

shell structure In building construction, a thin, curved plate structure shaped to transmit applied forces by compressive, tensile, and shear stresses that act in the plane of the surface. They are usually constructed of concrete reinforced with steel mesh (see SHOTCRETE). Shell construction began in the 1920s; the shell emerged as a major long-span concrete structure after World War II. Thin parabolic shell vaults stiffened with ribs have been built with spans up to about 300 ft (90 m). More complex forms of concrete shells have been made, including hyperbolic paraboloids, or saddle shapes, and intersecting parabolic vaults less than 0.5 in. (1.25 cm) thick. Pioneering thin-shell designers include FELIX CANDELA and PIER LUIGI NERVI.

Shelley, Mary Wollstonecraft *orig.* **Mary Wollstonecraft Godwin** (1797–1851) English Romantic novelist. The only daughter of WILLIAM GODWIN and MARY WOLLSTONECRAFT, she met and eloped with PERCY B. SHELLEY in 1814. They married in 1816 after his first wife committed suicide. Mary Shelley's best-known work is *Frankenstein* (1818), a narrative of the dreadful consequences of a scientist's artificially creating a human being. After her husband's death in 1822, she devoted herself to publicizing his writings and educating their son. Of her several other novels, the best, *The Last Man* (1826), is an account of the future destruction of the human race by a plague.

Mary Wollstonecraft Shelley, detail of an oil painting by R. Rothwell, first exhibited 1840; in the National Portrait Gallery, London.

BY COURTESY OF THE NATIONAL PORTRAIT GALLERY, LONDON

Shelley, Percy Bysshe (1792–1822) English Romantic poet. The heir to rich estates, Shelley was a rebellious youth who was expelled from Oxford in 1811 for refusing to admit authorship of *The Necessity of Atheism.* Later that year he eloped with Harriet Westbrook, the daughter of a tavern owner. He gradually channeled his passionate pursuit of personal love and social justice into poetry. His first major poem, *Queen Mab* (1813), is a utopian political epic revealing his progressive social ideals. In 1814 he eloped to France with Mary Wollstonecraft Godwin (see MARY SHELLEY); in 1816, after Harriet drowned herself, they were married. In 1818 the Shelleys moved to Italy. Away from British politics, he became less intent on social reform and more devoted to expressing his ideals in poetry. He composed the verse tragedy *The Cenci* (1819) and his masterpiece, the lyric drama *Prometheus Unbound* (1820), which was published with some of his finest shorter poems, including "Ode to the West Wind" and "To a Skylark." *Epipsychidion* (1821) is a Dantesque fable about the relationship of sexual desire to spiritual love and artistic creation. *Adonais* (1821) commemorates the death of JOHN KEATS. Shelley drowned at 29 while sailing in a storm off the Italian coast, leaving unfinished his last and possibly greatest visionary poem, *The Triumph of Life.*

Percy Bysshe Shelley, oil painting by Amelia Curran, 1819; in the National Portrait Gallery, London.

BY COURTESY OF THE NATIONAL PORTRAIT GALLERY, LONDON

shellfish Any aquatic MOLLUSK, CRUSTACEAN, or ECHINODERM that has a shell. OYSTERS, MUSSELS, SCALLOPS, and CLAMS rank among the most commercially important. Certain gastropod mollusks, such as ABALONE, WHELK, and CONCH, are also marketed. The main crustaceans are SHRIMP, LOBSTER, and CRAB. Among echinoderms, SEA URCHINS and SEA CUCUMBERS are locally popular. After being harvested, all shellfish are highly perishable. Many types are cooked live to protect the consumer against the effects of spoilage.

sheltie See SHETLAND SHEEPDOG

Shenandoah National Park National park, BLUE RIDGE MTNS., northern Virginia. Formed in 1935, it consists of 193,537 acres (78,322 hectares) and is noted for its scenery, which affords some of the widest views in the eastern states. It is heavily forested with hardwoods and conifers; wildlife includes deer, foxes, and numerous birds.

Shenandoah Valley Valley, chiefly in Virginia. It is about 150 mi (241 km) long and 25 mi (40 km) wide, and extends southwest from Harpers Ferry, W.V. It lies between the BLUE RIDGE MTNS. and the ALLEGHENIES. It is drained by the Shenandoah River. The Valley Pike, now an interstate highway, was used by Tuscarora and Shawnee Indians, and later become a main artery for westward expansion. It was the scene of military operations throughout the AMERICAN CIVIL WAR; today its many parks, limestone caverns, and scenic drives are tourist attractions.

sheng \'shəŋ\ (Chinese: "sage" or "saint") In Chinese belief, a mortal who attains extraordinary or supernatural powers by self-cultivation and serves as a model for others. CONFUCIUS used the term to refer to exemplary rulers of the past.

Shensi See SHAANXI

Shenyang *or* **Shen-yang** \'shən-'yäŋ\ *formerly* **Mukden** \'mu̇k-dən\ City (pop., 1991 est.: 4,540,000), capital of LIAONING province, northeastern China. An ancient city, it was the capital of the MANCHU empire 1625–44. After 1895 it was fought over by Russia and Japan in the struggle for MANCHURIA. It was occupied by the Japanese 1931–45. Taken by the Communist forces in 1948, it was a base for their conquest of the Chinese mainland. It is one of China's leading industrial cities; its manufactures include machinery, wires and cables, textiles, and chemicals. It is also a cultural and educational center.

Shepard, Alan B(artlett), Jr. (1923–1998) U.S. astronaut. Born in East Derry, N.H., he graduated from the U.S. Naval Academy and served in the Pacific during World War II. In 1959 he became one of the original seven MERCURY program astronauts. In May 1961, 23 days after YURY A. GAGARIN became the first human to orbit earth, Shepard made a 15-minute suborbital flight that reached an altitude of 115 mi (185 km). He later commanded the Apollo 14 flight (1971), the first to land in the lunar highlands.

Shepard, Roger N(ewland) (born 1929) U.S. psychologist and cognitive scientist. Born in Palo Alto, Cal., he received a PhD from Yale University and later worked at Bell Laboratories (1958–66) and taught at Stanford University (from 1968). He is known for his work in multidimensional scaling, the use of spatial models to show similarities and dissimilarities among data. He has also examined the phenomena of "mental rotation," a form of image transformation. He received the National Medal of Science in 1995.

Shepard, Sam *orig.* **Samuel Shepard Rogers** (born 1943) U.S. playwright and actor. Born in Fort Sheridan, Ill., he worked as an actor and rock musician before writing the early one-act dramas and experimental plays that were performed off-Broadway in the 1960s, winning several Obie awards. His successful full-length plays, noted for their often surreal images drawn from the American West, science fiction, and popular culture, include *The Tooth of Crime* (1972), *Curse of the Starving Class* (1976), *Buried Child* (1979, Pulitzer Prize), *True West* (1980), *Fool for Love* (1983; film, 1985), *A Lie of the Mind* (1985), and *Simpatico* (1996). He wrote the screenplay for *Paris, Texas* (1984) and has acted in numerous movies, including *Days of Heaven* (1978), *The Right Stuff* (1983), *Voyager* (1991), and *The Pelican Brief* (1993).

shepherd's purse Widespread lawn and roadside weed *(Capsella bursa-pastoris)* of the MUSTARD FAMILY, native to the Mediterranean and now found worldwide. Growing as high as 18 in. (45 cm), it is easily recognized by its flat, heart-shaped, green fruits, borne along the branching flower stalks, which arise from a dandelion-like rosette of deeply cut or almost entire leaves at the base and bear clusters of tiny white flowers. Shepherd's purse has been much studied to understand embryogenesis (development from zygote to seedling) in flowering plants.

Shepp, Archie (Vernon) (born 1937) U.S. saxophonist and composer, one of the principal figures of avant-garde jazz. Born in Fort Lauderdale, Fla., Shepp was originally inspired by JOHN COLTRANE. His playing increasingly demonstrated the influence of BEN WEBSTER, with a wide vibrato and gruff tone; his occasional eruptions of harsh screams and multiphonics (two notes played simultaneously) became trademarks of avant-garde saxophone technique. His first recordings were with free-jazz pianist Cecil Taylor in the early 1960s; thereafter he worked as leader of his own groups. Also a playwright and educator, Shepp became an eloquent spokesman for the new music and its social significance.

Sheraton, Thomas (died 1806) British cabinetmaker. A leading exponent of Neoclassicism, he gave his name to a style of furniture characterized by a firm feminine refinement of late Georgian and became probably the most powerful source of inspiration behind the furniture of the late 18th century. His four-part *Cabinet-Maker and Upholsterers' Drawing Book* (1791) greatly influenced British and U.S. design. At his best, Sheraton had a natural approach to contemporary design: he used wood for its own sake, rather than covering it with such disguises as gilt or modulating it excessively with ormolu mounts.

Sheridan, Philip H(enry) (1831–1888) U.S. Army officer. Born in Albany, N.Y., he graduated from West Point and served at frontier posts. In the Civil War he led a Union division in Tennessee and helped win the Battle of CHATTANOOGA with his cavalry charge up Missionary Ridge. In the East he became commander of the cavalry (1864) and led raids on Confederate forces around Richmond, Va. As commander of the Army of the Shenandoah, he drove Confederate forces under JUBAL EARLY from the Shenandoah Valley. He joined ULYSSES S. GRANT to help secure Union victories in the PETERSBURG CAMPAIGN. After the war he became general of the army (1883).

Sheridan, Richard Brinsley (Butler) (1751–1816) British playwright. Born in Dublin and educated at Harrow, he settled in London and rejected a legal career for the theater. His comedy *The Rivals* (1775) introduced the popular character Mrs. Malaprop and established him as a leading dramatist. He became manager and later owner of the DRURY LANE THEATRE (1776–1809), where his plays were produced. He won wide acclaim for his comedy of manners *The School for Scandal* (1777) and showed his flair for satirical wit again in *The Critic* (1779). His plays formed a link in the history of the comedy of manners between the Restoration drama and the later plays of OSCAR WILDE. In 1780 Sheridan became a member of Parliament, where he was a noted orator for the minority Whig party.

sheriff In the U.S., the chief law-enforcement officer for the courts in a county. The sheriff, who is ordinarily elected, may appoint a deputy. They have the power of police officers to enforce criminal law and may summon private citizens (the *posse comitatus,* or "force of the county") to help maintain the peace. The main judicial duty of the sheriff is to execute processes and WRITS of the courts. Officers of this name also exist in England, Wales, Scotland, and Northern Ireland. In England the office of sheriff existed before the Norman Conquest (1066).

Sherman, Cindy (born 1954) U.S. photographer. After graduating from the State University of New York at Buffalo, Sherman began work on *Untitled Film Stills* (1977–80), one of her best-known projects. The series of 8 x 10-inch black-and-white photographs features Sherman in a variety of roles reminiscent of FILM NOIR. Throughout her career she would continue to be the model in her photographs, donning wigs and costumes that evoke images from the realms of advertising, television, film, and fashion and that, in turn, challenge the cultural stereotypes about women supported by these media. During the 1980s Sherman's work featured mutilated bodies and reflected such concerns as eating disorders, insanity, and death. She returned to ironic commentary upon female identities in the 1990s, introducing mannequins and dolls to some of her photographs.

Sherman, John (1823–1900) U.S. politician. Born in Lancaster, Ohio, a brother of WILLIAM T. SHERMAN, he served in the U.S. House of Representatives 1855–61. A fiscal expert, he helped establish the national banking system (1863) and supported legislation that returned the U.S. to the gold-exchange standard. He served as U.S. secretary of the treasury 1877–81. In the U.S. Senate (1861–77, 1881–97), he proposed the SHERMAN ANTITRUST ACT and the

John Sherman.

BY COURTESY OF THE LIBRARY OF CONGRESS, WASHINGTON, D.C.

Sherman Silver Purchase Act (1890). He later served briefly as secretary of state (1897–98).

Sherman, Roger (1721–1793) American jurist and politician. Born in Newton, Mass., he became active in trade and law in Connecticut, and served as judge of the superior court (1766–85) and mayor of New Haven (1784–93). A delegate to the Continental Congress, he signed the Declaration of Independence and helped draft the Articles of Confederation. At the Constitutional Convention, he proposed a compromise on congressional representation that combined facets of the two opposing plans by the large and small states. The result, called the Connecticut (or Great) Compromise, provided for the bicameral legislature established in the U.S. Constitution.

Sherman, William Tecumseh (1820–1891) U.S. Army general. Born in Lancaster, Ohio, a brother of JOHN SHERMAN, he graduated from West Point, served in Florida and California, then resigned in 1853 to pursue a banking career. He rejoined the Union army when the American Civil War broke out. He fought in the Battle of Bull Run, then served under ULYSSES S. GRANT at Shiloh and was promoted to major general. With Grant he helped win the VICKSBURG CAMPAIGN and the Battle of CHATTANOOGA. As commander of the division of the Mississippi, he assembled 100,000 troops for the invasion of Georgia (1864). After engagements with Confederate troops under JOSEPH JOHNSTON, he captured and burned Atlanta and began his devastating March to the Sea to capture Savannah, leaving a trail of near-total destruction. In 1865 he marched north, destroying Confederate railroads and sources of supply in North and South Carolina. He accepted the surrender of Johnston's army on April 26. Promoted to general, he succeeded Grant as commander of the army (1869–84). Often credited with the saying "War is hell," he was a major architect of modern TOTAL WAR.

Sherman Antitrust Act (1890) First U.S. legislation enacted to curb concentrations of power that restrict trade and reduce economic competition. Proposed by Sen. JOHN SHERMAN, it made illegal all attempts to monopolize any part of trade or commerce in the U.S. Initially used against trade unions, it was more widely enforced under Pres. THEODORE ROOSEVELT. In 1914 Congress strengthened the act with the Clayton Antitrust Act and the formation of the FEDERAL TRADE COMMISSION. In 1920 the U.S. Supreme Court relaxed antitrust regulations so that only "unreasonable" restraint of trade through acquisitions, mergers, and predatory pricing constituted a violation. Later cases reinforced the prohibition against MONOPOLY control, including the 1984 break-up of AT&T. See also ANTITRUST LAW.

Sherpas Mountain-dwelling people of Nepal and of Sikkim state, India. Sherpas are of Tibetan culture and descent and speak a Tibetan dialect. Along with farming and cattle breeding, they make a living spinning and weaving wool. They have won fame as porters in the high Himalayas. They number about 120,000.

Sherrington, Charles Scott *later* **Sir Charles** (1857–1952) English physiologist. By studying animals whose cerebral cortexes had been removed, he showed that reflexes are integrated activities of the total organism, not based on isolated "reflex arcs." Sherrington's law states that when one set of muscles is stimulated, muscles opposing their action are inhibited. He showed that the role of proprioception in reflexes that maintain upright posture against gravity is independent of cerebral function and skin sensation. His work influenced the development of brain surgery and treatment of nervous disorders, and he coined the terms neuron and synapse. His classic work was *The Integrative Action of the Nervous System* (1906). In 1932 he shared a Nobel Prize with Edgar Adrian (1889–1977).

sherry Fortified WINE of Spanish origin. It takes its name from Jerez de la Frontera in Spain. Essential to its taste is the action of flor, a mildewlike growth encouraged by a slight exposure to air after FERMENTATION. Also unique is a system of blending wines of many vintage years. Sherry is fortified after fermentation with high-proof BRANDY, to 16–18% alcohol. It is served primarily as an aperitif, though sweeter, heavier sherries are used as dessert wines.

Sherwood, Robert E(mmet) (1896–1955) U.S. playwright. Born in New Rochelle, N.Y., he became a New York magazine editor and a member of the Algonquin Round Table. He examined the pointlessness of war in his first play, *The Road to Rome* (1927), and won wide acclaim for *The Petrified Forest* (1935). *Idiot's Delight* (1936), *Abe Lincoln in Illinois* (1938), and *There Shall Be No Night* (1940) won Pulitzer Prizes. In 1938 he cofounded the influential Playwrights' Company. During World War II he wrote speeches for Pres. FRANKLIN ROOSEVELT and headed the overseas branch of the Office of War Information (1941–44). His book *Roosevelt and Hopkins* (1948) won a Pulitzer Prize. Many of his plays were adapted for film; his original screenplays include *The Best Years of Our Lives* (1946, Academy Award).

Sherwood Forest Woodland and former royal hunting ground, NOTTINGHAMSHIRE, England. Known for its association with the legendary ROBIN HOOD, it formerly occupied almost all of western Nottinghamshire and extended into DERBYSHIRE. Today a reduced area of woodland remains between NOTTINGHAM and Worksop.

Shetland Islands *or* **Zetland Islands** Group of about 100 islands, Scotland. Lying 130 mi (210 km) north of the Scottish mainland and about 400 mi (640 km) south of the ARCTIC CIRCLE, the group comprises the Shetland administrative region; its headquarters is LERWICK. Fewer than 20 of the islands are inhabited. The northernmost point of Britain, the islands have fjordlike coasts and a climate warmed by the North Atlantic Current. The Norse ruled the Shetlands from the 8th to the 15th century. In 1472 the islands, with Orkney, were annexed to the Scottish crown. They are famous for their livestock, which includes the SHETLAND PONY and the Shetland sheep, whose fine wool is used in the distinctive Shetland and Fair Isle knitted patterns. The North Sea oil industry has contributed to the economy.

Shetland pony Breed of PONY that originated in Scotland's Shetland Islands. Well adapted to the islands' harsh climate and scant food supply, Shetlands were used as pack horses. Around 1850 they were taken to England to work in coal mines and to the U.S., where a more refined pony suitable for children was developed. Except for certain dwarf ponies, the Shetland is the smallest breed of HORSE. Its average height is about 40 in. (102 cm; Shetlands are not measured in hands). Shetlands are long-lived and need little care; they are gentle and even-tempered if properly trained.

Shetland sheepdog *or* **sheltie** Breed of SHEEPDOG developed from a Scottish WORKING DOG to herd the small sheep of the Shetland Islands. The sheltie resembles the rough-coated COLLIE but in miniature; it stands 13–16 in. (33–41 cm). Sturdy and agile, it is noted for its herding ability, intelligence, and affectionate nature. Its long, straight coat is generally black, brown, or blue-gray with black mottling.

Shetland sheepdog.
SALLY ANNE THOMPSON

Shevardnadze \ˌshe-vərd-ˈnäd-zə\, **Eduard (Amvrosiyevich)** (born 1928) Soviet-Georgian politician. He rose in the Komsomol hierarchy to become first secretary of its central committee in Georgia (1957–61). He later served as a member of the Soviet Union's Central Committee (1976) and a full member of the Politburo (1985). As foreign minister under MIKHAIL GORBACHEV (1985–90, 1991), he implemented the Soviet withdrawal from Afghanistan in 1988, new arms treaties with the U.S., and Russia's tacit acquiescence in the fall of the communist regimes of Eastern Europe (1989–90), while promoting the reform policies of GLASNOST and PERESTROIKA. After the Soviet Union's collapse, he returned to the newly independent republic of Georgia, where he has served as the elected head of state from 1992.

Shi Huangdi *or* **Shih Huang-ti** \ˈshir-ˈhwäŋ-ˈdē\ *orig.* **Zhao Zheng** (c. 260–210/9 BC) Founder of the QIN DYNASTY (221–206 BC). His father was king of Qin, which was regarded as barbarous by the central states of China but had developed a strong bureaucratic government under the philosophy of legalism (see HANFEIZI). Aided by LI SI, Zheng eliminated the other Chinese states until in 221 BC Qin ruled supreme. He proclaimed himself Qin Shi Huangdi ("First Sovereign Emperor of Qin") and initiated reforms designed to create a fully centralized administration. He was interested in magic and alchemy, hoping for an elixir of immortality; his reliance on magicians was strongly condemned by Confucian scholars, many of whom he executed. The scholars also advocated a return to old feudal ways; their obstinacy led him to order the burning of all nonutilitarian books. Traditional histories regarded him as the ultimate villain, cruel, uncultivated, and superstitious. Modern historians stress the endurance of his bureaucratic and administrative structure. Though the Qin dynasty collapsed after his death, future dynasties adopted his structures. He was buried in a massive tomb with an army of more than 6,000 terra-cotta soldiers and horses. See also QIN TOMB.

shiatsu See ACUPRESSURE

Shibusawa Eiichi \ˌshə-bü-ˈsä-wä-ˈā-i-chē\ (1840–1931) Japanese industrialist and government official. The son of wealthy peasants, he received samurai status from the SHOGUN Tokugawa Yoshinobu (1837–1913). On the overthrow of the TOKUGAWA SHOGUNATE in 1868, he worked in the finance ministry of the new government. In 1873 he left to become president of the First National Bank (now Dai-ichi Kangyo Bank). In 1880 he organized the Osaka Spinning Mill, a major industrial success. He also created a cotton-spinners' ZAIBATSU, or cartel, to help the industry and make mutually advantageous arrangements with shippers and merchandisers, a practice common in industrializing Japan. He helped create and manage many other companies, founded the Tokyo Chamber of Commerce and Bankers Assn., and, after retiring, was active in social-welfare causes.

shigella \shi-ˈgel-ə\ Any of the rod-shaped BACTERIA that make up the genus *Shigella,* which are normal inhabitants of the human intestinal tract and can cause DYSENTERY, or shigellosis. Shigellae are gram-negative (see GRAM STAIN), non-spore-forming, stationary bacteria. *S. dysenteriae,* spread by contaminated water and food, causes the most severe dysentery because of its potent toxin, but other species may also be dysentery agents.

shih tzu \ˈshē-ˈdzü\ Breed of TOY DOG developed in Tibet from the PEKINGESE and the LHASA APSO. Sturdily built and short-legged, it stands about 10 in. (26 cm) and weighs 18 lbs (8 kg) or less. It is longer than it is tall and has a short muzzle, hanging ears, and heavily haired tail, which it carries over its back. Its long, dense coat may be any of several colors and falls over the eyes, forming a beard.

Shiite \ˈshē-ˌīt\ Member of the Shia branch of ISLAM, which resulted from the first FITNAH, or split, within the religion over leadership. The Shiites supported ALI, MUHAMMAD's son-in-law, as the Prophet's heir; when the majority of Muslims (who constitute SUNNI Islam) rejected him, Shia became a religious movement. Ali's followers insisted that a CALIPH, or IMAM, be a lineal descendant of Ali and his wife, FATIMA. Shia's legal tradition is distinct from the four major schools of thought in Sunni Islam and is generally regarded as the most conservative. Though Shiites represent only about 10% of Muslims in the world, they are a majority in Iran and Iraq, and there are sizable populations in Yemen, Syria, Lebanon, East Africa, Pakistan, and northern India. The largest subdivision is the ITHNA ASHARIYA, or Twelvers, who recognized 12 historical imams (including Ali); other subsects include the ISMAILIS and the Zaydiya.

Shijiazhuang *or* **Shih-chia-chuang** \ˈshi-ˈjyä-ˈjwäŋ\ City (pop., 1991 est.: 1,320,000), capital of HEBEI province, northeastern China. Located on the edge of the North China plain at the foot of the Taihang Mtns., the site dates to pre-Han times (c. 206 BC). After it came under the TANG DYNASTY (7th–10th century AD), it was only a local market town. Its growth into one of China's major cities began in 1905, when the railway reached the area, stimulating trade and agriculture. Other rail connections and an extensive road network established it as a communications center. It developed into an industrial city with administrative functions at the end of World War II. It is now one of China's major industrial, cultural, and economic centers.

shikhara See SIKHARA

Shikoku \shē-ˈkō-kü\ Smallest main island (pop., 1990: 4,195,000) of Japan. It is located south of HONSHU and east of KYUSHU. Much of its 7,063 sq mi (18,292 sq km) is mountainous, and the population is concentrated in urban areas along the coast. Rice, barley, wheat, and mandarin oranges are among the island's major crops. Industries include petroleum, textiles, paper, and fishing.

Shillong \shi-ˈlȯŋ\ City (pop., 2001 prelim.: 132,876), northeastern India. It has been an administrative center since 1864, first as a district headquarters, later as the capital of ASSAM, and, since 1972, as the capital of MEGHALAYA state. It was completely rebuilt after an earthquake destroyed it in 1897. It is a resort area and an important agricultural trade center.

Shilluk \shi-ˈlük\ People living on the western bank of the Nile in Sudan. They are sedentary agriculturalists who keep cattle, sheep, and goats. Historically, they were united in a single tribal state headed by a divine king whose well-being was held to ensure the state's prosperity. In addition to several classes of royalty, the Shilluk were divided into royal retainers, commoners, and slaves. See also NILOTES.

Shiloh \ˈshī-lō\, **Battle of** (April 6–7, 1862) Second major engagement of the AMERICAN CIVIL WAR. Union forces under ULYSSES S. GRANT, including WILLIAM T. SHERMAN, camped on the Tennessee River at Pittsburg Landing, Tenn. (near Shiloh Church), in preparation for an offensive. Confederate forces under A. S. Johnston and P. G. T. BEAUREGARD attacked, surprising the Union troops and forcing their retreat, but Johnston was mortally wounded. A Union counterattack the next day regained the lost ground, and the Confederates withdrew to Corinth, Miss. Both sides claimed victory, but the battle was considered a Confederate defeat. Both sides suffered heavy casualties, about 10,000 each.

Shimabara Rebellion \shē-ˈmä-bä-rä\ (1637–38) Rebellion of some 20,000 Japanese peasants, supported by RONIN (masterless samurai), in protest at heavy taxation. Because the peasants were converts to Christianity, their rebellion strengthened government determination to isolate Japan from foreign influence and vigorously enforce its proscription of all Christian beliefs and activities.

Shimla See SIMLA

shimmy See CHEMIN DE FER

Shinano River \shē-ˈnä-nō\ River, HONSHU, Japan. The longest river in Japan, at 228 mi (367 km), it rises at the foot of Mount Kobushi and flows north-northeast to enter the Sea of JAPAN at Niigata. It has long served as an inland waterway, and has numerous river ports.

Shinbutsu shugo \ˈshēn-ˌbüt-sü-ˈshü-ˌgō\ Japanese amalgamation of BUDDHISM and SHINTO. The hybridization began on Buddhism's appearance in Japan (mid-6th century AD), and the practice of building Shinto and Buddhist shrines near each other developed in the 8th century. To separate the two religions, the government issued an edict in 1868 ordering Buddhist priests connected with Shinto shrines either to be reordained as Shinto priests or to return to lay life. Because the state religion was Shinto, the government abolished Buddhist ceremonies in the imperial household. Nevertheless, most Japanese incorporate elements of both religions in their lives, celebrating life-related events (birth, coming of age, marriage) at Shinto shrines but holding Buddhist funeral rites and memorial services.

shinden-zukuri \ˈshēn-ˌden-zü-ˈkü-rē\ Japanese architectural style of mansion-estates constructed in the HEIAN PERIOD (794–1185). The form consisted of a *shinden* (central building) to which subsidiary structures were connected by corridors. The shinden faced south on an open court, across which was a pond garden. The eastern and western *tainoya,* or subsidiary living quarters, were attached by *watadono* (wide corridors) from which narrow corridors extended south, ending in small pavilions. This layout resulted in a U-shaped arrangement around the court. See also SHOIN-ZUKURI.

shiner Any of several small freshwater fishes (genera *Notemigonus* and *Notropis,* family Cyprinidae). The common shiner *(Notropis cornutus)* is a blue and silver MINNOW up to 8 in. (20 cm) long. The golden shiner *(Notemigonus cryseleucas),* sometimes called the American ROACH, is a greenish and golden minnow, about 12 in. (30 cm) long and weighing 1.5 lbs (0.7 kg). It is edible and valuable as bait.

shingle Thin piece of building material made of wood, asphaltic material, slate, metal, or concrete, laid in overlapping rows to shed water. Shingles are widely used as roof covering on residential buildings and sometimes also for SIDING (see SHINGLE STYLE). Wood shingles in the U.S. are usually made of cypress, redwood, or Western red cedar.

Shingle style In the U.S., a style of wood-shingle-covered domestic architecture of the 1870s and '80s. Among the finest examples are HENRY HOBSON RICHARDSON's Sherman House (1874–75), Newport, R.I., and Stoughton House (1882–83), Cambridge, Mass. The style grew out of the QUEEN ANNE and STICK STYLES and was stimulated by a revived interest in colonial American architecture. The small size of the shingle made it easy to cover a variety of shapes. Like the Stick style, the Shingle style is characterized by a free-flowing, open plan; open porches and irregular roof lines contribute to the picturesque or rustic effect. The style had a significant influence on FRANK LLOYD WRIGHT.

shingles *or* **herpes zoster** \'hər-ˌpēz-'zäs-tər\ Acute viral skin and nerve infection. Groups of small blisters appear along certain nerve segments, most often on the back, sometimes after a dull ache at the site; pain becomes more severe when the blisters break out. Caused by the same virus as CHICKEN POX, it probably results from reactivation of seemingly inactive virus in a partially immune person. Spontaneous recovery from the infection usually occurs within two weeks, but NEURALGIA may last months or even years longer.

Shingon \'shēŋ-ˌgȯŋ, *Engl* 'shin-ˌgän\ Esoteric Japanese sect based on an interpretation of 9th-century Chinese BUDDHISM. It holds that the BUDDHA's secret wisdom can be developed through special ritual means (see YOGA) employing body, speech, and mind, including the use of symbolical gestures, mystical syllables, and mental concentration. The whole is intended to arouse a realization of the spiritual presence of the Buddha inherent in all living things. Shingon's main scripture, the Mahavairocana Sutra ("Great Sun Sutra"), is not canonical in other Buddhist schools. Shingon is properly considered a form of VAJRAYANA, though it was much modified and systematized by KUKAI.

Shining Path *Spanish* **Sendero Luminoso** Maoist movement in Peru dedicated to violent revolution. It was founded in 1970 by a philosophy professor, Abimael Guzmán Reynoso (born 1934), as a result of a split in the Peruvian Communist Party. The *senderistas* began their campaign among the impoverished Indians of the high Andes, attracting sympathizers by their emphasis on the empowerment of Indians at the expense of Peru's traditional elite. They gained control of large areas of Peru through violence and intimidation. By 1992, when Guzmán was captured and their influence began to wane, they had caused an estimated 25,000 deaths and seriously disrupted the Peruvian economy.

Shinran \'shēn-ˌrän\ *orig.* **Matsuwaka-Maru** (1173–1263) Japanese philosopher and religious reformer. He entered the priesthood at 9 and studied 20 years at the center founded by SAICHO on Mount Hiei. He later met HONEN, founder of the Jodo sect (see PURE LAND BUDDHISM). When Honen's movement was suppressed, he and Shinran were exiled. For more than 20 years, Shinran lived an academic and missionary life, compiling the six volumes of his teachings. In 1224 he established Jodo Shinshu ("True Pure Land Religion"). He refined the Pure Land teaching that salvation could be attained through chanting the name of the Buddha Amida (AMITABHA) by saying that even one such utterance, if made with true faith, was sufficient for salvation. He advocated marriage for his priests to minimize the distance between clergy and laity. Jodo Shinshu is the largest Buddhist denomination in modern Japan.

Shinto Indigenous religion of Japan, based on the worship of spirits known as *kami*. The term Shinto ("way of the *kami*") came into use to distinguish indigenous Japanese beliefs from Buddhism, which had been introduced into Japan in the 6th century AD. Shinto has no founder and no official SCRIPTURE, though its mythology is collected in the *Kojiki* ("Records of Ancient Matters") and *Nihon shoki* ("Chronicles of Japan"), written in the 8th century. At its core are beliefs in the mysterious creating and harmonizing power of *kami*. According to Shinto myths, in the beginning a certain number of *kami* simply emerged, and a pair of *kami*, IZANAGI AND IZANAMI, gave birth to the Japanese islands, as well as to the *kami* who became ancestors of the various clans. The Japanese imperial family claims descent from Izanagi's daughter, the sun goddess AMATERASU. All *kami* are said to cooperate with one another, and life lived in accordance with their will is believed to produce a mystical power that gains their protection, cooperation, and approval. Through veneration and observation of prescribed rituals at shrines (e.g., ritual purity), practitioners of Shinto can come to understand and live in accordance with divine will. See also SHINBUTSU SHUGO.

shinty or shinny Game similar to HURLING and FIELD HOCKEY, in which players (12 per team) use curved sticks to hit a small, hard ball into the opposing team's goal (hail). It is considered the national game of Scotland, where it originated before the 17th century.

ship Large floating vessel capable of crossing open waters. The term formerly was applied to sailing vessels with three or more masts; today it usually denotes a vessel of more than 500 tons' (450 metric tons') displacement. The largest ships today are enormous oil tankers, some of which are 500,000 tons (450,000 metric tons) deadweight. Other specialized ships (CONTAINERSHIPS) carry general freight in standardized containers that can be easily loaded, unloaded, and transferred. See also BATTLESHIP, BRIG, CLIPPER SHIP, CORVETTE, DHOW, FRIGATE, JUNK, LONGSHIP, OCEAN LINER, SCHOONER, YACHT.

ship money English tax levied by the crown on coastal cities for naval defense in time of war. First levied in medieval times, the tax required payment in the form of a number of warships or their equivalent in money. It was revived in 1634 by CHARLES I to raise extra revenue. He issued six annual writs (1634–39) that extended the imposition to inland towns and sought to establish it as a permanent tax. Its enforcement aroused widespread opposition and added to the discontent leading to the ENGLISH CIVIL WARS. In 1641 the tax was declared illegal by Parliament.

ship of the line Type of sailing warship, the principal vessel of the West's great navies from the mid-17th to the mid-19th century. It evolved from a tactic in naval warfare known as the line of battle, in which two opposing columns of ships maneuvered to fire their guns broadside against each other. Since the largest ships carrying the biggest guns usually won these battles, this led to the construction of more big line-of-battle ships, or ships of the line. These three-masted ships were often 200 ft (60 m) long, displaced 1,200–2,000 tons (1,100–1,800 metric tons), and had crews of 600–800 men; they usually had 60–110 cannons and other guns arranged along three decks. They eventually gave way to the steam-powered BATTLESHIP.

Shipka Pass Pass in the BALKAN MTNS., central Bulgaria. It is 4,376 ft (1,334 m) high. A main route between Bulgaria and Turkey, the pass was the site of fierce fighting during the RUSSO-TURKISH WAR; in one battle (1878) the Turks lost so many soldiers that their leader Suleyman earned the name the "Shipka butcher."

Shippen, William, Jr. (1736–1808) U.S. physician. Born in Philadelphia, he earned his MD in Edinburgh. In 1762 he established the first American maternity hospital, and in 1765, with JOHN MORGAN, he organized the first medical school in the American colonies, where he became the first systematic teacher of anatomy, surgery, and obstetrics. He was one of the first to use dissected human bodies to teach anatomy. He succeeded Morgan as head medical officer of the Continental Army in 1777. He was a founder and president of the College of Physicians of Philadelphia, the first American medical school.

shipping Act or business of transporting passengers and goods by water. Early civilizations, which arose by waterways, all utilized them for transport. The Egyptians were probably the first to use seagoing vessels (c. 1500 BC); the Phoenicians, Cretans, Greeks, and Romans also all relied on waterways. In Asia, Chinese ships equipped with multiple masts and a rudder were making sea voyages by c. AD 200; from as early as the 4th century BC the Chinese also relied heavily on internal waterways to transport food to their large cities (see GRAND CANAL). Japan, too mountainous to rely on roads for mass transport, also relied on internal and coastal waterways for shipping from early in its history. The spice trade was a great stimulus to shipping trade; Arabians were sailing to the spice islands before the Christian era and European merchant marines grew up largely because of it. The tea trade had a similar effect, as did the discovery of gold in the New World. From the 17th to the 19th century, the slave trade was a major feature of Atlantic shipping. The U.S. and England were the ascendant shipping nations in the 19th century; Germany, Norway, Japan, The Netherlands, and France joined them in the early 20th century. Today shipping remains a vital part of the world economy as the only viable way to transport large quantities of goods transoceanically. Many U.S. merchant ships are registered in a third nation to avoid heavy taxes. See also British EAST INDIA CO., Dutch EAST INDIA CO., French EAST INDIA CO.

shipworm *or* **pileworm** Any of approximately 65 species (family Teredidae) of common marine BIVALVES that can severely damage wooden structures, including ship hulls and wharves. Its anterior end is covered by a shell; the rest is a tubelike structure, sometimes up to 6 ft (1.8 m) long. File-like ridges on its white shell cut into wood at 8–12 rasping motions a minute. It secretes lime to line its burrow, and its tubelike portion extends back to the burrow opening. It ingests food particles and oxygen from the water; some wood is also ingested as food.

Shirakawa Hideki (b. 1936) Japanese chemist. Born in Tokyo, he earned a Ph.D. from the Tokyo Institute of Technology in 1966. After graduation he began teaching at the University of Tsukuba. In 1977 he started collaborating with ALAN J. HEEGER and ALAN G. MACDIARMID, conducting experiments on the polymer polyacetylene. Their work demonstrated that certain plastics can be chemically changed to conduct electricity almost as readily as metals. Other conductive polymers were later discovered, and the finding was expected to play a significant role in the emerging field of molecular electronics. With Heeger and MacDiarmid, Shirakawa was awarded the Nobel Prize for Chemistry in 2000.

Shiraz \shē-'räz\ Industrial and commercial city (pop., 1994: 1,043,000), southern central Iran. It was important during the Seleucid (312–175 BC), Parthian (247 BC–AD 224), and Sasanid (c. AD 224–651) periods, and reached its peak in the 10th–11th century. In the 14th century, TIMUR occupied Shiraz, which had become a Muslim center rivaling BAGHDAD. In 1724 it was sacked by Afghan invaders and later became the capital of the Zand dynasty (1750–94). Famous for its wine, gardens, shrines, and mosques, it was the birthplace of the Persian poets Sa'di and HAFEZ, whose tombs are there.

Shire River \'shir-ā\ River, southern Malawi and central Mozambique. The most important river in Malawi, it flows 250 mi (402 km) from the southern shore of Lake MALAWI into the ZAMBEZI RIVER. In Malawi it drops 1,260 ft (384 m) in a spectacular 50-mi (80-km) stretch of gorges and cataracts. A dam at Liwonde regulates flow from Lake Malawi and provides flood control.

Shirer \'shīr-ər\, **William L(awrence)** (1904–1993) U.S. journalist, historian, and novelist. Born in Chicago, he served as a foreign correspondent and radio broadcaster in Europe and India in the 1920s, '30s, and '40s. *Berlin Diary* (1941) collects his impressions of European political events. He was blacklisted in the McCarthy era as a leftist sympathizer. He is best known for *The Rise and Fall of the Third Reich* (1969, National Book Award), a massive study of Nazi Germany. His other major historical work is *The Collapse of the Third Republic* (1969), a study of France. *Gandhi* (1979) recalls interviews conducted in the 1930s.

shirk In Islam, idolatry and POLYTHEISM, both of which are regarded as heretical. The QURAN stresses that God does not share his powers with any partner *(sharik),* and warns that those who believe in idols will be harshly dealt with on the Day of Judgment. The concept of shirk has broadened considerably throughout the dogmatic development of Islam, and has come to be used as the opposite of *tawhid* (the oneness of God). Different grades of shirk have been distinguished by Islamic law; they include the belief in superstition, belief in the power of created things (e.g., reverencing saints), and belief in those who profess to know the future—all of which pale beside polytheism in seriousness.

Shirley, William (1694–1771) British-American colonial governor. A lawyer in England, he moved to Boston in 1731. He was appointed admiralty judge (1733), king's advocate general (1734), and governor of Massachusetts (1741–49, 1753–56). In KING GEORGE'S WAR he planned the British capture of Louisbourg (1745). He became commander of British forces in North America (1755) but was dismissed after the failure of his expedition against Fort Niagara. He served as governor of the Bahamas 1761–67.

Shiva *or* **Siva** \'shi-və, 'shē-və\ Major deity of HINDUISM, believed to have many manifestations. Like VISHNU he is the subject of an elaborate and sometimes contradictory mythology. He is both the destroyer and the restorer, the great ascetic and the symbol of sensuality, the benevolent herdsman of souls and the wrathful avenger. His female consort is known under various manifestations, including PARVATI, DURGA, and KALI. In SHAIVISM he is worshiped as the paramount lord.

Shiva, bronze statue, Madras, c. AD 900.

BY COURTESY OF THE GOVERNMENT MUSEUM, MADRAS; PHOTOGRAPH, ROYAL ACADEMY OF ARTS, LONDON

Shklovsky \'shklòf-skē\, **Viktor (Borisovich)** (1893–1984) Russian critic and novelist. From 1914 he was a major voice in the critical movement called Russian FORMALISM, to which he contributed the concept of *ostranenie,* or "making it strange." He argued that literature is a collection of devices that force readers to view the world afresh by presenting old ideas or mundane experiences in new, unusual ways. His earlier works include the acclaimed memoir *A Sentimental Journey* (1923) and *The Technique of the Writer's Craft* (1928). Official Soviet displeasure with Formalism later obliged him to write within the constraints of SOCIALIST REALISM, and he published historical novels, film criticism, and highly praised literary studies.

shock State in which the circulatory system fails to supply enough blood to peripheral tissues to meet basic requirements. Symptoms—weak, rapid PULSE; low BLOOD PRESSURE; and cold, sweaty skin—are not all present in every case. Causes include low blood volume, caused by bleeding or fluid loss from BURNS or DEHYDRATION; inability of the heart to pump enough blood, due to MYOCARDIAL INFARCTION, pulmonary EMBOLISM, or cardiac tamponade (compression of the heart by fluid in the membrane around it); and blood-vessel dilation as a result of SEPTICEMIA, allergy (including ANAPHYLAXIS), or drugs. All result in reduced capillary blood flow; reflexes increase heart rate and constrict small blood vessels to protect the blood supply to essential organs. Without treatment of the underlying cause, these mechanisms fail; since the cause is not always clear, cases tend to require different and occasionally contradictory treatment (e.g., intravenous fluids can save the life of a patient with massive blood loss but can overload a weakened heart).

shock absorber Device for controlling unwanted motion of a spring-mounted vehicle. On an automobile, the SPRINGS act as a cushion between the axles and the body and reduce the shocks produced by a rough road surface. Since some combinations of road surface and car speed may result in excessive up-and-down motion of the car body, shock absorbers—which today are hydraulic devices that oppose both compression and stretching of the springs—slow down and reduce the magnitude of these vibratory motions. See also DAMPING.

shock therapy Method of treating psychiatric disorders by inducing shock through drugs or electric current. Shock was formerly induced by administering increasingly large doses of insulin until the patient was thrown into a brief coma; insulin-shock therapy was used for the treatment of SCHIZOPHRENIA. Electroconvulsive, or electroshock, therapy involves passing an electric current through the patient's head between two electrodes placed over the temples and thus causing a convulsive seizure; it was used for BIPOLAR DISORDER and other types of DEPRESSION. Both forms of shock therapy were developed in the 1930s; their use has declined since the introduction of tranquilizing drugs and antidepressants.

Shockley, William B(radford) (1910–1989) U.S. engineer and teacher. Born in Palo Alto, Cal., he received his PhD from Harvard. He joined Bell Laboratories in 1936, where he began experiments that led to the development of the TRANSISTOR. During World War II he was director of research for the U.S. Navy's Antisubmarine Warfare Operations Research Group; later (1954–55) he was deputy director of the Defense Department's Weapons Systems Evaluation Group. He established the Shockley Semiconductor Laboratory at Beckman Instruments in 1955. In 1956 he shared a Nobel Prize with JOHN BARDEEN and WALTER H. BRATTAIN for his work on the transistor. He taught at Stanford University 1958–74. From the late 1960s he earned notoriety for his outspoken and controversial views on the intellectual capacity of blacks.

shoe Outer covering for the foot, usually of leather, with a stiff or thick sole and heel, and generally reaching no higher than the ankle (unlike a boot). Early examples from Mesopotamia were moccasinlike wraparounds of leather; not until the Hellenistic Age did shoes become luxurious. The Romans developed shoes fitted for the left and right feet, and differentiated according to sex and rank. In the 14th–15th century, shoes became extremely long and pointed, the points attaining a length of 18 in. (45 cm) or more. In the 16th century, the toes became extremely broad, like a duck's bill. In the 17th century, shoes had moderately high heels and were often decorated with large rosettes of lace and ribbons, which gave way to gold or silver buckles in the 18th century. The first shoe factory opened in 1760, in Massachusetts, but not until the development of modern machinery in the 19th century were shoes made quickly and inexpensively.

Shoemaker, Bill *or* **Willie Shoemaker** *orig.* **William Lee** (born 1931) U.S. jockey. Born in Fabens, Texas, he began his track career in

1949. He rode in 24 Kentucky Derbies and won four; he also won the Belmont Stakes five times and the Preakness twice. He rode more than 8,800 winners in his 41-year career, which ended in 1989, and is considered the greatest American jockey of the second half of the 20th century.

Shoemaker-Levy 9 COMET that collided with JUPITER in July 1994, discovered by Carolyn and Eugene Shoemaker and David Levy 16 months earlier. The comet was torn apart into more than 20 fragments during a close encounter with Jupiter in July 1992, resulting in a "string of pearls" that collided sequentially with Jupiter two years later over a period of a week, leaving dark spots larger than the earth at their impact sites in Jupiter's atmosphere.

shoen \'shō-'en\ In Japan (c. 8th–15th century), private, tax-free, often autonomous estates whose increase in numbers undermined the political and economic power of the central government and contributed to the growth of powerful local clans. Landowners would commend their parcels of land to powerful families or religious institutions with tax-free status, thereby obtaining that status for themselves. All people connected with the land—the powerful patron, the owner, the estate manager—had rights to part of the income from the land. Under the KAMAKURA SHOGUNATE, the warrior government asserted authority over the shoen by inserting its own stewards (JITO) into each estate to collect taxes. During Japan's WARRING STATES PERIOD, the shoen gave way to consolidated landholdings in the control of DAIMYO. See also SAMURAI.

shogi \'shō-gē\ Japanese chess played on a board of 81 squares, each player maneuvering 20 men. Two features differentiate it from European chess: (1) captured men are not dead but become part of the captor's forces, and (2) pawns capture in their normal move. The game's origin is obscure.

shogun \'shō-gən\ (Japanese: "barbarian-quelling generalissimo") In Japan during the HEIAN PERIOD, a title bestowed on occasion on a general after a successful campaign. MINAMOTO YORITOMO received the title in 1192 after gaining control of Japan and formed the KAMAKURA SHOGUNATE. Later Kamakura shoguns lost actual power to the HOJO FAMILY while remaining rulers in name. Ashikaga Takauji received the title of shogun in 1338 and established the ASHIKAGA SHOGUNATE, but his successors enjoyed even less control over Japan than had the Kamakura shoguns, and the country gradually fell into civil war (see ONIN WAR). TOKUGAWA IEYASU's shogunate (see TOKUGAWA SHOGUNATE) proved the most durable, but the Japanese penchant for removing actual power from its titular bearer prevailed, and a council of elders from the main branches of the Tokugawa clan ruled from behind the scenes. Since the title of shogun ultimately came from the emperor, he became a rallying point for those who brought down the shogunate in the MEIJI RESTORATION.

shoin-zukuri \'shō-ēn-zü-'kü-rē\ Style of Japanese domestic architecture. The name is taken from a feature called the *shoin,* a study alcove with a built-in desk. Other common features included the TOKO-NO-MA and *chigai-dana* (built-in shelves). The style, derived from Zen Buddhist monastic dwellings, gradually replaced the SHINDEN-ZUKURI style during the Muromachi period (1338–1573). It is characterized by a new modesty of scale (forced on the aristocracy by loss of income), asymmetry and an irregular flowing together of masses, and the use of solid wall construction and sliding SHOJI rather than the movable partitions that divided the main living space in the shinden.

Shoin-zukuri interior in the Ginkaku Temple, Kyoto, showing a *chigai-dana* (left background) and a *shoin* with *shoji* (right background), late 15th century.
OGURO PLANNING CO.—FPG

shoji \'shō-jē\ In Japanese architecture, sliding partition doors and windows made of a latticework wooden frame and covered with a tough, translucent white paper. When closed, they softly diffuse light throughout the house. In summer they can be slid back or removed, opening the house to the outside—a desirable arrangement in Japan because of the extreme humidity. Shoji are a feature of the SHOIN-ZUKURI style.

Sholem Aleichem \'shȯ-ləm-ə-'lā-k̲əm\ *orig.* **Sholem Yakov Rabinowitz** (1859–1916) Russian writer. Drawn to writing as a youth, he became a private tutor at 17 and later served as a government rabbi. Beginning in 1883 he published more than 40 widely translated volumes of novels, stories, and plays in Yiddish. English translations from his 14-vol. collected works include *Jewish Children* and *The Old Country.* His best-known character, Tevye the dairyman, was the subject of a volume of short stories that later was the basis for the musical *Fiddler on the Roof* (1964).

Sholes, Christopher Latham (1819–1890) U.S. inventor. Born in Mooresburg, Pa., his first experiments were with numbering and letter-writing machines. In 1868 he was granted a patent for a TYPEWRITER with Carlos Glidden and Samuel W. Soulé; later improvements brought him two more patents. In 1873 he sold his rights for $12,000 to the Remington Arms Co., which developed the machine that was marketed as the Remington Typewriter.

Sholokhov \'shȯl-ə-k̲əf\, **Mikhail (Aleksandrovich)** (1905–1984) Russian novelist. A native of the Don river region, he served in the Red Army and joined the Communist Party in 1932. He is best known for the huge novel *The Quiet Don,* translated in two parts as *And Quiet Flows the Don* (1934) and *The Don Flows Home to the Sea* (1940). A portrayal of the struggle between the Cossacks and Bolsheviks, it was heralded in the Soviet Union as a powerful example of SOCIALIST REALISM and became the most widely read novel in Russia. It became controversial when ALEKSANDR SOLZHENITSYN and others alleged that it was plagiarized from the Cossack writer Fyodor Kryukov (died 1920). Sholokov's later novels include *Virgin Soil Upturned* (1932–60). He received the Nobel Prize in 1965.

Shona Cluster of Bantu-speaking peoples living in eastern Zimbabwe and western Mozambique. Numbering about 8.5 million, they cultivate corn, millet, and sorghum and keep cattle. Their villages consist of mud-and-wattle huts, granaries, and common cattle kraals. Shona traditional culture, now fast declining under Christianizing and urbanizing influences, was noted for its ironwork, pottery, and music. Magic, witchcraft, and sorcery remain important.

shooting Sport of firing at targets with RIFLES, handguns (PISTOLS and REVOLVERS), and SHOTGUNS as an exercise in marksmanship. World-championship competitions are held for the small-bore rifle, free rifle, center-fire pistol, free pistol, rapid-fire pistol, air rifle, air pistol, and shotgun. Shooting has been an Olympic sport since the modern games began in 1896; women's events were established in 1984. See also SKEET SHOOTING, TRAPSHOOTING.

shooting star See METEOR

shopping mall *or* **shopping center** Collection of independent retail stores, services, and parking areas constructed and maintained by a management firm as a unit. It is a 20th-century adaptation of the historical marketplace. In the U.S., postwar migration from cities to suburbs and increased automobile use created a perceived need for centralized shopping facilities. The largest type, the regional center sited in a vast sea of parking lots, bears little resemblance to its ancestor, the smaller, urban shopping arcade. The arcade developed out of the need for shelter from the weather; Buffalo, N.Y., and Cleveland have charming trussed and glass-roofed examples. In recent years large shopping malls have attempted to revive an arcadelike atmosphere, often sporting atriums and balconies. Two of the world's largest malls are the West Edmonton Mall in Alberta, Canada and the Mall of America in Bloomington, Minn.

shore See COAST

Shore Temple Complex of elegant shrines (c. 700), one among a number of Hindu monuments at Mahabalipuram, on the coast of Tamil Nadu state, India. It is considered the finest early example of medieval southern Indian temple architecture. Unlike most of its neighbors at the site, it is built of cut stones rather than carved out of caves. It has two shrines, one dedicated to Shiva and the other to Vishnu. Its style is characterized by a pyramidal *kutina*-type tower, consisting of stepped stories topped by a cupola and finial, quite different from the northern Indian SIKHARA.

Short Parliament See LONG PARLIAMENT

short story Brief fictional prose narrative. It usually presents a single significant episode or scene involving a limited number of characters. The form encourages economy of setting and concise narration; character is disclosed in action and dramatic encounter but seldom fully developed. A short story may concentrate on the creation of mood rather than the telling of a story. Despite numerous precedents, it emerged only in the 19th century as a distinct literary genre in the works of writers such as E.T.A HOFFMANN, HEINRICH KLEIST, EDGAR ALLAN POE, PROSPER MERIMEE, GUY DE MAUPASSANT, and ANTON CHEKHOV.

Shorter, Frank (born 1947) U.S. runner. Born in Munich of American parents, he won his first marathon in 1970, finishing the race (in 2 hours 12 minutes 19.8 seconds) two minutes ahead of the second-place finisher. At the 1972 Olympic Games, Shorter became the first American in 64 years to win a gold medal in the marathon. At the 1976 Olympics he won the silver medal.

Shorter, Wayne (born 1933) U.S. saxophonist and composer. Born in Newark, N.J., he studied at NYU. He played with ART BLAKEY's group 1959–64, acting as its music director, then joined MILES DAVIS's remarkable mid-1960s group, including HERBIE HANCOCK, bassist Ron Carter (born 1937), and drummer Tony Williams (born 1945). In 1970, he and Joe Zawinul (born 1932) formed Weather Report, the most significant jazz-rock "fusion" band of the 1970s, with bassist Jaco Pastorius (1951–1987). He has written many distinctive jazz standards.

shorthair cat Breed of DOMESTIC CAT. Show standards call for a sturdily built cat with strong-boned legs, a round head, round eyes, and ears that are rounded at the tips. The coat must be short and may be of almost any color or pattern. Some colors, such as blue cream, are infrequently found in shorthairs; others, such as tabby (stripes and mottled patterns in silver, brown, blue, and red), are common.

shorthand *or* **stenography** \stə-'nä-grə-fē\ System for rapid WRITING that uses symbols or abbreviations for letters, words, or phrases. Employed since Greek and Roman times, shorthand has been used in England since the 16th century. Popular modern systems include Pitman, Gregg, and Speedwriting. Many are phonetic and call for writing words as they sound (e.g., in the Pitman system, *deal*, *may*, and *knife* are written *del*, *ma*, and *nif*). Shorthand has been used in reporting proceedings of legislative bodies and courts and in taking dictated business correspondence.

shorthorn *or* **Durham** Blocky, short-horned breed of beef CATTLE developed in the late 18th century by crossbreeding of local cattle in Durham Co., England. Color can be solid or white-marked red, white, or roan. The shorthorn is the only roan-colored modern cattle breed. It is popular throughout the world. Special strains are the milking, or dairy, shorthorn, raised for milk and beef, and the polled shorthorn, a hornless variety.

Shoshone \shə-'shō-nē\ Group of closely related North American Indian peoples that traditionally occupied the Great Basin region of the U.S. The Shoshone language belongs to the Numic group of the UTO-AZTECAN family. The Shoshone are usually divided into four groups: Western (unmounted) Shoshone, centered in eastern Nevada; Northern (mounted) Shoshone of northwestern Utah and southern Idaho; Wind River Shoshone in western Wyoming; and COMANCHE in western Texas. The Western Shoshone subsisted through hunting and gathering. The Northern Shoshone and Wind River Shoshone probably acquired horses by 1680, and adopted much of PLAINS INDIAN culture; they hunted buffalo, used TEPEES and skin clothing, and warred on other tribes. After splitting from the Wind River group, the COMANCHE moved south. Today the Shoshone number about 10,000; most live on reservations in territory they once held.

Shoshone River \shə-'shō-nē, shə-'shōn\ River, northwestern Wyoming. Formed by the uniting of two headstreams in the ABSAROKA RANGE in YELLOWSTONE NATIONAL PARK, it flows northeast 100 mi (160 km) to join the BIGHORN RIVER near the Montana border. It was named for the SHOSHONE Indian tribe.

Shostakovich \ˌshäs-tə-'kō-vich\, **Dmitri (Dmitrievich)** (1906–1975) Russian composer. Shaped by his intellectual parents and the political turmoil of his youth, he was admitted to the St. Petersburg Conservatory at 13. His Symphony No. 1 (1925) attracted international attention, displaying such distinctive traits as a convincing command of a large scale and an expressive palette ranging from unaffected lyricism to bitter satire to grand heroics. His next symphonies and such theater works as *The Nose* (1928), *The Age of Gold* (1930), and *Lady Macbeth of Mtsensk* (1932) were perhaps his most "modernistic" works. The denunciation of *Lady Macbeth* in *Pravda* (1936), perhaps by JOSEPH STALIN himself, led to his adopting a very different style. His wartime Symphony No. 7, thought to portray the German invasion, became a symbol of patriotism. After his music was denounced by the government in 1948, he was again devastated, and began putting his most personal feelings into chamber works, particularly the remarkable 15 string quartets. With the "thaw" of the late 1950s, he composed two outspokenly personal late symphonies, including no. 13, "Babi Yar" (1962). He is remembered as the greatest Russian composer to follow I. STRAVINSKY.

shot put Field event in which a metal ball is heaved for distance. It derives from the ancient event of "putting the stone"; later a shot (cannonball) was substituted. A 16-lb (7.3-kg) shot was adopted for men in the first modern Olympic Games (1896); an 8.8-lb (4-kg) weight is used by women.

shotcrete *or* **gunite** Concrete applied by spraying. Shotcrete is a mixture of PORTLAND CEMENT, aggregate, and water conveyed by compressed air to a spray gun. For structural uses, shotcrete is usually sprayed over a framework of reinforcing bars and steel mesh. Because it can take any shape, is easily colored, and can be sculpted after application, it is used for a variety of specialized structures, including artificial rock walls, zoo enclosures, canopies, shell structures, pools, and dams. It is sometimes used to bind the walls of tunnels.

shotgun Smoothbore shoulder weapon designed to fire a number of pellets, or shot, that scatter after they leave the muzzle. It is used mainly against small moving targets, especially birds. The earliest examples were the fowling pieces that appeared in 16th-century Europe. Repeating shotguns, in which several cartridges could be loaded at once, became available in the 1880s. The range of a modern shotgun is about 50 yards (45 m).

Shotoku Taishi \shō-'tō-kü-'tä-ē-shē\ (574–622) Japanese regent who promoted Buddhism and Confucianism, reinstituted embassies to China, and adopted the Chinese calendar and court ranks. He built HORYU-JI (the Horyu Temple) and is sometimes credited with writing the "Seventeen-Article Constitution," which describes Confucian ethical concepts and the Chinese bureaucratic system. Since his death he has been regarded as a Buddhist saint.

shoveler Any of four species (genus *Anas,* family Anatidae) of DABBLING DUCKS having a long, spoon-shaped bill. The migratory northern shoveler *(A. clypeata)* inhabits shallow marshes and lagoons in the Americas, Europe, Africa, and Asia. The male has a green head, white breast, chestnut belly and sides, and a blue patch on the forewing. It uses its bill to sift small organisms and seeds from the mud; in deeper waters, it skims the surface for plankton. The other species are the South American red shoveler *(A. platalea);* the Cape, or Smith's, shoveler *(A. smithii)* of South Africa; and the Australasian, or blue-winged, shoveler *(A. rhynchotis).*

show jumping Competitive riding of horses one at a time over a set course of obstacles in which the winner is judged according to jumping ability and speed. Individual and team jumping events have been part of the Olympic Games since 1912. The President's Cup is the world team championship.

Showa emperor See HIROHITO

Showa period \'shō-ə\ (1926–1989) Period of Japanese history corresponding to the reign of HIROHITO, the Showa emperor. The Showa period saw the militarism of the 1930s and Japan's disastrous participation in World War II, resulting in the nation's complete collapse and ultimate surrender. The postwar era was one of rehabilitation, marked by such successes as its joining the U.N. in 1956, hosting the 1964 Olympics, and holding the Osaka World Exposition in 1970. Japan experienced a so-called "economic miracle," with growth averaging 10% in 1955–60 and higher in the years following. In the 1980s, the Japanese economy became one of the world's largest and most sophisticated, with per capita income surpassing that of the U.S. Japanese society became increasingly urban, with one-tenth of the population living in Tokyo by the mid-1980s. U.S. influence on popular culture was very strong, and young Japanese emulated their U.S. counterparts in every way possible. The Showa period also saw more people living in nuclear families than in extended families, love marriages rather than arranged marriages, fewer children, and more opportunities for women. See also Heisei period, Occupation (of Japan).

shrapnel \'shrap-nᵊl\ Originally, a type of projectile invented by the British artillery officer Henry Shrapnel (1761–1842), containing small spherical bullets and an explosive charge to scatter the shot and fragments of the shell casing. A time fuse set off the explosive charge late in the shell's flight, when it was near opposing troops. The resulting hail of high-velocity debris was often lethal; it caused most of the artillery-inflicted wounds in World War I. In World War II a high-explosive bursting charge that fragmented the shell's iron casing made shrapnel balls unnecessary; the term shrapnel came to be used for the shell-casing fragments.

Shreve, Henry Miller (1785–1851) U.S. inventor and explorer. Born in New Jersey, he grew up on the western Pennsylvania frontier and began making trading voyages after his father's death in 1799. In the War of 1812 he was skipper of the *Enterprise*, the second steamboat on the Mississippi, carrying supplies for Andrew Jackson's army. Though it was the first steamboat to reach Louisville, Ky. (1815), the trip convinced Shreve of the need for a new design for river steamers. His design for the *Washington*—with a flat shallow hull, a steam engine on the main deck, and a second deck—established the Mississippi steamboat type. To clear rivers of debris, he later designed the first snag boat. His camp on the Red River in Louisiana grew into a permanent settlement as Shreveport.

Shreveport City (pop., 2000: 200,145), northwestern Louisiana. Founded in 1837 on the Red River on lands bought from the Caddo Indians, it became a Confederate state capital and army headquarters during the American Civil War. It developed rapidly after oil was discovered in 1906, and is now a commercial and industrial center for a three-state region. It is the site of Louisiana State Univ.

shrew Any of 290 small insectivore species (family Soricidae) of the Northern Hemisphere and the Andes. They resemble moles, and have tiny eyes and ears, a hanging snout, and long, hook-tipped incisors. Species are 1.5–11 in. (3.5–27 cm) long, excluding the 1–4-in. (2.5–10-cm) tail and weigh as little as 0.07 oz (2 g). The smallest shrews are the smallest of all mammals. Most species live in ground litter, but some live in burrows or trees and a few are semiaquatic. Because they are so small, shrews have the highest metabolic rates of any mammal (with pulses as high as 800 beats per minute) and can survive only a few hours without food. Their normal prey is invertebrates, though some will eat small mammals. Some species have toxic saliva (painful to humans). Raptors and snakes eat shrews, but mammals avoid them. Some authorities classify tree shrews (family Tupaiidae) with the primates.

Shrewsbury Town (pop., 1995 est.: 63,000), county seat of Shropshire, England. Located on the English–Welsh border, it is encircled by the Severn River. Founded in the 5th century AD by the Welsh kingdom of Powys, it became part of the Anglo-Saxon kingdom of Mercia at the end of the 8th century. An 11th-century grant to Roger de Montgomery, who founded its abbey, made it one of the first English earldoms. Prosperity came to the area in the late Middle Ages after centuries of fighting with the Welsh ended and trading in Welsh wool and flax began. It was the birthplace of Charles Darwin.

Shrewsbury, Duke of *orig.* **Charles Talbot** (1660–1718) English statesman. He inherited his father's title at 7 and was raised as a Catholic. He became a Protestant in 1679 and in 1688 was one of seven men who invited William of Orange to seize power from James II. After aiding the successful rebellion, Shrewsbury served William III as secretary of state (1689–90, 1694–99) and was created a duke in 1694. Shifting his allegiance from the Whigs, he served in a Tory administration as lord lieutenant of Ireland (1710–14) and was appointed by Queen Anne as lord high treasurer (1714). He obtained recognition of George I as the legitimate royal heir and assured the peaceful succession of the House of Hanover.

shrike Any of about 64 species of solitary, predatory songbirds (family Laniidae), especially any of the 25 species of the genus *Lanius*. Shrikes kill insects, lizards, mice, and birds with their bill or may impale their prey on a thorn (earning them the name butcher bird). Most species are gray or brownish and have a harsh call; several Eurasian species have reddish or brown markings. The great gray shrike *(L. excubitor)*, called northern shrike in Canada and the U.S., is about 10 in. (25 cm) long and has a black mask. The only other New World species is the similar but smaller loggerhead shrike *(L. ludovicianus)* of North America.

shrimp Any of approximately 2,000 decapod species (suborder Natantia) having a semitransparent body flattened from side to side and a flexible abdomen terminating in a fanlike tail. The appendages are modified for swimming, and the antennae are long and whiplike. Shrimps occur in shallow and deep ocean waters and in lakes and streams. Species range from less than an inch (a few millimeters) to about 8 in. (20 cm) long. Larger species are often called prawns. Shrimps swim backward by rapidly flexing the abdomen and tail. They eat small plants and animals; some species eat carrion. Many species are commercially important as food. See also fairy shrimp.

Peneus setiferus, an edible shrimp.
MARINELAND OF FLORIDA

Shropshire \'shräp-shir\ County (pop., 1995 est.: 420,000), western England. It is divided by the Severn River; its county seat is Shrewsbury. Remnants of Neolithic, Bronze Age, and early Iron Age inhabitants have been found in the region. In the 1st century AD, the Romans built a fortress at Viroconium, one of the largest towns in Roman Britain. The Saxon conquest brought the construction of Offa's Dyke, marking the England–Wales border. After the Norman Conquest of 1066, a double line of castles was established as fortification against the Welsh. In the 13th century the high quality of Shropshire wool brought prosperity to the region. In the early 18th century it became the greatest iron-producing area in England. Iron founding and agriculture remain important.

Shroud of Turin See Shroud of Turin

shrub Any woody plant that has several stems, none of which is dominant, and is usually less than 10 ft (3 m) tall. When much-branched and dense, it may be called a bush. Intermediate between shrubs and trees are arborescences, or treelike shrubs (10–20 ft, or 3–6 m, tall). Trees are generally defined as woody plants more than 20 ft (6 m) tall, having a dominant stem, or trunk, and a definite crown shape. These distinctions are not reliable, however; for example, under especially favorable environmental conditions, some shrubs may grow to the size of an arborescence or even a small tree.

Shu \'shü\ In Egyptian religion, the god of the air and supporter of the sky, created by the god Atum. Shu and his sister Tefnut (goddess of moisture) were the first couple of the group of nine gods called the Ennead of Heliopolis. Of their union were born Geb and Nut. Shu was portrayed in human form with an ostrich feather on his head. He was often represented supporting with uplifted arms the body of Nut arched above him. Later he was frequently termed the son of Re, and he was also identified with Onuris, a warrior god.

Shu (907–65) Ancient name for Sichuan and the name of two of the 10 kingdoms included in China's Ten Kingdoms period (907–c. 980), specifically the Qian (Former) Shu (907–25) and the Hou (Later) Shu (934–65). The kingdom of Shu was located in present-day Sichuan. Aside from 10 years of instability that occurred between the two Shu regimes, the area experienced peace and prosperity. Poetry flourished, as did Buddhism and Taoism. See also Five Dynasties, Three Kingdoms.

Shu jing *or* **Shu ching** \'shü-'jiŋ\ One of the Five Classics of Chinese antiquity. Documenting China's ancient history, the *Shu jing* contains the oldest Chinese writing of its kind. It consists of 58 chapters, of which 33 are generally considered authentic works of the 4th century BC or earlier. The first five chapters purport to preserve the sayings and recall the deeds of emperors who reigned during China's legendary golden age; the next four are devoted to the Xia dynasty; the next 17 chapters deal with the Shang dynasty; and the final 32 chapters cover the Western Zhou dynasty.

Shu Maung See U Ne Win

Shubert Brothers U.S. theatrical managers and producers. After emigrating from Russia with their parents in 1882, the two oldest brothers, Lee (1872?–1953) and Sam (c. 1875–1905), leased theaters and presented plays in Syracuse, N.Y., in the 1890s. By 1900 Jacob (1880–1963) had joined the business, and the brothers leased their first theaters in New York City. Coming into conflict with the Theatrical Syndicate, which controlled U.S. theatrical bookings, they led an independent movement to fight the syndicate and prevailed after a long legal battle. After Sam's death in 1905, Lee and Jacob built theaters across the U.S. and came to own over 60 legitimate houses and many vaudeville and movie theaters. They produced over 1,000 different shows, including 600 plays, revues, and musicals. Theatrical unions such as Actors' Equity were formed in response to their often sharp business practices. Charged with monopoly practices in 1950, they sold a number of theaters in 1956 but retained prestigious houses in many cities.

Shubra al-Khaymah \shu̇-'brä-el-'k̲ā-mə\ City (pop., 1992 est.: 834,000), Egypt. It is a northern suburb of CAIRO, on the eastern bank of the NILE RIVER. It was formerly a marketplace supplying Cairo with agricultural produce from the rich delta area. In the 1820s the Ottoman viceroy of Egypt built the country's first European-style factories and schools there, and it developed as an industrial center. The city lies west of the southern terminus of the Ismailia Canal, which links the SUEZ CANAL with the Nile.

shuffleboard Game in which two or four players use long-handled cues to shove disks into scoring areas of a diagram marked on a flat, smooth surface (6 by 52 ft, or 1.8 by 15.8 m). It was popular in England as early as the 15th century, especially with the aristocracy; it later became popular among travelers on ocean liners and cruise ships as a deck game. The current form of the game was defined at St. Petersburg, Fla., in 1924.

Shugen-do \shü-'gen-'dō\ Japanese religious tradition combining folk beliefs with SHINTO, BUDDHISM, and elements of TAOISM. The practitioner engages in spiritual and physical disciplines to attain power against evil spirits. Shugen-do flourished in the HEIAN PERIOD and allied itself with the esoteric schools of Buddhism, Tendai (TIANTAI), and SHINGON. Many Buddhist priests belonging to esoteric traditions regularly developed Shugen-do techniques, and Shugen-do practitioners often served as Shinto priests. The government abolished Shugen-do in 1872. After 1945, with the establishment of religious freedom, some Shugen-do groups attempted a revival, but the tradition's membership and influence remain greatly diminished.

Shula, Don(ald Francis) (born 1930) U.S. football coach. Born in Grand River, Ohio, he played football for John Carroll University and the Baltimore Colts and other NFL clubs. After coaching collegiate football, he became head coach of the Colts (1963–69); under Shula the team won 71 games, lost 23, and tied four. As coach of the Miami Dolphins (1970–96), he became the first NFL coach to win 100 games in 10 seasons; in 1972–73 the Dolphins became the first team to go undefeated through an entire season and the play-offs, culminating in a Super Bowl victory. Shula holds the all-time NFL record for victories, with 347.

Shull, George Harrison (1874–1954) U.S. botanist and geneticist. Born in Ohio, he acquired his doctorate in 1904 and worked thereafter primarily for the Carnegie Institute at Cold Spring Harbor, N.Y., and at Princeton University. He developed a method of breeding corn that made the seed capable of thriving under various soil and climatic conditions, as a result of which corn yields per acre were increased 25–50%. Shull developed his first hybrids before 1910, though commercial production did not begin until 1922. He founded the journal *Genetics* in 1916. See also EDWARD MURRAY EAST.

Shun \'shu̇n\ In Chinese mythology, one of the three legendary emperors, along with YAO and DA YU, of the golden age of antiquity (c. 23rd century BC), singled out by CONFUCIUS as models of integrity and virtue. Though his father repeatedly tried to murder him, Shun remained loyal to him. Because heaven and earth knew of his virtue, animals assisted him in all his labors. The emperor Yao bypassed his own son to select Shun as his successor, and gave him two daughters in marriage. Shun is credited with standardizing weights and measures, regulating waterways, and organizing the kingdom into provinces.

Shute, Nevil *orig.* **Nevil Shute Norway** (1899–1960) English-Australian novelist. Trained as an aeronautical engineer, Shute drew on technical detail in his fiction. His early works include *So Disdained* (1928) and *What Happened to the Corbetts* (1939), a foretaste of the bombing of civilians in World War II. After the war he settled in Australia, where he set his later novels. Reflecting a growing despair about the future of humanity, they include *A Town Like Alice* (1950; film, 1956) and his best-known work, *On The Beach* (1957; film, 1959), a vivid picture of the nuclear annihilation of the human race.

shuttle In the WEAVING of cloth, a spindle-shaped device used to carry the crosswise threads (weft) through the lengthwise threads (warp). Not all modern LOOMS use a shuttle; shuttleless looms draw the weft from a nonmoving supply. Shuttle looms fall into two groups according to whether the shuttle is moved by hand or automatically. The second kind is often described as an automatic loom, but except for shuttle movement it is no more automatic in its operation than the hand-moved or so-called nonautomatic loom. See also FLYING SHUTTLE.

Shwe Dagon \'shwā-ˌdä-gün\ PAGODA in Yangon (Rangoon) that is the center of Burmese religious life. A Buddhist temple complex begun in the 15th century, Shwe Dagon is constructed of brick in the form of a cone and is completely covered with gold. Raised over a relic chamber, it was rebuilt several times and was brought to its present height of 326 ft (99 m) in 1841 by King Tharrawaddy. The pagoda sits atop a hill that rises 168 ft (51 m) above the city.

Shymkent \shim-'kent\ *or* **Chimkent** City (pop., 1995 est.: 398,000), southern central Kazakhstan. It lies at an elevation of 1,680 ft (512 m) in the foothills of the Ugam Range, north of TASHKENT. Originally a settlement on the caravan route from central Asia to China, it dates to at least the 12th century. Destroyed by nomad attacks several times, it became part of the Khanate of QUQON in the early 19th century and was taken by Russia in 1864. It lies on the Turkistan-Siberian Railroad, and its population grew dramatically in the 20th century. It is now an industrial and cultural center.

SI system See INTERNATIONAL SYSTEM OF UNITS

Sia See HU, SIA, AND HEH

Siad Barre \'sē-ˌäd-'bär-ā\, **Mohamed** (1919?–1995) President of Somalia, 1969–91. He attended military school in Italy, and when Somalia achieved independence in 1960 he was made a colonel in its army. He seized power in a bloodless coup after the president's assassination in 1969. Under Siad Barre, Somali forces invaded a disputed area in southeastern Ethiopia in 1977, but were eventually repelled. His government was charged with widespread human-rights abuses, and from 1988 government forces repeatedly clashed with rebels. He fled into exile in Nigeria in 1991, leaving Somalia in a state of civil war and on the brink of mass starvation.

Siam See THAILAND

Siamese cat Breed of slender, short-haired DOMESTIC CAT that originated in Thailand (Siam). The Siamese has a pale fawn or gray body with dark points on the ears, face, legs, and tail. The points may be dark brown (seal point), blue-gray (blue point), milk-chocolate brown (chocolate point), pinkish gray (lilac point), or reddish orange (red point). The head is wedge-shaped. The blue eyes are slanted and may be crossed, though crossed eyes and kinked tail are discouraged by breeders of show animals. Siamese are considered highly intelligent and are very vocal, with a distinctive yowling mew.

Siamese fighting fish Freshwater tropical fish *(Betta splendens;* family Belontiidae, or Anabantidae), noted for the males' pugnacity toward one another. A native of Thailand, it was domesticated there for use in contests. Combat consists mainly of fin nipping and is accompanied by a display of extended gill covers, spread fins, and intensified coloring. This slender fish grows to about 2.5 in. (6.5 cm) long. In the wild, it is predominantly greenish or brown, with red fins; domesticated, it has been bred with long, flowing fins and in a variety of colors, such as red, green, blue, and lavender.

Siamese fighting fish (*Betta splendens*).
DOUGLAS FAULKNER

Siamese twins See CONJOINED TWINS

S
T
U
V

Sian See XI'AN

Siang River See XIANG RIVER

Sibelius \si-'bāl-yəs\, **Jean** *orig.* **Johan Julius Christian** (1865–1957) Finnish composer. He played violin and composed as a child, and later studied composition with Karl Goldmark (1830–1915). After initially concentrating on chamber music, he rapidly developed into an orchestral composer. He became involved with the movement for national independence from Russia, and his nationalism resulted in such works based on Finnish folklore as *Kullervo* (1892), the *Karelia* suite (1893), *Legends from the Kalevala* (1893), and *Finlandia* (1900). His major achievements were his seven symphonies (1899–1924), the violin concerto (1903), and *Tapiola* (1926). His works, marked by a sweeping but melancholy Romanticism, achieved huge international popularity. Out of sympathy with prevalent musical trends and perhaps damaged by years of heavy drinking, he wrote nothing in his last 30 years.

Siberia Region, northern central Asia, largely in Russia. It extends from the URAL MOUNTAINS to the Pacific Ocean and from the Arctic Ocean to central Kazakhstan and the boundaries of China and Mongolia; it covers about 5,000,000 sq mi (12,950,000 sq km). It is notorious for the length and severity of its almost snowless winters. Temperatures of –90°F (–68°C) have been recorded. The first settlers probably arrived in southern Siberia in the Paleolithic period. The area was under Chinese influence from c. 1000 BC, followed by the Turkic-Mongols in the 3rd century BC. Russian trappers and COSSACK explorers colonized it in the late 16th century, and by the mid-18th century most of Siberia was under Russian rule. It was connected to other parts of Russia by the TRANS-SIBERIAN RAILROAD. Eastern Siberia was the scene of the anti-Bolshevik government of ALEKSANDR KOLCHAK 1918–20. It was made part of the Russian S.F.S.R. in 1922. Russia exiled criminals and political prisoners there, and in the 1930s JOSEPH STALIN set up forced-labor camps that fueled industrial growth. When Russian factories were relocated there during World War II, it played an important role in the war effort. It has deposits of coal, petroleum, natural gas, diamonds, iron ore, and gold; its chief industrial products include steel, aluminum, and machinery. Southern Siberia produces wheat, rye, oats, and sunflowers. Its main cities include NOVOSIBIRSK, OMSK, KRASNOYARSK, and IRKUTSK.

Siberian husky Breed of dog developed in Siberia by the Chukchi people, who used it as a sled dog, companion, and guard. It was brought to Alaska in 1909 for sled-dog races and became established as a consistent winner. A graceful dog with erect ears and a dense, soft coat, it stands 20–24 in. (51–60 cm) and weighs 35–60 lbs (16–27 kg). It is usually gray, tan, or black and white; head markings may resemble a cap, mask, or spectacles. The breed, kept pure for hundreds of years in Siberia, is noted for intelligence and a gentle temperament.

Siberian peoples Any of a large number of small ethnic groups living in SIBERIA. Most engage either in reindeer herding or fishing, while some also hunt furbearing animals or farm and raise horses or cattle. In the past, many had both summer and winter dwellings, their winter homes sometimes being partially or entirely underground and their summer homes being various styles of tent. Shamanism was common, and the family was the basic societal unit. The Soviet government attempted to settle Siberian peoples on collective farms and to introduce new occupations, but some groups, such as the Koryak and the Nenets, still engage in their traditional pursuits. Other Siberian peoples include the Chuckchi, Evenki, Ket, Khanty, Mansi, YAKUT, and Yukaghir. See also PALEO-SIBERIAN LANGUAGES.

Siberut \,sē-bə-'rüt\ Island, Indonesia. The largest island in the Mentawai group, it lies off the western coast of SUMATRA, Indonesia. It is 25 mi (40 km) wide and 70 mi (110 km) long. The coast is low and swampy; the inland is savanna. Agriculture is the chief occupation.

Sibyl Prophetess of Greek legend. She was a figure of the mythical past whose prophecies, phrased in Greek hexameters, were handed down in writing. In the late 4th century BC, the number of sibyls multiplied, and the term sibyl was treated as a title. Sibyls were associated with various ORACLES, especially those of APOLLO, who was said to be their inspiration. They were typically depicted as extremely old women living in caves, who delivered their prophecies in an ecstatic frenzy. A famous collection of prophecies, the Sibylline Books, was traditionally kept in the temple of JUPITER, to be consulted only in emergencies.

Sichuan *or* **Szechwan** \'se-'chwän, 'sē-'chwän\ Province (pop., 1996 est.: 98,650,000), upper CHANG RIVER valley, southwestern China. Second-largest of China's provinces, it encompasses the central depression called the Red Basin; its capital is CHENGDU. It is one of China's most densely populated and ethnically diverse provinces. It was among the first areas to be settled by the Chinese in the first millennium BC. From the ZHOU DYNASTY (1122–221 BC) until the SONG AND S. SONG DYNASTIES (AD 960–1279), it was administered through various political subdivisions. It was established as a province during the QING dynasty (1644–1911). During the SINO-JAPANESE WAR, it served as the seat (at CHONGQING) of the Nationalist government; the Japanese never penetrated the area. It is China's leading producer of rice, corn, sweet potatoes, cattle, and pigs. The most industrialized province of southwestern China, it is a center for coal mining, petroleum refining, and chemical production.

Sicilian school Group of Sicilian, southern Italian, and Tuscan poets centered in the courts of FREDERICK II (r.1197–1250) and his son MANFRED of Sicily (died 1266). They established the vernacular, as opposed to Provençal, as the standard language for Italian love poetry and are also credited with inventing two major Italian poetic forms, the canzone and the SONNET. Some 125 of their poems are extant, many by Giacomo da Lentini, the school's senior poet. The Sicilian-school sonnet became, with variations, the dominant poetic form in Renaissance Italy and Elizabethan England, where it was modified to form the English, or Shakespearean, sonnet.

Sicilian Vespers (1282) Massacre of the French that began a Sicilian revolt against the Angevin king CHARLES I. Backed by PETER III of Aragon, the rising broke out when Sicilians killed some insulting French soldiers at vespers in the church of Santo Spirito in Palermo. The people of the city followed suit and massacred 2,000 of its French inhabitants. All of Sicily soon revolted and sought help from the Aragonese, and the war became a French-Aragonese struggle for possession of Sicily. The conflict was finally resolved when the Sicilians chose Frederick III, brother of the king of Aragon, as their ruler in 1302.

Sicilies, The Two Former kingdom, Italy. It united the southern part of the Italian peninsula with the island of SICILY. The region was conquered by the Normans in the 11th century but was divided in 1282 between the French on the mainland and the Spanish on the island, both with rulers claiming the title of king of Sicily. In 1442 ALFONSO V of Aragon reunited the two areas and took the title of king of the Two Sicilies. This title was sometimes used during the Spanish and Bourbon rule of the region in the 16th–19th century; it became official in 1816, when the administration of both areas was combined, and Sicily lost its autonomy. Conquered by GIUSEPPE DE GARIBALDI in 1860, the Two Sicilies became part of the kingdom of Italy.

Sicily \'si-sə-lē\ *Italian* **Sicilia** \si-'sil-yə\ Island and autonomous region (pop., 1996 est.: 5,095,000), Italy. It is separated from the mainland by the Strait of MESSINA. The largest island (9,830 sq mi, or 25, 460 sq km) in the Mediterranean Sea, it is also the site of Europe's highest active volcano, Mount ETNA. The capital is PALERMO. Its strategic location at the center of the Mediterranean has made the island a crossroads of history. The Greeks colonized it in the 8th–6th century BC, and in the 3rd century BC it became the first Roman province. It came under Byzantine rule in the 6th century AD, and in 965 fell to Arab conquest from North Africa. It was taken in 1060 by the NORMANS. In the 12th–13th century and again in the 18th century, it formed part of the kingdom of the Two SICILIES. During the 19th century it was a major center of revolutionary movements; in 1860 it was liberated from the Bourbons, and in 1861 it was incorporated into the kingdom of Italy. Agriculture is its economic mainstay; industries include oil refining, food processing, wine making, and shipbuilding.

sickle-cell anemia Serious HEMOGLOBINOPATHY seen mainly in persons of sub-Saharan African ancestry and their descendants, and in the Middle East, the Mediterranean area, and India. About one in 400 blacks worldwide has the disease, caused by inheriting two copies of a recessive gene that makes those with one copy of it (about one in 12 blacks worldwide) resistant to MALARIA. The gene specifies an abnormal HEMOGLOBIN (hemoglobin S or Hb S) that distorts ERYTHROCYTES into a rigid sickle shape. The cells become clogged in capillaries, damaging or destroying various tissues. Symptoms include chronic ANEMIA, shortness of breath, fever, and episodic "crises" (severe pain in the abdomen, bones, or muscles). Hydroxyurea treatment triggers production of fetal hemoglobin (Hb F), which does not sickle, greatly lessening severity of crises and increasing life expectancy, previously about 45 years.

Sicyon \'si-sē-ən\ Ancient city, northern PELOPONNESE, southern Greece. It is located 11 mi (18 km) northwest of CORINTH. It was influential in Greek history, attaining its greatest power in the 6th century BC under Cleisthenes, grandfather of CLEISTHENES OF ATHENS. During the 4th century BC it was celebrated for its school of painters and sculptors, which included LYSIPPUS. In the 3rd century BC it gained prominence under ARATUS, who brought it into the ACHAEAN LEAGUE.

Siddons, Sarah *orig.* **Sarah Kemble** (1755–1831) British actress. She acted with her father's traveling company and married actor William Siddons in 1773. She made her London debut as Isabella in *Fatal Marriage* at the DRURY LANE THEATRE in 1782 and was instantly acclaimed the leading tragedienne of the time. She played Shakespearean parts, notably Lady Macbeth, from 1785 until she retired in 1812. She was the subject of well-known portraits by THOMAS GAINSBOROUGH and JOSHUA REYNOLDS.

Sarah Siddons, chalk drawing by J. Downman, 1787; in the National Portrait Gallery, London.

BY COURTESY OF THE NATIONAL PORTRAIT GALLERY, LONDON

Side \'sē-də\ Ancient city, southwestern Turkey. The most important port of ancient Pamphylia, it originally was situated on the Mediterranean coast; it now lies inland. Though it was founded by Aeolian Greeks, a peculiar non-Greek language was spoken there. ALEXANDER THE GREAT occupied it; ANTIOCHUS III was defeated there in 190 BC. In the 1st century BC, pirates made it their chief slave market. The ruins include the remains of a colossal theater, built on arches and considered one of the finest in ASIA MINOR.

side horse *or* **pommel horse** Gymnastics event for men involving the use of a side (pommel) horse, a padded rectangular apparatus with two pommels (U-shaped handles) on the top and supported by legs. The gymnast performs various swinging and balancing feats, holding himself over the horse by means of the pommels or by grasping the front (neck), center (saddle), or rear (croup) of the horse. The apparatus stems from a wooden horse used by the Romans to teach mounting and dismounting.

sidereal period \sī-'dir-ē-əl\ Time required for a celestial body in the solar system to complete one revolution with respect to the fixed stars (as observed from a fixed point outside the system). A planet's sidereal period can be calculated from its SYNODIC PERIOD. The sidereal period of the moon or an artificial satellite of earth is the time it takes to return to the same position against the background of stars. See also DAY.

siderite \'sī-də-ˌrīt\ *or* **chalybite** \'ka-lə-ˌbīt\ Iron carbonate ($FeCO_3$), a widespread CARBONATE MINERAL that can be an ore of iron. The mineral commonly occurs in thin beds with shales, clay, or coal seams (as sedimentary deposits) and in hydrothermal metallic veins (as gangue, or waste rock).

sidewinder Species *(Crotalus cerastes)* of small, nocturnal RATTLESNAKE, found in sandy deserts of Mexico and the southwestern U.S. It is 18–30 in. (45–75 cm) long. It has hornlike scales above its eyes and is pale tan, pinkish, or gray, with an inconspicuous spotted pattern on the back and sides. It moves by looping itself obliquely across the sand, leaving a characteristic J-shaped trail. Its venomous bite is usually not fatal to humans.

Sidgwick, Henry (1838–1900) British philosopher. Educated at Cambridge, he remained there as a fellow (from 1859) and professor (from 1883). His *Methods of Ethics* (1874) is considered by some the most significant 19th-century ethical work in English. Drawing on JOHN STUART MILL's UTILITARIANISM and IMMANUEL KANT's CATEGORICAL IMPERATIVE, he proposed a system of "universalistic hedonism," which sought to reconcile the apparent conflict between the pleasure of self and that of others. His other writings include *Principles of Political Economy* (1883) and *Elements of Politics* (1891). He also cofounded the Society for Psychical Research (1882) and helped found Cambridge's first women's college.

siding Material used to surface the exterior of a building to protect against exposure to the elements, prevent heat loss, and visually unify the facade. The word siding implies wood units, or products imitative of wood, used on houses. There are many different types of siding, including CLAPBOARD, horizontal lap siding, vertical board siding, and SHINGLES. Board and batten siding, sometimes found in CARPENTER GOTHIC houses and very modest structures, differs from the common clapboard in that it consists of vertical wood boards with their butt joints covered by battens (narrow strips), imparting a seamed appearance. Both aluminum and polyvinyl-fluoride-coated siding (commonly called vinyl siding) were developed as maintenance-free alternatives to wood clapboard; they mimic its horizontal boards. Fiberboard, a pressed-wood-pulp product, is sometimes used, though its long-term durability is limited. In larger buildings, the exterior covering is called cladding, and may be of brick, glass in a metal framework, or stone, concrete, or metal panels.

Sidney, Sir Philip (1554–1586) English courtier, statesman, soldier, and poet. Born into an aristocratic family and educated to be a statesman and soldier, Sidney served in minor official posts and turned to literature as an outlet for his energies. *Astrophel and Stella* (1591), inspired by Sidney's passion for his aunt's married ward, is considered the finest Elizabethan SONNET cycle after WILLIAM SHAKESPEARE's sonnets. *The Defence of Poesie* (1595), an urbane and eloquent plea for imaginative literature, introduced the critical ideas of Renaissance theorists to England. His heroic romance *Arcadia,* though unfinished, is the most important work of English prose fiction of the 16th century. None of his works was published in his lifetime. Wounded in action while soldiering in the Netherlands, he died from an infection at 31, and was widely mourned as the ideal gentleman of his day.

Sidon \'sīd-ᵊn\ Seaport (pop., 1991 est.: 100,000), southwestern Lebanon. Located on the site of a city founded in the 3rd millennium BC, it was a principal city of PHOENICIA from the 2nd millennium BC and a parent city of TYRE. Ruled successively in ancient times by the Assyrians, Babylonians, and Persians, it was conquered by ALEXANDER THE GREAT c. 330 BC. Under Roman rule by the 1st century BC, it was an important center for the manufacture of glass and purple dyes. It changed hands several times during the CRUSADES, and fell to the Muslims in 1291. It flourished for a while under Turkish rule after 1517. It is now the Mediterranean terminal for a Saudi Arabian oil pipeline.

Sidra \'si-drə\, **Gulf of** *or* **Gulf of Sirte** \'sir-ˌtā\ Inlet of the Mediterranean Sea, northern central coast, Libya. It extends 275 mi (443 km). In August the gulf's water temperature reaches 88°F (31°C), the warmest in the Mediterranean. In World War II it was the scene of the Battle of Sirte, in which a British naval convoy thwarted attacks from Italian warships and German bombers.

SIDS See SUDDEN INFANT DEATH SYNDROME

Siegel \'sē-gəl\, **Bugsy** *orig.* **Benjamin** (1906–1947) U.S. gangster. Born in Brooklyn, N.Y., he began his career extorting money from Jewish peddlers on New York's Lower East Side. He joined with MEYER LANSKY and began operating bootlegging and gambling rackets; they later formed the forerunner of MURDER, Inc. In 1937 he was sent to develop rackets on the West Coast, and soon set up gambling dens and ships as well as narcotics smuggling and blackmail operations. In 1945 he built the Flamingo Hotel and Casino in Las Vegas. Originally budgeted at $1.5 million, its cost was driven to $6 million through his skimming. This angered Lansky and other bosses, and Siegel was shot down in his home.

Siegen \'zē-gən\, **Ludwig von** (1609–c. 1680) German painter and engraver. His earliest dated MEZZOTINT was a portrait of Amelia Elizabeth of Hesse-Kassel (1642); in its dedication he claimed the invention of the mezzotint process, which he described as engraving by dots rather than lines. To produce the dots he used a small roulette, a tool with a fine-toothed wheel. Seven known rouletted mezzotint plates by Siegen survive.

Siegfried \'sig-ˌfrēd, *German* 'zēk-ˌfrēt\ *Old Norse* **Sigurd** Hero of German and Old Norse mythology noted for his outstanding strength and courage. He is one of the heroes of the Poetic EDDA and the NIBELUNGENLIED, and he figures in many different, sometimes inconsistent, legends. In the earliest stories, Siegfried is presented as a boy of noble lineage who grew up without parental care, but other accounts provide elaborate detail of a courtly upbringing. One legend tells of his battle with a dragon, and another of his acquiring treasure; he also plays a part in the story of BRUNHILD, in which he meets his death. He is the hero of RICHARD WAGNER's operatic tetralogy *The Ring of the Nibelung.* See also KRIEMHILD.

Siemens \'sē-mənz\, **(Charles) William** *orig.* **Karl Wilhelm** *later* **Sir William** (1823–1883) German-British engineer and inventor. He emigrated to Britain in 1844. In 1861 he patented the open-hearth furnace (see OPEN-HEARTH PROCESS), which was soon being widely used in steelmaking and eventually replaced the earlier BESSEMER PROCESS. He also made a reputation and a fortune in the steel cable and TELEGRAPH industries, and was a principal in the company that laid the first successful transatlantic telegraph cable (1866). His three brothers were also eminent engineers and industrialists (see SIEMENS AG).

Siemens AG \'sē-mənz\ German electrical-equipment manufacturer. The first Siemens company, Siemens & Halske, was founded in Berlin in 1847 to build telegraph installations. Under Werner Siemens (1816–1892) and his three brothers (including WILLIAM SIEMENS), it expanded to produce dynamos, cables, telephones, electric power, and electric lighting. In 1903 Siemens & Halske transferred its power-engineering activities to the new Siemens-Schuckertwerke GmbH, and in 1932 Siemens-Reiniger-Werke AG was established to produce medical equipment. The companies expanded greatly during the Third Reich; after World War II, Siemens officials were charged with using slave labor and participating in the construction and operation of the AUSCHWITZ and BUCHENWALD camps. The Siemens companies flourished again in the 1950s, and by the 1966, when they merged to form Siemens AG (formed in 1966 by the merger of the three Siemens companies), were among the world's largest electrical suppliers. Siemens products include electrical components, computer systems, microwave devices, and medical equipment.

Siemens-Martin process See OPEN-HEARTH PROCESS

Siena \sē-'e-nä\ *ancient* **Saena Julia** City (pop., 1991: 56,969), western Italy. It is located south of FLORENCE. Founded by the ETRUSCANS, it later passed to the Romans and the Lombards; in the 12th century it became a self-governing commune. Rivalry with Florence made Siena the center of pro-imperial Ghibellinism in TUSCANY. It was conquered by Charles of Anjou, king of Naples and Sicily, in 1270 and joined the Guelph confederation (see GUELPHS AND GHIBELLINES). It was an important banking and commercial center until surpassed by Florence in the 13th–14th century. Conquered by the Holy Roman emperor CHARLES V in 1555, it was ceded to Florence in 1557. Modern Siena is a market town and tourist center; historic sites including the Gothic-Romanesque cathedral, the University of Siena (founded 1240), and the Piazza del Campo, where horse races originating in medieval times are still held.

Sienkiewicz \sh^{y}en-'k^{y}e-v^{y}ēch\, **Henryk (Adam Alexander Pius)** (1846–1916) Polish novelist. In 1869 he began to publish critical works showing the influence of POSITIVISM. He worked as a newspaperman and published successful short stories before producing the great trilogy consisting of *With Fire and Sword* (1884), *The Deluge* (1886), and *Pan Michael* (1887–88). Describing Poland's struggles against Cossacks, Tatars, Swedes, and Turks, the novels stress Polish heroism in a vivid style of epic clarity and simplicity. The widely translated *Quo Vadis?* (1896), set in Rome under Nero, established his international reputation. He received the Nobel Prize in 1905.

Sierra Club U.S. organization for the conservation of natural resources, headquartered in San Francisco. It was founded in 1892 by a group of Californians, including JOHN MUIR, who wanted to sponsor wilderness outings in Pacific Coast mountain regions. As its first president, Muir initiated the club's involvement in political action on behalf of nature conservation. With branches in all 50 states, it works to educate the public on environmental issues and lobbies local, state, and federal agencies for environmental legislation.

Sierra Leone \sē-ˌer-ə-lē-'ōn\ *officially* **Republic of Sierra Leone** Nation, western Africa. Area: 27,699 sq mi (71,740 sq km). Population (2002 est.): 4,823,000. Capital: FREETOWN. The Mende and Temne are the largest of about 18 ethnic groups. Languages: English (official), Krio (derived from English and a variety of African languages). Religions: Islam, traditional religious beliefs, Christianity. Currency: leone. Sierra

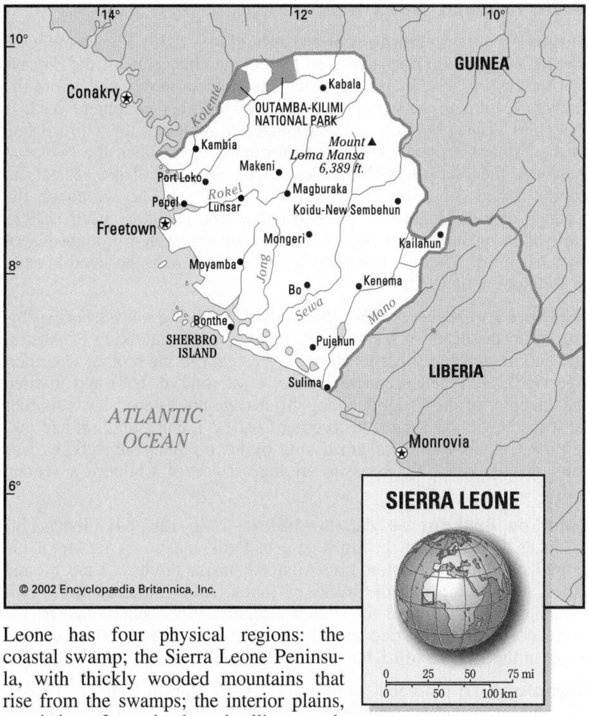

Leone has four physical regions: the coastal swamp; the Sierra Leone Peninsula, with thickly wooded mountains that rise from the swamps; the interior plains, consisting of grasslands and rolling wooded country; and the eastern plateau region, encompassing several mountains. More than one-fourth of the country is forest. Wildlife includes chimpanzees, tigers, crocodiles, and many species of birds. The economy is based largely on agriculture and mining; rice, cassava, coffee, cacao, and oil palm are major crops, and diamonds, iron ore, and bauxite are mined. Its head of state and government is the president. Its earliest inhabitants were probably the Bulom; the Mende and Temne peoples arrived in the 15th century. The coastal region was visited by the Portuguese in the 15th century, and by 1495 there was a Portuguese fort on the site of modern Freetown. European ships visited the coast regularly to trade for slaves and ivory, and the English built trading posts on offshore islands in the 17th century. British abolitionists and philanthropists founded Freetown in 1787 as a private venture for freed and runaway slaves. In 1808 the coastal settlement became a British colony. The region became a British protectorate in 1896. It achieved independence in 1961 and became a republic in 1971. Since independence Sierra Leone has suffered through the instability of a series of military coups. In the 1990s a civil war marked by horrific atrocities further devastated the country. Political and economic turmoil continued into the 21st century.

Sierra Madre Principal mountain system, Mexico. It includes the ranges of the Sierra Madre Occidental (west), the Sierra Madre Oriental (east), and the Sierra Madre del Sur (south). The Sierra Madre Occidental extends for about 700 mi (1,120 km), parallel with the Gulf of California and the Pacific Ocean; summits rise above elevations of 6,000 ft (1,800 m), with some exceeding 10,000 ft (3,000 m). the Sierra Madre Oriental originates in the barren hills of the RÍO GRANDE to the north and extends about 700 mi (1,120 km), roughly parallel with the Gulf of Mexico; it has an average elevation of about 7,000 ft (2,150 m) and rises to 12,008 ft (3,660 m) at the peak of Mount Peña Nevada. The sparsely inhabited Sierra Madre del Sur stretches through the southern Mexican states of GUERRERO and OAXACA, reaching elevations of about 6,500 ft (2,000 m), with a few peaks exceeding 10,000 ft (3,000 m).

Sierra Nevada Mountain range, eastern California. It extends more than 250 mi (400 km) from the MOJAVE DESERT to the CASCADE RANGE. It averages about 50 mi (80 km) in width. Its peaks are 11,000–14,000 ft (3,350–4,270 m) high; Mount WHITNEY is the highest. It is a year-round recreation center, accessible from the state's large urban areas.

Sierra redwood See BIG TREE

Sieyès \syā-'yes\, **Emmanuel-Joseph** (1748–1836) French political theorist. A Catholic priest, he rose to become chancellor of the diocese of Chartres in 1788. In sympathy with the reform movement before the French Revolution, he won great popularity with his pamphlet "What Is the Third Estate?" (1789) and was elected to represent the Third Estate in the Estates General. He led the movement to establish the NATIONAL ASSEMBLY, then served in the National Convention until the radical Jacobins seized control (1793). During the DIRECTORY, he served on the Council of Five Hundred (1795–99) and on the Directory itself (1799). He helped organize the Coup of 18–19 BRUMAIRE, which brought NAPOLEON to power. After the monarchy's restoration (1815), he lived in exile in Belgium until 1830.

Sigebert I \sēzh-'ber\ (535–575) Frankish king of the MEROVINGIAN DYNASTY. On the death of his father, CHLOTAR I, he became king of Austrasia, and he gained further territory on the death of his brother Charibert I (c. 567). He repelled attacks by the AVARS (562, c. 568) and married the daughter of the Visigothic king. To avenge his sister-in-law's murder he waged civil war against his brother CHILPERIC I, defeating him and taking most of his land. Acclaimed king by his brother's subjects, he was immediately killed by assassins in the service of Chilperic's second wife.

Siger de Brabant \sē-'zhā...bra-'bä^{n}\ (c. 1240–1281/84) French philosopher. He taught at the University of Paris and was a leader of the school of radical, or heterodox, Aristotelianism. From c. 1260 he and others gave lectures on the works of Greek, Arabic, and medieval philosophers without regard for church teaching. When summoned by the INQUISITION (1276), he fled to Italy. DANTE, in the *Divine Comedy*, put Siger in the Heaven of Light.

Sigismund \'si-jəs-mənd\ (1368–1437) Holy Roman Emperor (1433–37), king of Hungary (from 1387), German king (from 1411), king of Bohemia (from 1419), and Lombard king (from 1431). He became king of Hungary by marriage and pawned his German lands to raise funds for defense (1388). He pursued an expansionist policy that brought him into conflict with his brother WENCESLAS, whom he imprisoned (1402–3) in an abortive effort to seize Bohemia. As German king from 1411, Sigismund helped to end the Western SCHISM. He was twice defeated by the Turks (1396, 1428). He inherited the Bohemian crown in 1419, but wars against the HUSSITES delayed his coronation until 1436. He gained the imperial crown in 1433, becoming the last emperor of the House of Luxembourg.

Sigismund I *Polish* **Zygmunt Stary ("Sigismund the Old")** (1467–1548) King of Poland (1506–48). Son of CASIMIR IV, he became grand prince of Lithuania and king of Poland in 1506. After his army subdued the TEUTONIC ORDER in East Prussia, he established Polish suzerainty over the area, known as Ducal Prussia (1525). He added the duchy of Mazovia (now the province of Warsaw) to the Polish state in 1529. He established judicial and administrative reforms and encouraged a reform of the currency. A lover of the fine arts, he brought Italian artists to Poland and promoted the development of the Renaissance.

Sigismund II Augustus *Polish* **Zygmunt August** (1520–1572) King of Poland (1548–72). Son of SIGISMUND I, he was crowned coruler with his father in 1530 and ruled the duchy of Lithuania from 1544. After becoming king of Poland (1548), he supported the TEUTONIC ORDER in Livonia against Russia (1559) and by treaty incorporated Livonia into Lithuania (1561). Continued threats by Russia compelled Sigismund to unite the lands attached to the Polish crown, and by the Union of Lublin (1569) he united Poland and Lithuania and their respective dependencies. He died childless, which brought the end of the direct JAGIELLON DYNASTY.

Sigismund III Vasa *Polish* **Zygmunt Waza** (1566–1632) King of Poland (1587–1632) and of Sweden (1592–99). Son of King John III of Sweden (1537–1592) and Catherine, daughter of SIGISMUND I of Poland, he was elected king of Poland in 1587. On his father's death (1592), he accepted the Swedish throne and was crowned in 1594. He left his paternal uncle Charles (later CHARLES IX) as regent in Sweden and returned to Poland, but Charles later rose in rebellion, defeated Sigismund's army (1598), and deposed Sigismund (1599). Poland and Sweden fought intermittently from 1600 as Sigismund tried to regain the Swedish throne. He invaded Russia in the Time of TROUBLES and held Moscow 1610–12. In a renewal of the Polish–Swedish conflict in 1621, King GUSTAV II ADOLF seized most of Polish Livonia, which Sweden retained under the terms of a 1629 truce.

Sigismund III, detail of a painting, school of Rubens; in the Bayerische Staatsgemäldesammlungen, Munich.

BY COURTESY OF THE BAYERISCHE STAATSGEMALDESAMMLUNGEN, MUNICH

sign In marketing and advertising, a device placed on or before a premises to identify its occupant and the nature of the business done there or, placed at a distance, to advertise a business or its products. The ancient Egyptians and Greeks used signs for advertising purposes, as did the Romans, who also, in effect, created signboards by whitewashing convenient sections of walls for suitable inscriptions. Early shop signs were developed when tradesmen, dealing with a largely illiterate public, devised certain easily recognizable emblems to represent their trades. Modern sign designers use various forms of animation and light.

sign language Any means of communication through bodily movements, especially of the hands and arms, rather than through speech. It has long been used by speakers of mutually unintelligible languages—for example, various Plains Indians tribes in 19th-century North America communicated via a sign language—and is widely used for communication by the deaf. Charles-Michel, abbé de l'Épée (1712–1789), developed the first sign language for the deaf in the mid-18th cent; his system developed into French Sign Language (FSL), still used in France. Brought to the U.S. in 1816 by Thomas Gallaudet (1787–1851), it evolved into American Sign Language (ASL, or Ameslan), now used by more than half a million people. These and other national sign languages generally express concepts rather than elements of words and thus have more in common with each other than with their countries' spoken languages.

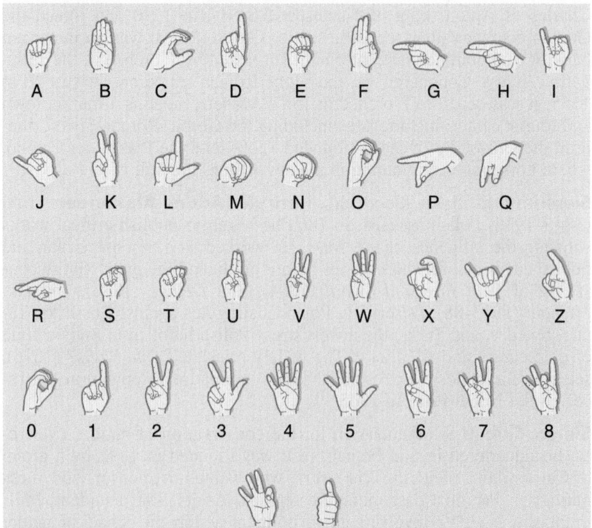

The alphabet and the numbers 0–10 in Amer. Sign Language.

© 2002 MERRIAM-WEBSTER INC.

Signac \sē-'nyák\, **Paul** (1863–1935) French painter. At 18 he gave up architecture to pursue painting in the Impressionist manner. In 1884 he became a founder of the SALON DES INDÉPENDANTS. With GEORGES SEURAT he developed an exact mathematical system of applying dots of color, which they called pointillism (see NEO-IMPRESSIONISM). He traveled extensively along the European coast painting landscapes and seascapes; in his later years he painted street scenes of Paris and other cities. He was a master of watercolor, in which he achieved great brilliance of color and a free, spontaneous style. His work had a great influence on HENRI MATISSE.

Signorelli \ˌsēn-yō-ˈrel-lē\, **Luca (d'Egidio di Ventura de')** *or* **Luca da Cortona** (c. 1445/50–1523) Italian painter. Highly influenced by the Florentine artists, he was probably a student of PIERO DELLA FRANCESCA. He went to Rome c. 1483, where he produced the *Testament of Moses* fresco in the Sistine Chapel. The dramatic action and depiction of great muscular effort in this and similar works mark him as essentially a Florentine naturalist. His masterpiece, the *End of the World* and *Last Judgment* frescoes in Orvieto Cathedral, with their many muscular nudes, greatly influenced MICHELANGELO.

Sigurd See SIEGFRIED

Sihanouk, Norodom See NORODOM SIHANOUK

Sikh Wars \ˈsēk\ (1845–46, 1848–49) Two wars fought between the Sikhs and the British. In the first war Sikhs invaded British India under the pretext of forestalling a British attack on the Sikh state in the PUNJAB (see RANJIT SINGH). They were defeated, the British annexed some of their lands, and British troops and a British resident were stationed in Lahore. The second war was a Sikh national revolt that ended in a British victory and annexation of the Punjab.

sikhara *or* **shikhara** \ˈshi-kə-rə\ Tower characteristic of Hindu temples of northern India. The sikhara over the sanctuary of a temple is usually tapered convexly, consisting of piled-up roof slabs of diminishing size. The surface is covered with vinelike *candrashala* (ogee arch) tracery; at the top is a cushion-shaped grooved disk *(amalaka),* and above that a pot with a crowning finial. The sikhara developed during the Gupta period (4th–6th century AD) and steadily grew taller and more elaborate, as in the soaring tower of the 11th-century Lingaraja Temple in BHUBANESWAR. In a variation of the basic form, half spires are added on either side of the sikhara; excellent examples are the 10th-century Laksmana and 11th-century Kandarya Mahadeva temples at Khajuraho, Madhya Pradesh. In addition to the curved sikhara, there is a smaller, rectilinear type frequently used above the temple *mandapa*s (halls).

A *sikhara* of the *bhumija* type, Udayesvara temple, Udayapur, Madhya Pradesh, India, 1059–82.
P. CHANDRA

Sikhism \ˈsē-ˌkiz-əm\ Indian monotheistic religion founded in the late 15th century by GURU NANAK. Most of its 18 million members, called Sikhs, live in the PUNJAB, the site of their holiest shrine, the GOLDEN TEMPLE, and the center of Sikh authority, the AKAL TAKHT. The ADI GRANTH is the canonical SCRIPTURE of Sikhism. Its theology is based on a supreme God who governs with justice and grace. Human beings, irrespective of CASTE and gender distinctions, have the opportunity to become one with God. The basic human flaw of self-centeredness can be overcome through proper reverence for God, commitment to hard work, service to humanity, and sharing the fruits of one's labor. Sikhs consider themselves disciples of the 10 Gurus. They accept the Hindu ideas of SAMSARA and KARMA, and they view themselves as the Khalsa, a chosen race of soldier-saints committed to a Spartan code of conduct and a crusade for righteousness. The emblems of the Khalsa, called the five Ks, are *kes* (uncut hair), *kangha* (a comb), *kachha* (long shorts), *kirpan* (a sword), and *karka* (a steel bracelet).

Sikkim \ˈsi-kəm\ State (pop., 1994 est.: 444,000), eastern HIMALAYAS, northeastern India. Mount KANCHENJUNGA, third-highest peak in the world, forms its western border. It has an area of 2,744 sq mi (7,107 sq km); the capital, GANGTOK, is the only urban center. As an independent country, it fought prolonged wars in the 18th and 19th century with Bhutan and Nepal. It first came under British influence in 1817, though it remained an independent buffer between British India and Tibet. In 1950 it became an Indian protectorate, and in 1975, a state of India. One of India's smallest states, it exports agricultural products and is one of the world's main producers of cardamom. Its mineral resources include copper, lead, zinc, coal, iron ore, and garnets.

Sikorski, Wladyslaw (Eugeniusz) (1881–1943) Polish general and politician. Born in Austrian Poland, he served in the Austrian army and in World War I was head of the Polish Legion, which joined with Austria against Russia. He served as prime minister of Poland 1923–24, and as minister of military affairs 1924–25. From 1928 he joined the opposition to the government controlled by JOZEF PILSUDSKI. After the German invasion of Poland (1939), he became prime minister of the Polish government-in-exile. When he asked JOSEPH STALIN to allow the Red Cross to investigate the KATYN MASSACRE, Stalin broke off Soviet–Polish diplomatic contact. Sikorski died in an airplane crash several months later.

Sikorsky, Igor (Ivan) (1889–1972) Russian-U.S. pioneer in aircraft design. After studying engineering in Kiev, he set up his own shop to develop the HELICOPTER. In 1910, after failing to build a workable model, he turned to fixed-wing airplane design, and in 1913 he built the first four-engine airplane, with an innovative enclosed cabin. He emigrated to the U.S. in 1919. In 1931 he produced the twin-engine amphibian aircraft that became the model for PAN AMERICAN WORLD AIRWAYS' "Clipper." In 1939 Sikorsky finally realized a viable helicopter design. He directed his company, a division of United Aircraft Corp., from 1929 to 1957.

Igor Sikorsky, Russian-born American aircraft designer.
BY COURTESY OF SIKORSKY AIRCRAFT

silage \ˈsī-lij\ *or* **ensilage** \ˈen-sə-lij\ FORAGE plants such as corn, legumes, and grasses that have been harvested at early maturity, finely chopped, packed tightly to exclude air, and stored in tower silos, pits, or trenches. Properly stored silage ferments slightly and keeps for several months. It is used as animal feed.

silane \ˈsi-ˌlān, ˈsī-ˌlān\ *or* **silicon hydride** Any of a series of inorganic compounds of SILICON and hydrogen with COVALENT BONDS, having the general chemical formula $Si_nH_{(2n+2)}$. Silanes are structural analogs of saturated (see SATURATION) HYDROCARBONS but are much less stable. All burn or explode when exposed to air and react readily with HALOGENS or hydrogen halides to form halogenated silanes and with OLEFINS to form alkylsilanes, products used as water repellents and as starting materials for SILICONES.

silenus See SATYR AND SILENUS

Silesia \si-ˈlē-zhə\ *Polish* **Shlask** \ˈshläsk\ *German* **Schlesien** \ˈshlā-zē-ən\ Historic region, eastern central Europe. It now lies mainly in southwestern Poland, with parts in Germany and the Czech Republic. It was originally a Polish province that became a possession of the Bohemian crown, and thus part of the HOLY ROMAN EMPIRE, in 1335. Due to succession disputes and the region's prosperity, there were at least 16 Silesian principalities by the end of the 15th century. It passed to the Austrian HABSBURGS in 1526; it was taken by Prussia in 1742. After World War I, it was divided between Poland, Czechoslovakia, and Germany. During World War II Polish Silesia was occupied by Germany and was the site of atrocities against the population by Nazi and, later, Soviet forces. In 1945 the Allied powers assigned virtually all of Silesia to Poland; today its nine Polish provinces contain almost one-fourth of Poland's population.

Silhak See PRACTICAL LEARNING SCHOOL

silhouette \ˌsi-lü-ˈet\ Outline image or design in a single solid, flat color, giving the appearance of a shadow cast by a solid figure. The term is usually applied to profile portraits in black against white (or vice versa), either painted or cut from paper, especially popular c. 1750–1850 as the least expensive method of portraiture. The name derives from Étienne de Silhouette, Louis XV's finance minister, notorious for his frugality and his hobby of making cut-paper shadow portraits. In 17th-century Europe, shadow portraits and scenes were produced by drawing the outline cast by candlelight or lamplight; when paper became widely available, they were often cut out freehand directly from life. Photography rendered silhouettes nearly obsolete, and they became a type of folk art practiced by itinerant artists and caricaturists.

Silhouette portrait by Charles Willson Peale; in the Library of Congress, Washington, D.C.

BY COURTESY OF THE LIBRARY OF CONGRESS, WASHINGTON, D.C.

silica mineral \'si-li-kə\ Any of the forms of silicon dioxide (SiO_2), including QUARTZ, tridymite, cristobalite, coesite, stishovite, melanophlogite, lechatelierite, and chalcedony. Various kinds of silica minerals have been produced synthetically.

silicate mineral Any of a large group of silicon-oxygen compounds that are widely distributed throughout much of the solar system. The silicates make up about 95% of the earth's crust and upper mantle, occurring as the major constituents of most IGNEOUS ROCKS and in appreciable quantities in SEDIMENTARY and METAMORPHIC rocks. They also are important constituents of lunar samples, meteorites, and most asteroids. In addition, planetary probes have detected them on the surfaces of Mercury, Venus, and Mars. Of the approximately 600 known silicate minerals, only the FELDSPARS, AMPHIBOLES, PYROXENES, MICAS, OLIVINES, FELDSPATHOIDS, and ZEOLITES are significant in rock formation.

siliceous rock \sə-'li-shəs\ Any of a group of SEDIMENTARY ROCKS that consist largely or almost entirely of silicon dioxide (SiO_2), either as QUARTZ or as CHERT, the most common siliceous rock. It occurs in beds and in nodules. Bedded cherts may be an original organic or inorganic precipitate. Nodular cherts appear to be produced by the alteration of preexisting sedimentary rock. In this process silica distributed throughout the rock dissolves and reprecipitates to form nodules.

silicon Nonmetallic to semimetallic chemical ELEMENT, chemical symbol Si, atomic number 14. Second only to oxygen in abundance in the earth's crust, it never occurs free but is found in almost all rocks and in sand, clay, and soils, combined with oxygen as silica (silicon dioxide, SiO_2) or with oxygen and metals as SILICATE MINERALS. It occurs in many plants and some animals. Pure silicon is a hard, dark gray solid with a metallic luster and the same CRYSTAL structure as DIAMOND. It is an extremely important SEMICONDUCTOR; doped (see DOPANT) with boron, phosphorus, or arsenic, it is used in various electronic circuit and switching devices, including computer chips, transistors, and diodes. Silicon is also used in metallurgy as a reducing (see REDUCTION) agent and in steel, brass, and bronze. Its usual VALENCE in compounds is 4. Silica is used as sand and clay for many purposes; as QUARTZ, it may be heated to form special GLASSES. Silicates are used in making glass, enamels, and ceramics; sodium silicates (water glass) are used in soaps, wood treatment, cements, and dyeing. See also SILANE, SILICONE.

silicon hydride See SILANE

Silicon Valley Industrial strip, western central California. Located between SAN JOSE and Palo Alto in the San Jose and Santa Clara valleys, it came into prominence in the early 1980s as a center of high-technology industries, including electronics and computer corporations. Its (unofficial) name derives from the electronics industry's extensive use of SILICON.

silicone *or* **polysiloxane** Any of a diverse class of POLYMERS manufactured as fluids, RESINS, or elastomers. They are partially organic compounds, but unlike most polymers, they have a backbone containing no carbon, composed of alternating SILICON and OXYGEN atoms. In most silicones, two organic groups, usually methyl or phenyl, are attached to each silicon atom. Silicones in general are exceptionally stable and inert. Silicone fluids are used in hydraulic fluids and emulsion-breaking compositions and as adhesives, lubricants, water repellents, and protective coatings. Silicone rubbers are used as electrical insulators in encapsulations, coatings, and varnishes; as gaskets; in specialized tubing; as automobile engine components; as flexible windows in face masks and air locks; for laminating glass cloth; and as surgical membranes and implants.

silicosis \ˌsi-lə-'kō-səs\ Common PNEUMOCONIOSIS caused by long-term inhalation of SILICA MINERAL dust. Known since the 18th century, it usually occurs after 10–20 years of exposure in jobs such as mining, stonecutting, grinding, or polishing. The smallest particles do the most damage, killing macrophages (see RETICULOENDOTHELIAL SYSTEM) that engulf them in the pulmonary alveoli. Dead cells accumulate, forming fibrous masses that reduce LUNG elasticity. Decreased lung volume and poor gas exchange lead to shortness of breath and then to coughing, difficulty in breathing, and weakness. Patients are vulnerable to TUBERCULOSIS, EMPHYSEMA, and PNEUMONIA. In the absence of effective treatment, control of silicosis depends on prevention with face masks, proper ventilation, and X-ray monitoring of workers' lungs.

Siljan \'sil-ˌyän\, **Lake** Lake, central Sweden. Covering 112 sq mi (290 sq km), it is Sweden's third-largest lake. It is fed by the Österdal River and extends into two bays. Its wooded shores are interspersed with meadows and quaint villages, making it an attractive tourist destination.

silk Animal fiber produced by certain insects as building material for cocoons and webs. In commercial use it refers almost entirely to filament from cocoons produced by the caterpillars of several moth species of the genus *Bombyx*, commonly called SILKWORMS. Silk is a continuous filament around each cocoon. It is freed by softening the cocoon in water and then locating the filament end; the filaments from several cocoons are unwound at the same time, sometimes with a slight twist, to form a single strand. In the process called throwing, several very thin strands are twisted together to make thicker, stronger YARN. Since World War II the substitution of such synthetic fibers as NYLON has greatly reduced the silk industry, but silk remains an important luxury material and is a major product of Japan, South Korea, and Thailand.

Silk Road Ancient trade route that linked China with Europe. Originally a CARAVAN route and used from c. 100 BC, the 4,000-mi (6,400-km) road started in XI'AN, China, followed the GREAT WALL to the northwest, climbed the Pamir Mtns., crossed Afghanistan, and went on to the eastern Mediterranean Sea, where goods were taken by boat to Rome. Silk was carried westward, while wool, gold, and silver were carried eastward. With the fall of Rome, the route became unsafe; it was revived under the Mongols, and MARCO POLO used it in the 13th century.

silkscreen *or* **serigraphy** \sə-'ri-grə-fē\ Sophisticated stenciling technique for surface printing, in which a design is cut out of paper or another thin, strong material and then printed by rubbing, rolling, or spraying paint or ink through the cutout areas. It was developed c. 1900 and originally used in advertising and display work. In the 1950s fine artists began to use the process. It got its name from the fine-mesh silk that, when tacked to a wooden frame, serves as a support for the cut-paper stencil, which is glued to it. To make a silkscreen print, the wooden frame holding the screen is hinged to a slightly larger wooden board, the printing paper is placed on the board under the screen, and the paint is pressed through the screen with a squeegee (rubber blade) the same width as the screen. Many colors can be used, with a separate screen for each color.

silkworm moth Any MOTH in the genus *Bombyx* (family Bombycidae). The Chinese silkworm *(B. mori)* has been used in commercial SILK production for centuries. The adult, which has a wingspan of about 2 in. (50 mm) and a thick, hairy body, lives only two or three days. The female lays 300–500 eggs. The pale, naked larvae are fed mulberry leaves until pupation be-

Silkworm larvae (*Bombyx*) feeding on mulberry leaves.

UPI

gins, when they are about 3 in. (75 mm) long. They spin a cocoon of one continuous white or yellow silken thread, about 1,000 yards (900 m) long. The pupa is killed with hot air or steam to preserve the thread intact. See also SATURNIID MOTH.

sill *or* **sheet** In geology, a tabular igneous intrusion emplaced parallel to the bedding of the enclosing rock. Although they may have inclined orientations, nearly horizontal sills are most common. Sills may range from a few inches to hundreds of feet thick and up to hundreds of miles long. They include rock compositions of all types.

Silla Kingdom of ancient Korea that in 668 unified Korea under the Unified Silla dynasty. Traditionally believed to have been founded by Hyokkose in 57 BC, Silla emerged as a full-fledged kingdom in the 6th century. In the reign of King Chinhung (540–76), a unique military corps, the *hwarang* (see HWARANGDO), was organized; allied with TANG DYNASTY China, it defeated the Korean state of PAEKCHE in 660 and KOGURYO in 668, then expelled the Tang forces to create a unified and independent Korean state. It adopted a Chinese bureaucratic structure, but its aristocracy was never replaced by a bureaucratic class based on merit. Silla art before unification shows a tendency toward abstraction; postunification art reflects Tang naturalism.

Sillanpää \'sēl-län-ˌpä\, **Frans Eemil** (1888–1964) Finnish novelist. The son of a farmer, he studied natural science but returned to the country to write. Shocked by the Finnish civil war of 1918, he produced his most substantial novel, *Meek Heritage* (1919), relating how a humble cottager becomes involved with the Red Guards. After several collections of short stories in the late 1920s, he published his best-known work, *The Maid Silja* (1931), about an old peasant family. *People in the Summer Night* (1934) is his most polished and poetic novel. In 1939 he became the first Finnish writer to win the Nobel Prize.

sillimanite \'si-lə-mə-ˌnīt\ *or* **fibrolite** \'fī-brə-ˌlīt\ Brown, pale green, or white glassy SILICATE MINERAL that often occurs in long, slender, needlelike crystals frequently found in fibrous aggregates. An aluminum silicate, Al_2OSiO_4, it occurs in high-temperature regionally metamorphosed clay-rich rocks (e.g., SCHISTS and GNEISSES). Sillimanite is found at many localities in France, Madagascar, and the eastern U.S.; a pale sapphire-blue gem variety occurs in the gravels of Sri Lanka.

Sillitoe \'si-li-ˌtō\, **Alan** (born 1928) English writer. The son of a tannery worker, he worked in factories from age 14. Many of his later novels and stories are brash and angry accounts of working-class life, beginning with his successful first novel, *Saturday Night and Sunday Morning* (1958; film, 1960). Perhaps his best-known work is the title story in the collection *The Loneliness of the Long-Distance Runner* (1959; film, 1962). His other works include the novels *The Death of William Posters* (1965), *The Widower's Son* (1976), and *The Open Door* (1989) and the story collections *The Ragman's Daughter* (1963; film, 1974) and *Second Chance* (1981).

Sills, Beverly *orig.* **Belle Silverman** (born 1929) U.S. soprano. Born in Brooklyn, N.Y., she sang on radio as a child and made her operatic debut in 1946. From 1955 she sang with the New York City Opera. After gaining attention for her coloratura performance in *Julius Caesar* (1966), she became one of the most celebrated opera stars in the world. After 25 years singing with the company, she served as its director 1979–89. She sang with the Metropolitan Opera as well (1975–80), though after her prime. An effervescent personality, she became popular among a wide public hosting broadcast concerts and opera performances.

Siloé \sē-lō-'ā\, **Diego de** (c. 1490–1563) Spanish sculptor and architect. Son of the sculptor Gil de Siloé (died 1501?), he probably trained with his father as well as in Italy. His works are considered among the finest of the Spanish Renaissance. His sculptural style is Plateresque, a mixture of Italian Renaissance, Gothic, and Mudéjar styles. His principal architectural work, the Granada Cathedral (begun 1528), combines the best features of those styles.

Silone \sē-'lō-nā\, **Ignazio** *orig.* **Secondo Tranquilli** (1900–1978) Italian novelist, short-story writer, and political leader. A founder of the Italian Communist party in 1921, he was active in the party until the fascists drove him into exile. In 1930 he settled in Switzerland, became disillusioned with communism, and began to write antifascist works. He became internationally famous with his first novel, *Fontamara* (1930), which was followed by the novels *Bread and Wine* (1937) and *The Seed Beneath the Snow* (1940) and the satire *The School for Dictators* (1938). After World War II he returned to Italian politics before retiring to write such works as *A Handful of Blackberries* (1952).

silt Sediment particles 0.00016–0.0024 in. (0.004–0.06 mm) in diameter, regardless of mineral type. Silt is easily transported by moving currents but settles in still water. An unconsolidated aggregate of silt particles is also called silt, whereas a consolidated aggregate is called SILTSTONE. Silt deposits formed by wind are known as LOESS. Sediments are seldom composed entirely of silt but rather are a mixture of clay, silt, and sand. Clay-rich silt, upon consolidation, frequently develops parting along bedding surfaces and is then called SHALE. If parting does not develop, the massive rock is called mudstone.

siltstone Hardened sedimentary rock that is composed primarily of angular silt-sized particles (see SILT) and that is not laminated or easily split into thin layers. Siltstones, which are hard and durable, occur in thin layers rarely thick enough to be classified as formations. They are intermediate between sandstones and shales but are not as common as either.

Silurian period \sī-'lu̇r-ē-ən\ Interval of geologic time, 443–417 million years ago. The third period of the PALEOZOIC ERA, the Silurian follows the ORDOVICIAN PERIOD and precedes the DEVONIAN. It marks the first appearance of land plants and jawed fishes. The continents were distributed as follows: Arctic Canada, Scandinavia, and Australia were probably in the tropics; Japan and the Philippines may have been inside the Arctic Circle; South America and Africa were likely near the South Pole, with either present-day Brazil or western Africa as the locus of the pole. The land surface was buried by an ice sheet, possibly as deep as that covering Antarctica today.

Silva, Luís (Ignácio da) *known as* **Lula** (born 1946) Leader of Brazil's leftist Workers' Party. A former factory worker, Lula helped build a labor-union movement into an important political party. In 1988 his party swept the municipal elections of São Paulo and other major cities. A leading contender for president in 1989, 1995, and 1998, proposing policies to help Brazil's working class, he lost each time to more conservative candidates. See also FERNANDO COLLOR DE MELLO.

Silvassa \ˌsil-vä-'sä\ Town (pop., 1991: 12,000), capital of DADRA AND NAGAR HAVELI Union Territory, western India. Located on the Daman Ganga River some 15 mi (25 km) from the Arabian Sea, it is the economic center of the territory, which produces rice, pulses, and fruit crops.

silver Metallic chemical ELEMENT, one of the TRANSITION ELEMENTS, chemical symbol Ag, atomic number 47. It is a white, lustrous precious METAL, valued for its beauty. It is also valued for its electrical conductivity, which is the highest of any metal. Between COPPER and GOLD in the PERIODIC TABLE, it is intermediate between them in many properties. Widely distributed in nature in small amounts, as the native metal and in ORES, it is usually recovered as a by-product of copper and lead production. Its use in bullion and coins was overtaken in the 1960s by demand for industrial purposes, especially photography. It is also used in printed electrical circuits, electronic conductors, and contacts. It is the CATALYST for converting ethylene to ethylene oxide, the precursor of many organic chemicals. Its use in ALLOYS in sterling (92.5% silver, 7.5% copper) and plated silverware, ornaments, and jewelry remains important; yellow gold used in jewelry is 25% silver, and gold dental alloys are about 10% silver. Silver dental fillings are an AMALGAM of silver and MERCURY. Silver in compounds, the most important of which is SILVER NI-

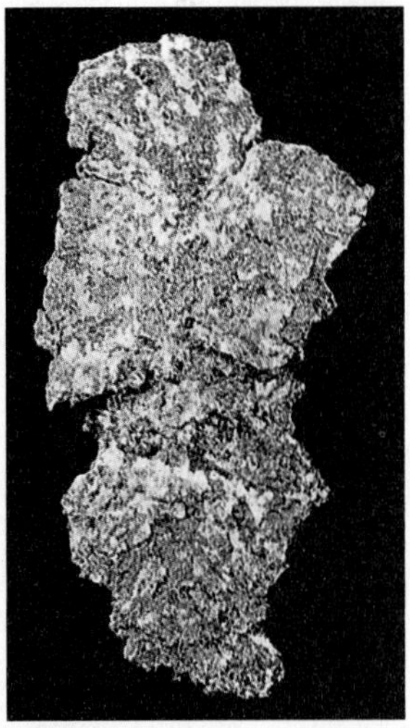

Dendritic (branching) silver from Ontario.

BY COURTESY OF JOSEPH AND HELEN GUETTERMAN COLLECTION; PHOTOGRAPH, JOHN H. GERARD

S T U V

TRATE, has VALENCE 1. Its chloride, bromide, and iodide are used in photography and its iodide in cloud seeding.

Silver, Horace (born 1928) U.S. pianist and composer, leader of one of the most influential ensembles in modern jazz. Born in Norwalk, Conn., Silver performed with STAN GETZ in 1950–51 before leading his own trio in 1952. With ART BLAKEY he led the Jazz Messengers from 1954, then formed his own quintet in 1956, performing his own compositions in arrangements that provided the template for much of the hard bop (see BEBOP) of the 1950s and '60s. Influenced by BUD POWELL and THELONIOUS MONK, Silver's music combines the sophistication of bebop with the earthiness of the BLUES in compositions such as "The Preacher," "Opus de Funk," and "Sister Sadie."

Silver Age In Latin literature, the period from c. AD 18 to 133, second only to the preceding Golden Age in literary achievement. SATIRE was the most vigorous literary form, exemplified by JUVENAL, MARTIAL, and PETRONIUS. Other figures included TACITUS and SUETONIUS in history, PLINY THE ELDER and PLINY THE YOUNGER in letter writing, and QUINTILIAN in literary criticism. Prose was characteristically elaborate and poetical in style, and many of the best works of the period were psychologically perceptive and humanist in tone. See also AUGUSTAN AGE.

silver nitrate Inorganic compound ($AgNO_3$), colorless, transparent crystals with a bitter, caustic, metallic taste. The most important SILVER compound, it is used to prepare other silver salts and as a reagent in ANALYSIS. Dilute solutions are effective against gonococcal bacteria and may be applied to newborns' eyes to prevent blindness from GONORRHEA. Eating silver nitrate causes violent abdominal pain and GASTROENTERITIS.

silver salmon See COHO

silver standard Monetary standard under which the basic unit of CURRENCY is defined as a stated quantity of silver. It is usually characterized by the coinage and circulation of silver, unrestricted convertibility of other MONEY into silver, and the free import and export of silver for the settlement of international obligations. No country now operates under a silver standard. In the 1870s most European countries adopted the GOLD STANDARD, and by the early 1900s only China, Mexico, and a few small countries still used the silver standard. In 1873 the U.S. Treasury stopped coining silver, which led to the FREE SILVER MOVEMENT, but the defeat of WILLIAM JENNINGS BRYAN ended agitation for free silver in the U.S. See also BIMETALLISM.

silverfish Species *(Lepisma saccharina)* of quick-moving, slender, flat, wingless insect having three tail bristles and silvery scales. Silverfish are found worldwide. Females deposit fertilized eggs in cracks and hidden places. The hatched young are scaleless and have short appendages. Silverfish normally live indoors and, because they eat starchy materials (e.g., paste, bookbindings, and wallpaper), can cause much damage. They live two to three years and molt throughout life.

Silverman, Fred (born 1937) U.S. television producer and executive. Born in New York City, he became vice president of programming at CBS (1970–75). As president of ABC's entertainment division (1975–78), he helped produce such popular sitcoms as *Laverne & Shirley*. As president of NBC-TV (1978–81), he helped create such hit series as *Hill Street Blues* and the cartoon series *Smurfs*. He formed his own production company in 1981 and coproduced the series *Matlock* (1986) and a series of Perry Mason television movies (1985–89).

silverpoint See METAL POINT

Silvers, Phil *orig.* **Philip Silversmith** (1912–1985) U.S. actor and comedian. Born in Brooklyn, N.Y., he began his career as a boy singer in vaudeville and a comedian in burlesque. After making his film debut in 1940, he appeared as comic relief in many feature films. He acted on Broadway in *High Button Shoes* (1947–50) and starred in *Top Banana* (1951–52, Tony award; film, 1954). He is best remembered for his role as Sgt. Bilko in the television series *The Phil Silvers Show* (1955–59). He appeared in the film version of *A Funny Thing Happened on the Way to the Forum* (1966) and its Broadway revival (1972, Tony award).

Silverstein, Shel(by) (1932–1999) American cartoonist, children's author, poet, songwriter, and playwright. Often compared to Dr. Seuss, Silverstein is best known for his children's stories and poems. Among his memorable characters are the protagonist in *Uncle Shelby's Story of Lafcadio, the Lion Who Shot Back* (1963), the boy-man and tree in *The Giving Tree* (1964), and the partial circle in *The Missing Piece*. Silverstein was credited with helping young readers develop an appreciation of poetry, and his serious verse reveals an understanding of common childhood anxieties and wishes.

Simcoe, John Graves (1752–1806) British soldier and colonial administrator in Canada. He served in the American Revolution as commander of the Queen's Rangers (1777–79). He was taken prisoner (1779) and released (1781) to return to England. After the Constitutional Act was passed, he served as the first lieutenant-governor of Upper Canada (now Ontario) 1792–96. He encouraged immigration and agriculture and supported defense and road building.

Simcoe, Lake Lake, southeastern Ontario. Located between GEORGIAN BAY and Lake ONTARIO north of TORONTO, it is 287 sq mi (743 sq km) in area. Numerous small streams and the Trent Canal feed the lake, which is 30 mi (48 km) long and contains several islands; the largest, Georgina, is an Indian reserve. The lake is a popular summer vacation area.

Simenon \sē-mə-ˈnō^{n}\, **Georges (Joseph Chrétien)** (1903–1989) Belgian-French novelist. During 1923–33 he wrote more than 200 pseudonymous books of pulp fiction. His first novel under his own name was *The Case of Peter the Lett* (1931), in which he introduced one of the best-known characters in detective fiction, the Parisian police official Inspector Maigret. He wrote some 80 more Maigret novels, as well as about 130 psychological novels, numerous short stories, and autobiographical works, and was one of the most prolific and widely published authors of the 20th century. The central theme running through his fiction is the isolated existence of the neurotic, abnormal individual.

Georges Simenon.
© JERRY BAUER

Simeon I \ˈsi-mē-ən\ *known as* **Simeon the Great** (864?–927) Czar of the first Bulgarian empire (925–27). The son of BORIS I, he succeeded his father in 893 after the short intervening reign (889–93) of his dissolute elder brother, Vladimir. Hoping to gain the imperial throne, he fought five wars with the Byzantine Empire between 894 and 923. He adopted the title "czar of all the Bulgarians" in 925. He extended his power over southern Macedonia, southern Albania, and Serbia but probably lost Bulgaria's dominion north of the Danube.

Simeon Stylites \stī-ˈlīt-ˌēz\, **St.** *or* **Simeon the Elder** (c. AD 390–459) Syrian ascetic. A shepherd, he entered a monastic community but was expelled for excessive austerity and became a hermit. His reputed miracle working drew such crowds that he took to living atop a 6-ft (2-m) pillar (Greek, *stylos*) c. 420, becoming the first of the stylites (pillar hermits). He remained atop a second, 50-ft (15-m) pillar until his death; a railing prevented his falling, and food was brought by disciples. He inspired other ascetics and is called Simeon the Elder to distinguish him from a 6th-century stylite of the same name. Stylites were documented as late as the 19th century in Russia.

Simic \ˈsim-ik\, **Charles** (born 1938) Yugoslavian-U.S. poet. When he was 15 he and his mother moved to Paris; a year later they joined his father in the U.S. After graduating from NYU, he translated Yugoslavian poetry into English. His first volume of poetry, *What the Grass Says* (1967) was recognized for its lively, surrealistic imagery; the collection *The World Doesn't End* (1989) won a Pulitzer Prize. He held a MacArthur Fellowship 1984–89. Since 1973 he has taught at the University of New Hampshire.

simile \ˈsi-mə-lē\ FIGURE OF SPEECH involving a comparison between two unlike entities. In a simile, unlike a METAPHOR, the resemblance is indicated by the words "like" or "as." Similes in everyday speech reflect simple comparisons, as in "He eats like a bird" or "She is slow as molasses." Similes in literature may be specific and direct or more lengthy and complex. The Homeric, or epic, simile, which is typically used in epic poetry, often extends to several lines.

Simla *or* **Shimla** City (pop., 2001 prelim.: 142, 161), capital of HIMACHAL PRADESH state, northwestern India. The city was built by the British after the Gurkha War (1814–16), on a ridge of the Himalayan foothills some 7,100 ft (2,200 m) high. It served as the British summer capital 1865–1939, and as the headquarters of PUNJAB 1947–53. Because of its cool climate and scenic setting, it is one of India's most popular hill resorts.

Simmel \'zim-əl\, **Georg** (1858–1918) German sociologist and philosopher. From teaching posts at the Universities of Berlin (1885–1914) and Strassburg (1914–18), Simmel did much to establish sociology as a basic social science in Germany. He sought to isolate the general forms or recurrent regularities of social interaction from the specific content of definite kinds of activity, such as political, economic, or aesthetic. He gave special attention to the problem of authority and obedience. In *The Philosophy of Money* (1900) he applied his principles to the subject of economics, stressing the role of a money economy in specializing social activity and depersonalizing individual and social relationships. His ideas became influential in the U.S. through the works of ROBERT E. PARK, Albion Small, and Ernest Burgess. See also INTERACTIONISM.

Simms, Willie (1870–1927) African American jockey, one of the first jockeys to be elected to the National Museum of Racing's Hall of Fame in Saratoga Springs, N.Y. Simms began racing in the North in 1887 and was one of the most successful early adopters of the short stirrup. Now ubiquitous, the short stirrup lifts the rider over the horse's withers (the ridge between the horse's shoulder bones) and thereby allows the animal better balance. In 1895 Simms became the first American jockey to win in England, where English sportswriters soon referred to the short stirrup and crouching posture as the "American seat." Simms won the Belmont Stakes in 1893 and 1894, the Kentucky Derby in 1896 and 1898, and the Preakness Stakes in 1898; he is the only African American to win all of the Triple Crown classics. Simms was the leading American jockey (on the basis of number of wins) in 1893 and 1894. He retired in 1901 with one of the best lifetime winning percentages in the sport, 24.8.

Simon \sē-'mōn\, **Claude (-Eugène-Henri)** (born 1913) French writer. Captured while fighting in World War II, he escaped to join the French Resistance. He completed his first novel during the war. His works, mixing narration and STREAM OF CONSCIOUSNESS in densely constructed prose, are representative of the *nouveau roman* ("new novel"), or French ANTINOVEL, that emerged in the 1950s. Perhaps most important is the cycle comprising *The Grass* (1958), *The Flanders Road* (1960), *The Palace* (1962), and *Histoire* (1967), with its recurring characters and events. His other novels include *The Wind* (1957), *Triptych* (1973), and *The Acacia* (1989). He received the Nobel Prize in 1985.

Simon \'sī-mən\, **Herbert (Alexander)** (1916–2001) U.S. social scientist. Born in Milwaukee, Wisconsin, he received his Ph.D. from the University of Chicago in 1943. At Carnegie-Mellon University (from 1949), he taught psychology and later computer science. In *Administrative Behavior* (1947) Simon argued for recognizing a multiplicity of factors (including psychological ones) in corporate decision-taking rather than emphasizing the achievement of maximum profits as the primary motivation. He was awarded the Nobel Prize in Economics in 1978. He subsequently worked in the field of ARTIFICIAL INTELLIGENCE using computer technology.

Simon, John Allsebrook *later* **Viscount Simon (of Stackpole Elidor)** (1873–1954) British politician. A successful lawyer, he served in the House of Commons 1906–18 and 1922–40. In the 1930s he led the Liberal National Party and served successively as foreign secretary (1931–35), home secretary (1935–37), and chancellor of the exchequer (1937–40). Favoring rapprochement with Germany, he supported the appeasement policy of NEVILLE CHAMBERLAIN and the MUNICH AGREEMENT.

Simon, (Marvin) Neil (born 1927) U.S. playwright. Born in New York City, he worked as a comedy writer for SID CAESAR in the 1950s. *Come Blow Your Horn* (1961) was the first of a long series of hit comedies, which included *Barefoot in the Park* (1963; film, 1967), *The Odd Couple* (1965; film, 1968), *Plaza Suite* (1968; film, 1971), *The Sunshine Boys* (1972; film, 1975), and *California Suite* (1976; film, 1978). His later plays include the autobiographical trilogy *Brighton Beach Memoirs* (1983), *Biloxi Blues* (1985, Tony award), and *Broadway Bound* (1986). His plays dealt humorously with the everyday conflicts of ordinary middle-class people, often in New York. For *Lost in Yonkers* (1991), he received a Tony award and a Pulitzer Prize. Simon also wrote screenplay adaptations of his plays and the books for several musicals, including *Sweet Charity* (1966) and *Promises, Promises* (1968).

Simon, Paul (Frederic) (born 1941) U.S. pop singer and songwriter. Born in Newark, N.J., Simon began performing with Art Garfunkel (born 1941) in the 1950s, using the name Tom and Jerry. After a break, the two reunited in 1964 as Simon and Garfunkel. Their first hit single was "Sounds of Silence" (1966); others over the next six years included "Mrs. Robinson" (for the film *The Graduate*) and "Bridge over Troubled Water." After the two parted company, Simon released several hit albums, including *Still Crazy after All These Years* (1975), and wrote and starred in the film *One Trick Pony* (1980). His *Graceland* (1986), recorded with African musicians, became the most successful and influential album of the new genre of "world music." African and Brazilian musics informed his later *The Rhythm of the Saints* (1990). With DEREK WALCOTT he wrote the Broadway musical *The Capeman* (1998).

Simon & Schuster \'shü-stər\ U.S. publishing company. It was founded in 1924 by Richard L. Simon (1899–1960) and M. Lincoln Schuster (1897–1970), whose initial project, the original crossword-puzzle book, was a best-seller. Among their other innovations was Pocket Books, the first U.S. paperback line, launched in 1939. The company came to publish a wide variety of books, including many best-sellers and prizewinners. In 1975 it was sold to Gulf and Western Inc., which, renamed Paramount Communications in 1989, was acquired by Viacom Inc. in 1994. With the 1998 sale of its educational, professional, international, and reference divisions, Simon & Schuster concentrated again on fiction and nonfiction for the general reader.

Simon de Montfort See Simon de MONTFORT

Simon Fraser University Privately endowed university in Burnaby, British Columbia, with a branch campus in Vancouver. It was established in 1963 and named after the explorer SIMON FRASER. It has faculties of arts, science, applied sciences, graduate studies, business administration, education, and continuing studies and a school for the contemporary arts. Total enrollment is about 17,000.

Simonde de Sismondi, J.-C.-L. See J.-C.-L. Simonde de SISMONDI

simony \'si-mə-nē, 'sī-mə-nē\ Buying or selling of church offices or powers. The name is taken from Simon Magus (Acts 8:18), who tried to buy the power of conferring the gifts of the HOLY SPIRIT. Simony became widespread in Europe in the 9th–10th century, as promotions to the priesthood or episcopate were bestowed by the wealthy and influential in return for money. Rigorously attacked by Pope GREGORY VII, the practice recurred in the 15th century, but after the 16th century its more flagrant forms disappeared.

simple harmonic motion Repetitive back-and-forth movement through a central, or EQUILIBRIUM, position in which the maximum displacement on one side is equal to the maximum displacement on the other. Each complete vibration takes the same time, the period; the reciprocal of the period is the FREQUENCY of vibration. The force that causes the motion is always directed toward the equilibrium position and is directly proportional to the distance from it. A PENDULUM displays simple harmonic motion; other examples include the electrons in a wire carrying ALTERNATING CURRENT and the vibrating particles of a medium carrying sound waves.

simplex method Standard technique in LINEAR PROGRAMMING for solving an OPTIMIZATION problem, typically one involving a FUNCTION and several constraints expressed as inequalities. The inequalities define a polygonal region (see POLYGON), and the solution is typically at one of the vertices. The simplex method is a systematic procedure for testing the vertices as possible solutions.

Simplon Pass \'sim-,plän\ Alpine pass and tunnel, southern Switzerland. It is situated between the Pennine and LEPONTINE ALPS at 6,581 ft (2,006 m) high. An important alpine route since the mid-13th century, it became a major link between central and southern Europe when NAPOLEON had a carriage road built there 1800–1807. A hospice, occupied by the AUGUSTINIANS and dating from 1235, is near the summit. When the pass is closed to road traffic in the winter, cars are transported by train through a 12.5-mi (20-km) tunnel below the pass that connects Brig, Switzerland, with Iselle, Italy.

Simpson, George Gaylord (1902–1984) U.S. paleontologist. Born in Chicago, he earned a doctorate at Yale University. His contributions to evolutionary theory include a detailed classification of mammals, based on his studies of mammalian evolution, which is still the standard. He is also known for his studies of intercontinental migrations of animal species, especially South American mammals, in past geologic times. His books include *Tempo and Mode in Evolution* (1944, 1984), *The Meaning of Evolution* (1949), *The Major Features of Evolution* (1953), and *The Principles of Animal Taxonomy* (1961).

Simpson, James Young *later* **Sir James** (1811–1870) Scottish obstetrician. He received his MD from the University of Edinburgh, where he became professor of obstetrics. After news of the use of ether in surgery in Boston reached Scotland, Simpson employed it in obstetrics to relieve labor pains (1847) and later substituted chloroform, which he continued to use despite opposition from obstetricians and the clergy. He also introduced iron-wire sutures, the use of pressure to stop bleeding, and Simpson's forceps (long obstetrical forceps).

Simpson, O(renthal) J(ames) (born 1947) U.S. football player. Born in San Francisco, he played tackle and fullback in high school. At USC as a running back (1965–68), Simpson set rushing records, was named All-American, and won the HEISMAN TROPHY (1968). He joined the Buffalo Bills in 1969, with whom he continued to set records and became a great box-office draw. Knee injuries led to his being traded in 1978 to the San Francisco 49ers; he retired after the 1979 season. Handsome and genial, he became a popular film and television actor, a successful advertising spokesman, and a well-regarded sports commentator. In 1994 his estranged wife, Nicole Brown Simpson, and her friend Ronald Goldman were stabbed to death outside her house. Charged with the murders, Simpson became the defendant in one of the most celebrated criminal trials in history, a long televised trial that attracted unprecedented public attention. A jury acquitted him of all charges in 1995, but in a separate civil trial in 1997 he was found guilty in the wrongful-death suit brought by the Brown and Goldman families.

Sims, William Sowden (1858–1936) U.S. naval officer. Born in Port Hope, Ontario, to U.S. parents, he graduated from Annapolis and later wrote a navigation textbook that became widely used. As naval attaché to U.S. embassies in Paris and St. Petersburg, he observed the superiority of foreign navies. As inspector of naval target practice (1902–9), he revolutionized U.S. naval gunnery. In World War I he commanded the U.S. fleet in Europe and helped secure use of the convoy system to protect Allied ships from German submarine attack. He was president of the Naval War College 1917–18 and 1919–22.

simulation, computer Use of a computer-generated system to represent the dynamic responses and behavior of a real or proposed system. A mathematical description of a system is developed as a computer program that uses equations to represent the functional relationships within the system. When the program is run, the resulting mathematical dynamics form an analog, usually represented graphically, of the behavior of the modeled system. Variables in the program can be adjusted to simulate varying conditions in the system. Computer simulations are used to study the behavior of objects or systems that cannot be easily or safely tested in real life, such as weather patterns or a nuclear blast. Simpler simulations performed by personal computers are business models and geometric models.

simultaneous equations See SYSTEM OF EQUATIONS

Sin \'sēn\ *Sumerian* **Nanna** In MESOPOTAMIAN RELIGION, the god of the moon. He was the father of SHAMASH and, in some myths, of ISHTAR. Sin was thought to confer fertility and prosperity on cowherds by governing the rise of waters and the growth of reeds, particularly in the marshes along the lower EUPHRATES RIVER, where his worship originated. In the 6th century BC, attempts were made to elevate Sin to a supreme position in the Babylonian pantheon.

sin Wrongdoing, particularly the breaking of moral or religious rules. In the OLD TESTAMENT, sin is viewed as a hatred of God or defiance of his commandments. The NEW TESTAMENT regards sinfulness as the inherent state of humanity, which JESUS came into the world to heal. Christian theologians divide sin into actual and ORIGINAL SIN. Actual sin, consisting of evil acts, words, and deeds, is in turn divided into mortal sin, in which the perpetrator deliberately turns away from God, and venial sin, a less serious transgression committed without full awareness of wrongdoing. In Islam, sin is a straying from God's path; the prophets were sent to guide people back to the true path. In Hinduism and Buddhism, the good and evil deeds one commits in this life affect one's rebirth in the next.

Sinai \'sī-ˌnī\ Peninsula, northeastern Egypt. Located between the gulfs of SUEZ and AQABA at the northern end of the Red Sea, it covers 23,500 sq mi (61,000 sq km). Its southern region is mountainous and includes Mount SINAI, while its northern two-thirds is an arid plateau known as the Sinai Desert. Inhabited since prehistoric times, it is famous as the route of the Israelite exodus from Egypt. For centuries, its northern coast was the main trade route between Egypt and Palestine. From the 1st century AD until its takeover by the Ottoman Turks in the 16th century, it was part of the Roman empire and the empire's successors. It was turned over to Egypt at the end of World War I. It was the scene of the principal campaign of the ARAB–ISRAELI WAR (1967) and occupied by Israel 1967–82; it was then returned to Egypt.

Sinai, Mt. *or* **Mount Horeb** Peak, southern central SINAI Peninsula, Egypt. It rises 7,497 ft (2,285 m). It is especially renowned as the site where MOSES received the TEN COMMANDMENTS. Though not positively identified as the place referred to in biblical texts, it is regarded as sacred in the Jewish, Christian, and Islamic traditions and is an important pilgrimage site. St. Catherine's, probably the world's oldest continuously inhabited Christian monastery, is at its northern base.

Sinaloa \ˌsē-nä-'lō-ä\ State (pop., 1995 est.: 2,426,000), northwestern Mexico. It is located on the Gulf of CALIFORNIA; its capital is CULIACÁN. The 22,521-sq-mi (58,328-sq-km) territory, which was made a state in 1830, consists of a tropical coastal plain that rises inland to the SIERRA MADRE Occidental. MAZATLAN is on its coast. It is primarily an agricultural area, producing wheat, cotton, tobacco, and sugarcane. Salt, graphite, manganese, and gold are mined.

Sinatra, Frank *orig.* **Francis Albert** (1915–1998) U.S. singer and actor. Born in Hoboken, N.J., Sinatra began his singing career in the mid-1930s and was discovered by HARRY JAMES, who immediately recruited him. He achieved sweeping national popularity in 1940–42 while singing with the TOMMY DORSEY Orchestra. He sang on the radio program "Your Hit Parade" 1943–45, while becoming a favorite performer in theaters and nightclubs. After 1953 he performed and recorded using arrangements by Nelson Riddle, Billy May, and Gordon Jenkins, reaching his peak in such albums as *In the Wee Small Hours* (1955), *Songs for Swingin' Lovers* (1956), *Come Fly with Me* (1958), and *Only the Lonely* (1958). He appeared in about 80 films; his performance in *From Here to Eternity* (1953, Academy Award) revived his flagging career, and he later starred in such film musicals as *Guys and Dolls* (1955), *High Society* (1956), and *Pal Joey* (1957), and such dramas as *The Man with the Golden Arm* (1955) and *The Manchurian Candidate* (1962). In 1961 he founded Reprise Records. His masterly performances, alternately swinging and affectingly melancholic, brought him a success unparalleled in the history of American popular music.

Sinclair, Upton (Beall) (1878–1968) U.S. novelist. Born in Baltimore, he was supporting himself as a journalist when an assignment led him to write *The Jungle* (1906), a best-selling muckraking exposé of conditions in the Chicago stockyards. A landmark among naturalistic, proletarian novels, it aroused great public indignation and resulted in the passage of the U.S. Pure Food and Drug Act. Many other topical novels followed, as well as the successful Lanny Budd series of 11 contemporary historical novels featuring an antifascist hero, beginning with *World's End* (1940) and including *Dragon's Teeth* (1942, Pulitzer Prize). In the 1930s Sinclair organized a socialist reform movement and won the Democratic nomination for governor of California.

Sind *or* **Sindh** Province (pop., 1983 est.: 20,312,000), southeastern Pakistan. It is bordered by the Arabian Sea to the south. The capital is KARACHI. The center of the ancient INDUS CIVILIZATION, it was annexed to the Persian Achaemenid empire in the 6th century BC. Conquered by ALEXANDER THE GREAT in 325 BC, it was part of the MAURYAN EMPIRE in the 3rd century BC. It fell to the Arabs c. AD 711. In the 16th–17th century it was ruled by the MUGHALS. It came under British control in 1843. After Pakistan's independence, it was integrated into the province of West Pakistan, but in 1970 it was reestablished as a separate province. It is arid except in the irrigated Indus River valley, where cotton, wheat, and rice are grown and where the population is concentrated.

sine See Trigonometric function

sines, law of Principle of trigonometry stating that the lengths of the sides of any triangle are proportional to the sines of the opposite angles. That is,

$$\frac{a}{\sin A} = \frac{b}{\sin B} = \frac{c}{\sin C}$$

when a, b and c are the sides and A, B and C are the opposite angles.

Singapore *officially* **Republic of Singapore** Island republic S.East Asia. Situated off the southern tip of the Malay Peninsula, it comprises Singapore island and 60 other islets. Area: 240 sq mi (622 sq km). Population (1997 est.): 3,104,000. Capital: Singapore. Three-fourths of the people are Chinese; most of the rest are Malays and Indians. Languages: English, Mandarin, Malay, Tamil (all official). Religions: primarily Confucianism, Buddhism, and Taoism; also Islam, Christianity, Hinduism. Currency: Singapore dollar. Nearly two-thirds of the island's hilly landscape lies less than 50 ft (15 m) above sea level; it has a hot, humid climate. Although only about 2% of its land is arable, it is among the most productive fruit and vegetable cropland in the world. The economy is based largely on international trade and finance. It has more than 100 commercial banks, most of which are foreign, and is the headquarters of the Asian Dollar Market. Its port is one of the largest in the world, and

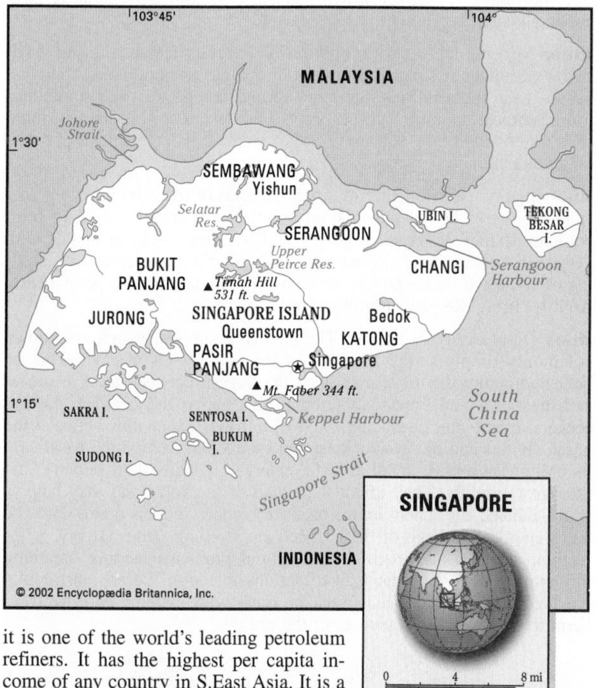

it is one of the world's leading petroleum refiners. It has the highest per capita income of any country in S.East Asia. It is a republic with one legislative house; its chief of state is the president, and the head of government is the prime minister. Long inhabited by fishermen and pirates, it was an outpost of the Sumatran empire of Shrivijaya until the 14th century, when it passed to Java and then Siam. It became part of the Malacca empire in the 15th century. In the 16th century the Portuguese controlled the area; they were followed by the Dutch in the 17th century. In 1819 it was ceded to the British East India Co., becoming part of the Straits Settlements and the center of British colonial activity in S.East Asia. The Japanese occupied the island 1942–45. In 1946 it became a crown colony. It achieved full internal self-government in 1959, became a part of Malaysia in 1963, and became independent in 1965. It is influential in the affairs of the Association of S.East Asian Nations. The country's dominant voice in politics for 30 years after independence was Lee Kuan Yew. Its economy was affected during the 1990s Asian economic crises, but it recovered more easily than many of its neighbors did.

Singapore City (metro. area pop., 1992 est.: 2,792,000), capital of the Republic of Singapore. A free port occupying the southern part of Singapore island, it so dominates the island that the republic is often called a city-state. Known as the Garden City for its many parks and tree-lined streets, it offers glimpses into the cultures brought to it by immigrants from all parts of Asia. Traditionally founded by a Shrivijayan prince, it was an important Malay city in the 13th century. Destroyed by the Javanese in the 14th century, it was refounded by Stamford Raffles of the British East India Co. in 1819. It became the capital of the Straits Settlements in 1833. It developed as a port and naval base, and today is one of the world's great commercial centers. Its thriving banking, insurance, and brokerage firms make it the chief trading and financial center of S.East Asia. It is home to the National University of Singapore (1980).

Singer, Isaac Bashevis *Yiddish* **Yitskhok Bashevis Zinger** (1904–1991) Polish-U.S. writer of novels, short stories, and essays. He received a traditional Jewish education at the Warsaw Rabbinical Seminary. After publishing his first novel, *Satan in Goray* (1932), he emigrated to the U.S. in 1935 and wrote for a Yiddish newspaper in New York. Though he continued to write mostly in Yiddish, he personally supervised the English translations. Depicting Jewish life in Poland and the U.S., his works are a rich blend of irony, wit, and wisdom, flavored distinctively with the occult and the grotesque. His works include the novels *The Family Moskat* (1950), *The Magician of Lublin* (1960), and *Enemies: A Love Story* (1972; film, 1989); the story collections *Gimpel the Fool* (1957), *The Spinoza of Market Street* (1961), and *A Crown of Feathers* (1973, National Book Award); and the play *Yentl the Yeshiva Boy* (1974; film, 1983). He was awarded the Nobel Prize in 1978.

Singer, Isaac Merritt (1811–1875) U.S. inventor and manufacturer. Born in Pittstown, N.Y., he became an apprentice machinist at 19. He patented a rock-drilling machine (1839) and a metal- and wood-carving machine (1849) before producing an improved version of Elias Howe's sewing machine in 1851 and soon thereafter founding I. M. Singer & Co. (see Singer Co.) to manufacture it. Howe's successful patent-infringement suit against him in 1854 did not prevent Singer from manufacturing his machine, and his company was soon the world's largest sewing-machine producer. He patented numerous further improvements in the technology; he also pioneered the use of installment credit plans.

Singer Co. U.S. sewing-machine manufacturer. The company began in 1851, when Isaac Merritt Singer (1811–1875) patented the first practical sewing machine for domestic use. By 1860 I. M. Singer & Co. was the largest maker of sewing machines in the world. In 1863 its business was taken over by the newly incorporated Singer Manufacturing Co. The company began mass-producing domestic electric machines in 1910 and pioneered marketing innovations such as the installment plan. It later expanded into power tools, floor-care products, furniture, and electronics; it adopted the name Singer Co. in 1963. Its sewing-machine and furniture operations were spun off into a separate company, SSMC Inc., in 1986. It was taken over by a corporate raider, Paul Bilzerian, in 1988 and its assets were sold; the new company, Bicoastal Corp., went bankrupt in 1991.

Singitic Gulf \sin-'ji-tik\ Inlet of the Aegean Sea, northeastern Greece. It is the larger and deeper of two gulfs (the other being Ierisoú Gulf) that extend into the peninsula of Greek Macedonia. The silted-up remains of a canal completed by Xerxes in 480 BC link the two gulfs. The main community on the gulf is Ouranópolis, a stop for tourists exploring Mount Athos.

single tax Tax on land values intended as the sole source of government revenues, replacing all existing taxes. Henry George proposed the single tax in his book *Progress and Poverty* (1879). The plan gained considerable support in subsequent decades but was never implemented. Advocates argued that since land is a fixed resource, the income it yields is a product of the economy's growth and not individual effort, and that it therefore can fairly be taxed to support the government. Critics protested that the single tax would take no account of an individual's ability to pay, since there is no correlation between land ownership and total wealth or income.

singspiel \'siŋ-ˌspēl, 'ziŋ-ˌshpēl\ German-language musical drama with spoken dialogue, songs, and choruses. Its main development follows the

1752 Leipzig performance of a translation of Charles Coffey's BALLAD OPERA *The Devil to Pay*. In Vienna it had a brief but intense flowering that resulted in W.A. MOZART's enduring *Abduction from the Seraglio* (1782) and *The Magic Flute* (1791). With its often folkloric subject matter and its frequently lower-class characters, singspiel led through transitional works such as LUDWIG VAN BEETHOVEN's *Fidelio* and C.M. VON WEBER's *Der Freischütz* to German Romantic opera. See also MUSICAL, OPERETTA, ZARZUELA.

Sinhalese \ˌsiŋ-gə-ˈlēz\ Largest ethnic group of Sri Lanka. Their ancestors are believed to have come from northern India. Most Sinhalese are agriculturalists and most adhere to THERAVADA Buddhism. Like other peoples of Sri Lanka, the Sinhalese have a caste society with a complex structure based largely on occupation. Today the Sinhalese number over 12 million.

Sinitic languages See CHINESE LANGUAGES

sinkhole *or* **sink** *or* **doline** \də-ˈlē-nə\ Depression formed as underlying limestone bedrock is dissolved by groundwater. Sinkholes vary greatly in area and depth and may be very large. The two main varieties are those caused by the collapse of a cavern roof, and those caused by the gradual dissolving of rock under a soil mantle. Collapsed sinkholes generally have steep rock sides and may receive streams that then flow underground. Soil-mantled sinkholes are generally shallower; they may become clogged with clay and hold a small lake.

Sinkiang Uighur See XINJIANG UYGUR

sinking fund Fund set aside by a corporation or government agency for the purpose of periodically redeeming BONDS, debentures, and preferred STOCKS. The fund is accumulated from earnings, and payments into the fund may be based on either a fixed percentage of the outstanding DEBT or a fixed percentage of PROFITS. Sinking funds are administered separately from the corporation's working funds by a trust company or trustee. The purpose of a sinking fund is to assure investors that provision has been made for the repayment of bonds at maturity.

Sinn Féin \ˈshin-ˈfān\ (Irish: "We Alone") Nationalist political party in Ireland. It was founded by ARTHUR GRIFFITH and others in 1902, and its policy involved passive resistance to the British, withholding of taxes, and establishing an Irish ruling council. The party had little impact until after the EASTER RISING, when the demand of its leader EAMON DE VALERA for a united, republican Ireland won the party 73 out of 105 seats in the 1918 election. Its power diminished after 1926, when de Valera founded FIANNA FÁIL, which absorbed most of Sinn Féin's membership. The party continued as the political arm of the IRISH REPUBLICAN ARMY, actively supporting Irish unification. Under the leadership of GERRY ADAMS in the 1980s and '90s, it participated in the peace talks on Northern Ireland.

Sino-French War (1883–85) Conflict between China and France over Vietnam that revealed the inadequacy of China's modernization efforts and aroused nationalistic sentiment in southern China. In 1880, when France began to extend its presence in Vietnam northward from the three southern provinces it controlled, China sent in troops and engaged in limited battles. The governor-general, LI HONGZHANG, negotiated an agreement whereby North Vietnam would be a joint protectorate, but a hard-line government faction in China rejected it. The French defeated Chinese reinforcements in 1883, and the new settlement was more strongly in France's favor. This too was rejected in China; further hostilities resulted in the new Chinese fleet of 11 steamers being destroyed, along with the Fuzhou shipyard. In 1885 China signed a peace treaty accepting the settlement of 1883.

Sino-Japanese War (1894–95) Conflict between China and Japan over Korea that marked the emergence of Japan as a world power and demonstrated the weakness of China. Though Korea had long been China's most important client state, Japan became interested in it for its natural resources and its strategic location. After Japan opened Korea to foreign trade in 1875, tensions between radical, pro-Japanese Koreans, who favored modernization, and conservative Korean government officials supported by China brought China and Japan into conflict. Foreign observers predicted an easy victory for the more massive Chinese forces, but Japan scored overwhelming victories on both land and sea. In the Treaty of Shimonoseki, China recognized the independence of Korea and ceded Taiwan, the Pescadores, and the Liaodong Peninsula (the last of which Japan was later forced to return) to Japan. China's resistance to Japan's aggression in Chinese territory from 1937 to 1945 is also referred to as the Sino–Japanese War (see MANCHUGUO, MARCO POLO BRIDGE INCIDENT, NANJING MASSACRE). See also TONGHAK UPRISING.

Sino-Tibetan languages \ˌsī-nō-tə-ˈbe-tən\ Superfamily of languages whose two branches are the Sinitic or CHINESE LANGUAGES and the Tibeto-Burman family, an assemblage of several hundred very diverse languages spoken by about 65 million people from northern Pakistan east to Vietnam, and from the Tibetan plateau south to the Malay Peninsula. western Tibeto-Burman languages include TIBETAN and the Bodish and Himalayan languages, spoken mainly in Nepal. Tibeto-Burman languages of northeastern India include the Bodo-Garo languages (spoken in ASSAM) and the northern Naga languages of NAGALAND; perhaps allied to these is Jinghpaw, spoken in northern Myanmar. Kuki-Chin and southern Naga languages are spoken in eastern India, eastern Bangladesh, and western Myanmar. Central Tibeto-Burman languages are spoken mainly in Arunachal Pradesh in India and in adjacent parts of China and Myanmar; they include Lepcha, an official language of SIKKIM. northeastern Tibeto-Burman comprises a heterogeneous group of languages spoken in western Sichuan and northwestern Yunnan in China. Burmese-Lolo, a geographically wide-ranging subgroup, includes Burmese, the national language of Myanmar (Burma). Loloish languages include the speech of the Yi or Lolo of Yunnan as well as several languages spread over Yunnan and parts of S.East Asia, including Lahu and Akha. Karen, spoken by the KAREN of Myanmar and Thailand, forms a distinct subgroup. Tibetan and Burmese are the only Tibeto-Burman languages with long literary traditions. Burmese is written in an adaptation of the Mon script (see MON-KHMER LANGUAGES). Most Tibeto-Burman languages have phonemic TONE and agglutinative MORPHOLOGY.

sinter Mineral deposit with a porous or vesicular texture (having small cavities). Siliceous sinter is a deposit of opaline or amorphous silica that occurs as an incrustation around hot springs and geysers and sometimes forms conical mounds (geyser cones) or terraces. Calcareous sinter, sometimes called tufa, calcareous tufa, or calc-tufa, is a deposit of calcium carbonate.

sintering WELDING together of small particles of METAL by applying heat at temperatures below the melting point. The process is used to form complex shapes, to produce alloys, and to allow work on metals with very high melting points. Sintering is also used in the preliminary molding of CERAMIC or GLASS powders into forms that can then be permanently fixed by firing. See also POWDER METALLURGY.

sinus Body cavity or hollow. The paranasal sinuses, which are known commonly simply as the sinuses, are any of four sets of cavities in the bones adjoining the nose: maxillary, the largest, between the eye socket and the PALATE and upper jaw; frontal, just above and between the eye sockets; ethmoidal, consisting of 3–18 thin-walled cavities between the nasal cavities and the eye sockets; and sphenoidal, behind the nasal cavity. All are absent or small at birth, enlarge gradually until puberty, and then grow rapidly. They affect the sound of the voice and may help to warm inhaled air. Their lining produces mucus, which drains into the nasal cavity. Blockage of their outlets by swelling (from allergy or infection; see SINUSITIS), POLYPS, or structural problems hamper breathing through the nose and can lead to serious infection. Severe obstruction may require surgery, which must be done with extreme care to avoid harm to nearby brain structures or the eyes.

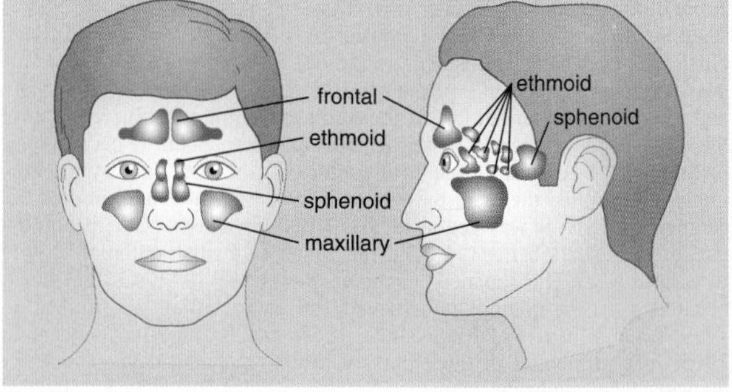

The paranasal sinuses.

sinusitis \ˌsī-nə-ˈsī-təs\ INFLAMMATION of the SINUSES. Acute sinusitis, usually due to infections such as the common COLD, causes localized pain and tenderness, nasal obstruction and discharge, and malaise. Nose drops or inhalations containing drugs that contract blood vessels help drain the sinuses. Antibiotics may be used for bacterial infections. Chronic sinusitis, with frequent colds, pus, obstructed breathing, loss of sense of smell, and sometimes headache, may follow repeated or untreated acute attacks, particularly with impaired breathing or drainage. If antibiotic therapy or repeated lavage (rinsing out) does not help, surgery to open passages for drainage may be needed.

Siouan languages \ˈsü-ən\ Family of North American Indian languages, located mainly west of the Mississippi River in the 17th–18th century. The principal languages and language groups at this time were Winnebago in Wisconsin, Chiwere (Iowa, Oto, and Missouri) in Iowa and northern Missouri, Dhegiha (Ponca, Omaha, Kansa, Osage, Quapaw) in an area extending from eastern Nebraska to Arkansas, Sioux or Dakota (a range of dialects including Santee or Dakota proper in Minnesota, Teton or Lakota in North and South Dakota, and Assiniboine in Canada), Hidatsa and Mandan on the middle Missouri River, and Crow in Wyoming and Montana. Separated from the main body of Siouan languages were the now-extinct languages Tufelo and Biloxi, near the Gulf of Mexico, and the distantly related Catawba, once spoken in South Carolina. The extant Siouan languages are now spoken mainly or solely by older adults.

Sioux \ˈsü\ *or* **Dakota** Group of PLAINS INDIAN peoples of SIOUAN LANGUAGE stock comprising the Santee (Eastern Sioux), Yankton, and Teton (Western Sioux), each of which in turn had lesser divisions (e.g., BLACKFOOT, Oglala). In the 17th century the Sioux lived in the area around Lake Superior, but attacks from the OJIBWA drove them west into Minnesota. They adopted a Plains way of life, hunting buffalo, living in TEPEES, emphasizing valor in warfare, and practicing the SUN DANCE. Sioux women were skilled at porcupine-quill and bead embroidery. The Sioux were resolute in resisting white incursions. In 1862, white treaty violations led the Santee to mount a bloody uprising under Little Crow; after their defeat, they were forced onto reservations in South Dakota and Nebraska. Serious fighting between U.S. troops and the Yankton and Teton Sioux in the 1860s and 1870s culminated in the Battle of LITTLE BIGHORN in 1876, a great Indian victory. Eventually, however, the Sioux surrendered and were forced onto reservations. In 1890 the GHOST DANCE religion inspired many Sioux to take up arms, leading to the massacre at WOUNDED KNEE. Today the Sioux number about 75,000; most live on reservations in North and South Dakota, Montana, and Nebraska. See also SITTING BULL.

Sioux Falls City (pop., 1996 est.: 113,000), southeastern South Dakota. Founded in 1857, it was abandoned in 1862 following an Indian uprising. With the establishment of Fort Dakota on the site in 1865, the settlers gradually returned. Now the state's largest city, it is a commercial and financial center in a livestock-farming region, with one of the largest livestock markets in the U.S. Nearby is one of the world's first commercial nuclear power plants. The Earth Resource Observation Systems (EROS) Data Center is located in the city.

Sippar \si-ˈpär\ Ancient city, BABYLONIA, southwest of present-day BAGHDAD on the EUPHRATES RIVER. From the 3rd millennium BC, it was a center of worship of the Sumerian sun-god SHAMASH. It was subject to the 1st dynasty of Babylon, but little else is known about the city before 1174 BC, when it was sacked by the Elamites. It recovered and was later captured by the Assyrians. Excavations, begun in 1882, have uncovered the remains of a large temple and thousands of religious and historic clay tablets.

Siqueiros \sē-ˈkā-rōs\, **David Alfaro** (1896–1975) Mexican painter. A Marxist activist from his youth, he fought in the Mexican Revolution alongside VENUSTIANO CARRANZA, who rewarded him by sponsoring his studies in Europe. Back in Mexico (1922), he began his lifework of decorating public buildings with murals and organizing unions of artists and workers. With DIEGO RIVERA and JOSE CLEMENTE OROZCO, he cofounded the renowned school of Mexican mural painting. His activism interrupted his career several times when he was imprisoned, chose self-imposed exile, and fought in the Spanish Civil War. His murals are marked by great dynamism, monumental size and vigor, and a limited color range subordinated to dramatic effects of light and shadow. His easel paintings (e.g., *Echo of a Scream,* 1937) helped establish his international reputation. In 1968 he became the first president of the Mexican Academy of Arts.

Siracusa See SYRACUSE

siren In GREEK MYTHOLOGY, a creature, half bird and half woman, who lures sailors to their doom with her sweet singing. HOMER placed sirens near the rocks of Scylla; in the *Odyssey,* Odysseus has his men plug their ears with wax and has himself tied to his ship's mast in order to hear their singing without endangering the ship. In one tale of JASON and the ARGONAUTS, ORPHEUS sings so sweetly that the crew do not listen to the sirens. According to later legend, the sirens committed suicide after one or the other of those failures.

Sirhindi \sir-ˈhin-dē\, **Shaykh Ahmad** (1564?–1624) Indian mystic and theologian. He traced his descent from UMAR IBN AL-KHATTAB. After a traditional Muslim education, he joined an important Sufi order and devoted himself to preaching against the tendencies of AKBAR and his successor, Jahangir, toward PANTHEISM and SHIITE Islam. His views are outlined in his most famous work, *Maktubat,* a compilation of his letters. His burial place at Sirhind is a site of pilgrimage.

Sirica \si-ˈri-kə\, **John** (1904–1992) U.S. jurist. Born in Waterbury, Conn., he served as an assistant U.S. attorney (1930–34) before establishing an active private practice in Washington, D.C. Appointed a district court judge for the District of Columbia (1957), he became the court's chief judge in 1971. He presided at the trial of the burglars in the WATERGATE SCANDAL; his questioning of witnesses led to the implication of staff members in RICHARD NIXON's administration. Sirica upheld the prosecution subpoena that required Nixon to deliver evidence, including the White House tape recordings. He also presided at the trials of JOHN MITCHELL, H.R. HALDEMAN, and JOHN D. EHRLICHMAN.

Sirius \ˈsir-ē-əs\ *or* **Dog Star** Brightest star in the night sky (apparent MAGNITUDE–1.5), a BINARY STAR about 8.6 light-years from the sun in the constellation Canis Major. The bright component of the binary is a blue-white star 23 times as luminous as the sun, about twice the size, and considerably hotter; its companion was the first WHITE DWARF STAR discovered. Its name probably comes from a Greek word meaning "sparkling" or "scorching." The ancient Egyptians used its predawn rising to predict the annual flooding of the Nile. The ancient Romans associated the rising of the Dog Star at dawn with the hottest part of the year, called the "dog days."

Sirk, Douglas *orig.* **Claus Detlef Sierck** (1900–1987) German-U.S. film director. He was artistic director of theaters in Bremen (1923–29) and Leipzig (1929–36) and made several films before fleeing Germany in 1937. He arrived in Hollywood in 1939 and received minor directing assignments until he joined Universal Pictures in 1950. There he directed comedy, western, and war movies but was best known for such popular melodramas as *Magnificent Obsession* (1954), *There's Always Tomorrow* (1956), *Written on the Wind* (1956), and *The Tarnished Angels* (1957). After directing his greatest success, *Imitation of Life* (1959), he retired to Germany.

sirocco *or* **scirocco** \sə-ˈrä-kō, shi-ˈrä-kō\ Warm, humid wind over the Mediterranean Sea and southern Europe, where it blows from the south or southeast and brings rain and fog. It is produced on the front sides of low-pressure centers that travel eastward over the southern Mediterranean. It originates over North Africa as a dry wind and picks up moisture as it crosses the Mediterranean.

Sirte, Gulf of See Gulf of SIDRA

sisal \ˈsī-səl\ Plant *(Agave sisalana)* of the AGAVE FAMILY, and the fiber from its leaves. The fiber is made into ropes and twines for marine, agricultural, shipping, and general industrial use, as well as into matting, rugs, hats, and brushes. Though sometimes referred to as sisal hemp, it is not related to true HEMP. Growing to a height of about 3 ft (1 m) and a diameter of about 15 in. (38 cm), the stalk bears fleshy, rigid, gray to dark-green, lance-shaped leaves in a dense rosette. Tanzania and Brazil are the main producers of sisal.

Siskind \ˈsis-kind\, **Aaron** (1903–1991) U.S. photographer, teacher, and editor. Born in New York City, he began to photograph in 1932 while teaching English in a public school. While documenting the Great Depression, he attended as closely to pure design as to his subjects. In the 1940s he began to photograph patterns and textures of such subjects as coiled ropes, footprints in sand, and weathered pavement and billboards. Though not immediately accepted by photographers, his abstract work was admired by WILLEM DE KOONING and FRANZ KLINE, with whom he later exhibited. He was most influential as a professor of photography and as coeditor of the magazine *Choice*.

Sisley \'siz-lē, sēs-'lā\, **Alfred** (1839–1899) British-French landscape painter. Born in Paris of English parents, he began painting as an amateur. His early style was much influenced by CAMILLE COROT. He became associated with CLAUDE MONET and AUGUSTE RENOIR, and with them became one of the founders of IMPRESSIONISM. His works are distinguished from those of his colleagues by their softly harmonious values. His family was ruined by the Franco-Prussian War and his life was a constant struggle against poverty. Not until after his death did his talent begin to be widely recognized.

Sismondi \sēs-mō^{n}-'dē, *Engl* sis-'män-dē\, **J(ean-) C(harles-) L(éonard) Simonde de** (1773–1842) Swiss economist and historian. He worked in a French bank from 1789, then moved to Tuscany in 1794 with his family to farm. Living in his native Geneva from 1800, he wrote his *History of the Italian Republics in the Middle Ages* (1809–18), which inspired the leaders of the RISORGIMENTO. In his influential *New Principles of Political Economy* (1819), he criticized capitalism and argued for regulation of economic competition and for a balance between production and consumption. He urged social reforms to improve working-class living conditions. His theories influenced such later economists as KARL MARX and JOHN MAYNARD KEYNES.

Sissle, Noble See Edward BLAKE

Sistan *or* **Seistan** \sē-'stän\ Extensive border region, eastern Iran and southwestern Afghanistan. Most of its sparse population and 40% of its area lie in Iran. It comprises a large marshland depression with a true desert climate. It is the reputed homeland of the legendary Kayanian dynasty of Persia, and played an important part in Persian history, especially under the SAFAVIDS (1502–1736). In the 19th century it was the center of a dispute between Persia and Afghanistan that led to the modern delimitation of their frontier.

Sistine Chapel \'sis-ˌtēn\ Papal chapel in the VATICAN PALACE, Rome, constructed 1473–81 by Giovanni dei Dolci for Pope SIXTUS IV (for whom it is named). It is the site of the principal papal ceremonies. Its exterior is drab and unadorned, but its interior walls and ceiling are decorated with frescoes by Florentine Renaissance masters, including PERUGINO, PINTURICCHIO, SANDRO BOTTICELLI, DOMENICO GHIRLANDAIO, and LUCA SIGNORELLI. Portions of the walls were once covered with tapestries designed by RAPHAEL (1515–19). The most important works are the frescoes by MICHELANGELO on the ceiling and the western wall behind the altar, considered among the greatest achievements of Western painting. The ceiling frescoes, depicting Old Testament scenes, were commissioned by Pope JULIUS II and painted 1508–12; the *Last Judgment* fresco on the western wall was painted 1536–41 for Pope Paul III. A controversial 10-year cleaning and restoration of the ceiling was completed in 1989, and of the western wall in 1994.

Sisyphus \'si-sə-fəs\ In GREEK MYTHOLOGY, the king of Corinth who was punished in Hades by having to roll a huge stone up a hill over and over again. He was the son of AEOLUS and the father of GLAUCUS. When Death came to fetch him, Sisyphus had him chained up so that no one died until ARES came to free Death. Before being taken to the underworld, Sisyphus asked his wife to leave his body unburied. When he reached Hades he was permitted to go back to earth to punish his wife, and he lived to a ripe old age before dying a second time. His trickery resulted in his punishment in Hades.

Sita, Mughal painting, c. 1600; in the collection of Bharat Kala Bhavan, Varanasi, India.
PRAMOD CHANDRA

Sita \'sē-ˌtä\ In Hindu mythology, the consort of RAMA. She sprang from a furrow when King Janaka was plowing his field, and Rama won her as his bride by bending SHIVA's bow. Her abduction by the demon king RAVANA and subsequent rescue are described in the *RAMAYANA*. She kept herself chaste during her long imprisonment, and on her return she proved her purity by undergoing an ordeal by fire. A symbol of the sufferings and strengths of women, she is one of the most revered figures in the Hindu pantheon.

sitar \si-'tär, 'si-ˌtär\ Long-necked STRINGED INSTRUMENT of northern India, the dominant instrument in Hindustani music. It is used as a solo instrument with the tamboura (drone-lute) and TABLA and in ensembles. It developed from the Middle Eastern tanbur. It has a deep pear-shaped gourd body, metal strings, front and side tuning pegs, a wide neck, and movable frets. It normally has four or five melody strings, which are plucked with a plectrum worn on the forefinger; several drone strings; and numerous sympathetic strings (strings caused to vibrate by the other strings' vibrations). A gourd resonator is attached to the top of the neck.

Sitka National Historical Park Park, southeastern Alaska. Located on Baranof Island in the Gulf of ALASKA, it was established in 1910 as a national monument; a national park since 1972, it covers 107 acres (43 hectares). It contains the ruins of the Indian fortress in which the TLINGIT Indians made their last stand against Russian settlers in 1804. It also has a collection of old HAIDA Indian totem poles, and the oldest intact Russian-American building in the U.S.

Sittang River \'si-ˌtäŋ\ River, eastern central Myanmar. It rises on the edge of the Shan Plateau and flows south 260 mi (420 km) to empty into the Gulf of Martaban of the ANDAMAN SEA. Though navigable only for a short distance, it is used to float timber (particularly teak) south for export. It was the scene of severe fighting during World War II.

Sitting Bull (1831?–1890) Teton SIOUX chief under whom the Sioux peoples united in their struggle for survival. Frequent skirmishes between the U.S. Army and Sitting Bull's warriors occurred in 1863–68, at the end of which the Sioux agreed to accept a reservation in southwestern South Dakota. When gold was discovered in the Black Hills in the mid-1870s, further outbreaks occurred. At the Battle of the Rosebud, troops under Gen. George Crook were forced to retreat; and at the Battle of LITTLE BIGHORN, Col. GEORGE CUSTER and his men were killed. In 1877 Sitting Bull led his followers into Canada, but, with the buffalo reduced to near-extinction, starvation eventually drove the Sioux to surrender. From 1883 Sitting Bull lived on Indian Agency lands, at one point (1885) traveling with Buffalo Bill's Wild West Show. During the GHOST DANCE movement, he was arrested; he was killed when his warriors tried to rescue him.

situation comedy *or* **sitcom** Radio or television comedy series that involves a continuing cast of characters in a succession of episodes. Often the characters are markedly different types thrown together by circumstance and occupying a shared environment such as an apartment building or workplace. Typically half an hour in length and either taped in front of a studio audience or employing canned applause, they are marked by verbal sparring and rapidly resolved conflicts.

Sitwell family British family of writers. Edith Sitwell (1887–1964) attracted attention when she joined her brothers in a revolt against GEORGIAN POETRY. Her early work, which emphasizes the value of sound, includes *Clowns' Houses* (1918) and *Façade* (1923), set to music by W. WALTON. Beginning with *Gold Coast Customs* (1929), her style became less artificial and experimental, and during World War II she emerged as a poet of some emotional depth. Her later poetry is informed by religious symbolism, as in *Gardeners and Astronomers* (1953) and *The Outcasts* (1962). She was famous for her formidable personality, Elizabethan dress, and eccentric opinions. Her brother Osbert (1892–1969) became famous, with his siblings, as a tilter at establishment windmills in literature and the arts. His best-known books are his memoirs, including *Left Hand! Right Hand!* (1944), *The Scarlet Tree* (1946), *Great Morning!* (1947), *Laughter in the Next Room* (1948), and *Noble Essences* (1950), which create with conscious nostalgia the portrait of a vanished aristocratic age. Their brother Sacheverell (1897–1988) is best known for his books on art, architecture, and travel. His *Southern Baroque Art* (1924) was the forerunner of much academic research. His poetry, including *The People's Palace* (1918) and *The Rio Grande*, was written mostly in traditional meters and reveals in its mannered style his interest in the arts and music.

Siva See SHIVA

Sivaji \'shi-vä-jē\ (1627/30–1680) Indian king (r.1674–80), founder of the Maratha kingdom of India. A devout Hindu, he grew up at a time when India was ruled by Muslims, and he found their religious persecution intolerable. Collecting a band of followers, he began c. 1655 to seize weak outposts of the sultan of Bijapur. In 1659 he lured the sultan's army to its destruction and, possessed of its horses and armaments, became overnight a formidable warlord. The Mughal emperor AURANGZEB sent out his most prominent general and an army of 100,000 to capture him, but Sivaji made a daring escape and soon was stronger than ever, adding a naval force to his military might. In 1674 he proclaimed himself an independent sovereign. He forged an alliance with the sultans in the south, thereby blocking the spread of Mughal rule. His rule was noted for its religious tolerance. See also MARATHA CONFEDERACY.

Siwa \'sē-wə\ *ancient* **Ammonium** Oasis (pop., 1986: 7,000), western Egypt, near the Libyan frontier. It is 6 mi (10 km) long and 4–5 mi (6–8 km) wide, with about 200 springs. Extremely fertile, it supports thousands of date palms and olive trees. It was the seat of the oracle temple of AMON; its fragmentary remains survive, with inscriptions dating from the 4th century BC, along with many Roman remains.

Six \'sēs\, **Les** (French: "The Six") Group of young French composers in the 1920s. Named by the critic Henri Collet (1885–1951), the composers were A. HONEGGER, D. MILHAUD, F. POULENC, Georges Auric (1899–1983), Louis Durey (1888–1979), and Germaine Tailleferre (1892–1983). Most of the group's members were attracted by the iconoclastic music of E. SATIE, and they benefited from the promotion of JEAN COCTEAU. As Les Six, they collaborated on a piano album and music for Cocteau's *Les mariés de la tour Eiffel*, then went their separate ways.

Six-Day War *or* **Arab-Israeli War of 1967** War between Israel and the Arab countries of Egypt, Syria, and Jordan. Palestinian GUERRILLA attacks on Israel from bases in Syria led to increased hostility between the two countries. A series of miscalculations by both sides followed. Syria feared that an invasion by Israel was forthcoming and appealed to Egypt for support. Egypt answered by ordering the withdrawal of United Nations peacekeeping forces from the SINAI PENINSULA and moving troops into the area. Amid increasingly belligerent language from both sides, Egypt signed a mutual defense treaty with Jordan. Israel, surrounded and fearing an Arab attack was imminent, launched what it felt was a preemptive strike against the three Arab states on June 5. Israeli forces captured the Sinai and the GAZA STRIP, the WEST BANK of the JORDAN RIVER and the Old City of JERUSALEM, and the GOLAN HEIGHTS. The status of these occupied territories subsequently became a major point of contention between the two sides.

Six Dynasties (AD 220–589) In China, the period between the end of the HAN DYNASTY and the foundation of the SUI. The name is derived from the six successive dynasties that had their capital at NANJING: the Wu (222–80), the Eastern JIN (317–420), the Liusong (420–79), the Southern Qi (479–502), the Southern Liang (502–57), and the Southern Chen (557–89). During this period northern China was ruled by a succession of kingdoms established by Central Asian invaders. Important among these were the NORTHERN WEI, Eastern Wei, Western Wei, Northern Qi, and Northern Zhou. Despite the chaos of the age, great advances were made in medicine, astronomy, botany, and chemistry. Buddhism and Taoism became great popular religions, and the translation of Buddhist texts focused Chinese attention on literature and calligraphy while also stimulating the erection of temples and monasteries.

Sixtus IV *orig.* **Francesco della Rovere** (1414–1484) Pope (1471–84). A Franciscan from Genoa, he enriched his family and the Papal States through SIMONY and heavy taxation. The PRAGMATIC SANCTION OF BOURGES caused strain with France, and Sixtus failed in his effort to unite the Russian and Roman churches. He endorsed the PAZZI CONSPIRACY, though not the attempt to kill LORENZO DE'MEDICI. He also incited Venice to attack Ferrara, then, in a turnabout, placed Venice under interdict (1483) as a rival to the Papal States. A patron of arts and letters, he built the SISTINE CHAPEL, which takes its name from him.

Sixtus V *orig.* **Felice Peretti** (1520–1590) Pope (1585–90). Elected pope at a time when the Papal States were in chaos, he restored order using harsh measures that won him many enemies. He raised vast sums through loans, taxes, and the sale of offices and carried out an extensive building program in Rome. He defined the Sacred College of CARDINALS (1586), reformed the ROMAN CURIA (1588), and became a founder of the COUNTER-REFORMATION. His foreign policy was aimed at combatting Protestantism; he excommunicated the Protestant Henry of Navarre (later HENRY IV of France) and promised subsidies in return for a Spanish invasion of England.

Sjaelland \'she-ˌlän\ *English* **Zealand** Largest and most populous island (pop., 1989 est.: 1,972,000), of Denmark, between the Kattegat and the BALTIC SEA. It covers 2,715 sq mi (7,031 sq km); COPENHAGEN is its major city. Two fjords break the irregular coastline, and fine beaches line the northern shore. It has many Stone Age and Viking relics, including the Viking fortress of Trælleborg (c. 1000), as well as medieval churches, castles, and manor houses. Grain and livestock farming, fishing, and tourism are major industries.

Sjahrir \'syä-ˌrir\, **Sutan** (1909–1966) Indonesian nationalist and prime minister. He received a Dutch education and returned to Indonesia, where he helped found a nationalist party in the 1930s. His party, which favored the adoption of Western constitutional democracy, opposed that of SUKARNO. He became prime minister after World War II, stripping power from then-president Sukarno, whose collaboration with the Japanese he feared would hurt the republic's image internationally. Sjahrir negotiated an agreement with the Dutch that established Indonesia's authority in Sumatra and Java. Twice forced to resign (1946, 1947), he then formed a socialist party (1948) that failed to win popular support. Sukarno banned it in 1960, and Sjahrir was arrested and imprisoned.

Sjöström \'shœ-strœm\, **Victor** *or* **Victor Seastrom** (1879–1960) Swedish film actor and director. Trained as a stage actor, he directed and starred in his first movie, *The Gardener,* in 1912. With such notable films as *Ingeborg Holm* (1913), *The Outlaw and His Wife* (1918), and *The Phantom Carriage* (1921), he established the artistic excellence of the Swedish silent film in the post-World War I era. In 1923 he moved to Hollywood, where he directed movies such as *The Scarlet Letter* (1926) and *The Wind* (1928). He returned to Sweden in 1930 and acted in numerous films, notably INGMAR BERGMAN's *Wild Strawberries* (1957).

Sjöström in *Wild Strawberries,* 1957.
BY COURTESY OF THE MUSEUM OF MODERN ART/FILM STILLS ARCHIVE, NEW YORK CITY

skaldic poetry \'sköl-dik\ Oral court poetry originating in Norway but developed chiefly by Icelandic poets (skalds) from the 9th to the 13th century. Skaldic poetry was contemporary with Eddic poetry (see EDDA), but differed from it in meter, diction, and style. Eddic poetry is anonymous, simple, and terse, often taking the form of an objective dramatic dialogue. Skalds were identified by name. Their poems were descriptive, occasional, and subjective, their meters strictly syllabic instead of free and variable, and their language ornamented with similes and metaphors. Formal subjects were the mythical stories engraved on shields, praise of kings, epitaphs, and genealogies.

Skanderbeg \'skän-dər-ˌbeg\ *orig.* **George Kastrioti** (1405–1468) Albanian leader. Son of the prince of Emathia, he was given early as a hostage to the Turkish sultan. He served in the Turkish army and was given the name Iskander and the rank of bey. In 1444 he abandoned the Turkish service and joined his Albanian countrymen against the Turks; organizing a league of Albanian princes, he was elected commander in chief. In 1444–66 he repulsed 13 Turkish invasions; his defeat of Murad II's armies in 1450 made him a hero in the Western world. After his death, however, Albania soon became part of the Ottoman empire. Skanderbeg is regarded as the national hero of Albania.

skandha \'skən-də\ In BUDDHISM, the five elements that constitute an individual's mental and physical existence. They are *rupa* (physical matter), *vedana* (feeling), *sanna* (perception), *sankharas* (mental formations), and *vinnana* (consciousness). The four mental aggregates are perceived to be the personality or ego, but are in fact only processes in a state of continuous change, subject to the effects of KARMA. At death the mental skandhas dissociate from the *rupa* and find a new physical base, resulting in a new birth.

Skara Brae \'skä-rä-'brā\ One of the most perfectly preserved STONE AGE villages in Europe, built c.2000–1500 BC, on the shore of the Bay of Skaill in Scotland's Orkney Islands. Formerly covered by a sand dune, its excavation began in the 1860s. Huts were of undressed, mortarless stone slabs, with stone furniture. They were linked by paved alleys; some had been covered by banking them with mixed sand, peat ash, and refuse, becoming stone-roofed tunnels. A sewer drained the whole. Inhabitants lived on the flesh and milk of their cattle and on shellfish; they probably wore skins. For tools they used stone, beach pebbles, and animal bones. Lozenges and similar rectilinear patterns were scratched on hut walls and along alleys. Pottery vessels, though of poor technique, show incised and relief designs, including the only example of a true spiral known from prehistoric Britain.

skarn In geology, a metamorphic zone developed in the contact area around IGNEOUS ROCK intrusions when carbonate SEDIMENTARY ROCKS are invaded by and replaced with chemical elements that originate from the igneous rock mass nearby. Many skarns also include ore minerals; productive deposits of copper or other base metals have been found in and adjacent to skarns. The typical rock of a skarn is hornfels, a fine-grained, flinty rock produced by the heat and solutions given off by the intruding magma.

skate Any of nine genera (suborder Rajoidea) of rounded to diamond-shaped RAYS. These bottom-dwellers are found from tropical to near-Arctic waters and from the shallows to depths of more than 9,000 ft (2,700 m). Most have spines on the upper surface, and some have weak electrical organs in their long, slender tails. Skates lay oblong, leathery eggs (called mermaid's purses), which are often found on beaches. Species vary from 20 in. (50 cm) to 8 ft (2.5 m) long. They swim with an undulating movement of their pectoral fins. They trap active mollusk, crustacean, and fish prey by dropping down on them from above. Skates' "wings" are edible.

skateboarding Form of recreation, popular among youths, in which a person rides standing balanced on a small board mounted on wheels. The skateboard first appeared in the early 1960s on paved areas along California beaches as a makeshift diversion for surfers when the ocean was flat. In the 1970s a faster, polyurethane wheel was developed. Eventually skateboard parks were built, providing a variety of slopes and banked surfaces for sudden turns and flamboyant stunts. The skateboarding craze contributed to the emergence of SNOWBOARDING as a winter youth sport.

skating Sport in which bladelike runners or sets of wheels attached to shoes are used for gliding on ice or on surfaces other than ice. See FIGURE SKATING, ICE DANCING, ICE HOCKEY, ROLLER-SKATING, SPEED SKATING.

skeet shooting Sport in which marksmen use shotguns to shoot at clay targets (pigeons) hurled into the air by spring devices called traps. It differs from TRAPSHOOTING in that skeet traps are set at two points on the field and targets may be thrown diagonally across the shooter's field of vision. Skeet shooting has been an Olympic event since 1968.

skeleton Bony framework of the body. It includes the SKULL, VERTEBRAL COLUMN, collarbone, shoulder blades, rib cage, and PELVIC GIRDLE and the BONES of the hands, arms, feet, and legs. The skeleton supports the body and protects its internal organs. It is held together by LIGAMENTS and moved at the JOINTS by the MUSCLES, which are attached to it. The skeletal system includes both bones and CARTILAGE. See illustration opposite.

skeleton dance See DANCE OF DEATH

skeleton sledding Winter sport similar to LUGEING in which a small sled is ridden downhill in a headfirst, prone position. The sport of skeleton sledding developed in the 1880s on the famed Cresta Run at Saint Moritz, Switz. The "bony" look of the early sleds gave the sport its name. Riders attain speeds of more than 80 miles (129 km) per hour. It was first contested at the Olympics in 1928.

Skelton, John (c. 1460–1529) English poet. Appointed court poet to Henry VII in 1489, Skelton became a tutor and eventually an adviser to Henry VIII. In 1498 he took holy orders. He wrote political and religious satires in an individual poetic style of short rhyming lines, called Skeltonics. Among his poems are *Bowge of Courte,* satirizing life at court; *Phyllyp Sparowe*, lampooning the liturgical office for the dead; and *Ware the Hawke,* attacking an irreverent priest. In 1516 he wrote the first secular MORALITY PLAY in English, *Magnyfycence. Speke, Parrot* (written 1521), *Collyn Clout* (1522), and *Why Come Ye Nat to Courte?* (1522) were directed against Cardinal WOLSEY and humanist learning.

Skelton, Red *orig.* **Richard Bernard** (1913–1997) U.S. comic actor. Born in Vincennes, Ind., he joined a touring medicine show at age 10, performed in minstrel shows, burlesque, and vaudeville, and was a hit on Broadway in 1937 with his trademark doughnut-dunking pantomime. His 1938 screen debut was followed by appearances in more than 35 film comedies. He starred in the popular *The Red Skelton Show* on radio (1941–44, 1945–53) and television (1951–71). Noted for his broad humor and warm personality, Skelton developed such characters as the Mean Widdle Kid, Clem Kadiddlehopper, and Freddie the Freeloader.

skene \'skē-nē\ In ancient Greek theater, a building behind the playing area that was originally a hut in which actors changed masks and costumes. It eventually became the scenic backdrop for the drama. First used c. 465 BC, the skene was a small wooden structure facing the circle of spectators. It developed into a two-story edifice decorated with columns, with three doors used for entrances and exits. It was flanked by wings (paraskenia). By the end of the 5th century BC, the wooden skene

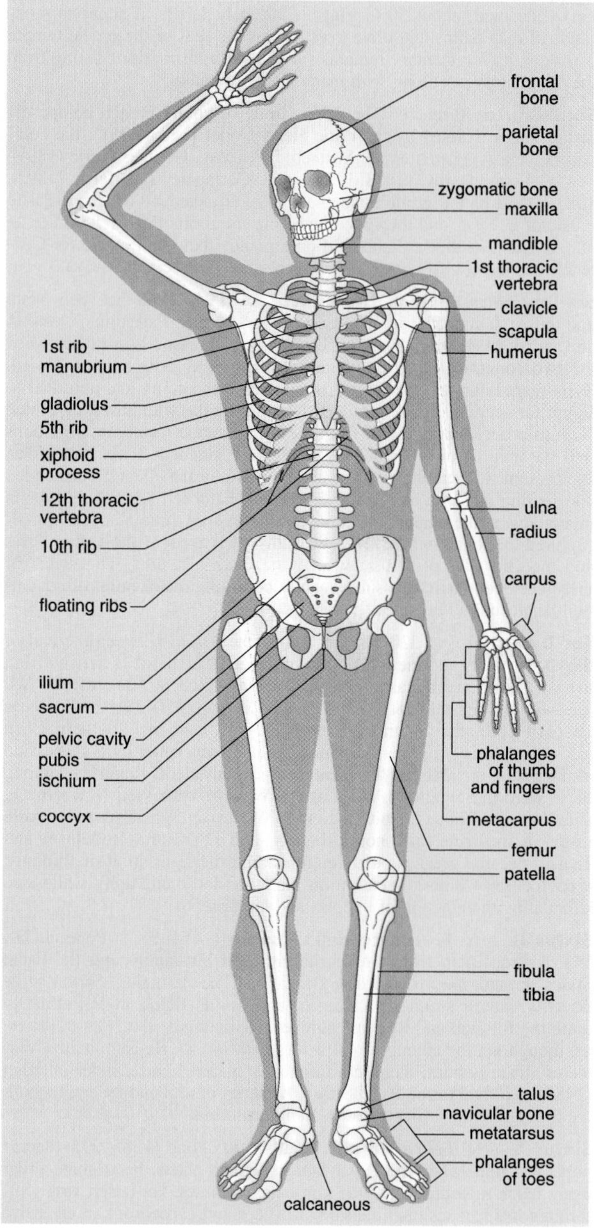

Major bones of the human skeleton.

was replaced by a permanent stone structure. In the Roman theater it was an elaborate building facade.

skepticism Philosophical doubting of knowledge claims in various areas. From ancient to modern times, skeptics have challenged accepted views in metaphysics, science, morals, and religion. Pyrrhon of Elis (c. 360–272 BC) sought mental peace by avoiding commitment to any particular view; his approach gave rise in the 1st century BC to Pyrrhonism, proponents of which sought to achieve suspension of judgment by systematically opposing various knowledge claims. One of its later leaders, Sextus Empiricus (2nd or 3rd century BC), strove for a state of imperturbability. Modern skeptical philosophers include MICHEL DE MONTAIGNE, PIERRE BAYLE, and DAVID HUME.

ski jumping Skiing event in which contestants ski down a steep ramp curved upward at the end and launch themselves into the air for distance. Using a crouch position, skiers can achieve ramp speeds of 75 mi (120 km) per hour. After takeoff, they lean far forward from the ankles with knees straight and skis held open at the tips to form a V, a position that minimizes wind resistance and maximizes lift. Scoring is based partly on distance and partly on form.

skiing Sport and mode of transportation involving moving over snow on a pair of long flat runners (skis) attached to shoes or boots. Skiing was born in Scandinavia; the oldest skis, found in Swedish and Finnish bogs, are 4,000–5,000 years old. The earliest skis were often short and broad. Skiing had reached northern China by the 7th century AD. Skiing was used in warfare in Scandinavia from the 13th century or earlier to the 20th century. Skis have continued to be used for transport and travel to the present day. The earliest mode of skiing developed into the sport now called CROSS-COUNTRY SKIING. Competitive cross-country skiing began in Norway in the 1840s and had reached California by the 1860s. Improvements on primitive bindings c. 1860 led to far wider recreational skiing. SKI-JUMPING competitions date from the 1870s. Downhill skiing was limited (in the absence of mountain railways or cable cars) by the need to climb the hill after skiing down; the building of ski lifts began in the 1930s. Skis were originally made of a single piece of wood, usually hickory; laminated construction began in the 1930s, plastic running surfaces were introduced in the 1950s, and no wood has been used in the construction of downhill skis for many decades. The business of skiing began its serious growth in the 1930s, which became explosive in the 1950s and '60s; huge resorts now dot the Austrian, Swiss, and Italian Alps, the Rocky Mtns., and other mountainous regions. See also ALPINE SKIING.

skin Surface covering of the body that protects it and receives external sensory stimuli, consisting of an epidermis over a thicker dermis. The epidermis contains cells involved in immune defenses, sensory receptors, pigment cells, and KERATIN-producing cells. The last harden and migrate to the surface to form a dead, relatively dry outer layer of horny tissue that constantly sloughs away. The dermis contains sensory nerves and blood vessels within CONNECTIVE TISSUE. COLLAGEN and elastin fibers give skin its tough, elastic quality. Cells scattered through it produce its components and take part in immune and other skin responses. A FAT layer under the dermis provides nutritional storage, cushioning, and insulation. Skin disorders range from DERMATITIS and ACNE to SKIN CANCER. Changes in skin color (e.g., JAUNDICE) or texture may be clues to systemic disorders. See also DERMATOLOGY, HAIR, INTEGUMENT, NAIL, PERSPIRATION, SEBACEOUS GLAND, SWEAT GLAND. See illustration opposite.

skin cancer Malignant tumor of the skin, including some of the most common human cancers. Though recognizable at an early stage, it has a significant death rate. Light-skinned people have the highest risk but can reduce it by limiting exposure to sunlight and to ionizing radiation. The most common types arise in the epidermis (outer skin layer) and have become more frequent with the thinning of the atmosphere's OZONE LAYER. The most serious form is MELANOMA, which is frequently fatal if not treated early with surgery. Cancers arising from the dermis are rare; the best known is KAPOSI'S SARCOMA.

skinhead Member of an international youth subculture characterized by hair and dress styles evoking aggression and physical toughness, such as shaved heads, combat boots, tattoos, and prominent body piercings. Skinheads first appeared in working-class areas of London in the 1960s; the skinhead phenomenon later spread to Australia, North America, and western continental Europe. In many countries, skinheads are known as right-wing nationalists who espouse racist views and engage in violent attacks on immigrants and racial minorities. This characterization does not apply to all members of the subculture.

skink Any of about 1,275 species (family Scincidae) of LIZARDS found throughout the tropics and in temperate regions of North America. Skinks have a cylindrical body, a conical head, and a long, tapering tail. Some species are 26 in. (66 cm) long, but most are under 8 in. (20 cm).

Striped broad-headed skink (*Eumeces laticeps*).
JOHN H. GERARD FROM THE NATIONAL AUDUBON SOCIETY COLLECTION/PHOTO RESEARCHERS

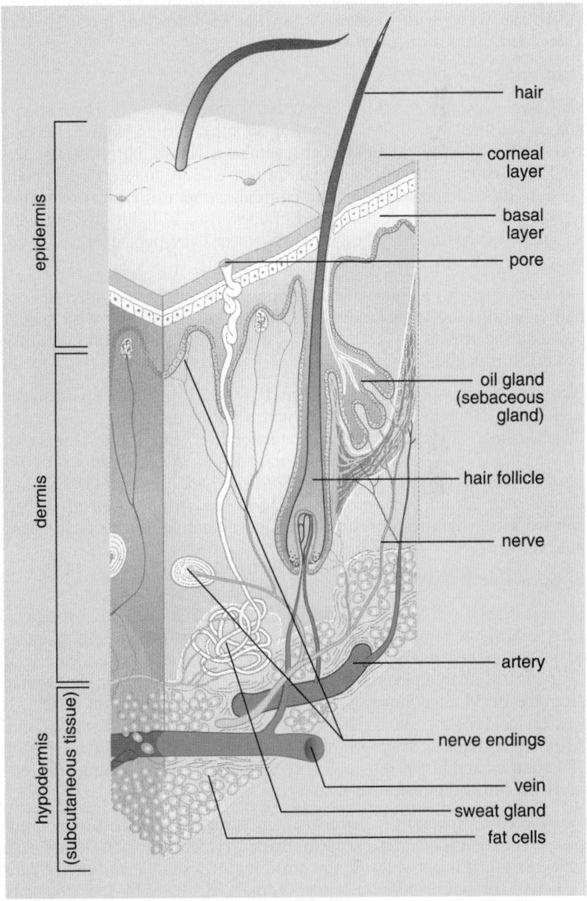

A section through the skin. The tough, dead cells of the outer epidermal surface (corneal layer) serve as a physical barrier and are continually replaced by cells produced in the basal layer. The thick supportive layer of dermis contains nerve endings, blood vessels, sweat glands, hair follicles, and oil glands. The hair follicle encloses the root of the hair. Oil glands associated with hair follicles secrete an oily substance (sebum) which lubricates the skin surface. The watery secretions of the tubular sweat glands are released onto the skin's surface through small pores. A layer of fat cells lies below the dermis.

S T U V

Some have small or no limbs and sunken eardrums. Most are ground-dwellers or burrowers; some are arboreal or semiaquatic. Skinks eat insects and other small invertebrates; large species are herbivorous. Some species lay eggs; others bear live young.

Skinner, B(urrhus) F(rederic) (1904–1990) U.S. psychologist and influential theorist of BEHAVIORISM. Born in Susquehanna, Pa., he received his PhD from Harvard University and first achieved notice with *The Behavior of Organisms* (1938). In the mid-1940s he presented his "Air-Crib," a soundproof, germ-free, air-conditioned box meant to serve as an optimal environment for the first two years of childhood. In *Walden Two* (1948), a controversial but popular work, he described a utopia based on behavioral engineering. He spent most of his teaching career at Harvard University (1948–74). His other works include *Science and Human Behavior* (1953), *Verbal Behavior* (1957), *Beyond Freedom and Dignity* (1971), and an autobiography (3 vols., 1976–83). He received the National Medal of Science in 1968.

Skinner, Cornelia Otis (1901–1979) U.S. actress and writer. Born in Chicago, she made her stage debut in *Blood and Sand* (1921) with her actor-father, Otis Skinner (1858–1942), who also collaborated on her first play, *Captain Fury* (1925). In the 1930s she wrote and staged one-woman monodramas, including *The Wives of Henry VIII* and *The Loves of Charles II*. She won acclaim in such plays as *Candida* (1939), *Lady Windermere's Fan* (1946), and *The Pleasure of His Company* (1958), which she wrote with Samuel Taylor. She also cowrote the best-seller *Our Hearts Were Young and Gay* (1942).

skip rope See JUMP ROPE

skipper Any of some 3,000 LEPIDOPTERAN species (family Hesperiidae) named for their fast (up to 20 mph, or 30 kph), darting flight. The head and stout body of the adult skipper resemble a MOTH's, but most skippers hold the first pair of wings vertically at rest, as BUTTERFLIES do. Most skippers are diurnal and lack the wing-coupling structures typical of moths. Larvae feed mostly on legumes and grasses, usually living inside folded or rolled leaves that may be woven together. They pupate in a thin cocoon of silk or silk and leaves.

skittles English ninepin bowling game played with a wooden disk or ball. The pins are set in a diamond formation; the player who knocks down all the pins in the fewest throws wins. Skittles has been played for centuries in public houses and clubs.

Skocpol \'skäch-ˌpōl\, **Theda** (born 1947) U.S. political scientist and sociologist. Born in Detroit, she earned her PhD at Harvard University. She has since taught at Harvard except for five years at the University. of Chicago (1981–86). Her books include *Social Revolutions in the Modern World* (1979), *Protecting Soldiers and Mothers* (1992), and *Boomerang: Health Reform and the Turn Against Government* (1997). Her work has significantly shaped the understanding of states and social policy.

Skopas See SCOPAS

Skopje \'skȯp-ye\ *Serbian* **Skoplje** \'skȯp-lye\ City (metro. area pop., 1994: 541,000), capital of Republic of Macedonia. The old city is located on a terraced riverbank dominated by an ancient fortress, north of which is a Roman aqueduct. Skopje was an important city in the Roman province of Moesia Superior and was a capital of medieval Serbia. It was under Turkish rule 1392–1913, then was incorporated into Serbia. After an earthquake destroyed 80% of the city in 1963, aid was sent by 78 countries and it was rebuilt. Today it is an industrial, commercial, educational, and administrative center.

skua \'skü-ə\ Species (*Catharacta skua,* family Stercorariidae) of predatory seabird, called great skua in Britain (where the JAEGERS are also called skua). It is about 24 in. (60 cm) long. It resembles a heavily built gull, with brownish body and large white wing patches. It is the only bird that breeds in both the Arctic and the Antarctic. The agile, swift skuas force other birds to disgorge food; they nest near penguins, petrels, murres, and terns, stealing their eggs and young. They also eat lemmings and carrion.

skull Skeletal framework of the head. With the exception of the lower JAW, its bones meet in immovable joints (sutures) to form a unit that encloses and protects the BRAIN and SENSE organs and gives shape to the FACE. The cranium, the upper part enclosing the brain, comprising the frontal, parietal, occipital, temporal, sphenoid, and ethmoid bones, is

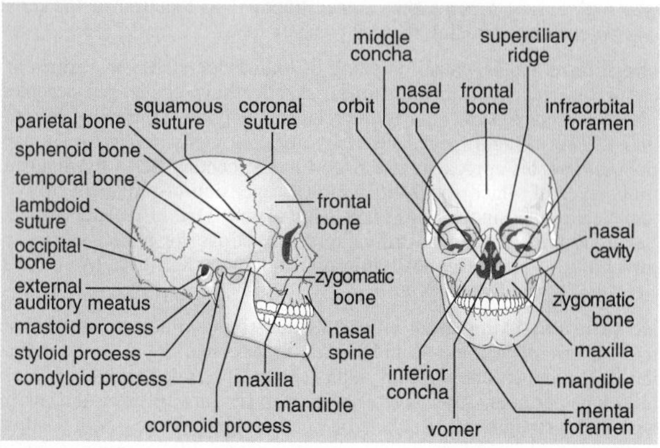

Front and side views of the human skull.

globular and relatively large compared to the facial portion. Its base has an opening through which the SPINAL CORD connects to the brain. The skull sits on the top vertebra (atlas), which permits back-and-forth motion. For side-to-side motion, the atlas turns on the next vertebra (axis). See also CRANIOSYNOSTOSIS, FONTANEL.

skunk Any of several black-and-white New World species in the CARNIVORE family Mephitidae that eject an odoriferous liquid (as far as 12 ft, or 3.7 m) when threatened. The liquid becomes a fine mist which causes tearing of the eyes and choking. Scent-gland secretions are used in perfume. Species vary in color pattern and size. Most are 18–37 in. (46–93 cm) long, including the bushy tail, and weigh 2–13 lbs (1–6 kg); the two species of spotted skunk (genus *Spilogale*) are much smaller. Skunks eat rodents, insects, eggs, birds, and plants. The striped, or common, skunk *(Mephitis mephitis)* occurs in most of North America. The seven species of hog-nosed skunk (genus *Conepatus*) have a long, naked snout. The hooded skunk *(Mephitis macroura)* has a neck ruff. The common skunk is a nocturnal feeder. With the scent glands removed, it is sometimes kept as a pet.

Striped skunk (*Mephitis mephitis*).

E.R. DEGGINGER

skunk bear See WOLVERINE

skunk cabbage Any of three species of plants that grow in temperate bogs and meadows, emitting unpleasant odors as they grow. The eastern North American skunk cabbage (*Symplocarpus foetidus,* of the ARUM FAMILY) has large fleshy leaves, purple-brown spathes, and a skunklike odor. The western, or yellow, skunk cabbage *(Lysichiton americanum),* also an arum, bears a large yellow spathe and is found from California to Alaska and eastward to Montana. The third species, *Veratrum californicum,* is the poisonous corn lily, or false HELLEBORE, of the LILY FAMILY, which grows from New Mexico and Baja California northward to Washington State.

skydiving Sport of jumping from an airplane at a moderate altitude (e.g., 6,000 ft, or 1,800 m) and executing various body maneuvers before pulling the rip cord of a PARACHUTE. Competitive events include jumping for style, landing with accuracy, and performing in teams (e.g., making free-fall formations). The sport parachute is designed to be more maneuverable than the safety parachute. See photograph opposite on following page.

Skylab U.S. space program that launched its first SPACE STATION (named Skylab) into earth orbit in 1973, by means of a SATURN V rocket. Three successive teams of astronauts conducted research and experiments from Skylab during its first 171 days in space. Skylab's orbit was then adjusted to an altitude believed sufficient to keep it in space until 1983, when it would again be adjusted for use in the SPACE-SHUTTLE program. Increased SUNSPOT activity caused greater atmospheric drag on Skylab than had been predicted, and the shuttle program was delayed. Skylab wandered from its orbit in 1978 and broke into earth's atmosphere in 1979; most of its pieces fell into the Indian Ocean.

skylark Species *(Alauda arvensis)* of Old World LARK particularly noted for its rich, sustained song and for singing in the air. It is about 7 in. (18 cm) long, with brown upper parts streaked with black and buffish white underparts. It breeds across Europe and has been introduced into Australia, New Zealand, Hawaii, and British Columbia.

skylight Roof opening covered with translucent or transparent glass or plastic designed to admit daylight. Skylights have found wide application admitting steady, even light in industrial, commercial, and residential buildings, especially those with a northern orientation. Installations range from purely functional daylighting to elaborate aesthetic forms. Flat-roofed buildings may have domed skylights; in others the skylight follows the slope of the roof. Often the skylight, or a portion of it, functions as an operating window to admit air.

skyscraper Very tall multistoried building. The term originally applied to buildings of 10–20 stories, but now generally describes HIGH-RISES of more than 40–50 stories. James Bogardus (1800–1874) built the pioneering Cast Iron Building, New York (1848), with a rigid iron frame providing the main support for upper-floor and roof loads. The refinement of the BESSEMER PROCESS for making steel (lighter and stronger than iron) made extremely tall buildings possible. Chicago's Home Insurance Co. Building (1884–85), by William Le Baron Jenney (1832–1907), was the first tall building to use a steel skeleton. Structurally, skyscrapers consist of a substructure supported by a deep foundation of PILES or CAISSONS beneath the ground, an aboveground superstructure of columns and girders, and a CURTAIN WALL hung on the structural framework. Tube structures, braced tubes, and trussed tubes were developed to give skyscrapers the ability to resist lateral wind and seismic forces. The bundled-tube system, developed by Fazlur Khan (1928–1982), uses narrow steel tubes clustered together to form exceptionally rigid columns, and has been used to build some of the world's tallest skyscrapers (e.g., SEARS TOWER). Skyscraper design and decoration have passed through several stages: LOUIS SULLIVAN emphasized verticality; the firm of McKim, Mead, & White (see CHARLES F. MCKIM, STANFORD WHITE) stressed Neoclassicism. The INTERNATIONAL STYLE was ideally suited to skyscraper design. Originally a form of commercial architecture, skyscrapers have increasingly been used for residential purposes as well. See also SETBACK.

slab In architecture, a flat, monolithic piece of stone or concrete used for a floor or roof. There are various forms of REINFORCED-CONCRETE slabs: one-way slabs cast with supporting beams, ribbed slabs cast with series of joists, two-way ribbed slabs (known as waffle slabs), flat plates reinforced in two or more directions without beams or girders, and flat slabs thickened at column supports with drop panels and/or column capitals. A waffle slab supports loads equally well along both axes and is thus most efficiently used to cover square modules.

Seven-man freefall hookup.
GUY SAUVAGE–AGENCE VANDYSTADT/PHOTO RESEARCHERS

slag By-product formed in SMELTING, WELDING, and other metallurgical and combustion processes from impurities in the metals or ores being treated. Slag consists mostly of mixed OXIDES of elements such as silicon, sulfur, phosphorus, and aluminum; ash; and products formed in their reactions with furnace linings and fluxing substances such as limestone. During smelting or refining, slag floats on the surface of the molten metal, protecting it from oxidation (see OXIDATION–REDUCTION) by the atmosphere and keeping it clean. Slag cools into a coarse aggregate used in certain concretes; it is used as a road-building material, as ballast, and as a source of available phosphate fertilizer.

slalom \ˈslä-ləm\ ALPINE SKIING event in which competitors race one at a time down a zigzag or wavy course past a series of flags or markers called gates. The course is carefully designed to test the skier's skill, timing, and judgment. A skier who misses a gate is disqualified unless he or she returns and passes through it from the proper side. Men's events use 55–75 gates, women's 45–65. The giant slalom has characteristics of both slalom and downhill skiing; giant-slalom gates are wider and set farther apart, and the course is longer than in the slalom. The supergiant slalom ("super-G") is closer to downhill; its course is steeper and straighter than that of the other slalom events and features longer, more sweeping turns taken at higher speed.

Skier competing in the giant slalom.
LAURA RILEY–STOCK, BOSTON

slander See DEFAMATION

slang Nonstandard vocabulary of extreme informality, usually not limited to any region. It includes newly coined words, shortened forms, and standard words used playfully out of their usual context. Slang is drawn from the vocabularies of limited groups: cant, the words or expressions coined or adopted by an age, ethnic, occupational, or other group (e.g., college students, jazz musicians); jargon, the shoptalk or technical terminology specific to an occupation; and argot, the cant and jargon used as a secret language by thieves or other criminals. Occupying a middle ground between standard and informal words accepted by the general public and the special words or expressions of these subgroups, slang often serves as a testing ground for words in the latter category. Many prove either useful enough to become accepted as standard or informal words or too faddish for standard use. *Blizzard*, *okay*, and *gas* have become standard, while *conbobberation* ("disturbance") and *tomato* ("girl") have been discarded. Some words and expressions have a lasting place in slang; for instance, *beat it* ("go away"), first used in the 16th century, has neither become standard English nor vanished.

slapstick Comedy characterized by broad humor, absurd situations, and vigorous, often violent action. It took its name from a paddlelike device, probably introduced by 16th-century COMMEDIA DELL'ARTE troupes, that produced a resounding whack when one comic actor used it to strike another. Slapstick comedy became popular in 19th-century music halls and vaudeville theaters and was carried into the 20th century by such silent-movie comedians as CHARLIE CHAPLIN, HAROLD LLOYD, and MACK SENNETT's Keystone Kops and later by LAUREL AND HARDY, the MARX BROTHERS, and the Three STOOGES.

slate Fine-grained, clayey METAMORPHIC ROCK that splits readily into thin slabs that have great tensile strength and durability. Some other rocks that occur in thin beds are improperly called slate because they can be used for roofing and similar purposes. True slates generally split not along the bedding plane but along planes of CLEAVAGE that may intersect the bedding plane at high angles. Slates may be black, blue, purple, red, green, or gray. Slate may be marketed either as dimension slate, used mainly for electrical panels, laboratory tabletops, roofing, and flooring, or as crushed slate, used on composition roofing, in aggregates, and as a filler.

Slater, Samuel (1768–1835) British-U.S. industrialist. Initially apprenticed to a partner of R. ARKWRIGHT, he emigrated to the U.S. in 1789, where he reproduced versions of Arkwright's spinning and CARDING MACHINES from memory and in 1793 established the first successful American COTTON mill at Pawtucket, R.I., the first of several plants. He founded the town of Slatersville, R.I. He is regarded as the founder of the U.S. cotton textile industry.

Slave Acts, Fugitive See FUGITIVE SLAVE ACTS

slave codes In U.S. history, laws governing the status of slaves, enacted by those colonies or states that permitted SLAVERY. Slaves were considered property rather than persons. They had few legal rights: in court, their testimony was inadmissible in cases involving whites; they could make no contract nor own any property; even if attacked, they could not strike a white person; they could not be away from their owner's premises without permission; they could not assemble unless a white person was present; they could not be taught to read or write; and they were not permitted to marry. Offenders were subject to punishment, including whipping, branding, imprisonment, and death. See also BLACK CODES.

Slave Lake, Lesser See LESSER SLAVE LAKE

slave narrative American literary genre consisting of slave memoirs of daily plantation life, including the sufferings and humiliations borne and the eventual escape to freedom. *A Narrative of the Uncommon Sufferings and Surprising Deliverance of Briton Hammon, a Negro Man* (1760) is often considered the first example. The major period of slave narratives was 1830–60. Some were factual autobiographies, while others were influenced or sensationalized by the writer's desire to arouse sympathy for the abolitionist cause. The genre reached its height with the autobiography of FREDERICK DOUGLASS (1845). In the 20th century, documentary narratives were compiled from recorded interviews with former slaves.

Slave River River, northern Alberta and southern Northwest Territories. Forming an integral part of the MACKENZIE RIVER waterway, it flows northward 258 mi (415 km) from Lake ATHABASCA before emptying into GREAT SLAVE LAKE near Fort Resolution. The PEACE RIVER and several small streams enter it along its course.

slave trade Capturing, selling, and buying of slaves. SLAVERY has existed throughout the world throughout history; trading in slaves has been equally universal. Slaves were taken from great population reservoirs: the Slavs and contiguous Iranians from antiquity to the 19th century, the sub-Saharan Africans during the Christian era, and the Germanic, Celtic, and Romance peoples during the Viking era. Elaborate trade networks developed: for example, in the 9th–10th century, Vikings might sell East Slavic slaves to Arab and Jewish traders, who would take them to Verdun and León, whence they might be sold throughout Moorish Spain and North Africa. The transatlantic slave trade is perhaps the best known. In Africa, women and children but not men were wanted as slaves for labor and for lineage incorporation; from c. 1500, captive men were taken to the coast and sold to Europeans. They were then transported to the Caribbean or Brazil, where they were sold at auction and taken throughout the New World. In the 17th–18th century, African slaves were traded in the Caribbean for molasses, which was made in the American colonies into rum and traded back to Africa for more slaves.

slavery Condition in which one human being is owned by another. A slave was considered in law as property, or chattel, and was deprived of most rights ordinarily held by free persons. Slavery has existed on nearly every continent and throughout most of recorded history. It typically occurs in societies whose economy is of a market type capable of producing surpluses: in that context the slave becomes a commodity who is bought and sold for profit. The Greeks and Romans accepted the institution of slavery, as did the Maya, Inca, and Aztecs. Europeans in the New World began importing slaves from Africa in the 16th century (see SLAVE TRADE). By the mid-19th century, the slave population in the U.S. had risen to more than 4 million. Most worked on plantations in the South, their status governed by SLAVE CODES. Following the rise of ABOLITIONISM, Britain abolished slavery in its colonies in 1833; France did the same in 1848. In the U.S. slavery was formally abolished by the EMANCIPATION PROCLAMATION (1863). Today slavery is not legally recognized by any government in the world. See also DRED SCOTT DECISION, FUGITIVE SLAVE ACTS, SERFDOM, UNDERGROUND RAILROAD.

Slavic languages \'slä-vik, 'sla-vik\ *or* **Slavonic languages** Branch of the Indo-European language family spoken by more than 315 million people in central and eastern Europe and northern Asia. The Slavic family is usually divided into three subgroups: West Slavic, comprising POLISH, SLOVAK, CZECH, and Sorbian (Lusatian, Wendish); East Slavic, comprising RUSSIAN, UKRAINIAN, and BELARUSIAN; and South Slavic, comprising SLOVENE, SERBIAN AND CROATIAN, Bulgarian, and Macedonian (see BULGARIAN LANGUAGE). Polish belongs to the Lechitic (Lekhitic) subgroup of West Slavic languages, which also includes Kashubian (Cassubian)—now spoken in western Poland by fewer than 150,000 people and regarded in Poland as a Polish dialect—and the several now-extinct languages. A distinctive feature of this subgroup is its preservation of the Proto-Slavic nasal vowels. Another remnant language is Sorbian, spoken by 60,000–70,000 people in eastern Germany. western Lechitic and Sorbian are all that remains of what was once a much greater Slavic speech area in central Europe; that area was gradually Germanized from about the 9th century. Among INDO-EUROPEAN LANGUAGES, Slavic is closest to the family of BALTIC LANGUAGES.

Slavic religion Beliefs and religious practices of the ancient Slavic peoples of East Europe, including the Russians, Ukrainians, Poles, Czechs, Slovaks, Serbs, Croats, and Slovenes. Most Slavic mythologies hold that God ordered the DEVIL to bring up a handful of sand from the bottom of the sea and created the land from it. Slavic religion was often characterized by DUALISM, with a Black God named in curses and a White God invoked to obtain protection or mercy. Lightning and fire gods were also common. The ancient Russians appear to have erected their idols outdoors, but the Baltic Slavs built temples and enclosed sacred places, where festivals were held and animal and human sacrifices occurred. Such festivals also often included communal banquets at which the flesh of sacrificial animals was consumed.

Slavonia Historical region, CROATIA. It lay between the SAVA RIVER on the south and the DRAVA and DANUBE rivers on the north and east. It was included in the kingdom of Croatia in the 10th century. As Slavonia–Crotia, it joins DALMATIA and ISTRIA as one of the three traditional regions of Croatia.

Slavophiles and Westernizers Opposing groups of intellectuals in 19th-century Russia. Prominent in the 1840s and '50s, the Slavophiles believed in the uniqueness of Russian culture and contended that Russia should rely on its own character and history to determine its future development. They hoped to restore the autocracy and the church to their ideal forms before PETER I THE GREAT introduced Western reforms, and also favored emancipation of the serfs and freedom of speech and the press. The Slavophile movement declined in the 1860s, but its principles were adapted and simplified by extreme nationalists, advocates of PAN-SLAVISM, and revolutionary POPULISTS. It was opposed by the Westernizers, who viewed Western Europe as a model for Russian modernization.

Slavs \'slävz\ Most numerous ethnic and linguistic body of peoples in Europe. They live chiefly in eastern and southeastern Europe but also extend across northern Asia to the Pacific. Slavs are customarily subdivided into eastern Slavs (Russians, Ukrainians, and Belarusians), western Slavs (Poles, Czechs, Slovaks, and Wends, or Sorbs) and southern Slavs (Serbs, Croats, Bulgarians, Slovenes, and Macedonians). Historically, western Slavs were integrated into Western Europe; their societies developed along the lines of other Western European nations. eastern and southern Slavs suffered Mongol and Turkish invasions and evolved more autocratic, state-centered forms of government. Religion (mainly Eastern Orthodoxy and Roman Catholicism) divides Slavs, as does the use of the CYRILLIC and LATIN alphabets. In the Middle Ages Slavic polities that left a rich cultural heritage developed in Bohemia, Poland, Croatia, Bosnia, Serbia, and Bulgaria, but by the end of the 18th century, all these states had been absorbed by powerful neighbors (the Ottoman empire, Austria, Hungary, Prussia, Russia). eastern Slavic history was marked by often unsuccessful attempts to repel Asian invaders until the 16th century, when Muscovy, later Russia, embarked on a course of expansion across northern and central Asia that eventually made it the most powerful Slavic state. PAN-SLAVISM in the 19th century had some influence on the formation of the new Slavic states after World War I, though by the end of the 20th century, Czechoslovakia and Yugoslavia—the two attempts to integrate different Slavic peoples into single polities—had both disintegrated, one peacefully and the other violently.

sled dog Any WORKING DOG used to pull a sled carrying people and supplies across snow and ice. The breeds most commonly used are the

ALASKAN MALAMUTE, Laika, SAMOYED, and SIBERIAN HUSKY. All are powerful dogs with a thick coat and high endurance. See also ESKIMO DOG.

sleep Natural periodic suspension of CONSCIOUSNESS during which the powers of the body are restored. Humans normally sleep at night, whereas nocturnal species sleep during the day. The average human sleep requirement is about 7.5 hours. Sleep is divided into two main types, REM (rapid-eye-movement) and NREM (non-REM); each recurs cyclically several times during a normal period of sleep. REM sleep is characterized by increased neuronal activity of the forebrain and midbrain, by depressed muscle tone, and by dreaming (see DREAM), rapid eye movements, and vascular congestion of the sex organs. NREM sleep is divided into four stages, the last of which is the deep, restorative, quiet sleep commonly associated with "a good night's rest." See also INSOMNIA, NARCOLEPSY.

sleeping sickness PROTOZOAL DISEASE transmitted by the bite of the TSETSE FLY. Two forms, caused by different species of the genus *Trypanosoma,* occur in separate regions in Africa. The parasite enters the bloodstream and invades the LYMPH NODES and SPLEEN, which become swollen, soft, and tender. Irregular fever and delayed pain sensation develop. In the Rhodesian form, the patient soon dies of massive toxemia. The Gambian type progresses to brain and spinal-cord invasion, causing severe headache, mental and physical fatigue, spastic or flaccid PARALYSIS, CHOREA, and profound sleepiness, followed over two or three years by emaciation, coma, and death. Some patients develop a tolerance but still carry the trypanosomes. The earlier drug treatment begins, the greater the chance of recovery. Sleeping sickness is still prevalent in parts of Africa despite heroic efforts to control it.

Slidell \slī-'del\, **John** (1793–1871) U.S. and Confederate diplomat. Born in New York City, he practiced law in New Orleans from 1819, then served in the U.S. House of Representatives (1843–45) and Senate (1853–61). In the Civil War he joined the Confederate foreign service. En route to France to seek support for the Confederacy, he and JAMES MURRAY MASON were removed from the British steamer *Trent* by a Union man-of-war. The ensuing TRENT AFFAIR led to their release.

Slim, William (Joseph) *later* **Viscount Slim (of Yarralumla and Bishopston)** (1891–1970) British general. He served with the British army in World War I and with the Indian army from 1920. In World War II he commanded Indian troops in East Africa and the Middle East (1940–41). As commander of the 1st Burma Corps (1942), he led a 900-mi (1,450-km) retreat from superior Japanese forces in Burma to India. In 1944 he led forces to repel a Japanese invasion of northern India; in 1945 he retook Burma from the Japanese. Promoted to field marshal (1948), he served as chief of the Imperial General Staff (1948–52) and later governor-general of Australia (1953–60).

slime mold Any of about 500 species of primitive organisms that contain true nuclei and resemble both PROTISTS and fungi (see FUNGUS). Originally grouped within the kingdom Fungi, some classification systems consider slime molds to be in the kingdom Protista. They typically thrive in dark, cool, moist conditions such as on forest floors. BACTERIA, YEAST, MOLDS, and fungi provide the main source of slime-mold nutrition. The complex life cycle of slime molds, exhibiting complete ALTERNATION OF GENERATIONS, may clarify the early evolution of both plant and animal cells. In the presence of water a tiny SPORE releases a mass of cytoplasm called a swarm cell, which later develops into an amoebalike creeping cell called a myxamoeba. Both swarm cells and myxamoebas can fuse in sexual union; the resulting fertilized cell, or plasmodium, grows through nuclear division and forms a spore case, which, when it dries, disintegrates and releases spores to begin the cycle again.

slippery elm *or* **red elm** Large-leaved ELM *(Ulmus rubra* or *U. fulva)* of eastern North America that has hard wood and fragrant inner bark. A gluelike substance in the inner bark has long been steeped in water as a remedy for throat ailments, powdered for use in poultices, and chewed as a thirst quencher, among other uses. It has received renewed attention in recent years as part of ALTERNATIVE MEDICINE's herbal pharmacopoeia, prescribed for a wide variety of ailments.

slipware POTTERY that has been treated with semiliquid clay, or slip. The technique was originally used to cover defects in body color, but later evolved into decorative techniques such as sgraffito, carving, painting, trailing, marbling, and inlay. In sgraffito a pattern is incised through the slip to reveal the different body color underneath. The Staffordshire potters in 17th-century Britain were famous for the decorative figures, flowers, and patterns they created by using dotted and trailed slip.

English slipware dish by Thomas Toft of northern Staffordshire, c. 1680; in the Victoria and Albert Museum, London.

Sloan, Alfred P(ritchard), Jr. (1875–1966) U.S. corporate executive. Born in New Haven, Conn., he began his career at the Hyatt Roller Bearing Co. in New Jersey and became its president at age 26. Hyatt was later acquired by GENERAL MOTORS CORP., and Sloan rose to become president and chief executive officer of GM in 1923. Under his leadership it surpassed FORD MOTOR CO. in sales and became the largest corporation in the world. He served as chairman of the board from 1937 to his retirement in 1956. A noted philanthropist, he endowed the Alfred P. Sloan Foundation and contributed to the Sloan-Kettering Cancer Center in New York and to the school of management at MIT.

Sloan, John (French) (1871–1951) U.S. artist. Born in Lock Haven, Pa., he worked as a commercial newspaper artist in Philadelphia, where he studied with ROBERT HENRI. He followed Henri to New York, where in 1908 with six others they exhibited as The EIGHT. Sloan's realistic urban paintings gave rise to the epithet ASH CAN SCHOOL. Such works as *Sunday, Women Drying Their Hair* (1912), *McSorley's Bar* (1912), and *Backyards, Greenwich Village* (1914) are sympathetic portrayals of working men and women; occasionally, as in *Wake of the Ferry* (1907), he evokes a mood of romantic melancholy.

Slocum, Joshua (1844–1909?) Canadian seaman and adventurer. Born in Wilmot Township, Nova Scotia, he worked his way up from ship's cook to captain of a trading vessel by 1869. Wrecked with his family on the Brazilian coast in 1886, he built a canoe from the wreckage and paddled back to New York. He set sail from Boston in 1895 in a 36-ft, 9-in. (11.1-m) fishing boat. In three years, two months, and two days, he sailed 46,000 mi (74,000 km) in a circuitous route ending in Newport, R.I, becoming the first man in recorded history to sail around the world singlehandedly. He wrote several books, including the classic *Sailing Alone Around the World.* In 1909 he set sail for Grand Cayman and was lost at sea.

Slonimsky, Nicolas (1894–1995) Russian-U.S. musicologist, conductor, and composer. Scion of a family of overachievers, he left the Soviet Union after studies at the St. Petersburg Conservatory and settled in the U.S. in 1923. In the 1930s he conducted premieres of works by C. IVES, E. VARESE, and others. In *Music Since 1900* (1937) he chronicled the century's musical life day by day. His *Lexicon of Musical Invective* (1952) collected wrongheaded musical criticism. His *Thesaurus of Scales and Melodic Patterns* (1947) was an inspiration to numerous composers. He edited four editions of *Baker's Dictionary of Music and Musicians* (1958–92). His commodious scholarship was undertaken with zest and humor, and near the end of his long life he was lionized by F. ZAPPA and other musicians.

slope Numerical measure of a line's inclination relative to the horizontal. In ANALYTIC GEOMETRY, the slope of any line, ray, or line segment is the ratio of the vertical to the horizontal distance between any two points on it ("slope equals rise over run"). In DIFFERENTIAL CALCULUS, the slope of a line tangent to the graph of a function is given by that function's DERIVATIVE and represents the instantaneous rate of change of the function with respect to change in the independent variable. In the graph of a position FUNCTION (representing the distance traveled by an object plotted against elapsed time), the slope of a TANGENT LINE represents the object's instantaneous velocity.

sloth Nocturnal, solitary, tree-dwelling MAMMAL (family Bradypodidae), found in South and Central America. About 2 ft (60 cm) long, sloths have a tiny tail, peglike teeth, long curved claws, and long forelimbs. A green alga grows in the shaggy fur. The four species of three-toed sloths, or ais, eat only leaves of the trumpet tree. The two species of two-toed sloths, or unaus *(Choloepus),* have two toes on the forelimbs; they eat fruits, stems, and leaves of various plants. Sloths cannot walk.

They cling upright to trunks, hang upside down (in which position they sleep some 15 hours a day), or move, extremely slowly (the source of their name), by pulling hand over hand. Their natural camouflage is their chief protection from predators.

Three-toed sloth (*Bradypus tridactylus*).
DES BARTLETT—BRUCE COLEMAN LTD.

Slovak language \'slō-ˌväk\ West SLAVIC LANGUAGE of Slovakia, spoken by about 5.6 million people there and in enclaves in the Czech Republic, Hungary, northern Serbia, and North America. Slovak was close to being an unwritten language until the later 18th century, largely because of the long political domination of Slovakia by Hungary and the much earlier literary cultivation of CZECH, Slovak's western linguistic neighbor. Present-day literary Slovak was effectively consolidated by the 1850s on the basis of Central Slovak dialects.

Slovakia *officially* **Slovak Republic** Nation, central Europe. Area: 18,933 sq mi (49,035 sq km). Population (1997 est.): 5,404,000. Capital: BRATISLAVA. About nine-tenths of the population are Slovak; Hungarians form the largest minority. Language: SLOVAK (official). Religion: Roman Catholicism, Protestantism, Orthodoxy. Currency: Slovak koruna. The CARPATHIAN MTNS. dominate Slovakia, with lowlands in the southwestern and southeastern regions. The MORAVA and DANUBE rivers form parts of the southern border. The country grows grain, sugar beets, and vegetable crops and raises pigs, sheep, and cattle, but the economy is based on mining and manufacturing; it has substantial deposits of iron ore, copper, magnesite, lead, and zinc. It is a republic with one legislative house;

its chief of state is the president, and the head of government is the prime minister. Slovakia was inhabited in the first centuries AD by Illyrian, Celtic, and Germanic tribes. Slovaks settled there around the 6th century. It became part of Great MORAVIA in the 9th century but was conquered by the MAGYARS c. 907. It remained in the kingdom of Hungary until the end of World War I, when the Slovaks joined the Czechs to form the new state of Czechoslovakia in 1918. In 1938 Slovakia was declared an autonomous unit within Czechoslovakia; it was nominally independent under German protection 1939–45. After the expulsion of the Germans, Slovakia joined a reconstituted Czechoslovakia, which came under Soviet domination in 1948. In 1969 a partnership between the Czechs and Slovaks established the Slovak Socialist Republic. The fall of the Communist regime in 1989 led to a revival of interest in autonomy, and Slovakia became an independent nation in 1993.

Slovene language \'slō-ˌvēn\ *or* **Slovenian language** South SLAVIC LANGUAGE spoken by more than 2.2 million people in Slovenia, in adjacent parts of Italy, Austria, and Hungary, and in small enclaves outside Europe. The oldest Slavic text in the LATIN ALPHABET, the Freising Fragments (c. 1000), are in a very early form of Slovene; the language is not attested again until the 16th century, when Lutheran reformers translated the Bible into Slovene. Slovene has a remarkable degree of dialect diversity considering the size of its speech area, probably enhanced by the country's Alpine geography and long period of domination by non-Slovene-speaking rulers.

Slovenia *officially* **Republic of Slovenia** Country, northwestern Balkans. Area: 7,821 sq mi (20,256 sq km). Population (1997 est.): 1,955,000. Capital: LJUBLJANA. The vast majority of the population is Slovene. Language: SLOVENE (official). Religion: Roman Catholicism (86%). Currency: Slovene tolar. Slovenia is predominantly mountainous

and wooded, with deep, fertile valleys and numerous rivers. One of the more prosperous regions of the Balkans, its economy is largely based on manufacturing. It mines coal, lead, and zinc; forestry, livestock, and crops, including potatoes, grains, and fruits are also important. It is a republic with two legislative houses; its head of state is the president, and the head of government is the prime minister. The Slovenes settled the region in the 6th century AD. In the 8th century it was incorporated into the Frankish empire of CHARLEMAGNE, and in the 9th century it came under Germany as part of the HOLY ROMAN EMPIRE. Except for 1809–13, when NAPOLEON ruled the area, most of the lands belonged to Austria until the formation of the kingdom of SERBS, CROATS, AND SLOVENES in 1918. It became a constituent republic of Yugoslavia in 1946, and received a section of the former Italian Adriatic coastline in 1947. In 1990 Slovenia held the first contested multiparty elections in Yugoslavia since before World War II. In 1991 it seceded from Yugoslavia; its independence was internationally recognized in 1992.

slug Any species of GASTROPOD that glides along on a broad tapered foot and has no shell or one that is merely an internal plate or a series of granules. Most slugs use the mantle cavity (see MOLLUSK) as a lung. Slugs have a soft, slimy body and live in moist habitats on land (except for one freshwater species). All are hermaphroditic. In temperate regions, the common slugs eat fungi and decaying leaves. Some tropical species eat plants, and some European species eat other snails and earthworms. See also NUDIBRANCH.

slum Densely populated area of substandard housing, usually in a city, characterized by unsanitary conditions and social disorganization. Rapid INDUSTRIALIZATION in 19th-century Europe was accompanied by rapid population growth and the concentration of working-class people in overcrowded, poorly built housing. England passed the first legislation for building low-income housing to certain minimum standards in 1851; laws for slum clearance were first enacted in 1868. In the U.S., slum development coincided with the arrival of large numbers of immigrants in the late 19th and early 20th century; laws concerning adequate ventilation, fire protection, and sanitation in urban housing were passed in the late 1800s. In the 20th century, government and private organizations built low-income housing and appropriated funds for urban renewal and offered low-interest home loans. Shantytowns, which often grow up around urban centers in developing countries as rural populations migrate to the cities in search of employment, are one sort of slum for which alleviating measures have yet to be successfully introduced. See also URBAN PLANNING.

slump, submarine See SUBMARINE SLUMP

Sluter \'slü-tər\, **Claus** (c. 1340/60–c. 1405) Early Netherlandish sculptor. He entered the service of PHILIP II THE BOLD in 1385 and became his chief sculptor in 1389. All his surviving sculptures were made for the Carthusian monastery of Champmol at Dijon, which Philip founded. Sluter moved beyond the prevailing French taste for graceful figures, delicate movement, and fluid falls of drapery and toward highly individual naturalistic forms. His works infuse realism with spirituality and monumental grandeur. His influence was extensive among both painters and sculptors of 15th-century northern Europe.

(From left) Zechariah, Daniel, and Isaiah from the "Well of Moses," marble sculpture by Sluter, 1395–1404/05; in the cloister of the Chartreuse de Champmol, Dijon, Fr.

FOTO MARBURG/ART RESOURCE, NEW YORK CITY

Small Computer System Interface See SCSI

small intestine Long, narrow, convoluted tube in which most DIGESTION takes place. It extends 22–25 ft (6.7–7.6 m), from the STOMACH to the LARGE INTESTINE. The mesentery, a membrane structure, supports it and contains its blood supply, lymphatics, and insulating fat. The AUTONOMIC NERVOUS SYSTEM supplies it with parasympathetic nerves that initiate PERISTALSIS and sympathetic nerves that suppress it. It is lined with minute fingerlike projections (villi) that greatly increase its surface area for ENZYME secretion and food absorption. Its three sections, the DUODENUM, jejunum, and ILEUM, have distinct characteristics. Food takes three to six hours to pass through the small intestine unless a disorder such as GASTROENTERITIS, diverticulosis, or obstruction impedes it.

smallpox *or* **variola** \və-'rī-ə-lə\ One of the world's most dreaded plagues before 1977. It was known in ancient China, India, and Egypt. It came to the Western Hemisphere with Europeans in the 16th century and devastated the native population, which lacked resistance. An infectious viral disease only of humans, it causes fever and then a rash of variable severity that blisters and dries up, leaving scars. It is not spread easily, but the virus can survive for long periods outside the body (e.g., in bedding). EDWARD JENNER developed a VACCINE from cowpox. The World Health Organization's eradication project reduced smallpox deaths from 2 million in 1967 to zero in 1977–1980. The virus now exists only in laboratories; in some countries it may be under development for purposes of BIOLOGICAL WARFARE.

Smalls, Robert (1839–1915) U.S. naval hero. Born to plantation slaves in Beaufort, S.C., he was taken to Charleston, where he worked as a hotel waiter. In the American Civil War he was impressed into the Confederate navy to serve on the armed frigate *Planter.* In 1862 he and 12 other slaves seized control of the ship in Charleston harbor and turned it over to the Union navy. He served as the ship's pilot and became its captain in 1863. After the war he served in the U.S. House of Representatives (1875–79, 1881–87).

Smalls.

BY COURTESY OF THE LIBRARY OF CONGRESS, WASHINGTON, D.C.

Smallwood, Joey *orig.* **Joseph Roberts** (1900–1991) Canadian politician. Born in Gambo, Newfoundland, he worked for socialist publications in New York (1921–25), then returned to Newfoundland to become a union organizer and radio broadcaster. An advocate of confederation with Canada, he was elected to a convention to decide Newfoundland's future (1946); his vigorous campaign helped effect its admission as a province (1948). He was elected its first premier in 1949 and retained leadership of government and the ruling Liberal Party until 1971.

smart bomb Bomb with a guidance system that directs its path toward a target. It is steered by fins or wings on the bomb that move in response to guidance commands. Guidance systems may be electro-optical, laser, or infrared. Electro-optical sensors send pictures of the target area to an air-crew member, who then locks the weapon onto the target or actively guides it to impact. Laser-guided weapons follow the reflections of a laser beam trained on the target from another source. Infrared guidance responds to heat generated by the target. Smart bombs and missiles, which permit far greater efficiency than the techniques of World War II, were extensively used in the Vietnam War.

Smarta Orthodox Hindu sect consisting of members of higher CASTES who worship all the gods of the Hindu pantheon and adhere to rules of ritual and conduct laid down in ancient SUTRAS. The sect was founded by SANKARA. The head of the monastery he established at Sringeri is the spiritual authority of the Smartas and one of the chief religious personages of India. The Smartas regard five gods as primary: SHIVA, VISHNU, Shakti (see SHAKTI), SURYA, and GANESHA. Active in all branches of learning, they have earned the honorary title *sastri* (Sanskrit: "men of learning").

Smeaton, John (1724–1792) British civil engineer. In 1756–59 he rebuilt the Eddystone Lighthouse (off Plymouth), during which he rediscovered hydraulic cement (lost since the fall of Rome) as the best mortar for underwater construction. He constructed the great Forth and Clyde Canal in Scotland; built bridges at Perth, Banff, and Coldstream; and completed the harbor at Ramsgate, Kent. He was a leader in the transition from wind-and-water to steam power; with his improvements, THOMAS NEWCOMEN's atmospheric STEAM ENGINE achieved its maximum performance. He designed atmospheric pumping engines for collieries, mines, and docks. In 1771 he founded the British Society of Civil Engineers (now the Smeatonian Society). He is regarded as the founder of the CIVIL-ENGINEERING profession in Britain.

smelt Any of certain slender, silvery, carnivorous, food fishes (family Osmeridae) having a small fleshy fin. Smelts live in cold northern seas, and most species spawn a short distance upstream. The American smelt *(Osmerus mordax),* introduced from the Atlantic to the Great Lakes, is the largest smelt, about 15 in. (38 cm) long. The European smelt *(O. eperlanus)* is similar. Among Pacific species are the rainbow herring, capelin, and eulachon, or candlefish, which is so oily at spawning time that it can be dried and burned as a candle. Silversides (see GRUNION) and other unrelated fishes are sometimes called smelts.

smelting Process by which a METAL is obtained from its ORE, either as the element or as a simple compound, usually by heating beyond the melting point, ordinarily in the presence of reducing agents such as COKE or oxidizing agents such as air (see OXIDATION–REDUCTION). A metal whose ore is an oxygen compound (e.g., iron, zinc, or lead OXIDE) is heated (reduction smelting) in a BLAST FURNACE (of designs that differ depending on the metal being won) to a high temperature; the oxide combines with the carbon in the coke, escaping as carbon monoxide or carbon dioxide. Other impurities are removed by adding FLUX, with which they combine to form SLAG. If the ore is a SULFIDE MINERAL (e.g., copper, nickel, lead, or cobalt), air or oxygen is blasted through (matte smelting) to oxidize the sulfide to sulfur dioxide and any iron to oxide slag, leaving the metal. See also METALLURGY, ORE DRESSING.

Smetana \'sme-tᵊn-ə\, **Bedrich** (1824–1884) Czech (Bohemian) composer. He determined to become a pianist, but his first concert (1847) ended his hopes, and he thereafter taught music, opening two schools of music. In the 1860s he turned to opera, becoming conductor of the national theater in 1866. His second opera was *The Bartered Bride* (1866), which gained lasting success after many revisions. *Dalibor* (1868) followed and also became popular; he would complete five more operas. Though rendered deaf by syphilis in 1874, in his last decade he wrote some of his most beloved music, including *Má vlast* (1875), with the famous "The Moldau," and the quartet "From My Life" (1876). He became insane in 1883 and died in an asylum. The strongly Czech character of his music made Smetana the preeminent Czech nationalist composer.

smew See MERGANSER

smilax \'smī-ˌlaks\ Any of about 300 species of woody or herbaceous vines, variously known as catbriers and greenbriers, that make up the genus *Smilax* (family Smilacaceae), native to tropical and temperate regions. The stems of many species are covered with prickles, the lower leaves are scalelike, and the leathery upper leaves have untoothed blades with three to nine large veins. White or yellow-green flowers are followed by clusters of red or bluish-black berries. Common catbrier *(S. rotundifolia)* and carrion flower *(S. herbacea)* of eastern North America are sometimes cultivated to form impenetrable thickets. See also SARSAPARILLA.

Smith, Adam (1723–1790) Scottish social philosopher and political economist. The son of a customs official, he studied at the Univs. of Glasgow and Oxford. A series of public lectures in Edinburgh (from 1748) led to a lifelong friendship with DAVID HUME and to Smith's appointment to the Glasgow faculty in 1751. After publishing *The Theory of Moral Sentiments* (1759), he became the tutor of the future Duke of Buccleuch (1763–66); with him he traveled to France, where he consorted with other eminent thinkers. In 1776, after nine years of work, Smith published *An Inquiry into the Nature and Causes of the Wealth of Nations,* the first comprehensive system of political economy. In it he argued in favor of an economic system based on individual self-interest that would be led, as if by an "invisible hand," to achieve the greatest good for all, and posited the DIVISION OF LABOR as the chief factor in economic growth. A reaction to the system of MERCANTILISM then current, it stands as the beginning of CLASSICAL ECONOMICS. *The Wealth of Nations* in time won him an enormous reputation, and would become virtually the most influential work on economics ever published. Though often regarded as the bible of CAPITALISM, it is harshly critical of the shortcomings of unrestrained free enterprise and monopoly. In 1777 Smith was appointed commissioner of customs for Scotland, and in 1787 rector of the University of Glasgow.

Smith, Alfred E(manuel) (1873–1944) U.S. politician. Born in New York City, he began his political career with a job from Tammany Hall (1895). In the state assembly (1903–15), he rose to speaker, then served in city political posts. He twice served as governor of New York (1919–20, 1923–28) and fought for improved housing, child welfare, and efficient government. In 1928 he won the Democratic nomination for U.S. president, the first Roman Catholic to be nominated, but lost to HERBERT HOOVER. He later opposed the NEW DEAL programs of FRANKLIN ROOSEVELT.

Smith, Bessie *orig.* **Elizabeth** (1894–1937) U.S. blues and jazz singer, one of the definitive stylists of classic blues and the most successful black entertainer of her time. Born in Chattanooga, Tenn., Smith sang popular songs as well as blues on the minstrel and vaudeville stage. She began recording in 1923 and appeared in the 1929 film *St. Louis Blues.* Her interpretations represent the fully realized transition of the rural folk tradition of the blues to its urbane structure and expressiveness. A bold, supremely confident artist with a powerful voice and precise diction, she became known as "Empress of the Blues." She died from injuries sustained in a car crash, having apparently been refused treatment for reasons of racial prejudice.

Smith, Cyril Stanley (1903–1992) British-U.S. metallurgist. He worked as a researcher at MIT and the American Brass Co. before joining the MANHATTAN PROJECT, where he determined the properties and technology of PLUTONIUM and URANIUM, the essential materials of the ATOMIC BOMB. He later taught at the University of Chicago (1946–61) and MIT (1961–69). He published many books on the history of metallurgy, including *A History of Metallography* (1960).

Smith, David (Roland) (1906–1965) U.S. sculptor. Born in Decatur, Ill., he learned to work with metal while employed at an automobile plant. In 1926 he went to New York and took various jobs while studying painting at the Art Students League. His sculptures grew out of his abstract paintings, to which he attached so many bits of wood, metal, and found objects that they became virtual bases for sculptural superstructures. He became the first U.S. artist to make welded metal sculpture. In 1940 he moved to Bolton Landing, N.Y., and there made his large yet seemingly weightless metal sculptures until his death in a car crash. His abstract biomorphic and geometric forms are remarkable for their erratic inventiveness, stylistic diversity, and high aesthetic quality.

Smith, Emmitt (born 1969) U.S. football player. Born in Pensacola, Fla., he set 58 school records at the University of Florida. As a running back for the Dallas Cowboys since 1990, he has accrued over 12,000 yards rushing and has helped his team win three Super Bowl games. In 1995 he set the all-time NFL record for touchdowns in a single season (25), and he holds the record for most career rushing touchdowns (125).

Smith, Frederick Edwin See Earl of BIRKENHEAD

Smith, George (1824–1901) British publisher. He took over his father's bookselling and publishing business in 1846. Under his leadership the firm issued works by such noted Victorian writers as JOHN RUSKIN, BRONTE FAMILY, CHARLES DARWIN, WILLIAM THACKERAY, ELIZABETH BARRETT BROWNING, WILKIE COLLINS, MATTHEW ARNOLD, HARRIET MARTINEAU, and ANTHONY TROLLOPE. His most important publication was the first edition of the *Dictionary of National Biography* (66 vols., 1885–1901), later continued by Oxford University Press. He also began the illustrated literary journal *Cornhill Magazine* (1860) and the *Pall Mall Gazette* (1865), a literary newspaper.

Smith, Gerrit (1797–1874) U.S. reformer and philanthropist. Born into a wealthy family in Utica, N.Y., he became active in the temperance movement (1828) and built one of the first U.S. temperance hotels at Peterboro, N.Y. From 1835 he was an active abolitionist, and he made his hotel a stop on the UNDERGROUND RAILROAD. He helped form the LIBERTY PARTY and was its unsuccessful presidential candidate in 1848 and 1852. He paid the legal expenses of many slaves arrested under the FUGITIVE SLAVE ACTS. He gave a farm to his friend JOHN BROWN and financed some of Brown's activities.

Smith, Hamilton O(thanel) (born 1931) U.S. microbiologist. Born in New York City, he received his MD from Johns Hopkins University. While studying the mechanism whereby the bacterium *Haemophilus influenzae* takes up DNA from a particular bacteriophage, Smith, WERNER ARBER, and DANIEL NATHANS discovered the first of what came to be called type II restriction enzymes. Whereas previously studied restriction enzymes cut DNA at unpredictable points, the type II enzymes' predictability allowed the scientists to cut DNA at a particular point. The enzymes have become valuable tools in the study of DNA structure and in recombinant-DNA technology. The three shared a 1978 Nobel Prize.

Smith, Hoke (1855–1931) U.S. politician. Born in Newton, N.C., he became publisher of the *Atlanta Journal* (1887–1900), which he used to promote progressive measures (except civil rights for blacks). He served as U.S. secretary of the interior 1893–96. As governor of Georgia (1907–9, 1911), he improved education, transportation, and prison conditions. Elected to the U.S. Senate (1911–21), he supported progressive legislation but opposed U.S. participation in the League of Nations.

Smith, Ian (Douglas) (born 1919) First native-born prime minister of the British colony of S. Rhodesia (1964–65). An ardent advocate of white rule, in 1965 he declared Rhodesia's independence and withdrew it from the Commonwealth. He faced guerrilla attacks from ROBERT MUGABE and JOSHUA NKOMO through most of the 1970s. In 1977 he was finally compelled to negotiate a transfer of power to the black majority, a process completed two years later. He continued to serve in Parliament until 1987.

Smith, John (1580–1631) English colonist. After a period as a military adventurer, he joined an English group preparing to establish a colony in North America. After the London Co. received its charter, the group set sail and arrived at Chesapeake Bay (1607) and established the first permanent English settlement in North America at Jamestown, of which Smith became the leader. On a river voyage to explore the surrounding region, he was captured by Indians of the Powhatan Confederacy and saved from death by Pocahontas. As president of the Jamestown colony, he oversaw its expansion. An injury forced his return to England in 1609. Eager for further exploration, he contacted the Plymouth Co. and sailed in 1614 to the area he named New England. He mapped the coast and wrote descriptions of Virginia and New England that encouraged others to colonize.

John Smith, engraving by Simon van de Passe, 1616.

BY COURTESY OF THE TRUSTEES OF THE BRITISH MUSEUM; PHOTOGRAPH, J.R. FREEMAN & CO. LTD.

Smith, John (born 1965) U.S. freestyle wrestler. Born in Del City, Okla., he attended Oklahoma State University and later coached wrestling there. He won six consecutive world championships (1987–92) and two Olympic gold medals (1988, 1992) in the featherweight class (136.5 lbs, or 62 kg).

Smith, Joseph (1805–1844) Founder of the Church of Jesus Christ of Latter-day Saints (Mormon Church). Born in Sharon, Vt., he began experiencing visions as a teenager in Palmyra, N.Y. In 1827 he claimed that an angel had directed him to buried golden plates containing God's revelation; these he translated into the *Book of Mormon* (1830). He led converts to Ohio, Missouri, and Illinois, where he established the town of Nauvoo (1839), which soon became the state's largest town. Imprisoned for treason after his efforts to silence Mormon dissenters led to mob violence, he was murdered at 38 by a lynch mob that stormed the jail where he was held. His work was continued by Brigham Young.

Joseph Smith, detail from an oil painting by an unknown artist; in the Heritage Hall Museum, the Auditorium, Independence, Mo.

BY COURTESY OF THE REORGANIZED CHURCH OF JESUS CHRIST OF LATTER DAY SAINTS, INDEPENDENCE, MO.

Smith, Kate *orig.* **Kathryn Elizabeth** (1909–1986) U.S. singer, long known as the "First Lady of Radio." Born in Virginia, Smith studied nursing before moving to New York, where she won a Broadway role as an overweight girl who was the butt of jokes. In 1931 she began her immensely popular radio show "Kate Smith Sings," which ran for 16 years; her theme song, "When the Moon Comes over the Mountain," became familiar to millions. In 1938 she created the news and gossip program "Kate Smith Speaks" and introduced Irving Berlin's "God Bless America." In the 1950s she hosted several TV shows. In 1982 she was awarded the U.S. Medal of Freedom.

Smith, Maggie *orig.* **Margaret Natalie** *later* **Dame Maggie** (born 1934) British actress. She first gained recognition on Broadway in *New Faces of 1956,* and after winning praise for her roles in *The Rehearsal* (1961) and *Mary, Mary* (1963), she joined the National Theatre, where she starred opposite Laurence Olivier in *Othello* (1964; film, 1965). Her later films include *The Prime of Miss Jean Brodie* (1969, Academy Award), *Travels with My Aunt* (1972), *California Suite* (1978, Academy Award), and *The Lonely Passion of Judith Hearne* (1987). Known for her nervous intensity, acid wit, and flawless timing, she has many great stage performances to her credit, notably in *The Way of the World* (1985) and *Lettice and Lovage* (1990, Tony award).

Smith, Margaret Chase (1897–1995) U.S. politician. Born in Skowhegan, Me., she served as secretary to her husband, Clyde Smith, after he was elected to Congress as a Republican in 1936. When he suffered a heart attack in 1940, he urged voters to elect her in his stead. She became the first woman to win election to both houses of Congress, serving in the House of Representatives (1940–49) and Senate (1949–73). Though a staunch anticommunist, she was the first of her party to condemn Joseph McCarthy's tactics, and she won respect for her rock-like integrity. She retired from politics after her defeat in 1972.

Smith, Red *orig.* **Walter Wellesley** (1905–1982) U.S. sports columnist. Born in Green Bay, Wis., Smith worked for various newspapers before his column, "Views of Sport," began appearing in the *New York Herald Tribune* in 1945; it was syndicated soon thereafter. He joined the *Times* in 1971. His writing, mostly about major spectator sports, shunned jargon and displayed literary craftsmanship, wry humor, and deep knowledge. He won a Pulitzer Prize in 1976. His columns were collected in five books, including *Out of the Red* (1950) and *Strawberries in the Wintertime* (1974).

Smith, Samuel (1752–1839) U.S. politician. Born in Carlisle, Pa., he became a merchant in Baltimore and fought in the American Revolution. He served in the U.S. House of Representatives (1793–1803, 1816–22) and Senate (1803–15, 1822–33). As brigadier general of the Maryland militia, he commanded U.S. troops that defended Baltimore from the British in the War of 1812. At 83, after leading the militia against rioters, he was elected mayor of Baltimore.

Smith, Stevie *orig.* **Florence Margaret** (1902–1971) British poet. She lived most of her life with an aunt in a London suburb and worked many years as a secretary. Her poetry, an unsentimental combination of the ludicrous and the pathetic, expresses an original and visionary personality. In the 1960s her poetry readings became popular, and she made radio broadcasts and recordings. Her *Collected Poems* (1975) is illustrated with her James Thurber-like sketches; it includes her first book, *A Good Time Was Had by All* (1937), and *Not Waving but Drowning* (1957), whose title poem appears in many anthologies.

Smith, Theobald (1859–1934) U.S. microbiologist and pathologist. Born in Albany, N.Y., he received his MD from Cornell University. He discovered that injected heat-killed cultures of the causative microorganisms can immunize animals against disease. His discovery that Texas cattle fever is caused by a parasite transmitted by ticks—the first definite proof of arthropods' role in spreading disease—helped the scientific community accept mosquitoes' role in malaria and yellow fever. Smith was the first to differentiate the bacteria that cause tuberculosis in cattle and in humans, and to notice anaphylaxis. He also improved laboratory production of vaccines.

Smith, W(illiam) Eugene (1918–1978) U.S. photojournalist. Born in Wichita, Kan., he worked as a photographer for local papers, then went to New York and worked for several magazines. In 1943–44, as a war correspondent for *Life* magazine, he covered many of the important battles of the Pacific theater. He produced a number of photo essays for *Life*, such as *Spanish Village* (1951), a study of villagers' daily struggle to draw life from exhausted soil. His most famous picture, *The Walk to Paradise Garden* (1947), showing his own children entering a forest clearing, concluded the landmark photographic exhibition *The Family of Man.*

Smith, William (1769–1839) English engineer and geologist, known as the founder of the science of stratigraphy. The son of a blacksmith, he was largely self-educated. He produced the first geologic map of England and Wales (1815), setting the style for modern geologic maps, and subsequently a series of geologic maps of the English counties. He introduced many techniques still used, including the use of fossils for the dating of layers. Current geologic maps of England differ from his primarily in detail, and many of the colorful names he applied to the strata are also used today.

Smith & Wesson U.S. gun manufacturers. The company has its roots in an 1852 partnership between Horace Smith (1808–1893) and Daniel B. Wesson (1825–1906), who designed and marketed a lever-action, repeating magazine handgun that held a self-contained cartridge. Their venture ran into financial difficulties and they were forced to sell it, but a second partnership in 1856, manufacturing their new revolving-cylinder handgun (now known as the .22 rimfire) proved more successful. The Civil War made Smith & Wesson a leading firearms manufacturer. In 1867 it began selling in Europe. It supplied the British in World War I and the Allies in World War II. In 1965 the Wesson family sold the company, which has since changed hands several times and is currently owned by the British firm Tomkins PLC.

Smith College Private liberal-arts college for women in Northampton, Mass. It was founded in 1871 through the bequest of Sophia Smith (1796–1870). Bachelor's degrees are granted in most major academic fields, and master's degrees are granted in education, biology, dance, theater, music, religion, and social work. Smith's school of social work also grants the PhD. The college belongs to a five-college cooperative with AMHERST, Hampshire, and MOUNT HOLYOKE colleges and the University of MASSACHUSETTS. Enrollment is about 2,800.

Smith Sound Channel between ELLESMERE ISLAND, Canada, and northwestern GREENLAND. About 30–45 mi (48–72 km) wide, it extends northward for 55 mi (88 km) from BAFFIN BAY to the Kane Basin. It was discovered by William Baffin in 1616 and named for Thomas Smythe (Smith), a promoter of voyages to find a NORTHWEST PASSAGE.

smithing Fabrication and repair of objects made of metal by hot and cold FORGING on an ANVIL or with a power hammer, or by WELDING and other means. Blacksmiths traditionally worked with IRON (anciently known as "black metal"), making agricultural and other tools, fashioning hardware (e.g., hooks, hinges, handles) for farm, home, and industry, and shoeing horses. The term "smithing" is also applied to work with precious metals (gold, silver) as well as other metals (e.g., tin, including tinplate).

Smithsonian Institution U.S. research institution. Enabled by the bequest of the English chemist James Smithson (1765–1829), it was established in Washington, D.C., by an 1846 act of Congress. The Smithsonian administers numerous bureaus, including the Freer Gallery of Art, the John F. Kennedy Center for the Performing Arts, the National Air and Space Museum, the National Gallery of Art, the National Museum of History and Technology, the National Museum of Natural History, the National Zoological Park, and the Smithsonian Astrophysical Observatory.

smog Polluted air over a community. The term, a combination of "smoke" and "fog," was popularized in the early 20th century and now commonly refers to the pall of automotive or industrial origin that lies over many cities. Sulfurous smog results from the use of sulfur-bearing fossil fuels, particularly coal, and is aggravated by dampness. Photochemical smog requires neither smoke nor fog. Nitrogen oxides and hydrocarbon vapors emitted from automobiles and other sources enter reactions in the presence of sunlight that produce a light brownish coloration of the atmosphere, reduced visibility, plant damage, irritation of the eyes, and respiratory distress.

smoking Breathing the fumes of burning plant material, especially tobacco, from a cigarette, cigar, or pipe. Despite social and medical arguments against tobacco use, the habit has spread worldwide. NICOTINE and related ALKALOIDS furnish the psychoactive effects and, along with tar (a residue containing resins and other by-products), the negative health effects. Those effects include LUNG CANCER, oral and throat cancers, HEART DISEASE, STROKE, EMPHYSEMA, chronic BRONCHITIS, and MACULAR DEGENERATION. Smoking also increases the effects of other risk factors (see ASBESTOSIS). Passive smoking (breathing the smoke from others' cigarettes) increases nonsmokers' risk of lung cancer and the risk of SUDDEN INFANT DEATH SYNDROME. Self-help and doctor-run programs, along with nicotine patches and gums that provide diminishing doses of nicotine, are among the aids available to help those who wish to quit smoking. Antismoking campaigns have greatly reduced smoking in the U.S. even as it rises in many other countries.

Smoky Mountains See GREAT SMOKY MTNS.

smoky quartz Common, coarse-grained variety of QUARTZ that ranges in color from nearly black through smoky brown. No distinct boundary exists between smoky and colorless quartz. Its abundance causes it to be worth considerably less than either AMETHYST or CITRINE. Heating bleaches the stone, the color sometimes passing through yellow; these yellow pieces are often sold as citrine.

Smolensk \smō-ˈlensk\ City (pop., 1995 est.: 355,000), western Russia. One of the oldest and most historic of Russian cities, it was a key stronghold on the DNIEPER RIVER by the 9th century and became a commercial center on the trade route between the BALTIC SEA and the BYZANTINE EMPIRE. Sacked by the TATARS c. 1240, it subsequently fell to Lithuania. Sieges led to its capture by Moscow in 1340 and recapture by Lithuania in 1408. It was fought over several times, then was finally taken by Russia in 1654. It was burned during NAPOLEON's invasion of Russia in 1812. The scene of heavy fighting in World War II, it was occupied by the Germans 1941–43. It is now a light-industry and educational center.

Smollett \ˈsmä-lət\, **Tobias (George)** (1721–1771) English satirical novelist. Throughout his life Smollett combined the roles of medical man and writer. He is best known for his novels, including the PICARESQUE NOVELS *Roderick Random* (1748), a graphic account of British naval life, and *Peregrine Pickle* (1751), a comic, savage portrayal of 18th-century society. In an active publishing career he did translations; wrote a *Complete History of England* (1757–58); edited periodicals, including *The Critical Review*; and compiled a 58-volume *Universal History*. In the mid-1760s, seriously ill with tuberculosis, he retired to France. In 1766 he published the irascible *Travels Through France and Italy*, his one nonfiction work that is still read. His finest work, *Humphry Clinker* (1771), is a humorous EPISTOLARY NOVEL.

Smollett, detail of an oil painting by an unknown artist, about 1770; in the National Portrait Gallery, London.

BY COURTESY OF THE NATIONAL PORTRAIT GALLERY, LONDON

Smoot-Hawley Tariff Act (1930) U.S. edict. It raised import duties by as much as 50%, adding considerable strain to the worldwide economic climate of the GREAT DEPRESSION. Despite a petition from 1,000 economists urging Pres. HERBERT HOOVER to veto the act, it was passed as a protective measure for domestic industries. It contributed to the early loss of confidence on Wall Street and signaled a U.S. isolationist stance. Other countries retaliated with similarly high protective tariffs, and overseas banks began to collapse. In 1934 Pres. FRANKLIN ROOSEVELT signed the Trade Agreements Act, which reduced such tariffs.

smrti \ˈsmri-tē, ˈsmər-tē\ Class of Hindu sacred literature that is based on human memory, as distinct from the VEDAS, which are considered to be divinely revealed. Smrti serves to elaborate, interpret, and codify Vedic literature. It is considered less authoritative than Vedic literature but tends to be more widely known. The term has come to refer particularly to texts pertaining to law and social conduct, including the Kalpa Sutras, the PURANAS, the BHAGAVADGITA, the *RAMAYANA*, and the *MAHABHARATA*.

smuggling Act of importing and exporting secretly and illegally to avoid paying duties or to evade enforcement of laws (e.g., drug- or firearms-control laws). Smuggling is probably as old as the first tax or regulation on trade. Two main methods exist: the undetected running of cargoes across frontiers, and the concealment of goods in unlikely places on ships or cars, in baggage or cargo, or on the person.

smut Disease of CEREALS, CORN, GRASSES, ONION, and SORGHUM, caused by many species of fungi (see FUNGUS). SPORES accumulate in sootlike masses (sori) that form within blisters in seeds, leaves, stems, flower parts, and bulbs. The sori usually break up into a black powder that is readily dispersed by wind. Many smut fungi enter embryos or seedling plants, develop throughout the plant, and appear externally only as the plants near maturity. Other smuts are localized, infecting actively growing tissues. Control includes growing resistant varieties in noninfested soil, treating seeds with fungicide, using disease-free transplants, and destroying infected plants or plant parts before the spores are released.

Smuts \ˈsmu̇ts\, **Jan (Christian)** (1870–1950) South African statesman, soldier, and prime minister (1919–24, 1939–48). An AFRIKANER, Smuts studied law at Cambridge University Returning to South Africa, he was appointed state attorney in Pretoria by Pres. PAUL KRUGER in 1897. He fought the British in the SOUTH AFRICAN WAR, and joined with LOUIS BOTHA to oppose ALFRED MILNER's implementation of the peace terms. By 1905 Smuts was reconciled to British control and sought to maintain South Africa within the Commonwealth. In World War I he joined again with Botha to suppress rebellion, conquer S.West Africa, and launch a campaign in eastern Africa. He attended the Versailles peace conference and helped promote the LEAGUE OF NATIONS. When Botha died, he became prime minister. He was defeated in 1924 by a NATIONAL PARTY coalition. In 1933 he helped J.B.M. HERTZOG force out the extreme nationalists, and in 1939 he replaced Hertzog as prime minister. Under his leadership, South Africa helped prevent Germany and Italy from conquering northern Africa. In 1948 he was defeated by DANIEL F. MALAN's Nationalists. He ended his life as chancellor of Cambridge Univ.

Smyrna See IZMIR

Smyth, Ethel (Mary) *later* **Dame Ethel** (1858–1944) British composer. Born into a military family, she studied at the Leipzig Conservatory and was encouraged by J. BRAHMS and A. DVORAK. She first gained notice with her sweeping Mass in D (1893). Her best-known work is *The Wreckers* (1906), the most admired English opera of its time. Her *March of the Women* (1911) reflected her strong involvement in the women's suffrage movement. Her comic opera *The Boatswain's Mate* (1916) enjoyed considerable success. Her work is notably eclectic, ranging from conventional to experimental. She wrote a multivolume autobiography, *Impressions That Remained* (1919–40).

Smythe \'smīth\, **Conn** *orig.* **Constantine Falkland Cary** (1895–1980) Canadian ice-hockey executive. Born in Toronto, he founded the Toronto Maple Leafs in 1927 and made them into a leading hockey club. Since 1965 the Conn Smythe Trophy has been given annually to the best player in the STANLEY CUP play-offs.

snail Any species of GASTROPOD that glides along on a broad tapered foot and has a high coiled shell into which it can withdraw. Snails are found in the ocean, in fresh waters, and on land. Most marine snails have gills in the mantle cavity (see MOLLUSK). Most land and freshwater snails have no gills; they use the mantle cavity itself as a lung. Snails may be either scavengers (of dead plant or animal matter) or predators. Some species are used as food, and the shells of some are used as ornaments. See also LIMPET, PERIWINKLE, SLUG, WHELK.

snail darter Rare species *(Percina tanasi)* of DARTER that originally was found only in the Little Tennessee River in the southeastern U.S. It became the subject of a legal controversy in 1978, when its status as an endangered species delayed for two years the construction of Tellico Dam. The situation was resolved when the fish was successfully introduced into the Hiwassee River.

snake Any member of about 11 REPTILE families (suborder Serpentes, order Squamata) that has no limbs, voice, external ears, or eyelids, only one functional lung, and a long, slender body. About 2,700 snake species are known to exist, most numerously in the tropics. Their skin is covered with scales. They have good eyesight, and they continually taste the surrounding air with their tongues. Though they lack any voice, they are capable of hissing. Most live on the ground, but some are arboreal or aquatic, and some are burrowers. They move by muscular contraction, aided by elongated scales on their abdomen. They are fearless predators, focusing 70% of their solitary existence on tracking, capturing, and digesting their living prey; the construction of their jaws and bodies enables them to swallow large prey whole. Mating and laying eggs or bearing live young are brief seasonal activities. About one-fifth of snake species are venomous; some can kill humans with their bite. Others kill their prey by constriction or simply ingesting. Species range from less than 5 in. (12 cm) to over 30 ft (9 m) long. Snakes grow continuously throughout their life, shedding their outgrown skin at each growth increment. They inhabit all continents, but few species are found on islands or in regions with long winters.

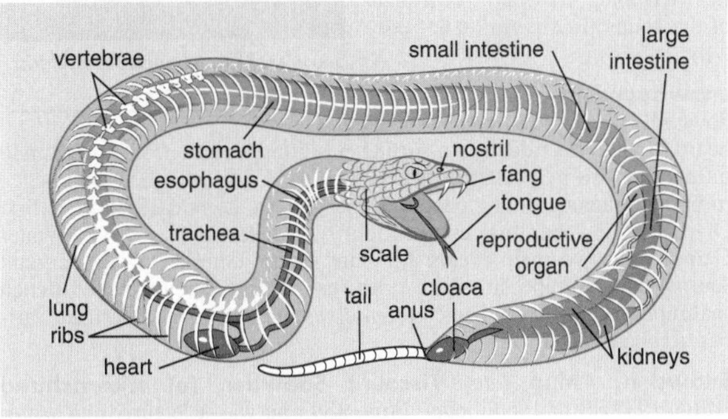

Internal and external features of a snake.

Snake River River, northwestern U.S. It is the largest tributary of the COLUMBIA RIVER and one of the most important streams in the Pacific Northwest. It rises in the mountains of YELLOWSTONE NATIONAL PARK in Wyoming and flows south through Idaho 1,040 mi (1,670 km) to enter the Columbia in southeastern Washington. The lower Snake flows through HELLS CANYON, the deepest river gorge in North America.

The lower Snake River in Hells Canyon National Recreation Area, between Oregon and Idaho.

GREG VAUGHN/TOM STACK & ASSOCIATES

snakebird See ANHINGA

snakebite Wound from the bite of a SNAKE, especially a venomous one. Nonvenomous snakes leave skin tears that may be treated like scratches. A person bitten by a venomous snake needs medical care as soon as possible. Antivenin must be specific to the type of VENOM, so the snake should be identified or accurately described. Different kinds of venom break down red blood cells or attack the nervous system, causing PARALYSIS. Local tissue destruction may lead to GANGRENE. First aid for snakebite seeks to keep the venom from spreading to the rest of the body. The bitten limb should be kept still below heart level with a broad, firm (not tight) bandage around it above the bite. Exertion and excitement should be avoided. Cutting, suction, tourniquets, and applying ice are not advised.

snapdragon family Family Scrophulariaceae, containing about 4,000 species of flowering plants in 190 genera, found worldwide. The family is notable for its many ornamental garden plants, including snapdragon (*Antirrhinum* species) and FOXGLOVE. *Antirrhinum* contains about 40 species native to western North America and the western Mediterranean. Other members of the family, including BUTTER-AND-EGGS, are wildflowers. Flowers of the family are tubular and bilaterally symmetrical (two-lipped).

snapper Any of about 250 species of valuable food fishes (family Lutjanidae), found throughout the tropics. These active schooling fishes have slender bodies, large mouths, sharp canine teeth, and blunt or forked tails. Many species grow to 2–3 ft (60–90 cm) long. Snappers eat crustaceans and other fishes. Some species, such as the Atlantic dog snapper, contain a toxin. The red snapper, a bright red fish, inhabits deep Atlantic waters. The emperor snapper is a red-and-white Indo-Pacific fish. The Atlantic yellowtail snapper has a broad yellow stripe from the nose to the wholly yellow tail.

Red spot snapper (*Lethrinus variegatus*).

DOUGLAS FAULKNER

snapping turtle Either of two species (family Chelydridae) of edible, omnivorous, freshwater TURTLES found in North and Central America. They are tan to black and have a rough upper shell, a small cross-shaped lower shell, a long tail, and a large head with hooked jaws. Known for their fierceness, they lunge at aggressors and prey and bite them with their powerful jaws. The common snapping turtle *(Chelydra serpentina)* has a shell 8–12 in. (20–30 cm) long and weighs 10–35 lbs (4.5–16 kg). The alligator snapping turtle *(Macrochelys,* or *Macroclemys, temmincki),* the largest freshwater turtle in the U.S., has a shell 16–28 in. (40–70 cm) long and weighs 40–155 lbs (18–70 kg). It lies quietly on the bottom of slow moving bodies of water, luring fishes by means of a wormlike appendage on the floor of its open mouth.

Snapping turtle (*Chelydra serpentina*).
WALTER DAWN

Snead, Sam(uel Jackson) (1912–2002) U.S. golfer. Born near Hot Springs, Va., he reportedly never took a golf lesson. Known for his straw hat and his flowing, powerful swing, "Slammin' Sammy" won the PGA championship three times (1942, 1949, 1951), the British Open (1946), the Masters three times (1949, 1952, 1954), and was a member of the U.S. RYDER CUP team 10 times. He won more PGA tournaments (81) than any other player in history, and his total number of world tournament wins is estimated at 135.

Snell's law Relationship between the path taken by a ray of light as it moves from one medium to another and the refractive indices of the two media. Discovered in 1621 by Willebrord Snell (1580–1626), the law went unpublished until its mention by CHRISTIAAN HUYGENS. If n_1 and n_2 represent the indices of refraction of two media, and θ_1 and θ_2 are the angles of incidence and REFRACTION that a ray of light makes with the line perpendicular to the boundary (the normal), Snell's law states that $n_1/n_2 = \sin\theta_2/\sin\theta_1$. Because the ratio n_1/n_2 is a constant for any given wavelength of light, the ratio of the two sines is also a constant for any angle.

snipe Any of about 20 species of birds (family Scolopacidae) that frequent wet meadows and marshes in temperate and warm regions worldwide. They are short-legged and chunky, with brown, black, and white stripes and bars. The wings are pointed and angular. The long, flexible bill is used to probe mud for worms. The common snipe *(Gallinago,* or *Capella, gallinago)* is about 12 in. (30 cm) long, including the bill.

Common snipe (*Gallinago gallinago*).
INGMAR HOLMASEN

snook Any of about eight species (genus *Centropomus*) of tropical marine fishes that are long and silvery and have two dorsal fins, a long head, and a large mouth with a projecting lower jaw. They are found along the North and South American Atlantic and Pacific coasts, often in estuaries and among mangroves and sometimes in fresh water. They range from 1.5 to 5 ft (0.5–1.5 m) long and are valued for food and sport.

snooker Variation of English BILLIARDS played with 15 red balls and six variously colored balls. Snooker arose, probably in India, as a game for soldiers in the 1870s. Players try to pocket first the red and then the nonred balls, scoring one point for each red ball and the number value of the others. "Snooker" refers to the position of the cue ball when it cannot hit a required ball.

Snorri Sturluson \'snōr-ē-'stūr-lū-sȯn\ (1179–1241) Icelandic poet, historian, and chieftain. Of an influential family, Snorri became the "lawspeaker," or president, of the Icelandic high court and a vassal of King Haakon IV of Norway. He was the author of the *Prose* EDDA and the *Heimskringla,* a history of Norwegian kings. His writings are remarkable for their scope and formal assurance; his genius lay in his power to present all that he perceived as a historian with the immediacy of drama. His relations with Haakon deteriorated, and he was assassinated on the king's order.

snout beetle See WEEVIL

snow Solid form of water that crystallizes in the atmosphere and falls to the earth, covering about 23% of the earth's surface either permanently or temporarily. Snowflakes are formed by crystals of ice that generally have a hexagonal pattern. Snow cover has a significant effect on climate and on plant, animal, and human life. By increasing the reflection of solar radiation and interfering with the conduction of heat from the ground, it induces a cold climate. The low heat conduction protects small plants from the effects of the lowest winter temperatures; on the other hand, late disappearance of snow in the spring delays the growth of plants.

Snow, C(harles) P(ercy) *later* **Baron Snow (of the City of Leicester)** (1905–1980) British novelist, scientist, and government administrator. Snow was a molecular physicist at Cambridge University for some 20 years and served as a scientific adviser to the British government. His 11-novel sequence *Strangers and Brothers* (1940–70), which analyzes bureaucratic man and the corrupting influence of power, includes *The Masters* (1951), *The New Men* (1954), and *Corridors of Power* (1964). *The Two Cultures and the Scientific Revolution* (1959) and later nonfiction works deal with the cultural separation between practitioners of science and literature.

C.P. Snow.
CAMERA PRESS—PICTORIAL PARADE/EB INC.

snow leopard *or* **ounce** Endangered species *(Leo,* or *Panthera, uncia;* sometimes regarded as the only member of the genus *Uncia)* of nocturnal, long-haired big CAT that inhabits the high mountains of central Asia and India. It is about 6 ft (1.8 m) long, including the 3-ft (1-m) tail, stands about 2 ft (0.5 m) high, and weighs 60–120 lbs (27–55 kg). Its dense, soft coat, consisting of an insulating undercoat and outer coat of 2-in. (5-cm) hairs, is pale grayish with dark rosettes and a dark streak along the spine. The whitish fur of the underparts may be 4 in. (10 cm) long. It preys on marmots, wild sheep and goats, birds, and other animals. It is hunted principally for the market in goods used in Asian traditional medicine.

snowberry Any of about 18 species of low shrubs that belong to the genus *Symphoricarpos* of the HONEYSUCKLE FAMILY. All are native to North America, except for one species in central China. All have bell-shaped, pinkish or white flowers and snow-white berries. The best-known ornamental species are *S. albus*, a shrub 3 ft (1 m) high, with delicate stems, oval leaves, and large, pulpy, white berries, and *S. rivularis,* slightly larger, with elliptical leaves and a profusion of berries. Creeping snowberry is a plant of the genus *Gaultheria* (HEATH FAMILY).

Snowberry (*Symphoricarpos rivularis*).
SVEN SAMELIUS

snowboarding Sport of sliding downhill over snow on a snowboard, a wide ski ridden in a surfing position. Derived from SURFING and influenced also by SKATEBOARDING as well as skiing, snowboarding began to burgeon among young people in the U.S. in the mid-1980s. The first Olympic snowboarding competition was held in the 1998 Winter Games. The two main events are giant slalom (similar to Alpine giant SLALOM) and halfpipe, in which riders use a large, snow-covered trench (halfpipe) to repeatedly launch themselves into the air and perform various acrobatic feats.

Snowden, Philip *later* **Viscount Snowden (of Ickornshaw)** (1864–1937) British politician. From 1893 he was a lecturer and writer for the socialist Independent Labour Party (ILP), then became its leader (1903–6). In the House of Commons (1906–18, 1922–31), he excelled in debates on social and economic questions. He served as chancellor of the exchequer in JAMES RAMSAY MACDONALD's governments (1924, 1929–31) and in 1931 secured Britain's abandonment of the gold standard.

Snowdonia National Park Park, northern Wales. Established in 1951, it has an area of 838 sq mi (2,171 sq km). It is best known for its mountains, composed largely of volcanic rock and cut by valleys that show the influence of Ice Age glaciers. Mount Snowdon, 3,560 ft (1,085 m) high, is the highest peak in England and Wales.

snowdrop Any of about 12 species and many variations of white-flowered, spring-blooming, bulbous Eurasian plants that make up the genus *Galanthus* of the AMARYLLIS FAMILY. Several species, including common snowdrop *(G. nivalis)* and giant snowdrop *(G. elwesii),* are cultivated as ornamentals for their nodding, sometimes fragrant flowers. They are among the earliest garden flowers to blossom in the spring. Similarly named but very different, the snowdrop tree, or silver bells (*Halesia carolina,* family Styracaceae), is a tall tree with clustered, bell-shaped flowers that grows in the southern U.S. The snowdrop bush *(Styrax officinalis)* of eastern Europe and Asia Minor, also unrelated, grows to about 18 ft (6 m).

Snowdrop (*Galanthus*).
DEREK FELL

snowshoe hare *or* **snowshoe rabbit** *or* **varying hare** Northern North American species *(Lepus americanus)* of HARE that undergoes an annual color change from brownish or grayish in summer to pure white in winter. The hind feet are heavily furred, and all four feet are large in proportion to body size, a snowshoe-like adaptation that enables the hare to travel over snow.

snowy egret White New World EGRET (*Egretta,* or *Leucophoyx, thula;* family Ardeidae). It is about 24 in. (60 cm) long and has filmy recurved plumes on the back and head. Formerly hunted for its plumes, it ranges from the U.S. to Chile and Argentina.

snowy owl White or barred brown-and-white typical OWL (*Nyctea scandiaca,* family Strigidae) of the Arctic tundra, sometimes found in Europe, Asia, and North America. Snowy owls are about 2 ft (60 cm) long and have broad wings and a round head without ear tufts. They are diurnal and eat small mammals, such as hares and lemmings, and birds. They nest on the ground in the open.

Snowy owl (*Nyctea scandiaca*).
W. SUSCHITZKY

Snyder, Gary (Sherman) (born 1930) U.S. poet. Born in San Francisco, Snyder worked as a forest ranger, logger, and seaman and studied Zen Buddhism in Japan 1958–66. His poetry, early identified with the BEAT MOVEMENT, is rooted in ancient, natural, and mythic experience. It initially contained images drawn from his outdoor work in the Pacific Northwest and later reflected his interest in Eastern philosophies. His volumes include *Turtle Island* (1974, Pulitzer Prize) and *Mountains and Rivers Without End* (1996). From the late 1960s he has been an important spokesman for communal living and ecological activism.

Soane, John *later* **Sir John** (1753–1837) British architect. He was appointed architect to the Bank of England in 1788. Various government appointments followed, and in 1806 he succeeded his mentor, George Dance (1741–1837), as professor of architecture at the Royal Academy. His work is characterized by a tendency to reduce classical elements to their structural essentials, use of linear instead of modeled ornamentation, frequent use of shallow domes and top lighting, and ingenious handling of interior space.

soap Organic compound, SALT of a FATTY ACID, usually stearic acid (with 18 carbon atoms) or palmitic acid (with 16 carbon atoms). The source may be any vegetable oil or animal fat. Soaps are emulsifying agents commonly used for cleaning; they have long been made from LYE and FAT. DETERGENTS are entirely synthetic and may or may not be soaps. Soaps of METALS heavier than sodium are not very soluble; the curdy precipitate made by soap in HARD WATER is the calcium or magnesium salt of the fatty acid in the soap. Heavy-metal soaps are used in lubricating greases, as gel thickeners, and in paints. NAPALM is an aluminum soap.

soap opera Broadcast serial drama, characterized by a permanent cast of actors, a continuing story, tangled interpersonal situations, and a melodramatic or sentimental style. Its name derived from the soap and detergent manufacturers who originally often sponsored such programs on radio. Soap operas began in the early 1930s as 15-minute radio episodes and continued on television from the early 1950s as 30-minute and later hour-long episodes. Usually broadcast during the day and aimed at housewives, they initially focused on middle-class family life, but by the 1970s their content was expanding to include a wider variety of characters and situations and a greater degree of sexual explicitness. In the 1980s similar series began to be aired in prime-time evening hours (e.g., *Dallas* and *Dynasty*). See also ANNE AND FRANK HUMMERT, CARLTON E. MORSE, IRNA PHILLIPS.

soaring *or* **gliding** Sport of flying a GLIDER or sailplane. The craft is towed behind a powered airplane to an altitude of about 2,000 ft (600 m) and then released. The glider pilot makes use of rising currents of warm air, such as those above a sunlit field, to maintain or gain altitude. Instruments used include the altimeter, airspeed indicator, compass, and turn-and-bank indicator. National soaring contests, which include events for altitude, speed, distance, and accuracy in returning to a starting point, are held annually.

Sobat River \'sō-ˌbat\ River, eastern central Africa. Formed by the confluence of the Baro and Pibor rivers on the Ethiopian border, it merges with the BAHR EL JEBEL in Sudan to form the White Nile. A major tributary of the NILE RIVER, it is 460 mi (740 km) long.

Sobukwe \sō-'bük-wā\, **Robert (Mangaliso)** (1924–1978) South African black nationalist leader. Sobukwe insisted that South Africa be returned to its indigenous inhabitants ("Africa for the Africans"). Charging the AFRICAN NATIONAL CONGRESS with being contaminated by non-African influences, he founded the Pan-Africanist Congress in 1959 and became a leader in the PAN-AFRICAN MOVEMENT. Arrested in 1960, he spent the rest of his life in prison or under house arrest.

soccer See FOOTBALL

social class See social CLASS

social contract Actual or hypothetical compact between the ruled and their rulers. The original inspiration for the notion may derive from the Biblical covenant between God and ABRAHAM, but it is most closely associated with the writings of THOMAS HOBBES, JOHN LOCKE, and J.-J. ROUSSEAU. Hobbes argued for a social contract that gave the rulers absolute power, in return for which they would protect the people from their natural state of warfare. Locke assumed a more benign natural state, and believed that rulers were obliged to protect not only the people but also their private property. Rousseau believed that, in surrendering individual freedom, people acquired a sense of moral and civic obligation, and that government must rest on the general will of the governed. The idea of the social contract influenced the shapers of the AMERICAN and FRENCH revolutions and the CONSTITUTIONS that followed them.

Social Credit Party Minor Canadian political party. It was founded 1935 by WILLIAM ABERHART and based on the social-credit theory of the British economist Clifford Douglas (1879–1952). By the late 1930s the party advocated employee profit sharing and shareholding. It led the government in Alberta 1935–71, and won several seats in the parliament in Ottawa between 1935 and 1980. It disbanded in the early 1980s.

social Darwinism Theory that persons, groups, and races are subject to the same laws of NATURAL SELECTION as CHARLES DARWIN had proposed for plants and animals in nature. Social Darwinists, such as HERBERT SPENCER and WALTER BAGEHOT in England and William Graham Sumner in the U.S., held that the life of humans in society was a struggle for existence ruled by "survival of the fittest," in Spencer's words. Wealth was said to be a sign of natural superiority, its absence a sign of unfitness. The theory was used from the late 19th century to support laissez-faire capitalism and political conservatism. Social Darwinism declined as scientific knowledge expanded.

social democracy Political ideology that advocates a peaceful, evolutionary transition of society from CAPITALISM to SOCIALISM, using established political processes. It rejects MARXISM's advocacy of social revolution. Social democracy began as a political movement in Germany in the 1870s. EDUARD BERNSTEIN argued (1899) that capitalism was overcoming many of the weaknesses KARL MARX had seen in it (including unemployment and overproduction) and that universal suffrage would lead peacefully to a socialist government. After 1945, social-democratic governments came to power in West Germany (see SOCIAL DEMOCRATIC PARTY), Sweden, and Britain (under the LABOUR PARTY). Social-democratic thought gradually came to regard state regulation (without state ownership) as sufficient to ensure economic growth and a fair distribution of income.

Social Democratic Party of Germany (SPD) German political party. Formed in 1875 as the Socialist Workers' Party and renamed in 1890, it is Germany's oldest and largest single party. Its influence grew until World War I, when centrists led by KARL KAUTSKY formed the Independent Social Democrats and leftists led by ROSA LUXEMBURG and KARL LIEBKNECHT formed the SPARTACISTS. Its right wing under FRIEDRICH EBERT helped crush the Soviet-style uprisings in Germany in 1918 and won 37% of the vote in the 1919 elections. The government's acceptance of the Treaty of VERSAILLES and Germany's severe economic problems caused a drop in support in the 1920s. Outlawed by the Nazis in 1933, the party revived after World War II in West Germany and grew steadily, receiving almost 46% of the vote in the 1972 elections. It formed coalition governments with the CHRISTIAN DEMOCRATIC UNION (1966–69) and the FREE DEMOCRATIC PARTY (1969–82). In 1990 it reunited with a newly independent SPD from the former East Germany.

Social Gospel Religious social-reform movement in the U.S., prominent from c. 1870 to 1920 among liberal Protestant groups. The movement focused on applying moral principles to improving industrialized society and particularly to reforms in child labor, wages and hours, and factory regulation. Many of its aims were incorporated in the labor movement and in NEW DEAL programs.

social history Branch of history that emphasizes social structures and the interaction of different groups in society rather than affairs of state. An outgrowth of economic history, it expanded as a discipline in the 1960s. It initially focused on disenfranchised social groups but later began to focus more attention on the middle and upper classes. As a field, it often borders on economic history on the one hand and on sociology and ethnology on the other.

social insurance Compulsory public-insurance program that protects against various economic risks (e.g., loss of income due to sickness, old age, or unemployment). Social insurance is considered one type of SOCIAL SECURITY, though the two terms are sometimes used interchangeably. The first compulsory national social-insurance programs were established in Germany under OTTO VON BISMARCK: HEALTH INSURANCE in 1883, WORKERS' COMPENSATION in 1884, and old-age and disability PENSIONS in 1889. Austria and Hungary soon followed Germany's example. After 1920, social insurance was rapidly adopted throughout Europe and the Western Hemisphere. The U.S. lagged behind until the passage of the SOCIAL SECURITY ACT in 1935. Social Security in the U.S. now provides retirement benefits, health care for persons over 65, and disability insurance. Social-insurance contributions are normally compulsory and may be made by the insured person's employer and the state as well as by the individual. Social insurance is usually self-financing, contributions being placed in specific funds for that purpose. See also UNEMPLOYMENT INSURANCE, WELFARE.

social learning In psychological theory, a change in behavior that is controlled by environmental influences rather than by innate or internal forces. In zoology, social learning is exhibited by innumerable species of birds and mammals, who modify their behavior by observing and imitating the adults around them. BIRDSONG is a socially learned behavior.

social psychology Branch of PSYCHOLOGY concerned with the PERSONALITY, ATTITUDES, MOTIVATIONS and behavior of the individual or group in the context of social interaction. The field emerged in the U.S. in the 1920s. Topics include the attribution of SOCIAL STATUS based on perceptual cues, the influence of social factors (such as peers) on a person's attitudes and beliefs, the functioning of small groups and large organizations, and the dynamics of face-to-face interactions.

Social Realism Trend in U.S. art, originating c. 1930, toward treating themes of social protest—poverty, political corruption, labor–management conflict—in a naturalistic manner. The movement was stimulated in part by the ASH CAN SCHOOL, the GREAT DEPRESSION, and the NEW DEAL's arts patronage programs, including the WPA FEDERAL ART PROJECT. Works in this vein include BEN SHAHN's *Passion of Sacco and Vanzetti* (1931–32) and William Gropper's *The Senate* (1935).

social science Any discipline or branch of science that deals with the sociocultural aspects of human behavior. The social sciences generally include CULTURAL ANTHROPOLOGY, ECONOMICS, POLITICAL SCIENCE, SOCIOLOGY, and SOCIAL PSYCHOLOGY. Comparative law and comparative religion (the comparative study of the legal systems and religions of different nations and cultures) are also sometimes regarded as social sciences.

social security Public provision for the economic security and social welfare of all individuals. Social-security programs are designed to protect individuals and their families from income losses due to unemployment, work injury, maternity, sickness, old age, and death and to improve their welfare through public services. The term encompasses not only SOCIAL INSURANCE but also health and welfare services and various income maintenance programs. The first organized cooperative efforts to provide for the economic security of individuals were instituted by workingmen's associations, mutual-benefit societies, and LABOR UNIONS; social security was not widely established by law until the 19th and 20th century. Almost all the developed nations now have social-security programs, which provide benefits or services through several major approaches, including social insurance and social assistance, a needs-based program that pays benefits only to the poor. See also SOCIAL SECURITY ACT, UNEMPLOYMENT INSURANCE, WELFARE, WORKERS' COMPENSATION.

Social Security Act (August 14, 1935) Legislation that established a national old-age pension system in the U.S. Dissatisfied with the government response to the GREAT DEPRESSION, about 5 million people joined "Townsend clubs" to support the plan of Francis E. Townsend (1867–1960) to demand a $200 monthly pension for everyone over 60. Pres. FRANKLIN ROOSEVELT set up a committee on economic security (1934), which recommended legislative action to the U.S. Congress. The act provided old-age benefits to be financed by a payroll tax on employers and employees. The system was later expanded to include dependents, the disabled, and others.

social settlement See SETTLEMENT HOUSE

social status Relative rank that an individual holds, with attendant rights, duties, and lifestyle, in a social hierarchy based on honor and prestige. Status is often ascribed on the basis of sex, age, family relationships, and birth, placing one into a particular social group irrespective of ability or accomplishments. Achieved status, on the other hand, is based on educational attainment, occupational choice, marital status, and other factors involving personal effort. Status groups differ from social CLASSES in being based on considerations of honor and prestige rather than purely economic position. Relative status is a major determinant of people's behavior toward one another, and competition for status seems to be a prime human motivator.

Social War *or* **Italic War** *or* **Marsic War** (90–89 BC) Rebellion waged by ancient Rome's Italian allies (Latin, *Socii*). The Italians had aided Rome in its wars, but were denied the privileges of Roman citizenship. The people of central Italy's hills organized a confederacy and began an uprising for independence, winning victories over Roman armies in the north and south. After Rome granted citizenship to those who had not revolted and those who would immediately lay down their arms, Italian interest in the struggle declined. SULLA defeated the weakened rebels in the south, and legislation was passed to unify Italy south of the Po River.

social welfare See WELFARE

social work Any of various professional activities or methods concerned with providing social services (such as investigatory and treatment services or material aid) to disadvantaged, distressed, or vulnerable persons or groups. The field originated in the charity organizations in Europe and the U.S. in the late 19th century. The training of volunteer workers by these organizations led directly to the founding of the first schools of social work and indirectly to increased government responsibility for the welfare of the disadvantaged. Social workers may serve the needs of children and families, the poor or homeless, immigrants, veterans, the mentally ill, the handicapped, victims of rape or domestic violence, and persons dependent on alcohol or drugs. See also WELFARE.

socialism System of social organization in which private property and the distribution of income are subject to social control; also, the political movements aimed at putting that system into practice. Because "social control" may be interpreted in widely diverging ways, socialism ranges from statist to libertarian, from Marxist to liberal. The term was first used to describe the doctrines of CHARLES FOURIER, HENRI DE SAINT-SIMON, and ROBERT OWEN, who emphasized noncoercive communities of people working noncompetitively for the spiritual and physical well-being of all (see UTOPIAN SOCIALISM). KARL MARX and FRIEDRICH ENGELS, seeing socialism as a transition state between CAPITALISM and COMMUNISM, appropriated what they found useful in socialist movements to develop their "scientific socialism." In the 20th century, the Soviet Union was the principal model of strictly centralized socialism, while Sweden and Denmark were well-known for their noncommunist socialism. See also COLLECTIVISM, COMMUNITARIANISM, SOCIAL DEMOCRACY.

Socialist International See SECOND INTERNATIONAL

Socialist Realism Officially sanctioned theory and method of artistic and literary composition in the Soviet Union from 1932 to the mid-1980s. Following the tradition of 19th-century Russian REALISM, Socialist Realism purported to serve as an objective mirror of life. Instead of critiquing society, however, it took as its primary theme the struggle to build socialism and a classless society and called for the didactic use of art to develop social consciousness. Artists were expected to take a positive view of socialist society and to keep in mind its historical relevance, requisites that seldom coincided with their real experiences and frequently undermined the artistic credibility of their works.

Socialist Revolutionary Party (SR) Russian political party. The ideological heir to the 19th-century POPULISTS, it was founded in 1901 by agrarian socialists and appealed mainly to the peasantry. It was the principal alternative to the RUSSIAN SOCIAL-DEMOCRATIC WORKERS' PARTY in the early 20th century. It relied on terrorist tactics and carried out hundreds of political assassinations. By 1917 it was Russia's largest socialist group; its members included ALEKSANDR KERENSKY, VIKTOR M. CHERNOV, and CATHERINE BRESHKOVSKY. The party split after the RUSSIAN REVOLUTION OF 1917, and its radical wing joined the BOLSHEVIK government. It was suppressed by VLADIMIR ILICH LENIN after the RUSSIAN CIVIL WAR.

Société Générale \sȯs-ye-'tā-zhā-nā-'rȧl\ Major French commercial bank, with headquarters in Paris. It was established in 1864 to offer banking and investment services, and was nationalized in 1946 along with several other large French banks. With subsidiaries and branches throughout the world, Société Générale provides general banking, investment advising, securities underwriting, foreign-currency exchange, and computer services.

Society Islands Archipelago (pop., 1988: 163,000), western FRENCH POLYNESIA. Its capital is PAPEETE, on its chief island of TAHITI. It comprises two groups, the Windward Islands and the Leeward Islands. The islands are volcanic in origin and mountainous. Claimed for Britain in 1767, the islands were visited in 1769 by Capt. JAMES COOK with a scientific expedition of the Royal Society (hence their name). They were claimed by France in 1768 and became a French protectorate in 1842, a French colony in 1881, and a part of French Oceania in 1903. Their chief products are copra and pearls.

sociobiology Systematic study of the biological basis of social behavior. The concept was popularized by EDWARD O. WILSON in his *Sociobiology* (1975) and by Richard Dawkins (born 1941) in *The Selfish Gene* (1976). Sociobiology attempts to understand and explain animal (and human) social behavior in the light of NATURAL SELECTION and other biological processes. A central tenet is that the transmission of GENES through successful reproduction is the central motivator in animals' struggle for survival, and that animals will behave in ways that maximize their chances of transmitting their genes to succeeding generations. Though sociobiology has contributed insights into animal behavior (such as altruism in social insects and male-female differences in certain species), it remains controversial when applied to human social behavior. See also ETHOLOGY.

sociocultural evolution Development of culture and society from simple to complex forms. Europeans had sought to explain the existence of various "primitive" societies, some believing that such societies represented the lost tribes of Israel, others speculating that primitive peoples had degenerated since the time of Adam from an originally "barbarous" to an even lowlier "savage" state. European society was taken to epitomize the highest state of existence, "civilization." In the late 19th century, EDWARD BURNETT TYLOR and LEWIS HENRY MORGAN elaborated the theory of unilinear evolution, specifying criteria for categorizing cultures according to their standing within a fixed system of growth of humanity as a whole and examining the modes and mechanisms of this growth. A widespread reaction followed; FRANZ BOAS introduced the "culture history" approach, which concentrated on fieldwork among native peoples to identify actual cultural and historical processes rather than speculative stages of growth. Leslie White, Julian Steward, and others sought to revive aspects of sociocultural evolutionism, positing a progression ranging from BANDS and TRIBES at one end to CHIEFDOMS and STATES at the other. More recently some anthropologists have adopted a general systems approach, examining cultures as emergent systems. Others continue to reject evolutionary thinking and look instead at historical contingencies, contacts with other cultures, and the operation of cultural SYMBOL systems. See also PRIMITIVE CULTURE, SOCIAL DARWINISM.

sociolinguistics Study of the sociological aspects of language. Sociolinguists attempt to isolate the linguistic features used in particular situations that mark the various social relationships among the participants and the significant elements of the situation. Factors influencing the choice of sounds, grammatical elements, and vocabulary may include age, gender, education, ethnic identity, occupation, and peer-group identification. See also INTERACTIONISM, LINGUISTICS, PRAGMATICS, SEMIOTICS.

sociology Science of society, social institutions, and social relationships, and specifically the systematic study of the development, structure, interaction, and collective behavior of organized human groups. It emerged at the end of the 19th century through the work of É. DURKHEIM in France, MAX WEBER and GEORG SIMMEL in Germany, and ROBERT E. PARK and Albion Small in the U.S. Today sociologists use observational techniques, surveys and interviews, statistical analysis, controlled experiments, and other methods to study such subjects as the FAMILY, ethnic relations, schooling, social CLASS, BUREAUCRACY, religious movements, deviance, the elderly, and social change.

sockeye salmon *or* **red salmon** Food fish *(Oncorhynchus nerka)* of the North Pacific that constitutes almost 20% of the commercial fishery of Pacific SALMON. It weighs about 6 lbs (3 kg) and lacks distinct spots on the body. It ranges from the northern Bering Sea to Japan and from Alaska to California. Sockeyes may migrate more than 1,000 miles (1,600 km) upriver to spawn in lakes or tributary streams. The young remain in freshwater one to five years. The kokanee is a small, nonmigratory, freshwater subspecies.

Male sockeye salmon (*Oncorhynchus nerka*) in spawning phase.

JEFF FOOTT—BRUCE COLEMAN INC.

Socotra \sə-'kō-trə\ Island, Yemen, in the Indian Ocean. Located about 210 mi (340 km) southeast of Yemen, it is about 1,400 sq mi (3,600 sq km) in area. Its interior is mountainous, with flora that includes myrrh, frankincense, and the dragon's blood tree. The island, mentioned in various legends, was long ruled by the Mahra sultans of southeastern Yemen, except for a brief Portuguese occupation 1507–11. In 1886 it came under British protection, and in 1967 became part of independent Yemen. Its chief town is Tamridah (formerly Hadibu).

Socrates (c. 470–399 BC) Greek philosopher, first of the great trio of ancient Greeks (with PLATO and ARISTOTLE) who laid the philosophical foundations of Western culture. Since Socrates wrote nothing, information about his personality and doctrine is found chiefly in PLATO's dialogues and XENOPHON's *Memorabilia*. Living during the chaos of the PELOPONNESIAN WAR, with its erosion of moral values, Socrates felt called to shore up the ethical dimensions of life by the admonition "know thyself" and by exploring the essence of virtue. After fighting in the war, he served in the Athenian boule. He lived in poverty, exemplifying his own moral teachings. His teaching method consisted largely of asking probing questions, which cumulatively revealed the students' unsupported assumptions and misconceptions (the "Socratic method"). The students who flocked to him, including Plato, ALCIBIADES, and Critias (c. 480–403 BC), were many of the finest in Athens. When Alcibiades became a traitor and Critias joined the Sparta-imposed THIRTY TYRANTS, Socrates was decried by many, including ARISTOPHANES. Accused of impiety and of corrupting the Athenian youth, he was condemned to death in 399 BC; Plato's *Phaedo* recounts his last day and the dignity with which he submitted to his sentence. Socrates influenced those now known as the "minor Socratics" (including the CYNICS, the CYRENAICS, and the MEGARIAN SCHOOL), but it was mainly through his influence on Plato that his efforts bore their full fruit for subsequent ages.

soda, caustic See CAUSTIC SODA

Soddy, Frederick (1877–1956) British chemist. He worked with ERNEST RUTHERFORD to develop a theory of the disintegration of radioactive elements. In 1912 he was among the first to conclude that elements might exist in forms (isotopes) of different ATOMIC WEIGHTS but indistinguishable chemically. In *Science and Life* (1920) he pointed out the value of isotopes in determining geologic age (see CARBON-14 DATING). For his investigations of radioactivity and isotopes, he received a 1921 Nobel Prize.

sodium Chemical ELEMENT, one of the ALKALI METALS, chemical symbol Na, atomic number 11. A very soft, silvery-white METAL, the sixth most abundant element on earth, it occurs mainly as HALITE, never free. Extremely reactive, it is used as a chemical reagent and raw material, in metallurgy, as a heat exchanger (in NUCLEAR POWER generators and certain types of engines), and in sodium-vapor lamps. Sodium is essential for life but rarely deficient in diets; high intake is linked to HYPERTENSION. Sodium in compounds, many of great industrial importance (including BICARBONATE OF SODA, CAUSTIC SODA, SALTPETER, and sodium chloride), has VALENCE 1. Sodium CARBONATE, one of the four most important basic chemical commodities, is used in making glass, detergents, and cleansers. Sodium hypochlorite, familiar as household BLEACH, is also used to bleach paper pulp and textiles, to chlorinate water, and in some medicines. The SULFATE is used in the KRAFT PROCESS and also used to make paperboard, glass, and detergents. The thiosulfate (hyposulfite, or "hypo") is used in developing photographs.

sodium bicarbonate See BICARBONATE OF SODA

sodium chloride *or* **table salt** Inorganic compound of SODIUM and CHLORINE, a SALT in which IONIC BONDS hold the two components in the familiar white crystals. Salt is essential to health as a source of sodium; blood and all other physiological fluids are dilute salt solutions. One of the most widely used materials of the chemical industry, it is used in manufacturing CHLORINE, CAUSTIC SODA, sodium CARBONATE, BICARBONATE OF SODA, SOAP, and chlorine BLEACH, as well as in ceramic glazes, metallurgy, food preservation, curing of hides, road de-icing, water softening, photography, and in many consumer products, including mineral waters, mouthwashes, and table salt itself. It is mined, extracted from sea water, and obtained from dry salt lakes called pans. See also HALITE.

Sodom and Gomorrah \'sä-dəm...gə-'mȯr-ə\ Legendary cities of ancient Palestine. According to the Old Testament book of Genesis, the notorious cities were destroyed by "brimstone and fire" because of their wickedness. The site of the cities is unknown, but may be in an area now beneath the waters of the DEAD SEA. Archaeological evidence shows that the area may once have been fertile, and could have drawn the biblical LOT to graze his flock. The cities' legendary wickedness has inspired many writers, including JEAN GIRAUDOUX and NIKOS KAZANTZAKIS.

sodomy Noncoital carnal copulation. The term is understood in several senses: (1) as male homosexual practices, (2) as anal intercourse, (3) as sexual relations with animals, and (4) as a number of other activities such as sexual contact with minors. Sodomy is a crime in some jurisdictions, and some sodomy laws provide severe penalties. The Wolfenden committee in Britain and the American Law Institute recommended abolition of criminal provisions, except in cases involving violence, children, or public solicitation. This position was adopted in England in 1967 and has been adopted in many U.S. states as well.

sofer *or* **sopher** \sō-'fer, 'sō-fər\ In JUDAISM, a scholar-teacher of the 5th–2nd century BC who transcribed, edited, and interpreted the BIBLE. The first sofer was EZRA, who, with his disciples, initiated a tradition of rabbinical scholarship that is still central in Judaism. It arose to meet the specific need of applying the idealistic aspirations of the TORAH and oral tradition to everyday life, thus in effect codifying Mosaic law. The soferim were important historically for having fixed the canon of the OLD TESTAMENT. Later the term sofer came to refer to one who taught the Bible to children or who was qualified to write Torah scrolls.

Sofia \'sō-fē-ə, sō-'fē-ə,\ *ancient* **Serdica** City (metro. area pop., 1996 est.: 1,193,000), capital of Bulgaria. Established as a Thracian settlement c. 8th century BC, it flourished under the Romans. Plundered by the Huns in the 5th century AD, it was rebuilt under the Byzantine empire. In 809 it became a Bulgarian town, but reverted to Byzantine rule 1018–1185, when the second Bulgarian empire was established. The Turks held it from 1382 until it was liberated by the Russians in 1878. In 1879 it was made the Bulgarian capital. It is the country's principal transportation and cultural center, and the site of many industries. Among its educational institutions is the University of Sofia (1888), Bulgaria's oldest university. Its historical monuments include the 6th-century Church of St. Sofia.

soft coal See BITUMINOUS COAL

soft drink Nonalcoholic beverage, usually carbonated, consisting of water (soda water), flavoring, and a sweet syrup. Attempts to reproduce the natural effervescence of certain spring waters for presumed health benefits began before 1700. JOSEPH PRIESTLEY's experiments with "fixed air" (carbon dioxide) led in the late 1790s to the successful preparation of carbonated "mineral water" by Jacob Schweppe of Geneva; by the early 1800s it was being bottled and sold commercially. Today there are hundreds of varieties of flavored soft drink. Some of the world's largest corporations (including COCA-COLA CO. and PEPSICO) founded their businesses on soft-drink manufacturing.

soft money Historically, paper money as contrasted with coins, or hard money; currently unregulated political donations. Soft-money advocates of the 19th and early 20th century were those who favored governmental deficit spending to stimulate consumption and employment. Fiscal conservatives (who put their trust in hard money) held the view that government should not spend beyond its resources. In late-20th-century political spending, strict regulations governed the source, amount, and use of donations to particular candidates (hard money), whereas contributions for the general promotion of a political party's message was relatively unregulated (soft money).

softball Game resembling BASEBALL but played on a smaller diamond with a larger ball (12 in., or 30.5 cm, in circumference), which is pitched underhand. Since the first standard set of rules was published in the 1920s, the game has been popular as an amateur sport in the U.S., and since the 1960s it has grown considerably in popularity outside of North America. In U.S. high schools and colleges it is a popular women's sport; a women's softball competition was added to the Olympic Games in 1996.

softshell turtle Any of more than 20 species (family Trionychidae) of swift-moving, carnivorous TURTLES found in North American, African, and Asian freshwaters with soft, muddy bottoms. They have a pancakelike, leathery shell; webbed feet; a long neck; and an elongated snout. They often lie buried in mud or sand and occasionally emerge to bask in the sun. Aggressive when captured, they can deliver rapid, vicious bites. The two North American species have a grayish or brown shell, 14–18 in. (35–45 cm) long. Two Old World species grow to 24 in. (60 cm) or more.

Softshell turtle (*Trionyx*).
E.R. DEGGINGER

software Instructions that tell a COMPUTER what to do. Software is the entire set of programs, procedures, and routines associated with the operation of a computer system, including the OPERATING SYSTEM. The term differentiates these features from HARDWARE, the physical components of

S T U V

a computer system. Two main types of software are system software, which controls a computer's internal functioning, and application software, which directs the computer to execute commands that solve practical problems. A third category is network software, which coordinates communication between computers linked in a network. Software is written by programmers in any number of PROGRAMMING LANGUAGES. This information, the source code, must then be translated by means of a COMPILER into MACHINE LANGUAGE, which the computer can understand and act on.

softwood Timber obtained from coniferous trees (mainly of the PINE and FIR families). With the exception of BALD CYPRESS, tamarack, and LARCH, softwood trees are EVERGREENS. Softwood is mostly obtained from the Baltic, Scandinavia, and North America and is the source of about 80% of the world's production of timber. The term sometimes imprecisely means all soft and hard woods used as construction wood in temperate regions. Softwoods of longleaf pine, DOUGLAS FIR, and YEW are much harder in the mechanical sense than several HARDWOODS.

Soga family Japanese aristocratic family preeminent in the 7th century and instrumental in introducing Buddhism to Japan. Soga Umako (died 626) overcame the powerful Mononobe and Nakatomi clans, who supported the native Shinto religion over Buddhism, and contrived to have his niece proclaimed empress, selecting one of his nephews to be her regent (see SHOTOKU TAISHI). The next generation alienated other aristocratic families with their high-handed ways, and after many intrigues and assassinations Soga power was crushed in 645 by a prince who was to become the future emperor Tenji, aided by Fujiwara Kamatari, founder of the FUJIWARA FAMILY. See also NARA PERIOD.

Sogdiana \ˌsäg-dē-ˈa-nə\ Province of the ancient Persian empire. It was centered in the fertile valley of the Zeravshan River, in modern Uzbekistan. It became a satrapy under DARIUS I in the 6th century BC, and was conquered by ALEXANDER THE GREAT in the 4th century. It asserted its independence from the SELEUCID DYNASTY c. 250 BC as part of the Bactrian kingdom (see BACTRIA), and fell to invading northern tribes in the 2nd century BC. It prospered until the Mongol invasions. Under the Samanid dynasty (9th–10th century AD), it was a focal point of Islamic civilization. See also BUKHARA.

Sogi \ˈsō-gē\ *orig.* **Iio Sogi** (1421–1502) Japanese poet. Sogi was a Zen monk in Kyoto before becoming, in his 30s, a professional *RENGA* (linked-verse) poet. He is considered the greatest master of *renga* because of two sequences, *Minase sangin hyakuin* (1488) and *Yuyama sangin hyakuin* (1491; "One Hundred Poems Composed by Three Poets at Yuyama"), in each of which poets led by Sogi took turns at composing short stanzas (links) to form a single poem with many shifts of mood and direction. The foremost poet of his age, he left more than 90 works, including anthologies, diaries, poetic criticism, and manuals.

Sogne Fjord \ˈsȯŋ-nə\ *or* **Sognefjorden** \ˈsȯŋ-nə-ˌfyȯr-dən\ Longest and deepest fjord in Norway. It extends 127 mi (204 km) inland from the Norwegian Sea and has a maximum depth of 4,291 ft (1,308 m). The fjord and its branches provide some of the most picturesque scenery in Norway.

soil Earthen material that covers land surfaces and is formed by the action of natural physical, chemical, and biological forces on the unconsolidated residue of rocks and minerals on the earth's surface. The most important constituents of soil are crystalline CLAY and organic matter. Soil is produced primarily by WEATHERING and LEACHING. Environmental factors such as rainfall, topography, and vegetation influence soil formation and properties, as do the activities of some animals, so that very different soils may be formed from the same parent material.

soil mechanics Study of soils and their utilization, especially in planning foundations for structures and highways. How the soil of a given site will support the weight of structures or respond to movement in the course of construction depends on a number of properties (e.g., compressibility, elasticity, and permeability). Examination techniques include trench-digging, boring, and pumping samples to the surface with water. Seismic testing and measurement of electrical resistance also yield helpful information. In road construction, soil mechanics helps determine which type of pavement (rigid or flexible) will last longer. The study of soil characteristics is also used to choose the most suitable method for excavating underground tunnels. See also FOUNDATION, SETTLING.

soil science See PEDOLOGY

Soka-gakkai \ˈsō-kä-ˈgäk-kī\ Lay religious and political group associated with the Buddhist sect Nichiren-sho-shu (see NICHIREN BUDDHISM). The most successful of Japan's new religious movements of the 20th century, it draws on the 13th-century teachings of NICHIREN. Like other movements in Nichiren Buddhism, it takes the LOTUS SUTRA as its chief scripture. Founded in 1930, Soka-gakkai came to prominence in the later 20th century, eventually developing a membership of over 6 million. In 1964 it established the Komeito (Clean Government Party), which by the 1980s was Japan's third-largest political party. It also conducts educational and cultural activities.

Sokhumi *formerly* **Sukhumi** \sü-ˈk̲ü-mē\ *ancient* **Dioscurias** Seaport (pop., 1991 est.: 120,000), Republic of Georgia. Located on the BLACK SEA, it was the site of an ancient Greek colony that was later held successively by the Romans, Byzantines, Turks, and Russians. It became a popular resort. After Georgia's independence (1991), it was the center of a rebellion for Abkhazian independence in the 1990s.

Sokolow \ˈsȯ-kȯ-lȯv\, **Anna** (1910–2000) U.S. modern dancer, choreographer, and teacher. She was born in Hartford, Conn. She studied with MARTHA GRAHAM and danced with her company 1930–38. She also taught and formed her own dance group in 1934, with which she performed until retiring in 1954. From 1939 to 1949 she spent part of each year as a teacher and choreographer in Mexico City, where she formed Mexico's first modern-dance group. She continued to choreograph for her own company, often on subjects of social concern.

Sokoto \sō-ˈkō-tō\ City (pop., 1996 est.: 205,000), northwestern Nigeria. It lies along the Sokoto River on a traditional caravan route that leads north across the SAHARA. It was the capital of the FULANI empire. Modern Sokoto is a major trade center for agriculture and leather crafts. A pilgrimage center, it is the site of mosques, a sultan's palace, and USMAN DAN FODIO's tomb and other holy shrines. Usman dan Fodio University was founded in 1975.

Sol \ˈsäl\ In ROMAN RELIGION, the name of two distinct sun gods at Rome. The original Sol, or Sol Indiges, had an annual sacrifice and shrines on the Quirinal and in the Circus Maximus. After the importation of various Syrian sun cults, ELAGABALUS built a temple to Sol Invictus on the Palatine and attempted to make his worship the principal religion at Rome. AURELIAN later reestablished the worship and erected a temple to Sol in the Campus Agrippae. The worship of Sol remained the chief imperial cult until the rise of CHRISTIANITY.

solar cell Any device that directly converts the ENERGY in LIGHT into electrical energy through the process of photovoltaics (see PHOTOVOLTAIC EFFECT). Solar cells do not use chemical reactions to produce electric power, and they have no moving parts. Most solar cells are designed for converting sunlight into ELECTRICITY. In large arrays, which may contain many thousands of individual cells, they can function as central electric power stations analogous to nuclear, coal-, or oil-fired power plants. Much smaller assemblies of solar cells are used to provide electric power in remote locations including space satellites; because they have no moving parts that could require service or fuels that would require replenishment, solar cells are ideal for providing power in space. See illustration on following page.

solar cycle Period in which several important kinds of solar activity repeat, discovered in 1843 by Samuel Heinrich Schwabe (1789–1875). Lasting about 22 years on average, it includes two 11-year cycles of SUNSPOTS, whose magnetic polarities alternate between the SUN's northern and southern hemispheres, and two peaks and two declines in the phenomena (e.g., SOLAR PROMINENCES, AURORAS) that vary in the same period. Attempts have been made to connect the solar cycle to various phenomena, including possible slight variations in the diameter of the sun, sequences of annual growth rings in trees, and even the stock market's rise and fall.

solar energy Radiation from the sun that can produce heat, generate electricity, or cause chemical reactions. Solar energy is inexhaustible and nonpolluting, but it is not an efficient energy source, since earth's atmosphere absorbs or scatters over 50% of incoming solar radiation. Solar collectors collect the radiation and transfer it as heat to a carrier fluid. It can then be used for heating. SOLAR CELLS convert solar radiation directly into electricity, by means of the PHOTOELECTRIC EFFECT.

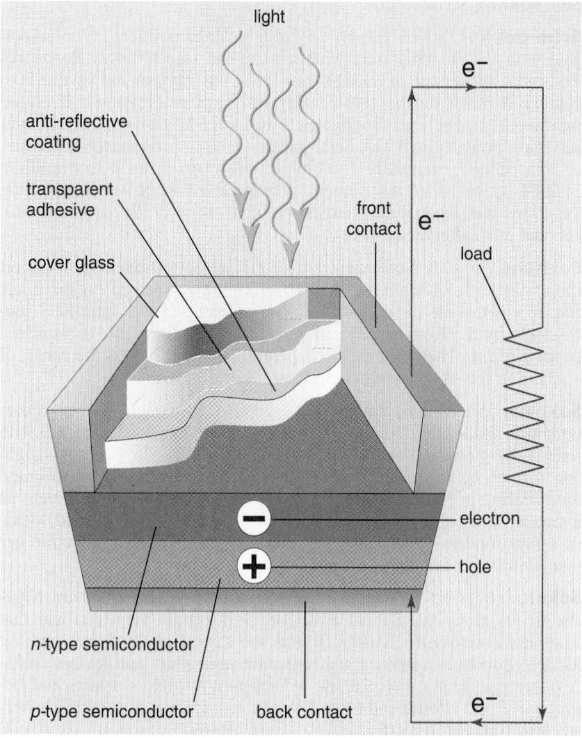

When sunlight strikes a solar cell, an electron is freed by the photoelectric effect. The two dissimilar semiconductors possess a natural difference in electric potential (voltage), which causes the electrons to flow through the external circuit, supplying power to the load. The flow of electricity results from the characteristics of the semiconductors, and is powered entirely by light striking the cell.

solar flare Sudden intense brightening of a small part of the SUN's surface, often near a SUNSPOT group. Flares develop in a few minutes and may last several hours, releasing intense X rays and streams of energetic particles. They appear to be connected with changes in the sun's magnetic fields during the SOLAR CYCLE. The ejected particles take a day or two to reach the vicinity of earth, where they can disrupt radio communications and cause AURORAS, and may pose a radiation hazard to astronauts.

solar heating Use of solar radiation to heat water or air in buildings. There are two types: passive and active. Passive heating relies on architectural design; the building's siting, orientation, layout, materials, and construction are utilized to maximize the heating effect of sunlight falling on it. A well-insulated building with a large south-facing window, for instance, can trap heat on sunny days and reduce reliance on gas, oil, or electricity. Brick, stone, or tile capacity walls are often incorporated to absorb the sun's energy and radiate it into the interior, usually after a time lag of several hours. In active solar heating, mechanical means are used to collect, store, and distribute solar energy. In liquid-based systems, a blackened metal plate on the exterior absorbs sunlight and traps heat, which is transferred to a carrier fluid. Alternatively, fluid may be pumped through a glass tube or volume of space onto which sunlight has been focused by mirrors. After picking up heat from the collector, the warm fluid is pumped to an insulated storage tank. The system can supply a home with hot water from the tank or provide space heating with the warmed water flowing through tubes in floors and ceilings.

solar nebula Gaseous cloud from which, in the nebular hypothesis of the origin of the SOLAR SYSTEM, the sun and planets formed by condensation. In 1755, IMMANUEL KANT suggested that a NEBULA in slow rotation, gradually pulled together by its own gravity and flattened into a disk, developed into the sun and planets. PIERRE-SIMON LAPLACE proposed a similar model in 1796. JAMES CLERK MAXWELL showed that if all the matter in the known planets had once been such a disk, shearing forces would have prevented condensation into individual planets. Another objection is that the sun has less ANGULAR MOMENTUM than the theory seems to require. For several decades most astronomers preferred the collision theory: that the planets formed as a result of a close approach to the sun by another star. Because objections to the collision theory were more convincing than those to the nebular hypothesis, a modified version of the latter has become the prevailing theory of the solar system's origin.

solar neutrino problem See solar NEUTRINO PROBLEM

solar prominence Arched stream of hot gas projecting from the SUN's surface into the CHROMOSPHERE or CORONA. Prominences can be hundreds of thousands of miles long, and can be visible to the naked eye during a total eclipse. They appear to lie along and are supported by loops in the sun's magnetic field, where they may remain for days.

solar system The SUN, its PLANETS and their natural SATELLITES, and the small bodies (see ASTEROID, CENTAUR OBJECT, COMET, KUIPER BELT, METEORITE, and OORT CLOUD) and interplanetary dust and gas under the sun's gravitational control. Another component of the solar system is the SOLAR WIND. The sun contains more than 99% of the mass of the solar system; most of the rest is distributed among the nine planets, with JUPITER containing about 70%. According to the prevailing theory, the solar system originated from the SOLAR NEBULA. See also EARTH, MARS, MERCURY, NEPTUNE, PLUTO, SATURN, URANUS, VENUS.

solar wind Flux of particles, chiefly PROTONS, ELECTRONS, and HELIUM nuclei, accelerated by the hot solar CORONA to speeds high enough to allow them to escape the sun. SOLAR FLARES increase its intensity. The solar wind deflects planets' MAGNETOSPHERES and the ion tails of COMETS away from the sun. The uninterrupted portion of the solar wind continues to travel to a distance of about 20 ASTRONOMICAL UNITS, where it cools and eventually diffuses into interstellar space.

soldering \'sä-dər-iŋ\ Process that uses METAL ALLOYS with low melting points to join metallic surfaces without melting them. Tin-lead solders, once widely used in the electrical and plumbing industries, are now replaced by lead-free alloys. Such alloys are also used to solder brass and copper automobile radiators. Solders are supplied in wire, bar, or premixed-paste form, depending on the application. Soldering can be carried out using a torch, a soldering iron, a flame heater, or an induction heater. See also BRAZING, FLUX.

sole Any of several FLATFISHES, especially about 100 species in the family Soleidae. Those found from Europe to Australia and Japan are marine; some New World species live in freshwater. The eyes are on the right side of the head. The Dover sole *(Solea solea),* found from estuaries to offshore waters in the eastern Atlantic and Mediterranean, grows to 20 in. (50 cm) long. The hogchoker *(Trinectes maculatus),* seldom over 10 in. (25 cm) long, is found in shallow coastal waters from New England to Central America and far inland in habitats associated with large rivers.

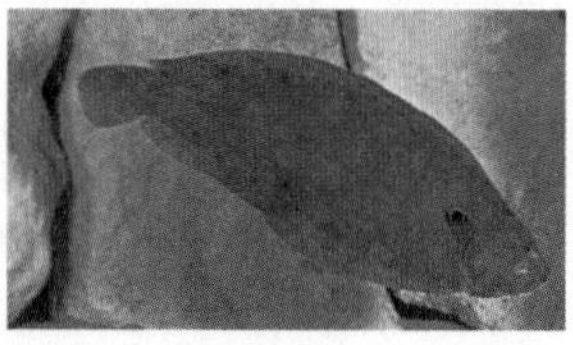

Dover sole (*Solea solea*).

JACQUES SIX

Solemn League and Covenant (1643) Agreement between the English and Scots in which the Scots agreed to support the English Parliamentarians in their disputes with the royalists, and both countries agreed to work for a civil and religious union of England, Scotland, and Ireland under a presbyterian-parliamentary system. The Scots sent an army to England in 1644, and CHARLES I surrendered to them in 1646. He later agreed to the covenant and received Scottish military assistance (1647). Neither OLIVER CROMWELL's Commonwealth nor CHARLES II (after the 1660 RESTORATION) honored the covenant, and it was not renewed. See also COVENANTERS.

Solent \'sō-lənt\, **The** Strait of the ENGLISH CHANNEL. It extends 15 mi (24 km) between mainland England and the Isle of WIGHT and varies in width from 2 to 5 mi (3 to 8 km). The submerged valley of a former eastward-flowing river, it is the scene of yacht races and is famous for the naval reviews off Spithead.

Soleri \sō-'ler-ē\, **Paolo** (born 1919) Italian-U.S. architect. After receiving a doctorate from Turin Polytechnic, he worked under FRANK

S | T | U | V

LLOYD WRIGHT in Arizona (1947–49). Beginning in 1959, he drew up plans for a series of compact urban centers that would extend vertically into space rather than horizontally along the ground. These megastructures were designed to conserve energy and resources (partly through reliance on solar energy and elimination of automobile use within the city), preserve natural surroundings, and condense human activities within integrated total environments. In 1970 he began constructing a prototype town called Arcosanti, for a population of 7,000, between Phoenix and Flagstaff, Ariz. The work, by students and volunteers, is still in progress.

solfeggio See SOLMIZATION

Solferino \ˌsäl-fə-ˈrē-nō\, **Battle of** (June 24, 1859) Engagement fought in Lombardy between Austria and an allied French and Piedmontese army. After its defeat at the Battle of MAGENTA, the Austrian army retreated eastward, where it unexpectedly met the allied army commanded by NAPOLEON III and VICTOR EMMANUEL II. The battle developed in a confused fashion until the French eventually broke the Austrian center line, but vigorous delaying actions left the allied army too exhausted to pursue the defeated Austrians. 14,000 Austrians and 15,000 French and Piedmontese were killed and wounded. The costly battle influenced Napoleon III to seek a truce (the Peace of VILLAFRANCA), which contributed to the unification of Italy.

Soli \ˈsō-ˌlī\ Ancient seaport, CILICIA, ASIA MINOR. It was located west of modern Mersin, southern central Turkey. Founded by Greek colonists from RHODES, it was conquered by ALEXANDER THE GREAT in 333 BC. Destroyed in the 1st century BC by Tigranes II of Armenia, it was rebuilt by the Roman general POMPEY. Traces of the port's artificial harbor and a portion of a long colonnade remain.

solicitation In CRIMINAL LAW, the act of asking, inducing, or directing someone to commit a crime. The person soliciting another becomes an accomplice to the crime. The term also refers to the act of obtaining bribes, as well as to the crime of a prostitute who offers sexual relations in exchange for money.

solicitor British lawyer who advises clients, represents them in the lower courts, and prepares cases for BARRISTERS to try in higher courts. The education required of a solicitor includes a law-school course and five years of apprenticeship with a practicing solicitor. In the U.S., the solicitor general represents the federal government in court, especially the U.S. Supreme Court.

solid One of the three basic states of MATTER. A solid forms from either a LIQUID or a GAS (the other two states of matter), because the energy of atoms is less when the atoms take up the relatively ordered, three-dimensional structure of a solid. All solids have the ability to support loads applied either perpendicular (normal) or parallel (shear) to a surface. Solids can be crystalline (as in metals), noncrystalline (as in plastics), or quasicrystalline (as in metal alloys), depending on the degree of order in the arrangement of the atoms.

solid solution Solid form of a liquid SOLUTION. As with liquids, a tendency for mutual solubility exists between any two coexisting solids (i.e., each can mix with the other); depending on the chemical similarities of the solids, mutual solubility of two substances may be 100% (as between silver and gold), or it may be near 0 (as between copper and bismuth).

solid-state device Electronic device that operates on the basis of the electric, magnetic, or optical properties of a solid material, especially one that uses a solid CRYSTAL in which an orderly three-dimensional arrangement of atoms, ions, or molecules is repeated throughout the entire crystal. Synthetic crystals of elements such as SILICON, gallium arsenide, and GERMANIUM are used in TRANSISTORS, rectifiers, and INTEGRATED CIRCUITS. The first solid-state device was the "cat's whisker" (1906), in which a fine wire was moved across a solid crystal to detect a radio signal. See also SEMICONDUCTOR.

solid-state physics Branch of physics concerned with the physical properties of solid materials. It deals with the properties of CRYSTAL-LATTICE arrangements of ATOMS, and dislocations and defects in the arrangements. These structures are especially important in the study of the conductance of heat and electricity through solid materials.

Solidarity *Polish* **Solidarność** Polish trade union. A workers' strike in 1980 at the Lenin Shipyards in Gdańsk inspired other labor strikes in Poland and compelled the government to agree to the workers' demands for independent unions. Solidarity was founded to unite the regional trade unions, and LECH WALESA was elected chairman. The movement won economic reforms and free elections before pressure from the Soviet Union forced the Polish government to suppress the union in 1981. The focus of worldwide attention, it continued as an underground organization until 1989, when the government recognized its legality. In the free elections of 1989, Solidarity candidates won most of the contested seats in the assembly and formed a coalition government. In the 1990s the union's role diminished as new political parties emerged in a free Poland.

soliloquy \sə-ˈli-lə-ˌkwē\ Dramatic monologue that gives the illusion of being a series of unspoken reflections. An accepted dramatic convention in the 16th–17th century, it was used artfully by WILLIAM SHAKESPEARE to reveal the minds of his characters. PIERRE CORNEILLE emphasized its lyricism, while JEAN RACINE favored it for dramatic effect. Overused in English Restoration plays (1660–85), it fell into disfavor. Rejected by prose dramatists such as HENRIK IBSEN, it was seldom used in late-19th-cent naturalist drama. Many 20th-century dramatists also avoided the soliloquy as artificial, though TENNESSEE WILLIAMS and ARTHUR MILLER, among others, adapted it by introducing narrators who alternately mused on the action and took part in it. It has been used by contemporary playwrights such as JOHN GUARE and BRIAN FRIEL, and the illusion that the characters are confiding in the audience has proved acceptable to a culture accustomed to the interview and the documentary film.

solmization \ˌsäl-mə-ˈzā-shən\ *or* **solfeggio** \säl-ˈfe-jē-ō\ Use of arbitrary syllables for singing as a guide for the singer. It may have been invented by GUIDO D'AREZZO when training his cathedral singers. Borrowing the syllables—*ut, re, mi, fa, sol, la*—from the first syllables of the lines of a hymn each of whose phrases began one note higher than the previous phrase, he claimed that his method made it possible for his singers to learn the chant for the entire church calendar in about two years. The syllables are still in use, though *ut* is usually replaced by the more singable *do,* and *ti* or *si* has been added for the seventh scale degree.

Solo River Longest river in JAVA, Indonesia. It rises on the slope of Mount Lawu volcano and flows 335 mi (539 km) north and east to discharge into the Java Sea. It is navigable for small craft in much of its upper course; its marshy delta is used for fish ponds.

Solomon (fl. mid-10th century BC) Son and successor of DAVID. Nearly all that is known about him comes from the BIBLE (1 Kings 1–11 and 2 Chronicles 1–9). Through the efforts of his mother, Bathsheba, and the prophet NATHAN, Solomon was anointed king while David was still alive. On accession to the throne, he liquidated his opponents ruthlessly and installed friends in key posts. He established Israelite colonies outside his kingdom's borders, cooperating with such friendly rulers as the Queen of SHEBA to increase commerce. Fortification of his far-flung empire necessitated a vast building program, the crowning achievement of which was the Temple of JERUSALEM. He reorganized the nation into 12 tribes with 12 administrative districts. He is said to have had a harem of 700 wives and 300 concubines. After the ascension to the throne of his son Rehoboam, the northern tribes seceded and formed their own kingdom of Israel, bringing an end to Solomon's empire. His legendary wisdom is recorded in the Book of PROVERBS, and he is traditionally named as the author of the biblical Song of Solomon. He was regarded as the greatest king of Israel.

Solomon Islands Island nation, South Pacific Ocean. It includes the islands of GUADALCANAL, MALAITA, SAN CRISTOBAL, Choiseul, Santa Isabel, Florida, and Rennell; the Russell, Shortland, Santa Cruz, and New Georgia island groups; and small islands and reefs. Area: 10,954 sq mi (28,370 sq km). Population (1997 est.): 411,000. Capital: HONIARA. The population is largely Melanesian. Languages: English (official); Pijin (an English-based pidgin), and more than 60 indigenous Melanesian languages. Religion: Christianity (mostly Protestantism). Currency: Solomon Islands dollar. The Solomons group consists of seven large volcanic islands arranged in two parallel chains that converge in the southeast. They consist mostly of heavily wooded, mountainous terrain drained by short, swift-flowing rivers. The climate is tropical. The economy is based on agriculture, fishing, and lumbering. Tourism is increasing as cruise ships and visitors to World War II battlefields stop at the islands. The nation is a constitutional monarchy with one legislative house; its chief of state is the British monarch represented by the governor-general, and the head of government is the prime minister. The Solomon Islands were probably settled c. 2000 BC by Austronesian people. Visited by the Spanish in 1568, they were subsequently explored and charted by the Dutch, French, and British. They were under British protection 1893–1900 and became the British Solomon Islands. The Japanese invasion of 1942 ignited three years of the most bitter fighting in the Pacific, particularly on Guadalcanal. The protectorate became self-governing in 1975 and fully independent in 1978. (Another island group named Solomon Islands, which includes BOUGAINVILLE, is part of Papua New Guinea.)

Solomon's seal Any of about 25 species of herbaceous perennials that make up the genus *Polygonatum* (LILY FAMILY), found throughout the Northern Hemisphere. Particularly common in the eastern U.S. and Canada, Solomon's seals flourish in damp, wooded areas and thickets. They have thick, creeping rhizomes and tall, drooping stems, and they bear clusters of white or greenish-white flowers in the axils of leaves, followed by drooping red berries. Similar plants of the genus *Smilacina,* known as false Solomon's seal, bear their flower clusters at the tips of the stems.

Solon \'sō-lən\ (c. 630–c. 560 BC) Athenian statesman, reformer, and poet, known as one of the Seven Wise Men of Greece. He was of noble descent but of moderate means. Though he held the office of ARCHON c. 594, he did not gain full power as a reformer and legislator until about 20 years later. He ended aristocratic rule and permitted participation by all citizens who had achieved a measure of wealth, eliminating any bloodline requirement. He replaced DRACO's code with more humane laws, freed citizens enslaved for debt and redeemed their land, encouraged professions, and reformed coinage and weights and measures. Despite complaints from all sides, the people abided by the changes. He apparently left Athens for 10 years on a series of travels; on his return, he warned Athens about his relative PEISISTRATUS, who would become TYRANT.

Solow \'sō-lō\, **Robert M(erton)** (born 1924) U.S. economist. Born in Brooklyn, N.Y., he received his PhD from Harvard Univ., and he began teaching at MIT in 1949. Solow developed a mathematical model that could show the relative contributions of various factors to sustained national economic growth. He demonstrated that, contrary to traditional economic thinking, the rate of technological progress is more important to growth than capital accumulation or increases in labor. From the 1960s on, his studies were influential in persuading governments to invest in technological research and development. In 1987 he was awarded the Nobel Prize.

solstice \'sȯl-stis\ Either of the two moments in the year when the sun's apparent path is farthest north or south from earth's equator; also, either of the two points along the ECLIPTIC that the sun passes through at these times. In the Northern Hemisphere the summer solstice occurs on June 21 or 22, the winter solstice on December 21 or 22. In the Southern Hemisphere, the seasons are reversed. See also EQUINOX.

Solti \'shȯl-tē\, **Georg** *later* **Sir Georg** (1912–1997) Hungarian-British conductor. After making his piano debut at 12, he studied piano with BELA BARTOK and composition with Z. KODALY. He was A. TOSCANINI's assistant at Salzburg (1936–37). In Switzerland when war broke out, he returned to piano, winning the 1942 Geneva International Competition. He was brought to Munich to lead the Bavarian State Opera (1945–52), then moved to Frankfurt (1952–61). As director of Covent Garden (1961–71), he made the first complete recording of RICHARD WAGNER's *Ring* cycle (1958–65), which remains one of the celebrated recordings of all time. Under Solti (1969–91), the Chicago Symphony Orchestra won extraordinary praise and success.

solubility Degree to which a substance dissolves in a SOLVENT to make a SOLUTION (usually expressed as grams of solute per liter of solvent). Solubility of one fluid in another may be complete (totally miscible; e.g., methanol and water) or partial (oil and water dissolve only slightly). In general, "like dissolves like" (e.g., AROMATIC hydrocarbons dissolve in each other but not in water). Some separation methods (ABSORPTION, extraction) rely on differences in solubility, expressed as the distribution coefficient (ratio of a material's solubilities in two solvents). Generally, solubilities of solids increase with temperature and those of gases decrease with temperature and increase with pressure. See also JOEL HILDEBRAND.

solution In chemistry, a homogeneous mixture of two or more substances in relative amounts that can vary continuously up to the limit of solubility (SATURATION), if any, of one in the other. Most solutions are LIQUIDS, but solutions of GASES and SOLIDS are possible—for example, AIR (composed primarily of oxygen and nitrogen) or BRASS (composed chiefly of copper and zinc). The liquid in a solution is the SOLVENT, and the substance added is the solute; if both are liquids, the one present in a smaller amount is usually considered the solute. If the saturation point is passed, excess solute separates out. Materials with IONIC BONDS (e.g., SALTS) and many with COVALENT BONDS (e.g., ACIDS, BASES, ALCOHOLS) undergo DISSOCIATION into IONS on dissolving and are called ELECTROLYTES. Their solutions can conduct ELECTRICITY and have other properties that differ from those of nonelectrolytes. Solutions are involved in most chemical reactions, refining and purification, industrial processing, and biological phenomena.

Solutrean industry \sə-'lü-trē-ən\ Short-lived STONE-TOOL INDUSTRY that flourished 17,000–21,000 years ago in southwestern France (including at La Solutré and Lougerie-Haute) and in nearby areas. The industry is of special interest because of its particularly fine workmanship. In addition to burins (engraving tools), scrapers, and borers, there are blades formed in the shape of laurel or willow leaves and various shouldered points. Some implements are so fine as to be useless as tools and may instead have been luxury items.

Solvay process \'säl-ˌvā\ *or* **ammonia-soda process** Modern method of manufacturing sodium carbonate (soda ash), devised and commercialized in Belgium by Ernest Solvay (1838–1922). Common salt (sodium chloride) is treated with ammonia and then carbon dioxide, under carefully controlled conditions, to form sodium bicarbonate and ammonium chloride. When heated, the bicarbonate yields sodium carbonate, the desired product; the ammonium chloride is treated with lime to produce ammonia (for reuse) and calcium chloride. The process proved of great commercial value, since large quantities of soda ash are used in making glass, detergents, and cleansers. See also CAUSTIC SODA.

solvent Substance, ordinarily a LIQUID, in which other materials dissolve to form a SOLUTION. Polar solvents (e.g., WATER) favor formation of IONS; nonpolar ones (e.g., HYDROCARBONS) do not. Solvents may be predominantly acidic, predominantly basic, amphoteric (both), or aprotic (neither). Organic compounds used as solvents include AROMATIC compounds and other hydrocarbons, ALCOHOLS, ESTERS, ETHERS, KETONES, AMINES, and nitrated and chlorinated hydrocarbons. Their chief uses are as industrial cleaners, in extractive processes, in pharmaceuticals, in inks, and in paints, varnishes, and lacquers.

Solway Firth Inlet of the IRISH SEA. On the border between northwestern England and southwestern Scotland, it extends inland for 38 mi (61 km). It is a traditional boundary between the two countries. HADRIAN'S WALL terminates on its southern shore.

Solzhenitsyn \ˌsōl-zhə-'nēt-sin\, **Aleksandr (Isayevich)** (born 1918) Russian novelist and historian. He fought in World War II but was arrested in 1945 for criticizing JOSEPH STALIN. He spent eight years in prisons and labor camps and three more in enforced exile. With *One Day in the Life of Ivan Denisovich* (1962), based on his labor-camp experiences, he emerged as an eloquent opponent of government repression. He was forced to publish later works abroad, including *The First Circle* (1968), *Cancer Ward* (1968), and *August 1914* (1971). Publication of the first volume of *The Gulag Archipelago* (1973), one of the greatest works in Russian prose, resulted in his being charged with treason. Expelled from the Soviet Union in 1974, he lived in the U.S., enjoying worldwide fame, until 1994, when he returned home. In the late 1980s glasnost brought renewed access to his work in Russia, but also a loss of interest in it and in the prophetic role he claimed for himself in Russian history. He was awarded the 1970 Nobel Prize.

soma In ancient Indian religion, an unidentified plant, the juice of which was an offering of the Vedic sacrifices. Its stalks were pressed, and its juice, filtered through wool, was mixed with water and milk. After being offered as a libation to the gods, the remainder of the soma was consumed by the priests and the sacrificer. It was highly valued for its exhilarating, probably hallucinogenic, effect. The plant was believed to have been delivered to the earth from heaven by an eagle. The personified deity Soma was the master of plants, healer of disease, and bestower of riches. See also VEDIC RELIGION.

Somalia Country, North Africa. Located in the Horn of Africa, it stretches from the equator to the Red Sea. Area: 246,000 sq mi (637,000 sq km). Population (1997 est.): 6,870,000 (excluding an estimated 450,000 refugees in other countries). Capital: Mogadishu. Most of the people are nomadic or seminomadic Somalis. Language: Somali, Arabic (both official). Religion: Islam (official). Currency: Somali shilling. Much of Somalia is semidesert. The central and southern regions are flat, while the northern region rises to form rugged mountain ranges. Only about 2% of its land is arable, though more than half is grazeable. Somalia has a developing, mixed economy largely based on livestock and agriculture. It is one of the poorest countries in the world. Muslim Arabs and Persians first established trading posts along the coasts in the 7th–10th century. By the 10th century Somali nomads occupied the area inland from the Gulf of Aden, and the south and west were inhabited by

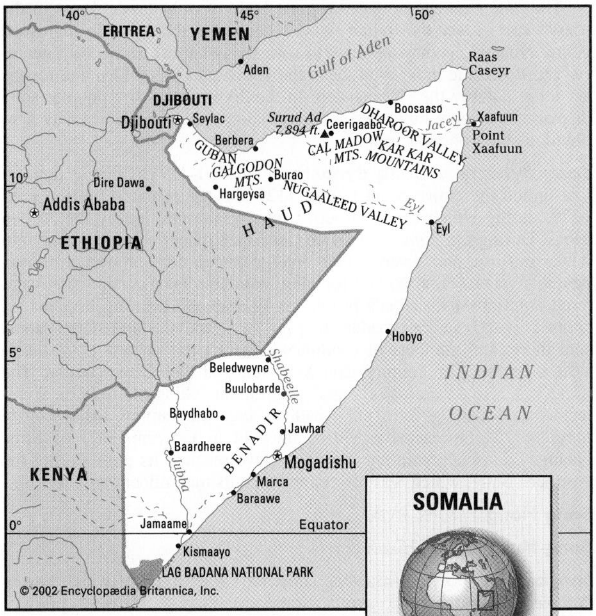

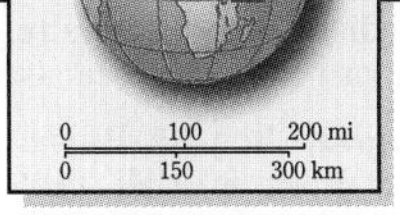

various groups of pastoral Oromo peoples. Intensive European exploration began after the British occupation of Aden in 1839, and in the late 19th century Britain and Italy set up protectorates in the region. During World War II the Italians invaded British Somaliland (1940); a year later British troops retook the area, and Britain administered the region until 1950, when Italian Somaliland became a U.N. trust territory. In 1960 it was united with the former British Somaliland, and the two became the independent Republic of Somalia. Since then it has suffered political and civil strife, including military dictatorship, civil wars, drought, and famine. In the 1990s no effective central government existed. In 1991, a proclamation of a Republic of Somaliland, on territory corresponding to the former British Somaliland was issued by a breakaway group. It did not receive international recognition, but it operated more smoothly than the area of traditional Somalia. A U.N. peacekeeping force intervened in 1992 to secure food supplies; fighting continued and the peacekeeping force left in 1995. The country remained in turmoil. Severe floods devastated the southern region in 1999.

Somaliland \sə-ˈmä-lē-ˌland\ Historical name for the region of eastern Africa between the equator and the Gulf of Aden that includes Somalia, Djibouti, and southeastern Ethiopia. It has an area of about 300,000 sq mi (777,000 sq km). The region probably formed part of the "Land of Punt" known to the ancient Egyptians. In the 7th–12th century AD, Muslim traders from Arabia and Iran settled on the coast, and formed sultanates. The nomadic Somalis, who occupied the northern part of the country in the 10th–15th century, adopted Islam and served in their armies. Gradually the sultanates themselves came under Somali control. In the late 19th century, France, Italy, and Britain partitioned the region among themselves. In 1960 British Somaliland and Italian Somaliland were united to form the Republic of Somalia. French Somaliland became independent as the Republic of Djibouti in 1977.

Somalis \sə-ˈmä-lēz\ People occupying all of Somalia and parts of Djibouti, Ethiopia, and Kenya. Their language is of the Cushitic branch of the Afroasiatic family. Numbering about 7 million, the Somalis are divided into northern, central, and southern groups. All have been Muslims since at least the 14th century. They are primarily nomadic herdsmen who, because of intense competition for scarce resources, have been extremely individualistic and frequently involved in blood feuds or wars with neighboring clans or peoples. A second category of Somalis are the townspeople and agriculturalists of the urban centers, especially along the coast of the Horn of Africa, many of whom act as commercial middlemen between the Arab world and the nomads of the interior.

somatotropin See GROWTH HORMONE

Somerset County (pop., 1995 est.: 481,000), southwestern England. Its county seat is Taunton. The remains of prehistoric villages are found in the region. The Romans mined lead and built villas; from the 7th century AD, Somerset formed the westernmost part of the kingdom of Wessex. A large part of western Somerset is made up of Exmoor National Park, and long stretches of coastline are protected. It is mainly an agricultural county and is known for its cider. Tourism draws visitors to its Bristol Channel resorts and historic mansions.

Somerset, Duke of *orig.* **Edward Seymour** (c. 1500–1552) English politician. After his sister, Jane Seymour, married Henry VIII in 1536, Somerset rose rapidly in royal favor. He commanded the English forces that invaded Scotland and sacked Edinburgh in 1544, and he decisively defeated the French at Boulogne in 1545. After Henry's death (1547), he was named Protector of England during the minority of Edward VI and acted as king in all but name. When the Scots rejected his appeal for a voluntary union with England, he invaded Scotland and won the Battle of Pinkie (1547). He introduced moderate Protestant reforms, but these provoked Catholic uprisings in western England. His land reforms were opposed by landowners and the duke of Northumberland, who had Somerset deposed from the protectorate in 1549. He was imprisoned in 1551 on a flimsy charge of treason and executed the next year.

Somerville \ˈsəm-ər-ˌvil\, **Edith (Anna Oenone)** (1858–1949) Irish novelist. She first met her cousin Violet Florence Martin (1862–1915) in 1886; three years later they published their first novel, *An Irish Cousin,* under the names E. Œ. Somerville and Martin Ross. They cowrote a total of 14 books, including a collection of short stories, *Some Experiences of an Irish R.M.* (1899), that, with its sequels, was their most popular work. Their works wittily and sympathetically portrayed Irish society in the late 19th century. After Martin's death, Somerville continued to write under the joint name.

Somme \ˈsȯm, ˈsäm, ˈsəm\, **Battle of the** (July 1–November 13, 1916) Allied offensive in World War I. British and French forces launched a frontal attack against an entrenched German army north of the Somme River in France. A weeklong artillery bombardment was followed by a British infantry assault on the still-impregnable German positions. Almost 60,000 British casualties (including 20,000 killed) occurred on the first day. The offensive gradually deteriorated into a battle of attrition, hampered by torrential rains in October that made the muddy battlefield impassable. By the time it was abandoned, the Allies had advanced only 5 mi (8 km). The staggering losses included 650,000 German casualties, 420,000 British, and 195,000 French. The battle became a metaphor for futile and indiscriminate slaughter.

Somme River \ˈsəm\ River, northern France. It rises near St.-Quentin and flows westward 152 mi (245 km) to the English Channel. Canals on its upper valley connect it with navigable waterways that link Paris and Flanders. Its upper basin was the scene of heavy fighting in World War I, particularly that of the Battle of the Somme (1916).

Somoza family \sō-ˈmō-sə\ Family that maintained political control of Nicaragua for more than 40 years. The dynasty's founder, Anastasio Somoza García (1896–1956), became head of Nicaragua's army in 1933 and, after deposing the elected president in 1936, ruled the country with a firm and grasping hand until he was assassinated. He was succeeded by his elder son, Luis Somoza Debayle (1922–1967), and later by his younger son, Anastasio Somoza Debayle (1925–1980), whose corrupt and brutal rule (1963–79) led to his overthrow by the Sandinistas. Somoza looted the country before fleeing to Miami; he was assassinated in Paraguay.

sonar Technique for detecting and determining the distance and direction of underwater objects by tracking acoustic echoes. The name derives from *so*und *na*vigation *r*anging. Sound waves emitted by or reflected from an object are detected by sonar apparatus and analyzed for information. In active sonar a sound wave is generated that spreads outward and is reflected back by a target object. Passive systems consist simply of receiving sensors that pick up the noise produced by the target (such as a submarine or torpedo). A third kind of sonar, used in communication systems, requires a projector and receiver at both ends. Sonar was first used to detect submarines in 1916. Modern nonmilitary uses include fish finding, depth sounding, mapping of the ocean floor, Doppler navigation (see DOPPLER EFFECT), and searching for wrecks or other artifacts in the oceans.

sonata Musical form for one or more instruments, usually consisting of three or four movements. The name, Italian for "sounded (on an instrument)," originally simply indicated nonvocal music, and was used for a confusing variety of genres into the late 17th century. In the 1650s two types of ensemble sonatas began to be codified, the sonata da chiesa (church sonata) and sonata da camera (chamber sonata). The former, intended for church performance, was generally in four movements, two of them slow; the latter was usually a SUITE of dances. The so-called solo sonata (for soloist—usually violin—and CONTINUO) and the TRIO SONATA (for two soloists and continuo) became standard. In the 1740s solo keyboard sonatas began to be written. C.P.E. BACH established the three-movement keyboard sonata as the norm, a status it would retain through the Classical era. Duo sonatas in the same form, usually for violin and keyboard, simultaneously became highly popular. Keyboard and duo sonatas have remained the standard types to the present day. From Bach's time onward, the first movement was generally in allegro tempo and in SONATA FORM. The second movement was usually slow. The last movement was generally a MINUET, RONDO, or THEME AND VARIATIONS. In a four-movement sonata, the third was usually a minuet or SCHERZO. In these respects the sonata paralleled such genres as the SYMPHONY and the STRING QUARTET.

sonata form *or* **sonata-allegro form** Form of most first movements and often other movements in such musical genres as the SYMPHONY, CONCERTO, STRING QUARTET, and SONATA. Sonata form evolved from two-part forms such as the dances of the baroque SUITE, each of whose parts was generally repeated. The second part, which initially tended to resemble the first part but reversed the order of its keys, gradually grew in size to become, in important respects, a three-part form. The first part, or exposition, presents the basic thematic material of the movement, which is often divided into two thematic groups, the second being in the dominant key or—if the movement is in a minor key—in the relative major key. The second section, or development, generally treats the earlier themes freely, often moving to various different keys. It leads to the final section, or recapitulation, when the tonic key returns and all the thematic material is repeated in the tonic. Sonata form was the most common form for instrumental works in Western art music from c. 1760 to the early 20th century.

Sonderbund \'zȯn-dər-ˌbu̇nt\ (German: "Separatist League") League formed in 1845 by the seven Catholic Swiss cantons. After the Protestant cantons sought to prevent the Jesuits' takeover of religious education in Luzern, the Catholic cantons formed the Sonderbund, which further angered the liberal cantons. In 1847 a reformist majority in the Swiss Diet voted to dissolve the Sonderbund and expel the Jesuits. In November 1847 the league took up arms, but its forces were quickly subdued. The new Swiss constitution adopted in 1848 strengthened the central government.

Sondheim \'sänd-ˌhīm\, **Stephen (Joshua)** (born 1930) U.S. composer and lyricist. Born in New York City, he studied piano and organ and at 15 wrote his first musical under the tutelage of O. HAMMERSTEIN, a family friend. After studies with M. BABBITT, he made his first mark on Broadway as lyricist for *West Side Story* (1957) and later *Gypsy* (1959). He wrote both music and lyrics for *A Funny Thing Happened on the Way to the Forum* (1962, Tony Award), *Company* (1970, Tony Award), *Follies* (1971), *A Little Night Music* (1973, Tony Award), *Sweeney Todd* (1979, Tony Award), *Sunday in the Park with George* (1984, Pulitzer Prize), and *Into the Woods* (1987), among other works. His stage works are known for their intellectuality, musical complexity, and frequently dark tone. He is a recipient of a Kennedy Center Honor (1993) and the National Medal of Arts (1997).

song Short and usually simple piece of music for voice, with or without instrumental accompaniment. Folk songs—traditional songs without a known composer transmitted orally rather than in written form—have existed for millennia, but have left few traces in ancient sources. Virtually all known preliterate societies have a repertory of songs. Folk songs often accompany religious ceremonies, dancing, labor, or courting; they may tell stories or express emotions; the music follows obvious conventions and is often repetitive. Songs written by a particular composer and poet generally are more sophisticated and are not attached to activities. In the West, the continuous tradition of secular art songs begins with the TROUBADOURS, TROUVÈRES, and MINNESINGERS of the 12th–13th century. Polyphonic songs, originating in the MOTET, begin to appear in the 13th century. The 14th century produced a great body of polyphonic songs in the FORMES FIXES. Later the Italian MADRIGAL becomes the most distinguished genre. Notated accompaniments to solo songs appear in the 16th century. The Romantic movement made the 19th century a golden age for the art song, notably the German LIED. In the 20th century the popular song displaced the more cultivated art song, and popular music is today synonymous with popular song.

Song dynasty *or* **Sung dynasty** \'su̇ŋ\ (960–1279) Chinese dynasty that united the entire country until 1127 and the southern portion until 1279, during which time northern China was controlled by the Juchen tribes. During the Song, commerce flourished, paper currency came into increasing use, and several cities boasted populations of over a million people. WANG ANSHI worked for more equitable taxation and state-centered solutions for China's problems. Widespread printing brought increased literacy and a broader elite; private academies and state schools sent increasing numbers of candidates through the CHINESE EXAMINATION SYSTEM. In the 12th century, ZHU XI systemized NEO-CONFUCIANISM. The Song was also an era of scholarship: groundbreaking treatises on architecture and botany were published, as was the famous history *Zizhi tongjian* ("Comprehensive Mirror for Aid in Government") of Sima Guang. Landscape painting is said to have reached its peak during the Northern Song, which was also famous for its magnificent architecture.

Song Hong See RED RIVER

Song Huizong See HUIZONG

songbird Any oscine PASSERINE (suborder Passere), all of which have a complex vocal organ, the syrinx. Some species (e.g., THRUSHES) produce melodious songs; others (e.g., CROWS) have a harsh voice; and some do little or no singing. See also BIRDSONG.

Songhai \'sȯŋ-ˌhī\ People inhabiting the area of the great bend in the Niger River in Mali, centered on the site of the old SONGHAI EMPIRE. Numbering about 700,000, the Songhai speak a NILO-SAHARAN LANGUAGE. Songhai society traditionally was highly structured, comprising a nobility, free commoners, artisans, griots (bards and chroniclers), and formerly slaves. They cultivate cereals in the rainy season (June–Nov.), and also engage in cattle raising and fishing. The Songhai have traditionally prospered from caravan trade. Many young Songhai have left home for the coast, especially Ghana.

Songhai empire *or* **Songhay empire** \'sȯŋ-ˌhī\ Ancient Muslim trading state, West Africa. Centered on the middle NIGER RIVER in what is now central Mali, it eventually extended to the Atlantic coast and into Niger and Nigeria. Established by the SONGHAI people c. AD 800, it reached its greatest extent in the 16th century before falling to Moroccan forces in 1591. Its important cities were Gao and Timbuktu (TOMBOUCTOU).

Songhua River *or* **Sung-hua River** \'su̇ŋ-'hwä\ *or* **Sungari River** \ˌsu̇ŋ-gə-'rē\ River, northeastern China. Rising in the Changbai Mtns., it is joined by its chief tributary, the NEN RIVER, before it enters the AMUR RIVER 1,197 mi (1,927 km) later. The Amur's largest tributary, it passes through a fertile plain and is navigable for much of its course.

Songjiang *or* **Sung-chiang** \'su̇ŋ-'jyäŋ\ Town (population 1985 est.: 100,000), SHANGHAI municipality, eastern China. It was a superior prefecture under the MING and QING dynasties. Originally a major rice-growing center, by the 18th century it had gained an international reputation for cotton textiles. During the TAIPING REBELLION (1850–64), it was badly damaged in the fighting to defend SHANGHAI; it is the burial place of the U.S. adventurer Frederick T. Ward, who commanded the "Ever-Victorious Army" in the rebellion. Shanghai's phenomenal 19th-century growth took away the town's role as a commercial center; in the 20th century it was completely dominated by Shanghai.

sonnet Fixed verse form having 14 lines that are typically five-foot iambics rhyming according to a prescribed scheme. The sonnet is unique among poetic forms in Western literature in that it has retained its appeal for major poets for five centuries. It seems to have originated in the 13th century among the SICILIAN SCHOOL of court poets. In the 14th century, PETRARCH established the most widely used sonnet form. The Petrarchan (or Italian) sonnet characteristically consists of an eight-line octave, rhyming *abbaabba,* that states a problem, asks a question, or expresses an emotional tension, followed by a six-line sestet, of varying rhyme schemes, that resolves the problem, answers the question, or resolves the tension. In adapting the Italian form, Elizabethan poets gradually developed the other major sonnet form, the Shakespearean (or English) sonnet. It consists of three quatrains, each with an independent rhyme scheme, and ends with a rhymed couplet.

Sonni Ali \sȯn-'ē-ä-'lē\ (died 1492) West African monarch who initiated the imperial expansion of the SONGHAI EMPIRE. His first major conquest (1468) was the city of TOMBOUCTOU, one of the chief anchors of the declining MALI EMPIRE. A seven-year siege of the city of Jenné (now Djenné) resulted in its conquest in 1473. He spent most of his reign repulsing attacks on his empire by the Dendi, the FULANI, the MOSSI, and the TUAREG. Little is known about his administration, but Arab chroniclers characterized him as a cruel and capricious tyrant.

Sonora \sə-'nōr-ə\ State (pop., 1995 est.: 2,086,000), northwestern Mexico. Bordering the U.S. and the Gulf of California, it covers 71,403 sq mi (184,934 sq km); its capital is HERMOSILLO. Explored by Spaniards in the 1530s, it became an important colonial mining district for copper, gold, and silver. It became a state in 1830, but the YAQUI Indian tribes were not finally subdued until the 20th century. It is generally arid and semiarid, and irrigation is used to grow winter vegetables, cereals, cotton, tobacco, and corn.

Sonoran Desert Arid region, western North America. It covers 120,000 sq mi (310,000 sq km) in southwestern Arizona, southeastern California, western SONORA state, Mexico, and northern Baja California; its subdivisions include the Colorado and Yuma deserts. Irrigation has produced many fertile agricultural areas, notably the COACHELLA and IMPERIAL VALLEYS. The warm winters attract tourists to its resorts, including PALM SPRINGS, TUCSON, and PHOENIX. Indian reservations (see PAPAGO and PIMA) are located there.

Sontag \'sän-ˌtag\, **Susan** *orig.* **Susan Rosenblatt** (born 1933) U.S. writer. Born in New York City, she studied at the University of Chicago and Harvard University and taught philosophy at several institutions. In the early 1960s she began contributing to such periodicals as the *New York Review of Books*, *Commentary*, and *Partisan Review,* her French-influenced essays being characterized by a serious philosophical approach to aspects of modern culture rarely taken seriously at the time, including films, popular music, and "camp" sensibility. Collections of her pieces include the influential *Against Interpretation* (1968) and *Styles of Radical Will* (1969). Her later critical works include *On Photography* (1977), *Illness as Metaphor* (1977), and *AIDS and Its Metaphors* (1988). She also has written screenplays and novels, including *The Volcano Lover* (1992).

Sony Corp. Major Japanese manufacturer of consumer electronics. Founded by Ibuka Masaru and AKIO MORITA in 1946 as Tokyo Telecommunications Engineering Corp., it adopted its present name in 1958. It began by making voltmeters, sound generators, and similar devices. Its first major consumer item was an audio tape recorder, introduced in 1950. Since then it has pioneered new technology for consumer products marketed worldwide, including the first pocket-sized transistor radio (1957) and a color video cassette recorder (1969), and the Walkman portable radio. Sony purchased CBS Records Group, the world's largest record company, in 1987–88 and Columbia Pictures Entertainment in 1989.

Soong family \'sůŋ\ Influential 20th-century Chinese family. Charlie Soong (1866–1918) trained in the U.S. to become a missionary. In China he made his fortune as a publisher, initially of Bibles, and became a supporter of SUN YAT-SEN, whose Nationalist Party (see GUOMINDANG) he helped finance. His first daughter married a businessman who also provided financial support to the Nationalists; his second daughter, Soong Ch'ing-ling (Song Qingling), married Sun Yat-sen; his third daughter, Soong Mei-ling, became CHIANG KAI-SHEK's second wife. A son, T. V. Soong, established the Central Bank of China and acted as finance minister for the Nationalist government in the 1920s and foreign minister in the 1930s. The 1949 Communist takeover divided the family: Ch'ing-ling, who had earlier denounced the Nationalists for betraying Sun Yat-sen's ideals, remained on the mainland and was named honorary chairman of the People's Republic in 1981. Mei-ling accompanied Chiang Kai-shek to Taiwan and publicized his cause in the West; as Madam Chiang, she became extremely popular in the U.S. T. V. Soong, once reputed the richest man in the world, moved to the U.S.

sopher See SOFER

Sophia \'sȯ-fyə\ *Russian* **Sofya Alekseyevna** (1657–1704) Regent of Russia (1682–89). Daughter of Czar ALEXIS, she objected to the succession of her half brother PETER I THE GREAT as czar (1682) and instigated an uprising by the STRELTSY (household troops). She arranged to have her brother IVAN V proclaimed coruler with Peter and assumed the role of regent. With help from her chief adviser and lover, VASILY GOLITSYN, she promoted the development of industry and concluded peace treaties with Poland (1686) and China (1689). After sponsoring two disastrous military campaigns against the Crimean Tatars (1687, 1689), she tried to regain her influence by inciting the streltsy to oust Peter and his advisers. She was instead overthrown by Peter in 1689 and forced to enter a convent.

sophists \'sä-fists\ Group of itinerant professional teachers, lecturers, and writers prominent in Greece in the later 5th century BC. The sophistic movement arose at a time when there was much questioning of the absolute nature of familiar values and ways of life. An antithesis arose between nature and custom, tradition, or law, in which custom could be regarded either as artificial trammels on the freedom of the natural state or as beneficial and civilizing restraints on natural anarchy. Both views were represented among the sophists, though the former was the more common. Their first and most eminent representative was PROTAGORAS; other notable sophists include Gorgias of Leontini, Prodicus, Hippias, Antiphon, Thrasymachus, and Critias. A later "second sophistic school" existed in the 2nd century AD.

Sophocles \'sä-fə-ˌklēz\ (496?–406 BC) Greek playwright. With AESCHYLUS and EURIPIDES, he was one of the three great tragic playwrights of classical Athens. A distinguished public figure in Athens, he served successively in important Athenian posts as a treasurer, commander, and adviser. He competed in dramatic festivals, defeating Aeschylus to win his first victory in 468 BC. He went on to achieve an unparalleled success, writing 123 dramas for dramatic competitions and winning over 20 victories. Only seven tragedies survive in their entirety, including *Antigone, Ajax, Electra, The Trachinian Women, Philoctetes, Oedipus at Colonus*, and *Oedipus the King,* his best-known work. He increased the size of the chorus and was the first to introduce a third actor onstage. For their supple language, vivid characterization, and formal perfection, his works are regarded as the epitome of Greek drama.

soprano Highest vocal register, ranging from about middle C to the second A above. Sopranos are normally female but may also include boy sopranos and (previously) castrati (see CASTRATO). Soprano voices are traditionally classified as dramatic (rich and powerful), lyric (lighter), and coloratura (high and very agile). The mezzo-soprano range is about a 3rd lower.

Sopwith, Thomas (Octave Murdoch) *later* **Sir Thomas** (1888–1989) British aircraft designer. He taught himself to fly in 1910 and won a prize for the longest flight to the European continent. In 1912 he founded his own aircraft company, which in World War I built such planes as the Camel, the Pup, and the Triplane. His firm produced the Hurricane fighter and the Lancaster bomber in World War II, and later the Harrier, a vertical-takeoff jet fighter. From 1935 to 1963, he was chairman of the Hawker Siddeley Group, successor to his original company.

Soranus of Ephesus \sȯ-'rā-nəs...'e-fə-səs\ (fl. 2nd century AD) Greek gynecologist, obstetrician, and pediatrician. A keen observer and unusually competent practitioner, he wrote works that influenced medical opinion for 1,500 years. His remarkable *On Midwifery and the Diseases* *of Women* describes contraceptive methods, obstetric techniques that were thought to be new in the 15th century, and what is now recognized as rickets. His suggested treatments for nervous disorders resemble aspects of modern psychotherapy. Soranus also wrote the first known biography of HIPPOCRATES.

Sorbs See WENDS

Sorby, Henry Clifton (1826–1908) British amateur scientist. Convinced of the value of the microscope to geology, Sorby began in 1849 to prepare thin sections of rocks, about 0.001 in. (0.025 mm) thick, for microscopic study. He developed a new type of spectrum microscope for analyzing the light of organic pigments (1865). His research on meteors led to studies of iron and steel, and his later studies included the origin of layered rocks, weathering, and marine biology. He published works dealing with the physical geography of geologic periods, rock breakdown and buildup, and the formation of river terraces. Sorby is considered the father of microscopical petrography and metallography.

sorcery See WITCHCRAFT AND SORCERY

Sorel \sȯ-'rel\, **Georges (-Eugène)** (1847–1922) French socialist and revolutionary syndicalist. Trained as a civil engineer, he was 40 before he became interested in social issues. He discovered MARXISM in 1893, but was disgusted by what he saw as the left's exploitation of the ALFRED DREYFUS case. He came to believe that society's decadence could be purged through revolutionary SYNDICALISM. In *Réflexions sur la violence* (1908), he wrote about myth and violence in the historical process, and on violence as necessary for revolutionary change. After 1909, disenchanted with syndicalism, he supported the French monarchist movement, which sought to reestablish a homogeneous and traditional moral order. After the RUSSIAN REVOLUTION OF 1917, he hoped the BOLSHEVIKS might bring about the moral regeneration of society. BENITO MUSSOLINI appropriated some of Sorel's ideas to support FASCISM.

sorghum \'sȯr-gəm\ CEREAL grain plant of the family Poaceae (or Gramineae), probably native to Africa, and its edible starchy seeds. All types raised chiefly for grain belong to the species *Sorghum vulgare,* which includes varieties of grain sorghums and grass sorghums (grown for hay and fodder), and broomcorn (used in making brooms and brushes). The strong grass usually grows 2–8 ft (0.5–2.5 m) or higher. The seeds are smaller than those of wheat. Though high in carbohydrates, sorghum is of lower feed quality than corn. Resistant to drought and heat, sorghum is one of Africa's major cereal grains. It is also grown in the U.S., India, Pakistan, and northern and northeastern China. Substantial quantities are also grown in Iran, the Arabian Peninsula, Argentina, Australia, and southern Europe. The grain is usually ground into meal for porridge, flatbreads, and cakes.

sorites \sə-'rī-tēz\ In philosophy, a chain of successive SYLLOGISMS in the first figure so related that either the conclusion of each is the minor premise of the next or the conclusion of each is the major premise of the next. If the conclusions of all the successive syllogisms (except the last) are suppressed and only the remaining premises and the final conclusion are stated, the resulting argument is a valid inference from the stated premises. (For example: Some enthusiasts show poor judgment; all who show poor judgment make frequent mistakes; none who makes frequent mistakes deserves implicit trust; therefore, some enthusiasts do not deserve implicit trust.) In general, there may be n + 1 premises, and analysis then yields a chain of n successive syllogisms. See also SORITES PROBLEM.

sorites problem PARADOX presented by the following reasoning: One grain of sand does not constitute a heap; if n grains of sand do not constitute a heap, then neither do n+1 grains of sand; therefore, no matter how many grains of sand are put together, they never constitute a heap. The problem is apt to arise in connection with any vague term. See also SORITES.

Sorokin \'sȯr-ə-kin\, **P(itirim) A(lexandrovitch)** (1889–1968) Russian-U.S. sociologist. Appointed the first professor of sociology at the University of Petrograd in 1919, he was exiled in 1922 for anti-Bolshevism. He emigrated to the U.S., where he founded the sociology department at Harvard University. He distinguished two kinds of society: the sensate (empirical, supportive of natural sciences) and the ideational (mystical, anti-intellectual, dependent on authority), and believed that the study of altruistic love as a science was necessary to avert worldwide chaos.

sororate See LEVIRATE AND SORORATE

Soros \'sȯr-ōs\, **George** (born 1930) Hungarian-U.S. financier. He left his native Hungary in 1944 and settled in London in 1947, where he studied and joined a merchant bank. He moved to New York in 1956 and initially worked as an analyst of European securities. By 1979 his daring investments and currency speculation brought large profits, some of which he used to found Soros Foundations, dedicated to creating open societies in many Eastern European countries and Russia. Other Soros programs have been dedicated to enlarging public debate on a wide range of controversial issues. In 1992 he reached new heights of wealth, making a profit of about $1 billion when Britain devalued the pound sterling, but in 1998 he suffered large losses from currency speculation in Russia.

sorrel Any of several hardy perennial herbs of the BUCKWHEAT family, widespread in temperate regions. Sheep sorrel *(Rumex acetosella),* a weed native to Europe and widespread in North America, is an attractive but troublesome invader in lawns, gardens, meadows, and grassy slopes. It has slender, triangular leaves and tiny yellow or reddish flowers. The pungent, sour leaves are used as a vegetable, as a flavoring in omelets and sauces, in soups, and, when young, in salads. Two related species are garden sorrel *(R. acetosa)* and French sorrel *(R. scutatus),* both found throughout Europe and Asia. Wood sorrels, unrelated plants, belong to the genus *Oxalis* (see OXALIS).

Sosa (Peralta), Sammy *orig.* **Samuel** (born 1968) U.S. (Dominican-born) baseball player. He came to the U.S. as a child, and he began playing organized baseball at 14. In 1985 he signed with the Texas Rangers, with whom he made his professional debut in 1989; he was soon traded to the Chicago White Sox, and in 1992 to the Chicago Cubs. In 1993 the right fielder became the Cubs' first player to hit 30 home runs and steal 30 bases in one season, a feat he repeated in 1994. In 1998 he dramatically battled MARK MCGWIRE for the all-time season home-run record; he finished the year with 66 home runs, earning him the National League's Most Valuable Player award. In 1999, with 63 homers, he became with McGwire the first player to hit over 60 homers in two seasons.

Soseki See NATSUME SOSEKI

Sotheby's \'sə-thə-bēz\ Art auction firm. Founded in London by the bookseller Samuel Baker in 1744, it was later managed by his nephew, John Sotheby, and by his successors until 1861. In the 19th and early 20th century, Sotheby's concentrated on books, manuscripts, and prints. After World War I it specialized in 19th- and 20th-century works, particularly Impressionist paintings. It opened an office in New York City in 1955, and in 1964 it acquired Parke-Bernet, the premier U.S. art auction house. A. Alfred Taubman purchased a controlling share of the company in 1983 and renamed it Sotheby's Holdings, Inc. In 2002 Taubman was convicted of price-fixing with rival auction house CHRISTIE'S, sentenced to a one-year jail term, and fined $7.5 million.

Sotho \'sō-ˌtō\ Cluster of Bantu-speaking peoples (numbering 10 million) occupying the high grasslands of southern Africa. They are culturally and historically distinct from the NGUNI peoples. The main Sotho groups are the Pedi and Lovedu in the north, the TSWANA in the west, and the Basuto of Lesotho. Most farm and raise livestock, though Christian missionary activity, urbanization, and detribalization have resulted in a breakdown of traditional culture patterns.

Soto, Hernando de See Hernando DE SOTO

soul Immaterial aspect or essence of a person, conjoined with the body during life and separable at death. The concept of a soul is found in nearly all cultures and religions, though the interpretations of its nature vary considerably. The ancient Egyptians conceived of a dual soul, one surviving death but remaining near the body, while the other proceeded to the realm of the dead. The early Hebrews did not consider the soul as distinct from the body, but later Jewish writers perceived the two as separate. Christian theology adopted the Greek concept of an immortal soul, adding the notion that God created the soul and infused it into the body at conception. In HINDUISM, each soul, or ATMAN, was created at the beginning of time and imprisoned in an earthly body; at death, the soul passes to a new body according to the laws of KARMA. BUDDHISM negates the idea of a soul, asserting that any sense of an individual self is illusory.

soul music Style of U.S. popular music sung and performed primarily by black musicians, having its roots in GOSPEL MUSIC and RHYTHM AND BLUES. The term was first used in the 1960s to describe music that combined rhythm and blues, gospel, JAZZ, and ROCK MUSIC and that was characterized by intensity of feeling and earthiness. In its earliest stages, soul music was found most commonly in the South, but many of the young singers who were to popularize it migrated to cities in the North. The founding of MOTOWN in Detroit and Stax-Volt in Memphis did much to encourage the style. Its most popular performers include JAMES BROWN, RAY CHARLES, SAM COOKE, and A FRANKLIN.

sound Mechanical disturbance that propagates as a longitudinal wave through a solid, liquid, or gas. A sound WAVE is generated by a vibrating object. The vibrations cause alternating compressions (regions of crowding) and rarefactions (regions of scarcity) in the particles of the medium. The particles move back and forth in the direction of propagation of the wave. The speed of sound through a medium depends on the medium's ELASTICITY, DENSITY, and TEMPERATURE. The FREQUENCY of a sound wave, perceived as PITCH, is the number of compressions (or rarefactions) that pass a fixed point per unit time. The audible frequencies range from approximately 20 hertz to 20 kilohertz. Intensity is the average flow of energy per unit time through a given area of the medium and is related to loudness. See also ACOUSTICS, EAR, HEARING, ULTRASONICS.

Sound, The See ØRESUND

sound barrier Sharp rise in aerodynamic drag that occurs as an aircraft approaches the speed of sound. The sound barrier was formerly an obstacle to supersonic flight. If an aircraft flies at somewhat less than sonic speed, the pressure waves (sound waves) it creates outspeed their sources and spread out ahead of it. Once the aircraft reaches sonic speed the waves are unable to get out of its way. Strong local shock waves form on the wings and body; airflow around the craft becomes unsteady, and severe buffeting may result, with serious stability difficulties and loss of control over flight characteristics. Generally, aircraft properly designed for supersonic flight have little difficulty in passing through the sound barrier, but the effect on those designed for efficient operation at subsonic speeds may become extremely dangerous. The first pilot to break the sound barrier was CHUCK YEAGER (1947), in the experimental X-1 aircraft.

sound card *or* **audio card** INTEGRATED CIRCUIT that generates an audio signal and sends it to a computer's speakers. The sound card can accept an analog sound (as from a microphone or audio tape) and convert it to digital data that can be stored in an audio file, or accept digitized audio signals (as from an audio file) and convert them to analog signals that can be played on the computer's speakers. On a personal computer, the sound card is usually a separate circuit board that is plugged into the motherboard.

sound effect Artificial imitation of sound to accompany action and supply realism in a dramatic production. Sound effects were first used in the theater, where they can represent a range of action too vast or difficult to present onstage, from battles and gunshots to trotting horses and rainstorms. Various methods were devised to reproduce sounds by backstage technicians (e.g., rattling sheet metal to create thunder); today most sound effects are produced by tape recordings. An important part of old-fashioned radio dramas, sound effects are still painstakingly added to television and movie soundtracks.

sound reception See HEARING

Souphanouvong \sü-'pä-nü-ˌvȯŋ\ (1909–1995) Leader of the revolutionary Pathet Lao movement and president of Laos (1975–86). Half brother of SOUVANNA PHOUMA, Souphanouvong was trained in civil engineering and built bridges and roads in Vietnam 1938–45. He fought the return of French colonial rule to Laos after World War II and broke with the Free Lao government-in-exile to ally himself with the VIET MINH, founding the communist-oriented Pathet Lao, which came to power in 1974–75.

sour gum See BLACK GUM

Souris River \'su̇r-əs\ River, Saskatchewan, Manitoba, and North Dakota. It rises in southeastern Saskatchewan, then flows southeast into North Dakota, where it turns north to reenter Canada, joining the ASSINIBOINE RIVER in Manitoba after a course of 600 mi (966 km). In North Dakota it is also called the Mouse River.

Sousa \'sü-zə\, **John Philip** (1854–1932) U.S. bandmaster and composer, known as "The March King." The son of an immigrant Portuguese father and a German mother, Sousa grew up in Washington, D.C., learning to play the violin and other instruments. He enlisted in the Marine Corps in 1868, and from 1880 to 1892 he directed the Marine Band, building it into a virtuoso ensemble. In 1892 he formed his own band, with which he toured internationally to great acclaim. He composed 136 military marches, including "Semper Fidelis" (the official march of the Marines), "The Washington Post," "The Liberty Bell," and "The Stars and Stripes Forever." He also wrote successful operettas, including *El Capitan* (1896), and dozens of other works. In the 1890s he developed the SOUSAPHONE.

sousaphone *or* **helicon** Spiral circular bass or contrabass TUBA. Traditionally made of brass, it is now often made of fiberglass for lightness. The helicon was probably first developed in Russia but was perfected in Vienna in 1849 by Ignaz Stowasser, who manufactured it in various sizes. J.P. SOUSA designed a removable and rotatable bell for the instrument in 1892, giving the new design his own name. Designed for portability, the instruments have become standard in marching bands.

Souter \'sü-tər\, **David H(ackett)** (born 1939) U.S. jurist. Born in Melrose, Mass., he graduated from Harvard Law School and soon joined the state attorney general's office. He was promoted to state attorney general in 1976, to the state's Superior Court in 1978, and to its Supreme Court in 1983. In 1990 he was appointed by Pres. GEORGE BUSH to the First U.S. Circuit Court of Appeals and later that year to the U.S. Supreme Court. His decisions, conservative at the outset, have generally moved toward the center on most issues.

South, University of the *known as* **Sewanee** Private university in Sewanee, Tenn., founded in 1857. Though affiliated with the Episcopal church, its teaching program is independent. It has a college of arts and sciences and a school of theology, which offers master's and doctoral programs. Its literary journal, *The Sewanee Review,* was founded in 1892. Current enrollment is about 1,300.

South Africa, Republic of *formerly* **Union of South Africa** Southernmost country on the African continent. The kingdom of LESOTHO lies

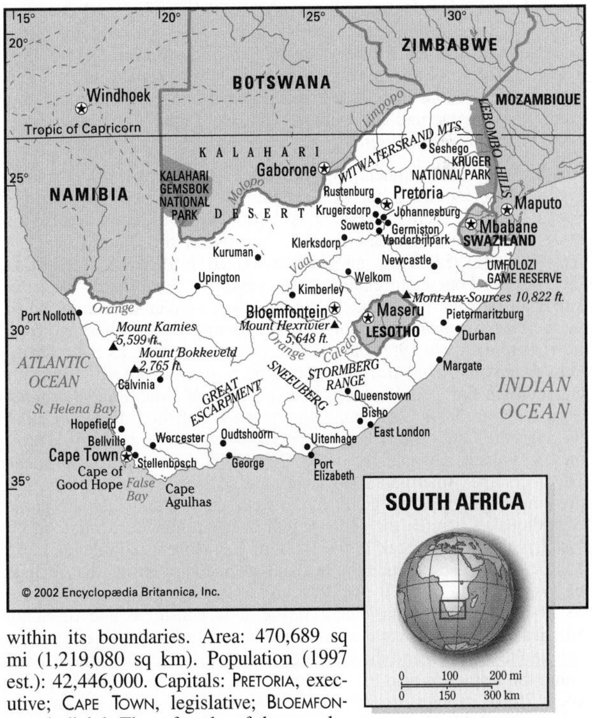

within its boundaries. Area: 470,689 sq mi (1,219,080 sq km). Population (1997 est.): 42,446,000. Capitals: PRETORIA, executive; CAPE TOWN, legislative; BLOEMFONTEIN, judicial. Three-fourths of the population are black Africans: they include the ZULU, XHOSA, SOTHO, and TSWANA; one-eighth are whites, and most of the remainder are of mixed race or Indian descent. Languages: Afrikaans, English, and nine BANTU

LANGUAGES (all official). Religions: Christianity, traditional beliefs. Currency: rand. South Africa has three major zones: the broad interior plateau, the surrounding mountainous Great Escarpment, and a narrow belt of coastal plain. It has a temperate subtropical climate. It is the world's largest producer of gold and a leading producer and exporter of coal, diamonds, platinum, and vanadium. It is a republic with two legislative houses; its head of state and government is the president. SAN and KHOIKHOI roamed the area as hunters and gatherers in the Stone Age, and the latter had developed a pastoralist culture by the time of European contact. By the 14th century, Bantu-speaking peoples had settled in the area and developed gold and copper mining and an active East African trade. In 1652 the Dutch established a colony at the Cape of GOOD HOPE; the Dutch settlers became known as Boers and later as AFRIKANERS, after their AFRIKAANS LANGUAGE. In 1795 British forces captured the Cape, and in 1830, to escape British rule, Dutch settlers made the GREAT TREK northward and established the independent Boer republics of ORANGE FREE STATE and the South African Republic (later the TRANSVAAL region), which the British annexed as colonies by 1902 (see SOUTH AFRICAN WAR). In 1910 the British colonies of Cape Colony, Transvaal, NATAL, and Orange River were unified into the new Union of South Africa. It became independent and withdrew from the COMMONWEALTH in 1961. Throughout the 20th century South African politics were dominated by the question of maintaining white supremacy over the country's black majority, and in 1948 South Africa formally instituted APARTHEID. Faced by increasing worldwide condemnation, it began dismantling the policy in the 1980s and ended it in 1989. In free elections in 1994, NELSON MANDELA became the country's first black president. High rates of AIDS and violent crime beset the nation's new leadership.

South African War *or* **Boer War** War fought between Great Britain and the two Boer (AFRIKANER) republics—the South African Republic (TRANSVAAL) and the ORANGE FREE STATE—from 1899 to 1902. It was caused by the refusal of the Boer leader PAUL KRUGER to grant political rights to Uitlanders ("foreigners," mostly English) in the interior mining districts, and by the aggressiveness of the British high commissioner, ALFRED MILNER. Initially the Boers defeated the British in major engagements and besieged the key towns of Ladysmith, MAFIKENG, and Kimberley; but British reinforcements under H. H. KITCHENER and F. S. Roberts relieved the besieged towns, dispersed the Boer armies, and occupied Bloemfontein, Johannesburg, and Pretoria (1900). Continuing Boer commando attacks led Kitchener to implement a scorched-earth policy: Boer farms were destroyed and Boer civilians were herded into concentration camps. More than 20,000 men, women, and children died as a result, causing international outrage. The Boers finally accepted defeat at the Peace of Vereeniging.

South America Continent, Western Hemisphere. The world's fourth-largest continent, it is bounded by the Caribbean Sea, the Atlantic Ocean, and the Pacific Ocean. It is separated from Antarctica by the DRAKE PASSAGE and is joined to North America by the Isthmus of Panama. Area: 6,895,000 sq mi (17,858,000 sq km). Pop., 2001 est.: 350,514,000. Four main ethnic groups have populated South America: American Indians, who were the continent's pre-Columbian inhabitants; the Iberians, Spanish, and Portuguese who dominated the continent from the 16th to the early 19th century; the Africans imported as their slaves; and the post-independence immigrants from overseas, mostly Germans and southern Europeans but also Lebanese, South Asians, and Japanese. The people are 90% Christian, with about 85% of those Roman Catholic. Spanish is the official language everywhere except in Brazil (Portuguese), French Guiana (French), Guyana (English), and Suriname (Dutch); some Amerindian languages are spoken. South America has three major geographic regions. In the west, the ANDES, which are prone to earthquakes, stretch the entire length of the continent; Mount ACONCAGUA is the highest peak in the Western Hemisphere. Highlands lie in the north and east, bordered by lowland sedimentary basins that include the AMAZON RIVER basin, the world's largest drainage basin, and the PAMPAS of eastern Argentina, whose fertile soils constitute one of South America's most productive agricultural areas. Important river systems include the Amazon and the ORINOCO. Four-fifths of South America lies within the tropics; it also has temperate, arid, and cold climatic regions. About 7% of its land is arable, producing mainly corn, wheat, and rice, and about one-fourth is under permanent pasture. About half is covered by forest, mainly the enormous but steadily diminishing Amazon Rain Forest. Almost one-fourth of all the world's known animal species live in the continent's rain forests, plateaus, rivers, and swamps. South America has one-eighth of the world's total deposits of iron and one-fourth of its copper reserves. Exploitation of these and numerous other mineral resources are important in many regions. Commercial crops include bananas, citrus fruits, sugar, and coffee; fishing is important along the Pacific coast. Most countries have free-market or mixed state and private-enterprise economies. Income tends to be unevenly distributed between large numbers of poor people and a small number of wealthy families, with the growing middle classes still a minority in most countries. Asiatic hunters and gatherers are thought to have been its first settlers, probably arriving less than 12,000 years ago. The growth of agriculture c. 2600 BC initiated a period of rapid cultural evolution whose greatest development occurred in the central Andes region and culminated with the INCA empire. European exploration began when CHRISTOPHER COLUMBUS landed in 1498; Spanish and Portuguese adventurers opened it for settlement. According to terms of the Treaty of TORDESILLAS, Portugal received the eastern part of the continent, while Spain received the rest. The native peoples were decimated and most of those who survived were reduced to a form of serfdom. The continent was free of European rule by the early 1800s except for the Guianas. Most of the countries adopted a republican form of government; social and economic inequalities or border disputes led to periodic revolutions in many of them. All joined the U.N. after World War II, and all joined the ORGANIZATION OF AMERICAN STATES in 1948. See map on following page.

South Asian art Visual arts of India, Pakistan, Bangladesh, and Sri Lanka. The art produced in South Asia is remarkable in its unity and consistency. Traditionally, artists produced works for patrons, and sacred written canons guided their works' proportions, iconography, and other artistic considerations. Wall paintings and miniatures, painted on palm leaves or paper, were prominent, but sculpture was the favored medium. Sculptures were largely religious and essentially symbolic and abstract. Works displaying Hindu and Buddhist imagery flourished in the Golden Age of India in the 4th–5th century. Islamic influences were incorporated into traditional styles after the Islamic invasions of the 12th century. At the end of the 19th century, rising Indian nationalism led to a conscious revival of native art traditions, though more recently artists have assimilated elements of European art styles.

South Australia State (pop., 2001 prelim.: 1,519,900), southern central Australia. It covers an area of 380,000 sq mi (984,381 sq km); its capital is ADELAIDE. The Dutch visited the coast in 1627. British explorers arrived in the early 1800s, and it was colonized as a British province in 1836. Its vast interior, a large part of which is barren, includes Lake EYRE and the FLINDERS RANGES. A major world source of opals, it also produces most of the wine and brandy consumed in the nation. It has the country's largest shipyards. It became a state of the Commonwealth of Australia in 1901. Its southeastern part has become industrialized since World War II.

South Bend City (pop., 2000: 107,789), northern Indiana. It is situated on the St. Joseph River. The French established a fur-trading post at the site in 1820, which was later promoted as a European settlement. Its highly industrialized economy has roots in the pioneering companies founded there in the 19th century, including Studebaker Brothers Manufacturing Co. (later an auto plant) and SINGER CO., a sewing machine manufacturer. Its center city has been dubbed Michiana because it serves as a trade and financial center for southern Michigan and northern Indiana. Nearby is the University of NOTRE DAME.

South Carolina State (pop., 2000: 4,012,012), southeastern U.S. It covers 31,113 sq mi (80,583 sq km) and is an original state of the Union; its capital is COLUMBIA. It comprises a broad coastal plain, with a rolling piedmont farther inland. At the time of European contact the area was inhabited by SIOUX, IROQUOIS, and Muskogean Indians. Spanish and French settlements were established and abandoned in the 16th century; the first permanent European settlement was made by the English in 1670 at Charles Town, moved to the present site of CHARLESTON in 1680. During the AMERICAN REVOLUTION there were several military campaigns in the state. In 1788 South Carolina was the eighth state to ratify the U.S. constitution. In 1860 it became the first state to secede from the Union. The initial action of the AMERICAN CIVIL WAR occurred there at FORT SUMTER. It was readmitted to the Union in 1868. Constitutional revisions in 1895 disenfranchised almost all the state's blacks, and a rigid policy of racial segregation persisted until the mid-1960s, when the national CIVIL RIGHTS MOVEMENT began to have some effect in ameliorating policies. South Carolina is a leader in U.S. textile manufacturing and

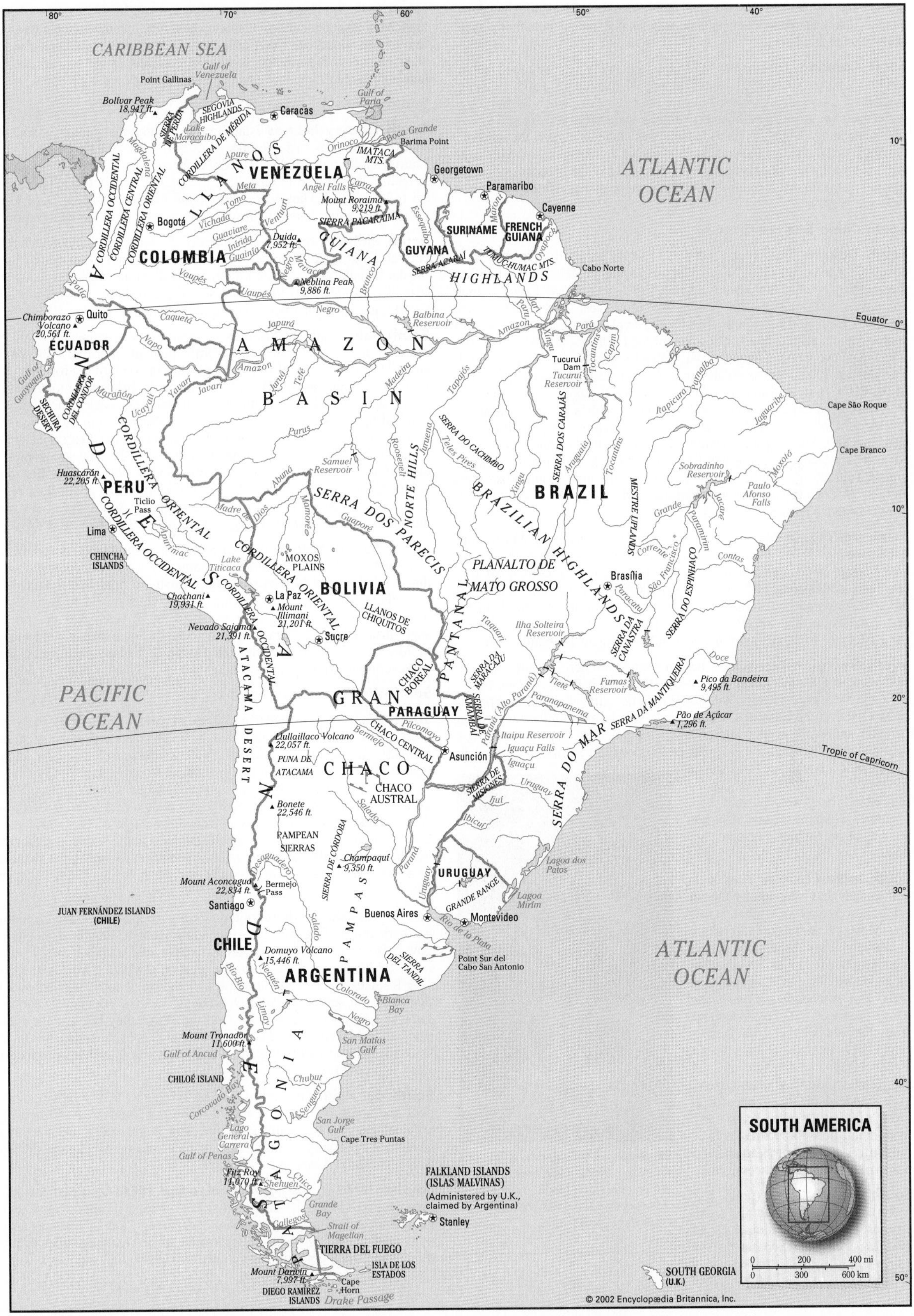
80°
70°
60°
50°
40°
10°
0°
10°
20°
30°
40°
50°
CARIBBEAN SEA
Gulf of Venezuela
Point Gallinas
Bolívar Peak 18,947 ft.
SIERRA DE PERIJÁ
SEGOVIA HIGHLANDS
Caracas
Lake Maracaibo
CORDILLERA DE MÉRIDA
Gulf of Paria
Boca Grande
Barima Point
Orinoco
IMATACA MTS.
Apure
LLANOS
VENEZUELA
Magdalena
CORDILLERA OCCIDENTAL
CORDILLERA CENTRAL
CORDILLERA ORIENTAL
Meta
Angel Falls
Caroní
Georgetown
Paramaribo
Cayenne
Mount Roraima 9,219 ft.
SIERRA PACARAIMA
Tomo
Vichada
Bogotá
Ventuari
Guaviare
Inírida
Guainía
Duida 7,952 ft.
GUIANA
Essequibo
SURINAME
FRENCH GUIANA
Maroni
Oyapock
GUYANA
SERRA ACARAÍ
TUMUCHUMAC MTS.
HIGHLANDS
COLOMBIA
Negro
Mavaca
Neblina Peak 9,886 ft.
Branco
Cabo Norte
Vaupés
Uaupés
Patía
ATLANTIC OCEAN
Chimborazo Volcano 20,561 ft.
Quito
Caquetá
Japurá
Negro
Balbina Reservoir
Amazon
Pará
Jari
Paru
Equator
ECUADOR
Napo
AMAZON
Xingu
Tocantins
Capim
Tucuruí Dam
Tucuruí Reservoir
Gulf of Guayaquil
CORDILLERA DEL CONDOR
Amazon
Juruá
Tefé
Madeira
Tapajós
Marañón
Javari
Yavarí
BASIN
Itapicuru
Parnaíba
Jaguaribe
Cape São Roque
SECHURA DESERT
Ucayali
CORDILLERA CENTRAL
Purus
SERRA DO CACHIMBO
SERRA DOS CARAJÁS
Araguaia
Tocantins
Cape Branco
Juruena
Teles Pires
Roosevelt
NORTE HILLS
Samuel Reservoir
Huascarán 22,205 ft.
PERU
CORDILLERA ORIENTAL
Abuná
Sobradinho Reservoir
Moxotó
Paulo Afonso Falls
BRAZIL
BRAZILIAN HIGHLANDS
Xingu
MESTRE UPLANDS
Ticlio Pass
Madre de Dios
Mamoré
SERRA DOS PARECIS
Grande
Paramirim
Jacaré
Lima
CORDILLERA OCCIDENTAL
Apurímac
Guaporé
Corrente
Contas
CHINCHA ISLANDS
Lake Titicaca
MOXOS PLAINS
São Francisco
SERRA DO ESPINHAÇO
Brasília
PLANALTO DE MATO GROSSO
CORDILLERA ORIENTAL
BOLIVIA
Paracatu
Chachani 19,931 ft.
La Paz
Mount Illimani 21,201 ft.
LLANOS DE CHIQUITOS
PANTANAL
Taquari
Ilha Solteira Reservoir
SERRA DA CANASTRA
Nevado Sajama 21,391 ft.
CORDILLERA OCCIDENTAL
Sucre
CHACO BOREAL
SERRA DA MARACAJU
Doce
Pico da Bandeira 9,495 ft.
ATACAMA DESERT
Tietê
Furnas Reservoir
PACIFIC OCEAN
GRAN
PARAGUAY
SERRA DE AMAMBAÍ
Paranapanema
Paraná (Alto Paraná)
SERRA DA MANTIQUEIRA
Pão de Açúcar 1,296 ft.
SERRA DO MAR
Pilcomayo
CHACO CENTRAL
Bermejo
Itaipu Reservoir
Iguaçu Falls
Llullaillaco Volcano 22,057 ft.
Asunción
Iguaçu
Tropic of Capricorn
PUNA DE ATACAMA
CHACO
SERRA DE MISIONES
Uruguay
CHACO AUSTRAL
Salado
Ijuí
Ibicuí
Bonete 22,546 ft.
PAMPEAN SIERRAS
Desaguadero
SIERRA DE CÓRDOBA
Champaquí 9,350 ft.
Paraná
Uruguay
Lagoa dos Patos
URUGUAY
Mount Aconcagua 22,834 ft.
Bermejo Pass
GRANDE RANGE
Lagoa Mirim
JUAN FERNÁNDEZ ISLANDS (CHILE)
Santiago
Salado
PAMPAS
Buenos Aires
Montevideo
Río de la Plata
CHILE
Domuyo Volcano 15,446 ft.
SIERRA DEL TANDIL
Point Sur del Cabo San Antonio
ATLANTIC OCEAN
Bío-Bío
Neuquén
ARGENTINA
Colorado
Blanca Bay
Limay
Negro
Mount Tronador 11,600 ft.
San Matías Gulf
Gulf of Ancud
ANDES
CHILOÉ ISLAND
Chubut
Corcovado Gulf
Senguerr
PATAGONIA
San Jorge Gulf
Lago General Carrera
Cape Tres Puntas
Gulf of Penas
Chico
FALKLAND ISLANDS (ISLAS MALVINAS) (Administered by U.K., claimed by Argentina)
Fitz Roy 11,070 ft.
Shehuen
Grande Bay
Stanley
Gallegos
Strait of Magellan
TIERRA DEL FUEGO
ISLA DE LOS ESTADOS
Mount Darwin 7,997 ft.
Cape Horn
DIEGO RAMÍREZ ISLANDS
Drake Passage
SOUTH GEORGIA (U.K.)
SOUTH AMERICA
0 200 400 mi
0 300 600 km

has a large industrial base. Tourism is its second largest industry. Agriculture also contributes to the economy; major crops include tobacco, soybeans, and cotton.

South Carolina, University of Public university system based in Columbia. Chartered in 1801, the first school opened in 1805 as South Carolina College. It was closed during the Civil War, when its buildings were used for a military hospital. Blacks were admitted from 1873 to 1877, when the flight of white faculty and students forced the school's closing; it reopened in 1880 as the College of Agriculture and Mechanic Arts. It took its present name in 1906. The system today comprises eight campuses, which offer more than 400 degree programs. Total enrollment is about 39,000.

South China Sea See CHINA SEA

South Dakota State (pop., 2000: 754,844), northern central U.S. It covers 77,116 sq mi (199,730 sq km); its capital is PIERRE. The state has three main regions: the eastern prairie; the central GREAT PLAINS, which contain the BADLANDS; and the BLACK HILLS to the west. The MISSOURI RIVER bisects it from north to south. The French explored the area in the 18th century, and sold it to the U.S. as part of the LOUISIANA PURCHASE in 1803. The LEWIS AND CLARK EXPEDITION spent about seven weeks there in 1804. The Dakota Territory was created in 1861, but settlement was sparse until the BLACK HILLS gold rush of 1875–76 swelled the population. Intermittent wars between the Indians and immigrant whites occurred until the massacre at WOUNDED KNEE in 1890. South Dakota became the 40th U.S. state in 1889. Farming and related industries form the state's economic base. It is a leader in cattle and hog production, and its main crops are grains. Tourism is a major industry; attractions include Mount RUSHMORE, and the WIND CAVE and BADLANDS national parks, and JEWEL CAVE NATIONAL MONUMENT.

South Dakota, University of Public university located in Vermillion. Established in 1862, its first classes were held in 1882. It is composed of a college of arts and sciences, a graduate school, a college of fine arts, and professional schools for law, medicine, education, and business. Research and academic units include the Institute of American Indian Studies and the Shrine to Music Museum and Center for Study of the History of Musical Instruments. Total enrollment is about 7,600.

South Georgia Mountainous, barren island, southern Atlantic Ocean. It is located 800 mi (1,300 km) east of the British FALKLAND ISLANDS, of which it is a dependency. With an Antarctic climate, it has perpetual snow covering three-fourths of the island. It is home to reindeer, several penguin and seal species, and abundant marine life. Capt. JAMES COOK claimed it for Britain in 1775, and ERNEST SHACKLETON first crossed it in 1916 while in search of aid for his ill-fated expedition; he died later on the island and was buried there. Formerly a whaling base, it is now the site of an Antarctic research station.

South Indian bronze Any of the cult images that rank among the finest achievements of Indian visual art. Most of the figures represent Hindu divinities, especially various iconographic forms of the god Shiva and Lord Vishnu, with their consorts and attendants. The images were produced in large numbers from the 8th to the 16th century, principally in the Thanjavur and Tiruchchirappalli districts of modern Tamil Nadu, and maintained a high standard of excellence for almost 1,000 years. The icons range from small household images to almost life-size sculptures intended to be carried in temple processions.

The god Shiva in the garb of a mendicant, South Indian bronze from Tiruvengadu, Tamil Nadu, early 11th century; in the Thanjavur Museum and Art Gallery, Tamil Nadu.
P. CHANDRA

South Island Island (pop., 2001 prelim.: 942,213), larger and southernmost of the two principal islands of New Zealand. Separated from NORTH ISLAND by COOK STRAIT, it has an area of 58,676 sq mi (151,971 sq km). Mountains, including the SOUTHERN ALPS, occupy almost three-quarters of the island. Its main cities are CHRISTCHURCH and Dunedin. FIORDLAND NATIONAL PARK in the southwest contains numerous coastal fjords and high lakes.

South Korea See KOREA, SOUTH

South Orkney Islands Island group, southern Atlantic Ocean, southeast of South America. Composed of two large islands (Coronation and Laurie) and many smaller islands, it forms part of the British Antarctic Territory. Barren and uninhabited, the islands have a total area of 240 sq mi (620 sq km). They were part of the FALKLAND ISLANDS Dependencies until 1962. Signy Island is used as a base for Antarctic exploration.

South Platte River River, Colorado and western Nebraska. It rises in central Colorado and flows southeast and then northeast across the Nebraska boundary to join the NORTH PLATTE RIVER and form the PLATTE RIVER. It is 442 mi (711 km) long. Its reservoirs and dams, particularly around DENVER, are used for flood control, irrigation, and power.

South Pole Southern extremity of the Earth's axis, located at 90°S latitude. It is the southern point from which all meridians of longitude start. The area around it is a lofty plateau in western central ANTARCTICA, with ice as much as 8,850 ft (2,700 m) thick. It has six months of complete daylight and six months of total darkness each year. It was first reached by the Norwegian explorer ROALD AMUNDSEN in 1911, one month before the expedition led by British explorer ROBERT FALCON SCOTT; U.S. explorer RICHARD E. BYRD flew to the pole in 1929. The geographic pole does not coincide with the magnetic South Pole, which lies on the Adélie Coast at about 66°00′ S, 139°06′ E; it moves about 8 mi (13 km) to the northwest each year. The geomagnetic South Pole also moves; during the early 1990s it was located at about 79°13′ S, 108°44′ E.

South Sea Bubble (1720) Speculation mania that caused financial ruin for many British investors. Parliament's acceptance of a proposal by the South Sea Co. to take over the British national debt resulted in an immediate rise in its stock. After soaring from 128½ to over 1,000 in nine months, the bubble of overvalued stock burst and the price per share dropped to 124, dragging other stocks down and leaving many investors ruined. An inquiry by the House of Commons found collusion by several government ministers.

South-West Africa See NAMIBIA

South-West Africa People's Organization (SWAPO) Party in S.-West Africa (now Namibia) that advocated immediate independence from South Africa. Founded in 1960, it used diplomacy to attain its goals until 1966, when it turned to armed struggle. Led by SAM NUJOMA and backed by the Angolan ruling party and the Soviet Union, SWAPO used Angola as a base for launching guerrilla attacks. From 1978, South Africa made periodic retaliatory strikes into Angola. That same year the U.N. recognized SWAPO as the Namibian people's sole representative. South Africa finally accepted a U.N. resolution requiring the withdrawal of South African troops in Namibia and the holding of free elections in 1988.

South Yorkshire Metropolitan county (pop., 1995 est. 1,304,000), northern central England. It lost its administrative functions in 1986, and now exists in name only; its administrative seat was BARNSLEY. It extends from the PENNINE moorlands in the west to lowland marshes in the east. The Romans built roads and forts in the area, and Anglian and later Scandinavian settlers cleared woodlands. In the 19th century the region grew as a major industrial area, and the Don valley became the focus of iron- and steelworks extending east from SHEFFIELD. Today South Yorkshire includes most of England's coalfields; its industries produce iron, steel, and cutlery.

Southeast Asia Vast region of Asia lying east of the Indian subcontinent and south of China. It includes the mainland area and a string of archipelagoes to the south and east, and is generally taken to include Myanmar, Thailand, Cambodia, Laos, Vietnam, Singapore, Malaysia, Indonesia, Brunei, and the Philippines.

Southeast Asia Treaty Organization (SEATO) Regional defense organization (1955–77) encompassing Australia, France, New Zealand, Pakistan, the Philippines, Thailand, Britain, and the U.S. It was founded as part of the S.East Asia Collective Defense Treaty in order to protect the region from communism. Vietnam, Cambodia, and Laos were not considered for membership, and other nations in the region preferred a policy of NONALIGNMENT. SEATO had no standing forces, but its members engaged in combined military exercises. Pakistan withdrew in 1968, and France suspended financial support in 1975. The organization was disbanded officially in 1977.

Southeast Asian architecture Buildings of Myanmar (Burma), Thailand, Laos, Cambodia, Vietnam, Malaysia, Singapore, Indonesia, and the Philippines. Most of S.East Asia's great temples were built by the 13th century. The Indian royal temple, which dominated S.East Asian culture, typically stood on a terraced PLINTH, upon which towered shrines could multiply. Construction was ideally of stone but could be brick sculpted with stucco. Exteriors displayed carved rhythmic moldings and figures. In c. 770 the Javanese Shailendra dynasty began its series of superb stonecut monuments, culminating in the huge Mahayana Buddhist BOROBUDUR and the Hindu Lara Jonggrang (c. 900–930). Around 800, the Cambodian king Jayavarman II built a brick mountain for a temple group. This plan was furthered when foundations were laid for Angkor, a scheme based on a grid of reservoirs and canals. Successive kings built more temple mountains there, culminating in ANGKOR WAT. Among S.East Asia's most impressive sites is the city of Pagan in Burma, with many brick and stucco Buddhist temples and STUPAS built 1056–1287. Burmese stupas (e.g., SHWE DAGON Pagoda) typically have a spreading, bell-shaped base topped by a dome and pointed spire. Burma and Thailand's many monasteries, like those of Laos and Vietnam, have been repeatedly enlarged and rebuilt. The architecture of the modified Hinduism of Bali is vigorously fantastical, with gilt paint and colored glass.

Southeast Asian arts Visual arts of Cambodia, Myanmar, Thailand, Vietnam, Laos, and Indonesia. The earliest arts of the region were wood carvings featuring supernatural and animal imagery developed and shared by the various tribal peoples. A second tradition emerged after Indian artists and artisans followed traders to S.East Asia in the first centuries AD. Within a short time, S.East Asians were producing their own distinctive local versions of Indian styles, sometimes rivaling Indian artists with their skill, finesse, and invention on a colossal scale. With the introduction of Hinduism and Buddhism, temple building, sculpture, and painting flourished from the 1st through the 13th century. Though affected by outside influences, the arts of S.East Asia retained a unique mix of fantasy and realism and an emphasis on the joyousness of human life.

Southeastern Indians Any AMERICAN INDIANS who inhabited what is now the southeastern U.S. Groups within this region included the CADDO, CATAWBA, CHEROKEE, CHICKASAW, CHOCTAW, CREEK, Natchez, and SEMINOLE.

Southend-on-Sea Resort (pop., 1994 est.: 166,000), Essex, southeastern England. It lies on the THAMES estuary and the NORTH SEA. The nearest seaside resort to LONDON, it attracts millions of visitors, and there are many resident commuters. It is noted for its 1.5-mi (2-km) pier as well as its beaches and gardens; yachting is popular. A 12th-century priory houses a museum.

Southern Alps Mountain range, SOUTH ISLAND, New Zealand. It extends almost the entire length of the island, and is the highest range in Australasia. It has elevations from 3,000 ft (900 m) to over 10,000 ft (3,050 m), culminating in Mount Cook at 12,349 ft (3,764 m) high. Glaciers descend from the permanently snow-clad top of the range. The range divides the island climatically: the forested western slopes and narrow coastal plain are much wetter than the eastern slopes and wide Canterbury Plains.

Southern California, University of (USC) Private university in Los Angeles, founded in 1880. It comprises a college of letters, arts, and sciences, a graduate school, and 18 professional schools. It offers undergraduate degrees in about 80 fields and graduate and professional degrees in about 125. It is especially well known for its programs in film, law, music, business, engineering, and social work. It operates more than 100 research institutes, including centers for the study of earthquakes, marine science, robotics and intelligent systems, and population. Its library contains a notable cinema collection. Total enrollment is about 28,000.

Southern Christian Leadership Conference (SCLC) U.S. nonsectarian agency founded by MARTIN LUTHER KING and others in 1957 to assist local organizations working for full equality of blacks. Operating primarily in the South, it conducted leadership-training programs, citizen-education projects, and voter-registration drives. It played a major role in the historic March on Washington in 1963 and in the campaigns to urge passage of the 1964 CIVIL RIGHTS ACT and the 1965 VOTING RIGHTS ACT. After King's assassination in 1968, RALPH ABERNATHY became president. The SCLC split in 1971 when JESSE JACKSON founded Operation PUSH in Chicago.

Southey \'sau̇-thē, 'sə-thē\, **Robert** (1774–1843) English poet and prose writer. In youth Southey ardently embraced the ideals of the French Revolution, as did SAMUEL TAYLOR COLERIDGE, with whom he was associated from 1794. Like Coleridge, he gradually became more conservative. Around 1799 he devoted himself to writing; later he was obliged to produce unremittingly to support both his and Coleridge's family. In 1813 he was appointed poet laureate. His poetry is now little read, but his prose style is masterly in its ease and clarity, as seen in such works as *Life of Nelson* (1813), *Life of Wesley* (1820), and *The Doctor* (1834–47), a fantastic, rambling miscellany.

Southampton City (pop., 1999: 215,000) and ENGLISH CHANNEL port, HAMPSHIRE, England. First settled by Romans, it was chartered (c. 1155) by King HENRY II and incorporated in 1445. In the Middle Ages it became a major British port. It declined in the 17th–18th century but revived in the 19th with the arrival of railways. Today it is England's second-largest port. Historic buildings include the 11th-century St. Michael's Church and the 12th-century King John's Palace, one of Britain's oldest domestic buildings.

Southampton, 1st Earl of *orig.* **Thomas Wriothesley** \'rät-slē, 'rī-əth-slē\ (1505–1550) English politician. He followed his father, a herald, into royal service and became personal secretary to THOMAS CROMWELL (1533), whom he succeeded as a secretary of state to HENRY VIII (1540). Wriothesley became one of Henry's leading councillors and was appointed lord chancellor of England (1544–47). After Henry's death, he was created earl of Southampton (1547) by the duke of SOMERSET but then deprived of the chancellorship. He supported Somerset's overthrow in 1549, but was excluded from the privy council in 1550.

Southampton, 3rd Earl of *orig.* **Henry Wriothesley** (1573–1624) English nobleman, patron of WILLIAM SHAKESPEARE. Grandson of the 1st earl of SOUTHAMPTON, he became a favorite of ELIZABETH I. He was a liberal patron of writers, including THOMAS NASHE. Shakespeare dedicated two long poems to him (1593, 1594), and he has often been identified as the noble youth addressed in most of Shakespeare's sonnets. He accompanied the 2nd earl of ESSEX on expeditions to Cádiz and the Azores (1596, 1597). For supporting the Essex rebellion (1601), he was imprisoned 1601–3; following JAMES I's accession, he regained his place at court. He became a privy councillor in 1619, but lost favor by opposing the 1st duke of BUCKINGHAM. He and his son volunteered to fight for the United Provinces against Spain, but soon after landing in the Netherlands they both died of fever.

Southampton Island Island, Keewatin region, Nunavut. Lying at the entrance to HUDSON BAY, it is roughly triangular and has an area of 15,913 sq mi (41,214 sq km). Its plateau in the northeast, with 1,000-ft (300-m) coastal cliffs, gradually slopes to lowlands in the south. Its coastal waters are noted for Arctic char fishing.

Southwest Indians Any AMERICAN INDIANS who inhabit what is now the southwestern U.S. The Southwest Indians divide roughly into four groupings: the YUMAN tribes, the PIMA and PAPAGO, the PUEBLO, and the NAVAJO and APACHE.

Soutine \sü-'tēn\, **Chaim** (1893–1943) Russian-French painter. After studying art in Vilnius, he went to Paris in 1913 to study at the École des Beaux-Arts. An art dealer enabled him to paint for three years in southern France, where his mature style emerged. Though a form of Expressionism, it is a highly individualistic style, characterized by thick impasto, agitated brushwork, convulsive compositional rhythms, and disturbing psychological content. Best known are his studies of choirboys and cooks, his series of pageboys, and his paintings of hung poultry and beef carcasses, which vividly convey the color and luminosity of putrescence.

Souvanna Phouma \sü-'vä-nä-'pü-mä\ (1901–1984) Premier of Laos (1951–54, 1960, 1962, 1974–75). Nephew of King Sisavangvong of Laos, Souvanna did not support his uncle's decision to welcome back French rule after the end of World War II. With his half brother SOUPHA-

NOUVONG, he joined the Free Laos movement and went into exile when the French reoccupied Laos. In 1949, when the French began to concede authority, he returned, and in 1951 he began his first stint as premier. Civil war broke out between the communist Pathet Lao and rightist members of government; Souvanna served as premier sporadically during that period. He tried to maintain Laotian neutrality during the VIETNAM WAR, but came to depend on U.S. military aid; Laos stabilized after the U.S. withdrawal from Vietnam. Souvanna remained an adviser to the government until his death.

Sovereign Council Administrative body that governed the colony of NEW FRANCE in Canada (1663–1702). It consisted of the governor and the bishop, who chose the additional five council members, an attorney general, and a clerk. The council named judges and minor officials, controlled public funds and commerce with France, and regulated the fur trade with the Indians. Decisions were subject to the governor's veto. From 1685 the intendant, a French administrative official, assumed many of the council's duties. The council was renamed the Superior Council in 1702.

sovereignty In political theory, the ultimate authority, in the decision-making process of the state and in the maintenance of order. In 16th-century France, JEAN BODIN used the concept of sovereignty to bolster the power of the king over his feudal lords, heralding the transition from feudalism to nationalism. By the end of the 18th century, the concept of the SOCIAL CONTRACT led to the idea of popular sovereignty, sovereignty by the people through an organized government. The HAGUE CONVENTIONS, the GENEVA CONVENTIONS, and the UNITED NATIONS all put restrictions on the powers of sovereign nations in the international arena, as does INTERNATIONAL LAW.

soviet Council that represented the primary unit of government in the Soviet Union. The first soviet was formed in St. Petersburg during the RUSSIAN REVOLUTION OF 1905 to coordinate revolutionary activities, but was suppressed. Socialist leaders formed the second soviet shortly before the abdication of NICHOLAS II, with one deputy for every 1,000 workers and every military company. After the RUSSIAN REVOLUTION OF 1917, the BOLSHEVIKS gradually gained a dominant position in soviets across the land. In 1918 a new constitution established soviets as the formal unit of local and regional government. The 1936 constitution created a directly elected bicameral Supreme Soviet, but the single candidate per district was chosen by the Communist Party.

Soviet law Law that developed in the Soviet Union after the RUSSIAN REVOLUTION OF 1917 and that, after World War II, was assimilated by other communist states. Legislative enactments, including the constitution of the U.S.S.R., were the principal sources of law in the Soviet legal system; these were then elaborated in codes of statutes by each union republic. No distinction between public and private law existed; all legal matters involved the state. Law was generally thought of as a force for restructuring society and advancing the nation toward COMMUNISM. Also known as socialist law, it was based on the writings of KARL MARX and FRIEDRICH ENGELS. In addition to criminal and civil offenses, "administrative offenses" constituted a large proportion of cases and were dealt with outside the court system.

Soviet Union See UNION OF SOVIET SOCIALIST REPUBLICS

sow bug \'saů\ *or* **wood louse** Any of certain terrestrial CRUSTACEANS of the order Isopoda, especially members of the genus *Oniscus*. Native to Europe, they have been introduced into North America. Sow bugs grow to 0.7 in. (18 mm) long. The oval, gray body is rather arched and is covered with broad, armorlike plates. Two elbowed antennae extend about half the length of the body, and there are seven pairs of limbs. The sow bug lives in moist places, especially under stones, in moist leaf litter, and in cellars. See also PILL BUG.

Sow bug (*Oniscus asellus*).
HUGH SPENCER

Soweto \sə-'wā-tō\ Township (pop., 1991 597,000), northeastern Republic of South Africa. It adjoins JOHANNESBURG on the southwest, and its name is an acronym derived from South-Western Townships. It was originally set aside by the South African white government for residence by blacks. The townships constituting Soweto grew out of shantytowns that arose with the arrival of black laborers from rural areas, especially between the World Wars. There is little industrial development; most of Soweto's residents commute to Johannesburg for employment. It is the country's largest black urban complex, and its residents were active in the protests that helped bring an end to APARTHEID by 1991.

Soya Strait *or* **La Pérouse Strait** \,lä-pā-'rüz\ International waterway between the Russian island of SAKHALIN and the Japanese island of HOKKAIDO. The strait, named after the French explorer comte de La Pérouse, separates the Sea of OKHOTSK from the Sea of JAPAN. It is 27 mi (43 km) wide at its narrowest part, and varies in depth from 167 to 387 ft (51 to 118 m). Noted for its extremely strong currents, it is closed by ice in the winter.

soybean Annual legume *(Glycine max,* or *G. soja)* of the pea family (see LEGUME) and its edible seed. The soybean plant has an erect, branching stem, white to purple flowers, and one to four seeds per pod. It was probably derived from a wild plant of East Asia, where it has been cultivated for some 5,000 years. Introduced into the U.S. in 1804, it began to be farmed widely as a livestock feed in the 1930s, and the U.S. is now the world's foremost soybean producer. Economically the world's most important BEAN, the soybean provides vegetable protein for millions of people and ingredients for hundreds of chemical products, including paints, adhesives, fertilizers, insect sprays, and fire-extinguisher fluids. Because soybeans contain no starch, they are a good source of protein for diabetics. Processed for food, soybean oil is made into margarine, shortening, and vegetarian cheeses and meats. Soybean meal serves as a high-protein meat substitute in many food products, including baby foods. Other food products include soybean milk, TOFU, salad sprouts, and soy sauce.

Soybeans (*Glycine max*).
J.C. ALLEN AND SON

Soyinka \shȯ-'yiŋ-kä\, **Wole** *orig.* **Akinwande Oluwole** (born 1934) Nigerian playwright. After studying in Leeds, England, he returned to Nigeria to edit literary journals, teach drama and literature at the university level, and found two theater companies. His plays, written in English and drawing on West African folk traditions, often focus on the tensions between tradition and progress. They include *A Dance of the Forests* (1960), *The Lion and the Jewel* (1963), *Death and the King's Horseman* (1975), and *From Zia, with Love* (1992). He has written several volumes of poetry; his best-known novel is *The Interpreters* (1965). A champion of Nigerian democracy, he has been repeatedly jailed and exiled. In 1986 he became the first African to be awarded the Nobel Prize for Literature.

Soyinka.
VERNON L. SMITH

Soyuz \sȯ-'yüz\ Any of a series of 40 Soviet spacecraft launched 1967–81. Soyuz 1 through Soyuz 10, carrying crews of one to three men, were launched into earth orbit. Most of the remaining 30 Soyuz flights involved the docking of a Soyuz capsule with an orbiting SALYUT space station and the transfer of its crew onto the space laboratory to conduct experiments for an extended period.

spa Spring or resort with thermal or mineral water for drinking and bathing. The word derives from a Belgian town whose springs reputedly had curative powers. Mineral springs usually contain various salts, trace minerals, and gases; many are naturally carbonated. Most thermal springs (see HOT SPRING) also contain minerals. Warm-water bathing aids relaxation (see HYDROTHERAPY), and high salt or sulfur content helps some skin conditions. Drinking mineral water is believed to aid digestion, and waters with specific minerals are used for particular conditions.

Spaak \'späk\, **Paul-Henri** (1899–1972) Belgian statesman. After practicing law 1921–31, he became a socialist member of the Chamber of Deputies in 1932. For most of the period 1936–66 he served as Belgium's foreign minister, and he twice served as its premier (1938–39, 1947–50). An advocate of European cooperation, he helped form the BENELUX ECONOMIC UNION (1944) and helped draft the U.N. charter, and in 1946 he served as the U.N. General Assembly's first president. He signed the BRUSSELS TREATY, helped form NATO, and served as NATO's secretary-general 1957–61. He also helped create the EUROPEAN ECONOMIC COMMUNITY and the EUROPEAN ATOMIC ENERGY COMMUNITY.

Spaatz \'späts\, **Carl (Andrews)** *orig.* **Carl Andrews Spatz** (1891–1974) U.S. air-force officer. Born in Boyertown, Pa., he flew as a combat pilot during World War I. During World War II he commanded the U.S. Strategic Air Forces in Europe (1944), directing the strategic bombing of Germany. In 1945, though personally opposed to using atomic bombs against cities, he directed the final bombing of Japan under orders of Pres. HARRY TRUMAN. In 1947 he became the first chief of staff of the independent Air Force.

space contraction See LORENTZ-FITZGERALD CONTRACTION

space exploration Investigation of the universe beyond earth's atmosphere by means of manned and unmanned SPACECRAFT. Study of the use of ROCKETS for spaceflight began early in the 20th century. Germany's research on rocket propulsion in the 1930s led to development of the V-2 MISSILE. After World War II, the U.S. and the Soviet Union, with the aid of relocated German scientists, competed in the "space race," making substantial progress in high-altitude rocket technology (see STAGED ROCKET). Both launched their first SATELLITES (see SPUTNIK, EXPLORER) in the late 1950s (followed by other satellites and unmanned lunar probes) and their first manned space vehicles (see VOSTOK, MERCURY) in 1961. A succession of longer and more complex manned space missions followed, most notably the U.S. APOLLO program, including the first manned lunar landing in 1969, and the Soviet SOYUZ and SALYUT missions. Beginning in the 1960s, U.S. and Soviet scientists also launched unmanned deep-space probes for studies of the planets and other solar system objects (see PIONEER, VENERA, VIKING, VOYAGER, GALILEO), and earth-orbiting astronomical observatories (see, for example, HUBBLE SPACE TELESCOPE), which permitted observation of cosmic objects from above the filtering and distorting effects of earth's atmosphere. In the 1970s and '80s the Soviet Union concentrated on the development of SPACE STATIONS for scientific research and military reconnaissance (see SALYUT, MIR). After the dissolution of the Soviet Union in 1991, Russia continued its space program, but on a reduced basis owing to economic constraints. In 1973 the U.S. launched its own space station (see SKYLAB), and since the mid-1970s it has devoted much of its manned space efforts to the SPACE SHUTTLE program and, more recently, to developing the INTERNATIONAL SPACE STATION in collaboration with Russia and other countries.

space frame Three-dimensional TRUSS based on the rigidity of the triangle and composed of linear elements subject only to compression or tension. Its simplest spatial unit is a tetrahedron having four joints and six members. A space frame forms a very strong, thick, flexible structural fabric that can be used horizontally or bent to a variety of shapes. The beauty of its open latticework web of lightweight tubular diagonals is only surpassed by its structural purity. R. BUCKMINSTER FULLER used this technology for some of his Dymaxion projects; in his Union Tank Car warehouse, Baton Rouge, La. (1958), a space frame reinforces an enormous geodesic dome.

space shuttle *formally* **Space Transportation System (STS)** Partially reusable rocket-launched vehicle developed by NASA to go into earth orbit, transport people and cargo between earth and orbiting spacecraft, and glide to a runway landing on earth. The first flight of a space shuttle into orbit took place in 1981. The shuttle consists of a winged orbiter that carries crew and cargo; an expendable external tank of liquid fuel and oxidizer for the orbiter's three main rocket engines; and two large, reusable solid-propellant booster rockets. The orbiter lifts off vertically like an expendable launch vehicle but makes an unpowered de-

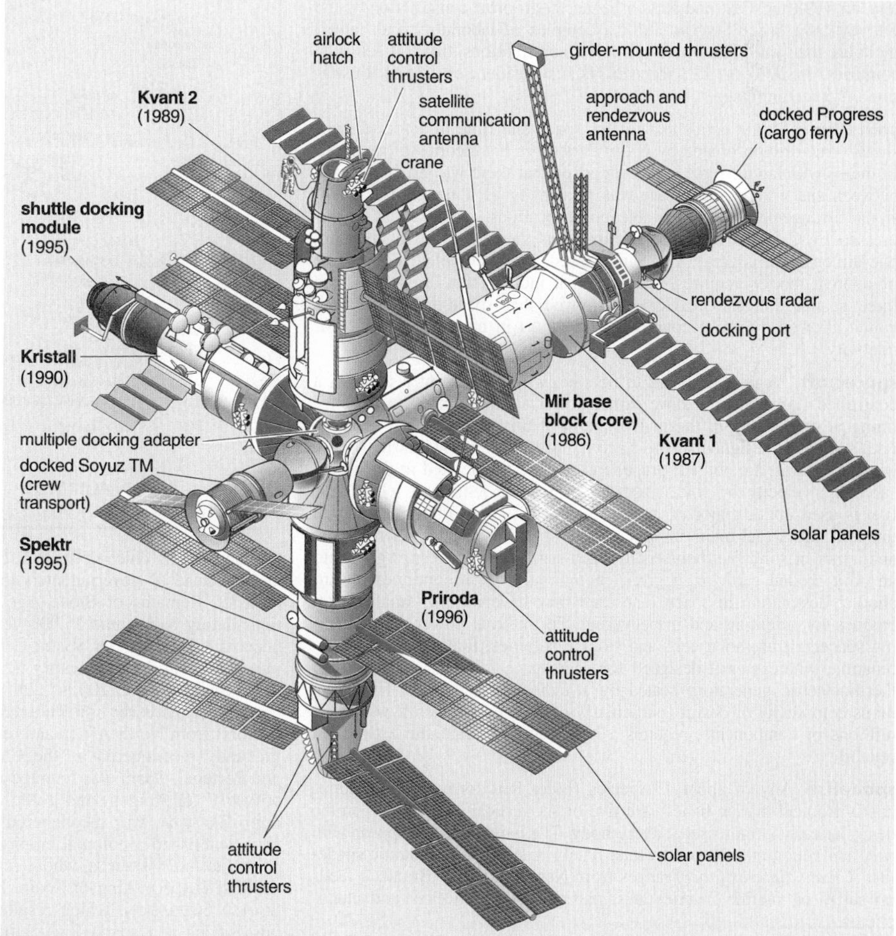

Modules and other components of space station Mir. The multiple docking adapter connected several modules together and allowed Soyuz spacecraft to dock with the station. The airlock allowed cosmonauts to exit Mir to work outside. Solar panels provided power. Date in parenthesis for each module is the year launched.

scent similar to a glider. Each orbiter was designed to be reused up to 100 times. For manipulating cargo and other materials outside the orbiter, astronauts use a remotely controlled robot arm or exit the orbiter wearing spacesuits. On some missions, the shuttle carries a European-built pressurized research facility called Spacelab in its cargo bay. Between 1981 and 1985, four shuttle orbiters were put into service: *Columbia* (the first in orbit), *Challenger, Discovery,* and *Atlantis.* CHALLENGER exploded in 1986, killing all seven astronauts aboard; it was replaced in 1992 by *Endeavour.* In 1995–98, NASA conducted shuttle missions to the Russian space station MIR to prepare for the construction of the INTERNATIONAL SPACE STATION (ISS). Beginning in 1998, the shuttle was used extensively to ferry components, supplies, and crews to the ISS.

space station Manned artificial structure designed to revolve in a fixed orbit as a long-term base for astronomical observations, study of the earth's resources and environment, military reconnaissance, and investigations of materials and biological systems in weightless conditions. As of 2001, nine space stations have been placed in a low earth orbit and occupied for varying lengths of time. The Soviet Union orbited the world's first space station, Salyut 1 (see SALYUT), designed for scientific studies, in 1971. From 1974 to 1982 five more Salyut stations—two outfitted for military reconnaissance—were successfully placed in orbit and occupied. In 1986 the U.S.S.R. launched the core module of MIR, a scientific station that was expanded with five additional modules over the next decade. The U.S. orbited its first space station in 1973; called SKYLAB, it was equipped as a solar observatory and medical laboratory. In 1998 the U.S. and Russia began the in-orbit construction of the INTERNATIONAL SPACE STATION (ISS), a complex of laboratory and habitat modules that would ultimately involve contributions from at least 16 countries. In 2000 the ISS received its first resident crew. See illustration on preceding page.

space-time Single entity that relates space and time in a four-dimensional structure, postulated by ALBERT EINSTEIN in his theories of RELATIVITY. In the Newtonian universe it was supposed that there was no connection between space and time. Space was thought to be a flat, three-dimensional arrangement of all possible point locations, which could be expressed by Cartesian coordinates; time was viewed as an independent one-dimensional concept. Einstein showed that a complete description of relative motion requires equations that include time as well as the three spatial dimensions. He also showed that space-time is curved, which allowed him to account for GRAVITATION in his general theory of relativity.

spacecraft Vehicle designed to operate, with or without a crew, in a controlled flight pattern above earth's lower atmosphere. Since streamlining is not needed in the high vacuum of this environment, a spacecraft's shape is designed according to its mission (see SPACE EXPLORATION). Most spacecraft are not self-propelled; they are accelerated to the necessary high velocity by STAGED ROCKETS, which are jettisoned when their fuel is used up. A major exception, the SPACE SHUTTLE orbiter, uses three onboard liquid-fuel main engines supplied by a disposable external tank and a pair of solid-fuel boosters to reach space. The spacecraft goes into an orbit around earth or, if given enough velocity, it continues toward another destination in space. The craft may have its own small rocket engines for orienting and maneuvering. For internal power, earth-orbiting spacecraft use solar cells and storage batteries, fuel cells, or a combination, whereas craft designed for deep-space missions usually carry thermoelectric generators heated by a radioactive element. The enormous complexity of design, particularly of manned spacecraft with their millions of components, requires a high degree of miniaturization and reliability.

spadefish Any of about 17 species (order Perciformes) of predominantly tropical marine fishes with five or six vertical black bands on the deep, laterally compressed, silvery body. The bands may disappear with age, and adults may be solid white, black, or silver. The Atlantic spadefish *(Chaetodipterus faber)* ranges from New England to Brazil. It feeds primarily on marine invertebrates, particularly crustaceans and ctenophores.

Spagnuolo, Pietro See Pedro BERRUGUETE

Spahn, Warren (Edward) (born 1921) U.S. baseball pitcher. Born in Buffalo, N.Y., he spent most of his career with the Boston (later Milwaukee) Braves (1942, 1946–64). He amassed 2,583 career strikeouts, giving him the third-highest total in baseball history when he retired. His feat of winning 20 or more games in each of 13 seasons was also a record, as was his striking out at least 100 batters each year for 17 consecutive seasons (1947–63). His total of 363 wins established a record for left-handers.

Spain *officially* **Kingdom of Spain** *Spanish* **España** Country, southwestern Europe. One of Europe's largest countries, it is located on the IBERIAN PENINSULA; it also includes the BALEARIC and CANARY islands. Area: 195,364 sq mi (505,990 sq km). Population (2000 est.): 40,128,000. Capital: MADRID. The people are predominantly Spanish, though there are populations of BASQUES, Catalans, and GYPSIES (Roma). Languages: Castilian Spanish (official), Catalan, Galician, and Basque. Religions: Roman Catholicism (two-thirds), Islam. Monetary unit: euro. Spain's large central plateau is surrounded by the EBRO RIVER valley, the mountainous CATALONIA region, the Mediterranean coastal region of VALENCIA, the GUADALQUIVIR RIVER valley, and the mountainous region extending from the PYRENEES to the Atlantic coast. It has a developed market economy based on services, light and heavy industries, and agriculture. Mineral resources include iron ore, mercury, and coal; agricultural products include grains and livestock. Spain is one of the world's major producers of wine. Tourism is also a major industry, especially along the southern Costa del Sol. It is a constitutional monarchy with two legislative houses. Its chief of state is the king, and the head of government is the prime minister. Remains of Stone Age populations dating back some 35,000 years have been found throughout Spain. Celtic peoples arrived in the 9th century BC, followed by the Romans, who dominated Spain from c. 200 BC until the Visigoth invasion in the early 5th century. In the early 8th century most of the peninsula fell to Muslims (Moors) from North Africa and remained under their control until it was gradually reconquered by the Christian kingdoms of CASTILE, ARAGON, and Portugal. Spain was reunited in 1479 following the marriage of FERDINAND V (of Aragon) and ISABELLA I (of Castile). The last Muslim kingdom, GRANADA, was reconquered in 1492, and around this time Spain also established a colonial empire in the Americas. In 1516 the throne passed to the HABSBURGS, whose rule ended in 1700 when PHILIP V became the first BOURBON king of Spain. His ascendancy caused the War of the SPANISH SUCCESSION, which resulted in the loss of numerous European possessions and sparked revolution within most of Spain's American colonies. It lost its remaining overseas possessions to the U.S. in the SPANISH-AMERICAN WAR (1898) (see CUBA, GUAM, PHILIPPINES, PUERTO RICO). Spain became a republic in 1931. The SPANISH CIVIL WAR (1936–39) ended in victory for the Nationalists under General FRANCISCO FRANCO, who ruled as dictator until his death in 1975. His successor as head of state,

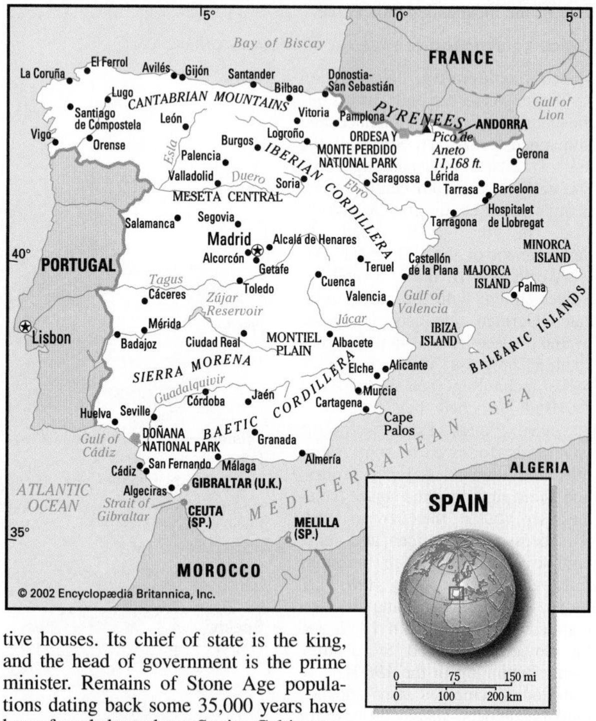

JUAN CARLOS I, restored the monarchy upon his accession to the throne; a new constitution in 1978 established a parliamentary monarchy. Spain joined NATO in 1982 and the EUROPEAN COMMUNITY in 1986. The 1992 quincentennial of CHRISTOPHER COLUMBUS's first voyage from Spain to the Americas was marked by a fair in SEVILLE and the staging of the OLYMPIC GAMES in BARCELONA. In the 1990s Spain developed closer ties to other European countries but continued to suffer internally as Basque separatists pressed their claims for independence.

Spalatin \'spä-lə-tən\, **Georg** *orig.* **Georg Burkhardt** (1484–1545) German humanist. He studied at the University of Erfurt and joined a band of humanist scholars in 1505. Ordained a priest in 1508, he was appointed tutor to the heir of Frederick the Wise, elector of Saxony. In 1511 he befriended MARTIN LUTHER at Wittenberg, and as librarian at Frederick's court from 1512 he influenced the elector to protect Luther during the controversy over indulgences. He championed the Reformation at the Diet of WORMS (1521) and under two subsequent electors of Saxony. In 1530 he helped PHILIPP MELANCHTHON prepare the text of the AUGSBURG CONFESSION. He was also influential in forming the SCHMALKALDIC LEAGUE in 1531. His many historical works include *Annals of the Reformation* (1718).

Spalding, A(lbert) G(oodwill) (1850–1915) U.S. baseball player, executive, and sporting-goods manufacturer. Born in Byron, Ill., he played with the Boston Red Stockings and later the Chicago White Stockings, which he later served as president (1882–91). In 1876 he and his brother founded, in Chicopee, Mass., the firm that, as A. G. Spalding & Bros., would become one of the premier American sporting-goods companies. He founded the annual *Spalding's Official Baseball Guide*, and wrote the history *America's National Game* (1911). He was elected to the Baseball Hall of Fame in 1939.

spandrel Roughly triangular area on either side of an ARCH, bounded by a line running horizontally through its apex, a line rising vertically from the springing of the arch, and the exterior curve of the arch. When arches adjoin, the entire area between their crowns and springing line is a spandrel. If filled in, as is ordinarily the case, the result is a spandrel wall; in medieval architecture this was usually ornamented. In buildings of more than one story, the spandrel is the area between the sill of a window and the head of the window below it. In steel or reinforced-concrete structures, a deep spandrel beam may span across this area. The triangular area of space beneath a stair is also known as a spandrel.

spaniel Any of several breeds of dogs used to flush game. Spaniels originated in Spain, but most modern breeds were developed in Britain. Breeds range from 14 to 20 in. (36–51 cm) and from 22 to 55 lbs (10–25 kg). The larger breeds are called springers, the smaller ones cockers. Breeds include the cocker spaniel, a round-headed, floppy-eared dog; the English and Welsh springer spaniels; the American water spaniel, a curly-coated, dark brown dog; the Brittany spaniel, a short-tailed French dog and the only spaniel that points; the Clumber spaniel, a low-slung, long-bodied dog; the Irish water spaniel, a water retriever; the Japanese spaniel; and the English toy spaniel.

Cocker spaniel.
SALLY ANNE THOMPSON

Spanish-American War (1898) Conflict between the U.S. and Spain that ended Spanish colonial rule in the New World. The war originated in Cuba's struggle for independence. The newspapers of WILLIAM RANDOLPH HEARST fanned U.S. sympathy for the rebels, which increased after the unexplained destruction of the *MAINE*. Congress passed resolutions declaring Cuba's right to independence and demanding that Spain withdraw its armed forces. Spain declared war on the U.S. in 1898. Commodore GEORGE DEWEY led the naval squadron that defeated the Spanish fleet in the Philippines (see Battle of MANILA BAY), and Gen. William Shafter led regular troops and volunteers (including THEODORE ROOSEVELT and his ROUGH RIDERS) in the destruction of Spain's Caribbean fleet near Santiago, Cuba (July 17, 1898). In the Treaty of Paris (December 10, 1898), Spain renounced all claim to Cuba and ceded Guam, Puerto Rico, and the Philippines to the U.S., marking the U.S.'s emergence as a world power.

Spanish Armada See Spanish ARMADA

Spanish Civil War (1936–39) Military revolt against the government of Spain. After the 1936 elections produced a Popular Front government supported mainly by left-wing parties, a military uprising began in garrison towns throughout Spain, led by the rebel Nationalists and supported by conservative elements in the clergy, military, and landowners as well as the fascist FALANGE. The ruling Republican government, led by the socialist premiers FRANCISCO LARGO CABALLERO and Juan Negrín (1894–1956) and the liberal president MANUEL AZANA Y DIAZ, was supported by workers and many in the educated middle class as well as militant anarchists and communists. Government forces put down the uprising in most regions except parts of northwestern and southwestern Spain, where the Nationalists held control and named FRANCISCO FRANCO head of state. Both sides repressed opposition; together, they executed or assassinated over 50,000 suspected enemies to their respective causes. Seeking aid from abroad, the Nationalists received troops, tanks, and planes from Nazi Germany and Italy, which used Spain as a testing ground for new methods of tank and air warfare. The Republicans (also called Loyalists) were sent matériel mainly by the Soviet Union, and the volunteer INTERNATIONAL BRIGADES also joined the Republicans. The two sides fought fierce and bloody skirmishes in a war of attrition. The Nationalist side gradually gained territory and by April 1938 succeeded in splitting Spain from east to west, causing 250,000 Republican forces to flee into France. In March 1939 the remaining Republican forces surrendered, and Madrid, beset by civil strife between communists and anti-communists, fell to the Nationalists on March 28. About 500,000 people died in the war, and all Spaniards were deeply scarred by the trauma. The war's end brought a period of dictatorship that lasted almost until Franco's death in 1975.

Spanish Guinea See EQUATORIAL GUINEA

Spanish Influenza Epidemic See INFLUENZA EPIDEMIC OF 1918–19

Spanish Inquisition See INQUISITION

Spanish language ROMANCE LANGUAGE spoken in Spain and in large parts of the New World. It has more than 332 million speakers, including over 23 million in the U.S. Its earliest written materials date from the 10th century, its first literary works from c. 1150. The Castilian dialect, the source of modern standard Spanish, arose in the 9th century in northern central Spain (Old Castile) and spread to central Spain (New Castile) by the 11th century. In the late 15th century the kingdoms of Castile, León, and Aragon merged, and Castilian became the official language of all Spain, with CATALAN and Galician (effectively a dialect of PORTUGUESE) becoming regional languages and Aragonese and Leonese reduced to a fraction of their original speech areas. Latin-American regional dialects are derived from Castilian but differ from it in PHONOLOGY. Spanish has almost completely lost the case system of Latin. Nouns and adjectives show masculine or feminine gender, and the verb system is generally regular, but complex.

Spanish Main Northern coast of South America roughly between the Isthmus of PANAMA and the delta of the ORINOCO RIVER when it was under Spanish control. The term also refers to the Caribbean Sea and adjacent waters, especially at the time the region was infested by pirates.

Spanish Mission style See MISSION STYLE

Spanish moss EPIPHYTE *(Tillandsia usneoides)* in the PINEAPPLE family, found in southern North America, the West Indies, and Central and South America. It often hangs in large, beardlike, silvery-gray masses from trees and other plants and even on telephone poles, but it is not parasitic or structurally intertwined with its host. It takes in carbon dioxide and rainwater or dew for PHOTOSYNTHESIS through tiny, hairlike scales that cover its threadlike leaves and long, threadlike stems. It absorbs nutrients from dust and solvents in rainwater, or from decaying organic matter around its aerial roots. Stalkless yellow flowers appear rarely. Spanish moss is sometimes used as a filler in packing boxes and upholstery, and around potted plants or floral arrangements.

Spanish Netherlands Spanish-held provinces in the southern Low Countries (roughly corresponding to modern Belgium and Luxembourg). In 1578 the diplomat ALESSANDRO FARNESE was sent to represent Spain in the Netherlands, and by 1585 he had reestablished Spanish control over the southern provinces, ending the union with the northern provinces that followed the Pacification of GHENT. In the 17th century the region saw a resurgence of economic and intellectual growth. As a buffer between Protestant and Catholic states, the region was the scene of constant warfare; areas were ceded to the Dutch Republic (1648) and France (1659). The territory began to decline in the late 17th century. Spanish control was lost after the War of the Spanish Succession, when the region passed to Emperor Charles VI and became the Austrian Netherlands.

Spanish Sahara See Western Sahara

Spanish Succession, War of the (1701–14) Conflict arising from the disputed succession to the throne of Spain after the death of the childless Charles II. The Habsburg Charles had named the Bourbon Philip, duc d'Anjou, as his successor; when Philip took the Spanish throne as Philip V, his grandfather Louis XIV invaded the Spanish Netherlands. The former anti-French alliance from the War of the Grand Alliance was revived in 1701 by Britain, the Dutch Republic, and the Holy Roman emperor, who had been promised parts of the Spanish empire by earlier treaties of partition (1698, 1699). The English forces, led by the duke of Marlborough, won a series of victories over France (1704–9), including the Battle of Blenheim, that forced the French out of the Low Countries and Italy. The imperial general, Eugene of Savoy, also won notable victories. In 1711 conflicts within the alliance led to its collapse, and peace negotiations began in 1712. The war concluded with the Peace of Utrecht (1713), which marked the rise of the power of Britain at the expense of both France and Spain, and the Treaties of Rastatt and Baden (1714).

spanner See wrench

Spark, Muriel (Sarah) *orig.* **Muriel Camberg** (born 1918) British writer. She spent several years in Central Africa, returning to Britain during World War II. Until 1957 she published only poetry and criticism, including studies of Mary Shelley and the Brontë family. Her fiction uses satire and wit to present serious themes, often questions about good and evil. *Memento Mori* (1959) is her most widely praised novel; the best known is *The Prime of Miss Jean Brodie* (1961; film, 1969). Her later novels, often more sinister in tone, include *The Abbess of Crewe* (1974), *A Far Cry from Kensington* (1988), and *Reality and Dreams* (1997).

spark plug Device that fits into the cylinder head of an internal-combustion engine and carries two electrodes separated by an air gap, across which current from a high-tension ignition system discharges, creating a spark and igniting the fuel. The electrodes and the insulator separating them must withstand high temperatures, as well as an electric stress of up to several thousand volts. Spark-gap length affects the energy of the spark, and the shape of the insulator affects the temperature of operation.

sparrow Any of numerous species of small, chiefly seed-eating songbirds having a conical bill, particularly members of the Old World family Ploceidae, the house sparrow, and most members of the New World family Fringillidae. Some species of Fringillidae are common. The trim-looking chipping and tree sparrows have a reddish brown cap. The finely streaked savanna and vesper sparrows inhabit grassy fields. The heavily streaked song and fox sparrows are woodland dwellers. The white-crowned and white-throated sparrows are larger than most species and have black-and-white crown stripes.

White-throated sparrow (*Zonotrichia albicollis*).
WILLIAM D. GRIFFIN

sparrow hawk Small hawk (usually genus *Accipiter*, family Accipitridae), found in Africa, Europe, and Asia. Sparrow hawks are gray above, barred-white below, and sometimes have white tail bars. They eat insects and small birds and mammals. The American kestrel is also called sparrow hawk.

Sparta *or* **Lacedaemon** \ˌla-sə-ˈdē-mən\ Ancient Greek city-state, capital of Laconia and chief city of the Peloponnese. Of Dorian origin, it was founded in the 9th century BC and developed as a strictly militaristic society. In the 8th–5th century BC, it subdued neighboring Messenia. From the 5th century, the ruling class of Sparta devoted itself to war, and forged the most powerful army in Greece. After a long contest with Athens in the Peloponnesian War (460–404 BC), it attained hegemony over all of Greece. Sparta's power was broken by Thebes at the battle of Leuctra in 371 BC. It lost its independence c. 192 BC when it was defeated by and forced to join the Achaean League. It was made part of the Roman province of Achaea in 146 BC. The Visigoths captured and destroyed the city in AD 396. The ruins of its acropolis, agora, theater, and temples remain.

Spartacists \ˈspär-tə-səsts\ *or* **Spartacus League** Revolutionary socialist group active in Germany (1914–18). It developed as an offshoot of the Social Democratic Party and was officially founded in 1916 by Karl Liebknecht, Rosa Luxemburg, and others who violently opposed Germany's role in World War I and called for a socialist revolution. The group encouraged demonstrations in December 1918 that led to the abortive Spartacus Revolt in January 1919, after which the leaders were murdered by members of the Freikorps. The league was then transformed into the Communist Party of Germany.

Spartacus \ˈspär-tə-kəs\ (died 71 BC) Leader in the Gladiatorial War against Rome (73–71). A Thracian, he served in the Roman army. He became a bandit, and was sold as a slave when caught. He escaped a gladiatorial school, where he had plotted a revolt with other gladiators, and set up camp on Mount Vesuvius, where he was joined by other runaway slaves and some peasants. With a force of 90,000, he overran most of southern Italy, defeating two consuls (72). He led his army north to the Cisalpine Gaul, where he hoped to release them to find freedom, but they refused to leave, preferring to continue the struggle. Returning south, he attempted to invade Sicily but could not arrange the passage. Marcus Licinius Crassus' legions caught the slave army in Lucania and defeated it; Spartacus fell in pitched battle. Pompey's army intercepted and killed many of those escaping north, and Crassus crucified 6,000 prisoners along the Appian Way.

Spartan Alliance See Peloponnesian League

Spassky, Boris (Vasilyevich) (born 1937) Soviet chess master. Born in Leningrad (now St. Petersburg), he attained the rank of international grand master in 1955. After a period of intermittent involvement with chess, he beat Tigran Petrosyan for the world title in 1969. In 1972 he lost it to Bobby Fischer.

spatial disorientation Inability to determine one's true body position, motion, and altitude (or, in water, depth) relative to the earth or one's surroundings. It may result from a brain or nerve disorder or from limitations in the normal sensory apparatus. Most clues to orientation are relayed from the eyes, ears, muscles, and skin. The senses may not perceive gradual changes in motion and may overestimate the degree of abrupt changes and overcompensate when motion stops. Airplane pilots and divers also contend with apparent changes in gravitational pull, which can lead to dangerous situations and must be overcome by training. See also inner ear, proprioception.

speaker See loudspeaker

Spearman, Charles E(dward) (1863–1945) British psychologist. He is known for his studies on human mental abilities, particularly intelligence, and especially for his statistical technique (factor analysis) for examining individual differences in psychological testing and identifying the underlying sources of these differences. His works include *Abilities of Man* (1927), *Creative Mind* (1931), and *Human Abilities* (1950).

spearmint Aromatic herb *(Mentha spicata)* of the mint family, the common garden mint widely used for culinary purposes. It has lax, tapering spikes of reddish-lilac flowers similar to peppermint flowers and sharply serrated leaves that are used fresh or dried to flavor many foods. The aroma and taste of spearmint are similar to those of peppermint but not as strong. Native to Europe and Asia, spearmint has been naturalized in North America.

special education Education for students (such as the physically disabled or mentally retarded) with special needs. An early proponent of education for the blind was Valentin Haüy, who opened a school in Paris in 1784; his efforts were followed by those of Louis Braille. Attempts to educate deaf children predate Haüy, but not until Friedrich Moritz Hill (1805–1874) developed an oral method of instruction did teaching to the deaf become established. The development of standardized sign languages further advanced instruction of the deaf. Scientific attempts to educate mentally retarded children began with the efforts of Jean-Marc-Gaspard Itard (1775–1838) to train a feral child known as the Wild Boy of Aveyron; Itard's work influenced such later theorists as Édouard Séguin (1812–1880) and MARIA MONTESSORI. Children with motor disabilities, once considered subjects for special education, are today usually integrated into the standard classroom, often by means of wheelchairs and modified desks. Children with LEARNING DISABILITIES and SPEECH problems usually require specialized techniques, often on an individual basis. For children with social and emotional problems, special therapeutic and clinical services may be provided.

special effects Artificial visual or mechanical effects introduced into a movie or television show. The earliest special effects were created through special camera lenses or through tricks such as projecting a moving background behind the actors. Greater flexibility came with the development of the optical printer, which made it possible to combine separate pieces of film and replace part of an image, thus allowing for such effects as characters flying through the air. Special effects have also been created mechanically on the set through the use of devices such as wires, explosives, and puppets and by building models to simulate epic scenes such as battles in miniature. The growing use of computer animation and computer-generated imagery has produced increasingly elaborate and realistic visual effects. Though each movie studio formerly had its own special-effects department, effects are now created by private companies such as GEORGE LUCAS's Industrial Light and Magic, formed to provide the revolutionary effects seen in *Star Wars* (1977) and later movies.

Special Forces See GREEN BERETS

Special Olympics International program to provide people with mental retardation year-round training and athletic competition in a variety of Olympic-type summer and winter sports. Inaugurated in 1968 through the efforts of Eunice Kennedy Shriver and the Chicago Park District, the Special Olympics was officially recognized by the International Olympic Committee in 1988. Games are held every two years, alternating between winter and summer sports. International headquarters are in Washington, D.C.

special prosecutor See INDEPENDENT COUNSEL

speciation \ˌspē-shē-ˈā-shən\ Formation of new and distinct SPECIES, whereby a single evolutionary line splits into two or more genetically independent ones. One of the fundamental processes of EVOLUTION, speciation may occur in many ways. Investigators formerly found evidence for speciation in the fossil record by tracing sequential changes in the structure and form of organisms. Genetic studies now show that such changes do not always accompany speciation, since many apparently identical groups are in fact reproductively isolated (i.e., they can no longer produce viable offspring through interbreeding). Polyploidy (see PLOIDY) is a means by which the beginnings of new species are created in just two or three generations.

Specie Circular \ˈspē-ˌshē\ (July 11, 1836) Executive order issued by Pres. ANDREW JACKSON. It required payment for purchases of public lands in gold or silver (specie means "money in coin"). The circular attempted to reduce the amount of paper money in circulation and limit land speculation. The result was deflationary and partly contributed to the economic crisis called the Panic of 1837. The U.S. Congress repealed the circular in 1838.

species \ˈspē-ˌshēz, ˈspē-ˌsēz\ Subdivision of biological classification composed of related organisms that share common characteristics and can interbreed. Organisms are grouped into species according to their outer similarities, but more important in classifying organisms that reproduce sexually is their ability to interbreed successfully. To be members of the same species, individuals must be able to mate and produce viable offspring. Because genetic variations originate in individuals which then pass on their variations only within the species, it is at the species level that EVOLUTION takes place (see SPECIATION). The international system of BINOMIAL NOMENCLATURE assigns new species a two-part name.

specific gravity *or* **relative density** Ratio of the DENSITY of a substance to that of a standard substance. For solids and liquids, the standard substance is usually water at 39.2°F (4.0°C), which has a density of 1.00 kg/liter. Gases are usually compared to dry air, which has a density of 1.29 g/liter at 32°F (0°C) and 1 atmosphere pressure. Because it is a ratio of two quantities that have the same dimensions (mass per unit volume), specific gravity has no dimension. For example, the specific gravity of liquid mercury is 13.6, because its actual density is 13.6 kg/liter, 13.6 times that of water.

specific heat Ratio of the quantity of heat required to raise the temperature of a body one degree to that required to raise the temperature of an equal mass of water one degree. The term is also used to mean the amount of heat, in calories, required to raise the temperature of one gram of a substance by one Celsius degree.

speckled trout See BROOK TROUT

spectacled bear *or* **Andean bear** Only South American species of BEAR (*Tremarctos ornatus,* family Ursidae), found in mountain forests, especially in the Andes. It feeds mainly on shoots and fruit and is an agile climber. It stands about 2 ft (60 cm) at the shoulder, is 4–6 ft (1.2–1.8 m) long, and has a 3-in. (7-cm) tail. Its shaggy coat is dark brown to black. Whitish to yellowish marks form its "spectacles" and often extend down the neck to the chest.

Spectacular Bid (foaled 1976) U.S. Thoroughbred racehorse. He won the Kentucky Derby and the Preakness Stakes in 1979 but lost in the Belmont Stakes. In 1980 he was syndicated for the record sum of $22 million, and later that year was put to stud.

Spectator, The Daily periodical published in London by RICHARD STEELE and JOSEPH ADDISON from March 1, 1711, to December 6, 1712, and revived by Addison in 1714 (for 80 issues). It succeeded *The Tatler*, launched by Steele in 1709. Aiming to "enliven morality with wit, and to temper wit with morality," *The Spectator* presented a fictional club whose imaginary members expressed the writers' ideas about society. It made serious discussion of letters and politics a normal pastime of the leisured class, set the pattern and established the vogue for the periodical in the 18th century, and helped create a receptive public for novelists.

spectrochemical analysis Any of a group of chemical ANALYSIS methods that depend on measurement of the WAVELENGTH and intensity of ELECTROMAGNETIC RADIATION. It is used chiefly to determine the arrangement of atoms and electrons in molecules on the basis of the amounts of ENERGY absorbed during changes in their structure or motion. In more common usage, it usually refers to ultraviolet (UV) and visible emission SPECTROSCOPY or to UV, visible, and infrared (IR) absorption SPECTROPHOTOMETRY.

spectrometer \spek-ˈträ-mə-tər\ Device for detecting and analyzing RADIATION, used for molecular SPECTROSCOPY. It includes a radiation source, a sample, and a detection and analysis device. Emission spectrographs excite MOLECULES of a sample to higher ENERGY states and analyze the radiation emitted when they decay to the original energy state. Absorption spectrometers pass radiation of known WAVELENGTH through a sample, varying the wavelengths to produce a spectrum of results; the detector system reveals to what extent each wavelength is absorbed. FOURIER-TRANSFORM spectrometers resemble absorption spectrometers but use a broad band of radiation; a computer analyzes the output to find the absorption spectrum. Different designs allow study of various kinds of samples over many frequencies, at different temperatures or pressures, or in an electric or magnetic field.

spectrophotometry \ˌspek-trō-fə-ˈtä-mə-trē\ Branch of SPECTROSCOPY dealing with measurement of radiant ENERGY transmitted or reflected by a body as a function of WAVELENGTH. The measurement is usually expressed as compared to that transmitted or reflected by a system that serves as a standard. Different types of spectrophotometers cover wide ranges of the ELECTROMAGNETIC SPECTRUM: ULTRAVIOLET (UV), visible LIGHT, INFRARED (IR), or MICROWAVE. UV spectrophotometry is particularly useful in detecting and quantifying colorless substances in SOLUTION. IR spectrophotometry is used mostly to study the molecular structures of complex organic compounds. See also COLORIMETRY.

spectroscopy \spek-ˈträ-skə-pē\ Branch of ANALYSIS devoted to identifying ELEMENTS and compounds and elucidating atomic and molecular structure by measuring the radiant ENERGY absorbed or emitted by a substance at characteristic WAVELENGTHS of the ELECTROMAGNETIC SPECTRUM (including GAMMA RAY, X RAY, ULTRAVIOLET, visible LIGHT, INFRARED, MICROWAVE, and RADIO-frequency radiation) on excitation by an external energy source. The instruments used are spectroscopes (for direct visual observation) or spectrographs (for recording spectra). Experiments involve a light source, a PRISM or grating to form the SPECTRUM, detectors (visual, photoelectric, radiometric, or photographic) for observing or recording its details, devices for measuring wavelengths and intensities, and interpretation of the measured quantities to identify chemicals identifications or give clues to the structure of atoms and molecules. HELIUM, CESIUM, and rubidium were discovered in the mid-19th century by spectroscopy of the sun's spectrum. Specialized techniques include Raman spectroscopy (see CHANDRASEKHARA VENKATA RAMAN), nuclear magnetic resonance (NMR), nuclear quadrupole resonance, dynamic reflectance spectroscopy, microwave and gamma ray spectroscopy, and ELECTRON SPIN RESONANCE (ESR). See also MASS SPECTROMETRY, SPECTROPHOTOMETRY.

spectrum Arrangement according to WAVELENGTH (or FREQUENCY) of ELECTROMAGNETIC RADIATION. The visible, "rainbow" spectrum is the portion of the ELECTROMAGNETIC SPECTRUM that is visible as light to the human eye. Some sources emit only certain wavelengths and produce an emission spectrum of bright lines with dark spaces between. Such line spectra are characteristic of the elements that emit the radiation. A band spectrum consists of groups of wavelengths so close together that the lines appear to form a continuous band. Atoms and molecules absorb certain wavelengths and so remove them from a complete spectrum; the resulting absorption spectrum contains dark lines or bands at these wavelengths.

speech Human communication through audible LANGUAGE. Speech sounds are made with air exhaled from the lungs, which passes between the vocal cords in the LARYNX and out through the vocal tract (PHARYNX and oral and nasal cavities). This airstream is shaped into different sounds by the articulators, mainly the TONGUE, PALATE, and lips (see ARTICULATION). Articulatory PHONETICS describes each sound in terms of the position and action of the articulators used to make it. Speech is also described in terms of SYNTAX, lexicon (inventory of words or MORPHEMES), and PHONOLOGY (sounds).

speech, figure of See FIGURE OF SPEECH

speech act theory Theory of meaning that holds that the meaning of linguistic expressions can be explained in terms of the rules governing their use in performing various speech acts (e.g., admonishing, asserting, commanding, exclaiming, promising, questioning, requesting, warning). In contrast to theories that maintain that linguistic expressions have meaning in virtue of their contribution to the truth conditions of sentences where they occur, it explains linguistic meaning in terms of the use of words and sentences in the performance of speech acts. Some exponents claim that the meaning of a word is nothing but its contribution to the nature of the speech acts that can be performed by using it. LUDWIG WITTGENSTEIN and J. L. AUSTIN provided important stimuli for the theory's development.

speech recognition *or* **voice recognition** Ability of COMPUTER systems to accept speech input and act on it or transcribe it into written language. Current research efforts are directed toward applications of automatic speech recognition (ASR), where the goal is to transform the content of speech into knowledge that forms the basis for linguistic or cognitive tasks, such as translation into another language. Practical applications include DATABASE-query systems, INFORMATION RETRIEVAL systems, and speaker identification and verification systems, as in telebanking. Speech recognition has promising applications in ROBOTICS, particularly development of robots that can "hear." See also PATTERN RECOGNITION.

speech synthesis Generation of speech by artificial means, usually by COMPUTER. Production of sound to simulate human speech is referred to as low-level synthesis. High-level synthesis deals with the conversion of written text or symbols into an abstract representation of the desired acoustic signal, suitable for driving a low-level synthesis system. Among other applications, this technology provides speaking aid to the speech-impaired and reading aid to the sight-impaired.

speech therapy Therapeutic treatment to correct defects in speaking. Such defects may originate in the brain, the ear (see DEAFNESS), or anywhere along the vocal tract and may affect the voice, ARTICULATION, language development, or ability to speak after language is learned. Therapy begins with diagnosis of underlying physical, physiological, or emotional dysfunction. It may involve training in breathing, use of the voice, and/or speaking habits. Some abnormalities that cause speech disorders (e.g., CLEFT PALATE, STROKE) can be corrected to various degrees before a speech therapist's work begins. See also APHASIA, STUTTERING.

speed skating Sport of racing on ice skates. The blade of the speed skate is longer and thinner than that of the hockey or figure skate. Two types of track are used in international competition. The long track is a 400-m flattened oval (straight sides and curved ends) on which two skaters race simultaneously. The short track, a more recent development, is a 111-m oval on which four to six skaters race during each heat. Long-track speed skating was included in the first Winter Olympics in 1924; short-track skating was added in 1992.

Speer \'shpār\, **Albert** (1905–1981) German Nazi official. He became an architect in 1927 and an active member of the Nazi Party in 1931. He impressed ADOLF HITLER with his efficiency and talent and was appointed chief architect of the Third Reich in 1933. He designed the parade grounds and banners of the Nazi rallies held for the party congresses, including the 1934 NUREMBERG RALLY filmed by LENI RIEFENSTAHL. In 1942 he became minister for armaments and war production and expanded the system of conscript and slave labor that maintained Germany's wartime productivity. Convicted at the Nuremberg Trials, he served 20 years in prison. He wrote the memoirs *Inside the Third Reich* (1969) and *Spandau* (1975).

Speke \'spēk\, **John Hanning** (1827–1864) British explorer, the first European to reach Lake VICTORIA. He was a member of RICHARD BURTON's expedition, and in 1858 Speke and Burton became the first Europeans to reach Lake TANGANYIKA. On the return trip he left Burton and struck out northward alone. In July 1858 he reached the great lake, which he named for the queen. His claim that it was the source of the NILE was questioned, but on a second expedition (1860–63) he found the Nile's exit from the lake.

Spelling, Aaron (born 1923) U.S. television producer. Born in Dallas, he wrote television scripts in the 1950s before producing the detective series *Burke's Law* (1963–66) and the police drama *Mod Squad* (1968–73). With Leonard Goldberg from 1972, he coproduced *Charlie's Angels* (1976–81) and *Family* (1976–80). Expert at creating escapist television that focused on sex, romance, and improbable plot lines, he later produced such successes as *The Love Boat* (1977–86), *Fantasy Island* (1978–84), *Dynasty* (1981–89), *Beverly Hills 90210* (1990–2000), and *Melrose Place* (1992–99).

spelling and grammar checkers Components of WORD-PROCESSING programs for PERSONAL COMPUTERS that identify apparent misspellings and grammatical errors by reference to an incorporated dictionary and a list of rules for proper usage. Spelling checkers cannot identify spelling errors that result in another legitimate word (e.g., "form" typed for "from") and are hard to use on documents that contain numerous words (e.g., foreign terms) not entered in the incorporated dictionary. Grammar checkers—which also generally check punctuation, sentence length, and other aspects of style—have been criticized for their reliance on oversimplified rules.

Spelman College Private, historically black, women's liberal-arts college in Atlanta. Its history is traced to 1881, when two Boston women began teaching 11 black women, mostly ex-slaves, in an Atlanta church basement. Donations from JOHN D. ROCKEFELLER, beginning in 1884, assured the school's growth; the school is named for Rockefeller's wife's mother. Spelman offers bachelor's degrees in more than 20 academic fields. It is one of six African-American institutions in the Atlanta area that share students, faculty, facilities, and curricula. Enrollment is about 2,000.

spelt Subspecies *(Triticum aestivum spelta)* of WHEAT that has lax spikes and spikelets containing two light-red kernels. *Triticum dicoccon* was cultivated by the ancient Babylonians and the ancient Swiss lakedwellers; it is now grown for livestock forage and used in baked goods and cereals.

Spencer, Christopher M(iner) (1833–1922) U.S. inventor and manufacturer. Born in Manchester, Conn., in 1860 he patented a repeating carbine whose seven cartridges could be fired in 18 seconds. It was quickly adopted by the U.S. government for cavalry use, and Spencer built his own factory, which produced 200,000 Spencer carbines and rifles during the Civil War. He also patented a breechloader and a magazine gun. He later contributed considerably to the technology of drop forging. His innovative screw-making lathes enabled the huge success of his Hartford Machine Screw Co. (established 1876).

Spencer, Herbert (1820–1903) British sociologist and philosopher, advocate of the theory of SOCIAL DARWINISM. His *System of Synthetic Philosophy* (9 vols., 1855–96) held that the physical, organic, and social realms are interconnected and develop according to identical evolutionary principles, a scheme suggested by the evolution of biological species. He saw human societies as evolving by means of increasing division of labor from undifferentiated hordes into complex civilizations. SOCIOCULTURAL EVOLUTION was thus a process of increasing "individuation," driven by the natural preeminence of the individual over society and of science over religion. Spencer's speculative sociology was soon superseded by the findings of CULTURAL ANTHROPOLOGY and a more empirically based SOCIOLOGY. He was one of the most argumentative and most discussed Victorian thinkers.

Spender, Stephen (Harold) *later* **Sir Stephen** (1909–1995) English poet and critic. While an undergraduate at Oxford, Spender met the poets W. H. AUDEN and C. DAY-LEWIS. In the 1930s they became identified with politically conscience-stricken, leftist "new writing." His poems, expressing a self-critical, compassionate personality, appear in volumes from *Poems* (1933) to *Dolphins* (1994). He was better known for his perceptive criticism, as in *The Destructive Element* (1935), *The Making of a Poem* (1955), and *The Struggle of the Modern* (1963), and for his association with the influential review *Encounter* (1953–67). He also wrote short stories, essays, and autobiography.

Spengler \'shpeŋ-glər\, **Oswald** (1880–1936) German philosopher. A schoolmaster before he turned to writing, Spengler is remembered for his influential *The Decline of the West* (2 vols., 1918–22), a study in the philosophy of history. He contended that civilizations pass through a life cycle, blossoming and decaying like natural organisms, and that Western culture is irreversibly past its creative stage and headed into eclipse. Though acclaimed by a public disillusioned in the wake of World War I, his work was criticized by both professional scholars and the Nazi Party, despite some affinities with its dogma.

Spengler, pencil drawing by K. Grossmann, 1920; in a private collection.

DEUTSCHE FOTOTHEK, DRESDEN

Spenser, Edmund (1552/53–1599) English poet. Little is known for certain about his life before he entered Cambridge University. His first important publication, *The Shepheardes Calender* (1579), can be called the first work of the English literary Renaissance. By 1580 he was apparently serving the Earl of Leicester and was part of a literary circle led by SIR PHILIP SIDNEY. In 1580 he became secretary to the lord deputy of Ireland, where he spent much of his remaining life; in 1588 or 1589 he took over a large property at Kilcolman, near Cork. In 1590 he published the first part of the long allegorical poem *The Faerie Queene* (first folio ed., 1609), an imaginative vindication of Protestantism and Puritanism and a glorification of England and Elizabeth I. The central poem of the Elizabethan period and one of the greatest poems in English, it was composed in a revolutionary nine-line stanzaic pattern, the "Spenserian stanza," that was used by many later poets. Of the 12 books he planned for the poem, he completed just over half. *Amoretti* (1595), a sonnet sequence, and *Epithalamion* (1595), a marriage ode, are among his other works. In the Irish uprising of 1598, Kilcolman was burned; Spenser, probably in despair, died shortly after.

Speransky \spyi-'rán-skē\, **Mikhail (Mikhaylovich)** *later* **Count Speransky** (1772–1839) Russian politician. After teaching at the seminary in St. Petersburg, he entered government service. He served as an assistant to Czar ALEXANDER I (1807–12), but his proposed financial and administrative reforms angered the nobles, who had him exiled (1812–16). He returned to government service, and served as governor-general of Siberia 1819–21. A member of the state council from 1821 under NICHOLAS I, he compiled the first complete collection of Russian law (1830). He was given the title of count in 1839.

sperm *or* **spermatozoon** \spər-,ma-tə-'zō-ən\ Male reproductive CELL. In mammals, sperm are produced in the TESTES and travel through the REPRODUCTIVE SYSTEM. At FERTILIZATION, one sperm of the roughly 300 million in an average ejaculation (see SEMEN) fertilizes an EGG (see OVARY) to produce an offspring. At PUBERTY, immature cells (spermatogonia) begin a maturation process (spermatogenesis). A mature human sperm has a flat, almond-shaped head, 4–5 by 2–3 microns, with a cap (acrosome) containing chemicals that help it penetrate an ovum. It is essentially a cell NUCLEUS, with 23 CHROMOSOMES (including either the X or Y that determines the child's sex). A 50-micron FLAGELLUM propels the sperm, which may live in a woman's reproductive tract for two to three days after SEXUAL INTERCOURSE, to the egg. Sperm may be frozen and stored for ARTIFICIAL INSEMINATION.

sperm whale *or* **cachalot** \'ka-shə-,lät, 'ka-shə-,lō\ Thickset, blunt-snouted TOOTHED WHALE *(Physeter catodon,* family Physeteridae) with small, paddlelike flippers and rounded humps on the back. Sperm whales have an enormous head, squarish in profile, and a narrow, underslung lower jaw with large conical teeth that fit into sockets in the toothless upper jaw when the mouth is closed. They are dark blue-gray or brownish. (HERMAN MELVILLE's Moby-Dick was presumably an albino.) The male grows to 60 ft (18 m). Herds of 15–20 live in temperate and tropical waters worldwide. They commonly dive to 1,200 ft (350 m), feeding primarily on cephalopods. The whales have been hunted for their spermaceti (a waxy substance in the snout, used in ointments and cosmetics) and for AMBERGRIS. The pygmy sperm whale (genus *Kogia*) is a black dolphinlike whale, about 13 ft (4 m) long, of the Northern Hemisphere that lacks commercial value.

spermatophyte See SEED PLANT

Sperry, Elmer (Ambrose) (1860–1930) U.S. inventor and industrialist. Born in Cortland, N.Y., the precociously gifted youth opened his own factory in Chicago at the age of 20 to make dynamos and arc lamps. He designed an electrical industrial locomotive and motor transmission machinery for streetcars, and later made electric automobiles powered by his patented battery. He invented processes for salvaging tin and producing white lead and for manufacturing fuse wire. His greatest inventions sprang from the GYROSCOPE (till then considered only a toy), which, once properly aligned, always points to true north. His gyrocompass was first installed on the battleship *Delaware* in 1911. He extended the gyro principle to guidance of torpedoes, to gyropilots for the steering of ships and for stabilizing airplanes, and finally to a ship stabilizer. In all, he founded eight manufacturing companies and took out more than 400 patents.

Sperry, Roger (1913–1994) U.S. neurobiologist. Born in Hartford, Conn., he earned a doctorate in zoology from the University of Chicago. He studied functional specialization in the hemispheres of the cerebral cortex, examining animals and then humans with epilepsy in whose brains the corpus callosum had been severed. His research showed that the left side of the brain is normally dominant for analytical and verbal tasks and the right for spatial tasks, music, and certain other areas. His techniques laid the groundwork for much more specialized explorations. He shared a 1981 Nobel Prize with DAVID HUBEL and TORSTEN WIESEL.

Spey River \'spā\ River, northeastern Scotland. It rises in the Corrieyairack Forest and flows 107 mi (172 km) northeast across the Highlands into the North Sea. It is noted for salmon fishing, and its valley is the site of high-quality whisky distilleries.

sphagnum See PEAT MOSS

sphalerite \'sfa-lə-,rīt\ *or* **blende** *or* **zincblende** Zinc sulfide (ZnS), the chief ore mineral of ZINC. It is found associated with GALENA in most important lead-zinc deposits. The most important deposits are in the Mississippi River valley (U.S.), Poland, Belgium, and North Africa. See also SULFIDE MINERAL.

Sphalerite from Baxter Springs, Kan.

BY COURTESY OF THE TED AND ELSIE BOENTE COLLECTION; PHOTOGRAPH, JOHN H. GERARD—EB INC.

sphere In geometry, the set of all points in three-dimensional space lying the same distance (the radius) from a given point (the center), or the result of rotating a circle about one of its diameters. The components and properties of a sphere are analogous to those of a circle. A diameter is any line segment connecting two points of a sphere and passing through its center. The circumference is the length of any great circle, the intersection of the sphere with any plane passing through its center. A meridian is any great circle passing through a point designated a pole. A geodesic, the shortest distance between any two points on a sphere, is an arc of the great circle through the two points. The formula for determining a sphere's surface area is $4\pi r^2$; its volume is determined by $(4/3)\pi r^3$. The study of spheres is basic to terrestrial geography and is one of the principal areas of EUCLIDEAN GEOMETRY and ELLIPTIC GEOMETRY.

sphere, celestial See CELESTIAL SPHERE

sphere of influence In international politics, a state's claim to exclusive or predominant control over a foreign area or territory. Legal claims gained currency in the 1880s, as European colonial powers rubbed shoulders in their overseas possessions. These consisted of promises not to interfere with one another's actions in mutually recognized spheres of influence. After colonial expansion reached its limits, geopolitical rather than legal claims to spheres of influence became common, examples being the U.S. claim to dominance in the Western Hemisphere under the much-earlier MONROE DOCTRINE, and the Soviet Union's expansion of its sphere of influence to Eastern Europe following World War II.

spherical coordinate system In geometry, a COORDINATE SYSTEM in which any point in three-dimensional space is specified by its angle with respect to a polar axis and angle of rotation with respect to a prime meridian on a sphere of a given radius. In spherical coordinates a point is specified by the triplet (r, θ, φ), where r is the point's distance from the origin (the radius), θ is the angle of rotation from the initial meridian plane, and φ is the angle from the polar axis (analogous to a ray from the origin through the North Pole).

sphinx Mythological creature with a lion's body and a human's head. It figures prominently in Egyptian and Greek art and legend. The winged sphinx of Thebes was said to have terrorized people by demanding the answer to a riddle taught to her by the MUSES—What is it that has one voice and yet becomes successively four-footed, then two-footed, then three-footed?—and devoured every person who answered incorrectly. When OEDIPUS correctly answered "man"—who crawls on all fours in infancy, walks on two feet when grown, and leans on a staff in old age—the sphinx killed herself. The earliest and most famous example in art is the Great Sphinx at Giza in Egypt, built c. 2500 BC. The sphinx appeared in the Greek world c. 1600 BC and in Mesopotamia c. 1500 BC.

The Great Sphinx at Giza, 4th dynasty.
E. STREICHAN—SHOSTAL ASSOC.

sphinx moth See HAWK MOTH

sphynx cat \'sfiŋks\ Breed of hairless DOMESTIC CAT, founded on two spontaneous mutations in shorthaired cats. The first occurred in 1975 when Jezabelle, a stray, produced a hairless female kitten, Epidermis, followed by another the next year. The second occurred in 1978, when a male and two female hairless kittens were rescued from the streets of Toronto. Sphynx cats must be bathed regularly to keep the skin free of the oils that the coat on a normal cat absorbs, and the very large ears must be cleaned regularly to rid them of dust and dirt and prevent wax buildup.

spice and herb Dried parts of various plants cultivated for their aromatic, savory, medicinal, or otherwise desirable substances. Spices are the fragrant or pungent products of such tropical or subtropical species as CARDAMOM, CINNAMON, CLOVES, GINGER, and PEPPER; spice seeds include ANISE, CARAWAY, CUMIN, FENNEL, POPPY, and SESAME. Herbs are the fragrant leaves of such plants as MARJORAM, MINT, ROSEMARY, and THYME. The most notable uses of spices and herbs in very early times were in medicine, in the making of holy oils and unguents, and as aphrodisiacs; they were also used to flavor food and beverages and to inhibit or hide food spoilage. Trade in spices, including TEA, has played a major role in human history. Important early trade routes, including those between Asia and the Middle East and between Europe and Asia, were initially forged to obtain exotic spices and herbs. The 15th-century voyages of discovery were launched largely as a result of the spice trade, and in the 17th century. Portugal and the British, Dutch, and French East India companies battled furiously for dominance (see British EAST INDIA CO., Dutch EAST INDIA CO., French EAST INDIA CO.)

spicebush Deciduous, dense shrub *(Lindera benzoin,* or *Benzoin aestivale)* of the LAUREL FAMILY, native to eastern North America. Found most often in damp woods, it grows 5–20 ft (1.5–6 m) tall. The shiny, oblong leaves (3–5 in., or 8–13 cm, long) are wedge-shaped near the base. Small, yellow flowers crowded in small, nearly stalkless clusters are followed by fleshy red fruit with a stony covering around the seed. Tea is sometimes brewed from young twigs, leaves, and fruit.

Spicebush (*Lindera benzoin*).
WALTER CHANDOHA

spider Any of some 34,000 predatory, mostly terrestrial, ARACHNID species in the order Araneida, abundant worldwide except in Antarctica. Spiders have two main body parts, eight legs, two pincerlike venomous appendages, and two spinnerets. Species range from less than an inch (2.5 mm) to about 3.5 in. (9 cm) long. The venom of a few species (e.g., BROWN RECLUSE) is harmful to humans. Most species catch insect prey in a web of silk extruded from the spinnerets. Spiders change little during growth, except in size. Species are classified largely on the basis of the number and arrangement of eyes and the type of web. See also BLACK WIDOW, TARANTULA, WOLF SPIDER.

spider crab Any species of sluggish marine CRAB in the widely distributed family Majidae (or Maiidae). Spider crabs have a beak-shaped head; thick, rounded body; and long, spindly legs. They use a muscuslike mouth secretion to fasten algae, sponges, and other organisms to the hairs, spines, and knobby projections covering the body. Most species are scavengers, especially of carrion. Their size varies greatly. The body of the European long-beaked spider crab *(Macropodia rostrata)* is less than 0.5 in. (1 cm) in diameter, whereas the Japanese giant crab *(Macrocheira kaempferi)*, whose outstretched claws can measure 13 ft (4 m) from tip to tip, is perhaps the largest known arthropod.

Spider crab (*Libinia*).
WALTER DAWN

spider mite *or* **red spider** Any plant-feeding MITE in the family Tetranychidae, common pests on houseplants and agriculturally important plants. Adult spider mites are tiny, about 0.02 in. (0.5 mm) long, and often red. They spin a loose silk webbing on infested plants. A heavy infestation can cause complete defoliation. Because of their increasing re-

S T U V

sistance to pesticides, they are difficult to control. One effective control is the use of another, predatory, mite species.

spider monkey Any of four species (family Cebidae) of diurnal, arboreal NEW WORLD MONKEYS found from Mexico to Brazil. Long-limbed and somewhat potbellied, they are 14–26 in. (35–66 cm) long and have thumbless hands and a heavily furred, prehensile 24–36-in. (60–92-cm) tail. The coat is gray, reddish, brown, or black. They swing through branches, using their tails and hands, or leap or drop spread-eagled from tree to tree. They eat fruit, nuts, flowers, and buds. They are used in laboratory studies of malaria, to which they are susceptible. Though sometimes kept as pets, adults are likely to throw tantrums and may be dangerous.

spider plant African plant of genus *Chlorophytum* (LILY FAMILY). This popular houseplant has long, narrow, grassy green-and-white-striped leaves. Periodically a flower stem emerges, and tiny white flowers (not always produced) are replaced by young plantlets, which can then be detached and rooted.

spiderwort Any of 20 or more erect to trailing, weak-stemmed herbs native to North and South America that make up the genus *Tradescantia* (family Commelinaceae). Several species are grown as indoor plants in baskets, especially the wandering Jews (*T. albiflora,* with green leaves, and *T. fluminensis,* with purplish underleaves). White velvet, or white-gossamer *(T. sillamontana),* has leaves and stems covered with a whitish fuzz. Chain plant *(T. navicularis)* has fleshy, narrow, lengthwise-folded leaves. Common spiderwort, or widow's tears *(T. virginiana),* is an upright, juicy-stemmed garden plant with white to purple flowers. Because they are easy to propagate, spiderworts are very popular indoor plants.

Spiegel \der-'shpē-gəl\, **Der** (German: "The Mirror") Weekly newsmagazine, preeminent in Germany and one of the best and most widely circulated in Europe. Founded in 1946 as *Diese Woche* ("This Week") and published in Hamburg since 1947, it is respected both for its news coverage and analysis and for its concise writing. It is especially renowned for its aggressive exposés of government malpractice and scandals and for its photography. It resembles *TIME* and *NEWSWEEK* in format, but is usually much thicker.

Spielberg, Steven (born 1947) U.S. film director and producer. Born in Cincinnati, he began making films in high school. As a director of television movies for Universal Pictures, he made the thriller *Duel* (1971), and in 1974 he directed the feature film *The Sugarland Express.* His shark-attack thriller *Jaws* (1975) became one of the highest-grossing movies ever, and he went on to direct such huge successes as *Close Encounters of the Third Kind* (1977), *Raiders of the Lost Ark* (1981), and *E.T.—the Extraterrestrial* (1982). His later movies include *Jurassic Park* (1993), *Schindler's List* (1993, Academy Award), *The Color Purple* (1985), *Empire of the Sun* (1987), *Amistad* (1997), and *Saving Private Ryan* (1998, Academy Award). His brisk editing, rich color cinematography, memorable sound tracks, and inventive special effects have made him, by some measures, the most successful filmmaker in the world. In 1994 he cofounded DreamWorks SKG, a film, animation, and television production company.

Spillane, Mickey *orig.* **Frank Morrison** (born 1918) U.S. writer of pulp detective fiction. Born in Brooklyn, N.Y., he initially wrote for pulp magazines and comic books in order to pay for his schooling. His first novel, *I, The Jury* (1947), introduced the detective Mike Hammer, who later appeared in works from *My Gun Is Quick* (1950) to *Black Alley* (1996). His other novels, all characterized by violence and sexual licentiousness, include *The Deep* (1961), a series with the international agent Tiger Mann beginning with *Day of the Guns* (1964), and *The Killing Man* (1989). At his height Spillane was perhaps the best-selling writer in the world.

spin Amount of ANGULAR MOMENTUM associated with a SUBATOMIC PARTICLE or NUCLEUS. It is measured in multiples of $\hbar$ (h-bar), equal to Planck's constant divided by 2π. ELECTRONS, NEUTRONS, and PROTONS have a spin of ½, for example, while pions and helium nuclei have zero spin. The spin of a complex nucleus is the vector sum of the orbital angular momentum and intrinsic spins of the constituent nucleons. For nuclei of even mass number, the multiple is an integral; for those of odd mass number, it is a half-integer. See also BOSE-EINSTEIN STATISTICS, FERMI-DIRAC STATISTICS.

spinach Hardy, leafy annual *(Spinacia oleracea)* of the goosefoot family (Chenopodiaceae), used as a vegetable. The edible leaves, somewhat triangular and either flat or puckered, are arranged in a rosette, from which a seedstalk emerges. Spinach requires cool weather and deep, rich, well-limed soil to give quick growth and maximum leaf area; sowing seed every two weeks from early spring to late summer provides a steady supply. A nutritious vegetable, spinach is rich in iron and vitamins A and C.

spinal column See VERTEBRAL COLUMN

spinal cord Body's major nerve tract, about 18 in. (45 cm) long, running from the base of the BRAIN through the VERTEBRAL COLUMN. It is covered by the MENINGES and cushioned by CEREBROSPINAL FLUID. It connects the peripheral nervous system (outside the brain and spinal cord) to the brain, and it and the brain thus constitute the central NERVOUS SYSTEM. Sensory impulses reach the brain via the spinal cord, and impulses from the brain travel down the spinal cord to motor neurons, which reach the body's muscles and glands via the peripheral nerves. The peripheral nerves are connected to the spinal cord via the spinal nerves. In humans there are 31 pairs of spinal nerves containing both sensory and motor fi-

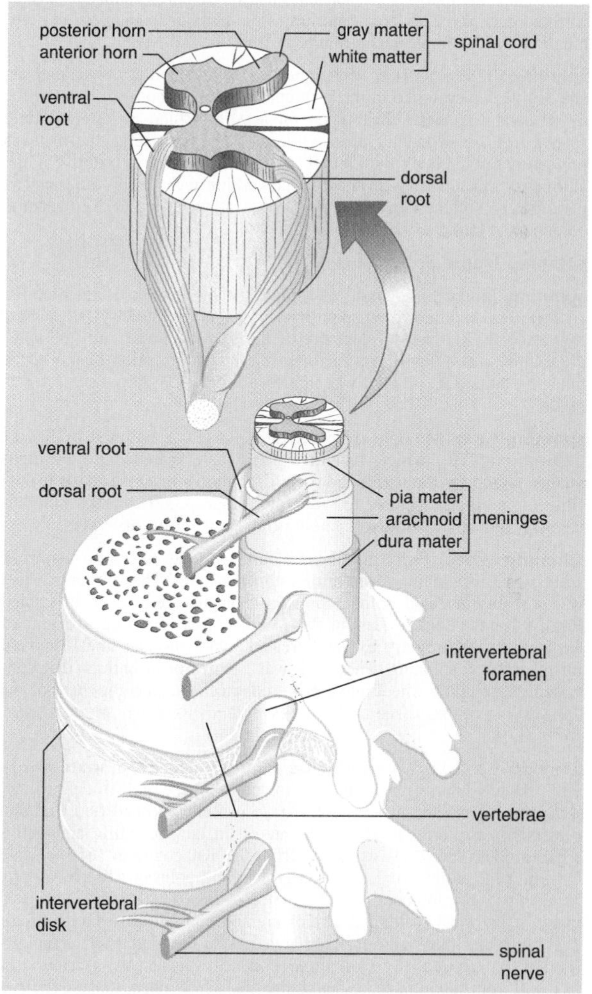

Section of a spinal cord. The anterior horn of the gray matter contains cell bodies from which the motor fibers of the spinal nerves arise. Its posterior horn contains cell bodies from which fibers pass to the brain carrying impulses brought by sensory fibers entering from the spinal nerves. Interneurons in the gray matter connect impulses within the cord. The white matter contains tracts of fibers which ascend to the brain with sensory impulses and descend from the brain carrying motor impulses. Nerve fibers emerge from the spinal cord through the foramina and form a dorsal root (containing fibers of sensory neurons) and a ventral root (containing fibers of motor neurons), which merge to form the spinal nerves.

S T U V

bers, which originate in the spinal cord and pass out between the vertebrae. These nerves branch and relay motor impulses to all parts of the body. Injury to the spinal cord may result in loss of communication between the brain and cause paralysis, loss of sensation, or weakness in the parts of the body served by areas below the injured region. Because nerve cells and fibers are unable to regenerate themselves, the effects are usually permanent.

spindle and whorl *or* **drop spindle** Earliest device for spinning fibers into thread or yarn. The spinster lets the spindle fall to draw out the fibers while the whorl keeps it rotating to apply the necessary twist. The spindle and whorl was replaced by the SPINNING WHEEL.

spinel \spə-ˈnel\ Mineral composed of magnesium aluminum oxide ($MgAl_2O_4$). Also called magnesia spinel, its color, due to various impurities, ranges from blood-red to blue, green, brown, and colorless. Spinel is found in basic igneous rocks, granite pegmatites, and contact metamorphic limestone deposits, often in association with corundum. Synthetic spinel has been manufactured since the early 20th century for use as imitation gem stones. Spinel may also refer more broadly to any of various mineral oxides of magnesium, iron, zinc, or manganese in combination with aluminum, chromium, or iron.

spinning In METALWORK, a technique for making hollow metal utensils and artifacts. Developed in the 19th century, the method can be used for most metals. A metal disk is set on a LATHE behind an appropriately shaped metal or wooden chuck; while the lathe is rotating, the metal is pressed onto the chuck with a tool. A typical modern spun object is the aluminum saucepan. As in most metalworking techniques, the metal is periodically softened by ANNEALING, or heating, when it has become hardened by being worked (see HARDENING).

spinning frame See DRAWING FRAME

spinning jenny Early multiple-spindle machine for spinning WOOL or COTTON. The hand-powered spinning jenny was patented by JAMES HARGREAVES in 1770. The development of the SPINNING WHEEL into the spinning jenny was a significant factor in the industrialization of the TEXTILE industry, though its product was inferior to that of R. ARKWRIGHT'S WATER FRAME.

spinning mule Multiple-spindle spinning machine invented by SAMUEL CROMPTON (1779), which permitted large-scale manufacture of high-quality THREAD for the textile industry. Crompton's machine made it possible for a single operator to work more than 1,000 spindles simultaneously, and was capable of spinning fine as well as coarse YARN.

spinning wheel Early machine for turning TEXTILE fiber into THREAD or YARN, which was then woven into cloth on a loom. The spinning wheel was probably invented in India, though its origins are unclear. It reached Europe via the Middle East in the Middle Ages. The improvement of the loom in 18th-century England created a yarn shortage and a demand for mechanical spinning. The result was a series of inventions that converted the spinning wheel into a powered, mechanized component of the INDUSTRIAL REVOLUTION (see DRAWING FRAME, SPINNING JENNY, SPINNING MULE, WATER FRAME).

Spinoza \spi-ˈnō-zə\, **Benedict de** *Hebrew* **Baruch Spinoza** (1632–1677) Dutch Jewish philosopher, a major exponent of 17th-century RATIONALISM. He was born in Amsterdam to parents who had fled Catholic persecution in Portugal. His early interest in new scientific and philosophical ideas led to his expulsion from the synagogue in 1656, and he thereafter made his living as a lens grinder and polisher. His philosophy represents a development of and reaction to that of RENE DESCARTES, and many of his most striking doctrines are solutions of Cartesian difficulties. He found three unsatisfactory features in the Cartesian metaphysics: the transcendence of God, mind–body DUALISM, and the ascription of free will both to God and to human beings. To Spinoza, those doctrines made the world unintelligible, since it was impossible to explain the relation between God and the world or between mind and body or to account for events occasioned by free will. In his masterpiece, *Ethics* (1677), he tried to construct a monistic system of metaphysics that would solve these problems in a fully intelligible and certain manner. Offered the chair of philosophy at the University of Heidelberg, he declined it, seeking to preserve his independence. His other major works are the *Tractatus Theologico-Politicus* (1670) and the unfinished *Tractatus Politicus*.

spiny anteater See ECHIDNA

spire Steeply pointed termination to a tower or roof. In GOTHIC ARCHITECTURE, the spire is a spectacular visual culmination of the building as well as a symbol of heavenly aspiration. The church spire originated in the 12th century as a simple, four-sided pyramidal roof capping a tower. Methods used to integrate an octagonal spire with a square tower below include broaches (sloping triangular sections of masonry added to the bottom of the four spire faces not coinciding with the tower sides), gabled dormers added to spire faces, and steep pinnacles (vertical ornaments of pyramidal or conical shape) added to tower corners. During the Decorated period (14th century) in England, a slender needle spire set in from the edge of the tower was popular; corner pinnacles and a low parapet around the tower's edge became customary. In the 20th century, architects tended to limit spires to rather elementary geometric shapes.

spirea \spī-ˈrē-ə\ Any of nearly 100 species of flowering shrubs in the genus *Spirea* (ROSE family), native to the northern temperate zone and commonly cultivated for their pleasing growth habit and attractive flower clusters. The most commonly grown, and possibly the most popular of all cultivated shrubs, is the Vanhouttei spirea, also called bridal wreath (a cross between *S. cantoniensis* and *S. trilobata*), which grows up to 6 ft (2 m) tall and has graceful arching branches that bear numerous white flowers in spring. Plants that resemble spirea are the shrubby false spireas (*Sorbaria* species, also rose family) and the perennial herbaceous spireas (*Astilbe* species, SAXIFRAGE family).

Spiraea.
E.R. DEGGINGER—EB INC.

spirillum \spi-ˈril-əm\ Any of the spiral-shaped BACTERIA that make up the genus *Spirillum,* which are aquatic except for one species that causes a type of rat-bite fever in humans. The term is used generally for any corkscrewlike species of bacteria (see SPIROCHETE). Spirilla are gram-negative (see GRAM STAIN) and move by means of tufts of flagella at each end.

spirits See DISTILLED LIQUOR

spiritual In North American white and black FOLK MUSIC, an English-language folk hymn. White spirituals derived variously, notably from the "lining out" of psalms, dating from at least the mid-17th century. Where congregations could not read, a leader intoned the psalm one line at a time, alternating with the congregation's singing of each line to a familiar melody; the tune, sung slowly, was ornamented with passing notes, turns, and other graces. A second source was the singing of hymns set to borrowed melodies, often secular folk tunes. Camp meetings and revivals were marked by spontaneous mass singing, often with call-and-response patterns and ornamented melodies. Themes included going home to the promised land, the defeat of Satan, and gaining ground against sin; typical refrains were "Roll, Jordan" and "Glory Hallelujah." The songs survive in oral tradition in isolated areas and also in SHAPE-NOTE SINGING. Black spirituals developed in part from white rural folk hymnody, but differ greatly in voice quality, vocal effects, rhythm, and type of rhythmic accompaniment. They were sung not only in worship but also as work songs, and the text imagery often reflects concrete tasks. Like the white gospel song, the modern black gospel song derives from the spiritual.

spiritualism Belief that the SOULS of the dead can make contact with the living, usually through a medium or during abnormal mental states such as trances. The basis of spiritualism is the conviction that spirit is the essence of life and that it lives on after the body dies. A medium is a person sensitive to vibrations from the spirit world, who may hold meetings known as séances in order to seek messages from spirits. A "control" is a spirit that gives messages to the medium, who in turn gives them to men and women on earth. Spirits may also manifest themselves through such means as rapping or levitating objects. Some spiritualists claim powers of paranormal healing. Scientific study of spiritualist phenomena has been the focus of the Society for Psychical Research, founded in Britain in 1882.

spirochete \'spī-rə-ˌkēt\ Any of an order (Spirochaetales) of spiral-shaped BACTERIA. Some are serious pathogens for humans, causing such diseases as SYPHILIS, YAWS, and RELAPSING FEVER. Spirochetes are gram-negative (see GRAM STAIN) and motile. They are unique in that their flagella, which number between two and more than 200 per organism, are contained within the cell. Most spirochetes are found in a liquid environment (e.g., mud and water, blood and lymph). Several species are borne by lice and ticks, which transmit them to humans.

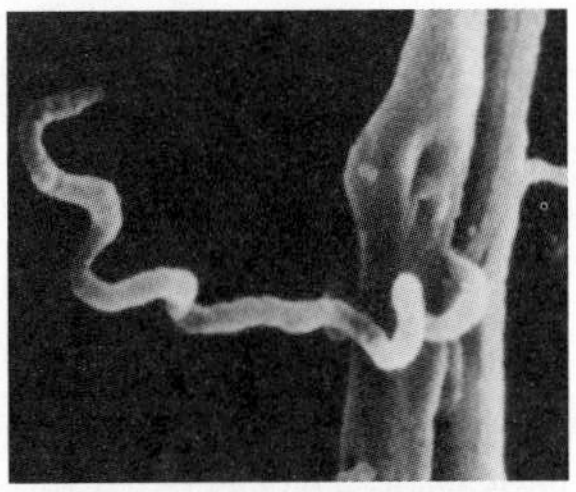

Scanning electron micrograph of the spirochete *Treponema pallidum* attached to testicular cell membranes.
ASM/SCIENCE SOURCE

spirulina \ˌspir-ü-'lē-nə\ Any CYANOBACTERIA in the genus *Spirulina*. A traditional food source in parts of Africa and Mexico, spirulina is an exceptionally rich source of vitamins, minerals, and protein, and one of the few nonanimal sources of vitamin B_{12}. It is now being widely studied for its possible antiviral, anticancer, antibacterial, and antiparisitic properties, and has been used for such medical conditions as allergies, ulcers, anemia, heavy-metal poisoning, and radiation poisoning. It is also used in weight-loss programs.

Spitfire *or* **Supermarine Spitfire** British FIGHTER AIRCRAFT in World War II. A low-wing monoplane first flown in 1936, it was adopted by the RAF in 1938. At that time one of the war's fastest single-seat fighters, it was used effectively during the Battle of BRITAIN. Later models allowed it to serve as a fighter-bomber and a photoreconnaissance plane. The 1938 version had a top speed of about 360 mph (580 kph) and was armed with eight .303-in. (7.7-mm) machine guns. The Spitfire XIV, one of the last models of the war, had a ceiling of 40,000 ft (12,200 m) and a top speed of 440 mph (710 kph). The RAF retired its last Spitfires in 1954.

Spitsbergen Norwegian archipelago, Arctic Ocean. The main group in the SVALBARD archipelago, it lies 360 mi (580 km) north of Norway. The chief islands are Spitsbergen (formerly West Spitsbergen), North East Land, Edge Island, and Barents Island. It was probably known to the Vikings. Its possession was disputed by several European nations in the 17th century over whaling rights, and in the 20th century over mining rights. Norway took formal possession in 1925. It has extensive coal deposits. Its chief settlement is Green Harbor.

Spitteler \'shpit-ə-lər\, **Carl** (1845–1924) Swiss poet. He was a private tutor in Russia and Finland before he wrote his first great poetic work, the mythical epic *Prometheus und Epimetheus* (1881). His second great work was the epic *Der olympische Frühling* (1900–1905; "The Olympic Spring"), in which he found full scope for bold invention and vividly expressive power. Late in life he rewrote his first epic as *Prometheus der Dulder* (1924; "Prometheus the Long-suffering"). Though known for his pessimistic yet heroic verse, he also wrote lyrical poems, stories, novels, and essays. He received the Nobel Prize in 1919.

spittlebug *or* **froghopper** Any of some 2,000 species of hopping insects (family Cercopidae, order Homoptera) with whitish nymphs that use a special abdominal valve to aerate an anal fluid secretion. The resulting frothy spittle protects the nymphs from enemies and desiccation. Adults are less than 0.6 in. (1.5 cm) long. The meadow spittlebug *(Philaenus leucophthalmus)*, of Europe and North America, resembles a frog and is a powerful leaper. It feeds extensively on clover and alfalfa, causing severe stunting that can result in the loss of up to 50% of a crop. Some African species occur in such enormous numbers that their spittle drips from tree branches like rain.

spitz Any of several northern dogs, including the CHOW CHOW, POMERANIAN, and SAMOYED, characterized by a dense, long coat, erect pointed ears, and a tail that curves over the back. In the U.S., the name is often given to any small, white, long-haired dog; it is also used for the American ESKIMO DOG. European breeds include the Finnish spitz, with a bright reddish brown coat, and the Lapland spitz, which has a white, brown, or blackish coat.

Spitz, Mark (Andrew) (born 1950) U.S. swimmer. Born in Modesto, Cal., he swam in college for Indiana University. At the 1968 Olympic Games he won two gold medals in team relay races. In the 1972 Olympics he won four individual men's events (setting world records in all four) and three team events (one world record); Spitz's feat of winning seven gold medals in a single Olympic Games remains unmatched.

spleen Lymphoid organ in the left side of the abdomen behind the stomach, the primary filtering element for the blood and site of red blood cell (ERYTHROCYTE) and PLATELET storage. It is one of four places where reticuloendothelial cells are found (see RETICULOENDOTHELIAL SYSTEM). Two types of tissue, red pulp and white pulp, are intermixed. The white pulp is LYMPHOID TISSUE containing LYMPHOCYTE production centers. The red pulp is a network of channels filled with blood where most of the filtration occurs, and is the major site of destruction of deteriorating erythrocytes and recycling of their HEMOGLOBIN. Both contain cells (see LEUKOCYTE) that remove foreign material and initiate an ANTIBODY-producing process. The spleen becomes enlarged in some infections. Its rupture in high-impact injuries may require surgical removal, which leaves the patient more susceptible to overwhelming infection.

Split *ancient* **Spalatum** Seaport (pop., 1991: 200,000), DALMATIA, Croatia. The Romans established the colony of Salonae nearby in 78 BC, and the emperor DIOCLETIAN lived at Split until his death in AD 313. After the Avars sacked the town in 615, the inhabitants built a new town within Diocletian's former palace, which has been continuously inhabited since it was built. It came under Byzantine rule in the 9th century. It passed to Venice in 1420. It was held by Austria in the 18th and 19th century. It came under Yugoslavia in 1918, and became part of independent Croatia in 1992. The port facilities were destroyed in World War II, but the old city was little damaged. It is a commercial, educational, and tourism center.

Spock, Benjamin (McLane) (1903–1998) U.S. pediatrician. Born in New Haven, Conn., he received his MD from Columbia University and later practiced pediatrics and taught psychiatry and child development. His *Common Sense Book of Baby and Child Care* (1946; 7th ed., 1998, as *Dr. Spock's Baby and Child Care*), which urged parental flexibility and reliance on common sense and discouraged corporal punishment, influenced generations of parents and has sold over 50 million copies in 39 languages, continually revised and updated to address new social and medical issues. In 1967 he ceased his practice to devote himself to the anti–Vietnam War movement. His advocacy late in life of a vegan (see VEGETARIANISM) diet for children aroused great controversy.

Spohr \'shpōr\, **Louis** *orig.* **Ludwig** (1784–1859) German composer and violinist. He was kapellmeister in Kassel from 1822, and remained there the rest of his life, eventually directing all the city's music. Highly prolific, he wrote 15 violin concertos, four clarinet concertos, many operas (including *Jessonda,* 1823), nine symphonies (including *Die Weihe der Töne,* 1832, and a *Historical Symphony,* 1839), and chamber music (including over 30 string quartets and a nonet). Considered a giant as a performer and composer in the 19th century, he has since been largely neglected.

spoils system *or* **patronage system** In U.S. politics, the practice by political parties of rewarding partisans and workers after winning an election. Proponents claim it helps maintain an active party organization by offering supporters jobs and contracts. Critics charge that it awards appointments to the unqualified and is inefficient because even jobs unrelated to public policy change hands after an election. In the U.S., the PENDLETON CIVIL SERVICE ACT (1883) was the first step in introducing the merit system in the hiring of government workers. The merit system has almost completely replaced the spoils system. See also CIVIL SERVICE.

Spokane \spō-'kan\ City (pop., 1996 est.: 187,000), eastern Washington. Situated at the falls of the Spokane River, it was settled on the site of a trading post established in 1810. It was incorporated in 1881 after the arrival of the NORTHERN PACIFIC RAILWAY. A fire in 1889 destroyed much of the city, but it soon was rebuilt and developed into a trade and shipping hub for the surrounding region. Completion of the Grand Coulee Dam Project (1941) assured industrial growth. It is home to Gonzaga University (1887) and is a gateway to the resorts of Mount Spokane and several national forests.

sponge Any of some 5,000 species (phylum Porifera) of permanently affixed (sessile), mostly marine, solitary or colonial INVERTEBRATES, found from shallow to deep (more than 30,000 ft, or 9,000 m) waters. Simple sponges are hollow cylinders with a large opening at the top through which water and wastes are expelled. A thin, perforated outer epidermal layer covers a porous skeleton, which is composed of interlocking spicules of calcium carbonate, silica, or spongin (found in 80% of all sponges), a proteinaceous material. The body, ranging in diameter or length from 1 in. (2.5 cm) to several yards, may be fingerlike, treelike, or a shapeless mass. Sponges lack organs and specialized tissue; flagellated cells move water into the central cavity through the perforations, and individual cells digest food (bacteria, other microorganisms, and organic debris), excrete waste, and absorb oxygen. Sponges can reproduce asexually or sexually. Larval forms are free-swimming but all adults are sessile. Since antiquity, sponges have been harvested for use in holding water, bathing, and scrubbing; because of overharvesting and newer technologies, most sponges sold today are synthetic.

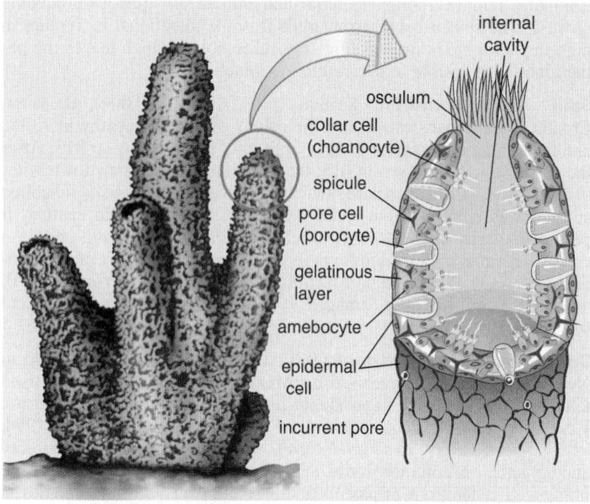

A simple saclike sponge. Its surface is perforated by small openings (incurrent pores) formed by tubelike cells (porocytes), which open into the internal cavity. A gelatinous middle layer contains the skeletal elements (spicules and spongin fibers) as well as amebocytes active in digestion, waste removal, and spicule and spongin formation. Flagellated collar cells (choanocytes) line the internal cavity, create currents to move water containing oxygen and food into the sponge, and engulf and digest food particles. Water and wastes are expelled through the ostium opening, whose size can be altered to regulate water flow through the sponge.

spontaneous abortion See MISCARRIAGE

spoonbill Any of six species (family Threskiornithidae) of long-necked, long-legged wading birds, inhabitants of Old and New World estuaries, saltwater bayous, and lakes. They are 24–32 in. (60–80 cm) long and have a short tail and a long, straight bill that is spatulate at the tip. Most species are white, sometimes rose-tinged; the roseate spoonbill *(Ajaia ajaja)* of North and South America is deep pink and strikingly beautiful. With a side-to-side motion of the bill, they sweep mud and shallow water for fishes and crustaceans. They fly with neck and legs extended and wings flapping steadily. Breeding colonies build stick nests in low bushes and trees. Some species, including the black-billed spoonbill, are endangered. See also IBIS.

spoonerism Reversal of the initial letters or syllables of two or more words, such as "I have a half-warmed fish in my mind" (for "half-formed wish") and "a blushing crow" ("a crushing blow"). The word is derived from the name of William Archibald Spooner (1844–1930), a distinguished Anglican clergyman and warden of New College, Oxford, a nervous man who committed many "spoonerisms." Such transpositions are often made intentionally for comic effect.

spore Reproductive cell capable of developing into a new individual without fusing with another reproductive cell. Spores thus differ from gametes, which must fuse in pairs in order to create a new individual. Spores are agents of nonsexual reproduction; gametes are agents of sexual reproduction. Spores are produced by BACTERIA, fungi (see FUNGUS), and green plants. Bacterial spores serve largely as a resting, or dormant, stage in the life cycle, preserving the bacterium through periods of unfavorable conditions. Many bacterial spores are highly durable and can germinate even after years of dormancy. Fungal spores serve a function similar to that of SEEDS in plants; they germinate and grow into new individuals under suitable conditions of moisture, temperature, and food availability. Among green plants (all of which have a life cycle characterized by ALTERNATION OF GENERATIONS), spores are the reproductive agents of the nonsexual generation (SPOROPHYTE), giving rise to the sexual generation (GAMETOPHYTE).

sporophyte \ˈspōr-ə-ˌfīt\ In many plants and algae, the nonsexual phase in the ALTERNATION OF GENERATIONS, or an individual representing the phase. The alternate, sexual phase is the GAMETOPHYTE. In the sporophyte phase, a diploid (see PLOIDY) plant body grows and eventually produces SPORES through MEIOSIS. These spores divide by MITOSIS to produce haploid gametophytes, which then can carry out sexual reproduction.

sports and games Recreational or competitive activities that involve physical skill, intellectual acumen, and often luck (especially in the case of games of chance). PLAY is an integral part of human nature. Throughout history, humans have invented sporting and gaming activities as a means to socialize, to display skills and prowess, and to entertain or offer excitement. The earliest games may have been based on hunting and gathering activities. In modern times, with the emergence of professional sports, games continue to serve as physical and emotional outlets, as diversions, and as enrichments to daily life while also playing a pronounced economic role.

sports-car racing Form of motor racing involving low, small, two-passenger automobiles designed for quick response, easy maneuverability, and high-speed driving. Unlike a Grand Prix car (see GRAND PRIX RACING), the sports car is usually series-produced, seldom handmade, and the reputation of the car maker (Porsche, Jaguar, etc) is thus put at stake. The most famous international sports-car race is that at LE MANS.

sports medicine Medical and paramedical supervision and treatment of athletes. It has four aspects. Preparation (conditioning) uses diet, exercises, and monitoring of practice sessions to improve performance. Prevention identifies any predisposition to injury or illness and covers warmup, stretching, and design and use of protective equipment. Many surgical techniques developed in sports medicine, particularly for knee injuries, are now used for the general population. Rehabilitation (see PHYSICAL MEDICINE AND REHABILITATION) prepares an injured or ill athlete to return to activity after initial treatment.

spotted fever See ROCKY MOUNTAIN SPOTTED FEVER

sprat *or* **brisling** Species *(Sprattus sprattus)* of edible fish in the HERRING family. Sprats are silver marine fishes that form enormous schools in western European waters. Less than 6 in. (15 cm) long, they are especially valuable for canning as SARDINES. They are eaten fresh, tinned in oil, pickled, or smoked. The term also refers to a small or young herring or similar fish (e.g., ANCHOVY).

Spratly Islands Group of reefs, CHINA SEA. The group is located midway between Vietnam and the Philippines, and claimed variously by Vietnam, China, Taiwan, Malaysia, Brunei, and the Philippines. Of the 12 main islets, the largest is the 90-acre (36-hectare) Itu Aba. Turtles and seabirds are the only permanent inhabitants. After World War II China established a garrison on Itu Aba, which the Chinese Nationalists maintained after their exile to Taiwan. Japan renounced its claim to the islands in 1951.

spraying and dusting Standard methods of applying pest-control chemicals and other compounds to plants, animals, soils, or agricultural products. For spraying, chemicals are dissolved or suspended in water or, less commonly, in an oil-based carrier. The mixture is then applied as a fine mist. In dusting, dry, finely powdered chemicals may be mixed with an inert carrier and applied with a blower. In fumigation, gases or the vapors of volatile compounds are held in contact with the materials to be treated. Sprays and dusts are used to control insects, mites, fungi, and bacterial diseases of plants; disease-spreading insects, such as lice and flies, on animals; and weeds. They are also used to apply mineral fertilizers, to increase or decrease fruit set, to delay the dropping of nearly mature fruits, and to defoliate plants to facilitate harvesting (e.g., of cotton; see DEFOLIANT). Sprays adhere to treated surfaces better than

S T U V

dusts do. Fumigation may be used to control insects and some diseases in stored products or to control insects and sometimes fungi and weeds in soil. Increasing use of spraying and dusting has prompted concern over their impact on the environment, the food chain, the water supply, and public health. New chemicals and precautions have only partially allayed these concerns. See also CROP DUSTER, FUNGICIDE, HERBICIDE, INSECTICIDE.

spreadsheet Computer SOFTWARE that allows the user to enter columns and rows of numbers in a ledgerlike format. Any cell of the ledger may contain either data or a formula that describes the value that should be inserted therein based on the values in other cells. When a change is made in one cell, the program recalculates the contents of all cells affected by the change. Spreadsheets are widely used for performing business calculations on PERSONAL COMPUTERS.

Spree River \'shprā\ River, northeastern Germany. Rising in the Lusatian Mountains near the Czech border, it flows north passing through BERLIN, where it joins the HAVEL RIVER after a course of 250 mi (403 km). Between Cottbus and Lübben it divides into a network of channels that form a marshy wooded region known as the Spree Forest. Much of this region is cultivated. It is a popular excursion area.

spring In hydrology, an opening at or near the earth's surface where water from underground sources is discharged. Springs discharge either at ground level or directly into the bed of a stream, lake, or sea. Water that emerges at the surface without a perceptible current is called a seep.

spring Elastic machine component able to deflect under load in a prescribed manner and to recover its initial shape when unloaded. The combination of force and displacement in a deflected spring is ENERGY, which may be stored when moving loads are being stopped or when the spring is wound up for use as a power source (e.g., in a WATCH). Though most springs are mechanical, hydraulic (liquid) and air springs exist.

Spring and Autumn Annals See CHUNQIU

Spring and Autumn period (770–476 BC) Period of the Chinese ZHOU DYNASTY named for one of the Confucian Classics, the *CHUNQIU* ("Spring and Autumn Annals"). During the Spring and Autumn period the imperial house's authority diminished as local nobles struggled for power in states which formed political and economic coalitions for military purposes as well as for drainage projects, canals, and other civil-engineering projects. Merchants and artisans began to assume some societal significance as well. Classical Chinese thought began in this period. See also CONFUCIUS, FIVE CLASSICS.

spring balance Weighing device that uses the relation between the applied load and the deformation of a SPRING. This relationship is usually linear; that is, if the load is doubled, the deformation is doubled. Spring balances are widely used commercially. Those with high load capacities are frequently suspended from crane hooks and are known as crane scales.

spring peeper Species *(Hyla crucifer)* of TREE FROG found in ponds, marshes, and other damp areas in the U.S. During the breeding season it can be found in woodland ponds; at other times it is seldom seen. It has a high, whistling call and is one of the first frogs to vocalize in spring. It is tiny (only 0.75–1.3 in. or 2–3.5 cm, long) and grayish, tan, or olive-brown, with an X-shaped or irregular brown mark on its back.

springbok *or* **springbuck** Species of ANTELOPE *(Antidorcas marsupialis),* native to treeless plains of southern Africa, the national emblem of South Africa. It stands about 30 in. (80 cm) high at the shoulder, and both sexes have ringed, lyre-shaped horns. A fold of skin from midback to rump can be opened to display a crest of white hair. The reddish brown upper body has a broad horizontal dark-brown band on each side; the underparts, head, tail, and rump are white. When excited, the springbok, with head down, hooves bunched, and back arched, makes a series of stiff-legged, vertical leaps up to 12 ft (3.5 m) high, an action called pronking. See photograph opposite.

Springfield City (pop., 2000: 111,454), capital of Illinois. It lies along the Sangamon River in the central part of the state. The first settler built a cabin in 1818; in 1837, largely through the efforts of ABRAHAM LINCOLN and other members of the Illinois legislature, the state capital was transferred there. Lincoln lived there until he became president in 1861; he is buried there. An educational and government services center, it also is a market center for a rich farming area.

Springfield City (pop., 2000: 152,082), southwestern Massachusetts, on the CONNECTICUT RIVER. Settled in 1636, it was incorporated in 1641. It was burned during KING PHILIP'S WAR (1675). It was the site of an arsenal during the AMERICAN REVOLUTION, which was a target of SHAYS' REBELLION in 1786. During the AMERICAN CIVIL WAR the U.S. Armory (see SPRINGFIELD ARMORY) first produced the Springfield muskets. It is home to several colleges and the Basketball Hall of Fame. It was the birthplace of THEODOR GEISEL (Dr. Seuss).

Springfield City (pop., 2000: 151,580), southwestern Missouri. Settled in 1829, it grew slowly until the U.S. period of heavy westward migration. Confederate forces held it briefly during the AMERICAN CIVIL WAR, and WILD BILL HICKOK lived there in the 1860s. Its agricultural-based economy is augmented by its educational institutions. The international headquarters of the ASSEMBLIES OF GOD church is in the city.

Springfield Armory Weapons factory established at SPRINGFIELD, Mass., by the U.S. Congress in 1794. It grew out of an arsenal established in Springfield by the revolutionary government in 1777, the site being chosen partly for its inaccessibility to British forces. The armory pioneered mass-production manufacturing techniques, and produced weapons ranging from smoothbore muskets in its earliest days to the famous SPRINGFIELD RIFLE and the M1 rifle of World War II, designed by JOHN GARAND. It closed in 1968 and is now a national historic site. See also ARMORY PRACTICE, THOMAS BLANCHARD.

Springfield rifle Any of several RIFLES that were standard infantry weapons of the U.S. Army from 1873 to 1936, all taking their name from the SPRINGFIELD ARMORY. The most famous began as the Model 1903 Springfield, an adaptation of the German Mauser. After modifications to accommodate Model 1906 ammunition, it entered history as the Springfield .30-06, one of the most reliable and accurate military firearms ever. The principal U.S. infantry weapon until 1936, it was replaced by the Garand (M1) rifle of World War II, also designed at the Springfield Armory. When the Springfield .30-06 was retired, it was widely modified into a sporting rifle that is still prized for its accuracy. See also M16 RIFLE.

Springsteen, Bruce (Frederick Joseph) (born 1949) U.S. singer and songwriter. Born in Freehold, N.J., he played guitar in several bar bands on the Jersey Shore before forming the E Street Band in the early 1970s. His third album, *Born to Run* (1975), a huge success, landed "The Boss" on the covers of *Time* and *Newsweek*. Even more successful was his *Born in the USA* (1984). Springsteen's sensitive lyrics, often voicing his working-class sympathies, and marathon concerts won a devoted following, whose concerns over the terrorist attacks of September 11, 2001, he addressed in *The Rising* (2002).

spruce Any of about 40 species of evergreen ornamental and timber trees that make up the genus *Picea* (PINE family), native to temperate and cold regions of the Northern Hemisphere. These pyramid-shaped trees have whorled branches and thin, scaly bark. The needlelike, spirally arranged leaves connect to their stems via a peglike woody base, which remains on the twig when the leaf falls. Tough, finely grained, resonant, and pliable, spruce wood is used for sounding boards in pianos and bod-

Springbok (*Antidorcas marsupialis*).
GEORGE HOLTON/PHOTO RESEARCHERS

ies of violins, as well as in construction, for boats and barrels, and as pulpwood. Common species throughout most of northern North America are black spruce *(P. mariana),* a source of spruce GUM, and white spruce *(P. glauca),* a source of good timber. Blue, or Colorado spruce *(P. pungens)* is used as an ornamental because of its bluish leaves and symmetrical growth habit.

Black spruce (*Picea mariana*).
GRANT HEILMAN—EB INC.

spruce budworm LARVA of a leaf roller MOTH *(Choristoneura fumiferana),* one of the most destructive North American pests. It attacks evergreens, feeding on needles and pollen, and can completely defoliate spruce and related trees, causing much loss for the lumber industry and damaging landscapes.

sprung rhythm Poetic rhythm designed to approximate the natural rhythm of speech. It is characterized by the frequent juxtaposition of single accented syllables and by the occurrence of feet with varying numbers of syllables whose sequence is interrupted by unstressed syllables that are not counted in the scansion. Because stressed syllables often occur sequentially, the rhythm is said to be "sprung." This system of PROSODY was developed by GERARD MANLEY HOPKINS, who saw it as the basis of such early English poems as WILLIAM LANGLAND's *Piers Plowman* and of nursery rhymes such as "*Ding, dong, bell / Pus*sy's *in* the *well*" (stressed syllables italicized).

spurge One of the largest flowering-plant genera *(Euphorbia),* with more than 1,600 species. It takes its common name from a group of annual herbs used as purgatives, or spurges. Many spurges are important as ornamentals or as sources of drugs; many others are weeds. One of the best-known is the POINSETTIA. *Euphorbia* is part of the family Euphorbiaceae, which contains about 7,500 species of flowering annual and perennial herbs and woody shrubs or trees in 275 genera; most are found in temperate and tropical regions. Flowers usually lack petals; those of *Euphorbia* are borne in cup-shaped clusters. The fruit is a CAPSULE. Leaves are usually simple. The stems of many species contain a milky latex. In addition to *Euphorbia,* economically important family members include the CASTOR-OIL PLANT, CROTON, CASSAVA, and RUBBER TREE.

Spurge (*Euphorbia venata*).
VALERIE FINNIS

Sputnik \'spu̇t-nik\ Any of a series of artificial earth satellites whose launching by the Soviet Union inaugurated the Space Age. Sputnik 1, the first satellite launched by humans (October 1957), remained in orbit until early 1958, when it fell back and burned in earth's atmosphere. Sputnik 2 carried a dog, Laika, the first living creature to orbit earth; since Sputnik 2 was not designed to sustain life, Laika did not survive the flight. Eight more missions with similar satellites carried out experiments on various animals to test life-support systems and reentry procedures and to furnish data on space temperatures, pressures, particles, radiation, and magnetic fields.

Spyri \'shpē-rē\, **Johanna** *orig.* **Johanna Heusser** (1829–1901) Swiss writer. Living in Zurich with her lawyer husband, Spyri wrote books, many widely translated, that are imbued with her love of homeland, feeling for nature, unobtrusive piety, and cheerful wisdom. She is best remembered for her popular novel *Heidi* (1880–81), a classic of children's literature about an orphan sent to live with her grandfather in the Swiss mountains.

SQL *in full* **Structured Query Language** Computer PROGRAMMING LANGUAGE used for retrieving records or parts of records in DATABASES and performing various calculations before displaying the results. SQL is particularly suitable for searching RELATIONAL DATABASES. It has a formal, powerful syntax and is able to accommodate logical operators. Its sentence-like structure resembles natural language except that its syntax is limited and fixed.

Squanto (died 1622) Pawtuxet Indian interpreter and guide. Squanto learned English after escaping an attempt to sell him into slavery and joining the Newfoundland Co. At Plymouth colony, he was made Gov. WILLIAM BRADFORD's Indian emissary; he also served as interpreter for EDWARD WINSLOW, the Pilgrim representative, during his negotiations with MASSASOIT, chief of the Wampanoags.

square In measurement, a device consisting of two straightedges set at a right angle. It is used by carpenters and machinists to check the correctness of right angles, as a guide when drawing lines on materials before cutting, or for locating holes. In mechanical drawing or drafting, a T-shaped instrument known as a T square is used to establish a horizontal reference on the drafting board.

square dance Dance for sets of four couples standing in square formation. The most popular type of U.S. folk dance, it derived from the QUADRILLE and was originally called a square dance to distinguish it from the contra, or longways, dance (for a double line of couples) and the round dance (for a circle of couples). The U.S. square dance progresses through specific patterns called or sung out to the dancers by a caller and accompanied by lively music played on instruments such as fiddle, banjo, accordion, guitar, and piano.

Square Deal Term used by Pres. THEODORE ROOSEVELT to describe his approach to social problems and the individual. He first used the term after the 1902 coal strike as the ideal of peaceful coexistence between big business and labor unions. The concept became part of the BULL MOOSE PARTY platform when Roosevelt became its candidate in 1912.

square of opposition See square of OPPOSITION

squash Any of various fruits of the genus *Cucurbita* in the GOURD family, widely cultivated as vegetables and for livestock feed. The principal species are *C. maxima* and certain varieties of *C. pepo.* Summer squash is a quick-growing, small-fruited, nontrailing or bush type of *C. pepo.* Diverse in form, color, and surface texture, the fruits do not store well and must be used soon after harvest (see ZUCCHINI). Winter varieties of squash, *C. maxima,* are long-vining, generally large-fruited, long-season types. Harvested fruits, in a wide range of sizes, shapes, and colors, can be stored many months if kept dry and well above freezing. The rinds are harder than those of summer squash and usually inedible. Examples include acorn squash and PUMPKIN. Native to the Americas, squash was widely cultivated by American Indians before Europeans arrived.

squash (rackets) Singles or doubles game played in a four-walled court with a long-handled racket and a rubber ball that can be hit off any number of walls (as long as it hits the front wall). A descendant of RACKETS, it probably originated in the mid-19th century at England's HARROW SCHOOL. The standard international game uses a relatively soft, slow ball; hardball squash, played in the U.S., is played on a narrower court with a harder, faster ball. The object of squash rackets is to bounce, or rebound, the ball off the front wall in such a way as to defeat an opponent's attempt to reach and return it.

squash bug *or* **leaf-footed bug** Any of more than 2,000 widely distributed insect species (family Coreidae), including many important plant pests. Most species are dull-colored and more than 0.4 in. (10 mm) long. Many have enlarged, flattened extensions on the legs. The North American squash bug *(Anasa tristis)* is an important pest of squash, melon, and pumpkin (plants in the GOURD family). It is basically yellow but is covered with black pits that make it look black. The larvae feed underground, and the piercing and sucking mouthparts of the adults enable them to attack the parts of plants that insecticides rarely penetrate.

squash tennis Singles racket game resembling SQUASH rackets, played with an inflated ball the size of a tennis ball. Played in virtually the same court as squash rackets, squash tennis makes fewer demands on the legs in pursuing the ball but puts a greater premium on agility and quickness of foot and reflexes in turning and spinning.

squatter sovereignty See POPULAR SOVEREIGNTY

Squaw Valley Valley, eastern California. It is located in the SIERRA NEVADA on the eastern slope of Squaw Peak, northwest of Lake TAHOE. A world-famous winter sports area, it has ice-skating facilities, ski lifts, and trails, and was the site of the 1960 Winter OLYMPIC GAMES.

Squibb, E(dward) R(obinson) (1819–1900) U.S. pharmaceutical manufacturer. Born in Wilmington, Del., he earned a medical degree and later worked on U.S. Navy ships; his work alerted him to the poor quality of the medicines supplied to the Navy, which he persuaded to manufacture its own drugs. At the Brooklyn Naval Hospital (from 1851) he devised a safe method for making anesthetic ether and also discovered processes for making chloroform, fluid extracts, and bismuth salts. In 1858 he set up his own Brooklyn laboratory; the Union Army during the Civil War relied heavily on his drugs, and by 1883 he was manufacturing 324 products and selling them around the world. A Quaker idealist, he refused to patent his medicines, and he crusaded for purity in drug manufacture; he did not live to see the culmination of his work in the Pure Food and Drug Act of 1904.

squid Any of numerous 10-armed CEPHALOPODS, found in both coastal and oceanic waters, that prey on fishes and crustaceans. Species range from less than 0.75 in. (1.5 cm) to more than 65 ft (20 m) long (in the case of the giant squid). Two of the 10 arms are long, slender tentacles; each has an expanded end and four rows of suckers with toothed, horny rings. An internal shell supports the slender tubular body of most species. Squid eyes, almost as complex as human eyes, are usually set into the sides of the head. Squids may be swift swimmers (propelling themselves by contracting and relaxing their mantle or by undulating their two fins) or mere drifters; water expelled from a funnel below the head can propel the squid backward. Like the OCTOPUS, it may emit an inky cloud from its ink sac when in danger from sperm whales, fishes, or humans, among other predators.

Squid (*Illex coindeti*) swimming forward.
DOUGLAS P. WILSON

squint See STRABISMUS

squirrel Any of about 260 species in 50 genera (family Sciuridae) of mostly diurnal RODENTS found almost worldwide. Many species are arboreal; some are terrestrial. All species have strong hind legs and a hairy tail. They vary widely in color and form and range in total length from the 4-in. (10-cm) African pygmy squirrel to the giant squirrels of Asia, about 35 in. (90 cm) long. Tree dwellers live in a tree hollow or nest, and most are active year-round. Ground dwellers live in burrows, and many become dormant in winter (hibernate) or summer (estivate). Most species are primarily vegetarian and are fond of seeds and nuts; some eat insects or supplement their diet with animal protein. See also CHIPMUNK, FLYING SQUIRREL, GROUND SQUIRREL, MARMOT, PRAIRIE DOG.

squirrel monkey Any of several species (genus *Saimiri*, family Cebidae) of arboreal, diurnal NEW WORLD MONKEYS, found in groups of up to several hundred in riverside forests of Central and South America. They eat fruit, insects, and small animals. They are 10–16 in. (25–40 cm) long and have a heavy, nonprehensile, black-tipped tail, 15–19 in. (37–47 cm) long. They have a small white face, large eyes, and large, usually tufted, ears. The short, soft coat is grayish to greenish, with yellow or orange arms, hands, and feet. The crown of the common squirrel monkey *(S. sciureus)* is olive or grayish; the red-backed *(S. oerstedii)* has a black crown and reddish back. They are often kept as gentle and affectionate pets.

Common squirrel monkey (*Saimiri sciureus*).
© GERRY ELLIS NATURE PHOTOGRAPHY

Sraosha \sraů-'shä\ In ZOROASTRIANISM AND PARSIISM, the divine being who is the messenger of AHURA MAZDA and the embodiment of the divine word. He serves as the mediator between the human and the divine. Zoroastrians believe that no ritual is valid without his presence. He is depicted as a strong and holy youth who lives in a celestial thousand-pillared house. He chastises the demons that harass people every night, and he leads the righteous soul through the ordeal of judgment three days after death. At the end of time, he will be the agent of the extermination of evil.

Sravasti \shrä-'vəs-tē\ Ancient city, northeastern UTTAR PRADESH, northern India. In Buddhist times (6th century BC–6th century AD), it was the capital of KOSALA and a prosperous trading center. It was also closely associated with the life of BUDDHA and with figures significant in later Buddhist history. Its ruins include those of a monastery.

Sri Lanka \ˌsrē-'läŋ-kə\ *officially* **Democratic Socialist Republic of Sri Lanka** *formerly* **Ceylon** Island country in the Indian Ocean, off the southeastern coast of India. Area: 25,332 sq mi (65,610 sq km). Population (2001): 19,399,000. Capitals: COLOMBO (executive), Sri Jayewardenepura Kotte (legislative and judicial). About 75% of the population is SINHALESE; other ethnic groups include TAMILS and Muslims. Languages: Sinhalese and Tamil (both official); English also widely spoken. Religions: Buddhism, Hinduism, Islam, Christianity. Currency: Sri Lanka rupee. Highlands make up Sri Lanka's southern central region

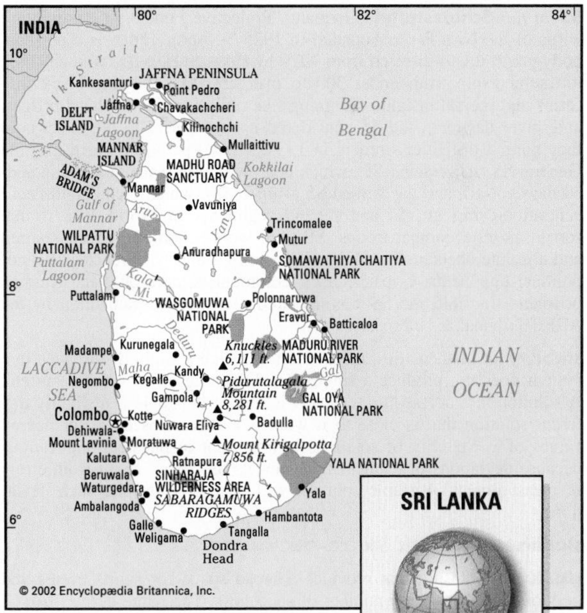

and heart, with gorges and deep river valleys. The surrounding lowlands include hills and fertile plains. It has a developing mixed economy, largely based on agriculture, services, and light industries. Tea, rubber, and coconuts are exported. The island is world-famous for its gemstones, which include sapphires, rubies, and topaz. It leads the world in the production of high-grade graphite. It is a republic with one legislative house; its head of state and government is the president, assisted by the prime minister. The Sinhalese people of Sri Lanka probably originated with aboriginal inhabitants blending with migrating Indo-Aryans from India c. 5th century BC. The Tamils were later immigrants from Dravidian India, migrating over a period from the early centuries AD to c. 1200. Buddhism was introduced during the 3rd century BC. As Buddhism spread, the Sinhalese kingdom extended its political control over Ceylon, but lost it to invaders from southern India in the 10th century AD. Between 1200 and 1505 Sinhalese power gravitated to southwestern Ceylon, while a southern Indian dynasty seized power in the north and established the Tamil kingdom in the 14th century. Foreign invasions from India, China, and Malaya occurred in the 13th–15th century. In 1505 the Portuguese arrived, and by 1619 they controlled most of the island. The Sinhalese enlisted the Dutch to help oust the Portuguese, and it eventually came under the control of the Dutch EAST INDIA CO., which relinquished it in 1796 to the British. In 1802 Ceylon became a crown colony, gaining independence in 1948. It became the Republic of Sri Lanka in 1972, and was renamed the Democratic Socialist Republic of Sri Lanka in 1978. Civil strife between Tamil and Sinhalese groups has beset the country in recent years, with the Tamils demanding a separate autonomous state in northern Sri Lanka.

Srinagar \srē-ˈnə-gər\ City (pop., 1990 est.: 850,000), summer capital of JAMMU AND KASHMIR state, northwestern India. It lies on the banks of the JHELUM RIVER in the Vale of Kashmir. Situated amid clear lakes and lofty mountains, it has long had a considerable tourist economy. Seven wooden bridges span the river, and the gondolas of Kashmir ply the adjacent canals and waterways. The floating gardens of Dal Lake are a famous attraction.

Srivijaya empire \ˌsrē-wi-ˈjō-yə\ (fl. 7th–13th century) Maritime and commercial kingdom in the Malay Archipelago. It originated on SUMATRA and soon came to control the Strait of MALACCA. Its power was based on its control of international sea trade; it had relations with other island states and with China and India. It was also a center for MAHAYANA Buddhism and a stopping place for Chinese pilgrims traveling to India. It was overcome by forces of the COLA DYNASTY in 1025 and lost power gradually thereafter.

SS *in full* **Schutzstaffel** (German: "Protective Echelon") Paramilitary corps of the NAZI PARTY. Founded in 1925 by ADOLF HITLER as a personal bodyguard, it was directed from 1929 by HEINRICH HIMMLER, who enlarged its membership from under 300 to over 250,000. Wearing black uniforms and special insignia (lightning-like runic S's, death's-head badges, and silver daggers), the SS considered itself superior to the SA, whom they purged on Hitler's orders in 1934. The corps was divided into the General SS *(Allgemeine-SS),* which dealt with police matters and included the GESTAPO, and the Armed SS *(Waffen-SS),* which included the concentration-camp guards and the 39 regiments in World War II that served as elite combat troops. SS men were schooled in racial hatred and absolute obedience to Hitler. They carried out massive executions of political opponents, Gypsies, Jews, communists, partisans, and Russian prisoners. In 1946 the SS was declared a criminal organization by the Allied Tribunal at Nuremberg.

stability In mathematics, a condition in which a slight disturbance in a system does not produce a significant disrupting effect on that system. A solution to a DIFFERENTIAL EQUATION is said to be stable if a slightly different solution that is close to it when $x = 0$ remains close for nearby values of x. Stability of solutions is important in physical applications because deviations in mathematical models inevitably result from errors in measurement. A stable solution will be usable despite such deviations.

stabilizer, economic See ECONOMIC STABILIZER

stadium Enclosure that provides a broad space for sports events and tiers of seats for a large number of spectators. The name derives from a Greek unit of measurement, the stade (about 607 ft, or 185 m), the length of the footrace in the ancient Olympics. Shapes of stadiums have varied depending on use: Some are rectangular with curved corners; others are elliptical or U-shaped. As a type of long-span structure, the stadium played a significant role in 20th-century construction technology. The building of large stadiums has been greatly facilitated by the use of reinforced concrete, steel, and MEMBRANE STRUCTURES, which have made possible daring new designs. The Houston Astrodome (see LAMELLA ROOF) was the first major fully roofed stadium. Cables contributed significantly to speed of construction, lightness of roof, and economy in covered stadiums. The enormous Hubert H. Humphrey Metrodome in Minneapolis (opened 1982) was built using a cable system.

Staël \ˈstäl\, **Germaine de** *orig.* **baronne (baroness) Anne-Louise-Germaine Necker de Staël-Holstein** *known as* **Madame de Staël** (1766–1817) French-Swiss writer, political propagandist, and salon hostess. Born in Paris, she early gained a reputation as a lively wit. She first became known for *Letters on the Works and the Character of J.-J. Rousseau* (1788). The most brilliant period of her career began in 1794, when she returned to Paris after the Reign of Terror; her salon, known for its literary and intellectual figures, flourished, and she published political and literary essays, notably *A Treatise on the Influence of the Passions upon the Happiness of Individuals and of Nations* (1796), an important document of European ROMANTICISM. In 1803 Napoleon, who resented her opposition, had her banished from Paris, and she made the family residence in Coppet, Switzerland, her headquarters. Probably her most important work is *Germany* (1810), a serious study of German manners, literature and art, philosophy and morals, and religion. Her other writings include novels, plays, moral essays, history, and memoirs.

Germaine de Staël, portrait by Jean-Baptiste Isabey, 1810; in the Louvre, Paris.

GIRAUDON—ART RESOURCE/EB INC.

Stafford Town (pop., 1994 est.: 123,000), county seat of STAFFORDSHIRE, western central England. Founded by the daughter of ALFRED the Great, the town had its own mint from the reign of Aethelstan to that of HENRY II. After being chartered in 1206, it grew as a market town. Parliamentarians demolished its 11th-century walls and castle in 1643 during the ENGLISH CIVIL WARS. It is situated on the London-Birmingham-Manchester road and rail route; its industries include electrical and mechanical engineering. It was the birthplace of IZAAK WALTON, and its Swan Hotel was associated with CHARLES DICKENS.

Staffordshire \ˈsta-fərd-ˌshir\ County (pop., 1995 est.: 802,000), central England. Its county seat is STAFFORD. Its northern moorlands form the southern tip of the PENNINES, and it encompasses the coalfield region known as The Potteries. Traces of Neolithic, Bronze Age, and Iron Age settlements remain. The Romans built roads through the area; it was the center of the kingdom of MERCIA in the 7th–9th century. The Danes ravaged it at the end of the 9th century. Staffordshire has mined coal and iron since the 13th century. Its pottery industry became famous in the 18th century with the innovations of JOSIAH WEDGWOOD.

Staffordshire figure Type of pottery figurine made in Staffordshire, England, beginning c. 1740. The figurines were made first in salt-glazed STONEWARE, later in lead-glazed EARTHENWARE. Subjects included musicians, animals, shepherds, classical deities, allegorical figures, portraits, theatrical and political personages, and even criminals. Staffordshire artists included the WOOD FAMILY of potters.

Staffordshire lead-glazed earthenware figure, c. 1780; in the Victoria and Albert Museum, London.

BY COURTESY OF THE VICTORIA AND ALBERT MUSEUM, LONDON; PHOTOGRAPH, EB INC.

Staffordshire terrier See PIT BULL TERRIER

stage design Aesthetic composition of a dramatic production as created by lighting, scenery, costumes, and sound. While such elements as painted screens and wheeled platforms were used in the Greek theater of the 4th century BC, most innovations in stage design were developed in the Italian Renaissance theater, where painted backdrops, perspective architectural settings, and numerous changes of scenery were common. Italian staging was introduced in England in 1605 by INIGO JONES for court masques. In the late 19th century, staging was influenced by the new naturalism, which called for historically accurate sets. In the 20th century, simplified stage design focused attention on the actor. Stage design has been greatly affected by advances in lighting, from the use of candles in the Renaissance to oil lamps in the 18th century and gas and electric lights in the 19th century. Modern stage lighting, which employs computerized control boards to achieve complex effects, can unify all the visual elements of a stage production.

stage machinery Devices designed for the production of theatrical effects, including rapid scene changes, lighting, sound effects, and illusions. Such devices had been in use since the 5th century BC, when the Greeks developed the DEUS EX MACHINA to lower an actor to the stage, as well as movable scenery mounted on wheels. Medieval mystery plays used trapdoors to allow the emergence of devils, and flying machines for angels. In the Italian Renaissance, elaborate machinery was used for spectacles produced in the churches on holy days. In the 17th century, the Italian Giacomo Torelli (1608–1678) invented a system for moving the stage wings that made it possible to change scenery quickly. In the 19th century, magical illusions were created with mirror devices and refined trapdoors. By the late 20th century, spectacle had fallen out of fashion except in musical theater, but hydraulic stage machinery allowed for swift and soundless scene changes.

stagecoach Public COACH pulled by horses regularly traveling a fixed route between stations or stages. Stagecoaches appeared in London by 1640 and in Paris by 1660. In the 19th cent. they were most widely used in the U.S. and in England, where in 1828 stagecoaches ran 12 times a day from Leicester to London. In the U.S. they were the only means of travel for long distances overland, carrying passengers and mail to locations especially in the West. As railroad travel became more common, stagecoach travel diminished except to remote locations.

staged rocket Vehicle driven by several ROCKET systems mounted in vertical sequence. The lowest, or first, stage ignites and lifts the vehicle at increasing speed until its propellants are used up. At that point the first stage drops off, making the vehicle lighter, and the second stage ignites and accelerates the vehicle further. Most space LAUNCH VEHICLES have three stages. See also SPACECRAFT.

Stagg, Amos Alonzo (1862–1965) U.S. college football coach. Born in West Orange, N.J., he played end for Yale and was chosen for the first All-America team in 1889. During his 41-year tenure at the University of Chicago (1892–1932), he devised the end-around play, the man in motion, the huddle (also credited to another), the shift play, and the tackling dummy. He later coached at three other colleges, not retiring until 1960. His 71 years of coaching represent the longest coaching career in the history of the sport. He died at 102.

Stahl, Franklin W(illiam) (born 1929) U.S. geneticist. Born in Boston and educated at Harvard University and the University of Rochester, he worked primarily at the University of Oregon. With MATTHEW STANLEY MESELSON he discovered and described (1958) the mode of replication of DNA. They found that the double-stranded helix breaks apart to form two strands, each of which directs the construction of a new sister strand.

stained glass Colored glass used to make decorative windows and other objects through which light passes. Stained glass is often made in large, richly detailed panels that are set together in a framework of lead. Like all colored glass, it acquires its color by the addition of metallic oxides to molten glass. A purely Western phenomenon, stained glass originated as a fine art of the Christian church, beginning in the 12th–13th century, when it was combined with GOTHIC ARCHITECTURE to create brilliant, moving effects. A decline set in after the 13th century, when stained-glass artists began to seek the realistic effects sought by Renaissance painters, effects to which the technique was less suited and which diverted artists from exploiting the all-important light-refracting quality of glass. More recently, stained-glass artists have again achieved high quality: during the 19th-century Gothic revival, in the Art Nouveau designs of LOUIS COMFORT TIFFANY, and in the work of such 20th-century artists as MARC CHAGALL.

stainless steel Any of a family of ALLOY STEELS usually containing 10–30% CHROMIUM. The presence of chromium, together with low carbon content, gives remarkable resistance to corrosion and heat. Other elements, such as nickel, molybdenum, titanium, aluminum, niobium, copper, nitrogen, sulfur, phosphorus, and selenium, may be added to increase corrosion resistance to specific environments, enhance resistance to oxidation (see OXIDATION–REDUCTION), and impart special characteristics.

stairway *or* **staircase** Series or flight of steps that provides a means of moving from one level to another. The earliest stairways seem to have been built with walls on both sides, as in Egyptian PYLONS dating from the 2nd millennium BC. The Romans were noted for their monumental stairs. The modern use of steel and reinforced concrete has made possible the curves and sweeps of contemporary design. Staircases have traditionally been built of wood, marble or stone, and iron or steel. A step's horizontal surface is called its tread, the vertical front its riser. Traditional wooden staircases are constructed with stringers, beams inclined to the angle of the staircase. Stringers are supported by newel posts, which also support the handrail, forming a balustrade.

Staked Plain See LLANO ESTACADO

stalactite and stalagmite \stə-ˈlak-ˌtīt...stə-ˈlag-ˌmīt\ Elongated forms of various minerals deposited from solution by slowly dripping water. A stalactite hangs like an icicle from the ceiling or side of a cavern. A stalagmite rises from the floor of a cavern. The two are not necessarily paired; when they are, continual elongation of one or both may eventually join them into a column. The dominant mineral in such deposits is CALCITE (calcium carbonate), and the largest displays are formed in caves of LIMESTONE and DOLOMITE.

stalactite work *or* **muqarnas** \mu̇-ˈkär-näs\ Honeycomb-like Islamic architectural ornamentation formed by the intricate corbeling (see CORBEL) of squinches (see BYZANTINE ARCHITECTURE), brackets, and inverted pyramids in overlapping tiers. It appeared in the early 12th century throughout the Islamic world; a frequent use was to overlay the transitional zone between domes and their supports. It reached its highest development in the 14th–15th century, when it became the usual decoration for door heads, niches, and the bracketing under cornices and minaret galleries. Rich examples are found in the ALHAMBRA and other Moorish works in Spain.

Stalin, Joseph *orig.* **Iosif Vissarionovich Dzhugashvili** (1879–1953) Soviet politician and dictator. Born in Georgia, the son of a cobbler, he studied at a seminary but was expelled for revolutionary activity in 1899. He joined an underground revolutionary group and sided with the BOLSHEVIK faction of the RUSSIAN SOCIAL-DEMOCRATIC WORKERS' PARTY in 1903. A disciple of VLADIMIR ILICH LENIN, he served in minor party posts and was appointed to the first Bolshevik Central Committee (1912). He remained active behind the scenes and in exile (1913–17) until the RUSSIAN REVOLUTION OF 1917 brought the Bolsheviks to power. Having adopted the name Stalin (from Russian *stal:* "steel"), he served as commissar for nationalities and for state control in the Bolshevik government (1917–23). He became secretary-general of the party's Central Committee from 1922, the post that later provided the power base for his dictatorship, and was also a member of the Politburo. After Lenin's death (1924), Stalin overcame his rivals, including LEON TROTSKY, GRIGORY Y. ZINOVYEV, LEV KAMENEV, NIKOLAY I. BUKHARIN, and ALEKSEY RYKOV, and took control of Soviet politics. In 1928 he inaugurated the FIVE-YEAR PLANS that radically altered Soviet economic and social structures and resulted in the deaths of many millions. In the 1930s he contrived to eliminate threats to his power through the PURGE TRIALS and through widespread secret executions and persecution. In WORLD WAR II he signed the GERMAN-SOVIET NONAGGRESSION PACT (1939), attacked Finland (see RUSSO-FINNISH WAR), and annexed parts of Eastern Europe to strengthen his western frontiers. When Germany invaded Russia (1941), Stalin took control of military operations. He allied Russia with Britain and the U.S.; at the TEHRAN, YALTA, and POTSDAM conferences, he demonstrated his negotiating skill. After the war he consolidated Soviet power in Eastern Europe and built up the Soviet Union as a world military power. He continued his repressive political measures to control internal dissent;

increasingly paranoid, he was preparing to mount another purge after the so-called DOCTORS' PLOT when he died. Noted for bringing the Soviet Union into world prominence, at terrible cost to his own people, he left a legacy of repression and fear as well as industrial and military power. In 1956 Stalin and his personality cult were denounced by NIKITA KHRUSHCHEV.

Stalin Peak See COMMUNISM PEAK

Stalinabad See DUSHANBE

Stalingrad See VOLGOGRAD

Stalingrad, Battle of (1942–43) Unsuccessful German assault on the Soviet city in World War II. German forces invaded the Soviet Union in 1941, and had advanced to the suburbs of Stalingrad (now Volgograd) by the summer of 1942. Met by a determined RED ARMY defense commanded by VASILY CHUIKOV, they reached the city's center after fierce street fighting. In November the Soviets counterattacked and encircled the German army led by FRIEDRICH PAULUS, who surrendered in February 1943 with 91,000 troops. The Axis forces (Germans, Romanians, Italians, and Hungarians) lost 800,000 dead; Soviet forces lost over 1 million dead. The battle marked the farthest extent of the German advance into the Soviet Union.

Stalinism Method of rule, or policies, of JOSEPH STALIN in the Soviet Union and his imitators elsewhere in the Soviet bloc. On taking power, Stalin brooked no dissent from party policies, of which he assumed the role of sole infallible interpreter. He postponed the struggle for world proletarian revolution, focusing instead on "socialism in one country." He decreed the wholesale collectivization of Russian agriculture and a program of rapid industrialization, which, though broadly effective, resulted in the deaths of many millions. Purges in the 1930s (see PURGE TRIALS) resulted in the deaths of millions more, as opponents were branded traitors and executed or sent to the GULAG. After Stalin's death NIKITA KHRUSHCHEV repudiated Stalinism (1956) as an aberration. See also LENINISM, TROTSKYISM.

Stalino See DONETSK

Stallone, (Michael) Sylvester (born 1946) U.S. film actor. Born in New York City, he began appearing in movies in 1970, including *The Lords of Flatbush* (1974) and *Capone* (1975). He wrote and starred in the surprise hit *Rocky* (1976), winning instant fame with his portrayal of a Philadelphia boxer who becomes a champion. He cowrote and acted in its four sequels (1979, 1982, 1985, 1990) and a series of violent action movies featuring the character Rambo, beginning with *First Blood* (1982). His other films include *Cliffhanger* (1993) and *Cop Land* (1997).

Stamboliyski \,stäm-bō-'lē-skē\, **Aleksandur** (1879–1923) Bulgarian politician and premier (1919–23). Editor of the Agrarian League's newspaper, he entered the National Assembly in 1908 as head of the Agrarian Union (Peasant Party). He opposed the pro-German king FERDINAND and supported the Allies in World War I, for which he was imprisoned 1915–18. He led the 1918 insurrection that forced Ferdinand's abdication, and was chosen premier of the new Bulgarian republic in 1919. Favoring a pro-agrarian policy, he redistributed land to the peasants and reformed the judicial system. His pacifist leanings and advocacy of a militia alienated the army, and he was overthrown in a military coup and executed.

stamen Male reproductive part of a FLOWER. Stamens produce POLLEN in terminal saclike structures called anthers. The number of stamens is usually the same as the number of petals. Stamens usually consist of a long slender stalk, the filament, with the anthers at the tip. Some stamens are similar to leaves, with the anthers at or near the margins. Small secretory structures called nectaries are often found at the base of the stamens and provide food rewards for insect and bird pollinators (see POLLINATION). See also PISTIL.

Stamford City (pop., 1996 est.: 110,000), southwestern Connecticut. It lies at the mouth of the Rippowam River on LONG ISLAND SOUND. Founded in 1641, it was a farming community until the railroad reached it in the 1840s. It was essentially a residential suburb of New York City until the early 1970s, when several major corporations moved their headquarters there, revitalizing the city's economic life. Its decaying downtown was razed and rebuilt with modern skyscrapers, and today it has one of the largest concentrations of corporate headquarters in the U.S.

Stamitz \'shtä-mits\, **Johann (Wenzel Anton)** (1717–1757) Hungarian-German composer and violinist. He joined the elector's court in Mannheim c. 1741, and soon became director of its orchestra, which he built into the finest in Europe. He wrote some 75 symphonies, in which he helped establish the four-movement form as the standard and introduced the orchestral crescendo to Germany from Italian music. He and his students (including his sons) made up what is called the "Mannheim School." His son Carl (1745–1801), also a composer and violinist, played in Mannheim, toured widely as a soloist, and wrote more than 50 symphonies.

stammering See STUTTERING

Stamp Act (1765) British parliamentary measure to tax the American colonies. To pay for costs resulting from the FRENCH AND INDIAN WAR, the British sought to raise revenue through a stamp tax on printed matter. A common revenue device in England, the tax was vigorously opposed by the colonists, whose representatives had not been consulted. Colonists refused to use the stamps, and mobs intimidated stamp agents. The Stamp Act Congress, with representatives from nine colonies, met to petition Parliament to repeal the act. Faced with additional protests from British merchants whose exports had been reduced by colonial boycotts, Parliament repealed the act (1766), then passed the DECLARATORY ACT.

"An Emblem of the Effects of the STAMP," a warning against the Stamp Act published in the Pennsylvania *Journal*, October 1765; in The New York Public Library.

RARE BOOKS AND MANUSCRIPTS DIVISION, THE NEW YORK PUBLIC LIBRARY, ASTOR, LENOX AND TILDEN FOUNDATIONS

stamp collecting See PHILATELY

Standard Generalized Markup Language See SGML

standard model In physics, the combination of two theories of PARTICLE PHYSICS into a single framework to describe all interactions of SUBATOMIC PARTICLES except those due to gravity (see GRAVITATION). The two theories, the ELECTROWEAK THEORY and the theory of QUANTUM CHROMODYNAMICS, describe the interactions between particles in terms of the exchange of intermediary particles. The model has proved highly accurate in predicting certain interactions, but it does not explain all aspects of subatomic particles. For example, it cannot say how many particles there should be or what their masses are. The search goes on for a more complete theory, and in particular a UNIFIED FIELD THEORY describing the STRONG, WEAK, and ELECTROMAGNETIC forces.

standard of living Level of material comfort that an individual or group aspires to or may achieve. This includes not only privately purchased goods and services but collectively consumed goods and services such as those provided by public utilities and governments. A standard of living determined for a group such as a country must be examined critically in terms of its constituent values. If the mean value increases over time, but at the same time the rich become richer and the poor poorer, the group may not be collectively better off. Various quantitative indicators can be used as measuring rods, including life expectancy, access to nutritious food and a safe water supply, and availability of medical care.

Standard Oil Co. and Trust U.S. company and corporate trust that held a near monopoly over the U.S. oil industry from 1870 to 1911. The company originated in 1863, when JOHN D. ROCKEFELLER joined a Cleveland refining firm, which, with other facilities, was incorporated as the Standard Oil Co. in 1870. By 1880, through elimination of competitors, mergers, and use of favorable railroad REBATES, it controlled the refining of 90–95% of all oil produced in the U.S. In 1882 Standard Oil and affiliated oil companies were combined in the Standard Oil Trust, which eventually included some 40 corporations. In 1892 the Ohio Supreme Court ordered the trust dissolved, but it continued to operate from headquarters in New York and later New Jersey. Its monopolistic practices were exposed in IDA TARBELL's *History of the Standard Oil Company* (1904), and after a lengthy antitrust suit by the U.S. government (see

ANTITRUST LAW), the Standard Oil empire was broken up in 1911. Standard Oil Co. (New Jersey) changed its name to EXXON CORP. in 1972; other corporations such as MOBIL, Amoco, and Chevron include companies that once belonged to the trust.

standard time Official local time of a region or country. Local mean solar time depends on longitude; it advances by four minutes per degree eastward. The earth can thus be divided into 24 standard time zones, each approximately 15° in longitude. The actual boundaries of each time zone are determined by local authorities and in many places deviate considerably from 15°. The times in different zones usually differ by an integral number of hours; minutes and seconds are the same. See also GREENWICH MEAN TIME.

standardbred Breed of light HORSE developed in the U.S., primarily for harness racing. The foundation sire was an English THOROUGHBRED imported in 1788; his progeny were bred with other breeds, especially the MORGAN, to produce speedy trotters and pacers. The standardbred's height is 15–16 hands (60–64 in., 152–163 cm); its weight is 900–1,000 lbs (410–450 kg). Color varies, but the most common is bay. "Standard" refers to a requirement imposed in 1871 that, to be registered, a horse must meet certain standards of speed (e.g., trotting a mile in 2.5 minutes).

standardization In industry, the development and application of standards that make it possible to manufacture a large volume of interchangeable parts. Standardization may focus on engineering standards, such as properties of materials, fits and tolerances, and drafting practices; or on product standards, which detail the attributes of manufactured items and are embodied in formulas, descriptions, drawings, or models. Adoption of standards makes it easier for firms to communicate with their suppliers. Standards are also used within industries to prevent conflict and duplication of effort. Governmental departments, trade associations, and technical associations help to set standards within industries; these are coordinated and promoted by organizations such as the American National Standards Institute (ANSI) and the INTERNATIONAL ORGANIZATION FOR STANDARDIZATION (ISO).

Standards and Technology, National Institute of See BUREAU OF STANDARDS

standing In law, the status of being qualified to bring a legal matter before a court because one has a sufficient and protectable interest in its outcome. The courts have ruled that a plaintiff who has suffered or is threatened with actual injury (physical, economic, or other) clearly has standing. A plaintiff who cannot demonstrate such injury will lack standing and therefore be unable to bring a case.

Standish, Myles (1584?–1656) British-American colonist. He fought in the Netherlands, where he met the Pilgrims, with whom he later sailed to North America on the *Mayflower* (1620). As the PLYMOUTH colony's military leader, he led several expeditions against hostile Indian tribes. He served as the colony's assistant governor and treasurer 1644–49. He was mythologized in HENRY W. LONGFELLOW's poem *The Courtship of Miles Standish* (1858); the story that he asked JOHN ALDEN to propose marriage for him has no historical basis.

Stanford, (Amasa) Leland (1824–1893) U.S. entrepreneur, a builder of the first transcontinental railroad. Born in Watervliet, N.Y., he practiced law in Wisconsin before settling in Sacramento, Cal., where he built a successful retail business in mining supplies and became active in local politics. He served as governor of California (1861–63). He invested heavily in the plan to build a transcontinental railroad, and when the CENTRAL PACIFIC RAILROAD was organized in 1861 he became its president (1861–93). During his tenure its track was built eastward to join that of the UNION PACIFIC at Promontory, Utah (1869), and he played a major role in further railroad development in California and the Southwest. From 1885 to 1893 he served in the U.S. Senate. He and his wife, Jane, founded STANFORD UNIV. in 1885.

Stanford University Private university in Stanford, Cal., near Palo Alto. It was founded in 1885 by LELAND STANFORD and his wife, Jane. The campus consists largely of the Stanfords' former farm. The buildings, designed by FREDERICK LAW OLMSTED, imitate old mission architecture. The university, consistently ranked as one of the finest in the U.S., is organized into schools of law, medicine, education, engineering, business, earth sciences, and humanities and sciences. Research facilities include the Food Research Institute, the HOOVER INSTITUTION ON WAR, REVOLUTION, AND PEACE, the Stanford Linear Accelerator Center (SLAC), and the Hopkins Marine Station. The university libraries hold over six million volumes. Total enrollment is about 14,000.

Stanhope, 1st Earl *orig.* **James Stanhope** (1673–1721) English soldier and statesman. He began a military career in 1691 and rose rapidly to become commander in chief of the English army in Spain in 1708 in the War of the SPANISH SUCCESSION. He was defeated and captured by the French (1710), then returned to England (1712) and regained his seat in the House of Commons (1701–21). He served in the Whig government as secretary of state and negotiated the QUADRUPLE ALLIANCE against Spain (1718). He served as first lord of the treasury 1717–18, but his ministry was discredited by the SOUTH SEA BUBBLE scandal.

Stanhope, 3rd Earl *orig.* **Charles Stanhope** (1753–1816) English politician and inventor. A member of the House of Commons (1780–86), where he was known as Lord Mahon until inheriting his father's title, he became chairman of the Revolution Society and favored parliamentary reform. He sympathized with the French republicans and opposed Britain's war with Revolutionary France. He was also an experimental scientist and invented calculating machines, a printing press and a microscope lens named for him, a stereotyping machine, and a steam carriage.

Stanislavsky \ˌsta-ni-ˈsläf-skē\, **Konstantin (Sergeyevich)** *orig.* **Konstantin Sergeyevich Alekseyev** (1863–1938) Russian director and actor. From age 14 he acted with his family's amateur dramatic group, and in 1888 he cofounded the Society of Art and Literature, with its permanent dramatic company. He won praise in 1891 for his first independent production, *The Fruits of Enlightenment.* In 1898 he and Vladimir Nemirovich-Danchenko (1858–1943) founded the MOSCOW ART THEATRE; it restaged ANTON CHEKHOV's *The Seagull* to great acclaim, and he continued to direct and act in many Russian plays, including Chekhov's *Uncle Vanya* (1899) and *The Cherry Orchard* (1904). He began training his actors to identify deeply with their characters, a technique that became known as the STANISLAVSKY METHOD. His company toured Europe and the U.S. (1922–24), where his method, described in his *My Life in Art* (1924) and *An Actor Prepares* (1926), influenced the later development of the GROUP THEATRE and the ACTORS STUDIO.

Stanislavsky method *or* **Method acting** Influential system of dramatic training developed by KONSTANTIN STANISLAVSKY. It requires that an actor use his emotion memory (i.e., his recall of past experiences and emotions) to identify with the character's inner motivation. The technique was developed in reaction to the histrionic acting styles of the 19th century. Noted American practitioners have included LEE STRASBERG, MARLON BRANDO, DUSTIN HOFFMAN, and Eli Wallach.

Stanislaw I \stä-ˈnē-släf\ *orig.* **Stanislaw Leszczynski** (1677–1766) King of Poland (1704–9, 1733). The son of a Polish noble, he became king when CHARLES XII of Sweden invaded Poland (1702), deposed King AUGUSTUS II, and placed Stanislaw on the throne (1704). When Sweden was defeated by the Russians in 1709, Augustus regained the throne and Stanislaw settled in France, where his daughter Marie married LOUIS XV. After Augustus's death (1733), Stanislaw was elected king of Poland, but Russia invaded to prevent an alliance with France, causing the War of the POLISH SUCCESSION. Deposed again, Stanislaw was granted the provinces of Lorraine and Bar, where he promoted economic development and made his court at Lunéville a cultural center.

Stanislaw II August Poniatowski \ˈpȯn-yä-ˈtȯf-skē\ *orig.* **Stanislaw Poniatowski** (1732–1798) King of Poland (1764–95). Son of a Polish noble, he was sent in 1757 to Russia to win support for Polish interests and became the lover of the future empress CATHERINE II. In 1764 Catherine used Russian troops and influence to ensure Stanislaw's election as king. He tried to introduce administrative reforms, but opposition from Polish nobles and from Catherine forced him to continue his rule as a pawn of Russia. He attempted to pass a new constitution but could not stop the Partitions of POLAND (1772, 1793, 1795), after which he abdicated.

Stanley, Francis Edgar and Freelan O. (1849–1918, 1849–1940) U.S. inventors of the steam-driven AUTOMOBILE. The twin Stanley brothers were born in Kingfield, Me. In 1883 they invented a dry-plate photographic process and conducted experiments with steam engines. In 1897 they built a steam-powered car, and in 1902 they established a company to manufacture their "Stanley Steamers." In 1906 they set a world record for the fastest mile, in 28.2 seconds. They retired in 1917; their company continued to manufacture cars until 1924, declining as gasoline-powered cars became easier to start and operate and steam cars became less popular.

Stanley, Henry Morton *later* **Sir Henry** *orig.* **John Rowlands** (1841–1904) British-U.S. explorer of central Africa. An illegitimate child, Stanley grew up partly in a British workhouse; he sailed to the U.S. as a cabin boy in 1859. After becoming a journalist for the *New York Herald* in 1867, he embarked (1871) on a journey to locate DAVID LIVINGSTONE, of whom little had been heard since his departure for Africa in 1866. On finding him at Ujiji on Lake TANGANYIKA, Stanley uttered the famous words "Dr. Livingstone, I presume?" He further explored central Africa for extended periods between 1874 and 1884, often in the service of LEOPOLD II of Belgium, for whom he paved the way for the creation of the Congo Free State. His last expedition (1888) was for the relief of MEHMED EMIN PASHA, who had been cut off by the Mahdist revolt in the Sudan; he escorted Emin and 1,500 others to the eastern coast. His highly popular books included *Through the Dark Continent* (1878) and *In Darkest Africa* (1890).

Sir Henry Morton Stanley, detail of a portrait by Sir Hubert von Herkomer; in the City Art Gallery, Bristol, England.

Stanley, Wendell Meredith (1904–1971) U.S. biochemist. Born in Ridgeville, Ind., he taught at UC–Berkeley from 1948 until his death. He is known for his work in the purification and crystallization of VIRUSES to demonstrate their molecular structure. He crystallized the tobacco mosaic virus and did important work on the INFLUENZA virus, for which he developed a vaccine. He shared a Nobel Prize in 1946 with JOHN H. NORTHROP and JAMES B. SUMNER.

Stanley brothers U.S. BLUEGRASS duo consisting of Ralph (Edmund) Stanley (born 1927) on banjo and Carter (Glen) Stanley (1925–1966) on lead guitar. Born and raised in Virginia's Shenandoah Valley, the brothers rose to fame performing traditional religious songs in a traditional Appalachian bluegrass style marked by close, high-pitched harmonies and strongly influenced by BILL MONROE. With their band, the Clinch Mountain Boys, they had several hit recordings. After Carter's death in a car crash, Ralph reorganized the band. He has recorded over 150 albums. In 1985 he became the first recipient of the National Endowment for the Humanities' Traditional American Music Award.

Stanley Cup Trophy awarded annually to the winning team of the NATIONAL HOCKEY LEAGUE championship. Named for its donor, the Canadian governor-general Frederick Arthur Stanley, Lord Stanley of Preston (1841–1908), the Stanley Cup was first awarded in the 1893–94 season. It is the oldest trophy that can be won by professional athletes in North America.

Stanleyville See KISANGANI

Stanovoy Range \ˌstä-nə-ˈvȯi\ Mountain range, eastern Russia in Asia. It is part of the watershed between the Pacific and Arctic oceans. The mountains are generally not high, although they reach 8,268 ft (2,520 m) in the east. They contain deposits of gold, coal, and mica.

Stanton, Edwin M(cMasters) (1814–1869) U.S. secretary of war (1862–68). Born in Steubenville, Ohio, he became a lawyer and abolitionist. He was appointed U.S. attorney general in 1861 and secretary of war in 1862. He ably administered the Union military effort in the Civil War, and later helped lead the investigation of ABRAHAM LINCOLN's assassination. Conflict with Pres. ANDREW JOHNSON over Reconstruction policy and his alliance with the Radical Republicans led to Stanton's dismissal by Johnson, in deliberate violation of the TENURE OF OFFICE ACT. Stanton refused to leave office, but he resigned after Johnson was acquitted in the impeachment trial.

Stanton, Elizabeth Cady *orig.* **Elizabeth Cady** (1815–1902) U.S. social reformer and women's suffrage leader. Born in Johnstown, N.Y., she married the abolitionist Henry B. Stanton in 1840 and began working to secure passage of a New York law giving property rights to married women. She and LUCRETIA MOTT organized the 1848 SENECA FALLS CONVENTION. She joined forces in 1850 with SUSAN B. ANTHONY in the WOMEN'S SUFFRAGE MOVEMENT, and later coedited the women's-rights newspaper *The Revolution* 1868–70. In 1869 she became the founding president of the National Woman Suffrage Association.

Stanwyck, Barbara *orig.* **Ruby Stevens** (1907–1990) U.S. film actress. Born in Brooklyn, N.Y., she was a chorus girl from age 15 and danced in revues until she won notice with her Broadway role in *The Noose* (1926). She made her screen debut in 1927 and went on to appear in over 80 films, often portraying strong-willed, independent women. Her movies include *Stella Dallas* (1937), *Union Pacific* (1939), *Ball of Fire* (1942), *Double Indemnity* (1944), *Sorry, Wrong Number* (1948), and *Executive Suite* (1954). She later starred in the television series *The Big Valley* (1965–69). She received an honorary Academy Award in 1981.

staphylococcus \ˌsta-fə-lō-ˈkä-kəs\ Any of the spherical BACTERIA that make up the genus *Staphylococcus.* The best-known species are present in great numbers on the mucous membranes and skin of all humans and other warm-blooded animals. The cells characteristically group together in grapelike clusters. Staphylococci are gram-positive (see GRAM STAIN) and stationary and do not require oxygen. Of significance to humans is the species *S. aureus,* an important agent of wound infections, boils, and other human skin infections, and one of the most common causes of FOOD POISONING. It also causes udder inflammation in domestic animals and breast infections in women. The largest cause of hospital infections (accounting for almost 15%), "staph" is often difficult to treat because of its increasing resistance to ANTIBIOTICS.

star Any massive, celestial body of gas that shines by radiant energy generated inside it. The MILKY WAY contains hundreds of billions of stars; only a very small fraction are visible to the unaided eye. The closest star is about 4.3 light-years from the sun; the most distant are in GALAXIES billions of light-years away. Single stars such as the SUN are the minority; most stars occur in pairs, multiple systems, or clusters (see BINARY STAR, GLOBULAR CLUSTER, OPEN CLUSTER). CONSTELLATIONS do not consist of such groupings but of stars in the same direction as seen from earth. Stars vary greatly in brightness (MAGNITUDE), color, temperature, mass, size, chemical composition, and age. In nearly all, HYDROGEN is the most abundant element. Stars are classified by their spectra (see SPECTRUM), from blue-white to red, as O, B, A, F, G, K, or M; the sun is a G-type star. Generalizations on the nature and evolution of stars can be made from correlations between certain properties and from statistical results (see HERTZSPRUNG-RUSSELL DIAGRAM). A star forms when a portion of a dense interstellar cloud of hydrogen and dust grains collapses inward from its own gravity. As the cloud condenses, its density and internal temperature increase until it is hot enough to trigger NUCLEAR FUSION in its core (if not, it becomes a BROWN DWARF). After hydrogen is exhausted in the core, the latter shrinks and heats up while the star's outer layers expand significantly and cool, making the star a red giant. The final stages of a star's evolution, when it no longer produces enough energy to counteract its own gravity, depend largely on its mass and whether it is a component of a close binary system (see BLACK HOLE, NEUTRON STAR, NOVA, SUPERNOVA, WHITE DWARF STAR). See also CEPHEID VARIABLE, DWARF STAR, ECLIPSING VARIABLE STAR, FLARE STAR, GIANT STAR, SUPERGIANT STAR, T TAURI STAR, VARIABLE STAR, POPULATIONS I AND II.

Star Chamber British PREROGATIVE COURT that exercised wide civil and criminal jurisdiction and was marked by secrecy, the absence of juries, and an inquisitorial rather than accusatorial system of justice. It met in a room in the palace of Westminster whose ceiling was decorated with stars. It was employed extensively under HENRY VIII because of its ability to enforce the law when other courts were unable to do so because of corruption and influence. When CHARLES I used it to enforce unpopular political and ecclesiastical policies, it became a symbol of oppression to his and Archbishop WILLIAM LAUD's parliamentary and Puritan opponents (though it never imposed the death penalty), and it was abolished by the Long Parliament in 1641.

Star of David See Star of DAVID

Star Wars See STRATEGIC DEFENSE INITIATIVE

S T U V

starch Any of several white, granular organic compounds produced by all green plants. They are POLYSACCHARIDES with the general chemical formula $(C_6H_{10}O_5)_n$, where *n* may range from 100 to several thousand; the constituent MONOSACCHARIDES are GLUCOSE units made in PHOTOSYNTHESIS. The glucose chains are unbranched in amylose and branched in amylopectin, which occur mixed in starches. Starch consumed by animals is broken down into glucose by ENZYMES during DIGESTION. Commercial starch is made mainly from corn, though wheat, tapioca, rice, and potato starch are also used. Starch has many uses in foods and the food industry, as well as in the paper, textile, and personal-care products industries and in adhesives, explosives, and oil-well drilling fluids and as a mold-release agent. Animal starch is another name for GLYCOGEN. See also CARBOHYDRATE.

stare decisis \ˌster-ē-di-ˈsī-səs\ (Latin: "to stand by things that have been settled") In COMMON LAW, the doctrine under which courts adhere to precedent on questions of law in order to ensure certainty, consistency, and stability in the administration of justice. Because no court decision can be universally applicable, the courts must often decide whether a previous decision is "in point." Departure from established precedent is permitted only for compelling reasons, such as to prevent the perpetuation of injustice.

starfish *or* **sea star** Any of 1,800 ECHINODERM species (class Asteroidea) that have regenerable arms surrounding an indistinct disk and that inhabit all oceans. Species range from 0.4 to 25 in. (1–65 cm) across, but most are 8–12 in. (20–30 cm) across. Their arms, usually five, are hollow and, like the disk, covered with short spines and pincerlike organs; on the lower side are tube feet, sometimes sucker-tipped, used for creeping or clinging to steep surfaces. Some species sweep organic particles into the mouth on the underside of the disk. Others either evert the stomach upon their prey for external digestion or swallow the prey whole.

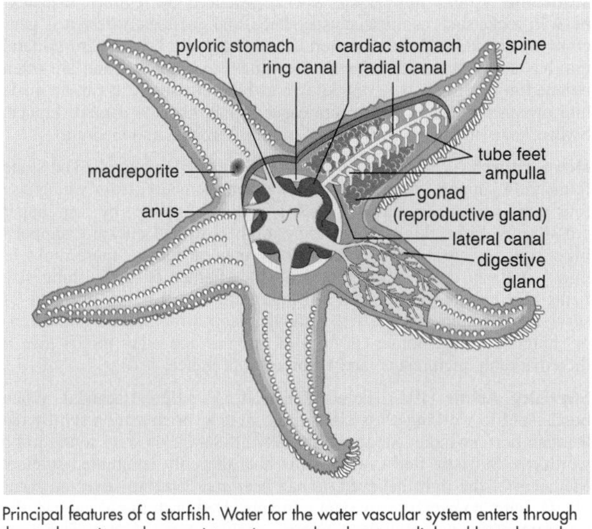

Principal features of a starfish. Water for the water vascular system enters through the madreporite and passes into a ring canal and on to radial and lateral canals, from which it enters the tube feet, which are connected to saclike ampullae on top. Contraction of the tube feet forces water into the ampullae, creating suction that allows suckers at the ends of the feet to hold to a surface. When the ampullae contract, water is forced into the feet, extending them and releasing the suction. These coordinated actions permit movement, attachment, and capture of prey. In many starfish, the cardiac stomach is everted through the mouth on the body's undersurface to envelop prey, and digestion may begin outside the body before the stomach is drawn back in.

Starhemberg \ˈshtär-əm-ˌberk\, **Ernst Rüdiger, Fürst (Prince) von** (1899–1956) Austrian politician. In 1930 he became leader of the fascist Austrian Heimwehr, a paramilitary defense force, and in 1932 he helped ENGELBERT DOLLFUSS form the right-wing coalition called the Fatherland Front. Appointed vice chancellor in 1934, he sought to maintain a fascist Austrian state that was independent of Nazi Germany. He fled Austria after the ANSCHLUSS (1938), and lived in Argentina 1942–55.

Stark, John (1728–1822) American Revolutionary officer. Born in Londonderry, N.H., he served in the French and Indian War with ROBERT ROGERS's Rangers (1754–59). In the AMERICAN REVOLUTION, he fought at the Battle of BUNKER HILL and in New Jersey. He commanded the militia that defeated the British at the Battle of Bennington, Vt. Promoted to brigadier general of the Continental Army, he helped force the British surrender at the Battle of SARATOGA and then served in Rhode Island. He was a member of the 1780 court-martial of Maj. JOHN ANDRE.

starling Any of about 168 species (family Sturnidae) of songbirds of temperate Eurasia, Africa, and Australia. The best-known is *Sturnus vulgaris,* an 8-in. (20-cm), chunky, iridescent black bird with a long sharp bill. It has been introduced from Eurasia to most parts of the world, except South America. The millions in North America are descendants of 100 birds released in New York City in 1890. Starlings search the ground for a wide range of plant and animal foods and fly in a tight flock. They are vocal year-round, mimicking other birds' notes and uttering wheezy sounds of their own.

Starling (*Sturnus vulgaris*).

GEORGE W. ROBINSON FROM ROOT RESOURCES

Starling, Ernest Henry (1866–1927) British physiologist. His studies of lymph secretion clarified the roles of different pressures in fluid exchanges between vessels and tissues. Starling and WILLIAM BAYLISS showed how nerve impulses control peristalsis and coined the term hormone. Starling also found that water and necessary chemicals filtered out by the kidneys are reabsorbed at the lower end of the nephron. His *Principles of Human Physiology* (1912), continually revised, remains a standard international text.

Starr, Belle *orig.* **Myra Belle Shirley** (1848–1889) U.S. outlaw. Born in Washington Co., Md., she lived on a farm near Dallas from 1863. She bore a child by the outlaw Cole Younger (1844–1916) and another by Jim Reed, with whom she rustled cattle and horses in Texas in 1869. She fashioned herself the "bandit queen," dressing in velvet and feathers or buckskin and moccasins. In 1880 she became the common-law wife of Sam Starr, and their Oklahoma ranch became an outlaws' hideout. Sam was killed in a gunfight in 1886, and Belle herself was later shot down near her ranch.

Stars and Stripes, The Newspaper for U.S. military personnel. It first appeared in single editions during the American Civil War and was revived as a weekly for troops in Europe at the end of World War I. Reestablished in 1942, first as a weekly and then a daily, it has been published since then in a European edition and since 1945 in a Pacific edition. It has carried the work of many outstanding writers, editors, cartoonists, and photographers. An authorized, unofficial publication of the Department of Defense, it is relatively free of military censorship and control.

START *in full* **Strategic Arms Reduction Talks** Negotiations between the U.S. and the Soviet Union aimed at reducing those countries' nuclear arsenals and delivery systems. Two sets of negotiations (1982–83, 1985–91) concluded in an agreement signed by GEORGE BUSH and MIKHAIL GORBACHEV committing the Soviet Union to a reduction from 11,000 to 8,000 nuclear weapons, and the U.S. to a reduction from 12,000 to 10,000. After the Soviet Union's collapse (1991), a supplementary agreement (1992) obligated Ukraine, Belarus, and Kazakhstan to either destroy the nuclear weapons on their soil or give them to Russia. Today, U.S. support for developing antimissile defenses threatens new complications for the arms control regime. See also SALT.

Stasi \ˈshtä-zē\ *officially* **Staatssicherheit** ("State Security") Secret police of East Germany (1950–90), established with Soviet help by German Communists in Soviet-occupied Germany after World War II. It was responsible for both domestic political surveillance and espionage. At its peak, it employed 85,000 officers full-time. Using hundreds of thousands of informers, it monitored one-third of the population. Most of its foreign focus was on West Germany (whose governing circles and military and intelligence services it successfully penetrated) and its NATO allies. It was disbanded after German reunification.

state Political organization of society, or the body politic, or, more narrowly, the institutions of government. The state is distinguished from other social groups by its purpose (establishment of order and security), methods (its laws and their enforcement), territory (its area of jurisdiction), and sovereignty. In some countries (e.g., the U.S.), the term also refers to nonsovereign political units subject to the authority of the larger state, or federal union.

state, equation of Any of a class of equations that relate the pressure P, volume V, and temperature T of a given substance in thermodynamic EQUILIBRIUM. For example, the equation $PV = nRT$, where n is the number of moles of gas and R is the universal gas constant, relates the pressure, volume, and temperature of a PERFECT GAS. Real gases, solids, and liquids have more complicated equations of state. See also THERMODYNAMICS.

State, U.S. Department of Federal executive division responsible for carrying out U.S. foreign policy. Established in 1789, and the oldest of the federal departments, it is the president's principal means of conducting treaty negotiations and forging agreements with foreign nations. Under its administration are the U.S. Mission to the U.N., the U.S. Foreign Service, and various offices of diplomatic security, foreign intelligence, policy analysis, international narcotics control, protocol, and passport services.

Staten Island Island in New York Harbor, a borough (pop., 1990: 379,000) of NEW YORK CITY. It has an area of almost 60 sq mi (155 sq km) and is connected with BROOKLYN by the Verrazano-Narrows Bridge and with New Jersey by several bridges; it is accessible to MANHATTAN by the Staten Island Ferry The Dutch attempted to colonize the island in 1630 but were thwarted by the Delaware Indian inhabitants until 1661, when the Dutch West India Co. granted the island to the French and settlements were established. Following the acquisition of New Netherland in 1664 by Britain, English and Welsh farmers established homes and farms on the island. As Richmond, it became a borough of New York City in 1898; Staten Island was made the official name in 1975. Mostly residential, it has some industry, including shipbuilding yards, printing plants, and oil storage tanks and refineries. It is the seat of Wagner College (1883, brought from Rochester in 1918).

States General See ESTATES GENERAL

states' rights All government rights or powers held by the individual states of a federal union under the provisions of a federal constitution. In some federally organized countries, these powers are those that remain after the powers of the central government are enumerated in the constitution. In others, the powers of both levels of government are defined in their respective constitutions. In the U.S., some states claimed in the 19th century the right to nullify federal authority and secede, which led to the AMERICAN CIVIL WAR. In the civil-rights era, the concept of states' rights was invoked by opponents of racial integration in public schools and the federal government's efforts to enforce such integration. The federal government can influence state policy even in areas that are constitutionally the purview of the states (e.g., education, local road construction) through withholding funds from states that fail to comply with its wishes. The 1996 welfare reforms in the U.S. reflected increasing attention to the prerogatives of states within a federal system of government.

statistical mechanics Branch of physics that combines the principles and procedures of STATISTICS with the laws of both classical MECHANICS and QUANTUM MECHANICS. It considers the average behavior of a large number of particles rather than the behavior of any individual particle, drawing heavily on the laws of probability, and aims to predict and explain the measurable properties of macroscopic (bulk) systems on the basis of the properties and behavior of their microscopic constituents.

statistics Branch of mathematics dealing with gathering, analyzing, and making inferences from data. Originally associated with government data (e.g., census data), the subject now has applications in all the sciences. Statistical tools not only summarize past data through such indicators as the mean (see MEAN, MEDIAN, AND MODE) and the standard deviation but can predict future events using FREQUENCY DISTRIBUTION functions. Statistics provides ways to design efficient experiments that eliminate time-consuming trial and error. Double-blind tests for polls, intelligence and aptitude tests, and medical, biological, and industrial experiments all benefit from statistical methods and theories. The results of all of them serve as predictors of future performance, though reliability varies. See also ESTIMATION, HYPOTHESIS TESTING, LEAST SQUARES METHOD, PROBABILITY THEORY, REGRESSION.

Statue of Liberty National Monument National monument, Liberty Island (formerly Bedloe's Island), New York Harbor, New York. Covering 58 acres (23 hectares), it includes the colossal statue "Liberty Enlightening the World," sculpted by F.-A. BARTHOLDI and dedicated in 1886, and the nearby Ellis Island Museum. The 302-ft (92-m) statue of a woman holding a tablet and upraised torch was given to the U.S. by France and commemorates the friendship of the two countries; a poem by EMMA LAZARUS is at the base. It was declared a national monument in 1924; in 1965 nearby ELLIS ISLAND was added to the monument.

Statute of Provisors See Statute of PROVISORS

Staubach \'stȯ-ˌbäk\, **Roger (Thomas)** (born 1942) U.S. football player. Born in Cincinnati, he compiled a notable record playing for the U.S. Naval Academy (1962–65), where he made All-American and won the HEISMAN TROPHY (1963). His professional career was spent as quarterback with the Dallas Cowboys (1969–79), which he helped make into a dominant team, leading them to the play-offs in every year but one (1974) and to four Super Bowl games.

Staupers, Mabel (Keaton) *orig.* **Mabel Doyle** (1890–1989) U.S. (Caribbean-born) nurse and executive. She joined two physicians to establish the first hospital in Harlem to treat U.S. blacks with tuberculosis (1920). As executive secretary of the National Association of Colored Graduate Nurses (NACGN), she campaigned to integrate the Armed Forces Nurse Corps; overwhelming public support led to full integration in 1945, and in 1948 NACGN succeeded in integrating the American Nurses Assn.

staurolite \'stȯr-ə-ˌlīt\ SILICATE MINERAL produced by regional METAMORPHISM in rocks such as mica schists, slates, and gneisses, where it is generally associated with other minerals. Staurolite is a brittle, hard mineral that has a dull luster. Its crystals are usually dark brown and are often twinned in cruciform patterns (known as fairy crosses) that can be made into ornaments. Staurolite occurs especially in Canada, Brazil, France, Switzerland, and the U.S. (North Carolina, Virginia, and Georgia).

stave church Type of medieval Norwegian wooden church. The stone foundation supports four horizontal wooden members, from which rise four corner posts, or staves, which are joined together by four upper crossbeams. From this boxlike frame, timbers extend outward, supporting a series of uprights, or masts. There may be four or more ranks of masts, with an equal number of triangular frames of diminishing size rising above them. The church at Borgund (c. 1150) is one of about 24 surviving examples. Its six tiers of double-sloped roofs, shell-like exterior shingles, and elaborate carvings of dragons and other motifs give it its remarkably picturesque and vigorous appearance.

Stavisky Affair (1934) French financial and political scandal. When bonds sold to working-class citizens by a credit organization run by the Russian-born swindler Serge A. Stavisky (1886–1934) were found to be worthless, Stavisky fled to Chamonix and allegedly committed suicide. Members of the right believed he had been murdered to cover up complicity with corrupt government officials. Demonstrations against the government by antirepublican groups, including the ACTION FRANÇAISE and the CROIX DE FEU, culminated in a riot on February 6, 1934, which killed 15 people. Two successive prime ministers were forced to resign; a centrist coalition was eventually formed to restore confidence.

STD See SEXUALLY TRANSMITTED DISEASE

Stead, Christina (Ellen) (1902–1983) Australian novelist. She traveled widely and at various times lived in London, Paris, and the U.S., where in the early 1940s she worked as a screenwriter for MGM. She returned to Australia in 1974. Her first published work was a collection of short stories, *The Salzburg Tales* (1934). She is best remembered for her famous novel *The Man Who Loved Children* (1940), the story of a disintegrating family living near Washington in the New Deal period.

steady-state theory Concept of an EXPANDING UNIVERSE whose average density remains constant, matter being continuously created throughout it to form new stars and galaxies at the same rate that old ones recede from sight. A steady-state universe has no beginning or end, and its average density and arrangement of galaxies are the same as seen from every point. Galaxies of all ages are intermingled. The theory was first put forward by W. Macmillan (1861–1948) in the 1920s and modified by Fred Hoyle to deal with problems that had arisen in connection with the big-bang model. Much evidence obtained since the 1950s contradicts the steady-state picture and supports the big-bang model.

stealth Any military technology intended to make vehicles or missiles nearly invisible to enemy radar or other electronic detection. Research in antidetection technology began soon after radar was invented. In World War II, the Germans coated their U-boat snorkels with radar-absorbent material. In the postwar era, researchers sought to learn the nature of radar echoes, beams of electromagnetic radiation bounced off surfaces. By the 1980s the U.S. had developed models of stealth technology, including a bomber. Though the bomber's details are classified, it is known that its surface materials and coatings can absorb radar transmissions and that its smooth, rounded shapes reduce radar echoes. Aircraft are less detectable when weapons are recessed into the aircraft structure, and shielding engine exhaust makes infrared detection more difficult.

steam Invisible gas consisting of vaporized water. When mixed with minute droplets of water, it has a white, cloudy appearance. In nature, steam is produced by the heating of underground water by volcanic processes and is emitted from hot springs, geysers, fumaroles, and some volcanoes. Steam also can be generated on a large scale by technological systems, such as those using fossil-fuel-burning boilers and nuclear reactors. Modern industrial society relies on steam power; water is heated to steam in power plants, and the pressurized steam drives turbines that produce electric current: thermal energy is converted to mechanical energy, which is converted into electricity.

steam engine Machine that uses steam power to perform mechanical work through the agency of heat (hence a prime mover). In a steam engine, hot steam, usually supplied by a boiler, expands under pressure, and part of the heat energy is converted into work. The rest of the heat may be allowed to escape, or, for maximum engine efficiency, the steam may be condensed in a separate apparatus, a condenser, at comparatively low temperature and pressure. For high efficiency, the steam must decrease substantially in temperature as it expands within the engine. The most efficient performance (i.e., the greatest output of work in relation to the heat supplied) is obtained by using a low condenser temperature and a high boiler pressure. See also Thomas Newcomen, James Watt.

steamboat *or* **steamship** Watercraft propelled by steam; more narrowly, a shallow-draft paddle-wheel steamboat widely used on rivers in the 19th century, particularly the Mississippi River and its tributaries. Though U.S. experiments with steam-powered boats began in 1787, the first regular steamboat service, operating on the Mississippi, was not established until 1812. Until c. 1870 the steamboat dominated the economy, agriculture, and commerce of the middle of the U.S. Because the paddle wheel created turbulence that eroded the banks of narrow channels, river steamboats worked best on broad rivers. The first ocean voyage of a steamboat occurred along the eastern coast of the U.S. in 1809, and Europeans soon developed steamboats capable of crossing Europe's stormy, narrow seas. The first transatlantic steamboat journey was made by the *Savannah* in 1819, and the first commercial shipping line, the Cunard Line (see Samuel Cunard), was established in 1840. The screw propeller replaced the paddle wheel in oceanic steamers in the later 19th century. See also ocean liner.

Steamers *Robert E. Lee* and the *Natchez* in the race from New Orleans to St. Louis, lithograph by Currier and Ives.
BBC HULTON PICTURE LIBRARY

Stebbins, G(eorge) Ledyard (1906–2000) U.S. botanist. Born in Lawrence, N.Y., he received his PhD from Harvard University and later taught in the University of California system. In *Variation and Evolution in Plants* (1950) he became the first biologist to apply the modern synthetic theory of evolution—a theory that distinguishes the basic processes of gene mutation and recombination, natural selection, changes in structure and number of chromosomes, and reproductive isolation—to higher organisms. Working with polyploid plants (new species that originated by a spontaneous doubling of the chromosomes of an existing species), he employed a technique for doubling a plant's chromosomal number artificially to produce successful artificial polyploids from wild-grass species, becoming the first person to artificially synthesize a plant species that could thrive under natural conditions.

Stedinger Crusade (1229–34) Crusade against the Stedinger, a body of peasants labeled as heretics by the archbishop of Bremen, who secured papal support for a crusade. In fact, the charge of heresy was unsubstantiated, and the "crusade" was an attack led by the archbishop's brother and other nobles of the region. In 1234 Pope Gregory IX was persuaded to summon a crusade with full privileges.

steel Alloy of iron and about 2% or less carbon. Pure iron is soft, but carbon greatly hardens it. Several iron-carbon constituents with different compositions and/or crystal structures exist: austenite, ferrite, pearlite, cementite, and martensite can coexist in complex mixtures and combinations, depending on temperature and carbon content. Each microstructure differs in hardness, strength, toughness, corrosion resistance, and electrical resistivity, so adjusting the carbon content changes the properties. Heat treating, mechanical working at cold or hot temperatures, or addition of alloying elements may also give superior properties. The three major classes are carbon steels, low-alloy steels, and high-alloy steels. Low-alloy steels (with up to 8% alloying elements) are exceptionally strong and are used for machine parts, aircraft landing gear, shafts, hand tools, and gears, and in buildings and bridges. High-alloy steels, with more than 8% alloying elements (e.g., stainless steels) offer unusual properties. Making steel involves melting, purifying (refining), and alloying, carried out at about 2,900°F (1,600°C). Steel is obtained by refining iron (from a blast furnace) or scrap steel by the basic oxygen process, the open-hearth process, or in an electric furnace, then by removing excess carbon and impurities and adding alloying elements. Molten steel can be poured into molds and solidified into ingots; these are reheated and rolled into semifinished shapes which are worked into finished products. Some steps in ingot pouring can be saved by continuous casting. Forming semifinished steel into finished shapes may be done by two major methods: hot-working consists primarily of hammering and pressing (together called forging), extrusion, and rolling the steel under high heat; cold-working, which includes rolling, extrusion, and drawing (see wire drawing), is generally used to make bars, wire, tubes, sheets, and strips. Molten steel can also be cast directly into products. Certain products, particularly of sheet steel, are protected from corrosion by electroplating, galvanizing, or tinplating.

steel drum Tuned gong made from the end, and part of the wall, of an oil barrel. The barrel's end surface is hammered into a concave shape, and several areas are outlined by chiseled grooves. It is heated and tempered, and bosses or domes are hammered into the outlined areas; the depth, curvature, and size of each boss determines its pitch. Melodies, complex accompaniments, and counterpoint can be played with rubber-tipped mallets on a single drum. The steel drum originated in Trinidad in the 1940s. It is usually played in ensembles, called steel bands, of widely varying sizes.

Steele, Richard *later* **Sir Richard** (1672–1729) English journalist, dramatist, essayist, and politician. He began his long friendship with Joseph Addison at school and attempted an army career before turning to writing. He launched and was the principal author (under the name Isaac Bickerstaff) of the essay periodical *The Tatler* (April 1709–January 1711), in which he created the mixture of entertainment and instruction in manners and morals that he and Addison would perfect in *The Spectator*. His attractive, often casual writing style was a perfect foil for Addison's more measured, erudite prose. He made many later ventures into journalism, some politically partisan, and held several government posts. In 1714 he became governor of DRURY LANE THEATRE, where he produced *The Conscious Lovers* (1723), one of the century's most popular plays and perhaps the best example of English sentimental comedy.

Steen \'stān\, **Jan (Havickszoon)** (1626–1679) Dutch painter. A brewer's son, he was enrolled at the University of Leiden in 1646 and in 1648 became a founding member of the Leiden painters' guild. One of the greatest Dutch genre painters, he is known for his humor and ability to capture subtle facial expressions, especially of children. His figures, which became larger and more individually characterized in his later works, were often shown playing cards or skittles, or carousing in inns and taverns. His paintings show great technical skill, particularly with color. His late paintings became increasingly elegant and somewhat less energetic.

steeplechase Either of two distinct sporting events: (1) a horse race over a closed course with obstacles, including hedges and walls; or (2) a footrace of 3,000 m over hurdles and a water jump. The name derives from impromptu races by fox hunters in 18th-century Ireland over natural country in which church steeples served as course landmarks. Equestrian steeplechase is popular in England, France, and Ireland, and to a lesser extent in the U.S. The most famous equestrian steeplechase is the GRAND NATIONAL. Track-and-field steeplechase dates back to a cross-country race at the University of Oxford in 1850. The course and distance were standardized at the 1920 Olympic Games.

Stefan Decansky \'ste-vän-de-'kän-skē\ *or* **Stefan Uros III** (fl. c. 1280–1330) King of Serbia (1322–31). After rebelling against his father, Stefan Uros II (r.1282–1321), he was blinded, so that he would be unfit to rule, and exiled (1314–20). He then showed he was not blind, claiming a miraculous cure, and was made king. He allied with the losing ANDRONICUS II PALAEOLOGUS in the civil war with ANDRONICUS III PALAEOLOGUS (1327–28) and was deposed by his son, STEFAN DUSAN.

Stefan Dusan \'dü-shän\ *or* **Stefan Uros IV** (1308–1355) King of Serbia (1331–46) and emperor of the Serbs and Greeks (1346–55). He deposed his father, STEFAN DECANSKY, in 1331. The greatest ruler of medieval Serbia, he began a war of conquest against Byzantium in 1334, gaining control of Albania and Macedonia by 1346 and Epirus and Thessaly by 1348. Dusan reformed the Serbian administration on the Byzantine model and introduced a law code. His rule over former Byzantine lands was threatened by JOHN VI CANTACUZENUS, and his empire broke apart soon after his death.

Stefan Nemanja *or* **Stephen Nemanja** \'ne-män-yä\ (died 1200) Founder of the Serbian state. He was grand *zupan* (clan leader) under Byzantine rule in 1169. He allied himself with Venice and was defeated by the avenging Byzantines, though he was later pardoned. After expanding Serbian territory, he abdicated in 1196 and entered a monastery.

Steffens, (Joseph) Lincoln (1866–1936) U.S. journalist and reformer. Born in San Francisco, he worked for New York newspapers (1892–1901) and was managing editor of *McClure's Magazine* (1901–6), where he began his famous muckraking articles—later published as *The Shame of the Cities* (1904)—exposing corruption in politics and big business. He lectured widely and aroused public interest in seeking solutions and taking action. He later supported revolutionary activities in Mexico and Russia and lived in Europe 1917–27. The success of his *Autobiography* (1931) returned him to the lecture circuit.

Stegner, Wallace (Earle) (1909–1993) U.S. writer. Born in Lake Mills, Iowa, Stegner studied at the University of Iowa and later taught at several universities, notably Stanford. *The Big Rock Candy Mountain* (1943), a novel about a family traveling around the West seeking their fortune, was his first critical and popular success. His later novels include *A Shooting Star* (1961), *Angle of Repose* (1971, Pulitzer Prize), and *The Spectator Bird* (1976, National Book Award). His nonfiction includes two histories of the settlement of Utah, *Mormon Country* (1942) and *The Gathering of Zion* (1964), and *Beyond the Hundredth Meridian* (1954), a biography of JOHN WESLEY POWELL.

stegosaur Any of the plated DINOSAURS, including *Stegosaurus* of the Late JURASSIC PERIOD (159–144 million years ago). Stegosaurs were four-legged herbivores that reached a maximum length of about 30 ft (9 m). The skull and brain were very small. The forelimbs were much shorter than the hind limbs, the back was arched, and the feet were short and broad. Stegosaurs had double rows of large, triangular, horn-covered bony plates along their backs and tail that may have been a temperature-regulating system. Two or three pairs of long, pointed bony spikes on the end of the tail were probably defensive weapons.

Steichen \'stī-kən\, **Edward (Jean)** *orig.* **Édouard Jean** (1879–1973) U.S. (Luxembourg-born) photographer. His family emigrated to the U.S. in 1881. Training in painting influenced his photography when he turned to that medium. He frequently used chemicals to achieve prints that resembled soft, fuzzy mezzotints or wash drawings. In 1902 he joined ALFRED STIEGLITZ in forming PHOTO-SECESSION, a group dedicated to promoting photography as a fine art. His style evolved from painterly impressionism to sharp realism after World War I. His portraits of artists and celebrities from the 1920s and '30s are remarkable evocations of character. In 1955 he organized the *Family of Man* exhibition of 503 photographs (selected from over 2 million), which was seen by more than 9 million people worldwide.

Edward Steichen, 1960.
JOANNA T. STEICHEN

Stein, Gertrude (1874–1946) U.S. avant-garde writer. Born to a wealthy family in Allegheny, Pa., Stein studied at Radcliffe College before moving to Paris, where from 1909 she lived with her companion Alice B. Toklas (1877–1967). Their home was a salon for leading artists and writers, including PABLO PICASSO, HENRI MATISSE, GEORGES BRAQUE, SHERWOOD ANDERSON, and ERNEST HEMINGWAY. An early supporter of Cubism, she tried to parallel its theories in her work, including the poetry volume *Tender Buttons* (1914). Her prose was characterized by a unique style employing repetition and fragmentation, especially in the immense novel *The Making of Americans* (written 1906–11, published 1928). Her only book to reach a wide public was *The Autobiography of Alice B. Toklas* (1933), actually Stein's own autobiography. Her other works include *Four Saints in Three Acts* (1934) and *The Mother of Us All* (1947), opera librettos scored by V. THOMSON.

Gertrude Stein, oil painting by Pablo Picasso, about 1906; in the Metropolitan Museum of Art, New York City.
BY COURTESY OF THE METROPOLITAN MUSEUM OF ART, NEW YORK CITY, BEQUEST OF GERTRUDE STEIN, 1946

Stein \'shtīn\, **(Heinrich Friedrich) Karl, Reichsfreiherr (Imperial Baron) vom und zum** (1757–1831) Prussian statesman. Born into the imperial nobility, he entered the civil service in 1780. As minister of economic affairs (1804–7) and chief minister (1807–8) to FREDERICK WILLIAM III, he introduced wide-ranging reforms in administration, taxation, and the civil service that modernized the Prussian government. He abolished serfdom, reformed the laws on land ownership, and helped reorganize the military. Anticipating war with France, he was forced to resign under pressure from NAPOLEON (1808) and fled to Austria. As an adviser to Czar ALEXANDER I (1812–15), he negotiated the Russo-Prussian Treaty of Kalisz (1813) that formed the last European coalition against Napoleon.

Stein-Leventhal syndrome See POLYCYSTIC OVARY SYNDROME

Steinbeck, John (Ernst) (1902–1968) U.S. novelist. Born in Salinas, Cal., Steinbeck intermittently attended Stanford University and worked as a manual laborer before his books attained success. He spent much of his life in Monterey Co., Cal. His reputation rests mostly on the naturalistic novels on proletarian themes that he wrote in the 1930s. Among them are *Tortilla Flat* (1935; film, 1942), *In Dubious Battle* (1936), *Of*

Mice and Men (1937; film 1939), and the acclaimed *The Grapes of Wrath* (1939, Pulitzer Prize; film, 1940), which aroused widespread sympathy for the plight of migratory farm workers. In World War II he served as a war correspondent. His later novels include *Cannery Row* (1945; film, 1982), *The Pearl* (1947; film, 1948), *The Wayward Bus* (1947; film, 1957), and *East of Eden* (1952; film, 1955). He received the Nobel Prize in 1962.

Steinbeck.

ENCYCLOPÆDIA, BRITANNICA, INC.

Steinberg, Saul *orig.* **Saul Jacobson** (1914–1999) Romanian-U.S. cartoonist and illustrator. He studied architecture in Milan, meanwhile publishing cartoons in Italian magazines. Settling in New York in 1942, he worked as a freelance artist, illustrator, and cartoonist, mainly for *The New Yorker.* His extraordinarily original and instantly recognizable works are often surrealistic or whimsically nightmarish visions of contemporary America and frequently employ odd versions of pop-culture icons.

Saul Steinberg, photograph by Arnold Newman, 1951.

© ARNOLD NEWMAN

Steinem, Gloria (born 1934) U.S. political activist, feminist, and editor. Born in Toledo, Ohio, she began her career as a writer and journalist in New York and became deeply involved in the WOMEN'S LIBERATION MOVEMENT in the late 1960s. In 1971 she was a founder of the National Women's Political Caucus, and in 1972 she founded *Ms.,* a trendsetting magazine that she subsequently edited, to treat contemporary issues from a feminist perspective. In the 1970s and '80s she founded or co-founded other women's organizations, including the NATIONAL ORGANIZATION FOR WOMEN. Her books include *Outrageous Acts and Everyday Rebellions* (1983), *Marilyn* (1986), and *Revolution from Within* (1992).

Steiner, (Francis) George (born 1929) French-U.S.-Swiss critic. Born in Paris, Steiner became a U.S. citizen in 1944 but has spent much of his time in Europe, teaching principally at Cambridge University and the University of Geneva. He has studied the relationship between literature and society, particularly in light of modern history, and his writings on language and the Holocaust have reached a wide nonacademic audience. Among his works are *The Death of Tragedy* (1960), *Language and Silence* (1967), essays on the dehumanizing effects of World War II on literature, *After Babel* (1975), on the intersection of culture and linguistics, *In Bluebeard's Castle* (1971), and *Real Presences* (1989).

Steiner, Max(imilian Raoul Walter) (1888–1971) Austrian-U.S. composer and conductor. A prodigy, he wrote an operetta at 14 that ran in Vienna for a year. He emigrated to the U.S. in 1914 and worked in New York as a theater conductor and arranger, then moved to Hollywood in 1929. He became one of the first and finest (if not subtlest) movie composers, establishing many techniques that became standard, with his scores for *King Kong* (1933), *The Informer* (1935, Academy Award), *Gone With the Wind* (1939), *Now, Voyager* (1942, Academy Award), *Since You Went Away* (1944, Academy Award), *The Big Sleep* (1946), *The Fountainhead* (1949), and many others.

Steiner \'shtī-nər\, **Rudolf** (1861–1925) Austrian-Swiss social and spiritual philosopher, founder of ANTHROPOSOPHY. He edited JOHANN W. VON GOETHE's scientific works and contributed to the standard edition of Goethe's complete works. Having helped found the German Theosophic Association (see THEOSOPHY), in 1912 he founded the Anthroposophical Society and in 1913 built his first Goetheanum, a "school of spiritual science," in Dornach, Switzerland. A progressive school he founded in 1919 for the workers at the Waldorf Astoria factory led to the international Waldorf School movement. Steiner's writings include *The Philosophy of Spiritual Activity* (1894), *Occult Science* (1913), and *Story of My Life* (1924).

Steinmetz \'shtīn-ˌmets, *Engl* 'stīn-ˌmets\, **Charles Proteus** *orig.* **Karl August Rudolf** (1865–1923) German-U.S. electrical engineer. Forced to leave Germany because of his socialist activities, he emigrated to the U.S. in 1889 and began working for General Electric Co. in 1893. He taught at Union College from 1902. His experiments led to the law of HYSTERESIS, which deals with power loss in electrical machinery when magnetic action is converted to unusable heat; the constant he calculated (by age 27) has remained a part of electrical engineering vocabulary. In 1893 he developed a simplified symbolic method of calculating alternating-current phenomena. He also studied electrical transients (changes of very short duration in electrical circuits, e.g., lightning); his theory of traveling waves led to development of devices to protect high-power transmission lines from lightning bolts, and to the design of a powerful generator. He patented over 200 inventions.

Steinmetz.

BY COURTESY OF UNION COLLEGE, SCHENECTADY, NEW YORK

Steinway German-U.S. piano-manufacturing firm. Henry E. Steinway, born Heinrich Engelhard Steinweg (1797–1871), was trained as an organ builder in his native Germany, and began building pianos in 1836. He and most of his family followed one of his sons to the U.S. in 1850. After working for other piano firms for several years to learn the American business, in 1853 father and sons founded their own company in New York City, which came to dominate the market. In 1865 he brought to the U.S. the sons who had kept the German business going. He himself became involved in research and development, and his improvements set the standard for the modern grand piano.

stele \'stē-lē, 'stēl\ *or* **stela** \'stē-lə\ Standing stone tablet used in the ancient world primarily as a grave marker but also for dedication, commemoration, and demarcation. Though the stele's origin is unknown, a stone slab was commonly used as a tombstone in Egypt, Greece, Asia, and the Mayan empire. In Babylon, the Code of HAMMURABI was engraved on a tall stele. The largest number of stelae were produced in ATTICA, chiefly as grave markers. The dead were represented on the stelae as they were in life: men as warriors or athletes, women surrounded by their children, children with their pets or toys.

Stella, Frank (Philip) (born 1936) U.S. painter. Born in Malden, Mass., he moved to New York after studying history at Princeton Univ., and there began his innovative "black paintings" (1958–60), incorporating symmetrical series of thin white stripes that replicated the canvas shape when seen against their black backgrounds. As a leading figure of MINIMALISM, in the mid-1960s he began using polychromy in an influential series marked by intersecting geometric curvilinear shapes and plays of vivid and harmonious colors. In the 1970s he began producing sensuously colored, mixed-media reliefs featuring more organic shapes. He was given retrospective exhibitions at the Museum of Modern Art in 1970 and 1987.

Steller's sea cow See SEA COW

S T U V

stem Plant axis that emerges from the roots, supports the branches, bears buds and shoots with leaves, and contains the vascular (conducting) tissues (XYLEM and PHLOEM) that transport water, minerals, and food to other parts of the plant. The pith (a central core of spongy tissue) is surrounded by strands (in dicots; see COTYLEDON) or bundles (in monocots) of conducting xylem and phloem, then by the cortex and outermost epidermis, or BARK. The CAMBIUM (an area of actively dividing cells) lies just below the bark. Lateral buds and leaves grow out of the stem at intervals called nodes; the intervals on the stem between the nodes are called internodes. In flowering plants, various stem modifications (RHIZOME, CORM, TUBER, BULB, STOLON) let the plant survive dormantly for years, store food, or sprout asexually. All green stems perform PHOTOSYNTHESIS, as do leaves; in plants such as the cacti (see CACTUS) and ASPARAGUS, the stem is the chief site of photosynthesis.

Stendhal \sta^{n}-'dål, *Engl* sten-'däl\ *orig.* **Marie-Henri Beyle** (1783–1842) French novelist. Born in Grenoble, he left for Paris in 1799 partly to escape his father's rule. By 1802 he was keeping a diary (posthumously published as his *Journal*) and writing other texts dealing with his intimate thoughts. From 1806 he served in Napoleon's army; after the French empire fell in 1814, he settled in Italy. As a result of political and romantic disappointments, he returned to Paris. During 1821–30, while leading an active social and intellectual life, he wrote works including the masterpiece *Rouge et noir* (1830; *The Red and the Black*), a powerful character study of an ambitious young man that is also an acute picture of Restoration France. His other major work, *The Charterhouse of Parma* (1839), is remarkable for its sophisticated rendering of human psychology and its subtly drawn portraits. His unfinished autobiographical works, *Memoirs of an Egotist* (1892) and *The Life of Henry Brulard* (1890), are among his most original achievements.

Stendhal, oil painting by Pierre-Joseph Dedreux-Dorcy; in the Bibliothèque Municipale de Grenoble, Fr.

BY COURTESY OF THE BIBLIOTHEQUE MUNICIPALE DE GRENOBLE, FR.; PHOTOGRAPH, STUDIO PICCARDY

Stengel, Casey *orig.* **Charles Dillon** (1891–1975) U.S. baseball player and manager. Born in Kansas City, he played outfield with the Brooklyn Dodgers (1912–17), Pittsburgh Pirates (1918–19), Philadelphia Phillies (1920–21), New York Giants (1921–23), and Boston Braves (1924–25). He became a coach and manager of the Dodgers and Braves, but achieved his greatest success with the New York Yankees (1949–61), leading the team to 10 pennants (five in consecutive years) and seven World Series championships (five in consecutive years) in 12 years. He later served as vice president and manager of the newly formed New York Mets (1962–65), which became noted for its dismal performance during these early years. Throughout his career Stengel was known for his showmanship and his idiosyncratic use and misuse of English (dubbed "Stengelese").

Stenmark, Ingemar (born 1956) Swedish Alpine skier. He trained with Sweden's junior national team from age 13 and won his first World Cup race in 1974. In 1976, 1977, and 1978 he was the overall victor in the World Cup (slalom, giant slalom, and downhill). In the 1980 Olympic Games he won gold medals in slalom and giant slalom. He turned professional later that year, and he retired in 1989. His lifetime total of 86 World Cup victories still stands as a record, and he is perhaps the greatest slalom and giant slalom skier of all time.

Steno \'stā-nō\, **Nicolaus** *Danish* **Niels Steensen** *or* **Niels Stensen** (1638–1686) Danish geologist and anatomist. An eminent physician, in 1660 he discovered the parotid salivary duct (Stensen's duct). In his geological observations, he was the first to realize that the earth's crust contains a chronologic history of geologic events that might be deciphered by careful study of rock strata and FOSSILS, which he identified as the remains of ancient living organisms. In 1669 he made the fundamental crystallographic discovery that all quartz crystals have the same angles between corresponding faces. He later abandoned science for religion and became a priest in 1675.

stenography See SHORTHAND

stenosis See AORTIC STENOSIS, ATRESIA AND STENOSIS, MITRAL STENOSIS

stenotypy \'ste-nə-,tī-pē\ System of machine SHORTHAND in which letters or groups of letters phonetically represent SYLLABLES, words, phrases, and PUNCTUATION marks. The machine, usually the commercial Stenotype or Stenograph, is often used in court reporting. Virtually noiseless, it can be operated at more than 250 words per minute. Several keys may be struck simultaneously to print a complete word with one stroke.

Stephen *or* **Stephen of Blois** \'blwä\ (1097?–1154) King of England (1135–54). The nephew of HENRY I, he pledged to support MATILDA but claimed the throne himself. In the civil strife that followed he was unable to win the loyalty of all the barons. Matilda invaded (1139), and in a display of chivalry Stephen had her escorted to Bristol. She gained control of most of western England and captured Stephen in battle (1141), but her arrogance provoked a rebellion, and she was forced to leave England (1148). An agreement was reached whereby Matilda's son Henry of Anjou (later HENRY II), who invaded England in 1153, was named as Stephen's successor.

Stephen *known as* **Stephen the Great** (1435–1504) Prince of MOLDAVIA (1457–1504).With the help of the Walachian prince VLAD III TEPES, Stephen secured the throne of Moldavia. He repelled a Hungarian invasion (1467) and later attacked Walachia (1471), by then under Turkish vassalage. He defeated invading Turks (1475, 1476) and contended with Polish and Hungarian designs on Moldavia. In 1503 Stephen signed a treaty preserving Moldavian independence at the cost of an annual tribute to the Turks.

Stephen, James Fitzjames *later* **Sir James** (1829–1894) British legal historian and judge. His *General View of the Criminal Law of England* (1863) was the first attempt since WILLIAM BLACKSTONE to explain the principles of English law. With the British viceroy's council in India (1869–72), he helped codify and reform INDIAN LAW. He later taught at the INNS OF COURT (1875–79) and served on the High Court of Justice (1879–91). His Indictable Offenses Bill, though never enacted, greatly influenced the reformation of criminal law in English-speaking nations.

Stephen, Leslie *later* **Sir Leslie** (1832–1904) British critic. After attending Eton College and Cambridge Univ., he gained entry to literary circles and in 1871 began an 11-year tenure as editor of *The Cornhill Magazine,* for which he wrote literary criticism. His greatest learned work was his *History of English Thought in the Eighteenth Century* (1876), but his most enduring legacy is the *Dictionary of National Biography,* which he edited 1882–91, personally writing many hundreds of its meticulous articles. He was the father of VIRGINIA WOOLF and the painter Vanessa Bell (1879–1961).

Stephen, St. (1st century) First Christian martyr. As told in the Acts of the Apostles, he was a foreign-born Jew who lived in Jerusalem and joined the church at an early date. He was one of seven deacons appointed by the Apostles to care for elderly women, widows, and orphans. As a Hellenized Jew he was strongly opposed to the Temple cult of Judaism, and for expressing his opposition he was brought before the SANHEDRIN. His defense of Christianity so outraged his hearers that he was condemned to be stoned to death. One of those who assented to the execution was Saul of Tarsus (later St. PAUL).

Stephen I *or* **St. Stephen** *orig.* **Vajk** (c. 970–1038) First king of Hungary (1000–38) and founder of the Hungarian state. The son of a Magyar chieftain, he was born a pagan but was later baptized as a Christian. After defeating his cousin to claim the throne, Stephen was crowned; his royal crown was a gift of Pope SYLVESTER II. His rule was peaceful except for an invasion by CONRAD II (1030) and minor disputes with Poland and Bulgaria, and he organized Hungarian government and church administration on German models. He is the patron saint of Hungary.

Stephen II (died 757) Pope (752–57). He freed the papacy from Byzantium and allied it with the Franks against the Lombards, who were threatening Rome. In Gaul he anointed PEPIN III, CHARLEMAGNE, and Carloman as kings of the Romans, and in return Pepin led his army against the Lombardic king Aistulf (754, 756). The victorious Franks granted the pope territory in Ravenna, Rome, Venetia, and Istria, thus establishing the PAPAL STATES under Stephen's rule.

Stephen Báthory \'bä-tòr-ē\ *Hungarian* **István Báthory** *Polish* **Stefan Batory** (1533–1586) Prince of Transylvania (1571–76) and king of Poland (1575–86). In 1571 he was elected prince of Transylvania by the Hungarians, and in 1575, as son-in-law of the late Sigismund I, he was elected king of Poland by the Polish nobility. A forceful and ambitious monarch, he successfully defended Poland's eastern Baltic provinces against Russian incursion and forced the cession of Livonia to Poland in 1582. He planned to unite Poland, Muscovy, and Transylvania and was preparing to renew the war against Russia when he died.

Stephen Decansky See Stefan Decansky

Stephen Dusan See Stefan Dusan

Stephen Nemanja See Stefan Nemanja

Stephens, Alexander H(amilton) (1812–1883) U.S. politician. Born in Wilkes Co., Ga., he served in the U.S. House of Representatives 1843–59, where he defended slavery but opposed dissolution of the Union. When Georgia seceded, he was elected vice president of the Confederacy. He supported constitutional government, opposed attempts by Jefferson Davis to infringe on individuals' rights, and advocated a program of prisoner exchanges. He led the delegation to the Hampton Roads Conference (1865). After the war he was held in Boston for five months. He later served again in the House (1873–82) and as governor of Georgia (1882–83).

Stephens, John Lloyd (1805–1852) U.S. traveler and archaeologist. Born in Shrewsbury, N.J., he practiced law before beginning his travels in the Middle East, which resulted in two books. With his illustrator friend Frederick Catherwood, he embarked for Honduras in 1839 to explore ancient Maya ruins rumored to exist. At Copán, Uxmal, Palenque, and elsewhere, they identified major new sites. They described their findings in *Incidents of Travel in Central America, Chiapas, and Yucatan* (1841), and recounted a second trip in *Incidents of Travel in Yucatan* (1843). Their books created a storm of popular and scholarly interest in the region.

Stephens, Uriah Smith (1821–1882) U.S. labor leader. Born in Cape May, N.J., he apprenticed as a tailor. He became involved in reform movements such as abolitionism and utopian socialism, and in 1862 he helped organize the Garment Cutters' Association of Philadelphia. In 1869 he cofounded the Noble Order of the Knights of Labor, the first national labor union in the U.S., and became its first leader (or grand master workman). The high calling of the union and the hostility of union-busters led Stephens to favor secrecy and ritual in its meetings, which became increasingly controversial, as did Stephens' opposition to strikes. In 1878 he resigned his post.

Stephenson, George (1781–1848) English engineer, principal inventor of the locomotive. Son of a coal-mine mechanic, he himself became chief mechanic at a coal mine, where his interest in steam engines led to experiments on a machine to pull coal-filled cars out of the mines. In 1815 he devised a powerful "steam blast" system that made the locomotive practical. In 1825 he built a steam locomotive for the first passenger railway, from Stockton to Darlington, which could carry 450 people at 15 mph (24 kph). In 1829, assisted by his son Robert Stephenson, he built his improved locomotive, the *Rocket,* which won a speed competition at 36 mph (58 kph) and became the model for later locomotives. His company built all eight locomotives for the new Liverpool–Manchester railway (1830).

George Stephenson, mezzotint by C. Turner after H.P. Briggs.

BY COURTESY OF THE SCIENCE MUSEUM, LONDON

Stephenson, Robert (1803–1859) British civil engineer and builder of long-span railroad bridges. The son of George Stephenson, he assisted his father in constructing the "Rocket" and several railways. Building a railway from Newcastle to Berwick, he spanned the Tyne River with a six-arch iron bridge. Called on to build a secure railroad bridge over the Menai Strait to the Welsh mainland, Stephenson conceived a unique tubular design, whose success led to his building other tubular bridges in England and elsewhere.

Steptoe, Patrick (Christopher); and Edwards, Robert (Geoffrey) (1913–1988, born 1925) British medical researchers. They perfected human in vitro fertilization, leading to the birth of the first "test-tube baby" in 1978. Steptoe had conducted research on sterilization and infertility and published *Laparoscopy in Gynaecology* (1967). Edwards succeeded in 1968 in fertilizing human ova outside the uterus. Their partnership, begun in 1968, resulted in the birth of more than 1,000 babies.

stereochemistry Term originated by Viktor Meyer c. 1878 for the study of stereoisomers (see isomer). Louis Pasteur had shown in 1848 that tartaric acid had optical activity and that this depended on molecular asymmetry, and Jacobus H. van't Hoff and Joseph-Achille Le Bel (1847–1930) had independently explained in 1874 how a molecule with a carbon atom bonded to four different groups has two mirror-image forms. Stereochemistry deals with stereoisomers and with asymmetric synthesis. John Cornforth (born 1917) and Vladimir Prelog (1906–1998) shared a 1975 Nobel Prize for work on stereochemistry and stereoisomerism of alkaloids, enzymes, antibiotics, and other natural compounds.

sterilization Any surgical procedure intended to end fertility permanently (see contraception). Such operations remove or interrupt the anatomical pathways through which the cells involved in fertilization travel (see reproductive system). They are relatively simple and more than 99% effective. The operations used in humans are vasectomy in men and tubal ligation (tying off and blocking or cutting of the fallopian tubes) in women. Though these operations are considered permanent, the development of microsurgery has improved the chances of reversal. Animals are sterilized by castration in males and spaying (removal of the ovaries) in females.

Sterkfontein \'sterk-fən-ˌtān\ One of three neighboring South African sites (the others being Kromdraai and Swartkrans) at which the remains of fossil hominids have been found, including those of *Australopithecus africanus, A. robustus,* and *Homo erectus*. In 1996 researchers uncovered the most complete australopithecine fossil skeleton since Lucy, that of an *A. africanus* individual with a humanlike pelvis but with limb proportions similar to those of a modern chimpanzee. At Makapansgat, 150 mi (240 km) to the north, the remains of about 40 individuals of *A. africanus* have been found.

Sterling, Bruce (born 1954) U.S. science-fiction writer. Born in Brownsville, Texas, he graduated from the University of Texas in 1976, the year his first story, "Man-Made Self," was published. A principal proponent of cyberpunk, science fiction dealing with harsh future urban societies dominated by computer technology, he edited *Mirrorshades: The Cyberpunk Anthology* (1986) and has published such novels as *Schismatrix* (1985), *Islands in the Net* (1988), *The Difference Engine* (1990; with William Gibson), and *Distraction* (1999).

Stern, Isaac (1920–2001) U.S. (Ukrainian-born) violinist. His family came to the U.S. when he was an infant. He first performed with the San Francisco Symphony in 1936, and he made his New York debut at 17. After the war, he began to tour extensively (including the Soviet Union in 1956). In 1960 he formed a famous trio with pianist Eugene Istomin (born 1925) and cellist Leonard Rose (1918–1984). He was instrumental in saving Carnegie Hall from demolition, helped establish the National Endowment for the Arts, and was a key presence in the musical life of Israel.

Stern Magazin \'shtern-mä-gä-'tsēn\ German weekly newsmagazine. Founded in 1948, it quickly became known for its outstanding photography and its blend of light and serious material. Its lively treatment of sex-oriented stories helped it achieve wide popularity. It features pictorial essays, celebrity profiles, interviews, and other material and combines sensational photographs with conventional news and pictures of current events.

Sternberg, Josef von *orig.* **Jonas Stern** (1894–1969) U.S. (Austrian-born) film director. Born into an Orthodox Jewish family in Vienna, he emigrated to New York as a boy. By 1923 he was a scriptwriter and cameraman in Hollywood. In 1927 he made the first serious gangster movie, *Underworld* (1927). His films became noted for their striking visual effects and atmospheric use of light and dark. In Germany he made *The Blue Angel* (1930), which made Marlene Dietrich an international star. She returned with Sternberg to Hollywood, where he directed her in *Morocco* (1930), *Shanghai Express* (1932), *Blonde Venus* (1932), *The Scarlet Empress* (1934), and *The Devil Is a Woman* (1935). His career thereafter declined, though his late films *Macao* (1952) and *The Saga of Anatahan* (1953) have been admired.

Josef von Sternberg editing a film.
CULVER PICTURES

Sterne, Laurence (1713–1768) English novelist and humorist. Sterne was a clergyman in York for many years before his talents became apparent when he wrote a Swiftian satire in support of his dean in a church squabble. Turning his parishes over to a curate, he began *Tristram Shandy* (1759–67), an experimental novel issued in nine parts in which the story is subordinate to its narrator's free associations and digressions. It is considered one of the most important ancestors of psychological and STREAM-OF-CONSCIOUSNESS fiction. Long afflicted with tuberculosis, Sterne fled the damp air of England and undertook the travels that inspired his unfinished *Sentimental Journey Through France and Italy* (1768), a comic novel that defies conventional expectations of a travel book.

Sterne, detail of an oil painting by Sir Joshua Reynolds, 1760; in the National Portrait Gallery, London.
NATIONAL PORTRAIT GALLERY, LONDON

steroid Any of a class of natural or synthetic organic compounds with 17 carbon atoms in a three-dimensional arrangement of four rings. The CONFIGURATION of the nucleus, the nature of the groups attached to it, and their positions distinguish different steroids. Hundreds have been found in plants and animals and thousands more synthesized or made by modifying natural steroids. Steroids are important in biology, chemistry, and medicine. Examples include many HORMONES (including the SEX HORMONES), BILE acids, sterols (including CHOLESTEROL), and oral contraceptives. DIGITALIS was the first steroid widely used in Western medicine. Corticosteroids (see CORTISONE) and their synthetic analogs are used to treat rheumatism and other inflammatory ailments. See also ANABOLIC STEROIDS.

Stettin See SZCZECIN

Stettinius \ste-ˈti-nē-əs\, **Edward Reilly, Jr.** (1900–1949) U.S. industrialist and statesman. Born in Chicago, he worked for General Motors Corp. and became a vice president in 1931. He joined U.S. Steel Corp. in 1934 and became chairman of the board in 1938. He served as chairman of the War Resources Board 1939–40, and as administrator of LEND-LEASE 1941–43. As U.S. secretary of state (1944–45), he advised Pres. FRANKLIN ROOSEVELT at the YALTA CONFERENCE. He led the U.S. delegation to the U.N. organizing conference in San Francisco and was the first U.S. delegate to the U.N. (1945–46).

Steuben \ˈstü-bən\, **Frederick William (Augustus)** (1730–1794) German-American Revolutionary officer. He joined the Prussian army at 16 and was a captain in the Seven Years' War; he claimed to have been created a baron. Recommended to GEORGE WASHINGTON, he arrived in America in 1777. Appointed to train the Continental forces at Valley Forge, Pa., he produced a disciplined fighting force that became the model for the entire Continental Army. He was appointed inspector general of the army and promoted to major general (1778), and he helped command at the Siege of YORKTOWN.

Stevens, George (1904–1975) U.S. film director. Born in Oakland, Cal., he acted in his father's touring theater company before becoming a Hollywood cameraman in 1921. He photographed many of LAUREL AND HARDY's comedies before turning to directing in 1933. Noted for his brilliant camera techniques and careful craftsmanship, he achieved fame with *Alice Adams* (1935) and *Swing Time* (1936). His later films include *Woman of the Year* (1942), *I Remember Mama* (1948), *A Place in the Sun* (1951, Academy Award), the classic western *Shane* (1953), and *Giant* (1956, Academy Award).

Stevens, John (1749–1838) U.S. engineer and inventor. Born in New York City, he served as a colonel in the American Revolution. To protect his boiler and engine designs, he submitted his outline for a PATENT law; the resulting Patent Law of 1790 formed the basis of the U.S. patent system. In 1802 he became the first person to employ a powered screw to propel a ship. In 1809 his steamship *Phoenix* became the world's first seagoing steamboat. In Philadelphia in 1811 he inaugurated the world's first steam-ferry service. In 1825, at age 76, he built the first American steam LOCOMOTIVE. He developed his New Jersey estate into the city of Hoboken. He was the father of ROBERT L. STEVENS. Another son, Edwin Augustus Stevens (1795–1868), was the inventor of the Stevens plow and a pioneer builder of ironclad warships, and established the Stevens Institute of Technology by a bequest. A third son, John Cox Stevens (1785–1857), headed the group that sent the yacht *America* to Britain, where it won the race that established the AMERICA'S CUP.

Stevens, John Paul (born 1920) U.S. jurist. Born in Chicago, he studied law at Northwestern University and clerked at the U.S. Supreme Court before joining a Chicago law firm, where he specialized in antitrust law while also teaching and serving on various public commissions. He was appointed to the U.S. Circuit Court of Appeals by Pres. RICHARD NIXON in 1970, and to the U.S. Supreme Court by Pres. GERALD FORD in 1975. An independent-minded justice, Stevens has become, with the departure of several colleagues, perhaps the Court's most liberal member.

Stevens, Robert Livingston (1787–1856) U.S. engineer and ship designer. Born in Hoboken, N.J., the son of JOHN STEVENS, he tested the first steamboat to use screw propellers. He designed the railway T-rail in 1830, and later the railroad spike. He found that rails laid on wooden ties, with crushed stone or gravel beneath, provided a roadbed superior to any known before; his construction remains in universal use.

Stevens, Thaddeus (1792–1868) U.S. politician. Born in Danville, Vt., he practiced law in Pennsylvania, defending fugitive slaves without fee. In the U.S. House of Representatives (1849–53, 1859–68), he opposed the extension of slavery into the western territories. After the Civil War he was a leader of the RADICAL REPUBLICANS and demanded strict criteria, including justice for blacks, for readmission of the seceded states. He helped establish the FREEDMEN'S BUREAU and secured passage of the 14th Amendment to the Constitution. He opposed the moderate Reconstruction policies of Pres. ANDREW JOHNSON and introduced the resolution for his impeachment.

Stevens, Wallace (1879–1955) U.S. poet. Born in Reading, Pa., Stevens practiced law in New York City before joining an insurance firm in Hartford in 1916; he rose to vice president, a position he held until his death. His poems began appearing in literary magazines in 1914. In *Harmonium* (1923), his first and most verbally brilliant book, he introduced the theme that occupied his creative lifetime and unified his thought: the relationship between imagination and reality. His later poetry, in such collections as *Ideas of Order* (1936), *The Man with the Blue Guitar* (1937), and *The Auroras of Autumn* (1950), continued to explore this theme with greater depth and rigor. His life was almost completely uneventful, and not until his late years was he widely read or recognized as a major poet by more than a few; he received a Pulitzer Prize only with his *Collected Poems* in 1955. He is now often considered America's greatest 20th-century poet.

Wallace Stevens, 1952.
© ROLLIE MCKENNA

Stevenson, Adlai E(wing) (1900–1965) U.S. politician and diplomat. Born in Christian Co., Ky., the grandson of a vice president, he practiced law in Chicago from 1926. During World War II he was assistant to the secretary of the navy (1941–44) and to the secretary of state

(1945). He was a delegate to the U.N. 1946–47. As governor of Illinois (1949–53), he introduced liberal reforms. Noted for his eloquence and wit, he was twice the Democratic candidate for president (1952, 1956) but lost both times to DWIGHT D. EISENHOWER. He later served as chief U.S. representative to the U.N. (1961–65).

Stevenson, Robert Louis (Balfour) (1850–1894) Scottish essayist, novelist, and poet. He prepared for a law career but never practiced. He traveled frequently, partly in search of better climates for his tuberculosis, which would eventually cause his death at 44. He became known for accounts such as *Travels with a Donkey in the Cévennes* (1879) and essays in periodicals, first collected in *Virginibus Puerisque* (1881). His immensely popular novels *Treasure Island* (1883), *Kidnapped* (1886), and *Dr. Jekyll and Mr. Hyde* (1886), and *The Master of Ballantrae* (1889) were written over the course of a few years. *A Child's Garden of Verses* (1885) is one of the most influential children's works of the 19th century. In his last years he lived in Samoa and produced works moving toward a new maturity, including the story "The Beach of Falesá" (1892) and the novel *Weir of Hermiston* (1896), his unfinished masterpiece.

Stevin \'stā-vin\, **Simon** (1548–1620) Flemish mathematician. In 1585 Stevin published a small pamphlet, *La Thiende* ("The Tenth"), in which he presented an account of decimal fractions and their daily use. Though he did not invent decimal fractions and his notation was clumsy, he established the use of decimals in day-to-day mathematics.

Stewart See House of STUART

Stewart, Ellen (born 1931) U.S. theater director. Born into a black family in Alexandria, La., she settled in New York, where she became known as the mother of Off-Off-Broadway theater. In 1961 she founded Café La Mama, an experimental theater specializing in total integration of music, dance, and drama. There she gave a start to many young actors and playwrights, including BETTE MIDLER and SAM SHEPARD. A European tour in 1965 made La Mama a mecca for European avant-garde directors. Its frequently distinguished productions have made La Mama a venerated institution and won over 50 Obie Awards.

Stewart, Henry See Lord DARNLEY

Stewart, James (Maitland) (1908–1997) U.S. film actor. Born in Indiana, Pa., he studied architecture at Princeton University and worked in a Massachusetts theater group before going to Hollywood. He made his film debut in 1935 and played endearingly simple and idealistic characters in FRANK CAPRA's *You Can't Take It with You* (1938) and *Mr. Smith Goes to Washington* (1939). After serving as a bomber pilot in World War II, he starred in *It's a Wonderful Life* (1946), which became a Christmas classic. His other movies include *Destry Rides Again* (1939), *The Philadelphia Story* (1940, Academy Award), *Harvey* (1950), *The Glenn Miller Story* (1954), *Bend of the River* (1952), *The Man from Laramie* (1955), *Anatomy of a Murder* (1959), and ALFRED HITCHCOCK's *Rope* (1948), *Rear Window* (1954), *The Man Who Knew Too Much* (1955), and *Vertigo* (1958).

James Stewart in *It's a Wonderful Life* (1946).
CULVER PICTURES

Stewart, J(ohn) I(nnes) M(ackintosh) (1906–1994) Scottish-English novelist, literary critic, and educator. Stewart began writing while working as a college professor. In his mystery novels, he created the character of Inspector John Appleby, a British detective known for his suave humor and literary finesse. Among the best of these mysteries, all published under the pseudonym of Michael Innes, are *Lament for a Maker* (1938), *The Journeying Boy* (1949), and *An Awkward Lie* (1971). Stewart wrote other works of fiction under his own name, as well as several works of literary criticism. His autobiography, *Myself and Michael Innes*, was published in 1987.

Stewart, Potter (1915–1985) U.S. jurist. Born in Jackson, Mich., he studied law at Yale University. He settled in Cincinnati after World War II and served on the city council and as vice mayor before his appointment to the U.S. Court of Appeals in 1954. In 1958 Pres. DWIGHT D. EISENHOWER appointed him to the U.S. Supreme Court, where he served until 1981. A moderate, he wrote the majority opinion in the *Shelton vs. Tucker* case, which held unconstitutional the requirement that teachers list all the associations to which they belong, and also wrote a memorable dissent in *MIRANDA VS. ARIZONA*.

Stibitz, George Robert (1904–1995) U.S. mathematician and inventor. Born in York, Pa., he received his PhD from Cornell University. In 1940 he and Samuel Williams, a colleague at Bell Labs, developed the Model I Complex Calculator, considered a forerunner of the digital computer. He accomplished the first remote computer operation by transmitting problems to be solved over a Teletype, and he pioneered computer applications in biomedical areas, such as the movement of oxygen in the lungs, brain cell anatomy, diffusion of nutrients and drugs in the body, and capillary transport. The holder of 38 patents, he was inducted into the Inventors Hall of Fame in 1983.

stibnite Antimony sulfide (Sb_2S_3), the principal ore of ANTIMONY. This SULFIDE MINERAL has a brilliant metallic luster, is lead or steel gray in color, and fuses (melts) readily. Stibnite occurs in low-temperature hydrothermal veins (see HYDROTHERMAL ORE DEPOSITS) and in REPLACEMENT DEPOSITS. Significant deposits have been found in China, Japan, and the U.S. (Idaho, California, and Nevada). Stibnite is used in making matches, fireworks, and percussion caps and was used by the ancients as a cosmetic (called kohl) to increase the apparent size of the eye.

Stick style Style of residential design popular in the U.S. in the 1860s and '70s, a precursor to the SHINGLE STYLE. The Stick style favored an imitation half-timbered effect, with boards attached to the exterior walls in grids suggestive of the underlying frame construction. Other characteristic features included attached open stickwork verandas, projecting square bays, steeply pitched roofs, and overhanging eaves. Angular and vertical elements were emphasized. Though associated with CARPENTER GOTHIC, the Stick style made less use of GINGERBREAD. The style also marked the beginning of greater openness of the floor plan. CHARLES S. AND HENRY M. GREENE succeeded admirably in reinterpreting the style in the early 20th century.

stickleback Any of about 12 species (family Gasterosteidae) of slender, scaleless fishes inhabiting temperate fresh- and saltwaters of the Northern Hemisphere. Sticklebacks grow to 6 in. (15 cm) long. They have a row of spines on the back, in front of a soft-rayed dorsal fin, and a sharp spine in each of the pelvic fins. They also have a slender tail base, a squared tail, and hard armor plates on their sides. The male builds a nest of plant materials and coaxes one or more females into it to lay eggs, fertilizes the eggs in the nest, and aggressively defends eggs and young.

Stickley, Gustav (1858–1942) U.S. furniture designer and maker. Born in Osceola, Wis., he learned to make furniture at a chair factory owned by an uncle. After taking over the factory, he moved it to New York state, first to Binghamton and then to Syracuse. Influenced by the ARTS AND CRAFTS MOVEMENT and by visits to old missions in the American Southwest, he introduced c. 1900 a highly original line of sturdy oak furniture. To spread his ideas and designs, he published the influential magazine *The Craftsman* 1901–16. In 1916 two younger brothers established a firm to produce furniture from his designs and gave the style the name Mission, by which name it is still popular today.

Stiegel \'stē-gəl, *German* 'shtē-gəl\, **Henry William** *orig.* **Heinrich Wilhelm** (1729–1785) German-U.S. ironmaster and glassmaker. After arriving in Philadelphia in 1750, he quickly became a prosperous ironmaster. In 1762 he bought a huge tract in Lancaster Co. and built the town of Manheim, where he established American Flint Glassworks, importing Venetian, German, and English glassworkers to make utilitarian vessels and high-quality blue, purple, green, and clear tableware. He owned three mansions, where his comings and goings were announced by a cannon salute and band music, but his lavish style and adverse economic conditions eventually bankrupted him.

Stieglitz \'stēg-lits\, **Alfred** (1864–1946) U.S. photographer and exhibitor of modern art. Born in Hoboken, N.J., he was taken to Europe by his wealthy family to further his education in 1881. In 1883 he abandoned engineering studies in Berlin for a photographic career. Returning to the U.S. in 1890, he made the first successful photographs in snow, in rain, and at night. In 1902 he founded the PHOTO-SECESSION group to establish photography as an art. His own best photographs are perhaps two series (1917–27), one of portraits of his wife, GEORGIA O'KEEFFE, and the other of cloud shapes corresponding to emotional experiences. His photographs were the first to be exhibited in major U.S. museums. He also was the first to exhibit, at his "291" gallery in New York, works of modern European and U.S. painters, five years before the ARMORY SHOW.

Alfred Stieglitz at his gallery "291" in 1934; behind him is a painting by his wife, Georgia O'Keeffe.
IMOGEN CUNNINGHAM

Stiernhielm \'shern-ˌyelm\, **Georg** *orig.* **Jöran Olofsson** *or* **Georgius Olai** *or* **Göran Lilia** (1598–1672) Swedish poet and scholar, often called "the father of Swedish poetry." Beginning about 1640 he was poet in attendance at the court of Queen CHRISTINA. His most important work is the allegorical, didactic epic *Hercules* (1658), a sermon on virtue and honor and a fine example of late-Renaissance classicism; it greatly influenced the development of Swedish poetry. His poems were collected in *Swedish Muses* (1668).

Stigand \'sti-gənd\ (died 1072) Archbishop of Canterbury (1052–70). He mediated the peace between EDWARD THE CONFESSOR and Earl Godwine (1052) and was made archbishop of Canterbury when the Norman archbishop fled. He was not accepted until 1058, and then only by the antipope Benedict X, after whose deposition Stigand was excommunicated by NICHOLAS II. His continuance in office was one of the reasons the pope supported WILLIAM I's invasion in 1066.

Stigler, George J(oseph) (1911–1991) U.S. economist. Born in Renton, Wash., he received his PhD from the University of Chicago. He taught at various institutions and in 1977 founded the Center for the Study of the Economy and the State at the University of Chicago. Stigler studied the economics of information, elaborating on the traditional understanding of how efficient markets operate. He also studied public regulation, concluding that it is usually detrimental to consumer interests. He won the Nobel Prize in 1982.

stigmata \stig-'mä-tə\ In Christian MYSTICISM, bodily marks, scars, or pains suffered in places corresponding to those of the crucified JESUS—on the hands and feet, near the heart, and sometimes on the head (from the crown of thorns) or shoulders and back (from carrying the cross and being whipped). They are often presumed to accompany religious ecstasy and are taken as signs of holiness. The first to experience the stigmata was St. FRANCIS OF ASSISI (1224). Of the more than 330 persons identified with stigmata since the 14th century, 60 were declared saints or the blessed by the Roman Catholic church.

Stijl \'stīl, 'stāl\, **De** (Dutch: "The Style") Group of Dutch artists founded in 1917, including THEO VAN DOESBURG and PIET MONDRIAN. The group advocated a utopian style: "the universal harmony of life." Its ideal of purity and order in life and society as well as art reflects the Calvinist background of its members. Through its journal, *De Stijl* (1917–31), it influenced painting, the decorative arts (including furniture design), typography, and especially architecture, where its aesthetic found expression at the BAUHAUS and in the INTERNATIONAL STYLE.

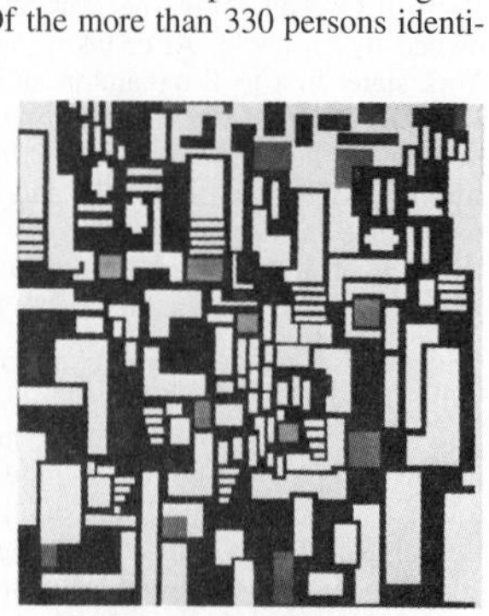
"Card Players," oil painting by De Stijl artist Theo van Doesburg, 1917; in the collection of the Haags Gemeentemuseum, The Hague.
BY COURTESY OF THE HAAGS GEMEENTEMUSEUM, THE HAGUE

Stikine River \sti-'kēn\ River, northwestern British Columbia and southeastern Alaska. It rises in the Stikine Ranges of British Columbia and flows in a wide arc west and southwest before emptying into the Pacific Ocean after a course of 335 mi (540 km). It served as a major access route during the KLONDIKE GOLD RUSH of 1896. Navigable for 168 mi (270 km), it is a chief route to the Cassiar Mountains mining region.

Still, Clyfford (1904–1980) U.S. painter. Born in Grandin, N.D., he studied at Spokane University and Washington State College. After experimenting with several styles he became involved in ABSTRACT EXPRESSIONISM and was a pioneer of the very large, monochromatic painting. Unlike the thin, unmodulated pigments of his colleagues BARNETT NEWMAN and MARK ROTHKO, he used thickly applied opaque paint (impasto) in expressively modulated, jagged forms to portray raw, aggressive power.

Still, William Grant (1895–1978) U.S. composer. Born in Woodville, Miss., he initially intended to be a doctor but instead studied music at Oberlin, learning clarinet, oboe, and violin. He played for the hit Broadway show *Shuffle Along* (1921) and studied composition with George Chadwick (1854–1931) and E. VARESE. His early style was avant-garde (*From the Black Belt*, 1926), but from c. 1930 he sought to develop a distinctive African-American art music in five symphonies (including Symphony No. 1, "Afro-American," 1930), ballets, operas, and choral and solo vocal works (*Songs of Separation*, 1949).

still-life painting Depiction of inanimate objects for the sake of their qualities of form, color, texture, composition, and sometimes allegorical or symbolical significance. Still lifes were painted in ancient Greece and Rome. In the Middle Ages they occur in the borders of illuminated manuscripts. The modern still life emerged as an independent genre in the Renaissance. Netherlandish still lifes often depicted skulls, candles, and hourglasses as allegories of mortality, or flowers and fruits to symbolize nature's cycle. Several factors contributed to the rise of still life in the 16th–17th century: an interest in realistic representation, the rise of a wealthy middle class that wanted artworks to decorate its homes, and increased demand for paintings of secular subjects other than portraits in the wake of the Reformation. Dutch and Flemish painters were the masters of still life in the 17th century. From the 18th century until the rise of nonobjective painting after World War II, France was the center of still-life painting.

Stillman, James (1850–1918) U.S. financier and banker. Born in Brownsville, Texas, he began his career in a New York mercantile house. He became president of the National City Bank (see CITIGROUP) in 1891, shortly after the Rockefeller family obtained a controlling interest in the bank. Under his leadership the bank prospered during the panic of 1893, more than doubling its deposits and becoming the leading U.S. bank. In 1897 it was the only bank capable of financing the reorganization of the UNION PACIFIC RAILROAD. At his death he left a huge personal fortune.

stilt Any of certain species of shorebirds (family Recurvirostridae) that have long thin legs and a long slender bill and inhabit warm regions worldwide. Stilts, 14–18 in. (35–45 cm) long, live around ponds, probing in mud and weedy shallows for crustaceans and other small aquatic animals. The common stilt *(Himantopus himantopus)* is variably black-and-white with pink legs and red eyes.

Black-necked stilt (*Himantopus himantopus mexicanus*).
G.W. ROBINSON—ROOT RESOURCES

Stilwell, Joseph W(arren) (1883–1946) U.S. Army officer. Born in Palatka, Fla., he graduated from West Point and served in World War I. He studied Chinese and served in Tianjin (1926–29) and as a military attaché in Beijing (1935–39). At the outbreak of World War II, he became chief of staff to Gen. CHIANG KAI-SHEK and commanded Chinese armies in Burma (1939–42). He became commander of U.S. forces in China, Burma, and India, and oversaw construction of the Ledo or STILWELL ROAD, a strategic military link with the Burma Road. Promoted to general (1944), he commanded the U.S. 10th Army in the Pacific (1945–46).

Stilwell Road *formerly* **Ledo Road** Former military highway, Asia. It was 478 mi (769 km) long and linked northeastern India with the BURMA ROAD. In World War II, U.S. Army engineers and Chinese troops constructed it to link the railheads of Ledo, India, and Mogaung, Burma. Named for Gen. JOSEPH STILWELL, it crossed into Burma (Myanmar) through the difficult Pangsau Pass of the Patkai Range.

Stimson, Henry L(ewis) (1867–1950) U.S. statesman. Born in New York City, he practiced law and served as U.S. secretary of war (1911–13), governor of the Philippines (1927–29), and U.S. secretary of state (1929–33). After the Japanese occupation of Manchuria (1931), he sent a diplomatic note to Japan refusing to recognize territorial changes and reaffirming U.S. treaty rights; this became known as the Stimson Doctrine. As secretary of war (1940–45), he oversaw the expansion and training of U.S. forces in World War II. He was the chief adviser on atomic policy to FRANKLIN ROOSEVELT and HARRY TRUMAN and recommended use of the atomic bomb on Hiroshima and Nagasaki.

stimulant Any drug that excites any bodily function; usually one that stimulates the central NERVOUS SYSTEM, inducing alertness, elevated mood, wakefulness, increased speech and motor activity, and decreased appetite. Their mood-elevating effects make some stimulants (e.g., AMPHETAMINES, CAFFEINE and its relatives, COCAINE, NICOTINE) potent drugs of abuse (see DRUG ADDICTION). Ritalin, prescribed for ATTENTION DEFICIT DISORDER in children, is a mild stimulant.

stingray *or* **whip-tailed ray** Any of various species (family Dasyatidae) of RAYS noted for their slender, whiplike tail with barbed, usually venomous spines. Most species inhabit warm seas; a few live in the rivers of South America. Species range in width from 10 in. (25 cm) to 7 ft (2 m). Stingrays eat worms, mollusks, and other invertebrates. These bottom-dwellers often lie partially buried in the shallows, lashing their tail when disturbed. Large stingrays can drive their tail spines into a wooden boat. The spines cause serious, extremely painful wounds that, if abdominal, may be fatal.

Stirling Burgh (pop., 1991: 27,984), southern central Scotland, on the River FORTH. It has evidence of early settlement by the British PICTS. Made a royal burgh c. 1130 and a royal residence in 1226, it was the birthplace of JAMES II of Scotland and site of the coronations of MARY, QUEEN OF SCOTS, and James VI of Scotland (later JAMES I of England). Two battles were fought nearby: the Battle of Stirling Bridge (1297), where Scottish troops routed the English, and the Battle of BANNOCKBURN (1314). It flourished until the mid-16th century and shared with EDINBURGH the privileges of a capital city. After the union of the Scottish and English crowns in 1603, it ceased to play an important national role. It is now a commercial center for an agricultural region, and the seat of the Central administrative region.

Stirling, Earl of See William ALEXANDER

Stirling, James (Frazer) *later* **Sir James** (1926–1992) Scottish architect. He began working (1956–63) in the New Brutalist style with his partner James Gowan. The engineering building at Leicester University (1963), with its precise crystalline forms, brought him early fame. From 1971 he worked with Michael Wilford. In the 1970s Stirling developed his own brand of POSTMODERNISM that made use of complex geometric abstraction, bold colors, and classical elements. The Neue Staatsgalerie (1977–84) in Stuttgart is among his finest statements. Stirling was the 1981 recipient of the Pritzker Architecture Prize.

stoa \'stō-ə\ In Greek architecture, a freestanding COLONNADE or covered walkway; also, a long open building, its roof supported by one or more rows of columns parallel to its rear wall. Stoas lined marketplaces and sanctuaries, and formed places of business and public promenades. Rooms might back onto the colonnade, and a second story was sometimes added. The Stoa of Attalus in Athens (2nd century BC), a large, elaborate, two-story building with a row of shops at the rear, was a prime example.

stochastic process \stə-'kas-tik\ In PROBABILITY THEORY, a family of RANDOM VARIABLES indexed to some other set and having the property that for each finite subset of the index set, the collection of random variables indexed to it has a joint probability distribution. It is one of the most widely studied subjects in probability. Examples include Markov processes (in which the present value of the variable depends only upon the immediate past and not upon the whole sequence of past events), such as stock-market fluctuations, and time series (in which temperature or rainfall measurements, for example, are taken at the same time each day over several days).

stock In finance, the subscribed capital of a corporation or limited-liability company, usually divided into shares and represented by transferable certificates. Many companies have only one class of stock, called common stock. Common stock, as a share of ownership in the company, entitles the holder to an interest in the company's earnings and assets. It carries voting rights that enable the holder to participate in the running of the company (unless such rights are specifically withheld, as in special classes of nonvoting shares). DIVIDENDS paid on common stock are often unstable because they vary with earnings; they are also usually less than earnings, the difference being used by the management to expand the firm. To appeal to investors who want to be sure of receiving dividends regularly, some companies issue preferred stock, which has a prior claim to dividends paid by the company and, in most cases, to the company's assets in case of its dissolution. Preferred-stock dividends are usually set at a fixed annual rate that must be paid before dividends are distributed to common stockholders. See also SECURITY, STOCK EXCHANGE.

stock-car racing Form of automobile racing, popular in the U.S., in which cars that conform externally to standard U.S. commercial models are raced, usually on oval, paved tracks. The National Association for Stock Car Auto Racing (NASCAR), founded in 1947 in Daytona Beach, Fla., gave the sport its first formal organization. The Daytona 500 is the sport's premier race.

stock exchange *or* **stock market** *or (in continental Europe)* **Bourse** Organized market for the sale and purchase of SECURITIES such as STOCKS and BONDS. Trading is done by members of the exchange, who serve as brokers, buying and selling for others and charging commissions. Stock exchanges give seats (the right to trade) to a limited number of members, who must conform to eligibility requirements. Stocks must likewise meet certain requirements to be listed. Stock exchanges differ from country to country in eligibility requirements and in the degree to which the government participates in their management. The LONDON STOCK EXCHANGE, for example, is an independent institution, free from government regulation. In the U.S., the NEW YORK STOCK EXCHANGE and the NASDAQ-Amex Market Group are not directly run by the government but are regulated by law. In Europe, members of the exchanges are often appointed by government officials and have semigovernmental status. See also TOKYO STOCK EXCHANGE.

Stock Market Crash of 1929 Economic event in the U.S. that precipitated the GREAT DEPRESSION. The U.S. stock market expanded rapidly in the late 1920s and reached a peak in August 1929, when prices began to decline while speculation increased. On October 18 the market fell sharply. On October 24, "Black Thursday," almost 13 million shares were traded. Banks and investment companies bought large blocks of stock to stem the PANIC, but on October 29, "Black Tuesday," 16 million shares were traded and prices collapsed. The crash began a 10-year economic slump that affected all the Western industrialized countries.

stock option Contractual agreement entitling the holder to buy or sell a share of STOCK at a designated price for a specified period of time, regardless of changes in its market price during that period. The various kinds of stock options include put and call options, which may be purchased in anticipation of changes in stock prices, as a means of speculation or HEDGING. A put gives its holder an option to sell, or put, shares to another party at a fixed price even if the market price declines. A call gives the holder an option to buy, or call for, shares at a fixed price even if the market price rises. U.S. corporations often issue stock options to executives as a form of compensation in addition to salary, on the theory that an option is an incentive to improve the company's business and thus raise the value of its stock; today such options may be far more valuable than the salary itself.

Stockhausen \'shtök-,haù-zən\, **Karlheinz** (born 1928) German composer. Orphaned during World War II, he supported himself with odd jobs (including jazz pianist) before entering Cologne's Hochschule in 1947. After hearing O. MESSIAEN's music at Darmstadt in 1951, he began pursuing "total serialism" and studied with Messiaen. His early works included *Kontrapunkte* and *Klavierstücke I–IV* (1952–53). He also became involved with musique concrète; his remarkable *Der Gesang der Jünglinge* (1956) used a highly processed recording of a boy soprano mixed with electronic sounds. His extensions of serialism continued in such pieces as *Zeitmasse* (1956) and *Gruppen* (1957), and he became a leading avant-garde spokesman. His *Momente* (1964) influentially applied serialism to groups of sounds rather than single pitches, and he began incorporating aleatory as well. From the late 1960s he conceived ever grander schemes, some incorporating literature, dance, and ritual, as in the *Licht* series (from 1978).

Stockholm City (metro. area pop., 1997 est.: 1,744,000), capital of Sweden. Built on numerous islands and peninsulas connected by old bridges and modern overpasses, it is regarded as one of the most beautiful capitals in the world. According to tradition, Swedish ruler Birger Jarl founded Stockholm c. 1250. In the Middle Ages it became Sweden's chief trade port, and in 1436 the capital. After years of conflict between the Swedes and Danes, GUSTAV I VASA liberated it from Danish rule in 1523. It developed rapidly in the mid-17th century as Sweden became a great power, and was Sweden's cultural center by the 18th century. It was extensively redeveloped in the 19th century. The second-largest port in Sweden, it is the country's leading cultural, commercial, financial, and educational center.

stocking frame KNITTING MACHINE invented in 1589 that produced a stocking stitch. Knitted fabrics are constructed by the interlocking of a series of loops made from one or more YARNS, with each row of loops caught into the previous row; the stocking frame allowed production of a complete row of loops at one time. The modern knitting industry, with its highly sophisticated machinery, has grown from this simple device.

Stockport City (pop., 1995 est.: 201,000), northwestern England, part of the metropolitan area of GREATER MANCHESTER. First chartered in 1220, the original settlement was built in a gorge where the Rivers Tame and Goyt meet to form the MERSEY RIVER; the modern town has spread over higher ground. Cotton spinning was important in the 19th century, and in the 20th century, diversification brought electronics and heavy engineering industries.

Stockton City (pop., 1996 est.: 233,000), central California, on the SAN JOAQUIN RIVER. Connected to SAN FRANCISCO BAY by the river's 78-mi (126-km) deepwater channel, it is one of the state's two inland ports. It was founded in 1847 and grew rapidly as a miners' supply point during the 1849 GOLD RUSH. With the introduction of irrigation and the arrival of the railroad, it grew as a market for farm produce and wines. The completion of the channel in 1933 made it a major port as well as a supply depot for U.S. Pacific military operations.

Stockton, Robert F(ield) (1795–1866) U.S. naval officer. Born in Princeton, N.J., he joined the navy and rose to the rank of commander (1838). When the Mexican War broke out, he took command of U.S. land and naval forces in present-day California and proceeded to capture Los Angeles, a Mexican stronghold, on August 13, 1846. Four days later, he set up a civil government and formally annexed California to the U.S., naming himself governor. He and Col. STEPHEN KEARNY's army troops defeated an uprising by native Mexicans and ceded the entire province to the U.S. In 1850 he resigned from the navy and was elected to the U.S. Senate. Stockton, Cal., is named in his honor.

stoichiometry \ˌstȯi-kē-ˈä-mə-trē\ Determination of the proportions (by weight or number of molecules) in which ELEMENTS or COMPOUNDS react with one another. The rules for determining stoichiometric relationships are based on the laws of conservation of MASS and ENERGY and the law of combining weights or volumes. The tools used are CHEMICAL FORMULAS, CHEMICAL EQUATIONS, ATOMIC WEIGHTS, and MOLECULAR or FORMULA weights. See also MOLECULE.

Stoicism \ˈstō-ə-ˌsi-zəm\ School of philosophy in Greco-Roman antiquity. Inspired by the teaching of SOCRATES and DIOGENES OF SINOPE, Stoicism was founded at Athens by ZENO OF CITIUM c. 300 BC and was influential throughout the Greco-Roman world until at least AD 200. It stressed duty and held that, through reason, mankind can come to regard the universe as governed by fate and, despite appearances, as fundamentally rational, and that, in regulating one's life, one can emulate the grandeur of the calm and order of the universe by learning to accept events with a stern and tranquil mind and to achieve a lofty moral worth. Its teachings have been transmitted to later generations largely through the surviving books of CICERO and the Roman Stoics SENECA, EPICTETUS, and MARCUS AURELIUS.

Stoker, Bram *orig.* **Abraham** (1847–1912) Irish writer. Though bedridden until he was 7, Stoker later became an outstanding athlete. He was in the civil service for 10 years and the manager of HENRY IRVING for 27 years, writing letters for his employer and accompanying him on tours. During this period he began writing fiction; his masterpiece was the immensely successful gothic novel *Dracula* (1897). Derived from vampire legends, the tale became the basis for a whole genre of literature and film. None of his other works, including *The Lair of the White Worm* (1911), approached its popularity or quality.

Stokes, William (1804–1878) Irish physician. He received his MD from the University of Edinburgh and returned to Dublin, where he continued ROBERT GRAVES's educational reforms, encouraging students to work, under faculty supervision, in hospital wards and to acquire a general as well as a medical education. He succeeded his father as Regius professor of medicine at Dublin University. His publications included *A Treatise on the Diagnosis and Treatment of Diseases of the Chest* (1837), *The Diseases of the Heart and Aorta* (1854), and one of the first English works on the stethoscope. He was considered one of the greatest European physicians of his time.

Stokowski, Leopold (Anthony) *orig.* **Antoni Stanislaw Boleslawowich** (1882–1977) British-U.S. conductor and organist. Despite his exotic accent, he was born in England and studied at the Royal College of Music and Oxford University. After holding organist positions and conducting a handful of concerts, he became conductor of the Cincinnati Symphony (1909–12), with great success. From there he moved to the Philadelphia Orchestra, and in the years 1912–38 made it a world-class ensemble, creating the lush "Philadelphia sound." He programmed much contemporary music, and he grasped very early the importance of recording. He made himself a star, appearing in WALT DISNEY's *Fantasia* (1940) and other films, and used his fame to help foster fledgling music organizations, including the American Symphony Orchestra, which he formed in 1962. His strong advocacy of new music did much to end the provinciality of American musical taste.

Stoller, Mike See Jerry LEIBER

stolon \ˈstō-lən\ *or* **runner** Slender stem that grows horizontally along the ground, giving rise to roots and aerial (vertical) branches at specialized points called nodes. Many annual and perennial GRASSES have creeping stolons (e.g., BENT GRASS).

Stolypin \stȯ-ˈlē-pyin\, **Pyotr (Arkadyevich)** (1862–1911) Russian politician. As governor of two Russian provinces (1902–3), he improved the welfare of the peasants while also subduing their rebellions. He gained the favor of Czar NICHOLAS II and was appointed minister of the interior and prime minister in 1906. He initiated agrarian reforms that gave the peasants greater freedom to choose representatives to the ZEMSTVO councils and to acquire land, which he believed would create a loyal and conservative class of farmers. His repressive measures against rebels and terrorists earned him the enmity of liberals. He dissolved the DUMA when it opposed his reforms, but later won support from moderates. He was assassinated by a revolutionary in 1911.

stoma *or* **stomate** Any of the microscopic openings or pores in the epidermis of leaves and young stems. They are generally more numerous on the undersides of leaves. They provide for the exchange of gases between the outside air and the interconnecting air canals within the leaf. A stoma opens and closes in response to TURGOR pressure within its two surrounding guard cells. Because the inner wall of each of these sausage- or bean-shaped cells is thicker than the outer wall, when they fill with water and become turgid they balloon outward, enlarging the stoma. A drop in carbon-dioxide levels to lower than normal also causes the guard cells to become turgid. Guard cells control excessive water loss from the plant, closing on hot, dry, or windy days and opening when conditions are more favorable.

stomach Digestive sac in the left upper ABDOMINAL CAVITY, which expands or contracts with the amount of food in it. It has four regions: the cardia leads down from the ESOPHAGUS; the fundus curves above it; the body is the largest part; and the antrum narrows to join the DUODENUM at the pyloric valve. Iron and very fat-soluble substances (e.g., alcohol, some drugs) are absorbed in the stomach. PERISTALSIS mixes food with ENZYMES and HYDROCHLORIC ACID from glands in its lining and moves the resulting CHYME toward the SMALL INTESTINE. The vagus nerve and sympathetic nervous system control the stomach's secretions and movements. Emotional stress affects its function. Common disorders include GASTRITIS, PEPTIC ULCER, hiatal HERNIA, and cancer. See also DIGESTION, GASTRECTOMY.

stomach cancer Malignant TUMOR of the STOMACH. The main risk factors include a diet high in salted, smoked, or pickled foods, *Helicobacter pylori* infection, tobacco and alcohol use, age (over age 60), and a family history of stomach cancer. Males develop stomach cancer at approximately twice the rate of females. Symptoms may be abdominal pain or swelling, unexplained weight loss, vomiting, and poor digestion. Surgery is the only method for treating stomach cancer, although radiation therapy or chemotherapy may be used in conjunction with surgery or to relieve symptoms.

stone, building Rock cut into blocks and slabs or broken into pieces. It comes as hard as granite and as soft as limestone or sandstone. Where available, stone has generally been the preferred material for monumental structures. Its advantages are durability, adaptability to sculpting, and the fact that it can be used in its natural state. But it is difficult to quarry, transport, and cut, and its weakness in tension limits its use. The simplest stonework is rubble, roughly broken stones bound in mortar. Ashlar work consists of regularly cut blocks with squared edges. Building stone is quarried by sawing if it is soft, and split apart with wedges or by blasting if hard. Many devices are used to shape and dress stone, from handheld tools to circular saws, surfacing machines, and lathes. Some stones are strong enough to act as monolithic (one-piece) supports and beams; and in some styles (e.g., ancient Egyptian temples) stone slabs are employed even for roofing, supported by many closely spaced columns. Before the ARCH, builders were handicapped by the tendency of stone to break under its own weight. But stone in compression has great strength, and the Romans built huge stone bridges and aqueducts. Though stone has generally been abandoned for structural use in the 20th century, it is widely used as a thin, nonbearing surface cladding. See also MASONRY.

Stone, Edward Durell (1902–1978) U.S. architect. Born in Fayetteville, Ark., he earned architecture degrees and traveled in Europe before joining the New York firm that designed Radio City Music Hall. In 1936 he organized his own architectural firm. A leading exponent of the INTERNATIONAL STYLE, he designed El Panamá Hotel in Panama City (1946), the U.S. embassy in New Delhi (1954), the U.S. pavilion at the Brussels World's Fair (1958), the KENNEDY CENTER FOR THE PERFORMING ARTS in Washington, D.C. (1964), and the Amoco Building in Chicago (1969). He also taught at NYU (1927–42) and Yale University (1946–52).

Stone, Harlan Fiske (1872–1946) U.S. jurist. Born in Chesterfield, N.H., he studied at Columbia Law School and later practiced law while serving as dean of the school (1910–23). Pres. CALVIN COOLIDGE appointed him U.S. attorney general in 1924; during his tenure he reorganized the FEDERAL BUREAU OF INVESTIGATION after its reputation had been tarnished by the TEAPOT DOME and other scandals. In 1925 Coolidge appointed him to the U.S. Supreme Court; in 1941 Pres. FRANKLIN ROOSEVELT promoted him to chief justice, a position he retained until his death. He wrote more than 600 opinions, many on important constitutional questions, and frequently sided with LOUIS BRANDEIS and OLIVER WENDELL, JR. HOLMES

Harlan Fiske Stone, 1929.
BY COURTESY OF THE LIBRARY OF CONGRESS, WASHINGTON, D.C.

Stone, I(sidor) F(einstein) *orig.* **Isidor Feinstein** (1907–1989) U.S. journalist. He worked on newspapers in his native Philadelphia and in New York and wrote for the leftist newspaper *PM* before starting his own investigative newsletter. From the outset *I. F. Stone's Weekly* (1953–67; *I. F. Stone's Bi-Weekly*, 1967–71) had an influence far greater than the size of its readership, which included some of the nation's most prominent politicians, academicians, and journalists. The sole author, Stone created a unique blend of wit, erudition, and pointed political commentary, and became known for his espousal of unpopular causes long before they were taken up by the liberal establishment.

Stone, Lucy (1818–1893) U.S. pioneer in the WOMEN'S SUFFRAGE MOVEMENT. Born in West Brookfield, Mass., she became a lecturer for the Massachusetts Anti-Slavery Society. She soon began speaking for women's rights and helped organize women's-rights conventions in the 1850s. She retained her own name after marriage to Henry Blackwell (1825–1909), as a protest against the unequal laws applicable to married women; other women who later chose to do the same called themselves "Lucy Stoners." In 1869 she and Blackwell helped establish the American Woman Suffrage Association and founded the influential suffrage magazine *Woman's Journal*, which they edited until their deaths. They were assisted by their daughter Alice Stone Blackwell (1857–1950), who served as chief editor 1893–1917.

Stone, Oliver (born 1946) U.S. film director. Born in New York City, he attended Yale University and served in Vietnam before studying filmmaking at NYU. He made his directorial debut with *Seizure* (1974) and wrote screenplays for several films marked by their rapid pace and violence, including *Midnight Express* (1978). He wrote and directed *Platoon* (1986, Academy Award), drawing on his Vietnam experience; it was followed by such movies as *Wall Street* (1987), *Born on the Fourth of July* (1989, Academy Award), *JFK* (1991), and *Natural Born Killers* (1994), some of them noted for their anti-establishment and even paranoiac interpretations.

Stone, Robert (Anthony) (born 1937) U.S. novelist. Born in New York City, he served in the U.S. Navy before attending New York and Stanford universities. *Dog Soldiers* (1974, National Book Award; film, *Who'll Stop the Rain?*, 1978), his second novel, brought home the corruption of the Vietnam War. His later works include the novels *A Flag for Sunrise* (1981), *Outerbridge Reach* (1992), and *Damascus Gate* (1998) and the short-story collection *Bear and His Daughter* (1997).

Stone Age First known period of prehistoric human culture, characterized by the use of stone tools. The term is little used by specialists today: see PALEOLITHIC PERIOD, MESOLITHIC PERIOD, NEOLITHIC PERIOD, STONE-TOOL INDUSTRY. See also BRONZE AGE, IRON AGE.

Stone of Scone See Stone of SCONE

stone-tool industry Any of several assemblages of artifacts displaying humankind's earliest technology. These stone tools have survived in great quantities and now serve as the major means of determining HOMINID activities. Archaeologists have classified distinct stone-tool industries on the basis of style and use, and named them after the site of their original identification. The major industries include (in chronological order) the OLDOWAN, ACHEULIAN, MOUSTERIAN, AURIGNACIAN, SOLUTREAN, and MAGDALENIAN.

stonefish See ROCKFISH

stonefly Any of some 1,550 INSECT species (order Plecoptera) with adults, about 0.25–2.5 in. (6–60 mm) long, that are generally gray, black, or brown. They have long antennae; weak, chewing mouthparts; and two pairs of membranous wings that, at rest, fold like a fan. The hind wings are generally broader but shorter than the forewings. Despite their well-developed wings, stoneflies are poor fliers. The female drops a mass of up to 6,000 eggs into a stream. Nymphs resemble adults but are wingless and may have external gills; they feed on plants, decaying organic matter, and insects. The nymphal stage lasts one to four years; adults live several weeks.

Stonefly (Plecoptera).
WILLIAM E. FERGUSON

Stonehenge Monumental circular arrangement of standing stones built in prehistoric times and located near Salisbury, Wiltshire, England. The stones are believed to have been put in place in three main phases c. 3100–c. 1550 BC. The reasons for the building of Stonehenge are unknown, but it is believed to have been a place of worship and ritual. Many theories have been advanced as to its specific purpose (e.g., for the prediction of ECLIPSES), but none have been proven. Stones erected during the second phase of construction (c. 2100 BC) were aligned with the sunrise at the summer SOLSTICE, suggesting some ritual connection with that event.

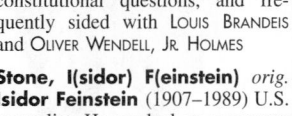

S T U V

Stonewall rebellion (June 28, 1969) Action by homosexuals in New York City. In response to the second raid in a week by police on the Stonewall Inn, a popular homosexual bar in Greenwich Village, about 1,000 homosexuals and others taunted police and threw debris; police responded with violence. Similar riots occurred on succeeding nights and were followed by protest rallies. The event marked the awakening of homosexual rights organizations throughout the U.S.; it is commemorated annually in Gay (later Gay and Lesbian) Pride Week.

stoneware POTTERY fired at a high temperature (about 2,200°F, or 1,200°C) until vitrified (made glass-like and impervious to liquid). Because stoneware is nonporous, glaze is applied only for decoration. Stoneware originated in China c. 1400 BC and was exported to Europe in the 17th century. This red to dark-brown stoneware was copied in Germany, England, and the Netherlands. See also BONE CHINA, PORCELAIN.

Salt-glazed stoneware *Bartmannkrug* with applied relief decoration, Cologne, c. 1540; in the Victoria and Albert Museum, London.

BY COURTESY OF THE VICTORIA AND ALBERT MUSEUM, LONDON; PHOTOGRAPH, WILFRID WALTER—EB INC.

Stono rebellion (1739) Largest slave uprising in early America. On the morning of September 9, near the Stono River 20 mi (30 km) from Charleston, S.C., slaves gathered, raided a firearms shop, and headed south, killing more than 20 whites as they went. Other slaves joined the rebellion until the group was about 60 strong. Whites set out in armed pursuit, and by dusk half the slaves were dead and half had escaped; most were eventually captured and executed. The slaves may have hoped to reach St. Augustine, Fla., where the Spanish were offering freedom and land to any fugitive. White colonists quickly passed a Negro Act that limited slave privileges even more seriously.

Stooges, Three Comedy team. It was originally formed as a vaudeville team in 1923 by brothers Moe and Shemp Howard (1897–1975, 1900–1955), who performed with "Ted Healy and His Stooges." In 1928 the brothers added Larry Fine (1911–1974) to the act, which appeared in Broadway revues. After Shemp left the act (1930), he was replaced by his brother Curly (1906–1952). After appearing in several feature films, in 1934 they began a series of comedy shorts that numbered over 200 before ending in 1958, consisting largely of violent slapstick, including hitting each other over the head with mallets and poking each other's eyes.

stools See FECES

Stoppard, Tom *orig.* **Tomas Straussler** (born 1937) British (Czech-born) playwright. After living in East Asia with his family in World War II, he moved to England and adopted his stepfather's name. His first play, *A Walk on the Water,* was televised in 1963, and he won fame with the absurdist *Rosencrantz and Guildenstern Are Dead* (1967). His later plays, marked by verbal brilliance, ingenious plotting, and a playful interest in pivotal historical moments, include *Jumpers* (1972), *Travesties* (1974), *Every Good Boy Deserves Favour* (1977; with music by A. PREVIN), *Undiscovered Country* (1980), *The Real Thing* (1982), and *Arcadia* (1993). He has also written radio plays, and screenplays for such films as *Empire of the Sun* (1987) and *Shakespeare in Love* (1998, Academy Award).

stored-program concept Storage of instructions in computer MEMORY to enable it to perform a variety of tasks in sequence or intermittently. The idea was introduced in the late 1940s by JOHN VON NEUMANN, who proposed that a program be electronically stored in binary-number format in a memory device so that instructions could be modified by the computer as determined by intermediate computational results. Other engineers, notably JOHN W. MAUCHLY and J. PRESPER ECKERT, contributed to this idea, which enabled DIGITAL COMPUTERS to become much more flexible and powerful. The first digital computer designed with internal programming capacity was EDVAC (1949).

stork Any of 17 species (family Ciconiidae) of voiceless, long-necked, mainly Old World birds. Storks are 2–5 ft (60–150 cm) tall, often with a totally or partially naked, brightly colored head and upper neck. They fly by alternately flapping and soaring, with neck outstretched and legs trailing. Most species are diurnal, feeding on small animals in shallow water and fields; some eat carrion. Usually found in flocks, storks pair off during the breeding season, and both parents incubate the eggs. Typical storks have a straight or nearly straight bill; the four species of wood stork have a curved bill. The only U.S. stork, the wood ibis *(Mycteria americana),* is white, with black wings and tail and a curved bill. See also IBIS, MARABOU.

storm petrel Any of about 20 species (family Hydrobatidae) of PETRELS that vary from 5 to 10 in. (13–25 cm) long. All are dark gray or brown, sometimes lighter below, often with a white rump. The relatively short wings are rounded at the tips. The toes are webbed, except for the small hind toe; the tail is square, forked, or wedge-shaped. Most species breeding in southern oceans "walk" over the water with wings spread, picking up minute marine organisms. Most northern species swoop over the water like tiny terns, occasionally alighting on the surface.

Storm Troopers See SA

Stornoway Seaport (pop., 1981: 14,000), Outer HEBRIDES ISLANDS, northern Scotland. Located on Lewis and Harris island, it grew from the 18th century as a fishing town; the chief industry now is the manufacture of Harris tweed. It is the headquarters of the Western Isles administrative region.

Story, Joseph (1779–1845) U.S. jurist. Born in Marblehead, Mass., he practiced law in Salem (1801–11) and served in the state legislature and U.S. Congress (1805–11). In 1811, though he was only 32 and lacked any judicial experience, he was appointed to the U.S. Supreme Court by Pres. JAMES MADISON. There he joined JOHN MARSHALL in construing the U.S. Constitution in favor of expanding federal power. His opinion in *Martin vs. Hunter's Lessee* (1816) established the Court's appellate authority over the highest state courts. While on the Court he taught at Harvard University (1829–45) and wrote an influential series of commentaries, including *Commentaries on the Constitution of the United States* (1833), *The Conflict of Laws* (1834), and *On Equity Jurisprudence* (1836). He and JAMES KENT are considered the founders of U.S. equity jurisprudence.

Stoss \'shtōs\, **Veit** (1445/50–1533) German sculptor and wood carver. Born in Germany, he worked mainly in Poland from 1477 to 1496; among his principal works is the majestic high altar in the Church of the Virgin Mary in Kraków (1477–89). After his return to Germany, he settled in Nuremberg and produced important wood and stone sculptures in churches there and in Bamberg. His nervous, angular forms, realistic detail, and virtuoso wood carving synthesized the sculptural styles of Flemish and Danubian art, and he exercised great influence on German late-Gothic sculpture.

"The Archangel Raphael," wood sculpture by Veit Stoss, 1516–18; in the German National Museum, Nürnberg.

BY COURTESY OF THE GERMANISCHES NATIONALMUSEUM, NURNBERG

Stour River \'stau̇r, 'stu̇r\ River, eastern England. It rises in eastern CAMBRIDGESHIRE, and flows eastward through East Anglia, forming most of the boundary between SUFFOLK and ESSEX, through country made famous by the paintings of JOHN CONSTABLE. After a course of 47 mi (76 km), it enters the North Sea at Harwich.

Stout, Rex (Todhunter) (1886–1975) U.S. writer. Born in Noblesville, Ind., he worked odd jobs until 1912, when he began to write. From 1927 he earned his living exclusively by writing. He is remembered for 46 genteel mystery novels and nov-

S T U V

elettes, beginning with *Fer-de-Lance* (1934), that revolve around Nero Wolfe, a brilliant, obese aesthete who solves crimes without leaving his New York City apartment. Stout endowed his detective with his own passions for haute cuisine and the growing of orchids.

Stowe \'stō\, **Harriet Beecher** *orig.* **Harriet Elizabeth Beecher** (1811–1896) U.S. writer and philanthropist. Born in Litchfield, Conn., Stowe was the daughter of the famous Congregationalist minister Lyman Beecher (1775–1863) and the sister of HENRY WARD BEECHER and CATHARINE ESTHER BEECHER. She taught school in Hartford and in Cincinnati, where she came into contact with fugitive slaves and learned about life in the South, and later settled in Maine with her husband, a professor of theology. Her antislavery novel *Uncle Tom's Cabin* (1852) had so great an impact that it has often been cited (by ABRAHAM LINCOLN, among others) among the causes of the American Civil War. Her other works include the novels *Dred* (1856), also against slavery, and *The Minister's Wooing* (1859).

Strabane \strə-'ban\ District (pop., 1995 est.: 36,000), western Northern Ireland. It is composed of river valleys, rolling lowlands, and moorlands of the Sperrin Mountains. Originally inhabited by the O'Neill clan of Ulster, the district was settled in the 17th century by Scots Protestants. Livestock grazing in the lowlands, salmon fishing in the many rivers, and textile manufacturing contribute to the economy. The market town of Strabane (pop., 1991: 12,000), located on the River Mourne, is its administrative seat.

strabismus \strə-'biz-məs\ *or* **squint** *or* **heterotropia** \ˌhet-ə-rə-'trō-pē-ə\ Failure of the EYES to align properly to focus on an object. The affected eye may deviate in any direction, including inward (cross-eye) or outward (walleye). Problems with PHOTORECEPTION or the nerves that relay images to the brain cause a constant degree of deviation (comitant); defects in the nerves that control the muscles that move the eyes cause deviation that varies with the direction of gaze (noncomitant). Both types impede development of a child's ability to focus the eyes and merge images from the two RETINAS into one (fusional reflex). The brain suppresses the image from the deviant eye, which may become functionally blind. Treatment may involve exercises to strengthen the weak eye or surgery or both.

Strabo \'strā-bō\ (64/63 BC–after AD 23?) Greek geographer and historian. Born in Asia Minor to a well-connected family, he studied under Aristodemus before moving to Rome (44 BC) to study with the Aristotelian school, then became a Stoic. Of his 47-volume *Historical Sketches*, covering the years 145–31 BC (published c. 20 BC), only a few quotations remain. His *Geographical Sketches* (after c. AD 14) is the only extant work on the range of peoples and countries known to Greeks and Romans during the reign of Caesar AUGUSTUS.

Strachey \'strā-chē\, **(Evelyn) John (St. Loe)** (1901–1963) British politician and writer. He was elected to Parliament in 1929 as a member of the Labour Party. A communist during the 1930s, he wrote several books on Marxism and socialism. After World War II he returned to Parliament, and he served in the Labour government as minister of food (1946–50) and war minister (1950–51). His later books included *Contemporary Capitalism* (1956), *The End of Empire* (1959), and *On the Prevention of War* (1962).

Strachey \'strā-chē\, **(Giles) Lytton** (1880–1932) English biographer and critic. After studying at Cambridge, he became a leader in the BLOOMSBURY GROUP. Though a self-identified homosexual, he was engaged for a time to VIRGINIA WOOLF. Adopting an irreverent attitude to the past, he opened a new era of biographical writing with his *Eminent Victorians* (1918), consisting of four sketches of Victorian idols whom he portrayed as multifaceted, flawed human beings. Fascinated by personality and motive, he treated his subjects idiosyncratically and somewhat cynically. He also published *Queen Victoria* (1921), *Elizabeth and Essex* (1928), *Portraits in Miniature* (1931), and critical writings, especially on French literature.

Stradivari \ˌsträ-dē-'vär-ē\, **Antonio** (1644–1737) Italian musical-instrument maker. An apprentice of NICOLA AMATI (from c. 1666), he established his own business in Cremona, eventually working with his sons Francesco (1671–1743) and Omobono (1679–1742). Though he made other instruments (including harps, lutes, mandolins, and guitars), few survive, and after 1680, he concentrated on violins. Moving away from the Amati style, he developed (c. 1690) the "long Strad." His later cellos were smaller, to abet the increased virtuosity of players, and have served as the model for most modern instruments. The period 1700–20 is considered the peak of his productivity and quality.

Strafford, Earl of See Thomas WENTWORTH

strain In the physical sciences and engineering, a number that describes the relative deformation of elastic, plastic, and fluid materials under applied forces. It arises throughout the material as the particles of the material are displaced from their usual position. Normal strain is caused by forces perpendicular to planes or cross sections of the material, such as in a volume that is under pressure on all sides. Shear strain is caused by forces that are parallel to, and lie in, planes or cross sections, such as in a short metal tube that is twisted about its longitudinal axis. See also DEFORMATION AND FLOW.

strain gauge Device for measuring the changes in distances between points in solid bodies that occur when the body is deformed. Strain gauges are used either to obtain information from which STRESSES in bodies can be calculated or to act as indicating elements on devices for measuring such quantities as FORCE, PRESSURE, and ACCELERATION.

Straits Question Recurrent controversy in the 19th–20th century over the passage of warships through the Bosporus and Dardanelles straits between the Black Sea and the Aegean and Mediterranean seas. Both straits were in Turkish territory, but when Russia gained control of the northern shore of the Black Sea, its ships were given free passage. Russia sought to control the passage of non-Turkish ships with the Treaty of UNKIAR-SKELESSI (1833), but it was reversed by the London Straits Convention (1841). The Treaty of LAUSANNE (1923) allowed free passage to all warships, until it was revised by the MONTREUX CONVENTION (1936) to reestablish Turkey's right to restrict access by navies of non–Black Sea states.

Straits Settlements Former British crown colony, on the Strait of MALACCA. It comprised three trade centers, PENANG, SINGAPORE, and Malacca, which were established or taken over by the British EAST INDIA CO. United in 1826 under Indian control, they were made a crown colony by the British in 1867. COCOS ISLANDS, Christmas Island, and Labuan were added in the early 20th century. Occupied by the Japanese during World War II, the colony was broken up in 1946 when Singapore became a separate colony. The remaining parts were ultimately ceded to Australia and Malaysia.

Strand, Mark (born 1934) U.S. (Canadian-born) poet and writer of short fiction. Educated in the U.S., he has taught at several American universities. His poetry, influenced by Latin-American surrealism and European writers such as FRANZ KAFKA, is known for its symbolic imagery and its minimalist sensibility. His volumes include the collections *Sleeping with One Eye Open* (1964), *The Story of Our Lives* (1973), and *Blizzard of One* (1998); *Dark Harbor* (1993), a book-length poem; and *Mr. and Mrs. Baby and Other Stories* (1985). He was named U.S. poet laureate in 1990.

Strand, Paul (1890–1976) U.S. photographer. Born in New York City, he studied photography with LEWIS WICKES HINE. At Hine's urging, he frequented ALFRED STIEGLITZ's "291" gallery; the avant-garde paintings by PABLO PICASSO, PAUL CEZANNE, and GEORGES BRAQUE that he saw there led him to emphasize abstract form and pattern in his photographs, such as *Wall Street* (1915). He rejected soft-focus pictorialism in favor of the minute detail and rich tonal range afforded by the use of large-format cameras. Much of his later work was devoted to North American and European scenes and landscapes. He collaborated on documentary films with Charles Sheeler and Pare Lorentz.

White Fence, photograph by Paul Strand, 1916.

BY COURTESY OF PAUL STRAND

Strasberg, Lee *orig.* **Israel Strassberg** (1901–1982) U.S. (Russian-born) theater director, teacher, and chief exponent of the STANISLAVSKY METHOD in the U.S. He emigrated to New York from Galicia (now Ukraine) with his family at age 7. After acting lessons with teachers who had studied under KONSTANTIN STANISLAVSKY, he became an actor and stage manager with the Theatre Guild. In 1931 he cofounded the GROUP THEATRE, where he directed such successful plays as *Men in White* (1933). After working in Hollywood (1941–48), he returned to New York to become artistic director of the ACTORS STUDIO, where he developed his form of Method acting and trained such students as MARLON BRANDO, MARILYN MONROE, DUSTIN HOFFMAN, GERALDINE PAGE, and JULIE HARRIS.

Strasbourg \'sträs-,bu̇rg\ *German* **Strassburg** \'shträs-,bu̇rk\ City (metro. area pop., 1999: 427,245), eastern France, on the Franco-German border. Originally a Celtic village, it became a garrison under the Romans. The FRANKS captured it in the 5th century, and in 842 the Oath of Strasbourg, uniting the West and East Franks, was concluded there. It became a free city within the HOLY ROMAN EMPIRE in 1262. It was seized by the French in 1681 and captured by Germany in the FRANCO-PRUSSIAN WAR. It reverted to France after World War I, but was occupied by Germany again during World War II, when it suffered considerable damage. A major river port and industrial center, it is the seat of the Council of EUROPE and an international communications center. Famous buildings include the restored medieval cathedral with its 14th-century astronomical clock. The EUROPEAN UNION's parliament has met there since 1979.

Strasser \'shträ-sər\, **Gregor and Otto** (1892–1934, 1897–1974) German politicians. The brothers joined the Nazi Party in the early 1920s. Gregor became the party's leader in the north and built a mass movement with the help of Otto and the young JOSEPH GOEBBELS, appealing to the lower middle classes and workers by advocating a socialism couched in nationalist and racist terminology. Otto resigned in 1930, disillusioned by ADOLF HITLER's nonsocialist goals. Gregor became head of the Nazi political organization, second only to Hitler in power, but came to share his brother's disillusionment and resigned in 1932. Gregor was murdered on Hitler's orders in 1934; Otto escaped into exile in Canada, then returned to Germany in 1955.

Strassmann, Fritz (1902–1980) German physical chemist. He helped develop the rubidium-strontium method of dating widely used in geochronology. Beginning in 1934 he joined OTTO HAHN and LISE MEITNER in their investigations of the radioactive products formed when uranium is bombarded by neutrons. In 1938 they discovered lighter elements produced from the neutron bombardment, which were the result of the splitting of the uranium atom into two lighter atoms (NUCLEAR FISSION). In 1946 he joined the faculty at the University of Mainz, where he established the Institute of Inorganic Chemistry (later the Institute of Nuclear Chemistry), and he directed the chemistry department at the Max Planck Institute for Chemistry 1945–53.

Strategic Arms Limitation Talks See SALT

Strategic Arms Reduction Talks See START

Strategic Defense Initiative (SDI) *or* **Star Wars** Proposed U.S. strategic defense system against nuclear attacks. Announced by Pres. RONALD REAGAN in 1983, SDI was intended to defend the U.S. from a full-fledged Soviet attack by intercepting ICBMs in flight. The interception was to be effected by technology then not yet developed, including space- and earth-based laser stations and air- and ground-based missiles. The space component of SDI led to its being derisively dubbed "Star Wars" after the popular film. Though Congress granted initial funding in the mid-1980s, the program aroused heated debate; widely criticized as unworkable, it was also decried for accelerating the arms race and undermining arms-control agreements. Early development efforts were largely unsuccessful, and after the fall of the Soviet Union the project was scaled back to focus on protecting the U.S. from a small attack by a rogue nation or a single accidentally launched missile. In 1999 the U.S. again announced its intent to implement a new antimissile defense program. See also ANTIBALLISTIC MISSILE.

strategus \strə-'tē-gəs\ In ancient Greece, a general, often functioning as a magistrate with wide powers. CLEISTHENES introduced an annual board of 10 strategi in Athens to be commanders of the army; one or more, all equal, were responsible for each operation. In the 5th century BC they gained political influence, in part because they were elected and could be reelected, thus able to entrench themselves in office. In the HELLENISTIC AGE they were the supreme magistrates in most federations and leagues. In Egypt (3rd century BC–4th century AD) they were civil governors.

strategy In warfare, coordinated application of all the forces of a nation to achieve a goal. In contrast to TACTICS, strategy's components include a long-range view, the preparation of resources, and planning for the use of those resources before, during, and after an action. The term has expanded far beyond its original military meaning. As society and warfare have steadily grown more complex, military and nonmilitary factors have become more and more inseparable in the conduct of war and in programs designed to secure peace. In the 20th century, the term grand strategy, meaning the art of employing all the resources of a nation or coalition of nations to achieve the objects of war (and peace), steadily became more popular in the literature of warfare and statecraft.

Stratemeyer \'stra-tə-,mī-ər\, **Edward** (1862–1930) U.S. writer of popular juvenile fiction. He began writing stories in imitation of HORATIO ALGER and other adventure writers, and later edited several publications and began writing series of books. In 1906 he founded the Stratemeyer Literary Syndicate, which would publish the Rover Boys, Hardy Boys, Tom Swift, Bobbsey Twins, and Nancy Drew series, written by himself and a stable of hack writers under a variety of names. After his death his company was largely directed by his daughter, Harriet Stratemeyer Adams (1893?–1982), who also wrote many books in several series.

Stratford, Viscount See Stratford CANNING

Stratford Festival Canadian summer theatrical festival. The foremost classical REPERTORY THEATER in North America, it was founded by Tom Patterson in Stratford, Ontario, in 1953. It includes three permanent theaters: the 220° open-stage Festival Theatre, the Avon Theatre, and the Tom Patterson Theatre, which is reserved for experimental works. The festival features productions of WILLIAM SHAKESPEARE's plays (Stratford was chosen as its locale because the town's name matched that of Shakespeare's birthplace) but also performs other classic dramatic works.

Stratford-upon-Avon Town (pop., 1995 est.: 28,000), WARWICKSHIRE, central England, on the AVON RIVER. The first royal charter was granted in 1553. For centuries a country market town, it became a tourist center because of its association with WILLIAM SHAKESPEARE, who was born and died there; his grave is in the parish church of Holy Trinity. The Shakespeare Centre includes a library and art gallery (opened 1881) and a theater (opened 1932). Every year from March until October, Shakespeare's plays are performed in the Royal Shakespeare Theatre.

Strathclyde Medieval Celtic kingdom, Scotland. Located south of the CLYDE RIVER, it was established in the 6th century. Its capital was Dumbarton. The Picts and Vikings ravaged the kingdom in the 8th–9th century. It suffered several defeats by the English who took it over in the early 10th century. The Anglo-Saxon king Edmund I leased it in 945 to the Scots king Malcolm I. It became a province of Scotland in the 11th century after the death of its king, who helped MALCOLM II defeat the English at Carham.

stratification Layering that occurs in most SEDIMENTARY ROCKS and in IGNEOUS ROCKS that are formed at the earth's surface, such as from lava flows and volcanic deposits. The layers (strata) may range from thin sheets that cover many square miles to thick lenslike bodies that are only a few feet wide.

stratigraphy \strə-'ti-grə-fē\ Scientific discipline concerned with describing rock successions and interpreting them in terms of a general time scale. It provides a basis for historical geology, and its principles and methods are applied in such fields as petroleum geology and archaeology. Stratigraphic studies deal primarily with SEDIMENTARY ROCKS but may also encompass layered igneous rocks (e.g., those resulting from successive lava flows) or metamorphic rocks formed either from such extrusive igneous material or from sedimentary rocks.

Stratofortress See B-52

stratosphere Layer of the ATMOSPHERE that is located above the TROPOSPHERE. The stratosphere extends from a lower boundary of about 11 mi (17 km) altitude to an upper boundary (the stratopause) at about 30 mi (50 km). The OZONE LAYER is a part of the stratosphere.

Straus family \'strau̇s\ German-U.S. merchandising family that distinguished itself in public service and philanthropy. The family originated in Bavaria, and the patriarch, Lazarus Straus, emigrated to the U.S. in 1852, followed by his wife and three sons: Isidor (1845–1912), Nathan (1848–1931), and Oscar Solomon (1850–1926). They established a merchandising firm that allowed them to gain an interest in MACY AND CO., which led to complete ownership in 1896. Isidor established the department-store chain of Abraham & Straus, served briefly in the U.S. Congress, and engaged in philanthropic works; he and his wife perished aboard the TITANIC after giving Mrs. Straus's place in a lifeboat to their maid. Nathan was noted for his philanthropy; he distributed food and coal in New York and supplied pasteurized milk to children in 36 cities during the 1892 depression, built the first tuberculosis preventorium for children (1909), and provided food for New York's poor during the harsh winter of 1914–15. He devoted the last years of his life to public-health work in Palestine. Oscar was appointed Secretary of Commerce and Labor by THEODORE ROOSEVELT, becoming the first Jewish Cabinet member (1906–9); he also served as emissary to Ottoman Turkey and as an adviser to Pres. WOODROW WILSON, and was a strong advocate for the protection of Jewish minorities in Europe.

Strauss \'shtraủs\, **Franz Josef** (1915–1988) German politician. He helped found the Bavarian Christian Social Union (CSU) in 1945 and was elected to the Bundestag in 1949. He served as minister of defense (1956–62) and minister of finance (1966–69). Head of the CSU from 1961, he was the party's unsuccessful candidate for chancellor in 1980. As premier of Bavaria (1978–88), he pursued economic policies that made it one of Germany's most prosperous states.

Strauss \'shtraủs, *Engl* 'straủs\, **Johann (Baptist), Jr.** (1825–1899) Austrian composer. His father, Johann Strauss, Sr. (1804–1849), was a self-taught musician who established a musical dynasty in Vienna. A violinist, he played in a dance orchestra from 1819; when it split in two (1824), he took over the second group, for which he began to write waltzes, galops, polkas, and quadrilles, eventually publishing more than 250 works. As bandmaster of a local regiment, he also wrote marches, including the *Radetzky March*. After he left his family (1842), Johann Jr. soon surpassed his father's popularity and productivity, becoming known as the "Waltz King." By inducing his brothers, Josef (1827–1870) and Eduard (1835–1916), to take over his conducting duties, he gained more time to compose the symphonic waltzes for which he is best known, including *The Beautiful Blue Danube* (1867) and *Tales from the Vienna Woods* (1868). His operettas include the popular *Die Fledermaus* (1874) and *The Gypsy Baron* (1885). Eduard's son Johann (1866–1939), a conductor and composer in Berlin, was the last of the dynasty.

Strauss, Richard (Georg) (1864–1949) German composer and conductor. Son of a horn player, Richard began composing at 6. Before he was 20, he had had major premieres of two symphonies and a violin concerto, In 1885 the conductor H. VON BULOW made him his successor. A convert to Wagnerism, he began to write programmatic orchestral tone poems, including *Don Juan* (1889), *Death and Transfiguration* (1890), *Till Eulenspiegel's Merry Pranks* (1895), *Thus Spake Zarathustra* (1896), *Don Quixote* (1897), and *Ein Heldenleben* (1898). After 1900 he turned to opera. His third opera, *Salome* (1905), was a succès de scandale, and with *Elektra* (1908) he began a productive collaboration with the poet HUGO VON HOFMANNSTHAL, with whom he wrote his greatest operas, including *Der Rosenkavalier* (1910), *Ariadne auf Naxos* (1912), and *Die Frau ohne Schatten* (1918). He later wrote eight more operas. He remained in Austria through World War II, but was later cleared of wrongdoing in connection with the Nazi regime. After many years writing lesser works, he produced several remarkable late pieces, including *Metamorphosen* (1945) and the *Four Last Songs* (1948).

Richard Strauss, portrait by Max Liebermann, 1918; in the National-Galerie, Berlin.

Stravinsky, Igor (Fyodorovich) (1882–1971) Russian-French-U.S. composer. Son of an operatic bass, he decided to be a composer at 20 and studied privately with N. RIMSKY-KORSAKOV (1902–8). His *Fireworks* (1908) was heard by SERGEY DIAGHILEV, who commissioned him to write the *Firebird* ballet (1910), which made him Russia's leading young composer. The great ballet score *Petrushka* (1911) followed. His next ballet, *The Rite of Spring* (1913), viscerally exciting and brutalist in its effect, was a landmark in music history; its Paris premiere caused a virtual riot, and Stravinsky's international notoriety was assured. He turned to smaller forces for the ballet *Les noces* (1923), and adopted a radically different style of restrained neoclassicism—employing often ironic references to older music—with his Octet (1923), as many were turning away from the excesses of the late 19th century, associated with the causes of World War I. His major neoclassical works included *Oedipus rex* (1927), the ballet *Apollo* (1928), the *Symphony of Psalms* (1930), the *Symphony in C* (1940), and the *Symphony in Three Movements* (1945), and culminated in the opera *The Rake's Progress* (1951). After A. SCHOENBERG's death, from 1954 he employed serialism, of which he soon devised his own version. His later works include *Agon* (1957)—the last of his many ballets choreographed by GEORGE BALANCHINE—*Threni* (1958), *Movements* (1959), and *Requiem Canticles* (1966).

straw Stalks of GRASSES, particularly CEREAL grasses such as wheat, oats, rye, barley, and buckwheat. Used collectively, the term means stalks aggregated into bales or piles after the drying and threshing of grain. Since ancient times, humans have used straw as litter and fodder for cattle, as a covering for floors, for coarse bedding, and even as clothing. It can also be woven into baskets, hats, floor mats, and furniture coverings. Thatched roofs consist of straw laid down approximately 1 ft (30 cm) thick and secured by strong cords, with the fibers running in the direction to be taken by rainwater. Chemically pulped straw is used in the manufacture of coarse paper and strawboard, a cardboard for cheap paper boxes.

strawberry Fruit plant of eight main species of the genus *Fragaria* (ROSE family), the chief cultivated varieties of which are *F. virginiana* and *F. chiloensis*, native to the Americas. The low-growing, herbaceous plant has a fibrous root system and a crown from which basal leaves arise. The leaves are compound, with three leaflets, sawtooth-edged and hairy. Small clusters of white flowers grow on slender stalks. Botanically, the strawberry fruit is not a BERRY or a single fruit, but is instead a greatly enlarged stem end that contains many partially embedded true fruits (achenes), popularly called seeds. The plant propagates by STOLONS as it ages. Strawberries are very perishable and require cool, dry storage. They are eaten fresh or prepared for use in desserts or preserves. Rich in vitamin C, they also provide iron and other minerals.

Strayhorn, Billy *orig.* **William** (1915–1967) U.S. pianist, composer, and arranger, DUKE ELLINGTON's musical collaborator for nearly three decades. Born in Dayton, Ohio, Strayhorn approached Ellington with a composition in 1938, and was soon contributing arrangements and original works to the band. His "Take the 'A' Train," recorded in 1941, became the band's theme song. His work so complemented Ellington's that it is often impossible to distinguish their respective contributions. Strayhorn made expressive ballads his specialty and became noted for the structural and harmonic sophistication of pieces such as "Lush Life," "Something to Live For," "Passion Flower," and "Day Dream."

streak Color of a mineral in its powdered form, usually obtained by rubbing the mineral on a hard, white surface (e.g., a tile of unglazed porcelain) to yield a streak of fine powder. The streak's color is usually constant for a given mineral, even if the mineral varies in color as it occurs in the field or if the streak is different from the color of the unpowdered mineral. Streak is diagnostically useful because it may distinguish between mineral species that are otherwise similar in appearance.

stream of consciousness Narrative technique in nondramatic fiction intended to render the flow of myriad impressions—visual, auditory, tactile, associative, and subliminal—that impinge on an individual consciousness. To represent the mind at work, a writer may incorporate snatches of thought and grammatical constructions that do not seem coherent because they are based on the free association of ideas and images. The term was first used by WILLIAM JAMES in *The Principles of Psychology* (1890). In the 20th century, writers attempting to capture the total flow of their characters' consciousness commonly used the techniques of interior monologue, which represents a sequence of thought and feeling. Novels in which stream of consciousness plays an important role include JAMES JOYCE's *Ulysses* (1922), WILLIAM FAULKNER's *The Sound and the Fury* (1929), and VIRGINIA WOOLF's *The Waves* (1931).

streambed *or* **stream channel** Any long, narrow, sloping depression on land that had been shaped by flowing water. Streambeds can range in width from a few feet for a brook to several thousand feet for the largest rivers. The channel may or may not contain flowing water at any given time; some carry water only occasionally. Streambeds may be cut in bedrock or through sand, clay, silt, or other unconsolidated materials.

streaming Method of transmitting a media file in a continuous stream of data that can be processed by the receiving computer before the entire file has been completely sent. Streaming, which typically uses DATA COMPRESSION, is especially effective for downloading large multimedia files from the INTERNET; it permits, for example, a video clip to begin playing on a user's computer as soon as it begins to be downloaded from a Web site. Even with improved modems and connection speeds, downloading and playing large audio and video files without the use of streaming techniques still takes an inconveniently long time. To accept streaming data, the receiving computer needs to be running a player, a program that decompresses the incoming data and sends the resulting signals to the display and speakers. The audio and video files may be prerecorded, but streaming can also accommodate a live feed over the Internet.

streamline In FLUID MECHANICS, the path of imaginary particles suspended in the fluid and carried along with it. In steady flow, the fluid is in motion but the streamlines are fixed. Where streamlines crowd together, the fluid speed is relatively high; where they open out, the fluid is relatively still. See also LAMINAR FLOW, TURBULENT FLOW.

Streep, Meryl *orig.* **Mary Louise** (born 1949) U.S. film actress. Born in Summit, N.J., she studied at Vassar College and the Yale School of Drama before appearing on Broadway and in the television films *The Deadliest Season* (1977) and *The Holocaust* (1978, Emmy award). An unusually versatile and expressive actress, she won stardom in *The Deer Hunter* (1978), *Manhattan* (1979), and *Kramer vs. Kramer* (1979, Academy Award). Her later films include *Sophie's Choice* (1982, Academy Award), *Silkwood* (1983), *Out of Africa* (1985), *A Cry in the Dark* (1988), *The Bridges of Madison County* (1995), and *Dancing at Lughnasa* (1998).

streetcar *or* **trolley car** Passenger-carrying vehicle that runs on rails laid in city streets. Streetcars in the 1830s were pulled by horses. Electric motors later supplied the power, with electricity transmitted by a trolley from overhead electric lines. From the 1890s to the 1940s, streetcars were widely used in cities around the world; they were gradually replaced by the AUTOMOBILE, the BUS, and the SUBWAY, and by the 1950s few remained. A variant, the cable car, invented in 1873 for use on San Francisco's steep hills, is drawn by a continuous cable set in a slot between the tracks.

Streicher \'shtrī-k̲ər\, **Julius** (1885–1946) German Nazi demagogue and politician. He joined the Nazi Party in 1921 and became a friend of ADOLF HITLER. In 1923 he founded the anti-Semitic weekly *Der Stürmer,* which provided a focus for Hitler's racial policies. As one of the most virulent advocates of persecution of the Jews, Streicher initiated the campaign that led to passage of the NUREMBERG LAWS in 1935. He was appointed gauleiter (district leader) of Franconia, but his sadistic excesses alienated party officials and he was stripped of his posts in 1940, though he remained editor of *Der Stürmer* owing to Hitler's protection. In 1945 he was arrested by the Allies, tried at Nuremberg, and hanged as a war criminal.

Streisand, Barbra *orig.* **Barbara Joan** (born 1942) U.S. singer and actress. Born in Brooklyn, N.Y., she sang in nightclubs before appearing on Broadway in *I Can Get It for You Wholesale* (1962), and became a major star with *Funny Girl* (1964; film and Academy Award, 1968). Her richly beautiful voice made her one of the world's most popular singers in the 1970s and '80s. An exuberant comic and dramatic actress, she starred in such movies as *Hello, Dolly!* (1969), *What's Up Doc?* (1972), *The Way We Were* (1973), and *A Star Is Born* (1976), and later directed and starred in *Yentl* (1983) and *The Prince of Tides* (1991).

streltsy (Russian: "musketeers") Russian military corps. Established in the mid-16th century, the streltsy formed the bulk of the Russian army for about 100 years and provided the czar's bodyguard. A hereditary military caste by the mid-17th century, they numbered about 55,000 and performed police and security duties in Moscow and the garrisoned border towns. In 1682 the corps became involved in the succession struggle that led to the regency of SOPHIA. When she was displaced (1689), they were forcibly disbanded by PETER I; hundreds were executed or deported. The corps was gradually absorbed into the regular army.

strength of materials ENGINEERING discipline concerned with the ability of a material to resist mechanical FORCES when in use. A material's strength in a given application depends on many factors, including its resistance to deformation and cracking, and it often depends on the shape of the member being designed. See also FRACTURE, IMPACT TEST, MATERIALS SCIENCE, TENSILE STRENGTH, TESTING MACHINE.

streptococcus \ˌstrep-tə-'kä-kəs\ Any of the spheroidal BACTERIA that make up the genus *Streptococcus.* The cells characteristically group together in chains resembling a string of beads. Streptococci are gram-positive (see GRAM STAIN) and stationary and do not require oxygen. Species are classified into four groups, mainly on the basis of their ability to cause red blood cells to burst. Some species cause infections, including RHEUMATIC FEVER, SCARLET FEVER, strep throat, and TONSILLITIS. Others are used in commercial starters for the production of butter, cultured buttermilk, and certain cheeses. See also PNEUMOCOCCUS.

streptomyces \ˌstrep-tə-'mī-sēz\ Any of the threadlike BACTERIA that make up the genus *Streptomyces,* occurring in soil and water. These gram-positive (see GRAM STAIN), oxygen-requiring bacteria form a branching net called a mycelium that bears chains of SPORES at maturity. Many species are important in the decomposition of organic matter in soil, contributing in part to the earthy odor of soil and decaying leaves and to the fertility of soil. Certain species produce broad-spectrum ANTIBIOTICS such as TETRACYCLINE and STREPTOMYCIN. See also ACTINOMYCETE.

streptomycin \ˌstrep-tə-'mī-sen\ ANTIBIOTIC synthesized by the ACTINOMYCETE *Streptomyces griseus,* found in soil. It was among the first antibiotics discovered (1943, by SELMAN WAKSMAN), after PENICILLIN, gramicidin, and tyrocidine. The first antibiotic effective against TUBERCULOSIS, it interferes with the tubercle bacillus's ability to synthesize certain vital proteins. Many other bacteria are sensitive to streptomycin, but it is seldom used for diseases other than tuberculosis because many strains have developed DRUG RESISTANCE and it occasionally causes nerve DEAFNESS.

Stresa Front \'strā-zä\ (1935) Coalition of France, Britain, and Italy formed at Stresa, Italy, to oppose ADOLF HITLER's announced intention to rearm Germany, which violated terms of the Treaty of VERSAILLES. When Italy invaded Ethiopia, France and Britain tried to reconcile the action with the need to remain united against Germany, but the coalition soon dissolved.

Stresemann \'shtrā-zə-ˌmän\, **Gustav** (1878–1929) German chancellor and foreign minister of the WEIMAR REPUBLIC. Noted as an expert on municipal affairs and a writer on economics, he was elected to the Reichstag (1907) as a member of the National Liberal Party. In 1918 he founded the GERMAN PEOPLE'S PARTY and sought to form coalitions with other democratic parties. As chancellor (1923) and foreign minister (1923–29), he worked to restore Germany's international status, pursuing a conciliatory policy with the Allied Powers. He negotiated the Pact of LOCARNO, supported the reparations revisions in the DAWES and YOUNG plans, and secured Germany's admission to the League of Nations. He shared the 1926 Nobel Peace Prize with ARISTIDE BRIAND.

Stresemann.

BY COURTESY OF BILDARCHIV PREUSSISCHER KULTURBESITZ BPK, BERLIN

stress In PHONETICS, an emphasis given to a SYLLABLE of speech by making it louder than the rest of the word. This emphasis may have no meaning; for example, Czech words are regularly stressed on the first syllable. It may, however, distinguish the meanings of similarly spelled but differently pronounced words; for example, *permit* is stressed on the first syllable as a noun and on the second as a verb. It may also be applied to a word to express its importance in a sentence. See also INTONATION.

stress In the physical sciences and engineering, the force per unit area within materials that arises from externally applied forces, uneven heating, or permanent deformation. Normal stress refers to the stress caused by forces that are perpendicular to a cross-section area of the material. Shear stress arises from forces that are parallel to the plane of the cross section. Stress is expressed as the quotient of a force divided by an area.

stress In psychology, a state of bodily or mental tension resulting from factors that tend to alter an existent equilibrium. Stress is an unavoidable effect of living and is an especially complex phenomenon in modern technological society. It has been linked to CORONARY HEART DISEASE, PSYCHOSOMATIC DISORDERS, and various other mental and physical problems. Treatment usually consists of a combination of COUNSELING or PSYCHOTHERAPY and medication.

strike Collective refusal by employees to work under the conditions set by employers. Strikes may arise from disputes over wages and working conditions. They may also be conducted in sympathy with other striking workers, or for purely political goals. Many strikes are organized by LABOR UNIONS; strikes not authorized by the union (wildcat strikes) may be directed against union leadership as well as the employer. The right to strike is granted in principle to workers in nearly all industrialized countries, and its use has paralleled the rise of labor unions since the 19th century. Most strikes are intended to inflict a cost on employers for failure to meet specific demands. Among Japanese unions, strikes are not intended to halt production for long periods of time and are more akin to demonstrations. In Western Europe and elsewhere, workers have carried out GENERAL STRIKES aimed at winning changes in the political system rather than concessions from employers. See also BOYCOTT, LOCKOUT.

strike In geology, the direction of the line formed by the intersection of a fault, bed, or other planar feature and a horizontal plane. Strike indicates the orientation of planar structural features such as faults, beds, joints, and folds.

Strindberg \'strin-ˌber^{y}, *Engl* 'strind-ˌbərg\, **(Johan) August** (1849–1912) Swedish playwright and novelist. While working as a journalist, he wrote the historical drama *Mäster Olof* (1872); though rejected by the national theater and not produced until 1890, it is now considered the first modern Swedish drama. He won fame with his novel *The Red Room* (1879), which satirized the Stockholm art world. His unhappy life included three marriages and episodes of mental instability. In his most creative period he moved restlessly around Europe for six years, writing his three major plays, *The Father* (1887), *Miss Julie* (1888), and *The Creditors* (1890)—works marked by bitterness and iconoclasm, which combined dramatic naturalism and psychology in portraying the battle of the sexes—as well as three novels. After a mental breakdown he experienced a religious conversion that inspired such symbolic dramas as *The Dance of Death* (1901), *A Dream Play* (1902), and five "chamber plays," including *The Ghost Sonata* (1907).

Strindberg, lithograph by Edvard Munch, 1896.
BY COURTESY OF THE MUNCH-MUSEET, OSLO; PHOTOGRAPH, O. VAERING

string quartet Ensemble consisting of two violins, viola, and cello, or a work written for such an ensemble. Since c. 1775 such works have been perhaps the predominant genre of CHAMBER MUSIC. It was principally developed (if not quite invented) by F.J. HAYDN, who wrote some 70 quartets between 1757 and 1803. W.A. MOZART, LUDWIG VAN BEETHOVEN, F. SCHUBERT, BELA BARTOK, and D. SHOSTAKOVICH are the preeminent subsequent quartet composers. Works called string quartets have traditionally observed the four-movement design of the SONATA and SYMPHONY. Like most chamber-music genres, quartet music was traditionally intended primarily for the private enjoyment of amateur musicians rather than for public performance.

string theory See SUPERSTRING THEORY

stringed instrument Any musical instrument that produces sound by the vibrations of strings. The strings may be of gut, metal, fiber, or plastic, and may be plucked, bowed, or struck. The orchestral stringed instruments include the VIOLIN, VIOLA, CELLO, DOUBLE BASS, and HARP. Keyboard stringed instruments include the CLAVICHORD, HARPSICHORD, PIANO, and VIRGINAL. See also AEOLIAN HARP, BALALAIKA, DULCIMER, GUITAR, KITHARA, KOTO, LUTE, LYRE, MANDOLIN, PIPA, SITAR, UD, UKULELE, VIOL, ZITHER.

strip mining *or* **surface mining** Removal of the soil and rock (overburden) above a seam of COAL or other mineral and extraction of the exposed mineral. The method is used to best advantage where the mineral is not deeply buried, though many modern strip mines employ equipment capable of removing overburden nearly 200 ft (60 m) thick. In Europe the technique is widely used for brown-coal deposits, while in the U.S. a large proportion of both ANTHRACITE and BITUMINOUS COAL is so mined. Strip mining is most economical where flat terrain and horizontal seams permit a large area to be stripped. Where deposits occur in rolling or mountainous terrain, a contour method is used that creates a shelf with a slope on one side and an almost vertical wall on the other. Strip mining has been criticized, especially in the U.S., for its damage to the local environment. See also PLACER MINING.

strobilus See CONE

stroboscope Instrument that repeatedly illuminates a rotating or vibrating object in order to study the motion of the object or to determine its rotation speed or vibration frequency. The effect is achieved by producing light in very short bursts timed to occur when the moving part is in the same phase of its motion. By use of the stroboscope, a machine part, for example, may be made to appear to slow down or stop.

Stroessner \'stres-nər\, **Alfredo** (born 1912) Military leader and president of Paraguay (1954–89). The son of a German immigrant, Stroessner joined the army in 1932 and rose to become commander in chief in 1951. He deposed Pres. Federico Chávez (1881?–1978) and was the sole candidate in the 1954 presidential elections. He stabilized the currency, moderated inflation, and provided some new schools and public health facilities, but spent half the national income on the military establishment in order to preserve his authority and harshly suppressed his political opponents. After his election to his eighth successive term, he was deposed in a coup d'état and went into exile.

"SS. Boris and Gleb," icon by a follower of Prokopy Chirin, Stroganov school, 17th century; in the State Tretyakov Gallery, Moscow.
NOVOSTI PRESS AGENCY, MOSCOW

Stroganov school \'strò-gə-nəf\ School of ICON painting named for its original patrons, the Stroganov family, that flourished in Russia in the late 16th and 17th century. The artists perfected their work in the service of the czar in Moscow. The paintings, designed for private use, were produced in a muted color range dominated by golden browns with gold and silver linear highlights. Small and exquisitely detailed, and embellished with frames and halos of beaten gold and silver, they represent the last vital stage of Russian medieval painting before the Westernization of Russian art at the end of the 17th century.

Stroheim \'shtrō-ˌhīm, *Engl* 'strō-ˌhīm\, **Erich von** *orig.* **Erich Oswald Stroheim** (1885–1957) Austrian-U.S. film director. Son of a Jewish hatmaker, he emigrated to the U.S. after his military service. He arrived in Hollywood in 1914, where he worked for D. W. GRIFFITH

Erich von Stroheim in *Foolish Wives*, 1922.
BROWN BROTHERS

S T U V

and acted in his trademark role as a Prussian officer. His directorial debut, *Blind Husbands* (1919), was followed by *The Devil's Passkey* (1920) and *Foolish Wives* (1922). *Greed* (1924), his masterpiece, was damagingly cut before its release; it was followed by *The Merry Widow* (1925), *The Wedding March* (1928), and *Queen Kelly* (1928). His extravagance and demand for artistic control scuttled his directing career, and he returned to acting, notably in *Grand Illusion* (1937) and *Sunset Boulevard* (1950).

stroke *or* **cerebrovascular accident (CVA)** Sudden impairment of BRAIN function due to HYPOXIA, which may cause death of brain tissue. HYPERTENSION, ARTERIOSCLEROSIS, SMOKING, high CHOLESTEROL, DIABETES, OLD AGE, ATRIAL FIBRILLATION, and genetic defects are risk factors. Strokes due to THROMBOSIS (the most common cause), EMBOLISM, or arterial spasm, which cause ischemia (reduced blood supply) must be distinguished from those due to hemorrhage (bleeding), which are usually severe and often fatal. Depending on its site in the brain, a stroke's effects may include APHASIA, ATAXIA, local PARALYSIS, and/or disorders of one or more senses. A massive stroke can produce one-sided paralysis, inability to speak, coma, or death within hours or days. ANTICOAGULANTS can arrest strokes caused by clots but worsen those caused by bleeding. If the cause is closure of the major artery to the brain, surgery may clear or bypass the obstruction. Rehabilitation and speech therapy should begin within two days to retain and restore as much function as possible, since survivors may live many more years. Transient ischemic attacks ("mini-strokes"), with short-term loss of function, result from blockage of blood flow to small areas. They tend to recur and may worsen, leading to multi-infarct dementia (see SENILE DEMENTIA) or stroke.

stromatolite \strō-'ma-tᵊl-ˌīt\ Layered deposit, mainly of LIMESTONE, formed by the growth of blue-green algae (see CYANOBACTERIA). These structures are usually characterized by thin, alternating light and dark layers that may be flat, hummocky, or dome-shaped. Stromatolites were common in PRECAMBRIAN TIME (more than 543 million years ago). Some of the first forms of life on earth are recorded in stromatolites in rocks 3.5 billion years old. Stromatolites continue to form in certain areas today, most abundantly in Shark Bay in western Australia.

Stromboli \'străm-bō-(ˌ)lē\ Volcano, Stromboli Island, off northeastern SICILY, Italy. One of Europe's most active volcanoes, it is 3,038 ft (926 m) high. Though the last serious eruption was in 1921, lava flows continuously from its crater to the sea. Tourists are attracted to the island by its volcano, climate, and beaches.

Strong, William (1808–1895) U.S. jurist. Born in Somers, Conn., he became a lawyer in Pennsylvania. He served in the U.S. House of Representatives 1847–51, and on the state supreme court 1857–68. In 1870 he was appointed to the U.S. Supreme Court by ULYSSES S. GRANT. In 1871 he spoke for the majority as the Court overturned the *Hepburn* decision, a reversal that allowed Congress the power to issue paper money as legal tender, a position favored by Grant. Strong retired from the court in 1880.

strong force *or* **strong nuclear force** Fundamental force acting between elementary particles of matter, mainly QUARKS. The strong force binds quarks together in clusters to form PROTONS and NEUTRONS and heavier short-lived particles. It holds together the atomic NUCLEUS and underlies interactions among all particles containing quarks. In strong interactions, quarks exchange gluons, carriers of the strong force, which are massless particles with one unit of intrinsic SPIN. Within its short range (about 10^{-15} m), the strong force appears to become stronger with distance. At such distances, the strong interaction between quarks is about 100 times greater than the ELECTROMAGNETIC FORCE.

strontium \'străn(t)-shē-əm, 'străn-tē-əm\ Chemical ELEMENT, one of the ALKALINE EARTH METALS, chemical symbol Sr, atomic number 38. A soft metal, it has a silvery luster when freshly cut but reacts rapidly with air. Both the metal and the compounds (in which it has VALENCE 2) resemble CALCIUM and BARIUM so closely that strontium has few uses that those elements cannot supply more cheaply. The nitrate and chlorate, very volatile, give off brilliant crimson flames and are used in flares, fireworks, and tracer bullets. The radioactive ISOTOPE strontium-90 (see RADIOACTIVITY), produced in nuclear explosions, is the principal health hazard in FALLOUT; it can replace some of the calcium in foods, concentrate in bones and teeth, and cause RADIATION INJURY.

structural geology Scientific discipline concerned with rock deformation on both small and large scales. Its scope ranges from submicroscopic lattice defects in crystals to fault structures and fold systems of the earth's crust. Depending on the scale, the general techniques used are the same as those used in PETROLOGY, field geology, and GEOPHYSICS. Furthermore, since the processes that cause rocks to deform can rarely be observed directly, computer models are also used.

structural system In building construction, the particular method of assembling and constructing structural elements of a building so that they support and transmit applied loads safely to the ground without exceeding the allowable stresses in the members. Basic types of systems include BEARING-WALL, post-and-beam, frame, membrane, and suspension. They fall into three major categories: low-rise, high-rise, and long-span. Systems for long-span buildings (column-free spaces of over 100 ft, or 30m) include tension and compression systems (subject to bending) and funicular systems, which are shaped to experience either pure tension or pure compression. Bending structures include the GIRDER and two-way grids and SLABS. Funicular structures include CABLE STRUCTURES, MEMBRANE STRUCTURES, and vaults and domes. See also FRAMED STRUCTURE, POST-AND-BEAM SYSTEM, SHELL STRUCTURE.

structuralism European critical movement of the mid-20th century. It is based on the linguistic theories of FERDINAND DE SAUSSURE, which hold that language is a self-contained system of signs (i.e., signifiers + signifieds), and the cultural theories of CLAUDE LEVI-STRAUSS, which hold that cultures, like languages, can be viewed as systems of signs and analyzed in terms of the structural relations among their elements. Central to structuralism is the notion that binary oppositions (e.g., male/female, public/private, cooked/raw) reveal the unconscious logic or "grammar" of a system. Literary structuralism views literary texts as systems of interlocking signs and seeks to make explicit the hidden logic governing the form and content of a work. The works of MICHEL FOUCAULT, JACQUES LACAN, ROMAN JAKOBSON, and ROLAND BARTHES have been prominent. Areas of study that have adopted and developed structuralist premises and procedures include SEMIOTICS and narratology. See also DECONSTRUCTION.

Structured Query Language See SQL

Struma River River, western Bulgaria and northeastern Greece. Rising in the RHODOPE MTNS. southwest of SOFIA, it courses 258 mi (415 km) southeast to the Aegean Sea. Its upper valley is a major source of brown coal for Bulgaria, and its lower course flows through a wide agricultural valley.

Struve \'shtrü-və\, **Friedrich Georg Wilhelm von** (1793–1864) German-Russian astronomer. He left Germany for Russia in 1808 to avoid conscription in Napoleonic armies, and joined the faculty at the University of Dorpat (now Tartu, Estonia), and became director of its observatory. The founder of the modern study of binary stars, in his survey of over 120,000 stars he measured over 3,000 binaries. He was also among the first to measure stellar parallax. In 1835, at the request of Czar NICHOLAS I, he went to Pulkovo to supervise construction of a new observatory, becoming its director in 1839. His son, Otto Struve (1819–1905), served as director of Pulkovo Observatory (1862–89); his grandson Gustav Wilhelm Ludwig Struve (1858–1920) was director of University of Kharkov observatory; OTTO STRUVE was his great-grandson.

Struve *Engl* 'strü-vē\, **Otto** (1897–1963) Russian-U.S. astronomer. Born in Ukraine, the great-grandson of FRIEDRICH G. W. VON STRUVE, he suspended his studies to serve in the Russian army in World War I before emigrating to the U.S. On the staff of the Yerkes Observatory, he made important contributions to stellar spectroscopy and astrophysics, notably the discovery of the widespread distribution of hydrogen and other elements in space. He served as director of Yerkes and later of McDonald Observatory in Texas, which he organized. He later taught at the University of Chicago in 1947 and UC–Berkeley, and he directed the National Radio Astronomy Observatory in Green Bank, W.V., 1959–62. A prolific writer, he published about 700 papers and several books.

Struve \'strü-və\, **Pyotr (Berngardovich)** (1870–1944) Russian economist and journalist. In 1894 he wrote a well-regarded Marxist analysis of Russian capitalism, and in 1898 a manifesto for the newly formed RUSSIAN SOCIAL-DEMOCRATIC WORKERS' PARTY. After his arrest and exile in 1901, he broke with revolutionary Marxism; he edited the illegal but widely read journal *Osvobozhdeniy* ("Liberation") (1902–5), calling for a constitutional monarchy. He returned to Russia in 1905, joined the

CONSTITUTIONAL DEMOCRATIC PARTY, and edited the moderate journal *Russkaya mysly* ("Russian Thought"). In 1917 he opposed the Bolshevik takeover and left Russia for Paris and (after 1928) Belgrade.

strychnine \'strik-ˌnīn\ Organic chemical, a poisonous ALKALOID obtained from seeds of the nux vomica tree of India and related plants of the genus *Strychnos.* It does not dissolve in water and not well in alcohol, and it has an intense bitter taste. It has been used in rodent POISONS. Within 20 minutes it causes painful muscle contractions and convulsions, pulling the head back and arching the back; death usually results from respiratory muscle spasms. It is used in small doses by veterinarians as a stimulant.

Stuart *or* **Stewart** *or* **Steuart, House of** Royal house of Scotland (1371–1714) and of England (1603–49, 1660–1714). The earliest members of the family were stewards in 11th-century Brittany, and one member who entered the service of DAVID I in Scotland received the title of steward. The 6th steward married the daughter of King ROBERT I the Bruce, and in 1371 their son became King Robert II (1316–1390), the first Stewart king of Scotland (r.1371–90). His descendants in the 15th–17th century included the Scottish monarchs JAMES I, JAMES IV, MARY, QUEEN OF SCOTS, and James VI (who inherited the English throne as JAMES I). The Stuarts (who eventually adopted the French-influenced spelling of their name) were excluded from the English throne after CHARLES I until the restoration of CHARLES II in 1660. He was followed by JAMES II, WILLIAM III and MARY II, and ANNE. The Stuart royal line ended in 1714 and the British crown passed to the House of HANOVER, despite later claims by James II's son JAMES EDWARD STUART and grandson CHARLES EDWARD STUART.

Stuart, Charles Edward (Louis Philip Casimir) *known as* **Bonnie Prince Charlie** (1720–1788) Claimant to the British throne. Born in Rome, he was the son of the royal pretender JAMES EDWARD STUART and grandson of the exiled JAMES II of England. Seeking to regain the throne, in 1745 the "Young Pretender" landed in Scotland, where he raised an army of 2,400 among the clans. After taking Edinburgh and routing the English at Prestonpans, he crossed the English border and reached Derby, but a lack of strong support from the JACOBITES and the French forced his retreat into Scotland. He was decisively defeated at the Battle of CULLODEN (1746) and, aided by Flora Macdonald (1722–1790) and disguised as her maid, escaped to France. He wandered about Europe trying to revive his cause, but his debauched behavior alienated his friends. He settled in Italy in 1766. He later became romanticized in ballads and legends.

Stuart, Gilbert (Charles) (1755–1828) U.S. painter. Born in North Kingston, R.I., he went to London in 1775 and worked six years with BENJAMIN WEST. He opened his own London studio in 1782 and enjoyed great success, but fled to Dublin in 1787 to escape his creditors. After six years there, he returned to the U.S. He developed a distinctively American portrait style, and quickly established himself as the nation's leading portraitist. Critics have praised his painterly brushwork, luminous color, and psychological penetration. Of his nearly 1,000 portraits, the most famous is an unfinished head of GEORGE WASHINGTON (1796).

Mrs. Richard Yates, oil painting by Gilbert Stuart, 1793–94; in the National Gallery of Art, Washington, D.C.

BY COURTESY OF THE NATIONAL GALLERY OF ART, WASHINGTON, D.C., ANDREW MELLON COLLECTION

Stuart, James (Francis) Edward (1688–1766) Claimant to the English and Scottish thrones. Son of the exiled JAMES II of England, he was raised in France as a Catholic. On the death of his father (1701), he was proclaimed king of England by the French king LOUIS XIV, but the English parliament passed a bill of attainder against him. He served with the French army in the War of the Spanish Succession. In the JACOBITE uprising (1715), James landed in Scotland, but within two months the uprising collapsed and he returned to France. He lived thereafter in Rome under the pope's patronage. He became known as the "Old Pretender" to distinguish him from his son, CHARLES EDWARD STUART.

Stuart, Jeb *orig.* **James Ewell Brown** (1833–1864) U.S. army officer. Born in Patrick Co., Va., he graduated from West Point and was an aide to Col. ROBERT E. LEE in the defeat of JOHN BROWN's raid on Harpers Ferry. In 1861 he joined the Confederate army and became brigadier general of a cavalry brigade. On scouting raids he obtained information on Union troop movements that contributed to Confederate victories at the Seven Days' Battle and the Second Battle of BULL RUN; Lee called Stuart the "eyes of the army." As major general, he helped win the battles of Fredericksburg and Chancellorsville. Before the Battle of GETTYSBURG, he was instructed by Lee to gather information on Union troop movements; he was delayed on a raid and arrived after the battle had begun. Though criticized for his action, he continued to provide intelligence to Confederate forces. He was mortally wounded in the Confederate defeat at Spotsylvania Courthouse.

Stuart style Style of visual arts produced in Britain during the reign of the house of STUART (1603–1714, excepting the interregnum of OLIVER CROMWELL). Though the period encompassed several specific stylistic movements, artists through much of the period looked for inspiration to contemporary movements (primarily the baroque) on the Continent, especially in Italy, Flanders, and France. Masters of the Stuart style included the architects INIGO JONES and CHRISTOPHER WREN. See also JACOBEAN AGE, QUEEN ANNE STYLE.

Stubbs, George (1724–1806) British animal painter and anatomical draftsman. Son of a prosperous tanner, he was briefly apprenticed to a painter but was basically self-taught. His masterly depictions of hunters and racehorses brought him innumerable commissions. Perhaps more impressive than the single portraits are his pictures of informal groups of horses, such as *Mares and Foals in a Landscape* (c. 1760–70). He also painted many other animals, including lions, tigers, giraffes, monkeys, and rhinoceroses, which he was able to observe in private menageries. His book *The Anatomy of the Horse* (1762), containing 18 masterfully engraved plates, was widely acclaimed.

stucco Exterior or interior plasterwork used as three-dimensional ornamentation, as a smooth paintable surface, or as a wet ground for fresco painting. Today the term is most often restricted to the rough plaster coating of exterior walls. Examples occur worldwide; stucco was applied to the temple walls of ancient Greece as early as 1400 BC. Roman architects stuccoed the rough stone or brick walls of monuments such as the baths at HADRIAN'S VILLA. Stucco was widely used in baroque and Renaissance architecture. Because of the many ways in which it can be treated, stuccowork has remained popular. In the warmer regions of the U.S., the 1920s stucco bungalow became virtually ubiquitous.

Studebaker family U.S. automobile manufacturers whose firm became the world's largest producer of horse-drawn vehicles and a leader in automobile manufacturing. In 1852 Clement Studebaker (1831–1901) started a blacksmith and wagon shop in South Bend, Ind., with his brother Henry (1826–1895). Later joined by their brothers John, Peter, and Jacob, the family business supplied vehicles to the U.S. government during the American Civil War and later helped outfit settlers moving west. By 1902 the company had built its first electric cars and, by 1904, gasoline-powered cars. In 1954 the Studebaker Corp. merged with the Packard Motor Car Co.; in 1966 it ceased production.

Students for a Democratic Society (SDS) Activist student organization in the U.S. Founded at the University of Michigan in 1960, its chapters were initially principally involved in the CIVIL RIGHTS MOVEMENT. Its "Port Huron Statement" of principles (1962) called for a new "participatory democracy." After organizing a national march in 1965 to protest U.S. involvement in the VIETNAM WAR, it became more militant, organizing student sit-ins to protest universities' participation in defense-related research. By 1969 the SDS had split into factions; the most notorious was the terrorist-oriented Weathermen, or Weather Underground. By the mid-1970s the group was defunct.

studio system System whereby U.S. movie companies controlled all aspects of production, distribution, and exhibition. In the 1920s such film studios as PARAMOUNT and MGM acquired theater chains to strengthen their vertical control of the industry, and WARNER BROTHERS, RKO, and TWENTIETH CENTURY–FOX built similar empires soon thereafter. Studio heads exerted control over the types of movies to be made and the direc-

S T U V

tors and actors to be hired; only a few directors maintained some independent control over their films. The studio system also developed the "star system," by which certain actors and actresses were groomed for stardom, with studio executives choosing their roles, publicizing their glamorized offscreen lives, and keeping them under control through long contracts. The system declined after a 1948 Supreme Court decision forced the large studios to sell their theater chains and increasing competition from television forced studios to limit their staffs, and by the 1960s it had effectively ended.

stupa Monument erected in memory of the BUDDHA or a Buddhist saint, often marking a sacred spot, commemorating an event, or housing a relic. Stupas are architectural symbols of the Buddha's death. A simple stupa may consist of a circular earthenware base supporting a massive solid dome, from which projects an umbrella, symbolizing protection. This basic design is the inspiration for other types of Buddhist monuments, including PAGODAS, seen throughout Asia. Worship consists of walking clockwise around a stupa. Many important stupas have become places of pilgrimage.

Stupa III and its single gateway, Sanchi, Madhya Pradesh state, India.
HOLLE BILDARCHIV

sturgeon Any of about 20 species (family Acipenseridae) of large fishes that are most abundant in southern Russia, Ukraine, and North America. Most species live in the sea and ascend rivers to spawn; a few live permanently in freshwaters. Four tactile barbels near the toothless mouth detect invertebrates and small fishes on the mud bottom. Sturgeon flesh and eggs, or roe (CAVIAR), are sold for food. The swim bladder is used in isinglass, a gelatin. The common Old World sturgeon *(Acipenser sturio)* and *A. oxyrhynchus,* found along the eastern coast of North America, are generally about 10 ft (3 m) long and weigh about 500 lbs (225 kg). See also BELUGA.

Sturges \'stər-jəs\, **Preston** *orig.* **Edmond Preston Biden** (1898–1959) U.S. film director. Born in Chicago, he took his last name from his bohemian mother's second husband. Initially a playwright, he wrote the Broadway hits *Strictly Dishonorable* (1929) and *Child of Manhattan* (1931). Moving to Hollywood, he became a noted screenwriter, winning an Academy Award for *The Great McGinty* (1940), the first film he directed. He went on to write and direct such distinctive satirical comedies as *Christmas in July* (1940), *The Lady Eve* (1941), *Sullivan's Travels* (1941), *The Palm Beach Story* (1941), *The Miracle of Morgan's Creek* (1944), *Hail the Conquering Hero* (1944), and *Unfaithfully Yours* (1948), characterized by their witty dialogue, rapid pace, and memorable minor characters.

Sturm und Drang \ˌshtu̇rm-u̇nt-'dräŋ, ˌstu̇rm-ənt-'dräŋ\ (German: "storm and stress") German literary movement of the latter half of the 18th century characterized by a revolt against the ENLIGHTENMENT cult of rationalism and the sterile imitation of French literature. It exalted nature, intuition, impulse, instinct, emotion, fancy, and inborn genius as the wellsprings of literature. Influenced by J.-J. ROUSSEAU, JOHANN GOTTFRIED HERDER, and others, it took its name from the title of a play by Friedrich von Klinger (1752–1831). Dramatic works were the movement's most characteristic product. Its most gifted representatives were FRIEDRICH SCHILLER and JOHANN W. VON GOETHE, whose *Sorrows of Young Werther* (1774) epitomizes its spirit.

Sturtevant \'stərt-ə-vənt\, **Alfred (Henry)** (1891–1970) U.S. geneticist. Born in Jacksonville, Ill., he received his PhD from Columbia University and taught principally at Caltech (1928–70). In 1912 he developed a technique for mapping the location of specific genes of the chromosomes in drosophila. He later proved that crossing-over (the exchange of genes between chromosomes) could be prevented in drosophila. He was one of the first to warn against the hazards of fallout as a consequence of nuclear-bomb testing.

Sturzo \'stürt-sō\, **Luigi** (1871–1959) Italian priest and political leader. Ordained a priest in 1894, he earned a doctorate in Rome, then returned to his native Sicily to help the oppressed miners and peasants. As mayor of Caltagirone (1905–20), he built community housing and other public works. In 1919 he founded the ITALIAN POPULAR PARTY and became its political secretary. Refusing to support BENITO MUSSOLINI, he went into exile in 1924. He returned in 1946, when his political movement was revived as the CHRISTIAN DEMOCRATIC PARTY. In 1952 he was appointed senator for life. He wrote several works of Christian social philosophy.

stuttering *or* **stammering** *or* **dysphemia** \dis-'fē-mē-ə\ Speech defect affecting the rhythm and fluency of speech, with involuntary repetition of sounds or SYLLABLES and intermittent blocking or prolongation of sounds, syllables, and words. Stutterers consistently have trouble with words starting with CONSONANTS, first words in sentences, and multisyllable words. Stuttering has a psychological, not a physiological, basis, tending to appear in children pressured to speak fluently in public. In earlier times, stutterers were subjected to often torturous efforts to cure them. Today it is known that about 80% recover without treatment, usually by early adulthood. This probably results from increased self-esteem, acceptance of the problem, and consequent relaxation. See also SPEECH THERAPY.

Stuttgart \'shtu̇t-ˌgärt\ City (pop., 1996 est.: 586,000), southwestern Germany, on the NECKAR RIVER. Originally a 10th-century stud farm, it became a town in the 13th century and passed to the counts of WÜRTTEMBERG, serving as their capital until the 19th century. The THIRTY YEARS' WAR, French invasions in the 17th century, and heavy bombing during World War II took a toll on the city. Many historic buildings have been rebuilt, including the 13th-century castle. It is a cultural, transportation, industrial, and publishing center. Stuttgart University was founded in 1829.

Stuyvesant \'stī-və-sənt\, **Peter** (1592?–1672) Dutch colonial governor. In 1643 he became director of the Dutch West India Co.'s Caribbean colonies, and in 1645 director general of all Dutch possessions in North America, including New Netherland and the Caribbean. He arrived in New Amsterdam (later New York City) in 1647 and soon faced conflict with the burghers' demands for self-government. He established a municipal government but continued to control it. He settled the boundary with Connecticut (1650), expelled the Swedes from New Sweden on the Delaware River, and incorporated the colony into Dutch territory (1655). Incursions from the New England colonies and a squadron sent by Charles II forced him to surrender New Netherland to the British (1664).

sty *or* **hordeolum** \hȯr-'dē-ə-ləm\ Infection of an eyelid gland. An external sty results from infection of a SEBACEOUS GLAND at the edge of the eyelid; tears flow and the eye feels tender, as if something is in it. The sty reddens and swells. Warm compresses help it break sooner. An internal sty is caused by infection of a meibomian gland under the eyelid lining. More painful than an external sty, it usually breaks through the inner lining of the lid when it discharges and may leave a painless cyst (chalazion) at the site. See also BOIL.

Style Moderne See ART DECO

stylistics Aspect of literary study that emphasizes the analysis of various elements of style (such as METAPHOR and diction). The ancients saw style as the proper adornment of thought. In this view, which prevailed throughout the Renaissance, devices of style can be catalogued and ideas can be framed with the help of model sentences and prescribed types of figures suited to the mode of discourse. In more recent theories, the relationship of style and the individual writer's unique vision of reality is emphasized.

stylolite \'stī-lə-ˌlīt\ Sedimentary structure consisting of a series of relatively small, alternating, interlocked, toothlike columns of stone; it is common in LIMESTONE, MARBLE, and similar rock. The individual columns never appear singly but occur as a succession of interpenetrations that in cross section make a zigzag suture across the face of the stone. Most geologists believe that they are of secondary origin; that is, they result from differential chemical solution as groundwater circulates along a parting in hardened rock.

Styne, Jule *orig.* **Julius Kerwin Stein** (1905–1994) U.S. (British-born) songwriter. Born to Ukrainian Jewish parents in London, he and his family settled in Chicago in 1912. His first hit song was published in 1926. Changing his name to avoid confusion with another performer, he moved to Hollywood in 1937 to write film musicals. In the 1940s he worked with S. CAHN, writing ballads for F. SINATRA, the film musical *Anchors Aweigh* (1945), and the Broadway musical *High Button Shoes* (1947). He collaborated with other lyricists on *Gentlemen Prefer*

Blondes (1949; film, 1953), *Bells Are Ringing* (1956; film, 1960), *Gypsy* (1959; film, 1962), *Do Re Mi* (1960), *Subways Are for Sleeping* (1961), and *Funny Girl* (1964; film, 1968). His songs include "Let It Snow," "The Party's Over," and "People."

Styria \'stir-ē-ə\ *German* **Steiermark** \'shtī-ər-ˌmärk\ State (pop., 1995 est.: 1,206,000), southeastern Austria. It has an area of 6,327 sq mi (16,387 sq km); its capital is GRAZ. Inhabited since the Stone Age, the region came under the Romans as part of the Celtic kingdom of NORICUM. Ruled by the Bavarians in the 8th century, it belonged to the duchy of CARINTHIA after 976 and was made a frontier territory of the Frankish empire in the 11th century. It became a duchy in 1180 and a HABSBURG crown land in 1282. After World War I, a southern portion was ceded to Yugoslavia.

Styron, William (born 1925) U.S. novelist. A native of Newport News, Va., educated at Duke Univ., Styron became part of the American expatriate community in Paris in the 1950s. His first novel, *Lie Down in Darkness* (1951), tells of a disturbed young woman who commits suicide. His fourth, the controversial *Confessions of Nat Turner* (1967, Pulitzer Prize), vividly evokes the slavery era. His later work includes *Sophie's Choice* (1979; film, 1982), examining ramifications of the Holocaust; and *Darkness Visible* (1990), a nonfiction account of his depression. His works often treat violent themes in a rich, Faulknerian style.

Styx \'stiks\ In GREEK MYTHOLOGY, a river of the underworld. The name comes from a Greek word that denotes both hatred and extreme cold, and it expresses loathing of death. In the epics of HOMER, the gods swore by the water of Styx as their most binding oath. HESIOD personified Styx as the daughter of Oceanus and the mother of Emulation, Victory, Power, and Might. The ancients believed that its water was poisonous and would dissolve any vessel except one made of the hoof of a horse or ass.

Su Song *or* **Su Sung** \'sü-'sůŋ\ (1020–1101) Chinese scholar and administrative and financial expert in the imperial bureaucracy. His *Illustrated Pharmacopoeia* (1070) revealed his knowledge of drugs, zoology, metallurgy, and related technology. An armillary clock that he built to serve as the basis of calendrical reform was housed in a 35-ft (11-m) tower and powered by a waterwheel and chain drive; its mechanism anticipated techniques that would not be used in Europe for hundreds of years.

Suárez \'swä-räth\, **Francisco** (1548–1617) Spanish theologian and philosopher. In his *Metaphysical Disputations* (1597), he drew on the works of ARISTOTLE, THOMAS AQUINAS, John DUNS SCOTUS, and Luis de Molina (1535–1600) in discussing the FREE WILL PROBLEM and other metaphysical topics. He is often considered the greatest Scholastic philosopher after Aquinas (see SCHOLASTICISM) and the major JESUIT theologian. His departures from Aquinas's positions have been considered significant enough to warrant the separate designation of his system as Suárezianism.

Suárez, Hugo Bánzer See Hugo BÁNZER SUÁREZ

subatomic particle *or* **elementary particle** Any of various self-contained units of matter or energy. Discovery of the ELECTRON in 1897 and of the atomic NUCLEUS in 1911 established that the ATOM is actually a composite of a cloud of electrons surrounding a tiny but heavy core. By the early 1930s it was found that the nucleus is composed of even smaller particles, called PROTONS and NEUTRONS. In the early 1970s it was discovered that these particles are made up of several types of even more basic units, named QUARKS, which, together with several types of LEPTONS, constitute the fundamental building blocks of all matter. A third major group of subatomic particles consists of BOSONS, which transmit the forces of the universe. More than 200 subatomic particles have been detected so far, and most appear to have a corresponding antiparticle (see ANTIMATTER).

subconscious See UNCONSCIOUS

subduction zone Oceanic trench area in which, according to the theory of PLATE TECTONICS, the seafloor underthrusts an adjacent plate, dragging the accumulated trench sediments downward into the earth's upper mantle.

Subic Bay Inlet of the CHINA SEA, southwestern LUZON, Philippines. From 1901 it was the site of the U.S.-operated Subic Bay Naval Station, the largest naval installation in the Philippines. The area suffered heavy damage in World War II and was occupied by the Japanese 1942–44. The base played a prominent supply and maintenance role in the VIETNAM WAR (1955–75). It was transferred to the Philippines in 1992; there were plans to redevelop it as a free-trade zone.

sublimation In physics, the change of state of a substance from a solid to a gas without first becoming liquid. One example is the vaporization of frozen carbon dioxide, or dry ice, at ordinary atmospheric pressure and temperature. The phenomenon occurs at pressures and temperatures (both relatively low) where solid and vapor PHASES coexist in equilibrium. Preservation of food by freeze-drying involves sublimation of water from the food in a frozen state under vacuum.

submachine gun Lightweight automatic small-arms weapon chambered for relatively low-energy pistol cartridges and fired from the hip or shoulder. Submachine guns usually have box-type magazines that hold 10–50 cartridges, or occasionally drums holding more rounds. A short-range weapon, they are rarely effective at more than 200 yards (180 m). They can fire 650 or more rounds per minute and weigh 6–10 lbs (2.5–4.5 kg). Important types include the Thompson submachine gun, or tommy gun (patented 1920), the British Sten gun of World War II, and the later Israeli UZI.

submarine Naval vessel capable of operating under water for sustained periods. In the 18th–19th century, American inventors such as David Bushnell (1742?–1824) and ROBERT FULTON experimented with submarines. In 1898 John P. Holland (1840–1914) launched the *Holland,* which had both internal-combustion engines (for surface locomotion) and electric motors (for submerged cruising); it was purchased by the U.S. government in 1900. The innovations of Simon Lake (1866–1945) were adopted first in Europe and later in the U.S. By the eve of World War I, all major navies had submarines; the German U-BOAT was an especially potent threat. World War II saw extensive submarine campaigns in all the world's oceans. The snorkel, adopted by the Germans in 1940, supplied fresh air to the diesel engine of the submerged craft, thus making it unnecessary to surface to recharge batteries. The shift to nuclear submarines began with the launching of the USS *NAUTILUS* in 1954. The abundant power provided by the uranium-fueled reactor meant that submarines could remain submerged and operate at high speed indefinitely. SONAR is widely used in navigation and to detect enemy vessels. Subs may be armed with cruise missiles and ballistic missiles fitted with nuclear warheads. Because they are so difficult to locate, they have been of great importance in the forces of nuclear-armed nations. See also DEPTH CHARGE, TRIDENT MISSILE.

submarine canyon Narrow, steep-sided underwater valley cut into a CONTINENTAL SLOPE. Submarine canyons resemble river canyons on land, usually having steep, rocky walls. They are found along most continental slopes. Those of the Grand Bahama Canyon, which are thought to be the deepest, cut nearly 3 mi (5 km) deep into the continental slope. Most submarine canyons extend only about 30 mi (50 km) or less, but a few are more than 200 mi (300 km) long.

submarine fan Accumulation of land-derived sediment on the seafloor; a fan is shaped like the section of a cone, with its apex at the mouth of a SUBBMARINE CANYON. The sediments consist largely of sandy material that drops from the canyon current in successively finer layers. Submarine fan valleys, with low relief and natural levees, often occur on submarine fans. Several fans may coalesce laterally.

submarine fracture zone Long, narrow, and mountainous submarine lineation that generally separates ocean-floor ridges differing in depth by as much as 1 mi (1.6 km). The largest fracture zones, in the eastern Pacific, are more than 1,000 mi (1,600 km) long and 60–125 mi (100–200 km) wide. Numerous shorter fracture zones in the Atlantic are associated with the MID-ATLANTIC RIDGE.

submarine mine In military and naval operations, a stationary explosive device placed in the water and designed to destroy ships that touch or approach it. Submarine mines have been used since the mid-19th century. They consist of an explosive charge fitted with a device that detonates the charge when a ship or submarine is nearby. Placed by vessels called minelayers or dropped by aircraft, they are anchored to the sea floor by a cable. Various types of submarine mines are detonated by contact, by an approaching ship's magnetic field, by changes in water pressure, or by the sound of a ship's propellers. The mine was the most effective antisubmarine weapon in World War I. Its role was even greater in World War II, when mines sank 1,118 Allied ships and 1,316 Axis ships. See also LAND MINE, MINESWEEPER.

submarine plateau See OCEANIC PLATEAU

submarine slump In a SUBMARINE CANYON or on a CONTINENTAL SLOPE, a relatively rapid and sporadic downslope moving mass composed of sediment and organic debris that has built up slowly into an unstable or marginally stable mass. After an individual slump in a canyon, however, the material tends to continue falling in a series of slumps until the sediment mass attains a shallower, more stable slope. A slumping episode may also trigger other slumps farther down the canyon.

subpoena \sə-ˈpē-nə\ In law, a WRIT commanding the person upon whom it has been served to appear in court or before a congressional committee, GRAND JURY, or some other body, under a penalty for failure to comply. Unlike a SUMMONS, a subpoena may command the recipient to produce evidence necessary to the resolution of a legal matter or controversy.

subsidy Financial assistance, either through direct payments or through indirect means such as price cuts and favorable contracts, to a person or group in order to promote a public objective. Subsidies to transportation, housing, agriculture, mining, and other industries have been instituted on the grounds that their preservation or expansion is in the public interest. Subsidies to the arts, sciences, humanities, and religion also exist in many nations where the private economy is unable to support them. Subsidies may be implemented through direct payments in cash or kind, through governmental provision of goods or services at prices below the normal market price, through governmental purchase of goods or services at prices above the market price, or through tax concessions. Though subsidies exist to promote the public welfare, they result in either higher taxes or higher prices for consumer goods. They may also encourage the preservation of inefficient producers. A subsidy is desirable only if its effects increase total benefits more than total costs (see COST-BENEFIT ANALYSIS).

subsistence farming Form of farming in which nearly all the crops or livestock raised are used to maintain the farmer and his family, leaving little surplus for sale or trade. Preindustrial agricultural peoples throughout the world practiced subsistence farming. As urban centers grew, agricultural production became more specialized and commercial farming developed, with farmers producing a sizable surplus of certain crops, which they traded for manufactured goods or sold for cash. Subsistence farming persists today in sub-Saharan Africa and other developing areas.

subsoil Layer (stratum) of earth immediately below the surface soil, consisting predominantly of minerals and leached materials such as iron and aluminum compounds. HUMUS remains and clay accumulate in subsoil, but the teeming macroscopic and microscopic organisms that make the topsoil rich with organic matter spend little time in the subsoil layer. Below the subsoil is a layer of partially disintegrated rock, and underlying bedrock. Stripping topsoil while clearing land for crop growth or commercial development exposes the subsoil and increases the rate of EROSION of soil minerals.

substantive law See PROCEDURAL LAW

subsurface water See GROUNDWATER

Subud \ˈsü-büd\ Indonesian religious movement based on spontaneous and ecstatic exercises. Founded in 1933 by Muhammad Subuh, a student of SUFISM, it was largely confined to Indonesia until it spread to Europe and the U.S. in the 1950s, chiefly because of the work of G. GURDJIEFF. The central feature of Subud is the *latihan,* a group spiritual activity in which practitioners allow the power of God to express itself through unrestrained spontaneous activity. Unprogrammed singing, dancing, shouting, and laughter are thought to give rise to feelings of rapture and release, and to promote psychological and physical healing.

subway Underground railway system used to transport passengers within urban and suburban areas. The first subway line, 3.75 mi (6 km) long, opened in London in 1863 and carried 9½ million passengers in its first year. The first electrified subway opened in 1890 in London (where it is called the underground or tube). Subways opened in Budapest in 1896 (the first on the European continent), Boston in 1897, Paris in 1900 (where it is called the *métro*), Berlin in 1902, New York in 1904, and later in Madrid (1919), Tokyo (1927), and Moscow (1935). Improvements in systems built from the 1970s on (including San Francisco, Washington, D.C., and Los Angeles) include computer technology to run subway trains by remote control, and refinements in track and car construction for faster, smoother, and quieter rides.

succubus See INCUBUS AND SUCCUBUS

succulent Any plant with fleshy, thick tissues adapted to water storage. Some succulents (e.g., the CACTUS) store water only in the stem and have no leaves or very small leaves; others (e.g., AGAVES) store water mainly in the leaves. Most have deep or broad root systems and are native to either deserts or regions that have a semiarid season. In succulents, the stomata (see STOMA) close during the day and open at night—the opposite of the usual pattern—in order to minimize TRANSPIRATION.

Suchow See YIBIN

sucker Any of 80–100 species (family Catostomidae) of freshwater food fishes found mostly in North America. Suckers can be distinguished from MINNOWS by the sucking mouth, with protrusible lips, on the underside of the head. Generally sluggish, they suck up detritus, invertebrates, and plants from the bottom of lakes and slow streams. The species vary greatly in size. The lake chubsucker *(Erimyzon sucetta)* grows to 10 in. (25 cm) long; the bigmouth buffalo fish *(Ictiobus cyprinellus)* grows to 35 in. (90 cm) and over 70 lbs (32 kg).

Sucker (*Catostomus*).
GRANT HEILMAN

suckerfish See REMORA

suckering Vegetative formation of a new stem and root system from an adventitious bud of a stem or root, either naturally or by human action. Such asexual reproduction is based on the ability of plants to regenerate tissues and parts. Examples of plants that spread by suckers include red RASPBERRY, FORSYTHIA, and LILAC. Suckering allows horticulturists and agriculturists to reproduce a desired plant over and over without significant variation.

sucking louse Any of more than 400 species (suborder Anoplura, order Phthiraptera) of small, wingless, flat ectoparasitic insects found worldwide. They have piercing and sucking mouthparts for extracting their food of mammals' blood and tissue fluids. The NYMPHS mature after several molts. Species are host-specific: *Pediculus* infests humans (see human LOUSE), whereas other sucking lice (genera *Haematopinus* and *Linognathus*) attack domestic animals, such as hogs, cattle, horses, and dogs.

suckling In MAMMALS, the drawing of milk into the mouth from the nipple of a mammary gland. In human beings, it is referred to as nursing or breast-feeding. The word also denotes an animal that has not yet been weaned—that is, whose access to milk has not yet been withdrawn, a process that gradually accustoms the young to accept an adult diet.

Suckling, Sir John (1609–1642) English CAVALIER POET, dramatist, and courtier. He inherited his father's considerable estates at 18 and became prominent at court as a gallant and a gamester; he is credited with inventing cribbage. After participating in a foiled plot to rescue the Earl of Strafford from the Tower of London, he fled to France and is believed to have committed suicide. He wrote four plays, the best being the lively comedy *The Goblins* (1638). His reputation as a poet rests on his lyrics, the best of which are easy and natural. His masterpiece is "A Ballad upon a Wedding," written in the style and meter of the contemporary street ballad.

Sucre \ˈsü-krā\ Constitutional capital (pop., 1993 est.: 145,000), Bolivia. Founded by the Spanish c. 1539 on the site of a Charcas Indian village, it became the capital of the Charcas territory of Upper Peru in 1561, and in 1609 the seat of an archdiocese. Many of its colonial churches survive. It was an early scene (1809) of the revolt against Spain. The Bolivian declaration of independence was signed there in 1825, and it became the capital in 1839. An effort to move the capital to LA PAZ in 1898 resulted in a civil war, which left the two cities sharing capital status. Sucre is also the seat of the national supreme court. It is a growing commercial center. The University of San Francisco Xavier, one of the oldest universities in South America, was founded there in 1624.

Sucre \'sü-krä\, **Antonio José de** (1795–1830) Liberator of Ecuador and first president of Bolivia (1826–28). A close ally of SIMON BOLIVAR, Sucre fought in the revolutionary struggles of Venezuela, Colombia, GRAN COLOMBIA (now Ecuador), Peru, and Upper Peru (now Bolivia), defeating royalist forces throughout the region. In 1826 he set up a Bolivian government and briefly served as president, but he soon retired to Gran Colombia. In 1829 he was called back into service to defend Gran Colombia against a Peruvian invasion. He was assassinated in 1830 at 35. He is remembered as one of the most respected leaders of the Latin-American wars for independence.

sucrose \'sü-ˌkrōs\ *or* **table sugar** Organic compound, colorless, sweet-tasting crystals that dissolve in water. Sucrose ($C_{12}H_{22}O_{11}$) is a disaccharide; HYDROLYSIS, by the ENZYME invertase, yields "invert sugar" (so called because the hydrolysis results in an inversion of the rotation of plane polarized light), a 50:50 mixture of FRUCTOSE and GLUCOSE, its two constituent MONOSACCHARIDES. Sucrose occurs naturally in sugarcane, sugar beets, sugar-maple sap, dates, and honey. It is produced commercially in large amounts (especially from sugarcane and sugar beets) and is used almost entirely as food.

Sudan *or* **the Sudan** Vast tract of open savanna plains, northern central Africa. Extending across 2 million sq mi (5 million sq km), it lies between the southern limits of the SAHARA and LIBYAN deserts and the northern limits of the equatorial rain forests. It extends from the western coast more than 3,500 mi (5,500 km) to the mountains of Ethiopia and the Red Sea. The SAHEL comprises the northern reaches.

Sudan \sü-'dan\ *or* **The Sudan** *officially* **Republic of the Sudan** Nation, North Africa. Area: 966,757 sq mi (2,503,890 sq km). Population (1997 est.): 32,594,000. Capital: KHARTOUM. Muslim Arab ethnic groups live in the northern and central two-thirds of the country, while Nilotic and Sudanic peoples live in the south. Languages: Arabic (official); 100 others spoken. Religions: Islam (official), animism, Christianity. Currency: Sudanese dinar. The largest country in Africa, the Sudan

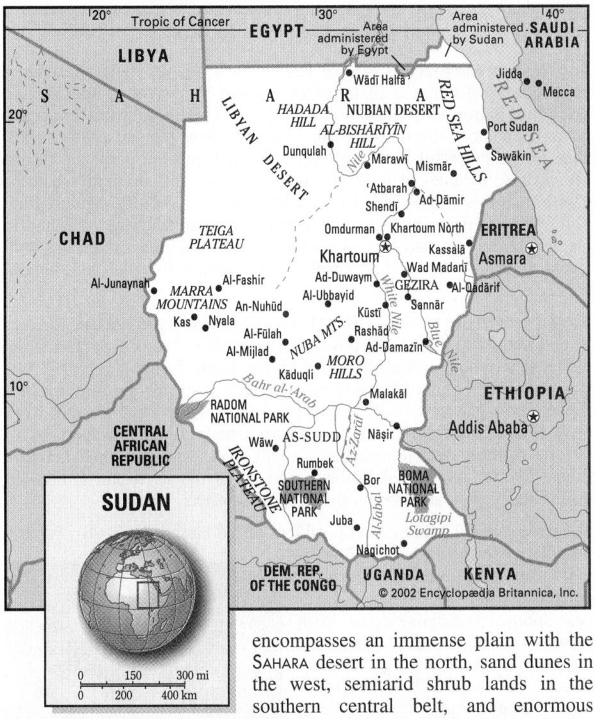

encompasses an immense plain with the SAHARA desert in the north, sand dunes in the west, semiarid shrub lands in the southern central belt, and enormous swamps and tropical rain forests in the south. The NILE RIVER flows the entire length of the country. Wildlife includes lion, leopard, elephant, giraffe, and zebra. It has a developing mixed economy based largely on agriculture. One of the largest irrigation projects in the world provides water to farms between the White and Blue Niles. Chief cash crops are cotton, peanuts, and sesame; livestock is also important. Major industries include food processing and cotton-ginning. It is ruled by an Islamic military regime. Evidence of inhabitation in the Sudan dates back tens of thousands of years. From the end of the 4th millennium BC, NUBIA (now northern Sudan) periodically came under Egyptian rule, and it was part of the kingdom of CUSH from the 11th century BC to the 4th century AD. Christian missionaries converted the Sudan's three principal kingdoms during the 6th century AD; these black Christian kingdoms coexisted with their Muslim Arab neighbors in Egypt for centuries, until the influx of Arab immigrants brought about their collapse in the 13th–15th century. Egypt had conquered all of the Sudan by 1874, and encouraged British interference in the region; this aroused Muslim opposition and led to the revolt of al-MAHDI, who captured Khartoum in 1885 and established a Muslim theocracy in the Sudan that lasted until 1898, when his forces were defeated by the British. The British ruled the country, generally in partnership with Egypt, until the Sudan achieved independence in 1956. Since then the country has fluctuated between ineffective parliamentary government and unstable military rule. The non-Muslim population of the south has engaged in ongoing rebellion against the Muslim-controlled government of the north, leading to famines and the displacement of some 4 million people in recent years.

sudden infant death syndrome (SIDS) *or* **crib death** Unexpected death of an apparently well infant. It occurs worldwide, almost always during sleep at night and usually at 2–4 months of age. Sleeping face-down and exposure to cigarette smoke have been implicated. It is more common in cases of premature birth, low birth weight, and poor prenatal care. Many cases that would once have been labeled SIDS prove to be due to suffocation in bedding or overheating. Some babies who die of SIDS have been found to have brain-stem abnormalities that interfere with their response to high carbon-dioxide levels in the blood.

Sudetenland \sü-'dā-tᵊn-ˌland\ Sections of northern and western Bohemia and northern Moravia around the Sudeten mountain ranges. Formerly part of Austria, the predominantly German-speaking area was incorporated into Czechoslovakia after World War I. Discontent among the Sudeten Germans was exploited in the mid-1930s by the NAZI PARTY and its local leader KONRAD HENLEIN. The inflammatory situation convinced Britain and France that, to avoid war, Czechoslovakia must be persuaded to give the region autonomy. ADOLF HITLER's demand that the region be ceded to Germany was initially rejected, but the cession was later accomplished by the MUNICH AGREEMENT. After World War II the region was restored to Czechoslovakia, which expelled its German inhabitants and repopulated the area with Czechs.

Sudra \'sü-drə, 'shü-drə\ Fourth and lowest of the VARNAS, or social classes, of Hindu India. Traditionally composed of artisans and laborers, it probably originally included all conquered peoples of the Indus civilization as they were assimilated into the CASTE system. Members are not permitted to participate in the UPANAYANA, and thus cannot study the VEDAS. The high end of the Sudra includes some landowners; at the low end are UNTOUCHABLES. See also BRAHMAN, KSHATRIYA, VAISHYA.

Suetonius \swē-'tō-nē-əs, ˌsü-ə-'tō-nē-əs\ *Latin* **Gaius Suetonius Tranquillus** (AD 69?–after 122) Roman biographer and antiquarian. Suetonius' family was of the knightly class. His writings include *De viris illustribus* ("Concerning Illustrious Men"), short biographies of literary figures that were the ultimate source of nearly all that is known about the lives of eminent Roman authors. *Lives of the Caesars*, his other major work, is seasoned with bits of gossip and scandal related to the first 11 emperors; it is largely responsible for the vivid picture of Roman society and its decadent leaders that dominated historical thought until modified in modern times by the discovery of nonliterary evidence.

Suez, Gulf of NW arm of the Red Sea, between Africa proper and the SINAI Peninsula. It is 195 mi (314 km) long and 12–20 mi (19–32 km) wide. Linked to the Mediterranean Sea by the SUEZ CANAL, it is an important shipping route. In the 1970s and '80s, oil was discovered at numerous locations in the gulf.

Suez Canal Ship canal, Isthmus of Suez, Egypt. Connecting the Red Sea with the eastern Mediterranean Sea, it extends 100 mi (160 km) from PORT SAID to the Gulf of SUEZ, and allows ships to sail directly between the Mediterranean and the Indian Ocean. Built by the French-owned Suez Canal Co., it was completed in 1869 after 11 years of construction. Its ownership remained largely in French and British hands until its nationalization by Egypt in 1956 set off an international crisis (see SUEZ CRISIS). It has a minimum width of 179 ft (55 m) and a depth

S T U V

of about 40 ft (12 m) at low tide. It is one of the world's most heavily used shipping lanes.

Suez Crisis (1956) International crisis that arose from Egyptian Pres. Gamal Abdel Nasser's nationalization of the Suez Canal in reaction to a broken promise of Western financial aid to build the Aswan High Dam. The French and British, who had controlling interests in the company that owned the canal, sent troops to occupy the canal zone. Their ally Israel seized the Sinai Peninsula. International opposition quickly forced the French and British out, and Israel withdrew in 1957. The incident led to the resignation of Britain's prime minister, Anthony Eden, and was widely perceived as heralding the end of Britain as a major international power. Nasser's prestige, by contrast, soared within the developing world. See also Arab–Israeli Wars.

Suffolk County (pop., 1995 est.: 657,000), eastern England. It is located on the North Sea; the county seat is Ipswich. Prehistoric flint mines are found in the north. During Anglo-Saxon times it formed part of the kingdom of E. Anglia; the Sutton Hoo ship burial dates from this time. Its medieval prosperity was based largely on the wool industry. Since then, agriculture has been the major economic activity; crops include cereals, sugar beets, and vegetables. Newmarket is famous for its racing stables, and the coast is dotted with holiday resorts.

Suffolk Breed of medium-wool, dark-faced, hornless sheep developed in England in the early 19th century by mating Norfolk horned ewes (females) with Southdown rams (males). Suffolks are prolific, early-maturing sheep with excellent mutton carcasses. They are energetic and have an alert carriage and great stamina. Introduced into the U.S. in 1888, the Suffolk is a popular lamb producer.

Suffolk, Earl of *orig.* **Thomas Howard** (1561–1626) English naval officer and politician. Son of the 4th duke of Norfolk, Howard held naval commands and distinguished himself in the attack on the Spanish Armada (1588). He led naval forays against the Spanish in the reign of Elizabeth I. Created earl of Suffolk in 1603, he served James I as lord chamberlain (1603–14) and lord high treasurer (1614–18). In 1618 he was deprived of his office on charges of embezzlement and was briefly imprisoned with his wife, who had taken bribes from Spain.

Sufism \'sü-ˌfi-zəm\ Mystical movement within Islam that seeks to find divine love and knowledge through direct personal experience of God. It consists of a variety of mystical paths that are designed to ascertain the nature of mankind and God and to facilitate the experience of divine love and wisdom in the world. Sufism arose as an organized movement after the death of Muhammad (AD 632) among different groups who found orthodox Islam to be spiritually stifling. The practices of contemporary Sufi orders and suborders vary, but most include the recitation of the name of God or of certain phrases from the Quran as a way to loosen the bonds of the lower self, enabling the soul to experience the higher reality toward which it naturally aspires. Though Sufi practitioners have often been at odds with the mainstream of Islamic theology and law, the importance of Sufism in the history of Islam is incalculable. Sufi literature, especially love poetry, represents a golden age in Arabic, Persian, Turkish, and Urdu languages. See also Ahmadiya, dervish, Malamatiya, tariqa.

sugar Any of numerous sweet, colorless organic compounds that dissolve readily in water and occur in the sap of seed plants and the milk of mammals. Sugars (whose names end in "-ose") are the simplest carbohydrates. The most common is sucrose, a disaccharide; there are numerous others, including glucose and fructose (both monosaccharides); invert sugar (a 50:50 mixture of glucose and fructose produced by enzyme action on sucrose); and maltose (produced in the malting of barley) and lactose (both disaccharides). Commercial production of sugar is almost entirely for food.

Sugar Act (1764) British legislation to raise revenue from North American colonies. A revision of the unenforced Molasses Act of 1733, it imposed new duties on sugar and molasses imported into the colonies from non-British Caribbean sources and provided for the seizure of cargoes violating the new rules. The act was the first attempt to recoup from the colonies the expenses of the French and Indian War and the cost of maintaining British troops in North America. The colonists objected to the act as taxation without representation, and some merchants agreed not to import British goods. Protests increased with passage of the Stamp Act.

sugar beet Variety of beet *(Beta vulgaris)* that accounts for about two-fifths of global sugar production, making it second only to sugarcane as a source of the world's sugar. Unlike sugarcane, sugar beets can be grown in temperate or cold climates in Europe, North America, and Asia; that is, within the densely populated, well-developed areas where much of the product is consumed. The sugar beet was grown as a garden vegetable and for fodder long before it was valued for its sugar content.

Sugar beet (*Beta vulgaris*).
GRANT HEILMAN

sugarcane Giant, thick, perennial grass (*Saccharum officinarum;* family Poaceae, or Gramineae), cultivated in tropical and subtropical regions worldwide for its sweet sap, a major source of sugar and molasses. The plant grows in clumps of solid stalks with regularly spaced nodes or joints, each with a bud that can be planted for commercial asexual propagation. Graceful, sword-shaped leaves, similar to those of the corn plant, fold in a sheath around the stem. Mature canes may be 10–20 ft (3–6 m) tall and 1–3 in. (2.5–7.5 cm) in diameter. Molasses, the syrup remaining after sugar is crystallized out of the juice, is used in cooking, in making rum, and as feed for farm animals. Residual cane fiber (bagasse) is burned as fuel or used as filler for paper and particleboard.

Sugarcane (*Saccharum officinarum*).
RAY MANLEY—SHOSTAL ASSOC.

Sugawara Michizane \sü-'gä-wä-rä-ˌmē-chə-'zä-nā\ (845–903) Japanese scholar of Chinese literature during the Heian period, later deified as Tenjin, patron of scholarship and literature. He was given important government posts by the emperor Uda, who saw him as a counterbalance to the powerful Fujiwara family. When Uda's son took the throne Michizane's fortunes were reversed, and he was sent into exile when the new emperor was persuaded that Michizane was plotting against him. Following his death in exile, calamities in the capital were attributed to his vengeful spirit, and he was posthumously reinstated. At shrines dedicated to Tenjin, schoolchildren often buy amulets for good luck on exams.

Suger \sūē-'zher\ (1081–1151) Abbot of St.-Denis and adviser to Louis VI and Louis VII. A peasant boy educated at the abbey of St. Denis, he was a schoolmate and close friend of the future Louis VI. In 1122 he was elected abbot, and he used popular veneration for the saint and for the church's banner to rally military support for the king. Suger's work on the church of St.-Denis was instrumental in the development of Gothic architecture. He arranged a treaty ending the civil war between Louis VII and his vassal Thibaut, and he served as regent (1147–49) during the King's absence on the Second Crusade.

Suharto (born 1921) Second president of Indonesia (1967–98). Suharto initially served with the Dutch colonial army, but after the Japanese conquest (1942) he joined a Japanese-sponsored defense corps. With Japan's surrender he joined the guerrilla forces seeking independence from the Dutch. When Indonesia became independent (1950), he was a lieutenant colonel. A strong anticommunist, he crushed an attempted communist coup d'état in 1965 with a brutal purge of communists and leftists throughout the country that left some 300,000 dead. He deposed the sitting presi-

Suharto.
AP/WIDE WORLD PHOTOS

dent, SUKARNO, and was himself appointed president in 1967. He established authoritarian rule, and was repeatedly elected without opposition. In 1975 he annexed EAST TIMOR, killing over 100,000 East Timorese. In 1998, a severe economic downturn focused public attention on his government's corruption, and this led to massive demonstrations that prompted his resignation after 31 years in power.

Suhrawardi \\ˌsu̇h-rȧ-ˈwär-dē\\, **al-** *in full* **Shihab al-Din Yahya ibn Habash ibn Amirak al-Suhrawardi** *known as* **al-Maqtul** (c. 1155–1191) Muslim theologian and philosopher. Born in Suhraward, Iran, he studied in Esfahan, a leading center of Islamic scholarship. His works fell into two categories: doctrinal and philosophical tracts, many of which took account of the ancient Greek philosophers, and shorter treatises intended to guide the mystic toward esoteric knowledge. His best-known work, *The Wisdom of Illumination*, held that existence is a single continuum that culminates in pure light, representing God. Charged with heresy by orthodox Islamic elders, he was executed by Malik al-Zahir, son of SALADIN.

Sui dynasty \\ˈswē\\ (581–618) Short-lived Chinese dynasty that unified northern and southern China after centuries of division. Under the Sui, the cultural and artistic renaissance that was to reach its height under the succeeding TANG DYNASTY was set in motion. The first Sui emperor established uniform institutions of government throughout the country, promulgated a new legal system, conducted a census, recruited officials through examinations, and reestablished Confucian rituals. It conducted three costly and unsuccessful campaigns against KOGURYO. The Sui capital at CHANGAN was, in design, six times the size of the modern city of Xi'an at the same site.

suicide Act of intentionally taking one's own life. Suicide may have psychological origins such as the difficulty of coping with DEPRESSION or other MENTAL DISORDERS; it may be motivated by the desire to test the affection of loved ones or to punish their lack of support with the burden of guilt. It may also stem from social and cultural pressures, especially those that tend to increase isolation, such as bereavement or estrangement. Attitudes toward suicide have varied in different ages and cultures; convicted criminals in ancient Greece were permitted to take their own lives, and the Japanese custom of SEPPUKU allowed SAMURAI to commit ritual suicide as a way of protecting honor and demonstrating loyalty. Jews committed suicide rather than submit to ancient Roman conquerors or crusading knights who intended to force their conversion. In the 20th century, members of new religious movements, notably the Peoples Temple and Heaven's Gate, committed mass suicide. Buddhist monks and nuns have also committed sacrificial suicide by self-immolation as a form of social protest. Japan's use of KAMIKAZE suicide bombers during World War II was a precursor to the suicide bombing that emerged in the late 20th century as a form of TERRORISM, particularly among Islamic extremists. Suicide, however, is generally condemned by Islam, Judaism, and Christianity, and attempts to commit suicide are still punishable by law in many countries. Some communities around the world have sought to legalize physician-assisted suicides for the terminally ill. EUTHANASIA was legalized in The Netherlands in 2001 and in Belgium in 2002, and it is openly practiced in Colombia. Since the 1950s suicide-prevention organizations have been established in many countries, with telephone hot lines serving as a source of readily available counseling.

Suir River \\ˈshu̇r\\ River, southeastern Ireland. It rises in northern Tipperary Co. and flows south and east. It is joined by the Barrow and the Nore before entering Waterford Harbor 114 mi (183 km) later. In the 1760s the river was made navigable to Clonmel.

suite Set of instrumental dances or dancelike movements. The suite originated in the paired dances of the 14th–16th century (pavane–galliard, basse danse–saltarello, etc.). In the 16th–17th century, German composers began to write sets of three or four dances, as in J.H. SCHEIN's *Banchetto musicale* (1617). In the late 17th century, a basic ordering of four dances—ALLEMANDE, COURANTE, SARABANDE, and GIGUE—became established as standard; other dances came to be interpolated between the sarabande and gigue. In the 19th century, the term came to refer to sets of instrumental excerpts from operas and ballets.

Sukarno (1901–1970) First president of Indonesia (1949–66). Son of a Javanese schoolteacher, he excelled in languages, mastering Javanese, Sundanese, Balinese, and modern Indonesian, which he did much to create. He emerged as a charismatic leader in the country's independence movement. When the Japanese invaded in 1942, he served them as a chief adviser, while pressuring them to grant Indonesia independence. Immediately following Japan's defeat, he declared independence; the Dutch did not transfer sovereignty until 1949. Once he became president, Indonesia made gains in health, education, and cultural self-awareness, but democracy and the economy foundered. His government was corrupt, inflation soared, and the country experienced a continuous state of crisis. An attempted coup by communists in 1965 led to a military takeover by SUHARTO and a purge of alleged communists left some 300,000 dead.

Sukhothai kingdom \\ˈsu̇-kə-ˈtī\\ Former kingdom, northern central Thailand. It was founded in the mid-13th century when a local Tai ruler led a revolt against KHMER rule. It remained only a small local power until its third ruler, RAMKHAMHAENG, inherited the kingdom c. 1279. He extended its power to the south onto the MALAY PENINSULA, to the west into what is now Myanmar, and to the northeast into modern Laos. On his death in 1298 the kingdom began to lose its power, and in 1438 it was absorbed into the kingdom of AYUTTHAYA.

Sukhothai style \\ˈsü-kə-ˈtī\\ Canonical style for Buddha icons developed probably in the kingdom of Sukhothai (modern Thailand), beginning in the 14th century. The Sukhothai Buddhas—typically either seated in the half-lotus posture with right hand performing the earth-touching gesture or walking with one foot forward and the right hand raised to the chest—have a boneless, weightless elegance. The parts of the body follow abstract ideals based on analogy with natural forms (e.g., shoulders like an elephant's trunk, torso like a lion). The head typically bears a flamelike protuberance above a cranial bump, which the faithful believe contains an extra brain cavity.

Sukhoy *officially* **OKB imeni P.O. Sukhoy** *formerly* **OKB-51** Russian aerospace design bureau that is the country's second most important producer of jet fighters (after MIG). The origin of Sukhoy dates to 1953, when the Soviet government allowed Pavel Sukhoy to reassemble his World War II aircraft-design team into a new bureau, which was designated OKB-51. In the 1950s and '60s OKB-51 planned and built a series of supersonic jet fighters, including the Su-7 and Su-9, which were later modified and used extensively by the U.S.S.R. and other WARSAW PACT countries. It improved the Su-9 into the Su-11 and Su-15 fighter-interceptors. After Sukhoy's death (1975) his name was added to that of the bureau. Perhaps the best known Sukhoy design was the versatile Su-27 air-superiority fighter (first flown 1977). In the 1990s the bureau introduced the Su-34 fighter-bomber and the redesigned Su-39 ground-attack aircraft. Its fifth-generation multirole S-37 Berkut air-superiority fighter (1997), had state-of-the-art electronics, forward-swept wings, and thrust vector control. In 1997 Russia formed the partially state-owned AVPK Sukhoy by combining the design bureau with its production plant and other affiliates. At the start of the 21st century Sukhoy began diversifying into the civilian market with sports aircraft, freight vehicles, and passenger aircraft.

sukiya style \\su̇-ˈkē-ə\\ Japanese architectural style developed in the Momoyama (1574–1603) and EDO (1603–1867) periods, originally used for teahouses and later also for private residences and restaurants. Based on an aesthetic of naturalness and rustic simplicity, buildings are intended to harmonize with their surroundings. Timber construction is employed, with wood left in a natural state, sometimes with the bark still on. Walls are typically of clay. Great attention is paid to detail and proportions, and the effect is one of refined simplicity. The architect Yoshida Isoya (1894–1974) pioneered a modern sukiya style using contemporary materials.

Sulaiman Range \\ˈsü-lī-ˌmän\\ Mountain range, central Pakistan, west of the INDUS RIVER. It extends about 280 mi (450 km), with summits averaging 6,000–7,000 ft (1,800–2,100 m) tall. The highest peaks, at the northern end, are the twin peaks called Solomon's Throne. The higher of the two, at 18,481 ft (5,633 m), is the site of a popular shrine.

Sulawesi \\ˌsü-lə-ˈwā-sē\\ *or* **Celebes** \\ˈse-lə-ˌbēz\\ Island (pop., 1999 est.: 14,768,400), Indonesia. One of the Greater SUNDA ISLES, it lies in the MALAY ARCHIPELAGO east of BORNEO and has an area of 72,775 sq mi (188,487 sq km). The island is mountainous; its tallest peak, Mount Rantekombola, reaches 11,335 ft (3,455 m). Muslims arrived in the 15th century. The Portuguese first visited in 1512 while developing the spice trade of the MOLUCCAS. The first foreign settlement in 1607 by the Dutch at Makasar (now Ujung Pandang) initiated a power rivalry with the native sultans that lasted into the 20th century. It joined Indonesia in 1950, though Communist rebellions against the central government have continued in recent years.

Süleyman I \sǖ-lā-ˈmän\ *known as* **Süleyman the Magnificent** (1495?–1566) Ottoman sultan (r.1520–66). He became sultan after serving as a provincial governor under his grandfather, BAYEZID II, and his father, Selim I. He immediately began leading campaigns against the Christians, taking Belgrade (1521) and Rhodes (1522). In 1529 he laid siege to Vienna, but failed to capture it. Campaigns in Hungary (1541, 1543) divided the nation between Habsburg-dominated and Ottoman-dominated areas. His first campaign against the Persian empire (1534–35) saw the capture of Iraq and Asia Minor; his second (1548–49) brought conquests in South Asia Minor around Lake Van; his third (1554–55) was unsuccessful. His navy, under BARBAROSSA, controlled the Mediterranean. In his realm he built mosques, bridges, and aqueducts, and he surrounded himself with great poets and legal scholars. His reign is considered a high point of Ottoman civilization. See also OTTOMAN EMPIRE.

sulfa drug Common term for sulfonamide drug, any member of a class of synthetic antibacterial drugs (e.g., sulfadiazine) with a particular chemical structure including both SULFUR and NITROGEN atoms. Their effectiveness against bacteria was discovered in 1932 by GERHARD DOMAGK, and they became the first chemical substances systematically used against human bacterial infections. Sulfa drugs inhibit the growth and multiplication of certain BACTERIA (but do not kill them) by interfering with certain ENZYME systems essential to their normal METABOLISM. Because of their toxicity and growing bacterial resistance, sulfa drugs are no longer in common use (except for urinary-tract infections), having been largely superseded by the less toxic ANTIBIOTICS.

sulfate Any of numerous chemical compounds related to SULFURIC ACID (H_2SO_4). The SALTS are inorganic compounds containing the sulfate ION (SO_4^{2-}), in IONIC BONDS with any of various CATIONS. The ESTERS are organic compounds in which the acid's hydrogen atoms are replaced by organic groups (e.g., methyl, ethyl, phenyl); a carbon atom in the organic group bonds to an oxygen atom, whose second bond is to the sulfur atom. (In sulfonates, a carbon atom bonds directly to the sulfur atom.) See also BONDING.

sulfide mineral *or* **sulphide mineral** Any member of a group of compounds of SULFUR with one or more metals. The metals that occur most commonly are iron, copper, nickel, lead, cobalt, silver, and zinc. They are the ore minerals of most metals used by industry (e.g., antimony, bismuth, copper, lead, nickel, and zinc). Other industrially important metals such as cadmium and selenium occur in trace amounts in numerous common sulfides and are recovered in refining processes.

Pyrite (iron disulfide) from Butte, Mont.

JOSEPH AND HELEN GUETTERMAN COLLECTION; PHOTOGRAPH JOHN H. GERARD

sulfur Nonmetallic chemical ELEMENT, chemical symbol S, atomic number 16. It is very reactive but occurs native in deposits, as well as combined in various ORES (e.g., PYRITE, GALENA, CINNABAR); in COAL, PETROLEUM, and NATURAL GAS; and in the water in sulfur springs. Sulfur is the third most abundant constituent of MINERALS and one of the four most important basic chemical commodities. Pure sulfur, a tasteless, odorless, brittle yellow solid, occurs in several crystalline and amorphous ALLOTROPES, including brimstone and flowers of sulfur. It combines, with VALENCE 2, 4, or 6, with nearly all other elements. Its most familiar compound is hydrogen sulfide, the poisonous gas that smells like rotten eggs. All metals except gold and platinum form sulfides, and many ores are sulfides. The OXIDES are SULFUR DIOXIDE and sulfur trioxide, which when dissolved in water make sulfurous acid and SULFURIC ACID, respectively. Several sulfur compounds with HALOGENS are industrially important. Sodium sulfite (Na_2SO_3) is a reducing agent used to pulp paper and in photography. Organic compounds with sulfur include several AMINO ACIDS, the SULFA DRUGS, and many insecticides, solvents, and substances used in making rubber and rayon.

Sulfur crystals from Sicily (greatly enlarged).

BY COURTESY OF THE ILLINOIS STATE MUSEUM; PHOTOGRAPH, JOHN H. GERARD

sulfur bacteria Any of a diverse group of BACTERIA that are capable of metabolizing SULFUR and its compounds and are important in the sulfur cycle. Members of the genus *Thiobacillus,* widespread in marine and terrestrial habitats, react with sulfur to produce sulfates useful to plants; in deep ground deposits they generate sulfuric acid, which dissolves metals in mines and corrodes concrete and steel. *Desulfovibrio desulfi-cans* reduces sulfates in waterlogged soils and sewage to hydrogen sulfide, a gas with the common rotten-egg odor.

sulfur butterfly See SULPHUR BUTTERFLY

sulfur dioxide Inorganic compound, heavy, colorless, poisonous GAS (SO_2). It has a pungent, irritating odor (the smell of a just-struck match). It occurs in volcanic gases and dissolved in the waters of some warm springs. Huge quantities are made industrially for use as a bleach, reducing agent, and as sulfites, which are food preservatives. It is a precursor of the trioxide (SO_3), used to make SULFURIC ACID. Sulfur dioxide is formed when sulfur-containing fuels are burned; measures to control sulfur dioxide AIR POLLUTION were widely adopted in the later 20th century.

sulfuric acid \ˌsəl-ˈfyu̇r-ik\ *or* **oil of vitriol** Dense, colorless, oily, corrosive liquid inorganic compound. A very strong ACID, it forms IONS of HYDROGEN or hydronium (H^+ or H_3O^+), hydrogen sulfate (HSO_4^-), and SULFATE (SO_4^{2-}). It is also an oxidizing (see OXIDATION-REDUCTION) and dehydrating agent and chars many organic materials. It is one of the most important industrial chemicals, used in various concentrations in manufacturing fertilizers, pigments, dyes, drugs, explosives, detergents, and inorganic salts and acids, in petroleum refining and metallurgical processes, and as the acid in lead–acid storage batteries. It is made industrially by dissolving sulfur trioxide (SO_3) in water, sometimes beyond the saturation point to make oleum (fuming sulfuric acid), used to make certain organic chemicals.

Sulla (Felix), Lucius Cornelius (138–78 BC) Victor in the Roman civil war (88–82) and DICTATOR (82–79). He fought alongside GAIUS MARIUS against JUGURTHA, whose capture through Sulla's trickery led to a break with Marius. After being made CONSUL, he was given command in the war against MITHRADATES VI; when Marius was named to replace him, he marched on Rome, and Marius fled. Though he succeeded in subduing Mithradates, the reigning popular party declared him a public enemy. From southern Italy he marched again successfully on Rome (83). Proclaimed DICTATOR with no time limit (at which time he took the name Felix, "Lucky"), he reestablished the power of the SENATE, increased the number of criminal courts, and passed new treason and citizen-protection laws, but became chiefly known for his ruthlessness. He resigned in 79.

Sulla, marble bust; in the Vatican Museum.

ALINARI—ART RESOURCE/EB INC.

Sullivan, Arthur (Seymour) *later* **Sir Arthur** (1842–1900) British composer. He attended the Royal Academy and the Leipzig Conservatory, then supported himself by teaching, playing organ, and composing for provincial festivals. He seemed destined to be an important composer, and his music for *The Tempest* (1861), Irish Symphony (1866), and songs (including "Onward, Christian Soldiers" and "The Lost Chord") were widely performed. In 1871 he first collaborated in comic opera with W.S. GILBERT, and in 1875 their *Trial by Jury* became a hit, setting the course for both their careers.

S T U V

Their collaboration continued with *The Sorceror* (1877), *H.M.S. Pinafore* (1878), *The Pirates of Penzance* (1879), *Patience* (1881), *Iolanthe* (1882), *Princess Ida* (1883), *The Mikado* (1885), *Ruddigore* (1887), *The Yeomen of the Guard* (1888), *The Gondoliers* (1889), and others, many of which would continue to delight international audiences for more than a century.

Sullivan, Ed(ward Vincent) (1901–1974) U.S. television host. Born in New York City, he began his career as a journalist and wrote a Broadway gossip column for the *Daily News.* Known for his talent at discovering interesting new performers, he was hired by CBS to host its variety program *Toast of the Town* (1948–55), later called *The Ed Sullivan Show* (1955–71), where he presented diverse entertainment (combining, for example, a concert pianist, a singing fireman, and a boxing referee with Hollywood celebrities in a single show) in a program that became a national institution for more than 20 years.

Sullivan, Harry Stack (1892–1949) U.S. psychiatrist. Born in Norwich, N.Y., he engaged in clinical research at the Pratt Hospital in Maryland 1923–30, pursuing his interest in the use of psychotherapy to treat SCHIZOPHRENIA, which he viewed as stemming from disturbed interpersonal relationships in early childhood. He asserted that psychiatric symptoms arise out of conflicts between the individual and his human environment and that personality development likewise stems from a series of interactions with other people. He helped establish the William Alanson White Psychiatric Foundation (1933) and the Washington School of Psychiatry (1936), and he also founded (1938) and served as editor of the journal *Psychiatry*. His works include *The Interpersonal Theory of Psychiatry* (1953) and *The Fusion of Psychiatry and Social Science* (1964).

Sullivan, John L(awrence) (1858–1918) U.S. heavyweight champion bareknuckle boxer. Born in Roxbury, Mass., he became heavyweight champion in 1882 by knocking out Paddy Ryan in nine rounds. His 75-round knockout of Jake Kilrain in 1889 was the last title bout under London Prize Ring (bareknuckle) rules. In his only championship defense under the QUEENSBERRY RULES, he was knocked out by Jim Corbett (1866–1933) in 21 rounds in 1892. From 1878 to 1905 Sullivan had 35 bouts, of which he won 31, 16 by knockouts. Some boxing historians regard him as a U.S. champion only, because he had only one international match of consequence and he refused to fight the great black Australian heavyweight Peter Jackson.

John L. Sullivan.
UPI—EB INC.

Sullivan, Louis H(enry) (1856–1924) U.S. architect, the father of modern U.S. architecture. Born in Boston, the young Sullivan was accepted at the École des Beaux-Arts in Paris but was a restless student. After working for several Chicago firms, he joined the office of Dankmar Adler (1844–1900) in 1879, becoming Adler's partner at age 24. Their 14-year association produced more than 100 buildings, many of them landmarks. Their first important work was the Auditorium Building (1889), a load-bearing stone structure with a 17-story tower, unadorned on the arcaded exterior and dazzlingly rich on the interior. Their most important skyscraper is the 10-story steel-framed Wainwright Building, St. Louis (1890–91); above its two-story base, the vertical elements are stressed and horizontals recessed, and it is capped by a decorative frieze and cornice. In 1895 Sullivan's partnership with Adler dissolved, and his practice began a steady decline. One of his few major commissions was Chicago's Carson Pirie Scott store (1899–1904), noted for its broad windows and exuberant ornamentation. Sullivan's ornamentation was based not on precedent but on geometry and natural forms. He considered it obvious that building design should indicate a building's functions and that, where the function does not change, the form should not change; hence his dictum "form follows function."

Sully \sue̅-'lē\, **duc (Duke) de** *orig.* **Maximilien de Béthune** (1560–1641) French statesman. Son of a French Huguenot noble, he was sent to the court of Henry of Navarre (later HENRY IV). He fought in the Wars of Religion and helped negotiate the Peace of Savoy (1601). As superintendent of finances from 1598, he instituted reforms in taxation and administration. A trusted agent to the king, he was rewarded with royal offices and created duc de Sully in 1606. He promoted a system of national improvements, encouraged agriculture, and strengthened the military. His political role ended with Henry's assassination (1610), and he resigned in 1611.

Sully Prudhomme \sue̅-lē-prue̅-'dȯm\ *orig.* **René-François-Armand Prudhomme** (1839–1907) French poet. Inspired at first by an unhappy love affair, he published fluent and melancholic verse in volumes beginning with *Stances et poèmes* (1865), containing his well-known "Le Vase brise." He later adopted the more objective approach of the PARNASSIAN POETS and attempted to represent philosophical concepts in verse. Among his best-known later works are *La justice* (1878) and *Le bonheur* (1888). In 1901 he was awarded the first Nobel Prize for Literature, over such greatly admired figures as LEO TOLSTOY.

Sully Prudhomme.
H. ROGER-VIOLLET

sulphide mineral See SULFIDE MINERAL

sulphur butterfly *or* **sulfur butterfly** Any of several species of BUTTERFLIES (family Pieridae) that are found worldwide. Adults have a wingspan of 1.5–2.5 in. (35–60 mm). The color and pattern of many species vary seasonally and between sexes, but they are generally bright yellow or orange. Some have two color patterns; for example, *Colias eurytheme* is usually orange with black wing margins, but some females are white with black margins. Pupae are attached to a twig by a posterior spine and a girdle of silk. The larvae feed on clover and may seriously damage crops.

Sulu Archipelago Volcanic and coral archipelago, southwestern Philippines, between MINDANAO and BORNEO. A double island chain, it extends 170 mi (270 km) and includes about 400 named islands and more than 500 unnamed ones; they cover an area of 1,038 sq mi (2,688 sq km). The islanders were converted to Islam by ABU BAKR in the mid-15th century. The Spanish tried, at first unsuccessfully, to subdue the inhabitants, whom they called MOROS. The islands finally became a Spanish protectorate in the 19th century, and in 1899 came under U.S. authority. The archipelago was ceded to the Philippines in 1940. The islands provide a haven for smugglers and pirates.

Sulzberger \'səlz-ˌbər-gər\, **Arthur Hays** (1891–1968) U.S. newspaper publisher. A son-in-law of ADOLPH OCHS, he joined the staff of *The* NEW YORK TIMES in 1918. He was the paper's publisher 1935–61, overseeing the extension of its news coverage into more specialized subject areas as well as important changes in technology and a growth in circulation. He was succeeded by his son, ARTHUR OCHS SULZBERGER.

Sulzberger, Arthur Ochs (born 1926) U.S. newspaper publisher. Grandson of ADOLPH OCHS and son of ARTHUR HAYS SULZBERGER, he spent a dozen years as a reporter and in other newspaper posts before becoming publisher of *The* NEW YORK TIMES in 1963. During his tenure he introduced many innovations that strengthened the paper's reputation while modernizing and streamlining the organization of its staff, including the unification of the daily *Times* with the Sunday edition in 1964 and an increase in coverage of such fields as economics, the environment, medicine, law, and science. In 1992 he was succeeded by his son, Arthur Sulzberger, Jr. (born 1951).

sumac \'shü-ˌmak, 'sü-ˌmak\ Any of certain species of shrubs and small trees in the genus *Rhus* of the family Anacardiaceae (the sumac, or cashew, family), native to temperate and subtropical zones. All sumacs have a milky or resinous sap, which in some species (e.g., POISON SUMAC) can irritate the skin. Used in the past as a source of dyes, medicines, and beverages, sumacs are now valued as ornamentals, soil binders, and cover plants. The sumacs grown for landscape use display a graceful form, spectacular fall color, or colorful fruit clusters. The smooth, or scarlet, sumac *(R. glabra),* native to the eastern and central U.S., is the most common.

Sumatra \sü-'mä-trə\ Island (pop., 1995 est.: 40,344,000), western Indonesia. It is one of the SUNDA ISLANDS and the second-largest island of Indonesia. It is 1,060 mi (1,706) long and 250 mi (400 km) wide; a chief city is PALEMBANG. Located on the seaborne trade routes, it had early contact with Hindu civilization. The SRIVIJAYA EMPIRE arose in the 7th century and came to dominate much of the island. It fell under the MAJAPAHIT EMPIRE in the 14th–16th century. First the Portuguese, then the Dutch and English established forts there beginning in the 16th century. It was occupied by Japan in World War II; in 1950 became part of the Republic of Indonesia. Its exports include rubber, tobacco, coffee, pepper, and timber products; mineral reserves include petroleum and coal.

Sumba \'süm-bə\ *English* **Sandalwood Island** Island (pop., 1990 est.: 445,000), Lesser SUNDA ISLANDS, Indonesia. The island, 140 mi (225 km) long and up to 50 mi (80 km) wide, is mainly a high plateau, with good harbors on the northern coast. Its chieftains were brought by treaty under Dutch control in 1756. It became part of independent Indonesia in 1950. It is known for the Sandalwood horse and Ongole cattle, and its woven cloth is famous for its design. Corn is the main crop; copra is exported.

Sumbawa \süm-'bä-wä\ Island (pop., 1990 est: 373,000), Lesser SUNDA ISLANDS, Indonesia. Its irregular coastline includes Bima Bay, one of the best harbors in Indonesia. The island, 175 mi (282 km) long and 55 mi (88 km) wide, is mountainous. Its highest point is volcanic Mount Tambora (9,354 ft, or 2,851 m), whose eruption in 1815 killed 50,000 people. It was once part of the MAJAPAHIT EMPIRE. In 1674 the Sumbawanese nobility signed agreements that gave the Dutch EAST INDIA CO. some power over the island; the Dutch gained direct control in the early 20th century. It became part of independent Indonesia in 1950. Agricultural products include rice, corn, coffee, and copra.

Sumer \'sü-mər\ Southern division of ancient BABYLONIA, southern MESOPOTAMIA, Tigris–Euphrates Valley, in what is now southern Iraq. It was first settled c. 4500–4000 BC by a non-Semitic people called the Ubaidians. They were the first civilizing force in Sumer, draining the marshes for agriculture and developing trade. The Sumerians, who spoke a Semitic language that came to dominate the region, arrived c. 3300 BC and developed the world's first known cities, which evolved into city-states. As rivalry among them increased, each adopted the institution of kingship, and eventually they were loosely united under one city or the other, beginning with KISH c. 2800 BC. Thereafter, Kish, ERECH, UR, NIPPUR, and LAGASH vied for ascendancy for hundreds of years. The area came under the ELAM (c. 2530–2450 BC) and later the AKKAD, led by the Akkadian king SARGON (r.2334–2279 BC). The city-states were largely independent after the Akkadian empire collapsed until they were reunified under the Third Dynasty of Ur (21st–20th century BC). This final Sumerian kingdom declined after foreign invasions, and the distinct Sumerian nation disappeared, becoming part of the Babylonian empire in the 18th century BC. The Sumerian legacy includes a number of technological and cultural innovations, including the first known wheeled vehicles and potter's wheels, a system of writing (see CUNEIFORM), and codes of law.

Summerhill School Experimental primary and secondary boarding school in Leiston, Suffolk, England. Founded in 1921 by Alexander Sutherland Neill (1883–1973), the school is self-governing (students and staff have a voice in policy matters) and emphasizes the student's own motivation to learn (class attendance is optional). Neill's highly influential and controversial book *Summerhill* (1960) stimulated much debate about alternatives to conventional schooling, particularly in the U.S.

summons In law, written notification that one is required to appear in court. In civil (noncriminal) cases, it notifies a defendant that he or she must appear and defend (e.g., by filing an answer) within a specified time or a default judgment will be rendered for the plaintiff. The summons is also used in cases involving minor criminal offenses (e.g., traffic violations) to call defendants to appear and answer to charges against them. See also SUBPOENA.

Sumner, Charles (1811–1874) U.S. politician. Born in Boston, he practiced law while crusading for abolition, prison reform, world peace, and educational reform. He was elected to the U.S. Senate (1852–74) and spoke out against slavery. He denounced the KANSAS-NEBRASKA ACT as the "crime against Kansas" and scorned its authors, Sen. STEPHEN A. DOUGLAS and Sen. Andrew P. Butler. In 1856 an incensed relative of Butler, a congressman from South Carolina, invaded the Senate and severely beat Sumner. He returned to the Senate in 1859, and as chairman of the foreign relations committee (1861–71) helped resolve the TRENT AFFAIR.

Charles Sumner.

BY COURTESY OF THE LIBRARY OF CONGRESS, WASHINGTON, D.C.

Sumner, James (Batcheller) (1887–1955) U.S. biochemist. Born in Canton, Mass., he taught at Cornell University 1929–55. In 1926 he became the first researcher to crystallize an ENZYME (urease); he later crystalled catalase and worked on purification of various other enzymes, which led to recognition that most enzymes are PROTEINS. This work earned him (with JOHN H. NORTHROP and WENDELL M. STANLEY) a 1946 Nobel Prize. In 1947 he became director of Cornell's laboratory of enzyme chemistry, established in recognition of his work.

sumo \'sü-mō\ Japanese form of wrestling in which a contestant loses if he is forced out of the ring (a 15-ft circle) or if any part of his body except the soles of his feet touches the ground. In sumo, a wrestler's weight, size, and strength are of the greatest importance, though speed and suddenness of attack are also useful. The wrestlers, who are fed a special protein diet and may weigh over 300 lbs (136 kg), wear only loincloths and grip each other by the belt. Sumo wrestling is an ancient sport with a complex system of ranking; at the top of the hierarchy is the *yokozuna* ("grand champion"). Lengthy rituals and elaborate posturings accompany the bouts, which are extremely brief, often lasting only a few seconds.

Sumter, Thomas (1734–1832) American Revolutionary officer. Born in Hanover Co., Va., he served in the French and Indian War and moved to South Carolina. In the American Revolution he was commissioned a brigadier general and escaped to North Carolina after the fall of Charleston (1780). He led the state militia to victories over the British in several engagements. He served in the U.S. House of Representatives (1789–93, 1797–1801) and the Senate (1801–10). Fort Sumter was named for him.

sun STAR around which the SOLAR SYSTEM revolves. About 5 billion years old, it is the dominant body of the system, with more than 99% of its mass. It converts 5 million tons of matter into energy every second by NUCLEAR FUSION reactions in its core, producing NEUTRINOS (see solar NEUTRINO PROBLEM) and solar radiation. The small amount of this energy that penetrates earth's ATMOSPHERE provides the light and heat that support life. Solar radiation can also supply electrical power (see SOLAR CELL). A sphere of luminous gas 864,950 mi (1.392 million km) in diameter, the sun has about 330,000 times the mass of earth. Its core temperature is close to 27,000,000°F (15,000,000°C) and its surface temperature about 10,000°F (6,000°C). The sun, a G-type (yellow) star, has fairly average properties for a main-sequence star (see HERTZSPRUNG-RUSSELL DIAGRAM). The sun rotates at different rates at different latitudes: One rotation takes 36 days at the poles but only 25 days at the equator. The PHOTOSPHERE is in constant motion, with the number and position of SUNSPOTS changing in a regular SOLAR CYCLE. Surface phenomena also include magnetic activity extending into the CHROMOSPHERE and CORONA, SOLAR FLARES, SOLAR PROMINENCES, and the SOLAR WIND. Effects on earth include AURORAS and disruption of radio communications and power-transmission lines. Despite this activity, the sun appears to have remained relatively unchanged for billions of years. See also ECLIPSE, HELIOPAUSE.

sun bear *or* **honey bear** Smallest member *(Helarctos,* or *Ursus, malayanus)* of the bear family (Ursidae), found in South Asian forests. Nocturnal and tree-climbing, the sun bear weighs 60–140 lbs (27–64 kg) and is 3–4 ft (1–1.2 m) long, with a 2-in. (5-cm) tail, large forepaws, and short black fur with an orange-yellow crescent on the chest. It uses its long, curved claws to tear or dig for insect nests, particularly those of bees and termites. It also eats fruit, honey, and small vertebrates. The sun bear is shy and intelligent; legends say that its chest crescent represents the sun.

sun dance Most spectacular and important religious ceremony of the 19th-cent. PLAINS INDIANS. Ordinarily held by each tribe once a year in early summer (hence the name), it was an occasion to reaffirm basic beliefs about the universe and the supernatural through rituals. The ceremony was most highly developed among the ARAPAHO, CHEYENNE, and Oglala SIOUX. The central rite involved dancers who, to fulfill a vow or seek "power" (spiritual energy and insight), danced for several days without stopping for food, drink, or sleep, their ordeal ending in frenzy and exhaustion. Among some tribes self-torture and mutilation were practiced.

sun worship Veneration of the sun or its representation as a deity. It appears in several early cultures, notably in ancient Egypt, Indo-Europe, and Mesoamerica, where urban civilizations were combined with a strong ideology of sacred kingship, in which kings ruled by the power of the sun and claimed descent from it. The imagery of the sun as the ruler of both the upper and the lower world, which he visits daily, was prominent. Sun heroes and deities also figure in many mythologies, including Indo-Iranian, Greco-Roman, and Scandinavian. In late Roman history, sun worship was of such importance that it was later called "solar monotheism." See also AMATERASU, RE, SHAMASH, SOL, SURYA, TONATIUH.

Sun Yat-sen \'sůn-'yät-'sen\ *or (pinyin)* **Sun Yixian** \'sůn-'ē-shē-'ən\ (1866–1925) Leader of the GUOMINDANG (Chinese Nationalist Party), known as the father of modern China. Educated in Hawaii and Hong Kong, Sun embarked on a medical career in 1892, but, troubled by the conservative QING DYNASTY's inability to keep China from suffering repeated humiliations at the hands of more advanced nations, he forsook medicine two years later for politics. A letter to LI HONGZHANG in which Sun detailed ways in which China could gain strength made no headway, and he went abroad to try organizing expatriate Chinese. He spent time in Hawaii, England, Canada, and Japan, and in 1905 became head of a revolutionary coalition, the Tongmeng hui ("Alliance Society"). The revolts he helped plot during this period failed, but in 1911 a rebellion in Wuhan unexpectedly succeeded in overthrowing the provincial government. Other provincial secessions followed, and Sun returned to be elected provisional president of a new government. The emperor abdicated in 1912, and Sun turned over the government to YUAN SHIKAI. The two men split in 1913; Sun headed a separatist regime in the south. In 1924, aided by Soviet advisers, he reorganized his Nationalist Party, admitted three Communists to its central executive committee, and approved the establishment of a military academy, to be headed by CHIANG KAI-SHEK. He delivered lectures on his doctrine, the Three Principles of the People (nationalism, democracy, and people's livelihood), but died the following year without having had the opportunity to put his doctrine into practice. See also WANG JINGWEI.

Sun Yat-sen.
BROWN BROTHERS

Sunbelt Region, south and southwestern U.S. It is characterized by a warm climate, rapid population growth since 1970, and relatively conservative voting patterns. Comprising 15 states, it extends from Virginia and Florida in the southeast through Nevada in the southwest, and includes southern California.

sunburn Acute skin INFLAMMATION caused by overexposure to ULTRAVIOLET RADIATION from sunlight or other sources. More common and severe in light-skinned people, it ranges from mild redness and tenderness to intense pain, EDEMA, and blistering, sometimes with shock, fever, and nausea. The process begins after 15 minutes in the sun, but redness starts 6–12 hours later and peaks within a day. Pigment cells in the skin increase MELANIN production ("tan"). Cold compresses and ANALGESICS reduce pain. Limiting sun exposure, using sunscreen, and wearing protective clothing can prevent severe sunburn. Long-term sun exposure can eventually cause SKIN CANCER, as well as skin wrinkling and thickening.

Sunda Isles Archipelago extending from the MALAY PENINSULA to the MOLUCCAS. The islands make up most of the land area of Indonesia, with only northern and northwestern BORNEO not under Indonesian political control. They include the Greater Sunda Islands (SUMATRA, JAVA, BORNEO, SULAWESI, and adjacent smaller islands), and the Lesser Sunda Islands (BALI, LOMBOK, SUMBAWA, SUMBA, and Flores, TIMOR, Alor, and adjacent smaller islands). Most of the islands are part of a geologically unstable and volcanically active ISLAND ARC. Malaysian cultures and languages predominate in the area.

Sunda Strait Channel between the islands of JAVA and SUMATRA. It is 16–70 mi (26–110 km) wide and links the Java Sea with the Indian Ocean. It contains several volcanic islands, the most famous of which is KRAKATAU.

Sundanese One of the three principal ethnic groups of the island of JAVA, Indonesia. They are a highland people of western Java, distinguished from the Javanese mainly by their language and their strict adherence to Islam. They are first mentioned in the 8th century AD. Once followers of Mahayana Buddhism, they converted to Islam in the 16th century under the influence of Muslim trade. Sundanese villages are ruled by a headman and a council of elders. Marriage, birth, and death ceremonies conform closely to the Javanese pattern, but are often mixed with Hindu elements. Modern developments have tended to erase differences between the Sundanese and other peoples of Java. Today they number about 26 million.

Sunday, Billy *orig.* **William Ashley** (1862/63–1935) U.S. revivalist. Born in Ames, Iowa, he became a professional baseball player with the Chicago White Sox in 1883 and later played for Pittsburgh and Philadelphia. In 1887 he underwent a conversion experience; he began preaching in 1897 and was ordained in the Presbyterian church in 1903. A flamboyant preacher of fundamentalist theology whose sermons reflected the social upheaval caused by the transition from a rural to an urban society, he advocated a strict morality and campaigned effectively for Prohibition. He conducted hundreds of revival meetings and reached an estimated 100 million people. His popularity faded in the 1920s, but he continued preaching until his death.

Sunderland Seaport (pop., 1999 est.: 289,040), northern England. Located at the mouth of the Wear River on the North Sea, it was known as Wearmouth in Saxon times; it formerly included Monkwearmouth, site of a monastery built in 674 where the Venerable BEDE studied. Sunderland itself (named for the part of Monkwearmouth "sundered" from the monastery by the river) was chartered in the late 12th century. The port grew rapidly as the coal trade developed in the 17th century, and by the mid-18th century it was a major shipbuilding center. Modern industries include glassware and automobile manufacturing.

Sunderland, Earl of *orig.* **Robert Spencer** (1641–1702) English statesman and chief adviser in the reigns of CHARLES II, JAMES II, and WILLIAM III. After a period in diplomatic service, he twice served as secretary of state (1679–81, 1683) and became the chief architect of Charles's pro-French foreign policy. He converted to Roman Catholicism to maintain his influence in James's reign. After William became king, Sunderland renounced his Catholicism and became the principal intermediary between the king and Parliament. He was appointed lord chamberlain in 1697, but Whig opposition soon forced him from office.

sundew Any of about 100 species of annual and perennial flowering CARNIVOROUS PLANTS in four genera, notably *Drosera,* that make up the family Droseraceae (sundew family). Sundews are found throughout tropical and temperate regions. Their leaves are usually in a basal rosette. Both leaf surfaces are generally covered with sticky, gland-tipped hairs and sensitive tentacles that trap insects. After the trapped prey has been digested by enzymes secreted by the tentacles, the leaf reopens, resetting the trap. The best-known sundew is the VENUS'S-FLYTRAP. See also PITCHER PLANT.

Sundiata \sůn-'jä-tə\ (died 1255) Monarch of the ancient MALI EMPIRE in western Africa. After organizing a private army and consolidating his position among his own MALINKE people, Sundiata launched attacks against neighboring states in the 1230s. In 1240 he seized and razed Kumbi, the last capital of the ancient empire of GHANA. During his reign over Mali he established its territorial base and laid the foundations for its future prosperity and political unity.

sunfish Any of numerous species of brightly colored North American carnivorous freshwater fishes placed with the CRAPPIES and BLACK BASSES in the family Centrarchidae. Usually less than 8 in. (20 cm) long, sunfishes are fine food and game fishes. The best known are the black-banded sunfish *(Enneacanthus chaetodon)* of the eastern U.S. and the bluegill *(Lepomis macrochirus),* which has an orange belly and blue markings. The longear sunfish has orange spots and wavy, bright blue streaks. The pumpkinseed, or common sunfish, has an orange belly and a red spot on its ear. The rock bass has irregular dark markings.

Pumpkinseed sunfish (*Lepomis gibbosus*).
JACQUES SIX

sunflower Any of 60 species of annual herbaceous plants in the genus *Helianthus* (COMPOSITE FAMILY), native mostly to North and South America. The common sunflower *(H. annuus)* has a rough, hairy stem 3–15 ft (1–4.5 m) high; broad, coarsely toothed, rough leaves 3–12 in. (7.5–30 cm) long; and large (3–6 in., or 7.5–15 cm, in diameter), flat, platelike compound flowers. Disk flowers swirl in a tight brown, yellow, or purple spiral; ray flowers are yellow. The leaves are used as fodder, the flowers yield a yellow dye, and the seeds contain oil and are used for food. The oil is used for cooking, as an ingredient of soaps and paints, and as a lubricant. Only a few species are cultivated, some for their spectacular size.

Sunflower (*Helianthus annuus*).
JOHN H. GERARD

Sung-chiang See SONGJIANG

Sung dynasty See SONG DYNASTY

Sung-hua River See SONGHUA RIVER

Sungari River See SONGHUA RIVER

sunna \'sù-nə\ Body of traditional social and legal custom and practice that constitutes proper observance of ISLAM. Early Muslims did not concur on what constituted sunna, owing to the wide variety of pre-Islamic practices among converted peoples that had to be assimilated, reconciled, or abandoned. In the 8th century, the sunna of MUHAMMAD, as preserved in eyewitness records, was codified as the HADITH by ABU ABD AL-LAH SHAFII. Later Muslim scholars strengthened the authority of sunna by devising a system for attesting the authenticity of various practices claimed as descending from Muhammad. See also ILM AL-HADITH, ISNAD, SHARIA, TAFSIR.

Sunni \'sù-nē\ Larger of the two major divisions of ISLAM, comprising 90% of the world's Muslims. Sunnis regard theirs as the mainstream and traditionalist branch of Islam, as distinguished from the minority branch, the SHIITES. Sunnis recognize the first four Umayyad caliphs (see UMAYYAD DYNASTY) as MUHAMMAD's rightful successors. Because the Sunnis understood Muhammad's theocratic state to have been an earthly, temporal dominion, they were willing to accept unexceptional and even foreign caliphs, provided order and religious orthodoxy were maintained. Sunni orthodoxy emphasizes consensus based on the views and customs of the majority of the community, thereby enabling them to incorporate various customs and usages that arose historically but that had no roots in the QURAN. Sunnis recognize the six authentic books of the HADITH and accept the four major schools of Islamic law. Today Sunni Muslims number about 1 billion.

Sunnyvale City (pop., 1996 est.: 125,000), western California, near SAN JOSE. Settled in 1850, it was incorporated in 1912. It was originally a fruit-processing center; its economic base shifted when the U.S. Navy built a dirigible base nearby in the 1930s and the Joshua Hendy Iron Works (later WESTINGHOUSE ELECTRIC CORP.) expanded in 1942. Its population grew rapidly in the 1960s. Chief manufactures include guided missiles.

Sunset Crater Volcano National Monument Preserve, northern central Arizona. Established in 1930, it covers 5 sq mi (13 sq km) and contains the brilliant-hued cinder cone of an extinct volcano that erupted c. 1064. It rises 1,000 ft (300 m) and has a crater 400 ft (120 m) deep and 1,280 ft (390 m) in diameter. The tract contains numerous lava flows, fumaroles, and lava beds.

sunspot Cooler-than-average region of gas on the SUN's surface associated with strong local magnetic activity. Sunspots appear as dark spots, but only in contrast with the surrounding PHOTOSPHERE, which is several thousand degrees hotter. Spots several times larger than earth are visible to the unaided eye (viewed through a filter); small ones are hard to see with a telescope. They come and go as part of the SOLAR CYCLE, usually in pairs or groups, and may last for months; their cause appears to be related to the magnetic field reversals that occur every 11 years. The reality of these apparent flaws in the sun was generally accepted only c. 1611. Periods of high sunspot activity are associated on earth with brighter AURORAS and interference with radio signals.

SUNY See State University of NEW YORK

Sunzi *or* **Sun-tzu** \'sün-'dzü\ (fl. 6th century BC) Chinese military strategist. A general who served the state of Wu late in the SPRING AND AUTUMN PERIOD (770–476 BC), he is traditionally regarded as the author of the earliest known treatise on war and military science, *The Art of War,* though it was more likely written early in the WARRING STATES PERIOD (475–221 BC). A systematic guide to STRATEGY and TACTICS, it discusses various maneuvers and the effect of terrain, stresses the importance of accurate information about the enemy's forces, and emphasizes the unpredictability of battle and the need for flexible responses. Its insistence on the close relationship between political considerations and military policy influenced modern strategists, notably MAO ZEDONG.

Super Bowl Annual championship game of the NATIONAL FOOTBALL LEAGUE, played by the winners of the league's American Football Conference and National Football Conference. The first Super Bowl competition was held in 1967. It normally falls in January, usually on the last Sunday, and is watched by more Americans than any other sporting event.

supercharger Air COMPRESSOR or blower used in piston-type INTERNAL-COMBUSTION ENGINES to increase the amount of air drawn into the cylinders by the movement of the pistons during each intake stroke. With the additional air, more fuel is burned, and the engine's power is increased. In aircraft engines, supercharging compensates for the reduced atmospheric pressure at high altitudes. Development of the gas TURBINE, which requires a constant flow of air and fuel, led to the turbosupercharger, a centrifugal blower driven by a small gas turbine powered by the exhaust gases from the engine cylinders.

supercomputer Any of a class of extremely powerful DIGITAL COMPUTERS. The term is commonly applied to the fastest high-performance systems available at a given time; current PERSONAL COMPUTERS are more powerful than the supercomputers of just a few years ago. Supercomputers are used primarily for scientific and engineering work. Unlike conventional computers, they usually have more than one CPU, often functioning in parallel (simultaneously); even higher-performance supercomputers are now being developed through use of massively parallel processing, incorporating thousands of individual processors. Supercomputers have huge storage capacity and very fast input/output capability, and can operate in parallel on corresponding elements of arrays of numbers rather than on one pair of elements at a time.

superconductivity Almost total lack of electrical RESISTANCE in certain materials when they are cooled to a temperature near ABSOLUTE ZERO. Superconducting materials allow low power dissipation, high-speed operation, and high sensitivity. They also have the ability to prevent external MAGNETIC FIELDS from penetrating their interiors and are perfect diamagnets (see DIAMAGNETISM). Since it was first discovered in mercury by HEIKE KAMERLINGH ONNES in 1911, similar behavior has been found in some 25 other chemical elements and in thousands of alloys and compounds. Superconductors have applications in medical imaging, magnetic energy-storage systems, motors, generators, transformers, computer components, and sensitive magnetic-field measuring devices.

superego In Freudian psychoanalytic theory, one of the three aspects of the human personality, along with the ID and the EGO. The last of the three elements to develop, the superego is the ethical component of the personality, providing the moral standards by which the ego operates. The superego is formed during the first five years of life in response to parental punishment and approval; children internalize their parents' moral standards as well as those of the surrounding society, and the developing superego serves to control aggressive or other socially unacceptable impulses. Violation of the superego's standards gives rise to feelings of guilt or anxiety.

superfluidity Unusual property of liquid HELIUM cooled below –455.75°F (–270.97°C). At such low temperatures, helium exhibits an enormous rise in heat conductivity and rapid flow through capillaries or over the rim of its container. To explain such behavior, the substance is described in terms of a "two-fluid" mixture model consisting of normal helium and superfluid helium. In normal helium the atoms are in excited states (see EXCITATION), whereas in superfluid helium they are in their ground state. As the temperature is lowered below –455.75°F, more of the helium becomes superfluid. It is assumed that the superfluid component can move through the container without FRICTION, thereby explaining the unusual behavior.

Superfund Government fund intended to pay for cleanup of hazardous-waste dump sites and spills. The 1980 act creating it called for its financing by a combination of general revenues and taxes on polluting industries. The ENVIRONMENTAL PROTECTION AGENCY was mandated to create a list of the most dangerous sites and either to compel the polluter to pay for their cleanup or to pay for the cleanup through Superfund and sue for reimbursement. By 1995 it had received $30 billion but had completed work on fewer than 100 sites, and was universally criticized for waste and mismanagement. See also LOVE CANAL.

supergiant star STAR of very great natural luminosity and relatively enormous size, typically several MAGNITUDES brighter and several times larger than a GIANT STAR. Like other classes of stars, they are distinguished in practice by examination of certain lines in their spectra (see SPECTROSCOPY). A supergiant may have a diameter several hundred times that of the sun and a luminosity nearly a million times as great. Supergiants live probably only a few million years, an extremely short life for a star.

Superior, Lake Lake, U.S. and Canada. The largest of the five GREAT LAKES, it is the world's largest freshwater lake. It is 383 mi (616 km) long and 160 mi (258 km) at its widest, with an area of 31,800 sq mi (82,362 sq km) and depths reaching 1,330 ft (405 m). It is known for its picturesque coastline and its numerous shipwrecks; its islands include Isle Royale. The head of the Great Lakes–ST. LAWRENCE SEAWAY system, it is connected to Lake HURON at its southeastern end via the SAULT STE. MARIE LOCKS. Ships transport grain, flour, and iron ore during the eight-month navigation season. The French Jesuit missionary Claude-Jean Allouez charted the lake in 1667. The region came under British control 1763–83 and remained in British hands until 1817, when the AMERICAN FUR CO. took over south of the Canadian border.

supermarket Large retail store operated on a self-service basis, selling groceries, produce, meat, bakery and dairy products, and sometimes nonfood goods. Supermarkets were first established in the U.S. during the 1930s as no-frills retail stores offering low prices. In the 1940s and '50s they became the major food marketing channel in the U.S.; the 1950s also saw them spread through much of Europe. Their growth is part of a trend in developed countries toward reducing cost and simplifying MARKETING. In the 1960s supermarkets appeared in developing countries in the Middle East, Asia, and Latin America, where they are patronized largely by the upper middle class.

supernova Any of a class of violently exploding stars whose luminosity after eruption suddenly increases to millions or even billions of times its normal level. Like NOVAS, supernovas undergo a tremendous, rapid brightening lasting a few weeks, followed by a slow dimming, and show blue-shifted emission lines on SPECTROSCOPY, implying that hot gases are blown outward. A supernova explosion is a catastrophic event for a star, leading to its collapse into a NEUTRON STAR or BLACK HOLE. Amounts of its matter equal to the mass of several suns may be blasted into space with such a burst of energy that the exploding star outshines its entire home galaxy. Only seven supernovas are known to have been recorded before the 17th century, the most famous in AD 1054; the latter's remnants are visible today as the CRAB NEBULA. Supernova explosions release not only tremendous amounts of RADIO energy and X RAYS but also COSMIC RAYS and many of the heavier ELEMENTS that make up the components of the solar system.

superstring theory Any of a number of theories in PARTICLE PHYSICS that treat elementary particles (see SUBATOMIC PARTICLE) as infinitesimal one-dimensional "stringlike" objects rather than dimensionless points in SPACE-TIME. Different vibrations of the strings correspond to different particles. Introduced in the early 1970s in attempts to describe the STRONG FORCE, superstring theories became popular in the 1980s when it was shown that they might provide a fully self-consistent QUANTUM FIELD THEORY that could describe gravity as well as the WEAK, strong, and ELECTROMAGNETIC forces. The development of a unified quantum field theory is a major goal in theoretical particle physics, but inclusion of gravity usually leads to difficult problems with infinite quantities in the calculations. The most promising superstring theories propose 10 dimensions; four correspond to the three ordinary spatial dimensions and time, while the rest are curled up and not perceptible.

supervenience \ˌsü-pər-ˈvēn-yəns\ In philosophy, the asymmetrical RELATION of ontological dependence that holds between two generically different sets of properties (e.g., mental and physical properties) if and only if every change in an object's properties belonging to the first set—the supervening properties—entails and is due to a change in properties belonging to the second set (the base properties). Supervenience has often been appealed to by philosophers who want to uphold physicalism while rejecting the IDENTITY THEORY: Though it may be impossible to identify mental properties with physical properties in a one-to-one fashion, mental properties may still supervene on, and thus be grounded in, physical properties. Thus, no two things that are physically alike can be mentally (or psychologically) different, and a being's mental properties will be determined by its physical ones.

supply and demand Relationship between the quantity of a commodity that producers have available for sale and the quantity that consumers are willing and able to buy. Demand depends on the PRICE of the commodity, the prices of related commodities, and consumers' incomes and tastes. Supply depends not only on the price obtainable for the commodity but also on the prices of similar products, the techniques of production, and the availability and costs of inputs. The function of the MARKET is to equalize demand and supply through the price mechanism. If buyers want to purchase more of a commodity than is available on the market, they will tend to bid the price up. If more of a commodity is available than buyers care to purchase, suppliers will bid prices down. Thus, there is a tendency toward an equilibrium price at which the quantity demanded equals the quantity supplied. The measure of the responsiveness of supply and demand to changes in price is their elasticity.

supply-side economics Theory that focuses on influencing the supply of labor and goods, using tax cuts and benefit cuts as incentives to work and produce goods. It was expounded by the U.S. economist Arthur Laffer (born 1940) and implemented by Pres. RONALD REAGAN in the 1980s. Supporters point to the economic growth of the 1980s as proof of its efficacy; detractors point to the massive federal deficits and speculation that accompanied that growth.

suprarenal gland See ADRENAL GLAND

Supremacy, Act of (1534) English act of Parliament that recognized HENRY VIII as the "Supreme Head of the Church of England." The act also required an oath of loyalty from English subjects that recognized his marriage to ANNE BOLEYN. It was repealed in 1555 under MARY I, but in 1559 Parliament adopted a new Act of Supremacy during the reign of ELIZABETH I.

Suprematism First movement of pure geometrical abstraction in art, introduced in Russia c. 1913. Originated by KAZIMIR MALEVICH and disseminated by EL LISSITZKY and the BAUHAUS school, it had far-reaching influence on Western art and design. Malevich aimed to convey the "supremacy of feeling in art," which he believed could be expressed through the simplest of visual forms. He exhibited the first Suprematist compositions in 1915, the year he issued the Suprematist manifesto. The purest embodiment of Suprematist ideals can be seen in his *White on White* series (1917–18).

Supreme Court of the United States Final court of APPEAL in the U.S. judicial system and final interpreter of the U.S. CONSTITUTION. The

Court was instituted by the Constitution in 1787 and granted authority to act in cases arising under the Constitution, laws, or treaties of the U.S.; in controversies to which the U.S. is a party; in controversies between states or between citizens of different states; in cases of admiralty and maritime jurisdiction; and in cases affecting ambassadors or other ministers or consuls. Its size, which is set by Congress, varied somewhat before stabilizing at nine in 1869. Appointments to the Court are made by the president with the advice and consent of the Senate. The Court has from an early date exercised the power of JUDICIAL REVIEW. Relatively few cases are brought in its original jurisdiction. The usual route to the Court is by appeal or CERTIORARI. Among the most important doctrinal sources used by the Court have been the COMMERCE, DUE-PROCESS, and EQUAL-PROTECTION clauses of the Constitution. It also has often ruled on controversies involving CIVIL LIBERTIES, including FREEDOM OF SPEECH and rights of PRIVACY. Much of its work consists of clarifying, refining, and testing the Constitution's philosophic ideals and translating them into working principles.

Supremes U.S. vocal trio, one of the most successful female groups in history. The original Supremes—Diana Ross (born 1944), Mary Wilson (born 1944), and Florence Ballard (1939–1976)—began recording for Motown (as The Primettes) on graduating from high school in Detroit. Their long string of MOTOWN hits in the mid-1960s, many written by BRIAN AND EDDIE HOLLAND and Lamont Dozier, began with "Where Did Our Love Go?" In 1966 Ballard was replaced with Cindy Birdsong (born 1939). Ross left the Supremes in 1969, and Wilson left in 1977. Ballard died in relative poverty of cardiac arrest. The group inspired the Broadway musical *Dreamgirls* (1981). Ross's highly successful solo career has included film roles (notably in *Lady Sings the Blues,* 1972) and a free 1983 Central Park concert that drew an audience of record-setting size.

Sur See TYRE

sura *or* **surah** Any chapter of the QURAN. Each of the 114 suras, which vary in length from several words to several pages, encompasses one or more revelations of MUHAMMAD. All but three are in the form of an address from God. The general tone is moralistic, demanding obedience to a transcendent but compassionate God. Except for the opening sura, known as *fatiha,* they are arranged in descending order of length and numbered serially. They carry conventional names (e.g., Cow, Spider, Blood Clot) deriving from some image contained in them that is not necessarily indicative of their meaning or theme.

Surabaya \ˌsu̇r-ə-ˈbī-ə\ Seaport city (pop., 1995 est.: 2,701,000), northeastern coast of JAVA, Indonesia. It is Indonesia's second-largest city and has been eastern Java's chief trading center since the 14th century. The Dutch gained control in the 18th century and built their main East Indies naval base there. Occupied by the Japanese in World War II, it suffered heavy damage; it was damaged again during Indonesia's war for independence (1945–49). It is the site of Indonesia's main naval base and a naval college, and of Airlangga University (1954).

Surat \ˈsu̇r-ət, sə-ˈrat\ City (metro. area pop., 2001 prelim.: 2,811,466), southeastern GUJARAT state, western central India. It is near the mouth of the TAPI RIVER and the Gulf of KHAMBHAT. A major seaport from the 16th century, it was conquered by the Mughals in 1573 and was twice sacked by the Marathas in the 17th century. It became a center for textile manufacturing and shipbuilding. The British established their first Indian trading station there c. 1612, marking the beginning of the British empire in India. It served as the seat of the British Indian government until the late 17th century, when the seat was moved to Bombay (now MUMBAI). It declined in the 18th century but prospered again with the opening of India's railways. Surat's cottons, silks, brocades, and objects of gold and silver are still famous.

surface In geometry, a two-dimensional collection of points (flat surface), a three-dimensional collection of points whose cross section is a CURVE (curved surface), or the boundary of any three-dimensional solid. In general, a surface is a continuous boundary dividing a three-dimensional space into two regions. For example, the surface of a sphere separates the interior from the exterior; a horizontal plane separates the half-plane above it from the half-plane below. Surfaces are often called by the names of the regions they enclose, but a surface is essentially two-dimensional and has an area, while the region it encloses is three-dimensional and has a volume. The attributes of surfaces, and in particular the idea of CURVATURE, are investigated in DIFFERENTIAL GEOMETRY.

surface Outermost layer of a material or substance. Because the particles (ATOMS OR MOLECULES) on the surface have nearest neighbors beside and below but not above, the physical and chemical properties of a surface differ from those of the bulk material; surface chemistry is thus a branch of PHYSICAL CHEMISTRY. The growth of CRYSTALS, the actions of CATALYSTS and DETERGENTS, and the phenomena of ADSORPTION, SURFACE TENSION, and CAPILLARITY are aspects of behavior at surfaces. The appearance of the surface, whether achieved with ELECTROPLATING, PAINT, OXIDATION–REDUCTION, bleaching (see BLEACH), or another means, is esthetically important.

surface integral In calculus, the INTEGRAL of a function of several variables calculated over a SURFACE. For functions of a single variable, definite integrals are calculated over intervals on the x-axis and result in areas. For functions of two variables, the simplest double integrals are calculated over rectangular regions and result in volumes. More generally, an integral calculated over a plane or curved surface results in a surface integral representing a volume, though it also has many nongeometric applications.

surface mining See STRIP MINING

surface tension Property of a liquid surface that causes it to act like a stretched elastic membrane (see ELASTICITY). Its strength depends on the forces of attraction among the particles of the liquid itself and with the particles of the gas, solid, or liquid with which it comes in contact. Surface tension allows certain insects to stand on the surface of water and can support a razor blade placed horizontally on the liquid's surface, even though the blade may be denser than the liquid and unable to float. Surface tension results in spherical drops of liquid, as the liquid tends to minimize its surface area.

surfing Sport of riding breaking waves toward the shore, especially with a surfboard. The sport originated prehistorically in the South Seas. In 1777 and 1778 Capt. JAMES COOK first reported seeing surfers in Tahiti and on Oahu. In 1821 surfing was banned by missionaries who thought it immoral. It was revived in the 1920s by the famous Hawaiian swimmer Duke Kahanamoku (1890–1968). Today surfing is enjoyed on beaches with breakers throughout the world, and several international championships are held. The goal is to maneuver on the unbroken face of the wave, preferably as far back toward the curl ("tube") as possible. In addition to surfboards, surfers can use belly- and kneeboards or kayaks, or they can bodysurf using no vehicle at all.

surgeonfish *or* **tang** Any of about 75 species (family Acanthuridae) of thin, deep-bodied, tropical marine fishes that are small-scaled, with a single dorsal fin and one or more distinctive, sharp spines on either side of the tail base. The spines resemble a surgeon's scalpel and may be either fixed or hinged at the rear so that they can be opened outward and directed forward. Surgeonfishes are mostly algae eaters and usually do not exceed 20 in. (50 cm) long. The yellow surgeon, or yellow tang *(Zebrasoma flavescens),* is an Indo-Pacific species, and the blue tang *(Acanthurus coeruleus)* is found in the Atlantic and Caribbean.

Surgeonfish *(Acanthurus leucosternon).*
JANE BURTON—BRUCE COLEMAN LTD.

surgery Branch of medicine concerned with treatment by physical means rather than drugs. In addition to operations requiring access to the inside of the body (open surgery), it includes manipulation from outside the body (e.g., setting of a broken bone, skin grafts). Modern surgery began in the mid-19th century with use of ANESTHETICS and ANTISEPTICS. Other important advances have included DIAGNOSTIC IMAGING, BLOOD TYPING, intubation to support breathing, intravenous administration of fluids and drugs, heart-lung machines (see ARTIFICIAL HEART), ENDOSCOPY, and devices that monitor body functions. Specialized instruments used in surgery include scalpels to cut tissue, forceps to hold blood vessels closed or grasp and manipulate structures, clamps to immobilize or crush tissues, gauze sponges to absorb fluids and keep an area dry, retractors to hold incisions open, and curved needles to suture them closed. Pre- and postoperative care is crucial to the success of surgery. See also MICROSURGERY, OPEN-HEART SURGERY, ORTHOPEDICS, PLASTIC SURGERY, TRANSPLANT.

Suriname \ˌsu̇-rə-ˈnä-mə\ *officially* **Republic of Suriname** *formerly* **Dutch Guiana** Nation, northern central coast of South America. Area: 63,251 sq mi (163,820 sq km). Population (1997 est.): 424,000. Capital: PARAMARIBO. The population includes East Indians, Creoles, Javanese, and smaller groups of blacks, Chinese, South American Indians, and Dutch. Languages: Dutch (official), English, Sranan (a creole), Hindi. Religions: Christianity; also Hinduism and Islam. Currency: Suriname guilder. The country has a low, narrow coastal plain, with inland savannas, a forested plateau region, and mountain ranges. Seven major rivers, including the COURANTYNE, MARONI, and SURINAME, cross it to empty into the Atlantic. Bauxite mining, aluminum production, and agriculture are the largest sectors of the economy. Exports include rice, bananas, sugar-

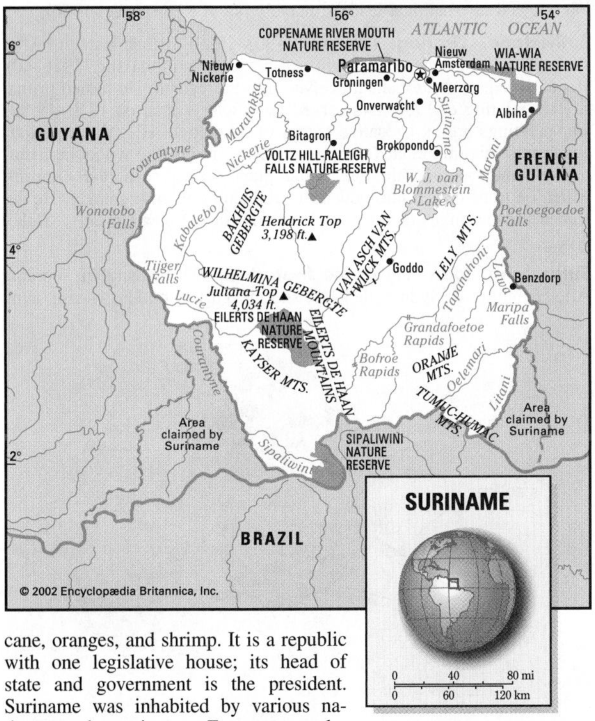

cane, oranges, and shrimp. It is a republic with one legislative house; its head of state and government is the president. Suriname was inhabited by various native peoples prior to European settlement. Spanish explorers claimed it in 1593, but the Dutch began to settle there in 1602, followed by the English in 1651. It was ceded to the Dutch in 1667, and in 1682 the Dutch West India Co. introduced coffee and sugarcane plantations and African slaves to cultivate them. Slavery was abolished in 1863, and indentured servants were brought from China, Java, and India to work the plantations, adding to the population mix. Except for brief interludes of British rule (1799–1802, 1804–15), it remained a Dutch colony. It gained internal autonomy in 1954 and independence in 1975. A military coup in 1980 ended civilian control until the electorate approved a new constitution in 1987. Military control resumed after a coup in 1990. Elections were held in 1992, followed by a resumption of democratic government.

Suriname River River, central and eastern Suriname. Rising in the highlands and flowing northeastward some 300 mi (480 km), it empties into the Atlantic Ocean just north of PARAMARIBO. It was dammed at Afobaka to create W. J. van Blommestein Lake, the largest in Suriname.

Surma River \ˈsu̇r-mə\ River, northeastern India and eastern Bangladesh. It rises in northern MANIPUR state, India, where it is called the Barak River, and flows west into Bangladesh. There it passes through a rich tea-growing valley and eventually enters an old channel of the BRAHMAPUTRA and becomes the MEGHNA RIVER, before entering the GANGES. It is 560 mi (900 km) long.

Surrealism Movement in the visual arts and literature that flourished in Europe between World Wars I and II. It developed in reaction against the "rationalism" that had led to World War I. The movement was founded in 1924 by ANDRE BRETON as a means of joining dream and fantasy to everyday reality to form "an absolute reality, a surreality." Drawing on the theories of SIGMUND FREUD, he concluded that the unconscious was the wellspring of the imagination. Breton was a poet, but Surrealism's major achievements were in painting. Surrealist painting is diverse, influenced by DADA, HIERONYMUS BOSCH, ODILON REDON, and GIORGIO DE CHIRICO. Some artists practiced organic, emblematic, or absolute Surrealism, expressing the unconscious through suggestive yet indefinite biomorphic images (JEAN ARP, MAX ERNST, ANDRE MASSON, JOAN MIRO). Others created realistically painted images, removed from their context and reassembled within a paradoxical or shocking framework (SALVADOR DALÍ, RENE MAGRITTE).

Surrey County (pop., 1995 est.: 1,044,000), southern England. It is located southwest of LONDON. Sheep raising was an important medieval activity, and by the 16th century a cloth trade was also growing. Its forested hills were a source of timber for charcoal, construction, and shipbuilding. Transport of these products, originally dependent on rivers, was facilitated in 1801 when the Surrey Iron Railway was established as the first public railway. During the 19th century, the world's densest network of suburban railways developed in northern Surrey. Suburban growth continued after World War II, proceeding under planning restraints.

Surrey, Earl of *orig.* **Henry Howard** (1517–1547) English poet. Because of his aristocratic birth and connections, Surrey was involved in the jockeying for place that accompanied HENRY VIII's policies. After returning to England in 1546 from a campaign abroad, he was accused of treason by his rivals. After his sister admitted he was still a Roman Catholic, he was executed at age 30. Most of his poetry was published 10 years later. With THOMAS WYATT, he introduced into England the styles and meters of the Italian humanist poets, laying the foundation of a great age in English poetry. He translated two books of VIRGIL's *Aeneid,* marking the first use in English of BLANK VERSE; and was the first to develop the SONNET form used by WILLIAM SHAKESPEARE.

surrogate motherhood Practice in which a woman (the surrogate mother) bears a child for a couple unable to produce children, usually because the wife is infertile or unable to carry a pregnancy to term. The surrogate is impregnated either through ARTIFICIAL INSEMINATION (usually with the sperm of the husband) or through the implantation of an in-vitro embryo. The surrogate traditionally gives up all parental rights, but in recent years this has been subject to legal challenge.

Surtees, Robert Smith (1803–1864) English novelist. Passionately addicted to riding to hounds from his youth, Surtees devoted nearly all his writings to horses and riding. In 1831 he launched *New Sporting Magazine*. His famous comic character Mr. Jorrocks, a blunt Cockney grocer entirely given over to fox hunting, appeared in *Jorrocks's Jaunts and Jollities* (1838), *Handley Cross* (1843), and *Hillingdon Hall* (1845). Among his other novels, which also portray the boredom, ill manners, discomfort, and coarse food of English provincial life, are *Hawbuck Grange* (1847) and *Mr. Facey Romford's Hounds* (1865).

Surtsey \ˈsərt-sē\ Volcanic island off southern Iceland. It emerged from the ocean in a fiery eruption in November 1963. Over four years its volcanic core built up an island 1 sq mi (2.5 sq km) in area, with elevations over 560 ft (170 m). Named for the fire god of Icelandic mythology, it is now a nature reserve and the site of a joint Icelandic-U.S. biological research program.

surveying Method of making relatively large-scale, accurate measurements of the earth's surfaces. Its principal modern uses are in the fields of transportation, building, land use, and communications. Surveying is divided into the categories of plane surveying (mapping small areas) and geodetic surveying (mapping large areas of the globe). The Romans are said to have used the plane table, which consists of a drawing board mounted on a tripod or other support and a straightedge along which lines are drawn. It was the first device capable of recording or establishing angles. With the publication of logarithmic tables in 1620, portable angle-measuring instruments, called topographic instruments, or theodolites, came into use; they included pivoted arms for sighting and could be used for measuring both horizontal and vertical angles. Two revolutionary 20th-century innovations were photogrammetry (mapping from aerial photographs) and electronic distance measurement, including the use of the laser.

Surveyor Any of a series of seven unmanned U.S. space probes sent to the MOON 1966–68. Surveyor 2 crashed on the moon, and radio contact with Surveyor 4 was lost minutes before landing, but the rest sent back thousands of photographs; some were equipped to sample and test lunar soil. Surveyor 6 made the first liftoff from an extraterrestrial body; Surveyor 7 landed in the lunar highlands and returned data showing that the landscape and soil there differ from those of lower areas. See also LUNA, PIONEER, RANGER.

Surya In HINDUISM, the sun and the sun god. Though once ranking with the major Hindu deities, he is now primarily worshiped only as one of the five important deities of the SMARTA sect and as the supreme deity by the small Savra sect. Nevertheless, he is still invoked by all orthodox Hindus in daily prayer, and his temples are found throughout India. He is the father of MANU, YAMA, and several other gods. The PURANAS record that the weapons of the gods were forged from pieces trimmed from Surya.

Surya, stone image from Deo-Barunarak, Bihar, India, 9th century AD.
PRAMOD CHANDRA

Suryavarman II \ˌsu̇r-yə-ˈvär-mən\ (died c. 1150) Cambodian king under whom ANGKOR WAT was built. Suryavarman established sole rule over Cambodia c. 1113, reuniting the country after 50 years of unrest. He expanded his country to include much of what is now Thailand, portions of Vietnam, and part of the Malay Peninsula. He promulgated VAISHNAVISM (a form of Hinduism), rather than the Buddhism of his predecessors, as the official religion. Construction of Angkor Wat, the world's largest religious structure, began under Suryavarman, and he figures prominently in its decorations. He died during a campaign against the kingdom of CHAMPA; the Chams eventually ravaged Angkor.

Susanna Figure in an apocryphal book of the Bible. The History of Susanna, set in Babylon during the Jewish exile, tells of a woman falsely accused of adultery by two elders who had earlier tried to seduce her. She is saved from death by DANIEL's intervention. The tale is one of a cycle of traditions added to the Book of Daniel when it was translated into Greek. The scene in which the elders spy on her at her bath was a popular subject for Renaissance artists.

Suslov \ˈsüs-ˌlȯf\, **Mikhail (Andreyevich)** (1902–1982) Soviet ideologue. He joined the Communist Party in 1921 and was sent to Moscow for his education, after which he taught economics. In the 1930s he helped supervise the Stalinist purges in the Urals and the Ukraine. Later a leading official in the Caucasus, he supervised the deportation of ethnic minorities in World War II. He was appointed to the Politburo in 1952, and from 1955 he held a pivotal position in the ruling clique. A political conservative, he helped NIKITA KHRUSHCHEV quell a conspiracy in the Politburo in 1957, but organized the bloodless coup in 1964 that ousted Khrushchev and substituted LEONID BREZHNEV.

suspension, automobile Elastic members designed to cushion the impact of road irregularities on a portion of an automotive vehicle. The members link the vehicle's tires with its suspended portion, and usually consist of springs and shock absorbers. Spring elements used for automobile suspension members include (in increasing order of ability to store elastic energy per unit of weight) leaf springs, coil springs, torsion bars, rubber-in-shear devices, and air springs. The springs absorb the energy of impacts of the tires along the road surface, and the shocks damp or dissipate that energy, using hydraulics, so that the suspended portion of the vehicle does not keep bouncing. See illustration opposite.

Susquehanna River \ˌsəs-kwə-ˈha-nə\ River, central New York, Pennsylvania, and Maryland. One of the longest rivers in the eastern U.S., it is about 444 mi (715 km) long. It rises in Otsego Lake, central New York, and winds through the APPALACHIAN MTNS. before flowing into northern CHESAPEAKE BAY. Though it was never an important waterway because of obstructions, including rapids, its valley was a significant land route to the OHIO RIVER system, and later a coal mining region.

Susskind \ˈsəs-ˌkīnd\, **David (Howard)** (1920–1987) U.S. television producer and host. Born in New York City, he worked as a publicist before forming the agency Talent Associates in 1952. He produced numerous television programs, including *Circle Theater* (1955–63) and *Dupont Show of the Month* (1957–64), but became best known as host of the talk shows *Open End* (1958–67) and *The David Susskind Show* (1967–86). Noted for his provocative discussions of such controversial issues as race relations, organized crime, and the Vietnam War, he also interviewed international leaders, notably NIKITA KHRUSHCHEV (1960).

Sutherland, Graham (Vivian) (1903–1980) British painter. After studying art in London, he taught and practiced printmaking (1926–40). His early representationalism evolved into Surrealism. He turned primarily to painting c. 1935, and served as official war artist 1940–45; his war paintings are an evocative record of desolation. His "thorn period" began with his important *Crucifixion* (1946); in his late works he incorporated anthropomorphic insect and plant forms, particularly thorns, which he transformed into powerful, frightening totemic images. He designed the enormous tapestry (c. 1955–61) for the new Coventry Cathedral.

Sutherland, Joan *later* **Dame Joan** (born 1926) Australian soprano. After debuting in Sydney in 1947, she moved to London. Having sung

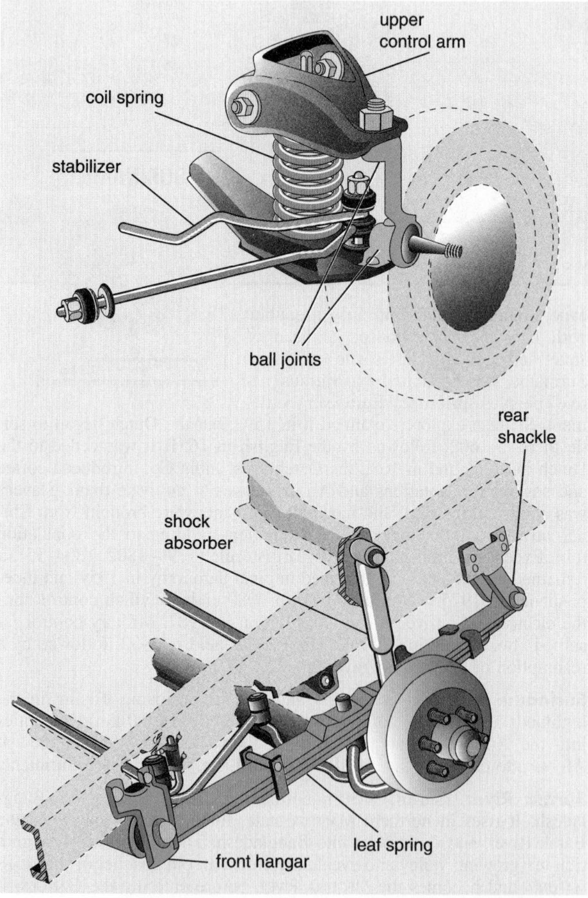

A vehicle is suspended over its wheels by springs, usually either coil or leaf springs. Irregularities in the road surface are transmitted mechanically to the springs. The energy in the compressed springs is dissipated by shock absorbers mounted inside coil springs or beside leaf springs.

minor roles at Covent Garden from 1952, she established her status as a major star in 1959 in *Lucia di Lammermoor*. She made her Metropolitan Opera debut in 1961, and her gloriously beautiful voice made her a favorite there and worldwide in bel canto roles until her retirement in 1991. She almost invariably performed under the baton of her husband, Richard Bonynge (born 1930).

Sutlej River \'sət-ˌlej\ River, Asia. The longest of the "Five Rivers" that give PUNJAB its name, it is 900 mi (1,450 km) long. It rises in southwestern Tibet and flows west through the HIMALAYAS, across HIMACHAL PRADESH and Punjab, India, then southwest across Punjab province of Pakistan. It forms 65 mi (105 km) of the Indo–Pakistani border. It joins the CHENAB RIVER in Pakistan to become the Panjnad, the link between the Five Rivers and the INDUS. Its middle course is used extensively for irrigation.

sutra \'sü-trə\ *Pali* **sutta** In HINDUISM, a brief aphoristic composition; in BUDDHISM, a more extended exposition of a subject and the basic form of the SCRIPTURE of both THERAVADA and MAHAYANA traditions. Since the early Indian philosophers did not work with written texts at all, and later philosophers often disdained them, there was a need for very brief explanatory works that could be committed to memory. The earliest sutras were expositions of ritual procedures, but their use spread, and eventually nearly all Indian philosophical systems had their own sutras. See also AVATAMSAKA-SUTRA, DIAMOND SUTRA, LOTUS SUTRA, TRIPITAKA.

Sutta Pitaka \'sůt-tə-'pi-tə-kə\ Major section of the TRIPITAKA, the canon of THERAVADA Buddhism, largely attributed to the BUDDHA himself. It is divided into five collections, or *nikayas:* the Digha nikaya ("Long Collection"), containing 34 lengthy SUTRAS, including some of the most important doctrinal expositions; the Majjhima nikaya ("Medium Collection"), containing 152 sutras dealing with a variety of subjects; the Samyutta nikaya ("Cluster Collection"), with more than 7,000 sutras arranged according to subject; the Anguttara nikaya ("Gradual Collection"), a numerical arrangement, for mnemonic purposes, of 9,557 terse sutras, and the KHUDDAKA NIKAYA. See also ABHIDHAMMA PITAKA, VINAYA PITAKA.

suttee *or* **sati** \'sə-ˌtē, ˌsə-'tē\ Indian practice whereby a widow burns herself to death either on the funeral pyre of her husband or soon after his death. The custom may be rooted in ancient beliefs that a husband needed his companions in the afterlife, though opponents point to it as an indication of a value system deeply hostile to women. Developed by the 4th century BC, it became widespread in the 17th–18th century but was banned in British India in 1829. Frequent instances of suttee continued to occur for many years thereafter, and occasional instances in remote areas are still reported today.

Sutter, John (Augustus) *orig.* **Johann August Suter** (1803–1880) U.S. (German-born) pioneer. Fleeing financial failures, he left his family in Switzerland and arrived in the U.S. in 1834. He obtained a land grant from the Mexican governor and established the colony of Nueva Helvetia (later SACRAMENTO, Cal.). On the American River he built Sutter's Fort, a frontier trading post, in 1841. When gold was found there in 1848, he tried to keep it a secret. In the resulting GOLD RUSH, squatters and gold seekers invaded his land and stole his goods and livestock. U.S. courts denied his claim to his Mexican land grant, and Sutter was bankrupt by 1852.

Sutton, Walter S(tanborough) (1877–1916) U.S. geneticist. Born in Utica, N.Y., he received a medical degree from Columbia University and practiced surgery the rest of his life. In 1902 he provided the earliest detailed demonstration that somatic chromosomes (those in cells other than sex cells) occur in distinct pairs of like chromosomes, hypothesizing that chromosomes carry the units of inheritance and that their behavior during meiosis is the physical basis of GREGOR MENDEL's law of heredity. In 1903 he concluded that chromosomes contain genes and that their behavior during meiosis is random. His work formed the basis for the chromosomal theory of HEREDITY.

Sutton Hoo Estate in Suffolk, England, the site of the grave or cenotaph of an Anglo-Saxon king. One of the richest Germanic burials ever found in Europe (1939), the Sutton Hoo site contained an 80-ft (24-m) wooden ship equipped for the afterlife (but no body). It displayed both pagan and Christian features, and its grave goods included solid gold and silver objects such as cups and bowls. The burial may have been for Raedwald (died 624?) or Aethelhere (died 654). Parallels to Swedish finds suggest a possible Swedish origin for the East Anglian royal dynasty.

Suva Seaport town (metro. area pop., 1996 est.: 167,000), capital of Fiji. It has one of the best harbors in the southern Pacific. Founded in 1849, it was made a city in 1952 and is now one of the largest urban centers in the South Pacific islands. It is Fiji's chief port and commercial center, and the site of educational and cultural institutions.

Suvorov \sü-'vò-ròf\, **Aleksandr (Vasilyevich)** (1729–1800) Russian army commander. Joining the army at 15, he became an officer in 1754 and served in the Seven Years' War. He wrote a battle-training manual that helped Russia win the Russo–Polish conflict of 1768–72 and a conflict with the Turks in 1773–74. He led the army in the Russo–Turkish War and was created a count. After crushing a revolt in Poland in 1794, he was promoted to field marshal. He commanded a Russo-Austrian force in Italy in 1799 and captured Milan, expelling most of the French army from Italy. Ordered to relieve a Russian force in Switzerland, he marched across the Alps; surrounded by a larger French force, he succeeded in breaking out and, repulsing the pursuing French, escaped with most of his army, a remarkable feat.

Suwannee River \sə-'wä-nē\ River, southeastern Georgia and northern Florida. It rises in the OKEFENOKEE SWAMP and enters the Gulf of MEXICO at Suwannee Sound after a course of 250 mi (400 km). All but 35 mi (56 km) of its course are in Florida. It is the Swanee River of S. FOSTER's famed "Old Folks at Home." In the 1780s the bays and inlets of Suwannee Sound were rendezvous points for pirates.

Suzdal \'süz-dəl\ Medieval principality, between the OKA RIVER and the Upper VOLGA, northeastern Russia. Ruled by a branch of the RURIK dynasty during the 12th–14th century, it united with ROSTOV, and in the 12th century with Vladimir. Suzdal-Vladimir achieved great political and economic importance, but disintegrated into small principalities in the 13th–14th century, which ultimately were absorbed by Moscow. See also VLADIMIR–SUZDAL SCHOOL.

Suzman \'sůz-män\, **Helen,** *orig.* **Helen Gavronsky** (born 1917) South African legislator. Born in the Transvaal to Lithuanian immigrants, she graduated from the University of Witwatersrand, where she later taught economic history (1945–52). Elected to Parliament in 1953, she and 11 others formed the Progressive Party to oppose APARTHEID. Suzman alone of the group was reelected in 1961; until 1974 she often cast the lone vote against an increasing number of apartheid measures. In 1978 she received the U.N. Human Rights award. Until her retirement in 1989, she remained a significant voice in the South African Parliament.

Svalbard \'sfäl-ˌbär\ Archipelago, Arctic Ocean, north of the Arctic Circle. It consists of nine main islands, including the SPITSBERGEN group. The islands are mountainous, with glaciers and snowfields covering nearly 60% of the area. The islands were first visited in modern times by the Dutch in 1596. In the early 20th century, many countries, including the U.S., debated ownership of mineral rights there. Officially a Norwegian possession since 1925, the islands have been the site of many scientific polar expeditions (beginning in 1773). The population changes seasonally but numbers about 3,000; there are no indigenous inhabitants. Longyearbyen is the administrative center.

Svealand \'svā-ə-ˌländ\ Region, southern central Sweden. Stretching across the breadth of the country, it covers an area of 31,212 sq mi (80,844 sq km). Settled as early as the Stone Age, it was the original home of the Svear, a people who gave Sweden its name, and was the political and cultural center from which Sweden developed and later secured its independence. Its diversified economy includes agriculture, manufacturing, forestry, and mining.

Svedberg \'svād-ˌbarʸ, *Engl* 'sved-ˌbərg\, **The(odor)** (1884–1971) Swedish chemist. He won a Nobel Prize in 1926 for his studies in the chemistry of COLLOIDS and for his invention of the ultracentrifuge (see CENTRIFUGE), which has become invaluable to research in biochemistry and other areas. Svedberg used it to determine precisely the MOLECULAR WEIGHTS of highly complex proteins (e.g., HEMOGLOBIN). Later he made studies in nuclear chemistry, contributed to the improvement of the CYCLOTRON, and helped his student Arne Tiselius (1902–1971) develop ELECTROPHORESIS.

Sverdlov \'svʸerd-lȯf\, **Yakov (Mikhaylovich)** (1885–1919) Soviet politician. He became a Bolshevik organizer and agitator in the Urals, for which he was often arrested and exiled. In the RUSSIAN REVOLUTION OF 1917, he headed the Bolshevik secretariat and helped plan and execute the October coup that brought the Bolsheviks to power. As titular head of state, he worked closely with VLADIMIR ILICH LENIN to consolidate power in the Communist Party's Central Committee. His untimely death at 33 from an infectious illness left a void in the party hierarchy that was filled by JOSEPH STALIN in 1922.

Sverdlovsk See YEKATERINBURG

Svevo \'zvā-vō\, **Italo** *orig.* **Ettore Schmitz** (1861–1928) Italian writer. Though family financial difficulties forced him to leave school and become a bank clerk, he read on his own and began to write. *A Life* (1892), revolutionary in its analytical, introspective treatment of an ineffectual hero, was ignored on publication, as was *As a Man Grows Older* (1898). He gave up writing until, encouraged by JAMES JOYCE (then living in Trieste), he produced his most famous novel, *Confessions of Zeno* (1923). He died in an auto accident. Two short-story collections, essays, dramatic works, correspondence with EUGENIO MONTALE, and his unfinished *Further Confessions of Zeno* (1969) were published after his death. He is regarded as a pioneer of the psychological novel.

Svyatoslav I \'svyȧ-tə-sləf\ (died 972) Grand prince of Kiev (945–72). The greatest of the Varangian princes of early Russian history, he defeated the KHAZARS and other peoples in the northern Caucasus (963–65) and conquered the Bulgars (967). Hoping to found a Russo-Bulgarian empire, he refused to cede his conquest to the Byzantines until their army defeated him and forced the surrender of Balkan territory (971). He was killed in an ambush on his way back to Kiev.

Swabia *German* **Schwaben** \'shväb-ᵊn\ Duchy, medieval Germany, nearly coextensive with modern Baden-Württemberg, Hesse, and western Bavaria states, as well as parts of eastern Switzerland and Alsace. The Suevi and Alemanni tribes occupied the area from the 3rd century AD, and the region was known as Alemannia until the 11th century. In the 7th century Irish missionaries began to introduce Christianity. From c. 10th century, it became one of the five great tribal duchies of early medieval Germany. It was ruled by the HOHENSTAUFEN DYNASTY c. 1077–1268, when the duchy was divided. Several alliances of Swabian cities, known as the Swabian Leagues, were formed in the 14th–16th century. The region comprised a territorial division of the HOLY ROMAN EMPIRE in the 16th–19th century. Its chief cities included AUGSBURG, FREIBURG, Konstanz, and Ulm.

swage \'swāj, 'swej\ Perforated cast-iron or steel block with grooved sides, used by metalworkers for shaping their work by holding it on the work (or the work on it) and striking with a HAMMER or sledge. Swage blocks are used in heading bolts and swaging bars by hand.

Swahili language \swä-'hē-lē\ BANTU LANGUAGE spoken in Tanzania, Kenya, Uganda, and Congo (Zaire) as a first language by more than 2 million people and as a second language by about 60 million. Standard Swahili is based on the Unguja (kiUnguja) dialect of Zanzibar, which was spread far inland in the 19th century by Zanzibari entrepreneurs seeking ivory and slaves. Its use was perpetuated by the European colonial governments that occupied East Africa toward the end of the century. Modern Swahili is usually written in the LATIN ALPHABET, though Swahili literature in Arabic script dates to the early 18th century. Among Bantu languages, Swahili is remarkable for the number of loanwords it has absorbed, especially from Arabic.

Common swallow (*Hirundo rustica*).
STEPHEN DALTON FROM THE NATURAL HISTORY PHOTOGRAPHIC AGENCY—EB INC.

swallow Any of 74 species (family Hirundinidae) of songbirds found nearly worldwide. Swallows are 4–9 in. (10–23 cm) long, with long, pointed, narrow wings; a short bill; small, weak feet; and sometimes a forked tail. The dark upper plumage may have a metallic blue or green sheen. Swallows capture insects on the wing. They nest in tree holes, burrow into sandbank, or plaster mud nests to walls. Some species (e.g., the common swallow, *Hirundo rustica*) are long-distance migrants; all have a strong homing instinct. The swallows of California's San Juan Capistrano Mission are cliff swallows *(Petrochelidon pyrrhonota)*. See also MARTIN.

swallowing *or* **deglutition** \ˌdē-ˌglü-'tish-ən\ Act that moves food from the mouth to the stomach. The TONGUE pushes liquid or chewed food mixed with SALIVA into the PHARYNX. REFLEX takes over as the soft PALATE rises to close off the nasal cavity; the LARYNX rises and the epiglottis covers the TRACHEA, interrupting breathing. Pressure in the mouth and pharynx pushes food toward the ESOPHAGUS, whose upper sphincter opens to let food in and closes to prevent backflow. Breathing resumes as the larynx lowers. As PERISTALSIS pushes food to the STOMACH, the lower esophageal sphincter opens and then closes to prevent reflux. Painful swallowing is usually caused by INFLAMMATION; other problems are caused by blockage or disorders affecting the motions of swallowing.

swallowtail butterfly Any of more than 500 species (genus *Papilio,* family Papilionidae) of BUTTERFLIES found worldwide except in the Arctic. Some have tail-like extensions of the hind wing. Color patterns vary with species, sex, season, and sometimes location (see TIGER SWALLOWTAIL). Most adults have yellow, orange, red, green, or blue markings on an iridescent black, blue, or green background. The brightly colored larvae eat foliage. Some have markings resembling a snake's head, and many discharge a bad-smelling substance when disturbed. The giant swallowtail *(P. cresphontes)*, with a wingspan of 4–5.5 in. (10–14 cm), is the largest butterfly in the U.S. and Canada.

swami See SADHU AND SWAMI

Swammerdam \'sväm-ər-ˌdäm\, **Jan** (1637–1680) Dutch naturalist. An adept microscopist, in 1658 he became the first person to observe and describe red blood cells. In his *General History of Insects* he accurately described and illustrated the life histories and anatomy of many insect species and classified insects into four major divisions, three of which have been more or less retained in modern classification. He studied tadpole and adult frog anatomy and described the ovarian follicles of mammals. His improved techniques for injecting wax and dyes into cadavers had important consequences for the study of human anatomy. His ingenious experiments showed that muscles alter in shape but not in size during contraction.

swamp Freshwater wetland ecosystem characterized by poorly drained mineral soils and plant life dominated by trees. Swamps have a sufficient water supply to keep the ground waterlogged, and the water has a high-enough mineral content to stimulate decay of organisms and to prevent the accumulation of organic materials. They are found throughout the world. See also MARSH.

swan Long-necked, heavy-bodied, big-footed WATERFOWL (genus *Cygnus,* family Anatidae). Among waterfowl, swans are the largest and fastest, both swimming and flying; at about 50 lbs (23 kg), the mute swan *(C. olor)* is the heaviest flying bird. Swans dabble in shallows for aquatic plants. Five all-white, black-legged species live in the Northern Hemisphere; a black and a black-necked species live in the Southern Hemisphere. Males (cobs) and females (pens) look alike. Swans mate for life. The cob keeps guard while the pen incubates, on average, six eggs on a heap of vegetation; the young (cygnets) are tended for several months. Their graceful form when swimming has made swans emblems of beauty for centuries.

Mute swan (*Cygnus olor*) and cygnet.
ARTHUR W. AMBLER—THE NATIONAL AUDUBON SOCIETY COLLECTION/PHOTO RESEARCHERS

Swan, Joseph (Wilson) *later* **Sir Joseph** (1828–1914) English physicist and chemist. By 1871 he had invented the dry photographic plate, an important improvement in photography. He had already produced an early electric lightbulb (1860), and in 1880, independently of THOMAS ALVA EDISON, he produced a carbon-filament incandescent electric lamp. He also patented a process for squeezing nitrocellulose through holes to form fibers, a process that became widely employed in the textile industry.

Swan River Ephemeral river, southwestern Western Australia. It flows 224 mi (360 km) west to the Indian Ocean. Called the Avon in its upper course, it is known as the Swan only along its lower 60-mi course. Perth lies near its mouth. The river is dry during much of the summer and autumn. In 1829, western Australia's first free settlement was made on its banks.

Swan River River, eastern Saskatchewan and western Manitoba. It flows northeast for about 110 mi (175 km) to empty into Swan Lake, which covers 118 sq mi (306 sq km). The town of Swan River (pop., 1991: 4,000), is located on the river. In the early 1800s there was intense fur-trading rivalry in the area between the Hudson's Bay Co. and the North West Co.

Swansea \'swän-zē\ *Welsh* **Abertawe** \ˌa-bər-'tau̇-ə\ Seaport (pop., 1999 est.: 229,700), southern Wales. Lying along the Bristol Channel, it is the second-largest city in Wales. It dates from the 12th century. Up to the early 18th century it was a small market town and coal port; thereafter, it grew steadily as an industrial center, and by the mid-19th century it was the center of the world copper trade. The city center was almost totally destroyed by German bombing in 1941 but has been redeveloped, and Swansea is now the chief shopping and service center for southwestern Wales. The poet Dylan Thomas was born there.

Swanson, Gloria *orig.* **Gloria May Josephine Svensson** (1899–1983) U.S. film actress. Born in Chicago, she played minor roles in comedies at the Mack Sennett studio before being hired by Cecil B. DeMille and achieving stardom in a series of farces, including *Male and Female* (1919), *Zaza* (1923), and *Madame Sans-Gêne* (1925). The glamorous queen of silent movies, she formed her own production company with backing from her lover Joseph P. Kennedy, making *Sadie Thompson* (1928) and then the disastrous *Queen Kelly* (1928). After retiring in 1934, she made an acclaimed comeback as an aging silent-film star in *Sunset Boulevard* (1950).

SWAPO See South-West Africa People's Organization

Swarthmore College Private liberal-arts college in Swarthmore, Pa., near Philadelphia. It was founded by a group of Quakers in 1864. Consistently ranked as one of the best colleges in the U.S., it offers bachelor's degree programs in a wide variety of disciplines. It participates in an exchange program with Bryn Mawr and Haverford colleges and the University of Pennsylvania. Enrollment is about 1,500.

swastika Equilateral cross with its arms bent at right angles, all in the same rotary direction, usually clockwise. It is used widely throughout the world as a symbol of prosperity and good fortune. In India, it continues to be the most common auspicious symbol of Hindus and Jains, as well as for Buddhists, for whom it symbolizes the Buddha's feet or footprints. In China and Japan, where it traveled with the spread of Buddhism, it has been used to denote plurality, prosperity, and long life. It occurs as a motif in early Christian and Byzantine art, as well as in Maya and Navajo art. The counterclockwise swastika, suggested as a general anti-Semitic symbol in 1910 by the German poet and nationalist Guido von List, was adopted as the symbol of the Nazi Party at its founding in 1919–20.

Swazi \'swä-zē\ *or* **Swati** \'swä-tē\ Bantu-speaking people inhabiting the grasslands of Swaziland and neighboring regions. With the Zulu and the Xhosa, the Swazi (numbering 2 million) form the southern Nguni ethnolinguistic group. They are chiefly agriculturalists and pastoralists. The highest traditional political, economic, and ritual powers are shared by a hereditary male ruler and his mother. The king's wives and children are settled in royal villages, diplomatically dispersed throughout the territory.

Swaziland *officially* **Kingdom of Swaziland** Nation, southern Africa. Area: 6,704 sq mi (17,364 sq km). Population (2002 est.): 1,124,000. Capitals: Mbabane (administrative); Lobamba (legislative). About nine-tenths of the population is Swazi and about one-tenth Zulu, with a small number of other minorities. Languages: Swazi, English (both official). Religions: Christianity, animism. Currency: lilangeni. The landlocked country is composed of high, middle, and low velds, culminating in the Lubombo escarpment in the east. Fauna includes hippopotamus, antelope, zebra, and crocodile. Four major rivers, including the Komati, flow through the country and irrigate citrus and sugarcane estates. Mineral resources include asbestos and diamonds. It is a monarchy with two legislative houses; its head of state and government is the king, assisted by the prime minister. Stone tools and rock paintings indicate prehistoric habitation in the region, but it was not settled until the Bantu-speaking Swazi people migrated there in the 18th century and established the nucleus of the Swazi nation. The British gained control in the 19th century after the Swazi king sought their aid against the Zulus. Following the South African War, the British governor of Transvaal administered Swaziland; his powers were transferred to the British high commissioner in 1906. In 1949 the British rejected the Union of South Africa's request to control Swaziland. The country gained limited self-government in 1963 and achieved independence in 1968. In the 1970s new constitutions were framed based on the supreme authority of the king and traditional tribal government. During the 1990s forces demanding democracy arose, but the kingdom remained in place.

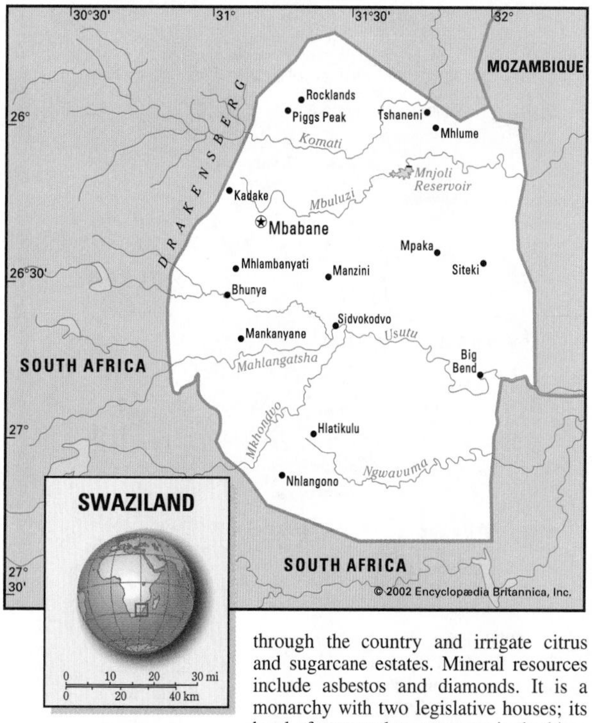

sweat gland Either of two types of perspiration glands in the skin. Eccrine sweat glands, controlled by the sympathetic nervous system, use evaporation to cool the skin by secreting water when body temperature rises. Apocrine sweat glands, usually associated with hair follicles, are concentrated in the underarms and genital region. Starting at puberty, hormones stimulate them to continuously secrete a fatty sweat. Certain specialized glands, such as mammary glands and wax-secreting glands of the ear canal, probably developed from this type of gland.

sweat lodge Hut or lodge used by American Indian peoples for ritual or therapeutic sweating. It is usually made of bent saplings and skin or blanket coverings and is heated by steam from water poured on hot stones. The ceremony typically surrounds the lodge's construction and use. Some groups believe the lodge becomes a symbolic center in which the six cardinal directions, the past and present, and the human and spiritual worlds are connected.

Sweden *officially* **Kingdom of Sweden** *Swedish* **Sverige** \'sve-rē-yə\ Nation, northern Europe, located on the Scandinavian Peninsula. Area: 173,732 sq mi (449,964 sq km). Population (2002 est.): 8,925,000. Capital: Stockholm. The population is largely homogeneous, although there are Finnish and Lappish minorities and 10% of the inhabitants are immigrants or their descendents. Language: Swedish (official). Religion: Church of Sweden (Lutheranism) (official). Currency: Swedish krona. Sweden has three regions. Mountainous Norrland covers about three-fifths of the country and has vast forests and large ore deposits. Svealand has undulating glacial ridges and contains most of the coun-

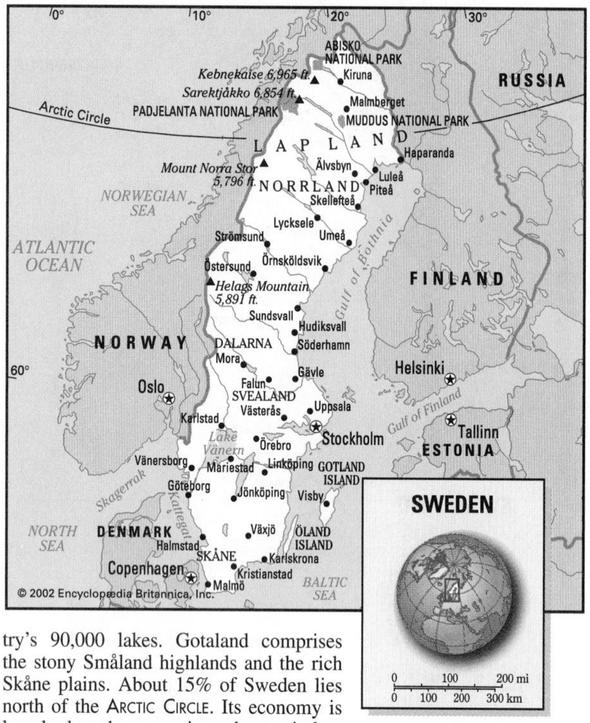

try's 90,000 lakes. Gotaland comprises the stony Småland highlands and the rich Skåne plains. About 15% of Sweden lies north of the ARCTIC CIRCLE. Its economy is largely based on services, heavy industries, and international trade. It has large deposits of iron ore; industries include mining, lumbering, steel manufacturing, and tourism. It raises grains, sugar beets, potatoes, and livestock. One of the world's richest countries, it is known for its comprehensive social welfare system. It is a constitutional monarchy with one legislative house; its chief of state is the king, and the head of government is the prime minister. The first inhabitants were apparently hunters who crossed the land bridge from Europe c. 12,000 BC. During the Viking era (9th–10th century), the Swedes controlled river trade in eastern Europe between the Baltic Sea and Black Sea and also raided western European lands. Sweden was loosely united and Christianized in the 11th–12th century. It conquered the Finns in the 12th century and in the 14th united with Norway and Denmark under a single monarchy. It broke away in 1523 under GUSTAV I VASA. In the 17th century it emerged as a great European power in the Baltic region, but its dominance declined after its defeat in the Second NORTHERN WAR (1700–21). It became a constitutional monarchy in 1809 and united with Norway 1815–1905; it acknowledged Norwegian independence in 1905. It maintained its neutrality during both World Wars. It was a charter member of the U.N., but abstained from membership in NATO and the EUROPEAN UNION until the 1990s. A new constitution drafted in 1975 reduced the monarch's powers to ceremonial head of state. In 1997 it decided to begin the controversial shutdown of its NUCLEAR POWER industry.

Swedenborg, Emanuel (1688–1772) Swedish scientist, theologian, and mystic. After graduating from the University of Uppsala, he spent five years abroad studying the natural sciences. On his return he began publication of Sweden's first scientific journal, *Daedelus Hyperboreas,* and CHARLES XIII appointed him assessor with the Royal Board of Mines. His writing gradually shifted toward philosophy of nature and metaphysics, as he became convinced that the universe had a basically spiritual structure. In 1744 he had a vision of Christ, and in 1745 he received a call to abandon worldly learning. He spent the rest of his career interpreting the Bible and relating what he had seen in his visions. He maintained that God was the power and life within all creatures, and that the Christian Trinity represented the three essential qualities of God: love, wisdom, and activity. He believed redemption consisted in mankind's being recreated in God's image through Christ's glorification. He published more than 30 works, including *The True Christian Religion* (1771). Societies were soon founded to propagate his pantheistic teaching, notably the New Jerusalem Church, established in London in 1787. Swedenborgians came to the U.S. in the 1790s.

Swedenborgians See NEW CHURCH

Swedish language National language of Sweden and one of two official languages of Finland, spoken by about 9 million people. It belongs to the East Scandinavian group of the GERMANIC LANGUAGES and is closely related to Norwegian and Danish. Its history from the Common Scandinavian period (600–1050) until c. 1225 is known chiefly from inscriptions in RUNIC WRITING. Modern Swedish is usually dated from 1526, when a translation of the New Testament was first printed. The standard language began to emerge in the 17th century, based largely on the Svea dialects spoken in Stockholm. Standard Swedish has no noun inflections except for the possessive and has only neuter and common genders; most dialects still have masculine, feminine, and neuter. Swedish, like Norwegian, has two tonal word accents.

Sweelinck \'swā-liŋk\, **Jan Pieterszoon** (1562–1621) Dutch composer. As organist at Amsterdam's Old Church from c. 1580, he became famous for his improvisations. Aside from occasional trips for organ consultation, he remained there, teaching S. SCHEIDT and other members of the North German school of organists (which would culminate in J.S. BACH). Many of his vocal works were published in *Psalms of David* (1604–14) and *Cantiones sacrae* (1619); he also published many keyboard fantasias, toccatas, and variation sets.

sweet pea Annual plant *(Lathyrus odoratus)* of the pea family (see LEGUME), native to Italy and widely cultivated elsewhere for its beautiful, fragrant flowers. The long (4–6 ft, or 1.2–2 m), vinelike stem climbs by means of tendrils and bears featherlike leaves. White, pink, red, violet, or purple flowers, reminiscent of butterflies in shape, are borne singly or in clusters of two to four. The fruit is a hairy pod about 2 in. (5 cm) long. Hundreds of varieties of sweet pea have been developed. The plant was the subject of important genetics experiments by REGINALD CRUNDALL PUNNETT and WILLIAM BATESON.

Sweet pea (*Lathyrus odoratus*).
SVEN SAMELIUS

sweet potato Food plant (*Ipomoea batatas;* family Convolvulaceae) native to tropical America and widely cultivated in tropical and warm temperate climates. Botanically unrelated to the white, or Irish, POTATO or the YAM, sweet potatoes are oblong or pointed oval, tuberous roots. Skin color ranges from light buff to brown to purplish-red; the pulp may be white (highest in starch) to orange (also high in CAROTENE) to purple. Long, trailing plant stems bear funnel-shaped flowers tinged with pink or rose violet. Sweet potatoes are served baked or mashed and used as pie filling.

sweet William Garden plant *(Dianthus barbatus)* in the PINK FAMILY, grown for its clusters of small, brightly colored flowers. It usually grows as a biennial, with seed sown the first year producing spring-flowering plants the second year. The plants grow about 2 ft (60 cm) high and produce numerous flowers with fringed petals in white, pink, or rose to violet, sometimes also bicolored.

Sweet William (*Dianthus barbatus*).
GRANT HEILMAN

sweetbrier *or* **eglantine** Small, prickly wild ROSE *(Rosa eglanteria,* or *R. rubiginosa)* with fragrant foliage and numerous small pink flowers, native to Europe and western Asia. Widely naturalized in North America, it grows along roadsides and in pastures from eastern Canada southwest to Tennessee and Kansas. The shrub form, which can grow 6 ft (2 m) high, is useful for screening out traffic noise and beautifying highways.

Sweyn I *or* **Sweyn Forkbeard** \'svān\ (died 1014) King of Denmark (c. 987–1014) and VIKING conqueror of Norway and England. He rebelled against his father, Harald Bluetooth (987), chasing him from Denmark. With Swedish and Norwegian allies he defeated OLAF I (c. 1000), becoming virtual ruler of Norway. Sweyn led raids on England in 1003–4 and became king after a successful military campaign in 1013, forcing ETHELRED II into exile. Norway reverted to Norwegian rule after Sweyn's death, but the Anglo-Danish empire continued under his son CANUTE THE GREAT.

swift Any of about 75 species (family Apodidae) of birds found almost worldwide. The fastest of small birds, swifts can fly at 70 mph (110 kph). They are 4–9 in. (9–23 cm) long and have long wings, a chunky dark body, a broad head, and a short, wide, slightly curved bill. The tail may be short or long and deeply forked. Swifts capture insects, drink, bathe, and sometimes mate on the wing. The feet, incapable of perching, are used to cling to vertical surfaces. Swifts use their sticky saliva to glue the nest to a cave wall, the inside of a chimney, or a tree hollow.

Swift, Gustavus Franklin (1839–1903) U.S. meatpacker. Born in West Sandwich (now Sagamore), Mass., Swift started as a butcher's helper at 14, and by 1859 was operating his own butcher shop. In 1872 he became the partner of a Boston meat dealer; three years later he transferred their cattle-buying operations to Chicago. Believing profits would increase if fresh meat rather than live cattle were shipped from Chicago, he had a refrigerator car designed and made his first shipment in 1877. With his brother he formed Swift & Co. (1885). Over his 18 years as president, its capitalization rose from $300,000 to $25 million. Like his rivals PHILIP D. ARMOUR and Nelson Morris, Swift was a leader in by-product utilization, entering related businesses such as soap, glue, fertilizer, and margarine.

Swift, Jonathan (1667–1745) Irish author, the foremost prose satirist in English. Swift was a student at Dublin's Trinity College during the anti-Catholic Revolution of 1688 in England. Irish Catholic reaction led him to seek security in England, where he spent various intervals before 1714. He was ordained an Anglican priest in 1695. His first major work, *A Tale of a Tub* (1704), comprises three satiric sketches on religion and learning; he also became known for religious and political essays and impish pamphlets written under the name "Isaac Bickerstaff." Reluctantly setting aside his loyalty to the Whigs, in 1710 he became the leading writer for the Tories because of their support for the established church. *Journal to Stella* (written 1710–13) consists of letters recording his reactions to the changing world. As a reward for writing and editing Tory publications, in 1713 he was awarded the deanery of St. Patrick's Cathedral, Dublin. He spent nearly all the rest of his life in Ireland, where he devoted himself to exposing English wrongheadedness and the unfair treatment of Ireland. His ironic tract "A Modest Proposal" (1729) proposes ameliorating Irish poverty by butchering children and selling them as food to wealthy English landlords. His famously brilliant and bitter satire *Gulliver's Travels* (1726), ostensibly the story of its hero's encounters with various races and societies in remote regions, reflects Swift's vision of humanity's ambiguous position between bestiality and rationality.

Jonathan Swift, detail of an oil painting by Charles Jervas; in the National Portrait Gallery, London.

BY COURTESY OF THE NATIONAL PORTRAIT GALLERY, LONDON

swimming In recreation and sports, the propulsion of the body through water by combined arm and leg motions. Swimming is popular as an all-around body developer and as competitive sport. It has been included in the modern Olympic Games since their inception in 1896. Events include freestyle (crawl-stroke) races at distances of 50, 100, 200, 400, 800, and 1,500 m; backstroke, breaststroke, and butterfly races at 100 and 200 m; individual medley races at 200 and 400 m; freestyle relays, 4×100 m and 4×200 m; and the medley relay, 4×100 m. Long-distance swimming competitions, usually of 15–37 mi (24–59 km), are generally held on lakes and inland waters.

swimming cat See TURKISH VAN CAT

Swinburne, Algernon Charles (1837–1909) English poet and critic. After attending Eton and Oxford, Swinburne lived on an allowance from his father. His verse drama *Atalanta in Calydon* (1865) first showed his lyric powers. *Poems and Ballads* (1866), containing some of his best work, displays his paganism and masochism and provoked controversy; a second series (1878) was less hectic and sensual. His verse is marked by emphatic rhythms, much alliteration and internal rhyme, and lush subject matter. His health collapsed in 1879 and he spent his last 30 years under a friend's guardianship. While his earlier poetry is noted for innovations in prosody, his later poetry is less important. Among his outstanding critical writings are *Essays and Studies* (1875) and monographs on WILLIAM SHAKESPEARE (1880), VICTOR HUGO (1886), and BEN JONSON (1889).

Swinburne, watercolour by Dante Gabriel Rossetti, 1862; in the Fitzwilliam Museum, Cambridge.

BY COURTESY OF THE FITZWILLIAM MUSEUM, CAMBRIDGE

swine fever See HOG CHOLERA

swing JAZZ played with a steady beat using the harmonic structure of popular songs and the BLUES as the basis for improvisations and arrangements. The popular music of the U.S. from about 1930 to 1945, swing is characterized by syncopated rhythmic momentum with equal stress accorded to the four beats of a measure. Larger jazz bands required some arranged material, and FLETCHER HENDERSON, DUKE ELLINGTON, and COUNT BASIE were the primary innovators of big-band swing. In smaller ensembles, improvised instrumental solos generally follow a rendering of the melody. See also SWING DANCE.

swing dance Social dance form dating from the 1940s. Danced in the U.S. to SWING music, the dance steps have distinct regional variations, including such forms as the West Coast swing, the East's jitterbug-lindy, the South's shag, and in Texas the push (Dallas) and whip (Houston). Performance versions include extreme athletic moves that distinguish them from everyday social swing dance. Though swing dance had largely disappeared by 1960, a revival began in the late 1980s and has since spread widely.

Swiss Bank Corp. Major Swiss bank. It was established in 1872 as the Basler Bankverein, specializing in investment banking. In a 1895 merger with Zürcher Bankverein, it became a COMMERCIAL BANK and changed its name to Basler und Zürcher Bankverein. After absorbing two other banks in 1897, it became Swiss Bank Corp. In 1998 it merged with Union Bank of Switzerland to form UBS.

Swiss chard See CHARD

switching theory Theory of CIRCUITS made up of ideal digital devices, including their structure, behavior, and design. It incorporates Boolean logic (see BOOLEAN ALGEBRA), a basic component of modern digital switching systems. Switching is essential to telephone, telegraph, data processing, and other technologies in which it is necessary to make rapid decisions about routing information. See also QUEUING THEORY.

Switzerland *officially* **Swiss Confederation** *French* **Suisse** \'swʸēs\ *German* **Schweiz** \'shvīts\ *Italian* **Svizzera** \'zvēt-tsā-rä\ *Romansh* **Helvetica** Landlocked country, central Europe. Area: 15,940 sq mi (41,284 sq km). Population (2002 est.): 7,282,000. Capital: BERN. The population is German, French, and Italian. Languages: German, French, and Italian (all official). Religions: Roman Catholicism (about 45%), Protestantism (40%). Currency: Swiss franc. Switzerland is divided into three regions: the meadow-covered JURA MTNS.; the central Mittelland, a rich agricultural and urbanized area; and the lofty crags of the ALPS. It is one of the world's major financial centers; its economy is based largely on international trade and banking, as well as light and heavy industries. Its manufactures include watches, precision instruments, machinery, and chemicals. Tourism and agriculture are also important; products include grains, fruits and vegetables, dairy products, chocolate, and wine. Despite diverse ethnic groups, religions, and languages, Switzerland has

S T U V

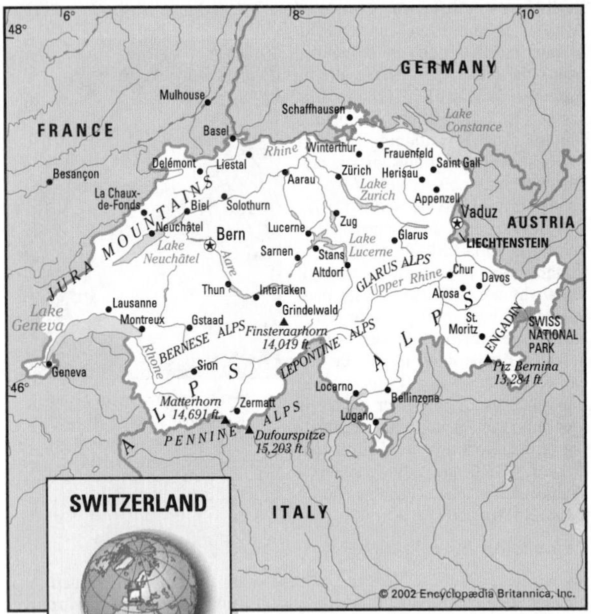

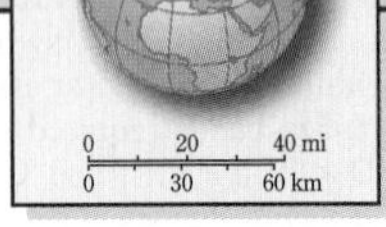

maintained the world's oldest democracy for some 700 years. It is a federal state with two legislative houses; its head of state and government is the president. The original inhabitants were the Helvetians, who were conquered by the Romans in the 1st century BC. Germanic tribes penetrated the region from the 3rd–6th century AD, and Muslim and Magyar raiders ventured in during the 10th century. It came under the FRANKS in the 9th century and the HOLY ROMAN EMPIRE in the 11th century. In 1291 three cantons formed an anti-Habsburg league that became the nucleus of the Swiss Confederation. It was a center of the REFORMATION, which divided the confederation and led to a period of political and religious conflict. The French organized Switzerland as the HELVETIC REPUBLIC in 1798. In 1815 the Congress of VIENNA recognized Swiss independence and guaranteed its neutrality. A new federal state was formed in 1848 with Bern as the capital. It remained neutral in both World Wars, and continued to guard this stance. With the formation of the EUROPEAN UNION, it began the effort to achieve provisional association with the European economic area. It joined the UN in 2002.

Swope, Gerard (1872–1957) U.S. business leader. After graduating from MIT, he joined WESTERN ELECTRIC in 1895 and became a director in 1913. He was made president of GENERAL ELECTRIC CO.'s international subsidiary in 1919 and greatly increased the company's foreign business. As president of General Electric (1922–39, 1942–44), he expanded its line of consumer products and pioneered PROFIT SHARING and other employee benefit programs. He also served on the Department of Commerce's Business Advisory Council, and his ideas and support underlay such important New Deal programs as the NATIONAL RECOVERY ADMINISTRATION and SOCIAL SECURITY.

sword Hand weapon consisting of a long metal blade fitted with a handle or hilt. Roman swords had a short, flat blade and a hilt distinct from the blade. Medieval European swords were heavy and equipped with a large hilt and a protective guard, or pommel. The blade was straight, double edged, and pointed. The introduction of firearms did not eliminate the sword but led to new designs; the discarding of body armor required the swordsman to be able to parry, and the rapier, a double-edged sword with a narrow, pointed blade, came into use. Swords with curved blades were used in India and Persia and were introduced into Europe by the Turks, whose scimitar, with its curved, single-edged blade, was modified in the West to the cavalry saber. Japanese swords are renowned for their hardness and extreme sharpness; they were the weapon of the SAMURAI. Repeating firearms ended the value of the sword as a military weapon, though its continued use in duels led to the modern sport of FENCING. See also KENDO.

sword dance Folk dance by men, with swords or two-handled blades, expressing themes such as human and animal sacrifice for fertility, battle mime, and defense against evil spirits. It originated in Greek and Roman times. A sword dance appeared in Germany in 1350 and later was part of the court ballet when mock battles were staged. The Scottish sword dance is a descendant of the early crossed-sword dances, and the MORRIS DANCE retains remnants of the sword dance. Outside of Europe, such dances are found in India, Borneo, and the Balkans.

swordfish Species *(Xiphias gladius)* of prized food and game fish, found in warm and temperate oceans worldwide. A slender, scaleless fish, it has a tall dorsal fin and a long sword, used for slashing at prey fishes, extending from its snout. The sword is flat, rather than rounded as in MARLINS. The swordfish is also distinguished by its lack of teeth and pelvic fins. It is purplish or bluish above, silvery below, and grows as large as 15 ft (4.5 m) and 1,000 lbs (450 kg). Though a popular food fish, it may concentrate dangerous levels of mercury in its flesh.

Sybaris \'si-bə-rəs\ Ancient Greek city, southern Italy, on the Gulf of Tarentum. Founded c. 720 BC by ACHAEANS and known for its wealth and luxury (hence, the English word *sybarite*), it was one of the oldest cities of MAGNA GRAECIA. Twice razed by the Crotoniates (510 BC and c. 448 BC), it attempted rebuilding and relocating but never regained its importance.

sycamore \'si-kə-ˌmȯr\ Any of several distinct trees called by the same name though in different genera and families. In the U.S. the term refers to the American PLANE TREE or buttonwood *(Platanus occidentalis)*, a hardy street tree. The sycamore MAPLE, or mock plane *(Acer pseudoplatanus),* is sometimes also called simply sycamore. The biblical sycamore, actually the sycamore FIG *(Ficus sycomorus),* was used by the ancient Egyptians to make mummy cases.

Sydenham \'si-dᵊn-əm\, **Thomas** (1624–1689) British physician. His *Observationes medicae* (1676) was a standard textbook for two centuries, noted for its detailed observations and the accuracy of its records. His treatise on gout (1683) is considered his masterpiece. He was among the first to explain the nature of hysteria and St. Vitus' dance (Sydenham's chorea) and to use iron to treat iron-deficiency anemia. Sydenham also named scarlet fever and differentiated it from measles, first used laudanum (a solution of opium in alcohol) as a medication, and helped popularize the use of quinine for malaria.

Sydney City (pop., 2001: 3,997,321), capital of NEW SOUTH WALES, Australia. Located on Australia's southeastern coast, it is the oldest and largest city in Australia and a major commercial and manufacturing center. It was founded in 1788 as a penal colony (see BOTANY BAY) and quickly became a major trading center. It is built on low hills surrounding one of the world's finest natural harbors, which supports extensive port facilities. It is dominated by Sydney Harbour Bridge, one of the biggest single-span bridges in the world, and the SYDNEY OPERA HOUSE. The city is widely known for its water sports, recreational facilities, and cultural life. It is the site of the universities of Sydney (1850) and New South Wales (1949), and Macquarie University (1964). Sydney was the host of the 2000 Summer Olympic Games.

Sydney Opera House Performing-arts center on the harbor in Sydney, Australia. Its dynamic, imaginative design, by the Danish architect Jørn Utzon (born 1918), placed first in a 1956 competition and brought him international fame. Construction posed a variety of problems, many resulting from the bold design, a series of organic, glittering white shell-shaped roofs. After several years of research, he gave the vaults a more spherical geometry, making them easier and more economical to build. The roofs are made up of PRECAST CONCRETE sections held together by cables. The center finally opened in 1973.

Sydow \'sē-dō, *Swed* 'sæ-dȯv\, **Max von** *orig.* **Carl Adolf von** (born 1929) Swedish actor. After studying at Stockholm's Royal Dramatic Theater School, he became a noted stage actor in Malmö and Stockholm. He is best known for his dour, brooding characterizations in INGMAR BERGMAN's films, notably *The Seventh Seal* (1957), *The Magician* (1958), *The Virgin Spring* (1960), *Winter Light* (1963), *Hour of the Wolf* (1968), *Shame* (1968), and *The Passion of Anna* (1969). His numerous U.S. and international movies include *The Greatest Story Ever Told* (1965), *The Exorcist* (1973), *Pelle the Conqueror* (1988), *Needful Things* (1993), and *Minority Report* (2002).

S
T
U
V

syllable Segment of speech usually consisting of a VOWEL with or without accompanying CONSONANT sounds (e.g., *a, I, out, too, cap, snap, check*). A syllabic consonant, like the final *n* sound in *button* and *widen*, also constitutes a syllable. Closed (checked) syllables end in a consonant, open (free) syllables in a vowel. Syllables play an important role in the study of SPEECH and in PHONETICS and PHONOLOGY.

syllogism \'si-lə-ˌji-zəm\ Form of argument that, in its most commonly discussed instances, has two CATEGORICAL PROPOSITIONS as premises and one categorical proposition as conclusion. An example of a syllogism is the following argument: Every human is mortal (every M is P); every philosopher is human (every S is M); therefore, every philosopher is mortal (every S is P). Such arguments have exactly three terms (human, philosopher, mortal). Here, the argument is composed of three categorical (as opposed to hypothetical) propositions, it is therefore a categorical syllogism. In a categorical syllogism, the term that occurs in both premises but not in the conclusion (human) is the middle term; the predicate term in the conclusion is called the major term, the subject the minor term. The pattern in which the terms S, M, and P (minor, middle, major) are arranged is called the figure of the syllogism. In this example, the syllogism is in the first figure, since the major term appears as predicate in the first premise and the minor term as subject of the second.

syllogistic \ˌsi-lə-'jis-tik\ Formal analysis of the SYLLOGISM. Developed in its original form by ARISTOTLE in his *Prior Analytics* c. 350 BC, syllogistic represents the earliest branch of formal logic. Syllogistic comprises two domains of investigation. Categorical syllogistic confines itself to categorical propositions and their variation with respect to MODALITIES. Noncategorical syllogistic is a form of logical inference using whole propositions as its units, an approach traceable to the Stoics but only fully developed by John Neville Keynes (1852–1949).

Sylvester II *orig.* **Gerbert of Aurillac** (c. 945–1003) First French pope (999–1003). Renowned as a scholar of logic and mathematics, he became archbishop of Reims (991) and of Ravenna (c. 998). As pope he worked closely with OTTO III, strengthening papal authority in distant states such as Kiev and Norway as well as in Italy. He denounced SIMONY, demanded clerical celibacy, and limited the power of the bishops. He wrote textbooks on mathematics, the sciences, and music and the philosophical work *De rationali et de ratione uti* ("Concerning the Rational and the Use of Reason").

Sylvius \'sil-vē-əs\, **Franciscus** *orig.* **Franz de le Boë** \ˌdā-lā-'bō-ā\ *French* **François du Bois** \dǖ-'bō-ä\ (1614–1672) German-Dutch physician, physiologist, anatomist, and chemist. He based his medical system on WILLIAM HARVEY's discovery of the circulation of the blood and felt that the most important life processes, both normal and pathological, took place in the blood. He proposed that chemical imbalances consist of an excess of either acids or alkalies in the blood and devised drugs to counteract them. An outstanding teacher, Sylvius had students instructed on hospital wards. He was the first to distinguish glands made up of smaller units with converging ducts from those forming a rounded mass. Several anatomical structures are named after him.

symbiosis Any of several living arrangements between members of two different species, including commensalism, mutualism, and PARASITISM. The species involved are called symbionts. In commensalism, one species (the commensal) obtains nutrients, shelter, support, or locomotion from the host species, which is substantially unaffected (e.g., REMORAS obtain locomotion and food from sharks). In mutualism, both species benefit. Many mutualistic relationships are obligative; neither species can live without the other (e.g., protozoans in the gut of TERMITES digest the wood ingested by the termites).

symbol Communication element intended to represent or stand for a person, object, group, process, or idea. Symbols may be presented graphically (e.g., the CROSS for Christianity, or the light/dark halved circle for YIN-YANG) or representationally (e.g., Uncle Sam standing for the U.S., or a lion standing for courage). They may involve associated letters (e.g., C for the chemical element carbon), or they may be assigned arbitrarily (e.g., the mathematical symbol for infinity or the dollar symbol). Symbols are not a LANGUAGE of and by themselves; rather they are devices by which ideas often too complex or highly charged to articulate in ordinary language are transmitted between people sharing a common CULTURE. Every society has evolved a symbol system that reflects a specific cultural logic; and every symbolism functions to communicate information between members of the culture in much the same way as, but more subtly than, conventional language. Though a symbol may take the discrete form of a wedding ring or a totem pole, symbols tend to appear in clusters and depend on one another for their accretion of meaning and value. See also SEMIOTICS.

symbolic interactionism See INTERACTIONISM

Symbolism In art, a loosely organized movement that flourished in the 1880s and '90s and was closely related to the SYMBOLIST MOVEMENT in literature. In reaction against both REALISM and IMPRESSIONISM, Symbolist painters stressed art's subjective, symbolic, and decorative functions, and turned to the mystical and occult in an attempt to evoke subjective states of mind by visual means. Though aspects of Symbolism appear in the work of PAUL GAUGUIN, VINCENT VAN GOGH, and the NABIS, its leading exponents were GUSTAVE MOREAU, ODILON REDON, and PIERRE PUVIS DE CHAVANNES. Though associated primarily with France, it flourished all over Europe, had great international impact, and influenced 20th-century art and literature.

Symbolist movement Literary movement that originated with a group of French poets in the late 19th century, spread to painting and the theater, and influenced Russian, European, and American literature of the 20th century. Reacting against the rigid conventions of traditional French poetry, as seen in the precise description favored by the PARNASSIAN POETS, Symbolist poets sought to convey individual emotional experience through the subtle, suggestive use of highly metaphorical language. The arcane and indirect meaning of the symbol is evoked as a substitute for the increasingly attenuated sense of collective and universal meanings. Principal Symbolist poets included STEPHANE MALLARME, PAUL VERLAINE, ARTHUR RIMBAUD, and É. VERHAEREN. Many Symbolists were also identified with the DECADENT movement. Just as Symbolist painters avoided concrete representation in favor of fantasy and imagination, Symbolist dramatists relied on myth, mood, and atmosphere to reveal only indirectly the deeper truths of existence.

Symington \'sī-miŋ-tᵊn\, **(William) Stuart** (1901–1988) U.S. politician. Born in Amherst, Mass., he became an executive in several industries (1927–45). He served as secretary of the air force 1946–50. Serving in the U.S. Senate from Missouri (1953–77), he advocated a strong national defense, but became an outspoken critic of U.S. involvement in the VIETNAM WAR, considering it unimportant to national security and damaging to the economy.

Symington \'sī-miŋ-tən\, **William** (1763–1831) British engineer. Educated for the ministry, he became a mechanic instead. He created a working model of a steam-driven road carriage in 1786 and first used steam for marine purposes the following year. In 1801–2 he developed a successful steam-driven paddle wheel and used it to propel one of the first practical steamboats, the *Charlotte Dundas.* Though his engine was used successfully on the Forth and Clyde Canal in 1802, cautious managers caused the project to be abandoned in 1803.

Symmachus \'si-mə-kəs\, **Quintus Aurelius** (c. AD 345–402) Roman statesman, orator, and writer. A leading opponent of Christianity, he struggled with St. AMBROSE to influence the increasingly Christian emperors GRATIAN (r.367–83) and Valentinian II (r.375–92) to tolerate paganism. As leader of the SENATE in 387, he congratulated the new emperor, Magnus Maximus, on having driven out Valentinian. When THEODOSIUS I reconquered Italy for Valentinian (388), Symmachus was forgiven and made CONSUL (391).

symmetry In geometry, the property by which the sides of a figure or object reflect each other across a line (axis of symmetry) or surface; in biology, the orderly repetition of parts of an animal or plant; in chemistry, a fundamental property of orderly arrangements of atoms in molecules or CRYSTALS; in physics, a concept of balance illustrated by such fundamental laws as the third of NEWTON'S LAWS OF MOTION. Symmetry in nature underlies one of the most fundamental concepts of beauty. It connotes balance, order, and thus, to some, a type of divine principle.

Symonds \'si-məndz\, **John Addington** (1840–1893) English essayist, poet, and biographer. He traveled extensively for his health, finally settling in Switzerland. His chief work, *Renaissance in Italy* (1875–86), is a series of extended essays on cultural history. His writings include translations, travel sketches, and studies of personalities such as PERCY B. SHELLEY, BEN JONSON, SIR PHILIP SIDNEY, MICHELANGELO, and WALT WHITMAN. His poetry served primarily as a release from his difficult emotional life.

A Problem in Greek Ethics (written 1871) and *A Problem in Modern Ethics* (1881) were among the first serious works treating homosexuality.

Symonds, chalk drawing by C. Orsi; in the National Portrait Gallery, London.

BY COURTESY OF THE NATIONAL PORTRAIT GALLERY, LONDON

Symons \'si-mənz\, **Arthur (William)** (1865–1945) English poet and critic. He contributed to *The Yellow Book*, an avant-garde journal, and edited *The Savoy* (1896). His *Symbolist Movement in Literature* (1899), the first English work championing the French SYMBOLIST MOVEMENT in poetry, summed up a decade of interpretation and influenced WILLIAM BUTLER YEATS and T. S. ELIOT. His poetry, mainly disillusioned in feeling, appears in such volumes as *Silhouettes* (1892) and *London Nights* (1895). He also translated poetry of PAUL VERLAINE and wrote travel pieces. After a nervous breakdown in 1908, he produced little apart from *Confessions* (1930), a moving account of his illness.

symphonic poem *or* **tone poem** Musical work for orchestra, usually in one movement, inspired by an extramusical story or idea, usually a literary text. It evolved from the concert OVERTURE (e.g., F. MENDELSSOHN's *Fingal's Cave). F.* LISZT, who coined the term, wrote 13 such works. Famous symphonic poems include B. SMETANA's *Moldau* (1879), C. DEBUSSY's *Prelude to The Afternoon of a Faun* (1894), P. DUKAS's *Sorceror's Apprentice* (1897), R. STRAUSS's *Don Quixote* (1897), and J. SIBELIUS's *Finlandia* (1900).

symphony Long musical composition for orchestra, usually in several movements. The term (meaning "sounding together") came to be the standard name for instrumental episodes, and especially overtures, in early Italian opera. The late-17th-century Neapolitan opera overture, or *sinfonia*, as established especially by ALESSANDRO SCARLATTI c. 1780, had three movements, their tempos being fast-slow-fast. Soon such overtures began to be performed by themselves in concert settings, like another forerunner of the symphony, the *CONCERTO GROSSO*. The two merged in the early 18th century in the symphonies of G. B. Sammartini. Around 1750, German and Viennese composers began to add a minuet movement. FRANZ JOSEPH HAYDN, the "father of the symphony," wrote over 100 symphonies of remarkable originality, intensity, and brilliance in the years 1755–95; since Haydn, it has been regarded as the most important orchestral genre. WOLFGANG AMADEUS MOZART wrote about 35 original symphonies. LUDWIG VAN BEETHOVEN's nine symphonies endowed the genre with enormous weight and ambition. Later symphonists include FRANZ SCHUBERT, FELIX MENDELSSOHN, ROBERT SCHUMANN, ANTON BRUCKNER, JOHANNES BRAHMS, ANTONÍN DVORAK, PIOTR ILYICH TCHAIKOVSKY, and GUSTAV MAHLER; their 20th-century successors include RALPH VAUGHAN WILLIAMS, JEAN SIBELIUS, and DMITRI SHOSTAKOVICH.

symposium In ancient Greece, an aristocratic banquet at which men met to discuss philosophical and political issues and recite poetry. It began as a warrior feast. Rooms were designed specifically for the proceedings. The participants, all male aristocrats, wore garlands and leaned on the left elbow on couches, and there was much drinking of wine, served by slave boys. Prayers opened and closed the meetings; sessions sometimes ended with a procession in the streets. In PLATO's famous *Symposium*, an imaginary dialogue takes place between SOCRATES, ARISTOPHANES, ALCIBIADES, and others on the subject of love. ARISTOTLE, XENOPHON, and EPICURUS wrote symposium literature on other subjects.

synagogue In Judaism, a community house of worship that also serves as a place for assembly and study. Though their exact origins are uncertain, synagogues flourished side by side with the ancient Temple cult and existed long before Jewish sacrifice and the established priesthood were terminated with Titus's destruction of the Second Temple (AD 70). Thereafter, synagogues took on even greater importance as the unchallenged focal point of Jewish life. There is no standard synagogue architecture. A typical synagogue contains an ark (where the scrolls of the Law are kept), an "eternal light" burning before the ark, two candelabra, pews, a *bimah* (see BEMA), and sometimes a ritual bath *(mikvah).*

synapse \'si-ˌnaps\ Site of transmission of electric nerve impulses between two nerve cells or between a nerve cell and a gland or muscle cell. At chemical synapses, impulses are transmitted across microscopic spaces via chemical substances called neurotransmitters. In electric synapses, direct communication between nerve cells whose membranes are fused is possible because ions flow between the cells through channels. Electric synapses are found mainly in invertebrates and lower vertebrates; they transmit messages faster than chemical synapses. Chemical transmission seems to have evolved in large, complex vertebrate nervous systems, in which multiple messages must be transmitted over long distances.

Synchromism \'siŋ-krə-ˌmi-zəm\ Art movement concerned with the purely abstract use of color. Founded in Paris in 1912–13 by the U.S. artists Stanton Macdonald-Wright (1890–1973) and Morgan Russell (1886–1953), Synchromism ("colors together") was based on theories of color with analogies to musical patterns. It has much in common with the ORPHISM of ROBERT DELAUNAY. The first Synchromist work, Russell's *Synchromy in Green* (1913), was exhibited at the Salon des Indépendants in 1913. Synchromism briefly attracted several other U.S. artists, including THOMAS HART BENTON.

synchronized swimming Swimming in which the movements of one or more swimmers are synchronized with a musical accompaniment so as to form changing patterns in the water. The sport developed in the U.S. in the 1930s and was admitted as an Olympic event (solo and duet only) in 1984; in 1996 the rules were changed to allow only teams of eight women. Teams are judged on compulsory and optional routines.

synchrotron \'siŋ-krə-ˌträn\ Cyclic PARTICLE ACCELERATOR in which the particle is confined to its orbit by a MAGNETIC FIELD. The strength of the magnetic field increases as the particle's MOMENTUM increases. An alternating ELECTRIC FIELD in synchrony with the orbital frequency of the particle produces acceleration. Synchrotrons are named according to the particles they accelerate. The proton synchrotron at the Fermi National Accelerator Laboratory in Illinois produces the highest particle energies achieved so far.

synchrotron radiation ELECTROMAGNETIC RADIATION emitted by charged particles that are moving at speeds close to that of light when their paths are altered. It is so called because it is produced by high-speed particles in a SYNCHROTRON. Such radiation is highly polarized (see POLARIZATION) and continuous. Its intensity and FREQUENCY depend on the strength of the MAGNETIC FIELD that alters the path of the particles, as well as on the energy of those particles. Synchrotron radiation at radio frequencies is emitted by high-energy ELECTRONS as they spiral through magnetic fields in space, such as those around Jupiter. Synchrotron radiation is emitted by a variety of astronomical objects, from planets to supernova remnants to quasars.

syncope \'siŋ-kə-pē\ Effect of temporary impairment of blood circulation to a part of the body. It is often used as a synonym for fainting, which is loss of consciousness due to inadequate blood flow to the brain. Paleness, nausea, sweating, and then pupil dilation, yawning, deep rapid breathing, and rapid heartbeat usually precede it. It lasts from under a minute to several minutes and may be followed by headache, confusion, and a weak feeling. The cause may be physical (e.g., AORTIC STENOSIS, HEART FAILURE, low blood sugar) or emotional (e.g., fear, anxiety). Abnormal vagus or autonomic nerve response can cause fainting (without preceding symptoms) triggered by ordinary activities such as urination, swallowing, coughing, or standing up or by pressure on the pulse point in the neck. Local syncope is coldness and numbness in a small area, especially the fingers, from diminished blood flow.

syndicalism \'sin-di-kə-ˌli-zəm\ Movement that advocated direct action by the working class to abolish the capitalist order, including the state, and replace it with a social order based on workers organized in production units. It evolved from French trade-union ANARCHISM at the end of the 19th century. It looked forward to victory in a class war, after which society would be organized around the *syndicat,* a free association of self-governing producers, who would keep in touch with other producers through a labor exchange, which would function as an employment and economic-planning agency. At the peak of its influence, before World War I, the movement had over a million members in Europe, Latin

America, and the U.S. After the war, syndicalists tended to drift toward the Soviet model of COMMUNISM or be lured by the prospects for working-class gains offered by LABOR UNIONS and democratic reforms. See also CORPORATISM.

Synge \'siŋ\, **John Millington** (1871–1909) Irish playwright. After studying languages and music in Dublin and France, he was inspired by WILLIAM BUTLER YEATS with enthusiasm for the Irish language and people. From 1899 to 1902 he spent his summers on the Aran Islands, and he based his first plays, *In the Shadow of the Glen* (1903) and *Riders to the Sea* (1904), on islanders' stories. His travels on the Irish west coast inspired his most famous play, *The Playboy of the Western World* (1907), whose unsentimental treatment of Irish character traits caused riots at its opening at the ABBEY THEATRE. His unfinished *Deirdre of the Sorrows* was performed in 1910. A poetic dramatist of great power, he was a leading figure of the IRISH LITERARY RENAISSANCE.

synodic period \sə-'nä-dik\ Time required for a body in the SOLAR SYSTEM to return to the same or about the same position relative to the sun as seen from earth. The moon's synodic period is the time between successive recurrences of the same phase (e.g., the period between one full moon and the next). A planet's synodic period is the time required for earth to overtake it as both go around the sun, or (in the case of fast-moving Mercury or Venus) for the other planet to overtake earth. See also SIDEREAL PERIOD.

syntax Arrangement of words in sentences, clauses, and phrases, and the study of the formation of sentences and the relationship of their component parts. In English, the main device for showing this relationship is word order; for example, "The girl loves the boy" follows standard subject-verb-object word order, and switching the order of such a sentence would change the meaning or make the sentence meaningless. Word order is much more flexible in languages like Latin, in which word endings indicate the case of a noun or adjective; such inflections make it unnecessary to rely on word order to know a word's function in the sentence.

synthesizer Machine that electronically generates and modifies sounds, frequently with the use of a digital computer, for use in the composition of electronic music and in live performance. The synthesizer generates wave forms and then subjects them to alteration in intensity, duration, frequency, and timbre. It may use subtractive synthesis (removing unwanted components from a signal containing a fundamental and all related overtones), additive synthesis (building tones from signals for pure sine-wave tones), or other techniques, most importantly whole-sound sampling (digital recording of sounds, usually from acoustic instruments). The first synthesizer was developed c. 1955 by RCA. Compact, commercially viable synthesizers, generally with pianolike keyboards, were produced in the 1960s by Robert Moog (born 1934), Donald Buchla (born 1937), and others. With transistor technology, these soon became portable and cheap enough for practical performance use, and such instruments became fixtures in rock bands, often displacing electric pianos and organs. See also MIDI.

synthetic ammonia process See HABER-BOSCH PROCESS

syphilis \'si-fə-ləs\ SEXUALLY TRANSMITTED DISEASE caused by the SPIROCHETE *Treponema pallidum.* Without treatment, it may progress through three stages: primary, characterized by a CHANCRE and low fever; secondary (weeks to months later; only half of those infected display symptoms), with a skin and mucous-membrane rash, LYMPH-NODE swelling, and bone, joint, eye, and nervous-system involvement; and tertiary. The tertiary stage follows a latency period that can last years, and only one-fourth of those infected display tertiary symptoms. These can be benign or incapacitating and even fatal; almost any part of the body may be attacked. Syphilis can be spread to a fetus from an infected mother. Other species of *Treponema* cause similar but milder, nonsexually transmitted forms of syphilis (see YAWS). Several blood tests can detect syphilis, even during latency. Antibiotic treatment is effective.

Syr Darya \ˌsir-dər-'yä\ *ancient* **Iaxartes** River, western central Asia, in Uzbekistan, Tajikistan, and Kazakhstan. Formed by the confluence of two headstreams in the fertile FERGANA VALLEY, it flows west-northwest 1,374 mi (2,212 km) to empty into the ARAL SEA. Its lower course is on the eastern edge of the KYZYL KUM desert. It is the longest river in central Asia, but carries less water than does the AMU DARYA. It is used extensively for hydroelectric power and irrigation.

Syracuse *Italian* **Siracusa** *ancient* **Syracusae** Seaport city (pop., 1996 est.: 126,000), eastern coast of Sicily. Founded in 734 BC by Greeks from CORINTH, it was seized by Hippocrates of Gela in 485 BC and ruled by tyrants until a revolution established a democratic government c. 465 BC. In 413 BC, during the PELOPONNESIAN WAR, it defeated an Athenian invasion force. Under the rule of DIONYSIUS I the Elder in 405–367 BC, it became the most powerful of the Greek cities, fighting three wars against rival CARTHAGE. It fell to Rome in 211 BC. It was sacked by Frankish invaders in AD 280 and captured by Arabs in 878; its importance waned in medieval times. Now the commercial center for an agricultural district, it is also a fishing port and tourist center. It has many examples of medieval and Renaissance architecture as well as Greek and Roman ruins. It was the birthplace of THEOCRITUS and ARCHIMEDES.

Syracuse City (pop., 1996 est.: 156,000), central New York. The site, at the southern end of Lake Oneida, was once the territory of the Onondaga Indians and headquarters of the IROQUOIS CONFEDERACY. It was visited by the French in the 17th century. Indian hostility and the swampy location precluded settlement until the establishment of a trading post in 1786. Soon a saltworks based on its brine springs began operation; it supplied most of the nation's salt until 1870. An important port on the ERIE CANAL, it serves as a distribution center for the central New York agricultural region. It also manufactures pharmaceuticals and electronics. It is the site of SYRACUSE UNIV. (1870) and the Everson Museum of Art (founded 1896).

Syracuse University Private university in Syracuse, N.Y., founded in 1870. It has colleges of arts and sciences, visual and performing arts, and human development and schools of architecture, engineering, nursing, communications (the S. I. Newhouse School), social work, information studies, management, and public affairs (the Maxwell School). Research facilities include centers for gerontology, computer applications, and science and technology. Enrollment is about 14,500.

Syria *officially* **Syrian Arab Republic** Country, South Asia, eastern coast of the Mediterranean Sea. Area: 71,498 sq mi (185,180 sq km). Population (2000 est.): 16,306,000. Capital: DAMASCUS. Arabs are the

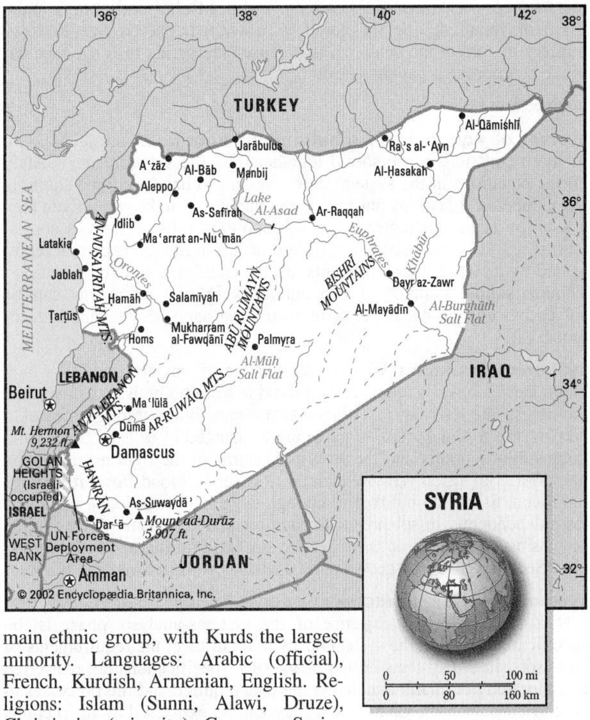

main ethnic group, with Kurds the largest minority. Languages: Arabic (official), French, Kurdish, Armenian, English. Religions: Islam (Sunni, Alawi, Druze), Christianity (minority). Currency: Syrian pound. Syria consists of a coastal zone, with abundant water supplies; a mountain zone that includes the ANTI-LEBANON MOUNTAINS; and a portion of the SYRIAN DESERT. The EUPHRATES RIVER is its most important water source and only navigable river. It has a mixed economy based on agri-

S T U V

culture, trade, and mining and manufacturing. Crops include cotton, cereals, fruits, tobacco, and livestock. Mineral resources include petroleum, natural gas, and iron ore; manufactures include textiles, cement, and shoes. It is a republic with one legislative house; its head of state and of government is the president, who by law must be a Muslim. The legal system is based largely on Islamic law. Syria has been inhabited for several thousand years. From the 3rd millennium BC, it has been under the control variously of Sumerians, Akkadians, Amorites, Egyptians, Hittites, Assyrians, and Babylonians. In the 6th century BC it became part of the Persian ACHAEMENIAN DYNASTY, which fell to ALEXANDER THE GREAT in 330 BC. SELEUCID rulers governed it 301–c. 164 BC; then Parthians and Nabataean Arabs divided the region. It flourished as a Roman province (64 BC–AD 300) and as part of the BYZANTINE EMPIRE (300–634), until Muslims invaded and established control. It came under the Ottoman empire in 1516, which held it, except for brief rules by Egypt, until the British invaded in World War I. After the war it became a French mandate; it achieved independence in 1944. It united with Egypt in the United Arab Republic (1958–61). During the SIX-DAY WAR (1967), it lost the GOLAN HEIGHTS to Israel. Syrian troops frequently clashed with Israeli troops in Lebanon during the 1980s and '90s. HAFIZ AL-ASSAD's long and harsh regime was marked also by antagonism toward Syria's neighbors Turkey and Iraq.

Syrian Desert Arid wasteland, South Asia. It extends over much of northern Saudi Arabia, eastern Jordan, southern Syria, and western Iraq. Largely covered by lava flows, it formed a nearly impenetrable barrier between the populated areas of the LEVANT and MESOPOTAMIA until modern times; several major highways and oil pipelines now cross it.

syringomyelia \sə-ˌriŋ-gō-mī-ˈē-lē-ə\ Disease characterized by the entrance of CEREBROSPINAL FLUID into the SPINAL CORD, where it forms a cavity (syrinx). The syrinx can expand and elongate over time, destroying the center of the spinal cord and causing symptoms that vary with the syrinx's size and location. It is often related to the presence of a congenital malformation of the cerebellum called a Chiari malformation, but may also arise as a complication of spinal trauma, meningitis, tumor, or other conditions. Symptoms include loss of sensitivity, especially to temperature, muscle weakness and spasticity, and headaches and chronic pain. Syringomyelia may be diagnosed with MAGNETIC RESONANCE IMAGING. Surgery to correct the condition that caused the syrinx to form may stabilize or improve a patient's health.

syrinx See PANPIPE

system of equations *or* **simultaneous equations** In algebra, two or more equations to be solved together (i.e., the solution must satisfy all the equations in the system). For a system to have a unique solution, the number of equations must equal the number of unknowns. Even then a solution is not guaranteed. If a solution exists, the system is consistent; if not, it is inconsistent. A system of linear equations can be represented by a MATRIX whose elements are the coefficients of the equations. Though simple systems of two equations in two unknowns can be solved by substitution, larger systems are best handled with matrix techniques.

systemic circulation \sis-ˈtem-ik\ Circuit of vessels through which blood carries oxygen to and carbon dioxide from body tissues other than the lungs. The left ventricle of the HEART pumps blood through the AORTA and ARTERIES to the CAPILLARIES; gases are exchanged in cells of tissues and organs; blood drains into the VEINS and returns to the right atrium of the heart. Arterial BLOOD PRESSURE maintains systemic blood flow; if it drops too much, tissues do not receive enough oxygen and nutrients. Flow varies independently in subcircuits to each organ and system—for example, increasing after meals in the digestive tract and during exercise in muscles. See also CARDIOVASCULAR SYSTEM, CIRCULATION, PULMONARY CIRCULATION.

S | T | U | V

systems analysis In INFORMATION PROCESSING, a phase of SYSTEMS ENGINEERING. The principal objective of the systems-analysis phase is the specification of what the system needs to do to meet the requirements of end users. In the systems-design phase such specifications are converted to a hierarchy of charts that define the data required and the processes to be carried out on the data so that they can be expressed as instructions of a computer program. Many information systems are implemented with generic software, rather than with such custom-built programs.

systems ecology Branch of ecosystem ecology (the study of energy budgets, biogeochemical cycles, and feeding and behavioral aspects of ecological communities) that attempts to clarify the structure and function of ECOSYSTEMS by means of applied mathematics, mathematical models, and computer programs. It concentrates on input and output analysis and has stimulated the development of applied ecology: the application of ecological principles to the management of natural resources, agricultural production, and problems of environmental pollution.

systems engineering Technique of using knowledge from various branches of engineering and science to introduce technological innovations into the planning and development stages of a system. Systems engineering was first applied to the organization of commercial telephone systems in the 1920s and '30s. Many systems-engineering techniques were developed during World War II in an effort to deploy military equipment more efficiently. Postwar growth in the field was spurred by advances in electronic systems and by the development of computers and information theory. Systems engineering usually involves incorporating new technology into complex, man-made systems, in which a change in one part affects many others. One tool used by systems engineers is the FLOWCHART, which shows the system in graphic form, with geometric figures representing various subsystems and arrows representing their interactions. Other tools include mathematical models, probability theory, statistical analysis, and computer simulations.

systems programming Development of computer SOFTWARE that is part of a computer OPERATING SYSTEM or other control program, especially as used in computer NETWORKS. Systems programming covers data and program management, including operating systems, control programs, network software, and DATABASE MANAGEMENT SYSTEMS.

Szczecin \ˈshchet-ˌsēn\ *German* **Stettin** \shte-ˈtēn\ Seaport (pop., 1996 est.: 414,000), northwestern Poland, near the mouth of the ODER RIVER. A Slavic fishing and commercial center for centuries, it was annexed to Poland by MIESZKO I in the 10th century. It joined the HANSEATIC LEAGUE in 1360. It passed to Sweden in 1648, and Prussia in 1720, remaining under German control until its transfer to Poland after World War II. During the war its port was completely destroyed and the city greatly depopulated. Under Polish administration the port and city were rebuilt, and it is now part of Poland's largest port complex. It is a cultural center of western Poland; several institutions of higher education are located there.

Széchenyi \ˈsā-chen-yi\, **István, Gróf (Count)** (1791–1860) Hungarian reformer and writer. Born to an aristocratic Hungarian family in Vienna, he traveled extensively in Europe. He returned to Budapest to found the Hungarian National Academy of Sciences (1825) and wrote several works that called for economic reforms and urged the nobility to pay taxes to modernize Hungary. He led projects that improved roads, made the Danube River navigable to the Black Sea, and built the first suspension bridge at Budapest. In the 1840s he lost his following to the more radical LAJOS KOSSUTH; he went insane in 1848.

Szechwan See SICHUAN

Szell \ˈsel, ˈzel\, **George** (1897–1970) Hungarian-U.S. conductor. He made his debut as a pianist at 11, and before his 20th birthday had appeared with the Berlin Philharmonic as pianist, conductor, and composer. He established himself as an opera conductor in various German cities, including Berlin (1924–30), and Prague (1930–36). When war broke out, he settled in the U.S., conducting at the Metropolitan Opera (1942–46) and then with the Cleveland Orchestra (1946–70). There he imposed stern discipline but won his players' devotion by his own fierce dedication. The legendary precision he obtained from the orchestra made it one of the world's finest.

Szent-Györgyi.
BOYER—H. ROGER-VIOLLET

Szent-Györgyi \sānt-ˈjȯrj, sānt-ˈjȯr-jē\, **Albert** (1893–1986) Hungarian-U.S. biochemist. His discoveries about the roles played by certain organic compounds, especially VITAMIN C, in the oxidation (see OXIDATION-REDUCTION) of nutrients by cells brought him a 1937 Nobel

Prize. He found and isolated an organic reducing agent from plant juices and adrenal gland extracts and showed it was identical to vitamin C. His work on intermediates in the cell laid the foundation for the elucidation of the TRICARBOXYLIC ACID CYCLE by HANS ADOLF KREBS. In later years he worked on the biochemistry of muscular action (demonstrating the role of ATP) and of CELL division.

Szilard \'zi-ˌlärd\, **Leo** (1898–1964) Hungarian-U.S. physicist. He taught at the University of Berlin (1922–33), then fled to England (1934–37) and the U.S., where he worked at the University of Chicago from 1942. In 1929 he established the relation between entropy and transfer of information, and in 1934 he helped develop the first method of separating isotopes of artificial radioactive elements. He helped ENRICO FERMI conduct the first sustained nuclear chain reaction and construct the first nuclear reactor. In 1939 he was instrumental in establishing the Manhattan Project, in which he helped develop the atomic bomb. After the first use of the bomb, he promoted the peaceful uses of atomic energy and the control of nuclear weapons, founding the Council for a Livable World. In 1959 he received the Atoms for Peace Award.

Szymanowski \ˌshi-mȧ-'nȯf-skē\, **Karol (Maciej)** (1882–1937) Polish composer. Born to a cultivated family, he studied music in Warsaw. Finding opportunities in Poland limited for new music, he traveled in Europe, Africa, and the Middle East, broadening his musical tastes. After losing all his possessions in World War I, he became a fervent nationalist, studying native Polish music and incorporating it into his own, including the opera *King Roger* (1924). Director of the Warsaw Conservatory (1927–29), he had to resign as his tuberculosis worsened. He wrote four symphonies, two violin concertos, a piano concerto, a *Stabat mater* (1926), the ballet *Harnasie* (1931), and many songs; his piano music includes *Metopes* (1915), *Masques* (1916), and 22 mazurkas.

Szymborska \shim-'bȯr-skə\, **Wislawa** (born 1923) Polish poet. From 1953 to 1981 Szymborska was on the staff of the weekly *Zycie Literackie* ("Literary Life"), gaining a reputation as a poet, book reviewer, and translator of French poetry. Her first two volumes of poetry were attempts to conform to SOCIALIST REALISM. Later poems, notable for their precise and concrete language and ironic detachment, express her dissatisfaction with communism and explore philosophical, moral, and ethical issues. A selection of her poems was published in English translation as *View with a Grain of Sand* (1995). She received the Nobel Prize in 1996.

T1 Type of broadband telecommunications connection (see BROADBAND TECHNOLOGY) used especially to connect INTERNET SERVICE PROVIDERS to the Internet's infrastructure. Developed by Bell Labs in the 1960s, the "T-carrier systems" offer entirely digital, full duplex exchange of data over traditional wire, coaxial cable, optical fiber, microwave relay, or other communications media. The T1 lines carry about 1.5 megabits of data per second, while the related T3 lines carry over 40. However, such systems are generally too expensive for individual network users, who turn instead to ISDN lines, CABLE MODEMS, DSL connections, or some form of wireless or satellite system for high-speed Internet access.

T cell With the B CELL, one of the two main types of white blood cell, essential parts of the immune system. T cells originate in the bone marrow, mature in the thymus, and travel in the blood to other lymphoid tissues, such as the spleen, tonsils, and lymph nodes. Through receptor molecules on their surfaces, T cells directly attack invaders (ANTIGENS) by binding to them and helping remove them from the body. Because the body contains millions of T and B cells, many of which carry unique receptors, it can respond to virtually any antigen. See also ANTIBODY, IMMUNOLOGY.

T Tauri star \'tē-'tȯr-ī\ Any of a class of very young STARS with masses less than about twice the sun's. Characterized by unpredictable changes in brightness, they represent an early stage in stellar evolution, having only recently been formed by the gravitational condensation of interstellar gas and dust. These young stars, now contracting more slowly, are relatively unstable and will remain so until their interior temperatures become high enough to support NUCLEAR FUSION for energy generation. More than 500 T Tauri stars have been observed.

Ta hsüeh See DA XUE

Ta-lien See DALIAN

T'a-li-mu Ho See TARIM RIVER

Ta-wen-k'ou culture See DAWENKOU CULTURE

Ta Yu See DA YU

Taaffe \'tä-fə\, **Eduard, Graf (Count) von** (1833–1895) Austrian politician and prime minister (1868–70, 1879–93). A boyhood friend of the future emperor FRANCIS JOSEPH, he entered the civil service in 1852 and rose rapidly, serving as governor of upper Austria, minister of the interior (1867, 1870–71, 1879), governor of Tirol (1871–79), and prime minister. In his second term as premier, he forged a conservative coalition that restored a degree of order among the Austrian empire's quarreling nationalities by granting concessions to the Polish and Czech nationalists and bringing them into the Habsburg civil service.

Taal \tä-'äl, 'täl\, **Lake** *formerly* **Lake Bombon** Lake, southwestern LUZON, Philippines. It covers an area of 94 sq mi (244 sq km) and occupies a volcanic crater less than 10 ft (3 m) above sea level. Volcano Island (984 ft or 300 m), which rises from the lake and is also called Taal Volcano, contains another small crater (Yellow Lake). The volcano has erupted 25 times since 1572, most recently in 1970. Located within a national park, the lake is a major tourist attraction.

Tabari \'tä-bȧ-rē\, **al-** *in full* **Abu Jafar Muhammad ibn Jarir al-Tabari** (839–923) Muslim scholar, Quranic commentator, and historian. Born in Amol, Tabaristan (Iran), he studied in Islamic centers of learning in Iraq, Syria, and Egypt. He wrote the *Quran Commentary,* annotating the Quran with all of the juridical, lexicographical, and historical explanations transmitted in the Hadith. His other major work was the *History of Prophets and Kings,* which began with the Creation and concluded with the fall of the UMAYYAD dynasty.

Tabasco \tə-'bas-kō\ State (pop., 1995 est.: 1,747,000), southeastern Mexico. It covers an area of 9,522 sq mi (24,662 sq km); its capital is VILLAHERMOSA. Pre-Columbian Indian cultures included those of the QUICHÉ, OLMEC, Tabasca, and NAHUA. The area was first visited by Europeans in 1518; in 1519 HERNAN CORTES first clashed with the Indians, who were partially subdued in the 1530s and 1540s. It became a state in 1824. Agriculture, forestry, beekeeping, fishing in the Gulf of Mexico, and cattle-raising provided much of the state's income before petroleum exploitation began in the 1960s. The state now has over 30 oil fields.

Tabernacle In Jewish history, the portable sanctuary constructed by MOSES as a place of worship for the Hebrew tribes during the period of wandering that preceded their arrival in the Promised Land. Elaborately described in EXODUS, it was divided into an outer room, the "holy place," and an inner room, the HOLY OF HOLIES, which housed the ARK of the Covenant. With the erection of the Temple of JERUSALEM, the Tabernacle no longer served a purpose. In modern ROMAN CATHOLICISM and EASTERN ORTHODOXY, the tabernacle is the receptacle on the church altar in which the consecrated elements of the EUCHARIST are stored.

tabes dorsalis \'tā-bēz-dȯr-'sā-ləs\ *or* **progressive locomotor ataxia** \,lō-kə-'mōt-ər-ə-'tak-sē-ə\ Rare neurologic form of tertiary SYPHILIS with spinal nerve root degeneration (see SPINAL cord). Untreated, it can weaken victims until they cannot walk unassisted. Symptoms, mainly in the legs, may take 25 years to appear, beginning with transient stabbing pains (lightning pain). Neurological deterioration then causes loss of TENDON reflexes; progressive ATAXIA; loss of pain and temperature senses and of PROPRIOCEPTION, with bladder incontinence, severe foot ULCERS, and knee and hip joint destruction. Tabes dorsalis is seldom fatal. Elimination of the bacteria with PENICILLIN can relieve pain but not reverse nerve degeneration.

tabla \'tä-blə\ Pair of small drums, the principal percussion in the chamber music of northern India. The higher-pitched *dahina* is a roughly cylindrical one-skinned drum, usually wooden, normally tuned to the RAGA's tonic. The *bahina* is a deep kettledrum usually of copper; its pitch varies with pressure from the heel of the player's hand. A disk of black tuning paste on the membrane of each drum gives it harmonic overtones.

table Article of furniture used in the Western world since at least the 7th century BC, consisting of a flat slab of stone, metal, wood, or glass supported by trestles, legs, or a pillar. Though tables were used in ancient Egypt, Assyria, and Greece, only during the Middle Ages, with the growing formality of life under feudalism, did tables increasingly take on social significance. Tables with attached legs appeared in the 15th century. The draw top was invented in the 16th century, making it possible to double the table length. Increasing contact with the East in the 18th century led to increasing specialization in the design of occasional tables.

Table Bay Inlet, Atlantic Ocean, forming the harbor of CAPE TOWN, South Africa. It is 12 mi (19 km) long and 8 mi (12 km) wide. Although less sheltered than other bays along the coast, it became a port of call for ships traveling to India and the East because of the availability of fresh water. The shore was permanently settled by the Dutch in 1652.

table tennis *or* **Ping-Pong** Game based on tennis that is played on a tabletop with wooden paddles and a small hollow plastic ball. The object is to hit the ball so that it goes over the net and bounces on the opponent's half of the table in such a way as to defeat the opponent's attempt to reach and return it. Both singles and doubles games are played. A match consists of the best of three or the best of five games, each game being won by the player or team that first reaches 21 points. Invented in England in the early 20th century, it soon spread throughout the world. Since the mid-1950s, East Asian countries have dominated the sport. It has been an Olympic sport for both men and women since 1988.

taboo Prohibition against touching, saying, or doing something for fear of immediate harm from a supernatural force. The term is of Polynesian origin and was first noted by Capt. JAMES COOK during his 1771 visit to Tonga, but taboos have been present in virtually all cultures. They may include prohibitions on fishing or hunting at certain seasons, eating certain foods, interacting with members of other social classes, coming into contact with corpses, and (for women) performing certain activities during menstruation. Though some taboos can be traced to evident risks to health and safety, there is no generally accepted explanation of most others, though there is broad agreement that they tend to relate to objects and actions that are significant for the maintenance of social order.

Tabriz \ta-'brēz\ City (pop., 1994 est.: 1,166,000), northwestern Iran. Earthquakes and invasions by Arabs, Turks, and Mongols have destroyed the city numerous times. The Turkish ruler TIMUR conquered it in 1392. During the next 200 years control passed several times between

Iran and Turkey. During the 18th–19th century, the Turks and Russians alternated occupation; they also fought over it in World War I. In the 1850s the BAB and 40,000 of his followers were executed there. Active in Iranian politics, it suffered bombing damage during the IRAN–IRAQ WAR (1980s). Notable ancient sites include the Blue Mosque (1465–66), renowned for the splendor of its blue tile decoration, and the remains of the 12-sided tomb of MAHMUD GHAZAN.

Tabriz school School of miniaturist painting founded by the Mongol Il-Khans early in the 14th century. Reflecting the penetration of East Asian traditions into Islamic painting, early Tabriz works were characterized by light, feathery brush strokes, gentle coloring, and an attempt to create the illusion of spatiality. The school reached its peak just as the Il-Khans were being conquered by the Islamic Timurids (1370–1506). It continued to be active in this period, though it was overshadowed by the workshops in Shiraz and Herat.

Tachism \'ta-ˌshi-zəm\ (from French, *tache:* "spot") Style of painting practiced in Paris after World War II and through the 1950s. Like its U.S. equivalent, ACTION PAINTING, it featured the intuitive, spontaneous gesture of the artist's brush stroke. The Tachists, including Hans Hartung (1904–1989) and Georges Mathieu (born 1921), produced large works of sweeping brush strokes and of drips, blots, stains, and splashes of color. Tachism was part of the postwar movement known as Art Informel, inspired by U.S. Abstract Impressionism.

tachycardia \ˌta-ki-'kär-dē-ə\ HEART rate over 100 (as high as 240) beats per minute. If a normal response to exercise or stress, it is no danger to healthy people, but when it originates elsewhere than the heart's natural PACEMAKER, it is a CARDIAC ARRHYTHMIA. Symptoms include fatigue, faintness, shortness of breath, and feeling the heart thumping. It may subside within minutes or hours with no lasting ill effects, but in serious heart, lung, or circulatory disease it can precede ATRIAL fibrillation or MYOCARDIAL infarction and demands immediate medical attention. Tachycardias can be treated by an electric shock to the heart, by antiarrhythmic drugs, and by antitachycardia pacemakers.

tachyon \'ta-kē-ˌän\ Hypothetical SUBATOMIC particle whose velocity is always greater than that of light. Its existence appears consistent with the theory of RELATIVITY. Just as an ordinary particle such as an electron can exist only at speeds less than that of light, a tachyon can exist only at speeds greater than that of light. At such speeds, its mass would be real and positive. On losing energy, a tachyon accelerates; the faster it travels, the less energy it has. The existence of tachyons has not been established experimentally.

Tacitus \'ta-sə-təs\ *Latin* **Publius Cornelius Tacitus** (AD 56?–120?) Roman orator and public official. After studying rhetoric, he began his career with a minor magistracy, eventually advancing to the proconsulate of Asia, the top provincial governorship (AD 112–113). In AD 98 he wrote *De vita Julii Agricolae,* a biographical account of his father-in-law, governor of Britain; and *De origine et situ Germanorum* (known as the *Germania*), describing the people of the Roman frontier on the Rhine. His works on Roman history are the *Histories*, concerning the empire from AD 69 to 96, and the later *Annals*, dealing with the empire from AD 14 to 68, which effectively diagnoses the decline of Roman political freedom he had described in the *Histories*. Only parts of each are extant. Tacitus is regarded as perhaps the greatest historian and one of the greatest prose stylists to write in Latin.

Tacoma Seaport (pop., 1996 est.: 179,000), western Washington, on PUGET SOUND. Settled in 1864, it grew to become a lumbering and port city. Docks and wharves line its waterfront. A boat-building center, it also has smelters, foundries, and electrochemical plants. It is a gateway to Mount RAINIER National Park and is connected by bridge to the Olympic Peninsula recreation areas. It is the seat of the University of Puget Sound (1888) and Pacific Lutheran University (1890).

Taconic orogeny \tə-'kä-nik-ȯ-'rä-jə-nē\ Mountain-building event that affected the APPALACHIAN GEOSYNCLINE along the eastern coast of the U.S. Evidence for the OROGENY is most pronounced in the northern Appalachian Mountains, but its effects can be noted as far away as Tennessee and Georgia. Events ascribed to it include the development of New York's Taconic Range and Vermont's Green Mountains. Originally thought to have occurred at approximately the Ordovician–Silurian boundary (c. 443 million years ago), it is now generally considered to have consisted of several pulses from the mid-Ordovician to the early Silurian period.

Taconic Range Part of the APPALACHIAN MOUNTAIN system, northeastern U.S. It extends 150 mi (240 km) from southern Vermont to northern New York. Mount Equinox (3,816 ft, or 1,163 m) in southwestern Vermont is the highest peak. In Massachusetts the mountains form the western section of the BERKSHIRE HILLS. Taconic State Park, in New York, is a popular mountain recreation area.

taconite \'ta-kə-ˌnīt\ Low-grade IRON formation (e.g., in Minnesota). Recovery of the iron requires fine grinding and concentration of iron-bearing phases (see ORE DRESSING), which are then formed into pellets suitable for BLAST furnaces. As high-grade deposits of iron ore have become depleted, taconite deposits have increased in importance.

tactics In warfare, the art and science of fighting battles. It is concerned with the approach to combat, placement of troops, use made of weapons, vehicles, ships, or aircraft, and execution of movements for attack or defense. In general, tactics deal with the problems encountered in actual fighting. Tactical thinking attempts to coordinate personnel with the existing weapons technology and apply both to the terrain and enemy forces in a way that uses the fighting force to best advantage. Deployment involves placing each type of weapon where it can do the most damage to the enemy or provide the most protection to one's own forces. Timing and direction of attack are also important considerations. At sea, direction was especially crucial in the era of wind-powered warships. In recent wars, timing has been a crucial factor in mounting airborne strikes that take advantage of the element of surprise. See also STRATEGY.

Tadema, Lawrence Alma- See Lawrence ALMA-TADEMA

Tadmor See PALMYRA

tadpole *or* **polliwog** Aquatic larval stage of FROGS and TOADS. Tadpoles have a short, oval body, broad tail, small mouth, and no external gills. Most are vegetarians, but those of some species are carnivorous or even cannibalistic. Tadpole METAMORPHOSIS follows a pattern of gradual development of forelimbs and hind limbs, resorption of the tail, shortening of the intestine, disappearance of the gills, and development of the lungs. On completion of metamorphosis, the young frog or toad emerges onto land.

tae kwon do \'tī-'kwän-'dō\ Korean MARTIAL ART resembling KARATE. It is characterized by the use of high standing and jump kicks as well as punches and is practiced for sport, self-defense, and spiritual development. In sparring, blows are stopped just short of contact. Based on earlier forms of Korean self-defense, tae kwon do was formalized and named in 1955. It became an Olympic sport in the year 2000.

Taegu \'ta-'gü\ City (pop., 1995: 2,449,000), southeastern South Korea. For centuries the administrative, economic, and cultural center of South Korea, it developed during the CHOSON dynasty (1392–1910) into one of the country's three big market cities. It has important textile industries, but is best known for the apples grown in the surrounding area, which are exported throughout East and Southeast Asia. The area attracts visitors to its several parks, ancient pagodas, and the 9th-century Buddhist temple containing the TRIPITAKA. It is home to many universities and colleges.

T'aejo See YI SONG-GYE

Taejon \'ta-'jȯn\ Special city (pop., 1995: 1,272,000) and capital of Ch'ungch'ong province, southeastern South Korea. It was a poor village until rail connections spurred development in the early 1900s. During the KOREAN WAR (1950–53), it was a temporary capital of the Republic of Korea, and 70% of the city was destroyed; it has since been rebuilt. The manufacture of cotton textiles, machinery, and chemicals has been developed. Chungnam National University and five other colleges are located there.

Taeuber \'tȯi-bər\, **Conrad and Irene Barnes-** *orig.* **Irene Barnes** (1906–1999, 1906–1974) U.S. demographers, statisticians, and social scientists. Born respectively in Hosmer, S.D., and Meadville, Mo., they worked for various government agencies. Their scholarly census work helped found the science of DEMOGRAPHY and made them authorities on population movements in the U.S. *The Changing Population of the United States* (1958) and *The Population of Japan* (1958) are considered classics in demography.

Taewon-gun \'tä-'wən-'gün\ (1821–1898). Father of the last ruling Korean king, Kojong (r.1864–1907), and regent 1864–73. As regent, Taewon-gun inaugurated reforms to strengthen the central government. He also modernized Korea's armies. He opposed concessions to Japan or the West but was kidnapped and held in China three years, during which time his power and many of his reforms were eliminated.

Taff Vale case (1900–1) Successful trial in Britain of a suit brought by the Taff Vale Railway Co. against the Amalgamated Society of Railway Servants (ASRS). In August 1900 the ASRS struck for higher wages but settled within two weeks when the company used strikebreakers. The company sued the union for violating the Protection of Property Act, and the courts held that a union could be sued for damages caused by a strike, effectively eliminating the strike as a weapon of organized labor. Opposition to the decision spurred the growth of the LABOUR PARTY and led to passage of the Trade Disputes Act of 1906, which nullified the decision's effect.

Tafilalt \,ta-fi-'lalt\ Oasis, southeastern Morocco. The country's largest Saharan oasis, it covers 533 sq mi (1,380 sq km). It comprises six fortified villages and palm groves stretching for 30 mi (50 km) along the Wadi Ziz. Its old capital was the prosperous BERBER stronghold of Sijilmassa, founded in AD 757 on the Saharan caravan route and finally destroyed in the 19th century. The oasis is noted for its dates.

tafsir \tȧf-'sēr\ Science of explanation and interpretation of the QURAN. It arose after the death of MUHAMMAD to deal with ambiguity, variant readings, defective texts, and apparent contradictions in the scripture. Starting from mere personal speculation, tafsir developed into a system of systematic EXEGESIS of the Quran's text, proceeding verse by verse and sometimes word by word. Early stages relied on the HADITH, later giving rise to a dogmatic type of tafsir. The most comprehensive tafsir was compiled by al-TABARI. Muslim modernists employ tafsir as a vehicle for their reformist ideas.

Taft, Robert A(lphonso) (1889–1953) U.S. politician. Born in Cincinnati, the son of WILLIAM H. TAFT, he served in the Ohio legislature before being elected to the U.S. Senate, where he served 1939–53. He became known as a strong advocate of traditional conservativism and earned the nickname "Mr. Republican." He opposed centralizing power in the federal government and cosponsored the TAFT-HARTLEY ACT to restrict organized labor. An isolationist, he opposed U.S. involvement in postwar international organizations. He was a favorite-son candidate at Republican national conventions, especially in 1948 and 1952, but internationalists in the party opposed his conservative views.

Taft, William Howard (1857–1930) 27th president of the U.S. (1909–13). Born in Cincinnati, he served on the state superior court (1887–90), as U.S. solicitor general (1890–92), and as U.S. appellate judge (1892–1900). He was appointed head of the Philippine Commission to set up a civilian government in the islands and was its first civilian governor (1901–4). He served as U.S. secretary of war (1904–8) under Pres. THEODORE ROOSEVELT, who supported Taft's nomination for president in 1908. He won the election but became allied with the conservative Republicans, causing a rift with party progressives. He was again the nominee in 1912, but the split with Roosevelt and the BULL MOOSE PARTY resulted in the electoral victory of WOODROW WILSON. Taft later taught law at Yale University (1913–21), served on the National War Labor Board (1918), and was a supporter of the League of Nations. As chief justice of the U.S. Supreme Court (1921–30), he introduced reforms that made it more efficient. He secured passage of the Judges Act of 1925, which gave the Court wider discretion in accepting cases. His important opinion in *Myers vs. U.S.* (1926) upheld the president's authority to remove federal officials. In poor health, he resigned in 1930.

William Howard Taft, 1909.
BY COURTESY OF THE LIBRARY OF CONGRESS, WASHINGTON, D.C.

Taft-Hartley Act *officially* **Labor-Management Relations Act** (1947) Legislation that restricted labor unions. Sponsored by Sen. ROBERT A. TAFT and Rep. Fred A. Hartley, Jr., the act amended much of the pro-union WAGNER ACT and was passed by a Republican-controlled Congress over the veto of Pres. HARRY TRUMAN. It allowed employees the right not to join unions (outlawing the CLOSED shop) and required advance notice of a labor strike, authorized an 80-day federal injunction when a strike threatened national health or safety, narrowed the definition of unfair labor practices, specified unfair union practices, restricted union political contributions, and required union officials to take an oath pledging they were not communists. See also LANDRUM-GRIFFIN ACT.

Tagalog \tə-'gä-ləg\ Largest cultural-linguistic group in the Philippines. They are the dominant population of Manila and of several provinces near the city. Most are Roman Catholic and most are farmers; their main cash crops are sugarcane and coconuts. The importance of Manila has given the urban Tagalog economic leadership in the Philippines. The TAGALOG LANGUAGE is the basis of Pilipino, the national language.

Tagalog language AUSTRONESIAN language of the Philippines, spoken as a first language by about 17 million people on the island of Luzon and by at least half a million immigrant Filipinos. As the language of Manila, the Philippines' capital and major metropolis, Tagalog has long had an importance outside its own speech area. With vocabulary enrichment from other Philippine languages, it has been made the basis of Pilipino, the national language; widely used in education and the media, Pilipino is now understood by more than 60% of the Philippine population. Though a script ultimately of South Asian origin was in use for Tagalog in the 16th century (see INDIC writing systems), all recent literature in the language has utilized adaptations of the LATIN ALPHABET.

Taglioni \täl-'yō-nē\, **Marie** (1804–1884) Italian ballet dancer whose delicate dancing typified the early-19th-century Romantic style. She trained with her dancer-choreographer father, Filippo Taglioni (1777–1871), making her debut in Vienna in 1822. Her father helped develop her unique technique, and she danced in his *La sylphide* at the Paris Opera in 1832 to great acclaim. She toured throughout Europe and danced with the Imperial Ballet in St. Petersburg 1837–42; she retired in 1847. She was one of the first to dance on pointe, to include floating leaps and the arabesque in her technical repertoire, and to dress in the full, light skirt that would evolve into the tutu.

Tagore \'tä-,gȯr, *Engl* tə-'gȯr\, **Debendranath** (1817–1905) Hindu philosopher and religious reformer. Born into a wealthy landowning family in Calcutta (now Kolkata), he was educated in both Eastern and Western philosophy. Striving to purge Hinduism of abuses, he spoke vehemently against SUTTEE and tried to bring education within the reach of all. He was active in the BRAHMO SAMAJ. In his zeal to erase idolatry and undemocratic practices, he rejected the VEDAS as deficient in dictating guidelines for human behavior. Failing to find a middle path between radical rationalism and Brahman conservatism, he retired from public life. He was known as the Great Sage. RABINDRANATH TAGORE was his son.

Tagore, Rabindranath (1861–1941) Bengali poet, writer, composer, and painter. The son of DEBENDRANATH TAGORE, he published several books of poetry, including *Manasi,* in his twenties. His later religious poetry was introduced to the West in *Gitanjali* (1912). Through international travel and lecturing, he introduced aspects of Indian culture to the West, and vice versa. He spoke ardently in favor of Indian independence; as a protest against the Massacre of AMRITSAR, he repudiated the knighthood he had received in 1915. He founded an experimental school in Bengal where he sought to blend Eastern and Western philosophies; it became Vishva-Bharati University (1921). He was awarded the 1913 Nobel Prize for Literature.

Rabindranath Tagore.
ENCYCLOPÆDIA BRITANNICA, INC.

Tagus River \'tā-gəs\ *Spanish* **Río Tajo** \'tä-hō\ *Portuguese* **Rio Tejo** \'rē-ü-'tā-zhü\ Longest waterway of the IBERIAN PENINSULA. It rises in eastern central Spain and flows west across Spain and Portugal for 626 mi (1,007 km) to empty into the Atlantic Ocean near LISBON. It covers the heart of the two nations, and is of vital economic importance. Dams harness it for irrigation and hydroelectric power, and large artificial lakes have been created. Navigable for about 100 mi (160 km) in its lower courses, it supplies a fine natural harbor at Lisbon.

Taha Hussein *or* **Taha Husayn** \'tä-hä-hü-'sān\ (1889–1973) Egyptian writer. Though blinded by illness at age 2, he became a professor of Arabic literature at the secular University of Cairo, where his bold views often enraged Islamic religious conservatives. An outstanding figure of the modernist movement in Egyptian literature, he wrote novels, stories, criticism, and social and political essays. Outside Egypt he is best known for his autobiography, *Al-Ayyam,* which appeared in English as *An Egyptian Childhood* (1932) and *The Stream of Days* (1943), and became the first modern Arab literary work to be acclaimed in the West.

Tahiti Island (pop., 1995 est.: 155,000), SOCIETY ISLANDS, FRENCH POLYNESIA. Located in the South Pacific Ocean, and the largest of the Society's eastern group, it occupies an area of 402 sq mi (1,042 sq km). PAPEETE is the capital. The island's interior is mountainous, rising to 7,339 ft (2,237 m) at Mount Orohena; its towns are located on the coastal plain. Long inhabited by Polynesians, it was visited by British Capt. Samuel Wallis in 1767, and in 1768 by L.-A. de BOUGAINVILLE, who claimed it for France. The first permanent European settlers were English missionaries who arrived in 1797. It became a French colony in 1880 and is now part of the self-governing overseas territory of French Polynesia. Continued French nuclear testing in the area angered the inhabitants and brought calls for independence in recent years. Tourism is economically important.

Tahoe, Lake Lake on the California–Nevada border. It occupies a fault basin in the northern SIERRA NEVADA and covers 193 sq mi (500 sq km). It is 22 mi (35 km) long by 10 mi (16 km) wide and lies at an elevation of 6,229 ft (1,899 m). Its water level has varied during seasons of drought in recent decades. Fed by numerous small streams, the intensely blue lake and the surrounding national forests have been developed as popular tourist resorts.

Lake Tahoe in Toiyabe National Forest, Nevada.
JOHN F. SHRAWDER—SHOSTAL/EB INC.

Tahtawi \täh-'tä-,wē\, **Rifaa Rafi al-** (1801–1873) Egyptian teacher and scholar. He spent five years in Paris as a religious teacher to a group of Egyptian students, and later headed a language school and a translation bureau in Cairo. He held that God established the social order, and that the ruler, as God's representative, should promote his citizens' well-being through education and other means. Material progress could be attained through harmony of government and society, with the aid of Western technology. As one of the first Egyptians to confront the question of adjusting to the West, he was exiled to Khartoum during the reign of Abbas I.

Tai \'tī\ Peoples of mainland S.East Asia, including the Thai, or Siamese (in Thailand), the Lao (in Laos and Thailand), the SHAN (in Myanmar), the Lü (primarily in Yunnan province, China), the Yunnan Tai (in Yunnan), and the tribal Tai (in Vietnam). All speak TAI LANGUAGES, and most are Buddhists of the THERAVADA school. None of the Tai peoples has a caste system, and the status of Tai women is high. Today the Tai number about 76 million.

Tai See SHAN

Tai, Lake *or* **Tai Hu** *or* **T'ai Hu** \'tī-'hü\ Lake, between ZHEJIANG and JIANGSU provinces, eastern China. Roughly crescent-shaped, it covers an area of 850 sq mi (2,200 sq km). It lies in a plain and is served by a maze of natural and man-made waterways, some dating from the 7th cent AD. Several islands in the eastern section were traditionally famous Taoist and Buddhist religious sites. The area's great natural beauty attracts many tourists.

t'ai chi ch'uan *pinyin* **taijiquan** \'tī-'jē-'chwän\ Ancient Chinese form of exercise or of attack and defense. As exercise, it is designed to provide relaxation in the process of body conditioning, which it accomplishes partly by harmonizing the principles of YIN–YANG. It employs flowing, deliberate movements with carefully prescribed stances and positions. As a mode of attack and defense, it resembles KUNG fu and is properly considered a MARTIAL ART. Dating to the 3rd century AD, t'ai chi ch'uan consists of two major schools, the Wu and the Yang. Depending on the school, the number of exercises varies from 24 to more than 100.

T'ai-chung \'tī-'chüŋ\ City (pop., 1997: 882,000), western central Taiwan. Most of the old town was torn down under the Japanese occupation (1895–1945) and replaced by a planned modern city. An agricultural center since the early 19th century, it is a major market for the rice, sugar, and bananas produced in the surrounding area. In the 1970s, an international seaport was developed west of the city, and T'ai-chung was designated an export-processing zone to encourage foreign investment. It is also a cultural center, with various institutions of higher education. In 1999 it suffered one of Taiwan's worst earthquakes.

Tai languages Family of closely related languages spoken in S.East Asia and southern China by more than 80 million people. According to a widely used classification, Tai comprises three branches. The Southwestern group includes Thai, the national language of Thailand; northeastern Thai (Isan) and Lao, spoken in eastern Thailand and Laos; Pak Tay (South Thai), spoken in southern Thailand; Shan, spoken in eastern and northern Myanmar; and Tai Dam (Black Tai) and Tai Don (Tai Khaw, or White Tai), spoken mainly in North Vietnam. The Central group includes Nung and South Zhuang, a dialect chain in northern Vietnam and China's Guangxi province; and Tay (Thô), spoken in the same area. The Northern group includes Buyi (Bouyei) and North Zhuang, a dialect chain spoken in Guangxi, Guizhou, and Yunnan, China. All Tai languages are TONE languages, and like Chinese and Vietnamese, the majority of MORPHEMES in the native vocabulary (at least historically) consist of single syllables. Most scholars believe the Tai family is related to a number of other languages spoken by minority peoples of southern China and northern Vietnam. Together with Tai, the entire group has been named the Kadai or Tai-Kadai family.

T'ai-nan \'tī-'nän\ *formerly* **Dainan** City (pop., 1997 est.: 712,000), southwestern Taiwan. It is one of the oldest urban settlements on the island. The Han Chinese settled there as early as 1590. The Dutch arrived in the city in 1623 and stayed until they were driven out in 1662 by ZHENG CHENGGONG, who made it his capital. It remained the island's capital when the QING dynasty reestablished Chinese control over Taiwan (1683). Under Chinese rule in the 19th century, it grew into a prosperous city and was the commercial and educational center of Taiwan. After the transfer of the capital to TAIPEI in 1891, it became primarily commercial. It expanded during the Japanese occupation (1895–1945). Today it is a major market and tourism center.

T'ai-tsu See TAIZU

T'ai-tsung See TAIZONG

Tai Xu *or* **T'ai Hsü** \'tī-'shü̅\ *orig.* **Lü Peilin** (1890–1947) Chinese Buddhist monk and philosopher. After training as a Buddhist monk near Ningbo, he helped organize the Association for the Advancement of Buddhism (1912). In 1921 he began publication of the influential journal *Haichaoyin* ("The Voice of the Sea Tide"). Heavily influenced by SUN YAT-SEN and the revolution of 1911, he sought to reform the education of monks and promoted social-welfare activities. From 1925 to 1941 he traveled extensively to promote the formation of national and international Buddhist organizations in Japan, Europe, the U.S., and South and Southeast Asia.

Taieri River \'tī-ə-rē\ River, southeastern SOUTH ISLAND, New Zealand. It rises in the Lammerlaw Range and flows 179 mi (288 km) north and southeast in a great arc, across plains and around the Rock and Pillar Range, to enter the Pacific Ocean near Dunedin. Gorges are found in both the upper and lower reaches.

taiga \'tī-gə\ *or* **boreal forest** Open coniferous forest (see CONIFER) growing on swampy ground that is commonly covered with LICHENS. It is the characteristic vegetation of the subpolar region of northern Eurasia (principally Russia, including Siberia, and Scandinavia) and northern North America, bounded by the colder TUNDRA to the north and the warmer temperate zone to the south. SPRUCES and PINES are the dominant trees. Soil organisms are PROTOZOANS, NEMATODES, and ROTIFERS; larger invertebrates (e.g., insects) that decompose plant litter are lacking, so HUMUS accumulates very slowly. The taiga is rich in fur-bearing animals (e.g., sable, fox, and ermine) and is home to elks, bears, and wolves. Siberian taiga alone accounts for 19% of the world's forested area and possibly 25% of total forest volume. Despite the remoteness of the taiga, it is a major source of lumber for construction, and huge expanses have been clear-cut.

Taiga, Ike no See IKE NO TAIGA

tail Extension of the VERTEBRAL column beyond the trunk, or any slender projection resembling such a structure. In fishes and other animals living completely or partly in water, it is very important to movement through water. Many tree-dwelling animals (e.g., squirrels) use the tail for balance and as a rudder when leaping; in some (e.g., certain monkeys), it is adapted for grasping. Birds' tail feathers aid in flight maneuverability. Other animals use their tails for defense (e.g., porcupines), social signals (e.g., dogs and cats), warning signals (e.g., deer and rattlesnakes), and hunting (e.g., alligators).

Táin Bó Cúailgne \'tänʸ-'bō-'kü-əlʸ-nʸə, 'tänʸ-'bō-'kü-lʸē\ *English* **The Cattle Raid of Cooley** Irish narrative, the longest of the ULSTER CYCLE. It was composed in prose with verse passages in the 7th–8th century, probably by an author acquainted with such epics as the *Aeneid*. Its hero is CÚ CHULAINN, who singlehandedly held off the Connaught army that invaded ULSTER to capture a famous and valuable brown bull. After three days of battle, Cú Chulainn gained victory, yet the Connaughts successfully captured the bull. Madb, the warrior-queen of Connaught, secured her superiority over her husband Ailill when the brown bull defeated Ailill's white-horned bull.

Taine \'ten\, **Hippolyte (-Adolphe)** (1828–1893) French thinker, critic, and historian. Taine came to believe as a youth that knowledge must be based on sense experience, observation, and controlled experiment, a conviction that guided his career. Teaching at the École des Beaux-Arts in Paris 1864–83, he earned a reputation as one of the most esteemed exponents of 19th-century French POSITIVISM with his attempts to apply the scientific method to the study of the humanities. His works include a *History of English Literature* (1863–64), containing an explanation of his approach to cultural and literary history and his scientific attitude toward criticism; *On Intelligence* (1871), a study in psychology; and his monumental historical analysis *Les origines de la France contemporaine* (3 vols., 1876–99).

Taino \'tī-nō\ ARAWAK Indians of the island of HISPANIOLA in the Caribbean Sea. They also inhabited Puerto Rico and the eastern tip of Cuba. They grew cassava and corn, hunted birds and small animals, and fished. They were skillful at working stone and wood. Their society consisted of three tiers—nobles, commoners, and slaves—and they were ruled by hereditary chiefs and subchiefs. Their religious beliefs centered on a hierarchy of nature spirits and ancestors. They became extinct within 100 years of the Spanish conquest.

Taipei \'tī-'pā\ City (pop., 2000 est.: 2,641,312), capital of Taiwan. Founded in 1708, it became an important center of the tea trade in the mid-19th century. When Taiwan was proclaimed a province of China in 1886, Taipei was later made the capital, retaining that designation under Japanese rule (1895–1945). In 1949 it became the capital of the Chinese Nationalist government. It is the commercial, financial, industrial, and transportation center of Taiwan. Its many educational institutions include the National Taiwan University (1928). The city's National Palace Museum houses one of the world's largest collections of Chinese artifacts.

Taiping Rebellion \'tī-'piŋ\ (1850–64) Large-scale rebellion against the QING dynasty in China that ravaged 17 provinces, took some 20 million lives, and left the Qing government unable to regain an effective hold over the country. The peasants, having suffered floods and famines in the late 1840s, were ripe for rebellion, which came under the leadership of HONG XIUQUAN. Hong's visions convinced him he was the younger brother of Jesus, and he saw it as his duty to free China from MANCHU rule. He preached the brotherhood and sisterhood of all people under God; property was to be held in common. His followers' militant faith unified a fiercely disciplined army that swelled to more than a million men and women (women were treated as equals by Taiping rebels). They captured Nanjing in 1853 and renamed it Tianjing ("Heavenly Capital"). Their attempts to capture Beijing failed, but an expedition into the Upper Chang (Yangtze) River valley scored many victories. Hong's idiosyncratic Christianity alienated both Western missionaries and the Chinese scholar-gentry. Without the gentry, the Taiping forces were unable to govern the countryside or supply their cities effectively. The leadership strayed from its original austerity and descended into power struggles that left Hong without competent help. In 1860 an attempt to take Shanghai was repelled by U.S.- and British-led forces, and by 1862 Chinese forces under ZENG GUOFAN had surrounded Nanjing. The city fell in 1864, but almost 100,000 of the Taiping followers preferred death to capture. Sporadic resistance continued elsewhere until 1868. See also LI HONGZHANG, NIAN REBELLION.

Taira Kiyomori \'tī-rä-ˌkē-yō-'mò-rē\ (1118–1181) Leader of the powerful Taira family and the first member of the warrior class to rule Japan. The Taira family had made itself useful to the imperial court quelling pirates on Japan's Inland Sea. In 1156, when the retired emperor Sutoku (see INSEI) enlisted the aid of the Minamoto warrior family to help in a rebellion against the reigning emperor Go-Shirakawa, Kiyomori supported Go-Shirakawa and defeated the Minamoto. The Minamoto staged a comeback in 1159–60, but Kiyomori defeated them again, executing all the Minamoto males except the children MINAMOTO YORITOMO and MINAMOTO YOSHITSUNE, who would later overthrow him. Temporarily victorious, Kiyomori received the highest court rank and manipulated the throne by marrying his daughters into the imperial family. The Taira forces took on the effete ways of the aristocrats and were no match for the frontier-hardy Minamoto, who defeated them in 1185. See also GEMPEI WAR, KAMAKURA shogunate.

Taisho democracy \'tī-'shō\ Term for Japan's continued moves toward broader representational government during the TAISHO PERIOD. The tax qualification for voting was reduced, enfranchising more voters, and eventually eliminated in 1925. Party politics flourished and legislation favorable to labor was passed.

Taisho period (1912–26) Period in Japanese history corresponding to the reign of the Taisho emperor, Yoshihito (1879–1926). It followed the MEIJI PERIOD and saw a continuation of Japan's rise on the international scene and liberalism at home (see TAISHO DEMOCRACY). Japan continued to push China for economic and political concessions and entered into treaties with Western nations that acknowledged its interests in Korea, Manchuria, and the rest of China. Rural Japan did not fare as well as urban Japan, and a domestic depression at the end of the Taisho period led to much suffering. See also SHOWA period.

Tait, Archibald C(ampbell) (1811–1882) English cleric. The son of Presbyterian parents, he became an Anglican while studying at Oxford University. In 1836 he became a deacon and for five years he was also a curate at two villages near Oxford. In 1842 he succeeded THOMAS ARNOLD as headmaster of Rugby School, and in 1849 he became dean of Carlisle Cathedral. He became bishop of London in 1856; in that position he stressed reconciliation between evangelical churchmen and those who supported the OXFORD MOVEMENT. As archbishop of Canterbury (from 1868) he oversaw the disestablishment of the Anglican Church in Ireland and the passage of the Burials Act (1880), which allowed non-Anglican burial services in Anglican churchyards.

Taiwan *officially* **Republic of China** *formerly* **Formosa** Island, off southeastern China. Both the Republic of China (Taiwan) and the People's Republic of China (mainland China) claim jurisdiction over it. Area: 13,971 sq mi (36,185 sq km), including its outlying islands. Population (2002 est.): 22,457,000. Capital: TAIPEI. Han Chinese constitute virtually the entire population. Languages: Mandarin Chinese (official), Taiwanese, Fukien, and Hakka dialects also spoken. Religions: Buddhism, Taoism, Confucianism; small minority, Christianity. Currency: new Taiwan dollar. Lying 100 mi (160 km) off the Chinese mainland, it is composed mainly of mountains and hills, with densely populated coastal plains in the west. It has one of the highest population densities in the world. It is a leading industrial power of the Pacific Rim, with an economy based on manufacturing industries, international trade, and services. Leading exports include electronic equipment, garments, and textiles. Agricultural exports include frozen pork, sugar, canned mushrooms, bananas, and tea. It is a major producer of Chinese-language motion pictures. It is a republic with one legislative branch; its chief of state is the president, and the head of government is the premier. Known to the Chinese as early as the 7th century, it was widely settled by them

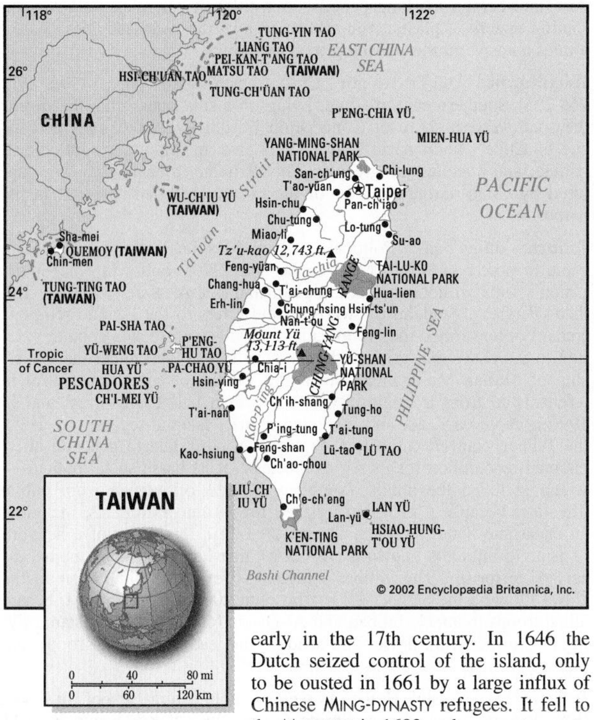

early in the 17th century. In 1646 the Dutch seized control of the island, only to be ousted in 1661 by a large influx of Chinese Ming-dynasty refugees. It fell to the Manchus in 1683 and was not open to Europeans again until 1858. In 1895 it was ceded to Japan following the Sino-Japanese War. A Japanese military center in World War II, it was frequently bombed by U.S. planes. After Japan's defeat, it was returned to China, which was then governed by the Nationalists. When the Communists took over mainland China in 1949, the Nationalist government fled to Taiwan and made it their seat of government, with Gen. Chiang Kai-shek as president. In 1954 he and the U.S. signed a mutual defense treaty, and Taiwan received U.S. support for almost three decades, developing its economy in spectacular fashion. It was recognized by many non-communist countries as the representative of all China until 1971, when it was replaced in the U.N. by the People's Republic of China. Martial law was lifted in Taiwan in 1987, and travel restrictions with mainland China in 1988. In 1989 opposition parties were legalized. The relationship with the mainland became increasingly close in the 1990s, though it again became strained when Chen Shui-bian (Ch'en Shui-pian), who advocated independence for Taiwan, was elected president in 2000.

Taiwan Strait *or* **Formosa Strait** Arm of the northwestern Pacific Ocean. Lying between the coast of China's Fujian province and the island of Taiwan, it is about 115 mi (185 km) wide. The strait connects the China Sea and East China Sea.

Taiyuan *or* **T'ai-yüan** \'tī-'ywän\ City (pop., 1990: 1,534,000), capital of Shanxi province, China, lying on the Fen River. Known since the time of the Zhou dynasty, it was a strategic center and administrative capital in the time of the Mongols (12th–14th century). It was the scene of a massacre in 1900 of foreign missionaries during the Boxer Rebellion, and was one of the first areas to oppose the emperor in 1911. Invaded by the Japanese in 1937, it was again besieged by Communist forces in 1948–49. One of the greatest industrial cities in China, it produces cement, iron and steel, and coal. It also is an education and research center. There are notable cave temples from the Tang and Yuan eras in the area.

Taizong *or* **T'ai-tsung** \'tī-'dzůŋ\ *orig.* **Li Shimin** (600–649) Second emperor of China's Tang dynasty. In his father's campaign against the Sui dynasty, Li Shimin was responsible for the conquest of Luoyang, the eastern capital. There he built up a regional administration and an entourage of talented officials. His brothers are said to have plotted to kill him; he did away with them instead, and his father soon abdicated in his favor. He restored normal civil administration to local government and created a unified civil service. He further developed the state schools created by his father and launched the editing of the Confucian Classics. On the frontiers, he fought eastern and western Turks and began to establish sovereignty over the oasis kingdoms of Xinjiang. An invasion of Koguryo failed, but he won great prestige for the Tang and came to be widely revered.

Taizu *or* **T'ai-tsu** \'tī-'dzü\ (927–976) First emperor of the Song dynasty, who began the unification of China, which his brother would complete. Initially a general for the founder of the Later Zhou dynasty (951–60), he was induced by his troops to take over when the dynasty was left in the hands of a child successor. An upright man, Taizu forgave minor faults while holding his officials to account in important matters. He had his ministers submit rough drafts of papers for his review, and he frequently traveled about incognito to observe conditions among his people. He reformed the Chinese examination system to prevent favoritism and began to award larger numbers of degrees. He gradually moved the administration of the prefectures from the military to civil officials. At his death, a good foundation had been laid for the future development of the dynasty.

Taj Mahal \'täzh-mə-'häl\ Mausoleum complex on the southern bank of the Yamuna River, outside Agra, India. It was built by the Mughal emperor Shah Jahan in memory of his wife, Mumtaz Mahal, who died in 1631. The Taj complex, begun c. 1632, took 22 years to complete. At its center lies a square garden area bounded by two smaller, oblong sections, one comprising the mausoleum and the other an entrance gateway. The mausoleum, of pure-white marble inlaid with semiprecious stones, is flanked by two red sandstone buildings, a mosque on one side and an identical building for aesthetic balance on the other. It stands on a high marble plinth with a minaret at each corner. It has four identical facades, each with a massive central arch 108 ft (33 m) high, and is surmounted by a bulbous double dome and four domed kiosks. Its interior, with fine, restrained stone decoration, centers on an octagonal chamber containing the marble tombs, enclosed by a perforated marble screen, with sarcophagi below. It is regarded as one of the world's most beautiful buildings.

Tajikistan \tä-ˌji-ki-'stan\ *officially* **Republic of Tajikistan** Country, southwestern central Asia. Area: 55,300 sq mi (143,100 sq km). Population (2002 est.): 6,327,000. Capital: Dushanbe. The majority of the population are Tajik (of Persian descent); Uzbeks make up a large minority. Language: Tajik (official). Religion: Islam (Sunni). Currency: Tajik ruble. An earthquake-prone mountainous country, about half of its territory lies above elevations of 10,000 ft (3,000 m), with the Pamirs dominating the east. The Amu Darya and Syr Darya rivers cross it

and are used for irrigation. Cotton, cattle, fruits, vegetables, and grain are raised. Heavy industries include coal mining, petroleum and natural-gas extraction, metalworking, and nitrogen fertilizer production. Light industries include cotton milling, food processing, and textiles. Tajikistan is a republic with one legislative house; its chief of state is the president, and the head of government is the prime minister. Settled by the Persians c. 6th century BC, Tajikistan was part of the empires of the Persians and of ALEXANDER THE GREAT and his successors. In the 7th–8th century AD, it was conquered by the Arabs, who introduced Islam. The Uzbeks controlled the region in the 15th–18th century. In the 1860s Russia took over much of Tajikistan. In 1924 it became an autonomous republic under the administration of the Uzbek Soviet Socialist Republic, and it gained republic status in 1929. It achieved independence with the collapse of the Soviet Union in 1991. Civil war raged through much of the 1990s between government forces and an opposition composed mostly of Islamic militants. Peace was reached in 1997.

Tajumulco Volcano \ˌtä-hü-ˈmül-kō\ Volcanic mountain, western Guatemala. Part of a mountain range that extends into Guatemala from southern Mexico, it is 13,845 ft (4,220 m) high. It is the highest peak in CENTRAL AMERICA.

Takemitsu \tä-ke-ˈmit-sü\, **Toru** (1930–1996) Japanese composer. In 1951 he founded Tokyo's Experimental Laboratory to promote an integration of Japanese music with contemporary European developments. Soon acknowledged as Japan's leading composer, he explored serialism, aleatory, graphic notation, and electronic music combined with traditional Japanese motives and instruments (e.g., *November Steps*, 1967, for biwa, shakuhachi, and orchestra), creating an individual sound world in which silence plays a large part.

Takfir wa al-Hijra \tåk-ˈfēr-wål-ˈhij-rə\ (Arabic: "Excommunication and [Holy] Flight") Name given by Egyptian authorities to a radical Islamic group calling itself the "Society of Muslims." It was founded in 1971 by a young agronomist, Shukri Mustafa, who had been arrested in 1965 for distributing MUSLIM BROTHERHOOD leaflets and was released from prison in 1971. Appealing to those who saw mainstream society—from which the group sought to flee (*Hijra:* i.e., HEGIRA)—as weak and corrupt, it engaged in acts of terrorism and was initially thought to be behind the assassination of ANWAR AL-SADAT.

Taklimakan *or* **Takla Makan** \ˌtä-klə-mə-ˈkän\ Desert, forming the greater part of the TARIM RIVER basin, western central China. One of the world's largest sandy wastes, it is about 600 mi (965 km) across, with an area of 105,000 sq mi (272,000 sq km). It is flanked by high mountain ranges, including the KUNLUN MTNS., whose rivers penetrate the desert 60–120 mi (100–200 km) before drying up in its sands. Its windblown sand cover is as much as 1,000 ft (300 m) thick and has formed such features as pyramidal dunes that can reach 1,000 ft (300 m) in height.

Taksin \ˈtäk-sin\ *or* **Phraya Taksin** (1734–1782) Thai general and later king (1767–82) who reunited Siam (Thailand) after its defeat by Myanmar. While Taksin was a provincial governor, his troops were among those besieged by the forces of Myanmar in 1766–67, but he escaped and raised new troops. He drove out the invaders and defeated other contenders for the throne, then extended his power into neighboring states. A better conqueror than ruler, he was deposed and probably executed in 1782.

Talbot, William Henry Fox (1800–1877) English chemist and pioneer photographer. In 1840 he developed the calotype; an early photographic process that improved on the daguerreotype, it involved the use of a photographic negative, from which multiple prints could be made. In 1835 he published his first article documenting a photographic discovery, that of the paper negative. His *The Pencil of Nature* (1844–46) was the first book with photographic illustrations. Talbot also published many articles in mathematics, astronomy, and physics, and was one of the first to decipher the cuneiform inscriptions of NINEVEH.

talc Common SILICATE mineral that is distinguished from almost all other minerals by its extreme softness. Its soapy or greasy feel accounts for the name soapstone, given to compact aggregates of talc with other rock-forming minerals. Soapstones have been used since ancient times for carvings, ornaments, and utensils. Resistant to most reagents and to moderate heat, they are especially suitable for sinks and countertops. Talc is also used in lubricants, leather dressings, toilet and dusting powders, and certain marking pencils; as a filler in ceramics, paint, paper, roofing materials, plastic, and rubber; as a carrier in insecticides; and as a mild abrasive in the polishing of cereal grains.

Talcahuano \ˌtäl-kä-ˈwä-nō\ City (metro. area pop., 1999 est.: 269,265), southern central Chile. Lying on a small peninsula that forms the southwestern shore of Concepción Bay, it is a major port and the site of Chile's main naval station. It is also an important commercial, fishing, and manufacturing center. The Peruvian ironclad *Huáscar*, captured by Chile during the War of the PACIFIC (1879), is moored in the harbor.

Taliban \ˌtå-lē-ˈbån\ Political and religious faction and militia that came to power in AFGHANISTAN in the mid-1990s. Following the Soviet Union's 1989 withdrawal from Afghanistan (see AFGHAN WARS), the Taliban (Persian: "Students")—whose name refers to the Islamic religious students who formed the group's main recruits—arose as a popular reaction to the chaos that gripped the country. In 1994–95 under the leadership of Mullah Mohammad Omar, the Taliban extended its control in Afghanistan from a single city to more than half the country, and in 1996 it captured KABUL and instituted a strict Islamic regime. By 1999, the Taliban controlled most of Afghanistan but failed to generate international recognition for its regime because of its harsh social policies—which included the almost complete removal of women from public life—and because it provided a haven for Islamic extremists, including an expatriate Saudi Arabian, OSAMA BIN LADEN, the leader of a network of Islamic militants known as AL-QAEDA that had engaged in numerous acts of terrorism. The Taliban's refusal to extradite bin Laden to the U.S. following the SEPTEMBER 11 ATTACKS in 2001 prompted the U.S. and allied troops to attack Taliban and Al-Qaeda forces in Afghanistan, driving the former from power and sending the leaders of both groups into hiding. See also ISLAMIC FUNDAMENTALISM.

Taliesin \ˌta-lē-ˈe-sin\ Home, as well as architectural school, of FRANK LLOYD WRIGHT. Located near Spring Green, Wis., it was begun in 1911 and was rebuilt after fires in 1914 and 1925. Taliesin West, near Scottsdale, Ariz., was begun in 1938 as a winter home for Wright and his students. Both structures were continually renovated and added to until Wright's death in 1959, after which they continued to be occupied by members of the Wright Foundation. Wright, of Welsh descent, named them after the renowned Welsh poet (fl. 6th century AD).

talk show Radio or television program in which a well-known personality interviews celebrities and other guests. The late-night programs hosted by JOHNNY CARSON, JAY LENO, DAVID LETTERMAN, and Conan O'Brien have emphasized entertainment, incorporating interludes of music or comedy. Other talk shows have focused on politics (see DAVID SUSSKIND), controversial social issues or sensationalistic topics (PHIL DONAHUE), and emotional therapy (OPRAH WINFREY). See also MERV GRIFFIN, LARRY KING, RUSH LIMBAUGH, JACK PAAR.

Tallahassee City (pop., 2000: 150,624), capital of Florida. Originally an Appalachee Indian village, it received Spanish settlers there after HERNANDO DE SOTO's visit in 1539. It became the capital of the Florida Territory in 1824 and of the state in 1845. In the AMERICAN CIVIL WAR, the secession resolution was adopted there in 1861; it was the only capital of a Confederate state east of the Mississippi not captured by Union forces. Today it is a wholesaling and distribution point for the surrounding lumbering, cotton, and cattle-raising region. Educational institutions include Florida State University (founded 1851).

Tallahatchie River River, northern Mississippi. It rises in Tippah Co. and flows southwest 230 mi (370 km) to join the Yalobusha River and form the YAZOO RIVER. It is navigable for about 100 mi (160 km). Its upper section is sometimes called the Little Tallahatchie River.

Tallapoosa River River, Georgia and Alabama. Rising in northwestern Georgia, it flows southwest for about 268 mi (431 km) before joining the larger COOSA RIVER just north of MONTGOMERY, Ala., to form the ALABAMA RIVER. Three private power dams have created reservoirs, including Lake Martin, for river control, power, and recreation.

Tallchief, Maria (born 1925) U.S. ballet dancer of Native American descent. Born in Fairfax, Okla., she studied with BRONISLAVA NIJINSKA before joining the BALLET RUSSE de Monte Carlo (1942–47). She joined the NEW YORK CITY BALLET in 1948 and became its prima ballerina, creating leading roles in many ballets choreographed for her by GEORGE BALANCHINE, her husband from 1946 to 1952, including *Symphonie concer-*

tante (1947), *Caracole* (1952), and *Pas de dix* (1955). She left the company in 1965, became artistic director of the Lyric Opera Ballet in Chicago, and founded the Chicago City Ballet in 1980.

Maria Tallchief in *Swan Lake*.
MARTHA SWOPE

Talleyrand (-Périgord) \tä-le-'rä^n\, **Charles-Maurice de** (1754–1838) French statesman. Ordained a priest, he became bishop of Autun in 1788. Elected to represent the clergy at the Estates General (1789), he became the "bishop of the Revolution" by calling for confiscation of church property to fund the new government and supporting the Civil Constitution of the Clergy. Excommunicated by the pope in 1790, he was sent to England as an envoy in 1792. He was expelled from France during the Reign of Terror, lived in the U.S. 1794–96, then returned to serve in the Directory as foreign minister (1797–99). He was forced to resign briefly for involvement in bribery scandals, including the XYZ Affair. Adept at political survival, he supported Napoleon and again became foreign minister (1799–1807) and later grand chamberlain (1804–7). He resigned in opposition to Napoleon's policy toward Russia but continued to advise him, arranging his marriage with Marie-Louise of Austria. As Napoleon faced defeat, Talleyrand secretly worked to restore the monarchy; in 1814 he was appointed foreign minister to Louis XVIII and represented France at the Congress of Vienna. Forced by ultraroyalists to resign (1815), he later became involved in the July Revolution of 1830 and served as ambassador to Britain 1830–34.

Tallinn \'ta-lən\ *formerly (until 1918)* **Revel** \'rā-vəl\ Seaport city (pop., 2000 est.: 404,000), capital of Estonia. It is located on the Gulf of Finland. A fortified settlement existed there from the late 1st millennium BC, and there was a town there in the 12th century. In 1219 it was captured by the Danes, who built a new fortress. Trade flourished after it joined the Hanseatic League in 1285. In 1346 it was sold to the Teutonic Order, and in 1561 it passed to Sweden. Russia captured it in 1710, and it remained a Russian city until it became the capital of independent Estonia from 1918 to 1940, when Estonia was annexed to the U.S.S.R. (1940–91). In World War II it was occupied by German forces 1941–44 and was severely damaged. Rebuilt, it became the capital of independent Estonia in 1991. It is a major commercial and fishing port, an industrial center, and the cultural center of Estonia, with numerous educational institutions. Historical structures include a medieval city wall and a 13th-century church.

Tallis \'ta-ləs\, **Thomas** (c. 1505–1585) British composer. An organist at abbeys and churches from 1532, by 1543 he was a Gentleman of the Chapel Royal, as both organist and composer. Though a Catholic, he was one of the first to write hymns in English for the Anglican church. During Mary I's Catholic reign, he wrote Latin masses, but he remained in favor after Elizabeth I's accession. His powerful *Lamentations of Jeremiah* are regarded as his greatest body of work; his 40-part motet *Spem in alium* is his most famous piece. He also wrote three masses and about 40 other motets. In 1575 Tallis and his pupil W. Byrd were given the first exclusive license to print music in England.

Talma \täl-'mä\, **François-Joseph** (1763–1826) French actor and theater manager. He made his debut at the Comédie-Française in 1787. Influenced by J.-L. David, he became an early advocate of historical costuming, and he created a sensation by appearing onstage in a Roman toga. After political dissension split the company (1789), the pro-republican Talma established a rival troupe. He developed realism in his staging and insisted on a naturalistic rather than a declamatory acting style. In 1799 his troupe was reunited with the Comédie-Française; as head of the company, he became recognized as the supreme tragedian of the era, winning the admiration of Napoleon.

Talmud \täl-'müd, 'tal-məd\ In Judaism, the systematic amplification and analysis of passages of the Mishna, the Gemara, and other oral law, including the Tosefta. Two Talmuds exist, produced by two different groups of Jewish scholars: the Babylonian Talmud (c. AD 600) and the Palestinian Talmud (c. AD 400). The Babylonian Talmud is more extensive and thus more highly esteemed. Both Talmuds formulate their own hermeneutics to convey their theological system by defining the Torah and by demonstrating its perfection and comprehensive character. The Talmud remains a text of central importance, particularly in Orthodox Judaism. Intensive modern Talmudic scholarship is pursued in Israel and the U.S. See also Halakhah.

Talmud Torah \täl-'müd-tō-'rä, 'tal-məd-'tō-rə\ Religious study of the Torah in search of the God who makes himself known in that work. It focuses on learning God's message for contemporary times through inquiry into the books of Hebrew scripture or those that record the original oral Torah of Sinai, the Mishna, Midrash, and Talmuds. Talmud Torah is also the name given to an elementary school under Jewish auspices that places special emphasis on religious education.

tamarin Any of about 25 species of long-tusked marmosets in the genera *Leontopithecus* (or *Leontideus,* according to some authorities) and *Saguinus.* Tamarins are 8–12 in. (20–30 cm) long, excluding the 12–16-in. (30–40-cm) tail. The emperor tamarin *(Saguinus imperator)* has long, grizzled gray fur; a reddish tail, and long white moustaches. The three species of *Leontopithecus* are endangered. See also golden lion tamarin.

tamarind \'ta-mə-rənd\ Evergreen tree *(Tamarindus indica)* of the pea family (see legume), native to tropical Africa and cultivated elsewhere as an ornamental and for its edible fruit. The tree grows about 80 ft (24 m) tall and has featherlike leaves. It bears small clusters of yellow flowers and plump pods that do not split open. The soft, brownish edible pulp contains 1–12 large, flat seeds that are used in Oriental foods, beverages, and medicines.

Tamarind (*Tamarindus indica*).
WALTER DAWN

Tamaulipas \,tä-maù-'lē-päs\ State (pop., 2000: 2,747,000), northeastern Mexico. Located on the Gulf of Mexico, it covers 30,822 sq mi (79,829 sq km). The capital is Ciudad Victoria. Though largely mountainous, it has extensive, fertile plains in the north and a sandy, lagoon-dotted coastal zone. Large areas are irrigated. Agriculture is the main industry; products include sorghum, soybeans, sugarcane, cotton, coffee, and fruit. Fisheries and copper mining also are important. It produces a third of Mexico's natural gas and increasing quantities of petroleum.

Tamayo \tə-'mī-ō\, **Rufino** (1899–1991) Mexican painter and graphic artist. He studied at Mexico City's School of Fine Arts and then taught at the National Museum of Archaeology (1921–26). He preferred easel painting to the monumental proportions and political rhetoric of Jose Clemente Orozco, Diego Rivera, and David A. Siqueiros. His distinctive style blended Cubism and Surrealism with Mexican folk-art subjects involving semiabstract figures, still lifes, and animals in vibrant colors. From 1936 he lived principally in New York. In 1950 an exhibition at the Venice Biennale brought him international recognition. He designed murals for Mexico City's Palace of Fine Arts (1952–53) and UNESCO's Paris headquarters (1958). In 1974 he donated his collection of pre-Hispanic art to his native Oaxaca.

Tambo, Oliver (1917–1993) President (1969–91) of South Africa's African National Congress (ANC). In 1944, with Nelson Mandela and others, he cofounded the Youth League of the ANC. He became the ANC's deputy president in 1958, and was forced into exile in Zambia when it was banned in 1960. He was elected ANC president in 1969 after the death of Albert Lutuli. He returned to South Africa in ill health in 1990 but yielded the party presidency to Mandela.

tambourine Small frame drum with one skin nailed or glued to a shallow circular frame, into which jingles or pellet bells are set. It is held with one hand and struck with the other, or simply shaken. Tambourines were played in ancient Mesopotamia, Greece, and Rome, especially in religious contexts, and have long been prominent in Middle Eastern folk and religious use. Crusaders brought them to Europe in the 13th century.

Tamburlaine See Timur

Tamerlane See Timur

Tamil language Dravidian language spoken by more than 63 million people. It is an official language of Tamil Nadu state in India and one of the official languages of Sri Lanka. Large Tamil-speaking communities also reside in Malaysia and Singapore, South Africa, and the Indian Ocean islands of Réunion and Mauritius. The earliest Tamil inscriptions date from c. 200 BC; literature in the language has a 2,000-year history. Tamil script is descended from the southern Indian Pallava script (see Indic writing systems). Tamil has several regional dialects, Brahman and non-Brahman caste dialects, and a marked division between literary and colloquial forms (see diglossia).

Tamil Nadu \'ta-məl-'nä-dü\ *formerly* **Madras** \mə-'dräs\ State (pop., 2001 prelim.: 62,110,839), southeastern India. The capital is Chennai (Madras). Bounded by the Bay of Bengal, it covers an area of 50,216 square miles (130,058 square km); its interior includes the fertile Kaveri River delta. By the 2nd century AD the region was occupied by Tamil kingdoms. They were followed by the Hindu kingdom of Vijayanagar, which ruled the southern regions 1336–1565. The Portuguese entered the area in 1498, only to be displaced by the Dutch in the 16th–17th century. The British established a settlement in 1611 and expanded outward to make the area a separate presidency, known as Madras, from 1653 to 1946. Made a state in 1956, it is one of India's most industrialized states; manufactures include vehicles, electrical equipment, and chemicals.

Tamils \'tä-məlz, 'ta-məlz\ People originally of southern India who speak the Tamil language. The Tamils have a long history of achievement; sea travel, city life, and commerce seem to have developed early among them. They traded with the ancient Greeks and Romans. They have the oldest cultivated Dravidian language and a rich literary tradition. They are mostly Hindus (the Tamil area in India is a center of traditional Hinduism). In Sri Lanka there are two separate Tamil populations, the Ceylon Tamils and the Indian Tamils. Tensions between the Ceylon Tamils and the Sinhalese Buddhist majority prompted a Tamil guerrilla insurgency in the 1980s and '90s. The Tamils number about 57 million, with 3.2 million living in Sri Lanka.

Tamiris \tə-'mir-əs\, **Helen** *orig.* **Helen Becker** (1905–1966) U.S. choreographer, modern dancer, and teacher. She was born in New York City. In 1930 she founded her own company and the School of American Dance, which she directed until 1945. Many of her own works, such as *Pioneer Memories* and *Walt Whitman Suite,* drew on American themes. From 1945 to 1957 she choreographed such Broadway musicals as *Show Boat, Annie Get Your Gun,* and *Fanny.* In 1960 she and her dancer-husband Daniel Nagrin founded the Tamiris-Nagrin Dance Co.

Helen Tamiris.
BY COURTESY OF THE DANCE COLLECTION, NEW YORK PUBLIC LIBRARY, ASTOR, LENOX AND TILDEN FOUNDATIONS

Tammany Hall \'ta-mə-nē\ Democratic Party's executive committee in New York City. The group was organized in 1789 in opposition to the Federalist Party's ruling "aristocrats." The Society of Tammany was incorporated in 1805 as a benevolent body; its name derived from a pre-Revolutionary association named after the benevolent Indian chief Tammanend. The group became identified with the city's Democratic Party. It was altered in 1817 when Irish immigrants forced their right to membership and benefits. By advocating extending the franchise to propertyless white males, it became popular with the working class. Gifts to the poor and political favors resulted in support for Tammany candidates at the polls. The rise of such bosses as William Marcy Tweed associated the group with political corruption. Its power was strongest in the late 19th and early 20th century; it declined in the 1930s under the reforms of Pres. Franklin Roosevelt and Mayor Fiorello La Guardia.

Tammuz \'tä-ˌmüz\ Mesopotamian god of fertility. He was the son of Enki, god of water, and Duttur, a personification of the ewe. Worship of Tammuz was centered around two yearly festivals, one in the early spring in which his marriage to the goddess Inanna symbolized the fertilization of nature for the coming year, and one in summer when his death at the hands of demons was lamented. He is thought to be the precursor of several later deities associated with agriculture and fertility, including Ninsun, Damu, and Dumuzi-Abzu.

Tammuz, alabaster relief from Ashur, c. 1500 BC; in the Staatliche Museen zu Berlin, Germany.
FOTO MARBURG—ART RESOURCE/EB INC.

tamoxifen \ta-'mäk-si-ˌfen\ Synthetic hormone, marketed as Nolvadex, that prevents the binding of estrogen to estrogen-sensitive breast cancer cells. Initially used to prevent recurrences of breast cancer after successful treatment, it was later found to prevent first occurrences in women at high risk. The most serious side effect is an increased risk of thrombosis, which may require patients to take an anticoagulant as well. Studies on its effectiveness against breast and other cancers continue.

Tampa City (pop., 1996 est.: 285,000), western central Florida, on the northeastern end of Tampa Bay. The U.S. Army established Fort Brooke on the site in 1824 to oversee the removal of the Seminole Indians. The town was incorporated in 1855. It developed as a cigar-making center after the town's first cigar factory was established (1886). It now has a wide range of industries and is a major distribution center. It is a winter and fishing resort and major tourist center; attractions include Busch Gardens.

Tampa Bay Inlet, Gulf of Mexico, western Florida. It is 25 mi (40 km) long and 7–12 mi (11–19 km) wide, and serves the recreational and commercial activities of St. Petersburg on the western shore and Tampa on the northeast. Hernando de Soto began his travels through the southeastern U.S. region when he reached Tampa Bay in 1539. It is spanned by the 15-mi (25-km) Sunshine Skyway Bridge.

Tampico \täm-'pē-kō\ Seaport (pop., 1990: 272,000), southeastern Tamaulipas state, northeastern Mexico. It lies on the Panuco River, almost surrounded by swampland and lagoons. It grew around a Franciscan monastery founded c. 1532. Destroyed by pirates in 1683, it was not resettled until 1823. It was occupied briefly by U.S. troops (1846) during the Mexican War and by the French in 1862. Until 1901 it was a second-rate port with a reputation for unsanitary conditions. It grew with the rapid exploitation of surrounding petroleum resources; it is now the most modern port in Mexico and one of the country's leading seaports. It is also a seaside resort.

Tan Cheng Lock \'tän-'cheŋ-'lȯk\ (1883–1960) Malaysian Chinese community leader and politician. Born to a wealthy Chinese family in Melaka (in present-day Malaysia), he campaigned against "pro-Malay" policies and in favor of equal rights for all ethnic groups, whether immigrant or indigenous. After World War II, he supported the British proposal for a unitary state with common citizenship, which the Malays rejected. During the Malayan Emergency, he cooperated with the British to promote national unity. In 1949 he was chosen to head the Malayan Chinese Assn., the first full-fledged centrist Malayan Chinese political party, and he continued as its head after Malayan independence in 1957.

Tan Malaka \'tän-mä-'lä-kä\, **Ibrahim Datuk (Headman)** (1894–1949) Indonesian communist leader. A schoolteacher, he became a communist after returning from Europe in 1919. Exiled by the Dutch for trying to incite a general strike in 1922, he returned to Java in 1944 and, competing with Sukarno for control of the Indonesian nationalist movement, he created a coalition that briefly came to power in 1946. He was imprisoned later that year on charges of attempting a coup. In 1948, while the Dutch and Indonesians were at war, he proclaimed himself head of Indonesia. Forced to flee the invading Dutch, within a few months he was captured and executed by Sukarno's supporters.

Tana, Lake Lake, Ethiopia. The country's largest lake, it is 47 mi (76 km) long and 44 mi (71 km) wide. It is the source of the Blue Nile (see NILE RIVER), which pours from it over a lava barrier, dropping 138 ft (42 m) to form Tisisat Falls. Coptic monasteries were built on two of its islands during the Middle Ages.

Tana River \'tä-nä\ River, Kenya. The country's longest river, it rises in the Aberdare Range and flows in a curve northeast, east, and south 440 mi (708 km) to the Indian Ocean. It is navigable by small craft for about 150 mi (240 km) upstream.

Tana River \'tä-nə\ River, northeastern Norway. It flows 224 mi (360 km) north and northeast to empty into Tana Fjord, an inlet of the ARCTIC OCEAN on the northeastern coast of Norway. The river forms a section of the boundary between Norway and Finland.

tanager \'ta-nə-jər\ Any of 200–220 species (family Emberizidae) of New World songbirds inhabiting forests and gardens. Most species are 4–8 in. (10–20 cm) long and have a short neck. Bills vary in shape, but all are slightly toothed and hooked. Tanagers have brilliant plumage in reds, yellows, greens, blues, and black, sometimes strikingly patterned. Most species are arboreal; most eat fruit, and some eat insects. The scarlet, summer, and western tanagers breed in temperate North America. The hepatic tanager breeds from Arizona to central Argentina. Most other species are chiefly tropical.

Tanagra \'ta-nə-grə, tə-'na-grə\ Ancient town, BOEOTIA, eastern central Greece. First occupied by an Athenian clan, it became the chief town of the eastern Boeotians, with lands extending to the Gulf of Euboea. It was the scene of the Athenian defeat by the Spartans in 457 BC during the first PELOPONNESIAN WAR. Finely modeled terra-cotta statuettes, known as TANAGRA FIGURES, were made there c. 340–150 BC and exported to Mediterranean countries.

Tanagra figure Any of the small terra-cotta figures dating primarily from the 3rd century BC and named after the site in Boeotia, Greece, where they were found. The statuettes, mostly of well-dressed young women standing or sitting, were all formed from molds and originally were covered with a white coating and then painted. On their discovery in the 19th century, they became enormously popular and were extensively and expertly forged.

Tanaka \'tä-nä-kä\, **Kakuei** (1918–1993) Prime minister of Japan 1972–74. As prime minister, Tanaka pushed through many government projects and was responsible for the economic revitalization of much of western Japan and for establishing diplomatic relations with the People's Republic of China. In 1976 he was charged with accepting, while prime minister, $2 million from Lockheed Aircraft Corp. to influence All Nippon Airways to buy Lockheed jets; he was convicted in 1983.

Tanaka, Tomoyuki (1910–1997) Japanese film producer. Tanaka was associated for nearly 60 years with Japan's Toho Studios, for which he produced more than 200 films. Of these, his best known were the 22 films in the Godzilla series, beginning with *Godzilla, King of the Monsters* in 1954 and ending with *Godzilla vs. Destroyer* in 1995. He also produced films for renowned director AKIRA KUROSAWA.

Tanana River \'ta-nə-,nȯ\ River, eastern central Alaska. Rising from two headstreams fed by glaciers high in the WRANGELL MTNS., it flows northwest 550 mi (885 km) to join the YUKON RIVER; it is the Yukon's chief southern tributary. It was first explored by Russian traders in the mid-19th century. Its valley was an important gold-producing area in the 1904 GOLD RUSH; it is also a lumbering district and one of Alaska's major farming regions. The ALASKA HIGHWAY follows it for nearly its entire course.

Tananarive See ANTANANARIVO

Tancred \'taŋ-krəd\ (died 1194) King of Sicily (1190–94), the last of the Norman rulers. He rebelled twice (1155, 1161) against his uncle William I of Sicily, and he gained the Sicilian throne after the death of William II. He gave in to the demand of RICHARD I the Lionheart (1191) for the legacy left him by William II and the return of the dowry of his sister Joan, William's widow, after Richard occupied Messina. Emperor HENRY VI sought to wrest the Sicilian throne from Tancred, unsuccessfully besieging Naples in 1191 and marching on Sicily again in 1194. Tancred died before his arrival, and Henry was crowned king.

Tandy, Jessica See Hume CRONYN and Jessica Tandy

Taney, Roger B(rooke) (1777–1864) U.S. jurist. Born in Calvert Co., Md., he practiced law (from 1801) and served in Maryland's legislature before being named state attorney general (1827–31). He was appointed U.S. attorney general in 1831 by Pres. ANDREW JACKSON, and achieved national prominence by opposing the BANK OF THE U.S. Jackson nominated him to the U.S. Supreme Court in 1835, but the Senate rejected the nomination. Later that same year he was named to succeed Chief Justice JOHN MARSHALL and was confirmed despite powerful resistance. His tenure as chief justice (1836–64) remains the second-longest in the Court's history. He is remembered principally for the DRED SCOTT decision. He is also noted for his opinions in *Ableman vs. Booth* (1858), which denied state power to obstruct the processes of the federal courts, and in *CHARLES RIVER BRIDGE VS. WARREN BRIDGE*. Though he considered slavery an evil, he believed its elimination should be brought about gradually and chiefly by the states where it existed.

Taney, photograph by Mathew Brady.

BY COURTESY OF THE LIBRARY OF CONGRESS, WASHINGTON, D.C.

tang See SURGEONFISH

Tang dynasty *or* **T'ang dynasty** \'täŋ\ (618–907) Chinese dynasty that succeeded the short-lived SUI and became a golden age for poetry, sculpture, and Buddhism. The Tang capital of CHANGAN became a great international metropolis, with traders and embassies from Central Asia, Arabia, Persia, Korea, and Japan passing through. A NESTORIAN Christian community also existed there, while mosques were established in Guangzhou. The economy flourished in the 8th–9th century, with a network of rural market towns growing up to join the metropolitan markets of Changan and Luoyang. Buddhism enjoyed great favor; there were new translations of the Buddhist scriptures and growth of indigenous sects, including Chan (see ZEN). Poetry was the greatest glory of the period; nearly 50,000 works by 2,000 poets survive. Foreign music and dance became popular and ancient orchestras were revived. The Tang government never completely controlled the northern Chinese border, where nomad tribes made constant incursions; periodic rebellions from the mid-8th century onward also weakened its power (see AN LUSHAN REBELLION). In its later years, the government's focus was on eastern and southeastern China rather than Central Asia. See also TAIZONG, WU HOU.

Tanganyika \,tan-gən-'yē-kə\, **Lake** Lake, central Africa. Located on the boundary between Tanzania and Congo (Zaire), it is the longest freshwater lake in the world, at 410 mi (660 km) long, and the second deepest, at 4,710 ft (1,436 m) deep. Fed by several rivers, it tends to be brackish. Oil palms and rice grow along its steep shores; hippopotamuses and crocodiles abound. It was first visited by Europeans, searching for the source of the NILE, in 1858.

Tange \'tän-gā\, **Kenzo** (born 1913) Japanese architect. Tange worked in the office of KUNIO MAEKAWA before setting out on his own. His best-known early work was the Peace Center, Hiroshima (1946–56). The Kagawa prefectural offices in Takamatsu (1955–58) were a particularly fine blend of the modern and traditional. In 1959 he and his students published the Boston Harbor project, launching the METABOLIST school. His work in the 1960s took more boldly dramatic form, and he became a master at manipulating complex geometries; his National Gymnasium for Tokyo's 1964 Olympic Games is exemplary. More recent works include the New Tokyo City Hall complex (1991). Also influential as a writer, teacher, and town planner, Tange was awarded the Pritzker Architecture Prize in 1987.

tangent See TRIGONOMETRIC FUNCTION

tangent line \'tan-jənt\ In geometry, a line that intersects a circle exactly once; in calculus, a line that touches a curve at one point and whose SLOPE is equal to that of the curve at that point. Particularly useful as approximations of curves in the immediate vicinity of the point of tangency, tangent lines are the basis of many ESTIMATION techniques, including LINEAR APPROXIMATION. The numerical value of the slope of the tangent line to the graph of a function at any point equals that of the function's DERIVATIVE at that point. This is one of the keystones of DIFFERENTIAL CALCULUS. See also DIFFERENTIAL GEOMETRY.

tangerine Small, thin-skinned variety of the mandarin ORANGE species *(Citrus reticulata deliciosa)* of the RUE, or citrus, family. Probably native to S.East Asia, today it is cultivated in subtropical regions worldwide, especially southern Europe and the southern U.S. The tree is smaller than other orange trees, with slender twigs and lance-shaped leaves. The fruit is slightly flattened at each end and has a loose, reddish-orange peel. Easily separated segments of tender, juicy, richly flavored pulp are abundant in vitamin C. Oil from the fragrant skin is a characteristic ingredient in several flavorings and liqueurs. Tangerines crossed with GRAPEFRUIT produce hybrids known as tangelos.

Tangerine (*Citrus reticulata deliciosa*).
GRANT HEILMAN—EB INC.

Tangier \tan-'jir\ *French* **Tanger** \tä^{n}-'zhā\ *Arabic* **Tanjah** \'tän-jə\ *ancient* **Tingis** Seaport (metro. area pop., 1994: 522,000), northern Morocco. Located at the western end of the Strait of GIBRALTAR, it was first known as an ancient Phoenician trading post, and later became a Carthaginian and then a Roman settlement. After five centuries of Roman rule, it was captured successively by the Vandals, Byzantines, and Arabs. It fell to the Portuguese in 1471; it later passed to the British, who gave it up to Morocco in 1684. When the rest of Morocco became a French protectorate in 1912, Tangier was granted special status; in 1923 it officially became an international city, governed by an international commission. It remained an international zone until it was integrated in 1956 with the independent kingdom of Morocco. It became a free port and royal summer residence in the 1960s. The old town is dominated by a Casbah and the Great Mosque. It is a busy port and trade center; industries include tourism, fishing, and textiles, especially carpets.

tango Spirited Spanish flamenco dance; also a South American BALLROOM dance. It evolved into a ballroom dance in Buenos Aires, possibly influenced by the Cuban habanera. It was made popular in the U.S. by VERNON AND IRENE CASTLE, and by 1915 it was being danced throughout Europe. Early versions were fast and exuberant; these were later modified to the smoother ballroom step, characterized by long pauses and stylized body positions and danced to music in 4/4 time.

Tango danced by Rudolph Valentino and partner from the motion picture *Four Horsemen of the Apocalypse,* 1921.
BY COURTESY OF METRO-GOLDWYN-MAYER INC., © 1921; PHOTOGRAPH, FROM THE MUSEUM OF MODERN ART FILM STILLS ARCHIVE

Tangun \'tän-'gün\ Mythological first king of the Koreans, whose reign began in 2333 BC. According to one legend, Tangun's father descended from heaven to rule earth from a mountaintop. When a bear and a tiger expressed the wish to become human, he ordered them into a cave for 100 days; after the tiger grew impatient and left, the bear was transformed into the beautiful woman who became Tangun's mother. Buddhism and Taoism credited Tangun with establishing a national religion and originating the Korean maxim *Hongik-ingan* ("Love humanity"). His birthday is a school holiday.

Tangut \'tän-'gu̇t\ People historically living in southern Inner Mongolia at the terminus of the SILK ROAD. They engaged in irrigated agriculture and pastoralism and acted as middlemen in trade between Central Asia and China. They adopted Buddhism as their state religion, created their own writing system, and in 1038 proclaimed their kingdom of XI XIA, which survived nearly 200 years.

Tanguy \tä^{n}-'gē\, **Yves** (1900–1955) French-U.S. painter. In 1923, after serving in the merchant marine, he was inspired to start painting when he saw the works of GIORGIO DE CHIRICO, though he had no formal art training. He joined the Surrealist group in 1925 and participated in all their major exhibitions. He developed a unique style, reminiscent of SALVADOR DALI's, depicting strange, amorphous creatures and unidentifiable objects set in barren, brightly lit landscapes with infinite horizons. Despite their smooth, painstaking detail, his pictures have a timeless, dreamlike quality (e.g., *The Invisibles*, 1951). He emigrated to the U.S. in 1939.

Tanimbar Islands \tə-'nim-,bär, 'ta-nəm-,bär\ Group of about 30 islands, southeastern MOLUCCAS, Indonesia. It includes the large island of Jamdena, 70 mi (113 km) long by 28 mi (45 km) wide, and the nearby islands of Larat and Selaru. Though there is a lack of fresh water, the soil supports corn, rice, coconut palms, and fruits. The Dutch claimed the group in 1639 but did not establish rule until 1900. After World War II, the islands became part of Indonesia.

Tanis \'tā-nəs\ *biblical* **Zoan** Ancient city, NILE RIVER delta, Egypt. Capital of a province of Lower Egypt and, at one time, of the whole country, it was important as one of the nearest ports to the Asian seaboard, and was a base for the 20th–22nd dynasties. In 1939 several intact royal tombs containing silver coffins, gold masks, and gold and silver jewelry were excavated within the ancient main temple enclosure.

Tanit \'tä-nit\ Chief goddess of CARTHAGE, the equivalent of ASTARTE. She first appeared around the 5th century BC. Though she seems to have had some connection with the heavens, she was also a mother goddess and symbol of fertility. She was the consort of Baal Hammon, chief god of Carthage, whose cult she eventually eclipsed. Archaeological evidence suggests that children, probably firstborn, were sacrificed both to her and to Baal Hammon. Outside Carthage, Tanit also enjoyed a following on Malta, on Sardinia, and in Spain.

Tanizaki Jun'ichiro \,tä-nē-'zä-kē-'jün-ē-,chē-rō\ (1886–1965) Japanese novelist. Though his earliest short stories have affinities with EDGAR ALLAN POE and the French DECADENTS, Tanizaki later turned to exploring more traditional Japanese ideals of beauty. His writings are characterized by eroticism and ironic wit. His novels include *Some Prefer Nettles* (1928–29), which tells of marital unhappiness that is in fact a conflict between the new and the old, with the implication that the old will win; and his masterpiece, *The Makioka Sisters* (1943–48), which describes, in the leisurely style of classical Japanese literature, the inroads of the harsh modern world on traditional society.

tank Heavily armed and armored combat vehicle that moves on two continuous metal chains called tracks. It is usually equipped with a CANNON mounted in a revolving turret as well as lighter automatic weapons. The British developed tanks during World War I to fill the need for an armored assault vehicle that could cross the muddy, uneven terrain of the trench battle zone. They first saw combat at the Battle of the SOMME (1916). In World War II, Germany's tank force was initially the most effective in Europe because it was organized into fast-moving massed formations with great striking power. After World War II, tanks became larger and more heavily armed. Most modern main battle tanks weigh more than 50 tons yet are capable of road speeds of 30–40 mph (50–70 kph). The standard main armament is a 120-mm gun, which fires armor-piercing projectiles; laser range-finders and infrared imaging devices aid in sighting.

Tannenberg \'tä-nən-,berk\, **Battle of** (July 15, 1410) Major Polish-Lithuanian victory over the Knights of the TEUTONIC ORDER. Fought near the villages of Grünfelde and Tannenberg in northeastern Poland (formerly East Prussia), the battle marked the end of the order's expansion along the southeastern coast of the Baltic Sea and the beginning of the decline of its power.

Tannenberg \'tä-nən-,berk\, **Battle of** (August 26–30, 1914) Battle in WORLD WAR I between Germany and Russia in modern northeastern Poland. Two Russian armies invaded German East Prussia but became separated. German forces under PAUL VON HINDENBURG attacked one of the isolated armies and forced its retreat, inflicting Russian casualties of over 30,000 and capturing over 90,000 men. German casualties were about 13,000. The battle was disastrous for Russia, but it forced Germany to divert troops from the attack on France.

Tanner, Henry Ossawa (1859–1937) U.S.-French painter. Born in Pittsburgh, he studied under THOMAS EAKINS at the Pennsylvania Academy of Fine Arts, where he was the only black student. He moved to Paris in 1891, and by 1894 his work was being exhibited at the annual Salons, where he was awarded honorable mention in 1896 for *Daniel in the Lions' Den* and won a medal in 1897 for his *Raising of Lazarus*. He gained international acclaim and many awards for his landscapes and his treatments of biblical themes. He was made a chevalier of the Legion of Honor in 1923, and in 1927 he became the first African-American granted full membership in the National Academy of Design.

Tannhäuser \'tän-ˌhȯi-zər\ (c. 1200–c. 1270) German lyric poet and legendary hero. A professional MINNESINGER, Tannhäuser served several noble patrons; a few of his works are extant. In the legend preserved in a popular ballad, *Danhauser,* he lives a life of pleasure but, torn by remorse, goes to Rome to seek remission of his sins. The pope tells him that, as his pilgrim's staff would never put on leaf again, so his sins can never be forgiven. Shortly afterward his discarded staff puts forth green leaves. The pope sends messengers to search for him, but he is never seen again. The legend, popular among 19th-century Romantic writers, was retold in RICHARD WAGNER'S *Tannhäuser* (produced 1845).

tannin *or* **tannic acid** Any of a group of pale yellow to light brown amorphous substances widely distributed in plants and used chiefly in TANNING leather, dyeing fabric, and making ink. Their solutions are acid and have an astringent taste. They are isolated from oak bark, sumac, myrobalan (an Asian tree), and galls. Tannins give TEA astringency, color, and some flavor. Tannins are used industrially to clarify wine and beer, reduce viscosity of oil-well drilling mud, and prevent scale in boiler water; they have also had medical uses.

tanning Chemical treatment of raw animal hides or skins to convert them into LEATHER. Vegetable tanning (using bark, wood, roots, or berries) has been practiced since prehistoric times. After removal of hair, flesh, or fat, a tanning agent displaces water from the interstices between the PROTEIN (mostly COLLAGEN) fibers in the skin and cements the fibers together. The agents most widely used are vegetable TANNIN, SALTS such as chromium sulfate, or fish or animal oil. The tanning of fair skin by sunlight is completely different: Ultraviolet light causes production and redistribution of MELANIN in epidermal cells.

tansy \'tan-zē\ Any of about 50 species of strong-smelling, poisonous herbs, especially common tansy *(Tanacetum vulgare,* or *Chrysanthemum vulgare),* of the COMPOSITE FAMILY, native to the northern temperate zone. *T. vulgare* has button-shaped yellow flower heads of disk flowers (no ray flowers) that are arranged in a flat-topped cluster, deeply cut leaves, and many stems. It is sometimes cultivated in herb gardens and was formerly used in medicines and insecticides. See also CHRYSANTHEMUM.

tantalum \'tan-tə-ləm\ Metallic chemical ELEMENT, one of the TRANSITION elements, chemical symbol Ta, atomic number 73. It is a dense, hard, unreactive, silvery-gray METAL with an extremely high melting point (5,425°F, or 2,996°C). Relatively rare, it occurs native in a few places. It is difficult to separate from niobium, the element above it in the PERIODIC TABLE, with which it shares many properties. The most important uses are in electrolytic capacitors, corrosion-resistant chemical equipment, dental and surgical instruments, tools, catalysts, components of electron tubes, rectifiers, and PROSTHESES. Its compounds are relatively unimportant commercially; tantalum carbide is used in machine tools and dies.

Tantalus \'tan-tᵊl-əs\ In GREEK MYTHOLOGY, the king of Sipylus (or Phrygia). An intimate friend of the gods, he was allowed to dine at their table until he offended them by repeating their secrets on earth. Another version of the myth held that he killed his son PELOPS and served him to the gods. In the underworld he was placed up to his neck in water, which flowed away every time he tried to drink, just as the branches overhead swung out of reach whenever he tried to pick the fruit from them.

tantra \'tən-trə\ In some Indian religions, a text that deals with esoteric aspects of religious teaching. There is considerable tantric literature and practice in HINDUISM, BUDDHISM, and, to a lesser extent, JAINISM. Because tantric practices typically represent teachings of relatively late development and incorporate elements of different traditions, they are often eschewed by orthodox practitioners. In Hinduism, tantras deal with popular aspects of the religion, such as spells, rituals, and symbols. Buddhist tantric literature, believed to date from the 7th century or earlier, has reference to numerous practices, some involving sexual activity, that have no basis in canonical literature.

Tanzania \ˌtan-zə-'nē-ə\ *officially* **United Republic of Tanzania** Country, eastern Africa. It includes the islands of ZANZIBAR, Pemba, and Mafia in the Indian Ocean. Area: 364,881 sq mi (935,037 sq km). Population (1997 est.): 29,461,000. Capital: DAR es Salaam; DODOMA, designated. There are about 120 identifiable ethnic groups; the largest, the Sukuma, are about one-fifth of the population. Languages: Swahili, English (both official). Religions: Islam, animism, Christianity. Currency: Tanzanian shilling. Although most of Tanzania consists of plain and plateau, it has some spectacular relief features, including Mount KILIMANJARO and Mount Lengai, an active volcano. All or portions of Lakes MALAWI, TANGANYIKA, VICTORIA, and RUKWA lie within it, as do the headwaters of the NILE, CONGO, and ZAMBEZI rivers. SERENGETI NATIONAL PARK is the most famous of its extensive game reserves. Important mineral deposits include gold, diamonds, gemstones, iron ore, coal, and natural gas. The centrally planned economy is based largely on agriculture; major crops include corn, rice, coffee, cloves, cotton, sisal, cashews, and tobacco. Industries include food processing, textiles, cement, and brewing. It is a republic with one legislative house; its head of state and government is the president. Inhabited from the 1st millennium BC, it was occupied by Arab and Indian traders and BANTU-speaking peoples by the 10th century AD. The Portuguese gained control of the coastline in the late 15th century, but they were driven out by the Arabs of OMAN and Zanzibar in the late 18th century. German colonists entered the area in the 1880s, and in 1891 the Germans declared the region a protectorate as GERMAN EAST AFRICA. In World War I Britain captured the German holdings, which became a British mandate (1920) under the name Tanganyika. Britain retained control of the region after World War II when it became a U.N. trust territory (1946). Tanganyika gained independence in 1961 and became a republic in 1962. In 1964 it united with Zanzibar under the name Tanzania. It experienced both political and economic struggles in recent years.

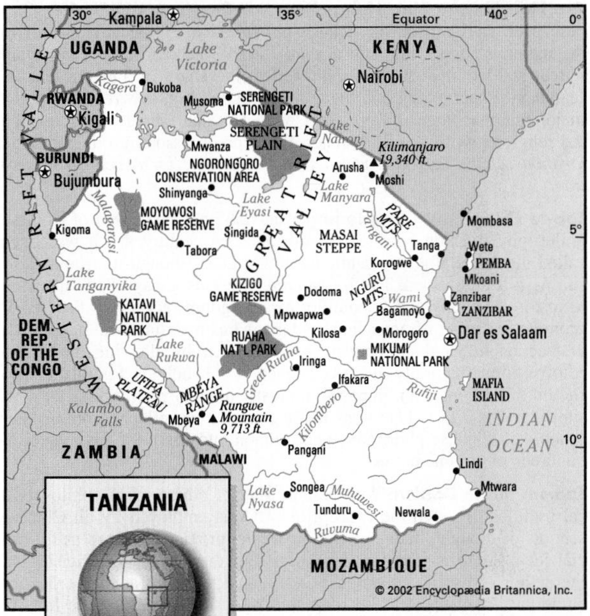

Tanzimat \ˌtän-zē-ˈmät\ (Turkish: "reorganization") (1839–76) Reforms undertaken in Ottoman Turkey to modernize society and reduce the influence of the Muslim clergy. The first set of reforms (1839) sought to secularize the government's treatment of people and property and to reform taxation and military conscription. Later reforms (1856) established a secular school system and a new law code. Efforts to centralize government administration ended by concentrating all authority in the sultan. The constitution of 1876, while promising democratic reforms, was intended to stave off European intervention. See also ABDÜLHAMID II, YOUNG TURKS.

tao *pinyin* **dao** \ˈdau̇\ In Chinese philosophy, a fundamental concept signifying the correct or divine way. In CONFUCIANISM, tao signifies a morally correct path of behavior. In TAOISM, the concept is more encompassing and includes the visible process of nature, by which all things change, as well as the principle underlying this process. This principle, known as Absolute Tao, can be only imperfectly understood by the practitioner but is the guiding principle in life. Taoists view life and death as stages of Absolute Tao and advocate a way of life that brings one closer to conformity with essential nature.

Tao Hongjing *or* **T'ao Hung-ching** \ˈtau̇-ˈhu̇ŋ-ˈjiŋ\ (AD 451–536) Chinese poet, calligrapher, physician, and naturalist. He became a tutor to the imperial court while still a youth. In 492 he retired to a mountain retreat at Mao shan to devote himself to the study of Taoism. His research in proper eating and living practices led him to write one of the major pharmacological works of China. He also edited and annotated the religious writings of his major Taoist predecessors, producing *Declarations of the Perfected* and *Secret Instructions for Ascent to Perfection.*

Tao-te ching *Pinyin* **Daode jing** \ˈdau̇-ˈdə-ˈjiŋ\ Classic text of Chinese philosophy. Written between the 6th and 3rd century BC, it was once called the *Laozi* after its traditional author LAOZI, though its true authorship is still unresolved. The *Tao-te ching* presents a way of life intended to restore harmony and tranquillity to a kingdom racked by disorder. It promotes a course of nonaction, understood as restraint from any unnatural action rather than complete passivity, thereby allowing the TAO to resolve things naturally. It was designed as a handbook for rulers, who should rule by inaction, imposing no restrictions or prohibitions on their subjects. The *Tao-te ching* has had a tremendous influence on all later schools of Chinese philosophy and religion and has been the subject of hundreds of commentaries.

Taoism *pinyin* **Daoism** \ˈdau̇-ˌiz-əm\ Major Chinese religio-philosophical tradition. Though the concept of TAO was employed by all Chinese schools of thought, Taoism arose out of the promotion of tao as the social ideal. LAOZI is traditionally regarded as the founder of Taoism and the author of its classic text, the *TAO-TE CHING*. Other Taoist classics include the *Zhuangzi* (4th–3rd century BC; see ZHUANGZI) and the *LIEZI*. In Taoism, tao is the force or principle about which nothing can be predicated, but that latently contains the forms, entities, and forces of all phenomena. This natural wisdom should not be interfered with; DE, or superior virtue, is acquired through action so entirely in accordance with the natural order that its author leaves no trace of himself in his work. The tradition holds that all beings and things are fundamentally one. Taoism's focus on nature and the natural order complements the societal focus of CONFUCIANISM, and its synthesis with BUDDHISM is the basis of ZEN. See also YIN-YANG.

Taos \ˈtau̇s\ Town (pop., 1996 est.: 5,000) and resort, northern New Mexico. Located on a branch of the RIO GRANDE in the SANGRE de Cristo Mtns., it is composed of three villages: Don Fernando de Taos (known as Taos), the pueblo of San Geronimo (Taos Pueblo), and the Ranchos de Taos. An early Spanish settlement, it was the scene of a revolt (1680) of Taos and other PUEBLO INDIANS against Spain, and later was an important commercial center on the SANTA FE TRAIL. In the 20th century artists and writers moved there, including D. H. LAWRENCE; his home and that of KIT CARSON are historic sites, and Carson's grave is in a memorial state park.

tap dance Style of American theatrical dance using precise rhythmical patterns of foot movement and audible foot tapping. It is derived from the traditional clog dance of northern England, the jigs and reels of Ireland and Scotland, and the rhythmic foot stamping of African dances. Popular in 19th-century minstrel shows, the "buck-and-wing" (danced vigorously in wooden-soled shoes) and "soft-shoe" (danced smoothly in soft-soled shoes) versions developed as separate techniques; by 1925 they had merged, and metal taps were attached to shoe heels and toes to produce a more pronounced sound. The dance was also popular in variety shows and early musicals.

Tapajos River \ˌtä-pä-ˈzhȯs\ River, northern Brazil. Formed by the confluence of the Teles Pires and the Juruena rivers, it flows northeast to empty into the AMAZON RIVER just above Santarém after a course of 807 mi (1,298 km). Though interrupted by rapids, its entire length is navigable. Several important rubber plantations lie along its banks.

tapas \ˈtə-pəs\ Ascetic practice carried out to achieve spiritual power or purification. In HINDUISM, it is associated with YOGA as a way of purifying the body in preparation for the more exacting spiritual exercises leading to liberation. In JAINISM, its practice is a central means of breaking the cycle of rebirths by preventing new KARMA from forming and by eliminating the old. Tapas can take many forms, including fasting, controlling the breath, and holding difficult and painful body postures. Extreme forms are carried out by SADHUS, many of whom earn alms for their unusual abilities or deprivations.

tape recorder Recording system that makes use of electromagnetic phenomena to record and reproduce SOUND waves. The tape consists of a plastic backing coated with a thin layer of tiny particles of magnetic powder. The recording head of the tape deck consists of a tiny C-shaped magnet with its gap adjacent to the moving tape. The incoming sound wave, having been converted by a microphone into an electrical signal, produces a time-varying magnetic field in the gap of the magnet. As the tape moves past the recording head, the powder is magnetized in such a way that the tape carries a record of the shape of the wave being recorded.

tapestry Heavy, reversible, patterned or figured hand-woven textile, usually in the form of a hanging or upholstery fabric. Tapestries are usually designed as single panels or as sets of panels related by subject and style and intended to be hung together. The earliest known tapestries were made from linen by the ancient Egyptians. Tapestry weaving was well established in Peru by the 6th century, and outstanding silk tapestries were made in China beginning in the TANG dynasty (AD 618–907). In Western Europe, tapestry making flourished from the 13th century. Among the greatest European tapestries are the 15th-century *Lady with the Unicorn* set and the 16th-century *Acts of the Apostles* set, based on cartoons by RAPHAEL. Tapestry art was revitalized in late-19th-century Britain with the ARTS and Crafts Movement. In the 20th century, abstract tapestries were produced at the BAUHAUS, and many painters, including PABLO PICASSO and HENRI MATISSE, allowed their paintings to provide the basis for tapestry art.

tapeworm Any of about 3,000 species (class Cestoda, phylum Platyhelminthes) of bilaterally symmetrical parasitic FLATWORMS found worldwide. Tapeworms range from 0.04 in. (1 mm) to more than 50 ft (15 m) long. The head bears suckers and often hooks for attaching to the liver or digestive tract of the host. Once attached, tapeworms absorb food through their body wall. The body is often divided into a head or scolex possessing the suckers and hooks, an unsegmented neck, and a series of proglottids (units containing both male and female reproductive organs) which continually form in a growth region at the base of the neck. Following fertilization, each mature proglottid containing thousands of embryos breaks off and is eliminated in the host's feces. The life cycle may require more than one host but otherwise somewhat resembles that of the roundworm TRICHINA. Many species that infest humans belong to the genus *Taenia;* the intermediate host is implied by the name (e.g., beef tapeworm, *T. saginata*). Human infestation is common in the southeastern U.S.; humans usually acquire tapeworms through fecal contamination of soil or water or inadequate cooking of meat or fish. See illustration on following page.

Tapi River \ˈtä-pē\ *or* **Tapti River** \ˈtäp-tē\ River, western central India. It flows west from the mountains of MADHYA PRADESH to the Gulf of KHAMBHAT and the Arabian Sea. It is about 435 mi (700 km) long and largely unnavigable.

Tápies \ˈtäp-yes\, **Antoni** (born 1923) Spanish (Catalan) painter. In 1946 he abandoned the study of law to devote his time to painting, which he taught himself. His early works were influenced by Surrealism, PAUL KLEE, and JOAN MIRO. In 1953, after seeing the works of JEAN DUBUFFET, he developed a unique blend of abstraction, assemblage, and

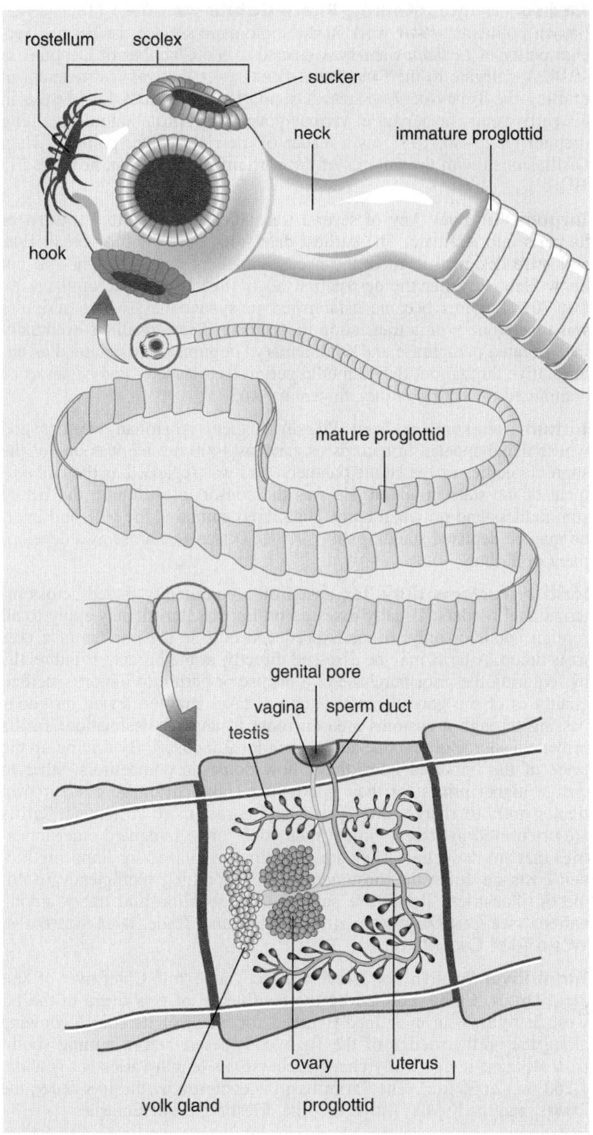

Principal features of the beef tapeworm. The head or scolex contains suckers and hooks for attaching to the human host. A series of reproductive organs (proglottids) continually form at the base of the neck, and following fertilization they mature and break off. Each proglottid, eliminated in the host's feces, contains thousands of embryos. If these are ingested by cattle (the intermediate host) grazing on food contaminated with feces, they develop into larvae, which bore through the intestinal wall into the circulatory system and are carried to muscle tissues, which they burrow into, forming a dormant cyst. When meat is inadequately cooked, humans become infected with the larvae, which attach to the intestinal wall.

impasto that established his international reputation. He has produced lithographs and illustrated books; his belief in the validity of commonplace materials has had worldwide influence. In 1990 the Tàpies Foundation, housing some 2,000 of his works, opened in Barcelona.

tapir \'tā-pər\ Any of four extant members (genus *Tapirus*) of the family Tapiridae, heavy-bodied, odd-toed UNGULATES, 6–8 ft (1.8–2.5 m) long and up to 3 ft (1 m) high. They have short ears and legs and a fleshy snout overhanging the upper lip. The feet have three functional toes. Body hair is usually short and sparse, but two species have a short, bristly mane. The Malayan tapir *(T. indicus)* has a black head, shoulders, and legs and white rump, back, and belly. The single Central and two South American species are plain brown or gray. Tapirs inhabit the deep forest or swamp.

Lowland tapir (*Tapirus terrestris*).

WARREN GARST—TOM STACK & ASSOCIATES

Tappan \'tap-ən\, **Arthur** (1786–1865) U.S. merchant and philanthropist. Born in Northampton, Mass., he operated various mercantile businesses, including a silk-importing firm in New York (1826–37) with his brother Lewis Tappan (1788–1873); they also founded the first commercial credit-rating service (1841). He used his wealth to support missionary societies and the abolitionist crusade, helping found the AMERICAN ANTI-SLAVERY SOCIETY and serving as its first president (1833–40). After breaking with WILLIAM LLOYD GARRISON, he created the American and Foreign Anti-Slavery Society (1840). The brothers later supported the UNDERGROUND RAILROAD.

taproot Main root of a primary-root system. It grows vertically downward. From the taproot arise smaller lateral roots (secondary roots), which in turn produce even smaller lateral roots (tertiary roots). Most dicotyledonous plants (see COTYLEDON), such as DANDELIONS, produce taproots. The system may be modified into a fibrous, or diffuse, system, in which the initial secondary roots soon equal or exceed the primary root in size and there is no well-defined single taproot. Fibrous root systems are generally shallower than taproot systems. Carrots and beets are tuberous roots modified from taproots.

taqiya \tə-'kē-ə\ In ISLAM, the practice of concealing one's faith and forgoing ordinary religious duties under threat of death or injury to oneself or one's fellow Muslims. Its basis is found in the QURAN, and MUHAMMAD is regarded as having set its first example when he chose to make the HEJIRA. Various rules governing its application are meant to ensure that taqiya does not become an excuse for cowardice or for failure to take appropriate action. Consideration of community rather than private welfare is generally stressed.

taqlid \ta-'klēd\ In Islamic law, the unquestioning acceptance of legal decisions without knowing their basis. The interpretation of taqlid varies widely among the major schools of Islamic law. Taqlid is compulsory for SHIITES; of the four SUNNI legal schools, the Shafi, Maliki, and Hanafi embrace taqlid, but the Hanbali reject it. Support for the practice is based mainly on the belief that early Muslim scholars, being closer in time to MUHAMMAD, were in the best position to derive authoritative legal opinions.

tar sand *or* **bituminous sand** Deposit of loose sand or partially consolidated SANDSTONE that is saturated with highly viscous BITUMEN. Oil recovered from tar sands, commonly referred to as synthetic crude, is a potentially significant form of FOSSIL FUEL. The largest known deposits of tar sands occur in Canada's Athabasca River valley, where commercial projects for synthetic oil production from tar sands are being carried out.

Tara \'tä-rä\ In BUDDHISM, a savior-goddess with numerous forms. Her worship is widely popular in Nepal, Tibet, and Mongolia. She is the feminine counterpart of AVALOKITESVARA. She came into existence when his tear fell to the ground and formed a lake; out of its waters rose a lotus, which, on opening, revealed the goddess. She is the protector of navigation and earthly travel, as well as of spiritual travel along the path to Enlightenment. In art she typically holds a lotus and has a third eye. She is represented in various colors, signifying different aspects of her powers.

White Tara, gilt copper repoussé statue from Nepal, 18th century; in the Asian Art Museum of San Francisco, The Avery Brundage Collection.

BY COURTESY OF THE ASIAN ART MUSEUM OF SAN FRANCISCO, THE AVERY BRUNDAGE COLLECTION; PHOTOGRAPH, MARTIN GRAYSON

Tarai See Terai

Tarantino, Quentin (born 1963) U.S. director and screenwriter. Born in Knoxville, Tenn., he trained as an actor before directing his first film, *Reservoir Dogs* (1993). His controversial *Pulp Fiction* (1994), which depicted similar violence with little moral perspective, won the Palme d'Or at Cannes. Oliver Stone's *Natural Born Killers* (1994), another film in the vein of fast-paced violence, was based on a story by Tarantino, and he wrote the screenplays for *True Romance* (1993) and *Jackie Brown* (1997). Though few in number, his films have been widely imitated.

Taranto \'tä-rän-ˌtō\ *ancient* **Tarentum.** Seaport (metro. area pop., 1996 est.: 212,000), Puglia region, southeastern Italy. Located on the Gulf of Taranto, the old city is on a small island, with newer areas on the adjacent mainland. Founded by Greeks from Sparta in the 8th century BC, it was called Taras and became one of the leading cities of Magna Graecia. It reached its zenith in the 4th century BC under Archytas. It came under Rome in 272 BC. Between the 5th–11th century AD it was taken by the Goths, Byzantines, Lombards, Arabs, and Normans. By the 15th century it was part of the kingdom of Naples. Part of the kingdom of the Two Sicilies from 1815, it joined the kingdom of Italy in 1861. It was an important stronghold of the Italian Navy in both world wars; it was heavily bombed in 1940 and was occupied by British forces in 1943. Still an important naval base, it is the site of extensive shipyards and a large iron- and steel-works.

tarantula \tə-ran-chə-lə\ Name that originally referred to the wolf spider but now covers any spider in the family Theraphosidae. It is found from the southwestern U.S. to South America. Many species live in a burrow, and most have a hairy body and long, hairy legs. They are nocturnal predators of insects and, occasionally, amphibians and mice. Certain South American tarantulas eat small birds. In the southwestern U.S., tarantulas of the genus *Aphonopelma* may have a body 2 in. (5 cm) long and a leg spread of nearly 5 in. (12 cm). They may inflict a painful bite if provoked. The most common U.S. species, *Eurypelma californicum,* may live up to 30 years.

American tarantula (*Aphonopelma*).
LYNAM—TOM STACK & ASSOCIATES

Tarascans Indian people of Michoacán state in central Mexico, a cool, arid area of high volcanic plateaus and lakes. Traditionally, they are primarily farmers, and they fish, hunt, trade, and work for wages as well. Each village tends to specialize in a craft (e.g., woodworking, weaving, pottery, net weaving, embroidering, or sewing). Their Roman Catholicism is only slightly influenced by pre-Columbian religion.They are gradually becoming assimilated to the mestizo culture, though their primary language remains Tarascan.

Tarawa \tə-'rä-wə, 'ta-rə-wä\ Coral atoll (pop., 1990: 28,800), Gilbert Islands, Kiribati. The site of Bairiki, the capital of Kiribati, it is made up of 15 islets along a reef 22 mi (35 km) long. Occupied by the Japanese during World War II, it was seized by U.S. Marines in 1943 after a costly battle. Now a commercial and educational center, it exports copra and mother-of-pearl and has an extension of the University of the South Pacific. It was the capital of Gilbert and Ellice Islands until 1975.

Tarbell \'tär-bəl\, **Ida M(inerva)** (1857–1944) U.S. investigative journalist, lecturer, and chronicler of American industry. Born in Erie Co., Pa., Tarbell went in 1891 to Paris, where she supported herself by writing for U.S. magazines. She became best known for *The History of the Standard Oil Company* (1904), an account of the rise of a business monopoly that first appeared serially in *McClure's Magazine* and led to the government's epochal antitrust suit against the company. For her work Tarbell became one of the journalists Theodore Roosevelt dubbed muckrakers. She also wrote for *American Magazine* (1906–15) and was its co-owner and coeditor for several years. Among her other works are popular biographies and an autobiography, *All in the Day's Work* (1939).

Tardieu \tär-'dyœ̄\, **André (-Pierre-Gabriel-Amédée)** (1876–1945) French politician. After work in the diplomatic service, he became foreign editor of *Le Temps* and was elected to the Chamber of Deputies in 1914. A delegate to the Paris Peace Conference, he was instrumental in drafting the Treaty of Versailles. A supporter of Georges Clemenceau in his early career, he served in various government posts before becoming premier (1929–30, 1932) as a leader of the right-center political wing. Disillusioned with the failures of the parliamentary system, he retired in 1936.

Targum \'tär-gəm\ Any of several translations of the Old Testament or its parts into Aramaic. The earliest date from after the Babylonian Exile and were designed to meet the needs of uneducated Jews who did not know Hebrew. After the destruction of the Second Temple of Jerusalem (AD 70), Targums became established in synagogues, where scripture was read aloud with a translation in Aramaic. These readings eventually incorporated paraphrase and commentary. Targums were regarded as authoritative throughout the Talmudic period (see Talmud), and began to be committed to writing in the 5th century AD.

Tarhun \'tär-ˌk̲ün\ *or* **Taru** \'tär-ˌü\ Ancient Anatolian weather god whose name appears in records as early as 1400 BC. He was one of the supreme deities of the Hittite pantheon and was regarded as the embodiment of the state in action. He was the consort of Arinnitti, the Hittite sun goddess and principal deity. His sacred animal is the bull, and in art he may be depicted standing on it. Jupiter Dolichenus arose as a development of Tarhun.

tariff *or* **customs duty** Tax levied on a commodity traded across international borders. Usually assessed on imports, tariffs may apply to all foreign goods or only to goods produced outside the borders of a customs union. A tariff may be assessed directly, at the border, or indirectly, by requiring the prior purchase of a license or permit to import specified quantities of the good. Transit duties or taxes may be levied on goods passing through a customs area en route to another destination. Tariffs provide a source of revenue and protect local industry. By driving up the price of the imported item, they allow domestic competitors either to charge higher prices for their goods or to take advantage of their own lighter taxes to charge lower prices and attract more customers. Tariffs are often used to protect "infant industries" or to safeguard older industries that are in decline. They are sometimes criticized for imposing hidden costs on domestic consumers and encouraging inefficiency in domestic industries. Tariffs are subject to negotiation and treaty among nations (see General Agreement on Tariffs and Trade, trade agreement, World Trade Organization).

Tarim River \'dä-'rēm\ *or* **T'a-li-mu Ho** \'tä-'lē-'mü\ Chief river of Xinjiang Uygur, China. Formed by the confluence of two rivers in the far west, it follows an undefined riverbed for much of its course, flowing along the northern edge of the Taklimakan desert before turning southeast. Because it frequently changes course, its length varies but is about 1,260 mi (2,030 km). The Tarim basin is enclosed by the Tian Shan, the Pamirs, and the Kunlun Mtns. It is the driest region of Eurasia.

tariqa \tä-'rē-kə\ In Sufism, the spiritual path toward direct knowledge of God or reality. For early Sufi mystics, the term referred to an individual's spiritual path; later it came to mean the path advocated by a particular school or order of Sufis, and then the order itself. Each mystic order claimed a chain of spiritual descent from Muhammad. Today Sufi tariqa number in the hundreds.

Tarkenton, Fran(cis Asbury) (born 1940) U.S. football quarterback. Born in Richmond, Va., he was an All-American at the University of Georgia (1958–61). Later, with the Minnesota Vikings (1961–66; 1972–78) and New York Giants (1967–71), he set all-time career records for most passes completed (3,686), most yards gained (47,003), and most touchdown passes (342) (all later broken by Dan Marino).

Tarkington, (Newton) Booth (1869–1946) U.S. novelist and dramatist. A native of Indianapolis, he became known for satirical and sometimes romanticized pictures of Midwesterners in humorous portrayals of boyhood and adolescence that include the young-people's classics *Penrod* (1914), *Seventeen* (1916), and *Gentle Julia* (1922). The trilogy *Growth* (1927) includes *The Magnificent Ambersons* (1918, Pulitzer Prize; film, 1942), which traces the decline of a once-powerful and prominent family. *Alice Adams* (1921) is perhaps his most finished novel. He also wrote many plays, including an adaptation of his popular romance *Monsieur Beaucaire* (1901).

Tarkovsky \tär-ˈkȯf-skē\, **Andrey (Arsenyevich)** (1932–1986) Russian film director. The son of a poet, he studied at the Soviet State Film School and won praise for his first feature film, *Ivan's Childhood* (1962). His religious and aesthetic concerns were reflected in *Andrei Rublev* (1966), about a medieval icon painter confronted with the brutality of war. His later films, noted for their striking visual images, visionary tone, and paucity of conventional plot, include *Solaris* (1972), *A Mirror* (1975), and *Stalker* (1978). Soviet authorities hindered domestic distribution of his films, and in 1984, after making *Nostalghia* (1983), he defected to the West, where he made his last film, the acclaimed *The Sacrifice* (1986).

Tarn River River, southwestern France. Rising in the Lozère Mtns., it flows west and southwest for 233 mi (375 km) into the GARONNE RIVER. Its magnificent gorges, which extend for more than 30 mi (48 km) through limestone plateaus, are popular tourist attractions.

taro \ˈtär-ō\ Herbaceous plant *(Colocasia esculenta)* of the ARUM family, probably native to S.East Asia, that spread to the Pacific islands. It is a staple crop cultivated for its large, starchy, spherical underground TUBERS, which, though poisonous raw, become edible with heating. They are consumed as a cooked vegetable or made into puddings, breads, or Polynesian poi (a thin, pasty, highly digestible mass of fermented taro starch). Poi is a staple food in Hawaii. The large leaves (also poisonous raw) of the taro are commonly eaten stewed.

tarot \ˈtar-ˌō\ Sets of cards used in fortune-telling and in certain card games. Their origins are obscure; cards approximating their present form first appeared in Italy and France in the late 14th century. Modern tarot decks consist of 78 cards, of which 22 have pictures representing forces, characters, virtues, and vices. The remaining cards are divided into four suits—(1) wands, batons, or rods, (2) cups, (3) swords, and (4) coins, pentacles, or disks—of 14 cards each. Each suit has 10 numbered cards and four court cards (king, queen, knight, and page). Modern PLAYING cards evolved from the latter. Initially used as playing cards, tarot cards were imbued with esoteric associations in the 18th century and are now used widely for fortune-telling. Each card's basic meaning is altered by the card's position in the spread of cards laid out by the fortune-teller, by the card's orientation, and by the cards that are near it.

Moon, the eighteenth card of the Major Arcana.
MARY EVANS PICTURE LIBRARY

tarpon Any of certain marine fish (family Megalopidae) having an elongated last dorsal fin ray and a bony throat plate between the sides of the protruding lower jaw. The scales are large, thick, and silvery. The Atlantic tarpon *(Tarpon,* or *Megalops, atlanticus)* is found inshore in warm parts of the Atlantic, on the Pacific side of Central America, and sometimes in rivers. It habitually breaks water and gulps air. It regularly grows to 6 ft (1.8 m) and 100 lbs (45 kg) or larger and is a favorite game fish. The Pacific tarpon *(M. cyprinoides)* is similar.

Young Atlantic tarpon (*Tarpon atlanticus*).
BY COURTESY OF MIAMI SEAQUARIUM

Tarquinia \tär-ˈkwēn-yä\ *formerly (until 1922)* **Corneto** Town (pop., 1991: 14,000), northern LAZIO region, central Italy. It developed out of the ancient Tárchuna, one of the chief cities of the Etruscan confederation. It was defeated by Rome in the 4th century BC and became a Roman colony (as Tarquinii) in the 1st century BC. It was moved to its present site after Lombard and Saracen invasions in the 6th–8th century AD. Remains of the ancient city include the foundations of a great Etruscan temple with a group of terra-cotta winged horses that is considered a masterpiece of Etruscan art. The famous necropolis contains the most important painted tombs in Etruscan Italy.

tarragon \ˈtar-ə-gən\ Bushy aromatic herb *(Artemisia dracunculus)* of the COMPOSITE FAMILY, the dried leaves and flowering tops of which are used to add tang to many culinary dishes. Tarragon is a common ingredient in seasoning blends, such as fines herbes. The fresh leaves are used in salads, and vinegar in which fresh tarragon has been steeped is a distinctive condiment. The plant is probably native to Siberia; a French variety is cultivated in Europe and North America.

tarsier \ˈtär-sē-ər, ˈtär-sē-ˌā\ Any of three species (genus *Tarsius,* family Tarsiidae) of nocturnal prosimian PRIMATES found on several South Asian islands. Tarsiers have large, goggling eyes and a round head that can be rotated 180°. The ears are large, membranous, and almost constantly in motion. Tarsiers are 4–6 in. (9–16 cm) long; the thin, tufted tail about twice that length serves as a balancer and prop. The gray to dark brown fur is thick and silky. Tarsiers cling vertically to trees and leap from trunk to trunk. They have greatly elongated hind limbs and disklike adhesive pads on the digit tips. Tarsiers prey mainly on insects. The well-furred newborn is born with eyes open.

Tarsus City (pop., 1995 est.: 230,000), southern central Turkey, near the Mediterranean coast. Settled from Neolithic times, it was razed and rebuilt c. 700 BC by the Assyrian king SENNACHERIB. Later, Achaemenid and Seleucid rule alternated with periods of autonomy. In 67 BC it was absorbed into the new Roman province of CILICIA, becoming its principal city. It was the site of the first meeting between Mark ANTONY and CLEOPATRA in 41 BC. It was the birthplace of St. PAUL. It remained a leading industrial and cultural center through the early Byzantine period. It came under various powers in the 10th–15th century, and passed to the Ottoman Turks in the early 16th century. Modern Tarsus is a prosperous agricultural and cotton-milling center.

tartan Cross-checkered repeating pattern (or "sett") of bands, stripes, or lines of various colors and of definite width and sequence, woven into woolen cloth, sometimes with silk added. Such patterns have existed for centuries in many cultures, but have come to be regarded as fundamentally Scottish and as a quasi-heraldic Scottish family or clan emblem. Though claims of great antiquity have been made for Scottish tartans, few seem to predate the 17th or even 18th century as clan emblems. The Scottish Tartans Society (founded 1963) maintains a register of all known tartans, numbering about 1,300.

Royal Stuart (Stewart) tartan.
THE SCOTTISH TARTANS SOCIETY/MUSEUM

Tartars See TATARS

Tartarus \ˈtär-tə-rəs\ In GREEK MYTHOLOGY, the lowest depths of the underworld. It was a region of eternal darkness where the evil were punished after death for having offended the gods. Here ZEUS confined the TITANS, who were prevented from escaping by hundred-armed giants. Later classical authors sometimes used Tartarus interchangeably with HADES to designate the entire underworld.

Tartikoff \ˈtär-ti-ˌkȯf\, **Brandon** (1949–1997) U.S. television executive. Born in New York City, he successfully promoted local ABC television stations before being hired by FRED SILVERMAN as ABC's director of dramatic development. From 1978 the two men worked together at NBC, and in 1980 Tartikoff became president of NBC entertainment, the youngest division chief in network history. He coordinated such dramatic series as *St. Elsewhere* and *Hill Street Blues* with such popular sitcoms as *Family Ties, The Cosby Show,* and *Cheers* to make NBC the top-rated network. He died of Hodgkin's disease.

Taru See TARHUN

tashbih \tȧsh-'bē, tȧsh-'bē-hə\ In ISLAM, the comparison of God to created things. The practice of attributing human characteristics to the deity is regarded as a sin in Islamic theology, as is its opposite, *tatil* (divesting God of all attributes). The difficulty of dealing with the nature of God in Islam arises from seemingly contradictory views in the Quran, which describes God as unique, yet also refers to him as having eyes, ears, hands, and face. Tashbih is forbidden out of the fear that its practice will lead to paganism and idolatry; *tatil* is feared to lead to atheism.

Tashkent \tash-'kent, tash-'kend\ City (pop., 1995 est.: 2,107,000), capital of Uzbekistan. Dating from about the 1st century BC, it was an important trade center on the caravan routes to Europe and the Orient. The Arabs conquered it in the early 8th century; it fell to the Mongols in the 13th century and was under Turkish control in the 14th–15th century. Taken by the Russians in 1865, it was made the administrative center of Turkistan in 1867, and a new European city grew up beside the old native one. The city was heavily damaged by an earthquake in 1966. Today it is the main economic and cultural center of central Asia. Its many institutions of higher education include the Uzbek Academy of Sciences (1943).

Tasman \'tás-män\, **Abel Janszoon** (1603?–1659?) Dutch explorer. In the service of the Dutch EAST INDIA CO., he made exploratory and trading voyages to East and Southeast Asia 1634–39. In 1642 he was sent by ANTHONY VAN DIEMEN, to find the hypothetical southern continent of the Pacific and a possible route to Chile. Sailing from Batavia (modern Jakarta), he reached 49° S at 94° E, then turned north and discovered land he named Van Diemen's Land (now Tasmania), then sailed along the coast of New Zealand, believing it to be the southern continent. He also discovered Tonga and the Fiji Islands. On his next voyage (1644) he sailed into the Gulf of Carpentaria and along the northern and western coasts of Australia.

Tasman Peninsula \'taz-mən\ Peninsula, southeastern TASMANIA, Australia. About 26 mi (42 km) long by 20 mi (32 km) wide, it has sea cliffs and unusual rock formations. First explored in 1642, it was not settled until a penal colony was established at Port Arthur in 1830. Its partly restored ruins are now a tourist attraction, and the peninsula is part of Australia's National Estate.

Tasman Sea Part of the South Pacific Ocean, between southeastern Australia and western New Zealand. About 1,400 mi (2,250 km) wide, it has maximum depths exceeding 17,000 ft (5,200 m) in the Tasman Basin. Explored by ABEL JANSZOON TASMAN in 1642 and by Capt. JAMES COOK in the 1770s, it is notoriously stormy. Economic resources include fisheries and petroleum deposits.

Tasmania \taz-'mā-nē-ə\ *formerly* **Van Diemen's Land** \'dē-mənz\ Island (pop., 1996: 460,000), state of Australia. Located off the southeastern corner of the continent, and separated from it by BASS STRAIT, the state also includes numerous smaller islands. HOBART is the capital. Originally inhabited by AUSTRALIAN ABORIGINES, it was explored and named Van Diemen's Land by ABEL JANSZOON TASMAN in 1642. Taken by the British in the early 1800s and made a colony in 1825, it was used as an auxiliary penal settlement until the 1850s. It was granted self-government and renamed Tasmania in 1856; it became a state of the Australian Commonwealth in 1901. Chief economic activities include copper, zinc, tin, and tungsten mining, and raising livestock, especially for wool.

Tasmanian devil MARSUPIAL species (*Sarcophilus harrisii* or *S. ursinus,* family Dasyuridae), now extinct on the Australian mainland, that survives in remote rocky areas of Tasmania. It is 30–40 in. (75–100 cm) long, with a stocky body, large head and jaws, and long bushy tail. The coat is usually black and brown with a white-marked breast. Named for its devilish expression and husky snarl, it is mainly a scavenger of wallaby and sheep carcasses but also eats beetle larvae and occasionally poultry. Its three or four young remain in the mother's pouch about five months.

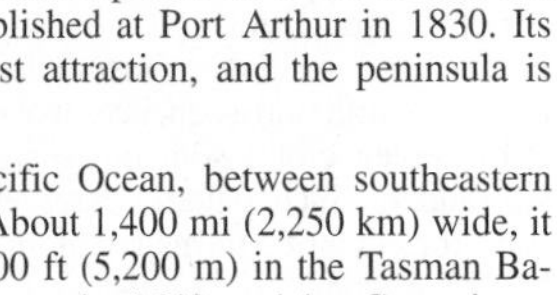

Tasmanian devil (*Sarcophilus harrisii*).
JOHN YATES–SHOSTAL

Tasmanian wolf *or* **Tasmanian tiger** Extinct, slender, fox-faced MARSUPIAL (*Thylacinus cynocephalus,* family Dasyuridae), 40–50 in. (100–130 cm) long. It was yellowish brown, with dark bars on the back and rump. It hunted at night for wallabies and birds. The female carried her young in a shallow pouch. Once found on the Australian mainland and New Guinea, it was confined to Tasmania in historical times, when competition with the DINGO led to its disappearance from the mainland. Europeans in Tasmania hunted it to protect their sheep; the last known individual died in captivity in 1936.

Tasmanians Extinct Australoid population of Tasmania. An isolate population of AUSTRALIAN ABORIGINES who entered Tasmania 25,000–40,000 years ago, they were cut off from the mainland when a general rise in the sea level flooded the Bass Strait c. 10,000 years ago. Subsistence was based on hunting land and sea mammals and collecting shellfish and vegetable food. The first permanent white settlement was made in Tasmania in 1803, and the settlers provoked a war in 1804. Of an estimated 4,000 Tasmanians when the Europeans first arrived, only 200 remained by the 1830s; moved to Flinders Island for their protection, they did not survive long in their new home, and the last full-blooded Tasmanian died in 1876.

Tass \'tás\ *in full* **Telegrafnoe Agentsvo Sovetskovo Soyuza ("Telegraph Agency of the Soviet Union")** Official news agency of the Soviet Union from 1925 to 1991. The main source of news for all Soviet newspapers and radio and television stations, it was also a major international wire service. Tass dispatches on matters of public policy and international affairs reflected the official position of the state. After the Soviet Union's 1991 breakup, Tass was reorganized into the Information Telegraph Agency of Russia (ITAR), reporting on news of Russia, and the Telegraph Agency of the Countries of the Commonwealth (Tass), reporting on news of other countries of the COMMONWEALTH OF INDEPENDENT STATES.

Tasso \'täs-sō\, **Torquato** (1544–1595) Italian poet. The son of a poet and courtier, Tasso became a courtier of Duke Alfonso II d'Este at Ferrara. In a period of intense poetic activity he produced the pastoral drama *L'Aminta* (1581; performed 1573), a lyrical idealization of court life. In 1575 he completed his celebrated masterpiece on the First Crusade, *Gerusalemme liberata* (1581; *Jerusalem Delivered*), a heroic epic in OTTAVA rima that blends historical events with imaginary romantic and idyllic episodes. He developed a persecution mania and from 1579 to 1586 was incarcerated in a hospital by order of the duke. *Gerusalemme liberata* was translated and imitated in many European languages, and Tasso was the subject of literary legend for centuries. He is regarded as the greatest Italian poet of the late Renaissance.

taste *or* **taste perception** Special SENSE for perceiving and distinguishing the sweet, sour, bitter, or salty quality of a dissolved substance, mediated by taste buds on the TONGUE. More than 9,000 taste buds on the tongue are responsible for the CHEMORECEPTION of taste. Some taste buds are also found on the roof of the mouth and throat. See illustration on following page.

Tatar language \'tä-tər\ *formerly* **Volga Tatar language** TURKIC language with some 8 million speakers. Its speakers include less than half the population of Tatarstan in Russia, with the remainder scattered in enclaves across eastern European Russian, Siberia, and the Central Asian republics. Tatar, like the closely related Bashkir language, is characterized by a remarkable series of vowel shifts that distinguish it (at least in its most characteristic varieties) from all other Turkic languages. It has numerous dialect distinctions; the conventional division is between a central group that includes the Tatar of most of Tatarstan and the literary language based on Kazan speech, a western group, and an eastern group. Crimean Tatar, belonging to the southwestern group of Turkic languages, and Chulym Tatar, belonging to the northeastern group, are not closely related to Tatar.

Tatar Strait \'tä-ˌtär\ Wide passage in the northwestern Pacific Ocean connecting the Sea of JAPAN to the Sea of OKHOTSK. Located between SAKHALIN island and the Russian mainland, it is generally shallow, with depths less than 700 ft (210 m). Ice impedes its ports for half the year.

Tatars \'tä-tərz\ *or* **Tartars** Turkic-speaking peoples who today live mainly in western central Russia east to the Ural Mountains, in Kazakhstan, and in western Siberia. They first appeared as nomadic tribes in northeastern Mongolia in the 5th century. Some joined the armies of

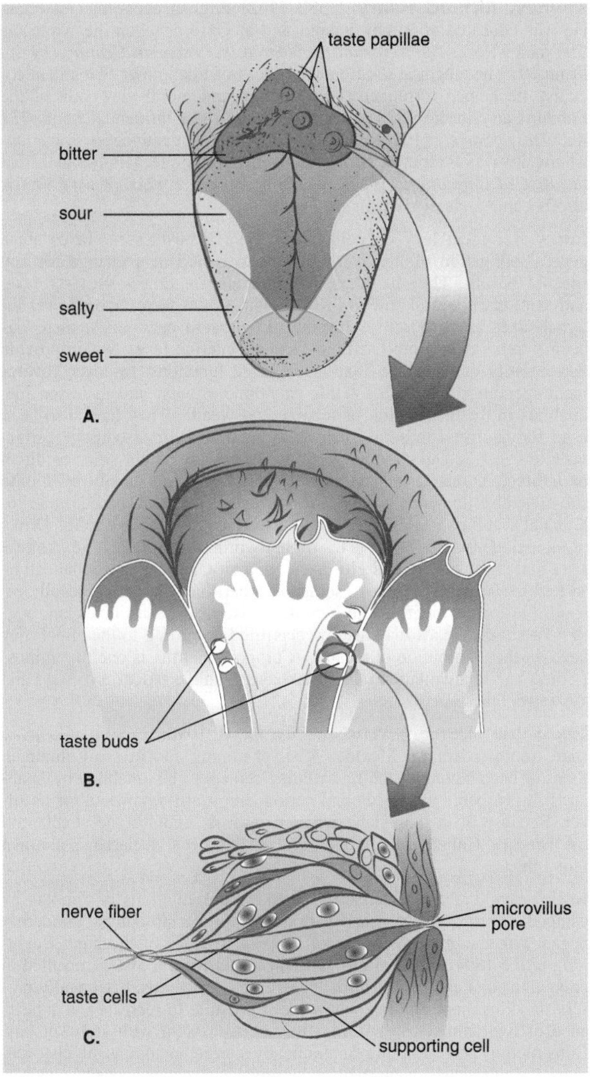

A. Taste centers on the tongue's surface. Taste buds on the tip of the tongue are most sensitive to sweet tastes, those on the sides to sour, those at the back to bitter, and those on the tip and sides to salty. B. Close-up of a papilla showing location of the taste buds. C. Structure of a taste bud. Each is composed of narrow modified epithelial taste cells with specialized hairs (microvilli) that project into a pore opening onto the tongue's surface and broader supporting cells. Impulses from the taste cells are carried by nerve pathways to the brain.

GENGHIS KHAN. Especially identified with the GOLDEN HORDE, they were converted to Islam in the 14th century. The Golden Horde soon became independent Tatar khanates (see KHAN). Their economy was based on mixed farming and herding, which remain central to their economy. They developed craftsmanship in wood, ceramics, leather, cloth, and metal and have been well known as traders. Today there are about 6 million Tatars in all regions; they constitute about half the population of the Russian republic of Tatarstan. See also TATAR LANGUAGE.

Tate, (John Orley) Allen (1899–1979) U.S. poet and novelist. Born in Winchester, Ky., he attended Vanderbilt Univ.; while there Tate helped found *The Fugitive* (1922–25), a poetry magazine concentrating largely on the South, and contributed to *I'll Take My Stand* (1930), a Fugitive manifesto defending the region's conservative agrarian society. From 1934 he taught at schools, including Princeton University and the University of Minnesota, becoming a leading exponent of the NEW CRITICISM. He emphasized the writer's need for tradition, which he found in Southern culture and later in Roman Catholicism, to which he converted in 1950. His best-known poem is "Ode to the Confederate Dead" (1926).

Tate, Nahum (1652–1715) Irish-English poet and playwright. After graduating from Trinity College, Dublin, Tate moved to London. Though he wrote plays of his own, he is best known for his adaptations of Elizabethan works, notably WILLIAM SHAKESPEARE's *King Lear,* with a happy ending, which was performed well into the 19th century. He wrote the libretto for H. PURCELL's *Dido and Aeneas* (1689?) and collaborated with Nicholas Brady in *A New Version of the Psalms of David* (1696). The best of his own poems is "Panacea: A Poem upon Tea" (1700). He became England's poet laureate in 1692.

Tate Gallery Art museum in London housing the national collection of British painting and sculpture and of modern British and European art since c. 1870. It is named after Sir Henry Tate (1819–1899), a sugar refiner and inventor of the sugar cube, who donated his collection of Victorian art to the nation in 1890. The Neoclassical building, designed by Sidney R. J. Smith, opened in 1897. Originally administered by the National Gallery, the museum became completely independent only in 1954. In 1987 the Clore Gallery was built to house the principal collection of J.M.W. TURNER's works. In 1988 a branch was opened in Liverpool. The Tate Modern, a converted power plant housing the modern collections, opened in 2000.

Tathagata \tə-'tä-gə-tə\ Epithet of the BUDDHA that he employed primarily when referring to himself. He also used it to refer to other buddhas who preceded him and who would follow. Tathagatha refers to one who has trod the path to full awakening and so reached the end of suffering and escaped SAMSARA. The implication is that the path is open to all who would follow it. In later MAHAYANA Buddhism, Tathagata came to mean the essential buddha nature found in everyone.

Tati \tà-'tē\, **Jacques** *orig.* **Jacques Tatischeff** (1908–1982) French film actor and director. A former professional rugby player, he became a popular music-hall entertainer in the 1930s with a pantomime act that caricatured athletes and referees. After appearing in comedy shorts, he wrote, directed, and starred in a series of comic feature films—*Jour de fête* (1949), *Monsieur Hulot's Holiday* (1953), *Mon oncle* (1958), *Playtime* (1968), *Traffic* (1971), and *Parade* (1974)—in which he became known for his inspired physical comedy and his accident-prone alter ego, Monsieur Hulot.

Tatlin \'tàt-lyin\, **Vladimir (Yevgrafovich)** (1885–1953) Ukrainian sculptor and painter. After a visit to Paris (1914), he became the leader of a group of Moscow artists who sought to apply engineering techniques to sculpture construction, a movement that developed into CONSTRUCTIVISM. He pioneered the use of iron, glass, wood, and wire in nonrepresentational constructions. His *Monument to the Third International,* commissioned by the Soviet government, was one of the first buildings conceived entirely in abstract terms, and was intended to be, at more than 1,300 ft (400 m), the world's tallest structure. A model was exhibited at the 1920 Soviet Congress, but the government disapproved of nonfigurative art and it was never built. After 1933 Tatlin worked largely as a stage designer.

tattoo Permanent mark or design made on the body by pigment introduced through ruptures in the skin. The term is also loosely applied to the inducement of scars (cicatrization). Tattooing has been practiced in most parts of the world, and examples have been found on Egyptian and Nubian mummies dating from 2000 BC. Decoration is perhaps the most common motive, though designs may also serve to identify rank, status, or membership and are thought by some to provide magical protection against sickness or misfortune. The word comes from Tahiti, where it was recorded by JAMES COOK's expedition in 1769. The first electric tattooing implement was patented in the U.S. in 1891.

Tatum \'tā-təm\, **Art(hur)** (1909–1956) U.S. pianist, one of the greatest technical virtuosos in jazz. Tatum was born in Toledo, Ohio, and was blind from birth. Influenced by FATS WALLER and EARL HINES, his playing represents a synthesis of stride and SWING piano traditions. He developed an unprecedented technical and harmonic control on the instrument, capable of astonishing speed and intricate elaborations of melody. By 1937, he was recognized as the outstanding pianist in jazz. He formed a trio with guitar and bass in 1943, but frequently made solo performances that showcased his unique mastery.

Tatum, Edward L(awrie) (1909–1975) U.S. biochemist. Born in Boulder, Col., he worked with GEORGE WELLS BEADLE at Stanford Univ., where they confirmed that all biochemical processes in organisms are ultimately controlled by genes, that these processes can be broken down into a series of individual sequential chemical reactions, each controlled by a single gene, and that mutation of a single gene changes the cell's ability to carry out only a single chemical reaction. Each gene was found to determine the structure of a specific ENZYME (the "one gene, one enzyme" hypothesis). With JOSHUA LEDERBERG, Tatum discovered the occurrence of genetic RECOMBINATION, or "sex," between certain bacteria. Largely because of their efforts, bacteria became the main source of information about genetic control of biochemical processes in the cell. Tatum, Beadle, and Lederberg shared the Nobel Prize in 1958.

Taunton Town (pop., 1995 est.: 55,000), county seat of SOMERSET, England. An Anglo-Saxon king founded it c. 710. Its castle was besieged during the ENGLISH CIVIL WARS, and subsequently dismantled. It later was the scene of the duke of MONMOUTH's rebellion (1685). It is in an agricultural region; tourism is important to the economy.

Taupo \'tau̇-pō\, **Lake** Lake, NORTH ISLAND, New Zealand. The largest lake in New Zealand, it is 234 sq mi (606 sq km) in area and covers the remains of several volcanic craters. The WAIKATO RIVER flows into and out of it. Numerous geothermal springs on the lake's borders are used for health resorts and for generating electricity.

Taurus (Latin: "Bull") In astronomy, the constellation lying between Aries and Gemini; in ASTROLOGY, the second sign of the ZODIAC, governing approximately the period April 20–May 20. Its symbol is a bull, a reference to the Greek myth in which ZEUS transformed himself into a white bull to abduct EUROPA.

Taurus Mountains Mountain chain, southern Turkey, running parallel to the Mediterranean coast. The system extends along a curve from Lake Egridir in the west to the upper reaches of the EUPHRATES RIVER in the east. It has many peaks 10,000–12,000 ft (3,000–3,700 m) high. The Cilician Gates pass, 38 mi (61 km) long and used by caravans and armies since antiquity, crosses the range north of TARSUS.

Taussig \'tau̇-sig\, **Helen Brooke** (1898–1986) U.S. physician. Born in Cambridge, Mass., she received her medical degree from Johns Hopkins in 1927. As head of a Baltimore heart clinic (1930–63), she studied "blue babies" (babies whose heart malformations cause low blood oxygen content) and pioneered use of fluoroscopy and X rays to pinpoint the defect responsible for each set of symptoms. The surgical treatment she devised with ALFRED BLALOCK saved thousands of such infants, and her research spurred development of other surgical treatments for heart disorders. Her *Congenital Malformations of the Heart* (2 vols., 1947) comprehensively described heart defects and diagnostic tools, techniques, and findings. She also played a key role in alerting U.S. physicians to the dangers of THALIDOMIDE.

tautog See WRASSE

tautology \tȯ-'tä-lə-jē\ In LOGIC, a statement that cannot be denied without inconsistency. Thus, "All bachelors are either male or not male" is held to assert, with regard to anything whatsoever that is a bachelor, that it is male or it is not male. In the PROPOSITIONAL CALCULUS, even complicated symbolic expressions such as $[(A \supset B) \wedge (C \supset \neg B)] \supset (C \supset \neg A)$ can be shown to be tautologies by displaying in a truth table every possible combination of T (true) and F (false) of its arguments A, B, C. A tautology can be purely formal (a statement form rather than a statement), and in some usages only such formal truths are tautologies.

tautomerism \tȯ-'tä-mə-ˌri-zəm\ Existence of two or more chemical COMPOUNDS (ISOMERS), with the same chemical composition but different structures, that convert easily from one to another. A major class of tautomeric reactions involves exchange of a HYDROGEN atom between two other atoms, in both cases with a COVALENT bond. For example, in keto–enol tautomerism, the hydrogen atom bonded to the carbon atom in a carbonyl (keto) group ($-CH-C{=}O$; see FUNCTIONAL GROUP) moves to the oxygen atom, making it an enol group ($-C{=}COH$). The keto form predominates in many ALDEHYDES and KETONES, the enol form in PHENOLS. SUGARS (e.g., GLUCOSE) exhibit tautomerism between open (chain) forms and closed (ring) forms. See also ISOMERISM.

Tawney, Richard Henry (1880–1962) English economic historian. He was educated at Rugby School and at Oxford, where he wrote his first major work, *The Agrarian Problem in the Sixteenth Century* (1912). From 1913 he taught at the London School of Economics. An ardent socialist, he helped formulate the economic and moral viewpoint of the Labour Party in the 1920s and '30s. In his most influential book, *The Acquisitive Society* (1920), he argued that the acquisitiveness of capitalist society was a morally wrong motivating principle. His *Religion and the Rise of Capitalism* (1926), which built on the work of MAX WEBER, also became a classic.

tax Government levy on persons, groups, or businesses. Taxes are a general obligation of taxpayers and are not paid in exchange for any specific benefit. They have existed since ancient times—PROPERTY TAXES and SALES taxes were known in Rome—but TARIFFS were favored over internal taxes as a source of revenue. In modern economies, there has been a trend away from tariffs in favor of internal taxes, which provide the majority of revenues. Taxes have three functions: to cover government spending, to promote stable economic growth, and to lessen inequalities in the distribution of income and wealth. They have also been used for nonfiscal reasons, such as to encourage or discourage certain activities (e.g., cigarette consumption). Taxes may be classified as direct or indirect. Direct taxes are those that the taxpayer cannot shift onto someone else; they are mainly taxes on persons and are based on an individual's ability to pay as measured by income or net wealth. Direct taxes include INCOME TAXES, taxes on net worth, death duties (i.e., INHERITANCE and ESTATE taxes), and gift taxes. Indirect taxes are those that can be shifted in whole or in part to someone other than the person legally responsible for payment. These include excise taxes, SALES taxes, and VALUE-ADDED TAXES. Taxes may also be classified according to the effect they have on the distribution of wealth. A proportional tax is one that imposes the same relative burden on all taxpayers, unlike PROGRESSIVE TAXES and REGRESSIVE taxes.

Taxco (de Alarcón) \'täs-kō\ City (pop., 1990: 87,000), GUERRERO state, southern central Mexico. A silver-mining site in pre-Columbian times, it became one of the first mining centers to be inhabited by Spaniards. It prospered in the colonial period, and is still renowned for its silver. Because of its colonial character, with its cobblestone streets and the baroque Church of Santa Prisca, it has been declared a national monument.

taxidermy Practice of creating lifelike representations of animals by using their prepared skins and various supporting structures. Taxidermy began with the ancient custom of keeping trophies of the hunt. Beginning in the 18th century, a growing interest in natural history resulted in collections and exhibits of birds, beasts, and curiosities. Chemically preserving skins, hair, and feathers made it possible to recreate the appearance of live animals by stuffing the sewed-up skin with straw or hay. Constructing and sculpting anatomically correct manikins of clay and plaster are the basis of modern taxidermy.

Taxila \'tak-sə-lə\ Ancient city, northwestern India. Its ruins, including temples and a fortress, lie west of RAWALPINDI, Pakistan. It was the capital of the Buddhist kingdom of Gandhara and a center of learning. Founded by Bharata, the younger brother of Rama, it came under Persian rule, and in 326 BC was surrendered to ALEXANDER THE GREAT. Ruled by a succession of conquerors, including Bactrians and Scythians, it became an important Buddhist center under King ASHOKA c. 261 BC. The apostle THOMAS reputedly visited in the 1st century AD. Its prosperity in ancient times resulted from its position at the junction of three great trade routes. When they declined, it sank into insignificance; it was finally destroyed by the Huns in the 5th century.

taxol \'taks-ȯl\ Organic compound with a complex multi-ring molecule that occurs in the bark of Pacific YEW trees *(Taxus brevifolia)*. It appears to be active against certain cancers of the lung, ovary, breast, head, and neck, disrupting CELL division and interfering with separation of the nuclear CHROMOSOMES. A semisynthetic process to make it from yew needles and twigs averted total destruction of yew forests, and total synthesis methods were later developed.

taxonomy \tak-'sä-nə-mē\ In biology, the classification of organisms into a hierarchy of groupings, from the general to the particular, that reflect evolutionary and usually morphological relationships: kingdom, phylum, class, order, family, genus, SPECIES. The black-capped chickadee, for example, is an animal (kingdom Animalia) with a dorsal nerve cord (phylum Chordata) and feathers (class Aves: birds) that perches (order Passeriformes: perching birds) and is small with a short bill (family Paridae), a song that sounds like "chik-a-dee" (genus *Parus*), and a black-capped head (species *atricapillus*). Most authorities recognize five kingdoms: monerans (PROKARYOTES), PROTISTS, fungi (see FUNGUS), PLANTS, and ANIMALS. CAROLUS LINNAEUS established the scheme of using Latin generic and specific names in the mid-18th century; his work was extensively revised by later biologists.

Tay River Longest river in Scotland. It rises on the northern slopes of Ben Lui and flows through Loch Tay to enter the NORTH SEA below DUNDEE after a course of 120 mi (193 km). It drains 2,400 sq mi (6,200 sq km), the largest drainage area in Scotland.

Tay-Sachs disease \'tā-'saks\ Recessive hereditary metabolic disorder, mostly in ASHKENAZI Jews, causing progressive mental and neurologic deterioration and death by age 5. A LIPID, ganglioside G_{M2}, accumulates in the brain due to inadequate activity of the enzyme that breaks it down, with devastating neurological effects. Infants appear normal at birth but soon become listless and inattentive, lose motor abilities, and develop seizures. Blindness and general paralysis usually precede death. Tests can detect the disease in fetuses and the Tay-Sachs gene in carriers. There is no treatment.

Taylor, Elizabeth (Rosemond) *later* **Dame Elizabeth** (born 1932) U.S. film actress. Born in London, she left with her American parents at the outset of World War II. Noted for her exceptional beauty from childhood, she was discovered by a talent scout in Beverly Hills. She made her screen debut in 1942, appeared in *Lassie Come Home* in 1943, and became a star with *National Velvet* in 1944. She was a glamorous adult star in *Father of the Bride* (1950), *A Place in the Sun* (1951), *Giant* (1956), *Cat on a Hot Tin Roof* (1958), *Suddenly Last Summer* (1959), *Butterfield 8* (1960, Academy Award), and *Cleopatra* (1963). In *Who's Afraid of Virginia Woolf* (1966, Academy Award) and other films, she starred opposite her husband, RICHARD BURTON. Her personal life and eight marriages were avidly followed in the popular press. In later years she campaigned energetically for AIDS research.

Taylor, Frederick W(inslow) (1856–1915) U.S. inventor and engineer. Born in Germantown, Pa., he worked at Midvale Steel Co. (1878–90), where he introduced TIME-AND-MOTION STUDY in order to systematize shop management and reduce manufacturing costs. Though his system provoked resentment and opposition from labor when carried to extremes, it had an immense impact on the development of MASS PRODUCTION techniques and has influenced the development of virtually every modern industrial country. Taylor is regarded as the father of scientific management. See also PRODUCTION MANAGEMENT, TAYLORISM.

Taylor, Geoffrey Ingram *later* **Sir Geoffrey** (1886–1975) British physicist. He taught at Cambridge University from 1911 to 1952. He made important discoveries in FLUID MECHANICS, as well as significant contributions to the theory of the elastostatic stress and displacement fields created by dislocating solids, the quantum theory of RADIATION, and the interference and diffraction of PHOTONS.

Taylor, John (1753–1824) American politician. Born in Caroline Co., Va., he served in the Continental Army (1775–79) and Virginia militia (1781) in the AMERICAN REVOLUTION. He served in the U.S. Senate 1792–94, 1803, and 1822–24. A strong advocate of states' rights, he opposed ratification of the U.S. Constitution. He introduced the VIRGINIA AND KENTUCKY RESOLUTIONS in the Virginia legislature (1798). A supporter of THOMAS JEFFERSON, he wrote essays on the importance of an agrarian democracy as a defense against a too-powerful central government.

Taylor, Joseph H(ooton), Jr. (born 1941) U.S. physicist. Born in Philadelphia, he received his PhD from Harvard University. While teaching at the University. of Massachusetts (1968–81), he and RUSSELL ALAN HULSE discovered the first binary PULSAR (1974). Their discovery provided evidence in support of ALBERT EINSTEIN's prediction that objects accelerated in a strong gravitational field will emit gravitational waves. With its enormous interacting gravitational fields, the binary pulsar should emit such waves, draining energy and reducing the distance between the two stars, as measured by a gradual reduction in the timing of the radio emissions. In 1978 they showed that the two stars are revolving ever faster and closer around each other at a rate agreeing precisely with Einstein's prediction. Their discoveries won the two men a 1993 Nobel Prize.

Taylor, Lawrence (Julius) (born 1959) U.S. football linebacker. Born in Williamsburg, Va., he played for the University of North Carolina, making All-American in 1980. During his 13-year career with the New York Giants (1981–94), he was twice named Defensive Player of the Year (1981, 1982) and once named Most Valuable Player (1986), only the second defensive player to be so honored. He set a career record for most quarterback sacks (132.5).

Taylor, Maxwell (Davenport) (1901–1987) U.S. Army officer. Born in Keytesville, Mo., he graduated from West Point and helped organize the army's first airborne division early in World War II. He commanded a parachute assault in the NORMANDY CAMPAIGN and in the Battle of the BULGE (1944). He served as commanding general of U.N. forces in Korea (1953), U.S. Army chief of staff (1955–59), and chairman of the Joint Chiefs of Staff (1962–64). He was appointed ambassador to South Vietnam (1964–65) and was a special consultant to Pres. LYNDON B. JOHNSON (1965–69). He advocated the maintenance of conventional infantry as a prudent alternative to nuclear weapons in war.

Taylor, Paul (Belville) (born 1930) U.S. modern dancer, choreographer, and director. Born in Pittsburgh, he joined MARTHA GRAHAM's company in 1953, where he was a leading soloist until 1960. In 1957 he established the Paul Taylor Dance Co., which has toured frequently in the U.S. and abroad. He has choreographed over 100 works in a variety of styles, including *Duet* (1957), *Aureole* (1962), *Orbs* (1966), *The Book of Beasts* (1971), and *Nightshade* (1979). He retired from performing in the 1970s but continues to direct his company.

Paul Taylor and Bettie de Jong in *Scudorama*, 1967.
JACK MITCHELL

Taylor, Peter (Hillsman) (1917–1994) U.S. short-story writer, novelist, and playwright. Born in Trenton, Tenn., Taylor studied in the 1930s under several poets associated with the Southern literary renaissance. He taught at various schools, including the University of Virginia (from 1967). He is best known for his short stories, which are usually set in contemporary Tennessee and which reveal conflicts between the old rural society and the industrialized "New South." The novella *A Woman of Means* (1950) is perhaps his finest work; his later works include *The Old Forest and Other Stories* (1985) and *A Summons to Memphis* (1986, Pulitzer Prize).

Taylor, Zachary (1784–1850) 12th president of the U.S. (1849–50). Born in Montebello, Va., he grew up on the Kentucky frontier. He fought in the War of 1812, the Black Hawk War (1832), and the Seminole War in Florida (1835–42), earning the nickname "Old Rough-and-Ready" for his indifference to hardship. Sent to Texas in anticipation of war with Mexico, he defeated the Mexican invaders at the battles of Palo Alto and Resaca de la Palma (1846). After the MEXICAN WAR formally began, he captured Monterrey and granted the Mexican army an eight-week armistice. Displeased, Pres. JAMES POLK moved Taylor's best troops to serve under WINFIELD SCOTT in the invasion of Veracruz. Taylor ignored orders to remain in Monterrey and marched south to defeat a large Mexican force at the Battle of BUENA VISTA (1847). He became a national hero and was nominated as the Whig candidate for president (1848). He defeated LEWIS CASS to win the election. His brief term was marked by a controversy over the new territories that produced the COMPROMISE OF 1850 and by a scandal involving members of his cabinet. He died, probably of cholera, after only 16 months in office and was succeeded by MILLARD FILLMORE.

Taylorism System of scientific management advocated by FRED W. TAYLOR. In Taylor's view, the task of factory management was to determine the best way for the worker to do the job, to provide the proper tools and training, and to provide incentives for good performance. He broke each job down into its individual motions, analyzed these to determine which were essential, and timed the workers with a stopwatch. With unnecessary motion eliminated, the worker, following a machinelike routine, became far more productive. See also PRODUCTION MANAGEMENT, TIME-AND-MOTION STUDY.

Taymyr Peninsula \tī-'mir\ Peninsula, northern central SIBERIA, northern Russia. It lies between the Kara Sea, the Laptev Sea, and the Vilkitsky Strait and includes Cape Chelyuskin, the northernmost point of Asia. Its central part is crossed by the Taymyra River, which is 400 mi (644 km) long.

Tbilisi \tə-bi-'lē-sē\ *formerly* **Tiflis** City (pop., 1997 est.: 1,253,000), capital of the Republic of Georgia, on the KURA RIVER. Founded c. AD 458 as the capital of the Georgian kingdom, its strategic position on trade routes between Europe and Asia led to its frequent capture. Under successive Persian, Byzantine, Arab, Mongol, and Turkish rule, it came under the Russians c. 1801. It was made the capital of the Transcaucasian Federation in 1921, the Georgian S.S.R. in 1936, and the independent Republic of Georgia in 1991. The Soviet military massacred civilians during an independence demonstration there in 1989. Some centuries-old structures still exist in the city, which is now a major cultural, educational, research, and industrial center and the site of a university (1918).

Tchaikovsky \chə-'kȯf-skē, chī-'kȯf-skē\, **Pyotr Ilyich** (1840–1893) Russian composer. Sensitive and interested in music from his early childhood, Tchaikovsky turned to serious composition upon his mother's death, when he was 14. In 1862 he began studying at the new St. Petersburg Conservatory, and by 1863 he was living by freelancing as a musician. From 1866 he taught at the Moscow Conservatory. His *Piano Concerto No. 1* (1875) was premiered by H. VON BULOW in Boston and became immensely popular. In 1875 he wrote *Swan Lake* on commission from the BOLSHOI BALLET. In 1877 came a commission from the wealthy Nadezhda von Meck (1831–1894), who became his patron and longtime correspondent (1877–90), though they agreed never to meet. The opera *Eugene Onegin* (1878) soon followed. Though homosexual, he married briefly; after three disastrous months of marriage, he attempted suicide. His composition was overshadowed by his personal crisis for years. His *Sleeping Beauty* ballet (1889) was followed by the opera *The Queen of Spades* (1890) and the great ballet *The Nutcracker* (1892). His *"Pathétique" Symphony* (1893) premiered four days before his death from cholera; claims that he was forced to commit suicide by noblemen outraged by his sexual liaisons are unfounded. His ballets were the greatest of the 19th century, and his symphonies have never lost their popularity. His music is characterized by tuneful, open-hearted melodies, impressive harmonies, and colorful, picturesque orchestration.

TCP/IP *in full* **Transmission Control Protocol/Internet Protocol** Standard INTERNET communications PROTOCOLS that allow DIGITAL COMPUTERS to communicate over long distances. The Internet is a packet-switched network, in which information is broken down into small packets, sent individually over many different routes at the same time, and then reassembled at the receiving end. TCP is the component that collects and reassembles the packets of data, while IP is responsible for making sure the packets are sent to the right destination. TCP/IP was developed in the 1970s and adopted as the protocol standard for ARPANET (the predecessor to the Internet) in 1983.

te See DE

Te Anau Lake \tā-'ä-naů\ Lake, southwestern SOUTH ISLAND, New Zealand. The largest of the Southern Lakes, it is 38 mi (61 km) long and 6 mi (10 km) wide, and a source of the Waiau River. In a superb alpine setting bordered by forested mountains, it is known for fishing and tourism.

Te Kanawa \te-'kä-nə-wə\, **Kiri (Janette)** *later* **Dame Kiri** (born 1944) New Zealand (half-Maori) soprano. After winning prizes at home, she went to London for further study in 1966 and made her Covent Garden debut in 1970. Soon moving into leading roles, she became especially admired as the Countess in *The Marriage of Figaro*. In 1974 she made a triumphal debut at the Metropolitan Opera, substituting at the last moment in G. VERDI's *Otello*. A glamorous and regally imperturbable presence with a rich voice, she was chosen to sing at the 1981 wedding of Prince Charles, and has made many recordings.

tea Beverage produced by steeping in freshly boiled water the young leaves and leaf buds of the tea plant, *Camellia sinensis,* a member of the family Theaceae, which contains 40 genera of trees and shrubs. Tea cultivation is first documented in China in AD 350; according to legend, it had been known there since c. 2700 BC. It was established in Japan by the 13th century and was spread to Java by the Dutch and to India by the English in the 19th century. Today tea is the most widely consumed drink in the world, drunk (either hot or cold) by half the world's population. Major tea types are classified by processing method: fermented, or black, tea produces an amber-colored, full-flavored beverage without bitterness; semifermented, or oolong, tea yields a slightly bitter, light brownish-green liquid; and unfermented, or green, tea, results in a mild, slightly bitter, pale greenish-yellow beverage. CAFFEINE is responsible for tea's stimulating effect. Green tea, long regarded as healthful in the Far East, has in recent years attracted much favorable attention in the West for a wide range of possible beneficial effects. Infusions and decoctions of the leaves, bark, and roots of many other, unrelated plants are commonly drunk as herbal or medicinal teas.

Tea Act (1773) British legislation giving a tea monopoly in the American colonies to the British East India Co. It adjusted the duty regulations to allow the failing company to sell its large tea surplus below the prices charged by colonial competitors. The act was opposed by colonists as another example of taxation without representation. Resistance to the act resulted in the BOSTON TEA PARTY.

tea ceremony Ritualized preparation and drinking of TEA developed in Japan. It involves a host and one or more guests; the tea, utensils, and movements of preparation, serving, and drinking the tea are all prescribed. When tea was introduced from Song-dynasty China by the Zen monk Eisai (1141–1215), it was drunk by Zen monks to help them stay awake. The laity enjoyed tea-tasting competitions that developed into a more refined, meditative form among the warrior aristocracy in the 15th century. The most famous exponent of the tea ceremony was Sen no Rikyu (1522–1591), tea master to TOYOTOMI HIDEYOSHI, who codified a style known as *wabi,* which favored rustic, rough-shaped tea bowls and spare, simple surroundings. Three popular schools of the tea ceremony trace their roots to Rikyu, and other schools exist as well; in the 20th century mastery of the tea ceremony was one accomplishment of a well-bred young woman.

Teach, Edward See BLACKBEARD

teaching Profession of those who give instruction, especially in an elementary or secondary school or a university. The teaching profession is a relatively new one. Traditionally, parents, elders, religious leaders, and sages were responsible for teaching children how to behave and think and what to believe. Germany introduced the first formal criteria for the education of teachers in the 18th century. In the 19th century, as society became more industrialized, the concept of schooling became more universal. In industrialized nations today, most teachers are university graduates. Teacher-training programs usually include both general and specialized academic, cultural, or vocational courses; the study of educational principles; and a series of professional courses combined with practical experience in a typical school setting. Most countries also require professional certification following formal training. See also AMERICAN FEDERATION OF TEACHERS, NATIONAL EDUCATION ASSN.

Teagarden, Jack *orig.* **Weldon Leo** (1905–1964) U.S. trombonist and singer, the greatest jazz trombonist of his time. Born in Texas, he worked with two of the most popular bands of the early SWING era, those of Ben Pollack (1928–33) and PAUL WHITEMAN (1933–38). After leading his own group 1938–47, he joined LOUIS ARMSTRONG's All Stars, and recorded and toured with them internationally until 1951. Teagarden's trademark relaxed, bluesy approach was evident in both his playing and singing, his engaging Texas accent seeming to color both.

teak Large deciduous tree *(Tectona grandis)* of the VERBENA family, and its wood, one of the most valuable and durable timbers. Teak has been widely used in India for more than 2,000 years; some temples contain teak beams more than 1,000 years old. The tree has a straight stem, often thickened at the base, a spreading crown, and four-sided branchlets. The rough leaves are opposite or sometimes whorled, and the branches end in many small white flowers. The unseasoned heartwood has a pleasant, strong aromatic fragrance and a beautiful golden-yellow color, which on seasoning darkens into brown, mottled with darker streaks. Resistant to the effects of water, teakwood is used for shipbuilding, fine furniture, door and window frames, wharves, bridges, cooling-tower louvers, flooring, and paneling. Its desirability has led to severe overcutting in tropical forests.

teal Any of about 15 species (genus *Anas,* family Anatidae) of small DABBLING ducks found on the major continents and many islands. Many are popular game birds. The Holarctic green-winged teal, usually found in a dense flock, is 13–15 in. (33–38 cm) long. The small blue-winged teal breeds across Canada and the northern U.S. and winters south of the U.S. The Hottentot teal of Africa frequently remains immobile among vegetation even when shots are fired nearby. Teal are primarily herbivorous, but some species eat small animals. Flocks of many species take off and change direction in unison.

Holarctic American green-winged teal drake (*Anas crecca carolinensis*).
© GORDON LANGSBURY–BRUCE COLEMAN INC.

Teamsters Union *officially* **International Brotherhood of Teamsters, Chauffeurs, Warehousemen and Helpers of America (IBT)** Largest labor union in the U.S., representing truck drivers and workers in related industries such as aviation. It was formed in 1903 with the merger of two team-drivers' unions, and local deliverymen using horse-drawn vehicles remained the core membership until the 1930s, when intercity truck drivers became predominant. From 1907 to 1952 the union was headed by Daniel J. Tobin, who built it up from 40,000 members in 1907 to more than one million in 1950. Disclosures of corruption in the leadership led to the Teamsters' expulsion from the AFL-CIO in 1957. Between 1957 and 1988 three Teamsters presidents—Dave Beck, JIMMY HOFFA, and Roy Williams—were convicted of various criminal charges and sentenced to prison terms. The union was readmitted to the AFL-CIO in 1987.

Teapot Dome scandal Secret leasing of U.S. government land to private interests. In 1922 oil reserves at Teapot Dome, Wyo., and Elk Hills, Cal., were improperly leased to private oil companies by Secretary of the Interior ALBERT FALL, who accepted cash gifts and no-interest loans from the companies. When the leases became known, Congress directed Pres. WARREN G. HARDING to cancel them. A later investigation revealed illegal actions by several government officials, thus the scandal became a symbol of government corruption.

tear duct and gland *or* **lachrymal duct and gland** \'lak-rə-məl\ Structures that produce, distribute, and carry away tears. An almond-shaped gland above the outer corner of each EYE secretes tears between the membrane (conjunctiva) lining the upper eyelid and that over the eyeball. Tears moisten and lubricate the conjunctiva and then flow into the barely visible openings (near the inner corners of the eyelids) of the tear ducts, which lead to the nasal cavity. Oil on the edge of the eyelid from SEBACEOUS glands keeps tears from spilling out unless secretion increases due to crying or a reflex triggered by stimuli such as eye irritation, bright lights, or spicy foods.

tear gas Any of a group of substances, most often synthetic organic HALOGEN compounds, that irritate the mucous membranes of the eyes, causing a stinging sensation and tears. They may also irritate the upper respiratory tract, causing coughing, choking, and general debility. Tear gas was first used in warfare in World War I, but since its effects are short-lasting and rarely disabling, it came into use by law-enforcement agencies as a means of dispersing mobs, disabling rioters, and flushing out armed suspects without the use of deadly force.

Teasdale, Sara *orig.* **Sara Trevor** (1884–1933) U.S. poet. Born in St. Louis, she made frequent trips to Chicago, where she eventually joined HARRIET MONROE's *POETRY* magazine circle. *Rivers to the Sea* (1915) established her as a popular poet, and *Love Songs* (1917) won the first Pulitzer Prize for poetry. Over time her verse became simpler and more austere. After her marriage ended in divorce in 1929, she moved to New York City, where she lived in virtual retirement. Many of the poems in her last book, *Strange Victory* (1933), foreshadow her death by her own hand at 48.

teasel \'tē-zəl\ Any of about 15 species constituting the genus *Dipsacus* of the family Dipsacaceae (the teasel family), native to Europe, the Mediterranean area, and tropical Africa. Many teasels are prickly, coarse biennials with tall-domed heads of numerous, four-lobed flowers that sit on a crownlike circle of spiny, narrow bracts. The spiny, dry fruiting heads of fuller's teasel *(D. sativus)* have been used since Roman times to raise the nap of woolen fabrics in a process known as fulling.

Tebaldi \tā-'bäl-dē\, **Renata** (born 1922) Italian soprano. After her 1944 debut in *Mefistofele*, she established herself at La Scala, performing with A. TOSCANINI for the 1946 reopening and over the next decade. Her debuts at Covent Garden (1950) and the Metropolitan Opera (1955) were both in the role of Desdemona, and she sang at the Met for 17 years in such roles as Tosca, Manon Lescaut, Mimi, and Violetta. Her voice was known for its great beauty and warmth. She retired in 1976.

technetium \tek-'nē-shē-əm\ Metallic chemical ELEMENT, one of the TRANSITION elements, chemical symbol Tc, atomic number 43. All its ISOTOPES are radioactive (see RADIOACTIVITY); some occur in trace amounts in nature as NUCLEAR FISSION products of URANIUM. Its isotope technetium-97 was the first element artificially produced (1937; see CYCLOTRON). Technetium-99, a fission product of nuclear reactors, is the most-used isotope in NUCLEAR MEDICINE. Technetium resembles platinum in appearance and manganese and rhenium in chemical behavior. It is used as a metallurgical tracer and in cryochemistry and corrosion-resistant products.

technical education Academic and vocational preparation of students for jobs involving applied science and modern technology. It emphasizes the practical application of principles of science and mathematics, rather than the attainment of proficiency in manual skills that is properly the concern of vocational education. See also EMPLOYEE training.

techno electronic dance music that began in the United States in the 1980s and became globally popular in the 1990s. It originated with Detroit deejay-producers who, inspired by European electro-pop, underlaid dreamy synthesizer melodies with rapid electronic rhythms. Imported to Europe, it was adopted by the burgeoning rave scene of all-night dance parties (often featuring the hallucinogen ECSTASY), and is celebrated in the annual Love Parade in Berlin.

technology Application of knowledge to the practical aims of human life or to changing and manipulating the human environment. Technology includes the use of materials, tools, techniques, and sources of power to make life easier and work more productive. Whereas science is concerned with how and why things happen, technology focuses on making things happen. Technology began to influence human endeavor as soon as people began using tools, and accelerated with the INDUSTRIAL REVOLUTION. Technological development has also had costs, in terms of pollution and other undesirable environmental effects.

tectonics Scientific study of the deformation of the rocks that make up the earth's crust and the forces that produce such deformation. It deals with the folding and faulting associated with mountain building; the large-scale, gradual, upward and downward movements of the crust; and sudden horizontal displacements along faults. Other phenomena studied include igneous processes and metamorphism. The chief working principle of tectonics is the concept of PLATE tectonics. See also CONTINENTAL DRIFT, SEAFLOOR SPREADING.

tectonism See DIASTROPHISM

Tecumseh \tə-'kəm-sə\ (1768–1813) SHAWNEE Indian chief. As a boy during the American Revolution, Tecumseh participated in combined British and Indian attacks on Americans. In 1794 he fought unsuccessfully against Gen. ANTHONY WAYNE. He eventually established a confederation made up of members of the CREEK and other nations. In 1811 his brother's attack on WILLIAM H. HARRISON's troops at TIPPECANOE ended in defeat. As the War of 1812 approached, Tecumseh assembled his followers under the British banner and captured Detroit. Several lesser successes followed, ending with his death at the Thames River in Ontario, marking the end of Indian resistance in the Old Northwest.

Tedder, Arthur William *later* **Baron Tedder (of Glenguin)** (1890–1967) British air marshal. He joined the British army in 1913, transferred to the Royal Flying Corps in 1916, and after World War I commanded a branch of the RAF. In World War II he commanded Allied air operations in North Africa and Italy, and in 1944 he was appointed head of Allied air operations in Western Europe. His policy of bombing German communications and providing close air support of ground operations contributed significantly to the success of the Normandy Campaign and the Allied advance into Germany. He later became the first peacetime chief of the air staff (1946–50).

Tees River \'tēz\ River, northern England. It rises in the northern PENNINES and flows 70 mi (110 km) east to the North Sea. There are falls and reservoirs along its course. Teesside, the urban area at the river's mouth, has seen large-scale industrial development since the railroad arrived in 1825.

Teflon Trademark name for POLYMERS of tetrafluoroethylene fluorocarbon (polytetrafluoroethylene, or PTFE) or fluorinated ethylene-propylene (FEP). Teflon is a tough, waxy, nonflammable organic compound with a slippery surface, attacked by very few chemicals and stable over a wide temperature range. Its qualities make it useful in gaskets, bearings, container and pipe linings, electrical insulation, parts for valves and pumps used for corrosive fluids, and protective coatings on cooking utensils, saw blades, and other articles.

Tegea \'tē-jē-ə\ Ancient city, eastern ARCADIA, southern Greece. It was under Spartan rule from the mid-6th century BC until THEBES' victory over SPARTA in the battle of Leuctra c. 371 BC. Afterward it joined a succession of leagues, and by the early 1st century AD was the only important town in Arcadia. It survived the Goth invasion in 395–396 and flourished under Byzantine and Frankish rule. It is the site of the Temple of Athena Alea, built by the city's traditional founder, Aleus, and rebuilt in the 4th century BC by the sculptor SCOPAS.

Tegernsee \'tā-gərn-ˌzā\ Lake, southern BAVARIA, southeastern Germany. Located in the foothills of the ALPS, it covers 3.5 sq mi (9 sq km). Surrounded by wooded mountains, it is a popular resort and recreation area. The castle of Maximilian I lies on the eastern shore.

Tegucigalpa \tā-ˌgü-sē-'gäl-pä\ City (metro. area pop., 1997 est.: 814,000), capital of Honduras. Located on hilly terrain hemmed in by mountains, it was founded in 1578 as a gold- and silver-mining center. It was made the permanent capital of Honduras in 1880. It produces textiles and sugar. Principal buildings include the presidential and legislative palaces, the National University of Honduras (1847), and an 18th-century cathedral.

Tehran *or* **Teheran** \ˌtā-(ə-)'rän\ City (pop., 1996: 6,758,845), capital of Iran. It is situated on the southern slopes of the ELBURZ MOUNTAINS. It was originally a suburb of ancient RHAGAE (Rey), which was destroyed by the Mongols in AD 1220 and was later the home of several SAFAVID rulers of Persia (16th–18th century). It became prominent after its capture by Agha Mohammad Khan, founder of the QAJAR DYNASTY, who made it his capital in 1785. It underwent rapid modernization after 1925 and especially after World War II. In 1943 it was the site of the TEHRAN CONFERENCE. In 1979, following the Islamic revolution in Iran, the U.S. embassy was seized and its staff taken hostage by Iranian militants (see IRAN HOSTAGE CRISIS). A transportation and industrial center, Tehran produces more than half of Iran's manufactured goods. It is the seat of several universities, including the University of Tehran (1934).

Tehran Conference (November 28–December 1, 1943) Meeting of FRANKLIN ROOSEVELT, WINSTON CHURCHILL, and JOSEPH STALIN in Tehran during World War II to discuss military strategy and political issues. Stalin agreed to launch a military offensive from the east to coincide with a planned invasion of German-occupied France from the west. Also discussed but not settled were Eastern Europe's postwar borders, including Poland's postwar status, and a postwar international organization.

Tehuantepec \tā-'wän-tā-ˌpek\, **Gulf of** Inlet of the Pacific Ocean, southeastern Mexico. It extends 300 mi (500 km) between OAXACA and CHIAPAS, and is 100 mi (160 km) wide at its mouth. Innumerable lagoons mark its shores, and the Tehuantepec River and numerous smaller streams flow into it. Its southern shore forms the Isthmus of Tehuantepec.

Teide \'tā-ˌthā\, **Pico de** *or* **Pico de Tenerife** \'pē-kō-dā-ˌtān-ə-'rēf-ə\ Volcanic peak on the island of Tenerife, CANARY ISLANDS. At 12,198 ft (3,718 m) tall, it is the highest point on Spanish soil. Vents within its crater and on its slopes eject hot gases. The peak is atop a volcanic cone on the upper reaches of El Teide, a conglomeration of several volcanoes; its last eruption was in 1789. It lies within a national park. Nearby is an international solar observatory.

Teilhard de Chardin \ˌtā-yär-də-shär-'da^{n}\, **(Marie-Joseph-) Pierre** (1881–1955) French philosopher and paleontologist. Ordained a Jesuit priest in 1911, he taught geology from 1918 at the Institut Catholique in Paris, and in 1929 he directed the excavations at the Peking Man site at ZHOUKOUDIAN. This and other geological work won him high honors, though it came to be disapproved by the Jesuit order. His philosophy was strongly informed by his scientific work, which he believed helped prove the existence of God. He is known for his theory that mankind is evolving, mentally and socially, toward a final spiritual unity that he called the Omega point. Though he wrote his major philosophical works, *The Divine Milieu* (1957) and *The Phenomenon of Man* (1955), in the 1920s and '30s, their publication was forbidden by the Jesuits in his lifetime.

Teilhard de Chardin.
© PHILIPPE HALSMAN

Tekakwitha \ˌtek-ə-'kwith-ə\, **Kateri** (1656–1680) First North American Indian considered for canonization. The daughter of an Algonquin Christian mother and a non-Christian Mohawk father, she was born in what is now Auriesville, N.Y., and was partially blinded by smallpox as a child. She was deeply impressed by the lives and words of three Jesuit missionaries she met at age 11, and at 20 she was baptized. Harassed and threatened with torture in her home village, she fled 200 mi (320 km) to a Christian Indian mission near Montreal, where she became known as the "Lily of the Mohawks" for her kindness, faith, and heroic suffering before her early death. She was beatified in 1980.

tektite Any of a class of small, natural glassy objects found on the earth's surface and associated with meteorite impacts. The extremely high temperatures and enormous pressures generated when a large meteorite, comet, or asteroid hits the earth melt the rocks at the site, producing masses of molten droplets that are blasted into and out of the earth's atmosphere. The droplets cool quickly to a glassy form and then fall back to the earth.

Tel Aviv-Jaffa \ˌtel-ə-'vēv-'jä-fə\ *or* **Tel Aviv-Yafo** \ˌtel-ə-'vēv-'yä-fō\ City (pop., 1997 est.: 353,000), on the Mediterranean Sea. The hub of Israel's largest urban center, it was formed in 1950 by the incorporation of the ancient port of Jaffa with Tel Aviv, its former suburb. Tel Aviv was founded in 1909 and was the capital of Israel 1948–50. It grew with Jewish immigration in the early 20th century, and by 1936 was the largest and most important city in Palestine. Jaffa was an old Canaanite city that was taken by Egypt in the 15th century BC, and occupied by the Israelite kings DAVID and SOLOMON. Over the centuries it was ruled by the Ptolemies, Syrians, and Romans, captured by the Crusaders, and razed by the Mamluks. The British occupied it in 1917; it surrendered to Jewish military forces during the first ARAB–ISRAELI WAR (1948). It is Israel's main business, communications, and cultural center. It is the site of more than half of Israel's industrial plants and the country's stock exchange. It is home to Tel Aviv University (1953) and the Bar-Ilan University (1953).

telecommunications Communication between parties at a distance from one another. Modern telecommunication systems—capable of transmitting TELEPHONE, FAX, data, RADIO, or TELEVISION signals—can transmit large volumes of information over long distances. Digital transmission is employed in order to achieve high reliability without noise or interference and because the cost of digital switching systems is much lower than the cost of analog systems. In order to use digital transmission, analog signals must be subjected to a process of analog-to-digital conversion. In data transmission the signals are already in digital form; most television, radio, and voice communications are analog and must be digitized before transmission. Transmission may occur over cables, wireless radio relay systems, or via satellite links.

telegraph Electromagnetic communication device. In 1832 SAMUEL F. B. MORSE made sketches of ideas for a system of electric telegraphy, and in 1835 he developed a code to represent letters and numbers (MORSE CODE). In 1837 he was granted a patent on an electromagnetic telegraph that transmitted signals along a wire. That same year British inventors patented a telegraph system that activated five needle pointers that could be made to point to specific letters and numbers on their mounting plate.

Public use of Morse's telegraph system began in 1844 and lasted more than 100 years. By the late 20th century the telegraph had been replaced in most applications in developed countries by digital data transmission systems based on computer technology. See also WESTERN UNION CORP.

Teleki \'te-le-ki\, **Pál, Gróf (Count)** (1879–1941) Hungarian politician. He was a delegate to the Paris Peace Conference, but withdrew from politics in 1921. An eminent geographer, he taught at Budapest Univ., then returned to office as minister of education (1938–39) and premier (1939–41). Hoping to use Germany's power to win back territories lost through the Treaty of TRIANON (1920), he initially cooperated with ADOLF HITLER. In 1941, caught between German demands for support after it invaded Yugoslavia (with whom Hungary had signed a friendship treaty in 1940) and British threats against helping Germany, he committed suicide.

Telemann \'tā-lə-ˌmän\, **Georg Philipp** (1681–1767) German composer. By age 10 he had learned several instruments, composing an opera at 12 before being ordered to stop by his mother. While studying law at Leipzig Univ., he organized student music groups and became music director of the Opera (1702), organist at the New Church (1704), and kapellmeister to a count (1705). Moving to Eisenach (c. 1708), where he met J.S. BACH, he composed French-style instrumental music and German-style sacred music. He moved to Gotha (1717), then Hamburg (1721), where he served as musical director of the Opera (1722–38), for which he wrote several dozen Italian-influenced works. He wrote some 600 cantatas, and a total of some 2,000 pieces, many of high quality.

telemetry \tə-'le-mə-trē\ Highly automated communications process by which data are collected from instruments located at remote or inaccessible points and transmitted to receiving equipment for measurement, monitoring, display, and recording. Transmission of the information may be over wires or, more commonly, by RADIO. The technique is used extensively for oil-pipeline monitoring and control systems and in oceanography and meteorology. Telemetry for rockets and satellites bloomed in the 1950s and has continued to grow in complexity and in breadth of application. Data can be transmitted from inside internal-combustion engines during tests, from steam turbines in operation, and from manned and unmanned spacecraft. Major scientific applications include biomedical research and remote observation of operations with highly radioactive material.

teleological argument See ARGUMENT FROM DESIGN

teleological ethics Theory that derives duty from what is valuable as an end, in a manner diametrically opposed to DEONTOLOGICAL ethics. Teleological ethics holds that the basic standard of duty is the contribution that an action makes to the realization of nonmoral values. Teleological theories differ on the nature of the nonmoral goods that actions ought to promote. EUDAEMONISM emphasizes the cultivation of VIRTUE in the agent as the end of all action. UTILITARIANISM holds that the end consists in the aggregate balance of pleasure to pain for all concerned. Other teleological theories claim that the end of action is survival and growth, as in evolutionary ethics (HERBERT SPENCER); power over others (NICCOLO MACHIAVELLI and FRIEDRICH NIETZSCHE); satisfaction and adjustment, as in PRAGMATISM (Ralph Barton Perry and JOHN DEWEY); and freedom, as in EXISTENTIALISM (J.-P. SARTRE).

teleology \ˌtē-lē-'ä-lə-jē\ Causality in which the effect is explained by an end (Greek, *telos*) to be realized. Teleology thus differs essentially from efficient causality, in which an effect is dependent on prior events. Aristotle's account of teleology declared that a full explanation of anything must consider its the final cause—the purpose for which the thing exists or was produced. Following Aristotle, many philosophers have conceived of biological processes as involving the operation of a guiding end. Modern science has tended to appeal only to efficient causes in its investigations. See also MECHANISM.

telephone Instrument designed for simultaneous transmission and reception of the human voice. It works by converting the sound waves of the human voice to pulses of electrical current, transmitting the current, and then retranslating the current back to sound. The U.S. patent granted to ALEXANDER GRAHAM BELL in 1876 for developing a device to transmit speech sounds over electric wires is often called the most valuable ever issued. Within 20 years, the telephone acquired a form that has remained fundamentally unchanged for more than a century. The advent of the TRANSISTOR (1947) led to lightweight, compact circuitry (see CELL PHONE). Advances in electronics have allowed the introduction of a number of "smart" features such as automatic redialing, caller identification, call waiting, and call forwarding. Telephone systems are also a primary access route for the INTERNET.

telescope Device that collects light from and magnifies images of distant objects, undoubtedly the most important investigative tool in ASTRONOMY. The first telescopes focused visible light by REFRACTION through LENSES; later instruments used REFLECTION from curved mirrors (see OPTICS). Their invention is traditionally credited to Hans Lippershey (1570?–1619?), who adapted A. VAN LEEUWENHOEK's use of lenses in MICROSCOPES. Among the earliest were Galilean telescopes, modeled after the simple instruments built by GALILEO, the first to use telescopes to study celestial bodies. In 1611 JOHANNES KEPLER proposed an improved version, which became the basis for modern refracting instruments. The reflecting telescope came into its own after HERSCHEL FAMILY used one to discover URANUS in 1781. Since the 1930s, RADIO TELESCOPES have been used to form images from radio waves emitted by celestial objects. More recently, telescopes have been designed to detect other parts of the ELECTROMAGNETIC SPECTRUM (see GAMMA-RAY ASTRONOMY, INFRARED ASTRONOMY, ULTRAVIOLET ASTRONOMY, X-RAY ASTRONOMY). Spaceflight has allowed telescopes to be launched into earth orbit to avoid the light-scattering and light-absorbing effects of the atmosphere (e.g., the HUBBLE SPACE TELESCOPE).

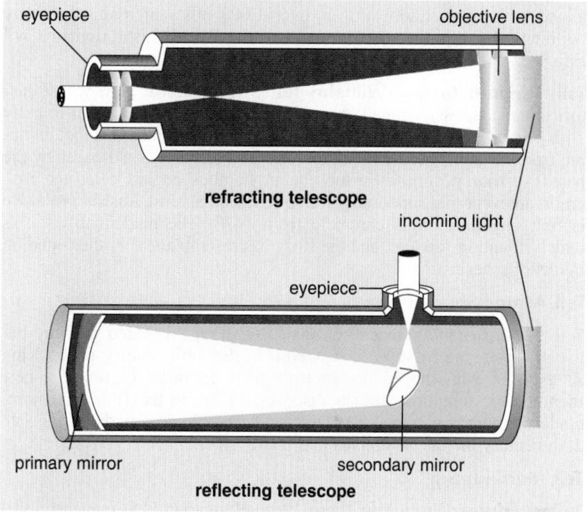

A refracting telescope forms an image by focusing light from a distant object using lenses. A reflecting telescope uses mirrors to focus the light. Both types use lenses in the eyepiece to magnify the image formed.

Teletype Telegraphic instrument that transmits and receives printed messages and data via telephone cables or radio relay systems. Teletypewriters (or teleprinters) became common for commercial use in the 1920s. In 1924 the Teletype Corp. introduced a series of teletypewriters that were so popular that the name Teletype became synonymous with teleprinters in the U.S. Coding schemes used for teleprinters included a variation of the BAUDOT code (1920s) and ASCII (1960s). Since the advent of high-speed DATA TRANSMISSION in the 1980s, teletype has given way to E-MAIL and FAX.

televangelism Evangelism through religious programs on television. Such programs are usually hosted by a fundamentalist Protestant minister, who conducts services and often asks for donations. BILLY GRAHAM became known worldwide through his TV specials from the 1950s on. Other prominent televangelists have included ORAL ROBERTS, Robert Schuller (born 1926), JERRY FALWELL, Jimmy Swaggart (born 1935), and PAT ROBERTSON.

television (TV) Electronic system for transmitting still or moving images and sound to receivers that project a view of the images on a picture tube or screen and recreate the sound. Early versions (1900–20) of the CATHODE-RAY (PICTURE) TUBE, methods of amplifying an electronic signal, and theoretical formulation of the electronic-scanning principle later became the basis of modern TV. RCA demonstrated the first all-electronic TV in 1932. Color TV (in the 1950s), CABLE TV systems (introduced in the 1960s), and recording or playback machines (in the 1980s; see VCR) followed. Digital high-definition (HDTV) systems (1990s) provide sharper, clearer pictures and sound with little interference or other imperfections, and have the potential to merge TV functions with those of computers.

television, cable See CABLE TELEVISION

telex International telegraphic message-transfer service consisting of a network of teleprinters. Subscribers to a telex service can exchange textual communications and data directly with one another. Telex systems originated in Europe in the early 1930s and were widely used for several decades. The ability to conduct high-speed digital communication over regular telephone lines led to a decline in the use of telex, but it is still used as a data transmission service for applications in which high transmission speeds are not necessary or in areas where more modern data equipment is not available.

Telford, Thomas (1757–1834) Scottish civil engineer. He built the Ellesmere, Caledonian, and Göta canals and the St. Katherine's Docks in London. His crowning achievement was the design and construction (1819–26) of the great Menai Bridge, a suspension bridge in Wales. In all he built some 1,200 bridges, over 1,000 miles of road, and many buildings. He was the first president of the British Institution of Civil Engineers (founded 1818).

Tell, William *German* **Wilhelm Tell** Swiss national hero whose historical existence is disputed. According to tradition, in the 13th or early 14th century he defied Austrian authority and was forced to shoot an apple from his son's head with a crossbow at a distance of 80 paces by the hated Austrian governor. He subsequently ambushed and killed the governor, an event that supposedly led to rebellion against Austrian rule. He is first mentioned in a chronicle from 1470. The marksman's test is widely found in folklore, and the story has resemblances to the founding myths of other nations.

Tell Asmar See ESHNUNNA

Tell el-Amârna Ancient city, NILE RIVER, Egypt. Located midway between THEBES and MEMPHIS, it was built in the 14th century BC by King AKHENATON, who moved his subjects there in order to found a new monotheistic religion. Artifacts discovered there in the 19th century included hundreds of CUNEIFORM tablets. Archaeological finds of the late 20th century include sculptures and paintings.

Tell Mardikh See EBLA

Teller, Edward *orig.* **Ede** (born 1908) Hungarian-U.S. nuclear physicist. Born to a prosperous Jewish family, he earned a PhD at the University of Leipzig (1930) before leaving Nazi Germany (1933), and settled in the U.S. in 1935. In 1941 he joined ENRICO FERMI's team in the effort to produce the first self-sustaining nuclear reaction, and in 1943 J. ROBERT OPPENHEIMER recruited him for the MANHATTAN PROJECT. At the war's end Teller advocated development of a fusion bomb, and he won permission after initial government resistance. With STANISLAW ULAM he developed a workable HYDROGEN BOMB in 1952. The same year he helped establish the Lawrence Livermore Laboratory (Livermore, Cal.), which became the U.S.'s chief factory for nuclear weapons. In 1954 he joined the opposition to Oppenheimer's continued security clearance. A staunch anticommunist, he devoted much energy to his crusade to keep the U.S. ahead of the Soviet Union in nuclear arms; he opposed nuclear-weapons treaties, and he was principally responsible for convincing Pres. R. Reagan of the need for the STRATEGIC DEFENSE INITIATIVE.

Teller.

BY COURTESY OF THE UNIVERSITY OF CALIFORNIA LAWRENCE BERKELEY LABORATORY, BERKELEY, CALIF.

Telloh See LAGASH

Telugu language \'te-lə-ˌgü\ DRAVIDIAN language spoken by more than 66 million people in South India and in immigrant communities elsewhere. It is the official language of the state of ANDHRA PRADESH. The earliest inscription entirely in Telugu is from the 6th century; literary texts begin in the 11th century. The Telugu script, derived from the writing of the CALUKYA DYNASTY, is closely akin to Kannada script (see INDIC writing systems). Like other major Dravidian languages, Telugu has very marked distinctions between formal or literary and colloquial registers and between social dialects.

telum figure *or* **tellem figure** \'te-ləm\ Small, devotional image carved from wood or stone, probably used in private ancestor worship in primitive societies. Telum figures are known from northwestern New Guinea and in the DOGON art of Sudan. Extant examples are rare, perhaps because they had less intrinsic value than the more carefully executed statues used in formal ceremonies of ancestor worship.

Tempe \'tem-pē, tem-'pē\ City (pop., 1996 est.: 163,000), southwestern central Arizona. It is located on the SALT RIVER, near PHOENIX. First settled in 1872, it was renamed in 1880 for the Vale of TEMPE. After World War II it experienced rapid residential and economic growth with light-industrial development. Arizona State University (founded 1885), located there, has an auditorium designed by FRANK LLOYD WRIGHT.

Tempe \'tem-pē\, **Vale of** *Greek* **Témbi** Narrow valley between Mount OLYMPUS and Mount Ossa, northeastern THESSALY, Greece. The PINIOS RIVER flows through the 6-mi (10-km) valley before emptying into the Aegean Sea. The ancient Greeks dedicated Tempe to the cult of APOLLO. Legends attribute its formation to a blow from POSEIDON's trident; however, geologists believe it was carved by stream action. Because it provides access from the coast of Greece to the Thessalian plain, it has been a traditional invasion route. Ruins of castles and fortifications, from the Roman period to the Middle Ages, mark its strong points.

tempera painting Painting executed with ground pigment mixed with a water-soluble material, such as egg yolk, gum, or wax. The special ground for tempera painting is a rigid wood panel coated with thin layers of gesso, a preparation usually made of plaster of Paris and glue. Tempera paint is resistant to water and allows overpainting with more color; the thin, transparent layers of paint produce a clear, luminous effect. The exclusive medium for panel painting in the Middle Ages and early Renaissance, it was largely superseded in the 15th century by oil paint.

temperament In the psychological study of PERSONALITY, an individual's characteristic or habitual inclination or mode of emotional response. The notion of temperament in this sense originated with GALEN, who developed it from an earlier theory regarding the four "humors": blood, phlegm, and black and yellow bile. The subject was taken up in the 20th century by ERNST KRETSCHMER and later theorists, including MARGARET MEAD. Today researchers emphasize physiological processes (including the ENDOCRINE and autonomic NERVOUS systems) and CULTURE and LEARNING.

temperament See TUNING AND TEMPERAMENT

temperance movement International social movement dedicated to the control of alcohol consumption through the promotion of moderation and abstinence. It began as a church-sponsored movement in the early 19th century in the U.S. and attracted the efforts of many women; by 1833 the U.S. had 6,000 local temperance societies. The first European temperance society was formed in Ireland in 1826. An international temperance movement began in Utica, N.Y., in 1851, and spread to Australasia, India, South and West Africa, and South America. See also CARRY NATION, PROHIBITION.

temperature Measure of hotness expressed in terms of any of several arbitrary scales, such as Fahrenheit, Celsius, or Kelvin. Heat flows from a hotter body to a colder one and continues to do so until both are at the same temperature. Temperature is a measure of the average energy of the molecules of a body, whereas heat is a measure of the total amount of THERMAL ENERGY in a body. For example, whereas the temperature of a cup of boiling water is the same as that of a large pot of boiling water (212°F, or 100°C), the large pot has more heat, or thermal energy, and it takes more energy to boil a pot of water than a cup of water. The most common temperature scales are based on arbitrarily defined fixed points. The Fahrenheit scale sets 32° as the freezing point of water and 212° as the boiling point of water (at standard atmospheric pressure). The Celsius scale defines the triple point of water (at which all three phases, solid, liquid, and gas, coexist in equilibrium) at 0.01° and the boiling point at 100°. The Kelvin scale, used primarily for scientific and engineering purposes, sets the zero point at ABSOLUTE ZERO and uses a degree the same size as those of the Celsius scale.

temperature inversion In meteorology, an increase of air temperature with altitude. Such an increase is a reversal of the normal temperature condition of the TROPOSPHERE, where temperature usually decreases with altitude. Inversions play an important role in determining cloud forms, precipitation, and visibility. An inversion acts as a lid, preventing the upward movement of the air below it. Where a pronounced inversion is present at a low level, convective clouds cannot grow high enough to produce showers and, at the same time, visibility may be greatly reduced by trapped pollutants (see SMOG). Because the air near the base of the inversion is cool, fog is frequently present there.

temperature stress Stress on the body from excessive heat or cold that can impair functioning and cause injury or death. It is a particular problem in AEROSPACE MEDICINE. See also ACCLIMATIZATION, FROSTBITE, HEAT EXHAUSTION, HEATSTROKE, HOMEOSTASIS, HYPOTHERMIA.

tempering Heat treating of metal ALLOYS, particularly STEEL, to yield specific properties. For instance, raising the temperature of hardened steel to 752°F (400°C) and holding it for a time before QUENCHING in oil decreases its hardness and brittleness and produces a strong and tough steel. Quench-and-temper HEAT TREATING is applied at many different cooling rates, holding times, and temperatures, and is a very important means of controlling the properties of steel.

Tempest, Marie *orig.* **Marie Susan Etherington** *later* **Dame Marie** (1864–1942) British actress. She began her career as an operetta singer, winning acclaim for her charming and high-spirited performances in *Dorothy* (1887) and *The Red Hussar* (1889) and touring the U.S. and Canada in the early 1890s in such works as *The Bohemian Girl* and *The Pirates of Penzance.* Turning to straight comedy in 1899, she appeared notably in *English Nell* (1900), *Becky Sharp* (1901), *Mrs. Dot* (1908), *Hay Fever* (1925), and *The First Mrs. Fraser* (1929).

Tempietto \tem-'pyet-ō\ Small monument built in 1502 to mark the crucifixion spot of St. Peter in Rome. Designed by DONATO BRAMANTE, it is a circular, domed, unadorned masterpiece of High Renaissance architecture. Its outer face is a colonnade of bare Tuscan Doric, the earliest modern use of this ORDER. Because of its proportions, the tiny temple has the majesty of a great monument.

Templar *or* **Knight Templar** \'tem-plər\ Member of a religious military order of knighthood established during the CRUSADES. At its beginning (c. 1119), the group consisted of eight or nine French knights who devoted themselves to protecting from Muslim warriors those on pilgrimage to Jerusalem. They were given quarters near the site of the former Temple of JERUSALEM, from which they derived their name. Taking vows of poverty and chastity, they performed courageous service, and their numbers increased rapidly, partly because of the propagandistic writing of St. BERNARD DE CLAIRVAUX, who also wrote their rule of life. They flourished for two centuries, expanding to other countries, growing in number to 20,000, and acquiring vast wealth and property. By 1304 rumors, probably false, of irreligious practices and blasphemies had made them the target of persecution. In 1307 PHILIP IV of France and Pope CLEMENT V initiated the offensive that culminated in the Templars' final suppression in 1312, including the confiscation of all their property and the imprisonment or execution of many members; their last leader, Jacques de Molay (1243–1314), was burned at the stake.

temple Edifice constructed for the worship of a deity. Features commonly include a sanctuary and an ALTAR. Ancient Egypt had two kinds of temple: mortuary temples for the cults of dead kings, with a chapel in which offerings were presented, and cult temples that held images of deities. The cult temple typically included a massive PYLON entrance with a court leading to a HYPOSTYLE hall and, at the heart of the temple, a shrine for the cult image. Most Classical Greek temples were rectangular and built of marble or other stone on a low stylobate (stepped platform). A gable roof was supported by columns, with a portico at each end (amphiprostyle temple), a colonnade extending all around (peripteral temple), or a double line of columns all around (dipteral temple). An inner CELLA housed the image of a deity, and an altar stood outside the temple. Roman temples were profoundly influenced by Greek style, but the altar was inside the temple and the colonnade was often reduced to a row of engaged columns. Hindu temples vary regionally, but generally consist of a towering shrine and a columned hall surrounded by an elaborate wall. Buddhist temples range from half-buried sanctuaries with richly carved entrances to single carved towers or statues. The Chinese and Japanese Buddhist temple is typically a one-story building of richly carved, painted, or tiled timber constructed around an atrium used for worship, though towering PAGODAS were sometimes built as temples over a shrine. In the Americas, Inca and Mayan temples were constructed of stone, often richly carved; they were generally stair-stepped pyramids, with the shrine at the top. See also SYNAGOGUE.

Temple, Shirley *later* **Shirley Temple Black** (born 1928) U.S. child actress. Born in Santa Monica, Cal., she was selected for a screen test from her dancing class and made her debut at 4. She won notice in *Stand Up and Cheer* (1934) and was featured in *Little Miss Marker* (1934) and *Bright Eyes* (1934), in which she sang "On the Good Ship Lollipop." A precocious performer known for her dimples and golden curls, she became the country's most popular female star in the Depression era. She received a special Academy Award in 1934. Her later films included *The Little Colonel* (1935), *Wee Willie Winkie* (1937), and *The Little Princess* (1939). As an adult she served as U.S. ambassador to Ghana (1974–76) and Czechoslovakia (1989–92).

Shirley Temple.
BROWN BROTHERS

Temple, William *later* **Sir William** (1628–1699) British statesman. As ambassador to The Hague (1668–70, 1674–79), he formulated England's pro-Dutch foreign policy and arranged the marriage between William of Orange and Princess Mary of England (later WILLIAM III and MARY II). After retiring from politics in 1681, he wrote numerous essays that were collected for publication by his secretary, JONATHAN SWIFT. He also wrote the acclaimed *Observations upon the United Provinces* (1673).

Temple of Heaven Large religious complex in the old outer city of Beijing, considered the supreme achievement of traditional Chinese architecture. Its layout symbolizes the belief that heaven is round and earth square. The three buildings are built in a straight line. The Hall of Prayer for Good Harvests (1420) has three concentric circles of massive wood columns symbolizing the four seasons, 12 months, and 12 daily hours; in a remarkable feat of engineering, they support the three roof levels and, in succession, a huge square brace (earth), circular architrave (heaven), and vast interior cupola. The Imperial Vault of Heaven (1530; rebuilt 1572) is a smaller circular building constructed without crossbeams; its dome is supported by complicated span work. The Circular Mound Altar (1530; rebuilt 1749) is a triple-tiered white stone terrace enclosed by two sets of walls that are square outside and round inside.

Tempyo style \'temp-yō\ Japanese sculptural style of the NARA period (710–784), greatly influenced by the Chinese imperial style of the TANG dynasty (618–907). Many supreme sculptural achievements of Japanese Buddhist art were created

Ashura, dry lacquer (*kanshitsu*) sculpture in the Tempyo style, Late Nara period (724–794); in the Kofuku-ji, Nara, Japan.
ASUKA-EN, JAPAN

during this era, often in unbaked clay, solid wood, and lacquered cloth molded on a removable core (a technique called *kanshitsu,* or dry lacquer). Tempyo style shows a closer fusion of parts into a unified whole than is found in works of the Early Nara period, giving a sense of activity and realistic observation; the new realism is especially notable in portrait sculpture.

Ten Commandments List of religious precepts sacred in JUDAISM and CHRISTIANITY. They include injunctions to honor God, the SABBATH, and one's parents, as well as bans on idolatry, blasphemy, murder, adultery, theft, false witness, and covetousness. In the Old Testament Book of EXODUS, they are divinely revealed to MOSES on Mount SINAI and engraved on two stone tablets. Most scholars propose a date between the 16th and 13th century BC for the commandments, though some date them as late as 750 BC. They were not regarded with deep reverence by Christians until the 13th century.

Ten Thousand Smokes, Valley of Volcanic region, southwestern Alaska. Located in KATMAI NATIONAL PARK, it covers 56 sq mi (145 sq km). It was created when the eruption of the Novarupta and Mount Katmai volcanoes in 1912 covered the valley in a flow of lava. When an expedition visited the site in 1915, they discovered tens of thousands of fissures spouting smoke, gas, and steam in the valley floor. The largest was 150 ft (46 m) in diameter; some had temperatures as high as 1,200°F (649°C). About 60 years later, there were fewer than 12 fumaroles. In the 1960s U.S. astronauts used the scarred region to train for moon landings.

tenant See LANDLORD AND TENANT

tenant farming Agricultural system in which landowners rent their land to farmers and receive either cash or a share of the product in return. Landowners may also contribute operating CAPITAL and management. Under one arrangement, known as sharecropping, the landowner furnishes all the capital and sometimes the food, clothing, and medical expenses of the tenant and may also supervise the work. The sharecropper then pays the landowner with a portion of the output grown on the land. In other forms of tenant farming, the tenant may furnish all the equipment and have substantial autonomy in the farm's operation. Tenants and their families probably constitute two-fifths of the world's population engaged in agriculture. Tenant farming can be highly efficient, as has been shown in England and Wales. Abuses occur when landowners' power is excessive and the tenants are poor or of inferior social status.

Tendai See TIANTAI

tendinitis *or* **tendonitis** \ˌten-dᵊn-ˈī-təs\ INFLAMMATION of a TENDON sheath, due to irritation of this thin, filmy tissue by overuse of the tendons, which slide within them, or to bacterial infection. It is often an occupational disease, affecting tendons used in repetitive motions on the job. The tendon becomes swollen and red, with pain that increases on motion. The swelling hampers the tendon's sliding within, causing stiffness. Treatment involves immobilization with a splint, cast, or bandage and gradually increasing motion after inflammation subsides, which may happen sooner with STEROID injections. Repeated episodes can permanently thicken the sheath, limiting motion.

tendon Tissue attaching a muscle to other body parts, usually bones, to transmit the mechanical force of muscle contraction to the other part. Much like LIGAMENTS, tendons are composed of dense, fibrous CONNECTIVE tissue with a high COLLAGEN content, which makes them remarkably tough and strong, with great tensile strength to withstand the stresses generated by muscle contraction.

tendril Plant organ specialized to anchor and support vining stems. A tendril is a slender, whiplike or threadlike strand, produced usually from the node of a stem and composed of either stem or leafstalk tissue, by which a VINE or other plant may climb. Sensitive to contact, the tendril turns toward any object it brushes against, wraps about it, and clings to it for as long as the stimulation persists. Later, strong mechanical tissue develops in the tendrils, making them strong enough to support the weight of the plant. Some tendrils have enlargements at the ends that flatten and produce an adhesive that firmly cements them to their support. Common examples of tendril plants are GRAPE, English IVY, SWEET PEA, GOURDS, and PASSIONFLOWERS.

Tenerife, Pico de See Pico de TEIDE

Teng Hsiao-p'ing See DENG XIAOPING

Teniers \tə-ˈnirs, tā-ˈnyā\, **David** Name of two Flemish painters. Little is known about the work of the elder Teniers (1582–1649) except that he painted primarily religious subjects. His more famous, highly prolific son (1610–1690) is best known for his genre scenes of peasant life, many of which were used for tapestry designs in the 18th century. He was brilliant at handling crowd scenes in an open landscape and adept at characterizing his figures with a warm, human, and often humorous touch. As court painter to the archduke Leopold William, he also made many small-scale copies of paintings in the archduke's collection; engraved and published as *Theatrum Pictorium* (1660), they constitute a valuable source as a pictorial inventory of a great 17th-century collection.

Tennessee State (pop., 1997 est.: 5,368,000), southeastern central U.S. It occupies 42,144 sq mi (109,153 sq km); its capital is NASHVILLE. The GREAT SMOKY MTNS. edge the eastern part of the state, while the MISSISSIPPI RIVER is on its western boundary. The TENNESSEE RIVER valley dominates much of the state. It has a moderate climate; about half is forested. American Indians, including Chickasaw, CHEROKEE, and Shawnee, inhabited the region when Spanish, French, and English explorers visited it in the 16th–17th century. It was included in the British charter of Carolina and in the French Louisiana claim, and was ceded to Great Britain after the FRENCH AND INDIAN WAR. The first permanent settlement was made c. 1770. It was part of North Carolina until 1785, when the area's settlers broke away and formed the free state of Franklin. North Carolina relinquished its claim in 1789, and Tennessee became the 16th U.S. state in 1796. In 1861 it seceded from the Union; the hard-fought AMERICAN CIVIL WAR battles of SHILOH, CHATTANOOGA, Stones River, and Nashville occurred there. In 1866 it was the first state readmitted to the Union. During the RECONSTRUCTION era, blacks lost what little power they had gained. After World War II, it became a testing ground for those involved in the CIVIL RIGHTS MOVEMENT. The state's economy is based on manufacturing. The TENNESSEE VALLEY AUTHORITY is the nation's largest electric-power generating system.

Tennessee, University of State university system based in Knoxville, with additional campuses at Memphis, Chattanooga, and Martin. It was founded in 1794 and received land-grant status in 1869. The main campus has colleges of liberal arts, agriculture, business administration, communications, education, engineering, nursing, law, and veterinary medicine, as well as schools of architecture, library science, and social work, among other fields. Enrollment is about 26,000. The Memphis campus is a comprehensive medical research and teaching institution.

Tennessee River Navigable river, Tennessee, northern Alabama, and western Kentucky. Formed by the confluence of the Holston and FRENCH BROAD rivers in eastern Tennessee, it flows 652 mi (1,049 km) before joining the OHIO RIVER in Kentucky. During the AMERICAN CIVIL WAR it served as a strategic invasion route into the western Confederacy. Its development as one of the world's greatest irrigation and hydropower systems began with the establishment in 1933 of the TENNESSEE VALLEY AUTHORITY. It is linked to the TOMBIGBEE RIVER by the Tennessee-Tombigbee Waterway.

Tennessee Valley Authority (TVA) U.S. government agency established in 1933 to control floods, improve navigation, and generate electrical power along the TENNESSEE RIVER and its tributaries. The TVA is a public corporation governed by a board of directors. It has jurisdiction over the entire basin of the river, which covers parts of seven states: Alabama, Georgia, Kentucky, Mississippi, North Carolina, Tennessee, and Virginia. Created by Congress as one of the major public-works projects of the NEW DEAL, the TVA built a system of dams to control the region's chronic flooding, deepened the channel to improve navigation, and encouraged the development of port facilities along the river. The projects greatly increased traffic on the river and provided cheap electricity, spurring the industrial development of what had been a chronically depressed regional economy. See also PUBLIC WORKS ADMINISTRATION.

Tennessee walking horse *or* **plantation walking horse** Breed of light HORSE with a distinctive, easy-to-sit gait, the running walk. It was developed for touring U.S. southern plantations. It averages 15.2 hands (62 in., 157 cm) high and weighs about 1,000 lbs (450 kg). Coat color varies. Its ancestors included any horse capable of a running walk, a natural gait that cannot be acquired, but the most influential stallion was a STANDARDBRED. The running walk, faster than a flat-footed walk, is a low, gliding, reaching action; the front foot strikes the ground an instant before the diagonal hind foot, which then oversteps the front footprint by several inches.

Tenniel \'ten-yəl\, **John** *later* **Sir John** (1820–1914) British illustrator and satirical artist. After attracting attention with his mural decorations, he was invited to contribute drawings to *Punch* magazine in 1850, and in time became its chief cartoonist. His drawings lent new dignity to the political cartoon. Of his many book illustrations, best known are those for LEWIS CARROLL's *Alice's Adventures in Wonderland* (1865) and *Through the Looking-Glass* (1872), remarkable for their subtlety and cleverness.

tennis Game played with rackets and a light, elastic ball by two players or pairs of players on a rectangular court divided by a low net. Tennis is played indoors and outdoors, on hard-surface, clay, and grass courts. The object is to hit the ball over the net and into the opponent's half of the court in such a way as to defeat the opponent's attempt to reach and return it. Each player serves for an entire game. Points are scored as 15, 30, 40, and game (the term "love" is used for 0). A tied score ("deuce") requires continued play until a two-point margin is achieved. The first player to win six games, with a lead of two games, takes the set. A match consists of the best two out of three (or three out of five) sets. Since the early 1970s, tiebreakers have been employed to eliminate marathon sets. Tennis developed in the 1870s in Britain from earlier racket-and-ball games. The first world lawn-tennis championship was held in 1877 at WIMBLEDON; clay- and hard-court competitions emerged later. Current international team tournaments include the DAVIS CUP for men and the Federation Cup (since 1963) for women's teams. The major tournaments for individual players constitute the "Grand Slam" of tennis: the national championships of Britain (Wimbledon), the U.S., Australia, and France.

Tennis Court Oath (June 20, 1789) Oath taken by deputies of the THIRD ESTATE in the FRENCH REVOLUTION. Believing that their newly formed NATIONAL ASSEMBLY was to be disbanded, the deputies met at a nearby tennis court when they were locked out of their usual meeting hall at Versailles. They vowed never to separate until a written constitution was established for France. Their solidarity forced LOUIS XVI to order the clergy and the nobility to join with the Third Estate in the National Assembly.

Tennyson \'te-nə-sən\, **Alfred** *later* **Baron Tennyson (of Aldworth and Freshwater)** *known as* **Alfred, Lord Tennyson** (1809–1892) English poet, the leading poet of the Victorian Age. While attending Cambridge Univ., Tennyson developed a deep friendship with Arthur Hallam and published *Poems, Chiefly Lyrical* (1830). Another volume, including "The Lotos-Eaters" and "The Lady of Shalott," was published in 1832 (dated 1833). When Hallam died suddenly in 1833, the severe shock prompted Tennyson to write poems that eventually became part of the vast *In Memoriam* (1850) and lyrics that later appeared in the brooding *Maud* (1855), his favorite poem. *Poems* (1842), including "Ulysses," "Morte d'Arthur," and "Locksley Hall," followed, then *The Princess* (1847), a long antifeminist fantasia that includes such lyrics as "Sweet and Low" and "Tears, Idle Tears." In 1850 he married and was named poet laureate of England. Among his subsequent works are "The Charge of the Light Brigade" (1855); *Idylls of the King* (1859), treating the ARTHURIAN legend; and *Enoch Arden* (1864). A consummate poetic artist who was inclined to melancholy, Tennyson was also regarded as a spokesman for the educated English middle class. His works often dealt with the difficulties of an age when traditional assumptions were increasingly called into question by science and modern progress.

Tenochtitlán \tā-ˌnȯch-tēt-'län\ Ancient capital of the AZTEC empire. Located at the site of modern MEXICO CITY, it was founded c. 1325 in the marshes of Lake TEXCOCO. It formed a confederacy with Texcoco and Tlacopán and was the Aztec capital by the late 15th century. Originally located on two small islands in Lake Texcoco, it gradually spread through the construction of artificial islands to cover more than 5 sq mi (13 sq km). It was connected to the mainland by several causeways. The population in 1519 was around 400,000 people, the largest concentration in Mesoamerican history. It contained the palace of MONTEZUMA II, said to consist of 300 rooms, as well as hundreds of temples. It was destroyed by the Spanish CONQUISTADORES under HERNAN CORTES in 1521.

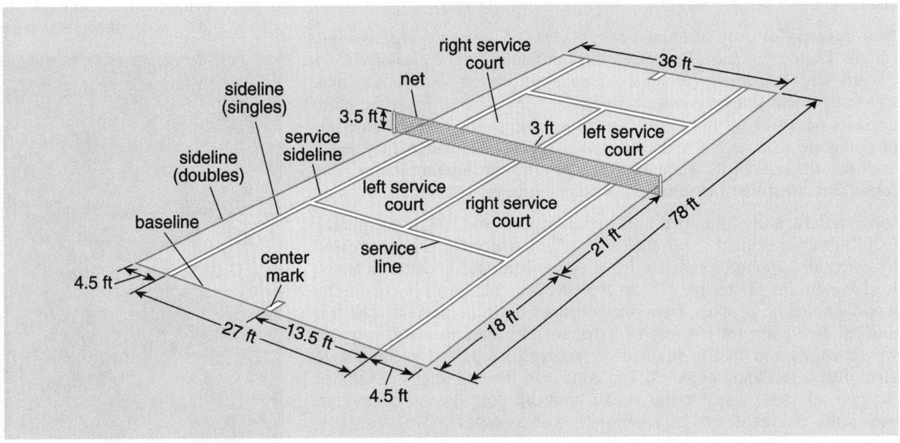

A professional tennis court. The person serving stands behind the baseline, alternately to the right and left of the center mark, and must land the ball alternately in the opposite left and right service court. A narrower portion of the court is used in singles tennis (one person on a side) than in doubles (two people on a side), though the size of the service court does not change. In doubles, the two partners alternate in serving, but both may otherwise roam freely over the entire court.

tenor High male voice range, extending from about the second B below middle C to the G above. In the polyphony of the 13th–16th century, the tenor was the part that held (Latin, *tenere:* "to hold") the CANTUS firmus. Tenor voices are often classified as dramatic, lyric, or heroic (heldentenor). In instrument families, tenor refers to the instrument whose central range is roughly that of the tenor voice (e.g., tenor saxophone).

tenor tuba See EUPHONIUM

tenpounder See LADYFISH

Tenrikyo \'ten-rē-ˌkyō\ Largest and most successful of the modern SHINTO sects in Japan. Its founder, Nakayama Miki (1798–1887), was a charismatic peasant who, at age 40, claimed to be possessed by a god of divine wisdom. She developed a form of worship characterized by ecstatic dancing and shamanistic practices, and a doctrine emphasizing charity and the healing of disease through mental acts of faith. Her writings and deeds were considered divine models. Tenrikyo was one of the most powerful religious movements in Japan immediately after World War II, and its membership reached about 2.5 million in the late 20th century.

tense In GRAMMAR, an inflected form of a verb indicating the time of a narrated event in relation to the time at which the narrator is speaking. Time is often perceived as a continuum with three main divisions, past, present, and future, defined in relation to the time when the event is described. Other categories, including MOOD and aspect, may further specify the action as definite or indefinite, completed or not completed, lasting or nonlasting, and recurring or occurring once.

tensile strength \'ten-səl\ Ratio of the maximum load a material can support without fracture when being stretched to the original area of a cross section of the material. When STRESSES less than the tensile strength are removed, a material completely or partially returns to its original size and shape. As the stress approaches that of the tensile strength, a material that has begun to flow forms a narrow, constricted region that is easily fractured. Tensile strengths are measured in units of force per unit area. See also DEFORMATION and flow.

Tenskwatawa See The PROPHET

tensor analysis Branch of mathematics concerned with relations or laws that remain valid regardless of the COORDINATE system used to specify the quantities. Tensors, invented as an extension of VECTORS, are essential to the study of MANIFOLDS. Every vector is a tensor, but tensors are more general and not easily pictured as geometrical objects. A tensor can be thought of as an abstract object defined as a set of components (like geometric coordinates) that, under a TRANSFORMATION of coordinates, undergo a specific type of transformation. While tensors were explored before ALBERT EINSTEIN, the success of his general theory of RELATIVITY led to their widespread exploration and use by mathematicians and physicists.

tent caterpillar Any MOTH larvae (see LARVA) of the genus *Malacosoma* (family Lasiocampidae). Tent caterpillars are often brightly colored. The eastern tent caterpillar *(M. americanum),* of eastern North America, spins huge, tent-shaped communal nests in tree crotches. Eggs the moth deposits on a tree in midsummer hatch in spring. The hatched caterpillars migrate to a crotch and construct a silken tent, which they leave each day throughout the summer to feed on the surrounding leaves. The forest tent caterpillar *(M. disstria)* is common in the southern U.S.

tent structure Building that uses masts or poles and tensile membrane (e.g., fabric or animal skin) enclosures. Tent structures are prestressed by externally applied forces so that they are held taut under anticipated load conditions. Tents have been the dwelling places of most of the world's nomadic peoples, from ancient times until the present. The traditional Bedouin tent consists of a rectangular membrane of strips of woven camel hair that is strained on webbing straps and secured with guys over a rectangle of poles. The American Plains Indians developed the conical TEPEE. The Central Asian nomadic pole dwelling, or yurt, uses skins and textiles as its covering. See also MEMBRANE STRUCTURE, POLE CONSTRUCTION.

Tenure of Office Act (1867) Law forbidding the U.S. president to remove civil officers without consent by the Senate. Passed by the RADICAL REPUBLICANS in the Congress over Pres. ANDREW JOHNSON's veto, it sought to prevent Johnson from removing cabinet members who supported Congress's harsh RECONSTRUCTION policies. When Johnson tried to dismiss his secretary of war, EDWIN M. STANTON, an ally of the Radical Republicans, they began IMPEACHMENT proceedings based on his defiance of the law. The law was partially repealed in 1869 and completely repealed in 1887; in 1926 it was found unconstitutional.

Tenzing Norgay \'ten-ˌziŋ-'nȯr-gē\ (1914–1986) Nepalese SHERPA mountaineer. Born in Solo Khumbu, he served on numerous expeditions before joining EDMUND HILLARY as sirdar, or organizer of porters. In 1953 he and Hillary became the first two people to reach the summit of Mount EVEREST. A devout Buddhist, he left an offering of food at Everest's summit.

teosinte \ˌtā-ō-'sin-tē\ Tall, stout, annual GRASS *(Zea mexicana* or *Euchlaena mexicana)* of the family Poaceae (or Gramineae), native to Mexico. Related to CORN, teosinte grows in large clumps, producing bundles of fruiting spikes enclosed in husks and with silk hanging from the upper ends, similar to corn ears. Species of corn have recently been crossed with teosinte to produce a perennial variety of corn.

Teotihuacán \ˌtā-ō-ˌtē-wä-'kän\ Largest (though not most populous) city of pre-Columbian central Mexico, about 30 mi (50 km) northeast of modern Mexico City. Teotihuacán wielded its greatest influence in the first 900 years AD, after which it was sacked by the TOLTECS. At its height, some 150,000 people lived in the city, which covered about 8 sq mi (21 sq km). Its plazas, temples, and palaces are dominated by the Pyramid of the Moon and the huge Pyramid of the Sun. Teotihuacán was the capital of one of the earliest MESOAMERICAN CIVILIZATIONS and some consider it also to have been the center of the Toltec civilization. See also TULA.

Tepe Gawra \'te-pā-gaů-'rä\ Ancient city, MESOPOTAMIA, near modern MOSUL, northwestern Iraq. It was continuously occupied from the mid-6th to the mid-2nd millennium BC and gave its name to the Gawra Period (c. 3500–2900 BC). Its remains include the earliest known temple decorated with pilasters and recesses, a style that remained dominant in Mesopotamia for centuries. Its archaeological record illustrates the transition from early Stone Age farming villages to complex settlements.

Tepe Yahya \'te-pā-'yä-yä\ Ancient trading city, southeastern Iran. Almost continuously occupied in the 5th–3rd millennium BC, it flourished as a center for the production and distribution of soapstone before being abandoned during the 2nd millennium. It was reoccupied from c. 1000 BC to c. AD 400.

tepee Tall tent dwelling used by the PLAINS INDIANS. It was suited to a nomadic life of buffalo hunting, being easily folded and dragged by a horse. It was made by stretching dressed and fitted buffalo skins over a skeleton of 20–30 wooden poles, all slanted in toward a central point and tied together near the top. A flap at the top allowed smoke to escape, and a flap at the bottom served as a doorway. The tepee became a popular symbol of all Indians, although the wigwam, wickiup, hogan, IGLOO, and LONGHOUSE were at least as important.

Tepees in Banff, Alta., Can.
ALPHA

Tepic \tā-'pēk\ City (pop., 1990: 238,000), capital of NAYARIT state, western central Mexico. It lies along the Tepic River, at the foot of an extinct volcano. Founded in 1542, much of the city retains its Spanish colonial atmosphere. Its isolation limited growth until construction of the railroad in 1912; since then it has become a commercial, industrial, and agricultural center. Nearby are TOLTEC ruins.

tequila \tə-'kē-lə\ DISTILLED liquor, usually clear in color and unaged, made from the fermented juice of the Mexican AGAVE plant. It contains 40–50% alcohol. It was developed soon after the Spaniards brought distillation to Mexico, and is named for the town of Tequila. It is mixed with lime juice and orange liqueur to make the Margarita cocktail, which is served in a glass rimmed with salt. Mescal, a stronger-flavored liquor, is made from a wild agave from Oaxaca.

Terai *or* **Tarai** \tə-'rī\ Region of northern India and southern Nepal. It runs parallel to the lower HIMALAYAN ranges and stretches from the YAMUNA RIVER to the BRAHMAPUTRA River. Numerous springs at its northern edge form several streams, including the GHAGHARA RIVER, that intersect the region and give it its marshy character. Much of the area's marshland, once malarial, has been drained and put under cultivation.

Terborch \tər-'bȯrk, *Engl* tər-'bȯrk\, **Gerard** *or* **Gerard ter Borch** (1617–1681) Dutch painter. After travels in England, Italy, Westphalia, and Spain, he returned home in 1648 and settled in Deventer in 1654. His works consist almost equally of portraits and genre paintings. By subtlety of tonal gradations and mastery of rendering diverse textures, he achieved extraordinarily rich effects with the clothing in his portraits. His superb color sense is seen to advantage in his interior genre pieces, in which he depicted with grace and fidelity the atmosphere of well-to-do middle-class life in 17th-century Holland.

Terbrugghen \tər-'brü-gən\, **Hendrik** *or* **Hendrick ter Brugghen** (c. 1588–1629) Dutch painter. He reportedly spent 10 years in Italy, and on his return to Utrecht in 1615 his work showed the strong influence of CARAVAGGIO. His two versions of *The Calling of St. Matthew* (c. 1617,

1621) reflect knowledge of Caravaggio's treatment of the same subject. He is most indebted to Caravaggio for his chiaroscuro, though his own light is more atmospheric and silvery, as in *The Flute Player* (1621). His masterpiece is *St. Sebastian Attended by Irene and Her Maid* (1625). With GERRIT VAN HONTHORST, he was a leader of the UTRECHT SCHOOL.

"The Flute Player," oil painting by Terbrugghen, 1621; in the Staatliche Kunstsammlungen, Kassel, Ger.

BY COURTESY OF THE STAATLICHE KUNSTSAMMLUNGEN, KASSEL, GER

Terence *orig.* **Publius Terentius Afer** (c. 195–159? BC) Roman comic dramatist. Born in Carthage as a slave, he was taken to Rome, where he was educated and later freed. His six extant verse plays are *The Woman of Andros, The Mother-in-Law, The Self-Tormentor, The Eunuch, Phormio,* and *The Brothers.* Produced between 166 and 160 BC, they were based on Greek originals (including four by MENANDER); Terence eliminated their original prologues, used contemporary colloquial Latin, and introduced a measure of realism. He influenced such later dramatists as MOLIÈRE and WILLIAM SHAKESPEARE.

Teresa (of Calcutta), Mother *orig.* **Agnes Gonxha Bojaxhiu** (1910–1997) Albanian-born nun, founder of the Roman Catholic Order of the Missionaries of Charity. The daughter of a grocer, she became a nun and went to India as a young woman. After studying nursing, she moved to the slums; in 1948 she founded her order, which served the blind, the aged, lepers, the disabled, and the dying. In 1963 the Indian government awarded her the Padmashri ("Lord of the Lotus") for her services to the people of India, and in 1971 Pope PAUL VI awarded her the first Pope John XXIII Peace Prize. In 1979 she received the Nobel Peace Prize. Although in her later years she suffered from a worsening heart condition, Mother Teresa continued to serve the poor and sick and also spoke out against divorce, contraception, and abortion. Her order included hundreds of centers in more than 90 countries with some 4,000 nuns and hundreds of thousands of lay workers. She was succeeded by the Indian-born Sister Nirmala. The process to declare her a saint began within two years of her death, and Pope JOHN PAUL II issued a special dispensation to expedite the process.

Teresa of Ávila, St. *orig.* **Teresa de Cepeda y Ahumada** (1515–1582) Spanish Carmelite nun, mystic, and saint. After entering a convent around the age of 20, she fell seriously ill. She underwent a religious awakening in 1555 and, despite her frail health, initiated the Carmelite Reform, leading the order's return to its original austere practices, including poverty and seclusion from the world. Against some opposition, she opened new convents (the first in 1562) under the reformed order throughout Spain. St. JOHN OF THE CROSS joined her in her efforts, establishing reformed Carmelite monasteries. Her doctrines have been accepted as the classical exposition of the contemplative life, and her spiritual writings are still widely read today, among them *The Interior Castle* (1588). In 1970 she became the first woman elevated to the position of Doctor of the Church.

Tereshkova \ˌter-əsh-ˈkȯ-və\, **Valentina (Vladimirovna)** (born 1937) Russian cosmonaut. An accomplished parachutist, she was accepted for the cosmonaut program in 1961. In 1963 she became the first woman in space, making 48 orbits in 71 hours aboard VOSTOK 6. She left the program after her flight and served in various governmental positions until the early 1990s. She was named a hero of the Soviet Union and twice awarded the Order of Lenin.

Terkel \ˈtər-kəl\, **Studs** *orig.* **Louis Turkel** (born 1912) U.S. radio personality and author. Born in New York City, he moved with his family to Chicago when he was 8. He gave up a legal career to become a radio disk jockey and interviewer, exposure that led to his own television show in 1950. In 1953, blacklisted from television for his leftist leanings, he returned to radio, continuing at the same station for 45 years. His books include *Division Street* (1967), about Chicago; *Hard Times* (1970), about the Depression; *Working* (1974), on Americans and their jobs; *The Good War,* on World War II (1984, Pulitzer Prize); and *Race* (1992), on American feelings about race.

Terman, Lewis M(adison) (1877–1956) U.S. psychologist. After joining the faculty of Stanford University in 1910, he revised the Binet-Simon intelligence scale and published the Stanford-Binet IQ test (1916), which soon was widely adopted in the U.S. During World War I he developed group intelligence testing for the U.S. Army, and in 1921 he launched a long-term program for the study of gifted children. He wrote *The Measurement of Intelligence* (1916) and coauthored *Genetic Studies of Genius* (5 vols., 1926–59).

termite Any of 1,900 species (order Isoptera) of mostly tropical, social, cellulose-eating insects that are usually soft-bodied and wingless. Intestinal microorganisms enable them to digest cellulose. Termite colonies consist of a fertile queen and king (reproductives), workers (the most numerous), and soldiers (see CASTE). Kings are less than an inch long (1–2 cm), but a queen may grow to more than 4 in. (11 cm). Workers and soldiers are sterile and blind. They survive two to five years; reproductives may live for 60–70 years. Termites live in a sealed, humid nest in wood or underground. Underground nests may be built up into a mound. Periodically, alates (winged, sighted forms) develop and leave the nest to start a new colony. Termites eat chiefly wood. Soil-dwelling termites attack wood that is in contact with the ground; wood-dwelling termites, requiring less humidity than soil-dwellers, attack trees, posts, and wooden buildings.

tern Any of about 40 species (subfamily Sterninae, family Laridae) of slender, web-footed, migratory water birds found almost worldwide. Species vary from 8 to 22 in. (20–55 cm) long. The plumage is white, black-and-white, or black; the sharply pointed bill is black, red, or yellow; and the feet are red or black. Most species have long, pointed wings and a forked tail. Terns plunge into the water to catch crustaceans and fishes. They breed colonially, usually on the ground on islands. See also ARCTIC TERN.

terneplate \ˈtərn-ˌplāt\ STEEL sheet with a coating of terne metal, an alloy of LEAD and TIN applied by dipping the steel in molten metal. The lead content gives terneplate a dull appearance, a noncorrosive surface, and solderability. The tin (12–50% of the alloy) wets the steel, making possible the union of lead and iron, which would otherwise not alloy. While it is still used for roofing, gutters and downspouts, casket linings, gasoline tanks, oil cans, and various containers, it has largely been replaced by other, more durable steel products that are easier to manufacture. See also GALVANIZING, TINPLATING.

terpene See ISOPRENOID

terra-cotta (Italian: "baked earth") Fairly coarse, porous clay that, when fired, assumes a color ranging from dull ochre to red. Terra-cotta objects are usually left unglazed and are often of a utilitarian kind, because of their cheapness, versatility, and durability. Small terra-cotta figures from 3000 BC have been found in Greece and others throughout the Roman empire from the 4th century BC. The use of terra-cotta virtually died out when the Roman empire collapsed, but it was revived in Italy and Germany in the 15th century.

"Virgin and Child," polychromed and gilded terra-cotta relief by Andrea del Verrocchio, c. 1470; in the Metropolitan Museum of Art, New York City.

BY COURTESY OF THE METROPOLITAN MUSEUM OF ART, NEW YORK CITY, ROGERS FUND 1909

Terranova Pausania See OLBIA

terrapin Any omnivorous aquatic TURTLE of the family Emydidae, especially the diamondback terrapin (*Malaclemys terrapin*). The diamondback inhabits salt marshes and coasts from New England to the Gulf of Mexico. It has raised diamond-shaped patterns on its brownish or black upper shell. The female attains a shell length of about 9 in. (23 cm); the male grows to about 6 in. (14 cm). The eight species of the turtle genus *Pseudemys* (or *Chrysemys*) are sometimes referred to as ter-

S T U V

rapins. They inhabit freshwaters from the northeastern U.S. to Argentina. The female's shell is 6–16 in. (15–40 cm) long. Infant red-eared turtles *(P. scripta elegans)* are sold in pet shops.

Diamondback terrapin (*Malaclemys terrapin*).

LEONARD LEE RUE III FROM THE NATIONAL AUDUBON SOCIETY COLLECTION/PHOTO RESEARCHERS—EB INC.

terrazzo \tə-ˈrät-sō, tə-ˈra-zō\ Type of flooring consisting of marble chips set in cement or epoxy resin that is poured and ground smooth when dry. Terrazzo was ubiquitous in the 20th century in commercial and institutional buildings. Available in many colors, it forms a hard, smooth, durable surface that is easily cleaned.

terrier Any of several dog breeds developed, mostly in England, to find and kill vermin and for use in the sports of foxhunting and dog fighting. Bred to fight and kill, they often were pugnacious but are now bred for a friendlier temperament. Because terriers had to fit in rodent burrows, most breeds are small and lean and have a rough, wiry coat that requires little maintenance. They have a long head, square jaw, and deep-set eyes. All terriers are vocal and inclined to chase and confront. Most breeds were named for the place where they were developed. See also AIREDALE terrier, BEDLINGTON terrier, BOSTON TERRIER, BULL TERRIER, DANDIE DINMONT terrier, FOX TERRIER, IRISH TERRIER, PIT BULL TERRIER, SCOTTISH TERRIER, YORKSHIRE TERRIER.

Terror, Reign of See REIGN OF TERROR

territorial behavior In zoology, the methods by which an animal, or group of animals, protects its territory from incursions by others of its species. Territorial boundaries may be marked by sounds (e.g., BIRDSONG), scents, or even by piles of dung. If such advertisement does not discourage intruders, chases and fighting follow. Territories may be seasonal (usually for nesting and feeding the young) or maintained permanently for hunting and living. Territorial behavior benefits the species by permitting mating and rearing young without interruption and by preventing overcrowding and minimizing competition for food.

territorial waters Waters under the sovereign jurisdiction of a nation or state, including both marginal sea and inland waters. The concept originated in the 17th-century controversy over the status of the sea. Though the doctrine that the sea must be free to all was upheld, a nation's jurisdiction over its coastal waters was also recognized. Nations subscribing to the Law of the SEA observe a territorial limit of 12 nautical mi (22 km) from shore. Territorial rights include the airspace above those waters and the seabed below them. See also HIGH SEAS.

terrorism Systematic use of violence to create a general climate of fear in a population and thereby to bring about a particular political objective. It has been used throughout history and the world by political organizations of both the left and the right, by nationalist and ethnic groups, and by revolutionaries. Though usually thought of as an instrument for destabilizing or overthrowing existing political institutions, terror has also been employed internally by governments against their own subjects to enforce adherence to the national ideology; examples include the reigns of certain Roman emperors, the French Revolution (see REIGN OF TERROR), Nazi Germany, and the Soviet Union in the Stalinist era. Terrorism's impact has been magnified by the deadliness and technological sophistication of modern-day weapons and the capability of modern media to disseminate news of such attacks instantaneously throughout the world. The deadliest terrorist attack ever occurred in September 2001, when suicide terrorists hijacked four commercial airplanes and crashed two of them into the twin towers of the WORLD TRADE CENTER complex and one into the PENTAGON building in Washington, D.C.; the fourth plane crashed near Pittsburgh, Pennsylvania. The crashes resulted in the collapse of much of the World Trade Center complex, the destruction of part of the southwest side of the Pentagon, and the deaths of 266 people aboard the planes and thousands more in the buildings or in nearby areas.

Terry, Eli (1772–1852) U.S. clockmaker. Born in East Windsor, Conn., he established a factory in Plymouth, Conn., in 1793. He made a specialty of one-day wooden shelf clocks, especially his "perfected wood clock" known as the "Terry clock" (1814). Using interchangeable parts made by mechanized techniques, his production rose to as high as 10,000–12,000 Terry clocks per year.

Terry, (Alice) Ellen (1847–1928) English actress. Born into a family of actors, she made her stage debut at 9. She acted with several companies before joining HENRY IRVING as his leading lady (1878–1902), playing a variety of Shakespearean roles in a notable partnership. Her warmth, gentleness, and beauty made her one of the most popular actresses in Britain and the U.S., and she continued to act until 1925. She conducted a famous correspondence with GEORGE BERNARD SHAW. (EDWARD) GORDON CRAIG was her son.

Tertiary period \ˈtər-shē-ˌer-ē\ Interval of geologic time, 65–1.8 million years ago. It constitutes the first of the two periods of the CENOZOIC era, the second being the QUATERNARY. The Tertiary has five subdivisions: (from oldest to youngest) the PALEOCENE, EOCENE, OLIGOCENE, MIOCENE, and PLIOCENE epochs. During most of the Tertiary, the spatial distribution of the major continents was largely similar to that of today. Emergence and submergence of land bridges between continents critically affected the distribution of both terrestrial and marine animals and plants. Virtually all the existing major mountain ranges were formed either partly or wholly during the Tertiary.

Tertullian \tər-ˈtəl-yən\ (c. AD 155–after 220) Early Christian theologian and moralist. Born and educated in Carthage, he became impressed by the courage, morality, and uncompromising monotheism of Christian martyrs, and converted to Christianity. He became a leading member of the African church and one of the early Apologists. He devoted himself to writing for 20 years, producing works on such topics as defense of the faith, prayer and devotion, and morality, as well as the first Christian book on baptism, *De baptismo*. Later, dismayed by the laxity he witnessed among even his orthodox contemporaries, he joined the prophetic movement known as MONTANISM, then left it to form his own sect, which survived in Africa until the 5th century.

terza rima \ˈtert-sə-ˈrē-mə\ Verse form consisting of tercets, or three-line stanzas, in which the second line of each rhymes with the first and third lines of the next. The series ends with a separate line that rhymes with the second line of the last stanza, so that the rhyme scheme is *aba*, *bcb*, *cdc*, . . ., *yzy*, *z*. DANTE, in *The Divine Comedy* (c. 1310–14), was the first to use terza rima in a long poem. A demanding form, it has not been widely adopted in languages less rich in rhymes than Italian. It was introduced into England by THOMAS WYATT in the 16th century. Poets who have experimented with terza rima include PERCY B. SHELLEY, ROBERT BROWNING, ELIZABETH BARRETT BROWNING, and W. H. AUDEN; DEREK WALCOTT's book-length *Omeros* is written in modified terza rima.

Teschen \ˈte-shən\ Former eastern European duchy. It was originally a principality linked to the Polish duchy of SILESIA, and passed in 1526 to the HABSBURGS. Though most of Silesia was seized by PRUSSIA in 1742, Teschen remained under Habsburg rule until the end of World War I. In 1920 Poland and Czechoslovakia contested and then divided the region; Poland received the eastern district, including the city of Teschen (now Cieszyn), while Czechoslovakia received the rest. The Czechs were forced to cede their section to Poland in 1938. Germany occupied the entire region until after World War II, when the 1920 borders were restored.

Tesla.

CULVER PICTURES

Tesla, Nikola (1856–1943) Croatian-U.S. inventor and researcher. He studied in Austria and Bohemia and worked in Paris before coming to the U.S. in 1884. He worked for THOMAS ALVA EDISON and GEORGE WESTINGHOUSE, but preferred independent research. His inventions made production and distribution of alternating-current electric power possible. He invented an induction coil that is still widely used in radio technology, the Tesla coil (c. 1890); his system was used by Westinghouse to light the 1893 World's Columbian Exposition. He established an electric-power station at Niagara Falls in 1893. He discovered terrestrial stationary waves (1899–1900), proving that the earth is a conductor. Due to lack of funds, many of his ideas remained in his notebooks, which are still examined by engineers for inventive clues.

Test Act (1673) Act passed by the British Parliament that required holders of civil and military offices to profess the established religion and to receive Holy Communion according to the rites of the Church of England. Though directed primarily against Roman Catholics, it extended in principle to all non-Anglicans; it was modified in 1689 to enable most non-Catholics to qualify. An act adopted in 1828 removed the test. In the U.S. Constitution, Article VI prescribes that "no religious test" shall be required for any officeholder. See also Catholic Emancipation.

testcross Experiment in which an organism with unknown genetic makeup is mated with an organism whose entire genetic makeup for a trait is known, to determine which genes are carried by the former. In a breed of dog, for example, in which the gene for black coat color is dominant over the gene for red coat color (see dominance), a dog with a black-colored coat may be pure (with two genes for black coat color) or hybrid (with one gene for black and one for red). When mated with a red-coated dog (which always has two genes for red coat color only), if all the offspring are black the black-coated parent must be pure, whereas if some of the young are red the parent must be hybrid.

testes *or* **testicles** Male reproductive organs (see reproductive system). Humans have two oval-shaped testes 1.5–2 in. (4–5 cm) long that produce sperm and androgens (mainly testosterone), contained in a sac (scrotum) behind the penis. Each testis is divided into 200–400 lobes containing three to 10 very thin coiled tubes (seminiferous tubules) each, which produce the sperm and contract to expel them through a complex network of canals to another structure in the scrotum, the epididymis, for temporary storage. The cells in the testes are undeveloped in early childhood; at puberty they are stimulated by hormones to develop into fertile sperm cells.

testing machine Machine used in materials science to determine the properties of a material. Machines have been devised to measure tensile strength, strength in compression, shear, and bending (see strength of materials), ductility, hardness, impact strength (see impact test), fracture toughness, creep, and fatigue. Standardization of machines and tests is the province of the International Organization for Standardization, American National Standards Institute, British Standards Institution, and many governmental bodies.

testosterone \tes-'tä-stər-ˌōn\ Masculinizing sex hormone produced by the testes. It is responsible for the development of the male sex organs and secondary sex characteristics (e.g., facial hair, masculine musculature, deep voice, and male-pattern baldness). Testosterone can be manufactured by modifying other, less expensive steroids. It is used in medicine to treat testicular insufficiency, certain types of breast cancer, and frigidity, as well as to suppress lactation.

tetanus \'te-tə-nəs\ *or* **lockjaw** Acute bacterial disease caused by *Clostridium tetani* (see clostridium). Spores of this organism are common, especially in soil; it thrives away from oxygen in deep wounds, especially punctures. Its toxin stimulates nerves, causing muscle rigidity with frequent spasms. This may occur around the site of the wound or, if the toxin reaches spinal motor ganglia via the bloodstream, throughout the body. The jaw muscles are almost always involved (lockjaw). Vaccination every four years is the best protection; an antitoxin prevents or delays symptoms in cases of suspect wounds but has limited value once they develop. Treatment usually includes antibiotics, sedatives, and muscle relaxants. Recovered patients are not immune.

Tetley (Jr.), Glen(ford Andrew) (born 1926) American dancer, choreographer, and ballet director. He trained in modern dance with Hanya Holm and Martha Graham. Between 1946 and 1962 he danced in Broadway musical productions as well as with dance companies such as the American Ballet Theatre. He became a choreographer in 1962, forming his own company and creating *Pierrot Lunaire.* Subsequently he staged works with most of the major dance companies throughout the world. Tetley's work helped to bring about a synthesis of modern dance and classical ballet. His creative staging and daring, often sexual, subject matter were sometimes controversial, but Tetley was praised for the passion and strong physicality of his work.

Teton Range \'tē-ˌtän\ Range of the northern Rocky Mtns., northwestern Wyoming. It extends 40 mi (64 km) across from the southern boundary of Yellowstone National Park to Teton Pass. Some foothills reach as far as southeastern Idaho. Many peaks exceed 12,000 ft (3,700 m); the highest point is Grand Teton (13,766 ft, or 4,196 m), which was first ascended in 1872. Much of the range lies within Grand Teton National Park.

tetra Any of numerous attractively colored freshwater South American and African fishes (family Characidae), often kept in home aquariums. Tetras are small, lively, hardy, and unaggressive. The slender neon tetra *(Paracheirodon,* or *Hyphessobrycon, innesi)* has gleaming red hind parts and a neonlike blue-green stripe on its sides. The glowlight tetra *(Hemigrammus erythrozonus)* has a shining red stripe along each side. The body of the silver tetra *(Ctenobrycon spilurus)* is flattened sidewise.

Glowlight tetras (*Hemigrammus erythrozonus*).

JANE BURTON—BRUCE COLEMAN LTD.

tetracycline Any of a class of broad-spectrum antibiotics with a common basic structure, including chlortetracycline (Aureomycin), tetracycline itself, and doxycycline. They may be isolated directly from several species of actinomycetes of the genus *Streptomyces* (see streptomyces) or modified from the compounds isolated. They are also effective against rickettsia, chlamydia, and mycoplasma. Overuse of these and other antibiotics has led to drug resistance in microorganisms.

Tetragrammaton \ˌte-trə-'gra-mə-ˌtän\ (Greek: "having four letters") Four Hebrew consonants *yod, he, vav,* and *he*—variously transliterated as JHVH, JHWH, YHWH, or YHVH—that together represent the name of God. Traditionally the tetragrammaton is not pronounced; Jehovah and Yahweh are two vocalizations of it.

tetrarch (Greek: "ruler of a quarter") In Greco-Roman antiquity, the ruler of a principality, originally the ruler of one-quarter of a region or province. The first tetrarchs ruled the four tetrarchies of Thessaly under Philip II of Macedonia. Tetrarchs ruled in Galatia (in Asia Minor) before the Roman conquest (169 BC), and still later in Hellenized Syria and Palestine, where the title denoted the semi-independent ruler of a divided kingdom or minor district. Herod the Great's realm after his death (4 BC) was ruled by his three sons, two of whom were called tetrarchs.

Teutoburg Forest \'tü-tə-ˌbərg\ *German* **Teutoburger Wald** \'tȯi-tə-ˌbu̇r-gər-ˌvält\ Range of forested hills, northern Germany. It was the scene of a battle in AD 9 in which German tribes defeated the Roman legions, thus establishing the Rhine River as the German–Latin border. The Hermannsdenkmal, a colossal statue commemorating the battle, stands outside Detmold. There are numerous health and holiday resorts in the forest's small hill towns.

Teutonic Order *or* **Teutonic Knights** \tü-'tä-nik\ *officially* **House of the Hospitallers of St. Mary of the Teutons** Religious order important in eastern Europe in the late Middle Ages. Founded in 1189–90 to nurse the sick in Palestine during the Third Crusade, it was militarized in 1198 and given land in Jerusalem and Germany. It transferred its base of operations to eastern Europe in the 13th century, gaining control of Prussia by 1283 and making Marienburg the center of a military principality (1309–1525). The order extended its influence until defeated at the Battle of Tannenberg (1410). Another Polish victory in 1466 forced the knights to cede land to Poland and become vassals of the Polish king. Napoleon dissolved the order in 1809 and redistributed its remaining lands. In 1834 the Austrian emperor refounded it as a charitable religious order, and it is now headquartered in Vienna.

Tewodros II \tā-'wȯ-drȯs\ *or* **Theodore II** (1818?–1868) Emperor of Ethiopia (1855–68), often called Ethiopia's first modern ruler. He came to the throne through the conquest of other chiefs. He reunified the various Ethiopian kingdoms into one empire, attempted to focus loyalty around the government rather than the Ethiopian church, and worked to abolish the feudal system. Though he failed in his aims, his example was followed by his successors. His reign ended when a British force under Robert Napier attacked in response to the imprisonment of several British citizens.

Texas State (pop., 1997 est.: 19,439,000), southwestern U.S. Occupying 266,807 sq mi (691,030 sq km), it is the second-largest state in both area and population. Its capital is AUSTIN. Plains and hills make up the terrain, which ranges from the fertile prairie of the Coastal Plains on the Gulf of MEXICO through the central GREAT PLAINS grasslands to the arid High Plains of the Panhandle. The forerunners of West Texas Indians inhabited the area as much as 37,000 years ago. Some of the tribes later formed the CADDO confederacy. Indians, including APACHES, lived in the region when the Spanish arrived in 1528. The first settlement was attempted in 1685 by the French, who claimed the region as part of Louisiana. In 1803 the U.S. acquired the French claim in the LOUISIANA PURCHASE, but relinquished it to Spain by treaty in 1819. It became part of Mexico at Mexican independence in 1821. In 1836 Texans declared independence from Mexico as the Republic of Texas (see STEPHEN AUSTIN, SAM HOUSTON). After a 10-year struggle to remain independent, Texas became the 28th U.S. state in 1845. Its boundary with Mexico was fixed after the MEXICAN WAR (1848). In the AMERICAN CIVIL WAR, it seceded from the Union (1861) and was readmitted in 1870. After the war, railroad building and increased shipping helped expand the economy, and the discovery of oil in 1901 transformed it. While Texas still leads all other states in oil and natural-gas production and in petroleum-refining capacity, its manufacture of electronics, aerospace components, and other high-technology items is increasingly important. It is also the U.S.'s leading cotton, beef-cattle and sheep producer.

Texas, University of State university system with 13 campuses throughout the state. It was founded in 1883. The main campus, at Austin, is the second most populous campus in the U.S. (enrollment 48,000). It is a comprehensive research and teaching institution, offering about 100 undergraduate programs and about 190 graduate degree programs. There are more than 85 organized research units on campus, including centers for biomedical research, economic geology, and cognitive science. The LYNDON B. JOHNSON Library and Museum is located there. Total enrollment for the University of Texas system is about 142,000.

Texas A&M University State university system based in College Station. The outgrowth of the Agricultural and Mechanical College of Texas (founded 1876), the system includes eight other branch campuses throughout the state. The College Station campus comprises 10 colleges and offers about five undergraduate, 15 graduate, and two professional degrees. The Health Science Center, which includes a college of medicine, was created in 1997. Enrollment at College Station is about 42,000. The Galveston campus specializes in marine science and maritime studies.

Texas Instruments, Inc. U.S. manufacturer of calculators, microprocessors, and digital signal processors. The direct antecedent to the company, which is headquartered in Dallas, Texas, was founded by John Karcher and Eugene McDermott in 1930 to provide seismographic data for the petroleum industry. In 1951 the company changed its name to Texas Instruments Inc. (TI), and the following year it purchased a license from Western Electric to manufacture transistors. From 1954 to 1958 TI was the only firm capable of producing silicon transistors in quantity. In 1958 Jack Kilby, a researcher at TI, coinvented the integrated circuit (IC), and TI received funding to develop ICs for use in ballistic missile guidance systems. In 1967 Kilby invented the basic design for handheld calculators. The 1970s saw continued growth in TI's semiconductor business, particularly after 1973, when the company began manufacturing dynamic random-access memory (DRAM, commonly shortened to RAM) chips for use in computers. In 1982 TI introduced the single-chip digital signal processor (DSP), whose market the company went on to dominate.

Texas Rangers Loosely organized police force in Texas. The first members were "minutemen" hired by U.S. settlers as protection against Indian attacks in the 1830s. They did not wear uniforms or salute their officers but were highly disciplined and known for their marksmanship, making the six-shooter (the Colt revolver) the weapon of the West. At their peak in the 1870s, the Rangers brought law and order to hundreds of miles of Texas frontier. In 1935 they were merged with the state highway patrol.

Texcoco \tās-'kō-kō\, **Lake** Lake, central Mexico. Originally one of the five lakes of the Valley of Mexico, Texcoco has been drained by channels and a tunnel to the PÁNUCO RIVER since the early 17th century. It now occupies only a small area surrounded by salt marshes just east of MEXICO CITY. TENOCHTITLÁN, the Aztec capital, stood on islands in old Lake Texcoco, connected to the mainland by causeways.

textile Any filament, fiber, or YARN that can be made into fabric or cloth, and the resulting material itself. The word originally referred only to woven fabrics but now includes knitted, bonded, felted, and tufted fabrics as well. The basic raw materials used in textile production are fibers, either obtained from natural sources (e.g., WOOL) or produced from chemical substances (e.g., NYLON and POLYESTER). Textiles are used for wearing apparel, household linens and bedding, upholstery, draperies and curtains, wall coverings, rugs and carpets, and bookbindings, in addition to being used widely in industry.

Tezcatlipoca \,tās-kät-lē-'pō-kə\ Omnipotent god of the AZTEC pantheon, and god of the constellation Ursa Major. The protector of slaves, he severely punished masters who ill-treated them. He is said to have put an end to the TOLTECS' golden age. Each year his worshipers selected a handsome prisoner of war who was allowed to live in princely luxury for a year before being sacrificed. Tezcatlipoca is represented in art with an obsidian mirror, in which he sees all, on his chest or in place of a foot.

Thackeray, William Makepeace (1811–1863) English novelist. He studied law and art but soon became a prolific writer for periodicals, using a variety of pen names. His early writings appear in such volumes as *The Book of Snobs* (1848), a collection of his articles from *PUNCH;* and *Miscellanies* (1855–57), which includes the historical novel *Barry Lyndon* (1844). His fame rests chiefly on the novels *Vanity Fair* (1847–48), a panoramic survey of English manners and human frailties set in the Napoleonic era, and *Henry Esmond* (1852), set in the early 18th century. *Pendennis* (1848–50) is a partly fictionalized autobiography. In his time he was regarded as the only possible rival of CHARLES DICKENS for his pictures of contemporary life, but his popularity declined in the 20th century.

Thackeray, detail of an oil painting by Samuel Laurence; in the National Portrait Gallery, London.

BY COURTESY OF THE NATIONAL PORTRAIT GALLERY, LONDON

Thailand \'tī-,land\ *officially* **Kingdom of Thailand** *formerly* **Siam** Kingdom, S.East Asia. Area: 198,115 sq mi (513,115 sq km). Population (1997 est.): 60,602,000. Capital: BANGKOK. The population is predominantly Thai, with significant Chinese, KHMER, and Malay minorities. Language: Thai (official). Religion: Buddhism (official). Currency: Thai baht. The country encompasses forested hills and mountains, a central plain containing the CHAO PHRAYA River delta, and a plateau in the northeast. Its market economy is based largely on services, light industries, and agriculture. It is a large producer of tungsten and tin. Among its chief agricultural products are rice, corn, rubber, soybeans, and pineapples; manufactures include clothing, canned goods, electrical circuits, and cement. Tourism is also important. It is a constitutional monarchy with two legislative houses; its chief of state is the king, and the head of government is the prime minister. The region of Thailand has been continuously occupied for 20,000 years. It was part of the MON and Khmer kingdoms from the 9th century AD. Thai-speaking peoples emigrated from China c. 10th century. During the 13th century two Thai states emerged: the SUKHOTHAI KINGDOM, founded c. 1220 after a successful revolt against the Khmer, and CHIANG MAI, founded in 1296 after defeating the Mon. In 1351 the Thai kingdom of AYUTTHAYA succeeded Sukhothai. The Burmese were its most powerful rival, occupying it briefly in the 16th century and destroying it in 1767. The CHAKRI dynasty came to power in 1782, moving the capital to Bangkok and extending the empire along the MALAY PENINSULA and into Laos and Cambodia. It was named Siam in 1856. Though Western influence increased during the 19th century, Siam's rulers avoided colonization by granting concessions to Eu-

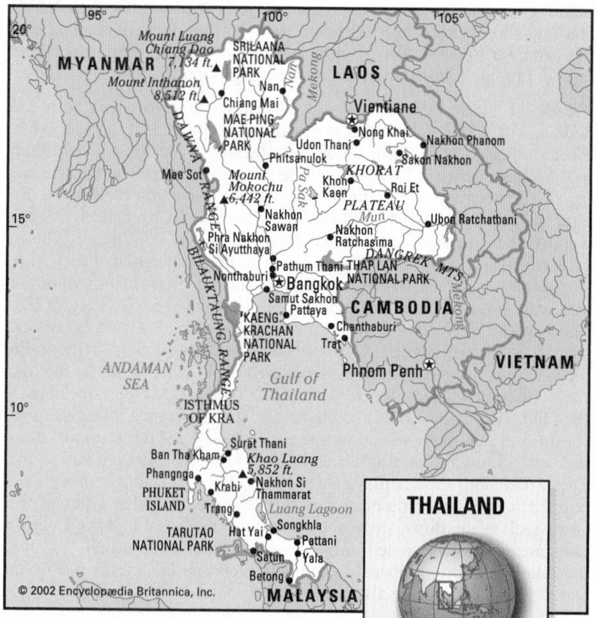

ropean countries; it was the only S.East Asian nation able to do so. In 1917 it entered World War I on the side of the Allies. It became a constitutional monarchy following a military coup in 1932 and was officially renamed Thailand in 1939. It was occupied by Japan in World War II. It participated in the KOREAN WAR as a U.N. forces member. It was allied with South Vietnam in the VIETNAM WAR. Along with other S.East Asian nations, it suffered from the 1990s regional financial crisis.

Thailand, Gulf of *formerly* **Gulf of Siam** Inlet of the CHINA SEA. Mostly bordering Thailand, though Cambodia and Vietnam form its southeastern shore, it is 300–350 mi (500–560 km) wide and 450 mi (725 km) long. Thailand's main harbors lie along its shores, and its waters are important fishing grounds.

Thalberg, Irving G(rant) (1899–1936) U.S. film executive. Born in New York City, he skipped college (because doctors had told him that a rheumatic heart condition would kill him before age 30), joined Universal Pictures, and soon became its studio manager in Hollywood. Hired by MGM as head of production in 1925, he became known as the "boy wonder of Hollywood." He tightly controlled MGM's output by supervising script selection and final film editing, and was responsible for the high quality of such movies as *The Barretts of Wimpole Street* (1934), *Mutiny on the Bounty* (1935), and *Romeo and Juliet* (1936) and for making stars of Nelson Eddy and Jeanette MacDonald with *Naughty Marietta* (1935). He died of pneumonia at 37.

Thales of Miletus \'thā-lēz...mī-'lē-təs\ (fl. 6th century BC) Greek philosopher. None of his writings survive, and no contemporary sources exist. The claim that Thales was the founder of Western philosophy rests primarily on ARISTOTLE, who wrote that he was the first to suggest a single material substratum for the universe, namely water. Thales' significance lies in his attempt to explain nature by the simplification of phenomena and in his search for causes within nature itself rather than in the caprices of anthropomorphic gods.

thalidomide \thə-'li-də-,mīd\ Drug formerly used as a sedative and to prevent morning sickness during pregnancy. Synthesized in 1954, it was introduced in almost 50 countries, including West Germany and Britain, where it became popular because it was effective and huge overdoses were not fatal. In 1961 it was found to cause CONGENITAL disorders; when it is taken in early pregnancy, some 20% of fetuses develop phocomelia (see AGENESIS) and other deformities; 5,000–10,000 such babies were born. It was never distributed for clinical use in the U.S. (see HELEN BROOKE TAUSSIG). Thalidomide appears effective against LEPROSY and certain late-stage AIDS symptoms, and is licensed for use in such treatments in some countries.

thallus \'tha-ləs\ Plant body of ALGAE, fungi (see FUNGUS), and similar simple, plantlike organisms. Composed of filaments or plates of cells, a thallus ranges in size from a single-celled structure to a complex treelike form. The photosynthetic and supportive cells tend to be organized linearly, but a thallus lacks such differentiated specialized structures as stem, leaves, and conducting tissue. Most thallus plants are currently classified as complex PROTISTS.

Thames \'temz\, **Battle of the** (October 5, 1813) Decisive U.S. victory over the British in the WAR OF 1812. After the British defeat in the Battle of Lake Erie, U.S. troops under Gen. WILLIAM H. HARRISON pursued retreating British soldiers across the Ontario peninsula. The British force of 600 regulars and 1,000 Indians under TECUMSEH met the 3,500 U.S. troops at the Thames River near Moraviantown, Ontario. The outnumbered British were quickly defeated, and Tecumseh was killed. The U.S. victory ended the Indian alliance with the British and made Harrison a national hero.

Thames River *ancient* **Tamesis** Principal river of England. It rises in the Cotswolds in GLOUCESTERSHIRE and winds 210 mi (338 km) eastward across southern central England into a great estuary, through which it empties into the North Sea. It is tidal for about 65 mi (104 km). Known by the Romans and by early English chroniclers, it has been celebrated by bards throughout history. One of the world's most important commercial waterways, it is navigable by large vessels to LONDON.

thanatology \,tha-nə-'tä-lə-jē\ Description or study of death and dying, and the psychological mechanisms of dealing with them. One influential model proposed in 1969 by the psychiatrist Elisabeth Kübler-Ross (born 1926) described five basic stages: denial, anger, bargaining, depression, and acceptance; however, not all dying persons follow a regular, clearly identifiable series of responses to their situation. Thanatology also examines attitudes toward death, the meaning and behaviors of bereavement and grief, and other matters.

Thanatos \'tha-nə-,täs\ Ancient Greek personification of death. He was the son of Nyx, goddess of night, and brother to Hypnos, god of sleep. He appeared to humans to carry them off to the underworld when the time allotted to them by the FATES had expired. Thanatos was once defeated by HERACLES, who wrestled him to save the life of ALCESTIS, and he was tricked by SISYPHUS, who wanted a second chance at life.

Thani dynasty \'tha-nē\ Ruling family of the emirate of Qatar. They are from the Tamim tribe of Arabia, which migrated eastward from the Jibrin oasis to the Qatar peninsula in the mid-19th century. There have been eight leaders from 1868 to the present. The second SHEIKH, Qassim bin Muhammad (1878–1913), is considered the emirate's founder. The seventh sheikh, Khalifa bin Hamad (r.1972–95), declared Qatar's independence from Britain in 1971 and became the first emir. The clan comprises about 40% of the native Qatari population.

Thanksgiving Day U.S. holiday. It originated in the autumn of 1621 when Plymouth governor WILLIAM BRADFORD invited neighboring Indians to join the Pilgrims for a three-day festival of recreation and feasting in gratitude for the bounty of the season, which had been partly enabled by the Indians' advice. Proclaimed as a national holiday in 1863, it is celebrated on the fourth Thursday in November; the traditional meal consists of New World foods. Canada adopted Thanksgiving as a national holiday in 1879; it is celebrated on the second Monday in October.

Thant, U (1909–1974) Third secretary-general of the UNITED NATIONS (1961–71), the first Asian to hold the post. Born in Myanmar (Burma), he was educated at the University of Yangon but had to leave before graduating. He taught high school before entering government service. Posted to the U.N. in 1952, he became Burma's U.N. ambassador in 1957. In 1961 he became acting secretary-general after DAG HAMMARSKJOLD's death; he became permanent secretary-general in 1962. In his two full terms (1962–71), he played a diplomatic role in the CUBAN MISSILE CRISIS, devised a plan to end the Congolese civil war (1962), and sent peacekeeping forces to Cyprus (1964).

Thapsus \'thap-səs\, **Battle of** (46 BC) Decisive battle in North Africa in the Roman civil war between Julius CAESAR and POMPEY (49–46). Caesar had laid siege to the seaport of Thapsus, near present-day Teboulba, Tunisia. Pompey was supported by the legions of his father-in-law,

S T U V

Quintus Metellus Scipio. When Caesar could not restrain his troops, they surged forward and overwhelmed the enemy, slaughtering about 10,000. It was the final blow delivered by Caesar against the forces of Pompey.

Thar Desert \'tär, 'tər\ *or* **Great Indian Desert** Region of hot, dry desert, northwestern India and southeastern Pakistan. Its undulating surface is composed of sand dunes separated by sandy plains and low, barren hills. Several saline lakes are found there. Covering 77,000 sq mi (200,000 sq km), it is bordered by the INDUS RIVER plain, the Aravalli Range, the Arabian Sea, and the PUNJAB plain.

Thargelia \thär-'gē-lē-ə, thär-'jē-lē-ə\ In GREEK RELIGION, a chief Athenian festival of APOLLO, celebrated on the sixth and seventh days of Thargelion (April–May). It was named after the first fruits or the first bread from the new wheat. On the first day, one or two men acting as SCAPEGOATS were led through Athens, whipped on the genitalia, and driven across the border. An official registration of adopted people took place on the second day.

Tharp, Twyla (born 1941) U.S. dancer, director, and choreographer. She was born in Portland, Ind. She danced with PAUL TAYLOR's company from 1963 to 1965, when she began to choreograph for various companies, creating such works as *Deuce Coupe* (1973), *Push Comes to Shove* (1976), *Baker's Dozen* (1979), *Nine Sinatra Songs* (1982), and *Fait Accompli* (1984). In 1965 she formed her own group, the Twyla Tharp Dance Co.; it disbanded in 1988. She was resident choreographer with the AMERICAN BALLET THEATRE 1988–91. She has also choreographed for the Broadway theater (including *The Catherine Wheel*, 1981) and several films (including *Amadeus*, 1984). Tharp is notable for her humor and particularly as one of the first American choreographers to use popular music.

Twyla Tharp.
© JACK MITCHELL

Thásos \'thä-,sȯs\ Island, northern AEGEAN SEA, northeastern Macedonia, Greece. It covers 146 sq mi (379 sq km). It was colonized c. 700 BC by Greeks from Paros, who exploited its gold mines and founded a school of sculpture. The Persians seized it in the early 5th century BC; it later came under Athens as a member of the DELIAN LEAGUE. A Macedonian dependency in 202 BC, it passed to Rome in 196 BC. The Turks ruled it from the mid-15th century AD until it was ceded to Greece in 1913. Its industries include boatbuilding, fishing, and tourism, and it has been a base for offshore oil exploration since the 1970s. Many 7th century BC–2nd century BC monuments have been found there.

Thatcher, Margaret *later* **Baroness Thatcher (of Kesteven)** *orig.* **Margaret Hilda Roberts** (born 1925) British politician and prime minister (1979–90). She earned degrees at Oxford Univ., then worked as a research chemist. After her marriage to Denis Thatcher (1951), she read for the bar and specialized in tax law. She was elected to Parliament in 1959 and served as secretary of state for education and science 1970–74. As a member of the Conservative Party's newly energetic right wing, she succeeded EDWARD HEATH as party leader in 1975. In 1979 she became Britain's first woman prime minister. She advocated individual initiative, confronted the labor unions, privatized national industries and utilities and attempted to privatize aspects of health care and education, pursued a strong monetarist policy, and endorsed a firm commitment to NATO. Her landslide victory in 1983 owed partly to her decisive leadership in the FALKLAND ISLANDS WAR. A split in party ranks over European monetary and political integration led to her resignation in 1990.

Margaret Thatcher, 1983.
AP/WIDE WORLD PHOTOS

theater Building or space in which performances are given before an audience. It contains an AUDITORIUM and stage. In ancient Greece, where Western theater began (5th century BC), theaters were constructed in natural hollows between hills. The audience sat in a tiered semicircle facing the orchestra, a flat circular space where the action took place. Behind the orchestra was the SKENE. The theaters of Elizabethan England were open to the sky, with the audience looking on from tiered galleries or a courtyard. The main innovation was the rectangular thrust stage, surrounded on three sides by spectators. The first permanent indoor theater was ANDREA PALLADIO's Olimpico Theater in Vicenza, Italy (1585). The Farnese Theater in Parma (1618) was designed with a horseshoe-shaped auditorium and the first permanent PROSCENIUM arch. Baroque European court theaters followed this arrangement, elaborating on the interior with tiered boxes for royalty. RICHARD WAGNER's Festspielhaus in Bayreuth, Germany (1876), with its fan-shaped seating plan, deep orchestra pit, and darkened auditorium, departed from the Baroque stratified auditorium and reintroduced classical principles that are still in use. The proscenium theater prevailed in the 17th–20th century; though still popular in the 20th century, it was supplemented by other types of theaters, such as the thrust stage and THEATER-IN-THE-ROUND. In Asia, stage arrangements have remained simple, with the audience usually grouped informally around an open space; notable exceptions are the NO drama and KABUKI of Japan. See also AMPHITHEATER, ODEUM.

theater Live performance of dramatic actions in order to tell a story or create a spectacle. The word derives from the Greek *theatron* ("place of seeing"). Theater is one of the oldest and most important art forms in cultures worldwide. While the script is the basic element of theatrical performance, it also relies in varying degrees on acting, singing, and dancing, as well as on technical aspects of production such as STAGE DESIGN and lighting. Theater is thought to have its earliest origins in religious ritual; it often enacts myths or stories central to the belief structure of a culture, or creates comedy through travesty of such narratives. In Western civilization, theater began in ancient Greece and was adapted in Roman times; it was revived in the medieval LITURGICAL dramas and flourished in the Renaissance with the Italian COMMEDIA dell'arte and in the 17th–18th century with such established companies as the COMÉDIE-FRANÇAISE. Varying theatrical forms may evolve to suit the tastes of different audiences (e.g., in Japan, the KABUKI of the townspeople and the NO drama of the court). In Europe and the U.S. in the 19th and early 20th century, theater was a major source of entertainment for all social classes, with forms ranging from BURLESQUE and VAUDEVILLE to serious dramas performed in the style of the MOSCOW ART THEATRE. Though the MUSICALS of BROADWAY and the FARCES of London's West End retain their popular appeal, the rise of television and movies has eroded audiences for live theater and tended to limit its spectators to an educated elite. See also LITTLE THEATER.

theater-in-the-round *or* **arena stage** Theater in which the stage is located in the center of the auditorium with the audience seated on all sides. The form evolved from Greek theater and was used in medieval times. From the 17th century the PROSCENIUM stage limited audience seating to the area directly in front of the stage. In the 1930s, plays at Moscow's Realistic Theater were produced in the round and the arena stage began to gain favor in Europe and the U.S. Its advantages are its informality and the rapport it creates between audience and actors, but it requires actors to constantly turn to address new sections of the audience.

theater of fact See theater of FACT

theater of the absurd See theater of the ABSURD

Theatre Guild U.S. theatrical society. Founded in New York in 1918 by Lawrence Langner (1890–1962) and others, the group proposed to produce high-quality, noncommercial plays. Its board of directors shared responsibility for choice of plays, management, and production. After the premiere of GEORGE BERNARD SHAW's *Heartbreak House* in 1920, the Guild became his U.S. agent and staged 15 of his plays. It also produced successful plays by EUGENE O'NEILL, MAXWELL ANDERSON, and ROBERT SHERWOOD and featured such actors as the LUNTS and HELEN HAYES. It helped develop the American MUSICAL by staging *Porgy and Bess* (1935), *Oklahoma!* (1943), and *Carousel* (1945), produced the radio series *The-*

S T U V

atre Guild on the Air (1945–53), and presented plays on television. In 1950 it became part of the American National Theatre and Academy (ANTA).

Théâtre National Populaire \tā-'ä-trᵊ-nȧ-syȯ-'nȧl-pȯ-pᵫ-'ler\ (TNP) French national theater created in 1920 to bring theater to the general public. Under the direction of its founder, Firmin Gémier (1869–1933), the TNP initially offered productions from the other national companies. In 1951 it established a permanent company under Jean Vilar 1951–63, which gave 150 performances a year in and around Paris, charging ticket prices competitive with the movies. By 1959 it was as popular as the COMÉDIE-FRANÇAISE. In 1972, in an effort to decentralize the theater, the government transferred its title to a subsidized theater company in Lyon.

theatricalism 20th-century theatrical movement that emphasized artifice in reaction to 19th-century naturalism. Marked by stylized acting, a stage projecting into the audience, and frank scenic artifices and conventions, it did not strive to create the illusion of reality but rather to remind the audience of their role as watchers and critics of the artwork in progress before them. Theatricalism was found in the Expressionist, Dadaist, and Surrealist drama of the early 20th century and has continued as a current in the modern theater.

Thebes \'thēbz\ *biblical* **No** Famed ancient city, northern Egypt, on the banks of the NILE RIVER. In early times it also included KARNAK and LUXOR; the Valley of the KINGS was nearby. The earliest monuments in the city itself date from the 11th dynasty, c. 21st century BC, when the rulers of Thebes united Egypt and made Thebes the capital of Upper Egypt. It remained the capital until the end of the Middle Kingdom (c. 18th century BC). It was obscured for two centuries under the rule of various foreign invaders; then the kings of Thebes restored Egyptian rule in the 16th century BC and again made it the capital. It flourished as Egypt's political and religious center throughout the New Kingdom period, well known for achievements in sculpture and architecture. It began to decline in the 12th century BC under RAMSES III. It was sacked by Assyrians in the mid-7th century BC, by Persians in the 6th–4th century BC, and by Romans c. 30 BC. Its ruins include great temples and tombs, including the Temple of Amon at Karnak (c. 20th century BC), the tomb of TUTANKHAMEN in the Valley of the Kings, and the great mortuary temples of RAMSES II and HATSHEPSUT.

Thebes *Greek* **Thívai** \'thē-ve\ Ancient city, BOEOTIA, eastern central Greece, one of the chief Greek city-states. Traditionally said to have been founded by CADMUS, it was the seat of the legendary OEDIPUS and the setting for many classic Greek tragedies. The building of its celebrated seven-gated wall is usually attributed to AMPHION. It was a center of MYCENAEAN power in the Bronze Age (c. 1500–1200 BC). Hostility to ATHENS led it to side with the Persians in the PERSIAN WARS and with SPARTA in the PELOPONNESIAN WAR. Thebes and Sparta subsequently clashed, and the victorious Sparta occupied it. It revolted c. 380 BC and defeated Sparta at the battles of Tegyra (375 BC) and Leuctra (371 BC). For the next 10 years it was the chief military power in Greece. It joined Athens against PHILIP II OF MACEDON and shared the defeat at the Battle of CHAERONEA in 338 BC. It was sacked by ALEXANDER THE GREAT in 336 and eventually fell to Rome in the 1st century BC. Among the few ancient remains are remnants of the city walls, the Mycenaean palace (c. 1450–1350 BC), and a temple of APOLLO.

theft In law, the crime of taking the property or services of another without consent. Under most statutes, theft encompasses the crimes of larceny, robbery, and BURGLARY. Larceny is the crime of taking and carrying away the goods of another with intent to steal. Grand larceny, or larceny of property of substantial value, is a felony, whereas petty larceny, or larceny of less valuable property, is a misdemeanor. The same principle applies to grand theft and petty theft, which need not necessarily involve the "carrying away" of property and may include the theft of services. Two offenses usually distinguished from theft are EMBEZZLEMENT and FRAUD.

theism View that all observable phenomena are dependent on but distinct from one supreme being. The view usually entails the idea that God is beyond human comprehension, perfect and self-sustained, but also peculiarly involved in the world and its events. Theists seek support for their view in rational argument and appeals to experience. Arguments for God's existence are of four principal types: cosmological, ontological, teleological, or moral. A central issue for theism is reconciling God, usually understood as omnipotent and perfect, with the existence of evil. See also AGNOSTICISM, ATHEISM, DEISM, MONOTHEISM, POLYTHEISM, THEODICY.

theme and variations Musical form in which a statement of a theme or melody or harmonic pattern is followed by a series of altered versions of the theme. The practice, originally involving use of a repeated bass line (basso ostinato, or ground bass), began in early-16th-century dance music in Italy and Spain. English keyboard composers were soon developing melodic variations extensively, as were J.P. SWEELINCK and his followers. Ground-bass forms include the chaconne and passacaglia, both of which usually employ a brief bass line repeated many times. In the 17th century, organ and harpsichord variations became a standard form in Germany. Keyboard variations in the 19th century often employed popular tunes or opera melodies; variation form was also commonly used in symphonies, quartets, and sonatas. It declined in importance after the Classical era, but has never ceased to be employed by important composers.

Themistocles \the-'mis-tə-ˌklēz\ (524?–c. 460 BC) Athenian politician and naval strategist. As ARCHON (493) he built defensible harbors at Piraeus. In 483 he persuaded the assembly to increase the navy, believing it represented Athens's best chance of warding off Persian invaders. When the invasion of the XERXES I did come, a Greek naval force at first yielded to Persia at Artemisium, but Themistocles lured Xerxes' remaining ships to their destruction at the Battle of SALAMIS. Despite his victory, Athens later ostracized the strongly democratic Themistocles (472) as the city's politics turned reactionary. When Sparta later accused him of complicity with Persia, he fled the Peloponnese, and served as governor of some Asian Greek cities still under Persian rule until his death.

theocracy \thē-'ä-krə-sē\ Government by those regarded as divinely guided. The government's leaders may be clergy, or the state's legal system may be based on religious law. Theocratic rule was a constant of early civilizations. The ENLIGHTENMENT marked the end of theocracy in most Western countries. Present-day examples include Saudi Arabia, Iran, Afghanistan, and the Vatican. See also CHURCH AND STATE, DIVINE kingship.

Theocritus \thē-'ä-krə-təs\ (c. 310–250 BC) Greek poet. Little is known of his life. His surviving poems consist of bucolics and mimes, set in the country, and epics, lyrics, and epigrams, set in towns. The bucolics, his most characteristic and influential works, introduced the PASTORAL convention into poetry and were the sources of VIRGIL's *Eclogues* and much Renaissance poetry and drama. Theocritus' best-known IDYLLS include *Thyrsis*, a lament for Daphnis, the shepherd poet of mythology, and *Thalysia* ("Harvest Festival"), which presents the poet's friends and rivals in the guise of rustics.

theodicy \thē-'ä-də-sē\ Argument for the justification of God, concerned with reconciling God's goodness and justice with the observable facts of evil and suffering in the world. Most such arguments are a necessary component of THEISM. Under POLYTHEISM, the problem is solved by attributing evil to a conflict of wills between deities. The solution is less simple in MONOTHEISM, and takes several forms. In some approaches, the perfect world created by God was spoiled by human disobedience or SIN. In others, God withdrew after creating the world, which then fell into decay. In general, however, God is understood to be the author of all that is good in the world and humans the source of evil.

Theodora, detail of a Byzantine mosaic in the Church of San Vitale, Ravenna, Italy.
ANDRE HELD—J.P. ZIOLO

Theodora (497?–548) Byzantine empress, wife of JUSTINIAN I. The daughter of a bear keeper at the circus in Constantinople, she became an actress and the mistress of Justinian. He married her in 525, and when he became emperor in 527 she was proclaimed empress. Probably the most powerful woman in

Byzantine history, she was her husband's most trusted adviser, sponsoring legal reforms and wielding great influence in diplomacy and internal politics. Her advice quelled the Nika revolt (532). She recognized the rights of women and ended persecution of Monophysite Christians, with whom she sympathized.

Theodorakis \ˌthē-ə-də-ˈrä-kis\, **Mikis** *orig.* **Michael George** (born 1925) Greek composer. He studied at the Athens and Paris conservatories. A member of the wartime resistance, he remained active in politics, serving several times in the Greek parliament. As a member of the Communist Party, he was arrested during the 1967 military coup and only released in 1970 under international pressure. He is best known outside Greece for his film scores, including *Zorba the Greek* (1964), *Z* (1969), and *State of Siege* (1972), but has also composed much concert music, including seven symphonies, four operas, ballets (including *Antigone*, 1959), and over 1,000 songs. He is esteemed in his homeland as a national hero.

Theodore I Lascaris \ˈlas-kə-rəs\ (1174?–1221) First emperor of NICAEA, the Byzantine government-in-exile during the crusaders' occupation of Constantinople. He distinguished himself during the sieges of Constantinople in the Fourth CRUSADE (1203–4). After the Byzantine capital fell, he gathered a band of refugees, first at Brusa and then at Nicaea, and formed a new Byzantine state. He took the title emperor in 1208 and successfully defended Nicaea against the crusaders, the Turks, and his rival emperor David Comnenus. He signed a treaty (c. 1214) with the Latin emperor of Constantinople defining Nicaea's boundaries, and betrothed his daughter to the heir to the Latin imperial throne.

Theodore II See TEWODROS II

Theodore of Canterbury, St. (602?–690) Seventh archbishop of Canterbury (668–90). Born in Tarsus in Asia Minor, he was sent from Rome to Canterbury, where he helped establish a famous school at the monastery later known as St. Augustine's. Theodore organized and centralized the English church, calling its first general synod (672) to end Celtic practices, affirm church doctrine, and divide dioceses. He deposed WILFRID as bishop of York in 677 but restored him in 686; he also made peace between King Aethelred of Mercia and King Ecgfrith of Northumbia.

Theodore of Mopsuestia \ˌmäp-sü-ˈes-chə\ (c. AD 350–428/29) Syrian theologian and spiritual head of the School of Antioch. He entered a monastery near Antioch, where he lived and studied until 378. He was ordained in 381 and became bishop of Mopsuestia c. 392. His exegetical writings exemplied scientific, critical, philological, and historical methods of analysis that anticipated modern scholarship. Theologically, he believed that Christ had two natures, divine and human, in some kind of union. He stressed the literal sense of scripture and opposed allegorical interpretations. The second Council of Constantinople (553) condemned his views, but he was venerated by the NESTORIAN church as "the Interpreter." He is said to have introduced into the Nestorian church the doctrine of universal salvation.

Theodore Roosevelt National Park Preserve, western central North Dakota. Established in 1947, it commemorates Pres. THEODORE ROOSEVELT's interest in the West. Its 110 sq mi (285 sq km) include several sites along the Little MISSOURI RIVER, including a petrified forest, Wind Canyon, eroded badlands, and Roosevelt's Elkhorn Ranch cabin.

Theodoret of Cyrrhus \thē-ˈäd-ə-rət\ (AD 393?–458/66?) Syrian theologian and bishop. A monk, he was bishop of Cyrrhus (near Antioch) by 423. Influenced by St. John CHRYSOSTOM and THEODORE OF MOPSUESTIA, he opposed allegorical interpretations of scripture and attributed a human nature to Christ. Accused of being a NESTORIAN heretic, he made conciliatory statements accepting the term "god-bearer" for Mary (thereby stressing Jesus' divinity). He was declared a heretic nevertheless (449), and sent into exile. He was partially vindicated by the Council of CHALCEDON (451), which agreed to declare him orthodox provided he condemn his friend NESTORIUS, and he reluctantly complied.

Theodoric *known as* **Theodoric the Great** (454?–526) King of the OSTROGOTHS and founder of the Ostrogothic kingdom in Italy. Sent by the Byzantine emperor ZENO to invade Italy in 488, he made himself sole ruler by 493 and murdered ODOACER by treachery. With Ravenna as his capital he staved off the Franks and Bulgarians, and he held sway over a kingdom that included Sicily, Dalmatia, and some German lands. An Arian (see ARIANISM), he tolerated Catholicism and promoted peace between GOTHS and Romans.

Theodosius I \ˌthē-ə-ˈdō-shē-əs\ *or* **Theodosius the Great** *in full* **Flavius Theodosius** (AD 347–395) Roman emperor of the East (379–92) and of East and West (392–95). Born in Spain of Christian parents, he served in the military under his father, a general. He distinguished himself against the SARMATIANS and was proclaimed coemperor by GRATIAN to rule in the eastern empire (379). To settle the contentious debate over true Christianity, he adopted the NICENE CREED as the Christian norm (380). He reached a treaty with the VISIGOTHS (382). When the Spanish general Maximus overthrew the new coemperor in the western empire (387), Theodosius defeated the usurper (388) and claimed supreme authority over the whole empire (392). He argued with St. AMBROSE over the role of the church in imperial affairs, but did not grant power to the church. In 392 forces advocating paganism led by Arbogast and Eugenius took power in Rome. In 394 Theodosius defeated them, and claimed the Christian God victorious over the pagan gods.

Theodosius I Boradiotes \ˌbȯr-ə-ˈdī-ə-ˌtēz\ (died after 1183) Greek Orthodox patriarch of Constantinople (1179–83). As patriarch he upheld stringent conversion requirements for converts from Islam against the wishes of Emperor MANUEL I COMNENUS. He also opposed Manuel's overtures to Pope ALEXANDER III and the Western church, refusing to cooperate with a proposed reunion of the two branches of Christianity. The succeeding emperor forced Theodosius to abdicate.

Theodosius II (AD 401–450) Eastern Roman emperor (408–50). In 402 he was made coemperor with his father, Arcadius (son of THEODOSIUS I), then became sole ruler of the East when he was 7, initially under a regency. A gentle, scholarly man, he allowed relatives and ministers to dominate his government. His generals twice repelled the Persians (422, 447) but failed to evict the VANDALS from Roman Africa (429) and to prevent ATTILA's invasions (441–43, 447). The NESTORIAN heresy caused internal upheaval. Theodosius was credited with building the wall around Constantinople (413), founding the University of Constantinople (425), and promulgating the Theodosian Code (438).

Theodosius of Alexandria (535–566) Patriarch of Constantinople (535–566). A moderate Monophysite, he was opposed by more extreme Monophysites and did not accept the orthodox position expressed by the Council of CHALCEDON (451). He was prevented from administering his patriarchate by his detention in Constantinople, but he influenced the independent churches in Antioch, Syria, and Egypt.

theology Study of the nature of God and the relationship of the human and divine. The term was first used in the works of PLATO and other Greek philosophers to refer to the teaching of myth, but the discipline expanded within CHRISTIANITY and has found application in all theistic religions (see THEISM). It examines doctrines concerning such subjects as SIN, faith, and GRACE and considers the terms of God's COVENANT with humankind in matters such as SALVATION and ESCHATOLOGY. Theology typically takes for granted the authority of a religious teacher or the validity of a religious experience. It is distinguished from PHILOSOPHY in being concerned with justifying and explicating a faith, rather than questioning the underlying assumptions of such faith, but it often employs quasi-philosophical methods.

Theophilus (Presbyter) \thē-ˈä-fə-ləs\ *originally probably* **Roger of Helmarshausen** (fl. 12th century) German monk and writer. He is known for his *De Diversis Artibus* (c. 1110–40), a thorough account of the techniques of almost all the known crafts of the early 12th century. From his writings it can be deduced that he was a practicing craftsman of the Benedictine order.

theorem In mathematics or logic, a statement whose validity has been established or proved. It consists of a hypothesis and a conclusion, beginning with certain assumptions that are necessary and sufficient to establish a result. A system of theorems that build on and augment each other constitutes a theory. Within any theory, however, only statements that are essential, important, or of special interest are called theorems. Less important statements, usually stepping-stones in PROOFS of more important results, are called lemmas. A statement proved as a direct consequence of a theorem is a corollary of the theorem. Some theorems (and even lemmas and corollaries) are singled out and given titles (e.g., GÖDEL'S THEOREM, fundamental theorem of ALGEBRA, fundamental theorem of CALCULUS, PYTHAGOREAN theorem).

theosophy \thē-ˈä-sə-fē\ Religious philosophy with mystical concerns that can be traced to the ancient world. It holds that God, whose essence pervades the universe as an absolute reality, must be experienced directly in mystical experience (see MYSTICISM). It is characterized by esoteric doctrine and an interest in occult phenomena. Theosophical beliefs are found in NEOPLATONISM, GNOSTICISM, and among students of the KABBALA, but JAKOB BOHME, who developed a complete theosophical system, is often called the father of modern theosophy. Today theosophy is associated with the Theosophical Society, founded by HELENA BLAVATSKY in 1875. See also ANNIE BESANT.

Thera See THÍRA

Theramenes \thē-ˈra-mə-ˌnēz\ (died 404/403 BC) Controversial Athenian leader in the last years of the PELOPONNESIAN WAR. In 411 BC he helped install the Council of the FOUR HUNDRED. Sent to quell an insurrection at Piraeus, he instead led the mutineers in deposing the Council. In 410 he helped ALCIBIADES defeat the Peloponnesian navy at Cyzicus. Under Alcibiades he taxed shipping from the Black Sea, helping Athens's economy to recover and helping restore full constitutional government. During the siege of Athens (405/404) he was sent to deal with LYSANDER, and negotiated terms of capitulation as Athens underwent three months of starvation. A leader of the THIRTY TYRANTS installed by Lysander, he fell out with Critias and was forced to drink poison hemlock.

Therapeutae \ˌther-ə-ˈpyü-tē\ (Greek: "Worshipers") Sect of Jewish ascetics believed to have settled along Lake Mareotis near ALEXANDRIA in the 1st century AD. Their origin and fate are unknown, and the only account of them is attributed to PHILO JUDAEUS. They shared with the ESSENES a dualistic view of the body and soul (see DUALISM), but differed from them in that their objective was "wisdom." They viewed the scriptures as allegorical. Devoting themselves entirely to prayer and spiritual exercise, members lived in isolation for six days of the week and met on the SABBATH for discourse and a common meal.

therapeutic radiology See RADIATION THERAPY

therapeutics \ˌther-ə-ˈpyü-tiks\ Treatment and care to combat disease or alleviate pain or injury. Its tools include drugs, surgery, radiation therapy, mechanical devices, diet, and psychiatry. Treatment may be active, to cure a disease (requiring no further treatment after recovery), treat it long-term, or heal a wound; symptomatic, to relieve symptoms until the IMMUNE system heals the body; supportive, to keep body functions going until the disease clears; or palliative, to minimize discomfort for patients with no chance of recovery. It almost always includes prevention, usually tertiary (see PREVENTIVE medicine). Therapeutic measures can be chosen, combined, and tailored based on accurate diagnosis to fit each patient. See also alternative medicine, CHEMOTHERAPY, HOLISTIC medicine, HYDROTHERAPY, NUCLEAR MEDICINE, OCCUPATIONAL THERAPY, PHYSICAL MEDICINE AND REHABILITATION, PSYCHOTHERAPY, RESPIRATORY THERAPY.

Theravada \ˌter-ə-ˈvä-də\ Major form of BUDDHISM, prevalent in Myanmar, Sri Lanka, Thailand, Cambodia, and Laos. It is the only survivor among the HINAYANA schools of Buddhism, and is generally regarded as the oldest, most orthodox, and most conservative form of Buddhism. It is relatively uninfluenced by other indigenous belief systems. It is believed to have survived intact from the 500 Elders, who followed in the tradition of the monks of the first Buddhist SANGHA. Theravada has no hierarchical authority structure, though seniority is respected in the sangha. It accepts the Pali canon (see TRIPITAKA) as authoritative scripture. Theravadins revere the historical BUDDHA but do not recognize the various celestial buddhas and ancillary gods associated with MAHAYANA BUDDHISM.

Theresa of Lisieux \lēz-ˈyœ\, **St.** *orig.* **Marie-Françoise-Thérèse Martin** (1873–1897) French Carmelite nun, doctor of the Roman Catholic church. Born into a religious family, she entered the convent at Lisieux at 15, where she was plagued by depression and guilt but was known for her sweetness of temper. At the insistence of the prioress, she wrote an account of her spiritual development, in which she called for an absolute and childlike surrender to God, which she called the Little Way. After her death from tuberculosis at 24, the book was published as *Story of a Soul* (1898) and became widely popular, and Theresa's burial site at Lisieux became a place of pilgrimage.

Theresienstadt \te-ˈrā-zē-ən-ˌshtät\ Nazi CONCENTRATION camp in WORLD WAR II. Originally a town in northern Bohemia (in the modern Czech Republic), it became a walled ghetto for Jews in 1941. After the small non-Jewish population was evacuated in 1942, Jewish captives were shipped there from Germany, Austria, Czechoslovakia, Denmark, and the Netherlands. Of the total number of inmates (about 141,000), about 33,500 died in the dense crowding of the ghetto, and 88,000 were shipped on to extermination camps, especially AUSCHWITZ. After the war, the town was resurrected under its Czech name, Terezín.

thermae \ˈthər-mē\ Public bathing complex of ancient Rome, designed for relaxation and social activity as well as bathing. The Romans developed public baths to a high degree of sophistication and standardization. They consisted of a large open garden surrounded by subsidiary club rooms and a main block that contained three large bath chambers—hot room, steam room, and warm room—and smaller bathrooms, cold room, and courts for exercise. Imperial thermae, such as the Baths of Caracalla (AD 216), were immense and opulently furnished. Service was supplied by slaves moving through underground passageways. Heating was accomplished by circulating heated air from a fire under the floor. Lighting of the enormous rooms was provided by an ingenious system of CLERESTORY windows.

thermal conduction Transfer of HEAT energy resulting from differences in temperature between adjacent bodies or adjacent parts of a body. In the absence of a HEAT PUMP, the energy will flow from a region of higher temperature to a region of lower temperature. The transfer of energy occurs as a result of collision among the particles of the matter involved. The rate of transfer of energy is proportional to the cross-sectional area of contact and to the difference in temperature between the two regions. A substance of high thermal conductivity, such as copper, is a good thermal CONDUCTOR; one with low thermal conductivity, such as wood, is a poor thermal conductor. See also CONVECTION, RADIATION.

thermal energy Internal energy of a system in thermodynamic equilibrium (see THERMODYNAMICS) by virtue of its temperature. A hot body has more thermal energy than a similar cold body, but a large tub of cold water may have more thermal energy than a cup of boiling water. Thermal energy can be transferred from one body, usually hotter, to a second body, usually colder, in three ways: conduction (see THERMAL CONDUCTION), CONVECTION, and RADIATION.

thermal expansion Increase in volume of a material as its temperature is increased, usually expressed as a fractional change in dimensions per unit temperature change. When the material is a solid, thermal expansion is usually described in terms of change in length, height, or thickness. If a crystalline solid has the same structural configuration throughout, the expansion will be uniform in all dimensions. Otherwise, there may be different expansion coefficients and the solid will change shape as the temperature increases. If the material is a fluid, it is more useful to describe the expansion in terms of a change in volume. Because the bonding forces among atoms and molecules vary from material to material, expansion coefficients are characteristic of elements and compounds.

thermal radiation Process by which energy is emitted by a warm surface. The energy is ELECTROMAGNETIC RADIATION and so travels at the speed of light and does not require a medium to carry it. Thermal radiation ranges in FREQUENCY from low-frequency infrared rays to high-frequency ultraviolet rays. The intensity and frequency distribution of the emitted rays are determined by the nature and temperature of the emitting surface; in general, the hotter the object, the shorter the wavelength. A hotter object is a better emitter than a cooler one, and a blackened surface is a better emitter than a silvered one. An example of thermal radiation is the heating of the earth by the sun.

thermal spring See HOT SPRING

Thermidorian Reaction (1794) Revolt in the FRENCH REVOLUTION against the REIGN of Terror that was initiated on 9 Thermidor (July 27). Weary of the mounting executions (1,300 in June alone), deputies in the NATIONAL CONVENTION decreed the arrest of MAXIMILIEN ROBESPIERRE, LOUIS DE SAINT-JUST, and other members of the COMMITTEE OF PUBLIC SAFETY. They and others were guillotined, inaugurating a brief "White Terror" against the radical JACOBIN CLUB. The DIRECTORY period followed soon afterward.

thermocouple *or* **thermal junction** *or* **thermoelectric thermometer** Temperature-measuring instrument consisting of two wires of different metals joined at each end. One junction is placed where the temperature is to be measured, and the other is kept at a constant lower (reference) temperature. A measuring instrument is connected in the electrical circuit. The temperature difference causes the development of an ELECTROMOTIVE force that is approximately proportional to the difference between the temperatures of the two junctions. Temperature can be read from standard tables, or the instrument can be calibrated to display temperature directly.

thermodynamics Study of the relationships among HEAT, WORK, TEMPERATURE, and ENERGY. Any physical system will spontaneously approach an EQUILIBRIUM that can be described by specifying its properties, such as PRESSURE, temperature, or chemical composition. If external constraints are allowed to change, these properties generally change. The three laws of thermodynamics describe these changes and predict the equilibrium state of the system. The first law states that whenever energy is converted from one form to another, the total quantity of energy remains the same. The second law states that, in a closed system, the ENTROPY of the system does not decrease. The third law states that, as a system approaches ABSOLUTE ZERO, further extraction of energy becomes more and more difficult, eventually becoming theoretically impossible.

thermoluminescence Emission of light from certain heated substances as a result of previous exposure to high-energy RADIATION. The radiation causes displacement of ELECTRONS within the CRYSTAL LATTICE of the substance. Upon heating, the trapped electrons return to their normal, lower-energy positions, releasing energy in the process. The longer the substance is exposed to radiation, the greater is the energy released. By measuring the amount of light given off, the duration of exposure to radiation can be determined; thus, thermoluminescence has been used to determine the age of various minerals and archaeological artifacts.

thermometry \thər-ˈmä-mə-trē\ Science of measuring the TEMPERATURE of a system or the ability of a system to transfer HEAT to another system. Temperature measurement is important to a wide range of activities, including manufacturing, scientific research, and medicine.

thermonuclear bomb See HYDROGEN BOMB

thermonuclear weapon See NUCLEAR WEAPON

Thermopylae \thər-ˈmä-pə-lē\, **Battle of** Battle in northern Greece (480 BC) in the PERSIAN WARS. The Greek forces, mostly Spartan, were led by LEONIDAS. After three days of holding their own against the Persian king XERXES I and his vast southward-advancing army, the Greeks were betrayed, and the Persians were able to outflank them. Sending the main army in retreat, Leonidas and a small contingent remained behind to resist the advance and were killed to the last man.

thermoreception Sensory capacity (see SENSE) to determine the temperature of the environment that also helps keep body temperature stable by regulating autonomic responses to temperature changes (see HOMEOSTASIS, TEMPERATURE STRESS). Temperature sensations are generated by separate heat and cold receptors (nerve endings) in the skin. Blood sucking insects and some snakes (e.g., the PIT VIPER) locate prey by its thermal radiation.

thermostat Device that detects TEMPERATURE changes for the purpose of maintaining the temperature of an enclosed area essentially constant. The thermostat generates signals, usually electrical, to activate relays, valves, switches, and so on when the temperature rises above or falls below the desired value. Thermostats are used to control the flow of fuel to a burner, of electric current to a heating or cooling unit, or of a heated or cooled gas or liquid into the area it serves. They are also used in fire-detection warning systems.

theropod \ˈthir-ə-ˌpäd\ Any species of bipedal, carnivorous SAURISCHIAN in the suborder Theropoda. The chicken-sized *Compsognathus,* the smallest known adult dinosaur, probably weighed 2–4 lbs (1–2 kg); the TYRANNOSAURS weighed tons. The theropods also included ALLOSAURUS, DEINONYCHUS, megalosaurus, oviraptor, and VELOCIRAPTOR. Theropod remains have been recovered from the Late TRIASSIC period through the Late CRETACEOUS period (227–65 million years ago) from all continents except Antarctica. Their well-developed hind legs provided support and locomotion; their short forelimbs had mobile hands, probably for grasping and tearing prey. Despite the group's name, which means "beast (i.e., mammal) foot," theropod feet usually resembled those of birds. It is widely believed that all modern birds are descended from one line of small theropods.

Theseum \thi-ˈsē-əm\ Temple in Athens dedicated to HEPHAESTUS and ATHENA as patrons of the arts and crafts. Built c. 450 BC, it is slightly older than the PARTHENON. Some of its sculptures represent the exploits of THESEUS (the source of its traditional name), though reconstructed fragments of its ornamentation reveal that its theme was actually the apotheosis of HERACLES. It is surrounded by a single row of Doric columns, with 13 at the sides and six at the ends. It is the world's best-preserved ancient Greek temple, largely because of its medieval conversion to a Christian church.

Theseus \ˈthē-sē-əs, ˈthēs-ˌyüs\ Hero of ancient Greek legend. He was the son of Aegeus, king of Athens. On his journey to Athens, he slew many legendary villains, including Sinis, Sciron, and Procrustes. In Athens he found Aegeus married to MEDEA; she recognized him before her husband did and tried to poison him but failed, and Aegeus declared him heir to the throne. In Crete Theseus met ARIADNE and slew the MINOTAUR; on returning to Athens he forgot to replace the ship's black sail with a white one signaling his victory, and Aegeus threw himself from the Acropolis in grief. Theseus went on to unite and extend the borders of ATTICA. He captured the AMAZON princess Antiope (Hippolyte), with the result that the Amazons attacked Athens and Antiope was killed while defending it. He abducted the child HELEN and attempted to steal PERSEPHONE from Hades, but was confined in the underworld until his rescue by HERACLES. He died when the king of Scyros threw him from a cliff.

thesis play See PROBLEM PLAY

Thesmophoria \ˌthez-mə-ˈfōr-ē-ə\ In GREEK RELIGION, a festival held in honor of Demeter Thesmophoros. The celebrants were free married women who had observed chastity for several days and abstained from certain foods. Pigs were thrown into an underground chamber, where they were eaten by snakes. The uneaten, rotted remains were brought up and laid on an altar; if mixed with seeds they were believed to ensure a good crop.

Thespiae \ˈthes-pē-ˌē\ Ancient town, BOEOTIA, eastern central Greece. It was the site of temples and festivals of the MUSES and of PRAXITELES' famous statue of Eros. It is important in Greek history chiefly as an enemy of nearby THEBES. Its citizens fought the Persians with Spartan forces under LEONIDAS at the battles of THERMOPYLAE in 480 BC and PLATAEA in 479. It served SPARTA as a base against Thebes 379–372 BC. The Thebans destroyed it in 371 BC, but it was soon rebuilt. It was an important Boeotian town under the Roman empire.

Thespis \ˈthes-pəs\ (fl. 6th century BC) Greek poet, often considered the "inventor of TRAGEDY." He is the first recorded winner of a prize for tragedy at the Great Dionysia, a drama festival, c. 534 BC. According to the rhetorician Themistius, ARISTOTLE said that tragedy in its earliest stage was entirely choral until the prologue and speeches were first introduced by Thespis. Thespis, according to Themistius' account, was thus the first "actor," and tragic dialogue began when he exchanged words with the leader of the chorus.

Thessaloniki \ˌthe-sä-lō-ˈnē-kē\ *formerly* **Salonika** \sə-ˈlä-ni-kə\ Seaport (pop., 1991: 378,000), Macedonia, Greece. Founded in 316 BC, it became the capital of the Roman province of Macedonia in 146 BC and grew to great importance. The apostle Paul (see St. PAUL) visited c. AD 49–50, and later addressed epistles to converts there. During the Byzantine empire, it prospered despite repeated attacks by Avars and Slavs. It was part of the Ottoman empire 1430–1912. The headquarters of the YOUNG TURK movement in 1908, it was returned to Greece in 1913. It was an important Allied base in World War I. It was occupied by the Germans in World War II. It is Greece's second-largest city and seaport.

Thessaly \ˈthe-sə-lē\ Historical region and current administrative region, eastern central Greece. The ancient region corresponded roughly to the modern one. It was the site of many cultures in the 3rd–2nd millennia BC; by c. 1000 BC Greeks had established power there. Incorporated into the Roman province of Macedon in the 2nd century BC, it was made a separate Roman province in the 4th century AD. In the 7th–13th century it was controlled by Slavs, Saracens, Bulgars, and Normans. In the late 14th century it passed to the Turks; it was returned to Greece in 1881. It saw heavy fighting between Allied and Axis forces in 1941. The site of Mount OLYMPUS, it is drained by the PINIOS RIVER.

Thetis \ˈthē-təs\ In GREEK MYTHOLOGY, a NEREID loved by both ZEUS and POSEIDON. When it was revealed that Thetis was destined to bear a son who would be mightier than his father, the two gods gave her to Peleus, king of the Myrmidons. Unwilling to wed a mortal, Thetis resisted Peleus' advances by changing into various shapes, but Peleus finally captured and married her. Their child was ACHILLES. Some legends relate that she bore seven children, all of whom perished either when she tried to render them immortal or when she killed them as the offspring of a forced marriage.

thiamine \'thī-ə-mən\ *or* **vitamin B$_1$** Organic compound, part of the VITAMIN B complex, necessary in the diet. It plays an important role in CARBOHYDRATE METABOLISM, in combined form as the COENZYME thiamine pyrophosphate. Its molecular structure includes a substituted PYRIDINE ring and a thiazole ring. Thiamine is found most abundantly in whole cereal grains and certain other seeds. It is removed in the refining process; deficiency leads to BERIBERI.

Thiers \tē-'er\, **(Louis-) Adolphe** (1797–1877) French politician and historian. He went to Paris in 1821 as a journalist and cofounded the opposition newspaper *National* in 1830. In the JULY REVOLUTION he supported LOUIS-PHILIPPE and served as minister of the interior (1832, 1834–36) and premier and foreign minister (1836, 1840). A leader of the conservative moderates, he crushed all insurrections. Following the FEBRUARY REVOLUTION, he helped elect Louis-Napoléon (later NAPOLEON III) president of the SECOND REPUBLIC. As a leader of the opposition 1863–70, he attacked Napoleon III's imperial policies. As president of the THIRD REPUBLIC 1871–73, he negotiated the end of the FRANCO-PRUSSIAN WAR and restored domestic order by crushing the PARIS COMMUNE. He also wrote major historical works, most importantly the huge *History of the French Revolution* (10 vols., 1823–27) and *History of the Consulate and the Empire* (20 vols., 1845–62).

Thimann \'thī-mən\, **Kenneth V(ivian)** (1904–1997) British-U.S. plant physiologist. He received his PhD from Imperial College in London. In 1934 he obtained and isolated pure AUXIN, an important plant-growth hormone and, with several coworkers, proved that auxin promotes cell elongation, formation of roots, and growth of buds, discoveries that led to the development of a widely used synthetic auxin, 2,4-D. Use of this and similar chemicals can prevent the premature falling of fruit and stimulate cut stems to grow abundant roots; because high concentrations of auxins are toxic to most plants, synthetic auxins are also effective weed killers.

Thimphu \thim-'pü\ Town (pop., 1993 est.: 30,000), capital of Bhutan. It lies on the Raidak River in the HIMALAYAS. It was designated the official seat of government in 1962. The Tashi Chho castle, a traditional fortified monastery and one of the finest examples of traditional Bhutanese architecture, houses the offices of the royal government. The local economy relies on agriculture and lumbering.

thin-layer chromatography (TLC) Type of CHROMATOGRAPHY using as the stationary phase a thin layer (0.01 inch, or 0.25 mm) of a special finely ground matrix (silica gel, alumina, or similar material) coated on a glass plate or incorporated in a plastic film. Solutions of the mixtures to be analyzed are spotted near one edge. Solutions of reference compounds are similarly applied. The edge of the plate is then dipped in a SOLVENT. The solvent travels up the matrix by CAPILLARITY, moving the components of the samples at various rates because of their different degrees of attachment to the matrix and solubility in the developing solvent. The components, visible as separated spots, are identified by comparing the distances they have traveled with those of the known reference materials. TLC is useful for biological mixtures, especially LIPIDS in animal or vegetable tissues and ISOPRENOIDS and ESSENTIAL oils found in flowers and plants. The matrices withstand strong solvents and developers better than the paper used in PAPER CHROMATOGRAPHY.

think tank Institute, corporation, or group organized for interdisciplinary research, usually conducted for governmental and commercial clients. Projects for government clients often involve social-policy planning and national defense. Commercial projects include developing and testing new technologies and new products. Funding sources include endowments, contracts, private donations, and sales of reports. See also BROOKINGS INSTITUTION, HOOVER INSTITUTION, RAND CORP.

thinking *or* **thought** Action of using one's mind to produce thoughts, or covert symbolic responses to stimuli. Theories of thought and thought processes have concentrated largely on directed thinking, including PROBLEM SOLVING. At the beginning of the 20th century, researchers focused on studying mental ASSOCIATIONS. Theorists of GESTALT psychology in the 1920s and '30s believed the elements of thought to be in the nature of patterns elicited from experience. Today these elements are often regarded as bits of information undergoing processing. See also COGNITIVE PSYCHOLOGY, INFORMATION PROCESSING.

Thíra \'thē-rä\ *ancient* **Thera** \'thir-ə\ *formerly* **Santorini** Island, southern CYCLADES, Greece. The remaining half of an exploded volcano, it surrounds a lagoon with volcanic cliffs rising to almost 1,000 ft (300 m). It was settled in the Bronze Age; MINOAN remains date to before 2000 BC. One of the largest known volcanic eruptions occurred on the island c. 1500 BC, depositing ash and pumice as far away as Egypt and Israel. The eruption has been linked to such phenomena as the miracles of the EXODUS and the sinking of ATLANTIS. Excavations have revealed a rich Minoan city buried under the volcanic debris. It was resettled by Dorian invaders c. 1000 BC.

Third Estate *French* **Tiers État** In French history, one of the three orders (with the nobility and the clergy) of the ESTATES GENERAL before the FRENCH REVOLUTION. The unprivileged order, it represented the great majority of the people. Its transformation with the TENNIS COURT OATH into a NATIONAL ASSEMBLY in 1789 marked the beginning of the Revolution.

Third International See COMINTERN

Third Reich \'rīk\ Official designation for the NAZI PARTY's regime in Germany from January 1933 to May 1945. The name reflects ADOLF HITLER's conception of his expansionist regime—which he predicted would last 1,000 years—as the presumed successor of the HOLY ROMAN EMPIRE (800–1806, the First Reich) and the German empire under the HOHENZOLLERN dynasty (1871–1918, the Second Reich).

Third Republic French government 1870–1940. After the fall of the SECOND EMPIRE and the suppression of the PARIS COMMUNE, the new CONSTITUTIONAL LAWS of 1875 were adopted, establishing a regime based on parliamentary supremacy. Despite its series of short-lived governments, the Third Republic was marked by social stability (except for the ALFRED DREYFUS affair), industrialization, and establishment of a professional civil service. It ended with the fall of France to the Germans in 1940. Presidents of the Third Republic included ADOLPHE THIERS (1871–73), MARIE EDME PATRICE DE MAC-MAHON (1873–79), JULES GREVY (1879–87), SADI CARNOT (1887–94), FELIX FAURE (1895–99), Émile Loubet (1899–1906), Armand Fallières (1906–13), RAYMOND POINCARE(1913–20), ALEXANDRE MILLERAND (1920–24), Gaston Doumergue (1924–31), and ALBERT LEBRUN (1932–40). Other notable leaders included LEON BLUM, GEORGES BOULANGER, ARISTIDE BRIAND, GEORGES CLEMENCEAU, EDOUARD DALADIER, JULES FERRY, LEON GAMBETTA, EDOUARD HERRIOT, JEAN JAURES, PIERRE LAVAL, PHILIPPE PETAIN, and PAUL REYNAUD.

Third Section *or* **Third Department** Office created in 1826 by Czar NICHOLAS I to conduct secret police operations. Designed and headed (1826–44) by Count Aleksandr Benckendorff (1783–1844), it gathered information on political dissidents and banished suspected political criminals to remote regions. It collaborated with the Corps of Gendarmes (formed in 1836), a military force that operated throughout Russia, and with a network of spies and informers. The department grew increasingly repressive, and in the 1870s it arrested many Populists who agitated among the peasantry. It was abolished in 1880, and its functions were transferred to the police of the interior ministry.

third world Political designation originally used (1963) to describe those states not part of the first world—the capitalist, economically developed states led by the U.S.—or the second world—the communist states led by the Soviet Union. The third world principally consists of the developing world, former colonies of Africa, Asia, and Latin America. With the end of the Cold War and the increased economic competitiveness of some developing countries, the term has lost its analytic clarity.

Thirteen Principles of Faith *or* **Thirteen Articles of Faith** Summary of the basic tenets of JUDAISM. It was formulated by MOSES MAIMONIDES in his commentary on the MISHNA, in an effort to put forth true concepts of God and faith as a tool in avoiding error. Though presented as dogma, his statement was a personal concept and has been much debated and revised. The principles state various doctrines concerning the nature of God, the law, and MOSES, and affirm that the MESSIAH is coming and that the dead will rise. All versions include the hymn *Yigdal,* which is part of most prayer services.

Thirty Tyrants (404–403 BC) SPARTAN-imposed oligarchy that ruled Athens after the PELOPONNESIAN WAR. Thirty commissioners were appointed to the oligarchy, which had an extremist conservative core, led by Critias. Their oppressive regime fostered a bloody purge, in which perhaps 1,500 residents were killed. Many moderates fled the city; gathering a force, they returned to defeat the tyrants' forces in a battle at Piraeus in 403. The thirty fled, and were killed off over the next few years.

Thirty Years' War (1618–48) Series of intermittent conflicts in Europe fought for various reasons, including religious, dynastic, territorial, and commercial rivalries. The overall war was mainly a struggle between the Habsburg-controlled Holy Roman Empire and the Protestant principalities that relied on the chief anti-Catholic powers of Sweden and the Netherlands. It also involved the rivalry of France with the Habsburg powers, which formed anti-French alliances. The conflicts began in 1618 when the future emperor FERDINAND II tried to impose Roman Catholicism on his domains and the Protestant nobles rebelled; the war was sparked by the Defenestration of PRAGUE. The battlefield centered on the principalities in Germany, which suffered severely from plundering armies. Early successes by the CATHOLIC LEAGUE were countered by military gains by Sweden. When the bloodshed ended with the Peace of WESTPHALIA (1648) , the balance of power in Europe had been radically changed. France emerged as the chief Western power and states of the Holy Roman Empire were granted full sovereignty, establishing a framework for a modern Europe of sovereign states.

thistle Weedy species of *Cirsium, Carduus, Echinops, Sonchus*, and other plant genera of the COMPOSITE FAMILY. The term usually refers to prickly leaved species of *Carduus* and *Cirsium*, which have dense heads of small, usually pink or purple flowers. Because they have spiny stems and flower heads without ray flowers, *Carduus* species are called plumeless thistles. Canadian thistle *(Cirsium arvense)* is an attractive but troublesome weed in agricultural areas of North America. The thistle is the national emblem of Scotland.

Thjórsá River \'thyȯr-ˌsaù\ River, Iceland. Carrying meltwater from several glaciers, it flows southwest for 143 mi (230 km) to discharge into the Atlantic Ocean. It is the country's longest river; its lower third flows through an extensive farming region. It is Iceland's main source of hydroelectric power

Thocmectony See Sarah Winnemucca HOPKINS

Thomas, Clarence (born 1948) U.S. jurist. Born in Pin Point, Ga., he graduated from Yale Law School and served as assistant attorney general in Missouri (1974–77), lawyer for Monsanto Co. (1977–79), legislative assistant to Sen. John Danforth (1979–81), assistant secretary in the U.S. Department of Education (1981–82), and chairman of the Equal Employment Opportunity Commission (1982–90). Pres. GEORGE BUSH appointed him to the U.S. Court of Appeals in 1990 and then to the U.S. Supreme Court to replace THURGOOD MARSHALL as the Court's second black justice. His 1991 confirmation hearings were complicated by accusations of SEXUAL HARASSMENT by Anita Hill, a law professor (born 1956), which attracted enormous public interest and controversy. He denied the charges, and the Senate narrowly voted to confirm him. Though a quiet presence on the Court, he has never swerved from a strong conservatism.

Thomas, Dylan (Marlais) (1914–1953) Welsh poet and prose writer. He left school at 16 to work as a reporter. His early verse, as in *The Map of Love* (1939), with rich metaphoric language and emotional intensity, made him famous. In the more accessible *Deaths and Entrances* (1946), with "Fern Hill," he often adopts a bardic, oracular voice. *In Country Sleep* (1952), containing "Do Not Go Gentle into That Good Night," and *Collected Poems* (1952) followed. Thomas's prose includes the comic *Portrait of the Artist as a Young Dog* (1940); a play, *Under Milk Wood* (1954); and the reminiscence *A Child's Christmas in Wales* (1955). His sonorous recitations contributed greatly to his fame. Debt and heavy drinking began taking their toll in the late 1930s, and he died of an alcohol overdose in New York while on tour.

Dylan Thomas, 1952.
ROLLIE MCKENNA

Thomas, George H(enry) (1816–1870) U.S. general. Born in Southampton Co., Va., he graduated from West Point. He remained loyal to the Union when the Civil War broke out and commanded in eastern Kentucky, where he won the first important Union victory in the west in 1862. At the Battle of CHICKAMAUGA he organized an unyielding defense, earning promotion to brigadier general and the nickname "the Rock of Chickamauga." In 1864 he defeated the Confederate forces of Gen. John B. Hood (1831–1879) in the Battle of Nashville, earning another promotion and the thanks of Congress.

Thomas, Helen (born 1920) U.S. journalist. Born to Lebanese immigrant parents, she grew up in Detroit and joined the UPI news agency in Washington, D.C., in 1943. A pioneer in overcoming the limitations on women in the news media, she became known for her bold and tireless pursuit of information. Assigned to the White House in 1961, she became UPI bureau chief there in 1974. She is best known as the reporter traditionally first recognized at presidential press conferences.

Thomas, Isaiah (Lord), III (born 1961) U.S. basketball player and executive. Born in Chicago, he played in college for Indiana University (1979–81). As a guard for the Detroit Pistons (1981–94), he amassed 9,061 career assists and helped the team win two NBA championships (1989, 1990); he is regarded as one of the greatest point guards of all time. He subsequently became general manager and part owner of the Toronto Raptors, and later worked as a television commentator.

Thomas, Lewis (1913–1993) U.S. physician and author. Born in Queens, N.Y., he attended medical school at Harvard and later taught at various universities. He was president of New York's Memorial Sloan-Kettering Cancer Center 1973–83. He translated his passionate interest in and wonder at the intricate mysteries of biology into lucid meditations and reflections on biology in award-winning essays. The best known of his widely read books is *The Lives of a Cell* (1974, National Book Award).

Thomas, Lowell (Jackson) (1892–1981) U.S. radio commentator, journalist, and author. A war correspondent in Europe and the Middle East while in his 20s, Thomas helped make T. E. LAWRENCE famous with his exclusive coverage and later with the book *With Lawrence in Arabia* (1924). He was a preeminent broadcaster with CBS from 1930; his radio nightly news was an American institution for nearly two generations, and he appeared on television from its earliest days. Out of his lifelong globetrotting came lectures, travelogues, and more than 50 books of adventure and comment, including *Kabluk of the Eskimo* (1932) and *The Seven Wonders of the World* (1956).

Lowell Thomas.
BROWN BROTHERS

Thomas, Norman (Mattoon) (1884–1968) U.S. social reformer and politician. Born in Marion, Ohio, he was ordained a Presbyterian minister and became pastor of New York's East Harlem Church. He joined the Socialist Party in 1918 and left his parish post to become secretary of the pacifist Fellowship of Reconciliation. He helped found the AMERICAN CIVIL LIBERTIES UNION, and served as codirector of the League for Industrial Democracy 1922–37. He was the Socialist Party's candidate for governor (1924), mayor of New York (1925, 1929), and U.S. president (1928–48), and headed the party from 1926. After World War II he pressed for nuclear disarmament as chairman of the Postwar World Council.

Thomas, St. (died AD 53?) One of the 12 DISCIPLES of Christ. He is best known for requiring physical proof of Jesus' resurrection before he could believe it; hence the phrase "doubting Thomas." When Jesus reappeared and had Thomas touch his wounds, Thomas became the first person to explicitly acknowledge Jesus' divinity, saying "My Lord and my God." His subsequent history is uncertain; he is said to have evangelized Parthia (modern Khorasan) and even India.

Thomas à Becket See St. Thomas BECKET

Thomas à Kempis *orig.* **Thomas Hemerken** (1379/80–1471) German monk and theologian. Born at Kempen in the Rhineland, he went to the Deventer, the Netherlands, c. 1392 and joined the Brethren of the Common Life, a community devoted to the care and education of the poor. In 1387 he entered the Augustinian monastery at Agnietenberg. He was ordained in 1413 and devoted himself to copying manuscripts and directing novices. He is credited with writing *The Imitation of Christ,* the most influential devotional work in Christian literature after the Bible. Noted for its simple language and style, it emphasizes spiritual over materialistic life and affirms the rewards of a life centered on Christ.

Thomas Aquinas \ə-'kwī-nəs\, **St.** (1224/25–1274) Foremost philosopher and theologian of the Roman Catholic church. Born of noble parents at Roccasecca, Italy, he studied at the University of Naples, joined the Dominicans, and taught at a Dominican school at the University of Paris. His time in Paris coincided with the arrival of Aristotelian science, newly discovered in Arabic translation; his great achievement was to integrate into Christian thought the rigors of ARISTOTLE's philosophy, just as the early church fathers had integrated PLATO's thought in the early Christian era. He held that reason is capable of operating within faith; while the philosopher relies solely on reason, the theologian accepts faith as his starting point and then proceeds to conclusion through the use of reason. This point of view was controversial, as was his belief in the religious value of nature, for which he argued that to detract from the perfection of creation was to detract from the creator. He was opposed by St. BONAVENTURE. In 1277, after his death, the masters of Paris condemned 219 propositions, 12 of them Thomas's. He was nevertheless canonized in 1323, named a Doctor of the Church in 1567, and declared the champion of orthodoxy during the modernist crisis at the end of the 19th century. A prolific writer, he produced more than 80 works, including *Summa contra Gentiles* (1261–64) and *Summa theologica* (1265–73). See also THOMISM.

Thomism \'tō-ˌmi-zəm\ Philosophical and theological system developed by St. THOMAS AQUINAS. It holds that the human SOUL is immortal and is a unique subsistent form, that human knowledge is based on sensory experience but also depends on the mind's reflective capacity, and that all creatures have a natural tendency to love God that can be perfected and elevated by GRACE and application. In the 20th century, Thomism was developed by Étienne Gilson (1884–1978) and JACQUES MARITAIN. After World War II, Thomists faced three major tasks: to develop an adequate philosophy of science, to account for phenomenological and psychiatric findings, and to evaluate the ontologies of EXISTENTIALISM and NATURALISM.

Thompson, Dorothy (1894–1961) U.S. journalist. Born in Lancaster, N.Y., she became a freelance correspondent in Europe after World War I. Her reporting on the Nazis so infuriated ADOLF HITLER that in 1934 she became the first U.S. correspondent expelled from Germany. Her column "On the Record" became hugely popular and was syndicated from 1941 to 1958 in as many as 170 daily newspapers. Her many books include *New Russia* (1928), *I Saw Hitler!* (1932), *Refugees* (1938), *Let the Record Speak* (1939), and *The Courage to Be Happy* (1957). From 1928 to 1942 she was married to the novelist SINCLAIR LEWIS.

Dorothy Thompson, 1934.

AP/WIDE WORLD PHOTOS

Thompson, E(dward) P(almer) (1924–1993) British historian. He served in Italy in World War II and taught at the Univs. of Leeds (1948–65) and Warwick (1965–71). He left the Communist Party in 1956 when Soviet troops crushed the Hungarian uprising, but remained a Marxist and socialist all his life. His best-known work is *The Making of the English Working Class* (1963), an acclaimed study of the period 1780–1832. Among his other books is *Whigs and Hunters* (1975). From the late 1970s he devoted much of his time to the antinuclear movement.

Thompson, Emma (born 1959) British actress. After graduating from Cambridge Univ., she acted on stage and television, winning acclaim in the miniseries *Fortunes of War* (1987). Married to KENNETH BRANAGH 1989–94, she appeared in several of his films, including *Henry V* (1989), *Dead Again* (1991), and *Much Ado About Nothing* (1993). She later starred in *Howards End* (1992, Academy Award), *The Remains of the Day* (1993), *Sense and Sensibility* (1995), for which she won an Academy Award for best screenplay, and *Primary Colors* (1998).

Thompson, Hunter S(tockton) (born 1939) U.S. journalist. Born in Louisville, Ky., he had run-ins with the law as a young man and served in the U.S. Air Force. In 1965 he infiltrated the Hell's Angels motorcycle gang, and published his account, *Hell's Angels,* in 1966. Other books include the psychedelic-drug romp *Fear and Loathing in Las Vegas* (1972; film, 1998), *Fear and Loathing on the Campaign Trail* (1973), and *The Great Shark Hunt* (1979). He created the genre known as "gonzo journalism," and his writing—idiosyncratic and subjective in the extreme, and often wildly funny—gained him a large underground following.

Thomson, J(ohn) Edgar (1808–1874) U.S. civil engineer and railroad executive. Born in Springfield Township, Pa., he joined the Pennsylvania engineer corps at 19. In 1847 he was hired as chief engineer of the newly incorporated Pennsylvania Railroad Co., which aimed to compete with trade lines to the west originating in New York and other eastern states. He became its president in 1852 and oversaw construction of a railway that crossed the Alleghenies without using inclined grades. Over the next 22 years, Thomson consolidated a network of lines from Philadelphia to Chicago, expanding the company's track from 250 to 6,000 mi. (400–10,000 km).

Thomson, J(oseph) J(ohn) *later* **Sir Joseph** (1856–1940) English physicist. Educated at Cambridge Univ., he taught at Cambridge's Cavendish Laboratory 1884–1918, which he developed into a world-renowned institution, and was master of Trinity College, Cambridge 1918–40. In 1897 he showed that cathode rays are rapidly moving particles, and by measuring their displacement by electric and magnetic fields determined that these particles were nearly 2,000 times less massive than the lightest known atomic particle. Originally called corpuscles by Thomson, the particles are now known as ELECTRONS. His discovery helped revolutionize the knowledge of atomic structure. In 1903 he suggested a discontinuous theory of light, foreshadowing ALBERT EINSTEIN's later theory of photons. He later discovered isotopes and invented mass spectrometry. In 1906 Thomson received a Nobel Prize for his research into the electrical conductivity of gases. Throughout his life he was noted as an outstanding teacher, and seven of his assistants would also become Nobel laureates.

Thomson, Roy Herbert *later* **Baron Thomson of Fleet** (1894–1976) Canadian-British publisher. A native of Ontario, Thomson began acquiring radio stations and newspapers there in the 1930s; later he expanded his interests to Britain and the U.S. and added television holdings. In 1952 he bought *The Scotsman* newspaper and went to Edinburgh to run it. In 1959 he purchased the Kemsley group of newspapers, the largest in Britain, which included the *Sunday Times.* In 1967 he made his most important purchase, *The* TIMES of London, and thereafter made a major investment in it, providing it financial stability. International Thomson is today one of the largest publishing conglomerates in the world.

Thomson, Virgil (1896–1989) U.S. composer and critic. Born in Kansas City, he attended Harvard Univ., intending to become a pianist and organist. Studying in Paris with N. BOULANGER (1921), he met Les SIX and their circle and began to compose. Resident in Paris 1925–40, he met GERTRUDE STEIN, with whom he wrote the operas *Four Saints in Three Acts* (1928) and *The Mother of Us All* (1946), affecting a charmingly naïve style. Back in New York, he served as music critic of the *Herald Tribune* (1940–54); his gracefully written criticism was respected for its concern with music rather than performers. Other works include the film scores *The Plow That Broke the Plains* (1936) and *The Louisiana Story* (1949, Pulitzer Prize).

Thonet \'tò-net\, **Michael** (1796–1871) German-Austrian pioneer in the industrialization of furniture manufacture. He developed a system of steam-bent veneers c. 1830 and created light, curvilinear chairs. By 1856 he had perfected the bending of solid beechwood with heat and began mass production of BENTWOOD furniture. He set up factories in Hungary and Moravia and opened salons from Moscow to Chicago. By 1870 he was producing furniture in hitherto unheard-of quantities. His furniture is still being manufactured today.

Thor Germanic deity who appeared as a great, red-bearded warrior of tremendous strength. The son of ODIN (according to some legends) and Jord, the earth goddess, he was the implacable foe of the harmful race of giants but was benevolent toward humans. His name is the Germanic word for thunder. His great weapon was his hammer, MJOLLNIR. His greatest enemy was the world serpent Jörmungand, which he was destined to kill, and be killed by, in the RAGNAROK. Thursday is named for Thor.

Thor with his hammer, Mjollnir, on his knees, bronze statuette from northern Iceland, c. AD 1000; in the National Museum of Iceland, Reykjavík.

BY COURTESY OF THE NATIONAL MUSEUM OF ICELAND, REYKJAVIK

Thor rocket MISSILE initially developed (1958) by the U.S. Air Force as an intermediate-range ballistic missile and later modified to serve as the first stage of launch vehicles for several spacecraft (see STAGED rocket). The Thor missile force was withdrawn in 1963. For space launching, three small auxiliary motors were strapped to a Thor rocket, resulting in a thrust nearly twice as powerful as the original.

thoracic cavity \thə-'ra-sik\ *or* **chest cavity** Second-largest hollow space of the body, enclosed by the ribs, VERTEBRAL column, and breastbone and separated from the ABDOMINAL CAVITY by the DIAPHRAGM. It contains the LUNGS and bronchi, part of the ESOPHAGUS and TRACHEA, and the HEART and major blood vessels. A membrane called the pleura lines the cavity (parietal pleura) and continues over the lung (visceral pleura) and the rest of the cavity's contents, defining a space called the mediastinum. Disorders include blood (hemothorax) or air (pneumothorax, which can lead to ATELECTASIS) in the pleural cavity, and inflammation of the pleura (pleurisy).

Thoreau \thə-'rō\, **Henry David** (1817–1862) U.S. thinker, essayist, and naturalist. Born in Concord, Mass., Thoreau graduated from Harvard University and taught school for several years before deciding to become a poet of nature. Back in Concord, he came under the influence of RALPH WALDO EMERSON and began to publish pieces in the Transcendentalist magazine *The Dial*. In the years 1845–47, to demonstrate how satisfying a simple life could be, he lived in a hut beside Concord's Walden Pond; essays recording his daily life were assembled for his masterwork, *Walden* (1854). His *A Week on the Concord and Merrimack Rivers* (1849) was the only other book he published in his lifetime. He reflected on a night he spent in jail protesting the Mexican-American War in the essay "Civil Disobedience" (1849), which would later influence such figures as MOHANDAS K. GANDHI and MARTIN LUTHER KING. In later years his interest in TRANSCENDENTALISM waned and he became a dedicated abolitionist. His many nature writings and records of his wanderings in Canada, Maine, and Cape Cod display the mind of a keen naturalist. After his death his collected writings were published in 20 volumes, and further writings have continued to appear in print.

Thoreau, portrait by Samuel Worcester Rowse, 1854; in the Concord Free Public Library, Massachusetts.

BY COURTESY OF THE CORPORATION OF THE FREE PUBLIC LIBRARY, CONCORD, MASS.

Thorez \tò-'rez\, **Maurice** (1900–1964) French communist politician. He began working as a coal miner at 12. He joined the FRENCH COMMUNIST PARTY c. 1920 and was arrested several times for agitation. After becoming local party secretary (1923), he rose to secretary-general of the party (1930). He served in the Chamber of Deputies 1932–39 and 1945–60, and helped form the POPULAR FRONT government in 1936. He lived in the Soviet Union 1943–44, then returned to France and served as a minister of state (1945) and deputy premier (1946, 1947). He remained a dedicated Stalinist even after NIKITA KHRUSHCHEV

Thorndike, Edward L(ee) (1874–1949) U.S. psychologist. Born in Williamsburg, Mass., he trained under WILLIAM JAMES and JAMES MCKEEN CATTELL and later taught at Columbia University (1904–40). A pioneer in the fields of animal learning and educational psychology, he developed a form of behaviorism known as connectionism, which holds that learning takes place through associative bonds. He contributed significantly to the development of quantitative experimental methods and to improving the efficiency of schooling. Among his writings are *Introduction to the Theory of Mental and Social Measurements* (1904), *Principles of Teaching Based on Psychology* (1906), *Animal Intelligence* (1911), and *The Psychology of Wants, Interests, and Attitudes* (1935).

Thorndike, (Agnes) Sybil *later* **Dame Sybil** (1882–1976) British actress. With the OLD VIC company in London (1914–18), she became a leading tragic actress. Noted for her versatility in modern and classical plays, she originated the title role in GEORGE BERNARD SHAW's *Saint Joan* (1924). She managed several London theaters, and often costarred with her husband, the actor-director Lewis Casson, in her more than five decades in the theater.

Thoroughbred Light breed of racing and jumping HORSE descended from three desert stallions brought to England between 1689 and 1724. Thoroughbreds have a delicate head, slim body, broad chest, and short back. Most are bay, chestnut, brown, black, or gray. They stand about 16 hands (64 in., 163 cm) high and weigh about 1,000 lbs (450 kg). They are sensitive and high-spirited and are often used to improve other stock.

Thorp, John (1784–1848) U.S. inventor. Probably born in Rehoboth, Mass., he invented the ring spinning machine in 1828. By the 1860s it had largely replaced SAMUEL CROMPTON's SPINNING MULE in the world's textile mills because of its greater productivity and simplicity.

Thorpe, Jim *orig.* **James Francis** (1888–1953) U.S. athlete. Born on an Indian reservation near Pargue, Okla., he was of predominantly American Indian (Sauk and Fox) descent. He trained as a football halfback under Pop WARNER while attending the Indian Industrial School in Carlisle, Pa. (1908–12), where he also excelled at baseball, basketball, boxing, lacrosse, swimming, and hockey. In 1912 he won the Olympic decathlon and pentathlon by wide margins, but he was deprived of his medals in 1913 after it was discovered he had played semiprofessional baseball. After playing outfield for several National League baseball teams (1913–19), he went on to become an early star of professional football (1919–26). In 1920–21 he served as first president of what would become the NATIONAL FOOTBALL LEAGUE. He had difficulty adjusting to his retirement and suffered near-poverty and bouts of alcoholism. His Olympic medals were restored posthumously in 1983. Thorpe is generally regarded as the greatest American athlete of the entire 20th century.

Jim Thorpe demonstrating the drop kick.

THE BETTMANN ARCHIVE

Thorvaldsen \'tȯr-ˌwȯl-sən, 'tůr-ˌväl-sən\, **Bertel** (1768/70–1844) Danish sculptor. Son of an Icelandic wood carver, he studied in Copenhagen and won a scholarship for travel to Rome, where he would remain over 40 years and pursue one of the most successful sculpting careers of the 19th century. His return to Copenhagen in 1838 was celebrated as a national event. Most of his sculptures are reinterpretations of classical figures and themes; he also did religious statues and portrait busts.

Thoth \'tōth, 'thōth, 'tōt\ Egyptian god of the moon and of reckoning, learning, and writing. He was the inventor of writing, the creator of languages, the representative of RE, and the scribe, interpreter, and adviser of the gods. In the myth of OSIRIS, Thoth protected the pregnant ISIS and healed the eye of her son HORUS. He judged the deceased and reported the results to Osiris. His sacred animals were the IBIS and the baboon, millions of which were mummified in his honor. He was often represented in human form with the head of an ibis. The Greeks identified Thoth with HERMES; as Hermes Trismegistos he was regarded as the author of the HERMETIC writings.

thought, laws of Traditionally, the three fundamental laws of logic: (1) the law of contradiction, (2) the law of excluded middle (or third), and (3) the principle of identity. That is, (1) for all propositions p, it is impossible for both p and not p to be true (symbolically, $\neg(p \wedge \neg p)$); (2) either p or not p must be true, there being no third or middle true proposition between them (symbolically $p \vee \neg p$); and (3) if a propositional function F is true of an individual variable x, then F is indeed true of x (symbolically, $(\forall x)\ [F(x) \supset F(x)]$). Another formulation of the principle of identity asserts that a thing is identical with itself, or $(\forall x)$ $(x = x)$.

Thousand and One Nights, The *or* **Arabian Nights' Entertainment** *Arabic* **Alf laylah wa laylah** Collection of Oriental stories of uncertain date and authorship. The frame story, in which the vengeful King Shahryar's plan to marry and execute a new wife each day is foiled by the resourceful Scheherazade, is probably Indian; the tales with which Scheherazade beguiles Shahryar, postponing and eventually averting her execution, come from India, Iran, Iraq, Egypt, Turkey, and possibly Greece. It is now believed that the collection is a composite work originally transmitted orally and developed over a period of several centuries. The first published version was an 18th-century European translation; Sir RICHARD BURTON's *Book of the Thousand Nights and a Night* (1885–88) has become the best-known English translation.

Thousand Islands Group of about 1,500 small islands extending 80 mi (128 km) in the ST. LAWRENCE RIVER between New York state and Ontario, Canada. Some belong to Canada and some to the U.S. They include summer resort facilities and the Canadian St. Lawrence Islands National Park, which was established in 1904 and covers 988 acres (400 hectares). The Thousand Islands International Bridge, which contains five spans linking some of the islands and is 8.5 mi (13,7 km) long, connects New York and Ontario.

Thrace Ancient and modern region, southeastern BALKAN PENINSULA. Its borders have varied at different periods. In ancient Greek times it was bounded by the DANUBE RIVER, the AEGEAN SEA, and the BLACK SEA. Modern Thrace corresponds to southern Bulgaria, the Greek province of Thrace, and European Turkey, including the GALLIPOLI peninsula. The Thracians were Indo-Europeans who settled in the region in the 2nd millennium BC; their culture was noted for its poetry and music, and their soldiers were known as superior fighters. Later colonized by Greeks in the 7th century BC, it became subject to Persia in the 6th century BC and to Macedon in the 4th century BC. Reduced to a Roman province in the 1st century AD, its northern part was annexed to MOESIA. It later became part of the Byzantine empire, and in 1453 part of the Ottoman empire. The northern part was annexed by Bulgaria in 1885; the eastern part passed to Turkey in 1923. The region harvests corn, rice, grapes, oysters, and eels; the chief cash crop is Turkish tobacco.

thrasher Any of 17 species (family Mimidae) of New World songbirds having a downcurved bill and noted for noisily foraging on the ground in dense thickets and for loud varied songs. Thrashers occur from northern Canada to central Mexico and the Caribbean. The brown thrasher *(Toxostoma rufum),* of North America east of the Rocky Mtns., is about 12 in. (30 cm) long and has red-brown plumage with streaked underparts. Long-tailed drab species are found in the arid southwestern U.S. and in Mexico.

Brown thrasher (*Toxostoma rufum*).
THASE DANIEL

thread Tightly twisted YARN consisting of several strands that has a circular cross-section and is used in commercial and home SEWING machines and for hand sewing. Thread is usually wound on spools, with thread size (degree of fineness) indicated on the spool end. COTTON thread can be used with fabrics made from yarn of plant origin, such as cotton and linen, and with rayon (made from cellulose, a plant substance). SILK thread is suitable for silks and wools, both of animal origin. NYLON and POLYESTER threads are appropriate for synthetics and for knits with a high degree of stretch.

thread cross Object made typically of two sticks bound together in the shape of a cross, with colored threads wound around their ends to resemble a cobweb, and used in Tibetan magical rituals to entrap evil spirits. Similar devices have been found in South Africa, Peru, Australia, and Sweden. They vary from simple diamond shapes to complex wheel- or box-shaped combinations reaching 11 ft (3 m) high. They are often highly decorated with wool, feather, and bits of paper.

Three Emperors' League *German* **Dreikaiserbund** Diplomatic alignment of the empires of Germany, Austria-Hungary, and Russia devised by OTTO VON BISMARCK in 1872. Its aim was to neutralize disagreement between Austria-Hungary and Russia over spheres of influence in the Balkans and to isolate Germany's enemy France. After the first Three Emperors' League (1872–78) collapsed, Bismarck succeeded in renewing it (1881, 1884). When Russia declined a third renewal, Bismarck negotiated a separate accord with Russia, the REINSURANCE TREATY (1887). See also AUSTRO-GERMAN ALLIANCE.

Three Gorges Dam Project Dam designed to span China's YANGTZE RIVER (Chang Jiang). On completion, scheduled for 2009, it would be the largest dam in the world, generating as much hydroelectricity as 15 coal-burning power stations. It would also create an immense deep-water reservoir that would allow 10,000-ton freighters to navigate 1,400 mi (2,250 km) inland from the East CHINA SEA. The extremely controversial project will require displacement of more than a million people and destruction of magnificent scenery and archaeological sites. Critics also fear potential pollution and silting of the reservoir and the possibility of the dam's collapse. Though construction began in 1993, a third of the National People's Congress either abstained or opposed it and the WORLD BANK would not advance funds, citing environmental and other concerns. Critics contend that smaller dams on Yangtze tributaries could accomplish the same purpose with fewer risks.

Three Henrys, War of the (1587–89) Last of the Wars of RELIGION in France, fought between King HENRY III, the ultra-Catholic Henri I de Lorraine, duc de GUISE, and the HUGUENOT leader Henry of Navarre (later HENRY IV). Early conflicts were won by the HOLY LEAGUE led by Guise, who forced Henry III to sign the Edict of Union in 1588, naming him lieutenant general of the kingdom. Humiliated, Henry III had Guise assassinated, but the League continued to wield power and Henry called for help from his cousin, Henry of Navarre. The royalist-Huguenot coalition forced the Leaguers to retreat, but Henry III was assassinated, and before he died he exhorted the future Henry IV to become a Catholic.

Three Kingdoms (AD 220–80) Trio of warring Chinese states that followed the demise of the HAN DYNASTY. CAO CAO put his son on the throne of the kingdom of Wei, which controlled northern China. The kingdom of Shu-Han was established in present-day Sichuan by Liu Bei and his adviser ZHUGE LIANG, and the kingdom of Wu was established in the south, with its capital at Nanjing. They were all subsumed into the JIN dynasty by AD 280. The 60 years of the Three Kingdoms have inspired Chinese literature, and especially historical fiction, ever since.

Three Mile Island Nuclear power station near Harrisburg, Pa., site of the most serious accident in the history of the U.S. nuclear power industry (March 28, 1979). Mechanical failures and human errors caused a partial meltdown of the nuclear core and the release of radioactive gases. Despite assurances that there had been little risk to people's health, the accident increased public fears about the safety of nuclear power and strengthened public opposition to its use, effectively stopping construction of nuclear reactors and further development of U.S. nuclear power plants.

3M See MINNESOTA MINING & MANUFACTURING CO.

threonine \'thrē-ə-ˌnēn\ One of the essential AMINO acids. It occurs in egg, milk, gelatin, and other PROTEINS and may be synthesized or obtained by hydrolyzing casein. It is used in nutrition and biochemical research and as a dietary supplement.

thresher shark Any of five species (family Alopiidae) of SHARKS with a long, scythelike tail that may constitute almost half their total length. They are found in tropical and temperate seas worldwide. They eat squid and schooling fishes, attacking after circling and herding their prey into small groups. They sometimes use their tail to stun their prey or, by thrashing the water, to frighten them. They are not considered dangerous to humans. The long-tailed thresher, or fox shark *(Alopias vulpinus),* is a big, dark fish that grows about 20 ft (6 m) long.

thrips Any of some 5,000 species (order Thysanoptera) of tiny winged insects that feed chiefly on plants, inhabiting temperate and tropical areas worldwide. Many species damage cultivated plants, by either sucking the sap or transmitting viral plant diseases. A few species are predators. Thrips reach a maximum length of about half an inch (15 mm). Most have two pairs of long, narrow, hair-fringed wings.

thrombocyte See PLATELET

thrombosis \thräm-'bō-səs\ Formation of a blood clot (thrombus) in the heart or a blood vessel. Contributing factors include injury to a blood vessel's lining from INFLAMMATION (thrombophlebitis) or atherosclerosis (see ARTERIOSCLEROSIS), blood flow that is turbulent (e.g., from an ANEURYSM) or sluggish (e.g., from prolonged bed rest), or COAGULATION abnormalities (e.g., from high numbers of PLATELETS or excessive FATS in the blood). Thrombosis, especially in deep veins of the leg, is a particular danger after major surgery. A thrombus can block blood flow at the point of clot formation or break free to block it elsewhere (EMBOLISM). See also LUNG INFARCTION.

throne Chair of state set on a dais and often surmounted by a canopy, representing the power of the dignitary who sits on it and sometimes conferring that power. In Greek history, thrones were identified as seats of the gods; soon the meaning of the word included the symbolic seats of those who held religious or secular power, a meaning common to virtually all cultures. The oldest surviving throne was built into the walls of Knossos (c. 1800 BC). Probably the most magnificent was the jewel-studded Peacock Throne of the rulers of Delhi, stolen from India by Persia in 1739 and thereafter the symbol of the Persian/Iranian monarchy. In the late 17th and 18th century, thrones were often made of silver, but later versions tend to be of gilded wood.

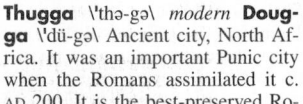

So-called throne of King Dagobert I, bronze, from the treasury of Saint-Denis, Paris, probably 8th century with 12th-century additions.

BY COURTESY OF THE BIBLIOTHEQUE NATIONALE, PARIS

throttle VALVE for regulating the supply of a fluid (as steam) to an engine, especially the valve controlling the volume of vaporized fuel delivered to the cylinders of an INTERNAL-COMBUSTION ENGINE. In an automobile engine, gasoline is held in a chamber above the CARBURETOR. Air flows down through the throat of the carburetor, past the throttle valve, and into the intake manifold. A throat is formed by the reduced diameter, and acceleration of the air through this smaller passage causes a decrease in pressure related to the amount of air flowing. This decrease in throat pressure results in fuel flow from the jet into the airstream. Any increase in airflow caused by change in engine speed or throttle position increases the pressure differential acting on the fuel and causes more fuel to flow. See also VENTURI tube.

thrush Any of about 300 species of songbirds (family Turdidae) that usually have a slender bill and "booted" lower legs (i.e., covered in front with one long scale instead of many short ones). Thrushes are 5–12 in. (13–30 cm) long. Most have dull plumage, often with patches of bright yellow, red, or blue. They are found virtually worldwide but are most diverse in the Old World, especially in Africa. The northern species are strong migrants. Occupying a wide range of arboreal and terrestrial habitats, thrushes eat insects and fruit; a few eat snails or earthworms. They lay three to six eggs in an open cup-shaped nest; a few occupy cavities. Some of the thrushes, including the hermit thrush and WOOD THRUSH, have notably beautiful songs. See also BLACKBIRD, BLUEBIRD, CHAT, OUZEL, REDSTART, ROBIN.

Thuan Thien See LE LOI

Thucydides \thü-'si-də-ˌdēz\ (c. 460–404? BC) Greatest of ancient Greek historians. An Athenian who commanded a fleet in the Peloponnesian War, Thucydides failed to prevent the capture of the important city of Amphipolis and consequently was exiled for 20 years. During that period he wrote his *History of the Peloponnesian War;* evidently he did not live to complete it, for it stops abruptly in 411 BC. It presents the first recorded political and moral analysis of a nation's war policies, treating the causes of the conflict, the characters of the two states, and the technical aspects of warfare in a carefully drawn, strictly chronological narrative of events, including some in which he took an active part.

Thucydides, detail of a Roman bust after a Greek original; in Holkham Hall, Norfolk, England.

BY COURTESY OF NATIONAL MONUMENTS RECORDS, LONDON

Thugga \'thə-gə\ *modern* **Dougga** \'dü-gə\ Ancient city, North Africa. It was an important Punic city when the Romans assimilated it c. AD 200. It is the best-preserved Roman site in Tunisia; its ruins include an arch in honor of Septimius SEVERUS, a forum, baths, villas, an aqueduct, a theater, and a temple of Jupiter, Juno, and Minerva. There is also a pre-Roman ruin of a 2nd-century-BC mausoleum.

thumb piano See MBIRA

Thunder Bay City (pop., 1991: 114,000), western central Ontario. It is located on the northwestern shore of Lake SUPERIOR. Its first settlement was a French fur trading post c. 1678. In the 1870s and 1880s silver strikes and the arrival of the Canadian Pacific Railway brought prosperity to the twin towns of Port Arthur and Fort William that had grown up there. Their rivalry was resolved with the unification of their harbor facilities in 1906; the towns merged in 1970 and created the city of Thunder Bay. It is one of Canada's busiest ports, with grain storage and transshipment depots; other industries include shipbuilding.

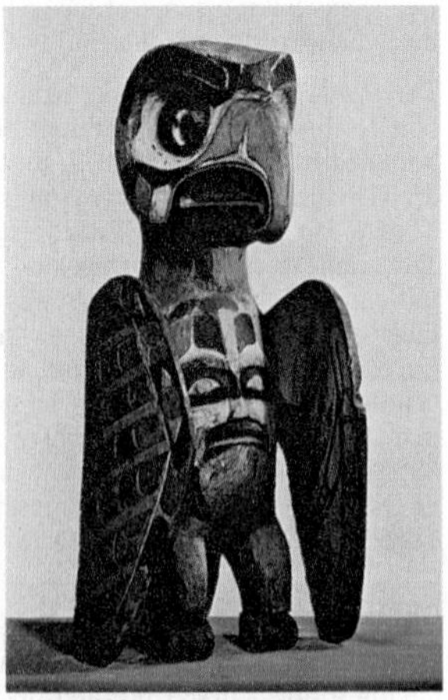

Wooden thunderbird of the Haida Indians, northwest coast of North America, 19th century; in the British Museum.

BY COURTESY OF THE TRUSTEES OF THE BRITISH MUSEUM

thunderbird In North American Indian mythology, a powerful spirit in the form of a bird that watered the earth and made vegetation grow. Lightning was believed to flash from its eyes or beak, and the beating of its wings was thought to represent rolling thunder. It was often portrayed with an extra head on its abdomen, particularly on TOTEM poles, and was frequently accompanied by lesser bird spirits. Though it is best known in North America, evidence of similar figures has been found throughout Africa, Asia, and Europe.

Thunderbolt See P-47

thunderstorm Violent, short-lived atmospheric disturbance, almost always associated with cumulonimbus clouds (very tall, dense rain clouds) and accompanied by thunder and LIGHTNING. Such storms usually generate strong, gusty winds and heavy rain, and occasionally HAIL or TORNADOES. Thunderstorms have been known to occur in almost every part of the world, although they are rare in the polar regions. In the U.S. the areas of maximum thunderstorm activity are the Florida peninsula and the coast of the Gulf of Mexico (70–80 days per year).

Thünen \'tue̅-nən\, **Johann Heinrich von** (1783–1850) German economist and agriculturalist. After carrying out research on his own estate into the relationship between the costs of commodity transportation and the location of production, he set forth his theories in *The Isolated State* (1826). He used an imaginary city, isolated in the middle of a fertile plain, to create a model of concentric zones of agricultural production. Heavy products and perishables would be produced close to the town, lighter and durable goods on the periphery; returns on the land would diminish as transport costs to the city increased. Thünen's model influenced many later writers on the subject.

Thurber, James (Grover) (1894–1961) U.S. writer and cartoonist. Born in Columbus, Ohio, he attended Ohio State University before moving to New York City in 1926. He was on the *New Yorker*'s staff 1927–33 and thereafter remained a leading contributor. His drawings illustrated his first book, *Is Sex Necessary?* (1929; with E.B. WHITE), and his cartoons became some of the most popular and recognizable in America. In 1940 failing eyesight forced him to curtail his drawing. His writings include *My Life and Hard Times* (1933), *Fables for Our Time* (1940), *The Thurber Album* (1952), the *New Yorker* memoir *The Years with Ross* (1959), and the children's book *The 13 Clocks* (1950). He is noted for his vision of the befuddled urban man who, like the hero of "The Secret Life of Walter Mitty" (1939; film, 1946), escapes into fantasy.

Thuringia \thu̇-'rin-jē-ə\ *German* **Thüringen** \'tue̅-riŋ-ən\ Historic region and state (pop., 1996 est.: 2,504,000), Germany. It includes the land around the Thuringian Forest in what was formerly southwestern EAST GERMANY. The capital is ERFURT. The Germanic Thuringians appeared after c. AD 350 and were conquered by the Huns in the mid-5th century. In 1485 it became part of SAXONY and was divided into several states; they joined the German empire in 1871 and were reunited after World War I. Following the partition of Germany in 1945, the state became part of East Germany; it was reconstituted as a state of the unified Germany in 1990. The economy is largely industrial.

Thurmond, (James) Strom (born 1902) U.S. politician and senator from 1955. Born in Edgefield, S.C., he served as a state senator (1933–38) and circuit court judge (1938–41). As governor (1947–51), he expanded the state educational system. At the 1948 Democratic convention he led a faction of Southern delegates opposed to the party's civil-rights policy; the so-called DIXIECRATS nominated Thurmond as their presidential candidate, and he won 39 electoral votes. In 1954 he was elected to the U.S. Senate; he would become its longest-serving member. Highly conservative, he advocated states' rights, opposed civil-rights legislation, and supported increases in military spending.

Thurstone, L(ouis) L(eon) (1887–1955) U.S. psychologist. Born in Chicago, he taught primarily at the University of Chicago (1927–52). Concerned with the measurement of people's attitudes and intelligence, he was instrumental in the development of psychometrics. His principal work, *The Vectors of the Mind* (1935; revised as *Multiple-Factor Analysis,* 1947), presented the technique of multiple-factor analysis to explain correlations between results in psychological tests.

Thutmose III \thüt-'mō-sə\ (died 1426 BC) Egyptian king of the 18th dynasty (r.1479–1426 BC), often regarded as the greatest PHARAOH of ancient Egypt. He ascended the throne around the age of 10, but his aunt, HATSHEPSUT, ruled first as his regent and then in her own right for the next 20 years. On her death he began military campaigns to reestablish Egyptian supremacy in Syria and Palestine. Later he attacked and defeated the kingdom of Mitanni, a powerful Mesopotamian rival of Egypt. He subdued the Nubian tribes to the south and employed them in the gold mines that became the basis of Egypt's wealth. He consolidated his victories with more campaigns and established a system whereby native rulers would pay yearly tribute to Egypt and send their heirs as hostages to Egypt, where they would be educated at court. At home he enlarged the temple of Amon at Karnak. His mummy was discovered in 1889 and his mortuary temple in 1962.

thyme \'tīm\ Pungent herb *(Thymus vulgaris)* of the MINT family, native to southern Europe, the Mediterranean, Asia Minor, and Central Asia, and cultivated in North America. A small, low-growing shrub, it has small, curled leaves that give off a fragrant odor when crushed. The dried leaves and flowering tops are used to flavor a wide range of foods. Bees are fond of thyme, and Sicily's thyme honey has been famous for centuries. The essential oil has antiseptic and anesthetic properties and is used as an internal medicine; it is also used in perfumes and toothpastes.

Thyme (*Thymus vulgaris*).
WALTER CHANDOHA

thymine \'thī-ˌmēn\ Organic compound of the PYRIMIDINE family, often called a base, consisting of a ring containing both nitrogen and carbon atoms, and a methyl group. It occurs in combined form in many important biological molecules, particularly DNA (where its complementary base is ADENINE). It or its corresponding NUCLEOSIDE or NUCLEOTIDE may be prepared from DNA by selective techniques of HYDROLYSIS.

thymus \'thī-məs\ Pyramid-shaped lymphoid organ (see LYMPHOID tissue) between the breastbone and the heart. Starting at puberty, it shrinks slowly. It has no lymphatic vessels draining into it and does not filter lymph; instead, stem cells in its outer cortex develop into different kinds of T (FOR THYMUS) CELLS (see BLOOD-CELL FORMATION, LYMPHOCYTES). Some migrate to the inner medulla and enter the bloodstream; those that do not may be destroyed to prevent autoimmune reactions. This process is most active during infancy. If a newborn's thymus is removed, not enough T cells are produced, the SPLEEN and LYMPH NODES have little tissue, and the immune system fails, causing a gradual, fatal wasting disease. Thymus removal in adults has little effect.

thyroid function test Clinical or laboratory test of the THYROID GLAND's efficiency in synthesizing its two most active HORMONES, THYROXINE (T_4) and triiodothyronine (T_3). Some tests measure the hormones' metabolic effects. Others assess some aspect of their synthesis, release, and transport, usually by measuring the uptake and distribution in the body of swallowed radioactive IODINE, which concentrates in the thyroid.

thyroid gland Endocrine gland in the throat that secretes HORMONES vital to metabolism and growth. Secretion of thyroid hormones—mostly THYROXINE (T_4)—is controlled by thyroid-stimulating hormone (TSH), released by the PITUITARY gland when their level in the blood drops below a certain threshold (see ENDOCRINE system). These hormones' primary action in adults is to regulate cellular oxygen consumption (metabolic rate). They also lower blood CHOLESTEROL and are necessary for normal growth and development of children, in whom deficiency causes CRETINISM. The thyroid also produces calcitonin, a hormone that stimulates deposition of calcium from the blood into the bones, balancing the action of parathyroid hormone. See also GOITER, GRAVES' DISEASE, IODINE DEFICIENCY, MYXEDEMA.

thyroxine \thī-'räk-ˌsēn\ *or* ***l*-tetraiodothyronine T_4** \'el-ˌte-trə-ī-ˌō-dō-'thī-rə-ˌnēn\ One of the two major HORMONES (along with the closely related *l*-triiodothyronine T_3) secreted by the THYROID GLAND. Its principal function is to stimulate OXYGEN consumption and thus METABOLISM in all cells and tissues in the body. Thyroxine is formed by the addition of IODINE to the amino acid TYROSINE while the latter is in a bound form. Thyroxine secretion is excessive in hyperthyroidism and deficient in hypothyroidism.

Thyssen \'tue̅-sən\, **Fritz** (1873–1951) German industrialist and financial backer of ADOLF HITLER. Thyssen entered the family iron, steel, and coal business and inherited his father's fortune and empire in 1926 (see THYSSEN KRUPP STAHL). He created a family business trust that came to

S
T
U
V

control over 75% of Germany's ore reserves and employ 200,000 workers. Distressed by the rise of socialism in Germany, he supported Hitler and helped finance his rise to chancellor. But Thyssen opposed Hitler's later policies and fled to Switzerland in 1939, which allowed Hitler to confiscate Thyssen's fortune (about $88 million). He was arrested in France (1941) and imprisoned by the Nazis. After the war, he was convicted as a "minor Nazi" and ordered to pay 15% of his property in restitution.

Thyssen Krupp Stahl \'tü̅-sən-'krůp-'shtäl\ German steel company. The Krupp firm began in 1811 when Friedrich Krupp (1787–1826) founded a steel plant in Essen, and it remained in family hands for a century and a half. Known for its high-quality steel and its cannons and other armaments, Krupp prospered with the rise of the German navy. It enjoyed a monopoly on arms manufacturing during World War I; one of its most potent weapons was "BIG BERTHA." After the war, Germany was forbidden to manufacture arms, and parts of the Krupp works were dismantled, though it remained a vast industrial empire. Krupp's factories were central to Germany's illegal rearmament under ADOLF HITLER in the 1930s. After World War II, Alfried Krupp (1907–1967) was convicted of war crimes for using slave labor and ordered to forfeit all his property, but with the outbreak of the Korean War he was granted amnesty and his property restored. In 1968, after his son renounced the Krupp name and fortune, the company went public. In 1992 it merged with Hoesch AG to become Fried Krupp AG Hoesch-Krupp. Thyssen AG originated as a rolling mill founded by August Thyssen (1842–1926). It merged with seven other steelworks to become Vereinigte Stahlwerke AG, but reassumed its own identity in 1953. In 1999 the rival companies merged to become Thyssen Krupp Stahl.

Tiamat \'tē-ä-ˌmät\ In Mesopotamian mythology, a primal goddess, a personification of salt water and the mother of the gods. When conflict between her husband, Apsu, and the other gods resulted in Apsu's death, Tiamat waged war on the other divinities, backed by an army of demons she had created. Her battle with, and defeat at the hands of, MARDUK forms the substance of the Babylonian creation epic *Enuma elish*. From her body Marduk fashioned the heavens and the earth.

Tian *or* **T'ien** \'tyen\ (Chinese: "sky, heaven") In indigenous Chinese religion, the supreme power reigning over humans and lesser gods. The term refers to a deity, to impersonal nature, or to both. As a god, Tian is an impersonal power, in contrast to the supreme ruler Shangdi, but the two are closely identified and their names are sometimes used synonymously. In later references, tian is likened to nature or fate. Scholars generally agree that Tian was the source of moral law, but long debated whether it responded to pleas, rewarding and punishing human actions, or whether events merely followed its order and principles.

Tian Shan *or* **Tien Shan** \'tyen-'shän\ Mountain chain (*shan*), Kyrgyzstan and XINJIANG UYGUR, western China. Its ranges and valleys stretch for about 1,500 mi (2,500 km) in an east–west direction. Its highest point is Pobeda Peak, at 24,406 ft (7,439 m) tall, in Kyrgyzstan; the peak was discovered in 1943 by a Soviet expedition. Most of the area's population lives in the FERGANA VALLEY.

Tiananmen Square \'tyán-'án-'men\ One of the largest public squares in the world, originally designed and built in Beijing in 1651 and enlarged in 1958. It is named for the massive stone "Gate of Heavenly Peace" (Tiananmen) at its northern end. It contains and is surrounded by halls, museums, and monuments, including the Mao Zedong Memorial Hall, where Mao's body rests in state. Tiananmen Square had been the rallying point for student demonstrations since 1919. In 1989 massive prodemocracy demonstrations there eventually attracted more than a million protesters, who occupied large sections of Beijing. Tanks were called in to disperse the crowds; hundreds were killed (the number is disputed) and thousands arrested, and the movement was effectively crushed. See also FANG LIZHI.

Tiancong See HONGTAIJI

Tianjin *or* **T'ien-chin** *or* **Tientsin** \'tyen-'jin\ Seaport and municipality with provincial status (pop., 1999 est.: city, 4,835,327; municipality, 9,590,000), on the HAI RIVER, northeastern China. Connected to the YANGTZE RIVER (Chang Jiang) by the GRAND CANAL, it is China's third-largest city. It has been a major transportation and trading center since the MONGOL DYNASTY in the 13th century. It was a garrison town during the MING DYNASTY (1368–1644). The British and French occupied it during the Second OPIUM WAR (1856–60); a treaty signed there in 1858 opened 11 Chinese ports to foreign trade. As a treaty port it developed rapidly. It was the scene of heavy fighting during the BOXER REBELLION (1900), after which it was placed under an international commission and its walls razed. It is the leading port in northern China and the country's second-largest manufacturing center. Educational institutions include Tianjin University (1895) and Nankai University (1919).

Tianshi Dao See FIVE PECKS OF RICE

Tiantai \'tyän-'dī\ *Japanese* **Tendai** \'ten-'dī\ Buddhist sect founded by ZHIYI in the 6th century AD. Its chief scripture is the LOTUS SUTRA, and the school is thus known as the Lotus school. Its basic philosophical doctrine is summarized as the Triple Truth: All DHARMAS lack ontological reality; nevertheless, they have a temporary existence; and they are simultaneously unreal and temporarily existing—an absolute truth that surpasses the others. In Tiantai, all Buddhist learning is arranged in a grand hierarchical scheme. In Japan, SAICHO attempted to incorporate ZEN meditation, monastic discipline, and esoteric cults. Amalgamation of SHINTO and Buddhism was also encouraged.

Tibbett \'tib-ət\, **Lawrence (Mervil)** *orig.* **Lawrence Mervil Tibbet** (1896–1960) U.S. baritone. Born in Bakersfield, Cal., he performed as a singing actor before moving into opera. After his 1923 Metropolitan Opera debut, he was a stalwart member of the company until his retirement in 1950, taking leading roles in such Met premieres as *The Emperor Jones*, *Merry Mount*, *Simon Boccanegra*, *Peter Grimes*, and *Khovanshchina*. He also starred in several musical films and appeared on radio's popular *Your Hit Parade*.

Tiber River \'tī-bər\ *Italian* **Tevere** \'tā-vā-rā\ River, Italy. The country's second-longest river, it rises in the Tuscan APENNINES, and flows south for 252 mi (405 km), ultimately passing through the city of ROME before entering the Mediterranean at OSTIA. It was an important navigation route for trade in Roman times. Despite sporadic dredging over the centuries, its persistent silting has limited its use in modern times.

Tiberias \tī-'bir-ē-əs\ *Hebrew* **Teverya** \tə-'ver-yə\ Town (pop., 1995: 35,291) and resort, Sea of GALILEE, northeastern Israel. At 689 ft (210 m) below sea level, it is one of the lowest-lying cities in the world. Founded c. AD 20 by HEROD ANTIPAS, it was named for TIBERIUS. After the destruction of Jerusalem by the Romans in AD 70 it became a center of Jewish learning and later the seat of SANHEDRIN and rabbinical schools. The TALMUD was edited there in the 3rd–6th century. SALADIN took the town from the Crusaders in 1187. The modern town was refounded under the British mandate in 1922, and it became part of independent Israel in 1948. Historic sites include the tomb of MOSES MAIMONIDES. It is one of the four holy cities of JUDAISM (see also HEBRON, JERUSALEM, ZEFAT).

Tiberias, Lake See Sea of GALILEE

Tiberius *in full* **Tiberius (Julius) Caesar Augustus** *orig.* **Tiberius Claudius Nero** (42 BC–AD 37) Second Roman emperor (AD 14–37). He was raised by AUGUSTUS, who had married his mother, Livia Drusilla. In his first military command, at 22, he recovered Roman legionary standards lost for decades in Parthia, and returned to great acclaim. He was forced to give up his beloved wife to marry Augustus' daughter JULIA (12 BC). Despite becoming TRIBUNE, he went into self-imposed exile on Rhodes (6 BC), becoming an angry recluse. By 4 BC Julia was exiled for promiscuity by Augustus, who recalled Tiberius and named him his heir. As emperor he initially ran the state efficiently and instituted some reforms, with only occasional severity, such as exiling Rome's Jewish population on a pretext. When his

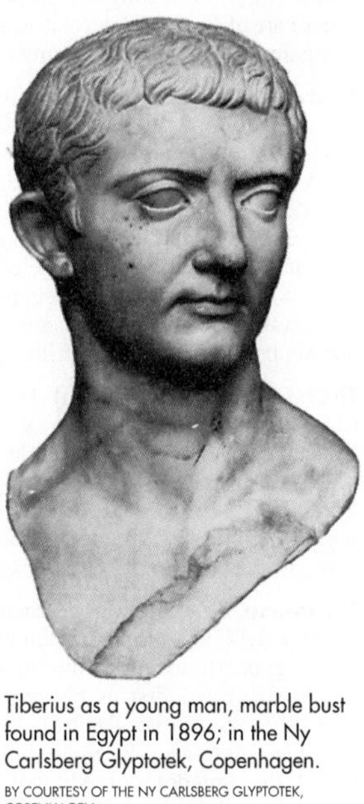

Tiberius as a young man, marble bust found in Egypt in 1896; in the Ny Carlsberg Glyptotek, Copenhagen.
BY COURTESY OF THE NY CARLSBERG GLYPTOTEK, COPENHAGEN

S T U V

son Drusus died mysteriously, he gave his trust to SEJANUS and was persuaded to move to Capri (27). He became increasingly violent, killing and torturing at a whim. After Sejanus became coconsul in 31, Tiberius became suspicious of his ambition and executed him, then named CALIGULA his heir. In 37 the PRAETORIAN GUARD declared its support for Caligula and killed Tiberius when he was sick in bed.

Tibet \ti-'bet\ *Tibetan* **Bod** \'bōd\ *Chinese* **Xizang** *or* **Hsi-tsang** \'shē-'dzäŋ\ Former country, now autonomous region (pop., 2000 est.: 2,620,000), western China. The capital is LHASA. Before the 1950s it was a unique entity with its own Buddhist culture and religion that sought isolation from the rest of the world. Situated on a plateau averaging 16,000 ft (4,900 m) above sea level, it is the highest region in the world. Its surrounding mountain ranges include the KUNLUN MTNS. and the HIMALAYAS; Mount EVEREST rises on its border with Nepal. Tibet emerged as a powerful Buddhist kingdom in the 7th–8th century AD. It came under the Mongols in the 13th century and under the MANCHU dynasty in the 18th century. After the 1911–12 Chinese revolution, it became independent under British influence. The Communist Chinese invaded and occupied the region in 1950 and harshly suppressed an anti-Chinese rebellion in 1959. In 1965 it was made a nominally autonomous region within Communist China. Its Buddhism-based culture was nearly destroyed during the Chinese CULTURAL REVOLUTION. Some religious and economic reforms have occurred since the late 1970s, but independence movements have increased since the late 1980s. Tibet's spiritual leader, the DALAI LAMA, set up a government-in-exile in India in 1959 and continued his attempt to rally world opinion for Tibetan independence.

Tibetan Buddhism Form of MAHAYANA BUDDHISM that evolved from the 7th century in Tibet. Based on MADHYAMIKA and YOGACARA philosophies, it incorporates the rituals of VAJRAYANA, the monastic disciplines of early THERAVADA, and the shamanistic features of BON. The predominant Tibetan sect for the past three centuries has been DGE-LUGS-PA. Its spiritual head is the DALAI LAMA. The Tibetan canon is divided into the *Bka'-'gyur* ("Translation of the Word"), consisting of canonical texts translated mostly from Sanskrit, and *Bstan-'gyur* ("Transmitted Word"), consisting of commentaries by Indian masters. After the Chinese Communist takeover in 1959, Tibetans began a massive emigration that has spread Tibetan Buddhism around the globe.

Tibetan language SINO-TIBETAN LANGUAGE spoken by more than 5 million people in Tibet (Xizang), Qinghai, Sichuan, and Gansu provinces in China; Bhutan; northern Nepal; and Jammu and Kashmir in India and Pakistan. Since the occupation of Tibet by China in 1959, enclaves of Tibetan-speakers have dispersed to India and other parts of the world. Spoken Tibetan comprises a very diverse range of dialects, conventionally divided into several groups: Western, including Balti and Ladakhi in Jammu and Kashmir; Central, including the speech of Lhasa and most of the Nepalese dialects (including Sherpa); Southern, including the dialects of Sikkim and Bhutan; Khams, or Southeastern, including the dialects of the interior plateau, southern Qinghai, eastern Tibet, and parts of western Sichuan; Amdo or Northeastern, including the dialects of northern Qinghai, southern Gansu, and northern Sichuan. Most Tibetans share a common literary language, written in a distinctive script of disputed origin first attested in the 8th century AD.

tic Sudden rapid, recurring MUSCLE contraction—usually a blink, sniff, twitch, or shrug—always brief, irresistible, and localized. Frequency decreases from head to foot. Unlike a spasm, a CRAMP, or the movements of CHOREA or EPILEPSY, it does not interfere with other movement and can be held off for a time. It can become ingrained as a habit of which the person (most often a nervous child 5–12 years old) is unaware. Most tics are probably psychological, but similar movements occur in some physical disorders (e.g., late-stage ENCEPHALITIS). People with tics have some control over the movement but feel impelled to go through with it to feel better. Tension increases the movement's likelihood, and distraction reduces it. Psychotherapy, relaxation training, and biofeedback training have had some success in treating tics.

Ticino River \tē-'chē-nō\ River, Switzerland and Italy. It rises on the slopes of the St. Gotthard range, winds south through Ticino canton, traverses Lake MAGGIORE, and continues south to the PO RIVER, for a total course of 154 mi (248 km). It is navigable below Lake Maggiore, and is an important source of hydroelectric power for Switzerland. HANNIBAL defeated the Romans on its banks in 218 BC.

tick Any of some 825 parasitic ARACHNID species (suborder Ixodida, order Parasitiformes), found worldwide. Adults may be slightly more than an inch (30 mm) long, but most species are much smaller. Hard ticks start and end each developmental stage—egg, larva, nymph, adult—on the ground; at the completion of each stage, they attach to a host (usually a MAMMAL), engorge on blood, then drop to the ground. Soft ticks feed intermittently, pass through several nymphal stages, and live in the host's den or nest. Hard ticks may draw large amounts of blood, secrete paralyzing or lethal neurotoxins, and transmit diseases. Soft ticks may also carry diseases. The deer tick is the principal vector of LYME disease.

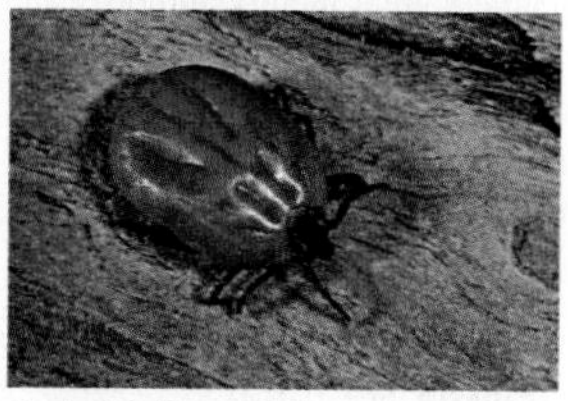

Cattle tick (*Boophilus*).

E.R. DEGGINGER

Ticonderoga \tī-,kän-də-'rō-gə\ Town (pop., 2000: 5,167) on Lake GEORGE, northeastern New York. In 1755 the French built Fort Carillon on nearby Lake CHAMPLAIN. Captured by the British in 1759, the fort was renamed Ticonderoga. In the AMERICAN REVOLUTION, ETHAN ALLEN and his Green Mountain Boys seized the fort in 1775. The British retook it in 1777 but abandoned it after the Battle of SARATOGA. The restored fort and the area around the town are now tourist attractions.

Ticonderoga, Battle of Conflict of the AMERICAN REVOLUTION. Held by the British since 1759, Fort Ticonderoga was overrun on the morning of May 10, 1775, in a surprise attack by the Green Mountain Boys under ETHAN ALLEN, assisted by BENEDICT ARNOLD. British artillery seized there was moved to Boston by HENRY KNOX, and formed the basis for the American artillery in the Revolution.

Ticunas See TUCUNAS

tidal flat Level muddy surface bordering an ESTUARY, alternately submerged and exposed to the air by changing tidal levels. In addition to the alternating submergence and exposure, the varying influences of fresh river water and salty marine waters cause physical conditions to vary more widely than in any other marine environment. The mud of a tidal flat is usually rich in dissolved nutrients, PLANKTON, and organic debris, and it supports large numbers of small animals such as crabs and worms. Vegetation is generally sparse, but mats of blue or blue-green algae (see CYANOBACTERIA) may be present.

tidal power Electricity produced by TURBINES operated by TIDE flow. Large amounts of power are potentially available from the tides in certain locations, such as Canada's Bay of FUNDY, where the tidal range reaches more than 50 ft (15 m), but this potential power is not continuous and varies with the seasons. The first working modern tidal power plant was built in France in 1961–67 and has 24 power units of 10,000 kilowatts each.

tidal wave See TSUNAMI

tide Regular, periodic rise and fall of the surface of the sea, occurring in most places twice a day. Tides result from differences in the gravitational forces exerted at different points on the earth's surface by another body (such as the moon). Although any celestial body (e.g., Jupiter) produces minute tidal effects, the majority of the tidal forces on the earth are raised by the sun (because of its enormous mass) and the moon (because of its proximity to earth). In fact, the tidal forces from the moon are about twice as strong as those from the sun. The largest tides (spring tides, exhibiting very large change in sea level between high and low tides) occur at the new and full moon, when the earth, the moon, and the sun are aligned and the sun's tidal forces are added to those of the moon. The smallest tides (neap tides) occur when the sun and moon are at right angles (from earth), when the tidal forces from the sun partially cancel those from the moon. The geometry of the coastline and of the water's basin also affects the range of the tides.

Tieck \'tēk\, **(Johann) Ludwig** (1773–1853) German writer and critic. He was educated at the Univs. of Halle, Göttingen, and Erlangen. His first works are associated with early Romanticism, the best appealing to the emotions rather than the intellect. *Volksmärchen* (1797) includes one of his best short novels, *Blond Eckbert*. This period culminated in the grotesque, lyrical plays *Life and Death of St. Genevieve* (1800) and *Emperor Octavian* (1804). Later his writing moved toward realism. While

S T U V

he was an adviser and critic at the Dresden theater (1825–42), he became a great literary authority and wrote 40 short novels.

T'ien See TIAN

Tien Chih See DIAN CHI

T'ien-chin See TIANJIN

Tien Shan See TIAN SHAN

T'ien-shih Tao See FIVE PECKS OF RICE

Tientsin See TIANJIN

Tiepolo \tē-ˈā-pə-lō\, **Giovanni Battista** *or* **Giambattista Tiepolo** (1696–1770) Italian painter and etcher. By the 1730s his fame had gone beyond his native Venice, and he accepted commissions to decorate two palaces in Milan (1731), the Cappella Colleoni in Bergamo (1731–32), and the Villa Loschi at Biron (1734). In the 1730s and '40s the Venetian clergy and nobility vied for his works. In 1750 he went to Würzburg with his sons and collaborators, GIOVANNI DOMENICO TIEPOLO and Lorenzo Tiepolo (1736–1776), to decorate the prince-archbishop's palace. His Würzburg frescoes and canvases are his most boldly luminous work. In 1762 he escaped the political disequilibrium of the Seven Years' War by accepting an invitation to paint ceilings in the royal palace in Madrid, again with his sons, his last great undertaking; he remained in Spain until his death. Though he initially used a melancholic chiaroscuro style, his later work is full of bright color and bold brush play; his luminous, poetic frescoes both extend the tradition of Baroque ceiling decoration and epitomize Rococo lightness and elegance.

Tiepolo \ˈtye-pō-lō\, **Giovanni Domenico** *or* **Giandomenico Tiepolo** (1727–1804) Italian painter and printmaker. He was apprenticed to his father, GIOVANNI BATTISTA TIEPOLO, in Venice in the early 1740s, and worked with him in Madrid from 1762 until the elder's death in 1770. His most notable early works are the chinoiserie decorations of the Villa Valmarana in Vicenza (1757). Back in Venice, he executed several frescoes and paintings of scenes from the commedia dell'arte. A talented genre painter and caricaturist, he was famous for his many engravings and etchings after his own and his father's designs.

Tierra del Fuego \tē-ˌer-ə-del-ˈfwā-gō\ Archipelago off the southern tip of South America. It is separated from the Antarctic Archipelago by the DRAKE PASSAGE. The southern and western parts are an extension of the ANDES, with peaks exceeding 7,000 ft (2,100 m). About two-thirds of the islands are Chilean and one-third Argentine. The main island, Tierra del Fuego, is divided between Chile (W half) and Argentina (E half); the Argentine city of Ushuaia there is the southernmost city in the world. Indigenous peoples were the undisputed occupants up to 1880, when colonization by Chilean and Argentine nationals was sparked by the discovery of gold. Chile's only oil field is there. The region's name (meaning "Land of Fire") refers to its many volcanoes.

Tietê River \tyā-ˈtā\ River, southeastern Brazil. Rising in the mountains near the Atlantic coast, it flows northwest about 700 mi (1,130 km) through central São Paulo state to join the PARANA RIVER. Several of the state's large cities, including SÃO PAULO, are located on or near it, but navigation is impeded by frequent falls and rapids.

Tiffany, Louis Comfort (1848–1933) U.S. painter, craftsman, philanthropist, decorator, and designer. Born in New York City, the son of the famous jeweler Charles Louis Tiffany (1812–1902), he studied painting there with GEORGE INNESS and in Paris, and was a recognized painter before he began to experiment with stained glass in 1875. He founded a glassmaking factory in Queens, N.Y., in 1878. There he developed an iridescent glass he called Favrile, which achieved widespread popularity in Europe. After 1900 Tiffany's firm ventured into lamps, jewelry, pottery, and bibelots. He is internationally recognized as one of the greatest forces of the ART NOUVEAU style.

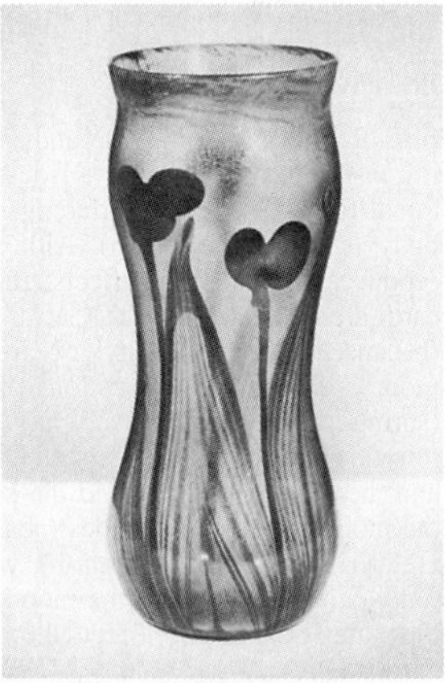

Vase of Favrile lustre glass made by Louis Comfort Tiffany, New York City, 1896; in the Victoria and Albert Museum, London.

BY COURTESY OF THE VICTORIA AND ALBERT MUSEUM, LONDON

Tiflis See TBILISI

tiger Reddish tan, striped, great CAT of forests, grasslands, and swamps in eastern Russia, parts of China, South Asia, and Sumatra. Tigers are solitary, nocturnal hunters, preying on medium-sized mammals (e.g., deer). Locality and subspecies determine size, color, and stripes. Southern tigers, such as the Bengal *(Panthera tigris tigris),* are smaller and more brightly colored than northern ones, such as the rare Siberian tiger *(P. t. altaica).* Males grow to over 3 ft (1 m) high and 7 ft (2.2 m) long, excluding the 3-ft (1-m) tail, and may weigh 350–640 lbs (160–290 kg). Tigers live about 11 years. The persistent use of tiger parts as tonics or medicines, despite evidence refuting their efficacy, is a manifestation of beliefs rooted in the awe that the cat has inspired for millennia. Though internationally protected, tigers are seriously endangered; their populations shrank by more than 90% in the last century, and three subspecies are now extinct.

Bengal tiger (*Panthera tigris tigris*).

© SILVESTRIS/AUSTRALASIAN NATURE TRANSPARENCIES

tiger beetle Any of some 2,000 species (family Cicindelidae) of voracious BEETLES, found worldwide but mostly in the tropics and subtropics. The larva waits at the top of its burrow (up to 2 ft, or 0.7 m, deep) and grasps approaching insect prey with sicklelike jaws. Hooks on the abdomen anchor it so that the struggling victim cannot pull away, and the prey is dragged into the burrow and eaten. The slender, long-legged adults, less than an inch (25 mm) long, have long jaws that can inflict a painful bite. Many are iridescent blue, green, orange, or scarlet.

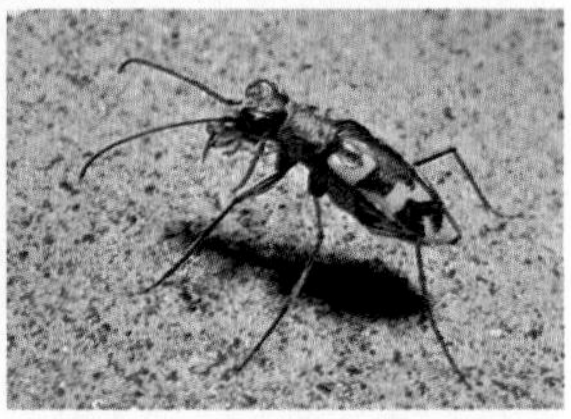

Tiger beetle (*Cicindela*).

WILLIAM E. FERGUSON

tiger moth Any of more than 3,500 species (family Arctiidae) of MOTHS, many with furry or hairy larvae called WOOLLY bears. Most adults have a thick body and white, orange, or green wings. At rest, the wings are folded rooflike over the body. The fall webworm *(Hyphantria cunea)* is a serious pest. The caterpillars construct webs over leaves, sometimes covering large areas with silken sheets. They pupate aboveground in a cocoon made of larval hairs and silk. The Isabella tiger moth *(Isia isabella)* attains a wingspan of 1.5–2 in. (37–50 mm). Black spots mark its abdomen and yellow wings.

tiger shark Potentially dangerous SHARK (*Galeocerdo cuvieri,* family Carcharhinidae), found worldwide in warm oceans, from the shoreline to the open sea. Up to 18 ft (5.5 m) long, the grayish tiger shark has a long, pointed upper tail lobe, and its large teeth are deeply notched along one side. This voracious shark eats fishes, other sharks, turtles, mollusks, birds, carrion, and garbage, including coal, tin cans, and clothing. It is a source of leather and liver oil. See also SAND SHARK.

tiger swallowtail Any of several North American species of black-and-yellow SWALLOWTAIL butterflies. The eastern tiger swallowtail *(Papilio glaucus)* is a large, widely distributed species. The yellow male has black margins and black stripes on the wings. The female is similarly marked in the north, where the black and distasteful pipevine swallowtail *(Battus philenor)* does not occur; in the south, where the two coexist, the female tiger swallowtail is very often all or mostly black.

tigereye *or* **tiger's-eye** Semiprecious quartz gem displaying chatoyancy, a vertical luminescent band like that of a cat's eye. Bands of parallel, blue asbestos (CROCIDOLITE) fibers are first altered to iron oxides and then replaced by silica. The gem has a rich yellow to yellow-brown or brown color and a fine golden luster when it is polished. The best stones come from South Africa. See also CAT'S-EYE.

Tiglath-pileser III \'tig-ˌlath-pī-'lē-zər\ (r.745–727 BC) King of Assyria who led the last and greatest phase of Assyrian expansion. On taking the throne, he immediately set about strengthening Assyria. He subdivided large provinces to quash independence movements, had officials report directly to him, and resettled tens of thousands of people to ensure loyalty. He defeated his northern neighbor, Uratu (743 BC), then subjected Syria and Palestine (734) and took over the throne of Babylon. See also ASHURBANIPAL, SARGON II.

Tiglath-pileser III, relief from Calah (Nimrud), 8th century BC; in the British Museum.
BY COURTESY OF THE TRUSTEES OF THE BRITISH MUSEUM

tigon \'tī-gən\ *or* **tiglon** \'tī-glən\ Zoo-bred offspring of a TIGER and a lioness. The opposite cross, of a LION and a tigress, produces a liger. Differences in behavior and habitat make interbreeding of the tiger and lion unlikely in the wild. The tigon and the liger have features of both parents, in variable proportions, but are generally larger and darker than either. It is thought that most, if not all, male tigons and ligers are sterile; the females may be able to produce young.

Tigray \'ti-ˌgrā\ Historic region of northern Ethiopia. Its dramatic landscape includes plateau regions over 10,000 ft (3,000 m) high and plains below sea level. Though vegetation is sparse, the population engages in agriculture and stock raising. Tigray contains the core of the ancient AKSUM kingdom, as well as Ethiopia's oldest town, the 3,000-year-old Yeha. It formerly controlled trade routes from the Red Sea to the empire in the south. Its status declined when it lost control of the coast in the 16th century; it was subsequently dominated by the south, and was later threatened by the Egyptian, Sudanese, British, and Italian armies. A rebellion begun in 1975 against the Ethiopian government aggravated the effects of a disastrous drought and famine in 1984–85. The rebels' victory in 1991 resulted in the installing of the chairman of the Tigray People's Liberation Front as prime minister. In 1999 Ethiopia's border war with Eritrea led to the displacement of over 300,000 people in Tigray, and famine loomed again.

Tigris River \'tī-grəs\ *Arabic* **Shatt Dijla** \ˌshät-'dij-lə\ *biblical* **Hiddekel.** River, southeastern Turkey and Iraq. It is 1,180 mi (1,900 km) long. It originates in the TAURUS MTNS. at Lake Hazar, Kurdistan, and flows southeast through Turkey and past BAGHDAD to unite with the EUPHRATES RIVER at Al Qurnah in southeastern Iraq; there it forms the SHATT al Arab. With the Euphrates it defined the ancient region of MESOPOTAMIA. Important for its irrigation capacity, it gave rise to sustained civilization. The ruins of many ancient cities lie on its banks, including those of NINEVEH, CALAH, ASHUR, CTESIPHON, and SELEUCIA.

Tijuana \tē-'hwä-nä\ City (pop., 1990: 699,000), northwestern BAJA CALIFORNIA, Mexico. It lies on the Tecate River near the Pacific Ocean, 12 mi (19 km) south of SAN DIEGO, Cal. It originated as a ranch settlement on a land grant in 1862 and developed as a border resort with gambling casinos. In the 20th century it became the main entry point to Mexico for U.S. tourists. It has many U.S.-owned assembly plants as well as food-processing plants and breweries.

Tikal \tē-'käl\ Ancient MAYA city, northern Guatemala. First occupied as a small village in a tropical rain forest c. 900–300 BC, it grew into an important ceremonial center. It flourished c. AD 600–900, with the building of its great plazas, pyramids, and palaces and with the flowering of Maya art in monumental sculpture. At its height it was the largest urban center in the southern Maya lowlands; the core city had a population of 10,000, with an outlying population of about 50,000. Its main structures covered about 1 sq mi (2.5 sq km). It was abandoned by the 10th century. Major excavation began in 1956; it is now part of Tikal National Park.

Tikhomirov \ˌtik-əm-'yir-ef\, **Vasily (Dmitrievich)** (1876–1956) Russian ballet dancer and teacher, considered one of the greatest teachers of Russian ballet. After training at the Bolshoi school, he joined the BOLSHOI BALLET in 1893. He soon became its principal dancer and created roles in a vigorous, athletic style which he later taught to students at the Bolshoi school. He was influential there as a teacher (from 1896) and as director (1924–37). With his wife, YEKATERINA GELTZER, he helped preserve the classic ballets after the 1917 Revolution.

Tikunas See TUCUNAS

Tilak \'tē-läk\, **Bal Gangadhar** (1856–1920) Indian scholar and nationalist. Born to a middle-class Brahman family, Tilak taught mathematics and in 1884 founded the Deccan Education Society to help educate the masses. Through two weekly newspapers, he voiced his criticisms of British rule in India, hoping to widen the popularity of the nationalist movement beyond the upper classes. In response to the Partition of BENGAL he initiated the boycotting of British goods and passive resistance, two forms of protest later adopted by MOHANDAS K. GANDHI. He left the INDIAN NATIONAL CONGRESS in 1907 when he was deported for sedition, but rejoined in 1916, in time to sign a Hindu–Muslim accord with MOHAMMED ALI JINNAH. Though militant in his opposition to foreign rule, late in life Tilak advocated a measure of cooperation with the British in order to achieve reforms.

tilapia \tə-'lä-pē-ə\ Any of numerous, mostly freshwater, fish species (genus *Tilapia,* family Cichlidae), native to Africa. They resemble North American sunfishes; one species grows to 20 lbs (9 kg). *Tilapia* species are easy to raise and harvest for food; they grow rapidly, resist disease, and eat readily abundant algae and zooplankton. They have been used in warm-water AQUACULTURE systems since the early Egyptian civilization and have been introduced into many freshwater habitats. See also CICHLID.

Tilden, Bill *orig.* **William Tatem** (1893–1953) U.S. tennis player who dominated the game in the 1920s. Born to a wealthy family in Philadelphia, he did not reach the finals of the U.S. singles championship until 1918. He went on to win seven U.S. men's singles championships (1920–25, 1929), three Wimbledon singles championships (1920–21, 1930), and two professional titles. He also won many doubles and mixed-doubles titles and 21 of 28 Davis Cup matches. His overpowering play and temperamental personality made him one of the most colorful sports figures of his time.

Bill Tilden.
CULVER PICTURES

Tilden, Samuel J(ones) (1814–1886) U.S. politician. Born in New Lebanon, N.Y., he became a leader in New York's Democratic Party; as state party chairman (1865–75), he effected the overthrow of the Tammany Hall boss WILLIAM MARCY TWEED. As governor (1875–76) he continued his reforms, exposing the Canal Ring, politicians and contractors who defrauded the state. In 1876 he was the Democratic nominee for president. The bitterly fought campaign ended in a popular-vote victory for Tilden, but Republicans contested the results in four states. To settle the controversy, Congress appointed the ELECTORAL COMMISSION, which awarded the election to RUTHERFORD B. HAYES. Unwilling to cause further conflict, Tilden accepted the decision and returned to his prosperous law practice. On his death he left his large fortune to establish a free public library for New York City.

tile Thin, flat slab or block used structurally or decoratively in building. Traditionally, tiles have been made of glazed or unglazed fired clay, but modern tiles are also made of plastic, glass, asphalt, and even cork. Ceramic tiles, used for walls, floors, and countertops, are usually machine-pressed, made of fine clays, and very hard. Quarry tiles (used for flooring) and terra-cotta, made of natural clays, are less hard and more porous but very popular for economic and aesthetic reasons. Structural tile, of fired clay, is a hollow tile containing parallel cells or cores, used for building partitions. Roof tiles of baked clay and of marble were used in ancient Greece. Tiles came to be widely used in Islamic architecture. Colored glazed tiles were common in Spain from an early period (see AZULEJO), and from there spread to Portugal and Latin America. By the 15th century tilework was used widely in northern Europe; blue-painted tiles from Delft were especially renowned. Modern clay roofing tiles may be flat or curved; around the Mediterranean, S-shaped tiles (pantiles), laid with alternate convex and concave surfaces uppermost, are common. Modern wall tiles may be highly glazed and semivitreous.

tilefish *or* **blanquillo** \bläŋ-'kē-,yō\ Any of 24 species (family Branchiostegidae, or Malacanthidae) of slender marine fishes found in shallow tropical and warm temperate seas. Tilefish are used as food, especially the large *Lopholatilus chamaeleonticeps,* a deepwater fish of the Atlantic and Gulf of Mexico with a fleshy appendage on the head and yellow spots on its upper body and some of its fins. Tilefish have a large oblique mouth with strong canines and one rather long dorsal fin with weak spines.

till In geology, the unsorted material deposited directly by glacial ice and showing no stratification. Till is sometimes called boulder clay because it is composed of clay, boulders of intermediate size, or both. The rock fragments are usually angular and sharp rather than rounded, because they are deposited from ice and have undergone little water transport. The pebbles and boulders may be faceted and striated from grinding while lodged in the glacier.

till-less agriculture See NO-TILL FARMING

Tillich \'ti-lik, *Engl* 'ti-lik\, **Paul (Johannes)** (1886–1965) German-U.S. Protestant theologian. He studied at Berlin, Tübingen, and Halle and was a chaplain with the German army during World War I. He taught successively at Marburg, Dresden, and Frankfurt am Main. In 1933 the Nazi takeover prompted him to emigrate to the U.S. With the aid of REINHOLD NIEBUHR, he joined the faculty of New York's Union Theological Seminary. He became respected for his lucid preaching and his *Systematic Theology* (3 vols., 1951–63). He moved to Harvard University in 1955 and to the University of Chicago in 1962. His theological system was an unusual combination of biblical, existentialist, and metaphysical elements, and he attempted to convey an understanding of God that depended neither on revelation nor on science. His other works include *The Courage to Be* (1952) and *Dynamics of Faith* (1957).

Tillman, Benjamin R(yan) (1847–1918) U.S. politician. Born in Edgefield Co., S.C., he worked as a farmer and in the 1880s became a spokesman for poor rural whites. As governor (1890–94), he introduced populist reforms that expanded public education, shifted the tax burden to the wealthy, and regulated the railroads. He also supported enactment of JIM CROW laws and considered lynching an acceptable law-enforcement measure. In the U.S. Senate (1895–1918), he pressed for agrarian reform. His attacks on his opponents earned him the nickname "Pitchfork Ben."

Tilly, Graf (Count) von *orig.* **Johann Tserclaes** (1559–1632) Bavarian general in the THIRTY YEARS' WAR. Born in the Spanish Netherlands, he served in its army under ALESSANDRO FARNESE (1585) and in 1594 joined the emperor Rudolf II's army against the Turks. Appointed by MAXIMILIAN I of Bavaria to reorganize the Bavarian army (1610), Tilly created an efficient force that became the spearhead of the CATHOLIC LEAGUE in the Thirty Years' War. He led the League's forces to victories in the Battle of WHITE MOUNTAIN (1620) and at Lutter (1626). In 1630 he added the imperial forces to his command. In 1631 he besieged the Protestant city of Magdeburg, but its destruction proved disastrous for him. Failing to stop the Swedish advance into Germany, he was defeated at Breitenfeld (1631) and was fatally wounded in a later battle.

Tilsit \'til-zit\, **Treaties of** (1807) Agreements that France signed separately with Russia and Prussia at Tilsit, northern Prussia (now Sovetsk, Russia). The treaties followed NAPOLEON's victories in the NAPOLEONIC WARS and established his supremacy in Western and central Europe. France and Russia became allies and divided Europe between them, reducing Prussia and Austria to helplessness. In secret provisions, Russia joined the CONTINENTAL SYSTEM against British trade. By 1810 Russian trade was hampered and the czar opened Russian ports to neutral ships, causing the alliance to fail and paving the way for Napoleon's invasion of Russia in 1812.

tilth Physical condition of SOIL, especially in relation to its suitability for planting or growing a crop. Factors that determine tilth include the formation and stability of aggregated soil particles, moisture content, degree of aeration, rate of water infiltration, and drainage. The tilth of a soil can change rapidly, depending on environmental factors such as changes in moisture. The objective of tillage (mechanical manipulation of the soil) is to improve tilth, thereby increasing crop production; in the long term, however, conventional tillage, especially plowing, often has the opposite effect, causing the soil to break down and become compacted.

timber framing Construction of frame or post-and-beam structures using large, heavy, wood members, specifically lumber 5 in. (13 cm) or more in the least dimension. The term implies stylistic features of a heavy nature. Half-timber work, in which the spaces between the heavy visible frames of interior and exterior walls are filled in with (nonstructural) material such as brick, plaster, or mud, was common in Asia and Europe. Half-timbering found its highest expression in the TUDOR STYLE. See also FRAMED structure, POST-AND-BEAM SYSTEM.

timbre \'tam-bər\ Quality of sound that distinguishes one instrument, voice, or other sound source from another. Timbre largely results from a characteristic combination of OVERTONES produced by different instruments. This distinctive combination (which usually varies across the range of pitches) is what principally permits a listener to distinguish a clarinet from a flute, an alto from a tenor, or even a Stradivarius violin from a Guarneri violin, when both are sounding the same pitch. One element of timbre results from the differing methods of producing the sounds (blowing, bowing, striking, etc.), especially audible at the moment a note begins.

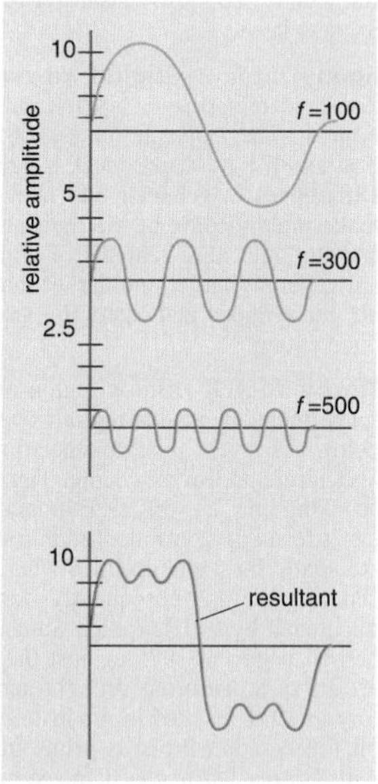

A mixture of three pure tones (top) yields a complex resultant tone (bottom), such as might be produced by an actual instrument, whose perceived quality or "color" is its timbre. The strong fundamental tone (top)—which would be perceived by the listener as the only tone played—has a frequency of 100. The other tones shown, with frequencies of 300 and 500, are weaker overtones of the fundamental; their relative loudness (amplitude), reflected in the complex resultant wave form, constitutes an essential aspect of the unique timbre the wave form represents.

Timbuktu See TOMBOUCTOU

time Measured or measurable period. More broadly, it is a continuum that lacks spatial dimensions. Philosophers have sought an understanding of time by focusing on the broad questions of the relation between time and the physical world and the relation between time and consciousness. Those who adopt an absolutist theory of time regard it as a kind of container within which the universe exists and change takes place, and believe that its existence and properties are independent of the physical universe. According to the rival relationist theory, time is nothing over and above change in the physical universe. Largely because of ALBERT EINSTEIN, it is now held that time cannot be treated in isolation from space (see SPACE-TIME). Some argue that Einstein's theories of RELATIVITY vindicate relationist theories, others that they vindicate the absolutist theory. The primary issue concerning the relation between time and consciousness is the extent, if any, to which time or aspects of time depend on the existence of conscious beings. Events in time are normally thought of in terms of notions of past, present, and future, which some philosophers treat as mind-dependent; others believe that time is independent of perception and hold that past, present, and future are objective features of the world. See also GEOLOGIC time, GREENWICH MEAN TIME, STANDARD TIME, UNIVERSAL TIME.

Time Major U.S. weekly newsmagazine, published in New York City. It was founded in 1923 by HENRY R. LUCE (as business manager) and Briton Hadden (as editor). It became the most influential newsmagazine in the U.S., with a format of short articles arranged in subject "departments," which became the standard for later general newsmagazines. After Hadden's death in 1929, Luce was long the magazine's guiding force, and it reflected his moderately conservative political viewpoint. By the 1970s it had assumed a more neutral, centrist stance in its reportage. It now appears in several foreign-language editions.

time-and-motion study Analysis of the time spent in going through the different motions of a job or series of jobs in the evaluation of industrial performance. Such studies were first instituted in offices and factories in the U.S. in the early 20th century. They were widely adopted as a means of improving work methods by subdividing the different operations of a job into measurable elements, and were in turn used as aids in STANDARDIZATION of work and in checking the efficiency of people and equipment.

time deposit Bank deposit that cannot be withdrawn unless the depositor gives advance notice or until a specific period of time has elapsed. Savings accounts sometimes function as time deposits, though the modest value of most ordinary savings accounts has led many banks to waive the advance-notice requirement on deposits by individuals. Another common type of time deposit is the CERTIFICATE of deposit, in which a sum of money is deposited for a stated period of time at a rate of interest usually higher than the rate paid on regular accounts.

time dilation In the theory of special RELATIVITY, the "slowing down" of a clock as perceived by an observer in relative motion with respect to that clock. Time dilation becomes noticeable only at speeds approaching that of LIGHT and has been accurately confirmed by the apparent increased lifetime of unstable SUBATOMIC particles traveling at nearly the speed of light and precise timing of atomic clocks carried on airplanes. See also LORENTZ-FITZGERALD CONTRACTION.

Time of Troubles See Time of TROUBLES

Time Warner Inc. Largest worldwide media and entertainment conglomerate, created by the 1989 merger of Time Inc. and Warner Communications. Time Inc. was founded in 1922 to publish *TIME* magazine, and grew with the founding of *Fortune* (1930), *LIFE* (1936), *Sports Illustrated* (1954), *Money* (1972), and *People* (1974). The company also founded Time-Life Books (1960) and acquired the publisher Little, Brown & Co. and the Book-of-the-Month Club. It bought an interest in American Television and Communications in 1971 (acquiring full ownership in 1978) and founded Home Box Office (HBO) in 1972. The 1989 merger included WARNER BROTHERS movie studio, a recording company, and a cable-television operator. In 1995 Time Warner bought two more cable-television companies and founded the WB broadcast network. In 1996 it acquired TED TURNER's Turner Broadcasting System. In 2001 it combined with AMERICA ONLINE, in the largest corporate merger to that date, to form AOL Time Warner.

Times, The Daily newspaper published in London, one of Britain's oldest and most influential, and one of the world's greatest newspapers. Founded by JOHN I. WALTER in 1785 as *The Daily Universal Register*, it became *The Times* in 1788, publishing commercial news and notices along with some scandal. By the mid-1800s it had developed into a widely respected national journal and daily historical record. Late in the 19th century its reputation and circulation declined, but it returned to financial security after being bought by Viscount NORTHCLIFFE (1908), and its preeminence in editorial matters and news coverage was reestablished under the editorship of WILLIAM HALEY (1952–67). In 1981 it was bought by RUPERT MURDOCH.

Times Literary Supplement (TLS) Weekly literary journal long famous for its coverage of all aspects of literature. Founded in 1902 as a supplement to *The Sunday Times* of London, the TLS sets the tone and standards of excellence in the field of literary criticism. It presents reviews of major books of fiction and nonfiction published in several languages, and its essays are written with sophistication and scholarly authority and in a lively style. It is also noted for its bibliographic thoroughness, for its topical essays by the world's leading scholars, and for the erudition of its readers' published letters to the editor. See also *The* TIMES.

Timiș River \'tē-ˌmēsh\ *Serbian* **Tamiš** \'te-ˌmesh\ River, western Romania and northeastern Yugoslavia. Rising in the southwestern CARPATHIANS, it flows in an arc to enter the DANUBE RIVER just below BELGRADE, Yugoslavia, after a course of 211 mi (340 km).

Timișoara \ˌtē-mē-'shwä-rä\ City (pop., 1994 est.: 328,000), western Romania. Located near the TIMIS RIVER, it was first settled in Neolithic and Roman times. It was sacked by the Tatars in the 13th century. Its citadel was rebuilt in the 14th century and for a few years became the residence of CHARLES I of Hungary. The Turks held the town from 1552 until the Austrians took it in 1716. Occupied by Serbia in 1919, it was allotted to Romania by the 1920 Treaty of TRIANON. Antigovernment demonstrations there in 1989 led to the execution of Pres. NICOLAE CEAUSESCU and the end of Communist rule in Romania. It is a manufacturing, commercial, and cultural center.

Timoleon of Corinth \ti-'mō-lē-ən\ (died after 335 BC) Greek statesman and general. When the city of SYRACUSE called to its mother city, CORINTH, for help in overthrowing its tyrant, Dionysius the Younger, Timoleon was chosen to lead the liberation force. By shrewd tactics he defeated the combined forces of the oppressor and his Carthaginian allies, who he confined to the western end of the island. He introduced constitutional safeguards and invited more Greek immigration. He retired in 337.

Timor \'tē-ˌmȯr, tē-'mȯr\ Island, southern MALAY ARCHIPELAGO. It is the easternmost of the Lesser SUNDA ISLANDS. Indonesian-Malay peoples live along the coast and Melanesian aboriginals in the mountains. The Portuguese began trading with Timor c. 1520. In 1613 the Dutch settled at the island's southwestern tip, and the Portuguese moved to the north and east. Treaties in 1860 and 1914 divided the island between them. Netherlands Timor (West Timor) was occupied by the Japanese in World War II; in 1950 the Dutch transferred it to Indonesia. Eastern Timor was held by the Portuguese until 1975, when Indonesian troops invaded and annexed the area; it was granted independence in 1999 (see EAST TIMOR).

Timoshenko \ˌti-mə-'sheŋ-kō\, **Stepan (Prokofyevich)** (1878–1972) Russian-U.S. civil engineer and educator. Born in St. Petersburg, he emigrated to the U.S. in 1922. He taught structural engineering at Stanford University (1936–54); his contributions to theoretical and applied mechanics included work on strength of materials, applied elasticity, and vibration in manufacturing.

timothy Perennial grass *(Phleum pratense)* of the family Poaceae (or Gramineae), native to Europe and widely cultivated as a HAY and pasture grass in North America. The stems grow in large clumps, are 1.5–3 ft (0.5–1 m) tall, and have swollen, bulblike bases. The flower clusters are long, dense, and cylindrical. Alpine, or mountain, timothy *(P. alpinum)* is about half as tall and occurs in wet areas from Greenland to Alaska, and at high altitudes in many other parts of North America and Europe.

timpani \'tim-pə-nē\ *or* **kettledrums** Large bowl-shaped drums with pedal mechanisms for altering their pitch by changing the membrane's tension. The timpani are the principal orchestral percussion instruments. Each drum usually has a range of a 5th; they are classically used in pairs. Until c. 1800 each

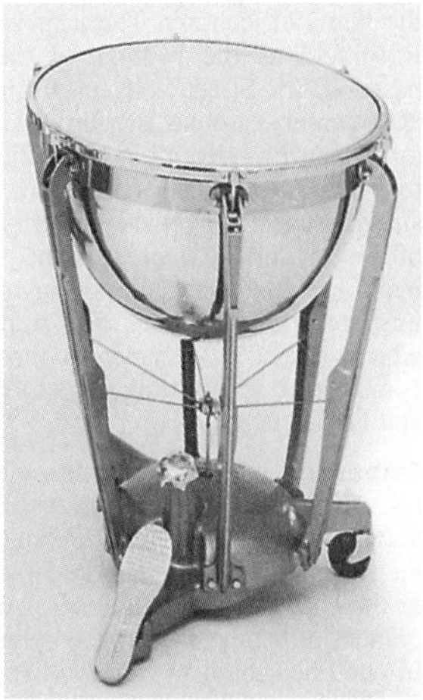

Modern timpani with pedal-controlled tension.

BY COURTESY OF LUDWIG INDUSTRIES, CHICAGO

S T U V

drum was tuned to a single pitch (usually tonic or dominant) that could not be altered in performance. Primitive kettledrums, or nakers, were played on horseback by Middle Eastern cavalry. In Europe they were primarily associated, in tandem with the trumpets, with court ceremony and the military. They entered the orchestra in the mid-17th century.

Timpanogos Cave National Monument \ˌtim-pə-'nō-gəs\ Preserve, Utah. Located on the northwestern slope of Mount Timpanogos (12,008 ft, or 3,660 m), the highest peak of the WASATCH MTNS., it was established in 1922; it occupies 250 acres (101 hectares). It centers around a three-chambered limestone cave noted for its pink and white crystal-filigreed walls and tinted formations.

Timur \tē-'mür\ *or* **Tamerlane** \'ta-mər-ˌlān\ *or* **Tamburlaine** (1336–1405) Turkic conqueror of Islamic faith whose conquests reached from India and Russia to the Mediterranean Sea. Born near SAMARQAND, he settled in Transoxania (modern Uzbekistan) after taking part in campaigns there with GENGHIS KHAN's descendant Chagatai. (Timur Lenk, or Tamerlane, means "Timur the Lame," reflecting the battle wounds he received.) Through machinations and treachery he took over TRANSOXANIA and proclaimed himself the restorer of the MONGOL empire. In the 1380s he began his conquest of IRAN (Persia), taking Khorasan and eastern Iran in 1383–85 and western Iran as far as Mesopotamia and Georgia in 1386–94. He occupied Moscow for a year. When revolts broke out in Iran, he ruthlessly suppressed them, massacring the populations of whole cities. In 1398 he invaded INDIA, leaving a trail of carnage. Next he marched on Damascus and Baghdad, deporting the artisans of the former to Samarqand and destroying all the monuments of the latter. In 1404 he prepared to march on China but died early in the march. Though Timur strove to make Samarqand the most splendid city in Asia, he himself preferred to be always on the move. His most lasting memorials are the architectural monuments of Samarqand and the dynasty he established, under which Samarqand became a center of scholarship and science.

tin Metallic chemical ELEMENT, chemical symbol Sn, atomic number 50. It is a soft, silvery-white METAL with a bluish tinge, employed since antiquity in BRONZE, its ALLOY with copper. It occurs chiefly as the OXIDE. Since it is nontoxic, ductile, malleable, and easily worked, it is used to plate steel cans ("tin cans") for food and to coat and plate other items. Pure tin is too weak to be used alone, but its many alloys include soft solder, PEWTER, BRONZE, and low-temperature casting alloys. It has VALENCE 2 or 4 in compounds, including stannous chloride (used in tin GALVANIZING and manufacturing polymers and dyes), stannous oxide (used to make tin salts for chemical reagents and plating), stannous fluoride (used in toothpastes), stannic chloride (a stabilizer for perfumes and a source of other tin salts), and stannic oxide (a catalyst and a polishing powder for steel). Tin bonds with carbon to form organotin compounds, used to stabilize PVC and in biocides and fungicides.

Tin Pan Alley Genre of U.S. POPULAR MUSIC that arose in New York in the late 19th century. The name was coined by the songwriter Monroe Rosenfeld as the byname of the street on which the industry was based—28th Street between Fifth Avenue and Broadway in the early 20th century, around Broadway and 32nd Street in the 1920s, and ultimately on Broadway between 42nd and 50th Streets. "Tin pan" referred to the sound of pianos furiously pounded by "song pluggers" demonstrating tunes to publishers. The genre comprised the commercial music of songwriters of ballads, dance music, and VAUDEVILLE songs, and its name eventually became synonymous with U.S. popular music. Its demise resulted from the rise of film, audio recording, radio, and TV, which created a demand for more and different kinds of music, and commercial songwriting centers grew up in such cities as HOLLYWOOD and NASHVILLE.

Tinbergen \'tin-ˌber-kən\, **Jan** (1903–1994) Dutch economist noted for his development of ECONOMETRIC models. For 40 years (1933–73) he taught at The Netherlands School of Economics. As economic adviser to the League of Nations (1936–38), he studied the economic development of the U.S. from 1919 to 1932, work that provided a basis for his development of business-cycle theory and methods of economic stabilization. In 1969 he shared with RAGNAR FRISCH the first Nobel Prize for Economics. NIKOLAAS TINBERGEN was his brother.

Tinbergen, Nikolaas (1907–1988) Dutch-British zoologist, a founder (with KONRAD LORENZ) of the science of ETHOLOGY. Brother of JAN TINBERGEN, he received his PhD from the University of Leiden and taught there until 1949, when he took a position at Oxford University. He emphasized the importance of both instinctive and learned behavior to survival and used animal behavior as a basis for speculation on human violence and aggression. His observations of seagulls led to important generalizations on courtship and mating behavior. From the 1970s he and his wife, Elizabeth, studied human behavioral disorders, particularly AUTISM. With Lorenz and KARL VON FRISCH he shared a Nobel Prize in 1973.

tincal See BORAX

Ting Ling See DING LING

Tinguely \ta^{n}-'glē\, **Jean** (1925–1991) Swiss sculptor and experimental artist. As a student of painting and sculpture in Basel, he showed interest in movement as an artistic medium, and in 1953 he moved to Paris and began to construct sophisticated KINETIC SCULPTURES. He created a sensation when his self-destroying *Homage to New York* (1960) failed to self-destruct at the Museum of Modern Art, but his *Study for an End of the World* (1961) detonated successfully. Tinguely's art satirized the mindless overproduction of material goods in advanced industrial society and expressed his conviction that the essence of both life and art consists of continuous change, movement, and instability.

tinplating Applying a coating of TIN to thin STEEL sheet either by dipping in molten metal or by electrolytic deposition (ELECTROPLATING); almost all tinplate is now produced by the latter process, in which the tin coating is applied without heat. Essentially a sandwich in which the core is strip steel, tinplate has the strength and formability of steel combined with the noncorrosive and nontoxic properties of tin, and additionally is easy to solder. It is used for containers for food and beverages, paints, oils, tobacco, and numerous other products, as well as in toys, baking equipment, and parts for radio and other electronic equipment. Modern materials, including stainless steel and plastics, have replaced tinplate in many common applications.

Tintoretto *orig.* **Jacopo Robusti** (1519–1594) Italian painter active in Venice. His father was a silk dyer (*tintore)*; hence the nickname Tintoretto ("Little Dyer"). His early influences include MICHELANGELO and TITIAN. In *Christ and the Adulteress* (c. 1545) figures are set in vast spaces in fanciful perspectives, in distinctly Mannerist style. In 1548 he became the center of attention of artists and literary men in Venice with his *St. Mark Freeing the Slave,* so rich in structural elements of post-Michelangelo Roman art that it is surprising to learn that he had never visited Rome. By 1555 he was a famous and sought-after painter, with a style marked by quickness of execution, great vivacity of color, a predilection for variegated perspective, and a dynamic conception of space. In his most important undertaking, the decoration of Venice's Scuola Grande di San Rocco (1564–88), he exhibited his passionate style and profound religious faith. His technique and vision were wholly personal and constantly evolving. Historians of modern art recognize him as the greatest representative of MANNERISM, interpreted in accordance with the great tradition of Venice.

Tipitaka See TRIPITAKA

Tippecanoe \ˌti-pə-kə-'nü\, **Battle of** (November 7, 1811) Victory by U.S. troops over the SHAWNEE. Gen. WILLIAM H. HARRISON led a U.S. force in pursuit of the Shawnee to destroy an intertribal alliance promoted by TECUMSEH and his brother, The PROPHET. At the Indian capital of Prophetstown on the Tippecanoe River, Ind., the Indians attacked the troops but were repulsed. Both sides suffered equal losses, but the battle was considered a victory for Harrison and helped establish him as a national figure.

Tippett \'tip-ət\, **Michael (Kemp)** *later* **Sir Michael** (1905–1998) British composer. Despite thorough musical training, he gave the impression of being self-taught because his music was so original. He devoted most of his energies to compositions with words (generally his own), including the cantatas *A Child of Our Time* (1941) and *The Mask of Time* (1984), and the operas *The Midsummer Marriage* (1952), *King Priam* (1961), *The Knot Garden* (1969), and *The Ice Break* (1976). His other works include four symphonies and five string quartets.

Tiranë *or* **Tirana** \ti-'rä-nə\ City (pop., 1999 est.: 279,000), capital of Albania. Founded in the early 17th century by a Turkish general, it gradually became a trading center at the junction of roads and caravan trails. It was named the capital of Albania in 1920. In World War II, it was occupied by Axis forces (1939–44). It is the nation's largest city and main industrial and cultural center, home to the national library and theater and site of the University of Tiranë (1957).

tire Rubber cushion that fits around a wheel and usually contains compressed air. Solid-rubber tires were used on road vehicles until they were replaced by air-filled pneumatic tires, which, although first patented by Robert Thomson (1822–1873) in 1845, came into common use only when John Dunlop (1840–1921) put them on bicycles in 1888 and the French manufacturer Michelin began to produce them for motor vehicles. The tire consisted of an inner tube containing compressed air that was covered by an outer rubber casing to provide traction. In the 1950s tubeless tires became standard on most automobiles. Improved tire construction produced the radial-ply tire.

Tiresias \tī-'rē-sē-əs\ In Greek mythology, a blind Theban seer. In Homer's *Odyssey* he retained his prophetic gifts even in the underworld, where Odysseus was sent to consult him. His prophecy led to the tragedy of Oedipus. It was said that he lived for seven generations, and that he was once turned into a woman for killing the female of two mating snakes; upon thereafter killing the male, he reverted to the male gender. According to one legend, he was blinded by Hera for arguing, on the basis of his unique experience, that women derive greater pleasure from sex than men do; his gift of prophecy was a compensatory gesture from Zeus.

Tirol *or* **Tyrol** \tə-'rōl, 'tī-ˌrōl\ State (pop., 1995 est.: 658,000), western Austria. It consists of North Tirol and East Tirol, separated by the state of Salzburg and the Italian region of Trentino-Alto-Adige. It is a mountainous region bordered by the Bavarian Alps and the Ötztaler Alps; its capital is Innsbruck. It came under Roman control in the 1st century BC. In the Middle Ages it was ruled by various counts and bishops until it passed to the Habsburgs in 1363. It was the scene of revolts in 1525 during the Reformation, and again in 1809 against French and Bavarian rule. The southern Tirol was transferred to Italy in 1919. Renowned for its skiing, it attracts many tourists.

Tirpitz \'tir-pəts\, **Alfred von** (1849–1930) German naval commander. As commander of a torpedo-boat flotilla, he devised new tactical principles. Promoted to rear admiral, he commanded a cruiser squadron in East Asia (1896–97). In 1897 he became secretary of state of the imperial navy department and reorganized the German navy into a formidable high-seas fleet. Promoted to grand admiral (1911), he favored unlimited submarine warfare in World War I, but opposition to his policy led to his resignation in 1916. In 1917 he cofounded the patriotic Fatherland Party.

Tirso de Molina \'tir-sō-dā-mə-'lē-nə\ *orig.* **Gabriel Téllez** (1584–1648) Spanish playwright. As a friar of the Mercedarian Order from 1601, he wrote its official history (1637). Inspired by Lope de Vega, he wrote a vast number of works, of which only about 80 have survived. His best-known play, the tragedy *The Seducer of Seville* (1630), introduced the legendary Don Juan. Noted for portraying the psychological conflicts of his characters, he also wrote the tragedy *The Doubted Damned* (1635) and *Antona García* (1635), which analyzed mob emotion. Though he also excelled in comedy, he was the greatest Spanish tragedian of his time.

tirtha \'tir-tə\ In Hinduism, a holy river, mountain, or other place made sacred through association with a deity or saint. Such sites are often the destination of pilgrims and the venue for large religious festivals. A Hindu will make such a pilgrimage as an act of devotion, to carry out a vow, to appease a deity, or to seek prosperity. On reaching a tirtha, the pilgrim will usually bathe, circle the temple or shrine, make an offering, have his name recorded by the tirtha priests, and listen to evening music and religious discourses.

Tirthankara \tir-'təŋ-kə-rə\ *or* **Jina** \'ji-nə\ In Jainism, a savior who has succeeded in crossing over life's cycle of rebirths and has made a path for others to follow. Each cosmic age produces 24 Tirthankaras; the first are giants, but as the age proceeds they decrease in stature and appear after shorter intervals of time. Of the 24 recorded Tirthankaras, each of whom is represented by a symbolic color and emblem, only Parsvanatha and Mahavira are considered actual historical figures. The Tirthankaras are not worshiped as gods but rather honored as exemplars. See also arhat, bodhisattva, samsara.

Tiryns \'tir-ənz, 'tīr-ənz\ Ancient city, eastern Peloponnese, southern Greece. Inhabited from Neolithic times, it developed as an important Mycenaean center in the Bronze Age, reaching its height c. 1400 BC. It declined as Argos grew in power after 1100 BC. The Argives destroyed it c. 468 BC. Ruins of its palace and massive walls date from the 15th–12th century BC. The term "Cyclopean masonry" derives from the huge stones used in its construction, supposedly by the Cyclops for Proteus. The city is also connected with Perseus and Heracles.

Tishtrya \'tish-trē-ə\ Ancient Iranian god identified with the star Sirius. His principal myth involves a battle with a demonic star named Apausha over rainfall and water. As one of the stars that cause rain, Tishtrya was intimately connected with agriculture.

tissue culture Biological research method in which tissue fragments (a cell, a population of cells, or all or part of an organ) are sustained in an artificial environment for examination and manipulation of cell behavior. It has been used to study normal and abnormal cell structure; biochemical, genetic, and reproductive activity; metabolism, functions, and aging and healing processes; and reactions to physical, chemical, and biological agents (e.g., drugs, viruses). A tiny sample of the tissue is spread on or in a culture medium of biological (e.g., blood serum or tissue extract), synthetic, or mixed origin having the appropriate nutrients, temperature, and pH for the cells being incubated. The results are observed with a microscope, sometimes after treatment (e.g., staining) to highlight particular features. Some viruses also grow in tissue cultures. Work with tissue cultures has helped identify infections, enzyme deficiencies, and chromosomal abnormalities; classify brain tumors; and formulate and test drugs and vaccines.

Tisza \'ti-sä\, **István, Gróf (Count)** (1861–1918) Hungarian politician. He entered the Hungarian parliament in 1886 and joined his father, Kalman Tisza, as a leader of the Liberal Party. A defender of the Austro-Hungarian dualist system of government and of Hungary's landed interests, he served as prime minister (1903–5, 1913–17). He opposed voting franchise reform and resigned over the king's 1917 decree for such reform. A supporter of the alliance with Germany in World War I, he was held responsible for his country's suffering and was assassinated by Magyar leftists.

Tisza, Kálmán (1830–1902) Hungarian politician and premier (1875–90). A member of an old landowning family, he took part in the struggle for Hungarian national autonomy within the Austro-Hungarian system of dual government. After the Compromise of 1867 he formed a coalition of the nobility, business interests, and small landowners into the new Liberal Party (1875) and became prime minister. His social, political, economic, and legal reforms helped Hungary develop into a modern state. He resigned over interference from the Austrian emperor but continued as leader of the Liberal Party, with his son, Istvan Tisza.

Tisza River *or* **Tisa River** \'ti-sä\ River, western Ukraine, eastern Hungary, and northern Yugoslavia. Rising in the Carpathian Mtns. of western Ukraine, it flows west, forming a section of the Ukraine–Romania border, then continues southwest across Hungary and into Yugoslavia to empty into the Danube River above Belgrade. It is 619 mi (996 km) long. The Tiszalök Dam (1954) forms the largest reservoir in Hungary. It is navigable for light-draft boats for about 450 mi (727 km).

tit Any of several woodland and garden songbird species in the genus *Parus* (family Paridae) having a rather stout, pointed bill. The great tit *(P. major),* found in Europe, North Africa, and Asia nearly to Java, is about 6 in. (14 cm) long. It has a white face, a black head, and a black center line on its underparts, which are yellow or buffy. The best-known North American species of crested tit is the tufted titmouse *(P. bicolor),* a 7-in. (17-cm) bluish gray bird with pinkish brown flanks. See also chickadee.

Tufted titmouse (*Parus bicolor*).

DAN SUDIO—THE NATIONAL AUDUBON SOCIETY COLLECTION

Titan \'tī-tən\ In Greek mythology, any of the children of Uranus and Gaea and their descendants. There were 12 original Titans: the brothers Coeus, Crius, Cronus, Hyperion, Iapetus, and Oceanus, and the sisters Mnemosyne, Phoebe, Rhea, Tethys, Thea, and Themis. Encouraged by Gaea, the Titans rebelled against their father. Cronus deposed Uranus by castrating him, and became king himself. Cronus' son Zeus rebelled against his father, launching a struggle in which most of the Titans sided with Cronus. Zeus and his siblings finally won after 10 years, and Zeus imprisoned the Titans in a cavity below TARTARUS.

Titan \ˈtī-tᵊn\ Largest moon of SATURN. Titan is the only satellite in the solar system known to have clouds and a dense atmosphere. It is believed to make one rotation for each revolution, always keeping the same hemisphere toward Saturn. With a diameter of 3,200 mi (5,150 km), Titan is, after Jupiter's Ganymede, the largest moon in the solar system. Its density implies that its interior is a mixture of rocky and icy materials, the latter probably including solid ammonia and methane as well as solid water. Its atmosphere is mainly nitrogen. An ocean of liquid methane and ethane may cover much of the surface.

Titan rocket Any of a series of U.S. rockets originally developed as intercontinental ballistic missiles (ICBMs) but also used as space launch vehicles. Titan I missiles (used 1962–65), designed to deliver a four-megaton nuclear warhead over 5,000 mi (8,000 km) to targets in the former Soviet Union, were stored in underground silos but had to be raised to ground level for launch, and fueling took at least 15 minutes. By 1965 they had been replaced by the much larger Titan II, which could be launched directly from its silo. With a nine-megaton warhead (the most powerful explosive ever mounted on a U.S. delivery vehicle), Titan II was the principal weapon in the land-based U.S. nuclear arsenal until the 1980s, when it was replaced by more accurate solid-fueled ICBMs (e.g., MINUTEMAN). NASA used the Titan II to launch GEMINI spacecraft in the 1960s. The Titan IV, developed in the late 1980s, has larger engines to lift heavy cargo like that carried by the SPACE SHUTTLE. At nearly 200 ft (60 m), it is the largest nonreusable launch vehicle used in the U.S.

Titanic British luxury passenger liner that sank on April 15, 1912, en route to New York from Southampton, England, on its maiden voyage. Over 1,500 of its 2,200 passengers were lost. The largest and most luxurious ship afloat, it had a double-bottomed hull divided into 16 watertight compartments. Because four of these could be flooded without endangering its buoyancy, it was considered unsinkable. Shortly before midnight on April 14, it collided with an iceberg southeast of Cape Race, Newfoundland; five compartments ruptured and the ship sank. As a result, new rules were drawn up requiring that the number of places in lifeboats equal the number of passengers (the *Titanic* had only 1,178 lifeboat places for 2,224 passengers) and that all ships maintain a 24-hour radio watch for distress signals (a ship less than 20 mi, or 32 km, away had not heard the *Titanic*'s distress signal because no one had been on duty). The International Ice Patrol was established to monitor icebergs in shipping lanes. In 1985 the wreck was found lying upright in two pieces at a depth of 13,000 ft (4,000 m) and was explored by American and French scientists using an unmanned submersible (see ROBERT BALLARD).

The *Titanic.*

THE BETTMANN ARCHIVE

titanium \tī-ˈtā-nē-əm\ Metallic chemical ELEMENT, one of the TRANSITION elements, chemical symbol Ti, atomic number 22. A silvery gray, lightweight, high-strength, low-corrosion structural METAL, it is found combined in almost all rocks and soils and in plants and animals, natural waters, and deep-sea dredgings. Its chief commercial ores are ILMENITE and RUTILE. Its alloys are used for parts for high-speed aircraft, spacecraft, missiles, and ships; in electrodes; in chemical, desalination, and food-handling equipment; and in prostheses. Its compounds, in which it has VALENCE 2, 3, or 4, include titanium trichloride (used as a catalyst in polypropylene production), titanium dioxide (extensively used as a PIGMENT—with the greatest hiding power of all white pigments—in paints, enamels, and lacquers), and titanium tetrachloride (used in skywriting, smoke screens, and as a catalyst).

Titchener, Edward Bradford (1867–1927) British-U.S. psychologist. Trained in Leipzig under WILHELM WUNDT, he later taught at Cornell University (1892–1927). He helped establish experimental psychology in the U.S., and also became the foremost exponent of structural psychology, a field concerned with the components and arrangement of mental states and processes. His principal work is *Experimental Psychology* (1901–5).

tithe Contribution of a tenth of one's income for religious purposes. Tithing dates to the Old Testament and was adopted by the Western Christian church. It was enjoined by eccesiastical law from the 6th century and enforced in Europe by secular law from the 8th century. After the Reformation, tithes continued to be imposed for the benefit of both the Protestant and Roman Catholic churches. They were eventually repealed in France (1789), Ireland (1871), Italy (1887), and England (1936); in Germany citizens must pay a church tax unless they formally renounce membership in a church. Tithing was never part of U.S. law, but certain sects (e.g., the MORMONS) require it and members of other churches may tithe voluntarily. Tithing was never accepted by the Eastern Orthodox churches.

Titian \ˈti-shən\ *orig.* **Tiziano Vecellio** (c. 1485/90–1576) Italian painter active in Venice. As a young man he was taught by BELLINI FAMILY and worked closely with GIORGIONE. His early works are so similar in style to Giorgione's as to be indistinguishable, but soon after Giorgione's early death Titian established himself as the leading painter of the Republic of Venice. Among his most important religious paintings is the revolutionary and monumental *Assumption* (1516–18) for Santa Maria dei Frari, in which the Virgin ascends to heaven in a blaze of color accompanied by a semicircle of angels. Titian was also interested in mythological themes, and his many depictions of Venus display his work's sheer beauty and inherent eroticism. *Bacchus and Ariadne* (1520–23), with its pagan abandon, is one of the greatest works of Renaissance art. Titian was sought after for his psychologically penetrating portraits, which include portrayals of leading Italian aristocrats, religious figures, and Emperor Charles V. He reached the height of his powers in *The Rape of Europa* (c. 1559–62), one of several paintings done for PHILIP II of Spain. He was recognized as supremely gifted in his lifetime, and his reputation has never declined.

Titicaca \ˌtē-tē-ˈkä-kä\, **Lake** Lake, Peru–Bolivia border. The world's highest navigable lake, it lies at 12,500 ft (3,810 m) in the ANDES. The second-largest lake of South America, it covers some 3,200 sq mi (8,300 sq km) and is 120 mi (190 km) long by 50 mi (80 km) wide. A narrow strait separates it into two bodies of water, which have 41 islands, some densely populated. The remains of one of the oldest known American civilizations have been found in the area. Temple ruins on Titicaca Island mark the spot where the legendary founders of the INCA were sent down to earth by the sun.

Tito \ˈtē-tō\ *orig.* **Josip Broz** (1892–1980) Yugoslav politician, premier (1945–53), and president (1953–80). Born in Croatia to a peasant family, he fought in the Austro-Hungarian army in World War I and was captured by the Russians in 1915. While in Russia, he took part in the JULY DAYS demonstrations (1917) and joined the BOLSHEVIKS. In 1920 he returned to Croatia, where he became a local leader of the Communist Party of Yugoslavia. He rose in the party hierarchy, interrupted by a prison term (1928–34), to become its secretary-general in 1939. In World War II, Tito (a pseudonym he adopted around 1935) proved an effective leader of Yugoslav partisans. As marshal from 1943, he strengthened communist control of Yugoslavia. As premier and president, he developed an independent form of socialist rule in defiance of the Soviet Union, pursued a policy of nonalignment, built ties with other nonaligned states, and improved relations with the Western powers. Within Yugoslavia, he set up a system of "symmetrical federalism" (1974) that established equality among the six republics and Serbia's autonomous provinces (including Kosovo), while maintaining tight control to prevent separatist movements. After his death, resentment of Serbian domination led gradually to a dissolution of the federal system.

Titograd See PODGORICA

S T U V

titration \tī-ˈtrā-shən\ Process of chemical ANALYSIS in which the quantity of some constituent of a sample is determined by adding an exactly known quantity of another substance with which it reacts in a definite, known proportion. The solution of known concentration is gradually added to the unknown solution from a burette (a long measuring tube with a stopcock at the bottom) until the equivalence point is reached. The amount of the unknown substance can then be calculated. The equivalence point is determined by a change of color in an indicator (e.g., LITMUS) or in an electrical property. Reactions used in titration include ACID–BASE reactions, precipitations (see SOLUTION), formation of complexes, and OXIDATION-REDUCTION reactions. See also PH.

Titus *in full* **Titus Vespasianus Augustus** ***orig.*** **Titus Flavius Vespasianus** (AD 39–81) Roman emperor (79–81). He commanded a Roman legion in Judaea under his father, VESPASIAN. After Vespasian became emperor (69), he gave Titus full command in Judaea, whereupon Titus captured and destroyed Jerusalem (70). He later took charge of the empire's general military operations. As emperor he developed goodwill in Rome for his extravagant spending; his projects included the completion of the Colosseum. He died suddenly, perhaps killed by DOMITIAN.

Tiv People living along the Benue River in Nigeria who speak a BENUE-CONGO LANGUAGE of the NIGER-CONGO family, numbering 2.3 million. They cultivate yams, millet, and sorghum. The Tiv family occupies a cluster of round huts; brothers usually live next to one another. Some Tiv have converted to Christianity, and a few have adopted Islam, but the traditional religion based on a creator-god remains strong.

Tivoli \ˈtē-vō-lē\ *ancient* **Tibur** Town (pop., 1991: 51,000), LAZIO, central Italy. The site has been continuously occupied since prehistoric times. Originally an independent member of the Latin League and a rival of nearby ROME, it came under Roman influence in the 4th century BC. It received Roman citizenship in 90 BC and attained prosperity as a summer resort under the early empire. Many wealthy Romans built villas and erected temples in the vicinity, and the buildings' remains are among the most impressive to survive from antiquity. They include HADRIAN'S VILLA and the poet HORACE's Sabine farm. It is also the site of the Villa d'Este (begun 1550), with its magnificent gardens and unrivaled Renaissance fountains.

Tiwanaku \ˌtē-ä-wä-ˈnä-kō\ *also spelled* **Tiwanacu** *Spanish* **Tiahuanaco** Major pre-Columbian ANDEAN CIVILIZATION known from the ruins of the same name near the southern shore of LAKE TITICACA in Bolivia. The Tiwanaku civilization spread throughout large areas of Bolivia and Peru and parts of Argentina and Chile. The main site's earliest remains may date from c. 200 BC–c. AD 200, and its major buildings date from c. AD 600 to 1000. Surviving artifacts include stelae, decorated pottery, and the famous Gateway of the Sun (Puerta del Sol), an ornamented doorway carved from a massive stone slab. Much of the culture's success was due to its raised-field farming technique: raised planting surfaces were separated by canals that retained the sun's heat during the cold nights and kept the crops from freezing. Algae that grew in the canals was used for fertilizer. The Tiwanaku culture vanished by 1200.

tjurunga *or* **churinga** \tyu̇-ˈrəŋ-gə\ In native AUSTRALIAN RELIGION, a ritual object that is a representation or manifestation of a mythical being. They are symbols of communication between humans and the DREAMING. Most tjurunga are used in men's secret and sacred rituals, though some small objects figure in women's rituals and still smaller objects in men's love magic. At initiation, a boy is introduced to the rituals and tjurunga of his local descent group. Later, he receives his own tjurunga, with which he has a personal bond. At a person's death, the tjurunga is sometimes buried with the corpse.

tlachtli \ˈtläch-tlē\ Ball court or field used for the ritual ball game *ollama,* played throughout pre-Columbian Mesoamerica. Some myths mention the game as a symbolic contest between day and night deities. The object of the game, played in teams, was to use elbows, knees, and hips to drive the ball through the opponent's goal. The game was accompanied by heavy betting. It was extremely violent and severe injuries were frequent, despite the players' protective clothing. Losing players were apparently sometimes sacrificed, and the ball may sometimes have consisted of a human head wrapped in latex.

Tlaloc \ˈtlä-lōk\ Aztec rain god, highly revered and feared for his ability to bestow or withhold prosperity. Five of the 18 months of the ritual year were dedicated to him, and children were sacrificed to him during two of the months. He could send out rain, provoke drought and hunger, and cause lightning and hurricanes. Dropsy, leprosy, and rheumatism were said to be caused by Tlaloc and his fellow deities. Those who died of such illnesses, or who had been killed by lightning, were granted an eternal and blissful life in his paradise, Tlalocan.

Tlaxcala \tlä-ˈskä-lä\ State (pop., 1995 est.: 884,000), central Mexico. The smallest Mexican state, it consists largely of plateau, covering 1,551 sq mi (4,016 sq km); the capital is TLAXCALA town. It occupies roughly the same area as the Indian principality of Tlaxcala, which was HERNAN CORTES principal Indian ally in the conquest of Mexico. Almost exclusively agricultural, it produces cereals, raises both dairy cows and fighting bulls, and has numerous handicrafts, notably the weaving of serapes and woolen cloth.

Tlaxcala Town (pop., 1990: 51,000), capital of TLAXCALA state, Mexico. It is located in a mountainous region at the foot of La Malinche volcano. Settled by a NAHUA people around the 14th century, it vied for power in the 15th–16th century with the AZTEC TENOCHTITLÁN (Mexico City). Though the inhabitants initially opposed HERNAN CORTES, they became his allies and aided in his conquest of MONTEZUMA II. It was a refuge for the Spaniards when they were driven out of Tenochtitlán in 1520. Cortés established the first Christian church (San Francisco) in the Americas there in 1521. The Sanctuary of Ocotlán and archaeological ruins are nearby.

Tlazoltéotl \ˌtlä-sōl-ˈtē-ō-tᵊl\ Important and complex Aztec earth-mother goddess. She was known in four guises, each associated with a different stage in life. As a young woman, she was a carefree temptress. In her second form, she was the destructive goddess of gambling and uncertainty. In middle age, she was able to absorb human wrongdoing. In her final manifestation, she was a terrifying hag preying on youths. She was thought to provoke carnal lust and illicit sexual activity, but she could also grant absolution and remove corruption from the world by eating sexual filth.

Tlingit \ˈtliŋ-gət\ Northernmost Indians of the northern Pacific Coast of North America, inhabiting the islands and coast of southern Alaska. The Tlingit language is thought to be related to ATHABASKAN. The basic social unit was the lineage, based on maternal lines of descent; clans and larger units (moieties) were also important. Each lineage had its own chief, owned and exploited lands of economic importance, and functioned as a ceremonial unit. The economy was based on salmon fishing, though sea and land mammals were also hunted. Wood, often decorated with stylized designs, was used for houses, TOTEM poles, canoes, dishes, and other objects. POTLATCHES marked a cycle of rituals mourning the death of a chief. Today the Tlingit number about 15,000.

TM See TRANSCENDENTAL MEDITATION

TNT *in full* **trinitrotoluene** \ˌtrī-ˌnī-trō-ˈtäl-yə-ˌwēn\ Pale yellow, solid organic compound made by adding NITRATE ($-NO_2$) groups to TOLUENE. Because TNT melts below the boiling point of water but explodes only above 464°F (240°C), it can safely be melted and poured into casings. It is relatively insensitive to shock and cannot be exploded without a detonator, making it the preferred chemical explosive, used in munitions and for demolition.

To-wang \ˈtō-ˈwäŋ\ *or* **Togtokhtör** \ˈtȯg-ˌtōk-ˈtu̇r\ 19th-century Mongolian prince. He opposed Manchu rule and hoped for Mongolia's independence from China. Concerned with education, he set up a primary school open to commoners, had Buddhist scriptures translated into Mongol, and codified practical advice for herdspeople in a book he circulated among them. To diversify the economy, he encouraged agriculture and the production of textiles and woolen goods. His plan to build a central temple to replace 11 local temples turned his people against him; higher authorities decided in his favor, but the temple project was canceled.

toad Any member of 26 genera (order Anura) of mainly terrestrial, nocturnal, tailless AMPHIBIANS. Toads have a squat body, short legs, external fertilization, and teeth in the up-

American toad (*Bufo americanus*).

GEORGE PORTER—THE NATIONAL AUDUBON SOCIETY COLLECTION/PHOTO RESEARCHERS

S T U V

per jaw. They eat insects or small animals. The more than 300 species of true toads *(Bufo)* are found almost worldwide. They are 1–10 in. (2–25 cm) long and have thick, dry, often warty skin. Poison secreted by glands on the back and warts irritates the eyes and mucous membranes of predators. Some species' poison can paralyze or kill animals as large as dogs, but toads do not cause warts. Toads reproduce by laying in water two long jelly tubes containing 600–30,000 eggs. The genus *Nectophrynoides* contains the only anurans that bear live young. See also FROG, HORNED TOAD.

toadfish Any of about 45 species (family Batrachoididae) of heavy-bodied, carnivorous, bottom-living fishes, found chiefly in the New World and mostly in warm seas. Toadfishes, up to 16 in. (40 cm) long, have a broad, flattened head, a large mouth, strong teeth, and small scales (if any). Most produce grunting or croaking sounds. The oyster toadfish *(Opsanus tau)* is common in shallow eastern North American coastal waters. Venomous toadfishes (genera *Thalassophryne* and *Daector*), of Central and South America, have venom-injecting spines on their dorsal fins and gill covers. Midshipmen (genus *Porichthys*), shallow-water American fishes, have rows of 600–840 buttonlike light organs along the body.

Oyster toadfish (*Opsanus tau*).
ROMAN VISHNIAC

toadflax See BUTTER-AND-EGGS

toadstool See MUSHROOM

Toba dynasty See NORTHERN WEI DYNASTY

tobacco Any of numerous species of plants in the genus *Nicotiana,* or the cured leaves of several of the species, used after processing in various ways for smoking, snuffing, chewing, and extracting of NICOTINE. Native to South America, Mexico, and the West Indies, common tobacco *(N. tabacum)* grows 4–6 ft (1–2 m) high and bears usually pink flowers and huge leaves, as long as 2–3 ft (0.6–1 m) and about half as wide. When CHRISTOPHER COLUMBUS reached the Americas, he reported natives using tobacco as it is used today, as well as in religious ceremonies. Believed to have medicinal properties, tobacco was introduced into Europe and the rest of the world, becoming the chief commodity that British colonists exchanged for European manufactured articles. Awareness of the numerous serious health risks posed by tobacco, including various cancers and a range of respiratory diseases, has led to campaigns against its use, but the number of tobacco users worldwide continues to rise. The World Health Organization estimates that smoking now causes three million deaths annually and within two decades will cause more deaths than any single disease.

Tobago See TRINIDAD AND TOBAGO

Tobey, Mark (1890–1976) U.S. painter. Born in Centerville, Wis., he studied at the Art Institute of Chicago. In 1918 he converted to the Baha'i religion and his work became inspired by Oriental art and thought. In the 1930s he achieved notoriety with his "white writing" paintings, consisting of a web of calligraphic marks painted in white on a gray or colored ground (e.g., *Broadway*, 1936), which soon displaced his representational work. His style is distinguished by his use of the small format and a refined execution in watercolor, tempera, or pastel. In the 1950s he exerted much influence abroad, especially on French TACHISM.

Tobit \'tō-bət\ Main character in the Bible's apocryphal *Book of Tobit.* Tobit, a pious Jew living in exile in NINEVEH, gives alms and buries the dead in accordance with Hebrew law, but is struck blind in spite of his good works. Sarah, daughter of a close relative, has had seven husbands, each of whom was killed by a demon on their wedding night. The two pray for deliverance, and the angel RAPHAEL intercedes for them. Tobit regains his sight, and Sarah marries Tobit's son Tobias. The book is an effort to reconcile the evil in the world with God's justice. See also APOCRYPHA.

tobogganing Sport of sliding down a snow-covered hill on a toboggan, a long, flat-bottomed sled made of thin boards curved up at the front end. The word is of Algonquian origin and probably refers to a towing sled. Tobogganing as a sport appears to have originated on the slopes of Mount Royal in Montreal in the late 19th century. In the early 20th century many tobogganing chutes (3-ft-wide wood- or ice-sided channels) were built.

Tobruk *ancient* **Antipyrgos** Port city (pop., 1988 est.: 110,000), northeastern Libya. The site of an ancient Greek agricultural colony, it later had a Roman fortress guarding the Cyrenaican frontier. For centuries it served as a way station on the coastal caravan route. An Italian military post by 1911, it was the scene of prolonged fighting during World War II (see NORTH AFRICA CAMPAIGN). The British captured it from the Italians in 1941; it fell to a German siege in 1942 and was recaptured by the British the same year. Rebuilt after the war, it was expanded in the 1960s to include a port terminal linked by pipeline to the Sarir oil field.

Tocantins River \,tō-käⁿ-'tēⁿs\ River, eastern central and northeastern Brazil. It rises in several headstreams, including the PARANÁ RIVER, and flows north and west to join the ARAGUAIA RIVER. It again turns north and flows into the PARÁ RIVER after a course of 1,677 mi (2,699 km). Frequently interrupted by rapids and waterfalls, it is mainly unnavigable.

Tocharian languages *or* **Tokharian languages** \tō-'kar-ē-ən\ Two extinct INDO-EUROPEAN LANGUAGES, Tocharian A and Tocharian B, formerly spoken in the TARIM RIVER basin in China. Documents date back to AD 500–700. Tocharian literature, written in a northern Indian syllabary derived from Brahmi (see INDIC writing system), was preserved in Buddhist monasteries. Spoken at the eastern frontier of the Indo-European world, Tocharian shows the influence of INDO-ARYAN and IRANIAN languages but seems closer to western Indo-European languages in vocabulary and grammar.

tocopherol See VITAMIN E

Tocqueville \'tōk-,vil, tȯk-'vēl\, **Alexis (-Charles-Henri-Maurice Clérel) de** (1805–1859) French political scientist, historian, and politician. Born into an aristocratic family, he entered government service by choice. After the July Revolution of 1830, his position became precarious because of his family's ties to the ousted king, and he undertook a nine-month study trip to the U.S. with his friend Gustave de Beaumont. Out of it came his best-known work, *Democracy in America* (4 vols., 1835–40), a highly perceptive and prescient analysis of the political and social system of the U.S. and of the vitality, excesses, and potential future of democracy, with attention to the situation in France. He was elected to the Chamber of Deputies in 1839 and held various political offices after the Revolution of 1848. *The Old Regime and the Revolution* (1856), a pessimistic analysis of French political tendencies, was the first volume of his unfinished study of the French Revolution.

Tocqueville, detail of an oil painting by T. Chassériau; in the Musée de Versailles.
H. ROGER-VIOLLET

Todai Temple \'tō-,dī\ *Japanese* **Todai-ji** Monumental temple of the KEGON sect located in Nara, Japan. The main buildings were constructed (745–52) under the emperor Shomu, marking the adoption of Buddhism as a state religion. The Great Buddha Hall, built within a 2-sq-mi (5-sq-km) enclosure, measured about 288 by 169 ft (88 by 52 m) and, as restored today, is the largest wooden building in the world. The 53-ft (16-m) Great Sun Buddha was installed in 752. The Shosoin is a repository for more than 9,000 works of art from the NARA period and more than 600 personal effects of Shomu.

Todos los Santos, Lake Lake, southern central Chile. It is located north of Puerto Montt. With neighboring Lake LLANQUIHUE it is the best known of Chilean lakes, and is in a popular resort area.

tofu Soft, bland, custardlike food product made from SOYBEANS. Believed to date from China's HAN DYNASTY (206 BC–AD 220), tofu is today an important source of protein in the cuisines of East and Southeast Asia. It is made from dried soybeans that are soaked in water, crushed, and boiled to produce a solid pulp and liquid soy "milk." Coagulants are then added to the milk to separate the curds from the whey. The resulting soft cakes are cut into squares and stored in water.

toga Loose, draped outer garment adopted by the Romans from the Etruscans. It was originally worn by both sexes of all classes, but was gradually abandoned by women, then by laborers, and finally by patricians, but throughout the history of the empire it remained the state dress, the garment of the emperor and high officials. Made from an oval-shaped piece of material, the toga had voluminous folds that made activity difficult, and thus became the distinctive garment of the upper classes. The color of the toga worn depended on class, age, and the character of such special events as mourning and triumphs.

Imperial Roman toga on Tiberius (reigned AD 14–37); in the Louvre, Paris.

GIRAUDON—ART RESOURCE/EB INC.

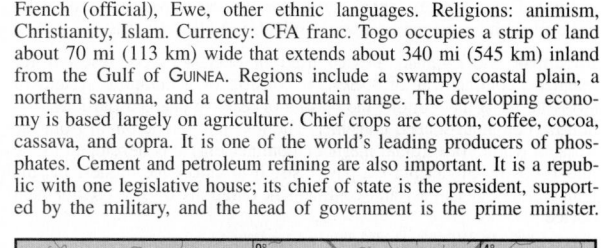

togavirus \ˌtō-gə-ˈvī-rəs\ Any of three genera of ARBOVIRUSES: *Alphavirus, Rubivirus* (which causes RUBELLA), and *Pestivirus* (which infects only animals). Some *Alphavirus* species produce a severe equine ENCEPHALITIS that has a mortality rate of up to 90% in horses and 10% in humans.

toggle mechanism Combination of solid, usually metallic links (bars), connected by pin (hinge) joints arranged so that a small FORCE applied at one point can create a much larger force at another point. See also LINKAGE.

Toghrïl Beg \tȯg-ˈrēl-ˈbeg\ (c. 990–1063) Founder of the SELJUQ dynasty. He and his brother Chagrï took refuge in Khwarezm in Central Asia after being defeated by MAHMUD of Ghazna. Later they entered KHORASAN (NE Iran), where they gradually built up a power base, defeating Mahmud's son in 1040. Chagrï took over Khorasan and Toghrïl prepared to conquer the rest of Iran. In the 1040s he extended his authority to Rayy, Hamadan, and Esfahan, and in 1055 he entered Baghdad, where he had been commissioned by the ABBASID dynasty to overthrow the Shiite FATIMID dynasty. A rebellion prevented the prompt accomplishment of this mission, but in 1060 Toghrïl crushed the rebellion and regained Baghdad.

Toghto \ˈtȯg-ˌtō\ (fl. 1340–55) High government official during the later years of China's YUAN DYNASTY (1368–1644). He followed his uncle as minister of the right (1340–44) and favored a centralized approach to government. Under him, positions that had been closed to the Chinese were reopened, many LITERATI returned to the capital, and the CHINESE EXAMINATION SYSTEM was restored. He was called back to office for another term (1349–55), during which time he oversaw the rerouting of the Huang (Yellow) River and the development of an apparatus for quelling the many popular uprisings of the 1350s.

Togliatti \tōl-ˈyä-tē\, **Palmiro** (1893–1964) Italian communist leader. After serving in World War I, in 1919 he helped found the left-wing weekly *L'Ordine Nuovo* ("New Order"), which became a rallying point for the breakaway communist wing of the Socialist Party (1921). He edited the Communist Party newspaper and was a member of the party's central committee from 1924. He was in Moscow when the party was banned in Italy (1926); he remained in exile and became a member of the COMINTERN secretariat (1935). He returned to Italy in 1944, and served in a coalition government as vice premier (1945). He advocated a national, democratically oriented form of communism and made the Italian Communist Party the largest in Western Europe.

Togo *officially* **Republic of Togo** Republic, western Africa. Area: 21,925 sq mi (56,785 sq km). Population (2001): 5,153,000. Capital: LOME. It has some 30 ethnic groups; the EWE are the largest. Languages: French (official), Ewe, other ethnic languages. Religions: animism, Christianity, Islam. Currency: CFA franc. Togo occupies a strip of land about 70 mi (113 km) wide that extends about 340 mi (545 km) inland from the Gulf of GUINEA. Regions include a swampy coastal plain, a northern savanna, and a central mountain range. The developing economy is based largely on agriculture. Chief crops are cotton, coffee, cocoa, cassava, and copra. It is one of the world's leading producers of phosphates. Cement and petroleum refining are also important. It is a republic with one legislative house; its chief of state is the president, supported by the military, and the head of government is the prime minister.

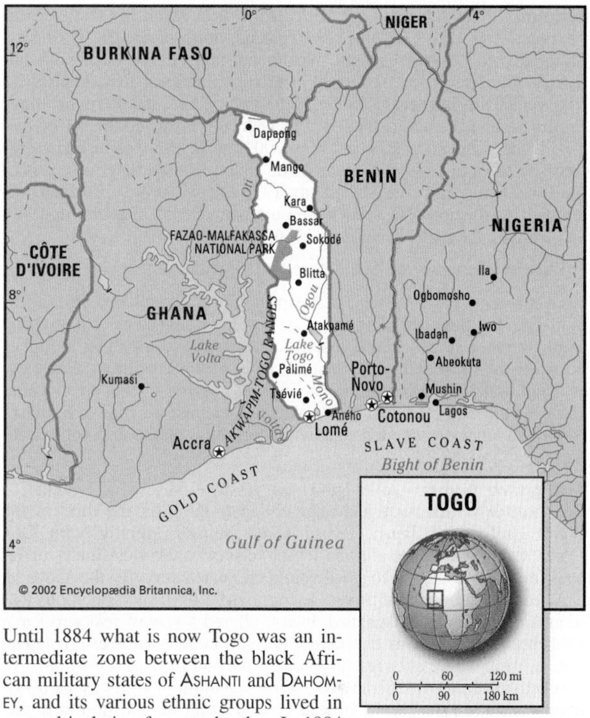

Until 1884 what is now Togo was an intermediate zone between the black African military states of ASHANTI and DAHOMEY, and its various ethnic groups lived in general isolation from each other. In 1884 it became part of the TOGOLAND German protectorate, which was occupied by British and French forces in 1914. In 1922 the League of Nations assigned eastern Togoland to France and the western portion to Britain. In 1946 the British and French governments placed the territories under U.N. trusteeship. Ten years later British Togoland was incorporated into the GOLD COAST and French Togoland became an autonomous republic within the French Union. Togo gained independence in 1960. It suspended its constitution 1967–80. A multiparty constitution was approved in 1992, but the political situation remained unstable.

Togoland Former German protectorate, western Africa. Now divided between Togo and Ghana, it covered an area between the British GOLD COAST colony and French Dahomey (now Benin). It was inhabited by a mixture of EWE and other peoples. Its coastal area became a political unit of Germany in 1884; hinterland boundaries were established in 1900. In 1914 it was captured by Anglo-French forces and divided into two administrative zones. The British zone was placed under control of the Gold Coast (now Ghana), with which it merged in 1956. The French zone became the independent Republic of Togo in 1960. Lingering sentiment for the reunification of Togoland, especially among Ewe people in Ghana, has occasionally strained relations between Togo and Ghana since independence.

Togtokhtör See TO-WANG

Tojo Hideki \ˈtō-jō-hē-ˈdä-kē\ (1884–1948) Army general and prime minister of Japan during most of World War II (1941–44). Under his direction, great victories were initially scored throughout S.East Asia and the Pacific, but prolonged reverses in the Pacific and the successful U.S. invasion of the Marianas resulted in his removal from office in 1944. He attempted suicide after Japan's surrender but was nursed back to health to be tried and executed as a war criminal. See also WAR CRIMES.

tokamak \'tō-kə-ˌmak\ Device used in NUCLEAR-FUSION research for magnetic confinement of PLASMA. It consists of a complex system of MAGNETIC FIELDS that confine the plasma of reactive charged particles in a hollow, doughnut-shaped container. The tokamak (an acronym from the Russian words for toroidal magnetic confinement) was developed in the mid-1960s by Soviet plasma physicists. It produces the highest plasma temperatures, densities, and confinement durations of any confinement device.

Tokelau \'tō-kə-ˌlaù\ *formerly (1916–46)* **Union Islands** Island territory (pop., 1992 est.: 2,000) of New Zealand, north of SAMOA. It consists of three coral atolls—Fakaofu, Nukunono, and Atafu—each with numerous low-lying islets. Originally settled by Samoans, the islands were first visited by Europeans in the 18th century. In 1863 Peruvian slave raiders abducted many islanders; the abductions and outbreaks of disease reduced the population to about 200. The British established a protectorate there in 1889. Under the name Union Islands, they were part of the GILBERT AND ELLICE ISLANDS colony 1916–26, when New Zealand was granted jurisdiction. The islands became part of New Zealand in 1948, and adopted the name Tokelau in 1976.

Tokharian languages See TOCHARIAN LANGUAGES

toko-no-ma \ˌtō-kə-'nō-mə\ In a Japanese room, an alcove with a low platform, used for the display of a flower arrangement and hanging scroll or other art objects. A feature of the SHOIN-ZUKURI style, the toko-no-ma is the focal point and spiritual center of the interior of almost every traditional Japanese house. It finds its origins in the private altar space of the Zen Buddhist monk, which contained a hanging Buddhist scroll and a narrow wooden table with an incense burner and votive candles.

Tokugawa Ieyasu \ˌtō-kù-'gä-wä-yä-'yä-sü\ (1543–1616) Founder of the TOKUGAWA SHOGUNATE and ruler of Japan 1603–16, the third of the Three Unifiers of Japan. Ieyasu allied himself initially with ODA NOBUNAGA; that alliance allowed Ieyasu to survive the vicissitudes of Japan's endemic wars and to slowly build up his territory. By the 1580s he had become an important DAIMYO in control of a fertile and populous HAN (domain). When Nobunaga died, Ieyasu offered a vow of fealty to TOYOTOMI HIDEYOSHI, who was extending his control over southwestern Japan; Ieyasu, meanwhile, enlarged his vassal force and increased his domain's productivity. In the 1590s he avoided participating in Hideyoshi's disastrous expeditions to Korea, instead consolidating his position at home. When Hideyoshi died, Ieyasu had the largest, most reliable army and the most productive and best-organized domain in all Japan; he emerged as victor from the ensuing power struggle. He confiscated his enemies' lands and gave them new domains away from Japan's heartland, much of which became Tokugawa property. He received the title of SHOGUN and two years later passed the title to his son, thereby establishing it as hereditary among the Tokugawa.

Tokugawa shogunate (1603–1867) Military government of Japan established by TOKUGAWA IEYASU with his assumption of the title of SHOGUN in 1603. The structures Ieyasu set in place were effective for governing Japan for the next 264 years. He established his capital at Edo (Tokyo) and assigned DAIMYO HAN (domains) according to their friendliness or hostility toward the Tokugawa: hostile daimyo received domains on the nation's periphery, while allies and collateral houses were given domains nearer to Edo. SANKIN kotai, a system of alternate attendance at Edo, also helped the shogunate keep control of the daimyo. To protect Japan from outside influences, particularly Christian missionaries, a new policy of national seclusion forbade Japanese to travel abroad and forbade foreigners to visit Japan (except for Chinese and Dutch traders, who were allowed to trade only at the port of Nagasaki). TOYOTOMI HIDEYOSHI's division of society into four fixed classes was preserved; the SAMURAI class became the civil bureaucrats, paid with a stipend in rice. Increased travel to Edo and other cities led to urban development and urban culture (see EDO period, GENROKU period); the merchant class flourished. By the mid-18th century the shogunate began to suffer financially; fiscal reform proved largely unsuccessful. During its last 30 years there were numerous peasant uprisings (see IKKI) and evidence of samurai unrest. It was overthrown by the domains of SATSUMA and CHOSHU in 1867. See also MEIJI RESTORATION, ODA NOBUNAGA.

Tokyo *formerly (until 1868)* **Edo** City (pop., 2000 prelim.: 8,130,408; metro. area pop.: 12,059,000), capital of Japan, southeastern HONSHU. The site has been inhabited since ancient times, and the small fishing village of Edo existed there for centuries before it became the capital of the TOKUGAWA SHOGUNATE in 1603. By the 19th century it was one of the largest cities in the world, with a population exceeding 1,000,000. Under the MEIJI RESTORATION, in 1868 it replaced KYOTO as the imperial capital, and Edo was renamed Tokyo. A devastating earthquake in 1923 destroyed most of the city and killed more than 100,000 people, but it was largely rebuilt by 1930. Much of it also had to be reconstructed after World War II due to U.S. bombing. The Summer OLYMPIC GAMES were held there in 1964. It is the administrative, cultural, financial, commercial, and educational center of Japan, and the center of an extensive complex of suburbs. Attractions include the Imperial Palace, encircled by stone-walled moats and broad gardens, and numerous temples and shrines. There are some 150 institutions of higher learning, including the University of TOKYO (1877).

Tokyo, University of State-financed university in Tokyo, the largest and most prestigious university in Japan. It was founded in 1877 and modeled on Western universities. It was destroyed in the great earthquake and fire of 1923, and reorganized following World War II. Today it has faculties of agriculture, economics, education, engineering, law, letters, medicine, pharmacology, and science, as well as a college of arts and sciences and a graduate school. Among its many research units are centers for the study of molecular and cellular biology, earthquakes, solid-state physics, cosmic radiation, oceanography, and Asian culture. Total enrollment is about 27,000.

Tokyo Bay Inlet, western Pacific Ocean. Located off the southeastern coast of HONSHU, Japan, it is about 30 mi (48 km) long and 23 mi (37 km) wide. It provides a spacious harbor area for several Japanese cities, including TOKYO, YOKOHAMA, and KAWASAKI. A highway connecting Kawasaki with Kisarazu (pop., 1995: 124,000) on the opposite side of the bay was constructed in the 1990s; it includes an undersea tunnel that is 31,000 ft (9,300 m) long.

Tokyo Rose *orig.* **Ikuko Toguri** (born 1916) U.S. broadcaster. Born in Los Angeles, she was visiting Japan when she was stranded at the outbreak of World War II. In 1943 she began radio announcing for a propaganda program beamed at U.S. troops, and eventually became one of 13 women announcers, all native speakers of American English, collectively known as Tokyo Rose. After the war she was convicted of treason and served six years in a U.S. prison. Mitigating information later came to light, and she was pardoned in 1977.

Tokyo Stock Exchange Main STOCK market of Japan, located in Tokyo. It opened in 1878 to provide a market for the trading of government bonds newly issued to former samurai. Government bonds and gold and silver currencies initially formed the bulk of trade on the exchange, but the trading of STOCKS came to predominate by the 1920s and '30s. It was closed from 1945 to 1949, when it opened after being reorganized by the occupying U.S. authorities. Today it accounts for more than 90% of all securities transactions in Japan, and it is one of the world's largest marketplaces for SECURITIES. The Nikkei index is the key stock-market index in Tokyo.

Toland \'tō-lənd\, **Gregg** (1904–1948) U.S. cinematographer. Born in Charleston, Ill., he began as an office boy at the Fox studio at 15 and soon became a cameraman, working for SAMUEL GOLDWYN and others in the 1930s and '40s. As director of photography for *Dead End* (1937), *Wuthering Heights* (1939, Academy Award), *The Grapes of Wrath* (1940), *Citizen Kane* (1941), and *The Best Years of Our Lives* (1946), he was noted for his lighting contrasts and his deep-focus camera work. He codirected the war documentary *December 7th* (1943) with JOHN FORD. He died of a heart attack at 44.

Toledo City (pop., 2000: 313,619), northwestern Ohio. It is the principal GREAT LAKES port, located at the southwestern end of Lake ERIE. The area was opened to white settlement after the 1794 Battle of FALLEN TIMBERS. Formed by the consolidation of two villages in 1833, it figured in the so-called Toledo War of 1835–36, a bloodless dispute between Michigan Territory and Ohio over the location of their common boundary. Industrial development was spurred in the 1830s and '40s by the arrival of canals and railroads. Glassmaking, now a major industry, was introduced in the late 1880s. A major commercial, industrial, and transportation center, it handles considerable foreign commerce and its port is one of the world's largest shippers of bituminous coal. Its educational institutions include the University of Toledo (1872).

Toledo \tə-'lē-dō, *Span* tō-'lā-t͟hō\ *ancient* **Toletum** City (pop., 1991: 60,000), capital of CASTILLA-LA MANCHA autonomous community, southern central Spain, on the TAGUS RIVER. It was the stronghold of the Carpentini, a powerful Iberian tribe, when it was conquered by Rome in 193 BC. In the 6th century AD it became the Visigoths' capital in Spain. Under the Moors (712–1085), it became a center of Hebrew and Arabic culture, and was noted for the manufacture of swords. Taken by ALFONSO VI in 1085, it became the capital of New Castile and, in 1230, of the united kingdoms of CASTILLA Y LEÓN. It was noted for its policy of religious tolerance toward Jews and Arabs during the 11th–15th century. It lost importance after PHILIP II moved the capital to MADRID in 1560. The French occupied it during the PENINSULAR WAR (1808–14), and Nationalist forces besieged it (1936) in the SPANISH CIVIL WAR. Known for its great wealth of notable architecture, the entire urban area is a national monument. It was the home of El GRECO.

Toledo, councils of Eighteen councils of the Visigothic church held in Toledo, Spain, from c. 400 to 702. Most attending were bishops, with some members of the lower clergy and the nobility. The decisions often affected civil and political affairs, and nearly all were convoked by kings. At the third Council of Toledo in 589, King Recared rejected his Arian faith and accepted Catholicism, an event that led to the unification of Visigothic Spain with Catholicism as the state religion.

Toleration Act (1689) Act of the British Parliament that granted freedom of worship to NONCONFORMISTS, allowing them their own places of worship and their own teachers and preachers. The act did not apply to Catholics and Unitarians and continued the existing social and political prohibitions, such as exclusion from political office, that applied to dissenters from the Church of England.

Tolkien \'täl-,kēn, *commonly* 'tōl-,kin\, **J(ohn) R(onald) R(euel)** (1892–1973) English (South African-born) novelist and scholar. A professor of Anglo-Saxon and of English language and literature at Oxford (1925–59), Tolkien achieved fame for his epic trilogy *The Lord of the Rings* (1954–56), consisting of *The Fellowship of the Ring*, *The Two Towers*, and *The Return of the King*. *The Hobbit* (1937) serves as an introduction to the series, *The Silmarillion* (1977) as a "prequel." Set in the mythical past, the richly inventive trilogy chronicles the struggle between good and evil kingdoms to possess a magic ring that controls the balance of power in the world. In the 1960s its popularity with young people made it a sociocultural phenomenon.

toll Sum levied on users of certain roads, canals, bridges, tunnels, and other such travel and transportation infrastructure, primarily to pay for construction and maintenance. Tolls were known in the ancient world and were widely used in medieval Europe as a means of supporting bridge construction. Canal building, which became extensive in Europe in the 18th–19th century, was financed chiefly by tolls, and many major roads were built by private companies with the right to collect tolls. The National Road, built in the U.S. beginning in 1806, was financed through the sale of public land, but maintenance problems soon caused Congress to authorize tolls. Toll roads passed out of fashion in the later 19th century, but the idea was revived with the Pennsylvania Turnpike in the 1930s, and after World War II many states built toll expressways. In the U.S. tolls are also used to finance long-span bridges and major tunnels. Canal tolls are still charged in some parts of the world, notably on the SUEZ and PANAMA canals.

Tolly, Mikhail Barclay de See Mikhail, Prince BARCLAY DE TOLLY

Tolman, Edward C(hace) (1886–1959) U.S. psychologist. Born in West Newton, Mass., he taught at UC–Berkeley 1918–54. Though a behaviorist, he considered classical behaviorism too reductive, and urged consideration of behavioral wholes and unmeasurable "intervening variables" over a strict focus on isolated reflexes. He also advanced the concept of "latent learning" (implicit, indirect learning). His major work was *Purposive Behavior in Animals and Men* (1932).

Tolstoy, Aleksey (Konstantinovich), Count (1817–1875) Russian poet, novelist, and dramatist. A distant relative of LEO TOLSTOY, he held various court posts. In the 1850s he began to publish comic verse, often satirizing government bureaucracy. Among his popular historical novels is *Prince Serebrenni* (1862). His dramatic trilogy about the 16th and 17th century—*The Death of Ivan the Terrible* (1866), *Czar Feodor Ioannovich* (1868), and *Czar Boris* (1870)—is written in blank verse and contains some of Russia's best historical dramatic writing. His lyric poetry includes many love and nature poems, as well as *Ioann Damaskin* (1859), paraphrasing a prayer for the dead.

Tolstoy, Aleksey (Nikolayevich), Count (1883–1945) Russian writer. Distantly related to LEO TOLSTOY, he supported the anti-Bolshevik White Army in the Russian Civil War, then emigrated to Western Europe, where he wrote one of his finest works, the nostalgic, partly autobiographical *Nikita's Childhood* (1921). In 1923 he returned to Russia as a supporter of the Soviet regime. He wrote many works that are purely entertaining and, in wartime, patriotic articles. He won three Stalin Prizes, for the novel trilogy *The Road to Calvary* (1920–41), the novel *Peter the First* (1929–45), and the play *Ivan the Terrible* (1943).

Tolstoy, Leo *Russian* **Lev Nikolayevich, Count Tolstoy** (1828–1910) Russian writer, one of the world's greatest novelists. The scion of prominent aristocrats, Tolstoy spent much of his life at his family estate of Yasnaya Polyana. After a somewhat dissolute youth, he served in the army and traveled in Europe before returning home and starting a school for peasant children. He was already known as a brilliant writer for the short stories in *Sevastopol Sketches* (1855–56) and the novel *The Cossacks* (1863) when *War and Peace* (1865–69) established him as Russia's preeminent novelist. Set during the Napoleonic Wars, it examines the lives of a large group of characters, centering around the partly autobiographical figure of the spiritually questing Pierre. Its structure, with its flawless placement of complex characters in a turbulent historical setting, is regarded as one of the great technical achievements in the history of the Western novel. His other great novel, *Anna Karenina* (1875–77), centers on an aristocratic woman who deserts her husband for a lover, and on the search for meaning by another autobiographical character, Levin. After its publication Tolstoy underwent a spiritual crisis and turned to a form of Christian anarchism. Advocating simplicity and nonviolence, he devoted himself to social reform. His later works include *The Death of Ivan Ilich* (1886), often considered the greatest novella in Russian literature, and *What Is Art?* (1898), which condemns fashionable aestheticism and celebrates art's moral and religious functions. He lived like a peasant on his great estate, practicing a radical asceticism. Finding his marriage unbearable, he departed suddenly for the local railway station, where he contracted a fatal pneumonia in the cold.

Toltecs Nahuatl-speaking people who held sway over what is now central Mexico from the 10th to the 12th century. Whether their urban center was TULA or TEOTIHUACÁN is a matter of dispute. In the 10th century they formed a number of small states of various ethnic origins into an empire. They introduced the cult of QUETZALCÓATL, and other Toltec religious and military influences spread through the Yucatán and were absorbed by the MAYA. They were noted as builders and craftsmen; artifacts include fine metalwork, gigantic statues, and carved human and animal standard-bearers. They were succeeded by the AZTECS. See also MESOAMERICAN CIVILIZATION.

Toluca (de Lerdo) \tō-'lü-kä\ City (pop., 1990: 488,000), capital of MEXICO state, central Mexico. At an elevation of 8,793 ft (2,680 m), it is one of the highest cities in North America. The site of the modern city, founded in 1530, was inhabited by the OTOMI Indians by the 13th century. It is a commercial and communications center in an agriculture and livestock region. Its oldest church was founded soon after the Spanish conquest and rebuilt in 1585. There are many archaeological sites in the area, including some influenced by AZTECS and TOLTECS.

toluene \'täl-yə-,wēn\ Colorless, flammable, toxic liquid HYDROCARBON AROMATIC compound, the methyl derivative of BENZENE. Found in coal-tar light oil and in PETROLEUM, it is obtained chiefly from the processing of petroleum fractions. It is used as a solvent, diluent, and thinner; as an antiknock additive in airplane gasoline; and as a raw material for TNT, benzoic acid and its derivatives, saccharin, dyes, photographic chemicals, and pharmaceuticals.

tomato Any fruit of the numerous cultivated varieties of *Lycopersicon esculentum*, a plant of the NIGHTSHADE family. The plant is generally much branched and has hairy, strongly odorous, feathery leaves. The drooping, clustered, yellow flowers are followed by red, scarlet, or yellow fruits, which hang from the many branches of one weak stem. The tomato fruit varies in shape from spherical to elongate and in size from 0.6 in. (1.5 cm) across to more than 3 in. (7.5 cm) across. The Spanish were bringing tomatoes from South America to Europe by the early 16th century; they were introduced to North America from Europe by the 1780s. Tomatoes are used raw, cooked as a vegetable or puree, and pickled, canned, and sun-dried. The term also applies to the fruit of *L. pimpinelli folium,* the tiny currant tomato.

Tomato (*Lycopersicon esculentum*).
GRANT HEILMAN

tomato fruitworm See CORN EARWORM

tomb Home or house for the dead. The term is applied loosely to all kinds of graves, funerary monuments, and memorials. Prehistoric tomb burial mounds, or barrows (artificial hills of earth and stones piled over the remains), were usually built around a hut containing personal effects for use in the afterlife. Burial mounds were a prominent feature of the Tumulus period in Japan (3rd–6th century); these often spectacular monuments consisted of earthen keyhole-shaped mounds surrounded by moats. Burial mounds, sometimes shaped like animals, were characteristic also of Indian cultures of eastern central North America c. 1000 BC–AD 700. With more advanced technology, brick and stone tombs appeared, often of imposing size. In Egypt tombs assumed great importance, especially in the form of PYRAMIDS. In medieval Christian thought, the tomb became a symbol of a heavenly home; this concept appeared in the Roman CATACOMBS, whose walls display scenes of paradise. Since the Renaissance, the idea of the tomb as a home has died out in the West, except as a faint reminiscence in the MAUSOLEUMS or vaults of modern cemeteries. See also BEEHIVE tomb, CENOTAPH, MASTABA, STELE.

Tomba, Alberto (born 1966) Italian Alpine skier. He was born near Bologna and learned to ski there. He has won three Olympic gold medals (1988, slalom and giant slalom; 1992, giant slalom), one Alpine World Cup championship (1995), and two World Championship of Skiing gold medals (1996, slalom and giant slalom), and has achieved rock-star fame for his flamboyance on and off the slopes.

Tombigbee River \täm-'big-bē\ River, Alabama. Formed by the confluence of the river's eastern and western forks near Amory, Miss., it crosses the Alabama border western of Carrollton and flows south nearly 400 mi (650 km) to join the ALABAMA RIVER and form the Mobile and Tensaw rivers. It is linked to the TENNESSEE RIVER by the Tennessee-Tombigbee Waterway.

Tombouctou \,tōⁿ-bük-'tü\ *or* **Timbuktu** Town (pop., 1987: 32,000), Mali, on the southern edge of the SAHARA near the NIGER RIVER. Founded c. AD 1100 by TUAREG nomads, it became an important post on the trans-Saharan caravan routes in the 12th century. After it was incorporated within the MALI EMPIRE, probably in the late 13th century, it became a center of Islamic culture (c. 1400–1600). It reached its height as a commercial and cultural center under SONGHAI rule c. 1500, but it declined rapidly after passing to Morocco in the late 16th century. The French captured it in 1893. It became part of independent Mali in 1960.

Tombstone City (pop., 1990: 1,220), southeastern Arizona. The site was named by Ed Schieffelin, who discovered silver there in 1877 after being told that all he would find would be his tombstone. By 1881 a silver rush had drawn such prospectors as DOC HOLLIDAY and Johnny Ringo, who brought the town a reputation for lawlessness. Feuds were common, including the 1881 gun battle at the O.K. Corral between the Earp (see WYATT EARP) and Clanton families. Tombstone was declared a national historic landmark in 1962.

tomography \tō-'mä-grə-fē\ Radiological technique for obtaining clear X-RAY images of internal structures by focusing on a specific plane within the body to produce a cross-sectional image. It allows the examination of structures that are obscured by overlying organs and soft tissues and do not show up clearly on conventional X-ray images. See also COMPUTED axial tomography.

Tompion \'täm-pē-ən\, **Thomas** (1639–1713) British clockmaker. Working closely with ROBERT HOOKE and Edward Barlow, he made one of the first English watches with a balance spring and patented the cylinder escapement. The most famous clockmaker of his time, he is remembered as the father of British clockmaking.

Bracket clock with oak case, ebony veneer, and gilt bronze mounts by Tompion, c. 1690; in the Victoria and Albert Museum, London.
BY COURTESY OF THE VICTORIA AND ALBERT MUSEUM, LONDON

Tompkins, Daniel D. (1774–1825) U.S. politician. Born in Scarsdale, N.Y., he served on the state supreme court 1804–7. As governor (1807–17), he initiated education and penal-code reforms and helped secure state legislation outlawing slavery. An opponent of banking interests, he blocked the chartering of a bank by calling an end to the legislature's session, the only such occurrence in New York history. He was twice elected vice president with Pres. JAMES MONROE (1817–25).

tonality Organization of music around a single pitch; more specifically, the Western system of KEYS that grew out of the modal music of the Renaissance in the 17th century. The term is often used to refer to the network of relationships implicit in the seven principal tones of a given key, each of which has the potential to become the tonic temporarily by means of MODULATION, whereby a new network of relationships arises. Because of its capacity to extend pitch relationships to remote lengths in an audibly comprehensible way, the tonal system permits the composition of music of enormous complexity.

Tonatiuh \tō-'nä-tē-ü\ Sun deity of the AZTECS and NAHUAS. According to most myths, there were four eras that preceded the era of Tonatiuh, each of which ended by cataclysm. He was viewed as a god constantly threatened by the awesome tasks of his daily birth at sunrise, arduous journey across the sky, and death at each sunset. He was the object of human sacrifice, which was thought necessary to sustain him. Generally represented by a colorful disk, he was depicted in the center of the Aztec calendar, with his eagle's claw hands clutching human hearts.

tone In LINGUISTICS, a variation in the pitch of the voice while speaking. The term is usually applied to languages (called tone languages) in which pitch differentiates words with an identical sequences of consonants and vowels. For example, *man* in Mandarin Chinese may mean either "deceive" or "slow," depending on its pitch. In tone languages, what matters is not absolute pitch but the pitch of one word relative to another or how pitch changes within a word.

tone See PITCH, TIMBRE

Tone, (Theobald) Wolfe (1763–1798) Irish republican and rebel. In 1791 he cofounded the Society of United Irishmen to work for parliamentary reform. He organized a Catholic convention of elected delegates that forced Parliament to pass the Catholic Relief Act in 1793. Seeking to overthrow English rule in Ireland, in 1796 he convinced France to send an invasion force of 43 ships and 14,000 men, but the ships were dispersed by a storm. In 1798, with only 3,000 men, he again attempted an invasion; captured and sentenced to hang, he committed suicide.

tone poem See SYMPHONIC POEM

Tone River \'tō-nä\ River, HONSHU, Japan. It rises in the volcanic area of northwestern Kanto region and flows 200 mi (320 km) southeast to enter the Pacific Ocean. No other river in Japan has been so modified by human activity; its course has been altered and its entire length is confined by dikes. It is an indispensable source for irrigation, industry, and hydroelectricity.

Tonga *officially* **Kingdom of Tonga** Nation, South Pacific Ocean. Area: 290 sq mi (750 sq km). Population (1997 est.): 101,000. Capital: NUKU'ALOFA. The people are of Polynesian ancestry. Languages: Tongan, English (both official). Religions: Free Wesleyanism, Roman Catholicism. Currency: pa'anga. Tonga comprises an archipelago of about 169

S T U V

islands that extends north to south in two parallel chains for about 500 mi (800 km). The eastern islands are low and formed of coral limestone; those in the west are mountainous and of volcanic origin, and four of the western islands have active volcanoes. The country has a developing free-market economy based mainly on agriculture. Chief products include fish, coconuts, sweet potatoes, and bananas. Tourism also is important. Tonga is a constitutional monarchy with one legislative house; the head of state and government is the king, assisted by the privy council. Tonga was inhabited at least 3,000 years ago by people of the LAPITA culture. The Tongans developed a stratified social system headed by a paramount ruler whose dominion by the 13th century extended as far as the Hawaiian Islands. The Dutch visited the islands in the 17th century, but effective contact dates from 1773, when Capt. JAMES COOK arrived and named the archipelago the Friendly Islands. The modern kingdom was established during the reign (1845–93) of King George Tupou I. It became a British protectorate in 1900. This was dissolved in 1970, when Tonga, the only ancient kingdom surviving from the pre-European period in Polynesia, achieved complete independence within the COMMONWEALTH.

Tonghak See CH'ONDOGYO

Tonghak Uprising (1894) Korean peasant rebellion that sparked the SINO–JAPANESE WAR. Despite persecution, impoverished peasants turned increasingly to Tonghak ("Eastern Learning," see CH'ONDOGYO), a syncretic, nationalistic religion that opposed Western culture and espoused equality before Heaven. When staged demonstrations met with a negative government response, the peasants rebelled, defeating government troops in southern Korea. The government called on China for aid; Japan sent in troops without being asked, and China and Japan clashed. The rebels laid down their arms to defuse tensions, but the Sino–Japanese War ensued nevertheless. The leaders of the uprising, including CH'OE SI-HYONG, were executed.

tongue Muscular organ on the floor of the MOUTH. It is important in motions of eating, drinking, and swallowing, and its complex movements shape the sounds of speech. Its top surface consists of thousands of raised projections (papillae). The receptors of TASTE (taste buds) are embedded in the papillae and are sensitive to four basic flavors: sweet, salty, sour, and bitter. More specific flavors are influenced by the sense of smell. The tongue's appearance (e.g., coated or red) can give clues to disease elsewhere. Disorders of the tongue include cancer (often caused by smokeless tobacco), leukoplakia (white patches), fungal infection, and CONGENITAL disorders. Different animals use the tongue to serve varied functions; for example, frogs have an elongated tongue adapted to capturing prey, the snake's tongue collects and transfers odors to a specialized sensory structure to help locate prey, and cats use their tongues for grooming and cleaning.

tongues, gift of *or* **glossolalia** Utterances approximating words and speech that are nonetheless generally unintelligible, usually produced during states of trance or delirium. The religious interpretation of the phenomenon is that the speaker is possessed by a supernatural spirit, is in conversation with divine beings, or is the channel of a divine proclamation. It occurred in ancient GREEK RELIGION, and is mentioned in both the Old and New Testaments. It first occurred among followers of JESUS at PENTECOST, and St. PAUL claimed to have been adept at it. Today it is mainly associated with charismatic Protestant movements such as PENTECOSTALISM.

Tonkin Former French protectorate, S.East Asia, now constituting the greater part of northern Vietnam. It was part of China from the 2nd century BC until the Vietnamese won independence in the 10th century AD. The French seized the area in 1883, making it a protectorate; it was joined with other regions controlled by France in 1887 to form FRENCH INDOCHINA. It was the chief focus in the area of anti-French fighting after World War II.

Tonkin, Gulf of Arm of the CHINA SEA, between northern Vietnam and HAINAN island, China. It is 300 mi (500 km) long and 150 mi (250 km) wide. In 1964 the Vietnamese reportedly fired on U.S. ships there, leading the U.S. Congress to adopt the GULF OF TONKIN RESOLUTION supporting increased U.S. involvement in the VIETNAM WAR.

Tonkin Gulf Resolution See GULF OF TONKIN RESOLUTION

Tonle Sap \tōn-'lā-'sap\ Lake, western Cambodia. The largest freshwater body in S.East Asia, it receives several tributaries as well as the floodwaters of the MEKONG RIVER. During the rainy season its area increases from 1,000 sq mi (2,600 sq km) to about 9,500 sq mi (25,000 sq km). At low water it is little more than a reed-infested swamp, with channels for fishing craft. A large carp-breeding and carp-harvesting industry there supports numerous floating fishing villages. The ruins of ANGKOR lie near its northwestern shore.

Tönnies \'tœn-yəs\, **Ferdinand (Julius)** (1855–1936) German sociologist. From 1881 he taught principally at the University of Kiel. In *Gemeinschaft und Gesellschaft* (1887; "Community and Society"), he explored the differences between the organic conception of society, or *Gemeinschaft* ("community," a social union based on traditional rules and a shared sense of solidarity), and the social-contract conception of society, or *Gesellschaft* ("society," a social union held together by rational self-interest). In practice, he argued, all societies show elements of both kinds of organization, because human conduct is neither wholly instinctive nor wholly reasoned.

tonsil Small mass of LYMPHOID tissue in the wall of the PHARYNX. The term usually refers to the palatine tonsils on each side of the oropharynx. They are thought to produce antibodies to help prevent respiratory and digestive-tract infection but often become infected themselves (see TONSILLITIS), mostly in children. There are also pharyngeal tonsils, better known as ADENOIDS, and lingual tonsils, at the base of the TONGUE. The last have more effective drainage than the others and are rarely infected.

tonsillitis Inflammatory INFECTION of the TONSILS, usually with hemolytic streptococci (see STREPTOCOCCUS) or VIRUSES. The symptoms are sore throat, trouble in swallowing, fever, and enlarged LYMPH NODES on the neck. The infection, which usually lasts about five days, is treated with bed rest and antiseptic gargling. SULFA drugs or other antibiotics are prescribed in severe bacterial infections to prevent complications. Streptococcal infection can spread to nearby structures. Complications may include ABSCESS, NEPHRITIS, and RHEUMATIC fever. Tonsils that become chronically inflamed and enlarged require surgical removal (tonsillectomy).

Tony awards Annual awards for distinguished achievement in the U.S. theater. Named for the actress-producer Antoinette (Tony) Perry (1888–1946), the annual awards were established in 1947 by the American Theatre Wing and are intended to recognize excellence in plays and musicals staged on BROADWAY. Awards are given for best play, best musical, best play revival, and best musical revival, and in such categories as acting, directing, music, choreography, set design, and costume design.

tool Device for making material changes on other objects, as by cutting, shearing, striking, rubbing, grinding, squeezing, measuring, or other process. A hand tool is a small manual instrument traditionally operated by the muscular strength of the user; a MACHINE TOOL is a power-driven mechanism used to cut, shape, or form materials such as wood and metal. Tools are the main means by which human beings control and manipulate their physical environment.

tool and die making Industrial art of manufacturing stamping DIES, plastics MOLDS, and JIGS and fixtures to be used in the mass production of solid objects. The making of dies for PUNCH presses constitutes most of the work done in tool and die shops, and most such pressworking dies are used in the manufacture of sheet-metal parts such as the panels of an automobile body. See also MACHINE TOOL.

tool steel Specialty STEELS that are produced in small quantities, contain expensive ALLOYS, and are often sold only by the kilogram and by their individual trade names. They are generally very hard, wear-resistant, tough, nonreactive to local overheating, and frequently engineered to particular service requirements. They must be dimensionally stable during hardening and tempering. They contain strong CARBIDE formers such as tungsten, molybdenum, vanadium, and chromium in different combinations, and often cobalt or nickel to improve high-temperature performance. See also HIGH-SPEED STEEL.

Toombs, Robert A(ugustus) (1810–1885) U.S. politician. Born in Wilkes Co., Ga., he became a plantation owner and lawyer. He served in the U.S. House of Representatives (1845–53) and Senate (1853–61), but resigned his Senate seat to help form the Confederate States of America. Disappointed not to be chosen its president, he served briefly as secretary of state (1861). He criticized JEFFERSON DAVIS's extralegal policies during the Civil War and after the war fled to England. He returned to

Georgia in 1867 to rebuild his law practice and to help revise the state constitution and restore white supremacy.

Toomer, Jean *orig.* **Nathan Eugene** (1894–1967) U.S. poet and novelist of the HARLEM RENAISSANCE. Born in Washington, D.C., he taught briefly before turning to writing. *Cane* (1923), considered his best work, is an experimental novel that depicts the experience of being black in the U.S.; it had a strong influence on younger black writers. He also wrote for *The Dial* and other small magazines. He visited the Gurdjieff Institute in France in 1926 and led Gurdjieff groups in Harlem and Chicago. He became a Quaker in 1940. Ambivalent about his mixed racial background and preoccupied with spiritual matters, he avoided race issues in subsequent works.

tooth Any of the hard structures in the MOUTH used for biting and chewing and in speech. Each consists of a crown above the GUM and one or more roots below it, embedded in the JAW. Its inner pulp contains the blood and nerve supply for the bonelike dentin, covered in the crown by enamel, the hardest tissue in the body. Twenty primary (baby) teeth come in by age 2 1/2 and fall out between ages 5 and 13 to be replaced by 32 permanent teeth. The incisors, in front, are shaped mostly for biting, the pointed canines for tearing, and the premolars and molars for grinding food. The teeth are subject to CARIES (decay), caused by acid from bacteria in plaque, a yellowish film that builds up on teeth. Misalignment of teeth between the upper and lower jaws can grind down the teeth and cause problems in chewing. Elsewhere, it is a cosmetic problem. Both can be treated with braces. See also DENTISTRY.

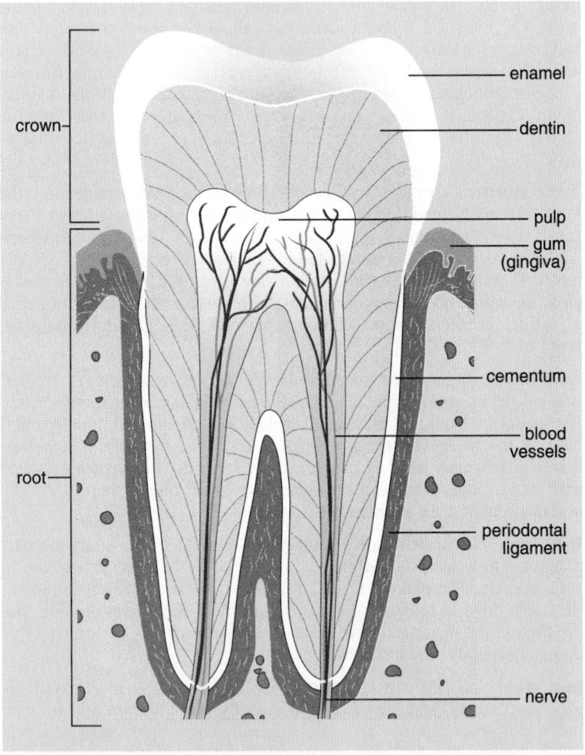

Cross section of an adult molar. The crown (the part of the tooth above the gum) is protected by a hard outer layer of enamel. The roots sit in a socket in the jawbone and are covered with cementum, a bonelike material. The periodontal ligament anchors the cementum in the jaw and cushions the tooth from the pressures of chewing. The tooth's main portion, the dentin, surrounds the soft pulp, which carries the blood vessels and nerves. Specialized cells of the pulp project threadlike extensions into the dentin through narrow channels and serve to form new dentin from minerals in the blood.

tooth decay See CARIES

toothed whale Common term for members of the CETACEAN suborder Odontoceti. Toothed whales have slicing teeth and a throat large enough to swallow chunks of giant squid, cuttlefish, and fish of all kinds. Included in this group are the BELUGA, KILLER whale, PILOT WHALES, SPERM WHALE, and mammalian DOLPHINS, PORPOISES, and NARWHALS.

Topa See NORTHERN WEI DYNASTY

topaz Aluminum SILICATE mineral, $Al_2SiO_4(F,OH)_2$, that is valued as a gemstone. It is formed by fluorine-bearing vapors given off during the last stages of the crystallization of IGNEOUS rocks. Pure topaz may be colorless and, when brilliant-cut, has been mistaken for diamond. It may also be various shades of yellow, blue, or brown. Imperial topaz, with vivid reddish orange color, from Minas Gerais, Brazil, is very highly valued.

Topaz from Minas Gerais state, Brazil.
LEE BOLTIN

Topeka \tə-'pē-kə\ City (pop., 1996 est.: 120,000), capital of Kansas, on the KANSAS RIVER. It was founded in 1854 by a group of antislavery colonists and was prominent in the political conflict between pro-slavery groups and the antislavery FREE SOIL PARTY. In 1859 it was the headquarters for the building of the ATCHISON, Topeka, and Santa Fe Railway system. It has been the capital since Kansas was admitted to the Union in 1861. The economy is based on agriculture, manufacturing, and governmental services. The MENNINGER family established its clinics there, making Topeka a national center for the treatment of mental illness.

Topeka Constitution (1855) Resolution to establish an antislavery territorial government in Kansas. To counter the proslavery government established after passage of the KANSAS-NEBRASKA ACT, antislavery settlers met in Topeka to draft a constitution that banned slavery. In January 1856 they elected a free-state governor and legislature, which created two governments. Pres. FRANKLIN PIERCE condemned the Topeka document and supported the proslavery government. The U.S. House of Representatives voted to admit Kansas under the Topeka Constitution, but the Senate blocked the move. The unresolved situation led to the conflict known as BLEEDING KANSAS.

topiary Art of training living trees and shrubs into artificial, decorative shapes. Topiary is known to have been practiced in the 1st century AD. The earliest topiary was probably the simple development of edgings, cones, columns, and spires to accent a garden scene. This architectural use gave way to elaborate shapes such as ships, hunters, and hounds. The fashion reached its height in Britain in the late 17th and early 18th century but was displaced by the so-called natural garden.

topology \tə-'pä-lə-jē\ In mathematics, the study of the properties of a geometric object that remains unchanged by deformations such as bending, stretching, or squeezing but not breaking. A sphere is topologically equivalent to a cube because, without breaking them, each can be deformed into the other as if they were made of modeling clay. A sphere is not equivalent to a doughnut, because the former would have to be broken to put a hole in it. Topological concepts and methods underlie much of modern mathematics, and the topological approach has clarified very basic structural concepts in many of its branches. See also ALGEBRAIC TOPOLOGY.

Torah \tō-'rä, 'tō-rə, 'tȯr-ə\ *or* **Pentateuch** \'pen-tə-ˌtük\ In JUDAISM, the divine revelations to Israel; specifically, the first five books of the BIBLE: GENESIS, EXODUS, Leviticus, Numbers, and Deuteronomy. By tradition their authorship has been ascribed to MOSES, but biblical scholarship has shown that they were written and compiled at a much later date, probably in the 9th–5th century BC, though drawing on much older traditions. The Scroll of the Torah (SEFER TORAH) is kept in the Synagogue Ark. The term Torah (but not Pentateuch) is often applied to the whole Hebrew Scripture (i.e., the later books of the OLD TESTAMENT), or, even more generally, to that and other Jewish sacred literature and oral tradition.

torana \'tōr-ə-nə\ Indian gateway, usually of stone, marking the entrance to a Buddhist shrine or STUPA or to a Hindu temple. Toranas typically consist of two pillars carrying two or three transverse beams that extend beyond the pillars on either side. Strongly reminiscent of wooden construction, toranas are often covered from top to bottom with exquisite sculpture. The four toranas of the Great Stupa at Sanchi (see SANCHI sculpture) are superb examples. See also TORII.

Tordesillas \ˌtȯr-dā-ˈsēl-yäs\, **Treaty of** (1494) Agreement between Spain and Portugal aimed at settling conflicts over lands explored by voyagers of the late 15th century. In 1493 Pope ALEXANDER VI had granted Spain all the lands west of a line 100 leagues west of the Cape Verde Islands, in return for an agreement to Christianize the peoples of the New World; Portuguese expeditions were to keep to the east. At Tordesillas (a village in Spain), ambassadors from Spain and Portugal moved that line west, thereby allowing Portugal to claim Brazil when it was discovered in 1500.

Tori style In Japanese art, a style of sculpture that emerged during the Asuka period (552–645) and lasted into the NARA period (710–784). Derived from the style of the Chinese NORTHERN WEI DYNASTY (AD 386–534), Tori was named after a sculptor of Chinese descent whose only known piece is a Buddhist triad (623). Works in the Tori style are characterized by slender, elegant bodies, a strong linear interest in drapery, and a tendency toward squatness in the proportion of the faces and also in the relation of the body to the feet.

Bronze triad of Shaka with attendant figures (left figure lost) in the Tori style, Asuka period, 623; in the Horyu-ji, Nara, Japan.

BY COURTESY OF THE HORYU-JI, NARA, JAPAN

torii \ˈtȯr-ē-ˌē\ Symbolic gateway marking the entrance to Shinto shrines or other sacred spots in Japan. It has many variations, but characteristically consists of two cylindrical posts topped by a crosswise rectangular beam extending beyond the posts on either side and a second crosswise beam a short distance below. The top beam often curves upward. Some authorities relate the torii to the Indian TORANA, others to Manchurian and Chinese gates. Often painted red, the torii demarcates the boundary between sacred and ordinary space.

Camphor wood *torii* at the shrine of Itsukushima, on Itsuku-shima, Japan.

PAOLO KOCH—RAPHO/PHOTO RESEARCHERS

Tormé \ˈtȯr-ˌmā\, **Mel(vin Howard)** (1925–1999) U.S. singer and composer, one of the most versatile singers of American popular song and jazz. Born in Chicago, Tormé began his career playing drums and singing with Chico Marx's band (1942–43). His vocal ensemble, the Mel-Tones, appeared with ARTIE SHAW (1945–46). Tormé became one of the great interpreters of ballads and swing in jazz, capable of inspired improvised scat singing. As a songwriter, he is best known for "The Christmas Song." His vocal timbre is reflected in his sobriquet, "the Velvet Fog."

tornado Violent low-pressure storm, relatively small in diameter but with very rapidly rotating winds and an intense updraft near the center. The relatively low pressure at the center of a tornado's funnel-like vortex causes cooling and condensation, making the storm visible as a revolving column of cloud, called the funnel. Tornadoes normally travel at 30–40 mph (50–65 kph). The winds around the vortex average nearly 300 mph (500 kph) and have been known to reach 500 mph (800 kph). Tornadoes often occur in groups.

Torne River \ˈtȯr-nə\ *Swedish* **Torneälv** \ˌtȯr-nē-ˈelv\ Northernmost river of Sweden. Issuing from Torne Lake near the Norwegian border, it flows southeast and south for 354 mi (570 km) to the Gulf of BOTHNIA. The lower course, strewn with rapids and mostly non-navigable, forms a section of the Sweden–Finland boundary. It is known for its salmon.

Toronto City (metro. area pop., 2001: 4,682,897), capital of ONTARIO. Canada's third-largest city, it lies on the northern shore of Lake ONTARIO. Originally inhabited by Seneca tribes, it occupies the site of a French trading post established c. 1750. It was founded in 1793 as York by Americans loyal to the British. U.S. troops sacked it twice during the WAR OF 1812. In 1834 it received its city charter and current name. It became capital of Ontario in 1867. In 1954 it formed a municipality with the adjoining towns of ETOBICOKE, EAST YORK, NORTH YORK, SCARBOROUGH, and YORK that has made it the most populous metropolitan area in Canada. It is Canada's financial and commercial center, the seat of the Toronto Stock Exchange, and a major international trading center, with access to Atlantic shipping via the ST. LAWRENCE SEAWAY and to major U.S. ports via the GREAT LAKES. It produces more than half of Canada's manufactured goods. Extensive immigration (1950–90) brought a variety of foreign cultures that transformed it into one of the liveliest cities on the continent. It is the site of the CN Tower (the world's tallest freestanding structure), the Hockey Hall of Fame, and the annual Canadian National Exhibition. Its educational institutions include the University of TORONTO (1827) and Victoria University (1836).

Toronto, University of Public university in Toronto. It was founded in 1843 and reorganized in 1853 and 1887. It comprises nine undergraduate colleges, three formerly independent but now federated universities, four affiliated theological colleges, and numerous other academic units. It offers undergraduate, graduate, and professional degrees in all major disciplines. Notable among its research units are centers for the study of medieval culture and society, religion, Russia and East Europe, international relations, drama, comparative literature, biomedical engineering, history of science and technology, and aerospace science. Total enrollment is about 55,000.

Toronto Star, The Canadian newspaper. Established in 1892 by 25 printers who had lost their jobs in a labor dispute, it became prosperous after its purchase in 1899 by a group of leading citizens, and maintained a liberal editorial outlook, pressing for social change while promoting stronger Canadian nationhood and a greater presence in international affairs. It established its own radio station in 1922. Its outspoken opposition to Nazism made it the first North American newspaper to be banned in Nazi Germany.

torpedo Cigar-shaped, self-propelled underwater MISSILE, launched from a SUBMARINE, surface vessel, or airplane and designed to explode on contact with the hulls of surface vessels and submarines. It contains devices to control depth and direction as well as a detonator for the explosive-filled warhead. Originally the word referred to any explosive charge, including the weapon now known as a SUBMARINE MINE. The first modern torpedo (1866) carried an 18-lb (8-kg) charge of dynamite in its nose and was powered by a compressed-air engine driving a single propeller; its range was 200–700 yards (180–640 m). Torpedoes were used successfully by submarines in both world wars, when many merchant ships were sunk, mostly by German U-BOATS. Torpedoes are now usually propelled by battery-powered electric motors.

torque *or* **moment** In physics, the tendency of a force to rotate the body to which it is applied. Torque is always specified with regard to the axis of rotation. It is equal to the magnitude of the component of the force lying in the plane perpendicular to the axis of rotation, multiplied by the shortest distance between the axis and the direction of the force component. Torque is the force that affects rotational motion; the greater the torque, the greater the change in this motion.

Torquemada, lithograph.

BY COURTESY OF THE BIBLIOTECA NACIONAL, MADRID

Torquemada \ˌtōr-kā-ˈmä-thä\, **Tomás de** (1420–1498) First grand inquisitor in Spain (1487–98). A Dominican prior, he became confessor and adviser to FERDINAND V and ISABELLA I. He guided the Spanish INQUISITION, directing its persecution of Jews, Moors, and others identified as heretics, sorcerers, or criminals. Torture was used to obtain evidence, and about 2,000 people were burned at the stake during Torquemada's tenure. He probably influenced Ferdinand and Isabella in their decision to expel the Jews from Spain (1492). His name has become synonymous with the cruel fanaticism of the Inquisition.

Torre, Víctor Raúl Haya de la See Víctor Raúl HAYA DE LA TORRE

Torres Bodet \'tōr-ās-bō-'det\, **Jaime** (1902–1974) Mexican poet, novelist, educator, and statesman. He held various diplomatic and government posts, including minister of public education (1943–46) and foreign minister (1946–48). His verse, which early on revealed the influence of MODERNISMO, often returned to the themes of loneliness, a search for identity, and a longing for death. *Cripta* (1937) is considered to include his most important poems. His poetry was collected in *Obra poética* (1967). Of six novels published between 1927 and 1937, *Sombras* (1937) is considered his best. Afflicted by cancer, he took his own life.

Torres Quevedo \'tòr-rās-kā-'vā-dō\, **Leonardo** (1852–1936) Spanish scientist. In 1890 he introduced an electromagnetic device capable of playing a limited form of chess. Though it did not always play the best moves and sometimes took much longer than a competent human player to win, it demonstrated the capability of machines to be programmed to follow specified rules (heuristics) and marked the beginnings of research into the development of ARTIFICIAL INTELLIGENCE.

Torres Strait \'tòr-iz\ Passage between the island of NEW GUINEA and Australia's Cape YORK Peninsula. It connects the CORAL SEA and the Arafura Sea. It was discovered in 1606 by Spanish navigator Luis Vaez de Torres. About 80 mi (130 km) wide, it has many reefs, shoals, and islands, including the TORRES STRAIT ISLANDS, and is treacherous to navigate.

Torres Strait Islands Island group (pop., 1981: 6,000), in the TORRES STRAIT. They are inhabited by a mixture of Polynesians, Melanesians, and Aborigines. They comprise three clusters: Western (high, rocky, and barren), Central (coral), and Eastern (volcanic, with dense vegetation); each has its own local government. The islands may be remnants of a land bridge that once linked Asia and Australia. They were annexed by QUEENSLAND in the 1870s. Pearls, fishing, and tourism are the main sources of income.

Torricelli \,tōr-rē-'chel-lē\, **Evangelista** (1608–1647) Italian physicist and mathematician, inventor of the BAROMETER. He served as secretary to GALILEO during the last three months of the latter's life, and was appointed to succeed him at the Florentine Academy. Two years later, pursuing a suggestion by Galileo, he filled a glass tube 4 ft (1.2 m) long with mercury and inverted the tube into a dish. He observed that some of the mercury did not flow out and that the space above the mercury in the tube was a vacuum. After much observation, he concluded that the variation of the height of the mercury from day to day was caused by changes in atmospheric pressure. He never published his findings. His work in geometry aided in the eventual development of integral calculus.

Torrijos (Herrera) \tòr-'ē-hōs\, **Omar** (1929–1981) Virtual dictator of Panama (1968–78). He entered the national guard in 1952 after military studies in Venezuela and the U.S., rose to the rank of general, and came to power in 1968 in a coup d'état. A nationalist and populist, he was one of the few Latin American heads of state to visit FIDEL CASTRO in Cuba, though he suppressed leftist labor agitators and students at home. In 1977 he achieved his supreme goal when Pres. JIMMY CARTER signed two treaties agreeing to transfer the PANAMA CANAL and CANAL ZONE to Panamanian sovereignty in 1999. He died in a plane crash while on a military inspection tour.

Tórshavn \'tòrs-,haùn\ Port town (pop., 1993 est.: 16,000) and capital of the FAEROE ISLANDS, Denmark. Located on Strømø Island, it was founded in the 13th century. During World War II the British occupied it as a defense against German forces in Denmark. It is home to about one-third of the population of the Faeroe Islands. Its main industries are fishing and knitwear.

torsion balance \'tòr-shən\ Device used to measure the gravitational acceleration at earth's surface. It consists essentially of two small masses at different elevations that are supported at opposite ends of a beam. The latter is suspended from a wire that twists because the masses are affected differently by the force of gravity. When the wire is twisted, an optical system indicates the angle of deflection, and the TORQUE, or twisting force, can be calculated. The torque is correlated with the gravitational force at the point of observation. Torsion balance may also refer to a device used in weighing, a type of equal-arm balance.

torsion bar Rod or bar that resists twisting (see TORQUE) and has a strong tendency to return to its original position when twisted. In an AUTOMOBILE, a torsion bar is a long spring-steel element with one end held rigidly to the frame and the other end twisted by a lever connected to the axle. It thus provides a SPRING action for the vehicle.

torsk See CUSK

tort Wrongful act, other than a breach of contract, that injures another and for which the law permits a civil (noncriminal) action to be brought. Relief may be obtained in the form of damages or an injunction. The term derives from Latin *tortum,* meaning "something twisted, wrung, or crooked." ASSAULT, DEFAMATION, MALPRACTICE, NEGLIGENCE, NUISANCE, product liability, property damage, and TRESPASS are all (apart from their potentially criminal and contractual aspects) torts.

tortoise Any of some 40 species (family Testudinidae) of slow-moving, terrestrial, herbivorous TURTLES, found in the Old and New Worlds but chiefly in Africa and Madagascar. Tortoises have a high, domed shell, heavy elephantlike hind legs, and hard-scaled forelegs. The four North American species (genus *Gopherus*) have a brown shell, about 8–14 in. (20–35 cm) long, and flattened forelimbs adapted for burrowing. The common, or European, tortoise *(Testudo graeca)* has a shell about 7–10 in. (18–25 cm) long. Most species of giant tortoises on the Galápagos and other islands are now rare or extinct. One captive Galápagos tortoise had a shell 4.25 ft (1.3 m) long and weighed 300 lbs (140 kg).

Galápagos tortoise (*Geochelone elephantopus*).
FRANCISCO ERIZE—BRUCE COLEMAN LTD.

torture Infliction of intolerable physical or psychological pain. Torture has been used by those in power for punishment, coercion, and intimidation, especially of enemies, and for extracting confessions and information. It was widely used by the Greeks and Romans; the practice was defended by ARISTOTLE but eloquently opposed by CICERO, SENECA, and St. AUGUSTINE. Its use in Europe increased in the 12th century as a means of obtaining confessions. It was common and sanctioned from the mid-14th through the 18th century; the Roman Catholic Church supported its use during the INQUISITION. Common instruments were the strappado (for repeatedly hoisting the body by the wrists behind the back and dropping it), the rack (for stretching the limbs and body), and the thumbscrew (for crushing the thumbs). By 1800 torture was illegal in most European countries, but it became common again in the 20th century, notably in Nazi Germany and the Soviet Union, and is still widely practiced in Latin America, Africa, and the Middle East. The belief that only sadists could be torturers was challenged by a U.S. study of the 1960s that found that ordinary people could be easily persuaded to inflict pain on others.

Tory Member of a political group in England, especially in the 18th century. Originally an Irish term for an outlaw, the name was applied as a term of abuse to those who supported the hereditary right of James, the Catholic duke of York (later JAMES II), to succeed to the throne of England. They were opposed by the WHIGS in that struggle (1679), but later modified their doctrine of divine-right absolutism. They came to represent the resistance, mainly by the country gentry, to religious toleration and foreign entanglements. The Tories' political power diminished after Viscount BOLINGBROKE, a leading Tory, fled to France in 1715; Tory sentiment subsequently survived in the unsuccessful JACOBITE movement. After 1784, WILLIAM PITT the Younger emerged as the leader of a new Tory party, representing the country gentry, merchants, and administrators. After 1815 the party gradually evolved into the CONSERVATIVE PARTY, whose members are still referred to as Tories.

Tosa \'tō-sä\ Region of the Japanese island of Shikoku whose history dates back at least to the HEIAN period, when Ki no Tsurayuki (868?–

945?), editor of Japan's first imperially commissioned poetry anthology, wrote a fictional diary drawing on his experiences as governor of Tosa. In 1571 it became a unified domain (HAN) whose DAIMYO opposed TOKUGAWA IEYASU; this historical enmity became important at the time of the MEIJI RESTORATION, when SAMURAI from Tosa, like those from SATSUMA and CHOSHU, helped overthrow the TOKUGAWA SHOGUNATE. See also ITAGAKI TAISUKE.

Toscanini \ˌtäs-kə-ˈnē-nē\, **Arturo** (1867–1957) Italian conductor. He entered a conservatory at 9, studying cello, piano, and composition. He began his professional life as a cellist. After substituting for an indisposed conductor in Verdi's *Aïda* (Buenos Aires, 1886), he conducted in various Italian opera houses, giving the premieres of *I Pagliacci* (1892) and *La Bohème* (1896). He served as music director of La Scala several times (1898–1903, 1906–8, 1920–29), and he opened the restored house in 1946. As musical director at the Metropolitan Opera (1908–15), he gave the world premiere of *The Girl of the Golden West*, and the U.S. premieres of *Boris Godunov* and J.-B. LULLY's *Armide*. In 1930 he became the first non-German to conduct at Bayreuth, but he stopped performing in Germany to protest Nazi policies. The NBC Orchestra was formed for him in 1937, and he conducted it until his retirement in 1954.

Tosefta \tō-sef-ˈtä, tō-ˈsef-tə\ Supplements to the MISHNA compiled c. AD 300. The Tosefta consists of laws attributed to the authorities named in the Mishna and generally follows the topical program and organization of the Mishna. Both works were the effort of Jewish scholars working mostly in Palestine who gathered, evaluated and correlated the most important traditions from a vast and heterogeneous mass of material that had developed from the time of EZRA. The Tosefta may have been meant to complement the Mishna by preserving material that appeared marginal or contradictory.

Tostig \ˈtäs-tig\ (died 1066) Anglo-Saxon earl of NORTHUMBRIA. He had strong ties with Norway and became earl of Northumbria in 1055; his severity in subduing the wild northern district stirred revolt in 1065. The rebels won the support of Tostig's brother Earl Harold (later HAROLD II) at Oxford, and Tostig went into exile. He gave his services to WILLIAM I THE CONQUEROR and harried the English coast, then joined Norway's king HARALD III SIGURDSSON in his invasion of England. Tostig was killed when his brother Harold defeated the invading army at Stamford Bridge.

total internal reflection Complete REFLECTION of a ray of light in a medium such as water or glass, from the surrounding surfaces back into the medium. It occurs when the angle of incidence is greater than a certain limiting angle, called the critical angle. In general, it takes place at the boundary between two transparent media when a ray of light in a medium of higher index of REFRACTION approaches another medium of lower index of refraction at more than the critical angle. At all angles less than the critical angle, both reflection and refraction occur. Total internal reflection is responsible for RAINBOWS, atmospheric halos, the sparkle of a diamond, and the path of light through optical fibers.

Total Quality Control (TQC) System for optimizing production based on ideas developed by Japanese industries from the 1950s on. The system, which blends Western and Eastern ideas, began with the concept of Quality Circles, in which groups of 10–20 workers were given responsibility for the quality of the products they produced. It gradually evolved into various techniques involving both workers and managers to maximize productivity and quality, including close monitoring of staff and excellent customer service. The concept of *kaizen*, the notion that improvement must involve all members of a company, is central to TQC. See also PRODUCTION MANAGEMENT.

Total Quality Management (TQM) Management practices designed to improve the performance of organizational processes in business and industry. TQM includes techniques for achieving efficiency, solving problems, imposing standardization and statistical control, and regulating design, housekeeping, and other aspects of business or production processes. See also INTERNATIONAL ORGANIZATION for Standardization (ISO), TOTAL QUALITY CONTROL.

total war Military conflict in which the contenders are willing to make any sacrifice in lives and other resources to obtain a complete victory. It is distinguished from the partial commitment of lives and resources in limited war. The modern concept of total war traces to CARL VON CLAUSEWITZ, who stressed the importance of crushing the adversary's forces in battle and described wars as tending constantly to escalate in violence toward a theoretical absolute. The classic 20th-century work is ERICH LUDENDORFF's *The Total War* (1935). World Wars I and II are usually regarded as total wars. After World War II, especially during the COLD WAR, the prospect of an all-out nuclear war made the major powers reluctant to engage in full-scale international warfare or allow their client states to do so.

totalitarianism Form of government that subordinates all aspects of its citizens' lives to the authority of the state, with a single charismatic leader as the ultimate authority. The term was coined in the early 1920s by BENITO MUSSOLINI, but totalitarianism has existed throughout history throughout the world (e.g., QIN-DYNASTY China). It is distinguished from DICTATORSHIP and AUTHORITARIANISM by its supplanting of all political institutions and all old legal and social traditions with new ones to meet the state's needs, which are usually highly focused. Large-scale, organized violence may be legitimized. The police operate without the constraint of laws and regulations. Where pursuit of the state's goal is the only ideological foundation for such a government, achievement of the goal can never be acknowledged. HANNAH ARENDT's *Origins of Totalitarianism* (1951) is the standard work on the subject.

totem pole Carved and painted vertical log, constructed by many NORTHWEST COAST INDIAN peoples. The poles display mythological images, usually animal spirits, whose significance is their association with the lineage. Each figure represents a type of family crest. Some poles relate a family legend in the form of pictographs. Poles are erected to identify the owner of a house or other property, welcome visitors, indicate a portal or passageway, mark a gravesite, and even ridicule persons. See also SYMBOL, TOTEMISM.

totemism Complex of ideas and practices based on the belief in kinship or mystical relationship between a group (or individual) and a natural object, such as an animal or plant. The term derives from the Ojibwa word *ototeman,* signifying a blood relationship. A society exhibits totemism if it is divided into an apparently fixed number of CLANS, each of which has a specific relationship to an animate or inanimate species (totem). A totem may be a feared or respected hunted animal or an edible plant. Very commonly connected with origin MYTHS and with instituted morality, the totem is almost always hedged about with TABOOS of avoidance or of strictly ritualized contact. Totem, taboo, and EXOGAMY seem to be inextricably intertwined. See also TOTEM pole.

Totonac \ˌtō-tə-ˈnäk\ North American Indians of eastern central Mexico. Some live on the cool, rainy high mesa, others in the hot, humid lowland. Both groups are farmers, but the highlanders engage in peddling and wage labor as well, and often work on lowland farms in the off-season. Most farm their own land and also perform required labor on land collectively owned by the village. They profess Roman Catholicism but have adapted it to their traditional beliefs.

toucan \ˈtü-ˌkan\ Any of about 40 species (family Ramphastidae) of large-billed, long-tailed Central and South American birds. Many species are black with a bold breast color; their thick, saw-edged bills are brightly and distinctively colored. Bands of toucans emit loud barks, bugling calls, and harsh croaks. They eat fruit, insects, lizards, and nestling birds. Toucans deposit two to four eggs in an unlined natural tree cavity or an abandoned woodpecker hole. *Ramphastos* species are up to 24 in. (60 cm) long, a third of which may be the bill. Smaller species (toucanets) are 10–14 in. (25–35 cm) long.

Gray-breasted mountain toucan (*Andigena hypoglauca*).
PAINTING BY JOHN P. O'NEILL

touch-me-not Either of two North American IMPATIENS, also known as jewelweed or snapweed, growing in moist areas. *Impatiens capensis,* also called *I. biflora,* typically has crimson-spotted orange flowers; *I. pallida* has yellow to white flowers, sometimes spotted with brownish-red. They are common weeds native to extensive regions of eastern North America. Their juice is said to be a remedy for POISON-IVY rashes.

S T U V

touch reception See MECHANORECEPTION

touchstone Black, silica-containing stone used in ASSAYING to determine the purity of GOLD and SILVER. The metal to be assayed is rubbed on the touchstone, and then a sample of metal of known purity is rubbed on the stone right next to it. The streaks of metal on the stone are treated with nitric acid, which dissolves impurities, thus increasing the contrast between the two samples when compared. Because other metals, such as copper, can be alloyed to silver without changing its color significantly, the touchstone method is not usually used now to assay silver, though it is still used to assay gold and provides a reasonably accurate guide to quality.

Toulon \tü-'lō^{n}\, **Siege of** (August 28–December 19, 1793) Military engagement in the FRENCH REVOLUTIONARY WARS. French royalists handed over the naval base and arsenal at Toulon, France, to an Anglo-Spanish fleet in August. The French Revolutionary army began a siege to recapture the port city, and after months of preparations successfully assaulted the allied-held forts commanding the anchorage. A battery of French guns, commanded by the young NAPOLEON BONAPARTE, fired on the British fleet and forced it to evacuate the inner harbor, though British and Spanish troops blew up the arsenal and burned 42 French ships before leaving. For his key role in the victory, Napoleon was promoted to brigadier general.

Toulouse \tü-'lüz\ *ancient* **Tolosa.** City (metro. area pop., 1990: 608,000), southern France, on the GARONNE RIVER. Founded in ancient times, it was taken from its Celtic inhabitants by the Romans in 106 BC. After 778 it became the seat of the feudal countship of Toulouse. Protestants were massacred there during the 16th-century Wars of RELIGION. In 1814 it was the scene of the British victory over the French in the last battle of the PENINSULAR WAR. A rail junction and canal port, it is a center of the French aviation industry. It has many historic buildings, including a Gothic cathedral, a Romanesque basilica, and the tomb of St. THOMAS AQUINAS. Its university, founded in 1224, is one of the oldest in the world.

Toulouse-Lautrec (-Monfa) \tü-'lüz-lō-'trek\, **Henri (-Marie-Raymond) de** (1864–1901) French painter and graphic artist. Born to an old aristocratic family, he developed his interest in art during lengthy convalescence after both his legs were fractured in separate accidents (1878, 1879) that left them permanently stunted and made walking difficult. In 1881 he resolved to become an artist; after taking instruction, he established a studio in the Montmartre district of Paris in 1884 and began his lifelong association with the area's cafés, cabarets, entertainers, and artists. He captured the effect of the movement of dancers, circus performers, and other entertainers by simplifying outlines and juxtaposing intense colors; the result was an art throbbing with life and energy. His lithographs were among his most powerful works, and his memorable posters helped define the possibilities of the genre. His pieces are often sharply satirical, but he was also capable of great sympathy, seen most poignantly in his studies of prostitutes (e.g., *At the Salon,* 1896). His extraordinary style helped set the course of avant-garde art for decades to come. A heavy drinker, he died at 36.

Toungoo dynasty \'tau̇ŋ-,gü\ Ruling house in Myanmar from the 15th or 16th century to the 18th century. The founder of the empire is considered to be either King Minkyinyo (r.1486–1531) or his son Tabinshwehti (r.1531–50), who expanded the empire and welded it together. Tabinshwehti's brother-in-law Bayinnaung (r.1551–81) extended the dynasty's reach to include much of Laos and Siam. No ruler ever managed to conquer Arakan (in southern Myanmar), though Tabinshwehti, Bayinnaung, and others tried. The empire slowly disintegrated after Bayinnaung's death, but the dynasty continued until 1752.

Tour, Georges de La See Georges de LA TOUR

Tour de France \,tür-də-'frä^{n}s\ Bicycle race held annually since 1903 on a 4,000-km (2,484-mi) course through France and Belgium, with occasional legs through adjoining countries. Considered the world's preeminent cycling event, it admits 120 or more professional male contestants. The race is divided into about 21 daily stages; each stage is timed, and the rider with the lowest aggregate time for all stages is the winner. A women's Tour de France was held from 1984 to 1989.

Touraine \tü-'ren\ Historical region, northwestern central France. It encompassed the former province of Touraine; its capital was at TOURS. In Roman times it was inhabited by the Gallic Turones. In the 5th century AD it was incorporated in the Visigothic kingdom, and it passed to the FRANKS in 507. Contested by various powers over the succeeding centuries, it came under French influence in the early 13th century. It began to decline c. 1700, and the province was abolished in 1789 during the FRENCH REVOLUTION. The region, which includes the LOIRE RIVER valley, known for its magnificent chateaus, is sometimes called the Garden of France.

Touré \tü-'rā\, **(Ahmed) Sékou** (1922–1984) First president of Guinea (1958–84) and a leading African politician. Touré, who claimed to be descended from SAMORI TURE, helped lead Guinea's campaign for independence in 1958. He actively supported KWAME NKRUMAH's program for African unity, and gave Nkrumah asylum when he was deposed in 1966. A member of the ORGANIZATION OF AFRICAN UNITY, he was viewed internationally as a moderate Islamic leader. After an unsuccessful invasion from neighboring Portuguese Guinea (now Guinea-Bissau) in 1971, he imposed harsh domestic measures and ruled with an iron hand.

Tourette's syndrome \tu̇-'rets\ Rare neurological disease that causes repetitive motor and vocal TICS. Named for Georges Gilles de la Tourette, who first described it in 1885, it occurs worldwide, is usually inherited, generally begins at age 2–15, and is three times more common in males. Motor tics occur first in about 80% of cases, compulsions to utter abnormal sounds in the rest. A compulsion to utter obscenities, once thought characteristic, is often absent. Repetition of words heard and spontaneous repetition of one's own words are two distinctive symptoms. Other vocal tics may include meaningless sounds. Motor tics may be virtually unnoticeable; more complex ones may appear intentional (e.g., hopping, clapping). Sleep, intense concentration, and exertion tend to suppress the tics; emotional stress worsens them. Unlike psychiatric compulsive disorders, Tourette's syndrome has a neurological origin and may improve with mind-altering drugs. Brain NEUROTRANSMITTER abnormalities may be involved, but the underlying cause remains uncertain.

tourmaline \'tər-mə-lən, 'tər-mə-,lēn\ Complex SILICATE mineral that is often used as a gemstone. Three types of tourmaline, distinguished by the presence of certain elements, are usually recognized: iron tourmaline (schorl) is black, magnesium tourmaline (dravite) is brown, and alkali tourmalines may be pink, green, blue, or colorless. Tourmaline is most common in granite PEGMATITES. Gem-quality stones are found especially in the U.S., Brazil, Russia, and Madagascar.

Tourneur \'tər-nər\, **Cyril** (c. 1575–1626) English dramatist. His early years were devoted to literature; after c. 1613 he served the government. His reputation rests largely on *The Atheist's Tragedie* (1611), a verse drama rich in macabre imagery. He may be the author of *The Revenger's Tragedie* (1607), often attributed to THOMAS MIDDLETON; though earlier than *The Atheist's Tragedie*, it is more mature in its structure and somber brilliance. He also wrote the poetical satire *The Transformed Metamorphosis* (1600).

Tours \'tür\ City (pop., 1990: 133,000), northwestern central France. Gallic tribes inhabited the site before the Roman conquest. In the 3rd century AD it was made an episcopal see, but the Christian community remained small until St. MARTIN became bishop in the 4th century; a magnificent basilica was raised above his tomb in the late 5th century, attracting pilgrims for hundreds of years. In the 5th century it became part of the Frankish dominion; CHARLES MARTEL defeated Moorish invaders nearby at the Battle of TOURS/POITIERS in 732. Under ALCUIN it developed as a center of learning. Though it prospered in the Middle Ages, it declined with the 17th-century emigration of the Protestant HUGUENOTS. It was the seat of French government during the siege of Paris (1870) in the FRANCO-PRUSSIAN WAR. The chief tourist center for the LOIRE valley, it has the remains of the old basilica of St. Martin. It was the birthplace of HONORE DE BALZAC.

Tours/Poitiers \pwä-'tyā\, **Battle of** (October 732) Victory won by the Frankish mayor of the palace CHARLES MARTEL over Muslim invaders from Spain. Charles led Frankish troops against a Muslim army seeking to gain control of Aquitaine. The Arab leader, Abd-al-Rahman al-Ghafiqi, was killed, and the Arabs retreated. The battle was decisive because it marked the end of the Muslim invasions of Frankish territory.

Toussaint-Louverture \'tü-,sa^{n}-'lü-vər-,tu̇r\ *orig.* **François Dominique Toussaint** (1743?–1803) Leader of the Haitian independence movement during the French Revolution. Born a slave, he was freed in 1777. In 1791 he joined a slave rebellion, and soon assembled an army of his own, which he trained in guerrilla warfare. When France and Spain went to war in 1793, he and other black commanders joined the Spaniards, but in 1794 he switched his allegiance to the French because France, unlike Spain, had recently abolished slavery. His revolt created the first independent nation in Latin America. He rose from lieutenant governor to governor-general of Saint-Domingue and gradually rid himself of nominal French superiors. Treaties with the British secured their withdrawal, and he began trade with them and the U.S. In 1801 he turned his attention to Santo Domingo, the Spanish-controlled portion of Hispaniola, driving out the Spanish and freeing the slaves there. He made himself governor-general for life. He was deposed by the French in 1802 and died in custody in France. See also J.-J. Dessalines.

Toutates See Teutates

Towada \tō-'wä-dä\, **Lake** Lake, northern Honshu, Japan. Occupying a volcanic crater, it is 27 mi (44 km) in circumference. The third-deepest lake in Japan, it is 1,096 ft (334 m) deep at its center. It lies in Towada-Hachimantai National Park, a popular recreation area.

tower Any freestanding or attached structure that is relatively tall in proportion to its base. The Romans, Byzantines, and medieval Europeans built defensive towers as part of the fortifications of their city walls (e.g., the Tower of London). Indian temple architecture uses towers of various types (e.g., the sikhara). Towers were an important feature of churches and cathedrals built in the Romanesque and Gothic periods. Some Gothic church towers were designed to carry a spire; others had flat roofs. The Italian campanile could either be attached to a church or freestanding. The use of towers declined somewhat during the Renaissance but reappeared in baroque architecture. The use of steel frames enabled buildings to reach unprecedented heights; the Eiffel Tower was the first structure to reveal the true vertical potential of steel construction.

Tower, Joan (born 1938) U.S. composer. Born in New Rochelle, N.Y., she studied piano as a child, attended Bennington College, and completed her music studies at Columbia University. In 1969 she formed the Da Capo Chamber Players, for which she played piano and wrote many pieces; she left the group in 1984. She is chiefly known for her colorful and often whimsical orchestral compositions, including *Sequoia* (1981), *Fanfare for the Uncommon Woman* (1987), and *Silver Ladder* (1987). Since 1972 she has taught at Bard College.

Tower of London Royal fortress on the northern bank of the River Thames. The central keep, or donjon, known as the White Tower because of its limestone, was begun c. 1078 by William I the Conqueror inside the Roman city wall. In the 12th–13th century the fortifications were extended beyond the wall, the White Tower becoming the nucleus of a series of concentric defenses. The only entrance from the land is at the southwestern corner; when the river was still a major highway, the 13th-century water gate was much used. Its nickname, Traitors' Gate, derives from the prisoners brought through it to the Tower, long used as a state prison; many were murdered or executed there.

towhee \'tō-ˌhē, 'tō-ˌē\ Any of several North American songbirds (passerine family Fringillidae, sometimes Emberizidae), long-tailed thicket-dwellers that noisily scratch the ground for food. The name is from the call of the rufous-sided towhee *(Pipilo erythrophthalmus)*, known as chewink in the southeastern U.S.; it ranges from Canada to Central America. About 8 in. (20 cm) long, it has a dark hood, white-cornered tail, and rusty flanks; western subspecies have white-spotted wings. The brown towhee *(P. fuscus)* of the western U.S. is a plain-looking bird. The green-tailed towhee *(Chlorura chlorura)*, also western, is gray, white, and greenish, with a red-brown cap.

Rufous-sided towhee (*Pipilo erythrophthalmus*).
JOHN H. GERARD FROM THE NATIONAL AUDUBON SOCIETY COLLECTION/PHOTO RESEARCHERS

town meeting Legislative assembly of a U.S. town in which all or some voters are empowered to conduct the community's affairs. Town meetings first appeared in New England in the colonial era and are still largely a New England phenomenon, partly because the region's towns tend to hold powers that are granted to counties elsewhere. They are normally held annually. Executive authority is usually held by a three- or five-member board of selectmen. Open town meetings, often regarded as an exceptionally pure form of democracy, allow all registered voters to vote on the articles listed on the agenda, or warrant; representative town meetings allow only elected members to vote.

Townes, Charles H(ard) (born 1915) U.S. physicist. Born in Greenville, S.C., he studied at Furman Univ., Duke Univ., and Caltech, and worked for Bell Labs before joining the faculty of Columbia University (1948). In the early 1950s he and his students constructed the first maser, and showed that a similar device producing visible light was also possible. For his role in the invention of the maser and later the laser, he shared a 1964 Nobel Prize with Aleksandr M. Prokhorov (born 1916) and Nikolay G. Basov (born 1922).

Townsend family U.S. cabinetmakers in Newport, R.I., of the 17th–18th century. The brothers Job (1699–1765) and Christopher (1701–1773) were the first generation involved in furniture making. Job's daughter married his apprentice John Goddard (see Goddard family). Five of Job's sons and two of Christopher's sons became cabinetmakers. The Goddard-Townsend group was best known for case furniture characterized by block fronts (divided into three panels, with the central panel recessed) and decorative carved shell motifs, frequently in the graceful and somewhat ornate style developed by Thomas Chippendale.

Townshend (of Rainham) \'tau̇n-zənd\, **Viscount** *orig.* **Charles Townshend** (1675–1738) British politician. He succeeded to his father's title in 1687, married the sister of Robert Walpole, and served as secretary of state 1714–16. With Walpole, he led the Whig Party and became president of the privy council (1720). Again secretary of state 1721–30, he formed the League of Hanover (1725), which allied Britain, France, and Prussia against Austria and Spain. He resigned when Walpole, by then the dominant minister, opposed an aggressive policy against Austria. Also interested in agricultural reform, Townshend developed the use of turnips in crop rotation, earning the nickname Turnip Townshend.

Townshend Acts (1767) British parliamentary measures to tax the American colonists. The series of four acts imposed duties on imports of lead, paint, glass, paper, and tea and established a board of customs commissioners to enforce collection. Colonial quartering of British troops was also revived. The colonists protested the new measures as taxation without representation and resisted compliance. Nonimportation agreements among colonial merchants cut British imports in half by 1769. In 1770 all the duties except the tax on tea were repealed.

toxic diffuse goiter See Graves' disease

toxic shock syndrome Bacterial disease caused by a toxin produced by *Staphylococcus aureus,* a common staphylococcus bacterium. It was first recognized in 1978 in women using superabsorbent tampons (no longer made). High fever, diarrhea, vomiting, and rash may progress to abdominal tenderness, drop in blood pressure, shock, respiratory distress, and kidney failure. The syndrome also has other causes, including post-surgical infection. Antibiotics are not effective. With intensive supportive therapy (see therapeutics), most patients recover in 7–10 days, but 10–15% die. Many patients have a milder recurrence within eight months.

toxicology Study of poisons and their effects, particularly on living systems. It overlaps with biochemistry, histology, pharmacology, pathology, and other fields. Its functions have expanded from identifying poisons and searching for treatments to include forensic toxicology (see forensic medicine) and testing and detection of a fast-growing number of new potentially toxic substances used in workplaces, in agriculture (e.g., insecticides, other pesticides, fertilizers), in cosmetics, as food additives, and as drugs (see medicinal poisoning). Perhaps the area of largest expansion is the study of toxic waste in the air, water, and soil, including chlorofluorocarbons, acid rain, dioxin, and radioactive isotopes.

toxin Any substance poisonous to an organism; often restricted to poisons produced by living organisms. In addition to those from such microorganisms as bacteria (see bacterial diseases), dinoflagellates, and algae, there are toxins in fungi (mycotoxins; see aflatoxin, mushroom poisoning), higher plants (phytotoxins), and animals (zootoxins, or venoms). The plants include nightshade (see nightshade family), poison hemlock, foxglove, mistletoe, and poison ivy. Many plant toxins (e.g., pyrethrins, nicotine, rotenone) apparently protect their producers against certain animals (especially insects) or fungi. Similar defensive secretions in animals may be widely distributed or concentrated in certain tissues, often with some sort of delivery system (e.g., spines, fangs). Animals such as spiders and snakes use venoms to catch prey and often for defense. Many normally edible fishes and shellfishes become poisonous after feeding on toxic plants or algae. See also ANTIDOTE, FOOD POISONING.

toxoid \'täk-ˌsȯid\ Bacterial TOXIN that has been made inactive but can still combine with or stimulate formation of ANTIBODIES. In many BACTERIAL diseases, the bacteria produce a toxin that causes the disease manifestations. Heating the toxin or treating it chemically converts it into a harmless toxoid that is injected into a person or animal to confer IMMUNITY from subsequent INFECTION. The VACCINES for TETANUS and DIPHTHERIA are toxoids.

toy Plaything for a child or infant. Toys survive from the remote past and from a great variety of cultures. They range from the simple to the complex, from a stick or piece of string that becomes a toy in a child's hands to complex mechanical and electronic devices. Perennial favorites include balls, jump ropes, dolls, drums, whistles, dice, jackstones, board games, marbles, play weapons, and costumes. In the modern era the toy industry has grown tremendously, especially with the advent of computer games.

toy dog Any of several breeds of DOGS that were bred to be small, portable, good-natured companions. Toy dogs were traditionally pampered and treasured by aristocracy around the world, and several breeds are ancient. They range from hairless (e.g., the Chinese crested dog) to profusely coated (e.g., the SHIH tzu). Some breeds, such as the PEKINGESE, could be owned only by royalty. The Cavalier King Charles spaniel was a favorite of English royalty. English toy spaniels and toy POODLES are popular in the U.S. The miniature pinscher resembles the DOBERMAN pinscher but has a different ancestry. Other toy dogs include the AFFENPINSCHER, MALTESE, PAPILLON, POMERANIAN, and YORKSHIRE TERRIER.

Toynbee, Arnold (Joseph) (1889–1975) English historian. Long a professor at the University of London and the Royal Institute of International Affairs, Toynbee also held positions with the British Foreign Office. He is best known for his 12-volume *A Study of History* (1934–61), which put forward a philosophy of history, based on an analysis of the development and decline of 26 civilizations. Criticisms of his *Study* include his use of myths and metaphors as being of comparable value to factual data and his reliance on a view of religion as a regenerative force. His other works include *Civilization on Trial* (1948), *East to West* (1958), and *Hellenism* (1959).

Toyota Motor Corp. Largest Japanese automobile manufacturer, parent company of the Toyota group. It was established in 1933 as a division of the Toyoda Automatic Loom Works, Ltd., and in 1937 it was incorporated as the Toyota Motor Co., Ltd. Since then Toyota has established several related companies, including Toyoda Machine Works, Ltd. (1941), and Toyota Auto Body, Ltd. (1945). In the 1960s and '70s the company expanded rapidly, exporting large numbers of cars to foreign markets. Its present name was adopted in 1982. Today it has assembly plants and distributors in many foreign countries, and it owns subsidiaries that produce cars and car parts, rubber and cork materials, steel, synthetic resins, automatic looms, and cotton and woolen goods. Its headquarters are in Toyota City.

Toyotomi Hideyoshi \ˌhē-de-'yō-shē\ (1536/7–1598) One of the Three Unifiers of Japan (with ODA NOBUNAGA and TOKUGAWA IEYASU) who brought the nation out of its WARRING STATES period. He began life as a peasant but was raised to the rank of samurai while a soldier for Nobunaga. After Nobunaga's death, he was appointed *kampaku* (chancellor to the emperor). Having concluded an alliance with his former rival Tokugawa Ieyasu, he became in 1590 the head of an alliance of DAIMYO that constituted a government of national unification. To stabilize society, he imposed the division of society into warriors, farmers, artisans, and tradesmen (an adaptation of ancient Chinese social divisions) and confiscated swords from all but the warriors. With visions of empire, he made two destructive but unsuccessful attempts to invade Korea (1592, 1597). After his death, power passed to Tokugawa Ieyasu.

TQC See TOTAL QUALITY CONTROL

TQM See TOTAL QUALITY MANAGEMENT

tracery In architecture, bars or ribs used decoratively in windows, especially the ornamental openwork in Gothic windows. In the earliest phase, two or three narrow, arched windows were placed close together under a single large arch, with the section of wall between the small and large arches pierced by a circular or four-lobed opening. The complexity of this plate tracery increased, reaching a climax in the magnificent windows of CHARTRES CATHEDRAL. After c. 1220 windows began to be subdivided by mullions, or upright bars, that continued at the head of the window to branch and form the patterns of bar tracery. Elaborate bar tracery soon became one of the most important elements of GOTHIC ARCHITECTURE and one of its finest achievements, as in the ROSE WINDOWS of the French RAYONNANT style. The bar tracery of the parallel English Decorated style formed netlike patterns based on the circle, arch, trefoil, and quatrefoil. By the late 14th century, the PERPENDICULAR style replaced curvilinear tracery with straight mullions extending to the top of the main arch, connected at intervals by horizontal bars.

trachea \'trā-kē-ə\ *or* **windpipe** Tube in the throat and upper THORACIC cavity through which air passes in RESPIRATION. It begins at the LARYNX and splits just above heart level into the two main bronchi, which enter the LUNGS. In adults it is about 6 in. (15 cm) long and 1 in. (2.5 cm) in diameter. Its structure—a membrane strengthened by 16–20 CARTILAGE rings open in the back, with their free ends connected by muscle bands—allows the trachea to stretch and contract in breathing. An inner mucous membrane has cilia (see CILIUM) that project inward to trap particles. Muscle fibers over and alongside the trachea contract in response to cold air or irritants in inhaled air; in coughing, the airway narrows to about one-sixth of its normal size to increase the speed and force of exhalation and to dislodge foreign bodies. Such diseases as DIPHTHERIA, SYPHILIS, TUBERCULOSIS, and TYPHOID often involve the trachea.

tracheitis \ˌtrā-kē-'ī-təs\ INFLAMMATION and infection of the TRACHEA. Inhaled irritants can injure the tracheal lining and increase the chance of infection (bacterial or viral). Acute infections, usually bacterial, produce fever, fatigue, and swelling of the tracheal lining but generally do no great damage. Chronic infections, promoted by irritants such as heavy smoking and alcohol abuse, cause progressive tissue degeneration and scarring.

tracheophyte See VASCULAR PLANT

trachyandesite See LATITE

trachyte \'tra-ˌkīt, 'trā-ˌkīt\ Light-colored, very fine-grained IGNEOUS rock composed chiefly of ALKALI FELDSPAR with only minor mafic minerals (BIOTITE, HORNBLENDE, or PYROXENE). Trachyte is commonly found in volcanic regions; like many volcanic rocks, it shows a streaked or banded structure due to flowing of the congealing lava.

track and field *British* **athletics** Variety of sport competitions held on a running track and on the adjacent field. It is the oldest form of organized sports, having been a part of the ancient OLYMPIC GAMES from c. 776 BC to AD 393. Modern events include various distance-running competitions (100-m dash, mile race, MARATHON, etc.), RELAY races, HURDLING, STEEPLECHASE, HIGH JUMP, POLE VAULT, LONG JUMP, TRIPLE jump, SHOT put, DISCUS throw, HAMMER THROW, JAVELIN throw, DECATHLON, PENTATHLON, and HEPTATHLON. CROSS-COUNTRY RUNNING and speed WALKING are usually considered adjuncts of track-and-field athletics. Events are held indoors and outdoors and records are kept separately; some events are modified or eliminated for indoor competition.

Tractarian movement See OXFORD MOVEMENT

tractor High-power, low-speed traction vehicle. The two main types are wheeled and continuous-track. Most modern tractors are powered by internal-combustion engines running on gasoline or diesel fuel. Tractors are used in agriculture, construction, and road building, for pulling equipment such as plows and cultivators, for pushing implements such as bulldozers and diggers, and for operating stationary devices such as saws and winches. The first tractors grew out of the STEAM ENGINES used on farms in the late 19th century; in 1892 an Iowa blacksmith, John Froehlich, built the first farm vehicle powered by a gasoline engine. The tractor revolutionized farming, displacing draft animals and many farm workers. By World War I the tractor inspired the TANKS built by the British and French.

Tracy, Benjamin F(ranklin) (1830–1915) U.S. public official. Born in Owego, N.Y., he served as a county district attorney (1853–59) and, after fighting in the Civil War, as U.S. attorney (1866–73). Appointed secretary of the navy (1889–93) by Pres. BENJAMIN HARRISON, he continued the expansion of the navy begun by WILLIAM C. WHITNEY, authorizing construction of new battleships and cruisers, and his departmental reforms and modernization helped build U.S. naval superiority.

Tracy, Spencer (1900–1967) U.S. film actor. Born in Milwaukee, he first starred on Broadway in *The Last Mile* (1930) and on film in *Up the River* (1930). Noted for his craggy features and his sincere, expert acting, he became one of the top stars of the 1930s and '40s, winning Academy Awards in *Captains Courageous* (1937) and *Boys Town* (1938) and being nominated for seven other roles, including *Inherit the Wind* (1960) and *Judgment at Nuremberg* (1961). He had a long relationship with KATHARINE HEPBURN, with whom he costarred in nine films, including *Woman of the Year* (1942), *Adam's Rib* (1949), and *Guess Who's Coming to Dinner* (1967).

trade, balance of See BALANCE OF TRADE

Trade, Board of *in full* **Lords Commissioners of Trade and Plantations** Advisory body that supervised American colonial affairs. Established in 1696 to replace the Lords of Trade (1675–96), it examined colonial legislation to ensure maximum benefit to British trade policies. The board nominated colonial governors, recommended laws affecting the colonies to Parliament, and heard complaints from the colonies about its administrators. It lacked executive or legislative powers, but it became the primary colonial policy-making body of the British government. It was abolished in 1782.

Trade, Board of Organized market for the exchange of commodity contracts (see COMMODITY EXCHANGE). The first grain-futures exchange in the U.S. was organized in Chicago in 1848. The Board of Trade began as a voluntary association of prominent Chicago grain merchants and was soon chartered by the Illinois legislature. Initially it sold grain by sample; later it introduced a system of inspection and grading to standardize the market and facilitate trading. By 1858 access to the trading floor was limited to members with seats on the exchange. It became the world's largest commodity exchange in terms of volume and value of business.

trade, restraint of See RESTRAINT OF TRADE

trade, terms of Relationship between the prices at which a country sells its exports and the prices paid for its imports. If a country's export prices rise relative to import prices, its terms of trade are said to have moved in a favorable direction, since, in effect, it now receives more imports for each unit of goods exported. The terms of trade, which depend on the world supply of and demand for the goods involved, indicate how the gains from international trade will be distributed among trading countries. An abrupt change in a country's terms of trade (e.g., a drastic fall in the price of its main export) can cause serious problems in its BALANCE OF PAYMENTS. See also COMPARATIVE ADVANTAGE.

trade agreement Any contractual arrangement between states concerning their trade relations. Trade agreements may be bilateral or multilateral, that is, between two states or more than two. For most countries international trade is regulated by unilateral barriers, including TARIFFS, nontariff barriers, and government prohibitions. Trade agreements aim to reduce such barriers and thus provide all parties with the benefits of increased trade. Reciprocity is a necessary feature of trade agreements, since neither state will be willing to sign the agreement unless it expects to gain as much as it loses. Another common feature is a most-favored-nation clause, which provides against the possibility that one of the parties to the current agreement will later offer lower tariffs to another country (see MOST-FAVORED-NATION TREATMENT). Agreements often include clauses providing for "national treatment of nontariff restrictions," meaning that both states promise not to duplicate the properties of tariffs with nontariff restrictions such as discriminatory regulations, selective excise taxes, quotas, and special licensing requirements. General multilateral agreements are sometimes easier to reach than separate bilateral agreements, since the gains to efficient producers from worldwide tariff reductions are large enough to warrant substantial concessions. The most important modern multilateral trade agreement was the GENERAL AGREEMENT on Tariffs and Trade (GATT), which reduced world tariff levels and greatly expanded world trade. See also NORTH AMERICAN FREE TRADE AGREEMENT, WORLD TRADE ORGANIZATION.

trade fair *or* **trade show** Temporary market organized to promote trade, where buyers and sellers gather to transact business. Trade fairs are organized at regular intervals, generally at the same location and time of year. They are especially common in Europe and Asia, where nearly every country has at least one major annual international exposition. They range in scope from those dealing with one industry or branch of industrial production to general exhibits of goods and merchandise. Fairs confined to a single industry or even to a specialized segment of an industry have become increasingly common.

trademark Mark used by a manufacturer or merchant to identify the origin or ownership of goods and distinguish them from others. Trademarks may be words or groups of words, letters, numerals, devices, names, the shape or other presentation of products or their packages, or combinations of colors. A trademark (indicated by ™ or, when registered, by the symbol ®) is considered the property of the holder and is protected by law from unauthorized use by others. A trademark or service mark (which identifies services, as opposed to goods) need not be registered with the U.S. Patent and Trademark Office or a state bureau in order for owners to enforce their rights in court, though registration often proves legally advantageous. See also COPYRIGHT.

Trades Union Congress (TUC) National organization of British labor unions. It was founded in 1868 to hold annual conferences of independent unions. It included only skilled workers until 1889, when unions of unskilled workers were admitted. In 1900 the TUC helped found a separate labor organization, the Labour Representation Committee, renamed the LABOUR PARTY in 1906. After World War I the TUC was governed by a General Council, which had powers to deal with interunion conflicts and intervene in disputes with employers. In the 1930s and '40s, it was the spokesman for industrial labor in dealings with the government. It continued to help formulate economic policy until 1979, when a Conservative government came to power, leading to a decline in TUC membership in the 1980s. In the late 1990s, under Labour prime minister TONY BLAIR, the TUC was encouraged to back "workplace partnerships" between unions and employers.

Trafalgar \trə-'fal-gər\, **Battle of** (October 21, 1805) Naval engagement in the NAPOLEONIC WARS that established British naval supremacy in Europe. It was fought west of Cape Trafalgar, Spain, between a Franco-Spanish fleet of 33 ships under Pierre de Villeneuve (1763–1806) and a British fleet of 27 ships under HORATIO NELSON. As Villeneuve tried to slip out of the besieged port of Cádiz, he was caught by Nelson. The French ships formed a single line and were attacked by the English at two points. After sending the famous signal "England expects that every man will do his duty," Nelson broke through the center of the French line and in the pell-mell battle captured Villeneuve and 20 ships. Near the end of the battle, Nelson was mortally wounded by a sniper. No British ships were lost and NAPOLEON abandoned his plan to invade England.

tragedy Drama of a serious and dignified character that typically describes the development of a conflict between the protagonist and a superior force (such as destiny, circumstance, or society) and reaches a sorrowful or disastrous conclusion. Tragedy of a high order has been created in three periods and locales, each with a characteristic emphasis and style: Attica, in Greece, in the 5th century BC; Elizabethan and Jacobean England (1558–1625); and 17th-century France. The idea of tragedy also found embodiment in other literary forms, especially the novel. See also COMEDY.

tragicomedy Literary genre consisting of dramas that combine elements of TRAGEDY and COMEDY. PLAUTUS coined the Latin word *tragicocomoedia* to denote a play in which gods and mortals, masters and slaves reverse the roles traditionally assigned to them. In the Renaissance and after, tragicomedy was mainly comic, though Elizabethan and Jacobean tragedies almost always include some comic or grotesque elements. Modern tragicomedy is sometimes used synonymously with absurdist drama, which suggests that laughter is the only response left to people faced with an empty and meaningless existence.

Traherne \trə-'hərn\, **Thomas** (1637–1674) English mystical poet and religious writer. He was ordained in the Anglican church in 1660. Most of his works were unknown for centuries. The discovery in 1896 in a London street bookstall of the manuscripts of *Poetical Works* (1903) and the prose *Centuries of Meditations* (1908) created a literary sensation.

Later the manuscript of *Poems of Felicity* (1910) was discovered in the British Museum. His poetry, though sometimes original and intense, is overshadowed by his vivid prose.

Trail of Tears Forced migration of the CHEROKEE Indians in 1838–39. In 1835, when gold was discovered on Cherokee land in Georgia, a small minority of Cherokee ceded all tribal land east of the Mississippi for $5 million. The U.S. Supreme Court invalidated the deal, but the ruling was ignored by state officials and Pres. ANDREW JACKSON refused to enforce it. The subsequent eviction and 116-day forced march of thousands of Cherokee to Oklahoma was badly mismanaged, and inadequate food supply, frigid weather, and the cruelty of escorting troops led to the death of about 4,000 Cherokees.

trailing arbutus \är-ˈbyü-təs\ *or* **mayflower** Trailing evergreen plant *(Epigaea repens)* of the HEATH family, native to sandy or boggy, acidic woodlands of eastern North America. Its leaves are oblong and hairy, and its white, pink, or rosy flowers grow in dense clusters. It is grown in shady wildflower gardens and as ground cover in terraria.

training, transfer of In psychology, the effect of having learned one activity on an individual's execution of other activities. Positive transfer occurs when a previously acquired skill enhances one's performance of a new one. Negative transfer occurs when the previously acquired skill impairs one's attempt to master the new one.

Trajan \ˈtrā-jən\ *in full* **Caesar Divi Nervae Filius Nerva Traianus Optimus Augustus** ***or*** **Caesar Nerva Traianus Germanicus** ***orig.*** **Marcus Ulpius Traianus** (AD 53–117) Roman emperor (98–117), the first born outside Italy. He had military commands in Asia and Europe before being named CONSUL in 91. In 97 he was adopted by NERVA as his successor. After Nerva's death in 98, he deified the former emperor and named himself Jupiter's representative on earth. He strengthened defenses along the northern frontier and weakened the PRAETORIAN GUARD at Rome. He gave the SENATE new authority, reduced taxes, supported the poor with government welfare, reformed provincial administration, and built public works, including a forum with Trajan's Column, a structure commemorating his Dacian Wars. He added Dacia, Mesopotamia, and Parthia to the empire. He was campaigning in Asia when revolts broke out in conquered territories. Discouraged and ill, he returned to Rome to die.

Trajan, detail of a marble bust; in the British Museum.

trampoline Resilient sheet or web (often of nylon) supported by springs in a metal frame and used as a springboard and landing area in tumbling. Trampolining is an individual sport of acrobatic movements performed after rebounding into the air from the trampoline. As a competitive sport, it was included in the Pan-American Games for the first time in 1955, and a world championship was established in 1964; competitors are scored on difficulty, execution, and form.

tranquilizer DRUG used to reduce anxiety, fear, tension, agitation, and related disturbed mental states. Major tranquilizers (antipsychotic agents, or neuroleptics) are used to treat SCHIZOPHRENIA and other PSYCHOSES; phenothiazines, including chlorpromazine, are the best known. They are thought to block the activity of the NEUROTRANSMITTER DOPAMINE in the brain. Minor tranquilizers (antianxiety agents, or anxiolytics) are used to treat anxiety and tension; they are usually benzodiazepines, including diazepam (Valium) and chlordiazepoxide (Librium). They have a calming effect and reduce both physical and psychological effects of anxiety, fear, and stress by enhancing the action of the neurotransmitter gamma-aminobutyric acid (GABA) in the brain.

Trans-Alaska Pipeline *or* **Alaska Pipeline** Oil pipeline running 800 mi (1,300 km) north–south across Alaska. Completed in 1977, it transports crude oil from the oil fields of PRUDHOE BAY on the Arctic Ocean to an ice-free port at Valdez. To avoid thawing the adjacent PERMAFROST, about half of the line is elevated.

Trans-Canada Highway World's longest national road, extending east–west for 4,860 mi (7,821 km) between Victoria, British Columbia, and St. John's, Newfoundland. Completed in 1965, it links many major Canadian cities and provides access to important national and provincial parks.

Trans-Siberian Railroad Longest single rail system in Russia, running from Moscow to Vladivostok, a distance of 5,778 mi (9,198 km). Conceived by Czar ALEXANDER III, its construction began in 1891 and proceeded simultaneously along its entire length, which traversed a section of Manchuria. It was completed in 1904, but the impending Japanese takeover of Manchuria compelled construction of a parallel section within Russian territory, completed in 1916. The railroad opened large areas of Siberia to settlement and industrialization by means of spur lines linking outlying areas with the main line. The complete trip takes about eight days.

Trans World Airlines, Inc. (TWA) Major U.S. airline. Formed in 1930 as Transcontinental & Western Air, Inc., from two smaller airlines, the company established the first coast-to-coast service that same year, flying from Newark, N.J., to Los Angeles in 36 hours. In 1946 TWA began flights between New York and Paris, and it expanded by the 1950s to routes through Europe, the Middle East, Africa, and Asia. It adopted its present name in 1950. HOWARD R. HUGHES was its principal stockholder and guiding genius from 1939 to 1960–61, when he lost control to a group of investors. Financially troubled since the 1980s, TWA continued to operate despite twice landing in bankruptcy court in the 1990s. It was acquired by American Airlines in 2001.

transcendental argument In philosophy, a form of argument that is supposed to proceed from a fact to the necessary conditions of its possibility. A transcendental argument is simply a form of deduction, with the typical pattern: Only if p then q; q is true; therefore, p is true. As this form of argument appears in philosophy, the interest, and the difficulty, reside not in the movement from premises to conclusions, which is routine, but in the setting up of the major premises—that is, in the kinds of things that are taken as starting points. For example, IMMANUEL KANT tried to prove the principle of causality by showing that it is a necessary condition of the possibility of making empirically verifiable statements in natural science.

transcendental function In mathematics, a FUNCTION not expressible as a finite combination of the algebraic operations of addition, subtraction, multiplication, division, raising to a power, and extracting a root. Examples include the functions $\log x$, $\sin x$, $\cos x$, e^x and any functions containing them. Such functions are expressible in algebraic terms only as INFINITE series. In general, the term *transcendental* means nonalgebraic. See also TRANSCENDENTAL NUMBER.

Transcendental Meditation (TM) Spiritual development technique developed and promoted by MAHARISHI MAHESH YOGI, a former Hindu ascetic. A movement that became popular in the West in the 1960s, it is based on specific MEDITATION techniques and is not strictly connected with any religious tradition, though the perspective behind it has roots in VEDANTA. Practice entails the mental repetition of a MANTRA in order to still the activity of thought and experience a deeper level of consciousness. Through this process, the practitioner finds deep relaxation, which can lead to inner joy, vitality, and creativity.

transcendental number Number that is not algebraic, in the sense that it is not the solution of an ALGEBRAIC EQUATION with rational-number coefficients. The numbers e and π, as well as any algebraic number raised to the power of an IRRATIONAL number, are transcendental numbers.

Transcendentalism Movement of 19th-century New England philosophers and writers who were loosely bound together by adherence to an idealistic system of thought based on a belief in the essential unity of all creation, the innate goodness of humankind, and the supremacy of vision over logic and experience for the revelation of the deepest truths. Part of ROMANTICISM, it developed around Concord, Mass., attracting such individualistic figures as RALPH WALDO EMERSON, HENRY DAVID THOREAU, MARGARET FULLER, and BRONSON ALCOTT. Transcendentalist writers and their contemporaries signaled the first flowering of American artistic genius and introduced the American Renaissance in literature. Some of the best writings by minor Transcendentalists appeared in *The Dial* (1840–44), a literary magazine.

transducer Device that converts one form of energy to another. A MICROPHONE is an acoustic transducer, converting sound waves into electrical signals. Different types of transducers act on heat, radiation, sound, strain, vibrations, pressure, and acceleration; they may output mechanical, electrical, pneumatic, or hydraulic signals. Examples include STRAIN GAUGES, LOUDSPEAKERS, PHOTOCELLS, TRANSFORMERS, and THERMOCOUPLES.

transept Area of a cruciform (cross-shaped) church lying at right angles to the principal axis. The bay at which the transept intersects the NAVE is called the crossing. The nave of a church with a cruciform plan usually extends west from the crossing, the choir and sanctuary east. The arms of the transept are designated by direction, as northern transept and southern transept.

transform See FOURIER TRANSFORM, INTEGRAL TRANSFORM, LAPLACE TRANSFORM

transformation In mathematics, a rule for changing a geometric figure or algebraic expression into another, usually accompanied by a rule for transforming it back. In geometry and TOPOLOGY, a transformation (e.g., flipping horizontally or vertically, rotating, or stretching vertically or horizontally) moves each point in a figure or graph to another position. A graph also undergoes a transformation when its COORDINATE system is changed. For example, the equations that establish a correspondence between the rectangular and polar coordinate systems constitute a transformation. In ANALYSIS, a transformation is a procedure that changes one function into another. Of special interest in many fields of mathematics are transformations forming a group, in which any two transformations applied successively produce the same result as another transformation in the group and each transformation has an inverse transformation (which undoes it) in the group. See also GROUP THEORY, INTEGRAL TRANSFORM, LINEAR TRANSFORMATION.

transformer Device that transfers electric energy from one ALTERNATING-CURRENT CIRCUIT to one or more other circuits, either increasing (stepping up) or reducing (stepping down) the voltage. Uses for transformers include reducing the line voltage to operate low-voltage devices (doorbells or toy electric trains) and raising the voltage from electric GENERATORS so that electric power can be transmitted over long distances. Transformers act through ELECTROMAGNETIC INDUCTION; current in the primary coil induces current in the secondary coil. The secondary voltage is calculated by multiplying the primary voltage by the ratio of the number of turns in the secondary coil to that in the primary.

transfusion See BLOOD TRANSFUSION

transistor SOLID-STATE SEMICONDUCTOR device for amplifying, controlling, and generating electrical signals. Invented at Bell Labs (1947) by JOHN BARDEEN, WALTER H. BRATTAIN, and WILLIAM B. SHOCKLEY, it displaced the VACUUM TUBE in many applications. Transistors consist of layers of different semiconductors produced by addition of impurities (such as arsenic or boron) to SILICON. These impurities affect the way electric current moves through the silicon. Transistors were pivotal in the advancement of electronics because of their small size, low power requirements, low heat generation, modest cost, reliability, and speed of operation. Single transistors were superseded in the 1960s and '70s by INTEGRATED CIRCUITS; present-day COMPUTER CHIPS contain millions of transistors. Today transistors perform many different functions in nearly every type of electronic equipment. See illustration opposite.

transition element Any chemical ELEMENT with valence ELECTRONS in two shells instead of only one. This structure gives them their outstanding ability to form IONS containing more than one ATOM (complex ions, or coordination compounds), with a central atom or ion (often a transition metal ion) surrounded by LIGANDS in a regular arrangement. Theories on the BONDING in these ions are still being refined. The elements in the PERIODIC TABLE from scandium to COPPER (atomic numbers 21–29), yttrium to SILVER (39–47), and lanthanum to GOLD (57–79, including the LANTHANIDE series) are frequently designated the three main transition series. (Those in the ACTINIDE series and beyond, 89–111, also qualify.) All are METALS, many of major economic or industrial importance (e.g., IRON, GOLD, NICKEL, TITANIUM). Most are dense, hard, and brittle, conduct heat and electricity well, have high melting points, and form ALLOYS with each other and other metals. Their electronic structure lets them form compounds at various VALENCES. Many of these are colored and paramagnetic (see PARAMAGNETISM) and often act as CATALYSTS.

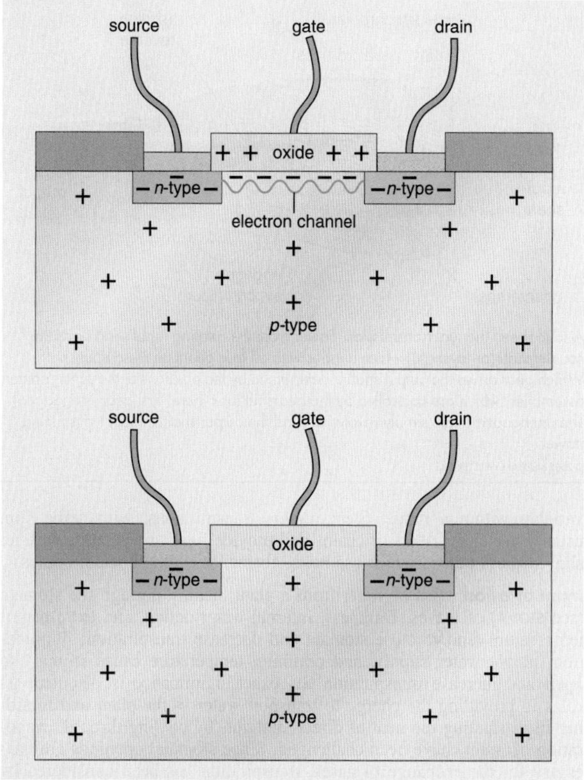

A transistor is a sandwich of dissimilar semiconductors to which are attached three electrodes. Because of the unique electrical properties that occur at *p-n* junctions, current between two of the electrodes may be turned on or off like a switch by varying the voltage applied to the third electrode. In the metal-oxide semiconductor field-effect transistor (MOSFET) shown, current flows between the source and drain electrodes and is regulated by the gate electrode. The *n*-type semiconductor regions have an excess of electrons, but are separated from each other by the *p*-type region, which has an excess of positive charge, called "holes." If a positive voltage is applied to the gate (top), electrons in the *p*-region will be attracted to the area under the oxide, forming a channel of negative charge between the source and drain. If a positive voltage is then applied to the drain, a current of electrons flows through the device and the transistor is on. If the gate voltage is removed (bottom), the electron channel is broken and the transistor is off.

transitive law Property of relationship that states that if A is in a given relation to B and B is in the same relation to C, then A is also in that relation to C. Equality, for example, is a transitive relation.

Transkei \'trans-'kā, 'trans-'kī\ Administrative region, Republic of South Africa. It borders on the Indian Ocean and Lesotho. It was created by South Africa in 1959 as the first Bantu homeland, a non-independent black state designated (together with CISKEI) for the Xhosa-speaking peoples (see XHOSA). It was made a nominally independent republic in 1976, and all black Africans with language ties to Transkei (whether or not they lived there) lost their South African citizenship and became citizens of the new country. Existing only as an element of the APARTHEID system, it never received international recognition. The region was reincorporated into South Africa in 1994 as part of Eastern Cape and KwaZulu/Natal provinces.

transmigration of souls See REINCARNATION

transmission System in an engine that transmits power generated by the engine to the point where it is to be used. Most mechanical transmissions function as rotary speed changers; the ratio of the output speed to the input speed may be either constant (as in a gearbox) or variable. On variable-speed transmissions, the speeds may be variable in individual steps (as on an automobile or some machine-tool drives) or continuously

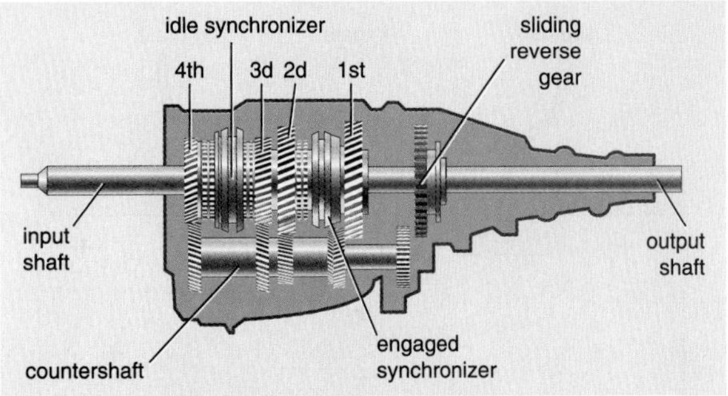

A four-speed manual transmission. Power from the rotating input shaft turns the countershaft (or layshaft), which meshes with all four gears on the output shaft. Which gear drives the output shaft is determined by the positions of the synchronizer assemblies, which are controlled by the gearshift stick (here, first gear is engaged). The unengaged gears simply revolve around the output shaft without transmitting power.

variable within a range. Step-variable transmissions, with some slip, usually use either Gears or chains and provide fixed speed ratios with no slip; stepless transmissions use belts, chains, or rolling-contact bodies.

transpiration Loss of water from a plant, mainly through the stomata (see Stoma) of leaves. Darkness, internal water deficit, and extremes of temperature tend to close stomata and decrease transpiration; illumination, ample water supply, and optimum temperature cause stomata to open and increase transpiration. Its exact significance is disputed; its roles in providing the energy to transport water in the plant and in aiding in dissipating the heat of direct sunlight (by cooling through evaporation of water) have been challenged. Since stomatal openings are necessary for the exchange of gases, transpiration has been considered by some to be merely an unavoidable phenomenon that accompanies the real functions of the stomata.

transplant *or* **graft** Partial or complete organ or other body part removed from one site and attached at another. It may come from the same or a different person or an animal. One from the same person—most often a skin graft—is not rejected. Transplants from another person or, especially, an animal are rejected unless they are unusually compatible or have no blood vessels (e.g., the cornea), or if the recipient's immune reaction is suppressed by lifelong drug treatment. Transplanted tissues must match (by blood tests) more closely than Blood transfusions. Monoclonal Antibodies targeting the cells that cause rejection hold great promise. Tests are now under way with monoclonal antibodies that react with antigens present only on T cells that are participating in rejection, sparing the rest. Rejection matters less in skin grafts, which may need to last only weeks, and bone grafts, whose structure remains after the cells die. In Bone-marrow transplants, the donor's marrow cells may attack the recipient's tissues, often fatally. Lung transplants have greater chance of success as part of a heart-and-lung transplant. See also Heart transplant, Kidney transplant.

transport In biochemistry, the movement of Molecules and particles across a cell membrane, a selective barrier that allows some substances (Fat-soluble molecules and some small molecules) to pass and blocks others (Ions and large, water-soluble molecules). Transport of these vital substances occurs via several systems. Open channels allow Diffusion (passive transport) of ions directly into cells; facilitators use a chemical change to help substances diffuse past the membrane; "pumps" force dilute substances through even when their concentration on the other side is higher (a form of active transport). Primary active transport is powered directly by energy released in cell Metabolism (see ATP, adenosine triphosphate). In secondary active transport, a molecule is linked to a different molecule that carries it across the membrane (cotransport) or is exchanged for a different molecule crossing in the other direction (countertransport). The membrane itself opens and closes to let larger particles in or out.

Transport and General Workers' Union (TGWU) British labor union. The Dockers' Union (founded 1889) took the lead in the merger of 14 unions to form the TGWU in 1922. The union grew rapidly under the leadership of eastern Bevin (1922–40). As a general union it was able to enroll workers excluded by the craft unions, and its membership included workers engaged in transportation industries (except the railroads) as well as in the automotive, construction, chemical, and textile industries. It exerted a strong influence on British labor policy and was the largest British union during much of the 20th century, reaching a peak of more than 2 million in the 1970s, though its membership declined thereafter. See also Labour Party, Trades Union Congress.

Transportation, U.S. Department of Federal executive agency responsible for programs and policies relating to transportation. Established in 1966, it controls the Federal Aviation Administration, Federal Highway Administration, Federal Railroad Administration, Federal Transit Administration, U.S. Coast Guard, Maritime Administration, and National Highway Traffic Safety Administration.

transsexualism Self-identification with one sex by a person who has the external genitalia and secondary sexual characteristics of the other sex. Early in life, such a person adopts the behavior characteristic of the opposite sex. Surgery and hormone therapy now allow permanent sex change, a procedure first performed in 1952. The male-to-female operation is more common because the genital reconstruction is more satisfactory. The male transsexual's penis and testes are removed and an artificial vagina created; breasts are created with implants or female sex hormones. Female transsexuals may undergo mastectomy and hormone treatments to produce male secondary sexual characteristics, but attempts to create an artificial penis have not been satisfactory.

transubstantiation In Christianity, the change by which the bread and wine of the Eucharist become in substance the body and blood of Jesus, though their appearance is not altered. This transformation is thought to bring the literal truth of Christ's presence to the participants. The doctrine was first elaborated by theologians in the 13th century and was incorporated into documents of the Council of Trent. In the mid-20th century, some Roman Catholic theologians interpreted it as referring to a change of meaning rather than a change of substance, but in 1965 Paul VI called for the retention of the original dogma.

transuranium element Any of the chemical Elements after Uranium in the Periodic table (with atomic numbers over 92). All are radioactive (see Radioactivity), with Half-lives ranging from tens of millions of years to fractions of a millisecond. Only two, neptunium (93) and Plutonium (94), occur in nature, and only in traces in uranium ores as a result of neutron irradiation. Elements with atomic numbers through 112, along with 114, 116, and 118, have been produced in laboratories. Each appears to resemble the elements above it in the periodic table; in particular, the Actinides, thorium (90) through lawrencium (103), are similar to the Lanthanides, cerium (58) through lutetium (71). The naming of the transuranium elements is fraught with controversy over which laboratory first made the discovery and should propose the name and over naming an element for a living person. See also Glenn Seaborg.

Transvaal \trans-'väl\ *formerly (1856–77, 1881–1902)* **South African Republic** Former province, northeastern South Africa. Located between the Limpopo and Vaal rivers, the region was inhabited c. 1800 chiefly by various Bantu-speaking peoples. The Boers (Afrikaners) began migrating there during the Great Trek of the 1830s. They established the short-lived South African Republic in 1856. Discoveries of diamonds and gold deposits (1868–74) heightened British interest in the region, and the British annexed the republic in 1877. A Boer rebellion restored it in 1881. Further discovery of gold in 1886 brought more foreigners, who eventually outnumbered the Boers. In 1895 Leander Starr Jameson attempted to incite them to overthrow the Boer government. In 1899 Transvaal joined with Orange Free State against Britain in the South African (Boer) War. It was taken in 1900, and in 1902, following the British victory, it became a crown colony. It was granted self-government in 1906, and joined the Union (now Republic) of South Africa in 1910. In 1994 the Transvaal was split into four provinces. The region is extremely rich in mineral and agricultural resources.

Transylvania Historic region, northwestern and central Romania. It comprises a plateau surrounded by the Carpathian Mtns. and the Transylvanian Alps. It formed the nucleus of the Dacian kingdom and was included in the Roman province of Dacia in the 2nd century AD. The Magyars (Hungarians) conquered the area at the end of the 9th century. When Hungary was divided between the Habsburgs and the Turks in the

16th century, Transylvania became an autonomous principality within the Ottoman empire. It was attached to Habsburg-controlled Hungary at the end of the 17th century. It was the scene of severe fighting in the Hungarian revolution against Austria in 1848. When Austria-Hungary was defeated in World War I, the Romanians of Transylvania proclaimed the land united with Romania. Hungary regained the northern portion during World War II, but the entire region was ceded to Romania in 1947.

Trapp family Austrian singers. Maria Augusta Kutschera (1905–1987), the family's best-known member, was an orphan and novitiate in a Benedictine convent in Salzburg. Later, as a governess, she won the hearts of the seven children of the widower Baron Georg von Trapp (1879?–1947) and of the baron himself. They married in 1927, had three children, and later began singing German and liturgical music under the Rev. Franz Wasner, with whom the family fled in 1938 from Nazi-dominated Austria to Italy, and finally to Stowe, Vt. They toured the world to great acclaim, disbanding in 1955. Their story was the subject of the musical *The Sound of Music* (1959).

trapshooting Shooting with a shotgun (usually 12-gauge) at clay disks (called pigeons) sprung from a trap into the air away from the shooter. A later variant is SKEET shooting. Trapshooting's origins date to the 18th century, when marksmen shot at live pigeons released from cages or box traps. The modern clay-pigeon variety has been included in Olympic Games competition since 1900. A single trap throws 25 targets at varying angles; each competitor fires four 25-target rounds.

Trasimeno \ˌträ-zē-ˈmā-nō\, Lake Lake, UMBRIA, central Italy. The largest lake of the Italian peninsula, it has an area of 49 sq mi (128 sq km) and is shallow, with a maximum depth of 20 ft (6 m). It is fed by small streams and has an artificial subterranean outlet (opened 1898) to the TIBER RIVER. In 217 BC HANNIBAL defeated a Roman army led by FLAMINIUS there in the Second PUNIC WAR. In World War II it was the scene of severe fighting (1944) between the British and German armies.

Travancore \ˈtra-vən-ˌkōr\ Former princely state, southwestern India. Now part of KERALA state, it was part of the kingdom of Kerala in the early centuries AD. In the 11th century it fell under the COLA empire; the Hindu kings of the VIJAYANAGAR empire held it briefly in the 16th century, after which it came under Muslim rule. In the mid-18th century it became the independent state of Travancore; then it was under British protection from 1795. After Indian independence, it merged with Cochin to form the state of Travancore-Cochin; boundaries were redrawn, and it was renamed Kerala in 1956.

Travelers Inc. Insurance company, now part of CITIGROUP. Founded in 1864 by the stonecutter James Batterson, the Travelers Insurance Co. was an innovative leader in its industry. It sold the first accident insurance in the U.S. in 1864, and in 1865 it began selling life insurance, becoming the first American company to offer more than one type of insurance. When Batterson died in 1901, Travelers was offering health, liability, and automotive insurance. In 1919 it became the first company to sell aviation insurance. In 1993, after suffering losses in real estate, it was acquired by the Primerica conglomerate, formed in 1987 from the non-packaging operations of the American Can Co., and the new company became known as the Travelers Group. In 1996 the Travelers Group bought the casualty and property insurance businesses of the Aetna Life and Casualty Co. In 1997 it bought Salomon Brothers Inc., which it merged with Smith Barney, Harris Upham & Co. and the Shearson brokerage business; the resulting firm, Salomon Smith Barney Holdings Inc., is one of the country's largest securities firms. In 1998 Travelers merged with Citicorp to form CITIGROUP.

Traven \ˈtrā-vən\, B. *orig.* **Hermann Albert Otto Macksymilian Wienecke** *or* **Ret Marut** (c. 1885?–1969) German-Mexican novelist. A recluse, he refused to disclose to publishers his parentage, nationality, and general identity, but he may have been forced to leave Germany for his participation in its short-lived communist revolution in 1919. Most of his books were written in German. He is noted for adventure stories and as a chronicler of rural life in Mexico, where he settled in the 1920s. Among his novels are *The Treasure of the Sierra Madre* (1927; film, 1948) and a series tracing the lives of impoverished Indians in southern Mexico, including *The Carreta* (1931) and *The Rebellion of the Hanged* (1936). His works are harsh and his themes compelling, and his lean prose has a hypnotic immediacy.

travertine \ˈtra-vər-ˌtēn\ Dense, banded rock composed of calcium carbonate, $CaCO_3$. Formed by rapid chemical precipitation of calcium carbonate from solution in surface and ground waters, it is a variety of LIMESTONE that has a light color and takes a good polish. It is often used for walls and interior decorations in public buildings and as a paving stone. Travertine is mined extensively in Italy; in the U.S., Yellowstone's Mammoth Hot Springs are actively depositing travertine. It also occurs in limestone caves in the form of STALACTITES AND STALAGMITES.

Travis, Merle (Robert) (1917–1983) U.S. COUNTRY-MUSIC singer and songwriter. Born in Rosewood, Ky., Travis learned banjo as a youth, later applying banjo technique to the guitar. He worked on radio in Cincinnati in the 1930s. Moving to California in 1944, he quickly rose to prominence on the strength of his guitar style and for writing and recording such honky-tonk classics as "Divorce Me C.O.D." and "No Vacancy" and the coal-mining protest songs "Sixteen Tons" and "Dark as a Dungeon."

Travolta, John (born 1954) U.S. film actor. Born in Englewood, N.J., he performed with the touring company of *Grease* before appearing on Broadway. He acted in the television series *Welcome Back, Kotter* (1975–78), where his cleft chin, blue eyes, and wide grin brought him an enthusiastic teenage following. He starred in the wildly successful *Saturday Night Fever* (1977), and later in *Grease* (1978) and *Urban Cowboy* (1980). His career faltered in the 1980s, but he returned to major stardom with QUENTIN TARANTINO's *Pulp Fiction* (1994). Subsequent films included *Michael* (1996) and *Primary Colors* (1998).

treason Offense of attempting to overthrow the government of one's country or of assisting its enemies in war. In the U.S., the framers of the Constitution defined treason narrowly—as the levying of war against the U.S. or the giving of aid and comfort to its enemies—in order to lessen the possibility that those in power might falsely or loosely charge their political opponents with treason. See also SEDITION.

Treasury, U.S. Department of the Federal executive division responsible for fiscal policy. Established in 1789, it advises the president on fiscal matters, serves as fiscal agent for the government, performs certain law-enforcement activities, manufactures currency and postage stamps, and supervises national banks. Among its agencies are the Bureau of ALCOHOL, Tobacco and Firearms, the U.S. Customs Service, the Bureau of Engraving and Printing, the INTERNAL REVENUE SERVICE, the U.S. Mint, and the U.S. Secret Service.

treasury bill Short-term U.S. government SECURITY with maturity ranging from one month to one year. Treasury bills are usually sold at auction on a discount basis with a yield equal to the difference between the purchase price and the maturity value. Because they are highly liquid (money not being tied up in them for long periods of time), their yield rate is normally lower than that of longer-term securities. Their prices do not usually fluctuate as much as those of other government securities but may be influenced by the purchase or sale of large quantities of bills by the CENTRAL BANK. First used extensively during World War I, treasury bills were initially regarded as an emergency source of revenue, but their flexibility and relatively low interest led to their adoption as a permanent element in the NATIONAL DEBT. From 1970 to 1998 the minimum order for treasury bills was $10,000, after which it was reduced to $1,000.

treaty Contract or other written instrument binding two or more states under INTERNATIONAL LAW. The term is generally reserved for the more important international agreements, usually requiring, in addition to the signatures of authorized persons, ratification by the governments involved. A treaty may be bilateral or multilateral; it usually contains a preamble, an enumeration of the issues agreed on, and clauses that discuss its ratification procedures, lifespan, and terms for termination. Treaties may be political, commercial, constitutional, or administrative, or they may relate to criminal and civil justice or codify international law.

Trebbia River \ˈtreb-byä\ River, EMILIA-ROMAGNA region, northern Italy. Rising northeast of GENOA, it flows 71 mi (115 km) northeast across the northern APENNINES and the Po lowland to enter the PO RIVER. It was the scene of two notable battles: a Roman defeat by HANNIBAL in 218 BC, and a French defeat by a Russo-Austrian army in 1799.

Treblinka \tre-ˈbliŋ-kä\ German Nazi CONCENTRATION camp. Located near the village of Treblinka, Poland, it opened in 1941 as a forced-labor camp. A larger and ultrasecret second camp a mile away, called T.II, opened in 1942 as an extermination camp for Jews. Victims were stripped and marched into "bathhouses," where they were gassed with carbon monoxide from ceiling pipes. Ukrainian guards and up to 1,500 Jewish prisoner-workers performed the executions. The total number killed has been estimated at 700,000–900,000. In 1943 a group of prisoner-workers rose in revolt and escaped, but most were soon killed or recaptured. The T.II camp was closed in October 1943, the labor camp in July 1944.

Tredgold \'tred-ˌgōld\, **Thomas** (1788–1829) British engineer and writer. Almost entirely self-taught, after some years of journeyman work he published *Elementary Principles of Carpentry* (1820), which became an enduring classic. It was followed by important treatises on cast iron and other metals (1822), ventilation and warming of buildings (1824), railroads and carriages (1825), and steam engines (1827).

tree Woody perennial plant. Most trees have a single self-supporting trunk containing woody tissues, and in most species the trunk produces secondary limbs called branches. Trees provide many valuable products, especially wood, one of the world's chief building materials, and wood pulp, used in papermaking. Wood is also a major fuel source. Trees also supply edible fruits and nuts. In addition, they help clean the air by taking in carbon dioxide and releasing oxygen during photosynthesis. Their root systems help conserve water and prevent floods and soil erosion. Trees provide homes and food for a wide variety of animals, and they beautify both natural and human-made landscapes. Growth rings in the trunk indicate the age of most trees. The tallest trees are the Pacific coast redwoods; the oldest are the bristlecone pines, some of which are over 4,000 years old. See also conifer, deciduous tree, evergreen, forest, shrub, softwood.

Tree, Herbert (Draper) Beerbohm *later* **Sir Herbert** (1853–1917) British actor-manager. A romantic actor with a gift for character roles and comedy, he made his London debut in 1878 and won favorable notice in *The Private Secretary* (1884). As manager of the Haymarket Theatre (1887–97), he directed and acted in lavish Shakespearean productions, which he continued as actor-manager of Her Majesty's Theatre (1897–1915). He produced notable stage versions of Charles Dickens's works. In 1904 he founded the Royal Academy of Dramatic Art. His half-brother, Max Beerbohm, wrote Tree's biography (1920).

tree fern Any of various ferns (especially those of the families Cyatheaceae and Marattiaceae) of treelike habit with a woody stem. Many attain heights over 50 ft (15.2 m). They are natives of humid mountain forests in the tropics and subtropics and of warm temperate regions of the Southern Hemisphere. The family Marattiaceae contains six genera; one species, *Angiopteris evecta,* has leaves (fronds) 15 ft (4.5 m) or more in length and stems of 2–6 ft (60–180 cm). Now-extinct members of the family date to the Carboniferous Period (354–290 million years ago). Members of the family Cyatheaceae are very large, terrestrial ferns with trunklike, upright rhizomes; the nearly 1,000 species are grouped into seven genera.

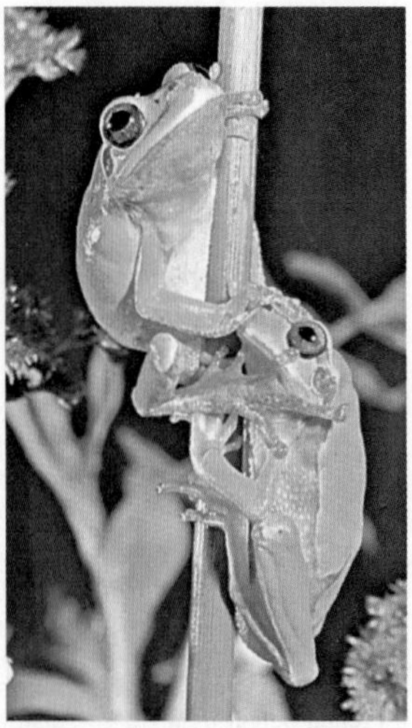

European green tree frogs (*Hyla arborea*).

JANE BURTON—BRUCE COLEMAN LTD.

tree frog *or* **tree toad** Any of some 550 species (family Hylidae) of mostly arboreal frogs, found worldwide but primarily in the New World. Most species are small, slender, and long-legged and have suckerlike adhesive disks on the finger and toe tips. Some do not climb well and live in water, on land, or in a burrow. Most species lay eggs in water. Young marsupial frogs (genus *Gastrotheca*), of South America, develop in a brood pouch on the female's back.

tree of heaven Rapid-growing tree *(Ailanthus altissima)* in the quassia family (Simaroubaceae), native to China and widely naturalized elsewhere, with several known varieties. Because of its resistance to pollution, freedom from insect predation and disease, and ability to grow in almost any soil, the tree of heaven is planted as a yard and street tree in urban centers. It grows to 60 ft (18 m) or more, producing long, compound leaves that emit an unpleasant odor when bruised. Male trees bear flowers with unpleasant scents. Female trees produce winged fruits which are tannish orange when ripe.

Treitschke \'trīch-kə\, **Heinrich von** (1834–1896) German historian and political writer. Son of a Saxon general, Treitschke studied at Bonn and Leipzig and then taught history and politics at a number of German universities. A member of the Reichstag 1871–84, he advocated authoritarian rulers unchecked by a parliament and disparaged Western European liberalism and American democracy. In 1886 he succeeded Leopold Ranke as official historiographer of Prussia. His major work is *Treitschke's History of Germany in the Nineteenth Century* (1879–94).

Trek, Great See Great Trek

trematode See fluke

trench warfare Warfare in which the opposing sides attack, counterattack, and defend from sets of trenches dug into the ground. It was developed by Sebastien Le Prestre de Vauban in the 17th century for laying siege to fortresses. Its defensive use was first institutionalized as a tactic during the American Civil War. It reached its highest development in World War I. Little used in World War II, it reappeared in the Iran–Iraq War. A typical construction was a series of two to four parallel trenches, dug in a zigzag, sandbagged, and floored with wooden planks. A perpendicular trench connected them. The first row was fronted by barbed wire and contained machine-gun emplacements. The rear trenches housed most of the troops. Increased use of tanks marked the end of trench warfare, since tanks were invulnerable to the machine-gun and rifle fire used by entrenched soldiers.

Trent, Council of (1545–63) 19th ecumenical council of the Roman Catholic church, which made sweeping reforms and laid down dogma clarifying nearly all doctrines contested by the Protestants. Convened by Pope Paul III at Trento in northern Italy, it served to revitalize Roman Catholicism in many parts of Europe. In its first period (1545–47) it accepted the Nicene Creed as the basis of Catholic faith, fixed the canon of the Old and New Testaments, set the number of sacraments at seven, and defined the nature and consequences of original sin; it also ruled against Martin Luther's doctrine of justification by faith. In its second period (1551–52) it confirmed the doctrine of transubstantiation and issued decrees on episcopal jurisdiction and clerical discipline. In the final period (1562–63) it defined the mass as a true sacrifice and issued statements on several other doctrinal issues. By the end of the 16th century, many of the abuses that had motivated the Protestant Reformation had disappeared, and the church had reclaimed many of its European followers.

Trent Affair (1861) Incident in the American Civil War involving freedom of the seas. On November 8, the Union frigate *San Jacinto* stopped the neutral British steamer *Trent* to seize Confederate commissioners John Slidell and James Murray Mason, who were en route to England and France to seek support for the Confederacy. Protests in Britain denounced the action and called for war. On December 26, William Seward admitted the Union's error in not bringing the ship into a U.S. port for adjudication, and the two men were soon released.

Trent Canal Canal, southeastern Ontario, linking Lake Huron with Lake Ontario. It extends from the southeastern shore of Georgian Bay up the Severn River to Lake Simcoe, connects several lakes of the Kawartha Lake region to Rice Lake, and passes down the Trent River to the Bay of Quinte and Lake Ontario. Its 242-mi (387-km) main course consists of 33 mi (53 km) of man-made channels and 42 locks. Construction began in 1833. The waterway once served a busy lumber trade; it is now a popular tourist attraction.

Trent River River, central England. It rises in Staffordshire and flows northeast 168 mi (270 km) to unite with the Ouse River west of Hull to form the Humber Estuary. It is navigable by barge for over half its length.

Trentino–Alto Adige \tren-'tē-nō-ˌäl-tō-'ä-dē-jā\ *formerly (until 1947)* **Venezia Tridentina** Autonomous region (pop., 1996 est.: 913,000), northeastern Italy. Its capital is Trento. A mountainous area, it has some of the highest peaks in Europe, cut through by passes into Switzerland

and Austria. Historically it included the medieval ecclesiastical principalities of Trento and Bressanone. Austria annexed it in 1815. It was the scene of much fighting during World War I, and was ceded to Italy at the end of the war. The population is a mix of German speakers in the north, and Italian speakers in the south; the regional parliament alternates German-speaking and Italian-speaking chairmen. The region grows grain and grapes, raises cattle, and mines zinc, lead, and other minerals. Tourism is a major industry.

Trento *English* **Trent** *ancient* **Tridentum** City (pop., 1991: 101,000), capital of TRENTINO–ALTO Adige region, northern Italy, on the ADIGE RIVER. Reportedly founded by the Raetians c. 4th century BC, it later became a Roman colony on the road to the Brenner Pass in the ALPS. In the Christian era it came under the Ostrogoths, Lombards, and FRANKS. It was the site of the Council of TRENT (1545–63). It came under the Napoleonic kingdom of Italy in the early 19th century, passed to Austria in 1814, and to Italy in 1918. An agricultural market center, it also has some light industry.

Trenton City (pop., 1996 est.: 85,000), capital of New Jersey. It lies at the head of navigation on the DELAWARE RIVER. Settled c. 1679 by English QUAKERS, it was incorporated in 1745. On Christmas night, 1776, GEORGE WASHINGTON led his army across the ice-choked Delaware River to attack Hessian troops quartered at Trenton (see battles of TRENTON AND PRINCETON). It served as temporary capital of the U.S. in 1784 and 1799, and was made the state capital in 1790. The completion of a canal and railroad line in the 1830s spurred Trenton's industrial development, and it remains an industrial city.

Trenton and Princeton, Battles of (1776–77) Engagements won by the Continental Army in the AMERICAN REVOLUTION. Defeats in New York forced the army under GEORGE WASHINGTON to retreat through New Jersey into Pennsylvania. On December 25, 1776, he led a force of 6,000 across the ice-filled Delaware River to surprise the 1,400 British-Hessian force at Trenton, N.J., capturing 900 men. A British force of 7,000 under CHARLES CORNWALLIS arrived to force the American army into retreat. At night Washington led his men around the British to defeat an outpost at Princeton, causing Cornwallis to retreat to New Brunswick and enabling Washington to lead his troops into winter quarters near Morristown. The victories restored American morale and renewed confidence in Washington.

trespass In law, unlawful entry onto land. Trespass was formerly defined as wrongful conduct causing injury or loss; today it is generally confined to issues involving real property (see REAL AND PERSONAL PROPERTY). Once a trespass is proved, the trespasser is usually held liable for any damages resulting, regardless of whether the trespasser was negligent or the damage was foreseeable. Criminal trespass, trespass to property that is forbidden by statute, is punishable as a crime.

Treurnicht \'trōir-,nikt\, **Andries (Petrus)** (1921–1993) South African politician. A preacher in the Dutch Reformed Church (1946–60), he later achieved high office in the NATIONAL PARTY as a strong supporter of APARTHEID. In 1976 his insistence that black children be taught Afrikaans lead to the Soweto uprising. In 1982 he left the National Party to form the Conservative Party, which opposed F.W. DE KLERK's decision to end apartheid. He came to support the idea of a separate white homeland within South Africa.

Trevelyan \tri-'vel-yən\, **G(eorge) M(acauley)** (1876–1962) English historian. He is known for books accessible to general readers that often show an appreciation of the Whig tradition in English thought and reflect a keen interest in the Anglo-Saxon element in the English constitution. They include three on GIUSEPPE DE GARIBALDI (1907, 1909, 1911), *England in the Age of Wycliffe* (1899), *British History in the Nineteenth Century (1782–1901)* (1922), *History of England* (1926), and *The Seven Years of William IV* (1952).

Trevino \trə-'vē-nō\, **Lee (Buck)** (born 1939) U.S. golfer. Born in Dallas, he placed a surprising fifth in the U.S. Open in 1967, then won it the next year. In 1971 "Super Mex" (the nickname reflects his Mexican-American parentage) became the first player to win the U.S., British, and Canadian Opens in a single year. He won the British Open in 1972 and the U.S. PGA in 1974. He underwent back surgery in 1982, but returned to win the PGA again in 1984.

Trevithick \'trev-ə-,thik\, **Richard** (1771–1833) British inventor of the first steam LOCOMOTIVE. With little formal education, in 1790 he became an engineer for several ore mines in Cornwall. In 1797 his experiments with high-pressure steam led him to develop a small, light engine to replace the large, low-pressure mine engines then used for hoisting ore. In 1801 he built the first steam carriage, which he later drove in London. In 1803 he built the first steam railway locomotive for an ironworks in Wales. He abandoned his locomotive projects in 1808 because the iron rails were too fragile to carry their weight. He adapted his engine to produce the first steam dredger in 1806. In 1816 he traveled to South America to deliver engines to Peruvian silver mines, hoping to become wealthy, but returned to England in 1827 penniless.

Trevithick, detail of an oil painting by John Linnell, 1816; in the Science Museum, London.

BY COURTESY OF THE SCIENCE MUSEUM, LONDON, THE WOODCROFT BEQUEST

Trevor, William *orig.* **William Trevor Cox** (born 1928) Irish-English writer. Educated at Trinity College, Dublin, he worked as a teacher, sculptor, and advertising copywriter before moving to England to write fiction full-time. His works focus largely on the psychology of eccentrics and outcasts. His second novel, *The Old Boys* (1964), tells the story of an "old boys" committee whose aging members plot against each other. His later novels include *Felicia's Journey* (1994) and *Death in Summer* (1998). He is perhaps best known for his acclaimed collections of short stories.

Trevor, 1982.

MARK GERSON

Triad Term used variously for secret societies in QING-DYNASTY China (and sometimes earlier), for modern Chinese crime gangs, and for crime gangs of other Asian nationals operating in their own countries or abroad. A secret society with the name Triad started operating in the early 19th century in southern China, where it took root and spread. In the 1850s Triad rebellions threatened Shanghai and Xiamen (Amoy) and contributed to the revolution of 1911. Chinese secret societies have in common the swearing of an oath to join, strict rules, a family relationship among members, the duty of mutual help, a hierarchy of functions, and hereditary membership within families.

triage \'trē-,äzh, trē-'äzh\ Division of patients for priority of care, usually into three categories: those who will not survive even with treatment; those who will survive without treatment; and those whose survival depends on treatment. If triage is applied, the treatment of patients requiring it is not delayed by useless or unnecessary treatment of those in the other groups. Triage originated in military medicine, when limited resources faced many wounded soldiers. It is used in civilian settings during disasters or epidemics, and in emergency rooms. Triage decisions are made after relatively quick examination; patients in lower-priority groups should be reexamined periodically.

trial In law, a judicial examination of issues of fact or law for the purpose of determining the rights of the parties involved. Attorneys for the plaintiff and the defendant make opening statements to a judge or jury, then the attorney for the plaintiff makes his case by calling witnesses, whom the defense attorney may cross-examine. Unless the case is then dismissed for lack of sufficient evidence, the defense attorney next takes a turn calling witnesses, whom the plaintiff's attorney cross-examines. Both sides make closing arguments. In a trial before a jury, the judge instructs the jury on the applicable laws, and the jury retires to reach a verdict. If the defendant is found guilty, the judge then hands down a sentence.

trial by ordeal See ORDEAL

triangle Geometric figure with three sides and three angles. Each two sides meet at a point called a vertex, and the three angles sum to 180°. A triangle with one 90° (right) angle is a right triangle. A triangle with all sides (and thus all angles) equal is equilateral, one with two sides equal is isosceles, and one with no two sides equal is scalene. Triangles are particularly useful in surveying, astronomy, and navigation. Two observation points (sight lines) form a triangle with a reference object serving as one vertex and the observation points as the other two. Knowing the angles of the sight lines and the distance between the observation points allows the calculation of the lengths of the other sides using the methods of TRIGONOMETRY.

Triangle Shirtwaist Co. fire (March 25, 1911) Industrial disaster that led to the enactment of many safety and labor laws. The fire in a New York City garment factory resulted in the deaths of 146 people, mostly young immigrant women. The sweatshop had few fire escapes and its doors were locked to prevent theft, forcing panicked workers to leap from upper-floor windows. Public outcry also led to new fire codes and child-labor laws and greater influence for the INTERNATIONAL LADIES' GARMENT WORKERS UNION.

Trianon \ˌtrē-ə-ˈnōn\, **Treaty of** (June 4, 1920) Treaty at the end of WORLD WAR I between Hungary and the Allied Powers, signed at the Trianon Palace at Versailles, France. By its terms, Hungary lost two-thirds of its former territory, which was divided among Czechoslovakia, Austria, the future Yugoslavia, and Romania. Hungary's armed forces were restricted to 35,000 lightly armed men, to be used only to maintain internal order.

Triassic period \trī-ˈa-sik\ Interval of geologic time, c. 248–206 million years ago, that marks the beginning of the MESOZOIC era. Many new vertebrates emerged during the Triassic, heralding the major changes that were to occur in both terrestrial and marine life forms during the Mesozoic era. The seas became inhabited by large marine reptiles. On land, ancestral forms of various modern amphibians arose, as did reptiles such as turtles and crocodilians. By the Late Triassic, ARCHOSAURS were becoming more and more dominant, and the first true mammals, small shrewlike omnivores, evolved. Seed ferns dominated the flora of southern GONDWANA, and GYMNOSPERMS including conifers, cycads, and ginkgos were common throughout much of PANGAEA.

triathlon Athletic long-distance race in three phases (such as swimming, bicycling, and running). The usual event includes an ocean swim of 3.8 km (2.4 mi), a bicycle tour of 180 km (112 mi), and a marathon run of 42.2 km (26.2 mi).

tribe Social group defined by traditions of common DESCENT and having temporary or permanent political integration above the family and CLAN levels as well as a shared language, CULTURE, and IDEOLOGY. Tribes are usually composed of a number of smaller local communities (e.g., BANDS or villages) and may be aggregated into higher-order clusters, sometimes called nations. Members typically share a tribal name and a contiguous territory; they work together in such joint endeavors as trade, agriculture, house construction, warfare, and ceremonial activities. Though applied more cautiously today than during the era of COLONIALISM, it remains the U.S. government term for American Indian groups and is commonly used among the groups themselves. See also ETHNIC group.

tribes (Greek, *phylai*; Roman, *tribus*) In ancient Greece and Rome, political and demographic subdivisions of the population. In Greece the groups divided into tribes were distinct by location, dialect, and tradition, and included the IONIANS, DORIANS, ACHAEANS, and Aetolians. In Attica, CLEISTHENES replaced the four Ionian tribes with 10 new tribes, each of which was named after a local hero; these came to develop political and civic functions, including the election of magistrates. The DEMES developed out of the tribal system. In Rome, the tribes formed the three (later four, and still later 35) original divisions of Roman citizens. These were the basis of military levies, property tax, census taking, and voting units in political assemblies.

tribology \trī-ˈbä-lə-jē\ Study of the interactions of sliding surfaces. It includes three subjects: FRICTION, wear, and LUBRICATION. Many manifestations of tribology are beneficial and make modern life possible. Many others are serious nuisances, and careful design is necessary to overcome problems caused by excessive friction or wear. Friction uses up, or wastes, a substantial amount of the energy generated by humans; in addition, a great deal of productive capacity is devoted to replacing objects that have worn out.

tribune In ancient Rome, any of various military and civil officials. Military tribunes were originally infantry commanders. In the early republic, there were six to a LEGION; some were appointed by CONSULS or military commanders, others elected by the people. During the Roman empire (from 27 BC), the emperor nominated military tribunes, the office of which was considered preliminary to a senatorial or equestrian career (see EQUES). Of the civil tribunes, the most important were the tribunes of the plebs (see PLEBEIAN), who were elected in the plebeian assembly. By 450 there were 10 plebeian tribunes, who were elected annually with the right to intervene in cases of unjust acts of consuls or magistrates by saying *Veto* ("I forbid it"). The office became powerful; its powers were curtailed by SULLA, but restored by POMPEY. Under the empire, the plebeian tribunes' power passed to the emperor.

tricarboxylic acid cycle \ˌtrī-ˌkär-bäk-ˈsil-ik\ *or* **Krebs cycle** *or* **citric-acid cycle** Last stage of the chemical processes by which living cells obtain energy from foodstuffs. Described by HANS ADOLF KREBS in 1937, the reactions of the cycle have been shown in animals, plants, microorganisms, and fungi, and is thus a feature of cell chemistry shared by all types of life. It is a complex series of reactions beginning and ending with the compound oxaloacetate. In addition to re-forming oxaloacetate, the cycle produces carbon dioxide and the energy-rich compound ATP. The enzymes that catalyze each step are located in mitochondria in animals, in CHLOROPLASTS in plants, and in the cell MEMBRANE in microorganisms. The hydrogen atoms and electrons that are removed from intermediate compounds formed during the cycle are channeled ultimately to oxygen in animal cells, or to carbon dioxide in plant cells.

Triceratops \trī-ˈser-ə-ˌtäps\ genus of large, plant-eating ORNITHISCHIAN DINOSAURS of the Late CRETACEOUS epoch (99–65 million years ago). *Triceratops* had a very long skull (some more than 6 ft, or 1.8 m, long); a large bony frill about the neck; a relatively short, pointed horn on the nose; a beaklike mouth; and two pointed horns, more than 3.3 ft (1 m) long, above the eyes. Adults weighed 4–5 tons (3.6–4.5 metric tons) and grew up to 30 ft (9 m) long. The limbs were very stout, and the hind limbs were more massive than the forelimbs.

trichina \tri-ˈkī-nə\ Species *(Trichinella spiralis)* of parasitic NEMATODE, found worldwide, that causes the disease TRICHINOSIS. Trichinae (or trichinas), 0.06–0.2 in. (1.5–4 mm) long, mate in the host's small intestine. Fertilized females penetrate the intestinal wall and release larvae, which the blood carries throughout the body. The larvae grow, mature, and become encysted within muscle tissue. The digestive juices of an animal that eats the muscle tissue break down the cyst, liberating the larvae for further development; the worms mature, and the cycle begins again.

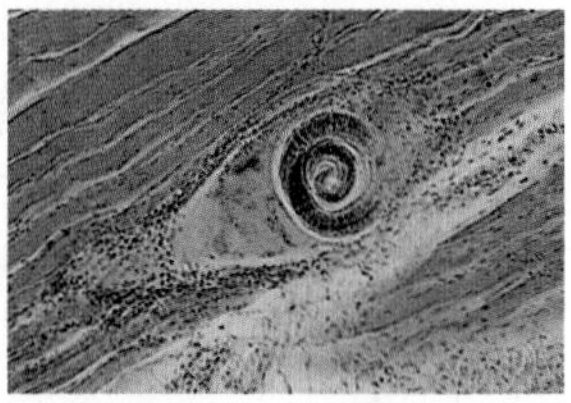

Trichina encysted in muscle.
RUSS KINNE—PHOTO RESEARCHERS/EB INC.

trichinosis \ˌtri-kə-ˈnō-səs\ Disorder caused by the roundworm TRICHINA, commonly acquired from undercooked infested PORK. Larval worms invade the small intestine, maturing within a week. Fertilized females deposit new larvae, which are carried by the blood, notably to the muscles (most often the diaphragm, eyes, throat, and tongue), where they encapsulate and may remain alive for years. Though trichinosis usually eventually subsides, it may be fatal if the heart and brain are involved. In the U.S. the incidence detected at autopsy is perhaps 15–20%. Few infected persons have sufficient parasites to produce symptoms (including diarrhea, nausea, and fever, followed by pain, stiffness, and swelling of various muscular structures). Anti-inflammatory drugs can relieve symptoms; thiabendazole may effectively destroy parasites in the intestine. There is no practical way to detect trichinous pork; the surest safeguard remains thorough cooking.

trichomonad \ˌtri-kə-ˈmō-ˌnad\ Any PROTOZOAN of the zooflagellate order Trichomonadida. Trichomonads have three to six flagella, and may have one or multiple nuclei. Most inhabit the digestive systems of animals. Three species occur in humans: *T. hominis* in the intestine, *T. vaginalis* in the vagina, and *T. buccalis* in the mouth.

trickster tale In oral traditions worldwide, a story of deceit, magic, and violence perpetrated by a mythical animal-human (trickster). The trickster-hero is both creator god and innocent fool, evil destroyer and childlike prankster. Coyote, the trickster of tales from American Indian peoples in California and the Southwest, is one of the most widely known. In the Pacific Northwest, the trickster is Raven. Many African peoples also have tales about tricksters (hare, spider, tortoise, etc.), which slaves brought to the New World. Tales involving the trickster Brer Rabbit were given literary form by JOEL CHANDLER HARRIS.

Trident missile U.S.-made SUBMARINE-launched ballistic missile. It succeeded the Poseidon and Polaris missiles of the 1980s and '90s. More accurate than most land-based ballistic missiles, Tridents posed a threat to missile silos and command bunkers in the former Soviet Union. Their extended range allows the submarines that carry them to patrol almost anywhere in the Atlantic and Pacific oceans, making detection extremely difficult.

Trieste \trē-'es-tā, trē-'est\ *in full* **Free Territory of Trieste** Former region, western ISTRIA, southern Europe, surrounding and including the city of TRIESTE. It was occupied by Yugoslavia in 1945. The U.N. established it as a free territory in 1947. It was divided for administrative purposes into two zones: Zone A in the north, including the city, was under the British and Americans; Zone B in the south was under the Yugoslavs. In 1954 most of the northern zone was incorporated into Italy; the southern zone went to Yugoslavia.

Trieste *ancient* **Tergeste** Seaport city (metro. area pop., 1996 est.: 224,000), capital of the FRIULI–VENEZIA Giulia region, northeastern Italy. It lies at the head of the ADRIATIC SEA on the Gulf of Trieste. It was under Roman control from the 2nd century BC until the collapse of the empire; then it was under episcopal rule 948–1202. It placed itself in 1382 under HABSBURG protection and became the prosperous main port of the AUSTRO-HUNGARIAN empire. After World War I it was ceded to Italy. Occupied by Germany in World War II and seized by Yugoslavia in 1945, it became the center of the Free Territory of TRIESTE in 1947. Returned to Italy in 1954, it became the regional capital in 1963.

triggerfish Any of about 30 species (family Balistidae) of shallow-water marine fishes, found worldwide in tropical seas. Triggerfishes are deep-bodied, usually colorful fishes with large scales, high-set eyes, and three dorsal-fin spines, which it uses for protection. When the fish is threatened, it darts into a coral crevice and erects its large and strong first spine, which it locks in place by the second (the "trigger"); when the trigger is later withdrawn, the first snaps back down. Though generally considered edible, some cause food poisoning. The largest grow to 2 ft (60 cm) long.

Triggerfish (*Balistes conspicillus*).
DOUGLAS FAULKNER

triglyceride \trī-'gli-sə-ˌrīd\ Any of an important class of naturally occurring LIPIDS, ESTERS in which three molecules of FATTY acids are linked to GLYCEROL. The three may be all the same, or different kinds. The types of triglycerides in animals vary with the species and the fats in their food. In mammals they are stored in ADIPOSE tissue until needed and then broken down to the glycerol and fatty acids. Many vegetable triglycerides (OILS) are liquid at room temperature, unlike those of animals, and tend to contain a greater variety of fatty acids. In ALKALI, triglycerides break down to form glycerol and three molecules of SOAP (saponification).

trigonometric function \ˌtri-gə-nə-'me-trik\ In mathematics, one of six functions (sine, cosine, tangent, cotangent, secant, and cosecant) that represent ratios of sides of right triangles. They are also known as the circular functions, since their values can be defined as ratios of the x and y coordinates (see COORDINATE system) of points on a circle of radius 1 that correspond to ANGLES in standard positions. Such values have been tabulated and programmed into scientific calculators and computers. This allows TRIGONOMETRY to be easily applied to surveying, engineering, and navigation problems in which one of a right triangle's acute angles and the length of a side are known and the lengths of the other sides are to be found. The fundamental trigonometric identity is $\sin^2\theta + \cos^2\theta = 1$, in which θ is an angle. Certain intrinsic qualities of the trigonometric functions make them useful in mathematical ANALYSIS. In particular, their DERIVATIVES form patterns useful for solving DIFFERENTIAL EQUATIONS.

trigonometry Mathematical discipline dealing with the relationships between the sides and ANGLES of triangles. Literally, it means triangle measurement, though its applications extend far beyond geometry. It emerged as a rigorous discipline in the 15th century, when the demand for accurate surveying techniques and navigational methods led to its use for the "solution" of right triangles, or the calculation of the lengths of two sides of a right triangle given one of its acute angles and the length of one side. The solution can be found by using ratios in the form of the TRIGONOMETRIC functions.

trikaya \tri-'kä-yə\ In MAHAYANA Buddhism, the concept of the three bodies, or modes of being, of the BUDDHA: the *dharmakaya* ("body of essence"), the unmanifested mode; the *sambhogakaya* ("body of enjoyment"), the heavenly mode; and the *nirmanakaya* ("body of transformation"), the earthly mode, or the Buddha as he appeared on earth in any form. The concept of trikaya applies to the Buddha Gautama and all other buddhas.

Trilling, Lionel (1905–1975) U.S. literary critic and teacher. Born in New York City, he taught at Columbia University from 1931 until his death. His collections of literary essays include *The Liberal Imagination* (1950), *Beyond Culture* (1965), *Sincerity and Authenticity* (1972), and *Mind in the Modern World* (1972). His other works include *Freud and the Crisis of Our Culture* (1955) and the novel *The Middle of the Journey* (1947). He was perhaps the most famous American literary critic of his time. His wife was the critic and writer Diana Trilling (1905–1996).

trillium \'tri-lē-əm\ Any of about 25 species of spring-flowering perennial herbaceous plants that make up the genus *Trillium* in the LILY FAMILY, native to North America and Asia. Whorls of oval leaves, flower parts, and fruits are arranged in groups of three. Each solitary white, greenish-white, yellow, pink, or purple flower is borne on a short stalk that arises from the whorl of leaves. Many species are cultivated in wildflower gardens. Wild trillium (also called wake-robin or birthroot) is a protected species.

trilobite \'trī-lə-ˌbīt\ Any of a group of ovate ARTHROPODS (subphylum Trilobita) that came to dominate the seas c. 540 million years ago and became extinct c. 245 million years ago. Trilobites had a chitinous exoskeleton and three body lobes: a raised middle lobe with a lower lobe on each side. The head, thorax, and tail were segmented; each segment bore two appendages. The forwardmost appendages were sense and feeding organs. Most species had two compound eyes, though some were eyeless. Some were predators, others were scavengers, and still others probably ate plankton. *Paradoxides harlani,* found near Boston, grew to 18 in. (45 cm) long and may have weighed 10 lbs (4.5 kg). Other species were small.

Trilobite.
LESLIE JACKMAN—NATURAL HISTORY PHOTOGRAPHIC AGENCY

Trimble, (William) David (born 1944) Leader of the Ulster Unionist Party (UUP) in Northern Ireland and corecipient with JOHN HUME of the Nobel Prize for Peace in 1998. He was elected to the British Parliament in 1990 and became leader of the UUP in 1995. He represented the UUP in multiparty peace talks beginning in September 1997. These talks, which included members of SINN FÉIN, the political wing of the IRISH REPUBLICAN ARMY (IRA), culminated in the Good Friday Agreement of April 1998, which aimed to restore self-government in Northern Ireland. Defying right-wing opposition, he signed the agreement and successfully campaigned for its acceptance in referenda in Northern Ireland and Ireland. In subsequent elections to the new Northern Ireland Assembly, he was elected first minister. Conflict with the IRA over decommissioning (disarmament) persisted and led to his resignation as first minister in 2001.

trimurti \tri-'mu̇r-tē\ In HINDUISM, the triad of the three great gods: BRAHMA, VISHNU, and SHIVA. Scholars consider the trimurti doctrine an attempt to reconcile different monotheistic approaches with one another and with the philosophic doctrine of ultimate reality. In trimurti symbolism, the three gods are collapsed into a single form with three faces. Each god is in charge of an aspect of creation, with Brahma as creator, Vishnu as preserver, and Shiva as destroyer; however, some sects ascribe all aspects of creation to their deity of choice. Though sometimes called the Hindu Trinity, trimurti has little similarity to the Holy Trinity of Christianity.

Trinidad and Tobago \'tri-nə-ˌdad...tə-'bā-gō\ *officially* **Republic of Trinidad and Tobago** Nation, comprising the islands of Trinidad and Tobago, in the Caribbean Sea off Venezuela. Area: 1,980 sq mi (5,128 sq km). Population (1997 est.): 1,276,000. Capital: Port-of-Spain. The people are mainly of East Indian and African ancestry. Language: English (official). Religions: Roman Catholicism, Protestantism, Hinduism, Islam. Currency: Trinidad and Tobago dollar. The islands are mostly flat or rolling, with narrow belts of mountainous highlands and luxuriant rain forests. The Caroni Swamp, an important bird sanctuary on Trinidad, supports flamingo, egret, and scarlet ibis. The country has large reserves of petroleum and natural gas, as well as the world's largest supply of natural asphalt. Other industries include agriculture, fishing, and tourism. Chief crops include sugarcane, citrus fruits, cocoa, and coffee.

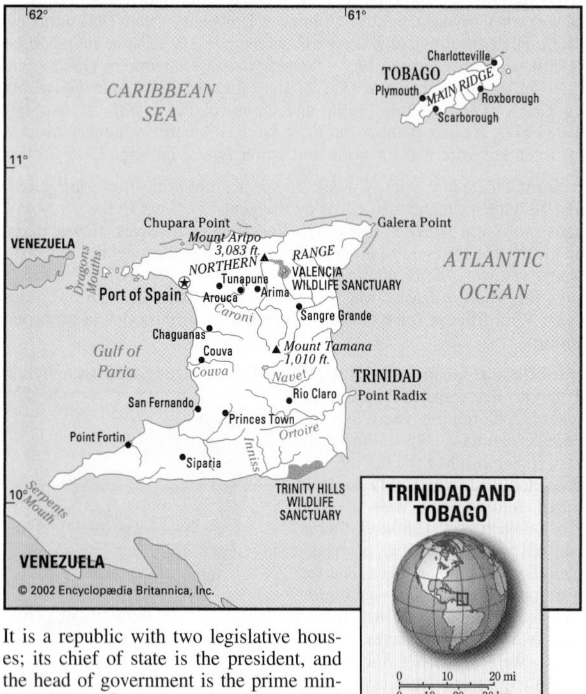

It is a republic with two legislative houses; its chief of state is the president, and the head of government is the prime minister. When Christopher Columbus visited Trinidad in 1498, it was inhabited by the Arawak Indians; Caribs inhabited Tobago. The islands were settled by the Spanish in the 16th century. In the 17th–18th century African slaves were imported for plantation labor to replace the original Indian population, which had been worked to death by the Spanish. Trinidad was surrendered to the British in 1797. The British attempted to settle Tobago in 1721, but the French captured the island in 1781 and transformed it into a sugar-producing colony. The British acquired it in 1802. After slavery ended in the islands 1834–38, immigrants from India were brought in to work the plantations. Trinidad and Tobago were administratively combined in 1889. Granted limited self-government in 1925, the islands became an independent state within the Commonwealth in 1962, and a republic in 1976. Political unrest was followed in 1990 by an attempted Muslim-fundamentalist coup against the government.

Trinity, Holy In Christian doctrine, the unity of the Father, Son and Holy Spirit as one God in three Persons. The word Trinity does not appear in the Bible. It is a doctrine formulated in the early church to interpret the way God revealed himself, first to Israel; then in Jesus as Savior; and finally as Holy Spirit, preserver of the church. The doctrine of the Trinity developed in the early centuries of the church and was explicitly stated at the Council of Nicaea in AD 325.

Trinity College See University of Dublin

Trinity College Private liberal-arts college in Hartford, Conn., founded in 1823. It is historically affiliated with the Episcopal church, though its curriculum is nonsectarian. It offers bachelor's degrees in about 35 majors and master's degrees in seven departments. It participates in a cooperative exchange program with 12 New England colleges and universities. Enrollment is about 2,100.

Trintignant \tra^{n}-tēn-'yä^{n}\, **Jean-Louis** (born 1930) French film actor. After leaving law school to study acting, he made his stage debut in 1951 and his film debut in 1956. He won favorable notice in *And God Created Woman* (1956) and gained international fame for his role as a race-car driver in *A Man and a Woman* (1966). Known for his reserved but intense screen persona, he conveyed the psychic conflicts of repressed characters in *My Night at Maud's* (1969), *Z* (1969), and, most strikingly, *The Conformist* (1970), among many other films.

trio sonata Principal chamber-music genre of the baroque era. Despite its name, it requires four performers: two melody instruments and continuo (usually a keyboard instrument and a bass instrument). It arose early in the 17th century as an instrumental version of the Italian vocal-duet ensemble. The two upper instruments, usually violins, generally wove their melodic, quasi-vocal lines high above the accompanying parts. Two standard forms emerged after 1750: the sonata da chiesa, or church sonata, standardized as a four-movement form (in slow-fast-slow-fast order); and the suite-like sonata da camera, or chamber sonata. By 1770 the genre had been abandoned in favor of the solo sonata.

Tripitaka \tri-'pi-tə-kə\ *Pali* **Tipitaka** Collective term for the three major divisions of the Pali canon, the canon of Theravada Buddhism. (The term means "Triple Basket.") It consists of the Abhidhamma Pitaka, the Sutta Pitaka, and the Vinaya Pitaka, which were transmitted orally by the sangha until they were committed to writing about 500 years after the Buddha's death. The texts appeared in two languages, Sanskrit and Pali, the Pali version being the better preserved. Sanskrit versions were translated into Tibetan, Chinese, and other languages.

Triple Alliance (1882) Secret agreement between Germany, Austria-Hungary, and Italy. It provided that Germany and Austria-Hungary would support Italy if it was attacked by France, that Italy would similarly assist Germany, and that Italy would remain neutral if Austria-Hungary was attacked by Russia. The alliance advanced Otto von Bismarck's efforts to isolate France. Conflicts between Italy and Austria-Hungary over their interests in the Balkans led Italy to reach an understanding of neutrality with France in 1902, which effectively nullified Italy's pledge to the members of the Triple Alliance, though the alliance was renewed in 1907 and 1912. See also Austro-German Alliance.

Triple Alliance, War of the See Paraguayan War

Triple Crown In U.S. horse racing, an unofficial championship attributed to a Thoroughbred horse that in a single season wins the Kentucky Derby, the Preakness Stakes, and the Belmont Stakes. First won in 1919 by Sir Barton, it has since been won 10 times, most recently by Secretariat (1973), Seattle Slew (1977), and Affirmed (1978).

Triple Entente \än-'tänt\ (1907) Association between Britain, France, and Russia. It developed from the Franco-Russian Alliance of 1894, the Anglo-French Entente Cordiale of 1904, and the Anglo-Russian Entente of 1907. Formed to settle mutual colonial disputes, the alignment became the nucleus of the Allied Powers in World War I.

triple jump *or* **hop, step, and jump** Track-and-field distance jump incorporating three distinct, continuous movements: a hop, in which the athlete takes off and lands on the same foot; a step, in which he or she lands on the other foot; and a jump, in which the athlete lands in any manner, usually with both feet together. It has been a modern Olympic event since the first games in 1896.

Tripoli \'tri-pə-lē\ *Arabic* **Tarabulus al-Sham** \tə-'rä-bə-ləs-al-'sham\ ("The Eastern Tripoli") Seaport (pop., 1991 est.: 240,000), northwestern Lebanon. Founded c. 700 BC, it became the capital of a federation of three Phoenician city-states: Sidon, Tyre, and Arvad. It was controlled by the Seleucids and Romans, and taken by the Muslims in the mid-7th century AD. Besieged and partially destroyed by crusaders in the early 12th century, it was rebuilt by the later crusaders. It was occupied by the Egyptians in the 1830s, the British in 1918, and the British and Free French in 1941. It became part of the Republic of Lebanon in 1946. A center of Christian–Muslim conflict, it was the scene of a siege in 1983 by Palestinian rebels against YASIR ARAFAT. It is a major port, a commercial and industrial center, and a popular beach resort. At the terminus of an oil pipeline from Iraq, it is an important oil storage and refining center.

Tripoli *Arabic* **Tarabulus al-Gharb** \tə-ˈrä-bə-ləs-al-ˈgärb\ ("The Western Tripoli") City (metro. area population 1995 est.: 1,682,000), capital of Libya. Located on the Mediterranean Sea, it is the nation's largest city and chief seaport. Founded by the PHOENICIANS c. 7th century BC, it was known as Oea in ancient times, and was one of the three cities of the region of TRIPOLITANIA. It was controlled by the Romans from the 1st century BC, and later by the Byzantines. It was conquered by the Arabs in 645. Conquered by the Turks in 1551, it was made a colonial capital of the Ottoman empire. It was under Italy's control 1911–43, after which it was occupied by the British until Libya's independence in 1951. The U.S. bombed it in 1983 in response to terrorist activity. Historical structures include numerous mosques and a Roman triumphal arch. In 1973 Al-Fateh University replaced the former University of Libya.

Tripolis \ˈtri-pə-ləs\ City (pop., 1991: 22,000), southern Greece, the commercial center of the central PELOPONNESE. It was founded in the 14th century AD as Drobolitza to replace the ancient cities of Pallantium, TEGEA, and MANTINEA. Rebuilt in 1770, it became the seat of the local Turkish pasha. The city prospered until 1828, when it was destroyed in the War of GREEK INDEPENDENCE. It was rebuilt after 1834.

Tripolitan War \tri-ˈpä-lə-tᵊn\ (1801–5) Conflict between the U.S. and Tripoli (now in Libya). The U.S. refused to continue paying tribute to the rulers of the North African BARBARY COAST states, which had bought immunity from pirate attacks in the Mediterranean. The pasha of Tripoli demanded greater tribute and then declared war on the U.S. (1801). A U.S. naval squadron was sent to Tripolitan waters and fought several skirmishes, including a raid by STEPHEN DECATUR. A U.S. naval blockade and an overland expedition from Egypt ended the war with a peace treaty favorable to the U.S.

Tripolitania \tri-ˌpä-lə-ˈtā-nē-ə\ Historical region, North Africa, now northwestern Libya. Colonized by the PHOENICIANS in the 7th century BC, it was named for its three chief cities—LEPTIS MAGNA, Oea (TRIPOLI), and SABRATA. It comprised the eastern part of Carthaginian territory by the 3rd century BC. It came under Numidian chieftains in the mid-2nd century BC. After the Numidian War (46 BC), it was attached to the Roman province of Africa Nova (see Roman AFRICA). It was ruled by successive Arab and Berber dynasties before becoming part of the Ottoman empire in 1551. It became independent in 1711. As one of the BARBARY COAST states, it plundered shipping in the Mediterranean, leading to the TRIPOLITAN WAR with the U.S. (1801–5). It came under Turkish administration again in 1835. The Italians acquired the region in 1912. It was the scene of fierce fighting between British and German forces in 1942. In 1951, with the provinces of CYRENAICA and FEZZAN, it formed the independent kingdom of Libya. The provinces were dissolved in 1963.

Trippe, Juan T(erry) (1899–1981) U.S. airline founder. Born in Sea Bright, N.J., he served as a pilot in World War I. After graduating from Yale University in 1922, he promptly established an air taxi service using government-surplus aircraft. He next formed Colonial Air Transport, which began the first airmail route between New York and Boston. In 1927 he founded PAN AMERICAN WORLD AIRWAYS. Under him the company introduced the first round-the-world air service (1947) and the first commercial jets (1955). He retired in 1968.

Tripura \ˈtri-pə-rə\ State (pop., 1994 est.: 3,065,000), northeastern India. It is bordered on three sides by Bangladesh; its capital is AGARTALA. It was an independent Hindu kingdom for more than 1,000 years before it became part of the Mughal empire in the 17th century. After 1808 it was under the influence of the British government. It became a union territory in 1956 and acquired full status as a state in 1972. The main economic activity is agriculture, with rice and jute the major crops.

trireme \ˈtrī-ˌrēm\ Oar-powered warship. Light, fast, and maneuverable, it was the principal naval vessel with which Persia, Phoenicia, and the Greek city-states vied for mastery of the Mediterranean from the Battle of SALAMIS (480 BC) through the end of the PELOPONNESIAN WAR (404). The Athenian trireme was about 120 ft (37 m) long, and was rowed by 170 oarsmen seated in three tiers along each side; it could reach speeds of more than 7 knots (8 mph, or 13 kph). Square-rigged sails were used when the ship was not engaged in battle. Armed with a bronze-clad RAM, it carried spearmen and bowmen to attack enemy crews. By the late 4th century BC, armed deck soldiers had become so important in naval warfare that it was superseded by heavier ships. See also GALLEY.

Tristan and Isolde Lovers in a medieval romance based on Celtic legend. The hero Tristan goes to Ireland to ask the hand of the princess Isolde for his uncle, King Mark of Cornwall. On their return the two mistakenly drink a love potion prepared for the king and fall deeply in love. After many adventures, they make peace with Mark, who marries Isolde. The distraught Tristan goes to Brittany, where he marries another noble Isolde. When he is wounded by a poisoned arrow, he sends for the first Isolde. His jealous wife tells him his true love has refused to come; he dies just before she arrives, and she dies in his arms. The original poem has not survived, but it exists in many later versions and even became part of ARTHURIAN legend. GOTTFRIED von Strassburg's 13th-century version, considered the masterpiece of medieval German poetry, was the basis for RICHARD WAGNER

Tristano, Lennie *orig.* **Leonard Joseph** (1919–1978) U.S. pianist, a major figure in the development of modern jazz. Born in Chicago and blind from childhood, Tristano performed and taught in New York from the 1940s. His recordings featured players who had studied with him, including saxophonists Lee Konitz and Warne Marsh. Although resistant to classification, Tristano's music displayed a rigor and virtuosity appropriate to BEBOP while its aesthetic foreshadowed much of cool jazz.

triticale \ˌtri-tə-ˈkā-lē\ WHEAT-RYE hybrid that has a high yield and rich protein content. The first cross was reported in 1875, the first fertile cross in 1888. The name triticale first appeared in scientific literature in 1935 and is attributed to ERICH TSCHERMAK VON SEYSENEGG von Seyseneg. In favorable environmental circumstances its yield equals that of wheat; under poor conditions its yield exceeds that of wheat. Its flour is not very suitable for breadmaking but can be blended with wheat flour. Major producers are Russia, the U.S., and Australia.

tritium \ˈtri-tē-əm, ˈtri-shē-əm\ Isotope of HYDROGEN, chemical symbol written as ^{3}H or T, with atomic number 1 but ATOMIC WEIGHT approximately 3. Its nucleus contains one PROTON and two NEUTRONS. Tritium is radioactive (see RADIOACTIVITY), with a HALF-LIFE of 12.32 years. Its occurrence in natural water at 10^{-18} the amount of natural hydrogen is probably due to the action of COSMIC RAYS. Some tritium is used in self-luminous phosphors and dials and as a radioactive tracer in chemical and biochemical studies. NUCLEAR FUSION of DEUTERIUM and tritium at high temperatures releases enormous amounts of ENERGY. Such reactions have been used in NUCLEAR WEAPONS. See also HEAVY WATER.

Triton \ˈtrī-tᵊn\ In GREEK MYTHOLOGY, a merman and a demigod of the sea. He was the son of POSEIDON and Amphitrite. According to HESIOD, Triton lived in a golden palace in the depths of the sea. He was represented as human to the waist, with the tail of a fish, and he had a spiral conch shell that he blew either to calm or raise the waves. Some traditions stated that there were many tritons.

Triton \ˈtrī-tᵊn\ Largest of Neptune's known moons. Its diameter is about 1,700 mi (2,700 km), somewhat less than that of earth's moon. Triton moves in a retrograde orbit, opposite the direction of Neptune's rotation, so slowly that each season lasts over 40 years. It has a very thin atmosphere of nitrogen and methane and a surface temperature of –400°F (–240°C). It is covered with enormous expanses of ice pitted by what appear to be a few meteorite craters. Plumes of gas observed by Voyager may be gas venting through fissures when the surface is warmed by sunlight.

triumph Ancient Roman ritual procession honoring a general who had won a major battle and killed at least 5,000 of the enemy. Senators and magistrates were followed by sacrificial animals, captured loot, and captives in chains. The general, in a purple-and-gold tunic, rode in a chariot, holding a laurel branch in his right hand and an ivory scepter in his left, while a slave held a golden crown over his head. Lastly came the soldiers, singing songs, which were sometimes ribald. Under the empire, only the emperor and members of his family celebrated triumphs.

triumphal arch Monumental structure, originating in Rome, pierced by at least one arched passageway and erected to honor an important person or commemorate a significant event. It usually spanned a street or roadway and was built astride the line of march of a victorious army during its triumphal procession. Most were built during the empire period. The basic form consisted of two piers connected by an arch and crowned by a superstructure, or attic, that served as a base for statues and bore inscriptions. The large central arch could also be flanked by two smaller arches. The Roman triumphal arch had a facade of marble columns, and the archway and sides were adorned with relief sculpture. Among those built since the Renaissance is the Arc de Triomphe in Paris.

triumvirate \trī-ˈəm-vir-ət\ In ancient Rome, usually a board of three officials who assisted higher magistrates in judicial functions, oversaw festival banquets, or ran the mint. The First Triumvirate (60 BC) of Pompey, Julius Caesar, and Crassus was an informal group of three strong leaders with no sanctioned powers. The Second Triumvirate (43 BC), consisting of Mark Antony, Lepidus, and Octavian (later Augustus)—formally *tresviri rei publicae constituendae* ("triumvirate for organizing the state")—held absolute dictatorial power.

Trivandrum \trə-ˈvan-drəm\ Seaport (pop., 1991: 524,000), capital of Kerala state, southwestern India. The community became prominent when it was made capital of the kingdom of Travancore in 1745. A large fort contains several palaces and a Vaishnava temple, which is a noted pilgrimage center. It also has cultural amenities and is the site of the University of Kerala (1937).

Troas \ˈtrō-ˌas\ *or* **The Troad** Ancient region surrounding the city of Troy. It was formed mainly by the northwestern projection of Asia Minor (modern Turkey) into the Aegean Sea. It extended from the Gulf of Edremit to the Sea of Marmara and the Dardanelles, and from the Ida Mountains to the Aegean. St. Paul visited the region on his missionary journeys.

Trobriand Islands \ˈtrō-brē-ˌand\ *or* **Kiriwina Islands** \ˌkir-ə-ˈwē-nə\ Group of small coral islands, Solomon Sea, South Pacific Ocean, Papua New Guinea. The islands are low-lying with coral reefs. The group has a total land area of about 170 sq mi (440 sq km). The largest, Kiriwina, is an atoll 30 mi (48 km) long and 3–10 mi (5–16 km) wide, covered largely with swamp; it served as an air and naval base for the Allies in 1943. Anthropologist Bronislaw Malinowski conducted research among the Trobriand islanders 1915–18.

Trobrianders Melanesian people of the Kiriwina (Trobriand) Islands, lying off eastern New Guinea. Their subsistence is based on yams and other vegetables, domesticated pigs, and fish. Trobrianders are noted for their elaborate intertribal trading system, the *kula,* by which red shell necklaces are traded between permanent trading partners in a clockwise direction around a ring of islands; white shell bracelets are traded counterclockwise. Among the Trobrianders wealth is extremely important as a sign of power. They were the subject of highly influential studies by Bronislaw Malinowski.

Troilus and Cressida \ˈtrȯi-ləs...ˈkre-si-də\ Lovers in medieval romance, based on characters from Greek mythology. In the *Iliad*, Troilus, son of Priam and Hecuba, is dead before the Trojan War starts. In non-Homeric legends he was said to have been killed during the war by Achilles. He was first turned into a romantic figure in the Middle Ages, when he was portrayed as an innocent young lover betrayed by the faithless Cressida, who abandoned him for the Greek warrior Diomedes. The first version of the story was written by the 12th-century trouvère Benoît de Sainte-Maure in the poem *Roman de Troie*. More-famous versions include Giovanni Boccaccio's *Il Filostrato*, Geoffrey Chaucer's *Troilus and Criseyde*, and William Shakespeare

Trojan asteroids Two groups of asteroids named for heroes of Greece and Troy in Homer's *Iliad*. These minor planets revolve around the sun at the Lagrangian points (see J.-L. Lagrange) in Jupiter's orbit. About 500 are known; Achilles, the first, was discovered in 1906. The known Trojans undoubtedly rank among the larger asteroids but appear faint because of their great distance from earth.

Trojan War Mostly legendary conflict between the Greeks and the people of Troy in western Asia Minor. It was dated by later Greeks to the 12th or 13th century BC. It is celebrated in Homer's *Iliad* and *Odyssey*, in Greek tragedy, and in Roman literature. In Homer's account, the Trojan prince Paris ran off with the beautiful Helen, wife of Menelaus of Sparta, whose brother Agamemnon then led a Greek expedition to retrieve her. The war lasted 10 years; its participants included Hector, Achilles, Priam, Odysseus, and Ajax. Its end resulted from a ruse: The Greeks built a large wooden horse in which a raiding party hid; when the Greeks pretended to leave, the Trojans brought the horse into the walled city and the Greeks swarmed out, opening the gates to their comrades and sacking Troy, killing the men and enslaving the women. The extent of the legend's actual historical content is not known; excavations have revealed human habitation from 3000 BC to AD 1200, and there is evidence of violent destruction about 1250 BC.

trolley car See streetcar

Trollope \ˈträ-ləp\, **Anthony** (1815–1882) English novelist. He worked for the post office 1834–67. Beginning in 1844 he produced 47 novels, writing mainly before breakfast at a fixed rate of 1,000 words an hour. His best-loved and most famous works are the six interconnected Barsetshire novels, including *Barchester Towers* (1857) and *The Last Chronicle of Barset* (1867). Depicting the social scene in an imaginary English county, they abound in memorable characters and atmosphere. The Palliser novels, dealing with political issues and featuring the character Plantagenet Palliser, include the sharply satirical *The Eustace Diamonds* (1872). Other works, such as *He Knew He Was Right* (1869), show great psychological penetration. *The Way We Live Now* (1875), with its ironic view of the Victorian upper classes, is especially highly regarded. His mother, Frances Trollope (1780–1863), won fame with her controversial *Domestic Manners of the Americans* (1832).

Trollope, oil painting by S. Laurence, 1865; in the National Portrait Gallery, London.

BY COURTESY OF THE NATIONAL PORTRAIT GALLERY, LONDON

trombone Brass instrument with an extendable slide with which the length of its tubing can be increased. It has a mostly cylindrical bore and a cup-shaped mouthpiece. The slide performs the same function as the valves in other brass instruments. Valve trombones, both with and without slides, were developed in the early 19th century; they provide increased agility but diminished tone quality. The trombone exists in several sizes; the tenor trombone in B-flat is the standard instrument, but the bass trombone is also used orchestrally. The trombone (long known as the sackbut) developed in the 15th century, and has changed little over 400 years. By the 16th century it had been adopted by town, court, church, and military bands; it was employed in early opera orchestras, but only began to be used in the symphony orchestra c. 1800. In the 20th century it became important in dance and jazz bands.

trompe l'oeil \trōⁿp-ˈlœi, *Engl* ˌtrȯmp-ˈləi\ (French: "deceive the eye") Style of representation in which a painted object is intended to deceive the viewer into believing it is the object itself. First employed by the ancient Greeks, trompe l'oeil was also popular with Roman muralists. Since the early Renaissance, European painters have used trompe l'oeil to create false frames from which the contents of still lifes or portraits seemed to spill, and to paint windowlike images that appeared to be actual openings in a wall or ceiling.

Trondheim \ˈtrȯn-ˌhām\ City (pop., 1997: 145,000), central Norway. It is located on Trondheim Fjord, an inlet of the Norwegian Sea that extends 80 mi (130 km) inland. It was founded by King Olaf I Tryggvason in 997 and was Norway's capital until the 14th century. It prospered as a trade center until the Hanseatic League made Bergen its chief port. The city declined until the late 19th century, when it was linked by rail to Oslo. Norway's third-largest city, it is a major Norwegian land and sea transport link and a manufacturing center.

Tropic of Cancer Parallel of latitude approximately 23°27′ north of the terrestrial equator. It is the northern boundary of the tropics, and it marks the northernmost latitude at which the sun can be seen directly overhead at noon.

Tropic of Capricorn Parallel of latitude approximately 23°27′ south of the terrestrial equator. It is the southern boundary of the tropics, and it marks the southernmost latitude at which the sun can be seen directly overhead at noon.

tropical cyclone Severe atmospheric disturbance in tropical oceans. Tropical cyclones have very low atmospheric pressures in the calm, clear center (the eye) of a circular structure of rain, cloud, and very high winds. In the Atlantic and Caribbean they are called hurricanes; in the Pacific they are known as typhoons. Because of the earth's rotation, tropical cyclones rotate clockwise in the Southern Hemisphere and counterclockwise in the Northern. They may be 50–500 mi (80–800 km) in diameter, and sustained winds in excess of 100 mph (160 kph) are common. In the eye, however, the winds drop abruptly to light breezes or even complete calm. The lowest sea-level pressures on earth occur in or near the eye.

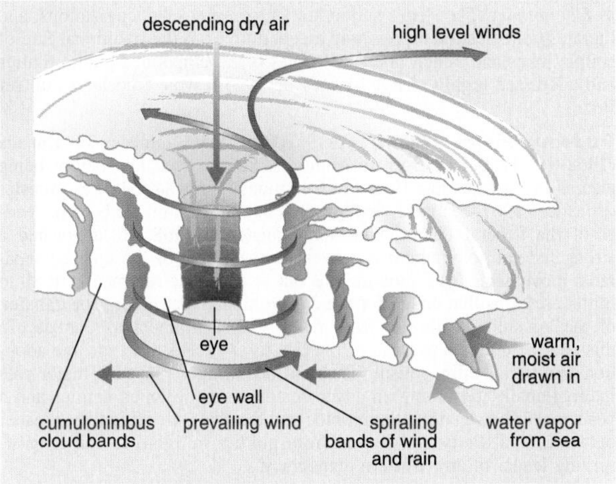

Cross section of a tropical cyclone. A cyclone derives its power from the warm air and water found at tropical latitudes. Its winds rotate around the low-pressure center, or "eye," where relative calm prevails. Wind and rain are usually most severe in or near the eye wall.

tropical fish Any of various small fishes of tropical origin often kept in aquariums. They are interesting for their behavior or showiness or both. Popular varieties include the ANGELFISH, GUPPY, kissing GOURAMI, SEA HORSE, SIAMESE FIGHTING FISH, and TETRA.

tropical medicine Science of diseases seen primarily in tropical or subtropical climates. It arose in the 19th century when European colonial doctors encountered infectious diseases unknown in Europe. The discovery that many tropical diseases (e.g., MALARIA, YELLOW FEVER) were spread by mosquitoes led to discovery of other vectors' roles (see SLEEPING sickness, PLAGUE, TYPHUS) and to efforts to destroy vector breeding grounds (e.g., by draining swamps). Later, antibiotics came to play an increasingly important role. Research institutes and national and international commissions were organized to control common tropical illnesses, at least in areas with Europeans. As colonies became independent, their governments took over most of these efforts, with help from the World Health Organization and the former colonizing countries.

troposphere \'trō-pə-ˌsfir\ Lowest region of the atmosphere, bounded by the earth below and the STRATOSPHERE above, with the upper boundary being about 6–8 mi (10–13 km) above the earth's surface. The troposphere is marked by decreasing temperature with height, which distinguishes it from the stratosphere. Most clouds and weather systems occur in the troposphere.

Troppau \'trȯ-ˌpau̇\, **Congress of** (1820) Meeting of the HOLY ALLIANCE powers held at Troppau in Silesia. Attended by representatives of Austria, Russia, and Prussia and by observers from Britain and France, the alliance signed a declaration of intention (the Troppau protocol) to take collective action against revolution. It also agreed that states having undergone revolutions would be excluded from the European alliance. The congress invited the king of the Two SICILIES to meet at the Congress of LAIBACH to discuss intervention against the revolution in Naples. Britain and France did not accept the protocol.

Trotsky, Leon *orig.* **Lev Davidovich Bronshtein** (1879–1940) Russian communist leader. Born in the Ukraine to Russian-Jewish farmers, he joined an underground socialist group and was exiled to Siberia in 1898 for his revolutionary activities. He escaped in 1902 with a forged passport using the name Trotsky. He fled to London, where he met VLADIMIR ILICH LENIN. In 1903, when the RUSSIAN SOCIAL-DEMOCRATIC WORKERS' PARTY split, Trotsky became a MENSHEVIK, allying himself with Lenin's opponents. He returned to St. Petersburg to help lead the RUSSIAN REVOLUTION OF 1905. Arrested and again exiled to Siberia, he wrote *Results and Prospects*, setting forth his theory of "permanent revolution." He escaped to Vienna in 1907, worked as a journalist in the Balkan Wars (1912–13), and moved around Europe and the U.S. until the RUSSIAN REVOLUTION OF 1917 brought him back to St. Petersburg (then Petrograd), where he became a BOLSHEVIK and was elected leader of the workers' soviet. He played a major role in the overthrow of the provisional government and the establishment of Lenin's communist regime. As commissar of war (1918–24), Trotsky rebuilt and brilliantly commanded the RED ARMY during the RUSSIAN CIVIL WAR. Though favored by Lenin to succeed him, he lost support after Lenin's death (1924) and was forced out of power by JOSEPH STALIN. After a campaign of denunciation, he was expelled from the Politburo (1926) and Central Committee (1927), then banished from Russia (1929). He lived in Turkey and France, where he wrote his memoirs and a history of the revolution. Under Soviet pressure, he was forced to move around Europe and eventually found asylum in 1936 in Mexico, where, falsely accused in the PURGE TRIALS as the chief conspirator against Stalin, he was murdered in 1940 by a Spanish communist.

Trotsky.

Trotskyism Marxist ideology based on the theory of permanent revolution first expounded by LEON TROTSKY. Trotsky believed that because all national economic development was affected by the laws of the world market, a revolution depended on revolutions in other countries for permanent success, a position that put him at odds with JOSEPH STALIN's "socialism in one country." After Trotsky's exile in 1929, Trotskyists continued to attack the Soviet bureaucracy as "Bonapartist" (based on the dictatorship of one man). In the 1930s Trotskyists advocated a united front with trade unions against FASCISM. After Trotsky's murder (1940), Trotskyism became a generic term for various revolutionary doctrines that opposed the Soviet form of COMMUNISM. See also LENINISM, MARXISM, STALINISM.

troubadour \'trü-bə-ˌdȯr, 'trü-bə-ˌdu̇r\ One of a class of lyric poets and poet-musicians, often of knightly rank, that flourished from the 11th through the 13th century, chiefly in Provence and other regions of southern France, northern Spain, and northern Italy. They wrote in the *langue d'oc* of southern France (see LANGUEDOC) and cultivated a lyric poetry intricate in meter and rhyme and usually of a romantic amatory strain reflecting the ideals of COURTLY love. Favored at courts, troubadours had great freedom of speech and were charged with creating around the court ladies an aura of pleasant cultivation. Their poetry, often set to music, was to influence all later European lyrical poetry. See also TROUVÈRE.

Troubles, Time of (1606–13) Period of political crisis in Russia. After the death of FYODOR I and the end of the RURIK dynasty (1598), the BOYARS opposed the rule of BORIS GODUNOV and after his death placed the nobleman Vasily Shuysky (1552–1612) on the throne in 1606. Shuysky's rule was weakened by revolts, challenges by the second False DMITRY, and the invasion of Russia by the Polish king SIGISMUND III VASA in 1609–10. The Russians finally rallied against the Polish invaders and succeeded in ousting them from their control of Moscow in 1612. A new representative assembly met in 1613 and elected MICHAEL ROMANOV as czar, commencing the 300-year reign of the ROMANOV dynasty.

Troughton \'trō-tən\, **Edward** (1753–1835) British maker of scientific instruments. At 17 he joined his brother's mechanician's shop in London, where he applied himself singlemindedly to inventing. His new mode of graduating arcs of circles (1778) would later be called "the greatest improvement ever made in the art of instrument-making." He constructed the first modern transit-circle in 1805, and in 1812 he erected a mural circle (for measuring polar distances) at the Greenwich Observatory. He invented numerous geodetical instruments; his sextants came to be used by navigators to the virtual exclusion of all others. A frugal and solitary man, he showed little interest in his many honors or in self-enrichment.

trout Any of several prized game and food fishes of the family Salmonidae, native to the Northern Hemisphere but widely introduced elsewhere. Though most species inhabit cool freshwaters, a few (called sea trout; e.g., CUTTHROAT trout) migrate to the sea between spawnings. Some WEAKFISH are also called sea trout. The genus *Oncorhynchus* includes SALMON and several trout species; *Salvelinus* contains trout species regarded as CHARS. Trout species vary greatly in anatomy, color, and habits. Most live among submerged objects or in riffles and deep pools, eating insects, small fishes and their eggs, and crustaceans. See also BROOK trout, BROWN TROUT, LAKE TROUT, RAINBOW TROUT.

trouvère \trü-'ver\ One of a school of poets that flourished in northern France from the 11th to the 14th century. Trouvères were the counterparts in the language of northern France (the *langue d'oïl*) to the Provençal TROUBADOUR. Of both aristocratic and humble origins, they were originally connected with feudal courts but later found middle-class patrons. Their works, including the CHANSONS DE GESTE, are generally narratives; their basic subject was COURTLY love. Trouvères pleased their audiences by combining stylized themes and traditional metrical forms rather than through originality of expression. The lyrics were intended to be sung, by the poet alone or accompanied by a hired musician.

Trowbridge \'trō-,brij\ Town (pop., 1995 est.: 30,000), WILTSHIRE, southern England. The county's administrative headquarters, it has some notable buildings including St. James parish church, which dates from the 14th century. GEORGE CRABBE was rector here toward the end of his life. The town is famous for its fine woolen cloth.

Troy *or* **Ilium** Ancient city in TROAS, northwestern ASIA MINOR. It holds an enduring place in both literature and archaeology. The archaeological site, a huge mound at modern Hissarlik on the MENDERES RIVER, was first excavated by HEINRICH SCHLIEMANN 1870–90. It consists of nine major layers dating from the Neolithic period to Roman times (c. 3000 BC–4th century AD). Whether it is the actual city of HOMER is still debated. In Greek legend, it was besieged and finally destroyed by the Greeks in the 10-year TROJAN WAR. The heroes of Troy were identified by Schliemann with the MYCENAEANS of the Greek Bronze Age, placing the war c. 1200 BC. Its story is told in HOMER's *Iliad* and *Odyssey* and VIRGIL's *Aeneid*.

Trubetskoy \,trü-byit-'skȯi\, **Nikolay (Sergeyevich), Prince** (1890–1938) Russian linguist. Born into a family of scholars, he held professorships in Russia and (from 1922) at the University of Vienna. One of the founders of the Prague school of LINGUISTICS, he was noted as the author of the school's most important work on PHONOLOGY, *Principles of Phonology* (1939). Influenced by FERDINAND DE SAUSSURE, Trubetskoy redefined the PHONEME functionally as the smallest distinctive unit within the structure of a language. He died of a heart attack after being persecuted by the Nazis for criticizing racist theory.

Trubetskoy family Russian noble family influential in the 19th century. One of its members, Sergey Petrovich Trubetskoy (1790–1860), was a leader in the DECEMBRIST revolt. Other notable members included the religious philosopher-brothers Sergey Trubetskoy (1862–1905) and Evgeny Trubetskoy (1863–1920) and Sergey's son, the linguist NIKOLAY S. TRUBETSKOY.

Truce of God Measure by the medieval Roman Catholic Church to suspend warfare on certain days of the week and for certain church festivals and Lent. It was instituted in France as early as 1027, and elsewhere in Europe (excluding England) during the next several decades. The popes later took its direction into their own hands, and the first decree of the Council of CLERMONT (1095) proclaimed a weekly truce for all Christendom, with an oath of adherence to be taken by all men over age 12. The truce was most powerful in the 12th century but was never entirely effective.

Trucial States See UNITED ARAB EMIRATES

truck Motor vehicle designed to carry freight or heavy articles. The first truck was built in Germany in 1896 by GOTTLIEB DAIMLER. By the 1920s trucks had become a major means of freight transportation. Gasoline engines for trucks were common until the 1940s, when DIESEL engines generally replaced them. Trucks may be either straight (all axles attached to the frame) or articulated (two or more frames connected by couplings); large articulated trucks consist of a towing tractor and a connected semitrailer. Air brakes were added to trucks in 1918 and four-wheel brakes in 1925; later improvements included power steering.

Trudeau \trü-'dō\, **Garry** *orig.* **Garretson Beekman** (born 1948) U.S. cartoonist. Born to a wealthy family in New York City, he studied art at Yale Univ., where his comic strip *Bull Tales* in the *Yale Daily News* acquired a loyal following. It was picked up by the Universal Press Syndicate in 1970 and began to appear in newspapers nationwide as *Doonesbury*. The strip's subtle humor, complex characterizations, and literate sophistication represented a departure from the traditional fare of simple jokes and punch lines, and it has often lampooned public figures and addressed highly charged issues. In 1975 it won Trudeau a Pulitzer Prize.

Trudeau, Pierre (Elliott) (1919–2000) Prime minister of Canada (1968–79, 1980–84). Born in Montreal, he practiced law before being elected to the Canadian House of Commons (1966–84). He was minister of justice (1967–68) in LESTER PEARSON's administration. He became leader of the Liberal Party and prime minister in 1968. He advocated a strong federal government and oversaw the defeat of the Quebec separatist movement. After nine months out of office, he returned in 1980 to initiate reforms that called for the constitutional "patriation," or transfer, of the amending authority from the British Parliament to Canada. To this end, he effected passage of the CANADA ACT. His term saw the adoption of official bilingualism. Trudeau increasingly played a major role internationally, becoming an advocate for underdeveloped nations and a peacemaker between the Soviet bloc and the West. He resigned as leader of the Liberal Party and retired from politics in 1984, as the longest-serving leader of any Western democracy.

Truffaut \trǖ-'fō, *Engl* trü-'fō\, **François** (1932–1984) French film director. After a troubled childhood and a stay in a reformatory, he became a film critic for the avant-garde *Cahiers du Cinéma*, becoming an advocate of the AUTEUR theory and helping establish the NEW WAVE movement. His first feature film was the semi-autobiographical *The 400 Blows* (1959), a portrait of a delinquent boy that won him international acclaim. Influenced by JEAN RENOIR and ALFRED HITCHCOCK, he made such varied and admired movies as *Shoot the Piano Player* (1960), *Jules and Jim* (1961), *Fahrenheit 451* (1966), *Stolen Kisses* (1968), *The Wild Child* (1969), *Day for Night* (1973, Academy Award), *The Story of Adele H.* (1975), and *The Last Metro* (1980).

truffle Edible, underground FUNGUS in the genus *Tuber* (class Ascomycetes, division Mycota), prized as a food delicacy since antiquity. Native mainly to temperate regions, truffles flourish in open woodlands on calcium-rich soil. The different species range from pea-sized to orange-sized. Truffles usually are associated with tree roots and are found up to about 1 ft (30 cm) below the soil surface. Experienced gatherers occasionally detect mature truffles by scent or by the morning and evening presence of hovering columns of small yellow flies, but more often with the help of trained pigs or dogs. The truffle is important in French cookery, and truffle gathering is an important industry in France. Truffles are among the most highly valued foods in the world. False truffles (genus *Rhizopogon*) form small, underground, potato-like structures under coniferous trees in parts of North America.

English truffle (*Tuber aestivum*).
S.C. PORTER—BRUCE COLEMAN INC.

Trujillo (Molina) \trü-'hē-yō\, **Rafael (Leónidas)** (1891–1961) Dictator of the Dominican Republic (1930–61). He entered the army in 1918 and rose through the ranks to become a general in 1927. In 1930 he seized power from Pres. Horacio Vásquez, and from then until his assassination he remained in absolute control of the country. Though he introduced a degree of economic modernization, its benefits were distributed inequitably, government corruption was rife, and Dominicans suffered the loss of civil and political liberties under his regime.

trullo Circular stone building roofed with a conical construction of dry stone masonry, unique to the region of PUGLIA in southeastern Italy and especially to the town of Alberobello, where trulli are used as dwellings. Trulli were built by piling circular courses of gray stone to a pinnacle on a whitewashed cylindrical wall. No mortar was used; the stones were held in place by gravity and pressure against one another.

Truman, Harry S. (1884–1972) 33rd president of the U.S. (1945–53). Born in Lamar, Mo., he worked at various jobs before serving with distinction in World War I. He became a partner in a Kansas City haberdashery; when the business failed, he entered Democratic Party politics with the help of THOMAS PENDERGAST. He was elected county judge (1922–24), and later became presiding judge of the county court (1926–34). His reputation for honesty and good management gained him bipartisan support. In the U.S. Senate (1935–45), he led a committee that exposed fraud in defense production. In 1944 he was chosen to replace the incumbent HENRY WALLACE as vice-presidential nominee and was elected with Pres. FRANKLIN ROOSEVELT. After only 82 days as vice president, he became president on Roosevelt's death (April 1945). He quickly made final arrangements for the San Francisco charter-writing meeting of the U.N., helped arrange Germany's unconditional surrender on May 8, which ended World War II in Europe, and in July attended the POTSDAM CONFERENCE. The Pacific war ended officially on September 2, after he ordered atomic bombs dropped on HIROSHIMA and NAGASAKI; his justification was a report that 500,000 U.S. troops would be lost in a conventional invasion of Japan. He announced the TRUMAN DOCTRINE to aid Greece and Turkey (1947), established the CENTRAL INTELLIGENCE AGENCY, and pressed for passage of the MARSHALL PLAN to aid European countries. In 1948 he defeated THOMAS DEWEY despite widespread expectation of his own defeat. He initiated a foreign policy of CONTAINMENT to restrict the Soviet Union's sphere of influence, pursued his POINT FOUR PROGRAM, and initiated the Berlin airlift (see BERLIN BLOCKADE AND AIRLIFT) and the NATO pact of 1949. In the KOREAN WAR he sent troops under Gen. DOUGLAS MACARTHUR to head the U.N. forces. Problems of pursuing the war occupied his administration until he retired. Though he was often criticized during his presidency, Truman's reputation grew steadily in later years.

Truman Doctrine Pronouncement by Pres. HARRY TRUMAN. On March 12, 1947, he called for immediate economic and military aid to Greece, which was threatened by a communist insurrection, and to Turkey, which was under pressure from Soviet expansion in the Mediterranean. Engaged in the COLD WAR with the Soviet Union, the U.S. sought to protect those countries from falling under Soviet influence after Britain announced that it could no longer give them aid. In response to Truman's message, Congress appropriated $400 million in aid.

Trumbull, John (1756–1843) U.S. painter, architect, and author. Born in Lebanon, Conn., son of Gov. Jonathan Trumbull (1710–1785), he served as an aide to GEORGE WASHINGTON during the American Revolution and later as secretary to JOHN JAY in London. In 1784 he studied painting in London with BENJAMIN WEST, and with West's encouragement he began the celebrated series of historical paintings and engravings he would work on throughout his life. In 1817 he was commissioned by Congress to paint the four large pictures that decorate the Capitol rotunda (completed 1826); most of the figures in the often-reproduced *Declaration of Independence* were painted from life.

Trumbull, Lyman (1813–1896) U.S. politician. Born in Colchester, Conn., he became a lawyer in Illinois and was elected to the U.S. Senate in 1855. Initially a Democrat, he switched to the Republican Party to support its antislavery policies. In 1864, as chairman of the Senate judiciary committee, he helped draft the 13th Amendment to the Constitution. Though a RADICAL REPUBLICAN, he voted to acquit Pres. ANDREW JOHNSON of impeachment charges. After retiring from politics to resume his law practice (1873), he returned to the Democratic Party and served as counsel for SAMUEL TILDEN in the disputed 1876 election.

Trump, Donald J(ohn) (born 1946) U.S. real-estate developer. Born in New York City, he joined his father's Trump Organization (1968) and expanded its holdings of rental housing. By the 1990s his properties included 25,000 rental and co-op apartment units, Trump Tower, and hotel-casinos in Atlantic City, N.J. Though an economic slump forced him to cede partial control of his properties to creditors, he later embarked on a vast building project on New York's West Side that was to include the world's tallest building. His personal life, political ambitions, and enjoyment of publicity combined to keep him in the public eye.

trumpet BRASS instrument with tubing twice-folded in an elongated shape. (In its broad sense, trumpet may refer to any lip-vibrated instrument.) The modern trumpet has a mostly cylindrical bore, three valves, and a cup-shaped mouthpiece, and is usually a B-flat or C instrument. The trumpet had taken its basic modern shape, with its ovoid loop, by c. 1500. In the 17th–18th century it employed crooks (removable lengths of tubing) to enable playing in different keys. The valved trumpet was developed in the 1820s. The trumpet has been associated with ceremonial and military uses since the 16th century. It joined the standard orchestra by c. 1700, though it was only selectively used, usually with the timpani. Its brilliant sound has since made it indispensable in a wide variety of ensembles. See also CORNET, FLUGELHORN.

trumpeter swan Black-billed species *(Cygnus cygnus buccinator)* of SWAN, named for its far-carrying, low-pitched call. About 6 ft (1.8 m) long, with a 10-ft (3-m) wingspan, it is the largest swan, though it weighs less than the mute swan. Once threatened with extinction (fewer than 100 were counted in the U.S. in 1935), it has made a strong comeback; though still listed as vulnerable, its population in western Canada and the northwestern U.S. now exceeds 5,000.

Truong Chinh \trü-'ȯŋ-'chin\ *orig.* **Dang Xuan Khu** (1907–1988) Vietnamese statesman, writer, and communist intellectual. He was an anticolonialist activist as a youth, joining HO CHI MINH in 1928. He became a teacher and joined the Indochinese Communist Party, becoming its secretary-general in 1941. With VO NGUYEN GIAP he developed the strategy that led to a Vietnamese victory over the Japanese occupation forces in 1945. With Le Duan (1908–1986) and Pham Van Dong (1906–2000) he ruled North Vietnam after Ho's death in 1969.

Truro City (pop., 1995 est.: 25,000), CORNWALL, southwestern England. Located on the Truro River at the head of Falmouth Harbor, it is the county seat of Cornwall and the Isles of SCILLY. Its industries include food processing and light engineering.

truss In building construction, a structural frame usually fabricated from pieces of metal or timber to form a series of triangles lying in a single plane. The linear members are subject only to compression or tension. The horizontal pieces forming the top and bottom of the truss are called the chords, and the sloping and vertical pieces connecting the chords are collectively called the web. Unlike a VAULT, the truss exerts no thrust but only downward pressure; supporting walls require no buttressing or extra thickening. Trusses have been used extensively in roofing and bridges. Wood trusses were probably first used in primitive dwellings c. 2500 BC. Wood was replaced by iron, which in turn was succeeded by steel.

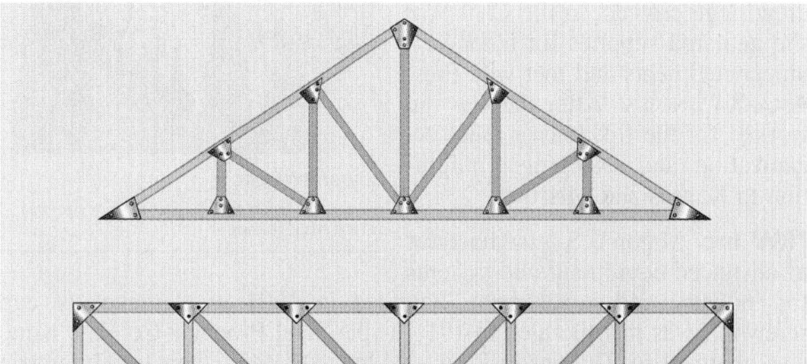

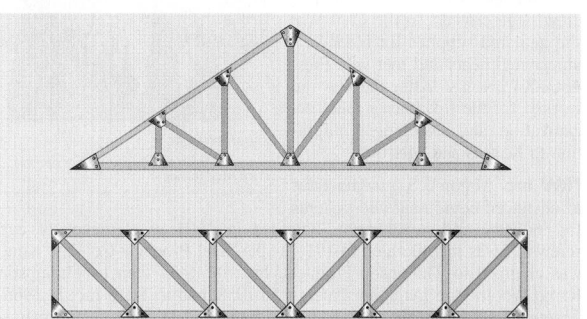

A truss's outer members are called the chords, its interior members are called the web members, and each triangular section is called a panel. A pitched truss (top) has inclined top chords; a flat truss (bottom) has parallel top and bottom chords.

trust In law, a relationship between parties in which one, the trustee or FIDUCIARY, has the power to manage property, and the other, the BENEFICIARY, has the privilege of receiving the benefits from that property. Trusts are used in a variety of contexts, most notably in family settlements and in charitable gifts. The traditional requirements of a trust are a named beneficiary and trustee, an identified property (constituting the principal of the trust), and delivery of the property to the trustee with the intent to create a trust. Trusts are often created for the sake of advantageous tax treatment (including exemption). A charitable trust, unlike most trusts, does not require definite beneficiaries and may exist in perpetuity. See also TRUST COMPANY.

trust company Company, often a COMMERCIAL bank, acting as trustee for individuals and businesses and providing related financial or estate-planning services. Trust services for individuals commonly include the administration of estates, living trusts (trusts that become effective during the lifetime of its maker, or settlor), and testamentary trusts (trusts originating in a will). Services for businesses include the administration of corporate bond indentures and corporate pension funds. Trust companies may also serve as corporate stock registrars and as paying agents for the distribution of dividends.

trust fund Property (e.g, money or securities) held in a trust; that is, property held legally by one party (the legal owner) for the benefit of another party (the equitable owner). The legal owner, or trustee, has the right of possession and the right of use of the property, but must exercise those rights to the benefit of the equitable owner, or beneficiary. In Anglo-American law, trust funds are set up principally for family settlements and for charitable giving. In the commercial sector, trust funds are often set up to provide for employee pensions and profit-sharing programs.

truth In philosophy, the property of statements, thoughts, or propositions that are said, in ordinary discourse, to agree with the facts or to state what is the case. At least four major types of truth theory have been proposed: correspondence theories (see REALISM), coherence theories (see COHERENTISM, IDEALISM), pragmatic theories (see PRAGMATISM), and deflationary theories. The latter group encompasses a wide variety of views, including the redundancy theory, the disquotation theory, and the prosentential theory.

Truth, Sojourner *orig.* **Isabella** (1797?–1883) U.S. evangelist and reformer. She was born into slavery in Ulster Co., N.Y., where she bore five children. After being freed, she worked as a domestic in New York City (1829–43) and began preaching on street corners with the evangelical missionary Elijah Pierson. Adopting the name Sojourner Truth, she left New York to obey a "call" to travel and preach. Adding abolitionism and women's rights to her religious messages, she traveled in the Midwest, where her magnetism drew large crowds. In the Civil War she gathered supplies for black volunteer regiments and met with Pres. ABRAHAM LINCOLN. After the war she worked for the freedmen's relief organization and encouraged migration to Kansas and Missouri.

Sojourner Truth.
BY COURTESY OF THE BURTON HISTORICAL COLLECTION, DETROIT PUBLIC LIBRARY

TRW Inc. Major U.S. manufacturer of advanced equipment and systems for industry and government. Founded in 1901 as a maker of cap screws, it was incorporated in 1916 as the Steel Products Co. The name was changed to Thompson Products, Inc., in 1926, then to Thompson Ramo Wooldridge Inc. after a merger in 1958, and to TRW Inc. in 1965. Through its various divisions and subsidiaries, TRW designs and manufactures a wide range of automotive parts and offers engineering and research services. It produces electronic systems for military aircraft and designs and builds spacecraft. Its information systems and services segments maintain databases for screening credit histories. Its headquarters are in Cleveland, Ohio.

tryptophan \'trip-tə-ˌfan\ One of the essential AMINO acids. It is a HETEROCYCLIC compound that is found in small amounts in most PROTEINS. It plays an important role in the growth and development of infants and in the biosynthesis of SEROTONIN and NIACIN (thus, deficiency of both niacin and tryptophan causes PELLAGRA). Its occurrence in milk is the reason milk helps people sleep. It is used in medicine and nutrition research, in enriched foods, and as a dietary supplement.

Ts'ai-shen See CAISHEN

Ts'ao Chan See CAO ZHAN

Ts'ao Ts'ao See CAO CAO

tsar See CZAR

Tsaritsyn See VOLGOGRAD

Tsavo National Park \'tsä-ˌvō\ Park, southeastern Kenya, east of Mount KILIMANJARO. Established in 1948, it covers 8,036 sq mi (20,812 sq km), and is Kenya's largest national park. It comprises semiarid plains covered by dormant vegetation (which blooms after a light rain), and acacia and baobab trees. Wildlife includes elephant, lion, rhinoceros, hippopotamus, hartebeest, and hundreds of bird species. Poaching and brush fires are constant problems.

Tschermak von Seysenegg \'cher-ˌmäk-fòn-'zī-zə-ˌnek\, **Erich** (1871–1962) Austrian botanist. He was one of the codiscoverers of GREGOR MENDEL's classic papers on heredity and the garden pea. Before running across Mendel's papers he had conducted his own breeding experiments with the garden pea, but found that Mendel's work duplicated and in some ways surpassed his own. In the same year that he reported his findings (1900), HUGO DE VRIES and CARL ERICH CORRENS also reported their discovery of Mendel's papers. See also WILLIAM BATESON.

Tselinograd See ASTANA

Tseng Kuo-fan See ZENG GUOFAN

tsetse fly \'tset-sē, 'tsē-tsē\ Any of about 21 species (genus *Glossina,* family Muscidae) of African bloodsucking DIPTERANS that are robust, sparsely bristled, and usually larger than a HOUSEFLY. They have stiff, piercing mouthparts. Only two species commonly transmit the protozoan parasites (trypanosomes) that cause human SLEEPING sickness: *G. palpalis,* found primarily in dense streamside vegetation, and *G. morsitans,* found in more open woodlands. The female requires a sufficient blood meal to produce viable larvae, but both sexes suck blood almost daily.

Tshombe \'chòm-bā\, **Moise (-Kapenda)** (1919–1969) President of the secessionist African state of Katanga (1960–63) and premier of the united Congo Republic (1964–65). After losing national elections to PATRICE LUMUMBA in 1960, Tshombe declared his Katanga province independent. When the U.N. intervened in 1963, he was forced into exile; he returned the following year as premier in JOSEPH KASAVUBU's government but was dismissed in 1965. See also MOBUTU SESE SEKO.

Tsimshian \'chim-shē-ən\ NORTHWEST COAST INDIAN people of PENUTIAN language stock from the Skeena and Nass river area in western central British Columbia and southern Alaska. The Tsimshian economy was based on fishing, with some hunting in winter. Large winter houses, made of wood and often carved and painted, symbolized family wealth. Descent was traced through the maternal line. Lineages functioned largely independently, but all participated in major ceremonies and in warfare. POTLATCHES marked various important events. At the turn of the 21st century the Tsimshian numbered in the thousands.

Tsinan See JINAN

Tsinghai See QINGHAI

Tso chuan See ZUO ZHUAN

Ts'u-hsi See CIXI

Tsugaru Strait \tsü-'gär-ü\ Strait, northwestern Pacific Ocean. It extends from the Sea of JAPAN to the open ocean between the islands of HONSHU and HOKKAIDO, Japan. It is 15–25 mi (24–40 km) wide. The Seikan Tunnel linking Aomori and Hakodate cities runs beneath the strait. Completed in 1988, it is the longest railway tunnel in the world; 14.3 mi (23.3 km) of its 33.4 mi (53.8 km) length lie under the strait.

tsunami \tsù-'nä-mē\ *or* **seismic sea wave** *or* **tidal wave** Catastrophic ocean WAVE, usually caused by a submarine earthquake with a magnitude greater than 6.5 on the RICHTER SCALE. Underwater or coastal landslides or volcanic eruptions also may cause tsunamis. The term tidal wave, frequently used for such a wave, is a misnomer, because the wave has no connection with the tides. Perhaps the most destructive tsunami ever occurred in 1703 at Awa, Japan, killing more than 100,000 people.

The spectacular underwater volcanic explosions that obliterated Indonesia's Krakatau island in 1883 created waves as high as 100 ft (30 m) and killed more than 36,000 people.

Tsushima \tsü-ˈshē-mä\, **Battle of** (May 27–29, 1905) Naval engagement in the RUSSO-JAPANESE WAR. As part of an assault on the Japanese navy, the Russian Baltic fleet was sent to join the Russian Pacific squadron at the besieged Port Arthur (Lüshun, China). Learning en route of the surrender of Port Arthur, the Russian admiral considered returning to Russia but sailed on to reach the China Sea seven months later. As the Russian fleet sailed for Vladivostok through the Tsushima Strait off southern Japan, the Japanese navy attacked. Its better-armed and speedier ships succeeded in sinking two-thirds of the Russian fleet. The decisive defeat crushed Russia's hope of regaining mastery of the sea and ended the war.

Tsvet \ˈtsvet\, **Mikhail (Semyonovich)** (1872–1919) Italian-Russian botanist and chemist. He is credited with the discovery (in 1903) and application of CHROMATOGRAPHY. In 1910 he described how he extracted plant PIGMENTS with ether and alcohol and percolated the solution through columns of calcium carbonate or powdered sugar; the different pigments appeared as separate colored bands. Tsvet discovered several new CHLOROPHYLLS and coined the words *chromatography* and *carotenoid.* His work was not discovered by mainstream Western scientists for nearly 30 years.

Tsvetayeva \tsvʸi-ˈtá-yə-və\, **Marina (Ivanovna)** (1892–1941) Russian poet. After spending most of her youth in Moscow, she began studies at the Sorbonne at 16. She published her first poetry collection in 1910. Her verses on the Russian Revolution glorify the anti-Bolshevik resistance, of which her husband was a part. She lived abroad 1922–39, mostly in Paris, writing varied works including poetry that increasingly reflected nostalgia for her homeland. Many of her best and most typical poetic qualities are displayed in the long verse fairy tale *Tsar-devitsa* (1922; "Tsar-Maiden"). Though little known outside Russia, she is considered one of the finest 20th-century poets in Russian.

Tswana \ˈtswä-nə\ Westerly division of the SOTHO peoples of South Africa and Botswana. The Tswana, numbering 4.1 million, live in a grassland environment in which they raise livestock and grow corn and sorghum. There is a seasonal migration of Tswana men, many of whom work in the mining and industrial centers of South Africa.

Tu Fu See DU FU

t'u-ti See TUDI

Tuamotu Archipelago \ˌtü-ə-ˈmō-tü\ Group of about 80 islands (pop., 1988: 12,000), FRENCH POLYNESIA. Its atolls and coral reefs are roughly dispersed as a double chain for over 900 mi (1,450 km). In 1947 THOR HEYERDAHL's Kon-Tiki expedition ended on the Raroia reef. Europeans visited the islands in the 16th–17th century. France occupied them in 1844 and annexed them in 1880 as a Tahitian dependency. They now form, with the GAMBIER ISLANDS, an administrative division of French Polynesia. France has used uninhabited atolls for nuclear testing.

Tuareg \ˈtwä-ˌreg\ Nomadic Berber-speaking people of the southwestern Sahara. Their feudal, matrilineal culture divides society into nobles, clergy, vassals, artisans, and laborers (once slaves). northern Tuareg live mainly in true desert; southern Tuareg live in steppe and savanna. They have traditionally engaged in herding, agriculture, convoying caravans across their territories, and raiding neighboring tribes. They combine many pre-Islamic rituals and customs with Sunni Muslim beliefs. Droughts in the 1970s and '80s reduced their numbers and eroded their traditional way of life.

tuatara \ˌtü-ə-ˈtä-rə\ Either of two species *(Sphenodon punctatus* and *S. guntheir)* of lizardlike, nocturnal REPTILES of the order Rhynchocephalia, found on certain islets of New Zealand. Up to 2 ft. (60 cm) long and weighing over 2 lbs (1 kg), tuataras have two pairs of well-developed limbs, a scaly crest down the neck and back, a third eyelid that closes horizontally, and a pineal eye between the two normal eyes. A bony arch behind the eyes distinguishes tuataras from lizards. They eats insects, other small animals, and birds' eggs. In spring, they lay 8–15 eggs away from their burrow. Tuataras may live about 100 years.

Tuatha Dé Danann \ˈtü-ə-hə-ˈdʸā-ˈdá-nən\ In Celtic mythology, a race inhabiting Ireland before the arrival of the Milesians, the ancestors of the modern Irish. Skilled in magic, they were banished from heaven because of their knowledge and descended on Ireland in a cloud of mist. They were thought to have disappeared into the hills when overcome by the Milesians. They were regarded as actual people by native historians up to the 17th century. Representative of the Celtic pantheon, they have become associated in popular legend with the numerous fairies still said to inhabit the Irish landscape.

tuba Deep-pitched valved BRASS INSTRUMENT with a widely expanding conical bore. Tubas vary in size and pitch. The tubing is coiled in an oblong shape, and the bell points upward or forward. Patented in Berlin in 1835, the tuba displaced the ophicleide to become the foundation of the brass section in the orchestra and in military and brass bands. See also EUPHONIUM, SOUSAPHONE.

Tubb, Ernest (Dale) (1914–1984) U.S. COUNTRY-MUSIC singer and songwriter. Born in Crisp, Texas, his first musical influence was the yodeling of JIMMIE RODGERS. He became one of the earliest exponents of honky-tonk with such hits as "I'm Walking the Floor over You" (1941). He joined the GRAND OLE OPRY in 1942, and became one of the first musicians to record in Nashville. He was a pioneer of the electric guitar in the early 1950s. His Nashville radio program, "Midnight Jamboree" (from 1947), helped launch such stars as the Everly Brothers and E. PRESLEY. In 1947 he starred in the first country-music show at Carnegie Hall.

tube worm Any of numerous species of sedentary, solitary or colonial, marine WORMS that spend their entire life in a tube made from special secretions or from sand grains glued together. Found worldwide, tube worms range from less than an inch (25 mm) to more than 20 ft (6 m) long. The bottom of the tube is attached to the seafloor; the mouth and tentacles are at the upper, open end. The worm breathes through gills, the tentacles, or the body wall. The tentacles, variously arranged, are used to filter-feed aquatic plants and animals. Tube worms occur in the ANNELID class Polychaeta and in the phyla Phoronida and Pogonophora. Many, mostly unnamed, forms live in deep-ocean vent communities.

tuber Short, thickened, mostly underground STEM that constitutes the resting stage of certain seed plants. It is often an organ of food storage, reproduction, or both. It bears minute scale leaves, each with a bud that has the potential for developing into a new plant. The common POTATO is a typical tuber; the much-reduced leaves and associated buds form its "eyes." The term is also used imprecisely but widely for fleshy roots or RHIZOMES that resemble tubers (e.g., the "tuber" of the DAHLIA, actually a tuberous root).

tuberculosis (TB) \tů-ˌbər-kyə-ˈlō-səs\ *formerly* **consumption** BACTERIAL disease caused by some species of MYCOBACTERIUM (tubercle BACILLUS). Mentioned in ancient Egyptian records and by HIPPOCRATES, it has occurred throughout history worldwide. In the 18th–19th century it reached near-epidemic proportions in the rapidly industrializing and urbanizing West, where it was the leading cause of death until the early 20th century. TB resurged in the 1980s, spreading from AIDS patients to others, especially in prisons, homeless shelters, and hospitals, since enclosed settings promote spread. It occurs worldwide and is still a major cause of death in many countries. The body isolates the bacilli by forming tiny tubercles (nodules) around them. This often arrests TB's progress, but if not treated, it may become active—and contagious—later. The primary form (mostly in children) is often mild but may spread through the body, producing tubercles in many organs; it can be fatal. The secondary form (mainly in young adults) starts with loss of energy and weight and persistent cough. Health deteriorates, with increasing cough, heavy sweating, and possibly pleurisy (see THORACIC cavity) and spitting up blood. Growing tubercle masses may destroy so much lung tissue that RESPIRATION cannot supply the body with enough oxygen. Other organs can be affected, with complications including MENINGITIS. A VACCINE with weakened bacteria has helped control infection, but preventing exposure by recognizing and treating active TB early is more effective. Because many strains are resistant to drugs, treatment requires at least two drugs to which the patient's strain is sensitive for at least six months; inadequate treatment lets resistant bacilli multiply. The acute disease caused by multidrug-resistant (MDR) strains is very hard to cure and usually fatal.

Tubman, Harriet (c. 1820–1913) U.S. abolitionist. Born into slavery in Dorchester Co., Md., she escaped north by the UNDERGROUND RAILROAD in 1849. She made frequent trips into the South to lead over 300 slaves to freedom, despite large rewards offered for her arrest. Known as the

"Moses of her people," she was admired by such abolitionists as JOHN BROWN, who called her General Tubman. In the Civil War, she served as a nurse, laundress, and spy for Union forces in South Carolina. She later settled in Auburn, N.Y., and was eventually granted a federal pension for her war work.

Tubman, William V(acanarat) S(hadrach) (1895–1971) President of Liberia, 1944–71. Tubman educated himself in law before entering public service, eventually ascending to the Supreme Court (1937–44). As president from 1944, he enacted suffrage and property rights for women, authorized participation in government by all ethnic groups, and established a nationwide public-school system.

Tuchman \'tək-mən\, **Barbara** *orig.* **Barbara Wertheim** (1912–1989) U.S. historian. Born in New York City, she wrote for *The Nation* and other publications before beginning to write most of the books that made her a leading popular historian. Marked by a masterly literary style and a powerful grasp of complex issues, they include *The Zimmermann Telegram* (1958); *The Guns of August* (1962, Pulitzer Prize), on the first month of World War I; *Stilwell and the American Experience in China, 1911–45* (1970, Pulitzer Prize), a study of the China–U.S. relationship; *A Distant Mirror* (1978), concerning 14th-century France; and *The March of Folly* (1984).

Barbara Tuchman.

© JERRY BAUER

Tucson \'tü-,sän\ City (pop., 2000: 486,699), southeastern Arizona. It lies along the Santa Cruz River on a SONORAN DESERT plateau rimmed by mountains. In 1700 the Spanish founded a mission nearby, and in 1776 the small walled pueblo of Tucson was made a Spanish presidio (fort). It remained the province's military headquarters under Mexican rule. The U.S. acquired the territory through the 1853 GADSDEN PURCHASE. It was the territorial capital 1867–77. It grew with the arrival of the railroad in 1880, and the discovery of silver at nearby TOMBSTONE and copper at Bisbee. Its dry, sunny climate and unique desert locale have made it a popular tourist and health resort and retirement community. It is the seat of the University of ARIZONA (1885).

Tucunas *or* **Ticunas** *or* **Tikunas** \tə-'kü-nəs\ South American Indian people living in Brazil, Peru, and Colombia. Traditional Tucunas live in the rain forest of the northwestern Amazon basin, cultivating cassava and corn, raising chickens, and hunting and gathering in the forest. They make baskets, pottery, and bark cloth, and trade animal hides and canoes for money and manufactured goods. They were once skilled hunters with blowguns, spears, and snares, but depletion of animal populations has altered old hunting patterns. They numbered about 25,000 in the late 1980s.

tudi *or* **t'u-ti** \'tü-'dē\ Type of Chinese god whose nature and functions are determined by local residents. Its chief characteristic is the limitation of its jurisdiction to a single place, such as a bridge, temple, or home. A tudi is subservient to the chenghuang, or municipal god. In most cases, a tudi originates as a person who in life aided the community. By deifying and offering sacrifices to them, residents hope to move them to show similar solicitude after death. If misfortunes visit a locality, the tudi is determined to have lost interest and a new patron is chosen.

Tudjman \'tüj-män\, **Franjo** (1922–1999) Croatian politician and president of Croatia (1990–99). He served with the partisans under Marshal TITO in World War II. He taught political science and history at the University of Zagreb 1963–67, and later wrote numerous books on history and politics. He was expelled from the Yugoslav Communist Party in 1967 for his nationalist writings, and he was imprisoned in 1972 and 1981. He became leader of the right-wing Croatian Democratic Union (1989). Elected president of Croatia, he proclaimed its independence from Yugoslavia in 1991, precipitating an armed conflict with Serbia. His excesses in the BOSNIAN CONFLICT and his autocratic rule earned Tudjman a reputation for brutality.

Tudor, Antony *orig.* **William Cook** (1908–1987) British-U.S. dancer, teacher, and choreographer. He joined MARIE RAMBERT's company in 1927, where he choreographed and danced such works as *The Planets* (1934) and *The Lilac Garden* (1936). In 1940 he moved to New York, joining the new Ballet Theatre (later AMERICAN BALLET THEATRE), where he stayed for 10 years and created many of his signature psychological ballets, including *Pillar of Fire* (1942) and *Shadow of the Wind* (1948). In the 1950s he taught at the Metropolitan Opera ballet school and at the Juilliard School. In 1974 he became associate director of the American Ballet Theatre.

Tudor, Henry See HENRY VII (England)

Tudor, House of English royal dynasty that gave five sovereigns to England (1485–1603). The Tudors originated in the 13th century but the dynasty's fortunes were established by Owen Tudor (c. 1400–1461), a Welsh adventurer who took service with HENRY V and married Henry's widow, Catherine of Valois (1401–1437). Owen and Catherine's son Edmund Tudor (c. 1430–1456) was created earl of Richmond and married Lady Margaret Beaufort (1443–1509), a descendant of John of Gaunt of the House of LANCASTER. Their son Henry Tudor claimed the English throne as HENRY VII in 1485 and cemented his claim with his marriage to Elizabeth of the House of YORK, daughter of EDWARD IV. The Tudor rose symbolized the union between the red rose of the Lancastrians and the white rose of the Yorkists. The Tudor dynasty continued in the 16th century with the reigns of HENRY VIII and his children EDWARD VI, MARY I, and ELIZABETH I. In 1603 the dynasty was succeeded by the House of STUART.

Tudor, Margaret See MARGARET TUDOR

Tudor, Mary See MARY I

Tudor style Architectural style in England (1485–1558) that made lavish use of half-timbering (see TIMBER framing), as well as ORIELS, GABLES, decorative brickwork, and rich plasterwork. Exposed diagonal bracing usually occurs at building corners, with the second story often sporting a picturesque overhang; this cantilevered construction partially counterbalances the load carried by the spanning portions of the beams.

tuff Relatively soft, porous rock that is usually formed by the compaction and cementation of volcanic ash or dust. Tuff may vary greatly not only in texture but also in chemical and mineralogical composition. In some eruptions, foaming MAGMA wells to the surface as an emulsion of hot gases and incandescent particles; the shredded pumice-like material spreads swiftly, even over gentle slopes, as a glowing avalanche (NUÉE ARDENTE) that may move many miles at speeds of 100 mph (160 kph).

Tufts University Private university in Medford, Mass., near Boston. It was established in 1852 and named after its founding benefactor, Charles Tufts. It offers bachelor's, master's, and doctoral degree programs in a wide variety of disciplines. Tufts also has schools of medicine, law and international relations (the Fletcher School), nutrition, dentistry, veterinary medicine, and biomedicine. Among its many research units are centers for the study of electro-optics and of hunger, poverty, and nutrition policy. Total enrollment is about 8,500.

Tugela River \tü-'gā-lə\ Principal river, KwaZulu/Natal province, South Africa. It rises in the Mont-aux-Sources plateau and hurtles 3,110 ft (948 m) down a series of waterfalls to cut through Tugela Gorge. It ends its 312-mi (502-km) course at the Indian Ocean. It was the scene of battles in the SOUTH AFRICAN WAR in 1899–1900. Historically, the Tugela marked the southern boundary of ZULULAND.

Tugwell, Rexford G(uy) (1891–1979) U.S. economist. Born in Sinclairville, N.Y., he joined the economics faculty of Columbia University in 1920, and in 1932 became a member of the BRAIN TRUST that advised FRANKLIN ROOSEVELT. Appointed undersecretary of agriculture, he helped formulate farm policy and other NEW DEAL economic reforms (1933–36). He chaired the New York City Planning Commission (1938–41), served as governor of Puerto Rico (1941–46), and taught at the University of Chicago (1946–57).

Tuileries Palace \'twē-lə-,rēz\ French royal residence, adjacent to the LOUVRE in Paris, destroyed by arson in 1871. The original palace, commissioned by CATHERINE DE MÉDICIS, was begun in 1564 by Philibert Delorme (c. 1515–1570); the next 200 years saw numerous additions and alterations by Jean Bullant (1520?–1578), Jacques du Cerceau (c. 1520–1585), Louis Le Vau (1612–1670), and others. The Tuileries Gardens have changed little since ANDRE LE NOTRE redesigned them in 1664. His design extended the central walkway beyond the gardens and out into the countryside to the hilltop west of the palace, where the ARC de Triomphe now stands.

Tukhachevsky \ˌtůk-ə-ˈchef-skē\, **Mikhayl (Nikolayevich)** (1893–1937) Soviet Red Army officer. In the Russian Civil War, he commanded the recapture of Siberia from ALEKSANDR KOLCHAK and led the Cossack forces against ANTON DENIKIN (1920). He thereafter played a leading role in military reform; from 1931 he directed the rearmament of the Soviet Union. He served as Soviet chief of staff (1925–28) and later as deputy commissar for defense (1931–37); he was made a marshal of the Soviet Union in 1935. A victim of the PURGE TRIALS in 1937, he was tried and executed with other top Red Army commanders.

Tukulor \ˌtü-kü-ˈlər\ Muslim people who inhabit Senegal and western Mali. Because of extended contacts with the FULANI, they speak a Fula dialect. In the 10th–18th century they were dominated by a succession of non-Tukulor groups in the kingdom of Tekrur. Around 1850 they established a empire of their own that conquered the BAMBARA kingdoms of Kaarta and Segu and extended to TOMBOUCTOU before being destroyed by the French in 1890. Today the Tukulor subsist on livestock raising, fishing, and cultivating millet and sorghum.

Tula Ancient city in Mexico, the capital of the TOLTECS, which flourished 10th–12th century. Its exact location is uncertain; the archaeological site now designated Tula, near the town of that name in Hidalgo state, has been the choice of historians, but other scholars identify Tula with what is now usually called TEOTIHUACÁN. The Tula site suggests a city that had a population in the tens of thousands. The major civic center consists of a plaza bordered by a five-stepped pyramid, two other pyramids, and two ball courts. Its art and architecture are strikingly similar to those of the AZTEC capital, TENOCHTITLÁN, and its artistic themes suggest that the Aztecs' concept of themselves as warrior-priests of the sun god was borrowed directly from Tula.

Tulane University Private university in New Orleans. It was founded in 1834 and later named for a major donor, Paul Tulane. It has a college of arts and sciences and schools of architecture, engineering, law, medicine, graduate studies, social work, and public health, among other divisions, and institutes for the study of political economy, Latin America, primates, and chemical engineering. Total enrollment is about 11,000.

tulip Any of almost 4,000 varieties of about 100 species of cultivated bulbous herbaceous plants making up the genus *Tulipa* in the LILY FAMILY, native to Eurasia. Among the most popular of all garden flowers, the tulip produces two or three thick, bluish-green leaves clustered at the base of the plant. The usually solitary inverted bell-shaped flowers have three petals and three sepals. Colors range from white through yellows and reds to brown and deep purple to almost black. Streaked blossoms get their streaks from a harmless virus infection that causes the color to disappear in patterns, letting white or yellow show through.

tulip tree *or* **tulip poplar** *or* **yellow poplar** Lofty North American ornamental and timber tree *(Liriodendron tulipifera)* of the MAGNOLIA family, not related to true POPLARS. It occurs in mixed HARDWOOD stands in eastern North America. It is taller than all other eastern broad-leaved trees (up to 197 ft, or 60 m), and its trunk often has a diameter greater than 7 ft (2 m). Long-stemmed, bright-green leaves have two to four side lobes and blunted tips. Yellowish-green tuliplike flowers have six petals, orange at their bases, and three bright-green sepals. Other characteristics include conelike clusters of winged fruits; aromatic, purplish-brown twigs; stunning golden-yellow autumn leaves; winter buds resembling a duck's bill; and resistance to pests and diseases. The wood is used to manufacture furniture parts, plywood panels, paper, boxes, and crates.

Tull, Jethro (1674–1741) British agronomist and inventor. Educated at Oxford, around 1701 he perfected a horse-drawn seed drill that economically sowed the seeds in neat rows, and later a horse-drawn hoe. He stressed the use of manure and the importance of breaking up the soil into small particles. Tull's methods, though initially attacked, were eventually adopted by many large landowners, and they helped form the basis of modern agriculture.

Tulsa City (pop., 1996 est.: 378,000), northeastern Oklahoma, on the ARKANSAS RIVER. It originated in 1836 as a settlement of Creek Indian immigrants; white settlement began in 1882 after the arrival of the railway. The discovery of oil nearby in the early 20th century launched an oil and gas boom, and phenomenal growth followed. Hundreds of major oil companies now have plants and offices in the city. It is the head of navigation for the Arkansas River Navigation System, a waterway that stretches 440 mi (708 km) to the junction of the Arkansas and MISSISSIPPI rivers. The commercial and financial center of a rich agricultural area, it is the seat of the University of Tulsa (1894) and Oral Roberts University (1965).

tumbleweed Plant that breaks away from its roots and is driven about by the wind as a light rolling mass, scattering seeds as it goes. Examples include pigweed (*Amaranth retroflexus,* a widespread weed in the western U.S.) and other AMARANTHS, tumbling mustard, Russian thistle, the steppe plant *Colutea arborea,* and the grass *Spinifex* of Indonesian shores and Australian steppes.

Tumen River \ˈtü-ˈmən\ River, Korea. It forms the northeastern frontier of North Korea with China and Russia. It originates on Mount Paektu, Korea's highest mountain, and flows generally north and northeast before turning southeast to enter the Sea of JAPAN. It is 324 mi (521 km) long, but navigable for only 53 mi (85 km). Many historic battle sites lie along its banks.

tumor *or* **neoplasm** Mass of abnormal tissue that arises from normal cells, has no useful function, and tends to grow. Cell abnormalities may include increased size or number, or loss of characteristics that differentiate their tissue of origin. Cells in malignant tumors (see CANCER) have a distorted size, shape, and/or structure. Less differentiated cells tend to grow faster. Malignant tumors invade tissues locally and spread (metastasize) in blood or lymph: the stronger the tendency to metastasize, the more malignant the tumor. Tumors may not cause pain until they press on or invade nerves. Both benign and malignant tumors can press on nearby structures, block vessels, or produce excess hormones, all of which can cause death. Benign tumors remain as a solid mass that can be removed by surgery if accessible; they can consist of various tissues and may become malignant; malignant tumors, though they may remain quiescent for a time, never become benign.

tuna Any of seven species (genus *Thunnus,* family Scombridae) of commercially valuable food fishes. Species range from the 80-lb (36-kg) ALBACORE to the bluefin tuna *(T. thynnus),* which grows to 14 ft (4.3 m) long and weighs up to 1,800 lbs (800 kg). Tunas have a slender, streamlined body and a forked or crescent-shaped tail. They are unique among fishes in having a vascular system modified to maintain a body temperature above the water temperature. Though slow swimmers, they migrate long distances over all the world's oceans. They eat fishes, squid, shellfish, and plankton.

tundra Treeless, level or rolling ground above the TAIGA in polar regions (Arctic tundra) or on high mountains (alpine tundra), characterized by bare ground and rock or by such vegetation as mosses, lichens, small herbs, and low shrubs. Animal species are limited by harsh environmental conditions. In the Arctic tundra they include lemmings, the Arctic fox, the Arctic wolf, caribou, reindeer, and musk-oxen. In the alpine tundra many animals, including mountain sheep and wildcats, descend to warmer zones during winter. The climate of alpine tundra is more moderate and has a higher amount of rainfall than does Arctic tundra. The freezing climate of the Arctic produces a layer of permanently frozen soil (PERMAFROST). An overlying layer of soil alternates between freezing and thawing with seasonal temperature variations. Alpine tundras have a freeze-thaw layer but no permafrost. Because Arctic tundras receive extremely long periods of daylight and darkness (lasting between one and four months), BIOLOGICAL RHYTHMS tend to be adjusted more to variations in temperature than to variations in sunlight. Arctic tundra covers about one-tenth of the earth's surface. Alpine tundras begin above the timberline of spruce and firs. Because of the small number of plant and animal species and the fragility of the food chains in tundra regions, natural or mechanical damage to any element of the habitat affects the whole ecosystem.

tuned circuit Electrically conducting pathway containing both INDUCTANCE and CAPACITANCE elements. When these elements are connected in series, the CIRCUIT presents low ELECTRICAL IMPEDANCE to ALTERNATING current of the same frequency as the resonance frequency of the circuit, and high impedance to current of other frequencies. The circuit's resonance frequency is determined by the values of inductance and capacitance. When the circuit elements are connected in parallel, the impedance is high at the resonance frequency and low at other frequencies. With their ability to pass only certain frequencies, tuned circuits are important in, for example, radio and television receivers.

Tung Ch'i-ch'ang See Dong Qichang

Tung Chung-shu See Dong Zhongshu

Tung-lin Academy See Donglin Academy

Tung-Pei See Manchuria

Tung-ting Hu See Dongting Hu

tungsten *or* **wolfram** \'wůl-frəm\ Metallic chemical element, one of the transition elements, chemical symbol W, atomic number 74. Exceptionally strong, white to grayish, and brittle, it has the highest melting point (6,170°F, or 3,410°C), greatest high-temperature strength, and lowest thermal expansion coefficient of any metal. Its chief uses are in steels to increase hardness and strength and in lightbulb filaments. It is also used in electrical contacts, rocket nozzles, chemical apparatus, high-speed rotors, and solar-energy devices. Tungsten is relatively inert, but compounds (in which it has various valences) are known. The most important, tungsten carbide, noted for its hardness, is used to increase the wear-resistance of cast iron and of tools' cutting edges.

tungsten-halogen lamp See halogen lamp

Tungusic languages See Manchu-Tungus languages

Tunguska event \tůŋ-'gü-skə\ (June 30, 1908) Enormous aerial explosion that flattened about 500,000 acres (2,000 sq km) of pine forest near the Stony Tunguska River in central Siberia. Its energy was equivalent to that of 10–15 megatons of TNT. Uncertain evidence suggests that a large comet fragment, composed mainly of ice and dust, may have disintegrated in the atmosphere high above earth's surface, creating a fireball and blast wave but no crater. Eyewitnesses spoke of a fireball lighting the horizon, initially visible from about 500 mi (800 km) away, followed by trembling ground and hot winds strong enough to throw people down and shake buildings. The object's vaporization scattered dust high into the atmosphere, causing abnormally bright nighttime skies in Siberia and Europe for some time afterward.

tunicate \'tü-ni-kət\ Any of some 2,000 species (chordate subphylum Tunicata, or Urochordata) of small marine invertebrates that are abundant worldwide. Tunicates are either sessile (permanently attached), free-swimming, or pelagic (floating). The name tunicate derives from a secreted protective covering (the tunic) containing cellulose. Pelagic species often form colonies that may be 13 ft (4 m) long. Some free-swimming species are too small to see. Adults filter-feed on microorganisms. Sessile forms growing on ships' hulls may be a nuisance, but some species are pharmaceutically useful. See also sea squirt.

tuning and temperament Two aspects of assuring that musical tones sound well together. Tuning assures a good sound for a given pair of tones; temperament compromises the tuning to assure a good sound for any and all pairs of tones. Two vibrating strings sound best together if the ratio between their lengths can be expressed by two small whole numbers. If two strings vibrate in a ratio of 2:1, the vibrations will always coincide and so reinforce each other. But if they vibrate in a ratio of 197:100 (very close to 2:1), they will cancel each other out three times per second, creating audible "beats." These beats are what make something sound "out of tune." Since a tone produced by one ratio will not necessarily agree with the same tone created by repeatedly applying another ratio, either some intervals must be mistuned to allow for the perfect tuning of others or all intervals must be slightly mistuned. Before 1700, several systems were used based on the former compromise, including "just intonation"; since then, the compromise represented by "equal temperament," in which the ratios represented by each pair of adjacent notes are identical, has prevailed.

Tunis \'tü-nəs\ City (pop., 1994: 674,000), capital of Tunisia. Situated on an isthmus between two lagoons, its port, Halq al-Wadi, is on the end of the eastern lagoon, the Lake of Tunis. Founded by Libyans, it later was a small town under Carthage; it became important after the Muslim conquest in the 7th century AD. It became the capital city under the Abbasid dynasty (9th century), and one of the leading cities of the Muslim world under the Hafsid dynasty (13th century). The Spanish and Turks held it during the 16th century. It was occupied by the Germans in 1942. It was made the national capital when Tunisia gained independence from France in 1956. It produces textiles, carpets, and olive oil, and has metallurgical industries. Tourism is also important.

Tunisia \tü-'nē-zhə\ *officially* **Republic of Tunisia** Nation, North Africa. Area: 59,664 sq mi (154,530 sq km). Population (1997 est.): 9,218,000. Capital: Tunis. The population is of Arab and Berber ancestry. Languages: Arabic (official), French. Religion: Islam (official). Currency: Tunisian dinar. Tunisia comprises a coastal region, mountains, an extensive plateau, a marshy area with shallow salt lakes, and a tract of the Sahara desert. The Medjerda is its largest (286 mi, or 460 km long) and only perennial river. Tunisia contains some of the largest phosphate and natural gas reserves in Africa, as well as substantial oil reserves. Major economic sectors are services, agriculture, light industries, and the production and export of petroleum and phosphates. Tourism, focusing on Tunisia's beaches and Roman ruins, is also important. Tunisia is a republic with one legislative house; its chief of state is the president, and the head of government is the prime minister. From the 12th century BC the Phoenicians had a series of trading posts on the North African coast. By the 6th century BC the Carthaginian kingdom encompassed most of present-day Tunisia. The Romans ruled from 146 BC until the Muslim Arab invasions in the mid-7th century AD. The area was fought over, won, and lost by many, including the Abbasids, the Almohads, Spain, and the Ottoman Turks, who finally conquered it in 1574 and held it until the late 19th century. For a time it maintained autonomy as the French, British, and Italians contended for the region. In 1881 it became a French protectorate. In World War II U.S. and British forces captured it in 1943 to end a brief German occupation. In 1956 France granted it full independence; Habib Bourguiba assumed power and remained in office until 1987.

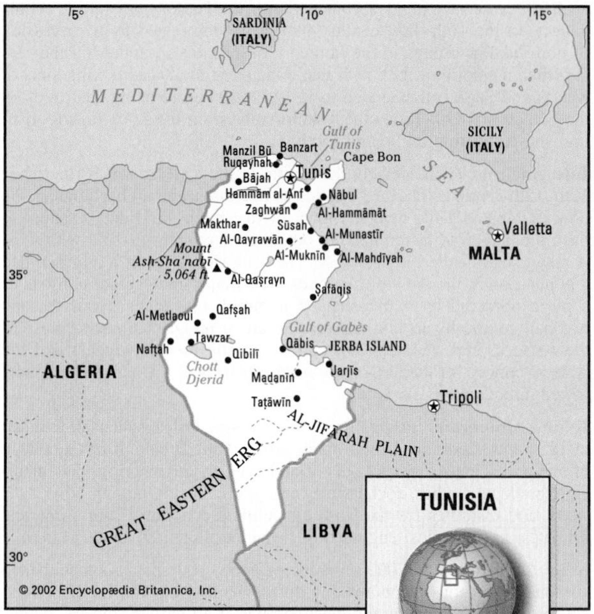

tunnel Horizontal or nearly horizontal underground or underwater passageway. Tunnels are used for mining, as passageways for trains and motor vehicles, for diverting rivers around damsites, for housing underground installations such as power plants, and for conducting water. Ancient civilizations used tunnels to carry water for irrigation and drinking, and in the 22nd century BC the Babylonians built a tunnel for pedestrian traffic under the Euphrates River. The Romans built aqueduct tunnels through mountains by heating the rock face with fire and rapidly cooling it with water, causing the rock to crack. The introduction of gunpowder blasting in the 17th century marked a great advance in solid-rock excavation. For softer soils, excavation is accomplished using devices such as the tunneling mole, with its rotating wheel that continuously excavates material and loads it onto a conveyor belt. Railroad transportation

S
T
U
V

in the 19th–20th century led to a tremendous expansion in the number and length of tunnels. Brick and stone were used for support in early tunnels, but in modern tunneling steel is generally used until a concrete lining can be installed. A common method of lining involves spraying SHOTCRETE onto the tunnel crown immediately after excavation.

tunneling *or* **barrier penetration** In physics, the passage of a particle through a seemingly impassable energy barrier. Though a particle's energy may be too low to surmount a barrier in classical physics, the particle may still cross the barrier as a consequence of its quantum-mechanical wave properties. An important application of this phenomenon is in the operation of the scanning tunneling microscope.

Tunney, Gene *orig.* **James Joseph** (1898–1978) U.S. boxer. Born in New York City, he boxed in the Marine Corps, earning the nickname "the Fighting Marine." He defeated JACK DEMPSEY in 1926 to become the world heavyweight champion. In a controversial rematch in Chicago in 1927, Dempsey knocked Tunney to the canvas in the seventh round but failed to retire immediately to a neutral corner, thus delaying the count; the "long count" allowed Tunney to rise and win the 10-round fight. He retired the next year with a record of 65 wins in 77 bouts.

Tupac Amarú \tü-'päk-ä-'mär-ü\ Revolutionary group in Peru, founded in 1983. It is best known for holding 490 people hostage in the Japanese embassy in Lima (1996) in an effort to gain release of jailed comrades. After a standoff of several weeks, soldiers stormed the embassy and killed all the guerrillas. Defections have apparently since decreased its membership to less than 100. The group takes its name from the Indian revolutionary Tupac Amarú II (*orig.* José Gabriel Condorcanqui, 1742?–1781), who in 1780 led Peruvian Indian peasants in the last widespread rebellion against Spain. The Indians identified him with his ancestor Tupac Amarú (died 1572), ATAHUALLPA's second successor as leader of the INCA, who was executed by the Spaniards.

Tupamaro \ˌtü-pə-'mä-rō\ Member of the National Liberation Movement, an Uruguayan leftist urban guerrilla organization founded c. 1963 and named for TUPAC AMARÚ. The earliest Tupamaro efforts involved robbing banks and businesses and distributing the goods to the poor, but in the late 1960s they mounted a wave of violence aimed at the authorities. The military government that seized power in 1973 launched an offensive against them, killing some 300 and imprisoning 3,000 others. When democratic rule returned in 1985, the Tupamaros were reorganized as a political party.

tupelo \'tü-pə-ˌlō\ Any of about seven species of trees that make up the genus *Nyssa* in the sour gum family (Nyssaceae). Five are found in moist or swampy areas of eastern North America, one in eastern Asia, and one in western Malaysia. They all have horizontal or hanging branches, broad leaves, and male and female flowers on different plants. North American species bear greenish-white flowers and small bluish-black or purple berries. The most widespread North American species is the BLACK GUM. Tupelo wood, most of which comes from the water tupelo *(N. aquatica)*, is pale yellow to light brown, fine-textured, and strong. It is used for crates and boxes, flooring, wooden utensils, and veneers.

Tupian languages \tü-'pē-ən\ Family of South American Indian languages with at least seven subgroups, spoken or formerly spoken in scattered areas from southern French Guiana south to southernmost Brazil and Paraguay and east to eastern Bolivia. About a third of the estimated 37 known Tupian languages are extinct. The largest subgroup, Tupí-Guaraní, includes the extinct language Tupinambá, the source for borrowings of many New World flora and fauna terms into Portuguese and hence other European languages. Another language of the subgroup, Guaraní, is spoken as a first or second language by more than 90% of Paraguayans, who consider it a token of Paraguayan identity.

Tupolev *officially* **ANTK imeni A.N. Tupoleva** *formerly* **OKB-156** Russian aerospace design bureau that is a major producer of passenger airliners and military bombers. It originated in 1922 as a group within the U.S.S.R's Central Aerohydrodynamics Institute to develop military aircraft. Under ANDREI TUPOLEV, it created the TB-1 (ANT-4) all-metal, cantilever-wing bomber (first flights 1925–26). After several years' confinement for political reasons, Tupolev was freed, and in 1943 he reestablished his team as the design bureau OKB-156. At the end of World War II, the bureau built the Tu-4 strategic bomber, a copy of the U.S. B-29. In the 1950s it produced the turboprop Tu-95 heavy bomber (NATO, "Bear"), which became a Soviet mainstay, and the first Soviet jetliner, the Tu-104 (first flown 1955). Between the late 1950s and early '80s, it introduced new supersonic bombers, including the variable-wing Tu-22M ("Backfire") and Tu-160 ("Blackjack"), and airliners such as the Tu-114 turboprop, Tu-154 trijet, and Tu-144 supersonic transport. In 1989, in honor of Tupolev (died 1972), the bureau was renamed ANTK imeni A.N. Tupoleva. After the dissolution of the U.S.S.R. in 1991, it became a joint stock company with the Russian government holding a limited financial interest. In the 1990s its projects involved jetliners such as the Tu-204 (in service 1996) and Tu-324.

Tupolev \'tü-pəl-yif\, **Andrei (Nikolayevich)** (1888–1972) Russian aircraft designer. In 1918 he cofounded the U.S.S.R.'s Central Aerohydrodynamics Institute, and in 1922 he became head of its design bureau (see TUPOLEV), producing airplanes of all-metal construction. Arrested in 1937 on charges of activities against the state, he was assigned to work on the design of military aircraft. Under confinement, he led a team that produced the Tu-2 twin-engine tactical bomber, which was widely used in World War II. Freed during the war, Tupolev and his reestablished design bureau replicated the U.S. B-29; the resulting Tu-4 became the Soviet Union's principal strategic bomber until the mid-1950s. After adapting jet propulsion to several piston-engine airframes, Tupolev introduced the swept-wing Tu-16 (NATO, "Badger") jet bomber (first flown 1952) and its civilian derivative Tu-104 (1955), one of the first jet transports to provide regular passenger service. Tupolev and his son Alexei headed the effort that produced the Tu-144 supersonic transport, the first passenger jet to exceed Mach 1 (1969).

Tura, Cosimo \'tü-rä\ *or* **Cosmè Tura** (c. 1430–1495) Italian painter. Court painter to the ESTE family at Ferrara, he was influenced by ANDREA MANTEGNA and PIERO DELLA FRANCESCA. A master of allegory and decorative painting, he was the founder and first significant figure of the school of Ferrara. His work is characterized by a mannered, nervous, and wiry line, carefully rendered detail, and brilliant color.

Turabi \tu̇-'rä-bē\, **Hassan abd Allah al-** (born 1932) Sudanese Muslim religious scholar and lawyer. He studied at London University and the Sorbonne. While teaching law at the University of Khartoum (1957–65), he participated in the 1958 revolution that ended military rule. He later served in the national legislature (1965–67). He supported the 1985 overthrow of GAAFAR MOHAMED EL-NIMEIRI. He is secretary general of the Popular Arab and Islamic Congress, the force behind the Sudanese government.

turbidity current Underwater current of abrasive sediments. Such currents appear to be relatively short-lived, transient phenomena that occur at great depths. They are thought to be caused by the slumping of sediment that has piled up at the top of the continental slope, particularly at the heads of submarine canyons. Slumping of large masses of sediment creates a dense slurry, which then flows down the canyon to spread out over the ocean floor and deposit a layer of sand in deep water. Repeated deposition forms submarine fans, analogous to the alluvial fans found at the mouths of river canyons.

turbine \'tər-bən, 'tər-ˌbīn\ Any of various devices that convert the ENERGY in a stream of fluid into mechanical energy by passing the stream through a system of fixed and moving fanlike blades and causing the latter to rotate. A turbine looks like a large wheel with many small radiating blades around its rim. There are four broad classes of turbine: water (hydraulic), steam, wind, and gas. The most important application of the first three is the generation of electricity; gas turbines are most often used in aircraft.

turbojet JET ENGINE in which a TURBINE-driven COMPRESSOR draws in and compresses air, forcing it into a combustion chamber into which fuel is injected. Ignition causes the gases to expand and to rush first through the turbine and then through a nozzle at the rear. Forward thrust is generated as a reaction to the rearward momentum of the exhaust gases. The turbofan or fanjet, a modification of the turbojet, came into common use in the 1960s. In the turbofan, some of the incoming air is bypassed around the combustion chamber and is accelerated to the rear by a turbine-operated fan. It moves a much greater mass of air than the simple turbojet, providing advantages in power and economy. See also RAMJET.

turboprop Hybrid engine that provides jet thrust and also drives a propeller. It is similar to the TURBOJET except that an added TURBINE, behind the combustion chamber, works through a shaft and speed-reducing gears to turn a propeller at the front of the engine. Because of improvements in turbojet design, the turboprop, which is less efficient at high speeds, lost much of its importance in the 1960s, though it is still used for relatively short-range aircraft.

turbot \'tər-bət\ Species (*Scophthalmus maximus*, family Scophthalmidae, or Bothidae) of broad-bodied European FLATFISH, a highly valued food fish. It lives along sand and gravel shores. It is left-sided (with eyes normally on the left side of the head) and scaleless; the head and body are studded with numerous bony knobs. Turbots grow to, at most, 40 in. (1 m) long and weigh about 55 lbs (25 kg). Color varies with the surroundings but is usually gray-brown or light brown with darker markings. A related species is the Black Sea turbot *(S. maeoticus).* Certain right-sided Pacific flatfish (genus *Pleuronichthys,* family Pleuronectidae) are also called turbot.

turbulence In FLUID MECHANICS, a flow condition (see TURBULENT flow) in which local speed and pressure change unpredictably as an average flow is maintained. Common examples are wind and water swirling around obstructions, or fast flow (REYNOLDS NUMBER greater than 2,100) of any sort. Eddies, vortices, and a reduction in DRAG are characteristics of turbulence. Lowered drag enables golf balls to travel farther than they would do otherwise, and the dimpled surface of golf balls is meant to encourage turbulence in the BOUNDARY layer. If swimsuits with rough surfaces help swimmers to move faster, as has been claimed, the same explanation may apply.

turbulent flow Fluid flow in which the fluid undergoes irregular fluctuations, or mixing. The speed of the fluid at a point is continuously undergoing changes in magnitude and direction, which results in swirling and eddying as the bulk of the fluid moves in a specific direction. Common examples of turbulent flow include atmospheric and ocean currents, blood flow in arteries, oil transport in pipelines, lava flow, flow through pumps and turbines, and the flow in boat wakes and around aircraft wing tips.

Turcoman See TURKMEN

Turenne \tü-'ren\, **vicomte (Viscount) de** *orig.* **Henri de La Tour d'Auvergne** (1611–1675) French military leader. He earned his reputation as a military leader in the Thirty Years' War, especially with the capture of Turin (1640). Made a marshal of France (1643), he commanded the French army in Germany and joined the Swedish army in conquering Bavaria (1648). In France he joined the aristocrats in the FRONDE (1649), but later he skillfully commanded the royal army to defeat the forces led by the prince de CONDÉ, who had allied himself with Spain, and to bring about the Peace of the PYRENEES (1659), which ended France's war with Spain. Appointed marshal-general (1660), Turenne marched alongside LOUIS XIV in joint command of the French armies in the War of DEVOLUTION (1667–68). His bold strategies won numerous victories against the imperial army in Germany (1672–75), but he was killed in action at Sasbach. He was buried with the kings of France at Saint-Denis and later moved to the Invalides by NAPOLEON, who esteemed Turenne as the greatest military leader in history.

Turenne, detail of a portrait by Charles Le Brun; in the Musée National de Versailles et des Trianons.
CLICHE DES MUSEES NATIONAUX, PARIS

turf In horticulture, the surface layer of soil with its matted, dense vegetation, usually GRASSES grown for ornamental or recreational use. Such turf grasses include Kentucky BLUEGRASS, creeping BENT grass, fine or red fescue, and PERENNIAL ryegrass among the popular cool-season types, and Bermuda grass, zoysia grass, and St. Augustine grass among the warm-season types. Turf grasses are often grown on turf, or sod, farms. Plugs, blocks, squares, or strips are cut and transplanted to areas where they quickly establish and grow. Lawns are fine-textured turfs that are mowed regularly and closely to develop into dense, uniformly green coverings that beautify open spaces and provide sports playing surfaces (e.g., tennis lawns, golf and bowling greens, and racing turfs).

Turgenev \tu̇r-'g^{y}ā-n^{y}if\, **Ivan (Sergeyevich)** (1818–1883) Russian novelist, poet, and playwright. His years at the University of Berlin convinced him of the West's superiority and the need for Russia to Westernize. He lived in Europe after c. 1862. He is known for realistic, affectionate portrayals of the Russian peasantry and for penetrating studies of the Russian intelligentsia who were attempting to move the country into a new age. His most famous early work is "The Diary of a Superfluous Man" (1850), which supplied the epithet "superfluous man" for the weak-willed intellectual common in 19th-century Russian literature. He gained fame with the short-story cycle *A Sportman's Sketches* (1852), which criticizes serfdom. His dramatic masterpiece, *A Month in the Country* (1855), and the novel *Rudin* (1856) followed. His interest in change and intergenerational differences is reflected in *On the Eve* (1860) and the controversial *Fathers and Sons* (1862), his greatest novel. *Smoke* (1867) caricatures both the left and right wings of the intelligentsia. The late *A Lear of the Steppes* (1870) and *Torrents of Spring* (1872) combine eloquent nostalgia with quasi-fantasy, while *Virgin Soil* (1877) focuses on populists who hope to sow revolution among the peasantry.

Ivan Turgenev.
FROM THE COLLECTION OF DAVID MAGARSHACK

turgor \'tər-gər\ Pressure exerted by fluid in a cell that presses the cell membrane against the cell wall. Turgor is what makes living plant tissue rigid. Loss of turgor, resulting from the loss of water from plant cells, causes flowers and leaves to wilt. Turgor plays a key role in the opening and closing of stomata (see STOMA) in leaves.

Turgot \tu̇r-'gō\, **Anne-Robert-Jacques** *later* **baron de l'Aulne** (1727–1781) French administrator and economist. He entered the royal administrative branch of the magistracy in 1753, then became intendant (governor) of Limoges (1761–74), where he instituted economic and administrative reforms. A PHYSIOCRAT, in 1766 he wrote his best-known work, *Reflections on the Formation and Distribution of Wealth.* In 1774 he was appointed comptroller general by LOUIS XVI and introduced his Six Edicts to expand economic reforms. His effort to abolish the CORVÉE (unpaid forced labor by peasants) was opposed by the privileged classes, and he was dismissed in 1776.

Turin *Italian* **Torino** City (pop., 1996 est.: 923,000), PIEDMONT region, Italy. Located on the PO RIVER, it was founded by the Taurini. It was partly destroyed by HANNIBAL in 218 BC. It was made a Roman military colony under Emperor AUGUSTUS. A part of the Lombard duchy in the 6th century AD, it became the seat of government under CHARLEMAGNE (742–814). It passed to the House of SAVOY in 1046. The capital of the kingdom of SARDINIA in 1720, it was occupied by the French during the NAPOLEONIC WARS. The political and intellectual center of the RISORGIMENTO movement, it served as the first capital of a united Italy 1861–65. During World War II it sustained heavy damage from Allied air raids, but was rebuilt. It is the center of Italy's automotive industry and an international fashion center. The Shroud of TURIN has been housed in its 15th century cathedral since the 16th century.

Turin, Shroud of Linen fragment that for centuries was said to be the burial garment of JESUS. It has been preserved since 1578 in the royal chapel of the Cathedral of San Giovanni Battista in Turin, Italy. Measuring 14 ft 3 in. by 3 ft 7 in. (4.3 m by 1.1 m), it appears to portray images of the back and front of a gaunt, sunken-eyed man. The images contain markings that correspond to the STIGMATA and stains presumed to be blood. It emerged historically in 1354 and went on exhibition in 1389, first as a representation of the true shroud and eventually as the genuine article. In 1988 independent tests determined that the cloth was made c. 1260–1390.

Turing \'tu̇r-iŋ\, **Alan (Mathison)** (1912–1954) English mathematician and logician. He studied at Cambridge University and at Princeton's Institute for Advanced Study. In his seminal 1936 paper "On Computable Numbers," he proved that there cannot exist any universal algorithmic method of determining truth in mathematics and that mathematics will always contain undecidable (as opposed to unknown) propositions. That paper also introduced the TURING MACHINE. He believed that computers eventually would be capable of thought indistinguishable from that of a human and proposed a simple test (see TURING TEST) to assess this capability. His papers on the subject are widely acknowledged as the foundation of research in ARTIFICIAL INTELLIGENCE. He did valuable work in CRYPTOGRAPHY during World War II; after the war he taught at the University of Manchester. His suicide at 41 followed an arrest for homosexual acts and extreme medical treatments aimed at changing his sexual orientation.

Turing machine Hypothetical computing device proposed by ALAN M. TURING (1936). Not actually a machine, it is an idealized mathematical model that reduces the logical structure of any computing device to its essentials. It consists of an infinitely extensible tape, a tape head that is capable of performing various operations on the tape, and a modifiable control mechanism in the head that can store instructions. As envisaged by Turing, it performs its functions in a sequence of discrete steps. His extrapolation of the essential features of INFORMATION PROCESSING was instrumental in the development of modern DIGITAL COMPUTERS, which share his basic scheme of an input/output device (tape and tape reader), central processing unit (CPU, or control mechanism), and stored MEMORY.

Turing test Test proposed by ALAN M. TURING to determine whether a computer can be said to "think." Turing suggested the "imitation game," wherein a remote human interrogator, within a fixed time frame, must distinguish between a computer and a human subject based on their replies to questions posed by the interrogator. A series of such tests would measure the computer's success at "thinking" by the probability of its being misidentified as the human subject. The test is performed today in competitions that test the success of ARTIFICIAL INTELLIGENCE.

Turkana, Lake *or* **Lake Rudolf** Lake, mainly in northern Kenya. The fourth-largest of the eastern African lakes, it lies 1,230 ft (375 m) above sea level in eastern Africa's GREAT RIFT VALLEY, and covers an area of 2,473 sq mi (6,405 sq km). The three main islands in the lake are volcanic. The lake is relatively shallow; its greatest recorded depth is 240 ft (73 m). Having no outlet, the lake's waters are brackish. Sudden storms are frequent, rendering navigation treacherous. It is a rich reservoir of fish.

Turkana remains See LAKE TURKANA REMAINS

turkey Either of two species of birds in the family Meleagrididae. The North American common turkey *(Meleagris gallopavo)* has been domesticated since pre-Columbian times. The adult male has a naked, bright-red head, a fleshy red ornament (snood) growing over the bill, and a fleshy wattle on the throat. The male (gobbler or tom) may be 50 in. (1.3 m) long and may weigh over 20 lbs (10 kg). Wild turkeys inhabit woodlands near water, eating seeds, insects, and an occasional frog or lizard. Males assemble a harem, and each hen lays 8–15 eggs in a hollow in the ground. An excellent source of meat and easily shot, the wild turkey was practically exterminated by European settlers; conservation efforts have reestablished it in much of its former range. The ocellated turkey *(Agriocharis,* or *Meleagris, ocellata)* of Central America has never been domesticated.

Male common turkey (*Meleagris gallopavo*), displaying.

S.C. BISSEROT—BRUCE COLEMAN INC.

Turkey *officially* **Republic of Turkey** Nation, western Asia and southeastern Europe. Area: 300,948 sq mi (779,452 sq km); about 97% lies in Asia. Population (2002 est.): 67,140,000. Capital: ANKARA. Ethnic groups include the Turks and Kurds. Languages: Turkish (official), Kurdish, Arabic. Religions: Islam (mostly Sunnite); Christianity and Judaism to a small extent. Currency: Turkish lira. Turkey is a mountainous country with an extensive plateau covering central ASIA MINOR. The highest peak is Mount ARARAT. The TAURUS MTNS. lie in the south. Its rivers include the TIGRIS, EUPHRATES, KIZIL IRMAK, and MENDERES. It is a major

producer and exporter of chromite, and also mines iron ore, coal, lignite, bauxite, and copper. It is the Middle East's leading steel producer. Chief agricultural products include wheat, barley, olives, and tobacco. Tourism also is important. It is a republic with one legislative house; its chief of state is the president, and the head of government is the prime minister. Turkey's early history corresponds to that of ASIA MINOR, the BYZANTINE EMPIRE, and the OTTOMAN EMPIRE. Byzantine rule emerged when CONSTANTINE THE GREAT made Constantinople (now ISTANBUL) his capital. The Ottoman Empire, begun in the 12th century, dominated for more than 600 years; it ended in 1918 after the YOUNG TURK revolt precipitated its demise. Under the leadership of MUSTAFA KEMAL ATATURK, a republic was proclaimed in 1923, and the caliphate was abolished in 1924. Turkey remained neutral throughout most of World War II, siding with the Allies in 1945. Since the war it has alternated between civil and military governments and has had several conflicts with Greece over CYPRUS. The 1990s saw political and civic turmoil between Islamicists and secularists and ongoing ethnic tension with Kurdish separatists.

turkey vulture *or* **turkey buzzard** Species *(Cathartes aura)* of long-winged, long-tailed VULTURE (family Cathartidae), about 30 in. (75 cm) long, with dark plumage, whitish beak and legs, bare red head covered with whitish bumps, and a 6-ft (1.8-m) wingspread. It uses its keen sense of smell to find carrion. It occurs throughout the Americas except in northern Canada; the northerly and southernmost populations are migratory.

Turkic languages Family of more than 20 ALTAIC languages spoken by some 135 million people from the Balkans to central Siberia. The traditional division of Turkic is into four groups. The southeastern or Uighur group comprises Uighur, spoken mainly in Xinjiang, China; and Uzbek, spoken mainly in Uzbekistan, other Central Asian republics, and northern Afghanistan. The southwestern or Oğuz (Oghuz) group includes TURKISH; Azerbaijani (Azeri), spoken in Azerbaijan and northwestern Iran; Crimean Tatar (Crimean Turkish), spoken mostly in Ukraine and Uzbekistan; and Turkmen, used in Turkmenistan, northern Iran, and northern Afghanistan. The northwestern or Kipchak group includes Kazakh, spoken in Kazakhstan, other Central Asian republics, and western China and Mongolia; Kyrgyz (Kirghiz), spoken in Kyrgyzstan, other Central Asian republics, and western China; TATAR; Baskhir, spoken in Bashkortostan and adjacent areas in Russia; Karachay-Balkar and Kumyk, spoken in the Russian Caucasus; and Karaim, with a few speakers in Lithuania and parts of southwestern Ukraine. The northeastern or Altai group comprises a group of languages and dialects spoken in Siberia northeast of the Irtysh River and in adjacent parts of Mongo-

S
T
U
V

lia, including Altai, Khakas, Shor, and Tuvan; and Yakut (Sakha), spoken in Yakutia and adjacent areas. Distinct from all the other languages is Chuvash, spoken in Russia's Chuvash Republic and adjacent areas. The earliest attestations of Turkic are a group of 8th-century funerary inscriptions of northern Mongolia, in a distinctive writing system called runic script, or Turkic runes. With the Islamicization of nearly all Turkic peoples southwest of the Irtysh beginning c. 900, Turkic languages began to adopt the ARABIC ALPHABET. Today the LATIN and CYRILLIC alphabets are more extensively used.

Turkish Angora cat Breed of longhaired DOMESTIC CAT that probably arose from a domesticated cat of Tatars who migrated to Turkey, where it is now regarded as a national treasure. It has a long body, fine bones, a pointed face, and a silky, medium-length coat. White is the most popular color, but it may be of any solid color or any pattern of two or more colors.

Turkish bath Bath originating in the Middle East, combining exposure to warm air, steam immersion, massage, and a cold bath or shower. The Turkish bath *(hammam)* reflects the fusion of the massage and cosmetic aspects of the Eastern bath tradition and the plumbing and heating techniques of the Romans. Turkish baths were smaller than the Roman THERMAE and more sparsely lit. The baths at Constantinople were domed, and rooms were richly decorated with marble or mosaics. Used for socializing and relaxation as well as bathing, the *hammam* was popular throughout the Islamic world; some baths are still in use. In the 19th century, the Turkish bath was adapted and imported to Europe and the U.S.

Turkish language TURKIC language of Turkey, spoken by about 90% of its population. Turkish has about 59 million speakers, with many enclaves in the Balkans and Cyprus (dating from Ottoman times) and in West Europe. Turkish was introduced into Anatolia with the invasion of Turkmen tribes in the 13th–14th century. Anatolian Turkish, written in the ARABIC ALPHABET, is first attested in the 13th century. Ottoman Turkish was so heavily influenced by Persian and Arabic that it lost some of its Turkic characteristics and was incomprehensible to lower social strata. Efforts to re-Turkicize the language began in the 18th century but did not make serious gains until the 20th century and the founding of the Turkish republic. Much Perso-Arabic vocabulary was removed, and the LATIN ALPHABET was adopted with the addition of diacritics to symbolize sounds peculiar to Turkish. Turkish is linguistically a typical Turkic language, with vowel harmony (correspondence of vowel features across syllables), agglutinative MORPHOLOGY, and subject-object-verb word order.

Turkish van cat Breed of semi-longhaired DOMESTIC CAT distinguished mainly by its unusual color pattern: white, with colored markings only on the head and tail. "Van" is a common term in the breed's native region, central and South Asia, used also to describe other cats with similar markings. The breed was brought to Europe by returning crusaders. A unique feature is its cashmere-like, waterproof coat; it loves water, and in its native region it has been called the swimming cat. They are large, active, and intelligent.

Turkistan *or* **Turkestan** Historical region, central Asia. The total area of more than 1,000,000 sq mi (2,600,000 sq km) was divided by the PAMIR and TIAN SHAN ranges into West and East Turkistan. West Turkistan, or Russian Turkestan, came under Russian rule in the 19th century; it included present-day Turkmenistan, Uzbekistan, Tajikistan, Kyrgyzstan, and southern Kazakhstan. East Turkistan, or Chinese Turkestan, was annexed by China in the 8th century; it included the former province of Sinkiang (now XINJIANG UYGUR).

Turkmen *or* **Turkoman** *or* **Turcoman** Muslim people belonging to the southwestern branch of the Turkic linguistic group. They number more than 4.3 million; most live in Turkmenistan (formerly part of the Soviet Union) and adjacent parts of Central Asia, while others live in Turkey, northern Iran, and Afghanistan, and there are pockets in northern Iraq and Syria. Initially a nomadic pastoral people living in tent villages, those under Soviet rule took up agriculture. They have traditionally divided themselves by economic function, each division being headed by a KHAN.

Turkmenistan Republic, western central Asia. Area: 188,500 sq mi (488,100 sq km). Population (1997 est.): 4,695,000. Capital: ASHGABAT. Turkmen make up more than 70% of the population, followed by Russians, Uzbeks, Kazaks, Tatars, Ukrainians, and Armenians. Language:

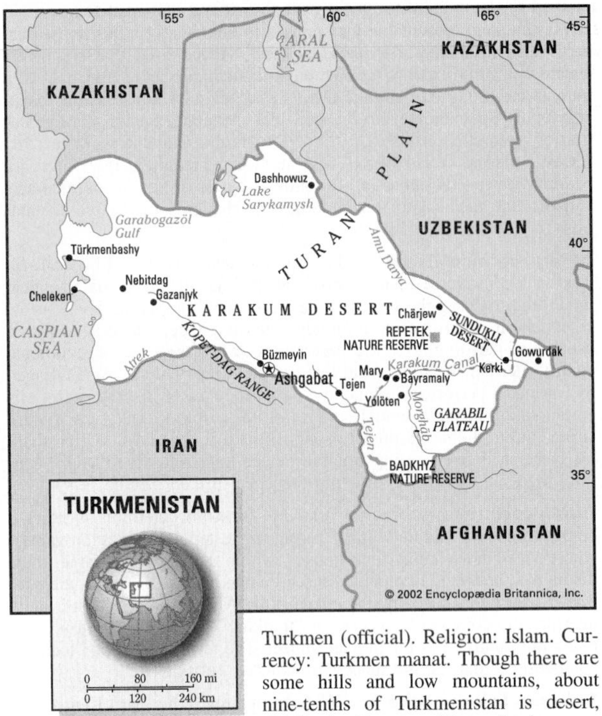

Turkmen (official). Religion: Islam. Currency: Turkmen manat. Though there are some hills and low mountains, about nine-tenths of Turkmenistan is desert, chiefly the KARAKUM. The main rivers are the AMU DARYA and MURGAB. Many irrigation canals and reservoirs have been built, including the Karakum Canal, which runs 870 mi (1,400 km) between the Amu Darya and the CASPIAN SEA. The country's chief products are oil and natural gas, cotton, silk, carpets, fish, and fruit. It is a republic with one legislative house; its head of state and government is the president, assisted by the People's Council. The earliest traces of human settlement in central Asia, dating back to Paleolithic times, have been found in Turkmenistan. The nomadic, tribal Turkmen probably entered the area in the 11th century AD. They were conquered by the Russians in the early 1880s and the region became part of Russian Turkestan. It was organized as the Turkmen Soviet Socialist Republic in 1924 and became a constituent republic of the U.S.S.R. in 1925. The country gained full independence from the Soviet Union in 1991 under the name Turkmenistan. The next decade was marked by economic struggles.

Turks *or* **Turkic peoples** Various peoples who speak TURKIC languages. They are connected with the T'u-chüeh, nomadic people who in the 6th century AD founded an empire stretching from Mongolia to the Black Sea. In the 11th century the SELJUQS created an extensive empire after defeating the Byzantines at the Battle of MANZIKERT (1071); the Turks then took Anatolia, base of the later OTTOMAN EMPIRE. Though overrun by the MONGOLS, the Turks succeeded in absorbing them after GENGHIS KHAN's death (1227). In the 14th century TIMUR held southwestern Central Asia and some of South Asia, but in the 15th century Russian expansion drove the Turks eastward into what is now Kazakhstan. Today the Turkic peoples live mostly in Turkey, Uzbekistan, Afghanistan, Kazakhstan, and Turkmenistan.

Turks and Caicos Islands \'kā-ˌkōs, 'kā-kəs\ British dependency (pop., 1993 est.: 13,000), WEST INDIES. It comprises two small island groups at the southeastern end of the BAHAMAS. The Turks group includes Grand Turk, Salt Cay, and lesser cays. The Caicos group includes South Caicos, East Caicos, Middle (or Grand) Caicos, North Caicos, Providenciales, West Caicos, and several smaller cays. The seat of government is at Cockburn Town on Grand Turk Island. When Spanish explorer JUAN PONCE DE LEON de León visited in 1512, the islands were inhabited by Indians. British colonists from BERMUDA arrived in 1678. The islands were at first placed under the government of the Bahamas, but in 1874 they were annexed to the colony of Jamaica. The Turks and Caicos Islands became a crown colony in 1962 and shared a governor with the

S T U V

Bahamas 1965–73. A new constitution was adopted in 1988. The chief industries are tourism and offshore financial services.

turmeric \'tər-mə-rik\ Perennial herbaceous plant (*Curcuma longa;* family Zingiberaceae), native to southern India and Indonesia. Its tuberous RHIZOMES have been used from antiquity as a condiment, as a textile dye, and medically as an aromatic stimulant. The rhizome has a pepperlike aroma and a somewhat bitter, warm taste. It colors and flavors prepared mustard and is used in curry powder, relishes, pickles, spiced butters and numerous culinary dishes. Paper tinged with turmeric turns from yellow to reddish-brown when an alkali is added to it, thus providing a test for alkalinity.

Turmeric (*Curcuma longa*).
W.H. HODGE

Turner, Frederick Jackson (1861–1932) U.S. historian. Born in Portage, Wisc., he taught at the University of Wisconsin and at Harvard University. Deeply influenced by his Wisconsin childhood, Turner rejected the doctrine that U.S. institutions could be traced mainly to European origins, and demonstrated his theories in a series of essays. In "The Significance of the Frontier in American History" (1893), he asserted that the American character had been shaped by frontier life and the end of the frontier era. Later he focused on sectionalism as a force in U.S. development. His essays were collected in *The Frontier in American History* (1920) and *Significance of Sections in American History* (1932, Pulitzer Prize).

Turner, J(oseph) M(allord) W(illiam) (1775–1851) British landscape painter. The son of a barber, he entered the Royal Academy school in 1789. In 1802 he became a full academician and in 1807 was appointed professor of perspective. His early work was concerned with accurate depictions of places, but he soon learned from RICHARD WILSON to take a more poetic and imaginative approach. *The Shipwreck* (1805) shows his new emphasis on luminosity, atmosphere, and romantic, dramatic subjects. After a trip to Italy in 1819, his color became purer and more prismatic, with a general heightening of key. In later paintings, such as *Sunrise, with a Boat Between Headlands* (1845), architectural and natural details are sacrificed to effects of color and light, with only the barest indication of mass. His compositions became more fluid, suggesting movement and space. In breaking down conventional formulas of representation, he anticipated French IMPRESSIONISM. His immense reputation in the 19th century was due largely to JOHN RUSKIN's enthusiasm for his early works; 20th-century critics celebrated the abstract qualities of his late color compositions.

Detail of a self-portrait by J.M.W. Turner, oil on canvas, 1798; in the Tate Gallery, London.
BY COURTESY OF THE TRUSTEES OF THE TATE GALLERY, LONDON

Turner, Lana *orig.* **Julia Jean Mildred Frances** (1920–1995) U.S. film actress. Born in Wallace, Idaho, she was allegedly discovered as a teenager at a Hollywood soda fountain and made her screen debut in 1937. A sultry, shapely blonde, publicized by MGM as the "Sweater Girl," she became a popular World War II pinup while starring in such movies as *Ziegfeld Girl* (1941), *Honky Tonk* (1941), and *Johnny Eager* (1942), and later *The Postman Always Rings Twice* (1946), *Peyton Place* (1957), and *Imitation of Life* (1959). Her tumultuous private life included eight marriages and the sensational 1958 stabbing death of her gangster boyfriend, Johnny Stompanato, by her 14-year-old daughter.

Turner, Nat (1800–1831) U.S. insurrectionist. Born into slavery in Southampton Co., Va., he became convinced of his mission to lead American slaves out of bondage and developed a scheme to capture the armory at Jerusalem, Va. He took an eclipse of the sun as a sign to act (1831) and began his insurrection by killing his master's family. He led 75 slaves as they killed about 60 whites on a two-day march to Jerusalem. About 3,000 state militia and local whites defeated the insurrectionists, who were captured or killed. Turner eluded arrest for six weeks but was found, tried, and hanged. Alarmed by the uprising, Southern states passed legislation forbidding the education, movement, or assembly of slaves.

Turner, Ted *orig.* **Robert Edward, III** (born 1938) U.S. broadcasting entrepreneur. Born in Cincinnati, he took over his father's Atlanta-based advertising firm after the latter's 1963 suicide and restored it to profitability. In 1970 he bought the Atlanta television station WJRJ (later WTBS), which in 1975 became the superstation of the Turner Broadcasting System, broadcasting via satellite to cable systems nationwide. In 1976 he bought the Atlanta Braves baseball team and in 1977 the Atlanta Hawks basketball team. In 1977 he piloted his yacht, *Courageous*, to victory in the AMERICA'S CUP race. He expanded his broadcasting empire with the 1980 launch of CNN and the 1986 purchase of MGM/UA Entertainment (MGM) and its library of over 4,000 old movies. He married JANE FONDA in 1991 (divorced 2001). In 1996 he merged his broadcasting system with the former TIME WARNER and became its vice-chairman. In 1997 he announced he would donate $1 billion to the U.N.

Turner's syndrome CHROMOSOMAL DISORDER (from the presence of only one SEX CHROMOSOME, X, in all or some of the body's cells) that causes abnormal sexual development in females. The syndrome may include absent or undeveloped ovaries, underdeveloped secondary sex characteristics, low hairline, webbed neck, shield-shaped chest with wide-spaced nipples, and kidney and heart malformations with coarctation (narrowing) of the aorta. It may not be recognized until a girl fails to undergo puberty at a normal age. ESTROGEN treatment results in puberty, adult appearance, and normal sex drive but not fertility. Surgery can correct malformations.

turnip Hardy biennial plant in the MUSTARD family, cultivated for its fleshy roots and tender leaves. There are two species, the turnip proper *(Brassica rapa)* and the Swedish turnip, or RUTABAGA. The true turnip probably originated in middle and eastern Asia and spread by cultivation throughout the temperate zone. Both species are cool-season crops. Turnips develop rapidly enough to have an early-spring or late-summer seeding produce a crop before, respectively, extremes of summer or late-fall weather occur.

turpentine Any resinous exudate or extract from CONIFERS, especially PINES. Semifluid mixtures of organic compounds consisting of RESINS dissolved in a volatile OIL, turpentines can be distilled (see DISTILLATION) into the volatile oil of turpentine (spirits of turpentine) and the nonvolatile rosin. A mixture of monoterpenes (see ISOPRENOID), chiefly pinene, turpentine is a colorless, odorous, flammable liquid that does not mix with water but is a good SOLVENT for many substances. Turpentine is favored over PETROLEUM solvents as a paint and varnish solvent and brush cleaner for oil paints. Its chief use is now as a raw material for resins, insecticides, oil additives, synthetic pine oil and CAMPHOR, and as a solvent.

turquoise Hydrated copper and aluminum phosphate mineral, $CuAl_6(PO_4)_4(OH)_8 \cdot 5H_2O$, that is used extensively as a gemstone. The color of turquoise ranges from blue through various shades of green to greenish and yellowish gray. A delicate sky-blue, which provides an attractive contrast with precious metals, is most valued for gem purposes. Numerous deposits of turquoise in the southwestern U.S. have been worked for centuries by American Indians. The mineral also occurs in Iran, northern Africa, Australia, and Siberia.

turtle Any of more than 250 species (order Chelonia) of REPTILES having a bony shell overlaid with horny shields; found in most parts of the world. Turtles have existed for 200 million years, making them the oldest of all surviving reptiles. Most species are aquatic or semiaquatic; some are terrestrial. Turtles eat plants, animals, or both. They are toothless, have a horny beak, and range from less than 4 in. (10 cm) to more than 7 ft (2 m) long. They have sturdy, sprawling limbs with short feet or paddlelike flippers (marine turtles). Some species bend the neck sideways, but most pull the head and neck backward into the shell. Almost half the known turtle species are rare, threatened, or endangered. See also BOX TURTLE, PAINTED TURTLE, SNAPPING turtle, SOFTSHELL turtle, TERRAPIN, TORTOISE.

turtledove Species (*Streptopelia turtur,* family Columbidae) of migratory European PIGEON that winters in northern Africa. It is about 11 in. (28 cm) long and has a reddish brown body, blue-gray head, and white-tipped tail. A ground feeder. it eats prodigious amounts of small seeds. The name is applied to other temperate and tropical Old World *Streptopelia* species of slim, fast-flying game birds. The ringed turtledove, or ringdove, has feral populations in California and Florida; the laughing and spotted doves have also been introduced outside their native habitats.

Tuscany *Italian* **Toscana** Autonomous region (pop., 2000: 3,536,392), western central Italy. Its capital is FLORENCE. Originally settled by ETRUSCANS c. 1000 BC, it came under Roman rule in the 3rd century BC. It was a Lombard duchy in the 6th century. It comprised several independent city-states in the 12th–13th century, which were subsequently united under the MEDICI dukes of Florence. It passed to the house of Lorraine in 1737 and to SARDINIA and the kingdom of Italy in the 1860s. The region suffered severe damage in World War II and extensive floods in 1966. Its mineral resources include the world-famous Carrara MARBLE, while its agricultural products include olives, olive oil, wines, and livestock. Tourism is important at its historical centers, including Florence and PISA.

Tusculum \'təs-kyə-ləm\ Ancient town, LATIUM, Italy. Located near ROME, it was a Latin settlement as early as the 1st millennium BC and probably was under ETRUSCAN influence. It was a favorite resort of wealthy Romans under the late republic and the empire (1st century BC–4th century AD), and was the home of orator MARCUS TULLIUS CICERO. Tourist attractions include a Roman forum, a 2nd-century amphitheater, and a medieval castle.

Tuskegee Airmen \tə-'skē-gē\ Black servicemen of the U.S. Army Air Forces (USAAF) who trained at Alabama's Tuskegee Army Air Field in World War II. They constituted the first African-American flying unit in the U.S. military. The first class trained at Tuskegee in 1941 became the 99th Pursuit Squadron, commanded by Lt. Col. BENJAMIN O. DAVIS, JR. They flew their first mission in the Mediterranean in 1943. Later that year the army activated three more squadrons; joined with the 99th in 1944, they constituted the 332nd Fighter Group. The latter was the USAAF's only escort group that did not lose a bomber to enemy planes. A second black flying group, the 477th Bombardment Group, was established near the end of the war. In all, the Tuskegee Airmen flew 1,578 missions, destroyed 261 enemy aircraft, and won over 850 medals.

Tuskegee University Private university in Tuskegee, Ala. Booker BOOKER T. WASHINGTON founded the school in 1881 as a teachers college for blacks, and it still has a predominantly African-American student body. GEORGE WASHINGTON CARVER conducted most of his research at Tuskegee (1896–1943), and Frederick D. Patterson, founder of the United Negro College Fund (1944), served as its president 1935–53. The infamous Tuskegee syphilis study, a U.S. Public Health Service project examining the course of untreated syphilis in black men, was based there from the 1930s. Today the university comprises schools of arts and sciences, agriculture, business, education, engineering and architecture, nursing, and veterinary medicine. Total enrollment is about 3,200.

Tussaud \tü-'sō\, **Marie** *orig.* **Marie Grosholtz** (1761–1850) French-British founder of Madame Tussaud's museum of wax figures in London. From 1780 until the French Revolution, she served as art tutor to Louis XVI's sister. During the Reign of Terror she made death masks from heads—frequently those of her friends—freshly severed by the guillotine. In 1802 she moved to Britain with her collection of wax models. Her museum contains a variety of historical figures, including the original models she made of her great contemporaries, including VOLTAIRE and BENJAMIN FRANKLIN.

tussock moth Typical member of the small European and New World LEPIDOPTERAN family Liparidae (formerly Lymantriidae). The large, hairy larvae of most species have hair tufts, or tussocks; many have stinging hairs. Several species, including the GYPSY moth, browntail moth, satin moth, and nun moth, damage trees. The larvae feed on foliage, sometimes foraging from a silken tent or a colonial nest of webbed leaves. Larvae pupate in a cocoon attached to a tree branch or trunk. Adult females range from white to brown; some, such as the white-marked tussock moth, are wingless. See also MOTH.

Tutankhamen \ˌtü-ˌtäŋ-'kä-mən\ *orig.* **Tutankhaten** (r.1333–1323 BC) Egyptian PHARAOH of the 18th dynasty. About 8 when he took the throne, he was advised to move back to Memphis from Akhetaton, the city of his father-in-law and predecessor, AKHENATON. During his reign the traditional religion was restored after the changes made by Akhenaton. Shortly before he died, still in his teens, he sent troops to Syria to aid an ally against HITTITE vassals. Because his name was among those stricken from the royal lists during the 19th dynasty, his tomb's location was forgotten and his burial chamber was not opened until 1922, when it was discovered by Howard Carter (1873–1939). Its treasures made Tutankhamen perhaps the best-known of the pharaohs despite his early death and few accomplishments.

Tutankhamen, gold funerary mask found in the King's tomb, 14th century BC; in the Egyptian Museum, Cairo.

Tutsi \'tüt-sē\ African ethnic group whose members, traditionally classed as NILOTES and numbering 1.5 million, live in Rwanda and Burundi. They represent a traditional aristocratic minority, which has dominated the more populous HUTU. Originally warrior-herders, the Tutsi entered the area in the 14th or 15th century and later, assisted by German and Belgian colonial regimes, cultivated a lord–vassal relationship with the Hutu. At the head of the pyramidal political structure was the *mwami* ("king"), considered to be of divine origin. Today Hutu and Tutsi cultures have largely become integrated, both speak Rwanda and Rundi and adhere to similar traditional and/or Christian religious beliefs. The Tutsi retained their dominant position over the Hutu in Rwanda until 1961, when the monarch was overthrown. An unsuccessful Hutu revolt in Burundi in 1972 led to 100,000 deaths, mostly Hutu. In 1993 in Burundi and in 1994 in Rwanda, further clashes occurred, the latter including a Hutu genocidal campaign in which over a million people in all were killed and 1–2 million Hutu forced into refugee camps in Zaire (now Congo) and Tanzania.

Tutu, Desmond (Mpilo) *later* **Sir Desmond** (born 1931) South African Anglican cleric. Born in the Transvaal, he studied theology at the University of South Africa and King's College, London. He became an Anglican priest in 1961, and bishop of Lesotho in 1976. In 1978 he became general secretary of the South African Council of Churches and an eloquent and outspoken advocate for the rights of black South Africans. He emphasized nonviolent protest and encouraged other countries to apply economic pressure to South Africa. In 1984 he received the Nobel Peace Prize for his role in opposing APARTHEID. In 1986 he was elected the first black archbishop of Cape Town and titular head of South Africa's 1.6-million-member Anglican Church. He retired from the primacy in 1996 and became chairman of the Truth and Reconciliation Commission, charged with hearing evidence of human-rights violations under white rule. Since 1988 he has been chancellor of the University of the Western Cape in Bellville, South Africa.

Tutub \'tü-tüb\ *modern* **Khafaje** \kä-'fä-jə\ Ancient Sumerian city-state. Located east of present-day BAGHDAD, Iraq, it was of greatest significance in the Early Dynastic Period (c. 2900–2334 BC). Important remains, such as the temple oval, have been found dating to that period.

Tutuola \ˌtü-tü-'wō-lä\, **Amos** (1920–1997) Nigerian writer. He had only six years of formal schooling. He wrote in English and outside the mainstream of Nigerian literature, incorporating Yoruba myths and legends into prose epics that improvise on traditional themes. His best-known work is *The Palm-Wine Drinkard* (1952), a classic quest tale that was the first Nigerian book to achieve international fame. His later works include the tale *The Witch-Herbalist of the Remote Town* (1981), *Yoruba Folktales* (1986), and *Village Witch Doctor* (1990).

Tuvalu \tü-'vä-lü\ *formerly* **Ellice Islands** \'e-lis\ Nation, western central Pacific Ocean. Area: 9.25 sq mi (23.96 sq km). Population (1997 est.): 10,000. Capital: Fongafale (on the FUNAFUTI atoll). The majority of the people are Polynesian. Language: Tuvalu; English is widely used. Religion: Church of Tuvalu (evolved from Congregational missions). Currency: Tuvalu dollar (equivalent to Australian dollar). Tuvalu is an island group comprising five atolls and four coral islands, all of them low-lying, with maximum elevations of less than 20 ft (6 m), and covered mainly with coconut palms, breadfruit trees, and grasses. The economy is based on subsistence agriculture and fishing. It is a constitutional monarchy with one legislative house; its chief of state is the British monarch represented by the governor-general, and the head of government is the prime minister. The original Polynesian settlers probably came mainly from SAMOA or TONGA. The islands were sighted by the Spanish in the 16th century. Europeans settled there in the 19th century and intermarried with Tuvaluans. During this period Peruvian slave traders, known as "blackbirders," decimated the population. In 1856 the U.S. claimed the four southern islands for guano mining. Missionaries from Europe arrived in 1865 and rapidly converted the islanders to Christianity. In 1892 Tuvalu joined the British GILBERT ISLANDS, a protectorate that became the GILBERT AND ELLICE ISLANDS colony in 1916. Tuvaluans voted in 1974 for separation from the Gilberts (now Kiribati), whose people are MICRONESIAN. Tuvalu gained independence in 1978, and in 1979 the U.S. relinquished its claims. Elections were held in 1981, and a revised constitution was adopted in 1986. In recent decades, the government has tried to find overseas job opportunities for its citizens.

Tuxtla (Gutiérrez) \'tüst-lä\ City (pop., 1990: 296,000), capital of CHIAPAS state, southeastern Mexico. The Spanish who arrived there in the 16th century were frequently beset by native Indians, and the town grew slowly. In 1892 it was made the state capital. It is now the major commercial and manufacturing center in the state, and an agricultural distributing point. There are archaeological remains of pre-Columbian culture in the region.

Tuzigoot National Monument \'tü-zi-ˌgüt\ National monument, central Arizona. Located in the Verde River valley, the 43-acre (17-hectare) park was established in 1939. Its outstanding feature is the ruin, excavated in 1933–34 and partially rebuilt, of a 110-room Sinagua Indian pueblo that was occupied by three cultural groups from AD 1100 to 1450.

Tuzla \'tüz-lä\ Town (pop., 1991: 132,000), northeastern Bosnia and Herzegovina. Deposits of rock salt are located nearby; in the 10th century the town was called Soli ("salts"), and its present name is from the Turkish *tuz,* "salt." It was a Turkish garrison town from 1510 until it passed to the Austro-Hungarian empire in the 19th century. It was incorporated into Yugoslavia in 1918. It is the center for a mining region, and agricultural district. It was a target during the war in Bosnia in the 1990s (see BOSNIAN CONFLICT).

TVA See TENNESSEE VALLEY AUTHORITY

Tver \'tver\, **Principality of** Medieval principality, eastern central Europe. It comprised the city of Tver and surrounding towns. Founded in 1246, it rivaled MOSCOW for supremacy in northeastern Russia during the 14th–15th century. It ultimately was annexed to Moscow under IVAN III in 1485.

TWA See TRANS WORLD AIRLINES, INC.

Twain, Mark *orig.* **Samuel Langhorne Clemens** (1835–1910) U.S. humorist, writer, and lecturer. Born in Florida, Mo., he grew up in nearby Hannibal, on the Mississippi River. At 13 he was apprenticed to a local printer. In 1856 he signed on as an apprentice to a steamboat pilot. He plied the Mississippi for almost four years before going to Nevada and California, where he wrote the story that made him famous, "The Celebrated Jumping Frog of Calaveras County" (1865). In 1863 he took his pseudonym, the riverman's term for water "two fathoms deep." He traveled widely as a successful lecturer and to obtain material for his writing, including the humorous narratives *The Innocents Abroad* (1869) and *Roughing It* (1872). He won a worldwide audience for his stories of youthful adventures, especially *Tom Sawyer* (1876), *The Prince and the Pauper* (1881), *Life on the Mississippi* (1883), and *Huckleberry Finn* (1884), one of the masterpieces of American fiction. The satirical *A Connecticut Yankee in King Arthur's Court* (1889) and increasingly grim works including *Pudd'nhead Wilson* (1894) and *The Man Who Corrupted Hadleyburg* (1900) followed. In the 1890s financial speculations bankrupted him and his eldest daughter died. After his wife's death (1904), he expressed his pessimism about human character in such late works as the posthumously published *Letters from the Earth* (1962).

tweed Medium- to heavy-weight fabric, rough in surface texture, and produced in a great variety of color and weave effects (see WEAVING). Most tweeds are made entirely of WOOL, but an increasing number are blends of wool with cotton, rayon, or other synthetic fibers. Most are woven from dyed YARNS, but some are dyed after being woven. Technical advances in dyeing raw stock, yarns, and fabrics, together with new techniques in finishing, have resulted in a wide variety of durable cloths.

Tweed, William Marcy *known as* **Boss Tweed** (1823–1878) U.S. politician. Born in New York City, he initially worked as a bookkeeper and volunteer firefighter. As city alderman (1851–56), he gained influence in TAMMANY HALL and obtained important positions in city government. He appointed political cronies to key city posts and built a group later called the Tweed ring. As head of Tammany's general committee (from 1860), he controlled the Democratic Party's nominations to all city positions. He opened a law office to receive payments for "legal services" from city contractors and corporations. Elected to the state senate (1868), he also became Tammany's grand sachem (leader) and controlled city and state political patronage. He gained control of the city treasury and plundered sums estimated at $30–200 million. Reformers and exposure by the press, including THOMAS NAST's cartoons in *Harper's Weekly*, brought prosecution, led by SAMUEL TILDEN, that convicted Tweed and sentenced him to prison (1873–75, 1876–78).

Boss Tweed.

BY COURTESY OF THE LIBRARY OF CONGRESS, WASHINGTON, D.C.

Tweed River River, southeastern Scotland and northeastern England. It rises in the Borders region of southeastern Scotland, then flows east, forming a section of the border between Scotland and England. It then crosses into England and empties into the NORTH SEA at Berwick. It is 97 mi (156 km) long.

Twelve Tables, Law of the Earliest codification of ancient ROMAN LAW, traditionally dated 451–450 BC. They were allegedly written at the demand of the plebeians, who were not satisfied to leave law in the hands of the patricians. Only random quotations from the Twelve Tables are extant; much knowledge of their contents derives from references in later juridical writings. Romans venerated the Twelve Tables as a prime legal source.

Twentieth Century–Fox Film Corp. U.S. movie studio. It was formed in 1935 by the merger of Twentieth Century Pictures (founded in 1933 by Joseph Schenck and DARRYL F. ZANUCK) and the Fox Film Corp. (founded in 1915 by William Fox). The new studio produced mainly westerns and musicals into the 1940s, as well as such notable films as *The Grapes of Wrath* (1940) and *The Snake Pit* (1948). In 1953 it introduced CinemaScope with *The Robe,* and later in the decade it made such hits as *The King and I* (1956) and *South Pacific* (1958). After the expensive failure of *Cleopatra* (1963), the studio recouped with *The Sound of Music* (1965), *Patton* (1970), and *Star Wars* (1977), the film industry's most profitable movie to that time. In 1981 the company was bought by the oil magnate Marvin Davis, who resold it in 1985 to RUPERT MURDOCH.

Twentieth Congress of the Communist Party of the Soviet Union (February 14–25, 1956) Meeting at which NIKITA KHRUSHCHEV repudiated JOSEPH STALIN and STALINISM. Khrushchev's secret speech denouncing the former Soviet leader was accompanied by his Report of the Central Committee to the Congress, which announced a new line in Soviet foreign policy. He based his new policy on "the Leninist principle of coexistence of states with different social systems." Khrushchev also used the Congress to promote his loyal supporters to high party office and to take control of the party from the Stalinist old guard.

twenty-one See BLACKJACK

twill One of the three basic TEXTILE weaves (see WEAVING), distinguished by diagonal lines. In the simplest twill, the weft crosses over two warp YARNS, then under one, the sequence being repeated in each succeeding shot (row), but stepped over, one warp either to the left or right. In regular twill, the diagonal line is repeated regularly, usually running upward from left to right at 45°. The weave can be varied in many ways—for example, by changing the direction of the twill line (as in herringbone twill) or its angle. Twill is much used for men's wear and many other clothing applications because it has stretch on both diagonals, which makes clothes comfortable even if closely fitted. DENIM and many TWEEDS are of twill weave.

Twining, Nathan F(arragut) (1897–1982) U.S. Air Force officer. Born in Monroe, Wis., he graduated from West Point and served as an army pilot from 1924. In World War II he commanded the air force in the South Pacific and directed the air war against Japan in the Solomon Islands and New Guinea (1943) and Japan (1945). In 1944–45 he led the strategic bombing campaign against Germany and the Balkans. He later became chief of staff of the U.S. Air Force (1953–57) and chairman of the Joint Chiefs of Staff (1957–60).

Two Sicilies See Two SICILIES

Tycho Brahe See Tycho BRAHE

Tyler, Anne (born 1941) U.S. writer. Born in Minneapolis, reared in North Carolina, and educated at Duke Univ., she worked as a bibliographer and librarian before settling in Baltimore in 1967 and beginning to write full-time. Her novels, comedies of manner marked by compassionate wit and precise details of domestic life, include *The Clock Winder* (1972), *Dinner at the Homesick Restaurant* (1982), *The Accidental Tourist* (1985; film, 1988), *Breathing Lessons* (1988, Pulitzer Prize), *Saint Maybe* (1991), *Ladder of Years* (1995), and *A Patchwork Planet* (1998). Several focus on eccentric middle-class people living in chaotic, disunited families in Baltimore.

Tyler, John (1790–1862) 10th president of the U.S. (1841–45). Born in Charles City Co., Va., he practiced law before serving in the state legislature (1811–16, 1823–25, 1839) and as governor of Virginia (1825–27). In the U.S. House of Representatives (1817–21) and Senate (1827–36), he was a states'-rights supporter. Though a slaveholder, he sought to prohibit the slave trade in the District of Columbia, provided Maryland and Virginia concurred. He resigned from the Senate rather than acquiesce to state instructions to change his vote on a censure of Pres. ANDREW JACKSON. After breaking with the Democratic Party, he was nominated by the WHIG PARTY for vice president under WILLIAM H. HARRISON. They won the 1840 election, carefully avoiding the issues and stressing party loyalty and the slogan "Tippecanoe and Tyler too!" Harrison died a month after taking office, and Tyler became the first to attain the presidency "by accident." He vetoed a national bank bill supported by the Whigs, and all but one member of the cabinet resigned, leaving him without party support. Nonetheless, he reorganized the navy, settled the second of the SEMINOLE WARS in Florida, and oversaw the annexation of Texas. He was nominated for reelection but withdrew in favor of JAMES POLK and retired to his Virginia plantation. Committed to states' rights but opposed to SECESSION, he organized the Washington Peace Conference (1861) to resolve sectional differences. When the Senate rejected a proposed compromise, Tyler urged Virginia to secede.

Tyler, Wat See PEASANTS' REVOLT

Tylor, detail of a chalk drawing by G. Bonavia; in the National Portrait Gallery, London.

BY COURTESY OF THE NATIONAL PORTRAIT GALLERY, LONDON

Tylor, Edward Burnett *later* **Sir Edward** (1832–1917) British anthropologist, often called the founder of CULTURAL ANTHROPOLOGY. He taught at Oxford University (1884–1909), where he became the first professor of anthropology. His *Primitive Culture* (2 vols., 1871), influenced by CHARLES DARWIN, developed the theory of an evolutionary relationship between primitive and modern cultures, stressing the cultural achievements that marked the progression of all humanity from a "savage" to a "civilized" state. At a time when there was still controversy over whether all human races belonged physically and mentally to a single species, Tylor was a powerful advocate of the unity of all humankind. He was instrumental in establishing anthropology as an academic discipline. See also ANIMISM, SOCIOCULTURAL evolution.

Tyne and Wear \'tīn...'wir\ Metropolitan county (pop., 1995 est.: 1,131,000), northeastern England. It was named for its two main rivers, the TYNE and the Wear. Settled since prehistoric times, the area was occupied by the Romans, who built HADRIAN'S WALL. Saxon, then Norman, settlement followed. From the 13th century to recent times, its economy was based on local coal reserves and on such coal-dependent industries as glass, pottery, and chemicals. Main industries now include shipbuilding and heavy electrical engineering.

Tyne River River, NORTHUMBERLAND, northern England. Formed by the confluence of the North Tyne and the South Tyne rivers, it flows east into the North Sea. It is 30 mi (48 km) long; with the North Tyne, it is 80 mi (129 km) long. It has shipped coal for at least six centuries. Its estuary is now lined with industry and large urban communities.

typeface See FONT

types, theory of In LOGIC, a theory introduced by BERTRAND RUSSELL and ALFRED NORTH WHITEHEAD in their *Principia Mathematica* (1910–13) to deal with logical PARADOXES arising from the unrestricted use of PROPOSITIONAL FUNCTIONS as variables. The type of a propositional function is determined by the number and type of its arguments (the distinct variables it contains). By not allowing propositional functions to be applied to arguments of equal or higher type, contradictions within the system are avoided.

typesetting Setting of type for use in any of various PRINTING processes. Type for printing, using woodblocks, was invented in China in the 11th cent, and movable type using metal molds had appeared in Korea by the 13th century. It was reinvented in Europe in the 1450s by JOHANNES GUTENBERG. For much of its history, typesetting and printing were often performed by the same person, who arranged movable type, one character at a time, in rows corresponding to the individual lines in the publication, and operated the hand press to imprint the image on paper. Typesetting was revolutionized in the 1880s with the invention of the "hot-metal" processes: Linotype (1884), in which the lines of type were assembled by use of a typewriter-like keyboard and each line was cast as a single slug of molten metal, and Monotype (1887), which also used a keyboard but cast each character separately. Photocomposition—the composition of text directly on film or photosensitive paper, using a rotating drum or disk with cutout type characters through which light could be directed onto the receiving surface—appeared in the early 20th century. Today characters are generated by computer; computer typesetting systems include a keyboard that produces magnetic tape for input, a computer for making hyphenation, layout, and other page-makeup decisions, and a typesetting unit for output, which transfers the images to light-sensitive paper or film by pulses from a laser beam, which forms each character in response to computer-generated electric pulses. Increasingly, typesetting projects are simply saved electronically and sent to the printer as electronic files rather than on paper or film. A computerized typesetter can set over 10,000 characters per second, and modern imagesetters can set complex layouts that include a variety of graphic matter in addition to type.

typewriter Machine for writing characters similar to those made by printers' types, especially a machine in which the characters are produced by steel types striking the paper through an inked ribbon, the types being activated by corresponding keys on a keyboard and the paper being held by a roller (the platen) that is automatically moved along with a carriage when a key is struck. The first practical typewriter was patented in 1868 by CHRISTOPHER L. SHOLES; commercial production began at the Remington firearms company in 1874. By the end of the century the typewriter had come to dominate the American office. The first electric typewriter for office use was introduced in 1920. From the 1970s typewriters began to be replaced by PERSONAL COMPUTERS and their associated printers.

S T U V

typhoid *or* **typhoid fever** Acute infectious disease resembling TYPHUS (and distinguished from it only in the 19th century). *Salmonella typhi,* usually ingested in food or water, multiplies in the intestinal wall and then enters the bloodstream, causing SEPTICEMIA. Symptoms begin with headache, aching, and restlessness. High fever gradually develops, with delirium. A rash appears on the trunk. The sites where the bacilli multiplied become inflamed and may ulcerate, leading to intestinal bleeding or PERITONITIS. Patients become exhausted and emaciated; up to 25% die if not treated. ANTIBIOTIC treatment is effective. Patients can carry typhoid for weeks to months (30%) or years (5%). Carriers can contaminate the food they handle. Prevention depends mainly on water and sewage treatment and excluding carriers from food-handling jobs.

Typhoid Mary *byname of* **Mary Mallon** (1870?–1938) U.S. carrier of TYPHOID. A 1904 typhoid epidemic on Long Island was traced to households where she had been a cook. She fled, but authorities finally caught up with her and isolated her on an island off the Bronx. In 1910 she was released after agreeing not to take a food-handling job again, but she did, causing more typhoid outbreaks. She was returned to the island for the rest of her life. Three deaths and 51 original cases were directly attributed to her.

Typhon In GREEK MYTHOLOGY, the youngest son of GAEA and TARTARUS. A grisly monster with a hundred dragons' heads, he was conquered and cast into the underworld by ZEUS but continued to be the source of destructive winds. In other accounts, he was confined in the land of the Arimi in Cilicia or under Mount ETNA, where he caused eruptions and was thus the personification of volcanic forces. Among his children were CERBERUS, CHIMERA, and the multiheaded Hydra. Later writers identified him with the Egyptian god SETH.

typhoon See TROPICAL CYCLONE

typhus Any of a group of related diseases caused by various species of RICKETTSIA that release TOXINS into the blood. Headache, chills, fever, and general pains begin suddenly and a rash soon after. The bacteria are transmitted by lice, fleas, mites, and ticks. Epidemic typhus, spread by the body louse, is the most severe. It is one of the great scourges of history, associated with crowded, filthy conditions. Improved hygiene has nearly eliminated it from the Western world, but it persists in many countries, despite modern vaccines and pesticides. Endemic typhus, spread by fleas on rats and other rodents, is milder (mortality under 5%). Scrub typhus, carried by mites, is usually classed as a separate disease. See also ROCKY MOUNTAIN SPOTTED FEVER, HANS ZINSSER.

typographic printing See LETTERPRESS PRINTING

typography Design or selection of letter forms to be organized into words and sentences and printed or displayed electronically. Typography originated after the invention of printing from movable type in the mid-15th century. The three major type families in the history of Western printing are ROMAN, italic, and BLACK LETTER (Gothic). All had their origin in the scripts of the calligraphers whose work was ultimately replaced by printing. In the succeeding centuries typographers have created some 10,000 typefaces (a complete set of letter forms of a particular design). Depending on the style of their letters, typefaces are categorized as old style, transitional, and modern. Commonly used typefaces include Caslon, Baskerville, Bodoni, Garamond, and Times New Roman. See also JOHN BASKERVILLE, GIAMBATTISTA BODONI, STANLEY MORISON.

tyrannosaur Any of a group of related carnivorous dinosaurs similar to the ALLOSAURS. *Tyrannosaurus rex* is the largest and best known, found as fossils in Late Cretaceous (99–65 million years ago) deposits of North America and eastern Asia. Some adults were more than 40 ft (12 m) long and 16–18 ft (over 5 m) tall and weighed 6 tons (5.4 metric tons) or more. Tyrannosaurs walked with a stooped posture, carrying the body forward and the long tail off the ground. They had a short, thick neck, a very large skull, and pointed teeth, up to 6 in. (15 cm) long, with serrated edges. Each small forelimb had two claws, perhaps for holding struggling prey. A nearly complete skeleton of *T. rex* called "Sue" is on display at the Field Museum in Chicago. Other tyrannosaurs include *Albertosaurus, Alectrosaurus,* and *Nanotyrannus.*

tyrant A cruel and oppressive absolute ruler, or, in ancient Greece, a ruler who seized power unconstitutionally or inherited such power. Though tyrants often replaced aristocratic regimes that were themselves unpopular, the Greeks resented their illegal autocracy, and those who killed tyrants received high honors.

Tyre \'tīr\ *Arabic* **Sur** \'sür\ Town (pop., 1994 est.: 80,000), southern Lebanon. In the 11th–6th century BC, it was a major commercial city, center of PHOENICIAN civilization, and a dominant sea power. It was noted for its silken garments and Tyrian purple dye. Probably founded before the 14th century BC, it is frequently mentioned in the Bible. It successfully resisted a 6th-century-BC siege of 13 years by the Babylonian king NEBUCHADNEZZAR II. It fell to ALEXANDER THE GREAT in 332 BC. Later under the SELEUCIDS, then the Romans, it passed to the Muslims in the 7th century AD. After its capture by the Crusaders in 1124, it became a chief city of the kingdom of Jerusalem. It fell again to the Muslims in 1291 and was destroyed. The modern town was included in Lebanon in 1920 and was occupied by Israeli forces 1982–85. Its main industry is fishing.

Tyrol See TIROL

Tyrone \tī-'rōn\ Former county, western central Northern Ireland. In the 1973 administrative reorganization of Northern Ireland, the county was divided into several smaller districts. The O'Nialls (or O'Neills) ruled the territory from the 5th to the 16th century AD. Subsequently the vast estates passed to the English crown and were divided and granted by the king under the scheme for the Plantation of Ulster. Royalist forces established fortifications, and the area was colonized.

Tyrone \'tī-rən\, **Earl of** *orig.* **Hugh O'Neill** (c. 1540–1616) Irish rebel. Born into the powerful O'Neill family of Ulster, he grew up in London, then returned to Ireland (1568) to assume his grandfather's title of earl of Tyrone. As chieftain of the O'Neills from 1593, he led skirmishes against the English and won the Battle of the Yellow Ford on the Blackwater River, Ulster, which sparked a countrywide revolt (1598). He received aid and troops from Spain (1601) but was defeated by the English at Kinsale and forced to surrender (1603). In 1607 he fled with about 100 chieftains and lived in Rome the rest of his life. The so-called "flight of the earls" brought an end to Gaelic Ulster, and the province was rapidly anglicized.

tyrosine \'tī-rə-ˌsēn\ One of the AMINO acids, not essential for humans unless they have PHENYLKETONURIA. It is the biochemical precursor of many important CATECHOLAMINES. It is found in small amounts in most PROTEINS, especially INSULIN and papain (found in PAPAYA). It is used in biochemical research and as a dietary supplement.

Tyrrhenian Sea \tə-'rē-nē-ən\ *Italian* **Mare Tirreno** \'mä-rā-tē-'re-nō\ Arm of the MEDITERRANEAN SEA. It is located between the western coast of Italy and the islands of CORSICA, SARDINIA, and SICILY. It is connected with the Ligurian Sea on the northwest through the Tuscan Archipelago and with the Ionian Sea on the southeast through the Strait of MESSINA. Chief inlets include the Bay of NAPLES.

Tyson, Mike *orig.* **Michael Gerald** (born 1966) U.S. boxer. Born in New York City, he was a street-gang member who spent time in reform school, where his talent was discovered. He turned professional in 1985 and won the title in 1986 by defeating Trevor Berbick, becoming at 20 the youngest heavyweight champion in history. He defended the title against LARRY HOLMES, Michael Spinks, and eight others before losing in an upset to James "Buster" Douglas in 1990. In 1992 he was convicted of rape and sentenced to six years in prison; he was released on parole in 1995. In 1996 he challenged but lost to EVANDER HOLYFIELD; in a 1997 rematch he was disqualified for biting off a piece of Holyfield's ear, and his license was revoked. In 1999 Tyson was relicensed and returned to the ring. In his bout against British heavyweight champion LENNOX LEWIS in 2002, Lewis twice knocked Tyson to the canvas before knocking him out in the eighth round.

tzaddiq See ZADDIK

Tzeltal \tsel-'täl\ Mayan Indian group of central Chiapas in southern Mexico. They are an agricultural people whose major crafts are pottery, weaving, and basketry. They profess Roman Catholicism, though pre-Columbian rituals are also practiced.

Tzotzil \tsōt-'sēl\ Mayan Indian group of central Chiapas in southern Mexico. They live at high altitudes where the climate is cool and precipitation is heavy during the rainy season. They raise sheep, primarily for wool, which they weave into ponchos for men and shawls for women. They practice slash-and-burn agriculture and grow peaches and other crops for the market. Some make pottery, leather, and fiber products or practice carpentry or stonework. Christian and native beliefs are intertwined in all Tzotzil areas.

U-2 Affair (1960) Confrontation between the U.S. and the Soviet Union. On May 1, 1960, the Soviet Union shot down a U.S. U-2 reconnaissance plane and called the flight an "aggressive act." The U.S. denied Soviet claims that the pilot, F. Gary Powers, had stated that his mission was to collect Soviet intelligence data. NIKITA KHRUSHCHEV declared that the Soviet Union would not take part in a scheduled summit conference with the U.S., Britain, and France unless the U.S. immediately stopped flights over Soviet territory, apologized, and punished those responsible. Pres. DWIGHT D. EISENHOWER agreed only to the first stipulation, and the conference was adjourned. Powers was tried in the USSR and sentenced to 10 years in prison; in 1962 he was exchanged for the Soviet spy Rudolf Abel.

U-boat *German* **Unterseeboot** German SUBMARINE ("undersea boat"). The first German submarine, the U-1, was built in 1905. By the eve of World War I, Germany possessed merchant U-boats over 300 ft. (90 m) long and capable of carrying 700 tons (635 metric tons) of cargo; these were fitted with TORPEDO tubes and deck guns for the war (by comparison, the "standard" submarine of World War I was only slightly over 200 ft, or 60 m, long.), and Germany became the first country to employ submarines in war. Its unrestricted U-boat warfare against merchant ships was largely responsible for U.S. entry into the war. In World War II the U-boat initially enjoyed great success, but Allied tactics eventually succeeded in rendering them less effective. Of the 1,162 U-boats built during World War II, 785 were destroyed.

Uaxactún \ˌwä-shäk-ˈtün\ Ruined ancient MAYA town, northern central Guatemala. One of the oldest known centers of Maya civilization, it was occupied in the 1st millennium BC; by 300 BC–AD 100 a number of ceremonial buildings had been erected, including a temple reminiscent of the more ancient OLMEC civilization. Major remains predate the Classic period (AD 100–900). In the 9th century it declined, as did other southern lowland Maya centers, and was abandoned in the 10th century.

Ubangi River \ü-ˈbaŋ-gē\ River, central Africa. Formed by the BOMU and Uele rivers on the central northern border of the Democratic Republic of the Congo, it flows west and south, forming part of the boundary with the Central African Republic and with the Republic of the Congo. It then empties into the CONGO RIVER. It is 700 mi (1,126 km) long; with its longest headstream, it is double that length.

Ubangi-Shari See CENTRAL AFRICAN REPUBLIC

Ubasti See BASTET

UC See University of CALIFORNIA

Ucayali River \ˌü-kä-ˈyä-lē\ River, central and northern Peru. The chief headstream of the AMAZON RIVER, it is formed by the junction of the APURIMAC and URUBAMBA rivers. It then meanders north to unite with the MARAÑÓN RIVER and form the Amazon. It is navigable for some 675 mi (1,086 km) of its 1,000-mi (1,610-km) length.

Uccello \ü-ˈche-lō\, **Paolo** *orig.* **Paolo di Dono** (1397–1475) Italian painter. Though apprenticed to the sculptor LORENZO GHIBERTI, he is not known to have worked in sculpture, and at 18 he was admitted to the painters' guild in Florence. *The Deluge*, one of his frescoes in the Chiostro Verde of Santa Maria Novella, demonstrates his intense study of perspective. He became so firmly identified with perspective that JOHN RUSKIN thought he had invented it. His three panels depicting the Battle of San Romano, like all the extant works of his mature years, combine the decorative late Gothic style with the new heroic style of the early Renaissance.

UCLA See University of CALIFORNIA

ud \üd\ Stringed instrument prominent in medieval and modern Islamic music, forerunner of the European LUTE. Dating from the 7th century, it has a pear-shaped body, a fretless fingerboard, a short neck, and a bent-back pegbox with the tuning pegs set in the sides. The gut strings, of which there are often four pairs, are plucked with a plectrum.

Udall \ˈyü-dəl, ˈyü-ˌdȯl\, **Nicholas** (1505?–1556) English playwright, translator, and schoolmaster. The headmaster of Eton College from 1534 and of Westminster from 1555, Udall was well known as a translator. He is credited with writing many plays, of which only one is extant, *Ralph Roister Doister* (performed c. 1553), the first known English comedy. About a braggart soldier-hero who is finally shown to be an arrant coward, it marks the emergence of comedy from the medieval morality plays, interludes, and farces.

Ufa \ü-ˈfä\ City (pop., 1996 est.: 1,100,000), western Russia. Lying at the confluence of the Belaya and Ufa rivers, it was founded as a fortress in 1574 to protect the trade route across the URAL MTNS. from KAZAN to Tyumen. It became a town in 1586. It developed as an industrial center from the late 19th century, and especially after World War II. Chief industries include electrical equipment, lumber and veneer, and oil refining.

Uffizi Gallery \ü-ˈfēt-sē\ Art museum in Florence, housing the world's finest collection of Italian Renaissance painting. The core collection derives from the MEDICI FAMILY of Tuscany. In 1559 Cosimo I de' MEDICI hired GIORGIO VASARI to design the Uffizi Palace (1560–80), originally for use as government offices *(uffizi)*. In 1565 Vasari built the corridor over the Ponte Vecchio connecting the Uffizi with the Pitti Palace. In 1737 Maria Ludovica, last of the Medici, bequeathed the family collections to Tuscany; the collection was given museum status and opened to the public in 1769. The building was restored and enlarged after bomb damage in World War II and flooding in 1966. In addition to Florentine paintings, it houses outstanding works of other Italian and non-Italian schools, antique sculpture, a gallery of self-portraits, and 100,000 prints and drawings.

UFO See UNIDENTIFIED FLYING OBJECT

Uganda \yü-ˈgan-də, yü-ˈgän-də\ *officially* **Republic of Uganda** Nation, eastern Africa. Area: 93,070 sq mi (241,040 sq km). Population (2001): 23,986,000. Capital: KAMPALA. There are dozens of African ethnic groups, as well as a small but influential Asian community. Languages: English (official), Swahili. Religions: Roman Catholicism, Protestantism, Islam, and indigenous beliefs. Currency: Ugandan shilling. A

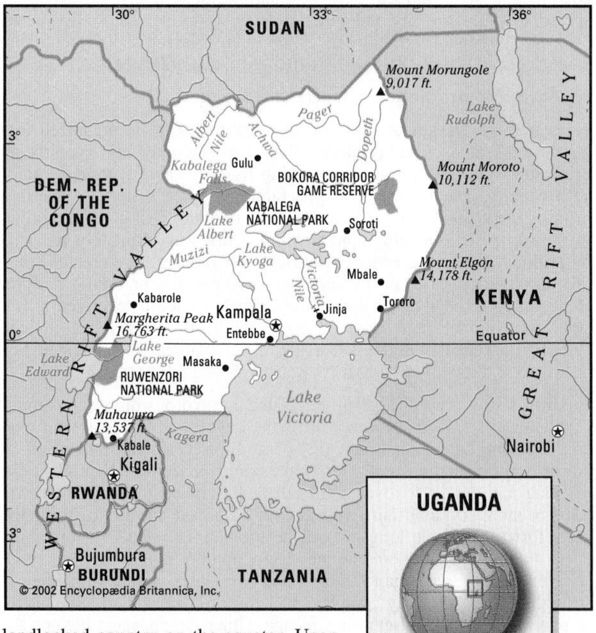

landlocked country on the equator, Uganda is largely situated on a plateau, with volcanic mountains edging its eastern and western borders; Mt ELGON is the highest peak. Part of Lake VICTORIA occupies virtually all of southeastern Uganda; other major lakes are Lakes ALBERT, KYOGA, EDWARD, George, and Bisina. The NILE RIVER traverses it. Huge

S T U V

tracts of land are devoted to national parks and game reserves. The economy is based largely on agriculture and food processing. Livestock raising and fishing are also important, and there is some manufacturing and mining. It is a republic with one legislative house; its head of state and government is the president. By the 19th century the region comprised several separate kingdoms inhabited by various peoples, including Bantu- and Nilotic-speaking tribes. Arab traders reached the area in the 1840s. The native kingdom of Buganda was visited by the first European explorers in 1862. Protestant and Catholic missionaries arrived in the 1870s, and the development of religious factions led to persecution and civil strife. In 1894 Buganda was formally proclaimed a British protectorate. As Uganda, it gained its independence in 1962, and in 1967 it adopted a republican constitution. The civilian government was overthrown in 1971 and replaced by a military regime under Idi Amin. His invasion of Tanzania in late 1978 resulted in the collapse of his regime. The civilian government was again deposed by the military in 1985, which in turn was overthrown in 1986. A constituent assembly enacted a new constitution in 1995.

Ugarit \yü-'gär-it, 'yü-gə-rit\ Ancient city on the site of modern Ras Shamra, Syria. Located on the eastern coast of the Mediterranean Sea, the earliest settlement was a small fortified town in the 7th millennium BC. It flourished in the 15th–12th century BC, when great royal palaces, temples, shrines, and libraries were built there. It was destroyed c. 1200 BC. Remains at the site include ancient records in cuneiform writing.

Uí Néill \ü-'nēl\ Major dynasty of medieval Ireland, which long dominated Ulster. It was founded by a shadowy figure known as Niall of the Nine Hostages (r.379–405). Divided into northern and southern branches, the Uí Néill ruled as high kings, to whom all other Irish kings owed deference. In the early 11th century the king of Munster, Brian Boru, challenged the high kings of the Uí Néill dynasty and ended their dominance.

Uighurs *or* **Uygurs** \'wē-ˌgu̇rz\ Turkic-speaking people of Central Asia who live largely in northwestern China. More than 7.7 million Uighurs live in China today, and some 300,000 in Uzbekistan, Kazakhstan, and Kyrgyzstan. They are among the oldest Turkic-speaking peoples of Central Asia, first mentioned in Chinese records from the 3rd century AD. They established a kingdom in the 8th century, which was overrun in 840. A Uighur confederacy (745–1209), established around the Tian Mtns., was overthrown by the Mongols. This confederacy came to the aid of China's Tang dynasty during the An Lushan Rebellion. The Uighurs of that time professed a Manichaean faith.

Uinta Mountains \yü-'in-tä\ Mountain range, southern central Rocky Mtns. They extend east more than 100 mi (160 km) from the Wasatch Mtns. across northeastern Utah and slightly into southwestern Wyoming. Many of the range's summits exceed 13,000 ft (4,000 m), including Kings Peak (13,528 ft, or 4,123 m), the highest point in Utah.

Ujung Pandang \'ü-ˌju̇ŋ-'pän-ˌdäŋ\ *formerly* **Macassar** \mə-'ka-sər\ City (pop., 1995 est.: 1,092,000), Sulawesi, Indonesia. Already a thriving port when the Portuguese arrived in the 16th century, it came under control of the Dutch, who built a trading station there in 1607 and finally deposed the sultan in 1667. It was made a free port in 1848 and the capital of the Dutch-sponsored state of Indonesia Timur (East Indonesia) in 1946. In 1949 it became part of the Republic of Indonesia. It is the site of Hasanuddin University (founded 1956).

ukiyo-e \ü-ˌkē-ō-'ā\ (Japanese: "pictures of the floating world") Dominant art movement of the Edo period in Japan. Screen paintings were the first works to be done in the style, which depicted aspects of the entertainment quarters ("floating world") of Edo (modern Tokyo) and other cities. The medium was most fully exploited by wood-block printmakers and such celebrated artists as Hiroshige Ando, Hokusai, and Utamaro. Favorite subjects included famous courtesans and prostitutes, kabuki actors in famous roles, and erotica; they were executed in flat, decorative colors and expressive patterns. A new interest in the urban everyday world sparked the development of *ukiyo-e* prints designed for mass consumption. The prints attracted much attention in Europe in the 19th century and had a great influence on avant-garde French artists.

Ukraine \yü-'krān\ Republic, southeastern Europe. Area: 233,100 sq mi (603,700 sq km). Population (1997 est.): 50,668,000. Capital: Kiev. Ethnic Ukrainians make up 70% of the population; minorities include Russians and Jews. Languages: Ukrainian (official), Russian, Romanian, Polish, Hungarian. Religions: Christianity, Judaism, Islam. Currency: hryvny. Ukraine consists of level plains and the Carpathian Mtns., which extend through the western region for more than 150 mi (240 km). The Bug, Dnieper, Donets, and Dniester are its major rivers. The Donets Basin in the eastern central region is one of the major heavy-industrial and mining-metallurgical complexes of Europe. It mines iron ore and coal, and produces natural gas, petroleum, iron, and steel. It is a major producer of winter wheat and sugar beets. It is a republic with one legislative body; its head of state is the president, and the head of government is the prime minister. Different parts of the area were invaded and occupied in the first millennium BC by the Cimmerians, Scythians, and Sarmatians, and in the first millennium AD by the Goths, Huns, Bulgars, Avars, Khazars, and Magyars. Slavic tribes settled there after the 4th century. Kiev was its chief town. The Mongol conquest in the mid-13th century decisively ended Kievan power. Ruled by Lithuania in the 14th century and Poland in the 16th century, it fell to Russian rule in the 18th century. The Ukrainian National Republic, established in 1917, declared its independence from Soviet Russia in 1918 but was reconquered in 1919; it was made the Ukrainian Soviet Socialist Republic of the U.S.S.R. in 1923. The northwestern region was held by Poland 1919–39. The Ukraine suffered a severe famine in 1932–33 under Soviet leader Joseph Stalin; over 5 million Ukrainians died of starvation in an unprecedented peacetime catastrophe. Overrun by Axis armies in 1941 in World War II, it was further devastated before being retaken by the Soviets in 1944. In 1986 it was the site of the Chernobyl accident, at a Soviet-built nuclear power plant. It declared independence in 1991. In recent years it has struggled both politically and economically.

Ukrainian language \yü-'krā-nē-ən\ *formerly* **Ruthenian language** \rü-'thē-nē-ən\ Slavic languages spoken by about 41 million people in Ukraine, Poland, Slovakia, Russia, and in enclaves around the world. Only about three-quarters of Ukrainians are first-language speakers of Ukrainian, but there are millions of first-language speakers in Russia, Belarus, and the Central Asian republics. Ukraine's premodern literary language was Church Slavic (see Old Church Slavic language). Ukrainian was one component in the chancery language of the Grand Duchy of Lithuania, which also mixed Church Slavic, Belarusian, and Polish. With the fall of the Zaporizhzhya Cossacks in the 18th century, Ukrainian-speakers were stateless and the status of the language, thought of as peasant speech by the nobility, was low. The language and orthography (using a form of the Cyrillic alphabet) were gradually standardized in the 19th century.

ukulele \ˌyü-kə-'lā-lē\ Small Hawaiian four-stringed guitar. It developed out of a similar Portuguese instrument introduced to Hawaii by sailors in the 1870s. It became highly popular in the U.S. after World War I, used in jazz and bluegrass ensembles and more widely as an amateur solo instrument.

Ulaanbaatar *or* **Ulan Bator** \ˌü-ˌlän-ˈbä-ˌtȯr\ City (pop., 1997 est.: 627,000), capital of MONGOLIA. Situated on a windswept plateau, it was founded in the mid-17th century as the residence of the Living Buddha *(bodgo-gegen)*. A century later it had become a trading center on caravan routes between Russia and China; it still is at the junction of principal Mongolian transportation routes. The Mongolian revolt for independence was centered there in 1911. It became the capital when the Mongolian People's Republic was established in 1924, and remained the capital when in 1992 the country's name was changed to Mongolia. It is Mongolia's main industrial center.

Ulam \ˈü-ləm\, **Stanislaw M(arcin)** (1909–1984) Polish-U.S. mathematician and atomic physicist. He received his doctoral degree in 1933 and was invited by JOHN VON NEUMANN to Princeton's Institute for Advanced Study in 1936. In 1943 he moved to LOS ALAMOS, where his early work included development (with von Neumann) of the MONTE CARLO METHOD of finding approximate solutions to problems. Later, working on a fusion bomb, he and EDWARD TELLER developed a two-stage radiation implosion design (the "Teller-Ulam configuration") that could generate an explosion capable of initiating nuclear fusion, a design that led to the creation of the HYDROGEN BOMB.

Ulanova \ü-ˈlä-nə-və\, **Galina (Sergeyevna)** (1910–1998) Russian ballet dancer, the first prima ballerina assoluta of the Soviet Union. She trained with A. VAGANOVA in Leningrad and joined the Kirov (formerly MARIINSKY) Theater company in 1928, where she began to dance leading roles and to develop the unique lyrical, dramatic style that won her wide acclaim. In 1944 she moved to the BOLSHOI BALLET and during the 1950s toured to great acclaim with the company in Europe and the U.S. She retired from dancing in 1962 but continued as ballet mistress and coach at the Bolshoi.

Ulbricht \ˈu̇l-ˌbrik̲t, *Engl* ˈu̇l-ˌbrikt\, **Walter** (1893–1973) German communist leader and head of East Germany (1960–73). He joined the German Communist Party after World War I and was elected to its central committee in 1923. He led the party in Berlin 1929–33, then fled abroad after the Nazi takeover. As an agent for the Comintern, he persecuted Trotskyites and other deviationists. In 1945 he returned to the Soviet-occupied zone of Germany, helped form the Socialist Unity Party in East Germany, and served as its general secretary 1950–71. He served as deputy premier of East Germany 1949–60, and as chairman of its council of state 1960–73. A constant foe of West Germany, he built the Berlin Wall in 1961. He exercised rigid control over East Germany while developing its industrial strength.

ulcer Concave sore on the skin or lining of an organ, with well-defined, sometimes raised edges. Erosion of surface tissue may extend to deeper layers. The main symptom is pain. The term most often refers to PEPTIC ULCER but also includes skin ulcer, common on legs with VARICOSE VEINS and the feet of people with DIABETES MELLITUS (when nerve damage has reduced sensation), and decubitus ulcer (bedsore or pressure sore). Other causes include INFECTION, trauma (e.g., BURN, FROSTBITE), improper nutrition (e.g., THIAMINE deficiency), and CANCER (likely in ulcers hard to the touch). Skin ulcers over a month old should be checked for cancer, especially after middle age.

Ullmann, Liv (born 1939) Norwegian-Swedish film actress. Raised mainly in Canada and the U.S., she returned to Norway and made her stage debut in Oslo. She became internationally famous in the films of INGMAR BERGMAN, including *Persona* (1966), *The Passion of Anna* (1969), *Cries and Whispers* (1972), *Scenes from a Marriage* (1973), and *Autumn Sonata* (1978). Noted for her expressive face and subtle acting, she also starred in other Swedish and international films, including *The Emigrants* (1971) and *The New Land* (1973), and appeared on stage in the U.S. and Europe. She directed and cowrote *Sofie* (1993) and directed *Private Confessions* (1999) from Bergman's screenplay.

Ulm, Battle of (September 25–October 20, 1805) Major victory by France over Austria at Ulm, Bavaria. In August 1805, Austria joined the Anglo-Russian alliance against NAPOLEON and on September 11 sent 72,000 troops under Baron Karl Mack (1752–1828) into Bavaria, an ally of France. Napoleon, hoping to crush the Austrians before Russian troops could join them, sent his Grand Army of 210,000 French troops across the Rhine River, marching 18 mi (29 km) a day to reach the Danube River on September 25. After several battles, he encircled the Austrians and forced them into the city of Ulm, where they faced French artillery attacks. Seeing little chance that his troops could hold out until Russian reinforcements arrived, Baron Mack surrendered on October 20 with about 50,000 men.

Ulmanis \ˈu̇l-mä-nis\, **Karlis** (1877–1942) Latvian independence leader and premier of Latvia (1918, 1919–21, 1925–26, 1931–32, 1934–40). An agronomist, he worked to improve farming in Latvia while becoming active in the Latvian independence movement. In 1905 he was forced into exile to the U.S., where he taught agriculture at the University of Nebraska until 1913. Returning to Latvia, he founded the Latvian Farmers' Union (1917) to press for independence from Russia. In 1918 he became premier of the newly independent republic. In his various terms of office he worked to resist internal dissension—instituting authoritarian rule in 1934—and military threats from Russia. Soviet occupation forced his resignation in 1940, and he was arrested and deported to Russia, where he died.

Ulster Historical province, northern IRELAND. It now forms Northern Ireland and Ulster province of Ireland. The ancient province was home to the Roman Catholic O'Neills (earls of TYRONE), who rebelled against English rule c. 1600. After they fled, most of the land was confiscated by British King JAMES I and settled with Protestant Scots, Welsh, and English. It was further colonized after Cromwellian settlement in the mid-17th century. In the early 20th century its opposition to Irish HOME RULE led to the formation of Northern Ireland.

Ulster cycle *or* **Ulaid cycle** \ˈü-lət̲h^y, ˈü-ləg^y\ In early Irish literature, a group of legends and tales dealing with the heroic age of the Ulaid, a people of northeastern Ireland from whom the name Ulster derives. The stories, set in the 1st century BC, were recorded from oral tradition between the 8th and 11th century and are preserved in the 12th-century manuscripts *The Book of the Dun Cow* and *The Book of Leinster* and later compilations. Reflecting the customs of a free pre-Christian aristocracy, they combine mythological and legendary elements. Among the stories are *Bricriu's Feast,* containing a beheading game that appeared in medieval narratives, and *The Tragic Death of the Sons of Usnech,* dramatized in the 20th century by WILLIAM BUTLER YEATS and JOHN MILLINGTON SYNGE.

ultra Member of the extreme right (ultraroyalist) wing of the royalist movement in the French BOURBON RESTORATION (1815–30). The ultras included large landowners, clericalists, and the former ÉMIGRÉ nobility. Opposed to the FRENCH REVOLUTION's secular and egalitarian principles, they called for restrictions on the press and greater power for the Catholic church. They controlled the Chamber of Deputies and the cabinet for most of the 1820s, especially during the reign of their leader CHARLES X. Their policies proved unpopular, and they lost power after 1827; with the JULY REVOLUTION (1830), the faction ceased to exist.

Ultra Allied intelligence system that, in tapping the very highest-level communications among the armed forces of Germany and Japan, contributed to the Allied victory in World War II. In the early 1930s Polish cryptographers first broke the code of Germany's cipher machine ENIGMA. In 1939 they turned their information over to the Allies, and Britain established the Ultra project at Bletchley Park to intercept and decipher Enigma messages. The Japanese also had a modified version of the Enigma, known as "Purple" by the Americans, who were able to duplicate it well before Pearl Harbor. The intercept of signals helped Allied forces win the Battle of Britain and the battles of the Coral Sea and Midway and led to the destruction of a large part of the German forces following the Allied landing in Normandy.

ultrasonics Vibrational or stress waves in elastic media that have a FREQUENCY above 20 kilohertz, the highest frequency of sound waves that can be detected by the human ear. The waves may be longitudinal (as in air or solids) or transverse (as in liquids). They can be generated or detected by piezoelectric transducers (see PIEZOELECTRICITY). High-power ultrasonics produce distortion in the medium; applications include ultrasonic welding, drilling, irradiation of fluid suspensions (as in wine clarification), cleaning of surfaces (such as jewelry), and disruption of biological structures. Low-power ultrasonic waves do not cause distortions; the uses include SONAR, structure testing, and medical imaging and diagnosis. Some animals, including BATS, employ ultrasonic ECHOLOCATION for navigation.

ultrasound *or* **ultrasonography** Use of ultrasonic waves to produce images of body structures. The waves travel through tissues and are reflected back where density differs (e.g., the border between a hollow organ's wall and its inside). The reflected echoes are received by an electronic apparatus that measures their intensity level and the position of the tissue reflecting them. The results can be displayed as still images or as a moving picture of the inside of the body. Unlike X RAYS or other ionizing radiation, ultrasound carries minimal if any risk. Most often used during pregnancy to examine the fetus, ultrasound imaging is also used on internal organs, the eye, breast, and major blood vessels. It can often show whether a growth is benign or malignant. See also DIAGNOSTIC IMAGING.

ultraviolet astronomy Study of the ultraviolet (UV) spectra of astronomical objects. It has yielded much information about chemical abundances and processes in interstellar matter, the sun, and certain other stellar objects, such as white dwarf stars. UV astronomy became feasible once rockets could carry instruments above earth's atmosphere, which absorbs most ELECTROMAGNETIC RADIATION of UV WAVELENGTHS. Since the early 1960s, several unmanned satellite observatories carrying UV telescopes, including the HUBBLE SPACE TELESCOPE, have collected UV-wavelength data on objects such as comets, quasars, nebulae, and distant star clusters. See also SPECTRUM.

ultraviolet radiation Portion of the ELECTROMAGNETIC SPECTRUM extending from the violet end of the visible light region to the X-RAY region. Ultraviolet (UV) radiation is divided into three bands: UVA (also called black light), UVB (responsible for the best-known effects on organisms), and UVC (which does not reach the earth's surface). Most UV rays from the sun are absorbed by the earth's OZONE LAYER. UV has low penetrating power, so its effects on humans are limited to the skin. These effects include stimulation of production of VITAMIN D, SUNBURN, suntan, aging signs, and carcinogenic changes. UV radiation is also used to treat jaundice in newborns, to sterilize equipment, and to produce artificial light.

Ulysses See ODYSSEUS

Umar ibn al-Khattab \'ù-mär-ˌib-nu̇l-k̲ät-'täb\ (586?–644) Second CALIPH (634–44). He initially opposed MUHAMMAD but became a Muslim c. 615. His daughter Hafsa married Muhammad in 625. He was nominated by ABU BAKR as his successor. As caliph he spread Islam to Egypt, Syria, and Persia. His innovations affected taxation, social welfare, and the empire's entire financial and administrative fabric, and he was noted for his justice, social ideals, and statesmanship.

Umar Tal \ˌù-mär-'tál\ *in full* **al-Hajj Umar ibn Said Tal** (1797?–1864) West African founder of the TUKULOR empire. Born in the Sénégal River valley, he became a mystic and set out to Mecca on a pilgrimage at 23. Through political and religious connections he made during and after his journey, he was appointed caliph for black Africa by the head of the Tijani brotherhood. He returned to Africa in 1833, and in 1854 he ordered a jihad to sweep away the pagans and bring back lapsed Muslims in the area of upper Guinea, eastern Senegal, and western and central Mali. He defeated the Bambara pagans of Mali, but they soon rebelled. Attacked by the Tuaregs, Moors, and Fulani in 1863, Umar's army was destroyed, and he was pursued and killed in an explosion. His empire lasted until 1897, when it was annexed by the French.

Umayyad dynasty \ù-'mä-yəd\ (661–750) First great Muslim dynasty. It was founded by MUAWIYAH I, who triumphed over Muhammad's son-in-law, ALI, to become the fifth caliph. He moved the capital to DAMASCUS and used the Syrian army to extend the Arab empire. The Umayyads' greatest period was under ABD AL-MALIK (r.685–705), when their empire extended from Spain to Central Asia and India. Their decline began with a defeat by the Byzantines in 717; intertribal feuding and the failure of financial reforms eventually led to their unseating by the ABBASID dynasty. See also ABD AL-RAHMAN III, ABU MUSLIM, HUSAYN IBN ALI.

Umberto I (1844–1900) King of Italy (1878–1900) and duke of Savoy. The son of VICTOR EMMANUEL II, he fought in the wars against Austria (1866). After ascending the throne in 1878, he led his country out of its isolation and into the TRIPLE ALLIANCE (1882). However, a tariff war with France led to economic difficulties (1888), and Umberto's colonial policy in Africa was ended by Italy's defeat by Ethiopia (1896). Facing increasing social unrest, he supported the imposition of martial law (1898) and created a period of turmoil that culminated in his assassination by an anarchist.

Umberto II (1904–1983) Prince of Savoy and briefly king of Italy (1946). Son of VICTOR EMMANUEL III, he commanded an Italian army division in World War II. In May 1946 his father abdicated in his favor, but Umberto was himself forced to abdicate in June after the Italian people voted for a republic. He and his male heirs were permanently banished from Italy, and he settled in Portugal.

Umbria Autonomous region (pop., 1996 est.: 826,000), central Italy. It is located in the APENNINES; its capital is PERUGIA. Originally inhabited by the ancient Italic Umbrian tribe, it came under Rome c. 300 BC and was made one of its administrative regions in the 1st century AD. During the Christian era it became part of the PAPAL STATES. It was the seat of the 15th–16th century Umbrian school of painting which included PERUGINO and PINTURICCHIO, and was the home of St. FRANCIS OF ASSISI. Agriculture is an economic mainstay, while its industries produce steel, chemicals, and textiles.

Umbrian language \'əm-brē-ən\ Ancient ITALIC LANGUAGE spoken in central Italy in the last few centuries BC. Umbrian was related closely to OSCAN and Volscian and more distantly to LATIN. It was displaced by Latin at an unknown date. Modern knowledge of the language is derived almost entirely from the IGUVINE TABLES (c. 300–90 BC).

Umbrians Ancient pre-Etruscan people pushed into central Italy (Umbria) by the ETRUSCANS and GAULS. They never fought an important war with the Romans. In the SOCIAL WAR they were among the first to make peace with Rome. They are described by ancient authors as being similar to their Etruscan enemies in culture. The Umbrian alphabet is undoubtedly of Etruscan origin. Their dialect was Indo-European.

U.N. See UNITED NATIONS

Un-American Activities Committee, House See HOUSE UN-AMERICAN ACTIVITIES COMMITTEE

Unabomber See Theodore KACZYNSKI

Unamuno (y Jugo) \ˌü-nä-'mü-nō\, **Miguel de** (1864–1936) Spanish philosopher and writer. He was rector of the University of Salamanca 1901–14 and 1931–36; he was dismissed first for espousing the Allied cause in World War I and later for denouncing FRANCISCO FRANCO's Falangists. Though he also wrote poetry and plays, he was most influential as an essayist and novelist. In *The Tragic Sense of Life in Men and Peoples* (1913), he stressed the role spiritual anxiety plays in driving one to live the fullest possible life. His most famous novel is *Abel Sánchez* (1917). *The Christ of Velázquez* (1920) is a superb example of modern Spanish verse.

uncertainty principle *or* **Heisenberg uncertainty principle** *or* **indeterminacy principle** Principle that states that the position and velocity of an object cannot both be measured exactly at the same time, and that the concepts of exact position and exact velocity together have no meaning in nature. Articulated by WERNER HEISENBERG in 1927, it applies only at the small scales of ATOMS and SUBATOMIC PARTICLES and is not noticeable for macroscopic objects, such as moving vehicles. Any attempt to measure the velocity of a subatomic particle precisely will displace the particle in an unpredictable way, thus invalidating any simultaneous measurement of its position. This displacement is a result of the wave nature of particles (see WAVE-PARTICLE DUALITY). The principle also applies to other related pairs of variables, such as energy and time.

James Montgomery Flagg's representation of Uncle Sam, which was first used on World War I recruiting posters.

BY COURTESY OF THE LIBRARY OF CONGRESS, WASHINGTON, D.C.

Uncle Sam Popular U.S. symbol, usually associated with a cartoon figure having long white hair and chin whiskers and dressed in a swallow-tailed coat, vest, tall hat, and striped trousers. The name probably originated with "Uncle Sam" Wilson, a businessman who provided beef to the army during the War of 1812. The "U.S." stamp on his barrels, meant to indicate government property, came to be associated with his nickname, which in time came to symbolize the U.S. government. The Uncle Sam figure evolved in the hands of British and U.S. cartoonists; its most familiar treatment appeared on recruiting posters during World Wars I and II with the caption "I want you."

unconscious *or* **subconscious** In PSYCHOANALYSIS, the part of the psychic apparatus that does not ordinarily enter the individual's awareness but may be manifested by slips of the tongue, DREAMS, or neurotic symptoms (see NEUROSIS). The existence of unconscious mental activities was first elaborated by SIGMUND FREUD and is now a well-established principle of PSYCHIATRY. The origin of many neurotic symptoms is said to depend on CONFLICTS that have been removed from CONSCIOUSNESS by REPRESSION and maintained in the unconscious through various DEFENSE MECHANISMS. Recent biopsychological explorations have shed light on the relationship between brain physiology and the levels of consciousness at which people retain memories.

Underground See RESISTANCE

underground See SUBWAY

Underground Railroad Secret system in northern U.S. states to help escaping slaves. Its name derived from the need for secrecy, using darkness or disguise, and the railway terms used in the conduct of the system. Various routes in 14 states, called lines, provided safe stopping places (stations) for the leaders (conductors) and their charges (packages) while fleeing north, sometimes to Canada. The system developed in defiance of the FUGITIVE SLAVE ACTS and was active mainly from 1830 to 1860. An estimated 40,000–100,000 slaves used the network. Assistance was provided mainly by free blacks, including HARRIET TUBMAN, and philanthropists, church leaders, and abolitionists. Its existence aroused support for the antislavery cause and convinced Southerners that the North would never allow slavery to remain unchallenged.

Undset \'ün-set\, **Sigrid** (1882–1949) Norwegian novelist. Her father was an archaeologist, and her home life was steeped in legend, folklore, and Norwegian history. Her early novels deal with the position of women in the contemporary lower middle class. Her masterpiece, the trilogy *Kristin Lavransdatter* (1920–22), is set in medieval Norway and depicts the spiritual growth of a strong woman. She converted to Roman Catholicism in 1924. Her later works, including the historical *The Master of Hestviken* (1925–27) and novels on contemporary themes, reflect her interest in religion. She received the Nobel Prize in 1928.

undulant fever See BRUCELLOSIS

unemployment Condition of a person who is able to work, is actively seeking work, but is unable to find any. Statistics on unemployment are collected and analyzed by government labor offices in most countries and are considered an important indicator of economic health. Since World War II full employment has been a stated goal of many governments. Full employment is not necessarily synonymous with a zero unemployment rate, since at any given time the unemployment rate will include some people who are between jobs and not unemployed in any long-term sense. In the U.S. an unemployment rate of 2% is often cited as a base rate. Underemployment is the term used to describe the situation of those who are able to find employment only for shorter than normal periods—for example, part-time workers and seasonal workers—and may also describe the condition of workers whose education or training makes them overqualified for their jobs.

unemployment insurance Form of SOCIAL INSURANCE designed to compensate workers for short-term, involuntary unemployment. It was created primarily to provide financial assistance to laid-off workers during a period deemed long enough to allow them to find another job or to be rehired at their original job. In most countries, workers who are permanently disabled or who have been unemployed for a long period of time are covered under other plans. In countries such as Canada and Britain, workers in any occupation may qualify for unemployment insurance; the U.S. denies coverage to certain workers, such as government employees and the self-employed. In most countries, benefits are related to earnings and are paid for a limited period of time. Funding may come out of general government revenues or from specific taxes placed on employers or employees.

UNESCO *in full* **United Nations Educational, Scientific, and Cultural Organization** Specialized agency of the U.N. created in 1946 to aid peace by promoting international collaboration in education, science, and culture. It supports member states' efforts to eliminate illiteracy, encouraging the extension of free education, and acts as a clearinghouse for the exchange of ideas and knowledge. In 1984 the U.S. (later followed by several other countries) withdrew from UNESCO to protest what it saw as UNESCO's politicization; it has not rejoined.

uneven parallel bars Event in women's gymnastics in which a pair of wooden bars supported horizontally above the floor at different heights is used to perform acrobatic feats. The apparatus allows a great variety of movements, but hanging and swinging exercises predominate. It became an Olympic event in 1936. See also PARALLEL BARS.

Ungaretti \,üŋ-gä-'rāt-tē\, **Giuseppe** (1888–1970) Egyptian-Italian poet. He lived in Alexandria until he was 24; the desert regions of Egypt provide recurring images in his work. While studying in Paris, he was strongly influenced by the poets of the SYMBOLIST MOVEMENT. He was the founder of HERMETICISM, which began with his *Il porto sepolto* (1916; "The Buried Port") and brought about a reorientation in modern Italian poetry. Though experimental, his poetry developed in a coherent direction in *Allegria di naufragi* (1919; "Gay Shipwrecks") and later collections. After World War II his works became more structured and acquired a more straightforward tone.

Ungava Bay \ən-'gä-və-\ Inlet, southern HUDSON STRAIT, northeastern Quebec. It is about 200 mi (320 km) long and 160 mi (260 km) wide at its mouth, with a maximum depth of 978 ft (298 m). Fed by several large rivers, including the Koksoak, Leaf, and Payne, it is ice-free only four months a year. At its mouth, Akpatok island (551 sq mi, or 1,427 sq km) rises to 930 ft (283 m).

Ungava Peninsula Northern part of New Quebec district, northern Quebec. It is bounded by HUDSON STRAIT, UNGAVA BAY, Labrador, Eastmain River, and HUDSON BAY. Physically, it is part of the CANADIAN SHIELD.

ungulate \'əŋ-gyə-lət\ Any hoofed, herbivorous, quadruped, placental mammal in three or four orders: Artiodactyla, the even-toed ungulates (including PIGS, CAMELS, DEER, and bovines); Perissodactyla, the odd-toed ungulates (including HORSES, TAPIRS, and RHINOCEROSES); Proboscidea (ELEPHANTS); and, by some authorities, Hyracoidea (see HYRAX). There are ten orders of extinct ungulates. The hoof is dermal tissue, comparable to the human fingernail, that extends over the end of a broadened terminal digit. See also RUMINANT.

UNICEF *in full* **United Nations Children's Fund** *formerly (1946–53)* **United Nations International Children's Emergency Fund** Special U.N. program devoted to the health, nutrition, education, and general welfare of children. It originally provided relief to children in need following World War II. After 1950 its efforts turned to general programs for improvement of children's welfare. It was awarded the Nobel Peace Prize in 1965. Much of its work has been in fields where small expenditures bring large returns, including health care, education, and surplus-food distribution. It is based in New York. It receives over 60% of its funds from governments and the rest through fundraising and card sales.

Unicode International character-encoding system designed to support the electronic interchange, processing, and display of the written texts of the diverse languages of the modern and classical world. The Unicode Worldwide Character Standard includes letters, digits, diacritics, punctuation marks, and technical symbols for all the world's principal written languages, using a uniform encoding scheme. Originally introduced in 1991, the most recent version contains almost 50,000 characters. Numerous encoding systems (including ASCII and EBCDIC) predate Unicode. With Unicode (unlike earlier systems), the unique number provided for each character remains the same on any system that supports Unicode.

unicorn Mythological animal resembling a white horse with a single horn on its forehead. The unicorn was depicted in Mesopotamian art and was referred to in the ancient myths of India and China. Its earliest description in Greek literature dates from c. 400 BC and probably refers to the Indian rhinoceros. The unicorn was believed to be fierce and difficult to capture, but if a virgin were brought before it, it would lay its head in the virgin's lap. Its horn was thought to offer protection against poison. Medieval writers associated the unicorn with Jesus, and the hunt for the unicorn was often represented in medieval art.

Unicorn, detail from "The Lady and the Unicorn" tapestry, late 15th century; in the Musée de Cluny, Paris.
GIRAUDON—ART RESOURCE

unidentified flying object (UFO) Aerial object or optical phenomenon not readily explainable to the observer. Interest in UFOs increased with developments in aeronautics and astronautics after World War II. A government panel investigating sightings in the 1950s reported that 90% coincided with astronomical or meteorological phenomena or sightings of aircraft, birds, or hot gases, sometimes under unusual weather conditions. Some remained unexplained, and in the mid-1960s a few scientists concluded that a small percentage indicated the presence of extraterrestrial visitors. This sensational hypothesis, promoted in the press, met with prompt resistance from other scientists. A U.S. Air Force UFO study begun in 1968 firmly rejected the extraterrestrial hypothesis, but a large fraction of the U.S. public, and a few scientists, still supported it. UFO reports vary widely in reliability. The unaided eye is easily fooled; radar sightings of UFOs, more reliable in some ways, may fail to distinguish physical objects from meteor trails, rain, or thermal discontinuities and are subject to radio interference. See also SETI.

Unification Church *officially* **Holy Spirit Association for the Unification of World Christianity** Religious movement founded (1954) in South Korea by Sun Myung Moon. Influenced by yin-yang principles and Korean shamanism, it seeks to establish divine rule on earth through the restoration of the family, based on the union of the Lord and Lady of the Second Advent (believed to be Moon and his wife, Hak Ja Han). It strives to fulfill what it asserts to be the uncompleted mission of Jesus—procreative marriage. The church has been criticized for its recruitment policies (said to include brainwashing) and business practices. Its mass marriage ceremonies have gained press attention. Its worldwide membership is about 200,000 in more than 100 countries.

unified field theory Attempt to describe all fundamental interactions between elementary particles in terms of a single theoretical framework (a "theory of everything") based on quantum field theory. So far, the weak force and the electromagnetic force have been successfully united in electroweak theory, and the strong force is described by a similar quantum field theory called quantum chromodynamics. However, attempts to unite the strong and electroweak theories in a grand unified theory have failed, as have attempts at a self-consistent quantum field theory of gravitation.

unified science *or* **unity-of-science view** In the philosophy of logical positivism, the doctrine holding that all sciences share the same language, laws, and method. The unity of language has been taken to mean either that all scientific statements could be restated as a set of protocol sentences describing sense-data or that all scientific terms could be defined using physics terms. The unity of law means that the laws of the various sciences must be deduced from some set of fundamental laws (e.g., those of physics). The unity of method means that the procedures for supporting statements in the various sciences are basically the same. The unity-of-science movement that arose in the Vienna Circle held to those three unities, and Rudolf Carnap's "physicalism" supported the notion that all the terms and statements of empirical science could be reduced to terms and statements in the language of physics.

uniform circular motion Motion of a particle moving at a constant speed on a circle. Though the magnitude of the velocity of such an object may be constant, the direction of the velocity is constantly changing, because the object's direction is constantly changing. Its direction at any given instant is perpendicular to a radius of the circle drawn to the point of location of the object on the circle at that time. The acceleration is strictly a change in direction and is a result of a force directed toward the center of the circle. This centripetal force causes centripetal acceleration.

Uniform Resource Locator See URL

uniformitarianism Doctrine in geology that physical, chemical, and biologic processes now at work on and within the earth have operated with general uniformity (in the same manner and with essentially the same intensity) through immensely long periods of time and are sufficient to account for all geologic change. In other words, the present is the key to the past. Although the term is no longer much used, the principle, originated by James Hutton, is fundamental to geologic thinking and underlies the whole development of the science of geology. See also Charles Lyell.

Unilever \ˈyü-nə-ˌlē-vər\ Either of two linked companies, Unilever PLC (based in London) and Unilever NV (based in Rotterdam). They are the holding companies for more than 500 firms worldwide that manufacture and sell soaps, foods, and other products. The modern Unilever was established in 1929 as an association between the British manufacturer Lever Bros. and several other European soap and margarine manufacturers. Today most Unilever sales are in household products, including soaps and detergents, margarines, cooking fats, dairy products, toiletries, and packaged and processed foods. The group also produces paper and plastic products, industrial chemicals, and animal feeds.

union See labor union

Union, Act of (May 1, 1707) Treaty that effected the union of England (and Wales) and Scotland under the name of Great Britain. The union benefited England's need for political safeguards against a possible Jacobite restoration through Scotland, and it gave Scotland economic security by freedom of trade with England. Under the treaty, initiated by Queen Anne, the two kingdoms adopted the Protestant succession, preserved Scots law and the law courts, and agreed to uniform taxation.

Union, Act of (January 1, 1801) Legislative agreement uniting Great Britain and Ireland under the name of the United Kingdom of Great Britain and Ireland. After the unsuccessful Irish revolt of 1798, the British prime minister, William Pitt, decided that the best solution to the Irish problem was a union to strengthen the connection between the two countries. The Irish parliament resisted the proposal, which called for its abolition, but votes bought by cash or honors ensured passage of the agreement in 1800. The union survived until the recognition of the Irish Free State (Ireland) in 1922.

Union Islands See Tokelau

Union League Association formed to inspire loyalty to the Union cause in the American Civil War. Ohio Republicans formed the first Union League of America (1862) to counteract the antiwar Copperheads. Leagues formed in other states to support the war effort and to revitalize the Republican Party. They also acted as social organizations, and some remain as clubs in cities such as New York and Washington. After the Civil War, leagues formed in the South to promote the Republican cause among free blacks.

Union of Soviet Socialist Republics (U.S.S.R.) *or* **Soviet Union** Former republic, eastern Europe and northern and central Asia. It consisted, in its final years, of 15 soviet socialist republics that gained independence at its dissolution: Armenia, Azerbaijan, Belorussia (now Belarus), Estonia, Georgia (now Republic of Georgia), Kazakhstan, Kirgiziya (now Kyrgyzstan), Latvia, Lithuania, Moldova, Russia, Tajikistan, Turkmenistan, Ukraine, and Uzbekistan. It also contained 20 autonomous soviet socialist republics: 16 within Russia, 2 within Georgia, 1 within Azerbaijan, and 1 within Uzbekistan. Area: 8,649,512 sq mi (22,402,235 sq km). Capital: Moscow. Stretching from the Baltic and Black seas to the Pacific Ocean, the Soviet Union comprised the largest country on the globe, having a maximum east–west extent of about 6,800 mi (10,940 km) and a maximum north–south extent of about 2,800 mi (4,505 km). It encompassed 11 time zones and had common boundaries with 6 European countries and 6 Asian countries. Its regions contained fertile lands, deserts, tundra, high mountains, some of the world's largest rivers, and large inland waters, including most of the Caspian Sea. The coastline on the Arctic Ocean extended 3,000 mi (4,825 km), while that on the Pacific was 1,000 mi (1,610 km) long. It was an agricultural, mining, and industrial power. Following the Russian

REVOLUTION OF 1917, four socialist republics were established on the territory of the former Russian empire: the Russian Soviet Federated Socialist Republic, the Transcaucasian Soviet Federated Socialist Republic, the Ukrainian Soviet Socialist Republic, and the Belorussian Soviet Socialist Republic. These four constituent republics established the Union of Soviet Socialist Republics in 1922, to which other republics were added over the years. A power struggle begun in 1924 with the death of Communist leader VLADIMIR LENIN ended in 1927 when JOSEPH STALIN gained victory. Implementation of the first of the FIVE-YEAR PLANS in 1928 centralized industry and collectivized agriculture. A purge in the late 1930s resulted in the imprisonment or execution of millions of persons considered dangerous to the state (see PURGE TRIALS). After World War II, with their respective allies, the U.S.S.R. and the U.S. engaged in the COLD WAR. In the late 1940s it brought about the establishment of Communist regimes throughout most of eastern Europe. The U.S.S.R. exploded its first atomic bomb in 1949, and its first hydrogen bomb in 1953. Following Stalin's death, it experienced limited political and cultural liberalization under NIKITA KHRUSHCHEV. It launched the first manned orbital space flight in 1961. Under LEONID BREZHNEV there was a partial reversal of the move towards liberalization. In the mid-1980s its leader MIKHAIL GORBACHEV instituted a liberal policy of PERESTROIKA. By the end of 1990 the Communist government had toppled, and a program to create a market economy was implemented. The U.S.S.R. was officially dissolved on December 25, 1991. (For further information, see independent republics mentioned above.)

Union Pacific Railroad Co. Company that extended the U.S. railway system to the Pacific Coast. Incorporated by an act of Congress in 1862, it was built westward 1,006 mi (1,620 km) from Omaha, Neb., to meet the CENTRAL PACIFIC RAILROAD, which was being built eastward from Sacramento, Cal. The two railroads were joined at Promontory, Utah, in 1869. The Union Pacific was largely financed by federal loans and land grants, but involvement in the CRÉDIT MOBILIER SCANDAL left it badly in debt, and the company went into receivership in 1893. It was reorganized in 1897 by EDWARD H. HARRIMAN, under whose leadership the railroad took part in the economic development of the West. In 1982 it merged with the Missouri Pacific Railroad Co. and the Western Pacific Railroad Co. Its acquisition of the Southern Pacific Rail Corp. in 1996 made it the largest railroad in the U.S., with control of almost all rail-based shipping in the western two-thirds of the U.S.

union shop Arrangement under which workers are required to join a particular union within a specified period of time after beginning employment. Such an arrangement differs from the CLOSED SHOP in that the employer's choice of new employees is not restricted to union members. Advocates of the union shop argue that it prevents workers from enjoying the benefits of unionism without bearing their share of the costs. Union shops are uncommon in most countries, but they are both legal and common in the U.S. and Japan. In the U.S., workers in an enterprise usually choose a single union to represent them by majority vote, though in some states RIGHT-TO-WORK LAWS prohibit requiring union membership as a condition of employment, thus forbidding both the union shop and the closed shop.

unit trust See MUTUAL FUND

Unitarianism Religious movement that stresses free use of reason in religion, holds that God exists in only one person, and denies the divinity of JESUS and the doctrine of the Holy TRINITY. Its modern roots are traced to several liberal, radical, and rationalist thinkers of the Protestant REFORMATION, who were in turn inspired by ARIUS. The mainstream of British and American Unitarianism grew out of Calvinist PURITANISM. The scientist JOSEPH PRIESTLEY was a founder of the English Unitarians, who became a force in Parliament and were noted advocates of social reform. In the U.S., Unitarianism developed out of New England CONGREGATIONALISM that rejected the 18th-century revival movement. TRANSCENDENTALISM injected Unitarianism with a new interest that attracted many more followers. See also CALVINISM, UNIVERSALISM.

Unitas \yü-ˈnī-təs\, **Johnny** *orig.* **John Constantine** (1933–2002) U.S. football quarterback. Born in Pittsburgh, he played for the University of Louisville; though selected in the NFL draft, he played semiprofessionally before signing with the Baltimore Colts. Playing with the Colts from 1957 to 1971, he led them to five league championship games (1958, 1959, 1964, 1968, 1970) and two Super Bowl games (1969, 1971). He later played for the San Diego Chargers (1971–73) before retiring. He passed for 40,239 yards and 290 touchdowns in his career and was elected to the Pro Football Hall of Fame in 1979.

Unité d'Habitation \ü̅-nē-ˈtā-dȧ-bē-tȧ-ˈsyōⁿ\ Residential block (18 stories high) in Marseille, France, that expressed LE CORBUSIER's ideal of urban family lodging. Completed in 1952, it is a vertical mixed-use community, with a shopping floor halfway up and other communal facilities on the roof. Two-story living rooms make for efficient use of volumes and permit the use of a "skip-stop" system in which elevators stop on every other floor. Each unit has front and rear balconies with sun protection provided by Le Corbusier's BRISE-SOLEIL. The concrete screen pierced with differently sized openings evokes tracery.

United Airlines, Inc. U.S. international airline. It began as United Aircraft and Transport Corp., which first operated transcontinental passenger flights in 1929. It became the first airline to introduce stewardesses in 1930. United Airlines, Inc., was established in Chicago in 1931 as a HOLDING COMPANY for the corporation's four constituent airlines. United expanded rapidly after World War II and became the largest air carrier in the Western world when it merged with Capital Airlines in 1961. United acquired PAN AMERICAN WORLD AIRWAYS' transpacific routes in 1986 and its Latin American and Caribbean routes in 1991. United employees purchased a controlling share of the airline in 1994, making it the largest employee-owned company in the U.S.

United Arab Emirates *formerly* **Trucial States** \ˈtrü-shəl\ Federation of seven states, eastern ARABIAN PENINSULA. They are the emirates of ABU DHABI, DUBAYY, Ajman, Al-Shariqah, Umm al-Qaywayn, Ras al-Khaymah, and Al-Fujayrah. Area: 32,280 sq mi (83,600 sq km). Population (2002 est.): 3,550,000. Capital: ABU DHABI. Indigenous inhabitants are Arabs, but a large part of the population is made up of Indian, Pakistani, Bangladeshi, and Iranian immigrant workers. Languages: Arabic (official), English, Persian, Urdu, Hindi. Religions: Islam (official), Christianity, Hinduism. Currency: U.A.E. dirham. The United Arab Emirates' low-lying desert plain is broken by the Al-Hajar Mountains along the MUSANDAM PENINSULA. Three natural deepwater harbors are located along the Gulf of OMAN. It has 10% of the world's petroleum reserves and 5% of its natural-gas reserves; their production makes up the principal industries. Other important economic activities include fishing, herding, and growing of dates. The federation has one appointive advisory board; its chief of state is the president and the head of government is the prime minister. In 1820 the British exacted a peace treaty with local rulers along the coast. The area formerly called the Pirate Coast became known as the Trucial Coast. In 1892 the rulers agreed

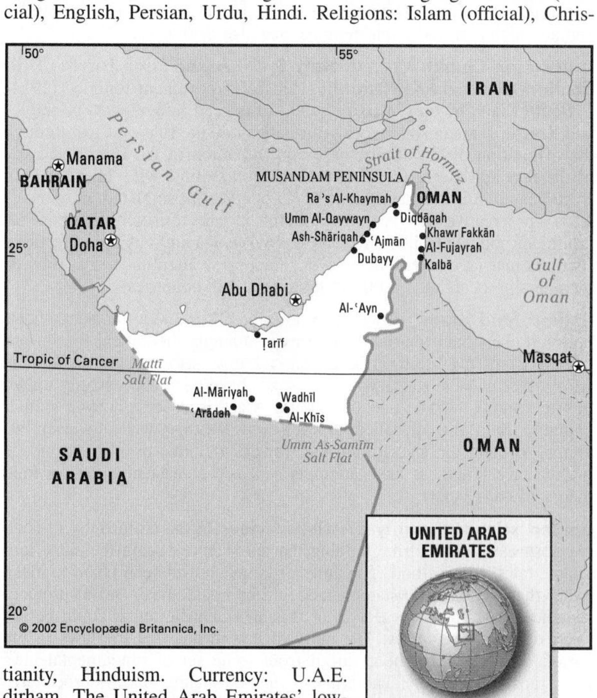

to restrict foreign relations to Britain. Though the British administered the region from 1843, they never assumed sovereignty; each state maintained full internal control. The states formed the Trucial States Council in 1960. In 1971 the sheiks terminated defense treaties with Britain and established the six-member federation. Ras al-Khaymah joined it in 1972. The U.A.E. aided coalition forces against Iraq in the PERSIAN GULF WAR (1991).

United Arab Republic See EGYPT

United Artists Corp. Former U.S. film company. It was founded in 1919 by CHARLIE CHAPLIN, MARY PICKFORD, DOUGLAS FAIRBANKS, and D.W. GRIFFITH in order to gain complete freedom to produce and distribute their own movies and to distribute other independently produced movies. The first major production company controlled by its artists, it prospered with the films of its founders, including *The Gold Rush* (1925), and those of such producers as SAMUEL GOLDWYN, HOWARD R. HUGHES, and ALEXANDER KORDA. After 1951 it became mainly a distributor, releasing such successful movies as *High Noon* (1952), *Some Like It Hot* (1959), and *West Side Story* (1961). It was sold to TransAmerica Corp. in 1967 and resold to MGM in 1981. The United Artists name disappeared when it was reorganized in 1992.

United Automobile Workers *in full* **United Automobile, Aerospace, and Agricultural Implement Workers of America (UAW)** U.S. industrial union of automotive and other vehicular workers, headquartered in Detroit. The UAW was founded in 1935, when the Committee for Industrial Organization (see AFL-CIO) began to organize automotive workers. The union successfully countered automakers' initial resistance with sit-down strikes and a 1937 Supreme Court decision upholding the right to organize as declared in the WAGNER ACT. GENERAL MOTORS CORP. was the first to recognize the UAW, and most other automakers followed suit, though FORD MOTOR CO. continued its resistance until 1941. Under WALTER REUTHER, the union won contracts providing for cost-of-living adjustments, health plans, and vacations. Reuther's friction with GEORGE MEANY led the UAW to withdraw from the AFL-CIO in 1968. A short-lived alliance with the TEAMSTERS was dissolved in 1972, and the UAW rejoined the AFL-CIO in 1981. Competition from foreign imports eroded the union's benefits in the 1980s and '90s.

United Brands Co. See CHIQUITA BRANDS INTERNATIONAL, INC.

United Fruit Co. U.S.-based fruit company. It was founded in 1899 in the merger of the Boston Fruit Co. and other companies that sold bananas grown in Central America, Colombia, and the Caribbean. Minor C. Keith, its principal founder, gained extensive land rights in Costa Rica in return for constructing railroads. United Fruit became the largest employer in Central America, developing vast tracts of jungle lands and building one of the largest private merchant navies in the world. Attacked in the Latin American press as *el pulpo* ("the octopus"), the company was widely accused of exploiting workers and influencing governments during the era of "dollar diplomacy" in the early to mid-20th century. Its later policies were more enlightened, and it transferred portions of its landholdings to individual growers. In 1970 United Fruit merged with AMK Corp. to form United Brands Co., which changed its name in 1990 to CHIQUITA BRANDS INTERNATIONAL, Inc.

United Kingdom of Great Britain and Northern Ireland *commonly shortened to* **United Kingdom** *or* **Great Britain** Kingdom, western Europe, comprising GREAT BRITAIN (ENGLAND, SCOTLAND, and WALES) and Northern IRELAND. Area: 94,248 sq mi (244,101 sq km). Population (2002 est.): 60,177,000. Capital: LONDON. The population is composed of the English (major ethnic group), Scots, Irish, and Welsh and immigrants from India, the West Indies, Pakistan, and Bangladesh. Languages: English (official), also Welsh and Scottish Gaelic. Religions: Churches of England and Scotland (established); no established church in Northern Ireland or Wales; Roman Catholicism, Protestant denominations, Islam, Judaism, Hinduism, Sikhism. Currency: pound sterling. The country has hill, lowland, upland, highland, and mountain regions. Tin and iron ore deposits, once central to the economy, have become exhausted or uneconomical, and the coal industry, long a staple of the economy, began a steady decline in the 1950s that worsened with pit closures in the 1980s. Offshore petroleum and natural gas reserves are significant. Chief crops are barley, wheat, sugar beets, and potatoes. Major manufactures include motor vehicles, aerospace equipment, electronic data-processing and telecommunication equipment, and petrochemicals. Fishing and publishing also are important economic activities. The

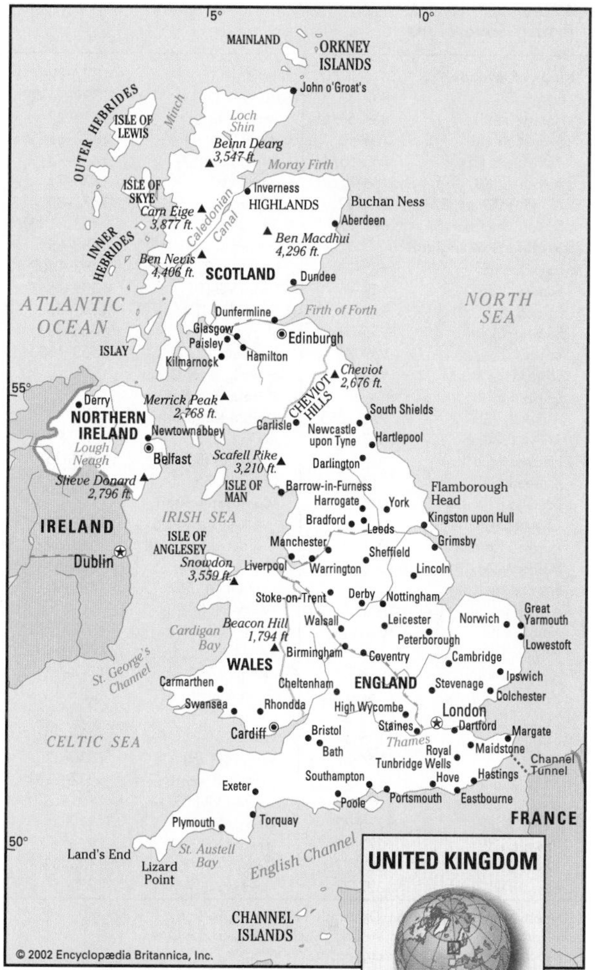

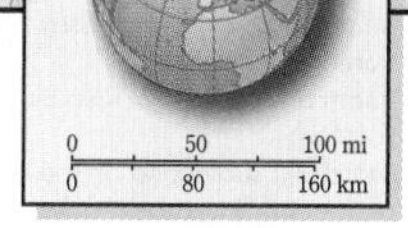

United Kingdom is a constitutional monarchy with two legislative houses; its chief of state is the sovereign, and the head of government is the prime minister. The early pre-Roman inhabitants of Britain (see STONEHENGE) were Celtic-speaking peoples, including the Brythonic people of Wales, the Picts of Scotland, and the Britons of Britain. Celts also settled in Ireland c. 500 BC. JULIUS CAESAR invaded and took control of the area 55–54 BC. The Roman province of Britannia endured until the 5th century and included present-day England and Wales. In the 5th century Nordic tribes of Angles, Saxons, and Jutes invaded Britain. The invasions had little effect on the Celtic peoples of Wales and Scotland. Christianity began to flourish in the 6th century. During the 8th–9th century, Vikings, particularly Danes, raided the coasts of Britain. In the late 9th century ALFRED the Great repelled a Danish invasion, which helped bring about the unification of England under Athelstan. The Scots attained dominance in Scotland, which was finally unified under MALCOLM II (1005–34). William of Normandy (see WILLIAM I) took England in 1066. The Norman kings established a strong central government and feudal state. The French language of the Norman rulers eventually merged with the Anglo-Saxon of the common people to form the English language. From the 11th century, Scotland came under the influence of the English throne. HENRY II conquered Ireland in the late 12th century. His sons RICHARD I and JOHN had conflicts with the clergy and nobles, and eventually John was forced to grant the nobles concessions in the MAGNA CARTA (1215). The concept of community of the realm developed during the 13th century, providing the foundation for parliamentary government. During the reign of EDWARD I, statute law developed to supplement English COMMON LAW, and the first PARLIAMENT was convened.

British Sovereigns

Kings of Wessex	
Egbert (S)	802–39
Aethelwulf (S)	839–56/58
Aethelbald (S)	855/56–60
Aethelberht (S)	860–65/66
Aethelred I (S)	865/66–71
Alfred the Great (S)	871–99
Edward the Elder (S)	899–924
Sovereigns of England	
Athelstan[1] (S)	925–39
Edmund I (S)	939–46
Eadred (S)	946–55
Eadwig (S)	955–59
Edgar (S)	959–75
Edward the Martyr (S)	975–78
Ethelred II the Unready (S)	978–1013
Sweyn Forkbeard (D)	1013–14
Ethelred II the Unready[2] (S)	1014–16
Edmund II Ironside (S)	1016
Canute (D)	1016–35
Harold I Harefoot (D)	1035–40
Hardecanute (D)	1040–42
Edward the Confessor (S)	1042–66
Harold II (S)	1066
William I the Conqueror (N)	1066–87
William II (N)	1087–1100
Henry I (N)	1100–35
Stephen (B)	1135–54
Henry II (P)	1154–89
Richard I (P)	1189–99
John (P)	1199–1216
Henry III (P)	1216–72
Edward I (P)	1272–1307
Edward II (P)	1307–27
Edward III (P)	1327–77
Richard II (P)	1377–99
Henry IV (P:L)	1399–1413
Henry V (P:L)	1413–22
Henry VI (P:L)	1422–61
Edward IV (P:Y)	1461–70
Henry VI[2]	1470–71
Edward IV[2]	1471–83
Edward V (P:Y)	1483
Richard III (P:Y)	1483–85
Henry VII (T)	1483–1509
Henry VIII (T)	1509–1547
Edward VI (T)	1547–53
Mary I (T)	1553–58
Elizabeth I (T)	1558–1603
Sovereigns of Great Britain and the United Kingdom	
James I (VI of Scotland) (St)	1603–25
Charles I (St)	1625–49
Commonwealth	
Oliver Cromwell	1653–58
Richard Cromwell	1658–59
Charles II (St)	1660–85
James II (St)	1685–88
William III & Mary II (O/St)	1689–1702[3]
Anne (St)	1702–14
George I (H)	1714–27
George II (H)	1727–60
George III (H)	1760–1820
George IV (H)	1820–30
William IV (H)	1830–37
Victoria (H)	1837–1901
Edward VII (SCG)	1901–10
George V (W)	1910–36
Edward VIII (W)	1936[4]
George VI (W)	1936–52
Elizabeth II (W)	1952–

Dynasty or house: S=Saxon, D=Danish, N=Norman, B=Blois, P=Plantagenet, L=Lancaster, Y=York, T=Tudor, St=Stuart, O=Orange, H=Hanover, SCG=Saxe-Coburg-Gotha, W=Windsor
[1]Athelstan was king of Wessex and the first king of all England.
[2]restored
[3]William and Mary, as husband and wife, reigned jointly until Mary's death in 1694.
[4]Edward VIII succeeded on the death of his father on January 20, 1936, but abdicated on December 11 before his coronation.

In 1314 Robert Bruce (see ROBERT I) won independence for Scotland. The TUDORS became the ruling family of England following the WARS OF THE ROSES (1455–85). HENRY VIII established the Church of England and incorporated Wales as part of England. The reign of ELIZABETH I began a period of colonial expansion; 1588 brought the defeat of the SPANISH ARMADA. In 1603 James VI of Scotland ascended to the English throne, becoming JAMES I, and established a personal union of the two kingdoms. The ENGLISH CIVIL WARS erupted in 1642 between Royalists and Parliamentarians, ending in the execution of CHARLES I (1649). After eleven years of Puritan rule under OLIVER CROMWELL and his son (1649–60), the monarchy was restored with CHARLES II. In 1707 England and Scotland assented to the ACT OF UNION, forming the kingdom of Great Britain. The Hanoverians ascended to the English throne in 1714, when George Louis, elector of HANOVER, became GEORGE I of Great Britain. During the reign of GEORGE III, Great Britain's American colonies won independence (1783). This was followed by a period of war with revolutionary France and later with the empire of NAPOLEON (1789–1815). In 1801 legislation united Great Britain with Ireland to create the United Kingdom of Great Britain and Ireland. Britain was the birthplace of the INDUSTRIAL REVOLUTION in the late 18th century, and it remained the world's foremost economic power until the late 19th century. During the reign of Queen VICTORIA, Britain's colonial expansion reached its zenith, though the older dominions, including Canada and Australia, were granted independence (1867 and 1901, respectively). The United Kingdom entered WORLD WAR I allied with France and Russia in 1914. Following the war, revolutionary disorder erupted in Ireland, and in 1921 the Irish Free State (see IRELAND) was granted dominion status. The six counties of ULSTER, however, remained in the United Kingdom as NORTHERN IRELAND. The United Kingdom entered WORLD WAR II in 1939. Following the war the Irish Free State became the Irish Republic and left the COMMONWEALTH. India also gained independence from the United Kingdom. Throughout the postwar period and into the 1970s, the United Kingdom continued to grant independence to its overseas colonies and dependencies. With U.N. forces, it participated in the KOREAN WAR (1950–53). In 1956 it intervened militarily in Egypt during the SUEZ CRISIS. In 1982 it defeated Argentina in the FALKLAND ISLANDS WAR. As a result of continuing social strife in Northern Ireland, it joined with Ireland in several peace initiatives, which eventually resulted in an agreement to establish an assembly in Northern Ireland. In 1997 referenda approved in Scotland and Wales devolved power to both countries, though both remained part of the United Kingdom.

United Mine Workers of America (UMWA) U.S. labor union. Founded in 1890, the UMWA grew rapidly under the leadership of John Mitchell (president 1898–1908) despite determined opposition from coal-mine operators. By 1920, when JOHN L. LEWIS took over, the union had half a million members. Lewis capitalized on the pro-labor climate of the NEW DEAL and led numerous strikes to win fair pay, safe working conditions, and benefits. The UMWA was a mainstay of the Congress of Industrial Organizations (see AFL-CIO) in its early years, but Lewis withdrew the union from the CIO in 1942. Unaffiliated for decades, the UMWA finally joined the AFL-CIO in 1989. The UMWA's importance declined in the later 20th century with the waning of the labor movement and the rise of alternative sources of fuel, and by the 1990s it had fewer than 200,000 members.

United Nations (U.N.) International organization founded (1945) at the end of World War II to maintain international peace and security, develop friendly relations among nations on equal terms, and encourage international cooperation in solving intractable human problems. A number of its agencies have been awarded the Nobel Prize for Peace, and the U.N. was the corecipient, with KOFI ANNAN, of the prize in 2001. The term originally referred to the nations opposing the Axis powers. An international organization was discussed at the YALTA CONFERENCE, and the U.N. charter was drawn up at the U.N. Conference on International Organization (1945). It has six principal organs: the Economic and Social Council, the U.N. GENERAL ASSEMBLY, the INTERNATIONAL COURT OF JUSTICE, the SECRETARIAT, the U.N. SECURITY COUNCIL, and the U.N. TRUSTEESHIP COUNCIL. It also has 14 specialized agencies—some inherited from its predecessor, the LEAGUE OF NATIONS (e.g., the INTERNATIONAL LABOR ORGANIZATION)—and a number of special offices (e.g., the Office of the UNITED NATIONS HIGH COMMISSIONER FOR REFUGEES), programs, and funds (e.g., UNICEF). The U.N. is involved with economic, cultural, and humanitarian activities and the coordination or regulation of international postal services, civil aviation, meteorological research, telecommunications, international shipping, and intellectual property. Its peacekeeping troops may be deployed for the long term (they have been in the disputed Kashmir region between India and Pakistan since 1949) or for limited stays. Its world headquarters are in New York City; its European headquarters are in Geneva. In 2000 the U.N. had 189 member nations. The principal administrative officer of the U.N. is the secretary-general, who is elected to a five-year renewable term by the General Assembly on the recommendation of the Security Council. Since the U.N.'s founding the secretaries-general and their periods in office have been TRYGVE LIE (1946–53), DAG HAMMARSKJÖLD (1953–61), U THANT (1961–71), KURT WALDHEIM (1972–81), JAVIER PÉREZ DE CUÉLLAR (1982–91), BOUTROS BOUTROS-GHALI (1992–96), and KOFI ANNAN (from 1997). See table on following page.

United Nations Children's Fund See UNICEF

United Nations Conference on Trade and Development (UNCTAD) Organ of the U.N. GENERAL ASSEMBLY created in 1964 to promote international trade. It meets every four years and is run by a Trade and Development Board (consisting of its member nations) when not in session. Its principal functions include promotion of trade between countries in different stages of development and with different economic systems, initiation of negotiations for trade agreements, and formulation of international trade policies.

U.N. Member States

1945	Argentina, Belarus, Brazil, Chile, China, Cuba, Denmark, Dominican Republic, Egypt, El Salvador, France, Haiti, Iran, Lebanon, Luxembourg, New Zealand, Nicaragua, Paraguay, Philippines, Poland, Russian Federation[3], Saudi Arabia, Syria, Turkey, Ukraine, United Kingdom, United States of America, Yugoslavia, Greece, India, Peru, Australia, Costa Rica, Liberia, Colombia, Mexico, S. Africa, Canada, Ethiopia, Panama, Bolivia, Venezuela, Guatemala, Norway, Netherlands, Honduras, Uruguay, Ecuador, Iraq, Belgium
1946	Afghanistan, Iceland, Sweden, Thailand
1947	Pakistan, Yemen[6]
1948	Burma (Myanmar)
1949	Israel
1950	Indonesia
1955	Albania, Austria, Bulgaria, Cambodia, Finland, Hungary, Ireland, Italy, Jordan, Laos, Libya, Nepal, Portugal, Romania, Spain, Sri Lanka
1956	Morocco, Sudan, Tunisia, Japan
1957	Ghana, Malaysia
1958	Guinea
1960	Benin, Upper Volta (Burkina Faso), Cameroon, Central African Republic, Chad, Congo, Democratic Republic of the Congo, Ivory Coast, Cyprus, Gabon, Madagascar, Niger, Somalia, Togo, Mali, Senegal, Nigeria
1961	Sierra Leone, Mauritania, Mongolia, Tanzania[5]
1962	Burundi, Jamaica, Rwanda, Trinidad and Tobago, Algeria, Uganda
1963	Kuwait, Kenya
1964	Malawi, Malta, Zambia
1965	Gambia, Maldives, Singapore
1966	Guyana, Botswana, Lesotho, Barbados
1968	Mauritius, Swaziland, Equatorial Guinea
1970	Fiji
1971	Bahrain, Bhutan, Qatar, Oman, United Arab Emirates
1973	Bahamas, Germany[2]
1974	Bangladesh, Grenada, Guinea-Bissau
1975	Cape Verde, Mozambique, São Tome and Principe, Papua New Guinea, Comoros, Suriname
1976	Seychelles, Angola, Samoa
1977	Djibouti, Vietnam
1978	Solomon Islands, Dominica
1979	Saint Lucia
1980	Zimbabwe, Saint Vincent and the Grenadines
1981	Vanuatu, Belize, Antigua and Barbuda
1983	Saint Kitts and Nevis
1984	Brunei Darussalam
1990	Namibia, Liechtenstein
1991	Estonia, N. Korea, S. Korea, Latvia, Lithuania, Marshall Islands, Micronesia
1992	Armenia, Kazakstan, Kyrgyzstan, Moldova, San Marino, Tajikistan, Turkmenistan, Uzbekistan, Azerbaijan, Bosnia and Herzegovina, Croatia, Slovenia, Georgia
1993	Czech Republic[1], Slovakia[1], Macedonia[4], Eritrea, Monaco, Andorra
1994	Palau
1999	Kiribati, Nauru, Tonga
2000	Tuvalu
2002	East Timor (Timor-Leste), Switzerland

[1]Czechoslovakia was an original member from 1945. The Czech Republic and the Slovak Republic obtained separate memberships in 1992.
[2]E. Germany and W. Germany were admitted as separate members in 1973; the two countries reunified in 1990.
[3]The seat held by the Soviet Union, a member from 1945, was assumed by Russia in 1991.
[4]Macedonia is referred to in the U.N. as "The former Yugoslav Republic of Macedonia" pending settlement of a dispute over its name.
[5]Tanganyika, a member from 1961, merged in 1964 with Zanzibar, a member from 1963, to form the new country of Tanzania.
[6]N. Yemen, a member from 1947, merged in 1990 with S. Yemen, a member from 1967.

United Nations Development Programme (UNDP) U.N. organization formed in 1965 by merging two older programs. Its Governing Council includes representatives from 48 nations (27 developing countries and 21 developed). Based in New York City, the UNDP helps low-income states develop their human capabilities and natural resources. It funds projects intended to attract development capital, train skilled workers, and institute modern technologies. It provides experts to study growth potentials and help provide facilities for scientific research.

United Nations Disaster Relief Coordinator Agency of the U.N. Secretariat, established in 1972 to coordinate international relief to countries struck by natural or other disaster. In 1992 the U.N. Department of Humanitarian Affairs was established to coordinate U.N. assistance in humanitarian crises. As part of the U.N. secretary-general's reform program, the department was renamed in 1998 the Office for the Coordination of Humanitarian Affairs (OCHA).

United Nations General Assembly One of six principal components of the UNITED NATIONS and the only one in which all U.N. members are represented. It meets annually or in special sessions. It acts primarily as a deliberative body; it may discuss and make recommendations about any issue within the scope of the U.N. charter. Its president is elected annually on a rotating basis from five geographic groups of members.

United Nations High Commissioner for Refugees, Office of the Office established in 1951 as successor to the International Refugee Organization to give legal, social, economic, and political aid to refugees. Its initial efforts focused on Europeans displaced by World War II; it has since assisted refugees in Africa, Asia, Latin America, and Yugoslavia. It is based in Geneva and financed by voluntary government contributions. The office won the Nobel Peace Prize in 1954 and 1981.

United Nations Relief and Rehabilitation Administration Administrative body (1943–47) for an extensive social-welfare program for war-ravaged nations. It distributed relief supplies and services, including shelter, food, and medicine, and helped with agricultural and economic rehabilitation. Its functions were later taken over by the International Refugee Organization, the WORLD HEALTH ORGANIZATION, and UNICEF.

United Nations Resolution 242 Resolution of the U.N. SECURITY COUNCIL that ended the 1967 SIX-DAY WAR. The Israelis supported the resolution because it called on the Arab states to accept Israel's right "to live in peace within secure and recognized boundaries free from threats or acts of force." All Arab states eventually accepted it (Egypt and Jordan accepted the resolution from the outset) because of its clause calling for Israel to withdraw from the territories conquered in 1967. The PALESTINE LIBERATION ORGANIZATION rejected it until 1988 because it lacked explicit references to Palestinians. Though never fully implemented, it was the basis of diplomatic efforts to end Arab–Israeli conflicts until the CAMP DAVID ACCORDS and remains an important touchstone in any negotiated resolution to the Arab–Israeli conflict.

United Nations Secretariat Administrative body that coordinates UNITED NATIONS activities. Its staff, recruited on the basis of merit, is composed of several thousand permanent professional experts from member states, including translators, clerks, technicians, administrators, project directors, and negotiators, who carry out the U.N.'s day-to-day operations and administer the policies and programs set by the other divisions. They are required to swear an oath of loyalty to the U.N. and must not take instructions from their home governments.

United Nations Security Council Division of the U.N. whose primary responsibility is to maintain international peace and security. It originally had five permanent members—Taiwan (succeeded in 1971 by China), France, England, the U.S., and the Soviet Union (succeeded in 1991 by Russia)—and six rotating members elected by the UNITED NATIONS GENERAL ASSEMBLY for two-year terms. In 1965 the nonpermanent membership was enlarged to 10 members. U.N. members agree to abide by the Security Council's resolutions when they join. It investigates disputes that may cause international friction and advises on how to resolve them. To prevent or stop aggression, it may impose diplomatic or economic sanctions or authorize the use of military force. The affirmative vote of all five permanent members is necessary to arrive at a decision on substantive matters, a requirement that has rendered the body toothless on innumerable occasions.

United Nations Trusteeship Council One of the main organs of the U.N., composed of the five permanent members of the Security Council. It supervised the administration of trust (non-self-governing) territories, including former colonies in Africa and the Pacific. The council's job was to send inspection missions to the territories, examine petitions, review reports, and make recommendations. It suspended operations after the last trust territory, Palau, gained its sovereignty in 1994.

United Netherlands, Republic of the See DUTCH REPUBLIC

United Provinces See UTTAR PRADESH

United States *officially* **United States of America** Federal republic, North America. It is comprised of 48 contiguous states occupying

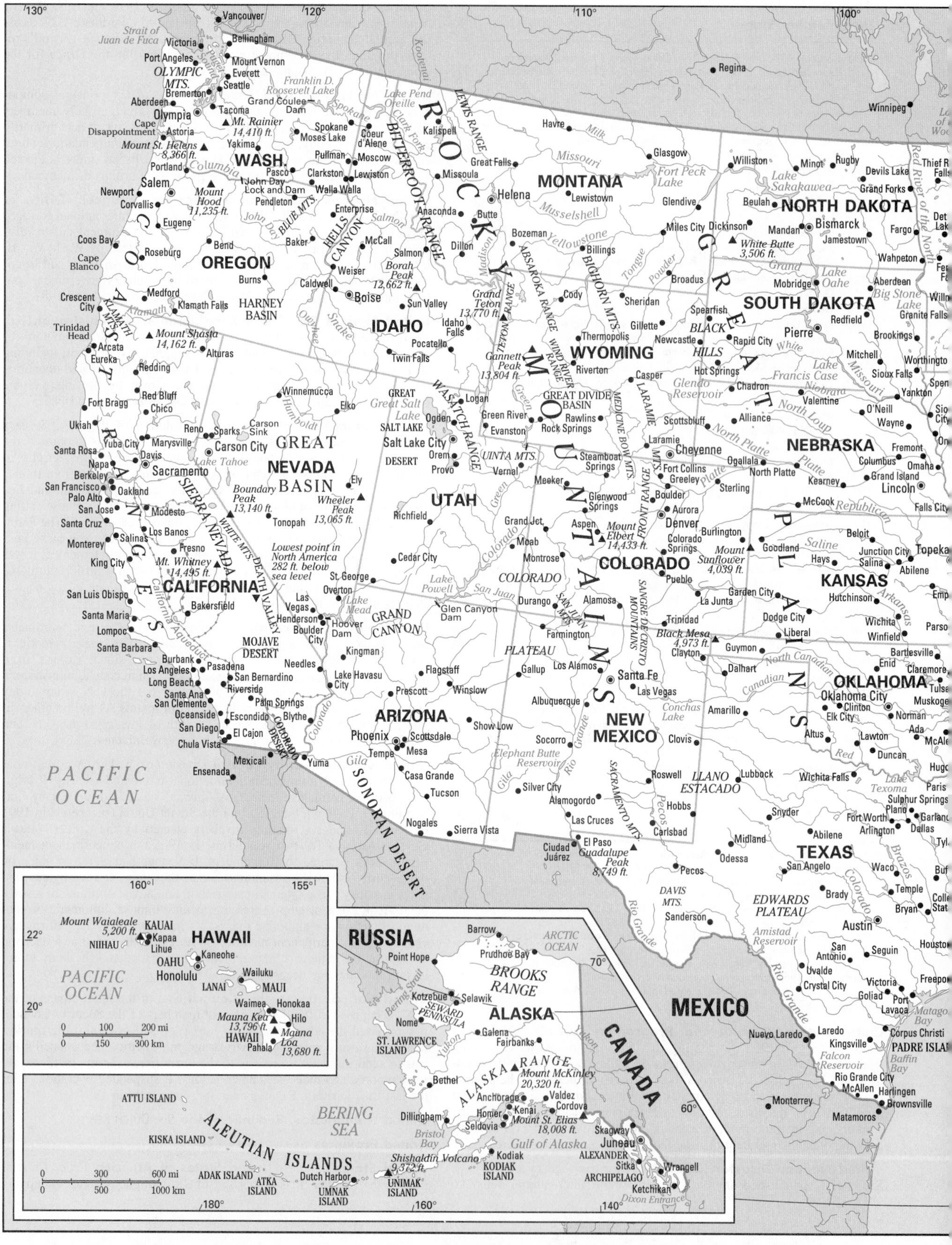

130°
120°
110°
100°
Strait of Juan de Fuca
Vancouver
Victoria
Bellingham
Port Angeles
Puget Sound
Mount Vernon
OLYMPIC MTS.
Everett
Seattle
Bremerton
Franklin D. Roosevelt Lake
Grand Coulee Dam
Aberdeen
Olympia
Tacoma
Mt. Rainier 14,410 ft.
Cape Disappointment
Astoria
Spokane
Moses Lake
Coeur d'Alene
Mount St. Helens 8,366 ft.
Yakima
WASH.
Pullman
Moscow
Portland
Columbia
Pasco
Clarkston
Lewiston
John Day Lock and Dam
Walla Walla
Salem
Newport
Mount Hood 11,235 ft.
Pendleton
Corvallis
Eugene
Enterprise
BLUE MTS.
HELLS CANYON
Coos Bay
Baker
Bend
McCall
Roseburg
Cape Blanco
OREGON
Weiser
Burns
Caldwell
Boise
Crescent City
Medford
Klamath Falls
HARNEY BASIN
KLAMATH MTS.
Trinidad Head
Mount Shasta 14,162 ft.
Arcata
Eureka
Alturas
Redding
Red Bluff
Chico
Fort Bragg
Ukiah
Reno
Sparks
Carson Sink
Carson City
Yuba City
Marysville
Santa Rosa
Napa
Davis
Sacramento
Lake Tahoe
Berkeley
San Francisco
Oakland
Palo Alto
San Jose
Modesto
Santa Cruz
Monterey
Salinas
Los Banos
Fresno
King City
Mt. Whitney 14,495 ft.
SIERRA NEVADA
WHITE MTS.
DEATH VALLEY
CALIFORNIA
San Luis Obispo
Bakersfield
Santa Maria
Lompoc
Santa Barbara
California Aqueduct
Burbank
Pasadena
Los Angeles
San Bernardino
Long Beach
Riverside
Santa Ana
San Clemente
Palm Springs
Oceanside
Escondido
Blythe
San Diego
El Cajon
Chula Vista
COLORADO DESERT
Mexicali
Yuma
Ensenada
PACIFIC OCEAN
COAST RANGES
Kootenai
Lake Pend Oreille
Clark Fork
Kalispell
LEWIS RANGE
BITTERROOT RANGE
Missoula
Great Falls
Helena
Anaconda
Butte
Salmon
Borah Peak 12,662 ft.
Sun Valley
Dillon
IDAHO
Idaho Falls
Pocatello
Twin Falls
Snake
Owyhee
Winnemucca
Humboldt
Elko
GREAT NEVADA BASIN
Ely
Boundary Peak 13,140 ft.
Wheeler Peak 13,065 ft.
Tonopah
Lowest point in North America 282 ft. below sea level
Las Vegas
Henderson
Boulder City
Hoover Dam
Lake Mead
MOJAVE DESERT
Needles
Kingman
Lake Havasu City
GRAND CANYON
St. George
Overton
Cedar City
Richfield
UTAH
GREAT SALT LAKE DESERT
Great Salt Lake
Logan
Ogden
Salt Lake City
Orem
Provo
WASATCH RANGE
UINTA MTS.
Vernal
Lake Powell
Glen Canyon Dam
San Juan
Flagstaff
Winslow
Prescott
ARIZONA
Phoenix
Scottsdale
Tempe
Mesa
Show Low
Gila
Casa Grande
Tucson
Nogales
Sierra Vista
SONORAN DESERT
ROCKY MOUNTAINS
Havre
Milk
Missouri
MONTANA
Lewistown
Musselshell
Glasgow
Fort Peck Lake
Glendive
Miles City
Bozeman
Yellowstone
Billings
ABSAROKA RANGE
BIGHORN MTS.
Tongue
Powder
Broadus
Madison
Cody
Sheridan
Grand Teton 13,770 ft.
TETON RANGE
Gillette
Thermopolis
WIND RIVER RANGE
WYOMING
Gannett Peak 13,804 ft.
Riverton
Casper
GREAT DIVIDE BASIN
Green River
Rawlins
Evanston
Rock Springs
LARAMIE MTS.
MEDICINE BOW MTS.
Laramie
Cheyenne
Steamboat Springs
Meeker
Fort Collins
Greeley
Boulder
FRONT RANGE
Glenwood Springs
Grand Jct.
Aspen
Mount Elbert 14,433 ft.
Denver
Aurora
Colorado Springs
Moab
Montrose
COLORADO
Pueblo
COLORADO PLATEAU
Durango
SAN JUAN MTS.
Alamosa
SANGRE DE CRISTO MOUNTAINS
Trinidad
Farmington
Gallup
Los Alamos
Santa Fe
Las Vegas
Albuquerque
NEW MEXICO
Rio Grande
Socorro
Elephant Butte Reservoir
Roswell
Silver City
Alamogordo
SACRAMENTO MTS.
Las Cruces
Pecos
Hobbs
Carlsbad
Ciudad Juárez
El Paso
Guadalupe Peak 8,749 ft.
Regina
Winnipeg
Williston
Minot
Rugby
Devils Lake
Lake Sakakawea
Grand Forks
Beulah
NORTH DAKOTA
Dickinson
Mandan
Bismarck
White Butte 3,506 ft.
Jamestown
Fargo
Wahpeton
Red River of the North
GREAT PLAINS
Lake Oahe
Mobridge
Aberdeen
Big Stone Lake
SOUTH DAKOTA
Spearfish
Redfield
BLACK HILLS
Rapid City
Pierre
Newcastle
Hot Springs
Brookings
Mitchell
Sioux Falls
Lake Francis Case
Glendo Reservoir
Chadron
Valentine
Yankton
Niobrara
North Loup
O'Neill
Scottsbluff
Alliance
Wayne
North Platte
NEBRASKA
Fremont
Ogallala
Columbus
Omaha
Platte
Kearney
Grand Island
Lincoln
Sterling
McCook
Republican
Burlington
Goodland
Beloit
Mount Sunflower 4,039 ft.
Saline
Junction City
Topeka
Hays
Salina
Abilene
KANSAS
Garden City
La Junta
Hutchinson
Arkansas
Dodge City
Wichita
Liberal
Winfield
Black Mesa 4,973 ft.
Clayton
Guymon
Dalhart
North Canadian
Bartlesville
Enid
Claremore
OKLAHOMA
Oklahoma City
Tulsa
Canadian
Conchas Lake
Amarillo
Clinton
Muskogee
Elk City
Norman
Clovis
Altus
Lawton
Ada
Red
Duncan
LLANO ESTACADO
Lubbock
Wichita Falls
Lake Texoma
Sulphur Springs
Snyder
Plano
Fort Worth
Arlington
Dallas
Abilene
Midland
Odessa
TEXAS
Pecos
San Angelo
Waco
Brazos
DAVIS MTS.
EDWARDS PLATEAU
Brady
Temple
Bryan
Sanderson
Austin
Amistad Reservoir
San Antonio
Seguin
Uvalde
Crystal City
Victoria
Goliad
Port Lavaca
Matagorda Bay
MEXICO
Nuevo Laredo
Laredo
Kingsville
Corpus Christi
Falcon Reservoir
Rio Grande City
McAllen
Harlingen
Brownsville
Monterrey
Matamoros
160°
155°
Mount Waialeale 5,200 ft.
KAUAI
Kapaa
Lihue
NIIHAU
22°
HAWAII
Kaneohe
OAHU
Honolulu
PACIFIC OCEAN
Wailuku
LANAI
MAUI
20°
Waimea
Honokaa
Mauna Kea 13,796 ft.
Hilo
Mauna Loa 13,680 ft.
HAWAII
Pahala
0 100 200 mi
0 150 300 km
RUSSIA
Barrow
ARCTIC OCEAN
Point Hope
Prudhoe Bay
70°
BROOKS RANGE
Bering Strait
Kotzebue
Selawik
SEWARD PENINSULA
ALASKA
Nome
Yukon
Galena
ST. LAWRENCE ISLAND
Fairbanks
CANADA
ALASKA RANGE
Mount McKinley 20,320 ft.
Bethel
Anchorage
Valdez
Cordova
60°
ATTU ISLAND
BERING SEA
Dillingham
Homer
Kenai
Mount St. Elias 18,008 ft.
Seldovia
Skagway
ALEUTIAN ISLANDS
KISKA ISLAND
Bristol Bay
Gulf of Alaska
Juneau
Shishaldin Volcano 9,372 ft.
Kodiak
KODIAK ISLAND
ALEXANDER ARCHIPELAGO
Sitka
Wrangell
ADAK ISLAND
ATKA ISLAND
Dutch Harbor
UMNAK ISLAND
UNIMAK ISLAND
Ketchikan
Dixon Entrance
0 300 600 mi
0 500 1000 km
180°
160°
140°

S
T
U
V

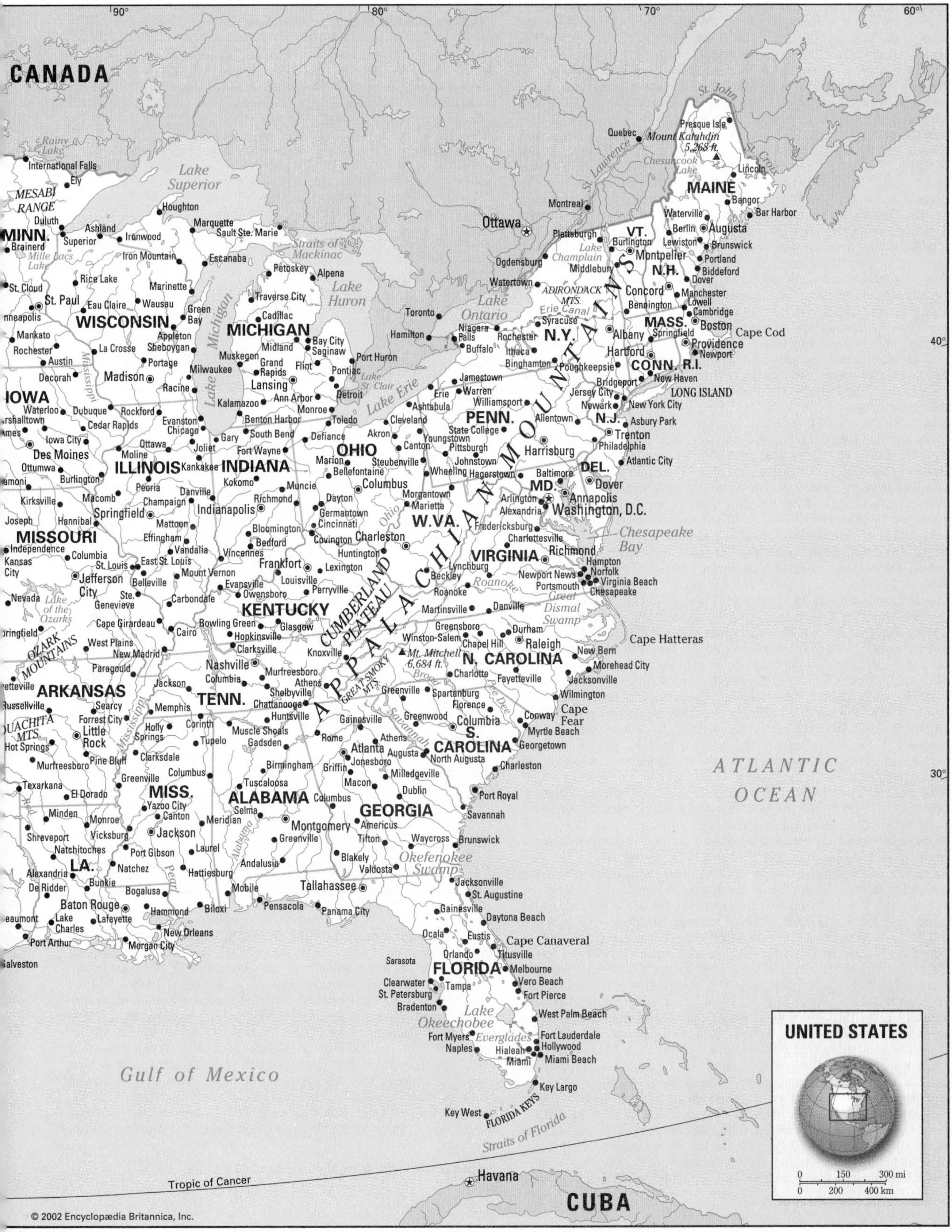

UNITED STATES
CANADA
CUBA
ATLANTIC OCEAN
Gulf of Mexico
Tropic of Cancer
Straits of Florida
Havana
90°
80°
70°
60°
40°
30°
0 150 300 mi
0 200 400 km
Lake Superior
Lake Michigan
Lake Huron
Lake Ontario
Lake Erie
Lake St. Clair
Straits of Mackinac
Rainy Lake
Mille Lacs Lake
MESABI RANGE
Lake of the Ozarks
OZARK MOUNTAINS
OUACHITA MTS.
APPALACHIAN MOUNTAINS
CUMBERLAND PLATEAU
GREAT SMOKY MTS.
ADIRONDACK MTS.
Erie Canal
Lake Champlain
Chesuncook Lake
Mount Katahdin 5,268 ft.
Mt. Mitchell 6,684 ft.
Chesapeake Bay
Great Dismal Swamp
Okefenokee Swamp
Lake Okeechobee
Everglades
FLORIDA KEYS
LONG ISLAND
Cape Cod
Cape Hatteras
Cape Fear
Cape Canaveral
St. John
St. Croix
St. Lawrence
Mississippi
Ohio
Roanoke
Savannah
Alabama
Pearl
Red
Broad
Pee Dee
MINN.
IOWA
MISSOURI
ARKANSAS
LA.
MISS.
WISCONSIN
ILLINOIS
MICHIGAN
INDIANA
OHIO
KENTUCKY
TENN.
ALABAMA
GEORGIA
FLORIDA
S. CAROLINA
N. CAROLINA
VIRGINIA
W.VA.
MD.
DEL.
N.J.
PENN.
N.Y.
CONN.
R.I.
MASS.
VT.
N.H.
MAINE
Washington, D.C.
Ottawa
Quebec
Montreal
Toronto
Hamilton
International Falls
Ely
Duluth
Superior
Ashland
Ironwood
Houghton
Marquette
Sault Ste. Marie
Iron Mountain
Escanaba
Petoskey
Alpena
Traverse City
Cadillac
Brainerd
St. Cloud
St. Paul
Minneapolis
Mankato
Rochester
Austin
Rice Lake
Eau Claire
Wausau
Marinette
Green Bay
Appleton
Sheboygan
La Crosse
Portage
Madison
Milwaukee
Racine
Decorah
Waterloo
Dubuque
Marshalltown
Ames
Cedar Rapids
Iowa City
Des Moines
Ottumwa
Burlington
Rockford
Evanston
Chicago
Gary
Joliet
Moline
Ottawa
Kankakee
Peoria
Macomb
Kirksville
Hannibal
St. Joseph
Springfield
Champaign
Danville
Mattoon
Effingham
Vandalia
Independence
Kansas City
Columbia
Jefferson City
St. Louis
East St. Louis
Belleville
Mount Vernon
Carbondale
Ste. Genevieve
Cape Girardeau
Cairo
Nevada
Springfield
West Plains
New Madrid
Paragould
Fayetteville
Russellville
Searcy
Forrest City
Little Rock
Hot Springs
Murfreesboro
Pine Bluff
Texarkana
El Dorado
Muskegon
Midland
Bay City
Saginaw
Flint
Port Huron
Pontiac
Grand Rapids
Lansing
Detroit
Kalamazoo
Ann Arbor
Monroe
Benton Harbor
South Bend
Toledo
Fort Wayne
Defiance
Kokomo
Muncie
Richmond
Indianapolis
Bloomington
Bedford
Vincennes
Evansville
Owensboro
Dayton
Germantown
Cincinnati
Covington
Marion
Bellefontaine
Columbus
Akron
Cleveland
Canton
Youngstown
Ashtabula
Erie
Steubenville
Wheeling
Morgantown
Marietta
Charleston
Huntington
Frankfort
Lexington
Louisville
Perryville
Bowling Green
Glasgow
Hopkinsville
Clarksville
Nashville
Murfreesboro
Columbia
Jackson
Memphis
Knoxville
Athens
Shelbyville
Chattanooga
Huntsville
Corinth
Tupelo
Holly Springs
Clarksdale
Greenville
Columbus
Muscle Shoals
Gadsden
Birmingham
Tuscaloosa
Rome
Atlanta
Athens
Griffin
Jonesboro
Augusta
North Augusta
Milledgeville
Macon
Dublin
Columbus
Montgomery
Selma
Yazoo City
Canton
Jackson
Meridian
Vicksburg
Monroe
Minden
Shreveport
Natchitoches
Port Gibson
Natchez
Laurel
Hattiesburg
Alexandria
De Ridder
Bunkie
Bogalusa
Baton Rouge
Lafayette
Hammond
Biloxi
Mobile
Pensacola
Beaumont
Lake Charles
Port Arthur
Galveston
Morgan City
New Orleans
Andalusia
Greenville
Americus
Tifton
Blakely
Valdosta
Waycross
Brunswick
Savannah
Port Royal
Tallahassee
Panama City
Jacksonville
St. Augustine
Gainesville
Daytona Beach
Ocala
Eustis
Orlando
Titusville
Sarasota
Clearwater
St. Petersburg
Tampa
Bradenton
Melbourne
Vero Beach
Fort Pierce
West Palm Beach
Fort Lauderdale
Hollywood
Fort Myers
Naples
Hialeah
Miami
Miami Beach
Key Largo
Key West
Charleston
Georgetown
Myrtle Beach
Conway
Columbia
Florence
Greenwood
Gainesville
Greenville
Spartanburg
Charlotte
Fayetteville
Wilmington
Jacksonville
Morehead City
New Bern
Raleigh
Durham
Chapel Hill
Greensboro
Winston-Salem
Martinsville
Danville
Roanoke
Beckley
Lynchburg
Charlottesville
Fredericksburg
Richmond
Hampton
Norfolk
Newport News
Portsmouth
Virginia Beach
Chesapeake
Arlington
Alexandria
Annapolis
Baltimore
Hagerstown
Johnstown
Pittsburgh
State College
Harrisburg
Williamsport
Allentown
Philadelphia
Trenton
Atlantic City
Dover
Asbury Park
Newark
Jersey City
New York City
Warren
Jamestown
Buffalo
Niagara Falls
Rochester
Ithaca
Binghamton
Syracuse
Watertown
Ogdensburg
Plattsburgh
Albany
Poughkeepsie
Bridgeport
New Haven
Hartford
Springfield
Providence
Newport
Boston
Cambridge
Lowell
Manchester
Concord
Bennington
Middlebury
Burlington
Montpelier
Dover
Biddeford
Portland
Brunswick
Lewiston
Berlin
Augusta
Waterville
Bangor
Bar Harbor
Lincoln
Presque Isle
© 2002 Encyclopædia Britannica, Inc.

S
T
U
V

the mid continent, Alaska at the northwestern extreme of North America, and the island state of Hawaii in the mid-Pacific Ocean. Area, including the U.S. share of the GREAT LAKES: 3,679,192 sq mi (9,529,063 sq km). Population (2002 est.): 287,602,000. Capital: WASHINGTON, D.C. The population is comprised of whites, African Americans, Hispanics, Asians, Pacific Islanders, American Indians (Native Americans), Eskimos, and Aleuts. Languages: English (predominant), Spanish. Religions: Protestantism, Roman Catholicism, Judaism, Islam. Currency: U.S. dollar. The country's regions encompass mountains, plains, lowlands, and deserts. Mountain ranges include the APPALACHIANS, OZARKS, ROCKY MOUNTAINS, CASCADES, and SIERRA NEVADAS. The lowest point is DEATH VALLEY, Cal. The highest point is Alaska's Mount MCKINLEY; within the coterminous U.S., it is Mount WHITNEY. Chief rivers are the MISSISSIPPI system, COLORADO, COLUMBIA, and RIO GRANDE. The GREAT LAKES, GREAT SALT LAKE, and OKEECHOBEE are the largest lakes. The U.S. is among the world's leading producers of several minerals, including copper, silver, zinc, gold, coal, petroleum, and natural gas; it is the chief exporter of food. Its manufactures include iron and steel, chemicals, electronic equipment, and textiles. Other important industries are tourism, dairying, livestock raising, fishing, and lumbering. It is a republic with two legislative houses; its head of state and government is the president. The territory was originally inhabited for several thousand years by numerous AMERICAN INDIAN peoples who had probably emigrated from Asia. European exploration and settlement from the 16th century began displacement of the Indians. The first permanent European settlement, by the Spanish, was at ST. AUGUSTINE, Fla., in 1565; the British settled JAMESTOWN, Va. (1607); PLYMOUTH, Mass. (1620); Maryland (1634); and Pennsylvania (1681). They took New York, New Jersey, and Delaware from the Dutch in 1664, a year after the Carolinas had been granted to British noblemen. The British defeat of the French in 1763 (see FRENCH AND INDIAN WAR) assured British political control over its 13 colonies. Political unrest caused by British colonial policy culminated in the AMERICAN REVOLUTION (1775–83) and the DECLARATION OF INDEPENDENCE (1776). The U.S. was first organized under the ARTICLES OF CONFEDERATION (1781), then finally under the CONSTITUTION (1787) as a federal republic. Boundaries extended west to the Mississippi River, excluding Spanish Florida. Land acquired from France by the LOUISIANA PURCHASE (1803) nearly doubled the country's territory. The U.S. fought the WAR OF 1812 with the British and acquired Florida from Spain in 1819. In 1830 it legalized removal of American Indians to lands west of the Mississippi River. Settlement expanded into the Far West in the mid-19th century, especially after the discovery of gold in California in 1848 (see GOLD RUSH). Victory in the MEXICAN WAR (1846–48) brought the territory of seven more future states (including California and Texas) into U.S. hands. The northwestern boundary was established by treaty with Great Britain in 1846. The U.S. acquired southern Arizona by the GADSDEN PURCHASE (1853). It suffered disunity during the conflict between the slavery-based plantation economy in the South and the free industrial and agricultural economy in the North, culminating in the AMERICAN CIVIL WAR, and the abolition of slavery under the 13th Amendment. After RECONSTRUCTION (1865–77), the U.S. experienced rapid growth, urbanization, industrial development, and European immigration. In 1877 it authorized allotment of Indian reservation land to individual tribesmen, resulting in widespread loss of land to whites. By the end of the 19th century, it had developed foreign trade and acquired outlying territories, including Alaska, Midway island, the Hawaiian Islands, the Philippines, Puerto Rico, Guam, Wake Island, American Samoa, the Panama Canal Zone, and the Virgin Islands. The U.S. participated in WORLD WAR I 1917–18. It granted suffrage to women in 1920 and citizenship to American Indians in 1924. The stock market crash of 1929 led to the GREAT DEPRESSION. The U.S. entered WORLD WAR II after the Japanese bombing of PEARL HARBOR (Dec. 7, 1941). Its explosion of the first ATOMIC BOMB on HIROSHIMA, Japan (Aug. 6, 1945), and the second on NAGASAKI, Japan (Aug. 9, 1945), brought about the end of the war, and made it the leader of the Western world, involved it in the reconstruction of Europe and Japan, and embroiled it in a rivalry with the Soviet Union that became known as the COLD WAR. It participated in the KOREAN WAR. In 1952 it granted autonomous commonwealth status to Puerto Rico. Racial segregation in schools was declared unconstitutional in 1954. Alaska and Hawaii were made states in 1959. In 1964 Congress passed the CIVIL RIGHTS ACT and authorized full-scale intervention in the VIETNAM WAR. The mid- to late-1960s were marked by widespread civil disorders, including race riots and antiwar demonstrations. The U.S. accomplished the first manned lunar landing in 1969. All U.S. troops were withdrawn from Vietnam in 1973. The U.S. led a coalition of forces against Iraq in the PERSIAN GULF WAR (1991), sent troops to Somalia (1992) to aid starving populations, and participated in NATO air strikes against Serb forces in the former Yugoslavia in 1995 and 1999. In 1998 Pres. WILLIAM J. CLINTON became only the second president to be impeached by the House of Representatives; he was acquitted by the Senate in 1999. Administration of the PANAMA CANAL was turned over to Panama in 1999. In 2000 GEORGE W. BUSH became the first person since 1888 to be elected president by the ELECTORAL COLLEGE despite having won fewer popular votes than his opponent, AL GORE. After terrorist attacks destroyed the WORLD TRADE CENTER and part of the PENTAGON on Sept. 11, 2001, the U.S. attacked Afghanistan's TALIBAN government for harboring and refusing to extradite the alleged mastermind of the TERRORISM, OSAMA BIN LADEN.

U.S. Presidents and Vice Presidents

President	Term	Vice president	Term
George Washington	1789–97	John Adams	1789–97
John Adams	1797–1801	Thomas Jefferson	1797–1801
Thomas Jefferson	1801–9	Aaron Burr	1801–5
		George Clinton	1805–9
James Madison	1809–17	George Clinton	1809–12*
		Elbridge Gerry	1813–14*
James Monroe	1817–25	Daniel D. Tompkins	1817–25
John Quincy Adams	1825–29	John C. Calhoun	1825–29
Andrew Jackson	1829–37	John C. Calhoun	1829–32**
		Martin Van Buren	1833–37
Martin Van Buren	1837–41	Richard M. Johnson	1837–41
William Henry Harrison	1841*	John Tyler	1841
John Tyler	1841–45		
James K. Polk	1845–49	George Mifflin Dallas	1845–49
Zachary Taylor	1849–50*	Millard Fillmore	1849–50
Millard Fillmore	1850–53		
Franklin Pierce	1853–57	William Rufus de Vane King	1853*
James Buchanan	1857–61	John C. Breckinridge	1857–61
Abraham Lincoln	1861–65*	Hannibal Hamlin	1861–65
		Andrew Johnson	1865
Andrew Johnson	1865–69		
Ulysses S. Grant	1869–77	Schuyler Colfax	1869–73
		Henry Wilson	1873–75*
Rutherford B. Hayes	1877–81	William A. Wheeler	1877–81
James A. Garfield	1881*	Chester A. Arthur	1881
Chester A. Arthur	1881–85		
Grover Cleveland	1885–89	Thomas A. Hendricks	1885*
Benjamin Harrison	1889–93	Levi Parsons Morton	1889–93
Grover Cleveland	1893–97	Adlai E. Stevenson	1893–97
William McKinley	1897–1901*	Garret A. Hobart	1897–99*
		Theodore Roosevelt	1901
Theodore Roosevelt	1901–9	Charles Warren Fairbanks	1905–9
William Howard Taft	1909–13	James Schoolcraft Sherman	1909–12*
Woodrow Wilson	1913–21	Thomas R. Marshall	1913–21
Warren G. Harding	1921–23*	Calvin Coolidge	1921–23
Calvin Coolidge	1923–29	Charles G. Dawes	1925–29
Herbert Hoover	1929–33	Charles Curtis	1929–33
Franklin D. Roosevelt	1933–45*	John Nance Garner	1933–41
		Henry A. Wallace	1941–45
		Harry S. Truman	1945
Harry S. Truman	1945–53	Alben W. Barkley	1949–53
Dwight D. Eisenhower	1953–61	Richard M. Nixon	1953–61
John F. Kennedy	1961–63*	Lyndon B. Johnson	1961–63
Lyndon B. Johnson	1963–69	Hubert H. Humphrey	1965–69
Richard M. Nixon	1969–74**	Spiro T. Agnew	1969–73**
		Gerald R. Ford	1973–74
Gerald R. Ford	1974–77	Nelson A. Rockefeller	1974–77
Jimmy Carter	1977–81	Walter F. Mondale	1977–81
Ronald Reagan	1981–89	George Bush	1981–89
George Bush	1989–93	Dan Quayle	1989–93
William J. Clinton	1993–2001	Albert Gore	1993–2001
George W. Bush	2001–	Richard B. Cheney	2001–

*Died in office. **Resigned from office.

United States, Bank of the See BANK OF THE U.S.

United States Air Force (USAF) Major component of the U.S. military organization, with primary responsibility for AIR WARFARE, air defense, and military space research. It also provides air services in coordination with the other military branches. U.S. military activities in the air began with army use of balloons for reconnaissance during the Civil War and the Spanish-American War; in 1907 the Aeronautical Division of the Signal Corps was created. In 1920 the Army Reorganization Act created the Air Service (after 1926, Air Corps) as a unit of the Army; in 1941 it became the Army Air Forces. In 1947 the independent U.S. Air Force was created and became part of the newly created Department of DEFENSE in 1949. The Department of the Air Force is headquartered at the PENTAGON. Separate operating agencies of the Air Force include the Air Force Reserve, the Air Force Intelligence Service, and the U.S. AIR FORCE ACADEMY. In 2000 there were over 350,000 Air Force personnel on active duty.

United States Air Force Academy Institution for the training of commissioned officers for the U.S. AIR FORCE, located in Colorado Springs, Col. Created by an act of Congress in 1954, it opened in 1955. Graduates receive a bachelor's degree and a second lieutenant's commission. Most physically qualified graduates go on to Air Force pilot-training schools. Candidates may come from the ranks of the Army or Air Force, be children of deceased veterans of the armed forces, or be nominated by U.S. senators or representatives or by the president or vice president, and must take a competitive entrance examination. Enrollment is about 4,000.

United States Army Major branch of the U.S. military forces, charged with preserving peace and security and defending the nation. The first regular U.S. fighting force, the Continental Army, was organized by the CONTINENTAL CONGRESS on June 14, 1775, to supplement local MILITIAS in the American Revolution. It was placed under the control of a five-member civilian board, and U.S. military forces have remained in civilian control ever since. The U.S. Constitution named the president as commander in chief, and in 1789 the civilian Department of War was established to administer the armed forces. The Continental Army was officially disbanded in 1783, and a small regular army was established. Thereafter, the army's size increased during times of crisis, swelled by CONSCRIPTION, and decreased during peacetime. The Department of the Army is organized as a military section of the Department of Defense and is headed by the Secretary of the Army. The Army Staff gives advice and assistance to the secretary and administers civil functions, including the civil-works program of the Corps of Engineers. The army also administers the U.S. MILITARY ACADEMY at West Point. In 2000 there were about 400,000 soldiers on active duty.

United States Coast Guard U.S. military service that enforces maritime laws. During peacetime it is under the jurisdiction of the Department of Transportation; in wartime it is part of the Department of the Navy. The Coast Guard enforces federal laws on the high seas and waters within U.S. territorial jurisdiction, develops and operates aids to navigation, and maintains a network of lifeboat and search-and-rescue stations using surface vessels and aircraft. It assists in the interdiction of illegal narcotics bound for the U.S. on or over coastal waters. It operates the International Ice Patrol (which maintains surveillance of icebergs in the North Atlantic shipping lanes), gathers data for the National Weather Service, and assists distressed ships and planes. Its wartime duties include ship escort, port security, and transport duty. In 2000 there were some 35,000 Coast Guard personnel on active duty.

United States Courts of Appeals In the U.S., the intermediate appellate courts included in the federal judicial system and created by act of Congress. Each Court of Appeals for the 11 numbered circuits is empowered to review the decisions of federal district courts (see U.S. DISTRICT COURT), as well as the divisions of the U.S. Tax Court within its jurisdiction and the U.S. Bankruptcy Courts. The District of Columbia has its own appellate court because so many cases are filed there. The U.S. Court of Appeals for the Federal Circuit (created in 1982) has jurisdiction over specialized courts, including the U.S. Court of Federal Claims (which has original jurisdiction over claims, other than TORT claims, against the U.S.) and the U.S. Court of International Trade (which has exclusive jurisdiction over civil actions under the tariff laws). The Federal Circuit may also review and enforce orders of various federal regulatory agencies, such as the FEDERAL TRADE COMMISSION, the SECURITIES AND EXCHANGE COMMISSION, and the NATIONAL LABOR RELATIONS BOARD. All Court of Appeals decisions are subject to review by the U.S. SUPREME COURT.

United States District Court In the U.S., any of the 90 trial courts of general jurisdiction in the federal judicial system. Each state, as well as the District of Columbia and the Commonwealth of Puerto Rico, has at least one federal district court. Each court has at least one district judge and can have more than a score of them, as well as a clerk, a U.S. attorney, a U.S. marshal, one or more U.S. magistrates, bankruptcy judges, probation officers, and other staff. District-court decisions are subject to appeal to a U.S. COURT OF APPEALS.

United States Marine Corps (USMC) Separate military service within the U.S. Department of the Navy (see U.S. NAVY), charged with providing marine troops for seizure and defense of advanced bases and with conducting operations on land and in the air in connection with naval campaigns. It is also responsible for providing detachments for service aboard certain types of naval vessels, as well as security forces for naval shore installations and U.S. diplomatic missions in foreign countries. The corps specializes in amphibious landings, such as those on Japanese-held islands in World War II. Marines have served in every major U.S. naval action since 1775, usually being the first or among the first to fight. In 2000 there were some 175,000 Marines on active duty.

United States Military Academy *known as* **West Point** Institution for the training of commissioned officers for the U.S. ARMY. Founded in 1802 at the fort at West Point, N.Y., it is one of the oldest service academies in the world. It was founded as an apprentice school for military engineers and, in effect, the first U.S. school of engineering. It was reorganized in 1812, and in 1866 its educational program was expanded considerably. Women were first admitted in 1976. The four-year course of college-level education and training leads to a bachelor of science degree and a commission as second lieutenant in the Army. West Point has trained such leaders as ULYSSES S. GRANT, WILLIAM T. SHERMAN, ROBERT E. LEE, STONEWALL JACKSON, JEFFERSON DAVIS, JOHN PERSHING, DWIGHT D. EISENHOWER, DOUGLAS MACARTHUR, OMAR BRADLEY, and GEORGE PATTON. Current enrollment is about 4,000.

United States Naval Academy *known as* **Annapolis** Institution for the training of commissioned officers for the U.S. NAVY and U.S. MARINE CORPS. It was founded at Annapolis, Md., in 1845 and reorganized in 1850–51. Women were first admitted in 1976. Graduates are awarded the degree of bachelor of science and a commission as ensign in the Navy or as second lieutenant in the Marine Corps. Annapolis has produced a long list of American notables, including GEORGE DEWEY, RICHARD E. BYRD, CHESTER NIMITZ, WILLIAM F. HALSEY, JR, A. A. MICHELSON, HYMAN RICKOVER, JIMMY CARTER, ROSS PEROT, and several astronauts. Current enrollment is about 4,000.

United States Navy Major branch of the U.S. military forces, charged with defending the nation at sea and maintaining security on the seas wherever U.S. interests extend. The Continental Navy was established by the CONTINENTAL CONGRESS in 1775. It was disbanded in 1784, but the harassment of U.S. merchant ships by Barbary pirates prompted Congress to establish the Department of the Navy in 1798. The navy took part in the WAR OF 1812 and was later important in the Union victory in the American Civil War. Sea victories during the Spanish-American War (1898) led to a period of steady growth. In World War I, its duties were limited to troop transport, minelaying, and escorting merchant ships. The Japanese attack on the naval base at Pearl Harbor (1941) led to U.S. entry into World War II, in which, in addition to antisubmarine and troop transport duties, the navy conducted AMPHIBIOUS assaults in the Pacific theater and along the European coast. AIRCRAFT CARRIERS proved decisive in battles with Japanese forces in the Pacific, and they are still the backbone of the navy's fleets. Since World War II it has remained the largest and most powerful navy in the world. The Department of the Navy, a branch of the Department of Defense, is headed by a secretary of the navy. The navy includes the U.S. MARINE CORPS and, during wartime, the U.S. COAST GUARD. In 2000 there were almost 400,000 Navy personnel on active duty, excluding the Marine Corps and Coast Guard. See also U.S. NAVAL ACADEMY.

United States service academies Group of institutions of higher education for the training of military and merchant marine officers: the U.S. MILITARY ACADEMY ("West Point"), the U.S. NAVAL ACADEMY ("Annapolis"), the U.S. AIR FORCE ACADEMY, the U.S. Coast Guard Academy (established 1876 near New London, Conn.; enrollment 800), and the U.S.

Merchant Marine Academy (established 1943 at Kings Point, Long Island, N.Y.; enrollment 900).

United States Steel Corp. Former U.S. corporation, now a subsidiary of USX Corp. It was founded in 1901 by CHARLES M. SCHWAB, ELBERT H. GARY, and J. P. MORGAN to consolidate ANDREW CARNEGIE's Carnegie Steel Co., Gary's Federal Steel Co., and other steel and metal companies. As chairman of the board, Gary dominated the corporation in its early years, organizing price agreements among steel producers and opposing unions. An antitrust suit against U.S. Steel went as far as the Supreme Court, which ruled in 1920 that it was not a monopoly in restraint of trade. The corporation recognized the UNITED STEELWORKERS OF AMERICA in 1936. The largest U.S. steel producer, U.S. Steel diversified into oil and gas in the later 20th century as well as into chemicals, mining, construction, and transportation. In 1986, the HOLDING COMPANY USX Corp. was established to oversee it and other operating units.

United Steelworkers of America (USWA) U.S. union of steel, aluminum, and other metallurgical workers. It grew out of the Steel Workers Organizing Committee (SWOC), established jointly in 1936 by the Committee for Industrial Organization (see AFL-CIO) and the Amalgamated Association of Iron, Steel, and Tin Workers. Under PHILIP MURRAY it developed into a powerful union. In 1942 SWOC became the United Steelworkers of America, of which Murray served as president until his death in 1952. The USWA absorbed the Aluminum Workers of America in 1944 and by the mid-1950s had over a million members. It won unprecedented benefits in the postwar period but saw its membership and power decline as the U.S. steel industry shrank from the 1970s onward. See also UNITED STATES STEEL CORP.

Unity (School of Christianity) Religious movement founded in 1889 by Charles (1854–1948) and Myrtle Fillmore (1845–1931) in Kansas City, Mo. Believing that spiritual healing had cured Myrtle of tuberculosis, the couple began to endorse spiritual healing. Until 1922, Unity was a member of the International New Thought Alliance. Unlike some NEW THOUGHT groups, Unity embraces practical CHRISTIANITY and modern medicine. It has no definite creed and is interdenominational. Its Silent Unity service helps people through counseling and prayer via mail and telephone, responding to 2.5 million requests for aid a year. Unity publishes magazines and books, and conducts classes for prospective Unity ministers at about 300 centers.

unity-of-science view See UNIFIED SCIENCE

universal In EPISTEMOLOGY and LOGIC, a general term representing a property, form, or principle of classification. The problem of universals concerns the question of what sort of being should be ascribed to such principles of classification (e.g., is there any such thing as an essence of redness that exists apart from particular red things?). The debate over the status of universals stems from PLATO's theory of FORMS. ARISTOTLE argued against Plato that forms (universals) exist only in the particulars in which they are exemplified. Though both were realists about universals (see REALISM), they differed over the existence of universals independently of their particular exemplars *(universalia ante rem).*

Universal Declaration of Human Rights Declaration on universal human rights adopted by the UNITED NATIONS GENERAL ASSEMBLY in 1948. It was adopted without dissent, but with eight abstentions. Among its 30 articles are definitions of civil and political rights (including freedom from slavery and the right to a nationality), as well as definitions of economic, social, and cultural rights (including the right to social security and to participation in the cultural life of one's community), all of which are owed by member states to those under their jurisdiction. It has acquired more juridical status than originally intended and has been widely used, even by national courts, as a means of judging compliance with the U.N.'s human-rights obligations. It has formed the basis for the work of such nongovernmental organizations as AMNESTY INTERNATIONAL.

Universal Negro Improvement Association (UNIA) Organization founded by MARCUS GARVEY in 1914. Organized in Jamaica, it was influential in urban black neighborhoods in the U.S. after Garvey moved north in 1916. It was dedicated to racial pride, economic self-sufficiency, and formation of an independent black nation in Africa. After Garvey's 1923 fraud conviction, the UNIA lost influence, but it proved to be a forerunner of BLACK NATIONALISM.

Universal Pictures U.S. film studio. Formed by CARL LAEMMLE in 1912, it became a top producer of popular, low-budget serials in the 1920s and of horror movies in the 1930s. Its later films included the ABBOTT AND COSTELLO comedies and the DORIS DAY–R. HUDSON bedroom farces. The studio was bought by MCA in 1962, and in 1966 it became a division of Universal City Studios, the largest packager of television series. It turned part of its Hollywood movie lot into the Universal Studios theme park, and later opened a second theme park in Orlando, Fla.

Universal Product Code (UPC) Standard BAR CODE used to identify grocery and other retail merchandise. In the UPC system, the five digits on the left are assigned to a particular manufacturer or maker and the five digits on the right are used by that manufacturer to identify a specific type or make of product.

Universal Resource Locator See URL

Universal Serial Bus See USB

Universal Time Mean (solar) time of the Greenwich meridian (0° longitude). Universal Time replaced the designation GREENWICH MEAN TIME in 1928; since 1972 it has been based on international atomic time, a uniform time derived from the frequences of certain atomic transitions and measured by an atomic clock. For most purposes, it is now identical to Greenwich Mean Time.

Universalism Belief in the SALVATION of all SOULS. Arising at various times in Christian history, the concept became an organized movement in America in the mid-18th century. It maintains the impossibility that a loving God would bestow salvation on only a portion of humankind while dooming the rest to eternal punishment. It stresses the use of reason in religion and the modification of belief in light of the discoveries of science. Thus, the miraculous elements of traditional CHRISTIANITY are rejected and JESUS, while a worthy teacher and model, is not held to be divine. Universalist and Unitarian churches in the U.S. merged in 1961 (see UNITARIANISM).

universe Whole cosmic system of matter and energy of which the earth is a part. Its main constituents are the GALAXIES, within which are STARS and stellar groupings, and nebulae (see NEBULA). Earth's sun is one star among the billions of stars in our galaxy, the MILKY WAY. All atoms, subatomic particles, and everything they compose are also part of the universe. The universe is governed by four fundamental forces: the STRONG FORCE, the WEAK FORCE, the ELECTROMAGNETIC FORCE, and GRAVITATION. Numerous theories have been proposed for the origin and structure of the universe. See also BIG BANG, COSMOLOGY, EXPANDING UNIVERSE, STEADY-STATE THEORY.

university Institution of higher education, usually comprising a liberal-arts-and-sciences college and graduate and professional schools that confer degrees in various fields. A university differs from a COLLEGE in that it is usually larger, has a broader curriculum, and offers advanced degrees in addition to undergraduate degrees. The first true university was the University of BOLOGNA, founded in the 11th century; the first in northern Europe was the University of PARIS, which served as a model for the universities of OXFORD, CAMBRIDGE, HEIDELBERG, and others. One of the first modern universities, in which secular objectivity and rationalism replaced religious orthodoxy, was the University of Halle (founded 1694 in Halle, Germany). The liberalism of Halle was adopted by GÖTTINGEN, BERLIN, and many other German universities. The German model of the university as a complex of schools and research institutes also exerted a worldwide influence. The growth of universities in the U.S., where most colleges had been established by religious denominations, was greatly spurred by the MORRILL ACT of 1862.

UNIX \'yü-niks\ OPERATING SYSTEM for DIGITAL COMPUTERS, developed by Ken Thompson of Bell Laboratories in 1969. It was initially designed for a single user (the name was a pun on the earlier operating system Multics). The C language was subsequently developed specifically for UNIX, and the system was rewritten almost entirely in C; it was improved by the addition of multiprogramming and time-sharing capabilities and enhanced portability. UNIX is very popular in universities, where it is used mostly on scientific and engineering workstations, and it is used on most of the SERVERS of INTERNET SERVICE PROVIDERS. Because its modular construction allows it to be easily modified, it has been improved in many ways by academic and industrial institutions (see LINUX).

Unkei \'ün-ˌkā\ (1151?–1223) Japanese sculptor. He established a style of realistic and dynamic Buddhist sculpture that had an immense impact on Japanese art for centuries. Commissioned by the KAMAKURA SHOGU-

S T U V

NATE, he made statues for the Kofuku and Todai temples in Nara and is best remembered for the nearly 26-ft (8-m) tall guardian figures at Todai temple's Great South Gate. He later produced many portrait sculptures.

Unkiar Skelessi \'ün-kyär-skə-'le-sē\, **Treaty of** (1833) Alliance between the Ottoman empire and Russia, signed at the village of Hunkar Iskelesi (Unkiar Skelessi), near Istanbul. In return for Russian military aid, the Ottoman sultan, Mahmud II, agreed to a secret article in their mutual defense treaty that closed the Dardanelles Strait to any foreign vessels of war except those of Russia. The treaty made the Ottoman empire a virtual protectorate of Russia. When other countries became suspicious of the agreement, Russia abandoned its Dardanelles privileges in 1841.

Unser, Bobby *orig.* **Robert William** *and* **Al(fred)** (born 1934, born 1939) U.S. automobile-racing drivers. The Unser brothers were born in Albuquerque, N.M., to a family of drivers, and began driving at an early age. Both won the Pikes Peak hill climb and various USAC races before racing in the INDIANAPOLIS 500, which Bobby won in 1968, 1975, and 1981, and Al in 1970, 1971, 1978, and 1987. Al's son Al Unser, Jr. (born 1962), won the same race in 1992 and 1994.

Unterwalden \'ün-tər-,väl-dən\ Former canton, central Switzerland. It was ruled after 1173 by the HABSBURG counts. In 1291, with Uri and Schwyz, it formed the Everlasting League, which became the nucleus of the Swiss Confederation. In 1340 it divided into two sovereign half cantons, Nidwalden and Obwalden; in 1803 they became demicantons having equal rights.

untouchable Former classification of various low-status persons and those outside the Hindu CASTE system in Indian society. The term Dalit is now used for such people (in preference to MOHANDAS K. GANDHI's term, harijan, which was considered condescending by the Dalit themselves), and their plight is recognized by the Indian constitution and by legislation. The groups traditionally considered untouchable included people whose occupations or habits of life involved activities considered to be polluting, such as taking life for a living (e.g., fishermen); killing or disposing of dead cattle or working with their hides; coming into contact with human excretions (e.g., sweepers); and eating flesh of cattle, pigs, or chickens. Many untouchables converted to other religions to escape discrimination.

upanayana \,ü-pə-'nə-yə-nə\ Hindu initiation ritual, restricted to the three upper VARNAS. It marks a male's entrance into the life of a student and his acceptance as a full member of the religious community. After a ritual bath, the boy, aged 5–24, is dressed as an ascetic and brought before his GURU, who invests him with various symbolic articles. The initiate receives a sacred thread, worn throughout his life, that identifies him as twice-born, the second birth being effected by receipt of a MANTRA. Observance of upanayana is decreasing and is now largely confined to the BRAHMAN class.

Upanishad \ü-'pä-ni-,shäd\ Any of 108 speculative texts of the VEDAS that contain elaborations in poetry and verse. They are believed to have been composed since 500 BC, based on teachings circulated since 1000 BC. They represent the final stage in the tradition of the Vedas, and the teaching based on them is called VEDANTA. Generally the Upanishads are concerned with the nature of reality, the individual soul (ATMAN), and the universal soul (BRAHMAN) and with the theory of the transmigration of souls and the nature of morality.

upasaka \ü-'pä-sə-kə\ Lay devotee of the BUDDHA. Originally the term applied to followers of the Buddha who were not ordained as BHIKSUS; today it is normally applied, mainly in S.East Asia, to pious individuals who visit the local monastery on the weekly holy days and who undertake special vows. They support the SANGHA with regular offerings and observe the five precepts expected of all Buddhists: to abstain from killing, stealing, sexual misconduct, lying, and using intoxicants.

UPC See UNIVERSAL PRODUCT CODE

Updike, John (Hoyer) (born 1932) U.S. writer. Born in Shillington, Pa., he attended Harvard University and in 1955 began a long association with the *New Yorker*. His works are known for careful craftsmanship and their subtle depiction of American middle-class life. His famous "Rabbit" tetralogy—*Rabbit, Run* (1960), *Rabbit Redux* (1971), *Rabbit Is Rich* (1981, Pulitzer Prize), and *Rabbit at Rest* (1990, Pulitzer Prize)—follows a very ordinary American man through the decades of the later 20th century. A Jewish novelist named Bech is the subject of three other novels. Updike's other fiction includes *The Centaur* (1963), *Of the Farm* (1965), *Couples* (1968), *The Witches of Eastwick* (1984; film, 1987), and *In the Beauty of the Lilies* (1996). He has also published short-story collections, including *Pigeon Feathers* (1962), several volumes of reviews and essays, and light verse.

Upper Canada See CANADA WEST

Upper Volta See BURKINA FASO

Uppsala \'üp-,sä-,lä\ City (metro. area pop., 1997 est.: 185,000), Sweden. Located north of STOCKHOLM, it lies near a village which was originally the capital of the ancient pre-Christian kingdom of Svea. By the 13th century it was an important commercial center. Relinquishing its political primacy to Stockholm, it remained the seat of the archbishop of Sweden; its Gothic cathedral (13th–15th century) is Sweden's largest. It is also an educational center, the site of Sweden's oldest university. In the 20th century it became an industrial city and transportation hub. CAROLUS LINNAEUS lived there.

Ur \'ər, ůr\ Ancient city and district, SUMER, southern BABYLONIA. It was situated on a former channel of the EUPHRATES RIVER. One of the oldest cities of MESOPOTAMIA, it was settled sometime in the 4th millennium BC. In the 25th century BC, it was the capital of southern Mesopotamia under its first dynasty. Though it declined, it again became important around the 22nd century BC. It is mentioned in the Bible (as Ur of the Chaldees) as the early home of Hebrew patriarch ABRAHAM in the 18th century BC. In subsequent centuries it was captured and destroyed by many, including the Elamites and Babylonians. NEBUCHADNEZZAR II restored it in the 6th century BC. Excavations, especially in the 1920s and 30s, uncovered remains of great archaeological value.

Northeastern facade (the ascents partly restored) of the ziggurat at Ur.
HIRMER FOTOARCHIV, MUNCHEN

uracil \'yůr-ə-,sil\ Organic compound of the PYRIMIDINE family, often called a base, consisting of a ring containing both nitrogen and carbon atoms. It occurs in combined form in many important biological molecules, including RNA and several COENZYMES active in CARBOHYDRATE metabolism. During synthesis of an RNA strand from DNA, uracil pairs with ADENINE. It or its corresponding NUCLEOSIDE or NUCLEOTIDE may be prepared from RNA by selective techniques of HYDROLYSIS.

Ural Mountains \'yůr-əl\ Mountain range, Russia and Kazakhstan. Constituting the boundary between Europe and Asia, the range extends south for 1,640 mi (2,640 km) from the Kara Sea to the URAL RIVER. The mountains average 3,000–4,000 ft (915–1,220 m) in height; the highest peak is Mount Narodnaya at 6,217 ft (1,895 m) tall. The Middle Urals contain one of the largest industrial regions of the COMMONWEALTH OF INDEPENDENT STATES, producing metal goods, chemicals, and machinery. During World War II, this region developed rapidly when many industrial plants were moved from the western U.S.S.R. to prevent their destruction by the Germans.

Ural River River, Russia and Kazakhstan. Rising at the southern end of the URAL MOUNTAINS, it flows southwest to cross through western Kazakhstan to the CASPIAN SEA at Atyrau. It is 1,509 mi (2,428 km) long and drains an area of 91,500 sq mi (237,000 sq km). Its lower course is navigable.

Uralic languages \yů-'ra-lik\ Family of more than 30 languages spoken by some 25 million people in central and northern Eurasia. A primary division is between the FINNO-UGRIC LANGUAGES, which account for most of the languages and speakers, and the Samoyedic languages.

Samoyedic languages have historically been spoken in the forest region of northern Siberia and in the tundra and coastal zones from the Ob to the White Sea and east into the Taymyr Peninsula. The known languages are Nganasan (Tavgy), Enets (Yenisei-Samoyed), Nenets (Yurak), Selkup (Ostyak-Samoyed), Kamas (Kamassian), and Mator (Motor). Mator became extinct in the 19th century and the last speaker of Kamas died in 1989. Of the others, Nenets, which has 25,000 speakers and is still being learned by children, is the most viable. They share little vocabulary with Finno-Ugric. Some specialists believe a remote genetic relation exists between Uralic and the Yukaghir languages (see PALEO-SIBERIAN LANGUAGES).

uraninite \yu̇-ˈrā-nə-ˌnīt\ Uranium dioxide (UO_2), a major OXIDE MINERAL of URANIUM. Uraninite is radioactive and usually forms black, gray, or brown crystals that are moderately hard and generally opaque. The elements uranium and radium were first extracted from uraninite ore from what is now the Czech Republic. It has also been mined in Germany and Canada, and in the Colorado Plateau (U.S.). See also PITCHBLENDE.

Uraninite in pitchblende from Great Bear Lake, Northwest Territories, embedded (for display) in a larger mass of feldspar from Grafton Center, N.H.

BY COURTESY OF THE FIELD MUSEUM OF NATURAL HISTORY, CHICAGO; PHOTOGRAPH, JOHN H. GERARD

uranium Chemical ELEMENT, RARE EARTH METAL of the ACTINIDE series (with many TRANSITION ELEMENT properties), chemical symbol U, atomic number 92. A dense, hard, silvery-white METAL that tarnishes in air, it is isolated from such ores as PITCHBLENDE. Until the discovery of the first TRANSURANIUM ELEMENT in 1940, uranium was believed to be the heaviest element. RADIOACTIVITY was discovered in uranium by A.-H. BECQUEREL. All its ISOTOPES are radioactive; several have HALF-LIVES long enough to permit determination of the age of the earth by URANIUM-THORIUM-LEAD DATING and URANIUM-234–URANIUM-238 DATING. NUCLEAR FISSION was discovered in 1938 in uranium bombarded with NEUTRONS, and the self-sustaining nuclear CHAIN REACTION, the ATOMIC BOMB, and the generation of NUCLEAR POWER followed. Uranium has various VALENCES in compounds, some of which have been used as colors in ceramic glazes, in lightbulb filaments, in photography, and as dyes and mordants.

uranium-234–uranium-238 dating Method of age determination that makes use of the radioactive decay of uranium-238 to uranium-234; the method can be used for dating sediments from either a marine or a PLAYA lake environment. Because this method is useful for the period c. 100,000–1.2 million years before the present, it helps in bridging the gap between the CARBON-14 DATING method and the POTASSIUM-ARGON DATING method.

uranium-thorium-lead dating *or* **common-lead dating** Method of dating very old rocks by means of the amount of common lead they contain. Common lead is any lead from a rock or mineral that contains a large amount of lead and a small amount of the radioactive precursors of lead (i.e., the isotopes uranium-235, uranium-238, and thorium-232). By this method, the age of the earth has been estimated to be c. 4.6 billion years. This figure is in good agreement with the age of meteorites and the age of the moon as determined independently.

Uranus *or* **Ouranus** \ˈyu̇r-ə-nəs, yu̇-ˈrā-nəs\ Ancient Greek personification of HEAVEN. When GAEA emerged from CHAOS, she produced Uranus, the mountains, and the sea. Her subsequent union with Uranus produced the TITANS, the Cyclopes, and the Hecatoncheires. Uranus despised his offspring and hid them in Gaea's body. In response to her appeal for vengeance, CRONUS castrated Uranus. From the drops of blood that fell on Earth were born the FURIES, the Giants, and the ash-tree NYMPHS called Meliai. His severed genitals floated on the sea, producing a white foam from which sprang APHRODITE. Uranus also consorted with Clymene, Hemera, HESTIA, and Nyx.

Uranus Seventh planet from the sun. It was discovered in 1781 by HERSCHEL FAMILY and named for the Greek god personifying heaven. A blue-green gas giant, it has almost 15 times the mass of earth and over 50 times its volume. It is less dense than earth; the gravity at the top of its atmosphere is 11% weaker. Its equatorial diameter is 31,800 mi (51,100 km). Uranus has 10 sharply defined, narrow, dark rings, with broad dust bands between them, consisting mainly of boulder-sized chunks of dark material. It also has at least 15 moons (most named after Shakespearean characters) and a magnetic field about as strong as earth's. The planet is estimated to rotate about every 17 hours, around an unusual horizontal axis, so it appears to spin on its side. It takes 84 years to orbit the sun, at a mean distance of 1.78 billion mi (2.87 billion km). Its interior is thought to consist of ice and gas, perhaps with a small rocky core. Its atmosphere appears to be thousands of miles deep, and its blue color comes from absorption of red light by methane in the atmosphere. The upper reaches of the atmosphere consist mainly of hydrogen and helium.

Urartu \u̇-ˈrär-ˌtü\ Ancient kingdom around Lake VAN, north of ASSYRIA, South Asia. Today the region is divided among Armenia, eastern Turkey, and northwestern Iran. The kingdom flourished c. 13th–7th century BC, enjoying considerable power in the Middle East in the 9th–8th century BC. Archaeological finds date from the time of King Shalmaneser I (c. 1274–1245) of Assyria. Repeatedly attacked by Assyrian kings, it declined in the late 8th century BC. It ceased to exist after invasions by Cimmerians, Scythians, and Medes in the 7th century BC.

Urban II *orig.* **Odo of Châtillon-sur-Marne** (c. 1035–1099) Pope (1088–99). The prior of a Cluniac monastery, he was made cardinal by GREGORY VII, whose reforms he furthered. Elected pope in 1088, Urban secured his authority against the antipope Clement III and strengthened the role of the papacy in the reform movement. He called for the First CRUSADE at the Council of CLERMONT (1095) in response to the appeal of ALEXIUS I COMNENUS, promoted the union of the Eastern and Western churches, and supported the Christian reconquest of Spain from the Moors.

Urban VI *orig.* **Bartolomeo Prignano** (1318?–1389) Pope (1378–89). Archbishop of Acerenza (1363) and Bari (1377), he became papal chancellor for Gregory XI, whom he was chosen to succeed. This election of an Italian appeased the Romans, who wanted to end the French-dominated AVIGNON PAPACY, but his harsh reforms soon angered the French cardinals, prompting them to elect the antipope Clement VII and beginning the Western SCHISM (1378). Europe was divided in its loyalties, and Urban warred with Naples when its queen backed Clement. Strife over the schism reduced the Papal States to anarchy, and Urban's death may have been from poisoning.

urban climate Any set of climatic conditions that prevails in a large metropolitan area and that differs from the climate of its rural surroundings. Urban climates are distinguished from those of less built-up areas by differences of air temperature, humidity, wind speed and direction, and amount of precipitation. These differences are attributable in large part to the altering of the natural terrain through the construction of artificial structures and surfaces. For example, tall buildings, paved streets, and parking lots affect wind flow, precipitation runoff, and the local energy balance.

urban planning Programs pursued in most industrialized countries in an attempt to improve the urban environment and achieve certain social and economic objectives. Evidence of urban planning can be found in the ruins of ancient cities, including orderly street systems and conduits for water and sewage. During the Renaissance, European CITY areas were consciously planned to achieve circulation of the populace and provide fortification against invasion. Such concepts were exported to the New World, where WILLIAM PENN developed the standard gridiron plan, the laying out of streets and plots of land adaptable to rapid change in land use. The modern urban planning and redevelopment movement arose in response to the disorder and squalor of the slums created by the Industrial Revolution. City planners imposed regulatory laws establishing standards for housing, sanitation, water supply, sewage, and public health conditions, and introduced parks and playgrounds into congested city neighborhoods. In the 20th century, zoning—the regulation of building activity according to use and location—came to be a key tool for city planners.

Urbino majolica \mə-ˈjä-li-kə\ Italian tin-glazed EARTHENWARE made in the city of Urbino, which dominated the market from c. 1520. Early wares, mostly dishes, are painted in a range of colors, dominated by brilliant yellow, orange, and brown, and decorated with narrative scenes typically covering the entire surface, a style known as *istoriato*. Scenes are taken from the Bible, mythology, classical and contemporary history, and poetry. Later wares were decorated in a style called grotesque, adapted from motifs found in Roman excavations. Production declined in the late 17th century. See also MAJOLICA.

Urdu language \'ür-dü\ INDO-ARYAN LANGUAGE used by Muslims in India and Pakistan. In the sociopolitical realm, Urdu and HINDI are different languages, but the colloquial basis of both is identical, and as a written language Urdu differs from Hindi principally in its greater acceptance of Perso-Arabic vocabulary and in some syntactic features. It is written in the ARABIC ALPHABET with modification of some letters to denote specifically Indo-Aryan sounds. As Pakistan's official language, Urdu has been promoted as a token of national unity, though less than 8% of Pakistanis—mainly immigrants and descendants of immigrants from India after the 1947 partition—speak it as a first language.

urea \yu̇-'rē-ə\ *or* **carbamide** One of the simplest organic compounds and the first synthesized from inorganic raw materials (see INORGANIC COMPOUND), by Friedrich Wöhler (1800–1882) in 1828. It is the diamide of carbonic acid (H_2NCONH_2; see AMIDE, CARBON DIOXIDE). The chief nitrogenous end product of PROTEIN breakdown in mammals and some fishes, it occurs not only in URINE but also in BLOOD, BILE, MILK, and PERSPIRATION. It is one of the industrial chemicals produced in largest quantities. With its high nitrogen content and low price, it is a major agricultural fertilizer and animal-feed ingredient. It is also used to make urea-formaldehyde PLASTICS (including foamed plastics; see POLYURETHANES), as well as to synthesize barbiturates, as a stabilizer in explosives, and in adhesives, hydrocarbon processing, and flameproofing.

uremia \yu̇-'rē-mē-ə\ Excess nitrogenous waste products in the blood and their toxic effects. Kidney impairment (see BRIGHT'S DISEASE, DIABETES MELLITUS, HYPERTENSION, KIDNEY FAILURE, NEPHRITIS) or disorders that hinder urine excretion (e.g., PROSTATIC DISORDERS) allow UREA and other protein waste products to accumulate. Symptoms usually start with fatigue and loss of concentration. They may include itching and muscle twitches; dry, flaky, yellowish skin; dry mouth, metallic taste, and ammonia breath; and nausea, vomiting, diarrhea, and constipation. Advanced stages affect the nervous, cardiovascular, and respiratory systems and can lead to HYPERTENSION, seizures, HEART FAILURE, and death. If the underlying disorder cannot be treated, DIALYSIS or KIDNEY TRANSPLANT may be required.

Urey \'yu̇r-ē\, **Harold C(layton)** (1893–1981) U.S. scientist. Born in Walkerton, Ind., he received his doctorate from the University of California at Berkeley and thereafter taught at various universities. He was awarded a Nobel Prize in 1934 for discovering DEUTERIUM and HEAVY WATER. He was a key figure in the development of the ATOMIC BOMB; his group worked on the gaseous DIFFUSION process for separation of uranium-235. He devised methods for estimating the temperature of ancient oceans, theorized on the compositions of primordial atmospheres, and studied the relative abundances of the elements, making fundamental contributions to a widely accepted theory of the origin of the earth and other planets (in *The Planets*, 1952).

Uriburu \ü-rē-'bü-rü\, **José Félix** (1868–1932) Argentine soldier and dictator. Nephew of a former president, he was a firm believer in class privileges. A visit to Germany made him an ardent admirer of Prussian militarism. In 1930 he led a coup against HIPOLITO IRIGOYEN's liberal regime, replacing the governing class with an elite representing the landed oligarchy, dissolving the legislature, and revising the laws to prohibit liberal-radicals from political participation. In 1931 he arranged a fraudulent election to ensure the oligarchy's continued control and stepped down in favor of a fellow officer, Agustín Justo.

uric acid \'yu̇r-ik\ HETEROCYCLIC COMPOUND of the PURINE type, the end product of METABOLISM of the purines in NUCLEIC ACIDS in many animals, including humans. It is excreted by reptiles and birds as the chief nitrogenous end product of PROTEIN breakdown. Small quantities are normally found in human blood; in GOUT, levels are abnormally high. Uric acid is used industrially in organic synthesis.

urinalysis \ˌyu̇r-ə-'na-lə-səs\ Laboratory examination of a URINE sample for clinical information. Abnormal concentrations of substances normally found in urine or presence of those that are not may indicate a disorder. Color, specific gravity, or volume changes may reveal a specific disease or injury. Significant findings include high glucose and acetone in DIABETES MELLITUS; various nitrogen compounds, pigments, amino acids, and their metabolic products in disorders of the ENZYMES that act on them; uric acid in GOUT; and UREA, ALBUMINS, and GLOBULINS in kidney disease. Hormones may be evidence of pregnancy or endocrine imbalance. Urinalysis can also detect poisons and drugs.

urinary system *or* **renal system** \'rē-nəl\ System that produces and discharges URINE to rid the body of waste products. It consists of the KIDNEYS, which balance ELECTROLYTES in blood, retaining and adding needed ones and removing unneeded or dangerous ones for excretion; the ureters, two thin muscular tubes 10–12 in. (25–30 cm) long that move the urine by PERISTALSIS; the hollow, muscular bladder, which receives and stores it; and the urethra, through which it leaves the body. In women the urethra is an inch or two long. In men it is longer (since it passes through the PENIS) and carries SEMEN from the PROSTATE GLAND as well as urine. Urinary disorders, which can lead to DEHYDRATION or EDEMA and to a dangerous buildup of waste and toxic substances, include KIDNEY FAILURE, TUMORS, INFECTION, INFLAMMATION, and bladder and KIDNEY STONES.

urination Process of excreting URINE from the bladder (see URINARY SYSTEM). Nerve centers in the spinal cord, brain stem, and cerebral cortex control it through involuntary and voluntary muscles. The need to void is felt when the bladder holds 3.5–5 oz (100–150 ml) of urine and becomes uncomfortable at a volume of 14–15 oz (350–400 ml). The detrusor contracts and the sphincter (muscular constriction) of the urethra relaxes to empty the bladder. Normally it empties completely, but bladder stones or PROSTATIC DISORDERS can block outflow; poor muscle tone (especially in older women) or certain nervous-system disorders can cause loss of control of urination (INCONTINENCE).

urine Liquid solution of metabolic wastes and other, often toxic, substances filtered from PLASMA. The fluid in the Bowman's capsule at the start of each NEPHRON (capsular urine) is essentially plasma without the large molecules (e.g., proteins). The concentrated fluid (final urine) that exits the KIDNEY consists of water, UREA, inorganic SALTS, URIC ACID, creatinine, AMMONIA, and broken-down blood pigments, including urochrome, which makes urine yellow, plus any unusual substances not reabsorbed into the blood. This is then excreted. See also HEMATURIA, URINALYSIS, URINARY SYSTEM, URINATION.

URL *in full* **Uniform Resource Locator** *or* **Universal Resource Locator** Address of a resource on the INTERNET. The resource can be any type of file stored on a server, such as a WEB page, a text file, a graphics file, or an application program. The address contains three elements: the type of PROTOCOL used to access the file (e.g., HTTP for a Web page, ftp for an FTP site); the DOMAIN NAME or IP address of the server where the file resides; and, optionally, the pathname to the file (i.e., description of the file's location). For example, the URL *http://www.britannica.com/heritage* instructs the browser to use the HTTP protocol, go to the www.britannica.com Web server, and access the file named *heritage*.

Urmia, Lake *Persian* **Daryacheh-ye Orumiyeh** \ˌdär-yä-'che-ye-u̇-ˌrü-'mē-yə\ Shallow saline lake, northwestern Iran. The largest lake in the Middle East, it covers an area that varies from 2,000 to 2,300 sq mi (5,200 to 6,000 sq km). It is about 87 mi (140 km) long and 25–35 mi (40–55 km) wide, with a maximum depth of 53 ft (16 m). There is a cluster of about 50 tiny islands at its southern part. Fed by three rivers, it has no outlet. It has been protected since 1967.

Urnfield culture Late BRONZE AGE culture of Europe, so called because its people placed their cremated dead in urns. It spread from eastern central Europe and northern Italy in the 12th century BC and later to Ukraine, Sicily, Scandinavia, France, and Spain. In some areas barrows marked the graves. The culture was warlike, with fortified settlements and bronze weapons, including the slashing sword. The uniformity of the culture and the persistence of certain pottery and metal forms apparently had great influence on Early IRON AGE culture.

urogenital malformation Defect in the organs or tissues of the URINARY SYSTEM or in the sex organs (genitals). In polycystic kidney disease (an inherited disease), CYSTS of varying size enlarge one or both KIDNEYS. Kidneys may have abnormal shapes or may be fused. In megaloureter, the ureter's diameter is enlarged. Males may have epispadias or hypospadias, in which the urethra opens on the upper surface or the underside, respectively, of the PENIS, or cryptorchidism (undescended testicles), in which one or both TESTES have not descended from the abdomen into the scrotum before birth. Female genital system malformations include AGENESIS of the OVARIES, VAGINA, or UTERUS and abnormally shaped uterus.

urology \yu̇-'rä-lə-jē\ Medical specialty dealing with the URINARY SYSTEM and male reproductive organs. It traces its origin to medieval lithologists, itinerant healers who specialized in surgical removal of bladder stones. The Spanish surgeon Francisco Díaz wrote the first treatises on urinary-tract disease (1588) and is regarded as the founder of modern urology. Most modern urological procedures originated in the 19th century. Today, urologists use bladder catheters (see CATHETERIZATION), the cystoscope (to view the inside of the bladder), and various DIAGNOSTIC IMAGING techniques; treat PROSTATIC DISORDERS; perform VASECTOMIES; and may surgically remove stones in the urinary tract and cancers of the kidneys, bladder, and testicles. Urology deals mostly with male patients; the urinary tract in females may be treated by gynecologists (see OBSTETRICS AND GYNECOLOGY).

Urquiza \ür-ˈkē-sä\, **Justo José de** (1801–1870) Argentinian soldier and statesman who helped overthrow JUAN MANUEL DE ROSAS. He became governor of Entre Ríos province in 1841, and allied himself with other provincial leaders to overthrow the dictatorial Rosas in 1852. As provisional dictator, he called a constitutional convention that sanctioned a constitution modeled on that of the U.S. All provinces accepted it, but the province of Buenos Aires, determined to lead the nation, refused to join the new union until 1859. Urquiza stepped down in 1860 and led the Argentinian army in the PARAGUAYAN WAR. He and his sons were assassinated by a political rival. See also BARTOLOME MITRE.

Ursula \ˈər-syu̇-lə\, **St.** Legendary leader of a band of virgins martyred by the Huns in the 4th century. The number of virgins was originally 11, but as the story was retold over the years it increased to 11,000. According to the 13th-century *Golden Legend* Ursula was an English princess who went on a pilgrimage to Rome with 11,000 virgins and was martyred with them on the homeward journey. Ursula is the patron saint of the order of St. Ursula (Ursulines), a congregation of nuns dedicated to educating girls.

Urubamba River \ˌü-rü-ˈbäm-bä\ River, central Peru. Part of the AMAZON drainage system, it rises in the ANDES and flows northwest for about 450 mi (725 km) to its junction with the APURIMAC RIVER, where it forms the UCAYALI RIVER. In the Gorge of Torontoy, the river plunges from 11,000 to 8,000 ft (3,400 to 2,400 m) in 20 mi (32 km).

Uruguay \ˌü-rü-ˈgwī, *Engl* ˈyu̇r-ə-ˌgwā\ *officially* **Oriental Republic of Uruguay** Country, southeastern South America. Area: 68,037 sq mi

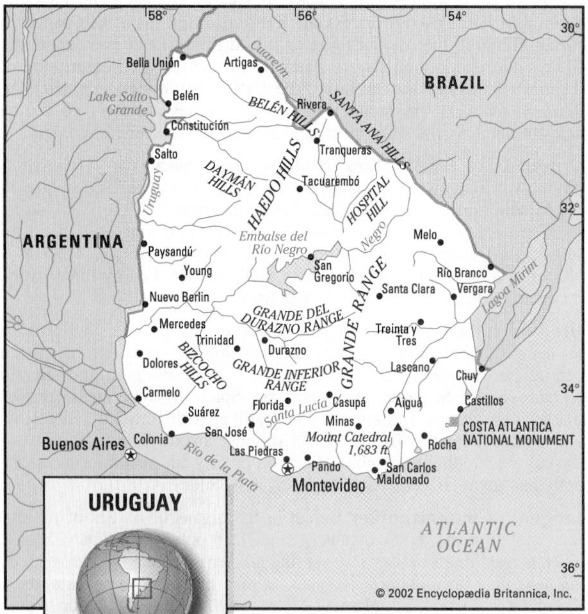

(176,215 sq km). Population (1997 est.): 3,185,000. Capital: MONTEVIDEO. Caucasians, mostly of Spanish and Italian origin, are the predominant ethnic group; the remainder are mestizos, mulattos, and blacks. Few Indians remain. Language: Spanish (official). Religions: Roman Catholicism, Protestantism, Judaism. Currency: Uruguayan peso. The only South American country lying entirely outside the tropics, its topography consists mainly of low plateaus and low hilly regions. The principal river is the NEGRO; the URUGUAY RIVER forms the country's entire western border with Argentina. Mineral and energy resources are limited. Pastures, covering almost four-fifths of the land area, support large herds of livestock for meat, leather goods, and wool. Chief crops include wheat, corn, oats, and barley. Other important industries are tourism, fishing, and the manufacturing of textiles, chemicals, and transportation equipment. It is a republic with two legislative houses; its head of state and government is the president. Prior to European settlement, Uruguay was inhabited mainly by the Charrúa Indians. The Spanish navigator Juan Díaz de Solís sailed into the Río de la PLATA in 1516. The Portuguese established Colonia in 1680. Subsequently, the Spanish established Montevideo in 1726, driving the Portuguese from their settlement; 50 years later Uruguay became part of the viceroyalty of RÍO DE LA PLATA. It gained independence from Spain in 1811. The Portuguese regained it in 1821, incorporating it into Brazil as a province. A revolt against Brazil in 1825 led to its being recognized as an independent state in 1828. It battled Paraguay 1865–70. For much of World War II it remained neutral. The presidential office was abolished in 1951 and replaced with a nine-member council. The country adopted a new constitution and restored the presidential system in 1966. A military coup occurred in 1973. It returned to civilian rule in 1985. The 1990s brought a general upturn in the economy.

Uruguay River River, southeastern South America. Rising in southern Brazil, it forms the Argentina–S Brazil border and the Uruguay–Argentina border. Above BUENOS AIRES, it combines with the PARANÁ RIVER to form the great estuary of the Río de la PLATA. Its 990-mi (1,593-km) course is interrupted by rapids, but it is navigable by ocean vessels for about 130 mi (210 km) from its mouth.

Uruk See ERECH

Urumqi \ u̇-ˈrœm-ˈchē\ *or* **Urumchi** \ü-ˈrüm-ˈchē\ *or* **Wu-lu-mu-ch'i** \ˈwü-ˈlü-ˈmü-ˈchē\ City (pop., 1999 est.: 1,258,457), capital of XINJIANG UYGUR autonomous region, northwestern China. Situated along the northern face of the TIAN SHAN, it first came under Chinese control in the 7th–8th century and became an important center for caravans en route to TURKISTAN. The UIGHURS had control from c. 750 until the resumption of Chinese rule in the 18th century. The city was held by Muslim rebels 1864–76. When the province of Sinkiang (later Xinjiang) was established in 1884, Urümqi became its capital. It grew rapidly into the greatest city and center of trade in central Asia. It is located in a coal-mining and petroleum-producing area; its chief manufactures include iron and steel, agricultural machinery, and chemicals.

Urundi See RUANDA-URUNDI

U.S. See UNITED STATES

U.S. News & World Report Weekly newsmagazine published in Washington, D.C. *U.S. News* was founded in 1933 by David Lawrence (1888–1973) to cover important domestic events; he founded *World Report* in 1945 to treat world news. The two magazines were merged in 1948. From its start, *U.S. News & World Report* had a somewhat more conservative editorial viewpoint than its larger rivals, *Time* and NEWSWEEK, and paid less attention to sports and the arts. In 1984 it was bought by Mortimer B. Zuckerman.

USA Today National U.S. daily general-interest newspaper, the first of its kind. Launched in 1982 by Allen Neuharth, head of the GANNETT CO. chain, it reached a circulation of 1 million within a year and surpassed 2 million in the 1990s. Initially considered gimmicky and insubstantial, it gradually developed a reputation for higher quality while increasing its circulation and advertising revenues at a time when few papers were experiencing growth. The features that originally set it apart—abundant colorful graphics, very brief stories, and a concentration on sports and celebrity—have influenced other newspapers.

USB *in full* **Universal Serial Bus** Type of serial BUS that allows peripheral devices (disks, modems, printers, digitizers, data gloves, etc.) to be easily connected to a computer. A "plug-and-play" interface, it allows a device to be added without an adapter card and without rebooting the computer (the latter is known as hot-plugging). The USB standard, developed by several major computer and telecommunications companies, supports data-transfer speeds up to 12 megabits per second, multiple data streams, and up to 127 peripherals.

USC See University of SOUTHERN CALIFORNIA

Usman dan Fodio \ü-'smän-'dän-fō-'dē-ō\ (1754–1817) FULANI mystic, philosopher, and revolutionary reformer. In a JIHAD (holy war) between 1804 and 1808, he created a new Muslim state, the Fulani empire, in what is now northern Nigeria. He stimulated the growth of Islam throughout the region and founded the important Sokoto caliphate. He also produced a large body of writings in Arabic and Fula that continue to enjoy wide circulation and influence.

U.S.S.R. See UNION OF SOVIET SOCIALIST REPUBLICS

Ussuri River \ü-'su̇r-ē\ River, western Asia. Formed by the confluence of two rivers in mountains at the extreme southern end of Primorsky Kray, Russia, it flows north, marking part of the border between Russia and China. Joining the AMUR RIVER near Khabarovsk it is 565 mi (909 km) long. In the 1960s, and especially in 1969, Soviet and Chinese forces clashed over large sections of the river border. In 1977 a limited agreement was reached on navigational use of the river.

Ustinov \'yüs-tə-ˌnȯf\, **Peter (Alexander)** *later* **Sir Peter** (born 1921) British actor and playwright. He made his film debut in *Hullo Fame* (1941). His film appearances include *Lola Montez* (1955), *Spartacus* (1960, Academy Award), *Topkapi* (1964, Academy Award), and a recurring role as Hercule Poirot in movies based on AGATHA CHRISTIE's mysteries, beginning with *Death on the Nile* (1978). He both starred in and directed *Billy Budd* (1962), among other films. He has written successful plays such as *The Love of Four Colonels* (1951) and *Romanoff and Juliet* (1956), and won Emmy awards for his television performances in *The Life of Samuel Johnson* (1957), *Barefoot in Athens* (1966), and *A Storm in Summer* (1970).

Usumacinta River \ˌü-sü-mä-'sēn-tä\ River, southeastern Mexico and northwestern Guatemala. Rising in western Guatemala, it flows northwest, forming a section of the Guatemala–Mexico boundary, before emptying into the Girijalva River in Mexico. Its upper course is known as the Chixoy or Salinas River; with the Chixoy, it is approximately 600 mi (1,000 km) long.

Usumbura See BUJUMBURA

usury \'yü-zhə-rē\ In law, the crime of charging an unlawfully high rate of INTEREST. In Old English law, the taking of any compensation whatsoever was termed usury. With the expansion of trade in the 13th century, the demand for credit increased, necessitating a modification in the definition of the term. In 1545 England fixed a legal maximum interest, a practice later followed by other Western nations.

Utah State, (pop., 2000: 2,233,169), western U.S. It covers 84,899 sq mi (219,888 sq km); its capital is SALT LAKE CITY. Utah contains the GREAT SALT LAKE and parts of the middle ROCKY MTNS. and UINTA MTNS. The western third of the state is a broad desert-like area. About 70% of the land is owned by either the federal or the state government. The region was inhabited as early as 10,000 BC. In c. AD 400 the PUEBLO INDIANS lived throughout Utah; they were followed by other groups, including the SHOSHONE, UTE, and PAIUTE Indians. Spanish missionaries visited there in the late 18th century. It passed to Mexico in 1821. While U.S. pioneer JIM BRIDGER discovered the Great Salt Lake in 1824, the area's first permanent settlers were MORMONS, who were led to the valley of the Great Salt Lake in 1847 by BRIGHAM YOUNG. The U.S. acquired the region after the MEXICAN WAR, and in 1850 organized the Utah Territory; it was reduced to the area of the present state by 1868. A conflict between Mormon authorities and the U.S. government known as the Utah War occurred in 1857–58, and statehood was denied until the Mormons renounced POLYGAMY. When they did, it entered the Union in 1896 as the 45th state. The Mormon Church has officially been politically neutral since the early 20th century and the influence of economic blocs has become more important. Utah has large reserves of coal and petroleum, and is the world's largest producer of beryllium. Major industries include agriculture and tourism.

Utah, University of Public university in Salt Lake City, founded in 1850. Through its 18 colleges and schools it offers more than 72 undergraduate degree programs and more than 90 graduate degree programs, as well as 50 teaching majors and minors. Notable among the university's research units are centers for the study of supercomputing, biomedical engineering, the human genome, politics, and the Middle East. Total enrollment is about 26,000.

Utamaro \ü-tä-'mä-rō\ *orig.* **Kitagawa Nebsuyoshi** (1753–1806) Japanese printmaker and painter. He moved from a provincial town to Edo (now Tokyo) in his youth; his early work included many illustrated books. One of the greatest UKIYO-E artists, he is known especially for his masterfully composed portraits of sensuous female beauties. Unlike other *ukiyo-e* artists, who favored prints of women in groups, Utamaro concentrated on half-length single portraits.

Ute \'yüt\ Shoshonean-speaking group of American Indians traditionally inhabiting western Colorado and eastern Utah (whose name derives from Ute). Until the 19th century, the Ute had no horses and lived in small family clusters, subsisting by food collecting. They were virtually indistinguishable from the Southern PAIUTE. After acquiring horses they became organized as loose bands of hunters, often targeting livestock. After the Indian wars of 1864–70 most Ute were settled on reservations. Today they number about 5,000.

uterine bleeding \'yü-tə-rən\ Abnormal bleeding from the UTERUS not related to MENSTRUATION. Most common in the first few years after menarche and as MENOPAUSE approaches, it is thought to occur when malfunctioning OVARIES reduce blood ESTROGEN levels. A malfunctioning HYPOTHALAMUS or PITUITARY GLAND may also cause hormonally induced uterine bleeding, as can birth-control pills or hormone replacement therapy. Some tumors produce estrogen and can alter the menstrual cycle, causing bleeding. Tumors in the uterus often bleed easily. Other causes include injury to the uterus, stress, obesity, chronic illness, psychological problems, and blood and cardiovascular disorders. Treatment is directed toward the underlying cause.

uterine cancer Malignant TUMOR of the UTERUS. Cancers affecting the lining of the uterus (endometrium) are the most common cancers of the female reproductive tract. Risk factors include absence of pregnancy, early age of first menstruation (before age 12), late onset of menopause (after age 52), obesity, diabetes, and estrogen replacement therapy. Additional risk factors are a personal history of breast or ovarian cancer, age (over age 40), and a family history of uterine cancer. Whites are more likely to develop uterine cancer than are blacks. The major symptom is vaginal bleeding or discharge. Treatment may begin with simple or radical HYSTERECTOMY. Some uterine cancers are treated in part by hormonal therapy, radiation therapy, or chemotherapy.

uterus *or* **womb** Inverted-pear-shaped organ of the female REPRODUCTIVE SYSTEM, in which the EMBRYO and FETUS develop during PREGNANCY. Lying over and behind the bladder, it is 2.5–3 in. (6–8 cm) long and about 2.5 in. (6 cm) across at the top, where the uterine (fallopian) tubes enter it; at the other end, the cervix extends down into the VAGINA. The uterine lining (endometrium), a moist mucous membrane, changes in thickness during the menstrual cycle (see MENSTRUATION), being thickest at ovulation (see OVARY) in readiness for a fertilized EGG. The uterine wall, about 1 in. (2.5 cm) thick, expands and becomes thinner as a fetus develops inside. The cervix expands to about 4 in. (10 cm) for delivery. Disorders of the uterus include infections, benign and malignant tumors, PROLAPSE, ENDOMETRIOSIS, and fibroids (leiomyomas; see MUSCLE TUMOR).

Uthman ibn Affan \üth-'män-ˌi-bən-af-'fan\ (died 656) Third CALIPH of the UMAYYAD DYNASTY. Born into the powerful Umayyad clan of Mecca, he became a wealthy merchant before converting to Islam and was the first convert of high social and economic standing. He married a daughter of MUHAMMAD. On the death of UMAR IBN AL-KHATTAB (644), Uthman was chosen as his successor. His reign as caliph was marked by nepotism and personal profit, and he made many enemies. His accomplishments included centralizing the administration of the caliphate and establishing an official version of the Quran. His death at the hands of rebels marked the beginning of the first FITNAH.

Utica \'yü-ti-kə\ Ancient Phoenician settlement, northern African coast. Traditionally considered the oldest settlement of PHOENICIA, it was located in what is now modern Tunisia. After its founding c. 8th cent. BC, it grew rapidly and was second in importance only to CARTHAGE. Made the capital of the Roman province of Africa after the Third PUNIC WAR (149–146 BC), it later declined after Emperor AUGUSTUS rebuilt Carthage. Excavations have uncovered Phoenician graves dating from the 8th century BC and a substantial residential section of the Roman city.

utilitarianism Ethical principle that action is right if it tends to maximize happiness, not only that of the agent but of everyone affected by his or her act. Thus, utilitarians focus on the consequences of an act rather than on its intrinsic nature or the motives of the agent (see CONSEQUENTIALISM). Classical utilitarianism is hedonist, but values other than, or in addition to, pleasure (ideal utilitarianism) can be employed, or—more neutrally, and in a version popular in economics—anything can be regarded as valuable that appears as an object of rational or informed desire (preference utilitarianism). The test of utility maximization can also be applied directly to single acts (act utilitarianism), or to acts only indirectly through some other suitable object of moral assessment, such as rules of conduct (rule utilitarianism). JEREMY BENTHAM's *Introduction to the Principles of Morals and Legislation* (1789) and JOHN STUART MILL's *Utilitarianism* (1863) are major statements of utilitarianism.

Uto-Aztecan languages \,yü-tō-'az-,te-kən\ Family of more than 30 American Indian languages spoken in pre-Columbian times from the northern Great Basin to Central America. Geographically, Uto-Aztecan can be divided into a northern and a southern branch. The northern branch, spoken from Oregon and Idaho to southern California and Arizona, includes the languages of the Northern and Southern PAIUTES, UTES, Northern and Eastern SHOSHONES, COMANCHES, and HOPI. The southern branch includes the languages of the O'odham (PIMA and PAPAGO) in Arizona, and of a number of Mexican Indian peoples, including the Tarahumara of Chihuahua, the Yaqui of northwestern Mexico and Arizona, and the Cora and Huichol of Nayarit and Jalisco; its southernmost extension includes NAHUATL.

utopian socialism Political and social idea of the mid-19th century. Adapted from such reformers as ROBERT OWEN and CHARLES FOURIER, utopian socialists drew from early communist and socialist ideas. Advocates included LOUIS BLANC, noted for his theory of worker-controlled "social workshops," and JOHN H NOYES, founder of the ONEIDA COMMUNITY in the U.S. Utopian settlements were also attempted by such religious groups as the MENNONITES, SHAKERS, and MORMONS. See also BROOK FARM.

Utrecht \'ue̅-,trekt, 'yü-,trekt\ City (pop., 1999 est.: 232,718), central Netherlands. The site of successive Roman, Frisian, and Frankish fortresses, it became an episcopal see in 696 under St. Willibrord. Its greatest prosperity was in the 11th–12th century, when it was an important commercial center. In 1527 it was transferred to Holy Roman Emperor CHARLES V and became part of the HABSBURG dominions. It was ruled by Spain until the 1570s when it became a center of Protestant resistance. It was the site of the signing of the Union of Utrecht (1579), which established a league of northern Netherlands provinces against Spain; the league was the basis for the future Netherlands kingdom. Occupied by the French 1795–1813, it was the residence of LOUIS BONAPARTE, king of Holland 1806–10. The only Dutch pope, Adrian VI, was born there. It is a transportation, financial, and insurance center.

Utrecht, Peace of (1713–14) Series of treaties concluding the War of the SPANISH SUCCESSION. One series was signed between France and other European powers; another series was signed between Spain and other powers. France concluded treaties with Britain, the Dutch Republic, Prussia, Portugal, and Savoy, in which it ceded various territories, including regions in Canada, to Britain. France also recognized Queen ANNE as the British sovereign, acknowledged FREDERICK I's royal title, and recognized VICTOR AMADEUS II as king of Sicily. Spain ceded Gibraltar to Britain. In a separate accord, the *asiento* agreement, Spain gave Britain the exclusive right to supply the Spanish colonies with African slaves for 30 years. Emperor CHARLES VI concluded a separate peace with France in the Treaty of RASTATT AND BADEN. The Spanish succession was settled in favor of the Bourbon PHILIP V. The treaties gave Britain the largest portion of colonial and commercial spoils and made it the leader in world trade.

Utrecht school Principally a group of three Dutch painters from UTRECHT—Dirck van Baburen (c. 1590–1624), GERRIT VAN HONTHORST, and HENDRIK TERBRUGGHEN—who were greatly influenced by CARAVAGGIO's art during travels to Rome. They used their newly learned technique in artwork with primarily religious subject matter, but also produced brothel scenes and pictures in sets, such as five works devoted to the senses. The numerous candles, lanterns, and other sources of artificial light in their paintings also differentiate them from Caravaggio, who never used such devices. Honthorst enjoyed the widest reputation at the time, but Terbrugghen is now considered the most talented and versatile of the group.

Utrillo \ue̅-trē-'yō, *Engl* yü-'tri-lō\, **Maurice** (1883–1955) French painter. When he became an alcoholic in his teens, his mother, the painter and artist's model Suzanne Valadon (1865–1938), encouraged him to take up painting as therapy; it soon became his obsession. He had no formal artistic training and was interested primarily in reproducing what he saw as faithfully as possible. Most of his compositions depict the old, deteriorating houses and streets of the Montmartre district of Paris. His best work is that of his "white period" (c. 1908–14), so called for his lavish use of zinc white in heavy layers to build up aging, cracked walls.

"Impasse Cottin," oil on cardboard, by Maurice Utrillo, c. 1910; in the National Museum of Modern Art, Paris.

Uttar Pradesh \'ü-tər-prə-'dāsh\ *formerly* **United Provinces (of Agra and Oudh)** State (pop., 2000: 166,052,859), northern India. It covers an area of 93,933 sq mi (243,286 sq km); its capital is LUCKNOW. The state, the most populous in the country, lies largely in the plains formed by the GANGES and YAMUNA rivers. The region was the setting of two great Sanskrit epics, the *MAHABHARATA* and *RAMAYANA*, and the scene of the rise of BUDDHISM after the 6th century BC. It was ruled by Mauryan King ASHOKA in the mid-3d century BC, the GUPTA DYNASTY c. 320–c. 425 AD, and King HARSA (606–647). The Mughals gained control in the 16th century, at which time the city of AGRA became a chief center. The British arrived in the late 18th century; by the 1830s they held sway and eventually formed the North-West Provinces, to which Oudh was later annexed. It was the main scene of the INDIAN MUTINY of 1857. The current province was formed in 1902, and became a state of India in 1947. In 2000 the northern portion of it was made into the state of UTTARANCHAL. Uttar Pradesh is the largest silica-producing state in the country, yet agriculture is by far its most important economic sector. Its noted tourist meccas are AGRA and VARANASI.

Uttaranchal State (pop., 2001: 8,479,562), northern India. It covers an area of 19,739 sq mi (51,125 sq km); its capital is Dehra Dun. The state lies in the HIMALAYAS, and some of India's highest peaks rise in its northern areas. The upper reaches of the GANGES and YAMUNA rivers flow southward through the state. In the south are found such hill resorts as Mussoorie, Naini Tal, and Ranikhet. The area now constituting Uttaranchal was a part of UTTAR PRADESH state after Indian independence in 1947 until it was made into a separate state in 2000. The population is mostly engaged in agriculture, although tourism is also important.

Uvarov \ü-'vär-əf\, **Sergey (Semyonovich), Count** (1786–1855) Russian administrator. After serving as head of the St. Petersburg educational district (1811–22), he became minister of education (1833–49) under Czar NICHOLAS I. In an influential report, Uvarov declared that education must adhere to the "principles of orthodoxy, autocracy, and nationality," which was adopted as an ideology rooted in loyalty to dynastic rule, traditional religious faith, and glorification of the Russian homeland.

uveitis \,yü-vē-'ī-təs\ INFLAMMATION of the uvea, the middle coat of the eyeball. Anterior uveitis, involving the iris or ciliary body (containing the muscle that adjusts the lens) or both, can lead to GLAUCOMA and blindness. Posterior uveitis, involving the choroid (which contains the eye's blood supply), can cause bleeding, lens clouding, and eyeball atrophy. Granulomatous uveitis (persistent inflammation with a grainy surface) causes vision impairment, pain, watery eyes, and sensitivity to light; nongranulomatous uveitis causes less pain and sensitivity, with a better chance of recovery. Causes include generalized infections and other diseases, allergic reactions, and injury. Rarely, the uninjured eye also has symptoms, with a risk of blindness in both eyes. Treatment aims to eliminate infection, reduce inflammation, and preserve vision.

Uxmal \üz-'mäl, üsh-'mäl\ Ancient city, YUCATÁN state, southeastern Mexico. It was the chief city of the later MAYA empire (600–c. 900 AD). After c. 1000, major construction in the city ceased, although it continued to be occupied and was a participant in the political League of Mayapan. When the league ended, Uxmal, like the other great cities of the north, was abandoned (c. 1450). Maya ruins include a pyramid, palace, and quadrangle.

Uygurs See UIGHURS

Uzbekistan \u̇z-ˌbe-ki-ˈstan\ *officially* **Republic of Uzbekistan** Nation, western central Asia. The Karakalpakstan Autonomous Republic is within its borders. Area: 172,700 sq mi (447,400 sq km). Population (1997 est.): 23,664,000. Capital: TASHKENT. The Uzbeks make up more than seven-tenths of the population; Russians, Tajiks, Kazaks, Tatars, and Karakalpaks make up the remainder. Languages: Uzbek (official), Russian, Tajik. Religions: Islam (Sunni), Russian Orthodoxy. Currency: sum. Uzbekistan lies in the heart of central Asia, largely between the AMU DARYA and the SYR DARYA rivers. Although it contains fertile oases and high mountain ranges in the south and east, almost four-fifths of the country consists of flat, sun-baked lowlands. Two-thirds of the ARAL SEA extends into Uzbekistan. It is a major producer and exporter of natural gas and has sizable reserves of petroleum, coal, and various metallic ores. It is one of central Asia's major cotton growers; it also grows fruits and vegetables and raises KARAKUL sheep. It is the main producer of machinery and heavy equipment in central Asia. It is a republic with one legislative body; its head of state is the president, and the head of government is the prime minister. GENGHIS KHAN's grandson Shibaqan received the territory as his inheritance in the 13th century AD. His Mongols ruled over nearly 100 mainly Turkic tribes, who would eventually intermarry with the Mongols to form the Uzbeks and other Turkic peoples of central Asia. In the early 16th century, a federation of Mongol-Uzbeks invaded and occupied settled regions, including an area called Transoxania that would become the Uzbeks' permanent homeland. By the early 19th century, the region was dominated by the khanates of Khiva, BUKHARA, and QUQON, all of which eventually succumbed to Russian domination. The Uzbek Soviet Socialist Republic was created in 1924. In June 1990 Uzbekistan became the first central Asian republic to declare sovereignty. It achieved full independence from the Soviet Union in 1991. During the 1990s, its economy was considered the strongest in central Asia, though its political system was deemed harsh. See map opposite.

Uzi submachine gun \ˈü-zē\ Compact automatic weapon used throughout the world as a police and special-forces firearm. It was named for its designer, Uziel Gal, an Israeli officer who developed it after the Arab-Israeli War of 1948. It is 25.6 in. (650 mm) long with its folding metal butt fully extended. The barrel is only 10 in. (260 mm) long. When loaded with a 25- or 32-round magazine of 9-mm pistol ammunition, it weighs about 9 lbs (4 kg). It has also been made in miniature versions as short as 18 in. (460 mm).

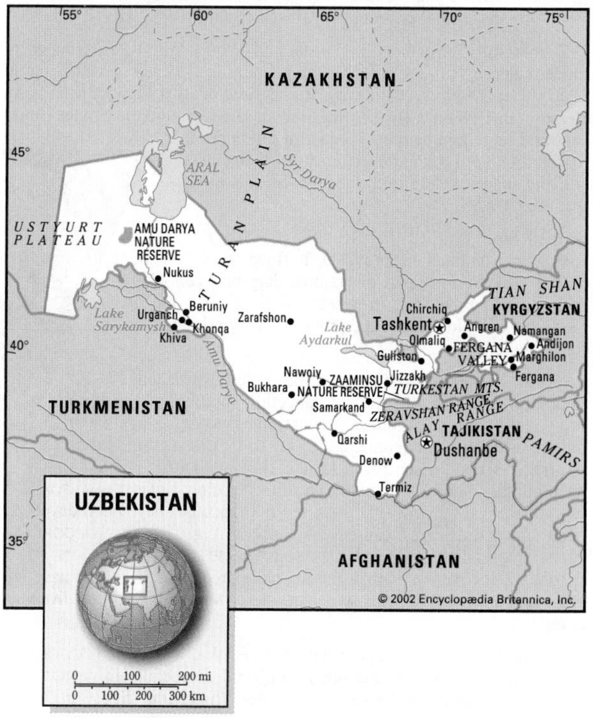

S T U V

V-1 missile *or* **flying bomb** *or* **buzz bomb** German missile of World War II. The forerunner of modern cruise missiles, it was about 25 ft (8 m) long and had a wingspan of about 18 ft (5.5 m). It was launched from catapult ramps or sometimes from aircraft; it carried an explosive warhead of almost 1,900 lbs (850 kg) and had an average range of 150 mi (240 km). More than 8,000 V-1s were launched against London in 1944–45, and a smaller number against Belgium. See also V-2 missile.

V-2 missile German ballistic missile of World War II, forerunner of modern space rockets and long-range missiles. Developed starting in 1936 under Wernher von Braun, it was fired against Paris, Britain, and Belgium in 1944 and 1945. After the war, the U.S. and the Soviet Union captured large numbers of V-2s and used them in research that led to the development of their missile and space-exploration programs. See also V-1 missile.

Vaal River \'väl\ River, Republic of South Africa. Rising in Mpumalanga province, it flows west 750 mi (1,210 km), forming part of the boundary between Mpumalanga and Free State provinces, to empty into the Orange River in Northern Cape province. It is primarily used for irrigation.

vaccine Preparation containing either killed or weakened live microorganisms, or a toxoid, introduced by mouth, by injection, or by nasal spray to stimulate production of antibodies against an infectious agent. This confers immunity to that agent, since the B lymphocytes remain sensitized to it and respond to later infection by producing more antibodies. The first vaccine, against smallpox, was introduced by Edward Jenner in 1798. Vaccines have been developed against diseases caused by bacteria (e.g., typhoid, whooping cough, tuberculosis) and by viruses (e.g., measles, influenza, rabies, poliomyelitis). Effectiveness varies, and a small percentage of people have adverse reactions. Those with immunodeficiency should not receive live vaccines.

vacuole \'vak-yə-ˌwōl\ Space within a cell that is empty of cytoplasm, lined with a membrane, and filled with fluid. Especially in protozoans, vacuoles perform functions such as storage, ingestion, digestion, excretion, and expulsion of excess water. The large central vacuoles often found in plant cells enable them to attain a large size without accumulating the bulk that would make metabolism difficult.

vacuum Space in which there is no matter or in which the pressure is so low that any particles in the space do not affect any processes being carried on there. It is a condition well below normal atmospheric pressure and is measured in units of pressure (the pascal). A vacuum can be created by removing air from a space using a vacuum pump or by reducing the pressure using a fast flow of fluid, as in Bernoulli's principle.

vacuum tube Electron tube consisting of a sealed glass or metal enclosure from which the air has been withdrawn. It was used in early electronic circuitry to control a flow of electrons. In the first half of the 20th century, vacuum tubes allowed the development of radio broadcasting, long-distance telephone service, television, and the first electronic digital computers, which were the largest vacuum-tube systems ever built. Transistors have replaced them in virtually all applications, but they are still occasionally used in display devices for television sets and computers (cathode-ray tubes), in microwave ovens, and as high-frequency transmitters on space satellites.

Vadim (Plemiannikov) \vȧ-'dēm\, **Roger** (1928–2000). French film director. After working briefly as a stage actor in the mid-1940s, he began his film career as an assistant on *Juliette* (1953). He directed and cowrote the highly successful erotic film *And God Created Woman* (1956), which established his wife, Brigitte Bardot, as a sex symbol. He duplicated this winning formula with two later wives, Annette Stroyberg in *Dangerous Liaisons* (1959) and Jane Fonda in *Barbarella* (1968), and his lover, Catherine Deneuve, in *Vice and Virtue* (1962).

Vadodara \və-'dō-də-ˌrä\ *or* **Baroda** \bə-'rō-də\ City (pop., 1991: 1,062,000), southeastern Gujarat state, western central India. It was known by many different names before receiving its present one in 1971. The earliest record of the city dates from a charter of AD 812, and during the succeeding centuries it came under various rulers, including those of the Muslim Delhi sultanate and the Mughal empire. Its varied products include cotton textiles, chemicals, machinery, and furniture.

Vaduz \fä-'düts\ City (pop., 1997 est.: 5,000), capital of Liechtenstein. Located on the Rhine River, it was greatly damaged in 1499 in a war between the Swiss and Holy Roman Emperor Maximilian I, but it was subsequently rebuilt. The Liechtenstein family gained possession in the early 18th century. It is a flourishing tourist center and the residence of the ruling prince, whose castle overlooks the town.

Vaganova \və-'gȧ-nə-və\, **Agrippina (Yakovlevna)** (1879–1951) Russian ballet dancer and teacher who developed a system of ballet instruction that combined classic technique with the athletic, acrobatic post-Revolution style. In 1897 she joined the Mariinsky Theater company, where she worked until 1917. She began teaching at the Leningrad Choreographic (formerly Imperial Ballet) school in 1921 and became its director in 1934. There she trained many of Russia's future leading dancers and teachers. Her textbook *Fundamentals of the Classic Dance* (1934) has been widely used worldwide.

vagina \və-'jī-nə\ Genital canal in females. Together with the cavity of the uterus, it forms the birth canal. In most virgins, its external opening is partially closed by a thin fold of tissue (hymen), which has various forms, not all of which significantly obstruct the opening. The vagina's lining thickens and thins during the menstrual cycle (see menstruation) in response to estrogen from the ovaries, being thickest and most elastic during ovulation and pregnancy. Its normally slightly acid environment discourages disease-causing microorganisms. Thick, elastic muscle walls accommodate movement of the penis during intercourse and passage of a child during delivery. A mucuslike fluid seeps through them for lubrication during sexual arousal. Vaginal disorders include bacterial and fungal infections (e.g., sexually transmitted diseases, candida), vaginitis, sores (see ulcer), and prolapse.

vaginitis \ˌva-jə-'nī-təs\ Inflammation of the vagina. The chief symptom is a whitish or yellowish vaginal discharge. Treatment depends on the cause: appropriate drugs for sexually transmitted diseases (often from *Gardnerella* bacteria or trichomonads) or yeast infections; estrogen cream for atrophy of the vaginal lining, which may dry out after menopause; and avoidance of any chemicals found to trigger irritation or allergy.

vagrancy Act of wandering about without employment or identifiable means of support. In the U.S., laws against vagrancy were used by police and prosecutors as a tool for proscribing a wide range of behavior. Most such laws have been struck down as unconstitutionally vague, and vagrancy has thus been largely decriminalized.

Vah River \'väk\ River, western Slovakia. Rising in the Tatra Mtns., it flows west and south for 242 mi (390 km) before entering the Danube River at Komárno. There are numerous hydroelectric-power stations along it.

Vail Town (pop., 1990: 3,600), western central Colorado. Located in the Rocky Mtns. west of Denver, it was founded as a resort town in 1962, and built in the style of an Alpine village. The skiable terrain around Vail Mountain extends for 15 sq mi (39 sq km), making Vail the largest ski resort in North America. It was host to the World Alpine Ski Championships in 1989.

Dainichi Nyorai ("Great Sun Buddha") by Unkei, lacquered wood sculpture, 1175; in the Enjo-ji, Nara, Japan.
ASUKA-EN

Vairocana \vī-'rō-chə-nə\ In Mahayana and tantric Buddhism, the supreme buddha who is the cosmic counterpart of Sakyamuni in his teaching mode. He is the most prominent of the five self-born buddhas, those who were born as humans to propagate the dharma. Though without canonical basis, Vairocana holds a special place in Tibetan Buddhism and has a special role in the Avatamsaka-sutra, in which he is the solar buddha who is both the ultimate reality of the cosmos and the one who pervades its component parts.

Vaisheshika \vī-'shā-shi-kə\ One of the six orthodox systems, or DARSHANS, of Indian philosophy. Founded c. 2nd–3rd century AD, it fused with NYAYA in the 11th century, forming the Nyaya-Vaisheshika school. Vaisheshika attempts to identify, inventory, and classify the entities that present themselves to human perception. It lists seven categories of being. It holds that the universe's smallest, indivisible, indestructible unit is the atom, which is made active through God's will, and that all physical things are a combination of the atoms of earth, water, fire, and air.

Vaishnavism \'vīsh-nə-,vi-zəm\ Worship of VISHNU as the supreme deity, as well as of his incarnations, mainly RAMA and KRISHNA. Vaishnavism is one of the major forms of modern HINDUISM, along with SHAIVISM and SHAKTISM, and is probably the most popular and most widely practiced. Characterized by an emphasis on BHAKTI, its goal is to escape from the cycle of birth and death in order to enjoy the presence of Vishnu. The philosophical schools into which Vaishnavism is divided are distinguished by their varying interpretations of the relationship between individual souls and God, and include aspects of MONISM and DUALISM.

Vaishya \'vīsh-yə\ Third-highest of the four VARNAS of India. Traditionally described as commoners, Vaishyas are connected with such productive labor as trade, agriculture, and pastoralism. According to legend, they sprang from the thighs of PRAJAPATI, after the BRAHMANS and the KSHATRIYAS but before the SUDRAS. Like the two higher classes, they are "twice-born"(see UPANAYANA). They are credited historically with favoring the rise of the reformist religious beliefs of BUDDHISM and JAINISM. In modern times they have become a symbol of middle-class prestige, and many rise to higher classes.

Vajiravudh \,vä-jē-rä-'vüd\ *or* **Phramongkutklao** \,prä-,mȯŋ-kủt-'klaủ\ *or* **Rama VI** (1881–1925) King of Siam (1910–25). Educated at Oxford, Vajiravudh undertook numerous social reforms as king, including making monogamy the only legal form of marriage. In 1921 he made primary education free and compulsory. He alienated both liberals and conservatives at home but was successful in foreign policy, restoring full fiscal autonomy to Siam. A prolific writer and translator, he introduced Western forms to Thai literature, translated WILLIAM SHAKESPEARE'S works, and composed about 50 original plays.

Vajpayee, Atal Bihari (born 1924) Leader of India's pro-Hindu BHARATIYA JANATA PARTY (BJP) and prime minister of India from 1998. Politically active as a teenager, he was briefly jailed by British colonial authorities. He was first elected to parliament in 1957 as a member of the Bharatiya Jan Sangh, a forerunner of the BJP. Vajpayee served as foreign minister in the late 1970s and helped formally establish the BJP in 1980. In 1992 he was one of the few Hindu leaders to speak out against the destruction of the historic Babri Masjid mosque by anti-Muslim extremists. Elected prime minister in May 1996, he was unable to form a government and resigned after 13 days. In 1998 and 1999 he was again elected prime minister as head of a BJP-led coalition. In May 1998 nuclear-weapons tests ordered by Vajpayee drew international condemnation and economic sanctions. In 2000 his government began an extensive program of divestment of public funds from several key state-run industries.

vajra \'vəj-rə\ Five-pronged ritual object extensively employed in the ceremonies of TIBETAN BUDDHISM. It is fashioned out of brass or bronze, the four prongs at each end curving around the central fifth to form a lotus-bud shape. In Sanskrit the word means both thunderbolt and diamond: like a thunderbolt it cuts through ignorance, and like a diamond it destroys but is itself indestructible. Originally a symbol of INDRA, it was used to conquer the non-Buddhist deities of Tibet. In ritual use, it is often employed in conjunction with a bell in the execution of MUDRAS.

Vajrayana \,vəj-rə-'yä-nə\ Form of tantric BUDDHISM that emerged in India in the first millennium AD and spread to Tibet, where it is the predominant tradition in TIBETAN BUDDHISM. Philosophically, Vajrayana is a blend of the YOGACARA and MADHYAMIKA disciplines. It aims to recapture the enlightenment experience of the BUDDHA Gautama, and it places special emphasis on the notion that enlightenment arises from the realization that seemingly opposite principles are in truth one. It introduced innovations involving the use of MANTRAS and MANDALAS as aids to meditation, and, in rare cases, the use of yogically disciplined sexual activities.

Vakataka dynasty \'vä-kə-tə-kə\ Indian ruling house that originated in the central Deccan in the mid-3rd century AD, the empire of which is believed to have extended from Malwa and Gujarat in the north to the Tungabhadra in the south and from the Arabian Sea in the west to the Bay of Bengal in the east. In the 4th century the Vakatakas were allied by marriage to the GUPTA DYNASTY, and Gupta cultural influence was significant. The Vakatakas are noted for having encouraged arts and letters.

Valdemar I \'vál-də-mär\ *known as* **Valdemar the Great** (1131–1182) King of Denmark (1157–82). On ascending the throne he ended more than 25 years of civil wars, and he defeated the Wends (Slavs) by 1169, freeing Danish ships from piracy. He acknowledged the overlordship of FREDERICK I BARBAROSSA and accepted his antipope Victor IV; he later acknowledged Pope ALEXANDER III (c. 1165) and rejected Frederick. He gained church approval for hereditary rule by his dynasty, the Valdemars, and in 1181 he allied with Frederick as an equal, aided by the marriage of their children.

Valdemar IV Atterdag \'át-tər-,dåg\ (c. 1320–1375) King of Denmark (1340–75). A son of King Christopher II, he sought to free Danish lands from foreign domination. He sold Estonia (1346), gained control of Zealand (1349), and subdued a revolt in Jutland (1350). By regaining Skåne from Sweden he completed the reunification of his father's kingdom (1360). His aggressive foreign policy led to conflict with Sweden, North German principalities, and the HANSEATIC LEAGUE, which defeated him in 1368, forcing him to concede trading privileges but allowing his kingdom to remain intact. The marriage of his daughter Margaret to the Norwegian king Haakon VI made possible the unification of Denmark and Norway.

Valdes, Peter See Peter WALDO

Valdés Leal \bäl-'dās-lē-'äl\, **Juan de** (1622–1690) Spanish painter. Son of a Portuguese father, he was educated in Córdoba and worked there and in Seville. After the death of BARTOLOME ESTEBAN MURILLO, he was Seville's leading painter. His early works are marked by exotic colors, dramatic lighting, and vigorous brush strokes. Later paintings such as *Vanitas* (1660) and *Triumph of Death* (1672) are characterized by their macabre subject matter, dynamic energy, and theatrical violence.

Vale of Tempe See Vale of TEMPE

Vale of the White Horse See Vale of the WHITE HORSE

valence \'vā-ləns\ Number of bonds (see BONDING) an ATOM can form. Hydrogen (H) always has valence 1, so other ELEMENTS' valences equal the number of hydrogen atoms they combine with. Thus, oxygen (O) has valence 2, as in water (H_2O); nitrogen (N) has valence 3, as in ammonia (NH_3); and chlorine (Cl) has valence 1, as in hydrochloric acid (HCl).

Valencia Autonomous community (pop., 2000 est.: 4,120,179), eastern Spain. Encompassing the provinces of Alicante, Castellón, and Valencia, it covers 8,979 sq mi (23,255 sq km); its capital is the city of VALENCIA. A generally mountainous region with salt lagoons on the coast, the area was conquered successively by Romans, Visigoths, and Moors. Part of the caliphate of CORDOBA (11th century), it subsequently became an independent Moorish kingdom. It was held by the Spanish commander El CID 1094–99; after his death it again was lost to the Moors, until King James I of ARAGON took it in 1238. One of the richest farming regions in the Mediterranean basin, it produces oranges, rice, grapes, and olives; it also has many manufacturing facilities.

Valencia City (metro. area pop., 2000 est.: 739,014), capital of the autonomous community of VALENCIA, eastern Spain. First mentioned as a Roman settlement in 138 BC, it was later taken by the Visigoths in AD 413 and the Moors in 714. It became the seat of the newly established independent Moorish kingdom of Valencia in 1021. After 1238 it was part of the dominions of the ARAGONS. The first Spanish printing press was established there in 1474; during the next two centuries the city was the seat of the Valencian school of painting. It was severely damaged in the PENINSULAR WAR, during the SPANISH CIVIL WAR, and by flood in 1957. Its port ships agricultural produce and manufactured items.

Valencia City (pop., 2000 est.: 1,338,833), northwestern Venezuela. It is located near the western shore of Lake VALENCIA. Founded in 1555, it rivaled CARACAS as the region's major city well into the 19th century. In 1814, during the struggle for Venezuela's independence, it was the site of a bloody battle between Spanish and opposition forces. It served as national capital in 1812, 1830, and 1858. One of Venezuela's principal industrial and transportation centers, it produces textiles, pharmaceuticals, and automobiles.

Valencia, Lake *formerly* **Tacarigua** \ˌtä-kä-ˈrē-gwä\ Lake, Carabobo and Aragua states, northern Venezuela. Its total area of 141 sq mi (364 sq km) makes it the second largest natural lake of Venezuela, after Lake MARACAIBO. It lies in an agricultural region and popular resort area.

Valens (AD 328–378) Eastern Roman emperor (364–78). His older brother, VALENTINIAN I, appointed Valens to be coemperor and assigned him to rule the eastern part of the empire, while Valentinian took the throne in the West. An Arian Christian, Valens persecuted Catholics and waged war on the pagan Procopius (366), the VISIGOTHS (367–369), and the Persians (c. 376). When the Visigoths again rebelled against the Romans, Valens' poor tactics led to his defeat and death in the great Battle of ADRIANOPLE.

Valentine's Day Lovers' holiday celebrated on February 14, the feast day of St. Valentine, one of two 3rd-century Roman martyrs of the same name. St. Valentine is considered the patron of lovers and especially of those unhappily in love. The feast day became a lovers' festival in the 14th century, probably as an extension of pagan love festivals and fertility rites celebrated in mid-February. Today it is marked by the exchange of romantic cards (valentines), flowers, and other gifts.

Valentinian I \ˌva-lən-ˈti-nē-ən\ *in full* **Flavius Valentinianus** (AD 321–375). Roman emperor (364–75). He served in the military in Africa under his father. Proclaimed emperor by the army, he made his brother VALENS ruler in the East while he ruled the West. Both showed religious toleration. Valentinian defeated the Alemanni in Gaul in 365, then moved to support the defense of Britain. He named his 9-year-old son GRATIAN coemperor (367) to ensure the succession. In Germany he fortified the Rhine; he went on to fight the Quadi in Pannonia, where he fell sick and died. Despite his achievements, he was known for his cruelty and poor choice of ministers.

Valentino, Rudolph *orig.* **Rodolfo Guglielmi di Valentina d'Antonguolla** (1895–1926) Italian-U.S. film actor. He emigrated to the U.S. in 1913 and worked as a dancer before moving to Hollywood in 1918. He played small parts in movies until his role in *The Four Horsemen of the Apocalypse* (1921) made him a star. Promoted by skillful press agents, his popularity soared among women as he played the handsome, mysterious lover in such romantic dramas as *The Sheik* (1921), *Blood and Sand* (1922), *The Eagle* (1925), and *The Son of the Sheik* (1926). His sudden death at 31 from a ruptured ulcer caused worldwide hysteria, several suicides, and riots at his funeral.

Valera, Eamon de See Eamon DE VALERA

Valerian *Latin* **Publius Licinius Valerianus** (died 260 AD) Roman emperor (253–260). He served as consul under SEVERUS ALEXANDER (r.222–235). Later a commander on the upper Rhine, he supported the emperor Gallus (r.251–53) in the conflict with a rival emperor but arrived with his legions too late to save Gallus from death at the hands of his own troops. Elected emperor by his soldiers (253), Valerian renewed the persecution of the Christians and executed Pope Sixtus II in 258. He appointed his son PUBLIUS LICINIUS GALLIENUS to rule the western part of the empire, then marched east to repel the Persian invasion. At first successful, he was later defeated by the Persian king Shapur I and died in captivity.

valerian Any of the more than 400 species of annual and perennial herbaceous plants in about 10 genera that make up the family Valerianaceae. A few are outstanding as ornamentals, salad or potherbs, or as sources of medicines and perfumes. Greek valerian is Jacob's ladder *(Polemonium caeruleum),* in the family Polemoniaceae. The true valerians (native to the temperate zones, the Andes Mtns., and Africa) have tubular flowers, often spurred at the base and clustered in tight heads. The largest genus, *Valeriana,* contains about 200 species and is best known for common valerian *(V. officinalis),* used by modern herbalists to calm the nerves.

Valéry \ˌva-lə-ˈrē\, **(Ambroise-) Paul (-Toussaint-Jules)** (1871–1945) French poet, essayist, and critic. A student of law, Valéry wrote many poems during 1888–91, some published in magazines of the SYMBOLIST MOVEMENT. After 1894 he wrote daily in his notebooks, later published as the famous *Cahiers.* He revised his early work to create his greatest poem, *La jeune parque* (1917). It was followed by *Album de vers anciens, 1890–1900* (1920) and *Charmes ou poèmes* (1922), containing "Le cimetière marin," which established him as the outstanding French poet of his time. He later became a prominent public personage, writing many essays and occasional papers on literary topics and taking a great interest in science and political problems.

Valéry.
EB INC.

Valhalla \val-ˈha-lə, väl-ˈhä-lə\ In GERMANIC RELIGION, the hall of slain warriors who live blissfully under the leadership of ODIN. Valhalla is depicted as a splendid palace, roofed with shields, where the warriors feast on the flesh of a boar slaughtered daily and made whole again each evening. They drink liquor that flows from the udders of a goat, and their sport is to fight one another every day, with the slain being revived in the evening. Thus they will live until the RAGNAROK, when they will leave Valhalla to fight at the side of Odin against the Giants. See also ASGARD, FREYJA, VALKYRIE.

validity In LOGIC, the property of an argument consisting in the fact that the truth of the premises logically guarantees the truth of the conclusion. Whenever the premises are true, the conclusion must be true, because of the form of the argument. Some arguments that fail to be valid are acceptable on grounds other than formal logic (e.g., inductively strong arguments), and their conclusions are supported with less than logical necessity. Where the support yields high probability of the conclusion relative to the premises, such arguments are sometimes called inductively valid. In other purportedly persuasive arguments, the premises actually provide no rational grounds for accepting the conclusion; such defective forms of argument are called fallacies (see FALLACY, FORMAL AND INFORMAL).

valine \ˈva-ˌlēn, ˈvā-ˌlēn\ One of the essential AMINO ACIDS, found in most PROTEINS. Produced industrially by HYDROLYSIS of proteins or by chemical synthesis, it is used in biochemical and nutritional research and as a dietary supplement.

Valium Trademark for a preparation of diazepam. A tranquillizing drug used to treat anxiety and as an aid in sedation, first introduced in 1963, it belongs to the group of chemically related compounds called benzodiazepines, the first of which was synthesized in 1933. Side effects include drowsiness and muscular incoordination; physical dependence can result after prolonged use. The discovery of Valium and similar drugs led to a new era in psychopharmacology.

Valkyrie \val-ˈkir-ē, ˈval-kə-rē\ In GERMANIC RELIGION, any of a group of maidens who are sent by ODIN to select slain warriors worthy of a place in VALHALLA. They rode to the battlefield on horses or, in some accounts, flew through the air and sea. Some had the power to cause the death of warriors they disliked; others guarded the lives and ships of those they favored. According to various myths, they were either purely supernatural or human with supernatural powers; they were associated with fairness, brightness, and gold as well as with bloodshed.

Valla \ˈväl-lä\, **Lorenzo** (1407–1457) Italian humanist, philosopher, and literary critic. Unable to find a post as a papal secretary, Valla left Rome in 1430 and spent five years traveling in northern Italy. He was royal secretary and historian for ALFONSO V of Aragon 1435–48. In his polemical style, he criticized the works of BOETHIUS, ARISTOTLE, and CICERO. Found heretical by the INQUISITION for his refusal to believe that the Apostles' Creed was composed by the 12 Apostles, he narrowly avoided being burned at the stake. His *Elegantiae linguae Latinae* (printed 1471; "Elegances of the Latin Language") was the first textbook of Latin grammar written since late antiquity. His *Annotations on the New Testament* (printed 1505) was his last major work.

Valladolid \ˌva-lə-də-ˈlid, *Span* ˌbäl-yä-t͟hō-ˈlēth\ City (metro. area pop., 1998: 319,946), capital of the autonomous community of

S T U V

CASTILLA Y LEÓN, Spain. First mentioned in 1074, it was the seat of the Castilian court until c. 1600. The Catholic monarchs ISABELLA of Castile and FERDINAND of Aragon were married there in 1469. It suffered heavy damage by fire in 1561 and by the French during the PENINSULAR WAR. Industry and commerce are economic mainstays. It has many medieval buildings, and its university (founded 1346) is one of Spain's oldest. CHRISTOPHER COLUMBUS died there in 1506.

Vallandigham \və-'lan-di-gəm\, **Clement L(aird)** (1820–1871) U.S. politician. Born in Lisbon, Ohio, he served in the U.S. House of Representatives (1857–63), where he became a leader of the antiwar COPPERHEADS and the secret Knights of the Golden Circle (later Sons of LIBERTY). As a result of his vociferous criticism of Pres. ABRAHAM LINCOLN's administration and its pursuit of the Civil War, he was arrested and found guilty of treasonable sentiments (1863) and was sentenced to exile in the South. He soon made his way to Canada, then illegally to Ohio, where he continued his antigovernment speeches.

Valle d'Aosta \ˌvä-lā-dä-'ȯs-tə\ Autonomous region (pop., 1996 est.: 119,000), northwestern Italy. It is enclosed on three sides by the ALPS; the capital is AOSTA. Originally the territory of the Celtic Salassi, it was annexed by the Romans. After the fall of the western Roman empire in the 5th cent, it formed part of the Burgundian and Frankish kingdoms. It was acquired in the 11th century by the house of SAVOY. The autonomous region of Valle d'Aosta was created in 1945, in recognition of the special French linguistic and cultural orientation of the area. It is important for dairy products and tourism.

Valle-Inclán \'bäl-yā-ēŋ-'klän\, **Ramón María del** *orig.* **Ramón Valle y Villanueva de Arosa** (1866–1936) Spanish novelist, playwright, and poet. Early on he was influenced by the Symbolist movement, and his first four works, collectively called the *Sonatas* (1902–5), are evocatively written in a tone of refined and elegant decadence. Some later plays and novels take an intentionally absurdist and cruelly satiric tone to express what he saw as the Spanish deformation of European civilization; representative are the play *Bohemian Lights* (1921) and the novel *The Court of Miracles* (1927).

Vallee \'val-ē\, **Rudy** *orig.* **Hubert Prior Vallée** (1901–1986) U.S. singer and entertainer. Born in Island Pond, Vt., he performed as a musician while at Yale University and in 1928 formed a dance band, the Yale Collegians (later the Connecticut Yankees). A singing bandleader, he used his trademark megaphone to amplify his suave, light-toned voice. He made his screen debut in *The Vagabond Lover* (1929) and evolved into a light comedian and character actor. On radio he hosted the first major network variety hour, *The Rudy Vallee Show* (1929–43), discovering such new talent as Alice Faye and EDGAR BERGEN.

Vallejo \və-'lā-ō\ City (pop., 1996 est.: 110,000), western California. It is located on San Pablo Bay, near OAKLAND. Settled in 1850, it served as the state capital for seven days in January 1852 and for a month in 1853. The Mare Island Naval Shipyard (established 1854, now closed) ensured the city's survival; area military installations are important to the economy. It is home to the California Maritime Academy (founded 1929).

Valletta \və-'le-tə\ Seaport city (pop., 1996 est.: 9,000), capital of MALTA. It is located on a rocky promontory with harbors on either side. Built after the Great Siege of Malta in 1565, which checked the advance of OTTOMAN power in southern Europe, it was named after Jean Parisot de la Valette, grand master of the KNIGHTS OF MALTA. It became the Maltese capital in 1570. After 1814 it was made the principal base of the British Mediterranean naval fleet and remained important through World War II, during which it suffered heavy damage from bombing raids. Several 16th-century buildings still exist. The city's economy relies mainly on trade and tourism.

valley Elongate depression of the earth's surface. Valleys are commonly drained by rivers and may be in a relatively flat plain or between ranges of hills or mountains. Valleys formed by rivers and slope denudation are typically V-shaped; those formerly occupied by glaciers are characteristically U-shaped. Valley evolution is controlled mainly by climate and rock type. Very narrow, deep valleys cut in resistant rock and having steep, almost vertical sides are called canyons. Smaller valleys of similar appearance are called gorges.

Valley Forge National Historical Park Preserve, southeastern Pennsylvania. The 3,468-acre (1,404-hectare) park commemorates the site where Gen. GEORGE WASHINGTON camped with his Continental Army in the winter of 1777–78 during the AMERICAN REVOLUTION. It was established in 1976.

Valley of Ten Thousand Smokes See Valley of TEN THOUSAND SMOKES

Valley of the Kings See Valley of the KINGS

Valois \vål-'wä\ Medieval county and duchy, northern France. It was under the Merovingian kings (c. 500–751) and their successors, the Carolingians, until it became a hereditary countship. In 1214 King PHILIP II AUGUSTUS annexed it to the royal domain. The duchy's last representative, Henry III, was succeeded in 1589 by the house of BOURBON. In 1790 it was abolished in the redivision of France into departments.

Valois, Ninette de See Ninette DE VALOIS

Valparaiso \ˌval-pə-'rī-zō\ City (pop., 1995 est.: 282,000) and seaport, central Chile. It was founded by the Spanish in 1536; few of its colonial buildings have survived a succession of pirate raids, severe storms, fires, and earthquakes (recently, 1906 and 1971). After Chilean independence in 1818, the city's port developed with the growth of the Chilean navy. In 1884 a treaty was signed here by which Bolivia ceded to Chile a coastal region containing principal nitrate deposits. As Chile's principal seaport, it handles the bulk of the country's imports. Still a naval facility, it also produces chemicals and textiles.

value-added tax Government levy on the amount a firm adds to the price of a commodity during production and distribution. In the most common method of calculation, the seller totals the sums of taxes he has collected on goods sold and paid on goods purchased; his net tax liability is the difference between the tax collected and the tax paid. The burden of the value-added tax, like that of other SALES TAXES, tends to be passed on to the consumer. To limit its regressiveness, most countries set lower rates for consumer necessities than for luxury items. In 1954 France became the first country to adopt the value-added tax on a large scale. Though complex to calculate, the tax served as an improvement on earlier systems by which a product was taxed repeatedly at every stage of production and distribution. It has since been adopted throughout most of Western Europe and in many countries in South America, Asia, and Africa. See also REGRESSIVE TAX.

valve In mechanical engineering, a device for controlling the flow of fluids (liquids, gases, slurries) in a pipe or other enclosure. It exerts control by means of a movable element that opens, shuts, or partially blocks an opening in a passageway. Valves are of seven main types: globe, gate, needle, plug (cock), butterfly, poppet, and spool. Some valves operate automatically; check (or nonreturn) valves, for example, are self-acting valves that permit flow in only one direction. Safety valves open

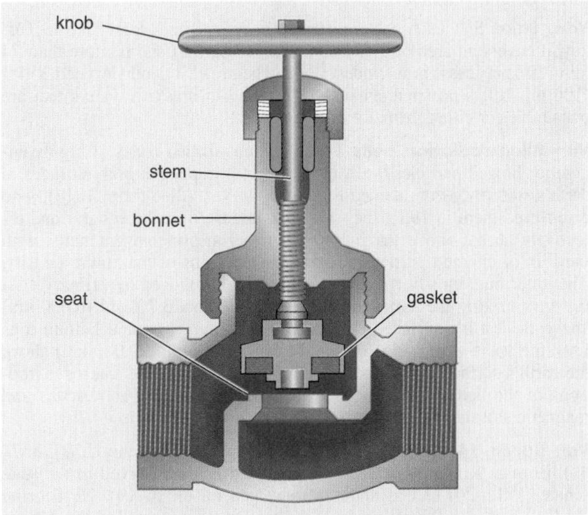

A globe valve controls the flow of a fluid through a pipe, inlet, or outlet. To stop the flow completely, the threaded stem is turned to lower a sealing gasket onto the seat.

at a predetermined pressure; the movable element usually has a weighted lever or a spring strong enough to hold the valve closed until a particular pressure is reached.

vampire In popular legend, a bloodsucking creature that rises from its burial place at night to drink the blood of humans, sometimes in the form of a bat. By daybreak it must return to its grave or to a coffin filled with its native earth. Tales of vampires are part of the folklore of many Asian and European countries, notably Hungary and other Slavic regions. The disinterment in Serbia in 1725 and 1732 of several fluid-filled corpses that villagers claimed were behind a plague of vampirism led to widespread interest and imaginative treatment of vampirism throughout Western Europe. Vampires are supposedly dead humans (originally suicides, heretics, or criminals) who maintain a kind of life by biting the necks of living humans and sucking their blood; their victims also become vampires after death. These "undead" creatures cast no shadow and are not reflected in mirrors. They can be warded off by crucifixes or wreaths of garlic and can be killed by exposure to the sun or by an oak stake driven through the heart. The most famous vampire was created by Bram Stoker in his *Dracula* (1897).

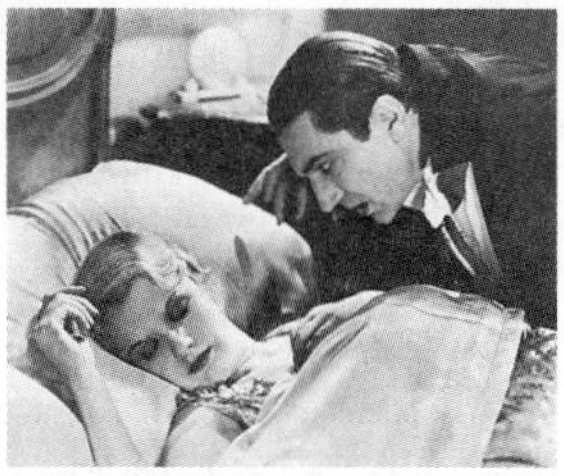

Bela Lugosi with Frances Dade in *Dracula* (1931).

BY COURTESY OF UNIVERSAL PICTURES; PHOTOGRAPH, THE BETTMANN ARCHIVE

vampire bat Any of three species (family Desmodontidae) of tailless, brown, blood-eating bats native to the New World tropics. They grow to 2–3.5 in. (6–9 cm) long and weigh 0.5–2 oz (15–50 g). They run swiftly and leap with agility. They live in colonies in caves, hollow trees, and culverts, leaving after dark to forage low on the ground. They feed on quietly resting birds and mammals, including the occasional human, making a small cut with their sharp incisor teeth, often without disturbing the prey, and lapping the blood. The wounds are not serious but may transmit rabies or other diseases.

Van City (pop., 1995 est.: 198,000), eastern Turkey, on the eastern shore of Lake Van. Stone building ruins there date from the 8th century BC when it was the chief center of the kingdom of Urartu. After the fall of Nineveh (612 BC), it was occupied in succession by the Medes, the kings of Pontus, Arabs (7th century AD), and Armenians (8th century AD). It fell to the Seljuq Turks after 1071 AD and to Ottoman Turks in 1543. Russian forces occupied it 1915–17 during World War I. It has a large Kurdish population. It once had a large Armenian population; for their nationalist aspirations, they were massacred during World War I. Van ships hides, grains, fruits, and vegetables.

Van, Lake Salt lake, eastern Turkey in Asia. The largest lake in Turkey, it covers an area of 1,434 sq mi (3,713 sq km) and is more than 74 mi (119 km) across at its widest point. The greatest depths exceed 330 ft (100 m). It has no apparent outlet, resulting in brackish waters that are unsuitable for either drinking or irrigation.

Van Allen radiation belts Two doughnut-shaped zones of highly energetic charged particles (see electric charge) trapped at high altitudes in earth's magnetic field. Named for James A. Van Allen (born 1914), who discovered them in 1958, they are most intense over the equator and effectively absent above the poles. The two zones merge gradually, with the flux of charged particles showing two regions of maximum density. The inner one, mostly protons thought to be produced by primary cosmic rays striking the atmosphere, is centered about 3,700 mi (6,000 km) above the earth's surface. The outer region includes some helium ions from the solar wind and is centered about 12,500 mi (20,000 km) above the earth's surface. Intense solar activity (see solar cycle) causes disruptions of the belts, linked in turn with such phenomena as auroras and magnetic storms.

Van Buren, Martin (1782–1862) Eighth president of the U.S. (1837–41). Born in Kinderhook, N.Y., he practiced law and served in the state senate (1812–20) and as state attorney general (1816–19). He became the leader of an informal group of political supporters, called the Albany Regency because they dominated state politics even while Van Buren was in Washington. He was elected to the U.S. Senate (1821–28), where he supported states' rights and opposed a strong central government. After John Quincy Adams became president, he joined with Andrew Jackson and others to form a group that later became the Democratic Party. He was elected governor of New York (1828) but resigned to become U.S. secretary of state (1829–31). He was nominated for vice president at the first Democratic Party convention (1832) and served under Jackson (1833–37). As Jackson's chosen successor, he defeated William H. Harrison to win the 1836 election. His presidency was marked by an economic depression, the Maine–Canada border dispute (see Aroostook War), the Seminole War in Florida, and debate over the annexation of Texas. He was defeated in his bid for reelection and failed to win the Democratic nomination in 1844 because of his antislavery views. In 1848 he was nominated for president by the Free Soil Party but failed to win the election and retired.

Van Cortlandt, Stephanus (1643–1700) American colonial official. Born in the Dutch colonial city of New Amsterdam (later New York City), he became a wealthy merchant. When the colony came under British rule (1664), he was appointed to the governor's council in 1674. He became the first native-born mayor of New York City (1677, 1686–87) and later served as associate justice and chief justice of the New York supreme court (1691–1700).

Van de Graaff, Robert J(emison) (1901–1967) U.S. physicist. Born in Tuscaloosa, Ala., he worked as an engineer, then as a physics researcher at Oxford University (1925–29). From 1931 he continued his research at MIT, as a professor 1934–60. He developed a high-voltage electrostatic generator (later called the Van de Graaff generator) that serves as a type of particle accelerator. In 1946 he cofounded the High Voltage Engineering Corp. to manufacture his accelerator. Widely used in atomic research, the device was also adapted to produce high-energy X rays for medical and industrial uses.

van de Velde, Henri See Henry van de Velde

van de Velde, Willem, the Elder See Willem van de Velde the Elder

van der Goes, Hugo See Hugo van der Goes

van der Rohe, Ludwig Mies See Ludwig Mies van der Rohe

van der Waals \'van-dər-ˌwȯlz\, **Johannes Diederik** (1837–1923) Dutch physicist. As professor at the University of Amsterdam (1877–1907), he extended the classical ideal-gas law (see gas laws) to describe the behavior of real gases, deriving the van der Waals equation of state in 1881. His work led to the liquefying of several common gases and made possible the study of temperatures near absolute zero. The van der Waals forces were named in his honor. He received a 1910 Nobel Prize.

van der Waals forces Relatively weak electrical forces that attract neutral (uncharged) molecules to each other in gases, liquefied and solidified gases, and almost all organic liquids and solids. Solids held together by van der Waals forces typically have lower melting points and are softer than those held together by ionic, covalent, and metallic bonds (see bonding). The forces arise because neutral molecules, though uncharged, are usually electric dipoles, which have a tendency to align with each other and to induce further polarization in neighboring molecules, resulting in a net attractive force. They are somewhat weaker than hydrogen bonds. See also Johannes D. van der Waals.

van der Weyden, Rogier See Rogier van der Weyden

Van Der Zee, James (Augustus Joseph) (1886–1983) U.S. photographer. Born in Lenox, Mass., he moved in 1906 with his family to Harlem in New York City. In 1915 he moved to Newark, N.J., to take a job in a portrait studio. He soon returned to Harlem to set up his own studio, and the portraits he took from 1918 to 1945 chronicled the Harlem Renaissance; among his many renowned subjects were Countee Cullen, Bill Robinson, and Marcus Garvey. After World War II his fortunes declined along with Harlem's, until the Metropolitan Museum of Art exhibited his photographs in 1969.

van Doesburg, Theo See Theo van Doesburg

Van Doren, Carl (Clinton) and Mark (1885–1950, 1894–1972) U.S. writers and teachers. The Van Doren brothers were born in Hope, Ill. Carl, who taught at Columbia University 1911–30, edited the *Cambridge History of American Literature* (1917–21) and journals. His critical works include the biography *Benjamin Franklin* (1938, Pulitzer Prize). Mark taught at Columbia 1920–59. He published more than 20 volumes of verse, including *Spring Thunder* (1924) and *Collected Po-*

ems (1922–38) (1939, Pulitzer Prize). He wrote three novels and several volumes of short stories and edited anthologies. His literary criticism includes works on JOHN DRYDEN, WILLIAM SHAKESPEARE, and NATHANIEL HAWTHORNE as well as *Introduction to Poetry* (1951), which examines shorter classic poems of English and American literature.

Van Dyck \van-'dīk\, **Anthony** *later* **Sir Anthony** (1599–1641) Flemish painter. Son of a well-to-do silk merchant, he was apprenticed to an Antwerp painter at 10. He soon came under the influence of PETER PAUL RUBENS, for his early works are painted in Rubens's melodramatic style, though with darker and warmer color, more abrupt chiaroscuro, and more angular figures. He was a master in the Antwerp artists' guild by 19, at which time he was also working with Rubens. He spent over five years in Italy (1621–27); on his return, he received many commissions for altarpieces and portraits. He also executed works on mythological subjects and was a fine draftsman and etcher, but he is chiefly known for his portraits, in which he idealized his models without sacrificing their individuality. In Britain in 1632, he was appointed court painter by CHARLES I. He gained a comfortable income from the many portraits he painted in Britain, and his life matched his clients' in luxury. His influence was pervasive and lasting; Flemish, Dutch, and German portraitists imitated his style and technique, and the 18th-century English portraitists, especially THOMAS GAINSBOROUGH and JOSHUA REYNOLDS, were deeply indebted to him.

Van Dyke, Dick *orig.* **Richard Wayne** (born 1925) U.S. actor and comedian. Born in West Plains, Mo., he played in nightclubs before making his Broadway debut in 1959. He starred in the musical *Bye Bye Birdie* (1960–61, Tony award; film, 1963), and then in the successful television comedy series *The Dick Van Dyke Show* (1961–66), winning several Emmy awards, *The New Dick Van Dyke Show* (1971–74), and the drama series *Diagnosis Murder* (1993–2001). He has starred in such movies as *Mary Poppins* (1964) and *Chitty, Chitty, Bang, Bang* (1968).

van Eyck, Jan See Jan van EYCK

van Gogh \vän-'ko̱k, *Engl* van-'gō\, **Vincent (Willem)** (1853–1890) Dutch painter. At 16 he was apprenticed to art dealers in The Hague, and he worked in their London and Paris branches 1873–76. After much personal turmoil, he began to draw and paint in watercolor (1880). He studied at the Brussels Academy and with Anton Mauve at The Hague (1881). His interest in art led him to join his brother Theo, an art dealer, in Paris, where he became acquainted with Impressionism and Postimpressionism. In 1888 he moved to Arles, in the southern of France; there he painted more than 200 canvases in 15 months. His favorite subjects were still lifes, landscapes, and peasant figures working in the countryside. Among his most famous paintings are *The Potato Eaters* (1885), *Starry Night* (1889), and *Self-Portrait with Pipe and Bandaged Ear* (1888; he had sliced off his ear after a quarrel with PAUL GAUGUIN). Living in poverty and suffering from recurrent depression, he entered an asylum but continued to paint; during his 12-month stay (1889) he completed 150 paintings and drawings. A move to Auvers-sur-Oise in 1890 was followed by another burst of activity, but he soon suffered a relapse and died that July of a self-inflicted gunshot wound. His 10-year artistic career produced more than 800 paintings and 700 drawings, of which he sold only one in his lifetime. His work had a powerful influence on the development of modern painting, and he is considered the greatest Dutch painter since REMBRANDT.

Van Heusen \van-'hyü-zən\, **Jimmy** *orig.* **Edward Chester Babcock** (1913–1990) U.S. songwriter. He began working in radio in his teens. In the early 1930s he worked in TIN PAN ALLEY, and later collaborated on such songs as "Darn That Dream" and "Polka Dots and Moonbeams." With Johnny Burke he wrote the songs for 23 BING CROSBY films. In 1954 he began collaborating with SAMMY CAHN. He composed 76 songs for his friend FRANK SINATRA, including "The Tender Trap" and "Come Fly with Me," and won Academy Awards for "Swinging on a Star," "All the Way," "High Hopes," and "Call Me Irresponsible."

van Ostade, Adriaen See Adriaen van OSTADE

vanadium \və-'nā-dē-əm\ Metallic chemical ELEMENT, one of the TRANSITION ELEMENTS, chemical symbol V, atomic number 23. A silvery-white, soft METAL found (always combined) in various minerals, coal, and petroleum, it is used in alloys with steel and iron for high-speed tool steel, high-strength low-alloy steel, and wear-resistant CAST IRON. Unalloyed, it is used in high-temperature applications, as a target for X rays, and as a catalyst. Its compounds, in which it has various VALENCES, have many beautiful colors in solution and are used as catalysts and mordants.

Vanbrugh \'van-,brük, van-'brü\, **John** *later* **Sir John** (1664–1726) English dramatist and architect. He began writing while serving as a soldier. His successful Restoration comedies of manners include *The Relapse* (1696) and *The Provok'd Wife* (1697). He also wrote lively adaptations from the French, more farce than comedy, including *The Country House* (performed 1703) and *The Confederacy* (1705). In 1702 he designed Castle Howard, Yorkshire, with Nicholas Hawksmoor (1661–1736). His masterpiece, again with Hawksmoor, was BLENHEIM PALACE (1705–16), Oxfordshire, which brought the English baroque style to its culmination.

Vance, Cyrus (Roberts) (1917–2002) U.S. public official. Born in Clarksburg, W.V., he served in World War II and later practiced law in New York City. He became general counsel for the U.S. Defense Department (1960–62), secretary of the army (1962), and deputy secretary of defense (1963–67) and actively supported prosecution of the VIETNAM WAR. He later urged Pres. LYNDON B. JOHNSON to stop the bombing of North Vietnam, and was sent to Paris in 1968 with W. AVERELL HARRIMAN to negotiate peace with the Vietnamese. As secretary of state (1977–80) under Pres. JIMMY CARTER, he worked to obtain the SALT II arms-control treaty and was instrumental in the CAMP DAVID ACCORDS. He resigned in 1980 in opposition to Carter's management of the IRAN HOSTAGE CRISIS.

Vancouver City (metro. area pop., 2001: 1,986,965), southwestern British Columbia. Located on a fine natural harbor, it originated as a lumber processing settlement in the 1870s. It recovered from a disastrous fire (1886) to become Canada's principal seaport. Its development was aided by completion of the transcontinental railroad in 1887 and the opening of the PANAMA CANAL in 1914, which made it economically feasible to export grain and lumber from Vancouver to the North American east coast and Europe. Economic activities also include producing lumber and plywood; oil refining; fishing; and shipbuilding.

Vancouver, George (1757–1798) English navigator. He entered the Royal Navy at 13 and sailed with JAMES COOK on his second and third voyages (1772–75, 1776–80). In 1791 he commanded an expedition that explored the coasts of Australia, New Zealand, Tahiti, and Hawaii before reaching the Pacific coast of North America in 1792, and over the next two years he meticulously mapped a major portion of the coast. In 1798 he published his maps and a lengthy account of his voyages.

Vancouver Island \'van-'kü-vər\ Island (pop., 2001: 705,000) off southwestern British Columbia. It is the largest island (12,076 sq mi, or 31,284 sq km) on the Pacific coast of North America. It has several peaks of more than 7,000 ft (2,100 m), as well as several fine harbors. The chief city is VICTORIA. It was inhabited by coastal Indians for several millennia before it was visited by early Spanish and English explorers, including Capt. JAMES COOK in 1778. It was surveyed in 1792 by GEORGE VANCOUVER and was held by the HUDSON'S BAY CO. until it was made a British crown colony in 1849. It united with British Columbia in 1866. The island's main industries include lumbering, fishing, agriculture, and tourism.

Vandals Germanic people who ruled a kingdom in North Africa from 429 to 534 and who sacked Rome in 455. Fleeing westward from the HUNS, they invaded Gaul before settling in Spain (409). Under King Gaiseric (r. 428–77) they migrated to North Africa and became federates of Rome (435). Four years later Gaiseric threw off Roman overlordship and captured Carthage. The Vandals later annexed Sardinia, Corsica, and Sicily, and their pirate fleets controlled much of the western Mediterranean. When they invaded Italy and captured Rome (455), they plundered the city and its artworks, and their name has remained a synonym for willful desecration and destruction. The Vandals were Arian Christians (see ARIANISM) who persecuted Roman Catholics in Africa. They were conquered when the Byzantines invaded North Africa (533–34).

Vandenberg, Arthur H(endrick) (1884–1951) U.S. politician. Born in Grand Rapids, Mich., he served as editor of the *Grand Rapids Herald* 1906–28. Elected as a Republican to the U.S. Senate (1928–51), he was a critic of Pres. FRANKLIN ROOSEVELT's foreign policy but revised his isolationist position after the attack on Pearl Harbor. In a 1945 Senate speech he advocated U.S. participation in international alliances, which gave valuable Republican support to the U.N., and he was a delegate to the

U.N. organizing conference. He led Republican congressional support for legislative measures introduced by Pres. HARRY TRUMAN, including the Marshall Plan, the Truman Doctrine, and NATO.

Vanderbilt, Cornelius (1794–1877) U.S. shipping and railroad magnate. Born in Port Richmond, Staten Island, N.Y., he began a passenger ferry business in New York harbor in 1810 with one boat, which he expanded to a small fleet in the War of 1812 to supply government outposts. He sold his boats to work as a steamship captain (1818–29), then started his own steamship company on the Hudson River. By cutting fares and offering luxury, he soon controlled the river traffic. He then provided transportation along the eastern seacoast. By 1846 he was a millionaire. He formed the Accessory Transit Co. to transport passengers and freight from New York to the California gold fields via Nicaragua. He again undercut his competitors, and they bought him out at a high price (1858). Turning to railroads, he acquired controlling stock in the New York and Harlem Railroad. After losing a battle for control of the Erie Railroad (1868), he bought and consolidated the Hudson River and the New York Central railroads (1869). After buying the Lake Shore and Michigan Southern Railroad (1873), he provided the first rail service between New York and Chicago. At his death, he left a fortune of over $100 million, the largest accumulated in the U.S. to that date. He gave $1 million to Central (later VANDERBILT) UNIV. He left almost all the rest to his son William H. Vanderbilt (1821–1885), who greatly expanded the New York Central network, acquired other railroads, and doubled the family fortune.

Vanderbilt University Private university in Nashville, Tenn. It was founded in 1873 and named after the philanthropist CORNELIUS VANDERBILT. Baccalaureate degrees are awarded through its college of arts and sciences, school of engineering, and school of music. About 40 master's, 40 doctoral, and several professional degree programs are offered through these schools and through its graduate school, divinity school, and schools of law, management, medicine, and nursing. Research institutes include centers for the study of education and human development, public policy, and the humanities. Total enrollment is about 10,000.

Vanderlyn, John (1775–1852) U.S. painter. Born in Kingston, N.Y., he studied with GILBERT STUART and later at the École des Beaux-Arts. He remained in Paris, where he enjoyed great popularity for his paintings in the Neoclassical style (including *Ariadne Asleep on Naxos*, 1812). At age 40 he returned to the U.S., but failing to receive the federal commissions he had anticipated, he retired embittered to Kingston. In 1832 he finally received a government commission for a full-length portrait of GEORGE WASHINGTON, and in 1839 another for *The Landing of Columbus* in the U.S. Capitol Rotunda.

Vane, Henry *later* **Sir Henry** (1613–1662) English politician. Son of the royal adviser Henry Vane the Elder (1589–1655), he was converted to Puritanism and in 1635 sailed to New England, where he served as governor of Massachusetts 1636–37. After returning to England, he became treasurer of the navy (1639), then served with his father in the LONG PARLIAMENT, where they helped secure the impeachment of THOMAS WENTWORTH. The chief English negotiator of the SOLEMN LEAGUE AND COVENANT, Vane became leader of the House of Commons (from 1643) and a member of the Commonwealth's Council of State (1649–53). After the RESTORATION, he was arrested, imprisoned (1660–62), and executed for treason.

Vänern \'va-nərn\ Lake, southwestern Sweden. The largest lake in Sweden and the third largest in Europe, it is about 90 mi (145 km) long, as much as 322 ft (98 m) deep, and covers an area of 2,156 sq mi (5,585 sq km). Fed by numerous rivers, it drains into the Kattegat strait via the Göta River.

Vanguard Any of three unmanned U.S. experimental test satellites. Vanguard I (1958), the second U.S. satellite placed in orbit around earth (after EXPLORER 1), was a tiny 3.25-lb (1.47-kg) sphere with two radio transmitters. Its flight path revealed that earth is almost imperceptibly pear-shaped, confirming earlier theories. Vanguard II (1959) carried light-sensitive PHOTOCELLS to provide information about earth's cloud cover, but its tumbling motion rendered the data unreadable. Vanguard III (1959) was used to map earth's MAGNETIC FIELD.

vanilla Any member of a group of tropical climbing ORCHIDS that make up the genus *Vanilla,* and the flavoring agent extracted from its seedpods. The plant has a long, fleshy climbing stem that attaches itself by aerial rootlets to trees; roots also penetrate the soil. Numerous flowers open a few at a time and last only a day. The fruit, a bean pod about 8 in. (20 cm) long at maturity, is harvested as soon as it turns golden green at the base. Curing and processing turn the pods a deep chocolate brown. Vanilla is used in a variety of sweet foods and beverages as well as in perfumery.

Vanir \'vä-ˌnir\ In GERMANIC RELIGION, the race of gods responsible for wealth, fertility, and commerce. They included NJÖRD and his children FREYR and FREYJA, among others. They were originally subordinate to the warlike AESIR, but after defeating the Aesir in battle they were granted equal status. The Vanir sent Njörd and Freyr to live with the Aesir and received Hoenir and MIMIR in exchange. The birth of KVASIR resulted from the peace ritual between the two races.

van't Hoff \vänt-'hȯf\, **Jacobus H(enricus)** (1852–1911) Dutch physical chemist. His early work on stereochemistry explained OPTICAL ACTIVITY in terms of the tetrahedral BONDING of CARBON atoms in organic molecules (see CONFIGURATION). His later work outlined the principles of chemical kinetics, applied the laws of THERMODYNAMICS to chemical equilibria, introduced modern concepts of chemical affinity, and advanced understanding of ELECTROLYTES. Equations relating osmotic pressure (see OSMOSIS) to mole fraction of solute and relating the equilibrium constant to temperature bear his name. In 1901 he was awarded the first Nobel Prize for Chemistry.

Vanua Levu \ˌvän-ˌwä-'lā-vü\ Island (pop., including adjacent islands, 1986: 129,000), Fiji. Fiji's second largest island, it is 2,137 sq mi (5,535 sq km) in area. Sighted by the Dutch navigator ABEL JANSZOON TASMAN in 1643, the volcanic Vanua Levu (meaning "Great Land") has a central mountain range, culminating at Mount Nasorolevu (3,386 ft, or 1,032 m), which divides the island into wet and dry sections. The chief river is the Ndreketi. There are several small coastal villages.

Vanuatu \ˌvan-wä-'tü\ *officially* **Republic of Vanuatu** *formerly* **New Hebrides** \'he-brə-ˌdēz\ Republic, consisting of a chain of 12 principal and 60 smaller islands, South Pacific Ocean. Area: 4,707 sq mi (12,190 sq km). Population (1997 est.): 176,000. Capital: PORT-VILA. The population is mainly indigenous Melanesian; there are also small numbers of French, Chinese, Vietnamese, and Pacific Islanders. Languages: Bislama, English, French (all official); Melanesian languages and dialects. Religion: Christianity, including Presbyterianism, Anglicanism, and Roman Catholicism. Currency: vatu. Extending for 400 mi (650 km), it includes the islands of ESPÍRITU SANTO, Malekula, Efate, Ambrim, Erromango, Tanna, Epi, Aneityum, Maéwo, and the Pentecost Islands. The larger islands are volcanic in origin and mountainous; there are several active volcanoes. Some of them, especially Efate and Malekula, have good harbors. The highest point is Mount Tabwémasana (6,165 ft or 1,879 m) on Espíritu Santo. The developing free-market economy is based mainly on agriculture, cattle raising, and fishing. Tourism is increasingly important. It is a republic with a single legislative house; its head of state is the president, and the head of government is the prime minister. The islands were inhabited for at least 3,000 years by Melanesian peoples before being discovered in 1606 by the Portuguese. They were rediscovered by French navigator L.-A. de BOUGAINVILLE in 1768, then explored by English mariner Capt. JAMES COOK in 1744 and named New Hebrides. Sandalwood merchants and European missionaries arrived in the mid-19th century; they were followed by British and French cotton planters. Control of the group was sought by both the French and British, who agreed in 1906 to form a condominium government. During World War II a major Allied naval base was on Espíritu Santo; the island group escaped Japanese invasion. New Hebrides became the independent Republic of Vanuatu in 1980. Much of the nation's housing was ravaged by a hurricane in 1987.

vapor lamp See ELECTRIC DISCHARGE LAMP

vaporization Conversion of a substance from the LIQUID or SOLID phase into the gaseous (see GAS), or vapor, phase. It includes boiling, in which vapor bubbles form in a liquid, and SUBLIMATION, in which a solid is converted directly to vapor. Vaporization requires that HEAT (the substance's LATENT HEAT of vaporization) be supplied to the liquid or solid; the same amount of heat is released in CONDENSATION, the reverse of vaporization. If the surroundings do not supply enough heat, the temperature of the remaining substance vaporizing drops. See also EVAPORATION.

Varanasi \vä-'rä-nə-sē,\ *or* **Benares** \'bə-'när-əs\ City (pop., 1995 est.: 1,000,000), UTTAR PRADESH, India. Located on the GANGES RIVER in southeastern Uttar Pradesh, it is one of the oldest continuously inhabited cities in the world and was the site of an Aryan settlement before the 2nd millennium BC. It is one of the seven sacred cities of Hinduism and has numerous shrines, temples, and palaces, and miles of steps for ritual bathing. More than a million Hindus visit the city each year. Just north of Varanasi is Sarnath, where the BUDDHA delivered his first sermon.

Vardan Mamikonian \'vär-dən-ˌma-mi-'kō-nē-ən\, **St.** (died 451) Armenian military commander. The Persian attempt to impose ZOROASTRIANISM on the Armenians provoked a rebellion, which ended when Vardan and his companions were slain at the Battle of Avarayr. Despite their victory the Persians renounced their plans to convert Armenia by force, and they deposed the traitorous Armenian governor.

Vardon, Harry (1870–1937) British golfer. Born in Grouville, Jersey, he learned golf on the island and turned professional at 20. A technical innovator, he won the British Open six times (1896, 1898, 1899, 1903, 1911, 1914) and the U.S. Open once (1900). The Vardon Trophy is awarded annually to the professional with the best scoring average.

Varèse \vá-'rez\, **Edgard (Victor Achille Charles)** (1883–1965) French-U.S. composer. Forbidden to study music by his father, he secretly continued his studies, and entered the Schola Cantorum with the help of his cousin the pianist Alfred Cortot (1877–1962). He soon moved to Berlin, where he met F. BUSONI and R. STRAUSS, musicians in tune with his forward-looking ideas. His *Bourgogne* (1907) caused a scandal because of its dissonance. His budding conducting career was interrupted by World War I, and he moved to the U.S. In 1921 he cofounded the International Composers Guild. His output was small, but every piece became a classic, including *Offrandes*, *Amériques* (both 1921), *Hyperprism*, *Octandre* (both 1923), *Arcana* (1927), and *Ionisation* (1931), works remarkable for the way they used instruments, especially percussion, to create blocks of sound. After World War II he composed *Déserts* (1954) and *Poème électronique* (1958), and it became evident that he had been waiting for technology to catch up with his imagination.

Edgard Varèse.
THE BETTMANN ARCHIVE

Vargas \'vär-gəs\, **Getúlio (Dorneles)** (1883–1954) President of Brazil (1930–45, 1951–54). He was elected governor of Rio Grande do Sul in 1928 and ran unsuccessfully for president in 1930, but later that year overthrew the government to become head of state. In 1937 he abolished the constitutional government and set up the totalitarian New State, under which the previously autonomous states became dependent on central authority. He enacted labor reforms and social-security laws, introduced extensive educational reforms, enfranchised women, and granted the secret ballot. Deposed by a coup in 1945, he was elected president again in 1951; restrained by a congress and public opinion, he was unable to hold support, and, faced with forced retirement, took his own life.

Vargas Llosa \'bär-gäs-'yō-sä\, **(Jorge) Mario (Pedro)** (born 1936) Peruvian writer. Vargas Llosa worked as a journalist and broadcaster before publishing *The Time of the Hero* (1963), his widely acclaimed first novel, which describes adolescents striving for survival in the hostile environment of a military school and reflects the malaise afflicting Peru. His commitment to social change is evident in his early novels, essays, and plays. He turned increasingly conservative, especially in the face of the SHINING PATH insurgency, and in 1990 he ran for president of Peru. His best-known works include *The Green House* (1965), *Aunt Julia and the Scriptwriter* (1977), and *The War of the End of the World* (1981), an account of a 19th-century Brazilian religious movement. He won the Cervantes Prize in 1994.

variable In ALGEBRA, a symbol (usually a letter) standing in for an unknown numerical value in an EQUATION. Commonly used variables include x and y (real-number unknowns), z (complex-number unknowns), t (time), r (radius), and s (arc length). Variables should be distinguished from coefficients, fixed values that multiply powers of variables in POLYNOMIALS and ALGEBRAIC EQUATIONS. In the QUADRATIC EQUATION $ax^2 + bx + c = 0$, x is the variable and a, b and c are coefficients whose values must be specified to solve the equation. In translating word problems into algebraic equations, quantities to be determined can be represented by variables.

variable, complex See COMPLEX VARIABLE

variable, random See RANDOM VARIABLE

variable star STAR whose observed brightness varies noticeably in intensity. Pulsating variables expand and contract in cycles, pulsating rhythmically in brightness and size. Explosive variables include NOVAS and SUPERNOVAS, which brighten rapidly due to sudden outbursts of radiant energy; the increased brightness lasts a short time, followed by relatively slow dimming. ECLIPSING VARIABLE STARS are variable only because light from one star is blocked by another in earth's direction. See also BINARY STAR, CEPHEID VARIABLE, FLARE STAR, PULSAR, T TAURI STAR.

variation In biology, any difference between cells, individual organisms, or groups of organisms within a species caused either by genetic differences (variation in GENOTYPE) or by the effect of environmental factors on the expression of genetic potentials (variation in PHENOTYPE). Variation may be shown in physical appearance, metabolism, fertility, mode of reproduction, behavior, learning and mental ability, and other obvious or measurable characters. Genotypic variations are caused by differences in number or structure of CHROMOSOMES or by differences in the GENES carried by the chromosomes. Eye color, body form, and disease resistance are genotypic variations. Phenotypic variations may result from factors such as climate, food supply, and actions of other organisms. Phenotypic variations also include stages in an organism's life cycle and seasonal variations in an individual. Because they do not involve hereditary alteration and in general are not transmitted to future generations, phenotypic variations are not important in EVOLUTION. See also POLYMORPHISM.

variations See THEME AND VARIATIONS

varicella See CHICKEN POX

varicose vein \'var-ə-ˌkōs\ *or* **varix** Twisted VEIN distended with blood. Varix also covers ARTERIES and lymphatic vessels (see LYMPHATIC SYSTEM). Varicose veins occur mostly in the legs, when malfunctioning valves let blood pool in veins near the skin. Causes include hereditary valve and vein wall weakness, and internal or external pressure on veins. Varices are common in pregnancy, suggesting that hormone abnormalities play a role. Symptoms include a heavy feeling, with leg cramps and swelling after standing a long time. Complications include skin ULCERS and THROMBOSIS. Treatment involves strong support hose, injection therapy, or surgery. Varices in the ESOPHAGUS, which often occur in liver disease, can ulcerate and bleed. See also HEMORRHOID.

variety theater See MUSIC HALL AND VARIETY THEATER

varing hare See SNOWSHOE HARE

variola See SMALLPOX

Varmus, Harold (Elliot) (born 1939) U.S. virologist. Born in Oceanside, N.Y., he joined the faculty of UC–San Francisco in 1970. With J. MICHAEL BISHOP, he discovered that, under certain circumstances, normal genes in healthy body cells can cause cancer. These oncogenes ordinarily control cell division and growth, but viruses or carcinogens can activate them. Their research superseded a theory that cancer is caused by viral genes, distinct from a cell's normal genetic material, that lie dormant until activated by carcinogens. For their work, the two shared a 1989 Nobel Prize. Varmus later served as director of the National Institutes of Health 1993–99, when he became president of Memorial Sloan-Kettering Cancer Center.

varna \'vər-nə\ Any of the four traditional social classes of Hindu India. One of the hymns of the RIG VEDA declares that the BRAHMAN, the KSHATRIYA, the VAISHYA, and the SUDRA issued forth at creation from the mouth, arms, thighs, and feet of PRAJAPATI. Traditional lawmakers specified a set of obligations, observed mainly in theory only, to each varna: the Brahman, to study and advise; the Kshatriya, to protect; the Vaishya, to cultivate; and the Sudra, to serve. An unofficial fifth class, the *panca-*

ma, was created to include certain UNTOUCHABLES and tribal groups falling outside this system. The relationship of the CASTE system to the class system is complex; individual castes, of which there are dozens, have sought to raise their social rank by identifying with a particular varna, demanding the associated privileges of rank and honor.

Varna Seaport city (population 1999 est.: 299,801), Bulgaria, on the Black Sea coast. Founded as Odessus by Milesian Greeks in the 6th century BC, it later was Thracian, Macedonian, and Roman. In AD 681 it became part of the first Bulgarian empire (c. 679–1018) and was named Varna. It came under OTTOMAN domination in 1391. In 1444 it was the scene of a battle between Turkish and Hungarian armies in which Wladyslaw III, king of Poland and Hungary, was killed. Varna was ceded to Bulgaria by the 1878 Treaty of Berlin (see Congress of BERLIN). It is an important administrative, economic, cultural, and resort center. Industries include exporting, shipbuilding, and manufacturing.

Varna, Battle of (November 10, 1444) Turkish victory over the Hungarians that marked the end of the European effort to protect Constantinople. The Hungarians under JANOS HUNYADI broke a truce and marched to Varna (in present-day Bulgaria), where they fought the Turks under Sultan Murad II and were defeated; the Hungarian king Ulászló I (also ruler of Poland) was killed in the battle. The victory enabled the Ottoman Empire to gain control of the Greek Peloponnese, conquer Constantinople (1453), and reabsorb Serbia (by 1459).

Varro \'var-ō\, **Marcus Terentius** (116–27 BC) Roman scholar and satirist. Varro was active in public life, rising to the office of praetor. He sided with POMPEY THE GREAT, but later reconciled with Julius CAESAR. A prolific writer, he sought in his writings to inculcate moral virtues and to link Rome's future with its glorious past. He is best known for his *Saturae Menippeae* ("Menippean Satires"), medleys in mixed prose and verse that mock the absurdities of modern times. He wrote some 75 works in more than 600 books on a wide range of subjects: jurisprudence, astronomy, geography, education, and literary history, as well as satires, poems, orations, and letters.

Varus \'var-əs\, **Publius Quintilius** (died AD 9) Roman general. He was born a patrician; his father was one of the murderers of Julius CAESAR. Varus crushed the rebellion in Judaea (4 BC) and reestablished Roman control. Assigned to the frontiers east of the Rhine, he tried to assert Roman jurisdiction, but was overwhelmed by a German attack in the TEUTOBURG FOREST and lost three legions. Disgraced, he killed himself by falling on his sword. His defeat led to the loss of all Roman possessions east of the Rhine.

varved deposit \'värvd\ Any form of repetitive sedimentary rock stratification that was deposited within a year. This annual deposit usually consists of paired contrasting layers (varves) of alternately finer (darker) and coarser (lighter) silt or clay, reflecting seasonal variations in SEDIMENTATION (winter and summer) within the year. Varved deposits are most commonly found in glacial lakes, but they can also be found in nonglacial lakes and marine settings.

Vasa dynasty Swedish (and Polish) royal dynasty. Its founder was Gustav Eriksson Vasa, regent of Sweden (1521) and king (1523) as GUSTAV I VASA. His descendants reigned in Sweden until 1818, the last being CHARLES XIII. A grandson of Gustav became king of Poland (1587–1632) as SIGISMUND III VASA, also ruling Sweden in the years 1592–99. He was succeeded as king of Poland by his sons, Wladyslaw IV Vasa (r.1632–48) and John II Casimir Vasa (r.1648–68), after which the dynasty ended in Poland.

Vasarely \ˌva-zə-'re-lē\, **Victor** *orig.* **Viktor Vásárhelyi** (1908–1997) Hungarian-French painter. Trained in Budapest in the Bauhaus tradition, he moved to Paris in 1930 and supported himself as a commercial artist. In the 1930s he was influenced by Constructivism, but by the 1940s he was painting animated surfaces of geometric forms and interacting colors. His style reached maturity in the mid-1950s and 1960s, with the use of more vibrant colors to increase the sense of movement through optical illusion, as in *Sirius II* (1954), and he became one of the leading figures of the OP ART movement.

Vasari \vä-'zä-rē\, **Giorgio** (1511–1574) Italian painter, architect, and writer. Though he was a prolific painter in the Mannerist style, he is more highly regarded as an architect (he designed the Uffizi Palace, now the UFFIZI GALLERY), but even his architecture is overshadowed by his writings. His *Lives of the Most Eminent Architects, Painters, and Sculptors* (1550) offers biographies of early to late Renaissance artists. His style is eminently readable and his material is well researched, though when facts were scarce he did not hesitate to fill in the gaps. In his view, GIOTTO had revived the art of true representation after its decline in the Dark Ages, and succeeding artists had brought that art progressively closer to the perfection achieved by MICHELANGELO. The work's second edition (1568) has proved an invaluable resource for art historians.

Vasari, self-portrait, oil painting; in the Uffizi, Florence.
SCALA—ART RESOURCE

Vasconcelos \ˌbäs-kōn-'sā-lōs\, **José** (1882–1959) Mexican educator, politician, essayist, and philosopher. A lawyer, he campaigned for the revolutionary candidates FRANCISCO MADERO and PANCHO VILLA. As minister of education (1920–24) he initiated major reforms in Mexico's school system, especially expansion of the rural school program. He ran unsuccessfully for president in 1929. His political activism forced him into exile several times. He regarded the indigenous Indian culture as transcending Western culture. His autobiography (5 vols., 1935–59), abridged as *A Mexican Ulysses* (1962), is one of the finest sociocultural studies of 20th-century Mexico.

vascular plant *or* **tracheophyte** \'trā-kē-ə-ˌfīt\ Any plant that has a specialized conducting system consisting mostly of PHLOEM (food-conducting tissue) and XYLEM (water-conducting tissue), collectively called vascular tissue. FERNS, GYMNOSPERMS, and FLOWERING PLANTS are all vascular plants. In contrast to the nonvascular BRYOPHYTES, the more conspicuous generation among vascular plants is the SPOROPHYTE (see ALTERNATION OF GENERATIONS). Because they have vascular tissues, these plants have true STEMS, LEAVES, and ROOTS, modifications of which enable species of vascular plants to survive in a variety of habitats under diverse, even extreme, environmental conditions. This ability to flourish in so many different habitats is the primary reason that vascular plants have become dominant among terrestrial plants.

vasectomy \və-'sek-tə-mē\ Severing of the vas deferens, which carries SPERM from the TESTES to the PROSTATE GLAND, to cause sterility or prevent infection. This relatively simple procedure, which can be performed in a doctor's office with local anesthetics, removes the ability to father children without affecting ability to achieve erection or orgasm. The vas is cut near its beginning, in the scrotum. The cut ends may be sealed off or left open. Reversal is more likely to succeed in the latter case; microsurgery has improved the success rate.

Vasily I \'va-sə-lē\ *Russian* **Vasily Dmitriyevich** (1371–1425) Grand prince of Moscow (1389–1425). After helping the Tatar khan Tokhtamysh fight TIMUR, he succeeded his father as grand prince of Moscow and Vladimir. He enlarged his realm to include Nizhniy Novgorod and Murom in the central Volga region, but his efforts to expand westward brought him into conflict with Lithuania and Novgorod. He prepared to fight Timur in 1395, but the Mongol leader withdrew from Russian lands without a battle. Vasily kept his state independent until the Tatars reasserted control in 1408.

Vasily II *Russian* **Vasily Vasilyevich** *known as* **Vasily the Blind** (1415–1462) Grand Prince of Moscow (1425–62). At age 10 he was named to succeed his father VASILY I, but for many years his uncle and cousins struggled to wrest the throne from him. Despite being blinded by his cousin Dmitry Shemyaka, he regained power in 1447 and ruled Muscovy for another 15 years. Vasily quelled internal strife in his realm by 1452 and enlarged his state's territory by absorbing nearby principalities. During his reign the Russian Church asserted its independence from the patriarch at Constantinople. Vasily signed a treaty with Lithuania (1449) but fought Tatar hordes on his southern and eastern borders.

vassal See FEUDALISM

Vassar College Private liberal-arts college in Poughkeepsie, N.Y. It was founded as a college for women by Matthew Vassar (1792–1868) in

1861, but did not open until 1865. It became coeducational in 1968. It offers undergraduate studies in most major disciplines, and has master's degree programs in biology, chemistry, and drama. The F. L. Loeb Art Center houses one of the oldest art collections in the U.S. Enrollment is about 2,500.

Vatican City *in full* **State of the Vatican City** Independent papal state, southern Europe, within the commune of ROME, Italy. Area: 108.7 acres (44 hectares). Population (1997 est.): 850. Its medieval and Renaissance walls form its boundaries except on the southeast at St. Peter's Square. Within the walls is a miniature nation, with its own diplomatic missions, newspaper, post office, radio station, banking system, army of more than 100 Swiss Guards, and publishing house. Extraterritoriality of the state extends to Castel Gandolfo and to several churches and palaces in Rome proper. Its independent sovereignty was recognized in the LATERAN TREATY of 1929. The POPE has absolute executive, legislative, and judicial powers within the city. He appoints the members of the Vatican's government organs, which are separate from those of the Holy See. Its many imposing buildings include ST. PETER'S BASILICA, VATICAN PALACE, and the VATICAN MUSEUMS. Frescoes by MICHELANGELO in the SISTINE CHAPEL and by PINTURICCHIO, and RAPHAEL's Stanze are also there. The Vatican Library contains a priceless collection of manuscripts from the pre-Christian and Christian eras.

Vatican Council, Second (1962–65) 21st ecumenical council of the Roman Catholic church, announced by Pope JOHN XXIII. It has come to symbolize the church's readiness to acknowledge the circumstances of the modern world. Among the most notable of the 16 documents enacted were the "Dogmatic Constitution on the Church," which treats church hierarchy and provides for greater involvement of laypeople in the church; the "Dogmatic Constitution of Divine Revelation," which maintains an open attitude toward scholarly study of the BIBLE; the "Constitution on the Sacred Liturgy," which provides for the use of vernacular languages in the MASS in place of Latin; and the "Pastoral Constitution on the Church in the World of Today," which acknowledges the profound changes humanity has experienced in the modern world and attempts to relate the church to contemporary culture. Observers from other Christian churches were invited to the council in a gesture of ECUMENISM.

Vatican Museums and Galleries Institutions and papal palaces in VATICAN CITY housing the art collections of the popes since the beginning of the 15th century. Among the many separate museums are the 18th-century Pio-Clementino Museum, which exhibits the collection of classical sculpture that originated in 1503–13 with JULIUS II; the exhibition rooms in the Vatican Library; and the SISTINE CHAPEL. The Vatican collections are most famous for their classical statues (including *Apollo Belvedere*, *Belvedere Torso*, *Laocoön*) but also contain important examples of Egyptian and Early Christian art. The Pinacoteca ("Picture Gallery"), founded by Pius VI in 1797, contains Italian religious paintings and Russian and Byzantine art. In 1956 a modern-art collection was begun with secular works by such artists as AUGUSTE RENOIR, GEORGES SEURAT, VINCENT VAN GOGH, HENRI MATISSE, and PABLO PICASSO. The Vatican collections are among the largest and most important in the world.

Vatican Palace Pope's residence since the late 14th century, located north of ST. PETER'S BASILICA in the Vatican. First enclosed in 850, the irregularly walled compound contains gardens (begun by NERO), courtyards, living quarters, galleries, the VATICAN MUSEUMS and Library, and other facilities. The residence, with more than 1,400 rooms, was begun in the 13th century by Pope Nicholas III. NICHOLAS V founded the Vatican Library. Under JULIUS II, Giovanni dei Dolci built the SISTINE CHAPEL, noted for its spectacular interior artwork including MICHELANGELO's ceiling, DONATO BRAMANTE completed the palace's northern facade and planned the immense Belvedere court, and RAPHAEL painted his masterpieces in the palace. ANTONIO DA SANGALLO THE YOUNGER, employed by PAUL III, designed the Sala Regia (Royal Hall) and Pauline Chapel, decorated by Michelangelo. Several chapels, along with Ottaviano Mascherino's famous Gallery of Maps, date from the late 16th century. Domenico Fontana added a wing of apartments and the present library building under SIXTUS V. In the baroque period, Urban VIII built the Matilda Chapel and, under Alexander VII, GIAN LORENZO BERNINI built the Scala Regia (Royal Stairway).

Vatnajökull \'vät-nä-ˌyœ-kü-tᵊl\ Extensive ice field, southeastern Iceland. It covers an area of 3,200 sq mi (8,400 sq km) and has an average ice thickness of more than 3,000 ft (900 m). It contains several mountains, including Hvannadalshnúkur (6,952 ft, or 2,119 m), the highest peak in Iceland. There are numerous active volcanoes throughout the ice field.

Vättern \'ve-tərn\ Lake, southern central Sweden, eastern of VÄNERN lake. With a length of 81 mi (130 km), a width of about 19 mi (31 km), and an area of 738 sq mi (1,912 sq km), it is Sweden's second largest lake, though only one-third the size of Vänern. Its maximum depth is 420 ft (130 m). Known for its dangerous currents, it is connected with the Baltic Sea by the Gota Canal.

Vauban \vō-'bäⁿ\, **Sébastien Le Prestre de** (1633–1707) French military engineer. After fighting with the forces of the CONDÉ FAMILY (1651–53), he switched to the royalist side and joined the newly formed engineer corps, becoming engineer in chief at the siege of Gravelines (1658). He designed fortifications for numerous French towns and outposts and devised tactics that led to many successes in the French wars of LOUIS XIV's reign; his innovations revolutionized the art of siege tactics and defensive fortification. He also introduced the tactic of ricochet gunfire and invented the socket bayonet. His treatises on fortification and siege-craft were studied for over 100 years. He was made a marshal of France in 1703.

Vaucanson \vō-käü-'sōⁿ\, **Jacques de** (1709–1782) French inventor. In 1739 he constructed an automaton, "The Duck," which imitated not only the motions of a live duck but also the motions of drinking, eating, and "digesting." An inspector of silk manufacture, Vaucanson automated the LOOM by means of perforated cards that guided hooks connected to the warp yarns (see WEAVING). His innovation was ignored for decades until J.-M. JACQUARD reconstructed and improved on it; the JACQUARD LOOM became one of the most important inventions of the INDUSTRIAL REVOLUTION.

Vaucheria \vō-'kir-ē-ə\ Genus of yellow-green ALGAE characterized by oil food reserves and tubular branches that have multiple nuclei and lack cross-walls except in association with reproductive organs or an injury. *Vaucheria* reproduce both asexually and sexually. The spherical female sex organ and the slender, hook-shaped male sex organ are usually produced on branches close to each other. After fertilization, the zygote may enter a resting phase for several weeks before developing into a new plant. Though most species occur in freshwater or are terrestrial, some are marine and others live in ice.

vaudeville \'vȯd-ˌvil\ Light entertainment popular in the U.S. in the late 19th and early 20th century. It consisted of 10–15 unrelated acts featuring magicians, acrobats, comedians, trained animals, singers, and dancers. The form developed from the coarse variety shows held in beer halls for a primarily male audience. TONY PASTOR established a successful "clean variety show" at his New York theater in 1881 and influenced other managers to follow suit. By 1900 chains of vaudeville theaters around the country included Martin Beck's Orpheum Circuit, of which New York's Palace Theater was the most famous (1913–32). Among the many entertainers who began in vaudeville were MAE WEST, W. C. FIELDS, WILL ROGERS, BUSTER KEATON, CHARLIE CHAPLIN, the MARX BROTHERS, BERENICE ABBOTT and LOU COSTELLO, MILTON BERLE, and BOB HOPE. See also MUSIC HALL AND VARIETY.

Vaugelas \vō-zhə-'lä\, **Claude Favre, seigneur (Lord) de, Baron de Pérouges** \pä-'rüzh\ (1585–1650) French grammarian. He played a major role in standardizing the French language of literature and of polite society. His *Remarks on the French Language, Useful for Those Who Wish to Speak Well and Write Well* (1647) became an authoritative guide to French usage, and his writings formed the basis of the rules for pure and elegant French promulgated by the ACADÉMIE FRANÇAISE, of which he was an original member.

Vaughan \'vȯn, 'vän\, **Henry** (1622–1695) Anglo-Welsh poet and mystic. Vaughan studied law but from the 1650s practiced medicine. After writing two volumes of secular poems, he read the religious poet GEORGE HERBERT and gave up "idle verse." He is chiefly remembered for the spiritual vision or imagination evident in his fresh and convincing religious verse, and is considered one of the major practitioners of METAPHYSICAL POETRY. Works that reveal the depth of his religious convictions include *Silex Scintillans* (1650, enlarged 1655; "The Glittering Flint") and the prose *Mount of Olives* (1652). He also translated short moral and religious works and two medical works.

Vaughan, Sarah (Lois) (1924–1990) U.S. singer, one of the most virtuosic and expressive in jazz. Born in Newark, N.J., Vaughan won an amateur contest at Harlem's Apollo Theater in 1942 and joined EARL HINES's big band as vocalist and second pianist the following year. Joining BILLY ECKSTINE in 1944, she gained exposure to the new music of BEBOP, and later recorded with DIZZY GILLESPIE and CHARLIE PARKER. Alternating between popular song and jazz, she worked as a soloist for the rest of her career. A vast range and wide vibrato in the service of her harmonic sensitivity enabled Vaughan to employ a seemingly instrumental approach when singing, often improvising as a jazz soloist.

Sarah Vaughan.

Vaughan Williams \vón-'wil-yəms\, **Ralph** (1872–1958) British composer. He moved from the Royal College of Music to Cambridge University and back, and studied in Berlin with MAX BRUCH before earning his doctorate from Cambridge. Having collected English folk song for his academic work, he combined folk melody with an excellent orchestral technique (acquired in part from studies with MAURICE RAVEL) and an interest in modern harmonic developments to forge a personal style that came to represent the core of English 20th-century music. His nine symphonies, including his *Sea Symphony* (1909), *London Symphony* (1913), *Pastoral Symphony* (1921), and *Sinfonia Antarctica* (1952), were his most exploratory works. Other popular pieces include *The Lark Ascending* (1914) and *Serenade to Music* (1938). He also wrote five operas, including *Riders to the Sea* (1936). He conducted extensively throughout his life, and he edited *The English Hymnal* (1906).

vault In building construction, an arched structure forming a ceiling or roof. The masonry vault exerts the same kind of thrust as the ARCH, and must be supported along its entire length by heavy walls with limited openings. The basic barrel vault, in effect a continuous series of arches, first appeared in ancient Egypt and the Middle East. Roman architects discovered that two barrel vaults intersecting at right angles (a groin vault) could, when repeated in series, span rectangular areas of unlimited length. Because the groin vault's thrusts are concentrated at the four corners, its supporting walls need not be massive. Medieval European builders developed the rib vault, a skeleton of arches or ribs on which the masonry could be laid. The fan vault, popular in the English PERPENDICULAR STYLE, used fan-shaped clusters of tracery-like ribs springing from PENDANTS or columns. The 19th century saw the use of large iron skeletons as frameworks for vaults of lightweight materials (see CRYSTAL PALACE). An important modern innovation is the reinforced-concrete shell vault, which, if its length is three or more times its transverse section, behaves as a deep beam and exerts no lateral thrust.

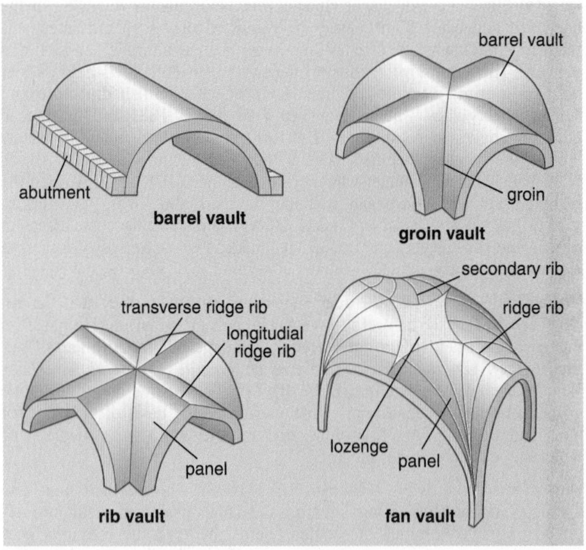

Four common types of vault. A barrel vault (also called a cradle vault, tunnel vault, or wagon vault) has a semicircular cross section. A groin (or cross) vault is formed by the perpendicular intersection of two barrel vaults. A rib (or ribbed) vault is supported by a series of arched diagonal ribs that divide the vault's surface into panels. A fan vault is composed of concave sections with ribs spreading out like a fan.

vaulting Gymnastics exercise in which the athlete leaps over a cylindrical form similar to the SIDE HORSE except that the pommels are absent. In men's vaulting, the horse is placed lengthwise; in women's vaulting, sideways. In both events the athlete runs toward the horse, rebounds off a springboard, and, coming into contact with the horse using his or her hands for support, vaults over it. A variety of acrobatic movements may be performed while airborne. Vaulting has been an Olympic event since 1896 for men and 1952 for women.

Vavilov \vəv-'yē-ləf\, **Nikolay (Ivanovich)** (1887–1943) Russian plant geneticist. Through expeditions to many parts of the world, Vavilov amassed an immense plant collection and conceived the theory that a cultivated plant's center of origin would be found in the region in which wild relatives of the plant showed maximum adaptiveness. He eventually proposed 13 world centers of plant origin. Though widely considered one of the greatest specialists in botanical populations, he was publicly condemned by TROFIM LYSENKO at successive plant-breeding congresses (1934–39) as peddling "Mendelist-Morganist genetics" (see GREGOR MENDEL, THOMAS HUNT MORGAN), and he died in a concentration camp.

vCard Electronic business card that automates the exchange of personal information typically found on a traditional business card. The vCard is a file that contains the user's basic business or personal data (name, address, phone number, URLs, etc.) in a variety of formats such as text, graphics, video clips, and audio clips. It can be attached to an E-mail or exchanged between computers or on the Internet, where, for example, the user can drag-and-drop his or her vCard to a registration or order form on a Web page so that it can automatically complete the form. It is used in such applications as voice mail, Web browsers, call centers, video conferencing, pagers, fax, and smart cards.

VCR *in full* **videocassette recorder** Electromechanical device that records, stores on a VIDEOTAPE cassette, and plays back on a TV set recorded images and sound. The first commercial VCRs were marketed by Sony Corp. in 1969. VCRs are used to record broadcast TV programs for later viewing and to play commercially recorded cassettes. They have from two to seven tape heads that read and inscribe video and audio tracks on magnetic tape. Home movies can be made with a camcorder system, a VCR connected to a simple video camera.

veal Meat of young calves. It is usually pale grayish white in color, firm and fine-grained, with a velvety texture. Calves bred to yield veal are usually raised indoors under controlled temperatures and intensively fed on milk, high-protein calf meal, or both. Herbaceous foods are excluded, resulting in an iron deficiency that produces the desirable light color in the meat. In recent decades, animal-rights groups have denounced calf farming for cruelty.

Veblen \'veb-lən\, **Thorstein (Bunde)** (1857–1929) U.S. economist. Born in Manitowoc County, Wisc., he grew up in Minnesota and earned a PhD in philosophy from Yale University. He taught economics at the University of Chicago and other universities but was unable to keep any position for long because of his unconventional ideas and the disorder in his personal life. In 1899 he published his classic work *The Theory of the Leisure Class*, which applied Darwin's evolutionary theories to the study of modern economic life, highlighting the competitive and predatory nature of the business world. With dry humor he identified the markers of American social class, and he coined the term "conspicuous consumption" to describe the display of wealth made by the upper class. His reputation was highest in the 1930s, when the GREAT DEPRESSION was seen as a vindication of his criticism of the business system.

vector In mathematics, a quantity characterized by magnitude and direction. Some physical and geometric quantities, called scalars, can be fully defined by a single number specifying their magnitude in suitable units of measure (e.g., mass in grams, temperature in degrees, time in seconds). Quantities like velocity, force, and displacement must be specified by a magnitude and a direction. These are vectors. A vector quantity can be visualized as an arrow drawn in a specific direction, whose length is equal to the magnitude of the quantity represented. A two-dimensional vector is specified by two coordinates, a three-dimensional vector by three coordinates, and so on. Vector analysis is a branch of mathematics that explores the utility of this type of representation and defines the ways such quantities may be combined. See also VECTOR OPERATIONS.

vector operations Extension of the laws of elementary algebra to VECTORS. They include addition, subtraction, and three types of multiplication. The sum of two vectors is a third vector, represented as the diagonal of the parallelogram constructed using the two original vectors as sides. When a vector is multiplied by a positive scalar (i.e., number), its magnitude is multiplied by the scalar and its direction remains unchanged (if the scalar is negative, the direction is reversed). The multiplication of a vector **a** by another vector **b** leads to the dot product, written $\mathbf{a} \cdot \mathbf{b}$, and the cross product, written $\mathbf{a} \times \mathbf{b}$. The dot product, also called the scalar product, is a scalar real number equal to the product of the lengths of vectors **a** ($|\mathbf{a}|$) and **b** ($|\mathbf{b}|$) and the cosine of the angle (θ) between them: $\mathbf{a} \cdot \mathbf{b} = |\mathbf{a}|\,|\mathbf{b}| \cos \theta$. This equals zero if the two vectors are perpendicular (see ORTHOGONALITY). The cross product, also called the vector product, is a third vector (**c**), perpendicular to the plane of the original vectors. The magnitude of **c** is equal to the product of the lengths of vectors **a** and **b** and the sine of the angle (θ) between them: $\mathbf{c} = |\mathbf{a}|\,|\mathbf{b}| \sin \theta$. The ASSOCIATIVE LAW and COMMUTATIVE LAW hold for vector addition and the dot product. The cross product is associative but not commutative.

vector space In mathematics, a collection of objects called VECTORS, together with the operations of addition and multiplication, satisfying four conditions: (1) the set is a commutative group (see GROUP THEORY) under addition, (2) the distributive law holds for multiplication by scalars, (3) the ASSOCIATIVE LAW holds for multiplication by scalars, and (4) the identity law holds, in that there exists a unit vector **1** such that $\mathbf{1v} = \mathbf{v}$ for any vector **v**. Vector spaces are very common in mathematics. The set of real numbers with ordinary addition and multiplication forms a vector space, as does the set of all POLYNOMIALS in one variable with real coefficients.

Ved-ava \'vā-dä-vä\ Divine ruler of the waters and their bounty, common to several Baltic and Finno-Ugric peoples traditionally dependent on fishing. She was also responsible for promoting fertility in humans and in livestock. In appearance, she resembled a mermaid, having long hair, large breasts, and a fishlike lower body. Fishermen sacrificed to her the first of their catch and observed numerous taboos while fishing. Seeing Ved-ava generally boded misfortune, most often drowning. She has been regarded as the spirit of a drowned person or simply as a personification of the water itself.

Veda \'vā-də\ Any of a group of sacred hymns and verses composed in archaic Sanskrit, probably in the period 1500–1200 BC. Together they form a body of liturgical literature that grew up around the cult of the SOMA ritual. They extol the hereditary deities that personified various natural and cosmic phenomena. The entire corpus of Vedic literature, including the UPANISHADS, was considered the product of divine revelation. The Vedas were handed down orally for many generations before being committed to writing. Even today, several are recited with intonation and rhythm associated with the early days of VEDIC RELIGION. See also RIG VEDA, VEDANTA.

Vedanta \vā-'dän-tə\ One of the six orthodox systems (DARSHANS) of Indian philosophy and the one that forms the basis of most modern schools of HINDUISM. Its three fundamental texts are the UPANISHADS, the BHAGAVADGITA, and the Brahma Sutras, which are very brief interpretations of the doctrine of the Upanishads. Several schools of Vedanta have developed, differentiated by their conception of the relationship between the self (ATMAN) and the absolute (BRAHMAN). They share beliefs in SAMSARA and the authority of the VEDAS as well as the conviction that Brahman is both the material and instrumental cause of the world and that the atman is the agent of its own acts and therefore the recipient of the consequences of action (see KARMA).

Vedic religion \'vā-dik\ *or* **Vedism** Ancient religion of India that was contemporary with the composition of the VEDAS and was the precursor of HINDUISM. The religion of the Indo-European-speaking peoples who entered India c. 1500 BC from the region of present-day Iran, it was a polytheistic system in which INDRA was the highest-ranked god. It involved the worship of numerous male divinities connected with the sky and natural phenomena. Ceremonies centered on ritual sacrifice of animals and on the use of SOMA to achieve trancelike states. These ceremonies, simple in the beginning, grew to be so complex that only trained BRAHMANS could carry them out correctly. Out of Vedism developed the philosophical concepts of ATMAN and Brahman. The spread (8th–5th century BC) of the related concepts of reincarnation, KARMA, and release from the cycle of rebirth through meditation rather than sacrifice marked the end of the Vedic period and the rise of Hinduism. The Hindu initiation ceremony, UPANAYANA, is a direct survivor of Vedic tradition.

Veeck \'vek\, **Bill** *orig.* **William Louis** (1914–1986) U.S. baseball-club executive and owner. He was born in Hinsdale, Ill., the son of a sportswriter and president of the Chicago Cubs (1919–33). He became co-owner of the minor-league Milwaukee Brewers (1941–45) and later the major-league Cleveland Indians (1946–48), St. Louis Browns (1949–53), and Chicago White Sox (1959–68; 1976–81). Believing that baseball was a form of entertainment and should not be treated like a business, he introduced many innovations in promotion and was almost always able to improve a team's attendance and usually its performance.

Vega \'vā-gə\, **Garcilaso de la** *known as* **El Inca** (1539–1616) One of the great Spanish chroniclers of the 16th century. Vega was the illegitimate son of a CONQUISTADOR and an INCA noblewoman. Raised in his father's household on a vast estate in Peru, he absorbed the traditions of both cultures. Going to Spain in 1560, he served as captain in the Spanish army against the Moors, then entered the priesthood. He is best known for *La Florida del Ynca* (an account of HERNANDO DE SOTO's expeditions north of Mexico) and his history of Peru. He was related to his namesake, the Spanish Golden Age poet Garcilaso de la Vega (1503–1536).

Vega \'vā-gə\, **Lope de** *in full* **Lope Félix de Vega Carpio** (1562–1635) Spanish playwright, the outstanding dramatist of the Spanish Golden Age. After serving with the Spanish Armada, he lived in Madrid, serving as secretary to a series of nobles, including the duke of Sessa (from 1605). Called the "Phoenix of Spain," the phenomenally prolific Vega wrote as many as 1,800 plays, of which 431 survive, and established the *comedia* (tragicomic social drama) that typified the new Golden Age drama. He wrote two major types of drama, both Spanish in setting: the historical play based on a national legend (e.g., *Peribáñez* and *El mejor alcalde, el rey*), and the "cloak-and-sword" drama of contemporary manners and intrigue, which turned on some "point of honor" (e.g., *El acero de Madrid*). He established the comic character, or *gracioso,* as a commentator on the follies of his social superiors. *All Citizens Are Soldiers* is his best-known work outside Spain. He also wrote 21 volumes of nondramatic works in verse and prose, including *The New Art of Writing Plays* (1609).

vegetable In the broadest sense, all plant life and plant products (vegetable matter); in common, narrow usage, the fresh edible portion of herbaceous plants (roots, stems, leaves, flowers, or fruit), either eaten fresh or prepared in some way. Almost all current vegetables were cultivated in ancient Old or New World civilizations, though some have been greatly modified. Vegetables are good sources of minerals (especially calcium and iron), VITAMINS (especially A and C), and dietary FIBER. All the amino acids needed to synthesize PROTEIN are available in vegetables. Fresh vegetables quickly age and spoil, but their storage life can be extended by such preservation methods as dehydration, canning, freezing, fermenting, and pickling.

vegetable oyster See SALSIFY

vegetarianism Theory or practice of eating only plants. The vegetarian diet includes grains, vegetables, fruits, and nuts; it excludes meat, poultry, and fish, but some vegetarians eat dairy products (lactovegetarians), egg products (ovovegetarians), or both (ovolactovegetarians). Those who eat no animal products (including honey) are called vegans. Motivations vary and include ethics (both unwillingness to kill animals and abhorrence of modern methods of raising animals for meat), self-denial or religious taboo, ecology (including concern about the wastefulness and environmental costs of beef farming), and health. Vegetarians point to the many health benefits of their diet, including low rates of heart disease, diabetes, colon cancer, and overweight. While obtaining sufficient protein is seldom a problem in affluent societies, vegetarians must be careful to consume enough iron and, especially for vegans, calcium and vitamins D and B_{12}. The most influential early proponent of vegetarianism was PYTHAGORAS, in the 6th century BC. Many Hindu sects and most Buddhists are vegetarian, and much of the world eats hardly any meat because it is unavailable. The Enlightenment led to a humane concern for animals; in the 19th century Britain became a major center of vegetarianism, and vegetarian movements soon arose in Germany, the U.S., and other countries.

Veii \'vē-yī, 'vā-yē\ Ancient ETRUSCAN town. It was located about 10 mi (16 km) northwestern of ROME, near modern Veio. As an important city of the Etruscan Confederation, and the foremost 6th-century producer of Etruscan terra-cotta sculptures, it had hegemony over Rome in the 7th–6th century BC. A subsequent series of wars ended in its destruction by Rome in 396 BC after a 10-year siege. Under AUGUSTUS it was made a municipium, and up to the 3rd century AD it continued as a religious center.

vein Vessel that carries blood to the heart. Except for the pulmonary veins (see PULMONARY CIRCULATION), veins bear deoxygenated blood from CAPILLARIES, which converge into threadlike venules and then veins, finally emptying into the venae cavae (see CARDIOVASCULAR SYSTEM, VENA CAVA). Blood moves through veins by contraction of the surrounding muscles. Backflow is prevented by valves in most veins' inner layer (tunica intima), which lacks the elastic membrane lining of ARTERIES. The thin middle layer (tunica media) is mostly COLLAGEN fibers and the thick outer layer (tunica adventitia) mostly CONNECTIVE TISSUE. See also CIRCULATION, VARICOSE VEIN.

Velasco (Alvarado) \bā-'läs-kō\, **Juan** (1910–1977) President of Peru (1968–75). Commander in chief of the army, he came to power by overthrowing Pres. Fernando Belaúnde Terry. His government was unusual among military regimes for its reformist and populist character. He nationalized transportation, communications, and electric power and converted millions of acres of private farms into workers' cooperatives. He defied the U.S. in nationalizing U.S.-owned oil fields and capturing and fining U.S. boats fishing within Peru's 200-mi (322-km) coastal limit. He was deposed in 1975 because of discontent with his restrictions on political participation.

Velasco Ibarra \bā-'läs-kō-ē-'bär-rä\, **José (María)** (1893–1979) Five-time president of Ecuador. Born into a wealthy family, he was first elected to the presidency in 1933. In response to Congress's lack of support for his LAND-REFORM program, he assumed dictatorial powers, imprisoning opposition leaders and censoring the press. Deposed by the army and forced into exile, he returned to the presidency in 1944, but his repressive policies alienated his liberal followers and again he was forced into exile. He returned and was elected three more times before his death in 1979, only once (1952–56) being permitted to serve out a full term.

Velázquez \və-'las-kəs, *Span* bā-'lath-kāth\, **Diego (Rodríguez de Silva)** (1599–1660) Spanish painter. Born in Seville, he was apprenticed to FRANCISCO HERRERA the Elder before being trained in the naturalistic style by Francisco Pacheco. His early works were mostly religious or genre scenes. After arriving in Madrid in 1623, he painted a portrait of PHILIP IV that won him immediate success and an appointment as court painter. His position gave him access to the royal collections, including works by TITIAN, the greatest influence on his style. A visit to Italy (1629–31) further advanced his style, and on his return to Madrid he entered his most productive period. He created a new type of informal royal portrait for Philip's hunting lodge, and his portraits of court dwarfs display the same discerning eye as those of his royal subjects. On a second visit to Rome (1649–51) he painted his fine portrait of Pope Innocent X. In his last years he created his masterpiece, *Las Meninas* (*The Maids of Honor,* 1656). In this casual scene, the artist is shown painting the king and queen in the presence of the infanta Margarita and her attendants; the nearly life-size figures create an illusion of reality unsurpassed by any other artist of his age. He is universally acknowledged as one of the giants of Western art.

Velde, Henri van de (1863–1957) Belgian architect, designer, and teacher. His most vital contributions to design were made as a teacher in Germany, where he became known through the interiors he exhibited at Dresden in 1897. Sharing the philosophy of WILLIAM MORRIS and the ARTS AND CRAFTS MOVEMENT in England, he carried these ideas to Weimar in 1902. There he directed and taught at the Weimar School of Arts and Crafts, which gave rise to the BAUHAUS. His architectural works included the Werkbund Theatre in Cologne (1914) and the Belgian pavilions at the international exhibitions in Paris (1937) and New York (1939).

Velde \'vel-də\, **Willem van de, the Elder** (1611–1693) Dutch marine painter. He sailed with the Dutch fleet and painted its engagements with the English. Settling in England in 1672, he continued to paint marine subjects, often in collaboration with his son, Willem the Younger (1633–1707), who became the foremost marine painter of his time. The latter was appointed court painter by CHARLES II in 1677 and was commissioned to paint England's naval battles; many of his works are housed in London's National Maritime Museum.

Velikovsky \ˌve-li-'kȯf-skē\, **Immanuel** (1895–1979) Russian-U.S. writer. He earned various degrees in Moscow and Edinburgh before moving to the U.S. in 1939. In his first book, *Worlds in Collision* (1950), he hypothesized, relying on legends of ancient peoples, that Venus and Mars had approached earth closely c. 1500 BC, disturbing its rotation, axis inclination, and magnetic field. His claim was widely discredited by astronomers, and the book's publication caused American scientists to threaten a boycott of his publisher.

Velociraptor \və-'lä-sə-ˌrap-tər\ Genus of clawed THEROPOD DINOSAUR (family Dromaeosauridae) that flourished in central and eastern Asia during the Late CRETACEOUS PERIOD (99–65 million years ago). It was related to an Early Cretaceous (144–99 million years ago) North American genus, *DEINONYCHUS*. Both genera had a sickle-shaped claw on each foot and ossified tendon reinforcements in the tail that enabled them to keep their balance while striking and slashing at prey. Swift, agile predators of small herbivores, they grew up to 6 ft (1.8 m) long and weighed up to 100 lbs (45 kg).

velocity Quantity that designates the speed and direction in which a body moves. It can be represented graphically by an arrow (pointing in the direction of the motion), the length of which is proportional to the magnitude, or speed. For an object in circular motion, the direction at any instant is tangential to the circle at that point, and so is perpendicular to the radius at that point. The instantaneous speed of a vehicle, such as an automobile, can be determined by a speedometer, or mathematically by DIFFERENTIAL CALCULUS. The average speed is the ratio of the distance traveled in any given time interval divided by the time taken.

velvet Fabric having a short, dense pile, used in clothing and upholstery. Velvet is made in the pile weave (see WEAVING), of SILK, COTTON, or synthetic fibers, and is characterized by a soft, downy surface formed by clipped YARNS (see SHEARING). Its "wrong" side is smooth and shows the weave used. Velvets can be made water-repellent and crush-resistant. They are also occasionally patterned or embossed.

vena cava \ˌvē-nə-'kā-və\ Either of two major VEINS that deliver oxygen-depleted blood to the right side of the heart. The superior vena cava drains the upper body, and the inferior vena cava drains the lower body. See also CARDIOVASCULAR SYSTEM, CIRCULATION.

Venda Bantu-speaking people who inhabit the northeastern corner of South Africa. The Venda, today numbering over 700,000, were the last of the peoples in the area to come under European control. Agriculture dominates their economy; cattle raising has increased in importance. Venda chiefs are traditionally custodians of the land, while local headmen permit household groups to occupy and work tracts of land.

Venda Former black enclave, northeastern Republic of South Africa. Located near the Zimbabwe border, it attracted the VENDA people who migrated into the region in the early 1700s from what is now Zimbabwe. Annexed to TRANSVAAL in 1898, it was a distinct administrative unit within South Africa when the country designated it a homeland for Venda-speaking people in 1962. The territory, whose capital was Thohoyandou, was granted partial self-government in 1973 and became an independent republic in 1979; it never received international recognition. After APARTHEID was abolished, Venda was reincorporated into South Africa in 1994, as part of the newly created Northern province.

Vendée \väⁿ-'dā\, **Wars of the** (1793–96) Insurrections in the west of France during the FRENCH REVOLUTION. In the religious and impoverished area known as the Vendée, discontent with the new government grew after it instituted strict controls over the Catholic church (1790). An uprising began in opposition to the conscription acts (1793) and spread throughout the region, where peasants were joined by royalists to form the Catholic and Royal Army. Led by the nobleman François Charette de La Contrie (1763–1796), the Vendéan army of 65,000 occupied several towns, but was defeated at Cholet by government troops and forced to retreat. After further defeats at Le Mans (about 15,000 rebels killed) and at Savenay, the general warfare ended in December 1793. Vicious reprisals by the government provoked further resistance, until an amnesty was announced (1794) and the Vendée was granted freedom from conscription (1795). Charette joined a British-backed landing of exiled French nobles in Brittany (1795), but after their defeat and his execution (1796) the counterrevolutionary struggle ended.

Vendémiaire \vä^{n}-dā-'myer\ First month in the FRENCH REPUBLICAN CALENDAR. It also was the name given to the event of 13 Vendémiaire of the year IV (October 5, 1795), when Gen. NAPOLEON Bonaparte led the French Revolutionary troops that stopped an insurrection of Parisians as they marched against the government.

vending machine Coin-activated machine through which various goods may be sold. The first vending machines were introduced in 18th-century England to sell snuff and tobacco. From the late 19th century they have been widely used in many countries. Vending service is typically provided by a company that owns the machines and places them in businesses, schools, and the like. These operators provide the products and service either without cost to the owner of the premises on which a machine is located or in return for a small servicing charge.

Vendsyssel-Thy \'ven-ˌsü̅-səl-'tü̅\ Island (pop., 1989 est.: 308,000), northern end of JUTLAND, Denmark. Its eastern section is called Vendsyssel and its western section, Thyland. The LIMFJORDEN separates it from the mainland, to which it was attached until 1825, when water erosion cut a channel through the narrow isthmus at Thyborøn. It has an area of 1,809 sq mi (4,686 sq km). Frederikshavn, the main port, lies on the east coast facing GÖTEBORG, Sweden. The island is a holiday resort.

veneer Extremely thin sheet of rich-colored wood (such as mahogany, ebony, or rosewood) or precious materials (such as ivory or tortoiseshell) cut in decorative patterns and applied to the surface of a piece of furniture. Though veneering was practiced in classical antiquity, its use lapsed in the Middle Ages. It was revived in the 17th century, reaching its apogee in France and spreading from there to other European countries. The considerable craftsmanship involved in artistic veneering is most evident in the 18th and early 19th century, when THOMAS CHIPPENDALE, GEORGE HEPPLEWHITE, and THOMAS SHERATON used mahogany and satinwood veneers. By the mid-19th century, mechanical saws allowed the veneering process to be used in mass production to cover defects in cheap furniture.

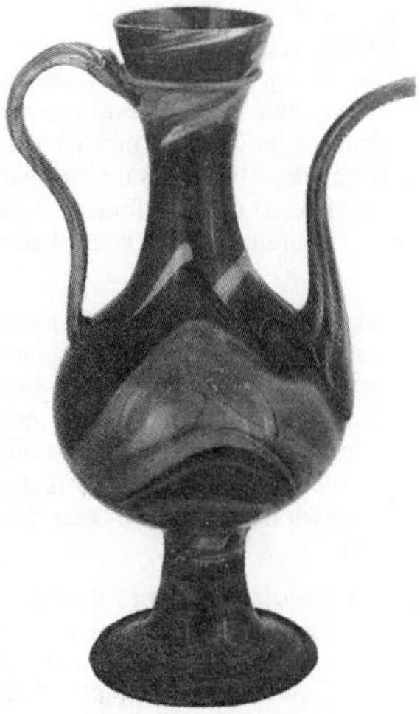

Ewer made of *calcedonio,* Venice, early 16th century; in the Museum für Kunsthandwerk, Frankfurt am Main, Ger.

BY COURTESY OF THE MUSEUM FUR KUNSTHANDWERK, FRANKFURT AM MAIN, GER.; PHOTOGRAPH, FOTO MARBURG–ART RESOURCE/EB INC.

Venera \vyi-'nyer-ə, *Engl* və-'nar-ə\ Any of a series of 16 unmanned Russian planetary probes sent to VENUS 1965–83. Venera 2 flew to within 25,000 miles (40,000 km) of Venus in 1966; Venera 3 crash-landed on its surface the following month, becoming the first spacecraft to strike another planet. Later missions analyzed Venus's atmosphere, made soft landings, detected certain long-lived radioactive ISOTOPES (chiefly uranium and thorium), sent back the first close-up photographs of the planet's surface, and mapped the surface of the northern hemisphere with radar.

Venetian glass Variety of glassware made in Venice from the 13th century to the present. In the 15th century, efforts were concentrated on the perfection of *cristallo* (clear glass that approximated rock crystal in appearance). By the 16th century, Venetian glassmakers mastered techniques of adding color and of removing the smoky tint produced by metal in the glass material. These and other secrets were guarded closely, and defecting workers were severely punished. But eventually many Venetian glassmakers did defect, and the techniques became common knowledge in France, Germany, the Netherlands, and England.

Venetian school Renaissance art and artists of VENICE, characterized by a love of light and color. J. BELLINI was the first in this influential line, followed by his son G. BELLINI, the instructor of Venice's great High Renaissance painters, including GIORGIONE and TITIAN. In due course Titian became the dominant force in Venetian painting, and his rich colors and painterly technique were widely imitated. Other 16th-century masters included VERONESE, known for his vast, brilliantly colored, pageantlike canvases, and TINTORETTO, who combined the Mannerists' rapidly receding diagonals and dramatic foreshortenings with the Venetian love of light as a means of defining form and heightening drama. GIOVANNI BATTISTA TIEPOLO was the last important Venetian figure painter and one of the greatest artists of the Rococo period.

Veneto \'ve-nə-ˌtō\ Autonomous region (pop., 1996 est.: 4,433,000), northern Italy. The capital is VENICE. Bordered by Austria, the Adriatic Sea, and Lake GARDA, the northern part is mountainous, while the southern part consists of a fertile plain. Parts were under Roman rule c. 2nd–1st century BC (see PADUA, VERONA) and later were subject to the Lombards. In the Middle Ages, several city-states gained importance, but most subsequently were subject to VENICE. The area began to slip from Venetian hold after the FRENCH REVOLUTION, and in the early 19th century came under Austrian rule. It was returned and joined to Italy in the 1860s. Agriculture is an economic mainstay, as are also the industrial works found around major cities.

Venezia Tridentina See TRENTINO–ALTO ADIGE

Veneziano, Domenico See DOMENICO VENEZIANO

Venezuela *officially* **Bolivarian Republic of Venezuela** Country, northern South America. Area: 352,144 sq mi (912,050 sq km). Population (2000 est.): 24,170,000. Capital: CARACAS. More than two-thirds of

the population is of mulatto-mestizo ancestry, followed by whites (about one-fifth), blacks (one-tenth), and Indians. Languages: Spanish (official), some 25 Indian languages. Religions: Roman Catholicism; some Protestantism. Currency: bolívar. Mountain ranges and plains dominate Venezuela's geography. In the west, a northeastern spur of the ANDES rises to PICO BOLÍVAR. The Llanos (plains) occupy one-third

S T U V

of the country's central region. The ORINOCO RIVER system covers almost the entire country and has an extensive and thickly wooded delta. The highest waterfall in the world, ANGEL FALLS, is in Venezuela. Lakes include MARACAIBO and VALENCIA. Principal mineral resources are petroleum and natural gas. Other mineral reserves include iron, bauxite, gold, and diamonds. Industries include steel, chemicals, textiles, and oil refining. Agricultural products, notably sugar, coffee, corn (maize), bananas, and cacao, are important. It is a republic with a unicameral legislature; its head of state and government is the president. Venezuela has been inhabited by indigenous peoples for millennia. In 1498 CHRISTOPHER COLUMBUS sighted it; in 1499 the navigators Alonso de Ojeda, AMERIGO VESPUCCI, and Juan de la Cosa traced the coast. A Spanish missionary established the first European settlement at Cumana c. 1520. In 1718 it was included in the viceroyalty of NEW GRANADA and was made a captaincy general in 1731. Venezuelan Creoles led by FRANCISCO DE MIRANDA and SIMÓN BOLÍVAR spearheaded the South American independence movement, and though Venezuela declared independence from Spain in 1811, it was not assured until 1821. Military dictators generally ruled the country from 1830 until the overthrow of MARCOS PÉREZ JIMÉNEZ in 1958. A new constitution adopted in 1961 marked the beginning of democracy. As a founding member of OPEC (ORGANIZATION OF PETROLEUM EXPORTING COUNTRIES), it enjoyed relative economic prosperity from oil production during the 1970s, and its economy has remained dependent on the world petroleum market. The government of Hugo Chavez promulgated a new constitution in 1999, the year in which a devastating rainstorm killed thousands in and around Caracas.

Venice *Italian* **Venezia** \vā-'nēt-syä\ City (pop., 1999: 66,945), capital of VENETO region, northern Italy. Built on the Lagoon of Venice, it encompasses some 118 islands, the whole 90-mi (145-km) perimeter of the lagoon, and two industrial mainland boroughs. Refugees from northern invasions of the mainland founded settlements in the 5th century AD that were built uniquely on islands as protection against raids. It was a vassal of the Byzantine empire until the 10th century. Beginning with control of a trading route to the Levant, it emerged from the Fourth CRUSADE (1202–4) as ruler of a colonial empire which included CRETE, EUBOEA, CYCLADES, the IONIAN ISLANDS, and footholds in Morea and EPIRUS. In 1381 it defeated GENOA after a century-long struggle for commercial supremacy in the Levant and eastern Mediterranean. In the 15th century, with the acquisition of neighboring regions, the Venetian Republic became an extensive Italian state. It gradually lost its eastern possessions to Ottoman Turks, with whom Venice fought intermittently 15th–18th century; it gave up its last hold in the Aegean in 1715. The republic dissolved and the territory was ceded to Austria in 1797. Incorporated into NAPOLEON's kingdom of Italy in 1805, it was restored to Austria in 1815. A revolt against Austria (1848–49) eventually resulted in Venice being ceded to Italy in 1866. It suffered little damage during World War II, but flooding along its many miles of canals caused severe damage in 1966. The waters of the lagoon rise and flood the city on a regular basis, complicating efforts to preserve its architecture, which includes representations of Italian, Arabic, Byzantine, and Renaissance styles. There are some 450 palaces and homes of major historic importance. Notable among its 400 bridges is the Bridge of Sighs, built c. 800, and among its churches, ST. MARK'S BASILICA. Most of the city's workers find employment in tourism and its related industries, though the city also plays a key market role within the vibrant economic system of the Veneto region.

Venice, Gulf of Northern section of the ADRIATIC SEA. It extends eastward for 60 mi (95 km) from the PO RIVER delta, Italy, to the coast of ISTRIA. Marshes, lagoons, and sandspits border the gulf's shores as far as TRIESTE, Italy. A northwest wind, called the bora, causes rough seas and creates shipping hazards in the gulf.

Venice, Peace of (1177) Agreement in which Holy Roman Emperor FREDERICK I BARBAROSSA acknowledged ALEXANDER III as the true pope. Frederick's decisive defeat by the LOMBARD LEAGUE at the Battle of Legnano (1176) had obliged him to abandon his Italian campaign and sign a truce. In the Peace of Venice, Frederick agreed to withdraw support from the antipope and to restore church property he had seized. He received the kiss of peace from the pope in front of St. Mark's.

Venice, Treaty of (1201) Treaty negotiated between crusaders in the Fourth CRUSADE and ENRICO DANDOLO of Venice to provide transport for 85,000 marks. The crusaders' failure to fulfill their monetary obligation was a major factor in the diversion of the crusade to ZARA and Constantinople.

Venice Biennale \,bē-en-'nä-lā\ International art exhibition held in the Castello district of Venice every two years and juried by an international committee. It was founded in 1895 as the International Exhibition of Art of the City of Venice to promote "the most noble activities of the modern spirit without distinction of country." The first Biennale, which achieved worldwide prestige, included artists from 16 nations; the committee included EDWARD BURNE-JONES, GUSTAVE MOREAU, and PIERRE PUVIS DE CHAVANNES. After World War II it became the leading showplace for the international avant-garde. Usually held in the summer months, it attracts many tourists and visitors.

Venizélos \,ven-yə-'ze-lôs\, **Eleuthérios (Kyriakos)** (1864–1936) Greek revolutionary leader. Son of a Cretan revolutionary, he served in the government of autonomous Crete as minister of justice (1899–1901), then led an insurrection that forced the autocratic high commissioner to leave Crete (1905). In Athens, he led the Military League opposition group and effected the union of Crete with Greece. As premier of Greece (1910–15) he helped form the BALKAN LEAGUE. During the BALKAN WARS, his policies doubled Greece's area and population. In World War I he supported the Allies; he resigned when opposed by the pro-German King CONSTANTINE, led the opposition that forced the king into exile, and again became premier (1917–20), aligning Greece with the Allies and successfully protecting Greek interests at the Paris Peace Conference. He served three more stints as premier (1924, 1928–32, 1933), but was forced into exile when the monarchy was restored in 1935.

venom POISON secreted by an animal, produced by specialized GLANDS often associated with spines, teeth, or stings. It may be primarily for paralyzing or killing prey or may be purely defensive. Some venoms also function as digestive fluids. Their effects can range from localized skin inflammation to almost immediate death; they include NERVOUS-SYSTEM excitation (CRAMPS, VOMITING, convulsions) or depression (PARALYSIS, respiratory or cardiac depression or arrest), HEMORRHAGE, red-blood-cell breakdown, circulatory collapse, and allergic reactions (including HIVES and inflammation). Many major groups of animals contain venomous species: snakes (COBRAS, MAMBAS, VIPERS, PIT VIPERS); fish (STINGRAYS, spiny SHARKS, certain CATFISH, puffers); lizards (GILA MONSTERS, beaded lizards); SCORPIONS; spiders (BLACK WIDOW spiders, BROWN RECLUSE SPIDERS); social insects (BEES, WASPS, some ANTS); and marine invertebrates (SEA ANEMONES, fire CORALS, JELLYFISH, SEA URCHINS). See also ANTIDOTE.

ventilating Natural or mechanically induced movement of fresh air into or through an enclosed space. The hazards of poor ventilation were not clearly understood until the early 20th century. Expired air may be laden with odors, heat, gases, or dust. Mechanical ventilation systems typically include a fan and filter to remove particles. A mechanically powered inlet of air, when combined with a natural exhaust, tends to cause a slight positive pressure within an enclosed space, so that the air leakage is outward. A mechanical exhaust with a natural air inlet causes a slight negative pressure, so that air moves inward. Such systems are often used to confine fumes or smells to a particular area of a building (e.g., laboratories, kitchens, bathrooms) and exhaust them to the outside.

ventricular fibrillation Uncoordinated contraction of the muscle fibers of the heart's ventricles (see CARDIAC ARRHYTHMIA). Causes include MYOCARDIAL INFARCTION, ELECTRIC SHOCK, anoxia, abnormally high potassium or low calcium in the blood, and DIGITALIS or EPINEPHRINE poisoning (see MEDICINAL POISONING). Death soon follows if CIRCULATION is not restored with electric shocks (defibrillation) or drugs, supplemented by chest compressions (as in CARDIOPULMONARY RESUSCITATION). See also ATRIAL FIBRILLATION.

ventriloquism Art of "throwing" one's voice in such a way that the sound seems to come from a source other than the speaker. A dummy or doll is commonly used to assist in the deception, with the ventriloquist moving the dummy's mouth while speaking through closed lips. Ventriloquists date from ancient times and include Eurycles of Athens. Such peoples as the Maoris, Zulus, and Eskimos are adept ventriloquists. The art was long a feature of puppet shows as well as of variety entertainment such as VAUDEVILLE. Notable ventriloquists included EDGAR BERGEN in the U.S. and Robert Lamouret in France.

Ventris \'ven-trəs\, **Michael (George Francis)** (1922–1956) British architect and cryptographer. At age 14 he heard a lecture on the continuing mystery of Linear B script (see LINEAR A AND LINEAR B) and resolved to decipher it. In 1952 he determined that Linear B was Greek in its oldest known form, dating from c. 1400–1200 BC. He collaborated with John Chadwick on *Documents in Mycenaean Greek* (1956), published a few weeks after his own death in an auto accident.

Venturi, Robert (Charles) (born 1925) U.S. architect. Born in Philadelphia, he studied at Princeton University and the American Academy in Rome. After working with EERO SAARINEN and LOUIS KAHN, he formed a partnership with his wife Denise Scott Brown and John Rauch. His philosophy, set forth in the influential books *Complexity and Contradiction in Architecture* (1966) and *Learning from Las Vegas* (1972), called for openness to the multiple influences of historical tradition, ordinary commercial architecture, and Pop art. His buildings often exhibit ironic humor. Important commissions include buildings for Princeton and the University of Pennsylvania, the Seattle Art Museum (1985–91), and the Sainsbury Wing of London's National Gallery (1986–91). He won the 1991 Pritzker Architecture Prize.

venturi tube \ven-'tu̇r-ē\ Short pipe with a constricted inner surface, used to measure fluid flows and as a pump. The effects of constricted channels on fluid flow were first investigated by Giovanni Battista Venturi (1746–1822), but it was Clemens Herschel (1842–1930) who devised the instrument in 1888. Fluid passing through the tube speeds up as it enters the tube's narrow throat, and the pressure drops. There are countless applications for the principle, including the automobile CARBURETOR, in which air flows through a venturi channel at whose throat gasoline vapor enters through an opening, drawn in by the low pressure. The pressure differential can also be used to measure fluid flow (see FLOW meter).

venue In law, the place or county in which the events giving rise to a legal action take place and from which a jury may be drawn to try the case. Venue statutes usually specify that a trial must take place in the district that has jurisdiction over the matter. The grounds for a change of venue are also specified; they include fear of biased jurors due to media coverage, danger of violence, and racial prejudice.

Venus Roman goddess of cultivated fields and gardens, later associated with APHRODITE. She was the daughter of JUPITER and Dione, the wife of VULCAN, and the mother of CUPID. She was famous for her romantic intrigues and affairs with both gods and mortals, and she became associated with many aspects of femininity. The planet Venus, originally the star of ISHTAR, came to be named for Venus through her association with Ishtar. She has been a favorite subject in art since ancient times, notably in the statue called *Venus de Milo* and SANDRO BOTTICELLI's painting *The Birth of Venus*.

Venus Second major PLANET from the sun. Named for the Roman goddess, Venus is, after the MOON, the most brilliant natural object in the night sky. It comes closer to earth—about 26 million mi (42 million km)—than any other planet. Its orbit around the sun is nearly circular at a distance of 67 million mi (108 million km) and takes 225 days; its rotation, in RETROGRADE MOTION, takes even longer (244 days). As viewed from earth, Venus undergoes phase changes similar to the moon's, going through one cycle of phases in 584 days and presenting nearly the same face to earth at each closest approach. It is seen only near sunrise or sunset and has long been known as both the morning and the evening star. Venus is a near twin of earth in size and mass but is completely enveloped by thick clouds of concentrated sulfuric-acid droplets. Its surface gravity is about 90% that of earth. Its atmosphere is over 96% carbon dioxide, with an atmospheric pressure about 90 times earth's. This and the thick cloud cover trap incoming solar energy so efficiently that Venus has the highest surface temperature of any of the sun's planets, about 860°F (460°C). Radar imaging indicates that most of Venus's surface consists of gently rolling plains and two large elevated regions analogous to continents on earth.

Venus's-flytrap *or* **Venus flytrap** Flowering perennial plant *(Dionaea muscipula),* sole member of its genus, in the SUNDEW family, notable for its unusual habit of catching and eating insects and other small animals (see CARNIVOROUS PLANT). Native to a small region of North and South Carolina, it is common in damp, mossy areas. Growing from a bulblike rootstock, the plant bears hinged leaves with spiny teeth along their margins and a round cluster of small white flowers at the tip of an erect stem 8–12 in. (20–30 cm) tall. When an insect alights on a leaf and stimulates its sensitive hairs, the leaf snaps shut in about half a second. Leaf glands secrete a red sap that digests the insect's body and gives the entire leaf a red, flower-like appearance. After 10 days of digestion, the leaf reopens. The trap dies after capturing three or four insects.

Venus's-flytrap (*Dionaea muscipula*).
JACK DERMID

Veracruz State (pop., 1995 est.: 6,737,000), eastern central Mexico. Bordering the Gulf of MEXICO, it occupies 28,114 sq mi (72,815 sq km); its capital is JALAPA. The state's low, sandy gulf area rises inland to a central plateau, where CITLALTÉPETL, Mexico's highest peak, is located. The area was inhabited by pre-Columbian cultures, including the OLMECS. The first European landing was made by HERNAN CORTES in 1519. A state since 1824, it has more than 25% of Mexico's petroleum reserves and several of the country's refineries. Its economy is supplemented by agriculture, forestry products, and manufacturing.

Veracruz (Llave) \,ver-ə-'krüz\ City (pop., 1990: 439,000) and port on the Gulf of MEXICO, eastern central Mexico. HERNAN CORTES founded La Villa Rica de la Veracruz as the first Mexican municipality in 1519, but the site was twice abandoned because of its unhealthy conditions; the present city dates from c. 1600. As the chief link between colonial Mexico and Spain, Veracruz prospered as a port and became the most "Spanish" of Mexican cities. It was attacked and captured repeatedly, first by privateers, then by French and U.S. forces (see VERACRUZ INCIDENT). It was renamed in honor of Gen. Ignacio de la Llave, governor of VERACRUZ state 1857–60. Both the 1857 and 1917 Mexican constitutions were proclaimed there. A revolt against Pres. FRANCISCO MADERO occurred there in 1912. It is one of Mexico's chief seaports and a commercial center for the Gulf coast.

Veracruz incident (1914) Occupation of Veracruz, Mexico, by U.S. Marines. In April, after the crew of a U.S. ship anchored in Tampico was briefly detained for landing in a forbidden area, Pres. WOODROW WILSON demanded an apology. When VICTORIANO HUERTA refused, Wilson sent a fleet to the Gulf of Mexico. He ordered the port of Veracruz seized after learning of an arms shipment to Huerta from Germany. The invasion caused 200 Mexican casualties and enabled the rival Constitutionalists under VENUSTIANO CARRANZA to take over the government.

Veralden-radien \'vä-ä-,räl-dän-'rä-dē-en\ Deity believed by the SAMI to be the closest to heaven. Because he is associated with the pillar supporting the heavens, he is also responsible for the continuance of life. He imparts the souls of unborn children to MADDERAKKA and takes the souls of the departed to the realm of the dead. He was also the subject of a phallic cult; each year the genitalia and blood of a bull reindeer were smeared on his statue. His worship has many Scandinavian features, which has led scholars to seek his origin in Norse mythology.

verbena \vər-'bē-nə\ Plant genus *(Verbena)* that contains about 250 species, almost all of them native to the New World tropics and subtropics. Two species are indigenous to the Old World. The familiar garden verbena *(V. hortensis,* or *V. hybrida)* is a creeping plant that has square stems and bears flat heads of phloxlike flowers, in a wide range of colors. Many U.S. species of *Verbena* are low-growing, small-flowered, somewhat weedy plants more commonly called vervains. The shrub lemon verbena *(Aloysia triphylla),* notable for its fragrant oil, is a member of the verbena, or vervain, family (family Verbenaceae), which contains more than 2,600 species in about 100 genera. Members of the family have opposite or whorled leaves that are usually undivided. The flowers, in spikes or clusters, usually consist of a tube flaring into four or five almost equally cut lobes. The family also includes TEAK.

Vercingetorix \,vər-sən-'je-tə-,riks\ (died 46 BC) Chieftain of the Gallic tribe of the Arverni. Julius CAESAR had almost subjugated Gaul (see GALLIC WARS) when Vercingetorix, acclaimed king of his people, led the GAULS against him (52 BC), using guerrilla tactics and picking battle sites favorable to his own forces. After winning a major victory at Gergovia, his later attack on the Roman army failed; besieged at Alesia, he was

S T U V

forced to surrender. Taken to Rome in chains, he was displayed in Caesar's TRIUMPH and executed six years later.

Verdi \'ver-dē\, **Giuseppe (Fortunato Francesco)** (1813–1901) Italian composer. An innkeeper's son, he showed talent early. While earning a living as an organist, he began to write operas in Milan; in 1839 his *Oberto* was successfully performed at La Scala, and it initiated Verdi's long association with the publisher Giulio Ricordi. His next opera, *Un giorno di regno* (1840), was a failure. Much worse, Verdi's two young daughters and his wife died. Ready to give up, he was manipulated into starting *Nabucco* (1842); it became his first big success, and was followed by the equally successful *I lombardi* (1843). For the rest of the decade he wrote a hit opera every year. Rejecting the prevailing structure of Italian opera—a patchwork of open-ended scenes and inserted arias, duets, and trios—he began seeking ways of maintaining momentum, and began conceiving of an opera as a series of integrated scenes, then as unified acts. Attracted to stories in which people's private and public lives come into conflict, he produced a series of masterworks, including *Rigoletto* (1851), *La traviata* (1853), *Simon Boccanegra* (1857), *Un ballo in mascara* (1859), *Don Carlos* (1867), and *Aïda* (1871). His long open liaison with the soprano Giuseppina Strepponi (1815–1897) attracted censure, which he rejected. A fervent nationalist, he became a great national figure. After composing his great *Requiem* (1874), he decided to retire, but when Giulio Ricordi brought him together with A. BOITO, initially to revise *Simon Boccanegra*, their mutual esteem led to the two great operas of Verdi's old age, *Otello* (1886) and *Falstaff* (1890).

Verdigris River \'vər-də-grəs\ River, southeastern Kansas and northeastern Oklahoma. It rises in eastern central Kansas and flows south across the Oklahoma border, emptying into the ARKANSAS RIVER northeast of Muskogee, Okla. It is 350 mi (560 km) long.

Verdun \vər-'dən\, **Battle of** (February 21–July, 1916) Major engagement of WORLD WAR I between Germany and France. As part of its strategy of war by attrition, Germany selected the fortress of Verdun as the site it believed France would defend to the last man. After a massive bombardment, the Germans advanced with little opposition for four days before the reinforced French army under PHILIPPE PETAIN slowed their advance. For two months the hills west of the Meuse River and north of Verdun were bombarded, attacked, and counterattacked. By July, Germany, which was also engaged in the Battle of the SOMME, had abandoned its strategy of attrition, and France gradually regained its forts and territory. The devastating losses included over 400,000 French casualties and nearly as many German casualties.

Verdun, Treaty of (843) Treaty partitioning the Carolingian empire among the three surviving sons of LOUIS I the Pious. It marked a first stage in the dissolution of CHARLEMAGNE's empire and a step toward the formation of the modern countries of Western Europe. LOTHAIR I received the imperial title and Francia Media, which included much of Italy as well as parts of several other present-day European countries. Louis the German received Francia Orientalis, the land east of the Rhine River, and CHARLES II THE BALD received Francia Occidentalis, the remainder of modern France.

Verga \'vär-gä\, **Giovanni** (1840–1922) Italian writer. Born to a family of Sicilian landowners, Verga became the most important of the Italian *verismo* (realist) school of novelists. His best works include the short stories of *Little Novels of Sicily* (1883), the novels *The House by the Medlar Tree* (1881) and *Mastro-Don Gesualdo* (1889), and the play *Cavalleria rusticana* (1884; "Rustic Chivalry"), the basis for a famous opera by PIETRO MASCAGNI. His influence on the post–World War II generation of Italian writers was particularly marked; LUCHINO VISCONTI's landmark Neorealist film *La terra trema* (1948) was based on *The House by the Medlar Tree.*

Vergennes \ver-'zhen\, **comte (Count) de** *orig.* **Charles Gravier** (1719–1787) French statesman. As ambassador to Ottoman Turkey (1754–68), he ably defended French policies during the Seven Years' War. As LOUIS XVI's minister of foreign affairs (1774–87), he advocated French financial and military support for the colonists in the American Revolution, concluded an alliance with them (1778), and helped negotiate the Treaty of Paris (1783). He also worked to establish a stable balance of power in Europe by mediating the peace in the War of the BAVARIAN SUCCESSION.

Verghina *or* **Vergina** \ver-'gē-nä\ Archaeological site and ancient capital of MACEDONIA, northern Greece. Built on a site in use from the Stone Age, it was first called Balla. The palace of Palatista, partly destroyed by fire, dates from the reign of Antigonus III Doson (c. 263–221 BC). An Iron Age cemetery that dates from the 10th–7th century BC is near the palace. The 4th-century-BC royal tomb of PHILIP II OF MACEDON also is at Verghina.

Vergil See VIRGIL

Verhaeren \ver-'hä-ren, ver-à-'ren\, **Émile** (1855–1916) Belgian poet. He wrote in French, producing more than 30 collections of poetry outstanding for its strength and range. His first book, *Les Flamandes* (1883), contains violently naturalistic poems. Later he began to show a growing concern for social problems. His major works include *The Sunlit Hours* (1896), *The Evening Hours* (1911), and *Belgium's Agony* (1915). His three main themes are Flanders, human energy, and his tender, understanding love for his wife. He also published plays and books on art. He was one of the group in Brussels who brought about the literary and artistic renaissance of the 1890s.

verifiability principle Criterion of meaningfulness associated with LOGICAL POSITIVISM and the VIENNA CIRCLE. Moritz Schlick's formulation "The meaning of a [declarative sentence] is the method of its verification" was close to the view held in PRAGMATISM, and later in OPERATIONALISM, that an assertion has factual meaning only if there is a difference in principle, open to test by observation, between the affirmation and the denial of the assertion. Thus, the statements of ethics, metaphysics, religion, and aesthetics were held to be meaningless. The verifiability criterion of meaningfulness was in part inspired by ALBERT EINSTEIN's abandonment of the ether hypothesis and the notion of absolute simultaneity.

Verlaine \ver-'len\, **Paul (-Marie)** (1844–1896) French lyric poet. After entering the civil service, he was first associated with the PARNASSIAN POETS, contributing to the first *Le Parnasse contemporain* (1866). His early collections, *Poèmes saturniens* (1866), *Fêtes galantes* (1869), *La bonne chanson* (1870), and *Romances sans paroles* (1874), show the intense lyricism and musicality that would mark all his verse. His marriage was shattered by his infatuation with ARTHUR RIMBAUD, and the two scandalized Paris with their behavior in 1872–73. While in prison in Belgium (1873–75) for shooting Rimbaud when the latter threatened to leave him, he converted to Catholicism and probably composed the famous "Art poétique," adopted in 1882 by the poets of the SYMBOLIST MOVEMENT. *Sagesse* (1880) expresses his religious faith and his emotional odyssey. He later taught French and English; he spent his late years in poverty, but just before his death he was sponsored for a major international lecture tour. His *Les poètes maudits* (1884; "The Accursed Poets") consists of short biographical studies of six poets, including STEPHANE MALLARME and Rimbaud. He is regarded as the third great member (after CHARLES BAUDELAIRE and Mallarmé) of the so-called DECADENTS.

Vermeer \vər-'mer, vər-'mir\, **Jan** *or* **Johannes Vermeer** (1632–1675) Dutch painter. He was born in Delft, where his parents kept a tavern, and spent his entire life there. He twice served as head of the Delft artists' guild but seems to have depended on his activities as an art dealer to support his family. He painted mainly interior genre subjects, depicting members of aristocratic and upper-middle-class society. About half of these paintings show solitary figures of women, absorbed in some ordinary, everyday activity. His interiors combine a microscopic observation of objects with a meticulous depiction of the gradations of daylight on varied shapes and surfaces. His masterpieces (none dated) include *View of Delft, Young Woman Reading a Letter,* and *Allegory of Painting,* his most symbolically complex work. He manages to be unique within a typically Dutch genre. Few foreign influences can be sensed in his work. His work was not widely appreciated in his own time, and he remained in obscurity until 1866, when Théophile Thoré celebrated his work and attributed 76 paintings to him; later authorities have reduced the number to between 30 and 35, while proclaiming him one of the greatest painters of all time.

Vermont State (pop., 2000: 608,827), northeastern U.S. One of the NEW ENGLAND states, it covers 9,614 sq mi (24,900 sq km); its capital is MONTPELIER. The GREEN MTNS. extend through the center of Vermont. The highest point is Mount Mansfield, at 4,393 ft (1,339 m) tall. Most of the rivers drain into Lake CHAMPLAIN. Settled originally by Abenaki Indians, the region was explored by SAMUEL DE CHAMPLAIN, who in 1609 discovered the lake that now bears his name. The French made the first permanent European settlement in 1666 on Isle La Motte. Both the Dutch and the British established settlements in the 18th century, but the area fell exclusively to the British in 1763. Disputes arose between New York and New Hampshire concerning jurisdiction of the area: New Hampshire had awarded grants to settlers. In 1770 ETHAN ALLEN organized the Green Mountain Boys to repel encroachers from western New York. When the AMERICAN REVOLUTION intervened, Allen and his group, fighting for the colonies, captured Fort TICONDEROGA from the British in 1775. Vermonters created an independent republic in 1777, and in 1791 it became the 14th U.S. state. In 1864 it was the site of the only AMERICAN CIVIL WAR action north of Pennsylvania when a band of Confederates raided St. Albans from Canada. Dairying and the mining of granite and marble contribute to the economy. In the 1930s the first ski runs were built and by the 1960s a winter tourist industry had developed.

Vermont, University of (UVM) Public university in Burlington. Established in 1791, it is one of the oldest state universities in the U.S. It became a land-grant institution in 1862. It comprises colleges of arts and sciences, agricultural and life sciences, engineering and mathematics, education and social services, graduate studies, and medicine, as well as schools of allied health, business administration, natural resources, and nursing. Total enrollment is about 10,000.

vernacular architecture Common domestic architecture of a region, usually far simpler than what the technology of the time is capable of maintaining. In highly industrialized countries such as the U.S., for example, barns are still being built according to a design employed in Europe in the 1st millennium BC. Vernacular structures are characterized by inexpensive materials and straightforwardly utilitarian design.

Verne, Jules (1828–1905) French writer. He studied law and wrote plays and stories before the success of *Five Weeks in a Balloon* (1863) encouraged him to produce other romantic adventures. His subsequent *voyages extraordinaires,* with increasingly fantastic but carefully conceived scientific wonders that often anticipated 20th-century technological achievements, include *A Journey to the Center of the Earth* (1864), *From the Earth to the Moon* (1865), *Twenty Thousand Leagues Under the Sea* (1870), *Around the World in Eighty Days* (1873), and *The Mysterious Island* (1874). Verne's work shaped the entire development of science fiction.

Vernet \ver-'nā\, **(Claude-) Joseph** (1714–1789) French painter. Son of a decorative painter, he catered to a new taste for idealized, somewhat sentimentalized landscapes. His shipwrecks, sunsets, and conflagrations reveal a subtle observation of light and atmosphere. His series of 15 *Ports of France* (1754–65), his finest works, constitute a remarkable record of 18th-century life. His son Carle (1758–1836) produced vast battle scenes for Napoleon, but his real talent was for intimate genre scenes and drawing. His long series of fashionable studies, often satirizing contemporary manners and costume, were widely reproduced as engravings. After the restoration of the monarchy, he became court painter to Louis XVIII. Carle's son Horace (1789–1863) developed a remarkable facility for working on a grand scale and became one of France's most important military painters, also known for his sporting subjects. A Bonapartist, he glorified the Napoleonic era, and after the restoration of the monarchy his studio was a center of political intrigue. He was later commissioned by Louis-Philippe and Napoleon III to produce the battle pieces at Versailles.

"The Mask of Joseph Vernet," chalk and pastel portrait by Maurice-Quentin de La Tour; in the Musée des Beaux-Arts, Dijon, Fr.
LAUROS–GIRAUDON FROM ART RESOURCE/EB INC.

vernier \'vər-nē-ər\ *or* **vernier caliper** Instrument for making very accurate linear or angular measurements. Introduced in 1631 by Pierre Vernier (c. 1580–1637), it uses two graduated scales: a main scale similar to that on a ruler, and a specially graduated scale, the vernier, that slides parallel to the main scale and enables readings to be made to a fraction of a division on the main scale.

Verona City (pop., 1996 est.: 254,000), northern Italy. Located on the ADIGE RIVER, it became a Roman colony in 89 BC and was the birthplace of the poet CATULLUS. It was captured by the Goths after the fall of the Roman empire and was the site of ODOACER's defeat by the Ostrogothic king THEODORIC in 489. It was occupied by CHARLEMAGNE in 774. It came under the della Scala family 1260–1387, the era recalled in WILLIAM SHAKESPEARE's *Romeo and Juliet.* It passed in 1405 to VENICE, which held it almost continuously until 1797, when it was ceded to Austria. It became part of the kingdom of Italy in 1866. It is noted for its ancient Roman amphitheater (1st century AD), now used for opera, and for Romanesque and Gothic buildings.

Verona, Congress of (1822) Last of the meetings held by the QUADRUPLE ALLIANCE (Russia, Prussia, Austria, and Britain). The congress met in Verona, Italy, to consider a request by the alliance's ally, France, to intervene in the revolutionary situation in Spain. The congress agreed to support France if it were attacked by Spain and authorized a French expedition into Spain. However, Britain threatened to use its sea power to prevent interference with the revolts in Spanish America. Increasing discord caused a breakdown in the congress system begun by the alliance in 1815.

Veronese \,ver-ə-'nā-sē\, **Paolo** *orig.* **Paolo Caliari** (1528–1588) Italian painter. Son of a stonecutter from Verona (the source of his nickname), he was apprenticed at 13 to a painter. After 1553, when he received the first of many commissions in Venice, he became a major painter of the 16th-century VENETIAN SCHOOL, known for his splendid use of color and pageantlike compositions. His first works in Venice, ceiling paintings for the Doges' Palace, employ skillful foreshortenings that make figures appear to be floating in space. He decorated the villas and palaces of the Venetian nobility and received many commissions for frescoes, altarpieces, and devotional paintings, including numerous "suppers" (e.g., *The Pilgrims of Emmaus* and *Feast in the House of the Pharisees*) that allowed him to compose large groups of figures in architectural settings. In decorating a villa built by PALLADIO at Maser (c. 1561), he brilliantly interpreted its architectural structure, breaking through the walls with illusionistic landscapes and opening the ceilings to blue skies with figures from classical mythology. Whimsical details in his *Last Supper* (commissioned 1573) caused him to be summoned before the Inquisition. Painters from the 16th century on were inspired by his use of color to express exuberance as well as to model form.

Verrazzano \,ver-ə-'zä-nō\, **Giovanni da** (1485–1528) Italian-French explorer. Educated in Florence, he moved to Dieppe, France, where he entered the maritime service. In 1524 he was sent to find a westward passage to Asia and reached North America. He explored the eastern coast from Cape Fear northward and became the first European to explore the sites of present-day New York harbor and Narragansett Bay. He sailed along the coast to Newfoundland, then returned to France. He later led expeditions to Brazil (1527) and to the Caribbean, where he was killed and eaten by cannibals.

Verres \'ver-,ēz\, **Gaius** (c. 115–43 BC) Roman magistrate notorious for corruption. As QUAESTOR, he embezzled funds. In Cilicia in Asia Minor, he helped the governor, Gaius Dolabella, plunder the province (80–78), then helped convict Dolabella at Rome. He became PRAETOR by bribery, and abused his power. As governor of Sicily (73–71) his corruption was extreme; he was prosecuted so effectively by CICERO (70) that his lawyer had no reply. He fled into exile but was murdered, perhaps at the orders of Mark ANTONY, who then acquired his art collection.

Verrocchio \və-'rō-kē-,ō\, **Andrea del** (1435–1488) Italian sculptor and painter. Little is certain about his early life. His most important works were executed in his final two decades, under the patronage of the Medici in his native Florence. His reputation as a master spread early, and many well-known artists studied at his studio, including LEONARDO DA VINCI and PERUGINO; the young Leonardo probably painted an angel and part of the distant landscape in Verrocchio's *Baptism of Christ* (c. 1470). Verrocchio's reputation as one of the great relief sculptors of the 15th century was established with his cenotaph in the cathedral at Pistoia; while it remained unfinished at his death and was later changed by others, the relief's arrangement of figures into a dramatically unified composition anticipates the baroque sculpture of the 17th century. His bronze statue of the military officer Bartolomeo Colleoni (commissioned 1483, erected in Venice 1496) is one of the greatest equestrian statues of the Renaissance.

Bartolomeo Colleoni, bronze statue by Andrea del Verrocchio, 1483–88; in Campo di Santi Giovanni e Paolo, Venice.

BROGI—ALINARI FROM ART RESOURCE

verruca See WART

vers de société \ˌver-də-sȯs-yā-ˈtā\ ("society verse") Witty, typically ironic, light verse, written with polish and ease of expression to amuse a sophisticated audience. It has flourished in cultured societies, particularly in court circles and literary salons, from the time of ANACREON (6th century BC). Trivial subjects are treated in an intimate, witty manner, and even when social issues form the theme, the light mood prevails. The poetry of OGDEN NASH, with its theme of self-ironic adult helplessness, is a 20th-century example.

Versace, Gianni (1946–1997) Italian fashion designer. He was born in Reggio Calabria, Italy, to a dressmaker mother. After working for several Italian ateliers in Milan, in 1978 Versace established his own company, Gianni Versace SpA. Throughout the 1980s and '90s he built a fashion empire by producing ensembles that oozed sensuality and sexuality. He staged his seasonal fashion shows like rock concerts at his lavish design headquarters in Milan. On July 15, 1997, Versace was shot and killed on the front steps of his Miami Beach, Florida, home, allegedly by the serial killer Andrew Cunanan. At the time of his death, many believed that the designer's 25-year career was at a peak.

Versailles \ver-ˈsī\, **Palace of** Baroque palace southwest of Paris built chiefly under LOUIS XIV. It was the principal residence of the French kings and the seat of government from 1682 to 1789, with some 1,000 courtiers and 4,000 attendants residing there. Originally a hunting lodge, it was enlarged by LOUIS XIII and Louis XIV. Louis Le Vau (1612–1670), with CHARLES LE BRUN and ANDRE LE NOTRE, began work on the palace in the 1660s. A masterpiece of formal grandeur intended as the visible expression of the glory of France, Versailles became the palatial ideal throughout Europe and the Americas. LE NÔTRE's inventive arrangement of earth forms, plantings, and fountains created vistas, terraces, formal gardens, and wooded areas that celebrated the delights of both open and intimate space. After Le Vau's death, Jules Hardouin-Mansart (1646–1708) was commissioned to triple the size of the palace and built the northern and southern wings, the Orangerie, and the Grand Trianon. Later additions include the classically restrained Petit Trianon, built 1761–64 for Louis XV and Madame de POMPADOUR. The first scenes of the French Revolution were enacted at Versailles, which had become a symbol of royal extravagance. In 1837 LOUIS-PHILIPPE restored the palace and turned it into a museum.

Versailles, Treaty of International agreement, signed in 1919 at the Palace of Versailles, that concluded WORLD WAR I. It was negotiated primarily by the U.S., Britain, and France, without participation by the war's losers. Germany was forced to accept blame for Allied losses and to pay major reparations. Its European territory was reduced by about 10%, its overseas possessions were confiscated, and its military establishment was reduced. Though some of the treaty's terms were eased in the 1920s, the bitterness it created led to the growth of FASCISM in Italy and the rise of the NAZI PARTY in Germany. The treaty also established the LEAGUE OF NATIONS, the INTERNATIONAL LABOR ORGANIZATION, and the Permanent Court of International Justice (later the INTERNATIONAL COURT OF JUSTICE). See also FOURTEEN POINTS.

vertebral column \vər-ˈtē-brəl, ˈvərt-ə-brəl\ *or* **spinal column** *or* **spine** *or* **backbone** Flexible column extending the length of the torso. In humans, it consists of 32–34 vertebrae, with different shapes and functions in each of five regions: seven cervical, in the neck (including the atlas and axis, modified for free movement of the SKULL); twelve thoracic, in the chest; five lumbar, in the lower back; five sacral (fused into the sacrum, part of the PELVIC GIRDLE); and three to five coccygeal (vestigial tailbones fused into the coccyx). The body of each vertebra is separated from its neighbors by cushioning intervertebral disks of CARTILAGE. Behind the body is a Y-shaped vertebral (neural) arch with structures extending up and down to form JOINTS with the adjacent vertebrae and to the back and sides to provide attachment points for MUSCLES and LIGAMENTS. The spine supports the torso and protects the SPINAL cord.

vertebrate Any animal of the CHORDATE subphylum Vertebrata, which includes the FISHES, AMPHIBIANS, REPTILES, BIRDS, and MAMMALS. Vertebrates have an internal skeleton formed of cartilage, bone, or both. The skeleton consists of a backbone (vertebral column), which partly encloses a spinal cord; a skull, which encloses the brain; and usually two pairs of limbs. Nerves extending from the spinal cord and brain permeate the skin, muscles, and internal organs. The muscular system consists primarily of bilaterally paired masses attached to bones or cartilage. Skin and scales, feathers, fur, or hair cover the outer surface. See also INVERTEBRATE.

vertical integration Form of business organization in which all stages of production of a good, from the acquisition of raw materials to the retailing of the final product, are controlled by one company. A current example is the oil industry, in which a single firm commonly owns the oil wells, refines the oil, and sells gasoline at roadside stations. In horizontal integration, by contrast, a company attempts to control a single stage of production or a single industry completely, which lets it take advantage of economies of scale but results in reduced competition.

vertigo \ˈvər-tə-ˌgō\ Feeling that one is spinning or that one's surroundings are spinning around one, causing confusion and difficulty keeping one's balance, sometimes accompanied by NAUSEA and VOMITING. Vertigo is normal after actual spinning, since INNER-EAR fluid continues to move once the body has stopped, producing a mismatch between visual and internal sensations. Lack of a stable visual reference point also contributes to this effect. Other causes include CONCUSSION and abnormalities of the inner ear (e.g., labyrinthitis; see OTITIS), of the nerves that carry signals from it, or of the brain centers that receive them (e.g., STROKE). Vertigo is often confused with a feeling of faintness (see SYNCOPE), since both are called dizziness. See also MOTION SICKNESS, PROPRIOCEPTION, SPATIAL DISORIENTATION.

vervain See VERBENA

vervet monkey *or* **vervet** Any of several African races of slim, arboreal, diurnal OLD WORLD MONKEYS of the guenon species *Cercopithecus aethiops* and *C. pygerythrus* (family Cercopithecidae). They have large cheek pouches. The arms and legs are long, and the nonprehensile tail is longer than the head-and-body length of 12–26 in. (30–65 cm). The soft, dense fur of many species has a speckled effect and bold markings of white or bright colors. The face, chin, hands, and feet of *C. aethiops* races are black.

Verwoerd \fər-ˈvürt\, **Hendrik (Frensch)** (1901–1966) South African (Dutch-born) prime minister (1958–66). He was taken to South Africa as an infant by his missionary parents. After studying at the University of Stellenbosch, he became a professor there, and in 1937 he became editor of the AFRIKANER nationalist daily in Johannesburg. Appointed senator (1948) and then minister of native affairs (1950), he was responsible for much of the country's new APARTHEID legislation. When he became prime minister in 1958, his apartheid program was strictly enforced, and he pushed through legislation resettling blacks in reservations. His policies provoked demonstrations, sometimes violent. In 1960 white voters approved his recommendation that South Africa leave the British Commonwealth, and his dream of a republic came true. He was stabbed to death in the parliamentary chamber by a mixed-race parliamentary messenger.

Very Large Array (VLA) Array of 27 radio telescopes operated on the plains of San Augustin near Socorro, N.M., by the National Radio Astronomy Observatory since 1980. Each telescope is 81 ft (25 m) in diameter and mounted on a transporter that can be moved along rails laid out in an enormous Y pattern whose arms are about 13 mi (21 km) long. The radio signals recorded by the dishes are integrated by computer, so the entire array acts as a single radio antenna (an interferometer). The VLA has a resolving power equal to that of the best ground-based optical telescopes, and has been responsible for producing many of the most detailed radio images of quasars, galaxies, supernovas, and the Milky Way's nucleus.

Vesalius \və-ˈsā-lē-əs\, **Andreas** *Flemish* **Andries van Wesel** (1514–1564) Flemish physician. Born into a family of physicians, he studied medicine at the University of Paris. He insisted on dissecting corpses himself, instead of relying on untrained assistants, to learn anatomy. Comparing his observations to ancient texts led him to question the theories of GALEN, at that time still considered authoritative. Vesalius' own complete textbook of human anatomy, *De humani corporis fabrica libri septem* (1543; "Seven Books on the Structure of the Human Body"), commonly called the *Fabrica,* was the most extensive and accurate description of the human body that had ever been published.

Vesey \ˈvē-zē\, **Denmark** (1767?–1822) U.S. insurrectionist. Born in the West Indies, he was sold to a Bermuda slaver captain. They settled in Charleston, S.C., and Vesey was allowed to purchase his freedom for $600 in 1800. After reading antislavery literature, he determined to relieve the oppression of slaves. He organized city and plantation blacks (up to 9,000 by some estimates) for an uprising in which they would free the slaves on surrounding plantations. After a house servant warned the authorities, the insurrection was forestalled and 130 blacks were arrested; Vesey was tried and hanged with 35 others.

Vespasian \ves-ˈpā-zhən\ *in full* **Caesar Vespasianus Augustus** *orig.* **Titus Flavius Vespasianus** (AD 9–79) Roman emperor (69–79), founder of the FLAVIAN DYNASTY. Though of humble birth, he won military glory in Britain and was awarded a TRIUMPH by CLAUDIUS. In 63 he became PROCONSUL of Africa. He reconquered Judaea except for Jerusalem (67–68), but stopped fighting on NERO's death (68). After GALBA's murder, Vespasian was proclaimed emperor by the legions, while VITELLIUS claimed the title in Cologne; his forces soon defeated Vitellius in Italy. Though he claimed absolute power and took every possible office for himself and his sons, he was a popular emperor and lived simply. He increased provincial taxation to pay for the deficits incurred by Nero and the civil wars, built the Temple of Peace and began the COLOSSEUM, and reformed the army and PRAETORIAN GUARD. He ended the Jewish war (70) and the Rhineland revolt, adding lands in Germany and Britain and pacifying Wales. He was succeeded by his son TITUS.

Vespasian, bust found at Ostia; in the Museo Nazionale Romano, Rome.
ANDERSON—ALINARI FROM ART RESOURCE/EB INC.

Vespucci \ves-ˈpü-chē\, **Amerigo** (1454–1512) Italian-Spanish navigator and explorer. Born in Florence, he entered the Medici family business and in 1491 was sent to Seville, where he helped outfit the ships for CHRISTOPHER COLUMBUS's expeditions. By 1496 he was manager of the Seville agency. He took part in two (or four—the number is disputed) voyages to the New World; he was navigator on a Spanish expedition (1499–1500) that probably discovered the mouth of the Amazon River, and he led a Portuguese expedition (1501–02) that discovered Guanabara Bay (Rio de Janeiro) and the Río de la Plata. In the accounts of the voyages (published 1507), the terms America and New World were first used to describe the lands visited by Amerigo Vespucci (in Latin, Americus Vespucius). As chief navigator for the Seville-based Commercial House for the West Indies (from 1508), he prepared maps of newly discovered lands from data supplied by ships' captains.

Vesta In ROMAN RELIGION, the goddess of the hearth, identified with the Greek HESTIA. Because maintaining a hearth fire was important in ancient times, she was worshiped in every household. Her state worship was elaborate: her temple in Rome had a perpetual fire that was attended by the VESTAL VIRGINS. The fire was officially extinguished and renewed annually on March 1st. See photograph opposite.

Vestal Virgin In ROMAN RELIGION, any of six priestesses, representing the daughters of the royal house, who tended the state cult of VESTA. They served for 30 years under a vow of chastity; violation of the vow was punishable by burial alive. Their duties included tending the perpetual fire in the Temple of Vesta, fetching water from a sacred spring, and officiating at the public worship of Vesta.

Vestris, (Marie-Jean-) Auguste (1760–1842) French ballet dancer. He was trained by his father, GAÉTAN VESTRIS, before making his formal debut in 1776. His dazzlingly athletic dancing set a new style of ballet. In his last years he was a revered teacher.

Vestris, Gaétan *orig.* **Gaetano Appolino Baldassare** (1729–1808) French ballet dancer and teacher. His style was flamboyant while respecting traditional courtly technique. Vestris later became renowned as the most distinguished teacher of his day. His most celebrated pupil was his son AUGUSTE VESTRIS.

Vesuvius Active volcano, eastern side of the Bay of NAPLES, southern Italy. It originated about 200,000 years ago; its current height of 4,198 ft (1,280 m) has varied considerably after each of its major eruptions; in 1900 it was 4,275 ft (1,303 m) high; in 1906, 3,668 ft (1,118 m) high; in the 1960s, 4,203 ft (1,281 m) high. The cone is half-encircled on the northern side by Mount Somma, part of the wall of a large crater in which the present cone has formed. There have been numerous destructive eruptions; in AD 79 POMPEII and HERCULANEUM were destroyed, and in 1631 about 3,000 people were killed.

vetch Any of about 150 species of herbaceous plants in the genus *Vicia* of the pea family (see LEGUME). A few species are cultivated as important fodder and COVER CROPS and as GREEN MANURE. Trailing or climbing stems grow 1–4 ft (0.3–1.2 m) tall, bearing compound leaves with several pairs of leaflets. Magenta, bluish-white, white, or yellow flowers are borne singly or in clusters. The pods contain 2–10 seeds. Like other legumes, vetches add nitrogen to the soil through NITROGEN FIXATION. See also CROWN VETCH.

Vetch (*Vicia cracca*).
WALTER DAWN

Veterans Affairs, U.S. Department of (VA) Federal executive division responsible for programs and policies relating to veterans and their families. Established in 1989, it succeeded the Veterans Administration (formed in 1930). The VA administers benefits for medical care, educational assistance and vocational rehabilitation, pensions and life insurance, and payments for disability or death related to military service.

Veterans Day U.S. holiday celebrated on November 11, honoring veterans of the U.S. armed forces and those killed in battle. Originally called Armistice Day, it began as a commemoration of the ending of WORLD WAR I on November 11, 1918. After World War II it was recognized as a day to pay tribute to all service members, and in 1954 it was designated as Veterans Day. It is usually observed with parades, speeches, and flowers placed on military graves and memorials. The holiday is called Remembrance Day in Canada and Remembrance Sunday (on the Sunday nearest to November 11) in Britain.

Vesta (seated on the left) with Vestal Virgins, classical relief sculpture; in the Palermo Museum, Italy.
BY COURTESY OF THE PALERMO MUSEUM, ITALY

veterinary science Medical field dealing with animals and with diseases that are contagious between animals and humans. It was a medical specialty in ancient Egypt and Babylonia but went through a period of virtual nonexistence in medieval Europe before reappearing in the mid-18th century with the founding of the first veterinary schools. Veterinarians earn a doctor of veterinary medicine (DVM) degree. They practice internal medicine, surgery, and preventive medicine, using the same techniques used on humans. Many specialize in either small animals (pets) or large ones (livestock); a few specialize in wild animals.

Viagra First oral drug for male IMPOTENCE, generic name sildenafil. Before the FDA approved Viagra in 1998, impotence was treated with surgical implants, suppositories, pumps, and drugs injected into the penis. Taken as a pill shortly before sexual intercourse, Viagra selectively dilates blood vessels in the penis, improving blood flow and allowing a natural sexual response. It works in about 70% of cases; it should not be used by anyone taking nitroglycerin or with heart problems, hypotension, hypertension, recent stroke, or certain eye disorders.

viatical settlement Arrangement by which a terminally ill patient's LIFE-INSURANCE policy is sold to provide funds while the insured (viator) is living. The buyer (funder), usually an investment company, pays the patient a lump sum of 50–80% of the policy's face value, pays the premiums until the patient dies, and receives the death benefit. Viatical settlements (from Latin, *viaticum:* "provisions for a journey") appeared in the 1980s, when people with AIDS had high medical bills and policies nominally sufficient to cover them, but whose funds would not be available until they died.

vibraphone *or* **vibraharp** Percussion instrument with tuned metal bars, arranged keyboard-style like the XYLOPHONE, which are struck with mallets. Each bar has a resonating tube suspended vertically below it to sustain the tone; small electrically powered spinning disks at the top of the resonators produce a vibrato effect by rapidly closing and opening the resonators. Invented c. 1920, it soon became a popular jazz instrument.

vibration Periodic back-and-forth motion (see PERIODIC MOTION) of the particles of an elastic body or medium. It is usually a result of the displacement of a body from an EQUILIBRIUM condition, followed by the body's response to the forces that tend to restore equilibrium. Free vibrations occur when a system is disturbed but immediately allowed to move without restraint. Because all systems are subject to FRICTION, they are also subject to DAMPING. One example of free vibration is the motion of a weight suspended by a spring. If the weight is pulled down and then released, it continues to bounce up and down, the amplitude of each vibration being less than that of the preceding one until eventually it comes to rest. See also RESONANCE.

vibrio \'vib-rē-ō\ Any of a group of aquatic, comma-shaped BACTERIA in the family Vibrionaceae. Some species cause serious diseases in humans and other animals. They are gram-negative (see GRAM STAIN), highly capable of movement (with one to three flagella at one end), and do not require oxygen. Their cells are curved rods, single or strung together in S-shapes or spirals. Two species are of significance to humans: one causes CHOLERA, the other acute bacterial diarrhea.

viburnum \vī-'bər-nəm\ Any of about 200 shrubs and small trees that make up the genus *Viburnum* in the HONEYSUCKLE FAMILY, native to temperate and subtropical Eurasia and North America. Many species are cultivated for their ornamental foliage, fragrant clusters of usually white flowers, and colorful blue-black fruits. Familiar garden shrubs in this family include Chinese snowball *(V. macrocephalum* variety *sterile)* and Japanese snowball *(V. plicatum),* each with large balls of white to greenish-white flowers.

Vicente \vē-'sāⁿn-tə\, **Gil** (1465?–1536?) Portuguese playwright. His first plays were produced in 1502, and for the next 34 years acted as court dramatist and poet laureate, staging his plays to celebrate great events and religious occasions. Regarded as the founder of Portuguese drama, he wrote in both Portuguese and Spanish. His 44 extant plays included tragicomedies, farces, and *autos sacramentales* (short biblical plays) that reflected the change and upheaval of his era. His works include *Exhortation to War* (1513), *The Forge of Love* (1524), and *The Pilgrimage of the Aggrieved* (1533).

Vichy France \'vē-shē\ *officially* **French State** *French* **État français** (July 1940–September 1944) French regime in WORLD WAR II after the German defeat of France. The Franco-German armistice (June 1940) divided France into two zones: one under German military occupation and one under nominal French control (the southeastern two-fifths of the country). The National Assembly, summoned at Vichy to ratify the armistice, was persuaded by PIERRE LAVAL to grant PHILIPPE PETAIN authority to assume full powers in the "French State." The antirepublican Vichy government collaborated with the Germans and became increasingly a tool of German policy, especially after the Germans occupied the whole of France in 1942. By early 1944 the RESISTANCE movement against the GESTAPO and Vichy militias created a period of civil war in France, and after the liberation of Paris the Vichy regime was abolished.

Vicksburg Campaign (1862–63) Engagements fought at Vicksburg, Miss., in the AMERICAN CIVIL WAR. Confederate forces held the fortified city against Union naval bombardment from the Mississippi River (1862) and attempts to attack by land. In April 1863 ULYSSES S. GRANT used the Union ships to ferry troops across the river at night. He quickly took nearby Port Gibson and Grand Gulf to prevent Confederate forces under JOSEPH JOHNSTON from aiding those in the city. Unable to take Vicksburg directly, Grant besieged the city for six weeks. On July 4 Gen. John Pemberton (1814–1881) surrendered his force of 30,000, leaving the Mississippi River completely under Union control and splitting the Confederacy in half.

Vico \'vē-kō\, **Giambattista** (1668–1744) Italian philosopher of cultural history and law. In his major work *New Science* (1725), Vico attempted to bring about the convergence of history and the more systematic social sciences, so that their interpenetration could form a single science of humanity. He had his own vision of mankind and the universe, and he posed the modern problem of the meaning of life and history. He affirmed that Providence must right the course of history so that humanity would be engulfed in successive cataclysms. Increasingly recognized as one of the important figures in European intellectual history, Vico is seen today as a forerunner of the founders of CULTURAL ANTHROPOLOGY.

Victor III *orig.* **Dauferi** (1027–1087) Pope (1086–87). As abbot of MONTE CASSINO from 1058, he promoted manuscript illumination, established a school of mosaic, and reconstructed the abbey. He served as papal vicar in southern Italy, negotiating peace between the Normans and the papacy. He was proclaimed pope against his will and was soon driven from Rome by supporters of Emperor HENRY IV and the antipope Clement III. In 1087 Victor resumed his papal authority, and after sending an army to defeat the Saracens at Tunis (1087), he called a synod at Benevento and excommunicated Clement. He fell ill and returned to Monte Cassino, where he died.

Victor Amadeus II \,äm-ə-'dā-əs\ *Italian* **Vittorio Amedeo** (1666–1732) King of Sicily (1713–20) and of Sardinia (1720–30). The son of Charles Emmanuel II, he inherited his father's title as duke of Savoy in 1675 and grew up under a regency headed by his mother, who pursued a pro-French policy. In the War of the SPANISH SUCCESSION he sided with France, but in 1703 he shifted to the Habsburg side. With the French defeat at Turin (1706) he secured his position in Italy. The Treaty of UTRECHT (1713) gave him the title of king of Sicily, which he was obliged to exchange for Sardinia in 1720. As the first king of Sardinia, which also included Piedmont and Savoy, he established the foundation for the future Italian national state.

Victor Emmanuel I *Italian* **Vittorio Emanuele** (1759–1824) King of Sardinia (1802–21). Son of Victor Amadeus III and great-grandson of VICTOR AMADEUS II, he led Sardinian forces against the French (1792–97). He became duke of Savoy and king of Sardinia in 1802 when his brother Charles Emmanuel IV abdicated. His kingdom, except for the island of Sardinia, was occupied by France (1802–14), then restored with the addition of Genoa by the Congress of VIENNA (1815). He abdicated in 1821 in favor of his brother Charles Felix (1765–1831).

Victor Emmanuel II.
ALINARI—ART RESOURCE/EB INC.

Victor Emmanuel II *Italian* **Vittorio Emanuele** (1820–1878) King of Sardinia (1849–61) and first king of a united Italy (1861–78). The son of CHARLES ALBERT, he took part in the war against Austria (1848) and became king when his father abdicated in 1849. Assisted by his minister CAMILLO CAVOUR, he strengthened the kingdom and supported the RISORGIMENTO movement

S T U V

for unity. In the war with Austria (1859–61), he commanded troops to victories in the Battles of MAGENTA and SOLFERINO. He secretly encouraged GIUSEPPE DE GARIBALDI in the conquest of Sicily and Naples and led the invasion of the Papal States. He assumed the title of king of Italy (1861) and later acquired Venetia (1866) and Rome (1870).

Victor Emmanuel III *Italian* **Vittorio Emanuele** (1869–1947) King of Italy (1900–1946). Son of UMBERTO I, he came suddenly to the throne on his father's assassination (1900). He accepted a Liberal cabinet and readily agreed to Italy's war against Turkey (1911–12) and entry into World War I. After the war, he failed to prevent the rise of BENITO MUSSOLINI and the Fascist seizure of power, which turned him into a figurehead sovereign. In 1943, after disastrous Italian military losses and the Allied invasion of Sicily, he had Mussolini arrested and replaced by PIETRO BADOGLIO as premier. In 1944 he relinquished power to his son Umberto and, in an unsuccessful attempt to preserve the monarchy, abdicated in Umberto's favor in 1946 (see UMBERTO II). When the Italian republic was declared in 1946, father and son went into exile.

Victoria *orig.* **Alexandrina Victoria** (1819–1901) Queen of the United Kingdom of Great Britain and Ireland (1837–1901) and Empress of India (from 1876). The only child of Edward, duke of Kent, she succeeded her uncle, WILLIAM IV, in 1837. She was first guided as queen by the Whig prime minister Lord MELBOURNE and then by her husband, Prince ALBERT, whom she married in 1840. Devoted to him, she accepted his decisions on all issues in the period sometimes called the "Albertine monarchy." They had nine children, through whose marriages descended many of the royal families of Europe. From 1861 Victoria deeply mourned Albert's death and thereafter made royal decisions as she believed he would have advised. She was frequently at odds with Prime Minister WILLIAM E. GLADSTONE and welcomed his replacement by BENJAMIN DISRAELI in 1874. Her reign, called the Victorian age, was marked by a period of British expansion and a restoration of dignity and popularity to the monarchy, as shown by her Jubilees of 1887 and 1897. She remains the longest-reigning monarch in British history.

Victoria State (pop., 1996: 4,374,000), southeastern Australia. It covers an area of 87,900 sq mi (227,600 sq km); its capital is MELBOURNE. The state's western and northwestern parts are sandy desert and lowland, while the central and eastern parts are highlands forming the southern end of the AUSTRALIAN ALPS. The southwestern coastal region is known as GIPPSLAND. The MURRAY RIVER forms almost the entire boundary between the state and NEW SOUTH WALES. AUSTRALIAN ABORIGINES had lived in the region for at least 40,000 years before contact with Europeans. Some 60 years after Capt. JAMES COOK first sighted its coastline (1770), the area was settled by immigrants from TASMANIA, who brought in their wake diseases which decimated much of the aboriginal population. Victoria became a separate colony in 1851. In 1901 it became a state of the Commonwealth of Australia. Boosting its economy is a very productive agricultural inland.

Victoria City (metro. area pop., 1996 est.: 304,000), capital of British Columbia. It is located on the southeastern tip of VANCOUVER ISLAND, overlooking JUAN DE FUCA STRAIT. It was founded in 1843 by the HUDSON'S BAY CO. as a fur-trading post known as Fort Camosun; it was later renamed Fort Victoria to honor the English queen. It was selected as the capital in 1866 when Vancouver Island united with British Columbia. It is now one of the province's largest business centers and, a tourist resort and retirement community. A major port, it is the Pacific headquarters of the Canadian navy.

Victoria Seaport city, capital of HONG KONG, China. It lies on the northern shore of Hong Kong island (pop., 1996: 1,313,000). It has extensive wharves and is connected to the Chinese mainland by ferry, and by automobile and railway tunnels. It is the chief administrative, commercial, and cultural center of Hong Kong and is the headquarters for numerous international banks and corporations.

Victoria Town (pop., 1993 est.: 25,000), capital of the Republic of Seychelles. Located on the northeastern coast of Mahé Island, in the Indian Ocean, it is the only port of the archipelago and the only town of any size in Seychelles. It is the country's business and cultural center.

Victoria, Lake *or* **Victoria Nyanza** Largest lake in Africa and chief reservoir of the NILE RIVER, eastern central Africa. The southern half lies in Tanzania, the northern half in Uganda; it borders Kenya in the northeast. With an area of 26,828 sq mi (69,484 sq km), it is the second largest freshwater lake in the world (after Lake SUPERIOR in North America). It is about 210 mi (337 km) long, 150 mi (240 km) wide, and up to 270 ft (82 m) deep. Though the KAGERA RIVER is the largest of the lake's tributaries, its most important source is rainfall. Its only outlet is the VICTORIA NILE. JOHN HANNING SPEKE, searching for the source of the Nile in 1858, was the first European to sight it. He named it for Queen VICTORIA; the Arabs had called it Ukerewe. HENRY MORTON STANLEY circumnavigated it in 1875. It became a reservoir when the water level was raised after completion of Owen Falls Dam in 1954.

Victoria, Tomás Luis de (1548–1611) Spanish composer. He went to Rome c. 1565 as an organist and singer, and may have studied with G.P. DA PALESTRINA, eventually becoming chapel master for a Jesuit congregation (1573–77). Ordained a priest (1575), he was associated with St. Philip NERI's group 1578–85. During this time, he published his books of motets, masses, Magnificats, and hymns. In 1587 he returned to Spain as chaplain to the king's sister, in whose convent he served as organist and choirmaster until his death. He wrote 20 masses (including a *Pope Marcellus Mass*), 18 Magnificats, and 52 motets (including *O magnum mysterium*). His music is mystical, impressive, and moving, and he was renowned as the greatest Spanish composer of the Renaissance.

Victoria, University of Public university in Victoria, British Columbia, founded in 1903. It has faculties of arts and sciences, education, engineering, fine arts, graduate studies, human and social development, and law, as well as schools of business, music, nursing, and other specializations. Total enrollment is about 17,000.

Victoria and Albert Museum Museum of decorative arts in London. It was conceived by Prince ALBERT as a way to improve the standards of British design by making the finest models available for study. The core collection, consisting of objects purchased at the 1851 CRYSTAL PALACE exhibition, was originally called the Museum of Ornamental Art and was opened by Queen VICTORIA in 1857. A new building was later designed by Sir Aston Webb, and the museum was renamed when Victoria laid the cornerstone in 1899; it was opened to the public by EDWARD VII in 1909. It houses vast collections of European sculpture, ceramics, furniture, metalwork, jewelry, textiles, and musical instruments from medieval times to the present; remarkable Chinese ceramics, jade, and sculpture; the premier collection of Italian Renaissance sculpture outside Italy; and the outstanding national collection of British watercolors, miniatures, prints, and drawings. It is regarded as the world's greatest decorative-arts museum. Its branch museums include the Bethnal Green Museum of Childhood, the Theatre Museum, and the Wellington Museum.

Victoria Desert See GREAT VICTORIA DESERT

Victoria Falls Waterfall, at the border between Zambia and Zimbabwe. Approximately twice as wide and twice as deep as NIAGARA FALLS, the falls span the entire breadth of the ZAMBEZI RIVER at one of its widest points (more than 5,500 ft, or 1,700 m). There, the river plunges over a precipice, split by islands and promontories, to a drop of 355 ft (108 m). Two national parks, Victoria Falls in Zimbabwe, and Mosi-oa-Tunya in Zambia are adjacent to the falls. Victoria Falls was designated a WORLD HERITAGE SITE in 1989. The first European sighting of the falls was in 1855 by DAVID LIVINGSTONE, who named them after Queen VICTORIA.

Victoria Falls See IGUAZÚ FALLS

Victoria Island Third-largest island of the ARCTIC ARCHIPELAGO, Canada. About 320 mi (515 km) long and 170–370 mi (270–600 km) wide, it has an area of 83,896 sq mi (217,291 sq km). Discovered in 1838 by Thomas Simpson, it was named for Queen VICTORIA and was first explored by John Rae in 1851. Formerly part of the NORTHWEST TERRITORIES, a portion of it was transferred to NUNAVUT in 1999.

Victoria Nile River that forms the upper section of the NILE RIVER. Some 260 mi (420 km) long, it issues from the northern end of Lake VICTORIA, then flows over the Owen Falls Dam, through Lake KYOGA, and over Kabalega Falls (118 ft, or 36 m) before entering the northeastern corner of Lake ALBERT. It is about 300 mi (480 km) long.

Victoria River Longest river in NORTHERN TERRITORY, Australia. It flows northwest for about 350 mi (560 km) to enter Joseph Bonaparte Gulf of the Timor Sea. Its last 100 mi (160 km) are tidal. Captain J. C. Wickham of the HMS *Beagle* reached the river in 1839 and named it in honor of Queen VICTORIA.

Victoria Strait Channel of the ARCTIC OCEAN. It is located between southeastern VICTORIA ISLAND and King William Island, off the northern Canada mainland in NUNAVUT. At about 100 mi (160 km) long and from 50–80 mi (80–130 km) wide, it connects Queen Maud Gulf with McClintock Channel and Franklin Strait.

Victorian architecture Building style of the GOTHIC REVIVAL that marks the movement from a sentimental phase to one of greater exactitude. Its principles, especially honesty of expression, were first laid down in *The True Principles of Pointed or Christian Architecture* (1841) by Augustus Pugin (1812–1852). Much Victorian design consisted of adapting the decorative details and rich color combinations of Italian and especially Venetian Gothic. Though ornamentation could be elaborate, it was usually not superficially applied but grew rationally out of the form and material used.

vicuña \vi-'kün-yə, vī-'kü-nə\ South American lamoid (see ALPACA), the smallest species *(Lama,* or *Vicugna, vicugna)* in the CAMEL family, found in semiarid grasslands of the central Andes at altitudes of 12,000–16,000 ft (3,600–4,800 m). The remarkably long, soft, lustrous coat is cinnamon to white; a dense, silky, white fleece hangs from the flanks and base of the neck. Vicuñas are about 36 in. (90 cm) high and weigh over 100 lbs (50 kg). Small bands of females, led by a male, graze on low grasses, ruminate while at rest, and spit often and noisily. They mark their territory with communal dung heaps. Vicuñas are untamable but have been hunted for centuries; they are now protected as an endangered species.

Vidal \'vē-,däl, vē-'däl\, **Gore** *orig.* **Eugene Luther** (born 1925) U.S. novelist, playwright, and essayist. Born into a wealthy family in West Point, N.Y., Vidal began publishing his writings soon after his wartime army service. Though he has written stage plays and television and film screenplays, he is best known for his irreverent and intellectually adroit novels. *The City and the Pillar* (1948) became notorious for its homoerotic subject matter. *Myra Breckenridge* (1968) was acclaimed for its wild satire. His other novels, many of them historical and most of them best-sellers, include *Julian* (1964), *Washington, D.C.* (1967), *Burr* (1974), *1876* (1976), and *Lincoln* (1984). He has also published several essay collections and the memoir *Palimpsest* (1996). Known for his iconoclastically leftist political analyses, he has twice run unsuccessfully for Congressional office.

video card INTEGRATED CIRCUIT that generates the video signal sent to a computer display. The card is usually located on the computer motherboard or is a separate circuit board, but is sometimes built into the computer display unit. It contains a digital-to-analog module, as well as MEMORY chips that store display data. All video cards (also known as video adapters, video boards, and video controllers) adhere to a display standard, such as SVGA or XGA.

videocassette recorder See VCR

videodisc Rigid circular plate of either metal or plastic used to record video and audio signals for playback. It resembles a phonograph record and can be played on a machine attached to a conventional television receiver. There are two major classes of videodiscs, magnetic and nonmagnetic. Magnetic videodiscs have an oxide-coated surface onto which input signals are recorded as magnetic patterns in spiral tracks. Nonmagnetic videodiscs use either a mechanical recording system analogous to that used in phonograph records, or optical technology that uses a laser to read data coded as a sequence of pits on the disc. The most common type of videodisc today is the DVD.

videotape Magnetic tape used to record visual images and sound, or the recording itself. There are two types of videotape recorders, the transverse (or quad) and the helical. The transverse unit uses four heads rotating on an axis perpendicular to the direction in which the tape is fed. The transverse format achieves 1,500-in.-per-minute head-to-tape speed, necessary for high picture quality. The helical unit uses tape traveling around a drum in the form of a helix. VCRs use a helical format, known as VHS (Video Home System), consisting of two helical bands and tape 1/2 in. (1 cm) wide.

Vidor \'vē-dȯr\, **King (Wallis)** (1894–1982) U.S. film director. Born in Galveston, Texas, he worked in Hollywood as an extra and studio clerk before directing his first feature film, *The Turn in the Road* (1919). He won acclaim for *The Big Parade* (1925) and for *The Crowd* (1928), considered a silent-movie classic. Noted for his realistic portrayals of contemporary life, he directed the first all-black film, *Hallelujah!* (1929), as well as *Our Daily Bread* (1934) and *The Citadel* (1938). His later movies included the western epic *Duel in the Sun* (1946), *The Fountainhead* (1949), and *War and Peace* (1956).

Vieira \'vyā-ē-rə\, **António** (1608–1697) Brazilian (Portuguese-born) missionary, orator, diplomat, and writer. Born in Lisbon, he was raised in Brazil, where he became a Jesuit priest. His sermons exhorting all races to join in repelling Dutch invaders are considered the first expression of the Brazilian concept of forming a new race of mixed blood. He worked among the Indians and black slaves until 1641, mastering several of their languages. Returning to Portugal, he became an important figure in the court of John IV, where he advocated toleration for Jewish converts to Christianity. He was imprisoned by the Inquisition 1663–68, but returned to Brazil in 1681.

Vienna City (pop., 1992 est.: 1,560,000), capital of Austria. Located on the DANUBE RIVER, it was founded by the Celts; it became a Roman military station in the 1st century BC. Ruled by many, including the Franks in the 6th century AD and the Magyars in the 10th century, it was an important trade center during the CRUSADES. It was the seat of the HOLY ROMAN EMPIRE 1558–1806, of the Austrian (and HABSBURG) empire 1806–67, and of the Austro-Hungarian empire until 1918. In 1814–15 it was the seat of the Congress of VIENNA. The administrative center of German Austria 1938–45, it was frequently bombed during World War II by the Allies, and was taken by Soviet troops in 1945. It was under joint Soviet-Western Allied occupation 1945–55. The Strategic Arms Limitations Talks (SALT) between the U.S. and U.S.S.R. took place there in the 1970s. The commercial and industrial center of Austria, it also is a cultural center renowned for its architecture and music. It was the birthplace of the composers F. SCHUBERT, JOHANN, JR. STRAUSS, and A. SCHOENBERG, and the home of W.A. MOZART, LUDWIG VAN BEETHOVEN, J. BRAHMS, and G. MAHLER. It also was the home of SIGMUND FREUD, GUSTAV KLIMT, OSKAR KOKOSCHKA, and JOSEF HOFFMANN.

Vienna, Congress of (1814–15) Assembly that reorganized Europe after the NAPOLEONIC WARS. The powers of the QUADRUPLE ALLIANCE had concluded the Treaty of CHAUMONT just before Napoleon's first abdication and agreed to meet later in Vienna. There they were joined by Bourbon France as a major participant and by Sweden and Portugal; many minor states also sent representatives. The principal negotiators were KLEMENS, FURST VON METTERNICH, representing FRANCIS II (Austria); ALEXANDER I (RUSSIA); FREDERICK WILLIAM III and KARL AUGUST, FURST VON HARDENBERG (Prussia); VISCOUNT CASTLEREAGH (Britain); and CHARLES MAURICE DE TALLEYRAND (France). The Congress reduced France to its 1789 borders. A new kingdom of Poland was established, under Russian sovereignty. To check possible future aggression by France, its neighbors were strengthened: the kingdom of the Netherlands acquired Belgium, Prussia gained territory along the Rhine River, and the Italian kingdom acquired Genoa. The German states were joined loosely in a new GERMAN CONFEDERATION, subject to Austria's influence. For its part in the defeat of Napoleon, Britain acquired valuable colonies, including Malta, the Cape of Good Hope, and Ceylon. The Vienna settlement was the most comprehensive treaty that Europe had ever seen, and the configuration of Europe established at the congress lasted for over 40 years.

Vienna, Siege of (July 17–September 12, 1683) Attempted capture of Vienna by Ottoman Turkey. On appeal from the Hungarian Calvinists to attack the Habsburg capital, the Turkish grand vizier, Kara Mustafa (1634–1683), and his army of 150,000 laid siege to Vienna in July 1683, after capturing its outer fortifications. Pope Innocent XI convinced JOHN III SOBIESKI of Poland to lead a combined army of 80,000 to relieve the siege. On September 12, 1683, Sobieski, aided by Charles of Lorraine, led the attack from the surrounding hills and after 15 hours drove the Turks from their trenches around the city. Thousands were slaughtered or taken prisoner. The event marked the beginning of the decline of Turkish domination in eastern Europe.

Vienna, University of State-financed university at Vienna. Founded in 1365 on the model of the University of PARIS, it is the oldest university in the German-speaking world. It was reorganized in 1384, becoming particularly noted for its faculties of medicine, law, and theology. It was a center of revolution during the uprising of 1848, when Prince Metternich was forced from power. The modern university includes faculties of theology, social sciences and economics, medicine, sciences, mathematics, and natural sciences. Total enrollment is about 72,000.

Vienna Circle *German* **Wiener Kreis** \'vē-nər-'krīs\ Group of philosophers, scientists, and mathematicians formed in the 1920s that met regularly in Vienna to investigate scientific language and Scientific Method. It formed around Moritz Schlick (1882–1936), who taught at the University of Vienna; its members included Gustav Bergmann, Philipp Frank, Rudolf Carnap, Kurt Godel, Friedrich Waismann, Otto Neurath, Herbert Feigl, and Victor Kraft. The movement associated with the Circle has been called Logical Positivism. Its members' work was distinguished by their attention to the form of scientific theories, their formulation of a Verifiability Principle of meaning, and their espousal of a doctrine of Unified Science. The group dissolved after the Nazis invaded Austria in 1938.

Vientiane \ˌvyen-'tyän\ *Laotian* **Viangchan** \ˌvyeŋ-'chän\ City (metro. area pop., 1999 est.: 534,000), capital of Laos. It is located north of the Mekong River. Founded in the late 13th century, it was made the administrative center of an early Laotian kingdom in the mid-16th century. In 1778 it came under Siamese control; in 1828 it was destroyed when the Laotian king revolted against the Siamese. The French made it the capital of their colony on their takeover of the region in the 1890s; it remained the administrative center after Laos gained independence in 1953. It is the commercial center of the region, and Laos's principal port of entry.

Vierordt \'fēr-ˌȯrt\, **Karl von** (1818–1884) German physician. He started a medical practice in 1842 and began teaching at the University of Tübingen in 1849. He discovered a way to make an exact red-blood-cell count (see Blood Analysis) and invented the sphygmograph, the first instrument to produce a pulse tracing, and the hemotachometer, which monitors blood-flow velocity.

Viet Cong *in full* **Viet Nam Cong San** Guerrilla force that sought to reunify North and South Vietnam under communist leadership from the late 1950s through 1975. Originally a collection of various groups opposed to the government of South Vietnam's Pres. Ngo Dinh Diem, the Viet Cong became the military arm of the National Liberation Front (1960) and later of the Provisional Revolutionary Government (PRG; 1969). Members were recruited largely from South Vietnam, but they received guidance, weapons, and reinforcements from the north. The Viet Cong's guerrilla war against the South Vietnamese government and its powerful U.S. allies was successful; the U.S. withdrew its troops from Vietnam between 1969 and 1973 and the PRG assumed power in South Vietnam in 1975, following a full-scale invasion.

Viet Minh \'vyet-'min\ *in full* **Viet Nam Doc Lap Dong Minh Hoi** Organization that led the struggle for Vietnamese independence from French rule. Formed in 1941 by Ho Chi Minh, it was a national organization open to people of all political leanings, though it was led by communists. In 1943 the Viet Minh began guerrilla operations against the occupying Japanese; when the Japanese surrendered to the Allies, the Viet Minh seized Hanoi and proclaimed Vietnam's independence. In the First Indochina War that followed, the Viet Minh (and the Lien Viet and Lao Dong who succeeded them) defeated the French. Elements of the Viet Minh also joined the Viet Cong to fight the U.S. in the Vietnam War. See also Vo Nguyen Giap.

Vietnam *officially* **Socialist Republic of Vietnam** Nation, South Asia. Area: 127,816 sq mi (331,041 sq km). Population (2001): 79,939,000. Capital: Hanoi. Almost 90% of the total population is Vietnamese; minorities include Chinese, Hmong, Thai, Khmer, and Chan. Languages: Vietnamese (official), French, Chinese, English, Khmer. Religions: Buddhism, Taoism, Confucianism, Roman Catholicism, Islam, Protestantism. Currency: New dong. Vietnam is about 1,025 mi (1,650 km) long, 210–340 mi (340–550 km) wide at its widest parts, and 35 mi (56 km) wide at its narrowest part. Northern Vietnam is mountainous where Fan-si-pan, the country's highest peak, rises to 10,306 ft (3,141 m). The Red River is the principal river. Southern Vietnam is dominated by the Mekong River Delta. A low-lying, narrow coastal plain about 620 mi (1,000 km) long connects the two major river deltas. The densely forested Annamese Cordillera extends through western central Vietnam and covers two-thirds of the total land area. Northern Vietnam is rich in mineral resources, especially anthracite and lignite coal. Some petroleum deposits exist off the southern coast. Significant food crops include

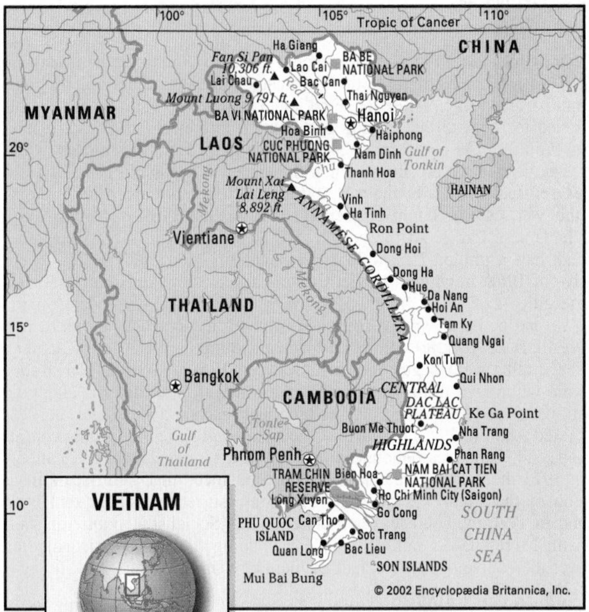

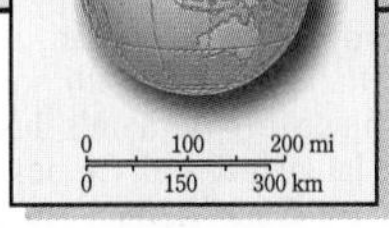

rice, sugarcane, coffee, tea, and bananas. Food processing and fishing are important industries, as are the manufacture of steel and phosphates. It is a socialist republic with one legislative house; its chief of state is the president, and its head of government is the prime minister. A distinct Vietnamese group began to emerge c. 200 BC in the independent kingdom of Nam Viet, which was later annexed to China in the 1st century BC. The Vietnamese were under continuous Chinese control until the 10th century AD. The southern region was gradually overrun by Vietnamese from the north in the late 15th century. The area was divided into two parts in the early 17th century, with the northern part known as Tonkin, and the southern part as Cochin China. In 1802 the northern and southern parts of Vietnam were unified under a single dynasty. Following several years of attempted French colonial expansion in the region, the French captured Saigon in 1859 and later the rest of the area, controlling it until World War II (see French Indochina). The Japanese occupied Vietnam 1940–45 and declared it independent at the end of World War II, a move the French opposed. They fought the First Indochina War until French forces with U.S. financial backing were defeated at Dien Bien Phu in 1954; evacuation of French troops ensued. Following an international conference at Geneva, Vietnam was partitioned along the 17th parallel, with the northern part under Ho Chi Minh, and the southern part under Bao Dai; the partition was to be temporary, but the reunification elections scheduled for 1956 were never held. Bao Dai declared the independence of South Vietnam (Republic of Vietnam), while the Communists established North Vietnam (Democratic Republic of Vietnam). The activities of North Vietnamese guerrillas and pro-communist rebels in South Vietnam led to U.S. intervention and the Vietnam War. A cease-fire agreement was signed in 1973, and U.S. troops were withdrawn. The civil war soon resumed, and in 1975 North Vietnam invaded South Vietnam and the South Vietnamese government collapsed. In 1976 the two Vietnams were united as the Socialist Republic of Vietnam. From the mid-1980s, the government enacted a series of economic reforms and began to open up to Asian and western nations. In 1995 the U.S. officially normalized relations with Vietnam.

Vietnam Veterans Memorial Monument in Washington, D.C., designed by Maya Lin. It consists of two low, black granite walls that meet to form a wide V shape. Engraved on the mirrorlike surface are the names of the more than 58,000 U.S. dead and missing-in-action who served in the Vietnam War, listed by date of casualty. When Lin's abstract design was announced, several veterans groups and others protested; eventually a traditional statue depicting three servicemen with a flag was commissioned, to stand at the entrance to the site. Since its dedication in 1982, the controversial wall has become one of the city's most visited and most affecting tourist attractions.

Vietnam War (1955–75) Protracted effort by South Vietnam and the U.S. to prevent North and South Vietnam from being united under communist leadership. After the First INDOCHINA WAR, Vietnam was partitioned to separate the warring parties until free elections could be held in 1956. HO CHI MINH's popular VIET MINH party from the north was expected to win the elections, which the leader in the south, NGO DINH DIEM, refused to hold. In the war that ensued, fighters trained in the north (the VIET CONG) fought a guerrilla war against U.S.-supported South Vietnamese forces. At the height of U.S. involvement, there were more than half a million U.S. military personnel in Vietnam. The Tet Offensive of 1968, in which the Viet Cong attacked 36 major South Vietnamese cities and towns, marked a turning point in the war. Many in the U.S. had come to oppose the war on moral and practical grounds, and Pres. LYNDON B. JOHNSON decided to shift to a policy of "de-escalation." Peace talks were begun in Paris. Between 1969 and 1973 U.S. troops were withdrawn from Vietnam, but the war was expanded to Cambodia and Laos in 1970. Peace talks, which had reached a stalemate in 1971, started again in 1973, producing a cease-fire agreement. Fighting continued, and both sides denounced the other for numerous truce violations. In 1975 the North Vietnamese became convinced that a full-scale invasion of the south was possible. The south surrendered later that year, and in 1976 the country was reunited as the Socialist Republic of Vietnam. More than 2 million people (including 58,000 Americans) died over the course of the war, half of them civilians.

Vietnamese language MON-KHMER LANGUAGE, the native language of 60–65 million people in Vietnam and a second language for many members of Vietnam's more than 50 minority ethnic groups, with some 2 million speakers outside the country. For much of Vietnam's history, Classical CHINESE was the dominant literary language, and Chinese vocabulary given a Vietnamese pronunciation ("Sino-Vietnamese") remains a significant part of the language's lexicon. By the 13th century, Chinese characters were adapted to write native Vietnamese words. In the 17th century, Roman Catholic missionaries introduced a system of writing Vietnamese in the LATIN ALPHABET with diacritics distinguishing vowel qualities and tones, a system widely adopted only in the 20th century.

Viganò \vē-'gä-nō\, **Salvatore** (1769–1821) Italian dancer and choreographer. He studied dance with his father and toured in Spain (1788) and Vienna (1793–95, 1799–1803), where he began to choreograph works in a style synthesizing dance and mime, similar to J.-G. NOVERRE's *ballet d'action,* which he called "coreodramma." He created over 40 works, including *The Creatures of Prometheus* (1801), *Gli strelizzi* (1809), *Otello* (1818), and *I titani* (1819). In 1811 he became ballet master at La Scala in Milan, where he promoted the development of ballet in Italy.

Vigée-Lebrun \vē-'zhā-lä-'brœ^{n}\, **(Marie-Louise-) Elisabeth** (1755–1842) French painter. Taught first by her father, a pastel portraitist, she was also advised by JOSEPH VERNET. In 1779 she was summoned to Versailles to paint MARIE-ANTOINETTE, whom she would paint at least 25 more times. At the outbreak of the French Revolution, she left France and traveled abroad, painting portraits of such notables as Lord BYRON and GERMAINE DE STAEL and playing a leading role in society. Her paintings are notable for their freshness, charm, and sensitivity, and she was one of the most technically fluent portraitists of her era.

Vigny \vē-'nyē\, **Alfred-Victor, comte (count) de** (1797–1863) French poet, dramatist, and novelist. Vigny embarked on a military career but turned to writing well-received Romantic poetry. His *Cinq-Mars* (1826) was the first important historical novel in French. Growing disillusioned, he wrote *Stello* (1832), on separating the poetic and political life. *Chatterton* (1835), his best play and one of the finest Romantic dramas, glorifies the anguish of the misunderstood artist. His pessimism was manifest also in *The Military Necessity* (1835), whose first and third stories are his prose masterpieces. His later writings include poetry collected posthumously in *Les destinées* (1864). In middle age he withdrew from Paris society.

Vigo \vē-'gō\, **Jean** (1905–1934) French film director. The son of a militant anarchist who died in prison under suspect circumstances, he spent an unhappy childhood in boarding schools. After contracting tuberculosis he settled in Nice, where he directed his first film, the satiric social documentary *À propos de Nice* (1930). He explored the subject of freedom versus authority in his celebrated *Zero for Conduct* (1933), which was branded "anti-French" by the censors and withdrawn from theaters. His last film, *L'Atalante* (1934), is also regarded as a masterpiece. He died of leukemia at 29.

Vijayanagar \,vi-jə-yə-'nə-gər\ Former Hindu kingdom, southern India, south of the KRISHNA RIVER. Founded in 1336 by leaders of the Kanarese people, it became the greatest empire of southern India and for more than two centuries served as a barrier against Muslim raiders from the north. It was an important center of BRAHMAN culture and Dravidian art. Its downfall began with the defeat at Talikota (1565) by a confederacy of Deccan Muslim sultans; the empire dissolved c. 1614. The kingdom's capital, Vijayanagar, was destroyed in 1565. Its ruined site is located at modern Hampi, in southeastern KARNATAKA.

Vijnanavada See YOGACARA

Viking Either of two unmanned U.S. spacecraft launched by NASA in 1975. After 10 months, Vikings 1 and 2 entered orbits around MARS and released landers that touched down on the planet and relayed measurements of properties of its atmosphere and soil and color photographs of its surface. Experiments designed to detect evidence of living organisms provided no convincing evidence of life on the surface. The orbiters transmitted photographs of large expanses of the Martian surface.

Viking 2 lander (foreground) on Mars, photographed by one of the spacecraft's own cameras, 1976.

BY COURTESY OF THE JET PROPULSION LABORATORY/NATIONAL AERONAUTICS AND SPACE ADMINISTRATION

Viking ship See LONGSHIP

Vikings *or* **Norsemen** Scandinavian seafaring warriors who raided and colonized areas of Europe in the 9th–11th century. Overpopulation at home, ease of conquest abroad, and their extraordinary capacity as shipbuilders and sailors inspired their adventures. In 865 Vikings conquered East Anglia, Northumbria, and much of Mercia. Wessex under ALFRED the Great made a truce in 878 that led to Danish control of much of England. Alfred defeated fresh Viking armies 892–99, and his son continued his reconquest, recovering lands in Mercia and East Anglia by 924; Viking Northumbria fell in 954. Renewed raids in 980 brought England into CANUTE'S empire until 1042, when native rule was restored. The Scandinavians permanently affected English social structure, dialect, and names. In the western seas, Scandinavians had settled in Iceland by 900, whence they traveled to Greenland and North America. They invaded Ireland in 795, establishing kingdoms at Dublin, Limerick, and Waterford. The Battle of Clontarf (1014) ended the threat of Scandinavian rule. France suffered periodic Viking raids but no domination. In Russia Vikings briefly dominated Novgorod, Kiev, and other centers, but were quickly absorbed by the Slav population. As traders they made commercial treaties with the Byzantines (912, 945), and they served as mercenaries in Constantinople. Viking activity ended in the 11th century.

Vikramaditya See CANDRA GUPTA II

Vila See PORT-VILA

villa Country estate, complete with house, grounds, and subsidiary buildings. The term particularly applies to the suburban summer residences of the ancient Romans and their later Italian imitators. Roman villas frequently were asymmetrical in plan and built with elaborate terracing on hillsides; they had long colonnades, towers, gardens with reflecting pools and fountains, and extensive reservoirs. In Britain the term has come to mean a small detached or semidetached suburban home. See also HADRIAN'S VILLA, ANDREA PALLADIO.

Villa \'vē-yə\, **Pancho** *orig.* **Doroteo Arango** (1878–1923) Mexican guerrilla leader. Orphaned at a young age, he spent his adolescence as a fugitive, having murdered a landowner in revenge for an assault on his sister. An advocate of radical LAND REFORM, he joined FRANCISCO MADERO's uprising against PORFIRIO DIAZ. His *División del Norte* joined forces with VENUSTIANO CARRANZA to overthrow VICTORIANO HUERTA (1854–1916), but he soon broke with the moderate Carranza and in 1914 was forced to flee with EMILIANO ZAPATA. In 1916, to demonstrate that Carranza did not control the north, he raided a town in New Mexico. A U.S. force led by Gen. JOHN PERSHING was sent against him, but his popularity and knowledge of his home territory made him impossible to capture. He was granted a pardon after Carranza's overthrow (1920) but was assassinated three years later. See also MEXICAN REVOLUTION, ALVARO OBREGON.

Villa-Lobos \ˌvē-lə-ˈlō-bōsh\, **Heitor** (1887–1959) Brazilian composer. He was exposed to the folk music as a child, and his later extensive ethnomusicological studies (1905–12) had great influence on his own works. Self-taught as a composer, he met D. MILHAUD in 1917, and ARTHUR RUBINSTEIN later promoted his music and helped support him. A "week of modern art" in São Paulo (1922) brought his music to national attention, and he was given a grant to go to Paris (1923–30), where his music was received enthusiastically. On his return, he became a leader in musical education—founding the Ministry of Education conservatory (1942) and the Brazilian Academy of Music (1945)—and Brazil's semiofficial ambassador to the world. His many works include his nine *Bachianas brasileiras* for various ensembles, and his 14 *Chôros*, based on a popular form of street music.

Villafranca \ˌvē-lä-ˈfräŋ-kä\, **Peace of** (1859) Preliminary peace treaty between France's NAPOLEON III and Austria's emperor FRANCIS JOSEPH that ended the Franco-Piedmontese war against Austria. Napoleon III made peace after the costly Battle of SOLFERINO without consulting the Piedmontese king, VICTOR EMMANUEL II. By the peace terms, Lombardy was ceded to France and then to Piedmont, and the dukes of Parma, Modena, and Tuscany were restored to their thrones after being deposed by nationalists. Though decried by Italian nationalists, the peace marked the beginning of Italy's unification under Piedmontese leadership.

Villahermosa \ˌbē-yä-er-ˈmō-sä\ City (pop., 1990: 261,000), capital of TABASCO state, southeastern Mexico. Founded in 1596 as Villa Felipe II, it has also been known as San Juan de Villa Hermosa and as San Juan Bautista; it was given its present name in 1915. The city's cathedral was built in 1614; its archaeological museum is one of the best in Mexico. It is the state's chief distributing, processing, and agricultural city. There are MAYA archaeological ruins in the area.

Villanovan culture \ˌvi-lə-ˈnō-vən\ Early IRON AGE culture in Italy, named after the village where the first site was found in 1853. It appeared in the 10th or 9th century BC as a branch of the URNFIELD CULTURES. Its dead were cremated and the ashes put in a decorated pottery two-story urn covered with a bowl or a helmet-shaped lid, or in a so-called hut urn, a terra-cotta vessel. Expert metalworkers, the Villanovans controlled Tuscany's copper and iron mines. In the later 8th century BC, their art and burials were influenced by Greece. Their culture began to fade in the 7th century.

Villard \və-ˈlärd\, **Henry** *orig.* **Ferdinand Heinrich Gustav Hilgard** (1835–1900) German-U.S. journalist and financier. In 1853 he emigrated to the U.S., where he first found work with German-language newspapers. During the Civil War he was a correspondent for two New York newspapers. In 1881 he purchased the *Nation* magazine and the *New York Evening Post*. In the 1870s he organized several railroads in Oregon, and from 1881 to 1884 he was president of the NORTHERN PACIFIC, a transcontinental railroad completed under his management despite large cost overruns; he later served as chairman of the board (1888–93). He bought two Edison companies and created the Edison General Electric Co. in 1889, serving as president until its reorganization in 1892 as the GENERAL ELECTRIC CO.

Villard de Honnecourt \vē-ˈlår-də-ò-nə-ˈkür\ (c. 1225–c. 1250) French architect. He is remembered mainly for the sketchbook he compiled while traveling in search of work as a master mason, containing sketches and writings concerning architectural practices of the time. He includes sections on technical procedures and mechanical devices, as well as notes on the buildings and monuments he had seen, offering insights into the variety of interests and work of the 13th-century master mason and providing an explanation for the spread of GOTHIC ARCHITECTURE in Europe.

Villars \vi-ˈlär\, **Claude-Louis-Hector, duc (Duke) de** (1653–1734) French soldier. He distinguished himself in France's war against the Dutch (1672–78) and in the War of the Grand Alliance. After leading French forces to early victories in the War of the Spanish Succession, he was made a marshal of France (1702) and a duke (1705). He continued successful military campaigns in Germany (1705–8), inflicted heavy losses on the duke of MARLBOROUGH's forces at Malplaquet (1709), and defeated EUGENE OF SAVOY at Denain (1712). He served on the regency council for the young LOUIS XV. At the outbreak of the War of the Polish Succession, he was given the exceptional title of marshal-general of France (1733) and sent to attack Austrian lands in northern Italy.

Villella \vi-ˈle-lə\, **Edward** (born 1936) U.S. ballet dancer, choreographer, and director, considered one of the outstanding U.S. male dancers. Born in New York City, he trained at the School of American Ballet and joined the NEW YORK CITY BALLET in 1957, becoming a principal dancer in 1960. He danced leading roles in many of GEORGE BALANCHINE's ballets, notably *The Prodigal Son* (1960), displaying a powerful technique. After retiring from dancing in 1983, he became artistic director of Ballet Oklahoma (1983–86). In 1986 he founded the Miami City Ballet, where he continues as artistic director.

Villella in *The Prodigal Son.*
MARTHA SWOPE

Villemin \vēl-ˈmaⁿ\, **Jean Antoine** (1827–1892) French physician. As an army doctor he observed that healthy young men often developed TUBERCULOSIS (TB) living in the close quarters of the barracks. Aware that a similar disease in horses was transmitted by inoculation, he gave TB to rabbits by inoculating them with material from sick humans and cows, proving that it was an infectious disease. His contagion theory, published in 1867, was initially ignored but was later corroborated by other scientists' experiments.

Villiers, George See 1st Duke of BUCKINGHAM

Villon \vē-ˈyōⁿ, vē-ˈlòn\, **François** *orig.* **François de Montcorbier** *or* **François des Loges** (1431–after 1463) French lyric poet. Villon was a rigorously trained scholar who led a life of criminal excess; he killed a priest in 1455, then joined a criminal organization and became involved in robbery, theft, and brawling. Incarcerated several times, in 1462 he received a death sentence that was commuted to banishment. He was never heard from again. His works, published posthumously, include *Le petit testament* (1489), ironic bequests to friends and acquaintances; *Le testament* (1489), which reviews his life with great emotional and poetic depth; and various ballades, chansons, and rondeaux. His verse, which ranges from themes of drunkenness and prostitution to a humble ballade-prayer to the Virgin written at his mother's request, makes a direct, unsentimental appeal to the emotions but also displays remarkable control of rhyme and disciplined composition.

Vilnius \ˈvil-nē-əs\ City (pop., 1996 est.: 573,000), capital of Lithuania. Founded in the 10th century, it became the capital of Lithuania in 1323. It was destroyed in 1377 by the Teutonic Knights, but was rebuilt. It passed to Russia in 1795, and for several centuries was a noted European center for Jewish learning. It was occupied by the Germans in World Wars I and II and suffered heavy damage. In 1920–39 it was included in Poland; it was taken by Soviet troops in 1939 and restored to Lithuania, which the Soviets annexed in 1940. One result of the World War II German occupation was the decimation of the city's Jewish population. In 1991 it became the capital of the newly independent Lithuania. An important industrial center, it also has many historic buildings representing Gothic, Renaissance, and baroque styles of architecture.

Vilnius dispute Conflict between Poland and Lithuania over possession of the city of Vilnius. After World War I, the new Lithuanian government established itself at Vilnius. It was forced out by Soviet forces in 1919, and the city was then occupied by Polish forces (1919) and again by the Soviets, which ceded it to Lithuania in 1920. An armistice was arranged by the League of Nations, but Poland took Vilnius in 1920 and controlled the city and its surrounding region until they were restored to Lithuania in 1939.

Vilyui River *or* **Vilyuy River** \vil-ˈyü-ē\ River, eastern central Siberia. The longest tributary of the LENA RIVER, it is 1,647 mi (2,650 km) long. It joins the Lena about 200 mi (320 km) northwest of Yakutsk. It is navigable for about 900 mi (1,448 km). In 1954 rich diamond deposits were discovered near the river.

Viña del Mar \'bēn-yä-del-'mär\ City (metro. area pop., 1995 est.: 322,000), central Chile. A residential suburb of VALPARAISO and located on the Pacific Ocean, it is a resort city with a gaming casino, beaches, museums, and theaters. Army and navy garrisons, and petroleum depots add to the city's economic base.

Vinaya Pitaka \'vi-nə-yə-'pi-tə-kə\ Oldest and smallest division of the TRIPITAKA. It lays out the 227 rules of monastic life for BHIKSUS, along with an account of the occasion that led the BUDDHA to formulate the rule. It varies less from school to school than does the SUTTA PITAKA or the ABHIDHAMMA PITAKA. It includes an exposition of the rules, which are divided into classes according to the severity of the punishment for breaking them; texts that deal with such matters as admission to and expulsion from the order; and a classified digest of the rules in the other Vinaya texts.

Vincennes ware \vaⁿ-'sen\ Pottery made at Vincennes, France, from 1740 until 1756 (three years after it had become the royal manufactory), when the enterprise moved to Sèvres, near Versailles. Typical Vincennes pottery included biscuit (white, unglazed soft-paste) figures and soft-paste flowers on wire stems or applied to vases. From 1756 to 1770 pottery continued to be made at Vincennes, both tin-glazed earthenware (officially) and soft-paste porcelain (clandestinely, in defiance of a Sèvres monopoly). See also SÈVRES PORCELAIN.

Vincent de Paul, St. (1581–1660) French religious leader. Educated by the Franciscans at Dax, he was ordained in 1600 and graduated from the University of Toulouse in 1604. It is said that he was captured at sea by Barbary pirates but escaped. In 1625 he founded the Congregation of the Mission (also called Lazarists or Vincentians) in Paris as a preaching and teaching order. He also established Confraternities of Charity, associations of laywomen who nursed the sick. With St. Louise de Marillac he cofounded the Daughters of Charity (Sisters of Charity of St. Vincent de Paul).

Vincent of Beauvais \bō-'vā\ (c. 1190–1264) French scholar and encyclopedist. A Dominican priest (c. 1220), he became lector and chaplain to the court of King LOUIS IX. By 1244 he had compiled *Speculum majus* ("Great Mirror"), an 80-book compendium of knowledge from the Creation to the time of Louis IX that included human history, natural history and science known to the West, and a compendium of European literature, law, politics, and economics. His work influenced scholars and poets up to the 18th century. See also ENCYCLOPEDIA.

Vinci, Leonardo da See LEONARDO DA VINCI

vine Plant whose stem requires support and that climbs by TENDRILS or twining or creeps along the ground, or the stem of such a plant. Examples include BITTERSWEET, most GRAPES, some HONEYSUCKLES, IVY, LIANAS, and MELONS.

vinegar Sour liquid obtained by FERMENTATION of dilute alcoholic liquids. Probably first made from WINE (French *vinaigre* means "sour wine"), vinegar may also be made from malted BARLEY, RICE, or other substances. The source substance, which must contain sugar, is fermented by YEAST to produce alcohol. The alcohol is then aerated, causing it to convert, through the action of *Acetobacter* bacteria, to acetic acid, water, and various other compounds. Vinegar is used in pickling meat, fish, fruits, and vegetables and in creating marinades, dressings, and other sauces.

Vingt \'vaⁿ\, **Les** *or* **Les XX** ("The Twenty") Group of Symbolist artists, including JAMES ENSOR, Fernand Khnopff, and Henry van de Velde, who exhibited in Belgium 1891–93. Belgian Symbolist painting employed simplified forms, heavy outlines, a subjective use of color, and a heightened spiritual content inspired by religious, exotic, and primitive cultures. The styles of various members of Les Vingt eventually merged into the new ART NOUVEAU style.

Vinland Wooded land in North America visited and named by LEIF ERIKSSON THE LUCKY c. AD 1000. It was probably located along the Atlantic coast of what is now eastern or northeastern Canada. The Vikings' visits to Vinland (named "wine land" for its wild grapes) are recorded in the Norse SAGAS. Leif Eriksson is said to have led the first expedition, and his brother Thorvald, a second one c. 1003. A colonizing expedition of 130 Vikings c. 1004 was abandoned after warfare with the native Indians. The final expedition was led c. 1013 by ERIK THE RED's daughter Freydis. In 1963 the remains of a Norse settlement were discovered at L'ANSE AUX MEADOWS, at the northernmost tip of NEWFOUNDLAND.

Vinson, Fred(erick Moore) (1890–1953) U.S. jurist. Born in Louisa, Ky., he served in Congress from 1923 to 1938 with one two-year absence. He served on the U.S. Court of Appeals (1938–1943), after which he held high executive positions, including secretary of the treasury under Pres. HARRY TRUMAN. He helped establish the INTERNATIONAL BANK FOR RECONSTRUCTION AND DEVELOPMENT and the INTERNATIONAL MONETARY FUND. He was appointed chief justice of the U.S. Supreme Court by Truman in 1946, and served until 1953. During his tenure he favored Truman's internal-security policies and upheld the rights of minorities to equal protection.

Vinson Massif Mountain, Sentinel Range, central Ellsworth Mtns., western Antarctica. It is 16,066 ft (4,897 m) high and the highest mountain on the continent. It was discovered in 1935 by U.S. explorer Lincoln Ellsworth.

vinyl chloride *or* **chloroethylene** Colorless, flammable, toxic gas, belonging to the family of organic compounds of HALOGENS. It is produced in very large quantities and used principally to make PVC, as well as in other syntheses and in adhesives.

viol \'vī-əl, 'vī-,ōl\ *or* **viola da gamba** \vē-,ō-lə-də-'gäm-bə\ Bowed STRINGED INSTRUMENT of the 16th–18th century. The viols are distinguished from the VIOLIN family particularly by a fretted fingerboard, sloping shoulders, flat back, six strings, and milder tone. They exist in four sizes: treble, tenor, bass, and double bass (violone). They are played vertically, the body being held between the legs or rested on the knee. The viol family appeared in the late 15th century and soon became widely popular and acquired a large repertory. Throughout the baroque era, the bass viol joined the harpsichord in the basso CONTINUO. The contemporaneous violin family, with their more penetrating tone, gradually displaced the viols in the 18th century.

viola \vī-'ō-lə, vē-'ō-lə\ STRINGED INSTRUMENT, the tenor member of the VIOLIN family. In appearance it is almost identical to the violin but slightly larger; its strings are tuned a 5th lower. It is a member of many chamber-music ensembles, and the modern orchestra uses six to 10 violas. Its tone is darker, warmer, and less powerful than the violin's, and it is rarely employed as a solo instrument. The viola d'amore is an 18th-century instrument with six or seven melody strings and several sympathetic strings strung under the melody strings which resonate in concord with the sounded pitches.

violet Any of the approximately 500 species of herbaceous plants or low shrubs that make up the genus *Viola,* which includes the small, solid-colored violets and the larger-flowered, often multicolored violas and PANSIES. Many *Viola* species have two types of flowers: the showy spring flower is infertile; the less conspicuous summer flower is self-fertilizing. The best-known species of *Viola* have heart-shaped leaves. The popular florist's violets, consisting of several hybrids (many of them *V. odorata*), are usually called sweet violets. The family Violaceae, to which *Viola* belongs, has members worldwide; they are typically small trees and shrubs that grow as low vegetation beneath the taller trees of forests. The so-called AFRICAN VIOLET belongs to the GESNERIAD family. See also DOGTOOTH VIOLET.

violin Family of bowed STRINGED INSTRUMENTS consisting of the violin, VIOLA, CELLO, and DOUBLE BASS. The instrument called the violin is the family's highest-pitched member. It has a fretless fingerboard, four strings, and a distinctively shaped wooden body whose "waist" permits freedom of bowing. It is held on the shoulder and bowed with the right hand. It has a wide range of over four octaves. It evolved in Italy in the 16th century from the medieval fiddle and other instruments. Its average proportions were settled by the 17th century, but innovations in the 18th–19th century increased its tonal power. With its brilliance, agility, and singing tone, the violin has been immensely important in Western art music, and it has the largest and most distinguished repertoire of any stringed instrument, including thousands of concertos. From the mid-17th century it has been the foundation of the symphony orchestra, which today usually includes 20–26 violins, and is also widely used in chamber music and as a solo instrument. It is played as a folk instrument in many countries, folk violins being often called fiddles.

Viollet-le-Duc \ˌvē-ə-ˈlā-lə-ˈdük\, **Eugène-Emmanuel** (1814–1879) French GOTHIC REVIVAL architect, restorer, and writer. After studying architecture and training as an archaeologist, he was placed in charge of restoring the abbey church at Vézelay (1840). He assisted in restoring the Sainte-Chapelle (1840) and NOTRE-DAME DE PARIS (1845), and supervised the restoration of many other medieval buildings, including Amiens Cathedral (1849) and the fortifications of Carcassonne (1852). In his later restorations he often added new elements of his own design, for which he was criticized in the 20th century. He is most distinguished for his writings, which include the *Dictionnaire raisonné de l'architecture française du XIe au XVIe siècle* (1854–68) and *Entretiens sur l'architecture* (1858–72). His theories of rational architectural design linked the revivalism of the Romantic period to 20th-century FUNCTIONALISM and influenced the architects of the CHICAGO SCHOOL.

Viollet-le-Duc.
ARCHIVES PHOTOGRAPHIQUES, PARIS

violoncello See CELLO

vipassana \vi-ˈpä-sə-nə\ In THERAVADA Buddhism, a method of insight meditation. It aims at developing understanding of the nature of reality by focusing a sharply concentrated mind on physical and mental processes. The meditator comes to understand, through personal experience, the truths of *dukkha* (suffering), *anicca* (impermanence), and *anatta* (lack of an enduring self). It is a process of mental purification that leads to the abandonment of the roots of unwholesome actions, eradication of ignorance, and attainment of NIRVANA.

viper Any of about 200 species (family Viperidae) of venomous snakes in two subfamilies: Viperinae (Old World vipers of Europe, Asia, and Africa) and Crotalinae (PIT VIPERS). Two long, hollow, venom-injecting fangs attached to the movable bones of the viper's upper jaw can be folded back in the mouth when not in use. Vipers range in length from less than 12 in. (30 cm) to more than 10 ft (3 m). They eat small animals and hunt by striking, then trailing, their prey. Many Old World vipers are terrestrial; a few are arboreal or burrowers. Most bear live young.

Viracocha \ˌbē-rä-ˈkō-chä\ Creator god of the pre-Inca inhabitants of Peru, later assimilated into the Inca pantheon. A god of rain, he was believed to have created the sun on the waters and foam of Lake TITICACA. After forming the rest of the heavens and the earth, he wandered through the world teaching humankind the arts of civilization. At Manta (Ecuador) he walked westward across the Pacific Ocean, promising to return one day. His cult was extremely ancient, and he is probably the weeping god sculpted in the megalithic ruins at TIAHUANACO.

viral diseases \ˈvī-rəl\ Diseases caused by VIRUSES. Long-term IMMUNITY usually follows viral CHILDHOOD DISEASES. The common COLD recurs into adulthood because many different viruses cause its symptoms, and immunity against one does not protect against others. Some viruses mutate fast enough to reinfect people after recovery (see INFLUENZA) or to keep the IMMUNE SYSTEM from fighting them off (see AIDS). Certain CANCERS are caused by viruses. VACCINES can prevent some viral diseases. Most recently developed antiviral drugs work only against specific viruses; antibiotics are ineffective against viral diseases. See also POLIOMYELITIS, SMALLPOX.

Virchow \ˈfir-ḵō\, **Rudolf (Carl)** (1821–1902) German pathologist, anthropologist, and statesman. In 1847 he cofounded the pathology journal now named for him *(Virchows Archiv)*. He held the first chairs of pathological anatomy at the Univs. of Würzburg (1849–56) and Berlin (1856–1902). In 1861 he was elected to the Prussian Diet and founded the Progressive Party. He coined the terms thrombosis and embolism while disproving the theory that PHLEBITIS causes most diseases. His work supported emerging ideas on cell division and metabolism, pointing out that cell division accounted for the multiplication of cells to form tissues. His rejection of the theory that bacteria causes disease and of IGNAZ SEMMELWEIS's advocacy of antisepsis delayed the use of antiseptics. Virchow also founded two anthropological societies and accompanied HEINRICH SCHLIEMANN to TROY (1879) and Egypt (1888).

vireo \ˈvir-ē-ˌō\ Any of 42 species (family Vireonidae) of New World songbirds with a stout, slightly notched, hook-tipped bill that has fine bristles at the base. Vireos are 4–7 in. (10–18 cm) long and are plain gray or greenish, with white or yellow touches. They glean insects from foliage in woodlands and thickets, repeating loud short phrases over and over. The nest is a cuplike structure suspended from a small fork in a branch. The red-eyed vireo *(Vireo olivaceus),* which breeds from southern Canada to Argentina, is 6 in. (15 cm) long and has a black-outlined, white eye stripe that contrasts with its gray crown.

Virgil *or* **Vergil** \ˈvər-jil\ *Latin* **Publius Vergilius Maro** (70–19 BC) Greatest of Roman poets. The well-educated son of a prosperous provincial farmer, Virgil led a quiet life, though he eventually became a member of the circle around Octavian (later Caesar AUGUSTUS) and was patronized by MAECENAS. His poetry reflects the turbulence in Italy during a period of civil war and the subsequent trend toward stability. His first major work, the 10 pastoral *Eclogues* (42–37 BC), may be read as a prophecy of tranquility, and one has even been read as a prophecy of Christianity. The *Georgics* (37–30 BC) point toward a Golden Age in the form of practical goals: the repopulation of rural Italy and the rehabilitation of agriculture. His great epic, the *Aeneid* (begun c. 29 BC, but unfinished at his death), is one of the masterpieces of world literature; a celebration of the founding of Rome by the legendary AENEAS at the request of Augustus, whose consolidation of power in 31–30 BC unified the Roman world, it also explores the themes of war and the pathos of unrequited love. In later centuries his works were regarded in the Roman empire as virtually sacred, and he was taken up reverently by Christians as well, including DANTE, who made Virgil his guide through hell and purgatory. Virgil's influence on European literature is perhaps second only to HOMER's.

Virgin Birth Fundamental doctrine of orthodox Christianity that JESUS had no natural father but was conceived by MARY through the power of the HOLY SPIRIT. Based on the infancy narratives in the GOSPELS of Matthew and Luke, the doctrine was universally accepted in the Christian church by the 2nd century. It remains a basic article of belief in Roman Catholicism, Eastern Orthodoxy, most Protestant churches, and Islam. A corollary of its dogma is the doctrine of Mary's perpetual virginity, accepted by the Orthodox and Roman Catholic churches and by some Lutheran and Anglican theologians. See also IMMACULATE CONCEPTION.

Virgin Islands, British Dependent territory (pop., 1993 est.: 18,000) of the United Kingdom, eastern Caribbean Sea. Part of the island chain of the Virgin Islands, which are divided between the U.K. and the U.S., it consists of four larger islands (Tortola, Anegada, Virgin Gorda, and Jost Van Dyke) and many smaller uninhabited islands. The chief town and port is Road Town on Tortola. The majority of British Virgin Islanders are black or mulatto, the descendants of African slaves. English is the chief language and Protestantism is the chief religion. The islands are generally hilly, and many have lagoons with coral reefs and barrier beaches. Tourism is the mainstay of the economy. For the early history, see VIRGIN ISLANDS OF THE U.S. The islands were an early haunt for pirates, and Tortola was held by Dutch buccaneers until it was taken by English planters in 1666; it was annexed by the British-administered LEEWARD ISLANDS in 1672. The English sugar plantations declined after slavery was abolished in the 19th century. The islands were part of the Colony of the Leeward Islands from 1872 until 1956, when the British Virgin Islands became a separate colony.

Virgin Islands National Park Conservation area, St. John, U.S. VIRGIN ISLANDS. Covering 14,696 acres (5,947 hectares), it has steep mountains, white beaches, and coral reefs. Though most of the tree cover was removed for sugarcane cultivation in the 17th–18th century, the land has reverted to forest. Some 100 species of birds and the only native land mammal, the bat, can be found there. It has remains of ARAWAK Indian villages.

Virgin Islands of the U.S. Unincorporated U.S. island territory, at the eastern end of the Greater ANTILLES, northeastern CARIBBEAN SEA. It consists of the islands of ST. CROIX, St. John, and ST. THOMAS and about 50 small islets. Area: 136 sq mi (352 sq km). Population, 1990 est.: 102,000. Capital: CHARLOTTE AMALIE. About 80% of the population is black or mulatto; most of the remainder are Hispanic (mainly Puerto

Rican) or recent white immigrants. The people are U.S. citizens and elect a nonvoting representative to the U.S. House of Representatives, but they do not vote in U.S. national elections. Languages: English (official), French, Spanish. Religions: Protestantism, Orthodox Judaism. The islands are hilly and surrounded by coral reefs. Tourism dominates the economy. They probably were originally settled by ARAWAK Indians, but they were inhabited by the CARIBS when CHRISTOPHER COLUMBUS landed on St. Croix in 1493. St. Croix was occupied by the Dutch, English, French, and Spanish, and at one time owned by the Knights of Malta. Denmark occupied St. Thomas, St. John, and St. Croix and established them as a Danish colony in 1754. The U.S. purchased the Danish West Indies in 1917 for $25 million and changed the name to the Virgin Islands. They were administered by the U.S. Department of the Interior from 1931. In 1954 the Organic Act of the Virgin Islands created the current governmental structure, and in 1970 the first popularly elected governor took office. The area suffered extensive damage by hurricane in 1995.

virginal *or* **virginals** Small rectangular HARPSICHORD with a single set of strings and a single manual. The derivation of its name is uncertain. The virginal's strings run parallel to the keyboard, which occupies only a portion of the longer side. Combination virginals include a smaller portable virginal that can be placed on top of the larger keyboard to create a two-manual instrument. The virginal was particularly popular in 16th–17th-century England, where much music was written for it by W. BYRD, T. MORLEY, THOMAS WEELKES, and others.

English virginal (with jack rail removed) made by Robert Hatley, London, 1664; in the Benton-Fletcher Collection, the National Trust, Hampstead, London.

FROM THE BENTON-FLETCHER COLLECTION AT THE NATIONAL TRUST PROPERTY, FENTON HOUSE, HAMPSTEAD, LONDON

Virginia State (pop., 1997 est.; 6,734,000), eastern U.S. Located on the central Atlantic seaboard, it covers an area of 40,767 sq mi (105,586 sq km); its capital is RICHMOND. The coastal plain, also known as the Tidewater, lies in the east, the Piedmont, in mid-state, and the BLUE RIDGE and APPALACHIAN MOUNTAINS in the west. The POTOMAC, SHENANDOAH, JAMES, and ROANOKE rivers flow through the state. It was inhabited by American Indians when futile attempts were made by English navigator Sir WALTER RALEIGH to found settlements 1584–87. Britain's first American colony was founded there in 1607 at JAMESTOWN. On the eve of the AMERICAN REVOLUTION, it was the largest of the 13 colonies and one of the first to resist the British STAMP ACT. Its citizens were among the leaders of the Revolutionary period and later contributed four of the country's first five presidents. In 1788 it became the 10th state to ratify the U.S. Constitution. Though slavery was outlawed, it continued to be an important part of Virginia's economy, and helped precipitate NAT TURNER's insurrection (1831). It passed an ordinance of secession in 1861, but the western part of the state refused to secede: it split off to become West Virginia in 1863. Virginia, whose capital of Richmond was also the capital of the Confederacy, bore the brunt of military action during the AMERICAN CIVIL WAR. It was readmitted to the Union in 1870. Strife over state debt took over political life for the next decades, but after World War I the state's prosperity increased. World War II brought thousands to its military camps and caused the NORFOLK area to boom. The federal government is Virginia's largest employer, while manufacturing is the second largest. Its port of HAMPTON ROADS is one of the nation's leading ports. Tourism is important; its many historical sites include Colonial WILLIAMSBURG, GEORGE WASHINGTON'S MOUNT VERNON, THOMAS JEFFERSON'S MONTICELLO, the Civil War battlefields, and Gen. ROBERT E. LEE's house, now in Arlington National Cemetery. The College of WILLIAM AND MARY (founded 1693) is the country's second oldest college; the University of VIRGINIA was largely the creation of T. Jefferson.

Virginia, University of Public university founded in Charlottesville by THOMAS JEFFERSON. It was chartered in 1819 and opened in 1825. Jefferson designed its famously beautiful campus and buildings, planned the curriculum, and selected the faculty. By the time of the Civil War, the university was second only to Harvard in size of faculty and student body. It first admitted women in 1970. In addition to its College of Arts and Sciences, it has schools of architecture, education, engineering and applied sciences, and nursing, as well as a business school, a graduate school, and schools of law and medicine. Total enrollment is about 22,000.

Virginia and Kentucky Resolutions Measures passed by the legislatures of Virginia and Kentucky in 1798–99 as a protest against the ALIEN AND SEDITION ACTS. Drafted by JAMES MADISON and THOMAS JEFFERSON (though this was not known at the time), they protested limitations on civil liberties and declared the right of states to decide on the constitutionality of federal legislation. Though their authors applied the resolutions to the specific issues of the day, Southern states later used the measures to support the theories of NULLIFICATION and SECESSION.

Virginia Beach City (pop., 1996 est.: 430,000), southeastern Virginia. It is situated on the Atlantic Ocean and CHESAPEAKE BAY. Founded in 1887, it developed as a resort after a railroad was built linking it with NORFOLK. After World War I it became an important base in the national coastal defense system. In 1963 it and the former Princess Anne county merged to become the City of Virginia Beach. Its economy is based on tourism and military installations. Cape HENRY Memorial is in the city and the Cape Henry Lighthouse (1791) is nearby.

Virginia Declaration of Rights Measure adopted by the colony of Virginia (June 12, 1776). Drafted by GEORGE MASON, it stated that "all men are by nature equally free and independent and have certain inherent rights" and specified such civil liberties as freedom of the press and freedom of religion. It became a model for the BILL OF RIGHTS.

Virginia deer See WHITE-TAILED DEER

Virginia Polytechnic Institute and State University Public institution of higher learning in Blacksburg, Va., western of Roanoke. Founded in 1872, it is a comprehensive, land-grant university. It comprises colleges of agriculture and life sciences, architecture and urban studies, arts and sciences, business, education, engineering, forestry and wildlife resources, human resources, and veterinary medicine. It operates 12 agricultural stations throughout the state. Total enrollment is about 25,000.

Virgo \'vər-gō\ (Latin: "Virgin, Maiden") In astronomy, the constellation lying between Leo and Libra; in ASTROLOGY, the sixth sign of the ZODIAC, governing approximately the period August 23–September 22. Its symbol is a maiden carrying a sheaf of wheat. She has been identified with fertility goddesses such as ISHTAR or with PERSEPHONE.

Virgo cluster Closest large CLUSTER OF GALAXIES at a distance of about 50 million light-years in the direction of the constellation Virgo. Its gravitational influence has decelerated the motion of the LOCAL GROUP away from the cluster center by about 125 mi/second (200 km/second) since the BIG BANG. About 200 bright galaxies and thousands of faint ones reside in the cluster. The giant elliptical galaxy M87 (or Virgo A), near its center, is one of the strongest radio sources in the sky and also a powerful X-ray source. Images of M87's ACTIVE GALACTIC NUCLEUS, obtained in 1994, revealed gas orbiting at such high speeds that astronomers believe a supermassive BLACK HOLE must be present.

virion \'vī-rē-ˌän\ Entire VIRUS particle, consisting of an outer protein shell (called a capsid) and an inner core of NUCLEIC ACID (either RNA or DNA). The core gives the virus infectivity, and the capsid provides specificity (i.e., determines which organisms the virus can infect). In virions whose capsids are further encased by a fatty membrane, the virion can be inactivated by exposure to a solvent such as ether or chloroform. Many virions have capsids with 20 triangular faces and the nucleic acid densely coiled within; others have capsids consisting of surface spikes, with the nucleic acid loosely coiled within. Virions of most plant viruses are rod-shaped.

viroid \'vī-ˌrȯid\ Infectious particle that is smaller than any of the known VIRUSES. The particle consists of an extremely small circular RNA molecule that lacks the protein coat of a virus. Viroids appear to be transmitted mechanically from one cell to another through cellular debris. They are of much interest because of their subviral nature and their unknown mode of action. Viroids are agents of certain plant diseases; whether they occur in animal cells is uncertain.

virology \vī-'rä-lə-jē\ Branch of microbiology that deals with the study of VIRUSES. Viruses were not closely examined until 1892, when a Russian bacteriologist observed that the agent of tobacco mosaic disease could pass through a filter that did not permit the passage of bacteria. Modern virology began in the early 20th century, when the existence of bacteriophages was discovered. Direct visualization of viruses became possible after the electron microscope was introduced (c. 1940).

virtual reality Use of computer modeling and simulation to enable a person to interact with an artificial three-dimensional visual or other sensory environment. A computer-generated environment simulates reality by means of interactive devices that send and receive information and are worn as goggles, headsets, gloves, or body suits. The illusion of being in the created environment (telepresence) is accomplished by motion sensors that pick up the user's movements and adjust his or her view accordingly, usually in real time. The basis of the technology emerged in the 1960s in simulators that taught how to fly planes, drive tanks, shoot artillery, and generally perform in combat. It came of commercial age in the 1980s and is now used in games, exhibits, and aerospace simulators. It has potential for use in many fields, including entertainment, medicine and biotechnology, engineering, design, and marketing.

virtue Practical dispositions in conformity with standards of excellence or with principles of practical reason. The seven cardinal virtues of the Christian tradition include the four "natural," or cardinal, virtues, those inculcated in the old pagan world that spring from the common endowment of humanity, and the three "theological" virtues, those specifically prescribed in Christianity and arising as special gifts from God. The natural virtues are prudence, temperance, fortitude, and justice; this enumeration, said to go back to Socrates, is found in Plato and Aristotle. To these St. Paul added the theological virtues of faith, hope, and love—virtues which, in Christian teaching, do not originate naturally in humanity but are instead imparted by God through Christ and then practiced by the believer. See also virtue ethics.

virtue ethics Approach to ethics that takes the notion of virtue (often conceived as excellence) as fundamental. Virtue ethics is primarily concerned with traits of character that are essential to human flourishing, not with the enumeration of duties. It falls somewhat outside the traditional dichotomy between deontological ethics and consequentialism: It agrees with consequentialism that the criterion of an action's being morally right or wrong lies in its relation to an end that has intrinsic value, but more closely resembles deontological ethics in its view that morally right actions are constitutive of the end itself and not mere instrumental means to the end. See also eudaemonism.

Virunga Mountains \vē-ˈrüŋ-gä\ Volcanic range, eastern central Africa. Located north of Lake Kivu, it extends for about 50 mi (80 km) along the borders of Congo (Zaire), Rwanda, and Uganda. Of its eight major volcanic peaks, the highest is Karisimbi, while Nyiragongo is at the western end of the chain; in 1861 John Hanning Speke was the first European to spot them. Parts of the range are in Virunga National Park, Volcanoes National Park (NW Rwanda), and Gorilla National Park (Uganda).

Virunga National Park *formerly* **Albert National Park** Game preserve and gorilla sanctuary, northeastern Congo (Zaire). Established in 1925, it has an area of 3,012 sq mi (7,800 sq km). Its southern tip touches the northern shore of Lake Kivu and much of its central region is occupied by Lake Edward. The Virunga Mtns. lie between the two lakes.

virus Microscopic, simple infectious agent that can multiply only in living cells of animals, plants, or bacteria. Viruses are much smaller than bacteria, and consist of a single- or double-stranded nucleic acid (DNA or RNA) surrounded by a protein shell called a capsid; some viruses also have an outer envelope composed of lipids and proteins. They vary in shape. The two main classes are RNA viruses (see retrovirus) and DNA viruses. Outside of a living cell, a virus is an inactive particle, but within an appropriate host cell it becomes active, capable of taking over the cell's metabolic machinery for the production of new virus particles (virions). Some animal viruses produce latent infections, in which the virus persists in a quiet state, becoming periodically active in acute episodes, as in the case of the herpes simplex viruses. An animal can respond to a viral infection in various ways, including fever, secretion of interferon, and attack by the immune system. Many human diseases, including influenza, the common cold, and AIDS, as well as many economically important plant and animal diseases, are caused by viruses. Successful vaccines have been developed to combat such viral diseases as measles, mumps, poliomyelitis, smallpox, and rubella. Drug therapy is generally not useful in controlling established viral infections, since

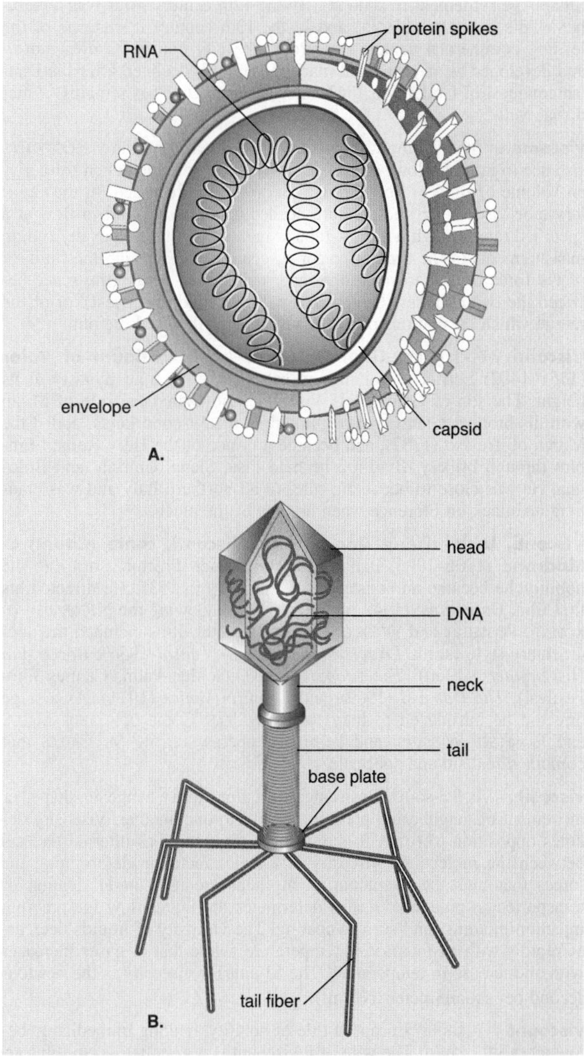

A. Influenza virus. The influenza virus possesses both a protein shell (capsid) and a lipid and protein envelope. The protein spikes of the envelope facilitate adherence and entry into the host cell. The capsid proteins determine the influenza type (A, B, C), and the highly variable proteins of the spikes and envelope determine the different strains within each type. B. Bacteriophage (bacterial virus). This bacteriophage has a capsid shaped like an icosahedron (with 20 sides). The tail fibers attach the virus to the bacterium, bringing the base plate into contact with the surface. The tail contracts and DNA from the head is injected into the host.

drugs that inhibit viral development also inhibit the functions of the host cell. See also adenovirus, arbovirus, bacteriophage, picornavirus, plant virus, poxvirus.

virus, computer See computer virus

Visayan Islands \vi-ˈsī-ən\ Group of islands, central Philippines. Covering 23,944 sq mi (62,015 sq km), they are surrounded by the Visayan, Samar, and Camotes seas. The main islands are Bohol, Cebu, Leyte, Masbate, Negros, Panay, and Samar. These islands and their smaller neighbors make up the central group of the Philippine archipelago. Agriculture and fishing are important. The major urban centers are Cebu city on Cebu, and Iloilo city on Panay.

Visby City (pop., 1990 est.: 21,000), southeastern Sweden. Located on the northwestern coast of the island of Gotland, it was the site of a

Stone Age settlement c. 2000 BC. By the 12th century AD it was a member of the HANSEATIC LEAGUE, and in the 13th century it was one of the leading commercial centers of Europe; the city coined its own money and developed an international maritime code. It declined after the Danish conquest of Gotland in 1361. A seaside resort, it has remains of medieval walls.

viscometer \vis-'kä-mə-tər\ Instrument for measuring the VISCOSITY (resistance to internal flow) of a FLUID. In one type, the time taken for a given volume of fluid to flow through an opening is recorded. In the capillary-tube viscometer, the pressure needed to force the fluid to flow at a specified rate through a narrow tube is measured. Other types depend on measurements of the time taken for a sphere to fall through the fluid, or of the force needed to rotate the inner cylinder of a pair (the space between the two cylinders being filled with the fluid under test), or of the rate at which oscillations of a disk vibrating in the fluid die out.

Visconti \vēs-'kōn-tē\, **Gian Galeazzo** *known as* **Count of Valor** (1351–1402) Leader of Milan who brought the Visconti dynasty to its height. The son of Galeazzo II Visconti, who shared the rule of Milan with his brother, Gian Galeazzo united all the Visconti lands, added the March of Treviso (1387), and became a prince of the Holy Roman Empire through bribery. By 1402 he held Pisa, Siena, Umbria, and Bologna. He was close to becoming ruler of all northern Italy and was planning an attack on Florence when he died of the plague.

Visconti, Luchino *orig.* **Don Luchino Visconti, conte (Count) di Modrone** (1906–1976) Italian film and theater director. Born into the nobility, he became an assistant to JEAN RENOIR in 1935. He directed his first film, *Ossessione* (1942), in a style foreshadowing the NEOREALISM of ROBERTO ROSSELLINI and VITTORIO DE SICA. His later films included the documentary-style drama *La terra trema* (1948), *Senso* (1954), *Rocco and His Brothers* (1960), *The Leopard* (1963, Golden Palm, Cannes Film Festival), *The Damned* (1969), and *Death in Venice* (1971). As a stage director, he introduced to Italy works by JEAN COCTEAU, ARTHUR MILLER, and TENNESSEE WILLIAMS, and he staged operas starring M. CALLAS that combined realism and spectacle.

viscosity \vis-'kä-sə-tē\ Resistance of a fluid to a change in shape, or movement of neighboring portions relative to one another. Viscosity denotes opposition to FLOW. It may also be thought of as internal FRICTION between the molecules. Viscosity is a major factor in determining the forces that must be overcome when fluids are used in lubrication or transported in pipelines. It also determines the liquid flow in spraying, injection molding, and surface coating. The viscosity of liquids decreases rapidly with an increase in temperature, while that of gases increases with an increase in temperature. The SI unit for viscosity is the newton-second per square meter ($N\text{-}s/m^2$).

viscount \'vī-ˌkau̇nt\ European title of nobility, ranking immediately below a COUNT, or earl. The wife of a viscount is a viscountess. In the Carolingian period, the *vicecomes* were deputies or lieutenants of the counts *(comes),* whose official powers they exercised by delegation. In the 11th century most of Normandy was divided into *vicomtés,* but the viscountcy was not introduced into the English peerage until nearly 400 years after the Norman conquest.

Viscount Melville Sound \'vī-ˌkau̇nt-'mel-ˌvil\ *formerly* **Melville Sound** Body of water, northern Canada. Located in the ARCTIC ARCHIPELAGO, between MELVILLE and VICTORIA islands, it is 250 mi (400 km) long and 100 mi (160 km) wide. Its discovery, when reached from the east (1819–20) by William E. Parry and from the west (1850–54) by Robert McClure, proved the existence of the NORTHWEST PASSAGE. The sound is navigable only under favorable weather conditions.

vise Device consisting of two parallel jaws for holding a workpiece. One of the jaws is fixed, and the other can be moved by a SCREW, LEVER, or CAM. Vises used for holding a workpiece during hand operations (such as filing, hammering, or sawing) are usually permanently bolted to a bench. In vises designed to hold metallic workpieces, the faces of the jaws are hardened steel plates, often removable, with teeth that grip the workpiece. Woodworking vises have smooth jaws, often of wood, and rely on friction alone rather than on teeth.

Vishnu \'vish-nü\ Principal Hindu deity worshiped as the protector and preserver of the world and restorer of DHARMA. He is known chiefly through his AVATARS, particularly RAMA and KRISHNA. In theory, he manifests himself anytime he is needed to fight evil, and his appearances are innumerable, but in practice 10 are most common. His various names, numbering about 1,000, are repeated as acts of devotion by his worshipers.

Visigoths \'vi-zə-ˌgäths\ Western division of the GOTHS. Separated from the OSTROGOTHS (E Goths) in the 4th century AD, they were driven from Dacia by the HUNS (376) and crossed the Danube into the Roman empire. Oppressed by Roman taxation, they revolted and plundered the Balkan provinces, defeating VALENS and his army at the Battle of ADRIANOPLE (378). THEODOSIUS I settled them in Moesia (382) to defend the frontier. Converted to Arian Christianity, they left Moesia in 395 under ALARIC and invaded Greece and Italy, sacking Rome (410) and settling in southern Gaul and Spain (415). Recalled from Spain by Constantius III, they lost their first king, Theodoric I, in a battle against ATTILA (451). They were federates of Rome until King Euric declared independence (475). He extended their kingdom from the Loire to the Pyrenees and the lower Rhône, including most of Spain. In 507 they were defeated by the FRANKS under CLOVIS; retaining only SEPTIMANIA (a strip from the Pyrenees to the Rhône), they held it and much of Spain until defeated by the Muslims in 711.

vision See PHOTORECEPTION

vision, computer See COMPUTER VISION

vision quest Among American Indian peoples of the eastern woodlands and Great Plains, an essential rite of PASSAGE for adolescent boys. The youth was sent out from the camp on a solitary vigil involving fasting and prayer in order to gain some sign, often through a dream, of the presence and nature of his guardian spirit. Upon receiving these visions he returned home and communicated them to a SHAMAN or elder, who helped interpret them.

Visistadvaita \vi-'shish-täd-'vī-tə\ Principal school of VEDANTA. Its seminal figure was RAMANUJA, the first Vedanta thinker to establish as the cornerstone of his system the identification of a personal God with the BRAHMAN of the UPANISHADS. For him, soul and matter depended on God for their existence. Exclusive devotion to God can elicit his grace, assisting the devotee in gaining release from the cycle of rebirth. After Ramanuja, a schism developed over the role of grace, giving rise to different schools. The spread of Visistadvaita was important in the devotional renaissance of VAISHNAVISM. In southern India the philosophy remains a major intellectual influence.

Vistula River \'vis-chə-lə\ *Polish* **Wisla** \'vē-swä\ River, Poland. It rises on the northern slope of the CARPATHIAN MTNS. in southwestern Poland, flows in a curve through WARSAW and Torun, then empties into the BALTIC SEA at GDANSK. Most of its 651 mi (1,047 km) are navigable. The nation's largest river, its tributaries include the BUG and DUNAJEC rivers.

visual-field defect Blind spot (scotoma) or area in the normal field of vision. It may be persistent, or temporary and shifting, as in a MIGRAINE aura. The field may narrow, as in GLAUCOMA. The normally small blind spot corresponding to the point where the optic nerve enters the EYE can enlarge if fluid accumulates at that point (papilledema). METHANOL or QUININE poisoning, diseases of the nerve sheaths, deficiency diseases, and atherosclerosis (see ARTERIOSCLEROSIS) can also cause blind spots. TUMORS pressing on the optic nerves in different locations can cause loss of different halves or quarters of the visual field of each eye. See also MACULAR DEGENERATION.

visual purple See RHODOPSIN

visualization, scientific See SCIENTIFIC VISUALIZATION

vitamin Organic compound required in small amounts in the diet to maintain normal metabolic functions. The term "vitamine" (1911) was changed to "vitamin" when it was realized that not all vitamins were AMINES (i.e., not all contained nitrogen). Many vitamins act as or are converted to COENZYMES. They neither provide energy nor are incorporated into tissues. Water-soluble vitamins (VITAMIN B COMPLEX, VITAMIN C) are excreted quickly. Fat-soluble vitamins (VITAMIN A, VITAMIN D, VITAMIN E, and VITAMIN K) require BILE salts for absorption and are stored in the body. The normal functions of many vitamins are known. Deficiency of specific vitamins can lead to diseases (including BERIBERI, NEURAL TUBE DEFECT, PERNICIOUS ANEMIA, RICKETS, and SCURVY). Excess amounts, especially of fat-soluble vitamins, can also be dangerous: too much vitamin A causes liver damage, an effect not seen with beta-carotene, which the body converts into vitamin A. Several vitamins are now known to support the IMMUNE SYSTEM. Most vitamins are adequately supplied by a balanced diet, but people with higher requirements may need supplements.

vitamin A Fat-soluble ALCOHOL, most abundant in fish and especially in fish-liver oils. The chief vitamin A is retinol. It is not found in plants, but many vegetables and fruits contain CAROTENES, which are readily converted in the body to vitamin A. It functions directly in vision, especially night vision. A derivative, retinal, is a component of the visual PIGMENTS, including RHODOPSIN, in the RETINA. Humans require vitamin A in very small amounts (1 mg a day is recommended for adults). Unlike carotenes, it is toxic in large amounts and is readily destroyed by exposure to heat, light, or air.

vitamin B complex Water-soluble organic compounds with loosely similar properties, distribution in natural sources, and physiological functions. Most are COENZYMES, and all appear essential to the metabolic processes of all animal life. They include THIAMINE (B_1), RIBOFLAVIN (B_2), NIACIN (B_3), pyridoxine (B_6), PANTOTHENIC ACID, FOLIC ACID, BIOTIN, and cyanocobalamin (B_{12}); some authorities also include CHOLINE, carnitine, lipoic acid, myoinositol, and *para*-aminobenzoic acid. Vitamin B_6 is needed for metabolism of amino acids and prevention of skin and nerve disorders. Good sources are vegetable fats, whole-grain cereals, legumes, yeast, muscle meats, liver, and fish. Vitamin B_{12} prevents PERNICIOUS ANEMIA and is involved in nucleic-acid synthesis, fat metabolism, conversion of carbohydrate to fat, and metabolism of amino acids. Sources are milk, meat, liver, eggs, and fish.

vitamin C *or* **ascorbic acid** Water-soluble organic compound resembling a six-carbon SUGAR, important in animal METABOLISM. Most animals produce it in their bodies, but humans, other primates, and guinea pigs need it in the diet to prevent SCURVY. How it works is not clearly understood, but it is essential in COLLAGEN synthesis, wound healing, blood-vessel maintenance, IRON absorption, metabolism of certain AMINO ACIDS, synthesis or release of ADRENAL GLAND HORMONES, and IMMUNITY. It can shorten and reduce the symptoms of the COMMON COLD and is now widely recognized to prevent colds as well. It works as an ANTIOXIDANT in the body and is used as a preservative. It is easily destroyed by heat or oxygen. Excellent sources are citrus fruits and dark-green vegetables.

vitamin D Any of a group of fat-soluble ALCOHOLS (ergosterol, cholecalciferol, ergocalciferol) important in CALCIUM METABOLISM in animals to form strong bones and teeth and prevent RICKETS and OSTEOPOROSIS. In humans, vitamin D is formed by action of sunlight on sterols (see STEROID) in the SKIN. It occurs in fish-liver oils and is added to margarine, milk, and cereals for the benefit of those in nontropical areas who may not get enough sunlight in winter. About 10 micrograms/day appear adequate for children. Because the body cannot excrete it, prolonged high intake can cause a toxic reaction including fatigue, nausea, and abnormal calcium accumulation.

vitamin E *or* **tocopherol** \tō-ˈkä-fə-ˌrōl\ Any of a group of related fat-soluble organic compounds (α-, β-, γ-, and δ-tocopherol) with two rings and 26–29 carbon atoms. Alpha, the most potent, occurs in certain plant oils and leaves of green vegetables. Vitamin E acts as an ANTIOXIDANT in body tissues and may prolong life by slowing oxidative destruction of MEMBRANES. Certain rodents require it for normal reproduction. Besides uses in foods and in nutritional research and supplements, tocopherols are used to retard rancidity in FATS, especially vegetable oils.

vitamin K Any of several fat-soluble compounds essential for the clotting of blood. A deficiency of vitamin K in the body leads to an increase in clotting time. In 1929 a previously unrecognized fat-soluble substance present in green leafy vegetables was found to be required for coagulation of the blood; its letter name comes from Danish *koagulation.* A pure form was isolated and analyzed structurally in 1939; several related compounds having vitamin-K activity have since been isolated and synthesized. Vitamin K1, the compound recognized in 1939, is synthesized by plants, whereas vitamin K2 is of microbial origin and is the important form in mammalian tissue. All other forms of vitamin K are converted to vitamin K2 in the body. Besides the natural compounds, many synthetic compounds having vitamin-K activity are used to decrease blood-clotting time.

Vitellius \vi-ˈtel-ē-əs\, **Aulus** (AD 15–69) Roman emperor (69), the last of NERO's three short-lived successors. He was commander of the Lower German army when Nero died, and was proclaimed emperor by his troops. When he marched on Italy, Otho, a rival emperor, committed suicide. Vitellius entered Rome but had to contend with VESPASIAN, whose army had also proclaimed him emperor, and his troops lost to Vespasian's. Vitellius' PRAETORIAN GUARD prevented him from abdicating, whereupon his own soldiers murdered him.

Viti Levu \ˈvē-tē-ˈlā-vü\ Island (pop., 1986 est.: 341,000), Fiji, South Pacific Ocean. It has an area of 4,011 sq mi (10,388 sq km). SUVA, the Fijian capital, is situated on the island's southeastern coast. It was sighted by Capt. WILLIAM BLIGH in 1789. It is split by a central mountain range which also divides the island into wet and dry sections. Mount Tomanivi, the highest point in Fiji, rises to 4,341 ft (1,323 m). Islanders grow sugar, pineapples, cotton, rice, and tobacco. There is a goldfield in the northern central part of the island.

vitiligo \ˌvit-ᵊl-ˈī-gō\ *or* **leukoderma** Skin disorder manifested by smooth, white spots on various parts of the body. Though the pigment-making cells of the skin, or melanocytes, are structurally intact, they have lost the ability to synthesize the pigment. The reason for the condition is unclear. Individuals with vitiligo (about 1% of the adult population) are usually in good general health, but vitiligo presents a cosmetic problem that can be serious in dark-skinned individuals. Normal skin color rarely returns, and there is no known cure.

Vitória \vē-ˈtōr-yə\ City (pop., 1991: 258,000), eastern Brazil. Located on the western side of Vitória island in Espírito Santo bay, it was founded by the Portuguese in 1535, and was made a provincial capital in 1823. It was Brazil's leading iron-ore port until the 1960s. Its economy is based now on textile factories, sugar refineries, and other small manufacturing plants as well as on the shipment of coffee. It is the seat of a university (founded 1961).

Vitoria \vē-ˈtōr-ē-ə\ City (pop., 1995 est.: 215,000), capital of BASQUE COUNTRY autonomous community, northeastern Spain. Founded as Victoriacum by the Visigothic king Leovigild in 581, it was granted a charter in the 12th century. In 1200 Alfonso VIII captured it and incorporated it into his kingdom. In 1813 it was the scene of a battle in which allied forces under English Gen. Arthur Wellesley (later duke of WELLINGTON) defeated the French, driving them from Spain and leading to the end of the PENINSULAR WAR. A rapidly growing manufacturing center, it retains several medieval buildings.

vitriol, oil of See SULFURIC ACID

Vitruvius \və-ˈtrü-vē-əs\ *in full* **Marcus Vitruvius Pollio** (fl. 1st century BC) Roman architect, engineer, and author of the celebrated treatise *De architectura,* a handbook for Roman architects. Little is known of his life except what can be gathered from his writings. The treatise is divided into 10 books covering almost every aspect of architecture and city planning. His wish was to preserve the Classical Greek tradition in the design of temples and public buildings, and his prefaces contain many pessimistic remarks about the architecture of the time. His work was the chief authority on ancient CLASSICAL ARCHITECTURE throughout the antique revival of the Renaissance, the classical phase of the baroque, and the Neoclassical period.

Vitsyebsk \ˈvēt-syipsk\ *or* **Vitebsk** \ˈvē-tipsk\ City (pop., 1996 est.: 365,000), northeastern Belarus. First mentioned in 1021, it was a major fortress and trading center and was the chief town of an independent principality for some 200 years. It passed to Lithuania in 1320, later to Poland, and then to Russia in 1772. Over the years it suffered destruction by the Poles, the Swedes, Napoleon in 1812, and the Germans in World War II. A major industrial center, it produces machine tools, electrical instruments, and a range of consumer goods.

Vittorini \ˌvēt-ˈtō-ˈrē-nē\, **Elio** (1908–1966) Italian novelist, translator, and critic. He left school at 17 and later learned English while working as a proofreader. He became, with CESARE PAVESE, a pioneer in translating the works of U.S. and English writers into Italian. His novels of NEOREALISM mirror Italy's experience of fascism and the social, political, and spiritual agonies of the 20th century. *Conversation in Sicily* (1941), which clearly expresses his antifascist feelings, is his most important novel.

Vivaldi \vi-ˈväl-dē\, **Antonio (Lucio)** (1678–1741) Italian composer. Taught violin by his father, he was ordained a priest in 1703, and became known as the "Red Priest" for his red hair. He spent most of his career teaching violin and leading the orchestra at a Venetian girls' orphanage. After c. 1718 he became more involved in opera as both composer and impresario. His concertos were highly influential in setting the genre's three-movement (fast–slow–fast) form, with a returning theme *(ritornello)* for the larger group set off by contrasting material for the soloists, and he popularized such effects as pizzicato and muting. His *L'estro armonico* (1711), a collection of concerti grossi, attracted international attention. His *La stravaganza* (c. 1714) was eagerly awaited, as were its successors, including *The Four Seasons* (1725). In all he wrote over 500 concertos. His most popular sacred vocal work is the *Gloria* (1708). Though often accused of repeating himself, Vivaldi was in fact highly imaginative, and his works exercised a strong influence on J.S. BACH.

Vivarini family \ˌvē-vä-ˈrē-nē\ Family of 15th-century Venetian painters. Antonio Vivarini (c. 1415–c. 1480) collaborated from 1441 with his brother-in-law, Giovanni d'Alemagna (died 1450), on altarpieces, four of which survive in the churches of San Zaccaria (1443) and San Pantalon (1444), and on a large three-part canvas in the Accademia (1446). Their large-scale polyptychs feature stiff, archaic figures and heavily ornamented frames. In 1447–50 they lived in Padua and worked with ANDREA MANTEGNA on a cycle of frescoes for the Church of the Eremitani (destroyed in World War II). Antonio's younger brother and pupil Bartolomeo (1432?–after 1500) collaborated with Antonio after 1450. His work, more progressive than his brother's, was imitative of Mantegna. From 1459 he worked independently. His most distinguished works include the altarpieces in the churches of SS. Giovanni e Paolo (1473), Santa Maria dei Frari (1474), and San Giovanni Bragora (1478) and in the Accademia (1477). Antonio's son Alvise (c. 1445–c. 1505) came under the influence of the BELLINI FAMILY, with whom he worked on paintings (now lost) for the Doges' Palace (1488). The overlapping careers of Antonio, Bartolomeo, and Alvise recapitulate the overall development of Venetian painting from the late Gothic period to the threshold of the High Renaissance.

Vivekananda \ˈvē-vā-kə-ˈnən-də\ *orig.* **Narendranath Datta** (1863–1902) Hindu spiritual leader and reformer. Born in Calcutta (now Kolkata), he received a Western education. He later joined the BRAHMO SAMAJ and became the most notable disciple of RAMAKRISHNA. By stressing the universal and humanistic aspects of the VEDA and emphasizing service over dogma, he attempted to infuse vigor into Hinduism. He was a motivating force behind the VEDANTA movement in the United States and England, lecturing and proselytizing in both countries. In 1897 he founded the Ramakrishna Mission, which carries out extensive educational and philanthropic work in India and expounds Vedanta in Western countries.

vivisection Operation on a living animal for experimental rather than healing purposes; more broadly, all experimentation on live animals. It is opposed by many as cruelty and supported by others on the ground that it advances medicine; a middle position is to oppose unnecessarily cruel practices, use alternatives when possible, and restrict experiments to necessary medical research (as opposed, for example, to cosmetics testing). Surgery on animals without anesthesia was once common; many people, most significantly RENE DESCARTES, claimed that animals did not really feel pain. Testing chemicals on animals to find the lethal dose still occurs despite alternative methods (computer simulations, TISSUE CULTURE tests). An antivivisection movement in the late 19th century broadened its scope to include prevention of all cruelty to animals and later gave rise to the animal rights movement.

vizier \və-ˈzir\ *Arabic* **wazir** Chief minister of the ABBASID caliphs, and later a high government official in various Muslim countries. The office was originally held and defined by the BARMAKIDS in the 8th century; they acted as the caliph's and later the sultan's representative to the public. In the OTTOMAN EMPIRE, the title could be held by several people at once; under MEHMED II the position of grand vizier, the absolute representative of the sultan, was created. In pharaonic Egypt, a vizier was a civil officer who held viceregal power.

Vlad III Tepes \ˈvläd...ˈtse-pesh\ *or* **Vlad the Impaler** (1431?–1476) Ruler of WALACHIA (1448, 1456–62, 1476). He succeeded his father, Vlad II Dracul ("dragon"). He gained the throne decisively in 1456 with the help of JANOS HUNYADI. He fought the Turkish invasions of Walachia and built many fortifications to hold them back, including the fortress of Poenari with its stairway of 1,400 steps. He was imprisoned 12 years in Hungary by MATTHIAS I, from whom he had sought aid after being overthrown by the Ottomans. He was killed by an Ottoman-supported prince. Though an effective administrator and military leader, he was notorious for cruel depravities. In establishing his domination over the Walachian nobility, he apparently tortured to death 20,000 men, women, and children by impaling them upright on thin stakes. His epithet Dracula ("son of the dragon") was used by BRAM STOKER for the Romanian vampire count in his famous novel.

Vladimir I \ˈvla-də-ˌmər,vlə-ˈdē-mir\, **St.** *Russian* **Vladimir Svyatoslavich** (956?–1015) Grand prince of Kiev (980–1015). He became prince of Novgorod in 970, and after his father's death in 972 he seized Kiev from his brother. He consolidated the Kievan realm from Ukraine to the Baltic Sea by 980 and fortified its frontiers against Baltic and Eastern nomads. Originally a pagan, Vladimir made a pact (c. 987) with BASIL II, providing him with military aid in exchange for marriage to Basil's sister and promising to convert to Christianity. He adopted the Byzantine rite for his realm, forcibly converting Kiev and Novgorod and ordering pagan idols cast into the Dnieper River.

Vladimir-Suzdal school \ˈvla-də-mər-ˈsüz-dəl\ School of Russian medieval mural and icon painting, with origins in Kievan Byzantine art, that flourished in the 12th–13th century around the cities of Vladimir and Suzdal, in northeastern Russia. Its works, while maintaining Byzantine illusionistic modeling and solid proportions that lack the elongation that characterizes all later Russian art, move toward a more Russian expression: the emotion is intensely ascetic, the anatomy of the figures is uncertain and the hands are typically small, and the facial expressions portray a range of emotions. This brilliant artistic development ended with the mid-13th-century Mongol invasions.

"The Archangel Michael," icon by an anonymous artist of the Vladimir-Suzdal school, egg tempera on panel, c. 1300; in the State Tretyakov Gallery, Moscow.
NOVOSTI PRESS AGENCY, MOSCOW

Vladivostok \ˌvla-də-və-ˈstäk, ˌvla-də-ˈväs-ˌtäk\ Seaport city (pop., 1999 est.: 613,100), southeastern Russia in Asia. Founded in 1860 as a Russian military outpost, it became the main Russian naval base on the Pacific Ocean in 1872. It became a free commercial port in 1904 and grew rapidly as a military base after the RUSSIAN REVOLUTION OF 1917. During the Soviet era it was the home of the Pacific fleet; its military importance was such that it was closed to foreign shipping from the late 1950s. After the collapse of the U.S.S.R. in 1991, it reemerged as a commercial port, with such industries as ship repair and fish and meat processing. It is the eastern terminus of the TRANS-SIBERIAN RAILROAD and the cultural center of the Russian Far East.

Vlaminck \vlə-ˈmaŋk\, **Maurice de** (1876–1958) French painter. Noted for his brash temperament as well as his flair for landscapes, he began in 1900 to share a studio with ANDRE DERAIN, a friend from childhood. In 1905 he first exhibited at the Salon des Indépendants. His experiments with pure, intense color applied in thick daubs earned him association with FAUVISM, but by 1908 he had turned to painting landscapes of thickly applied whites, grays, and deep blues, and his style moved closer to that of PAUL CEZANNE. He began c. 1915 to develop a personal, strongly stated style that placed him solidly in the realm of French EXPRESSIONISM.

Vlissingen \ˈvli-siŋ-ə\ Seaport city (pop., 2001 est.: 44,776), southwestern Netherlands. As a medieval trading town, its importance lay in its strategic position to ANTWERP. In 1572 it was the first Netherlands town to rebel against Spanish rule. It was turned into a naval base by NAPOLEON during the French occupation (1795–1814). It was heavily damaged during World War II when the area was flooded in 1944 by the

Allies to clear the way to Antwerp. Since rebuilt, it is now a commercial port, fishing harbor, seaside resort, and naval base.

Vltava River \'vəl-tə-və\ *German* **Moldau** River, Czech Republic. It rises in southwestern BOHEMIA from two headstreams in the Bohemian Forest, then flows southeast, and north across Bohemia to empty into the ELBE RIVER. At 270 mi (435 km), it is the nation's longest river.

Vo Nguyen Giap \'vò-'ŋüē-ən-'zyȧp, *Engl* 'vō-en-gī-'en-jē-'ap\ (born 1912) Vietnamese military leader. He began to work for Vietnamese autonomy as a youth and attended the same high school as HO CHI MINH. As a professor of history in Hanoi, he converted many colleagues and students to his political views. He fled to China in 1939 when the French banned the Indochinese Communist Party, but returned in 1941. In 1945 he led the VIET MINH forces that defeated the Japanese, who occupied Vietnam during World War II. He brought French colonial rule to an end at the Battle of DIEN BIEN PHU (1954) in the First INDOCHINA WAR, and he led the forces of the north that defeated the U.S. and South Vietnam in the VIETNAM WAR (1955–75). He served in various roles in the postwar government of Vietnam.

vocal cord Either of two folds of mucous membrane that extend across the interior cavity of the LARYNX and are primarily responsible for voice production. Sound is produced by the vibration of the folds in response to the passage between them of air exhaled from the lungs. The pitch of sound varies with the degree of vocal-cord tension. Sounds are then modified by the tongue, palate, and lips to produce speech. When at rest, the vocal cords lie apart, forming a V-shaped opening (glottis) through which air is breathed. The folds located just above the vocal cords are termed the vestibular or false vocal cords because they are not involved in voice production. Inflammation (as from excessive use) limits the normal contraction of the vocal cords, resulting in hoarseness.

vodka Colorless DISTILLED LIQUOR of neutral spirits usually made from a grain mash (generally RYE or WHEAT). Potato vodka originated in Russia in the 14th century. Today most vodka is distilled from cereal grains. It is highly neutral, most flavoring substances being eliminated during distillation and filtration, the latter process employing charcoal purifiers. Distilled water is usually added before bottling in order to lower alcohol content to 40–43% by volume (80–86 proof). Vodka is not aged. It is traditionally consumed unmixed and chilled, in small glasses; in the U.S. and elsewhere it is often used in mixed drinks.

vodun \vō-'dün\ *or* **voodoo** National folk religion of Haiti. It combines theological and magical elements of AFRICAN RELIGIONS and ritual elements of ROMAN CATHOLICISM. Practitioners profess belief in a supreme God but give more attention to a large number of spirits called the *loa,* which can be identified as local or African gods, deified ancestors, or Catholic saints. The *loa* demand ritual service and attach themselves to individuals or families. In turn, they act as helpers, protectors, and guides. In ritual services, a priest or priestess leads devotees in ceremonies involving song, drumming, dance, prayer, food preparation, and animal sacrifice. The *loa* possess worshipers during services, dispensing advice, performing cures, or displaying special physical feats. A well-known aspect of vodun is the ZOMBIE. See also MACUMBA, SANTERÍA.

voice In GRAMMAR, the form of a verb indicating the relation between the participants (subject, object) in a narrated event and the event itself. English grammar distinguishes between the active voice ("The hunter killed the bear") and the passive voice ("The bear was killed by the hunter"). In the active voice, the emphasis is on the subject of the active verb (the agent performing the action named), whereas the passive voice indicates that the subject receives the action.

voice box See LARYNX

voice mail Electronic system for recording oral messages sent by telephone. Typically, the caller hears a prerecorded message and then has an opportunity to leave a message in return. The person called can then retrieve the message at a later time by entering specific codes on his or her telephone. Voice mail is distinguished from an answering machine by its ability to provide service to multiple phone lines and by the more sophisticated functions that it offers in addition to recording messages.

Voice of America Radio broadcasting network of the U.S. government. Its function is to promote understanding of the U.S. and spread democratic values. Its daily broadcasts include news reports, editorials, and discussions of U.S. political and cultural events. Its first broadcast, in German, took place in 1942 to counter Nazi propaganda. By the end of World War II, it was broadcasting 3,200 programs in 40 languages every week. During the Cold War it focused its message at the communist countries of eastern and central Europe. It became part of the U.S. Information Agency when that agency was formed in 1953.

voice recognition See SPEECH RECOGNITION

voir dire \'vwär-'dir\ (Anglo-French: "to speak the truth") In law, the act or process of questioning prospective jurors to determine which are qualified and suited for service on a JURY. The questioning attorneys may dismiss a juror for cause, such as when bias or preconceived notions of guilt or innocence are in evidence, and also have a limited number of peremptory challenges that they can use to dismiss a juror for any or no reason.

Vojvodina \'vòi-vò-ˌdē-nä\ Province (pop., 1996 est.: 1,983,000), Yugoslavia, within the republic of SERBIA. Its chief city is NOVI SAD. Slavs settled there in the 6th–7th century, followed by Hungarian nomads in the 9th–10th century. Ottoman Turks controlled the region from the early 16th century to the late 18th century, when it became part of the Austrian HABSBURG empire. By then it was a center of Serbian Orthodox culture. In 1849 portions of the historical regions of Backa and Banat were united as Vojvodina under Croatia-Slavonia. In 1867 it reverted to Hungary, and in 1918 it was made part of the kingdom of Serbs, Croats, and Slovenes (later Yugoslavia). In 1945 it became an autonomous province of the Serb republic, but in 1989 SLOBODAN MILOSEVIC rescinded this status. In 1999, after receiving tens of thousands of Serbian refugees from KOSOVO, it demanded restoration of its autonomy.

volcanic glass Any glassy rock formed from LAVA or MAGMA that has a chemical composition close to that of GRANITE. Such molten material may reach very low temperatures without crystallizing, but its viscosity may become very high. Because high viscosity inhibits crystallization, the combination of sudden cooling and loss of volatiles, as when lava extrudes from a volcanic vent, tends to chill the material to a glass rather than crystallize it.

volcanism \'väl-kə-ˌni-zəm\ *or* **vulcanism** Any of various processes and phenomena associated with the surface discharge of molten rock or hot water and steam, including VOLCANOES, GEYSERS, and FUMAROLES. Most active volcanoes occur where two plates converge and one overrides the other (see PLATE TECTONICS). Volcanism can also occur along the axis of an OCEANIC RIDGE, where the plates move apart and magma wells up from the mantle. A few volcanoes occur within plates, far from margins. Some of these are thought to occur as a plate moves over a "hot spot" from which magma can penetrate to the surface; others appear to result from an extremely slow form of plate spreading.

volcano Vent in the crust of the earth from which molten rock, debris, and steam issue. Volcanoes are commonly divided into two broad types. Fissure volcanoes occur along fractures in the crust and may extend for many miles; LAVA is ejected relatively quietly and continuously and forms enormous plains or plateaus of volcanic rock. Central volcanoes have a single vertical lava pipe and tend to develop a conical profile; lava flows from the throat and follows the easiest path downhill. Often in these volcanoes highly viscous lava clogs the throat, causing a pressure buildup that is relieved only by violent explosion and eruption. Such eruptions may completely remove the top of the cone and occasionally also part of its interior. See illustration on following page.

Volcano Islands Group of three small volcanic islands, western Pacific Ocean, southern of BONIN ISLANDS, Japan. After they were visited by Japanese fishermen and sulfur miners in 1887, the three islands of Kita Iwo, IWO JIMA (the largest), and Minami Iwo were claimed by Japan in 1891. After World War II, Japan retained residual sovereignty over the islands, but the U.S. administered them from 1951 until their return to Japan in 1968.

volcanology *or* **vulcanology** Scientific discipline concerned with all aspects of volcanic phenomena. Volcanology deals with the formation, distribution, and classification of VOLCANOES, as well as their structure and the kinds of materials ejected during an eruption (e.g., lava, dust, ash, and gas). It also involves research on the relationships between volcanic eruptions and other large-scale geologic processes, such as mountain building and earthquakes. One of its chief aims is to determine the nature and causes of volcanic eruptions in order to predict them. Another practical concern is obtaining data that may aid in locating commer-

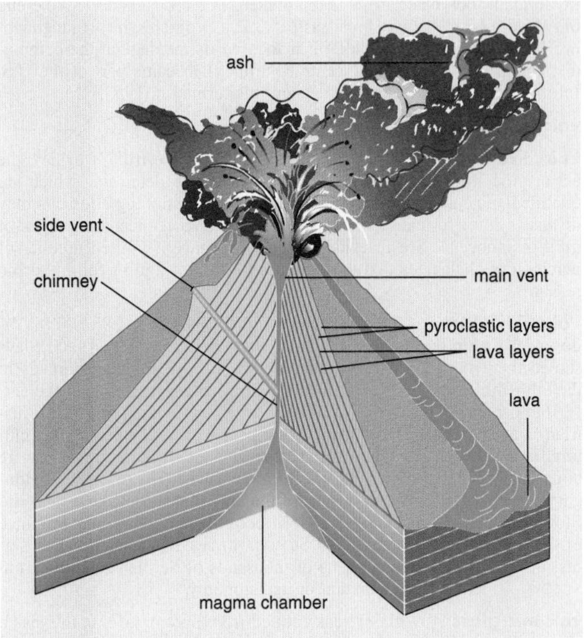

A volcano forms when magma beneath the earth's crust forces its way to the surface. Alternating layers of solidified lava and pyroclastic materials (ash and cinders) build up the typical cone-shaped volcano as they are ejected through the central vent during eruptions.

cially valuable deposits of ores, particularly those of certain metallic sulfides.

Volcker, Paul A(dolph) (born 1927) U.S. economist. Born in Cape May, N.J., he worked as an economist for the Chase Manhattan Bank 1957–61 and 1965–68. As an undersecretary at the U.S. Treasury Department (1969–74), he was the chief architect of the U.S.'s abandonment of the gold-exchange standard and the devaluations of the U.S. dollar (1971, 1973). After serving as president of the Federal Reserve Bank (1975–79), he was appointed head of the Federal Reserve System in 1979 by Pres. JIMMY CARTER, and served until 1987. To end a period of very high inflation, he slowed the growth of the money supply and allowed interest rates to rise, causing a recession (1982–83) but dramatically reducing inflation.

vole Any burrowing RODENT (family Cricetidae) with a blunt snout, small ears, and short limbs. Most species are herbivorous and are found throughout North America and Eurasia. The approximately 45 species of the genus *Microtus,* also called meadow mice, are 4–10 in. (10–26 cm) long, including the tail. Their long, shaggy fur is grayish brown. About 10 species of pine voles inhabit swamps, fields, and hardwood forests. Red-backed voles inhabit forests in cold regions. Water voles are found only in Eurasia and usually live near a stream, ditch, or lake.

Vole (*Microtus pennsylvanicus*).
JUDITH MYERS

Volga-Baltic Waterway Series of rivers and canals, Russia in Europe. The navigable system links the VOLGA RIVER with the BALTIC SEA. It includes the NEVA RIVER, a canal along the southern shore of Lake LADOGA, and the Sheksna River past Cherepovets through the RYBINSK RESERVOIR. Its total length is about 700 mi (1,120 km). The system was expanded and improved at various intervals, including major reconstruction in 1964 that included installation of seven automatic locks.

Volga River River, western Russia. Europe's longest river and the principal waterway of western Russia, it rises in the Valdai Hills northwest of MOSCOW and flows 2,193 mi (3,530 km) southeastward to empty into the CASPIAN SEA. It is used for power production, irrigation, flood control, and transportation. The river has played an important part in the life of the Russian people, and in Russian folklore it is characteristically named "Mother Volga."

Volga Tatar language See TATAR LANGUAGE

Volgograd *formerly (until 1925)* **Tsaritsyn** *(1925–61)* **Stalingrad** City (pop., 1995 est.: 1,003,000), southwestern Russia. Located on the VOLGA RIVER, it was founded as the fortress of Tsaritsyn in 1589. During the RUSSIAN CIVIL WAR (1918–20), JOSEPH STALIN organized the city's defense against the White Russian armies, and it was later renamed in his honor. During World War II it was reduced to rubble in the Battle of STALINGRAD; it was rebuilt in the postwar era. Its manufactures include steel and aluminum, engineering products, timber goods, building materials, and foodstuffs. A major railroad junction and river port, it is the eastern terminus of the Volga-Don Ship Canal.

Volhynia \väl-ˈhi-nē-ə\ Historical region, northwestern Ukraine. Located around the headstreams of the PRIPYAT and BUG rivers, it originally was a Russian principality (10th–14th century), west of KIEV. In the 14th century it became part of the Grand Duchy of Lithuania but was ruled largely by its own aristocracy. It passed to Poland in 1569. In 1793 it was transferred to Russia under the second partition of Poland. The Treaty of RIGA (1921) divided it between Poland and the U.S.S.R. The U.S.S.R. took the Polish section in 1939 and made it part of the Ukrainian S.S.R. after World War II.

Volkswagen AG Major German automobile manufacturer. It was founded in 1937 by the Nazi government to mass-produce a low-priced "people's car" *(Volkswagen).* After World War II it was rebuilt with Allied help, and within a decade it was producing half of West Germany's motor vehicles. U.S. sales of the small, rounded car were initially low, but an advertising campaign marketing it as the Beetle massively increased sales in the 1960s, making it the leading auto import in the U.S. Competition from other foreign compact cars brought Volkswagen near bankruptcy by 1974, but it rebounded with newer, sportier models such as the Rabbit. In 1998 it introduced a new version of the Beetle. With its affiliates Volkswagen operates plants worldwide; it also owns several other auto companies, including Audi and ROLLS-ROYCE.

volleyball Game played by two teams of six players each, in which an inflated ball is volleyed over a high net. Each team tries to make the ball touch the court within the opposing side's playing areas before it can be returned. A team is allowed to touch the ball three times before returning it. The team that first scores 15 points wins the game. Volleyball was invented in 1895 by William G. Morgan in Holyoke, Mass. It soon proved to have wide appeal for both sexes in schools, playgrounds, the armed forces, and other settings. International competition began in 1913, and volleyball became an Olympic sport in 1964. Beach volleyball, a variation with two players on a side, has grown increasingly popular and became an Olympic sport in 1996.

Volsci \ˈvȯl-skē, ˈväl-ˌsī\ Ancient Italic people prominent in the history of Roman expansion in the 5th century BC. They belonged to the Osco-Sabellian group of tribes and lived (c. 600 BC) in the valley of the upper Liris River (then in southern Latium). They fought the Romans and the Latins intermittently for about 200 years. The Romans established several colonies to stem the Volsci advance. In 340 they joined the Latin revolt against Rome, but were defeated. After submitting to Rome by 304, they quickly became fully Romanized.

Volstead Act See PROHIBITION

Völsunga saga \ˈvœl-su̇ŋ-ə, ˈvōl-su̇ŋ-ə\ ("Saga of the Volsungs") Best of the Icelandic sagas known as *fornaldar sögur* ("sagas of antiquity"). Dating from roughly 1270, it is the first of the *fornaldar sögur* to have been written down. It contains the Northern version of the story told in the *NIBELUNGENLIED.* The saga was based on the heroic poems in the *Poetic EDDA* and is especially valuable because it preserves in prose form some of the poems from the Edda that were lost. It became one of the sources of RICHARD WAGNER's operatic *Ring* tetralogy..

Volta \ˈvȯl-tə\, **Alessandro (Giuseppe Antonio Anastasio)** (1745–1827) Italian scientist. In 1775 he invented the electrophorus, a device used to generate static electricity. He taught physics at the University of Pavia 1779–1804. After LUIGI GALVANI in 1780 produced an electric current by connecting two different metals with the muscle of a frog, Volta began experimenting in 1794 with metals alone and found that animal tissue was not needed to produce current. He demonstrated the first electric battery in 1800. In 1801 he demonstrated the battery's generation of current before Napoleon, who made him a count and senator of the kingdom of Lombardy. In 1815 he was appointed director of the philosophical faculty at the University of Padua. The volt was named in his honor in 1881.

Volta, Lake Lake, Ghana. One of the world's largest artificial lakes, it was formed in 1965 when the Akosombo Dam dammed the VOLTA RIVER and created a reservoir that extends about 250 mi (400 km) upstream to beyond the former confluence of the Black Volta and WHITE VOLTA rivers. It covers 3,283 sq mi (8,502 sq km), or 3.6% of Ghana's area. It is a major fishing ground and provides irrigation water for farmland in the ACCRA plains. The dam generates enough hydroelectric power to supply most of Ghana's electricity needs.

Volta River \'väl-tə, 'vōl-tə\ River, Ghana, western Africa. The nation's chief river, it flows from Lake VOLTA, and receives the Black Volta and the WHITE VOLTA rivers. It flows southward through Ghana to the Bight of BENIN in the Gulf of GUINEA. The river system is 1,000 mi (1,600 km) long.

Voltaic languages See GUR LANGUAGES

Voltaire \vōl-'ter\ *orig.* **François-Marie Arouet** (1694–1778) French writer, one of the greatest 18th-century European authors. Voltaire studied law but abandoned it to become a writer. He made his name with classical tragedies and continued to write for the theater all his life. He was twice sent to the Bastille for his remarks and in 1726 was exiled to England, where his philosophical interests deepened; he returned to France in 1728 or 1729. His epic poem *La Henriade* (1728) was well received, but his lampoons of the Regency and his liberal religious opinions caused offense. *Lettres philosophiques* (1734), in which he spoke out against established religious and political systems, caused an uproar. He fled Paris and settled at Cirey in Champagne with Mme du Châtelet, who became his patroness and mistress, and there turned to scientific research and the systematic study of religions and culture. After her death he spent periods in Berlin and Geneva; in 1754 he settled in Switzerland. In addition to his many works on philosophical and moral problems, he wrote *contes* ("tales") including *Zadig* (1747), *Micromégas* (1752), and his best-known work, *Candide* (1759), a satire on philosophical optimism. He kept up an immense correspondence and took an interest in any cases of injustice, especially those resulting from religious prejudice, that came to his notice. He is remembered as a crusader against tyranny and bigotry and noted for his wit, satire, and critical capacity.

Volturno River \väl-'tür-nō\ River, southern central Italy. It flows southeast from the Abruzzese APENNINES, then turns west to empty into the Gulf of Gaeta. It is 109 mi (175 km) long and has a dam for flood control and irrigation. During the wars for Italian unity, the Italian nationalist leader GIUSEPPE DE GARIBALDI defeated a Neapolitan army there in 1860. During World War II, German forces in southern Italy used it as their line of defense after the fall of NAPLES; after severe fighting, the Allies crossed the river in October 1943.

volume See LENGTH, AREA, AND VOLUME

voluntarism \'vä-lən-tə-ˌri-zəm\ Metaphysical or psychological system that assigns a more predominant role to the will (Latin, *voluntas*) than to the intellect. Christian philosophers who have been described as voluntarist include St. AUGUSTINE, John DUNS SCOTUS, and BLAISE PASCAL. A metaphysical voluntarism was propounded in the 19th century by ARTHUR SCHOPENHAUER, who took will to be the single, unconscious force behind all of reality and all ideas of reality. An existentialist voluntarism was present in FRIEDRICH NIETZSCHE's doctrine of the overriding "will to power" whereby man would eventually recreate himself as "superman." And a pragmatic voluntarism is evident in WILLIAM JAMES's reference of belief, knowledge, and truth to purpose and to practical ends.

vomiting Forcible ejection of the stomach contents from the mouth, usually following NAUSEA. Causes include illness, MOTION SICKNESS, certain drugs, INNER-EAR disorders, and head injury. Vomiting may occur without nausea (e.g., after extreme exertion). Two centers in the brain's medulla oblongata are believed to control it; the vomiting center initiates and controls a series of muscle contractions beginning at the small intestine and moving through the stomach and esophagus. This reaction may be set off by the chemoreceptor trigger zone, stimulated by many toxins and drugs, to rid the body of them, or by stimuli from various parts of the body that may be stressed or diseased. Severe vomiting may cause dehydration, malnutrition, or esophageal wall rupture. Vomiting of blood may be a sign of bleeding ULCER or other upper digestive tract disorders. See also BULIMIA.

von Neumann \vän-'nȯi-män\, **John** *orig.* **Johann** (1903–1957) Hungarian-U.S. mathematician. After receiving his PhD from the University of Budapest, he emigrated to the U.S. to teach at Princeton University (1930), and was among the original faculty of the Institute for Advanced Study (from 1933). He solved one of DAVID HILBERT's 23 theoretical problems and collaborated on developing an algebraic RING with profound applications in quantum physics. During World War II he participated in the development of the ATOMIC BOMB. After the war he made major contributions to the development of high-speed computers; one of his computers was essential to the creation of the HYDROGEN BOMB. As coauthor of *Theory of Games and Economic Behavior* (1944), he was one of the founders of GAME THEORY. He coined the term cybernetics.

Vondel \'vȯn-dəl\, **Joost van den** (1587–1679) Dutch poet and dramatist. Of Mennonite parents, Vondel early showed a preference for using Christian mythology as subject matter of his plays. He also wrote lampoons and satirical poems against the Dutch church and government. His dramatic tragedies, with their lyrical language and grandeur of conception, are his most important achievement. *The Passover* (1612) is his most notable early work. He first modeled plays on ancient Latin drama but later turned to the Greek model for plays including his masterpiece, the trilogy comprising *Lucifer* (1654), *Adam in Exile* (1664), and *Noah* (1667), which influenced JOHN MILTON's *Paradise Lost.*

Vonnegut \'vä-nə-ˌgət\, **Kurt, Jr.** (born 1922) U.S. novelist. Born in Indianapolis, he attended Cornell University and the University of Chicago. He was captured by the Germans during World War II and survived the Allied firebombing of Dresden, an experience he made part of *Slaughterhouse-Five* (1969; film, 1972). His pessimistic and satirical novels use fantasy and science fiction to highlight the horrors and ironies of 20th-century civilization. They include *Player Piano* (1952), *Cat's Cradle* (1963), *Breakfast of Champions* (1973), *Galápagos* (1985), *Hocus Pocus* (1990), and *Timequake* (1997). He also has written plays, including *Happy Birthday, Wanda June* (1970), and collections of short stories, including *Welcome to the Monkey House* (1968).

voodoo See VODUN

Voronezh \və-'rō-nish\ City (pop., 1995 est.: 908,000), western Russia. It lies along the Voronezh River above its confluence with the DON. It was founded in 1586 as a fortress. PETER I THE GREAT built a naval flotilla in Voronezh for use in his campaigns against the Turks. With the agricultural development of the region it became a center for the grain trade. Occupied by the Germans and largely destroyed in World War II, it was rebuilt in the postwar era. It has a range of engineering, chemical, and food-processing industries. Its university was established in 1918.

Vorontsov \və-rənt-'sȯf\, **Mikhail (Illarionovich)** (1714–1767) Russian statesman. At 14 he was appointed a page in the court of Yelizaveta Petrovna (later ELIZABETH). In 1742 he helped her overthrow Czar IVAN VI and become empress. As Elizabeth's vice chancellor (1744–58) and chancellor (1758–62), he played a major role during her reign, especially in his pro-French foreign policy.

Voroshilov \ˌvȯr-ə-'shē-ˌlȯf\, **Kliment (Yefremovich)** (1881–1969) Soviet military and political leader. A notable military commander in World War I and later in the Russian Civil War, he led the defense of Tsaritsyn (now Volgograd). A close associate of JOSEPH STALIN, he was appointed people's commissar for defense (1925) and a member of the Politburo (1926). Named a marshal of the Soviet Union (1935), he reorganized the Soviet general staff, mechanized the army, and developed the air force. After the initial Soviet defeats in World War II, he was removed as defense commissar but appointed to the committee for state defense (1941–44). He later chaired the Presidium of the Supreme Soviet (1953–57).

Vorster \'fȯr-stər\, **John** *orig.* **Balthazar Johannes** (1915–1983) South African prime minister (1966–78). Vorster was arrested in 1942 for supporting Germany in World War II. In the 1948 elections he was rejected by the NATIONAL PARTY as too extreme, but his support grew in the 1950s. As minister of justice (1961–66) under Hendrik Freusch Verwoerd (1901–1966), he rigidly enforced APARTHEID. When Verwoerd was assassinated, Vorster was chosen to replace him. In the 1970s he sent troops into Angola against its Soviet- and Cuban-supported government. He resigned in 1978 and took the ceremonial post of president, but a scandal forced his resignation.

Vorticism \'vȯr-ti-ˌsi-zəm\ Literary and artistic movement that flourished in England 1912–15. Founded by WYNDHAM LEWIS, it attempted to relate art to industrialization. It opposed 19th-century sentimentality and extolled the energy of the machine and machine-made products, and it promoted something of a cult of sheer violence. In the visual arts, Vorticist compositions were abstract and sharp-planed, showing the influence of CUBISM and FUTURISM. Artists involved in the movement included the poet EZRA POUND and the sculptor JACOB EPSTEIN.

Võrts-Järv *or* **Võrtsjärv** \'vərts-ˌyarv\ Lake, southern central Estonia. With an area of 110 sq mi (280 sq km), it is the largest lake in Estonia. It forms part of the 124-mi (200-km) course of the Ema River, which enters the lake from the south and drains it north and east into Lake PEIPUS.

Vostok \vü-'stȯk, *Engl* 'väs-ˌtäk\ Any of a series of six manned Russian spacecraft launched 1961–63. Vostok 1 (1961) carried the first human (YURY A. GAGARIN) into space. Vostok 3 set a new time record in space of 94 hours. Vostoks 5 and 6 were launched two days apart and traveled very close together, at times only 3 mi (5 km) apart, setting the stage for future dockings between orbiting vehicles. The first woman in space, VALENTINA TERESHKOVA, flew aboard Vostok 6.

Voting Rights Act Act passed by the U.S. Congress in 1965 to ensure the voting rights of African-Americans. While the Constitution's 15th Amendment had guaranteed the right to vote regardless of race since 1870, blacks in the South faced efforts to disenfranchise them (including poll taxes and literacy tests) as late as the 1960s, when the CIVIL RIGHTS MOVEMENT focused national attention on the need to protect blacks' voting rights; Congress responded with the Voting Rights Act, which prohibited many Southern states from using literacy tests to determine eligibility to vote. Later laws prohibited literacy tests in all states and made poll taxes illegal in state and local elections.

Voto, Bernard De See Bernard DE VOTO

Vouet \'vwe, *Engl* vü-'ā\, **Simon** (1590–1649) French painter. He formed his style in Italy, where he lived 1614–27. His early work was influenced by CARAVAGGIO, but works done after 1620 display more idealized figures and use more evenly diffused white light. He returned to Paris in 1627 to become first painter to Louis XIII. Thereafter he won almost all the important commissions and dominated the city artistically for the next 15 years. He introduced the Italian baroque style in France with such paintings as *St. Charles Borromeo* (c. 1640). His late works display the soft, idealized modeling, sensuous forms, and bright colors for which he is best known.

vowel SPEECH sound in which air from the lungs passes through the mouth with minimal obstruction and without audible friction, like the *i* in *fit*. The word also refers to a letter representing such a sound *(a, e, i, o, u,* and sometimes *y).* In articulatory PHONETICS (see ARTICULATION), vowels are classified by tongue and lip position; for example, high vowels like the *i* in *machine* and the *u* in *flute* are both pronounced with the tongue arched high in the mouth, but in *u* the lips are also rounded. Single vowel sounds are monophthongs; two vowel sounds pronounced as one syllable, like the *ou* in *round,* are diphthongs.

Voyager Either of two unmanned U.S. interplanetary probes launched in 1977 to gather information about the sun's outer planets. Voyager 1 flew by JUPITER in 1979 and reached SATURN in 1980. Voyager 2 traveled more slowly, flying by Jupiter, Saturn, and URANUS to reach NEPTUNE in 1989. Data and photographs from both probes revealed new details about these giant planets, their moons, and their rings. They will continue into deep space, beyond the outer edge of the solar system. Voyager 2 is expected to operate until c. 2020, periodically transmitting data on the HELIOPAUSE.

Voyageurs National Park \ˌvwä-yä-'zhər\ National park, northern Minnesota. Located along the Canadian border, it was established in 1975, and was named for the mostly French-Canadian fur-trading frontiersmen (voyageurs) of the 18th–19th century. It occupies an area of 217,892 acres (88,178 hectares) and consists of a network of streams and lakes, the largest of which is RAINY LAKE.

Voznesensky \vəz-nʸi-'sʸen-skē\, **Andrey (Andreyevich)** (born 1933) Russian poet. His childhood experience of World War II was later vividly reflected in his poetry, including "Goya" (1960), his best-known poem. He became a protégé of BORIS PASTERNAK and a star attraction at poetry readings until a 1963 Soviet crackdown on "excessively experimental" artists and writers. He later returned to partial favor. His most characteristic poems are apolitical celebrations of art, freedom, and the unrestrained human spirit. His works were collected in the bilingual *An Arrow in the Wall* (1987) and in *On the Edge* (1991).

Vuillard \vwē-'yär\, **(Jean-) Edouard** (1868–1940) French painter, printmaker, and decorator. With PIERRE BONNARD he developed the Intimist style, characterized by small paintings of daily home life, such as *Woman Sweeping* (c. 1892). He was an original member of the NABIS; his *Jardins de Paris* (*Public Gardens,* 1894), a series of decorative panels that use pale light and neutral colors to create a mood of restful calm, are typical of his mature work as a Nabi. He received numerous commissions to decorate public buildings, including murals in the Palais de Chaillot (1937) and in the League of Nations building in Geneva (1939), and also designed for the BALLETS RUSSES.

"Under the Trees," tempera on canvas panel from "Jardin de Paris," by Édouard Vuillard, c. 1894; in the Cleveland Museum of Art, Cleveland.

BY COURTESY OF THE CLEVELAND MUSEUM OF ART, CLEVELAND, GIFT OF HANNA FUND

Vulcan Ancient Roman god of fire. He was the counterpart of the Greek HEPHAESTUS. Vulcan was especially associated with the destructive aspects of fire, such as volcanoes or conflagrations, and for this reason his temples were usually located outside the city. His chief festival, the Volcanalia, was marked by a rite in which the heads of Roman families threw fish into the fire. Often invoked to avert fire, he was addressed with epithets such as Mulciber ("Fire Allayer").

Vulcan Hypothetical planet within the orbit of MERCURY, predicted in 1859 by Urbain-Jean-Joseph Le Verrier (1811–1877) to account for an unexplained precession of Mercury's orbit. Sightings were reported between 1859 and 1878, but these were not confirmed subsequently by observations made either during solar eclipses or when Vulcan was predicted to cross the sun. The anomalies of Mercury's orbit were later explained by ALBERT EINSTEIN's general theory of RELATIVITY.

vulcanism See VOLCANISM

vulcanization Chemical process, discovered by CHARLES GOODYEAR (1839), by which the physical properties of natural or synthetic RUBBER are improved. It consists principally of heating rubber with sulfur; other substances (accelerators, carbon black, antioxidants, etc.) are also added. The sulfur does not simply dissolve or disperse in the rubber, but rather combines chemically, mostly in the form of cross-links (bridges) between the long-chain molecules; however, the reactions are not fully understood. Vulcanized rubber has higher tensile strength and resistance to swelling and abrasion, and is elastic over a greater range of temperatures.

Vulcano \vül-'kä-nō\ Island of the LIPARI ISLANDS, off northeastern SICILY. There are three volcanoes on the island, whose area is 8 sq mi (21 sq km). Although the last major eruptions were in 1888–90, one volcano is still active.

vulcanology See VOLCANOLOGY

Vulci \'vəl-ˌsī\ Ancient ETRUSCAN city, northwest of ROME. It grew out of a number of Villanovan villages and flourished chiefly in the 6th–4th century BC, largely as a result of trade, and the manufacture of bronze objects, including jugs and tripods. The important center of a large city-state, after the 6th century BC it gradually came under Roman rule. The site, excavated in the 1950s, is noted for its bronze and pottery, much of which has been found in a huge necropolis. There also are Roman ruins.

vulture Any of 20 species of bare-headed, keen-sighted BIRDS OF PREY found in temperate and tropical regions. New World vultures (family Cathartidae) are 24–28 in. (60–70 cm) long. Old World vultures (family Accipitridae) include the smallest (20 in., or 50 cm, long) and the largest vulture species. The cinereous, or black, vulture *(Aegypius monachus),* one of the largest living birds of flight, grows to about 40 in. (100 cm) long, weighs almost 30 lbs (13 kg), and has a 9-ft (2.7-m) wingspread. Most species eat carrion, garbage, and excrement but will occasionally eat a live animal. See also CONDOR, MARABOU, TURKEY VULTURE.

vulvitis \vəl-'vī-təs\ INFLAMMATION of the vulva (female external genitalia), with red, swollen, itchy skin that may turn white, crack, or blister. The vulva provides a moist, warm breeding ground, particularly for yeast infection (see CANDIDA) but also for other fungi, bacteria, or viruses, especially if underwear is tight, nonporous, and nonabsorbent and if hygiene is poor. Pantyhose, synthetic underwear, detergents, vaginal sprays, and deodorants may cause allergy or irritation. Drying and thinning of tissues after MENOPAUSE make them more susceptible to irritation and infection. Treatment ranges from wearing loose, absorbent cotton underwear, to creams that kill the infective microorganisms.

Vychegda River \'vi-chəg-də\ River, northwestern Russia. It rises on the slopes of the Timan Ridge and joins the Northern DVINA RIVER near Kotlas. Its 702-mi (1,130-km) course is frequently marked by marshes, lakes, and sandbanks, but it is navigable for 596 mi (960 km).

Vygotsky \vi-'gȯt-skē\, **L(ev) S(emyonovich)** (1896–1934) Soviet psychologist. He studied linguistics and philosophy at the University of Moscow before becoming involved in psychological research. While working at Moscow's Institute of Psychology 1924–34, he became a major figure in post-revolutionary Soviet psychology. He studied the role of social and cultural factors in the making of human consciousness; his theory of signs and their relationship to the development of speech influenced such psychologists as A.R. LURIA and JEAN PIAGET. His best-known work, *Thought and Language* (1934), was briefly suppressed as a threat to Stalinism. He died of tuberculosis at 38.

Vyshinsky \və-'shin-skē\, **Andrey (Yanuaryevich)** (1883–1954) Soviet politician and diplomat. A public prosecutor, he taught at Moscow State University Appointed chief prosecutor of the Soviet Union (1935), he gained worldwide notoriety for his zeal in prosecuting the PURGE TRIALS. As deputy commissar of foreign affairs, he supervised the annexation of Latvia (1940) and established a communist regime in Romania (1945). He later served as Soviet foreign minister (1949–53) and representative to the U.N. (1949–54), where he frequently launched bitter attacks on the U.S.

Vytautas the Great \vē-'tau̇-täs\ *Lithuanian* **Vytautus Didysis** (1350–1430) Lithuanian national leader. Continuing a family struggle for control of Lithuania, he fought his cousin WLADYSLAW II JAGIELLO but made peace in 1384. His popularity grew until Wladyslaw was obliged to make him vice regent (1392), an office that allowed him to become effective ruler of Lithuania. He subdued rebellious nobles but was defeated by Mongols in the east (1399). He and Wladyslaw united Lithuania and Poland (1401) and waged war on the TEUTONIC ORDER, defeating them at the Battle of TANNENBERG (1410). Vytautas was named king of Lithuania in 1429, but died before he could be crowned.

W particle Electrically charged subatomic particle that transmits the weak force that governs radioactive decay (see radioactivity) in some atomic nuclei and the interactions between hydrogen nuclei that initiate nuclear fusion in the sun and other stars. The electroweak theory explains that the electromagnetic force and the weak force are manifestations of the same interaction. The weak force is exchanged via three types of particles, two charged and one neutral. The charged particles are designated W^+ and W^- according to the sign of their charge. The W particle has a mass about 90 times that of the proton, which gives the weak force a very short range. See also Z particle.

Waals, Johannes Diederik van der See Johannes D. van der Waals

Wabash River \'wȯ-ˌbash\ River, Indiana and Illinois. Rising in western Ohio, it flows southwest across Indiana, then forms the 200-mi (320-km) southern section of the Indiana–Illinois boundary below Terre Haute, Ind. It empties into the Ohio River in southwestern Indiana after a course of 475 mi (764 km). During the 18th century the French used it as a transportation link between Louisiana and Quebec. After the War of 1812, its basin was rapidly developed by settlers. After the coming of the railroads in the 1850s, navigation almost disappeared except for barge traffic on its lower course.

WAC See Women's Army Corps

Wace \'wās, 'wäs\ (c. 1100–after 1174) Anglo-Norman poet. He is known for his two verse chronicles, the *Roman de Brut* (1155) and the *Roman de Rou* (1160–74), named respectively after the reputed founders of the Britons and Normans. The *Brut* is a romanticized account of Geoffrey of Monmouth's *Historia regum Britanniae.* Its many fanciful additions (including the story of Arthur's Round Table) were important in the development of the Arthurian legend, and its literary style influenced later verse romances. The *Rou*, commissioned by Henry II of England, is a history of the Norman dukes c. 911–1106.

Waco \'wā-kō\ City (pop., 2000: 113,726), northern central Texas. Located on the Brazos River, it was founded in 1849 on the site of an Indian village. After 1865 it became a river-bridge crossing on cattle trails; later its economy was based on cotton. Its diversified economy now includes manufacturing and tourism. A tornado devastated Waco in 1953, killing 114 persons. On April 19, 1993, after a 51-day standoff with federal agents, some 80 members of the Branch Davidians perished in a fire at their compound near Waco.

Wadai \wä-'dī\ Historical African kingdom, central Africa. Located east of Lake Chad and west of Darfur, it was founded in the 16th century. A Muslim dynasty was established there c. 1630, and though long subordinate to Darfur, it became independent by the 1790s and began a period of rapid expansion. It came under French influence in 1899 and French control 1912–14. The area is now largely in eastern Chad.

Wade, Benjamin F(ranklin) (1800–1878) U.S. politician. Born in Springfield, Mass., he practiced law in Ohio before serving in the U.S. Senate (1851–69), where he opposed the extension of slavery and the Kansas-Nebraska Act. In the Civil War he joined the Radical Republicans in demanding vigorous prosecution of the war and headed a joint congressional committee to investigate the Union military effort. He cosponsored the Wade-Davis Bill, which brought him into conflict with Abraham Lincoln. Opposed to Pres. Andrew Johnson's Reconstruction policies, he voted for impeachment and, as Senate president pro tem, prepared to succeed Johnson. Disappointed by the trial's outcome, he was later defeated for reelection.

Wade-Davis Bill (1864) Measure passed by the U.S. Congress to set Reconstruction policy. It was cosponsored by Sen. Benjamin Wade and Rep. Henry W. Davis (1817–1865) to counter Pres. Abraham Lincoln's lenient plans for readmitting Southern states after the Civil War. Supported by the Radical Republicans, the bill called for provisional military government of the seceded states, an oath of allegiance from a majority of the state's whites, and new state constitutions that would abolish slavery and disqualify Confederate officials from holding office. Lincoln considered the bill too harsh and by pocket veto allowed it to expire.

wage-price control Setting of government guidelines to limit increases in wages and prices. It is one of the most extreme approaches to incomes policy. By controlling wages and prices, governments hope to control inflation and prevent extremes in the business cycle. Countries with highly centralized methods of setting wages tend to have the greatest degree of public or collective regulation of wage and price levels. For example, wage settlements in The Netherlands must be approved by the government, and price increases are investigated by the Ministry of Economic Affairs. Other countries, including the U.S., have also made efforts at restraining wage and price increases, usually seeking the voluntary cooperation of management and labor. In the U.S., wage-price controls were instituted by Pres. Franklin Roosevelt during World War II and by Pres. Richard Nixon in the early 1970s, when high inflation combined with rising unemployment to create instability.

Wagner \'wag-nər\, **Honus** *orig.* **John Peter** (1874–1955) U.S. baseball player. Born in Mansfield (now Carnegie), Pa., he played principally for the Pittsburgh Pirates (1900–17), and coached the team from 1933 to 1951. The right-handed hitter led the National League in batting average in eight seasons (1900, 1903–4, 1906–9, 1911) and in stolen bases five seasons. His total of 252 three-base hits remains a National League record. Nicknamed the "Flying Dutchman" for his speed, Wagner is considered one of the greatest shortstops and all-around players in baseball history.

Wagner \'väg-nər\, **Otto** (1841–1918) Austrian architect and teacher. In 1893 his general plan (not executed) for Vienna won a major competition, and in 1894 he was appointed Academy professor. Among his notable works are a number of stations for the City Railway of Vienna (1894–97) and the Postal Savings Bank (1904–6). The latter, which had little decoration, is recognized as a milestone in the history of modern architecture, particularly for the curving glass roof of its central hall. Wagner's lectures were published in 1895 as *Moderne Architektur*.

Wagner \'väg-nər\, **(Wilhelm) Richard** (1813–1883) German composer. His childhood was divided between Dresden and Leipzig, where he had his first composition lessons; his teacher refused payment because of his talent. His first opera, *Die Feen* (1834), was followed by *Der Liebesverbot* (1836); the premiere performance was so unprepared that the event was a fiasco, and he henceforth determined not to settle for modest productions. The success of *Rienzi* (1840) led him to be more adventurous in *The Flying Dutchman* (1843), and even more so in *Tannhäuser* (1845). Caught up in the political turmoil of 1848, he was forced to flee Dresden for Zurich. During this enforced vacation, he wrote influential essays, asserting (following G. W. F. Hegel) that music had reached a limit after Ludwig van Beethoven, and that the "artwork of the future" would unite music and theater in a *Gesamtkunstwerk* ("total artwork"). In 1850 he saw *Lohengrin* produced. He had begun his most ambitious work, *The Ring of the Nibelung*, a four-opera cycle. The need for large-scale unity brought him to the concept of the leitmotiv. He ceased work on the *Ring*'s third opera, *Siegfried,* in the throes of an adulterous love with Mathilde Wesendonk, and wrote an opera of forbidden love, *Tristan und Isolde* (1859), which also seemed to break the bonds of tonality. He published the *Ring* librettos in 1863, asking if some German prince would support his artistic dreams, and Ludwig II of Bavaria responded. Shortly thereafter, Cosima Liszt von Bülow became the mother of the first of his children; they married in 1870, after his own wife's death. From the late 1860s to the early 1880s, Wagner completed work on *Die Meistersinger*, *Siegfried*, *Götterdämmerung*, and the long-deferred *Parsifal*, as he also oversaw the building of the great festival theater at Bayreuth (1872–76) that would be dedicated to his operas. His astonishing works made Wagner one of the most influential and consequential figures in the history of Western music, and indeed of Western culture.

Wagner \'wag-nər\, **Robert F(erdinand)** (1877–1953) U.S. (German-born) politician. He emigrated with his family to New York City in

1885. He became active in Democratic politics, serving in the state legislature (1904–19) and as a justice of the state court of appeals (1919–26). In the U.S. Senate (1927–49), he became an ally of Pres. Franklin Roosevelt, and introduced New Deal labor and social-reform legislation, including the National Industrial Recovery Act (1933), the National Labor Relations Act (known as the Wagner Act), and the Social Security Act. He cosponsored the Wagner-Steagall Act (1937), which created the U.S. Housing Authority. His son, Robert F. Wagner, Jr. (1910–1991), served as mayor of New York 1954–65.

Wagner Act *or* **National Labor Relations Act** (1935) Labor legislation passed by the U.S. Congress. Sponsored by Sen. Robert F. Wagner, the act protected workers' rights to form unions and to bargain collectively. A three-member National Labor Relations Board was established to supervise union elections and prohibit employers from engaging in unfair labor practices. The act, considered the most important piece of labor legislation in the 20th century, helped ensure union support for Pres. Franklin Roosevelt in the 1936 election.

Wagner-Jauregg \'väg-nər-'yau̇-rek\, **Julius** *orig.* **Julius Wagner, Ritter (Knight) von Jauregg** (1857–1940) Austrian psychiatrist and neurologist. Having observed that patients with some nervous disorders improved after infections with fever, and knowing that malaria could be controlled with quinine, he treated syphilis patients with central-nervous-system disorders by inducing malaria, the first form of shock therapy. For thus controlling an incurable fatal disease, he was awarded a 1927 Nobel Prize. Though antibiotics replaced this treatment for syphilis, it led to the development of fever therapy and shock therapy for other mental disorders.

wagon Four-wheeled vehicle designed to be drawn by draft animals. Wagons have been used from the 1st century BC.; early examples used spoked wheels with metal rims, pivoted front axles, and linchpins to secure the wheels. Ninth-century improvements in suspension made the wagon preferable to the two-wheeled cart, especially for carrying freight and agricultural produce.

Wagram \'vä-ˌgräm\, **Battle of** (July 5–6, 1809) Victory by French forces under Napoleon against Austria. In an attempt to break French control of Germany, Austria's 158,000 troops under Archduke Charles (1771–1847) were deployed along a 14-mi (23-km) front on either side of the village of Wagram, near Vienna. The attack by Napoleon and his 154,000 French troops split the center of the Austrian line. By the time reinforcements arrived, Charles's army was in retreat, and four days later he asked for an armistice. Heavy use of artillery (the heaviest in any war to that time) caused over 40,000 Austrian casualties and about 34,000 French.

wagtail Any of 7–10 passerine species in the genus *Motacilla* and the forest wagtail *(Dendronanthus indicus)* of Asia. Wagtails continually pump their long tail up and down; the forest wagtail wags its entire body from side to side. They inhabit beaches, meadows, and streamsides, nesting on the ground and roosting in trees. Males of the white, or pied, wagtail *(M. alba),* common across Eurasia, are white and gray or white and black. The only New World species, the yellow wagtail *(M. flava),* breeds in Alaska and migrates to Asia.

Gray wagtail (*Motacilla cinerea*).

H. REINHARD—BRUCE COLEMAN INC.

Wahhab \wȧ-'hȧb\, **Muhammad ibn Abd al-** (1703–1792) Islamic theologian and founder of the Wahhabi movement. Born in Arabia and educated in Medina, he spent several years teaching in Iraq and Iran. He reacted against what he perceived as the extremism of various sects of Sufism, setting out his ideas in the *Book of Unity* (1736). He stressed the traditional and conservative observation of Islam, as enunciated by Muhammad. He rejected polytheism, condemning reverence of saints and the decoration of mosques. His views were controversial; eventually he settled in Najd, where, in alliance with Ibn Saud, his teachings found favor and grew dominant.

Wahhabi \wȧ-'hȧb-ē\ Member of a Muslim puritan movement founded in the 18th century by Muhammad ibn Abd al-Wahhab. Members call themselves *Muwahhidun,* a name derived from their emphasis on the absolute oneness of God. They reject all acts implying polytheism, including the veneration of saints, and advocate a return to the original teachings of Islam as found in the Quran and the Hadith. They stress literal belief in the canonical texts of Islam and the establishment of a Muslim state based on Islamic law. Adopted by the ruling Saudi family in 1744, the movement controlled all of Nejd by the end of the 18th century. It was assured of dominance on the Arabian Peninsula with the creation of the kingdom of Saudi Arabia in 1932.

wahoo \'wä-ˌhü\ Species *(Acanthocybium solanderi)* of swift-moving, powerful, predacious food and game fish found worldwide, especially in the tropics. A slim, streamlined fish, it has sharp-toothed, beaklike jaws and a tapered body ending in a crescent-shaped tail. Gray-blue above and paler below, it is marked with a series of vertical bars and, like the related tunas, has a row of small finlets behind the dorsal and anal fins. It may grow to 6 ft (1.8 m) long and weigh more than 120 lbs (55 kg).

Waigeo \wī-'gā-ō\ Island, northeastern Moluccas, Indonesia. Located off northwestern Irian Jaya, it is 80 mi (130 km) long and 30 mi (48 km) wide. Its rocky and generally steep coastline is almost bisected by a narrow inlet of the Dampier Strait; its central areas are mountainous, rising to 3,300 ft (1,000 m), and are heavily forested. Islanders raise cattle and export tortoiseshells and fish.

Waikato River \wī-'kä-tō\ River, North Island, New Zealand. Rising on the slopes of Mount Ruapehu as the Tongariro River, it flows north through Lake Taupo, then northwest to enter the Tasman Sea. The nation's longest river, it is 264 mi (425 km) long and is a major source of hydroelectric power. It was the scene of several skirmishes between the British and the Waikato tribes in 1863–65.

Waikiki \ˌwī-kə-'kē\ Resort area, southern coast of Oahu island, Hawaii. Located in the southeastern section of Honolulu, near Diamond Head, its famous beach is lined with luxury hotels; it has water-sports facilities as well as an aquarium, a zoo, gardens, and the International Market Place. Waikiki is also the site of Fort DeRussy, a military recreation area. The area was once a favorite resort of island monarchs.

Wailing Wall See Western Wall

Wailuku Valley See Iao Valley

Waimakariri River \wī-ˌmä-kə-'rir-ē\ River, eastern central South Island, New Zealand. It rises in the Southern Alps and flows 100 mi (160 km) southeast to Pegasus Bay of the Pacific Ocean. Its delta constitutes a major portion of Banks Peninsula and part of the Canterbury Plains.

Wairau River \'wī-ˌrau̇\ River, northern South Island, New Zealand. It rises in the Spenser Mountains and flows for 105 mi (169 km) to enter Cloudy Bay of Cook Strait. In 1843 it was the site of the Wairau Affray, a battle between the New Zealand Co. and local Maori chiefs.

Waite, Morrison (Remick) (1816–1888) U.S. jurist. Born in Lyme, Conn., the son of a judge, he moved to Ohio to practice law; in his most notable case he prosecuted the *Alabama* claims. In 1874 he was appointed chief justice of the U.S. Supreme Court by Pres. Ulysses S. Grant; he would remain on the Court until his death. The Waite Court hindered civil rights with such decisions as *U.S. vs. Cruikshank,* in which he stated that the 15th Amendment did not give blacks the right to vote because "the right to vote comes from the states." In his most famous opinion, *Munn vs. Illinois* (1877), he upheld legislation fixing maximum rates chargeable by grain elevators and railroads, saying that when a business or private property was "affected with a public interest" it was subject to governmental regulation.

Waitemata Harbor \ˌwī-tə-'mä-tə\ Harbor, northern North Island, New Zealand. The harbor for Auckland, it opens into Hauraki Gulf through Stanley Bay. Its shore has many lesser embayments; several tidal rivers empty into the western part.

waiting-line theory See queuing theory

Waitz, Grete *orig.* **Grete Andersen** (born 1953) Norwegian marathon runner. She set world records in the 3000-m event (1975, 1976), and became the world women's marathon champion in 1983. She won the women's silver medal in the marathon at the 1984 Olympic Games. She won the New York marathon nine times in the years 1978–88 and was the first woman to finish that race in under 2½ hours.

wakan \wä-'kän\ Among some American Indian tribes, a spiritual power of supernatural origin belonging to some natural objects, people, horses, and celestial and terrestrial phenomena. Wakan can be conceived of as weak or strong powers; the weak can be ignored but the strong must be placated. Wakan beings are the immortal supernatural powers who bestow wakan; they too may be weak or strong, but are all believed to enjoy music and smoke from pipes. Poisonous plants and reptiles can contain wakan, as can intoxicating drinks. The concept of wakan is similar to that of MANA.

Wakatipu Lake \ˌwä-kə-'tē-pü\ Lake, southern central SOUTH ISLAND, New Zealand. The S-shaped lake measures 48 mi (77 km) by 3 mi (5 km) and has an area of 113 sq mi (293 sq km) and a maximum depth of 1,240 ft (378 m). It receives the Dart, Rees, Greenstone, and Von rivers and empties by the Kawarau, a tributary of the CLUTHA RIVER.

Wake Forest University Private university in Winston-Salem, N.C. Founded in 1834, it is affiliated with the Baptist church. It consists of an undergraduate college, a graduate school, and schools of business and accountancy, law, management, and medicine. Research facilities include a primate center and a laser physics laboratory. Total enrollment is about 6,000.

Wake Island Atoll, central Pacific Ocean. An unincorporated territory of the U.S., it comprises three low-lying coral islets (Wilkes, Peale, and Wake) that surround a lagoon and occupy a total land area of 2.5 sq mi (6.5 sq km). It was claimed by the U.S. in 1899. The U.S. Navy began construction of an air and submarine base in 1939; it was half-completed when Wake was attacked and occupied by Japanese forces in December 1941 after a 15-day resistance by a small contingent of U.S. marines. Now administered by the U.S. Air Force, it has been used since 1974 as a commercial aircraft emergency stopover. It is also the site of weather research stations.

Wakefield City (metro. area pop., 1995 est.: 317,000), administrative center for WEST YORKSHIRE, England. Originally part of a royal manor, it became a baronial holding after 1086. It was the scene of the Wars of the ROSES at which Richard, duke of York, was captured and beheaded by Lancastrians. In the 15th century the Wakefield Plays, one of the collections of English MIRACLE PLAYS, were presented there. The town was attacked and taken by the Parliamentarian general Baron FAIRFAX in 1643 during the ENGLISH CIVIL WARS. Known as a textile center since the 16th century, it specializes in wool and synthetic knitting yarns.

Wakefield, Edward Gibbon (1796–1862) British colonizer of South Australia and New Zealand. After viewing the problems of the penal system, including the forcible removal of convicts to British colonies, he wrote *A Letter from Sydney* (1829) and proposed colonization by the sale of small landholdings to ordinary citizens. He influenced the founding of South Australia as a nonconvict settlement. As organizer and manager of the New Zealand Land Co. (1838–49), he sent colonists to settle New Zealand and forced the British government to recognize the colony. As an adviser to the earl of DURHAM, he influenced the report that led to the union of Upper and Lower Canada. He founded a Church of England settlement at Canterbury, New Zealand (1847).

Waksman, Selman (Abraham) (1888–1973) Ukrainian-U.S. biochemist. He became a U.S. citizen in 1916 and spent most of his career at Rutgers University. After the discovery of penicillin, he played a major role in initiating a calculated, systematic search for antibiotics (a term he coined in 1941) among microorganisms. His 1943 discovery of streptomycin, the first specific agent effective in the treatment of tuberculosis, brought him a 1952 Nobel Prize. Waksman also isolated and developed several other antibiotics, including neomycin, that are used in treating many infectious diseases of humans, domestic animals, and plants.

Walachia \wä-'lā-kē-ə\ Former principality, southern central Europe, between the DANUBE RIVER and Transylvania Alps, Romania. It was founded in 1290 by Radu Negru, a vassal of Hungary, and achieved independence from Hungary in 1330. Its capital in the 14th–17th century was Targoviste. Walachia was under the Turks in the 15th century, though some princes resisted, notably Vlad Dracul (1436–47) and VLAD III TEPES, who are often cited as the historical basis for the Dracula vampire tales. Walachia annexed MOLDAVIA and TRANSYLVANIA in the late 16th cent. Russian influence grew in the 18th century, and in 1774 it came under Russia's protection, though it continued to recognize Turkish suzerainty. Russia's protectorate ended after the CRIMEAN WAR, and in 1859 Walachia united with Moldavia to form Romania.

Walcott \'wȯl-ˌkät\, **Derek (Alton)** (born 1930) Saint Lucian poet and playwright. Of mixed black, Dutch, and English descent, Walcott has lived in his native Saint Lucia, Jamaica, Grenada, Trinidad, and the U.S. Most of his works explore the Caribbean cultural experience. He is best known for his poetry; in volumes such as *In a Green Night* (1962), *The Gulf* (1969), *Another Life* (1973), *The Star-Apple Kingdom* (1979), *The Fortunate Traveller* (1981), and *The Bounty* (1997), Walcott's erudition is submerged in sweeping rhythmic and sensuous sonorities. His epic *Omeros* (1990) is a retelling of the *Odyssey* in Caribbean terms. Of his approximately 30 plays, the best known are *Dream on Monkey Mountain* (produced 1967), *Ti-Jean and His Brothers* (1958), and *Pantomime* (1978). In 1992 he became the first Caribbean writer to be awarded the Nobel Prize.

Wald, George (1906–1997) U.S. biochemist. Born in New York City, he taught at Harvard University from 1934. His outstanding contributions were on the importance of VITAMIN A, the mechanisms of the PHOTOCHEMICAL REACTIONS in the rod cells that enable night vision, and the identification of the color-sensitive pigments in the cone cells (see PHOTORECEPTION, RETINA). He shared the Nobel Prize in 1967 with HALDAN KEFFER HARTLINE and RAGNAR ARTHUR GRANIT. He was a prominent opponent of the Vietnam War.

Waldeck \'väl-ˌdek\ Former state, Germany. Now a part of HESSE, its capital was Arolsen. A county in the Middle Ages, it became a principality in 1712 and part of Prussia in 1867. A republic and constituent state of the WEIMAR REPUBLIC 1918–29, it later formed part of the Prussian Hesse-Nassau province until 1945.

Waldeck-Rousseau \väl-dek-rü-'sō\, **(Pierre-Marie-) René** (1846–1904) French politician. A conservative lawyer, he served in the Chamber of Deputies 1879–89, and served as minister of the interior 1881–82 and 1883–85. In 1884 he sponsored the law that legalized French trade unions. After returning to his prosperous law practice, he became a senator in 1894. In the upheaval over the ALFRED DREYFUS affair, he was appointed premier (1899–1902) and formed a coalition cabinet that persuaded the president to pardon Dreyfus.

Waldenses \wȯl-'den-ˌsēz\ *French* **Vaudois** \vō-'dwä\ *Italian* **Valdesi** \val-'dā-zē\ Members of a Christian movement that originated in 12th-century France. Devotees sought to follow the example of JESUS by living in poverty and simplicity. The movement's reputed founder, PETER WALDO, was eventually condemned by the archbishop of Lyon for his use of a non-Latin Bible and other unorthodox activities. After being placed under ban by Pope Lucius III (1184), Waldo and his followers departed from ROMAN CATHOLICISM by rejecting such concepts as PURGATORY and the veneration of the saints. Rome responded with active persecution and execution of Waldenses, and their numbers diminished by the end of the 15th century. In the 16th century they adopted the church organization of Genevan Protestantism. Intermittently persecuted, they have remained a small movement within Christianity, surviving today in Argentina, Uruguay, and the U.S.

Waldheim, 1971.
UPI

Waldheim \'vält-ˌhīm\, **Kurt** (born 1918) Fourth secretary-general of the UNITED NATIONS (1972–81). After military service in the German army before and during World War II, he entered the foreign service and served successively as ambassador to Canada (1958–60) and the U.N. (1964–68, 1970–71) and as foreign minister (1968–70). Elected U.N. secretary-general to succeed U THANT, he served two terms, during which he oversaw disaster relief in Bangladesh, Nicaragua, and Guatemala and peacekeeping missions in Cyprus, the Middle East, Angola, and Guinea. Denied a third term, he returned to Austria and ran for president in 1986. His candidacy became controversial when it was learned that he had lied about the nature of his military service and his membership in the Nazi Party. Elected nonetheless, he was diplomatically isolated throughout his term (1986–92).

Waldo, Peter *or* **Peter Valdès** \vål-'des\ (died before 1218) French religious leader. Around 1170 he began to preach a doctrine of voluntary poverty in Lyon. In 1179 his vow of poverty was confirmed by Pope ALEXANDER III, but he was forbidden to continue preaching. In 1184 he and his followers, called Paupers, were excommunicated and banished from Lyon. Later influenced by the CATHARI and others, the so-called WALDENSES were severely persecuted from 1197.

Wales *Welsh* **Cymru** \'kəm-rē\ Principality, constituting an integral part of the United Kingdom. It occupies a peninsula on the western side of the island of GREAT BRITAIN. Area: 8,015 sq mi (20,758 sq km). Population (2001 est.): 2,949,000. Capital: CARDIFF. The population is of Celtic, Anglo-Saxon, and Anglo-Norman ancestry. Languages: English, Welsh. Religion: Methodism. Wales is almost entirely an upland area generally known as the Cambrian Mountains. The highest peak in England and Wales, Mount Snowdon, is found in SNOWDONIA NATIONAL PARK. The SEVERN, WYE, and Dee are the longest rivers. The country mines coal, slate, and lead; imports and refines petroleum; and manufactures consumer electronics. Tourism is an important industry. In prehistoric times, tribal divisions of the British Celtic speakers who dominated all of Britain south of the Firth of Forth and the Firth of Clyde inhabited the region. The Romans ruled from the 1st century AD until the 4th–5th century. Welsh Celts fought off incursions from the Anglo-Saxons. A number of kingdoms arose there, but none was successful in uniting the area. The Norman conquerors of England brought all of southern Wales under their rule in 1093. English King EDWARD I conquered northern Wales and made it a principality in 1284. Since 1301 the heir to the English throne has carried the title Prince of Wales. It was incorporated with England in the reign of HENRY VIII. It became a leading international coal-mining center during the 19th century. The Welsh Nationalist Party was founded in 1925, but its influence did not gather force until the 1960s, when Welsh nationalist aspirations rose. In 1997 a referendum approved the devolution of power to an elected assembly, which first convened in 1999.

Wales, Prince of Title of the heir apparent to the British throne. In 1301 EDWARD I of England granted it to his son Edward after conquering Wales and executing the last native Welsh prince (1283). Since that time most of the eldest sons of English sovereigns have been given the title. The title ceases to exist when a Prince of Wales becomes king, until a monarch bestows it on a son.

Walesa \vä-'len-sə, *Polish* vä-'weⁿ-sə\, **Lech** (born 1943) Polish labor leader and president of Poland (1990–95). An electrician, he worked in the Lenin Shipyard at Gdańsk, Poland 1967–76, but was fired for his antigovernment activities. In 1980 he joined workers in a strike and soon became leader of the SOLIDARITY trade union. The union was banned in 1981, and he was detained into 1982. In 1983 he was awarded the Nobel Peace Prize. He continued to direct the outlawed union until it received legal recognition in 1988. Though he refused to serve as premier, he won Poland's first direct presidential election by a landslide in 1990, and helped guide Poland into a free-market economy. His confrontational style eroded his popularity, and he was narrowly defeated in his bid for reelection in 1995.

Wali Allah \wä-'lē-ä-'lä\, **Shah** (1702/3–1762) Indian Islamic theologian. He received a traditional Islamic education, and after a pilgrimage to Mecca in 1732 he remained in the Hejaz to study theology. Living in a time of disillusionment following the death of AURANGZEB, he believed that Muslim polity could be restored only through religious reform that would harmonize Islam with India's changing social and economic conditions. He was steadfastly monotheistic but otherwise much more liberal than most Islamic theologians that had preceded him. His best-known work is *The Secrets of Belief*. His synthesis of theology, philosophy, and mysticism so reinvigorated Islam that it became prevalent among Islamic scholars in India until the 20th century.

Walker, Alice (Malsenior) (born 1944) U.S. writer. Born in Eatonton, Ga., Walker moved to Mississippi after attending Spelman and Sarah Lawrence colleges and became involved with the civil-rights movement. Her works are noted for their insightful treatment of African-American culture. Her third and most popular novel, *The Color Purple* (1982, Pulitzer Prize; film, 1985), depicts a black woman's struggle for racial and sexual equality. Her later novels include *The Temple of My Familiar* (1989) and *Possessing the Secret of Joy* (1992). She has also written essays, some collected in *In Search of Our Mothers' Gardens* (1983); several books of poetry; short stories; and children's books.

Walker, David (1785–1830) U.S. abolitionist. Born in Wilmington, N.C., to a slave father and a free mother, he was educated and traveled widely before settling in Boston, where he became an abolitionist lecturer and wrote for the antislavery *Freedom's Journal.* In his pamphlet *Appeal to the Colored Citizens of the World* (1829), he called for armed revolt. He smuggled it into the South by hiding copies in clothing that he sold to sailors from his used-clothes store in Boston. Southern states banned all abolitionist literature, and Walker was warned to flee for his life to Canada. He refused, and his body was found soon after; many believed he was poisoned.

Walker, Jimmy *orig.* **James John** (1881–1946) U.S. politician. Born in New York City, he entered politics after graduating from New York Law School, becoming a member of the Assembly (1909) and then of the State Senate (1914). Backed by Gov. ALFRED E. SMITH and Tammany Hall, he was elected mayor in 1925 and later reelected. A popular figure known for his charm and wit but particularly for his enthusiastic participation in the high life typical of the era, he made improvements in sanitation, hospitals, and subways. In 1931 the state legislature, investigating the city's affairs, charged Walker with corruption; he resigned in 1932.

Walker, Sarah Breedlove *orig.* **Sarah Breedlove** (1867–1919) U.S. businesswoman and philanthropist, the first black female millionaire in the U.S. Born near Delta, La., she was a widowed washerwoman with a daughter to support in 1905 when she developed a method for straightening curly hair. She founded the Madame C. J. Walker Manufacturing Co. to sell her treatment, and her door-to-door saleswomen became familiar figures in the black communities of the U.S. and the Caribbean. In 1910 she moved her company to Indianapolis. She augmented her earnings with shrewd real-estate investments, and she donated two-thirds of her fortune to charitable and educational institutions. Her daughter, A'Lelia Walker Kennedy, hosted salons where artists and cultural figures mingled during the HARLEM RENAISSANCE.

Walker, William (1824–1860) U.S. military adventurer. Born in Nashville, Tenn., he moved to California in 1850. His interest in colonizing Baja California developed into a filibustering (insurrection) scheme. He landed at La Paz (1853) and proclaimed Lower California and Sonora an independent republic, but Mexican resistance forced him back to the U.S. In 1855 he sailed to Nicaragua, where he effectively established himself as leader. There, officers of CORNELIUS VANDERBILT's Accessory Transit Co. promised him financial assistance in a plot to take the company away from Vanderbilt. Walker seized the company and turned it over to them, then made himself president of Nicaragua (1856). In 1857 Vanderbilt induced five Central American republics to drive Walker out. In 1860 he attempted a filibuster in Honduras, where he was captured and executed.

Walker Cup Trophy awarded to the winner of a golf competition between amateur men's teams from the U.S. and Britain. It has been held biennially since 1922 on sites alternating between the two countries. The cup is named for the event's organizer, George H. Walker, a president of the U.S. Golf Association Contests consist of four 18-hole foursome matches and eight 18-hole singles matches on each of two days, with one point awarded to the winning side in each match.

walking In TRACK AND FIELD, a form of racing in which the competitor's advancing foot must touch the ground before the rear foot leaves it. Walking as a sport dates from the later 19th century. Walking races of 10 mi and 3,500 m were added to the men's Olympic program in 1908, but since 1956 the Olympic distances have been 20 km and 50 km. A women's 10-km walk was introduced in 1992.

walking catfish Species *(Clarias batrachus)* of Asian and African CATFISH that can progress remarkable distances over dry land. It uses its pectoral-fin spines as anchors to prevent jackknifing as its body musculature produces snakelike movements. Treelike respiratory structures extending above the gill chambers enable it to breathe. It has been introduced into southern Florida, where it now poses a serious threat to native fauna.

walking leaf See LEAF INSECT

wall Any of various upright constructions used to divide or enclose a room or building. In traditional masonry construction, BEARING WALLS supported the weight of floors and roofs, but modern steel and reinforced-concrete frames, as well as heavy timber and other skeletal structures, require exterior walls only for shelter. Some urban buildings dispense with walls on the ground floor, extending outdoor plazas under the building and permitting easier access to elevators, escalators, and stairs. In masonry construction, all types of floors and roofs except domes are most easily supported on straight, parallel walls. Nonbearing walls, used when loads are carried by girders, beams, or other members, can be either CURTAIN WALLS or infill of brick, block, or other material. See also CAVITY WALL, RETAINING WALL, SHEAR WALL.

Wall Street Street in New York City where many major U.S. financial institutions are located. The street, in southern Manhattan, is narrow and short and extends only about seven blocks from Broadway to the East River. It was named for an earthen wall built by Dutch settlers in 1653 to repel an expected English invasion. Even before the Civil War it was recognized as the nation's financial capital, and it remains a worldwide symbol of high finance. The Wall Street, or financial, district contains the NEW YORK STOCK EXCHANGE, the AMERICAN STOCK EXCHANGE, and the Federal Reserve Bank of New York. The district is also the headquarters for many INVESTMENT BANKS, securities dealers, utilities and insurance companies, and brokerage firms.

Wall Street Journal, The Daily business newspaper, the most influential U.S. business-oriented paper and one of the most respected dailies in the world. Founded in 1889 by Charles H. Dow, founder of Dow Jones & Co., it quickly won success. Beginning in the Great Depression, it began to feature more articles, reviews, and opinion on other subjects. Published in New York City and in four regional editions printed in 10 plants across the U.S., it has the highest daily circulation of any U.S. newspaper. It is also published in Asian, European, and other special editions.

wallaby \ˈwä-lə-bē\ Any of about 25 species of medium-sized KANGAROOS, found chiefly in Australia. Brush wallabies (11 species) are built like the big kangaroos but differ in dentition. Rock wallabies live among rocks, usually near water. Nail-tailed wallabies, named for a horny growth on the tail tip, rotate their forelimbs while hopping. The small hare wallabies resemble HARES in movement and some habits. The small, stocky scrub wallabies, hunted for meat and fur, have short hind limbs and pointy noses. The similar short-tailed scrub wallaby occurs only on two offshore islands of western Australia. Several wallaby species have been exterminated, and several others are endangered.

Bridled nail-tailed wallaby (*Onychogalea fraenata*).

Wallace, Alfred Russel (1823–1913) British naturalist. Though trained as a surveyor and architect, he became interested in botany and traveled to the Amazon in 1848 to collect specimens. In 1854–62 he toured the Malay Archipelago, augmenting his collection. His observations of the islands led to his developing a theory of the origin of species through natural selection independently of, and simultaneously with, CHARLES DARWIN, though Darwin developed his own theory in much greater detail, provided far more evidence for it, and was mainly responsible for its acceptance. Unlike Darwin, Wallace insisted that the higher mental capacities of humans could not have arisen by natural selection but that some nonbiological agency must have been responsible. He hypothesized a boundary (Wallace's line) running between the islands of the Malay Archipelago, between the oriental and Australasian faunal regions, many animals abundant on one side being absent on the other. In the realm of public policy he supported socialism, pacifism, land nationalization, and women's suffrage. His works include *Contributions to the Theory of Natural Selection* (1870), *Geographical Distribution of Animals* (2 vols., 1876), and *Darwinism* (1889).

Wallace, (William Roy) DeWitt and Lila Acheson *orig.* **Lila Bell Acheson** (1889–1981, 1889–1984) U.S. publishers. Born in St. Paul, Minn., De Witt Wallace began an index of favorite magazine articles while he was briefly a student of the University of California, and developed the idea of a pocket-sized digest of popular articles while recuperating from wounds suffered in World War I. Lila Acheson, a minister's daughter born in Virden, Manitoba, worked in social services during the war. The two were married in 1921. After various publishers rejected the digest idea, they began publishing *READER'S DIGEST* themselves on a low budget, and had rapid success. DeWitt Wallace served as editor until 1965. They supported numerous philanthropic causes; the Lila Wallace–Reader's Digest Fund has been a major benefactor of the arts and culture.

Wallace, (Richard Horatio) Edgar (1875–1932) British novelist, playwright, and journalist. He held odd jobs, served in the army, and was a reporter before producing his first success, *The Four Just Men* (1905). With works such as *Sanders of the River* (1911), *The Crimson Circle* (1922), *The Flying Squad* (1928), and *The Terror* (1930), he virtually invented the modern "thriller"; the plots of his detective and suspense stories are complex but clearly developed and end in exciting climaxes. His output (including 175 books) was prodigious and his rate of production so great as to be the subject of humor.

Wallace, George C(orley) (1919–1998) U.S. politician. Born in Clio, Ala., he practiced law and served in the state legislature 1947–53. As a circuit court judge (1953–59), he was known for his resistance to federal investigation of racial discrimination. Campaigning as a segregationist, he was elected governor in 1963 and kept his pledge "to stand in the schoolhouse door" to prevent enrollment of black students at the University of Alabama. He yielded only in the face of the federalized National Guard. Further confrontations made him a nationwide symbol of intransigence toward racial integration. He formed the American Independent Party and was its presidential candidate in 1968, winning 13% of the popular vote. He again served as governor 1971–79. While campaigning for the 1972 Democratic presidential nomination, he was shot in an assassination attempt and left partly paralyzed. In the 1980s he renounced his segregationist views, and he won his last term as governor (1983–87) with support from black voters.

Wallace, Henry A(gard) (1888–1965) U.S. politician. Born in Adair Co., Iowa, he became an agricultural expert and succeeded his father as editor of *Wallace's Farmer* (1924–33). In 1932 he helped FRANKLIN ROOSEVELT win Iowa. As U.S. secretary of agriculture (1933–40), he shaped the administration's farm policy, including the AGRICULTURAL ADJUSTMENT ADMINISTRATION. He served as vice president in Roosevelt's third term but was replaced in 1944 by HARRY TRUMAN. He was later secretary of commerce (1945–46). Very liberal in his views, he helped form the PROGRESSIVE PARTY in 1948 and was its candidate against Truman in the presidential election, winning over 1 million votes. He wrote several books, including *Sixty Million Jobs* (1945).

Wallace, Lew(is) (1827–1905) U.S. writer. Born in Brookville, Ind., the son of the state's governor, he served in the Mexican War and in the American Civil War, in which he rose to major general. Later he returned to law practice, interrupted by two diplomatic postings. His reputation rests on three historical novels: *The Fair God* (1873), on the Spanish conquest of Mexico; *The Prince of India* (1893), on the Byzantine empire; and the enormously popular *Ben-Hur* (1880; films, 1925,

1959), a romantic tale set in the Roman empire during the time of Christ.

Wallace, Mike *orig.* **Myron Leon** (born 1918) U.S. television interviewer and reporter. Born in Brookline, Mass., he worked as an announcer and newscaster on radio from 1939 and on television from 1946, and hosted several television quiz shows in the 1950s. He joined CBS as a reporter in 1963 and was coeditor of the long-running *60 Minutes* from its first program in 1968. Noted for his aggressive interviewing style, he has won numerous Emmy awards.

Lew Wallace.

BY COURTESY OF THE LIBRARY OF CONGRESS, WASHINGTON, D.C.

Wallace, William *later* **Sir William** (c. 1270–1305) Scottish national hero. Son of a small landowner, he began his attacks on English settlements and garrisons in 1297, after EDWARD I declared himself ruler of Scotland. His army defeated a much larger English force at Stirling Bridge, captured Stirling Castle, and then ravaged northern England, for which Wallace was knighted and proclaimed guardian of the Scottish kingdom. In 1298 Edward I invaded Scotland and defeated Wallace at the Battle of Falkirk. Disgraced, Wallace resigned his guardianship and was replaced by the future ROBERT I, but apparently continued to fight a guerrilla war. In 1305 he was arrested by the English and hanged, then disemboweled, beheaded, and quartered. The next year Robert raised the rebellion that eventually won independence for Scotland.

Wallack, James William (1795–1864) British-U.S. actor-manager. Born into a London stage family, he acted in Shakespearean roles from age 12 and made his U.S. debut as Macbeth in 1818. He performed in London and New York until 1852, crossing the Atlantic 35 times. In 1837–39 he comanaged New York's National Theater with his brother Henry John Wallack (1790–1870), the company's leading player. In 1852–62 he comanaged the Lyceum Theater (renamed Wallack's Lyceum) with his son Lester (1820–1888) as stage manager. Succeeding his father as general manager, Lester staged polished productions of English plays and trained most of the major 19th-century U.S. stage performers, including his cousin James William Wallack II (1818–1873). In 1882 Lester built another Wallack Theater, which he managed until 1887.

wallaroo \ˌwä-lə-ˈrü\ *or* **euro** \ˈyu̇r-ˌō\ One of the three largest species of KANGAROO. The wallaroo *(Macropus robustus)* is smaller and stockier than the other two species (also in the genus *Macropus*); its color varies from dark gray to pinkish brown. It lives in rocky country throughout Australia except in Victoria.

Wallenberg \ˈwä-lən-ˌbərg, *Swed* ˈwä-lən-ˌber-ē\, **Raoul** (1912–1947?) Swedish businessman and humanitarian. The scion of a family of bankers, industrialists, and diplomats, in 1936 he became the foreign representative of a Hungarian trading company whose president was Jewish. When the Nazis sent troops to round up Jews in Hungary (1944), Wallenberg asked to be sent to Budapest as a diplomat. There he rescued thousands of Hungarian Jews by sheltering them in "protected houses" under the Swedish flag or securing their passage out of Hungary through bribes or counterfeit documents. Soon after Soviet troops occupied Budapest (1945), he was arrested on suspicion of espionage. He was sent to Moscow, where he allegedly died of a heart attack in prison in 1947. Unconfirmed reports from freed Soviet prisoners reported him alive in 1951, 1959, and 1975.

Wallenda \vä-ˈlen-dä, *Engl* wȯ-ˈlen-də\, **Karl** (1905–1978) German-U.S. circus acrobat. He founded the Great Wallendas acrobatic troupe, which achieved fame in Europe for its four-man pyramid and cycling on the high wire without a safety net. His wife, Helen Kreis (1910–1996), joined the troupe in 1926 and later was balanced at the peak of the seven-person pyramid, the most famous of the Wallendas' acts. The troupe traveled with the U.S. RINGLING BROS. and Barnum & Bailey Circus 1928–46, then performed as freelancers. Karl's nephew Gunther (1927–1996) trained on the wire from age 5; when a pyramid collapsed in 1962, Gunther was the only member left standing and rescued three who were clinging to the wire; two others were killed and one was paralyzed. Two troupe members died in accidents in 1963 and 1972. Karl died in a fall from a wind-whipped wire 123 ft (37 m) above a street in San Juan, Puerto Rico.

Wallenstein \ˈvä-lən-ˌshtīn, *Engl* ˈwä-lən-ˌstīn\, **Albrecht Wenzel Eusebius von** *later* **Herzog (Duke) von Mecklenburg** (1583–1634) Austrian general. A noble of Bohemia, he served with the future Habsburg emperor FERDINAND II in the campaign against Venice in 1617. He remained loyal to Ferdinand when other Bohemian nobles revolted (1618–23) and was made governor of Bohemia and allowed to acquire vast holdings in confiscated estates. Created duke of Friedland (1625), he commanded the imperial armies in the Thirty Years' War. After successes in the war against Denmark (1625–29), he was awarded the principality of Sagan (1627) and the duchy of Mecklenburg (1629). Under pressure from the German princes, Ferdinand was forced to dismiss Wallenstein. Recalled to imperial command in 1631, he drove the Swedish army from Bavaria and Franconia but was defeated at the Battle of Lützen (1632). Believing he had the support of his generals, he mounted a revolt against the emperor (1634) and was assassinated.

Waller, Edmund (1606–1687) English poet. As a member of Parliament during the political turmoil of the 1640s, he was arrested for his part in a plot to establish London as a stronghold of the king; by betraying his colleagues and by lavish bribes, he avoided death. He later wrote poetic tributes to both OLIVER CROMWELL (1655) and CHARLES II (1660). Rejecting the dense verse of METAPHYSICAL POETRY, he adopted smooth, regular versification, preparing the way for the heroic couplet's emergence by the end of the 17th century as the dominant form of English poetry. His lyrics include the famous "Go, lovely Rose!"

Waller, Fats *orig.* **Thomas Wright** (1904–1943) U.S. pianist, singer, and composer, one of the most popular and charismatic figures in jazz. Born in New York City, Waller was influenced early by stride pianist JAMES P. JOHNSON. He became an important exponent of stride piano by the late 1920s, recording solo piano pieces such as "Handful of Keys." From 1934 he recorded with a small ensemble, Fats Waller and His Rhythm, integrating his vocals and unique comic timing with instrumental finesse. His rhythmically contagious performances of his own songs, such as "Ain't Misbehavin'" and "Honeysuckle Rose," are timeless classics of jazz. A notorious bon vivant, Waller died of pneumonia following a heavy touring schedule.

walleye *or* **walleyed pike** Species *(Stizostedion vitreum)* of pike-perch (family Percidae), carnivorous food and game fishes found in clear, cool lakes and rivers of eastern North America. Walleyes are slender and darkly mottled. They have two dorsal fins and generally weigh less than 10 lbs (4.5 kg), though some may weigh up to 24 lbs (11 kg). They are at most 35 in. (90 cm) long. Walleyes are not true PIKES.

Wallis, Barnes (Neville) *later* **Sir Barnes** (1887–1979) British aeronautical designer and military engineer. He invented the innovative "dambuster" bombs used in World War II by the RAF to destroy the Möhne and Eder dams in Germany's industrial Ruhr area, producing heavy floods that slowed industrial production. He also produced the 12,000-lb (5,400 kg) "Tallboy" and the 22,000-lb (10,000 kg) "Grand Slam" bombs and was responsible for the bombs that destroyed the German warship *Tirpitz,* the V-rocket sites, and much of Germany's railway system. In 1971 he designed an aircraft that could fly five times the speed of sound.

Wallis and Futuna Islands Island group, South Pacific Ocean. It is a self-governing overseas territory (pop., 1993 est.: 14,000) of France; it includes the two groups of WALLIS ISLANDS and FUTUNA ISLANDS. The administrative seat is the village of Matautu, on Uvea island. Until 1961 it was a protectorate under French authority attached to NEW CALEDONIA.

Wallis Islands Island group (pop., 1990: 9,000), forming the north-eastern part of the French overseas territory of Wallis and Futuna, South Pacific Ocean. It comprises the main island of Uvea and eight islets, all enclosed in one coral reef, and has an area of 23 sq mi (60 sq km). Visited in 1767 by the British navigator Capt. Samuel Wallis, the islands were occupied by the French in 1842. They became a French protectorate in 1887 and part of the overseas territory in 1959.

wallpaper Ornamental and utilitarian covering for walls made from long sheets of paper that have been stenciled, painted, or printed with abstract or narrative designs. Wallpaper developed soon after the introduction of papermaking to Europe in the late 15th century, originally as a substitute for tapestry, painted cloth, and wood paneling, and the first wallpapers were esteemed for the cleverness with which they mimicked the more costly wall coverings. In the 18th century, designs such as chintz patterns and stripes began to express the medium's decorative possibilities. In the mid-19th century, the wallpapers of WILLIAM MORRIS, featuring stylized, naturalistic patterns, created a revolution in wallpaper design. Plastic coating now improves wallpaper's durability and maintenance.

Hand-printed wallpaper by Jean-Baptiste Réveillon, c. 1780–90; in the Victoria and Albert Museum, London.

BY COURTESY OF THE VICTORIA AND ALBERT MUSEUM, LONDON; PHOTOGRAPH, THE COOPER-BRIDGEMAN LIBRARY, LONDON

walnut Any of about 20 species of DECIDUOUS TREES in the genus *Juglans,* family Juglandaceae. Black walnut *(J. nigra)* of eastern North America and English, or Persian, walnut *(J. regia),* native to Iran, are valuable timber trees that produce edible NUTS. The butternut *(J. cinerea)* of eastern North America also produces an edible nut. The walnut family contains an additional seven genera of flowering plants, found mainly in the northern temperate zone in a variety of habitats. PECAN and HICKORY are among the many family members that are prized for both their edible nuts and their strong, attractive woods, especially noted for their grain patterns and luster. Leaves of the walnut family are featherlike; tiny, resinous scales that look like yellow dots on the undersurface of the leaflets give *Juglans* species a pungent aroma.

Walnut Canyon National Monument National monument, northern central Arizona. Established in 1915, and covering an area of 3 sq mi (8 sq km), it preserves more than 300 pre-Columbian dwellings built by the PUEBLO INDIANS in shallow caves on the canyon walls. Main occupancy was from AD 1000 to 1200.

Walpole, Horace *orig.* **Horatio** *later* **Earl of Orford** (1717–1797) English writer, connoisseur, and collector. The son of ROBERT WALPOLE, he had an undistinguished career in Parliament. In 1747 he acquired a small villa at Twickenham that he transformed into a pseudo-Gothic showplace called Strawberry Hill. His literary output was extremely varied. He became famous for *The Castle of Otranto* (1765), the first GOTHIC NOVEL in English. He is especially remembered for his private correspondence of more than 3,000 letters, most addressed to Horace Mann, a British diplomat. Intended for posthumous publication, they constitute a survey of the history, manners, and taste of his age.

Horace Walpole, detail of an oil painting by Sir Joshua Reynolds, 1757; in the City of Birmingham Museum and Art Gallery, England.

BY COURTESY OF BIRMINGHAM MUSEUMS AND ART GALLERY

Walpole, Hugh (Seymour) *later* **Sir Hugh** (1884–1941) British novelist, critic, and dramatist. A natural storyteller, Walpole turned to writing and reviewing books after unsuccessful attempts at teaching and lay reading in the Anglican church. Among his important novels is the semiautobiographical series that includes *Jeremy* (1919), *Jeremy and Hamlet* (1923), and *Jeremy at Crale* (1927). The "Herries Chronicle," about an English country family, comprises *Rogue Herries* (1930), *Judith Paris* (1931), *The Fortress* (1932), and *Vanessa* (1933). He also wrote critical works on ANTHONY TROLLOPE, WALTER SCOTT, and JOSEPH CONRAD.

Walpole, Robert *later* **Earl of Orford** (1676–1745) English statesman generally regarded as the first British prime minister. Elected to the House of Commons in 1701, he became an active Whig parliamentarian. He served as secretary at war 1708–10, and as treasurer of the navy 1710–11. He was also a member of the KIT-CAT CLUB. The Tory government sought to remove his influence by impeaching him for corruption, and he was expelled from the Commons in 1712. With the accession of GEORGE I (1714), he regained his position and rose rapidly to become first lord of the treasury and chancellor of the exchequer (1715–17, 1721–42). Though associated with the SOUTH SEA BUBBLE scandal, he restored confidence in the government and maintained the Whigs in office. He cultivated the support of GEORGE II from 1727 and used royal patronage for political ends, skillfully managing the House of Commons to win support for his trade and fiscal programs, including the SINKING FUND. With his consolidation of power, he effectively became the first British prime minister. He avoided foreign entanglements and kept England neutral until 1739, but was forced into the War of JENKINS' EAR. He resigned under pressure in 1742 and was created an earl. His acclaimed art collection, sold to Russia in 1779, became part of the Hermitage Museum collection.

Robert Walpole, detail of an oil painting by Sir Godfrey Kneller, c. 1710–15; in the National Portrait Gallery, London.

BY COURTESY OF THE NATIONAL PORTRAIT GALLERY, LONDON

Walpurgis Night Night before May 1. The name comes from the 8th-century St. Walburga (or Walpurgis), an English missionary who ran an important early convent in Germany, May 1 being one of her feast days. In Sweden it is celebrated with bonfires as the beginning of spring. In Germany, as Walpurgisnacht, it was the night witches were supposed to meet in the Harz Mountains (see BROCKEN), though the association of witches with St. Walburga is only coincidental. See also BELTANE.

Walras \väl-ˈrä\, **(Marie-Esprit-) Léon** (1834–1910) French-Swiss economist. An advocate of COOPERATIVES as an alternative to revolution, he ran a bank for producers' cooperatives with Léon Say (grandson of J.-B. SAY) from 1865 to 1868. At the Academy of Lausanne, Switzerland (1870–92), he began the school of economics later known (under VILFREDO PARETO) as the Lausanne school. Walras's *Elements of Pure Economics* (1874–77) was one of the first comprehensive mathematical analyses of general economic equilibrium. Assuming an environment of free competition, he constructed a mathematical model in which productive factors, products, and prices automatically adjust in equilibrium. He thus tied together the theories of production, exchange, money, and capital.

walrus Only living species *(Odobenus rosmarus)* of the PINNIPED family Odobenidae. Larger than the related SEALS, walrus males grow up to 12 ft (3.7 m) long and weigh up to 2,800 lbs (1,270 kg). Both sexes have long, downward-pointing tusks that may grow to 3 ft (1 m) long and weigh 12 lbs (5.4 kg) each. They have no external ears. The grayish skin is deeply folded over the shoulders. They live on ice

Atlantic walrus (*Odobenus rosmarus rosmarus*).

FRANCISCO ERIZE/BRUCE COLEMAN LTD.

floes, in groups of up to 100, on relatively shallow water in arctic seas of Eurasia and North America. They may dive to great depths in search of food, mostly shellfish. On land and ice, they move on all four limbs. They generally follow the ice line south in winter and north in summer. Traditionally important to native humans as sources of food and clothing, they have also been hunted commercially for centuries, which has resulted in serious depletion of their numbers. Commercial hunting is now generally banned.

Walsh, Raoul (1887–1980) U.S. film director. Born in New York City, he became a screen actor and assistant to D. W. GRIFFITH in 1912 and appeared in *The Birth of a Nation* (1915). In his 50-year career, he directed over 200 films, including many outdoor action movies noted for their brisk pacing; they included *What Price Glory?* (1926), *The Roaring Twenties* (1939), *They Drive by Night* (1940), *They Died with Their Boots On* (1941), *High Sierra* (1941), *White Heat* (1949), *The Naked and the Dead* (1958), and *A Distant Trumpet* (1964).

Walsingham, Francis *later* **Sir Francis** (1532?–1590) English statesman and adviser to Queen ELIZABETH I (1573–90). A member of Parliament from 1563, he became ambassador to the French court (1570–73) and established friendly relations between France and England. He was admitted to the Privy Council in 1573 and became secretary of state to Elizabeth I. Though not allowed to pursue an independent policy, he faithfully executed Elizabeth's foreign policy. He proved invaluable in uncovering conspiracies by Catholics against Elizabeth's life, including the plots by Francis Throckmorton (1583) and ANTHONY BABINGTON (1586) to free MARY, QUEEN OF SCOTS.

Walter, Bruno *orig.* **Bruno Walter Schlesinger** (1876–1962) German-U.S. conductor. An associate of G. MAHLER, he was long a faithful proponent and interpreter of Mahler's music, giving the world premieres of *Das Lied von der Erde* and the Symphony No. 9. He held positions in Munich (1913–22) and at Covent Garden (1924–31), but thereafter served more often as a guest conductor than a music director. After moving to the U.S. in 1939, he often conducted the New York Philharmonic (recording as the Columbia or CBS Symphony), the Metropolitan Opera, the Philadelphia Orchestra, and the Los Angeles Philharmonic, and was admired for the warmth of his interpretations.

Walter, John (1739–1812) English newspaper publisher. Initially a coal dealer and marine-insurance underwriter, Walter acquired the patent for a printing system in 1783, and in 1785 in London began to publish the *Daily Universal Register.* He renamed it *The* TIMES in 1788. Though neither outstanding nor honest as a journalist, he turned from scandal to more serious reportage and organized (while in prison for libeling members of the royal family) a news service from the European continent, thereby launching *The Times* toward its later preeminence in foreign news coverage. Walter's family owned *The Times* for almost 125 years.

Walters, Barbara (born 1931) U.S. television journalist. Born in Boston, she worked in television as a writer-producer (1952–58), interviewer (1964–74), and cohost (1974–76) of NBC's *Today* show. In 1976–78, for an unprecedented $1 million a year, she was coanchor of the *ABC Evening News*, the first woman to anchor a network newscast. From 1976 she hosted the series of *Barbara Walters Specials*, interviewing celebrities and world leaders. From 1984 she also cohosted ABC's *20/20* news magazine program.

Walther von der Vogelweide \ˈväl-tər-fȯn-der-ˈfō-gəl-ˌvī-də\ (c. 1170–c.1230) Greatest German lyric poet of the Middle Ages. Of knightly birth, Walther was educated at a monastery school. He served masters in several courts. His poetry goes far beyond the artificial conventions followed by other MINNESINGERS by introducing an element of realism. He emphasizes the virtues of the balanced life, in both the social and the personal spheres. More than half of his approximately 200 extant poems are political, moral, or religious; the rest are love poems, among them the popular "Unter der Linden."

Walton, Izaak (1593–1683) English biographer and author. A prosperous ironmonger with only a few years of schooling, he read widely, developed scholarly tastes, and associated with men of learning. A friend and fishing companion of JOHN DONNE, he contributed "An Elegie" to the posthumous publication of Donne's poetry (1633) and wrote biographies of Donne (1640), GEORGE HERBERT (1670), and others. His classic *The Compleat Angler* (1653), a pastoral discourse on the joys and stratagems of fishing, is one of the most frequently reprinted works in English literature, most often in a revision (1676) with additions by Charles Cotton (1630–1687).

Walton, Sam(uel Moore) (1918–1992) U.S. retail magnate, founder of Wal-Mart Stores, Inc. Born in Kingfisher, Okla., he attended the University of Missouri and then trained with the J.C. PENNEY Co. In 1945 he started a chain of variety stores in Arkansas, and in 1962 he opened his first Wal-Mart store in Rogers, Ark., offering a wide selection of discount merchandise. Whereas other discount-store chains were usually situated in or near large cities, Walton based his stores in small towns where there was little competition from such chains. Using this strategy the chain expanded to 800 stores by 1985. In 1983 he opened the first Sam's Wholesale Club. Walton stepped down as chief executive officer of Wal-Mart Stores in 1988 but remained chairman until his death, by which time there were over 1,700 stores and Walton's family was the wealthiest in the U.S. In the 1990s Wal-Mart became controversial for depleting downtown districts of their commercial life by siting stores nearby. Today it is the world's largest retailer.

Walton, William (Turner) *later* **Sir William** (1902–1983) British composer. His parents were musicians, and he learned to sing and play piano and violin early. He made a splash at age 19 by setting SITWELL FAMILY's whimsical verse in the jazzy *Facade* (1923), premiered with the poet reading her poetry through a megaphone. Later works include *Belshazzar's Feast* (1931), two symphonies (1935, 1960), and concertos for viola, violin, and cello (1929, 1939, 1956), marking him as E. ELGAR's successor. His scores for LAURENCE OLIVIER's films of *Henry V* (1944), *Hamlet* (1947), and *Richard III* (1955) became well known; he also wrote coronation marches for GEORGE VI and ELIZABETH II.

waltz Ballroom turning dance evolved from the LÄNDLER in the 18th century. It is characterized by a step, slide, and step in 3/4 time. It was highly popular in the 19th and early 20th century. Variations include the rapid, whirling Viennese waltz and the slower, dipping Boston waltz, modified by VERNON AND IRENE CASTLE as the hesitation waltz. Many 19th-century composers wrote waltz music, most notably F. SCHUBERT, F. CHOPIN, J. BRAHMS, and JOHANN STRAUSS, JR.

Walvis Bay Town (pop., 1985: 17,000), western central Namibia, on the Atlantic Ocean. A mid-19th-century rush for GUANO deposits on nearby islands was followed by British annexation of the bay and the adjacent land in 1878. It was incorporated into Britain's Cape Colony in 1884. In 1910 it was included in the newly united South Africa. Administered as part of South West Africa 1922–77, it was then governed directly by South Africa, which retained the enclave after Namibia reached independence in 1990. The two countries administered the enclave jointly 1992–94; then South Africa transferred it to Namibia. Its harbor serves as Namibia's chief port.

wampum Tubular shell beads assembled into strings or woven into belts or embroidered ornaments. The ALGONQUIAN word (short for *wampumpeag)* translates as "string of white (shell beads)." Before contact with white settlers, Indians used wampum primarily ceremonially or in GIFT EXCHANGES. In the early 17th century it came to be used as money in trade with whites because of a shortage of European currency.

Wanaka \ˈwä-nə-kə\, **Lake** Lake, western central SOUTH ISLAND, New Zealand. It covers an area of 75 sq mi (193 sq km) and is some 1,000 ft (300 m) deep. Fed by the Makarora and Matukituki rivers, it is the source of the CLUTHA RIVER. Its outlet is harnessed for hydroelectric power.

Wang Anshi *or* **Wang An-shih** \ˈwäŋ-ˈän-ˈshir\ (1021–1086) Chinese poet and government reformer of the SONG DYNASTY. His "New Policies" of 1069–76 sparked academic controversy that continued for centuries. He created a fund for agricultural loans to farmers to spare them the exorbitant demands of moneylenders; he also replaced corvée labor with a hired-service system financed by a graduated tax levied on all families. He enabled officials to purchase supplies at the cheapest price in the most convenient market. He established a village militia system (see BAOJIA), reorganized the HANLIN ACADEMY, and restructured the civil-service examinations. His reforms were unpopular and Wang was forced to resign in 1074, returning in 1075 with less political power. After the emperor's death an antireform clique came to power; they had dismantled Wang's reforms by his death in 1086. Today he is seen as totalitarian by some and as a socially minded crusader by others. See also FAN ZHONGYEN.

Wang Chong *or* **Wang Ch'ung** \'wäŋ-'chu̇ŋ\ (AD 27–100?) Chinese philosopher of the HAN DYNASTY. A rationalistic naturalist, he paved the way for the critical spirit of the next philosophical period and prepared China for the advent of Neo-Taoism. He opposed the superstitious element of CONFUCIANISM, declaring that natural events occur spontaneously and are not influenced by the actions of humans, who have no exceptional position in the universe. He also insisted that theories be supported by concrete evidence and experimental proof. Though never greatly popular in China, he attracted new interest in the 20th century for his foreshadowing of RATIONALISM and the SCIENTIFIC METHOD.

Wang Jingwei *or* **Wang Ching-wei** \'wäŋ-'jiŋ-'wā\ (1883–1944) Chinese leader, head of the regime established by the Japanese in 1940 to govern their conquests in China. A leading polemicist for SUN YAT-SEN's revolutionary party, in 1910 he tried to assassinate the imperial regent and was caught; his courage in the face of execution resulted in his sentence being reduced. He was released the following year after the Republican Revolution. In the 1920s he served as a major official in the Nationalist Party (see GUOMINDANG). After Sun's death, he chaired the party while CHIANG KAI-SHEK led the NORTHERN EXPEDITION against China's WARLORDS. Chiang and Wang vied for party control; in a compromise in 1932, Wang became president and Chiang headed the military. After war erupted with Japan, Wang flew to Hanoi and issued a statement calling on the Chinese to work out a peaceful settlement. In 1940, in cooperation with the Japanese, he became head of a regime that governed the Japanese-occupied areas centered on Nanjing. Though Wang had hoped to be granted virtual autonomy, the Japanese continued to exercise military and economic dominance. He died while undergoing medical treatment in Japan.

Wang Mang \'wäŋ-'mäŋ\ (45 BC–AD 23) Founder of the short-lived Xin dynasty (AD 9–25), an interlude between the two halves of the HAN DYNASTY in China. Wang's family was well connected to the Han imperial family and in 8 BC Wang was appointed regent, only to lose the position when the emperor died. When the new emperor died in 1 BC, Wang returned as regent and married his daughter to the subsequent emperor, who also died. Wang picked the youngest of more than 50 eligible heirs to follow him and was named acting emperor. In AD 9 he ascended the throne and proclaimed the Xin dynasty. His dynasty might have endured had the Huang (Yellow) River not changed course twice before AD 11, resulting in massive devastation and attendant famines, epidemics, and social unrest. Peasants banded together in ever larger units. One such group, the RED EYEBROWS, set the capital on fire, forced their way into the palace, and killed him.

Wang Yangming *or* **Wang Yang-ming** \'wäŋ-'yäŋ-'miŋ\ (1472–1529) Chinese scholar and official whose idealistic interpretation of NEO-CONFUCIANISM influenced philosophical thinking in East Asia for centuries. Son of a high government official, he was both a secretary to the Ministry of War and a lecturer on Confucianism by 1505. The next year, he was banished to a post in remote Guizhou, where hardship and solitude led him to focus on philosophy. He concluded that investigation of the principles of things should occur within the mind rather than through actual objects, and that knowledge and action are codependent. Named governor of southern Jiangxi in 1516, he suppressed several rebellions and implemented governmental, social, and educational reform. By the time he was appointed war minister (1521), his followers numbered in the hundreds. His philosophy spread across China for 150 years and greatly influenced Japanese thought during that time. From 1584 he was offered sacrifice in the Confucian temple under the title Wencheng ("Completion of Culture").

Wankel \'väŋ-kəl\, **Felix** (1902–1988) German engineer and inventor. In 1954 he completed the design of his distinctive engine, with an orbiting rotor in the shape of a curved equilateral triangle, which does the work done by the moving pistons in other internal-combustion engines. Its advantages include light weight, few moving parts, compactness, low initial cost, fewer repairs, and relatively smooth performance. The first unit was tested in 1957. The Japanese automobile company Mazda produced and developed the engine, introducing it to the U.S. market in 1971.

Wankie National Park See HWANGE NATIONAL PARK

Wannsee Conference \'vän-ˌzā\ (January 20, 1942) Meeting of Nazi officials in the Berlin suburb of Grossen-Wannsee to plan the "final solution" to the "Jewish question." The meeting of 15 Nazi bureaucrats, including ADOLF EICHMANN, was led by REINHARD HEYDRICH, who had been ordered in 1941 to prepare such a plan. An earlier idea to deport Europe's Jews to Madagascar was rejected as impractical. In the final plan, all Jews were to be rounded up, transported eastward, and organized into labor gangs. The expected harsh living conditions would produce a "natural diminution" of Jews, and those that survived would be "treated accordingly." The conference report did not explicitly mention extermination, but within months of the meeting, the first gas chambers were installed at AUSCHWITZ and TREBLINKA. See also HOLOCAUST.

wapiti \'wä-pə-tē\ Species *(Cervus canadensis)* of North American DEER, often considered the same species as the RED DEER. Once common, the wapiti is now confined to the Rocky Mountains and southern Canada. It is the second-largest living deer species (the MOOSE is first). Males may stand taller than 5 ft (1.5 m) at the shoulder and weigh up to 1,100 lbs (500 kg). The coat is brown, pale on the rump, and long and shaggy on the shoulders and neck. The male's five-tined antlers tower almost 4 ft (1.2 m) above his head. Wapiti live in large bands in winter and in small groups in summer. See also ELK.

Male wapiti (*Cervus canadensis*).
ALAN CAREY

war State of conflict, generally armed, between two or more entities. It is characterized by intentional violence on the part of large bodies of individuals organized and trained for that purpose. On the national level, some wars are fought internally between rival political factions (civil war); others are fought against an external enemy. Wars have been fought in the name of religion, in self-defense, to acquire territory or resources, and to further the political aims of the aggressor state's leadership.

War Communism (1918–21) Soviet economic policy applied by the BOLSHEVIKS during the RUSSIAN CIVIL WAR. Its chief features were the expropriation of private business and the nationalization of industry, as well as the forced requisition of surplus grain and other food products from the peasantry. These measures caused a rapid decline in agricultural production, labor productivity, and industrial output. Real wages declined by two-thirds and uncontrolled inflation made paper currency worthless. By 1921 public discontent resulted in strikes and protests, culminating in the KRONSHTADT REBELLION. In response, the Bolsheviks adopted the less-radical NEW ECONOMIC POLICY.

war crime Any violation of the laws of WAR, as laid down by international customary law and certain international TREATIES. Three categories of war crime were established following World War II: conventional war crimes (including murder, ill treatment, or deportation of the civilian population of occupied territories), crimes against peace, and crimes against humanity (political, racial, or religious persecution against any civilian population). Conventional war crimes have been punishable throughout history; the London Agreement of 1945 listed the additional two categories and provided for an international military tribunal to try major Axis war criminals. It further stated that a defendant's position as head of state would not free him from accountability, nor would having acted on orders or out of military necessity. See also GENEVA CONVENTIONS, GENOCIDE, HAGUE CONVENTIONS, NUREMBERG TRIALS.

War Hawks Members of the U.S. Congress who advocated war with Britain (1811). The term was applied by opponents to newly elected Southern and Western congressmen who strongly promoted U.S. expansion into the Northwest and Canada and vigorously protested British aid to Indians. The anti-British fervor of the War Hawks, who included HENRY CLAY and JOHN C. CALHOUN, helped cause the WAR OF 1812.

War of 1812 U.S.–British conflict arising from U.S. grievances over oppressive British maritime practices in the NAPOLEONIC WARS. To enforce its blockade of French ports, the British boarded U.S. and other neutral ships to check cargo they suspected was being sent to France and to impress seamen alleged to be British navy deserters. The U.S. reacted by passing such legislation as the EMBARGO ACT (1807); Congress's

WAR HAWKS called for expulsion of the British from Canada to ensure frontier security. When the U.S. demanded an end to the interference, Britain refused, and the U.S. declared war on June 18, 1812. Despite early U.S. naval victories, notably the duel between the *CONSTITUTION* and the *Guerrière*, Britain maintained its blockade of eastern U.S. ports. A British force burned public buildings in Washington, D.C., including the WHITE HOUSE, in retaliation for similar U.S. acts in York (Toronto), Canada. The war became increasingly unpopular, especially in New England, where a separatist movement originated at the HARTFORD CONVENTION. On December 24, 1814, both sides signed the Treaty of Ghent, which essentially restored territories captured by each side. Before news of the treaty reached the U.S., its victory in the Battle of NEW ORLEANS led it to later proclaim the war a U.S. victory. See also Battles of CHATEAUGUAY, CHIPPEWA, the THAMES; ISAAC HULL, FRANCIS SCOTT KEY, OLIVER PERRY.

War of Independence, U.S. See AMERICAN REVOLUTION

War of the Three Henrys See War of the THREE HENRYS

War Powers Act (November 7, 1973) U.S. edict. Passed by the U.S. Congress over the veto of Pres. RICHARD NIXON, it restrained the president's ability to commit U.S. forces overseas by requiring the executive branch to consult with and report to Congress before involving U.S. forces in foreign hostilities. Generally considered a measure to help prevent "future Vietnams," it nonetheless met with some resistance from subsequent presidents and was not always strictly interpreted by Congress.

Warbeck, Perkin (1474?–1499) Flemish impostor, pretender to the throne of HENRY VII. While working as a servant in Ireland in 1491, he was misidentified as royalty while dressed in his master's rich silks, and was soon persuaded to impersonate Richard, duke of York, who was presumed to have been murdered with his brother in the Tower of London in 1483. Encouraged by several monarchs and other Yorkist enemies in both England and Europe, he gathered forces and supporters on the continent for an invasion. After abortive attempts in 1495 and 1496, he landed in Cornwall in 1497 but was captured and hanged when he tried to escape.

warble fly Any of several DIPTERAN species (BOTFLY family Oestridae or the family Hypodermatidae), widespread in Europe and North America. The warble flies *Hypoderma lineatum* and *H. bovis,* also called cattle grubs or heel flies, are large, heavy, and beelike. They deposit their eggs on cattle legs. The larvae penetrate the skin, migrate through the body, and produce a lump, or warble, on the animal's back. Mature grubs emerge and drop to the ground to pupate. Warbles contains breathing holes, which reduce the hide's commercial value. One species *(Oedemagena tarandi)* is a reindeer pest that also causes economic losses.

warbler Any songbird of almost 350 Old World species (family Sylviidae) or about 120 New World species (family Parulidae, see WOOD WARBLER). Old World warblers, found in gardens, woodlands, and marshes, have a slender bill adapted for gleaning insects from foliage. They occur mainly from Europe and Asia to Africa and Australia, but a few (e.g., the GNATCATCHER) live in the Americas. They are drab greenish, brownish, or black and 3.5–10 in. (9–26 cm) long. See also BLACKCAP, BLACKPOLL WARBLER, GNATCATCHER, WOOD WARBLER.

Warburg \'vär-,bu̇rk, *Engl* 'wȯr-,bərg\, **Otto (Heinrich)** (1883–1970) German biochemist. In the 1920s, after earning doctorates in chemistry and medicine, he investigated the process by which oxygen is consumed in the cells of living organisms, introducing the technique of measuring changes in gas pressure for studying the rates at which slices of living tissue take up oxygen. His search for the cell components involved in oxygen consumption led to identification of the role of the cytochromes. He was awarded a 1931 Nobel Prize for his research. He was the first to observe that the growth of cancer cells requires much less oxygen than that of normal cells.

Warburg family *orig.* **Del Banco family** Family of eminent bankers, philanthropists, and scholars. A Jewish family apparently of Italian origin, they settled in the German town of Warburgum in 1559, and branches subsequently settled in Scandinavia, the U.S., and Britain. Simon Elias Warburg (1760–1828) founded the first Jewish community in Sweden. Among the family's bankers were Moses Marcus Warburg (died 1830) and his brother Gerson (died 1825), who founded the Hamburg bank of M. M. Warburg & Co. (1798), and James Paul Warburg (1896–1969), a member of Pres. FRANKLIN ROOSEVELT'S BRAIN TRUST. The family's scholars included OTTO WARBURG. Among the U.S. philanthropists were Frieda Schiff Warburg (1876–1958) and her sons, patrons of art and music.

Ward, Barbara (Mary) *later* **Baroness Jackson** (of Lodsworth) (1914–1981) British economist and writer. After studying economics at Oxford Univ., she became a writer and editor at *The Economist* (from 1939). She married Sir Robert Jackson in 1950. She was an influential adviser to the Vatican, the U.N., and the World Bank, and she wrote numerous articles and books on the worldwide threat from poverty among third-world nations and the importance of conservation; her books, which reached a wide audience, included *The Rich Nations and the Poor Nations* (1962), *Spaceship Earth* (1966), *Only One Earth* (with RENE DUBOS, 1972), and *Progress for a Small Planet* (1980).

warfare See AIR WARFARE, AMPHIBIOUS WARFARE, BIOLOGICAL WARFARE, CHEMICAL WARFARE, ECONOMIC WARFARE, HOLY WAR, NAVAL WARFARE, PSYCHOLOGICAL WARFARE, TOTAL WAR, TRENCH WARFARE

warfarin \'wȯr-fə-rən\ ANTICOAGULANT drug, marketed as Coumadin. Originally developed to treat thromboembolism (see THROMBOSIS), it interferes with the liver's metabolism of VITAMIN K, leading to production of defective COAGULATION factors. Warfarin therapy risks uncontrollable HEMORRHAGE, either spontaneously or from any cut or bruise; it requires frequent checks to maintain the proper level in the blood. In high concentrations, warfarin is used as a rodent poison, causing death by internal bleeding.

Warfield, Paul (born 1942) U.S. football player. Born in Warren, Ohio, he compiled an outstanding record at Ohio State University. As a wide receiver for the Cleveland Browns (1964–69, 1976–77), he helped lead them to four league championship games. With the Miami Dolphins (1970–74) he won three Super Bowl games. In his 13-year career, he caught 427 passes for 8,565 yards, averaging a near-record 20.1 yards per catch.

Warhol, Andy *orig.* **Andrew Warhola** (1928–1987) U.S. artist, filmmaker, and leading exponent of the POP ART movement. He was born to Czech immigrant parents in Pittsburgh, where he studied pictorial design at the Carnegie Institute of Technology. He then worked in New York as a commercial illustrator. An adroit self-publicist, he conceived the idea of the artist as celebrity. In 1962 he achieved notoriety when he exhibited paintings of Campbell's Soup cans, Coca-Cola bottles, and wooden replicas of Brillo soap-pad boxes. In later work he used the photographic silkscreen technique to print numerous variations of garishly colored celebrity portraits. In the 1960s he devoted more of his energy to making underground films known for their plotlessness, inventive eroticism, and inordinate length. Throughout the 1970s and until his death, he continued to produce prints depicting celebrities and was involved in a range of advertising and other commercial projects. His death resulted from a botched operation. He was one of the most famous and important American cultural figures of the later 20th century, and the effects of his work on conceptions of art continue to be felt.

warlord In China, an independent military commander in the early 20th century. Warlords, supported by provincial military interests or foreign powers, ruled various parts of China following the death of YUAN SHIKAI, first president of the Republic of China. In southeastern China, SUN YAT-SEN and the Nationalist Party gained the backing of a warlord based in Guangzhou. In northern China three leading warlords emerged: ZHANG ZUOLIN, a Japanese-backed bandit in Manchuria; Wu Peifu, a traditionally educated officer in central China; and Feng Yuxiang, who seized Beijing in 1924. The Nationalist Party consolidated its control in the south and, under CHIANG KAI-SHEK, swept northward, reuniting the country in 1928. Numerous local warlords continued to exert de facto power over their own domains until the Japanese invasion during what became World War II. See also NORTHERN EXPEDITION.

Warner, Pop *orig.* **Glenn Scobey** (1871–1954) U.S. college football coach. Born in Springfield, N.Y., he excelled in several sports at Cornell University. As a coach at the Carlisle (Pa.) Indian School (1898–1904, 1906–15), he trained JIM THORPE. Other schools where he coached included the University. of Pittsburgh (1915–23) and Stanford University. (1924–32). Warner perfected the single- and double-wing formations (now rarely used); this and other innovations helped refine the modern game. In 46 seasons (1895–1940) his teams won 312 games, lost 104, and tied 32.

Warner, W(illiam) Lloyd (1898–1970) U.S. sociologist and anthropologist. Born in Redlands, Cal., he studied with ALFRED L. KROEBER and A. R. RADCLIFFE-BROWN, and later taught at the Univs. of Chicago and Michigan. His studies of the American class system have been widely influential. In the late 1930s he produced a five-volume study of Newburyport, Mass.; his other books include *A Black Civilization* (1937), *The Social Life of a Modern Community* (1941), and *The Living and the Dead* (1959).

Warner Brothers U.S. film studio. Beginning in Pennsylvania as movie distributors and theater owners in 1903, the four Warner brothers started producing their own films in 1913 and moved to Hollywood in 1917. They founded Warner Brothers Pictures Inc. in 1923, with Harry (1881–1958) as president in New York, Albert (1884–1967) as treasurer, and Sam (1888–1927) and Jack (1892–1978) as studio managers in Hollywood. In the mid-1920s they helped develop the important Vitaphone sound process. With the release of *The Jazz Singer* (1927), the first feature film with synchronized music and dialogue, the studio's success was assured. Warner Brothers went on to produce gangster films starring JAMES CAGNEY and EDWARD G. ROBINSON, adventure movies with ERROL FLYNN, and mystery dramas with HUMPHREY BOGART. After his brothers retired, Jack became president (1956–72). See also TIME WARNER.

warrant In law, authorization in writing empowering a person to perform an act or execute an office. Arrest warrants are necessary (except in certain circumstances) for an arrest to be considered legal. Search warrants entitle the holder to enter and search a property. Both are classes of judicial warrants. To obtain them, a complainant must provide an affidavit setting forth facts sufficient to satisfy the belief that a crime has been committed and that the accused is the guilty party (or, in the case of the search warrant, that the place to be searched will yield the expected evidence). Nonjudicial warrants include tax warrants (which provide the authority to collect taxes) and land warrants (which entitle the holder to a specific tract of public land).

Warrau \wə-'raù\ *or* **Guarauno** Group of nomadic South American Indians who in modern times inhabit the swampy Orinoco River delta in Venezuela and areas eastward into Guyana. Some live in Suriname. They subsist mainly by fishing, hunting, and gathering, though they practice some agriculture in the drier regions. The Mauritia palm is a staple: they make a fermented drink from its sap and bread from its pith, eat its fruit, and fashion its fiber into clothing and hammocks. Their priestly ceremonies and complex social classes are unusual among hunters and gatherers. They currently number about 20,000.

Warren Town (pop., 2000: 11,360), eastern Rhode Island. Located near PROVIDENCE, it was settled in 1632 and was originally part of Massachusetts. In 1747 Rhode Island annexed it. It was pillaged and burned by the British during the AMERICAN REVOLUTION. It is now a summer resort.

Warren, Earl (1891–1974) U.S. jurist and politician. Born in Los Angeles, he graduated from law school at the University of California, then served as a county district attorney (1925–39) and as state attorney general (1939–43) before winning three terms as governor (1943–53). He was criticized for interning Japanese citizens in concentration camps during World War II. His only electoral defeat came in 1948 when he ran for vice president on the Republican ticket with THOMAS DEWEY. In 1953 Pres. DWIGHT D. EISENHOWER appointed Warren chief justice of the U.S. Supreme Court, in which post he would remain until 1969. The Warren Court proved to be strongly liberal, and the era saw sweeping changes in U.S. constitutional law. Among Warren's notable opinions are those in *BROWN VS. BOARD OF EDUCATION*; *Reynolds vs. Sims*, the "one man, one vote" decision that required state legislative reapportionment (1964); and *MIRANDA VS. ARIZONA*. After the assassination of Pres. JOHN F. KENNEDY he chaired the so-called WARREN COMMISSION.

Earl Warren, 1953.

UPI—EB INC.

Warren, Harry *orig.* **Salvatore Guaragna** (1893–1981) U.S. songwriter. The youngest of 12 children, the Brooklyn-born Warren was self-taught musically. He toured with brass bands and carnivals from age 15. After a few years as a song plugger on TIN PAN ALLEY, he began contributing tunes to Broadway musicals, including "You're My Everything" and "I Found a Million Dollar Baby in a Five-and-Ten-Cent Store." In 1932 he moved to Hollywood, where he collaborated on such films as *Gold Diggers of 1933, 42nd Street* (1933), *Down Argentine Way* (1940), and *Sun Valley Serenade* (1941; with "Chattanooga Choo-Choo"), and he received Academy Awards for "Lullaby of Broadway," "You'll Never Know," and "On the Atchison, Topeka and the Santa Fe." Between 1935 and 1950 he wrote more top-10 hit songs than any other songwriter.

Warren, Joseph (1741–1775) American Revolutionary leader. Born in Roxbury, Mass., he became a physician in Boston. He was active in patriot causes after passage of the Stamp Act (1765) and helped draft the Massachusetts colonial grievances called the Suffolk Resolves (1774). As a member of the Massachusetts Committee of Public Safety, he sent PAUL REVERE on his ride to Lexington. He was made a major general in the Revolutionary army, and died in the Battle of BUNKER HILL.

Warren, Mercy Otis *orig.* **Mercy Otis** (1728–1814) U.S. writer. Born in Barnstable, Mass., the sister of JAMES OTIS, she received no formal education but nevertheless became a woman of letters and a friend and correspondent of the leading political figures of her day. She commented on the issues of the day in political satires, plays, and pamphlets. Though a defender of the American Revolution, she opposed the Constitution, arguing instead that power should rest with the states. Her most significant work, *History of the Rise, Progress, and Termination of the American Revolution* (3 vols., 1805), covered the period 1765–1800.

Warren, Robert Penn (1905–1989) U.S. novelist, poet, and critic. Born in Guthrie, Ky., Warren attended Vanderbilt Univ., where he joined the Fugitives, a group of poets who advocated the agrarian way of life in the South. Later he taught at several colleges and universities and helped found and edit *The Southern Review* (1935–42). His writings often treat moral dilemmas in a South beset by the erosion of its traditional rural values. His best-known novel is *All the King's Men* (1946, Pulitzer Prize; film, 1949). The short-story volume *The Circus in the Attic* (1948) contains the notable "Blackberry Winter." He won Pulitzer Prizes for poetry in 1958 and 1979 and became the first U.S. poet laureate in 1986.

Warren Commission (1963–64) *officially* **President's Commission on the Assassination of President John F. Kennedy** Group appointed by Pres. LYNDON B. JOHNSON to investigate the circumstances surrounding JOHN F. KENNEDY's slaying and the shooting of his assassin, LEE HARVEY OSWALD. It was chaired by EARL WARREN and included two U.S. senators, two U.S. congressmen, and two former public officials. After months of investigation it reported that Kennedy was killed by Oswald's firing of a rifle from the Texas School Book Depository and that Oswald's murder by Jack Ruby two days later was not part of a conspiracy to assassinate Kennedy. Its findings have been questioned in many books and articles, but no conclusive contradictory evidence has been found.

Warring States period In China and later in Japan, a period in which small feuding kingdoms or fiefdoms struggled for supremacy. The Chinese Warring States period (475–221 BC) was dominated by six or seven small feuding Chinese kingdoms; it was the age of Confucian thinkers MENCIUS and XUNZI. In Japan's Warring States period (1482–1558), rival DAIMYO sought to consolidate and increase their landholdings.

Wars of the Roses See Wars of the ROSES

Warsaw City (pop., 1999: 1,618,468), capital of Poland, on the VISTULA RIVER. Founded c. 1300, it flourished as a trade center, came under Polish control in 1526, and became the capital in 1596. During the late 18th century it expanded rapidly, but it was destroyed in 1794 by the Russians. In 1807 it was made the capital of the Grand Duchy of WARSAW by NAPOLEON. Taken by the Russians in 1813, it was the center of Polish insurrection in 1830–31 and 1860. It was occupied by the Germans in WORLD WAR I and again in WORLD WAR II, when its large Jewish population revolted in the WARSAW GHETTO UPRISING (1943). After the unsuccessful WARSAW UPRISING in 1944, the Germans virtually destroyed the city. Modern Warsaw, rebuilt after the war, now houses government bodies, including the Sejm (parliament); it is also an industrial and educational center. Among its historic buildings are a 14th-century Gothic cathedral and a medieval castle.

Warsaw, Grand Duchy of Independent Polish state (1807–15), created by NAPOLEON. Established by the Treaties of Tilsit in 1807 after the Poles had helped Napoleon defeat Prussia, it consisted originally of the major portion of the central Polish provinces that Prussia had taken in the 1790s. For Napoleon's second war against Russia (1812), it supplied nearly 98,000 men, but Napoleon's defeat in Russia also sealed the fortunes of the duchy. In 1813 the Russians assumed control of it. Later, the Congress of VIENNA divided it into three parts: the Grand Duchy of POZNAN; the free Republic of KRAKOW; and the Congress Kingdom of Poland, which was joined to Russia by making the Russian emperor its king.

Warsaw Ghetto Uprising (April 19–May 16, 1943) Revolt by Polish Jews under Nazi occupation against deportation to TREBLINKA. By July 1942 the Nazis had herded 500,000 Jews from surrounding areas into the ghetto in Warsaw. Though starvation killed thousands each month, the Nazis began transferring over 5,000 Jews a day to rural "labor camps." When word reached the ghetto in early 1943 that the destination was actually the gas chambers at Treblinka, the underground Jewish combat group ZOB attacked the Nazis, killing 50 in four days of street fighting and causing the deportations to halt. On April 19 HEINRICH HIMMLER sent 2,000 SS men and army troops to clear the ghetto of its remaining 56,000 Jews. For four weeks the Jewish ZOB and guerrillas fought with pistols and homemade bombs, destroying tanks and killing several hundred Nazis, until their ammunition ran out. All the Jews were either killed or deported, and on May 16 the SS chief declared "The Warsaw Ghetto is no more."

Warsaw Pact *or* **Warsaw Treaty Organization** Military alliance of the Soviet Union, Albania (until 1968), Bulgaria, Czechoslovakia, East Germany, Hungary, Poland, and Romania, formed in 1955 in response to West Germany's entry into NATO. Its terms included a unified military command and the stationing of Soviet troops in the other member states. Though its ostensible goal was to protect against NATO attack, the only occasions on which Warsaw Pact troops were called into action were to suppress uprisings in Poland (1956), Hungary (1956), and Czechoslovakia (1968). The alliance was dissolved in 1991 after the collapse of the Soviet bloc, and the Soviet troops departed.

Warsaw Uprising (Aug.–October 1944) Insurrection in Warsaw in WORLD WAR II that failed to prevent the pro-Soviet Polish administration from gaining control of Poland. In July 1944, as Soviet troops approached Warsaw, the Polish underground was encouraged to stage an uprising against the Germans. Though wary of Soviet promises of self-government, the Polish home army of 50,000 troops attacked the weakened German force and gained control of most of Warsaw in four days. German reinforcements then bombarded the city with air and artillery attacks for 63 days. The approaching Red Army halted, and the Soviets refused to allow aid from the Allies to the beleaguered Poles, who were forced to surrender when their supplies ran out in October; the Germans then deported the rest of the city's population and destroyed most of the city itself. By allowing the Polish home army to be eliminated, the Soviets diminished potential resistance to their establishing political domination of Poland in 1945.

wart *or* **verruca** \və-'rü-kə\ Well-defined small growth on the skin, usually caused by a PAPILLOMAVIRUS, which triggers overproduction of epidermal cells. This may lead to a single long-standing wart, profuse local spread (especially in moist areas), or warts in various parts of the body. The most common type is a round bump with a dry, rough surface. Warts are usually painless except in pressure areas, such as the sole of the foot (plantar wart). Genital warts are merely a nuisance unless they become large or numerous enough to interfere with urination, defecation, or childbirth, but some viral strains are associated with cancer. Warts are considered contagious. Treatment to remove warts includes applying acids or subfreezing chemicals (cryotherapy), or surgery; they sometimes disappear spontaneously.

Warta River \'vär-tä\ River, western central Poland. It rises northwest of KRAKOW and flows northwest 502 mi (808 km) before joining the ODER RIVER. It is the second longest river lying entirely in Poland; about half its length is navigable. Its lower course, formerly in Germany, is in a region assigned to Poland by the POTSDAM CONFERENCE in 1945.

Wartenburg, Johann Yorck von See Johan, Graf YORCK VON WARTENBURG

warthog Large-headed species *(Phacochoerus aethiopicus)* of PIG (UNGULATE family Suidae), inhabiting open and lightly forested areas of Africa. Warthogs, about 30 in. (76 cm) high, are blackish or brown, with a coarse mane from the neck to the midback. The male has two pairs of bumps (warts) on the face. Both sexes have tusks. The tusks on the lower jaw are weapons; those on the upper jaw curve upward and inward in a semicircle, growing to more than 24 in. (60 cm) in some males. The long tufted tail is held high when the animal runs. Warthogs live in groups, feeding on grass and other vegetation.

Warthog (*Phacochoerus aethiopicus*).
KARL H. MASLOWSKI

Warwick \'wär-ik\ Town (metro. area pop., 1994 est.: 120,000), county seat of WARWICKSHIRE, central England. Known for its historic castle, it grew up at a crossing place on the River AVON and was fortified c. 915. By 1086, it was a royal borough, and WILLIAM I ordered the castle to be enlarged. The present-day castle dates mainly from the 14th–15th century. With its virtually intact structure and its fine collections of paintings and armor, the castle has become a major tourist attraction. The town, which grew around the castle, is a market center and has light industry.

Warwick \'wär-ik\, **Earl of** *orig.* **Richard Neville** (1428–1471) English nobleman influential in the Wars of the ROSES. Son of the earl of Salisbury, he became through marriage (1449) the earl of Warwick and acquired vast estates. With his father, he helped the Yorkists win the Battle of St. Albans (1455). Appointed captain of Calais, in 1460 he crossed to England to defeat and capture HENRY VI at Northampton. In 1461 he was routed by the Lancastrians, but he recovered to march on London with York's son Edward, soon crowned EDWARD IV. Warwick was the virtual ruler during Edward's early reign (1461–64), but tensions between the two mounted, and in 1469 Warwick engineered a revolt in northern England that forced Edward to flee to Flanders in 1470. Warwick joined the Lancastrians and restored Henry VI to the throne, earning his later nickname "the Kingmaker." He was killed by Edward's forces at the Battle of Barnet.

Warwickshire \'wär-ik-ˌshir\ County (pop., 1995 est.: 499,000), central England. Its county seat is WARWICK. In Saxon times it formed a border zone between the kingdoms of WESSEX and MERCIA. During the Middle Ages two major centers grew up, at Warwick and Kenilworth. Historical structures surviving in the area include Norman and early English churches, and buildings at STRATFORD-UPON-AVON associated with WILLIAM SHAKESPEARE. The Battle of Edgehill (1642), the first serious clash of the ENGLISH CIVIL WARS, was fought in Warwickshire near the OXFORDSHIRE border. Farming, dairy farming, fruit growing, market gardening, and coal mining are important economic activities.

Wasatch Mountains \'wȯ-ˌsach\ Range of the southern central ROCKY MTNS. They extend about 250 mi (400 km) from southeastern Idaho to central Utah. Mount Timpanogos (12,008 ft, or 3,660 m) is the highest peak. The TIMPANOGOS CAVE NATIONAL MONUMENT is within the range.

Washington State (pop., 1997 est.: 5,610,000), northwestern U.S. It covers an area of 68,139 sq mi (176,479 sq km); its capital is OLYMPIA. The state contains the CASCADE RANGE, which includes Mount RAINIER and Mount ST. HELENS, and the OLYMPIC MTNS. The Strait of JUAN DE FUCA and PUGET SOUND extend inland into the state from the Pacific Ocean. Cape Alva, the most westerly point of the coterminous U.S., is in Washington, as is the COLUMBIA RIVER. The area was inhabited by Pacific coast Indians, including the CHINOOK and NEZ PERCÉ, when the region was visited by Spanish, Russian, British, and French explorers 1543–1792. Claimed by the Spanish and British, it was crossed by the LEWIS AND CLARK EXPEDITION in 1805. Spain surrendered to the U.S. its territories north of California in 1819. Until the 1840s international agreement permitted citizens of both the U.S. and Britain to settle in what was known as Oregon Country. An 1846 treaty with Great Britain set the present Washington–Canada boundary; the Oregon Country was added to the U.S., and renamed the Territory of Oregon in 1848. Washington received territorial status in

1853 and was reduced to its present size in 1863. It was admitted to the Union as the 42nd state in 1889. In the late 1890s it was the main staging point for gold miners going to the Alaskan and Yukon strikes. The greatest stimulus to its 20th century progress came with the development of hydroelectric power and the work on the Bonneville and Grand Coulee dams. Its important manufactures include aircraft and shipbuilding. Expanding trade with Pacific Rim countries, high technology, and tourism add to the economy.

Washington, Booker T(aliaferro) (1856–1915) U.S. educator and black-rights leader. Born into slavery in Franklin Co., Va., he moved with his family to West Virginia after emancipation. He worked from age 9, then attended (1872–75) and joined the staff of the Hampton (Va.) Normal and Agricultural Institute. In 1881 he was selected to head the Tuskegee Normal and Industrial Institute, a new teacher-training school for blacks, and he successfully transformed it into a thriving institution (later TUSKEGEE UNIV.). He became perhaps the most prominent black leader of his time. His controversial conviction that blacks could best gain equality in the U.S. by improving their economic situation through education rather than by demanding equal rights was termed the ATLANTA COMPROMISE. His books include *Up from Slavery* (1901).

Washington, D.C. City (pop., 2000: 572,059), capital of the U.S. It is coextensive with the DISTRICT OF COLUMBIA. Situated at the navigational head of the POTOMAC RIVER, between Maryland and Virginia, it has an area of 69 sq mi (179 sq km). The site was chosen by GEORGE WASHINGTON in 1790, as a political compromise that satisfied both Northern and Southern states. Designed by P.-C. L'ENFANT, it is one of the few cities in the world planned expressly as a national capital. The federal government occupied it in 1800. British troops burned the city (1814) during the WAR OF 1812. With the annexation of Georgetown in 1878, the city became coterminous with the District of Columbia. Significant buildings include the Capitol, WHITE HOUSE, and LIBRARY OF CONGRESS. The WASHINGTON MONUMENT, Lincoln Memorial, Jefferson Memorial, and VIETNAM VETERANS MEMORIAL are among the most famous of the city's more than 300 memorials and statues. The SMITHSONIAN INSTITUTION is in Washington, as are numerous other cultural and educational institutions, and foreign embassies. The economy is based on national and international political activities, scientific research, and tourism.

Washington, Denzel (born 1954) U.S. film actor. Born in Mount Vernon, N.Y., he began his career as a stage actor. Featured in the television series *St. Elsewhere* (1982–88), he also appeared in movies from 1981 and won acclaim for his roles in *Cry Freedom* (1987), *Glory* (1989, Academy Award), and *Mississippi Masala* (1991). Praised for his portrayal of the title character in SPIKE LEE's *Malcolm X* (1992), he also starred in such films as *The Pelican Brief* (1993), *Philadelphia* (1993), *Crimson Tide* (1995), *He Got Game* (1998), and *The Hurricane* (1999).

Washington, Dinah *orig.* **Ruth Lee Jones** (1924–1963) U.S. singer, one of the most versatile in American music. Born in Tuscaloosa, Ala., Washington participated in church choirs as a child. She joined LIONEL HAMPTON's band in 1943, embarking on a solo career in 1946. Her recordings encompassed a wide variety of idioms including rhythm-and-blues, jazz, and country music; her 1959 "What a Difference a Day Makes" was a pop hit. Known as "Queen of the Blues," her precise diction and intonation combined with an alternately gentle and brassy vocal timbre, and her voice was remarkable for its clarity and projection. She died from an accidental overdose of sleeping pills.

Washington, George (1732–1799) American Revolutionary commander-in-chief (1775–83) and first president of the U.S. (1789–97). Born into a wealthy family in Westmoreland Co., Va., he was educated privately and worked as a surveyor from age 16. In 1752 he inherited his brother's estate at MOUNT VERNON, including 18 slaves whose ranks grew to 49 by 1760, though he disapproved of slavery. In the FRENCH AND INDIAN WAR he was commissioned a colonel and sent to the Ohio Territory. After EDWARD BRADDOCK was killed, Washington became commander of all Virginia forces, entrusted with defending the western frontier (1755–58). He resigned to manage his estate and in 1759 married Martha Dandridge Custis (1731–1802), a widow. He served in the House of BURGESSES 1759–74, where he supported the colonists' cause, and in the Continental Congress 1774–75. In 1775 he was elected to command the Continental Army. In the ensuing AMERICAN REVOLUTION, he proved a brilliant commander and stalwart leader despite several defeats. With the war effectively ended by the capture of YORKTOWN (1781), he resigned his commission and returned to Mount Vernon (1783). He was a delegate to and presiding officer of the CONSTITUTIONAL CONVENTION (1787) and helped secure ratification of the Constitution in Virginia. When the state electors met to select the first president (1789), Washington was the unanimous choice. He formed a cabinet to balance sectional and political differences but was committed to a strong central government. Elected to a second term, he followed a middle course between the political factions that became the FEDERALIST PARTY and DEMOCRATIC PARTY. He proclaimed a policy of neutrality in the war between Britain and France (1793) and sent troops to suppress the WHISKEY REBELLION (1794). He declined to serve a third term, setting a 144-year precedent, and retired in 1797 after delivering his "Farewell Address." Known as the "father of his country," he is universally regarded as one of the greatest figures in U.S. history.

Washington, Harold (1922–1987) U.S. politician and mayor of Chicago (1983–87). Born in Chicago, he practiced law and served as a city attorney 1954–58. He was elected successively to the Illinois legislature (1965–76), state senate (1976–89), and U.S. House of Representatives (1980–83). After a hard-fought campaign for reform and an end to city patronage, he was elected mayor of Chicago, becoming the first black to hold that post. He was reelected to a second term in 1987 but died soon after.

Washington, Mt. Peak in the Presidential Range of the WHITE MTNS., northern New Hampshire. At 6,288 ft (1,917 m), it is the highest point in the northeastern U.S. It is noted for its extreme weather conditions; the world's highest wind velocity (231 mph, or 372 kph) was recorded there in 1934. It is the site of Mount Washington Observatory; the area is included in the White Mountain National Forest.

Washington, University of Public university in Seattle, founded in 1861. It is a comprehensive research university with sea-grant status. It consists of colleges of architecture and urban planning, arts and sciences, education, engineering, forestry, and oceanography as well as schools of business, dentistry, drama, communications, international studies, law, library science, music, medicine, nursing, pharmacy, public affairs, and social work. Campus facilities include an alcohol and drug abuse institute, a marine science laboratory, and two research forests. Total enrollment is about 35,000.

Washington and Lee University Private university in Lexington, Va. Founded as an academy in 1749, it is one of the oldest institutions of higher learning in the U.S. It is named after GEORGE WASHINGTON, who presented the academy with a gift of $50,000 in 1796, and ROBERT E. LEE, who served as its president 1865–70. It became coeducational in 1984. It has an undergraduate college, a law school, and a school of commerce, economics, and politics. Among its offerings are programs in engineering, environmental studies, and journalism. Total enrollment is about 2,000.

Washington Birthplace National Monument, George See GEORGE WASHINGTON BIRTHPLACE NATIONAL MONUMENT

Washington Conference *officially* **International Conference on Naval Limitation** Conference held in Washington, D.C. (1921–22), to limit the naval arms race and negotiate Pacific security agreements. The Four-Power Pact (signed by Britain, Japan, France, and the U.S.) stipulated mutual consultation regarding any issue in the Pacific and affirmed respect for one another's Pacific territories. The Five-Power Naval Limitation Treaty (which Italy also signed) negotiated proportional limits to the number of warships each signatory nation could maintain and mandated some actual disarmament; it lapsed in 1936 when Japan was refused equality with the U.S. and Britain. Another agreement signed by the five regulated the use of submarines and outlawed poison gas in warfare. A Nine-Power Pact (with the Netherlands, Portugal, Belgium, and China) affirmed China's sovereignty.

Washington Monument Memorial to GEORGE WASHINGTON, in Washington, D.C. Based on a design by Robert Mills (1781–1855), it was built between 1848 and 1884. A granite OBELISK faced with Maryland marble, it is over 555 ft (169 m) high. Inserted in the interior walls are 192 carved stones presented by various individuals, cities, states, and foreign nations. It is located on grounds that are a westward extension of the Mall. The top can be reached by elevator or an interior iron stairway. It underwent a major restoration project in the 1990s and reopened in 2001.

Washington Post, The Morning daily newspaper published in Washington, D.C., the dominant paper in the U.S. capital and one of the nation's great newspapers. Established in 1877 as a Democratic Party organ, it changed orientation and ownership several times and faced constant economic problems until the financier Eugene Meyer purchased it in 1933. Under Meyer (to 1946), Philip L. Graham (1946–63), KATHERINE GRAHAM (1963–79), and Donald E. Graham (from 1979) it acquired domestic and international prestige, becoming known for its sound and independent editorial stance and thorough, accurate reporting.

Washington University Private university in St. Louis. It was founded as a seminary in 1853 and became a university in 1857. It is a comprehensive research and teaching institution, with one of the leading medical schools in the U.S. It has a college of arts and sciences, a graduate school, and schools of architecture, business (the Olin School), engineering and applied science, fine arts, law, and social work. Research facilities include a space science center, a center for the study of Islamic culture and society, and an institute for the deaf. Total enrollment is about 11,000.

Washita River See OUACHITA RIVER

Washita River \'wä-shi-ˌtȯ\ River, western and southern central Oklahoma. It rises in northwestern Texas and flows east across the Oklahoma boundary, then southeast to southern central Oklahoma, and south into the RED RIVER. It is 626 mi (1,007 km) long. The Battle of the Washita (November 1868), in which Gen. GEORGE CUSTER attacked a CHEYENNE Indian encampment, took place near Cheyenne, Okla.

wasp Any of more than 20,000, usually winged, insect species in the order Hymenoptera. The abdomen is attached to the thorax by a slender petiole, or "waist," and the female's abdomen has a formidable stinger. Most species are solitary; about 1,000 species are highly social; and some may be either social or solitary. Adults feed primarily on nectar. Most solitary wasps nest in tunnels in the ground and feed larvae with paralyzed insects or spiders. The paperlike nest of social wasps (family Vespidae) consists of chewed plant material mixed with saliva and arranged in adjacent hexagonal cells. The female lays one egg in each cell and provisions it with a macerated caterpillar. Successive generations may enlarge the nest and care for the young.

Wassermann \'vä-sər-ˌmän, *Engl* 'wä-sər-mən\, **August von** (1866–1925) German bacteriologist. With Albert Neisser (1855–1916) he developed a test for the antibody to the spirochete that causes syphilis in 1906. That test, along with other procedures, is still used to diagnose syphilis. He is also noted for developing tests for tuberculosis. With Wilhelm Kolle he wrote the major *Handbook of Pathogenic Microorganisms* (6 vols., 1903–9).

Wassermann \'vä-sər-ˌmän, *Engl* 'wä-sər-mən\, **Jakob** (1873–1934) German novelist. After an unsettled youth, he became well known with such works as *The Jews of Zirndorf* (1897), *Caspar Hauser* (1908), and *The World's Illusion* (1919). His popularity was greatest in the 1920s and '30s, when he wrote *The Maurizius Case* (1928), treating the theme of justice with the carefully plotted suspense of a detective story, and extended the tale of a post–World War I youth into a trilogy with *Etzel Andergast* (1931) and *Kerkhoven's Third Existence* (1934). He is frequently compared to FYODOR DOSTOYEVSKY in both his moral fervor and his tendency to sensationalism.

Wasserstein \'wä-sər-ˌstīn\, **Wendy** (born 1950) U.S. playwright. Born in Brooklyn, N.Y., she earned a graduate degree at the Yale School of Drama and wrote her first play in 1973. She won favorable notice for *Uncommon Women and Others* (1977), which was followed by *Isn't It Romantic* (1981) and *The Heidi Chronicles* (1988, Tony award, Pulitzer Prize), and became noted for her comic gift and her portrayals of single women. Her later plays include *The Sisters Rosensweig* (1992) and *An American Daughter* (1997), and she wrote the screenplay for *The Object of My Affection* (1998).

Wat Tyler's Rebellion See PEASANTS' REVOLT

watch Portable timepiece designed to be worn on the wrist or carried in the pocket. The first watches appeared shortly after 1500, when the mainspring (see SPRING) was invented as a replacement for weights in driving CLOCKS. The progressive miniaturization of electronic components in recent decades has made possible the development of all-electronic watches, in which the necessary transistors, resistors, capacitors, and other elements are all on one or several miniature INTEGRATED CIRCUITS, or chips. Such circuitry enables them to perform several timekeeping functions and also makes possible digital readouts of the time.

water Inorganic compound composed of HYDROGEN and OXYGEN (H_2O), existing in LIQUID, GAS (STEAM, water vapor), and SOLID (ICE) states. At room temperature, water is a colorless, odorless, tasteless liquid. One of the most abundant compounds, water covers about 75% of the earth's surface. Life depends on water for virtually every process, its ability to dissolve many other substances being perhaps its most essential quality. Life is believed to have originated in the world's oceans, and living organisms use aqueous solutions (including blood and digestive juices) as mediums for carrying out biological processes. Because water molecules are asymmetric and therefore ELECTRIC DIPOLES, HYDROGEN BONDING between molecules in liquid water and in ice is important in holding them together. Many of water's complex physical and chemical properties (high melting and boiling points, VISCOSITY, SURFACE TENSION, greater density in liquid than in solid form) arise from this extensive hydrogen bonding. Water undergoes DISSOCIATION to the IONS H^+ (or H_3O^+) and OH^-, particularly in the presence of salts and other solutes; it may act as an ACID or as a BASE. Water occurs bound (water of hydration) in many SALTS and MINERALS. It has myriad industrial uses, including as a suspending agent (papermaking, coal slurrying), SOLVENT, diluting agent, coolant, and source of hydrogen; it is used in filtration, washing, steam generation, hydration of lime and cement, textile processing, sulfur mining, HYDROLYSIS, HYDRAULICS, as well as in beverages and foods. See also HARD WATER, HEAVY WATER.

water bloom Dense aquatic accumulation of microscopic organisms produced by an abundance of nutrient salts in surface water, coupled with adequate sunlight for PHOTOSYNTHESIS. The microorganisms or the toxic substances they release may discolor the water, exhaust its oxygen content, poison aquatic animals and waterfowl, and irritate the skin and respiratory tract of humans. Single species of ALGAE, DIATOMS, or DINOFLAGELLATES, reproducing every few hours, may dominate a blooming population; the number of individuals per quart (liter) of water, normally about 1,000, can increase to 60 million. Blooms of the dinoflagellate genus *Gymnodinium* cause RED TIDES. The Red Sea is named for the occasional blooms of the alga *Trichodesmium erythraeum.* See also WATER POLLUTION.

water buffalo *or* **Indian buffalo** Either of two types of oxlike BOVID (species *Bubalus bubalis*) domesticated in Asia from earliest recorded times. Its name derives from its suitability for work on waterlogged land and in humid climates. It stands 5–6 ft (1.5–1.8 m), is up to 9 ft (2.8 m) long, and may weigh over 2,000 lbs (1,000 kg). The dull black or dark gray body has little hair. The horns spread outward and upward, measuring up to 7 ft (2 m) across. One type, the swamp buffalo, is the principal draft animal of southern China and southeast Asia. The other, the river buffalo, is used for dairy and meat production and draft work in southern and southwestern Asia and Egypt.

water chestnut Any of several perennial water plants of the genus *Trapa* (family Trapaceae), native to Europe, Asia, and Africa, or their edible, nutlike fruit. The water caltrop *(T. natans)* has two sets of leaves: long, feathery, rootlike submerged leaves, and a loose rosette of floating leaves attached to leafstalks 2–4 in. (5–10 cm) long. The small fruit usually has four spiny angles. The Chinese water chestnut *(Eleocharis tuberosus)* is a member of the SEDGE FAMILY.

water clock *or* **clepsydra** \'klep-sə-drə\ Ancient device for measuring time by the gradual flow of water. One form, used by North American Indians and some African peoples, consisted of a small boat or floating vessel that shipped water through a hole until it sank. In another form, water escaped through a hole in a vessel marked with graduated lines; specimens from Egypt date from the 14th century BC. The Romans invented a clepsydra consisting of a cylinder into which water dripped from a reservoir; a float provided readings against a scale on the cylinder wall. GALILEO used a mercury clepsydra to time his experimental falling bodies. See also CLOCK.

water flea Any of about 450 species (order Anomopoda) of microscopic, mostly freshwater, CRUSTACEANS distributed worldwide. Species in the genus *Daphnia* are ubiquitous in Europe and North America. Water fleas have a discrete head that bears antennae. The carapace (shell) encloses all or most of the body, except on the predatory giant *Leptodora* (up to 0.7 in., or 18 mm, long), whose carapace is just a small brood sac. Most species swim by powerful strokes of the antennae, sometimes producing a hopping-and-sinking motion. All but a few predatory species use specialized thoracic limbs to filter organic matter from the water. See also COPEPOD.

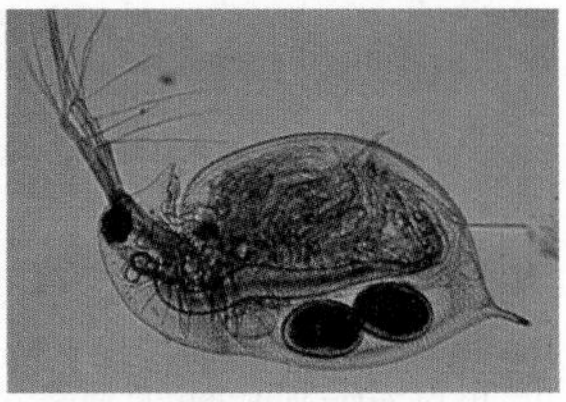

Water flea of the genus *Daphnia* (magnified about 30×).
ERIC V. GRAVE—PHOTO RESEARCHERS

water frame In textile manufacture, a spinning machine powered by water that produced a cotton YARN suitable for warp (lengthwise threads). Patented in 1769 by R. ARKWRIGHT, it represented an improvement on JAMES HARGREAVES's SPINNING JENNY, which produced weaker thread suitable only for weft (filling yarn).

water hyacinth Any of about five species of aquatic plants that make up the genus *Eichhornia* of the pickerelweed family (Pontederiaceae), native mainly to the New World tropics. Some species float in shallow water; others are rooted in muddy stream banks and lakeshores. All have slender rootstocks, feathery roots, rosettes of stalked leaves, and flowers arranged in spikes or clusters. The common water hyacinth *(E. crassipes)* is the most widespread species. Its leafstalk is spongy and inflated, and the upper lobes of its purple flowers have blue and yellow markings. It reproduces quickly, often clogging slow-flowing streams. It is used as an ornamental in outdoor pools and aquariums.

Common water hyacinth (*Eichhornia crassipes*).
W.H. HODGE

water lily Any of the freshwater plants in eight genera that make up the family Nymphaeaceae, native to temperate and tropical regions. All are perennial except those in the genus *Euryale.* Most have rounded, floating, waxy-coated leaves growing atop long stalks that contain many air spaces. Thick, fleshy, creeping underwater stems are buried in the mud. In some species, the leaves are also submerged. Showy, solitary, cuplike flowers with numerous spirally arranged petals are borne at or above the water surface on long stalks. The genus *Nymphaea* includes the water lilies proper (or water nymphs). The common North American white water lily, pond lily, or toad lily is *N. odorata.* The lotus of ancient Egyptian art was usually the blue lotus *(N. caerulea).* The largest water lilies are two species that make up the tropical South American genus *Victoria;* the Santa Cruz water lily *(V. cruziana)* has leaves 2–6 ft (60–180 cm) in diameter. Water lilies provide food for fish and wildlife but sometimes cause drainage problems because of their rapid growth. Many varieties have been developed for ornamental use in garden pools and conservatories.

Santa Cruz water lily (*Victoria cruziana*).
GOTTLIEB HAMPFLER

water moccasin *or* **cottonmouth moccasin** Species *(Agkistrodon piscivorus)* of PIT VIPER that inhabits marshy lowlands of the southeastern U.S. It is called cottonmouth because it threatens with the mouth open, showing the white interior. It is up to 5 ft (1.5 m) long and is completely black or brown with darker crossbands. A dangerous snake with a potentially lethal bite, it tends to stand its ground when alarmed. It will eat almost any small animal, including turtles, fishes, and birds. See also COPPERHEAD.

water ouzel See DIPPER

water pollution State resulting when substances are released into a body of water, where they become dissolved or suspended in the water or deposited on the bottom, accumulating to the extent that they overwhelm its capacity to absorb, break down, or recycle them, and thus interfering with the functioning of aquatic ecosystems. Contributions to water pollution include substances drawn from the air (see ACID RAIN), silt from soil erosion, chemical FERTILIZERS and PESTICIDES, runoff from septic tanks, outflow from livestock feedlots, chemical wastes (some toxic) from industries, and sewage and other urban wastes from cities and towns. A community far upstream in a watershed may thus receive relatively clean water, whereas one farther downstream receives a partly diluted mixture of urban, industrial, and rural wastes. When organic matter exceeds the capacity of microorganisms in the water to break it down and recycle it, the excess of nutrients in such matter encourages algal WATER BLOOMS. When these algae die, their remains add further to the organic wastes already in the water, and eventually the water becomes deficient in oxygen. Organisms that do not require oxygen then attack the organic wastes, releasing gases such as methane and hydrogen sulfide, which are harmful to the oxygen-requiring forms of life. The result is a foul-smelling, waste-filled body of water. See also EUTROPHICATION.

water polo Goal game, similar to soccer, that is played in water by teams of swimmers (seven per side) using a ball resembling a soccer ball. The name derives from a mid-19th-century version of the sport in which players rode barrels and struck the ball with sticks. A rough and demanding game, it is played by both men and women. Modern water polo was introduced as an Olympic sport in 1900.

water resource Any of the entire range of natural waters (vapor, liquid, or solid) that occur on the earth and that are of potential use to humans. These resources include the waters of the oceans, rivers, and lakes; groundwater and deep subsurface waters; and glaciers and permanent snowfields. Continuing increase in water use has led to growing concern over the availability and quality of water supplies.

water snake Any of 65–80 SNAKE species (genus *Natrix,* family Colubridae) and similar snakes, found worldwide except in South America, and members of several New World genera, especially *Nerodia.* Most species have a stout body, with dark blotches or streaks, and ridged scales. They kill fishes and amphibians with a nonvenomous bite. The New World species live in or near water and bear live young; European species are less water-dependent and lay eggs. All are bad-tempered; in defense, they inflate the head, strike, and release a foul secretion. They average about 3 ft (1 m) long; some Old World species reach 6 ft (1.8 m).

water-supply system Facilities for the collection, treatment, storage, and distribution of water. Ancient systems included wells, storage reservoirs, CANALS and AQUEDUCTS, and water-distribution systems. Highly advanced systems appeared c. 2500 BC and reached their peak in the Roman aqueduct system. In the Middle Ages, water supplies were largely neglected and epidemics caused by waterborne organisms were common. In the 17th–18th century, distribution systems utilizing cast-iron pipes, aqueducts, and pumps began to be installed. The link between polluted water and disease came to be understood in the 19th century, and treatment methods such as slow sand filtration and disinfection with chlorine were introduced. Modern reservoirs are formed usually by constructing DAMS near the collection point of mountain-water runoff or across rivers. After the water reaches collection points, it is treated to improve its quality; it is then pumped either directly into a city or town's distribution system or to an elevated storage location, such as a water tank. See also PLUMBING.

water table *or* **groundwater table** Surface of a body of underground water below which the soil or rocks are permanently saturated with water. The water table separates the groundwater zone (zone of saturation) that lies below it from the zone of aeration that lies above it. The water table fluctuates both with the seasons and from year to year because it is affected by climatic variations and by the amount of precipitation used by vegetation. It also is affected by withdrawing excessive amounts of water from wells or by recharging them artificially. See also AQUIFER. See illustration on following page.

W X Y Z

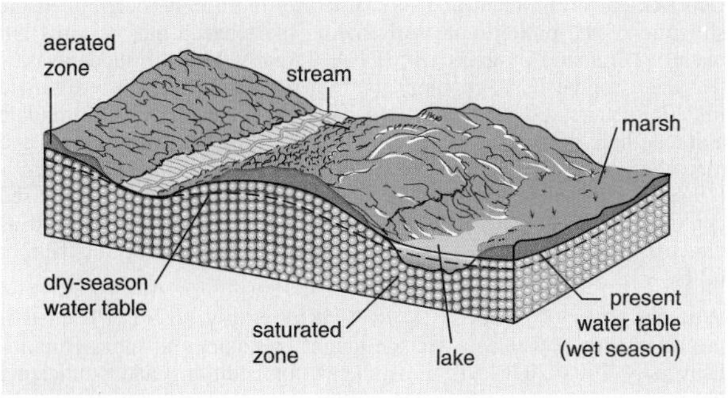

Diagram showing seasonal variations in groundwater levels, which rise and fall with precipitation and drought.

waterbuck Species of ANTELOPE *(Kobus ellipsiprymnus)* that lives in herds, usually near water, on plains and floodplains and in woodlands and swamps of sub-Saharan Africa. Waterbucks are almost 5 ft (1.5 m) high at the shoulder. Males have long, heavily ridged horns that curve backward and then upward. The coarse, shaggy coat is grayish, and the rump has a white ring.

Waterbury City (pop., 1996 est.: 106,000), western Connecticut, on the Naugatuck River. Established as Mattatuck Plantation in 1674, it was incorporated as the town of Waterbury in 1686 and as a city in 1853. In the 19th century it became the nation's largest producer of brass products. Other manufactures include clocks, watches, and chemicals. It is the financial and commercial center of western Connecticut.

watercolor Painting made with a pigment ground in gum, usually gum arabic, and applied with brush and water to a surface, usually paper. The pigment is ordinarily transparent but can be made opaque by mixing with a whiting to produce GOUACHE. Transparent watercolor allows for freshness and luminosity. Whereas oil paintings achieve their effects by a building up of color, watercolors rely on what is left out, with empty, unpainted spaces being an integral part of the work.

watercress Perennial plant *(Nasturtium officinale)* of the MUSTARD FAMILY, native to Eurasia and naturalized throughout North America. It grows submerged, floating on the water, or spread over mud surfaces in cool flowing streams. White flowers are followed by small, beanlike seedpods. Cress is often cultivated in tanks for its young shoots, which are used in salads. The delicate, light-green, peppery-flavored leaves are rich in vitamin C. Since watercress grown near cattle and sheep feedlots can become contaminated by feces containing cysts of the liver fluke worm, agent of the illness fascioliasis (liver rot), regulations specify that commercial watercress beds be protected from such pollution.

Wateree River River, central South Carolina. It enters the state from North Carolina as the CATAWBA RIVER, but is known as the Wateree in South Carolina. It joins the Congaree River to form the SANTEE RIVER. The Wateree-Catawba River is 395 mi (636 km) long. The Wateree flows through a series of lakes and reservoirs, the largest of which is Wateree Lake, 15 mi (24 km) long.

waterfall Area where flowing river water drops abruptly and nearly vertically. A waterfall may also be termed a falls, or, when large volumes of water are involved, a cataract. Waterfalls of small height and less steepness or a series of small falls are called cascades. Still gentler stretches of river that exhibit turbulent flow and white water are called rapids.

Waterford glass Heavy cut glassware produced in Waterford, Ireland, from the 1720s to the present, characterized by thick walls, deeply incised geometric cutting, and brilliant polish. Characteristic Waterford products include Rococo chandeliers, wall lamps, sconces, bowls, and vases. After c. 1770 Waterford glassmakers gradually abandoned the Rococo style in favor of the more restrained Neoclassical style popular in England.

waterfowl Any member of the family Anatidae, web-footed birds with a broad bill containing fine plates, or lamellae; usually stocky and often long-necked, including DUCKS, geese (see GOOSE), and SWANS. Waterfowl feed by dabbling, diving, or grazing. Most species are social and have an array of formal displays and group cohesion signals. Almost all breed in water. The female usually selects the nest site, builds the nest from any vegetation within reach, and incubates the 3–12 eggs. Shortly after hatching, the young imprint on their mother (see IMPRINTING). Many species are migratory.

Watergate scandal (1972–74) Political scandal involving illegal activities by Pres. RICHARD NIXON's administration. In June 1972 five burglars were arrested after breaking into the Democratic Party's national headquarters at the Watergate Hotel complex in Washington, D.C. The White House denied any connection to the burglary, and Nixon was reelected. In January 1973 the trial of the burglars was held before Judge JOHN SIRICA, whose direct questioning of witnesses revealed details of a cover-up by H.R. HALDEMAN, JOHN D. EHRLICHMAN, and JOHN W. DEAN. They and Attorney General Richard G. Kleindienst resigned in April. The new attorney general, Elliot L. Richardson (1920–1998), appointed Archibald Cox (born 1912) as special prosecutor. A Senate committee under SAMUEL ERVIN held televised hearings and learned of the existence of tapes of conversations in the president's office. Cox and Ervin subpoenaed the tapes, but Nixon refused to relinquish them and ordered Cox fired (October 20). Richardson resigned in protest, and the public outcry, Sirica's order to provide the tapes, and the new special prosecutor, LEON JAWORSKI, forced Nixon to surrender the tapes (December 8), which revealed clear signs of his involvement. The House of Representatives began inquiry into impeachment, and in July its judiciary committee passed three articles of impeachment. On August 5 Nixon supplied three tapes that clearly implicated him in the cover-up. While insisting he had not committed any offenses, he resigned on August 8, 1974. He was pardoned a month later by his successor, GERALD FORD.

Waterloo, Battle of (June 18, 1815) Final defeat of NAPOLEON and French forces in the NAPOLEONIC WARS. The battle was fought near Waterloo village, south of Brussels, by Napoleon's 72,000 troops against the duke of WELLINGTON's combined Allied army of 68,000 aided by 45,000 Prussians under GEBHARD VON BLÜCHER. After the French defeated the Prussians at Ligny and held Wellington at Quatre-Bras in secondary battles on June 16, Napoleon's marshals, including MICHEL NEY, failed to eliminate either enemy while they were separated. Napoleon delayed his attack at Waterloo until midday, to allow the ground to dry, which enabled Blücher's main force to escape the pursuing French and join Wellington. Four French attacks on the Allied center failed to break through, and Napoleon had to move troops to meet the Prussian flanking attack. When Ney succeeded in capturing a farmhouse at the center of the Allied line, his call to Napoleon for reinforcements was refused. Wellington and his forces, though vulnerable after heavy losses, repulsed the final French assault and turned to advance against the French, forcing them into a disorganized retreat. The French suffered 25,000 casualties, Wellington's army suffered 15,000, and Blücher's suffered 8,000. Four days later, Napoleon abdicated for the last time.

Waterloo, University of Public university in Waterloo, Ontario, founded in 1957. It has faculties of applied health sciences, arts, engineering, environmental studies, mathematics, and science, as well as schools of accounting, architecture, optometry, and urban and regional planning. Special facilities include museums of optometry and of games. Total enrollment is about 22,000.

watermelon Succulent fruit of *Citrullus lanatus* (formerly *C. vulgaris*), in the GOURD family, native to tropical Africa and cultivated on every continent except Antarctica. The vines spread across the ground with branched tendrils, deeply cut leaves, and light-yellow flowers. Each vine bears 2–15 large, reddish, white, or yellow, sweet, very juicy fruits with flat black seeds. Varieties differ in flesh color, shape, and rind thickness. The rind may be preserved as a pickle.

waterpower POWER produced by a stream of water as it turns a wheel or similar device. The WATERWHEEL, probably invented in the 1st century BC, was widely used throughout the Middle Ages and into modern times for grinding grain, operating bellows for furnaces, and other purposes. The more compact water TURBINE, which passes water through a series of fixed and rotating blades, was introduced in 1827. Water turbines, used originally for direct mechanical drive for irrigation, now are used almost exclusively to generate HYDROELECTRIC POWER.

W
X
Y
Z

Waters, Ethel (1896?–1977) U.S. blues and jazz singer and actress. Born in Chester, Pa., she was a professional singer by 17, and she recorded with such jazzmen as Duke Ellington and Benny Goodman in the 1930s. She made her Broadway debut in the *Africana* revue (1927), and later had a lead role in *Blackbirds* (1930). In 1933 she appeared in Irving Berlin's *As Thousands Cheer,* in which she sang "Heat Wave" and "Suppertime." Later stage successes included *Cabin in the Sky* (1940; film, 1943) and *The Member of the Wedding* (1950; film, 1952). Her other films included *Pinky* (1949) and *The Sound and the Fury* (1959).

Waters, Muddy *orig.* **McKinley Morganfield** (1915–1983) U.S. blues guitarist and singer. He grew up in the cotton country of Mississippi and taught himself harmonica as a child. He later took up guitar, eagerly absorbing the styles of Rafer Johnson and Son House. He was first recorded in 1941 by Alan Lomax (see John Lomax). In 1943 he moved to Chicago; there he broke with the country blues style by playing over a heavy dance rhythm, adopting the electric guitar and adding piano and drums while retaining a moan-and-shout vocal style and lyrics that were by turns mournful, boastful, and sexual. The result came to be known as urban blues, from which sprang in large part such later forms as rock music and soul music. A surge in interest in the roots of popular music in the early 1960s brought Waters widespread fame, and he performed internationally into the 1970s.

waterskiing Sport of planing and jumping on water skis, broad skilike runners that a rider wears while being towed by a motorboat. The sport originated in the U.S. in the 1920s. International competitions have been held since 1946. Single-ski slalom competition is held on a course consisting of a specified number of buoys around which the skier must negotiate. Jumping competitions employ a ramp; skiers are judged for distance and style. Barefoot and trick skiing are also part of some competitions.

Waterton Lakes National Park National park, western Canada. Located in southern Alberta, it was created in 1895. A mountain recreational area, it covers 129,920 acres (52,618 hectares). It adjoins the U.S. border and Glacier National Park in the U.S.; the two parks together compose the Waterton-Glacier National Peace Park, dedicated in 1932.

waterwheel Machine for tapping the energy of running or falling water (hence a prime mover) by means of a set of paddles or buckets mounted around a wheel. The force of the moving water against the paddles, or the weight of water poured into the buckets, rotates the wheel. The resulting power is transmitted to machinery via the shaft of the wheel. The waterwheel was perhaps the earliest source of mechanical energy to replace that of humans and animals, and it was first used for such tasks as raising water and grinding grain. See also waterpower.

Watie \'wä-tē\, **Stand** *orig.* **De Gata Ga** (1806–1871) American Indian leader. Born in Rome, Ga., he learned English at a mission school and helped publish the *Cherokee Phoenix,* a tribal newspaper. In 1835 he joined three other Cherokee chiefs to sign the Treaty of New Echota, which surrendered Cherokee lands in Georgia and forced the tribe to move to Indian Territory in present-day Oklahoma. In the Civil War he raised a mounted Cherokee rifle regiment and joined the Confederate army. He directed cavalry raids on fields and property of Indians who backed the Union. Promoted to brigadier general (1864), he remained loyal to the Confederacy even after the tribe ended its alliance.

Watling Street Ancient Roman road in Britain. Extending from London to Wroxeter, it was one of the great arterial roads of Roman Britain. In the 9th century it divided Mercia. Later the name was applied to other main roads, including the London–Dover road that ran through Canterbury.

Watson, Doc *orig.* **Arthel Lane** (born 1923) U.S. country-music singer, banjoist, and guitarist. Blind from birth, Watson grew up on a farm in North Carolina and learned to play guitar, banjo, and harmonica as a child. Though he did not record professionally until he was in his late thirties, he quickly rose to prominence with his renditions of traditional and popular tunes backed by his virtuoso flat-picking guitar style. He appeared at the 1963 Newport Folk Festival to great acclaim. He performed for many years with his son Merle (1949–1985).

Watson, James D(ewey) (born 1928) U.S. geneticist and biophysicist. Born in Chicago, he earned his PhD at Indiana University in 1950. Using X-ray diffraction techniques, he began work in Britain with Francis Crick on the problem of DNA structure. In 1952 he determined the structure of the protein coat surrounding the tobacco mosaic virus but made no dramatic progress with DNA. In early 1953 he suddenly saw that the essential DNA components, four organic bases, must be linked in definite pairs, a discovery that enabled Watson and Crick to formulate a double-helix molecular model for DNA. In 1962 the two scientists and Maurice Wilkins shared the Nobel Prize. Watson's *The Double Helix* (1968), a best-selling personal account of the DNA discovery, aroused controversy. He taught at Harvard University (1955–76) and served as director of the Carnegie Institute's laboratory at Cold Spring Harbor (1968–94). See also Rosalind Franklin.

Watson, John B(roadus) (1878–1958) U.S. psychologist. Trained at the University of Chicago, Watson taught psychology at Johns Hopkins University 1908–20. He is remembered for codifying and publicizing behaviorism. In his epoch-making article "Psychology as a Behaviorist Views It" (1913), he asserted that psychology should restrict itself to the objective, experimental study of the relations between environmental events and human behavior. In *Behavior* (1914) he argued for the use of animal subjects in studying reflexes and conditioned responses, and in *Psychology from the Standpoint of a Behaviorist* (1919) he extended the principles and methods he employed in animal experiments. In 1920 he left academia to enter the advertising business.

Watson, Thomas J(ohn), Sr. (1874–1956) U.S. industrialist. Born in Campbell, N.Y., he went to work for the National Cash Register Co. in 1899. In 1914 he became president of the company that in 1924 became International Business Machines (IBM), which he built into the world's largest manufacturer of electric typewriters and data-processing equipment. Backing an aggressive research-and-development program, he assembled a highly motivated, well-trained, and well-paid staff, gave pep talks, enforced a strict dress code, and posted the famous "Think" sign in company offices. In the 1930s and '40s he pursued international trade, extending IBM's influence worldwide. Active in civic affairs, he was noted for his efforts on behalf of the arts and world peace. His son Thomas John Watson, Jr. (born 1914), succeeded him as president (1952), chairman (1961), and CEO (1972).

Watson, Tom *orig.* **Thomas Sturges** (born 1949) U.S. golfer. Born in Kansas City, he attended Stanford University and turned professional in 1971. He became one of the sport's dominant figures in the mid-1970s, winning the British Open (1975, 1977, 1980, 1982, 1983), the Masters (1977, 1981), and the U.S. Open (1982).

Watson-Watt, Robert Alexander *later* **Sir Robert** (1892–1973) Scottish physicist. He began as a meteorologist working on devices for locating thunderstorms. As head of the radio department of Britain's National Physical Laboratory (1935) he worked on aircraft radio location and could locate planes at a distance of about 80 mi (110 km) by beaming radio waves at them, receiving reflections of the waves, and calculating distance by elapsed time. This led to the design of the world's first practical radar system, a vital element in the defense of Britain against German air raids (1940). His other contributions include a cathode-ray direction finder used to study atmospheric phenomena, research in electromagnetic radiation, and inventions used for flight safety.

Watt, James (1736–1819) Scottish engineer and inventor. Though largely self-taught, he began work early as an instrument maker and later as an engineer on the Forth and Clyde Canal. Watt's major improvement to Thomas Newcomen's steam engine was the use of a separate condenser (1769), which reduced the loss of latent heat and greatly increased its efficiency. With Matthew Boulton he began manufacture of his new engine in 1775. In 1781 he added rotary motion (a so-called sun-and-planet gear) to replace the up-and-down action of the original engine. In 1782 he patented the double-acting engine, in which

Watt, oil painting by H. Howard; in the National Portrait Gallery, London.

the piston pushed as well as pulled. This engine required a new method of rigidly connecting the piston to the beam, a problem he solved in 1784 with an arrangement of connected rods that guided the piston rod in a perpendicular motion. His application of the centrifugal governor for automatic control of the speed of the engine (1788) and his invention of a PRESSURE GAUGE (1790) virtually completed the Watt engine, which had immense consequences for the INDUSTRIAL REVOLUTION. He introduced the concept of HORSEPOWER; the watt, a unit of power, is named for him.

Watteau \vȧ-'tō, *Engl* wä-'tō\, **(Jean-) Antoine** (1684–1721) French painter. Son of a roof tiler in Valenciennes, he was apprenticed to a local artist. At 18 he moved to Paris, where he worked for a series of painters; one of them was a theatrical scenerist, and much of Watteau's work consequently embraced the artifice of the theater, particularly the COMMEDIA DELL'ARTE and the ballet. His works typified the lyrically charming and graceful Rococo style. The greatest, his *Pilgrimage to the Island of Cythera,* depicting pilgrims setting out for (or departing from) the mythic island of love, was his presentation piece when he was inducted into the Academy in 1717. The academicians, unable to fit him into any of the recognized categories, welcomed him as a painter of "elegant festivities," or *fêtes galantes,* an important new genre of painting to which countless later Rococo pictures belong.

wattle See ACACIA

Watts, André (born 1946) U.S. (German-born) pianist. Born in Nuremberg, son of an African-American soldier and a Hungarian mother, he made his debut at 9 at a Philadelphia Orchestra children's concert. He attracted wide attention when at 16 he performed on television under LEONARD BERNSTEIN. Though already a mature musician, he chose to continue study with Leon Fleischer (born 1928) rather than try to exploit his celebrity. He toured the world under State Department auspices in 1967, and a 1976 concert was the first live television broadcast of a solo recital in history.

Watts, Isaac (1674–1748) English Nonconformist minister, regarded as the father of English hymnody. Watts studied at the Dissenting Academy at Stoke Newington, London, and later became pastor of Mark Lane Independent (i.e., Congregational) Chapel. His collections of sacred lyrics include *Horae Lyricae* (1706), *Hymns and Spiritual Songs* (1707), and *The Psalms of David Imitated in the Language of the New Testament* (1719). His hymns, numbering more than 600, became known throughout Protestant Christendom; they include "When I Survey the Wondrous Cross," "O God, Our Help in Ages Past," "Joy to the World," and "Jesus Shall Reign." A man of great erudition, he published books on a range of subjects.

Watusi See TUTSI

Waugh \'wȯ\, **Evelyn (Arthur St. John)** (1903–1966) English novelist. After an Oxford education, he devoted himself to solitary observant travel and the writing of novels, soon earning a wide reputation for sardonic wit and technical brilliance. His finest satirical novels are *Decline and Fall* (1928), *Vile Bodies* (1930), *Black Mischief* (1932), *A Handful of Dust* (1934), *Scoop* (1938), and *The Loved One* (1948). He converted to Roman Catholicism in 1930, and his Catholicism is insistently reflected in his novels from then on. After service in World War II he led a retired life, growing increasingly conservative and misanthropic; his later works, intended to be more serious but written with less élan, include *Brideshead Revisited* (1945) and the *Sword of Honour* trilogy—*Men at Arms* (1952), *Officers and Gentlemen* (1955), and *Unconditional Surrender* (1961).

Evelyn Waugh, photograph by Mark Gerson, 1964.
CAMERA PRESS

wave Propagation of disturbances from place to place in a regular and organized way. Most familiar are surface WAVES that travel on water, but sound, light, and the motion of SUBATOMIC PARTICLES all exhibit wavelike properties. In the simplest waves, the disturbance oscillates periodically (see PERIODIC MOTION) with a fixed FREQUENCY and WAVELENGTH. Mechanical waves, such as sound, require a medium through which to travel, while electromagnetic waves (see ELECTROMAGNETIC RADIATION) do not require a medium and can be propagated through a vacuum. Propagation of a wave through a medium depends on the medium's properties. See also SEISMIC WAVE.

wave In oceanography, a ridge or swell on the surface of a body of water, normally having a forward motion distinct from the motions of the particles that compose it. Ocean waves are fairly regular, with an identifiable WAVELENGTH between adjacent crests and with a definite frequency of oscillation. Waves result when a generating force (usually the wind) displaces surface water and a restoring force returns it to its undisturbed position. SURFACE TENSION alone is the restoring force for small waves. For large waves, gravity is more important.

wave-cut platform *or* **abrasion platform** Gently sloping rock ledge that extends from the high-tide level at a steep cliff base to below the low-tide level. It develops as a result of wave abrasion; beaches protect the shore from abrasion and therefore prevent the formation of platforms. A platform is broadened as waves erode a notch at the base of the sea cliff, causing overhanging rock to fall. As the sea cliffs are attacked, weak rocks are quickly eroded, leaving the more resistant rocks as protrusions.

wave front Imaginary surface that represents corresponding points of waves vibrating in unison. As identical waves from the same source travel through a homogeneous medium, corresponding crests and troughs are in PHASE at any instant; that is, they have completed the same fraction of their PERIODIC MOTION. Any surface drawn through all points of the same phase constitutes a wave front.

wave function Variable quantity that mathematically describes the WAVE characteristics of a particle. It is related to the likelihood of the particle being at a given point in space at a given time, and may be thought of as an expression for the amplitude of the particle wave, though this is strictly not physically meaningful. The square of the wave function is the significant quantity, as it gives the probability for finding the particle at a given point in space and time. See also WAVE-PARTICLE DUALITY.

wave-particle duality Principle that SUBATOMIC PARTICLES possess some wavelike characteristics, and that electromagnetic WAVES, such as light, possess some particlelike characteristics. In 1905, by demonstrating the PHOTOELECTRIC EFFECT, ALBERT EINSTEIN showed that light, which until then had been thought of as a form of electromagnetic wave (see ELECTROMAGNETIC RADIATION), must also be thought of as localized in packets of discrete energy (see PHOTON). In 1924 LOUIS-VICTOR BROGLIE proposed that ELECTRONS have wave properties such as WAVELENGTH and FREQUENCY; their wavelike nature was experimentally established in 1927 by the demonstration of their DIFFRACTION. The theory of QUANTUM ELECTRODYNAMICS combines the wave theory and the particle theory of electromagnetic radiation.

waveguide Device that constrains the path of electromagnetic WAVES (see ELECTROMAGNETIC RADIATION). It can be used to transmit power or signals in the form of waves while minimizing power loss. Common examples are metallic tubes, COAXIAL CABLES, and optical fibers (see FIBER OPTICS). Waveguides transmit energy by propagating transmitted electromagnetic waves through the inside of a tube to a receiver at the other end. Metal waveguides are used in such technologies as MICROWAVE OVENS, RADAR systems, radio relay systems, and RADIO TELESCOPES.

wavelength Distance between corresponding points of two consecutive waves. "Corresponding points" refers to two points or particles that have completed identical fractions of their PERIODIC MOTION. In transverse waves, wavelength is measured from crest to crest or from trough to trough. In longitudinal waves, it is measured from compression to compression or from rarefaction to rarefaction. Wavelength, λ, is equal to the speed v of a wave in a medium divided by its FREQUENCY f, or $\lambda = v/f$.

Wavell \'wā-vəl\, **Archibald Percival** *later* **Earl Wavell (of Eritrea and of Winchester)** (1883–1950) British army officer. Recognized as an excellent trainer of troops, he became British commander in chief for the Middle East in 1939. In World War II he was noted for his defeat of the numerically superior Italian armies in North Africa (1940–41) but was unable to stop the German force under ERWIN ROMMEL in the NORTH AFRICA CAMPAIGN. As commander in chief of Southeast Asia (1941–43), he failed to stop the Japanese conquests of Malaya, Singapore, and Burma (1942). Promoted to field marshal, he served as viceroy of India 1943–47.

wax Any of a class of pliable substances, organic compounds of animal, plant, mineral, or synthetic origin, less greasy, harder, and more brittle than FATS. Waxes contain mostly compounds of high MOLECULAR WEIGHT (FATTY ACIDS, ALCOHOLS, and saturated HYDROCARBONS). Many melt at moderate temperatures and form hard films that can take a high polish. Animal and plant waxes are ESTERS of fatty acids and either a sterol (see STEROID) or a straight-chain higher ALCOHOL (e.g., cetyl alcohol). Animal waxes include BEESWAX; wool wax (lanolin), used in pharmaceuticals and cosmetics; and sperm oil and spermaceti (from SPERM WHALES), used as lubricants. Plant waxes include CARNAUBA WAX, candelilla wax, and SUGARCANE wax, used in polishes. About 90% of the waxes in commerce are recovered by dewaxing PETROLEUM. There are three main types: PARAFFIN (used in candles, crayons, paper coating, and industrial polishes and as a protective sealant, lubricant, insulating agent, and antifrothing agent), microcrystalline wax (used in paper coating), and petrolatum (used in ointments and cosmetics). Synthetic waxes (carbowaxes), derived from ETHYLENE GLYCOL, are commonly blended with petroleum waxes.

wax sculpture Figures modeled or molded in beeswax, either as finished pieces or for use as forms for casting metal (see LOST-WAX CASTING) or creating preliminary models. At ordinary temperatures, beeswax can be cut and molded easily, it melts at a low temperature, it mixes with any coloring matter and takes surface tints well, and its texture can be modified by a variety of additives. The ancient Egyptians used wax figures of deities in their funeral rites, and the Romans used wax images as presents in the Saturnalia. MICHELANGELO used wax models in making preliminary sketches for his statues. Wax medallion portraits, popular in the 16th century, enjoyed renewed popularity in the 18th century. JOHN FLAXMAN made many wax portraits and relief figures which JOSIAH WEDGWOOD translated into pottery. Exhibitions of wax figures are still popular, the most famous being those of MARIE TUSSAUD in London.

waxwing Any of three species (family Bombycillidae) of elegant-looking songbirds named for shiny red beads on the tips of the secondary wing feathers. All species are gray-brown and have a tapering crest. The common, or Bohemian, waxwing *(Bombycilla garrulus)* is 8 in. (20 cm) long and has yellow, white, and red wing markings. It breeds in northern forests of Eurasia and America. The cedar waxwing *(B. cedrorum),* smaller and less colorful, breeds in Canada and the northern U.S. Flocks of waxwings may invade city parks and gardens in winter, searching for berries. The Japanese waxwing *(B. japonica)* is restricted to northeastern Asia.

Wayne, Anthony (1745–1796) American Revolutionary officer. Born near Paoli, Pa., he owned a tannery before he was commissioned a colonel in the Continental Army (1776). He covered the American retreat from Canada and was given command of Fort Ticonderoga (1776). Promoted to brigadier general (1777), he led troops in the battles of the Brandywine, Paoli, and Germantown. He led the successful storming of the British fort at Stony Point, N.Y. (1779), and earned the nickname "Mad Anthony" for his boldness. He served in the siege of Yorktown and later defeated the Indians allied with the British in Georgia. In 1792 Pres. GEORGE WASHINGTON sent Wayne to fight the Indians in the Ohio Territory, and he decisively ended Indian resistance at the Battle of FALLEN TIMBERS (1794).

Wayne, John *orig.* **Marion Michael Morrison** (1907–1979) U.S. film actor. Born in Winterset, Iowa, he worked as a propman at the Fox studio before meeting JOHN FORD, who cast him in small parts from 1928. After his leading role in *The Big Trail* (1930), he played in more than 80 low-budget movies before winning acclaim for his role in Ford's *Stagecoach* (1939). Noted for his image as the strong, silent man, Wayne, nicknamed "Duke," became one of the top box-office attractions in movie history. He starred in such other westerns (many directed by Ford) as *Red River* (1948), *She Wore a Yellow Ribbon* (1949), *Rio Grande* (1950), *The Searchers* (1956), *Rio Bravo* (1959), and *True Grit* (1969, Academy Award), as well as in *The Quiet Man* (1952), *The Alamo* (1960), which he also directed, *Hatari!* (1962), and *The Green Berets* (1968), which he codirected.

WCTU See WOMAN'S CHRISTIAN TEMPERANCE UNION

weak force *or* **weak nuclear force** Fundamental interaction that underlies some forms of RADIOACTIVITY and certain interactions between SUBATOMIC PARTICLES. It acts on all elementary particles that have a SPIN of ½. The particles interact weakly by exchanging particles that have integer spins. These particles have masses about 100 times that of a PROTON, and it is this relative massiveness that makes the weak force appear weak at low energies. For example, in radioactive decay, the weak force has a strength about 1/100,000 that of the ELECTROMAGNETIC FORCE. However, it is now known that the weak force has intrinsically the same strength as the electromagnetic force, and the two are believed to be only different manifestations of a single electroweak force (see ELECTROWEAK THEORY).

weakfish *or* **sea trout** Any of several species (genus *Cynoscion*) in the DRUM family (Sciaenidae), carnivorous bottom-dwelling fishes along warm and tropical seashores. The name weakfish refers to their delicate mouth, which is easily torn by fishhooks. About six species inhabit North American coasts. The weakfish, or sea trout *(Cynoscion regalis),* is a sport fish but is usually less than 2 ft (60 cm) long. Weakfish are caught commercially along the Middle Atlantic coastal states and are considered the most economically important species in the family. The spotted sea trout *(C. nebulosus)* is found along Florida's Atlantic and Gulf coasts. Sea trouts resemble but are not related to true TROUTS.

weapons system Any integrated system for the control and operation of a specific type of weaponry. Weapons are usually divided into two categories, strategic and tactical. Strategic weapons strike at the seat of an enemy's military, economic, and political power, targeting cities, factories, military bases, transportation and communications networks, and seats of government. NUCLEAR WEAPONS are part of strategic weapons systems. Tactical weapons are designed instead for offensive or defensive use at relatively short range; for example, GUIDED MISSILES are intended as antiaircraft and antitank weapons, or other weapons used in aerial and naval combat. Only a few nations operate strategic weapons systems; tactical weapons systems exist in almost every country.

weasel Any of several genera (CARNIVORE family Mustelidae) of voracious nocturnal predators found throughout the Americas, Africa, and Eurasia. Weasels have slender bodies and necks, small flat heads, short legs, clawed toes, dense short fur, and slim pointed tails. The size and relative length of the tail vary among species. Their total length is 7–20 in. (17–50 cm), and they may weigh 1–12 oz (30–350 g). The approximately 10 New World and Eurasian species of *Mustela* are reddish brown; in cold regions, their winter coat turns white, and the pelt, especially of the stoat *(M. erminea),* is called ERMINE. Weasels generally hunt alone, feeding on rodents, fish, frogs, and birds' eggs.

Long-tailed weasel (*Mustela longicauda*).

JOHN H. GERARD—EB INC.

weather State of the atmosphere at a particular place during a short period of time. It involves day-to-day changes in such atmospheric phenomena as temperature, humidity, precipitation (type and amount), air pressure, wind, and cloud cover. Most weather occurs in the TROPOSPHERE, but phenomena of the higher regions of the atmosphere, such as JET STREAMS, and geographic features, most notably mountains and large bodies of water, also affect it. See also CLIMATE.

weather forecasting Prediction of the weather through application of the principles of physics and METEOROLOGY. Weather forecasting predicts atmospheric phenomena and changes on the earth's surface caused by atmospheric conditions (snow and ice cover, storm tides, floods, etc.). Scientific weather forecasting relies on empirical and statistical techniques, such as measurements of temperature, humidity, atmospheric pressure, wind speed and direction, and precipitation, and computer-controlled mathematical models.

weather modification Deliberate or inadvertent alteration of atmospheric conditions by human activity, sufficient to modify the weather on a local or regional scale. Deliberate alterations include covering plants to keep them warm at night, seeding clouds to induce or augment precipitation, and firing silver-iodide particles into clouds to suppress or mitigate hail and to reduce fog at airports. Inadvertent alterations are the result of industrialization and urbanization, which have added billions of tons of carbon dioxide and other gases to the atmosphere (see ACID RAIN, GLOBAL WARMING, GREENHOUSE EFFECT).

weathering Physical disintegration and chemical decomposition of rocks, minerals, and immature soils at or near the earth's surface. Physical, chemical, and biological processes induced or modified by wind, water, and climate cause the changes. Weathering is distinguished from EROSION in that no transportation of material is involved. A broader application of erosion, however, includes weathering as a component. Weathering is also distinguished from METAMORPHISM, which usually takes place deep in the crust at much higher temperatures and elevated pressures.

Weaver, James B(aird) (1833–1912) U.S. politician. Born in Dayton, Ohio, he became an advocate of the Greenback movement and was elected to the U.S. House of Representatives from Iowa (1879–81, 1885–89). He helped form the People's Party (see POPULIST MOVEMENT) and was its candidate for president in 1892, winning over 1 million popular votes and 22 electoral votes. After helping effect the party's merger with the Democratic Party, he retired to Iowa.

Weaver, John (1673–1760) English dancer and teacher, known as "the father of English pantomime." From 1700 to 1736 he performed and produced his dance dramas in the Drury Lane and Lincoln's Inn Fields theaters. His libretto for *The Loves of Mars and Venus* (1717) was the first published dance drama and displayed the integration of plot and dance that was later developed by J.-G. NOVERRE and GASPARO ANGIOLINI as the *ballet d'action.*

Weaver, Warren (1894–1978) U.S. mathematician. Born in Reedsburg, Wisc., he studied at the University of Wisconsin, taught there 1920–32, and directed the Rockefeller Foundation's Natural Science Division 1932–55. He is considered the first person to propose using electronic computers for the translation of natural languages. In a 1949 memo, he proposed that statistical techniques from the field of information theory could be used to enable computers to translate text from one natural language to another automatically. His proposal was based on the assumption that a document in a human language can be viewed as having been written in code, which can be broken like other codes.

weaving Production of fabric by interlacing two sets of YARNS so that they cross each other, normally at right angles, usually accomplished with a hand- or power-operated LOOM. In weaving, lengthwise yarns are called warp and crosswise yarns are called weft, or filling. Most woven fabrics are made with their outer edges finished in a manner that avoids raveling (because the weft yarn turns around instead of ending in a cut end). These edges, called selvages, run lengthwise, parallel to the warp yarns. The three basic weaves are plain or tabby (weft threads go over one warp thread, then under one), TWILL, and SATIN. Fancy weaves, such as pile, Jacquard, dobby, and leno, require more complicated looms or special loom attachments. See also NAVAJO WEAVING.

Web See WORLD WIDE WEB

Web site Collection of files and related resources accessible through the WORLD WIDE WEB and organized under a particular DOMAIN NAME. Typical files found at a Web site are HTML documents with their associated graphic image files (GIF, JPEG, etc.), scripted programs (in PERL, CGI, JAVA, etc.), and similar resources. The site's files are usually accessed through HYPERTEXT or hyperlinks embedded in other files. A Web site may consist of a single HTML file, or it may comprise hundreds or thousands of related files. A Web site's usual starting point or opening page, called a home page, usually functions as a table of contents or index, with links to other sections of the site. Web sites are hosted on one or more Web SERVERS, which transfer files to client computers or other servers that request them using the HTTP protocol. Although the term "site" implies a single physical location, the files and resources of a Web site may actually be spread among several servers in different geographic locations. The particular file desired by a client is specified by a URL that is either typed into a BROWSER or accessed by selecting a hyperlink.

Webb, Sidney (James) and Beatrice (1858–1943, 1859–1947) British socialist reformers. Sidney was a civil-service clerk when GEORGE BERNARD SHAW induced him to join the FABIAN SOCIETY in 1885. He wrote the first Fabian tract, *Facts for Socialists* (1887), and took to lecturing on socialism. In 1891 he met Beatrice (born Martha Beatrice Potter), author of *The Cooperative Movement in Great Britain* (1891), and they were married in 1892. Together they wrote the influential *The History of Trade Unionism* (1894) and *Industrial Democracy* (1897). As a member of the London County Council (1892–1910), Sidney effected extensive reforms in public education. The Webbs cofounded the London School of Economics and helped reorganize the University of London. As a member of the Poor Laws commission (1905–9), Beatrice wrote a report that anticipated the WELFARE STATE. In 1914 they joined the Labour Party, and Sidney wrote its influential policy statement, *Labour and the New Social Order* (1918). He served in Parliament 1922–29, and served as colonial secretary 1929–31, having been ceated Baron Passfield of Passfield Corner in 1929. Impressed by the Soviet Union after their trip in 1932, the Webbs wrote *Soviet Communism: A New Civilisation?* (1935).

Webber, Andrew Lloyd See Andrew LLOYD WEBBER

Weber \'vā-bər\, **Carl Maria (Friedrich Ernst) von** (1786–1826) German composer. Son of a musician and theater manager, and first cousin to W.A. MOZART's wife, he was born with a deformed hip and was never strong. He had composition lessons with Michael Haydn (1737–1806) and with Abbé Vogler (1749–1814), who recommended him for a post in Breslau (1804–6). His operas began to have success, and took over direction of the Prague Opera (1813–16), which he saved from ruin, but finding little time for composition, he resigned. Showing signs of the tuberculosis that would kill him, he began to compose more prolifically. Appointed kapellmeister for life in Dresden, he began work on his masterpiece, *Der Freischütz* (1821), whose premiere made him an international star. The libretto for his next opera, *Euryanthe* (1823), was so bad that its admirable music never succeeded, and his final opera, *Oberon* (1826), composed for London, was a success there but not elsewhere. He died in England at 39.

Weber \'vā-bər\, **Max** (1864–1920) German sociologist and political economist. Son of a wealthy liberal politician and a Calvinist mother, Weber was a compulsively diligent scholar who suffered occasional nervous collapses. Insights derived from his own experience inform his most famous and controversial work, *The Protestant Ethic and the Spirit of Capitalism* (1904–5), which examines the relationship between Calvinist (or Puritan) morality, compulsive labor, BUREAUCRACY, and economic success under capitalism (see PROTESTANT ETHIC). Weber also wrote penetratingly on social phenomena such as charisma and mysticism, which he saw as antithetical to the modern world and its underlying process of rationalization. His efforts helped establish sociology as an academic discipline in Germany, and his work continues to stimulate scholarship. Through his insistence on the need for objectivity and his analysis of human action in terms of motivation, he profoundly influenced sociological theory. His voluminous writings, mostly published posthumously, include *Economy and Society* (2 vols., 1922–25) and *General Economic History* (1923).

Webern \'vā-bərn\, **Anton (Friedrich Wilhelm von)** (1883–1945) Austrian composer. He learned piano and cello as a child and earned a doctorate in musicology at the University of Vienna, specializing in the music of H. ISAAC. In 1904 he and A BERG began composition lessons with A. SCHOENBERG, and he was soon combining atonality with complex counterpoint in the manner of Isaac, producing works distinctive for their extreme brevity and delicacy. As Schoenberg was working on the twelve-tone method, Webern was independently moving in a similar direction, and after Schoenberg laid out the system for him, Webern embarked on such relatively extended pieces as the *Symphony* (1928), *Concerto* (1934), and *Variations for Piano* (1936), but the character of his works remained radically different from those of any contemporary. He earned a living most of his life as a conductor. During Austria's occupation at the end of World War II, he absentmindedly stepped outside during a curfew and was shot by an American soldier. Though he was little appreciated during his lifetime, his works became hugely influential internationally in the postwar decades.

Weber's law \'vā-bərz\ *or* **Weber-Fechner law** \'fek-nər\ In PSYCHOPHYSICS, a historically important law quantifying the perception of change in a given stimulus. Originated by the German physiologist Ernst Heinrich Weber (1795–1878) in 1834 and elaborated by his student GUSTAV

Theodor Fechner, the law states that the change in a stimulus that will be just noticeable is a constant ratio of the original stimulus. It was later shown not to hold for extremes of stimulation.

Webster, Ben(jamin Francis) (1909–1973) U.S. tenor saxophonist, one of the most influential saxophone soloists of the swing era. He was born in Kansas City. Influenced by Coleman Hawkins and Johnny Hodges, he played in several important swing bands before joining Duke Ellington in 1940. After 1943 he worked mostly as the leader of small ensembles. He moved to Copenhagen in 1964. His sensual, breathy tone and wide vibrato were his trademarks, and he became one of the master interpreters of ballads in jazz.

Webster, Daniel (1782–1852) U.S. lawyer and politician. Born in Salisbury, N.H., he was elected to the U.S. House of Representatives (1813–17). After moving to Boston (1816), he built a prosperous law practice and represented Massachusetts in the House 1823–27. He argued several precedent-setting cases before the U.S. Supreme Court, including the Dartmouth College case, *McCulloch vs. Maryland*, and *Gibbons vs. Ogden*. Elected to the U.S. Senate (1827–41, 1845–50), he became famous as an orator in supporting the Union and opposing the nullification movement and its advocates, John C. Calhoun and Robert Y. Hayne. As U.S. secretary of state (1841–43, 1850–52) he negotiated the Webster-Ashburton Treaty to settle the Canada–Maine border dispute.

Daniel Webster, daguerreotype by A.S. Southworth and J.J. Hawes.

BY COURTESY OF THE METROPOLITAN MUSEUM OF ART, NEW YORK CITY, GIFT OF I.N. PHELPS STOKES, EDWARD S. HAWES, ALICE MARY HAWES, MARION AUGUSTA HAWES,

Webster, John (c. 1580–c. 1625) British playwright. Little is known of his life, but he may have been an actor who began writing plays later in his career. He collaborated with several leading dramatists, including Thomas Dekker. He is best remembered for the revenge tragedies *The White Devil* (1612) and *The Duchess of Malfi* (1623), both of which concern the murders and bloody deeds that arise out of family quarrels among the Italian nobility. They are often considered the greatest 17th-century English tragedies apart from those of William Shakespeare.

Webster, Lake See Lake Chargoggagoggmanchauggauggagoggchaubunagungamaugg

Webster, Noah (1758–1843) U.S. lexicographer and writer. Born in West Hartford, Conn., he attended Yale University and studied law. While working as a teacher in New York, he began his lifelong efforts to promote a distinctively American education. His first step was publishing *A Grammatical Institute of the English Language*, including *The American Spelling Book* (1783), the famed "Blue-Backed Speller" that went on to sell some 100 million copies (making it perhaps the best-selling book in American history) and provided much of his income for the rest of his life. An ardent Federalist, he founded two pro-Federalist newspapers (1793) and wrote articles on politics and many other subjects. In 1821 he cofounded Amherst College. He produced his first dictionary in 1806; in 1807 he began work on his landmark *American Dictionary of the English Language* (1828; 2nd edition 1840). Reflecting his principle that spelling, grammar, and usage should be based on the living, spoken language, it was instrumental in establishing the dignity and vitality of American English. The rights to the dictionary were purchased from his estate by George and Charles Merriam, whose firm developed the Merriam-Webster dictionary series.

Webster-Ashburton Treaty (1842) Treaty between the U.S. and Britain establishing the northeastern boundary of the U.S. Negotiated by U.S. secretary of state Daniel Webster and Britain's ambassador Lord Ashburton, it also provided for Anglo-U.S. cooperation in the suppression of the slave trade. It fixed the present boundary between Maine and New Brunswick, granted the U.S. navigation rights on the St. John River, provided for extradition in nonpolitical criminal cases, and established a joint naval system for suppressing the slave trade off the African coast.

Wedekind \ˈvā-də-ˌkint\, **Frank** *orig.* **Benjamin Franklin** (1864–1918) German actor and playwright. He lived in Switzerland (1872–84), then in Munich, where he worked at various jobs, including journalist and cabaret performer. He wrote plays from 1891, when his tragedy *The Awakening of Spring* created a scandal with its theme of awakening adolescent sexuality. In his "Lulu" cycle, *Earth Spirit* (1895) and *Pandora's Box* (1904), he extended the theme of sex to the underworld of society and introduced the amoral Lulu. His plays used episodic scenes, fragmented dialogue, distortion, and caricature, prefiguring the theater of the absurd and forming a transition from realism to expressionism.

Wedemeyer \ˈwe-də-ˌmī-ər\, **Albert C(oady)** (1897–1989) U.S. Army officer. Born in Omaha, Neb., he graduated from West Point and served in China, the Philippines, and Europe until World War II. As a staff officer in the war-plans division of the U.S. War Department (1941–43), he was the principal author of the 1941 Victory Program for U.S. entry into the war and helped plan such strategies as the Normandy Campaign. He became chief of staff to Gen. Chiang Kai-shek and commander of U.S. forces in China (1944–46). He retired in 1951 and was promoted to general in 1954.

wedge In mechanics, a device that tapers to a thin edge, usually made of metal or wood, and used for splitting, lifting, or tightening, such as to secure a hammer head onto its handle. The wedge is considered one of the five simple machines. Wedges have been used since prehistoric times to split logs and rocks; for rocks, wooden wedges, caused to swell by wetting, have been used. In terms of its mechanical function, the screw may be thought of as a wedge wrapped around a cylinder.

Wedgwood, Josiah (1730–1795) British pottery designer and manufacturer. His family had been potters since the 17th century. After an apprenticeship with his elder brother, he formed a partnership with another potter and finally went into business for himself. He took a scientific approach to pottery making and was so successful that the makers of even Meissen and Sèvres porcelain found their trade affected. His many innovations include development of a green glaze still popular today, the perfection of creamware, and the invention of the pyrometer. His daughter Susannah was the mother of Charles Darwin. See also Wedgwood ware, Wood family.

Wedgwood ware English stoneware made by Staffordshire factories originally established by Josiah Wedgwood. Creamware appealed to the middle class because of its high quality, durability, and affordability. Black basaltes (from 1768), unglazed stoneware of fine texture that was ideal for imitating antique and Renaissance objects, appealed to antiquarians. Also in the Neoclassical tradition was jasperware (from 1775), a white, matte, unglazed stoneware that could be stained. White ornaments were applied to the colored body, achieving the look of an antique cameo. With the help of such artists as John Flaxman, Wedgwood copied many antique designs. Production of fine Wedgwood ware continues to the present day.

Wedgwood jasperware vase, Staffordshire, England, c. 1785; in the Victoria and Albert Museum, London.

BY COURTESY OF THE VICTORIA AND ALBERT MUSEUM, LONDON; PHOTOGRAPH, WILFRID WALTER—EB INC.

weed Any plant growing where it is not wanted. On land under cultivation, weeds compete with crops for water, light, and nutrients. On rangelands and in pastures, weeds are those plants that grazing animals dislike or that are poisonous. Many weeds are hosts of plant disease organisms or of insect pests.

W X Y Z

Some originally unwanted plants later were found to have virtues and came under cultivation, while some cultivated plants, when transplanted to new climates, escaped cultivation and became weeds in the new habitat.

Weed, Thurlow (1797–1882) U.S. journalist and politician. Born in Cairo, N.Y., he worked on various newspapers in upstate New York. A leader in the ANTI-MASONIC MOVEMENT, he was the founding editor of the *Albany Evening Journal* (1830–63). He helped form the Whig Party in New York and was instrumental in WILLIAM SEWARD's election as governor (1838) and in the presidential election of WILLIAM H. HARRISON (1840). He later became active in the Republican Party and was a staunch supporter of Pres. ABRAHAM LINCOLN. In 1861 he was sent to England to win support for the Union.

Weelkes \'wēlks\, **Thomas** (c. 1575–1623) British composer and organist. He published his first book of madrigals in 1597, and was appointed organist at Winchester College the following year. His next two books of madrigals, his greatest, were soon published (1598, 1600), and a final volume in 1608. His settings are often marked by strong chromaticism for expressive purposes.

weevil *or* **snout beetle** Any of about 40,000 BEETLE species in the largest family of beetles, Curculionidae, also the largest family in the animal kingdom. Most weevils have long, elbowed antennae that may fold into special grooves on the prominent snout. Many species are wingless. Most species are less than 0.25 in. (6 mm) long, are plainly colored and marked, and feed exclusively on plants. Some species are more than 3 in. (80 mm) long. The larvae may feed on only a certain part of a plant or a single plant species; adults are less specialized. The family includes many destructive pests, including the BOLL WEEVIL.

Wegener \'vā-gə-nər\, **Alfred (Lothar)** (1880–1930) German meteorologist and geophysicist. After earning a PhD in astronomy (1905), he became interested in paleoclimatology and traveled to Greenland to research polar air circulation. He formulated the first complete statement of the CONTINENTAL DRIFT hypothesis, which he presented in *The Origin of Continents and Oceans* (1915). His theory won some adherents, but by 1930 most geologists had rejected it because of the implausibility of his postulations for the driving force behind the continents' movement. It was resurrected in the 1960s as part of the theory of PLATE TECTONICS. Wegener died during his fourth expedition to Greenland.

Wei Mengbian *or* **Wei Meng-Pien** \'wā-'məŋ-'pyen\ (fl. AD 340) Chinese mechanical engineer. He devised numerous wheeled vehicles, including a hodometer (for measuring distance) and a south-pointing carriage. He also built a wagon mill in which rotation of the wheels drove a set of millstones and hammers that automatically processed grain. His mechanisms anticipated those later used by European engineers.

Wei River \'wā\ River, northern central China. It rises in the mountains of southeastern GANSU province and flows east through SHAANXI province to join the HUANG RIVER. It is 537 mi (864 km) long. Its valley was the earliest center of Chinese civilization and until the 10th century AD was the site of a succession of capital cities. In the 3rd century BC, the area around the junction of the Ching and Wei rivers was the site of the first ambitious irrigation works in China.

Wei Zhongxian *or* **Wei Chung-hsien** \'wā-'jùŋ-shē-'ən\ (1568–1627) EUNUCH who dominated the Chinese government 1624–27. As a close companion to the nurse of the future Tianji emperor (r.1620–27), Wei captured the young prince's trust. Once on the throne, the weak and indecisive emperor let Wei become the actual ruler. Wei levied crushing taxes on the provinces, ruthlessly exploited the population, hounded his enemies, terrorized the official class, and filled the government with sycophants and opportunists. He fell from power when the emperor died, and hanged himself to avoid trial. He is considered the most powerful eunuch in Chinese history.

Weidman \'wīd-mən\, **Charles** *orig.* **Charles Edward Weidman, Jr.** (1901–1975) U.S. modern dancer, teacher, and choreographer. He was born in Lincoln, Neb. He studied at the Denishawn school and was a member of its company in the 1920s. In 1928 he cofounded with DORIS HUMPHREY the Humphrey-Weidman school and dance company, for which he choreographed many works. In 1945 he established his own school and in 1948 founded the Theater Dance Co., for which he choreographed his major work, *Fables for Our Time*. He continued to teach, choreograph, and dance into the 1970s.

Weierstrass \'vī-ər-ˌshträs\, **Karl (Theodor Wilhelm)** (1815–1897) German mathematician. He taught principally at the University of Berlin (from 1856). After many years of working in isolation, an article in 1854 initiated a string of important contributions, which he disseminated mainly through lectures. He is known for his work on the theory of FUNCTIONS, and he is called the father of modern ANALYSIS. His greatest influence was felt through his students, many of whom went on to make important contributions to mathematics.

weight Gravitational force of attraction on an object, caused by the presence of a massive second object, such as the earth or moon. It is a consequence of the universal law of GRAVITATION. At the same location, more massive (see MASS) objects weigh more. The farther an object is from the earth, the less it weighs. Though the mass of a given object remains constant, its weight varies according to its location. For example, an object's weight on the moon is about one-sixth of its weight on earth, because the moon has less mass and a smaller radius. Weight W is the product of an object's mass m and the acceleration of gravity g at the location of the object, or $W = mg$. Since weight is a measure of force rather than of mass, the units of weight are newtons (N).

weight lifting Sport in which barbells are lifted competitively or as an exercise. The two main events are (1) the snatch, in which the barbell is lifted from the floor to arm's length overhead in a single, continuous motion; and (2) the clean and jerk, in which it is lifted first to the shoulders and then, after a pause, to arm's length overhead. Contestants are divided into 10 body-weight categories ranging from flyweight to superheavyweight. Lifts may range to over 1,000 lbs (455 kg) in the heavyweight divisions. The origins of modern competition are to be found in 18th- and 19th-century strongman contests. The first three Olympic Games (1896, 1900, 1904) included weight lifting, as have all games after 1920.

weight training System of conditioning involving lifting weights, especially for strength and endurance. It may include the use of barbells and dumbbells, a Nautilus or similar machines, or a combination of these. Athletes use it to improve their performance, nonathletes use it for general conditioning or bodybuilding, and those recovering from an injury may use it as part of an overall rehabilitation program.

weights and measures Standard quantities by which comparisons are made between an object to be measured and a known quantity of the same kind (see MEASUREMENT). Weights and measures are fundamental to the sciences, to engineering, building, and other technical matters, and to much everyday activity. See also FOOT, GRAM, INTERNATIONAL SYSTEM OF UNITS, METER, METRIC SYSTEM, POUND. See table on following page.

Weil \'vey\, **Simone** (1909–1943) French mystic and social philosopher. After graduating from the École Normale Supérieure, she taught philosophy in secondary schools and labored in factories, sharing her wages with the poor and living in poverty. She assisted the anti-Franco forces in the Spanish Civil War and worked in the French Resistance in World War II. Though born Jewish, she became a Roman Catholic in the 1940s. She died at 34 of tuberculosis complicated by self-imposed starvation undertaken out of sympathy for those suffering in occupied France. Her posthumously published works, including *Gravity and Grace* (1947), *The Need for Roots* (1949), *Waiting for God* (1950), and *Notebooks* (3 vols., 1951–56), which particularly influenced French and English social thought, explore her own religious life while analyzing the individual's relation with the state and God, the spiritual shortcomings of modern industrial society, and the horrors of totalitarianism.

Weill \'vīl\, **Kurt (Julian)** (1900–1950) German-U.S. composer. Son of a cantor, by 15 he was working as a theater accompanist. He studied composition briefly with E. HUMPERDINCK, and a conductor's post gave him wide experience. For a master class with F. BUSONI (1920), he wrote his first symphony. He gained attention with his one-act opera *Der Protagonist* (1925), whose sparse and spiky style prefigured that of his greatest works. In 1927 he teamed with BERTOLT BRECHT to write *The Threepenny Opera* (1928) in a new "cabaret" style; the musical had enormous success in Berlin and elsewhere. In 1929 the two produced *Happy End*, and in 1930 *The Rise and Fall of the City of Mahagonny*. When the Nazis took power in 1933, he fled to Paris with his wife, L. LENYA, where he wrote *The Seven Deadly Sins* (1933). In 1935 they emi-

UNIT	ABBREVIATION OR SYMBOL	EQUIVALENTS IN OTHER UNITS OF SAME SYSTEM	METRIC EQUIVALENT
Weights and Measurements[1] (British Imperial System/U.S. Customary System)			
WEIGHT			
Avoirdupois[2]			
ton			
short ton		20 short hundredweight, 2000 pounds	0.907 metric ton
long ton		20 long hundredweight, 2240 pounds	1.016 metric ton
hundredweight	cwt		
short hundredweight		100 pounds, 0.05 short tons	45.359 kilograms
long hundredweight		112 pounds, 0.05 long ton	50.802 kilograms
pound	lb *or* lb avdp *also* #	16 ounces, 7000 grains	0.454 kilogram
ounce	oz *or* oz avdp	16 drams, 437.5 grains, 0.0625 pound	28.350 grams
dram	dr *or* dr avdp	27.344 grains, 0.0625 ounce	1.772 grams
grain	gr	0.037 dram, 0.002286 ounce	0.0648 gram
Troy			
pound	lb t	12 ounces, 240 pennyweight, 5760 grains	0.373 kilogram
ounce	oz t	20 pennyweight, 480 grains, 0.083 pound	31.103 grams
pennyweight	dwt *also* pwt	24 grains, 0.05 ounce	1.555 grams
grain	gr	0.042 pennyweight, 0.002083 ounce	0.0648 gram
Apothecaries'			
pound	lb ap	12 ounces, 5760 grains	0.373 kilogram
ounce	oz ap	8 drams, 480 grains, 0.083 pound	31.103 grams
dram	dr ap	3 scruples, 60 grains	3.888 grams
scruple	s ap	20 grains, 0.333 dram	1.296 grams
grain	gr	0.05 scruple, 0.002083 ounce, 0.0166 dram	0.0648 gram
CAPACITY			
U.S. liquid measure			
gallon	gal	4 quarts (231 cubic inches)	3.785 liters
quart	qt	2 pints (57.75 cubic inches)	0.946 liter
pint	pt	4 gills (28.875 cubic inches	473.176 milliliters
gill	gi	4 fluid ounces (7.219 cubic inches)	118.294 milliliters
fluid ounce	fl oz	8 fluid drams (1.805) cubic inches)	29.573 milliliters
fluid dram	fl dr	60 minims (0.226 cubic inch)	3.697 milliliters
minim	min	1/60 fluid dram (0.003760 cubic inch)	0.061610 milliliter
U.S. dry measure			
bushel	bu	4 pecks (2150.42 cubic inches)	35.239 liters
peck	pk	8 quarts (537.605 cubic inches)	8.810 liters
quart	qt	2 pints (67.201 cubic inches)	1.101 liters
pint	pt	½ quart (33.600 cubic inches)	0.551 liter
British imperial liquid and dry measure			
bushel	bu	4 pecks (2219.36 cubic inches)	36.369 liters
peck	pk	2 gallons (554.84 cubic inches)	9.092 liters
gallon	gal	4 quarts (277.420 cubic inches)	4.546 liters
quart	qt	2 pints (69.355 cubic inches)	1.136 liters
pint	pt	4 gills (34.678 cubic inches)	568.26 milliliters
gill	gi	5 fluid ounces (8.669 cubic inches)	142.066 milliliters
fluid ounce	fl oz	8 fluid drams (1.7339 cubic inches)	28.412 milliliters
fluid dram	fl dr	60 minims (0.216734 cubic inch)	3.5516 milliliters
minim	min	1/60 fluid dram (0.003612 cubic inch)	0.059194 milliliter
LENGTH			
mile	mi	5280 feet, 1760 yards, 320 rods	1.609 kilometers
rod	rd	5.50 yards, 16.5 feet	5.029 meters
yard	yd	3 feet, 36 inches	0.9144 meter
foot	ft *or* ′	12 inches, 0.333 yard	30.48 centimeters
inch	in *or* ″	0.083 foot, 0.028 yard	2.54 centimeters
AREA			
square mile	sq mi *or* mi^2	640 acres, 102,400 square rods	2.590 square kilometers
acre		4840 square yards, 43,560 square feet	0.405 hectare, 4047 square meters
square rod	sq rd *or* rd^2	30.35 square yards, 0.00625 acre	25.293 square meters
square yard	sq yd *or* yd^2	1296 square inches, 9 square feet	0.836 square meter
square foot	sq ft *or* ft^2	144 square inches, 0.111 square yard	0.093 square meter
square inch	sq in *or* in^2	0.0069 square foot, 0.00077 square yard	6.452 square centimeters
VOLUME			
cubic yard	cu yd *or* yd^3	27 cubic feet, 46,656 cubic inches	0.765 cubic meter
cubic foot	cu ft *or* ft^3	1728 cubic inches, 0.0370 cubic yard	0.028 cubic meter
cubic inch	cu in *or* in^3	0.00058 cubic foot, 0.000021 cubic yard	16.387 cubic centimeters

[1]For U.S. equivalents of the metric unit see Metric System table. [2]The U.S. uses the avoirdupois units as a common system of measuring weight.

W X Y Z

grated to the U.S.; there he collaborated on such musicals as *Knickerbocker Holiday* (1938), *Lady in the Dark* (1941), *One Touch of Venus* (1943), and *Lost in the Stars* (1949).

Weimar Republic \'vī-ˌmär\ Government of Germany 1919–33, so named because the assembly that adopted its constitution met at Weimar in 1919. In its early years, the Weimar Republic was troubled by postwar economic and financial problems and political instability, but it had recovered considerably by the late 1920s. Its major political leaders included presidents FRIEDRICH EBERT (1919–25) and PAUL VON HINDENBURG (1925–34), as well as GUSTAV STRESEMANN, who was chancellor (1923) and foreign minister (1923–29). With the GREAT DEPRESSION, its political and economic collapse enabled ADOLF HITLER to rise to power and become chancellor (1933), after which he suspended the Weimar constitution.

weimaraner \ˌvī-mə-'rä-nər, 'wī-mə-ˌrä-nər\ Dog breed developed in the early 19th century by German nobles of the court of Weimar. First used to hunt big game, the breed was later used as a bird dog and retriever. A graceful dog, it has hanging ears; blue, gray, or amber eyes; and a short, sleek, mouse- or silver-gray coat. It stands 23–27 in. (58–69 cm) and weighs 70–85 lbs (32–39 kg). It is characterized by an alert, well-balanced stance and is valued as an aggressive hunter and a good companion and watchdog.

Weingartner \'vīn-gärt-nər\, **(Paul) Felix, Edler (Lord) von Münzberg** (1863–1942) German conductor and composer. After studies in Leipzig, he came to the attention of F. LISZT, who arranged the premiere of his first opera at Weimar (1884). He held conducting posts at Danzig, Hamburg, and Mannheim, and became conductor of the Berlin Opera in 1891. He succeeded G. MAHLER at the Vienna Opera (1908–11), and stayed on with the Vienna Philharmonic until 1927. He also directed the Basel Conservatory (1927–33) and was a distinguished writer on music.

Weir \'wir\, **Peter (Lindsay)** (born 1944) Australian film director. After working as a cameraman and producer for an Australian film studio, he began directing films in 1973. He won an international audience with the haunting and atmospheric *Picnic at Hanging Rock* (1975), which was followed by *The Last Wave* (1977), *Gallipoli* (1981), and *The Year of Living Dangerously* (1982). His later movies, made in Hollywood, include *Witness* (1985), *The Mosquito Coast* (1986), *Dead Poets Society* (1989), and *The Truman Show* (1998).

Weiser \'vī-zər\, **Johann Conrad** (1696–1760) American (German-born) colonial Indian agent. He emigrated to New York in 1710 and lived briefly among the IROQUOIS before becoming a farmer and serving as an Indian interpreter. In 1729 he moved to Pennsylvania, where he worked with the colony's Indian agent. He arranged agreements between Iroquois tribes and colonial governments that helped form a British-Indian alliance against the French.

Weisgall, Hugo (David) (1912–1997) U.S. (Czech-born) composer. Son of an opera singer, cantor, and composer, he was raised in Baltimore from 1920. He studied composition with R. SESSIONS and conducting with FRITZ REINER, also earning a doctorate in German literature from Johns Hopkins University. He is considered one of the most important U.S. opera composers for the literary quality of his chosen texts and the individuality and effectiveness of his music; his works include *The Tenor* (1950), *The Stronger* (1952), and *Six Characters in Search of an Author* (1956); his last completed opera, *Esther* (1993), won wide acclaim.

Weiss \'vīs\, **Peter (Ulrich)** (1916–1982) German playwright. After fleeing Germany in 1934, his family settled in Sweden. He painted and made avant-garde films in the 1950s, then turned to fiction and drama, establishing a reputation in Germany with his novel *Exile* (1962). Preoccupied with revolution and violence, he won international acclaim for his play *The Persecution and Assassination of Jean-Paul Marat as Performed by the Inmates of the Asylum of Charenton Under the Direction of the Marquis de Sade* (1964). Associated with the theater of FACT movement, he also wrote the documentary dramas *The Investigation* (1965), *The Song of the Lusitanian Bogey* (1967), and *Discourse on Vietnam* (1968).

Weissmuller \'wīs-ˌməl-ər\, **Johnny** *orig.* **Peter John** (1904–1984) U.S. freestyle swimmer and actor. Born in Pennsylvania, he was reared in Chicago, where he attended the University of Chicago and developed into a champion swimmer. He won five Olympic gold medals (three in 1924, two in 1928) and set 67 world records. He later became even more famous as an actor, starring as Tarzan of the Apes in 12 films (1932–48) and later creating the role of the comic-book character Jungle Jim for film and television.

Weizmann \'vīts-män\, **Chaim (Azriel)** (1874–1952) Russian-Palestinian chemist and first president of Israel (1949–52). Born in present-day Belarus, he earned a doctorate in chemistry and patented several dyestuffs before moving to England to teach in 1904. His 1912 discovery of a bacterium that could convert car-bohydrate to acetone proved of great value to the British armaments industry in World War I, and in return the government aided his negotiations for the BALFOUR DECLARATION (1917). In 1919 he obtained an agreement on Jewish-Arab coexistence in Palestine from Emir Faysal ibn Husayn, and in 1920 he became president of the World Zionist Organization, a post from which he was ousted in 1931. Despite conflicts with more extreme Zionists, he was sent to the U.S. to secure support for Israel in 1948, and in 1949 he was elected Israel's first president.

Welch, William Henry (1850–1934) U.S. pathologist. Born in Norfolk, Conn., he studied pathology in Germany before returning to open the nation's first pathology laboratory at Bellevue Hospital Medical College (1879). From 1893 he directed the rise of Johns Hopkins Univ., where he developed the country's first true university department of pathology. He recruited WILLIAM OSLER and WILLIAM S. HALSTED for the faculty and was the medical school's first dean (1893–98). His curriculum revolutionized U.S. medicine by demanding that students study physical sciences and be actively involved in clinical duties and laboratory work. Welch also demonstrated the effects of diphtheria toxin and discovered bacteria involved in wound fever and gas gangrene.

Weld, Theodore Dwight (1803–1895) U.S. reformer. Born in Hampton, Conn., he left his divinity studies to become an agent for the AMERICAN ANTI-SLAVERY SOCIETY (1834). His pamphlets *The Bible Against Slavery* (1837) and *Slavery as It Is* (1839) helped convert such figures as JAMES BIRNEY, HENRY WARD BEECHER, and HARRIET BEECHER STOWE to the antislavery cause. He married his coworker SARAH GRIMKE (1838), and they directed schools and taught in New Jersey and Massachusetts. In 1841–43 Weld organized an antislavery reference bureau in Washington, D.C., to assist congressmen seeking to repeal the GAG RULES.

welding Technique for joining metallic parts, usually through the application of heat. Discovered in the 1st millennium AD during attempts to manipulate IRON into useful shapes, the technique produced a strong, tough blade. Welding traditionally involved interlayering relatively soft and tough iron with high-carbon material, followed by hammer FORGING. Modern welding processes include gas welding, arc welding, and resistance welding. More recently, electron-beam welding, laser welding, and several solid-phase processes such as diffusion bonding, friction welding, and ultrasonic joining have been developed. See also BRAZING, SOLDERING.

Welensky, Roy *later* **Sir Roy** (1907–1991) Rhodesian politician. Born in Salisbury, Southern Rhodesia (now Zimbabwe), he worked on the railways as a youth, later becoming head of the Railway Workers Union. He held the heavyweight boxing title for Rhodesia 1925–27. He began his political career with election to Northern Rhodesia's legislature in 1938. A strong supporter of the Federation of RHODESIA and Nyasaland (now Malawi), he was elected to its first parliament and became prime minister in 1956. He served until the Federation broke up in 1963, when Southern Rhodesia declared independence.

Welf dynasty \'velf\ Dynasty of German nobles and rulers. They descended from Count Welf of Bavaria (early 9th century), whose daughters married LOUIS I THE PIOUS and Louis the German. The Welfs were linked to the House of ESTE in the 11th century. They supported the papal party against Emperor HENRY IV and were rivals of the HOHENSTAUFENS in central Europe and in Italy (where their name was Guelpho; see GUELPHS AND GHIBELLINES). As part of the House of HANOVER, they became rulers of Britain.

welfare *or* **social welfare** Any of a variety of governmental programs that provide assistance to those in need. Programs include PENSIONS, disability and UNEMPLOYMENT INSURANCE, family allowances, survivor benefits, and national health insurance. The earliest modern welfare laws were enacted in Germany in the 1880s (see SOCIAL INSURANCE), and by the 1920s and '30s most Western nations had adopted similar programs. Most industrialized countries require firms to insure workers for disability (see WORKERS' COMPENSATION), so that they have income if they are injured, whether temporarily or permanently. For disability from illness unrelated to occupational injury, most industrial nations pay a short-term benefit followed by a long-term pension. Many countries pay a family allowance to reduce the poverty of large families or to increase the birthrate. Survivor benefits, provided for widows below pension age left with a dependent child, vary considerably among nations and generally cease if the woman remarries. Of the wealthier nations, only the U.S. fails to provide national health insurance other than for the aged and the poor (see MEDICARE AND MEDICAID).

welfare economics Branch of economics that seeks to evaluate economic policies in terms of their effects on the community's well-being. It was first established as a well-defined branch of economic theory in the 20th century. Early writers defined welfare as the sum of the satisfactions accruing to an individual through an economic system. Believing it was possible to compare the well-being of two or more individuals, they argued that a poor man would derive more satisfaction than a rich man from an increase in income. Later writers objected that making such comparisons with any precision was impossible. A new and more limited criterion was later developed: one economic situation was deemed superior to another if at least one person had been made better off without anyone else being made worse off. See also CONSUMER'S SURPLUS, VILFREDO PARETO.

Welfare Island See ROOSEVELT ISLAND

Welfare Party See REFAH PARTY

welfare state Concept of government in which the state plays a key role in protecting and promoting the economic and social well-being of its citizens. It is based on the principles of equality of opportunity, equitable distribution of wealth, and public responsibility for those who lack the minimal provisions for a good life. The term may be applied to a variety of forms of economic and social organization. A basic feature of the welfare state is SOCIAL INSURANCE, intended to provide benefits during periods of greatest need (e.g., old age, illness, UNEMPLOYMENT). The welfare state also usually includes public provision of education, health services, and housing. Such provisions are less extensive in the U.S. than in Western Europe, where comprehensive health coverage and state-subsidized university-level education are common. In socialist countries the welfare state also covers employment and administration of consumer prices. As the concept of LAISSEZ-FAIRE declined in popularity in the 20th century, most nations instituted at least some of the measures associated with the welfare state. Britain adopted comprehensive social insurance in 1948, and in the U.S., social-legislation programs such as the NEW DEAL and the Fair Deal were based on welfare-state principles. Scandinavian countries provide state aid for the individual in almost all phases of life.

Welk, Lawrence (1903–1992) U.S. bandleader and television performer. Born in Strasburg, N.D., a German-speaking village, he played the accordion and formed two musical groups that opened for bands and orchestras in the Midwest. He moved to Los Angeles, where his television dance-band program *The Lawrence Welk Show* (1955–71) became a huge success. It continued as *Memories with Lawrence Welk* (1971–82). Known for his unpretentious warmth and his trademark phrase "Wunnerful, wunnerful," he played light, nostalgic "champagne music" and featured such smiling performers as the Lennon Sisters.

well-field system Communal land organization supposedly in effect early in the ZHOU DYNASTY (c. 1111–255 BC). It is mentioned in the writings of MENCIUS, who advocated it. In the well-field system, one unit of land was divided among eight peasant families. A shared field was surrounded by eight fields, each worked by an individual family. The field in the center was worked jointly by the families for their lord. Later reformers referred to the concept to justify their land-redistribution systems or to criticize government land practices.

well-made play *French* **pièce bien faite** Play constructed according to strict technical principles that produce neatness of plot and theatrical effectiveness. The form was developed c. 1825 by E. SCRIBE and became dominant on 19th-century European and U.S. stages. It called for complex, artificial plotting, a buildup of suspense, a climactic scene in which all problems are resolved, and a happy ending. Scribe's hundreds of successful plays were imitated all over Europe; other such playwrights included VICTORIEN SARDOU, GEORGES FEYDEAU, and ARTHUR WING PINERO, who brought the form to the level of art with *The Second Mrs. Tanqueray* (1893).

Weller, Thomas H(uckle) (born 1915) U.S. physician and virologist. Born in Ann Arbor, Mich., he studied at Harvard Medical School. For culturing poliomyelitis virus, which led to the development of polio vaccines, he shared a 1954 Nobel Prize with John Enders (1879–1985) and Frederick Robbins (born 1916). He was the first (with Franklin Neva) to culture rubella virus and to isolate chicken-pox virus from human cell cultures. He served as director of Harvard Univ.'s Center for the Prevention of Infectious Diseases 1966–81.

Welles \'welz\, Gideon (1802–1878) U.S. politician. Born in Glastonbury, Conn., he cofounded and edited the *Hartford Times* (1826–36). In 1856 he founded one of the first Republican Party newspapers in New England, the *Hartford Evening Press*. In 1861 he was appointed secretary of the navy by Pres. ABRAHAM LINCOLN, and in the Civil War he built a large Union navy from a few ships, supported development of the IRONCLADS, and helped form the strategic naval blockade. His *Diary of Gideon Welles* (published 1911), gives valuable insights into the Civil War.

Welles, (George) Orson (1915–1985) U.S. film director, actor, and producer. Born in Kenosha, Wis., he began acting on stage at 16 and made his Broadway debut in 1934. He directed an all-black cast in *Macbeth* for the Federal Theater Project. In 1937 he and JOHN HOUSEMAN formed the Mercury Theatre, creating a series of radio dramas, attempting to mount MARC BLITZSTEIN's *The Cradle Will Rock* in the face of determined opposition, and winning notoriety with their panic-producing broadcast of *War of the Worlds* (1938). Welles then moved to Hollywood, where he cowrote, directed, produced, and acted in the classic *Citizen Kane* (1941), noted for its innovative narrative technique and atmospheric cinematography and considered the most influential movie in film history. His other films include *The Magnificent Ambersons* (1942), *Journey into Fear* (1943), *The Stranger* (1946), *The Lady from Shanghai* (1948), *Othello* (1952), *The Trial* (1963), *Touch of Evil* (1958), and *Chimes at Midnight* (1966). His problems with Hollywood studios curtailed future productions, and he moved to Europe. He was also notable as an actor in *Jane Eyre* (1944), *The Third Man* (1949), and *Compulsion* (1959).

Wellesley (of Norragh), Marquess *orig.* **Richard Colley Wellesley** (1760–1842) British statesman. He inherited his father's Irish title as earl of Mornington and sat in the Irish House of Lords from 1781. He served in the British House of Commons 1784–97. As governor of Madras and governor-general of Bengal (1797–1805), he used military force and annexation to greatly enlarge the British empire in India, but was recalled by the East India Co. for his vast expenditures. In 1809 he went to Spain to make diplomatic preparations for the Peninsular War; he served as foreign secretary 1809–12. As lord lieutenant of Ireland (1821–28, 1833–34) he tried to reconcile Protestants and Catholics. Despite his own achievements, he became increasingly jealous of his younger brother, the duke of WELLINGTON.

Wellesley College Private women's college in Wellesley, Mass., chartered in 1870. Long one of the most eminent women's colleges in the U.S., it was the first to provide scientific laboratories. It grants bachelor's degrees in humanities, including Chinese, Japanese, and Russian languages; in social science, including African studies, religion, and economics; and in science and mathematics, including computer science. Among its facilities are an advanced science center and an observatory. Enrollment is about 2,300.

Wellington City (pop., 2001 prelim.: 165,945), port, and capital of New Zealand. It is located in southern NORTH ISLAND, on Port Nicholson. Founded in 1840, it became a municipality in 1853. In 1865 the capital was transferred there from AUCKLAND. It is the financial, commercial, and transportation center of New Zealand. Wellington produces transportation equipment, machinery, metal products, textiles, and printed materials. It is the site of the major government buildings and the headquarters of many cultural, scientific, and agricultural organizations.

Wellington, Duke of *orig.* **Arthur Wellesley** (1769–1852) British general. Son of the Irish earl of Mornington, he entered the army in 1787 and served in the Irish Parliament 1790–97. Sent to India in 1796, he commanded troops to victories in the Maratha War (1803). Back in England, he served in the British House of Commons and as chief secretary in Ireland 1807–9. Commanding British troops in the Peninsular War, he won battles against the French in Portugal and Spain and invaded France to win the war in 1814, for which he was promoted to field

W X Y Z

marshal and created a duke. After NAPOLEON renewed the war against the European powers, the "Iron Duke" commanded the Allied armies to victory at the Battle of WATERLOO (1815). Richly rewarded by English and foreign sovereigns, he became one of the most honored men in Europe. After commanding the army of occupation in France (1815–18) and serving in the Tory cabinet as master general of ordnance (1818–27), he served as prime minister 1828–30, but lost his office for opposing parliamentary reform. He was honored on his death by a monumental funeral and burial in St. Paul's Cathedral alongside HORATIO NELSON.

Wellman, William (Augustus) (1896–1975) U.S. film director. Born in Brookline, Mass., he was a flying ace in World War I and later a barnstorming stunt pilot. He acted in *Knickerbocker Buckeroo* (1919) with DOUGLAS FAIRBANKS, then turned to directing. Known as "Wild Bill," he made the aerial dogfight classic *Wings* (1929, Academy Award), setting standards for documentary realism, and launched a gangster movie trend with *Public Enemy* (1931), starring JAMES CAGNEY. His other films include *A Star Is Born* (1937), *Nothing Sacred* (1937), *Beau Geste* (1939), *The Ox-Bow Incident* (1942), *The Story of GI Joe* (1945), and *The High and the Mighty* (1954).

Wells, H(erbert) G(eorge) (1866–1946) English novelist, journalist, sociologist, and historian. While studying science under T.H. HUXLEY in London, Wells formulated a romantic conception of the subject that would inspire the inventive and influential science-fiction and fantasy novels for which he is best known, including the epochal *The Time Machine* (1895), *The Invisible Man* (1897), and *The War of the Worlds* (1898). He simultaneously took on a public role as an agitator for progressive causes, including the League of Nations. He later abandoned science fiction and drew on memories of his lower-middle-class early life in works including the novel *Tono-Bungay* (1908) and the comic *The History of Mr. Polly* (1910). World War I shook his faith in human progress, prompting him to promote popular education through nonfiction works including *The Outline of History* (1920). *The Shape of Things to Come* (1933) was an antifascist warning. Though a sense of humor reappears in *Experiment in Autobiography* (1934), most of his late works reveal a pessimistic, even bitter outlook.

Wells, Ida B(ell) *or* **Ida Bell Wells-Barnett** (1862–1931) U.S. advocate for blacks' and women's rights. Born to slaves in Holly Springs, Miss., she was a teacher until she turned to journalism in the late 1880s, writing articles for black-owned newspapers on such issues as the education of black children. In 1892, after she denounced the lynching of three of her friends, her newspaper office was destroyed by whites. She lectured and founded anti-lynching societies and black women's clubs throughout the U.S. In 1895 she married Ferdinand Barnett and began writing for his newspaper, the *Chicago Conservator.* In 1910 she cofounded the Chicago Negro Fellowship League. She also founded Chicago's Alpha Suffrage Club, perhaps the first black women's-suffrage group.

Wells, Kitty *orig.* **Muriel Ellen Deason** (born 1919) U.S. COUNTRY-MUSIC singer and songwriter. Born in Nashville, Deason sang gospel in church as a child. In the 1930s she made her radio debut, taking her name from a CARTER FAMILY song. She married Johnny Wright in 1937, and they have performed together off and on ever since. Her first major hit was the classic "It Wasn't God Who Made Honky Tonk Angels" (1952). Her extensive repertory made her the top-ranking female country artist for some 15 years, paving the way for such later stars as P. CLINE and LORETTA LYNN.

Wells Fargo & Co. U.S. company formerly involved in both express transport and banking. Founded in 1852, Wells, Fargo transported gold between the west and east coasts in the wake of the California GOLD RUSH. By 1866 it had gained control of almost all stagecoach business in the West. In 1905 its banking operations were separated from its express operations. The express carrier disappeared by the mid-1920s, its domestic business taken over by the firm later known as the RAILWAY EXPRESS AGENCY and its foreign express business by AMERICAN EXPRESS CO. Its security services still exist under the name Wells Fargo Armored Service Corp., a subsidiary of Baker Industries. The Wells Fargo Bank's holding company, Wells Fargo & Co., was established in 1968. Headquartered in San Francisco, the bank has subsidiaries and affiliates worldwide. In 1998 Wells Fargo & Co. merged with Norwest Corp.

Welsh corgi \'kȯr-gē\ Either of two cattle dog breeds. The Cardigan Welsh corgi was developed from Celtish relatives of the DACHSHUND that were brought to Wales c. 1200 BC. The Pembroke Welsh corgi is descended from sled-dog stock brought to Wales about 1100 by Flemish weavers. Both have short legs, a foxlike head, and erect ears; both stand 10–12 in. (25–30 cm) and weigh 25–38 lbs (11–17 kg). The Cardigan has a long tail and rounded ears; the Pembroke has a short tail and pointed ears. The Cardigan's coarser coat can be solid-colored, tricolored, or mottled; the Pembroke is solid- or bicolored.

Welsh language CELTIC LANGUAGE of Wales. Besieged for centuries by English, Welsh continues to be spoken by 18–20% of the population of Wales, or more than half a million people, though estimates of the actual number of first-language speakers vary widely. Welsh is traditionally divided into three periods: Old Welsh (c. 800–1150), attested mainly in glosses and short textual passages; Middle Welsh (c. 1150–1500), with a rich medieval literature including poetic texts originally composed much earlier; and Modern Welsh (from c. 1500). Modern literary Welsh was largely fixed by WILLIAM SALESBURY's Bible translation. Vernacular Welsh, split along dialectal lines, has long been diverging from literary Welsh; many modern speakers cannot write or easily understand the traditional written language. The issue of an acceptable modern standard remains unresolved.

Welsh literary renaissance Literary activity in Wales and England in the mid-18th century that attempted to stimulate interest in the Welsh language and in the classical bardic verse forms of Wales. It was centered on the Morris family of Welsh scholars, who preserved ancient texts and encouraged contemporary poets to use the strict meters of the ancient Welsh BARDS. The movement gave rise to many publications and helped reestablish local EISTEDDFODS and, in the early 19th century, the National Eisteddfod. A second revival, centered in the newly established University of Wales, occurred at the end of the 19th century.

Welty, Eudora (1909–2001) U.S. short-story writer and novelist. A native of Jackson, Miss., Welty focused her work on a small town that resembled her birthplace and the Delta country. Her main subject is the intricacies of human relationships. She first gained attention for the story collection *A Curtain of Green* (1941), containing the widely admired "Petrified Man" and "Why I Live at the P.O." Other stories appear in *The Wide Net* (1943), *The Golden Apples* (1949), and *The Bride of the Innisfallen* (1955). Her novels include *Delta Wedding* (1946), *The Ponder Heart* (1954), *Losing Battles* (1970), and *The Optimist's Daughter* (1972, Pulitzer Prize). She also published books of her photographs, including those she took while working for the government during the Depression.

Wenceslas (1361–1419) King of BOHEMIA (as Wenceslas IV, 1363–96) and German king and Holy Roman Emperor (1378–1400). The son of the emperor CHARLES IV, he was a weak ruler whose reign was plagued by wars and princely rivalries. He spent most of his time in Prague to the detriment of Germany, which suffered a decade of anarchy until peace was established by the diet at Eger (1389). He was deposed by rebellious princes in 1400.

Wenceslas I \'wen-sə-ˌslȯs\ (1205–1253) King of BOHEMIA (1230–53). He prevented Mongol armies from attacking Bohemia in 1241, but could not defend Moravia. He gained control of Austria and forced the Austrian estates to accept his son Premysl Otakar II as their duke in 1251. Bohemia prospered under his reign, and an influx of German colonists and craftsmen enriched the country.

Wenceslas II (1271–1305) King of BOHEMIA (1278–1305). He inherited the throne from his father at age 7, but his cousin Otto IV of Brandenburg served as his regent until 1283. Wenceslas gained full control of the country only after suppressing a dissident faction and executing his ambitious stepfather in 1290. A capable ruler who extended the boundaries of his kingdom, he annexed most of Upper Silesia and occupied Kraków (1291). He became king of Poland in 1300 but declined to become king of Hungary in 1301, instead placing his son Wenceslas on the Hungarian throne (1301–4).

Wenders \'ven-dərs\, **Wim** (born 1945) German film director. He directed short films from 1967 and made features from 1973, including *Alice in the Cities* (1974) and *Kings of the Road* (1976). He won acclaim in the U.S. for *Paris, Texas* (1984) and *Wings of Desire* (1987). Noted for his themes of alienation and anxiety, he later directed *Far Away, So Close* (1993), *Lisbon Story* (1994), *The End of Violence* (1997), and the documentary *Buena Vista Social Club* (1999).

Wendi *or* **Wen-ti** \'wən-'dē\ Chinese god of literature. His chief heavenly task is to keep a register of men of letters so that he can mete out rewards and punishments to each according to merit. He had 17 reincarnations, during the ninth of which he appeared on earth as Zhang Ya. His writing earned him canonization during the TANG DYNASTY.

Wendi *or* **Wen-ti** \'wən-'dē\ *orig.* **Liu Heng** (died 157 BC) Fourth emperor of the Chinese HAN DYNASTY. His long reign (180/179–157 BC) was one of good government and peaceful consolidation of power. Under his rule, China's economy prospered and its population expanded. To later ages Wendi epitomized the virtues of frugality and benevolence in a Chinese ruler.

Wendi *or* **Wen-ti** *orig.* **Yang Jian** (541–604) Founder of the Chinese SUI DYNASTY, which reunified China after centuries of instability. He was born into a powerful family in northern China, an area controlled by the non-Chinese Northern Zhou dynasty (557–81). When the Zhou emperor died unexpectedly, Wendi seized the throne, overcame his rivals, and in 581 proclaimed the Sui dynasty. Intending to build a strong, centralized state, he designed a huge new capital at CHANGAN and attacked entrenched local interests. Families with hereditary local power were replaced with officials selected by examination, who were forbidden to serve in the areas from which they came and were rotated frequently. Wendi conquered the dynasties of southern China and breaking the power of the Turkish empires in Turkistan and Mongolia. He put the EQUAL-FIELD SYSTEM into practice and produced a new legal code. His government brought in tax revenues and maintained price-regulating granaries. In old age he became deeply involved with BUDDHISM, building shrines and dedicating relics. See also YANG DI.

Wends Group of Slavic tribes that by the 5th century AD had settled in the area between the ODER and ELBE rivers in what is now eastern Germany. They occupied the eastern borders of the domain of the Franks and other Germanic peoples. From the 6th century the Franks warred sporadically against the Wends; under CHARLEMAGNE in the early 9th century they began a campaign to subjugate the Wends and forcibly convert them to Christianity. German annexation of Wendish territories began in 929, but collapsed during a Wendish rebellion in 983. A German crusade against the Wends in 1147, authorized by the church and led by Henry the Lion, inflicted great loss of life. The Wends thereafter offered little opposition to German colonization of the Elbe-Oder region; themselves enserfed, they were gradually assimilated by the Germans, except for a minority in the traditional region of Lusatia (in eastern Germany) now known as Sorbs.

Wentworth, Thomas *later* **Earl of Strafford** (1593–1641) English politician and leading adviser to CHARLES I. Though an outspoken member of the opposition, he switched his support to the crown when offered a barony in 1628. As lord president of the north (1628–33), he quelled defiance to the crown. As lord deputy of Ireland (1633–39), he consolidated the royal authority, extended English settlement, reformed the administration, and increased revenues for the crown. He was recalled to command Charles's army against a Scottish revolt, but the costly war was opposed by the LONG PARLIAMENT; as a target representing the king's authority, he was impeached and executed.

Wenwang *or* **Wen-wang** \'wən-'wäŋ\ (c. 12th century BC) King Wen, father of WUWANG, the founder of the ZHOU DYNASTY, and one of the sage rulers regarded by Confucian historians as a model king. He is traditionally credited as author, with ZHOUGONG, of the hexagrams of the *YI JING (I CHING)*, which he is supposed to have written during his imprisonment by the last ruler of the SHANG DYNASTY. See also CONFUCIANISM, FIVE CLASSICS.

werewolf In European folklore, a man who changes into a wolf at night and devours animals, people, or corpses, returning to human form by day. Some werewolves are thought to change shape at will; others, who inherited the condition or acquired it by being bitten by a werewolf, are transformed involuntarily under the influence of a full moon. Belief in werewolves is found throughout the world and was especially common in 16th-century France. Humans who believe they are wolves suffer from a mental disorder called lycanthropy.

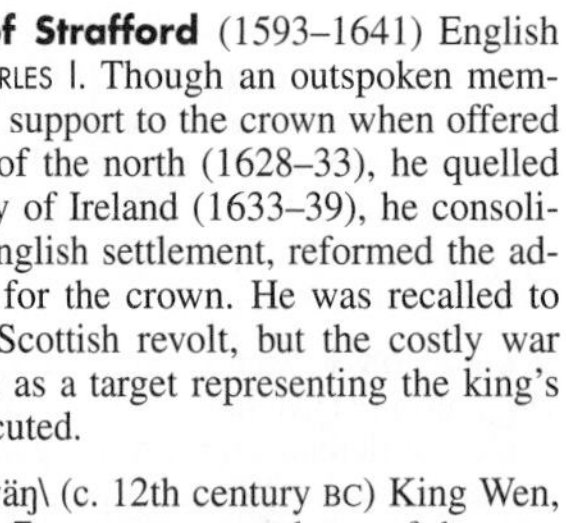

Lon Chaney, Jr., as a werewolf in *The Wolf Man* (1941).

BY COURTESY OF UNIVERSAL PICTURES; PHOTOGRAPH, LINCOLN CENTER LIBRARY OF THE PERFORMING ARTS, NEW YORK PUBLIC LIBRARY

Werner \'ver-nər\, **Abraham Gottlob** (1750–1817) German geologist. In opposition to the Plutonists, or Vulcanists, who argued that granite and many other rocks were of igneous origin, he founded the Neptunist school, which proclaimed that all rocks resulted from precipitation from oceans that had, he theorized, once completely covered the earth. He rejected UNIFORMITARIANISM. His brilliant lecturing and personal charm won him many students, who, though many eventually discarded his theories, would not renounce them while Werner lived.

Wertheimer \'vert-,hī-mər\, **Max** (1880–1943) German psychologist. He taught at the Univs. of Frankfurt and Berlin (1916–29) before emigrating to the U.S. to teach at the New School for Social Research (1933–43). With WOLFGANG KOHLER and Kurt Koffka (1886–1941), he was instrumental in establishing Gestalt psychology. Much of his work dealt with perception, though he also explored thinking and problem solving. His *Productive Thinking* was published posthumously in 1945.

Wertmüller \'vert-,mü-lər\, **Lina** *orig.* **Arcangela Wertmuller von Elgg** (born 1928) Italian film director. After working as a puppeteer and stage actress and director, she became an assistant to FEDERICO FELLINI and began writing and directing her own films in 1963. She achieved international fame with *The Seduction of Mimi* (1972), a satire on sexual hypocrisy, and *Love and Anarchy* (1972). Her most controversial works were the witty *Swept Away* (1974) and the morally ambiguous *Seven Beauties* (1976), about a man scrabbling to survive in a Nazi concentration camp. Her later movies, including *Ciao Professore* (1994), were less successful.

Weser River \'vā-zər\ River, western Germany. Formed by the union of the FULDA and Werra rivers at Münden, it flows northward into the NORTH SEA through a large estuary. It is 273 mi (440 km) long. There are several hydroelectric dams on the Weser, and it is linked with numerous canals.

Wesley, John (1703–1791) Anglican clergyman, evangelist, and cofounder of METHODISM. The 15th child of a former Nonconformist minister, he graduated from Oxford University and became a priest in the Church of England in 1728. From 1729 he participated in a religious study group in Oxford organized by his brother Charles (1707–1788), its members being dubbed the "Methodists" for their emphasis on methodical study and devotion. Its numbers grew, and it began to undertake social and charitable activities. After a largely unsuccessful mission to the North American colony of Georgia (1735–37), they returned to London, where they came under the influence of the MORAVIAN CHURCH. In 1738, inspired by the theology of MARTIN LUTHER, both men had a religious experience that convinced them that salvation was possible through faith alone. Zealous evangelists, they had great success in preaching to the masses in the succeeding decades. In 1784 John began ordaining ministers himself when the bishop of London refused to do so (despite Charles's disapproval) and declared his independence from the Church of England. The two wrote several thousand hymns, including "Hark, the Herald Angels Sing" and "Christ the Lord Is Ris'n Today."

Wesleyan University Private university in Middletown, Conn. It was founded in 1831 by Methodists, but has been dedicated from its inception to nonsectarian education. It offers 50 major fields of undergraduate and graduate study, including 11 master's degree programs and doctoral programs in music and sciences. Campus facilities include centers for African-American and East Asian studies, an astronomical observatory, and the Center for Humanities and Arts. Enrollment is about 3,300.

Wessex Ancient Anglo-Saxon kingdom, southern Britain. Its area approximated that of the modern counties of HAMPSHIRE, DORSET, WILTSHIRE, SOMERSET, BERKSHIRE, and AVON; its capital was WINCHESTER. The kingdom is traditionally thought to have been founded by Saxon invaders of Britain c. 494. It conquered Kent and Sussex and, in the 9th century, under King ALFRED the Great, kept the Danes from conquering England south of the DANELAW. By 927 it had reconquered the Danelaw, and Alfred's grandson, Athelstan, became the king of all England; thereafter all kings of Wessex were kings of England. The region figures prominently in legends of King Arthur (see ARTHURIAN LEGEND), and the designation "Wessex" was used by THOMAS HARDY to represent the region of southwestern England in which he set his works of fiction.

West, Benjamin (1738–1820) U.S.-British painter. After studying painting in his native Philadelphia, he established himself as a portraitist in New York. He sailed to Italy in 1760 and visited most of its art centers before settling in London in 1763. The patronage of GEORGE III freed him of the need to paint portraits for a living, and he became known for historical, religious, and mythological subjects. His *Death of General Wolfe* (1771) aroused controversy for its depiction of modern dress rather than the flowing robes expected in a history painting, but was one of his most popular works. He never returned to the U.S., but through such pupils or followers as WASHINGTON ALLSTON, GILBERT STUART, CHARLES WILLSON PEALE, and JOHN SINGLETON COPLEY he exerted considerable influence on the development of U.S. art in the 19th century.

West, Jerry *orig.* **Jerome Alan** (born 1938) U.S. basketball player, coach, and manager. Born in Cheylan, W.V., he became a two-time All American at the University of West Virginia. As a guard for the Los Angeles Lakers (1960–74), he compiled a career scoring average of 27 points (fourth in all-time standings); his jump shot was particularly well known. As the Lakers' head coach (1976–79), he led them to 145 wins and 101 losses. He later became the team's general manager and executive vice president.

West, Mae (1892–1980) U.S. film actress. Born in Brooklyn, N.Y., she was appearing on the national vaudeville circuit by 1907 and made her Broadway debut as a singer and dancer in 1911. In 1926 she began to write, produce, and star in her own Broadway plays, including the sensation-creating *Sex* (1926), *Diamond Lil* (1928), and *The Constant Sinner* (1931), productions that mired her in legal battles. Her frank sensuality, regal postures, and suggestive wisecracks became her trademarks in such popular movies as *She Done Him Wrong* (1933), *Belle of the Nineties* (1934), *I'm No Angel* (1933), and *My Little Chickadee* (1940). In World War II Allied soldiers called their inflatable life jackets "Mae Wests" in honor of her hourglass figure.

West, Nathanael *orig.* **Nathan Weinstein** (1903–1940) U.S. writer. Born in New York City, he attended Brown University and was supporting himself as a hotel manager, giving free or low-rent rooms to struggling fellow writers, when he wrote the novella *Miss Lonelyhearts* (1933), about an advice columnist whose attempts to solace his correspondents end in ironic defeat. *A Cool Million* (1934) mocks the American success dream popularized by HORATIO ALGER. His last novel, *The Day of the Locust* (1939), depicts the savagery lurking beneath the Hollywood dream. Though not widely read until after his death in an auto accident at 37, West is now considered a major American novelist.

West, Rebecca *later* **Dame Rebecca** *orig.* **Cicily Isabel Fairfield** (1892–1983) British journalist, novelist, and critic. Trained as an actress, from 1911 West contributed to the left-wing press and made a name as a fighter for woman suffrage. She had a 10-year love affair with H.G. WELLS (1913–23). Her novels, including *The Judge* (1922), *The Thinking Reed* (1936), and *The Birds Fall Down* (1966), attracted less attention than her social and cultural writings. Her admired reports on the NUREMBERG TRIALS were collected in *A Train of Powder* (1955). Her history of Yugoslavia, *Black Lamb and Grey Falcon* (1942), is regarded as one of the century's finest nonfiction works. Later books include *The Meaning of Treason* (1949) and *The New Meaning of Treason* (1964).

West Atlantic languages See ATLANTIC LANGUAGES

West Bank Area (pop., 2000 est.: 2,184,000), Palestine, west of the JORDAN RIVER. Covering an area of about 2,270 sq mi (5,900 sq km), the territory, excluding East Jerusalem, is also known within Israel by its biblical names, Judaea and Samaria. Settlements include Nabulus, HEBRON, BETHLEHEM, and JERICHO. Under a 1947 U.N. agreement it was to become Palestinian when the State of Israel was formed. Arabs denounced the partition plan and attacked Israel (see ARAB-ISRAELI WARS). Following a truce, Jordan annexed it in 1950 and governed it until Israel occupied it during the SIX-DAY WAR of 1967. During the 1970s and '80s, Israel established settlements there, provoking Arab resentment. Arab uprisings began in 1987 in the GAZA STRIP and spread to the West Bank (see INTIFADA). Jordan relinquished its claims in 1988, ceding them to the PALESTINE LIBERATION ORGANIZATION (PLO). Secret meetings between the PLO and Israel in 1993 led to an end of violence and an agreement granting Palestinian self-rule in parts of the West Bank and Gaza Strip. Further negotiations to resolve outstanding issues proceeded intermittently in the 1990s but broke down amid renewed violence in late 2000.

West Bengal State (pop., 2001 prelim.: 80,221,171), northeastern India. Its capital is KOLKATA (Calcutta). It encompasses two broad natural regions, the Gangetic Plain in the south and the HIMALAYAS in the north, and covers an area of 34,267 square miles (88,752 square km). From the 3rd century BC, it formed part of ASHOKA's empire. In the 4th century AD, it was absorbed into the Gupta empire. From the 13th century it was under Muslim rule, until it came under the British in 1757. At Indian independence in 1947, it was partitioned, with the eastern sector becoming East Pakistan (later Bangladesh) and the western sector, India's West Bengal. The state is important for its mineral output, but agriculture is its main economic activity. It is noted for its artistic endeavors, including filmmaking.

West Indies Islands, enclosing the Caribbean Sea. Lying between southeastern North America and northern South America, they may be divided into the following groups: the Greater ANTILLES, including CUBA, JAMAICA, HISPANIOLA (HAITI and the DOMINICAN REPUBLIC), and PUERTO RICO; the Lesser Antilles, including the VIRGIN ISLANDS, WINDWARD ISLANDS, LEEWARD ISLANDS, BARBADOS, and the islands in the southern Caribbean Sea north of Venezuela (generally considered to include TRINIDAD AND TOBAGO); and the BAHAMAS. Although physiographically not a part of the West Indies, BERMUDA is often included.

West Irian See IRIAN JAYA

West Midlands Metropolitan county (pop., 1999 est.: 2,626,500), western central England. Its main center is BIRMINGHAM. Its administrative functions have been dispersed, and it has existed in name only since 1986. Early settlement was sparse until SAXON colonists arrived; COVENTRY was the region's only significant town by the late 14th century. Small metalworking industries began in Birmingham in the 16th century, and by the 18th century the area's coalfields were important for ironworking. Many of the West Midlands' traditional metallurgical and manufacturing industries have persisted into the 20th century, alongside the growth of electrical engineering and the manufacture of motor vehicles, aircraft, and synthetic fibers.

West Nile virus Virus belonging to the family Flaviviridae that can cause encephalitis (inflammation of the brain). West Nile is predominantly a fatal infection of birds but can be transmitted to humans by mosquitoes. Most human infections are inapparent or mild, causing a flu-like illness that lasts only a few days. A minority develop encephalitis, characterized by headache, fever, neck stiffness, and muscle weakness, that has proved fatal in some cases. The virus was originally confined to Africa, the Middle East, and Southeast Asia but has spread to Europe and North America. There is no treatment, and, in severe cases, intensive medical care is necessary.

West Papua See IRIAN JAYA

West Point See UNITED STATES MILITARY ACADEMY

West River See XI RIVER

West Schelde See WESTERSCHELDE

West Sussex County (pop., 1999 est.: 760,700), southeastern England. It borders the ENGLISH CHANNEL; its county seat is CHICHESTER. There is evidence of settlements dating from prehistoric times in the region. A dynasty of British chieftains was in the area just before the Roman invasion. After the Romans left, Saxon invaders conquered Sussex in the late 5th century. They were overcome by the peoples of neighboring WESSEX, and later by the Normans, who built castles and monasteries. Since the beginning of the 14th century, the growth of seaside resorts has been important in the development of the area's coast; inland, much of it remains rural.

West Virginia State (pop., 2000 prelim.: 1,808,344), eastern central U.S. It covers an area of 24,232 sq mi (62,760 sq km); its capital is CHARLESTON. The OHIO RIVER forms a large section of the upper western boundary, while the POTOMAC forms a section of the northern boundary. The Great KANAWHA, Little Kanawha, MONONGAHELA, and Shenandoah rivers cross the state. It contains the APPALACHIAN MTN. system, and is generally rugged land. The highest elevation is Spruce Knob (4,861 ft, or 1,482 m). Long occupied by Indian hunters, it was home to the ADENA, or Mound Builders, who left archaeological traces. They were succeeded by the IROQUOIS and the CHEROKEE. The first permanent white settlement was in the 1730s. The English controlled the region during the 1750s and 1760s. Though eastern Virginia was rapidly settled, the area's western rugged terrain restricted settlement there. After the AMERICAN REVOLU-

TION, largely nonslaving settlers moved west; they grew dissatisfied with the Virginia government. With the outbreak of the AMERICAN CIVIL WAR, residents from western Virginia voted against the ordinance of secession in 1861. In 1863 it was admitted to the Union as the 35th state. Its industrial emergence, encouraged by railroad expansion, began in the 1870s when its natural resources, including coal and gas, contributed to the growth of the U.S. In the 20th century, recreation and tourism became economically important.

West Virginia University One of two state universities of West Virginia (the other being Marshall Univ.). A land-grant university founded in 1867, it is located on two campuses in Morgantown. It has about 175 degree programs, including over 30 doctoral programs, and awards professional degrees in dentistry, law, medicine, and pharmacy. It also operates experimental farms and a geology camp. Enrollment is about 23,000.

West Yorkshire Metropolitan county (pop., 1995 est.: 2, 106,000), northern England. Its main center is WAKEFIELD. Its administrative functions have been dispersed, and it has existed in name only since 1986. Anglo-Saxons and Scandinavians from the east established the first settlements. While baronial power was strong in the medieval period, anarchic conditions often prevailed, and the area was the site of several 15th century battles. In the same period, the wool textile industry developed. In the 18th and 19th century abundant waterpower, and later steam power based on locally mined coal, stimulated factory-based industry. Worsted and woolen industries remain important, while an engineering industry has developed.

western Genre of novels and short stories, motion pictures, and television and radio shows set in the American West, usually during 1850–1900, when the area was opened to white settlers. Though basically a U.S. creation, it has counterparts in the GAUCHO LITERATURE of Argentina and in tales of the settlement of the Australian outback. Conflicts between white pioneers and Indians and between cattle ranchers and fence-building farmers form two basic themes. Cowboys, the town sheriff, and the U.S. marshal are staple figures, and lawlessness and gun violence are standard. OWEN WISTER'S *The Virginian* (1902) is regarded as the seminal western novel; the genre's great popularity was in the early and middle decades of the 20th century and declined somewhat thereafter.

Western Australia State (pop., 1996: 1,726,000), western Australia. Covering an area of 975,100 sq mi (2,525,500 sq km), it constitutes one-third of the continent, but has less than one-tenth of Australia's population; its capital is PERTH. The extensive interior region has three deserts: GREAT SANDY, GIBSON, and GREAT VICTORIA. The coast along the Timor Sea and Indian Ocean has only a few good harbors; notable inlets are JOSEPH BONAPARTE and EXMOUTH gulfs. AUSTRALIAN ABORIGINES have occupied Western Australia for about 40,000 years. The western coast was first visited in 1616 by the Dutch; it was later explored by Englishman William Dampier in 1688 and 1699. In 1829 Capt. James Stirling led the first group of settlers there to establish Australia's first nonconvict colony. The discovery of gold in 1886 prompted a movement for constitutional autonomy, which was granted in 1890. In 1900 it was the last state to ratify the newly constituted Commonwealth of Australia. Initially it suffered from slow growth, but in recent decades its economy, fueled by agriculture and mining, has been expanding.

Western Electric Co. Inc. Former U.S. telecommunications company. Founded in 1869 by Elisha Gray and Enos N. Barton, the firm was incorporated in Chicago in 1872 as the Western Electric Manufacturing Co. It manufactured a series of new products, including the world's first commercial typewriters and incandescent lamps. Bell Telephone bought a controlling interest in the company in 1881; the next year it was reincorporated as Western Electric Co., becoming part of the Bell system (see AT&T CORP.). It became a major manufacturer of telephone equipment and communications satellites, in addition to producing radar and missile systems. In 1983, with the breakup of AT&T, the company was dissolved as a separate subsidiary. Its factories were taken over by AT&T Technologies, and its brand name continued to be used.

Western European Union (WEU) Association of 10 nations in Europe to coordinate matters of European security and defense. The WEU was formed in 1955, as an outgrowth of the BRUSSELS TREATY of 1948. Composed of Belgium, France, Germany, Greece, Italy, Luxembourg, the Netherlands, Portugal, Spain, and Britain, it works in cooperation with NATO and is administered by a council of the foreign affairs and defense ministers of the member nations. Headquartered in London, it meets at least twice yearly to discuss problems of mutual concern.

Western Hemisphere Part of the earth comprising North and South America and surrounding waters. Longitudes 20° W and 160° E are often considered its boundaries.

Western Indian bronze Style of metal sculpture that flourished in India from the 6th to the 12th century and later, mainly in the area of modern Gujarat and Rajasthan states. Most of the bronzes are associated with JAINISM; they include representations of savior figures and ritual objects such as incense burners and lamp bearers. Most are small, as they were intended for private worship. They were made by LOST-WAX CASTING, and the eyes and ornaments are frequently inlaid with silver and gold.

Rsabhanatha, Western Indian bronze from Chahardi, western Khandesh, Maharashtra state, 9th century AD; in a private collection.
P. CHANDRA

Western Isles See HEBRIDES ISLANDS

Western Ontario, University of Public university in London, Ontario, founded in 1878. It has faculties of applied health sciences, arts, business administration, dentistry, education, engineering, graduate studies, journalism, law, library science, medicine, music, nursing, science, and social science as well as a graduate school of journalism. Total enrollment is about 24,000.

Western Reserve Tract of land, northeastern Ohio. Located on the southern shore of Lake ERIE, it formed part of the western lands of Connecticut not surrendered to Congress in 1786. It covered about 3,500,000 acres (1,417,500 hectares), and was sold in part to immigrants from Connecticut 1786–1800. Ceded in 1800 to Ohio, it was later divided into several counties.

Western Sahara *formerly* **Spanish Sahara** Territory, North Africa. Area: 102,703 sq mi (266,000 sq km). Population (1993 est.): 213,000. Capital: EL AAIÚN. Little is known of the area's prehistory, though rock engravings in southern locations suggest a succession of nomadic groups. In the 4th century BC there was trade between it and Europe across the Mediterranean; this did not last, and later there was little European contact until the 19th century. In 1884 Spain claimed a protectorate over the RÍO DE ORO region. Boundary agreements with France were concluded in 1900 and 1912. Spain formally united the area's northern and southern parts into the overseas province of the Spanish Sahara in 1958. In 1976 Spain relinquished its claim and the region was divided between Mauritania, which gave up its claim in 1979, and Morocco, which later occupied the whole territory. Separatists based in Algeria declared a government-in-exile called the Saharan Arab Democratic Republic in 1976; the issue of Western Sahara's status was still unresolved in 2001. Western Sahara has vast phosphate deposits, and some potash and iron ore deposits.

Western Samoa See SAMOA

Western Schism See Western SCHISM

Western Union Corp. Former U.S. telecommunications company. It was founded in 1851 to build a telegraph line from Buffalo, N.Y., to St. Louis. In 1856 the expanding business was reorganized as the Western Union Telegraph Co. By the end of 1861 Western Union had built the first transcontinental TELEGRAPH line. It continued to grow and to absorb competitors, including Postal Telegraph Inc. in 1943. As telegraphy was superseded by other methods of telecommunication, Western Union diversified into teletypewriter services, money orders, and mailgrams. In 1988 the company was reorganized as Western Union Corp. to handle money transfers and related services. After declaring bankruptcy in 1993, it sold its financial-services arm to First Financial Management Corp., which merged with First Data in 1995.

Western Wall *or* **Wailing Wall** Place of prayer in JERUSALEM sacred to the Jewish people. It is the only remnant of the Second Temple of JERUSALEM. Because it now forms part of a larger wall surrounding the Muslim DOME OF THE ROCK and al-Aqsa Mosque, Jews and Arabs have long fought over its control. When Israel captured the Old City in the fighting of 1967, the Jews once more gained control of the site.

Westernizers See SLAVOPHILES AND WESTERNIZERS

Westerschelde \'ves-tər-ˌsk̲el-də\ *or* **West Schelde** Estuary, southwestern Netherlands. An inlet of the North Sea at the mouth of the SCHELDE RIVER, it flows west for about 30 mi (50 km) through the Delta Islands to the North Sea. It has been an important transportation route since the 16th century, when Holy Roman emperor CHARLES V designated VLISSINGEN as his port of embarkation from the Netherlands. It continues to operate as an important shipping route to many destinations, including ANTWERP.

Westinghouse, George (1846–1914) U.S. inventor and industrialist. Born in Central Bridge, N.Y., he served in the American Civil War. His first major invention was an air brake (patented 1869), which was eventually made compulsory on all American trains. He developed a railway signaling system, and later introduced many innovations in piping natural gas. His major achievement was the adoption by the U.S. of alternating current for electric power transmission. The electrical system being developed in the U.S. in the 1880s used direct current (DC), though alternating-current (AC) systems were being developed in Europe. Westinghouse purchased the patents for NIKOLA TESLA's AC motor and hired Tesla to improve and modify the motor for use in his power system. In 1886 he incorporated the predecessor of WESTINGHOUSE ELECTRIC CORP. He eventually prevailed over powerful opposition from advocates of DC power, and in 1893 his company was hired to light the World's Columbian Exposition at Chicago. He also obtained the rights to develop the great falls of the Niagara River with AC generators. See also ELECTRIC CURRENT.

Westinghouse.

BY COURTESY OF WESTINGHOUSE ELECTRIC CORPORATION

Westinghouse Electric Corp. U.S. television and radio broadcasting company, formerly an electrical-equipment manufacturer. It was founded in 1886 as the Westinghouse Electric Co. by GEORGE WESTINGHOUSE to make and sell alternating-current electrical systems. The company became a major supplier to the electric-utility industry, producing machinery used to generate and distribute electricity. It adopted the name Westinghouse Electric Corp. in 1945. After World War II Westinghouse also manufactured nuclear reactors and defense electronics. In the 1990s it bought television and radio stations throughout the U.S., and in 1995 it acquired the television network CBS Inc. It sold its defense-electronics unit in 1996, changed its name to CBS Corp. in 1997, and announced the sale of its nuclear operations in 1998.

Westminster, Statute of (1931) Parliamentary statute that effected the equality of Britain and the then-dominions of Canada, Australia, New Zealand, South Africa, Ireland, and Newfoundland. It confirmed declarations made at British imperial conferences in 1926 and 1930 that the self-governing dominions were to be regarded as "autonomous communities within the BRITISH EMPIRE." United in their allegiance to the crown, the nations individually controlled their own domestic and foreign affairs as equal members of the British COMMONWEALTH of Nations.

Westminster Abbey Church in London. It was originally a Benedictine monastery. EDWARD THE CONFESSOR built a Norman-style church (consecrated 1065) on the site of an older church there; this was pulled down in 1245 by Henry III (except for the nave) and replaced with the present Gothic-style abbey church. The rebuilding of the nave was begun by 1376 and continued intermittently until Tudor times. The chapel of Henry VII (begun c. 1503) is noted for its exquisite fan vaulting. ELIZABETH I refounded the church as the Collegiate Church of St. Peter in Westminster (1560). The western towers (1745), by Nicholas Hawksmoor and John James, were the last addition. Every British sovereign since William the Conqueror has been crowned in the abbey except Edward V and Edward VIII. Many are also buried there, and it is crowded with the tombs and memorials to other famous Britons. Part of the southern transept is known as the Poets' Corner, while the northern transept has memorials to statesmen.

Westminster Confession Confession of faith of English-speaking Presbyterians, representing a theological consensus of international CALVINISM. Produced by the Westminster Assembly, it was completed in 1646 and approved by Parliament in 1648. When the monarchy was restored in 1660, the episcopal form of church government was reinstated and the Confession lost official status in England, but it had already been adopted by the Church of Scotland (1647) and various other churches. Consisting of 33 chapters, it states that the sole doctrinal authority is scripture, restates the doctrines of the Holy TRINITY and JESUS, and gives reformed views of the SACRAMENTS, the ministry, and GRACE. See also PRESBYTERIANISM.

Weston, Edward (1886–1958) U.S. photographer. Born in Highland Park, Ill., he was a camera enthusiast from boyhood. In his early work he imitated Impressionist paintings by suppressing detail and manipulating the image in the darkroom, but in 1915 an exhibition of modern art inspired him to emphasize abstract form and sharp resolution of detail. The result was sharp and realistic pictures that convey the beauty of natural objects through skillful composition and subtleties of tone, light, and texture. He is best known for his photographs of nudes and nature taken in California.

Edward Weston at Point Lobos, Carmel Bay, Calif., 1945.

IMOGEN CUNNINGHAM

Westphalia Former province of PRUSSIA, now part of Germany. Settled by Saxons called Westphalians c. AD 700, it was created a duchy in 1180, which, for several centuries, was administered for the archbishop of COLOGNE. The Peace of WESTPHALIA (1648) was signed at MUNSTER. In 1807 NAPOLEON created for his brother, Jerome BONAPARTE, the kingdom of Westphalia; its capital was Kassel. Reorganized by the Congress of VIENNA in 1815, it became a province of Prussia in 1816, with its capital at Munster. Its cities suffered severe bombings in World War II. In 1946 it was divided among the North Rhine-Westphalia, Lower Saxony, and Hesse states of West Germany.

Westphalia, Peace of (1648) European settlements that ended the THIRTY YEARS' WAR, negotiated in the Westphalian towns of Münster and Osnabrück. The deliberations began in 1644 and ended in 1648 with two assemblies that produced the treaty between Spain and the Dutch (signed January 30) and another among Emperor FERDINAND III, the other German princes, France, and Sweden (signed October 24). Territorial changes gave Sweden control of the Baltic Sea, ensured France a firm frontier west of the Rhine River, and provided their allies with additional lands. Independence was confirmed for the United Provinces of the Netherlands and for the Swiss Confederation. The treaties also confirmed the Peace of AUGSBURG and extended the religious toleration of Lutherans to include toleration of the Reformed (Calvinist) Church. The Holy Roman Empire was forced to recognize its German princes as absolute sovereigns in their own dominions, which greatly weakened its central authority.

Wetar \'we-ˌtär\ Island, Indonesia. Lying 35 mi (56 km) north of EAST TIMOR, it is 80 mi (130 km) long, 28 mi (45 km) wide, and has an area of 1,400 sq mi (3,600 sq km). In its interior, rugged mountains covered with tropical rain forests rise to 4,632 ft (1,412 m). Subsistence farming and fishing are the main occupations of the few islanders.

Weyden \'vī-dᵊn, 'vā-dᵊn\, **Rogier van der** (1399/1400–1464) Flemish painter. He seems to have begun his painting career at the rather advanced age of 27, when he entered the studio of ROBERT CAMPIN. In early paintings, he combined Campin's bold style with the elegance and subtle visual refinements he admired in the art of Jan van Eyck. By 1435 he moved to Brussels and the next year was appointed city painter. During that period (c. 1435–40) he executed the celebrated panel of the *Descent from the Cross* for the chapel of the Archers' Guild of Louvain. His international reputation grew, his work being particularly admired in Italy. Though most of his work was religious, he produced secular paintings (now lost) and some sensitive portraits. His art affected generations of Flemish artists and introduced the Flemish style throughout Europe.

Weyerhaeuser \ˈwī-ər-ˌhau̇-zər\, **Frederick** *orig.* **Friedrich** (1834–1914) German-U.S. lumber magnate. He emigrated to the U.S. at 18 and found work in an Illinois sawmill, which he and his brother-in-law bought in 1857. He traveled constantly to buy stands of timber and acquired an interest in many logging and milling operations. In 1872 he organized the Mississippi River Boom and Logging Co., a huge confederation that handled all the logs milled on the Mississippi. In 1900 he bought 900,000 acres of timberland in the Pacific Northwest and founded the Weyerhaeuser Timber Co. (now Weyerhaeuser Co.), centered in Tacoma, Wash. During his lifetime the company bought almost two million acres of land.

Weygand \vā-ˈgä^{n}\, **Maxime** (1867–1965) French (Belgian-born) army officer. He was educated in France and taught at the French cavalry school. He served as chief of staff to Gen. Ferdinand Foch (1914–23), high commissioner in Syria (1923–24), and inspector general of the army (1931–35), and retired in 1935. In May 1940 he was recalled to take command of the French armies; unable to prevent a German victory, he advised capitulation in June. He tried to join the Allied forces in North Africa (1942) but was arrested and detained by the Germans until 1945. Arrested by the French, he was released in 1948 and later exonerated by Charles de Gaulle.

whale Any of several species of exclusively aquatic mammals found in oceans, seas, rivers, and estuaries worldwide but especially numerous in the Antarctic Ocean. Whales are commonly distinguished from the smaller porpoises and mammalian dolphins and sometimes from narwhals, but they are all cetaceans. See also baleen whale, toothed whale.

whale shark Species *(Rhincodon typus)* of gigantic but harmless shark found worldwide but mainly in the tropics. The largest of living fishes, it often grows to about 30 ft (9 m) long and may reach twice that size. It is gray or brown with a pale undersurface and is distinctively marked with small spots and narrow vertical lines of yellow or white. It has tiny teeth, and eats plankton and small fishes. A sluggish animal, it generally swims slowly near the surface and has been hit by ships.

Whales, Bay of Former inlet of the Ross Sea, Ross Ice Shelf, Antarctica. It was first seen by the British explorer James C. Ross in 1842. The bay was the continent's most southerly open harbor in summer, and the site of several important bases for Antarctic exploration. More than 10 mi (16 km) wide in 1911, it gradually narrowed as advancing ice sheets collided. It disappeared entirely in 1987, when an iceberg 99 mi (159 km) long broke off from the Ross Ice Shelf.

whaling Hunting of whales for food, oil, or both. Whaling dates to prehistoric times, when Arctic peoples used stone tools to hunt whales. They used the entire animal, a feat not accomplished by Western commercial whalers until the advent of floating factories in the 20th century. The Basque were the first Europeans to hunt whales commercially; when seaworthy oceangoing vessels began to be made, they took to the open seas (14th–16th cent). They were followed by the Dutch and the Germans in the 17th century and the British and their colonists in the 18th century. In 1712 the first sperm whale was killed; its oil proved more valuable than that of the right whale, which had hitherto been the object of whaling ventures. Whaling expeditions in pursuit of the free-ranging sperm whale could last for four years. The discovery of petroleum (1859), overfishing, vegetable oil, and steel-boned corsets led to a steep decline in whaling in the later 19th century, but Norwegian innovations made hunting the hitherto "wrong" whales (including the blue whale and the sei whale; so called because they sank when killed) commercially feasible, and the number of whales killed rose from under 2,000 to over 20,000 between 1900 and 1911. The Norwegians and British dominated whaling into the mid-20th century, when overfishing again made it unprofitable for most nations, though not Japan and the Soviet Union, which became the chief whaling nations. Concern over the near-extinction of many species led to the establishment in 1946 of the International Whaling Commission. Commercial whaling was prohibited altogether in 1986, but several nations, notably Japan, Norway, and the Soviet Union, initially refused to comply.

Wharton, Edith (Newbold) *orig.* **Edith Newbold Jones** (1862–1937) U.S. novelist and short-story writer. Born in New York City into upper-class society, Wharton began writing a few years after her marriage in 1885. Her works examine the barriers of social convention, especially in the upper class, that stand in the way of individual happiness. Her close friendship with the older Henry James did much to support and shape her work. The critical and popular success of her novel *The House of Mirth* (1905) established her as a leading writer. She is best known for *Ethan Frome* (1911), which exploits the grimmer possibilities of New England farm life. Her other books, of which she wrote almost 50, include the novels *The Custom of the Country* (1913), *The Age of Innocence* (1920, Pulitzer Prize), and *The Buccaneers* (1938).

wheat Any of various cereal grasses in the genus *Triticum* of the Poaceae (or Gramineae) family, one of the oldest and most important of the cereal crops. More of the world's farmland is devoted to wheat than to any other food crop; China is the largest wheat producer. The plant has long, slender leaves, hollow stems in most varieties, and flowers grouped together in spikelets. Of the thousands of varieties known, the most important are *T. aestivum,* used to make bread; *T. durum,* used in making pasta; and *T. compactum* (club wheat), a softer type used for cake, crackers, cookies, pastries, and household flours. Winter wheat (sown in fall) and spring wheat (sown in spring or, where winters are mild, sometimes fall) are the two major types. The greatest portion of wheat flour is used for breadmaking. Small quantities are used in the production of starch, malt, gluten, alcohol, and other products. Inferior and surplus wheats and various milling by-products are used for livestock feeds.

Wheatley, Phillis (1753?–1784) First U.S. black woman poet. Probably born to a Fulani family in Senegal, she was sold from a slave ship in 1761 to John Wheatley, a Boston merchant. The Wheatleys taught her to read and write English and Latin. At about 14 she began writing poetry modeled on Alexander Pope and other Neoclassical writers. Her verse, largely on conventional subjects, attracted much attention. *Poems on Various Subjects, Religious and Moral* (1773), published in England, spread her fame to Europe. Freed in 1773, she married a free black man. She worked as a servant in her final years and died in poverty.

wheel Circular frame of hard material capable of turning on an axle. Wheels may be solid, partly solid, or spoked. The oldest known wheel was a wooden disk of planks held together by crosspieces. A pottery wheel or turntable was developed c. 3500 BC in Mesopotamia. The spoked wheel appeared c. 2000 BC on chariots in Asia Minor. Later developments included iron hubs that turned on greased axles. Perhaps the most important invention in human history, the wheel was essential to developing civilizations, and has remained essential to power generation, transportation, industrial manufacturing, and countless other applications.

wheel lock Device for igniting the powder in a firearm such as a musket. Developed c. 1515, the wheel lock struck a spark to ignite powder in the pan of a musket by means of a holder that pressed a shard of flint or a piece of iron pyrite against an iron wheel with a milled edge; the wheel rotated and sparks flew. The principle was used in the design of the flint-and-wheel cigarette lighter. See also flintlock.

whelk Any marine snail of the family Buccinidae, or a snail having a similar shell; found worldwide. Some whelks are called conchs. The sturdy shell of most species in the family is slender and has a wide opening in the first whorl. The animal feeds on other mollusks through its long proboscis; some species also kill fishes and crustaceans caught in commercial traps. Most are cold-water species; tropical species are smaller and more colorful. The common northern whelk *(Buccinum undatum)* has a stout pale shell about 3 in. (8 cm) long and is abundant in North Atlantic waters.

Northern whelk (*Buccinum undatum*).
INGMAR HOLMASEN

W X Y Z

Whewell \'hyü-əl\, **William** (1794–1866) British philosopher and historian. He spent most of his career at Cambridge Univ., where he taught mineralogy (1828–32) and moral philosophy (1838–55) and served as college master (1841–66). He is remembered primarily for his work on the theory of INDUCTION. He stressed the need to see scientific progress as a historical process, asserting that inductive reasoning could be employed properly only if its use throughout history was closely analyzed. He is best known for his *History of the Inductive Sciences* (3 vols., 1837) and *Philosophy of the Inductive Sciences* (1840).

Whewell, plaster cast of bust by Edward Hodges Baily, 1851; in the National Portrait Gallery, London.

BY COURTESY OF THE NATIONAL PORTRAIT GALLERY, LONDON

Whig Member of a political faction in England, particularly in the 18th century. Originally a term for Scottish Presbyterians, the name came to imply nonconformity and rebellion and was applied in 1679 to those who wanted to exclude James, the Catholic duke of York (later JAMES II), from succession to the throne of England. The Whigs were opposed by the TORY faction in that struggle but later represented the aristocratic, landowning families and financial interests of the wealthy middle classes. They maintained power through patronage and connections in Parliament, but there was no distinct party until 1784, when CHARLES JAMES FOX represented the interests of religious dissenters, industrialists, and others who sought parliamentary reform. After 1815 and following various party realignments, the political group became the LIBERAL PARTY. See also WHIG PARTY.

Whig Party (1834–54) U.S. political party. Organized by opponents to Pres. ANDREW JACKSON, whom they called "King Andrew," it took its name from the British antimonarchist party. The U.S. Whigs favored a program of national development and supported the Second BANK OF THE U.S., espoused by HENRY CLAY. It also included members of the former Anti-Masonic Party. The party's candidate, WILLIAM H. HARRISON, won the 1840 presidential election, but his premature death halted enactment of the Whig nationalistic program. Clay was the party's unsuccessful candidate in the 1844 election. In 1848 it nominated ZACHARY TAYLOR, who won the election. The party began to split into the "conscience" (antislavery) and "cotton" (proslavery) Whigs and was further divided by the COMPROMISE OF 1850. Its nominee in the 1852 election, WINFIELD SCOTT, failed to win wide support as most Southern Whigs joined the DEMOCRATIC PARTY. In 1854 most Northern Whigs joined the new REPUBLICAN PARTY; some joined the KNOW-NOTHING PARTY.

whip-tailed ray See STINGRAY

whippet Breed of HOUND dog developed in 19th-century Britain to chase rabbits in an arena. It was developed from TERRIERS and English and Italian GREYHOUNDS, which it resembles. It stands 18–22 in. (46–56 cm), weighs about 28 lbs (13 kg), and has a smooth coat of gray, tan, or white. Capable of speeds up to 35 mph (56 kph), it is used for racing and for hunting small game. It is typically quiet and even-tempered.

Whippet.

SALLY ANNE THOMPSON—EB INC.

Whipple, George H(oyt) (1878–1976) U.S. pathologist. Born in Ashland, N.H., he studied medicine at Johns Hopkins University. He and GEORGE MINOT discovered that raw liver fed to chronically bled dogs reversed ANEMIA; this led to liver treatment of pernicious anemia, for which the two men shared a 1934 Nobel Prize with William Murphy (1894–1987). Whipple's study of bile pigments led to an interest in how the body makes HEMOGLOBIN (hemoglobin being important in bile pigment production). His experiments in artificial anemia (1923–25) established iron as the most potent inorganic factor in red-blood-cell formation.

whippoorwill Species *(Caprimulgus vociferus)* of nocturnal North American bird, similar to the NIGHTJAR, named for its resonant "whip-poor-will" call (first and third syllables accented), which it may repeat 400 times without stopping. It lives in woods near open country, where it catches insects on the wing around dusk and dawn. By day it sleeps on the forest floor or perches lengthwise on a branch. About 10 in. (25 cm) long, it has mottled brownish plumage; the male has a white collar and white tail corners. It winters as far south as Costa Rica.

whiskey Any of several DISTILLED LIQUORS made from a fermented mash of CEREAL grains. Whiskeys are distinctive because of differences in raw materials and production methods. All are aged in wooden containers. The earliest direct account of whiskey making is found in Scottish records from 1494. Scotch whisky (this spelling is also used by Canadians) is usually somewhat light in body, with a distinctive smoky MALT flavor; it is made primarily from malted BARLEY that has been heated over a peat fire, fermented, distilled, and blended with similar whiskeys made by different distillers. Irish whiskeys, lighter-bodied and lacking any smoky flavor, are not malt-fired and may be mixed with neutral grain spirits. Canadian whisky, light in color and flavor, is a blend of highly flavored and neutral grain whiskeys. In the U.S., the largest producer and consumer of whiskey, both straight (at least 51% single-mash) and blended whiskeys are produced, derived from both sour and sweet mashes. (Sour mashes are fermented with both fresh and previously fermented yeast; sweet mashes employ only fresh yeast.) Bourbon, first produced in Bourbon Co., Ky., is a full-bodied unblended whiskey derived from a sour mash of corn grain. Whiskeys are consumed both unmixed and mixed in cocktails, punches, and other beverages.

Whiskey Rebellion (1794) American uprising to protest a federal liquor tax. Farmers in western Pennsylvania rebelled against paying a tax on their locally distilled whiskey and attacked federal revenue collectors. After 500 armed men burned the home of the regional tax inspector, Pres. GEORGE WASHINGTON ordered 13,000 federal troops to the area. The rebellion quickly dissolved, with no fighting. The event established the authority of federal law within the states and strengthened support for the FEDERALISTS' advocacy of a strong central government.

Whiskey Ring (1875) Group of U.S. whiskey distillers who defrauded the government of taxes. The ring operated mainly in St. Louis, Milwaukee, and Chicago and kept liquor taxes after bribing Internal Revenue officials in Washington, D.C. A secret investigation by the U.S. Treasury Department resulted in 238 indictments and 110 convictions. While not involved, Pres. ULYSSES S. GRANT was tarnished by the scandal; his private secretary, Orville E. Babcock, was indicted but acquitted on Grant's testimony. The Republican Party allegedly received some of the illegally held tax money.

whist Card game, the original of modern BRIDGE. Whist originated in 17th-cent England. It is played with a 52-card deck by four players in two partnerships. The object is to take tricks, each of which consists of one card played by each player. One point is scored for each trick in excess of six.

whistler See GOLDENEYE

Whistler, James (Abbott) McNeill (1834–1903) U.S.-British painter, etcher, and lithographer. Born in Lowell, Mass., he attended West Point but soon abandoned the army for art. In 1855 he arrived in Paris to study painting and adopted a bohemian lifestyle. In 1863 he moved to London, where he had considerable success, becoming widely famous for his wit and large public presence. An articulate theorist, he expounded on the "correspondences" between the arts, especially painting and music, and helped introduce Britain to modern French painting and Japanese art. From the 1870s on he concentrated on portraits. His most famous work is *Arrangement in Grey and Black, No. 1: The Artist's Mother* (1871–72), known as *Whistler's Mother*. In 1877 he brought a libel suit against JOHN RUSKIN for attacking his *Nocturne in Black and Gold: The Falling Rocket* (1875); he won his case but received damages of only a farthing, and the costs of the suit bankrupted him. A commission for etchings took him to Venice in 1880, and the 50-odd works he produced there won him success again in London on his return.

whistling swan Species *(Olor,* or *Cygnus, columbianus)* of North American SWAN that calls with a soft, musical note. It has a black bill, usually with a small yellow spot near the eye. It breeds in the Arctic tundra and winters in shallow fresh or salt water, especially along eastern and western U.S. coasts.

Whitby, Synod of Meeting of the Christian church of the Anglo-Saxon kingdom of Northumbria in 663–64 to decide whether to follow Celtic or Roman usages. Though Northumbria had been mainly converted by Celtic missionaries, the king decided for Rome, believing that Rome followed the teaching of St. PETER, holder of the keys to heaven. The decision led to the acceptance of Roman usage elsewhere in England and brought the English church into close contact with the rest of Europe.

White, Byron R(aymond) (1917–2002) U.S. jurist. Born in Fort Collins, Col., he was an accomplished athlete, playing football with the Pittsburgh Pirates (now Steelers) and the Detroit Lions. He was a Rhodes scholar at Oxford before studying law at Yale. He clerked for FRED M. VINSON and later practiced corporate law in Colorado. He was named deputy U.S. attorney general by Pres. JOHN F. KENNEDY in 1961 and was appointed to the U.S. Supreme Court the next year. His opinions and votes on the court were generally moderate to conservative. He retired in 1993.

White, E(lwyn) B(rooks) (1899–1985) U.S. essayist and literary stylist. Born in Mount Vernon, N.Y., White attended Cornell University and in 1927 joined *The New Yorker*; he would contribute to it and later to *Harper's* magazine over several decades. He collaborated with JAMES THURBER on *Is Sex Necessary?* (1929). His *Stuart Little* (1945), *Charlotte's Web* (1952), and *The Trumpet of the Swan* (1970) are classics of children's literature; *Charlotte's Web* ranks among the most successful American children's books of all time. His revision of *The Elements of Style* (1959) by his professor William Strunk became a standard style manual for writers. He received a Pulitzer Prize special citation in 1978.

White, James (Springer) and Ellen (Gould) *orig.* **Ellen Gould Harmon** (1821–1881, 1827–1915) Cofounders of the Seventh-Day Adventists. James was a schoolteacher and then a minister who accepted the ADVENTIST views of William Miller (1782–1849). He married Ellen Harmon in 1846; she had become a Millerite in 1840, at 13. A visionary, Ellen had more than 2,000 visions before she died; these helped guide the Seventh-Day Adventist Church, which was formed in 1863. They preached together until James's death. Ellen continued, speaking on many subjects, notably temperance, and was regarded by some as a prophet. Of her many books, the best known is *Steps to Christ*.

White, John (died 1593?) British artist, explorer, and North American colonist. He sailed on an expedition to Greenland in 1577 and returned to England with sketches of the land and its people. His 1585 trip to colonize ROANOKE was sponsored by Sir WALTER RALEIGH. White's paintings and sketches illustrated a report of the region after the colony was abandoned (1586). He was appointed governor of a second colony and arrived at Roanoke with 100 colonists (1587). He returned to England for supplies that year but was unable to send a relief expedition to Roanoke until 1590; it found no trace of the colonists, including White's granddaughter, VIRGINIA DARE.

White, Minor (1908–1976) U.S. photographer and editor. Born in Minneapolis, he began to photograph seriously in 1938 when he went to work for the WORKS PROGRESS ADMINISTRATION. In 1946 he studied with EDWARD WESTON and ALFRED STIEGLITZ before moving to San Francisco, where he worked closely with ANSEL ADAMS. He succeeded Adams as head of the photography department at the California School of Fine Arts and later taught at MIT. He founded and edited (1952–76) the photography magazine *Aperture* and also edited *Image* (1953–57). His efforts to extend photography's range of expression made him one of the century's most influential photographers.

White, Patrick (Victor Martindale) (1912–1990) Australian writer. As a youth White moved between Australia and England, where he attended Cambridge University, returning after World War II to Australia, which he saw as a country in a volatile process of growth and self-definition. His somewhat misanthropic novels, which often explore the possibilities of savagery in that context, include *The Aunt's Story* (1946), *The Tree of Man* (1955), *Voss* (1957), *Riders in the Chariot* (1961), *The Eye of the Storm* (1973), and *The Twyborn Affair* (1979). His other works include plays and short stories, the latter collected in *The Burnt Ones* (1964) and *The Cockatoos* (1974). He was awarded the Nobel Prize in 1973.

White, Stanford (1853–1906) U.S. architect. Born in New York City, he trained with HENRY HOBSON RICHARDSON. In 1880 he formed an architectural firm with CHARLES F. MCKIM and William R. Mead that soon became the most famous in the country, known especially for its Shingle-style country and seaside mansions. The firm later led the U.S. trend toward Neoclassical architecture. White's design for the Casino (1881) at Newport, R.I., exhibited the gracefully proportioned structures with Italian Renaissance ornamentation at which he excelled. His New York commissions included Madison Square Garden (1891) and the Washington Arch (1891). A versatile artist, he also designed jewelry, furniture, and interiors. An extrovert noted for his lavish entertainments, he was shot to death at Madison Square Garden by Harry Thaw, the husband of the showgirl Evelyn Nesbit, with whom White had had a love affair.

White, T(erence) H(anbury) (1906–1964) English (Indian-born) novelist, social historian, and satirist. Educated at Cambridge University, White was working as a teacher when he attained his first critical success with the autobiographical *England Have My Bones* (1936). He later devoted himself to writing, studying subjects such as ARTHURIAN LEGEND while living a largely reclusive life. He is best known for his adaptation of SIR THOMAS MALORY'S *Le Morte Darthur* in the tetralogy *The Once and Future King* (1958), comprising *The Sword in the Stone* (1938), *The Queen of Air and Darkness* (originally *The Witch in the Wood,* 1939), *The Ill-Made Knight* (1940), and *The Candle in the Wind* (1958).

White, Theodore H(arold) (1915–1986) U.S. journalist, historian, and novelist. Born in Boston, White became one of *Time*'s first foreign correspondents, serving in East Asia 1939–45 and later as a European correspondent. He is best known for his astute, suspenseful accounts of two presidential elections, *The Making of the President, 1960* (1961, Pulitzer Prize) and *The Making of the President, 1964* (1965), which were followed by similar analyses of the 1968 and 1972 campaigns. His later books include *Breach of Faith* (1975) and the autobiographical *In Search of History* (1978).

White, William Allen (1868–1944) U.S. journalist. Born in Emporia, Kan., White purchased the *Emporia Daily and Weekly Gazette* in 1895. His editorial writing was a mixture of tolerance, optimism, liberal Republicanism, and provincialism. His widely circulated 1896 editorial "What's the Matter with Kansas?" was credited with helping elect WILLIAM MCKINLEY president. He also wrote fiction, biographies, and an autobiography. His son and successor, William Lindsay White (1900–1973), wrote the best-selling World War II book *They Were Expendable* (1942).

white blood cell See LEUKOCYTE

white butterfly Any of several LEPIDOPTERAN species (family Pieridae) found worldwide. Adults have a wingspan of 1.5–2.5 in. (37–63 mm); the wings are white, with black marginal markings. The pattern and color of many species vary with sex and season. Many of the green, slender larvae, most of which are covered with a short down, or pile, are pests of garden crops. The pupae are attached to a twig by a posterior spine and a girdle of silk. See also CABBAGE WHITE.

White butterfly (*Pieris brassicae*).
CHR LEDERER–BAVARIA-VERLAG

white cedar In the lumber trade, the American ARBORVITAE, some species of false cypress (genus *Chamaecyparis*) and McNab cypress, incense cedar *(Calocedrus decurrens),* and California juniper, all in the CYPRESS family. Nonconiferous trees that are called white cedar include the chinaberry (*Melia azedarach,* MAHOGANY FAMILY) and some members of the plant families Bignoniaceae (trumpet creepers), Celastraceae (staff trees), Myristicaceae (nutmegs), Burseraceae, and Dipterocarpaceae. Botanically, white cedar is *Chamaecyparis thyoides*, a picturesque tree with purple cones, native to North America and East Asia. The wood is used for carpentry, pencils, storage chests, interiors, and fence posts.

white dwarf star Any of a class of small, faint STARS representing the end point of the evolution of stars without enough mass to become NEU-

TRON STARS or BLACK HOLES. Named for the white color of the first ones discovered, they actually occur in a variety of colors depending on their temperature. They are extremely dense, typically containing the mass of the sun within the volume of the earth. White dwarfs have exhausted all their nuclear fuel and cannot produce heat by NUCLEAR FUSION to counteract their own gravity, which compresses the electrons and nuclei of their atoms until they prevent further gravitational contraction. When a white dwarf's reservoir of thermal energy is exhausted (after several billion years), it stops radiating and becomes a cold, inert stellar remnant, sometimes called a black dwarf. White dwarf stars play an essential role in the outbursts of NOVAS, and if mass transfer increases their mass above 1.4 times the sun's mass (the CHANDRASEKHAR limit), they collapse and generate a SUPERNOVA explosion.

white-footed mouse See DEER MOUSE

White Horse, Vale of the Valley, OXFORDSHIRE, England. It is named from the *White Horse,* a gigantic (374 ft or 114 m long) prehistoric figure of a horse formed by cutting away the turf on the side of a chalk hill. A number of other prehistoric remains are in the vicinity, including the megalith known as Wayland's Smithy. Wantage, an ancient market town in the valley, is said to be the birthplace of ALFRED the Great.

White House Official residence of the U.S. president, in Washington, D.C. It has been the home of every president since JOHN ADAMS. In 1791 James Hoban (1762–1831) won the commission to build the presidential residence with his plan for a Georgian mansion in the style of ANDREA PALLADIO. The structure, to be built of gray sandstone, was to have more than 100 rooms. The British burned it in 1814, but it was rebuilt and enlarged under Hoban's direction. In the 1820s, Hoban added eastern and western terraces as well as a semicircular southern portico and a colonnaded northern portico. The later addition of the West Wing (1902) and East Wing (1942) provided additional office space. THEODORE ROOSEVELT adopted "White House" as the building's official name in 1902. Its public areas are toured by about 1.5 million people every year.

White Lotus In 12th-century China, a pious vegetarian group dedicated to the worship of the Buddha AMITABHA. It developed into a millenarian organization active in rebellions at the end of the YUAN DYNASTY. The White Lotus Rebellion (1796–1804), in the mountains of central China, consisted of uncoordinated roving bands using hit-and-run guerrilla tactics that were hard to combat, especially as much of the government money allocated to fighting the rebels was embezzled. It was eventually put down by peasants organized into local militia defense corps. Later Chinese governments came to use the term White Lotus for all illegal millenarian groups. The NIAN REBELLION of 1852 may have been a new manifestation of the White Lotus Society, as was the secret society behind the BOXER REBELLION.

White Monk See CISTERCIAN

White Mountain, Battle of (1620) Decisive battle near Prague at the beginning of the THIRTY YEARS' WAR. The Catholic forces of MAXIMILIAN I, duke of Bavaria, commanded by Graf von TILLY, defeated the Protestant forces of FREDERICK V, king of Bohemia. By the defeat, Bohemia lost its independence and Protestantism was exterminated until 1648.

White Mountains Segment of the APPALACHIAN MTNS. It extends 87 mi (140 km) across northern central New Hampshire and into western Maine. Containing the highest elevations in the northeastern U.S., its loftiest peaks, mostly 5,000–6,000 ft (1,500–1,800 m) high, occur in a series of summits that are named for U.S. presidents and make up the Presidential Range. The highest point is Mount WASHINGTON. Most of the White Mountains lie within the White Mountain National Forest. It is a popular summer and winter resort area.

White Nile See NILE RIVER

White River River, Arkansas. It rises in the Boston Mountains in northwestern Arkansas, flows north into southern Missouri, then bends southeast and reenters Arkansas. It continues south to join the ARKANSAS RIVER near its confluence with the MISSISSIPPI RIVER. It is 685 mi (1,102 km) long.

White Sands National Monument National monument, southern central New Mexico. Established in 1933, it covers 225 sq mi (583 sq km), and lies between the San Andres and the Sacramento mountains. Its white gypsum sand constantly drifts into dunes 10–60 ft (3–18 m) high. The San Andres National Wildlife Refuge, White Sands Missile Range, and Holloman Air Force Base are nearby.

White Sea Sea, extension of the Arctic Ocean, northwestern Russia. Almost landlocked, it is connected to the more northerly BARENTS SEA by a long, narrow strait known as the Gorlo. It covers an area of approximately 35,000 sq mi (90,000 sq km) and has a maximum depth of 1,115 ft (340 m). Rivers, including the Northern DVINA and Onega, flow into it. An important transportation route, it remains navigable year-round, with the help of icebreakers in winter. ARKHANGELSK is one of the principal ports.

white shark See GREAT WHITE SHARK

white-tailed deer *or* **Virginia deer** Common reddish brown DEER *(Odocoileus virginianus),* an important game animal found alone or in small groups from southern Canada to South America. The tail, white on the underside, is held aloft when the deer is alarmed or running. The male has forwardly curved antlers with several unbranched tines. Northern white-tailed deer grow up to 3.5 ft (107 cm) tall and weigh up to 400 lbs (180 kg). The white-tailed deer lives in open woodlands (young and cutover forests) and on the fringes of urban areas and farmlands, and eats leaves, twigs, fruits, nuts, lichen, and fungi.

White-tailed deer buck (*Odocoileus virginianus*).
KARL H. MASLOWSKI

White Volta River River, Burkina Faso and Ghana, western Africa. It rises in Burkina Faso (where it is known as the Nakanbe) and flows southwest for about 400 mi (640 km) to empty into Lake VOLTA in Ghana. It is a headstream of the VOLTA RIVER.

whitefish Any of several silvery food fishes (family Salmonidae, or Coregonidae), inhabiting cold northern lakes of Europe, Asia, and North America. Whitefish weigh about 2–5 lbs (1–2 kg); they eat insect larvae and other small animals. The Lake Superior whitefish *(Coregonus clupeaformis),* also called whiting or shad, is the largest of the lake whitefishes. Ciscoes, or lake herring *(Leucichthys,* or *Coregonus, artedi),* are herringlike food and sport fishes. The best sport fishes of the family are the Rocky Mountain whitefish *(Prosopium williamsoni)* and other round whitefishes.

whitefly Any sap-sucking member of the insect family Aleyrodidae (order Homoptera). Nymphs are flat, oval, and usually covered with a cottony substance. Adults, 0.08–0.12 in. (2–3 mm) long, are covered with a white opaque powder and resemble moths. Whiteflies are abundant in warm climates, on houseplants, and in greenhouses. The greenhouse whitefly is one of the most abundant and destructive members of the family. The citrus whitefly and citrus blackfly damage fruit and other crops by sucking sap and producing honeydew, a by-product of digestion on which grows a sooty fungus that ruins fruit and reduces the host plant's ability to photosynthesize.

Whitehead, Alfred North (1861–1947) British mathematician and philosopher. He taught principally at Cambridge University (1885–1911) and Harvard (1924–37). His *Treatise on Universal Algebra* (1898) extended Boolean symbolic logic. He collaborated with BERTRAND RUSSELL on the epochal *Principia Mathematica* (1910–13). He later developed a comprehensive metaphysical theory. In *Process and Reality* (1929), he proposed that the universe consists entirely of becomings, each a process of appropriating and integrating the infinity of items provided by the antecedent universe and by God. Other works include "On Mathematical Concepts of the Material World" (1905), *An Introduction to Mathematics* (1911), "The Aims of Education" (1916), *Enquiry Concerning the Principles of Natural Knowledge* (1919), *The Concept of Nature* (1920), *Science and the Modern World* (1925), and *Religion in the Making* (1926). He received the Order of Merit in 1945.

Whitehorse City (pop., 2001: 19,058), capital of Yukon Territory. Located on the YUKON RIVER, it was founded during the KLONDIKE GOLD RUSH (1897–98) as a staging and distribution center. ROBERT SERVICE got much of his inspiration for his ballads while working there. The territorial capital since 1952, it is an important transportation center on the ALASKA HIGHWAY, as well as an outfitting base for anglers and hunters.

Whiteman, Paul (1890–1967) U.S. musician, the best-known bandleader of the 1920s. Born in Denver, Whiteman made his first records in 1920. His instrumental concept, known as "symphonic jazz," featured lush harmonies and simplified jazz rhythms but little improvisation; he nevertheless became known as "The King of Jazz." Whiteman commissioned GEORGE GERSHWIN's *Rhapsody in Blue* and conducted its premiere in 1924. The Whiteman band featured, among others, BING CROSBY, BIX BEIDERBECKE, Frankie Trumbauer, Bunny Berigan, and J. TEAGARDEN. Active as a bandleader into the 1950s, he later served as music director for ABC.

whiting Species *(Gadus,* or *Merlangius, merlangus)* of common marine food fish of the COD family (Gadidae), found in European waters and especially abundant in the North Sea. It feeds on invertebrates and small fishes. It has three dorsal and two anal fins; a chin barbel (a slender, fleshy feeler), if present, is very small. Whitings grow to less than 30 in. (70 cm) long. They are silvery, with a distinctive black blotch near the base of each pectoral fin. Several species of the family Sciaenidae are also called whiting. See also WHITEFISH.

Whitman, Marcus (1802–1847) U.S. missionary and pioneer. Born in Rushville, N.Y., he became a physician and Congregational missionary and was sent to the Oregon region. In 1836 he and his wife founded a mission among the Cayuse Indians near present-day Walla Walla, Wash. He helped the Indians build houses and a corn-grinding mill; his wife opened a mission school. In 1842 he traveled east to encourage settlement of the Oregon country. On his return he joined a caravan of 1,000 immigrants to the Columbia River valley. He cared for Indian children in an 1847 measles epidemic, but was accused of sorcery when many died while white children survived. The Indians attacked the whites and massacred 14, including the Whitmans. Their deaths led Congress to organize the Oregon Territory in 1848.

Whitman, Walt(er) (1819–1892) U.S. poet, journalist, and essayist. Born in West Hills, Long Island, N.Y., Whitman lived in Brooklyn as a boy and left school at 12. He went on to hold a great variety of jobs, including writing and editing for periodicals. His revolutionary poetry dealt with extremely private experiences (including sexuality) while celebrating the collective experience of an idealized democratic American life. His *Leaves of Grass* (first ed., 1855), revised and much expanded in successive editions that incorporated his subsequent poetry, was too frank and unconventional to win wide acceptance in its day, but was hailed by such figures as RALPH WALDO EMERSON and exerted a strong influence on American and foreign literature. Written without rhyme or traditional meter, such poems as "I Sing the Body Electric" and "Song of Myself" assert the beauty of the human body, physical health, and sexuality; later editions included "Crossing Brooklyn Ferry," "Out of the Cradle Endlessly Rocking," and the elegies on ABRAHAM LINCOLN "O Captain! My Captain!" and "When Lilacs Last in the Dooryard Bloom'd." Whitman served as a volunteer in Washington hospitals during the Civil War. The prose *Democratic Vistas* (1871) and *Specimen Days & Collect* (1882–83) drew on his wartime experiences and subsequent reflections. His powerful influence in the 20th century can be seen in poets as diverse as PABLO NERUDA, FERNANDO PESSOA, and ALLEN GINSBERG.

Walt Whitman, photograph by Mathew Brady.

BY COURTESY OF THE LIBRARY OF CONGRESS, WASHINGTON, D.C.

Whitney, Amos (1832–1928) U.S. manufacturer. Born in Biddeford, Me., he was apprenticed at age 13. In 1860, with FRANCIS PRATT, he founded the firm of Pratt and Whitney, originally to manufacture thread spoolers. It later diversified into the manufacture of innovative designs of guns, cannons, sewing machines, and typesetting machines; instruments for measurement developed there proved of great value to science and industry. Today a separate company formed from the toolworks produces aircraft engines and space-propulsion systems.

Whitney, Eli (1765–1825) U.S. inventor, engineer, and manufacturer. Born in Westboro, Mass., he is best remembered as the inventor of the COTTON GIN (1793), which led to greatly increased production of the short-staple cotton grown in much of the South, making the region prosperous. The most important innovation credited to Whitney may be the concept of MASS PRODUCTION of INTERCHANGEABLE PARTS. His idea of manufacturing quantities of identical parts for assembly into muskets, after undertaking in 1797 to supply the U.S. government with 10,000 muskets in two years, helped inaugurate the vastly important AMERICAN SYSTEM OF MANUFACTURE.

Whitney, Gertrude Vanderbilt (1875–1942) U.S. sculptor and art patron. Great-granddaughter of CORNELIUS VANDERBILT, she was born to great wealth in New York City, and she studied sculpture there and in Paris. Among her major works were the *Titanic Memorial* in Washington, D.C. (1914–31), and *Victory Arch* in New York (1918–19). All her works were simple, direct, and traditional. In 1929 she offered to donate her collection of about 500 works by modern American artists to the Metropolitan Museum of Art, but was refused by the traditionalist director. The next year she founded the Whitney Museum of American Art, which opened in 1931; today it is the foremost museum of American art.

Whitney, John Hay (1904–1982) U.S. multimillionaire and sportsman. Born in Ellsworth, Me., the son of Harry Payne Whitney and GERTRUDE VANDERBILT WHITNEY, "Jock" Whitney attended Yale University and later Oxford, which he left to manage the family fortune on his father's death. He became an internationally ranked polo player, his stables produced notable racehorses, he invested in successful films and Broadway plays, and he boasted one of the finest art collections in the U.S. As a combat-intelligence captain in World War II, he was captured in France but escaped; he was later awarded the Legion of Merit. He served as ambassador to Britain 1956–61. As publisher and (from 1961) editor in chief of the *New York Herald Tribune*, he tried to revitalize the paper, but it folded in 1966. He founded the John Hay Whitney Foundation in 1946.

Whitney, Mt. Peak in the SIERRA NEVADA, southeastern central California. Located in SEQUOIA NATIONAL PARK, it is 14,494 ft (4,418 m) high, the highest point in the continental U.S. outside of Alaska. It was first climbed in 1873.

Whitney, William C(ollins) (1841–1904) U.S. politician. Born in Conway, Mass., he practiced law in New York City, where he helped SAMUEL TILDEN overthrow the corrupt WILLIAM MARCY TWEED and served as corporation counsel for the city (1875–82). As U.S. secretary of the navy (1885–89), he rebuilt the neglected fleet with a major shipbuilding program that included the battleship *Maine.* He returned to New York, where he became co-owner of the city's first rapid-transit system.

Whittier, John Greenleaf (1807–1892) U.S. poet and reformer. A Quaker born on a farm near Haverhill, Mass., Whittier had limited education but was early acquainted with poetry. He became involved in journalism and published his first volume of poems in 1831. During 1833–42 he embraced the abolitionism of WILLIAM LLOYD GARRISON and became a prominent antislavery crusader. Thereafter he continued to support humanitarian causes while publishing further poetry volumes. After the Civil War he was noted for his vivid portrayals of rural New England life. His best-known poem is the nostalgic pastoral "Snow-Bound" (1866); others include "Maud Muller" (1854) and "Barbara Frietchie" (1863).

Whittington, Richard *known as* **Dick Whittington** (died 1423) Lord mayor of London (1397–99, 1406–7, 1419–20). The son of a knight, he earned a vast fortune as a merchant and made loans to HENRY IV and HENRY V, then entered city politics and served three terms as lord mayor. In legend he is portrayed as an orphan, who ventures his only possession, a cat, as an item to be sold on one of his master's trading ships. Ill-treated by the cook, he runs away, but at the edge of the city he hears the bells say, "Turn again, Whittington, lord mayor of great London." He returns to find that his cat has been sold for a great sum to a Moorish ruler plagued by rats. He becomes a wealthy merchant and later lord mayor.

Whittle, Frank *later* **Sir Frank** (1907–1996) British aviation engineer and pilot who invented the JET ENGINE. He obtained his first patent for a TURBOJET engine in 1930, and in 1936 he cofounded Power Jets Ltd. The outbreak of World War II spurred the British government to support Whittle's work, and the first jet-powered aircraft took off in 1941. He was knighted in 1948 and awarded the Order of Merit in 1986.

Whitworth, Joseph *later* **Sir Joseph** (1803–1887) British mechanical engineer. Working for HENRY MAUDSLAY, he devised a scraping technique for making a true plane surface. He followed this with a measuring machine and a system of accurate dimensional standards or master gauges to go with it, and screws with standardized threads (1841), among other innovations. His machine tools became internationally known for their accuracy and quality.

WHO See WORLD HEALTH ORGANIZATION

wholesaling Selling of merchandise to anyone other than a retail customer. The term may include sales to a retailer, wholesaler, or business enterprise. Wholesaling usually involves sales in quantity and at a cost significantly lower than the average retail price. It has become especially necessary since the introduction of MASS PRODUCTION and mass marketing techniques in the 19th century. Without wholesalers, large manufacturers would have to market their products directly to a huge number of retailers or consumers at high unit costs, and retailers or consumers would have to deal with an inconveniently large number of manufacturers. There are three major categories of wholesalers. Merchant wholesalers, the most important category, are independent businesses that buy merchandise in great quantities from manufacturers and resell it to retailers. Manufacturers' sales branches are businesses founded by manufacturers to sell directly to retailers. Merchandise agents and brokers represent various manufacturers; they usually do not buy the merchandise they handle but instead arrange for shelf space and the display of merchandise. See also RETAILING.

whooping cough *or* **pertussis** Acute, very contagious CHILDHOOD DISEASE, typically with bouts of coughing followed by a long, loud inhalation (whoop) and ending with mucus expulsion and often vomiting. Caused by the bacterium *Bordetella pertussis,* it initially resembles a cold with a short dry cough. Within one or two weeks, coughing bouts begin; this phase usually lasts four to six weeks. Serious complications include bronchopneumonia (PNEUMONIA involving the bronchi), asphyxia, and rarely, seizures and signs of brain damage. Treatment is supportive. Antibiotics are ineffective against the disease but can combat additional infections. The pertussis vaccine is usually combined with tetanus and diphtheria toxoids as part of routine childhood immunizations.

whooping crane Migratory North American bird *(Grus americana)* and one of the world's rarest birds, on the verge of extinction. The tallest North American bird, it is almost 5 ft (150 cm) tall and has a wingspread of about 7 ft (210 cm). It is white with black-tipped wings, black legs, and a bare red face and crown. Its shrill, whooping call can be heard for 2 miles (3 km). Almost exterminated in the early 20th century, it became the object of intensive conservation efforts; by century's end there were still fewer than 300 wild and captive individuals. See also SANDHILL CRANE.

Whooping crane (*Grus americana*).
H. WILLIAM BELKNAP

Whorf \'wȯrf\, **Benjamin Lee** (1897–1941) U.S. linguist. Born in Winthrop, Mass., he worked professionally as a fire-prevention authority. The concept he developed (under EDWARD SAPIR's influence) of the equation of culture and language became known as the Whorf (or Sapir-Whorf) hypothesis. He maintained that a language's structure tends to condition the ways its speakers think—for example, that the way a people views time and punctuality may be influenced by the types of verb TENSES in its language. Whorf was also noted for his studies of UTO-AZTECAN LANGUAGES, especially Hopi, and MAYAN HIEROGLYPHIC WRITING.

Whymper \'hwim-pər\, **Edward** (1840–1911) British mountaineer and artist. He became a mountaineer after making sketches for a book on the Alps. In 1865 he made the first ascent of the MATTERHORN; an accident on the descent caused the death of four of his companions. His *Scrambles Amongst the Alps* (1871) and *Travels Amongst the Great Andes* (1892) describe his experiences and are illustrated with his own engravings.

Wicca Modern Western witchcraft movement. Some practitioners consider Wicca the religion of pre-Christian Europe, forced underground by the Christian church. That thesis is not accepted by historians, and modern Wicca is usually dated to the work of Gerald B. Gardner (1884–1964) and Doreen Valiente (1922–1999), who, after the repeal of the last Witchcraft Act in England (1951), went public with their cult of witchcraft, which centered on a horned god of fertility and a great earth goddess. Gardner is credited with introducing the term Wicca. So-called "Dianic" Wicca focuses on the Goddess as the supreme being and usually excludes men. Wiccans share a belief in the importance of the feminine principle, a deep respect for nature, and a pantheistic and polytheistic worldview. They practice some form of ritual magic, almost always considered good or constructive. Some are solitary practitioners; others belong to covens.

Wichita \'wi-chə-ˌtȯ\ City (pop., 1996 est.: 320,000), southern central Kansas, on the ARKANSAS RIVER. Founded in 1864 as a trading post on the site of a Wichita Indian village, it developed with the Texas cattle trade along the CHISHOLM TRAIL, and the rapid spread of agricultural settlement along the ATCHISON, TOPEKA AND SANTA FE RAILROAD CO. In the 1870s it was a major cattle-shipping center. It developed as a center of the aircraft industry in the 1920s. Aircraft construction continues; other economic activities include oil refining, grain processing and storage, and livestock marketing.

Wideman, John Edgar (born 1941) U.S. writer. Born in Washington D.C., he grew up in Homewood, Pa. After graduating from the University of Pennsylvania, he became the second African-American to receive a Rhodes scholarship to Oxford University. He published his first novel, *A Glance Away,* in 1967. He won PEN/Faulkner Awards for *Sent for You Yesterday* (1983) and *Philadelphia Fire* (1990), a fictional account of the bombing of the militant black group MOVE combined with an examination of his relationship with his son, now in prison. A recent novel is *The Cattle Killing* (1996). He has taught at the University of Massachusetts since 1985.

Wieland \'vē-ˌlänt\, **Heinrich Otto** (1877–1957) German chemist. He won a 1927 Nobel Prize for research on BILE acids that showed that the three acids then isolated had similar structures and were also structurally related to CHOLESTEROL. He also found that different forms of nitrogen in organic compounds can be detected and distinguished from each other, an important contribution to structural organic chemistry. Wieland's theory that oxidation in living tissues occurs through removal of hydrogen atoms, not addition of oxygen (see OXIDATION-REDUCTION), was of great importance to physiology, biochemistry, and medicine.

Wiener \'wē-nər\, **Norbert** (1894–1964) U.S. mathematician. Born in Columbia, Mo., he earned a PhD from Harvard at 18. He joined the faculty of MIT in 1919. His work on generalized harmonic analysis and Tauberian theorems (which deduce the convergence of an infinite series) won the American Mathematical Society's Bôcher Prize in 1933. The origin of CYBERNETICS as an independent science is generally dated from the 1948 publication of his *Cybernetics.* He made contributions to such areas as stochastic processes, quantum theory, and, during World War II, gunfire control. Crater Wiener on the Moon is named for him.

Wiener.
BY COURTESY OF THE LIBRARY OF CONGRESS, WASHINGTON, D.C.

Wiener Werkstätte \'vē-nər-'verk-ˌshtet-ə\ *English* **Vienna Workshops** Cooperative enterprise for crafts and design founded

W X Y Z

in Vienna in 1903. Inspired by WILLIAM MORRIS and the English ARTS AND CRAFTS MOVEMENT, it was founded by Koloman Moser (1868–1918) and JOSEF HOFFMANN with the goal of restoring the values of hand craftsmanship to an industrial society in which such crafts were dying. It had close ties to the artists of the Vienna SEZESSION and the ART NOUVEAU movement. Its work in jewelry, furnishings, interior design, fashion, and other areas, which often celebrated the beauty of geometry, became widely known for elegance and innovation, and this "square style" influenced the work of the BAUHAUS craftsmen in the 1920s as well as the work of FRANK LLOYD WRIGHT.

Wiesbaden \'vēs-,bä-dən\ City (pop., 1999 est.: 268,200), capital of HESSE, southern Germany, situated on the RHINE RIVER. The Romans fortified it in the 1st century AD; it has been noted since then for its hot saline springs. Made an imperial city in 1241, it passed to the counts of Nassau in 1255. It was capital of the duchy of Nassau 1806–66, then passed to Prussia. After World War I it was the seat of the Rhineland Commission under French and British occupation (1918–29). In 1946 it became the capital of the newly created state of Hesse. It was particularly noted for its spa in the 18th–19th century, when it was frequented by JOHANN W. VON GOETHE, J. BRAHMS, and FYODOR DOSTOYEVSKY. It continues to be a popular resort. It has printing firms, publishing houses, and film studios; it is noted for its Sekt (German champagne).

Wiesel \vē-'zel\, **Elie** *orig.* **Elizer** (born 1928) Romanian-U.S. novelist. Living in a small Hasidic community, Wiesel and his family were deported in 1944 to Auschwitz and then to Buchenwald; his parents and sister were killed. All his works reflect his experiences as a survivor of the Holocaust and his attempt to resolve the ethical torment of why it happened and what it revealed about human nature. They include *Night* (1958), *A Beggar in Jerusalem* (1968), *The Testament* (1980), and *The Forgotten* (1989). A noted lecturer, he was awarded the 1986 Nobel Peace Prize for his universal condemnation of violence, hatred, and oppression.

Wiesel \'vē-səl\, **Torsten (Nils)** (born 1924) Swedish neurobiologist. After earning his medical degree in Sweden, he moved to the U.S., where he joined DAVID HUBEL in investigating brain function. By analyzing the flow of nerve impulses from the eye in laboratory animals, they detected many structural and functional details of the visual cortex, in the occipital lobes of the cerebral cortex. Their studies of the effects of visual impairments in young animals lent strong support to the view that prompt surgery is crucial to correct certain eye defects in newborn children. The two shared a 1981 Nobel Prize with ROGER SPERRY.

wig Manufactured head covering of real or artificial hair worn in the theater, as personal adornment, disguise, or symbol of office, or for religious reasons. Ancient Egyptians, Assyrians, Phoenicians, Greeks, and Romans used wigs, often as protection from the sun. In the West, the wig first became an acceptable form of adornment or corrective for nature's defects in the 16th century, and men's perukes, or periwigs, came into widespread use in the 17th century. Men's wigs were common through the 18th century. Women wore wigs surreptitiously in the 18th–19th century; after the development of inexpensive synthetic wigs in the 20th century, women's wigs increased in popularity. In the Orient, wigs have been used rarely except in the Chinese and Japanese theater.

Wigan \'wi-gən\ Town (pop., 1999 est.: 306,521), northwestern GREATER MANCHESTER, England. It lies along the River Douglas and the Leeds and Liverpool Canal. Coal was mined from the 14th century, and textiles were produced in the area as early as the 16th century. Industrialization in the late 18th century was accelerated by the building of canals and railways. Coal and textiles are still important products; other industries include food processing and electrical engineering. Tourism was spurred by GEORGE ORWELL's *Road to Wigan Pier.*

wigeon *or* **widgeon** Any of four species of DABBLING DUCKS, popular game and food birds. The male European wigeon *(Anas,* or *Mareca, penelope)* has a reddish head, cream forehead, and gray back. The male American wigeon, or baldpate *(A. americana),* has a white crown, green eye stripe, and brown back. Baldpates often graze on young grasses. The Cape wigeon *(A. capensis)* of Africa is a nocturnal feeder.

Wiggin, Kate Douglas *orig.* **Kate Douglas Smith** (1856–1953) U.S. novelist. Born in Philadelphia, she moved to San Francisco, where she established the Silver Street Kindergarten (1878), the first free kindergarten in the West. She wrote novels for both adults and children, but is best remembered for the children's classic *Rebecca of Sunnybrook Farm* (1903).

Wight, Isle of Island and county (pop., 1999 est.: 128,300) off the southern coast of England, in the ENGLISH CHANNEL. Separated from HAMPSHIRE Co. on the mainland by The SOLENT, the island has an area of 147 sq mi (381 sq km); the county seat is NEWPORT. The backbone of the Isle of Wight is a chalk ridge that extends across its entire breadth, the thickest bed of chalk in the British Isles. The Needles are three detached masses of chalk that lie off the island's westernmost point and rise to about 100 ft (30 m). Three rivers, the Eastern Yar, the Medina, and the Western Yar, flow northward into The Solent. The island's warm, sunny climate has made it a popular vacation spot.

Wightman, Hazel Hotchkiss *orig.* **Hazel Virginia Hotchkiss** (1886–1974) U.S. tennis player. Born in Healdsburg, Cal., she graduated from the University of California at Berkeley. She was a dominant competitor in the pre–World War I years, winning nine national tennis titles in the years 1909–11 alone. She won a lifetime total of 45 U.S. titles, the last at age 68. She was instrumental in establishing an annual match between British and U.S. women's teams; the Wightman Cup competition, first held in 1923, continued until 1989. She served as captain of the U.S. team from its inception until 1948.

Wigner, Eugene (Paul) *orig.* **Jenó Pál** (1902–1995) Hungarian-U.S. physicist. After studies at the University of Berlin, he emigrated to the U.S. in 1930 and joined the faculty of Princeton University. He was instrumental in getting the MANHATTAN PROJECT started and was present when ENRICO FERMI initiated the first chain reaction. He determined that the nuclear force is short-range and does not involve an ELECTRIC CHARGE, using GROUP THEORY to investigate atomic structure. His name was given to several formulations, including the Breit-Wigner formula, which describes resonant nuclear reactions. He won a 1963 Nobel Prize (shared with MARIA G. MAYER and Hans Jensen (1907–1973), who won for unrelated work) for his insights into QUANTUM MECHANICS, especially principles governing interaction of protons and neutrons in the nucleus and his formulation of the law of conservation of PARITY (see CONSERVATION LAW). In addition to his many scientific awards, he received numerous awards for his work for peace.

wigwam American Indian dwelling, characteristic of the ALGONQUIAN-speaking nomadic tribes of what is now the northeastern U.S. It is constructed of saplings driven into the ground in a circle and tied together at the top, then covered with mats of woven rushes or sewn bark. See also IGLOO, LONGHOUSE, TEPEE.

Wilberforce, William (1759–1833) British politician. He entered the House of Commons in 1780, where he supported parliamentary reform and Catholic emancipation. Converted to evangelical Christianity (1785), he agitated against the slave trade and cofounded the Anti-Slavery Society. His sponsorship of antislavery legislation led to passage of a bill abolishing the slave trade in the British West Indies (1807). From 1821 he agitated for emancipation of all slaves and was joined in Parliament by Thomas F. Buxton (1786–1845), who continued to sponsor legislation after Wilberforce retired (1825). The Slavery Abolition Act was passed one month after Wilberforce's death in 1833.

Wilbur, Richard (Purdy) (born 1921) U.S. poet, critic, editor, and translator. Born in New York City, he studied literature at Harvard University and established himself as an important young writer with the collections *The Beautiful Changes* (1947) and *Ceremony* (1950). His urbane, well-crafted verse later appeared in such volumes as *Things of This World* (1956, Pulitzer Prize), *Walking to Sleep* (1969), and *The Mind Reader* (1976). He also has translated plays (notably those of MOLIÈRE) and written children's books and criticism, some collected in *Responses* (1976). He served as U.S. poet laureate in 1987–88.

Wilbye \'wil-bē\, **John** (1574–1638) British composer. He spent his entire life in the employ of the Kytson family, as a domestic musician at Hengrave Hall, and then in Colchester (from 1628). One of the finest of the English madrigalists, he published only two collections (1598, 1609). His madrigals are less chromatic than those of his contemporary THOMAS WEELKES, but he made subtle use of varying textures for expression.

wild boar See BOAR

wild carrot See QUEEN ANNE'S LACE

W
X
Y
Z

wild pig See BOAR

wild rice Coarse annual GRASS *(Zizania aquatica)* of the family Poaceae (or Gramineae) whose grain, now often considered a delicacy, has long been an important food of American Indians. Despite its name, the plant is not related to RICE. Wild rice grows naturally in shallow water in marshes and along the shores of streams and lakes in northern central North America. Cultivated varieties are now grown in Minnesota and California. The plant, about 3–10 ft (1–3 m) tall, is topped with a large, open flower cluster. The ripened grains, dark brown to purplish-black, are slender rods 0.4–0.8 in. (1–2 cm) long.

Wild West Show Theatrical extravaganza produced by WILLIAM F. (BUFFALO BILL) CODY. First performed in 1883, the show reached New York's Madison Square Garden in 1887 with a cast of 100 Indians, the sharpshooter ANNIE OAKLEY, other trick riders and ropers, and such wild animals as buffalo, elk, bear, and deer. The four-hour spectacle, including Indian war dances and an attack on a stagecoach, toured Europe to great success in the 1890s and continued touring the U.S. until 1916.

wildcat Wild species *(Felis silvestris)* of CAT (family Felidae) native to Eurasian forests. Very similar to the domestic yellowish tabby, it will interbreed with DOMESTIC CATS (of which it is presumably an ancestor). It is 20–32 in. (50–80 cm) long, excluding the 10–14-in. (25–35-cm) tail. It stands 14–16 in. (35–40 cm) and weighs 6–20 lbs (3–10 kg). Solitary and nocturnal, it preys on birds and small animals. In North America the name is used for the BOBCAT and LYNX; in Africa it refers to the Caffre cat.

wildcat bank In the U.S., an unsound bank chartered under state law during the period of state banking control (1816–63). Such banks distributed currency backed by questionable SECURITIES and were located in inaccessible areas to discourage note redemption. Note circulation by state banks ended with the passage of the National Bank Act of 1863, which provided for the incorporation of NATIONAL BANKS and the issue of banknotes on the security of government BONDS. The term wildcat bank was later applied to any unstable bank.

Wilde, Oscar (Fingal O'Flahertie Wills) (1854–1900) Irish poet and dramatist. Son of an eminent surgeon, Wilde attended Trinity College, Dublin, and later Oxford University, becoming widely known for his wit while still an undergraduate. A spokesman for AESTHETICISM, in the early 1880s he gave a lecture tour in the U.S. and established himself in London circles by his wit and flamboyance. His only novel, *The Picture of Dorian Gray* (1891) combines gothic elements with mockery of bourgeois morality. His macabre play *Salomé* (1893) was later adapted as the libretto of RICHARD STRAUSS's opera; his other plays, all successes, include *Lady Windermere's Fan* (1893), *A Woman of No Importance* (1893), and *An Ideal Husband* (1895). His greatest work was the comedy *The Importance of Being Earnest* (1899), a satire of Victorian social hypocrisy. Two critical dialogues, "The Decay of Lying" and "The Critic as Artist," are admired as equally brilliant. Though happily married, in 1891 he began an intimate relationship with the young Lord Alfred Douglas, son of the marquess of Queensberry. Accused by the latter as a sodomite, Wilde sued him and lost, then was arrested for sodomy and convicted in a trial that became internationally notorious. Imprisoned at Reading Gaol 1895–97, he wrote a recriminatory letter to his lover that was edited and published as *De Profundis* (1905). After his release, he moved to Paris; his only later work was *The Ballad of Reading Gaol* (1898), on inhumane prison conditions. He died suddenly of acute meningitis at 46.

Wilde, 1882.

BY COURTESY OF THE WILLIAM ANDREWS MEMORIAL LIBRARY OF THE UNIVERSITY OF CALIFORNIA, LOS ANGELES

wildebeest See GNU

Wilder, Billy *orig.* **Samuel** (1906–2002) Austrian-U.S. film director and screenwriter. Working as a reporter in Vienna and Berlin, he wrote screenplays for German films. He fled Germany in 1933 and arrived in Hollywood a year later. He cowrote screenplays with Charles Brackett and established his reputation as a director with *Double Indemnity* (1944). Noted for his humorous treatments of controversial subjects and his biting indictments of hypocrisy, he also directed *The Lost Weekend* (1945, Academy Award), *Sunset Boulevard* (1950, Academy Award for best screenplay), *Stalag 17* (1953), and *The Apartment* (1960, Academy Award). His acclaimed comedies include *Sabrina* (1954), *The Seven Year Itch* (1955), *Some Like It Hot* (1959), and *Kiss Me, Stupid* (1964).

Wilder, Laura Ingalls *orig.* **Laura Ingalls** (1867–1957) U.S. children's author. Born in Lake Pepin, Wis., she led the pioneer life with her family, living in Kansas, Minnesota, Iowa, and South Dakota, where she married. With her husband she finally settled in Missouri, where she edited the *Missouri Ruralist* for 12 years before being encouraged by her daughter to write down her childhood memories, and the internationally popular *Little House* books (1932–1943), eight (or nine) in all, were the result. They were the basis of a popular television series (1974–84).

Wilder, Thornton (Niven) (1897–1975) U.S. playwright and novelist. Born in Madison, Wis., he attended Yale University. He earned wide acclaim for his second novel, *The Bridge of San Luis Rey* (1927, Pulitzer Prize). His *Our Town* (1938, Pulitzer Prize), which became one of the most enduringly popular of all American plays, was followed by the successful *The Skin of Our Teeth* (1942, Pulitzer Prize). In them he rejected naturalism, often discarding props and scenery, using deliberate anachronisms, and having the characters address the audience directly. His *The Matchmaker* (1954) was adapted into the musical *Hello, Dolly!* (1964). His later novels include *The Eighth Day* (1967) and *Theophilus North* (1973).

Wilderness, Battle of the (May 5–7, 1864) Engagement in the AMERICAN CIVIL WAR. When ULYSSES S. GRANT planned a Union campaign to capture Richmond, Va., and advanced with 115,000 troops, he was met by a Confederate army of 62,000 under ROBERT E. LEE in dense thickets called the Wilderness. After two days of intense fighting and an indecisive outcome, heavy Union casualties outnumbered those of the Confederacy. Grant moved on to Spotsylvania Courthouse, forcing Lee back toward Richmond.

wildflower Any FLOWERING PLANT that grows without intentional human aid. Wildflowers are the source of all cultivated garden varieties of flowers. Thousands of the approximately 250,000 species of flowering plants are wildflowers. Wildflowers can be divided into three categories by location: those found in the tropics and subtropics, those in temperate regions, and those that grow on the summits of mountain chains and in the Arctic and Antarctic.

wildlife conservation Regulation of wild animals and plants in such a way as to provide for their continuance. Efforts are aimed at preventing the depletion of present populations and ensuring the continued existence of the habitats targeted species need to survive. Techniques involve establishment of sanctuaries and controls on hunting, use of land, importation of exotic species, pollution, and use of pesticides. See also BIODIVERSITY, CONSERVATION, ENDANGERED SPECIES.

Wilfrid, St. *or* **Wilfrid of York** (634–709?) English bishop who established close relations between the Anglo-Saxon church and the papacy. At the Synod of WHITBY he successfully advocated the adoption of Roman over Celtic usages. As bishop of York, he built a monastery at Hexham and introduced the Benedictine Rule to the kingdom. A quarrel over the division of his diocese obliged Wilfrid to take refuge in Sussex, where he Christianized the people and founded a monastery at Selsey; he later served as bishop of Mercia. He traveled twice to Rome to address controversies over his jurisdiction (679, 704).

Wilhelmina (Helena Pauline Maria) (1880–1962) Queen of the Netherlands (1890–1948). Daughter of King WILLIAM III, she became queen on his death, under her mother's regency until 1898, and soon gained wide popular approval. She helped maintain her country's neutrality in World War I. After Germany invaded the Netherlands in 1940, she left with her family for London. Throughout World War II she made radio broadcasts to maintain the morale of the Dutch people, becoming a symbol of Dutch resistance to the German occupation. In 1948 she abdicated in favor of her daughter, JULIANA.

Wilkes, John (1725–1797) English politician. His early life was profligate, and he bribed voters to win election to the House of Commons

(1757). For an attack on the government in his journal the *North Briton* (1763), he was prosecuted for libel and expelled from Parliament. Reelected, he continued to print his attacks on the government, and was again tried for libel and expelled (1764). Regarded as a victim of persecution and a champion of liberty, he gained widespread popular support. He was again elected to Parliament and again expelled (1769). He become lord mayor of London in 1774. Back in the House of Commons 1774–90, he supported parliamentary reform and freedom of the press.

Wilkes, Maurice V(incent) (born 1913) British computer-science pioneer. Among his many accomplishments, he helped build the EDSAC computer (1949), invented microprogramming (1950), cowrote the first book on computer programming (1951), wrote the first paper on cache memories (1964), and pioneered client-server architecture computing (1980). He won the Turing Award in 1967 and the Kyoto Prize in 1992. In 1995 he published *Memoirs of a Computer Pioneer.*

Wilkins, Maurice (Hugh Frederick) (born 1916) New Zealand-British biophysicist. Educated in Birmingham and Cambridge, he participated in the Manhattan Project, working on the separation of uranium isotopes for use in the atomic bomb. On his return to Britain, he began a series of investigations that led ultimately to his studies of DNA. His X-ray diffraction studies of DNA proved crucial to the determination of DNA's molecular structure by James D. Watson and Francis Crick, for which the three were awarded a 1962 Nobel Prize. He later applied X-ray diffraction techniques to the study of RNA. See also Rosalind Franklin.

Wilkins, Roy (1901–1981) U.S. civil-rights leader. Born in St. Louis, he became a reporter and later managing editor of the black-owned *Kansas City Call.* In 1931 he joined the staff of the NAACP and was editor (1934–49) of its official publication, *The Crisis.* In 1955 he began a 22-year tenure as executive director of the NAACP, which he set on a course to seek equal rights through legal redress. He helped organize the 1963 March on Washington, and he served as chairman of the U.S. delegation to the International Conference on Human Rights in 1968.

Wilkinson, David (1771–1852) U.S. inventor. Born in Smithfield, R.I., the son of a blacksmith, in 1797 he invented a gauge and sliding lathe for turning iron and brass, which proved valuable to the U.S. government in constructing machines for its armories. He produced much of the manufacturing machinery used by Samuel Slater, and apparently built the first American steamboat 16 years before Robert Fulton.

Wilkinson, James (1757–1825) American army officer and double agent. Born in Calvert Co., Md., he served in the American Revolution under Horatio Gates and was involved in the Thomas Conway cabal. He settled in Kentucky in 1784 and schemed to ally the Kentucky region with Spain, while in fact working against Spain. He served as governor of part of the Louisiana territory 1805–6. He allegedly planned to conquer the Mexican provinces of Spain and conspired with Aaron Burr to establish an independent government; when he betrayed Burr's plan, he was investigated but cleared. In the War of 1812 he commanded U.S. forces on the Canadian border, but his campaign against Montreal failed.

James Wilkinson, portrait by J.W. Jarvis; in the Filson Club Collection, Louisville, Ky.

BY COURTESY OF THE FILSON CLUB, LOUISVILLE, KY.

Wilkinson, John (1728–1808) British industrialist. Known as "the great Staffordshire ironmaster," he found many new applications for iron, developed a boring machine whose precision enabled James Watt to perfect his steam engine, and used Watt's first steam engine to drive a huge air pump in his factory for the large-scale manufacture of wrought iron.

will In law, a formal declaration, usually in the form of an executed document, of a person's wishes regarding the disposal of his or her property after death. It is valid if it meets the formalities of the law, which usually requires that it be witnessed. It may be considered invalid if, among other instances, the testator was mentally incapable of disposing of his or her property, if it imposes unreasonable or cruel demands as a condition of inheritance, or if the testator did not have clear title to the bequeathed assets. Any party who contests a will must bring the claim within a time specified by statute and must bear the burden of proof in demonstrating that the will is faulty. See also probate.

Willamette River River, northwestern Oregon. It flows north for 300 mi (485 km) into the Columbia River near Portland. Oregon's most populous cities are in its valley. The Fremont Bridge, a steel arch with a main span of 1,225 ft (366 m), crosses the river at Portland.

Willemstad \'vi-ləm-ˌstät\ City (pop., 1999 est.: 123,000), capital of the Netherlands Antilles, West Indies. Located on the southern coast of Curaçao, it was founded in 1634. It has many Dutch-Colonial buildings and the oldest (1732) synagogue in the western Hemisphere. It became a major oil-refining center after 1918; other industries include banking and tourism.

William I *known as* **William the Conqueror** (1028?–1087) Duke of Normandy (1035–87) and king of England (1066–87). Though illegitimate, he succeeded his father as duke of Normandy, subduing rebellions and becoming the mightiest feudal lord in France. In 1051 Edward the Confessor promised to make him heir to the English throne, but on Edward's death in 1066, Harold, earl of Wessex (Harold II), was accepted as king. Determined to assert his right to the throne, William sailed from Normandy with an invasion force, defeated Harold at the Battle of Hastings, and was crowned king. The Norman Conquest was thus completed, though English rebellions continued until 1071. To secure England's frontiers, he invaded Scotland (1072) and Wales (1081). In 1086 he ordered the survey summarized in the Domesday Book. He divided his lands among his sons, giving Normandy and Maine to Robert II and England to William II.

William I *German* **Wilhelm Friedrich Ludwig** (1797–1888) King of Prussia (1861–88) and German emperor (1871–88). Son of Frederick William III of Prussia, he fought in the war against Napoleon (1814) and thereafter devoted himself to the Prussian army and military affairs. He advocated the use of force against the rebels in 1848. Military governor of Rhineland province from 1849, he succeeded his brother on the Prussian throne in 1861. A supporter of military reform, he appointed Otto von Bismarck prime minister (1862). Though conservative, he cautiously supported Bismarck's policies in the Seven Weeks' War and the Franco-Prussian War. Proclaimed German emperor in 1871, he oversaw the continued rise of Germany as a European power.

William I *Dutch* **Willem** *known as* **William the Silent** (1533–1584) First stadtholder of the United Provinces of the Netherlands (1572–84). Son of William, count of Nassau-Dillenburg, he inherited the principality of Orange and other vast estates from his cousin in 1544. He was educated at the Habsburg imperial court in Brussels, then appointed by Philip II to the council of state (1555). He helped negotiate the Treaty of Cateau-Cambrésis, earning his byname for keeping silent about secret policy decisions, and was named stadtholder (governor) in Holland, Zeeland, and Utrecht in 1559. Increasingly opposed to Philip's strict ordinances against Protestants, he led a revolt in 1568 that proved unsuccessful, but in 1572 he succeeded in uniting the northern provinces. He was proclaimed their stadtholder, and his position was solidified by the Pacification of Ghent (1576). He sought help from France in the revolt against Spain, and in 1579 he was outlawed by Philip. A reward was offered for his assassination, and in 1584 he was shot by a fanatical Catholic.

William I *Dutch* **Willem Frederik** (1772–1843) King of the Netherlands and grand duke of Luxembourg (1815–40). Son of William V, prince of Orange, he married in 1791 and emigrated with his family to England after the French invasion of the Dutch Republic (1795). He sided with Prussia against Napoleon and lived in exile at the Prussian court until 1812. After the Dutch revolt against French rule, he became sovereign prince of the Dutch Republic (1813) and king of the United Netherlands (1815), which included Belgium, Liège, and Luxembourg. He led an economic recovery program that sparked a commercial revival, but his autocratic methods and imposition of Dutch as the official language provoked a revolt by Belgium (1830) that led to its independence. In 1840 he abdicated in favor of his son, William II.

William I *known as* **William the Lion** (1143–1214) King of Scotland (1165–1214). He succeeded his father as earl of Northumberland (1152) but was forced to relinquish his earldom to England's HENRY II in 1157. He succeeded his brother, Malcolm IV, as king of Scotland and in 1173 joined a revolt of Henry's sons in an attempt to regain Northumberland. Captured in 1174, he was released after submitting to Henry's overlordship. He bought his release from subjection in 1189. He continued to agitate for the restoration of Northumberland but was forced to renounce his claim by King JOHN in 1209. William created many of the major burghs of modern Scotland.

William II *or* **William Rufus** (1056?–1100) King of England (1087–1100) and de facto duke of Normandy (1096–1100). He inherited England from his father, WILLIAM I, and quelled a rebellion by barons (1088) loyal to his brother ROBERT II. A tyrannical ruler, he brutally punished the leaders of a second revolt (1095). He forced St. ANSELM, archbishop of Canterbury, to leave England and seized his lands (1097). He reduced the Scottish kings to vassals (1093), subjugated Wales (1097), and waged war on Normandy (1089–96), gaining control when Robert mortgaged the duchy. His death in a hunting accident may have been an assassination ordered by his brother Henry (later HENRY I).

William II *German* **Friedrich Wilhelm Viktor Albert** *known as* **Kaiser Wilhelm** (1859–1941) German emperor (kaiser) and king of Prussia (1888–1918). Son of the future Frederick III and grandson of Britain's Queen VICTORIA, William succeeded his father to the throne in 1888. Two years later, he forced the resignation of OTTO VON BISMARCK. He was characterized by his frequently militaristic manner and by his vacillating policies that undermined those of his chancellors, including LEO VON CAPRIVI and BERNHARD, PRINCE VON BÜLOW. From 1897 he encouraged Adm. ALFRED VON TIRPITZ to strengthen the German fleet and challenged France's position in Morocco (see MOROCCAN CRISES). He sided with Austria-Hungary in the crisis with Serbia (1914), and in World War I he encouraged the grandiose war aims of the generals and politicians. After Germany's defeat, he fled to the Netherlands, ending the monarchy in Germany, and lived in exile until his death.

William II *Italian* **Guglielmo** *known as* **William the Good** (1154–1189) Last Norman king of Sicily (1166–89). His mother served as regent until 1171, after which he ruled alone, winning a reputation for clemency and justice. His friendship with MANUEL I COMNENUS ended when the Byzantine emperor thwarted William's proposed marriage to his daughter. Turning against the Byzantines, William allied with FREDERICK I BARBAROSSA. He agreed to his aunt's marriage to Frederick's son Henry (later HENRY VI), giving Henry a claim to Sicily. He attacked the Byzantines (1185) with early success but was defeated within sight of Constantinople.

William II *Dutch* **Willem** (1626–1650) Prince of Orange, count of Nassau, and stadtholder of the Netherlands (1647–50). The son of FREDERICK HENRY, prince of Orange, he succeeded to his father's offices in 1647, which included the stadtholdership of all the provinces of the Netherlands except Friesland. Despite the treaty with Spain in 1648 that recognized the independence of the United Provinces, he planned to conquer part of the Spanish Netherlands (modern Belgium). He imprisoned members of the assembly of Holland who opposed his war policy, but died of smallpox before his influence could be tested.

William II *Dutch* **Willem Frederik George Lodewijk** (1792–1849) King of the Netherlands and grand duke of Luxembourg (1840–49). Son of WILLIAM I, he lived in exile with his family in England from 1795. He commanded Dutch troops in the Battle of WATERLOO (1815). Sent by his father to Belgium in 1830 to appease the rebels, he failed to stop the independence movement. In 1840 he became king of the Netherlands on his father's abdication. As king, he helped stabilize the economy. In 1848 he oversaw passage of a new liberal constitution that expanded the authority of the ministers and assembly, established direct elections, and secured basic civil liberties.

William III *Dutch* **Willem Hendrik** (1650–1702) Stadtholder of the United Provinces of the Netherlands (1672–1702) and king of England (1689–1702). Son of WILLIAM II, Prince of Orange, and Mary, daughter of CHARLES I of England, he was born in The Hague soon after his father's death. The Act of Seclusion (1654) that barred the House of Orange from power in the United Provinces was rescinded in 1660, and William was appointed captain-general and named stadtholder by popular acclaim in 1672. He successfully defended his country against CHARLES II of England and LOUIS XIV of France. In 1677 he married Mary (later Queen MARY II), daughter of the English duke of York (later JAMES II). In 1688 William was invited by James's opponents to intervene against the Catholic ruler, and he landed with a Dutch army in Devon, England. He and Mary were proclaimed joint rulers of England in 1689; he ruled alone after Mary's death in 1694. He directed the European opposition to Louis XIV, which led to the War of the GRAND ALLIANCE. In Britain he secured religious toleration and strengthened Parliament, granting independence to the judiciary in the Act of SETTLEMENT.

William III *Dutch* **Willem Alexander Paul Frederik Lodewijk** (1817–1890) King of the Netherlands and grand duke of Luxembourg (1849–90). Son of WILLIAM II, he succeeded to the throne on his father's death in 1849. Opposed to the liberal constitution of 1848, he adopted an anti-Catholic posture and in the years 1862–68 was able to rule through the cabinet. He tried to sell his sovereignty over Luxembourg to France (1867), but yielded to Prussia's demand that the area be independent. Following this crisis, his influence over parliament declined. On his death, he was succeeded by his daughter, WILHELMINA.

William IV (1765–1837) King of Great Britain and Ireland and of Hanover (1830–37). The son of GEORGE III, he entered the royal navy at 13, fought in the American Revolution, and served in the West Indies, leaving the navy as a rear admiral in 1790 (he was later called "the Sailor King"). He angered his father by his numerous love affairs and fathered 10 illegitimate children by the actress Dorothea Jordan (1761–1816). In 1830 he succeeded his brother GEORGE IV as king. Opposed to parliamentary reform, William delayed consideration of the REFORM BILL OF 1832, but his prime minister, Earl GREY, persuaded him to promise to create enough peers in the House of Lords to carry it, forcing its passage. On William's death, the British crown passed to his niece, VICTORIA, and the Hanoverian crown to his brother Ernest Augustus, duke of Cumberland (1771–1851).

William and Mary, College of State-supported college in Williamsburg, Va. The second-oldest institution of higher education in the U.S. (after HARVARD UNIV.), it was chartered in 1693 by King WILLIAM III and Queen MARY II. Its alumni include THOMAS JEFFERSON, JOHN MARSHALL, JAMES MONROE, JOHN TYLER, and Gen. WINFIELD SCOTT. GEORGE WASHINGTON was the college's first American chancellor, from 1788 to 1799. The honor society Phi Beta Kappa was organized as a social FRATERNITY there in 1776. The modern college has a faculty of arts and sciences and schools of business administration, education, law, and marine science. Enrollment is about 8,000.

William of Auvergne \ō-'vernʸ, ō-'vərn\ *French* **Guillaume d'Auvergne** (c. 1180–1249) French philosopher and theologian. Named bishop of Paris in 1228, William was a reformer who defended the rising mendicant orders against attacks by the secular clergy. After the church condemned the works of ARISTOTLE, he became one of the first Western scholars to attempt to incorporate into Christianity whatever in Aristotle's thought was compatible with it. He was influenced by AVICENNA and by the NEOPLATONISM of St. AUGUSTINE. His principal work, written 1223–40, is *Magisterium divinale* ("The Divine Teaching").

William of Auxerre \ō-'ser\ *French* **Guillaume d'Auxerre** (1150?–1231) French philosopher and theologian. After a long career at the University of Paris, he was appointed in 1231 by Pope GREGORY IX to a council to censor the works of ARISTOTLE (which in 1210 had been deemed corruptive of Christianity) included in the university's curriculum. Seeing no reason to avoid the rational analysis of Christian revelation, he was on the verge of reorganizing the curriculum when he died. In his principal work, usually called the *Summa aurea* (written 1215–20), he treated such matters as God's triune nature, the problem of human choice, and the nature of virtue.

William of Ockham See William of OCKHAM

William Rufus See WILLIAM II (ENGLAND)

William Tell See William TELL

William the Conqueror See WILLIAM I (ENGLAND)

William the Good See WILLIAM II (SICILY)

William the Silent See WILLIAM I (NETHERLANDS)

Williams, Daniel Hale (1858–1931) U.S. surgeon. Born in Hollidaysburg, Pa., he graduated from Chicago Medical College. In 1891 he founded Provident Hospital in Chicago, the first interracial hospital in the U.S., to provide training for black interns and nurses. There in 1893 he performed the first successful heart surgery; the patient lived at least 20 years after Williams opened the thoracic cavity, sutured a wound of the pericardium (the sac around the heart), and closed the chest. In 1913 he became the only black charter member of the American College of Surgeons.

Williams, (George) Emlyn (1905–1987) Welsh actor and playwright. He made his acting debut in 1927 and won acclaim in London and New York for his performance in his own play, the macabre *Night Must Fall* (1935; film, 1964). His most popular play was the autobiographical *The Corn Is Green* (1938; film, 1945), the story of a boy and his teacher in a Welsh mining town. Also a film actor, he was renowned for his public readings from CHARLES DICKENS, SAKI, and DYLAN THOMAS.

Williams, Eric (Eustace) (1911–1981) First and longtime prime minister of independent Trinidad and Tobago (1962–81). He received a doctorate from Oxford University and served on the faculty of Howard University in the U.S. before founding the People's National Movement (PNM) in 1956 and taking his nation into the Federation of the West Indies in 1958, only to withdraw in favor of independence in 1962. He stressed social services and education and stimulated development by cautiously attracting foreign investment. Oil reserves helped boost the nation's income and Williams remained popular until 1970, when an economic downturn led to unsuccessful revolts. He served as prime minister until his death.

Williams, Hank *orig.* **Hiram King** (1923–1953) U.S. singer and guitarist. Born into poverty in Georgiana, Ala., Williams began playing guitar at 8, made his radio debut at 13, and formed his first band, Hank Williams and his Drifting Cowboys, at 14. With the help of FRED ROSE, his "Lovesick Blues" became a smash hit in 1949, and he joined the GRAND OLE OPRY that year after an extraordinary debut appearance. Among his best-selling recordings were "I'm So Lonesome I Could Cry," "Jambalaya," "Your Cheatin' Heart," and "Hey, Good Lookin'." He wrote almost all the songs he recorded. His death from heart failure at 29 may have resulted from drug and alcohol abuse. He remains perhaps the most revered figure in the history of COUNTRY MUSIC. His son Hank Williams, Jr. (born 1949) has had an exceptional recording career, and his grandson Hank Williams III (born 1972) is also active.

Williams, Jody (born 1950) American activist who in 1992 helped found the International Campaign to Ban Landmines (ICBL). In 1997 she and the campaign were named corecipients of the Nobel Prize for Peace. She lectured widely on the dangers of land mines, publicizing the presence of about tens of millions of unexploded land mines in more than 70 countries. In December 1997 the Mine Ban Treaty was signed by more than 100 countries in Ottawa, Ont., Can., and by 2002 some 125 countries had ratified the treaty, but not the major mine-producing ones, such as the United States, Russia, and China. Williams was coauthor, with Shawn Roberts, of *After the Guns Fall Silent: The Enduring Legacy of Landmines* (1995).

Williams, Joe *orig.* **Joseph Goreed** (1918–1999) U.S. singer, one of the most popular interpreters of ballads and BLUES in jazz. Born in Georgia, Williams worked with COLEMAN HAWKINS and LIONEL HAMPTON before joining COUNT BASIE's band in 1954. The success of "Every Day I Have the Blues" established Williams as a sophisticated blues singer with a powerful bass-baritone voice. After leaving the Basie band in 1961 Williams led small ensembles singing popular songs and blues.

Williams, John (Towner) (born 1932) U.S. composer and conductor. Born in Queens, N.Y., Williams studied music at UCLA and Juilliard. He began his career as a jazz pianist, but began to compose for TV and film in the 1960s. He has scored over 75 films, including *Jaws* (1975), the *Star Wars* trilogy, *Close Encounters of the Third Kind* (1977), *E.T.* (1982), *Schindler's List* (1993), and *Harry Potter and the Sorcerer's Stone* (2001) and has won five Academy Awards. He has also written many concert works. From 1980 to 1993 he was conductor of the Boston Pops.

Williams, Mary Lou (1910–1981) U.S. pianist, composer, arranger, and bandleader. Born in Atlanta, Williams wrote arrangements for many swing bands, including Andy Kirk and DUKE ELLINGTON, beginning in 1929. Her *Zodiac Suite* was performed by the New York Philharmonic in 1946. A pianist with strong roots in the BLUES and early jazz, Williams embraced the innovations of BEBOP and later free jazz, performing with musicians as diverse as DIZZY GILLESPIE and Cecil Taylor. Her *Mary Lou's Mass* was choreographed by ALVIN AILEY.

Williams, Ralph Vaughan See Ralph VAUGHAN WILLIAMS

Williams, Robin (born 1952) U.S. film actor and comedian. Born in Chicago, he worked as a stand-up comedian in West Coast clubs, then won favorable notice as an extraterrestrial in the television series *Mork and Mindy* (1978–82). A nervous, creative comic with a gift for rapid-fire improvisation, he has appeared in films from 1980, playing comic and serious roles in such movies as *Good Morning Vietnam* (1987), *Dead Poets Society* (1989), *The Fisher King* (1991), *Mrs. Doubtfire* (1993), and *Good Will Hunting* (1997, Academy Award).

Williams, Roger (1603?–1683) British-American clergyman and founder of Rhode Island. He arrived in Boston in 1631 and became pastor of the separatist Plymouth colony (1632–33). Banned from the MASSACHUSETTS BAY COLONY for his beliefs, including support for religious toleration and the rights of Indians and opposition to civil authority, he founded the colony of Rhode Island and the town of Providence (1636) on land purchased from the Narragansett Indians. The colony established a democratic government and separation of church and state, and became a haven for Quakers and others seeking religious liberty. He obtained a charter for the colony (1643) and served as its first president, maintaining friendly relations with the Indians and acting as peacemaker for nearby colonies.

Williams, Ted *orig.* **Theodore Samuel** (1918–2002) U.S. baseball player, one of the great hitters of all time. Born in San Diego, he began playing professionally at 17. He became an outfielder with the Boston Red Sox in 1939, and remained with the team until his retirement in 1960. Tall and thin, he was dubbed "the Splendid Splinter," but was also known more simply as "the Kid." A left-handed hitter, he compiled a lifetime batting average of .344, the fifth-highest on record. He batted .406 in 1941, becoming the last .400 hitter of the century. His career slugging percentage (.634) is second only to that of BABE RUTH. He is the only player besides ROGERS HORNSBY to have twice won the batting triple crown (best average, most home runs, and most runs batted in). Despite losing five years of his career to service as a flyer in World War II and the Korean War, he hit a total of 521 home runs (tenth-highest in history), capping his career with a home run in his final at-bat. After retiring as a player he managed the Washington Senators (1969–72).

Williams, Tennessee *orig.* **Thomas Lanier** (1911–1983) U.S. playwright. The son of a traveling salesman and a clergyman's daughter, he was born in Columbus, Miss., and lived in St. Louis from age 12. He attended several colleges, graduating from the University of Iowa. He won recognition by the GROUP THEATRE for his one-act plays *American Blues* (1939). Wider success came with *The Glass Menagerie* (1944) and mounted with *Summer and Smoke* (1948), *A Streetcar Named Desire* (1947, Pulitzer Prize; film, 1951), *Camino Real* (1953), and *Cat on a Hot Tin Roof* (1955, Pulitzer Prize; film, 1958). His plays, which also included *Suddenly Last Summer* (1958; film, 1959), *Sweet Bird of Youth* (1959; film, 1962), and *The Night of the Iguana* (1961; film, 1964), described a world of repressed sexuality and violence thinly veiled by gentility. He also wrote the novel *The Roman Spring of Mrs. Stone* (1950; film, 1961) and the screenplays for *The Rose Tattoo* (1955, adapted from his 1951 play) and *Baby Doll* (1956). A chronicler of fragile illusions, he is regarded as one of the greatest American playwrights.

Williams, Venus and Serena (born 1980 and 1981, respectively) U.S. tennis players. The sisters were introduced to the sport by their father, who early on recognized their talent. Venus turned professional in 1994, and Serena followed suit a year later. Possessing powerful groundstrokes and superb athleticism, the sisters were soon dominating women's professional tennis. Serena won the U.S. Open in 1999. Venus won Wimbledon and the U.S. Open in 2000 and 2001. In 2002 Serena won the French and U.S. opens and Wimbledon, defeating Venus in the finals of each tournament.

Williams, William Carlos (1883–1963) U.S. poet. Trained as a pediatrician, Williams spent a lifetime writing poetry and practicing medicine in his hometown of Rutherford, N.J. He is noted for making the ordinary appear extraordinary through clear and discrete imagery and a powerful evocation of the world of common objects, as in the fresh impressions of the sensuous world expressed in "The Red Wheelbarrow," from *Spring and All* (1923). *Paterson* (1946–58), a five-part long poem, evokes a complex vision of modern American life. His other poetry includes *Pictures from Brueghel* (1962, Pulitzer Prize). His numerous prose works include essays, a trilogy of novels, short stories, drama, and autobiography.

Williams College Private liberal-arts college in Williamstown, Mass. Established in 1793 by the Congregational Church, it is now nondenominational. Consistently rated as one of the best colleges in the U.S., it offers bachelor's and master's degree programs in fine and applied arts and sciences. Campus facilities include notable collections of American, contemporary, and South Asian art and materials relating to U.S. history. Enrollment is about 2,200.

William's War, King See KING WILLIAM'S WAR

Williamsburg City (pop., 1995 est.: 13,000), southeastern Virginia. Located on a tidewater peninsula between the JAMES and York rivers, it was settled in 1633 as Middle Plantation and served as a refuge from Indian attacks. The College of WILLIAM AND MARY was founded there in 1693. After the burning of nearby JAMESTOWN in 1699, it became the capital of Virginia until 1780, when the capital was moved to RICHMOND. During the AMERICAN CIVIL WAR, Confederate forces were defeated at the Battle of Williamsburg in 1862. Colonial Williamsburg, an extensive restoration of several hundred colonial buildings, was begun in 1926 and became part of the COLONIAL NATIONAL HISTORICAL PARK in 1936.

Willkie, Wendell L(ewis) (1892–1944) U.S. politician. Born in Elwood, Ind., he moved to New York in 1929 as an attorney for the Commonwealth and Southern Corp., of which he was president 1933–40. He led the opposition of utilities companies to competition from the federally funded Tennessee Valley Authority. His criticism of Pres. FRANKLIN ROOSEVELT led to his dark-horse victory at the 1940 Republican presidential convention. After a vigorous campaign, he won only 10 states but received over 22 million popular votes, the largest number received by a Republican to that time. After a worldwide tour, he wrote *One World* (1943), a best-selling plea for postwar international cooperation.

willow Any shrub or tree of the genus *Salix*, family Salicaceae, native mostly to northern temperate regions, and common in lowland and marshy areas. Willows are valued as ornamentals and for their shade, erosion control, and timber. Certain species yield salicin, the source of SALICYLIC ACID used in pain relievers. All species have alternate, usually narrow leaves, catkins, and seeds with long, silky hairs. Pussy willows, the male form of several shrubby species, have woolly catkins that form before the leaves appear and are considered one of the first signs of spring. Weeping willows have long drooping branches and leaves. Several species grow as small matted woody plants on the tundra.

Weeping willow (*Salix babylonica*).
A TO Z BOTANICAL COLLECTION

willow herb Any of about 200 plants that make up the genus *Epilobium,* of the EVENING-PRIMROSE family, especially FIREWEED (also called great willow herb). The young parts of some species can be cooked and eaten as potherbs. The plants are sometimes cultivated but must be carefully confined. The hairy willow herb, or codling-and-cream *(E. hirsutum),* is similar to fireweed but has hairy leaves and stalks and notched flower petals; it is found in waste places in eastern North America. Rock fringe *(E. obcordatum)* is a low-growing form from the western U.S.

Wills, Bob *orig.* **James Robert** (1905–1975) U.S. COUNTRY-MUSIC fiddler, singer, and songwriter. Born in Kosse, Texas, Wills learned fiddle from his father. In Tulsa in 1934 he formed the Texas Playboys; their radio performances made him a star in the Southwest, and in 1942 the group moved to California, performing in dance halls and films. They pioneered the "western swing" genre, which blended traditional hoedown fiddling with big-band SWING and BLUES. Wills's best-known compositions include "San Antonio Rose" and "Panhandle Rag.".

Wills, Helen (Newington) *or* **Helen Wills Moody** *in full* **Helen Newington Wills Moody Roark** (1905–1998) U.S. tennis player. Born in Centerville, Cal., she won the first of seven U.S. singles titles in 1923. She took the gold medal in both singles and doubles at the 1924 Olympic Games. So overpowering was her game that from 1927 to 1932 she won every set she played in U.S. singles play. She took the Wimbledon title eight times (1927–30, 1932, 1933, 1935, 1938), a record only broken in 1990 by MARTINA NAVRATILOVA.

Wilmington City (pop., 1996 est.: 72,000), northern Delaware. Located at the junction of the DELAWARE and Christina rivers, it is the state's largest city and its industrial, financial, and commercial center and main port. The oldest permanent settlement in the Delaware Valley, it was settled by Swedes in 1638. Called Fort Christina, it was captured by PETER STUYVESANT's Dutch forces in 1655; they were ousted by the English in 1664. A prosperous port after the Quakers moved there in the 1730s, it was renamed Wilmington in 1739. During the AMERICAN REVOLUTION, the Battle of the BRANDYWINE was fought nearby. In 1802 E. I. du Pont de Nemours established a gunpowder mill there (see DU PONT CO.).

Wilmot Proviso \prə-ˈvī-ˌzō\ (1846) Proposal in the U.S. Congress to prohibit the extension of slavery to the territories. Offered by Rep. David Wilmot (1814–1868) as an amendment to a bill that purchased territory from Mexico, it prohibited slavery in the new territory. The proviso provoked a national debate that reflected the growing sectional discord between North and South. Though never approved by both houses of Congress, it became a basic tenet of the REPUBLICAN PARTY on its founding.

Wilson, Alexander (1766–1813) Scottish-U.S. ornithologist. In Scotland he wrote poetry while working as a weaver and peddler; in 1792 his satirical works led to a fine and imprisonment. Impoverished, he emigrated in 1794 to the U.S., where he became a teacher. Influenced by WILLIAM BARTRAM, he decided c. 1804 to write on North American birds, and began studying art and ornithology in his leisure time. His pioneering work *American Ornithology* (9 vols., 1808–14) established him as a founder of the field. After publication of its first volume, he spent much of his time selling subscriptions for the expensive work and collecting specimens for the remaining volumes.

Wilson, August (born 1945) U.S. playwright. Born in Pittsburgh, he was largely self-educated. A participant in the BLACK AESTHETIC MOVEMENT, he cofounded and directed Pittsburgh's Black Horizons Theater (1968), published poetry in black journals, and produced several plays, including *Jitney* (1982), before his *Ma Rainey's Black Bottom* opened on Broadway in 1984. Inspired by the colloquial language, music, folklore, and storytelling tradition of black Americans, he continued his cycle of plays, each set in a different decade of the 20th century, with *Fences* (1986, Pulitzer Prize), *Joe Turner's Come and Gone* (1988), *The Piano Lesson* (1990, Pulitzer Prize), *Two Trains Running* (1992), and *Seven Guitars* (1996).

Wilson, C(harles) T(homson) R(ees) (1869–1959) Scottish physicist. His invention of the Wilson cloud chamber, a device that became widely used in the study of radioactivity, X rays, cosmic rays, and other particle phenomena, also led to the later development of the BUBBLE CHAMBER. He shared the 1927 Nobel Prize for Physics with ARTHUR COMPTON.

Wilson, Colin (Henry) (born 1931) British writer. Born into a working-class family, he initially thought of a career in science, then gravitated toward writing. At 24 he published *The Outsider* (1957), a study of 20th-century alienation that had a phenomenal success. His next books were dismissed as unoriginal or superficial, but his first two novels, *Ritual in the Dark* (1960) and *Adrift in Soho* (1961), helped repair his reputation. Many of his more than 70 books deal with the psychology of crime, the occult, human sexuality, and his own existential philosophy. *Alien Dawn* (1998) discusses the UFO phenomenon.

Wilson, Edmund (1895–1972) U.S. critic and essayist. Born in Red Bank, N.J., he attended Princeton University and initially worked as a reporter and magazine editor.

Edmund Wilson.
EB INC.

Much of his writing, in which he probed diverse subjects with scholarship and common sense in clear and precise prose, appeared in the *New Republic* and the *New Yorker*. Among his influential critical works are *Axel's Castle* (1931), a survey of the Symbolist poets; *To the Finland Station* (1940), a study of the thinkers who set the stage for the Russian Revolution; and *Patriotic Gore* (1962), analyzing American Civil War literature. His other writings include plays, poetry, the short-story collection *Memoirs of Hecate County* (1946), and five volumes of posthumously published journals. He was widely regarded as the leading critic of his time.

Wilson, Edmund B(eecher) (1856–1939) U.S. cell biologist. Born in Geneva, Ill., he joined the Columbia University faculty in 1891, where he became established as an outstanding pioneer in work on cell lineage (tracing the formation of different kinds of tissues from individual cells). His interests later extended to internal cellular organization and the problem of sex determination, leading to a series of papers (1905) on the role of chromosomes. Recognizing the importance of GREGOR MENDEL's findings, he realized that the role of chromosomes went far beyond the determination of sex, and envisioned their function as important components in heredity as a whole, ideas that were a powerful force in shaping future genetic research.

Wilson, Edward O(sborne) (born 1929) U.S. biologist. Born in Birmingham, Ala., he received his PhD from Harvard Univ., where he taught from 1956. Recognized as the world's leading authority on ants, he discovered their use of pheromone for communication. His *The Insect Societies* (1971) was the definitive treatment of the subject. In 1975 he published *Sociobiology*, a highly controversial and influential study of the genetic basis of social behavior in which he claimed that even a characteristic such as unselfish generosity may be genetically based and may have evolved through natural selection, that preservation of the gene rather than the individual is the focus of evolutionary strategy, and that the essentially biological principles on which animal societies are based apply also to human social behavior. In *On Human Nature* (1978, Pulitzer Prize) he explored SOCIOBIOLOGY's implications in regard to human aggression, sexuality, and ethics. With Bert Hölldobler he wrote the major study *The Ants* (1991, Pulitzer Prize). In *The Diversity of Life* (1992) he traced how the world's species became diverse and examined the massive extinctions caused by 20th-century human activities.

Wilson, (James) Harold *later* **Baron Wilson (of Rievaulx)** (1916–1995) British politician and prime minister (1964–70, 1974–76). While at Oxford Univ., he collaborated with WILLIAM H. BEVERIDGE on work that led to the latter's 1942 report. In World War II he was drafted into the civil service and produced a study of the mining industry. His book *New Deal for Coal* (1945) was the basis for the Labour Party's plan to nationalize the coal mines. He was elected to the House of Commons in 1945 and appointed president of the Board of Trade (1947–51). Elected leader of the Labour Party in 1963, he became prime minister in 1964. He widened the party's voting majority in 1966 but faced economic problems after the devaluation of the pound in 1967. In his second term, he confirmed Britain's membership in the EUROPEAN ECONOMIC COMMUNITY (1975). He resigned unexpectedly in 1976 and was created a life peer in 1983.

Wilson, Harriet E. *orig.* **Harriet Adams** (1828?–1863?) U.S. writer, probably the first African-American to publish a novel in English in the U.S. Little is known of her history until 1850. She may have been an indentured servant in Milford, N.H., before becoming a domestic in Massachusetts. In 1851 she married a fugitive slave who ran off to sea before the birth of their son. Her one book, written to make money to reclaim her son from foster care, is *Our Nig* (1859), a largely autobiographical novel that treats racism in the pre–Civil War North.

Wilson, J(ohn) Tuzo (1908–1993) Canadian geologist and geophysicist. Born in Ottawa, he was the first graduate of a Canadian university in the field of geophysical studies (1930). After World War II he became a professor of geophysics at the University of Toronto. He established global patterns of faulting and the structure of the continents, and in the 1960s he became the world's leading spokesman for the theory of CONTINENTAL DRIFT. His studies also were important for the SEAFLOOR SPREADING hypothesis and the theory of convection currents within the earth. A range of mountains in Antarctica is named for him.

Wilson, James (1742–1798) Scottish-American lawyer and politician. He arrived in Philadelphia in 1765, where he practiced law after studies with JOHN DICKINSON. In 1774 he published a widely read treatise proposing a commonwealth of British colonies. He was a member of the Committee of Correspondence, a delegate to the Continental Congress (1775–77), and a signer of the Declaration of Independence. He helped draft the U.S. Constitution and the Pennsylvania state constitution, delivering lectures that became landmarks in American jurisprudence. He served on the U.S. Supreme Court 1789–98.

Wilson, Lanford (Eugene) (born 1937) U.S. playwright. Born in Lebanon, Mo., he began writing plays in 1962 and became cofounder and director of the off-Broadway Circle Repertory Co. (1969–95). His plays include *Lemon Sky* (1970), the long-running hit *The Hot l Baltimore* (1973), *The Mound Builders* (1975), *The 5th of July* (1978), *Talley's Folly* (1979, Pulitzer Prize), *Talley and Son* (1985), *Burn This* (1987), *Redwood Curtain* (1993), and *By the Sea* (1996).

Wilson, Richard (1713/14–1782) Welsh landscape painter. He worked as a portraitist for many years, but after a lengthy stay in Italy (1750–57) he worked almost exclusively in landscape, except for numerous drawings of Roman sites and buildings that he used in composing Italianate landscapes. A set of drawings made for Lord Dartmouth (dated 1754) show that he tempered his delicate observation of light and distance with the discipline of such 17th-cent classicists as NICOLAS POUSSIN. The landscapes he produced after his return to Britain influenced J.M.W. TURNER and JOHN CONSTABLE.

Wilson, Robert W(oodrow) (born 1936) U.S. radio astronomer. Born in Houston, he joined Bell Labs in 1963 and headed its Radio Physics Research Department 1976–94. With his colleague ARNO PENZIAS, he detected the COSMIC BACKGROUND RADIATION, a discovery for which the two men shared a 1978 Nobel Prize with Pyotr Kapitsa (1894–1984).

Wilson, Teddy *orig.* **Theodore Shaw** (1912–1986) U.S. pianist and bandleader, the principal piano stylist in the SWING era. Born in Austin, Texas, he began recording as the leader of small groups in 1935. These recordings, often featuring BILLIE HOLIDAY, are classics of small-group swing. Wilson joined BENNY GOODMAN's trio in 1936. After 1940 he worked primarily as a leader of small ensembles or as a solo pianist, showcasing his tasteful and refined amalgam of the styles of FATS WALLER, EARL HINES, and ART TATUM.

Wilson, William Julius (born 1935) U.S. sociologist. Born in Derry Twp., Pa., he spent 24 years on the University of Chicago faculty before moving to Harvard University in 1996. He has contended that entrenched black poverty was due neither to RACISM nor to welfare dependency, but rather primarily to changes in the global economy that pulled low-skilled manufacturing jobs out of the inner city, and that only "race-neutral" programs such as universal health care and government-financed jobs could alleviate the problems of the underclass.

Wilson, (Thomas) Woodrow (1856–1924) 28th president of the U.S. (1913–21). Born in Staunton, Va., he earned a law degree and later received his doctorate from Johns Hopkins University. He taught political science at Princeton University. 1890–1902. As its president (1902–10), he introduced various reforms. With the support of progressives, he was elected governor of New Jersey. His reform measures attracted national attention, and he became the Democratic presidential nominee in 1912. His campaign emphasized the progressive measures of his New Freedom policy, and he defeated THEODORE ROOSEVELT and WILLIAM H. TAFT to win the presidency. As president, he approved legislation that lowered tariffs, created the FEDERAL RESERVE SYSTEM, established the FEDERAL TRADE COMMISSION, and strengthened labor unions. In foreign affairs he promoted self-government for the Philippines and sought to contain the Mexican civil war. From 1914 he maintained U.S. neutrality in WORLD WAR I, offering to mediate a settlement and initiate peace negotiations. After the sinking of the *LUSITANIA* (1915) and other unarmed ships, he obtained a pledge from Germany to stop its submarine campaign. Campaigning on the theme that he had "kept us out of war," he was narrowly reelected in 1916, defeating CHARLES EVANS HUGHES. Germany's renewed submarine attacks on unarmed passenger ships caused Wilson to ask for a declaration of war in April 1917. In a continuing effort to negotiate a peace agreement, he presented the FOURTEEN POINTS (1918). He led the U.S. delegation to the PARIS PEACE CONFERENCE, where he attempted to stand on his original principles but was forced to compromise by the demands of various countries. The Treaty of VERSAILLES faced opposition in the Senate from the Republican majority led by HENRY C. LODGE. In search of popular support for the treaty and its LEAGUE OF NATIONS, Wilson began a cross-country speaking tour, but he collapsed and returned to Washington, D.C. (September 1919), where a stroke left him partially paralyzed. He rejected any attempts to compromise his version of the League of Nations and urged his Senate followers to vote against ratification of the treaty, which was defeated in 1920. He was awarded the 1919 Nobel Peace Prize.

Wilson's disease *or* **hepatolenticular degeneration** \'hi-ˌpat-ə-lən-ˌtik-yə-lər\ Recessive hereditary defect (see RECESSIVENESS) that impairs ability to metabolize copper, which accumulates in the basal ganglia (see GANGLION) of the brain (involved in control of movement), causing progressive degeneration; forms a brownish ring at the margin of the cornea of the eye; and is deposited in the liver, gradually leading to CIRRHOSIS. It usually appears in the teens or twenties. Symptoms include tremor, lack of coordination, and personality changes. Early diagnosis and treatment with a high-protein, low-copper diet and a substance to chelate copper can reverse the effects and prevent permanent brain and liver damage.

Wilson's Promontory Southernmost point of the Australian mainland, southern VICTORIA, Australia. The peninsula, 22 mi (35 km) long with a maximum width of 14 mi (23 km), projects into BASS STRAIT and is almost an island. Its highest point is Mount Latrobe (2,475 ft, or 754 m). Visited in 1798 by the English explorer George Bass, it was first called Furneaux Land; it was renamed for Thomas Wilson, an English merchant. In 1905 it was made a national park.

Wiltshire \'wilt-ˌshir\ County (pop., 1995 est.: 417,000), southern England. It is located in a watershed separating the basins of the BRISTOL CHANNEL, the ENGLISH CHANNEL, and the River THAMES; its administrative seat is TROWBRIDGE. Chalk uplands constitute much of the county, and in prehistoric times they were the most heavily populated parts of England; Wiltshire has many prehistoric monuments, including STONEHENGE and Iron Age hill forts. The town of Salisbury has long been an ecclesiastical center and is renowned for its cathedral. There is an industrial center at Swindon; otherwise, agriculture is the most important economic activity.

Wimbledon Municipal center in the Greater London borough of Merton, known as the site of the annual lawn-tennis All-England Championships. Held in late June and early July, the tournament is the oldest (founded 1877) and most prestigious in the world. It is one of four tournaments that make up the Grand Slam of tennis, and the only one still played on natural grass. Competition was opened to professionals in 1968.

Winchell, Walter *orig.* **Walter Winchel** (1897–1972) U.S. journalist and broadcaster. Born in New York, he entered vaudeville at 13 and eventually began contributing tidbits to the *Vaudeville News*. Later, as a full-time gossip columnist, he moved to the *New York Daily Mirror*, where his widely syndicated column appeared until 1963. He had a weekly radio program from 1932 until the early 1950s. A prolific phrase-maker, he was noted for his slangy Broadway idiom. His opinionated news reports brought him a massive audience and great influence from the 1930s through the 1950s.

Winchester City (pop., 1995 est.: 39,000), county seat of HAMPSHIRE, England. Initially founded by Celtic peoples, it became important as Venta Belgarum under Roman rule. It was the capital of WESSEX and a center of learning under ALFRED the Great; later it was the seat of the Danish king CANUTE's government. It remained important under the Norman kings until the emergence of LONDON as the sole capital of England late in the 12th century. It is known for its cathedral (11th–14th century) and for Winchester College, founded in 1382.

Winchester, Oliver (Fisher) (1810–1880) U.S. manufacturer of guns and ammunition. Born in Boston, he initially set up a factory to manufacture dress shirts, and his success enabled him to purchase the Volcanic Repeating Arms Co. (1857), which became the Winchester Repeating Arms Co. (1867). His chief gun designer, B. T. Henry, designed the lever-action Henry repeating rifle (patented 1860). Widely used in the American Civil War, it was the forerunner of a long line of Winchester guns, including the famous Model 73, a favorite weapon of the settlers in the U.S. West.

Winckelmann \'viŋ-kəl-ˌmän, *Engl* 'wiŋ-kəl-mən\, **Johann (Joachim)** (1717–1768) German archaeologist and art historian. The son of a cobbler, he studied theology and medicine before he discovered Greek art. His essay *Reflections on the Painting and Sculpture of the Greeks* (1755) became a manifesto of the Greek ideal in education and art and was soon translated into several languages. After converting to Catholicism he moved to Rome (1755) and held important posts in the Vatican. There he wrote *History of the Art of Antiquity* (1764), which inaugurated the study of art history as a discipline and of archaeology as a humane science. His writings reawakened the popular taste for classical art and were instrumental in generating the Neoclassical movement in the arts.

Winckelmann, oil painting by Anton Raphael Mengs, 1758; in the Metropolitan Museum of Art, New York City.

BY COURTESY OF THE METROPOLITAN MUSEUM OF ART, NEW YORK CITY, HARRIS BRISBANE DICK FUND, 1948

wind Movement of air relative to the surface of the earth. Wind is an important factor in determining and controlling climate and weather. It is also the generating force of most ocean and freshwater waves. Wind occurs because of horizontal and vertical differences in atmospheric pressure. The general pattern of winds over the earth is known as the general circulation, and specific winds are named for the direction from which they originate (e.g., a wind blowing from west to east is a westerly). Wind speeds are often classified according to the Beaufort scale.

Beaufort Scale

No.	Name	Wind speed, mph (kph)	Description
0	Calm	<1 (<1)	Calm; smoke rises vertically
1	Light air	1–3 (1–5)	Direction of wind shown by smoke but not by wind vanes
2	Light breeze	4–7 (6–11)	Wind felt on face; leaves rustle; wind vane moves
3	Gentle breeze	8–12 (12–19)	Leaves and small twigs in constant motion; wind extends light flag
4	Moderate breeze	13–18 (20–28)	Wind raises dust and loose paper; small branches move
5	Fresh breeze	19–24 (29–38)	Small-leaved trees begin to sway; crested wavelets form on inland waters
6	Strong breeze	25–31 (39–49)	Large branches move; overhead wires whistle; umbrellas difficult to control
7	Moderate gale or near gale	32–38 (50–61)	Whole trees sway; walking against wind is difficult
8	Fresh gale or gale	39–46 (62–74)	Twigs break off trees; moving cars veer
9	Strong gale	47–54 (75–88)	Slight structural damage occurs; shingles may blow away
10	Whole gale	55–63 (89–102)	Trees uprooted; or storm considerable structural damage occurs
11	Storm or violent storm	64–72 (103–117)	Widespread damage occurs
12	Hurricane	>72 (>117)	Widespread damage occurs

Wind Cave National Park National park, southwestern South Dakota. Established in 1903 to preserve limestone caverns and unspoiled prairie grassland in the BLACK HILLS, it covers an area of 28,292 acres (11,449 hectares). Its basic cave contains 83 mi (134 km) of explored passages and has beautiful rock formations called boxwork, formed by CALCITE deposition in unique patterns. The park is also a wildlife refuge.

wind chill Still-air temperature that would have the same cooling effect on exposed skin as a given combination of temperature and wind speed. As the wind speed increases, the wind chill equivalent temperature decreases; e.g., as shown in the chart, an air temperature of 30°F (–1.1°C) with a wind speed of 20 mph (32.2 kph) produces a wind chill of 17°F (–8°C). Wind chill is often included in weather reports to describe how cold it feels.

wind speed (mph) \ temperature (°F): calm	40	35	30	25	20	15	10	5	0	–5	–10	–15	–20	–25	–30	–35	–40	–45
5	36	31	25	19	13	7	1	–5	–11	–16	–22	–28	–34	–40	–46	–52	–57	–63
10	34	27	21	15	9	3	–4	–10	–16	–22	–28	–35	–41	–47	–53	–59	–66	–72
15	32	25	19	13	6	0	–7	–13	–19	–26	–32	–39	–45	–51	–58	–64	–71	–77
20	30	24	17	11	4	–2	–9	–15	–22	–29	–35	–42	–48	–55	–61	–68	–74	–81
25	29	23	16	9	3	–4	–11	–17	–24	–31	–37	–44	–51	–58	–64	–71	–78	–84
30	28	22	15	8	1	–5	–12	–19	–26	–33	–39	–46	–53	–60	–67	–73	–80	–87
35	28	21	14	7	0	–7	–14	–21	–27	–34	–41	–48	–55	–62	–69	–76	–82	–89
40	27	20	13	6	–1	–8	–15	–22	–29	–36	–43	–50	–57	–64	–71	–78	–84	–91
45	26	19	12	5	–2	–9	–16	–23	–30	–37	–44	–51	–58	–65	–72	–79	–86	–93
50	26	19	12	4	–3	–10	–17	–24	–31	–38	–45	–52	–60	–67	–74	–81	–88	–95
55	25	18	11	4	–3	–11	–18	–25	–32	–39	–46	–54	–61	–68	–75	–82	–89	–97
60	25	17	10	3	–4	–11	–19	–26	–33	–40	–48	–55	–62	–69	–76	–84	–91	–98

wind chill (°F) = $35.74 + 0.6215T - 35.75(V^{0.16}) + 0.4275T(V^{0.16})$ T = air temperature (°F)

frostbite times: 30 minutes; 10 minutes; 5 minutes V = wind speed (mph)

Source: U.S. National Weather Service; Meteorological Services of Canada

wind power Use of the energy in winds to produce power. Though wind is irregular and spread out, it contains tremendous amounts of energy. Sophisticated wind TURBINES have been developed to convert this energy to electric power. The use of wind-energy systems grew considerably in the 1980s and '90s. Germany today produces more wind energy than any other country. Some 15,000 wind turbines are now in operation in California. See also WINDMILL.

Wind River Range Mountain range, central ROCKY MTNS., western central Wyoming. It extends for 100 mi (160 km) northwest–southeast to the Sweetwater River and is part of the CONTINENTAL DIVIDE. It contains many peaks above 12,000 ft (3,658 m); the highest is Gannett Peak at 13,804 ft (4,207 m). The OREGON TRAIL ran through the historic South Pass (7,743 ft, or 2,360 m). Parts of Bridger and Shoshone national forests and Wind River Indian Reservation are in the range. The Wind River flows from the eastern side into the BIGHORN RIVER; the GREEN RIVER rises on its western slopes.

wind shear Rate of change of wind velocity with distance perpendicular to the wind direction. A very narrow zone of abrupt velocity change is known as a shear line. Wind shear is observed near the ground and in jet streams, where it may be associated with clear-air turbulence. Vertical wind shear is closely associated with the vertical flux of momentum, heat, and water vapor.

wind tunnel Device for producing a controlled stream of air to study the effects on objects such as aircraft moving through air or the effects of moving air on models of stationary objects such as buildings. Applications of wind-tunnel research range from testing of airframes (the structures of aircraft and spacecraft) to research on the BOUNDARY LAYER, TURBULENCE, DRAG, and LIFT. Measurements of air pressure and other characteristics at many points on the model yield information about how the total wind load is distributed. In addition to testing the effects of wind on aircraft and spacecraft, studies in wind tunnels have been used to solve design problems in automobiles, boats, trains, bridges, and buildings. See also AERODYNAMICS.

Windermere Lake, northwestern England. Located in the southeastern LAKE DISTRICT, it is the country's largest lake, 10.5 mi (17 km) long and 1 mi (1.6 km) wide; its area is 6 sq mi (16 sq km). It has a maximum depth of 219 ft (67 m). Part of the Lake District National Park, it is a popular tourist center.

Windhoek \'vint-ˌhu̇k\ Town (pop., 1997 est.: 169,000), capital of Namibia. Located in the central part of the country, the area was originally settled by African peoples. In 1890 the site of the present town was claimed for the German government. In 1915 South African forces occupied it and initiated their claim to the country, then known as South West Africa. When Namibia became independent in 1990, Windhoek became its capital. It is the country's main commercial and transportation center.

Windischgrätz \ˌvin-dish-'grets\, **Alfred, Fürst (Prince) zu** (1787–1862) Austrian field marshal. He entered the Habsburg imperial army as an officer (1804) and rose through the ranks to become military commander for Bohemia (1840). In the REVOLUTIONS OF 1848, he suppressed the Czech rebels in Prague and crushed the insurrection in Vienna, where he was noted for his harsh military rule. Appointed field marshal (1848), he occupied Budapest in 1849 and drove the Hungarian rebels beyond the Tisza River. He was recalled after disagreements with the Habsburg prime minister FELIX, FURST ZU SCHWARZENBERG and retired to Bohemia.

windmill Machine for harnessing the energy of the wind using sails mounted on a rotating shaft. The sails are mounted at an angle or are given a slight twist, so that the force of wind against them has two components, one of which, in the plane of the sails, causes rotation. Like WATERWHEELS, windmills were among the original prime movers that replaced human beings as a source of power. Their most important traditional use was for grinding grain, though in certain areas their use in land drainage and water pumping was equally important. Windmill use became increasingly widespread in Europe (particularly the Netherlands) from the 12th century to the early 19th century, but thereafter slowly declined. Interest in windmills for generating electric power revived in the 1970s. See also WIND POWER.

window Opening in the wall of a building for light and air, and sometimes to frame a view. Since early times, the openings have been filled with stone, wooden, or iron grilles, with panes of glass, or with other translucent material such as mica or, in the Far East, paper. A window in a vertically sliding frame is called a sash window: a single-hung sash has only one half that moves; in a double-hung sash, both parts slide. A casement window swings open on hinges attached to the upright side of the frame. Awning windows swing outward on hinges attached to the top of the frame; hopper windows swing inward on hinges attached to the bottom of the frame. Large, fixed (nonoperating) areas of glass are commonly called picture windows. A bay window (see ORIEL) is an exterior projection of a BAY of a building which also forms an interior recess, providing better light and view than would a window flush with the building line. See also DIOCLETIAN WINDOW, ROSE WINDOW, SHOJI.

Windows Family of software products developed by MICROSOFT CORP., mainly for PERSONAL COMPUTERS and workstations, that began as a GRAPHICAL USER INTERFACE and developed into an OPERATING SYSTEM. Version 1.0 (1985) provided a graphical user interface, MULTITASKING, and virtual MEMORY management; it ran on top of MS-DOS and was supported on Intel-based personal computers. Version 3.1 (1992) sold over 3 million copies in its first two months and helped establish Microsoft's dominance of the operating-system market for microcomputers. Windows 95 and Windows 98 (named for the years of their release) continued its success. Windows NT (1993), which can run on RISC-based computers as well as traditional Intel-based systems, is a high-end version of Windows intended for more powerful personal computers, workstations, and servers. Windows CE (1996) is an embedded operating system for PALM PCs and other handheld devices. Microsoft continues to release new versions of its operating system: Windows 2000 for corporate-oriented computers, Windows Me (2000) for consumer-oriented computers, and in 2001 a version for both environments, Windows XP. Today Windows runs on more than 90% of all personal computers.

windpipe See TRACHEA

Windsor City (pop., 1991: 191,000), southern Ontario. Located on the southern bank of the DETROIT RIVER, opposite DETROIT, Mich., it was settled by French farmers shortly after 1701, when a fort was established at Detroit. It was known first as "the Ferry" and later as Richmond, before it was renamed in 1836. With its strategic location opposite Detroit, it became an industrial center, an important railway terminus, and a busy port in GREAT LAKES shipping. Its manufactures include motor vehicles and parts, foods and beverages, and medicines. It is Canada's leading port of entry from the U.S.

Windsor, Duchess of *orig.* **Bessie Wallis Warfield** (1896–1986) U.S.-British wife of the duke of Windsor (formerly EDWARD VIII). Born in Blue Ridge Summit, Pa., she became a Baltimore socialite and married Earl Spencer in 1916. After their divorce (1927), she married Ernest Simpson (1928) and moved with him to London. As a member of fashionable British society, she met Edward, Prince of Wales, and the two gradually fell in love. She filed for divorce in 1936 with the intention of marrying Edward (by then King Edward), but as a woman twice divorced, she was unacceptable as a prospective British queen. Edward renounced the throne, and after she received her divorce they were married in 1937. The two thereafter lived a well-publicized international social life, residing mainly in France.

Windsor, House of *formerly (1901–17)* **House of Saxe-Coburg-Gotha** Royal house of Britain, which succeeded the House of HANOVER on the death of its last monarch, Queen VICTORIA. The dynastic name of Saxe-Coburg-Gotha was that of Victoria's German-born husband, Prince ALBERT. The dynasty included EDWARD VII, GEORGE V, EDWARD VIII, GEORGE VI, and ELIZABETH II. In view of the anti-German atmosphere of World War I, George V proclaimed in 1917 that all British male descendants of Queen Victoria would adopt the surname of Windsor.

Windsor Castle Principal British royal residence, on the River Thames in Windsor, Berkshire, southern England. It comprises two quadrilateral building courts, or upper and lower wards, separated by the Round Tower (erected by HENRY II), a massive structure built on a mound and visible for many miles. The present-day complex has been reworked repeatedly since WILLIAM THE CONQUEROR first constructed a stockade on the site. The lower ward includes the Albert Memorial Chapel and St. George's Chapel, the burial place of 10 sovereigns. The upper ward, part of which was damaged by fire in 1992, includes the monarch's private apartments, visitors' apartments, and the royal library.

windsurfing Sport of riding a sailboard, a modified surfboard with a movable mast that is sailed by one person standing up. Sailboards are capable of moderately high speeds and are usually used on lakes, or close to shore—sometimes within the surf zone—on the ocean. The sport originated in the U.S. in the late 1960s and quickly grew in popularity. It was introduced at the Olympic Games in 1984.

Windward Islands Island group, Lesser ANTILLES, West Indies. Located at the eastern end of the CARIBBEAN SEA, they include DOMINICA (sometimes classified as part of the LEEWARD ISLANDS), MARTINIQUE, ST. LUCIA, ST. VINCENT, GRENADA, and the chain of small islands known as the GRENADINES. Though near the general area, TRINIDAD AND TOBAGO and BARBADOS are usually not considered part of the group.

wine ALCOHOLIC BEVERAGE made from the fermented juice of GRAPES. Though known by the ancients, wine was not drunk in its matured form until the development of the bottle and cork in the late 17th century. In wine manufacture, grapes are crushed and strained and the juice (called must) is sealed in vats along with YEAST *(Saccharomyees ellipsoideus)* and often sulfur dioxide, which suppresses wild yeasts and organisms. FERMENTATION continues for several weeks, then the wine is drawn off ("racked") into wooden barrels or other containers for a second fermentation ("aging"). It is clarified and bottled before undergoing final maturation. Wines may be classified according to color as red, rosé (pink), or white; color depends on whether the skins of red grapes are allowed to ferment with the juice. Wine taste is described as sweet or dry, sweet wines being high in sugar content and dry wines containing little or no sugar. Sparkling wines, such as CHAMPAGNE, contain suspended carbon dioxide, the result of bottling the wine before fermentation is complete. Fortified wines, such as PORT and SHERRY, contain added brandy. The leading wine-producing countries are France, Italy, Germany, the U.S., Spain, Portugal, and Chile.

Winfrey, Oprah (born 1954) U.S. television talk-show host and actress. Born in Kosciusko, Miss., she endured an impoverished and troubled childhood. She worked as a television reporter and anchor in Baltimore, where she cohosted her first talk show (1977–83), then hosted *A.M. Chicago* (1984), which became the city's highest-rated morning show. The renamed *Oprah Winfrey Show* was syndicated in 1986, making her the first black woman to host a successful national daytime talk show. Initially sensationalist, the enormously popular show gradually took on an uplifting and therapeutic tone. In 1996 she introduced "Oprah's Book Club" to foster reading by endorsing certain books. She appeared in the movies *The Color Purple* (1985) and *Beloved* (1998).

wing In zoology, one of the paired structures certain animals use for flying. Bat and bird wings are modifications of the VERTEBRATE forelimb. In birds, the fingers are reduced and the forearm is lengthened. The primary flight feathers propel the bird forward, and the secondaries (on the upper wing) provide lift. Bat wings consist of a membrane stretched over slender, elongated arm and hand bones. Insect wings are folds of integument ("skin"). Most insects have two pairs of wings; DIPTERANS (flies) have only one developed pair, and BEETLES have two but use only one for flying. The two wings on a side usually move together, but DRAGONFLY wings work independently.

Winnebago \ˌwi-nə-ˈbā-gō\ SIOUAN-speaking North American Indian people who before the 17th century lived in what is now eastern Wisconsin. By the early 19th century, as a result of their participation in the fur trade, they had expanded into southwestern Wisconsin and northwestern Illinois. They lived in villages of dome-shaped wigwams, cultivated corn, squash, beans, and tobacco, and hunted bison. Their major ceremony was the Medicine Dance, in which both men and women participated. CLANS were important units in social life. The Winnebago were involved in the BLACK HAWK War of 1832, after which most of the tribe was removed to other Midwestern states. Today they number about 7,500.

Winnemucca, Sarah Hopkins See Sarah Winnemucca HOPKINS

Winnipeg City (metro. area pop., 1996: 667,000), capital of Manitoba. Located at the confluence of the RED RIVER OF THE NORTH and ASSINIBOINE RIVER, it was settled as a French fur-trading post in 1738. In the early 19th century THOMAS DOUGLAS founded a Scottish settlement there. Development ensued with the arrival of Canada's first transcontinental railroad in 1881. Following disastrous floods in 1950, much of the city was rebuilt. The fourth-largest city in Canada, it is a cultural, financial, commercial, industrial, and government center.

Winnipeg, Lake Lake, southern central Manitoba. Fed by many rivers, including the SASKATCHEWAN, RED RIVER OF THE NORTH, and WINNIPEG, it is drained to the northeast by the NELSON RIVER. It is 264 mi (425 km) long, up to 68 mi (109 km) wide, and has an area of 9,416 sq mi (24,387 sq km). The Canadian explorer PIERRE LA VERENDRYE visited the lake in 1733. With an average depth of 50 ft (15 m), it is important for shipping, commercial fishing, and recreation.

Winnipeg River River, southeastern Manitoba and southwestern Ontario. It issues from the Lake of the WOODS and flows northwest for about 200 mi (320 km) before entering the southeastern part of Lake WINNIPEG. It served as a route for early European explorers and fur traders. There are numerous hydroelectric power plants along its course.

Winnipegosis \ˌwi-nə-pə-ˈgō-səs\, **Lake** Lake, western Manitoba. Located west of Lake WINNIPEG, it is a remnant of glacial Lake Agassiz. Numerous streams feed the 2,075-sq-mi (5,374-sq-km) lake, which drains southeastward into Lake MANITOBA. It is more than 150 mi (240 km) long, up to 32 mi (51 km) wide, and has a maximum depth of 833 ft (254 m). It was explored in 1739 by PIERRE LA VERENDRYE and later served as part of a fur-trading route. It now is important for commercial fishing.

Winnipesaukee \ˌwi-nə-pə-ˈsȯ-kē\, **Lake** Lake, eastern central New Hampshire. The state's largest lake, it covers an area of 71 sq mi (184 sq km) and is 20 mi (32 km) long by 12 mi (19 km) wide. It is dotted with 274 islands. Its outlet, the Winnipesaukee River, flows about 20 mi (32 km) southwest to enter the MERRIMACK RIVER. It is a popular summer recreation area.

Winogradsky \vyin-ə-ˈgrät-skē\, **Sergey (Nikolayevich)** (1856–1953) Russian microbiologist. In studying the physiology of sulfur bacteria, he showed that the colorless ones oxidize hydrogen sulfide to sulfur and then to sulfuric acid in the absence of light (1887). He discovered (1889–90) two groups of microbes, each involved in one step of nitrification (oxidation of ammonia to nitrites and nitrites to nitrates), and established a new genus for each. He also proposed new ways to study soil microorganisms, particularly those symbiotic with legumes.

Winslow, Edward (1595–1655) British-American colonist. In 1620 he sailed on the *Mayflower* to New England, where he was a founder of the Plymouth colony. He served on the governor's council 1624–47, and was governor of the colony 1633–34, 1636–37, and 1644–45. He traded with the Wampanoag Indians and won the friendship of their chief, Massasoit. As a commissioner of the United Colonies of New England, he often went to England to represent the interests of the Massachusetts Bay and Plymouth colonies. In 1646 he returned to England and held minor offices under Oliver Cromwell.

Winslow, Josiah (1629?–1680) American colonist. Born in Plymouth colony, Mass., the son of Edward Winslow, he succeeded Myles Standish as commander of its military forces in 1656. He was appointed assistant governor of the colony (1657–73) and served as a member of the New England Confederation's directorate. He was elected governor of Plymouth colony (1673–80), the first native-born colonial governor, and established its first public school. In King Philip's War he was commander in chief of the confederation's military forces (1675–76).

Winsor \'win-zər\, Justin (1831–1897) U.S. librarian and historian. A freelance writer in his native Boston, Winsor was appointed a trustee of the Boston Public Library and served as its superintendent 1868–77. He was a founder of the American Library Association (1876) and its first president. From 1877 he was librarian of Harvard University. He edited the *Narrative and Critical History of America* (1884–89) and wrote several books.

Winsor, engraving by J.A.J. Wilcox.

BY COURTESY OF THE LIBRARY OF CONGRESS, WASHINGTON, D.C.

Winston-Salem City (pop., 1996 est.: 154,000), northern central North Carolina. With High Point and Greensboro it forms a tri-city industrial area. Salem was laid out by Moravian colonists in 1766. R. J. Reynolds founded his tobacco company there in 1875 (see RJR Nabisco, Inc.). Winston was founded in 1849 and named for an American Revolutionary soldier. The two towns were consolidated as Winston-Salem in 1913. Tobacco dominates its diversified industries, which include the manufacture of cigarettes, textiles, beer, rubber, leather, and petroleum.

Winter War See Russo-Finnish War

wintergreen Any of several evergreen plants in the heath order (Ericales). They grow as woodland wildflowers and are cultivated as garden ground cover. They are also grown as a source of oil of wintergreen, a volatile, pungent oil used to flavor candies and chewing gum and to soothe muscular aches. Wintergreen is an alternative common name for several woodland herbs: *Pyrola* (shinleaf), about 12 species of creeping perennials; and *Gaultheria* species, especially *G. procumbens* (also called teaberry and checkerberry; see also snowberry), with white berries and spicy red berries.

Wintergreen (*Gaultheria procumbens*).

ROGER AND JOY SPURR—BRUCE COLEMAN INC./EB INC.

Winthrop, John (1588–1649) British-American political leader, first governor of the Massachusetts Bay Colony. In 1629 he joined the Massachusetts Bay Co., and he was elected governor of the colony that was to be established by the company in New England. An ardent Puritan, he envisioned a colony based on his religious beliefs. He guided the colonists on his arrival in North America in 1630, and was elected governor 12 times during 1631–48. Though widely respected, he was criticized for opposing the formation of a representative assembly (1634), and Roger Williams and Anne Hutchinson decried the colony's limitations on religious expression. His son, John Winthrop (1606–1676), was an influential governor of Connecticut (1659–76).

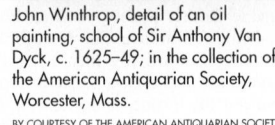

John Winthrop, detail of an oil painting, school of Sir Anthony Van Dyck, c. 1625–49; in the collection of the American Antiquarian Society, Worcester, Mass.

BY COURTESY OF THE AMERICAN ANTIQUARIAN SOCIETY, WORCESTER, MASS.

wire drawing Making of wire, generally from a rod or bar. The wire-drawing process consists of pointing the rod, threading the pointed end through a die, and attaching the end to a drawing block. The block, made to revolve by an electric motor, pulls the lubricated rod through the die, reducing it in diameter and increasing its length. Fine wire is made by a multiple-block machine, because the reduction cannot be performed in a single draft.

wire service See news agency

wireless communications System using radio-frequency, infrared, microwave, or other types of electromagnetic or acoustic waves in place of wires, cables, or fiber optics to transmit signals or data. Wireless devices include cellular phones, two-way radios, remote garage-door openers, television remote controls, and GPS receivers (see Global Positioning System). Wireless modems, microwave transmitters, and satellites make it possible to access the Internet from anywhere in the world. A Wireless Markup Language (WML) based on XML is intended for use in such narrow-band devices as cellular phones and pagers, for the transfer and display of text.

Wisconsin State (pop., 1997 est.: 5,170,000), northern Midwest, U.S. It covers an area of 56,153 sq mi (145,436 sq km), including part of Lake Michigan; its capital is Madison. With many unique landforms, including the Door Peninsula between Lake Michigan and Green Bay, its northern area has one of the greatest concentration of lakes in the world. The Mississippi and the Wisconsin rivers cross the state. Forests cover about 45% of it. Originally inhabited by the Adena, or Mound Builders, the region was home to several different Indian tribes, including the Ojibwa, Menominee, and Winnebago, when Europeans arrived. The French explorer Jean Nicolet visited Wisconsin in 1634; the first permanent European settlement was established in 1717. The area remained under French control until 1763, when France ceded it to Great Britain after the French and Indian War. After the American Revolution the region was ceded to the U.S. The Europeans dispossessed the Indians of their land (see Black Hawk), and settled the region. It became the Wisconsin Territory in 1836. It was admitted to the Union as the 30th state in 1848. The Progressive movement (see Progressive Party) began in Wisconsin c. 1900, resulting in the passage of legislation that made the state a leader in social reform. It is the major milk, butter, and cheese producer in the U.S. Tourism and recreation also are economically important. Wisconsin ports handle much of the Great Lakes domestic freight shipping.

Wisconsin, University of State system of higher education comprising 13 four-year colleges or university campuses and an equal number of two-year institutions. The main campus was founded at Madison in 1849. In 1971 it was merged with the Wisconsin State Universities system, creating one of the largest such systems in the nation (total enrollment 150,000). The Madison campus is a comprehensive research and academic center. It has colleges of letters and science and of engineering; undergraduate schools of agriculture and life sciences, health professions, business, education, environmental studies, and consumer sciences; and graduate or professional schools of law, pharmacy, medicine, veterinary medicine, and nursing. Enrollment at Madison is about 40,000.

Wisconsin River River, central and southwestern Wisconsin. It rises near the Wisconsin–Michigan border and flows south through central Wisconsin, then turns west and enters the MISSISSIPPI RIVER after a course of 430 mi (690 km). It is navigable for small craft for about 200 mi (320 km) from its mouth. Lake Wisconsin is formed by a hydroelectric dam on the river near Prairie du Sac.

Wise, Isaac Mayer (1819–1900) Rabbi and organizer of REFORM JUDAISM in the U.S. Emigrating from Bohemia, in 1854 he accepted a pulpit in Cincinnati, a post he held the rest of his life. He propagandized tirelessly for centralized Reform institutions, and was instrumental in the formation of the Union of American Hebrew Congregations and of the Central Conference of American Rabbis, both of which he presided over. In 1857 he compiled a standard Reform prayer book, *Minhag America.* Though he failed to unite American Jews of all persuasions, he did bring about unanimity among Reform Jews.

Wise, Stephen Samuel (1874–1949) U.S. (Hungarian-born) Reform rabbi, political activist, and Zionist leader. His family emigrated to the U.S. when he was an infant. He earned his PhD at Columbia University in 1901 and was trained as a rabbi. In 1907, after declining a post at an influential congregation because of inadequate assurances of free speech in the pulpit, he founded the Free Synagogue. In 1898 he attended the Second Zionist Congress and helped found the Zionist Organization of America. A prominent member of the Democratic Party, he helped win U.S. government approval of the BALFOUR DECLARATION. In 1922 he founded the Jewish Institute of Religion, a seminary for liberal rabbis, which merged with Hebrew Union College in 1950.

Wister, Owen (1860–1938) U.S. novelist. Born in Philadelphia, he spent his summers in the West from 1885. After practicing law two years, he devoted himself to a literary career. His novel *The Virginian* (1902), the story of a cattle-ranch foreman, was a great popular success and helped establish the cowboy as an American folk hero and stock fictional character. His other major work was *Roosevelt* (1930), detailing his long acquaintance with his Harvard classmate THEODORE ROOSEVELT.

Wister.
BY COURTESY OF THE LIBRARY OF CONGRESS, WASHINGTON, D.C.

wisteria *or* **wistaria** \wis-ˈtir-ē-ə\ Any of the twining, usually woody vines that make up the genus *Wisteria,* of the pea family (see LEGUME), native mostly to Asia and North America. The leaves are pinnately compound (feathery). They are widely cultivated for their attractive spreading growth and beautiful, profuse flowers (blue, purple, rose, or white), which grow in large, drooping clusters. American wisteria *(W. frutescens)* and Kentucky wisteria *(W. macrostachya)* are native to the U.S.

witan \ˈwi-tän\ *or* **witenagemot** \ˈwi-tᵊn-ə-gə-ˌmōt\ Council of the Anglo-Saxon kings in medieval England. Usually attended by high-ranking nobles and bishops, the witan was expected to advise the king on all matters on which he chose to ask its opinion. It attested his grants of land to churches or laymen, consented to his issue of new laws, and helped him deal with rebels and disaffected subjects. Its composition and time of meeting were determined at the king's pleasure.

witch-hazel family Family Hamamelidaceae, composed of 23 genera of shrubs and trees, native to tropical and warm temperate regions. The six species of the genus *Hamamelis* include such ornamentals as witch hazel, winter hazel, and *Fothergilla,* which are outstanding for their early flowering and fall leaf color. Members are characterized by simple leaves and by flowers with four or five petals and sepals each. American, or common, witch hazel *(H. virginiana)* flowers in fall and retains yellow, cuplike calyxes (collections of sepals) through the winter. The common name refers to the forked twigs that were sometimes used for water-witching, or DOWSING, to locate underground water. The fragrant liniment witch hazel is made from the dried leaves and sometimes from twigs and bark. Brilliant autumn leaf color is an outstanding trait of the IRONWOOD *Parrotia persica.* Another genus, *Altingia,* has seven species, all Asian and all valued for their timber. *A. excelsa* is one of the largest trees of the Asian tropics, sometimes reaching a height of 82 ft (25 m).

witchcraft and sorcery Use of alleged supernatural powers, usually to control people or events. Sorcery is sometimes distinguished from witchcraft in that it may be practiced by anyone with the appropriate knowledge, using charms, spells, or potions; whereas witchcraft is considered to result from inherent mystical power and to be practiced by invisible means. Modern witches, however, claim that their craft is learned, and therefore another distinction between witchcraft and sorcery is that sorcery is always used with evil intent. Both witchcraft and sorcery occur widely but are especially prevalent in close-knit communities experiencing decline or misfortune and embroiled in petty social conflict and scapegoating. In ancient Greece witchcraft was mentioned as early as Homer (see CIRCE). The best-known sorceress in classical times was the legendary MEDEA. The Roman Horace describes two witches in his *Satires.* The Bible contains several references to witches, notably the Witch of Endor consulted by Saul (I Sam. 28). The early Church Fathers held that witchcraft was a delusion and denounced its practice. In the Middle Ages, witchcraft was believed to involve demonic possession. It was also associated with heresy and so came within the scope of the INQUISITION. In the witch-hunts of the 16th–17th century, European courts frequently regarded witches and sorcerers alike as candidates for burning. Although estimates of the number killed vary widely, it is likely that between 40,000 and 60,000 people were executed and many more were tortured and imprisoned during the witch-hunts. See also MAGIC, SALEM WITCH TRIALS.

Witherspoon, John (1723–1794) Scottish-American clergyman. Ordained a Presbyterian minister (1745), he served in Scottish parishes until 1768, when he was sent to become president of the College of New Jersey (later Princeton Univ.), where he expanded the curriculum and increased enrollment. An advocate for colonists' rights, he was a member of the local COMMITTEE OF CORRESPONDENCE (1775–76) and the Continental Congress (1776–79, 1780–82), and was the only clergyman to sign the DECLARATION OF INDEPENDENCE. He helped organize the American Presbyterian Church as a national body (1785–89).

Witt \ˈvit, ˈwit\, **Katarina** (born 1965) German figure skater. Born in Karl-Marx-Stadt (now Chemnitz), she won the first of six European championships in 1983, and went on to win two Olympic gold medals (1984, 1988) and four World Championships (1984, 1985, 1987, 1988). She was popular with audiences, who prized her grace and elegance as much as her technical abilities. She turned professional in 1988.

Witte \ˈvi-tə\, **Sergey (Yulyevich), Count** (1849–1915) Russian statesman and premier (1905–6). He entered the imperial administrative service in 1871 and served as minister of finance 1892–1903. He improved communications, promoted construction of the TRANS-SIBERIAN RAILWAY, and planned to modernize the Russian empire. He represented Russia in the negotiations that ended the RUSSO-JAPANESE WAR. Though opposed to constitutionalism, he persuaded Czar NICHOLAS II to issue the OCTOBER MANIFESTO in 1905 and was appointed the first constitutional premier. He repressed further civil disruption and restored Russian finances with loans from European banks. In 1906 the czar, favoring a more conservative regime, replaced him with PIOTR STOLYPIN.

Wittelsbach \ˈvi-təls-ˌbäk\, **House of** German noble family that ruled in Bavaria from the 12th to the 20th century. In 1124 Otto V, count of Scheyern (died 1155), moved the family residence to the castle of Wittelsbach and took its name. In 1180 his son Otto VI became OTTO I, duke of Bavaria. In 1214 Otto II obtained the Palatinate of the Rhine. A descendant, LOUIS IV, as Holy Roman emperor divided the lands, granting the Palatinate to his nephew, Rupert, who obtained the title of elector (r.1353–90). Several divisions of ducal Bavaria were reunited under Albert IV (died 1508). The Bavarian dukes became electors from 1623, and the last direct line died out in 1777. The Palatine branch united with Bavaria in 1799 under Duke Maximilian IV Joseph, who became king of Bavaria (1806) as MAXIMILIAN I. His descendants (including LUDWIG I and LUDWIG II) were kings until the abdication of Ludwig III in 1918.

Wittgenstein \ˈvit-gən-ˌshtīn\, **Ludwig (Josef Johann)** (1889–1951) Austrian-British philosopher, one of the most influential figures in 20th-century philosophy. The son of an immensely wealthy and cultivated Viennese industrialist, he studied mechanical engineering in Berlin and Manchester. The works of BERTRAND RUSSELL led to his increasing interest in mathematics, and he later studied under Russell at Cambridge (1912–13). He produced two original and influential systems of philosophical thought, his logical theories and later his philosophy of language. He served in the Austrian army in World War I, and completed his great *Tractatus Logico-Philosophicus* in a prisoner-of-war camp. It dealt with the question of how language expresses meaning; his solution was that a sentence that says something (a proposition) must be "a picture of reality." It exerted great influence on the VIENNA CIRCLE and the school of LOGICAL POSITIVISM. Thereafter, he gave away all of his fortune and worked in an odd variety of jobs, before returning to Cambridge as a fellow in 1929. Through his lectures and the wide circulation of notes taken by his students, he came to exert a powerful influence on English-language philosophy. *Philosophical Investigations* (1953) crowned this second period of activity, in which he strove to show how language is linked to actions and reactions, with the aim of demonstrating that its significance is due not to an intangible realm of mind but to the human forms of life in which it plays a role. Several other works were edited posthumously. See also ANALYTIC PHILOSOPHY.

Witz \'vits\, **Konrad** (c. 1400–1445/46) German-Swiss painter. Born in Germany, in 1434 he entered the painters' guild in Basel, where he worked most of his life. Little else is known of his life. His masterpiece, *The Miraculous Draft of Fishes* (1444), from an altarpiece for the cathedral of Geneva, exemplifies such precise realism that the light reflected off the water's surface is carefully distinguished from the light reflected off the stones beneath the shallow water. He was one of the first German painters to show the influence of Early Netherlandish art, and one of the first European artists to incorporate realistic landscapes into religious paintings.

"The Miraculous Draft of Fishes," tempera on panel by Konrad Witz, 1444; in the Museum of Art and History, Geneva.

©MUSEE D'ART ET D'HISTOIRE, GENEVA; PHOTOGRAPH, YVES SIZA

Wladyslaw II Jagiello \vlȧ-'dis-lȧf...yȧg-'yel-lō\ (1351?–1434) Grand duke of Lithuania (1377–1401) and king of Poland (1386–1434), founder of the JAGIELLON DYNASTY. He had to defeat rivals, including his cousin VYTAUTAS, in order to secure his rule in Lithuania. He married the Polish queen Jadwiga (1386) after agreeing to Christianize Lithuania and unite it with Poland. He regained Ruthenia from Hungary (1387) and made the prince of Moldavia his vassal. He signed a treaty (1401) recognizing Vytautas as duke on the condition that Poland and Lithuania pursued a common foreign policy, and together they broke the power of the TEUTONIC ORDER.

Wobblies See INDUSTRIAL WORKERS OF THE WORLD

Wodehouse \'wu̇d-ˌhau̇s\, **P(elham) G(renville)** *later* **Sir Pelham** (1881–1975) English-U.S. novelist, short-story writer, lyricist, and playwright. He lived for long periods in the U.S. and France after 1909, and settled in the U.S. after World War II. He is best known as the creator of Bertie Wooster and his supreme "gentleman's gentleman," Jeeves, who appeared in comic stories and novels from "Extricating Young Gussie" (1915) to *Much Obliged, Jeeves* (1971). He wrote more than 90 books and 20 film scripts and collaborated on more than 30 plays and musical comedies, writing lyrics for J. KERN (*Leave It to Jane,* 1917; *Show Boat,* 1927), GEORGE GERSHWIN (*Oh, Kay!,* 1926), and others.

Wolcott, Oliver (1726–1797) American public official. Born in Windsor, Conn., he was a member of the Connecticut council (1771–86), a delegate to the Continental Congress (1775–76, 1778, 1780–84), and a signer of the DECLARATION OF INDEPENDENCE. He raised a local militia to fight in the American Revolution and led troops in the defense of Connecticut (1779). As a commissioner of northern Indian affairs, he negotiated the Treaty of FORT STANWIX. He served as lieutenant governor (1787–96) and later governor (1796–97) of Connecticut.

wolf Either of three extant species of wild DOG. The gray, or timber, wolf *(Canis lupus)* is the ancestor of all domestic dogs. It once had the largest distribution of any mammal except human beings, but it is now found primarily in Canada, Alaska, the Balkans, and Russia. Wolves are intelligent and social. Their primary prey are deer, moose, and caribou, though they feed on many smaller animals as well. Because wolves have killed livestock, they have been persecuted by farmers and ranchers. A male gray wolf may be 7 ft (2 m) long and weigh up to 175 lbs (80 kg); it is the largest living wild canid. Gray wolves live in hierarchical packs whose territories cover at least 38 sq mi (100 sq km) and hunt mostly at night. The much smaller red wolf *(C. rufus),* once widespread in the southern central U.S., has been bred in captivity and reintroduced. The Abyssinian wolf *(C. simensis)* of Ethiopia was formerly considered a JACKAL. See also DIRE WOLF.

Wolf \'vȯlf, *Engl* 'wu̇lf\, **Christa** *orig.* **Christa Ihlenfeld** (born 1929) German novelist, essayist, and screenwriter. Wolf was reared in a middle-class, pro-Nazi family; after Germany's defeat in 1945, she moved with her family to East Germany. Her work reflects her experiences during World War II and her postwar life in a communist state. Her novels include *Divided Heaven* (1963), which brought her political favor; *The Quest for Christa T.* (1968), severely attacked in East Germany; *A Model Childhood* (1976); *Cassandra* (1983), her most widely read book, linking nuclear and patriarchal power; and *What Remains* (1990), on government surveillance and her own links to the East German Stasi.

Wolf \'vȯlf\, **Hugo (Filipp Jakob)** (1860–1903) Austrian composer. He entered the Vienna Conservatory at 15, but, as a rabid Wagnerian, he lost patience with his teachers' conservatism and soon left. By 18 he probably already had the syphilis that would kill him, making him mentally unstable, and his volatile personality made it difficult to keep private students. As a critic (1884–87), he attracted attention for his vituperative comments. His productivity came in bursts; in 1888–89 he produced the remarkable songs of the *Mörike Lieder*, the *Eichendorff Lieder*, the *Goethe Lieder*, and much of the *Spanish Songbook*—more than half his total output. After beginning the *Italian Songbook* in 1891, he wrote nothing for three years, then quickly composed the opera *Der Corregidor* (1896) and finished the *Italian Songbook* (1896). In 1897 he suffered a complete breakdown, and he thereafter lived largely in an asylum.

wolf spider Name that originally referred to a species of southern European SPIDER *(Lycosa tarentula)* but now refers to more than 175 spider species (family Lycosidae) found in North America, Europe, and north of the Arctic Circle. The body of *L. tarentula,* the largest species, is about 1 in. (2.5 cm) long. Most species have a long, broad, hairy brown body; stout, long legs; and strong, prominent jaws. Wolf spiders chase and pounce upon their prey, hunting mostly at night. Most species build a silk-lined, tubular nest in the ground, which they dig with their heavy front legs. A few species spin webs. The bite of *L. tarentula* produces no ill effects in humans.

Wolfe, Elsie de See Elsie DE WOLFE

Wolfe \'wu̇lf\, **James** (1727–1759) British army commander. After a distinguished military career in Europe, in 1758 he helped lead Gen. JEFFERY AMHERST's successful expedition against the French on Cape Breton Island. In 1759 he was appointed commander of the British army on its mission to capture Quebec from the French. In the ensuing Battle of QUEBEC, he defeated the French in a battle lasting less than an hour. He died of his third wound received in the battle, but after having learned of Quebec's surrender.

James Wolfe, painting attributed to J.S.C. Schaak; in the National Portrait Gallery, London.

BY COURTESY OF THE NATIONAL PORTRAIT GALLERY, LONDON

Wolfe \'wu̇lf\, **Thomas (Clayton)** (1900–1938) U.S. writer. Born in Asheville, N.C., Wolfe studied at the University of North Carolina and moved to New York City in 1923 and taught at NYU while working at writing plays. *Look Homeward, Angel* (1929), his first and best-known novel, and *Of Time and the River* (1935) are thinly veiled autobiography. In *The Story of a Novel* (1936) he describes the close working relation with MAXWELL PERKINS that shaped the chaotic manuscripts for both books into publishable form. His short stories were collected in *From Death to Morning* (1935). After his death at 37 from tuberculosis, the novels *The Web and the Rock* (1939) and *You Can't Go Home Again* (1940) were among the works extracted from the manuscripts he left.

Wolfe, Tom *orig.* **Thomas Kennerly Wolfe, Jr.** (born 1930) U.S. journalist and novelist. Born in Richmond, Va., he earned a doctorate from Yale Univ., then wrote for newspapers and worked as a magazine editor, becoming known as a proponent of New Journalism, the application of fiction-writing techniques to journalism. *The Electric Kool-Aid Acid Test* (1968) chronicled the life of a traveling group of hippies. *The Right Stuff* (1979; film, 1983) examined the first U.S. astronaut program. Other controversial nonfiction books attacked fashionable 1960s leftism, modern abstract art, and international architectural styles. His novel *The Bonfire of the Vanities* (1987), mocking the pieties of the New York liberal establishment, was a huge best-seller. A second novel, *A Man in Full,* was published in 1998.

Wolff \'vȯlf\, **Christian, Freiherr (baron) von** (1679–1754) German philosopher, mathematician, and scientist. He was a pupil of G. W. LEIBNIZ. He wrote numerous works in theology, psychology, botany, and physics, but is best known as the German spokesman of Enlightenment RATIONALISM. His essays, all beginning under the title *Rational Ideas,* covered many subjects and expounded Leibniz's theories in popular form. He applied the rational thought of Leibniz and RENE DESCARTES in developing his own philosophical system, which was partly based on mathematical methodology, and his ideas became a major force in the development of German philosophy.

Wölfflin \'vœlf-lin\, **Heinrich** (1864–1945) Swiss art historian. He was educated at the Univs. of Basel, Berlin, and Munich, and his doctoral thesis already showed the approach he was later to develop: an analysis of form based on a psychological interpretation of the creative process. His chief work, *Principles of Art History* (1915), synthesized his ideas into a complete aesthetic system that was to become of great importance in art criticism. He eschewed the popular anecdotal approach and emphasized the formal stylistic analysis of drawing, composition, light, color, subject matter, and other pictorial elements as they were handled similarly by the painters of a particular period or national school.

wolfram See TUNGSTEN

Wolfram von Eschenbach \'vȯlf-räm-fȯn-'esh-ən-ˌbäk\ (c. 1170–c. 1220) German poet. An impoverished Bavarian knight, Wolfram apparently served a succession of lords. The epic *Parzival,* one of his eight surviving lyric poems, is one of the masterpieces of the Middle Ages; likely based on a romance by CHRÉTIEN DE TROYES, it introduced the theme of the Holy Grail into German literature. RICHARD WAGNER used it as the basis for his last opera, *Parsifal* (1882). Wolfram's influence on later poets was profound, and, with HARTMANN VON AUE and GOTTFRIED VON STRASSBURG, he is one of the three great Middle High German epic poets.

Wollaston Lake \'wä-ləs-tən\ Lake, northeastern Saskatchewan. It is 70 mi (113 km) long and 25 mi (40 km) wide, with an area of 1,035 sq mi (2,681 sq km). It drains through two outlets: one northwestward through Fond du Lac River to Lake ATHABASCA and the MACKENZIE RIVER system, the other northeastward via Cochrane River to Reindeer Lake and the CHURCHILL RIVER system. It was used as a link between the two river systems after it was discovered by Peter Fidler about 1800. It is noted for its fishing.

Mary Wollstonecraft (Godwin), detail, oil on canvas by John Opie, c. 1797; in the National Portrait Gallery, London.
NATIONAL PORTRAIT GALLERY, LONDON

Wollstonecraft \'wəl-stən-ˌkraft\, **Mary** (1759–1797) English writer. She taught school and worked as a governess and for a London publisher. In 1797 she married WILLIAM GODWIN; she died days after the birth of their daughter, MARY SHELLEY, that same year, at the age of 38. She is noted as a passionate advocate of educational and social equality for women. Her early *Thoughts on the Education of Daughters* (1787) foreshadowed her mature work on the place of women in society, *A Vindication of the Rights of Woman* (1792), whose core is a plea for equality of education for men and women. The *Vindication* is widely regarded as the founding document of modern feminism.

Wolof \'wō-lȯf\ Muslim people of Senegal and Gambia speaking a language of the ATLANTIC branch of the NIGER-CONGO family. In the 14th–16th century the Wolof maintained a powerful empire. Traditional Wolof society was highly stratified, consisting of royalty, an aristocracy, a warrior class, commoners, slaves, and members of despised artisan castes. Today most Wolof (numbering 4.5 million) are farmers, but many live and work in Dakar and Banjul. Wolof women are renowned for their elaborate hair styles, abundant gold ornaments, and voluminous dresses.

Wolper, David (Lloyd) (born 1928) U.S. television and film producer. Born in New York City, he worked for a production company that made TV movies (1950–54), then formed Wolper Pictures in 1960. His numerous television programs and specials have included *The Making of the President* (1964) and the miniseries *Roots* (1977).

Wolsey \'wu̇l-zē\, **Thomas, Cardinal** (1475?–1530) English prelate and statesman. He served as chaplain to HENRY VII and later HENRY VIII, for whom he organized the successful campaign against the French (1513). On Henry's recommendation, the pope made Wolsey successively bishop of Lincoln (1514), archbishop of York (1514), cardinal (1515), and papal legate (1518). In 1515 Henry appointed him lord chancellor of England, which added to his power and wealth. Wolsey sought to bring peace to Europe, but in 1521 he allied with Emperor CHARLES V against France. Though he introduced judicial and monastic reforms, he became unpopular for raising taxes. In 1529 he failed to persuade the pope to grant Henry an annulment of his marriage to CATHERINE OF ARAGON, for which he soon lost favor and was stripped of his offices except the archbishopric of York. In 1530 he was arrested for treason for corresponding with the French court, and he died on his way to face the king.

wolverine *or* **skunk bear** Solitary, voracious, nocturnal carnivore *(Gulo gulo)* that inhabits northern timberlands worldwide. Wolverines are 26–36 in. (65–90 cm) long and 14–18 in. (36–45 cm) high, and weigh 20–65 lbs (9–30 kg); the bushy tail is 5–10-in. (13–26-cm) long. They have short bowed legs, hairy soles, and long, sharp claws. Their long, coarse hair, used to trim parkas, is blackish brown, with a light horizontal strip. The anal glands secrete an unpleasant-smelling fluid. A cunning, fearless predator, the wolverine will attack almost any animal, including sheep, deer, and small bears.

Wolverine (*Gulo gulo*).
ALAN G. NELSON—ROOT RESOURCES

Woman's Christian Temperance Union (WCTU) U.S. TEMPERANCE-MOVEMENT organization. Founded in Cleveland, Ohio, in 1874, it used educational, social, and political means to promote legislation. Its president (1879–98) was Frances Willard (1839–1898), an effective speaker and lobbyist who also led the World's Woman's Christian Temperance Union from its founding in 1883. The WCTU was instrumental in promoting nationwide temperance and in the eventual adoption of PROHIBITION.

womb See UTERUS

wombat Either of two species (family Phascolomyidae, or Vombatidae) of nocturnal Australian MARSUPIALS that are heavily built, 28–47 in. (70–120 cm) long, and tailless. The single newborn develops in the mother's pouch for about five months. Wombats eat grasses, tree bark, and shrub roots. They make a grassy nest at the end of a long burrow. The common wombat *(Phas-*

Common wombat (*Vombatus ursinus*).
WARREN GARST—TOM STACK AND ASSOCIATES

colomis, or *Vombatus, ursinus)* of southeastern Australia and Tasmania, considered a pest, has coarse dark hair and short ears. The rare Queensland hairy-nosed wombat *(Lasiorhinus barnardi)* has fine fur and longer ears; protected by law, the population lives principally in a national park.

Women's Army Corps (WAC) U.S. Army unit. It was established (as the Women's Auxiliary Army Corps) by Congress to enlist women for auxiliary noncombat duty in WORLD WAR II. Its first head was OVETA C. HOBBY. By 1945 nearly 100,000 women had served. After the war the government requested reenlistment to meet employment needs of army hospitals and administrative centers. The WAC became part of the regular army with the passage of the 1948 Women's Armed Services Integration Act. In 1978 it was dissolved as a separate unit and fully integrated into the army.

women's movement Diverse social movement, largely based in the United States, seeking equal rights and opportunities for women in their economic activities, their personal lives, and politics. It is recognized as the "second wave" of the larger feminist movement. While first-wave FEMINISM of the 19th and early 20th centuries focused on women's legal rights, such as the right to vote, the second-wave feminism of the "women's movement" peaked in the 1960s and '70s and touched on every area of women's experience—including family, sexuality, and work. A variety of American women's groups, including the NATIONAL ORGANIZATION FOR WOMEN, sought to overturn laws that enforced discrimination in matters such as contract and property rights and employment and pay. The movement also sought to broaden women's self-awareness and challenge traditional stereotypes of women as passive, dependent, or irrational. An effort in the 1970s to pass the EQUAL RIGHTS AMENDMENT failed, but its aims had been largely achieved by other means by the end of the 20th century.

women's suffrage movement Movement to grant women the right by law to vote. Women's voting rights became an issue in the 19th century, especially in Britain and the U.S. In the U.S. the women's-suffrage movement arose from the antislavery movement (see ABOLITIONISM) and the emergence of such leaders as LUCRETIA MOTT and ELIZABETH CADY STANTON, who believed that equality should extend to women as well as blacks and organized the SENECA FALLS CONVENTION (1848). In 1850 LUCY STONE established the movement's first national convention. Stanton and SUSAN B. ANTHONY formed the National Woman Suffrage Association in 1869 to secure an amendment to the Constitution, while Stone founded the American Woman Suffrage Association to seek similar amendments to state constitutions; in 1890 the two organizations merged as the National American Woman Suffrage Association. Following Wyoming's lead in 1890, states began adopting such amendments; by 1918 women had acquired suffrage in 15 states. After a women's-suffrage amendment was passed by Congress, a vigorous campaign brought ratification, and in August 1919 the 19th Amendment became part of the Constitution. In Britain, the first women's-suffrage committee was formed in Manchester in 1865. In the 1870s suffragists submitted petitions with almost 3 million signatures. Despite growing support, suffrage bills were continually defeated; in frustration, some suffragists became militant activists under the leadership of EMMELINE AND CHRISTABEL PANKHURST. Parliament finally passed the REPRESENTATION OF THE PEOPLE ACT in 1918. Women had already won voting rights in New Zealand (1893), Australia (1902), Finland (1906), Norway (1913), and the Soviet Union (1917). They were followed by Poland (1918), Sweden (1919), Germany (1919), and Ireland (1922); France, Italy, India, and Japan passed women's-suffrage laws after World War II.

Wonder, Stevie *orig.* **Steveland Judkins** *later* **Steveland Morris** (born 1950) U.S. SOUL-MUSIC singer, songwriter, and musician. Born in Saginaw, Mich., he was blind virtually from birth. He was a skillful performer on the piano and other instruments by age 8. The family moved to Detroit, and at 10 he signed with the fledgling MOTOWN label. His first hit, "Fingertips, Part 2" (1963), was followed by many top-selling singles, including "Up-Tight" and "I Was Made to Love Her." After studying composition at USC, he continued to enjoy enormous success in the 1970s and '80s with such albums as *Talking Book* (1972) and *Songs in the Key of Life* (1976) and such hits as "Superstition," "Ebony and Ivory," and "I Just Called to Say I Love You." He has spoken out against nuclear war, worked to end apartheid in South Africa, and raised funds for his eye-disease facility, Wonderland.

Wonders of the World, Seven See SEVEN WONDERS OF THE WORLD

Wonhyo Daisa \'wən-'hyō-'da-ˌsä\ (617–686) Korean Buddhist priest. He was the first to systematize Korean Buddhism, bringing the various Buddhist doctrines into a unity that served both philosophers and laypeople. He advocated maintaining harmony between the real and the ideal in life to pursue spiritual goals. His works, mainly in the form of commentaries on MAHAYANA SUTRAS, had profound influence on Chinese, Japanese, and Korean Buddhists. He is considered the greatest of the ancient Korean religious teachers and one of the Ten Sages of the Ancient Korean kingdom.

wood Hard, fibrous material formed by the accumulation of secondary XYLEM produced by the vascular CAMBIUM. It is the principal strengthening tissue found in the stems and roots of TREES and SHRUBS. Wood forms around a central core (pith) in a series of concentric layers called GROWTH RINGS. A cross section of wood shows the distinction between heartwood and sapwood. Heartwood, the central portion, is darker and composed of xylem cells that are no longer active in the life processes of the tree. Sapwood, the lighter area surrounding the heartwood, contains actively conducting xylem cells. Wood is one of the most abundant and versatile natural materials on earth, and unlike coal, ores, and petroleum, is renewable with proper care. The most widely used woods come from two groups of trees: the CONIFERS, or SOFTWOODS (e.g., PINE, SPRUCE, FIR), and the broadleaves, or HARDWOODS (e.g., OAK, WALNUT, MAPLE). Trees classified as hardwoods are not necessarily harder than softwoods (e.g., BALSA, a hardwood, is one of the softest woods). Density and moisture content affect the strength of wood; in addition to load-bearing strength, other variable factors often tested include elasticity and toughness. Wood is insulating to heat and electricity and has desirable acoustical properties. Some identifying physical characteristics of wood include color, odor, texture, and grain (the direction of the wood fibers). Some 10,000 different wood products are commercially available, ranging from lumber and plywood to paper, from fine furniture to toothpicks. Chemically derived products from wood and wood residues include cellophane, charcoal, dyestuffs, explosives, lacquers, and turpentine. Wood is also used for fuel in many parts of the world.

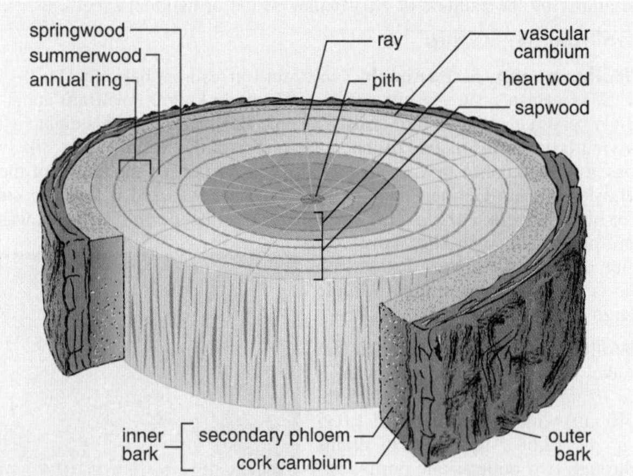

Cross section of a tree trunk. Wood is formed by the accumulation of secondary xylem produced by growth of the vascular cambium tissue. Each growth layer is distinguished by early or springwood, composed of large thin-walled cells produced during the spring when water is usually abundant, and the denser late or summerwood, composed of small cells with thick walls. Growth rings vary in width as a result of differing climatic conditions; in temperate climates, a ring is equivalent to one year's growth. The dark heartwood consists of xylem that has been infiltrated by gums and resins and has lost its ability to conduct water, unlike the actively functioning sapwood. Certain conducting cells form rays that conduct water and dissolved substances laterally across the xylem. Bark is composed of the tissues outside the vascular cambium, incl. secondary phloem, cork cells, and cork-producing cells (cork cambium). The outer bark, composed of dead tissue, protects the inner region from injury, disease, and desiccation.

Wood, Grant (1891–1942) U.S. painter. Born near Anamosa, Iowa, he was trained as a craftsman and designer as well as a painter. On a visit to Germany in 1928, he was strongly influenced by the sharp detail of 15th-century German and Flemish paintings, and he soon abandoned his Impressionist manner for the detailed, realistic manner he is known for. His *American Gothic* caused a sensation when exhibited in 1930. A telling portrait of the sober, hardworking Midwestern farmer, it has become one of the best-known icons of U.S. art, though it is often misinterpreted: the woman is not the man's wife but the familiar figure of the unmarried daughter designated to stay on the farm to assist her widowed father.

Wood, Leonard (1860–1927) U.S. Army officer. Born in Winchester, N.H., he studied medicine and became a contract surgeon with the U.S. Army. In the Spanish–American War he and his friend THEODORE ROOSEVELT recruited and commanded the volunteer ROUGH RIDERS. Promoted to brigadier general, Wood served as military governor of Cuba 1899–1902, and organized a modern civil government. After service in the Philippines, he served as chief of staff of the U.S. Army (1910–14). He advocated preparedness for war, but as a Republican he was passed over for a command post in World War I by the Democratic administration. He later served as governor general of the Philippines (1921–27).

Wood, Natalie *orig.* **Natasha Gurdin** (1938–1981) U.S. film actress. Born in San Francisco, she began appearing in movies at age 5. A dark-haired beauty of Russian-French extraction, she moved easily into teenage and adult leading roles in *Rebel Without a Cause* (1955), *Splendor in the Grass* (1961), *West Side Story* (1961), *Love with the Proper Stranger* (1963), *Inside Daisy Clover* (1966), and *Bob & Carol & Ted & Alice* (1969). She drowned in a boating accident.

wood alcohol See METHANOL

Wood Buffalo National Park Park, western Canada. Situated between ATHABASCA and GREAT SLAVE lakes, it was established in 1922; it occupies an area of 17,300 sq mi (44,807 sq km). The world's largest park, it is a vast region of forests and plains, crossed by the PEACE RIVER and dotted with lakes. The habitat of the largest remaining herd of wood buffalo (BISON) on the North American continent, as well as of bear, caribou, moose, and beaver, it also provides nesting grounds for the endangered WHOOPING CRANE.

wood duck North American DUCK (*Aix sponsa,* family Anatidae); a popular game bird. Wood ducks, 17–21 in. (43–52 cm) long, nest in a tree cavity up to 50 ft (15 m) off the ground; they have long-clawed toes for perching. Both sexes have a head crest in winter. The beautifully colored male has a purple and green head, red-brown breast flecked with white, and bronze sides; the female has a white eye ring and duller coloring. Ducklings eat aquatic insects and other small organisms; adults prefer acorns or other nuts. Hunted nearly to extinction for its flesh and feathers, it has been restored to healthy populations by strong conservation efforts.

Drake wood duck (*Aix sponsa*).
GRANT HEILMAN

Wood family English family of Staffordshire potters, a major force in the development of Staffordshire wares from peasant pottery to an organized industry. Its most prominent members were Ralph Wood (1715–1772), his brother Aaron (1717–1785), and his son Ralph Jr. (1748–1795). Ralph Jr. was related through his mother to JOSIAH WEDGWOOD, and the two names were often linked professionally. The elder Ralph became famous for his extremely well-modeled figures with colored glazes, and he is credited with introducing the Toby mug. Ralph Jr. produced a variety of figures, coloring them with enamel rather than glazes, and supplied some of them to Wedgwood. Aaron's son William (1746–1808) was employed as a modeler by Wedgwood. His brilliant brother Enoch (1759–1840) apprenticed with Wedgwood but by 1783 was established as an independent potter in partnership with his cousin Ralph Jr. In 1818 he continued his firm as Enoch Wood & Sons. Much of his earthenware was exported to the U.S. The firm closed in 1846. See also STAFFORDSHIRE FIGURE.

wood louse See PILL BUG, SOW BUG

wood mouse See FIELD MOUSE

wood rat *or* **pack rat** Any of 22 species (genus *Neotoma,* family Cricetidae) of RODENTS that are nocturnal vegetarians of North and Central American deserts, forests, and mountains. Wood rats are buff, gray, or reddish brown, usually with white undersides and feet. They have large ears and are 9–19 in. (23–47 cm) long, including the 3–9-in. (8–24-cm) furry tail. The nest, up to 3 ft (1 m) across and usually built of twigs or cactus, is placed in a protected spot (e.g., under a rock ledge). Wood rats are sometimes called pack rats because they collect material to deposit in their dens.

wood thrush One of the 11 species of THRUSHES (in the genus *Hylocichla,* or *Catharus*) called nightingale thrushes because of their rich songs. *H. mustelina* is common in eastern U.S. broadleaf forests; it is 8 in. (20 cm) long and has drab, spotted plumage and a rusty-colored head.

wood warbler Any of about 120 species of lively North and Central American songbirds in the family Parulidae. Wood warblers superficially resemble the true WARBLERS of the Old World but are usually more brightly colored (at least in the breeding season) and smaller (about 5 in., or 13 cm, long). They commonly inhabit woodlands and sometimes marshes and dry scrub. Their songs are buzzy and monotonous. The usual nest is a tidy cup in a bush or tree. They lay two to five speckled eggs. See also BLACKPOLL WARBLER, CHAT, REDSTART.

woodbine Any of many species of vines belonging to various flowering-plant families, especially the Virginia creeper (*Parthenocissus quinquefolia,* family Vitaceae) of North America and the Eurasian woodbine HONEYSUCKLE (*Lonicera periclymenum,* family Caprifoliaceae). The Virginia creeper, also called American ivy, attaches to walls, fences, and large tree trunks by means of disk-tipped tendrils. Its leaves display spectacular fall color from yellow to red-purple. Woodbine honeysuckle has grayish-green leaves and fragrant, yellowish-white flowers.

woodchuck *or* **groundhog** Reddish brown or brown species *(Marmota monax)* of solitary MARMOT inhabiting fields and forest edges in Alaska, Canada, and the eastern and central U.S. Woodchucks are 17–20 in. (42–52 cm) long, have a 4–6-in. (10–15-cm) tail, and weigh 4–14 lbs (2–6 kg). They are good diggers, swimmers, and climbers. Their burrows have a main entrance and an escape tunnel. See also GROUNDHOG DAY.

woodcock Any of five species (family Scolopacidae) of plump, sharp-billed migratory birds of damp, dense woodlands in North America, Europe, and Asia. With eyes set far back on the head, a woodcock has a 360° field of vision. The buffy-brown, mottled plumage provides camouflage. A solitary bird, most active at dusk, it drums its feet to coax earthworms to the surface and then extracts them with its long, forceps-like bill; it may eat twice its weight in worms each day. The female American woodcock *(Scolopax,* or *Philohela, minor)* is about 11 in. (28 cm) long; the male is slightly smaller. The male's striking courtship display includes a long, repeated spiraling and dropping sequence. Woodcocks have been popular game birds.

woodcut Design printed from a plank of wood incised parallel to the vertical axis of the wood's grain. One of the oldest methods of making prints, it was used in China to decorate textiles from the 5th century. Printing from wood blocks on textiles was known in Europe from the early 14th century, but developed little until paper began to be manufactured in France and Germany at the end of the 14th century. In the early 15th century, religious images and playing cards were first made from wood blocks. Black-line woodcut reached its greatest perfection in the 16th century with ALBRECHT DÜRER and his followers. In the late 19th and early 20th century, artists such as EDVARD MUNCH, PAUL GAUGUIN, and the German Expressionists rediscovered the expressive potential of woodcuts. Woodcuts have played an important role in the history of Japanese art (see UKIYO-E).

Woodhull, Victoria *orig.* **Victoria Claflin** (1838–1927) U.S. social reformer. Born in Homer, Ohio, she was raised in a family of traveling spiritualists with her sister Tennessee Claflin (1845–1923). After Victoria's marriage (1853) to Canning Woodhull ended in 1864, the sisters opened a successful brokerage firm in New York. They founded *Woodhull and Claflin's Weekly* (1870), which advocated equal rights for women, a single standard of morality for both sexes, and free love. A splinter group of radical suffragists formed a political party in 1872 and nominated Woodhull for president with FREDERICK DOUGLASS as vice president. In 1872 the sisters published the first English translation of the *Communist Manifesto*. For printing news of an alleged adulterous affair by HENRY WARD BEECHER, they were charged with libel but acquitted (1873). They moved to England (1877), where they lectured, worked for charities, and married wealthy Englishmen. Woodhull and her daughter published the eugenics journal *Humanitarian* (1892–1910).

Woodland cultures Prehistoric cultures of eastern North America dating from the 1st millennium BC. They included the ADENA and HOPEWELL cultures, and were characterized by the raising of corn, beans, and squash, the fashioning of distinctive pottery, and the building of burial mounds. Most of these cultures were replaced by the MISSISSIPPIAN CULTURE in the 1st millennium AD.

woodpecker Any of about 180 species (family Picidae) of mostly nonmigratory, solitary birds found nearly worldwide. Woodpeckers spiral up tree trunks, probing for insects, and chisel nest holes in dead wood by means of rapidly repeating blows of the beak. Though they spend their entire life in trees, only the few ground-feeding species can perch. Some species eat fruits and berries or tree sap. Woodpeckers are usually silent, except in spring, when males call loudly and drum on hollow wood. Species range from 6 to 18 in. (15–47 cm) long. All have a straight chisel-like bill, and most are patterned in black, white, or yellow and bright colors. See also FLICKER, IVORY-BILLED WOODPECKER, SAPSUCKER.

Woods, Lake of the Lake astride the Canadian–U.S. boundary, southwestern Ontario, southeastern Manitoba, and northern Minnesota. Irregular in shape, it is 70 mi (110 km) long and up to 60 mi (95 km) wide. It has an area of 1,727 sq mi (4,472 sq km), of which 642 sq mi (1,663 sq km) are in U.S territory. It has an estimated 25,000 mi (40,000 km) of shoreline and more than 14,000 islands. It receives the Rainy River from the southeast and drains north through the WINNIPEG RIVER into Lake WINNIPEG. Visited by French explorers in 1688, it became an important fur-trading route between the GREAT LAKES and western Canada. The Northwest Angle, the northernmost point of the coterminous U.S., is separated from the rest of Minnesota by a part of the lake.

Woods, Tiger *orig.* **Eldrick** (born 1975) U.S. golfer. Born in Cypress, Cal., to a Thai mother and a black U.S. Army officer, he won the first of three consecutive U.S. Junior Amateur Championships (1991–93) when he was 15. In 1994 he became the youngest winner (at 18) of the U.S. Amateur competition, which he also won in 1995 and 1996. After two years at Stanford Univ., in 1997 Woods became the youngest player (at 21) ever to win the Masters Tournament, winning by a record margin of 12 strokes. Winner of five other PGA tournaments in 1997, Woods became the youngest player ever ranked no. 1 in world golf competition. In 2000 he became, at 24, the youngest player ever to win a career Grand Slam.

Woodson, Carter G(odwin) (1875–1950) U.S. historian. Born into a poor Virginia family, he supported himself as a coal miner and was unable to enroll in high school until he was 20. He went on to receive a PhD from Harvard University. In 1915 he founded the Association for the Study of Negro Life and History to encourage the study of the black past; he also edited the association's *Journal of Negro History.* In the early 1920s he founded Associated Publishers to bring out books on black life and culture. Among his works dealing with the black experience was the college text *The Negro in Our History* (1922).

Woodstock *in full* **Woodstock Art and Music Fair** ROCK festival held near Bethel, N.Y. (its site was to have been the nearby town of Woodstock), on August 15–17, 1969. It attracted about 450,000 young rock fans, and featured such performers as the GRATEFUL DEAD, Jefferson Airplane, J. HENDRIX, the Who, and J. JOPLIN. The festival, whose participants exhibited extraordinary good feeling in the face of rain and organizational chaos, marked the high point of U.S. youth counterculture in the 1960s. It was documented in the film *Woodstock* (1970). It was revived with mixed success on its 25th and 30th anniversaries.

Woodward, C(omer) Vann (1908–1999) U.S. historian. Born in Vanndale, Ark., he graduated from Emory University in 1930. He received his PhD from the University of North Carolina. His writings on the American South and the Civil War, including *The Strange Career of Jim Crow* (1955) and *The Burden of Southern History* (1961), transformed the nation's understanding of the region. He edited *Mary Chesnut's Civil War* (1981; Pulitzer Prize) and *The Oxford History of the United States.* At his death he was professor emeritus at Yale Univ.

Woodward, Joanne (born 1930) U.S. actress. Born in Thomasville, Ga., she acted in Broadway plays and in TV dramas before turning to films. She starred as a schizophrenic in *The Three Faces of Eve* (1957, Academy Award), and also gave distinguished performances in such films as *The Long Hot Summer* (1958) and *Rachel, Rachel* (1968), directed by her husband, PAUL NEWMAN. Her later films include *Mr. and Mrs. Bridge* (1990).

Woodward, Robert B(urns) (1917–1979) U.S. chemist. Born in Boston, he attended MIT and taught at Harvard University 1938–79. Recognizing that physical measurement revealed molecular structure better than chemical reaction, in 1940–42 he developed "Woodward's rules" for determining structure by ultraviolet spectroscopy. In 1945 his methods finally clarified the structure of penicillin and of many more complex natural products. He proposed the correct biosynthetic pathway of steroid hormones. He was the most accomplished synthesist of complex organic compounds, including quinine (1944) and vitamin B12 (1971, in over 100 reactions), a task that led to the fundamental concept of conservation of orbital symmetry. He received a 1965 Nobel Prize, and in 1963 the new Woodward Research Institute in Basel, Switzerland, was named for him.

woodwind instruments Wind instruments that produce sound by either directing a stream of air against the edge of a hole or by making a reed or a double reed vibrate (see REED INSTRUMENTS). In BRASS INSTRUMENTS, by contrast, the airstream passes directly from the player's vibrating lips into the air column. The orchestral woodwinds include the FLUTE, piccolo, CLARINET, OBOE, ENGLISH HORN, and BASSOON. Other woodwinds include the SAXOPHONE, RECORDER, PANPIPE, SHAKUHACHI, and SHAWM.

wool Animal fiber that is the protective covering, or fleece, of SHEEP or such other hairy mammals as goats and camels. Wool is readied by washing (lanolin is the by-product), CARDING, sometimes combing, then spinning. Coarser than such textile fibers as cotton, linen, silk, and rayon, wool is resilient after limited stretching or compression, so fabrics and garments made from wool tend to retain shape, drape well, and resist wrinkling. Wool is warm and lightweight and takes dyes well. Woolen YARNS, usually made from shorter fibers, are thick and full and are used for such items as TWEED fabrics and blankets. WORSTEDS usually are made from longer fibers.

Woolf \'wu̇lf\, **(Adeline) Virginia** *orig.* **Adeline Virginia Stephen** (1882–1941) British novelist and critic. Daughter of LESLIE STEPHEN, she and her sister became the early nucleus of the BLOOMSBURY GROUP. She married Leonard Woolf in 1912; in 1917 they founded the Hogarth Press. Her best novels include *Mrs. Dalloway* (1925), *To the Lighthouse* (1927), which use vividly metaphoric presentation of an individual consciousness meditating on apparently insignificant events to present a whole life and a whole historical period. *Orlando* (1928) is a historical fantasy about the experiences of a single character from the Elizabethan era to the present day, and *The Waves* (1931), perhaps her most radically experimental work, uses interior monologue and recurring images to trace the inner lives of six characters. Such works confirmed her place among the major figures of literary modernism. Her best critical studies are collected in *The Common Reader* (1925, 1932). Her long essay *A Room of One's Own* (1929) addressed the status of women, and women artists in particular. Her other novels include *Jacob's Room* (1922), *The Years* (1937), and *Between the Acts* (1941). Her health and mental stability were delicate throughout her life; in a recurrence of mental illness, she drowned herself. Her diaries and correspondence have been published in several editions.

Woollcott \'wu̇l-kət\, **Alexander (Humphreys)** (1887–1943) U.S. author, critic, and actor. He joined the *New York Times* in 1909 and became its drama critic in 1914. Known for his acerbic wit, he became the self-appointed leader of the Algonquin Round Table, the informal luncheon club at New York's Algonquin Hotel in the 1920s and '30s. that included Groucho MARX, DOROTHY PARKER, ROBERT SHERWOOD, and GEORGE S. KAUFMAN. He later wrote for the *New Yorker,* wrote such books as *Two Gentlemen and a Lady* (1928) and *While Rome Burns* (1934), and was the inspiration for the play *The Man Who Came to Dinner* (1939).

woolly bear *or* **wooly bear** CATERPILLAR of a TIGER MOTH. The larva of the Isabella tiger moth *(Isia isabella),* known as the banded woolly bear, is brown in the middle and black at both ends. The width of the black bands is purported to predict the severity of the coming winter: the narrower the bands, the milder the weather will be.

Woolworth Co. U.S. merchandising company. F. W. Woolworth (1852–1919) founded his first "five- and ten-cent" store in 1879. By 1904 there were 120 stores in 21 states. The company's New York headquarters, the Woolworth building (1913), was once the world's tallest skyscraper. By 1929 Woolworth had about 2,250 outlets. Its stores continued to proliferate in the U.S. and Britain, and it acquired other chains dealing in sportswear, shoes, and children's wear. From 1992 it began closing down hundreds of stores and selling off subsidiaries; in 1998 it changed its name to Venator Group, Inc., and announced its intention to focus on sporting goods. In 2001 the company name changed to Foot Locker, Inc.

wootz (steel) \'wüts\ STEEL produced by a method known in ancient India. The process involved preparation of porous IRON, hammering it while hot to release SLAG, breaking it up and sealing it with wood chips in a clay container, and heating it until the pieces of iron absorbed carbon from the wood and melted. The steel thus produced had a uniform composition of 1–1.6% carbon and could be heated and forged into bars for later use in fashioning articles, such as the famous medieval Damascus swords. See also BLOOMERY PROCESS.

Worcester City (pop., 1995 est.: 91,000), county seat of HEREFORD AND WORCESTER, England. Located on the SEVERN RIVER, it was settled before AD 680. During the Middle Ages it was an important wool town and also became known for its glove making. OLIVER CROMWELL and his Parliamentarian army routed CHARLES II and his Scottish army in the Battle of Worcester, effecting an end to the ENGLISH CIVIL WAR. In 1751 John Wall founded the porcelain industry for which the town is now famous, and in 1838 the condiment known as Worcestershire sauce was introduced there by Lea & Perrins. The town's noted cathedral (11th–14th century) contains the tombs of King JOHN and Prince Arthur, the eldest son of HENRY VII.

Worcester \'wu̇s-tər\ City (pop., 1996 est.: 166,000), central Massachusetts, on the BLACKSTONE RIVER. The original settlement (1673) was disbanded during KING PHILIP'S WAR (1675–76) and a later settlement was established in 1713. Textile manufacturing began in 1789; the first corduroy cloth in the U.S. was produced there. Industrial development occurred after the opening (1828) of the Blackstone Canal. An early abolitionist center, Worcester became an important stop on the UNDERGROUND RAILROAD. It is a commercial and industrial center and the state's second-largest city. Among its institutions of higher education are College of the HOLY CROSS and Clark University (1887).

word processing Preparation of textual documents on computer. A word-processing system typically consists simply of a PERSONAL COMPUTER linked to a computer PRINTER, but may instead employ a terminal linked to a MAINFRAME computer. Word processing differs from typewriter typing in numerous ways. Electronic text can be moved around at will; misspelled terms can be corrected throughout the document by means of a single command; SPELLING AND GRAMMAR CHECKERS can automatically alert the user to apparent errors of spelling, punctuation, and syntax; and the document's format, layout, and type fonts and sizes can be changed repeatedly until a satisfactory design is achieved. Since all editing ideally occurs on-screen, word processing can result in decreased paper usage and simplified editing. When the final draft is ready, the document can be printed out (in multiple copies if necessary), sent as an E-MAIL attachment, shared on a computer NETWORK, or simply stored as an electronic file.

Worde \'wȯrd\, **Wynkyn de** *orig.* **Jan van Wynkyn** (died 1534/35) British printer. Born in Alsace, he was employed at WILLIAM CAXTON's press from its founding in 1476 until Caxton's death, when he took over the concern. Unlike Caxton and other contemporaries, he did not edit or translate. An astute businessman, he published at least 600 titles after 1501, and was the first printer in England to use italic type (1524).

Wordsworth, Dorothy (1771–1855) English writer. An inspiring influence on her brother WILLIAM WORDSWORTH, she lived with him from 1795. Her *Alfoxden Journal 1798* (1897)—from the period when he and SAMUEL TAYLOR COLERIDGE produced *Lyrical Ballads* (1798)—and *Grasmere Journals 1800–03* (1897) are intimate records of their lives. Both are appreciated for their imaginative descriptions of nature, their perfection of style, and their revelation of her personality as well as for the light they throw on her brother. In 1829 severe illness left her an invalid, and her mind was clouded in her last 20 years.

Wordsworth, William (1770–1850) English poet. Orphaned at 13, Wordsworth attended Cambridge Univ., but remained rootless and virtually penniless until 1795, when a legacy made possible a reunion with his sister DOROTHY WORDSWORTH. He became friends with SAMUEL TAYLOR COLERIDGE, with whom he wrote *Lyrical Ballads* (1798), the collection often considered to have launched the English Romantic movement. Wordsworth's contributions include "Tintern Abbey" and many lyrics controversial for their common, everyday language. Around 1798 he began writing the epic autobiographical poem that would absorb him intermittently for the next 40 years, *The Prelude* (1850). His second verse collection, *Poems, in Two Volumes* (1807), includes many of the rest of his finest works, including "Ode: Intimations of Immortality." His poetry is perhaps most original in its vision of the almost divine power of the creative imagination reforging the links between man and man between humankind and the natural world. The most memorable poems of his middle and late years were often cast in elegaic mode; few match the best of his earlier works. By the time he became widely appreciated by the critics and the public, his poetry had lost much of its force and his radical politics had yielded to conservatism. In 1843 he became England's poet laureate. He is regarded as the central figure in the initiation of English ROMANTICISM.

work In economics and sociology, the activities and labor necessary for the survival of society. As early as 40,000 BC, hunters worked in groups to track and kill animals, while younger or weaker members of the tribe gathered food. When agriculture replaced hunting and gathering, the resulting surplus of food allowed early societies to develop, with some members pursuing crafts such as pottery making, textiles, and metallurgy. The establishment of towns led to the creation of new occupations in commerce, law, medicine, and defense. Early civilizations were characterized by rigid social hierarchies. Nobles, clergy, merchants, artisans, and peasants pursued occupations defined largely by hereditary social class. Craft GUILDS, influential in the economic development of medieval Europe, limited the supply of labor in each profession and controlled production. The coming of the INDUSTRIAL REVOLUTION, spurred by technological advances such as steam power, changed working life profoundly. Factories divided the work once done by a single craftsman into a number of distinct tasks performed by unskilled or semiskilled workers (see DIVISION OF LABOR). Manufacturing firms grew larger in the 19th century as standardized parts and machine tools came into use, and ever more specialized positions for managers, supervisors, accountants, engineers, technicians, and salesmen were necessary. The trend toward specialization continued through the 20th century, giving rise to a number of disciplines concerned with the management and design of work, including PRODUCTION MANAGEMENT, INDUSTRIAL RELATIONS, personnel administration, and SYSTEMS ENGINEERING. By the turn of the 21st century, automation and technology had spurred tremendous growth in SERVICE INDUSTRIES.

work In physics, the measure of energy transfer that occurs when an object is moved over a distance by an external force, some component of which is applied in the direction of displacement. For a constant force, work W is equal to the magnitude of the force f times the displacement d of the object, or $W = fd$. Work is also done by compressing a gas, by rotating a shaft, and by causing invisible motions of particles within a body by an external MAGNETIC FORCE. No work is accomplished by simply holding a heavy stationary object because there is no transfer of energy and no displacement. Work done on a body is equal to the increase in energy of the body. Work is expressed in units called joules (J). One joule is equivalent to the energy transferred when a force of one newton is applied over a distance of one meter.

workers' compensation Social-welfare program through which employers bear some of the cost of their employees' work-related injuries and occupational diseases. It was first introduced in Germany in 1884. In Britain and the U.S. in the late 19th century, there was a movement to secure the right of injured workers to compensation and improve working conditions through court decisions, employer liability statutes, and safety codes. By the mid-20th century most countries in the world had adopted some sort of workers' compensation. Some systems take the form of compulsory SOCIAL INSURANCE; in others the employer is legally required to provide certain benefits, but insurance is voluntary. The system of workers' compensation serves as an economic incentive for employers to prevent accidents and illness among employees, since liability for medical costs and the income lost by having workers in a hazardous environment can easily exceed the costs of establishing safe working conditions.

Workers' Opposition (1920–21) Group within the Soviet Union's COMMUNIST PARTY that championed workers' rights and trade-union control over industry. It was formed in 1919 to resist the central party's increasing control over local party units and trade unions. In 1920 it objected to LEON TROTSKY's plan to transform trade unions into state organs. Led by ALEKSANDRA KOLLONTAY and others, the group insisted that the unions, as true representatives of the proletariat, should control the national economy. At the 10th Party Congress (1921), its platform was rejected and it was ordered to disperse.

workfare Form of WELFARE requiring able-bodied adults to work. In 1994 various U.S. states were already experimenting with workfare programs when Pres. WILLIAM JEFFERSON CLINTON proposed a similar national scheme, including a welfare payment cutoff after two years, coupled with aggressive programs of job training and retraining. The final bill, passed in 1996, replaced the existing 60-year-old program with block grants to the states, which were to run their own programs. Most recipients were required to work within two years of receiving benefits and were limited to a lifetime maximum of five years on welfare rolls. The law provided for job training and child-care assistance, though in a more limited form than originally proposed, and denied noncitizens access to a variety of services.

working dog Any of various breeds of dog bred as guard, herding, draft, or rescue animals. Breeds range from medium to large, but all are sturdy and muscular, intelligent and loyal. Guard breeds include the AKITA, BOXER, bullmastiff, DOBERMAN PINSCHER, giant and standard SCHNAUZERS, GREAT DANE, MASTIFF, and ROTTWEILER. Livestock guard breeds include the Great Pyrenees, komondor (Hungary), kuvasz (Tibet), and Pyrenean mountain dogs (Britain). Herding dogs include the GERMAN SHEPHERD, SHETLAND SHEEPDOG, and WELSH CORGI. Breeds developed for hauling and rescue work include the BERNESE MOUNTAIN DOG, Portuguese water dog, NEWFOUNDLAND, ST. BERNARD, and SLED DOG.

Workingmen's Party First labor-oriented U.S. political party. It was formed in Philadelphia (1828) and New York (1829) by craftsmen, skilled journeymen, and reformers who demanded a 10-hour workday, free public education, abolition of debtor imprisonment, and an end to competition from prison contract labor. Leaders included Thomas Skidmore, FANNY WRIGHT, ROBERT DALE OWEN, and GEORGE H. EVANS. Factional disputes split the party in the 1830s, and many in New York joined the reform LOCOFOCO PARTY.

Works Progress Administration *later (1939–43)* **Work Projects Administration (WPA)** U.S. work program for the unemployed. Created in 1935 under the NEW DEAL, it aimed to stimulate the economy during the GREAT DEPRESSION and preserve the skills and self-respect of unemployed persons by providing them useful work. During its existence, it employed 8.5 million people on the construction of 650,000 mi (1,046,000 km) of roads, 125,000 public buildings, 75,000 bridges, 8,000 parks, and 800 airports. The WPA also administered the WPA FEDERAL ART PROJECT, the Theater Project, and the Writers' Project, providing jobs for unemployed artists, actors, and writers. In 1943, with the virtual elimination of unemployment by the wartime economy, the WPA was terminated.

workstation Computer intended for use by one person, but with a much faster processor and more memory than an ordinary PERSONAL COMPUTER. Workstations are designed for powerful business applications that do large numbers of calculations or require high-speed graphical displays; the requirements of CAD/CAM systems were one reason for their initial development. Because of their need for computing power, they are often based on RISC processors and generally use UNIX as their operating system. An early workstation was introduced in 1987 by Sun Microsystems; workstations introduced in 1988 from Apollo, Ardent, and Stellar were aimed at 3D graphics applications. The term workstation is also sometimes used to mean a personal computer connected to a MAINFRAME computer, to distinguish it from "dumb" display terminals with limited applications.

World Bank Specialized agency of the U.N. system, established at the BRETTON WOODS CONFERENCE for postwar reconstruction. It is the principal international-development institution. Its five divisions are the INTERNATIONAL BANK FOR RECONSTRUCTION AND DEVELOPMENT (its main component), the International Development Association (IDA), the International Finance Corp. (IFC), the Multilateral Investment Guarantee Agency (MIGA), and the International Center for Settlement of Investment Disputes (ICSID). The IDA (founded 1960) makes interest-free loans to the bank's poorest member countries. The IFC (founded 1956) lends to private businesses in developing countries. The MIGA (founded 1985) supports national and private agencies that encourage foreign direct investment by offering insurance against noncommercial risks. The ICSID (founded 1966) was developed to relieve the IBRD of the burden of settling investment disputes. See also INTERNATIONAL MONETARY FUND.

World Council of Churches (WCC) Christian ecumenical organization founded in 1948 in Amsterdam. It functions as a forum for Protestant and Eastern Orthodox denominations, which cooperate through the WCC on a variety of undertakings and explore doctrinal similarities and differences. It grew out of two post-World War I ecumenical efforts, the Life and Work Movement (which concentrated on practical activities) and the Faith and Order Movement (which focused on doctrinal issues and the possibility of reunion). The impetus for these two organizations sprang from the International Missionary Conference in Edinburgh in 1910, the first such cooperative effort since the REFORMATION. The Roman Catholic church, though not a member of the WCC, sends representatives to its conferences. The more fundamentalist Protestant denominations have also refused to join.

World Court See INTERNATIONAL COURT OF JUSTICE

World Cup Any of three major international sporting competitions and their trophies. The World Cup of soccer (football) is a tournament involving the 16 best national teams, culminating in a match between the two top teams. It has been held every fourth year since 1930 (except during World War II). Followed and watched by billions of people worldwide, it has by far the greatest audience of any single sporting event in the world. The World Cup of skiing, held annually since 1967, is an Alpine-skiing contest (downhill, slalom, and giant slalom) held at designated meets throughout the winter. The winners are the male and female skiers with the highest point totals. The World Cup of golf (founded in 1953 as the Canada Cup) is an annual competition for two-man professional teams representing nations.

World Food Programme (WFP) Food-aid organization of the U.N., founded in 1961. The world's largest food-aid organization, it feeds people in emergencies brought about by wars or natural disasters, targets pregnant and breast-feeding women and school-aged children in countries with chronic hunger, and promotes self-reliance through food-for-work programs. It receives only voluntary contributions, which it accepts from nongovernmental organizations, donor nations, corporations, and private individuals. It also assists in land reclamation, de-mining, and irrigation projects. Its headquarters are in Rome.

World Health Organization (WHO) Public-health agency of the U.N., established in Geneva in 1948 to succeed two earlier agencies. Its mandate is to promote "the highest possible level of health" in all peoples. Its work falls into three categories. It provides a clearinghouse for information on the latest developments in disease and health care and establishes international sanitary standards and quarantine measures. It sponsors measures for the control of epidemic and endemic disease (including immunization campaigns and assistance in providing sources of pure water). Finally, it encourages the strengthening of public-health programs in member nations. Its greatest success to date has been the worldwide eradication of SMALLPOX (1980).

World Heritage site Any of various areas or objects designated as having "outstanding universal value" under the Convention Concerning the Protection of the World Cultural and Natural Heritage. This convention, adopted by UNESCO in 1972, provides for international cooperation in preserving and protecting cultural and natural treasures throughout the world. Each site on the list is under strict legal protection by the government of the nation in which it is situated. Among the cultural

Selected UNESCO World Heritage sites

site*	country	notes
Africa		
Abu Ruwaysh	Egypt	archaeological remains
Aksum	Ethiopia	historic monuments
Carthage	Tunisia	remains of ancient city
Dahshur	Egypt	pyramids and funerary complex
Giza	Egypt	pyramids and funerary complex
Gorée Island	Senegal	slave-trading depot
Great Zimbabwe	Zimbabwe	ruins of Shona capital
Hadar	Ethiopia	early hominid remains
Karnak	Egypt	Theban temple ruins
Kilimanjaro	Tanzania	montane national park and reserve
Kings, Valley of the	Egypt	Theban necropolis
Lalibela	Ethiopia	rock-hewn medieval churches
Leptis Magna	Libya	remains of Roman architecture
Luxor	Egypt	Theban ruins
Marrakech	Morocco	historic medina
Memphis	Egypt	remains of ancient city
Mount Kenya	Kenya	national park and forest reserve
Ngorongoro	Tanzania	wildlife conservation area
Olduvai Gorge	Tanzania	early hominid remains
Philae	Egypt	Nubian monuments
Saqqarah	Egypt	step pyramid and funerary complex
Serengeti	Tanzania	national park, wildlife refuge
Thebes	Egypt	ruins of ancient Egyptian capital
Timbuktu	Mali	medieval center of Islamic culture
Victoria Falls	Zambia and Zimbabwe	national parks, cataracts, Zambezi River, rainforest, and wildlife
Virunga	Congo (Kinshasa)	national park, diversity of habitats
Asia		
Ajanta Caves	India	rock-cut Buddhist monasteries
Angkor	Cambodia	archaeological remains
Ayutthaya	Thailand	ruins of capital complex
Baikal, Lake	Russia	unique freshwater environment
Borobudur	Indonesia	Buddhist temple compound
Chogha Zanbil	Iran	ruins of Elamite city
Damascus	Syria	historic city center
Delhi	India	historic monuments and tomb
Elephanta Island	India	Hindu cave temple
Ellora Caves	India	Hindu, Buddhist, Jaina cave temples
Everest, Mount	Nepal	montane national park
Forbidden City	China	imperial palace in Beijing
Great Wall of China	China	extensive fortification
Ha Long Bay	Vietnam	picturesque island group
Hatra	Iraq	ruins of Parthian city
Hiroshima	Japan	peace memorial
Horyu Temple	Japan	Buddhist monuments
Hue	Vietnam	imperial citadel
Jerusalem	Israel	Jewish, Islamic, Christian holy city
Kandy	Sri Lanka	sacred Buddhist city
Khiva	Uzbekistan	Islamic architecture
Kyoto	Japan	historic imperial capital
Lahore	Pakistan	Mughal fortress, palace, gardens
Palmyra	Syria	ruins of ancient city
Petra	Jordan	remains of ancient city
Potala Palace	China	former residence of the Dalai Lama, in Lhasa, Tibet
Qin tomb	China	archaeological site, terra-cotta army
San'a'	Yemen	historic architecture
Sundarbans	Bangladesh and India	national park (India), sanctuary, mangrove forest and wetlands
Taj Mahal	India	monumental funerary complex
Tyre	Lebanon	ruins of three millennia of habitation
Ujong-Kulon	Indonesia	national park and reserve on Java
Zhoukoudian	China	early hominid habitation
Australia and Oceania		
Great Barrier Reef	Australia	marine national park
Lord Howe Island	Australia	diversity of habitats
Rennell Island	Solomon Islands	unique island ecosystem
Shark Bay	Australia	rare marine and terrestrial life-forms
Uluru (Ayers Rock)	Australia	national park, sandstone monolith

site*	country	notes
Europe		
Acropolis of Athens	Greece	complex of monuments
Alhambra	Spain	Moorish palace and fortress
Altamira	Spain	prehistoric cave paintings
Amiens Cathedral	France	Romanesque and Gothic styles
Arles	France	Roman, Romanesque monuments
Auschwitz	Poland	Nazi concentration camp
Avebury	England	prehistoric megalith group
Bergen	Norway	Hanseatic wharf
Bern	Switzerland	medieval city center
Canterbury	England	cathedral and abbey
Chartres Cathedral	France	Gothic architecture
Delphi	Greece	remains of sanctuary complex
Ferrara	Italy	Renaissance architecture
Florence	Italy	historic city center
Fontainebleau	France	royal château and gardens
Giant's Causeway	Northern Ireland	coastal rock formations
Granada	Spain	Moorish, Andalusian structures
Hadrian's Wall	England	Roman fortification
Herculaneum	Italy	ruins of Vesuvius-destroyed town
Istanbul	Turkey	numerous historic sites
Kraków (Cracow)	Poland	medieval city center
Lascaux Grotto	France	prehistoric cave paintings
Lübeck	Germany	Hanseatic architecture
Luxembourg city	Luxembourg	fortifications and old city
Meteóra	Greece	Orthodox Christian monasteries
Mont-Saint-Michel	France	medieval village and abbey
Moscow	Russia	Kremlin and Red Square
Naples	Italy	historic city center
Olympia	Greece	ruins of ancient sacred city
Palatine Chapel (Aachen Cathedral)	Germany	imperial chapel of Charlemagne, Carolingian and Gothic styles
Paris	France	banks of Seine River
Pompeii	Italy	ruins of Vesuvius-destroyed town
Porto (Oporto)	Portugal	historic city center
Prague	Czech Republic	historic city center
Reims Cathedral	France	High Gothic architecture
Rhodes	Greece	medieval city center
Rila Monastery	Bulgaria	cradle of Bulgarian "National Revival"
Saint Petersburg	Russia	historic city center and monuments
Salzburg	Austria	historic city center
Samos	Greece	ancient port and temple remains
Santiago	Spain	old city and pilgrimage route
Segovia	Spain	old town and Roman aqueduct
Split	Croatia	Roman palace, other monuments
Stonehenge	England	prehistoric megalith group
Tallinn	Estonia	historic city center
Toledo	Spain	historic structures
Transylvania	Romania	Saxon fortified churches, villages
Vatican City	Vatican City	seat of Roman Catholic church
Venice	Italy	island city and surrounding lagoon
Versailles	France	royal palace and park
Visby	Sweden	historic Hanseatic town
North America		
Banff	Canada	national park, Rocky Mountains
Chaco Canyon	United States	historical park, Pueblo ruins
Chichén Itzá	Mexico	Mayan-Toltec architecture
Cocos Island	Costa Rica	national park, forest and marine life
Copán	Honduras	remains of major Mayan city
Glacier Bay	United States	subarctic national park, preserve
Grand Canyon	United States	national park
Havana	Cuba	colonial city center
Hawaii Volcanoes	United States	national park
Jasper	Canada	national park, Rocky Mountains
Kluane	Canada	subarctic national park
Kootenay	Canada	national park, Rocky Mountains
L'Anse aux Meadows	Canada	remains of medieval Norse settlement in Newfoundland
Mammoth Cave	United States	cave system and national park
Mesa Verde	United States	prehistoric cliff dwellings
Mexico City	Mexico	historic city center
Palenque	Mexico	national park, Mayan city

Selected UNESCO World Heritage sites (continued)

site*	country	notes
North America (continued)		
Santo Domingo	Dominican Rep.	colonial city
Statue of Liberty	United States	national monument
Teotihuacán	Mexico	extensive pre-Hispanic ruins
Tikal	Guatemala	national park, Mayan ruins
Uxmal	Mexico	Mayan city and ceremonial center
Wrangell-St. Elias	United States	subarctic national park, preserve
Xochimilco	Mexico	Aztec canals and floating gardens
Yellowstone	United States	national park, geothermal formations
Yoho	Canada	national park, Rocky Mountains
South America		
Arequipa	Peru	colonial architecture
Brasília	Brazil	urban planning and architecture
Cartagena	Colombia	colonial port, fortresses, monuments
Chan Chan	Peru	ruins of pre-Inca Chimú capital
Colonia del Sacramento	Uruguay	Portuguese, Spanish colonial architecture
South America (continued)		
Córdoba	Argentina	Jesuit institutions and estates
Coro	Venezuela	Spanish, Dutch, local architecture
Cuzco	Peru	Inca and colonial architecture
Easter Island	Chile	monumental sculptures
Galapagos Islands	Ecuador	national park, unique ecosystem
Huascarán, Mount	Peru	montane national park
Iguaçu (Iguazú)	Brazil and Argentina	national parks, waterfalls, subtropical rainforests
Los Kaitos and Darién	Colombia and Panama	national parks on the frontier, rainforest, wetlands
Machu Picchu	Peru	Inca ruins
Nazca Lines	Peru	extensive geoglyphs
Pantanal	Brazil	freshwater wetland ecosystem
Potosí	Bolivia	colonial industrial city
Quito	Ecuador	colonial city center
Valdés Peninsula	Argentina	seals, whales

*The spelling or styling of place-names in this table may differ from those given on the World Heritage List; in addition, some place-names represent one or more constituent parts of larger World Heritage sites.

sites are many of the world's most famous buildings. The ratio of cultural to natural sites on the list is roughly three to one.

world music Musical genre incorporating diverse styles from Africa, eastern Europe, Asia, South and Central America, the Caribbean, and nonmainstream Western folk sources. First defined largely by the sudden increase of recordings in non-English languages that were released in Great Britain and the United States in the 1980s, by the early 1990s world music had become a bona fide musical genre and counterpoint to the increasingly synthetic sounds of Western pop music. Initially African popular music and world music were virtually identical, and the genre's biggest stars included Nigerians King Sunny Ade, Fela Anikulapo Kuti, and Senegalese Youssou N'Dour. Moreover, one of its earliest advocates was the Cameroonian-born Frenchman Francis Bebey. By the 21st century world music encompassed everything from Pakistani singer Nusrat Fateh Ali Khan and the pop-flamenco of the French group the Gipsy Kings to "ambient-global" projects that merged so-called ethnic voice samples with state-of-the-art rhythm programming.

World Series Annual championship of U.S. major-league baseball, played between the top team of the American League (AL) and that of the National League (NL). First held in 1903, it was canceled the following year after the New York Giants (NL) refused to play Boston (AL). The series resumed in 1905 and continued annually until a players' strike in 1994 forced its cancellation that year. A seven-game series has been standard since 1922.

World Trade Center Complex formerly consisting of seven buildings around a central plaza, near the southern tip of Manhattan. Its huge twin towers (completed 1970–72) were designed by Minoru Yamasaki (1912–1986). At 1,368 ft (417 m) and 1,362 ft (415 m) tall, they were the world's tallest buildings until surpassed in 1973 by the Sears Tower in Chicago. The towers were notable for the relationship of their simple, light embellishment to their underlying structure. In 1993 a bomb planted by terrorists exploded in the underground garage, killing several people and injuring some 1,000. A much more massive attack occurred on Sept. 11, 2001, when first One World Trade Center and then Two World Trade Center were struck by hijacked commercial airliners deliberately flown into them. Shortly thereafter both of the heavily damaged towers, as well as adjacent buildings, collapsed into enormous piles of debris. The attacks—the deadliest terrorist assault in history—claimed the lives of some 2,800 victims. Thousands more were injured. See September 11 attacks.

World Trade Organization (WTO) International organization based in Geneva that supervises world trade with the intention of making it flow as smoothly, predictably, and freely as possible. It was created by 104 members in 1995 to replace the General Agreement on Tariffs and Trade (GATT). Like its predecessor, it aims to lower trade barriers and encourage multilateral trade. It monitors members' adherence to all GATT agreements and negotiates and implements new agreements. Critics of the WTO, including many opponents of economic globalization, have charged that it infringes upon national sovereignty by promoting the interests of large multinational corporations and that in developing countries the trade liberalization the WTO encourages leads to environmental damage and declining living standards for low-skilled workers.

World War I *or* **First World War** (1914–18) International conflict between the Central Powers—Germany, Austria-Hungary, and Turkey—and the Allied Powers—mainly France, Britain, Russia, Italy, and (from 1917) the U.S. After a Serbian nationalist assassinated Archduke Francis Ferdinand of Austria in June 1914, a chain of threats and mobilizations resulted in a general war between the antagonists by mid-August. Prepared to fight a war on two fronts, based on the Schlieffen Plan, Germany first swept through neutral Belgium and invaded France. After the First Battle of the Marne (1914), the Allied defensive lines were stabilized in France, and a war of attrition began. Fought from lines of trenches and supported by modern artillery and machine guns, infantry assaults gained little ground and were enormously costly in human life, especially at the Battles of Verdun and the Somme (1916). On the Eastern front, Russian forces initially drove deep into East Prussia and German Poland (1914), but were stopped by German and Austrian forces at the Battle of Tannenberg and forced back into Russia (1915). After several offensives, the Russian army failed to break through the German defensive lines. Russia's poor performance and enormous losses caused widespread domestic discontent that led to the Russian Revolution of 1917. Other fronts in the war included the Dardanelles Campaign, in which British and Dominion forces were unsuccessful against Turkey; the Caucasus and Iran (Persia), where Russia fought Turkey; Mesopotamia and Egypt, where British forces fought the Turks; and northern Italy, where Italian and Austrian troops fought the costly Battles of the Isonzo. At sea, the German and British fleets fought the inconclusive Battle of Jutland, and Germany's use of the submarine against neutral shipping eventually brought the U.S. into the war in 1917. Though Russia's armistice with Germany in December 1917 released German troops to fight on the Western Front, the Allies were reinforced by U.S. troops in early 1918. Germany's unsuccessful offensive in the Second Battle of the Marne was countered by the Allies' steady advance, which recovered most of France and Belgium by October 1918 and led to the November Armistice. Total casualties were estimated at 10 million dead, 21 million wounded, and 7.7 million missing or imprisoned. See also Battles of Caporetto, Vimy Ridge, and Ypres; Fourteen Points; Lusitania; Paris Peace Conference; Treaties of Brest-Litovsk, Neuilly, Saint-Germain, Sèvres, Trianon, and Versailles; Edmund H. H. Allenby, Ferdinand Foch, John

FRENCH, DOUGLAS HAIG, PAUL VON HINDENBURG, JOSEPH-JACQUES-CESAIRE JOFFRE, ERICH LUDENDORFF, JOHN PERSHING.

World War II *or* **Second World War** (1939–45) International conflict principally between the AXIS POWERS—Germany, Italy, and Japan—and the ALLIED POWERS—France, Britain, the U.S., and the Soviet Union. Political and economic instability in Germany, combined with bitterness over its defeat in WORLD WAR I and the harsh conditions of the Treaty of VERSAILLES, allowed ADOLF HITLER and the NAZI PARTY to rise to power. In the mid-1930s, Hitler began secretly to rearm Germany, in violation of the treaty. He signed alliances with Italy and Japan to oppose the Soviet Union and intervened in the SPANISH CIVIL WAR in the name of anticommunism. Capitalizing on the reluctance of other European powers to oppose him by force, he sent troops to occupy Austria in 1938 (see ANSCHLUSS) and to annex Czechoslovakia in 1939. After signing the GERMAN–SOVIET NONAGGRESSION PACT, Germany invaded Poland on September 1, 1939. Two days later, France and Britain declared war on Germany. Poland's defeat was followed by a period of military inactivity on the Western front (see PHONY WAR). At sea Germany conducted a damaging submarine campaign by U-BOAT against merchant shipping bound for Britain. By early 1940 the Soviet Union had divided Poland with Germany, occupied the Baltic states, and subdued Finland in the RUSSO–FINNISH WAR. In April 1940 Germany overwhelmed Denmark and began its conquest of Norway. In May German forces swept through the Netherlands and Belgium on their BLITZKRIEG invasion of France, forcing it to capitulate in June and establish the VICHY FRANCE regime. Germany then launched massive bombing raids on Britain in preparation for a cross-Channel invasion, but after losing the Battle of BRITAIN Hitler postponed the invasion indefinitely. By early 1941 Hungary, Romania, and Bulgaria had joined the Axis, and German troops quickly overran Yugoslavia and Greece in April. In June Hitler abandoned his pact with the Soviet Union and launched a massive surprise invasion of Russia, reaching the outskirts of Moscow before Soviet counterattacks and winter weather halted the advance. In East Asia, Japan expanded its war with China and seized European colonial holdings. In December 1941 Japan attacked U.S. bases at Pearl Harbor and in the Philippines, and the U.S. declared war on Japan and all the Axis Powers. Japan quickly invaded and occupied most of S.East Asia, Burma, the Netherlands East Indies, and many Pacific islands. After the crucial U.S. naval victory at the Battle of MIDWAY (1942), U.S. forces began to advance up the chains of islands toward Japan. In the NORTH AFRICA CAMPAIGNS, the British defeated Italian and German forces by 1943. The Allies then invaded Sicily and Italy, forcing the overthrow of the Fascist government in July 1943, though fighting against the Germans continued in Italy until 1945. In the Soviet Union, the Battle of STALINGRAD (1943) marked the end of the German advance, and Soviet reinforcements in great numbers gradually pushed the German armies back. The massive Allied invasion of Western Europe began with the NORMANDY CAMPAIGN in western France (1944), and the Allies' steady advance ended in the occupation of Germany in 1945. After Soviet troops pushed German forces out of the Soviet Union, they advanced into Poland, Czechoslovakia, Hungary, and Romania, and had occupied the eastern third of Germany by the time the surrender of Germany was signed on May 8, 1945. In the Pacific, an Allied invasion of the Philippines (1944) was followed by the successful Battle of LEYTE GULF and the costly Battles of IWO JIMA and OKINAWA (1945). The war in the Pacific ended quickly after atomic bombs were dropped on HIROSHIMA and NAGASAKI in August 1945. Japan's formal surrender on September 2 ended the war. Estimates of total military and civilian casualties varied from 35 million to 60 million killed, including about 6 million Jews who died in the HOLOCAUST. Millions more civilians were wounded and made homeless throughout Europe and East Asia. See also ANTI-COMINTERN PACT; ATLANTIC CHARTER; Battles of EL ALAMEIN, the ATLANTIC, the BULGE, GUADALCANAL, and the PHILIPPINE SEA; CASABLANCA, POTSDAM, TEHRAN, and YALTA conferences; DUNKIRK EVACUATION; LEND-LEASE; MUNICH AGREEMENT; NUREMBERG TRIALS; Siege of LENINGRAD; SINO–JAPANESE WARS; OMAR BRADLEY, WINSTON CHURCHILL, DWIGHT D. EISENHOWER, DOUGLAS MACARTHUR, BERNARD LAW MONTGOMERY, BENITO MUSSOLINI, GEORGE PATTON, ERWIN ROMMEL, FRANKLIN ROOSEVELT, JOSEPH STALIN, YAMAMOTO ISOROKU, GEORGY K. ZHUKOV.

World Wide Web (WWW) *or* **Web** Leading information-exchange service of the INTERNET. It was created by TIM BERNERS-LEE and his colleagues at CERN and introduced to the world in 1991. The Web gives users access to a vast array of documents that are connected to each other by means of HYPERTEXT or hyperlinks. A hypertext document with its corresponding text and hyperlinks is written in HTML and is assigned an on-line address, or URL. The Web operates within the Internet's basic CLIENT-SERVER ARCHITECTURE. Individual HTML files with unique electronic addresses are called Web pages, and a collection of Web pages and related files (such as graphics files, scripted programs, and other resources) sharing a set of similar addresses (see DOMAIN NAME) is called a WEB SITE. The main or introductory page of a Web site is usually called the site's home page. Users may access any page by typing in the appropriate address, search for pages related to a topic of interest by using a SEARCH ENGINE, or move quickly between pages by clicking on hyperlinks incorporated into them. Though introduced in 1991, the Web did not become truly popular until the introduction of Mosaic, a BROWSER with a graphical interface, in 1993. Subsequently, browsers produced by Netscape and Microsoft have become predominant.

World Wildlife Fund *or* **World Wide Fund for Nature** Largest privately supported international conservation organization in the world. Founded in 1961 by a small group of European scientists, naturalists, and business and political leaders, including PETER MARKHAM SCOTT, the organization raises funds and channels them to other conservation groups. It directs its efforts toward protecting endangered environments such as coral reefs, saving endangered species, and addressing global threats such as pollution. It has helped establish and manage parks and reserves, and was instrumental in saving the giant panda (whose image it uses as its symbol) and other endangered species.

world's fair Specially constructed attraction showcasing the science, technology, and culture of participating countries and enterprises. World fairs have often featured outstanding architectural designs and introduced significant inventions. The first was held in England in 1756; more than 300 have been held since. The most notable include the 1851 CRYSTAL PALACE Exhibition (London), the 1876 U.S. International Centennial Exposition (Philadelphia), the 1893 World's Columbian Exposition (Chicago), the 1901 Pan-American Exposition (Buffalo, N.Y.), the 1904 St. Louis World's Fair, the 1910 Brussels World's Fair, the 1933–34 Century of Progress (Chicago), the 1939–40 Golden Gate Exposition (San Francisco), the 1939–40 New York World's Fair, the 1964–65 New York World's Fair, the 1967 Montreal Exposition, and the 1998 World Exposition (Lisbon).

worm Any of thousands of species of unrelated INVERTEBRATE animals that typically have a soft, slender, elongated body with no appendages. The major phyla are Platyhelminthes (FLATWORMS), Annelida (ANNELIDS, or segmented worms), Nemertea (ribbon worms), Acanthocephala (spiny-headed worms), and Aschelminthes (NEMATODES and others). There are several minor phyla. Length ranges from microscopic (e.g., some aschelminths) to more than 100 ft (30 m) (some ribbon worms). Worms are found worldwide on land and in water. They may be parasitic or free-living and are important as soil conditioners, parasites, and a link in the food chain in all ecosystems. See also FLUKE, PINWORM, POLYCHAETE, ROTIFER, TAPEWORM, TUBE WORM.

Wormley Conference (February 26, 1877) Meeting to resolve the disputed U.S. presidential election of 1876 between SAMUEL TILDEN and RUTHERFORD B. HAYES. Leaders of both parties met at Wormley's Hotel in Washington, D.C., to reach a compromise that would forestall the Democrats' protest of the ELECTORAL COMMISSION's decision. In return for awarding the election to Hayes, Republicans promised to withdraw troops from the South, end RECONSTRUCTION and Northern interference in Southern politics, and vote for railroad construction and other internal improvements in the South. The compromise satisfied the Southern Democrats, and Hayes was declared the winner on March 2, 1877.

Worms \'vȯrms, *Engl* 'wərmz\, **Concordat of** (1122) Compromise between Pope CALIXTUS II and Emperor Henry V (r.1106–25) to settle the INVESTITURE CONTROVERSY, reached at Worms, Germany. It marked the end of the first phase of conflict between Rome and the HOLY ROMAN EMPIRE and made a clear distinction between the spiritual side of a prelate's office and his position as a landed magnate and vassal of the crown. Bishops and abbots were to be chosen by the clergy, but the emperor was to decide contested elections. Those selected were to be invested first with the powers and privileges of their office as vassal (granted by the emperor) and then with their ecclesiastical powers and lands (granted by church authority).

Worms, Diet of Meeting of the assembly (Diet) of the HOLY ROMAN EMPIRE at Worms, Germany, in 1521, where MARTIN LUTHER's defended the principles of the REFORMATION. Luther had already been excommunicated by Pope LEO X, but Emperor CHARLES V granted him safe conduct to a hearing at the Diet. On April 17, 1521, Luther refused to recant his views. Disorder broke out, the emperor adjourned the proceedings, and Luther was obliged to go into hiding. In May the Diet issued the Edict of Worms declaring Luther an outlaw and a heretic and banning his writings.

worsted \'wu̇s-təd, 'wər-stəd\ WOOL YARN made of long-staple fibers that have been combed to remove unwanted short fibers and make them lie parallel. In the spinning operation, which gives the necessary twist to hold the fibers together, worsted yarns are more tightly twisted than are the bulkier woolen yarns. The soft, heavy yarn is strong and durable and is often used for sweaters. Worsteds are also used for fine dress fabrics and suit material.

Worth, Charles Frederick (1825–1895) British-French fashion designer. In 1845 he left England, where he had been a bookkeeper, and worked in a Paris dress accessories shop. In 1858 he opened his own ladies' tailor shop and soon gained the patronage of the empress EUGÉNIE. He was a pioneer of the "fashion show" (the preparation and showing of a collection), the first man to become prominent in the field of fashion, and the first designer to create dresses intended to be copied and distributed throughout the world. He became the dictator of Paris fashion and was especially noted for his elegant Second Empire gowns. He invented the bustle, which became standard in women's fashion in the 1870s and '80s.

Charles Frederick Worth, detail of an engraving.
BBC HULTON PICTURE LIBRARY

Wotan See ODIN

Wouk \'wōk\, **Herman** (born 1915) U.S. novelist. Born in New York City, he served aboard a destroyer-minesweeper in World War II. That experience provided material for *The Caine Mutiny* (1951, Pulitzer Prize; film, 1954), a drama of naval tradition that presented the unforgettable character Captain Queeg. His *The Winds of War* (1971) and *War and Remembrance* (1978) together represent a two-volume novel of the war. His other novels include *Marjorie Morningstar* (1955), *The Hope* (1993), and *The Glory* (1994).

wound *or* **trauma** Break in any body tissue due to external action (including surgery). It may be closed (blunt trauma) or open (penetrating trauma). Blood vessels, nerves, muscles, bones, joints, and internal organs may be damaged. A closed wound can be caused by impact, twisting, bending, or deceleration (as in a car crash). It can range from a minor bruise or sprain to a skull fracture with brain damage or a spinal-cord injury with paralysis. In an open wound, foreign matter such as bacteria, dirt, and clothing fragments entering through broken skin or mucous membrane may result in INFECTION. Other factors affecting severity include depth, surface area, degree of tearing, and structures damaged. Minor wounds need only first aid. For others, after examination and perhaps diagnostic imaging and exploratory surgery, treatment may include fluid replacement or drainage, sterilization and antibiotics, tetanus antitoxin, and repair of damaged structures. A closed wound may need to be opened or an open one sutured closed. See also BURN, COAGULATION, CRUSH INJURY, DISLOCATION, SCAR.

Wounded Knee Hamlet and creek in southwestern South Dakota, the site of two conflicts between the SIOUX Indians and the U.S. government. In 1890 the Sioux had been inspired by the GHOST DANCE movement to take up arms and reclaim their heritage, but federal military intervention quelled the rebellion. On December 29 a young brave, while surrendering, became involved in a scuffle and a trooper was killed. Soldiers fired at the Indians, killing more than 200 men, women, and children. Thirty soldiers also died. The so-called Battle of Wounded Knee is regarded as the final episode in the conquest of the North American Indian. In 1973 some 200 members of the AMERICAN INDIAN MOVEMENT took the reservation hamlet by force, declared it an independent nation, and vowed to stay until the government agreed to address Indian grievances; a siege by federal marshals ended when the Indians surrendered in exchange for a promise of negotiations.

Wovoka \wō-'vō-kə\ (1858–1932) PAIUTE religious leader. In 1889 Wovoka announced that during a trance God had told him that his people's ancestors would rise from the dead, buffalo would return to the plains, and the white man would vanish if the people would perform a ritual dance, the GHOST DANCE. The cult quickly spread to other tribes, notably the militant SIOUX, and Wovoka was worshiped as a new messiah. After the WOUNDED KNEE massacre, Wovoka's following dissipated and the movement died out.

Wozniak, Stephen G(ary) (born 1950) U.S. computer engineer. Born in San Jose, Cal., he designed electronic devices and games while still in his teens. In the 1970s he worked for Hewlett-Packard. In 1976 he and STEVEN JOBS founded Apple Computer, Inc. Badly injured in a 1981 plane crash, he took a leave from Apple, but he returned to work on the revolutionary Macintosh computer. He left Apple for good in 1985, the year he was awarded the National Medal of Technology. He has since taught in elementary school.

WPA See WORKS PROGRESS ADMINISTRATION

WPA Federal Art Project Extensive visual-arts project, part of the WORKS PROGRESS ADMINISTRATION established by FRANKLIN ROOSEVELT during the GREAT DEPRESSION. It employed artists from relief rolls with a wide range of experience and styles, and had great influence on subsequent U.S. movements. At its peak in 1936, it provided work for more than 5,000 artists. Over the eight years of its existence, its employees produced 2,566 murals, more than 100,000 easel paintings, about 17,700 sculptures, and nearly 300,000 fine prints. The project also developed an audience by establishing more than 100 community art centers and galleries in regions where art was generally unknown. The total federal investment was about $35 million. It was the first major attempt at U.S. government patronage of the visual arts.

Wrangel, Pyotr (Nikolayevich), Baron (1878–1928) Russian general who led the anti-Bolshevik forces in the RUSSIAN CIVIL WAR. He served in the Russian imperial guards and commanded a Cossack division in World War I. After the Russian Revolution of 1917, he joined the anti-Bolshevik "White" forces of ANTON DENIKIN. After capturing Tsaritsyn (now Volgograd) in 1919, he became commander of the Whites in April 1920 and tried to rally support from the peasants and Cossacks. He launched an offensive in the Ukraine in June, but by November the RED ARMY had defeated the Whites and forced them to retreat to the Crimea. After evacuating his troops to Constantinople, he lived in exile in Western Europe.

Wrangel Island Island, northeastern Russia in Asia. Located in the Arctic Ocean, it is crossed by the 180th meridian. It has an area of some 2,800 sq mi (7,300 sq km). Although it reaches an altitude of 3,596 ft (1,096 m) at Sovetskaya Mtn., there are no glaciers. Russian explorer Ferdinand P. von Wrangel looked unsuccessfully for it in the early 1820s. Russian fur traders subsequently visited the island, and it was sighted by U.S. vessels in 1867 and 1881. The Soviet Union annexed it and began permanent occupation in 1926. Wrangel Island State Reserve, established in 1976, occupies 1,730,000 acres (700,000 hectares).

Wrangell Mountains Range, southern Alaska. It extends south for about 100 mi (160 km), from the Copper River to the ST. ELIAS MTNS. near the Yukon border. Many peaks exceed 10,000 ft (3,000 m); the highest are Mount Blackburn (16,390 ft or 4,990 m), Mount Bona (16,500 ft or 5,029 m), and Mount Sanford (16,237 ft, or 4,950 m). Most of the summits are extinct volcanoes. Snowfields drain into glaciers as long as 45 mi (72 km). The range forms a major part of WRANGELL–ST. ELIAS NATIONAL PARK.

Wrangell–St. Elias National Park National park, southeastern Alaska. Proclaimed a national monument in 1978, the area underwent boundary and name changes in 1980. The largest unit in the U.S. national park system, it has an area of 12,318,000 acres (4,987,000 hectares). At the convergence of the Chugach, WRANGELL, and ST. ELIAS mountain ranges, it includes the largest assemblage of glaciers and the greatest collection of peaks above 16,000 ft (4,880 m) on the continent.

wrasse \'ras\ Any of some 300 species (family Labridae) of slender, often brilliantly colored, fishes, found worldwide in tropical and temperate seas, often on coral reefs. Species range from 2 in. to 7 ft (5 cm to 2

m) long. Wrasses have thick lips, large scales, long fins, and large, often protruding, canine teeth. Most eat invertebrates; some species, called cleaner wrasses, pick off and eat the external parasites of larger fishes. The tautaug *(Tautoga onitis)* is an edible species.

wren Any of 59 species (family Troglodytidae) of chunky songbirds, found in the Western Hemisphere. One species, *Troglodytes troglodytes,* has spread to the Old World; typical of the family, it is about 4 in. (10 cm) long and dark-barred brown, with a short, slightly downcurved bill, short rounded wings, and short cocked tail. Common throughout the Western Hemisphere is the house wren. The largest U.S. species (8 in., or 20 cm, long) is the cactus wren of southwestern deserts. Wrens hunt insects in marshes, rocky wastes, or shrubbery, revealing their presence by chatter and loud song. They nest in holes, in thickets, or on ledges.

Wren, Christopher *later* **Sir Christopher** (1632–1723) British architect, astronomer, and geometrician. He taught astronomy at Gresham College, London (1657–61) and Oxford (1661–73), and did not turn to architecture until 1662, when he was engaged to design the Sheldonian Theater at Oxford. Though classical in form, the theater was roofed with novel wood trusses that were the product of Wren's scholarly and empirical approach. As King's Surveyor of Works (1669–1718), he had a hand in the rebuilding of more than 50 churches destroyed in the GREAT FIRE OF LONDON. Meanwhile, he was evolving designs for ST. PAUL'S CATHEDRAL, a work that occupied him until its completion in 1710. Other works include the classical Trinity College library, Cambridge (1676–84), additions to Hampton Court (begun 1689), and Greenwich Hospital (begun 1696). Wren was buried in St. Paul's; nearby is the famous inscription: "Reader, if you seek a monument, look around."

Sir Christopher Wren, detail of an oil painting by Sir Godfrey Kneller, 1711; in the National Portrait Gallery, London.

BY COURTESY OF THE NATIONAL PORTRAIT GALLERY, LONDON

wrench *or* **spanner** Tool, usually operated by hand, for tightening bolts and nuts. A wrench basically consists of a lever with a notch at one or both ends for gripping the bolt or nut so that it can be twisted by a pull at right angles to the axes of the lever and the bolt or nut. Open-end wrenches have ends with straight-sided slots that fit over the part being tightened; box-end wrenches have ends that enclose the nut and have six, eight, 12, or 16 points inside the head. A socket wrench is essentially a short pipe with a square or hexagonal hole and either a permanent or a removable handle.

wrestling Sport in which two competitors grapple with and strive to trip or throw each other down or off-balance. It is practiced in various styles, including freestyle wrestling, in which contestants can use holds above and below the waist, and GRECO-ROMAN WRESTLING, which allows only holds above the waist. Sambo is a style of Russian origin employing judo techniques. SUMO wrestling is a specialized Japanese variety. U.S. professional wrestling is today among the most popular of all spectator sports, though it principally involves wildly flamboyant showmanship, including such nonclassical moves as kicks to the head that would be lethal if they were not actually pulled.

Wright, Almroth Edward *later* **Sir Almroth** (1861–1947) British bacteriologist and immunologist. While teaching at the Army Medical School in Netley (from 1892), he developed a TYPHOID immunization that used killed typhoid bacilli. It made Britain the only country with troops immunized against typhoid at the start of World War I, the first war in which fewer British soldiers died of infection than from trauma. He also developed VACCINES against enteric tuberculosis and pneumonia. He was well known for advancing autogenous vaccines (vaccines prepared from a patient's own bacteria).

Wright, Fanny *orig.* **Frances** (1795–1852) Scottish-American social reformer. After travels in the U.S., she published *Views of Society and Manners in America* (1821). Returning to the U.S. in 1824, she bought and freed slaves and settled them at Nashoba, a socialist, interracial community she established in Tennessee (1825–28). She worked with ROBERT DALE OWEN in New York (1829) and defied convention by lecturing widely, attacking slavery, religion, traditional marriage, and unequal treatment of women. She was a co-leader of the WORKINGMEN'S PARTY. After marrying and living in France 1831–35, she returned to the U.S. and became a supporter of ANDREW JACKSON and the Democratic Party.

Wright, Frank Lloyd (1867–1959) U.S. architect. Born in Richland Center, Wis., he studied engineering briefly at the University of Wisconsin. He worked for the firm of Dankmar Adler (1844–1900) and LOUIS SULLIVAN before opening his own Chicago practice in 1893. Wright became the chief practitioner of the PRAIRIE SCHOOL, building about 50 Prairie houses from 1900 to 1910. Early nonresidential buildings included the forward-looking Larkin Building in Buffalo, N.Y. (1904; destroyed 1950), and Unity Temple in Oak Park, Ill. (1906). In 1911 he began work on his own house, TALIESIN. The lavish Imperial Hotel in Tokyo (1915–22, dismantled 1967) was significant for its revolutionary floating cantilever construction, which made it one of the only large buildings to withstand the earthquake of 1923. In the 1930s he designed his low-cost Usonian houses, but his most admired house, Fallingwater, in Bear Run, Pa. (1936), was an extravagant country retreat cantilevered over a waterfall. His Johnson Wax Building (1936–39), an example of humane workplace design, touched off an avalanche of major commissions, including the GUGGENHEIM MUSEUM. Often considered the greatest U.S. architect, Wright became famous for "organic architecture," buildings that harmonize both with their inhabitants and their environment.

Wright, Mickey *orig.* **Mary Kathryn** (born 1935) U.S. golfer. She was born in San Diego and attended Stanford University Noted for her classic swing, her long drives, and her superior iron play, she won a record number of LPGA tournaments (82), including an unmatched 13 in one season (1963), and remains the only four-time winner of the LPGA championship (1958, 1960, 1961, 1963). Twice named Woman Athlete of the Year by the Associated Press (1963, 1964), she has been called the greatest woman golfer of all time.

Wright, Richard (1908–1960) U.S. novelist and short-story writer. Born near Natchez, Miss., he grew up in poverty. After migrating north he joined the Federal Writers' Project in Chicago, then moved to New York in 1937. He was a member of the Communist Party in the years 1932–44. He first came to wide attention with a volume of novellas, *Uncle Tom's Children* (1938). His novel *Native Son* (1940), though considered shocking and violent, became a best-seller. The fictionalized autobiography *Black Boy* (1945) vividly describes his often harsh childhood and youth. After World War II he settled in Paris. He is remembered as one of the first African-American writers to protest white treatment of blacks.

Wright, Sewall (1889–1988) U.S. geneticist. Born in Melrose, Mass., he earned his doctorate at Harvard University. His earliest studies included investigation of the effects of inbreeding and crossbreeding on guinea pigs, animals he later used in studying the effects of gene action on coat and eye color. With J.B.S. HALDANE and R. A. FISHER, he developed a mathematical basis for evolutionary theory using statistical techniques. He originated a theory that could guide the use of inbreeding and crossbreeding in livestock improvement. He is perhaps best known for his concept of GENETIC DRIFT.

Wright, Wilbur and Orville (1867–1912, 1871–1948) U.S. inventors who achieved the first powered, sustained, and controlled airplane flight. Born respectively near Millville, Ind., and in Dayton, Ohio, the brothers first worked in printing-machinery design and later in bicycle manufacturing, which financed their early experiments in airplane design. To test flight control, essential to successful powered flight, they built and flew three biplane gliders (1900–2). Propeller and engine innovations led to their first powered airplane, *Flyer I* (now called the *Kitty Hawk*), which Orville flew successfully for 12 seconds and Wilbur later flew for 59 seconds at Kill Devil Hills, North Carolina (near the village of Kitty Hawk), in 1903. Their *Flyer III,* built in 1905, could turn, bank, circle, and remain airborne for over 35 minutes. They demonstrated their planes in Europe and the U.S.; in 1908 Wilbur gave over 100 exhibition flights in France, setting a duration record of 2 hours and 20 minutes. They established an aircraft company and produced planes for the U.S. Army; it later merged with the company of GLENN H. CURTISS. After Wilbur's death from typhoid, Orville established a new aeronautical research company.

Wriothesley, Thomas See 1st Earl of SOUTHAMPTON

writ In COMMON LAW, an order issued in the name of a sovereign or court commanding a person to perform or refrain from performing a specified act. It was a vital official instrument in Old English law. A plaintiff would commence a suit by choosing the proper form of action and obtaining a writ appropriate to the remedy sought; its issuance forced the defendant to comply or to appear in court. Writs were also constantly in use for financial and political purposes of government. Though the writ no longer governs civil pleading and has lost many of its applications, the extraordinary writs, especially of HABEAS CORPUS, mandamus (commanding the performance of a ministerial act), prohibition (commanding an inferior court to stay within its jurisdiction), and CERTIORARI, reflect its historical importance as an instrument of judicial authority.

writing System of human visual communication using signs or symbols associated by convention with units of LANGUAGE—meanings or sounds—and recorded on materials such as paper, stone, or clay. Its precursor was PICTOGRAPHY. Logography, in which symbols stand for individual words, typically develops from pictography. Logography requires thousands of symbols for all possible words and names. In phonographic systems, the symbol associated with a word also stands for similar- or identical-sounding words. Phonographic systems may evolve to the point where symbols represent syllables, constituting a syllabary. An ALPHABET provides symbols for all the consonants and vowels.

Writs of Assistance See Writs of ASSISTANCE

Wroclaw \'vrȯt-ˌswäf\ *German* **Breslau** City (pop., 1996 est.: 643,000), southwestern Poland. Located on the ODER RIVER, it originated in the 10th century at the crossroads of the trade route linking the Black Sea to western Europe. In 1138 it became the first capital of SILESIA. The Tartars destroyed it in 1241. Rebuilt, it passed to BOHEMIA with the rest of Silesia in 1335 and in 1526, to the HABSBURGS. In 1741 it fell to Prussia under the rule of FREDERICK II THE GREAT and eventually became part of Germany. During World War II it was besieged (1945) by Soviet troops. The city was assigned to Poland by the POTSDAM CONFERENCE of 1945. Heavily damaged during the war, it was rebuilt, and is now a major commercial city.

wrought iron One of the two forms in which IRON is obtained by SMELTING. Wrought iron is a soft, easily worked, fibrous metal. It usually contains less than 0.1% CARBON and 1–2% SLAG. It is superior for most purposes to CAST IRON, which is hard and brittle because of its higher carbon content. In antiquity, iron was smelted directly by heating ore in a forge with charcoal, which served both as fuel and reducing agent. While still hot, the iron-and-slag mixture was removed as a lump and worked (wrought) with a hammer to expel most of the slag and weld the iron into a coherent mass. Wrought iron began to take the place of bronze (being far more available) in Asia Minor in the 2nd millennium BC; its use for tools and weapons was established in China, India, and the Mediterranean by the 3rd century BC. Later, in Europe, wrought iron was produced indirectly from cast iron (see PUDDLING PROCESS). With the invention of the BESSEMER PROCESS and OPEN-HEARTH PROCESS, STEEL supplanted wrought iron for structural purposes, and its use in the 20th century has been principally decorative.

wu Fundamental Taoist philosophical concept. Wu ("Not-being"), *you* ("Being"), *wuming* ("the Nameless"), and *youming* ("the Named") are interdependent and grow out of one another. Wu and *you* are two aspects of the TAO. Not-being does not mean nothingness, but rather the absence of perceptible qualities; in LAOZI's view, it is superior to Being. It is the Void that harbors in itself all potentialities and without which even Being lacks its efficacy. According to the scholar He Yan (died AD 249), wu is beyond name and form, and hence absolute, complete, and capable of accomplishing anything. See also TAOISM.

Wu Chengen *or* **Wu Ch'eng-en** \'wü-'chəŋ-'ən\ (c. 1500–1582?) Chinese novelist and poet. He received a traditional Confucian education and became known for his clever poetry and prose composition in the classical style. Interested in bizarre stories, he used oral and written folktales as the basis of the novel *Xiyou ji* ("Record of a Journey to the West" ; translated in English as *Monkey*), published anonymously in 1592. It relates the comic mishaps and adventures of the 7th-century monk XUANZANG, who traveled to India looking for sacred texts, and his entourage of three animal spirits: a monkey, a pig, and a fish. It satirizes Chinese society and government and contains religious and philosophical elements drawn from Buddhism, Taoism, and Neo-Confucianism. Only two volumes of his other writings have survived.

Wu Hou \'wü-'hō\ *or* **Wu Zetian** \'wü-dzə-'tyan\ (625–705) Empress of China of the TANG DYNASTY. She began her career as the concubine of the emperor TAIZONG but became the consort of his son. She eliminated her female rivals and became empress in 655. By 660 she had eliminated those who opposed her through dismissal, exile, and execution. Because the emperor was sickly, she was able to rule in his name; after his death she ruled in the name of her sons, at last declaring herself ruler in her own name in 690. To support her reign, she claimed to be an incarnation of the bodhisattva MAITREYA. Though long vilified for her cruelty and her methods of maintaining power, she supported the development of a scholarly bureaucracy to replace rule by aristocratic families and she stabilized the dynasty.

Wu-lu-mu-ch'i See ÜRÜMQI

Wu Sangui *or* **Wu San-kuei** \'wü-'sän-'gwā\ (1612–1678) Chinese general who invited the MANCHUS into China and helped them establish the QING DYNASTY. Though he had for many years battled the Manchus on China's northeastern frontier, he turned to them for aid when the MING-DYNASTY capital at Beijing fell to LI ZICHENG. The Manchu forces defeated Li and then set up their own dynasty, in which Wu served many years. Only when he was put in charge of eliminating the remnants of Ming resistance in southwestern China did he break away, creating his own state in the area of Yunnan and Guizhou. Two other commanders had set up similar states in neighboring southern provinces; in 1673 Wu led the three in rebellion. After Wu's death, his grandson continued the rebellion until 1681, when it was finally crushed. See also DORGON.

Wuchang *or* **Wu-ch'ang** \'wü-'chäŋ\ Industrial city, central China, part of the tri-city conurbation of WUHAN. It is the oldest of the Wuhan cities, probably dating from the HAN DYNASTY. It was the capital of the kingdom of Wu in the 3rd century AD, as well as capital of an administrative district under the YUAN DYNASTY (1279–1368), and later of HUBEI province (until 1950). In 1911 it was the starting point of a revolution against the imperial regime. The Japanese occupied the city 1938–45; the Chinese Communists took it in 1949. It became part of Wuhan in 1950.

Wudi *or* **Wu-ti** \'wü-'dē\ *orig.* **Liu Che** (156–87/86 BC) Emperor of the Chinese HAN DYNASTY who vastly increased its authority and its influence abroad and made CONFUCIANISM China's state religion. Under Wudi, China's armies drove back the nomadic XIONGNU tribes that plagued the northern border, incorporated southern China and northern and central Vietnam into the empire, and reconquered Korea. Their farthest expedition was to Fergana (in modern Uzbekistan). Wudi's military campaigns strained the state's reserves; seeking new income, he decreed new taxes and established state monopolies on salt, iron, and wine.

Wuhan *or* **Wu-han** \'wü-'hän\ City (pop., 1999 est.: 3,911,824), capital of HUBEI province, eastern central China. It is located at the confluence of the HAN and YANGTZE (Chang) rivers, and is a conurbation of three cities that merged in 1950: Hankou, on the northern bank of the Yangtze; Hanyang, across the Han; and WUCHANG, on the southern bank of the Yangtze. The chief industrial and commercial center of central China, it is a hub of maritime, river, rail, and road transportation. It serves as the collection and distribution point for the products of the middle Yangtze valley and for western and southwestern China. It has numerous industries, including iron- and steel-producing complexes. It is the seat of Wuhan University and the Central China Technical University.

Wundt \'vu̇nt\, **Wilhelm** (1832–1920) German physiologist and psychologist, the founder of EXPERIMENTAL PSYCHOLOGY. After earning a medical degree, he studied briefly with JOHANNES PETER MULLER and later assisted HERMANN VON HELMHOLTZ. At the University of Heidelberg in 1862, following publication of his *Contributions to the Theory of Sense Perception* (1858–62), he gave the first course in scientific psychology. In *Principles of Physiological Psychology* (1873–74) he claimed that psychology must be based directly on experience and that its proper method was that of controlled introspection. At the University of Leipzig (1875–

Xhosa women dancing as they return from the fields to their village.
AUTHENTICATED NEWS INTERNATIONAL

mercial center. MARCO POLO visited in the 13th century. It was an entry point in the 1920s for Communist ideology from the Soviet Union. In 1936 the kidnapping of CHIANG KAI-SHEK there (see XI'AN INCIDENT) united the Communist-Nationalist front against Japanese invaders. It is the site of several educational institutions and numerous temples and pagodas. It has become an important tourist destination with the discovery of the nearby tomb of Emperor SHI HUANGDI, with its army of 6,000 life-size terracotta warriors.

Xi'an Incident *or* **Sian Incident** \'shyan\ (1936) Seizure of CHIANG KAI-SHEK by one of his generals, Chang Hsüeh-liang (Zhang Xueliang) (1898–2001), in order to persuade Chiang to postpone his war on the Chinese Communists until the invading Japanese had been defeated. As a result of the incident, the Nationalists and Communists formed an alliance that turned its attention to the Japanese in Manchuria. See also MANCHUGUO, PEOPLE'S LIBERATION ARMY.

Xiang River *or* **Hsiang River** *or* **Siang River** \'shyäŋ\ River, HUNAN province, southeastern China. One of the principal tributaries of the CHANG (YANGTZE) RIVER, it flows 500 mi (800 km) from the mountains in northern GUANGXI Zhuangzu, through Hunan province, into DONGTING HU (lake), and then into the Chang. Large vessels from the Chang can reach as far as CHANGSHA via the Xiang. The river has been a north–south trade route for centuries.

Xiang Yu *or* **Hsiang Yü** \shē-'äŋ-'yü̅\ (232–202 BC) Chinese aristocratic general and cultural hero. He overthrew the QIN DYNASTY and tried to return China to a pre-Qin ruling system. His forces were overwhelmed by LIU BANG, founder of the HAN DYNASTY, and Xiang Yu chose suicide over capture. His heroism has been glorified in Chinese stories and poetry.

xiao *or* **hsiao** \'shyau̇\ *Chinese:* **"filial piety"** In CONFUCIANISM, the attitude of obedience, devotion, and care toward one's parents and other elders considered fundamental to moral conduct. Originally rooted in the hierarchical ideology of Chinese feudalism, it was raised to a moral precept by CONFUCIUS, who cited it as the basis of REN. It is seen as the basis not only of family harmony but of social and political stability.

Xin See WANG MANG

Xingkai Hu See Lake KHANKA

Xingu River \'shēŋ-'gü\ River, central and northern Brazil. Formed by several headstreams, it flows north through northeastern MATO GROSSO state and central Pará state into the AMAZON RIVER near its mouth. Though approximately 1,300 mi (2,100 km) long, it is navigable for only about 125 mi (201 km); its central part is a series of rapids 400 mi (644 km) long. In the 1950s Xingu National Park was designated as a preserve for Brazil's Indians, including the Tchikao, who were threatened by extinction.

Xining *or* **Hsi-ning** \'shē-'niŋ\ City (pop., 1999 est.: 604,812), capital of QINGHAI province, western China. Located in a valley of the HUANG RIVER, on what was traditionally the main trade route from northern China into Tibet, the region was a frontier county under the HAN DYNASTY and again under the SUI and TANG. In 763 it was taken by Tibetans and called Qingtangeheng. It was recovered by the SONG DYNASTY in 1104 and renamed Xining (meaning "peace in the west"). It became an important religious center under the Tibetans, and Qinghai's largest lamasery was nearby. It was named provincial capital when Qinghai became an independent province in 1928. Its industries include leather processing plants and steelworks.

Xinjiang Uygur *or* **Sinkiang Uighur** \'shin-'jyäŋ-'wē-'gu̇r\ *or* **Xinjiang** Autonomous region (pop., 2000 est.: 19,250,000), northwestern China. China's largest political unit, it covers some 635,900 sq mi (1,646,900 sq km). The capital is ÜRÜMQI. Inhabited since early times by nomad tribes, it is an area of rugged mountains and desert basins. The SILK ROAD traversed the region. It came under the control of local leaders with the fall of the HAN DYNASTY in the 3rd century AD, and was regained by China in the 7th century. It was successively subject to the Tibetans, Uighurs, and Arabs, and was conquered by GENGHIS KHAN in the 13th century. Again under Chinese rule during the MANCHU dynasty, it was established as Xinjiang province c. 1884. It came under Chinese Communist rule in 1949. It was reconstituted as an autonomous region in 1955. It has mineral resources, heavy industry, including iron and steel works, and some agricultural production.

Xiongnu *or* **Hsiung-nu** \shē-'u̇ŋ-'nü\ Nomadic pastoral people who at the end of the 3rd century BC formed a great tribal league that was able to dominate much of Central Asia for more than 500 years. Their threat to the northern Chinese frontier throughout this period led to China's eventual conquest of northern Korea and southern Manchuria during the HAN DYNASTY. Excavation of Xiongnu graves has revealed remains of Chinese, Iranian, and Greek textiles, indicating a wide trade with distant peoples.

Xipe Totec \'shē-pā-'tō-tek, 'hē-pā-'tō-tek\ Pre-Columbian Mexican god of spring and of new vegetation; he is also the patron of precious metals. Originating with the ZAPOTEC Indians, he was adopted by the AZTECS. A symbol of new vegetation, he is always depicted in art wearing a freshly flayed skin, representing the "new skin" that covers the earth in spring. In the second ritual month of the Aztec calendar, priests sacrificed human victims by removing their hearts or shooting them with arrows, flayed the bodies, and put on the skins, which were dyed yellow and called "golden clothes."

Xiuhtecuhtli \ˌshē-ü-'tā-ku̇t-lē\ Aztec god of fire and creator of all life. With Chantico, his feminine counterpart, he was believed to be a representation of OMETECUHTLI. Xiuhtecuhtli's festivals coincided with the two extremes in the climatological cycle, the heat of August and the cold of January. He was also the center of a ritual transfer of fire from temple to temple that occurred once every 52 years at the end of the Aztec calendar cycle.

XML *in full* **Extensible Markup Language** MARKUP LANGUAGE developed to be a simplified and more structural version of SGML. It incorporates features of HTML (e.g., HYPERTEXT linking), but is designed to overcome some of HTML's limitations. For example, it is designed to be extensible (i.e., designed to allow the creation of customized markup tags), which HTML is not. It is also designed to represent data by meaning rather than by layout (as it is represented in HTML). Like SGML, it is a metalanguage (a language for dealing with languages); it allows users to create a language tailored specifically to their needs.

Xochicalco \ˌsō-chē-'käl-kō\ Ancient TOLTEC city known for its impressive ruins and feathered-serpent pyramid. It is located on several hilltops near CUERNAVACA, Mexico. Built mainly in the 8th–9th century, it became an important trading center and religious center, and it was turned into a defensive stronghold before the Spanish conquest (c. 1520). The main temple pyramid is known for its lower facing of intricately carved stones. The reliefs, which show a strong Mayan influence, portray plumed serpents, priests with elaborate headdresses, squatting warriors, calendar glyphs, and fire symbols.

Xuanxue *or* **Hsüan-hsueh** \'shwän-'shwe\ *Chinese:* **"Dark Learning"** Intellectual movement in China in the 3rd–4th century AD during a period of disenchantment with CONFUCIANISM. Founded by Wang Bi (AD

226–249), the movement drastically reinterpreted Confucian sources and incorporated aspects of TAOISM. Wang Bi and his followers tried to determine whether the nature of ultimate reality was Being or Nothingness and sought to discover if the principle underlying a thing was universal or particular. The movement played an important role in the development of Chinese BUDDHISM.

Xuanzang *or* **Hsüan-tsang** \'shwän-'dzäŋ\ (602–664) Chinese Buddhist monk and pilgrim to India. He received a classical Confucian education before converting to Buddhism. Troubled by discrepancies in the sacred texts, he left for India in 629 to study the religion at its source. He traveled by foot across Central Asia and reached India in 633. After study at the famous Nalanda monastery, he returned home in 645 to a hero's welcome, bringing back hundreds of Buddhist texts, including some of the most important Mahayana scriptures, and spent the rest of his life at translating. Influenced by the YOGACARA school, he established the Weishi ("Ideation Only") school of Buddhism, which won many followers in Japan as the Hosso school. The classic novel *Xiyou ji* was inspired by his life.

Xuanzong *or* **Hsüan Tsung** \'shu̅e̅n-'dzu̇ŋ\ *orig.* **Li Longji** (685–762) Sixth emperor of the TANG DYNASTY of China, which during his reign achieved its greatest prosperity and cultural brilliance. Xuanzong reformed the bureaucracy, increased tax revenues through reregistering the population, improved the transportation system, and established a permanent military force along China's northern frontiers. Toward the end of his reign, he withdrew more and more from government and came under the influence of his consorts, including the notorious beauty Yang Guifei. The AN LUSHAN REBELLION of 755 forced him to flee the capital, CHANGAN, and he soon abdicated in favor of the heir apparent.

Xunzi *or* **Hsün-tzu** \'shu̅e̅n-'dzə̇\ (c. 300 BC–c. 230 BC) Chinese scholar and philosopher. He belonged to the academy of philosophy in the state of Qi before becoming magistrate of a district in Chu in 255. His major work, the *Xunzi,* taught that humanity is evil by nature and can only become good through rigorous training. This view provoked much controversy because it was opposed to the teachings of MENCIUS, who believed in innate human goodness. Xunzi's teachings were later eclipsed when the *Mencius* became a Confucian classic. He is regarded as one of the three great philosophers of the classical period of Confucianism in China.

XX, Les See Les VINGT

xylem \'zī-ləm\ Part of a plant's vascular system that conveys water and dissolved minerals from the roots to the rest of the plant and furnishes mechanical support. Xylem constitutes the major part of a mature woody stem or root and the wood of a tree, and consists of specialized water-conducting tissues made up mostly of several types of narrow, elongate, hollow cells. Xylem formation begins when the actively dividing cells of growing root and shoot tips give rise to primary xylem. Eventually the primary xylem is covered by secondary xylem produced by the CAMBIUM. The primary xylem cells die, forming a hard skeleton that supports the plant but loses its conducting function. Thus, only the outer part of the wood (secondary xylem) serves in water conduction.

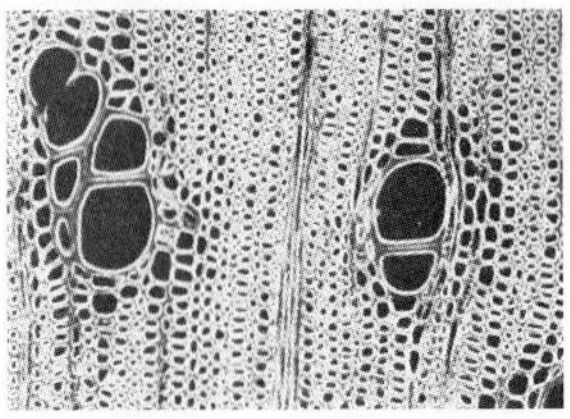

Cross section of oak xylem.

J.M. LANGHAM

xylophone Percussion instrument consisting of a set of tuned wooden bars that are struck with mallets. Primitive xylophones may consist of logs of graded length laid across two supporting logs; a pit may be dug underneath to serve as a resonator. The xylophone has long been one of the principal instruments of African music; it is also important in the Indonesian GAMELAN. The Latin American xylophone is the MARIMBA. In the modern orchestral xylophone, the bars are laid out on a stand in keyboard arrangement, with vertical resonating tubes suspended under each bar. See also GLOCKENSPIEL, VIBRAPHONE.

African log *amadinda* xylophone; property of the Uganda Museum, Kampala.

HILLEGEIST/KUBIK

XYZ Affair (1797–98) Diplomatic incident between the U.S. and France. Pres. JOHN ADAMS sent special envoys ELBRIDGE GERRY and JOHN MARSHALL to France to help CHARLES C. PINCKNEY negotiate an agreement to protect U.S. shipping from French privateers. Before the three could meet with CHARLES MAURICE DE TALLEYRAND, they were approached by three of his agents—called X, Y, and Z in diplomatic correspondence to Adams—who suggested a bribe of $250,000 to Talleyrand and a loan of $10 million to France as preconditions for negotiations. Adams rejected the French demands and reported the mission had failed. When he was forced to reveal the correspondence, public outrage was followed by calls for war with France. The ALIEN AND SEDITION ACTS were passed to restrict potential French sympathizers. The Convention of 1800 ended a period of undeclared naval warfare between the U.S. and France.

Y2K bug *or* **Year 2000 bug** *or* **millennium bug** Potential problem in computers and computer networks at the beginning of the year 2000. Until the 1990s, most computer programs used only the last two digits to designate the year, the first two digits being fixed at 19. As the year 2000 approached, many programs had to be partly rewritten or replaced to prevent interpretation of "00" as 1900 rather than 2000. It was feared that such a misreading would lead to software and hardware failures in computers used in such important areas as banking, utilities systems, government records, and so on, with the potential for widespread chaos on and following January 1, 2000. Up to $600 billion may have been spent to upgrade computers and application programs to be Y2K-compliant. Despite international alarm, few major failures occurred, partly because these measures were effective and partly because the likely incidence of failure was exaggerated.

Ya-lung River See YALONG RIVER

yacht \'yät\ Sail- or motor-driven vessel used for racing or recreation. The term is popularly applied to large recreational engine-powered boats; the sailboats known as yachts and used for racing are usually light and comparatively small. Until the mid-19th century, yachts were designed along the lines of naval craft such as SCHOONERS and cutters. Yacht design was greatly affected by the 1851 success of the *America* in the race that established the AMERICA'S CUP. In the 20th century, notably after World War II, smaller racing and recreational craft became more common. See also SAILING.

yachting See SAILING

Yagoda \yə-'gò-də\, **Genrikh (Grigoryevich)** (1891–1938) Soviet politician. A leader of the Cheka secret police (1920–24) and its successor, the OGPU (1924–34), and a close associate of JOSEPH STALIN, he organized the Soviet's forced-labor camps from 1930 and became a member of the Communist Party's Central Committee in 1934. As head of the Commissariat of Internal Affairs, or NKVD, he prepared the first of the PURGE TRIALS (1936). In 1937 he was replaced as police chief by NIKOLAY YEZHOV and himself became a victim of the widespread purges. Accused of conspiracy, he was convicted at the third purge trial (1938) and executed.

yahrzeit *or* **jahrzeit** \'yär-ˌtsīt\ In JUDAISM, the anniversary of the death of a parent or close relative, commonly observed by burning a candle for an entire day. On that day, the KADDISH is recited in the synagogue and the TORAH is read. Some mark the anniversary by studying portions of the MISHNA, choosing those sections from the sixth division that begin with letters from the name of the deceased. Yahrzeit developed from an early Jewish custom of fasting on the anniversaries of deaths of certain leaders, and some Jews still fast on this day.

Yahweh See TETRAGRAMMATON

yak Massive OX *(Bos grunniens mutus)* of high Tibetan plateaus. Bulls grow to 6 ft (1.8 m) at the shoulder hump. The wild yak's hair is black and short, except for a long, shaggy fringe on the flanks and tail. The horns spread outward and upward; the head is held low. Wild females and young live in large herds; mature bulls form smaller groups. Yaks graze on grass and require much water, eating snow in winter. Wild yaks are now endangered. Domestic yaks, which breed freely with domestic cattle, are used as pack, draft, milk, and beef animals. The hide provides leather; the tail, fly whisks; the fringe hair, ropes; the dried dung, fuel.

Yak (*Bos grunniens*).
RUSS KINNE—PHOTO RESEARCHERS/EB INC.

Yakima River \'ya-kə-ˌmò, 'ya-kə-mə\ River, southern central Washington. Rising in the CASCADE RANGE, it flows southeast for about 200 mi (320 km) to join the COLUMBIA RIVER near Kennewick. The Yakima and its tributaries irrigate about 460,000 acres (190,000 hectares) in the river valley. The Yakima Indian name probably means "runaway," referring to the rushing waters of the river.

Yakovlev \yə-'kòv-lyef\, **Aleksandr N(ikolayevich)** (born 1923) Soviet economist. He served in the Red Army in World War II and joined the Communist Party in 1944. He held administrative positions in the party and served as head of the propaganda department 1965–73. He was Soviet ambassador to Canada 1973–83, then became chief aide to MIKHAIL GORBACHEV. As a member of the Politiburo 1987–90, he was instrumental in developing Gorbachev's policies of GLASNOST and PERESTROIKA.

Yakut \yə-'küt\ *or* **Sakha** Siberian people who speak a TURKIC LANGUAGE. Most were formerly seminomadic, raising cattle and horses. They lived in winter settlements of earth-covered log huts and summer camps of conical birch-bark tents near pasturage and sources of hay for winter fodder. Through assimilation, many southern Yakut turned to farming while northern Yakut adopted reindeer breeding from the Evenki. The Yakut were noted for their ironwork (supernatural power was attributed to blacksmiths) and also made pottery; traditional arts such as ivory and wood carving are still practiced. Filmmaking has become popular more recently. The Yakut number about 380,000. See also SIBERIAN PEOPLES.

yakuza \'yä-kü-zə\ Japanese gangsters. Yakuza, who trace their roots back to RONIN, often adopt samurai-like rituals and identify themselves with elaborate body tattoos. They engage in such organized-crime pursuits as extortion, blackmail, smuggling, prostitution, drugs, and gambling, and they control many restaurants, bars, trucking companies, and taxi fleets in Japanese cities. Their numbers today exceed 150,000; they are organized into more than 2,000 gangs, most affiliated under the umbrella of one of a dozen or fewer conglomerate gangs. Yakuza gangs are rigidly hierarchical, and the price for disappointing the gang is often to be forced to cut off one's own finger.

Yale University Private university in New Haven, Conn., a traditional member of the IVY LEAGUE. Founded in 1701, it is the third-oldest institution of higher learning in the U.S. Yale's initial curriculum emphasized classical studies and strict adherence to orthodox Puritanism. Medical, divinity, and law schools were added in 1810, 1822, and 1824. The geologist Benjamin Silliman (1779–1864), who taught at Yale 1802–53, did much to expand the experimental and applied sciences. Beginning in the mid-19th century, schools of graduate studies, art, music, forestry, nursing, drama, management, and architecture were organized. Yale's library, with more than 10 million volumes, is one of the largest in the U.S. Its extensive art galleries were established in 1832. The Peabody Museum of Natural History houses important collections of paleontology, archaeology, and ethnology. Yale is one of the most highly regarded schools in the nation; its graduates have included five U.S. presidents. Total enrollment is about 11,000.

Yalong River *or* **Ya-lung River** \'yä-lüŋ\ River, SICHUAN province, southern China. It rises in mountains at an elevation of nearly 16,500 ft (5,000 m) in QINGHAI province and flows into the YANGTZE RIVER on the YUNNAN border. It is 822 mi (1,323 km) long. It is torrential for most of its course and is unnavigable.

Yalow \'ya-lō\, **Rosalyn (Sussman)** *orig.* **Rosalyn Sussman** (born 1921) U.S. medical physicist. Born in New York City, she received a PhD in physics from the University of Illinois. She developed the technique of radioimmunoassay (RIA) by combining techniques from radioisotope tracing and immunology. RIA proved a very sensitive and simple way to measure tiny concentrations of biological substances or drugs in blood or other body fluids. She originally applied RIA to study blood insulin levels in diabetes mellitus (1959), but the method soon found hundreds of other applications. In 1976 she became the first woman awarded the Albert Lasker Prize, and in 1977 she shared a Nobel Prize with ANDREW V. SCHALLY and ROGER C.L. GUILLEMIN.

Yalta City (pop., 1991 est.: 89,000), southern CRIMEA, Ukraine. It faces the BLACK SEA on the southern shore of the Crimean Peninsula. Settlement on the site dates from prehistoric times, but modern Yalta developed only in the early 19th century, becoming a town in 1838. Its mild winters and scenic location between sea and mountains have made it one of the most popular vacation and health resorts of Ukraine. In 1945 during World War II it was the site of the Allied leaders' YALTA CONFERENCE.

Yalta Conference (February 4–11, 1945) Conference of Allied leaders at Yalta to plan Germany's final defeat in World War II. FRANKLIN ROOSEVELT, WINSTON CHURCHILL, and JOSEPH STALIN discussed the postwar occupation of Germany, postwar assistance to the German people, German disarmament, war-crimes trials, the fate of the defeated or liberated states of Eastern Europe, voting in the future U.N. Security Council, and German reparations. Stalin agreed to enter the war against Japan after the German surrender. Roosevelt died two months later, and Stalin broke his promise to allow democratic elections in Eastern Europe. See also POTSDAM CONFERENCE, TEHRAN CONFERENCE.

Yalu River *or* **Ya-lü River** \'yä-lü\ *Korean* **Amnok River** \'äm-ˌnək\ River between northeastern China and North Korea. Some 491 mi (790 km) long, it rises on the northern border of North Korea, then flows to Korea Bay. It is an important source of hydroelectric power and is navigable by smaller vessels for most of its course. It became a political boundary in the 14th century. During the KOREAN WAR, as U.N. forces battled toward it in 1950, Chinese troops crossed it, in effect marking their entry into the war.

yam Any of several plant species of the genus *Dioscorea* (family Dioscoreaceae, or yam family), native to warmer regions of both hemispheres. A number of species are cultivated for food in the tropics; in certain tropical cultures, notably of West Africa and New Guinea, the yam is the primary agricultural commodity and the focal point of elaborate ritual. The edible tuberous roots, which vary in taste from sweet to bitter to tasteless, are eaten as cooked starchy vegetables. Often boiled and then mashed, they may also be fried, roasted, or baked. True yams are botanically distinct from the SWEET POTATO, though in the U.S. the names are commonly interchanged. *Dioscorea mexicana* contains a chemical that can suppress ovulation in humans and is used as the basis for birth-control pills. The so-called yam bean is the legume JICAMA.

Yama \'yə-mə\ In Indian mythology, the lord of death. The VEDAS describe him as the first man who died. The son of the sun god SURYA, he presides over the resting place of the dead. In the Vedas, he was a cheerful king of the departed ancestors, but in later mythology he became known as the just judge who punished the deceased for their sins.

Yamagata Aritomo \ˌyä-mə-'gä-tə-ˌär-ē-'tō-mō\ (1838–1922) First prime minister under Japan's parliamentary regime (1889–91, 1898–1900). As a SAMURAI youth in CHOSHU, Yamagata was among those who answered the foreign threat with the slogan *Sonno joi,* "Honor the emperor and expel the barbarians." Bombardment of the Choshu coast in 1864 convinced him of the need for modern armaments. After participating in the MEIJI RESTORATION, he went abroad to research military institutions. He became commander of an Imperial Guard of 10,000 troops. When he introduced conscription, bearing arms ceased to be the exclusive prerogative of a warrior class. His forces defeated SAIGO TAKAMORI's troops in 1877. In politics he was more conservative than his contemporary ITO HIROBUMI, favoring a strong executive. As prime minister, his policies were expansionist; Japan sent the largest of all foreign forces to China to quell the BOXER REBELLION. He increased the autonomy of the military and tried to suppress an incipient social-labor movement. After retirement, he continued to wield power as a GENRO (elder statesman). See also MEIJI CONSTITUTION, MEIJI PERIOD.

Yamal \yə-'mäl\ Peninsula between Kara Sea and Gulf of Ob, northwestern SIBERIA, western central Russia. It has a total length of 435 mi (700 km), a maximum width of 150 m (240 km), and an area of 47,100 sq mi (122,000 sq km). Large natural-gas deposits are on its western coast.

Yamamoto Isoroku \ˌyä-mä-'mō-tō-ˌē-sō-'rō-kü\ (1884–1943) Japanese naval officer. He fought in the Russo-Japanese War and thereafter rose to become commander in chief of Japan's Combined Fleet in 1941. When war with the U.S. was decided on, Yamamoto asserted that the only chance for a Japanese victory lay in a surprise attack that would cripple U.S. naval forces in the Pacific and conceived of the surprise attack on PEARL HARBOR. He then sought to destroy the remnants of the U.S. fleet, principally its aircraft carriers, but the Japanese lost the resulting Battle of MIDWAY. His campaign in the Solomon Islands was also unsuccessful. He was killed when the U.S. broke the Japanese communications codes, discovered his whereabouts, and shot down his plane over Bougainville island.

Yamasee War \'yä-mə-sē\ (1715–16) Conflict between Indians and American colonists. Indian resentment of colonial settlers and traders in South Carolina led a group of Yamasee Indians to kill 90 whites in 1715. Other tribes soon joined the Yamasee in their raids on trading posts and plantations. Colonial military assistance from neighboring colonies and war supplies from New England helped end the raids. Many defeated Indians escaped to Florida, where they joined runaway black slaves and other Indians in the Seminole tribe.

Yamato Takeru \yä-'mä-tō-tä-'ke-rü\ Japanese folk hero who may have lived in the 2nd century AD. The son of the 12th emperor, Keiko, he was responsible for expanding the territory of the Yamato court. In stories, he subdued two Kumaso warriors by disguising himself as a woman and killing them while they were drunk. With a miraculous sword he then cut away the burning grass fire set by the Ainu tribesmen and escaped. On the plains of Tagi, he became ill, changed into a white plover, and disappeared. His tomb at Ise is known as the Mausoleum of the White Plover.

Yamazaki Ansai \'yä-mä-ˌzä-kē-'än-ˌsī\ (1619–1682) Japanese exponent of the philosophy of the Chinese Neo-Confucianist ZHU XI. Early in life he was a Buddhist monk, but he gradually rejected Buddhism in favor of Confucianism, which he began to teach to thousands of students. He reduced NEO-CONFUCIANISM to a simple moral code, which he then blended with native Shinto religious doctrines. He equated Neo-Confucian principles and theories with Shinto legends and divinity, creating a philosophical system that took on greater authority than its sources possessed alone. His thought was one of the sources of the extreme nationalism and emperor worship that developed later in Japan.

Yamm \'yäm\ Ancient West Semitic deity who ruled the oceans, rivers, lakes, and underground springs. At the beginning of time, Yamm was awarded the divine kingship by EL, the head of the pantheon. One day, Yamm's messengers requested that the gods send BAAL to become Yamm's servant. Baal refused to go, and engaged Yamm in battle. After a furious fight, Yamm was slain and the kingship was given to Baal. Yamm may have been the same deity as Lotan (Hebrew: "Leviathan"), who was represented as a dragon or serpent.

Yamoussoukro \ˌyä-mü-'sü-krō\ Town (pop., 1995 est.: 110,000), capital designate of Ivory Coast. From 1960 to 1993, it served as the country's "second capital" because it was the birthplace, home, and unofficial headquarters of President FELIX HOUPHOUET-BOIGNY. It was designated the official capital in 1983 and shares some of the functions of the former national capital, ABIDJAN. Fishing and forestry are important to its economy. It is the site of the world's largest Christian church.

Yamuna River \'yə-mə-nə\ River, northern central India. Rising in the HIMALAYAS, it flows south and southeast 855 miles (1,376 km) into the GANGES RIVER at PRAYGRAJ (Allahabad); their confluence is a sacred place to Hindus. The Yamuna's upper course forms a long section of the Uttar Pradesh–Haryana state border.

Yancey, William Lowndes (1814–1863) U.S. politician. Born in Warren Co., Ga., he served in the U.S. House of Representatives 1844–46. In response to the WILMOT PROVISO, he drafted the Alabama Platform (1848), which asserted slaveholders' rights to take their chattel with them to the new territories. He later added secession to the platform. He helped create the League of United Southerners (1858) and supported the Southern Democrats in their nomination of JOHN C. BRECKINRIDGE for president (1860). He drafted Alabama's secession ordinance and served in the Confederate government 1861–63.

Yang, Chen Ning *known as* **Frank Yang** (born 1922) Chinese-U.S. theoretical physicist. He emigrated to the U.S. in 1945 and studied with EDWARD TELLER at the University of Chicago. He showed that PARITY is violated when elementary particles decay. This and other work in PARTICLE PHYSICS earned him and Tsung-Dao Lee (born 1926) a 1957 Nobel Prize. His research focused mostly on interactions involving the WEAK FORCE among ELEMENTARY PARTICLES. He also worked in STATISTICAL MECHANICS.

Yang Di *or* **Yang Ti** \'yäŋ-'dē\ *orig.* **Yang Guang** (569–618) Second ruler of the Chinese SUI DYNASTY. Under Yang Di canals were built and great palaces erected. In 608 he built a great canal linking the rice-producing areas in the south with the densely populated north, and he extended this system in 610, contributing to what was to become the GRAND CANAL network. He embarked on military campaigns in Vietnam and Inner Asia. Three expeditions to Korea were so disastrous that the

Chinese people turned against him; he was assassinated in southern China. One of his former officials reunited the empire and established the TANG DYNASTY. See also WENDI.

yangban \'yäŋ-ˌban\ (Korean: "two groups") Highest social class of the Korean CHOSON dynasty (1392–1910). It consisted of both *munban* (civilian officials) and *muban* (military officials). Though the term originated in the KORYO dynasty (935–1392), it was only later applied to the highest of four social classes. The yangban were granted land and stipends and were the only social class permitted to take the civil-service examinations. The yangban system was discarded in 1894.

Yangon \ˌyäŋ-'gōn\ *formerly* **Rangoon** City (metro. area pop., 1996 est.: 4,000,000), principal seaport, and capital of Myanmar, on the Yangon River. It was a fishing village until the present city was founded c. 1755 by Burmese King Alaungpaya, and developed into a port. The British occupied it 1824–26 during the First ANGLO-BURMESE WAR and again took it in 1852 during the Second Anglo-Burmese War. After the British annexation of all of Burma (Myanmar) in 1886, Rangoon became the capital city. During World War II the Japanese occupied it and it suffered severe damage. In 1988 it was the scene of severe repression of antigovernment demonstrators by the military. It handles more than 80% of the Myanmar's foreign commerce.

Yangshao culture \'yäŋ-'shau̇\ (5000–3000 BC) Prehistoric culture of China's Huang (Yellow) River basin, represented by several sites at which painted pottery has been uncovered. In Yangshao culture, millet was cultivated, some animals were domesticated, chipped and polished stone tools were used, silk was produced, and pottery was fired in kilns dug into the ground. See also BANPO.

Yangtze Gorges Dam Project See THREE GORGES DAM PROJECT

Yangtze River \'yäŋ-'tsə\, *or* **Chang Jiang** \'chäŋ\, *or* **Ch'ang Chiang** River, China. Rising in the eastern KUNLUN MOUNTAINS in western China, it flows southeast, continuing east across YUNNAN and then across the rest of China to the CHINA SEA near SHANGHAI. It is known as the JINSHA in its upper course. At 3,434 mi (5,525 km) long, it is the world's third-longest river. Navigable for 585 mi (940 km), it becomes harder to navigate above Yichang because of the gorges that occur between CHONGQING, at 650 ft (200 m), and Yichang, at 130 ft (40 m). Its chief tributaries are the YALONG, MIN, Jialing, HAN, and Wu rivers. Several large cities, including Shanghai, NANJING, WUHAN, and Chongqing lie in the river's basin, which is known as the granary of China. The controversial THREE GORGES DAM PROJECT, first discussed in the 1920s, and promoted in the 1950s by MAO ZEDONG, was inaugurated in 1994. Located west of Yichang, it will enable freighters to navigate 1,400 mi (2,250 km) inland from the East China Sea to Chongqing.

Yanofsky \ya-'nȯf-skē\, **Charles** (born 1925) U.S. geneticist. Born in New York City, he received his PhD from Yale University. He was part of the research team that first demonstrated that certain mutant genes produce inactive proteins. Later, working with *E. coli,* he showed that the sequence of the nitrogenous bases that form part of the structure of the genetic material corresponds to the amino-acid sequence of proteins. Investigating the biochemical actions of suppressor mutations (changes in a gene that reverse the visible effects of mutation in a second gene), he found that suppression restored the ability to form an active enzyme in a mutant that had previously produced an inactive protein.

Yanomami *or* **Yanomamö** South American Indians who live in the remote forest of the Orinoco River basin in southern Venezuela and the northern reaches of the Amazon basin in Brazil. They are hunters and gatherers who also grow crops in gardens cleared by slashing and burning. Their reputation as a "fierce people" perpetually at war has been challenged in recent years. Because their survival was threatened by incursions of Brazilian miners, in 1991 the Brazilian government set aside an area of 36,000 sq mi (93,000 sq km) as a homeland. They number about 10,000.

Yao \'yau̇\ Various Bantu-speaking peoples inhabiting southern Tanzania, northern Mozambique, and southern Malawi. In the colonial era the Yao were prominent as slave traders. They were never completely united but lived as small groups ruled by chiefs. By 1900 they had come under German, Portuguese, or British rule. Today numbering 2.2 million, the Yao practice slash-and-burn horticulture. Most are Muslims.

Yao \'yau̇\ In Chinese mythology, one of three legendary emperors, along with SHUN and DA YU, of the golden age of antiquity (c. 24th century BC). All three were exalted by CONFUCIUS as models of virtue, righteousness, and unselfish devotion.

Yao, imaginative portrait by an artist of the Ch'ien-lung period (1735–96); in the Metropolitan Museum of Art, New York City.

BY COURTESY OF THE METROPOLITAN MUSEUM OF ART, NEW YORK, GIFT OF MRS. EDWARD S. HARKNESS, 1947

Yaoundé \yau̇n-'dā\ City (pop., 1992 est.: 800,000), capital of Cameroon. It was founded in 1888 while Cameroon was a German protectorate. The area came under French control, and it was declared the capital of French Cameroun in 1922. In 1940–46 it was replaced as the capital by DOUALA, but after Cameroon achieved independence in 1960, it again became the seat. It contains several small manufacturing and processing industries (sawmills and printing presses) and is the area's agricultural market.

Yaqui \'yä-kē\ American Indian people centered in southern Sonora on the western coast of Mexico. They were settled agriculturalists who offered stubborn resistance to the first Spanish invaders and only gradually came under mission influence. In the 19th century they fought against Mexican encroachment on their fertile lands, and were finally quelled with difficulty in 1887. Thousands were subsequently deported. In the 1930s much of their land was returned to them. Irrigation projects have led to a shift from subsistence agriculture to cash cropping (wheat, cotton, and crops for vegetable oil). They number about 25,000 in Mexico and several thousand in Arizona.

Yarborough \'yär-ˌbu̇r-ō\, **Cale** *orig.* **William Caleb** (born 1939) U.S. stock-car racer. Born in Timmonsville, S.C., he began racing stock cars in the early 1960s. He was the first to win the NASCAR championships three consecutive years (1976–78). He also won the Daytona 500 three times (1968, 1977, 1983) and the Atlanta 500 four times (1967, 1968, 1974, 1981).

yard Unit of length, equal to 36 INCHES or 3 ft (see FOOT) in the U.S. system, or to 0.9144 m (see METER) in the INTERNATIONAL SYSTEM OF UNITS. A cloth yard, used to measure cloth, was 37 in. long. (A cloth yard was also the standard length for arrows.) In casual speech, a yard (e.g., of concrete, gravel or topsoil) may refer to a cubic yard.

Yarmuk River \yär-'mük\ River, northwestern Jordan. It rises in southwestern Syria and flows southwest to its confluence with the JORDAN RIVER. For most of its course of about 50 mi (80 km), it forms the boundary between Syria and Jordan. It was the scene of a major battle between Arabs and Byzantines in 636 AD that established Muslim dominance there. That dominance, broken only by the period of the CRUSADES (1099–1291), lasted until World War I. Since the SIX-DAY WAR of 1967, the lower river valley has been under Israeli control.

yarn Continuous strand of fibers grouped or twisted together and used to construct TEXTILE fabrics. Yarns are made from both natural and synthetic fibers, in filament or staple form. Filament is very long fiber, including the natural fiber SILK and the synthetic fibers. Most fibers that occur in nature are fairly short, or staple, and synthetic fibers may be cut into short, uniform lengths to form staple. Spinning is the process of drawing out and twisting a mass of cleaned, prepared fibers. Filament yarns generally require less twist than do staple yarns. More twist produces stronger yarn; low twist produces softer, shinier yarn. Two or more single strands may be twisted together to form ply yarn. Knitting yarns have less twist than weaving yarns. THREAD, used for sewing, is a tightly twisted ply yarn.

Yaroslav \yə-rə-'slȧf\ *known as* **Yaroslav the Wise** (980–1054) Grand prince of Kiev (1019–54). A son of VLADIMIR I, he defeated his brother Svyatopolk the Accursed to become ruler of Kiev. He consolidated the state through administrative reforms and military campaigns, codified laws, and promoted the spread of Christianity. He also built many fortifications and churches in the Byzantine style, including the Cathedral of St. Sophia. Yaroslav regained Galicia from the Poles and expanded Kievan possessions in the Baltic region, but his military campaign against Constantinople was a failure (1043).

Yarqon River \yär-'kōn\ River, western central Israel. It rises near Rosh ha-Ayin and flows westward for about 16 mi (26 km) to the Mediterranean in northern TEL AVIV-JAFFA. It marks the boundary between the Plain of SHARON and the coastal lowlands. Since the construction and expansion of the Yarqon-Negev Project in the 1950s (see NEGEV), the water level has gone down and pollution has increased. During World War I it was the site of several important British victories over the Turks in their conquest of Palestine.

yarrow \'yar-ō\ Any of about 80 species of perennial herbs that make up the genus *Achillea* in the COMPOSITE FAMILY, native mainly to the northern temperate zone. Some species are cultivated as garden ornamentals. They have toothed, often finely cut, sometimes aromatic leaves. Many small white, yellow, or pink flowers are often grouped into flat-topped clusters, which can be dried for winter bouquets.

Yarrow (*Achillea millefolium* variety *lanulosa*).
DENNIS E. ANDERSON

Yasin \yȧ-'sēn\, **Abd al-Salam** (born 1928) Moroccan religious leader of the banned Charity and Justice Party. A former school inspector fluent in English and French, he has been under house arrest since 1989. He enjoys immense popularity among Morocco's Islamists, and international human-rights groups regard him as a prisoner of conscience.

yaws *or* **frambesia** \fram-'bē-zhə\ Contagious tropical disease, caused by SPIROCHETES indistinguishable from those of SYPHILIS, which may be a subspecies. Yaws spreads mainly by discharge from skin sores, not sexual activity. It is common in children, who usually become immune. In the first stage, a skin sore starts as a wartlike thickening, cracks open, leaks fluid, and bleeds easily. A month or more later, multiple sores erupt. The third stage (much rarer than in syphilis) involves destruction of skin, mucous membranes, and bones. PENICILLIN cures early-stage yaws. Prevention requires isolation and prompt treatment, and personal and group hygiene.

Yayoi culture \'yä-,yȯi\ (c. 250 BC–c. AD 250) Prehistoric culture of Japan subsequent to JOMON CULTURE. It arose on the island of Kyushu and spread northeastward across Honshu. The Yayoi people mastered bronze and iron casting, wove hemp, and employed a Chinese method of wet-paddy rice cultivation. Yayoi pottery is unglazed; early examples have incised decorations, but pieces produced in the last stage of the period are often undecorated. Chinese-style bronze mirrors and coins indicate contact with HAN-DYNASTY China.

Yazid I \yȧ-'zēd\ (c. 645–683) Second CALIPH of the UMAYYAD DYNASTY. His victory at the Battle of KARBALA (680) led to the permanent split of Islam into Sunni and Shiite sects. He succeeded his father, MUAWIYAH I, as caliph (680–83), keeping his father's advisers and retaining most of his policies, while reforming the financial system, adjusting tax policy, and improving the irrigation system of the Damascus oasis. See also ALI, FITNAH, HUSAYN IBN ALI.

Yazidi \'yä-zi-dē\ Middle Eastern religion, a syncretic combination of Zoroastrian, Manichaean, Jewish, Nestorian Christian, and Islamic elements. Its adherents, numbering less than 100,000, are found in Iraq, Turkey, Syria, Armenia, the Caucasus, and Iran. Most speak Kurdish. They believe that they were created separately from the rest of mankind and segregate themselves from the rest of society. In Yazidi belief, seven angels, subordinate to a supreme but uninvolved God, rule the universe. The belief that God restored the devil to his position as chief of the angels upon the devil's repentance has led to an undeserved reputation as devil worshipers. Their chief saint is Shaykh Adi, a 12th-century Muslim mystic. Their name derives from YAZID I (c. 645–683), from whose supporters they may be descended.

Yazoo land fraud \ya-'zü\ (1795–1814) Scheme to sell land in Georgia. After legislators were bribed to sell Georgia's western land claims around the Yazoo River to four land companies for $500,000, public anger forced a newly elected Georgia legislature to rescind the act (1796) and return the money. Much of the land had meanwhile been resold to third parties, who refused the money and maintained their claim to the property. The state ceded its claim to the U.S. in 1802. In 1810 the U.S. Supreme Court ruled that the 1796 rescinding law was an unconstitutional infringement on a contract. By 1814 the U.S. government assumed possession of the territory and awarded the claimants over $4 million.

Yazoo River \ya-'zü\ River, western central Mississippi. Formed by the confluence of the TALLAHATCHIE and Yalobusha rivers north of Greenwood, Miss., it meanders 189 mi (304 km) south and southwest to join the MISSISSIPPI RIVER above Vicksburg. Its basin is protected from flooding by an extensive system of levees.

Yeager \'yā-gər\, **Chuck** *orig.* **Charles Elwood** (born 1923) U.S. test pilot.Born in Myra, W.V., he served as a pilot in World War II and became a flight instructor and test pilot after the war. Chosen to test-fly the secret experimental X-1 aircraft, in 1947 he became the first person to break the sound barrier in flight, with a speed of 670 mph (1,079 kph). A brash and colorful personality, he retired with the rank of brigadier general in 1975 and received the Presidential Medal of Freedom in 1985.

year Time required for the earth to travel once around the sun, slightly less than $365\frac{1}{4}$ days. This fractional number makes necessary the periodic adjustment of days in any calendar that is to be kept in step with the seasons. In the GREGORIAN CALENDAR, a common year contains 365 days, and every fourth year is a leap year of 366 days.

Year 2000 bug See Y2K BUG

yeast Any of certain economically important single-celled fungi (see FUNGUS), most in the class Ascomyetes, a few in Basidiomycetes. Found worldwide in soils and on plant surfaces, yeasts are especially abundant in sugary mediums such as flower nectar and fruits. The types commonly used in the production of bread, beer, and wine are selected strains of *Saccharomyces cerevisiae.* The small cakes and packets used in food and beverage processing contain billions of individual yeast cells, each of which can ferment approximately its own weight of glucose per hour. Yeast is 50% protein and is rich in B vitamins; brewer's yeast is sometimes taken as a vitamin supplement. Some yeasts are mild to dangerous pathogens of humans and other animals (e.g., *Candida albicans,* which irritates mouth and vaginal linings; and *Histoplasma* and *Blastomyces,* which cause persistent lung infections).

Yeats \'yāts\, **William Butler** (1865–1939) Irish poet, dramatist, and prose writer. The son of a well-known painter, Yeats early developed an interest in mysticism and visionary traditions as well as in Irish peasant folklore, and both interests would continue to be sources of poetic imagery for him. His early volumes include the poetry volume *The Wanderings of Oisin* (1889) and the essay collection *The Celtic Twilight* (1893). In 1889 he fell in love with Maud Gonne, a brilliant, beautiful Irish patriot who inspired his involvement in Irish nationalism but did not reciprocate his feelings. With Lady AUGUSTA GREGORY and others, he founded the theater that became the ABBEY THEATRE; throughout his life he would remain one of its directors. He contributed plays to its repertoire, including *The Countess Cathleen* (1899), *On Baile's Strand* (1905), and *Deirdre* (1907). His poetry changed decisively in the years 1909–14: the otherworldly, ecstatic atmosphere of the early lyrics cleared and his work gained in concreteness and complexity, often dealing with political themes, though his interest in mysticism and his passion for Maud Gonne continued unabated. With *Responsibilities* (1914) and *The Wild Swans at Coole* (1917) he began the period of his highest achievement. Some of his greatest verse appears in *The Tower* (1928), *The Winding Stair* (1929), and *Last Poems* (1939), whose individual poems are largely held together by the system of symbolism he developed in *A Vision* (1925), which used astrological images to link individual psychology with the larger patterns of history. He was a member of the Irish Senate 1922–28. He won the Nobel Prize in 1923, and he is regarded by some as the greatest English-language poet of the 20th century.

Yeh-lü Ch'u-ts'ai See YELÜ CHUCAI

Yekaterinburg \yi-ˌkä-ti-rən-ˈbu̇rk\ *formerly (1924–91)* **Sverdlovsk** \sfyird-ˈlȯfsk\ City (pop., 1996 est.: 1,300,000), western central Russia. An ironworks was established in 1721 and a fortress, named after Empress CATHERINE I, was founded there in 1722. It grew as the center for all the ironworks of the URAL MTNS. region and its importance increased with the building of a highway (1783) and the TRANS-SIBERIAN RAILROAD. It achieved notoriety as the place where Czar NICHOLAS II and his family were held prisoner and executed by the BOLSHEVIKS (1918). In 1924 it was renamed Sverdlovsk in honor of YAKOV SVERDLOV. The city reverted to its original name after the breakup of the U.S.S.R. in 1991. It is a major Russian industrial center, especially for heavy machinery.

Yelizavetpol See GÄNCÄ

Yellow Emperor See HUANGDI

yellow fever Acute infectious tropical disease, sometimes occurring in temperate zones. Abrupt onset of headache, backache, fever, nausea, and vomiting is followed by either recovery with immunity, or by higher fever, slow pulse, and vomiting of blood. Patients may die in a week. JAUNDICE is common (hence the name). One of the world's great plagues for 300 years, it is caused by a virus transmitted by several species of mosquitoes. CARLOS FINLAY suggested and WALTER REED proved this means of spread, leading to near-elimination of the disease through mosquito control (see WILLIAM GORGAS). Treatment consists of supportive care (see THERAPEUTICS), particularly fever reduction. Control of mosquitoes near cities and live-virus vaccines—developed by Max Theiler (1899–1972), who won a 1951 Nobel Prize for his work—have made yellow fever completely preventable.

yellow jacket Any of 35–40 species (genus *Dolichovespula* or *Vespula*) of social WASPS, principally of the Northern Hemisphere, named for the black bands on its yellow abdomen. They differ from other wasps in having their wings folded longitudinally when at rest. *Dolichovespula* species typically build exposed nests. *Vespula* species build concealed nests underground or in protected cavities; when a nest is stepped on, the colony may erupt in an angry, stinging swarm. Nest size varies widely; some nests can be held in one hand, whereas nests in warmer climates may weigh half a ton.

yellow journalism Use of lurid features and sensationalized news in newspaper publishing to attract readers and increase circulation. The phrase was coined in the 1890s to describe tactics employed in the furious competition between two New York papers, JOSEPH PULITZER's *World* and WILLIAM RANDOLPH HEARST's *Journal*. When Hearst hired away from Pulitzer a cartoonist who had drawn the immensely popular comic strip "The Yellow Kid," another cartoonist was hired to draw the comic for the *World,* and the rivalry excited so much attention that the newspapers' competition was dubbed "yellow journalism." Techniques of the period that became permanent in U.S. journalism include banner headlines, colored comics, and copious illustrations.

yellow poplar See TULIP TREE

Yellow River See HUANG RIVER

Yellow Sea *Chinese* **Huang Hai** \ˈhwäŋ-ˈhī\ Large inlet of the western Pacific Ocean, between northeastern China and the Korean peninsula. Famous for its fishing grounds, it connects with the CHINA SEA on the south; the SHANDONG PENINSULA extends into it from the west. It has an area of 180,000 sq mi (466,200 sq km) and a maximum depth of 338 ft (103 m). It derives its name from the color of the silt-laden water discharged into it by the HUANG and other major Chinese rivers, including the CHANG and LIAO. Leading port cities include SHANGHAI and TIANJIN in China, INCHON in South Korea, and Nampo in North Korea.

Yellow Turbans Chinese secret society founded during a time of pestilence (2nd century AD). The rebels' yellow headdresses signified their association with the earth element, which they believed would succeed the (red) fire element that represented Han rule. The sect was Taoist in inspiration, like the contemporaneous FIVE PECKS OF RICE sect. Its rebellion (AD 184–204?) against the tyrannical eunuchs who influenced the emperor contributed to the fall of the HAN DYNASTY. See also TAOISM.

yellowhammer *or* **yellow bunting** Songbird species (*Emberiza citrinella,* family Emberizidae) found from Britain to central Asia. The name is derived from the German *Ammer* ("bunting"). Yellowhammers are 6 in. (16 cm) long and have a streaked brown body, yellow-tinged head and breast, and a rapid song. In the southern U.S., the yellow-shafted FLICKER is called yellowhammer because of its drumming.

Yellowknife City (pop., 1991: 15,000), capital of Northwest Territories. Lying on the northwestern shore of GREAT SLAVE LAKE near the mouth of the Yellowknife River, it was founded in 1935, one year after gold was discovered in the area; it took its name from the Yellowknife band of Athabascan Indians. Gold mining remains the chief economic activity. There are also reserves of diamonds in the region. The capital since 1967, it is the largest community and the chief administrative, commercial, and educational center in the territories.

yellowlegs Either of two species (family Scolopacidae) of shorebirds with a trim, gray-brown and white streaked body; long bill; and long, bright-yellow legs. Both species breed in Canada and winter in South America and eat small fish and other aquatic creatures. The lesser yellowlegs *(Tringa flavipes),* about 10 in. (25 cm) long, appears in sizable flocks on mudflats during migration; it has a flat call of one or two notes. The less-common greater yellowlegs *(T. melanoleuca),* about 14 in. (35 cm) long, has a longer, stouter, slightly upturned bill; its call is a clear three-note whistle.

Lesser yellowlegs (*Tringa flavipes*).
MARY M. TREMAINE–ROOT RESOURCES

Yellowstone Lake Lake, YELLOWSTONE NATIONAL PARK, northwestern Wyoming. It lies at 7,731 ft (2,356 m) above sea level, the largest body of water in North America at so high an altitude. It is fed and drained by the YELLOWSTONE RIVER. About 20 mi (32 km) long and 14 mi (23 km) wide, it has a maximum depth of 390 ft (119 m) and a surface area of 137 sq mi (354 sq km). It is a haven for rare species of waterbirds, including TRUMPETER swans, and is prized for trout fishing.

Yellowstone National Park National preserve, northwestern Wyoming, southern Montana, eastern Idaho. The oldest national park in the U.S, and in the world, it was established by the U.S. Congress in 1872; it covers 3,468 sq mi (8,983 sq km). The Gallatin Range, ABSAROKA RANGE, Snow Mtns., and TETON RANGE extend into it. Yellowstone has unusual geologic features, including fossil forests and eroded basaltic lava flows. It also has 10,000 hot springs, which erupt as steam vents, fumaroles, and geysers. Old Faithful, the park's most famous geyser, erupts every 33 to 93 minutes. It has many lakes and rivers, including YELLOWSTONE LAKE, Shoshone Lake, the SNAKE RIVER, and the YELLOWSTONE RIVER. In 1988 an extensive series of forest fires temporarily laid waste large areas of the park.

Yellowstone River River, northwestern Wyoming and southern and eastern Montana. It rises in Wyoming, flows north through YELLOWSTONE LAKE and YELLOWSTONE NATIONAL PARK, then continues north into Montana. There it flows northeast into the MISSOURI RIVER on the Montana–North Dakota boundary. It is 692 mi (1,114 km) long, and has been developed extensively for irrigation. Its principal tributaries are the BIGHORN, Tongue, and POWDER rivers. It was first explored in 1806 during the LEWIS AND CLARK EXPEDITION.

Yeltsin, Boris (Nikolayevich) (born 1931) Russian politician and president of Russia (1990–99). After attending the Urals Polytechnic Institute, he worked at construction projects in western Russia 1955–68. He became Communist Party leader in Sverdlovsk in 1976, and an ally of MIKHAIL GORBACHEV. He was ap-

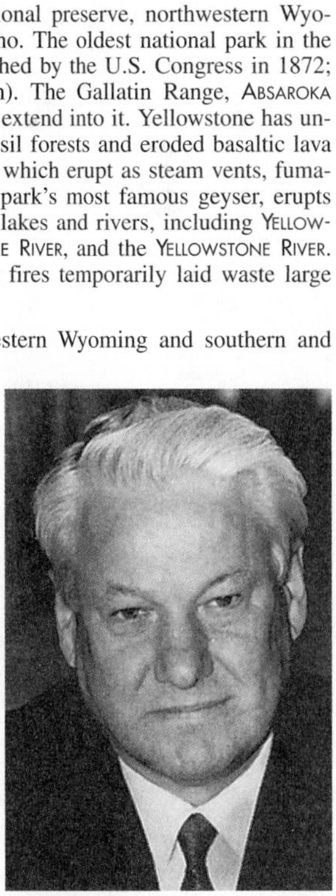

Boris Yeltsin, 1991.
VARIO PRESS/CAMERA PRESS FROM GLOBE PHOTOS

W X Y Z

pointed by Gorbachev to eliminate corruption in the Moscow party organization, and as first secretary (mayor) of Moscow (1985–87) he proved a determined reformer. His criticism of the slow pace of reform led to a break with Gorbachev, and Yeltsin lost his position. In 1989 he was elected to the new Soviet parliament by a landslide, then became president of the Russian Republic (1990) and resigned from the Communist Party. In 1991 he won the presidency again in the first popular election in Russian history. When communist hard-liners staged a coup against Gorbachev, Yeltsin successfully opposed it, facing down its leaders with a dramatic outdoor speech in Moscow. He led the establishment of the COMMONWEALTH OF INDEPENDENT STATES (1991) and began to transform Russia's economy into one based on free markets and private enterprise. He faced opposition from hard-liners, who staged an unsuccessful coup in 1993. When Chechnya unilaterally declared independence, Yeltsin sent troops to fight the rebels (1994). The Chechnya situation and Russia's deepening economic distress depressed his popularity, but he won reelection in 1996. He spent months recovering from a heart attack; he rejected suggestions that he resign the presidency, despite his increasingly erratic behavior as well as the deterioration of civil order and rampant corruption, but continuing poor health led to his resignation on December 31, 1999. He was succeeded by VLADIMIR PUTIN.

Yelü Chucai *or* **Yeh-lü Ch'u-ts'ai** \'ye-'lǖ-'chüt-'sī\ (1190–1244) Chinese statesman of Khitan extraction, adviser to GENGHIS KHAN and his son ÖGÖDEI. He established a formal bureaucracy and rationalized taxation system for the Mongol-controlled portions of China. By persuading Ögödei to spare the inhabitants of northern China in order to utilize their wealth and skills, Yelü gave the Mongols access to the Chinese weapons that later enabled them to conquer the SONG DYNASTY. See also MONGOL, YUAN DYNASTY.

Yemen \'ye-mən\ *officially* **Republic of Yemen** Country, southwestern Arabian Peninsula. It also includes SOCOTRA Island in the Indian Ocean and the Kamaran group in the RED SEA. Area: 203,849 sq mi (527,969 sq km). Population (2001): 18,078,000. Capital: SANAA. The population is mainly Arab. Language: Arabic (official). Religions: Islam (official); remnants, Christianity, Hinduism, Judaism. Currency: Yemeni rial. From the Gulf of ADEN and the RED SEA, a narrow coastal plain leads to highlands that cover most of the country. The northern region covers the southern and southwestern parts of the RUB AL-KHALI. Mineral resources include iron ore, salt, oil, and natural gas, all of which are exploited. Agriculture is important; industries include food processing and salt production. It is a republic with one legislative house; its head of state is the president, and the head of government is the prime minister. Yemen was the home of ancient Minaean, Sabaean, and Himyarite kingdoms. The Romans invaded the region in the 1st century AD. In the 6th century it was conquered by Ethiopians and Persians. Following conversion to Islam in the 7th century, it was ruled nominally under a caliphate. The Egyptian AYYUBID DYNASTY ruled there from 1173 to 1229, after which the region passed to the Rasulids. From 1517 through 1918, the OTTOMAN EMPIRE maintained varying degrees of control, especially in the northwestern section. A boundary agreement was reached in 1934 between the northwestern imam-controlled territory, which subsequently became the Yemen Arab Republic (North Yemen), and the southeastern British-controlled territory, which subsequently became the People's Democratic Republic of Yemen (South Yemen). Relations between the two Yemens remained tense and were marked by conflict throughout the 1970s and 1980s. Reaching an accord, the two officially united as the Republic of Yemen in 1990. Its 1993 elections were the first free, multiparty general elections held in the Arabian Peninsula, and they were the first in which women participated. In 1994, after a two-month civil war, a new constitution was approved.

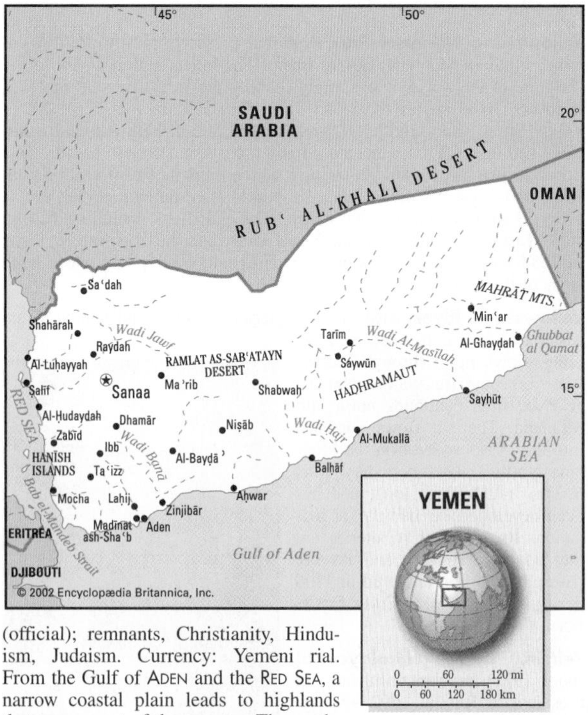

Yenisey River \yi-ni-'sā\ River, western Russia. One of the longest rivers on the Asian continent, it rises in the borderland of southern central Russia and Mongolia and flows along the western Siberian Plain to empty into the Kara Sea. Along its course it receives numerous tributaries, including the ANGARA RIVER. Approximately 1,900 mi (3,000 km) of the river's 2,540-mi (4,090-km) course are navigable.

yerba maté See MATÉ

Yerevan *formerly* **Erivan** \ˌyer-ə-'vän\ City (pop., 1995 est.: 1,249,000), capital of Armenia. Fortified since the 8th century BC, and part of Armenia since the 6th century BC, it developed as an important center of the caravan trade. Over the centuries, it was ruled by many, including the Romans, Arabs, Turks, and Russians, falling to the last in 1827. In 1920 it became the capital of independent Armenia, and remained so during Soviet rule and renewed independence. Its industries include producing chemicals, aluminum, cars, and electrical machinery.

Yermak *orig.* **Yermak Timofeyevich** (died 1584?) COSSACK leader. In 1579 he was enlisted by the merchant Stroganov family to defend its possessions against attacks by Siberian tribesmen. He set out with an expeditionary force of 840 Cossacks and reached the central Tatar khanate of Sibir in 1582. With their firearms, Yermak and his army defeated the numerically superior forces of Khan Kuchum and occupied the capital, Sibir. Though later killed in a revolt of Kuchum's forces, Yermak was considered the conqueror of Siberia and became a hero of Russian folklore.

Yesenin \yi-'sʸenʸ-in\, **Sergey (Aleksandrovich)** *or* **Sergey Aleksandrovich Esenin** (1895–1925) Russian poet. From a peasant family, he celebrated traditional "wooden Russia" over modern, industrialized society in works beginning with *Radunitsa* (1916), and he believed the Revolution of 1917 would lead to the peasant millennium he envisioned. Taking up the life of a rowdy and blasphemous exhibitionist, he wrote cynical, swaggering tavern verse such as *Confessions of a Hooligan* (1921). In 1922 he married ISADORA DUNCAN, though neither could speak the other's language. His efforts to adjust to the revolutionary era were unsuccessful, and he hanged himself at 30. Though frowned on by the authorities, he was very popular in Russia both during his life and afterward.

yeshiva \yə-'shē-və\ Academy of higher Talmudic learning. Through its biblical and legal exegesis and application of scripture, the yeshiva has defined and regulated JUDAISM for centuries. Traditionally, it is the setting for the training and ordination of RABBIS. Following the destruction of the Second Temple of JERUSALEM, a series of yeshivas were set up around the Levant to codify and explain centuries of Jewish scholarship. In medieval times, yeshivas flourished in Europe, wherever there were large populations of Jews. The first yeshiva in the U.S., Etz Hayyim (1886), later became YESHIVA UNIV. (1945).

Yeshiva University Private university in New York City. It was established in 1886 as Yeshiva Eitz Chaim; in 1915 it merged with a Jewish theological seminary. Today the university is independent, though its curriculum emphasizes Jewish culture and history. Yeshiva consists of a liberal-arts college, a college for women, a college of Hebraic studies, and the Albert Einstein College of Medicine, as well as schools of Judaic studies, Talmudic studies, business, law (the Cardozo School), social work, education, and graduate studies, among others. Total enrollment is about 5,500.

Yeti See ABOMINABLE SNOWMAN

Yevtushenko \yif-tü-'shen-kə\, **Yevgeny (Aleksandrovich)** (born 1933) Russian poet. The descendant of Ukrainians exiled to Siberia, he grew up in Moscow and in the small town that is the setting of his first important narrative poem, *Zima Junction* (1956). He became the spokesman for the post-Stalin generation of Russian poets with his internationally publicized demands for greater artistic freedom, which signaled an easing of Soviet control over artists in the late 1950s and '60s. He revived brash, slangy language and such traditions as love lyrics and personal lyrics, and became famous worldwide for his passionate declamations of the contents of such volumes as *Baby Yar* (1961) and *The Bratsk Station* (1965) in public recitals.

yew Any of about eight species of ornamental evergreens in the genus *Taxus,* family Taxaceae (the yew family), distributed throughout the Northern Hemisphere. Two species are always shrubby, but the others may reach heights of 77 ft (25 m). The plants have many branches, covered with needlelike leaves. Yew wood is hard, fine-grained, and heavy, with white or creamy sapwood and amber to brown heartwood. Once popular for cabinetwork, implements, and archery bows, it is used more today for articles either carved or turned on a lathe. Other trees called yew but not in this family are the plum-yew (family Cephalotaxaceae) and Prince Albert yew (family Podocarpaceae).

Yezhov \yi-'zhôf\, **Nikolay (Ivanovich)** (1895–1939?) Soviet secret-police chief. By 1927 he was a functionary for the Moscow party's central committee and a favorite of JOSEPH STALIN. He became a member of the party's Central Committee (1934) and succeeded GENRIKH YAGODA as chief of the Soviet security police, or NKVD (1936). He instituted the most severe stage of the Great Purge (see PURGE TRIALS), known as *Yezhovshchina.* By 1938 he had become the object of Stalin's suspicions and was replaced by LAVRENTY P. BERIA as head of the NKVD. He disappeared in 1939 and was probably executed.

Yggdrasill \'ig-drə-ˌsil\ In Norse mythology, the WORLD TREE. One of its roots extended into the underworld, another into the land of the giants, and the third into ASGARD. At its base were three wells: the Well of Fate, from which the tree was watered by the Fates; the Roaring Kettle, in which dwelt Nidhogg, the monster that gnawed the tree's roots; and Mimir's Well, the source of wisdom, for whose water ODIN sacrificed an eye. After the RAGNAROK, Yggdrasill, though badly shaken, is to be the source of new life.

Yi dynasty See CHOSON DYNASTY

Yi Hwang \'ē-'hwäŋ\ (1501–1570) Korean religious leader, the foremost Korean Confucian. He helped shape the character of Korean Confucianism through his creative interpretation of ZHU XI's teaching. His *Discourse on the Ten Sagely Diagrams,* an aid for educating the king, offered a depiction of all the major concepts in SONG-DYNASTY learning. He elevated the level of Confucian dialogue to a new height of intellectual sophistication through his correspondence with Ki Taesung (1527–1572). In their so-called four-seven debate, they discussed the relationship between MENCIUS' four basic human feelings (commiseration, shame, modesty, and right vs. wrong) and seven emotions.

Yi jing *or* **I ching** \'ē-'jiŋ\ (Chinese: "Book of Changes") Ancient Chinese text, one of the FIVE CLASSICS of Confucianism. The main body of the work, traditionally attributed to Wen Wang (fl. 12th century BC), contains a discussion of the divinatory system used by wizards in the ZHOU DYNASTY. A supplementary section of "commentaries," believed to date from the WARRING STATES PERIOD (475–221 BC), is a philosophical exposition that attempts to explain the world and its ethical principles. The book's cosmology, which involves humans and nature in a single system, has made it universally popular.

Yi Song-gye \'yē-'səŋ-'gye\ *or* **T'aejo** \'tī-'jō\ (1335–1408) Founder of the Korean CHOSON DYNASTY (1392–1910). A military leader in the KORYO dynasty, he rose through the ranks by battling invading forces. He defeated his rivals and drove out the last king of the Koryo dynasty, taking the throne in 1392. He established his capital at Hanyang (now Seoul). He and his successors redistributed land, which had been concentrated in the hands of a few high-ranking bureaucrats, throughout the various levels of officialdom. In a break with the past, he made Neo-Confucianism the state religion, replacing Buddhism. Farming was made the center of the economy. In foreign relations, he maintained a close relationship with China's MING DYNASTY.

Yi Sun-shin \'yē-'sün-'shin\ (1545–1598) Korean admiral and national hero. He worked on developing the *kobukson* ("turtle ship"), thought to be the first ironclad battleship. As a result of Yi's preparations, his forces, unlike most of the Korean military, were ready to fight when the Japanese under TOYOTOMI HIDEYOSHI invaded in 1592. His sea victories effectively cut off the Japanese troops in Korea from their supplies. In 1597 he was falsely accused of disloyalty and demoted to the rank of common soldier. When the Japanese launched a second invasion and largely destroyed the Korean navy, Yi was reinstated and soon restored Korea's control of the seas. He was killed by a stray bullet as he pursued the retreating Japanese.

Yibin *or* **I-pin** \'ē-'bin\ *formerly* **Suchow** \'sü-'jō\ City (pop., 1999 est.: 288,039), southern SICHUAN province, southern central China. It is located at the junction of the MIN and CHANG rivers. A county administration was set up there in the 2nd century BC. It first received the name Yibin in AD 742. The Chinese hold expanded there during the SONG DYNASTY. By the QING DYNASTY (1644–1911), it was Hsü-chou superior prefecture, known to Europeans as Suifu. In 1912 it reverted to Yibin. In 1913 steamship communication with CHONGQING was opened, and Yibin grew into a major collection and distribution center. It has long been known for its salt deposits, which now supply a large chemical plant.

Yichang *or* **I-ch'ang** \'ē-'chäŋ\ City (pop., 1999 est.: 481,277), western HUBEI province, eastern central China. An ancient city, it is located at the head of navigation on the CHANG RIVER, below the entrance to the gorges of the Daba Mountains. As the gateway to the rich province of SICHUAN, it was often disputed during times of Chinese political turmoil. It was made a treaty port for foreign trade in 1877; a Western quarter grew beside it, and many Western commercial firms established branches there. It was occupied by the Japanese and badly damaged during World War II, but the city and its shipyards have been rebuilt. It is now an industrial center and a distribution point for the region's manufactured goods.

Yiddish drama Productions of the professional Yiddish theater. European Jewish drama originated in the Middle Ages, when dancers and jesters entertained at PURIM celebrations. By the 16th century, elaborate plays were being performed for the occasion in Yiddish. The professional Yiddish theater dates from 1876, when Abraham Goldfaden (1840–1908) wrote a well-received musical sketch in Romania and organized a troupe to perform his songs and plays. In 1883 anti-Semitic laws in Russia that forbade Yiddish plays compelled many actors and playwrights to emigrate to England and the U.S. The playwright Jacob Gordin (1853–1909) brought new material and adaptations to the U.S. Yiddish theater, including *The Jewish King Lear* (1892), starring Jacob P. Adler, founder of a family of Yiddish- and English-speaking actors. In 1918 Maurice Schwartz founded and directed the Yiddish Art Theatre, which trained such actors as Jacob Ben-Ami and Muni Weisenfreund (later known as Paul Muni). World War II destroyed most Yiddish culture in Eastern Europe, and by the late 20th century only a few Yiddish theaters survived in such cities as New York, London, Bucharest, and Warsaw.

Yiddish language Language of Ashkenazic Jews and their descendants (see ASHKENAZI), written in the HEBREW ALPHABET. Yiddish developed from southeastern dialects of Middle High German carried into central and eastern Europe from the 12th century on; it has been strongly influenced by Hebrew and ARAMAIC, from which it draws 12–20% of its lexicon. The isolation of eastern European speakers from High German, and their exposure to SLAVIC LANGUAGES, particularly POLISH and UKRAINIAN, led to a primary distinction between West and East Yiddish dialects. From the late 18th century, most Jews remaining in central Europe gave up Yiddish in favor of German; it has now virtually died out. East Yiddish dialects differ markedly in realization of vowels; there are central, NE, and southeastern dialects. A flourishing literary language in the 19th and early 20th century, Yiddish declined dramatically due to massive migration, assimilation, and Nazi genocide. Today Yiddish may still be spoken by 3 million people worldwide, but most of its speakers are middle-aged or older.

Yima \ya-'mä, 'yē-mə\ In ancient Iranian religion, the first man, son of the sun, and progenitor of the human race. In one legend, Yima became king in a golden age in which need, death, disease, aging, and extremes of temperature were banished from the earth because of his virtue. This golden age ended when AHURA MAZDA foretold a terrible winter. Yima was instructed to build an underground domain, take in the best individuals from each species to preserve their seed, and then reemerge after the winter to repopulate the earth. In Zoroastrian legends, Yima was replaced by GAYOMART.

Yin dynasty See SHANG DYNASTY

yin-yang In East Asian thought, the two complementary forces or principles that make up all aspects and phenomena of life. Yin is earth, female, dark, passive, and absorbing; it is present in even numbers and in valleys and streams, and is represented by the tiger, the color orange, and a broken line. Yang is heaven, male, light, active, and penetrating; it is present in odd numbers and mountains, and is represented by the dragon, the color azure, and an unbroken line. Together they express the interdependence of opposites.

Yinchuan *or* **Yin-ch'uan** \'yin-'chwän\ City (pop., 1999 est.: 469,180), capital of NINGXIA Huizu autonomous region, northern central China. It is located near the western end of the GREAT WALL. Originally a county in the 1st century BC, it became the capital of the XI XIA dynasty in 907 AD. In 1227 it came under the MONGOL dynasty, and was later under the MING and the QING dynasties. In 1928 it became the capital of the newly formed Ning-hsia province. In 1954 when Ning-hsia province was abolished, it became part of GANSU province. With the establishment of the Ningxia autonomous region in 1958, it once again became the capital. Largely nonindustrial, it is the chief agricultural market and distribution center for the area.

ylang-ylang *or* **ilang-ilang** \ˌē-ˌläŋ-'ē-ˌläŋ\ South Asian evergreen tree *(Cananga odorata)* of the CUSTARD APPLE family. The name means "flower of flowers" in the Tagalog language. Tall (77 ft, or 25 m) and slim, it has smooth bark and is covered year-round with drooping, long-stalked, rich-scented flowers that have six narrow, greenish-yellow petals. The pointed oval leaves have wavy edges. Clustered, oval black fruits hang from long stalks. Leis are made from the blooms, and a delicate fragrance is distilled from the flowers. The woody ylang-ylang vine *(Artabotrys odoratissimus),* in the same family, is popular on trellises and patios in warm, moist climates.

YMCA *in full* **Young Men's Christian Association** Nonsectarian, nonpolitical Christian lay movement that aims to develop high standards of Christian character among its members. It originated in London in 1844 when 12 young men formed a club to improve the spiritual condition of young tradesmen. The first U.S. club was formed in Boston in the 1850s. YMCA programs include sports and physical education, camping, formal and informal education, and citizenship activities. It also runs hotels, residence halls, and cafeterias. National councils are members of the World Alliance of YMCAs (established 1855), headquartered in Geneva. The YMCA was charged with sponsoring educational and recreational facilities in prisoner-of-war camps by the GENEVA CONVENTION of 1929. It now operates in dozens of countries. The Young Women's Christian Association (YWCA) was founded in Britain (1877) to address the needs of women from rural areas who came to the cities to find work; in the U.S. (founded 1906), it has championed racial equality. The Young Men's and Young Women's Hebrew Association (YM-YWHA) developed in the mid-19th century from Jewish men's literary societies in the U.S. and now exists in some 20 other countries worldwide.

Ymir See AURGELMIR

Yoga One of the six orthodox systems (DARSHANS) of Indian philosophy, which has had widespread influence on many schools of Indian thought. It is better known through its practical aspect than its intellectual content, which is largely based on the philosophy of SAMKHYA. Holding that the evolution of the world occurred in stages, Yoga attempts to reverse this order so that a person reenters his or her state of purity and consciousness. Generally, the Yoga process involves eight stages, which may require several lifetimes to pass through. The first two stages are ethical preparations emphasizing morality, cleanliness, and devotion to God. The next two stages are physical preparations that condition the body to make it supple, flexible, and healthy; the physical aspects of Yoga have been most successfully popularized in the West. The fifth stage involves control of the mind and senses to withdraw from outward objects. The remaining three stages entail the cultivation of increasingly concentrated states of awareness, which will ultimately lead to release from the cycle of rebirth. See also CHAKRA, KUNDALINI.

Yogacara \'yō-gä-'chä-rä\ *or* **Vijnanavada** \vij-ˌnä-nə-'vä-də\ Idealistic school of MAHAYANA Buddhism. It rejects the complete realism of THERAVADA Buddhism and the practical realism of the MADHYAMIKA school, preferring a more complicated position in which the reality perceived by humans does not exist, but only appears to do so by virtue of the capacity of the mind to perceive patterns of continuity and regularity. Yogacara emerged in India about the 2nd century AD and was introduced into China in the 7th century by XUANZANG. It was transmitted to Japan in the mid-7th century as Hosso.

yogurt Semisolid, fermented, often flavored MILK food. Yogurt is known and consumed in almost all parts of the world. It is traditionally made by adding common strains of *Streptococcus* and *Lactobacillus* bacteria to raw milk. The culture is produced by taking a portion of a previous batch. In modern yogurt making, a blend of concentrated sterilized milk and milk solids is inoculated with the two bacteria; sometimes *L. acidophilus* or a lactose-fermenting YEAST is also added. The product is then incubated four or five hours at 110–112°F (43–44°C) until curd forms. Various flavors and sweetening may be added.

Yoho National Park National park, southeastern British Columbia. It occupies 507 sq mi (1,313 sq km) of the western and central slopes of the ROCKY MTNS. and is adjacent to BANFF and KOOTENAY national parks. Known for the BURGESS SHALE archaeological site, geologic treasures, diverse wildlife, and scenic landscape, it was established as a national park in 1886. Features include glaciers, ice fields, steep mountains, and broad valleys. Black and grizzly bears, moose, mule deer, wapiti (elk), and mountain goats inhabit the park.

Yojoa \yō-'hō-ä\, **Lake** Lake, central Honduras. The nation's largest inland lake, it has an area of 110 sq mi (285 sq km). It is volcanic in origin and sits at an elevation of 2,133 ft (650 m). It and the surrounding region are popular with tourists.

Yokohama Seaport city (pop., 2000 prelim.: 3,426,506), southeastern HONSHU, Japan, on western TOKYO BAY. It was a small fishing village when U.S. naval officer MATTHEW PERRY visited in 1854 to negotiate Japanese trading possibilities. It was opened for foreign settlement and trade in 1859. It was destroyed by earthquake and fire in 1923 and severely damaged by U.S. air raids in 1945 during World War II, but it was rebuilt both times. It is Japan's principal port and part of the Tokyo urban-industrial region. It produces textiles, chemicals, ships, machinery, petroleum products, and automobiles.

Yom Kippur \ˌyōm-kē-'pu̇r, ˌyäm-'ki-pər\ *English* **Day of Atonement** Jewish religious holiday, observed on the 10th day of the lunar month of Tishri (in late September or early October). It concludes the 10 days of repentance that begin with ROSH HASHANAH. Its purpose is to purify the individual and community by forgiving the sins of others and by repenting one's own sins against God. Before the destruction of the Temple of JERUSALEM, the high priest performed a sacrificial ceremony that concluded with the death of a SCAPEGOAT. Today it is marked by fasting and abstention from sex. Its eve, when the KOL NIDRE is recited, and the entire day of Yom Kippur, are spent in prayer and meditation.

Yongjo \'yȯŋ-jō\ (r.1724–76) King of the Korean CHOSON DYNASTY. A reformer, Yongjo reinstated the universal military service tax, but then reduced it by half, making up the deficiency with other taxes. He adopted an accounting system and reduced an onerous cloth tax. Yongjo upgraded the status of the offspring of commoners, but his social reforms could not keep up with the speed of societal change.

Yongle emperor *or* **Yung-lo emperor** \'yu̇ŋ-'le\ *orig.* **Zhu Di** (1360–1424) Third emperor of China's MING DYNASTY, which he raised to its greatest power. Son of the HONGWU EMPEROR, founder of the Ming, he was his father's favorite. He was enfeoffed as the Prince of Yan (the region around present-day Beijing) and spent his youth patrolling the northern frontier and keeping the MONGOLS fragmented. When his nephew succeeded to the throne, Zhu Di rebelled and became emperor in 1403. As emperor, he worked to extend China's sway. He sent out ships of exploration, most notably under ZHENG HE; these returned with envoys bearing tribute to acknowledge China's overlordship. He became the only ruler in Chinese history to be acknowledged suzerain by the Japanese. A foray into Annam (now Vietnam), which he attempted to incorporate into China, led to years of guerrilla warfare. He five times led large armies north to the Gobi Desert, forestalling the creation of a Mongol confederation that might have threatened China. He transferred China's capital from Nanjing to Beijing. He built the FORBIDDEN CITY and repaired the GRAND CANAL so that Beijing could be provisioned without relying on sea transport. He sponsored the compilation and publication of the Confucian Classics and the preparation of the 11,000-volume compendium the *Yongle dadian* ("Great Canon of the Yongle Era").

yoni \'yō-nē\ In HINDUISM, a representation of the female sexual organ and feminine generative power, the symbol of the goddess Shakti (see SHAKTI). The yoni is often associated with the phallic LINGA, the symbol of the god SHIVA. The linga is depicted in art as resting in the yoni, their union representing the eternal process of creation and regeneration.

Yonkers City (pop., 1996 est.: 190,000), southeastern New York. It is located on the HUDSON RIVER north of NEW YORK CITY. Once the site of an American Indian village, it was part of a purchase made by the Dutch West India Co. from the Indians in 1639. In 1646 it was included in a grant of land made to "Jonkheer" Adriaen van der Donck. The southern portion of old Yonkers was annexed to what later became the BRONX in 1874. Industry is well diversified and includes printing and publishing, and the manufacture of elevators, chemicals, electronic components, and clothing.

Yonne River \'yȯn\ River, northern central France. It flows north out of Nièvre department into the SEINE RIVER at Montereau-faut-Yonne. It is 182 mi (293 km) long and is navigable for 70 mi (113 km) downstream from Auxerre.

Yorck von Wartenburg \'yȯrk-fȯn-'vär-tən-ˌbu̇rk\, **Johann (David Ludwig), Graf (Count)** (1759–1830) Prussian army commander. After serving with the Prussian army (1772–79) and Dutch army (1779–87), he rejoined the Prussian army and fought in Poland (1794) and later in the war against France (1806). Promoted to major general, he helped reorganize the army, developing the tactics of the infantry scout and the line of skirmishes. In 1812 he led the Prussian contingent of NAPOLEON's invading army into Russia. During the French retreat, he concluded an accord with Russia that opened the way for Prussia to join the Allied powers against Napoleon. He was made a count in 1814 and a field marshal in 1821.

Yoritomo See MINAMOTO YORITOMO

York City (pop., 1991: 141,000), southeastern Ontario. It forms part of the municipality of Metropolitan Toronto, along with the cities of TORONTO, ETOBICOKE, SCARBOROUGH, and NORTH YORK and the borough of EAST YORK. Occupying an area of 9 sq mi (23 sq km), York was established in 1967, through the amalgamation of the former township of York and the town of Weston. The original York township was formed in 1793.

York *ancient* **Eboracum** City (pop., 1994 est.: 104,000), NORTH YORKSHIRE, England. Located at the confluence of the OUSE and Foss rivers, it is the cathedral city of the archbishop of York and was historically the ecclesiastical capital of northern England. It was also the seat of the former county of YORKSHIRE. It was a Celtic, then Roman, settlement. CONSTANTINE I was proclaimed Roman emperor there in 306 AD. Later, it was ruled by Danes, then Normans. During the Middle Ages it was a prosperous wool-trading town and the site of the performance of the YORK PLAYS. It has a manufacturing economy and a tourist industry fostered by its medieval sites.

York, Alvin C(ullum) (1887–1964) U.S. World War I hero. Born in Pall Mall, Tenn., he worked as a blacksmith, and was drafted into the U.S. Army in 1917 after being denied conscientious-objector status. In the Meuse-Argonne offensive (October 1918), his patrol of 17 men was ordered to attack a German machine-gun nest. Pinned down behind enemy lines, he advanced alone to attack the enemy gunners, killing 25 and forcing the others to surrender. As he marched them back to U.S. lines, he captured more German soldiers for a total of 132 prisoners. He received the Congressional Medal of Honor, and his autobiography (1928) was the basis of the movie *Sergeant York* (1941).

York, Cape Northern point of Cape York Peninsula, QUEENSLAND, Australia. Australia's most northern point, it is about 15 mi (25 km) long and 12 mi (19 km) wide, and juts into TORRES STRAIT. It was named in 1770 by Capt. JAMES COOK for the duke of York, brother of King GEORGE III.

York, House of Younger branch of the PLANTAGENET dynasty, descended from EDWARD III's fifth son, Edmund of Langley (1341–1402), 1st duke of York. In the 15th century the Yorkists took the throne from the House of LANCASTER; the Yorkist kings were EDWARD IV, Edward V, and RICHARD III. The Wars of the ROSES between the two houses continued until Richard's death at the Battle of BOSWORTH FIELD. The marriage of HENRY VII, the first Tudor king, to the daughter of Edward IV, merged the House of York with the House of Tudor.

York plays Cycle of 48 plays, dating from the 14th century, of unknown authorship, which were performed in the Middle Ages by craft guilds in York, England, on the summer feast day of Corpus Christi. The cycle covers the story of the Fall of Man and his redemption, from the creation of the angels to the Final Judgment. The plays were given in chronological order, on pageant wagons proceeding from one selected place to another. See also MYSTERY PLAY.

York University Privately endowed university in North York, Ontario, founded in 1959. It has faculties of administrative studies, arts, education, environmental studies, fine arts, and graduate studies as well as schools of law and of pure and applied science. Among its research units are centers for the study of refugees, atmospheric chemistry, law and public policy, and computers in education. Total enrollment is about 40,000.

Yorke Peninsula Promontory, southeastern SOUTH AUSTRALIA, Australia. It is located between Spencer Gulf to the west and Gulf ST. VINCENT and Investigator Strait to the east and south. It extends southward for 160 mi (260 km) and is 20–35 miles (32–56 km) wide. Sighted by the English in 1802, it was named after Charles P. Yorke, first lord of the admiralty.

Yorkshire \'yȯrk-ˌshir\ Former county, northern England. Historically, it was divided into three administrative counties—North Riding, East Riding, and West Riding—and the city of YORK. For most purposes the ridings were separate administrative units for a thousand years; Yorkshire and the ridings, comprising the country's largest county, ceased to exist with the administrative reorganization of 1974. It was an agricultural, fishing and manufacturing center. Its main cities and towns include LEEDS, SHEFFIELD, HULL, BRADFORD, and WAKEFIELD.

Yorkshire terrier *or* **Yorkie** Breed of TOY DOG developed in the mid-19th century in Yorkshire and Lancashire, England. Its lineage appears to include TERRIERS, such as the Skye and DANDIE DINMONT. Its outstanding feature is its straight, silky coat, parted on the back from nose to tail and long enough to sweep the ground. Its coat color is dark blue-gray, with tan on the head and chest. It may grow to 9 in. (23 cm) tall and weigh up to 7 lbs (3 kg).

Yorktown, Siege of (1781) American-French campaign against the British that virtually ended the AMERICAN REVOLUTION. About 7,500 British troops under CHARLES CORNWALLIS occupied defensive positions at the coastal port of Yorktown, Va., on August 1, 1781. They were opposed by a smaller American force under the Marquis de LAFAYETTE, assisted by ANTHONY WAYNE and FREDERICK STEUBEN. From New York, GEORGE WASHINGTON ordered Lafayette to prevent Cornwallis's escape by land. French troops under COMTE DE ROCHAMBEAU joined Washington's forces and marched south. Linking up with a French fleet at the head of Chesapeake Bay, they joined Lafayette's forces on September 28, and the 14,000-man force besieged the British position. Cornwallis waited for British reinforcements under HENRY CLINTON to arrive by sea; but now outnumbered, outgunned, and running low on food, he surrendered his 8,000 men and 240 guns on October 19.

Yoruba \'yȯr-ə-bə\ One of Nigeria's two largest ethnic groups, numbering 22 million. The many dialects comprising the Yoruba language belong to the BENUE-CONGO branch of the NIGER-CONGO family. The Yoruba states, including the OYO EMPIRE, were built in the 11th–16th century. Yorubaland remains divided into politically autonomous kingdoms, each centered on a capital city or town and headed by a hereditary king (*oba),* traditionally considered sacred. Most Yoruba men are farmers, growing yams, corn, and millet as staples; cocoa is a cash crop. Yoruba women control much of the complex market system. Craftsmen work in blacksmithing, weaving, leatherworking, glassmaking, bronze casting, and ivory- and woodcarving. Though some Yoruba are now Christians or Muslims, belief in their traditional religion continues (see SANTERÍA). The Yoruba language has an extensive literature of poetry, short stories, myths, and proverbs.

Yorubaland \'yȯr-ü-bə-ˌland\ Name for an area of western Africa, in present-day Nigeria. It once comprised several kingdoms headed by individual YORUBA kings. It flourished for centuries before disputes between minor rulers, difficulties in maintaining trade routes, and invasions led to its decline, beginning in the late 18th century. Cyo, Ife, and OSHOGBO are cities with historical Yoruba background.

Yosemite Falls \yō-'se-mə-tē\ Two waterfalls, YOSEMITE NATIONAL PARK, central California. Formed by creeks tumbling into the Yosemite River valley, the upper falls drop 1,430 ft (436 m) and the lower, 320 ft (98 m). With the cascades between, the total drop from the crest of the upper to the base of the lower is 2,425 ft (739 m), one of the world's longest cataracts.

Yosemite National Park National preserve, central California. Made a national park in 1890, it encompasses 761,320 acres (308,106 hectares) in the SIERRA NEVADA range. Its many features include giant REDWOOD groves with trees thousands of years old, YOSEMITE FALLS, Bridalveil Fall (620 ft, or 189 m), and huge domes and peaks; the greatest of these is El Capitan, a granite buttress that is 3,604 ft (1,098 m) high.

Yoshida Shigeru \'yō-shē-dä-shē-'ge-rü\ (1878–1967) Japanese prime minister after World War II. He served as ambassador to Britain in the 1930s. He was arrested in 1945 for his attempts to force an early Japanese surrender and was not freed until the OCCUPATION began in September. He first became prime minister in 1946, and between 1946 and 1954 he formed five separate cabinets. He guided Japan back to economic prosperity and set a course for postwar cooperation with the U.S. and Europe. In 1951 he negotiated the peace treaty that ended World War II; he also negotiated a security pact between Japan and the U.S. He retired from politics in 1955. See also SHOWA PERIOD.

Yoshida Shoin \'yō-shē-dä-'shō-ēn\ (1830–1859) Japanese teacher of military tactics in the domain of CHOSHU. He studied "Dutch learning" (European studies) in Nagasaki and Edo and was deeply influenced by the pro-emperor thinkers in the domain of MITO. His radical pro-emperor stance influenced young SAMURAI in Choshu to overthrow the TOKUGAWA SHOGUNATE. He was executed for an assassination plot against the SHOGUN's representative in Kyoto. See also KIDO TAKAYOSHI.

Yoshitsune See MINAMOTO YOSHITSUNE

Youghiogheny River \ˌyä-kə-'gā-nē\ River, northeastern West Virginia, northwestern Maryland, and southwestern Pennsylvania. It rises in West Virginia, near the western edge of Maryland, and flows north through northwestern Maryland into Pennsylvania to enter the MONONGAHELA RIVER at McKeesport, Pa., after a course of 135 mi (217 km). It is the only river in western Maryland that does not flow south into the POTOMAC RIVER.

Youmans \'yü-mənz\, **Vincent (Millie)** (1898–1946) U.S. songwriter. Born in New York City, he started writing songs while in the navy during World War I, and later worked as a song plugger on TIN PAN ALLEY. He collaborated with such lyricists as IRA GERSHWIN and O. HAMMERSTEIN on the Broadway musicals *Wildflower* (1923), *No, No, Nanette* (1925), *Hit the Deck* (1927), *Great Day* (1928), and the first FRED ASTAIRE-G. ROGERS vehicle, *Flying Down to Rio* (1933). His standards included "Tea for Two," "More Than You Know," "Time on My Hands," and "Carioca."

Young, Andrew *in full* **Andrew Jackson Young, Jr.** (born 1932) U.S. politician. Born in New Orleans, he earned a divinity degree in 1955 and became a pastor at Southern black churches. Active in the civil rights movement, he worked with MARTIN LUTHER KING and RALPH ABERNATHY in the SOUTHERN CHRISTIAN LEADERSHIP CONFERENCE (1961–70). He served in the U.S. House of Representatives 1972–77. An early supporter of JIMMY CARTER, he was appointed U.S. ambassador to the U.N. (1977–79), the first black to hold the post. He served as mayor of Atlanta 1982–89.

Young, Brigham (1801–1877) U.S. religious leader, second president of the MORMON church. Born in Whitingham, Vt., he settled in Mendon, N.Y., in 1829 and was baptized into JOSEPH SMITH's Church of Jesus Christ of Latter-Day Saints in 1832. In 1834 he joined the Mormons in Missouri, and when they were driven out in 1838, he organized their move to Nauvoo, Ill. He established a Mormon mission in England in 1839. After Smith's murder in 1844, Young took over the church. He led the persecuted Mormons from Illinois to Utah (1846–48), choosing the site of Salt Lake City for the new Mormon headquarters. Elected president of the Mormons in 1847, he became governor of the provisional state of Deseret in 1849 and of the territory of Utah in 1850. His dictatorial autonomy and legalization of polygamy led Pres. JAMES BUCHANAN to replace him as governor in 1857 and send the army to assert federal supremacy in the so-called Utah War, but Young remained head of the Mormon church until his death. He took more than 20 wives and fathered 47 children.

Brigham Young.
BY COURTESY OF UTAH STATE HISTORICAL SOCIETY

Young, Coleman (1918–1997) U.S. politician. Born in Tuscaloosa, Ala., he moved with his family to Detroit in 1923. At Ford Motor Co. he became involved in union activities and civil-rights activism. In World War II, he served with the Tuskegee Airmen. He later cofounded the National Negro Labor Council, which he disbanded in the 1950s to avoid turning over its membership list during an investigation by the House Un-American Activities Committee. He was elected to the Michigan senate in 1964, and in 1968 he became the Democratic National Committee's first black member. As mayor of Detroit from 1973, he focused on revitalizing the crime-ridden city by attracting new businesses and reinforcing the police department. He retired in 1993 after an unprecedented five terms.

Young, Cy *orig.* **Denton True** (1867–1955) U.S. baseball pitcher. Born in Gilmore, Ohio, he was a powerful 6-ft 2-in. (1-m 88-cm) right-handed thrower. He began his major-league career in 1890 with the Cleveland Indians (National League); after his Cleveland years (1890–98), he pitched for the St. Louis Cardinals (1899–1900), the Boston Red Sox (1901–8), the Cleveland Indians again (American League, 1909–11), and the Boston Braves (1911). In each of 16 seasons he won more than 20 games; in five he won more than 30. Though many early records are in dispute, he won more major-league games (509 or 511) than any other pitcher in history. Among his other records are games started (816 or 818), completed starts (750 or 751), and innings pitched (7,356 or 7,377). In 1904 he pitched the first perfect game (no player reaching first base). The annual Cy Young award, instituted in 1956, originally honored the best major-league pitcher; since 1967 it has been given to the best pitcher in each league.

Young, Lester (Willis) (1909–1959) U.S. tenor saxophonist, one of the most innovative and influential musicians of the SWING era. Born in Mississippi, Young joined COUNT BASIE in 1936 and was recognized as a major new stylist on the instrument dominated by the influence of COLEMAN HAWKINS. His small-group recordings from the late 1930s with Basie and BILLIE HOLIDAY are classics. Nicknamed Prez by Holiday (short for "President of the saxophone"), Young's subtle harmonies and unconventional rhythmic independence influenced both BEBOP and cool-jazz musicians; his gentle tone and ethereal lyricism inspired an entire school of jazz saxophone playing.

Lester Young, c. 1955.
REPRINTED WITH PERMISSION OF DOWN BEAT MAGAZINE

Young, Neil (born 1945) Canadian rock singer and songwriter. Born in Toronto, he began his career as a folksinger in Winnipeg and later moved to Los Angeles, where he formed the rock group Buffalo Springfield with Stephen Stills. In 1968 he released a solo album; in 1969 he joined Stills, David Crosby, and Graham Nash, to form Crosby, Stills, Nash and Young. With a new band, Crazy Horse, he had great success with such albums as *Harvest* (1972) and *Comes a Time* (1978). In the 1980s he experimented with rockabilly and electronic music.

Young, Thomas (1773–1829) English physicist. Trained as a physician, he practiced medicine at St. George's Hospital from 1811 until his death, but spent much of his time on scientific research. He was the first to describe and measure astigmatism (1800–1), and the first to explain color sensation in terms of retinal structures corresponding to red, green, and violet (1801). He established the principle of interference of light, thus resurrecting the century-old wave theory of light (1801). He explained capillarity independently of Pierre-Simon Laplace. Investigating elasticity, he proposed Young's modulus, a numerical constant that describes the elastic properties of a solid undergoing tension or compression. His other work included measuring the size of molecules and surface tension in liquids. With J.-F. Champollion, he helped decipher the inscriptions on the Rosetta Stone (1813–14).

Young Algerians Pre–World War I Algerian nationalists. A loosely organized group of French-educated workers in the modernized French sector, the Young Algerians were "assimilationists" willing to consider permanent union with France on the condition that native Algerians be given the full rights of French citizens. In the years following the war, such gradualist reformers found themselves in opposition to radical nationalists demanding complete independence. See also Ferhat Abbas, Association of Algerian Reformist Ulama, National Liberation Front.

Young America movement U.S. political concept popular in the 1840s. Inspired by European youth movements of the 1830s (see Young Italy), the U.S. group was formed as a political organization in 1845 by Edwin de Leon and George H. Evans. It advocated free trade, expansion southward into the territories, and support for republican movements abroad. It became a faction in the Democratic Party in the 1850s. Sen. Stephen A. Douglas promoted its nationalistic program in an unsuccessful effort to compromise sectional differences.

Young Italy *Italian* **Giovine Italia** Movement founded by Giuseppe Mazzini in 1831 to work for a united, republican Italian nation. In contrast to earlier independence movements of the Carbonari, Young Italy was to be based on support from the Italian people, who would be educated in their political role. To propagate his ideas, Mazzini published the journal *Giovine Italia* (1832–34). The movement spread in northern Italy and by 1833 included over 50,000 members. It staged revolts in the 1830s and '40s, but failed to win popular support for insurrection. In 1848 Mazzini replaced Young Italy with the Italian National Committee. After 1850 his influence declined as leadership of the movement for Italian unification passed to Camillo Cavour. See also Risorgimento.

Young Men's Christian Association See YMCA

Young Plan (1929) Renegotiation of Germany's World War I reparations payments by a committee chaired by the U.S. lawyer Owen D. Young (1874–1962) in Paris. The Young Plan, a revision of the Dawes Plan, reduced the amount due from Germany to $26.3 billion, to be paid over 59 years, and ended foreign controls on German economic life. It went into effect in 1930, but the world depression affected Germany's ability to pay. When Adolf Hitler came to power in 1933, he repudiated the obligations of the Treaty of Versailles, including reparations.

Young Tunisians Political party formed in 1907 by French-educated Tunisian intellectuals to oppose French rule. They demanded complete control of the country's government and administration and full citizenship rights for both Tunisians and Frenchmen. They protested the Italian invasion of Libya (1911) and rioted against French actions at home. The French exiled party leaders, driving the party underground until 1920, when it reemerged and reorganized itself as the Destour Party, which remained active until 1957. See also Habib Bourguiba.

Young Turks *Turkish* **Jöntürkler** Coalition of young dissidents who ended the Ottoman sultanate. Consisting of college students and dissident soldiers, the group succeeded in 1908 in forcing Abdülhamid II to reinstitute the 1876 constitution and recall the legislature. They deposed him the following year, reorganized the government, and began modernizing and industrializing Turkish society. They joined the Central Powers during World War I. Facing defeat in 1918, they resigned a month before the war ended. See also Mustafa Kemal Ataturk, Enver Pasa, Midhat Pasa, Ottoman empire.

Younghusband, Francis Edward *later* **Sir Francis** (1863–1942) British army officer and explorer. He forced the conclusion of the Anglo-Tibetan Treaty (1904) that gained Britain long-sought trade concessions. His two initial attempts to negotiate trade and frontier issues with Tibet failed despite British military action; he then marched to Lhasa with British troops and forced the conclusion of a trade treaty, though the Dalai Lama, Tibet's leader, had fled. See also amban.

Youngstown City (pop., 1996 est.: 87,000), northeastern Ohio. Located on the Mahoning River, near the Pennsylvania border, it was founded in 1797. Ohio's first furnace to produce iron was built nearby in 1805. In 1855 the Sault Ste. Marie locks were opened, making the rich iron ores from the upper Great Lakes region available; railroad lines were later built to transport ores and coal to Youngstown. By 1920 it had become one of the largest steel-producing centers in the U.S. Its products now include aluminum, rubber, and paper products. Youngstown State University was established in 1908.

Yourcenar \yür-sə-'när\, **Marguerite** *orig.* **Marguerite de Crayencour** (1903–1987) Belgian-French-U.S. novelist, essayist, and short-story writer. Independently wealthy after her father's death, she led a nomadic life until World War II, when she settled in the U.S. with the American woman who would be her lifelong companion and translator. Her works are noted for their rigorously classical style, their erudition, and their psychological subtlety. Her masterpiece is *Memoirs of Hadrian* (1951), a historical novel of the 2nd-century Roman empire. Other works include the novels *Coup de grâce* (1939) and *The Abyss* (1968), *Oriental Tales* (1938), and the prose poem *Fires* (1936). In 1980 she became the first woman in history to be elected to the Académie Française.

Marguerite Yourcenar, 1971.

youth hostel Supervised shelter providing inexpensive overnight lodging, particularly for young people. Often located in scenic or historic areas, hostels range from simple farmhouses to hotels able to house several hundred people. Guests often cook their own meals, make their own beds, and do other chores; in return they receive lodging at much less than the usual commercial rate. Hostels place limits on the length of stay, and formerly set a maximum age limit for guests. The hosteling movement was founded by Richard Schirrmann, a German schoolteacher concerned about the health of young people breathing polluted air in industrial cities. Common in Germany in the early 1900s, youth hostels spread through Europe and other parts of the world after World War I. An international organization was formed in 1932; today known as Hostelling International, its membership includes national federations in more than 70 countries, comprising some 5,000 hostels. Upper age limits are no longer imposed.

Ypres \'ēprᵊ\, **Battles of** Three costly battles in World War I in western Flanders. In the first battle (October 12–November 11, 1914), the Germans were stopped on their march to the sea, but the Allied forces were then surrounded on three sides. The second battle (April 22–May 25, 1915) marked the Germans' first use of poison gas as a weapon. In the third and longest battle (July 31–November 6, 1917), also called the Battle of Passchendaele, the British were initially successful in breaking through the left wing of the German lines. The seasonal rains soon turned the Flanders countryside into an impassable swamp, but Gen. Douglas Haig persisted in his offensive. On November 6 his troops, including the Canadian Corps, occupied the ruins of Passchendaele, barely five miles from the start of the offensive. Over 325,000 British soldiers were lost in the battles.

Ypsilanti family \ˌip-sə-'lan-tē\ Greek family prominent in the 19th century. Early members were Greek Phanariots (residents of the Greek quarter of Constantinople) distinguished in the Ottoman imperial service. Constantine Ypsilanti (1760–1816) was governor of Moldavia (1799–1801) and Walachia (1802–6) when he encouraged Serbians to rebel against Turkey. He was forced to flee to Russia, where his son Alexander Ypsilanti (1792–1828) became an officer in the Russian imperial guard. As the leader of the secret Greek organization Philikí Etaireía (1820), he promoted the cause of Greek freedom and led an unsuccessful attack on the Turks at Dragasani (1821). His brother, Demetrios Ypsilanti (1793–1832), carried on the cause in the War of GREEK INDEPENDENCE and served as commander of the Greek forces 1828–30.

Yrigoyen, Hipólito See Hipólito IRIGOYEN

Yser River \ē-'zer\ River, northern France and Belgium. Rising in northern France, it flows through western Belgium and enters the North Sea near Nieuwpoort after a course of 48 mi (77 km). Its estuary was probably as far inland as Loo into the 10th century, but gradual land reclamation has since reduced it to a narrow tidal creek. During World War I (1914) the German advance toward CALAIS and the ENGLISH CHANNEL coast was halted at the river when Nieuwpoort sluices were flooded; this checked the German advance and allowed the Allies to set up an impregnable position.

Yuan Chiang See RED RIVER

Yuan dynasty *or* **Yüan dynasty** \yü-'än\ *or* **Mongol dynasty** (1206–1368) Dynasty established in China by MONGOL nomads. GENGHIS KHAN occupied northern China in 1215, but not until 1279 did KUBLAI KHAN take control of southern China. The Mongols established their capital at Beijing (then called Dadu). They rebuilt the GRAND CANAL and put the roads and postal stations in good order. Paper money, which had had limited circulation under the SONG, came to be used throughout the empire. Advances were made in astronomy, medicine, and mathematics, and trade was carried out throughout the Mongol empire from the plains of eastern Europe across the steppes to Mongolia and China. Many foreigners came to China (notably MARCO POLO) and many Chinese traveled to Iran, Russia, and even western Europe. The Chinese resented the Mongol conquerors, whose governmental system discriminated against them (see KUBLAI KHAN). Chinese artists demonstrated passive resistance by withdrawing and turning to personal expression. LITERATI painting became very popular; the novel developed, and new dramatic forms also appeared. Disputes over succession weakened the central government from 1300 on, and rebellions were frequent, many connected with secret societies such as the RED TURBANS. The dynasty was overthrown in 1368 by the future HONGWU EMPEROR. See also MING DYNASTY.

Yuan River \'ywen, 'ywän\ River, southeastern central China. It rises in GUIZHOU, then flows northeast in HUNAN province to DONGTING HU. It is 537 mi (864 km) long and is navigable for most of its course.

Yuan Shikai *or* **Yüan Shih-kai** \yü-'än-'shir-'kī\ (1859–1916) Chinese army leader and first president of the Republic of China (1912–16). He began his military career serving in Korea in the 1880s. In 1885 he was made Chinese commissioner at Seoul; his promotion of China's interests contributed to the outbreak of the SINO-JAPANESE WAR. The war destroyed China's navy and army, and the task of training a new army fell to Yuan. When his division was the only one to survive the BOXER REBELLION, his political stature increased. He played a decisive part in China's modernization and defense programs and enjoyed the support of CIXI. On her death he was dismissed, only to be called back following the overthrow of the QING DYNASTY in 1911–12, when he became the first president of the new republic. Impatient with the new National Assembly, he ordered the assassination of Song Jiaoren, leader of the Nationalist Party (see GUOMINDANG) in 1913. He quelled a subsequent revolt, but his efforts to found his own dynasty (1915–16) failed. See also SUN YAT-SEN.

yuca See CASSAVA

Yucatán \yü-kä-'tän\ State (pop., 2000: 1,658,200), northern YUCATÁN PENINSULA, southeastern Mexico. Covering an area of 16,749 sq mi (43,380 sq km), its capital is MÉRIDA. Yucatán occupied the entire peninsula when it became a state in 1824, but the secession of CAMPECHE (1858), loss of QUINTANA ROO (1902), and later boundary changes reduced it to its present size. Long occupied by rural Maya Indians who speak little Spanish, it is the site of ancient MAYA ruins.

Yucatán Peninsula Peninsula, northeastern CENTRAL AMERICA. It lies between the Gulf of MEXICO and the CARIBBEAN SEA; its 76,300-sq-mi (197,600-sq-km) territory includes the Mexican states of CAMPECHE, QUINTANA ROO, and YUCATÁN and, in the south, large parts of Belize and Guatemala. It is about 200 mi (320 km) wide and has a coastline of about 700 mi (1,100 km). It came under TOLTEC influence c. 1000, and later was the seat of MAYA civilization. In 1525 HERNAN CORTES traversed its inland part. Spanish rule was subsequently established, but since then many independent Maya have kept to its inland rural areas and resisted central governmental authority. Its coastal area, with beaches and resorts, and its ancient archaeological sites, including CHICHÉN ITZÁ, UAXACTUN, and UXMAL, are major tourist destinations, as is CANCÚN.

yucca \'yə-,kə\ Any of about 40 species of SUCCULENT plants (genus *Yucca*) of the LILY FAMILY, native to southern North America. Most species lack a stem and have a rosette of stiff, sword-shaped leaves at the base and clusters of waxy white flowers. The Joshua tree *(Y. brevifolia)* has a stem more than 33 ft (10 m) high. Commonly cultivated as ornamentals for their unusual appearance and attractive flower clusters are the aptly named Spanish bayonet *(Y. aloifolia),* Spanish dagger *(Y. gloriosa),* and Adam's needle, or bear grass *(Y. filamentosa).* Yucca moths (genus *Tegeticula*) inhabit yucca bushes, each moth species adapted to a particular yucca species. The yucca can be fertilized by no other insect, and the moth can use no other plant to raise its larvae.

Yucca.
BY COURTESY OF THE NEW MEXICO DEPARTMENT OF DEVELOPMENT

Yudenich \yü-'dye-nyich\, **Nikolay (Nikolayevich)** (1862–1933) Russian commander of anti-Bolshevik forces in the RUSSIAN CIVIL WAR. A career army officer, he commanded in the RUSSO-JAPANESE WAR and was promoted to general in 1905. In World War I he led Russian troops in the Caucasus (1914–15, 1917). After retiring to Estonia, he organized anti-Bolshevik forces there and launched an unsuccessful offensive toward Petrograd (St. Petersburg). He renewed his offensive in coordination with other White forces but was stopped by the Red Army and forced to retreat to Estonia, where he disbanded his army (1920). He fled to France, where he died in exile.

Yue Fei *or* **Yüeh Fei** \yᴂ-'e-'fā\ (1103–1141) One of China's greatest generals and national heroes. When the Juchen overran northern China and captured the SONG-DYNASTY capital at Kaifeng, Yue Fei accompanied the future Gaozong emperor into the south, where the Southern Song was established. Yue Fei prevented the advance of the Juchen in the south and was able to recover and secure some of the occupied territory in central China. His attempt to push north and recover all the lost territory was opposed by the minister QIN GUI, who had Yue executed. Yue has been extolled for his resistance to foreign domination.

yuga \'yü-gə\ Unit of the cosmic cycle in Hindu cosmology. Each yuga is progressively shorter than the preceding one, corresponding to a decline in the moral and physical state of humanity. Four such yugas make up a mahayuga; 2,000 mahayugas make up the basic cosmic cycle, the kalpa. The first yuga was an age of perfection that lasted 1,728,000 years. The fourth and most degenerate yuga began in 3102 BC and will last 432,000 years. At the close of this yuga, the world will be destroyed, to be recreated after a period of quiescence as the cycle resumes.

Yugoslavia *officially* **Federal Republic of Yugoslavia** Federated country, western central BALKAN PENINSULA, consisting of the republics of SERBIA and MONTENEGRO. Area: 39,449 sq mi (102,173 sq km). Population (2002 est.): 10,663,806. Capital: BELGRADE. The population comprises Serbian, Albanian, Montenegrin, Hungarian, and other ethnic groups. Languages: Serbo-Croatian (official), Albanian. Religions: Serbian Orthodoxy, Islam, Catholicism, Protestantism. Currency: Yugoslav new dinar. The southern two-thirds of Yugoslavia is mountainous, with the Dinaric Alps in the west and the BALKAN MTNS. in the east. Rivers include the DANUBE, Ibar, MORAVA, TIMIS, and TISZA. The country has oil, gas, coal, copper, lead, zinc, and gold deposits. Its industries include machine building, metallurgy, mining, electronics, and petroleum products, while its agricultural products include corn, wheat, potatoes, and fruit. It is a federal republic with two legislative houses; its chief of state is the federal president, and the head of government is the prime minister. The Kingdom of the Serbs, Croats, and Slovenes was created after the collapse of AUSTRIA-HUNGARY at the end of World War I. The country signed

treaties with Czechoslovakia and Romania 1920–21, marking the beginning of the LITTLE ENTENTE. In 1929 an absolute monarchy was established, the country's name was changed to Yugoslavia, and it was divided without regard to ethnic boundaries. Axis powers invaded Yugoslavia in 1941, and German, Italian, Hungarian, and Bulgarian troops occupied it for the rest of World War II. In 1945 the Socialist Federal Republic of Yugoslavia was established; it included the republics of BOSNIA AND HERZEGOVINA, CROATIA, MACEDONIA, Montenegro, Serbia, and SLOVENIA. Its independent form of Communism under TITO's leadership, provoked the U.S.S.R. and led to its expulsion from the COMINFORM in 1948. Internal ethnic tensions flared up in the 1980s, causing the country to collapse. In 1991–92 independence was declared by Croatia, Slovenia, Macedonia, and Bosnia and Herzegovina; the new Federal Republic of Yugoslavia (containing roughly 45% of the population and 40% of the area of its predecessor) was proclaimed by Serbia and Montenegro. Still fueled by long-standing ethnic tensions, hostilities continued into the 1990s (see BOSNIAN CONFLICT). Despite the approval of the Dayton peace accord (1995), sporadic fighting continued and was followed in 1998–99 by Serbian repression and expulsion of ethnic populations in Kosovo (see KOSOVO CONFLICT). In 2002 the two constituent republics agreed to create a new constitution under the name Serbia and Montenegro.

Yukaghir See SIBERIAN PEOPLES

Yukon *or* **Yukon Territory** Territory (pop., 2001 est.: 30,000), northwestern Canada. Bounded by Alaska, its capital is WHITEHORSE. Drained by the YUKON RIVER system, it has some of the highest mountains in North America, notably the ST. ELIAS MTNS. and Mount LOGAN, Canada's highest peak. It was originally settled by American Indians and the Inuit (ESKIMO). The first European visitor (1825) was British explorer John Franklin, who was seeking the NORTHWEST PASSAGE. Sporadic settlement occurred thereafter. The discovery of gold in the 1870s later resulted in the KLONDIKE GOLD RUSH. In 1898 it was separated from the NORTHWEST TERRITORIES and given territorial status. The economic boost from the gold rush soon abated, and the exploitation of other minerals expanded and continued throughout the 20th century. Its economic mainstays, though, are government services and tourism.

Yukon River River, northwestern North America. Formed by the confluence of the LEWES and Pelly rivers in southwestern Yukon Territory, it is 1,980 mi (3,190 km) long. It flows northwest across the Yukon border into Alaska, then southwest across central Alaska to the BERING SEA. It is the third-longest river in North America; its entire course of 1,265 mi (2,035 km) in Alaska is navigable. It attracted attention following the rich gold strikes in 1896 on one of its Canadian tributaries, the Klondike River (see KLONDIKE GOLD RUSH).

Yuman \'yü-mən\ Any of various Native American groups who traditionally lived in the lower Colorado River valley and adjacent areas in Arizona, California, and Mexico and who spoke related languages of HOKAN stock. The river Yuman (including the MOJAVE, Yuma, and Maricopa) lived along the lower Colorado and middle Gila rivers; the upland Yuman (including the Hualapai and Havasupai) inhabited western Arizona south of the Grand Canyon. The river Yuman were primarily farmers; the upland Yuman also practiced hunting and gathering. Both lacked settled villages. Yuman religion is characterized by belief in a supreme creator, faith in dreams, and ritual use of song narratives. Today the Yuman number over 4,000.

Yung-lo emperor See YONGLE EMPEROR

Yung-ning See NANNING

Yungang caves *or* **Yün-kang caves** \'yuen-'gäŋ\ Series of magnificent Chinese Buddhist cave temples, created in the 5th century AD during the SIX DYNASTIES period. There are about 20 major cave temples and many smaller niches and caves, stretching for over half a mile. They are among the earliest remaining examples of the first flowering of Buddhist art in China. The predominant sculptural style is a synthesis of various foreign influences, including Persian, Byzantine, and Greek, with elements ultimately derived from the Buddhist art of India.

Yunnan *or* **Yün-nan** \yūē-'nän\ Province (pop., 2000 est.: 42,880,000), southern China. The capital is KUNMING. Its population is one of China's most ethnically mixed, comprising more than 20 nationalities. The terrain is very mountainous, especially in the north and west. It is crossed by three major river systems—the YANGTZE (known there as the Jinsha), the MEKONG, and the SALWEEN—and is the source of two others—the HONGSHUI and the YUAN. Because of its isolation, the region was independent during the historical development of China. The Mongols overran it the 13th century. In 1855–73 it was the scene of the great Panthay (Muslim) revolt. Part of the province was seized by the Japanese in World War II. It is now noted for its agricultural production, especially of rice, as well as for having an extensive mining industry.

Yunnan See KUNMING

YWCA See YMCA

Z particle Electrically neutral carrier of the WEAK FORCE and the neutral partner of the W PARTICLE. It is nearly 100 times more massive than the PROTON and has a lifetime of only about 10^{-25} second. Study of the decay of Z particles shows a natural variation in mass that is related to the particle's lifetime through the UNCERTAINTY PRINCIPLE. Measurements show that when Z particles decay to neutrino-antineutrino pairs (see PAIR PRODUCTION), they produce only three types of lightweight neutrino, indicating that there are only three sets each of LEPTONS and QUARKS.

Zab River \'zäb\ Two tributaries of the TIGRIS RIVER that double the river's flow during the floods of March and April. The Great Zab, or Zab al-Kabir, rises in the mountains of Kurdistan and flows about 260 mi (420 km) south and southwest through southeastern Turkey and northern Iraq, joining the Tigris below Mosul, Iraq. The Little Zab, or Zab al-Asfal, flows about 230 mi (370 m) through northwestern Iran and northern Iraq before entering the Tigris about 50 mi (80 km) below the Great Zab.

Zacatecas \ˌsä-kä-'tā-käs\ State (pop., 1995 est.: 1,336,000), northern central Mexico. It covers an area of 28,973 sq mi (75,040 sq km); its capital is ZACATECAS city. Located within a central plateau, it is traversed by several mountain ranges, whose average elevation is 7,700 ft (2,350 m). Its mineral wealth was discovered soon after the Spanish conquest, and some of its mines, still worked, date from the mid-16th century. Agriculture, livestock-raising, and meat processing are also important to the economy.

Zacatecas City (pop., 1990: 100,000), capital of ZACATECAS state, Mexico. It lies in a deep, narrow ravine, 8,189 ft (2,496 m) above sea level. Founded in 1548, two years after silver was discovered in the area, it was given city status in 1585. Until the 19th century, the mines around Zacatecas yielded one-fifth of the world's silver. Still a mining center, it is also a commercial and manufacturing center. Noted for its cathedral, it is located near the extensive Indian ruins of Chicomóztoc, southwest of the city.

zaddik *or* **tzaddiq** \'tsä-dik, tsä-'dēk\ One who embodies the religious ideals of Judaism. The term is used repeatedly in the OLD TESTAMENT and in the TALMUD, which asserts that the continued existence of the world is due to the merits of 36 righteous men. In HASIDISM, it came to refer to a religious leader who was viewed as a mediator between humankind and God. Initially the zaddikim traveled widely and engaged in social activities to strengthen the community's spiritual life. Toward the end of the 18th century, they ceased this practice and became available at home for those seeking advice.

Zadkine \zȧd-'kēn\, **Ossip** (1890–1967) Russian-French sculptor. Educated in England, he moved to Paris in 1909 and studied at the École des Beaux-Arts. Influenced by both Cubism and classical Greek sculpture, he developed a unique figurative style featuring concave and convex forms, lines, and parallel planes. During World War II he taught at New York's Art Students League. His large bronze *To a Destroyed City* (1951–53), an homage to Rotterdam, is regarded as a masterpiece. In 1950 he received the grand prize for sculpture at the Venice Biennale, and in the 1960s he received commissions for statues in Jerusalem, Amsterdam, and elsewhere.

Zadokite Fragments See DAMASCUS DOCUMENT

Zaghlul \zag-'lül\, **Sad** (1857–1927) Egyptian statesman. Initially cooperative with the occupying British, his attitude changed on his election to the Legislative Assembly in 1912. When Britain declared martial law and dissolved the Legislative Assembly during World War I, he led a delegation that demanded recognition as the people's representatives and called for abolition of the British protectorate. When their requests were turned down, widespread disorder broke out that was not quelled even when Zaghlul, who had been deported to Malta, was brought back and swept into power as prime minister in 1924 by the first elections under a new constitution. He resigned after the murder of a number of British officials and Egyptian "collaborators," but later served as president of the Chamber, where he was able to exercise some control over his more extreme followers.

Zagreb \'zä-ˌgreb\ City (pop., 1991: 868,000), capital of CROATIA. It was first mentioned in 1093, when a Roman Catholic bishopric was established there. In medieval times, the area also contained a civil and an ecclesiastical settlement. Rivals until the 19th century, they were joined when a spate of new building occurred and expanded onto the SAVA RIVER floodplain. At the time of the Croatian national revival in the 19th century, it was the center of both a pan-Yugoslav movement and a Croatian independence movement. During the civil war following Croatia's secession from Yugoslavia in 1991, it sustained heavy damage. It is Croatia's principal industrial center.

Zagreus \'zā-grē-əs, 'za-grē-əs\ In GREEK MYTHOLOGY, the son of ZEUS and his daughter PERSEPHONE. Zeus intended to make Zagreus his heir and bestow on him unlimited power, but a jealous HERA urged the TITANS to attack the child. They tore Zagreus to pieces and consumed all but his heart, which ATHENA managed to save and bring to Zeus, who swallowed it. Zeus then begot a son with SEMELE, and this child, made from the heart of Zagreus, was DIONYSUS.

Zaharias \zə-'har-ē-əs\, **Babe Didrikson** *or* **Babe Didrikson** *orig.* **Mildred Ella Didrikson** (1914–1956) U.S. athlete, sometimes called the greatest woman athlete of the 20th century. Born in Port Arthur, Texas, she became a remarkable performer in basketball and track and field, and later a leading golfer. In 1930–31 she was a member of the women's All-America basketball team. In national track-and-field competition in 1930–32, she won eight events and tied for a ninth. In the 1932 Olympics she won gold medals in the 80-m hurdles and javelin throw; she was deprived of the high-jump gold medal for using a then-unorthodox method. As a golfer from 1946, she won numerous championships, including the U.S. and British women's amateur tournaments (1946, 1947) and the U.S. Women's Open (1948, 1950, 1954); her last Open victory followed cancer surgery in 1953.

zaibatsu \zī-'bät-sü\ (Japanese: "financial clique") Large capitalist enterprises of pre-World War II Japan, similar to CARTELS or trusts but usually organized around a single family. One zaibatsu might operate companies in many areas of economic importance; all zaibatsu owned their own banks, which they used as a means for mobilizing capital. After the war the zaibatsu were dissolved: stock owned by the parent companies was put up for sale and individual companies were freed from the control of parent companies. After the signing of the peace treaty in 1951, many companies began associating into what became known as enterprise groups; these differed from zaibatsu primarily in the informal manner that characterized policy coordination and in the limited degree of financial interdependency between member companies. Modern-day *keiretsu* are similar.

zaim \zȧ-'ēm\ Political leader, either an officeholder or power broker. The term has been used especially in Lebanon, where it designated the power brokers of the various sectarian communities.

Zaire See Democratic Republic of the CONGO

Zaire River See CONGO RIVER

Zakharov \'zä-k̲ə-rəf\, **Rostislav (Vladimirovich)** (1907–1984) Russian ballet dancer, choreographer, teacher, and director. He studied at the Leningrad State (formerly Imperial) Ballet School and joined the Kiev Ballet in 1926. He later choreographed ballets for the Kirov Theater and various other companies, applying the STANISLAVSKY METHOD to ballet by emphasizing its dramatic aspects. He was director of the BOLSHOI BALLET school (1946–49) and was a founding member of the choreography faculty at the Theater Institute in Moscow from 1958.

Zama \'zā-mə\, **Battle of** (202 BC) Engagement in which the Romans under SCIPIO AFRICANUS THE ELDER decisively defeated the Carthaginians led by HANNIBAL, ending the Second PUNIC WAR. As the Romans marched on Carthage, Hannibal returned from Italy to defend the city. He was overwhelmed by a combined force of Romans and Numidians under MASINISSA. Carthage ceded Spain to Rome, gave up most of its ships, and began paying a 50-year indemnity to Rome.

Zambezi River \zam-'bē-zē\ River, southern central and South Africa. It rises in northwestern Zambia, flows south across eastern Angola and western Zambia to the border of Botswana, then turns east and forms the Zambia–Zimbabwe border. It then crosses central Mozambique and empties into the MOZAMBIQUE CHANNEL at Chinde. About 2,200 mi (3,500 km) long, it is navigable in three long stretches, separated by rapids and by VICTORIA FALLS. It drains the entire southern central region of the continent. Its many tributaries include the KWANDO, KAFUE, and SHIRE. It was explored by DAVID LIVINGSTONE in the early 1850s.

Zambia *officially* **Republic of Zambia,** *formerly* **Northern Rhodesia** Landlocked country, southern central Africa. Area: 290,586 sq mi (752,614 sq km). Population (1997 est.): 9,350,000. Capital: LUSAKA. The population is composed almost entirely of BANTU-speaking African ethnic groups. Languages: English (official); some 80 local languages and dialects also spoken. Religions: Christianity (predominant), Islam, Hinduism, and indigenous beliefs. Currency: kwacha. The country consists of tableland through which the ZAMBEZI (including VICTORIA FALLS), KAFUE, and Luangwa rivers flow. Lake BANGWEULU is within northern Zambia, while lakes MWERU and TANGANYIKA touch its northern boundaries. The Bangweulu Swamps form one of the largest inland wetlands in the world. The Muchinga Mountains in the east include the highest point (7,100 ft, or 2,200 m) in the country. There are valuable forests of Zambezi teak in the southwest. Zambia's economy is heavily dependent

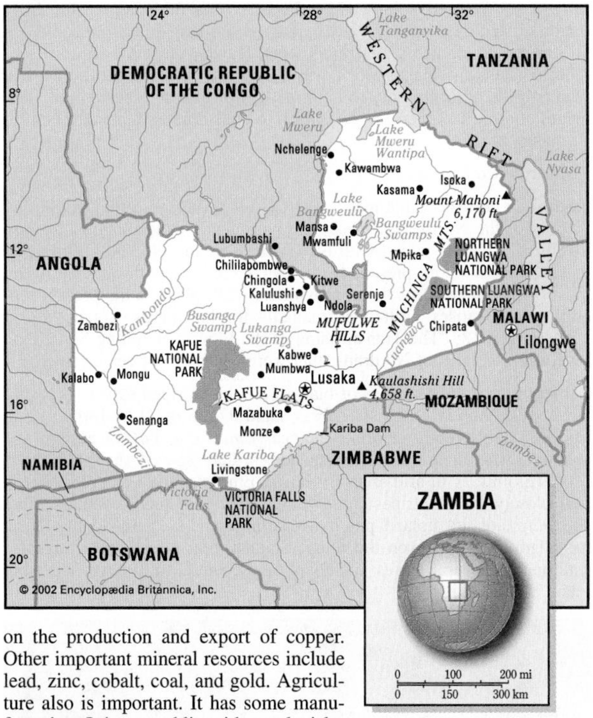

on the production and export of copper. Other important mineral resources include lead, zinc, cobalt, coal, and gold. Agriculture also is important. It has some manufacturing. It is a republic with one legislative house; its head of state and government is the president. Archaeological evidence suggests that early humans roamed present-day Zambia 1–2 million years ago. Ancestors of the modern Tonga tribe reached the region early in the 2nd millennium AD, but other modern peoples from Congo (Zaire) and Angola reached the country only in the 17th–18th century. Portuguese trading missions were established early in the 18th century. Emissaries of CECIL RHODES and the British South Africa Co. concluded treaties with most of the Zambian chiefs during the 1890s. The company administered the region known as Northern Rhodesia until 1924, when it became a British protectorate. It was part of the Central African Federation of Rhodesia and Nyasaland 1953–63. In 1964 Northern Rhodesia became the independent republic of Zambia. A constitutional amendment was passed in 1990 allowing opposition parties; the following years were filled with political tension.

Zamboanga \ˌzäm-bō-ˈwäŋ-gä\ Port city (pop., 1994 est.: 464,000), western MINDANAO, Philippines. Founded in 1635 as a fort by the Spanish, it later became the chief market of the southern Philippines. In World War II it was a Japanese defense headquarters that was taken by U.S. troops in 1945. It exports rubber, pearls, copra, and mahogany, and is a center for Moro brassware and bronzeware. It is also a tourist resort.

Zamora, Niceto Alcalá See Niceto ALCALÁ ZAMORA

Zamyatin \ˌzə-ˈmya-tʸin\, **Yevgeny (Ivanovich)** (1884–1937) Russian novelist, playwright, and satirist. Educated as a naval engineer, he combined a scientific career with writing. A chronic dissenter, he was a Bolshevik before the Russian Revolution of 1917 but disassociated himself from the party afterward. His ironic criticism of literary politics kept him out of official favor. His most ambitious work, the novel *We* (1924; first published in the Soviet Union 1989), was the first anti-utopian novel and the literary ancestor of ALDOUS HUXLEY's *Brave New World* and GEORGE ORWELL's *Nineteen Eighty-four.*

Zande See AZANDE

Zangwill \ˈzaŋ-gwil\, **Israel** (1864–1926) English novelist, playwright, and Zionist leader. The son of Eastern European immigrants, Zangwill drew on his own experience in *Children of the Ghetto* (1892), which aroused great interest. Other works of Jewish content include *The King of Schnorrers* (1894), a picaresque novel about an 18th-century rogue, and *Dreamers of the Ghetto* (1898), essays on famous Jews. The metaphor of America as a crucible wherein various nationalities are transformed into a new race comes from his play *The Melting Pot* (1908). He is remembered as one of the earliest English interpreters of Jewish immigrant life.

Zanuck \ˈza-nək\, **Darryl F(rancis)** (1902–1979) U.S. film producer and executive. Born in Wahoo, Neb., he became a screenwriter for Warner Brothers in 1924. After writing scripts for more than 35 movies, he was made a producer. He promoted the conversion to sound by producing *The Jazz Singer* (1927). In 1933 he cofounded Twentieth Century Pictures, which soon merged with the Fox Film Corp. As the controlling executive of TWENTIETH CENTURY–FOX, he produced such films as *The Grapes of Wrath* (1940), *Gentleman's Agreement* (1947), and *Viva Zapata!* (1952). He resigned in 1956, but later returned as president (1962) to effect the company's financial recovery with such hits as *The Longest Day* (1962), *The Sound of Music* (1965), and *Patton* (1970). He retired as chairman in 1971.

Zanzibar Chief island (pop., 1988: 375,000), Tanzania. Located in the Indian Ocean, off eastern central Africa, it has an area of 637 sq mi (1,651 sq km). Zanzibar city (pop., 1988: 158,000), the island's principal port and commercial center, is on the western side. Both Zanzibar and Pemba islands are believed to have once formed part of the African continent. In the late 17th century it came under the control of Omani Arabs, and the sultan of Oman made Zanzibar city his capital in 1832. In 1861 Zanzibar was separated from Oman and became an independent sultanate composed of the island, Kenya, Mafia Island, and the coasts of Tanzania and Somalia. Under Sultan Barghash (r.1870–88), most of the mainland territories were lost to European powers. In 1890 the British proclaimed a protectorate over Zanzibar and Pemba islands. In 1963 the sultanate regained its independence and became a member of the COMMONWEALTH. The sultanate was overthrown in 1964 and a republic was established. It then joined with Tanganyika to form the Republic of Tanzania. The economy depends on agriculture and fishing.

Zapata \sä-ˈpä-tä\, **Emiliano** (1879–1919) Mexican revolutionary and champion of the rural poor. A mestizo peasant, he was orphaned at 17 and took responsibility for his brothers and sisters. He led his neighbors in protests against the hacienda that had appropriated their land, and eventually led them in taking the land by force. He organized a small force to help FRANCISCO MADERO unseat PORFIRIO DIAZ. Dissatisfied with the pace of LAND REFORM under Madero, Zapata led a guerrilla campaign that took land back from the haciendas and returned it to the communal Indian EJIDOS. He was instrumental in the defeat of Gen. VICTORIANO HUERTA after Huerta deposed and assassinated Madero. With PANCHO VILLA he

Zapata, 1912.
ARCHIVO CASASOLA

occupied Mexico City and began to implement land reform, but was tricked, ambushed, and killed by the forces of VENUSTIANO CARRANZA, whom the U.S. had recognized as president.

Zapopan \ˌsä-pō-ˈpän\ City (pop., 1990: 668,000), northern central JALISCO state, western central Mexico. Located in the Guadalajara River valley, it is a commercial and manufacturing center for an agricultural area that produces corn, sugarcane, cotton, fruits and vegetables, and livestock. Apiculture and tourism also contribute to the economy. The 17th-century Basilica of Zapopan is the site of annual pilgrimages.

Zaporizhzhya \ˌzäp-ə-ˈri-zhə\ *formerly (until 1921)* **Aleksandrovsk** City (pop., 1996 est.: 882,000), southeastern Ukraine, on the DNIEPER RIVER. In 1770 the fortress of Aleksandrovsk was built to ensure government control over the Zaporizhzhya COSSACKS, whose headquarters were nearby. The settlement became a town in 1806. The city expanded during the 1927–32 construction of the Dnieper hydroelectric station, then the largest in the world. The dam was destroyed in World War II but was later rebuilt. It has a major iron and steel plant; automobiles are also manufactured.

Zapotec \ˌzä-pə-ˈtek\ Indian population living in the state of Oaxaca, in southern Mexico. Early Zapotec civilization, centered on MONTE ALBÁN (near the modern city of Oaxaca), produced the first writing in Mesoamerica and devised the 52-year round calendar later borrowed by other groups. Present-day traditional Zapotec society is largely agricultural, and slash-and-burn clearing techniques are used in cultivation. The major crafts include pottery and weaving. The Zapotecs profess Roman Catholicism, but belief in spirits and myths persists. See also MESOAMERICAN CIVILIZATION.

Zappa, Frank *orig.* **Francis Vincent** (1940–1993) U.S. rock musician and composer. Born in Baltimore, Zappa grew up in California and taught himself drums and guitar. He wrote film scores in the early 1960s. In 1964 he began working with the Soul Giants, which eventually became the Mothers of Invention. He became known for his musical virtuosity and wildly eccentric wit on such albums as *Freak Out!* (1966), *We're Only in It for the Money* (1967), *Lumpy Gravy* (1967), *Absolutely Free* (1967), *Sheik Yerbouti* (1979), and *Jazz from Hell* (1988). His greatest commercial success was "Valley Girl," featuring his daughter Moon Unit.

Zara, Siege of (1202) Major episode of the Fourth CRUSADE, the first attack on a Christian city by a crusading army. Zara (modern Zadar, Croatia), a vassal city of Venice, had rebelled and placed itself under Hungary's protection in 1186. Over the objections of INNOCENT III, the Venetians diverted the Fourth Crusade from Palestine and Egypt, using financial pressure to persuade the cruaders to besiege Zara. The city soon surrendered, and the army went on to attack Constantinople in 1203–4.

Zaragoza See SARAGOSSA

Zarathustra See ZOROASTER

Zaria \ˈzär-ē-ə\ *formerly* **Zazzau** Historic kingdom and traditional emirate, northern Nigeria. It was founded in the 11th century and was the southernmost of the original seven HAUSA Bakwai states. Islam was introduced c. 1456, and there were Muslim Hausa rulers in the early 16th century. A SONGHAI warrior conquered Zazzau c. 1512. By the end of the century it was renamed Zaria and was in decline. It became a tributary state (c. 1734–1804) of the BORNU kingdom. In 1804 it came under the FULANI Muslims. The Zaria emirate was created in 1835. It remains one of Nigeria's largest traditional emirates, and it is one of the nation's leading producers of cotton for export.

Zarlino \dzär-ˈlē-nō\, **Gioseffo** (1517–1590) Italian music theorist and composer. He received the tonsure in 1532 and played organ at the local cathedral. In 1541 he moved to Venice to study with Adrian Willaert (c. 1490–1562), then took over as chapel master at St. Mark's Basilica, where his students included Vincenzo Galilei (c. 1528?–1591) and Claudio Merulo (1533–1604). His influential treatise *Le institutioni harmoniche* (1558) argued for more stringent control of dissonance (while accepting several previously dissonant intervals as consonances) and stricter adherence to unity of mode in a composition. *Dimonstrationi harmoniche* (1571) renumbered the church modes, starting with C instead of the traditional A, thus acknowledging the growing relevance of tonality.

zarzuela \ˌzär-ˈzwā-lə\ Spanish musical play consisting of spoken dialogue, songs, choruses, and dances. Zarzuela originated in the 1650s as an aristocratic entertainment, the first being performed at the royal residence of La Zarzuela near Madrid. The principal early composer was Juan Hidalgo (1614–1685); early librettists included LOPE DE VEGA and PEDRO CALDERON DE LA BARCA. As Italian opera rose in popularity, the zarzuela adopted aspects of *opera seria* style but suffered a decline. It was revived in the late 18th century in more popular style; it was revived again c. 1840 as a satirical treatment of everyday life incorporating folk music, dance, and improvisation, and the next hundred years saw the production of thousands of zarzuelas. Since 1940 few new works have been written.

Zátopek \ˈtsä-tō-ˌpek\, **Emil** (1922–2000) Czech long-distance runner. He won his first Olympic gold medal in 1948 in the 10,000-m race. At the 1952 Olympics he won gold medals in the 5,000-m, 10,000-m, and marathon. From the mid-1940s to the mid-1950s he set 18 world records, and he held the record for the 10,000-m from 1949 to 1954.

zazen \ˈzä-ˈzen\ Sitting meditation as practiced in ZEN Buddhism. The disciple sits in a quiet room, breathing rhythmically and easily, with legs fully or half crossed, spine and head erect, hands folded one palm above the other, and eyes open. Logical, analytic thinking is suspended, as are all desires, attachments, and judgments, leaving the mind in a state of relaxed attention. The practice was brought to prominence by DOGEN, who considered it not only to be a method of moving toward enlightenment but also, if properly experienced, to constitute enlightenment itself. See also KOAN.

Zealand See SJAELLAND

Zeami *or* **Seami** \zā-ˈä-mē\ (1363/64–1443) Japanese playwright and theorist of the No theater. Under the patronage of the shogun ASHIKAGA Yoshimitsu, Zeami joined with his father, Kan'ami (1333–84), to create the NO DRAMA in its present form. He is credited with about 90 (and most of the greatest) of the approximately 230 plays in the present repertoire. In treatises written as manuals for his pupils, notably *Fushi kaden* (1400–18; "The Transmission of the Flower of Acting Style"), he set forth principles of No drama that were followed for centuries.

zebra Any of three species of black-and-white-striped EQUINES that subsist almost entirely on grass. Zebras stand 47–55 in. (120–140 cm) tall. The Burchell's zebra, or bonte quagga *(Equus quagga),* of eastern and southern African grasslands, has wide, widely spaced stripes. Grevy's zebra *(E. grevyi),* of arid areas in Kenya, Ethiopia, and Somalia, has narrow, closely spaced stripes and a white belly. The small mountain zebra *(E. zebra),* of dry upland plains in Namibia and western South Africa, has a gridlike pattern on the rump. Small zebra groups consisting of a stallion and several mares and foals may coalesce into large herds but retain their identity.

Burchell's zebra, or bonte quagga (*Equus quagga*).
LEONARD LEE RUE III

zebra fish Any member of two unrelated groups of fishes: freshwater species in the genus *Brachydanio* (family Cyprinidae) and saltwater species in the genus *Pterois* (family Scorpaenidae). The zebra danio *(Brachydanio rerio),* a popular freshwater aquarium fish originally from Asia, is up to about 1.5 in. (4 cm) long and has dark-blue and silvery longitudinal stripes. The distinctive saltwater zebra fishes *(Pterois),* used in marine aquariums, have extremely large pectoral fins, numerous extremely poisonous spines, and colorful vertical stripes. Some species are more commonly known as LIONFISH and turkeyfish.

zebra mussel Either of two species of tiny MUSSELS (genus *Dreissena*) that are prominent freshwater pests. They proliferate quickly and adhere in great numbers to virtually any surface. The voracious mussels disrupt food webs by wiping out PHYTOPLANKTON, and their massive clustering on water-intake valves and pipes, bridge abutments, and other structures can cause severe commercial damage. They made their first known attack on Europe in the early 19th century and were carried (probably in ship water ballasts) to North America c. 1986; their invasion of all the Great Lakes has had devastating effects on the lakes' native mussel and fish populations.

zebu See BRAHMAN

Zechariah \ˌzek-ə-ˈrī-ə\ (fl. 520–518 BC) One of the 12 Minor Prophets of the OLD TESTAMENT, whose prophecies are recorded in the Book of Zechariah. (The work is part of a larger book, The Twelve, in the Jewish canon.) His visions concern the return of the Jews to Jerusalem after the BABYLONIAN EXILE, the rebuilding of the Temple of JERUSALEM, and the world's recognition of Israel's God. The book also includes his apocalyptic visions of the end of time.

Zedillo (Ponce de León) \sā-ˈdē-yō\, **Ernesto** (born 1951) President of Mexico (1994–2000). Raised in a working-class family, he joined Mexico's ruling party in 1971 and earned a PhD in economics from Yale University. As secretary of the Ministry of Programming and Budget he controlled Mexico's huge foreign debt, reduced inflation, and balanced the budget. Elected president after the assassination of the original PRI candidate, Luis Donaldo Colosio, he undertook reforms to reduce poverty, root out corruption, and continue democratizing the electoral system. His devaluation of the peso in 1994 led to an economic crisis that was turned around with massive U.S. aid. A rebellion in CHIAPAS plagued his administration, which was charged with human-rights abuses in that region.

Zee, James Van Der See James VAN DER ZEE

Zeeman effect \ˈzā-ˌmän\ Splitting of a spectral line (see SPECTRUM) into two or more lines of different FREQUENCIES. The effect occurs when the light source is placed in a MAGNETIC FIELD. It has helped identify the energy levels in atoms; it also provides a means of studying atomic nuclei and electron paramagnetic resonance (see MAGNETIC RESONANCE), and is used in measuring the magnetic field of the sun and other stars. It was discovered in 1896 by Pieter Zeeman (1865–1943); he shared the second Nobel Prize for Physics (1902) with HENDRIK ANTOON LORENTZ, who had hypothesized that a magnetic field would affect the frequency of the light emitted.

Zefat \ˈtse-ˌfät\ City (pop., 1990 est.: 17,000), northern Israel. Located near the Sea of GALILEE, it is one of the four Jewish holy cities of Palestine. It was fortified in the 1st century AD by FLAVIUS JOSEPHUS, and in the Middle Ages by the Crusaders. It was the seat of an important school of medieval Jewish mysticism (see KABBALA). It was taken from the Arabs in 1948 by Jewish forces. It is now an artists' colony; its economy is based on light industry and tourism.

Zeffirelli \ˌze-fə-ˈre-lē\, **Franco** *orig.* **Gianfranco Corsi** (born 1923) Italian director, producer, and stage designer. In 1946 he joined LUCHINO VISCONTI's Morelli-Stoppa Co. as an actor and stage director. After serving as Visconti's assistant on such films as *La Terra Trema* (1948), he turned to stage design. His major operatic productions, noted for their visual richness, began with *L'Italiana in Algeri* (1952–53) and have included *Lucia di Lammermoor* (1959) and *La Bohème* (1963, 1981), among many others; he directed films of *La traviata* (1983) and *Otello* (1986). His other films have included *The Taming of the Shrew* (1967), *Romeo and Juliet* (1968), *Endless Love* (1981), *Jane Eyre* (1996), and *Tea with Mussolini* (1999).

Zeiss \ˈtsīs, *Engl* ˈzīs\, **Carl** (1816–1888) German industrialist. In 1846 Zeiss opened a workshop for producing microscopes and other optical instruments. He later formed a partnership with the physicist and mathematician Ernst Abbe (1840–1905). The chemist Otto Schott developed about 100 new kinds of optical glass and numerous types of heat-resistant GLASS for the company. After Zeiss's death, Abbe donated the firm and his share in the glassworks to the Carl Zeiss Foundation; in 1923 Schott added his share in the glassworks.

Zemes mate \ˈze-mes-ˈmä-te\ In BALTIC RELIGION, the female aspect of nature and the source of all life. Together with DIEVS, she stimulates and protects the power of life. Libations of beer were offered to her at the opening of every festival, and bread, ale, and herbs were buried in the ground, thrown into rivers and lakes, or tied to trees in her honor. Her various functions were eventually assumed by demigoddesses of forests, fields, stones, animals, water, and, in the Christian era, by the Virgin MARY.

zemstvo \ˈzemst-və\ Rural elected assembly in the Russian empire. Established by Czar ALEXANDER II in 1864 to provide social and economic services, the zemstvos became a liberal influence in imperial Russia. The assemblies, formed at the district and province levels, were composed of delegates representing the landed proprietors and the peasant village communes. They expanded education, improved roads, and provided health care. From the 1890s they agitated for constitutional reform, and they stimulated activity in the Russian Revolutions of 1905 and 1917 (see RUSSIAN REVOLUTION OF 1905, RUSSIAN REVOLUTION OF 1917). They were abolished after the BOLSHEVIKS came to power.

Zen Important school of BUDDHISM that claims to transmit the experience of enlightenment achieved by the BUDDHA Gautama. Arising as Chan in China in the 6th century (introduced by BODHIDHARMA), it divided into two schools, the Southern school, which believed in sudden enlightenment, and the Northern school, which believed in gradual enlightenment. By the 8th century only the Northern school survived. Zen developed fully in Japan by the 12th century and had a significant following in the West by the later 20th century. Zen teaches that the potential to achieve enlightenment is inherent in everyone but lies dormant because of ignorance. It is best awakened not by the study of scripture, the practice of good deeds, rites and ceremonies, or worship of images, but by breaking through the boundaries of mundane logical thought. Methods employed vary among different schools and may emphasize the practice of ZAZEN (in the Soto school), the use of KOANS (in the Rinzai school), or the continual invocation of Amida (in the Obaku school; see AMITABHA).

Zend-Avesta See AVESTA

Zeng Guofan *or* **Tseng Kuo-fan** \ˈdzən-ˈgwō-ˈfän\ (1811–1872) Chinese military leader most responsible for suppressing the TAIPING REBELLION, thus staving off the collapse of the QING DYNASTY. Having passed the highest examinations in the CHINESE EXAMINATION SYSTEM, Zeng entered the HANLIN ACADEMY and worked successfully as a bureaucrat. In 1852 he was asked to help combat the Taiping rebels, who had reached the Chang (Yangtze) River valley and were threatening the dynasty's survival. The imperial troops being weak, Zeng and other members of the scholar-gentry organized local militias. His army seized the rebels' supply areas along the upper Chang and besieged and captured their capital, Nanjing, in 1864. In 1865 he was called on to help suppress the NIAN REBELLION; a year later he asked that LI HONGZHANG take over the campaign. See also ZHANG ZHIDONG.

Zenger, John Peter (1697–1746) American printer and journalist. He emigrated from Germany to New York at 13 and was indentured to a printer before starting his own printing business in 1726. In 1733 he began publishing the *New York Weekly Journal.* Arrested for libel in 1734 for his attacks on the policies of the colonial governor, he was acquitted on the ground that his charges were based on fact (a key consideration in libel cases since that time) in the first important victory for freedom of the press in Britain's North American colonies.

Zeno \ˈzē-nō\ *orig.* **Tarasicodissa** (died AD 491) Eastern Roman emperor (474–91). A military leader, he married the daughter of Emperor Leo I (c. 466), and their son reigned briefly as Leo II (474). On the boy's early death, Zeno became emperor. Obliged to flee to Isauria to escape a coup d'état, he returned to Constantinople in 476. He made peace with the VANDALS in Africa, put down a rebellion in Asia Minor (484), and persuaded the OSTROGOTHS to leave the Eastern Empire by making THEODORIC king of Italy (489). Seeking to reconcile orthodox Christians and MONOPHYSITES, he caused a schism with Rome (484–519).

Zeno of Citium \'zē-ˌnō...'si-sh(ē-)əm\ (c. 335–263? BC) Greek philosopher, founder of STOICISM. He attended lectures in Athens by the Cynics Crates of Thebes (fl. late 4th century BC) and Stilpon of Megara (c. 380–300 BC) and lectures at the Academy before beginning to teach in the Stoa Poikile ("Painted Colonnade"). His system included logic and theory of knowledge, physics, and ethics. He taught that happiness lay in conforming the will to the divine reason, which governs the universe. In logic and the theory of knowledge he was influenced by Antisthenes (c. 445–365 BC) and Diodorus Cronus (fl. 4th century BC), in physics by HERACLEITUS. Only fragmentary quotations from his many treatises have survived.

Zeno of Elea \'ē-lē-ə\ (c. 495–430 BC) Greek philosopher and mathematician. He was called by ARISTOTLE the inventor of dialectic. He is best known for his paradoxes (see PARADOXES OF ZENO). As a pupil and friend of PARMENIDES, he took it on himself to reply to those who thought that Parmenides' MONISM was inconsistent. He tried to show that the assumption of the existence of a plurality of things in time and space carried with it more serious inconsistencies.

Zenobia \zə-'nō-bē-ə\ *in full* **Septimia Zenobia** (died after AD 274) Queen of the Roman colony of PALMYRA (AD 267?–272). Her husband, a Roman client ruler of Palmyra, was assassinated after recapturing several of Rome's eastern provinces from the Persians. She became her son's regent but called herself queen. In 269 she seized Egypt and much of Asia Minor and declared her independence from Rome. AURELIAN defeated her armies and besieged Palmyra; she and her son were captured and taken to Rome (272), where she later married a senator. A second revolt, without her leadership, brought the destruction of Palmyra (273).

Zenobia, portrait bust; in the Vatican Museum, Rome.
ANDERSON—GIRAUDON FROM ART RESOURCE

zeolite \'zē-ə-ˌlīt\ Any member of a family of hydrated aluminosilicate minerals that have a framework structure enclosing interconnected cavities occupied by large metal cations (positively charged ions)—generally sodium, potassium, magnesium, calcium, and barium—and water molecules. The ease of movement of ions and water within the framework allows reversible dehydration and cation exchange, properties that are exploited in water softeners and molecular sieves for pollution control, among other uses.

zeolitic facies \ˌzē-ə-'li-tik-'fā-shēz\ One of the major divisions of the mineral facies classification of METAMORPHIC ROCKS, encompassing rocks that formed at the lowest temperatures and pressures associated with regional metamorphism. Typical minerals in these facies include the ZEOLITES, ALBITE, and QUARTZ.

Zephaniah (7th century BC) One of the 12 Minor Prophets of the OLD TESTAMENT, traditional author of the Book of Zephaniah. (The work is part of a larger book, The Twelve, in the Jewish canon.) He prophesied in the reign of JOSIAH, denouncing the worship of foreign gods, which suggests that he preached before the reforms instituted by Josiah. His dominant theme is the coming "day of the Lord," a time of divine judgment for Judah's sins.

zeppelin Rigid AIRSHIP of a type designed by the German builder Ferdinand, Graf (Count) von Zeppelin (1838–1917). It was a cigar-shaped, trussed, and covered frame supported by internal gas cells, below which hung two external cars with an engine geared to two propellers. The first zeppelin flew in 1900. In World War I zeppelins were used as bombers by Germany. In 1928 the *Graf Zeppelin* inaugurated transatlantic flight service; it had completed 590 flights by 1937, when the *HINDENBURG* DISASTER halted such flights.

zero NUMBER and numeral of critical importance in mathematics. As a number, it has the property that any number added to it remains the same and any number multiplied by it becomes zero. (By an important law of EQUATION solving, if the product of two numbers is zero, at least one of them must equal zero.) Division by zero is undefined. As a numeral indicating an empty space, it was first used by the ancient Babylonians. The symbol 0 dates from about 150 BC, when PTOLEMY began using the Greek letter omicron (the first letter of the Greek word for "nothing") to indicate the absence of a digit at the end of a number. Zero was not widely accepted as a number in Western mathematics until the 16th century.

Zero *in full* **Mitsubishi A6M Zero** Japanese FIGHTER AIRCRAFT of World War II. A single-seat, low-wing monoplane made by Mitsubishi, it was introduced in 1940, the 2,600th anniversary of the crowning of Japan's legendary first emperor, JIMMU, and named for the "zero-year" celebration. It had a top speed of 350 mph (565 kph) at nearly 20,000 ft (6,000 m). When it first appeared, it could outmaneuver every plane it encountered; Allied fighters could not defeat it until 1943. Many Zeros became KAMIKAZE craft in the war's closing months.

zero-point energy Vibrational energy retained by molecules even at a temperature of ABSOLUTE ZERO. Since temperature is a measure of the intensity of molecular motion, molecules would be expected to come to rest at absolute zero. However, if molecular motion were to cease altogether, the atoms would each have a precisely known location and VELOCITY (zero), and the UNCERTAINTY PRINCIPLE states that this cannot occur, since precise values of both position and velocity of an object cannot be known simultaneously. Thus, even molecules at absolute zero must have some zero-point energy.

Zeroual \zer-'wäl\, **Liamine** (born 1941) President of Algeria (1994–99). After a military education, he rose through the ranks to become Land Forces Chief in 1989 and defense minister in 1993. In 1994 he was appointed transitional president by the military-dominated High Council of State, which had taken over the government after the cancellation of elections in 1992 and the assassination of Pres. MUHAMMAD BOUDIAF. Elected for a full term in 1995, he was replaced in 1999 by Abdelaziz Bouteflika.

Zetkin \'tset-kən\, **Clara** *orig.* **Clara Eissner** (1857–1933) German communist leader. She joined the Social Democratic Party in 1881, and later married a Russian revolutionary exile, Ossip Zetkin (1848–1889). From 1892 she edited the Socialist women's newspaper *Die Gleichheit* ("Equality") in Stuttgart. A friend of VLADIMIR ILICH LENIN and ROSA LUXEMBURG, Zetkin was a cofounder of the SPARTACISTS (1916) and later joined the new Communist Party of Germany (1919). In 1921 she was elected to the presidium of the Third International. Her influence waned after Lenin's death in 1924.

Zeus \'züs\ In GREEK RELIGION, the chief deity of the pantheon, a sky and weather god. His Roman counterpart was JUPITER. Zeus was regarded as the bearer of thunder and lightning, rain, and winds, and his traditional weapon was the thunderbolt. The son of CRONUS and RHEA, he was fated to dethrone his father. He divided dominion over the world with his brothers POSEIDON and HADES. As ruler of heaven, Zeus led the gods to victory against the TITANS. From his home atop Mount OLYMPUS, he dispensed justice and served as protector. Known for his amorousness, a source of perpetual discord with his wife, HERA, he had many love affairs with mortal and immortal women, giving rise to such offspring as APOLLO, ARES, ARTEMIS, ATHENA, DIONYSUS, HELEN, HEPHAESTUS, and PERSEPHONE. In art he was represented as a bearded, dignified, and mature man.

Zeus hurling a thunderbolt, bronze statuette from Dodona, Greece, early 5th century BC; in the Staatliche Museen zu Berlin, Germany.
BY COURTESY OF THE STAATLICHE MUSEEN ZU BERLIN, ANTIKENABTEILUNG

Zeuxis \'zük-səs\ (fl. late 5th century–early 4th century BC) Greek painter. Though none of his work survives, his style and subject matter were recorded by ancient writers. He advanced the trend toward illu-

W X Y Z

sionism through the use of shadow to produce a rudimentary form of chiaroscuro. Apparently he was a panel painter rather than a wall painter. He preferred small compositions, often a single figure; his subjects were gods and heroes and such genre figures as an old woman, an athlete, and a still life.

Zhang Daoling *or* **Chang Tao-Ling** \'jäŋ-'daù-'liŋ\ (34?–156? AD) Founder and first patriarch of the Chinese Taoist church. Zhang composed a Taoist work that attracted many followers among Chinese and indigenous groups in Sichuan to his cult. Like contemporary Taoists he promised longevity and physical immortality, but unlike others he emphasized the importance of religious organization. He founded the FIVE PECKS OF RICE movement. Zhang, his son, and grandson are known as the Three Zhangs. While the *TAO-TE CHING* was the basic text, Zhang's Xing'er commentary interpreted it to suit the church's needs.

Zhang Heng *or* **Chang Heng** \'jäŋ-'həŋ\ (AD 78–139) Chinese mathematician, astronomer, and geographer. His seismoscope for registering earthquakes was apparently cylindrical in shape, with eight dragons' heads arranged around its upper circumference, each with a ball in its mouth. Below were eight frogs, each directly under a dragon's head. When an earthquake occurred, a ball dropped and was caught by a frog's mouth, generating a sound.

Zhang Juzheng *or* **Chang Chü-cheng** \'jäŋ-'jü-'jəŋ\ (died 1582) Powerful Chinese minister of the MING DYNASTY under the Longqing and Wanli emperors. His benevolent rule and strong foreign and economic policies are considered to have brought the Ming dynasty to its peak. He is credited with centralizing government, limiting special privileges, and reclaiming tax-exempt land.

Zhang Yimou \'jäŋ-'yē-'mō\ (born 1950) Chinese film director. He began his film career as a cinematographer, and his work for Chen Kaige's *The Yellow Earth* (1983) helped launch the "Fifth Generation," filmmakers who brought back sensuality and emotion to Chinese movies. Zhang made his directorial debut with *Red Sorghum* (1987), which starred Gong Li in the first of her acclaimed roles. Noted for his technical mastery, he also directed such films as *Ju Dou* (1990), *Raise the Red Lantern* (1991), *The Story of Qiu Ju* (1992), *To Live* (1994), and *Shanghai Triad* (1995).

Zhang Zai *or* **Chang Tsai** \'jäŋ-'dzī\ (1020–1077) Realist philosopher of the SONG DYNASTY. The son of a magistrate, he studied Buddhism and Taoism before being inspired by the Confucian classics. In his *Correct Discipline for Beginners,* he declared the universe a unity with myriad aspects and all existence an eternal integration and disintegration. REN (humaneness) is the basic virtue, and morality consists in doing one's duty as a member of society and of the universe.

Zhang Zhidong *or* **Chang Chih-tung** \'jäŋ-jir-'dúŋ\ (1837–1909) Chinese classicist and one of the foremost reformers of his time. From 1862 to 1882 he was a scholar and educational director; from 1882 to 1907 he rose from a provincial to a national leader. He supported the dowager empress CIXI, who in turn favored him with many promotions. Concerned with the rejuvenation of China, he searched for a way for China to survive in the modern world that could accommodate Western knowledge but preserve traditional ways. His launching of China's first iron-and-steel works failed, but he later built a railway from Hankou to near Beijing, and founded a mint, tanneries, tile and silk factories, and paper, cotton, and wool mills. In response to China's defeat in the SINO-JAPANESE WAR, Zhang turned his attention to education, encouraging study abroad for Chinese students, establishment of a school system, translation of Western and Japanese books, and acquisition of knowledge from foreign newspapers. He also urged the abolition of the civil-service examinations, which occurred in 1905. See also ZENG GUOFAN.

Zhang Zuolin *or* **Chang Tso-lin** \'jäŋ-dzò-'lin\ (1873–1928) Chinese warlord. After fighting in the SINO-JAPANESE WAR, Zhang organized a self-defense militia in his native district. By 1912 he was in command of a division, and he set out to dominate Manchuria, relying on the tacit support of the Japanese, to whom he granted concessions in Manchuria. In 1918 he became inspector general of Manchuria's three provinces, which he ruled as a virtually autonomous state. In 1920 he pushed south into China proper; in 1924 he took Beijing. His troops had to abandon their position in the face of CHIANG KAI-SHEK's 1927 NORTHERN EXPEDITION. Zhang was killed by a bomb planted by Japanese extremists who hoped his death would provoke the Japanese into occupying Manchuria.

Zhdanov \'shtä-nóf\, **Andrey (Aleksandrovich)** (1896–1948) Soviet politician. He joined the Bolsheviks in 1915 and became a leading member of the Politburo (1939) and Communist Party secretary in Leningrad. A close associate of JOSEPH STALIN, he formulated the extreme anti-Western cultural policy known as "Zhdanovism" (1946), which imposed strict government control on art and literature and soon affected all intellectual activity in the Soviet Union. In 1947 he founded the propaganda bureau COMINFORM.

Zhejiang *or* **Chekiang** \'jə-'jyäŋ\ Province (pop., 2000 est.: 46,770,000), eastern China. It is bounded by the CHINA SEA and FUJIAN, JIANGXI, ANHUI, and JIANGSU provinces; its capital is HANGZHOU. One of China's smallest provinces, it is one of the most densely populated. Its northern part lies just south of the CHANG (YANGTZE) RIVER delta. Occupying parts of various kingdoms until the 13th century AD, it was divided in the 1270s into eastern and western regions. Foreign penetration began in the 1840s. After the Chinese revolution (1911–12), it became a power base for the Nationalist Party of CHIANG KAI-SHEK, who was born in the province. Occupied by the Japanese during World War II, it was little affected by the 1946–49 civil war. In addition to its agricultural importance, it has a thriving fishing industry. Its hydroelectric power plants have spurred more growth.

Zheng Chenggong *or* **Cheng Ch'eng-kung** \'jəŋ-'chəŋ-'gùŋ\ *or* **Koxinga** \käk-'siŋ-ə\ (1624–1662) Chinese hero of the late MING and early QING dynasties. After the Ming dynasty fell to the MANCHU, Zheng refused Manchu offers of rank and power, and launched a military campaign against the new dynasty in 1659, taking a large force from his base in Fujian up the Chang (Yangtze) River. Initial success turned to failure, but undaunted, Zheng took Taiwan from the Dutch in 1662 to use as a secure rear base area. Further glory was cut short by his death later that year. He became a popular deity and cultural hero to the Chinese on Taiwan, and even the Qing court honored him as a paragon of loyalty. In Japan, CHIKAMATSU MONZAEMON celebrated him on the stage (Zheng had a Japanese mother), and in the 20th century both Chinese Communists and Nationalists embraced him as a national hero.

Zheng He *or* **Cheng Ho** \'jəŋ-'he\ *orig.* **Ma Sanbao** (1371?–1435) Eunuch admiral and diplomat who helped extend Chinese maritime and commercial influence throughout the region bordering on the Indian Ocean. Zheng was named commander in chief of missions to the "Western Oceans" by the YONGLE EMPEROR. He first set sail in 1405; this mission visited Champa (S Vietnam), Siam, Malacca, and Java, then traveled through the Indian Ocean as far as Ceylon (Sri Lanka), returning to China in 1407. Subsequent voyages took him to Arabia, the eastern coast of Africa, S.East Asia, and India. Chinese emigration increased in the wake of these missions, resulting in Chinese colonization of S.East Asia and consequent tributary trade that lasted into the 19th century.

Zhengzhou *or* **Cheng-chou** \'jəŋ-'jō\ *formerly (1913–49)* **Cheng-hsien** \'jəŋ-'shyen\ City (pop., 1999 est.: 1,465,069), capital of HENAN province, eastern central China. Located south of the HUANG RIVER, it is an important rail center. There were Neolithic settlements in the area, and the SHANG Bronze Age culture (fl. c. 1500 BC) was centered there on a walled city. ZHOU-DYNASTY tombs have also been discovered. The city was first called Cheng-chou (Zhengzhou) in AD 605, and it has been known by that name virtually ever since. It achieved its greatest importance in the 6th–12th century, when it was the terminus of a canal that joined the Huang to the north. In the early 20th century it became a rail junction and a regional agricultural center. After 1949, its industrial base was greatly expanded.

Zhivkov \'zhiv-,kóf\, **Todor (Khristov)** (1911–1998) Bulgarian politician. A member of the outlawed Communist Party, he organized a resistance movement in World War II. After the war, he held posts in the Soviet-sponsored government, including head of the People's Militia. He became first secretary of the Bulgarian Communist Party in 1954, the youngest leader in the Soviet bloc, then served as premier (1962–71) and president (1971–89). He hewed closely to the Soviet line but encouraged industrialization and improved the country's living standard. When democratization reached Bulgaria, Zhivkov resigned (1989). Convicted of embezzlement, he was sentenced to house arrest in 1992.

Zhiyi *or* **Chih-i** \'jir-'ē\ (538–597) Chinese Buddhist monk who founded the eclectic TIANTAI sect. Orphaned at 17, he studied with the Buddhist master Huisi for seven years. He was associated with the imperial governments of the Chen dynasty in southern China and the SUI DYNASTY, which reunified China. He reconciled the various strains of Buddhism by regarding all Buddhist doctrines as true and present in the mind of the enlightened BUDDHA, who unfolded his teachings in periods, to accommodate his listeners' capacities. He considered the LOTUS SUTRA the highest teaching and helped establish it as the most popular scripture in East Asia.

Zhong yong *or* **Chung yung** \'jùŋ-'yùŋ\ *or* **Doctrine of the Mean** One of four ancient Confucian texts known as the FOUR BOOKS, published together in 1190 by ZHU XI. Its metaphysics had interested Buddhists and earlier Neo-Confucianists. Zhu Xi attributes the work to CONFUCIUS' grandson Zi Si, though it was actually part of *Li ji* ("Book of Rites"), one of the FIVE CLASSICS. *Zhong yong* expresses an ideal of moderation, rectitude, and lack of prejudice that should encompass virtually every relationship and activity in life.

Zhou dynasty *or* **Chou dynasty** \'jō\ (c. 1050–256/255 BC) Ancient Chinese dynasty that gave China its historically identifying political and cultural characteristics. The period before 771 BC is known as the Western Zhou; the period from 771 BC on is called the Eastern Zhou, and is further divided into the SPRING AND AUTUMN PERIOD (770–476) and the WARRING STATES PERIOD (475–221). During the Zhou dynasty, iron, ox-drawn plows, crossbows, and horseback riding were introduced; large-scale irrigation projects were instituted; the CHINESE WRITING SYSTEM was further developed; and the great Chinese philosophers of antiquity, including CONFUCIUS, MENCIUS, and ZHUANGZI, lived and taught. Pottery and bronzework expanded on the traditions of the earlier SHANG DYNASTY, as did work in jade and lacquer.

Zhou Enlai *or* **Chou En-lai** \'jō-'en-'lī\ (1898–1976) Chinese Communist leader, premier from the founding of the People's Republic until his death (1949–76). Zhou became a Communist during his studies abroad in France and was an organizer for the CHINESE COMMUNIST PARTY in Europe. Like other Communists, he worked with the Nationalists in the early 1920s and escaped capture when CHIANG KAI-SHEK purged his former allies in 1927. He joined ZHU DE and MAO ZEDONG in Jiangxi (Kiangsi) and became political commissar of the Red Army. In the 1930s he negotiated a tactical alliance with the Nationalists to resist Japanese aggression. When the Communists prevailed over the Nationalists in 1949, Zhou became premier of the new People's Republic of China. During the CULTURAL REVOLUTION, Zhou helped restrain Maoist extremists; with its waning in the early 1970s, he sought to restore DENG XIAOPING and other moderates to power. He is credited with arranging the historic meeting between Pres. RICHARD NIXON and Mao that paved the way for U.S. recognition of the Communist government.

Zhougong *or* **Chou-kung** \'jō-'gùŋ\ (fl. 12th century BC) Political figure who solidified the power of the ZHOU DYNASTY. On the death of his brother WUWANG, founder of the Zhou dynasty, he resisted the temptation to seize the throne and chose instead to serve as counselor to his nephew, the second Zhou ruler. When Zhougong stepped down after seven years, the Zhou political and social system had been stabilized. CONFUCIUS admired Zhougong's wisdom and virtue as a minister, holding him up as a model for rulers of his own time to emulate.

Zhoukoudian \'jō-kōd-yən\ Cave lying 37 mi (60 km) southwest of Beijing, at which have been found fossil remains of the extinct hominid *HOMO ERECTUS*. So-called "Peking man" was identified as a new fossil human in 1927 and variously classified as *Pithecanthropus* and *Sinanthropus* before being assigned to *H. erectus*. Partial remains of about 40 individuals along with over 100,000 artifacts have been uncovered, making Zhoukoudian one of the most important *H. erectus* sites in the world. Its strata date to 460,000–230,000 years ago. Ancient hearths and other evidence indicate that the Zhoukoudian hominids had a well-developed communal culture, practiced hunting, and used fire domestically.

Zhu De *or* **Chu Teh** \'jü-'de\ (1886–1976) Founder of the Chinese Communist Army. Educated at Yunnan Military Academy, Zhu began his military career in the armies of warlords in southern China. He became a Communist in the early 1920s but hid his affiliation to become an officer in the Nationalist army. In 1927 he took part in the Communist-led Nanchang Uprising, an event celebrated annually in China as the birth of the PEOPLE'S LIBERATION ARMY. When the uprising was defeated, Zhu led his troops south to join MAO ZEDONG's small guerrilla forces. He became commander in chief of the Communist forces, a position he held through World War II and the civil war with the Nationalists, only stepping down in 1954. With Mao, Zhu is credited with elevating guerrilla warfare to a major strategic concept.

Zhu Rongji \'jü-róŋ-'jē\ (born 1928) Premier of the State Council of China. In the 1950s he was denounced as a rightist, and he was purged again in the 1970s, but once his party membership was restored he rose rapidly. In 1988 he became mayor of Shanghai, and in 1991 a vice-premier of the State Council. He was governor of the People's Bank of China 1993–95, and became director of the Institute for Economic Management at Qinghua University in 1994. He was appointed premier of the State Council in 1998. In the face of the Asian economic crisis at the end of the 1990s, he worked to cut back government bureaucracy drastically.

Zhu Xi *or* **Chu Hsi** \'jü-'shē\ (1130–1200) Chinese philosopher and proponent of NEO-CONFUCIANISM. The son of a minor government official, he was educated in the Confucian tradition and entered government service. In 1189 he began a commentary on the *DA XUE*; he continued working on the *Da xue* all his life. Philosophically, his thought incorporated the ideas of CHENG HAO AND CHENG YI, Zhou Dunyi (1017–1073), and ZHANG ZAI, whose works he compiled. His commentaries on the FOUR BOOKS, notably on the *LUNYU (ANALECTS)* of CONFUCIUS and on *MENCIUS* (both 1177), were enormously influential.

Zhu Yuanzhang See HONGWU EMPEROR

Zhuangzi *or* **Chuang-tzu** \'jwäŋ-'dzə\ (369?–286 BC) Most significant early Chinese interpreter of TAOISM, and the purported author of the Taoist classic that bears his name. A minor official and a contemporary of MENCIUS, he drew on the sayings of LAOZI but took a broader perspective. He taught that enlightenment comes from the realization that everything is One, the TAO, but that the tao has no limitations or demarcations and whatever can be known or said of the tao is not the tao. He held that things should be allowed to follow their own course and that no situation should be valued over any other.

Zhukov \'zhü-ˌkȯf\, **Georgy (Konstantinovich)** (1896–1974) Soviet army commander in World War II. He joined the Red Army in the RUSSIAN CIVIL WAR and rose to become head of Soviet forces in Manchuria (1938–39). In World War II he was chief of staff of the Red Army and organized the defense of Leningrad and Moscow (1941). He directed the offensive that broke the siege in the Battle of STALINGRAD (1943) and was named a marshal of the Soviet Union. After helping win the Battle of KURSK, he directed the Soviet offensive through Belorussia (now Belarus) and commanded the final assault on Berlin (1945). After the war Zhukov's great popularity caused JOSEPH STALIN to assign him to obscure regional commands. After Stalin's death he was appointed minister of defense (1955) and attempted to make the army more autonomous, but opposition from NIKITA KHRUSHCHEV caused his dismissal in 1957.

Zia-ul-Haq \'zē-ə-əl-'häk\, **Mohammad** (1924–1988) President of Pakistan (1978–88). He served with the British in S.East Asia at the end of World War II; after Pakistan's independence, he held various staff and command appointments for 19 years. He became a major general in 1972 and army chief of staff in 1976. The following year he seized power from ZULFIKAR ALI BHUTTO, and in 1978 he assumed the presidency. After having the popular Bhutto executed in 1979, he tightened his grip on the government, suspending political parties and declaring martial law, and worked for the Islamization of Pakistan's political and cultural life. He died in an airplane crash.

Zia (ur-Rahman), Begum Khaleda *orig.* **Khaleda Majumdar** (born 1945) Politician who served as prime minister of Bangladesh from 1991 to 1996 and from 2001. In 1959 she married Zia ur-Rahman, a leader in the fight for the independence of Bangladesh, then part of India. Her husband became president of Bangladesh in 1977, and after his assassination in 1981 Zia became politically active. In 1984 she assumed the leadership of the Bangladesh Nationalist Party. Zia was arrested repeatedly during the dictatorship of Hossain Mohammad Ershad in the 1980s, but in 1991 she led the opposition to victory and became prime minister. Her overwhelming reelection victory in February 1996 was tainted by an opposition-led boycott of the voting, and, after a wave of strikes and protests, she resigned the following month. In 2001, Zia was again elected prime minister.

Ziegfeld \'zig-ˌfeld, 'zēg-ˌfeld\, **Florenz** (1869–1932) U.S. theatrical producer. Born in Chicago, he worked as a publicist for Sandow the strongman before turning to theatrical management in 1896, and his press releases promoting the French beauty Anna Held set a pattern of star-making publicity. In 1907 in New York he produced the first of his *Ziegfeld Follies*, REVUES which combined seminudity, pageantry, and comedy in a formula that he repeated successfully for 23 years. Under the slogan "Glorifying the American Girl," he made the revue an extravagant spectacle and developed such talent as WILL ROGERS and FANNY BRICE. He also produced the hit musical *Show Boat* (1927).

Ziegler \'tsē-glər\, **Karl** (1898–1973) German chemist. He held academic appointments at the Univs. of Frankfurt am Main, Heidelberg, and Halle, and in 1943 he became director of the Kaiser Wilhelm (later Max Planck) Institute. He was the first to explain the reactions involved in the synthesis of rubber (c. 1928). His most important work, in the 1950s, led to the discovery that certain catalysts permitted the fast polymerization of ethylene at atmospheric pressure to a linear polymer of high molecular weight having valuable plastic properties. His work formed the basis of nearly all later developments in the production of long-chain polymers of hydrocarbons from such olefins as ethylene and butadiene; the resulting products came into widespread use as plastics, fibers, rubbers, and films. He shared a 1963 Nobel Prize with Giulio Natta (1903–1979).

ziggurat \'zi-gə-ˌrät\ Pyramidal, stepped temple tower characteristic of the major cities of Mesopotamia between 2200 and 500 BC. It was built with a core of mud brick and an exterior covered with baked brick. It had no internal chambers and was usually square or rectangular. Some 25 ziggurats are known, located in SUMER, BABYLONIA, and ASSYRIA. The best-preserved ziggurat is at UR, and the largest is at ELAM. The legendary Tower of BABEL has been associated with the ziggurat of the great temple of MARDUK in BABYLON.

Zimbabwe \zim-'bä-bwā, zim-'bä-bwē\ *officially* **Republic of Zimbabwe** *formerly* **Rhodesia** Landlocked country, southern central Africa. Area: 150,873 sq mi (390,759 sq km). Population (2001 est.): 11,365,000. Capital: HARARE. The SHONA make up about 70% of the population, the NDEBELE about 16%, and whites about 2%. Languages: English (official); BANTU LANGUAGES of the Shona and Ndebele much more widely spoken. Religions: Christianity, indigenous beliefs, Islam. Currency: Zimbabwe dollar. A vast plateau sloping southwest–northeast, whose central part lies at an elevation of 4,000–5,000 ft (1,200–1,500 m), dominates Zimbabwe's landscape. The ZAMBEZI RIVER forms the country's northwestern boundary and contains VICTORIA FALLS, as well as a major dam (completed 1959) that created Lake Kariba, which, at more than 2,000 sq mi (5,200 sq km), is one of the world's largest man-made lakes. The LIMPOPO and SAVE river basins are in the southeast. Agricultural products, raising livestock, and working the mineral reserves, including gold, are all economically important. It is a republic with one legislative house; its head of state and government is the president. Remains of Stone Age cultures dating back 500,000 years have been found in the area. The first Bantu-speaking peoples reached it during the 5th–10th century AD, driving the Bushmen inhabitants into the desert. A second migration of Bantu-speakers began c. 1830. During this period the British and Afrikaners moved up from the south, and the area came under the administration of the British South Africa Co. 1889–1923. Called Southern Rhodesia (1911–64), it became a self-governing British colony in 1923. The colony united in 1953 with Nyasaland (Malawi) and Northern Rhodesia (Zambia) to form the Central African Federation of Rhodesia and Nyasaland. The federation dissolved in 1963, and Southern Rhodesia reverted to its former colonial status. In 1965 it issued a unilateral declaration of independence considered illegal by the British government, which led to economic sanctions against it. The country, which proclaimed itself a republic in 1970, called itself Rhodesia 1964–79. In 1979 it instituted limited majority rule and changed its name to Zimbabwe Rhodesia. It was granted independence by Britain in 1980 and became Zimbabwe. A multiparty system was established in 1990. During recent years, there has been increased tension between white farmers and black government leaders as the government has tried to introduce policies offering blacks redress for discrimination suffered during the nation's colonial days.

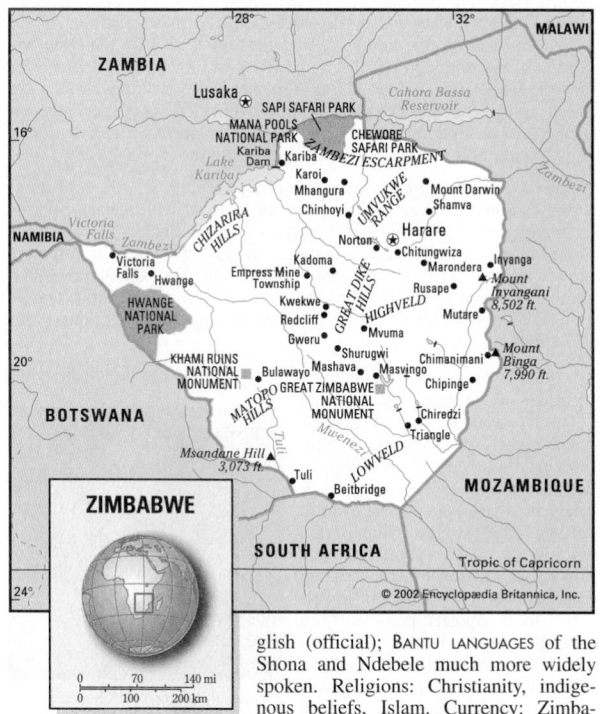

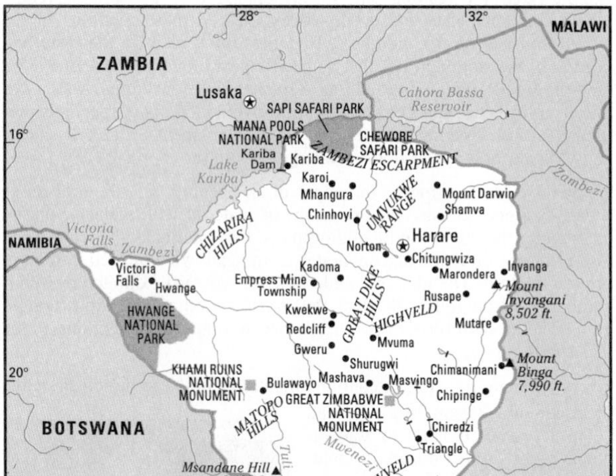

Zimbabwe *or* **Great Zimbabwe** Extensive stone ruins, South Africa. Located southeast of Nyanda, Zimbabwe, it is the largest of many such ruins in southern Africa. Extending over more than 60 acres (24 hectares), the ruins comprise a hilltop fortress and walls of stone monoliths. Its oldest parts date from the 8th century AD, though the site had been occupied for about 600 years before that. The center of a great inland empire ruled by the Karanga people who traded on the shores of the Indian Ocean, it flourished between the 11th and 15th century. The rediscovery of the ruins in 1867 attracted much archaeological research. A smaller and more recent group of ruins (Little Zimbabwe) is located about 8 mi (13 km) away.

Zimmermann \'tsi-mər-ˌmän\, **Arthur** (1864–1940) German diplomat. He became foreign minister of Germany in 1916. With Germany's decision to resume unrestricted submarine warfare, he planned to reduce the possible U.S. intervention in Europe by embroiling it in war with Mexico. On January 16, 1917, he sent a coded telegram to the German ambassador in Mexico, proposing a German-Mexican alliance that would allow Mexico to "reconquer her lost territory in Texas, New Mexico, and Arizona." It was intercepted and decoded by British naval intelligence, then published in the U.S. on March 1, causing public outrage. The "Zimmermann telegram" became a key factor in the U.S. declaration of war against Germany on April 6. Zimmermann was forced to resign in 1917.

zinc Metallic chemical ELEMENT, chemical symbol Zn, atomic number 30. Zinc is a bluish silver METAL, ductile when very pure but brittle otherwise. It forms BRASS (with COPPER) and many other ALLOYS. Its major use is in GALVANIZING iron, steel, and other metals. Zinc is an essential trace element, particularly in red blood cells; in snails, it corresponds to iron in the blood of vertebrates. Zinc oxide is used as a PIGMENT, ultraviolet light absorber (to prevent sunburn), dietary supplement and seed treatment, and photoconductor. Zinc's many other compounds (in which it has VALENCE 2 or, rarely, 1) are used in industrial and consumer applications, including as pesticides, pigments, mordants (see DYE), fluxes, and wood preservatives.

zincblende See SPHALERITE

Zinder, Norton (David) (born 1928) U.S. biologist. Born in New York City, he received his PhD from the University of Wisconsin. He discovered genetic transduction (the transfer of genes from one type of microorganism to another by an agent such as a bacteriophage) in salmonella bacteria. Using this transduction, later experimenters were able to show that bacterial genes affecting certain physiological processes were grouped together in what are now known as operons. His experiments also led to the discovery of the only known bacteriophage containing RNA as its genetic material.

Zinkernagel \'tsiŋ-kər-ˌnä-gəl, *Engl* 'ziŋ-kər-ˌnā-gəl\, **Rolf M(artin)** (born 1944) Swiss immunologist and pathologist. He received his PhD from the Australian National University Studying T CELLS in mice infected with a meningitis virus, he and PETER DOHERTY found that those from one infected mouse would destroy infected cells from another only if the mice belonged to the same genetic strain: no immune response occurs unless the T cells recognize two signals, those of the virus and those identifying the cell as "self." In 1992 he became head of the University of Zurich's Institute of Experimental Immunology. In 1996 he and Doherty shared a Nobel Prize.

Zinnemann \'zin-ə-mən\, **Fred** (1907–1997) Austrian-U.S. film director. After studying law in his native Vienna, he learned cinematography in Paris and worked in Berlin. In 1929 he moved to Hollywood, and in 1934 he codirected his first feature, *The Wave,* which was initially followed largely by documentaries and short subjects. His feature films, many of which focused on a moral crisis, include *The Search* (1948), *The Men* (1950), the classic western *High Noon* (1952), *From Here to Eternity* (1953, Academy Award), *Oklahoma!* (1955), *The Nun's Story* (1959), *A Man for All Seasons* (1966, Academy Award), *The Day of the Jackal* (1973), and *Julia* (1977).

zinnia Any of about 22 species of herbaceous plants and shrubs that make up the genus *Zinnia* (COMPOSITE FAMILY), native mainly to North America. Where native, they are perennial; elsewhere they are annual. Zinnias have stiff, hairy stems and oval or lance-shaped leaves arranged opposite each other and often clasping the stem. The numerous garden varieties grown for their showy, solitary flowers come from the species *Z. elegans.* Garden zinnias range from dwarf compact plants (less than 1 ft, or 30 cm, tall), with flowers 1 in. (2.5 cm) in diameter, to giant forms (up to 3 ft, or 1 m, tall), with flowers up to 6 in. (15 cm) across.

Zinnia elegans.
KENNETH AND BRENDA FORMANEK

Zinovyev \zyi-'nȯf-yif\, **Grigory (Yevseyevich)** *orig.* **Ovsel Gershon Aronov Radomyslsky** (1883–1936) Soviet politician. An early activist with the Bolsheviks (1903), he became VLADIMIR ILICH LENIN's close collaborator in exile (1909–17) and in the RUSSIAN REVOLUTION OF 1917, helping win public support for the Bolshevik regime. By 1921 he was head of the Petrograd (St. Petersburg) soviet and a member of the Politburo. He was chairman of the Comintern 1919–26, and helped JOSEPH STALIN oust LEON TROTSKY. He was removed from power by Stalin in 1926. In 1935 he was arrested for conspiracy and sentenced to prison; the next year he was retried in the first of the PURGE TRIALS and executed.

Zinsser, Hans (1878–1940) U.S. bacteriologist and epidemiologist. Born in New York City, he taught principally at the Columbia (1913–23) and Harvard (1923–40) medical schools. He isolated the bacteria that cause the European type of typhus, developed the first antityphus vaccine, and, with colleagues, found a way to mass-produce it. He recognized that cases of mild typhuslike symptoms in lice-free persons are recurrences after a latent period (Brill-Zinsser disease). His best-known book, *Rats, Lice and History* (1935), recounts the effects of typhus on mankind (he believed disease had destroyed more civilizations than war) and efforts to eradicate it.

Zion Easternmost of the two hills of ancient JERUSALEM, where DAVID established his royal capital. In the OLD TESTAMENT, the name Zion frequently refers to Jerusalem as a whole; it is overwhelmingly a poetic and prophetic designation. Mount Zion is the place where Yahweh (God) dwells and is the scene of his messianic salvation. The name came to mean the Jewish homeland, symbolic of Judaism or Jewish national aspirations, and thus was the source of the term ZIONISM. Though the name is rare in the NEW TESTAMENT, it has been frequently used in Christian literature and hymns as a designation for the heavenly city or for the earthly city of Christian faith and fraternity.

Zion National Park National park, southwestern Utah. It covers an area of 229 sq mi (593 sq km); its principal feature is Zion Canyon, which was named by the MORMONS who discovered it in 1858. Part of the area was first set aside as the Mukuntuweap National Monument in 1909. Enlarged and renamed Zion National Monument in 1918, it was established as a national park in 1919. Zion Canyon was carved by the Virgin River and is about 15 mi (24 km) long and 0.5 mi (0.8 km) deep. Rocky domes dot the canyon walls, which contain an abundant fossil record. Excavation has yielded evidence that prehistoric peoples once inhabited the area.

Zionism \'zī-ə-ˌni-zəm\ Jewish nationalism movement with the goal of establishing a Jewish state in Palestine. In the 16th–17th century, a number of "messiahs" tried to persuade the Jews to return to Palestine, but by the late 18th century interest had largely faded. POGROMS in Eastern Europe led to formation of the "Lovers of Zion," which promoted the settlement of Jewish farmers and artisans in Palestine. In the face of persistent anti-Semitism, THEODOR HERZL advocated a Jewish state in Palestine. He held the first Zionist Congress in Basel in 1897. After World War I the movement picked up momentum with the issuing of the BALFOUR DECLARATION. The Jewish population in Palestine increased from 90,000 in 1914 to 238,000 in 1933. The Arab population resisted Zionism, and the British tried unsuccessfully to reconcile Jewish and Arab demands. Zionism achieved its goal with the creation of Israel in 1948. See also ALLIANCE ISRAÉLITE UNIVERSELLE, DAVID BEN-GURION, HAGANA, VLADIMIR JABOTINSKY, IRGUN ZVAI LEUMI.

Zionist church Any of several prophet-healing groups in southern Africa that arose early in the 20th century from the fusion of African culture with the Christian message brought by U.S. Protestant missionaries. Their common features include: origination from a mandate received by a PROPHET in a dream or vision; a chieflike leader who is succeeded by his son and who is occasionally regarded as a MESSIAH; healing through CONFESSION, repeated BAPTISM, purification rites, and EXORCISM; revelation and power from the HOLY SPIRIT through prophetic utterances and pentecostal phenomena; Africanized worship characterized by singing, dancing, clapping, and drumming; and repudiation of traditional magic, medicines, DIVINATION, and ancestor cults, though these are often replaced with Christianized equivalents.

zip code System of postal-zone codes (zip stands for "zone improvement plan") introduced in the U.S. in 1963 to improve mail delivery and exploit electronic reading and sorting capabilities. The original code, which corresponds to the postal codes used in most countries in the world, consists of five numbers. The first three identify the state and portion of the state, the last two a specific post office or zone. In 1983 a nine-digit code (created by adding a hyphen and four digits) was introduced to further speed delivery; the first two added digits specify a particular "sector," the last two an even smaller "segment" (e.g., one side of a city block, or a single floor in a large building).

zipper Device for binding the edges of an opening, as on a garment or a bag. A zipper consists of two strips of material with metal or plastic teeth along the edges, and a sliding piece that interlocks the teeth when moved in one direction and separates them again when moved in the opposite direction. The idea of a slide fastener was first exhibited by Whitcomb L. Judson (died 1909) at the World's Columbian Exposition of 1893. The modern form of the zipper began to appear on clothing in the late 1920s.

zircon Silicate mineral, zirconium silicate, $ZrSiO_4$, the principal source of zirconium. Zircon is widespread as an accessory mineral in acid igneous rocks; it also occurs in metamorphic rocks and, fairly often, in detrital deposits. It occurs in beach sands in many parts of the world, particularly Australia, India, Brazil, and Florida, and is a common heavy mineral in sedimentary rocks. Gem varieties occur in stream gravels and detrital deposits, particularly in Indochina and Sri Lanka, but also in Myanmar, Australia, and New Zealand. Zircon forms an important part of the syenite of southern Norway and occurs in large crystals in Quebec.

Zircon with quartz from Cheyenne Canyon, Colorado.
BY COURTESY OF THE FIELD MUSEUM OF NATURAL HISTORY, CHICAGO; PHOTOGRAPH, JOHN H. GERARD—EB INC.

zirconium Metallic chemical ELEMENT, one of the TRANSITION ELEMENTS, chemical symbol Zr, atomic number 40. The METAL is hard and brittle when impure, soft and ductile when highly purified. It is relatively abundant, occurring as zircon (which can be a semiprecious gemstone) and baddeleyite. Highly transparent to NEUTRONS, zirconium became important in the 1940s in NUCLEAR-ENERGY applications. Other uses are in ALLOYS, fireworks, and flashbulbs and as a scavenger for oxygen and other gases. Its compounds, in most of which it has VALENCE 4, are important industrial materials. Zirconia (the OXIDE) is used in piezoelectric crystals (see PIEZOELECTRICITY), high-frequency induction coils, colored glazes and glasses, heat-resistant fibers, and preparations to cure the rash of poison ivy.

zither Plucked or struck STRINGED INSTRUMENT with a shallow soundbox. The common Austrian zither is roughly rectangular and has 30–40 strings; it is placed on the player's knees or on a table. Several melody strings pass over a fretted fingerboard; the player's left hand stops these strings, while the right hand plucks with the fingers and a thumb plectrum. The larger zither family includes such instruments as the AEOLIAN HARP, autoharp, cimbalom, DULCIMER, KOTO, and even the CLAVICHORD, HARPSICHORD, and PIANO.

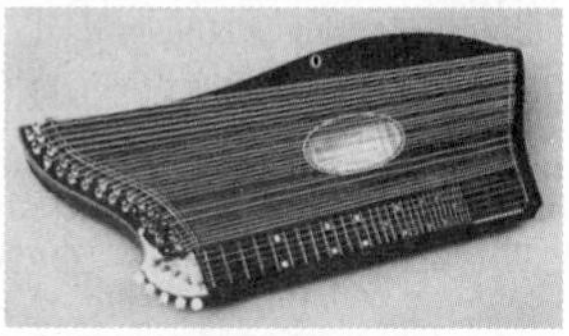

Zither made in Vienna.

Zoan See TANIS

zodiac \'zō-dē-ˌak\ Belt around the heavens extending about 9° on either side of the ECLIPTIC. The orbits of the moon and the major planets (except Pluto) lie entirely within the zodiac. In ASTROLOGY, each of 12 CONSTELLATIONS along this circle is considered to occupy 1/12 (30°) of it. The positions of the sun and planets when a person is born and their motion through these constellations are said to exert influence on his or her life, though precession of the EQUINOXES has shifted the constellations eastward and the sun no longer passes through them on the traditional dates: ARIES, the ram (March 21–April 19); TAURUS, the bull (April 20–May 20); GEMINI, the twins (May 21–June 21); CANCER, the crab (June 22–July 22); LEO, the lion (July 23–August 22); VIRGO, the virgin (August 23–September 22); LIBRA, the balance (September 23–October 23); Scorpius (see SCORPIO), the scorpion (October 24–November 21); SAGITTARIUS, the archer (November 22–December 21); Capricornus (see CAPRICORN), the goat (December 22–January 19); AQUARIUS, the water bearer (January 20–February 18); PISCES, the fish (February 19–March 20).

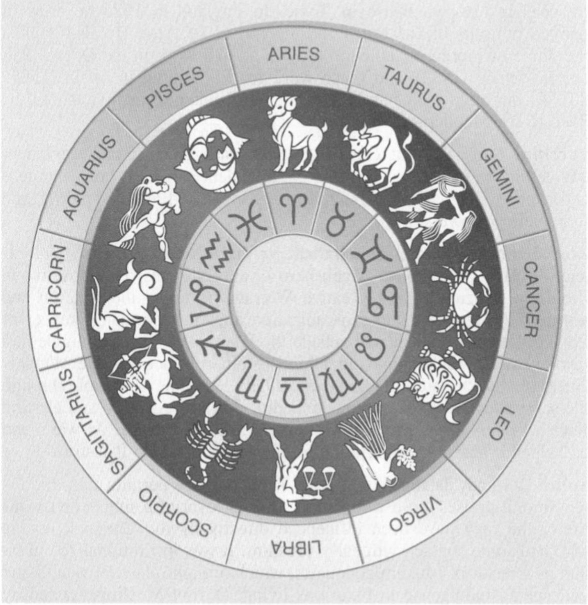

The astrological images and symbols of the zodiac.

zodiacal light \zō-'dī-ə-kəl\ Band of very faint light in the night sky, thought to be sunlight reflected from dust and meteoroids (see METEOR), mostly in the plane of the ZODIAC, or ECLIPTIC. Seen in the west after twilight and in the east before dawn, it is most clearly visible in the tropics, where the ecliptic is approximately perpendicular to the horizon. In midnorthern latitudes, it is best seen evenings in February and March and mornings in September and October (vice versa in midsouthern latitudes). The light can be followed visually to a point about 90° from the sun. It continues to the region opposite the sun, where a slight enhancement, the GEGENSCHEIN, is visible.

Zoe \'zō-ē\ (978?–1050) Byzantine empress. The daughter of Constantine VIII, she married ROMANUS III ARGYRUS in 1028. He died in 1034, perhaps poisoned by her, and she married her lover and chamberlain, who became Michael IV. After his death in 1041, his successor, Michael V, banished Zoe to a convent; she was recalled by public outcry and Michael was deposed, blinded, and exiled (1042). Zoe and her sister became uneasy corulers, and she married CONSTANTINE IX MONOMACHUS to secure her throne. Her court was known for its intellectual brilliance. The SCHISM OF 1054 followed soon after her death.

Zog I *Albanian* **Ahmed Bey Zogu** (1895–1961) President (1925–28) and king of Albania (1928–39). After serving in the Austrian army in World War I, he became a leader of Albania's reformist Popular Party. He held ministerial posts in the government (1920–24) and was elected head of the Albanian republic in 1925. Proclaimed king in 1928, he pursued a policy of close collaboration with Italy. Unable to resist BENITO MUSSOLINI's increasing control of the country's finances and army, he was forced into exile when Italy invaded and made Albania a protectorate (1939). After World War II Albania became a communist republic, and Zog formally abdicated in 1946.

Zola \'zō-lə, *French* zō-'lä\, **Émile (-Édouard-Charles-Antoine)** (1840–1902) French novelist and critic, the founder of NATURALISM in literature. Raised in straitened circumstances, Zola worked at a Paris publishing house for several years during the 1860s while establishing himself as a writer. In the gruesome novel *Thérèse Raquin* (1867), he put his "scientific" theories of the determination of character by heredity and environment into practice for the first time. In 1870 he began the ambitious project for which he is best known, the *Rougon-Macquart Cycle* (1871–93), a sequence of 20 novels documenting French life through the lives of the violent Rougon family and the passive Macquarts. It includes *L'assommoir* (1877), a study of alcoholism that is among his most successful and popular novels; *Nana* (1880); *Germinal* (1885), his masterpiece; and *La bête humaine* (1890). Among his other works are two shorter novel cycles and treatises explaining his theories on art, including *The Experimental Novel* (1880). He is also notable for his involvement in the ALFRED DREYFUS affair, especially for his open letter, "J'accuse" (1898), denouncing the French army general staff. He died under suspicious circumstances, overcome by carbon-monoxide fumes in his sleep.

Zollverein \'tsȯl-ver-ˌīn\ (German: "Customs Union") Free-trade area throughout much of Germany established in 1834 under Prussian leadership. The customs union developed from the 1818 Prussian tariff law that abolished internal customs dues and the customs union set up in 1828 in southern Germany by Bavaria and Württemberg. By 1834 other German states had joined, for a total of 18 members; more joined in subsequent years. The Zollverein represented an important step in German unification. See also FRIEDRICH LIST.

zombie In VODUN, a dead person who is revived after burial and compelled to do the bidding of the reviver, including criminal acts and heavy manual labor. It is believed that actual zombies are living persons under the influence of powerful drugs, including burundanga (a drug reportedly used by Colombian criminals) and drugs derived from poisonous toads and puffer fish.

Zonca \'tsȯŋ-kä\, **Vittorio** (1568–1603) Italian mechanical engineer. His *New Theater of Machines and Buildings* (1607) showed designs for numerous practical machines and mechanisms, including a water mill running silk-spinners, a water-powered grain mill operated on a boat moored in a river, and a barbecue spit turned by gears and a windmill.

zone melting Any of a group of techniques used to purify an element or a compound or to control its composition by melting a short region (called a zone) and causing this liquid zone to travel slowly through a relatively long INGOT, or charge, of the solid. In zone refining, the most important of the zone-melting techniques, a solid is refined by multiple molten zones being passed through it in one direction. Each zone carries a fraction of the impurities to the end of the solid charge, thereby purifying the remainder. Zone refining is particularly important as a method of purifying crystals, especially for use in SEMICONDUCTOR devices.

zone of avoidance See zone of AVOIDANCE

zoning Legislative method of controlling land use by regulating such considerations as the type of buildings that may be erected and the population density. German and Swedish cities first applied zoning regulations in the late 19th century to address the problems of urban congestion and building height. The earliest U.S. zoning ordinances date from the beginning of the 20th century and were motivated by the need to regulate the location of commercial and industrial activities. New York City's 1916 ordinance was the first comprehensive zoning law; it and other early regulations were designed to protect property values and preserve light and air. Modern zoning regulations divide land use into three types: residential, commercial, and industrial. Within each designation, more specific aspects of development (e.g., building proximity, height, type) are also determined. Zoning is often used to maintain the distinctive character of a town or city; an adverse consequence of such zoning is economic segregation. The U.S. Supreme Court ruled against such zoning in 1977 when it declared the zoning regulations of one Chicago suburb discriminatory.

zoo *or* **zoological garden** Place where wild and sometimes domesticated animals are exhibited in captivity. Marine zoological gardens are called aquariums. The first zoos were perhaps associated with domestication. Pigeons were kept in captivity as early as 4500 BC; other animals (e.g., elephants and antelopes) have also been kept in captivity since antiquity. Animal collections were kept by CHARLEMAGNE and other European monarchs. HERNAN CORTES described a zoo in Mexico (1519) so large that it required a staff of 300. Modern zookeeping started in 1752 with the founding of the Imperial Menagerie at Vienna's Schönbrunn Palace. Open-range zoos were first established in the early 1930s, some so large that visitors drive through in cars, as on an African safari. There are now more than 1,000 animal collections (incl., in the U.S., the BRONX ZOO and SAN DIEGO ZOO) open to the public throughout the world.

zoology Branch of biology concerned with members of the animal kingdom and with animal life in general. The science originated in the works of HIPPOCRATES, ARISTOTLE, and PLINY. The contributions of individuals such as WILLIAM HARVEY (the circulation of blood), CAROLUS LINNAEUS (system of nomenclature), G.-L. de BUFFON (natural history), GEORGES CUVIER (comparative anatomy), and CLAUDE BERNARD (homeostasis) greatly advanced the field. The 1859 publication of CHARLES DARWIN's *On the Origin of Species by Means of Natural Selection* was a major turning point. Since that time, the study of genetics has become essential in zoological studies.

zooplankton \,zō-ə-'plaŋk-tən\ Small floating or weakly swimming animals that drift with water currents and, with PHYTOPLANKTON, make up the planktonic food supply on which almost all oceanic organisms ultimately depend (see PLANKTON). Included are many animals, from single-celled radiolarians to the eggs or larvae of herrings, crabs, and lobsters. Permanent plankton (holoplankton), such as PROTOZOANS and COPEPODS, spend their lives as plankton. Temporary plankton (meroplankton), such as young starfish, clams, worms, and other bottom-dwelling animals, live and feed as plankton until they become adults.

Zorn, John (born 1953) U.S. saxophonist and composer, one of the most eclectic musicians in the avant-garde of JAZZ. Born in New York City, he has worked there since. He exhibits influences from the most diverse elements of music and culture: free jazz, KLEZMER MUSIC, PUNK ROCK, cartoon music, film scores, and contemporary classical music. His game pieces involve rules, understood by his musicians and cued by hand signals, which determine the flow of the music, placing emphasis on the process rather than the result of the performance.

Zoroaster \'zōr-ə-,was-tər\ *or* **Zarathustra** \,zar-ə-'thüsh-trə\ (628?–551? BC) Iranian religious reformer and prophet, founder of ZOROASTRIANISM AND PARSIISM. He was a priest in his tribal religion, with which he eventually became disillusioned. Having received a vision, he began teaching that AHURA MAZDA was the highest god, who alone was worthy of worship, a concept that went against the polytheism of Iranian religion. He forbade the orgiastic rites that accompanied animal sacrifice, common in his time, but preserved the ancient cult of fire worship. After converting a king called Vishtaspa to his teachings, Zoroaster remained at the royal court. He became the subject of legends and a model for various occupations. The Greeks regarded him as a philosopher, mathematician, astrologer, or magician; Jews and Christians viewed him as an astrologer, magician, prophet, or heretic.

Zoroastrianism and Parsiism Ancient religion that originated in Iran based on the teachings of ZOROASTER. Founded in the 6th century BC, it influenced the monotheistic religions Judaism, Christianity, and Islam. It rejects POLYTHEISM, accepting only one supreme god, AHURA MAZDA. In early Zoroastrianism, the struggle between good and evil was seen as an eternal rivalry between Ahura Mazda's twin sons, Spenta Mainyu (good) and Angra Mainyu (evil). Later Zoroastrian cosmology made the rivalry between Ahura Mazda himself (by then called Ormazd) and Ahriman. This later cosmology identifies four periods of history; the last began with the birth of Zoroaster. Zoroastrian practice includes an initiation ceremony and various rituals of purification intended to ward off evil spirits. Fire worship, a carryover from an earlier religion, survives in the sacred fire that must be kept burning continually and must be fed at least five times a day. The chief ceremony involves a sacrifice of haoma, a sacred liquor, accompanied by recitation of large parts of the AVESTA, the primary scripture. Zoroastrianism enjoyed status as an official religion at various times before the advent of ISLAM, but Zoroastrians were persecuted in the 8th–10th century, and some left Iran to settle in India. By the 19th century these Indian Zoroastrians, or PARSIS, were noted for their wealth and education. The small group of Zoroastrians remaining in Iran are known as the GABARS.

Zorrilla (y Moral) \thōr-'rēl-yä\, **José** (1817–1893) Spanish poet and dramatist. Zorrilla first gained notice in 1837 with his recitation of an elegy at the funeral of the satirist Mariano José de Larra. The major figure of the nationalist wing of the Spanish Romantic movement, he made his name with verse *leyendas* ("legends") about remote times and places, notably in *Cantos del trovador* (1841). His greatest success was *Don Juan Tenorio* (1844), the most popular play of 19th-century Spain. His works are considered quintessentially Spanish in style and tone. In 1889 he was crowned the national poet.

Zuccaro \'tsü-kär-ō\, **Federico** *or* **Federico Zuccari** \'tsü-kär-ē\ (1540/42–1609) Italian painter and art theorist. In 1565 he worked in Florence with GIORGIO VASARI. He codified the theory of MANNERISM in *The Idea of Painters, Sculptors, and Architects* (1607) and in a series of frescoes in his own house in Rome. In England in 1575 he drew or painted portraits of ELIZABETH I and the earl of LEICESTER. He also painted the dome of Florence Cathedral (1574), a large work in the Doges' Palace in Venice (1582), and much work for El Escorial in Spain (1585–88). At one time the central figure of the Roman Mannerist school, he lived to see Mannerism become extinct.

zucchini Subspecies of *Cucurbita pepo*, dark green elongate summer SQUASH in the GOURD family, of great abundance in U.S. home gardens and supermarkets. The creeping vine has five-lobed leaves, tendrils, and large yellow flowers.

Zuckerman \'tsu̇k-ər-,män\, **Itzhak** *or* **Yizhak Cukierman** \'tsu̇k-ər-,män\ (1915–1981) Polish-Israeli hero of anti-Nazi resistance. Active in Zionist organizations in his native Warsaw, he urged the creation and arming of a Jewish defense organization after the German takeover of Poland. He used his contacts outside the Warsaw Ghetto to smuggle in a few arms. He took command after the other leaders of the WARSAW GHETTO UPRISING were killed, and eventually led some 75 people through the sewers to safety. He continued leading Jewish resistance and alerting Jewish leaders elsewhere to the situation in Nazi Europe. At war's end he helped organize transportation for Jewish refugees to Palestine.

zuhd \'zu̇-həd\ Islamic ASCETICISM. Though ISLAM permits unforbidden pleasure, it praises those who shun luxury in favor of a simple and pious life. Zuhd may have been influenced directly by the Christian HERMITS who had some contact with early Muslims. It was institutionalized in Islam as a result of Muslim conquests, which brought material wealth and widespread indulgence in luxurious living. Devout Muslims reacted by calling for a return to the way of life of MUHAMMAD, who spent long periods in solitary vigil, fasting and praying. See also SUFISM.

Zuider Zee \ˌzī-dər-ˈzā, ˌzī-dər-ˈzē\ Former inlet of the NORTH SEA, northern coast of the Netherlands. From the 13th to the 20th century, it penetrated the Netherlands and occupied some 2,000 sq mi (5,000 sq km); it was separated from the NORTH SEA by an arc of former sandflats that are now the West Frisian Islands. Frisian peoples inhabited the sandflats from c. AD 400 and built the first seaworks, considered engineering marvels, to stem rising sea levels. Controlling water levels within the dikes developed into the reclamation of lowland (polders) from the water. In 1927–32 a dam 19 mi (30 km) long was built across the Zuider Zee, separating it into the Waddenzee and the IJsselmeer. By the early 1980s four polders (of five proposed), largely agricultural land, had been created.

Zulu Nguni-speaking people living in KwaZulu/Natal province in South Africa. Numbering about 9.5 million, they are South Africa's largest ethnic group. Traditionally grain farmers, they also kept large herds of cattle. European settlers wrested grazing and water resources from the Zulu in prolonged warfare during the 19th century; with much of their wealth lost, modern Zulu depend largely on wage labor on farms owned by whites or work in the cities. The Zulu provide the main support for the INKATHA FREEDOM PARTY. Many Zulu belong to independent or separatist African churches, though the traditional religion, based on ancestor worship and belief in a creator-god, witches, and sorcerers, remains strong. See also SHAKA.

Zululand Historical region, eastern Republic of South Africa. It was the home of the ZULU people when Chief SHAKA established dominance over what is now KwaZulu-Natal. His state fought the Boers in the 1840s; it later lost parts of its territory to them. The British moved into nearby NATAL and annexed it in 1843. The Zulus resisted British rule in 1878, but were overcome in 1879. The British made Zululand a crown colony in 1887 and annexed it to Natal in 1897. Under the APARTHEID system, a Bantu Homeland named KwaZulu, composed of parts of the historical Zululand, was established for the Zulus in the 1970s. With the abolition of the apartheid system, KwaZulu in 1994 was reincorporated into Natal province, which was renamed KwaZulu-Natal.

Zuni \ˈzü-nē\ PUEBLO INDIAN people of western central New Mexico. Their origin and early history are uncertain. When first encountered by 16th-century Spanish explorers, they were living in seven separate towns (the fabled Seven Cities of CÍBOLA); under the Spaniards they were crowded into a single PUEBLO. The traditional occupation was corn farming; basketry and pottery were also well developed. Religious life centered on gods or spirits called KACHINAS. Today the Zuni number about 6,000.

Zunz \ˈtsu̇nts\, **Leopold** *Hebrew* **Yom-Tob Lippmann** (1794–1886) German historian of Jewish literature. After taking his doctorate at Halle, he spent much of his life in a precarious struggle with poverty. Following the publication of his seminal work, *On Rabbinic Literature* (1818), he started (1819) the movement called Wissenschaft des Judentums ("Science of Judaism"), which stressed the analysis of Jewish literature and culture with the tools of modern scholarship. His *On History and Literature* (1845) places Jewish literary activity in the context of European literature and politics. Zunz is often considered the greatest Jewish scholar of the 19th century.

Zuo zhuan *or* **Tso chuan** \ˈdzwȯ-ˈjwän\ Ancient commentary on the *CHUNQIU* ("Spring and Autumn Annals"). It provides extensive narrative accounts and background materials concerning events covered in the *Chunqiu,* as well as authentic historical documents and written evidence of the philosophical schools of the time. Finally, it provides a comprehensive account of the principal political, social, and military events of the period. It was once believed to have been written by Zuo, an ancient historian about whom virtually nothing is known, but modern scholarship attributes it to an anonymous author of the period 475–221 BC.

Zurbarán \ˌzu̇r-bə-ˈrän\, **Francisco** (1598–1664) Spanish painter. He was apprenticed in 1614 to a painter in Seville, where he lived until 1658, when he moved to Madrid. He had a few royal commissions but remained throughout his life a provincial painter of religious pictures. His apostles, saints, and monks are painted with almost sculptural modeling, and his emphasis on the minutiae of their dress lends verisimilitude to their miracles, visions, and ecstasies. This distinctive combination of naturalism with religious sensibility conforms to the guidelines for Counter-Reformation artists outlined by the Council of Trent. He had many commissions from monasteries and churches throughout southern Spain, and many of his works were sent to Lima, Peru. His late devotional paintings show the influence of BARTOLOME ESTEBAN MURILLO.

Zurich \ˈzu̇r-ik\ *or* **Zürich** \ˈtsue̅-rik̲\ City (pop., 1996 est.: 344,000), Switzerland. Located at the northwestern end of Lake ZURICH, the site was occupied first by prehistoric lake dwellers and later by the Celtic Helvetii before the Romans conquered the area c. 58 BC. It subsequently was held by the Alamanni, then the FRANKS. It grew as a trade center, and in 1218 it became a free imperial city; in 1351 it joined the Swiss Confederation. Under the leadership of HULDRYCH ZWINGLI it became the center of the Swiss reformation in the 16th century. Attracting refugees from the COUNTER-REFORMATION, it established a liberal democratic order during the 1830s. Long an industrial center, and Switzerland's largest city, it is also an important financial center and a major tourist destination.

Zurich, Lake *or* **Zürichsee** \ˈtsue̅-rik̲-ˌzā\ Lake, northern central Switzerland. Extending southeast from the city of ZURICH, it lies at an altitude of 1,332 ft (406 m) and has an area of about 34 sq mi (88 sq km). It is 18 mi (29 km) long and has a maximum depth of 469 ft (143 m). The Linth River flows into it and emerges as the Limmat.

Zuse \ˈtsü-zə\, **Konrad** (1910–1995) German engineer. In 1941 he constructed the first fully operational program-controlled electromechanical binary calculating machine, or DIGITAL COMPUTER, called the Z3. The machine predated HOWARD H. AIKEN Harvard Mark I but was destroyed by bombing during World War II. In 1945 he designed Plankalkül, one of the first attempts at a high-level PROGRAMMING LANGUAGE, which was never implemented. In his later years, he became an accomplished abstract artist.

Zweig \ˈtsvīk\, **Arnold** (1887–1968) German writer. A Jew, Zweig was exiled from Germany by the Nazis in 1933 and lived as an émigré in Palestine until returning to East Germany in 1948. He is best known for the novel *The Case of Sergeant Grischa* (1927), which depicts the German army in World War I through a Russian prisoner's tragic encounter with the Prussian military bureaucracy. Later works, including *Education Before Verdun* (1935) and *The Crowning of a King* (1937), follow characters introduced in *Sergeant Grischa.*

Zweig, Stefan (1881–1942) German writer. His interest in psychology and the teachings of SIGMUND FREUD is reflected in his subtle portrayal of character. His essays include studies of HONORE DE BALZAC, CHARLES DICKENS, and FYODOR DOSTOYEVSKY, in *Three Masters* (1920); and FRIEDRICH HOLDERLIN, HEINRICH KLEIST, and FRIEDRICH NIETZSCHE, in *Master Builders* (1925). He achieved popularity with *The Tide of Fortune* (1928), five historical portraits in miniature. He also wrote biographies, poetry, short stories, dramas, and a novel. Driven into exile by the Nazis in 1934, Zweig and his wife went to England and then Brazil, where, lonely and disillusioned, they committed suicide.

Zwicky \ˈtsvik-ē\, **Fritz** (1898–1974) Swiss-U.S. astronomer and physicist. He received his PhD from the Swiss Federal Institute of Technology and moved to the U.S. in 1925 to work at Caltech, where he remained until 1972. In 1934, with Walter Baade (1893–1960), he proposed that SUPERNOVAS are a class of stellar explosion completely different from NOVAS. He conducted an extensive search of neighboring galaxies for supernovas, and discovered 18; only about 12 had been recorded previously in the entire history of astronomy. In the years 1943–46 he developed some of the earliest jet engines.

Zwilich \ˈzwi-lik\, **Ellen Taaffe** (born 1939) U.S. composer. Born in Miami, she was trained as a violinist, studying with Ivan Galamian (1903–1981). She studied composition with E. CARTER and R. SESSIONS at Juilliard. Her straightforward and expressive music, written in 20th-century tonality, has won wide recognition; her Symphony no. 1 (1983) was the first composition by a woman to win a Pulitzer Prize.

Zwinger \ˈtsviŋ-ər\ ROCOCO-STYLE building complex (1709–32), on the southern bank of the Elbe in Dresden, Germany, designed by Matthäus Daniel Pöppelmann (1662–1736). Originally planned as the forecourt for a castle, it is considered one of the finest works of its style in the world. It comprises one- and two-story buildings surrounding an immense square court. Its festive air is accented by bold, richly sculpted and ornamented facades and gates and by dramatic contrasts between its low arcades and high pavilions.

Zwingli \ˈzwiŋ-lē, *German* ˈtsviŋ-lē\, **Huldrych** (1484–1531) Major reformer in the Protestant REFORMATION in Switzerland. Educated in Vienna and Basel, he was ordained a priest in 1506. Influenced by the ideas of his contemporary, MARTIN LUTHER, he began preaching reformist ideas in Zurich in 1518 and became increasingly active in challenging the ritualism, decadence, and hierarchy of the Roman Catholic church. The main contentions of his *67 Articles* (1523) were adopted by most priests in Zurich. As his movement spread, he made a number of unorthodox assertions, declaring that Jesus alone is head of the church, that the mass is an affront to Christ, and that there is no biblical foundation for the intercession of the dead or for purgatory. He also rejected the notions of transubstantiation (which put him at odds with Luther) and priestly celibacy. He was killed in a battle between Protestants and Catholics while serving as an army chaplain.

Zwingli, detail of an oil portrait by Hans Asper, 1531; in the Kunstmuseum Winterthur, Switz.

Zworykin \ˈzvȯrʸ-kyin, *Engl* ˈzwȯr-i-kən\, **Vladimir (Kosma)** (1889–1982) Russian-U.S. electronic engineer and inventor. He emigrated to the U.S. in 1919. While with Westinghouse Electric Corp. (1920–29), he filed patent applications for his inventions of the iconoscope (a TV transmission tube, 1923) and the kinescope (TV receiver, 1924), which formed the first all-electronic TV system. In 1929 he became director of electronic research at RCA, where he developed a color TV system (patented 1928). His electron image tube, sensitive to infrared light, was the basis for devices first used in World War II for seeing in the dark.

zydeco \ˈzī-də-ˌkō\ Form of Creole dance music from southern Louisiana, with roots in 19th-century French (see CAJUN), African, and Caribbean styles. The name comes from the song title "Les haricots sont pas salés." The music usually features guitar, accordion, and washboard played to a driving beat. It became widely popular in the 1980s through the performances of Clifton Chenier, Queen Ida, Buckwheat Zydeco, Boozoo Chavis, Beau Jocque, and others.

zymogen \ˈzī-mə-jən\ *or* **proenzyme** Any of a class of PROTEINS that are secreted by cells and are inactive precursors of ENZYMES. Transformation into active enzymes occurs as one or more PEPTIDE bonds in the zymogen are cleaved. Examples include trypsinogen and chymotrypsinogen, secreted by the PANCREAS and converted by PROTEOLYSIS in the SMALL INTESTINE into the active enzymes trypsin and chymotrypsin; and numerous COAGULATION factors.

W X Y Z

Encyclopædia Britannica

Merriam-Webster

The following is the editorial staff of Merriam-Webster that contributed to *Merriam-Webster's Collegiate Encyclopedia:*

Editor: Mark A. Stevens; ***Associate Editors:*** Jocelyn White Franklin, Francesca M. Forrest, Kathleen M. Doherty; ***Art Coordinator:*** Lynn Stowe Tomb; ***Pronunciation Editor:*** David B. Justice

Merriam-Webster Consultants: Anne Agur (University of Toronto), Robert Audi (University of Nebraska), Carol Berkin (Baruch College, City University of New York), Paul Bottino (University of Maryland), Brian Burrell (University of Massachusetts), Louis P. Cain (Loyola University Chicago, Northwestern University), Francis D. K. Ching (University of Washington), Dale F. Eickelman (Dartmouth College), John A. Garraty (Columbia University [emeritus]), Robert B. Gordon (Yale University), James J. Jenkins (University of South Florida), John W. Johnson (University of Northern Iowa), Daniel Kaiser (Sarah Lawrence College), Cornelis Klein (University of New Mexico), Joel Krieger (Wellesley College), James M. Powell (Syracuse University [emeritus]), Edwin D. Reilly, Jr. (SUNY-Albany [emeritus]), Conrad Schirokauer (Columbia University), Stephen L. Schneider (University of Massachusetts), Thomas E. Skidmore (Brown University), Fredric P. Smoler (Sarah Lawrence College), Graham Speake (Oxford University), William C. Summers (Yale University), Christine Sutton (Oxford University), Birdsall S. Viault (Winthrop University [emeritus]), David K. Wyatt (Cornell University), Mark J. Zucker (Louisiana State University)

Merriam-Webster Editorial Staff: Michael G. Belanger, Susan L. Brady, Deanna Chiasson, Jennifer N. Cislo, Robert D. Copeland, Joanne M. Despres, Florence A. Fowler, Daniel J. Hopkins, Joan I. Narmontas, Kara L. Noble, Madeline L. Novak, Seán O'Mannion-Espejo, Roger J. Pease, Stephen J. Perrault, Thomas F. Pitoniak, James L. Rader, Donna L. Rickerby, Michael D. Roundy, Maria A. Sansalone, Adrienne M. Scholz, Michael Shally-Jensen, Peter A. Sokolowski, Karen L. Wilkinson

Particular acknowledgment is due to Jennifer Cislo, who fact-checked the great majority of the encyclopedia's entries; Mike Roundy, who advised on a range of scientific and technical subject areas; Deanna Chiasson, who coordinated the provision of pronunciations; Jim Rader, who served as language consultant; Steve Perrault, who served as sports consultant; Dan Hopkins, who acted as in-house cartography coordinator; Roger Pease, who drew up the botany and zoology entry lists; Joan Narmontas, who oversaw creation of the biological diagrams; Seán O'Mannion-Espejo and Peter Sokolowski, who wrote many of the music articles; Karen Wilkinson, who prepared many of the tables; Robert Copeland, who handled the file conversions; and Adrienne Scholz, who proofread virtually the entire volume. Mike Shally-Jensen contributed valuable analyses and many hundreds of articles in the project's early stages.

Merriam-Webster Freelance Staff: Michael J. Anderson, Cynthia Susan Ashby, Arlene Bensam, Frank Calvillo, May K. Chapman, Mary Wood Cornog, Lori Dirks, Jennifer Goss Duby, Elizabeth Morris Ewell, Amy Fass, Sharon Goldstein, Mary Catherine Hager, Helen Downs Haller, Orin K. Hargraves, Stephanie Hiebert, Betty B. Hoskins, Patricia Hurley Jarden, Anthony P. Johnson, Frances Kianka, Mark L. Koontz, Polly Kummel, Lynne Lackenbach, Ellen S. Leach, Arthur Maisel, Danny Marcus, Marvin Martin, Doris Maxfield, Wayne F. Moquin, Caroline Power, Margo Quinto, Mary H. Russell, Barbara H. Salazar, Fran Shonfeld Sherman, Elizabeth Stevens, Jeri Stolk, Barbara R. Tepperman, Deborah J. Untener, Helen M. Webber, Holly Isabella Webber

The project owes special thanks to Mike Anderson, Susan Ashby, Amy Fass, Mary Catherine Hager, Helen Haller, Stephanie Hiebert, Polly Kummel, Lynne Lackenbach, Barbara Salazar, and Holly Webber for their unusually extensive work.

Other Contributors: Tech-Graphics Corporation of Atlantic Highlands, N.J., produced the encyclopedia's diagrams. John Nelson provided its maps. Susana Darwin and Amor Montes de Oca selected and prepared the photographs from the Encyclopædia Britannica collection. Mark Diller drew up the religion entry list. Ellen Sullivan Farley and Loree Hany assisted in technical preparation of the art. Dale Good served as consultant on project management. Ted Atanowski provided computer assistance. The text was typeset by the Clarinda Co. of Clarinda, Iowa, under the exemplary direction of Dee Hughes. Finally, John M. Morse, publisher of Merriam-Webster, conceived the encyclopedia more than 20 years before its publication and offered indispensable support and encouragement throughout its development.